Oxford
Collocations
Dictionary
for students of English

Second edition

Chief editor	Colin McIntosh
Editors	Ben Francis
	Richard Poole

OXFORD
UNIVERSITY PRESS

OXFORD
UNIVERSITY PRESS

Great Clarendon Street, Oxford OX2 6DP

Oxford University Press is a department of the University of Oxford.
It furthers the University's objective of excellence in research, scholarship,
and education by publishing worldwide in

Oxford New York

Auckland Cape Town Dar es Salaam Hong Kong Karachi
Kuala Lumpur Madrid Melbourne Mexico City Nairobi
New Delhi Shanghai Taipei Toronto

With offices in

Argentina Austria Brazil Chile Czech Republic France Greece
Guatemala Hungary Italy Japan Poland Portugal Singapore
South Korea Switzerland Thailand Turkey Ukraine Vietnam

OXFORD and OXFORD ENGLISH are registered trade marks of
Oxford University Press in the UK and in certain other countries

First published 2002
Second edition 2009

2012 2011 2010
7 6 5 4 3

Photocopying

The Publisher grants permission for the photocopying of those pages
marked 'photocopiable' according to the following conditions. Individual
purchasers may make copies for their own use or for use by classes that they
teach. School purchasers may make copies for use by staff and students, but
this permission does not extend to additional schools or branches

Under no circumstances may any part of this book be photocopied for resale

ACKNOWLEDGEMENTS

We would like to thank the following for their permission to reproduce photographs:
Getty Images, Inc. paint and brush (p138), keyboard and mouse (p149), salt
and pepper (p338), basketball (p795), man walking in desert (S7); Jupiter
Images (UK) Ltd. coins (p93), man hiding behind wall (S4); Ingram Publishing
fruit selection (p350), table and chairs (p515), violin (p541).

ISBN: 978 0 19 432538 7   (BOOK AND CD-ROM PACK)
ISBN: 978 0 19 431724 5   (BOOK IN PACK)
ISBN: 978 0 19 432539 4   (CD-ROM IN PACK)

Text capture and typesetting by Oxford University Press

Printed in China

Contents

Editorial teams

Second edition

Chief editor — Colin McIntosh

Editors — Ben Francis
Richard Poole

Contributors — Rosalind Combley
Andrew Delahunty
Lucy Hollingworth
Janet Gough
Lisa Isenman
Laura Wedgeworth

First edition

Managing editors — Jonathan Crowther
Sheila Dignen
Diana Lea

Editors — Margaret Deuter
James Greenan
Joseph Noble
Janet Phillips

Preface

This new edition of the *Oxford Collocations Dictionary* has been completely revised and updated using the Oxford English Corpus, a database of almost two billion words of text in English taken from up-to-date sources from around the world. This has ensured that the information we have about word behaviour is as accurate as possible, and that the evidence upon which the work is based is as full and reliable as possible. In particular, it has allowed us to include information about American English on an equal footing with British English.

I would like to thank the editors, designers and technical specialists who worked on the current and previous editions. I would also like to thank my former colleagues Sally Wehmeier and Judith Willis for their advice and support in bringing this new edition to fruition. Thanks are also due to all colleagues, teachers and students who have given feedback on the previous edition and on sample material for the current one.

We hope that the many students and teachers who already know and love the *Collocations Dictionary* will enjoy exploring the wealth of new information it contains, and that new users will come to appreciate what a valuable and unique learning resource it is.

Colin McIntosh

Introduction:
Using the *Oxford Collocations Dictionary*

What is collocation?

Collocation is the way words combine in a language to produce natural-sounding speech and writing. For example, in English you say *strong wind* but *heavy rain*. It would not be normal to say *heavy wind* or *strong rain*. And whilst all four of these words would be recognized by a learner at pre-intermediate or even elementary level, it takes a greater degree of competence with the language to combine them correctly in productive use.

Why is collocation important?

Collocation runs through the whole of the English language. No piece of natural spoken or written English is totally free of collocation. For the student, choosing the right collocation will make his or her speech and writing sound much more natural, more native-speaker-like, even when basic intelligibility does not seem to be at issue. A student who talks about *strong rain* may make himself or herself understood, but it requires more effort on the part of the listener and ultimately creates a barrier to communication. Poor collocation in exams is also likely to lead to lower marks.

But, perhaps even more importantly than this, language that is collocationally rich is also more precise. This is because most single words in the English language – especially the more common words – embrace a whole range of meanings, some quite distinct, and some that shade into each other by degrees. The precise meaning in any context is determined by that context: by the words that surround and combine with the core word – by collocation. A student who chooses the best collocation will express himself or herself much more clearly and be able to convey not just a general meaning, but something more precise. Compare, for example, the following two sentences:

> *This is a good book and contains a lot of interesting details.*
> *This is a fascinating book and contains a wealth of historical detail.*

Both sentences are perfectly 'correct' in terms of grammar and vocabulary, but which communicates more? Clearly, the second, which is also more likely to engage the reader with its better style.

Why use a Collocations Dictionary?

A normal dictionary, whether monolingual or bilingual, splits up meaning into individual words; it has a lot of power in dissecting the meaning of a text. Its power is more limited when it comes to constructing texts. Good learners' dictionaries give as much help as they can with usage, with grammar patterns clearly explained, register labels and example sentences showing words in context. Modern dictionaries are increasingly giving attention to collocation. But they are still hampered by trying to provide a whole range of information about any word besides its collocations. A collocational dictionary doesn't have to generalize to the same extent: it covers the entire language (or a large part of it!) on a word by word, collocation by collocation basis. It manages this by not attempting to account for every possible utterance, only for what is most typical.

By covering the language systematically from A-Z, a collocations dictionary allows students to build up their own collocational competence on a 'need-to-know' basis, starting from the words they already know – or know in part.

Which collocations are included in this dictionary?

The approach taken to this question was pragmatic, rather than theoretical. The questions asked were: is this a typical use of language? Might a student of English want to express this idea? Would they look up this entry to find out how? The aim was to give the full range of collocation – from the fairly weak (*see a movie, an enjoyable experience, extremely complicated*), through the medium-strength (*see a doctor, direct equivalent, highly intelligent*) to the strongest and most restricted (*see reason, burning ambition, blindingly obvious*) – for around 9,000 headwords.

Totally free combinations are excluded and so, for the most part, are idioms. Exceptions to this rule are idioms that are only partly idiomatic. An idiom like *not see the wood for the trees* has nothing to do with wood or trees, and is therefore excluded; but *drive a hard bargain* is very much about bargaining, even if the expression as a whole can be considered to be idiomatic.

Typical use of language

The first question (Is this a typical use of language?) required that all the collocations be drawn from reliable data. The main source used was the Oxford English Corpus. A corpus is a collection of texts of written or spoken language stored in electronic form. It provides us with the evidence of how language is used in real situations, which we use as the basis for our dictionary entries. The Oxford English Corpus is a database of almost two billion words of text in English taken from up-to-date sources from around the world, ensuring that we have the most accurate information about word behaviour possible.

By analysing the corpus and using special software, we can see words in context and find out how they combine with other words. Compilers of the dictionary were able to check how frequently any given combination occurred, in how many (and what kind of) sources, and in what particular contexts. The corpus also helped in the preparation of example sentences, most of which were based on the authentic texts included in the corpus, with minor modifications to make them more accessible (but without, of course, altering any collocations).

A productive dictionary

The second question asked (Might a student of English want to express this idea?) led to a focus on current English: language that students not only need to understand but can be expected to reproduce. Consideration was given to the kind of texts that students might wish to write. Primary attention was given to what might be called 'moderately formal language' – the language of essay and report writing, and formal letters – treating all subjects – business, science, history, sport, etc. at the level of the educated non-specialist. In addition, the dictionary includes some of the most important collocations from some specialist areas, such as law, medicine, politics, current affairs and sport; collocations from fiction, particularly useful in treating more personal subjects such as feelings and relationships; and informal collocations and those very frequent in spoken language and Internet communication (blogs, emails, etc.). Technical, informal and journalistic uses are labelled as such.

Looking up a collocation in the dictionary

The third question asked (Would a student look up this entry to find this expression?) led to the exclusion of noun collocates from verb and adjective entries. When framing their ideas, people generally start from a noun. You might think of **rain** and want to know which adjective best describes rain when a lot falls in a short time. You would be unlikely to start with the adjective **heavy** and wonder what you could describe with it (*rain, breathing, damage, gunfire?*) Similarly, you might be looking for the verb to use when you do what you need to do in response to a challenge. But you would not choose **meet** and then choose what to meet (*a challenge, an acquaintance, your death, the expense*).

Types of combination

The dictionary covers the following types of word combination:

Noun entries
adjective + noun: *bright/harsh/intense/strong* **light**
quantifier + noun (... of): *a beam/ray of* **light**
verb + noun: *cast/emit/give/provide/shed* **light**
noun + verb: **light** *gleams/glows/shines*
noun + noun: *a* **light** *source*
preposition + noun: *by the* **light** *of the moon*
noun + preposition: *the* **light** *from the window*

Verb entries
adverb + verb: **choose** *carefully*
verb + verb: *be free to* **choose**
verb + preposition: **choose** *between two things*

Adjective entries
verb + adjective: *make/keep/declare sth* **safe**
adverb + adjective: *perfectly/not entirely/environmentally* **safe**
adjective + preposition: **safe** *from attack*

In addition, short phrases including the headword are included: *the speed of* **light**, *pick and* **choose**, **safe** *and sound*.

Sets of words

Most of the collocations in the dictionary can be called 'word collocations', that is, these are the precise words that combine with each other: *small fortune* cannot be changed to *little fortune*, even though *small* and *little* would seem to be synonymous. There is another area of collocation that might be called 'category collocation', where a word can combine with any word from a readily definable set. This set may be quite large, but its members are predictable, because they are all words for nationalities, or measurements of time, for example. At the entry for **walk**, one of the groups of collocates is given as *three-minute, five minutes'*, etc.: the 'etc.' is to indicate that any number may be substituted for 'three' or 'five' in these expressions. At the entry for **passport**, the collocates given include *Canadian, Mexican, Swiss*, etc., indicating that any nationality may be used with *passport*.

Modifiers

With adjectives, often a wide range of modifying adverbs can be used. To indicate that the adjective can be used with a full range of modifiers, the adverbs section gives *extremely, fairly, very, etc.* The main modifiers which are used in this way are:

extremely
fairly
pretty
quite
rather
really
somewhat
very

Quite is used especially in British English, but is also used in American English, where the meaning is similar to 'very'. *Somewhat* is used especially in American English. *Rather* is used in British English more than in American English. *Pretty* is mainly used informally in both British and American English.

Another group of modifiers is indicated by *a little, slightly, etc.*:

a bit
a little
slightly

A bit is often informal and is used especially in British English.

Defined sets

It also happens that certain sets of words share all or most of their collocations. This is particularly true of very strictly defined sets such as days of the week, months and points of the compass, but it also applies to slightly less rigid, but still limited sets such as currencies, weights and measures, and meals. In order to show how these collocations are shared by a number of headwords, the dictionary includes 25 usage notes, each treating the collocations of a particular set. The entries for the individual members of the set include a cross-reference to the usage note. In cases where all the collocations are shared (months, for example) the cross-reference replaces all other information in the entry. In cases where some of the collocations are shared, but others apply only to an individual member of the set (for example, seasons), the individual collocations are given at the entry, and a cross-reference directs the user to the shared collocations in the usage note. A full list of the usage notes and where they may be found is given on page xii. The 9,000 headwords include most of the commonest words in the language that upper-intermediate students will already know, plus some words that they will start to encounter as they move to a more advanced level of English. Some very common words – such as the verbs *make* and *do* – do not merit entries of their own. This is because these verbs have no real collocates of their own. They themselves are the collocates of lots of nouns, and appear in the entries for those nouns. There are also two pages of exercises in the central study section addressing this notorious area of difficulty.

How to use this dictionary

This dictionary is intended for productive use, most typically for help with writing. The collocations in each entry are divided according to part of speech; within each part of speech section they are grouped according to meaning or category. For example, at the entry for **pollution**, *avoid*, *eliminate* and *prevent* are roughly synonymous, as are *combat*, *control*, *fight* and *tackle*, and so on. The groups are arranged in an order that tries to be as intuitive as possible: in this case from the 'strongest' form of action (*avoid/eliminate/prevent*) to the 'mildest' (*monitor*). Many collocate groups have illustrative examples showing one or more of the collocations in context.

Because this is a type of dictionary that may be totally new to many students, it is recommended that users familiarize themselves with how the dictionary works by working through some of the exercises in the photocopiable study section in the centre of the dictionary. The first of these aims to show the overall concept of the dictionary by looking at a single entry (**idea**) in some detail. The next few exercises take users systematically through the different sections of the entries for nouns, verbs and adjectives. Two pages of exercises get students thinking about the common verbs *make*, *do*, *have*, *give* and *take*; and the remaining exercises range across the whole dictionary, testing collocations linked to various themes, including politics, jobs and money.

British and American English

The dictionary includes the most frequent and useful British and American collocates for the 9,000 British and American headwords. Where appropriate, headwords, meanings and collocations are labelled to show that they are used only, or especially, in one variety of English or the other. The labels used are:

AmE   *BrE*   *esp. AmE*   *esp. BrE*

The labels *esp. AmE* and *esp. BrE* indicate that the headword or collocation is used especially in that variety. It may be used in the other variety, but is significantly less frequent. Other collocations may be more frequently used to express the same idea, or it may have a special meaning in one variety but not in the other.

For example, the headword **pavement** is labelled *BrE*. All the collocates given at this entry are also therefore to be understood as British English. A cross-reference to **sidewalk** indicates the American equivalent of the headword.

A word may be labelled as British English or American English, but may include some collocations which are actually found in both varieties. An example is the entry **shop**, which is labelled *esp. BrE*. *Gift shop*, *pet shop* and *souvenir shop*, however, are used in American English as well as British English, so these are labelled *BrE, AmE*.

These labels always refer to the preceding collocate only. The labels *all BrE*, *all AmE*, etc. and *both BrE*, *both AmE*, etc. indicate that all or both of the collocations in that group are British English or American English.

Example sentences may also be followed by a *BrE* or *AmE* label where that particular usage is more restricted than the collocate itself is.

Where a collocate has different spellings in British and American English it is given as a slashed alternative: *colour/color*.

Some collocations are used far more frequently in British or American English simply because they refer to institutions that are particular to the UK or the US. High schools are found in the US, not normally in the UK; but the term may be used in British English to refer to this type of US school. Collocates like this are labelled *in the UK* or *in the US*. Collocates referring to particular sports, etc. that are more popular in one country than another are labelled *in cricket*, *in baseball*, etc., but are not given a geographical label.

Other information in this dictionary

The focus of this dictionary is very much on collocation. In order to make the collocational information as comprehensive and accessible as possible, non-collocational information has largely been excluded. Definitions of headwords are given only insofar as they are necessary to distinguish different senses of the same word, when they have different collocations and need to be treated separately. These are not full definitions, but rather 'sense discriminators', just detailed enough to allow the senses to be distinguished.

Formal and informal

Register information (whether a word is formal or informal) is given when any pair of words in combination takes on a different register from the two words separately. Examples would be *do drugs* (*informal*) – though neither *do* nor *drugs* is informal in itself – or *hear a lecture* (*formal*). Collocations are also labelled if they belong to a particular field of language such as law or medicine. For a full list of the usage labels used in this dictionary, see inside the front cover. In addition to these labels, more specific usage restrictions such as *in football* or *used in journalism* are given in brackets.

Figurative use

The most frequent usage label used in the dictionary is *figurative*. It is a feature of English that when the meaning of a word is extended and used in a non-literal sense, the collocations of the literal sense are often carried over: that is, both literal and figurative meanings of a word may share collocations. The dictionary indicates where this is so: for example, at **way**, the collocation *lose* is given, followed by the examples: *She lost her way in the fog* and *This project seems to have lost its way* (*figurative*). This shows that *lose your way* can be used in both a literal and a figurative way. With strong collocations that are slightly idiomatic, a short explanation of the meaning may be given. For example, at **bargain**, the phrase *drive a hard bargain* has the gloss (= *force sb to agree to the arrangement that is best for you*).

Special pages

The dictionary also includes ten special pages on different topics such as business, meetings and sport. These pull together collocations from the different topics and can be used as the basis for topic work in class, or for brainstorming vocabulary for an essay, for example. A full list of special topic pages and where to find them is given on page xii.

It is hoped that this dictionary will be of use not only to students of English of upper-intermediate level and above, but also to teachers (both non-native speaker and native-speaker teachers, looking for ways to present collocations to their students), translators, academics, business people, and all who wish to write fluent and idiomatic English. The Guide to the Entries (pages x–xi) is there as a quick reference, to give help as needed, but the whole dictionary has been designed to be accessible, and (we hope) enjoyable to use.

Guide to the entries

Nouns

adjectives, or nouns that function like adjectives, that collocate with **store**

Collocates are grouped according to meaning or category.

words that refer to a group, number or amount of the headword

verbs that come before **store**

verbs that come after **store**

nouns that come after **store**

prepositions that come before or after **store**

common phrases that include **store**

Sense numbers and short definitions indicate the different senses of **store**.

---

store *noun*

1 place where you can buy things → See also SHOP

ADJ. **big, large, major** (*esp. BrE*) | **small** | **retail** | **department** | **high-street** (*BrE*), **local, village** (*esp. BrE*) | **chain** | **online** ◊ *You can buy music from an online* ~. | **discount** | **convenience, corner** (*esp. BrE*), **general** | **specialty** (*AmE*) | **outlet** | **DIY** (*esp. BrE*), **electrical** (*esp. BrE*), **grocery** (*esp. AmE*), **hardware** (*esp. AmE*), **health-food** (*esp. AmE*), **liquor** (*AmE*), **record, toy, video, etc.** | **dime** (*AmE*) | **thrift** (*AmE*) | **flagship** ◊ *Ralph Lauren's flagship* ~ *on Madison Avenue*

... OF STORES **chain**

VERB + STORE **go to, visit** | **close, open** ◊ *The company plans to open two new* ~*s in Dublin.* | **operate, run** ◊ *The company operates four* ~*s in Maryland.* | **hit** ◊ *The CD will hit* ~*s in January.*

STORE + VERB **carry sth, offer sth, sell sth** ◊ *The* ~ *offers a comprehensive line of auto parts.* | **close, open**

STORE + NOUN **chain** | **account** (*AmE*), **card** (*BrE*) | **shelf, window** (*both esp. AmE*) ◊ *The new book has been flying off* ~ *shelves.* | **brand** (*esp. AmE*) ◊ *Buying* ~ *brands certainly works out cheaper.* | **sales** (*esp. AmE*) | **clerk, employee** (*both AmE*) | **manager, owner** | **detective** (*esp. BrE*)

PREP. **at a/the** ~, **in a/the** ~

PHRASES **the back of a/the** ~, **the front of a/the** ~

2 supply for future use

ADJ. **good, great, large, vast** | **small** | **food** | **energy, fat** ◊ *your body's fat* ~*s*

VERB + STORE **have, keep** | **build up**

STORE + NOUN **cupboard** (*BrE*), **room** (usually *storeroom*)

PREP. ~ **of** ◊ *a vast* ~ *of knowledge*

Verbs

adverbs that collocate with **rest**

verbs that come before **rest**

prepositions that come after **rest**

common phrases that include **rest**

Phrasal verbs are treated separately at the end of the entry.

---

rest *verb*

ADV. **casually, gently, lightly, loosely, softly** | **heavily** | **comfortably** ◊ *Her head was* ~*ing comfortably against his chest.* | **peacefully, quietly** | **safely** ◊ *He could* ~ *safely in this place.* | **lazily** ◊ *His hand was* ~*ing lazily against the steering wheel.* | **briefly, momentarily** | **awhile**

VERB + REST **let sth** ◊ *She let his hand* ~ *heavily on hers.* | **have to, need to** | **want to, would like to** | **stop to** ◊ *I stopped to* ~ *on one of the benches.*

PREP. **against** ◊ *She* ~*ed the ladder against the wall.* | **atop** (*esp. AmE*) ◊ *Her thin hands were* ~*ing atop the quilted bed cover.* | **in** ◊ *I settled back, my hands* ~*ing in my lap.* | **on, upon** ◊ *His hands* ~*ed lightly on her shoulders.*

PHRASES ~ **easy** ◊ *I can* ~ *easy* (= stop worrying) *knowing that she's safely home.*

PHR V **rest on/upon sth**

ADV. **solely, squarely** ◊ *It is rare for the responsibility for causing conflict to* ~ *solely on one side.* | **entirely** ◊ *The decision* ~*s entirely upon how good a fighter you think she is.*

Adjectives

verbs that come before **economical**

adverbs that collocate with **economical**

prepositions that come after **economical**

common phrases that include **economical**

---

economical *adj.*

VERBS **be, seem** ◊ *Solid fuel would be more* ~.

ADV. **extremely, fairly, very, etc.** | **highly, remarkably** ◊ *This new oven is highly* ~.

PREP. **in** ◊ *This arrangement is more* ~ *in its use of staff.* | **of** ◊ *more* ~ *of time and resources* | **with** ◊ *This arrangement is more* ~ *with space.*

PHRASES ~ **with the truth** ◊ *She accused him of being* ~ *with the truth* (= not telling the truth).

American English and British English

Driving licence is used only in British English.
Driver's license is the equivalent expression in American English.

This collocation is more common in British English than in American English.

This collocation is used only in American English.

This collocation is used only in British English.

driving licence (*BrE*) (*AmE* **driver's license**) *noun*
ADJ. **valid** | **current** | **clean** (*esp. BrE*) | **full** (*BrE*) | **commercial** (*AmE*) | **provisional** (*BrE*)
VERB + DRIVING LICENCE/DRIVER'S LICENSE **have, hold** | **get, obtain** | **lose** | **issue**

All the collocates in this group are used only in American English.

Both of the collocates in this group are only used in British English.

Examples of British or American English have labels.

packet *noun*
ADJ. **empty** | **cereal, cigarette** (*cigarette pack* in *AmE*), **cornflake, crisp** (*all BrE*) | **ketchup, mustard, sugar** (*all AmE*) | **seed** | **pay, wage** (*both BrE*) ◇ *a weekly pay ~ (= wage) of £200* | **math** (= work to do in the the holiday/vacation) (*AmE*) ◇ *My kids have summer math ~s from their schools.*
VERB + PACKET **open**
PACKET + VERB **contain sth** ◇ *a ~ containing seeds*
PACKET + NOUN **soup**
PREP. **on a/the ~** ◇ *Follow the instructions on the ~.* | **~ of** ◇ *a ~ of crisps* (*BrE*) ◇ *a ~ of sugar* (*AmE*)

Truant and its collocates are especially common in British English.

This collocation is used only in British English.

This collocation is equally common in British and American English.

truant *noun* (*esp. BrE*)
ADJ. **persistent** | **school**
VERB + TRUANT **play** (*BrE*) ◇ *She often played ~ and wrote her own sick notes.*
TRUANT + NOUN **officer** (*BrE, AmE*)

Labels such as (*in the UK*) or (*in the US*) indicate cultural differences between the UK and the US rather than differences of language.

These organizations are found only in the UK.

This job title is found only in the UK.

This job title is found only in the US.

borough *noun*
ADJ. **county, metropolitan** (*both in the UK*) | **outer**
BOROUGH + NOUN **council, councillor** (*in the UK*), **president** (*in the US*) | **resident** | **park, school**

Other features of the entries

'etc.' shows that similar words also collocate with **undergraduate**.

When a label appears after 'etc.' it refers to the entire group.

undergraduate *noun*
ADJ. **college, university** | **Harvard, Oxford, etc.** | **first-year, second-year, etc.** (*esp. BrE*) | **chemistry, history, etc.** | **full-time, part-time**

a short explanation of the meaning of this phrase

Register labels give information about how a collocation is used.

planet *noun*
ADJ. **distant** | **alien, unknown** | **inner, outer** ◇ *the outer ~s of our solar system* | **extrasolar** (= outside our solar system) (*technical*) ◇ *Hubble has found around 100 new extrasolar ~s.* | **Earth-like** ◇ *the search for Earth-like ~s* | **rocky** ◇ *rocky ~s like Venus and Mars* | **another, different** (*figurative, humorous*) ◇ *He looked like something from another ~!*

a cross-reference to a related enrty.

'~' replaces **pantyhose** in examples and phrases.

a cross-reference to a special page at **clothes**, which has more collocations for clothes

pantyhose *noun* (*AmE*) → See also TIGHTS
ADJ. **sheer** | **fishnet** | **control-top**
... OF PANTYHOSE **pair** ◇ *a pair of black ~*
VERB + PANTYHOSE **wear**
PREP. **in ~**
→ Special page at CLOTHES

List of usage notes

List of special pages

A a

abandon verb

1 leave sb/sth

ADV. **hastily** ◊ *The town had been hastily ~ed.*
PHRASES **~ sb to their fate | be left ~ed | be found ~ed** ◊ *The car was found ~ed in a nearby town.*

2 stop doing/supporting sth

ADV. **altogether, completely, entirely, totally** ◊ *The government does not propose to ~ the project altogether.* | **effectively, largely, virtually** ◊ *This principle has now been effectively ~ed.* | **eventually, finally | simply** ◊ *Traditional policies were simply ~ed.* | **formally | abruptly** (*esp. AmE*), **immediately, quickly | gradually | quietly** ◊ *The plans for reform were quietly ~ed.* | **temporarily | voluntarily**
VERB + ABANDON **be forced to, have to | decide to**
PREP. **for** ◊ *He ~ed the army for politics.* | **in favour/favor of** ◊ *She ~ed her teaching career in favour/favor of singing.*

abashed adj.

VERBS **be | look**
ADV. **a little, slightly, etc. | suitably** ◊ *He glanced at Juliet accusingly and she looked suitably ~.*

abbreviation noun

ADJ. **common, standard**
VERB + ABBREVIATION **use** ◊ *Abbreviations are used in the text to save space.*
ABBREVIATION + VERB **stand for** ◊ *The ~ PC stands for 'personal computer'.*
PREP. **~ for** ◊ *AC is the standard ~ for 'air conditioning'.* | **~ of** ◊ *Ad lib is an ~ of the Latin phrase 'ad libitum'.*

abhorrent adj.

VERBS **be | become | find sth**
ADV. **absolutely, totally, utterly** ◊ *I find the idea absolutely ~.* | **morally**
PREP. **to** ◊ *Such a savage punishment is ~ to a civilized society.*

ability noun

1 skill/power to do sth

ADJ. **exceptional, extraordinary, great, outstanding, re-markable, uncanny | inherent, innate, natural** ◊ *It's important to discover the natural abilities of each child.* | **proven | academic, acting, artistic, athletic, creative, intellectual, linguistic, mathematical, musical, psychic, reading, technical | mental, physical**
... OF ABILITY **level** ◊ *She showed a high level of ~ as a runner.*
VERB + ABILITY **have, possess | retain | demonstrate, show** ◊ *Both players demonstrated their ~ to hit the ball hard.* | **acquire, develop, enhance, improve | lack | lose** ◊ *I seem to have lost my ~ to attract clients.* | **affect, hamper, hinder, impair, impede, limit, undermine | appreciate, recognize** ◊ *Fox's abilities were soon recognized.* | **doubt, question | overestimate, underestimate**
PREP. **~ in** ◊ *She showed great ~ in mathematics.*
PHRASES **to the best of your ~** ◊ *We will keep you informed to the best of our ~.*

2 speed with which sb learns

ADJ. **high** ◊ *The school does nothing for children of high ~.* | **limited, low | average, mixed** ◊ *It is much more difficult to teach a mixed-ability class.*
VERB + ABILITY **assess, measure, test**
ABILITY + NOUN **level | range**
PHRASES **a range of ~, a range of abilities** ◊ *I taught a wide range of abilities.*

ablaze adj.

VERBS **be | set sth** ◊ *Truck after truck was set ~ as the fire spread.*
ADV. **well** (*BrE*) ◊ *By the time firefighters were called, the house was well ~.*
PREP. **with** ◊ *Every window was ~ with light.*

able adj.

1 able to do sth having the ability to do sth

VERBS **be, feel, prove, seem**
ADV. **fully, perfectly, quite, well** ◊ *He is well ~ to take care of himself.* | **better, more** ◊ *Once you've had some sleep you'll feel better ~ to cope.* | **uniquely** ◊ *Humans are uniquely ~ to use true language.* | **just** ◊ *I was just ~ to make out a dark figure in the distance.* | **barely, hardly, scarcely** | **financially, physically** ◊ *She was not physically ~ to take care of herself.*

2 intelligent; doing your job well

VERBS **be, seem** ◊ *She seems very ~.*
ADV. **extremely, fairly, very, etc. | reasonably | less** ◊ *less ~ students*

abolish verb

ADV. **altogether** (*esp. BrE*), **completely, entirely, totally** ◊ *Some say the tax should be ~ed entirely.* | **virtually | largely** ◊ *Foreign exchange controls were largely ~ed.* | **effectively** ◊ *The new immigration act effectively ~es quotas on immigrants.*
VERB + ABOLISH **seek to | decide to, vote to**

abortion noun

ADJ. **legal, legalized | elective | early** (*esp. BrE*), **early-term** (*esp. AmE*) **| late** (*esp. BrE*), **late-term** (*esp. AmE*) **| induced, spontaneous, therapeutic | back-alley** (*esp. AmE*), **back-street, illegal**
VERB + ABORTION **have** ◊ *She decided to have an ~.* | **obtain, procure | carry out, do** (*informal*), **perform** ◊ *Some nurses wanted the right to refuse to perform ~s.* | **legalize | ban, prohibit, restrict**
ABORTION + NOUN **clinic, counselling/counseling | pill | law, legislation** ◊ *the country's strict ~ laws* | **debate, issue** ◊ *The ~ issue is political dynamite.*
PHRASES **~ on demand** (= the right to have an abortion if you want one) ◊ *Women's groups are calling for free contraception and ~ on demand.*

abscess noun

VERB + ABSCESS **have | develop, get** ◊ *I developed an ~ on my neck.* | **cause | drain | treat**
ABSCESS + VERB **burst** ◊ *Once an ~ has burst it should be bathed with antiseptic liquid.*

absence noun

1 fact of not being present

ADJ. **extended, lengthy, long, prolonged | brief, temporary | frequent | excused** (*AmE*) **| unauthorized, unexplained**
... OF ABSENCE **period** ◊ *You will not be paid for the full period of ~.*
VERB + ABSENCE **have** ◊ *Your son has had too many ~s from school.* | **notice** ◊ *Nobody had noticed her ~.* | **explain**
PREP. **during sb's ~, in sb's ~** (= while sb is not there) ◊ *My father did all the cooking in my mother's ~.* | **~ from** ◊ *from work*
PHRASES **conspicuous by your ~, notable by your ~** (*esp. BrE*) ◊ *When it came to clearing up after the party, Anne was conspicuous by her ~* (= very obviously absent when she should have been present). | **leave of ~** (= permission to be absent) ◊ *He asked for leave of ~ from his job.*

2 lack

ADJ. **complete, total | virtual | conspicuous, notable** ◊ *a conspicuous ~ of evidence*

PREP. **in the ~ of** ◊ *In the ~ of stone, most houses in the area are built of wood.*

absent *adj.*

VERBS **be** | **remain**
ADV. **completely, entirely, quite, totally, wholly** | **almost, virtually** | **largely** | **temporarily** | **conspicuously, markedly, notably, noticeably, strikingly** ◊ *Local people were conspicuously ~ from the meeting.* | **curiously, strangely** ◊ *He now played with a passion that had been strangely ~ from his previous performance.*
PREP. **from** ◊ *He was ~ from work for two weeks.*
PHRASES **~ without leave** (= without permission) ◊ *soldiers who go ~ without leave*

absorb *verb*

1 liquid, gas, energy, etc.
ADV. **quickly, rapidly** | **directly, easily, readily**
PREP. **into** ◊ *Nutrients are ~ed into the bloodstream.*
2 make part of sth larger
ADV. **gradually**
PHRASES **be ~ed into sth** ◊ *These committees were gradually ~ed into the local government machine.*
3 information/atmosphere
ADV. **easily, readily** ◊ *The information is presented so that it can be readily ~ed.* | **fully** | **passively**
4 interest
ADV. **completely, totally, utterly** ◊ *His work ~ed him completely.* | **deeply**

absorbed *adj.*

VERBS **appear, be, look, seem** | **become, get** | **keep sb** ◊ *A crossword can keep me ~ for hours.*
ADV. **very** | **completely, fully, totally, utterly** ◊ *He was totally ~ in his book.* | **increasingly**
PREP. **in** ◊ *~ in thought*

abstract *adj.*

VERBS **be**
ADV. **extremely, fairly, very, etc.** | **highly** | **entirely, purely** ◊ *purely ~ drawing* | **increasingly**

absurd *adj.*

VERBS **be, look, seem, sound** | **become** | **find sth** ◊ *She found the whole concept faintly ~.*
ADV. **absolutely, completely, quite** (*esp. BrE*) **, totally, utterly** | **clearly, manifestly** (*BrE*) **, patently, simply** ◊ *Such beliefs are patently ~.* | **rather, somewhat** | **a little, slightly, etc.** | **faintly**
PHRASES **a sense of the ~** ◊ *His sense of the ~ kept him from becoming too solemn.*

abundance *noun*

ADJ. **great, rich, sheer** ◊ *We were amazed by the sheer ~ of food.* | **relative** | **high, low**
VERB + ABUNDANCE **have** ◊ *The country has an ~ of natural resources.* | **produce, provide**
PREP. **in ~** ◊ *Mushrooms grew there in great ~.* ◊ *Exotic plants are found in ~.* | **~ of** ◊ *The brochure promised beautiful walks with an ~ of wildlife.*

abuse *noun*

1 wrong/bad use of sth
ADJ. **alcohol, drug, solvent, substance** (= drugs, etc.) | **systematic, widespread** | **flagrant**
VERB + ABUSE **prevent, stop** | **investigate, report** | **be open to** ◊ *The legal system is open to ~.*
PREP. **~ of** ◊ *~ of prisoners*
PHRASES **the ~ of power**

2 bad, usually violent treatment of sb
ADJ. **emotional, physical, psychological, sex, sexual** | **child, elder** (*esp. AmE*) **, prisoner, spousal** (*esp. AmE*) ◊ *victims of child ~* | **human rights ~s** ◊ *allegations of human rights ~s* | **alleged, suspected**
...OF ABUSE **case** ◊ *six cases of suspected child ~*
VERB + ABUSE **commit** | **subject sb to** ◊ *She was subjected to regular sexual ~.* | **experience, suffer, take** ◊ *The child had taken a lot of emotional ~.* | **allege, suspect sb of**
ABUSE + VERB **happen, occur, take place**
ABUSE + NOUN **victim**
PHRASES **an allegation of ~** ◊ *allegations of child ~* | **a perpetrator of ~** | **a victim of ~**
3 insulting words
ADJ. **verbal** | **personal, racial** (*esp. BrE*) **, racist**
...OF ABUSE **stream, torrent** ◊ *He was subjected to a torrent of personal ~.*
VERB + ABUSE **hurl, scream, shout, shower sb with, subject sb to** | **endure** ◊ *They had to endure continual racist ~.*
PHRASES **heap ~ on sb/sth** ◊ *Abuse and scorn were heaped on the proposals.* | **a target for ~, a target of ~** ◊ *The team who lost became a target of ~ for angry fans.* | **a term of ~** ◊ *Calling someone stupid is definitely a term of ~.*

abuse *verb*

ADV. **emotionally, mentally, physically, sexually, verbally** ◊ *All the children had been physically and emotionally ~d.* | **badly, severely**

abusive *adj.*

VERBS **be** | **become, get**
ADV. **extremely, very** | **rather** | **openly** ◊ *He became openly ~.* | **emotionally, physically, sexually, verbally**

academic *adj.*

VERBS **be** | **become**
ADV. **merely, purely, strictly** ◊ *The distinction being made is purely ~.* | **largely, rather, somewhat** | **overly** (*esp. AmE*) ◊ *The writers' approach is not overly ~.*

academy *noun*

ADJ. **military, naval, police** | **training**
VERB + ACADEMY **attend, be at, enter, go to, join** | **graduate from, leave**
PREP. **at an/the ~** ◊ *He specialized in naval history at the Naval Academy.*

accelerate *verb*

1 go faster
ADV. **hard, quickly** | **smoothly** ◊ *The runners ~d smoothly around the bend.* | **suddenly** | **away** (*esp. BrE*) ◊ *The car purred into life and ~d away.*
2 develop quickly
ADV. **dramatically, greatly, rapidly, sharply** ◊ *The epidemic is accelerating dramatically.* | **significantly**

acceleration *noun*

1 increase in speed
ADJ. **rapid, sudden** | **gradual**
PREP. **~ in** ◊ *There has been a rapid ~ in the growth of industry.*
2 ability of a car to accelerate
ADJ. **fast, good** ◊ *This model has the best ~ of any available sports car.* | **poor, slow**

accelerator *noun*

VERB + ACCELERATOR **depress, floor, hit, press, put your foot (down) on, step on** ◊ *She put her foot on the ~ and we sped through the traffic lights.* | **take your foot off**
ACCELERATOR + NOUN **pedal**

accent noun

ADJ. **broad** (*esp. BrE*), **heavy, marked, pronounced, strong, thick** ◊ *She had a pronounced Southern ~.* | **slight** | **country, foreign, local, regional** (*esp. BrE*) | **American, British** (*AmE*), **English, French, etc.** | **northern, southern, etc.** | **middle-class** (*BrE*) | **cut-glass** (*BrE*), **posh** (*BrE*), **public-school** (*BrE*), **RP** ◊ *He spoke with a cut-glass English ~.* | **cockney, hick** (*informal, esp. AmE*), **Midwestern, Valley Girl, etc.**
... OF ACCENT **hint, trace** ◊ *Her French was excellent, without a trace of an ~.*
VERB + ACCENT **have, speak in, speak with** | **acquire** (*esp. BrE*) | **adopt, affect, assume, put on** ◊ *She put on a Southern ~ when she answered the phone.* | **fake, imitate, mimic** | **cultivate** | **drop, lose** ◊ *He lost his ~ after moving to the capital.* | **place** ◊ *Where are you from? I can't place your ~.*
PREP. **in an ~** ◊ *She spoke in a strong Jamaican ~.* | **with an ~, without an ~** ◊ *a tall man with a Canadian ~*

accept verb

1 take/receive

ADV. **eagerly, gladly, graciously, gratefully, willingly** ◊ *She graciously ~ed my apology.* | **reluctantly**
VERB + ACCEPT **be glad to, be happy to** | **be reluctant to, be unwilling to** | **be unable to** ◊ *I am unfortunately unable to ~ your kind invitation.*
PREP. **from** ◊ *She ~ed a bribe from an undercover policeman.*

2 agree/admit

ADV. **happily, readily** ◊ *Some people readily ~ that they may have to pay for medical treatment.* | **fully** | **blindly, uncritically, unquestioningly** | **grudgingly**
VERB + ACCEPT **be happy to, be prepared to, be ready to, be willing to** | **be reluctant to, be unwilling to** | **be unable to, refuse to** | **can, will** | **cannot, will not** ◊ *The college cannot ~ responsibility for items lost or stolen on its premises.* | **be forced to, have to** | **learn to**
PHRASES **be commonly ~ed, be generally ~ed, be universally ~ed, be widely ~ed** ◊ *It is generally ~ed that people are motivated by success.* | **~ sth at face value** ◊ *These figures should not be ~ed at face value.* | **have no choice but to ~** ◊ *I had no choice but to ~ the committee's decision.*

acceptable adj.

VERBS **be, prove, seem** | **become** | **make sth** ◊ *an attempt to make the reforms ~ to both sides* | **consider sth, deem sth, find sth** ◊ *We must come up with a solution that our customers will find ~.*
ADV. **highly, very** ◊ *Most people found the drink's taste to be highly ~.* | **completely, entirely, fully, perfectly, quite, totally** ◊ *Yogurt is a perfectly ~ substitute for cream in cooking.* | **fairly, reasonably** | **(not) remotely** ◊ *These actions cannot be considered remotely ~ in a civilized society.* | **generally, universally, widely** | **easily, readily** | **equally** ◊ *Are all political groups equally ~?* | **minimally** (*esp. AmE*) | **mutually** | **publicly** | **commercially, culturally, environmentally, ethically, grammatically, morally, politically, socially** ◊ *a grammatically ~ sentence* ◊ *socially ~ terminology*
PREP. **to** ◊ *a compromise that is ~ to both sides*
PHRASES **the boundaries of acceptable..., the bounds of acceptable..., the limits of acceptable...** ◊ *This crosses the boundaries of ~ conduct.*

acceptance noun

ADJ. **complete, full, total, unconditional, wholehearted** | **conditional, grudging, reluctant** | **gradual** | **greater, growing, increasing** ◊ *Alternative medicines are now winning greater ~ among doctors.* | **broad, general, universal, wide, widespread** | **popular, public** | **blind, easy, immediate, ready, uncritical, unquestioning** ◊ *Their attitude was condemned as blind ~ of authority.* | **implicit, passive, tacit** | **formal, official** | **cultural, social, societal** (*esp. AmE*) | **mainstream** | **consumer, market, user**
VERB + ACCEPTANCE **achieve, find, gain, win** ◊ *The idea was slow to gain general ~.* | **seek** ◊ *The group is now seeking formal ~.*
ACCEPTANCE + NOUN **address, speech** | **letter**
PREP. **~ among** ◊ *These concepts have gained broad ~ among scientists.* | **~ of** ◊ *society's ~ of homosexuality*

access noun

ADJ. **direct, easy, free, full, good, ready, unfettered, unlimited, unrestricted** ◊ *Students have easy ~ to libraries.* | **limited, poor, restricted** ◊ *Access to this information is severely restricted.* | **unauthorized** | **greater, improved** | **fast, immediate, instant, quick, rapid** | **secure** | **equal** ◊ *Men and women should have equal ~ to education and employment.* | **universal** ◊ *universal ~ to education* | **public** | **vehicle, vehicular** (*BrE*), **wheelchair** | **broadband, dial-up, Internet, network, remote, Wi-Fi, wireless** ◊ *high-speed Internet ~*
VERB + ACCESS **have** | **gain, get** | **give (sb), offer (sb), provide (sb with)** ◊ *The computer provides ~ to all the information.* | **demand, require, seek, want** | **control** | **allow (sb), grant (sb)** | **block, deny sb, limit, prevent, refuse (sb), restrict** ◊ *Some people are being denied ~ to adequate medical care.*
ACCESS + NOUN **point** | **road, route** | **code** | **course** (= *helping people without qualifications to study*) (*BrE*)
PREP. **~ for** ◊ *improved ~ for disabled visitors* | **~ to** ◊ *He was finally granted ~ to the medical records.*

accessible adj.

VERBS **be** | **become** | **remain** | **make sth**
ADV. **highly, very** ◊ *a very ~ account of Korean history* | **directly, easily, freely, immediately, readily** ◊ *It is written in simple language, immediately ~ to the reader.* | **widely** | **publicly** | **universally** | **instantly** | **fully**
PREP. **by** ◊ *The museum is easily ~ by public transport.* (*BrE*) ◊ *The museum is easily ~ by public transportation.* (*AmE*) | **for** ◊ *All the buildings are ~ for people in wheelchairs.* | **to** ◊ *The beach should be ~ to everyone.* ◊ *The cartoon strips are designed to make Shakespeare ~ to children.*

accessory noun

1 extra item

ADJ. **essential, must-have** | **optional** | **fashionable, stylish** | **perfect, ultimate** ◊ *This silk scarf is the perfect ~ for stylish summer evenings.* | **fashion, hair** | **bathroom, car, travel**

2 person who helps in crime

PREP. **~ to** ◊ *an ~ to murder*
PHRASES **an ~ before/after the fact** (= *a person who knows about a crime before/after it was committed and protects the criminal*) (*law*)

accident noun

1 unexpected event that causes damage/injury

ADJ. **bad, dreadful** (*esp. BrE*), **horrible, horrific** (*esp. BrE*), **major, nasty, serious, terrible, tragic, unfortunate** | **deadly** (*AmE*), **fatal** ◊ *a fatal road ~* | **minor, slight, small** | **bizarre, freak** ◊ *Their boat sank in a freak ~.* | **hit-and-run** | **industrial, nuclear** | **auto** (*AmE*), **automobile** (*AmE*), **bike, car, highway** (*AmE*), **motor** (*BrE*), **motorbike** (*BrE*), **motorcycle, motor-vehicle, road, traffic** ◊ *The woman was involved in a road traffic ~.* (*BrE*) | **aircraft, airplane** (*AmE*), **plane** (*esp. AmE*) | **boating, climbing, hunting, riding, skiing**
VERB + ACCIDENT **be involved in, have, meet with** (*BrE*), **suffer** ◊ *She met with an ~ while skiing in Colorado.* | **cause** | **avoid, prevent** | **survive** | **recover from**
ACCIDENT + VERB **happen, occur, take place**
ACCIDENT + NOUN **black spot** (*BrE*) | **victim** | **prevention** | **investigation, report** | **rate, statistics**
PREP. **in an/the ~**
PHRASES **an ~ involving** ◊ *He was badly hurt in an ~ involving two cars and a van.* | **an ~ waiting to happen** (= *a situation which is likely to become dangerous*) | **the scene**

of the ~ ◊ *The ambulance took only six minutes to reach the scene of the ~.*

2 sth not planned in advance

ADJ. **mere, pure, sheer** ◊ *By pure ~ he had come across the very man who could solve the mystery.* | **happy** | **historical**
PREP. **by ~** ◊ *We met by ~ at the airport.*
PHRASES **an ~ of birth** (*esp. BrE*) | **an ~ of history** ◊ *It's just an ~ of history that the city became part of the Soviet Union.* | **be no ~ that …** ◊ *It is no ~ that men fill most of the top jobs.* | **by ~ or design** ◊ *It happened, whether by ~ or design, that Steve and I were the last two people to leave.*

accidental adj.

VERBS **be**
ADV. **completely, entirely, purely** | **almost**

acclaim noun

ADJ. **great** | **general, universal, wide, widespread** | **popular, public** | **critical** ◊ *Her latest novel has won great critical ~.* | **international, national, worldwide**
VERB + ACCLAIM **deserve, earn (sb), gain (sb), garner** (*esp. AmE*), **meet with, receive, win** ◊ *His discoveries earned him wide ~.*
PREP. **to … ~** ◊ *The play opened last week to universal ~.* | **~ for** ◊ *She received international ~ for her performance.* | **~ from** ◊ *~ from the critics*

acclaim verb

PHRASES **be critically ~ed, be highly ~ed, be internationally ~ed, be widely ~ed** ◊ *This book has been widely ~ed as a modern classic.*

accolade noun

ADJ. **great, high** (*esp. BrE*), **prestigious, top** (*esp. BrE*), **ultimate** (*esp. BrE*) ◊ *Four restaurants have been awarded the highest ~ of a three-star rating.* | **critical** | **industry, media** ◊ *a long list of industry ~s*
VERB + ACCOLADE **earn, garner, get, receive, win** | **award (sb), bestow, give sb, grant (sb)** | **deserve**

accommodate verb

ADV. **comfortably, easily, readily** ◊ *It was a large hall, where a lot of people could be comfortably ~d.*
VERB + ACCOMMODATE **be able to, can** ◊ *The garage can ~ three cars.*

accommodation noun

1 (*BrE*) place for sb to live/stay

ADJ. **comfortable, decent, good, suitable** | **inadequate, poor, substandard** | **excellent, luxurious** | **overnight, temporary** ◊ *The family is staying in temporary ~ until their house is rebuilt.* | **permanent** | **free** | **private, rented** ◊ *She lived on her own in rented ~.* | **holiday, hotel** | **living, residential** | **sleeping** | **bed-and-breakfast** | **furnished** | **sheltered** ◊ *Many old people choose to live in sheltered ~.* | **secure** ◊ *We need more secure ~ for young prisoners.* | **student**
VERB + ACCOMMODATION **have** ◊ *The council should be able to help families who have no ~.* | **look for, seek** | **find, get, secure** | **offer (sb), provide (sb with)** ◊ *It is the duty of the local community to provide ~ for the homeless.*
ACCOMMODATION + NOUN **costs**
PREP. **in ~**

2 accommodations (*AmE*) place for sb to live/stay, often providing food, etc.

ADJ. **overnight, sleeping** | **guest, hotel, tourist** | **living** | **public** | **comfortable, de luxe, luxurious, luxury, upscale**
VERB + ACCOMMODATIONS **offer (sb), provide (sb with)** ◊ *The boat provides reasonable overnight ~s for four adults.* | **arrange, book** ◊ *You should book your travel ~s and flights quickly.*

3 satisfactory arrangement

VERB + ACCOMMODATION **come to** (*esp. BrE*), **make, reach, work out** | **seek**
PREP. **~ between** ◊ *Some ~ between conservation and tourism is essential.* | **~ to** ◊ *~ to the harsh circumstances of rural life* | **~ with** ◊ *They were forced to reach an ~ with the rebels.*

accompaniment noun

1 things that go or happen together

ADJ. **essential, ideal, perfect** | **delicious, good**
VERB + ACCOMPANIMENT **be, make**
PREP. **to the ~ of** ◊ *The women's medical school opened in 1874, to the ~ of much ridicule.* | **with the ~ of** ◊ *The sun was back, with its ~ of dust and flies.* | **~ for, ~ to** ◊ *These wines also make a good ~ for vegetarian dishes.*

2 music played to go with singing, etc.

ADJ. **instrumental, musical, orchestral** | **piano, string, etc.**
VERB + ACCOMPANIMENT **provide**
PREP. **to the ~ of** ◊ *She sang to the ~ of a guitar.*

accomplice noun

ADJ. **willing** | **unwitting** | **alleged**
PREP. **~ in** ◊ *She became his unwitting ~ in the robbery.* | **~ to** ◊ *an ~ to murder*

accomplish verb

ADV. **successfully** ◊ *A rather difficult task had been successfully ~ed.* | **easily**

accomplished adj.

VERBS **be** | **become**
ADV. **highly, very** | **technically** ◊ *a technically ~ musician*
PREP. **at** ◊ *Sarah had become ~ at running the house.* | **in** ◊ *He came to New York in 1976, already ~ in English.*

accomplishment noun

ADJ. **amazing, big, considerable, great, huge, impressive, major, remarkable, significant** ◊ *If this works, it will be a major ~.* | **scientific, technical** ◊ *Her technical ~ on the piano is impressive.*
VERB + ACCOMPLISHMENT **celebrate** | **recognize**
PREP. **of … ~** ◊ *a work of real ~* | **~ in** ◊ *The award recognizes extraordinary ~ in the field of medicine.*
PHRASES **a feeling of ~, a sense of ~** ◊ *There is a real sense of ~ when everything goes right.* | **quite an ~** ◊ *It would be quite an ~ if we could get this finished in time.*

accord noun

ADJ. **peace, trade** | **international**
VERB + ACCORD **negotiate, reach** ◊ *A peace ~ was reached in March.* | **sign**
PREP. **~ between** ◊ *a trade ~ between Europe and the United States* | **~ on** ◊ *an ~ on environmental protection* | **~ with** ◊ *They signed a trade ~ with the Chinese.*

accord verb

ADV. **fully**
PREP. **with** ◊ *His version of events does not ~ fully with the facts.*

account noun

1 description

ADJ. **brief, short** | **blow-by-blow** (*informal*), **comprehensive, detailed, full, graphic** ◊ *He gave us a blow-by-blow ~ of the incident.* | **fascinating, vivid** | **accurate, clear, factual, true** | **eyewitness, first-hand, personal** | **glowing, good** ◊ *She received a glowing ~ of her son's progress.* | **media, news** (*AmE*), **newspaper** ◊ *the newspaper ~ of the trial* | **fictional, fictionalized** | **autobiographical** | **historical** | **biblical**
VERB + ACCOUNT **give (sb), offer, provide (sb with), write (sb)** ◊ *Can you give us an ~ of what happened?* | **publish**
PREP. **in an/the ~** ◊ *Dr Richards describes this very well in his ~ of the events.*

PHRASES **by all ~s** (= according to what people say) ◊ *I've never been there, but it's a beautiful place by all ~s.* | **by sb's own ~** ◊ *By his own ~ he had an unhappy childhood.*

2 arrangement with a bank

ADJ. **bank, building-society** (*BrE*) | **checking** (*AmE*), **cheque** (*BrE*), **current** | **deposit** (*BrE*), **investment, savings** | **personal** | **business** | **individual, joint, separate** ◊ *My husband and I have separate ~s.* | **numbered, private** (*esp. AmE*) ◊ *They have a numbered ~ in Switzerland.* | **high-interest, interest-bearing, tax-free** | **offshore** | **brokerage** (*esp. AmE*), **money-market, trust** | **retirement** (*esp. AmE*)
VERB + ACCOUNT **have, hold** ◊ *Go and see the manager of the bank where your ~ is held.* | **close, open** ◊ *She opened a savings ~ at the bank.* | **credit sth to, pay sth into** (*esp. BrE*), **put sth into** ◊ *The money will be credited to your ~ tomorrow.* | **debit (sth from), draw sth out of, pay sth from, take sth out of, withdraw sth from** ◊ *She had taken all her money out of her ~.* | **access** | **empty, overdraw** ◊ *Your ~ is overdrawn.*
ACCOUNT + NOUN **number** | **holder** | **balance**
PREP. **at** ◊ *He opened an ~ at a bank in Germany.* | **~ with** ◊ *I have an ~ with another bank.*

3 (usually **accounts**) record of money earned/spent

ADJ. **profit and loss ~** | **~s payable, ~s receivable**
VERB + ACCOUNT **do, keep** ◊ *Try to keep accurate ~s.* | **audit, check, look at** | **submit** ◊ *Your ~s will need to be submitted to the tax office.* | **publish**
ACCOUNT + VERB **be in order** ◊ *The ~s are all in order.*
ACCOUNT + NOUN **~ book** | **~ balance**
→ Special page at BUSINESS

4 arrangement with a shop/store, etc.

ADJ. **expense** (= an arrangement to charge expenses to your own employers) ◊ *Clients are often taken for expense ~ lunches.* | **charge** (= an arrangement with a shop/store to pay bills for goods or services at a later time) (*AmE*), **credit** (*BrE*) | **email, user**
VERB + ACCOUNT **have** | **create, open** ◊ *I'd like to open an ~, please.* | **close** | **pay off, settle** ◊ *It is best to settle the ~ each month.* | **charge sth to, debit (sth from), put sth on** ◊ *Charge this to my ~, please.* | **credit sth to**
PREP. **on** ◊ *Call a cab on ~.* | **~ at, ~ with** ◊ *an ~ with a large store*

account *verb*

PHR V **account for sth**
ADV. **fully** ◊ *The increase can be fully ~ed for.* | **partly** ◊ *The differences in achievement between the students are partly ~ed for by differences in age.* | **adequately, properly**

accountability *noun*

ADJ. **greater, increased** | **local, public** ◊ *demands for greater public ~ in the police service* | **individual, personal** | **direct** | **moral** | **corporate, financial, professional** | **democratic, government, parliamentary** (*esp. BrE*), **political** | **police**
VERB + ACCOUNTABILITY **enhance, improve, increase, strengthen** | **reduce, weaken** ◊ *This process of centralization further reduces ~.* | **ensure** | **demand**
PREP. **~ for** ◊ *to ensure ~ for decisions made* | **~ to** ◊ *police ~ to the public*
PHRASES **a lack of ~** ◊ *the apparent lack of ~ of the security forces* | **a need for ~** ◊ *There is a need for increased professional ~.*

accountable *adj.*

VERBS **be** | **become** | **make sb** | **hold sb** ◊ *The directors are held ~ by the shareholders.*
ADV. **fully, properly** | **personally** | **directly** ◊ *Senior managers are directly ~ to the Board of Directors.* | **ultimately** ◊ *Someone has to be held ultimately ~ for the accident.* | **publicly** ◊ *Local authorities should be publicly ~ to the communities they serve.* | **democratically** ◊ *democratically ~ leaders* | **financially, legally, politically**
PREP. **for** ◊ *In the end, we are all ~ for our actions.* | **to** ◊ *The real power lies with a bureaucracy that is not ~ to the public.*

accountancy (*esp. BrE*) (*AmE usually* **accounting**) *noun*

ADJ. **chartered** (*BrE*) | **public** (*AmE*) | **creative** ◊ *It had taken considerable creative ~ on my part to produce a set of figures that showed us making any profit at all.*
ACCOUNTANCY/ACCOUNTING + NOUN **firm, practice** (*BrE*) | **body** (*BrE*) ◊ *the members of the different professional ~ bodies* | **profession**
→ Note at SUBJECT (for more verbs and nouns)

accountant *noun*

ADJ. **certified public** (*AmE*), **chartered** (*BrE*) | **professional, qualified** (*esp. BrE*) | **trainee** (*BrE*) | **independent, self-employed** (*esp. BrE*) | **company, corporate** | **tax** | **chief** ◊ *We talked to the company's chief ~.* | **management** (*esp. BrE*)
→ Note at PROFESSIONAL (for verbs)

accumulate *verb*

ADV. **gradually, slowly** | **steadily** | **quickly, rapidly**
VERB + ACCUMULATE **begin to** | **be allowed to** ◊ *Dirt must not be allowed to ~.* | **tend to** ◊ *Toxic chemicals tend to ~ in the body.*
PHRASES **~ over the years, ~ over time**

accumulation *noun*

ADJ. **rapid** | **gradual, steady** ◊ *the steady ~ of evidence by the police* | **slow** | **great, large, massive** ◊ *a massive ~ of facts about the motor industry* | **capital** (*finance*)
VERB + ACCUMULATION **lead to** | **reduce** | **prevent**
PHRASES **the rate of ~** ◊ *The rate of ~ has slowed dramatically.*

accuracy *noun*

ADJ. **absolute, complete, deadly, perfect, pinpoint, total, unerring** ◊ *The needle has to be positioned with pinpoint ~.* | **amazing, considerable, great, high** (*technical*), **remarkable, uncanny** ◊ *He predicted the election results with uncanny ~.* | **reasonable, sufficient** | **improved, increased** | **factual, historical, scientific, technical** ◊ *The film-makers went to great lengths to achieve historical ~ in every detail.*
...OF ACCURACY **degree, level** ◊ *The missiles are capable of a very high degree of ~.*
VERB + ACCURACY **achieve** ◊ *Digital techniques achieve exceptionally high ~.* | **improve, increase** ◊ *We are hoping to improve the ~ of our forecasts.* | **ensure** ◊ *Great care is taken to ensure the ~ of research data.* | **doubt, question** ◊ *Many people began to question the ~ of his statement.*
PREP. **with ~** ◊ *It is possible to predict the outcome with reasonable ~.*

accurate *adj.*

VERBS **be, prove** ◊ *His predictions proved ~.*
ADV. **extremely, fairly, very, etc.** | **deadly, highly** | **amazingly, remarkably, surprisingly, uncannily** ◊ *Her assessment turned out to be remarkably ~.* | **completely, perfectly, totally** | **not completely, not entirely, not quite, not strictly, not wholly** ◊ *The figures he gave were not strictly ~.* | **partially** | **broadly, generally, largely, reasonably, sufficiently** | **factually, historically, scientifically, statistically, technically** ◊ *Although this book is historically ~, it is not a history book.*
PREP. **to** ◊ *Results are ~ to within 0.2 seconds.*
PHRASES **full and ~** ◊ *He gave a full and ~ account of his movements.*

accusation *noun*

ADJ. **serious** | **baseless, false, unfounded, unsubstantiated** | **ridiculous, wild** | **bitter** | **mutual** ◊ *They sank into mutual ~ and recrimination.* | **public** | **veiled** ◊ *She made a lot of thinly veiled ~s.* | **renewed, repeated**
VERB + ACCUSATION **hurl, level at, make** ◊ *They have the nerve to level these ~s against one of our most respected members.* | **face** ◊ *Their father now faces an ~ of murder.* | **deny,**

dismiss, refute, reject | prove, substantiate, support ◇ *New evidence has emerged which supports the ~ against her.*
ACCUSATION + VERB **fly, fly around** ◇ *There seem to be a lot of wild ~s flying around.*
PREP. **amid ~s** ◇ *He fled the country amid ~s of fraud.* | **~ against** ◇ *You made a public ~ of misconduct against Saunders.* | **~ of** ◇ *He was forced to defend himself against ~s of plagiarism.*
PHRASES **bring an ~ against sb** ◇ *She rejected all the ~s brought against her.*

accuse *verb*

ADV. **falsely, unjustly, wrongfully, wrongly | angrily | openly, publicly** ◇ *They openly ~d her of dishonesty.* | **practically, virtually** ◇ *She practically ~d me of starting the fire!*
VERB + ACCUSE **cannot** ◇ *You couldn't ~ him of being selfish.*
PREP. **of** ◇ *No one could ever ~ this government of not caring about the poor.*
PHRASES **stand ~d of** ◇ *He stands ~d of murdering his wife and children.*

accustomed *adj.* **accustomed to sth**

VERBS **be | become, get, grow** ◇ *She had grown ~ to his long absences.*
ADV. **quite, well** ◇ *He was well ~ to hard work.*

ace *noun*

1 playing card
→ Note at CARD

2 winning first hit in tennis
VERB + ACE **serve** ◇ *Nadal has served 15 ~s in the match so far.*

3 person who is very good at sth
ADJ. **fighter, flying, goal** (*BrE*)**, soccer, tennis | staff** (*AmE*) ◇ *Staff ~ Robert Robson helped the team to its first win this season.*

ache *noun*

ADJ. **constant, deep** (*figurative*)**, dull, nagging, throbbing | familiar | muscular, stomach, tummy**
VERB + ACHE **be aware of, feel, have** ◇ *She kept feeling the nagging ~ in her heart.* ◇ *I felt the familiar ~ in my lower back.* | **ease** ◇ *He changed his position once again to ease the ~ in his back.*
ACHE + VERB **throb** ◇ *A dull ~ throbbed at the back of David's head.*
PREP. **~ in** ◇ *a nagging ~ in her knee* ◇ *She could hardly speak for the ~ in her heart.* | **~ inside | ~ of** ◇ *the ~ of loneliness inside him*
PHRASES **~s and pains** ◇ *He was always complaining about his various ~s and pains.*

ache *verb*

ADV. **badly, really, terribly** ◇ *My feet ~d badly.* | **a little, slightly, etc.** ◇ *My left foot ~d a little.*
PREP. **from** ◇ *I still really ~ from all that running yesterday.*
PHRASES **~ all over** ◇ *Her head felt hot and she was aching all over.*

achieve *verb*

VERB + ACHIEVE **fail to** ◇ *The present law has failed to ~ its objectives.* | **be able to | try to | be designed to | be difficult to, be easy to, be impossible to, be possible to**

achievement *noun*

1 thing done successfully
ADJ. **amazing, considerable** (*esp. BrE*)**, extraordinary, fine, great, important, impressive, major, monumental, no mean** (*esp. BrE*)**, notable, outstanding, real, remarkable, significant, tremendous** ◇ *It's a monumental ~ for such a young athlete.* ◇ *This was no mean ~ for the government.* |

rare | unique | positive | crowning, main, supreme ◇ *He regarded that victory as the crowning ~ of his career.* | **lasting | personal | math, mathematics, reading** (*all AmE*) ◇ *low reading ~ in children* | **artistic, athletic** (*esp. AmE*)**, cultural, economic, educational, engineering, literary, scientific, sporting** (*esp. BrE*)**, technical, technological** ◇ *Rutherford was knighted in recognition of his scientific ~s.*
VERB + ACHIEVEMENT **be, constitute, represent** ◇ *This conference in itself represents a solid ~.* | **celebrate, honour/ honor, recognize** ◇ *This award honours/honors the ~s of American women in medicine.*
PREP. **~ in** ◇ *She was given a prize for her ~s in textile design.*
PHRASES **quite an ~** ◇ *To be offered this job is quite an ~.*

2 act of achieving sth
ADJ. **high** ◇ *two years of consistently high ~* | **individual, personal | human** ◇ *The moon landing of 1969 was seen as a high point of human ~.* | **academic, educational, intellectual** ◇ *Winners are selected on the basis of high academic ~.* ◇ *Success should not be measured solely by educational ~.*
...OF ACHIEVEMENT **level, standard**
VERB + ACHIEVEMENT **measure** ◇ *standards by which to measure human ~*
ACHIEVEMENT + NOUN **gap** ◇ *the ~ gap between white and minority schoolchildren* | **award** ◇ *He won a lifetime ~ award for cinematography.* | **test** (*esp. AmE*) ◇ *amazing ~ test scores*
PHRASES **a feeling of ~, a sense of ~** ◇ *Climbing the mountain gave him a tremendous sense of ~.* | **a lack of ~ | a record of ~** ◇ *an impressive record of ~*

acid *noun*

1 chemical compound
ADJ. **concentrated, strong | dilute, weak | acetic, citric, folic, hydrochloric, lactic, nitric, sulphuric/sulfuric, etc.** ◇ *the increasingly painful build-up of lactic ~ in your muscles* | **amino, nucleic | fatty, trans-fatty** ◇ *fish that are rich in omega-3 fatty ~s* | **stomach**
VERB + ACID **produce | neutralize**
ACID + VERB **burn sth** ◇ *The ~ burned a hole in her coat.* | **break sth down** ◇ *Stomach ~s can break down the poison.*

2 illegal drug
VERB + ACID **drop** ◇ *They smoke joints and drop ~.*
PREP. **on ~** ◇ *He described the music as 'Brahms on acid'.*
→ Note at DRUG

acknowledge *verb*

ADV. **fully | freely, readily | grudgingly, reluctantly | clearly, explicitly | implicitly, tacitly** ◇ *The peace settlement effectively ~d the country's independence.* | **formally, officially | openly, publicly** ◇ *He ~d publicly that he might have made a mistake.* | **privately | gratefully | barely | duly** ◇ *The company duly ~d receipt of the letter.* | **hereby** ◇ *I hereby ~ receipt of your letter of July 25.*
VERB + ACKNOWLEDGE **fail to, refuse to | be forced to** ◇ *Mental illness can exist for years before families are forced to ~ the truth.*
PHRASES **be generally ~d, be universally ~d, be widely ~d** ◇ *a truth that is universally ~d*

acknowledgement *noun*

ADJ. **brief | explicit | tacit | open, public | formal, official**
VERB + ACKNOWLEDGEMENT **amount to, be** ◇ *This amounted to an ~ that she had been wrong.* | **get, receive** ◇ *I wrote to them but never got any ~.* | **grunt, nod, wave** ◇ *She merely nodded ~ of his statement.*
PREP. **in ~ (of)** ◇ *He raised his hand to her in ~.* | **~ from** ◇ *She is still waiting for some ~ from her fellow academics.*

acne *noun*

ADJ. **bad, severe, terrible**
VERB + ACNE **have, suffer from** ◇ *He had terrible ~ when he was younger.* | **develop, get** ◇ *A lot of teenagers develop ~.* | **cause | cure, treat** ◇ *Doctors can treat ~ with creams.*
ACNE + VERB **clear, clear up** ◇ *Acne often clears up by itself.*

acquaintance *noun*

1 person you know

ADJ. **casual** ◇ *I ran into a casual ~ in town.* | **new** | **close, old** | **business, childhood, mutual, personal, social**
VERB + ACQUAINTANCE **bump into** (*esp. BrE*), **meet, run into** | **greet** ◇ *He greeted all his old ~s.*
PHRASES **friends and ~s**

2 knowledge of sb/sth

ADJ. **nodding, passing, slight** ◇ *a man with whom I had a passing ~* | **brief, short** | **close, intimate** | **chance**
VERB + ACQUAINTANCE **make sb's/sth's** (= become acquainted with sb/sth) ◇ *I first made his ~ in 2006.* | **strike up** ◇ *I first met Simon in 1998 and struck up an ~ with him.* | **renew**
PREP. **of sb's ~** (*formal*) ◇ *He introduced me to a reporter of his ~.* | **~ with** ◇ *her ~ with modern philosophy*
PHRASES **have an ~ with** ◇ *They have little ~ with colloquial English.* | **on close ~, on closer ~** | **on first ~** ◇ *On first ~ she seemed a little odd.*

acquainted *adj.* familiar with sth

VERBS **be** | **become, get** ◇ *I would like to get ~ with her.*
ADV. **fully, intimately, well** | **personally** ◇ *I am not personally ~ with her.*
PREP. **with** ◇ *Are you fully ~ with the facts?*

acquisition *noun*

1 thing you have obtained

ADJ. **latest, new, recent**

2 act of obtaining sth

ADJ. **data, language, property** ◇ *Language ~ begins in the first months of a baby's life.*
VERB + ACQUISITION **make**

3 company bought by another company; act of buying a company

ADJ. **big, major, substantial** | **small** | **strategic** | **possible, proposed**
VERB + ACQUISITION **complete, make** ◇ *The company has just made another ~.*

acquittal *noun*

VERB + ACQUITTAL **return** (*BrE*), **vote for** (*AmE*) ◇ *The jury returned an ~ after only 22 minutes.* | *She claimed she had been intimidated into voting for ~.* | **direct** (*BrE*), **order** ◇ *The trial judge ordered an ~.* | **obtain, secure** (*esp. BrE*), **win** (*AmE*) | **lead to, result in** ◇ *The trial resulted in an ~.* | **uphold** ◇ *The judge upheld their ~.*

acre *noun* → Note at MEASURE

act *noun*

1 thing that sb does

ADJ. **charitable, kind** | **heroic, selfless** ◇ *a heroic ~ of bravery* | **aggressive, barbaric, hostile, provocative, terrorist, violent** ◇ *He was arrested on suspicion of planning terrorist ~s.* | **appalling** (*esp. BrE*), **cowardly, despicable, heinous, horrific, immoral, outrageous, terrible, unspeakable** ◇ *horrific ~s of violence* | **criminal, delinquent** (*esp. AmE*), **illegal, unlawful, wrongful** | **careless** (*esp. BrE*), **foolish, impulsive** | **conscious, deliberate, intentional, positive, voluntary, wilful/willful** ◇ *The company says that the explosion was no accident but a deliberate ~ of sabotage.* | **private, public** ◇ *a private ~ of revenge* | **creative, dramatic, physical, political, symbolic** | **homosexual, sex, sexual** | **random** ◇ *random ~s of violence*
VERB + ACT **carry out, commit** (*law*), **perform, perpetrate** ◇ *images of African Americans performing heroic ~s* | **condemn** | **condone, justify** | **prevent** | **witness**
PREP. **in the ~ of** (= while doing something) | **~ of** ◇ *For Jane, the ~ of writing was always difficult.*
PHRASES **an ~ of faith, an ~ of love, an ~ of violence, an ~ of will, an ~ of worship** | **a hard ~ to follow, a tough ~ to follow** ◇ *Their contribution will prove a hard ~ to follow.* | **catch sb in the ~ (of doing sth)** ◇ *He was caught in the ~ of*

stealing. | **the simple ~ of doing sth, the very ~ of doing sth** ◇ *The very ~ of writing out your plan clarifies what you need to do.*

2 law made by a government

VERB + ACT **bring in** (*BrE*), **introduce, pass** ◇ *The Act was passed by a majority of 175 votes to 143.* | **amend** | **repeal** ◇ *The old ~ has now been repealed.* | **breach** (*esp. BrE*), **contravene** (*BrE*), **violate** (*esp. AmE*) ◇ *The company had violated the Data Security Act of 2006.*
ACT + VERB **become law, come into force** (*BrE*) ◇ *The new Children's Act will become law next year.* | **contain sth, say sth, state sth** ◇ *The ~ contains regulations for financial institutions.* | **apply to sth** ◇ *The 1995 ~ applies only to food and not to dietary supplements.* | **require sth** | **prohibit sth**
PREP. **under an/the ~** ◇ *He was charged under the Firearms Act.*

3 entertainment; entertainers

ADJ. **class** (*informal*) (used for sb who does sth well) ◇ *Their new player looks a class ~.* | **solo** | **double** ◇ *comedy double ~ French and Saunders* | **live** ◇ *their reputation as one of rock's most impressive live ~s* | **main, support** ◇ *The main ~ will come on at about ten o'clock.* | **opening** | **cabaret, circus, comedy, dance, drag, music, musical, novelty, stage, stand-up, variety** ◇ *The club offers live music and cabaret ~s.* ◇ *The group is merely a novelty ~ (= an act that is only interesting because it is strange or unusual).* | **hip-hop, pop, rock, etc.** | **balancing, disappearing, juggling, vanishing** (*all figurative*) ◇ *The cat had done a disappearing ~.* ◇ *The UN must perform a difficult balancing ~ between the two sides in the conflict.*
VERB + ACT **do, perform** ◇ *He does a little novelty ~.* | **rehearse, work on** ◇ *I have to work on my ~.*

4 division of a play

ADJ. **opening** | **final, last** | **first, second, etc.**
PREP. **in (the) ~** ◇ *The king is killed in the opening ~.*

5 insincere actions

VERB + ACT **put on** ◇ *Don't take any notice—she's just putting on an ~!*

act *verb*

1 do sth/behave

ADV. **at once, immediately, promptly, quickly, swiftly** ◇ *The government must ~ promptly to change this law.* | **appropriately, correctly, legally, properly** | **dishonestly, illegally, improperly, inappropriately, unconstitutionally, unlawfully, wrongly** ◇ *The country's highest court ruled that police had ~ed unlawfully.* | **rationally, reasonably, responsibly, sensibly** (*esp. BrE*), **wisely** ◇ *All citizens have a duty to ~ responsibly and show respect to others.* | **irrationally, irresponsibly, rashly, unreasonably** | **oddly, strangely, suspiciously** ◇ *Jenny has been ~ing rather strangely recently.* | **bravely, heroically** | **decisively** ◇ *The government was criticized for failing to ~ decisively.* | **aggressively, independently, unilaterally** | **effectively** | **in self-defence/self-defense** ◇ *The jury accepted that he had ~ed in self-defence/self-defense.* | **accordingly** ◇ *George knew about the letter and ~ed accordingly.*
PREP. **against** ◇ *The government needs to ~ against the sale of these dangerous toys.* | **for sb, on behalf of sb** ◇ *His lawyers are continuing to ~ for him.* | **like** ◇ *Stop ~ing like a spoiled child.* ◇ *hormones in the brain that ~ like natural painkillers* | **on** ◇ *Alcohol ~s quickly on the brain.* | **out of** ◇ *I suspected that he was ~ing out of malice.*
PHRASES **~ as if** ◇ *She was ~ing as if she owned the place.* | **~ in sb's best interests** ◇ *We are all ~ing in the best interests of the children.* | **~ in good faith** ◇ *His excuse was that he had ~ed in good faith.*

2 perform in a play, film/movie, etc.

ADV. **brilliantly, well** ◇ *The play is well ~ed.* | **badly, poorly**

acting noun

ADJ. **brilliant, excellent, good, superb | bad, poor, wooden** ◇ *The movie is spoiled by some very wooden ~.* | **voice** ◇ *The game's voice ~ is excellent.* | **method**
VERB + ACTING **do** ◇ *I did a lot of ~ when I was in college.*
ACTING + NOUN **career, profession | class**

action noun

1 process of doing sth

ADJ. **decisive, effective, firm, strong, vigorous** ◇ *He urged the government to take decisive ~ against music piracy.* | **aggressive, violent | immediate, prompt, swift, urgent | appropriate** ◇ *Unless appropriate ~ is taken, our sales will decline.* | **drastic, emergency** ◇ *The situation calls for drastic ~.* | **collective, concerted, joint, united** (*esp. BrE*) | **direct, positive, unilateral | corrective, evasive, remedial | pre-emptive, preventative, preventive | disciplinary, legal, military, strike** ◇ *Disciplinary ~ will be taken against students who cheat.* (see also *industrial action*) | **congressional** (*esp. AmE*), **government, governmental, legislative, political, state** (*esp. AmE*) | **affirmative** (*esp. AmE*) ◇ *Affirmative ~ was most successful in creating opportunities for college-educated women.*
VERB + ACTION **take** ◇ *We'll take whatever ~ is necessary.* | **call for | agree on** ◇ *The leaders have agreed on joint ~ to combat terrorism.* | **leap into, spring into, swing into** ◇ *The emergency services swung into ~ as soon as the disaster was reported.* | **carry out, perform** ◇ *Only the priest can perform these ~s.* | **galvanize sb into, prod sb into, spur sb into** ◇ *We have to galvanize people into ~.* | **bring sth into, put sth into** ◇ *We need to put these ideas into ~.* | **keep sb/sth out of, put sb/sth out of** ◇ *A fire has put the factory out of ~.*
PREP. **in** ~ ◇ *I have not yet seen the machines in ~.* | **out of ~** ◇ *He is out of ~ following an ankle injury.* | **~ against** ◇ *~ against drug dealers* | **~ on** ◇ *The government is taking strong ~ on refugees.*
PHRASES **~s speak louder than words** (*saying*) | **a course of ~** ◇ *Is this the best course of ~ to follow?*

2 legal case

ADJ. **court | civil, criminal, libel, tort | class** (*AmE*)
VERB + ACTION **bring, file, initiate, take** ◇ *I considered taking legal ~.* ◇ *They took out a libel ~ against the newspaper's owners.* ◇ *Her husband brought a civil ~ against her after their divorce.*
PREP. **~ against**

3 fighting

ADJ. **combat** (*esp. AmE*), **enemy** ◇ *He was killed during enemy ~.* | **terrorist | covert** ◇ *paramilitary covert ~ teams working overseas*
VERB + ACTION **see** ◇ *I never saw ~ during the war.*
PHRASES **killed in ~, missing in ~, wounded in ~** ◇ *He was reported missing in ~.*

active adj.

VERBS **be | become | keep (sb), remain, stay** ◇ *Try to keep ~ in the cold weather.*
ADV. **extremely, fairly, very, etc. | highly** ◇ *a highly ~ volcano* | **increasingly | mentally, physically** ◇ *It's important to remain mentally ~ after retirement.* | **sexually** ◇ *By the age of 18, 65% of teenagers report being sexually ~.* | **economically, politically** ◇ *When did you first become politically ~?*
PREP. **against** ◇ *drugs that are ~ against cancers* | **in** ◇ *She has been ~ in local politics for some years.*

activity noun

ADJ. **frantic, frenetic, heightened, increased, intense** ◇ *The scene was one of frenetic ~.* | **criminal, illegal, subversive, suspicious, terrorist** ◇ *His income was derived from criminal ~.* | **class** (*esp. AmE*), **classroom, group | after-school, extra-curricular, leisure, leisure-time, outdoor, recreational, social** ◇ *Shopping is now a leisure ~.* | **mental,**

physical, sexual ◇ *They had engaged in sexual ~ in the past three months.* | **aerobic, strenuous | business, commercial, cultural, economic, industrial, intellectual, political, scientific | government, military, police, union | human | electrical, seismic, volcanic** ◇ *The islands were formed by volcanic ~.*
...OF ACTIVITY **burst, flurry** ◇ *There was a flurry of ~ as the movie star appeared on the balcony.* | **level** ◇ *Newspapers report a higher level of ~ in the foreign-exchange markets.*
VERB + ACTIVITY **conduct, do, perform** ◇ *Here's an ~ you can do with mixed-ability classes.* | **be involved in, engage in, participate in, take part in, undertake** ◇ *We suspect he may be involved in illegal activities.* ◇ *Teachers here are not allowed to engage in any political ~.* | **stop, suspend, terminate** ◇ *The party's activities have been suspended.* | **stimulate** ◇ *It will only be possible to stimulate business ~ with an injection of public funds.* | **curb, inhibit | coordinate, regulate | measure, monitor | resume | bustle with, buzz with** ◇ *The room was buzzing with ~.*
PHRASES **a hive of ~** (= a very busy place) ◇ *The classroom was a hive of ~ as the children prepared for the concert.* | **a sign of ~** ◇ *Police watched the house all day, but there was no sign of ~.*

actor, actress noun

ADJ. **accomplished, brilliant, consummate, experienced, fine, good, great, talented, wonderful** ◇ *He's a brilliant actor!* ◇ *I just signed a talented young actor.* | **celebrated, famous, leading, principal, star, veteran, well-known | successful | Oscar-winning** ◇ *Marlon Brando, the two-times Oscar-winning actor* | **A-list, B-list, etc. | main | bit-part, struggling, unknown | amateur, non-professional | professional | serious, trained | aspiring, wannabe, would-be** ◇ *The college is offering aspiring actors the opportunity to work with a professional cast.* | **out-of-work, unemployed** (*esp. BrE*) | **character, classical, comedy** (*esp. BrE*), **comic, dramatic, Shakespearean, straight** ◇ *Olivier was hailed as the leading classical actor of his generation.* | **film** (*esp. BrE*), **Hollywood, movie** (*esp. AmE*), **screen | television, TV | stage, theatre/theater | child | supporting** ◇ *the award for best supporting actor*
VERB + ACTOR/ACTRESS **hire | audition, cast**
ACTOR/ACTRESS + VERB **act (sth), perform (sth), play (sb/sth), portray sb/sth** ◇ *The same actor plays three different parts in the movie.* | **rehearse (sth) | audition** ◇ *He was one of many actors who auditioned for the part of Hamlet.*
→ Note at JOB

acumen noun

ADJ. **considerable, great | business, commercial** (*BrE*), **financial, legal, political, technical**
VERB + ACUMEN **demonstrate, show** ◇ *He had demonstrated considerable business ~.* | **have, possess** ◇ *She has great financial ~.* | **lack**

ad noun (informal)

ADJ. **display, full-page | classified, small** (*BrE*), **want** (*AmE*) ◇ *They put classified ~s in local papers.* | **magazine, newspaper, print, radio, television, TV | banner, button, online, pop-up | campaign** (*esp. AmE*) | **cereal, detergent, job, etc.**
VERB + AD **place, put, take out** ◇ *She took out a full-page ~ in a women's magazine.* | **air, publish, run, show | post | pull | answer, reply to, respond to**
AD + VERB **appear** ◇ *The ~ appeared on all major channels.* | **say sth, show sth | feature sb/sth**
AD + NOUN **campaign | agency | exec, executive | revenue**
PREP. **in an/the ~** ◇ *A lot of claims are made in the ~.* | **~ for** ◇ *TV ~s for cars*

adapt verb

1 change your way of behaving

ADV. **successfully, well** ◇ *The children have ~ed well to the heat.* | **quickly | easily, readily** ◇ *The company can easily ~ to changing demand.* | **accordingly** ◇ *We need to assess the new situation and ~ accordingly.*

VERB + ADAPT **be able to, can | be unable to, cannot | have to, must | need to | learn to**
PREP. **to**
PHRASES **the ability to ~** ◇ *Some animals have a remarkable ability to ~ to changing environments.* | **find it difficult to ~, find it hard to ~** ◇ *A lot of companies have found it hard to ~ to the new system.*

2 change a thing

PREP. **for** ◇ *to ~ a book for television* | **from** ◇ *The radio play had been ~ed from a novel.*
PHRASES **specially ~ed** ◇ *The classroom has been specially ~ed to take wheelchairs.*

adaptable *adj.*

VERBS **be, prove | make sb/sth**
ADV. **extremely, fairly, very, etc. | highly** ◇ *The company provides highly ~ business systems.* | **easily, readily | endlessly, infinitely**
PREP. **to** ◇ *The vehicles are large and not easily ~ to new uses.*

adaptation *noun*

1 a change/the process of changing

ADJ. **successful | special | evolutionary**
VERB + ADAPTATION **make** ◇ *plans for making ~s to your home*
ADAPTATION + VERB **occur** ◇ *Adaptations in plants occur over thousands of years.*
PREP. **~ for** ◇ *The Antarctic species have few special ~s for polar life.* | **~ of** ◇ *the ~ of buildings for military purposes* | **~ to** ◇ *~ to the workplace*
PHRASES **a process of ~** ◇ *The process of ~ to a new school is difficult for some children.*

2 for cinema/movies, TV, etc.

ADJ. **cinematic, film** (*esp. BrE*), **movie** (*esp. AmE*), **screen, stage, television, TV** ◇ *He specializes in screen ~s of classic novels.* | **comic, musical | faithful**
VERB + ADAPTATION **develop | direct, film, make, produce, shoot, stage**
PREP. **~ of** ◇ *a screen ~ of 'The Lord of the Rings'*

add *verb*

ADV. **hastily, hurriedly, quickly | softly** ◇ *He ~ed softly, 'I missed you.'* | **thoughtfully | bitterly, pointedly**
VERB + ADD **hasten to** ◇ *I hasten to ~ that I knew nothing of the fraud at the time.*

addict *noun*

ADJ. **cocaine, drug, heroin, etc. | computer, television, etc.** ◇ *Many young boys become computer ~s.*

addicted *adj.*

VERBS **be | become, get**
ADV. **totally | hopelessly**
PREP. **to** ◇ *She had become ~ to painkillers.*

addiction *noun*

ADJ. **alcohol, cocaine, drug, etc.**
VERB + ADDICTION **become, turn into** ◇ *A habit can easily become an ~.* | **have | cause, lead to | feed** ◇ *He stole money from his parents to feed his ~.* | **treat | beat, cure, overcome** ◇ *He was struggling to beat his heroin ~.*
PREP. **~ to** ◇ *She had an ~ to heroin.*

addictive *adj.*

VERBS **be | become**
ADV. **extremely, highly, very** ◇ *Cocaine is a highly ~ drug.*

addition *noun*

1 sth that is added; process of adding sth

ADJ. **useful, valuable, welcome, worthy | important, major, notable, significant | latest, new, recent**
VERB + ADDITION **make** ◇ *We have made several ~s to the collection recently.*

PREP. **in ~** ◇ *There is, in ~, one further point to make.* | **~ to** ◇ *the latest ~ to the family* (= a new baby)

2 process of adding numbers/amounts

ADJ. **simple** ◇ *He worked it out through simple ~.*
VERB + ADDITION **do** ◇ *She can do ~, but she hasn't learned subtraction yet.*

3 (*AmE*) **part added to a building** → See also EXTENSION

ADJ. **building, room | two-story, three-story, etc. | 490-square-foot, 2 000-square-foot, etc.**
VERB + ADDITION **build | design** ◇ *a 22 000-square-foot ~ designed by a Japanese architect*
PREP. **~ to** ◇ *a family-room ~ to his home*

address *noun*

1 where you live/work

ADJ. **home, private | business | contact** ◇ *Please leave a contact ~.* | **forwarding, return** ◇ *There was no return ~ on the back of the envelope.* | **mailing, postal** (*esp. BrE*), **snail-mail | billing | full** ◇ *Please write your full postal ~.* | **false, wrong** ◇ *He gave a false ~ to the police.* | **correct, right | useful | secret**
VERB + ADDRESS **give, leave, write**
ADDRESS + NOUN **book**
PREP. **at a/the ~** ◇ *I'm afraid there's nobody called Williams at this ~.*
PHRASES **a change of ~** ◇ *Please inform us of any change of ~.* | **name and ~ | no fixed ~** ◇ *a man of no fixed ~*

2 in computing

ADJ. **email** ◇ *What's your email ~?* | **Internet, Web, website**

3 speech

ADJ. **short | commencement** (*AmE*), **farewell** (*esp. AmE*), **inaugural, keynote, opening | welcoming | public** ◇ *a public ~ system* | **radio, televised, television | election | presidential**
VERB + ADDRESS **deliver, give** ◇ *The Secretary General delivered the keynote ~ at the conference.*
PREP. **in a/the ~** ◇ *He gave details of the policy in an ~ to party members.* | **~ by** ◇ *an ~ by the Dean of the University* | **~ to** ◇ *a radio ~ to the nation*

address *verb*

1 write name and address

ADV. **correctly, properly** (*BrE*) | **personally** ◇ *The president did not reply to my letter although I ~ed it to him personally.*
PREP. **to**

2 say sth to sb

ADV. **by name, directly** ◇ *She did not ~ him by name.* ◇ *He never ~ed her directly.*
PREP. **to** ◇ *He ~ed his comments to the chairman.*

3 deal with problem

ADV. **directly, explicitly, specifically | fully | adequately** ◇ *These concerns were not adequately ~ed in the report.* | **successfully**
VERB + ADDRESS **seek to** ◇ *the problems we are seeking to ~* | **fail to**
PHRASES **~ yourself to sth** ◇ *The authors of the book ~ themselves to the question of unemployment.*

adept *adj.*

VERBS **be, seem | become**
ADV. **extremely, fairly, very | highly | equally** ◇ *She is equally ~ in the pop and classical fields.* | **especially, particularly | technically, technologically**
PREP. **at** ◇ *He was highly ~ at avoiding trouble.*

adequate *adj.*

VERBS **be, prove, seem | remain | consider sth, think sth** ◇ *These measures are not considered ~ by conservationists.*
ADV. **really, very | perfectly, quite, totally | more than** ◇

The system is more than ~ to deal with any problems. | **barely, hardly, less than, not entirely, not wholly** ◇ *The financial assistance given to students is less than ~.* | **merely | more or less** ◇ *The amount of money we have been given is more or less ~.* | **no longer**
PREP. **for** ◇ *The old software is still perfectly ~ for most tasks.*

adhere *verb*

ADV. **properly** (*BrE*), **well** ◇ *The tiles may not ~ well if you do not use the correct glue.*
PREP. **to** ◇ *The glue would not ~ to the metal surface.*
PHR V **adhere to**
ADV. **closely, firmly, rigidly, rigorously, scrupulously, strictly** ◇ *This principle must be strictly ~d to.* | **fully, properly** (*esp. BrE*) ◇ *The guidelines were not always fully ~d to.*

adherence *noun*

ADJ. **blind, close, faithful, firm, rigid, slavish, strict**
PREP. **~ to** ◇ *strict ~ to a diet*

adjacent *adj.*

VERBS **be, be situated, lie, stand** ◇ *The vineyards of Verzy lie ~ to those of Verzenay.*
ADV. **directly, immediately** ◇ *There is a row of houses immediately ~ to the factory.*
PREP. **to** ◇ *The miller's house stands ~ to the mill.*

adjective *noun*

ADJ. **attributive, predicative** ◇ *Attributive ~s precede the noun.* | **comparative, superlative | gradable, non-gradable | possessive** ◇ *'My' is a possessive ~.*
VERB + ADJECTIVE **apply** ◇ *'Enterprising' is not an ~ you would apply to him!*
ADJECTIVE + VERB **describe** ◇ *~s describing texture* | **modify, qualify** ◇ *Adjectives qualify nouns.* | **follow** ◇ *Predicative ~s follow the noun.* | **precede**

adjourn *verb*

ADV. **indefinitely, sine die** (*law*) ◇ *The trial was ~ed indefinitely.*
PREP. **for** ◇ *The case was ~ed for a week.* | **pending** ◇ *The inquest was ~ed pending further investigations.* | **to** ◇ *Shall we ~ to your office?*

adjust *verb*

1 change sth slightly
ADV. **slightly | finely** ◇ *It is important to have equipment that can be finely ~ed.* | **automatically | carefully | accordingly** ◇ *Children are sensitive to family attitudes and ~ their attitudes accordingly.* | **downwards/downward, upwards/upward** ◇ *This estimate may have to be ~ed downwards/downward.*
PREP. **for** ◇ *Salaries are ~ed for inflation.*
2 get used to new situation
ADV. **quickly, rapidly | gradually, slowly**
VERB + ADJUST **be difficult to, be hard to | need time to, take time to** ◇ *It may take a little time to ~ to the climate here.* | **try to**
PREP. **to** ◇ *She will gradually ~ to her new role.*

adjustable *adj.*

VERBS **be**
ADV. **fully** ◇ *The straps are fully ~ to fit any size.*

adjustment *noun*

1 small change made
ADJ. **delicate, fine, minor, slight, small | important, major, significant | appropriate, necessary | automatic | financial**
VERB + ADJUSTMENT **make** ◇ *The mechanic made the necessary*

~s to the engine. | **need, require** ◇ *The dosage may need ~ to suit the individual.*
PREP. **~ for** ◇ *a cut of 1.5% in real terms (after ~ for inflation)* | **~ in** ◇ *~s in the exchange rates* | **~ to** ◇ *a few minor ~s to the schedule*
2 process of changing
ADJ. **successful | emotional, personal, social**
PREP. **~ to** ◇ *The company's ~ to the new markets has been successful.*
PHRASES **a period of ~** ◇ *There was a long period of ~ under the new boss.* | **the process of ~** ◇ *The process of ~ to life in another country can be very difficult.*

administer *verb*

ADV. **effectively, efficiently | centrally, locally** ◇ *The legislation was to be centrally ~ed by the Board of Education.* | **jointly**
VERB + ADMINISTER **be difficult to, be easy to, be simple to | be cheap to, be expensive to**

administration *noun*

1 organizing how sth is done
ADJ. **effective, efficient, good | poor** ◇ *The college loses a lot of money through poor ~.* | **day-to-day, routine | general | office | bureaucratic | central | arts, business, educational, financial, justice, social | government, public**
VERB + ADMINISTRATION **be in charge of, be responsible for**
ADMINISTRATION + NOUN **costs**
2 people who manage an organization
ADJ. **college, hospital, prison, etc.**
3 government
ADJ. **colonial, federal, local, municipal, provincial, regional, state** ◇ *the handover of sovereignty by the British colonial ~* | **civil, imperial, royal | Conservative, Labour, etc. | Democratic, Republican, etc. | Bush, Clinton, etc. | caretaker, interim, temporary** ◇ *the role of the UN in the setting-up of an interim ~* | **coalition, joint | minority | civilian, military**
VERB + ADMINISTRATION **form** ◇ *On September 27 a new coalition ~ was formed.*
4 giving a drug
ADJ. **intravenous, oral | drug**

admirable *adj.*

VERBS **be | find sb/sth**
ADV. **very | wholly** ◇ *She had acted in ways that he found wholly ~.* | **truly**

admiral *noun*

ADJ. **rear, vice**
PHRASES **Admiral of the Fleet** (*BrE*), **Fleet Admiral** (*AmE*) → Note at RANK

admiration *noun*

ADJ. **deep, genuine, great, sincere, tremendous | frank, open | sneaking** (*BrE*) ◇ *Inwardly, I had a sneaking ~ for them.* | **grudging, reluctant | mutual**
VERB + ADMIRATION **be filled with, be full of, feel, have** ◇ *I'm full of ~ for him.* ◇ *I have the greatest ~ for the nurses.* | **express, show** ◇ *She wrote to him expressing her ~.* | **compel, draw, fill sb with, gain, win** ◇ *a dignity that compels ~* ◇ *The way he dealt with the crisis filled me with ~.* ◇ *He gained the ~ of thousands of people.* | **be worthy of** ◇ *As a writer she is certainly worthy of ~.* | **lose** ◇ *He never lost the ~ of his students.*
PREP. **in ~** ◇ *She stared at him in open ~.* | **with ~** ◇ *He gazed at her with ~.* | **~ for** ◇ *~ for his work*
PHRASES **a gasp of ~** (*esp. BrE*) ◇ *The picture was greeted with gasps of ~.* | **have nothing but ~ for sb/sth** ◇ *I have nothing but ~ for the way she tackled those bullies.*

admire *verb*

1 have high opinion of sb/sth

ADV. **deeply, enormously, greatly, hugely, particularly, really** ◇ *He ~s you enormously.* | **rather** | **clearly, openly** | **secretly** ◇ *She secretly ~d and envied him.*
VERB + ADMIRE **have to** ◇ *You have to ~ their dedication and commitment.*
PREP. **about** ◇ *What do you most ~ about her?* | **for** ◇ *I rather ~ him for his determination.*
PHRASES **be generally ~d, be widely ~d** ◇ *He is widely ~d as a journalist.* | **can't help admiring, can't help but ~** ◇ *I couldn't help but ~ his determination.* | **you can only ~ sb/sth** ◇ *You can only ~ her courage and determination.*

2 look at sth attractive

VERB + ADMIRE **pause to, stop to** | **stand back to, step back to** ◇ *He stood back to ~ his handiwork.*

admirer *noun*

ADJ. **ardent, devoted, fervent, great, keen** (*esp. BrE*) | **secret** ◇ *Perhaps the flowers were sent by a secret ~!*
... OF ADMIRERS **band, circle, host** ◇ *She was always surrounded by a circle of ~s.*
VERB + ADMIRER **have** | **gain, win** ◇ *She soon gained ~s in England and France.*
PHRASES **friends and ~s** ◇ *The funeral was attended by the singer's friends and ~s.*

admission *noun*

1 entrance

ADJ. **free, half-price** | **emergency** ◇ *emergency ~s to hospital* | **cinema** (*BrE*), **theatre/theater** | **accident and emergency** (abbreviated to **A & E**) (*BrE*), **emergency-room** (abbreviated to **ER**) (*AmE*), **hospital** ◇ *70% of hospital ~s are associated with alcohol.* | **college, law-school, school, university** | **graduate, undergraduate** (*both esp. AmE*) | **open, selective** (*both esp. AmE*)
VERB + ADMISSION **apply for, seek** ◇ *He's applied for ~ to the local college.* | **gain** ◇ *to gain ~ to one of the best schools* | **grant sb** | **refuse sb**
ADMISSION + NOUN **charge, fee, price** | **criteria, policy** | **procedure** | **rate** ◇ *hospital ~ rates* | **~s department, ~s office** | **~s director, ~s officer** | **process** | **~s requirements** (*esp. AmE*)
PREP. **on ~** ◇ *On ~ to hospital you will be examined by a doctor.* | **~ to**

2 statement admitting sth

ADJ. **clear, frank, full** ◇ *This is a clear ~ that you were wrong.* | **tacit** | **grudging**
VERB + ADMISSION **make**
PREP. **~ of** ◇ *She has made no ~ of any involvement in the plot.*
PHRASES **an ~ of defeat, an ~ of failure, an ~ of guilt, an ~ of liability** ◇ *She saw his leaving the company as an ~ of failure.* | **by sb's own ~** ◇ *By his own ~ he should never have driven so fast.*

admit *verb*

ADV. **freely, readily** ◇ *He freely admitted that he had taken bribes.* | **frankly, honestly** | **openly** | **privately** ◇ *Some ~ privately that unemployment could continue to rise.* | **grudgingly, reluctantly** ◇ *In the end he'd done a good job, Carol admitted grudgingly.*
VERB + ADMIT **be forced to, have to, must** ◇ *I must ~ that the results were disappointing.* | **refuse to** | **be honest enough to, be prepared to, be the first to, be willing to, dare (to), have the courage to** ◇ *He was honest enough to ~ his mistake in the end.* ◇ *She would be the first to ~ that she is very difficult to work with.* ◇ *She dared not ~ her fear.* | **be ashamed to, be embarrassed to, be loath to, be reluctant to, be unwilling to, hate to, not care to** ◇ *I hate to ~ it, but I think he is right.* ◇ *He had caused her more pain than she cared to ~.*
PREP. **to** ◇ *He admitted to feeling a little tired.*
PHRASES **I don't mind admitting** ◇ *I was scared and I don't mind admitting it.*

admittance *noun*

VERB + ADMITTANCE **gain** ◇ *They were unable to gain ~ to the hall.* | **allow sb** | **deny sb, refuse sb**
PREP. **~ to** ◇ *The ticket will allow you ~ to the concert.*

adolescence *noun*

ADJ. **early, late**
VERB + ADOLESCENCE **reach**
PREP. **during ~, in ~** ◇ *She developed the problem in early ~.*

adolescent *noun*

ADJ. **young** | **pimply** (*AmE*), **spotty** (*BrE*) | **awkward** | **disturbed, troubled**

adopt *verb*

1 child

ADV. **legally** ◇ *The child has now been legally ~ed.*
PHRASES **have sb ~ed** ◇ *She was forced to have her baby ~ed.*

2 take and use sth

ADV. **formally, officially** ◇ *The policy has not yet been formally ~ed.*
VERB + ADOPT **tend to** | **decide to** | **be forced to**

adoption *noun*

1 of child

VERB + ADOPTION **offer sb for, place sb for, put sb up for** ◇ *She has decided to put the child up for ~.* | **be available for** ◇ *When will the child be available for ~?*
ADOPTION + VERB **go through** ◇ *They were so happy when the ~ went through successfully.*
ADOPTION + NOUN **agency**

2 taking/using sth

ADJ. **general, widespread** | **formal** ◇ *The widespread ~ of new information technology could save $162 billion a year.* ◇ *The party announced the formal ~ of George Smith as their election candidate.* (*BrE*)
VERB + ADOPTION **recommend, urge** ◇ *The committee recommended the ~ of new safety procedures.*

adore *verb*

ADV. **absolutely, simply** ◇ *She absolutely ~s her grandchildren.* | **clearly, obviously**

adrenalin *noun*

ADJ. **pure**
... OF ADRENALIN **burst, flow, rush, surge** ◇ *He felt a surge of pure ~ as he won the race.*
VERB + ADRENALIN **feel**
ADRENALIN + VERB **course, flow, pump, surge** ◇ *The ~ was coursing through his system.*
ADRENALIN + NOUN **rush**
PHRASES **get the ~ flowing, get the ~ going** ◇ *We'll start with some dancing to get the ~ going.*

adrift *adj.*

VERBS **be** | **come** ◇ *I nearly suffocated when the pipe of my breathing apparatus came ~.* | **go** (*figurative*) ◇ *Our plans had gone badly ~.* | **cast sb/sth, cut sb/sth, set sb/sth** ◇ *Their boat had been set ~.*
PREP. **from** ◇ *He had been cut ~ from everything he knew.* (*figurative*) | **in** ◇ *She felt cast ~ in a vulgar, materialistic society.* (*figurative*) | **of** (*BrE*) ◇ *The team are now just six points ~ of the leaders* (= behind their score).

adult *noun*

ADJ. **young** ◇ *This book will definitely appeal to teenagers and young ~s.* | **single** ◇ *The number of single-adult households has doubled in the past 30 years.* | **consenting** ◇ *What consenting ~s do in private is their own business.* |

responsible ◇ *I simply can't believe that responsible ~s allowed a child to wander the streets.*
ADULT + NOUN **education, literacy** | **population**

adultery noun

VERB + ADULTERY **be guilty of, commit** | **accuse sb of** | **admit**
PREP. **~ with** ◇ *He admitted ~ with several women.*

adulthood noun

ADJ. **early, young**
VERB + ADULTHOOD **attain, reach** ◇ *children who lose their parents before reaching ~* | **make it to, survive into, survive to**
PREP. **during ~, in ~** ◇ *His problems began in early ~.* | **into ~** ◇ *Her childhood problems persisted into ~.* | **towards/toward ~** ◇ *a step towards/toward ~*

advance noun

1 forward movement

ADJ. **rapid** | **Allied, British, German, etc.**
VERB + ADVANCE **make** ◇ *The regiment made an ~ on the enemy lines.* | **order** ◇ *The general ordered an ~ to the front line.* | **halt, resist, stop**
PREP. **~ on** ◇ *the ~ on Madrid* | **~ to, ~ towards/toward** ◇ *the Russian ~ towards/toward Berlin*

2 development

ADJ. **big, considerable, dramatic, enormous, great, spectacular, substantial, tremendous** ◇ *Hindu science made great ~s in astronomy and mathematics.* | **important, major, notable, remarkable, significant** ◇ *Recent years have seen significant ~s in our understanding of the human genome.* | **rapid, steady** ◇ *rapid ~s in science and technology* | **recent** | **economic, educational, medical, political, scientific, social, technical, technological** ◇ *The design incorporates the most recent technological ~s.* | **theoretical**
VERB + ADVANCE **make** ◇ *We need more money if we are to make any further ~s in this area of science.*
PREP. **~ in** ◇ *two major ~s in medical science* | **~ on** ◇ *an ~ on the existing techniques* | **~ towards/toward** ◇ *an ~ towards/toward a better understanding of God*

3 money

ADJ. **large** | **cash**
VERB + ADVANCE **give, pay** ◇ *The publishers have paid me an ~.* | **get, receive**
PREP. **~ of** ◇ *an ~ of $10 000* | **~ on** ◇ *He was paid £5 000 as an ~ on royalties.*

4 advances sexual

ADJ. **amorous** (*humorous*), **sexual**
VERB + ADVANCES **make** ◇ *He made amorous ~s to one of his students.*
PREP. **~ to**

advance verb

1 move forward

ADV. **quickly, rapidly** | **cautiously, slowly**
PREP. **from** ◇ *troops advancing from the south* | **into** ◇ *The troops ~d into central Europe.* | **on, upon** ◇ *The army ~d on the capital.* | **towards/toward** ◇ *He ~d towards/toward me in aggressive style.*

2 develop

ADV. **considerably, greatly, significantly** | **rapidly**
PREP. **beyond** ◇ *Society needs to ~ beyond prejudice and superstition.*

advanced adj.

VERBS **be**
ADV. **extremely, fairly, very, etc.** | **highly** ◇ *a highly ~ economy* | **relatively** | **industrially, technically, technologically** | **far, well** ◇ *The disease was too far ~ for doctors to operate.*

advancement noun

ADJ. **individual, personal** | **collective** | **career** | **social** | **material** ◇ *society's need for material ~* | **economic, scientific, technical, technological**
PREP. **~ in** ◇ *~s in science* ◇ *~ in the profession* | **~ to** ◇ *her ~ to the position of Supervisor*
PHRASES **an opportunity for ~** ◇ *There are good opportunities for ~ within the company.*

advantage noun

1 thing that helps

ADJ. **big, considerable, enormous, great, huge, overwhelming** | **clear, decided, decisive, definite, distinct, material, obvious, positive, real** ◇ *The new design gives us a clear ~ over our competitors.* | **important, key, main, major, significant** | **dubious** | **unfair** ◇ *The company has an unfair ~ over its competitors.* | **added, additional** ◇ *These computers have the added ~ of being cheap.* | **special** | **potential** | **comparative, relative** | **mutual** ◇ *The plan would be to our mutual ~.* | **natural** ◇ *the natural ~s of a fertile soil* | **commercial, competitive, economic, educational, electoral, financial, military, personal, political, practical, psychological, social, strategic, tactical, technical, technological** ◇ *The company was able to gain a competitive ~ over its rivals by reducing costs.* | **cost, price, speed, tax**
VERB + ADVANTAGE **have** | **gain, get** ◇ *He would gain considerable ~ from staying in that job.* | **bring (sb), give sb, offer (sb)** ◇ *Another qualification would give me a big ~ at job interviews.* | **press home** ◇ *The commanders were anxious to press home their ~ with a further offensive in the north.* | **outweigh** ◇ *They argue that the possible risks attached to such vaccines vastly outweigh any ~s.*
PREP. **to sb's ~** ◇ *It is to your ~ to delay things for as long as possible.* | **~ in** ◇ *There may be some ~ in laying down a clearer procedure.* | **~ over** ◇ *East coast resorts have the ~ over west coast ones.* | **~ to** ◇ *the ~ to both countries of closer economic ties*
PHRASES **to good ~, to sb/sth's best ~** ◇ *The bright lighting showed the jewels to their best ~.*

2 take advantage of make use of

ADJ. **complete** (*esp. AmE*), **full, maximum** ◇ *We took full ~ of the hotel facilities.* ◇ *I took complete ~ of the situation.*

advantageous adj.

VERBS **be, prove** ◇ *It may be ~ to buy in bulk.* ◇ *Membership of the union could prove ~.* | **become** | **make sth** ◇ *Lower fares make it ~ to travel in winter.* | **consider sth, deem sth, find sth** ◇ *You may find it ~ to wait a few weeks before replying.*
ADV. **extremely, fairly, very, etc.** | **highly, particularly** | **mutually** ◇ *This trade arrangement could be mutually ~.* | **economically, financially** | **politically**
PREP. **for** ◇ *This plan could be ~ for people on low incomes.* | **to** ◇ *The new tax system is ~ to small businesses.*

adventure noun

ADJ. **big, epic, exciting, great, wonderful** | **little** ◇ *We had a little ~ yesterday.* | **dangerous, perilous** | **hair-raising** ◇ *I had some hair-raising ~s when I was backpacking.* | **romantic** | **fantasy, foreign, historical, military, sexual**
VERB + ADVENTURE **embark on, have** | **be looking for, want** ◇ *Those of you looking for ~ can shoot the rapids.* | **offer** ◇ *Perhaps the army offered ~, a chance to travel.*
ADVENTURE + NOUN **film** (*esp. BrE*), **movie** (*esp. AmE*), **novel, story** | **holiday** (*BrE*), **tour** (*AmE*), **vacation** (*AmE*) | **playground** (*BrE*)
PHRASES **quite an ~** (= *very exciting*) ◇ *Our trip to Mexico was quite an ~ for the children.* | **a sense of ~, a spirit of ~** ◇ *The trip began with a sense of ~.*

adverb noun

ADJ. **interrogative, sentence**
ADVERB + VERB **modify sth, qualify sth** ◇ *Adverbs qualify verbs.*

adversary noun

ADJ. **fearsome, formidable** | **worthy** ◊ *The British considered him a worthy ~.* | **old** ◊ *The two of them were old adversaries.*

adversity noun

VERB + ADVERSITY **be faced with, meet with** ◊ *When faced with ~ she was never tempted to give up.* | **overcome, triumph over**
PREP. **in ~** ◊ *patience in ~*
PHRASES **in the face of ~** ◊ *courage in the face of ~*

advert noun (BrE)

ADJ. **classified, front-page, full-page** | **magazine, newspaper, television, TV** | **chocolate, job, etc.** | **banner, pop-up** ◊ *How can I block those annoying pop-up ~s?*
VERB + ADVERT **place, put, take out** ◊ *I put an ~ in the local newspaper.* ◊ *She took out a full-page ~ in a magazine.* | **carry, publish, run, show** ◊ *The paper ran our ~ last week.* | **find, see, spot** ◊ *I saw the ~ in 'The Times'.* | **answer, reply to, respond to**
ADVERT + VERB **appear** ◊ *The ~ appeared in 'The Guardian'.* | **say sth, show sth, state sth** | **feature sb/sth** ◊ *The ~ featured a dolphin swimming around a goldfish bowl.*
PREP. **in a/the ~** ◊ *A lot of claims are made in the ~.* | **~ for** ◊ *an ~ for jeans*

advertise verb

ADV. **heavily** ◊ *These products have been ~d very heavily.* | **widely** ◊ *There are plans to ~ the job more widely.* | **locally, nationally**
PREP. **for** ◊ *We are advertising for a babysitter.*

advertisement noun

ADJ. **good** | **discreet** | **misleading** | **classified, front-page, full-page** ◊ *The classified ~s are on page 25.* | **magazine, newspaper, press, television, TV** | **banner, online, pop-up** | **cigarette, job, political, etc.** | **walking** ◊ *He's a walking ~ for healthy living.*
VERB + ADVERTISEMENT **place, put, take out** ◊ *We placed ~s in a number of national newspapers.* | **carry, display, publish, run, show** ◊ *Television and radio refused to carry ~s for the album.* | **find, see, spot** | **answer, reply to, respond to**
ADVERTISEMENT + VERB **appear** | **say sth, show sth, state sth** | **feature sb/sth**
PREP. **in a/the ~** ◊ *A lot of claims are made in the ~.* | **~ for**

advice noun

ADJ. **constructive, excellent, good, helpful, practical, sensible, sound, useful, valuable** ◊ *That's very sound ~.* | **bad, wrong** ◊ *I think my lawyer gave me the wrong ~.* | **unsolicited** ◊ *I will refrain from giving unsolicited ~.* | **clear** | **general** | **detailed** | **conflicting** | **confidential** | **impartial, independent** | **free** ◊ *The website gives free, impartial ~ on all aspects of saving energy.* | **expert, professional, specialist** ◊ *It is essential to seek expert ~ from a mental health professional.* | **financial, legal, medical** ... OF ADVICE **bit, piece, word** ◊ *Can I give you a friendly word of ~?*
VERB + ADVICE **give (sb), offer (sb), pass on, provide (sb with)** ◊ *I hope I can pass on some useful ~.* | **get, obtain, receive, take** ◊ *I think you need to take legal ~.* | **ask, ask for, go to sb for, seek, turn to sb for** ◊ *Go to your doctor and ask for ~.* ◊ *She asked her mother's ~.* | **accept, act on, follow, heed, listen to, take** ◊ *I wished that I had followed her ~.* | **disregard, ignore, reject**
ADVICE + NOUN **centre** (BrE) ◊ *The Local Authority runs an ~ centre in the town.* | **column** ◊ *She writes a weekly ~ column in the local paper.*
PREP. **against sb's ~** ◊ *Permission was given against the ~ of the planning officers.* | **on sb's ~** ◊ *On the ~ of his experts he bought another company.* | **~ about** ◊ *~ about bringing up children* | **~ for** ◊ *Here is some ~ for pregnant women.* | **~ on** ◊ *Can you give me some ~ on where to buy good maps?* | **~ to** ◊ *My ~ to you would be to wait a few months.*

advisable adj.

VERBS **be, seem** | **consider sth, deem sth, think sth** ◊ *We thought it ~ to seek police assistance.*
ADV. **always** ◊ *It is always ~ to make a will.*

advise verb

1 tell sb what you think they should do

ADV. **strongly** ◊ *I strongly ~ you not to do this.* | **badly, wrongly** ◊ *We were badly ~d by our lawyer.* | **properly** | **legally**
PREP. **about** ◊ *We can ~ parents about education.* | **against** ◊ *They ~d me against visiting the troubled south of the country.* | **on** ◊ *We will be happy to ~ on any financial matters.*
PHRASES **be ill ~d to do sth, be well ~d to do sth** ◊ *John would be ill ~d to rely on their support.* ◊ *You would be better ~d to consult an accountant.*

2 inform sb of sth

VERB + ADVISE **be pleased to** ◊ *I am pleased to ~ you that your application has been accepted.* | **regret to**
PREP. **of**
PHRASES **keep sb ~d** ◊ *Please keep me ~d of new developments in this case.*

adviser (also advisor) noun

ADJ. **chief, principal, senior, special, top** ◊ *the government's chief economic ~* | **close, trusted** ◊ *the president's most trusted ~* | **personal** | **expert** (esp. BrE), **professional** | **independent** | **government, presidential** | **economic, medical, military, policy, political, scientific, security, technical** ◊ *top foreign policy ~s* | **campaign** (esp. AmE), **public relations** (BrE) | **business** (esp. BrE), **financial, investment, legal, tax** | **careers** (BrE), **faculty** (AmE) ◊ *Students can sit down with a careers ~ and discuss what to do next.* | **thesis** (AmE)
VERB + ADVISER **act as** | **appoint, appoint sb (as)** | **have** ◊ *Do you have a financial ~?* | **consult, consult with** (AmE), **see, speak to, talk to** ◊ *You ought to consult an independent legal ~.*
PREP. **~ on** ◊ *an ~ on environmental issues* | **~ to** ◊ *She acts as an ~ to the president.*

advocate noun

1 sb who supports sth

ADJ. **ardent, effective, firm** (esp. BrE), **great, outspoken, powerful, staunch, strong, tireless** (esp. AmE), **vocal** ◊ *She's a staunch ~ of free trade.* | **chief, leading, prominent** | **long-standing**
ADVOCATE + VERB **argue, claim, say**
PREP. **~ for** ◊ *He is one of the leading ~s for a more modern style of worship.* | **~ of** ◊ *an ~ of pacifism*

2 lawyer

ADJ. **solicitor** (BrE) | **judge**
→ Note at PROFESSIONAL (for verbs)

advocate verb

ADV. **strongly** ◊ *Heart specialists strongly ~ low-cholesterol diets.* | **openly, publicly**
PHRASES **be widely ~d** ◊ *These policies have been widely ~d.*

aerial (BrE) noun → See also ANTENNA

ADJ. **radio, television, TV**
AERIAL + VERB **transmit sth** | **pick sth up, receive sth** ◊ *The ~ receives signals from the ground.*

aeroplane (BrE) (AmE airplane) noun → See also PLANE

ADJ. **model, paper, toy**
AEROPLANE/AIRPLANE + NOUN **engine**

affair noun

1 event/situation

ADJ. **whole** ◇ She saw the whole ~ as a great joke. | **glittering, grand** ◇ I knew that the wedding would be a grand ~. | **intimate, low-key, simple** | **community, local** | **messy, sad, sordid, sorry** (esp. BrE), **squalid** (esp. BrE) ◇ the newspaper article that exposed this whole sordid ~

VERB + AFFAIR **deal with, handle** ◇ Many people have criticized the way the government handled the ~. | **be involved in** | **investigate**

PHRASES **sb's involvement in the** ~ ◇ He has tried to play down his involvement in the ~. | **a state of** ~**s** ◇ How did this state of ~s come about? | **wash your hands of the** ~ (= to refuse to be responsible for sth or involved in sth)

2 sexual relationship

ADJ. **brief, casual** | **clandestine, illicit, secret** | **adulterous, extramarital** ◇ He had an extramarital ~ with his secretary. | **passionate, steamy, torrid** | **scandalous** | **unhappy** | **love, romantic, sexual** ◇ a torrid love ~ | **gay, homosexual, lesbian** | **alleged**

VERB + AFFAIR **carry on, conduct, have** ◇ He's having an ~ with a colleague. | **cover up, deny** | **expose**

AFFAIR + VERB **go on** ◇ How long has the ~ been going on?

PREP. ~ **between** ◇ It's the story of a secret ~ between a married teacher and her teenage student. | ~ **with** ◇ an ~ with a married man

3 sth that concerns one person/small group

ADJ. **family, sb's own, personal, private** ◇ It's a family ~.

VERB + AFFAIR **interfere in, meddle in**

PHRASES **sb's** ~ ◇ What I do at home is my ~. | **no** ~ **of sb's** ◇ That's no ~ of yours.

4 affairs important matters

ADJ. **current** ◇ a current-affairs magazine | **public** | **human** | **domestic, home, internal, national** | **civic, community, local** | **external, foreign, global, international, world** ◇ the minister for foreign ~s | **business, financial, legal** | **commercial, consumer, cultural, economic, environmental, military, political, religious, social**

VERB + AFFAIRS **administer, arrange, attend to, conduct, manage, run** ◇ I am trying to arrange my father's financial ~s. | **get in order, put in order, set in order, settle, wind up** ◇ She went back home to put her ~s in order before she died.

PHRASES ~**s of state** ◇ The Cabinet will be discussing certain ~s of state. | **a state of** ~**s** ◇ the current state of ~s in schools

affect verb

1 influence

ADV. **dramatically, greatly, materially, radically** (esp. BrE), **significantly** | **positively** | **barely, hardly, not unduly** ◇ Sales did not seem unduly ~ed. | **slightly** | **clearly, directly, indirectly** | **disproportionately** | **adversely, badly, negatively, seriously, severely**

VERB + AFFECT **be likely to** ◇ developments that are likely to ~ the environment

2 make sb sad/angry

ADV. **deeply, profoundly** ◇ Her death ~ed him deeply.

affection noun

ADJ. **deep, genuine, great, real, special, strong, warm** | **mutual** | **brotherly, marital** | **physical** (esp. AmE)

VERB + AFFECTION **feel, have, hold sb in** (esp. BrE), **retain** (formal) ◇ He has a great ~ for animals. | **display, express, give sb, show (sb)** | **get, receive** | **return** | **crave, need, want** ◇ He just wants a bit of ~. | **gain, win** ◇ She had tried hard to win his ~. | **develop** ◇ She had developed a real ~ for him.

PREP. **with** ~ ◇ He'll be remembered with genuine ~. | ~ **for** ◇ I have a deep ~ for his mother. | ~ **to,** ~ **towards/toward** ◇ The teacher showed ~ to all her students.

PHRASES **a display of** ~ ◇ I don't go in for public displays of ~.

| **a feeling of** ~ ◇ a strong feeling of ~ | **love and** ~ ◇ I yearn for the love and ~ I once had. | **the object of sb's** ~**s** ◇ The object of his ~s was a young opera singer. | **a show of** ~, **a sign of** ~

affinity noun

ADJ. **close, great, real, special, strong** ◇ I felt a great ~ with the people of the islands. | **natural** ◇ He has a natural ~ with numbers.

... OF AFFINITY **degree, level**

VERB + AFFINITY **feel, have, share** ◇ It's important that you share an ~ with your husband. ◇ A house design should have some ~ with the surrounding architecture. | **display, show** ◇ His work shows some ~ with current trends in design.

PREP. ~ **between** ◇ an ~ between the two women ◇ There is a close ~ between these two species. | ~ **for** ◇ Many girls do show an ~ for craft skills. | ~ **towards/toward** ◇ Jo feels a great ~ towards/toward Pamela. | ~ **with** ◇ an ~ with animals ◇ She felt an ~ with earlier poets.

afflict verb

ADV. **badly, severely**

PHRASES **be** ~**ed with** ◇ He's badly ~ed with a skin disorder.

afford verb

ADV. **easily, well** ◇ She can well ~ to pay for herself. | **barely, hardly, ill, just, not really, only just** ◇ an amount which we could ill ~ to pay

VERB + AFFORD **be able to, can** ◇ We can ~ to go to Miami this year. | **be unable to, cannot** ◇ I couldn't possibly ~ to eat in that restaurant.

affront noun

ADJ. **personal**

VERB + AFFRONT **regard sth as, see sth as, take sth as** ◇ He took his son's desertion as a personal ~.

PREP. ~ **to** ◇ This remark caused ~ to many people.

afloat adj.

1 floating on water

VERBS **be** | **keep, remain, stay** | **set sth** ◇ The children set their new boat ~ on the lake. | **keep sth** ◇ They were struggling to keep the vessel ~.

2 able to survive financially

VERBS **keep, stay** ◇ He is struggling to keep ~ after a series of emotional and health problems. | **keep sth** ◇ They had to sell their assets to keep the business ~.

afraid adj.

VERBS **be, feel** | **look, seem, sound** | **become, grow** | **make sb** ◇ What has made you so deeply ~ of your boss?

ADV. **extremely, rather, very** | **deeply, desperately, mortally, terribly** | **really, truly** | **almost** ◇ She was tense, almost ~ to open the letter. | **a little, slightly, etc.** | **half** ◇ He was half ~ to look at her. | **just, simply** ◇ You do know, don't you? You are just ~ to tell me. | **genuinely** | **suddenly** ◇ He stopped abruptly, suddenly ~ to say the words out loud. | **physically**

PREP. **for** ◇ Roger was very ~ for her. | **of** ◇ Charlie is ~ of marriage.

PHRASES **nothing to be** ~ **of** ◇ Don't worry. There's nothing to be ~ of.

aftermath noun

ADJ. **immediate** ◇ The president visited the region in the immediate ~ of the disaster.

VERB + AFTERMATH **cope with, deal with** ◇ How does a country cope with the ~ of war?

PREP. **in the** ~ **of** ◇ He first took office in the ~ of the civil war.

afternoon noun

ADJ. **this, tomorrow, yesterday** | **Friday, Saturday, etc.** | **early, late** | **April, May, etc.** | **spring, summer, etc.** | **long**

◇ the long sunny ~s | golden, hot, sunny, warm | grey/gray, rainy, wet
VERB + AFTERNOON **spend** ◇ We spent the ~ sitting by the pool.
AFTERNOON + VERB **progress, wear on** ◇ As the ~ wore on he began to look unhappy.
AFTERNOON + NOUN **snack, tea** ◇ Afternoon tea is served on the terrace. | **heat, light, sun, sunlight, sunshine** ◇ The ~ sun shone full on her. | **nap**
PREP. **by ~, during the ~, in the ~, on Monday, etc. ~**
PHRASES **an/the ~ off** ◇ You deserve an ~ off.

age noun

1 how old sb/sth is → See also OLD AGE

ADJ. **early, tender, young** ◇ He was sent away to school at an early ~. | **advanced, great, old, ripe** ◇ He was still active even at the advanced ~ of 87. ◇ White hair is a sign of great ~. ◇ She dreaded old ~. | **advancing, increasing | middle, third** (BrE) ◇ a pleasant woman in early middle ~ | **childbearing, pensionable** (BrE), **retirement, school, school-leaving** (BrE) ◇ children of school ~ | **drinking, voting, working | mental, reading** (esp. BrE)
VERB + AGE **attain, get to, live to, reach** ◇ When you get to my ~ you get a different perspective on life. ◇ She lived to the ~ of 75. | **act, feel, look** ◇ Act your ~! ◇ She was beginning to feel her ~ (= feel that she was getting old). | **lower, raise** ◇ The voting ~ was lowered from 21 to 18 years.
AGE + NOUN **group, range | limit**
PREP. **at a/the ~** ◇ At your ~ I had already started work. | **between the ~s** ◇ children between the ~s of five and eleven | **by the ~** ◇ He could read by the ~ of four. | **for sb's ~** ◇ He's quite a big boy for his ~. | **over (the) ~** ◇ Twelve million people are over retirement ~. | **under ~** ◇ It is illegal to sell alcohol to children who are under ~ (= not legally old enough). | **under the ~** ◇ It is illegal to sell alcohol to children under the ~ of 18. | **with ~** ◇ A lot of wines improve with ~. | **~ of** ◇ He left school at the ~ of 18.
PHRASES **the ~ of consent** ◇ The general ~ of consent for sexual activity is 16. | **sb's own ~** ◇ She needs a friend of her own ~ to play with. | **years of ~** ◇ He's 20 years of ~.

2 period of history

ADJ. **another, bygone, different** ◇ This exquisite little hotel seemed to belong to a different ~. | **Bronze, Ice, Stone | computer, digital, industrial, modern, nuclear, etc. | Elizabethan, Victorian, etc. | golden** ◇ the golden ~ of Hollywood
PREP. **during the ... ~** ◇ He lived during the Victorian ~. | **in a/the ~** ◇ She lived in an ~ when few women became politicians. | **through the ~s** ◇ an exhibition of Islamic art through the ~s | **~ of** ◇ the ~ of the computer
PHRASES **in this day and ~** (= in the period we now live in) ◇ Why dress so formally in this day and ~?

3 ages/an age (esp. BrE) **a very long time**

VERB + AGES/AN AGE **spend, take** ◇ It took an ~ for us all to get on the boat.
PHRASES **absolutely ~s** ◇ I've been sitting here for absolutely ~s. | **~s ago** ◇ Carlos left ~s ago. | **for ~s** ◇ We had to wait for ~s!

age verb

ADV. **a lot, really** ◇ The shock has ~d her a lot. ◇ My mother has really ~d since she got sick. | **a little** ◇ He had put on weight and ~d a little. | **quickly, rapidly** ◇ a rapidly ageing/aging population | **prematurely | gracefully, well** ◇ This wine has not ~d well.

agency noun

ADJ. **official | federal, government, governmental, public, state | regulatory | UN | external, independent, outside | commercial, private | voluntary** (esp. BrE), **volunteer** (esp. AmE) | **international, local | adoption, dating, travel | estate** (BrE), **real estate** (AmE) | **aid, health, relief, welfare** (esp. AmE) | **news, press | employment, recruitment** (esp. BrE) | **temp** (esp. AmE), **temping** (BrE) ◇ She was hired from a temp ~. ◇ I've signed up with a temping ~. | **intelligence, law enforcement** (esp. AmE), **police** (esp. AmE) | **ad, advertising,**

marketing | appropriate ◇ Details of the problem will be logged by the Help Desk staff who will then contact the appropriate ~.
PREP. **through an/the ~** ◇ He found a job through an ~.
→ Note at ORGANIZATION (for verbs)

agenda noun

ADJ. **five-point, etc.** ◇ An 18-point ~ was drawn up for the meeting. | **hidden, secret** ◇ He accused the government of having a hidden ~. | **real | full** ◇ We have a very full ~ of issues to discuss. | **broad, narrow** ◇ The party has a rather narrow political ~. | **clear** ◇ A clear ~ will win votes in the next election. | **agreed** (esp. BrE) | **ambitious, radical | public | personal | domestic, international, national | economic, ideological, legislative, policy, political, research, social | conservative, liberal, progressive**
VERB + AGENDA **have | agree on, draw up** (esp. BrE), **establish, set** ◇ The college needs to establish an ~ for change. | **follow, pursue** ◇ They were pursuing their own ~. | **advance, further, push** ◇ I'm not trying to push any ~ here. | **add sth to, put sth on** ◇ I will put this on the ~ for the next meeting. | **remove sth from, take sth off** ◇ The question of pay had been taken off the ~. | **circulate**
AGENDA + NOUN **item**
PREP. **on a/the ~** ◇ Safety at work is on the ~ for next month's meeting. | **off the ~** ◇ Child poverty has been pushed off the ~. | **~ for** ◇ We have an agreed ~ for action.
PHRASES **firmly on the ~** (esp. BrE), **high on the ~** ◇ In our company, quality is high on the ~. | **an item on the ~, a point on the ~ | next on the ~** ◇ Next on the ~ is deciding where we're going to live. | **top of the ~** ◇ Improving trade between the two countries will be top of the ~ at the talks.
→ Special page at MEETING

agent noun

1 works in an agency

ADJ. **booking, ticket, travel | election** (BrE), **parliamentary** (BrE) | **advertising, press, publicity | land** (BrE), **leasing** (AmE), **letting** (BrE), **managing** (esp. BrE), **rental** (AmE) | **estate** (BrE), **real estate** (AmE) ◇ They were advised by the real estate ~ that their house would not be saleable. | **border-patrol, law enforcement | insurance | literary, sports, talent | local** ◇ The company has developed sales through local ~s in key markets.
VERB + AGENT **employ, have, use** ◇ I have an ~ who deals with all my contracts. | **appoint, get (sb), hire** (esp. AmE) ◇ If you want to get published, get yourself an ~! | **act as | fire, sack** (BrE)
PREP. **through an ~** ◇ She got the work through an ~. | **~ for an ~** for a shipping company
→ Note at JOB

2 spy

ADJ. **intelligence | enemy, foreign | federal, government | covert, secret, special, undercover | double** ◇ As a double ~, he worked for the Americans and the Russians.

3 person/thing that has an effect

ADJ. **chief, main, primary, prime, principal | effective | human | moral, rational | free** ◇ I told him I couldn't stop him and that he was a free ~.
PREP. **~ for** ◇ The charity is an ~ for social change.
PHRASES **an ~ for change, an ~ of change**

aggravate verb

ADV. **seriously, severely** ◇ Their negative reactions have greatly ~d the situation. | **slightly | further**

aggression noun

ADJ. **naked, open, overt** ◇ a display of naked ~ | **pent-up** ◇ ways of releasing pent-up ~ | **unprovoked | physical, sexual, verbal | external, foreign** ◇ The president announced that the country would not tolerate foreign ~. | **American, British, etc. | armed, military**

... OF AGGRESSION **act** ◊ *Acts of ~ against against gays and lesbians are not always reported.*
VERB + AGGRESSION **display, exhibit, express, show** ◊ *the brutality and ~ displayed by the soldiers* | **channel, direct** ◊ *He manages to channel his ~ into football.* | **control, deter** | **release** | **encourage** ◊ *Do toy guns encourage ~?*
PREP. **~ against, ~ by** ◊ *Aggression by one nationality against another often leads to war.* | **~ towards/toward** ◊ *It showed no ~ towards/toward other dogs.*

aggressive adj.

VERBS **be, look, seem, sound** | **become, get, grow** (*esp. AmE*), **turn** | **make sb** ◊ *Watching violence on TV makes some children more ~.*
ADV. **extremely, fairly, very, etc.** | **highly, particularly, really** ◊ *the company's highly ~ marketing techniques* | **increasingly** | **openly** ◊ *Her mood became openly ~ when his name was mentioned.* | **physically, verbally** | **sexually**
PREP. **towards/toward** ◊ *He warned that his dog was ~ towards/toward strangers.* | **with** (*esp. AmE*) ◊ *Dogs of this breed can be ~ with other dogs.*

agility noun

ADJ. **amazing, considerable, great, surprising** | **mental, physical** ◊ *I admired his considerable mental ~.*
VERB + AGILITY **have** | **demonstrate, show** ◊ *She shows great ~ on the tennis court.* | **lack**
PREP. **with ~** ◊ *He jumped over the wall with surprising ~.*

agitated adj.

VERBS **be, feel, look, seem, sound** ◊ *He sounded very ~ on the phone.* | **become, get, grow** | **make sb**
ADV. **extremely, fairly, very, etc.** | **highly** | **increasingly** | **a little, slightly** | **obviously, visibly**
PREP. **about** ◊ *She's ~ about getting there on time.* | **at** ◊ *She started to grow ~ at the sight of the spider.*
PHRASES **in an ~ state** ◊ *By now he was in a very ~ state.*

agitation noun

1 worry/excitement

ADJ. **acute, extreme**
VERB + AGITATION **show** ◊ *She was trying not to show her ~.* | **conceal, hide** ◊ *He could not hide his ~.*
PREP. **in sb's ~** ◊ *He knocked his glass over in his ~.* | **with ~** ◊ *She was wriggling on the seat with ~.*
PHRASES **a feeling of ~, a state of ~**

2 public protest

ADJ. **growing** | **mass, popular, public** | **political**
VERB + AGITATION **engage in, turn to** ◊ *The organization is turning to political ~ in order to achieve its aims.* | **stir up**
PREP. **~ against** ◊ *There has been mass ~ against the president.* | **~ for** ◊ *There is growing ~ for reform of local government.*

agony noun

ADJ. **excruciating, extreme, intense** | **absolute, pure, sheer, utter** | **exquisite** | **mental, physical** | **death** ◊ *The little creature squirmed in its death agonies.*
VERB + AGONY **endure, go through, suffer** ◊ *He endured the agonies of loneliness.* ◊ *They went through ~ in the search for their missing relatives.* | **cause, inflict** ◊ *She was causing David a great deal of ~.* | **prolong** ◊ *Don't prolong the agony—just tell me the result!*
PREP. **in ~** ◊ *The soldier died in ~.* | **in an ~ of** ◊ *She mumbled an apology in an ~ of embarrassment.*
PHRASES **a groan of ~, a scream of ~** | **groan in ~, scream in ~** | **be contorted in ~, writhe in ~** ◊ *His face was contorted in ~ as he tried to lift himself out of the chair.*

agree verb

1 share opinion

ADV. **emphatically, heartily, strongly, very much** ◊ *I very much ~ with your point.* | **absolutely, completely, entirely,**
fully, quite, totally, wholeheartedly ◊ *I ~ entirely with what you have said.* | **basically, broadly, generally, largely** ◊ *It is generally ~d that more funding is needed for education.* | **unanimously** | **privately, secretly**
VERB + AGREE **cannot** | **have to** ◊ *I would have to ~ with you there.* | **be inclined to, tend to** ◊ *I'm inclined to ~ there's nothing we can do.*
PREP. **about** ◊ *We don't always ~ about everything.* | **on, upon** ◊ *Are we all ~d on this?* | **with** ◊ *Do you ~ with me that the plan won't work?*
PHRASES **I couldn't ~ more** ◊ *I couldn't ~ more with what has just been said.* | **I quite ~** | **I'm sure you will ~** ◊ *I'm sure you'll ~ that this issue is vitally important to the success of the company.*

2 say yes; decide

ADV. **happily, readily, voluntarily, willingly** ◊ *She suggested a walk in the open air and he readily ~d.* | **grudgingly, reluctantly** | **graciously, kindly** ◊ *Ms Harlow has kindly ~d to help.* | **secretly, tacitly** | **expressly** (*BrE*) | **provisionally** (*esp. BrE*) ◊ *It was provisionally ~d that August 12 was to be the date.*
VERB + AGREE **be unable to, fail to** ◊ *The two countries were unable to ~ on a common strategy.*
PREP. **to** ◊ *He ~d to our proposals.*
PHRASES **~ to differ, ~ to disagree** ◊ *We must just ~ to disagree on this point.* | **(be) mutually ~d** ◊ *We are working towards/toward mutually ~d goals.* | **internationally ~d, nationally ~d** ◊ *nationally ~d guidelines*

agreeable adj. (formal)

1 pleasant

VERBS **be, look, sound** ◊ *It all sounds very ~.* | **find sb/sth** ◊ *He finds her very ~.* | **make yourself** ◊ *She did her best to make herself ~.*
ADV. **extremely, fairly, very, etc.** | **most** ◊ *It was a most ~ evening.* | **mutually** ◊ *We tried to negotiate a mutually ~ solution.*

2 willing to accept/do sth

VERBS **be**
ADV. **perfectly, quite**
PREP. **to** ◊ *He was perfectly ~ to the idea.*

agreement noun

1 contract/decision

ADJ. **draft** ◊ *The draft ~ will be available before the meeting.* | **formal, signed, written** | **binding, legal** ◊ *The ~ will be legally binding.* | **tentative** | **informal, verbal** | **tacit, unspoken** | **voluntary** | **definitive** | **bilateral, international, multilateral** | **ceasefire, peace** | **trade** | **contractual, licensing** | **prenuptial** ◊ *The Hollywood stars signed a prenuptial ~ before marrying last year.* | **confidentiality** | **credit, hire-purchase** (*BrE*), **lease, rental**
VERB + AGREEMENT **negotiate, work out** ◊ *They are working out a formal ceasefire ~.* | **conclude, enter into, reach, sign** ◊ *After hours of talks the government and the union have reached an ~.* | **have** ◊ *We have an ~ to always tell each other the truth about everything.* | **be bound by** ◊ *We signed the ~ so we are now bound by it.* | **adhere to, honour/honor, keep to, stick to** ◊ *You have not kept to our ~.* | **break, go back on, renege on, violate** ◊ *Some employers reneged on ~s once the recession set in.*
PREP. **in an/the ~** ◊ *a clause in the ~* | **under an/the ~** ◊ *Under the ~, the farmer is not allowed to use this field.* | **~ between** ◊ *an ~ between the company and the unions* | **~ on** ◊ *They signed two ~s on improving economic cooperation.* | **~ with** ◊ *a trade ~ with China*
PHRASES **breach of ~** (*esp. BrE*) ◊ *He sued the company for breach of ~.* | **the terms of the ~** ◊ *The terms of the ~ do not allow such exports.*

2 state of agreeing

ADJ. **absolute, complete, full, total** | **broad, general, widespread** | **mutual**
VERB + AGREEMENT **arrive at, come to, reach** ◊ *I am hopeful that we can come to an ~.* ◊ *The two sides failed to reach ~.* |

nod ◇ He nodded his ~. | **get** ◇ We will need to get the ~ of local organizations.
PREP. **by** ~ ◇ The separation is by mutual ~. | **in** ~ ◇ I think we are all in ~ that prices should be kept low. | **in** ~ **with** ◇ I am in ~ with you that she should be given more responsibilities. | **with** ~ ◇ With the ~ of all members of the club, we decided to organize a trip. | ~ **among** ◇ There is ~ among teachers that changes need to be made. | ~ **between** ◇ As yet there is no ~ between the two sides. | ~ **on** ◇ As yet there is no ~ on policies.
→ Special page at MEETING

agriculture noun

ADJ. **modern** | **intensive** | **organic** | **sustainable** | **conventional, traditional** | **large-scale, small-scale** | **peasant** | **subsistence** | **slash-and-burn**
VERB + AGRICULTURE **be employed in, be engaged in, work in** | **be dependent on, depend on** ◇ 50% of the country's population depends on ~.

aid noun

1 money, food, etc.
ADJ. **emergency** | **humanitarian** | **cash** (esp. BrE), **development, economic, financial, food, legal, medical, military, reconstruction, relief** ◇ Legal ~ is a fundamental part of our system of justice. | **federal, government, state** | **foreign, international, overseas** ◇ The country relies on foreign ~.
VERB + AID **appeal for, call for** ◇ The country's president has appealed for international ~ in the wake of the disaster. | **extend, give (sb), provide (sb with), send (sb)** | **get, receive** | **depend on, rely on** | **promise** | **cut, cut off, suspend, withdraw, withhold** ◇ The government has now suspended humanitarian ~ to the area.
AID + NOUN **agency, worker** | **budget, package, programme/program** ◇ a $240 million ~ package

2 help
VERB + AID **ask for, enlist** ◇ We enlisted the ~ of John and his family. | **come to sb's, go to sb's** (= to help someone) ◇ She screamed loudly and two people came to her ~.
PREP. **in** ~ **of** (esp. BrE) ◇ We were collecting money in ~ of charity. | **with the** ~ **of, without the** ~ **of** ◇ She is now able to get around with the ~ of a walking stick.

3 person/thing that helps → See also FIRST AID
ADJ. **effective, essential, useful, valuable** | **teaching, training, visual** | **hearing, walking** (BrE) | **memory** | **navigational** | **sleep** (AmE) | **buoyancy** (BrE)
PREP. ~ **to** ◇ Dictionaries are essential ~s to learning.

aide noun

ADJ. **close, trusted** ◇ one of the President's closest ~s | **senior, top** | **congressional, legislative** (AmE), **personal, presidential, royal**
VERB + AIDE **act as, serve as, work as**
PREP. ~ **to** ◇ He served as an ~ to the former president.

AIDS (BrE usually Aids) noun

ADJ. **full-blown** ◇ Not all of those infected will develop full-blown ~.
... OF AIDS **case** ◇ Six cases of ~ have been reported.
VERB + AIDS **be infected with, fight, have, suffer from** ◇ people fighting ~ | **become infected with, contract, develop, get** | **die of** | **diagnose**
AIDS + NOUN **patient, sufferer, victim** | **virus** | **epidemic** | **prevention**
PHRASES **the spread of** ~ ◇ a worldwide campaign to prevent the spread of ~
→ Special page at ILLNESS

ailment noun

ADJ. **common, minor, trivial** | **chronic, serious** | **childhood** | **physical** | **mysterious** | **heart, respiratory, stomach**
VERB + AILMENT **be afflicted with, get, have, suffer, suffer from** ◇ I got all the usual childhood ~s. | **cure, heal, treat** | **cause**

aim noun

1 purpose/goal
ADJ. **broad, general, overall** | **basic, central, fundamental** | **chief, first, key, main, major, overriding, primary, prime** (BrE), **principal** | **sole** ◇ His sole ~ in life is to enjoy himself. | **clear, explicit, specific** ◇ It is important to have a clear ~ in view. | **ambitious** | **high, noble, worthy** (esp. BrE) ◇ Simple truth must be the highest ~ of any real investigation. | **limited, modest** | **legitimate** | **common** ◇ I want to see a strong and united country in which people work together with common ~s. | **immediate, initial** | **original** | **eventual, ultimate** ◇ His ultimate ~ was to force the chairman to resign. | **long-term, short-term** | **avowed, declared, express, expressed, stated** ◇ The express ~ of the treaty is to keep the whole region free from nuclear weapons. | **war** | **policy, political, strategic**
VERB + AIM **have** | **set (yourself)** | **accomplish, achieve, fulfil/fulfill** ◇ You will have to work hard to achieve your ~. | **further, pursue** ◇ They were intent on furthering their ~s. ◇ The country is still pursuing its ~ of joining the EU.
PREP. **with the** ~ **of** ◇ She started the organization with the ~ of helping local people.
PHRASES ~**s and objectives** ◇ What are the ~s and objectives of this visit?

2 pointing weapon, etc.
ADJ. **careful, direct, steady** ◇ I'll take more careful ~ next time. | **poor** ◇ His ~ was poor and he missed the target.
VERB + AIM **take** | **adjust**
PREP. ~ **at** ◇ He took ~ at the target and fired.

aim verb

1 try/plan to achieve sth
PREP. **at** ◇ She's ~ing at a scholarship this year. | **for** ◇ He is ~ing for a win in this race.
PHRASES ~ **high** (= to attempt to achieve a lot) ◇ a young man who is prepared to ~ high

2 intend sth for sb
ADV. **clearly, directly, squarely** | **deliberately** | **largely, mainly, mostly, primarily, principally** | **particularly, specifically** | **solely**
PHRASES **be** ~**ed at** ◇ educational courses ~ed particularly at older people

3 point/direct sth at sb
ADV. **directly, straight** | **carefully, deliberately**
PREP. **at** ◇ She ~ed the gun straight at the intruder. | **for** ◇ Aim for his legs, not his body.

air noun

1 gas/space
ADJ. **hot, warm** | **chill, cold, cool, crisp** | **clean, clear, fresh, pure** ◇ There are regulatory requirements for clean ~ and water. ◇ We need some fresh ~ in this stuffy room! | **sweet** ◇ The ~ was sweet with incense. | **foul, foul-smelling, polluted, stale** ◇ the polluted ~ of our cities ◇ the musty smell of stale ~ | **damp, humid, moist** | **dry** | **still** ◇ Nothing moved in the still ~. | **thin** ◇ It's difficult carrying such heavy loads in the thin ~ of the mountains. | **thick** ◇ The ~ was thick with cigarette smoke. | **compressed** ◇ They have developed an engine powered by compressed ~. | **country, mountain, sea** | **evening, morning, night** ◇ Music filled the night ~.
... OF AIR **blast, gust, rush** ◇ We felt a blast of cold ~ as she opened the door. | **current** ◇ warm currents of ~ | **breath** ◇ He drew in another breath of ~.
VERB + AIR **breathe** ◇ Land crabs breathe ~ and cannot swim. | **breathe in, gulp in, inhale, suck in** ◇ She gulped in the fresh mountain ~. ◇ I sat for a moment, inhaling the fresh forest ~. | **fight for, gasp for** ◇ She was gasping for ~ as she ran out of the burning house. | **smell, sniff** ◇ The dog stretched and sniffed the ~. | **fill, hang in** ◇ The tang of some wild herb hung in the ~. | **blow** | **pollute** | **clear** (figurative) ◇ The

argument helped to clear the ~ between them. | **punch** ◊ He punched the ~ in triumph. | **pierce** ◊ Suddenly a scream pierced the ~.

AIR + VERB **blow, circulate, flow, rise, rush, waft** ◊ The cool night ~ wafted in through the open windows.

AIR + NOUN **pollution** | **quality** ◊ equipment to monitor ~ quality | **pressure** | **current** | **temperature** | **conditioning** | **conditioner**

PREP. **in the ~, into the ~** ◊ I kicked the ball high into the ~. | **through the ~** ◊ Spicy smells wafted through the ~.

PHRASES **in the open ~** (= outside) ◊ The market is held in the open ~.

2 for planes

AIR + NOUN **travel** | **fare** | **traffic** ◊ We are cleared by Air Traffic Control to taxi and take off. | **crash, disaster** | **attack, defence/defense, raid, strike** ◊ Three buildings were bombed last night in an ~ strike on the city.

PREP. **by ~** (= by plane) ◊ It only takes three hours by ~. | **from the ~** ◊ The hideout is clearly visible from the ~.

3 impression

VERB + AIR **have, retain** ◊ You have an ~ of authority. | **add, bring, give (sth)** ◊ A stone balcony gives the building an ~ of elegance. | **lend**

PREP. **with an/the ~** ◊ He leaned over to Melissa with an ~ of confidentiality. | **~ of** ◊ He had an ~ of mystery about him.

air verb

ADV. **in public, openly, publicly** ◊ The issues were openly ~ed and discussed by the group.

aircraft noun

ADJ. **fixed-wing, jet, light, low-flying, supersonic** ◊ Three men were flying in a light ~ at low altitude when a passenger jet approached. | **single-engined, twin-engined** | **manned, unmanned** ◊ The army is using unmanned ~ to survey the area. | **microlight** (BrE), **ultralight** (AmE) | **cargo, civil, civilian, commercial, passenger, private** | **attack, combat, fighter, military, reconnaissance, stealth, strike, surveillance, transport** | **enemy** | **model** (esp. BrE) ◊ His passion is making model ~.

VERB + AIRCRAFT **fly, operate, pilot** ◊ The ~ was flown by a young American pilot. | **land** | **board** ◊ The passengers boarded the ~. | **hijack** | **destroy, shoot down** ◊ To be an ace you had to shoot down five enemy ~.

AIRCRAFT + VERB **fly, operate** ◊ There are approximately 6 700 commercial ~ operating in the United States. | **land, take off** ◊ The ~ is due to take off at midnight. | **crash** | **carry sth** | **attack sth, bomb sth**

AIRCRAFT + NOUN **industry** | **production** | **manufacturer** | **maintenance** | **engine, parts** | **engineer** | **commander** | **hangar** | **carrier** ◊ a US Navy ~ carrier | **noise** ◊ Significant progress has been made in reducing ~ noise.

airline noun

ADJ. **big, large, major** | **domestic, international, national, regional** | **commercial, private** ◊ He operates a private ~. | **state, state-owned** (both BrE) | **charter, scheduled** ◊ Prices on charter ~s are usually lower. | **budget** (esp. BrE), **discount** (esp. AmE), **low-cost, low-fare** (esp. AmE), **no-frills** (esp. BrE) ◊ He's the founder of Europe's biggest no-frills ~.

VERB + AIRLINE **operate, run** | **fly** (esp. AmE), **fly with** ◊ I'll never fly this ~ again.

AIRLINE + VERB **fly, operate** ◊ The ~ operates mainly between Florida and Puerto Rico.

AIRLINE + NOUN **business, company, industry** ◊ From 1984 to 1996 the international ~ industry grew dramatically. | **flight, service** ◊ All scheduled ~ services will be affected by the strike. | **employee** (esp. AmE), **pilot, staff** (esp. BrE) | **passenger** | **reservation, ticket** | **strike**

airplane noun (AmE) → See AEROPLANE

airport noun

ADJ. **big, large, major** | **small** | **busy** | **domestic, international, local, regional** | **hub** ◊ Most major hub ~s have three or four runways. | **commercial, military** | **departure, destination** ◊ The pilot made the decision to return to the departure ~.

VERB + AIRPORT **depart from, fly from, take off from** ◊ We fly from Guarulhos ~. | **arrive at, land at, touch down at** ◊ The plane touched down at Narita ~ just before midday. | **pass through, use** | **leave**

AIRPORT + NOUN **building, terminal** | **check-in, lounge** | **hotel** | **screener** (AmE), **security** ◊ Airport screeners failed to spot the fake bomb. | **employee** (esp. AmE), **official, staff** (esp. BrE), **worker**

PREP. **at an/the ~** ◊ They were waiting at the ~.

airspace noun

ADJ. **controlled, restricted** | **international, national** | **enemy** | **British, French, US, etc.**

VERB + AIRSPACE **cross, cross into, enter, fly in, fly into, penetrate, stray into, use, violate** ◊ The jet had crossed into Russian ~. | **leave** | **close, open** ◊ They have decided to open their ~ to commercial aircraft. | **control, defend**

PREP. **in …~** ◊ The glider was in Dutch ~. | **out of ~** ◊ They were now out of controlled ~.

PHRASES **a violation of ~** ◊ The president said that all future violations of our ~ would result in serious consequences.

ajar adj.

VERBS **be, stand** ◊ The office door stood ~. | **leave sth** ◊ She had left the kitchen door slightly ~.

ADV. **slightly**

akin adj. akin to sth

VERBS **be, seem**

ADV. **closely, much** ◊ This game is closely ~ to hockey. | **somewhat** ◊ A balalaika is an instrument somewhat ~ to a guitar.

PHRASES **something ~ to sth** ◊ She was wearing something ~ to a pineapple on her head.

alarm noun

1 fear/worry

ADJ. **considerable, great** | **growing** | **sudden** | **public** ◊ There is growing public ~ at this increase in crime. | **unnecessary**

VERB + ALARM **cause, create, provoke** ◊ The incident created serious public ~. | **express** ◊ Many people have expressed ~ at the plans.

PREP. **in ~** ◊ He shouted out in ~. | **to sb's ~** ◊ To her parents' ~, she announced that she intended to travel the world. | **with ~** ◊ The news has been greeted with ~. | **~ about, ~ at, ~ over** ◊ There has been considerable ~ about the new proposals.

PHRASES **cause for ~** ◊ I see no cause for ~, as she often arrives late.

2 warning of danger

ADJ. **false** ◊ The police were called, but it was a false ~.

VERB + ALARM **give, raise, sound** ◊ The guard raised the ~ when he discovered that six prisoners had escaped.

ALARM + NOUN **call** ◊ Many birds give ~ calls to warn of danger.

3 device

ADJ. **fire, smoke** | **burglar, intruder, security** | **car** | **panic** (esp. BrE), **personal, rape** (BrE) ◊ Carry a personal ~ with you and make sure you know how to use it. | **radio**

VERB + ALARM **set** ◊ I set my ~ for 6.30. | **activate, set off, trigger, trip** ◊ Unfortunately any little noise can set off the ~. | **disable, switch off, turn off** | **be fitted with** (BrE) ◊ The fire brigade recommends that every house is fitted with a smoke ~. | **fit** (BrE), **install** | **test**

ALARM + VERB **go off, ring, sound** ◊ The ~ went off at 7 o'clock.

◇ Suddenly the ~ sounded and they all had to leave the building.
ALARM + NOUN **bell, clock, system** | **call** (*BrE*) (***wake-up call*** in *AmE*) ◇ *Book an ~ call if you need to make an early start.*

alarmed *adj.*

VERBS **be, feel, look, seem, sound** | **become, get, grow** ◇ *She began to grow ~ when she realized how late it was.*
ADV. **extremely, fairly, very, etc.** | **seriously** | **increasingly** | **a little, slightly, etc.** | **(not) unduly** ◇ *The government is not unduly ~ by these figures.*
PREP. **at** ◇ *She was ~ at the prospect of being alone.* | **by** ◇ *I was slightly ~ by what Susan told me.*
PHRASES **nothing to be ~ about** ◇ *The doctors have decided to keep him overnight but there is nothing to be ~ about.*

alarming *adj.*

VERBS **be, seem** | **find sth** ◇ *I find the prospect of being without work extremely ~.*
ADV. **extremely, fairly, very, etc.** | **particularly** | **a little, slightly, etc.**

album *noun*

1 book

ADJ. **family, wedding** | **photo, photograph** | **stamp**
PREP. **in an/the ~** ◇ *I keep the photographs in an ~.*

2 music

ADJ. **best-selling, good, great** ◇ *Their best-selling ~ has won three awards.* | **debut, first** | **double** | **live, studio** | **concept** | **solo** ◇ *It's the singer's first solo ~.* | **compilation** | **latest, new** ◇ *Their new ~ has been getting good reviews.* | **greatest-hits**
VERB + ALBUM **make, produce, record** ◇ *The singer recorded her second ~ in Los Angeles.* | **put out, release** ◇ *She has not put out a new ~ this year.* | **download** ◇ *You can download an entire ~ with a click of a mouse.*
ALBUM + VERB **come out** ◇ *His latest ~ comes out in the spring.*
ALBUM + NOUN **chart** | **track** | **cover, sleeve**

alcohol *noun*

ADJ. **excess, excessive** ◇ *the dangers of excessive ~* | **pure** ◇ *Is it possible for cars to run on pure ~?* | **strong** (*AmE*) | **grain** (*AmE*) | **rubbing** (*AmE*)
...OF ALCOHOL **drop** | **unit** (*esp. BrE*) ◇ *You need to be careful how many units of ~ you drink in a week.* | **bottle, glass** | **level** ◇ *The driver had more than the permitted level of ~ in his blood.*
VERB + ALCOHOL **consume, drink** | **avoid, not touch, stay away from** (*esp. AmE*), **stay off** ◇ *I haven't touched a drop of ~ for three weeks.* | **abuse** (*formal*) ◇ *Most drinkers do not abuse ~ at all.* | **serve**
ALCOHOL + NOUN **content, level** ◇ *It can take a long time for blood ~ levels to fall.* | **consumption, intake, use** | **abuse, addiction, dependence, misuse** | **problem** ◇ *People can find it hard to admit they have an ~ problem.* | **prohibition**
PHRASES **under the influence of ~** ◇ *He had been driving while under the influence of ~.*

alcoholic *noun*

ADJ. **chronic** | **raging** (*AmE, informal*) | **recovering** | **recovered** (*esp. AmE*), **reformed**
VERB + ALCOHOLIC **become** ◇ *Taylor was becoming an ~ because of the stress of his job.*
ALCOHOLIC + VERB **recover** ◇ *I don't think an ~ can recover without proper medical help.*

alcoholism *noun*

ADJ. **chronic**
VERB + ALCOHOLISM **suffer from** ◇ *Three people in the family suffer from ~.* | **treat** | **battle, combat, overcome**
→ Special page at ILLNESS

alert *noun*

ADJ. **heightened, high** ◇ *The country has put its troops on high ~.* | **full** | **amber, orange, red, yellow** ◇ *His sudden*

disappearance triggered a red ~ among his friends. | **nationwide** | **bomb, fire, flood, pollution, security, terror** ◇ *A security ~ was issued after four men escaped from the prison.* | **email** ◇ *Receive regular email ~s about breaking news.*
VERB + ALERT **issue, put out, raise, sound** ◇ *They rang the bells to sound the ~.* | **spark** (*esp. BrE*), **trigger** | **call off** ◇ *The ~ was called off when it was found that the bomb was not live.*
ALERT + VERB **go out** ◇ *A nationwide ~ went out for three escaped prisoners.*
PREP. **on the ~** | **~ for** ◇ *You should always be on the ~ for anyone who looks suspicious.*
PHRASES **be on full ~** ◇ *The security forces are now on full ~.* | **place sb on ~, put sb on ~** ◇ *Thousands of police were put on full ~ at all main roads leading to the city.* | **keep sb on ~** | **a state of ~** ◇ *The army was yesterday placed on a state of ~ in case of more riots.*

alert *adj.*

VERBS **be, look, seem** | **become** | **remain, stay** | **keep sb** ◇ *The machine should help to keep the pilot ~.*
ADV. **extremely, fairly, very, etc.** | **fully** | **immediately, instantly, suddenly** ◇ *There was a noise outside and he was suddenly ~.* | **always, constantly** | **mentally** ◇ *He was as mentally ~ as a man half his age.*
PREP. **to** ◇ *Climbers need to be ~ to possible dangers.*

alias *noun*

ADJ. **known** ◇ *One of his known ~es is Ed Neil.* | **email, online** ◇ *On his website he uses the online ~ 'Maddox'.*
VERB + ALIAS **adopt, assume, go by, use** ◇ *After her escape from prison she adopted the ~ Daryl Crowe.*
PREP. **under an/the ~** (= using another name) ◇ *Five years ago he had lived in France under an ~.*

alibi *noun*

ADJ. **cast-iron** (*BrE*), **good, ironclad** (*AmE*), **perfect, solid** ◇ *She was in the office all of Wednesday and so has a solid ~.* | **false**
VERB + ALIBI **have** | **establish, provide, supply** ◇ *They relied on witnesses to establish ~s for the accused.* | **concoct** (*esp. BrE*), **create, invent** ◇ *It was alleged that the accused had created an ~ to save himself.*
PREP. **~ for** ◇ *The accused was not able to provide an ~ for the evening.*

alien *noun*

1 non-citizen

ADJ. **enemy** ◇ *During the war, he was imprisoned as an enemy ~.* | **illegal, undocumented** (*AmE*) ◇ *Illegal ~s are usually deported to their country of origin.* | **criminal** (*AmE*) | **undesirable** | **resident**
VERB + ALIEN **deport** ◇ *The provisions would broaden the government's ability to deport ~s.* | **apprehend, arrest, detain** (*all esp. AmE*) | **hire** (*esp. AmE*) ◇ *It is illegal for employers to hire ~s not authorized for employment.* (*AmE*)

2 creature from another planet

ADJ. **space** ◇ *Do you genuinely believe that space ~s have landed on our planet?* | **giant** | **intelligent** ◇ *Few movies represent intelligent ~s as physically different from humans.*
ALIEN + VERB **abduct, kidnap** ◇ *He was convinced that he'd been abducted by ~s.* | **invade** ◇ *In the movie ~s invade Earth.*

alien *adj.*

VERBS **be, feel, seem** | **become** | **find sth** ◇ *It was an act of violence that she found ~ and shocking.*
ADV. **so, very** | **completely, entirely, totally, utterly** | **quite, somewhat** | **essentially** ◇ *What is it like to live in an essentially ~ culture?*
PREP. **to** ◇ *They spoke a language totally ~ to him.*

alienation noun

ADJ. **growing, increasing | widespread | cultural, political, social** ◊ *Such policies foster social ~ and discontent.*
VERB + ALIENATION **experience | express**
PREP. **~ from** ◊ *his growing ~ from his family*
PHRASES **a feeling of ~, a sense of ~** ◊ *There is a growing feeling of ~ among young people.*

alight adj.

VERBS **be | catch** (*esp. BrE*) ◊ *His clothing caught ~.* | **remain, stay** (*both esp. BrE*) ◊ *The fire should remain ~ overnight.* | **set sth** ◊ *The building had been set ~ by the killer.* | **keep sth** ◊ *The fires had to be kept ~ each night.*
ADV. **well** (*esp. BrE*) ◊ *The fire should be well ~ by now.*
PHRASES **~ with excitement, laughter, pleasure, etc.** (*figurative*) ◊ *The children's eyes were ~ with excitement.*

align verb

ADV. **accurately, closely, correctly, perfectly, properly | fully | roughly | horizontally, vertically**
PREP. **along** ◊ *The house is ~ed along an east-west axis.* | **with** ◊ *This pillar is roughly ~ed with the others.*
PHR V **align yourself with sb/sth**
ADV. **closely, firmly** ◊ *The group does not want to ~ itself too closely with the government.*

alignment noun

1 arrangement in correct position
ADJ. **correct, proper**
VERB + ALIGNMENT **bring sth into**
PREP. **in ~ (with sth)** ◊ *The door needs to be in ~ with the frame before you start work on it.* | **out of ~** ◊ *A few of the tiles were clearly out of ~.*

2 political support
ADJ. **close | military, political**
VERB + ALIGNMENT **establish, form | maintain**
PREP. **~ between** ◊ *It has been very difficult to maintain the ~ between the two countries since the trade dispute.* | **~ to** ◊ *IT needs to have a closer ~ to business.* | **~ with** ◊ *China has formed a close ~ with some African countries.*

alike adj.

VERBS **be, look, seem**
ADV. **remarkably, very, very much | exactly** ◊ *Though Pedro and Paulo look exactly ~, they act differently.*
PREP. **in** ◊ *The two towns are very much ~ in size and population.*

alive adj.

1 living
VERBS **be, seem | remain, stay** ◊ *Lost and so far from other human life, he faced a desperate struggle to stay ~.* | **escape, get out** ◊ *He considered himself lucky to escape ~.* | **return** ◊ *They had little chance of returning ~.* | **keep sb** ◊ *Doctors fought to keep her ~.* | **be buried, be burned, be eaten | found, be left** ◊ *Five people were found ~ in the wreckage.* | **be captured, be taken**
ADV. **very much** ◊ *The old rascal is still very much ~.* | **barely, only half** ◊ *For four days he seemed barely ~.* | **still** ◊ *I wasn't sure if he was still ~.*
PHRASES **~ and kicking** ◊ *My mother is still ~ and kicking.* | **~ and well** ◊ *At any moment he may turn up ~ and well.* | **dead or ~** ◊ *The police are desperate to catch this man dead or ~.* | **lucky to be ~** ◊ *It was a very narrow escape and we are lucky to be ~.* | **more dead than ~** ◊ *Poor child, she looks more dead than ~.*

2 full of life
VERBS **be, feel, seem** ◊ *I feel really ~ in the country!* | **come** ◊ *The city comes ~ at night.* | **bring sb/sth** ◊ *The wealth of detail in his book really brings it ~.*
ADV. **really, truly, very | fully | intensely | only half** ◊ *She*

realized that she had only been half ~ for the last four years. | **suddenly** ◊ *His eyes were suddenly ~ with excitement.*
PREP. **with** ◊ *The hall was ~ with the sound of voices.*

3 continuing to exist
VERBS **be | remain | keep sth** ◊ *The people try to keep the old traditions ~.*
ADV. **very much** ◊ *The old customs are still very much ~ in this region.*
PHRASES **~ and well** ◊ *The art of debate is ~ and well in our schools.*

4 aware of sth
VERBS **be | become | remain**
ADV. **very much**
PREP. **to** ◊ *He remained very much ~ to the dangers.*

allegation noun

ADJ. **damaging, serious | baseless, false, spurious** (*esp. BrE*), **unfounded, unproven, unsubstantiated, untrue, wild | malicious | defamatory | credible, true** ◊ *The defendants in the libel case maintain that their ~s are true.* | **fresh, further, new** ◊ *There have been fresh ~s of atrocities.* | **widespread | corruption, fraud, rape**
VERB + ALLEGATION **level** (*esp. BrE*), **make, publish, report | retract** (*esp. BrE*), **withdraw** ◊ *I advise you to withdraw your ~ before I contact my lawyer.* | **be at the centre/center of, be confronted with, face** ◊ *the school at the centre/center of these ~s* | **admit** ◊ *She refused to admit the ~s.* | **deny, dismiss, dispute, reject | answer, contest, counter, refute** ◊ *The president has the right to answer specific ~s.* ◊ *He will need to counter ~s that he accepted money from criminals.* | **confirm, prove, support** ◊ *The committee found no evidence to support ~s of smuggling.* | **disprove** ◊ *It took over two months to disprove the ~.* | **give rise to, lead to, prompt** (*esp. BrE*), **provoke** ◊ *The sudden collapse of the business led to ~s of corrupt deals.* | **examine, investigate, look into, probe** (used in journalism) ◊ *The governor of the prison is investigating ~s that a prisoner was attacked and beaten by a prison warden.*
PREP. **amid ~** ◊ *He has resigned amid corruption ~s.* | **~ about, ~ concerning** ◊ *~s about the president's private life* | **~ against** ◊ *He has made certain ~s against the company.*

allegiance noun

ADJ. **full, strong** ◊ *We will give our full ~ to the party.* | **traditional | shifting** ◊ *It is hard to keep up with the shifting ~s between the various political parties.* | **national, political, religious | blind** ◊ *Love of one's country does not mean blind ~ to a regime.* | **true** ◊ *He keeps everyone guessing about his true ~.* | **primary | class, party**
VERB + ALLEGIANCE **give, owe** ◊ *He owed his ~ to the organization that had given him all his opportunities.* | **declare, pledge, profess** (*esp. BrE*), **swear** ◊ *The rebels now have to swear ~ to a leader they hate.* | **show | feel | abandon** ◊ *Many people have abandoned their traditional party ~s.* | **change, shift, switch, transfer | claim** ◊ *The various splinter groups all claim ~ to the true spirit of the movement.* | **claim, command** ◊ *Catholicism claims ~ from more than 80% of the population.* | **retain** ◊ *The union needs to retain the ~ of all its members for the strike to succeed.*
PREP. **~ to** ◊ *He is now very rich but his ~ to his working-class origins is still strong.*
PHRASES **an oath of ~, a pledge of ~** ◊ *New officers take an oath of ~ to their country.* ◊ *Every day the children say the Pledge of Allegiance.* (*in the US*)

allergy noun

ADJ. **food | milk, nut, peanut, penicillin, pollen, etc. | respiratory | bad, life-threatening, serious, severe**
VERB + ALLERGY **have, suffer from | develop | diagnose | cause, trigger** ◊ *Hair and feathers can trigger allergies.* | **prevent, treat**
ALLERGY + NOUN **sufferer | specialist** ◊ *You may wish to consult a food ~ specialist for help in planning your diet.* | **symptom | attack | test | drug, medication** (*esp. AmE*), **medicine** (*esp. AmE*), **shot** (*AmE*) ◊ *In severe cases your doctor may recommend ~ shots.* | **season**

alleviate verb

ADV. **considerably, greatly, significantly** (*esp. BrE*) ◇ *These problems have been greatly ~d by the passing of the new Act.* | **partially, partly, somewhat**
VERB + ALLEVIATE **be designed to, help (to)** ◇ *These measures are designed to ~ the situation.* | **do little to, do nothing to** ◇ *Her words did little to ~ his fears.*

alley noun

ADJ. **dark, darkened** | **deserted, empty** (*esp. AmE*) | **little, narrow** ◇ *a maze of narrow ~s* | **cobbled** (*esp. BrE*) | **back, side** | **blind** (*figurative*) ◇ *Over-reliance on statistics has led us down a blind ~.*
ALLEY + VERB **lead onto sth, lead to sth** ◇ *The ~ leads to the restaurant kitchen.*
ALLEY + NOUN **cat**
PREP. **along an/the ~, down an/the ~, up an/the ~** ◇ *I walked back along a side ~.* ◇ *a bar down a little ~* | **in an/the ~** ◇ *They had cornered him in an ~.* | **through an/the ~** ◇ *She wandered through the back ~s.*

alliance noun

ADJ. **broad** ◇ *The organization is a broad ~ of many different groups.* | **grand** | **close** | **powerful, strong** | **fragile, loose, uneasy** ◇ *a loose ~ of opposition groups* | **shifting** ◇ *the shifting ~s among the various political groups* | **formal, informal** | **strategic, working** | **unholy** ◇ *an unholy ~ between the Fascists and the Communists* | **unlikely** | **temporary** | **global, transatlantic, Western** | **defensive, military** | **electoral** (*esp. BrE*), **political** | **opposition** | **marriage**
VERB + ALLIANCE **have** ◇ *They have ~s with other companies.* | **seek** | **announce** | **build, build up, create, develop, enter into, establish, forge, form, make, strike up** ◇ *The government has tried to forge ~s with environmentalists.* | **join** ◇ *Seven more countries have been invited to join the ~.* | **cement, strengthen** ◇ *The marriage was meant to cement the ~ between the two countries.* | **maintain** | **seek**
PREP. **in ~ with** ◇ *The government, in ~ with the army, has decided to ban all public meetings for a month.* | **~ against** ◇ *old ~s against enemies that no longer exist* | **~ between** ◇ *an ~ between the USSR and India* | **~ with** ◇ *an ~ with China*
PHRASES **~ of convenience** ◇ *It was an ~ of convenience, not of conviction.*

allied adj.

VERBS **be**
ADV. **closely** | **loosely** ◇ *an offensive by seven loosely ~ guerrilla groups*
PREP. **to** ◇ *The US remains closely ~ to Saudi Arabia.* | **with** ◇ *The party is ~ with the Communists.*

allocate verb

ADV. **randomly** | **efficiently** ◇ *Local authorities have to learn to ~ resources efficiently.*
PREP. **according to, by** ◇ *Millions of dollars were ~d by the government.* | **for** ◇ *More money should be ~d for famine relief.* | **to** ◇ *More funds will now be ~d to charitable organizations.*

allocation noun

1 process of giving sth out
ADJ. **efficient, inefficient** | **random** | **fair** | **asset, budget, budgetary** (*esp. BrE*), **grant** (*esp. BrE*), **housing** (*esp. BrE*), **land, resource, time**
VERB + ALLOCATION **make** ◇ *The ~ must be made according to a strict set of criteria.* | **announce** ◇ *He announced the ~ of additional funds for the campaign.*

2 amount given to sb
ADJ. **total** | **fair**

VERB + ALLOCATION **get, receive** | **increase** ◇ *The charity is trying to get its ~ increased for next year.* | **cut, reduce**

allowance noun

1 amount of sth that you are allowed
ADJ. **baggage** | **tax** | **holiday** (*BrE*)
VERB + ALLOWANCE **be entitled to, get, have** ◇ *You're entitled to a baggage ~ of 28 kilos.*
PHRASES **recommended daily ~** ◇ *The recommended daily ~ of vitamin C is 60–90 milligrams.*

2 amount of money sb receives regularly
ADJ. **generous, large** | **meagre/meager** (*esp. BrE*), **small** | **annual, daily, monthly, weekly** | **attendance, child, disability, family** (*esp. BrE*) | **clothing, housing, travel**
VERB + ALLOWANCE **be entitled to** ◇ *You may be entitled to a clothing ~ if your job requires it.* | **get, receive** | **claim** | **give sb, grant** ◇ *The company gives me a travel ~.* | **spend** ◇ *She spends her ~ on clothes.*
PREP. **~ of** ◇ *an ~ of $25* | **~ for** ◇ *The weekly ~ for each child is £15.*

allusion noun

ADJ. **clear, direct** | **frequent** | **indirect, subtle, vague, veiled** ◇ *She was made uncomfortable by his veiled ~ to the previous night.* | **biblical, classical, cultural, historical, literary, Shakespearean**
VERB + ALLUSION **contain, include** | **make** ◇ *He makes several ~s to these events in his latest book.*
PREP. **~ to**

ally noun

ADJ. **great, important, key, powerful, strong** | **close** ◇ *Charles remained a close ~ of the French king.* | **loyal, reliable, staunch, trusted** | **natural, strategic, useful, valuable** | **long-time** (*esp. AmE*), **old, traditional** ◇ *Portugal is a traditional ~ of England.* | **erstwhile, former** | **wartime** | **potential** | **European, NATO, Western, etc.** | **political**
VERB + ALLY **have** ◇ *Lois felt that she had an ~.* | **find, gain, get** | **alienate, lose**
PREP. **~ against** ◇ *He now had an ~ against his boss.*
PHRASES **find an ~ in sb, have an ~ in sb** ◇ *She had found an ~ in her old teacher.* | **a friend and ~** ◇ *a friend and ~ of the president*

alone adj.

VERBS **be, feel, sit, stand** ◇ *These islands are too small to stand ~ as independent states.* | **feel** ◇ *I've never felt so ~ as I do now.* | **leave sb, let sb** ◇ *Don't touch me! Leave me ~!*
ADV. **very much** ◇ *I felt vulnerable and very much ~.* | **all, completely, entirely, quite, utterly** ◇ *Carol felt all ~ in the world.* ◇ *He felt lost and completely ~.* | **together** ◇ *Finally the two of us were ~ together.*
PREP. **with** ◇ *She did not want to be ~ with him.*

aloof adj.

VERBS **be, look, seem** | **find sb** ◇ *Some people find her ~ and unfriendly.* | **hold (yourself), keep (yourself), remain, stand** ◇ *Some thought that Britain was standing ~ from Europe.*
ADV. **somewhat** | **a little, slightly, etc.**
PREP. **from** ◇ *He has remained somewhat ~ from the business of politics.*

alphabet noun

ADJ. **Arabic, Cyrillic, Greek, Hebrew, Latin, Roman, etc.** | **phonetic**
VERB + ALPHABET **know, learn** | **recite**
PREP. **in the ~** ◇ *How many letters are there in the Greek ~?*
PHRASES **the letters of the ~**

altar noun

ADJ. **high, main** | **makeshift, portable** | **sacrificial**

alter

VERB + ALTAR **approach, go up to** ◇ *The bride approached the ~.* | **face** | **decorate** ◇ *The ~s were decorated with images.* | **dedicate** ◇ *an ~ dedicated to Saint John* | **build** ◇ *He built an ~ to God and made a sacrifice.*

ALTAR + NOUN **boy** | **cloth, frontal** | **rail** | **table** | **call** (*esp. AmE*) ◇ *He accompanied his friend to the front during an ~ call.*

PREP. **at an/the ~** ◇ *Helen and Tony knelt at the ~.* | **before an/the ~** ◇ *He lay prostrate before the high ~.* | **on an/the ~** ◇ *He placed the candles on the ~.* | **~ of** ◇ *the high ~ of the church*

alter *verb*

ADV. **completely, considerably** (*esp. BrE*), **dramatically, drastically, fundamentally, greatly, profoundly, radically, significantly, substantially** ◇ *He had not ~ed greatly in the last ten years.* | **slightly** | **forever, irreversibly, irrevocably, permanently**

PHRASES **not ~ the fact that** ◇ *Unemployment has come down slightly but this does not ~ the fact that it is still a major problem.*

alteration *noun*

ADJ. **dramatic, extensive, fundamental, major, radical, significant, substantial** (*esp. BrE*) | **minor, slight, small, subtle**

VERB + ALTERATION **carry out, do, make** | **cause** | **undergo** | **need, require** ◇ *The leaflets require no ~ from year to year.*

PREP. **~ in** ◇ *There will be no ~ in the level of subsidy.* | **~ to** ◇ *We will have to make a slight ~ to the plans.*

alternative *noun*

ADJ. **attractive, effective, good, radical** | **acceptable, reasonable, suitable** | **available, credible, practical, real, realistic, serious, viable** ◇ *Is there a viable ~ to prison?* | **clear, obvious** | **cheap, healthy, interesting, safe** ◇ *a healthier ~ to fried chicken*

VERB + ALTERNATIVE **have** ◇ *We have two ~s.* | **offer, provide** ◇ *His idea seemed to offer a possible ~.* | **develop, find, seek** ◇ *We'll have to find an ~.* ◇ *They are seeking ~s to fossil fuels.* | **consider, discuss, explore** | **present, propose, suggest**

ALTERNATIVE + VERB **be available, exist**

PREP. **~ for** ◇ *There is no ~ for those with no car of their own.* | **~ to** ◇ *Is there an ~ to surgery for this complaint?*

PHRASES **have little ~ (but to), have no ~ (but to)** ◇ *She had no ~ but to do as he said.* | **leave sb with no ~ (but to)** ◇ *He was left with no ~ but to hobble to the nearest hospital.*

altitude *noun*

ADJ. **extreme, great, high** | **low** | **maximum, minimum** | **cruising** ◇ *The plane took off and climbed to cruising ~.*

VERB + ALTITUDE **cruise at, fly at, maintain** ◇ *The aircraft maintained an ~ of 28 000 feet.* | **reach, rise to** ◇ *The aviators reported the columns of smoke rising to an ~ of 2 000 feet.* | **gain** | **lose** ◇ *The plane suddenly started to lose ~.*

ALTITUDE + NOUN **sickness** | **training** ◇ *She plans to carry out ~ training before going to the Olympics.*

PREP. **at (an/the) ~** ◇ *No trees will grow at that ~.* ◇ *people who lived at high ~s* ◇ *It's harder to breathe at ~.* | **~ of** ◇ *They fly at ~s of up to 15 000 feet.*

amateur *noun*

1 sb who does an activity for pleasure, not money

ADJ. **gifted, talented, top** | **enthusiastic** (*esp. BrE*), **keen** (*BrE*) | **gentleman** (*BrE*) ◇ *International affairs today are no longer for gentleman ~s.*

PREP. **as an ~** ◇ *I was competing as an ~.*

2 sb who is not very good at sth

ADJ. **bumbling** (*esp. BrE*), **complete, rank** ◇ *The others had often been skiing before and made her feel like a rank ~.*

...OF AMATEURS **bunch** ◇ *They're just a bunch of ~s.*

amazed *adj.*

VERBS **be, look, seem, sound, stand**

ADV. **absolutely, completely, just, pretty** (*esp. AmE*), **quite, really, totally, truly, utterly** | **genuinely** | **always, constantly, continually** | **still** ◇ *I am still ~ that she won first prize.*

PREP. **at** ◇ *Frances was ~ at her sudden strength.* | **by** ◇ *I was totally ~ by the brilliance of her paintings.*

PHRASES **continue to be ~, never cease to be ~** ◇ *I never cease to be ~ at the way people hurt one another.* | **shocked and ~** ◇ *I was shocked and ~ at what I was seeing.*

amazement *noun*

ADJ. **complete, sheer, utter** | **stunned, wide-eyed** | **mock** ◇ *She raised her eyebrows in mock ~.*

VERB + AMAZEMENT **express**

PREP. **in ~** ◇ *He stared at the animal in ~.* | **to sb's ~** ◇ *To her ~, she got the job.* | **with ~** ◇ *Laura looked around her with ~.* | **~ at** ◇ *He expressed ~ at being left out of the game.*

amazing *adj.*

VERBS **be, look, sound, taste** | **find sb/sth**

ADV. **absolutely, pretty, rather** (*esp. AmE*), **really, simply, truly, utterly** ◇ *a truly ~ achievement* | **just, quite** ◇ *He remembered our names from ten years ago— isn't that just ~?* | **most** ◇ *I saw the most ~ movie yesterday!*

PHRASES **be nothing short of ~** (*esp. AmE*) ◇ *The results of the treatment were nothing short of ~.*

ambassador *noun*

ADJ. **former** | **British, French, US, etc.** | **unofficial** | **special** | **roving** ◇ *She served as a roving ~, with 51 trips to foreign countries by 1999.* | **goodwill**

VERB + AMBASSADOR **act as, serve as** | **appoint, appoint sb (as), make sb** ◇ *She's been appointed ~ to the UN.* | **send** ◇ *The King sent an ~ to Paris.* | **recall, withdraw** ◇ *The US ~ was recalled to Washington in protest.* | **expel**

PREP. **~ in** ◇ *the Israeli ~ in London* | **~ for** (*often figurative*) ◇ *He's a great ~ for the sport of bodybuilding.* | **~ to** ◇ *He served as ~ to Syria.*

ambiguity *noun*

ADJ. **certain, possible, potential** ◇ *The poem contains a certain ~.* | **moral, sexual** | **inherent** ◇ *the inherent ~ of language*

...OF AMBIGUITY **degree, element** ◇ *There is a degree of ~ in this statement.*

VERB + AMBIGUITY **lead to** ◇ *Incorrect choice of words leads to ~ for the reader.* | **avoid** ◇ *The document has been carefully written to avoid ~.* | **clarify, reduce** | **eliminate, remove, resolve** ◇ *They had to change some of the wording in the document to resolve the ~.*

AMBIGUITY + VERB **arise, occur** ◇ *Ambiguity arises when students' spoken English is very limited.* | **surround** ◇ *the ~ surrounding the concept of 'reality'*

PREP. **~ about** ◇ *There will always be some ~ about what actually happened.* | **~ in** ◇ *There was some ~ in what he said.*

PHRASES **a source of ~**

ambiguous *adj.*

VERBS **be** | **remain** | **leave sth, make sth, render sth** ◇ *The paragraph is rendered ~ by the writer's careless use of pronouns.*

ADV. **highly, very** | **rather, slightly, somewhat** | **deliberately, intentionally** ◇ *I suspected that he was being deliberately ~.* | **morally, sexually** ◇ *He is portrayed as a dark and somewhat morally ~ character.*

ambition *noun*

1 strong desire to be successful

ADJ. **driving** (*esp. BrE*), **great, naked** ◇ *She's a woman of driving ~.* | **personal**

VERB + AMBITION **have** ◇ *He has no ~.* | **lack**

AMBITION + VERB **burn** ◇ *Ambition burned within her.*

2 sth you very much want to have/do

ADJ. **big, burning, driving** (esp. BrE), **great, high, main** (esp. BrE), **ultimate** (esp. BrE) ◇ Her biggest ~ was to climb Everest. | **lifelong, life's** ◇ At last he had realized his life's ~. | **long-held, long-standing** (both esp. BrE) | **grandiose, lofty** | **modest** (esp. BrE) | **personal** | **secret** | **youthful** | **frustrated, thwarted, unfulfilled** ◇ This is a tale of jealousy and thwarted ~s. | **artistic, career, literary, political, presidential, social, sporting** (BrE) | **global, imperial, imperialist, nuclear, territorial** ◇ the company's global ~s
VERB + AMBITION **cherish, harbour/harbor, have, nurture** (esp. BrE) ◇ He had only one ~ in life. | **abandon, give up** | **achieve, fulfil/fulfill, realize** | **limit** | **frustrate, thwart** ◇ He felt great resentment at having his ~ frustrated.

ambitious adj.

1 determined to be successful

VERBS **be, seem**
ADV. **extremely, fairly, very, etc.** | **highly** ◇ He is a highly ~ politician. | **fiercely, ruthlessly** | **politically, socially**
PREP. **for** ◇ She is very ~ for her four children.

2 difficult to achieve

VERBS **be, seem**
ADV. **extremely, fairly, very, etc.** | **hugely, wildly** | **overly** ◇ Phases 2 and 3 seem overly ~.
PREP. **in** ◇ The book is ~ in scope.

ambivalence noun

ADJ. **deep, profound** ◇ She feels a profound ~ about her origins. | **moral, sexual**
VERB + AMBIVALENCE **feel** | **express, reflect, show** ◇ The document expressed some ~ over the doctrine of predestination. | **resolve**
PREP. **with** ~ ◇ She viewed her daughter's education with ~. | ~ **about** ◇ their ~ about supporting the government | ~ **in** ◇ There is a sexual ~ in her public image. | ~ **over** ◇ his ~ over money | ~ **towards/toward** ◇ She felt a certain ~ towards/toward him.

ambivalent adj.

VERBS **be, feel, seem, sound** | **remain**
ADV. **extremely, fairly, very, etc.** | **deeply, highly, profoundly** ◇ The party's position on nuclear weapons is deeply ~. | **morally, sexually** ◇ In his latest film, he plays a sexually ~ bartender.
PREP. **about** ◇ He feels rather ~ about his role as teacher.

ambulance noun

ADJ. **air, field, land** ◇ He had to be flown by air ~ to a Las Vegas hospital. | **emergency** (esp. BrE) | **waiting** ◇ I was put straight into a waiting ~ and rushed to the hospital.
VERB + AMBULANCE **call (for), get, phone (for)** (esp. BrE), **ring (for)** (BrE), **telephone (for)** (BrE) ◇ Quick, call an ~! | **send** ◇ An ~ was sent to the scene of the accident. | **load sb into** (esp. AmE), **put sb in, put sb into** ◇ He was put into an ~ and taken away. | **drive**
AMBULANCE + VERB **be on its way** ◇ Don't worry—the ~ is on its way. | **arrive, come** ◇ When the ~ came, I carried her out to it.
AMBULANCE + NOUN **service** (esp. BrE) | **crew, personnel** (BrE), **staff** (BrE) | **driver** | **man, paramedic, technician, worker** (all BrE) | **chief, spokesman** (both BrE) | **station** (BrE) | **trust** (BrE) ◇ the region's three ~ trusts | **chaser** (figurative, esp. AmE) ◇ Her attorney is nothing more then an ~ chaser.
PREP. **by** ~ ◇ She was rushed to hospital by ~. | **in an/the** ~ ◇ He went in the ~ with Louise.

ambush noun

ADJ. **deadly** | **enemy**
VERB + AMBUSH **lay, prepare, set up** ◇ The soldiers set up an ~ on the road. | **carry out, spring, stage** ◇ They staged an ~ on an army patrol. | **be caught in, run into, walk into** ◇ We ran into an ~ in the valley.
AMBUSH + VERB **take place**

PREP. **in an/the** ~ ◇ Twelve men were killed in the ~. | ~ **on** ◇ an ~ on an army patrol
PHRASES **lie in** ~, **wait in** ~ ◇ The soldiers lay in ~ for the enemy troops.

amenable adj.

VERBS **be, prove** | **seem** | **find sb/sth** | **render sth**
ADV. **highly, most, particularly** ◇ The manager was most ~. Nothing was too much trouble.
PREP. **to** ◇ You should find him ~ to reasonable arguments.

amendment noun

ADJ. **important, major, significant** ◇ A major ~ was introduced into the legislation. | **minor, slight, small** | **draft, proposed** | **subsequent** | **constitutional** | **balanced-budget** (AmE), **budget** (esp. AmE) | **congressional, federal** (both in the US) | **Lords, parliamentary** (both in the UK) | **rebel** (BrE) ◇ In total 217 MPs backed the rebel ~ opposing the government. | **Fifth Amendment, First Amendment, etc.** (= of the US Constitution) ◇ He is simply exercising his First-Amendment rights.
VERB + AMENDMENT **introduce, make** | **draft** ◇ The committee does not adequately consult others when drafting ~s. | **move** (BrE), **offer** (AmE), **propose, put forward** (esp. BrE), **suggest, table** (BrE) ◇ He moved an ~ limiting capital punishment to certain very serious crimes. | **add** ◇ The Senate added numerous ~s to the bill. | **withdraw** ◇ She withdrew her ~ and left the meeting. | **repeal** (esp. AmE) ◇ a call to repeal the 22nd ~ to the Constitution | **back, endorse** (AmE), **support** | **accept, adopt, approve, pass, ratify, vote for** ◇ The Senate accepted the ~ and the bill was eventually passed. ◇ On a free vote, the ~ was carried by 292 votes to 246. | **oppose, vote against** | **defeat, reject**
AMENDMENT + VERB **pass (sth)** (esp. AmE) ◇ The ~ passed in 2001. | **ban sth, outlaw sth, prohibit sth** (all esp. AmE) ◇ a constitutional ~ banning same-sex marriage | **guarantee, protect** (both esp. AmE)
PREP. **without** ~ ◇ The new clause was accepted without ~. | ~ **to** ◇ They have proposed an ~ to the federal constitution.

amenity noun

ADJ. **excellent** | **basic** | **local** (BrE) ◇ The campsite is close to all local amenities. | **modern** ◇ a hotel with all modern amenities | **public** ◇ The building will be developed as a public ~. | **cultural, environmental, leisure** (esp. BrE), **lifestyle** (esp. AmE), **natural** (esp. AmE), **recreational, social** ◇ the diverse cultural amenities of cities
VERB + AMENITY **have** ◇ The hotel has excellent amenities. | **offer, provide** ◇ They will provide an ~ for local residents. | **lack** ◇ All of the houses lacked basic amenities. | **improve** (esp. BrE)

amiable adj.

VERBS **be, look, seem, sound**
ADV. **extremely, fairly, very, etc.** | **perfectly** (esp. BrE) ◇ a perfectly ~ young man | **enough** ◇ I've only met Annie once but she seems ~ enough.

ammunition noun

ADJ. **live** | **blank** (esp. BrE) | **artillery**
... OF AMMUNITION **round**
VERB + AMMUNITION **carry, have** | **load** | **fire, use** | **be out of, run out of** ◇ A few of the jeeps had run out of ~.
AMMUNITION + NOUN **depot, dump, store** (esp. BrE)

amnesty noun

ADJ. **blanket** (esp. AmE), **general** | **political** | **tax** (esp. AmE) | **firearms, gun, knife** (all BrE)
VERB + AMNESTY **give sb, grant, offer** ◇ The government granted an ~ to all political prisoners. | **announce, declare** | **oppose, support**
AMNESTY + NOUN **program** (AmE) ◇ the President's ~ program for illegal aliens

PREP. **~ for** ◇ *They announced a general ~ for crimes committed during the war.*

amount noun

ADJ. **considerable, copious ~s, enormous, huge, immense, incredible, large, massive, significant, substantial, tremendous, vast** ◇ *a considerable ~ of money* ◇ *He drank copious ~s of beer.* | **high, low** ◇ *exposure to high ~s of oxygen* | **adequate, reasonable** | **disproportionate, excessive, inordinate** | **increasing** | **decent, fair, good** (*esp. AmE*) ◇ *There was a fair ~ of traffic on the roads.* | **certain** | *You have a certain ~ of freedom to explore new techniques.* | **limited, minimal, minute, moderate, negligible, small, tiny** | **full, total** ◇ *You must pay back the full ~ of money that you owe.* | **maximum, minimum** ◇ *He aimed to cause the maximum ~ of embarrassment.* | **exact** | **right** ◇ *The sauce has just the right ~ of salt.* | **equal, equivalent** ◇ *Mix the ingredients in equal ~s.* ◇ *an ~ equivalent to 3% per annum* | **varying** ◇ *Tap water also contains varying ~s of rust and grit.*
VERB + AMOUNT **double, increase** | **decrease, limit, reduce** ◇ *They want to limit the ~ of cash available.*
AMOUNT + VERB **double, increase** ◇ *The ~ of reclaimed glass used in industry has doubled in the last five years.* | **decrease, fall** ◇ *The average ~ of sunshine fell this year.*
PREP. **~ of**

amuse verb

ADV. **greatly, no end** (*BrE*), **to no end** (*AmE*) ◇ *Her discomfort ~d him greatly.* ◇ *His impersonation of the President ~d me (to) no end.* | **always**
VERB + AMUSE **seem to** ◇ *The thought of me on the stage seemed to ~ him.* | **try to** | **never cease to, never fail to** ◇ *It never fails to ~ me how excited people can get about winning a game.*
PREP. **with** ◇ *He ~d us with his stories.*

amused adj.

VERBS **be, look, seem, sound** ◇ *She looked faintly ~.* | **keep sb** ◇ *He kept the children ~ for hours.*
ADV. **extremely, fairly, very, etc.** | **greatly, highly, much, thoroughly, vastly** ◇ *He was much ~ by all this talk.* | **not at all** ◇ *I was not at all ~ to find they had eaten all the cake.* | **a little, slightly, etc.** | **faintly, mildly, vaguely** | **clearly** ◇ *Mr Stopes was clearly ~ by the confusion.* | **genuinely** | **quietly** | **easily** ◇ *I am very easily ~.*
PREP. **at** ◇ *Tony was very ~ at the story.* | **by** ◇ *She seemed greatly ~ by his jokes.*

amusement noun

1 feeling of wanting to laugh

ADJ. **great, much** (*esp. BrE*) | **faint, mild** | **quiet** | **ironic, wry** | **genuine, obvious, real** | **personal** ◇ *He kept the diaries for his own personal ~.*
... OF AMUSEMENT **glimmer** | **hint, note, trace** ◇ *There was a note of ~ in her voice.*
VERB + AMUSEMENT **afford sb** (*formal*), **cause** (*esp. BrE*), **provide** | **derive, find, get** ◇ *He seemed to be deriving ~ from her discomfort.* | **show** | **conceal, hide**
AMUSEMENT + VERB **show** ◇ *A glimmer of ~ showed in her eyes.*
PREP. **for (sb's) ~** ◇ *What do you do for ~ around here?* ◇ *The play was written for the ~ of the other students.* | **in ~** ◇ *Her wide mouth twitched in ~.* | **to sb's ~** ◇ *Much to their ~, I couldn't get the door open.* | **with ~** ◇ *She chuckled with ~.*
PHRASES **a source of ~** ◇ *His son was a constant source of ~ to him.*

2 sth that makes time pass pleasantly

ADJ. **popular** ◇ *She disapproved of popular ~s such as fairs.*
AMUSEMENT + NOUN **arcade** (*BrE*), **park** ◇ *an amusement-park ride* | **machine** (*BrE*)

amusing adj.

VERBS **be, sound** | **find sth, think sth**

ADV. **extremely, fairly, very, etc.** | **highly, most** (*esp. BrE*), **particularly** | **mildly, slightly, vaguely** (*esp. BrE*)
PHRASES **not remotely ~, nothing remotely ~** ◇ *There is nothing even remotely ~ about the situation.*

anaesthetic (*BrE*) (*AmE* anesthetic) noun

ADJ. **general, local**
VERB + ANAESTHETIC/ANESTHETIC **administer, give sb, inject** ◇ *He was given a general ~.* ◇ *A local ~ is injected in an area over your lower spine.* | **use** ◇ *The operation was completed in ten minutes using only local ~.* | **have** ◇ *She had a local ~ to stop the pain.* | **come around from, come round from** (*BrE*), **recover from**
ANAESTHETIC/ANESTHETIC + VERB **take effect, work** ◇ *The ~ began to take effect.* | **wear off**
PREP. **under (an/the) ~** ◇ *It would have to be done under ~.* | **without (an/the) ~** ◇ *They had to operate without ~.*

analogous adj.

VERBS **be** | **appear, seem**
ADV. **closely** | **directly, exactly** | **broadly, roughly, somewhat** (*esp. AmE*) ◇ *The two situations are roughly ~.*
PREP. **to** ◇ *The company is in a position closely ~ to that of its main rival.* | **with** ◇ *The national debt is ~ with private debt.*

analogy noun

ADJ. **appropriate, apt, good, useful** | **close, obvious, perfect** (*esp. AmE*) ◇ *A close ~ with the art of singing can be made.* | **simple** | **bad, false** | **historical, musical, sporting** (*BrE*), **sports** (*AmE*), **etc.**
VERB + ANALOGY **draw, make, suggest, use** ◇ *She drew an ~ between running the economy and a housewife's weekly budget.*
ANALOGY + VERB **fit, hold** ◇ *The Wild West ~ does not fit here.*
PREP. **by ~, by ~ to, by ~ with** ◇ *We can understand this theory by ~ with human beings.* | **~ between** ◇ *She suggested an ~ between the human heart and a pump.* | **~ for** ◇ *The computer is a useful ~ for the brain.* | **~ with** ◇ *There is an ~ here with the way an engine works.*
PHRASES **argument by ~, argument from ~** ◇ *Argument from ~ is not always valid.*

analyse (*BrE*) (*AmE* analyze) verb

ADV. **carefully, critically, fully, in depth, in detail, painstakingly, systematically** ◇ *The results must be ~d in detail.* | **quantitatively, statistically**
VERB + ANALYSE/ANALYZE **attempt to, try to** | **be difficult to, be impossible to** ◇ *The precise reasons for the disaster are difficult to ~.* | **be possible to**

analysis noun

ADJ. **careful, close, comprehensive, detailed, in-depth, serious, systematic, thorough** | **brief** | **objective** | **comparative, critical, qualitative, quantitative, statistical, theoretical** ◇ *We performed a comparative ~ of genes from different species.* | **cost-benefit, critical, economic, financial, historical, legal, linguistic, political, strategic, structural** | **content, data, discourse** ◇ *Researchers identified themes from the content ~ of interviews.* | **chemical, genetic, sequence** ◇ *a DNA sequence ~*
VERB + ANALYSIS **carry out, conduct** (*esp. AmE*), **do, make, perform** (*esp. BrE*) ◇ *They carried out an in-depth ~ of the results.* | **give (sb)** ◇ *She gave a brief ~ of the present economic situation.*
ANALYSIS + VERB **indicate sth, reveal sth, show sth** ◇ *Analysis of the wine showed that it contained dangerous additives.*
PREP. **in an/the ~** ◇ *In his ~ of the novel he discusses various aspects of the author's own life.*
PHRASES **in the final ~, in the last ~** ◇ *In the final ~, the people were stronger than the generals.*

analyst noun

ADJ. **leading, principal, senior** (*esp. AmE*) ◇ *a leading business ~* | **business, computer, data, financial, industry, intelligence, investment, legal** (*esp. AmE*), **market, media,**

military, policy, political, research (*esp. AmE*), retail, security, systems | CIA, Wall Street, etc.
PREP. **~ of** ◇ *He was a shrewd ~ of players' strengths and weaknesses.*
→ Note at JOB

anarchy *noun*

ADJ. **complete, total** | **near, virtual** ◇ *The high number of strikes resulted in near ~.* | **moral** | **international**
VERB + ANARCHY **bring, cause, create, lead to, result in** ◇ *The defeat of the government would lead to ~.* | **collapse into, descend into, slide into** ◇ *If prices rise, the country could slide into ~.* | **prevent, save sth from** ◇ *The parties joined forces to save the country from ~.*
ANARCHY + VERB **reign** ◇ *Anarchy reigned in the countryside as bandits attacked government convoys.*
PHRASES **the brink of ~, the edge of ~** ◇ *The strikes brought the city to the brink of ~.*

anatomy *noun*

ADJ. **animal, human** | **female, male** | **comparative**
VERB + ANATOMY **study** ◇ *I'm studying human ~.*
PHRASES **a part of your ~** (*often humorous*) ◇ *He was hit in a rather sensitive part of his ~.* | **~ and physiology** ◇ *a college-level course in ~ and physiology*

ancestor *noun*

ADJ. **direct** ◇ *The builder of the house was a direct ~ of the present owner.* | **immediate** | **ancient, distant, early, remote** ◇ *a distant ~ of mine* ◇ *Our earliest ~s lived in a world fraught with danger.* | **common** ◇ *The two species share a common ~.* | **ape-like, human** | **illustrious** ◇ *The Romans built these monuments to glorify their illustrious ~s.* | **literary, spiritual, etc.** (*figurative*) ◇ *He claims as his literary ~s such giants as Henry James and William Faulkner.*
VERB + ANCESTOR **be descended from, have, share** ◇ *A lot of the people there are descended from a common ~.* | **trace** (*esp. BrE*) ◇ *He can trace his ~s back to the reign of Elizabeth I.* | **honour/honor** ◇ *They honour/honor their ~s and believe in the spirits of nature.*

ancestry *noun*

ADJ. **common, shared** ◇ *The two species have developed from a common ~.* | **African, Japanese, etc.**
VERB + ANCESTRY **claim, have, share** ◇ *Humans share a common ~ with chimpanzees.* | **trace** ◇ *We can trace our ~ back to the 17th century.*
ANCESTRY + VERB **go back to** ◇ *The company claims an ~ going back to 1727.*
PHRASES **be of Irish, German, etc. ~** ◇ *He is of Chinese ~.*

anchor *noun*

VERB + ANCHOR **cast, drop, lower** ◇ *The ship cast ~ in the bay.* ◇ *We dropped ~ off a small island.* | **raise, weigh** ◇ *We raised the ~ and set sail.* ◇ *We weighed ~ next morning and sailed south.* | **lie at, ride at** ◇ *The ship lay at ~ in the bay.*
PREP. **at ~** ◇ *the ships at ~ in the bay*

anchor *verb*

ADV. **firmly, securely, well** ◇ *The crane is securely ~ed at two points.*
PREP. **to** ◇ *The ropes were ~ed to the rocks.*

ancient *adj.*

VERBS **be, look**
ADV. **extremely, fairly, very, etc.** | **incredibly** | **positively** ◇ *The man looked positively ~.*

anecdote *noun*

ADJ. **amusing, entertaining, humorous, interesting** | **telling** ◇ *The biographer provides a telling ~ about the President's actions at this time.* | **personal**
VERB + ANECDOTE **recount, relate, tell** ◇ *She is good at telling ~s.* | **exchange, share, swap**
PREP. **~ about** ◇ *We swapped ~s about old friends.*

anesthetic *noun* (*AmE*) → See ANAESTHETIC

angel *noun*

1 heavenly being

ADJ. **guardian** | **avenging** ◇ *He liked to think of himself as an avenging ~ fighting for justice.* | **fallen** ◇ *a book about anti-heroes and fallen ~s* | **snow** (*AmE*) ◇ *We lay back in the snow and made snow ~s.*
... OF ANGELS **choir, host** ◇ *a whole host of ~s*
VERB + ANGEL **look like** ◇ *She looks like an ~.*
ANGEL + NOUN **wings** ◇ *She wore a white costume with big furry ~ wings.*
PHRASES **the face of an ~, the voice of an ~** ◇ *a singer who has the voice of an ~*

2 good/kind person

ADJ. **absolute, little, perfect** (*esp. AmE*) ◇ *Deborah's children are little ~s.* | **ministering** ◇ *I could hardly see Lisa in the role of ministering ~.*
ANGEL + NOUN **investor** ◇ *An ~ investor provided the start-up capital.*
PHRASES **be an ~** (*esp. BrE*) ◇ *Be an ~ and make the tea, will you?* | **be no ~** ◇ *I'm no ~, but I wouldn't dream of doing a thing like that.*

anger *noun*

ADJ. **bitter, deep, fierce, great, intense, seething** | **genuine, real** | **growing, mounting, rising** ◇ *mounting ~ among teachers and parents* | **sudden** | **righteous** ◇ *Catherine appeared in the doorway, shaking with righteous ~.* | **controlled, pent-up, suppressed** | **popular, public** | **widespread** (*esp. BrE*)
... OF ANGER **burst, fit, flash, outburst** ◇ *He slammed the door in a fit of ~.* ◇ *She felt a brief flash of ~.*
VERB + ANGER **be filled with, feel, seethe with, shake with, tremble with** ◇ *His eyes were filled with ~.* ◇ *She was trembling with ~.* | **express, release, show, vent, voice** ◇ *Children express their ~ in various ways.* | **channel, direct** ◇ *He tried to channel his ~ into political activism.* ◇ *Much of the public's ~ was directed at the government.* | **control, hide, suppress** ◇ *It is not healthy to suppress your ~.* | **arouse, cause, fuel, provoke, stir up** ◇ *His words only served to fuel her ~.* | **change to, give way to, turn into, turn to** ◇ *His joy soon turned to ~ when he heard the full story.*
ANGER + VERB **boil over, boil up, bubble up, build up, flare, flare up, grow, mount, rise, well up** ◇ *Hank stood up, his ~ rising.* | **abate, drain, evaporate, fade, subside** ◇ *The ~ drained from his face.* ◇ *Her ~ subsided as quickly as it had flared up.*
ANGER + NOUN **management** ◇ *You could probably benefit from ~ management classes.*
PREP. **in ~** ◇ *He raised his voice in ~.* | **with ~** ◇ *His face was flushed with ~.* | **~ against** ◇ *her feelings of ~ against the murderer* | **~ at** ◇ *I felt a sudden ~ at his suggestion.* | **~ over** ◇ *There is much ~ over plans to close the hospital.* | **~ towards/toward** ◇ *her ~ towards/toward her parents*
PHRASES **a feeling of ~** | **in a moment of ~** ◇ *He had walked out in a moment of ~.*

anger *verb*

ADV. **deeply, greatly** ◇ *I was deeply ~ed by their lack of concern.* | **easily** ◇ *He is not easily ~ed.*

angle *noun*

1 space between lines/surfaces that meet

ADJ. **acute, oblique, obtuse, right** | **45-degree, 90-degree, etc.** | **external, internal** | **narrow, sharp, steep** ◇ *The plane started descending at a steep ~.* | **shallow, slight, wide** ◇ *The instrument has a wide ~ of view.* | **awkward, crazy, odd, unnatural, weird** ◇ *The calf's legs were splayed out at awkward ~s.* | **jaunty** ◇ *He wore his hat at a jaunty ~.*
VERB + ANGLE **form, make** ◇ *The vertical line makes an ~ with the horizontal line.* | **draw** ◇ *Draw a 130° ~ in your*

notebooks. | **adjust, alter, change** ◇ *She adjusted the ~ of the legs to make the table stand more firmly.* | **increase, reduce** | **calculate, measure** | **move through, rotate through** ◇ *Each joint can move through an ~ of 90°.*
PREP. **at an ~** ◇ *The tower of Pisa leans at an ~.* | **~ between** ◇ *the ~ between these two lines*

2 position from which you look at or consider sth

ADJ. **interesting, strange, unusual** ◇ *The subject is considered from an unusual ~.* | **camera** ◇ *The variety of camera ~s gives her photographs interest.* | **viewing**
VERB + ANGLE **take** ◇ *He took a different ~ on the story.*
PREP. **from an ~** ◇ *Seeing herself from this ~, she realized how much like her mother she looked.*
PHRASES **~ of vision** ◇ *How you see the building depends on your ~ of vision.* | **from all ~s, from every conceivable ~, from every possible ~** ◇ *You need to consider the question from all ~s.* ◇ *We've looked at the problem from every possible ~ but still haven't found a solution.*

angry *adj.*

VERBS **appear, be, feel, look, seem, sound** | **become, get, grow, turn** (*esp. AmE*) | **remain, stay** ◇ *She couldn't stay ~ with him for long.* | **get sb** (*esp. AmE*), **make sb** ◇ *That man makes me ~ every time I see him.*
ADV. **extremely, fairly, very, etc.** | **bitterly, furiously, incredibly, terribly** | **a little, slightly, etc.** | **increasingly** | **suddenly** | **clearly, visibly** | **understandably** ◇ *They are understandably ~ that some workers will be fired.*
PREP. **about** ◇ *Local people are very ~ about the plans to close another hospital.* | **at** ◇ *The members of the group are frustrated and ~ at their lack of power.* | **with** ◇ *I got terribly ~ with him.*
PHRASES **have every reason to be ~, have every right to be ~, have a right to be ~** ◇ *She had every right to be ~ about the damage to the house.* | **have no reason to be ~, have no right to be ~**

anguish *noun*

ADJ. **bitter, deep, great, real** | **inner, personal, private** | **emotional, mental, physical, spiritual**
VERB + ANGUISH **cause** ◇ *The loss of a pet can cause some people real ~.* | **experience, feel, suffer** ◇ *He suffered the ~ of watching his son go to prison.*
PREP. **in (sb's) ~** ◇ *to cry out/groan/scream in ~* ◇ *In her ~, she turned to her father for help.* | **with ~** ◇ *His mouth felt dry with ~.* | **~ at, ~ over** ◇ *his ~ at the death of his son*
PHRASES **a cry of ~, a scream of ~** | **pain and ~** ◇ *All the pain and ~ inside her rose like a tidal wave.*

animal *noun*

ADJ. **dead, live, living** ◇ *the export of live ~s for slaughter* | **cold-blooded, warm-blooded** | **higher, lower** | **dumb** | **stuffed** ◇ *glass cases of stuffed ~s* ◇ *She sleeps with lots of stuffed ~s.* | **furry** | **dangerous** | **endangered, rare** | **extinct** | **social, solitary** | **tame, feral, stray, wild** | **exotic** | **non-human** (*technical*) ◇ *research with humans and non-human ~s* | **caged, trapped, wounded** (*often figurative*) ◇ *He was pacing the room like a caged ~.* | **barnyard** (*AmE*), **companion, domestic, domesticated, farm, lab** (*informal, esp. AmE*), **laboratory, zoo** | **aquatic, forest, land, marine** | **draught/draft, pack** ◇ *pack ~s such as mules*
VERB + ANIMAL **have, keep** ◇ *In court he was banned from keeping ~s.* | **breed, raise, rear** (*esp. BrE*) ◇ *~s bred in captivity* | **clone** ◇ *Most cloned ~s die at a premature age.* | **feed** ◇ *The ~s were fed only on pasture.* | **tame, train** ◇ *This ~ can be trained to follow simple orders.* | **hunt, trap** | **butcher, kill, slaughter** | **sacrifice**
ANIMAL + NOUN **life, species** | **behaviour/behavior, instinct** | **lover** | **husbandry** | **experimentation, experiments, testing, tests** ◇ *protests against ~ experiments* | **cruelty** | **rights, welfare** | **fat, products**
PHRASES **the ~ kingdom, the ~ world** ◇ *the wonders of the ~ kingdom* | **a species of ~**

animosity *noun*

ADJ. **personal** | **long-standing**
VERB + ANIMOSITY **bear, feel, have, hold** (*esp. AmE*) ◇ *Despite everything, she bore her former boss no ~.* | **arouse, create, stir up**
PREP. **without ~** ◇ *They managed to discuss their past disagreements without ~.* | **~ between** ◇ *The two rivals for party leadership insist that there is no ~ between them.* | **~ towards/toward** ◇ *I feel no ~ towards/toward the military.*

ankle *noun*

ADJ. **bad, broken, injured, sprained, swollen, twisted** ◇ *I had a broken ~.* | **slender, slim, well-turned** ◇ *She has long legs and slender ~s.*
VERB + ANKLE **break, fracture, hurt, injure, sprain, turn, twist**
ANKLE + NOUN **injury, sprain** | **bone, joint, ligament** | **boots, socks** (*BrE*) | **bracelet**

annex *verb*

ADV. **formally, officially** ◇ *The region was formally ~ed in 1892.* | **illegally**
PREP. **to** ◇ *The territory had been ~ed to Poland.*

annihilation *noun*

ADJ. **complete, total** | **nuclear**
VERB + ANNIHILATION **face** ◇ *They were to surrender immediately or face total ~.* | **threaten, threaten sb/sth with** ◇ *The two superpowers threatened each other with nuclear ~.* | **avoid, escape**

anniversary *noun*

ADJ. **first, second, etc.** | **wedding** | **diamond, golden, silver, etc.** ◇ *The event celebrates its silver ~ this summer.*
VERB + ANNIVERSARY **celebrate, commemorate, honour/honor** (*esp. AmE*), **mark** ◇ *They held celebrations to mark the ~ of Mozart's death.*
ANNIVERSARY + VERB **be, fall** ◇ *The ~ of the founding of the charity falls in November.* | **approach, come up** ◇ *Our 20th ~ is coming up.*
ANNIVERSARY + NOUN **celebration, party** | **edition, issue** ◇ *the 100th ~ edition of this classic novel* | **year** ◇ *the 200th ~ year of Darwin's birth*
PREP. **~ of** ◇ *the ~ of their son's death* | **on an/the ~** ◇ *on the 20th ~ of his death* ◇ *He bought her a diamond ring on their tenth wedding ~.*

announce *verb*

ADV. **formally, officially, publicly** | **happily, proudly, triumphantly** ◇ *The company proudly ~d the launch of its new range of cars.* | **loudly** ◇ *'I'm hungry!' he loudly ~d.*
VERB + ANNOUNCE **be expected to, expect to** ◇ *We expect to ~ details of the plan later this week.* | **be delighted to, be pleased to, be proud to** ◇ *Mr and Mrs James are pleased to ~ the engagement of their daughter, Louise.* | **regret to** ◇ *We regret to ~ the death of our chairman, Tony Rossi.*
PREP. **to** ◇ *He ~d to the crowd that the war was over.*

announcement *noun*

ADJ. **formal, official** | **public** | **public-service** (*AmE*) ◇ *They placed public-service ~s on TV about bullying.* | **government** | **dramatic, startling, stunning, surprise, surprising** ◇ *Phillips issued his surprise ~ after two hours of talks.* | **earnings, merger** (*both esp. AmE*) ◇ *His resignation follows a disappointing earnings ~ by the company.* | **birth, retirement, wedding** (*all AmE*) ◇ *We can produce personalized birth ~s.*
VERB + ANNOUNCEMENT **issue, make** ◇ *We will make a formal ~ tomorrow.* | **greet, welcome** ◇ *The ~ of the ceasefire was greeted with relief.* | **await, expect** ◇ *We are still awaiting an ~ on the possible closure of the plant.* | **hear** ◇ *We heard a security ~.* | **delay** ◇ *He wanted to delay the ~ until after the holidays.*
ANNOUNCEMENT + VERB **come** ◇ *The ~ of further job losses comes at a bad time.*
PREP. **in a/the ~** ◇ *In an ~ to the press, the spokesperson said*

that the peace negotiations would continue. | **~ about** ◇ *an official ~ about the disaster* | **~ by, ~ from** ◇ *an ~ from the president*

announcer *noun*

ADJ. **continuity** (*BrE*), **radio, television, TV** | **baseball, basketball, sports, etc.** (*esp. AmE*) | **public address** (abbreviated to *PA*) ◇ *The PA ~ called out the score.*
→ Note at JOB

annoy *verb*

ADV. **intensely, really** ◇ *His air of calm superiority ~ed her intensely.* ◇ *It really ~s me when people forget to say thank you.*
VERB + ANNOY **be beginning to, be starting to** ◇ *The wasps were beginning to ~ me.*
PHRASES **do sth just to ~ sb, do sth only to ~ sb** ◇ *I only stay out late to ~ my parents.*

annoyance *noun*

1 feeling of being annoyed

ADJ. **great, intense** ◇ *A look of intense ~ crossed his face.* | **obvious** ◇ *She tapped the table with her pen in obvious ~.* | **mild, slight** ◇ *He had a look of mild ~ on his face.* | **mock** ◇ *She rolled her eyes in mock ~.* | **pure, sheer, utter** ◇ *He wore an expression of pure ~.*
...OF ANNOYANCE **flicker** ◇ *A flicker of ~ crossed his face.*
VERB + ANNOYANCE **cause** ◇ *He had been causing ~ to the other guests.* | **feel** ◇ *I felt some ~ when he told me his plans.* | **express, show** ◇ *She tried not to show her ~.* | **hide**
PREP. **in ~** ◇ *He shook his head in ~.* | **with ~** ◇ *Her cheeks flushed with ~.* | **~ at, ~ over, ~ with** ◇ *her ~ with him over his failure to cooperate*
PHRASES **a look of ~** ◇ *There was a look of ~ on his face.* | **to sb's ~, much to sb's ~** ◇ *I dropped out of college, much to the ~ of my parents.*

2 thing that annoys

ADJ. **minor, petty** ◇ *A leaking roof is just one of life's petty ~s.*

annoyed *adj.*

VERBS **be, feel, look, seem, sound** | **become, get** | **make sb** ◇ *His attitude made me extremely ~.*
ADV. **extremely, fairly, very, etc.** | **highly** | **thoroughly** | **increasingly** | **a little, slightly, etc.** | **mildly, vaguely** | **clearly, obviously, visibly**
PREP. **about** ◇ *I was a little ~ about the whole thing.* | **at** ◇ *We enjoyed the game but were rather ~ at being beaten.* | **by** ◇ *I was ~ by her remarks.* | **with** ◇ *Lianne felt slightly ~ with herself.*

annoying *adj.*

VERBS **be, prove** | **become, get** ◇ *Please stop making that noise—it's getting ~.* | **make sth** | **find sth** ◇ *I found it really ~ not to be able to communicate.*
ADV. **extremely, fairly, very, etc.** | **highly, incredibly, etc.** | **a little, slightly, etc.** | **mildly** | **especially, particularly**
PREP. **to** ◇ *The background hum of the fan may be ~ to some users.*

anonymity *noun*

ADJ. **complete, total** | **relative** ◇ *This Canadian author has chosen to live in relative ~ on a Pacific island.*
VERB + ANONYMITY **assure, ensure, guarantee** | **maintain, preserve, protect** ◇ *Our company promises to preserve the ~ of all its clients.* | **demand, insist on, prefer, request, seek** ◇ *Some people prefer the ~ of life in a big city.*

anonymous *adj.*

VERBS **be** | **become** | **remain, stay**
ADV. **completely, entirely** (*esp. BrE*), **totally** | **largely, relatively** ◇ *the largely ~ perpetrators of terrorist acts*
PHRASES **prefer to remain ~, wish to remain ~** ◇ *My client wishes to remain ~.*

answer

answer *noun*

1 sth that you say/write/do as a reply

ADJ. **brief, one-word, quick, short** ◇ *The short ~ to your question is that he has acted completely illegally.* | **blunt, direct, straight, straightforward** ◇ *I expect a straight ~ to a straight question.* | **clear** | **detailed, full, precise** | **definite** ◇ *I cannot give you a definite ~ just yet.* | **immediate** | **final** | **affirmative, positive** | **negative** | **honest, truthful** | **serious** | **real, reasonable, satisfactory, sensible** | **unclear, vague**
VERB + ANSWER **get, have, receive** ◇ *Did you ever get an ~ to your letter?* | **demand, want** ◇ *I want some ~s before I agree to anything.* | **need** | **await, wait for** | **expect** ◇ *He was clearly expecting a different ~.* | **deserve** ◇ *The question deserves a proper ~.* | **give sb, offer, provide, supply** ◇ *Please give her your ~, so she can make the necessary arrangements.* ◇ *We can provide ~s to any questions you may have about the system.* | **formulate** ◇ *I struggled to formulate an ~.* | **guess, know** ◇ *I think you can guess the answer—they won't lend us the money.* | **dread, fear** ◇ *'Is it true?' she asked, dreading the ~.* | **hear** ◇ *He left without waiting to hear her ~.*
ANSWER + VERB **come** ◇ *She pounded on the door, but no ~ came.*
PREP. **in ~ to** ◇ *In ~ to your question, I can only say that we did not find her work of a satisfactory standard.* | **~ to** ◇ *her ~ to his question*

2 solution to a problem

ADJ. **easy, instant, pat, ready, simple, straightforward** ◇ *There are no easy, pat ~s.* | **clear, clear-cut, obvious** ◇ *The obvious ~ would be to cancel the party.* | **logical, plausible, reasonable, sensible** | **adequate, real, satisfactory** | **complete, convincing, definitive, effective, good, perfect** | **long-term** | **partial**
VERB + ANSWER **have, know** ◇ *We are aware of this problem, but we do not have the ~.* | **look for, seek** | **arrive at, come up with, discover, find** ◇ *We have arrived at an ~ which we hope will satisfy everyone.* | **give sb, offer, provide, suggest, yield** ◇ *If you really want to save time, this machine will provide the ~.*
ANSWER + VERB **come to sb** ◇ *The ~ came to him in a flash.* | **depend on sth, lie in sth** ◇ *The ~ lies in a combination of factors.*
PREP. **~ to** ◇ *There is no easy ~ to the problem.*
PHRASES **have all the ~s, know all the ~s** ◇ *He's so arrogant, he thinks he knows all the ~s.*

3 to questions in a test/competition

ADJ. **acceptable, appropriate, correct, right** | **incorrect, wrong** | **written** ◇ *This part of the exam requires a written ~.* | **long, short** (*both esp. AmE*) ◇ *the short-answer section of the test*
VERB + ANSWER **give, submit** | **guess** ◇ *It's not worth guessing the ~, as you may lose points.* | **know** | **find** ◇ *The students are allowed to use textbooks to find the right ~.* | **print, write** ◇ *Please print the ~s to questions 1 and 2.*
PREP. **~ to** ◇ *Do you know the ~ to the question?*

answer *verb*

ADV. **affirmatively, in the affirmative** ◇ *She ~ed in the affirmative.* | **in the negative, negatively** | **honestly, truthfully** ◇ *He tried to ~ as honestly as he could.* | **correctly** | **fully** ◇ *What he told me does not fully ~ the question of what his motives were.* | **satisfactorily** | **evasively, vaguely** (*esp. AmE*) | **confidently, firmly** | **immediately, promptly, quickly** | **finally** | **hesitantly** (*esp. AmE*), **nervously, slowly** | **coldly, coolly, curtly, shortly** | **bluntly, flatly** | **calmly, matter-of-factly** | **quietly, softly** | **simply** ◇ *She ~ed simply, 'No.'* | **drily, sarcastically** | **politely** | **casually, nonchalantly** | **cheerfully** | **sheepishly**

antagonism noun

ADJ. **great, strong** (esp. AmE) | **mutual** | **class, personal, racial**
VERB + ANTAGONISM **feel, have** ◇ She felt nothing but ~ towards/toward her boss. ◇ He seems to have an ~ to the local people. | **express** | **arouse, cause, create, lead to** ◇ The new rules will create a lot of ~.
PREP. **~ between** ◇ the ~ between the two brothers | **~ to** ◇ an attitude of ~ to the legal profession | **~ towards/toward** ◇ her ~ towards/toward her mother

antenna noun

1 of an insect
ANTENNA + VERB **quiver, twitch** (often figurative) ◇ Certain words make reporters' antennae quiver.
2 (esp. AmE) for radio, TV, etc. → See also AERIAL
ADJ. **radio, television, TV | GPS, microwave, radar, satellite** (all BrE, AmE) | **dish** (BrE, AmE) | **Wi-Fi, wireless** (both BrE, AmE) | **rooftop**
VERB + ANTENNA **install, mount** ◇ They installed a dish ~ on the roof.

anthology noun

ADJ. **literary | horror, poetry, short-story, etc.**
VERB + ANTHOLOGY **compile, edit, publish, put together** ◇ We have put together an ~ of children's poetry.
PREP. **in an/the ~** ◇ The essay first appeared in an ~ of feminist criticism. | **~ of**

antibiotic noun

ADJ. **effective | oral | broad-spectrum**
...OF ANTIBIOTICS **course, dose** ◇ The doctor put her on a course of ~s.
VERB + ANTIBIOTIC **be on, take** ◇ Did you remember to take your ~s? | **be given, receive** ◇ Meat from animals that receive ~s could not be classified as organic. | **administer, give sb, prescribe, put sb on, treat sth with** ◇ The doctor prescribed ~s. | **overprescribe, overuse**
PREP. **~ for** ◇ I got an ~ for my ear infection.

anticipate verb

PHRASES **be eagerly ~d, be highly ~d, be hotly ~d, be keenly ~d** (esp. BrE) ◇ one of the most eagerly ~d arts events of the year | **be widely ~d** ◇ It is widely ~d that she will resign.

anticipation noun

ADJ. **great, keen** (esp. BrE) | **breathless, eager, excited** ◇ We look forward to your lecture with eager ~. ◇ Following weeks of breathless ~, the winner was announced. | **anxious, nervous | growing** ◇ There is growing ~ that the chairman will have to resign.
VERB + ANTICIPATION **be full of** ◇ We are full of ~, and can't wait to visit you. | **heighten** ◇ These brief glimpses heightened their ~ of when they could be together.
PREP. **in ~ of** ◇ People are buying extra groceries in ~ of heavy snowstorms.
PHRASES **a feeling of ~, a sense of ~** ◇ There was a sense of ~ in the audience as the curtain went up for the premiere. | **a shiver of ~, a thrill of ~** ◇ The unexpected news sent a thrill of ~ through the group.

antics noun

ADJ. **amusing, crazy, playful | wacky, zany** (both informal, esp. AmE) | **childish**
VERB + ANTICS **get up to** (esp. BrE), **perform** ◇ The youngsters got up to all sorts of amusing ~. ◇ a comic who performs wacky ~ on his TV show | **be amused by, enjoy, laugh at, smile at** ◇ She was laughing at his ~.

antidote noun

1 against poison/disease
ADJ. **effective | natural**
VERB + ANTIDOTE **administer, give** ◇ The doctor administered an ~.
PREP. **~ for** ◇ Quinine is a natural ~ for this fever. | **~ to** ◇ We do not have an effective ~ to this poison.
2 thing that takes away the effects of sth unpleasant
ADJ. **effective, good, perfect, potent, powerful | bracing, refreshing, welcome**
VERB + ANTIDOTE **act as, serve as | offer, provide** ◇ The resort offers the perfect ~ to the pressures of modern life.
PREP. **~ for** ◇ I think that stricter punishment is the best ~ for crime. | **~ to** ◇ Creative activity serves as an effective ~ to depression.

antipathy noun

ADJ. **deep, strong | growing | mutual** ◇ They have a mutual ~ to each other. | **personal** ◇ Despite his personal ~ to me, he was still able to be polite. | **natural** ◇ a natural ~ for people in authority
VERB + ANTIPATHY **feel, have | express**
PREP. **~ between** ◇ There was a lot of ~ between the two doctors. | **~ for** ◇ his ~ for his boss | **~ to, ~ towards/toward** ◇ I feel a profound ~ to using any weapon. ◇ His ~ towards/toward swimming dates back to childhood.

antique noun

ADJ. **fine | genuine | precious, priceless, valuable**
VERB + ANTIQUE **collect**
ANTIQUE + NOUN **dealer | ~ shop, ~s store** (AmE) | **~s fair**

antiquity noun

1 ancient times
ADJ. **classical, Greek, Roman, etc.** ◇ legends from Greek ~ | **late | remote**
VERB + ANTIQUITY **date back to, go back to, survive from | be lost in** ◇ The origins of this ancient structure are lost in ~.
PREP. **from ~** ◇ a study of urban life from ~ to the present day | **in ~** ◇ vases that were manufactured in late classical ~
2 a work of art, etc. from ancient times
ADJ. **classical, Egyptian, Greek, Roman, etc. | priceless | looted, stolen**
VERB + ANTIQUITY **collect** ◇ He collects Egyptian antiquities.
ANTIQUITIES + NOUN **antiquities dealer**
3 great age
ADJ. **considerable, great** ◇ the considerable ~ of the rocks in this region

antiseptic noun

ADJ. **powerful | mild** ◇ Mint is a mild ~.
VERB + ANTISEPTIC **apply, put on** ◇ You should put some ~ on that cut.

antithesis noun

ADJ. **absolute, complete, exact, very**
VERB + ANTITHESIS **be, represent**
PREP. **~ between** ◇ the sharp ~ between their views | **~ of** ◇ The company represented the ~ of everything he admired.

anxiety noun

ADJ. **acute, considerable, deep, great | chronic, constant, nagging | free-floating** (esp. AmE), **generalized** ◇ We seem to live in a state of free-floating ~ that can attach itself to anything. | **growing, increasing, mounting | understandable** (esp. BrE) | **needless** (BrE), **unnecessary | public | castration, separation, etc.** (psychology)
...OF ANXIETY **level** ◇ the high level of ~ created by entering a new environment
VERB + ANXIETY **arouse, bring, cause, create, provoke | lead to | experience, feel, suffer from** ◇ She felt a nagging ~ that could not be relieved. | **express, share** ◇ The mothers were able to share their anxieties with each other. | **betray,**

reflect ◇ *His face betrayed his ~.* | **cope with, deal with, overcome** ◇ *skills to cope with ~* | **allay, alleviate, assuage, dispel, ease, lessen, quell, reduce, relieve, soothe** ◇ *The aim is to reduce ~ and help the patients relax.* | **exacerbate, heighten, increase**
ANXIETY + VERB **grow** ◇ *The more reports I study the more my ~ grows.* | **arise, arise from sth, arise out of sth, surface** ◇ *A few anxieties surfaced during the meeting.* | **surround** ◇ *A lot of ~ surrounds the issue of human cloning.*
ANXIETY + NOUN **attack** | **disorder** ◇ *patients suffering from an ~ disorder* | **dream** ◇ *I keep having this ~ dream where I've forgotten to do something important.* | **level**
PREP. **~ about** ◇ *her growing ~ about her health* | **~ at** ◇ *~ at the deterioration of relations between the powers* | **~ for** ◇ *deep ~ for the whole family* | **~ over** ◇ *There are anxieties over the effects of unemployment.*
PHRASES **~ and depression** ◇ *Physical activity can help reduce ~ and depression.* | **fear and ~** ◇ *They were encouraged to express their fears and anxieties.*

anxious *adj.*

VERBS **appear, be, feel, look, seem, sound** | **become, get, grow** ◇ *The bus was late and Sue began to get ~.* | **make sb** ◇ *The delays only made him more ~.*
ADV. **extremely, fairly, very, etc.** | **desperately, incredibly, terribly** | **increasingly** ◇ *She was watching the clock and becoming increasingly ~.* | **a little, slightly, etc.** | **naturally** (*esp. BrE*), **understandably** ◇ *Students are understandably ~ about getting work after graduation.* | **overly** (*esp. AmE*), **unduly** ◇ *There's no need to get unduly ~ on my account.*
PREP. **about** ◇ *I'm becoming very ~ about my son.* | **for** ◇ *We are extremely ~ for her safety.*

apartment *noun*

1 (*esp. AmE*) a flat

ADJ. **large, spacious** | **cramped, small, tiny** | **cozy** (*AmE*) | **comfortable, luxury** | **dingy, shabby** ◇ *Colin lives in a dingy one-room ~ with his pet turtles.* | **modern** | **one-bedroom, two-bedroom, etc., one-bedroomed, two-bedroomed, etc.** (*BrE*) | **studio** | **first-floor, second-floor, etc.** | **downstairs, upstairs** ◇ *the people who live in the upstairs ~* | **basement, loft, penthouse** | **high-rise** ◇ *Larger cities have many high-rise ~s.* | **rental** (*AmE*), **rented** | **empty** | **holiday, self-catering** (*both BrE*)
VERB + APARTMENT **buy** | **lease, rent, sublet** ◇ *We will be renting the ~ for a year.* | **live in, share, stay in** ◇ *I share an ~ with two friends.* | **look for** ◇ *I'm looking for an ~ on the east side of the city.* | **find** | **move into, move out of** | **clean, decorate, furnish, renovate**
APARTMENT + NOUN **block** (*BrE*), **building** (*AmE*), **complex, house** (*AmE*) ◇ *high-rise ~ buildings* | **living** | **dweller** ◇ *Apartment dwellers can participate in community gardens.*

2 apartments (*BrE*) set of rooms

ADJ. **private, royal, state** ◇ *the private ~s of the imperial family*

apathy *noun*

ADJ. **general, widespread** | **political, public, voter**
VERB + APATHY **suffer from** | **fall into, sink into** ◇ *Once defeated, he sank into ~.* | **lead to** ◇ *Such attitudes can only lead to ~.*
PREP. **~ among** ◇ *widespread ~ among students* | **~ towards/ toward** ◇ *a general ~ towards/toward politics*

apologetic *adj.*

VERBS **be, feel, look, sound**
ADV. **extremely, fairly, very, etc.** | **profusely** | **genuinely, sincerely** | **almost** ◇ *Leroy sounded almost ~.* | **a little, slightly, etc.** | **vaguely** | **suitably** (*BrE*) ◇ *I hope she was suitably ~ afterwards.*
PREP. **about** ◇ *He was profusely ~ about the mistake.* | **for** ◇ *She was ~ for taking so long.*

apologize (*BrE also* -ise) *verb*

ADV. **sincerely** | **profusely** ◇ *He ~d profusely for the damage*

he had caused. | **humbly, meekly, sheepishly** ◇ *I do ~ most humbly.* (*formal*) | **formally, personally, publicly** ◇ *The president of the company ~d personally for the tragic accident.* | **hastily, immediately, quickly**
VERB + APOLOGIZE **ought to, should** | **want to, wish to, would like to** ◇ *I would like to ~ most sincerely for any embarrassment caused.*
PREP. **for** ◇ *She ~d for being late.* | **to** ◇ *He ~d to his colleagues.*
PHRASES **I do ~, I must ~** ◇ *I must ~ for not letting you know sooner.*

apology *noun*

ADJ. **abject** (*esp. BrE*), **humble, profuse** ◇ *It was a mistake. My profuse apologies.* | **heartfelt, profound, sincere** | **half-hearted** ◇ *He mumbled a half-hearted ~ and quickly left.* | **full** | **formal, official** | **public** | **written**
VERB + APOLOGY **convey, give sb, issue, make, offer (sb), publish, send (sb)** ◇ *The newspaper has issued an ~ to those concerned.* | **get, receive** | **demand, deserve, expect, want** ◇ *We expect a full written ~.* | **owe sb** ◇ *She certainly owes you an ~.* | **mumble, murmur, mutter, whisper** ◇ *John muttered an ~ then went back to his book.* | **stammer, stutter** | **accept** ◇ *Please accept my sincere apologies.* | **reject** ◇ *She rejected my ~, saying it was not enough.*
PREP. **without** ◇ *He backed out arrogantly and without ~.* | **~ for** ◇ *an ~ for arriving late* | **~ from** ◇ *Apologies have been received from the Browns.* | **~ to** ◇ *my apologies to your wife*
PHRASES **extend your apologies** (*formal*) ◇ *If anyone has been offended, I extend my sincere apologies.* | **a letter of ~** | **make no ~ for, make no apologies for** ◇ *I make no apologies for bringing this issue to your attention once again.*

appalling *adj.*

VERBS **be, look, sound**
ADV. **really, truly** | **absolutely, the most, quite, utterly** ◇ *They had to wait for hours in the most ~ weather.*

apparatus *noun*

ADJ. **breathing, electrical, experimental, scientific** | **administrative, bureaucratic, ideological, legal, party, security, state** ◇ *the state's powerful security ~* | **repressive**
... OF APPARATUS **piece** ◇ *a very sophisticated piece of laboratory ~*
PHRASES **the ~ of government, the ~ of the state**

apparent *adj.*

VERBS **be, seem** | **become** ◇ *It soon became ~ that the company was losing money.* | **make sth** ◇ *He made it ~ that he was very annoyed.*
ADV. **glaringly, particularly, strongly, very** | **fully, quite** | **increasingly** | **all too** ◇ *His unhappiness was all too ~.* | **quickly, soon** | **immediately, instantly** ◇ *The extent of their injuries was not immediately ~.* | **easily, readily** | **clearly** | **painfully** ◇ *Local suspicion of the incomers was painfully ~.*
PREP. **to** ◇ *His lack of experience was quite ~ to everyone.*

appeal *noun*

1 attraction/interest

ADJ. **considerable, great, growing, obvious, powerful, special, strong** | **immediate, instant** (*esp. BrE*) ◇ *the book's immediate ~ to young children* | **enduring, lasting, timeless** ◇ *Her charming children's stories have timeless ~.* | **limited, little** | **broad, crossover, mainstream, mass, popular, populist, universal, wide, widespread** ◇ *a publication designed for mass ~* | **aesthetic, commercial, electoral, emotional, intellectual, visual** ◇ *Unfortunately the movie lacks commercial ~.* | **sex**
VERB + APPEAL **have, hold** ◇ *His views hold no ~ for me.* | **retain** | **lose** | **broaden, extend, widen** ◇ *We are trying to broaden the ~ of classical music.* | **boost, enhance, increase**
APPEAL + VERB **lie in sth** ◇ *His considerable ~ lies in his quiet, gentle manner.*
PREP. **~ for** ◇ *College lost its ~ for her in the second year.*

2 serious request for sth you need/want very much

ADJ. **desperate, emergency** (*esp. BrE*), **emotional, urgent** | **direct, personal** | **fresh** (*BrE*) ◇ *a fresh ~ for witnesses to come forward*
VERB + APPEAL **issue, make** ◇ *They made a direct ~ to the government for funding.*
PREP. **~ for** ◇ *an ~ for help* | **~ to** ◇ *an ~ to reason*

3 formal request to sb in authority

ADJ. **formal** (*esp. BrE*) | **court, legal** ◇ *She won the right to make another court ~.* | **further** ◇ *There is a possibility of a further ~ to a higher court.*
VERB + APPEAL **bring, file** (*AmE*), **lodge** (*BrE*), **make** ◇ *He's bringing an ~ against the size of the fine.* | **drop** ◇ *They have agreed to drop the ~.* | **exhaust** ◇ *All ~s have been exhausted and his execution is imminent.* | **win** | **lose** | **consider** ◇ *His lawyer is considering an ~ to the Supreme Court.* | **allow** (*formal*), **hear** ◇ *The judge has agreed to allow his ~.* ◇ *The court will hear the ~ on June 10.* | **uphold** (*esp. BrE*) ◇ *His ~ was upheld and he was released immediately.* | **deny, dismiss, reject, throw out** | **turn down** (*esp. BrE*)
APPEAL + VERB **fail** | **succeed**
APPEAL + NOUN **~ court** (*BrE*), **~s court** (*AmE*) | **tribunal** (*BrE*) | **hearing** | **~ judge** (*BrE*), **~s judge** (*AmE*) | **~s procedure, ~s process** | **system** (*esp. BrE*)
PREP. **on ~** ◇ *On ~ it was held that the judge was correct.* ◇ *The case was upheld on ~.* | **under ~** ◇ *a case currently under ~* | **~ against** ◇ *an ~ against his conviction of fraud* | **~ for** ◇ *an ~ for leniency* | **~ to** ◇ *an ~ to the High Court*
PHRASES **court of ~** (*BrE*), **court of ~s** (*AmE*) | **grounds of ~** (*BrE*) | **a right of ~** ◇ *You have the right of ~ to the Constitutional Court.* | **pending ~** ◇ *The players have been suspended pending ~.*

4 event for raising money

ADJ. **charity** (*esp. BrE*), **fund-raising**
VERB + APPEAL **hold, launch** ◇ *An ~ is to be launched on behalf of the refugees.* | **back, support**
APPEAL + VERB **raise sth** (*esp. BrE*) ◇ *The ~ raised over three million pounds.*
APPEAL + NOUN **fund** (*BrE*)

appeal verb

1 make serious request for sth

ADV. **directly** ◇ *He went over the heads of union officials, ~ing directly to the workforce.*
PREP. **for, to** ◇ *Police ~ed to the public for information about the crime.*

2 to sb in authority

ADV. **successfully, unsuccessfully** | **directly**
PREP. **against** ◇ *She ~ed unsuccessfully against her conviction for murder.* | **to** ◇ *He has decided to ~ to the European Court.*
PHRASES **give sb leave to ~, grant sb leave to ~** (*both BrE*)

3 be attractive/interesting to sb

ADV. **really, strongly** ◇ *The prospect of teaching such bright children ~ed to her enormously.* ◇ *The idea of retiring early really ~s to me.* | **directly** | **primarily** ◇ *Computer games used to ~ primarily to boys.*
PREP. **to** ◇ *These characters will ~ directly to children's imaginations.*

appealing adj.

VERBS **be, look, seem, sound** | **make sth** ◇ *The large salary made their offer even more ~ to him.* | **find sth** ◇ *I find his manner very ~.*
ADV. **extremely, fairly, very, etc.** | **enormously** | **especially, particularly** | **immediately** | **aesthetically, visually**
PREP. **to** ◇ *These toys are not immediately ~ to children.*

appear verb

1 come into sight/existence

ADV. **suddenly** ◇ *A man suddenly ~ed in the doorway.* | **from nowhere, magically** ◇ *A police officer ~ed as if from nowhere and ordered us to halt.* | **first, initially, originally** ◇ *Modern contact lenses first ~ed in the 1940s.* | **usually** ◇ *Symptoms usually ~ within two to three days.* | **recently** ◇ *Some exciting new products have recently ~ed on the market.*

2 perform/be seen in public

ADV. **currently** | **frequently, occasionally, often** ◇ *The Senator has ~ed frequently on this show.* | **rarely** ◇ *She rarely ~s in public.* | **briefly** ◇ *He ~s briefly in the movie as a waiter.*
PREP. **at** ◇ *She is currently ~ing at the Playhouse.*
PHRASES **~ on television** ◇ *She regularly ~s on television.*

3 in court

PREP. **at** (*BrE*) ◇ *He will ~ at Manchester Crown Court next week.*
PHRASES **~ before a court, ~ before a judge, ~ before a magistrate** ◇ *The man will ~ before magistrates later today.* | **~ in court** ◇ *A man has ~ed in court charged with the murder of seven women.*

appearance noun

1 way that sb/sth looks

ADJ. **attractive, handsome, youthful** | **distinctive, odd, strange, striking** | **dishevelled/disheveled, scruffy** (*esp. BrE*), **unkempt, unprepossessing** ◇ *With his dishevelled/disheveled ~ he often looks as though he's just fallen out of bed.* | **external, outer, outward, physical, surface, visual** ◇ *In outward ~ the two types of tomato are similar.* | **personal** ◇ *attention to personal ~ and hygiene* | **general, overall** ◇ *attempts to improve the general ~ of the town*
VERB + APPEARANCE **have** ◇ *Inside, the house had the ~ of a temple.* | **take on** ◇ *Towns merged to take on the ~ of a city.* | **create, give** ◇ *The report gives an ~ of scientific credibility.* | **alter, change** ◇ *Shaving off his beard changed his ~ dramatically.* | **check** ◇ *He stopped at the mirror to check his ~.* | **enhance, improve** | **mimic** ◇ *man-made materials that mimic the ~ of wood* | **avoid** ◇ *We must avoid any ~ of impropriety.* | **keep up, maintain, preserve** ◇ *They tried to maintain the ~ of normality.*
PREP. **in ~** ◇ *rather bird-like in ~*
PHRASES **contrary to ~s, despite ~s** ◇ *The American president, despite ~s, has only limited power.* | **judge (sb/sth) by ~s** ◇ *To judge by ~s, Roger was rather embarrassed.* | **keep up ~s** (= hide the true situation and pretend that everything is going well) ◇ *When she lost all her money, she was determined to keep up ~s.*

2 arrival of sb/sth

ADJ. **abrupt, dramatic, sudden, surprise, unexpected** | **brief** | **first, initial** ◇ *Since its first ~ in the 19th century, cholera has killed millions.*
VERB + APPEARANCE **make, put in** ◇ *She made a sudden ~ just as we were about to leave.* ◇ *I feel I must put in at least a brief ~ at the party.* | **mark** ◇ *This marked the ~ of a new genre in American music.*

3 act of appearing in public

ADJ. **first, second, etc.** ◇ *her first ~ on the stage* | **final, last** | **frequent, occasional, rare, regular** | **recent** | **live, personal** | **public** | **cameo, guest** | **court, radio, stage, television, TV** ◇ *one of the actor's rare television ~s* | **scheduled** ◇ *The singer had to cancel her scheduled ~.*
VERB + APPEARANCE **make** ◇ *She made a cameo ~ in the movie.* | **cancel** ◇ *She was forced to cancel her ~ as keynote speaker at the event.*
APPEARANCE + NOUN **fee, money** (*both sports, esp. BrE*)

appendix noun

ADJ. **burst, inflamed, perforated, ruptured** ◇ *He was taken to the hospital with a burst ~.*
VERB + APPENDIX **remove, take out** ◇ *Doctors had to take out his ~.* | **have out** ◇ *She might have to have her ~ out.*
APPENDIX + VERB **burst, rupture** ◇ *If the condition is not treated, the ~ can rupture.*

appetite noun

1 desire for food

ADJ. **big, enormous, gargantuan, good, healthy, hearty, huge, insatiable, large, ravenous** ◇ *special double-decker sandwiches for big ~s* | **poor, small** ◇ *The symptoms of depression can include poor ~.* ◇ *I have always had a small ~.* | **jaded** (*BrE*) ◇ *magnificent meals to tempt the most jaded ~s*
VERB + APPETITE **have** ◇ *She had no ~ and began to lose weight.* | **lose** | **build, build up, develop, work up** ◇ *I went for a walk to work up an ~ for breakfast.* | **get back, regain** ◇ *After a week she had regained her ~.* | **give sb** ◇ *All that digging has given me an ~.* | **increase, stimulate** ◇ *The cold air had given an edge to my ~.* | **control, curb, decrease, reduce, suppress, take away, take the edge off** (*esp. BrE*) ◇ *Some drugs can suppress the ~.* | **ruin, spoil** | **satisfy** ◇ *This meal will satisfy even the healthiest ~.*
APPETITE + VERB **grow, increase** | **come back, return** ◇ *His ~ has returned to normal.*
PHRASES **a lack of ~, a loss of ~** ◇ *The symptoms include aching limbs and a loss of ~.*

2 strong desire for sth

ADJ. **enormous, great, huge, insatiable, voracious** ◇ *an insatiable ~ for books* | **growing** ◇ *The airport cannot accommodate the growing ~ for flights.* | **public** ◇ *The website recognizes the public ~ for serious information.* | **sexual** | **intellectual** ◇ *The website has enough good content to satisfy its users' intellectual ~.*
VERB + APPETITE **have** | **lose** | **give sb** | **feed, fuel, increase, whet** ◇ *Reading the first story whetted my ~ for more.* | **dull** | **sate, satisfy** ◇ *He sated her ~ for adventure and intrigue.* | **indulge** ◇ *We get into debt to indulge our ~ for consumer goods.*
APPETITE + VERB **grow, increase**
PREP. **~ for** ◇ *His ~ for power had grown.*

applaud verb

1 clap your hands

ADV. **enthusiastically, heartily, loudly, wildly** ◇ *The audience ~ed loudly.* | **politely**

2 praise sb/sth

ADV. **warmly, widely** ◇ *The decision to save the company has been warmly ~ed.*
PHRASES **is to be ~ed, should be ~ed** ◇ *His efforts to help people should be ~ed.*

applause noun

ADJ. **deafening, loud, thunderous, tumultuous** (*esp. BrE*) | **enthusiastic, rapturous, warm, wild** | **prolonged** (*esp. BrE*), **sustained** | **spontaneous** ◇ *a little burst of spontaneous ~* | **muted** (*esp. BrE*), **polite** ◇ *To muted ~ a small flag was raised over the building.*
... OF APPLAUSE **burst** (*esp. BrE*), **ripple** (*esp. BrE*), **roar, round** ◇ *The crowd gave them a round of ~.*
VERB + APPLAUSE **be greeted with, draw, earn, get, receive, win** ◇ *The speech drew loud ~.* | **break into, burst into** ◇ *The audience broke into ~.* | **hear** | **acknowledge** ◇ *She stood back and acknowledged the ~ of the crowd.* | **deserve** ◇ *He deserves the respect and ~ of his colleagues.*
APPLAUSE + VERB **break out, erupt, greet sb/sth** ◇ *A great roar of ~ broke out.* | **Wild ~ greeted this remark.** | **echo** ◇ *Applause echoed around the hall.* | **grow** | **die away, die down, subside** ◇ *The ~ died down as the curtain closed.*
PREP. **to ~** ◇ *He left the stage to thunderous ~.* | **~ for** ◇ *There was a ripple of ~ for the speaker.* | **~ from** ◇ *This remark brought ~ from the audience.*

apple noun

ADJ. **sweet** | **sharp, sour, tart** ◇ *Add some sugar to the stewed apple—it's still a little tart.* | **juicy** | **crisp** | **green, red** | **shiny** | **cider, cooking, dessert, eating** | **windfall** (*BrE*) | **baked** | **candy** (*AmE*), **caramel** (*AmE*), **toffee** (*BrE*) | **bruised** ◇ *The ~s were all bruised after being dropped on the floor.* | **rotten**
VERB + APPLE **bite into, eat, munch, munch on** ◇ *He just sat there munching on an ~.* | **core, grate, peel, slice**

application

APPLE + NOUN **crisp** (*AmE*), **crumble** (*BrE*), **pie, tart** | **juice** | **core** | **pip** (*esp. BrE*), **seed** | **slice** | **orchard, tree**
→ Special page at FRUIT

appliance noun

ADJ. **modern** | **energy-efficient** | **faulty** (*esp. BrE*) | **electric, electrical, electronic, gas** | **cooking, heating** | **combustion** (*AmE*) ◇ *Turn off all combustion ~s such as water heaters.* | **domestic, home, household, kitchen** | **stainless-steel** | **major** ◇ *All major ~s such as refrigerators must have an energy guide label.* | **surgical** (*BrE*)
VERB + APPLIANCE **switch on, turn on** | **switch off, turn off** ◇ *Always switch off ~s that are not in use.* | **plug in, unplug** | **run, use** ◇ *Many household ~s are expensive to run.*

applicable adj.

VERBS **be, prove, seem** ◇ *new developments that could prove directly ~ to the treatment of some cancers* | **become** | **make sth**
ADV. **broadly, generally, widely** | **universally** | **directly** | **immediately** | **equally** ◇ *The rules have now been made equally ~ to all members.* | **easily, readily** ◇ *The theory does not seem easily ~ in this case.* | **very** (*esp. AmE*) ◇ *His message is very ~ to high-school students.* | **especially, particularly**
PREP. **for** ◇ *The offer is only ~ for flights during the week.* | **to** ◇ *The law is ~ to everyone.*

applicant noun

ADJ. **potential, prospective** | **eligible, qualified, suitable** (*BrE*) ◇ *Grant payments will be made to suitably qualified ~s.* (*BrE*) | **lucky** (*esp. BrE*), **successful** | **unsuccessful** ◇ *Unsuccessful ~s may appeal against the decision.* | **black, minority, white** | **college, student** | **job** | **visa** | **asylum**
VERB + APPLICANT **seek** ◇ *The company will seek ~s nationwide.* | **attract** ◇ *The advertisement attracted a number of ~s.* | **shortlist** (*esp. BrE*) ◇ *Eight ~s were shortlisted.* | **evaluate, screen** ◇ *software that lets employers screen job ~s* | **interview** | **admit** (*esp. AmE*), **appoint** (*BrE*), **select** | **reject, turn away** (*esp. AmE*), **turn down**
APPLICANT + VERB **apply** ◇ *All ~s should apply in writing.*
PREP. **~ for** ◇ *There were over fifty ~s for the job.*

application noun

1 written request

ADJ. **formal, written** | **successful** ◇ *I am pleased to tell you that your ~ for the position has been successful.* | **unsuccessful** | **grant, job, membership, patent, planning** (*BrE*), **visa, etc.** ◇ *There has been a drop in visa ~s.*
VERB + APPLICATION **file, lodge** (*BrE*), **make, send, send in, submit** ◇ *The applicant must file a written ~ to the court.* | **fill in** (*BrE*), **fill out** ◇ *Prospective members fill out an online ~.* | **withdraw** | **consider, examine, process, review, screen** ◇ *It takes time to process each ~.* | **invite** (*esp. BrE*) ◇ *Applications are invited for the post of Lecturer in French.* | **accept** ◇ *We accept permit ~s year-round.* | **approve, grant** (*law*) ◇ *His ~ for bail was granted.* | **refuse** (*law*), **reject, turn down**
APPLICATION + NOUN **form** | **guidelines** | **deadline** | **fee** | **procedure, process**
PREP. **by ~** (*formal*) ◇ *Admission is obtained by written ~.* | **on ~** ◇ *A permit is available on ~ to the company.* | **~ for** ◇ *an ~ for a new permit* | **~ to** ◇ *an ~ to the authorities*

2 practical use

ADJ. **practical, real-world** ◇ *What are the practical ~s of this work?* | **general** ◇ *The program is designed for general ~.* | **wide** | **potential** ◇ *The research has a wide range of potential ~s.* | **agricultural, clinical, commercial, industrial** | **therapeutic** ◇ *the reported therapeutic ~s of bee venom*

3 computing

ADJ. **software** | **database, multimedia** | **e-business, e-commerce** | **desktop** | **Web, Web-based** | **business-critical, mission-critical** | **stand-alone** | **interactive** |

mobile, wireless | **killer** (usually ***killer app***) ◊ *I believe email is the one single killer app since the invention of computers.*
VERB + APPLICATION **launch, run, use** ◊ *You can run several ~s at the same time.* | **download** | **install** | **access** ◊ *Users access the ~s via the Web.* | **build, create, develop, write** | **integrate** ◊ *an operating system that can integrate other ~s*
APPLICATION + VERB **run**
APPLICATION + NOUN **program, software** | **developer** | **development** | **performance**
→ Special page at COMPUTER

apply *verb*

1 be relevant

ADV. **equally** ◊ *These principles ~ equally in all cases.*
PREP. **to** ◊ *These restrictions do not ~ to us.*
PHRASES **the same applies** ◊ *US companies are subject to international laws and the same applies to companies in Europe.*

2 put/spread on a surface

ADV. **directly** | **evenly** | **liberally** | **sparingly** ◊ *Apply the insecticide sparingly.* | **carefully** ◊ *I carefully applied a creamy foundation.* | **externally**
PREP. **over** ◊ *Apply the glue evenly over both surfaces.* | **to** ◊ *Never ~ the cleaning liquid directly to the surface.*

appointment *noun*

1 agreement to meet sb

ADJ. **important, urgent** | **first, initial** | **follow-up** | **scheduled** | **missed** ◊ *Patients may be charged for missed ~s.* | **business** | **dental, dentist** | **doctor's, medical** | **hospital, outpatient** (*both esp. BrE*) ◊ *The hospital needs to allow more time for outpatient ~s.* | **hair, nail** | **therapy** (*esp. AmE*)
VERB + APPOINTMENT **have** | **arrange, book, fix** (*esp. BrE*), **make, schedule** (*esp. AmE*), **set up** ◊ *I'd like to make an ~ to see the doctor, please.* | **reschedule** | **get** ◊ *I didn't know if I would get an ~ at such short notice.* | **give sb** ◊ *Tom has been given an ~ at the local hospital.* | **attend, keep** ◊ *He failed to keep his ~.* | **forget, miss** ◊ *She has already missed three ~s.* | **cancel**
APPOINTMENT + NOUN **book, calendar** (*AmE*) ◊ *The receptionist checked the ~ book.* | **time** ◊ *I assume he'll come at his usual 10 a.m. ~ time.*
PREP. **by ~** ◊ *Viewing is only allowed by ~.* | **with an ~, without an ~** ◊ *He called without an ~.* | **~ with** ◊ *an ~ with a doctor*

2 (*esp. BrE*) **job/position**

ADJ. **permanent, temporary** | **lifetime** (*AmE*) | **tenured** (*AmE*) | **full-time, part-time** | **senior** | **public** (*BrE*) | **court,** (*AmE*) | **judicial** (*both BrE, AmE*) | **cabinet** (*BrE, AmE*), **federal** (*AmE*), **government** (*BrE*), **ministerial** (*BrE*), **political** (*BrE, AmE*) | **executive** | **academic** (*BrE, AmE*), **faculty** (*AmE*), **university**
VERB + APPOINTMENT **hold** ◊ *Employees may not hold any other ~s.* | **give sb, offer sb** ◊ *He was offered an ~ in the English Department.* | **accept** | **get, obtain, receive** | **take up** ◊ *He takes up his ~ in January.* | **resign, resign from** ◊ *Ms Green resigned her ~ as our regional representative.* | **terminate** ◊ *The college terminated the ~s of six professors.* | **secure** ◊ *The President secured the ~ of a close friend.*

3 choosing sb for job

ADJ. **key** ◊ *The company has made five key ~s at its Chicago office.* | **formal** (*esp. BrE*), **official** | **presidential** (*AmE*) | **staff** (*esp. BrE*) | **recent** ◊ *the recent ~ of Lars Nittves as director* | **new** ◊ *They announced a series of new ~s of key security officials.*
VERB + APPOINTMENT **make** | **announce** | **confirm** ◊ *The board has confirmed the ~ of Howard Kendall as Sales Manager.* | **approve** | **block**
APPOINTMENT + NOUN **process**
PREP. **~ to** ◊ *the first ~s to the new government*

appraisal *noun*

ADJ. **honest, realistic** | **detailed, full** ◊ *A detailed ~ of the plan will now be carried out.* | **independent** | **critical** | **economic, financial** (*both esp. BrE*) | **project** (*BrE*) | **performance, staff, teacher** (*all BrE*) ◊ *a formal system of performance ~*
VERB + APPRAISAL **carry out** (*esp. BrE*), **give, make** ◊ *He was asked to give an independent ~.* ◊ *She made an ~ of the other guests.*
APPRAISAL + NOUN **interview** (*BrE*) ◊ *We are holding staff ~ interviews.*

appreciate *verb*

1 recognize good qualities

ADV. **really, truly** | **fully, properly** ◊ *The sound quality was poor so we couldn't fully ~ the music.* | **especially, particularly** ◊ *Teachers will especially ~ the lists at the back of the book.*

2 be grateful

ADV. **deeply, genuinely, greatly, highly, really, sincerely, totally** (*esp. AmE*), **truly, very much** ◊ *We do really ~ your help.* | **especially, particularly** ◊ *Younger kids might especially ~ a trip to the zoo.*

3 understand

ADV. **fully, totally** ◊ *I fully ~ your concern. We will do all in our power to help.* | **easily, readily** ◊ *The problems should be easily ~d.*
VERB + APPRECIATE **fail to** ◊ *The government failed to ~ the fact that voters were angry.*
PHRASES **be generally ~d, be widely ~d** ◊ *It is generally ~d that the rail network needs a complete overhaul.*

appreciation *noun*

1 understanding and enjoyment of sth

ADJ. **deep, great, real** | **aesthetic** | **art, music** | **new-found** ◊ *his new-found ~ for art* | **renewed** ◊ *a renewed ~ of traditions once branded as primitive* | **public**
VERB + APPRECIATION **have** ◊ *They have little ~ of the arts.* | **share** ◊ *He doesn't share my ~ for opera.* | **show** | **develop, gain** ◊ *I have now developed an ~ of poetry.* | **foster** ◊ *We hope the course will help foster a lifelong ~ of music.* | **enhance, increase**
PREP. **in ~** ◊ *She gazed in ~ at the scene.* | **~ for, ~ of** ◊ *They had a new-found ~ for Japanese music.*

2 feeling of being grateful for sth

ADJ. **deep, genuine, heartfelt, sincere**
VERB + APPRECIATION **express, show** ◊ *I would like to express my ~ and thanks to you all.* | **extend** (*formal, esp. AmE*) ◊ *The authors extend their sincere ~ to everyone who contributed to the book.*
PREP. **in ~ (of)** ◊ *I'll be sending them a donation in ~ of their help.* | **with ~** ◊ *'Thank you,' she murmured, with heartfelt ~.* | **~ for** ◊ *his ~ for all the work she had done*
PHRASES **a lack of ~** | **a token of your ~** ◊ *As a token of our ~ we would like to offer you this small gift.*

3 understanding of what sth involves

ADJ. **better, clear, deep, full, great, keen, real, true, wider** | **growing** ◊ *There is a growing ~ of the need for change.* | **new** ◊ *The article gave me a new ~ for the work which went into the album.*
VERB + APPRECIATION **have** | **gain** ◊ *The course helped me to gain a deeper ~ of what scientific research involves.*
PREP. **~ of** ◊ *She had no ~ of the difficulties we were facing.*

apprehension *noun*

ADJ. **considerable** (*esp. AmE*), **great, growing** | **slight**
VERB + APPREHENSION **be filled with, be full of, feel** ◊ *They were filled with ~ as they approached the building.* | **express, show** | **sense** ◊ *Marisa seemed to sense my growing ~.* | **cause** ◊ *The change in the law has caused ~ among many people.*
PREP. **with ~** ◊ *School reports are always received with some ~.* | **~ about, ~ over** ◊ *her ~ about being in the hospital* | **~ at** ◊ *She felt some ~ at the thought of seeing him again.*

apprehensive *adj.*

VERBS **be, feel, look, seem, sound** | **become, get, grow** | **remain** | **make sb** ◇ *The long delay had made me quite ~.*
ADV. **extremely, fairly, very, etc.** | **deeply** (*esp. BrE*) | **a little, slightly, etc.**
PREP. **about** ◇ *She was extremely ~ about her future.* | **of** ◇ *He was rather ~ of failure.*

approach *noun*

1 way of dealing with sb/sth

ADJ. **conventional, orthodox, traditional** | **alternate** (*AmE*), **alternative, different, fresh, new, novel** ◇ *We need to try alternative ~es to the problem.* | **cautious, conservative** | **proactive** ◇ *The company is taking a proactive ~ to easing the energy crisis.* | **creative, innovative** | **flexible** | **eclectic** | **balanced, common-sense, no-nonsense, positive, practical, pragmatic, problem-solving, rational, sensible, straightforward, useful** ◇ *a pragmatic ~ to the role of religion in politics* | **direct, hands-on** | **hands-off, indirect** | **wait-and-see** | **step-by-step** | **one-size-fits-all** ◇ *He criticized the one-size-fits-all ~ to learning.* | **piecemeal** | **formal, informal** | **aggressive** | **low-key** | **right, wrong** | **basic, general** | **analytical, disciplined, scientific, structured, systematic, theoretical** | **methodological** | **holistic, integrated** ◇ *The therapy takes a holistic ~ to health and well-being.* | **interdisciplinary, multidisciplinary** | **two-pronged** | **bottom-up, top-down** | **simplistic** | **comprehensive**
VERB + APPROACH **have** ◇ *Some teachers have a more traditional ~ to teaching.* | **adopt, apply, develop, employ, follow, implement, pursue, take, try, use, utilize** ◇ *We need to adopt a more pragmatic ~.* | **pioneer** ◇ *The US army pioneered this ~.* | **advocate, favour/favor, prefer** ◇ *Next time I'd advocate the direct ~.* | **change, modify, rethink** ◇ *He challenges teachers to rethink their ~.* | **abandon** | **evaluate** | **describe, outline** | **test** ◇ *I spent some time testing this ~.* | **extend** ◇ *This ~ can be extended to other fields.*
APPROACH + VERB **allow sth, enable sth** ◇ *This ~ allows students to learn at their own pace.* | **offer sth, yield sth** ◇ *This ~ offers many advantages.* ◇ *Taking a fresh ~ often yields interesting results.* | **fail, work** ◇ *This ~ works for me.*
PREP. **~ to** ◇ *I liked her ~ to the problem*

2 act of coming nearer

ADJ. **shallow, steep**
VERB + APPROACH **make** ◇ *The aircraft had to make a steep ~ to the landing strip.* | **signal** ◇ *The swishing of the grass signalled the ~ of a person.*
APPROACH + NOUN **speed** | **route**
PREP. **at the ~ of** ◇ *The children fell silent at the ~ of their teacher.* | **with the ~ of** ◇ *The weather turned warmer with the ~ of spring.* | **to** ◇ *The plane crashed during its ~ to the runway.*

3 discussion with sb in order to ask them for sth

VERB + APPROACH **make** | **have, receive** (*esp. BrE*)
PREP. **~ from** ◇ *We've received an ~ from the director of a rival company.* | **~ to** ◇ *We'll have to make an ~ to the chief executive.*

approach *verb*

1 come nearer

ADV. **slowly** | **carefully, cautiously, warily, with caution**
PREP. **from** ◇ *The army ~ed from the south.*

2 come nearer in time

ADV. **fast, quickly, rapidly, swiftly** ◇ *The time is fast ~ing when we will have to replace these old machines.*

3 speak to sb, usually to ask for sth

ADV. **directly** ◇ *It's best to ~ her directly.*
VERB + APPROACH **be easy to** | **be difficult to** ◇ *She found her father difficult to ~.*
PREP. **about** ◇ *Have you ~ed John about doing a concert?* | **for** ◇ *I ~ed the bank for a loan.*

4 come close in amount/quality/style

ADV. **closely** ◇ *Here Wordsworth's verse movement closely ~es that of Gray.* | **not remotely** ◇ *There is no other player even remotely ~ing her.*

appropriate *adj.*

VERBS **be, seem** | **consider sth, deem sth, feel sth, think sth** ◇ *It was thought ~ to award her the prize.*
ADV. **extremely, fairly, very, etc.** | **entirely, perfectly** | **culturally**
PREP. **for** ◇ *It might be ~ for him to attend the course.* | **to** ◇ *Tutors can construct tests ~ to individual students' needs.*

approval *noun*

ADJ. **full, warm** (*esp. BrE*), **wholehearted** ◇ *The plan did not win wholehearted ~.* | **grudging, qualified** | **general, overwhelming, popular, public, unanimous, universal** | **23%, etc.** (*esp. AmE*) ◇ *The latest poll has him at 47% ~ and 49% disapproval.* | **final, initial, preliminary, prior** ◇ *All development requires the prior ~ of the planning authority.* | **tacit** | **written** | **formal, official** | **legislative** (*esp. AmE*), **regulatory** | **board, congressional, court, federal, government, judicial, parliamentary, presidential, royal, Senate** | **shareholder, voter** | **parental** | **social** | **drug** ◇ *We need to streamline the process for new drug ~.*
VERB + APPROVAL **need, require** | **seek, submit sth for** ◇ *We have submitted a design for ~.* | **await** | **have** ◇ *We already have ~ for six products.* | **gain, get, meet, meet with, obtain, receive, secure, win** ◇ *You are not allowed to build without first obtaining the ~ of the planners.* | **earn** ◇ *I could tell I had earned her ~.* | **recommend** ◇ *The committee is expected to recommend ~ of the new drug.* | **give, grant** ◇ *The government has now given its ~ for the new examinations.* | **refuse** (*esp. BrE*), **withhold** | **express, nod, nod in, roar, show, voice** ◇ *The people listening nodded ~.* ◇ *The crowd roared its ~ for the song.*
APPROVAL + NOUN **process** | **rating** ◇ *The president's ~ ratings were slipping.*
PREP. **on ~** ◇ *The goods were supplied on ~ (= they could be sent back if they were not satisfactory).* | **with ~** ◇ *Jane's father regards her fiancé with ~.* | **with sb's ~, without sb's ~** ◇ *You may not decorate without the landlord's ~.* | **for ~** ◇ *He won ~ for his project.* | **~ from** ◇ *We're waiting for ~ from the authorities.*
PHRASES **a nod of ~** ◇ *She gave him a nod of ~.* | **a roar of ~** ◇ *There was a roar of ~ from the crowd.* | **sb's seal of ~, sb's stamp of ~** ◇ *The government has given its seal of ~ to the project.* | **subject to ~** ◇ *The offer is subject to ~ at the Annual General Meeting.*

approve *verb*

1 like sb/sth

ADV. **fully, heartily, strongly, thoroughly** (*esp. BrE*), **very much, wholeheartedly** (*esp. BrE*) ◇ *I wholeheartedly ~ of his actions.* | **personally** ◇ *I don't personally ~ but I'm willing to live with it.*
PREP. **of** ◇ *I very much ~ of these new tests.*

2 agree to sth

ADV. **formally, officially** ◇ *His appointment has not been formally ~d yet.* | **federally** (*AmE*) ◇ *The chemical has never been federally ~d as a pesticide.* | **personally** ◇ *He personally ~d a huge contract for 20 jets.* | **overwhelmingly, unanimously** | **narrowly** ◇ *The Legislature narrowly ~d an amendment to the Massachusetts Constitution.*

approximation *noun*

ADJ. **accurate, close, good, nearest, reasonable** ◇ *This is the nearest ~ of cost that they can give us.* | **crude, rough** ◇ *This is only a crude ~ of the actual conditions in the area.*
VERB + APPROXIMATION **make** ◇ *We do not have the true figures so we will have to make some ~s.* | **give (sb), provide (sb with)**

April *noun* → Note at MONTH

aptitude *noun*

ADJ. **great, intrinsic** (*esp. AmE*), **natural, special** ◇ *He has a natural ~ for this work.* | **mathematical, musical, etc.**
VERB + APTITUDE **have** | **display, show** ◇ *children who show an ~ for music*
APTITUDE + NOUN **test**
PREP. **~ for** ◇ *an ~ for mathematics*

arbitrary *adj.*

VERBS **be, seem**
ADV. **completely, entirely, purely, quite** (*esp. BrE*), **totally, wholly** | **fairly, rather, somewhat** | **essentially** | **apparently, seemingly**

arbitration *noun*

ADJ. **binding** ◇ *Both sides have agreed that the ~ will be binding.* | **independent** (*esp. BrE*), **international** | **salary** (*esp. AmE*)
VERB + ARBITRATION **agree to, go to, submit to** (*esp. BrE*) ◇ *Both parties agreed to independent ~.* ◇ *The matter will go to ~.* | **refer sth to** (*BrE*), **submit sth to** (*esp. BrE*), **take sth to** | **offer sb** (*esp. AmE*) | **determine sth by, settle sth by** (*both BrE*) ◇ *The matter will be settled by ~.*
ARBITRATION + NOUN **procedure** (*esp. BrE*), **process, scheme** (*BrE*), **service** (*BrE*), **system** | **case** | **hearing** | **panel** | **award** ◇ *He had won an ~ award against the company.*

arch *noun*

ADJ. **pointed, round, rounded** | **brick, steel, stone, etc.** | **monumental** (*esp. BrE*), **triumphal** | **Gothic, Romanesque, etc.** | **proscenium** ◇ *a performance space with a traditional proscenium ~* | **railway** (*BrE*) ◇ *Homeless people slept under the railway ~es.* | **graceful** ◇ *the graceful ~es of the bridge*
VERB + ARCH **build, erect** ◇ *This huge triumphal ~ was erected at the beginning of this century.* | **form, make** ◇ *The branches of the trees formed an ~ over the bench.*
PREP. **beneath an/the ~, through an/the ~, under an/the ~** ◇ *He rode under the ~.*

archaeologist (*AmE also* archeologist) *noun*

ADJ. **amateur, professional**
ARCHAEOLOGIST + VERB **excavate sth** | **dig sth up, discover sth, find sth, uncover sth, unearth sth** ◇ *examples of life thousands of years ago, unearthed by ~s*
→ Note at JOB

archaeology (*AmE also* archeology) *noun*

ADJ. **Anglo-Saxon, classical, medieval, etc.** | **industrial, marine, underwater**
→ Note at SUBJECT (for verbs and nouns)

archbishop *noun*

ADJ. **Anglican, Roman Catholic** | **cardinal** (*AmE*)
VERB + ARCHBISHOP **be appointed (as), be consecrated, become, be enthroned (as)** (*BrE*), **be made, succeed sb as** ◇ *He was enthroned as ~ in Canterbury Cathedral in 1980.*
PREP. **~ of** ◇ *He was made Archbishop of Milan.*

architect *noun*

ADJ. **famous, great, leading, master** (*esp. AmE*), **noted, prominent, renowned, well-known** | **chief, executive** (*esp. AmE*), **senior** | **licensed, registered** (*both AmE*) | **practising/practicing** | **local** | **contemporary, modern, modernist** | **design** (*esp. AmE*) | **church, city, landscape, naval, residential** (*AmE*)
VERB + ARCHITECT **appoint** (*esp. BrE*), **commission, employ** (*esp. BrE*), **hire** (*esp. AmE*) | **consult**
ARCHITECT + VERB **design sth, draw up plans (for sth)** ◇ *The*

house was designed by ~ Louis Kahn. | **create sth** ◇ *The ~s created an elevated lake.* | **specify sth**
→ Note at PROFESSIONAL (for more verbs)

architecture *noun*

1 style/design of a building
ADJ. **classical, contemporary, medieval, modern, modernist, traditional** | **vernacular** | **colonial, Gothic, Victorian, etc.** | **sustainable** | **church, domestic, landscape, naval, residential** (*esp. AmE*)
PHRASES **a school of ~, a style of ~**
→ Note at SUBJECT (for verbs and nouns)

2 design and structure of a computer system
ADJ. **client-server, hardware, information, network, processor, software**

archive *noun*

ADJ. **extensive, massive, rich, vast** | **historical** | **data, film, news, newspaper, photo, photographic, sound** ◇ *The recordings are preserved in the museum's sound ~s.* | **digital, electronic, online** | **searchable** | **email, Internet, Web** | **county** (*esp. BrE*), **family, local, national, personal, private, public, state**
VERB + ARCHIVE **build, build up, create, set up** ◇ *We are collecting documents to build up an ~.* | **house, keep, maintain** ◇ *the person responsible for keeping the ~s* ◇ *the building which houses the state ~s* | **open** ◇ *There were ambitious plans to open the ~s to the public.* | **access** | **check, consult, examine, look through, search**
ARCHIVE + VERB **contain sth, hold sth, include sth**
ARCHIVE + NOUN **collection** | **film** (*esp. BrE*), **footage** ◇ *~ footage of the victory celebrations* | **material** | **file, page** (*both computing*)
PREP. **among the ~s** ◇ *There are many clues hidden among the ~s of the local museum.* | **from an/the ~** ◇ *some photographs from the library's ~s* | **in an/the ~** ◇ *No record of this letter exists in the ~s.* ◇ *The data is now held in the company ~s.*

area *noun*

1 part of place
ADJ. **huge, large, vast, wide** | **small** | **immediate, local** ◇ *She knows the local ~ very well.* | **surrounding** ◇ *The storms hit Boston and the surrounding ~.* | **central** | **geographical** | **isolated, outlying, remote, secluded** ◇ *We were in a secluded ~ far away from the rest of the school.* | **rural** | **built-up, downtown** (*AmE*), **inner-city** (*BrE*), **metro** (*AmE, informal*), **metropolitan, suburban, urban, urbanized** ◇ *the widening economic gap between urban and rural ~s* | **industrial** | **residential** | **populated, unpopulated** | **coastal, forested, mountain, wilderness, wooded** | **low-lying, mountainous** ◇ *The storm surges have brought significant flooding to low-lying coastal ~s.* | **natural** | **conservation, protected, sensitive** ◇ *environmentally sensitive ~s* | **grassy** | **ski** ◇ *the Mount Sunapee ski ~ in New Hampshire* | **deprived** (*esp. BrE*) ◇ *people living in socially deprived ~s* | **high-crime** | **disaster**
VERB + AREA **inhabit, live in** | **move into, move to** ◇ *A lot of new people have moved into the ~ recently.* | **leave, move away from** | **cover** | **be scattered over, be spread over** ◇ *Wreckage from the plane was scattered over a large ~.* | **patrol** ◇ *Police patrol the ~ regularly.* | **survey** ◇ *He slowly turned around, surveying the ~.* | **search** | **visit** ◇ *Thousands of tourists visit the ~ every year.* | **explore, tour** ◇ *I explored the ~ on my day off.*
AREA + NOUN **manager, office** | **hospital, hotel, restaurant** (*all AmE*) ◇ *Search for ~ hotels on the website.* | **code** (= in a telephone number) (*esp. AmE*)
PREP. **in an/the ~** ◇ *Few homes in the ~ had electricity.* | **outside an/the ~** ◇ *I live outside the metropolitan ~.* | **within an/the ~** | **~ around, ~ round** (*esp. BrE*) ◇ *the ~ around San Francisco*

2 space
ADJ. **dining, lounge, reception** | **picnic, play** | **waiting** | **seating** | **landing** | **storage** ◇ *Keep storage ~s locked.* |

outdoor ◇ *The hotel has an outdoor ~ that rivals any Las Vegas hotel.* | **no-smoking, smoking** | **VIP** ◇ *He was shown to a table in the VIP ~.* | **penalty** (in football/soccer) | **designated** ◇ *You can only smoke in designated ~s.* | **enclosed** ◇ *Do not use the spray in enclosed ~s.*
PREP. **in an/the ~** ◇ *I'll meet you in the reception ~.*

3 subject/activity

ADJ. **broad** | **important, key, main** | **complex, difficult, problem, sensitive** ◇ *Taxation is a very complex ~.* | **growth** ◇ *The big growth ~ of recent years has been in health clubs.* | **content, subject** | **grey/gray** ◇ *The proposals contain too many grey/gray ~s* (= aspects that are not clear).
VERB + AREA **cover** ◇ *The course covers two main subject ~s.* | **explore** ◇ *The research explores three ~s.* | **identify** ◇ *The primary need is to identify problem ~s.*
PREP. **in an/the ~** ◇ *There have been some exciting new developments in this ~.*
PHRASES **an ~ of activity, an ~ of life** ◇ *People with this disability can cope well in most ~s of life.* | **an ~ of concern, an ~ of difficulty** ◇ *We are generally pleased with the results but there are a few ~s of concern.* | **an ~ of interest, an ~ of research, an ~ of study**

4 measurement

ADJ. **large** | **small** | **total** | **floor, surface** ◇ *A building with a floor ~ of 100 square feet.*
VERB + AREA **cover, have** ◇ *The estate covers an ~ of 106 acres.*

arena noun

1 for sports/entertainment

ADJ. **Olympic** | **sports** | **training** | **basketball, hockey, rodeo, showjumping, etc.** | **ice** | **indoor, outdoor** | **home** (*esp. AmE*) ◇ *The Hurricanes have a new home ~.* | **10 000-seat, etc.**
VERB + ARENA **build** | **leave** ◇ *He left the ~ to loud applause.*
ARENA + NOUN **floor**
PREP. **in an/the ~, into an/the ~**

2 area of activity

ADJ. **global, international, national, world** | **domestic, foreign** ◇ *the challenges faced by farmers in the international and domestic ~s* | **wider** ◇ *Unions are also active in the wider ~ of the state.* | **public** | **academic, commercial, cultural, economic, financial, legal, legislative, political, social** | **policy** ◇ *This observation also applies in the environmental policy ~.* | **digital, online** ◇ *the challenges of bringing a business into the online ~* | **competitive**
VERB + ARENA **create, provide** ◇ *The conference should provide an ~ for marketing our products.* | **emerge into, enter, move into** ◇ *He had no desire to enter the political ~.* | **dominate**
PREP. **in an/the ~, within an/the ~** ◇ *The company has been very successful in the commercial ~.* | **outside an/the ~** ◇ *I want to work outside the ~ of competition.*

argue verb

1 disagree

ADV. **bitterly, fiercely, furiously, heatedly** | **loudly** | **constantly, endlessly** | **back** ◇ *Magda walked out of the room before her husband could ~ back.*
PREP. **about** ◇ *They ~ endlessly about money.* | **over** ◇ *They were arguing over who should have the car that day.* | **with** ◇ *She's always arguing with her mother.*

2 give reasons to support opinion

ADV. **forcefully, passionately, strenuously** (*esp. AmE*), **strongly, vehemently, vigorously, vociferously** | **cogently, compellingly, convincingly, effectively, persuasively, plausibly, powerfully, successfully** ◇ *The report ~s convincingly that economic help should be given to these countries.* | **correctly, reasonably, rightly** | **eloquently** | **easily** ◇ *You could easily ~ that this policy will have no effect.*
VERB + ARGUE **wish to** (*formal*) ◇ *I would wish to ~ that appreciation of the arts should be encouraged for its own sake.* | **be prepared to** ◇ *Are you prepared to ~ that killing is sometimes justified?* | **attempt to, try to** | **go on to** ◇ *In her paper she goes on to ~ that scientists do not yet know enough*

about the nature of the disease. | **be possible to** ◇ *It is possible to ~ that the rules are too strict.* | **be difficult to**
PREP. **against** ◇ *She ~d against a rise in interest rates.* | **for** ◇ *The general ~d for extending the ceasefire.* | **in favour/favor of** ◇ *They ~d in favour/favor of stricter punishments.*

argument noun

1 discussion

ADJ. **bitter, heated, violent** | **big** ◇ *I had a big ~ with my mother this morning.* | **little, petty, pointless, silly, stupid** | **age-old**
VERB + ARGUMENT **become involved in, get into, get involved in, have** ◇ *I don't want to get into an ~ with her.* | **cause, provoke, start** | **lose, win** ◇ *I was determined to win the ~.* | **settle** ◇ *Jory was always the one who settled ~s between us.*
ARGUMENT + VERB **arise, break out, develop, erupt** ◇ *Minutes later a violent ~ erupted.* | **ensue** ◇ *He felt offended by the suggestion, and a violent ~ ensued.* | **rage** ◇ *the bitter ~s raging about who was the real winner*
PREP. **~ about** ◇ *We had an ~ about what we should buy.* | **~ between** ◇ *an ~ between her parents* | **~ over** ◇ *The ~ over decentralization will probably continue for ever.* | **~ with** ◇ *an ~ with his wife*
PHRASES **brook no ~** ◇ *'You'll come home with me.' His voice brooked no ~.*

2 reason supporting opinion

ADJ. **basic, general** | **central, main** | **closing** ◇ *In her closing ~, the prosecutor said that the hairs found on the defendant matched those of the victim.* | **forceful, good, major, powerful, sound, strong, valid** | **cogent, compelling, conclusive, convincing, persuasive** ◇ *The author makes a compelling ~ for the use of hydrogen as a fuel.* | **credible, plausible** ◇ *Their ~ sounds plausible, but is it really valid?* | **substantive** (*formal, esp. AmE*) | **bogus, fallacious** (*formal*), **slippery-slope** (*AmE*), **specious** (*formal*), **spurious, weak** | **ridiculous** | **circular** | **legitimate, reasonable** | **logical, rational, reasoned, well-reasoned** | **opposing** | **economic, legal, moral, philosophical, political, theoretical, etc.**
VERB + ARGUMENT **advance, deploy, make, mount, offer, present, put forward, use** ◇ *He put forward some very convincing ~s.* | **articulate** | **develop** ◇ *This ~ is developed further in the next chapter.* | **build, construct, formulate, frame** ◇ *the language used to frame the legal ~s* | **reiterate, repeat** | **bolster, buttress, illustrate, reinforce, strengthen, support, underline** ◇ *Do you have any evidence to support your ~?* | **consider, hear, listen to** | **address** ◇ *I'll briefly address each ~.* | **accept, agree with** | **dismiss, reject** ◇ *The company dismissed his ~s as alarmist.* | **counter, discredit, rebut, refute** ◇ *She tried to think how to refute the ~ on moral grounds.* | **demolish, undercut, undermine, weaken** | **summarize** | **apply** ◇ *This ~ can be applied to other contexts.*
ARGUMENT + VERB **be based on sth** ◇ *The government's ~ is always based on how much such a plan would cost.* | **depend on sth, rely on sth, rest on sth, revolve around sth** | **boil down to sth** ◇ *As I see it, his ~ boils down to a combination of two basic points.* | **go, run** ◇ *Centralized government, so the ~ goes, is too far removed from the problems of ordinary citizens.* | **apply (to sth)** ◇ *The same ~ applies to adoption.* | **justify sth** | **support sth** | **imply sth, suggest sth** ◇ *These ~s suggest that the medical establishment had an interest in suppressing the research.* | **show sth** | **assume sth**
PREP. **~ against** ◇ *the ~s against lowering taxes* | **~ concerning** ◇ *~s concerning the nature of morality* | **~ for** ◇ *There is a very good ~ for increasing spending.* | **~ in favour/favor of** ◇ *What are the ~s in favour/favor of change?*
PHRASES **all sides of an ~, both sides of an ~** ◇ *He was able to see both sides of the ~.* | **a flaw in the ~** ◇ *I can see no flaw in your ~.* | **a line of ~** ◇ *I can see a few problems with this line of ~.*

arise verb

ADV. **naturally, spontaneously** | **directly** | **commonly,**

frequently, often | typically ◇ *Violence typically ~s out of anger.* | initially | inevitably
VERB + ARISE **may, might** | **be likely to, be unlikely to**
PREP. **from** ◇ *Some learning difficulties ~ from the way children are taught.* | **out of** ◇ *The current debate arose out of the concerns of parents.*

aristocracy noun

ADJ. **British, French, etc.** | **landed, landowning** | **local**
PHRASES **a member of the ~**

arithmetic noun

ADJ. **basic, simple** | **mental** ◇ *a test of mental ~*
VERB + ARITHMETIC **do** ◇ *By the age of ten, the children can do simple ~.*

arm noun

ADJ. **left, right** | **upper** ◇ *the muscles of the upper ~* | **muscular, powerful, strong** | **bony, skinny, slender, thin** | **short** | **hairy** | **good** ◇ *He used his good ~ to support his weight.* | **aching, bad, bleeding, broken, bruised, injured, sore, weak** ◇ *I have a sore ~, so I'm afraid I can't help you.* | **bandaged** | **prosthetic** | **raised, upraised** | **extended, open** (often figurative), **outstretched** ◇ *They're sure to welcome you with open ~s.* | **comforting, loving, protective** ◇ *He placed a comforting ~ around her shoulder.* | **waiting, welcoming** ◇ *Kris collapsed into her mother's waiting ~s.* | **crossed, folded** ◇ *He stood there with crossed ~s, looking angry.* | **shaking, trembling** | **flailing** ◇ *She ducked his flailing ~s.* | **bare** | **tanned** | **tattooed**
VERB + ARM **bend, flex, move** | **lift, lower, raise** ◇ *The figure in the boat raised an ~.* | **flap, swing, wave** ◇ *He was running forward, waving his ~s.* | **break, dislocate, hurt, twist** | **amputate** | **extend, hold out, open, stretch out** ◇ *He held out his ~s with a broad smile.* | **cross, fold** ◇ *She folded her ~s and stared at him.* | **uncross, unfold** | **hook, link** ◇ *The couple linked ~s and set off along the beach.* | **catch, catch at, catch hold of, clutch, grab, grasp, take** ◇ *A hand reached out and caught hold of her ~.* ◇ *She moved closer to her father and took his ~.* | **grip, hold, pat, squeeze, touch** | **fall into** ◇ *They fell into each other's ~s.* | **draw sb into, gather sb into, pull sb into, take sb in** ◇ *He pulled her into his ~s and kissed her.* | **hold sb in**
ARM + VERB **drop** | **bend** | **dangle, hang** ◇ *His ~ hung awkwardly against his side.* | **circle, slide, wave** ◇ *His ~s slid around her.* | **cradle sb/sth** | **clutch sb/sth** ◇ *His ~s clutched his stomach.* | **rest** ◇ *Her ~s were resting on the table.* | **tighten** ◇ *Her ~s tightened convulsively around the child.* | **shake, tremble** | **flail, swing, wave**
ARM + NOUN **injury** | **muscle** | **motion, movement** | **gesture** | **stroke, swing** | **workout**
PREP. **by the ~** ◇ *The officer grabbed him by the ~ (= grabbed his arm).* | **in sb's ~s** ◇ *The child lay in its mother's ~s.* | **on the ~** ◇ *She touched him gently on the ~.* | **on your ~** ◇ *Lucy felt the warm sun on her bare ~s.* ◇ *He walked in with a tall blonde on his ~ (= next to him and holding her arm).* | **under an/one/your ~** ◇ *She carried the dog under one ~.*
PHRASES **~ in ~** ◇ *They walked along ~ in ~ (= with the arm of one person linked with the arm of the other).* | **at arm's length** ◇ *He held the dirty rag at arm's length (= as far away from his body as possible).* | **the crook of an/sb's ~** ◇ *She lay curled up in the crook of his ~.* | **fling your ~s around sb/sth, put your ~s around sb/sth, throw your ~s around sb/sth** ◇ *He ran up to her and flung his ~s around her.* | **in each other's ~s** ◇ *They fell asleep in each other's ~s (= holding each other).* | **with ~s akimbo** (= with your arms bent and your hands on your hips) ◇ *She stood looking at him with ~s akimbo.*

armaments noun

ADJ. **conventional, nuclear**
VERB + ARMAMENTS **manufacture, produce**
ARMAMENTS + NOUN **industry**

armchair noun

ADJ. **big, deep, large** | **comfortable, comfy** (informal) | **plush** | **old** | **overstuffed** | **leather, upholstered**
VERB + ARMCHAIR **be seated in, be slumped in, be sprawled in, sit in** | **collapse into, flop into, throw yourself into** | **curl up in, ease yourself into, settle into** ◇ *He eased himself into the big ~.*

armed adj.

VERBS **be**
ADV. **heavily, well** | **lightly** | **fully**
PREP. **with** ◇ *The soldiers were all ~ with automatic rifles.*

armour (BrE) (AmE armor) noun

ADJ. **full, heavy, thick** | **light** | **body** ◇ *police officers in full body ~* | **battle, combat** | **protective** | **chain-mail, leather, metal, steel** | **shiny**
VERB + ARMOUR/ARMOR **have on, wear** | **don, put on** | **remove, take off** | **penetrate, pierce** ◇ *An arrow had pierced his ~.*
PREP. **in ~** ◇ *warriors in full ~*
PHRASES **a suit of ~** ◇ *He wore a suit of heavy ~ and carried a sword.*

armoured (BrE) (AmE armored) adj.

VERBS **be**
ADV. **heavily** ◇ *a convoy of heavily ~ vehicles* | **lightly** | **fully** ◇ *a fully ~ model with bulletproof windows*

arms noun

ADJ. **nuclear** | **small** ◇ *fighters using small ~ and home-made grenades*
VERB + ARMS **bear, carry** ◇ *The right to bear ~ is enshrined in the Constitution.* | **call sb to** (formal) ◇ *He called his comrades to ~ (= urged them to fight).* | **take up** (formal) ◇ *The people took up ~ to defend their country.* | **lay down** (formal) ◇ *They called on the rebels to lay down their ~ and surrender.* | **supply** ◇ *He was accused of supplying ~ to terrorists*
ARMS + NOUN **build-up, race** ◇ *The country's economic growth could fuel an ~ build-up.* | **control, embargo** | **reduction** | **agreement, treaty** | **exports, shipment** | **deal, industry, sales, trade** | **dealer, merchant** | **manufacturer** | **inspection** | **inspector**
PREP. **under ~** (formal) ◇ *There were more than a million men under ~ during the American Civil War.*

army noun

1 group of soldiers

ADJ. **great, huge, large, massive, mighty, powerful** | **small** | **ragtag** (informal) | **professional, regular, standing** ◇ *The taxes were used to maintain a standing ~ of around 55 000 troops.* | **reserve** | **conscript** | **all-volunteer, volunteer** | **mercenary** | **modern** | **allied** | **enemy, opposing** | **foreign** | **national** | **imperial, royal** | **private** | **guerrilla** | **rebel, revolutionary** | **advancing, approaching, invading, occupying, victorious** ◇ *Their city fell victim to an invading ~.* | **defeated, retreating**
VERB + ARMY **have** | **enter, go into, join** ◇ *After finishing school, Mike went into the ~.* | **leave** | **desert** | **be in command of, command, lead** ◇ *He was in command of the British Army in Egypt.* ◇ *He led the ~ into battle.* | **march** ◇ *He marched a foreign ~ into the capital.* | **drill, train** | **amass, build up, form, gather, raise, recruit** ◇ *The king was unable to raise an ~.* | **maintain** | **equip, supply** | **mobilize** | **deploy, field** | **fight** ◇ *those who fought the Soviet ~ in Afghanistan* | **face** | **crush, decimate, defeat, destroy, put to flight, rout** ◇ *The ~ was finally defeated in the spring.* | **disband, dissolve** (esp. AmE)
ARMY + VERB **gather** | **advance, march** ◇ *A huge ~ marched on the city.* | **camp** | **enter sth, invade (sth)** ◇ *The German ~ entered Austria in March 1938.* | **attack, clash, fight** ◇ *The two opposing armies clashed in battle.* | **kill sb** | **defeat sth** | **occupy sth** | **flee, move out, pull back, retreat, withdraw**
ARMY + NOUN **captain, chief of staff, colonel, commander, general, lieutenant, officer, sergeant** | **soldiers, troops** |

chaplain, engineer, medic, nurse, surgeon | leader, official, personnel ◇ *The companies recruit mostly retired ~ personnel.* | battalion, command, corps, division, unit | reserve, reservist | recruiter (*esp. AmE*) | career | deserter | veteran | barracks, base, camp, depot, headquarters, post ◇ *He grew up on an ~ base in the 1960s.* | patrol | checkpoint | intelligence | logistics | helicopter, tank, truck | hospital | boots, fatigues, uniform | surplus ◇ *He bought the jacket at an ~ surplus store.* | wife
PREP. in the ~ ◇ *Her husband is in the ~.*

2 large group

ADJ. vast ◇ *a vast ~ of personnel* | veritable ◇ *The singer was surrounded by a veritable ~ of reporters.* | small ◇ *a small ~ of volunteers* | growing, increasing
VERB + ARMY create ◇ *He created an ~ of loyal customers.* | employ, hire (*esp. AmE*) ◇ *Actresses now hire armies of hairdressers and stylists.* | maintain ◇ *NASA maintains a small ~ of engineers.* | organize ◇ *Who will organize the ~ of volunteers?*
PREP. ~ of ◇ *There was an ~ of technicians ready to help.*

aroma noun

ADJ. pungent, rich, strong ◇ *The pungent ~ of hay and horse manure filled his nostrils.* | heady | distinctive | faint, subtle | delicious, pleasant, wonderful | appetizing, mouth-watering ◇ *the mouth-watering ~ of prawns cooked in garlic* | spicy, sweet
VERB + AROMA inhale, savour/savor, smell ◇ *I immediately smelled the distinctive ~ of fresh coffee.* | be filled with, have ◇ *The room was filled with a strong ~ of woodsmoke.*
AROMA + VERB linger, waft ◇ *The ~ of fresh baking wafted through the air.* | fill sth ◇ *A pleasant ~ filled the house.*

arrange verb

1 plan/organize sth

ADV. easily | hastily, quickly | secretly | specially
VERB + ARRANGE try to | be able to, can ◇ *Todd will be able to ~ matters.* | be difficult to, be easy to ◇ *These matters are easy to ~.* | be possible to
PREP. for ◇ *Can you ~ for this work to be carried out?*

2 put in order; make neat/attractive

ADV. carefully, neatly, perfectly ◇ *Her red hair was carefully ~d and her face made up.* | artfully | haphazardly, randomly | alphabetically, chronologically, symmetric-ally, systematically, thematically ◇ *The books are ~d alphabetically by author.*
PREP. in ◇ *She ~d the chairs in neat rows.* | into ◇ *She took the list of visitors' names and ~d them into groups of four.* | according to ◇ *The clothes were ~d according to size.*
PHRASES ~ sth in … order ◇ *The names are ~d in alphabetical order.*

arrangement noun

1 plans/organization

ADJ. alternative, better, different, new, other ◇ *It may be necessary to make alternative ~s.* | final | practical | satisfactory, sensible, suitable (*all esp. BrE*) | careful, detailed | flexible | unusual | special ◇ *There are special ~s for people working overseas.* | formal | necessary, proper (*esp. BrE*) | administrative, organizational | social | childcare, domestic, funeral, holiday (*BrE*), living, pension (*BrE*), seating, security, sleeping, travel ◇ *Their domestic ~s were considered unconventional at the time.* | working ◇ *Flexible working ~s are catching on.*
VERB + ARRANGEMENT make | complete, confirm, finalize ◇ *Arrangements for the trip have now been completed.* | discuss ◇ *We are just discussing the final ~s for the concert.* | upset ◇ *All her careful ~s had been upset!* | change ◇ *We'll have to change our travel ~s.*
ARRANGEMENT + VERB stand ◇ *As far as I know, the ~ still stands.* | fall through ◇ *The catering ~s for the conference fell through at the last minute.*
PREP. ~ for ◇ *Arrangements for the funeral are complete.* | ~ with ◇ *I have made ~s with the store for the goods to be delivered here.*

2 agreement

ADJ. business, contractual, financial ◇ *It's purely a business arrangement—there's no need to get emotionally involved.* | constitutional | power-sharing | custody ◇ *Joint custody ~s do not work for all parents.* | special | formal, informal | voluntary | private | reciprocal | long-standing, long-term, permanent | interim, temporary
VERB + ARRANGEMENT have ◇ *The company has a special ~ with the bank.* | accept, agree, come to, make ◇ *She made an ~ with her employer whereby she worked a reduced number of hours.* | develop, establish, negotiate
PREP. by (an/the) ~ ◇ *Viewing of the property is only possible by ~ with the owner.* ◇ *They have an ~ by which they each contribute equally to the cost of the house.* | under an/the ~ ◇ *Under this ~ you can pay for the goods over a longer period.* | ~ between ◇ *an ~ between the two men* | ~ with ◇ *He finally came to an ~ with his landlord.*
PHRASES by prior ~ (*esp. BrE*) ◇ *A tour of the library is available by prior ~.*

3 group of things placed together

ADJ. complex, complicated ◇ *a complex ~ of rods and cogs* | physical, spatial ◇ *Even the physical ~ of the classroom can influence the way children learn.* | floral, flower
VERB + ARRANGEMENT design, do ◇ *Who did this beautiful flower ~?*

array noun

ADJ. broad, endless, extensive, full, huge, large, vast, wide ◇ *a seemingly endless ~ of options* | whole ◇ *Florists have access to a whole ~ of flowers.* | diverse | bewildering, confusing, dizzying | complex | amazing, astonishing, colourful/colorful, dazzling, fascinating, fine, formidable, impressive, incredible, rich, staggering, stunning, wonderful ◇ *a dazzling ~ of talent* | usual ◇ *The city has the usual ~ of social problems.*
VERB + ARRAY boast, carry, contain, display, feature, have, offer, provide ◇ *The store offers a bewildering ~ of gardening tools.* | comprise, cover, include ◇ *Her writing covers a wide ~ of topics.* | be faced with ◇ *The customer is faced with a formidable ~ of products.* | choose from, select from ◇ *It is difficult to choose from the vast ~ of wines.*

arrest noun

ADJ. false, wrongful | arbitrary | mass | citizen's ◇ *He grabbed the intruder by the arm and said, 'I am making a citizen's ~.'* | house ◇ *Following the coup, the leaders were put under house ~.* | drug, drug-related, marijuana (*esp. AmE*) | drunk-driving, felony (*both AmE*)
VERB + ARREST make | place sb under, put sb under | order ◇ *Some members of the Convention ordered the ~ of Robespierre.* | lead to ◇ *A reward has been offered for information that leads to the ~ of the murderer.* | face ◇ *She faced ~ and prison if she returned to the country.* | avoid, escape, evade (*esp. BrE*) | resist ◇ *He was charged with resisting ~.* | protest (*AmE*)
ARREST + NOUN warrant | record (*AmE*) ◇ *Many of the teenagers in the neighborhood already have ~ records.* | rate ◇ *The country's juvenile crime ~ rate increased by 25%. (esp. AmE)*
PREP. under ~ ◇ *The man is now under ~ in Rio.* | ~ for ◇ *They made ten ~s for possession of drugs.*
PHRASES the power of ~ ◇ *The government may remove the power of ~ from military police.* | a warrant for sb's ~

arrival noun

1 act of arriving

ADJ. early | late | on-time (*AmE*), scheduled ◇ *Which airline has the worst on-time ~s?* | timely ◇ *the timely ~ of the letter* | sudden, unexpected | expected, imminent, impending ◇ *I told her of my brother's expected ~.* | safe ◇ *Security escorts will ensure their safe ~.*
VERB + ARRIVAL make ◇ *At 11 p.m. Jody made his timely ~.* |

announce, herald, mark, signal ◇ *a frost in the air which marked the ~ of winter* | expect | anticipate, await ◇ *a crowd awaiting the ~ of the movie star* | greet ◇ *The staff greeted the ~ of the new boss with excitement.* | celebrate, welcome | delay | hasten

ARRIVAL + NOUN date, time

PREP. on (sb's) ~, upon (sb's) ~ ◇ *Guests receive dinner upon ~ at the hotel.* | with the ~ ◇ *With the ~ of John's friends, the party livened up.* | ~ at ◇ *his ~ at the airport* | ~ in ◇ *their ~ in Dallas*

PHRASES ~ on the scene ◇ *They were saved by the ~ on the scene of another boat.* | ~s and departures ◇ *There are 120 ~s and departures every day.* | time of ~ ◇ *Our estimated time of ~ is 7.15.*

2 sb/sth that arrives

ADJ. early, first | late ◇ *Someone should stay here to meet the late ~s.* | latest, new, recent ◇ *The club has a dinner to welcome new ~s to the town.* ◇ *We're expecting a new ~ (= a baby) in the family soon.*

VERB + ARRIVAL meet, welcome

arrive verb

ADV. early, late | shortly, soon ◇ *We should be arriving shortly.* | eventually, finally ◇ *We finally ~d at our destination late that evening.* | on time, promptly, punctually | safe and sound, safely | unannounced, unexpectedly ◇ *My uncle ~d unannounced yesterday evening.*

VERB + ARRIVE be due to ◇ *We are due to ~ in Sydney at ten o'clock.* | fail to ◇ *The package failed to ~.*

PREP. at ◇ *We ~d at the hotel late.* | in ◇ *I should ~ in Boston tomorrow morning.*

PHRASES the first to ~, the last to ~

arrogance noun

ADJ. breathtaking, sheer, supreme | intellectual

VERB + ARROGANCE have ◇ *She had the ~ to believe the law did not apply to her.* | display, show

arrow noun

1 weapon

ADJ. poison, poisoned

... OF ARROWS hail, volley ◇ *A hail of ~s descended from the tower.*

VERB + ARROW fire, release, shoot | draw ◇ *He drew two ~s and placed them in the bow.* | fit, string ◇ *She strung an ~ to her bow.* | aim

ARROW + VERB fly, shoot, whizz ◇ *An ~ whizzed past his head.* | hit sb/sth, pierce sb/sth, strike sb/sth ◇ *The ~ hit its target.* | land | rain, rain down | miss (sb/sth) ◇ *She aimed carefully at the tree but the ~ missed.*

ARROW + NOUN head (usually **arrowhead**), point, tip | shaft | slit ◇ *the ~ slits in the castle's battlements* | wound

PHRASES a bow and ~ ◇ *The people used bows and ~s for hunting.*

2 symbol

ADJ. left, right | down, up ◇ *The down ~ indicates rain.* | horizontal, vertical | broken, curved, dashed, shaded, solid ◇ *The old road is shown on the map by broken ~s.*

VERB + ARROW follow ◇ *Follow the red ~s to get to the camp reception.*

ARROW + VERB denote sth, indicate sth, mark sth, point, represent sth, show sth ◇ *You will see an ~ pointing to the left.*

ARROW + NOUN key ◇ *You can scroll through the text using the up and down ~ keys.*

art noun

1 paintings, drawings, etc.

ADJ. great, high | commercial, fine | abstract, conceptual, figurative, representational, visual | ancient, classical, medieval, modern, modernist, postmodern | animation, digital, graphic, installation, performance, pop | cinematic, video | erotic, sacred | avant-garde, contemporary, cutting-edge | 20th-century, etc. | original | folk, traditional | public | African, Japanese, Western, etc. | comic, cover ◇ *He created cover ~ and illustrations for the magazine.* | clip (*computing*)

VERB + ART create, produce | display, exhibit, feature, showcase ◇ *The museum normally showcases Western ~.* | buy, purchase | collect | view | appreciate

ART + NOUN gallery, museum | exhibit (*AmE*), exhibition, show | collection ◇ *The castle houses one of the finest ~ collections in Britain.* | buyer, collector, consultant, critic, curator, dealer, director, historian, professional, publisher ◇ *He was a noted ~ collector.* | aficionado, connoisseur, enthusiast, expert, lover | object, treasure, work (usually **artwork**) | book, magazine, print | academy, college, school | studio | form ◇ *Cinema gradually became accepted as an ~ form.* | style ◇ *His ~ style was less radical than his contemporaries.* | movement ◇ *the Impressionist ~ movement* | history | market | auction, fair | community, scene, world ◇ *the New York ~ scene* ◇ *Many people from the ~ world attended the funeral.* | therapy

PHRASES life imitates ~ ◇ *Will real life ever imitate ~ the way Hollywood wishes it would?*

2 (the) arts art, music, drama, literature, etc.

ADJ. creative, culinary, decorative, dramatic, performing, plastic, visual | applied | martial

ARTS + NOUN administrator, patron

PHRASES ~s and crafts ◇ *an exhibition of Peruvian ~s and crafts* | funding for the ~s, sponsorship of the ~s | a patron of the ~s

3 arts not sciences

ADJ. liberal (*esp. AmE*)

ARTS + NOUN subject (*esp. BrE*) | degree ◇ *an ~s degree (BrE)* ◇ *a liberal ~s degree (AmE)*

PHRASES ~s and sciences

4 ability/skill

ADJ. lost ◇ *Social interaction is increasingly becoming a lost ~.*

VERB + ART master, perfect ◇ *I've never mastered the ~ of making bread.*

PREP. ~ of ◇ *Television has ruined the ~ of conversation.*

PHRASES have sth down to a fine ~ (= know how to do it very well) (*esp. BrE*) ◇ *She has the business of buying presents down to a fine ~.*

NOTE

Works of art

a piece/work of art ◇ *Picasso's Guernica is a magnificent work of art.*

collect... ◇ *She collects photographic portraits.*

display..., exhibit..., show... ◇ *The works will be displayed in the new museum.*

... is (put) on display/exhibition/show, ...goes on display/exhibition/show ◇ *paintings put on show for the first time* ◇ *The photographs are on exhibition until the end of September.*

house... ◇ *A new wing was built to house the sculptures.*

a series of... ◇ *a series of paintings by Van Gogh*

a collection of..., an exhibition of..., an exhibit of... (*AmE*) ◇ *an exhibition of 20th-century French masterpieces*

an art/photographic/photography exhibition, an art/photographic/photography exhibit (*AmE*) ◇ *The open art exhibition will allow new artists to exhibit their work.*

by... ◇ *a kinetic sculpture by Alexander Calder*

---

artery noun

ADJ. main, major | blocked, clogged | narrowed | severed

VERB + ARTERY block, clog | constrict, narrow | dilate, open, widen | sever | damage

ARTERY + VERB clog up ◇ *Too much fatty food will make your arteries clog up.* | supply sth ◇ *an ~ supplying your heart with blood*

ARTERY + NOUN **wall** | **blockage**
PHRASES **hardening of the arteries** (= a disease of the arteries) ◇ *She suffers from hardening of the arteries.*

article noun

1 piece of writing

ADJ. **brilliant, excellent, fascinating, good, great, informative, insightful, interesting, must-read** (*informal, esp. AmE*), **thoughtful, thought-provoking** | **well-researched, well-written** | **influential, major, seminal** | **controversial, critical, provocative** | **in-depth** | **lengthy** | **brief, short** | **timely** (*esp. AmE*) | **news** | **feature, front-page, lead, leading, op-ed** (*AmE*), **review** ◇ *A leading ~ in 'The Times' accused the minister of lying.* | **occasional** (= not part of a series) ◇ *It was her job to commission occasional ~s.* | **follow-up, related** | **accompanying** | **how-to** (*esp. AmE*) ◇ *The magazine includes a how-to ~ on building a greenhouse.* | **published** | **academic, scholarly, scientific** | **peer-reviewed** | **journal, magazine, newspaper, press** | **online**
... OF ARTICLES **series**
VERB + ARTICLE **author** (*formal*), **co-author, do, pen, write** ◇ *I'm doing an ~ about ways of preventing pollution.* | **research** | **commission** | **adapt** | **edit** | **excerpt** (*AmE*) ◇ *an ~ excerpted from 'CAD Principles'* | **contribute, email, submit** | **post** | **read, see** ◇ *Did you see the ~ on China in today's paper?* | **cite, quote, reference** | **review** | **carry, feature, print, publish, reprint, run** ◇ *The magazine refused to print his ~.* | **clip** (*AmE*), **clip out** (*esp. AmE*), **cut out** ◇ *He always clips and saves ~s about people he knows.*
ARTICLE + VERB **appear** ◇ *The ~ appears in this week's edition of 'Time'.* | **contain sth, feature sth** ◇ *The ~ contains a good deal of information about the software.* | **describe sth, detail sth, explain sth, mention sth, outline sth, point sth out, present sth, report sth, reveal sth, say sth, state sth, talk about sth** | **demonstrate sth, illustrate sth, indicate sth, show sth** | **address sth, analyse/analyze sth, deal with sth, discuss sth, examine sth, explore sth, focus on sth, look at sth** ◇ *The ~ looks at two questions.* | **emphasize sth, highlight sth** | **review sth** | **allege sth, argue sth, assert sth, claim sth, imply sth, suggest sth** | **propose sth** | **attack sb/sth, criticize sb/sth** | **cite sb/sth, quote sb/sth** | **conclude sth**
PREP. **in an/the ~** ◇ *She admitted she was wrong in an ~ in the newspaper.* | **~ about, ~ on** ◇ *an ~ on the dangers of sunbathing* | **~ by** ◇ *an ~ about wine by Alison Waters*
PHRASES **an ~ called sth, an ~ entitled sth, an ~ headed sth, an ~ headlined sth, an ~ titled sth** (*esp. AmE*) ◇ *an ~ entitled 'Think Yourself Thin'*

2 part of law

ADJ. **key** ◇ *the key ~s of the constitution*
VERB + ARTICLE **be in breach of** (*esp. BrE*), **breach** (*esp. BrE*), **contravene** (*esp. BrE*), **infringe** (*BrE*), **violate** ◇ *The actions of the organization violate Article 12 of the treaty.*
ARTICLE + VERB **provide sth** (*formal*), **specify sth, state sth** ◇ *Article 10 provides that all businesses must be registered correctly.*
PREP. **under an/the ~** ◇ *The judge ordered the child's return home under Article 12 of the Convention.*
PHRASES **the terms of an ~** ◇ *The terms of Article 3 will be changed by the new government.*

3 thing

ADJ. **finished** ◇ *The finished ~ takes two months to manufacture.* | **the genuine** ◇ *Fake designer watches are sold at a fraction of the price of the genuine ~.* | **offending** | **household, toilet**
VERB + ARTICLE **make, manufacture, produce**
PHRASES **an ~ of clothing**

4 grammar

ADJ. **definite, indefinite**
VERB + ARTICLE **take** ◇ *Names of countries in English do not usually take an ~.*

articulate verb

1 pronounce sth carefully

ADV. **carefully, clearly, well** ◇ *She spoke slowly, articulating each word clearly.*

2 express sth

ADV. **clearly, well** ◇ *She cannot ~ her feelings very well.* | **explicitly** (*esp. AmE*), **fully**

articulate adj.

VERBS **be** | **become**
ADV. **extremely, fairly, very, etc.** | **highly** ◇ *a highly ~ woman*
PREP. **about** ◇ *The teachers help the children to be more ~ about their lives.*

artificial adj.

VERBS **be, look, seem**
ADV. **extremely, fairly, very, etc.** | **highly** | **completely, entirely, totally** | **a little, slightly, etc.**

artillery noun

ADJ. **field** | **heavy** ◇ *The enemy has enough heavy ~ to win the war.* | **anti-aircraft** | **air-defence/air-defense** | **rocket** | **long-range** | **enemy**
ARTILLERY + NOUN **attack, barrage, bombardment, fire, strike** | **system** | **piece, shell** | **ammunition, cannon, gun, projectile, rocket, weapon** | **round** | **battalion, battery, brigade, regiment, train, unit** ◇ *The soldiers of the ~ train had panicked.* ◇ *nuclear ~ units* | **commander, officer**

artist noun

1 person who creates works of art

ADJ. **accomplished, gifted, great, talented** | **celebrated, distinguished, established, famous, influential, leading, major, master** (*esp. AmE*), **renowned, successful, top-selling, well-known, world-renowned** | **aspiring, budding, emerging, up-and-coming** ◇ *She set up the gallery so that up-and-coming ~s could exhibit their work.* | **lesser-known, struggling, unknown** | **amateur, professional** | **freelance** | **self-taught** | **serious** ◇ *He is a serious ~, and totally committed to his work.* | **prolific** | **local** | **creative** | **real, true** ◇ *My husband is a real ~ in the kitchen.* (*figurative*) | **fine** | **commercial** | **folk** | **abstract, conceptual, figurative, performance, visual** | **ceramic, graphic, mixed-media, watercolour/watercolor** | **Impressionist, pop** | **landscape, war** (*esp. BrE*), **wildlife** | **graffiti, pavement** (*BrE*), **sidewalk** (*AmE*) | **make-up, tattoo** | **comic, comic-book** | **avant-garde, contemporary, living, modern** | **19th-century, etc.**
VERB + ARTIST **commission** ◇ *In 1942 the city commissioned war ~ John Piper to paint its bombed cathedral.* | **feature, showcase** ◇ *The museum's featured ~s include Degas, Cézanne and Renoir.* ◇ *an exhibition featuring wildlife ~ Emma Gray* | **promote, represent** ◇ *The agency began to represent Chinese ~s.* | **inspire** ◇ *Artists are inspired by beauty.*
ARTIST + VERB **create sth, design sth, draw (sth), paint (sth), produce sth** ◇ *an ~ who paints in oils* | **work** ◇ *~s who work in different media* | **experiment with sth, explore sth** ◇ *The ~s explored common themes.* | **depict sb/sth, portray sb/sth** | **specialize in sth** ◇ *a group of ~s who specialize in jazz-themed art* | **exhibit sth, show sth** ◇ *Local ~s are currently exhibiting their work at the gallery.*
PHRASES **an ~ in residence** ◇ *the new ~ in residence at the Tate Gallery*

2 a professional entertainer

ADJ. **guest** ◇ *The Blue Note Quartet will be the guest ~s tomorrow night.* | **solo** | **recording** | **escape, mime** (*esp. BrE*), **trapeze** | **hip-hop, rap, reggae, etc.** | **spoken-word** (*esp. AmE*)
VERB + ARTIST **feature** ◇ *The festival featured up-and-coming young ~s.* | **promote, represent** | **sign**

ARTIST + VERB **perform (sth)** | **work** | **record (sth)**
→ Note at JOB

ascend *verb*

ADV. **gently** | **steeply** | **quickly, rapidly** | **slowly**
PREP. **from** ◊ *The road ~s steeply from the beach.*

ascent *noun*

1 act of climbing/moving up

ADJ. **gradual, slow**
VERB + ASCENT **make** ◊ *The climbers made their ~ of the mountain without oxygen.* | **begin, start** | **continue**
PREP. **~ from** ◊ *the ~ from the valley* | **~ to** ◊ *their ~ to the summit*

2 upward path/slope

ADJ. **steep** | **long**
VERB + ASCENT **climb** ◊ *They climbed the steep ~ on to the plateau.*

3 becoming more important or powerful

ADJ. **rapid** | **gradual**
PREP. **~ to** ◊ *her rapid ~ to power*

ash *noun*

1 powder that is left after sth has burned

ADJ. **glowing, hot, red-hot, smouldering/smoldering** ◊ *the glowing ~es of the dying fire* | **cold** ◊ *The fire had died to cold ~es.* | **fine** ◊ *Fine ~ covered the hill near the volcano.* | **grey/gray** | **cigarette, volcanic, wood**
... OF ASH **cloud** ◊ *A cloud of ~ rose from the volcano.*
VERB + ASH **flick, tap** (used about cigarette ash) ◊ *He flicked ~ into the ashtray.* | **reduce sth to, turn to ~es** ◊ *a town reduced to ~es by war* | *All her dreams had turned to ~es.* (figurative)
ASH + VERB **fall** ◊ *Ash from the volcano fell over a wide area.*
PHRASES **rise from the ~es** (figurative) ◊ *The party had risen from the ~es of electoral disaster.*

2 ashes remains of a dead body

VERB + ASHES **scatter, spread** ◊ *His ~es were scattered on his beloved farm.* | **bury**

ashamed *adj.*

VERBS **be, feel, look, seem, sound** | **make sb** ◊ *His foul-mouthed way of speaking made me ~ of him.*
ADV. **deeply, really, very** | **thoroughly** | **rather, somewhat** | **a little, slightly, etc.** | **almost**
PREP. **about** ◊ *I've done nothing to be ~ about.* | **at** ◊ *He was slightly ~ at having run away.* | **of** ◊ *She was ~ of what she had done.*

ask *verb*

1 put a question to sb

ADV. **gently, quietly, softly** ◊ *'How do you feel?' she ~ed softly.* | **conversationally, politely, sweetly** ◊ *'Did you sleep well?' he ~ed politely.* | **eagerly, excitedly** | **angrily, bluntly, coldly, crossly** (esp. BrE), **impatiently, irritably, sarcastically, sharply, slyly** | **calmly, casually, coolly, drily, innocently, nonchalantly** ◊ *'Oh, Sue went too, did she?' I ~ed innocently* (= pretending I did not know that this was important). | **curiously, doubtfully, incredulously, inquisitively, pointedly, quizzically, sceptically/skeptically, suspiciously, warily** | **anxiously, apprehensively, concernedly, fearfully, nervously, timidly, worriedly** ◊ *'Will he be all right?' Sabrina ~ed anxiously.* | **cautiously, hesitantly, tentatively, uncertainly** | **hopefully** ◊ *'Do you still want to go out tonight?' she ~ed hopefully.* | **jokingly, teasingly** | **legitimately** ◊ *Voters can legitimately ~ whose interests are being served by the new legislation.*
VERB + ASK **want to** ◊ *I wanted to ~ him a question.* | **dare (to)** ◊ *I wondered how old she was but I didn't dare ~.* | **forget to** ◊ *I completely forgot to ~ his name.*
PREP. **about** ◊ *He ~ed about her family.*

PHRASES **get ~ed sth** ◊ *I often get ~ed that.* | **if you don't mind me ~ing, if you don't mind my ~ing** ◊ *How old are you—if you don't mind my ~ing?*

2 request sth

ADV. **nicely** ◊ *If you ~ her nicely, she'll give you a hand.* | **specifically** ◊ *He specifically ~ed for information on the subject.*
PREP. **for** ◊ *I'm not ~ing for money.*

asleep *adj.*

VERBS **be, lie, seem** ◊ *The baby lay peacefully ~ in its cradle.* ◊ *All the houses seemed ~.* | **fall** ◊ *I fell ~ almost immediately.* | **remain, stay**
ADV. **deeply, fast, sound, soundly** ◊ *The children were all sound ~ in bed.* | **almost, half, nearly** ◊ *At the end of the afternoon they were exhausted and half ~.* | **peacefully** | **still**

aspect *noun*

ADJ. **central, crucial, essential, fundamental, important, key, main, major, principal, significant, vital** | **basic, broad, general** ◊ *Questions also cover much broader ~s of general health.* | **appealing, attractive, beneficial, encouraging** (esp. BrE), **exciting, fascinating, interesting, pleasing** (esp. BrE), **positive** | **controversial, difficult, disappointing** (esp. BrE), **disturbing, negative, problematic, sinister, troubling, unfortunate, worst** ◊ *the worst ~s of tourism* | **bizarre, curious, intriguing, puzzling, unusual** | **distinctive, noteworthy, remarkable, striking** | **unique** | **subtle** | **mundane** | **neglected** | **certain, specific, various** ◊ *They provided assistance on various ~s of the job.* | **formal, functional, practical, theoretical** ◊ *the theoretical ~s of the course* | **business, commercial, cultural, economic, environmental, ethical, financial, historical, human, legal, military, moral, physical, political, psychological, religious, scientific, social, spiritual, technical**
VERB + ASPECT **have** ◊ *The project has two main ~s.* | **take on** ◊ *Events began to take on a more sinister ~.* | **address, consider, cover, deal with, discuss, emphasize, examine, explore, focus on, highlight, investigate, look at, study** ◊ *We will be looking at many different ~s of pollution.* | **demonstrate, illuminate, illustrate, reveal** ◊ *a unique collection illustrating ~s of art history* | **ignore, neglect, overlook**
PREP. **from the ... ~** ◊ *This plan is very good from the social ~.* | **~ to** ◊ *the positive ~s of retirement*
PHRASES **all ~s of sth, every ~ of sth** | **in every ~ (of sth)** ◊ *The service was excellent in every ~.*

aspiration *noun*

ADJ. **high, lofty** ◊ *He has high ~s and wants to improve his qualifications.* | **human, personal, social** | **career, professional** | **political, presidential** | **academic, artistic, cultural, educational, literary** | **democratic, national**
VERB + ASPIRATION **have** | **achieve, fulfil/fulfill, meet, realize, satisfy** ◊ *a political party that realizes the ~s of the people*
PREP. **~ for** ◊ *an ~ for personal power* | **~ to** ◊ *the country's ~s to independence* | **~ towards/toward** ◊ *~s towards/toward starting his own business*
PHRASES **dreams and ~s, goals and ~s, hopes and ~s** ◊ *She talked about her hopes and ~s.*

aspirin *noun*

ADJ. **soluble** | **low-dose** | **baby** (esp. AmE) | **coated** (esp. AmE)
... OF ASPIRIN **dose**
VERB + ASPIRIN **take** ◊ *She took an ~ and went to bed.* | **give sb** ◊ *Never give ~ to a child under twelve.* | **dissolve** ◊ *Dissolve two ~ in water.*

assassin *noun*

ADJ. **attempted, would-be** | **hired, professional** ◊ *He was killed by a hired ~.* | **trained** | **deadly**
VERB + ASSASSIN **hire**

assassinate verb

VERB + ASSASSINATE **attempt to, try to** | **plan to, plot to** ◊ *He was executed in 1887 for plotting to ~ the Tsar.*
PHRASES **an attempt to ~ sb** | **a plot to ~ sb**

assassination noun

ADJ. **attempted** | **targeted** | **political** ◊ *Three local leaders have been killed in political ~s.* | **character** ◊ *a vicious campaign of character ~*
VERB + ASSASSINATION **carry out** | **plan, plot** ◊ *It is believed that they plotted the ~ of the rebel leader.* | **order**
ASSASSINATION + NOUN **attempt, plot** ◊ *He has survived several ~ attempts.* ◊ *a failed ~ attempt* | **target** | **squad**

assault noun

1 crime of attacking sb

ADJ. **brutal, ferocious, savage, vicious, violent** | **armed** | **criminal** | **common** (*BrE, law*) | **aggravated** (*law*), **serious** | **felonious, felony, misdemeanor** (*all AmE, law*) | **alleged** | **attempted** | **indecent, physical, racial** (*esp. BrE*), **sexual** ◊ *He was convicted of rape and another six counts of indecent ~.* | **domestic**
... OF ASSAULTS **series, wave**
VERB + ASSAULT **carry out** (*esp. BrE*), **commit** ◊ *~s committed by teenagers* | **be the victim of, suffer** | **report** ◊ *He reported the ~ to the police.*
ASSAULT + VERB **happen, occur, take place**
PREP. **~ against** ◊ *Better street lighting has helped reduce the number of ~s against women.* | **~ on, ~ upon**
PHRASES **allegations of ~** ◊ *allegations of police ~ on the boy* | **~ and battery** (*law*)
→ Note at CRIME (for more verbs)

2 military/verbal attack

ADJ. **all-out, direct, frontal, full-scale, major, massive** ◊ *After an all-out ~ the town was captured by the enemy.* | **deadly, fierce** | **fresh, further** | **sustained** ◊ *She used the article to make a sustained ~ on her former political allies.* | **relentless** | **initial** | **final** | **successful** | **aerial, air, airborne, amphibious, ground** ◊ *air ~s by fighter planes* | **military** | **terrorist** | **verbal** | **legal** ◊ *a two-year legal ~ on alleged tax fraud*
... OF ASSAULTS **series**
VERB + ASSAULT **begin, carry out, conduct, launch, lead, make, mount** ◊ *Enemy troops launched an ~ on the town.* | **launch into** ◊ *He launched into a verbal ~ on tabloid journalism.* | **come under, face** ◊ *The factory came under ~ from soldiers in the mountains.* | **survive, withstand** ◊ *The garrison was built to withstand ~s.*
ASSAULT + NOUN **course** (*BrE*) ◊ *They took part in a vigorous army ~ course.* | **operation** | **gun, rifle, weapon** | **force, team, troops** | **helicopter, ship, vehicle**
PREP. **under ~** ◊ *Today these values are under ~.* | **~ on** ◊ *a series of ~s on enemy targets*

assault verb

ADV. **brutally, seriously** (*esp. BrE*), **violently** (*esp. BrE*) | **indecently** (*BrE*), **physically, sexually, verbally** | **allegedly**

assemble verb

ADV. **carefully** | **hastily, quickly** ◊ *a hastily ~d force of warriors* | **easily** | **already** ◊ *I bought the desk already ~d.* | **together**
VERB + ASSEMBLE **begin to** ◊ *I've already begun to ~ my team for the job.* | **manage to** | **be easy to, be possible to** | **be difficult to**
PREP. **for** ◊ *We had ~d for the first rehearsal.* | **into** ◊ *the force that permits atoms to ~ into molecules*
PHRASES **fully ~d, partially ~d** ◊ *The shelves are available in kit form or fully ~d.*

assembly noun

1 elected group

ADJ. **elected, representative** | **constitutional, consultative, general, legislative** | **local, national, provincial, regional, state**
VERB + ASSEMBLY **create, form, set up** (*BrE*) | **elect, vote for** ◊ *South Korea voted for its National Assembly this week.* | **dissolve**
ASSEMBLY + VERB **meet** ◊ *Provincial assemblies meet once a year.* | **vote** ◊ *The ~ voted to delay the legislation to allow further consultation to take place.*
ASSEMBLY + NOUN **member** | **seat** | **building, room**
PREP. **in an/the ~** ◊ *These issues have been discussed in the local assemblies.*
PHRASES **a meeting of the ~, a session of the ~**
→ Note at ORGANIZATION

2 group gathered together

ADJ. **public** | **peaceful** | **unlawful**
VERB + ASSEMBLY **hold** ◊ *They demanded the right to hold peaceful assemblies.* | **call**
ASSEMBLY + NOUN **point** ◊ *When the fire alarm sounds, leave the building and proceed to your ~ point.*
PHRASES **freedom of ~, the right of ~** (= the right to gather freely)

3 at school

ADJ. **school** | **morning**
VERB + ASSEMBLY **have, hold** ◊ *We hold an ~ every morning.* | **attend, go to**
ASSEMBLY + NOUN **hall**
PREP. **at ~, during ~, in ~** ◊ *The announcement was made during morning ~.*

4 putting parts together

ADJ. **easy** | **final** ◊ *This factory deals with final ~ and testing.*
VERB + ASSEMBLY **require** ◊ *Some ~ is required.*
ASSEMBLY + NOUN **line** ◊ *workers on the ~ line* | **area, plant** ◊ *The company has twenty ~ plants in Europe.* | **operation, process, work**

assert verb

1 say sth clearly and firmly

ADV. **boldly, confidently, emphatically, forcefully, strongly** ◊ *The report ~s confidently that the industry will grow.* | **directly, explicitly** | **merely, simply** ◊ *He had no real evidence—he simply ~ed that what he said was true.* | **repeatedly** | **correctly, rightly**

2 make other people recognize your rights/authority

VERB + ASSERT **need to** | **be determined to, wish to** ◊ *She wished to ~ her independence from her parents.* | **seek to, try to** | **be able to** ◊ *He was able to ~ his power over the media.* | **be unable to, fail to**

assertion noun

ADJ. **bold, confident, strong** | **dogmatic, general, sweeping** ◊ *sweeping ~s about the role of women in society* | **simple** ◊ *The argument needs to progress beyond the simple ~ that criminals are made not born.* | **factual** | **false, unsubstantiated, unsupported** | **repeated**
VERB + ASSERTION **make** ◊ *How can you make such an ~?* | **justify, prove, support** ◊ *Your ~ is not supported by the facts.* | **accept, agree with** | **challenge, dispute, question** ◊ *Researchers have recently challenged these ~s.* | **reject** | **contradict, refute** | **repeat**
PREP. **~ about** ◊ *~s about human nature*

assess verb

1 form an opinion

ADV. **fully** | **accurately, correctly, properly** | **carefully** ◊ *She carefully ~ed the situation.* | **quickly** | **directly** | **independently** ◊ *The studies were independently ~ed by several researchers.* | **critically**
VERB + ASSESS **attempt to, try to** | **help to** | **be difficult to** ◊ *It is difficult to fully ~ the damage.*
PREP. **for** ◊ *She decided to get her daughter ~ed for dyslexia.*

2 amount/value

ADV. **accurately, correctly, properly**

VERB + ASSESS **attempt to, try to** | **be difficult to** ◇ *It is difficult to ~ the building's value properly without seeing it.* PREP. **at** ◇ *The legal costs have been ~ed at $75 000.*

assessment *noun*

ADJ. **broad, general, overall** | **individual** | **continuous, regular** ◇ *Examination is by continuous ~.* | **quick, rapid** | **external, internal** | **initial** | **final** | **follow-up** | **accurate, balanced, fair, good, honest, proper, realistic** | **careful, comprehensive, detailed, formal, quantitative, systematic, thorough** | **independent, objective** | **personal, subjective** ◇ *He was shrewd in his personal ~s.* | **adequate** | **critical** | **optimistic, pessimistic** | **course** | **tax** | **damage, health, impact, intelligence, needs, performance, quality, risk, threat** ◇ *Needs ~ is crucial if the hospital is to deliver effective health care.* | **clinical, educational, financial** (*esp. BrE*), **medical, psychiatric, psychological, scientific**
VERB + ASSESSMENT **carry out, complete, conduct, do, make, perform, undertake** ◇ *The new manager carried out an ~ of the sales department.* | **give, offer, provide**
ASSESSMENT + NOUN **methods, procedures, technique, tools** | **criteria** | **process, system**
PHRASES **a form of ~, a method of ~**

asset *noun*

1 useful person/thing

ADJ. **big, considerable, great, important, invaluable, precious, priceless, real, tremendous, useful, valuable** ◇ *The teachers are the school's biggest ~.* | **best, main, major, principal, prize, prized** | **cultural** ◇ *The country's cultural ~s should be made more accessible.* | **natural** ◇ *Scotland's mountain areas are a natural ~ to be proud of.* | **military, strategic**
PREP. **~ to** ◇ *She will be an ~ to any school she attends.*

2 what a company owns

ADJ. **combined, total** | **gross, net** ◇ *The company's net ~s are worth millions.* | **business, company, corporate** | **commercial, financial** | **current, disposable, liquid** ◇ *Liquid ~s can be sold more quickly.* | **capital, fixed, fund, non-cash** (*esp. BrE*), **non-monetary, physical, property** | **intangible, tangible** | **wasting** | **hidden** ◇ *They have hidden ~s in banks around the world.* | **foreign, overseas** | **personal** | **national, public, state**
VERB + ASSET **have, hold, own, possess** ◇ *~s held by the company in Asia.* | **transfer** ◇ *He transferred all his ~s into his wife's name.* | **accumulate, acquire, buy, purchase** | **dispose of, realize, sell** ◇ *The business disposed of all its capital ~s.* | **value** | **increase, reduce** ◇ *The company has increased its UK ~s.* | **freeze** ◇ *The courts can order a company's ~s to be frozen.* | **release** | **seize** ◇ *The authorities have the power to seize the ~s of convicted drug dealers.* | **protect** | **manage, use**
ASSET + VERB **be worth sth** | **appreciate, grow, increase** ◇ *Net ~s have grown to $169 million.* | **decline, depreciate**
ASSET + NOUN **price, value** | **management** | **sale**
PHRASES **~s and liabilities**

assignment *noun*

1 task

ADJ. **special** | **important** | **dangerous, difficult, tough** | **job** (*esp. AmE*), **work** | **modelling/modeling, photographic**
VERB + ASSIGNMENT **accept, take on** ◇ *Why did you take on this ~ if you're so busy?* | **get, have, receive** | **carry out** | **refuse** ◇ *If you refuse this ~ you risk losing your job.* | **complete, finish** | **give sb**
PREP. **on** ◇ *The photographer is on ~ in China at the moment.*

2 piece of school/college work

ADJ. **reading, writing, written** | **homework** | **class, group** (*both esp. AmE*)
VERB + ASSIGNMENT **give, hand out, set** (*esp. BrE*) ◇ *The teacher gave us an ~ on pollution.* | **get, receive** (*esp. AmE*) | **do,**

write (*esp. AmE*) | **read** | **complete, finish** | **hand in** ◇ *The students handed in their ~s.*
PREP. **~ on** ◇ *an ~ on modern lifestyles*

assimilate *verb*

1 learn/understand

ADV. **easily, quickly, rapidly, readily** ◇ *Children ~ new information very quickly.*

2 become/make sb part of sth

ADV. **completely, fully, thoroughly** (*esp. AmE*) ◇ *Many new immigrants have not yet ~d fully into the new culture.*
PREP. **into**

assist *verb*

ADV. **greatly, materially** (*esp. AmE*) ◇ *We have been greatly ~ed by individuals and organizations.* | **ably** ◇ *She was ably ~ed by a team of volunteers.* | **actively**
VERB + ASSIST **be designed to** ◇ *measures designed to ~ people with disabilities*
PREP. **in** ◇ *He had to ~ her in opening the gates.* | **with** ◇ *She offered to ~ with the marketing of the product.*

assistance *noun*

ADJ. **considerable, great, real, substantial** | **limited** | **invaluable, valuable** | **practical** | **special** | **direct, emergency, immediate** ◇ *People in the flooded areas are in need of direct ~.* | **mutual** ◇ *The treaty pledged mutual ~ in the event of an attack on either country.* | **expert, professional** | **external, outside** | **foreign, international** | **federal, government** ◇ *They argued the case for extra government ~ for the poorest regions.* | **public, social, welfare** ◇ *the stigma attached to receiving social ~* | **personal** ◇ *disabled people who need personal ~ to enable them to live in their own homes* | **humanitarian** | **development** | **economic, financial, legal, material, medical, military, research, technical**
VERB + ASSISTANCE **give sb, lend (sb), offer (sb), provide, render** ◇ *The government is willing to lend ~ to victims of the flooding.* ◇ *We provide ~ if your car breaks down.* | **get, obtain, receive** ◇ *Did you receive any ~ from the authorities?* | **pledge, promise (sb)** ◇ *The World Bank promised ~ of $5 million.* | **be in need of, need, require** | **expect** | **ask for, call for, request, seek** ◇ *I advise you to seek ~ from the police.* | **turn to sb for** ◇ *She had no one to turn to for ~.* | **be of, come to sb's** ◇ *Do let us know if we can be of any ~ to you.* ◇ *A sympathetic passer-by came to his ~.* | **welcome** | **acknowledge**
PREP. **with ~, without ~** ◇ *The work was completed with the ~ of local carpenters.* | **~ for** ◇ *humanitarian ~ for refugees* | **~ from** ◇ *~ from friends and family* | **~ in** ◇ *~ in finding a place to stay* | **~ with** ◇ *~ with rent for people on a low income*

assistant *noun*

ADJ. **chief, senior** | **deputy** | **personal** ◇ *I'll ask my personal ~ to deal with this.* | **special** | **administrative, care** (*esp. BrE*), **catering** (*BrE*), **checkout** (*BrE*), **clerical** (*esp. BrE*), **executive** (*esp. AmE*), **graduate** (*esp. AmE*), **laboratory, library, physician** (*AmE*), **production, research, sales** (*BrE*), **shop** (*BrE*), **teaching, technical** ◇ *She took up a post as research ~ in the Department of Pharmacology.*
VERB + ASSISTANT **employ (sb as), have** ◇ *She had an ~ to do her paperwork.* | **get, hire (sb as)** (*esp. AmE*), **recruit (sb as)** ◇ *I'm getting a new ~ next month.* | **fire** (*esp. AmE*), **sack** (*esp. BrE*)
PREP. **~ to** ◇ *She is ~ to the Production Manager.*
→ Note at JOB

associate *noun*

ADJ. **close** ◇ *a close ~ with whom he started a business* | **former, old** ◇ *Her former ~s refused to see her.* | **long-time** | **business, political**

association noun

1 an organization

ADJ. **international, local, national, regional, state** | **non-profit** (*esp. AmE*), **private, public, voluntary** | **arts, business, community, constituency** (*in the UK*), **consumer, housing, industry, library, neighbourhood/neighborhood, parent-teacher, political, professional, student, trade,** etc.
ASSOCIATION + VERB **meet** ◊ *The ~ meets four times a year.* → Note at ORGANIZATION (for more verbs)
PREP. **~ for** ◊ *a professional ~ for music teachers*

2 relationship between people/organizations

ADJ. **close** | **free** ◊ *It was to be a free ~ of equal partners.* | **loose** ◊ *a loose ~ of sovereign states* | **long, long-standing** | **personal**
VERB + ASSOCIATION **form** | **maintain** ◊ *They have maintained a close ~ with a college in the US.*
PREP. **in ~ with** (= together with) ◊ *The book was published in ~ with the university.* | **~ between** ◊ *the ~ between the two countries* | **~ with** ◊ *His ~ with such criminals can only destroy him.*
PHRASES **freedom of ~**

3 connection between things

ADJ. **clear, close, direct, intimate, strong** ◊ *a close ~ between the two nations* | **loose** | **early, long, traditional** | **formal** | **free** ◊ *the technique of free ~, in which the patient is encouraged to say the first thing that comes to mind*
VERB + ASSOCIATION **have** ◊ *The city has had a long ~ with the mining industry.* | **form** ◊ *The dog forms an ~ between the action and the reward.* | **demonstrate, find, prove, show** ◊ *The research showed an ~ between diet and various diseases.* | **examine, observe**
PREP. **by ~** ◊ *Dogs learn mainly by ~.* | **in ~ with** (= together with) ◊ *We are working in ~ with several NGOs.* | **~ between** ◊ *a clear ~ between good health and regular exercise* | **~ with** ◊ *the traditional ~ of the Democrats with minority interests*
PHRASES **guilty by ~, tainted by ~** ◊ *He was considered tainted by ~ with the corrupt regime.*

4 associations feelings/memories

ADJ. **strong** | **happy, pleasant, positive** | **negative** | **cultural, historical, literary** ◊ *Tourists visit the city for its historical ~s.*
VERB + ASSOCIATIONS **have, hold** (*BrE*) ◊ *Does the name 'Baxter' have any ~s for you?* | **evoke, trigger** ◊ *The smell of fresh bread triggers all kinds of ~s for me.*
PREP. **~ for**

assortment noun

ADJ. **large, rich, vast, wide** | **diverse, varied** | **motley** ◊ *a motley ~ of characters* | **odd, strange** ◊ *She was wearing an odd ~ of clothes.* | **usual**
PREP. **~ of** ◊ *an ~ of nuts*

assume verb

ADV. **automatically, naturally** ◊ *I automatically ~d that you knew about this.* | **reasonably, safely** ◊ *I think we can safely ~ that this situation will continue.* | **commonly, generally, usually, widely** ◊ *It is generally ~d that they were lovers.* | **implicitly**
VERB + ASSUME **can, might** | **tend to** | **be fair to, be reasonable to, be safe to** ◊ *It is reasonable to ~ that the economy will continue to improve.* | **be a mistake to, be wrong to** | **be easy to** ◊ *It's all too easy to ~ that people know what they are doing.*
PHRASES **let us ~** ◊ *Let us ~ for a moment that the plan succeeds.*

assumption noun

ADJ. **basic, fundamental, key** | **hidden, implicit, tacit, underlying, unspoken** ◊ *There is an underlying ~ that the unemployed are reluctant to work.* | **common, commonly held, conventional, general, shared, widely held, widespread** ◊ *shared ~s between teachers and parents* | **correct, reasonable, safe, valid** | **erroneous, false, flawed, incorrect, mistaken, questionable, wrong** | **cultural**
... OF ASSUMPTIONS **number, series, set** ◊ *Your argument is based on a set of questionable ~s.*
VERB + ASSUMPTION **make** ◊ *She's always making ~s about how much money people have.* | **base sth on, start from, work on, work under** ◊ *We are working on the ~ that the techniques are safe.* | **accept** | **challenge, question, test** | **support** ◊ *Lots of evidence supports this ~.*
ASSUMPTION + VERB **underlie sth, underpin sth** ◊ *the ~s underlying their beliefs*
PREP. **on the ~ that** ◊ *I set the table for eight people, on the ~ that Jo would come.* | **~ about** ◊ *~s about how women should behave*

assurance noun

1 promise

ADJ. **absolute, categorical** (*BrE*), **clear** (*esp. BrE*), **firm, full** | **reasonable** | **further, repeated** | **formal, official, personal, verbal, written** ◊ *He gave me his personal ~ that the vehicle was safe.*
VERB + ASSURANCE **have** ◊ *We now have a firm ~ of support from the government.* | **give sb, make, offer sb, provide** | **gain, get, obtain, receive** | **ask for, demand, need, seek, want** | **accept** ◊ *They accepted his ~ that patients would be treated as soon as possible.* | **go back on** ◊ *He accused the president of going back on ~s given earlier.*
PREP. **~ about** ◊ *an ~ about the safety of this equipment* | **~ by, ~ from** ◊ *~s from the manager*
PHRASES **despite ~s** ◊ *Despite ~s from the government, the chemicals are known to be dangerous.*

2 feeling of calm and confidence

ADJ. **calm, quiet** ◊ *She spoke with calm ~.* | **great**
VERB + ASSURANCE **have** | **show** ◊ *Even at a very young age she showed a great deal of ~.*

assure verb

VERB + ASSURE **can** | **hasten to** ◊ *He hastened to ~ us that the press would not be informed.*
PREP. **of** ◊ *We can ~ you of our full support.*
PHRASES **let me ~ you** ◊ *Let me ~ you that I will try to help you.*

assured adj.

1 confident

VERBS **be, feel, look, rest, seem** ◊ *You can rest ~ that your children are in good hands.*
ADV. **very** ◊ *Although the situation was tense, her voice was calm and very ~.*

2 certain to happen

VERBS **be, look, seem**
ADV. **virtually**

asthma noun

ADJ. **severe** | **acute, chronic** | **bronchial**
VERB + ASTHMA **have, suffer from** | **develop** ◊ *children who develop ~* | **treat**
ASTHMA + NOUN **attack** | **symptoms** | **sufferer** | **case** ◊ *We have thousands of ~ cases a year.*
→ Special page at ILLNESS

astonished adj.

VERBS **be, look, seem, sound**
ADV. **absolutely, quite**
PREP. **at** ◊ *She was quite ~ at his rudeness.* | **by** ◊ *He was ~ by the amount of junk in the house.*

astonishing adj.

VERBS **be, seem** | **find sth** ◊ *I find his attitude absolutely ~.*
ADV. **really, truly** | **absolutely, quite** | **simply**

astonishment

astonishment *noun*

ADJ. **great** | **absolute, complete, utter** | **mild** (*esp. BrE*) ◊ *an air of mild ~* | **blank** (*esp. BrE*) ◊ *a look of blank ~*
VERB + ASTONISHMENT **express** | **hide** ◊ *She simply could not hide her ~.*
PREP. **in ~** ◊ *She gazed at him in ~.* | **to sb's ~** ◊ *Then, to my great ~, he started to cry.* | **with ~** ◊ *Everyone gasped with ~.* | **at** ◊ *He expressed ~ at the results.*
PHRASES **a gasp of ~, a look of ~**

astute *adj.*

VERBS **be**
ADV. **very** | **financially, politically**

asylum *noun*

1 protection given by a government

ADJ. **political** | **temporary**
VERB + ASYLUM **apply for, claim, request, seek** ◊ *She fled the country, and is now seeking ~ in Sweden.* | **give sb, grant sb, offer sb** | **get, receive** | **deny sb, refuse sb** ◊ *Over 400 people have been refused ~.*
ASYLUM + NOUN **seeker** ◊ *bogus/genuine ~ seekers* | **application, case, claim**
PHRASES **an application for ~** | **the right of ~, the right to ~** ◊ *Those fleeing from the war have the right to ~.*

2 mental hospital

ADJ. **insane, lunatic, mental**
PREP. **in an/the ~** ◊ *He spent three years in an ~.*

atheist *noun*

ADJ. **avowed, committed**

athlete *noun*

ADJ. **elite, fine, good, great, Olympic, outstanding, talented, top, world-class** ◊ *one of the greatest ~s of all time* | **natural** ◊ *She has the build and strength of a natural ~.* | **all-around** (*AmE*), **all-round** (*BrE*), **track, track-and-field** | **endurance** | **amateur, professional** | **college, high-school, student** (*all esp. AmE*)
ATHLETE + VERB **train** ◊ *The ~s are training hard for the Olympics.* | **compete, perform** ◊ *Our field ~s have performed well.* | **play** (*AmE*) ◊ *~s playing pro football*

athletics *noun*

1 (*BrE*) sports such as running, jumping, etc. → See also TRACK AND FIELD

ADJ. **indoor, outdoor** | **junior, senior** | **amateur, schools** | **international, world**
VERB + ATHLETICS **compete in, do, take part in** ◊ *My daughter wants to compete in ~.* | **take up** ◊ *She didn't take up ~ until she was 20.* | **quit**
ATHLETICS + NOUN **championships, competition, event, meet, meeting** | **stadium** | **star** | **coach** | **club, team** | **federation** | **official** | **career** ◊ *the hardest event of her ~ career* | **circuit, scene, world** ◊ *How long has she been competing on the international ~ circuit?*

2 (*AmE*) any sports

ADJ. **collegiate, intercollegiate** | **college, high-school** | **amateur, competitive, professional**
ATHLETICS + NOUN **program** | **department**
→ Special page at SPORTS

atmosphere *noun*

1 general feeling in a place

ADJ. **calm, comfortable, congenial, convivial, cosy/cozy, family, friendly, great, happy, homely** (*BrE*), **informal, nice, pleasant, positive, relaxed, warm, welcoming** ◊ *The bar has a relaxed, friendly ~.* | **charged, emotional, heavy, highly charged, hostile, oppressive, strained, tense** | **carnival, electric, festive, heady, lively, party** ◊ *Before the parade, the ~ was electric.* | **intimate, romantic** | **gloomy** |

rarefied, unique ◊ *the rarefied ~ of academic life* | **general, whole** ◊ *The whole ~ in the stadium changed dramatically.* | **political**
VERB + ATMOSPHERE **create, establish** (*esp. AmE*), **maintain, provide** ◊ *She tries to create an ~ of calm and security for her children.* | **have** ◊ *The restaurant has a comfortable ~.* | **poison, ruin, sour** (*esp. BrE*), **spoil** ◊ *His blunt comments ruined the ~.* | **improve, lighten** ◊ *His funny remarks lightened the ~.* | **sense** ◊ *She could sense the hostile ~ in the room.* | **enjoy**
ATMOSPHERE + VERB **be charged (with sth)** ◊ *The ~ was charged with excitement.* | **pervade sth, prevail, surround sth** ◊ *A relaxed ~ prevails in the club.*
PREP. **~ between** ◊ *Since their argument there had been a strained ~ between them.*

2 the air

ADJ. **heavy, humid, oppressive, polluted, smoky, stuffy**
VERB + ATMOSPHERE **poison, pollute** ◊ *Pesticides can kill wildlife and pollute the ~.* | **clear** ◊ *Last night's storm had cleared the ~.*

3 gases around the earth/a planet

ADJ. **lower, upper** | **thick, thin**
VERB + ATMOSPHERE **enter, leave, re-enter** ◊ *The spaceship should re-enter the earth's ~ later today.* | **be released into, escape into** ◊ *Dangerous gases have escaped into the ~.*
PREP. **in the ~** ◊ *levels of radiation in the ~*

atom *noun*

ADJ. **charged, unstable** ◊ *positively charged ~s* | **carbon, nitrogen, etc.**
VERB + ATOM **split** ◊ *the first person to split the ~*
ATOM + NOUN **bomb**

atrocity *noun*

ADJ. **appalling** (*esp. BrE*), **terrible, worst** ◊ *one of the worst atrocities of the war* | **alleged** | **human rights** | **terrorist**
VERB + ATROCITY **be responsible for, carry out, commit, perpetrate** ◊ *In the war, both sides committed atrocities.*
ATROCITY + VERB **occur, take place**
ATROCITY + NOUN **stories**
PREP. **~ against** ◊ *atrocities against the civilian population* | **~ by** ◊ *reports of atrocities by gunmen*
PHRASES **accounts of atrocities, allegations of atrocities, reports of atrocities**

attach *verb*

ADV. **firmly, securely** | **loosely**
PREP. **to** ◊ *He ~ed the rope securely to a tree.*

attached *adj.*

1 full of affection

VERBS **be** | **become, get, grow** ◊ *We've grown very ~ to this town and wouldn't want to move.* | **remain**
ADV. **deeply, strongly, very** | **quite** | **emotionally**
PREP. **to** ◊ *George is obviously very ~ to you.*

2 joined to sth

VERBS **be** | **remain, stay**
ADV. **firmly, securely** ◊ *Make sure all the wires remain firmly ~.* | **loosely** | **directly** | **permanently** | **physically**
PREP. **to** ◊ *The ball was ~ to a chain.*

attachment *noun*

1 strong feeling of affection

ADJ. **close, deep, passionate, special, strong** | **enduring, lasting** | **emotional, personal, romantic, sentimental**
VERB + ATTACHMENT **feel, have** ◊ *I feel no ~ to the countryside.* | **develop, form** ◊ *Prisoners can develop ~s to their guards.*
PREP. **~ to** ◊ *her strong ~ to her mother*

2 document sent using email

ADJ. **email** | **unsolicited** | **infected**
VERB + ATTACHMENT **include, send** ◊ *No ~ was included.* | **open**

attack *noun*

1 violence against sb

ADJ. **brutal, frenzied, horrific, savage, serious, vicious, violent** | **unprovoked** ◊ *Stephen had died in an unprovoked racist ~.* | **homophobic, racist** | **arson, gun, knife** ◊ *an increase in knife ~s on police officers* | **sexual**
... OF ATTACKS **series, spate, wave**
VERB + ATTACK **carry out** ◊ *Two teenagers carried out a frenzied ~ on a taxi driver.* | **be subjected to** ◊ *He was subjected to a violent ~.* | **block, dodge**
ATTACK + VERB **happen, occur, take place** ◊ *Where did the ~ happen?*
PREP. **~ against** ◊ *vicious ~s against senior citizens* | **~ by** ◊ *an ~ by an armed gang* | **~ on** ◊ *an ~ on a bus driver*
PHRASES **a victim of an ~**

2 act of violence in war

ADJ. **all-out, full-scale, major** | **sustained** | **deadly, devastating** | **horrific** | **sneak, surprise** ◊ *the sneak ~ on Pearl Harbor* | **retaliatory** | **pre-emptive** ◊ *The administration may launch a pre-emptive ~ against terrorist bases.* | **mock, direct, flank, frontal** | **enemy, guerrilla, insurgent, terror, terrorist** | **suicide** | **air, bomb, missile, mortar, nuclear, rocket** | **biological, chemical**
... OF ATTACKS **series** ◊ *The border towns have suffered a series of ~s.*
VERB + ATTACK **carry out, launch, lead, make, mount, spearhead** ◊ *The soldiers mounted an all-out ~ on the town.* | **come under, suffer** ◊ *They came under sustained ~ from the air.* | **repel, repulse, resist** | **prevent, stop** | **survive, withstand** ◊ *Most of the population would stand little chance of surviving a nuclear ~.* | **press** (*esp. AmE*), **press home** (*esp. BrE*), **renew** ◊ *Bombers renewed their ~, causing severe damage to bridges.* | **plan**
ATTACK + VERB **come, happen, occur, take place** ◊ *The ~ took place under cover of darkness.* | **continue** | **fail, succeed**
PREP. **under ~** ◊ *The province has been under ~ from the rebels.* | **~ against** ◊ *~s against civilians* | **~ by** ◊ *an ~ by rebel forces* | **~ on** ◊ *an ~ on enemy positions*

3 criticism

ADJ. **bitter, blistering, devastating, fierce, outspoken** (*BrE*), **savage, scathing, scurrilous, stinging, vigorous** | **personal** ◊ *It was seen as a personal ~ on the president.* | **concerted** | **direct** | **verbal**
VERB + ATTACK **deliver, go on the, launch, make, mount, unleash** ◊ *Doctors have gone on the ~, accusing the government of incompetence.* | **come under, provoke** ◊ *All politicians come under ~ for their views.*
PREP. **~ on, ~ upon** ◊ *an ~ on my integrity*
PHRASES **a/the line of ~** ◊ *The first line of ~ is often name-calling.* | **open to ~** ◊ *He has laid himself wide open to ~.*

4 sudden illness

ADJ. **acute, sudden** | **bad, nasty, severe** | **fatal** | **mild, slight** | **recurrent** | **asthma, heart, panic** ◊ *a fatal heart ~*
VERB + ATTACK **experience, have, suffer, suffer from** ◊ *He suffers from ~s of anxiety.* | **bring on, cause, trigger** ◊ *a heart ~ brought on by stress*
ATTACK + VERB **happen, occur, take place**
PREP. **~ of** ◊ *a sudden ~ of nerves*

attack *verb*

1 use violence

ADV. **brutally, savagely, viciously, violently** ◊ *They were brutally ~ed by two men.* | **physically** | **repeatedly**
PREP. **with** ◊ *He ~ed her with a knife.*

2 criticize

ADV. **fiercely, savagely, strongly, vigorously** | **repeatedly** | **directly**
PREP. **for** ◊ *The police have been strongly ~ed for not taking immediate action.*

attempt *noun*

ADJ. **successful** | **abortive, botched, failed, fruitless, futile, ill-fated, misguided, unsuccessful, vain** ◊ *her vain ~ to save her son's life* | **conscious, deliberate** | **bold, brave,**

concerted, determined, serious, valiant | **blatant** | **feeble, half-hearted, lame, pathetic, weak** ◊ *She smiled at my feeble ~ at humour/humor.* ◊ *I made a half-hearted ~ at cleaning my apartment.* | **clumsy, crude** | **desperate, frantic, last-ditch** ◊ *a desperate ~ to find survivors* | **repeated** ◊ *repeated ~s to break through enemy lines* | **first** ◊ *That's not bad for a first ~.* | **assassination, coup, escape, rescue, suicide** ◊ *Rescue ~s were stopped because of bad weather.*
VERB + ATTEMPT **make** ◊ *She has made no ~ to contact her mother.* | **succeed in** ◊ *He succeeded in his ~ to break the world record.* | **abandon, fail in, give up** ◊ *He abandoned his ~ to reach the summit.* | **foil, thwart** ◊ *Their ~ to break out of prison was foiled.* | **resist** ◊ *The board said it would resist any ~ to take control of the company.*
ATTEMPT + VERB **succeed** | **fail**
PREP. **in an/the ~** ◊ *In an ~ to ward off criticism, the government has made education a priority.* | **~ at** ◊ *He made a feeble ~ at a smile.* | **~ by** ◊ *an ~ by workers to prevent job losses*
PHRASES **an ~ on sb's life** (= an attempt to kill sb) | **at the first, second, etc. ~** (*esp. BrE*), **in the first, second, etc. ~** (*AmE*) ◊ *I passed my test at/in the first ~.*

attend *verb*

ADV. **regularly** ◊ *to ~ church regularly*
VERB + ATTEND **be able to, be unable to** | **be asked to, be invited to** ◊ *He was invited to ~ a seminar in Chicago.*
PHRASES **sparsely ~ed** ◊ *Her lectures were generally rather sparsely ~ed.* | **well ~ed** ◊ *The event was well ~ed.*

attendance *noun*

ADJ. **good, large, record** ◊ *It was a record ~ for a midweek game.* | **low, poor, sparse** (*esp. AmE*), **spotty** (*AmE*) | **falling** ◊ *Despite falling ~s, the zoo will stay open.* | **average** ◊ *The average ~ at sports events increased last year.* | **daily, weekly** ◊ *Average daily school ~ was only 75%.* | **total** | **constant, frequent, regular** ◊ *Regular ~ at lectures is important.* | **compulsory, mandatory** (*esp. AmE*) | **church, cinema** (*BrE*), **college, movie** (*AmE*), **school, etc.**
VERB + ATTENDANCE **boost, improve, increase** ◊ *Building a new stadium has boosted ~s by 40%.*
ATTENDANCE + VERB **decline, drop, fall, go down, plummet** ◊ *Attendances at the pool always fall in winter.* | **go up, increase, soar** ◊ *Movie ~ soared during the war.*
ATTENDANCE + NOUN **figures, numbers** (*esp. AmE*), **rate, record** ◊ *Attendance figures were up this year.*
PREP. **in ~** ◊ *The ambulances were in ~ within 22 minutes.* | **~ at** ◊ *~ at the meetings*
PHRASES **take ~** (*AmE*) (**take the register** in *BrE*) ◊ *Mrs Sakamoto had finished taking ~.*

attendant *noun*

ADJ. **car-park** (*BrE*), **garage, gas-station** (*AmE*), **parking, parking-lot** (*AmE*), **petrol-pump** (*BrE*) | **flight** | **cloakroom** (*BrE*), **lavatory** (*BrE*), **restroom** (*AmE*), **washroom** (*AmE*) | **museum, pool** (*both BrE*) ◊ *Pool ~s kept a constant watch on the swimmers.*
→ Note at JOB

attention *noun*

1 act of watching/listening/showing interest

ADJ. **full, rapt, undivided** ◊ *They listened with rapt ~.* | **careful, close, meticulous, scrupulous, serious** | **insufficient, little, scant** ◊ *Policy-makers paid scant ~ to the wider issues.* | **urgent** | **considerable** ◊ *The issue of climate change has received considerable ~ in recent times.* | **extra, particular, special** ◊ *Please pay extra ~ to what I'm about to tell you.* | **constant, sustained** ◊ *She attracts constant media ~.* | **unwanted, unwelcome** | **undue** | **international, national, worldwide** | **critical, media, public, scholarly** ◊ *His music deserves more scholarly ~.*
VERB + ATTENTION **devote, direct, give (sb/sth), pay** ◊ *How*

many times do I have to ask you to pay ~? | **gain, garner** (esp. AmE), **get, have, receive** ◇ Can I have your ~, please? ◇ These poems have received a lot of critical ~. | **attract, call, capture, catch, command, compel, demand, draw, grab** ◇ I tried to attract the waiter's ~. ◇ Wherever he goes, he commands ~. ◇ She doesn't like to draw ~ to her illness. | **deflect, distract, divert, draw** ◇ The government is trying to divert ~ away from the economy. | **hold, keep, rivet** ◇ There was something in the way he spoke that riveted her ~. | **concentrate, confine, focus** ◇ In this chapter we confine our ~ to non-renewable energy sources. | **refocus, shift, transfer, turn** ◇ The company decided to refocus its ~ back onto its traditional strengths and expertise. ◇ He then turned his ~ to the report. | **deserve, merit, need, require, warrant** ◇ a matter requiring urgent ~ | **compete for, jostle for, vie for** ◇ dozens of concerns jostling for your ~ ◇ She was surrounded by men all vying for her ~. | **repay** ◇ an interesting essay that repays close ~ | **bring sth to** ◇ My boss was grateful that I had brought the matter to her ~. | **come to** | **avoid, escape** ◇ Her primary aim was to avoid the ~s of the newspapers.

ATTENTION + VERB **focus** ◇ Media ~ focused today on the prince's business affairs. | **shift, turn** ◇ Attention has now shifted to the presidential elections. | **drift, drift off, wander** ◇ I felt my ~ wandering during the lecture.

ATTENTION + NOUN **span**

PREP. **for sb's ~** ◇ a letter for the ~ of your doctor

PHRASES **~ to detail** ◇ He is a designer known for his meticulous ~ to detail. | **care and ~** ◇ It 's clear that a great deal of care and ~ was put into the movie sets. ◇ He was convicted of driving without due care and ~. (BrE, law) | **the centre/center of ~** ◇ Some children love being the centre/center of ~. | **the focus of ~** ◇ The focus of ~ must now be how to improve the economy. | **force your ~s on sb** ◇ A man like Luke had no need to force his ~s on unwilling women. | **not pay much ~ to sth, pay little ~ to sth, pay no ~ to sth** (= not take something very seriously) ◇ Pay no ~ to what Bill said—he's a liar!

2 care

ADJ. **constant** | **individual, personal, special** ◇ The child needs special ~. | **immediate** ◇ His injuries required immediate ~. | **medical**

VERB + ATTENTION **devote, give, lavish** ◇ He devoted all his ~ to his mother. ◇ She lavishes ~ on those silly little dogs. | **be in need of, demand, need, require, want** ◇ a patient requiring ~

attic noun

ADJ. **cluttered, cramped, little, small, tiny** | **converted** (esp. BrE) ◇ Her photography studio was a converted ~. | **dark, dusty, musty** (esp. AmE)

ATTIC + NOUN **apartment** (AmE), **bedroom, flat** (BrE), **room** | **stairs, steps** | **window**

attitude noun

ADJ. **carefree, good, healthy, positive, right, upbeat** ◇ I try to have a healthy, positive ~ to life. ◇ She seems to have the right ~ for the job. | **conciliatory, favourable/favorable, friendly, sympathetic** | **bad, negative, wrong** | **aggressive, belligerent, critical, hostile, racist** | **arrogant, cavalier, cocky, condescending, dismissive, patronizing** ◇ She shares his somewhat cavalier ~ to the law (= does not take it as seriously as she should). | **casual, flexible, irreverent, laid-back, laissez-faire, lax, liberal, nonchalant, permissive, relaxed, tolerant, wait-and-see** (esp. AmE) ◇ The teachers seem to have a very relaxed ~ to discipline. | **responsible, serious** | **conservative, inflexible, rigid, uncompromising** (esp. BrE) | **ambivalent** | **changing** | **general, prevailing, public** ◇ The general ~ of the public is sympathetic. | **cultural, mental, moral, racial, sexual** | **parental** | **social, societal** (esp. AmE) ◇ Newspapers reflect social ~s.

VERB + ATTITUDE **adopt, cultivate, have, maintain, take** ◇ The government has taken a positive ~ to this problem. ◇

Sometimes it's essential for doctors to cultivate a detached ~. | **display, express** ◇ He displayed a condescending ~ towards/toward his co-workers. | **change, influence, shape** ◇ The experience changed his ~ to religion. | **reflect** ◇ The policy reflects a caring ~ towards/toward employees. | **foster, instil/instill, reinforce** ◇ efforts to foster positive ~s to learning | **give** ◇ Don't give me any ~ (= don't treat me disrespectfully)!

ATTITUDE + VERB **exist, persist, prevail** ◇ This sort of ~ exists among certain groups of people. | **permeate sth, pervade sth** ◇ A playful ~ pervades all his work. | **change, shift**

ATTITUDE + NOUN **problem** ◇ At school he was thought to have an ~ problem. | **adjustment, shift** (both esp. AmE) ◇ Changing conditions require an ~ adjustment on the part of business.

PREP. **~ about** ◇ changing ~s about death | **~ of** ◇ an ~ of confidence and trust | **~ to, ~ towards/toward** ◇ There has been a marked change in ~ towards/toward the war.

PHRASES **a change in ~, a change of ~** | **with ~** (= having a confident, aggressive attitude that challenges what people think) (informal) ◇ a rock band with ~

attorney noun (AmE)

ADJ. **defense, prosecuting** | **district** | **assistant** | **practicing** ◇ He is a practicing family law ~ with years of experience. | **bankruptcy, civil, criminal, immigration, malpractice, patent, etc.** | **corporate** | **court-appointed** ◇ He fired his court-appointed ~ and began representing himself. | **famed, high-profile, prominent, renowned, senior** ◇ He hired a high-profile defense ~ to represent him.

VERB + ATTORNEY **hire, retain** | **appoint, assign** ◇ The assistant district ~ was assigned to prosecute the case. | **consult** ◇ Consult an ~ whenever you make a major decision affecting your estate.

ATTORNEY + VERB **represent sb** | **practice sth, specialize in sth** ◇ an ~ specializing in entertainment law | **file sth** ◇ Her ~ filed a motion for an injunction. | **argue sth, argue for sth** ◇ Attorneys argued that prosecutors never proved who sent the email. ◇ Army ~s argued for a general discharge. | **advise sb/sth** ◇ Your ~ may advise you to accept a cash settlement.

attraction noun

1 fact of attracting/being attracted

ADJ. **fatal, irresistible, obvious, powerful, strong** | **mutual** ◇ They shared a powerful mutual ~. | **erotic, physical, same-sex, sexual** | **gravitational, magnetic**

VERB + ATTRACTION **feel** ◇ the strong ~ that she felt for him | **see** ◇ I could now see the ~ of a steady job and regular income. | **have, hold** ◇ Long flights hold no ~ for me. | **deny** ◇ They could no longer deny the ~ between them. | **resist** ◇ I struggled to resist the ~. | **exert** ◇ All matter exerts a gravitational ~.

PREP. **~ between** ◇ the ~ between two people | **~ to, ~ towards/toward** ◇ His ~ to you is obvious.

PHRASES **the centre/center of ~** (esp. BrE) ◇ Susan was plainly the centre/center of ~ in the room.

2 sth that attracts people

ADJ. **added, big, chief, great, main, major, obvious, special, star** ◇ The main ~ of the place is the nightlife. | **popular, tourist**

VERB + ATTRACTION **have** ◇ A freelance career has the ~ of flexibility. | **be, prove** ◇ Feeding the animals proved a popular ~ for visitors to the farm.

PREP. **~ for** ◇ The lack of heat was an ~ for cyclists.

attractive adj.

VERBS **be, look** ◇ She looked ~ and beautifully dressed. | **become, grow** ◇ He had grown more ~ with age. | **make sb/sth** | **find sb/sth** ◇ This is an idea that I find very ~.

ADV. **extremely, fairly, very, etc.** | **incredibly, particularly** | **strikingly, stunningly** ◇ a stunningly ~ woman | **irresistibly** | **physically, sexually, visually** ◇ He no longer found her physically ~. ◇ a visually ~ display | **economically** ◇ This is not an economically ~ option for many farmers. | **superficially** ◇ The policy is superficially ~, but unlikely to work.

PREP. **to** ◊ *Schools must try to make science more ~ to youngsters.*

attribute *noun*

ADJ. **chief, great, key, main** | **defining, distinguishing, essential, necessary** ◊ *Patience is an essential ~ for a teacher.* | **desirable, desired, important, positive, useful, valued** | **common** | **unique** | **divine, human** | **feminine, masculine** | **cultural, personal, physical, social** ◊ *His physical ~s were much admired.*
VERB + ATTRIBUTE **embody, have, possess**

attribute *verb*

ADV. **directly** | **solely** | **largely, mainly** | **in part, partially, partly** | **erroneously, falsely, incorrectly, mistakenly, wrongly** ◊ *a quote that has often been falsely ~d to George Patton*
PREP. **to** ◊ *They claim that one in twenty deaths can be directly ~d to air pollution.*
PHRASES **be commonly ~d to, be generally ~d to, be usually ~d to, be widely ~d to** ◊ *Climate change is widely ~d to the build-up of greenhouse gases.*

auction *noun*

ADJ. **public** | **charity** | **Internet, online** | **reverse** (*esp. AmE*), **sealed-bid** (*esp. AmE*), **sealed-offer** (*AmE*), **silent** ◊ *In a reverse ~, the price is driven steadily down.* | **art, cattle, furniture,** etc.
VERB + AUCTION **hold** ◊ *The estate is holding an ~ to raise money.* | **conduct** ◊ *My father will be conducting the ~ tomorrow.* | **attend, go to** ◊ *He regularly attended ~s.* | **put sth up for** ◊ *The horse will be put up for public ~.* | **be up for, come up for, go up for** ◊ *The paintings will come up for ~ next month.*
AUCTION + VERB **take place**
AUCTION + NOUN **house, room** (*esp. BrE*) | **item** | **catalogue** | **price** | **market, mart** (*BrE*), **sale**
PREP. **at ~** ◊ *I try to buy furniture at ~s because it is cheaper that way.* ◊ *The house was sold at ~ for half a million pounds.* | **by ~** ◊ *The goods were put up for sale by ~.*

audible *adj.*

VERBS **be** | **become, grow**
ADV. **clearly, perfectly** ◊ *The shot was clearly ~ in the silence.* | **barely, hardly, scarcely** | **faintly, just** ◊ *The singer's voice was just ~.* | **almost**
PREP. **above** ◊ *The noise was ~ even above the roar of the engines.* | **to** ◊ *The sounds made by bats are not ~ to the human ear.*

audience *noun*

1 group of people watching/listening to sth

ADJ. **big, capacity, large, mass, packed, vast** | **broad, diverse, wide** ◊ *The museum is trying to attract a wider ~.* | **select, small** | **appreciative, enthusiastic, receptive, sympathetic** | **hostile** | **captive** | **general, lay, mainstream** ◊ *Most movies are designed to appeal to a mainstream ~.* | **core** ◊ *His core ~ is over the age of 35.* | **intended, potential, target, targeted** | **listening, viewing** | **cinema** (*BrE*), **live, movie** (*esp. AmE*), **radio, studio, television, TV** | **international, Western, worldwide** ◊ *These artists remain relatively unknown to Western ~s.*
VERB + AUDIENCE **address, perform to, play to** ◊ *He prefers playing to live ~s.* | **regale** ◊ *She regales her ~ with funny stories.* | **attract, draw, pull in** ◊ *Such a well-known politician should draw a big ~.* | **reach** ◊ *We want to reach a younger target ~.* | **captivate, delight, engage, grip, thrill, wow** (*informal*) ◊ *The movie has thrilled ~s throughout the country.* | **move** ◊ *The ~ was visibly moved.* | **educate, inform** | **convince, persuade** ◊ *He was trying to convince his ~ of his seriousness.* | **alienate** ◊ *Some scenes in the movie risk alienating a female ~.*
AUDIENCE + VERB **applaud, cheer, clap** ◊ *The ~ cheered loudly.* | **boo, jeer** | **laugh, roar** ◊ *The ~ roared with laughter.* | **gasp** | **react, respond**
AUDIENCE + NOUN **participation** | **member**

PREP. **before an/the ~, in front of an/the ~** ◊ *He felt nervous standing up in front of the large ~.*

2 formal meeting with a very important person

ADJ. **private**
VERB + AUDIENCE **have** | **ask for, request, seek** | **give sb, grant sb** ◊ *The Pope granted him an ~.*
PREP. **~ with** ◊ *She sought a private ~ with the Japanese emperor.*

audition *noun*

ADJ. **ballet, singing** | **band** | **TV**
VERB + AUDITION **do, get, go for, have** ◊ *I did an ~ for the part of the queen.* | **give sb, hold** ◊ *We're holding ~s for new actors.* | **schedule** | **pass** | **fail**
AUDITION + NOUN **tape**
PREP. **~ for** ◊ *an ~ for a place at drama school* | **~ with** ◊ *an ~ with Houston Ballet*

auditor *noun*

ADJ. **company, company's** | **internal** | **external, independent, outside** | **county** (*AmE*), **district, government** (*BrE*)
VERB + AUDITOR **appoint** (*BrE*), **hire** (*AmE*)
PREP. **~ of** ◊ *She is one of the nation's leading ~s of public companies.* | **~ to** (*BrE*) ◊ *His firm has been appointed the ~s to the company.*
PHRASES **an auditors' report**
→ Note at PROFESSIONAL (for verbs)

auditorium *noun*

ADJ. **huge, vast** | **200-seat, 200-seater** (*BrE*), etc. | **crowded, packed** | **empty** | **darkened** | **school** (*esp. AmE*)
VERB + AUDITORIUM **fill**
AUDITORIUM + VERB **hold sb, seat sb** ◊ *The ~ seats over a thousand people.* | **be filled with sth** ◊ *The darkened ~ was filled with muttering.*

August *noun* → Note at MONTH

aunt *noun*

ADJ. **elderly** | **maiden** (*esp. BrE*), **spinster** (*esp. AmE*), **unmarried** | **widowed** | **maternal, paternal** | **great** (usually **great-aunt**) (= the sister of one of your grandparents) ◊ *Great-Aunt Emily*

aura *noun*

ADJ. **magical** | **faint**
VERB + AURA **be surrounded by, emanate, emit, exude, have, radiate, retain** ◊ *He exuded an ~ of wealth and power.* | **take on** ◊ *The picture seemed to take on the ~ of an ancient work of art.* | **create, give sb/sth** ◊ *The sunlight created an ~ of beauty around her.* | **lose**
AURA + VERB **emanate from sb/sth, radiate from sb/sth, surround sb/sth** ◊ *I felt an evil ~ radiating from him.*
PREP. **~ about, ~ of** ◊ *There was always a faint ~ of mystery about her.*

austerity *noun*

ADJ. **post-war, wartime** (*esp. BrE*) | **economic, fiscal** (*esp. AmE*)
AUSTERITY + NOUN **measures, plan, policies, programme/program**

authenticity *noun*

VERB + AUTHENTICITY **cast doubt on, dispute, doubt, question** ◊ *Some have cast doubt on the ~ of the official version of events.* | **ascertain, check, test** | **certify, confirm, establish, prove, validate, verify**
PHRASES **a certificate of ~** ◊ *Despite its certificate of ~, the painting was a fake.* | **a debate over the ~ of sth** ◊ *There has been some debate over the ~ of his will.* | **of doubtful ~** (*esp. BrE*), **of dubious ~** (*esp. AmE*), **of questionable ~** (*esp. AmE*) ◊ *a document of doubtful ~*

author

48

PREP. ~ on ◇ She's a leading ~ on genetics.

author noun

ADJ. best-selling | prolific | famous, well-known |
published ◇ Her ambition was to become a published ~. |
anonymous ◇ the anonymous ~ of this pamphlet |
children's ◇ Primarily a children's ~, she has also written
books for adults. | contributing, joint (esp. BrE) ◇ He is a
contributing ~ to many school textbooks. | sole | lead,
senior (esp. AmE) ◇ the lead ~ of the report | favourite/
favorite
VERB + AUTHOR read ◇ Stephen King is an ~ I've never read. |
cite, quote
AUTHOR + VERB write (sth) ◇ The ~ was writing in the 17th
century. | argue sth, conclude sth, note sth, suggest sth ◇
The study's ~s conclude that there is insufficient evidence to
justify the policy.

authoritarian adj.

VERBS be | become
ADV. extremely, fairly, very, etc. | highly | increasingly

authority noun

1 (often authorities) people with responsibility for
making decisions

ADJ. central, district, federal, local, municipal, regional |
government, public | civil, civilian, military, religious,
secular | education, health, housing, immigration, law
enforcement, planning (BrE), regulatory, tax ◇ The
government is urging education authorities to spend less
money. ◇ the right of law enforcement authorities to take
and retain photographs | appropriate, competent, proper,
relevant, statutory ◇ He had permission from the proper
authorities.
VERB + AUTHORITY alert, contact, inform, notify ◇ The system
notifies the authorities when a security breach occurs.
AUTHORITY + VERB agree sth, claim sth, decide sth, deny sth,
promise sth, recommend sth ◇ The health ~ denied
negligence. | allow (sb) sth, approve sth, give (sb) sth, grant
(sb) sth ◇ The local ~ has not granted planning permission. |
refuse (sb) sth ◇ Immigration authorities refused him entry
to the country. | arrest sb, detain sb, seize sb/sth ◇ German
authorities arrested the author of the computer virus.

2 power/right to give orders

ADJ. absolute, complete, full | highest, supreme, ultimate
◇ The commander-in-chief exercises supreme ~ within his
zone. | constitutional, governmental, judicial, legal,
political, presidential, regulatory | divine, religious ◇
These men denied the divine ~ of the Church. | parental |
moral | lawful, legitimate ◇ He acted without any
legitimate ~.
VERB + AUTHORITY have, possess ◇ Parents have the ~ to
discipline their children. | assume ◇ He assumed full ~ as
tsar in 1689. | give sb, grant sb | assert, demonstrate,
establish, exercise, exert, show, use, wield ◇ The new
manager obviously felt the need to demonstrate her ~. | lack
| delegate, transfer | cede, give up, relinquish | abuse,
exceed, overstep ◇ Some legal experts think the agency may
have exceeded its ~. | accept, recognize, respect |
challenge, defy, deny, question, rebel against, reject,
undermine ◇ She had challenged my ~ once too often. |
usurp
AUTHORITY + NOUN figure ◇ adult ~ figures such as parents and
teachers
PREP. in ~ ◇ I need to talk to someone in ~. | under the ~ of ◇
Border security will fall under the ~ of the department. |
without ~ ◇ He took the car without ~. | ~ over ◇ He refuses
to relinquish ~ over the design process.
PHRASES an air of ~ ◇ He bore an air of ~. | a position of ~ ◇
She holds a position of ~ in the local church.

3 person with special knowledge

ADJ. foremost, leading, respected, world
VERB + AUTHORITY cite, invoke ◇ He justified his innovation by
citing respected authorities.

authorization (BrE also -isation) noun

ADJ. formal, official, written | congressional (in the US) ◇
They secured congressional ~ for a new hydro-electric dam. |
prior ◇ You will need prior ~ from your bank. | explicit,
express ◇ We cannot act without the explicit ~ of the board.
VERB + AUTHORIZATION need, require | ask for, request, seek
◇ He asked for ~ to proceed with the plan. | get, have, obtain
| give sb, grant (sb) | refuse (sb) ◇ The government will
probably refuse ~ under these conditions. | revoke
PREP. with ~, without ~ ◇ You cannot take a day off without
~. | ~ for ◇ Formal ~ for the trip was given last week. | ~
from ◇ The change of plan would require ~ from the
president.

autobiography noun

VERB + AUTOBIOGRAPHY pen, work on, write | publish | read
PREP. in an/the ~ ◇ In his ~, he recalls the poverty in which he
grew up.

autograph noun

VERB + AUTOGRAPH give sb, sign ◇ He signed his ~ for the little
girl. | ask for, want ◇ She was surrounded by fans wanting
~s. | get, have ◇ Can I have your ~, please?
AUTOGRAPH + NOUN book | hunter (esp. BrE)

automatic adj.

1 working by itself
VERBS be ◇ The machine is fully ~.
ADV. completely, fully

2 certain to happen
VERBS be
ADV. almost, virtually ◇ Promotion was almost ~ after two or
three years.

automobile noun (esp. AmE)

ADJ. luxury | vintage | gasoline-powered (AmE), hydrogen-
powered, etc.
VERB + AUTOMOBILE drive ◇ Learning to drive an ~ is not easy. |
power ◇ Compressed natural gas can be used to power ~s.
AUTOMOBILE + NOUN engine, exhaust, tyre/tire, windshield
(AmE) | emissions | accident | dealer, dealership, show-
room | industry, manufacture | factory, manufacturer |
assembly line, assembly plant

autonomous adj.

VERBS be | become
ADV. completely, entirely, fully | essentially, largely |
partially | fairly, relatively
PREP. from ◇ Higher education is relatively ~ from the
government.

autonomy noun

ADJ. considerable, substantial | greater, increased,
increasing, more | absolute, complete, full | relative |
limited ◇ The Act granted limited ~ to the republics. |
individual, personal | local, national, regional | admin-
istrative, cultural, economic, financial, managerial, pol-
itical, professional, etc. | patient, teacher, worker, etc.
... OF AUTONOMY degree, level, measure ◇ a high degree of ~
VERB + AUTONOMY enjoy, have ◇ The subsidiary companies will
now have more ~. | assert, exercise ◇ an individual's right
to exercise ~ | maintain, preserve, retain ◇ The cantons and
communes of Switzerland have preserved their ~. | gain |
seek, struggle for, want | give sb, grant (sb) ◇ Head office is
giving the regional offices more ~. | reduce
PREP. ~ from ◇ Schools have gained greater ~ from
government control.
PHRASES a demand for ~ ◇ demands for cultural ~

autopsy noun

VERB + AUTOPSY carry out, conduct, do, perform | request |
undergo

avoidable

AUTOPSY + VERB **find sth, reveal sth, show sth** ◇ *The ~ revealed that he had been poisoned.* | **confirm sth** ◇ *The diagnosis was confirmed by ~.*
AUTOPSY + NOUN **findings, report, results**
PREP. **~ on** ◇ *They carried out an ~ on the victim.*

autumn (*esp. BrE*) *noun* → See also FALL

ADJ. **last, this past** (*esp. AmE*) | **the following, next, this, this coming** | **early, late** | **wet**
AUTUMN + NOUN **weather** | **sun, sunlight, sunshine** | **frost, rain** | **gale, wind** | **landscape, sky** | **colours/colors** ◇ *Now is the time when the ~ colours/colors are at their best.* | **leaf** ◇ *the sound of ~ leaves rustling* | **equinox** | **term** (*BrE*) ◇ *classes to be held for schoolchildren during the ~ term* | **collection, exhibition** ◇ *their ~ collection of dresses*
→ Note at SEASON (for more collocates)

availability *noun*

ADJ. **easy, ready** ◇ *the easy ~ of many illegal drugs* | **general, wide, widespread** | **greater, increased, increasing** | **continuous, unlimited** ◇ *the seemingly unlimited ~ of mortgage credit* | **limited** | **land, staff, ticket, etc.**
VERB + AVAILABILITY **check, ensure** ◇ *Check the ~ of bottled water before you set off.* | **expand, increase, maximize** | **limit, reduce, restrict** ◇ *They want to restrict the ~ of abortions.*
PHRASES **subject to ~** ◇ *All holiday bookings are subject to ~.*

available *adj.*

1 that you can get, buy, use, etc.

VERBS **be** | **become** | **make sth** ◇ *The product will now be made ~ throughout the market.*
ADV. **easily, freely, readily** | **commonly, generally, publicly, universally, widely** | **locally** ◇ *The houses are built using locally ~ materials.* | **commercially** | **currently, now** | **immediately, instantly** ◇ *He has $10 000 of immediately ~ funds.*
PREP. **for** ◇ *Grants should be ~ for most students.* ◇ *The DVDs are ~ for purchase.* | **from** ◇ *Details are ~ from the above address.* | **to** ◇ *This information is freely ~ to anyone wishing to see it.*

2 free to be seen, talked to, etc.

VERBS **be** | **become** ◇ *She's in a meeting, but I'll let you know as soon as she becomes ~.*
PHRASES **not ~ for comment** ◇ *The chairman was not ~ for comment.*

avalanche *noun*

1 large amount of snow falling

VERB + AVALANCHE **trigger**
AVALANCHE + VERB **happen** | **wipe out sth/sb** | **kill sb** ◇ *They were killed by an ~ in the Swiss Alps.*
PREP. **in an/the ~** ◇ *They died in an ~.*

2 large number/amount of sth

VERB + AVALANCHE **be buried under**
PREP. **~ of** ◇ *We've been almost buried under the ~ of letters.*

avenue *noun*

1 wide street

ADJ. **broad, wide** | **leafy** (*esp. BrE*), **tree-lined**
AVENUE + VERB **be lined with sth** ◇ *an ~ lined with elms*
PREP. **along an/the ~, down an/the ~, up an/the ~** ◇ *We were strolling down a tree-lined ~.* | **in an/the ~** (*BrE*), **on an/the ~** (*esp. AmE*) ◇ *a house in Acacia Avenue* ◇ *an office building on Fifth Avenue*

2 way of doing/getting sth

ADJ. **possible, potential, promising** | **fruitful, productive**
VERB + AVENUE **explore, pursue, try** ◇ *We need to explore every possible ~.* | **exhaust** ◇ *After two months of negotiations we had exhausted all ~s.* | **open, open up, provide**
AVENUE + VERB **be open to sb** ◇ *There was only one ~ open to him.*
PREP. **~ for** ◇ *to provide a new ~ for research* | **~ of** ◇ *We will*

need to seek other ~s of growth. ◇ *the two main ~s of enquiry* (*BrE*) | **~ to** ◇ *an ~ to success*

average *noun*

ADJ. **annual, five-year, monthly, etc.** | **national** ◇ *The national ~ is just over two children per family.* | **overall** | **career, lifetime** (*esp. AmE*) | **moving, weighted** (*both technical*) | **batting, bowling, scoring, slugging** (*AmE*) (*all sports*) | **grade, grade point** (*both AmE*) ◇ *the student with the best grade point ~ in his class*
VERB + AVERAGE **arrive at, calculate, compute, find, work out** ◇ *You'll have to calculate the ~.* | **exceed**
PREP. **above ~, below ~** ◇ *His test results are well above ~.* | **on ~** ◇ *On ~, prices have risen 6%.*

aversion *noun*

ADJ. **strong** ◇ *He has a strong ~ to dogs.* | **natural** | **pathological**
VERB + AVERSION **have** | **develop** | **overcome**
AVERSION + NOUN **therapy** ◇ *I underwent ~ therapy for smoking.*
PREP. **~ to** ◇ *People can be helped to overcome their ~ to snakes.*

avert *verb*

1 prevent sth

ADV. **narrowly** ◇ *Disaster was narrowly ~ed when two airliners almost collided above Detroit.*
VERB + AVERT **try to** | **be able to, manage to** ◇ *He managed to ~ the closure of the factory.* | **fail to**
PHRASES **an attempt to ~ sth, an effort to ~ sth**

2 turn sth away

ADV. **quickly** ◇ *They quickly ~ed their faces to hide their giggles.*
VERB + AVERT **try to**
PHRASES **~ your eyes (from sth/sb), ~ your gaze (from sth/sb)** ◇ *He looked up, and she quickly ~ed her gaze.*

avoid *verb*

1 prevent sth; choose not to do sth

ADV. **altogether** ◇ *It is sometimes impossible to ~ conflict altogether.* | **actively, assiduously, carefully, consciously, deliberately, intentionally, purposefully, purposely, scrupulously, studiously** ◇ *The two men carefully ~ed one another.* ◇ *I scrupulously ~ artificial additives when I buy food.* | **barely, narrowly** ◇ *They narrowly ~ed defeat in the semi-final.* | **deftly, wisely** ◇ *He deftly ~ed answering the question.* | **pointedly** ◇ *She pointedly ~ed looking at him when she spoke.* | **easily, successfully** ◇ *Most of these problems could have been easily ~ed.* | **generally, largely** ◇ *As someone who generally ~s teen movies, I didn't expect to enjoy this.* | **at all costs** ◇ *Getting involved in a court case is something to be ~ed at all costs.*
VERB + AVOID **be anxious to, want to, wish to** ◇ *They are anxious to ~ any further misunderstandings.* | **attempt to, try to** | **be careful to, take care to** ◇ *He was careful to ~ any sentimentality in his speech.* | **help (to)** | **be able to, manage to** | **be possible to** | **be difficult to, be impossible to**
PHRASES **an attempt to ~ sth, an effort to ~ sth** ◇ *He failed in his attempt to ~ having to pay.*

2 not hit sb/sth

ADV. **narrowly** ◇ *He braked hard and narrowly ~ed a parked van.*
VERB + AVOID **brake to, slow to, slow down to** | **swerve to** ◇ *She swerved to ~ a bicycle.* | **duck to, duck down to** ◇ *They ducked to ~ a low branch.*

avoidable *adj.*

VERBS **be** ◇ *Most accidents are easily ~.*
ADV. **completely, entirely** (*esp. BrE*), **wholly** | **easily**

await verb
ADV. **anxiously, breathlessly** (*AmE*), **nervously** ◇ *She is anxiously ~ing a decision on her future.* | **eagerly, keenly** (*BrE*), **with interest** (*esp. BrE*) ◇ *The outcome of the appeal is ~ed with interest.* | **patiently** | **impatiently**
PHRASES **long ~ed** ◇ *her long ~ed return to professional tennis*

awake verb
ADV. **early, late** ◇ *She awoke early the next morning.* | **abruptly** (*esp. AmE*), **suddenly** ◇ *He awoke suddenly in a cold sweat.* | **slowly**
PREP. **from** ◇ *I awoke from a deep sleep at six o'clock.*

awake adj.
VERBS **be, lie** ◇ *At night he lay ~ beside her.* | **come** (*esp. AmE*), **jerk** ◇ *Claudia came ~ slowly.* ◇ *Stephen jerked ~ from a nightmare.* | **keep, remain, stay** ◇ *He was struggling to stay ~.* | **jerk sb, jolt sb, nudge sb, shake sb** ◇ *A few hours later Benjamin shook me ~.* | **keep sb** ◇ *The noise had kept her ~.*
ADV. **fully, wide** ◇ *By now, the baby was wide ~.* | **barely, only half** ◇ *It was very early and I was only half ~.* | **still** ◇ *The children were still ~ when we went out.*

awaken verb
ADV. **early, late** | **abruptly, suddenly** (*both esp. AmE*) | **slowly** (*esp. AmE*)
PREP. **from** ◇ *She was just ~ing from sleep.*
PHRASES **be rudely ~ed** ◇ *He was rudely ~ed by the sound of drilling.*

awakening noun
ADJ. **rude, sudden** ◇ *If they expected a warm welcome, they were in for a rude ~.* | **political, religious, sexual, spiritual** ◇ *the political ~ that followed the crisis*
PREP. **~ from** ◇ *Kerry's ~ from slumber* | **~ to** ◇ *the story of one boy's ~ to his sexuality*

award noun
1 prize that sb gets for doing sth well
ADJ. **annual** | **national** | **coveted, highest, major, prestigious, special, top** | **cash** ◇ *The winning designers will receive cash ~s.* | **bravery** (*esp. BrE*), **design, lifetime achievement, literary, merit, teaching, etc.** ◇ *He won a lifetime achievement ~ for his civil rights campaigning.*
VERB + AWARD **announce, bestow, give sb, hand out, make (sb), present (sb with)** ◇ *The ~ was made for his work in cancer research.* ◇ *the numerous ~s bestowed on him in his lifetime* | **carry off** (*BrE*), **earn (sb), garner, get, receive, win** ◇ *Stephen's quick thinking has earned him a bravery ~.* | **deserve** ◇ *The movie deserved all the ~s it received.* | **accept** | **sponsor** ◇ *a business ~ sponsored by the Chamber of Commerce*
AWARD + VERB **go to sb** ◇ *The best documentary ~ went to Ugyen Wangdi for 'Price of Letter'.*
AWARD + NOUN **~s banquet** (*esp. AmE*), **~s ceremony, ~s dinner, ~s luncheon** (*esp. AmE*) ◇ *The ~s ceremony was intended to celebrate the achievements of young artists.* | **scheme** (*BrE*) | **recipient** (*esp. AmE*), **winner** | **citation** (*esp. AmE*), **nomination**
PREP. **~ for** ◇ *the ~ for best actor* | **~ from** ◇ *She received an ~ from the PPS Foundation.*
2 money given to sb
ADJ. **compensatory** (*esp. BrE*), **discretionary** (*BrE*) | **pay** (*esp. BrE*) ◇ *The union is unhappy with this year's pay ~.* | **compensation** (*esp. BrE*), **damages, libel** (*esp. BrE*), **malpractice**
VERB + AWARD **get, receive** | **grant, make** ◇ *The judge has the power to make damages ~s.*

award verb
ADV. **automatically** | **jointly** ◇ *He was jointly ~ed the Nobel Prize with Alex Mueller.* | **posthumously** | **annually** ◇ *The prize is ~ed annually for the best new building.*
PREP. **to** ◇ *Promotions were automatically ~ed to senior officials.*

aware adj.
1 conscious
VERBS **be, seem** | **become** | **make sb** ◇ *We need to make people more ~ of these problems.* | **remain, stay** ◇ *Citizens need to remain ~ of the danger.*
ADV. **acutely, intensely, keenly, very, very much, well** ◇ *I am very much ~ that not everyone agrees with me.* | **fully, perfectly** ◇ *Mr Moore did not appear fully ~ of the importance of this act.* | **consciously** ◇ *Even before you are consciously ~ of being afraid, your body may be reacting.* | **dimly, vaguely** | **suddenly** ◇ *She was suddenly ~ that she was being watched.* | **barely, hardly, not really** ◇ *He was not really ~ of what he was doing.* | **horribly, painfully, uncomfortably** ◇ *Moran was painfully ~ of Luke's absence.*
PREP. **of** ◇ *The police are well ~ of the dangers.*
2 informed
VERBS **be** | **become**
ADV. **very** | **increasingly** ◇ *Food manufacturers are dealing with increasingly ~ consumers.* | **environmentally, politically, socially**

awareness noun
ADJ. **full** | **greater, heightened, increased** | **dawning, growing, increasing** ◇ *a growing ~ of healthy living* | **acute, deep, intense, keen, strong** | **conscious, direct** | **intuitive** | **sudden** | **general, public** | **brand, consumer** ◇ *a marketing campaign to increase brand ~* | **emotional, sensory, spatial** | **cultural, ecological, environmental, moral, political, racial, sexual, social, spiritual**
VERB + AWARENESS **have** ◇ *Politicians now have much greater ~ of these problems.* | **build, create, develop, encourage, enhance, foster, heighten, increase, promote, raise** ◇ *The group is trying to raise public ~ about homelessness.*
AWARENESS + VERB **increase, spread** ◇ *Environmental ~ has increased over the years.*
AWARENESS + NOUN **campaign, programme/program, training** ◇ *All staff receive mental health ~ training.*
PREP. **~ among** ◇ *the emergence of a new social ~ among young people* | **~ of** ◇ *an increased ~ of the risks*
PHRASES **a lack of ~**

awe noun
ADJ. **great**
VERB + AWE **be in, hold sb in, stand in** ◇ *Most people hold him in some ~.* | **feel** | **inspire, instil/instill** ◇ *Everest has always inspired ~ and respect among climbers.*
PREP. **in ~, with ~** ◇ *We gazed in ~ at the massive building.* | **~ at** ◇ *What I mostly felt was ~ at her achievement.*
PHRASES **in ~ of sb/sth** ◇ *I stared at the clouds, in ~ of their beauty.* | **a sense of ~** ◇ *They experienced a tremendous sense of ~ in the cathedral.*

awesome adj.
VERBS **be, seem**
ADV. **really, simply, totally** (*informal, esp. AmE*), **truly** ◇ *The Niagara Falls are a truly ~ sight.* | **pretty, quite** (*esp. BrE*)

awful adj.
VERBS **be, feel, look, smell, sound, taste** ◇ *I felt ~ when I realized what I'd done.* ◇ *The fish tasted ~.*
ADV. **just, quite, really, simply, truly** ◇ *a truly ~ book* | **absolutely, the most** ◇ *She's the most ~ snob.* | **pretty, rather**

awkward adj.
1 difficult
VERBS **be, look, seem** | **make sth**
ADV. **extremely, fairly, very, etc.** ◇ *She asked some rather ~ questions.* | **incredibly, terribly** | **a little, slightly, etc.**

PHRASES **make things ~** ◇ *He could make things very ~ for me if he wanted to.*

2 not relaxed

VERBS **be, feel, look, sound** ◇ *He always sounded ~ on the phone.* | **become** | **make sb** ◇ *He was embarrassed, which made him ~.*

ADV. **extremely, fairly, very, etc.** | **a little, slightly, etc.** | **painfully** ◇ *As a teenager he was painfully ~ in company.* | **socially** ◇ *I was the most socially ~ person you could imagine.*

PREP. **about** ◇ *They felt ~ about having to leave so soon.* | **with** ◇ *She is ~ with people she doesn't know.*

axe *(esp. BrE)* *(AmE usually* **ax***) noun*

1 tool

VERB + AXE **brandish** *(esp. BrE)*, **carry, heft** *(esp. AmE)*, **hold, wield** ◇ *A man used to wielding an ~ fought best on foot.* | **use** | **swing** | **sharpen**

AXE + VERB **fall** ◇ *The executioner's ~ fell.*

PREP. **with an/the ~** ◇ *to chop a tree down with an ~*

PHRASES **a blow from an ~, a blow of an ~** ◇ *With a few swift blows of the ~, she severed the cable.*

2 the axe complete loss of sth/big reduction in sth

VERB + THE AXE **be given, get** ◇ *His prime-time TV show is likely to get the ~.* | **swing, wield** *(both esp. BrE)* ◇ *Wielding the ~ on the prison plan would be one way of saving money.* | **face** *(BrE)* ◇ *Up to 300 workers are facing the ~ at a struggling Merseyside firm.* | **save sb/sth from** ◇ *Patients are delighted their local hospital has been saved from the ~.*

THE AXE + VERB **fall** ◇ *We were expecting bad news but had no idea where the ~ would fall (= where the loss would be).*

axis *noun*

ADJ. **horizontal, vertical** | **x, y, z**

PREP. **along an/the ~** ◇ *the speed is measured along the horizontal ~* | **on an/the ~** ◇ *The earth spins on its ~.*

PHRASES **an ~ of rotation** ◇ *the earth's ~ of rotation* | **an ~ of symmetry**

B b

baby *noun*

ADJ. **new, newborn, tiny** | **low-birthweight, small, tiny** ◇ *Smoking in pregnancy increases the risk of producing a low-birthweight ~.* | **big** | **full-term** | **premature, preterm** *(esp. BrE)* | **stillborn** | **unborn** | **little, young** | **three-day-old, six-week-old, ten-month-old, etc.** | **beautiful, bonny** *(BrE)*, **cute, lovely** *(esp. BrE)* | **bouncing** *(informal)*, **healthy, normal** | **contented** *(esp. BrE)*, **good, perfect** | **colicky, crying, screaming** | **sleeping** | **growing** ◇ *He took an interest in the growing ~ even before it was born.* | **bottle-fed, breastfed** | **illegitimate** | **test-tube** | **abandoned, unwanted** | **war** (= born during the war)

VERB + BABY **have** ◇ *I want to have a ~.* | **want** ◇ *She's not sure if she wants a ~.* | **conceive, make** *(informal, humorous)* | **carry, expect** ◇ *She's not sure yet how many babies she's carrying.* ◇ *She's expecting a ~ in July.* | **give birth to, produce** | **deliver** ◇ *The ~ was delivered by a midwife.* | **lose** ◇ *She lost her ~ (= had a miscarriage) three months into her pregnancy.* | **name** ◇ *They named the ~ Charlie.* | **care for, look after** *(esp. BrE)* | **feed** | **bottle-feed** | **breastfeed, nurse** | **burp** ◇ *The ~ needed burping after every bottle.* | **wean** ◇ *You can start weaning your ~ when it's four months old.* | **change** ◇ *The ~ needs changing again (= needs a clean nappy/diaper).* | **bath** *(BrE)*, **bathe** *(esp. AmE)* | **comfort, cradle, cuddle, hold, pick up, rock, take** ◇ *She rocked the ~ to sleep in her arms.* ◇ *Can you take the ~ while I unlock the door?* | **kiss** | **swaddle** | **play with** | **adopt** ◇ *They would like to adopt a newborn ~.* | **have adopted, put up for adoption** ◇ *She decided to put her ~ up for adoption.* | **abandon**

BABY + VERB **be due** ◇ *The ~ is due in October.* | **arrive, be born** ◇ *Their first ~ arrived exactly nine months after the wedding.* | **bawl, cry, scream, wail** | **babble, coo, gurgle** ◇ *The ~ cooed happily on the rug.* | **feed, nurse** *(esp. AmE)*, **suck** ◇ *Babies nurse more at night in the first three weeks.* | **be sick, dribble, drool, spit up** *(AmE)* ◇ *Babies drool a lot when they are teething.* | **be teething** | **crawl, sit up, take his/her first steps, toddle, walk** | **grow, grow up** ◇ *The doctor said the ~ was growing nicely.* | **kick, move** ◇ *I could feel the ~ moving inside me.* | **sleep**

BABY + NOUN **boy, girl** | **brother, daughter, sister, son** | **bird, rabbit, etc.** | **clothes** | **food, formula** *(esp. AmE)*, **milk** *(esp. BrE)* | **lotion, oil, powder** | **buggy** *(BrE)*, **carrier, stroller** *(AmE)* (see also **baby carriage**) | **alarm** *(BrE)*, **monitor** | **bath** | **talk** | **unit** *(esp. BrE)* ◇ *the hospital's ~ unit* | **shower** *(AmE)* | **boom** (= a period when many more babies are born than usual), **boomer** (= a person born during such a period)

PHRASES **sleep like** ◇ *He was so tired after all his exertions, he slept like a ~.*

baby carriage *noun (AmE)* → See also PRAM

VERB + BABY CARRIAGE **push** ◇ *He saw a woman pushing a ~.*

PREP. **in a/the ~** ◇ *There's an old photo of me in a ~.*

bachelor *noun*

ADJ. **confirmed, lifelong** ◇ *He was 38, and a confirmed ~.* | **eligible** ◇ *one of the country's most eligible ~s*

BACHELOR + NOUN **days, life** | **apartment** *(AmE)*, **flat** *(BrE)*, **pad** | **status** | **party** *(AmE)*

back *noun*

1 part of the body

ADJ. **broad** | **slender** | **muscular, strong** | **bent** | **straight** | **lower, upper** | **bare** ◇ *The sun beat down on their bare ~s.* | **aching, bad, sore, stiff** ◇ *He's in bed with a bad ~.* | **broken** ◇ *He spent six months recovering from a broken ~.*

VERB + BACK **bend, hunch** *(esp. AmE)* ◇ *He hunches his ~ when he walks.* | **straighten** | **stretch** ◇ *He yawned and stretched his ~ as he got out of bed.* | **break, hurt, injure** | **arch** ◇ *The cat arched its ~ and hissed at the dog.* | **lean** ◇ *He leaned his ~ against the bar.* | **support** | **caress, massage, pat, rub, stroke** *(esp. BrE)* | **scratch**

BACK + VERB **arch** | **stiffen, straighten** ◇ *His ~ stiffened as he saw the photographers waiting.* | **ache, hurt**

BACK + NOUN **injury, pain, trouble** | **muscles** | **support** ◇ *a seat with good ~ support* | **massage, rub** ◇ *Would you give me a ~ rub?*

PREP. **behind sb's ~** ◇ *They tied his hands behind his ~.* ◇ *People say bad things about him behind his ~, but never to his face. (figurative)* | **flat on your ~** ◇ *I was flat on my ~ for six weeks when I broke my leg.* | **on your ~** ◇ *He was carrying a small child on his ~.* ◇ *She was lying on her ~ on the sofa.* | **in the/your ~** ◇ *I have a nagging pain in my lower ~.* | **~ to** ◇ *He was standing with his ~ to the fire.*

PHRASES **sb's ~ is turned** ◇ *The boss was certain that the staff would stop working as soon as his ~ was turned. (figurative)* | **~ to** ◇ *The children sat ~ to ~.* | **a pat on the ~, a slap on the ~** ◇ *He smiled and gave me a hearty slap on the ~.* ◇ *She deserves a pat on the ~ for her efforts. (figurative)* | **the small of your ~** ◇ *She felt a sharp pain in the small her ~.* | **turn your ~ (on sb/sth)** ◇ *Actors should never turn their ~s on the audience.* ◇ *She decided to turn her ~ on Paris and return home. (figurative)* | **watch your ~** (= be careful because people may want to harm you.) ◇ *I warned her she should watch her ~.*

2 part furthest from the front

PREP. **around ~** *(AmE)*, **around the ~** *(BrE)*, **round the ~** *(BrE)* (= to the area behind the house, etc.) ◇ *Come around ~ and I'll show you the pool.* ◇ *If you'd like to come round the ~, I'll show you the garden.* | **at the ~** ◇ *We could only get seats at the ~.* | **down the ~** ◇ *My money's all fallen down the ~ of the cushion.* | **in ~** *(AmE)* ◇ *There's room for three people in ~.* | **in the ~** *(BrE)* ◇ *Two passengers sat in the ~ of the car.* |

to the ~ ◇ *The cup had been pushed to the ~ of the cupboard.* | **towards/toward the ~** ◇ *The arts page is usually towards/ toward the ~ of the newspaper.*
PHRASES **~ to front** (*BrE*) ◇ *I had my pullover on ~ to front.*

back verb

1 move back

ADV. **hastily, hurriedly, immediately, quickly** ◇ *She ~ed away hurriedly.* | **slowly** ◇ *He ~ed slowly out of the room.* | **instinctively** ◇ *They instinctively ~ed away from the intense heat.* | **cautiously, nervously** ◇ *He took a step forward and she nervously ~ed away.* | **away, in, off, up** ◇ *Try ~ing the car in—it's easier that way.* ◇ *Back off! There's no need to yell at me.* ◇ *Can you ~ your car up so that I can get through?*
VERB + BACK **try to** ◇ *He tried to ~ away.*
PREP. **across** ◇ *She ~ed across the room.* | **away from** ◇ *The children ~ed away from him in fear.* | **into** ◇ *She ~ed into the garage.* | **out of** ◇ *He ~ed out of the drive.*

2 support sb/sth

ADV. **strongly** ◇ *Teachers are strongly ~ing the new educational policies.* | **fully** | **overwhelmingly** | **unanimously** | **openly, publicly** | **financially** ◇ *his election bid was financially ~ed by a soft drinks company.* | **up** ◇ *I'll ~ you up if they don't believe you.*

PHR V back down

VERB + BACK DOWN **will (not)** ◇ *He will never ~ down.* | **refuse to** | **be forced to** (*esp. BrE*), **have to**
PREP. **from** ◇ *The government was forced to ~ down from implementing these proposals.* | **over** ◇ *The committee finally ~ed down over the issue of spending cuts.*

backdrop noun

ADJ. **dramatic, magnificent** (*esp. BrE*), **perfect, picturesque, romantic, scenic** ◇ *The beautiful gardens provided a scenic ~ for the wedding ceremony.* | **economic, historical, political** ◇ *Their lives played out against a historical ~ of conflict.* | **painted** ◇ *The photographer poses his subjects against painted ~s.*
VERB + BACKDROP **have** | **create, form, provide** ◇ *Worsening economic conditions have created an unfavorable ~ for global markets.* | **paint** ◇ *She painted the ~s for school plays.*
PREP. **against a/the ~ of** ◇ *The conference begins this week against a ~ of unmitigated gloom.* | **~ for** ◇ *The ocean provided the perfect ~ for a romantic dinner.* | **~ of** ◇ *The large bay has a superb ~ of mountains.* | **~ to** ◇ *War is more than just a dramatic ~ to the novel.*

backfire verb

ADV. **badly, spectacularly, totally** | **ultimately** ◇ *He pretended to be sick, a ploy which ultimately ~d.*
PREP. **on** ◇ *The surprise I had planned ~d on me.*

background noun

1 type of family, social class, etc. sb comes from

ADJ. **family** ◇ *Can you tell me something about your family ~?* | **broad** ◇ *It is important to have a broad educational ~.* | **different, diverse, mixed, varied, various** ◇ *We work with clients from diverse ~s.* | **similar** ◇ *I think we get on well because we're from similar ~s.* | **privileged, wealthy** | **deprived, disadvantaged, poor** (*esp. BrE*) | **middle-class, upper-class, working-class** | **solid, stable, strong** ◇ *She has a good solid ~ in management.* | **criminal** ◇ *She wanted to know about his criminal ~.* | **engineering, military, musical, professional, scientific, technical** ◇ *Children from a military ~ often move around a lot.* ◇ *Even people with a technical ~ will struggle to understand some of the jargon.* | **Christian, Jewish, Muslim, etc.** | **class, cultural, ethnic, genetic, linguistic, racial, religious, social, socio-economic** | **academic, educational** ◇ *Her academic ~ includes a degree in education.*
VERB + BACKGROUND **come from, have** ◇ *He came from a very*

privileged ~.* | **be drawn from** ◇ *The students are drawn from very mixed social ~s.*
BACKGROUND + VERB **be in sth** ◇ *Her ~ was in biology and medicine.*
BACKGROUND + NOUN **check** ◇ *In the future, we will require ~ checks on airport employees.*
PREP. **from a ~** ◇ *children from deprived ~s* | **with a ~** ◇ *an economist with a ~ in business* | **~ in**
PHRASES **a range of ~s, a variety of ~s**

2 facts connected with a situation/event

ADJ. **general** | **factual** | **cultural, economic, historical, political**
VERB + BACKGROUND **describe, explain, give (sb), outline, provide (sb with)** ◇ *The book provides the ~ to the revolution.* | **form** ◇ *Those discussions formed the ~ to the decision.*
BACKGROUND + NOUN **briefing, info** (*informal*), **information, knowledge, reading** ◇ *~ information on the country*
PREP. **against the ~** ◇ *Against that general ~, let me give you a more detailed view of current practice.* | **~ to** ◇ *the technical ~ to the report* | **~ of** ◇ *the historical ~ of the project*

3 part of a view/picture behind the main parts

ADJ. **black, blue, grey/gray, etc.** | **dark** | **neutral**
VERB + BACKGROUND **blend in with, match** ◇ *The wolves' coats turn white to match their snowy ~.*
BACKGROUND + NOUN **colour/color** ◇ *Most paintings look good against a neutral ~ colour/color.*
PREP. **against a/the ~** ◇ *The areas of water stood out against the dark ~.* | **in the ~** ◇ *The mountains in the ~ were capped with snow.* | **on a/the ~** ◇ *bright blue on a red ~*

4 position in which sb/sth is not important/noticed

VERB + BACKGROUND **blend into, fade into, melt into, recede into, retreat into, slip into** ◇ *The dispute over the new contract allowed her other problems to fade into the ~.* ◇ *He had learned how to melt invisibly into the ~.*
BACKGROUND + NOUN **music, noise, radiation** | **vocals** ◇ *Who did the ~ vocals on that track?* | **distortion, hiss** ◇ *The signal was very clear, with no ~ hiss or distortion.*
PREP. **in the ~** ◇ *There was a radio on in the ~.* ◇ *I could see my secretary hovering in the ~.* ◇ *He prefers to remain in the ~ and let his assistant deal with the press.*

backing noun

ADJ. **solid, strong** | **full, unanimous** (*esp. BrE*), **wholehearted** (*BrE*) ◇ *The teachers have the full ~ of the parents.* | **financial, legal** (*esp. BrE*) | **government, official** (*esp. BrE*), **popular**
VERB + BACKING **have** | **gain, get, receive, secure, win** ◇ *They have won financial ~ from the EU.* | **need, seek** | **lack** | **give sb, provide (sb with)** ◇ *Who's going to provide the ~?*
BACKING + VERB **come from sb/sth** ◇ *The ~ will come from the government.*
PREP. **with the ~, without the ~** ◇ *They brought the legal action with the ~ of their doctor.* | **~ for** ◇ *They want ~ for more research.* | **~ from** ◇ *~ from management*

backlash noun

ADJ. **conservative** ◇ *a conservative ~ against the feminism of the 80s* | **anti-American, anti-feminist, anti-war, etc.** | **political** | **public** | **inevitable**
VERB + BACKLASH **cause, create, engender, fuel, produce, provoke, spark, trigger** ◇ *Such a decision may provoke a ~ from their supporters.* | **risk** | **expect, fear** | **face**
PREP. **~ against** ◇ *a ~ against any reforms* | **~ from** ◇ *They face a ~ from shareholders.*

backlog noun

ADJ. **big, huge, large**
VERB + BACKLOG **be faced with, have** ◇ *We are faced with a ~ of orders we can't deal with.* | **catch up on, clear, deal with, eliminate, reduce**
BACKLOG + VERB **build up** (*esp. BrE*) ◇ *A huge ~ of work had built up.*

backpack noun (*esp. AmE*) → See also RUCKSACK

ADJ. **leather** | **bulging, loaded, overstuffed, stuffed**

VERB + BACKPACK **grab, shoulder** | **drop, heave, hoist, throw, toss** ◇ *He threw his ~ into the car.* | **sling, swing** ◇ *She swung her ~ over her shoulder.* | **wear** | **pack, pack up** | **close, open** | **unzip, zip**

backstroke noun → Note at STROKE

backward adj.
VERBS **be, seem**
ADV. **extremely, fairly, very, etc.** ◇ *a rather ~ part of the country* | **economically, educationally, technologically**

bacon noun
ADJ. **lean** (*esp. BrE*) | **streaky** (*BrE*) | **back** (*esp. BrE*) | **crisp, crispy** ◇ *Fry the ~ until crisp.* | **smoked** (*esp. BrE*), **smoky, unsmoked** (*BrE*) | **turkey** (*AmE*)
...OF BACON **bit, piece, rasher** (*esp. BrE*), **slice** ◇ *I'll have two rashers of ~ and a fried egg.* | **side** (*BrE*) ◇ *A whole side of ~ was hanging from a hook on the ceiling.*
VERB + BACON **cook, fry, grill** (*esp. BrE*), **sauté** (*esp. AmE*) | **cure** (*esp. BrE*)
BACON + NOUN **fat, grease** (*esp. AmE*), **rind** (*esp. BrE*) | **butty** (*BrE*), **sandwich** (*esp. BrE*)
PHRASES **~, lettuce and tomato** (abbreviated to *BLT*) ◇ *a BLT sandwich*
→ Special page at FOOD

bacteria noun
ADJ. **dangerous, harmful** | **beneficial, healthy**
VERB + BACTERIA **attack, destroy, fight, fight off, get rid of, kill** ◇ *Neither chilling nor freezing kills all ~.*
PHRASES **a strain of ~**

bad adj.
1 not good; serious
VERBS **be, look, sound** | **get** ◇ *The weather got very ~ later in the day.*
ADV. **extremely, fairly, very, etc.** ◇ *John's in a pretty ~ mood this morning.* | **appallingly** (*esp. BrE*), **incredibly, terribly, truly, unbelievably** | **embarrassingly, laughably** (*esp. BrE*) ◇ *The service was laughably ~.* | **especially, particularly** ◇ *He is particularly ~ at remembering names.* | **notoriously** ◇ *Jim was a notoriously ~ driver.* | **enough** ◇ *Things are ~ enough without our own guns shelling us.* | **equally** ◇ *The problem is equally ~ in many other countries.* | **inherently** ◇ *Watching television is not inherently ~ for children.*
PREP. **at** ◇ *He's really ~ at languages.* | **for** ◇ *Smoking is very ~ for you.*
PHRASES **not half ~** (= good) ◇ *I saw him yesterday, and he wasn't looking half ~.*
2 not safe to eat
VERBS **be, look, smell, taste** ◇ *The sausages tasted ~.* | **go, turn** ◇ *This meat has gone ~.*
3 guilty/sorry
VERBS **feel**
ADV. **extremely, fairly, very, etc.** | **enough** ◇ *I feel ~ enough without you constantly telling me how it was all my fault!*
PREP. **about** ◇ *She felt pretty ~ about leaving him.*

badge noun
ADJ. **name** | **police** (*esp. AmE*) | **merit** (*esp. AmE*) | **cap** (*BrE*) | **blazer, lapel** (*both BrE*) | **button** (*BrE*)
VERB + BADGE **wear** | **display, flash, pull out** (*esp. AmE*) ◇ *The police officer flashed his ~.* | **earn** (*esp. AmE*) ◇ *Gates earns a merit ~ for his ideas on surviving the recession.* (*figurative*)
BADGE + NOUN **holder** (= an object for holding a badge) (*esp. BrE*) | **holder** (= a person who has a badge) (*esp. BrE*) ◇ *parking for disabled ~ holders*
PHRASES **a ~ of honour/honor** (*figurative*) ◇ *His scars are ~s of honour/honor.* | **a ~ of office** (*esp. BrE*) ◇ *His ~ of office, a large gold key, hung around his neck.*

bad-tempered adj.
VERBS **be, look, seem, sound** | **become, grow** | **make sb** ◇ *It is his illness that makes him ~.*
ADV. **extremely, fairly, very, etc.** | **increasingly** ◇ *He grew increasingly ~ as the afternoon wore on.*

baffled adj.
VERBS **be, feel, look, sound** | **remain**
ADV. **completely, totally, utterly**
PREP. **about** ◇ *Officials say they're ~ about the cause of the gas explosion.* | **as to** ◇ *The referee remains ~ as to why his decision caused so much anger.* | **by** ◇ *The doctors are completely ~ by her illness.*

bag noun
ADJ. **strong** | **heavy** | **empty** | **small** | **burlap** (*AmE*), **canvas, cloth, leather, mesh** (*esp. AmE*), **paper, plastic, polythene** (*BrE*), **string** | **brown** (*esp. AmE*) ◇ *He brought his lunch every day in a brown ~.* | **carrier** (*BrE*), **grocery** (*esp. AmE*), **shopping** | **freezer, Ziploc™** (*AmE*), **bin** (*BrE*), **dustbin** (*BrE*), **garbage** (*esp. AmE*), **rubbish** (*BrE*), **trash** (*AmE*) | **clutch** (*esp. BrE*), **shoulder, tote** (*AmE*) ◇ *Her crocodile skin shoulder ~ matched her shoes.* | **drawstring, duffel** | **evening** | **carry-on** (*esp. AmE*) ◇ *New airline regulations banned scissors in carry-on ~s.* | **overnight, travel, travelling** (*BrE*) | **make-up, sponge** (*BrE*), **toilet** (*BrE*), **toiletry** (*AmE*), **wash** (usually **washbag**) (*BrE*) | **changing** (*AmE*), **diaper** (*AmE*) ◇ *a baby changing ~* | **book, school** | **beach, camera, golf, gym, sports** | **messenger** (*esp. AmE*) ◇ *a cyclist with his laptop in a messenger ~ slung across his chest* | **kit** (usually *kitbag*) (*esp. BrE*) | **medical** | **lunch** (*esp. AmE*), **sandwich** | **crisp** (*BrE*) | **body** ◇ *The dead soldiers were put on the plane in body ~s.* | **barf** (*AmE*), **sick** (*esp. BrE*) (= a paper bag for a person to vomit into on a plane, boat, etc.) | **doggy** (= for taking uneaten food home from a restaurant) | **gift, goody** (= a bag given as a gift with a variety of things in it) ◇ *We're giving away a free goody ~ with every children's meal.* | **sleeping** | **bean** (usually *beanbag*) | **saddle** (usually *saddlebag*) | **money** ◇ *He could not convince those who held the money ~s that his idea was viable.* (*figurative*) | **diplomatic** (= an official government container that may not be opened by customs officials) (*BrE*) | **mail** (usually *mailbag*), **post** (usually *postbag*) (*BrE*)
VERB + BAG **open, unzip** | **close, zip up** | **fill, pack** | **empty, unpack** | **cram sth in/into, push sth in/into, put sth in/into, shove sth in/into, slip sth in/into, stuff sth in/into** ◇ *The camera caught him slipping a CD into his ~.* | **draw sth out of, produce sth from, pull sth out of/from, take sth from/out of** | **delve into** (*esp. BrE*), **dive into, fumble in, reach into, rummage in** ◇ *I rummaged in my ~ for a pen.* | **clutch, hold** | **carry, drag, haul, lug** ◇ *I had to lug my ~s up the stairs.* | **heave, hoist, lift** | **shoulder** ◇ *He shouldered his ~ and left.* | **fling, sling, throw, toss** ◇ *He tossed his ~ onto an empty seat.* | **drop, dump, put down** | **deposit, drop off, leave** ◇ *We dropped our ~s off at the hotel and went straight out.* | **check** (*AmE*), **check in** (*BrE*) ◇ *You can check ~s of up to 70 pounds for free.* | **grab, snatch** ◇ *She grabbed her ~ and ran out of the door.* ◇ *Two youths snatched her ~ as she was walking home.* | **swing** ◇ *He was walking along swinging his school ~.* | **load into sth, load onto sth** ◇ *She helped me load my ~s into the car.* | **unload** | **look in, search** | **gather** ◇ *They were gathering their ~s, preparing to leave.* | **retrieve** ◇ *I opened the trunk of the car to retrieve my ~s.*
BAG + VERB **bulge (with sth)** ◇ *The ~ bulged with papers and letters.* | **contain sth, hold sth** | **be crammed with sth, be full of sth, be stuffed with sth** | **dangle, hang, swing** ◇ *She had a heavy ~ swinging from each hand.*
PREP. **in a/the ~** ◇ *The mushrooms are sealed in a ~ for freshness.* | **inside a/the ~** | **~ of** ◇ *a ~ of groceries*
PHRASES **the contents of a ~** ◇ *The customs officer asked him to empty out the contents of his ~.* | **have your ~s packed** ◇ *You need to have your ~s packed and be ready to go by six.* | **sling your ~ over your shoulder** ◇ *She stepped down off the bus with her ~ slung over her shoulder.*

baggage

baggage noun (esp. AmE)

ADJ. **carry-on, hand** (BrE) | **checked** (esp. AmE), **checked-in** (BrE) ◊ Any sharp objects must go in your checked ~. | **excess** ◊ At the airport I found that I had 20 kg of excess ~. | **cultural, emotional, ideological** (all figurative) ◊ She's still carrying all that emotional ~ from her first marriage.
...OF BAGGAGE **piece**
VERB + BAGGAGE **carry, lug** | **go through, screen, search** | **check** (AmE), **check in** (BrE) ◊ Where do we check (in) our ~? | **claim** (AmE), **collect, pick up** ◊ Let's collect our ~ first. | **jettison, shed** (both figurative) ◊ The party has shed its ideological ~.
BAGGAGE + NOUN **allowance** | **screening** | **cart** (AmE), **trolley** (esp. BrE) | **handler** | **claim** (AmE), **reclaim** (BrE) ◊ the ~ reclaim hall | **train** | **car** (AmE)

bail noun

ADJ. **conditional, unconditional** (both BrE) | **police** (BrE)
VERB + BAIL **apply for** (esp. BrE) | **allow sb, give sb, grant (sb)** ◊ She has been granted conditional ~. | **set** ◊ The judge set ~ at £50 000. | **get** ◊ For very serious crimes, it is hard to get ~. | **oppose** (esp. BrE) ◊ The police were successful in opposing ~. | **deny, refuse (sb), revoke** | **post, put up, stand** ◊ A wealthy businessman has stood ~ for him. | **free sb on, release sb on, remand sb on** (BrE) ◊ They were released on police ~ pending further enquiries. | **jump, skip** (= not return for your trial after bail has been granted)
BAIL + NOUN **application** (esp. BrE) | **hearing** | **bond** | **conditions** (esp. BrE) | **bondsman** (esp. AmE) | **jumper** (esp. AmE) | **hostel** (BrE) ◊ He was sent to a ~ hostel until the case came to court.
PREP. **on ~** ◊ He committed another robbery while out on ~. | Rosenthal is currently free on ~. | **without ~** ◊ The accused were held without ~.
PHRASES **an application for ~** (BrE)

bait noun

ADJ. **fresh, live** ◊ He used maggots as live ~.
VERB + BAIT **dangle** (often figurative), **put out, set out** ◊ We'll put out the ~ and see what happens. | **use sth as** | **nibble, nibble at, rise to, swallow, take** (all often figurative) ◊ We hope that potential investors will take the ~. | **resist**

bake verb

PHRASES **freshly ~d, newly ~d** ◊ The house was filled with the scent of freshly ~d bread.

balance noun

1 even combination/distribution

ADJ. **correct, equal, even, exact, ideal, necessary, optimal, optimum, perfect, proper, right** ◊ With children, it is important to achieve the right ~ between love and discipline. | **comfortable, excellent, good, happy, harmonious, healthy** ◊ a healthy ~ of foods | **acceptable, appropriate, fair, reasonable, sensible** (BrE) ◊ How do you find an acceptable ~ between closeness and distance in a relationship? | **careful, delicate, fine** (esp. BrE), **subtle** ◊ Being a good boss requires a fine ~ between kindness and authority. | **fragile, precarious, uneasy** | **overall** ◊ It is the overall ~ of the diet that is important. | **ecological, natural** ◊ Pulling up all the plants will disturb the natural ~ of the pond. | **hormonal, nutritional** | **work-life** | **ethnic, gender, racial, social** ◊ There is an even gender ~ among staff and students.
VERB + BALANCE **require** | **seek** | **achieve, attain, create, find, strike** ◊ We need to strike a ~ between these conflicting interests. | **keep, maintain, preserve, sustain** ◊ You have to maintain a ~ in your life or else you'll go crazy. | **improve** ◊ ways to improve your work-life ~ | **disrupt, disturb, upset** ◊ Tourists often disturb the delicate ~ of nature on the island. | **redress, re-establish, restore** | **affect** | **adjust, alter, change, shift**
BALANCE + VERB **change, shift**
PREP. **on ~** (= after considering all the information) ◊ On ~,

the company has had a successful year. | **in ~** ◊ It is important to keep the different aspects of your life in ~. | **~ between** ◊ the ~ between academic and practical work | **~ of** ◊ the ~ of animals and plants in the environment
PHRASES **the ~ of nature**

2 division of power/influence

ADJ. **changing, shifting** | **military, political** | **competitive**
VERB + BALANCE **affect** | **change, shift** | **swing** (esp. BrE), **tilt, tip** ◊ In an interview, good presentation can tip the ~ your way.
BALANCE + VERB **change, shift, swing, tilt** ◊ He argues that the ~ has swung too far in favour/favor of capitalism.
PHRASES **the ~ of advantage** (esp. BrE) ◊ The ~ of advantage has shifted from the unions to employers. | **the ~ of forces** ◊ They assessed the ~ of forces between Israel and other countries. | **the ~ of power** ◊ Who holds the ~ of power in this relationship? ◊ There was a dramatic shift in the ~ of power. | **checks and ~s** ◊ Democracy depends on a system of checks and ~s.

3 of the body

ADJ. **excellent, good** | **poor**
VERB + BALANCE **have** ◊ Gymnasts have excellent ~. | **affect** ◊ Tightness in one set of muscles will affect your whole ~. | **improve** ◊ Yoga improves ~ as well as flexibility. | **keep** ◊ I struggled to keep my ~ on my new skates. | **lose** ◊ She lost her ~ and fell. | **catch** (esp. AmE), **recover, regain** | **adjust** ◊ He set his feet wider and adjusted his ~. | **knock sb off, throw sb off** ◊ The sudden movement threw him off ~.
BALANCE + NOUN **beam** (esp. AmE) ◊ The gymnasts finish with floor exercises and the ~ beam.
PREP. **off ~**
PHRASES **a sense of ~** ◊ Cats have a very good sense of ~.

4 money

ADJ. **account, bank** | **cash, money** | **credit, favourable/favorable, healthy, positive** | **debit, negative** | **cleared** (BrE), **net** | **opening** | **final** (esp. BrE), **outstanding** | **trade**
VERB + BALANCE **have** ◊ Everyone likes to have a healthy bank ~. | **ask for, request** ◊ He asked the cashier for the ~ of his current account. | **check** ◊ I'll need to check my bank ~ before I spend so much money. | **show** | **be due** ◊ The final ~ is due six weeks before departure. | **pay** ◊ I'll pay the ~ later. | **use** ◊ The ~ of the proceeds will be used for new equipment. | **bring forward, carry forward** ◊ the ~ brought forward from the previous year
BALANCE + NOUN (see also **balance sheet**)
PHRASES **the ~ of payments, the ~ of trade**

balance verb

1 keep steady

ADV. **carefully, delicately, precariously**
PREP. **on** ◊ He ~d the glasses carefully on the tray.

2 compare two things; give them equal value

ADV. **beautifully, delicately, evenly, finely, nicely, perfectly** ◊ The song perfectly ~s melody and rhythm.
VERB + BALANCE **have to, need to** | **seek to, try to** ◊ The plan seeks to ~ two important objectives. | **manage to** | **fail to**
PREP. **against** ◊ We have to ~ the risks of the new strategy against the possible benefits. | **with** ◊ She tries to ~ the needs of her children with those of her employer.

balanced adj.

VERBS **be** | **remain**
ADV. **properly, well** ◊ The report was accurate and well ~. ◊ a properly ~ diet | **completely, perfectly** ◊ a perfectly ~ design | **equally, evenly** | **fairly, reasonably** | **carefully, closely, delicately, finely** (esp. BrE), **nicely** ◊ The issues are finely ~ and there is no simple answer to the question. | **beautifully** ◊ a beautifully ~ recording | **precariously**
PREP. **between** ◊ an investment portfolio ~ between gas and oil

balance sheet noun

ADJ. **healthy, strong** | **weak** | **company** (esp. BrE), **corporate** (esp. AmE) | **bank** (AmE)

banana

VERB + BALANCE SHEET **bolster, expand** (*AmE*), **improve, strengthen**

bald *adj.*

VERBS **be** | **go** ◇ *He started to go ~ in his twenties.*
ADV. **completely, quite, totally** | **almost, nearly** | **half, partially** | **prematurely** ◇ *young men who go prematurely ~*

balding *adj.*

VERBS **be** ◇ *He's in his twenties but already ~.*
ADV. **already, prematurely**

ball *noun*

1 round object in games

ADJ. **bowling, cricket, golf, ping-pong/Ping-Pong™, rugby, soccer** (*esp. AmE*), **tennis, etc.** | **beach** | **match, practice** | **rubber**
VERB + BALL **play with** | **head, hit, kick** ◇ *The kids love to kick a ~ against my wall.* | **throw, toss** | **bowl, pitch** | **bat, blast, drive, pound, strike** | **roll** | **bounce, dribble** | **chip, volley** | **clear, cross, pass** | **move, run** | **catch, stop** ◇ *He caught the ~.* | **control, trap** | **get, grab, steal** | **chase** | **retrieve, run down** | **return** ◇ *The fielders try to retrieve the ~ quickly and return it to the bowler.* | **miss** ◇ *The catcher missed the ~.* | **drop, let go of** | **handle, touch** | **give away** (*BrE*), **lose** | **win** (*esp. BrE*) | **keep, retain** (*BrE*)
BALL + VERB **go, travel** | **float, fly, roll, sail, soar** ◇ *The ~ flew over the fence.* | **spin** | **hit, land, strike** ◇ *The ~ hit me on the head.* | **bounce, rebound, ricochet**
BALL + NOUN **game** | **control, handling, skills** ◇ *His ~ control was excellent.* | **carrier, handler** (*both AmE*) ◇ *He's an excellent ~ handler.*
→ Special page at SPORTS

2 (*AmE*) baseball

ADJ. **college** | **pro, professional**
VERB + BALL **play**
BALL + NOUN **player** | **team** | **cap**

3 kick/hit of a ball

ADJ. **loose** | **high, low** ◇ *He sent over a high ~.* | **long, short** | **quick, slow** | **good, great, superb** (*all esp. BrE*) | **bad** (*esp. BrE*) | **curve** (= that changes direction unpredictably) (*esp. AmE*) ◇ *The plot throws a few curve ~s along the way to keep you guessing.* (*figurative*) | **foul** | **hand** (usually *handball*) (in football/soccer) ◇ *He was penalized for handball.*
VERB + BALL **play, send** | **pick up, pounce on, punish** ◇ *He pounced on a loose ~ and scored.*
PREP. **~ from** ◇ *a great ~ from Rooney*

4 round object like a ball

ADJ. **tight** | **fiery** ◇ *The sun was a fiery ~, low on the hills.* | **crystal** ◇ *Without a crystal ~ it's impossible to say where we'll be next year.* | **cannon** | **wrecking** | **cotton** (*AmE*) | **disco** | **medicine** (= heavy ball used as a weight)
VERB + BALL **curl (up) into, roll (up) into** ◇ *The little girl curled up into a ~ in her mother's arms.* | **form sth into, make sth into, roll sth (up) into, screw sth (up) into, shape sth into** ◇ *He screwed the letter up into a tight ~.*
PHRASES **a ~ and chain** (*figurative*) ◇ *The responsibility was a ~ and chain around my ankle.*

5 party

ADJ. **charity** (*esp. BrE*) | **college** (*BrE*) | **hunt** (*BrE*) | **costume, fancy-dress** (*esp. BrE*), **masked** ◇ *We're going to a masked ~.*
VERB + BALL **have, hold, organize** ◇ *We're organizing a charity ~.* | **attend, go to**
BALL + NOUN **dress, gown**
PREP. **at a/the ~** ◇ *She met him at the ~.*

ballet *noun*

ADJ. **classical, contemporary, modern, romantic** | **19th-century, 20th-century, etc.** | **narrative** | **one-act, two-act, etc.** | **full-length**
VERB + BALLET **learn, study, teach** ◇ *He's studying classical ~.* | **compose, create, write** | **stage** | **choreograph** | **dance, perform**
→ Note at PERFORMANCE (for more verbs)

BALLET + NOUN **music** | **dancer** | **company, troupe** | **shoe, slipper** | **class, lesson, school** | **master, mistress, teacher** | **director**

balloon *noun*

1 toy

ADJ. **helium** ◇ *helium ~s for the children's party* | **water** | **colourful/colorful** | **party**
VERB + BALLOON **blow up, inflate** | **burst, pop** | **tie** ◇ *They tied the ~s to the back of the car.*
BALLOON + VERB **burst, pop**

2 in the sky

ADJ. **barrage, hot-air, weather**
VERB + BALLOON **go up in** ◇ *We went up in a ~.* | **launch, release**
BALLOON + VERB **float by, float over, float up**
BALLOON + NOUN **flight** | **race**
PREP. **in a ~** ◇ *She crossed the Atlantic in a hot-air ~.*

ballot *noun*

ADJ. **secret** | **open** | **postal** (*BrE*) | **absentee** (*esp. AmE*) | **provisional** | **electronic, paper** | **national** | **first, second** | **leadership** | **strike** | **spoiled** (*BrE*)
VERB + BALLOT **carry out, hold** | **organize** | **cast** ◇ *Only 40% of eligible voters cast their ~s.* | **count, recount** | **spoil** (*BrE*) | **mark** | **mail** (*AmE*), **post** (*BrE*)
BALLOT + NOUN **box** | **form, paper** (*BrE*) | **rigging** | **measure** (*AmE*)
PREP. **at/the ~** ◇ *They voted against him at the second ~.* | **by ~** ◇ *The jury cast their vote by secret ~.* | **in a/the ~** ◇ *The club members decided in a ~ to suspend the captain.* | **on a/the ~** ◇ *I voted for her on the first ~.* | **~ for** ◇ *a ~ for the party leadership* | **~ on** ◇ *a ~ on the new contracts* | **~ over** ◇ *a ~ over strike action*

ban *noun*

ADJ. **blanket** (*esp. BrE*), **complete, outright, total** | **partial** | **temporary** | **overtime** | **advertising** | **blanket advertising ~ on tobacco** | **driving** | **smoking** | **test** ◇ *a nuclear test ~ treaty* | **constitutional** (*AmE*) | **federal** (*AmE*)
VERB + BAN **enact** (*esp. AmE*), **impose, introduce** (*esp. BrE*), **place, put** ◇ *They have imposed a ~ on the import of seal skins.* | **enforce** | **lift, overturn, remove** | **uphold** | **tighten** | **ease** ◇ *The ~ on exports has now been eased.* | **call for, demand, support** | **oppose, reject** | **comply with** | **defy** (*esp. BrE*) ◇ *The students took to the streets, defying a ~ on political gatherings.*
BAN + VERB **come into force, start** | **apply to sth, cover sth** ◇ *The ~ only covers tropical hardwood.* | **affect sth** ◇ *The ~ will affect all public and work premises.*
PREP. **~ on** ◇ *a ~ on smoking in public places*

ban *verb*

ADV. **effectively** | **formally, officially** | **completely**
VERB + BAN **attempt to, seek to, try to** | **vote to** ◇ *Congress has voted to ~ online gambling.*
PREP. **from** ◇ *The weightlifter was banned from the Olympics for failing a drugs test.* ◇ *He has been banned from driving for a year.* (*BrE*)
PHRASES **an attempt to ~ sth, a move to ~ sth** (*esp. BrE*) ◇ *a move to ~ tobacco advertising* | **a decision to ~ sth**

banana *noun*

ADJ. **ripe** | **overripe** | **green** | **mashed**
... OF BANANAS **bunch** ◇ *I bought a small bunch of ~s.*
VERB + BANANA **eat, have** | **pick** | **mash** | **slice** | **peel**
BANANA + NOUN **peel, skin** (*figurative*) ◇ *The company has acquired an unhappy knack of slipping on ~ skins* (= being led into making mistakes that make it look stupid). | **plant, tree** | **leaf** | **grove, plantation** | **bread, cake**
→ Special page at FRUIT

band noun

1 group of musicians

ADJ. **big** | **brass, string, wind** | **backing** ◇ He was accompanied onstage by his backing ~. | **blues, dance, indie, jazz, pop** (esp. BrE), **rock, etc.** | **boy, girl** ◇ Boy ~s are not usually known for their musical talent. | **cover, tribute** (esp. BrE) ◇ They hired a Beatles tribute ~ to play at the reception. | **garage** ◇ He formed a garage ~ with his friends. | **marching, military, regimental** | **school** | **live** ◇ the excitement of seeing a live ~ | **one-man** (often figurative) ◇ He runs the business as a one-man ~.
VERB + BAND **form, start** | **join, play in, sing in** ◇ She plays in a rock ~. | **quit** | **conduct, lead** | **front**
BAND + VERB **perform (sth), play (sth)** | **strike up** ◇ We heard a ~ strike up in the park.
BAND + NOUN **leader** | **member** | **practice**
PREP. **in a/the ~** ◇ a singer in a rock ~ | **with a/the ~** ◇ a drummer with a jazz ~
PHRASES **a member of the ~**

2 group of people

ADJ. **select** (esp. BrE), **small** ◇ He is one of a select ~ of top class players. | **dwindling** | **growing** | **merry** | **ragtag**
VERB + BAND **join**
PREP. **~ of** ◇ a ~ of rebels

3 range

ADJ. **age, price, tax** ◇ the 25–35 age ~
VERB + BAND **be in, fall into** ◇ Which tax ~ do you fall into?

bandage noun

ADJ. **tight** | **loose** | **makeshift** | **compression** | **adhesive** (AmE) | **crepe, elastic, gauze** | **clean, sterile** | **fresh, new**
VERB + BANDAGE **put on, wind, wrap** ◇ Wrap the ~ firmly around the injured limb. | **tie** | **have on, wear** | **change, remove, take off, undo**
PREP. **~ around, ~ round** (esp. BrE) | **~ on** ◇ She had a ~ on her arm.
PHRASES **be in ~s, be swathed in ~s, be wrapped in ~s** ◇ He'll be in ~s for a few weeks.

Band-Aid™ noun (esp. AmE) → See also PLASTER

VERB + BAND-AID **apply, put on** | **need**
BAND-AID + NOUN **approach, solution** (both figurative) ◇ It's just a Band-Aid solution and is unlikely to work long-term.

bandwagon noun

VERB + BANDWAGON **climb on, join, jump on** ◇ Competitors have jumped on the ~ and started building similar machines.
BANDWAGON + VERB **be rolling, gather momentum, gather pace, sweep along** (all esp. BrE) ◇ The globalization ~ is gathering momentum.
BANDWAGON + NOUN **effect** ◇ There is now a ~ effect with more and more companies following the trend.
PREP. **on board a/the ~**

bang noun

1 sudden loud noise

ADJ. **almighty** (esp. BrE), **big, enormous** (esp. BrE), **huge** (esp. BrE), **loud, massive** (esp. BrE), **resounding**
VERB + BANG **hear** ◇ We suddenly heard an almighty ~ from the kitchen.
BANG + VERB **echo**
PREP. **with a ~** ◇ She slammed the door with a loud ~.

2 sudden hard hit

ADJ. **nasty** ◇ He got a nasty ~ on the head.
VERB + BANG **get, have**

3 bangs (AmE) hair → See also FRINGE

ADJ. **blond, brown, etc.** | **long, short** | **messy, overgrown, shaggy, wispy**
VERB + BANG **blow, brush, pull back, push, sweep** ◇ She blew her ~s out of her face.

bang verb

1 hit noisily

ADV. **hard, loudly** | **repeatedly**
PREP. **against** ◇ He kept ~ing his chair against the wall. | **on** ◇ She ~ed loudly on the table.
PHRASES **~ (sth) down, ~ (sth) open, ~ (sth) shut** ◇ The bedroom door ~ed shut. ◇ She ~ed the door shut.

2 part of the body/person

ADV. **badly, hard** ◇ I ~ed my head badly.
PREP. **into** ◇ He ~ed into me in the corridor. | **on** ◇ I ~ed my leg on the table.

bank noun

1 for money

ADJ. **big, large, major** | **small** | **central, clearing** (in the UK), **commercial, international, investment, issuing, national, reserve, savings** ◇ The central ~ has put up interest rates. ◇ The bond will be priced by the issuing ~. ◇ She has her money in one of the largest savings ~s. | **private** | **foreign, international, overseas** | **offshore**
VERB + BANK **go to** | **borrow (sth) from** | **rob** | **owe** ◇ The company owes the ~ more than €4 million. | **bail out** ◇ The government has refused to bail out the ~.
BANK + VERB **pay sb sth** | **lend sb sth** ◇ The ~ lent her money to buy a car. | **underwrite sth** ◇ A group of ten international ~s is to underwrite and sell the bonds. | **charge sb/sth** ◇ The ~ charged him a monthly $5 fee. | **issue sth** ◇ Many of these ~s issue both credit and debit cards. | **collapse, crash** ◇ Investors lost millions when the ~ crashed.
BANK + NOUN **account, balance, deposit, loan, statement** | **charges** (esp. BrE), **fees** (AmE) | **credit** | **manager** | **teller** | **robber** | **heist, robbery**
PREP. **from a/the ~** ◇ He got a large loan from the ~. | **in a/the ~** ◇ I'll put half the money in the ~ and spend the rest. | **out of a/the ~** ◇ I need to get some money out of the ~.

2 by a river/canal

ADJ. **far, opposite, other** ◇ We could see them waving on the opposite ~. | **canal, river**
VERB + BANK **burst, overflow** ◇ The river had burst its ~s after torrential rain.
PREP. **along a/the ~** ◇ We strolled along the river ~. | **on a/the ~** ◇ a picnic on the ~s of the river

3 area of sloping ground

ADJ. **steep** | **grassy** | **muddy**
PREP. **down a/the ~** ◇ The children rolled down the grassy ~. | **up a/the ~**

4 mass of cloud, etc./row of machines, etc.

ADJ. **huge, vast** ◇ a huge ~ of switches and buttons | **cloud** (esp. AmE)
PREP. **~ of** ◇ a vast ~ of cloud

banking noun

ADJ. **business, commercial, corporate** | **central** | **investment, merchant** | **retail, wholesale** | **private** | **domestic, national** | **offshore** | **global, international** | **electronic, Internet, online** ◇ At first consumers were wary of online ~.
BANKING + NOUN **system** | **market** | **group** | **business, industry, sector** | **community** ◇ the international ~ community | **service** ◇ I mainly use the Internet ~ service.
PREP. **in ~** ◇ This software is used in ~.

bankrupt adj.

VERBS **be** | **become, go** ◇ Hundreds of companies went ~ during the recession. | **declare sb, make sb** ◇ She had to pay the mortgage after her husband was declared ~.
ADV. **almost, nearly, virtually** | **economically, ideologically, intellectually, morally**
PREP. **of** (figurative) ◇ a government ~ of new ideas

bankruptcy noun

ADJ. **consumer, personal** | **corporate** | **intellectual, moral**
VERB + BANKRUPTCY **face** ◇ Small travel operators are facing ~. | **avoid** | **cause** | **be close to, be on the brink of, be on the**

verge of | be driven into (*esp. AmE*), be forced into, enter
(*AmE*), go into | file for, petition for ◇ *The company has
been forced to file for ~.* | declare ◇ *It is the only country to
have declared ~.* | be saved from, escape, escape from, exit
(*AmE, formal*)
BANKRUPTCY + NOUN filing, order, proceedings ◇ *The
defendant has a ~ order against him.* | protection | bill (*esp.
AmE*), law, legislation | court | judge
PHRASES the threat of ~

banner noun

VERB + BANNER drape, hang, hang out | carry, hold | wave |
unfurl | display, fly, hoist
BANNER + VERB hang | flutter, fly, wave ◇ *~s waving in the
wind* | bear sth ◇ *The demonstrators carried ~s bearing
various slogans.* | advertise sth, demand sth, proclaim sth,
read sth, say sth ◇ *Banners demanded the leader's
resignation.* | be strung across sth ◇ *A ~ strung across the
road read, 'Welcome home, boys!'*
BANNER + NOUN ad | headline | year (*AmE*) ◇ *1999 was a ~
year for the US economy.*

banquet noun

ADJ. grand, great, lavish, sumptuous | five-course, six-
course, etc. | formal, official | royal, state | awards (*AmE*),
farewell, wedding ◇ *The winners will be announced at the
annual awards ~.* | medieval | annual (*esp. AmE*)
VERB + BANQUET give, hold | organize, prepare, prepare for
◇ *The kitchens are preparing for a lavish ~.* | attend ◇ *The
president attended a state ~ last night.* | enjoy
PREP. at a/the ~ | ~ for ◇ *a ~ for the president*
PHRASES a ~ in sb's honour/honor, a ~ in honour/honor of
sth ◇ *Over 1600 people attended a ~ in his honour/honor.*

banter noun

ADJ. easy, friendly, good-natured, light, light-hearted,
lively, pleasant | idle | witty
VERB + BANTER hear | enjoy | exchange | be engaged in,
engage in (*both esp. BrE*) ◇ *She engages in friendly ~ with her
customers.*

bar noun

1 for drinks/food

ADJ. licensed (*BrE*) | crowded | open | lounge, public (*BrE*),
saloon (*esp. BrE*) | hotel | gay, lesbian, singles | karaoke |
beer (*AmE*), cocktail, wine | breakfast, burger, coffee,
juice, salad, sandwich, snack, sushi | local | popular,
trendy | favourite/favorite | dive (*AmE*) ◇ *It was supposed
to be a restaurant but seemed more like a dive ~.*
VERB + BAR enter, frequent, go to, hang out (*informal, esp.
AmE*), hit (*informal*), stop at, visit ◇ *He often drops into a ~
on the way home from work.* | manage, own, run
BAR + NOUN food, menu, snacks | stool | manager, owner |
staff | counter | area
PREP. in a/the ~ ◇ *There were not many people in the ~.* | at
a/the ~ ◇ *We met at a ~ called the Anvil.*

2 counter

ADJ. breakfast
VERB + BAR be propping up (*humorous*)
PREP. at the ~ ◇ *They were chatting at the ~.* | behind the ~
◇ *The barmaid stood behind the ~.*

3 (BrE) in music → See also MEASURE

VERB + BAR hum, play, sing ◇ *She played a few ~s on the
piano.*
PREP. in a/the ~ ◇ *the notes in the first ~*
PHRASES two, four, etc. beats to the ~

bar verb

ADV. effectively | legally | permanently
PREP. from ◇ *The curfew has effectively barred migrant
workers from their jobs.*

bare adj.

VERBS be, look | remain | leave sth ◇ *You shouldn't have left*

the wires ~. | lay sth, strip sth ◇ *The earth had been laid ~.* ◇
The walls have been stripped ~.
ADV. very | completely, quite ◇ *The room was completely ~.* |
almost, rather
PREP. of ◇ *The house was almost ~ of furniture.*

barefoot adj., adv.

VERBS be, dance, go, run, stand, walk ◇ *The children had to
go ~ because there was no money for shoes.* ◇ *He danced ~ on
the carpet.*

bargain noun

1 sth sold at a lower price

ADJ. absolute, amazing, excellent, good, great, incredible,
real
VERB + BARGAIN find, get, pick up ◇ *I picked up a really good ~
in the market.*
BARGAIN + NOUN buy (*esp. BrE*), price, rate | hunter, hunting
| basement ◇ *The shop sells books at bargain-basement
prices.* | bin

2 agreement

ADJ. grand (*esp. AmE*)
VERB + BARGAIN make, strike
PREP. ~ between ◇ *A ~ was struck between the employers and
the unions.* | ~ with ◇ *I'll make a ~ with you.*
PHRASES drive a hard ~ (= force sb to agree to the
arrangement that is best for you) | sb's half of the ~, sb's
part of the ~, sb's side of the ~ ◇ *Her part of the ~ was to
provide the food.* | keep (to) your half of the ~, keep (to)
your part of the ~, keep (to) your side of the ~ ◇ *You
haven't kept your side of the ~.*

bargain verb

ADV. hard ◇ *He ~ed hard and was stubborn.* | collectively ◇
the right of workers to ~ collectively
PREP. about ◇ *He was prepared to ~ about money.* | for ◇ *to ~
for a better salary* | over ◇ *crowds of men ~ing over horses* |
with ◇ *He tried to ~ with her.*

bargaining noun

ADJ. hard ◇ *There will be some hard ~ before an agreement is
reached.* | collective ◇ *Unions were insistent on the right to
collective ~.* | institutional | political
BARGAINING + NOUN position, power ◇ *We are now in a strong
~ position.* | chip, counter (*BrE*)

barge noun

ADJ. brightly painted | canal, river | sailing (*BrE*) | floating |
cargo, coal, etc.
VERB + BARGE pull, tow | load (sth into), unload (sth from) |
moor, tie up
BARGE + VERB be loaded with sth, carry sth
PREP. by ◇ *They travel by ~.* | in a/the ~, on a/the ~ ◇ *We
spent the summer cruising the canals of France in a ~.*

baritone noun

ADJ. pleasant, rich | deep, low
BARITONE + NOUN voice | solo
PREP. in a... ~ ◇ *He sang in his rich ~*

bark noun

1 on a tree

ADJ. rough | tree | birch, pine, willow, etc.
VERB + BARK peel off, remove, strip ◇ *The people strip the ~
and use it in medicines.*
BARK + VERB peel off ◇ *The ~ peels off in summer.*
BARK + NOUN chippings (*BrE*), chips, mulch

2 of a dog

ADJ. loud, noisy
VERB + BARK give ◇ *The dog gave a loud ~.*

3 loud sound/voice

ADJ. short | harsh, sharp (*esp. AmE*)
VERB + BARK give ◇ *He gave a harsh ~ of laughter.*
PHRASES a ~ of laughter

bark *verb*

ADV. angrily, excitedly, frantically, furiously, happily, loudly, madly, wildly
PREP. at ◇ *The dog was ~ing furiously at a cat.*

barley *noun*

ADJ. malted, malting | roasted | pearl | wild | feed ◇ *Feed ~ prices are set to rise.* | spring, winter
... OF BARLEY ear | field
VERB + BARLEY grow | sow | cut, harvest | thresh | grind
BARLEY + VERB grow | ripen
BARLEY + NOUN harvest | field | grain | soup (*esp. AmE*)

barometer *noun*

1 instrument that measures air pressure

ADJ. aneroid
VERB + BAROMETER check, read | tap ◇ *He tapped the ~ and noted where the needle was pointing.*
BAROMETER + VERB rise | drop, fall

2 sth that shows the state of sth

ADJ. accurate, good, reliable, sensitive, useful (*esp. BrE*) ◇ *Infant mortality is a highly sensitive ~ of socio-economic conditions.* | cultural, moral, political
PREP. ~ of

baron *noun*

1 noble

→ Note at PEER

2 powerful businessman

ADJ. media, newspaper, press, railroad (*AmE*) | cocaine, drug, oil ◇ *the oil ~s of Texas* | robber

baroness, baronet *noun* → Note at PEER

barracks *noun*

ADJ. army, marine, military, police | fortified | wooden
VERB + BARRACKS live in | be confined to ◇ *He was confined to ~ for three weeks as a punishment.* | attack, bomb | build | leave ◇ *The soldiers are searched before they are allowed to leave ~.* | go back to, return to, withdraw to ◇ *Troops are being withdrawn to ~ to avoid further clashes.*

barrage *noun*

1 firing of guns

ADJ. heavy, intense, massive | artillery, missile, mortar, rocket
VERB + BARRAGE fire, launch, let loose, send, unleash
BARRAGE + NOUN balloon
PREP. ~ of ◇ *Troops unleashed a ~ of grenades.*

2 large number of questions, etc.

ADJ. constant, continuous, daily, endless, non-stop, relentless, steady
VERB + BARRAGE be faced with, endure, face, withstand | unleash | keep up ◇ *The reporters kept up a constant ~ of questions.*
PREP. ~ of ◇ *a ~ of questions* ◇ *a ~ of abuse (esp. BrE)* ◇ *a ~ of complaints (esp. BrE)* ◇ *The president is facing a ~ of criticism over his handling of the crisis.*

barrel *noun*

1 container

ADJ. beer, whisky/whiskey, wine, etc. | oak, wooden
VERB + BARREL fill ◇ *They filled the ~s with cider.*
BARREL + VERB contain sth

PREP. a ~, per ~ ◇ *The price of oil had fallen to $16 per ~.* | by the ~ ◇ *Beer is sold by the ~.* | ~ of ◇ *a ~ of oil*

2 of a gun

ADJ. gun, rifle, shotgun ◇ *I felt the gun ~ at my head.* | rifled | 7.5-inch, 26-inch, etc.
VERB + BARREL look down, peer down ◇ *She found herself looking down the ~ of a gun.*
BARREL + VERB point
PHRASES the ~ of a gun

barren *adj.*

VERBS appear, be | become | make sth ◇ *The years of growing cotton had made the land completely ~.*
ADV. completely | almost | fairly (*esp. BrE*), largely, rather, very

barricade *noun*

ADJ. human | police | makeshift | burning | concrete, metal, steel, wooden, etc.
VERB + BARRICADE build, construct, erect, put up, set up | form ◇ *The protesters formed a human ~.* | dismantle, remove, take down | breach, smash, storm ◇ *The army used tanks to storm the ~s.* | man ◇ *There were six strikers manning the ~s.*
PREP. behind a/the ~, over a/the ~ ◇ *The two sides watched each other over the ~s.* | ~ across ◇ *a ~ across the main road* | ~ against ◇ *Students built a ~ against the police.* | ~ in front of ◇ *Police had formed a ~ in front of the gates.* | ~ of ◇ *a ~ of wooden benches*

barrier *noun*

1 fence/gate

ADJ. physical | crash, crush (*BrE*), flood, police, protective, safety (*esp. BrE*), security, ticket (*BrE*) | concrete | sound (*figurative*) ◇ *the first plane to break the sound ~*
VERB + BARRIER build, erect, install | jump | break through ◇ *The crowd managed to break through the ~s.*
PREP. at a/the ~ ◇ *Please show your ticket at the ~. (BrE)* | behind a/the ~ ◇ *The police waited behind the ~s.* | through a/the ~ ◇ *There was a slow trickle of people through the ~s.*

2 thing that causes problems

ADJ. effective, formidable, major | class, colour/color, cultural, institutional, language, racial, trade | invisible | artificial | impenetrable, insurmountable
VERB + BARRIER build, create, erect, put up, set up ◇ *The old laws created ~s to free trade.* | break, break down, eliminate, lift, lower, reduce, remove | identify | cross ◇ *They believe that music can cross any ~s.* | be faced with, encounter, face | overcome, transcend
PREP. ~ against ◇ *The country has set up ~s against imports.* | ~ between ◇ *a class ~ between the two families* | ~ to ◇ *a formidable ~ to communication*

3 physical object that prevents sb/sth passing

ADJ. impassable, impenetrable | natural
VERB + BARRIER form
PREP. ~ between ◇ *The mountains form a natural ~ between the two countries.*

barrister *noun* (*BrE*)

ADJ. brilliant, eminent, good, leading, prominent, senior, successful, top | practising, qualified | junior, trainee | criminal, tribunal | former | defence | prosecuting, prosecution
PREP. ~ for ◇ *the ~ for the ferry company*
→ Note at PROFESSIONAL (for verbs)

base *noun*

1 lowest part

ADJ. firm, solid, strong | circular, flat, rounded, square | concrete, granite, steel, etc.
VERB + BASE have ◇ *The statue has a solid concrete ~.*

2 original idea/situation

ADJ. firm, secure, solid, sound, strong | economic,

VERB + BASE **form, have** | **establish, give sb, provide (sb with)** ◇ *These policies give us a solid ~ for winning the next election.* | **use sth as**
PREP. **~ for** ◇ *He used the notes as a ~ for his lecture.*

3 of support/income/power

ADJ. **solid, sound** | **broad, narrow** ◇ *These policies have a broad ~ of support.* | **power** ◇ *a politician with a rural power ~* | **democratic** | **asset, commercial, economic, financial, industrial, manufacturing, political, resource, revenue, tax** ◇ *The country has a sound commercial ~.* | **client, customer, subscriber, user**
VERB + BASE **create, form, have, provide** | **broaden, develop, expand, improve, increase** ◇ *The company is trying to expand its customer ~.* | **maintain**
BASE + VERB **grow** | **shrink**

4 main place

ADJ. **excellent, ideal, perfect**
VERB + BASE **have** ◇ *The company has its ~ in New York.* | **establish, set up** ◇ *The company has set up its new ~ in the north.*
BASE + NOUN **camp**
PREP. **~ for** ◇ *an ideal ~ for mountain expeditions*

5 for army, navy, etc.

ADJ. **foreign** ◇ *Demonstrators demanded the removal of foreign ~s.* | **air, air-force, military, missile, naval**
VERB + BASE **have** | **build, establish** ◇ *The Americans established a naval ~ on the island in the 1960s.* | **attack** | **destroy** | **defend** | **occupy**
PREP. **at a/the ~** ◇ *equipment kept at the ~* | **on a/the ~** ◇ *people living on the air force ~* | **to (the) ~** ◇ *The planes have all returned to ~.*

base *verb*

PHRV **base sth on/upon sth**
ADV. **closely, firmly** | **broadly, loosely, partly** ◇ *The novels are all loosely ~d on the author's life.* | **entirely, largely, mainly, mostly, primarily** ◇ *Their research was ~d largely on anecdotal evidence.* | **exclusively, purely, solely**

baseball *noun*

1 game

ADJ. **major-league, minor-league** | **Little League** | **pro** (*esp. AmE*), **professional** | **organized** | **college, high-school** | **fantasy**
VERB + BASEBALL **play** | **coach** | **follow** | **watch**
BASEBALL + NOUN **game, play-off** | **player** | **batter, pitcher, slugger** | **team** | **fan** | **coach, manager, commissioner, official, umpire** | **season** | **league** | **diamond, field, park, stadium** | **bat, glove, mitt** | **jersey, shirt, uniform** (*AmE*) | **cap, hat** | **practice** | **legend, star** | **career** | **world** | **tickets** | **card** (= for collecting)

2 ball

VERB + BASEBALL **pitch, throw, toss** | **hit** | **catch**

basement *noun*

ADJ. **dark, unlit, windowless** | **damp, dank** | **cold, cool** | **flooded** | **finished, unfinished** (*both AmE*) | **bargain** (*usually figurative*) ◇ *bargain-basement prices*
BASEMENT + NOUN **apartment** (*esp. AmE*), **bar, flat** (*BrE*), **kitchen, room, studio** | **door, floor, stairs, steps, wall, window** | **car park** (*BrE*)
PREP. **in a/the ~** ◇ *The canteen is down in the ~.*

bash *noun*

1 strong hit

VERB + BASH **give sb/sth** | **get**
PREP. **~ on** ◇ *She got a ~ on the head.*

2 party

ADJ. **big** | **birthday, charity, farewell**
VERB + BASH **give, host, throw** (*esp. BrE*) ◇ *They're throwing a big ~ to celebrate their anniversary.* | **attend** | **plan**

bash *verb*

PREP. **on** ◇ *Someone ~ed him on the nose.* | **with** ◇ *She ~ed him with her book.*
PHRASES **~ sb about, ~ sb up** (*both BrE*) ◇ *He had been attacked and ~ed about a bit.*

basics *noun*

VERB + BASICS **grasp, know, learn, master, pick up, understand** | **explain, outline, teach** | **cover, review** ◇ *The book covers the ~ of massage.* | **concentrate on, stick to** ◇ *It's best to stick to ~ when planning such a large party.* | **get back to, get down to, go back to** ◇ *It's time our education system got back to ~.*
PHRASES **get the ~ right** ◇ *The important thing is to get the ~ right.*

basis *noun*

1 starting point

ADJ. **firm, solid, sound**
VERB + BASIS **form, provide**
PREP. **~ for** ◇ *The proposal provides a sound ~ for a book.*
PHRASES **have no ~ in sth** ◇ *These allegations have no ~ in fact.*

2 principle/reason

ADJ. **whole** | **consistent, factual, rational, scientific, theoretical**
PREP. **on the ~ of** ◇ *We took our decision on the ~ of the information we had.* | **~ for** ◇ *The whole ~ for your argument is false.*

3 way sth is done/organized

ADJ. **regular** | **annual, daily, day-to-day, monthly, weekly, yearly, etc.** ◇ *Staff are employed on a monthly ~.* | **permanent, temporary** | **casual, part-time, voluntary** | **ongoing** | **ad hoc, case-by-case** ◇ *Each application is considered on a case-by-case ~.* | **commercial**
PREP. **on a … ~**

basket *noun*

1 container

ADJ. **bamboo, plastic, straw, wicker, wire, woven, etc.** | **laundry, sewing** | **bread, food, fruit, shopping** | **waste** (*AmE*), **waste-paper** (*BrE*) ◇ *She threw the letter into the waste ~.* ◇ *I decided to empty the waste-paper ~.* | **cat, dog** | **bicycle** ◇ *She was cycling along with her bicycle ~ full of groceries.* | **picnic** | **flower, hanging** ◇ *hanging ~s full of summer flowers*
VERB + BASKET **make, weave** | **fill, load (sth into), pack (sth into), put sth in** | **take sth from, take sth out of, unpack** | **carry, heave, pick up** ◇ *She heaved the huge ~ onto the table.* | **swing** | **put down, set down**
BASKET + VERB **be filled with sth, be full of sth, contain sth** ◇ *a ~ filled with delicious fruit*
PHRASES **in a/the ~, into a/the ~** ◇ *The cat lay curled in its ~.* | **~ of** ◇ *a ~ of flowers/fruit*

2 in basketball

VERB + BASKET **shoot** | **make, score, sink**

basketball *noun*

ADJ. **college, high-school** (*esp. AmE*), **pro** (*esp. AmE*), **professional, varsity** (*esp. AmE*) | **wheelchair**
… OF BASKETBALL **game**
VERB + BASKETBALL **play** | **watch**
BASKETBALL + NOUN **championship, competition** (*esp. AmE*), **game, match** (*BrE*), **tournament** | **league** | **court** | **coach, player, star, team** | **fan** | **referee**
→ Special page at SPORTS

bass *noun* lowest part in music

ADJ. **loud, pounding, throbbing, thumping**

VERB + BASS turn down, turn up ◇ *He always plays his stereo with the ~ turned right up.*
→ Special page at MUSIC

bassoon *noun* → Special page at MUSIC

bat *noun*

1 in games

ADJ. baseball, cricket, table-tennis (*BrE*) (*Ping-Pong™ paddle* in *AmE*) | aluminium (*BrE*), aluminum (*AmE*), wooden | left-handed, right-handed
VERB + BAT grip, hold | carry | swing | wield

2 small flying animal

ADJ. fruit, vampire, etc.
BAT + VERB flutter, fly | hang, roost ◇ *~s hanging upside down* | squeak

bat *verb*

VERB + BAT go in to (*BrE*), go to (*AmE*), put sb in to ◇ *Hick went in to ~ after Hussain.* ◇ *He went to ~, two runs down, with his team about to lose.* ◇ *India won the toss and put England in to ~.* ◇ *She really went to ~ for me* (= supported me).
PREP. for (*BrE*) ◇ *Smith was first to ~ for Warwickshire.*

batch *noun*

1 number of people/things

ADJ. large, small | whole ◇ *A whole ~ of original drawings will be on sale.* | fresh, new ◇ *He baked a fresh ~ of rolls.* ◇ *Each summer a new ~ of students tries to find work.* | latest ◇ *the latest ~ of opinion polls*
PREP. in a/the ~ ◇ *How many books are there in each ~?* ◇ *We deliver the goods in ~es.* | ~ of ◇ *a ~ of letters*

2 in computing

BATCH + NOUN job ◇ *to process a ~ job* | file, program | process, processing | mode ◇ *to run in ~ mode*

bath *noun*

1 (*BrE*) (*also* bathtub *AmE, BrE*) large container for washing your body

ADJ. free-standing, sunken | cast-iron, tin
VERB + BATH/BATHTUB fill | lie in, soak in
BATH/BATHTUB + NOUN faucet (*AmE*), tap (*BrE*) ◇ *~ taps* (*BrE*) ◇ *bathtub faucets* (*AmE*)
PREP. in the ~ ◇ *I'm in the ~!* (*BrE, AmE*) ◇ *I'm in the bathtub!* (*AmE*)

2 water in the bathtub; act of washing your body

ADJ. hot, warm | cold | long | quick | luxurious, nice, relaxing, soothing | bubble, mud, steam, Turkish ◇ *I lay soaking in a hot bubble ~.* | bed (*BrE*), blanket (*BrE*), sponge (*AmE*)
VERB + BATH draw (*AmE*), prepare (*AmE*), run ◇ *Could you run a ~ for me?* | have (*esp. BrE*) | take (*esp. AmE*) | give sb | need
BATH + NOUN mat, towel | oil, salts | time ◇ *It's the children's ~ time.*

bathroom *noun*

ADJ. steamy | large, spacious | tiny | main, master (*esp. AmE*) | luxurious, luxury (*esp. BrE*) | fitted (*BrE*) | tiled | adjoining, en suite ◇ *The master bedroom also has an en suite ~.* | communal, shared | unisex | private ◇ *The best boats have cabins with private ~s.* | public (*AmE*) | downstairs, upstairs
VERB + BATHROOM go to, use (= go to the toilet) | clean, scrub | decorate, redo (*AmE*), remodel (*AmE*) | hog ◇ *Sorry I'm late! Dad was hogging the ~.*
BATHROOM + NOUN cabinet, cupboard | accessories, fittings (*esp. BrE*), fixtures (*esp. AmE*), suite (*esp. BrE*) | faucet (*AmE*), mirror, sink, tap (*BrE*) | tile | door, floor | counter,

countertop (*both AmE*) | scale (*AmE*), scales (*BrE*) ◇ *I weigh myself on the ~ scale(s) every day.* | facilities | stall (*AmE*)

baton *noun*

1 (*esp. BrE*) used by police/soldiers

ADJ. wooden | police
VERB + BATON carry, hold | draw (*BrE*), use ◇ *The police were ordered to draw their ~s and disperse the crowd.*
BATON + NOUN charge (*BrE*) ◇ *Five people were injured in the ~ charge.*

2 used by a conductor

VERB + BATON raise, tap, wave ◇ *He tapped his ~ on the music stand to get everyone's attention.*
PREP. under the ~ of ◇ *The orchestra made the recording under the ~ of a young German conductor.*

3 used in a relay race

VERB + BATON hand, pass ◇ *Each runner passes the ~ to the next.* | take, take up | drop

4 used by a drum majorette

VERB + BATON swing, twirl

batsman *noun* in cricket → See also BATTER

ADJ. opening | home | left-handed, right-handed
VERB + BATSMAN dismiss ◇ *Five of their top six batsmen were dismissed by Kershaw.*
BATSMAN + VERB make sth, score sth ◇ *The next four batsmen made just 21 between them.* | hit sth ◇ *Each ~ hit an early six.*

batter *noun*

1 mixture of eggs, milk and flour → See also MIXTURE

ADJ. smooth, thick | crispy, light (*both esp. BrE*) | remaining | crêpe, pancake | brownie, cake, cookie (*all AmE*) | chocolate (*AmE*) | beer, tempura
VERB + BATTER mix, stir ◇ *I started mixing the ~ for the pancakes.* | pour, spoon, transfer (*esp. AmE*) ◇ *Pour the ~ into a prepared pan.*

2 in baseball → See also BATSMAN

ADJ. left-handed, right-handed | first, lead-off | next | opposing ◇ *Opposing ~s are fooled by Madsen's delivery.*
VERB + BATTER face sb ◇ *Rivera faced seven ~s and retired six.* | retire sb, strike sb out, walk sb ◇ *Jimmy struck out the first ~ with ease.* ◇ *He has walked just eight ~s all year.*
BATTER + VERB step in, step into the box | swing | strike out ◇ *The first ~ struck out.* | hit sth ◇ *I heard the fans groan as the ~ hit a grand slam.*

battered *adj.*

VERBS be, feel, look | become, get
ADV. extremely, fairly, very, etc. | badly | a little, slightly, etc. | emotionally ◇ *She felt emotionally ~.*
PHRASES ~ and bruised, bruised and ~ ◇ *The team is feeling a little ~ and bruised right now.* | ~ old ◇ *She carried a ~ old suitcase.*

battery *noun*

1 for electricity

ADJ. dead, flat ◇ *The car won't start—the battery's flat.* | rechargeable | disposable | removable | spare | car, flashlight (*AmE*), laptop, phone, torch (*BrE*) | alkaline, lithium | AA, AAA, etc. | 9-volt, 48-volt, etc. | storage (*AmE*)
VERB + BATTERY charge, recharge | drain ◇ *Don't leave the radio on—it'll drain the car ~.* | change, replace | remove | connect, disconnect ◇ *Is the ~ connected correctly?* | be powered by, run on, use, work on ◇ *The machine can also run on batteries.*
BATTERY + VERB die, give out (*esp. BrE*), go dead, run down, run out ◇ *After about six hours, the ~ will run down.*
BATTERY + NOUN power | life ◇ *With our product you get longer ~ life.* | failure | compartment ◇ *The ~ compartment is at the back of the unit.* | charger, recharger | pack ◇ *The lights have rechargeable ~ packs.* | acid

PHRASES **battery-operated, battery-powered** ◇ *a small battery-powered car*

2 large group of similar things

ADJ. **full, whole**
PREP. **~ of** ◇ *I had to answer a whole ~ of questions.*
PHRASES **a ~ of tests**

3 number of large guns

ADJ. **artillery, gun, howitzer** (*esp. AmE*) | **anti-aircraft**

battle *noun*

1 between armies

ADJ. **bloody, fierce** | **intense, pitched** ◇ *The two armies fought a pitched ~ on the plain.* | **climactic, decisive, final** ◇ *Iwo Jima was for many the climactic ~ of World War II.* | **epic, famous, great, historic, important, major** | **land, naval, sea** | **coming, upcoming** (*AmE*) ◇ *The squadron was getting ready for the coming ~.*
VERB + BATTLE **fight** | **win** | **lose** | **do, enter, give, go into, join, wage** ◇ *Charles V refused to give ~.* ◇ *The two armies joined ~.* | **send sb into** ◇ *Many young men were sent into ~ without proper training.* | **survive**
BATTLE + VERB **begin, ensue, take place** | **rage** | **continue, unfold** ◇ *The leaders anxiously watched the ~ unfold.* | **be over, end**
PREP. **at a/the ~** ◇ *Napoleon was defeated at the Battle of Waterloo.* | **in (a/the) ~** ◇ *He died in ~.*

2 violent fight between two groups

ADJ. **fierce** | **pitched** | **running** | **gun** | **turf** (*esp. AmE*) ◇ *A turf ~ among competing drug cartels has claimed several lives.*
VERB + BATTLE **fight**
BATTLE + VERB **erupt**
PREP. **~ against** ◇ *Police fought a pitched ~ against demonstrators.* | **~ between** ◇ *a gun ~ between police and drug smugglers* | **~ with** ◇ *Scores of people have been hurt in running ~s with police.*

3 struggle

ADJ. **bitter, fierce, heated, intense, tough** ◇ *a heated ~ between the oil industry and environmentalists* | **real** ◇ *There's now a real ~ at the top of the First Division.* | **constant, continuing, epic, long, long-running, ongoing, prolonged, running** ◇ *The college president fought a running ~ with the editors of the student newspaper.* | **coming, upcoming** (*AmE*) ◇ *The upcoming political ~ could be for the allegiance of the young.* | **losing, uphill** ◇ *We seem to be fighting a losing ~.* | **successful** | **court, custody, legal**
VERB + BATTLE **do, engage in, fight** ◇ *Are you prepared to do ~ with your insurance company over the claim?* | **be engaged in** | **face** | **win** | **lose** | **end** ◇ *She saw a way to end the prolonged legal ~.*
BATTLE + VERB **rage** ◇ *A policy ~ is raging in Washington.* | **begin, ensue** ◇ *A ten-month legal ~ ensued.* | **be brewing, be looming, loom** ◇ *A ~ is brewing between ecologists and big business.* | **be over, end**
PREP. **~ against** ◇ *his long ~ against cancer* | **~ between** ◇ *a fierce ~ between developers and the local community* | **~ for** ◇ *the ~ for human rights* | **~ over** ◇ *The government now faces a new ~ over tax increases.* | **~ with** ◇ *They are engaged in a long-running legal ~ with their competitors.*
PHRASES **a ~ of ideas, a ~ of words** | **a ~ of wills, a ~ of wits** | **a ~ royal** (= a major battle in which all available forces take part) | **fight your own ~s** ◇ *My parents believed in leaving me to fight my own ~s.* | **pick your ~s** (= decide which things are worth fighting or disagreeing about) ◇ *As a parent, you have to pick your ~s.*

battle *verb*

ADV. **ferociously, fiercely, hard** | **bravely, gamely, valiantly** ◇ *The child ~d bravely for her life.* | **in vain, unsuccessfully** ◇ *Doctors ~d in vain to save his life.* | **constantly** | **away** ◇ *We'll keep battling away and hope that the goals start to come.*
PREP. **against** ◇ *Rescuers ~d against torrential rain and high winds.* | **for** ◇ *factions battling for control of the party* | **over** ◇ *Residents are battling over plans for a new airport runway.*

| **through** ◇ *We ~d through the snowstorm.* | **with** ◇ *Riot police ~d with 4 000 students.* ◇ *He ~d with cancer for many months.*
PHRASES **~ it out** ◇ *Competitors ~d it out against the clock.* | **~ your way** ◇ *He ~d his way to the bar.*

bay *noun*

1 part of a coast

ADJ. **sheltered** | **shallow** | **sandy** (*esp. BrE*)
VERB + BAY **overlook** ◇ *apartments overlooking the ~*
PREP. **across the ~** ◇ *Lights twinkled across the ~.*

2 area used for a particular purpose

ADJ. **cargo, docking, hangar, landing, loading, shuttle** | **disabled, parking** (*both BrE*) | **sick**

beach *noun*

ADJ. **beautiful, fine** (*esp. BrE*), **lovely** | **palm-fringed** (*esp. BrE*), **sun-drenched** (*esp. BrE*), **sun-kissed** (*esp. BrE*), **sunny, tropical** | **golden, sandy, white, white-sand** | **pebble, rocky, shingle** (*BrE*) | **bathing, pleasure** (*both esp. BrE*) | **deserted, empty, private, secluded** | **pristine, unspoiled** ◇ *The island group has over 230 miles of pristine tropical ~es.* | **nude** (*esp. AmE*), **nudist** (*esp. BrE*)
VERB + BEACH **overlook** ◇ *They sat on a grassy hill overlooking the ~.*
BEACH + VERB **stretch** ◇ *a beautiful golden ~ stretching for miles*
BEACH + NOUN **towel, umbrella** | **house, hut** | **volleyball** | **holiday** (*BrE*), **vacation** (*AmE*) | **resort**
PREP. **along a/the ~** ◇ *He walked along the ~.* | **at a/the ~** ◇ *They met at the ~.* | **on a/the ~** ◇ *She lay on the ~ and read her book.*

bead *noun*

1 small piece of glass, wood, etc.

ADJ. **amber, glass, wooden, etc.** | **prayer, rosary** | **worry**
... OF BEADS **strand, string** ◇ *a string of wooden ~s*
VERB + BEAD **wear** | **string, thread** ◇ *She threaded the ~s carefully.*
BEAD + VERB **hang** ◇ *A strand of coral ~s hung around her neck.*
BEAD + NOUN **bracelet, necklace** | **curtain**

2 small drop of liquid

PHRASES **a ~ of moisture, perspiration, sweat, etc.**

beak *noun*

ADJ. **short, small** | **large, long** | **curved, hooked, pointed, sharp** | **powerful**
VERB + BEAK **open** | **close**

beam *noun*

1 ray of light

ADJ. **light** | **bright, intense, powerful** | **narrow, thin** | **flashlight** (*AmE*), **searchlight, torch** (*BrE*) | **electron, infrared, laser, X-ray** | **full** (*BrE*), **high** (*AmE*) ◇ *a car with its headlights on full ~* ◇ *a car with its high ~s on* | **dipped** (*BrE*), **low** (*AmE*)
VERB + BEAM **emit, fire, shoot** | **direct, focus, point, send, shine** ◇ *They focus a high-powered X-ray ~ on the affected area.* | **deflect, reflect** | **catch sb/sth in** ◇ *He was suddenly caught in the full ~ of a searchlight.*
BEAM + VERB **shine** | **illuminate sth, light sth up**
PREP. **~ from** ◇ *the ~ from the lighthouse* | **~ of** ◇ *A ~ of sunlight shone in through the window.*

2 long piece of wood/metal

ADJ. **timber** (*esp. BrE*), **wooden** | **oak** | **iron, metal, steel** | **old, original** (*esp. BrE*) ◇ *a cottage with original ~s and a thatched roof* | **exposed** ◇ *an old house with exposed oak ~s* | **horizontal, vertical**
BEAM + VERB **support sth**

beam *verb*

ADV. **broadly** ◊ *He ~ed broadly at them, clearly very pleased to see them.* | **positively** ◊ *She positively ~ed with satisfaction.* | **brightly, happily, proudly**
PREP. **at** ◊ *She ~ed happily at Maxim.* | **with** ◊ *His face ~ed with pleasure.*

bean *noun*

1 vegetable

ADJ. **broad** (*esp. BrE*), **butter** (*esp. BrE*), **chilli** (*BrE*), **fava** (*AmE*), **French** (*BrE*), **garbanzo** (*AmE*), **green, haricot** (*BrE*), **kidney, mung, navy** (*AmE*), **pinto, red** (*AmE*), **runner** (*esp. BrE*), **soy** (*AmE*), **soya** (*BrE*), **string** | **canned, dried, refried** | **baked** ◊ *baked ~s on toast* (*BrE*)
VERB + BEAN **plant** | **grow** ◊ *She grows her own broad ~s.* | **drain** | **soak** ◊ *If using dried ~s, soak them overnight first.*
BEAN + NOUN **curd** | **sprout**
→ Special page at FOOD

2 seed of other plants

ADJ. **castor, cocoa, coffee, vanilla**
VERB + BEAN **roast** | **grind**

bear *verb*

1 accept/deal with sth

VERB + BEAR **be able to, can** ◊ *Don't leave me alone. I wouldn't be able to ~ it.* ◊ *How can you ~ this awful noise?* | **be unable to, cannot** | **can hardly, can scarcely** ◊ *We could hardly ~ to be outdoors in the blinding sunlight.*

2 be responsible for sth

VERB + BEAR **have to, must** ◊ *Do parents have to ~ the whole cost of tuition?* ◊ *You must ~ at least some responsibility for what has happened.*

PHR V **bear on/upon sb/sth**
ADV. **heavily** ◊ *The burden of the tax bore most heavily on the poor.* | **directly** ◊ *information not ~ing directly on (= not directly relevant to) his argument*

bearable *adj.*

VERBS **be** | **become** | **make sth** ◊ *The camaraderie among fellow employees made the tedious work just ~.* | **find sth** ◊ *He found the dullness of his work hardly ~.*
ADV. **almost** | **quite, somewhat** (*AmE*) | **just**
PREP. **for** ◊ *The money made life more ~ for her.*

beard *noun*

ADJ. **bushy, flowing, full, shaggy** | **neat, neatly clipped, neatly trimmed, trim** | **patchy, scraggly** (*AmE*), **scruffy, straggly** (*BrE*), **unkempt, wispy** | **goatee** (*esp. BrE*) (usually just *goatee* in *AmE*) | **pointed** | **ginger** (*BrE*), **grey/gray, reddish, white, etc.** | **greying/graying, grizzled** | **fake, false** (*esp. BrE*)
VERB + BEARD **grow** | **have, sport, wear** ◊ *He sported a pointed ~.* | **clip, cut, trim** | **shave, shave off** | **pull, pull at, rub, scratch, stroke, tug, tug at** ◊ *Jim stroked his ~ reflectively.*
BEARD + VERB **grow** ◊ *My beard's grown a lot.* | **be streaked with sth** ◊ *His ~ is streaked with white.*
BEARD + NOUN **growth, stubble** ◊ *He had two days' ~ growth.*
PREP. **with a/the ~** ◊ *She's scared of men with ~s.*
PHRASES **a three-day, etc. growth of ~** | **a three-day-old, etc. ~**

bearing *noun*

1 way in which sth is related

ADJ. **direct, important, significant** ◊ *The rise in interest rates had a direct ~ on the company's profits.*
VERB + BEARING **have**
PREP. **~ on**
PHRASES **have little ~ on sth, have no ~ on sth** ◊ *You are describing ideal conditions that have little ~ on the real world.*

2 direction/position

ADJ. **compass**
VERB + BEARING **check** ◊ *He checked his ~s on the map in the car.* | **find, gain, get** ◊ *Everything was in darkness and it was difficult to get my ~s.* | **keep** ◊ *Keeping your ~s in a sandstorm is impossible.* | **regain** ◊ *He took a moment to regain his ~s.* | **lose** ◊ *She lost her ~s in the thick forest.*
PHRASES **take a (compass) ~ on sth** ◊ *Take a compass ~ on that mountain.*

beast *noun* animal

ADJ. **ferocious, ravenous, savage, snarling, wild** ◊ *Savage ~s once roamed these forests.* | **fearsome, foul** (*literary*), **hideous, monstrous** ◊ *The princess came face-to-face with a hideous ~.* | **exotic, fantastic, legendary, mythical, rare, strange** ◊ *paintings of mythical ~s* | **prehistoric** ◊ *the fossilized skeletons of prehistoric ~s* | **great, huge, magnificent, mighty** | **winged** ◊ *Legend had it he flew through the air on a winged ~.*
PHRASES **a ~ of burden, a ~ of prey**

beat *noun*

1 rhythm

ADJ. **regular, rhythmic, steady** | **pounding** | **disco, funky, hip-hop, techno, etc.** ◊ *He chants his lyrics over an infectious disco ~.* | **drum** (usually *drumbeat*) | **heart** (usually *heartbeat*) | **hoof**
VERB + BEAT **clap to, dance to, sway to** ◊ *They danced to the rhythmic ~ of the music.* | **feel** ◊ *She felt the ~ of his heart.* | **hear** ◊ *We heard the ~ of distant drums.* | **count** ◊ *Count four ~s and then start singing.*
PHRASES **two, three, four, etc. ~s to the bar** (*BrE*) ◊ *The piece has four ~s to the bar/measure.* | **sb's heart misses a ~, sb's heart skips a ~** (= sb feels very nervous) ◊ *As I opened the letter, my heart missed a ~.*

2 of a police officer

VERB + BEAT **pound, walk** (both *BrE*) ◊ *We have two officers walking the ~ after midnight.*
PREP. **on the ~** ◊ *officers on the ~*

beat *verb*

1 in sports, business, politics, etc.

ADV. **comfortably** (*BrE*), **comprehensively** (*BrE*), **convincingly** (*esp. BrE*), **easily, handily** (*AmE*), **hands down, soundly** ◊ *He ~ her hands down.* | **consistently** ◊ *a higher-rated player who consistently ~ her* | **narrowly** ◊ *He was narrowly beaten by his opponent.*
PREP. **at** ◊ *She ~ him at chess.* | **by** ◊ *I ~ her by just three points.*
PHRASES **~ sb into second, third, etc. place** ◊ *He was beaten into second place by the American.*

2 hit sb

ADV. **badly, brutally, mercilessly, savagely, severely, soundly, violently** | **constantly, repeatedly, routinely** ◊ *His stepfather repeatedly ~ his mother.*
PREP. **with** ◊ *She was beaten with a metal bar.*
PHRASES **~ sb about the head** (*BrE*), **~ sb over the head** ◊ *He had been beaten over the head with a rock.* | **~ sb to death** | **~ sb unconscious**

3 of heart/wings

ADV. **fast, frantically, furiously, painfully, rapidly, wildly** ◊ *I could feel my heart ~ing wildly.* | **loudly**

4 mix

ADV. **thoroughly, well** ◊ *Beat the mixture well, until it is light and creamy.* | **lightly** ◊ *Add three eggs, lightly beaten.*

beating *noun*

ADJ. **brutal, savage, severe, terrible, vicious**
VERB + BEATING **get, receive, suffer, take** ◊ *The team took a terrible ~.* | **administer, give sb/sth** ◊ *They caught him and gave him a violent ~.*

beautiful adj.

VERBS **be, feel, look, seem, sound** | **become, grow** | **make sb/sth** ◇ *We did all we could to make the room ~.* | **find sb/sth** ◇ *He found her exquisitely ~.* | **be considered** ◇ *She was never considered ~ at school.*

ADV. **extremely, fairly, very, etc.** | **exceptionally, extraordinarily, outstandingly, really, remarkably, supremely** (*esp. BrE*), **truly, very** | **absolutely, perfectly, quite, utterly** | **just, simply** ◇ *'They're just ~,' breathed Jo, when she saw the earrings.* | **almost** ◇ *I remember her as pretty, almost ~.* | **amazingly, astonishingly, breathtakingly, impossibly, incredibly, spectacularly, staggeringly, startlingly, strikingly, stunningly, unbelievably** | **naturally** ◇ *She didn't need make-up. She was naturally ~.* | **uniquely** | **exquisitely** | **serenely** | **classically, conventionally** ◇ *Her features were classically ~, with perfectly structured high cheekbones.* | **achingly, eerily, hauntingly, heartbreakingly, painfully, strangely** ◇ *a hauntingly ~ melody*

beauty noun

1 quality of being beautiful

ADJ. **breathtaking, exquisite, great, majestic, outstanding** (*esp. BrE*), **sheer, stunning** ◇ *an area of breathtaking ~* | **classical** ◇ *the classical ~ of her face* | **timeless, unspoiled** ◇ *the timeless ~ of this ancient landscape* | **stark** ◇ *There is a stark ~ to the desert terrain.* | **ethereal** ◇ *They were captivated by the ethereal ~ of the music.* | **natural** | **feminine** ◇ *Her art challenges conventions of feminine ~.* | **aesthetic, physical** | **inner** ◇ *The film argues that inner ~, not physical appearance, is most important.* | **scenic**

VERB + BEAUTY **admire, appreciate, enjoy** ◇ *They took a walk, enjoying the ~ of the landscape.* | **enhance** | **preserve** | **mar** ◇ *Advertising hoardings mar the ~ of the countryside.* | **capture, convey** ◇ *The film-maker magnificently captures the ~ of the changing seasons.* | **be awed by, be captivated by, be enchanted by, be entranced by, be mesmerized by, be transfixed by**

BEAUTY + VERB **amaze sb, overwhelm sb** ◇ *The ~ of the city amazed her.* | **last** | **fade** ◇ *Her ~ faded as she got older.*

BEAUTY + NOUN **competition** (*esp. BrE*), **contest, pageant** (*AmE*) ◇ *She was a contestant in the Miss World ~ pageant.* | **contestant, queen** | **parlour/parlor, salon** ◇ *She works in a ~ salon.* | **makeover** (*esp. AmE*), **product, regime** (*BrE*), **regimen** (*AmE*), **routine, treatment** | **rest** (*AmE*), **sleep** | **spot**

2 beautiful person or thing

ADJ. **great** ◇ *She was known as a great ~ in her time.* | **blonde, dark-haired, etc.** ◇ *He met a blonde ~ named Cindy.* | **exotic** ◇ *an exotic ~ with raven hair* | **radiant** ◇ *She was still a radiant ~.* | **absolute, real** ◇ *My new car's a real ~!* | **little** ◇ *Isn't she a little ~?*

bed noun

1 piece of furniture for sleeping on

ADJ. **single** | **double** | **king-size, king-sized** | **queen-size, queen-sized** (*both AmE*) | **twin** | **bunk, camp** (*esp. BrE*), **canopy** (*esp. AmE*), **feather, four-poster, hospital, sofa** ◇ *I slept in the bottom bunk of a set of bunk ~s.* | **comfortable, comfy** (*informal*), **cosy/cozy, soft, warm** | **unmade** ◇ *a messy room, with an unmade ~ and clothes on the floor* | **empty** ◇ *He came home to find an empty ~.* | **makeshift** (*esp. AmE*) ◇ *He slept on a makeshift ~ of blankets and cushions.* | **marital, marriage** | **tanning** (*esp. AmE*)

VERB + BED **make, make up** | **strip** ◇ *Please strip the ~s and put the sheets in the washing machine.* | **climb into, crawl into, get into, go to, tumble into** ◇ *She crawled into ~ exhausted.* | **climb out of, get out of, leap out of** | **lie (down) on, lie in, sit on** ◇ *He lay in ~, reading his book.* ◇ *Elizabeth was sitting on her ~ writing a letter.* | **put sb to, tuck sb up in** ◇ *It's your turn to put the children to ~.* | **occupy, sleep in** ◇ *All the hospital ~s were occupied.* | **share** ◇ *He and his brother had to share a ~.* | **wet** ◇ *Don't punish a child who wets the ~.*

BED + NOUN **clothes, linen** (usually *bedclothes, bedlinen*) | **sheet** | **sore** (usually *bedsore*)

PREP. **in ~** ◇ *I like to be in ~ before 11 o'clock.* | **out of ~** ◇ *Are you out of ~ yet?*

PHRASES **~ and breakfast** ◇ *We stayed at a comfortable ~ and breakfast.* ◇ *Bed and breakfast accommodation is available.* (*BrE*) | **the edge of the ~, the foot of the ~, the head of the ~, the side of the ~** | **get sb into ~** (= persuade sb to have sex) | **go to ~ with sb** (= have sex with sb) (*esp. BrE*) | **take to your ~** (= go to bed because you are ill) (*old-fashioned*) | **time for ~** ◇ *Come on, children, it's time for ~.*

2 piece of ground for growing flowers, vegetables, etc.

ADJ. **flower, rose, strawberry, etc.** | **garden, planting** (*both AmE*) | **raised**

PREP. **~ of** ◇ *ornamental ~s of roses*

bedroom noun

ADJ. **comfortable, cosy/cozy** | **big, large, spacious** | **little, small, tiny** | **double, single, twin** | **en suite** (*BrE*) | **main, master, principal** ◇ *an en suite master ~* (*BrE*) | **study** (*BrE*) | **attic, back, front, loft** (*esp. AmE*), **upstairs** | **downstairs, ground-floor** (*BrE*) | **first-floor, second-floor, etc.** | **guest, spare** ◇ *I told him he could sleep in the spare ~.* | **separate** ◇ *All the children had separate ~s.* | **hotel**

VERB + BEDROOM **share** ◇ *I used to share a ~ with my brother.* | **convert** ◇ *They converted the spare ~ into an office.* | **decorate, furnish, paint, redecorate**

BEDROOM + NOUN **closet** (*AmE*), **furniture, mirror, suite** | **door, floor, wall, window** | **slippers** | **scene** ◇ *The actress refused to appear naked in the ~ scenes.*

PREP. **around a/the ~** ◇ *There were dirty clothes strewn around the ~.* | **in a/the ~**

bedside noun

VERB + BEDSIDE **be called to, be summoned to** ◇ *The doctor was summoned to his ~.* | **stay at, stay by** | **leave** ◇ *His wife never left his ~.*

BEDSIDE + NOUN **cabinet, lamp, light, table** (*esp. BrE*)

PREP. **at sb's/the ~, by sb's/the ~** ◇ *I like to keep a glass of water by my ~.*

bedtime noun

ADJ. **normal, regular** (*esp. AmE*), **usual**

BEDTIME + NOUN **ritual, routine** | **reading, story** | **prayer** (*esp. AmE*) | **drink, snack** (*AmE*)

PREP. **at ~, before sb's ~, past sb's ~** ◇ *It's well past my normal ~.*

bee noun

1 flying insect

ADJ. **bumble** (usually *bumblebee*), **honey, killer** | **queen, worker** | **angry** ◇ *He was stung by thousands of angry ~s.* … OF BEES **swarm**

VERB + BEE **attract** ◇ *Lavender attracts ~s.*

BEE + VERB **buzz, hum** ◇ *A ~ buzzed in my ear.* | **sting (sb)** | **fly, swarm** ◇ *The ~s swarmed around the hive.* | **pollinate sth** ◇ *Butterflies, flies, and ~s pollinate flowers.*

BEE + NOUN **hive** (usually *beehive*) | **sting** | **keeper** (usually *bee-keeper*)

2 (*AmE*) meeting in a group

ADJ. **quilting, spelling**

beef noun

ADJ. **fresh** | **lean** | **fatty** | **tender** | **tough** | **choice** (*AmE*), **prime** | **organic** | **medium, rare, well done** ◇ *'How would you like your ~?' 'Rare, please.'* | **roast** | **ground** (*AmE*), **minced** (*esp. BrE*), **shredded, sliced** | **chipped** (*AmE*), **corned, dried, salt, salted** … OF BEEF **bit, piece, slice** | **fillet, joint, rib** (*all esp. BrE*) | **side** | **cut** ◇ *cuts of ~ that are suitable for roasting*

VERB + BEEF **eat** | **boil, braise, cook, fry, roast, stew** (*esp. BrE*) | **carve, cut** ◇ *Dad stood up to carve the ~.* | **produce, sell**

BEEF + NOUN **broth** (*esp. AmE*), **jerky** (*esp. AmE*), **stew, stock, stroganoff** | **brisket** (*AmE*), **burger** (usually *beefburger*), patty (*esp. AmE*), steak (usually *beefsteak*), tenderloin | cattle, cow | farmer (*esp. BrE*) | industry, production

beer noun

ADJ. **good, great, quality** | **cheap** | **strong** | **alcohol-free, light, low-alcohol, no-alcohol, non-alcoholic** | **cold, ice-cold** | **warm** | **black, blonde, dark** | **wheat** | **craft, specialty** (*both AmE*) | **domestic** (*esp. AmE*), **imported, local** | **bottled, cask** (*BrE*), **draught/draft, keg** | **flat** (= that the gas has gone out of) | **stale** ◇ *The bar smelled of stale ~.* | **home-brewed** | **ginger, root** (*AmE*)
... OF BEER **pint** (*BrE*) ◇ *I ordered half a pint of ~ with my sandwich.* | **barrel, bottle, can, keg, pitcher** (*AmE*) | **cup** (*AmE*), **glass, mug** (*AmE*), **tankard** | **case** (*esp. AmE*), **crate** (*esp. BrE*), **six-pack**
VERB + BEER **drink** ◇ *Do you drink ~?* | **have** ◇ *Will you have a ~?* | **get, grab** (*esp. AmE*) | **down** ◇ *He downed his ~ in one go.* | **chug** (*AmE*), **gulp, gulp at, guzzle, sip, sip at, swig** | **take a gulp of, take a sip of, take a swig of** | **draw, pour** (**sb**) ◇ *This ~ should be drawn slowly.* ◇ *He poured us all a ~.* | **spill** | **buy** (**sb**), **order** ◇ *I saw him at the bar ordering a ~.* | **sell, serve** | **go for** (*BrE*), **go out for** ◇ *I'm going (out) for a ~ with Carl tonight.* | **brew** | **chill**
BEER + VERB **chill** ◇ *I have some ~s chilling in the cooler.* | **go flat** | **flow** (*figurative*) ◇ *The ~ flowed freely after the game.* | **spill** ◇ *He slammed his glass down and the ~ spilled over the sides.*
BEER + NOUN **drinker, lover** | **maker** | **barrel, bottle, can, crate** (*esp. BrE*), **glass, keg, mug, stein** (*AmE*), **tankard** | **coaster** (*AmE*), **mat** (*BrE*) | **cooler** (*esp. AmE*) | **festival** | **consumption, production, sales** | **ad** (*informal*), **advertisement, commercial** | **cellar** (*BrE*), **garden** ◇ *Children are welcome in the ~ garden.* | **belly, gut** (*both informal*) ◇ *He's only twenty but he already has a ~ belly.* | **money** ◇ *Singing in bars keeps him in ~ money* (= earns him a little money).

beg verb

1 ask sb for food, money, etc.

VERB + BEG **be forced to, have to**
PREP. **for** ◇ *They were forced to ~ for food.* | **from** ◇ *He had to ~ food from passers-by.*

2 ask for sth with great emotion

ADV. **almost, practically** ◇ *In the end they almost begged him to take the job.* | **humbly** ◇ *We humbly ~ you to show mercy.* | **silently** ◇ *Don't leave me, he begged her silently.* | **desperately, frantically**
VERB + BEG **be forced to, have to**
PREP. **for** ◇ *We went to him to ~ for forgiveness.* | **of** (*formal*) ◇ *Do not do that, I ~ of you.*

begin verb

ADV. **again, all over again, anew** (*esp. AmE*) ◇ *Once it has finished, the DVD automatically ~s again.* ◇ *We had to ~ all over again.* | **immediately, quickly, suddenly** ◇ *Research into the problem began immediately.* | **gradually, slowly** ◇ *He took a deep breath and slowly began.* | **shortly, soon** ◇ *The concert will ~ shortly.* | **finally** ◇ *Work on the building finally began in the summer.*
VERB + BEGIN **be due to, be expected to, be scheduled to** ◇ *The entertainment was due to ~ at 8.30.* | **be ready to** | **be about to, be going to** ◇ *A new life was about to ~ for him.*
PREP. **by** ◇ *Let's ~ by writing down a few ideas.* | **with** ◇ *We will ~ with a brief discussion of the problems.* ◇ *Can you think of a word beginning with V?*
PHRASES **~ at the beginning** ◇ *OK, let's just ~ at the beginning.* | **be just beginning, be only beginning** ◇ *Their troubles are only beginning.*

beginner noun

ADJ. **absolute, complete** | **advanced**
VERB + BEGINNER **teach** ◇ *The driving course teaches ~s the basics.*

beginning noun

ADJ. **new** ◇ *She spoke of a new ~ for the nation.* | **auspicious, hopeful, promising** ◇ *It was an auspicious ~ to his long career.* | **inauspicious, unpromising** (*esp. BrE*)
VERB + BEGINNING **herald, mark, represent, signal, signify, spell, symbolize** ◇ *This invention marked the ~ of the modern age.* | **see, witness** ◇ *2001 saw the ~ of a period of rapid growth.* | **trace** ◇ *a custom that traces its ~s to the 15th century*
PREP. **at the ~** (**of sth**) ◇ *I'm paid at the ~ of each month.* | **from the ~** ◇ *Tell me the whole story, right from the ~.* | **in the ~** ◇ *In the ~ I found the course very difficult.*
PHRASES **the ~ of the end** ◇ *That day was the ~ of the end of our friendship.* | **early ~s, first ~s** ◇ *The society had its early ~s in discussion groups.* | **from ~ to end** ◇ *The play was nonsense from ~ to end.* | **from humble ~s, from modest ~s, from small ~s** ◇ *From these small ~s it grew into the vast company we know today.* | **be just the ~, be only the ~** ◇ *These changes are just the ~: much more is to come.* | **the very ~** ◇ *I disliked her from the very ~.*

behave verb

ADV. **impeccably** (*esp. BrE*), **perfectly, well** | **honourably/honorably** | **aggressively, badly, disgracefully** (*esp. BrE*), **outrageously** (*esp. BrE*) ◇ *Children who ~ badly are rejecting adult values.* | **appropriately, correctly, properly, responsibly** ◇ *The officers investigated whether soldiers had ~d correctly.* | **improperly** (*esp. BrE*), **inappropriately, irresponsibly** | **rationally, reasonably** | **irrationally, stupidly, unreasonably** (*esp. BrE*) | **normally** | **erratically, oddly, strangely, suspiciously** (*esp. BrE*) | **differently** ◇ *I know I should have ~d differently.* | **similarly** ◇ *Humans and machines sometimes ~ similarly.* | **accordingly** ◇ *Children, if they are used to being treated with respect, will ~ accordingly.* | **naturally** ◇ *the freedom to ~ naturally*
PREP. **according to** ◇ *People ~ according to their own understanding of situations.* | **as if, as though** ◇ *He ~d as if nothing out of the ordinary had happened.* | **like** ◇ *Stop behaving like a three-year-old!* | **towards/toward** ◇ *He had always ~d in a friendly manner towards/toward us.*

behaviour (*BrE*) (*AmE* behavior) noun

ADJ. **exemplary, good** ◇ *He had his jail term cut for good ~.* | **acceptable** | **normal** | **bizarre, strange, suspicious** ◇ *a report of suspicious ~* | **antisocial, bad, inappropriate, unacceptable, undesirable** | **addictive, delinquent, deviant, problem** ◇ *Teachers can't always respond effectively to problem ~.* | **abusive, aggressive, criminal, disruptive, violent** | **high-risk, impulsive, risk-taking, risky, self-destructive, suicidal** | **adolescent, animal, human, sexual, social** ◇ *the study of human behavior* | **courtship, maternal, mating, parental, parenting, territorial** ◇ *Some birds display courtship behavior throughout the year.*
VERB + BEHAVIOUR/BEHAVIOR **affect, control, influence, regulate, shape** ◇ *Parents can influence the ~ of their children.* | **alter, change, modify** | **display, exhibit, show** ◇ *Animals in zoos often display disturbed ~.* | **analyse/analyze, examine, observe, study** ◇ *I know you were upset, but that doesn't excuse your ~.* | **mimic, model** | **reinforce, reward** ◇ *Parents should reinforce good ~.*
BEHAVIOUR/BEHAVIOR + NOUN **pattern** | **modification** | **issues, problem** | **disorder, therapy** (*both esp. AmE*)
PREP. **~ towards/toward** ◇ *his ~ towards/toward his parents*
PHRASES **~ and attitudes** ◇ *a new study looking at the ~ and attitudes of young men* | **be on your best ~** (= to behave very well in order to impress sb) | **a code of ~** | **a pattern of ~** | **standards of ~**

being noun

1 living creature

ADJ. **human, living** ◇ *the rights of all human ~s* | **intelligent, rational, sentient** (*formal*) ◇ *I work on the assumption that people are rational ~s.* | **alien, magical, strange, supernatural** | **divine, supreme**

VERB + BEING **be brought into, come into** (= to start to exist) ◇ *How do you think the world came into ~?*

belief *noun*

ADJ. **absolute, deep-seated, deeply held, fervent, firm, passionate, profound, strong, strongly held, unshakable, unwavering** | **genuine, sincere** ◇ *She was strict with her children in the genuine ~ that it was the right thing to do.* | **common, commonly held, general, popular, widely held, widespread** | **mutual, shared** ◇ *They had a shared ~ in the power of education.* | **growing** | **long-held, long-standing** | **basic, central, core, fundamental** ◇ *the basic ~s of Christianity* | **personal, private** ◇ *I think the rights and wrongs of eating meat are a matter of personal ~.* | **rational, reasonable** | **irrational, superstitious** | **paranormal, supernatural** | **instinctive** | **naive** | **strange** | **conflicting, contradictory** | **erroneous, false, misguided, mistaken** ◇ *I took the job in the mistaken ~ that I would be able to stay in Philadelphia.* | **ancient, folk, traditional** ◇ *The people still follow their traditional ~s.* | **orthodox** | **cultural, moral, philosophical, political, religious, spiritual, theological** ◇ *They were persecuted for their religious ~s.* | **Catholic, Christian, pagan, etc.**
... OF BELIEFS **set, system** ◇ *Each religion has its set of ~s.*
VERB + BELIEF **espouse, have, hold** ◇ *I have very firm ~s about moral issues.* | **share** ◇ *He shared his father's ~ that people should work hard for their living.* | **adhere to, cherish, cling to, follow, hold on to, stick to** ◇ *She clung to the ~ that he would come back to her.* ◇ *The party must stick to its ~s.* | **abandon, give up, renounce** | **lose** ◇ *She has lost her ~ in God.* | **affirm, assert, declare, express, state** | **emphasize, stress** | **encourage, foster, fuel** ◇ *The exam results encouraged the ~ that he was a good teacher.* | **confirm, justify, reaffirm, reinforce, strengthen, support, validate** ◇ *This latest evidence strengthens our ~ that the government is doing the right thing.* | **reconcile** ◇ *an attempt to reconcile apparently opposite ~s* | **contradict** | **challenge, question, shake, shatter, undermine, weaken** ◇ *The child's death shook her ~ in God.* | **respect** ◇ *You must respect other people's ~s.* | **impose** ◇ *He tried to impose his ~s on other people.* | **beggar** (*esp. BrE*), **defy** ◇ *It defies ~ how things got this bad.*
BELIEF + VERB **persist** ◇ *Belief in the magical properties of this herb persisted down the centuries.*
BELIEF + NOUN **system**
PREP. **beyond ~** (= too great, difficult, etc. to be believed) ◇ *Dissatisfaction with the government has grown beyond ~.* ◇ *icy air that was cold beyond ~* | **in the ~ that** ◇ *She did it in the ~ that it would help her career.* | **~ about** ◇ *~s about the origin of the universe* | **~ among** ◇ *There is a ~ among young people that education is a waste of time.* | **~ in** ◇ *a ~ in God*
PHRASES **contrary to popular ~** (= in spite of what people think) ◇ *Contrary to popular ~, deserts are not always hot.*

believable *adj.*

VERBS **be, sound** | **find sth**
ADV. **very** ◇ *All the characters were very ~.* | **completely, entirely, totally** ◇ *Her character comes across as entirely ~.* | **hardly** ◇ *I find her story hardly ~.*

believe *verb*

ADV. **deeply, fervently, firmly, passionately, really** ◇ *He firmly ~d that he was right.* | **genuinely, honestly, sincerely, truly** | **completely, fully** | **seriously** (only used with negatives) ◇ *No one seriously ~s that this war will happen.* | **personally** ◇ *I personally ~ that it's important.* | **long** ◇ *I've long ~d that a good reputation is the most valuable asset you can have in business.* | **secretly** | **rightly** | **erroneously** (*formal*), **falsely, incorrectly, mistakenly, wrongly** | **foolishly, naively** | **otherwise** ◇ *Paul thinks he's happy, but his mother ~s otherwise.*
VERB + BELIEVE **cannot** ◇ *I couldn't ~ what I was hearing.* | **be hard to** ◇ *It's hard to ~ that this campaign has been going on for ten years.* | **give sb to** (*BrE*) ◇ *The boss gave me to ~ that we would be paid soon.* | **have reason to** ◇ *We have reason to ~ that the escaped prisoner may be hiding in this house.* | **be inclined to** ◇ *I'm inclined to ~ you.* | **lead sb to** ◇ *The ad led us to ~ that all prices had been cut.*
PHRASES **can hardly ~ sth, can scarcely ~ sth** | **not ~ a word of sth** ◇ *I didn't ~ a word of what he said.*

believer *noun*

1 sb who has religious faith
ADJ. **devout, genuine, true** | **religious** | **Christian, Muslim, etc.** | **fellow** | **new** | **ordinary** (*esp. AmE*)
2 sb who believes that sth is good
ADJ. **avid** (*esp. AmE*), **fervent, firm, great, passionate, staunch, strong** | **big, huge** (*both informal*)
PREP. **~ in** ◇ *I'm a firm ~ in the benefits of exercise.*

bell *noun*

1 hollow metal object that rings
ADJ. **church, temple** | **wedding** (*often figurative*) ◇ *Their friends could already hear wedding ~s* (= were sure they would get married). | **cow** (usually **cowbell**) | **sleigh** | **distant** | **brass, silver**
VERB + BELL **ring** | **hear**
BELL + VERB **chime, clang, jangle** (*esp. AmE*), **jingle** (*esp. AmE*), **peal, ring, ring out, sound, tinkle, toll** ◇ *The ~s on the harness tinkled softly.* ◇ *The church ~ tolled for the funeral.*
BELL + NOUN **tower** | **pull, rope** | **ringer, ringing** (usually **bell-ringer**, etc.)
PHRASES **a chime of ~s** ◇ *the faint chime of ~s* | **a peal of ~s** ◇ *She heard a peal of church ~s.* | **a sound of ~s** ◇ *The sound of ~s echoed across the valley.*
2 other object that rings
ADJ. **bicycle, door** (usually **doorbell**) | **dinner, lunch, school** | **second-period, third-period, etc.** (*AmE*) | **electric** | **alarm, warning** (*both often figurative*) ◇ *Alarm ~s were ringing inside Stuart's head.* | **closing, opening** | **final** | **dismissal** (*AmE*) | **late, tardy** (= to indicate that classes are about to start) (*both AmE*) | **loud, shrill**
VERB + BELL **press, ring, sound** | **answer** ◇ *She hurried to answer the doorbell.*
BELL + VERB **go, ring, sound** ◇ *The school ~ goes at three every afternoon.* | **signal sth** | **interrupt sb/sth**
BELL + NOUN **pull, push** (*BrE*)
PHRASES **saved by the ~** ◇ *Saved by the ~! I thought I'd have to sit here listening to you two argue forever.* | **~s and whistles** ◇ *The laptop has all the latest ~s and whistles* (= attractive extra features).

bellow *noun*

ADJ. **great, loud** | **angry**
VERB + BELLOW **give, let out** ◇ *She gave a great ~ of laughter.* | **hear**
PREP. **~ of**
PHRASES **a ~ of laughter, a ~ of rage**
→ Note at SOUND

belly *noun*

ADJ. **empty, full** | **flat** | **round** | **big, huge, large** | **fat, pot** ◇ *Since he turned 30 he's started to develop a pot ~.* | **bulging, protruding** | **bloated, distended, swollen** | **bare** | **beer** (= from drinking too much beer) | **pregnant** (*esp. AmE*)
VERB + BELLY **pat, rub, scratch** | **fill** ◇ *I filled my ~ with a sausage sandwich.* | **expose** ◇ *Kayla lifted up her shirt to expose her round ~.*
BELLY + VERB **bulge** | **hang** ◇ *He's so fat, his ~ hangs over his shorts.* | **swell**
PREP. **in sb's ~** ◇ *She felt the child in her ~ kick.*

belongings *noun*

ADJ. **personal** | **meagre/meager**
VERB + BELONGINGS **collect, collect together, collect up), gather, gather together, gather up), pack, pack up** ◇ *She collected up her personal ~ and left.* | **retrieve** ◇ *Kyle came*

back out to retrieve his ~. | **grab** ◇ *She grabbed her ~ and shoved them in her bag.* | **steal** | **lose** | **go through, look through, rifle through, search** ◇ *In her absence, someone had gone through her ~.* | **sort through** ◇ *He was trying to sort through his ~.*

beloved *adj.*

VERBS **be**
ADV. **dearly, much** ◇ *the death of his much ~ wife*
PREP. **by** ◇ *an area ~ by artists* | **of** ◇ *She ran one of the little cafes so ~ of tourists.*

belt *noun*

1 narrow piece of leather, etc. worn around the waist

ADJ. **narrow, wide** | **thick** | **leather** | **chain, studded** ◇ *a studded leather ~* | **matching** | **pants** (*AmE*), **trouser** (*BrE*) | **garter** (*AmE*), **suspender** (*BrE*) ◇ *She was wearing a garter ~ and stockings.* | **money, utility** (*esp. AmE*) | **ammo** (*informal, esp. AmE*), **ammunition, cartridge, gun** | **bomb, explosive, suicide** | **sword**
VERB + BELT **buckle, do up, fasten** | **unbuckle, undo, unfasten** | **tighten** | **loosen** | **adjust**
BELT + NOUN **buckle, loop** | **holster** | **clip**
→ Special page at CLOTHES

2 in a machine

ADJ. **conveyor, drive, fan, timing**

3 area of land

ADJ. **broad, wide** | **narrow, thin** | **central** | **coastal, mountain** | **corn, cotton, wheat** | **green** (= open land around a city where building is strictly controlled), **industrial** ◇ *New roads are cutting into the green ~.* | **rust** (= an area where industries have closed) | **Bible** (= where many people have strong Christian beliefs) (*in the US*) | **hurricane** | **radiation** ◇ *The space mission provided new data on the Earth's radiation ~s.* | **commuter, stockbroker** (*both BrE*)
PREP. **~ of** ◇ *a narrow ~ of trees*

bemused *adj.*

VERBS **be, look, seem, sound** | **become**
ADV. **a little, slightly, etc.** | **totally** (*BrE*) ◇ *Sarah looked totally ~.* | **quite** (*esp. BrE*), **rather, somewhat** ◇ *I was beginning to feel slightly ~.*
PREP. **by** ◇ *Connie was rather ~ by all the attention she was getting.*

bench *noun*

1 long seat

ADJ. **empty** | **long** | **narrow** | **hard** | **cushioned, padded** | **metal, stone, wood, wooden** | **garden, park** | **picnic** | **replacements', subs'** (*informal*), **substitutes'** (*all BrE, sports*) ◇ *They have several top players on the subs' ~.* | **piano** (*AmE*)
VERB + BENCH **sit (down) on**
BENCH + NOUN **seat**
PREP. **on a/the ~** ◇ *She often sleeps on park ~es.* ◇ *He's sick of spending every game on the ~* (= not playing).

2 (*BrE*) in Parliament

ADJ. **government, Opposition** | **Conservative, Labour, etc.** | **back, front** (Government ministers and the most important members of the Opposition sit on the *front benches*. *Backbench* MPs have no official position besides that of MP.)
VERB + BENCH **be on, sit on**
PREP. **from the … ~s** ◇ *There were cheers from the Labour ~es.* | **on the … ~s** ◇ *Some MPs on the government back ~es are starting to question the government's handling of the war.*

3 long narrow table that people work at

ADJ. **work** (usually *workbench*) | **carpenter's, lab** (*informal*), **laboratory** | **kitchen** (*esp. AmE*)
PREP. **at a/the ~** ◇ *He was working at his ~.*

bend *noun*

ADJ. **gentle, slight, wide** | **hairpin** (*BrE*), **sharp, tight** ◇ *Some of the hairpin ~s had Ruth clinging to her seat.* | **dangerous** | **blind** (*BrE*) ◇ *mountain roads with steep gradients and blind ~s* | **left-hand, right-hand** | **final, last, opening** (= in a race) ◇ *He had a winning lead off the final ~.*
... OF BENDS **series** ◇ *a series of dangerous ~s*
VERB + BEND **come around, come round** (*esp. BrE*), **negotiate, round, take, turn** ◇ *He slowed down to negotiate the ~.*
PREP. **around a/the ~, round a/the ~** (*esp. BrE*) ◇ *The car vanished around a ~.* | **into a/the ~** ◇ *I inched the car into the ~.* | **off a/the ~** ◇ *He came off the ~ in the lead.* | **on a/the ~** ◇ *Slow down on the tight ~s.* | **~ in** ◇ *a wide ~ in the river*

bend *verb*

ADV. **slightly** | **quickly, swiftly** | **slowly** | **back, backwards/backward, forward** | **down, over** ◇ *I bent down and tied my shoelace.* | **close, nearer** ◇ *Sarah bent close to him.* | **double** ◇ *I had to ~ double to get under the table.*
PREP. **at** ◇ *Avoid ~ing at the waist when lifting heavy objects.* | **towards/toward** ◇ *He came closer and bent towards/toward her.*

benefactor *noun*

ADJ. **generous** | **wealthy** | **great, major** | **anonymous, mysterious, mystery** | **private** | **public** ◇ *He was a great public ~ and gave land for building the sea wall.*
BENEFACTOR + VERB **donate sth, give sth** ◇ *A private ~ donated $20 000.*
PREP. **~ to** ◇ *She was a generous ~ to the library.*

beneficial *adj.*

VERBS **be, prove** ◇ *Some alternative treatments may prove highly ~.* | **consider sth**
ADV. **extremely, very** | **highly** | **entirely, wholly** | **especially, particularly** | **clearly** | **potentially** | **mutually** ◇ *The arrangement was mutually ~.* | **economically, environmentally, socially**
PREP. **for** ◇ *I think it would be ~ for each committee member to have a copy.* | **to** ◇ *Exercise is extremely ~ to health.*

benefit *noun*

1 advantage

ADJ. **considerable, enormous, great, huge, immense, major, real, significant, substantial, tremendous** ◇ *This could bring real ~s for teachers.* | **clear, obvious, tangible** | **positive** | **perceived** ◇ *Consumers choose organic meat for a number of reasons, including perceived health ~s.* | **apparent, supposed** | **proven** | **maximum** | **added, additional** ◇ *The method has many additional ~s.* | **mutual** ◇ *The different environmental groups could work together to their mutual ~.* | **direct, indirect** | **potential** | **unexpected** | **long-term, short-term** | **lasting** | **practical** | **public** | **personal** | **clinical, economic, educational, environmental, financial, material, nutritional, psychological, social, therapeutic** | **fitness, health**
VERB + BENEFIT **enjoy, experience, have** ◇ *The industry will be one of the first to enjoy the ~s of the recovery.* ◇ *children who have the ~ of a stable home background* | **derive, gain, get, obtain, reap, receive** ◇ *The company derived substantial ~ from the deal.* ◇ *I reaped the ~s of all my early training.* | **bring, confer, deliver, offer, produce, provide, yield** ◇ *The new factory will bring considerable ~s to the area.* ◇ *This deal will offer major ~s to industrialists and investors.* | **maximize** ◇ *If you want to maximize the ~s of blueberries, eat them raw.* | **highlight** | **extol, promote, tout** (*esp. AmE*) ◇ *a marketing campaign which promotes the cosmetic ~s of vitamin E* | **appreciate, recognize, see** ◇ *I can see the ~s that such games give children.* | **evaluate, weigh** ◇ *Weigh the ~s of hiring help before hiring new employees.* | **extend** ◇ *These ~s will now be extended to agency workers.* | **deny sb** ◇ *He had been denied the ~s of a good education.*
BENEFIT + VERB **accrue** ◇ *the ~s that accrue from a good education* | **arise from sth, result from sth** ◇ *A number of ~s*

better

arise from having a fitter body. | **outweigh sth** ◇ *The ~s easily outweigh the cost.*
PREP. **for sb's ~** ◇ *We shall do this for the ~ of the patients.* | **of ~ to** ◇ *This arrangement will be of great ~ to you both.* | **to sb's ~** ◇ *It will be to everyone's ~.* | **with the ~ of, without the ~ of** ◇ *They somehow manage to work without the ~ of modern technology.* | **~ for** ◇ *the ~s for companies* | **~ from** ◇ *the ~s from tourism* | **~ of** ◇ *the ~ of a steady income* | **~ to** ◇ *What are the ~s to investors?*

2 financial advantages given by a company, the government, etc.

ADJ. **fringe** (= extra things that an employer gives as well as a salary) ◇ *The fringe ~s include free health insurance.* | **tax** | **employee, retiree** (*both AmE*) | **domestic-partner** (*esp. AmE*)
VERB + BENEFIT **give** | **receive** | **extend** ◇ *These ~s will now be extended to agency workers.* | **deny sb** ◇ *Same-sex couples were denied the ~s given to married couples.*
BENEFIT + NOUN **plan** (*esp. AmE*) | **~s package**

3 (*BrE*) money

ADJ. **welfare** | **state** | **insurance** | **means-tested, universal** | **cash** | **generous** | **child, disability, health-care, housing, maternity, sickness, social-security** | **pension, retirement** | **jobless, unemployment**
... OF BENEFIT **amount, level**
VERB + BENEFIT **be eligible for, be entitled to, qualify for** | **claim** ◇ *You may be able to claim housing ~.* | **collect, draw, get, receive** ◇ *He receives unemployment ~.* | **be dependent on** | **lose** ◇ *She is worried that if she takes on a job she will lose her ~s.* | **cut, reduce, slash** ◇ *The government has cut unemployment ~.* | **increase**
BENEFIT + VERB **be paid** ◇ *Benefit is paid monthly.*
BENEFIT + NOUN **~s agency** | **office** | **payment** | **system** | **cut**
PREP. **on ~** ◇ *He's on social security ~.*

benefit *verb*

ADV. **considerably, enormously, greatly, immensely, really, significantly, substantially, tremendously** | **fully** | **clearly, obviously, undoubtedly** ◇ *The new law clearly ~s those earning the most money.* | **ultimately** | **equally** | **disproportionately** | **mainly, primarily** | **personally** | **directly, indirectly** ◇ *We ~ed directly from the reorganization.* | **economically, financially** ◇ *We both ~ed financially from the arrangement.*
PREP. **from**

benign *adj.*

VERBS **be, look, seem**
ADV. **fairly, rather, relatively** ◇ *The effects of this chemical are fairly ~.* | **seemingly** | **environmentally** ◇ *We are looking for an environmentally ~ alternative to bleach.*

bent *noun*

ADJ. **natural** | **artistic, intellectual, literary, philosophical, political, scientific**
VERB + BENT **have** ◇ *She has an artistic ~.* | **show** ◇ *He showed a literary ~ from a young age.*
PREP. **with ~** ◇ *a child with a scientific ~* | **~ for** ◇ *a natural ~ for languages*

bent *adj.*

VERBS **be, look** | **become, get** ◇ *The post got ~ in the crash.*
ADV. **slightly** ◇ *He stood with knees slightly ~.*
PHRASES **~ double** ◇ *The man shuffled back a few paces, ~ almost double.*

bequest *noun*

ADJ. **generous, large** ◇ *The library has received a generous ~ from a local businessman.* | **charitable**
VERB + BEQUEST **leave (sb), make (sb)** ◇ *In his will he made a substantial ~ to his wife.* | **receive**
PREP. **~ from** ◇ *a ~ from the late Jack Dawkins* | **~ to** ◇ *a ~ to his son*

bereaved *adj.*

VERBS **be**
ADV. **newly, recently** ◇ *a recently ~ family*

bereavement *noun*

ADJ. **recent** | **family**
VERB + BEREAVEMENT **suffer** ◇ *He has suffered a ~.* | **come to terms with, cope with, get over**
BEREAVEMENT + NOUN **counselling/counseling, counsellor/ counselor** | **leave** (*esp. AmE*)
PHRASES **the pain of ~, the shock of ~**

berry *noun*

ADJ. **ripe** | **fresh** | **frozen** | **wild** | **poisonous** | **holly, juniper, etc.**
VERB + BERRY **have, produce** ◇ *Does this bush have berries?* | **pick** ◇ *We picked a few of the berries.* | **eat**
BERRY + VERB **ripen** | **drop off**
→ Special page at FRUIT

berth *noun*

ADJ. **empty** | **upper** | **lower**
VERB + BERTH **have** | **book, get, take** ◇ *I've managed to get ~s on the overnight ferry.*

best *adj.*

VERBS **be** | **consider sth, deem sth, judge sth, think sth** ◇ *Owen judged it ~ to make no reply.*
ADV. **very** ◇ *We aim to give our guests the very ~ attention.* | **by far, easily** ◇ *This is by far the ~ restaurant in the town.*
PREP. **at** ◇ *Who in the class is ~ at history?* | **for** ◇ *I'm only trying to do what's ~ for you.*

bet *noun*

ADJ. **good, safe, sure** | **fair** | **bad** | **risky** | **outside** (= with a very small chance of winning) | **stupid** ◇ *I wish I hadn't agreed to that stupid ~.* | **winning** | **big, huge, large** ◇ *I was tempted to place a large ~.* | **small**
VERB + BET **have, make, place, put** ◇ *I'm going to place a ~ on that white horse.* | **accept, take** ◇ *We are now taking ~s on the election result.* | **win** | **lose**
PREP. **~ on** ◇ *I had a ~ on the three o'clock race.* | **~ with** ◇ *I made a ~ with a friend.*
PHRASES **do sth for a ~** | **it is my ~ (that)... , my ~ is (that)...** ◇ *My ~ is that Canada will win.*

betrayal *noun*

ADJ. **personal** | **ultimate** ◇ *His defection to the other side was the ultimate ~.*
VERB + BETRAYAL **regard sth as, see sth as, view sth as** ◇ *The business community regarded the measures as a ~ of election promises.*
PREP. **~ of** ◇ *a ~ of his friends* ◇ *The decisions were a ~ of everything my father stood for.*
PHRASES **an act of ~** | **a ~ of (sb's) trust** | **a feeling of ~, a sense of ~**

better *adj.*

1 comparative of 'good'

VERBS **be, feel, look, seem** | **get** ◇ *Cars are getting ~ all the time.* | **make sth** ◇ *We must make our inner cities ~ to live and work in.* | **consider sth, deem sth, judge sth, think sth** ◇ *I thought it ~ to tackle him outside of business hours.*
ADV. **considerably, even, far, infinitely, a lot, markedly, much, significantly, still, substantially, vastly** ◇ *His latest book is very much ~ than the one before.* | **a good deal, a great deal** | **somewhat** | **ten times, a thousand times, etc.** | **a little, slightly, etc.** | **marginally** | **arguably** | **inherently**
PHRASES **no ~** ◇ *The new situation is no ~ than the old.* | **nothing ~ than** ◇ *There's nothing ~ than a nice juicy peach!*

2 recovered from an illness

VERBS be, feel, look, seem | get ◇ *I hope you get ~ soon.* | get sb, make sb ◇ *The doctor will soon make you ~.* | kiss sth ◇ *Did you hurt yourself? Come here and let me kiss it ~.*
ADV. a lot, much | a good deal, a great deal | a little, slightly, etc.

bewildered adj.

VERBS be, feel, look, seem, sound | become | leave sb ◇ *She packed her bags and left—leaving Matthew ~ and confused.*
ADV. very | completely, quite, thoroughly, totally, utterly | rather, somewhat | a little, slightly, etc.
PREP. at ◇ *He was rather ~ at seeing her there.* | by ◇ *She was totally ~ by his message.*

bewildering adj.

VERBS be, seem | find sth ◇ *I found the experience quite ~.*
ADV. very ◇ *It was all very ~.* | completely, quite, totally ◇ *a totally ~ array of different wines* | a little, slightly, etc.

bias noun

ADJ. clear, definite, marked, obvious, significant, strong | blatant | slight | possible, potential ◇ *The data was checked for potential ~es.* | alleged | conservative, left-wing, liberal, right-wing ◇ *He claims that America's media has a liberal ~.* | cultural, political, racial | class, gender | personal | inherent, systematic | media
VERB + BIAS have ◇ *The newspaper has a clear ~ towards/toward the party.* | demonstrate, display, exhibit, reveal, show | avoid, eliminate, minimize, prevent, reduce | address, correct, overcome ◇ *We have now tried to correct the ~ in our original report.* | be free from ◇ *The newspaper was free from political ~.*
BIAS + VERB creep in, exist, occur ◇ *Bias often creeps in through the wording of questions.* | result in sth | affect sb/sth | favour/favor sb
PREP. with ~, without ~ ◇ *All material must be selected and presented without ~.* | with a ~ ◇ *a newspaper with a strong left-wing ~* | ~ against ◇ *a ~ against women* | ~ in favour/favor of, ~ towards/toward ◇ *a ~ towards/toward small companies*

biased (also biassed) adj.

VERBS be
ADV. extremely, very | heavily, hopelessly, strongly | a little, slightly, etc. | naturally | inherently | ideologically, politically | racially
PREP. against ◇ *Fate was strongly ~ against him.* | in favour/favor of ◇ *The methods they employed were heavily ~ in favour/favor of the rich.* | towards/toward ◇ *Managers are naturally ~ towards/toward projects showing a quick return.*

Bible noun

ADJ. Holy
VERB + BIBLE read, study
BIBLE + VERB say sth, teach sth, tell sb sth ◇ *The ~ teaches that all people are equal before God.*
BIBLE + NOUN reading, story, verse | camp (*esp. AmE*), school | study
PREP. in the ~ ◇ *You can read the story of Noah in the ~.*

bibliography noun

ADJ. brief, select, selective, short | complete, comprehensive, detailed, extensive, full ◇ *an extensive ~ of books and articles* | useful | annotated
VERB + BIBLIOGRAPHY compile, put together | contain, include, provide | publish | consult ◇ *Consult the ~ for further reading on the subject.*
PREP. in a/the ~ ◇ *You'll find the professor's book in the ~.* | ~ of ◇ *The book includes a selective ~ of works on French art.*

bicycle noun

VERB + BICYCLE ride | get on, mount ◇ *He mounted his ~ and rode off.* | get off | come off, fall off ◇ *She came off her ~ when it skidded on some wet leaves.* | pedal ◇ *She tried to pedal her ~ up the track.* | push, wheel ◇ *I dismounted and began to push my ~ up the hill.* | park | hire (*esp. BrE*), rent (*esp. AmE*)
BICYCLE + NOUN ride | rider (*AmE*) | chain, frame, pump, seat, tyre/tire, wheel | helmet | rack, shed | hire (*esp. BrE*), rental (*AmE*) | lane, path (*both AmE*) | accident | race | messenger (*AmE*)
PREP. by ~ ◇ *Did you come by ~?* | on a/the ~ ◇ *We watched the boys on their ~s.*
PHRASES lean a ~ against sth, prop a ~ against sth

bid noun

1 offer of a sum of money to buy sth

ADJ. high ◇ *The highest ~ was only $200.* | low | opening, starting | final | competing | winning | sealed | competitive | cash
VERB + BID make, place, put in, submit ◇ *He made a cash ~ for the company.* | withdraw | call for, invite, solicit (*AmE*) ◇ *They have invited ~s for the property.* | get, receive | increase, raise | accept | reject
BID + NOUN price | process
PREP. by, ~ from ◇ *a $24 million ~ by a rival company* | ~ for ◇ *a ~ for the chair* | ~ of ◇ *a ~ of £100* | ~ on (*AmE*) ◇ *I placed a ~ on a repossessed Ferrari.*

2 attempt

ADJ. successful | failed, unsuccessful | strong ◇ *The party made a strong ~ to seize power at the ballot box.* | serious | desperate | first | final | comeback | election, re-election | gubernatorial (*AmE*), presidential | Olympic | hostile, takeover (*both business*)
VERB + BID launch, make, mount (*esp. BrE*) ◇ *A German company launched a takeover ~ for the company.* | succeed in, win | fail in, lose ◇ *They failed in their ~ to buy the company.* | support ◇ *College presidents supported his ~ for the position.* | reject
BID + VERB succeed (*esp. BrE*) | fail
PREP. in a/the ~ ◇ *He attacked his guards in a desperate ~ for freedom.* | ~ by ◇ *a ~ by the president to boost his popularity* | ~ for ◇ *This play was her last ~ for recognition.*
PHRASES a ~ for freedom | a ~ for power | a ~ to escape

bid verb

1 offer money for sth

PREP. against ◇ *Two dealers ~ against each other for the table.* | for ◇ *She ~ $10 000 for the painting.*

2 offer to do work

ADV. successfully | competitively
PREP. for (*BrE*) ◇ *We have successfully ~ for the contract.* | on (*AmE*) ◇ *We have successfully ~ on the contract.*

big adj.

VERBS be, look, seem | become, get, grow
ADV. extremely, fairly, very, etc. ◇ *This is a fairly ~ decision to make.* ◇ *We were hoping the show would be a really ~ success.* ◇ *This house is rather ~ for us. We need something smaller.* | incredibly | awfully | a little, slightly, etc. | potentially ◇ *a potentially ~ drawback*
PHRASES ~ fat ◇ *The whole story is just a ~ fat lie.* | great ~ ◇ *He was a short man with great ~ glasses.*

bike noun

ADJ. dirt, mountain, racing, recumbent, road, touring, town, trail | exercise | electric
VERB + BIKE ride | get on, mount ◇ *He got on his ~ and rode off.* | get off | come off, fall off ◇ *She came off her ~ when it skidded on some wet leaves.* | knock sb off | pedal ◇ *She tried to pedal her ~ up the track.* | push, walk, wheel ◇ *We had to push our ~s up the hill.* | straddle | park | lock | hire (*esp. BrE*), rent (*esp. AmE*)
BIKE + NOUN ride | race | tour, trip | rider | racer | bell,

chain, frame, seat, tyre/tire | helmet, lock | rack, shed, stand | lane (*AmE*) | path, trail | accident
PREP. **by** ~ ◇ *Did you come by ~?* | **on a/the** ~ ◇ *We watched the boys on their ~s.*
PHRASES **lean a** ~ **against sth, prop a** ~ **against sth**

bikini *noun*

ADJ. **skimpy, tiny** | **string** (*esp. AmE*)
BIKINI + NOUN **bottoms, briefs** (*AmE*), **top** | **line** | **wax** (= treatment to remove hair which shows around a bikini)
→ Special page at CLOTHES

bilingual *adj.*

VERBS **be** | **become**
ADV. **fully**
PREP. **in** ◇ *He is virtually ~ in Spanish and Portuguese.*

bill *noun*

1 showing money owed for goods/services
ADJ. **big, hefty, high, huge, large, massive** | **outstanding, unpaid** | **itemized** ◇ *Customers receive an itemized monthly phone ~.* | **legal, medical** | **electricity, energy, fuel, gas, heating** | **utility** ◇ *Many people struggle to pay their rent and utility ~s.* | **grocery, hospital, hotel, phone, telephone, etc.** | **tax** | **credit-card** | **repair**
VERB + BILL **get, receive** ◇ *I've just received a huge tax ~.* | **be landed with, face** ◇ *The company could now face higher fuel ~s.* | **run up** ◇ *We ran up a very large hotel ~.* | **foot, pay, pick up, settle** ◇ *Don't worry—the company will pick up the ~.* | **cover** ◇ *Use the money in the account to cover the ~s.* | **present sb with, send sb, submit** ◇ *They presented us with a very large ~.* | **cut, lower, reduce** ◇ *We need to cut our electricity ~s.* | **share** ◇ *We share the gas and electricity ~s.*
BILL + VERB **arrive, come in** | **amount to, come to** ◇ *The ~ amounted to $850.*
BILL + NOUN **payment** | **collector** (*AmE*)
PREP. ~ **for** ◇ *Who is going to foot the ~ for the damage?*

2 (*esp. BrE*) showing money owed for food and drinks
→ See also CHECK
VERB + BILL **ask for** | **bring** | **get, have** ◇ *Could I have the ~, please?* | **pay** | **split** ◇ *We decided to split the ~.*
BILL + VERB **arrive, come** | **come to** ◇ *The ~ came to £120.*

3 (*AmE*) paper money → See also NOTE
ADJ. **five-dollar, twenty-dollar, etc.** | **crisp** | **counterfeit**
VERB + BILL **count, count out**

4 proposal for a new law
ADJ. **controversial** | **comprehensive, sweeping** (*AmE*) ◇ *a sweeping ~ that will reform the nation's immigration system* | **emergency** | **draft** | **proposed** | **pending** (*AmE*) | **bipartisan** (*AmE*) | **private member's** (*in the UK*) | **congressional, federal, Treasury** (*in the US*) | **budget, spending** (*both AmE*) | **reform** | **anti-terrorism, education, immigration, intelligence, etc.**
VERB + BILL **bring forward, bring in, introduce, propose, put forward, submit** ◇ *The ~ will be brought before Parliament next year.* ◇ *The government has put forward an emergency ~ to limit the powers of the police.* | **bring before Parliament** (*BrE*), **bring to the floor** (*AmE*), **bring to a vote** (*esp. AmE*) ◇ *The ~ will be brought before Parliament next year.* ◇ *The ~ was brought to the floor of the House last summer.* | **force through** (*BrE*), **push through, rush through** (*BrE*) ◇ *Republicans will try to push the ~ through Congress.* ◇ *The opposition will try to force the ~ through Parliament.* | **draft, prepare, write** | **sponsor** | **amend** | **debate** | **adopt, approve, pass, sign** | **back, endorse, support, vote for** | **block, defeat, kill** (*AmE*), **reject, throw out, veto** | **oppose, vote against** | **shelve, withdraw**
BILL + VERB **become law** ◇ *The ~ became law in June.* | **contain, include sth** ◇ *The ~ included a gradual phase-out of estate tax.* | **propose sth** | **ban sth, prohibit sth** | **allow sth**

5 programme/program of entertainment
ADJ. **double**
VERB + BILL **head, top** ◇ *Rufus Wainwright is topping the ~.* | **share**

PREP. **on a/the** ~ ◇ *Also on the ~ are Hot Chip.*

bin *noun*

ADJ. **litter, rubbish, waste, waste-paper** (*all BrE*) ◇ *She threw the letter in the waste-paper ~.* | **recycling** | **storage** | **compost** | **pedal, wheelie** (*both BrE*) | **recycle** (= on a computer screen)
VERB + BIN **put sth in** | **chuck sth in/into, throw sth in/into** (*both esp. BrE*)
BIN + NOUN **bag, liner** (*both BrE*) | **man** (*BrE*)
PREP. **in a/the** ~ ◇ *Put the bottles in the recycling ~.*

bind *verb*

1 tie with rope/fabric
ADV. **tightly** ◇ *They bound his hands together tightly.* | **loosely** | **together**
PREP. **to** | **with** ◇ *The sails are bound to the mast with rope.*
PHRASES ~ **and gag sb,** ~ **sb hand and foot** ◇ *She found herself bound hand and foot.*

2 make sb do sth
ADV. **contractually, legally, morally**

3 book
PHRASES **be beautifully bound, be handsomely bound, be richly bound** | **be bound in sth** ◇ *two volumes bound in leather*

binding *adj.*

VERBS **be** | **become**
ADV. **absolutely** | **legally, morally**
PREP. **on, upon** ◇ *The decisions of the European Court are ~ on the United Kingdom.*

binge *noun*

ADJ. **drinking, drunken** | **eating** | **buying, spending** | **drug**
VERB + BINGE **go on, have** ◇ *He went on a drunken ~ when he heard the bad news.*
BINGE + NOUN **drinking, eating** | **drinker**

binoculars *noun*

ADJ. **high-powered, powerful**
... OF BINOCULARS **pair**
VERB + BINOCULARS **use** | **look through** | **focus** ◇ *He focused his ~ on the building in the distance.* | **adjust** | **lift, raise** ◇ *She raised her ~ to the distant road across the valley.* | **lower**
PREP. **through** ~ ◇ *We watched the race through ~.*

biography *noun*

ADJ. **authorized, official** | **unauthorized, unofficial** | **brief, potted** (*BrE*), **short** ◇ *The book gives potted biographies of all the major painters.* | **full-length** | **detailed** | **definitive** | **new, recent** | **celebrity**
VERB + BIOGRAPHY **work on, write** | **produce, publish** | **read** | **research**
PREP. ~ **by** ◇ *a ~ by Antonia Fraser* | ~ **of** ◇ *a ~ of the former president*

biologist *noun*

ADJ. **distinguished, prominent, senior** | **professional** | **field, research** ◇ *She's a research ~ for a pharmaceutical company.* | **developmental, evolutionary, forensic, marine, molecular** | **cell, fishery, plant, wildlife** | **conservation**
→ Note at JOB

biology *noun*

ADJ. **cellular, developmental, environmental, evolutionary, marine, molecular, population, reproductive** | **cell, human, plant, wildlife** | **conservation** | **modern**
→ Note at SUBJECT (for verbs and nouns)

bird *noun*

ADJ. **wild** | **caged** | **exotic, rare** | **common** | **endangered** |

game | predatory | migratory | native | aquatic, forest, grassland, land, marine, sea (usually *seabird*), tropical, wading, woodland ◊ *Seabirds flocked above our heads.* | song (usually *songbird*) | backyard (*AmE*), garden (*BrE*) | pet | breeding, nesting | flightless | adult, baby | extinct
... OF BIRDS **flock**
BIRD + VERB **circle, flit, fly, glide, soar, swoop, swoop down** ◊ *We watched a ~ of prey swoop down on a mouse.* | **hop** | **flap its wings, flutter** | **land (on sth)** ◊ *A ~ landed on my shoulder.* | **perch on sth** | **flock** | **migrate** ◊ *The ~s migrate in September.* | **chirp, sing, twitter, warble** | **peck** ◊ *~s pecking at the corn* | **feed on sth** | **build a nest, nest** ◊ *~s nesting on the roof of the church* | **breed, lay eggs** | **moult/ molt**
BIRD + NOUN **species** | **call, song** (usually *birdsong*) | **bird's nest** | **sanctuary** | **conservation** | **habitat** | **life** ◊ *an area with a very varied ~ life* | **population** | **watcher, watching** (usually *birdwatcher, birdwatching*) | **enthusiast, lover** | **feeder** | **table** (*BrE*) ◊ *They set up a ~ table in the garden.* | **bath** | **cage** (usually *birdcage*) | **seed** (usually *birdseed*) | **droppings, poo** (*BrE, informal*), **poop** (*AmE, informal*) | **feathers** | **dog** (= used in hunting) (*AmE*) | **flu** | **strike** (= when a bird hits a plane)
PHRASES **a ~ of passage** (= a migratory bird), **a ~ of prey** | **a breed of ~, a species of ~, a type of ~**

birth *noun*

ADJ. **live** ◊ *Better living conditions mean more live ~s and fewer stillbirths.* | **normal** | **difficult** | **breech** | **Caesarean, vaginal** | **natural** (= without the use of drugs) | **premature, preterm** | **multiple** | **illegitimate, out-of-wedlock** (*AmE*) | **home, hospital** | **water** (= in water)
VERB + BIRTH **give** ◊ *She gave ~ to a baby boy.* | **register** | **celebrate** ◊ *They recently celebrated the ~ of their second daughter.* | **await** ◊ *He was anxiously awaiting the ~ of his child.* | **announce** | **attend** ◊ *A doctor and three midwives attended the ~.*
BIRTH + NOUN **certificate** | **records** | **date** | **place** (usually *birthplace*) | **weight** (usually *birthweight*) | **process** | **complications** | **defect** | **canal** ◊ *the mother's ~ canal* | **mother** | **attendant** (= person who assists a woman giving birth) | **partner** (= person a woman chooses to be with when giving birth) | **plan** ◊ *You should prepare a ~ plan with your obstetrician.* | **announcement** | **rate** ◊ *a low/ high ~ rate* (see also **birth control**)
PREP. **at ~** ◊ *The baby weighed seven pounds at ~.* | **at a/the ~, during a/the ~** ◊ *The child's father was present at the ~.* | **by ~** ◊ *He was American by ~, but lived in France.*
PHRASES **~s, deaths and marriages** (*AmE*), **~s, marriages and deaths** ◊ *announcements of ~s, marriages and deaths* | **your date of ~, your place of ~** | **of low ~, of noble ~** (both old-fashioned) | **the moment of ~**

birth control *noun*

ADJ. **effective**
VERB + BIRTH CONTROL **practise/practice, use**
BIRTH-CONTROL + NOUN **method** | **pill**
PHRASES **a form of ~, a method of ~**

birthday *noun*

ADJ. **last, next** ◊ *I'll be 28 on my next ~.*
VERB + BIRTHDAY **have** ◊ *I hope you have a nice ~.* | **spend** ◊ *She spent her 50th ~ in Paris.* | **celebrate** | **mark** ◊ *an exhibition to mark the artist's 70th ~* | **forget, remember** | **approach** ◊ *He is approaching his 40th ~, and thinking of retiring from the sport.* | **reach** ◊ *I reached my 86th ~ this year.* | **share** ◊ *They share the same ~.*
BIRTHDAY + NOUN **gift, present** | **card** | **cake** | **bash** (*informal*), **celebration, party** | **surprise** ◊ *He had a portrait painted as a ~ surprise for his daughter.* | **treat** (*esp. BrE*) ◊ *We're taking him to see the new movie for his ~ treat.* | **boy, girl** ◊ *Here comes the ~ girl!*
PREP. **for your ~** ◊ *What do you want for your ~?* | **on your ~** ◊ *She'll be 34 on her next ~.*

PHRASES **happy ~!** | **wish sb a happy ~** ◊ *Wish John a happy ~ from me.*

biscuit *noun* → See also COOKIE

ADJ. **dry, hard** (*both BrE*) | **flaky** (*AmE*) | **stale** | **fresh** | **chocolate, coconut, ginger, etc.** (*all BrE*) | **digestive, shortbread, wafer** (*all BrE*) | **home-made** | **breakfast** (*AmE*) | **hot** (*AmE*) | **dog**
... OF BISCUITS **box, packet, tin** (*all BrE*) ◊ *a packet of coconut ~s*
VERB + BISCUIT **eat, have** | **nibble** (*esp. BrE*) | **dunk** (*BrE*) ◊ *Frank always dunks his ~s in his tea.* | **bake, make** | **cut out** (*BrE*) ◊ *He was cutting ~s out and putting them on a baking tray.*
BISCUIT + NOUN **barrel, tin** (*both BrE*) | **crumbs** ◊ *He brushed the ~ crumbs from his jacket.*
PHRASES **cheese and ~s** (*BrE*) | **~s and gravy** (*AmE*) → Special page at FOOD

bishop *noun*

ADJ. **Anglican, Catholic, Orthodox, etc.** | **diocesan** ◊ *He's the diocesan ~ and he has three suffragan ~s to help him.* | **assistant, suffragan**
VERB + BISHOP **appoint, appoint sb (as), be elected, consecrate, make sb, ordain** | **succeed sb as**
PREP. **~ of** ◊ *He was appointed Bishop of Palm Beach.*

bit *noun* (*esp. BrE*)

1 a bit small amount

ADJ. **little, teensy** (*informal*), **wee** (*esp. BrE*) ◊ *He helped me a little ~ in the afternoon.*
PHRASES **just a ~** ◊ *I'm still just a ~ confused.* | **not the least ~** ◊ *I'm not the least ~ interested in football.*

2 a bit large amount

ADJ. **fair, good** ◊ *It rained a fair ~ during the night.* ◊ *We made a good ~ of progress.*
VERB + A BIT **take** ◊ *The new system will take quite a ~ of getting used to* (= it will take a long time to get used to).
PHRASES **quite a ~** ◊ *It rained quite a ~ during the night.* | **just a ~** (*ironic*) ◊ *'Has it been difficult for you at work?' 'Just a ~* (= it has been very difficult).'

3 part/piece of sth

ADJ. **little, small, tiny** | **big, large** ◊ *A big ~ of stone had fallen off the wall.* | **good, nice** ◊ *The best ~ of the trip was seeing the Grand Canyon.* ◊ *I've bought a nice ~ of fish for dinner.* | **boring, interesting** ◊ *I read it, but I skipped the boring ~s.* | **odd** ◊ *He managed to get odd ~s of work, but no regular job.*
VERB + BIT **pick out, pick up** ◊ *Listen to the interview again and pick out the ~s you want to use in the article.* ◊ *I picked up a ~ of information that might interest you.*
BIT + VERB **fall off** ◊ *I'm worried because ~s keep falling off my car.*
PREP. **~ of**
PHRASES **~s and bobs, ~s and pieces** (= small items of various kinds) (*both BrE, informal*) ◊ *My mother has some ~s and pieces to give you.* | **blow sth to ~s, pull sth to ~s, smash sth to ~s** ◊ *All the crockery had been smashed to ~s.* | **do your ~** (= do your share of a task) (*informal*) ◊ *We can finish this job on time if everyone does their ~.* | **fall to ~s** (*BrE*) ◊ *My briefcase eventually fell to ~s.*

bite *noun*

1 act of biting/amount of food

VERB + BITE **have, swallow, take**
PREP. **between ~s** ◊ *She tried to talk between ~s.* | **~ from** ◊ *I took a ~ from the apple.* | **~ of** ◊ *Can I have a ~ of your sandwich?* | **~ out of** ◊ *She took a ~ out of the slab of cake.*

2 of an insect/animal

ADJ. **dog, insect, mosquito, snake, etc.** | **nasty**
VERB + BITE **get** ◊ *I got a lot of mosquito ~s last night.*
BITE + NOUN **mark**
PREP. **~ from** ◊ *a ~ from a poisonous snake*

3 small amount to eat

ADJ. **quick**

VERB + BITE **grab, have** ◇ *We managed to grab a ~ at the airport.*
PREP. **~ of** ◇ *a quick ~ of lunch*
PHRASES **a ~ to eat** ◇ *We'll have a ~ to eat in town.*

bite *verb*

1 use your teeth

ADV. **badly** ◇ *Their cat was badly bitten by a dog.* | **off** ◇ *He bit off a chunk of bread.*
PREP. **at** ◇ *He bit at his lower lip.* | **down on** ◇ *She bit down on her bottom lip.* | **into** ◇ *She bit into the apple.* | **through** ◇ *The dog had bitten right through its rope.*
PHRASES **~ sth in half, ~ sth in two**

2 have an effect

ADV. **deep, hard** ◇ *As the recession ~s harder, many small companies are going bankrupt.*
VERB + BITE **begin to, start to** ◇ *After two cold months, the coal shortage was beginning to ~.*

bitter *adj.*

1 angry/unhappy

VERBS **be, feel, seem, sound** | **become, grow, turn** ◇ *He had grown ~ as the years passed.* ◇ *Loving relationships can turn ~.* | **remain** | **leave sb, make sb** ◇ *The divorce had left her ~.*
ADV. **extremely, fairly, very, etc.** | **slightly** | **increasingly**
PREP. **about** ◇ *She still seems ~ about it.* | **towards/toward** ◇ *I felt very ~ towards/toward them.*

2 very cold

VERBS **be** | **become, turn** ◇ *The weather turned ~.* | **remain**
ADV. **extremely, fairly, very, etc.**

3 having a sharp taste

VERBS **be, taste** ◇ *The drink tasted ~.*
ADV. **extremely, fairly, very, etc.** | **a little, slightly, etc.**

bitterness *noun*

ADJ. **considerable, deep, great, real** | **lingering**
... OF BITTERNESS **edge, hint, touch, trace**
VERB + BITTERNESS **feel** ◇ *She feels no ~ towards/toward him.* | **express, show** ◇ *He's never shown any ~.* | **hide** ◇ *She smiled and tried to hide her ~.* | **cause, create**
PREP. **with ~, without ~** ◇ *She spoke slowly and with some ~.* | **~ about, ~ over** ◇ *their ~ over the strike* | **~ against, ~ towards/toward** ◇ *his ~ towards/toward his own father* | **~ among** ◇ *the ~ among nurses about this pay deal* | **~ between** ◇ *There is no ~ between them.* | **~ in** ◇ *The ~ in her voice was evident.*

bizarre *adj.*

VERBS **be, look, seem, sound** | **become** | **find sth** ◇ *I found the whole situation very ~.*
ADV. **extremely, fairly, very, etc.** ◇ *It's a pretty ~ movie.* | **most** (*esp. BrE*), **truly** ◇ *He walked off in a most ~ fashion.* | **frankly** (*esp. BrE*) | **downright, totally** ◇ *He made some totally ~ comments.* | **increasingly** | **a little, slightly, etc.**

black *adj., noun*

ADV. **very** ◇ *The sky looks very ~.* | **all, completely, entirely** ◇ *His hands were all ~ from messing with the car.* | **almost, nearly**
ADJ. **deep, jet, pitch** (used about the night) ◇ *She had beautiful jet-black hair.* ◇ *It was pitch-black outside.*
→ Special page at COLOUR

blacklist *noun*

VERB + BLACKLIST **place sb on, put sb on** | **compile, create, draw up** | **update** | **maintain**
PREP. **on a/the ~** ◇ *She was on the company's ~.*

blackmail *noun*

ADJ. **emotional, moral** | **economic, nuclear, political**
BLACKMAIL + NOUN **attempt, threat** | **plot, scheme** |
→ Note at CRIME (for verbs)

blank

blackmail *verb*

ADV. **effectively, virtually** ◇ *Voters were effectively ~ed into voting 'Yes'.* | **emotionally** ◇ *Don't let him emotionally ~ you.*
VERB + BLACKMAIL **attempt to, try to**
PREP. **into** ◇ *She says she was virtually ~ed into giving up her claim to the property.*

black market *noun*

ADJ. **thriving** | **lucrative**
BLACK-MARKET + NOUN **activity, trade** ◇ *a thriving black-market trade in antiquities*
PREP. **on the ~** ◇ *You could buy anything you needed on the ~.* | **~ in** ◇ *During the war, there was a thriving ~ in food.*

bladder *noun*

ADJ. **full** | **irritable, weak**
VERB + BLADDER **empty, relieve** | **control**
BLADDER + NOUN **control** | **cancer, infection, problem** ◇ *He died of ~ cancer.*

blade *noun*

ADJ. **sharp** | **blunt, dull** (*esp. AmE*) | **curved, pointed, serrated, thin** | **metal, stainless-steel, steel** | **knife, razor, saw, scalpel, sword** | **rotor, turbine** ◇ *a helicopter's rotor ~s* | **rotary**
VERB + BLADE **sharpen** | **draw** | **sheathe** | **swing** ◇ *He swung the ~ with all his strength.*

blame *noun*

VERB + BLAME **get** ◇ *My brother broke the window, but I got the ~.* | **accept, bear, shoulder, take** ◇ *The company refused to accept any ~ for the damage.* | **apportion** (*esp. BrE*), **attach, attribute, lay, pin, place, put** ◇ *They placed the ~ squarely on the doctor.* | **share** ◇ *The government must share the ~ for this confusion.* | **escape, shift** ◇ *They tried to shift the ~ onto someone else.* | **absolve sb from, absolve sb of** ◇ *He was absolved of all ~.*
BLAME + VERB **fall on sb, lie with sb, rest with sb** ◇ *The ~ lies with the police, who failed to act quickly enough.*
PREP. **~ for** ◇ *He tried to escape ~ for what he did.*
PHRASES **lay the ~ at sb's door** (*BrE*) ◇ *The government tried to lay the ~ at the door of the unions.* | **part of the ~, a share of the ~**

blame *verb*

ADV. **unfairly, unjustly** | **partly** | **not really** ◇ *You can't really ~ them for not telling you.* | **widely** ◇ *He is widely ~d for masterminding the attacks.*
VERB + BLAME **can't, don't** ◇ *'I just slammed the phone down when he said that.' 'I don't ~ you!'* | **can hardly** ◇ *You can hardly ~ Peter for being angry with her.*
PREP. **for** ◇ *I don't ~ Jack for the mistake.* | **on** ◇ *Whenever something goes wrong, everyone ~s it on me.*
PHRASES **be to ~** (**for sth**) ◇ *A spokesman said that bad weather was partly to ~ for the delay.* | **be widely ~d for sth** ◇ *The government has been widely ~d for the crisis.*

blameless *adj.*

VERBS **be**
ADV. **completely, entirely** ◇ *She herself was entirely ~.* | **far from, not entirely** ◇ *Johnson himself was far from ~.*

blank *noun*

1 empty space on paper

VERB + BLANK **fill in** ◇ *In the test, we had to fill in the ~s.* | **leave** ◇ *If you don't know the answer, just leave a ~.*

2 cartridge for a gun

VERB + BLANK **fire** ◇ *Soldiers fired ~s into the sky.*

blank *adj.*

1 with nothing written, recorded, etc. on

VERBS **be** | **go** ◇ *The screen's gone ~.* | **remain** | **leave sth** ◇ *I left the third column ~.*
ADV. **completely, entirely**

2 without emotion/interest/understanding

VERBS **be, look** ◇ *Gina looked ~; then understanding dawned.* | **go, turn** (*esp. AmE*) ◇ *What if my mind goes completely ~ with panic?* ◇ *Kevin's expression turned ~.* | **remain**
ADV. **completely, totally** | **studiously** ◇ *His expression remained studiously ~.*

blanket *noun*

ADJ. **heavy, thick** | **thin** | **warm** | **soft** | **wool, woollen/ woolen** | **electric** | **security** (*figurative*) ◇ *For her, money was like a security ~.*
VERB + BLANKET **cover sb with, drape over sb/sth, tuck around sb, wrap sb in** | **draw up, pull up** ◇ *She pulled the ~ up and went to sleep.* | **kick off, push off, throw off** | **clutch, grab** | **spread out**
PREP. **beneath a/the ~, under a/the ~** ◇ *They shivered under their thin ~s.*
PHRASES **a wet ~** (*figurative*) ◇ *I hate to be a wet ~, but I thought the show was terrible.*

blasphemy *noun*

VERB + BLASPHEMY **commit, speak, utter**
BLASPHEMY + NOUN **law** (*esp. BrE*)
PREP. **~ against** ◇ *His writings were branded as obscene and a ~ against God.*
PHRASES **a charge of ~**

blast *noun*

1 explosion

ADJ. **huge, loud, massive, powerful** | **bomb, grenade, nuclear, shotgun**
VERB + BLAST **survive** | **cause** ◇ *Officials say they do not know what caused the ~.*
BLAST + VERB **hit sth, rip through sth, rock sth** ◇ *A huge bomb ~ rocked Jakarta last night.* | **occur** ◇ *The ~ occurred at about 9 a.m.* | **injure sb, kill sb** | **damage sth, destroy sth** | **blow sth** ◇ *The ~ blew a hole in the front of the building.*
PREP. **in a/the ~** ◇ *Twenty people were killed in the ~.*

2 sudden rush of air/wind

ADJ. **hot, icy** ◇ *She felt an icy ~ of air.*
PREP. **~ of** ◇ *a ~ of cold air*

3 sudden loud sound

ADJ. **long** | **short** | **loud, shrill** | **trumpet**
VERB + BLAST **give** | **hear**
PREP. **~ on** ◇ *He gave a short ~ on his trumpet.*

blaze *noun*

ADJ. **fierce, huge** (*esp. BrE*), **intense, massive**
VERB + BLAZE **attend** (*BrE*), **battle, fight, tackle** (*esp. BrE*) ◇ *The fire brigade attended the ~.* ◇ *Firefighters are battling those ~s in five counties.* | **start** ◇ *An electrical overload may have started the ~.* | **bring under control, control, get under control** | **extinguish, put out**
BLAZE + VERB **spread, sweep through sth** ◇ *The ~ swept through the whole building.*
PREP. **in a/the ~** ◇ *The antiques were destroyed in a ~ last year.*

bleak *adj.*

1 without hope

VERBS **appear, be, look, seem** | **become** | **remain**
ADV. **extremely, fairly, very, etc.** ◇ *Prospects for the industry are extremely ~.* | **increasingly**

2 bare/empty/without pleasant features

VERBS **be, look, seem** ◇ *The landscape looked ~ and desolate in the rain.* | **become**
ADV. **very** | **rather** ◇ *It was a rather ~ and dismal place.*

bleed *verb*

ADV. **badly, heavily, profusely** | **internally** | **easily** ◇ *The small blood vessels in the nose ~ easily.*
PREP. **from** ◇ *She was ~ing heavily from a head wound.*
PHRASES **~ to death**

bleeding *noun*

ADJ. **excessive, heavy, major, massive, severe** | **uncontrollable** | **internal**
VERB + BLEEDING **have, suffer from** | **cause** | **control, staunch, stem, stop**
PREP. **~ from** ◇ *Some drugs can cause ~ from the small intestine.*

blemish *noun*

ADJ. **minor, slight** | **ugly, unsightly** | **skin**
VERB + BLEMISH **have** ◇ *The police say the suspect has a slight ~ on his left cheek.* | **cover, hide**
PREP. **without (a) ~** (*figurative*) ◇ *He was criticized, but she escaped without ~.* | **not a single ~** ◇ *There wasn't a single ~ on his skin.*

blend *noun*

ADJ. **delightful** (*esp. BrE*), **good, nice, perfect, right** ◇ *just the right ~ of work and relaxation* | **curious, special, strange, subtle, unique** ◇ *a scarf with a subtle ~ of shades* | **seamless** ◇ *The band's music is a seamless ~ of funk, reggae and rock.*

blend *verb*

1 mix

ADV. **together** ◇ *Blend all the ingredients together.* | **well** ◇ *Add the fruit and cream and ~ well.*
PREP. **into** ◇ *Blend the cocoa into the eggs.* | **with** ◇ *Blend a little milk with two tablespoons of syrup.*

2 combine well

ADV. **happily, harmoniously, perfectly, seamlessly, well** | **in** ◇ *The carpet doesn't ~ in with the rest of the room.*
PREP. **with** ◇ *The ornamental pool ~s perfectly with its surroundings.*

blessing *noun*

1 thing that brings happiness/improves your life

ADJ. **great, real** | **mixed** (= a thing that has advantages and disadvantages)
PREP. **~ for** ◇ *A TV can be a real ~ for old people.*
PHRASES **a ~ in disguise** (= a thing that seems unfortunate, but is later seen to be fortunate), **count your ~s** (= to be grateful for the good things you have)

2 approval/support

ADJ. **full** | **official**
VERB + BLESSING **have** | **give sb/sth** ◇ *The government has given its official ~ to the project.* | **get, receive** ◇ *She received the full ~ of her employers.*
PREP. **with sb's ~, without sb's ~** ◇ *He went off to Latin America with his mother's ~.*

3 prayer

ADJ. **traditional** | **papal** | **divine, spiritual**
VERB + BLESSING **bestow, give, make, pronounce, say** ◇ *The ~ was said in Hebrew.* | **ask, ask for** | **receive**
PREP. **~ on** ◇ *They asked God's ~ on their pastoral work.*

blind *noun* → See also SHADE

ADJ. **window** | **roller, venetian**
VERB + BLIND **open, pull up, raise** | **close, draw, lower, pull down, shut** (*esp. AmE*)
PREP. **through a/the ~** ◇ *She saw a figure through the ~s.*

blind *verb*

ADV. **almost, nearly** ◇ *The strong light almost ~ed him.* | **momentarily, temporarily** | **completely**

blind *adj.*

1 unable to see

VERBS **be, be born** | **be registered (as)** | **go** ◇ *She went ~ at the age of ten.* | **make sb**
ADV. **completely, totally** | **almost, nearly, virtually** | **partially** | **temporarily** | **legally** (*AmE*)
PHRASES **as ~ as a bat** | **be ~ in one eye** ◇ *He is almost ~ in one eye.*

2 blind to sth not willing to notice/admit sth

VERBS **be, seem** | **become** | **make sb**
ADV. **completely, totally** ◇ *His own problems have made him completely ~ to the sufferings of others.* | **wilfully/willfully** ◇ *Is the public wilfully/willfully ~ to what is going on?*

blink *verb*

ADV. **hard** ◇ *He ~ed hard and forced a smile.* | **furiously, quickly, rapidly** | **slowly**
PREP. **at** ◇ *She ~ed at him, astonished.* | **in, with** ◇ *He ~ed in surprise.*
PHRASES **~ away a tear, ~ back tears** ◇ *She had to ~ back her tears before she continued her story.* | **~ your eyes, your eyes ~**

bliss *noun*

ADJ. **pure, sheer, total** ◇ *The first six months of marriage were sheer ~.* | **domestic** | **romantic** | **marital, married, wedded** ◇ *They're celebrating 25 years of wedded ~.* | **eternal** | **ignorant**
PHRASES **sb's idea of ~** ◇ *My idea of ~ is a hot day and an ice-cold beer.*

blitz *noun*

1 campaign; sudden, great effort

ADJ. **advertising, marketing, media, PR, promotional, propaganda, safety** | **all-out** ◇ *an all-out ~ on crime*
VERB + BLITZ **conduct, have, launch, mount** ◇ *We decided to have a ~ on the kitchen* (= to clean the kitchen thoroughly). | **plan**
PREP. **~ on** ◇ *a ~ on illegal parking*

2 (*esp. BrE*) sudden military attack, often by air

ADJ. **bombing** | **wartime**
VERB + BLITZ **carry out**
PREP. **during a/the ~, in a/the ~** ◇ *Many people died in the London Blitz.* | **~ on** ◇ *Enemy bombers carried out a ~ on the city.*

blizzard *noun*

ADJ. **blinding** (*esp. AmE*), **fierce, heavy, howling, raging** | **winter** | **snow**
VERB + BLIZZARD **brave** | **blow** (*BrE*) ◇ *After a short while it began to blow a ~.*
BLIZZARD + VERB **hit (sth), strike (sth)** ◇ *The ~ struck while we were still on the mountain.* | **blow, rage**
BLIZZARD + NOUN **conditions**
PREP. **in ~, into ~** ◇ *We got stuck in a howling ~.* | **through ~** ◇ *He fought his way through the ~.*

bloc *noun*

ADJ. **large, solid, substantial** ◇ *A solid ~ of members supported the decision.* | **economic, military, regional, trade, trading, voting** | **Communist, Eastern, European, Soviet, etc.** ◇ *Eastern ~ countries*
PREP. **in a/the ~, within a/the ~** ◇ *There have been growing tensions within the trading ~.*

block *noun*

1 solid piece of sth

ADJ. **big, huge, large, massive** | **small** | **solid** | **cement, concrete, ice, stone, wood, wooden** | **building** | **rect-**

angular | starting (for a runner) ◇ *I was aiming to be first out of the starting ~s.* | **stumbling** (*figurative*) ◇ *The issue has been a major stumbling ~ in trade negotiations.* | **breeze** (*BrE*), **cinder** (*AmE*)
PHRASES **on the chopping ~** ◇ *I'm not putting my head on the chopping ~* (= putting myself at risk) *for you.*

2 (*BrE*) large building divided into offices, etc.

ADJ. **high-rise, tower** | **tenement** (*BrE*) | **administration, apartment, cell, office** ◇ *The prisoners had been transferred to a different cell ~.*
PREP. **in a/the ~** ◇ *She lives in a modern apartment ~.* | **~ of** ◇ *a ~ of flats*

3 group of buildings with streets around it

ADJ. **city** ◇ *The hotel occupies an entire ~.*
PREP. **around the ~, round the ~** (*esp. BrE*) ◇ *People were queueing round the ~ to get in.* (*BrE*) ◇ *Fans lined up around the ~ to get tickets for the show.* (*AmE*) | **~ from** (*AmE*) ◇ *We're about four ~s from my house.* | **~ down** (*AmE*) ◇ *They walked a few ~s down the street.*

4 temporary loss of abilities

ADJ. **mental, writer's** ◇ *The author denies that she is experiencing writer's ~.*
VERB + BLOCK **experience, have, suffer from** ◇ *I suddenly had a mental ~ and couldn't remember his name.*

block *verb*

1 make it difficult to pass

ADV. **completely** | **almost** | **partially, partly** | **off, up** ◇ *The old route is completely ~ed off.* ◇ *Don't ~ up the corridor with all these boxes.*
VERB + BLOCK **try to** | **move to** ◇ *One of the men moved to ~ their path.*
PREP. **with** ◇ *The exit was ~ed with beer crates.*

2 prevent sth being done

ADV. **successfully** | **effectively** ◇ *The new rules would effectively ~ protesters' attempts to assert their rights.*
VERB + BLOCK **attempt to, seek to, try to** | **move to** ◇ *The group has moved to ~ the government's proposals.*

PHR V **block sth out**
ADV. **completely** ◇ *Black clouds had completely ~ed out the sun.* | **almost**

blockade *noun*

ADJ. **complete, total** | **tight** | **partial** | **economic, military, naval** | **road** | **effective**
VERB + BLOCKADE **impose** | **end, lift, remove** | **enforce, maintain** | **tighten** | **ease, relax** | **break, break through, get through, run** ◇ *They attempted to break the ~ by using submarines.* | **form** ◇ *The group then formed a ~ across the road.*
PREP. **~ against** ◇ *the need to enforce a naval ~ against the country* | **~ around, ~ round** (*esp. BrE*) ◇ *a ~ around the city* | **~ by** ◇ *the ~ by Western nations* | **~ of** ◇ *a complete ~ of the island*

blockage *noun*

ADJ. **complete** | **partial**
VERB + BLOCKAGE **cause, create** | **prevent** | **clear, remove** ◇ *They used chemicals to clear the ~.*
PREP. **~ in** ◇ *a ~ in a major artery*

blog *noun*

ADJ. **favourite/favorite, popular** | **group, personal** | **academic, corporate, political** | **baseball, food, news, etc.**
VERB + BLOG **read, visit** | **post, write** | **update** | **create, launch, start** | **keep, maintain, run** ◇ *I'm making my students keep ~s this semester.* | **find**
BLOG + NOUN **entry, post** | **reader** | **site** | **posting**
PREP. **~ about** ◇ *a ~ about music* | **in a/the ~, on a/the ~** ◇ *You can read about my trip in my ~.*

blog

blonde noun

ADJ. **attractive, beautiful, gorgeous, pretty, sexy, stunning** | **blue-eyed** | **dumb** ◊ *She's not just a dumb ~.* | **natural** ◊ *She was slender and a natural ~.* | **bottle** | **ash, platinum, strawberry** ◊ *a tall strawberry ~ with stunning legs*

blonde (also blond) adj., noun

VERBS **be, look** | **go, turn** | **dye sth**
ADV. **very** | **quite**
ADJ. **ash, dark, dirty, golden, light, pale, platinum, sandy, strawberry** ◊ *ash-blond hair*

blood noun

ADJ. **cold, hot, warm** | **clotted, congealed, dried** | **fresh** | **arterial, venous** | **menstrual** | **contaminated** | **aristocratic, blue, noble, pure, royal** ◊ *I doubt if I have a single drop of aristocratic ~ in my veins.* | **African, Irish, Mediterranean, etc.** | **animal, human** | **fake**
... OF BLOOD **drop, pool, trickle** ◊ *The body lay in a pool of ~.* ◊ *A thin trickle of ~ ran down from a cut above her eye.* | **spots, traces** ◊ *He worked to remove all traces of ~.*
VERB + BLOOD **lose** ◊ *She'd lost a lot of ~ and doctors decided to do a transfusion.* | **shed, spill** (*literary*) ◊ *He was a hot-headed youth, always too quick to shed ~.* | **donate, give** ◊ *The hospital appealed for more people to donate ~.* | **pump** ◊ *The heart pumps ~ around the body.* | **collect, draw** ◊ *Samples of ~ were drawn using sterile syringes.* | **choke on** ◊ *He choked on his own ~ after being shot in the throat.* | **smear, wipe** ◊ *There was ~ smeared down his shirt.*
BLOOD + VERB **dribble, drip, flow, gush, ooze, run, seep, splash, spurt, stream, trickle, well, well up** ◊ *Blood oozed slowly from the corner of his mouth.* | **spread** ◊ *The ~ spread rapidly from where he lay.* | **spatter, splatter** ◊ *Blood spattered the seats of the vehicle.* | **soak sth, soak into sth** | **cake sth, stain sth** ◊ *Dried ~ caked his hands.* | **clot, coagulate, congeal** | **circulate** ◊ *He rubbed his limbs vigorously to get the ~ circulating.* | **course, rush, surge** ◊ *I felt the ~ coursing in my veins as I ran.* ◊ *The ~ rushed to her face as she realized her error.* | **pound, pulse** ◊ *The ~ pounded in her ears.* | **drain** ◊ *The ~ drained from his face when I told him the news.* | **freeze, run cold, turn cold, turn to ice** ◊ *Our ~ ran cold at the thought of how easily we could have been killed.*
BLOOD + NOUN **cell** | **group, type** (*esp. AmE*) ◊ *What ~ group are you?* (*BrE*) ◊ *What ~ type do you have?* (*AmE*) | **sample, test** | **count** ◊ *Her white ~ cell count is slightly elevated.* | **loss** | **donation, donor** | **bank** | **circulation, flow, supply** (see also *blood pressure, blood vessel*) | **clot, coagulation** | **disease, disorder, poisoning** | **cholesterol, glucose, sugar** | **transfusion**
PREP. **in ~** ◊ *His shirt was soaked in ~.* | **in sb's/the ~** ◊ *Traces of an illegal substance were found in his ~.* | **~ from** ◊ *My handkerchief was soaked in ~ from my nose.*
PHRASES **caked in ~, caked with ~** ◊ *The dog's fur was caked in ~ when we found him.* | **covered in ~, covered with ~** ◊ *He was lying on the floor, covered in ~.* | **in cold ~** ◊ *He shot them in cold ~ (= in a way that was planned and deliberately cruel).*

blood pressure noun

ADJ. **elevated** (*esp. AmE*), **high, low, normal, raised**
VERB + BLOOD PRESSURE **check, measure** | **control** | **decrease, increase, reduce**
BLOOD-PRESSURE + NOUN **medication**

bloodshed noun

ADJ. **further** | **massive, widespread** | **little** ◊ *Their aims were achieved quickly and with relatively little ~.* | **unnecessary**
VERB + BLOODSHED **cause, end in, lead to** ◊ *This election result could well lead to further ~.* | **end, halt, stop** | **avoid, prevent**

bloodstream noun

VERB + BLOODSTREAM **enter** | **absorb sth into** ◊ *The drug is quickly absorbed into the ~.*
PREP. **in sb's/the ~** ◊ *Traces of banned substances were detected in his ~.* | **into sb's/the ~** ◊ *Bacteria was introduced into his ~ through an unsterile needle.* | **through sb's/the ~** ◊ *Red blood cells transport oxygen through the ~.*

blood vessel noun

ADJ. **major** | **broken, burst**
VERB + BLOOD VESSEL **block, constrict** | **dilate, enlarge** | **burst** ◊ *He burst a ~ in a fit of coughing.* | **damage**
BLOOD VESSEL + VERB **carry sth, supply sth** ◊ *~s supplying nutrition to the skin* | **burst** | **dilate, enlarge** | **contract**

bloom noun

ADJ. **beautiful, glorious, perfect** ◊ *a tree with exquisite ~s* | **fragrant** | **exotic** | **bright** | **summer** | **single** | **huge**
VERB + BLOOM **bear** (*formal, esp. AmE*), **have, produce** | **encourage** (*esp. AmE*)
BLOOM + VERB **appear** ◊ *The small white ~s appear in May.* | **fade** ◊ *The ~s have started to fade now.*
PREP. **in ~** ◊ *banks of rhododendrons in ~*
PHRASES **in full ~** ◊ *The roses are now in full ~.* | **burst into ~, come into ~** ◊ *The spring flowers have come into ~.*

blossom noun

ADJ. **beautiful, lovely** | **pale, pink, white** ◊ *a tree with pale pink ~s* | **apple, peach, etc.** | **fragrant** | **spring**
VERB + BLOSSOM **bear** (*formal, esp. AmE*), **have, produce** ◊ *Hopefully the tree will produce some ~ next year.* | **see, smell** ◊ *In the spring visitors come to see the ~s at their peak.*
BLOSSOM + VERB **be out** ◊ *The cherry ~ is out.* (*BrE*) ◊ *The cherry ~s are out.* (*AmE*) | **come out** | **fall**
PREP. **in ~** ◊ *He loves it when the apple trees are in ~.*
PHRASES **in full ~** ◊ *The plum tree is in full ~.*

blouse noun

ADJ. **long-sleeved, short-sleeved, sleeveless** | **high-necked, low-cut** | **loose, tight** | **cotton, silk, etc.** | **embroidered, frilly** | **light, pale** | **see-through** | **school** | **peasant**
VERB + BLOUSE **button, button up** | **unbutton**
→ Special page at CLOTHES

blow noun

1 hard knock that hits sb/sth

ADJ. **hard, heavy, nasty, painful, powerful, severe, sharp, stinging, violent** | **deadly, fatal, final, mortal** | **physical** | **glancing, light** ◊ *Jack caught him a glancing ~ on the jaw.* | **single** ◊ *He killed the man with a single ~ of the hammer.*
... OF BLOWS **flurry**
VERB + BLOW **get, receive, suffer, take** ◊ *He suffered a severe ~ to the head.* | **catch sb, deal sb, deliver, give sb, land, rain (down), strike sb** ◊ *It was the gardener who delivered the fatal ~.* ◊ *She landed a nasty ~ on his nose.* ◊ *He rained heavy ~s on the old woman.* | **exchange** ◊ *The demonstrators exchanged ~s with the police.* | **aim** ◊ *She aimed a ~ at Lucy.* | **avoid, block, deflect, dodge, parry, ward off** | **feel** ◊ *He felt a stinging ~ across the side of his face.*
BLOW + VERB **fall, land** ◊ *The ~ landed on my right shoulder.* | **knock sb down, over, etc.** ◊ *The ~ knocked him to the ground.* | **knock sb out**
PREP. **~ of** ◊ *two ~s of the hammer.* | **~ on** ◊ *a nasty ~ on the head* | **~ to** ◊ *a ~ to the victim's chest*
PHRASES **come to ~s** ◊ *The children came to ~s over the new toy.* | **the force of the ~** ◊ *The force of the ~ knocked him out.*

2 sudden shock/disappointment

ADJ. **big, great, huge, major, serious, severe, terrible** | **bitter, crippling, cruel, crushing, devastating, knockout** | **double** | **decisive, mortal** ◊ *a mortal ~ to local industry* | **body**
VERB + BLOW **deal (sb/sth), deliver, strike** ◊ *His defeat dealt a crushing ~ to the party.* | **receive, suffer** | **cushion, soften** ◊

to soften the ~ of tax increases | **come as** ◇ *The news came as a bitter ~ to the staff.*
BLOW + VERB **come, fall** ◇ *The ~ came at a meeting yesterday.*
PREP. **~ for** ◇ *A tax on books would be a body ~ for education.* | **~ to** ◇ *Her decision to leave home was a terrible ~ to her parents.*
PHRASES **a bit of a ~** (*esp. BrE*)

blow *verb*

1 of wind/air, etc.

ADV. **hard, strongly** | **gently**
PREP. **from** ◇ *a gale ~ing from the west* | **off** ◇ *The wind blew the papers off the table.*
PHRASES **~ sth off course** ◇ *The ship was blown off course in the storm.* | **see which way the wind is ~ing** (*figurative*) ◇ *They won't commit themselves until they see which way the wind is ~ing.*

2 send air out of your mouth

ADV. **hard** | **softly**
PREP. **on** ◇ *He blew on his soup to cool it.*

blowout *noun* → See also PUNCTURE

ADJ. **tyre/tire**
VERB + BLOWOUT **have** ◇ *What are the chances of having a ~ in a new car?*

blue *adj., noun*

ADJ. **aqua** (*esp. AmE*), **azure, baby, cerulean** (*esp. AmE*), **cobalt, electric, ice, icy, midnight, navy, pastel, powder, royal, sapphire, sky, teal** (*AmE*), **turquoise** (*esp. AmE*) ◇ *a navy ~ sweater*
→ Special page at COLOUR

blueprint *noun*

ADJ. **detailed** | **original** | **new** | **genetic** ◇ *DNA carries the genetic ~ which tells any organism how to build itself.*
VERB + BLUEPRINT **have** ◇ *The government does not have a ~ for reform.* | **create, develop, draw up** | **follow** | **act as, offer, provide, serve as** ◇ *The charter should serve as a ~ for cooperation.*
PREP. **~ for** ◇ *a ~ for change*

blues *noun*

1 music

VERB + BLUES **play, sing** ◇ *He plays ~ on the harmonica.* ◇ *She sings the ~ in smoky bars.*
BLUES + NOUN **band, musician, singer** | **song**

2 the blues state of feeling sad/depressed

VERB + THE BLUES **have** | **get, suffer from** | **banish** (*esp. BrE*), **beat, cure** ◇ *I'm planning a cruise as a way to beat the ~.*

blunder *noun*

ADJ. **big, colossal, great, huge, major** ◇ *one of the greatest policy ~s in history* | **serious, terrible, tragic** | **strategic, tactical** | **policy, political** | **administrative, bureaucratic** (*both esp. BrE*)
... OF BLUNDERS **series**
VERB + BLUNDER **commit, make** ◇ *The president has made a series of political ~s.*

blur *noun*

ADJ. **dim, faint, pale** ◇ *The object was a dim ~ in the moonlight.*
PREP. **~ of** ◇ *a ~ of fire and smoke*
PHRASES **be all a bit of a ~, be all a ~, be just a ~** ◇ *I can't remember that day very well. It's all a bit of a ~.*

blush *noun*

ADJ. **crimson, deep** | **faint, slight**
VERB + BLUSH **hide** ◇ *She tried to hide her fiery ~.*
BLUSH + VERB **deepen** | **colour/color sb's cheeks, creep, rise, spread** ◇ *A deep ~ spread from her head to her neck.*

PREP. **with a ~, without a ~** ◇ *She lowered her eyes with a deep ~.* | **~ of** ◇ *a ~ of embarrassment*
PHRASES **a ~ comes to sb's cheeks, a ~ comes to sb's face** | **bring a ~ to sb's cheeks, bring a ~ to sb's face** | **save sb's ~es, spare sb's ~es** (= to save sb from an embarrassing situation) (*BrE*)

blush *verb*

ADV. **deeply, furiously, hotly, profusely** | **faintly, a little, slightly** | **angrily, guiltily** | **shyly**
VERB + BLUSH **make sb** ◇ *Stop teasing—you're making him ~.*
PREP. **at** ◇ *He ~ed at the mention of her name.* | **with** ◇ *She ~ed crimson with embarrassment.*
PHRASES **~ crimson, ~ pink, ~ red, ~ scarlet** ◇ *Lia ~ed a deep shade of red.*

board *noun*

1 flat piece of wood, plastic, etc.

ADJ. **bulletin** (*AmE*), **drawing, poster** (*AmE*) | **ironing** | **diving** | **circuit** | **chopping** (*BrE*), **cutting** (*AmE*) | **emery**
BOARD + NOUN **game**
PREP. **on a/the ~** ◇ *There's a notice on the ~.*

2 group of people who control an organization

ADJ. **advisory, editorial, executive, governing, management, review** | **health, parole, school, etc.**
VERB + BOARD **be on, serve on, sit on** ◇ *He sits on the company's management ~.* | **join** | **appoint sb to, elect sb to** | **resign from** | **go to** ◇ *The project will go to the ~ for consideration.* | **submit sth to, take sth to** ◇ *She took her ideas to the ~.*
BOARD + NOUN **member** | **meeting**
PREP. **~ of** ◇ *the company's ~ of directors*
PHRASES **at ~ level** ◇ *The issue has been discussed at ~ level.* | **chairman of the ~** | **a member of the ~** | **a seat on the ~** ◇ *She was promoted and offered a seat on the ~.*

3 meals that are provided when you stay in a hotel

ADJ. **full** (*BrE*) (*American plan* in *AmE*) | **half** (*BrE*) (*European plan* in *AmE*)
PHRASES **~ and lodging** (*esp. BrE*), **room and ~** (*esp. AmE*)

boardroom *noun*

ADJ. **company, corporate, executive**
BOARDROOM + NOUN **battle, coup, shake-up** (*esp. BrE*), **showdown** (*AmE*) | **table** | **pay** (*BrE*) ◇ *The massive ~ pay awards were criticized by the workers.*
PHRASES **in a/the ~** ◇ *The directors were working overtime in the ~.*

boast *noun*

ADJ. **proud** | **empty, idle**
VERB + BOAST **make**
PREP. **~ about** ◇ *a ~ he made about his achievements* | **~ of** ◇ *her ~ of having seen all the countries of Africa*

boast *verb*

1 talk with too much pride

ADV. **openly**
PREP. **about, of** ◇ *He openly ~ed of his talents.*

2 have sth good/impressive

ADV. **proudly** ◇ *This is a region which proudly ~s its own distinct culture.*

boat *noun*

ADJ. **little, small** | **open** ◇ *He was adrift in an open ~ for three days.* | **flat-bottomed, glass-bottomed** | **inflatable, rubber** | **wooden** | **motor, power, speed, steam** (usually *motorboat, powerboat,* etc.) | **sail** (usually *sailboat*) (*AmE*), **sailing** (*BrE*) | **paddle, row** (usually *rowboat*) (*AmE*), **rowing** (*BrE*) | **canal, river** ◇ *We hired a canal ~ in France.* ◇ *a Mississippi river ~* | **pleasure, recreational, tour** | **banana, cargo, charter, ferry, passenger, patrol, pilot** (*esp. BrE*),

pontoon (*AmE*), **rescue, torpedo** | **flying** | **fishing, shrimp** (*AmE*) | **model, toy** | **stricken** (*esp. BrE*) ◊ *The lifeboat was preparing to go to the aid of the stricken ~.* | **capsized, upturned** (*BrE*)
... OF BOATS **fleet, flotilla** ◊ *a flotilla of small ~s*
VERB + BOAT **take out** ◊ *You couldn't take a ~ out in that wild sea.* | **take sb out in** ◊ *My brother took us all out in his new ~.* | **get into, get on, get onto** | **get off, get out of** | **launch, lower** ◊ *A new type of patrol ~ was launched yesterday.* | **push out** ◊ *I pushed the ~ out into the middle of the river.* | **propel, row, sail** ◊ *The ~ is propelled by a powerful outboard motor.* ◊ *Where did you learn to sail a ~?* | **guide, steer, turn, turn around** | **captain, pilot, skipper** (*esp. BrE*) | **crew** (*esp. BrE*) ◊ *Normally the ~ is crewed by five people.* | **beach** ◊ *He beached the ~ and the children leaped out to explore.* | **dock** (*esp. AmE*), **moor, tie up** | **untie** | **anchor, berth** (*esp. BrE*) ◊ *Boats were anchored two and three abreast.* | **board** | **load, unload** | **charter, rent** | **rock** ◊ *Sit down, you're rocking the ~.* ◊ *She was told to keep her mouth shut and not rock the ~* (= not take unnecessary action that would cause problems). (*figurative*) | **capsize, overturn** | **build, design** | **catch, take** ◊ *They crossed the island to catch a ~ for islands south of Skye.* | **miss** (*often figurative*) ◊ *If you don't buy now, you may find that you've missed the ~* (= cannot take advantage of this offer because it is too late).
BOAT + VERB **go, head, sail** ◊ *The ~ headed upriver.* ◊ *The ~ sailed out to sea.* | **arrive, come in, dock** | **return** | **bob** ◊ *~s bobbing up and down in the estuary* | **drift, float, pass** | **lurch** (*esp. AmE*), **pitch, rock, roll** ◊ *The ~ pitched violently from side to side.* | **fill** ◊ *The ~ slowly filled with icy water.* | **capsize, sink** | **operate, ply** ◊ *Ferry ~s ply regularly between all the resorts on the lake.* | **carry sth, ferry sth, hold sth, take sth**
BOAT + NOUN **cruise, excursion, ride, trip** | **race** | **club** (*esp. BrE*) | **house** (usually *boathouse*) | **train** (= the train scheduled to connect with a particular sailing) (*BrE*) ◊ *the 7.30 p.m. ~ train to Harwich* | **crew, operator, owner** | **people** (= refugees who arrive by boat)
PREP. **by ~** ◊ *The cave can only be reached by ~.* | **in a/the ~** ◊ *I took them in my ~.* | **on a/the ~** ◊ *They ate on the ~.* | **~ from, ~ to** ◊ *a ~ from Jamaica to Trinidad*

bob *verb*
ADV. **gently, slightly** | **about, along** ◊ *An old cigarette pack bobbed along in the current.*
PHRASES **~ up and down** ◊ *The small boats bobbed gently up and down in the bay*

body *noun*
1 whole physical form of a person/an animal
ADJ. **entire, whole** ◊ *Her whole ~ trembled.* | **lower, upper** | **healthy** | **human** | **female, male** | **naked, nude** | **fit, lithe, muscular, perfect, toned** | **frail, lean, slender, slim, thin, tiny** | **fat** | **limp, unconscious**
VERB + BODY **rack** ◊ *Pain racked her ~.*
BODY + VERB **ache** | **shake, tremble** | **convulse** | **stiffen, tense**
BODY + NOUN **heat, temperature** | **mass, shape, size, weight** ◊ *to maintain your ideal ~ weight* | **fat, fluids** | **parts** | **odour/odor** | **armour/armor** | **piercing** | **image** | **language**
PREP. **in the/your ~** ◊ *Extreme heat may cause changes in the ~.* | **on the/your ~** ◊ *She still had the marks from the ropes on her ~.*
PHRASES **part of the ~, sell your ~** (= to work as a prostitute)
2 dead human body
ADJ. **dead, lifeless** | **mangled, mutilated** | **decomposed, decomposing** | **bloated**
VERB + BODY **discover, find, recover** | **examine** | **bury, cremate, embalm** | **exhume**
BODY + NOUN **count** (= the number of people killed) ◊ *The ~*

count is growing all the time.* | **bag** ◊ *soldiers who come home in ~ bags*
PREP. **on a/the ~** ◊ *A diary was found on the ~.*
3 amount of sth
ADJ. **growing, large, substantial, vast** ◊ *a substantial ~ of evidence*
PHRASES **a ~ of water** ◊ *The two islands are separated by a large ~ of water.*
4 main part of sth
ADJ. **main** ◊ *The bar is in the main ~ of the hotel.*
5 group of people who work/act together
ADJ. **advisory, corporate, executive, governing, legislative, professional, public, regulatory, sanctioning** (*esp. AmE*), **statutory** (*BrE*) | **international, national** | **government, governmental** | **student** | **independent** | **voluntary** (*esp. BrE*) | **elected** | **politic** (always after *body*) ◊ *Freedom of speech is necessary for the health of the ~ politic.*
VERB + BODY **create, establish, form**
6 object
ADJ. **foreign** ◊ *They removed a foreign ~ from her eye.* | **celestial, heavenly** ◊ *Stars are celestial bodies.*

bodyguard *noun*
ADJ. **armed** | **personal** ◊ *He never goes anywhere without his personal ~s.*
VERB + BODYGUARD **have, keep** ◊ *She has to have an armed ~ wherever she goes.* | **hire**
BODYGUARD + VERB **protect sb**
PREP. **~ to** ◊ *a former ~ to the prince*
→ Note at JOB

bog *noun*
ADJ. **vast** | **stagnant** | **peat**
VERB + BOG **sink into** ◊ *The more she struggled the deeper she sank into the ~.*
PREP. **in a/the ~** ◊ *He found himself in a vast stagnant ~.* | **through a/the ~** ◊ *I found myself walking through a ~.*

bogus *adj.*
VERBS **be, seem** | **dismiss sth as** ◊ *75 paintings which art experts dismiss as ~*
ADV. **completely, entirely, totally** | **largely**
PHRASES **turn out to** ◊ *The dinosaur bones turned out to be ~.*

boil *noun*
1 state of boiling
ADJ. **rolling** (*AmE*) ◊ *Bring the water to a rolling ~.*
VERB + BOIL **bring sth to** ◊ *Bring the soup to the ~.* (*BrE*) ◊ *Bring the soup to a ~.* (*AmE*) | **come to** ◊ *When it comes to the ~, reduce the heat.* (*BrE*) ◊ *When it comes to a ~, reduce the heat.* (*AmE*) | **go off** (*BrE, usually figurative*) ◊ *He played brilliantly for the first set but then went rather off the ~.*
2 infected spot
VERB + BOIL **lance** ◊ *The doctor lanced the ~.*

boil *verb*
ADV. **furiously, rapidly, vigorously** ◊ *Boil the beans rapidly for ten minutes.*
VERB + BOIL **put sth on to** ◊ *I'll put the kettle on to ~.*

boiler (*BrE*) *noun* device to provide heating and hot water in a building → See also FURNACE
ADJ. **gas, oil-fired** | **central-heating** (*esp. BrE*) | **industrial**
VERB + BOILER **install, put in** | **service**
BOILER + VERB **explode**
BOILER + NOUN **system** | **room**

boiling point *noun*
VERB + BOILING POINT **reach** ◊ *Kate's anger was reaching ~.* (*BrE*) ◊ *Kate's anger was reaching the ~.* (*AmE*) | **bring sth to, heat sth to** ◊ *Bring the sauce to ~.* (*BrE*) ◊ *Bring the sauce to the ~.* (*AmE*)

bold *adj.*

VERBS **be, feel** | **become, grow** | **make sb** ◇ *The exciting news had made him* ~.
ADV. **extremely, fairly, very,** etc.

bolt *noun*

1 for fastening things together

VERB + BOLT **tighten, tighten up** | **loosen** | **remove, undo, unscrew**
PHRASES **nuts and ~s**

2 for fastening a door

VERB + BOLT **draw back, pull back, slide back** | **push home, slide home** ◇ *She closed the door quickly and pushed the ~s home.*

bolt *verb*

ADV. **firmly, securely** ◇ *Make sure that the rails are securely ~ed in place.* | **together** ◇ *The two parts are ~ed together.*
PREP. **to** ◇ *The yacht's keel is ~ed to the hull.*

bomb *noun*

ADJ. **big, huge, large, massive** | **small** | **cluster, fire** (usually *firebomb*), **high-explosive, incendiary, mortar, nail, petrol** (*BrE*), **smoke** | **atom, atomic, hydrogen, neutron, nuclear** | **bouncing** (*BrE*), **flying** | **terrorist** | **home-made** | **unexploded** | **stray** (*esp. BrE*) ◇ *Their truck was hit by a stray* ~. | **dummy** (*esp. BrE*), **fake** ◇ *The suspect was apprehended for planting a fake* ~ *in a bus terminal.* | **car, roadside** | **letter, parcel** (*BrE*) | **dirty** | **smart** (= one that is controlled by an electronic device) | **suicide** | **time** (*figurative*) ◇ *He described global warming as 'an environmental time bomb'.*
VERB + BOMB **place, plant, put** ◇ *Police suspect terrorists planted the* ~. | **carry** ◇ *The plane had been adapted to carry* ~s. | **drop, release** ◇ *Enemy planes dropped* ~s *on the airport.* | **defuse, disarm** | **detonate, explode, set off** | **build, construct, develop, test** (These verbs are only used about countries.) ◇ *India started to build a nuclear* ~. | **make** ◇ *He used a clock to make a home-made* ~. | **strap, strap on** ◇ *The* ~s *were strapped to their chests.*
BOMB + VERB **fall, rain, rain down** ◇ *Eighty people died when* ~s *rained down on the city's crowded streets.* | **hit sth** | **detonate, explode, go off** | **blow sb/sth to pieces, blow sth up, destroy sth, kill sb, rip through sth** ◇ *Fifteen people were blown to pieces by the car* ~. ◇ *A terrorist* ~ *ripped through the station.* | **target sb/sth** | **be ticking away**
BOMB + NOUN **attack, blast, explosion** | **alert** (*esp. BrE*), **scare, threat, warning** (*BrE*) | **plot** | **hoax** (*BrE*) | **disposal, squad** | **shelter** | **crater** ◇ *The land was scarred with* ~ *craters.* | **damage** | **site** | **factory** | **victim** | **suspect** | **test** ◇ *the fallout from atomic* ~ *tests*

bomb *verb*

ADV. **heavily** ◇ *The city had been very heavily* ~ed. | **accidentally, mistakenly**

bombard *verb*

1 attack with bombs

ADV. **heavily** ◇ *The city has been heavily* ~ed *for the last three days.*

2 direct a lot of things at sb

ADV. **constantly, continually**
PREP. **with** ◇ *We're all constantly* ~ed *with television ads.*

bombardment *noun*

ADJ. **constant, continuous** | **heavy, intense, massive** | **aerial, air, artillery, naval**
VERB + BOMBARDMENT **launch** | **stop** | **be subjected to, be under, come under, suffer** ◇ *The city has been under constant* ~ *for three days.* | **survive, withstand** ◇ *They have withstood heavy* ~ *for many months.*
BOMBARDMENT + VERB **begin, start** | **continue** | **end, stop**
PREP. **during a/the** ~, **in a/the** ~ ◇ *Many people were killed in the* ~. | **~ against** ◇ *The army launched artillery* ~s *against*

enemy positions. | **~ from** ◇ *~ from the air* | **~ with** ◇ *a three-hour ~ with rockets and mortars*

bombing *noun*

ADJ. **aerial, roadside** ◇ *the aerial ~ of ports* | **pinpoint, precision** | **accidental** | **heavy, massive** | **deadly, horrific** | **area, carpet, indiscriminate, saturation** | **strategic** | **terror, terrorist** | **suicide**
BOMBING + NOUN **attack** | **campaign** | **mission, raid, run, sortie** ◇ *He was shot down during a ~ raid over the south.* | **target** | **victim**

bombshell *noun*

VERB + BOMBSHELL **be, come as** (*BrE*) ◇ *His revelation was a ~.* ◇ *The news came as a ~.* | **drop** ◇ *Then she dropped the bombshell—she was pregnant.*
BOMBSHELL + VERB **come**

bond *noun*

1 feeling of friendship

ADJ. **close, strong** | **common** | **special** | **natural** | **emotional, spiritual** ◇ *A strong spiritual ~ exists between them.*
VERB + BOND **be linked by, feel, have, share** ◇ *She felt a ~ of affection for the other girls.* | **create, develop, establish, forge, form** | **strengthen** | **loosen, weaken** | **break, sever**
BOND + VERB **exist** | **link sb** ◇ *the ~ that links us*
PREP. **~ between** ◇ *We try to forge ~s between the different communities.* | **~ of** ◇ *~s of friendship*

2 certificate for money you have lent

ADJ. **high-yield, long-term** | **corporate, government, municipal** (*AmE*), **savings, treasury** | **convertible** | **junk** ◇ *the high yield on junk ~s*
VERB + BOND **buy, invest in, purchase, put money into** ◇ *I decided to invest in some government ~s.* | **cash, cash in, redeem** ◇ *The ~s were redeemed in 2002.* | **issue, sell**
BOND + NOUN **market**

bone *noun*

ADJ. **delicate, fine** ◇ *the delicate ~s of her face* | **healthy, strong** | **brittle, fragile** ◇ *She was diagnosed as having brittle ~s.* | **broken, cracked, splintered** | **weary** | **bleached, dry** | **ankle, hip, leg, shin, thigh,** etc. | **animal, human** | **chicken, dinosaur, fish,** etc.
VERB + BONE **break, chip, crack, fracture, shatter** | **rest** ◇ *He longed to get home to bed and rest his weary ~s.*
BONE + NOUN **structure** ◇ *The black-and-white photographs emphasized her fine ~ structure.* | **marrow** ◇ *a ~ marrow transplant* | **cancer, disease** | **graft, transplant**
PHRASES **every ~ in sb's body** ◇ *The shock shook every ~ in his body.* | **skin and ~** ◇ *He's all skin and ~ after his illness.*

bonfire *noun*

ADJ. **blazing, roaring**
VERB + BONFIRE **build, have, make** | **light, start** | **put out**
BONFIRE + VERB **blaze, burn**

bonnet *noun*

1 hat

ADJ. **Easter** | **straw** | **matching**
→ Special page at CLOTHES

2 (*BrE*) part of a vehicle covering the engine → See also HOOD

ADJ. **car**
VERB + BONNET **close, open** | **hit** ◇ *The child hit the ~ and was flung through the air.* | **dent**
PHRASES **the ~ of a/the car**

bonus *noun*

1 money added to salary, etc.

ADJ. **big, huge, large** | **extra, special** | **cash** | **annual,**

Christmas (*esp. BrE*), **year-end** (*AmE*) ◇ *All employees get an annual ~ before the holidays.* | **loyalty** (*BrE*), **performance, retention** (*AmE*), **roster** (*AmE*) | **no-claims** (*BrE*)
VERB + BONUS **award (sb), give sb, pay sb** | **earn, get, receive** ◇ *You will receive a ~ for high levels of productivity.*
BONUS + NOUN **payment, scheme** (*BrE*) ◇ *Some employees will receive discretionary ~ payments.*
PREP. **~ of** ◇ *He was awarded a cash ~ of $2 500.*

2 sth extra that is good

ADJ. **great, huge, major, real** | **added, extra, special** ◇ *The house is comfortable, and as an added ~, it's near my work.* | **unexpected** | **nice, welcome** (*esp. BrE*)
PREP. **~ for** ◇ *The sunshine on the final day was a welcome ~ for the spectators.*

boo *noun*

ADJ. **loud**
VERB + BOO **be greeted with, be met with** ◇ *His speech was met with ~s.*
PREP. **~ from** ◇ *There were loud ~s from the audience.*
PHRASES **~s and hisses** ◇ *~s and hisses from the crowd*

book *noun*

1 for reading

ADJ. **latest, new, recent** | **best-selling** | **forthcoming, upcoming** (*esp. AmE*) | **hardback, hardcover** (*esp. AmE*), **leather-bound, paperback** | **printed** ◇ *one of the earliest printed ~s* | **rare** | **second-hand** (*esp. BrE*), **used** (*AmE*) | **excellent, fascinating, fine, good, great, interesting, readable, remarkable, terrific, useful, wonderful** ◇ *There's nothing like curling up with a mug of tea and a good ~.* | **famous, important, influential** | **controversial** ◇ *a controversial ~ about the royal family* | **favourite/favorite** ◇ *a survey to find the nation's favourite/favorite children's ~* | **library** | **audio** | **children's, colouring/coloring, comic, picture, reading, story** (usually **storybook**) | **cook** (usually **cookbook**), **cookery** (*BrE*) | **guide** (usually **guidebook**), **travel** | **phrase, reference** | **coffee-table, illustrated** | **how-to, self-help, tell-all** | **school, set** (*BrE*), **text** (usually **textbook**) | **history, science, etc.** | **address, autograph, exercise, order** | **phone, telephone** | **holy, hymn, prayer**
... OF BOOK **copy** ◇ *How many copies of the ~ did you order?*
VERB + BOOK **flick through** (*esp. BrE*), **flip through** (*esp. AmE*), **look at, read, skim through** | **be deep in, be engrossed in, be immersed in** | **study** | **look up from, put down** ◇ *She looked up from her ~ and smiled at him.* ◇ *I couldn't put the ~ down.* | **close, open** | **author, co-author, write** | **bring out, publish, put out** | **reprint** | **edit, proofread, revise** | **translate** | **illustrate** | **bind** | **ban, censor** | **dedicate, inscribe** ◇ *The ~ is dedicated to his mother.* ◇ *Her name was inscribed in the ~.* | **review** | **recommend** | **borrow, check out** (*esp. AmE*), **have out, take out** (*esp. BrE*) (= from a library) ◇ *How many ~s can I borrow?* | **return, take back** (= to a library) | **renew** ◇ *Do you want to renew any of your library ~s?*
BOOK + VERB **appear, come out** ◇ *His latest ~ will appear in December.* | **be out of print, go out of print**
BOOK + NOUN **title** | **review, reviewer** | **club** | **token** (*BrE*) | **bag** (*AmE*)
PREP. **in a/the ~** ◇ *These issues are discussed in his latest ~.* | **~ about, ~ on** ◇ *She's busy writing a ~ on astrology.* | **~ by** ◇ *a ~ by Robert Grout* | **~ of** ◇ *a ~ of walks in London*

2 books company records

ADJ. **account**
VERB + BOOKS **do, keep** ◇ *She does the ~s for us.* | **audit, check** | **cook** (*informal*) ◇ *Someone was cooking the ~s* (= falsifying the accounts).
PREP. **on the ~s** ◇ *We have fifty people on the ~s* (= working for us).

book *verb*

ADV. **ahead, early, in advance** ◇ *Seats go quickly, so it is essential to ~ in advance.* | **online** ◇
PREP. **with** ◇ *Book with Suntours and kids go free!*
PHRASES **be ~ed solid** (= be fully booked), **be ~ed up, be fully ~ed**

booking *noun*

1 (*esp. BrE*) arrangement that you make in advance to buy a ticket, etc.

ADJ. **advance, early** | **late** | **priority** | **double** (= two bookings for the same time) | **block** (= a large number of seats booked together) | **hotel** (*BrE, AmE*), **travel** (*esp. AmE*) | **online** (*BrE, AmE*), **postal** (*BrE*), **telephone**
VERB + BOOKING **make** ◇ *I made the ~ through a travel agent.* | **cancel** | **confirm** | **change** | **accept, take** ◇ *We also accept telephone ~s.*
BOOKING + NOUN **fee, form, system** | **office** | **agent** (*BrE, AmE*)
PREP. **~ for** ◇ *a ~ for the Saturday performance*

2 (*BrE*) punishment in football/soccer

VERB + BOOKING **collect, earn, pick up** ◇ *Drummond earned a ~ for arguing with the official.*

bookkeeping *noun*

ADJ. **double-entry**
VERB + BOOKKEEPING **do** ◇ *I run the hotel and do the ~.*
BOOKKEEPING + NOUN **entry** | **method, system**

boom *noun*

1 period of sudden increase

ADJ. **great** | **post-war** | **consumer, credit, economic, inflationary, investment, spending** | **stock-market** | **building, housing, property** (*esp. BrE*), **real estate** (*esp. AmE*) | **oil** | **baby** ◇ *the baby ~ generation* | **dotcom, high-tech, Internet, tech**
VERB + BOOM **cause, create, fuel, lead to** ◇ *Demand for consumer products helped fuel the ~.* | **experience**
BOOM + NOUN **period, time, year** | **town**
PREP. **during a/the ~, in a/the ~** ◇ *He was born during the post-war baby ~.* | **~ in** ◇ *a ~ in real estate*
PHRASES **~ and bust** ◇ *the ordinary business cycle of ~ and bust*

2 deep hollow sound

ADJ. **big, loud** | **deep** | **sonic** ◇ *We heard the sonic ~ of a jet overhead.*
VERB + BOOM **hear**
BOOM + VERB **echo** ◇ *The deep ~ of a foghorn echoed across the bay.*
PREP. **with a ~**

boon *noun*

ADJ. **great, huge, real**
VERB + BOON **be, prove**
PREP. **~ for** ◇ *High productivity has been a ~ for corporate profits.* ◇ *The contracts come as an enormous ~ for the building industry.* | **~ to** ◇ *These machines have proved a real ~ to disabled people.*

boost *noun*

ADJ. **big, enormous, great, huge, major, significant, tremendous** | **much-needed, welcome** ◇ *The new factory will provide a much-needed ~ to the local economy.* | **extra, unexpected** | **confidence, ego, financial, morale, psychological** | **energy, performance**
VERB + BOOST **give sb, provide (sb with)** | **get, receive**
PREP. **~ for** ◇ *The Olympics provided a ~ for Chinese products.* | **~ in** ◇ *a big ~ in sales* | **~ to** ◇ *a ~ to the economy*

boost *verb*

ADV. **considerably, dramatically, greatly, significantly, substantially** | **artificially**
VERB + BOOST **help (to)** ◇ *The new service helped ~ profits by 10%.*

boot *noun*

1 strong shoe

ADJ. **heavy** | **light, lightweight** | **high, knee-length, thigh-high, thigh-length** | **ankle, desert** | **calf-high, calf-length** | **muddy** | **polished** | **leather, plastic, suede** | **rain** (*AmE*), **rubber** (*esp. AmE*), **snow, wading, waterproof, Wellington** (*BrE*) | **lace-up** | **high-heeled** | **hobnail, hobnailed, thick-soled** | **steel-capped** (*BrE*), **steel-toecapped** (*BrE*), **steel-toed** (*esp. AmE*) | **work** | **army, combat** | **baseball, football, rugby** (*all BrE*) (**cleats** in *AmE*) | **climbing, cowboy, hiking, riding, ski, walking** (*BrE*)

... OF BOOTS **pair** ◇ *a pair of heavy walking ~s*

VERB + BOOT **have on, wear** | **put on** | **pull off, remove, take off** | **lace up, unlace** | **polish**

BOOT + NOUN **polish**

PHRASES **as tough as old ~s** (*esp. BrE*) ◇ *The meat was as tough as old ~s.* | **the toe of sb's ~** ◇ *She kicked at the snow with the toe of her ~.*

→ Special page at CLOTHES

2 (*BrE*) of a car, etc. → See also TRUNK

ADJ. **car**

VERB + BOOT **open** | **close, shut**

PREP. **in the ~** ◇ *What have you got in the ~?*

booth *noun*

ADJ. **DJ, photo, tanning, ticket** | **phone, telephone** | **polling, voting**

PREP. **in a/the ~** ◇ *She waited in the phone ~.*

booze *noun*

ADJ. **cheap** | **free** ◇ *There was free ~ at the party.*

VERB + BOOZE **smell** ◇ *I could smell ~ on his breath.* | **bring, take** ◇ *We need to take some ~ to the party.* | **turn to** ◇ *He turned to ~ (= started drinking a lot of alcohol) when his wife died.* | **kick** ◇ *She's still trying to kick the ~ (= stop drinking so much alcohol).*

BOOZE + NOUN **problem** | **cruise** (= trip to buy cheap alcohol) (*BrE*) | **cruise** (= party on a boat where alcohol is drunk) (*AmE*)

PREP. **off the ~** (= not drinking alcohol) ◇ *She's been off the ~ for a month now.* | **on the ~** (= drinking alcohol) ◇ *He was dry for years but now he's back on the ~.*

border *noun*

1 line that divides two countries

ADJ. **open** | **closed** | **porous** | **common** ◇ *Brazil has a common ~ with most South American countries.* | **disputed** | **northern, southern, etc.** | **international, national**

VERB + BORDER **arrive at, reach, stop at** | **cross, drive across, drive over, slip across, slip over** ◇ *They slipped across the ~ at nightfall.* | **escape across, escape over, flee across, flee over** | **form, mark** ◇ *A river forms the ~.* | **draw, draw up, establish, fix** | **guard, patrol** | **open | close, seal | secure | share** ◇ *Ethiopia shares its longest ~ with Somalia.*

BORDER + NOUN **crossing, post** | **region, town** | **control, guard, troops** | **clash, dispute, war** | **raid** | **clash, incident, skirmish**

PREP. **across a/the ~, over a/the ~** ◇ *to smuggle goods across the ~.* | **along a/the ~** ◇ *There has been fighting along the ~.* | **at a/the ~, on a/the ~** ◇ *We were stopped on the ~.* | **on the ~ of** ◇ *a farm on the ~ of Cumbria and Yorkshire* | **up to the ~** ◇ *He drove us right up to the Russian ~.* | **~ between, ~ of** ◇ *the ~ between Austria and Switzerland* | **~ with** ◇ *the ~ with Mexico*

PHRASES **north of the ~, south of the ~** | **on both sides of the ~, on one side of the ~** ◇ *There has been fighting on both sides of the ~.*

2 decorative band/strip around the edge of sth

ADJ. **wide** | **narrow** | **decorative**

VERB + BORDER **have** ◇ *The tablecloth has a narrow lace ~.* | **draw**

PREP. **with a/the ~** ◇ *a white handkerchief with a blue ~* | **~ around, ~ round** (*esp. BrE*) ◇ *She drew a decorative ~ around the picture.*

bore *noun*

1 person

ADJ. **awful, crashing, dreadful** (*esp. BrE*), **real, terrible** ◇ *Her husband is a crashing ~.* | **complete, total**

PHRASES **a bit of a ~**

2 a bore sth that you have to do

ADJ. **real, terrible** ◇ *It's a real ~ having to meet my aunt for lunch.*

bore *verb*

ADV. **easily** ◇ *I'm very easily ~d.*

PREP. **with** ◇ *I won't ~ you with too many details.*

PHRASES **~ sb rigid** (*BrE*), **~ sb silly** (*BrE*), **~ sb stiff, ~ sb to death, ~ sb to tears** ◇ *That lecture ~d me to tears!* | **~ sb out of their brains** (*AmE*), **~ sb out of their mind, ~ sb out of their tiny mind** (*BrE*)

bored *adj.*

VERBS **be, feel, look, seem, sound** | **become, get, grow** ◇ *Some children get ~ very quickly.* | **remain**

ADV. **extremely, fairly, very, etc.** | **terribly, thoroughly** | **a little, slightly, etc.**

PREP. **at** ◇ *~ at the prospect of going shopping* | **by** ◇ *He seemed slightly ~ by the whole process.* | **with** ◇ *He was ~ with their conversation.*

PHRASES **~ rigid** (*BrE*), **~ silly** (*BrE*), **~ stiff, ~ to death, ~ to tears** ◇ *I remember being ~ stiff during my entire time at school.* ◇ *She was alone all day and ~ to death.* | **~ out of your brains** (*AmE*), **~ out of your mind, ~ out of your tiny mind** (*BrE*) ◇ *He walked along, ~ out of his mind.*

boredom *noun*

ADJ. **pure** (*esp. AmE*), **sheer, utter** | **terminal**

VERB + BOREDOM **prevent** | **alleviate, avoid, combat, relieve** ◇ *An MP3 player can relieve the ~ of running.* | **die of, go mad with** (*BrE*) ◇ *I'd die of ~ if I lived in the country.* | **drive sb mad with** (*BrE*) ◇ *Unemployment can drive you mad with ~.*

PHRASES **a low ~ threshold** (*esp. BrE*) ◇ *Sorting mail is not a job for people with a low ~ threshold.*

boring *adj.*

VERBS **be, look, seem, sound** | **become, get** | **make sth** ◇ *Try not to make the diet ~.* | **consider sb/sth, find sb/sth, think sb/sth** ◇ *She found her job ~.*

ADV. **extremely, fairly, very, etc.** | **awfully** (*esp. BrE*), **dead** (*BrE*), **incredibly, terribly** | **completely, downright, utterly** | **a little, slightly, etc.**

PREP. **for** ◇ *The game was ~ for the spectators.*

PHRASES **~ old** ◇ *Green is much better than ~ old white.*

born *verb* be born

ADV. **prematurely**

PREP. **into** ◇ *She was ~ into a wealthy family.* | **of** (*formal*) ◇ *to be ~ of noble parents* | **to** ◇ *babies who are ~ to very young mothers* | **with** ◇ *Their child was ~ with a serious medical problem.*

PHRASES **be ~ alive, be ~ dead** | **be ~ and bred, be ~ and brought up** (*esp. BrE*), **be ~ and raised** (*esp. AmE*) ◇ *I was ~ and bred in Texas.* | **be ~ blind, deaf, etc.** | **be ~ out of wedlock, be ~ outside marriage** (*esp. BrE*), **be ~ outside of marriage** (*esp. AmE*)

borough *noun*

ADJ. **county, metropolitan** (*both in the UK*) | **outer**

BOROUGH + NOUN **council, councillor** (*in the UK*), **president** (*in the US*) | **resident** | **park, school**

PREP. **in a/the ~, throughout a/the ~, within a/the ~** ◇

There are factories scattered throughout the ~. | *~ of* ◇ *the New York ~ of Queens* ◇ *the London ~ of Lewisham*

borrow verb

1 money/things

ADV. **heavily** ◇ *He ~ed heavily to set the company up.*
PREP. **from** ◇ *She ~ed some money from her mother.* | **off** (*informal, esp. BrE*) ◇ *I ~ed £50 off my mum.*

2 ideas, etc.

ADV. **freely**
PREP. **from** ◇ *His designs ~ freely from the architecture of ancient Egypt.*

bosom noun

ADJ. **ample, full, large**
BOSOM + VERB **heave** ◇ *Her ~ heaved with every breath.*
PHRASES **clutch sb/sth to your ~** (*literary*) ◇ *She clutched her son tightly to her ~.*

boss noun

ADJ. **big** | **company, crime, party, union**

bother noun

VERB + BOTHER **have** (*esp. BrE*) ◇ *I had a little ~ finding your house.* | **cause, give sb** (*both esp. BrE*) ◇ *Your little boy didn't give me any ~.* | **go to** ◇ *I wouldn't go to the ~ of making the cakes myself.* | **put sb to** (*BrE*) ◇ *I'd love to come and stay with you, but I don't want to put you to any ~.* | **save sb** ◇ *Getting a taxi will save you the ~ of picking me up from the station.*
PREP. **without any ~** (*esp. BrE*) ◇ *We found the hotel without any ~.* | **~ to** ◇ *I don't mind taking care of your dog—it's no ~ to me.* | **~ with** ◇ *He's having a little ~ with his computer.*
PHRASES **a bit of ~, a little ~, a lot of ~, a spot of ~** (*all esp. BrE*) ◇ *He's in a bit of ~ with the police.* | **no ~** ◇ *It was no ~ having the children to stay.*

bothered adj.

VERBS **be, look, seem, sound** | **get** ◇ *He never got too ~ about the mess.*
ADV. **not at all, not in the least** (*both esp. BrE*) ◇ *I'm not in the least ~ about the price.* | **not all that, not particularly, not really, not that, not too** (*all esp. BrE*) ◇ *He is not that ~ about his appearance.* ◇ *They're not really ~ about what you do.*
PREP. **about** ◇ *He wasn't too ~ about the slight leak.* | **by** ◇ *He was still ~ by a persistent leg injury.* | **with** ◇ *They did not want to be ~ with her problems.*
PHRASES **can't be ~** ◇ *He couldn't even be ~ to get dressed.* | **hot and ~** ◇ *She got herself all hot and ~ about the test.*

bottle noun

ADJ. **full** | **empty** | **broken** | **recyclable, returnable** | **beer, medicine, milk, etc.** | **glass, plastic** | **hot-water** | **feeding** | **Thermos™** (*usually just* **Thermos**) (*AmE*)
VERB + BOTTLE **fill** ◇ *She filled the ~ with water.* | **empty** | **open, uncork** | **break open, crack open** (*both used only about alcoholic drinks*) ◇ *Let's crack open a ~ of champagne to celebrate.* | **drink, have, wash sth down with** ◇ *We washed the food down with a ~ of cheap red wine.* | **share** | **bring** (= *to bring a bottle of wine to a party*) | **throw** ◇ *a crowd of youths throwing ~s and stones*
BOTTLE + NOUN **cap, top** | **opener** | **bank** (*BrE*) | **feeding**
PREP. **over a/the ~** ◇ *We discussed the problem over a ~ of wine.* | **~ of**
PHRASES **be on the ~** (= *to be an alcoholic*) | **hit the ~, take to the ~** (*esp. BrE*) (= *to start drinking alcohol heavily*)

bottom noun

1 lowest part of sth

ADJ. **false** ◇ *a case with a false ~*
VERB + BOTTOM **arrive at, fall to, get to, reach, sink to** ◇ *He reached the ~ of the steps in no time.* ◇ *The boat sank to the ~ of the sea.* | **touch** ◇ *She could only just touch the ~ (= of a swimming pool, etc.).* | **cover, line** ◇ *Line the ~ of the cage with newspaper.*
BOTTOM + NOUN **end, half**
PREP. **along the ~** ◇ *We rode along the ~ of the valley.* | **at the ~** ◇ *at the ~ of the hill* | **from the ~** ◇ *strange sounds from the ~ of the well* | **in the ~** ◇ *in the ~ of my bag* | **on the ~** ◇ *on the ~ of the box* | **near the ~, towards/toward the ~** ◇ *near the ~ of the page*

2 least important position

VERB + BOTTOM **start at, work up from** ◇ *He started at the ~ and worked his way up through the company.*
PREP. **at the ~, near the ~, towards/toward the ~** ◇ *He's near the ~ of the class.*

3 (*esp. BrE*) part of the body

ADJ. **bare**
VERB + BOTTOM **slap, smack, spank**

4 basic cause of sth/truth about sth

VERB + BOTTOM **be at, lie at** ◇ *I'd love to know what lies at the ~ of all this.* | **get to** ◇ *The only way to get to the ~ of it is to confront the chairman.*

boulevard noun

ADJ. **broad, wide** | **tree-lined**
BOULEVARD + VERB **be lined with sth** ◇ *a ~ lined with cafes*
PREP. **along, down, up, etc. a/the ~** ◇ *They sauntered along the tree-lined ~.*

bounce verb

ADV. **high** ◇ *The ball ~d high and she missed it.* | **back, off** ◇ *The stone hit the window but ~d off.*
PREP. **against, around, down, off, on, towards/toward ~** *Short sound waves ~ off even small objects.* ◇ *The idea had been bouncing around in my head for some time.*

bound adj.

1 bound to do sth certain to do sth

VERBS **be, seem**
ADV. **almost** ◇ *These problems were almost ~ to arise.*

2 bound (to do sth) obliged to do sth

VERBS **be, feel** | **become** | **remain** | **hold sb** ◇ *The country will not be held ~ by a treaty signed by the previous regime.*
ADV. **absolutely** | **irrevocably** | **by law, contractually, legally** ◇ *Officials are ~ by law to investigate any possible fraud.* ◇ *He was legally ~ to report them to the authorities.* | **morally** ◇ *I felt morally ~ to report the incident.*
PREP. **by** ◇ *We are legally ~ by this decision.*

3 going in a particular direction

VERBS **be**
ADV. **homeward, outward**
PREP. **for** ◇ *tourists who are ~ for Europe*

4 bound up closely connected

VERBS **be** | **become**
ADV. **closely, intimately** | **inevitably, inextricably** | **together** ◇ *A person's name and their sense of their own identity are often closely ~ up together.*
PREP. **with** ◇ *From that moment my life became inextricably ~ up with hers.*

boundary noun

1 line that marks the limits of a place

ADJ. **common** | **northern, southern, etc.** | **national, state** | **territorial** | **district, parish** (*esp. BrE*) | **geographic** (*esp. AmE*), **geographical**
VERB + BOUNDARY **have** | **form, mark** ◇ *The river forms the ~.* | **share** | **draw, establish, fix, set** ◇ *The ~ was fixed just south of the farm.* | **redraw**
BOUNDARY + NOUN **fence, hedge** (*esp. BrE*), **line, wall** | **dispute** ◇ *a dispute between Brazil and Paraguay*
PREP. **across the ~, over the ~** ◇ *They drove across the ~.* | **along the ~** ◇ *We continued along the southern ~ of the*

county. | **at the ~**, **on the ~** ◇ *We had to stop at the ~.* ◇ *on the ~ of the two countries* | **beyond the ~** ◇ *She had never strayed beyond the city boundaries.* | **within the ~s** ◇ *within the boundaries of the old city walls* | **~ between** ◇ *the ~ between Sussex and Surrey* | **~ with** ◇ *The state has a ~ with Ontario.*

2 limit

ADJ. **traditional**
VERB + BOUNDARY **cross** ◇ *This job crosses the traditional ~ between social work and health care.* | **extend**, **push**, **push back** ◇ *research which extends the boundaries of human knowledge* | **overstep** | **establish** | **define** | **blur** ◇ *The Internet has blurred the ~ between news and entertainment.*
PREP. **across ~s** ◇ *His policies appeal across party political boundaries.* | **beyond the ~s** ◇ *This goes beyond the boundaries of what is accepted.* | **on the ~** ◇ *on the ~ of physics and chemistry* | **within the ~s** ◇ *the importance of keeping within the boundaries of the law* | **~ between** ◇ *the ~ between sanity and insanity*
PHRASES **the boundaries of taste** ◇ *In her performance she had clearly overstepped the boundaries of good taste.* | **sb/sth knows no boundaries** ◇ *His passion for the arts knows no boundaries.*

bouquet noun

ADJ. **huge, large** | **small** | **bridal, wedding**
VERB + BOUQUET **carry, hold** | **catch, throw** ◇ *She caught the bride's ~.* | **send (sb)** | **place** ◇ *They walked up and placed their ~ of flowers on the grave.*
PREP. **in a/the ~** ◇ *Are there any roses in your ~?* | **~ of** ◇ *He sent her a large ~ of wild flowers.*

bout noun

ADJ. **bad, nasty, prolonged, serious, severe** ◇ *I got a bad ~ of flu last winter.* ◇ *I got a bad ~ of the flu last winter.* (*AmE*) | **mild** | **occasional** | **sudden** | **drinking**
VERB + BOUT **get, have, suffer, suffer from**
PREP. **during a/the ~** | **~ of** ◇ *a ~ of flu* (*BrE*) ◇ *a ~ of the flu* (*AmE*) | **~ with** (*AmE*) ◇ *a ~ with the flu*

boutique noun

ADJ. **chic, elegant, exclusive, smart** (*esp. BrE*), **trendy** | **fashion** | **designer** | **expensive**
VERB + BOUTIQUE **open** | **run**

bow¹ noun

1 act of bowing

ADJ. **deep, low** | **little, slight, small** | **formal, stiff**
VERB + BOW **give, make** ◇ *He gave a formal ~ and left the room.* | **take** (= used about a performer) ◇ *The song ended and Albert took a ~.* ◇ *The boss takes his final ~* (= is retiring) *today.* (*figurative*)
PREP. **~ to** ◇ *He made a deep ~ to the king.*

2 front part of a ship

ADJ. **port, starboard** ◇ *There's a small boat on the port ~.*
VERB + BOW **cross** ◇ *A whale crossed our ~s.* (*BrE*) ◇ *A whale crossed our ~.* (*AmE*)
PREP. **across the, our, etc. ~** (*AmE*), **across the, our, etc. ~s** (*BrE*) ◇ *They fired a shot across our bow/bows.* | **in the ~** (*esp. AmE*), **in the ~s** (*BrE*) ◇ *We left two men in the ~ to receive the cargo.* | **off the, our, etc. ~** ◇ *100 yards off our ~* | **on the, our, etc. ~** ◇ *The ship's name was printed on her ~.* | **over the, our, etc. ~**, **over the, our, etc. ~s** (*both BrE*) ◇ *There were huge waves breaking over the ~s.*

bow² verb

ADV. **deeply, low** ◇ *He swept off his hat and ~ed deeply.* | **slightly** | **quickly** | **politely, respectfully** | **gracefully** | **down**
PREP. **before** ◇ *The Emperor's subjects ~ed down before him.* | **to** ◇ *The pianist stood up and ~ed to the audience.*

bow³ noun

1 knot with two loops

ADJ. **neat** | **double**
VERB + BOW **tie (sth into)** ◇ *Can you tie a ~?* ◇ *She tied the ribbon into a neat ~.*

2 weapon for shooting arrows

VERB + BOW **be armed with, carry, have, hold** | **aim, draw, raise** ◇ *She drew and aimed her ~.* | **shoot** | **lower**
PHRASES **a ~ and arrow**

bowel noun

ADJ. **large, small** | **irritable** ◇ *irritable ~ syndrome*
VERB + BOWEL **empty, evacuate, move** (*esp. AmE*), **open**
BOWEL + NOUN **action, function, habit, movement** ◇ *Patients are asked to report any change in ~ habit.* ◇ *He's been having painful ~ movements.* | **frequency** | **wall** | **cancer, disease, disorder, obstruction, problems** | **biopsy, surgery**
PREP. **in the ~**

bowl noun

ADJ. **deep, shallow** | **empty, full** | **ceramic, china, crystal, cut-glass, earthenware, enamel, glass** | **food** | **cereal, dessert** (*AmE*), **pudding** (*BrE*), **salad, soup** | **fruit, punch** (usually *punchbowl*), **sugar** | **water** ◇ *I refilled the dog's water ~.* | **mixing, serving** | **washing-up** (*BrE*) ◇ *a washing-up ~ full of dirty dishes* | **finger** (= for washing your fingers at the table) | **begging** (*figurative*) ◇ *The school is always having to get out the begging ~ for books and basic equipment.* | **goldfish** | **lavatory** (*BrE*), **toilet**
VERB + BOWL **fill, pour (sb), pour sth into** ◇ *He poured himself a ~ of soup.* | **empty** | **eat** ◇ *I ate a ~ of cereal.*
BOWL + VERB **contain sth, hold sth** ◇ *a ~ containing flour* ◇ *This ~ holds about four pints.* | **overflow** ◇ *The ~ was overflowing.*
PREP. **from a/the ~** ◇ *I helped myself to an apple from the ~.* ◇ *The cat drank some milk from the ~.* ◇ *The boy was drinking milk out of a ~.* | **in a/the ~, into a/the ~** ◇ *Mix the ingredients in a deep ~.* ◇ *Sieve the flour into a ~.* | **~ of** ◇ *a ~ of cherries*

bowler noun in cricket → See also PITCHER

ADJ. **fast, pace, quick** | **slow** | **strike** ◇ *England's number-one strike ~* | **spin** | **left-arm, right-arm**
BOWLER + VERB **bowl (sth)** ◇ *Australia's fast ~s bowled well.* | **take sth** ◇ *The Pakistani pace ~ took six wickets for 60.*

bowling noun

1 indoor game

ADJ. **pro** (*AmE*), **professional** (*esp. AmE*) | **duckpin** (*AmE*), **tenpin** (*esp. BrE*) | **lawn** (*esp. AmE*)
VERB + BOWLING **go** ◇ *Let's go ~ on Saturday.*
BOWLING + NOUN **ball** | **pin** (*esp. AmE*) | **alley, centre/center** | **club** | **green** (*esp. BrE*)
→ Special page at SPORTS

2 in the game of cricket

ADJ. **fast, pace, quick** | **slow** | **seam, spin, swing** | **accurate, tight**
VERB + BOWLING **open** ◇ *McArthur opened the ~ on the first day of the match.*
BOWLING + NOUN **attack** ◇ *England were no match for the Indian ~ attack.* | **average** | **crease**

box noun

1 container

ADJ. **rectangular, square** | **upturned** (*esp. BrE*) ◇ *They were sitting around the fire on upturned ~es.* | **empty** | **cardboard, metal, plastic, wooden, etc.** | **storage** | **cereal, chocolate, cigar, egg** (*BrE*) (*egg carton* in *AmE*), **pizza** | **jewel, jewellery/jewelry, shoe, tool** (usually *toolbox*) | **CD, DVD** | **gift** | **lunch, sandwich** (*BrE*) | **first-aid** | **safe deposit, safety deposit, security** ◇ *There is a safety deposit ~ in every*

room of the hotel. | **cash, money** (*esp. BrE*) ◊ *The cash ~ was kept in a safe.* | **collection, donation** ◊ *The exhibition is free, but there is a collection ~ for donations.* | **ballot** | **letter** (*BrE*), **mail** (usually *mailbox*) (*AmE*) | **nest, nesting**
... OF BOXES **pile, stack**
VERB + BOX **fill, pack** ◊ *She filled the ~ with old clothes.* | **pack sth in, pack sth into, put sth away in, put sth in, put sth into, store sth in** ◊ *We packed all the books into ~es.* | **remove sth from, take sth out of** | **empty, unpack** | **open** | **close, shut** | **lock** | **place, stack**
BOX + VERB **be filled with sth, be full of sth, contain sth, hold sth** ◊ *This ~ holds ten 10 candles and costs $21.40.* | **be labelled/labeled sth, be marked sth** ◊ *a ~ marked 'fragile'* | **be covered in sth, be covered with sth, be lined with sth** ◊ *The dog sleeps in a ~ lined with an old blanket.*
PREP. **in a/the ~, inside a/the ~** | **into a/the ~** | **out of a/the ~** | **~ of** ◊ *a ~ of chocolates*
PHRASES **the lid of a ~**

2 enclosed area

ADJ. **soundproof** | **call, phone, telephone** (*all BrE*) | **jury, witness** | **commentary** (*BrE*), **press** ◊ *There was a babble of languages in the commentary ~ when the race began.* | **director's, executive, hospitality** (*all BrE*) ◊ *They drank champagne as they watched the game from the executive ~.* | **private, royal** ◊ *a private ~ at the opera* | **signal** (*BrE*) | **horse** (usually *horsebox*) (*BrE*)
PREP. **in a/the ~, into a/the ~**

3 square on a form/screen

ADJ. **appropriate, relevant** (*esp. BrE*) ◊ *Tick the appropriate ~ below.* | **dialog** ◊ *Click on 'open file' in the dialog ~.* | **check, tick** (*BrE*) (usually *checkbox, tickbox*)
VERB + BOX **check** (*esp. AmE*), **fill in, mark** (*esp. AmE*), **put sth in, tick** (*BrE*), **write (sth) in** ◊ *Put a cross in the ~ if you agree with the comments.*
PREP. **in a/the ~, into a/the ~**
PHRASES **tick all the ~es** (= do exactly the right things to please sb) (*BrE, informal*) ◊ *The house we would like to buy ticks all the ~es.*

boxing *noun*

ADJ. **heavyweight, lightweight, middleweight, welterweight, etc.** | **amateur, professional, unlicensed** ◊ *Unlicensed ~ can be very dangerous.* | **world** ◊ *the most respected coach in world ~* | **kick, Thai** | **shadow** (usually *shadow-boxing*) (= boxing with an imaginary opponent) ◊ *The two candidates engaged in shadow-boxing before the election.* (*figurative*)
VERB + BOXING **do** ◊ *He does ~ in his spare time.*
BOXING + NOUN **glove** | **boot** (*BrE*), **shoe** (*AmE*) | **competition, match, tournament** | **title** | **champion** | **ring** | **skill, technique** | **coach, promoter** | **career** | **fan** | **writer** | **circles** ◊ *He is highly respected in ~ circles.*
→ Special page at SPORTS

box office *noun*

BOX-OFFICE + NOUN **draw, hit, smash, success** | **failure, flop** | **gross** (*AmE*), **numbers, receipts, takings** (*esp. BrE*) ◊ *Box-office receipts for the movie have hit $50 million.*
PREP. **at a/the ~** ◊ *Tickets are available at the ~.*
PHRASES **do badly, well, etc. at the ~** ◊ *The musical has done very well at the ~* (= a lot of tickets have been sold).

boy *noun*

ADJ. **big** ◊ *Your ~ is big for his age.* ◊ *Don't cry—you're a big ~ now.* | **little, small** ◊ *A little ~ rode by on a tricycle.* ◊ *Their ~ is small for his age.* | **young** ◊ *Our youngest ~ is just starting school.* | **elder, eldest, older** ◊ *How old is your eldest ~?* | **baby** | **five-year-old, etc.** | **adolescent, teenage** | **good** ◊ *Eat up your greens—there's a good ~.* | **bad, naughty** | **bright, clever** (*esp. BrE*), **smart** (*esp. AmE*)
VERB + BOY **have** ◊ *They've had a baby ~.* ◊ *I have three ~s.*

boycott *noun*

ADJ. **mass, total, worldwide** | **academic, consumer, economic, trade** ◊ *a consumer ~ of GM foods*
VERB + BOYCOTT **declare, impose, introduce** ◊ *Opposition groups declared a ~ of the elections.* | **call for, threaten, urge** ◊ *Lawyers threatened a ~ of the courts.* | **lead, organize** | **support** | **end, lift** ◊ *Politicians want to end their ~ of the talks.* | **join** ◊ *There is pressure on the biggest union to join the ~.*
BOYCOTT + NOUN **campaign**
PREP. **~ by** ◊ *a ~ by international singers* | **~ of** ◊ *The group is calling for a mass consumer ~ of these products.* | **~ on** ◊ *The US has imposed a ~ on some European goods.*

boycott *verb*

VERB + BOYCOTT **threaten to** | **call on sb to, urge sb to** ◊ *They have urged people to ~ foreign products.*

boyfriend *noun*

ADJ. **current, latest, new** | **former, old, previous** | **first** | **last** | **long-standing, long-term, serious, steady** | **live-in** | **abusive, jealous** | **jilted** ◊ *She was stalked by a jilted ~.*
... OF BOYFRIENDS **string, succession** ◊ *She had a string of wealthy ~s before she finally married.*
VERB + BOYFRIEND **have** ◊ *Do you have a ~?* | **meet** | **live with** | **sleep with** | **kiss** | **marry** | **dump** (*informal*), **leave**
BOYFRIEND + NOUN **trouble** ◊ *She's been having ~ trouble.*

bra *noun*

ADJ. **padded, push-up, strapless, underwire** (*AmE*), **underwired** (*BrE*), **uplift** | **maternity, nursing** (*AmE*) | **training** (*esp. AmE*) | **sports**
VERB + BRA **put on** | **wear** | **take off** | **do up** | **undo, unhook**
BRA + NOUN **strap**
→ Special page at CLOTHES

brace *noun*

1 for supporting a part of the body

ADJ. **knee, leg, neck, shoulder**
VERB + BRACE **have, wear** ◊ *I used to wear a ~.*
PREP. **~ on** ◊ *He had a ~ on his teeth.* (*BrE*) ◊ *He had ~s on his teeth.* (*AmE*)

2 braces (*BrE*) for holding trousers/pants up → See also SUSPENDERS

BRACES + VERB **hold sth up, support sth** ◊ *The ~s held up his trousers.*
→ Special page at CLOTHES

bracket *noun*

1 brackets (*esp. BrE*) marks around extra information in writing → See also PARENTHESIS

ADJ. **angle** (*BrE, AmE*), **curly** (also *braces*, esp. in *AmE*), **round, square** (just *brackets* in *AmE*)
VERB + BRACKETS **enclose sth in, give sth in, put sth in** ◊ *The prices are given in ~s.*
PREP. **in ~s, inside ~s, within ~s** ◊ *The words in ~s should be deleted.* | **outside ~s** ◊ *The numbers outside the curly ~s are the sales figures.*

2 range

ADJ. **age, income, price, tax** | **high, higher, top, upper** | **middle** | **low, lower**
PREP. **in a/the ~, within a/the ~** ◊ *These machines are in the higher price ~.* | **outside a/the ~** ◊ *people outside this age ~*

brain *noun*

1 part of the body

ADJ. **human** | **left, right** ◊ *The left ~ controls the right-hand side of the body.*
BRAIN + NOUN **cell, tissue** | **region** | **stem** (usually *brainstem*) | **function, process** | **activity** | **damage, death, disease, disorder, failure, haemorrhage/hemorrhage, illness, injury, tumour/tumor** | **scan** ◊ *He had a ~ scan to*

search for possible damage. | **surgeon, surgery** | activity, function, waves (usually *brainwaves*)

PREP. **in the/your ~** ◊ *Doctors tried to reduce the swelling in his ~.* | **on the/your ~** ◊ *He was found to have a blood clot on his ~.* ◊ *He has sex on the ~ (= thinks about nothing but sex).*

PHRASES **blow your ~s out** ◊ *He put a gun to his head and threatened to blow his ~s out.*

2 ability to think/intelligence

ADJ. **fertile, fine, good, great, quick** | **muddled, tired** ◊ *My tired ~ couldn't cope with such a complex problem.* | **analytical**

VERB + BRAIN **rack** ◊ *We racked our ~s but we couldn't come up with a solution.* | **pick sb's** (= ask sb for information because they know more about a subject than you) ◊ *I need to pick your ~s: what can you tell me about credit unions?* | **take** ◊ *It doesn't take much ~ to work out that both stories can't be true.* | **use**

BRAIN + VERB **function, tick over, work** ◊ *It's important to keep your ~ ticking over.* | **reel** ◊ *His ~ reeled as he realized the implication of his dismissal.* | **register sth** ◊ *The stopping distance includes the time taken for the ~ to register the need to stop.*

BRAIN + NOUN **power** (usually *brainpower*) | **drain** (= the movement of skilled people to other countries)

PREP. **~ behind** ◊ *He was the ~s behind the robberies.*

PHRASES **~s, not brawn, etc.** ◊ *They relied on ~s rather than brawn (= intelligence, not strength).* | **have a ~ for sth** ◊ *She has a good ~ for mathematics.*

brake *noun*

ADJ. **defective, faulty** | **front, rear** | **emergency** (*AmE*), **foot** (usually *footbrake*), **hand** (usually *handbrake*) (*esp. BrE*), **parking** (*AmE*) | **air, anti-lock, disc, drum, vacuum**

VERB + BRAKE **apply, hit, jam on, put on, slam on, use** ◊ *She slammed on the ~s to try to avoid the dog.* | **put your foot on, slam your foot on** | **keep your foot on** | **let off, release, take your foot off** ◊ *He released the ~ and sped off.*

BRAKE + VERB **work** ◊ *My ~s are not working properly.* | **fail** ◊ *The car crashed after its ~s failed.* | **screech, squeal** | **be off, be on** ◊ *Is the ~ on?*

BRAKE + NOUN **failure** | **cable, fluid, lights, pads, pedal, pipes, shoes** (*esp. AmE*)

PHRASES **act as a ~ on sth, serve as a ~ on sth** (both figurative) | **put a ~ on sth, put the ~s on sth** (figurative) ◊ *The need to earn some money put the ~s on my wilder ambitions.* | **a screech of ~s, a squeal of ~s** ◊ *We heard the screech of ~s, followed by a loud crash.*

brake *verb*

ADV. **hard, heavily** (*esp. BrE*), **sharply** (*esp. BrE*), **suddenly**

PHRASES **~ to a halt** ◊ *The train ~d to a shuddering halt.* | **~ to avoid sth** ◊ *She ~d suddenly to avoid a cat.*

branch *noun*

1 part of a tree

ADJ. **top, topmost** | **low, low-hanging, overhanging** ◊ *Be careful of overhanging ~es.* | **bare, dead** ◊ *the bare ~es of a tree in winter* | **flowering, leafy** | **broken** | **fallen** | **pine, willow, etc.**

VERB + BRANCH **cut, prune, remove, trim**

2 part of a larger organization

ADJ. **central, high-street** (*BrE*), **local, regional** | **foreign** (*esp. BrE*), **overseas** | **executive, judicial, legislative**

VERB + BRANCH **establish, open, set up** ◊ *The store is opening more local ~es.* | **close, close down**

BRANCH + NOUN **chairman** (*BrE*), **chief** (*AmE*), **manager, member, office, representative, secretary**

→ Special page at BUSINESS

brand *noun*

1 type of product made by a particular manufacturer

ADJ. **leading, major, premium, principal, top** ◊ *the world's leading ~ of vodka* | **famous, favourite/favorite, name, popular, well-known** | **new** | **generic** | **own** (*BrE*), **store**

(*AmE*) ◊ *Supermarkets make a lot of profit on their own ~s.* ◊ *You pay less for the store ~.* ◊ *own-brand/store-brand products*

BRAND + NOUN **identity, image, name, value** ◊ *The company owes its success to ~ image.* ◊ *The company's core ~ value is consistency in quality and service.* | **awareness** | **leader** | **loyalty** | **manager**

PREP. **~ of** ◊ *a well-known ~ of toothpaste*

2 particular type of sth

ADJ. **particular, peculiar, special, unique** ◊ *His designs have a unique ~ of stylishness.* | **~ of** ◊ *his particular ~ of comedy*

brandy *noun*

ADJ. **double, large** | **single, small** | **stiff, strong** ◊ *a stiff ~ and soda* (= containing a lot of brandy and not much soda) | **neat** (*BrE*), **straight** (*AmE*) | **cherry, plum, etc.**

... OF BRANDY **drop** (*esp. BrE*), **measure** (*BrE*), **shot, tot** (*esp. BrE*) ◊ *He added a shot of ~ to his coffee.* ◊ *She poured herself a large measure of ~.* | **bottle, flask, glass, snifter** (= a glass) (*AmE*)

VERB + BRANDY **drink** ◊ *Do you drink ~?* | **have** ◊ *I'll have some ~, please.* | **pour (sb)** | **sip** | **gulp, swig** | **down, finish** | **distil, produce**

BRANDY + NOUN **bottle** | **glass** ◊ *He sat cradling his ~ glass.*

brass *noun*

1 metal

ADJ. **gleaming, polished, shiny** | **solid**

VERB + BRASS **be made from/in/of/out of** ◊ *candlesticks made of solid ~*

PREP. **in ~** ◊ *The door knocker was a female figure in ~.*

2 musical instruments made of brass

BRASS + NOUN **band** | **instrument** | **section** ◊ *the ~ section of the orchestra*

→ Special page at MUSIC

bravado *noun*

ADJ. **sheer** | **mere** | **false, forced** | **macho, male** | **typical** (*esp. BrE*), **usual**

PREP. **out of ~** ◊ *He behaved aggressively out of ~.* | **with ~** ◊ *'I'll be fine on my own,' she said with ~.*

PHRASES **a display of ~, a show of ~**

brave *adj.*

VERBS **be, feel, seem, sound** | **make sb** ◊ *The vodka had made me ~.*

ADV. **extremely, fairly, very, etc.** | **exceptionally, terribly** (*esp. BrE*) | **amazingly, incredibly**

bravery *noun*

ADJ. **exceptional, extraordinary, great, outstanding**

VERB + BRAVERY **demonstrate, display, show** | **admire, praise** (*esp. BrE*) | **salute** | **require** ◊ *The decision requires great ~ and commitment.*

BRAVERY + NOUN **award** (*esp. BrE*), **medal**

PREP. **with ~** ◊ *The men fought with great ~.*

PHRASES **an act of ~**

brawl *noun*

ADJ. **drunken** | **bar** (*AmE*), **barroom, pub** (*BrE*), **street** | **mass** | **all-out** (*esp. BrE*) ◊ *The game turned into an all-out ~.*

VERB + BRAWL **provoke, spark** (*esp. BrE*), **start** | **become/get involved in, get caught up in, get into** | **be caught up in, be involved in**

PREP. **in a/the ~** ◊ *They got caught up in a street ~.* | **~ between** ◊ *a ~ between different gangs* | **~ over** ◊ *a ~ over a woman*

breach *noun*

1 breaking of a law, agreement, rule, etc.

ADJ. **clear, fundamental, grave, serious** | **deliberate,**

flagrant ◇ *He refused to shake hands, in deliberate ~ of etiquette.* | **minor** | **security** | **alleged** (*esp. BrE*) | **gross, major**
VERB + BREACH **constitute** ◇ *Such actions constitute a ~ of confidentiality.* | **commit** | **remedy** | **prevent**
PREP. **in ~ of** ◇ *The court's decision is in ~ of the Convention.* | **~ of** ◇ *a minor ~ of discipline*
PHRASES **a ~ of confidence, a ~ of trust** | **(a) ~ of confidentiality, ~ of contract** ◇ *He was sued for ~ of contract.* | **a ~ of security** | **a ~ of the peace**

2 break in friendly relations
VERB + BREACH **cause, lead to** | **heal, repair**
PREP. **~ between** ◇ *What caused the ~ between the two brothers?* | **~ with** ◇ *She left home following the ~ with her family.*

bread noun

ADJ. **fresh** | **hard, mouldy/moldy, soggy, stale** ◇ *This ~ is going stale.* | **crusty** ◇ *loaves of crusty French ~* | **sliced** | **unleavened** | **organic** | **home-baked, home-made** | **fried** (*esp. BrE*), **toasted** | **banana, garlic** | **black, brown, corn, granary, naan** (*esp. AmE*), **rye, soda, sourdough, wheat, white, wholegrain, wholemeal** (*BrE*), **wholewheat** | **seven-grain, etc.**
...OF BREAD **loaf** | **package** (*AmE*) | **chunk, crumb, crust, hunk, morsel, piece, slice** ◇ *She tore off a large hunk of ~.*
VERB + BREAD **bake, make** ◇ *the smell of freshly baked ~* | **cut, slice** | **butter, put sth on, spread** ◇ *~ thickly spread with peanut butter* | **toast**
BREAD + NOUN **dough** | **pudding** (*esp. BrE*), **roll, sauce** (*esp. BrE*) | **basket, bin** (*BrE*), **box** (*AmE*), **knife**
PREP. **on ~** ◇ *What would you like on your ~?*
PHRASES **~ and butter, ~ and margarine** ◇ *a plate of ~ and butter* | **~ and cheese, ~ and jam** (*esp. BrE*), **~ and water** ◇ *He had to live on ~ and water for two weeks.* | **~ and wine** (= in the Christian Communion service) ◇ *People started going up to receive the ~ and wine.*
→ Special page at FOOD

breadth noun

1 distance between two sides of sth
PREP. **in ~** ◇ *The pool is 15 feet in ~.*
PHRASES **the length and ~ of sth** ◇ *He travels the length and ~ of* (= all over) *the country.*

2 great extent or variety
ADJ. **full, great, sheer**
PHRASES **~ of experience** ◇ *I need a greater ~ of experience.* | **~ of interest, knowledge, understanding, etc., ~ of mind, ~ of vision**

break noun

1 short rest; short holiday/vacation
ADJ. **little, quick, short** | **coffee, dinner** (*esp. BrE*), **lunch, tea** (*BrE*) | **Christmas, Easter, holiday** ◇ *Are you going away for the Easter ~?* | **spring, summer, winter** | **weekend** (*esp. BrE*) ◇ *I won a weekend ~ in Paris.* | **10-minute, two-week, etc.** ◇ *We have a 15-minute ~ in the morning.*
VERB + BREAK **have, take** ◇ *We'll take a ~ now and resume in an hour.* | **need, want** | **deserve** | **enjoy**
BREAK + NOUN **time** (= between lessons at school) (*BrE*)
PREP. **at ~** (*BrE*) ◇ *I'll see you at ~.* | **during (a/the) ~** ◇ *I had a word with John during the ~.* | **without a ~** ◇ *We worked all day without a ~.* | **~ for** ◇ *a ~ for lunch* | **~ from** ◇ *a ~ from caring for the children*

2 change/interruption in sth
ADJ. **clean, complete, sharp** | **career** | **commercial** (*esp. AmE*) | **nice, welcome** (*esp. BrE*)
VERB + BREAK **make** ◇ *His new work makes a ~ with the past.* ◇ *I wanted to leave but was nervous about making the ~.*
PREP. **~ from** ◇ *a ~ from tradition* | **~ in** ◇ *a ~ in the weather* | **~ with**

3 opportunity
ADJ. **big, lucky**
VERB + BREAK **get** ◇ *I always knew I would get my lucky ~ one day.* | **give sb** ◇ *He's the director who gave her her first big ~.*

break verb

ADV. **easily** | **in half, in two** ◇ *She broke the bar in two and gave a piece to me.* | **apart, up** ◇ *She broke the chocolate up into small pieces.*
PREP. **into** ◇ *The glass broke into hundreds of pieces.*

PHR V **break down**
1 fail
ADV. **completely, irretrievably** ◇ *Their marriage had broken down irretrievably.* | **eventually**
2 start crying
PHRASES **~ down and cry, ~ down in tears** ◇ *She broke down in tears as she spoke to reporters.*

break off
ADV. **abruptly, immediately** ◇ *He broke off abruptly when Jo walked in.*
PREP. **from** ◇ *She broke off from the conversation to answer the telephone.*

breakdown noun

1 mechanical failure
ADJ. **mechanical**
BREAKDOWN + VERB **occur**
BREAKDOWN + NOUN **service** (*BrE*) ◇ *Most ~ services give priority to women travelling alone.* | **truck, vehicle** (*both BrE*) | **lane** (*AmE*)

2 failure/end of sth
ADJ. **serious** | **complete, irretrievable, total** ◇ *the irretrievable ~ of the marriage* | **communication, family, marital, marriage, relationship, social**
VERB + BREAKDOWN **cause, lead to** | **prevent**
PREP. **~ in, ~ of** ◇ *a ~ in negotiations*

3 collapse of mental health
ADJ. **emotional, mental, nervous, psychological** | **complete, serious**
VERB + BREAKDOWN **have, suffer**
PHRASES **the brink of a nervous ~, the edge of a nervous ~, the verge of a nervous ~** ◇ *The stress of her job had brought her to the brink of a nervous ~.*

4 list of the details of sth
ADJ. **detailed, full** | **cost** | **statistical**
VERB + BREAKDOWN **prepare** ◇ *I have prepared a detailed cost ~ for the project.* | **give sb, provide (sb with)**
PREP. **~ by, ~ of** ◇ *Please provide us with a ~ of expenditure by department.*

breakfast noun

ADJ. **big, full, good, hearty, large, proper, solid, substantial** | **light, modest** | **cooked, fried** (*esp. BrE*) | **American-style, continental, English** ◇ *a full English ~ of cereal, bacon and eggs and toast* | **hot** | **buffet** | **pancake** (*AmE*) | **hasty, hurried, quick** | **leisurely, long** | **early, late** | **healthy** | **working** | **champagne**
BREAKFAST + NOUN **cereal** | **dishes, things** ◇ *Would you clear away the ~ things?* | **bar, nook** (*AmE*) | **meeting** | **show, television** | **food** ◇ *Low-fat cheeses and yogurt are good ~ foods.*
PHRASES **~ in bed** ◇ *He treated his wife to ~ in bed on her birthday.*
→ Note at MEAL (for verbs)

break-in noun

ADJ. **attempted** | **recent** | **factory, house, etc.**
BREAK-IN + NOUN **happen, take place**
PREP. **~ at** ◇ *a ~ at the factory*

breakthrough noun

ADJ. **big, crucial, great, historic, huge, important, major,**

real, significant | new, recent | diplomatic, medical, political, scientific, technological
VERB + BREAKTHROUGH **be, represent | achieve, make** ◇ *We have achieved a real ~ in the search for peace.*
BREAKTHROUGH + VERB **come, happen** ◇ *The crucial ~ came almost by accident.*
PREP. **~ for** ◇ *The new deal represents a major ~ for the company.* | **~ in** ◇ *a significant ~ in computer design*
PHRASES **the latest ~** ◇ *the latest ~ in biotechnology*

breakup *noun*

ADJ. **family, marital, marriage, relationship | bad, messy, painful**
VERB + BREAKUP **cause, initiate** (*esp. AmE*)**, lead to | get through, go through | survive**

breast *noun*

1 part of a woman's body

ADJ. **ample, big, enormous, full, heavy, large | little, small | bare, exposed, naked | firm, perky, pert, pointed | round, shapely | pendulous, sagging | tender | fake**
BREAST + NOUN **cancer, lump, tumour/tumor | examination | surgery | clinic | screening | milk** ◇ *The protective benefits of ~ milk are numerous for both mother and baby.* | **size | implant | augmentation, enlargement, reduction** ◇ *She had breast-augmentation surgery.* | **tissue**

2 your chest

PHRASES **beat your ~** (= say publicly how sorry you are) | **clutch sb/sth to your ~, hold sb/sth to your ~** ◇ *He held the letter to his ~.*

breaststroke *noun* → Note at STROKE

breath *noun*

ADJ. **big, deep, heavy, long, slow | quick, shallow, sharp, short | shaky, shuddering | hot, warm | bad** (= bad-smelling) ◇ *Smoking gives you bad ~.*
VERB + BREATH **draw, draw in, inhale, suck in, take** ◇ *He spoke solidly for twenty minutes, barely pausing to draw ~.* ◇ *Take a deep ~ and try to relax.* | **exhale, let out, release** ◇ *He let out a long ~.* | **feel** ◇ *She could feel his warm ~ against her cheek.* | **hold** ◇ *How long can you hold your ~ for?* | **get back** (*BrE*)**, regain** ◇ *I needed a few minutes to get my ~ back after the run.* | **catch** ◇ *She paused to catch her ~.* | **gasp for** ◇ *He came up out of the water gasping for ~.* | **pause for** ◇ *She poured out her story, hardly pausing for ~.* | **save** (*figurative*) ◇ *It's useless talking to him—you may as well save your ~.* | **waste** (*figurative*) ◇ *Don't waste your ~. He never listens to advice.*
BREATH + VERB **come in gasps, pants, puffs, etc.** ◇ *His ~ came in short gasps.*
PREP. **on sb's ~** ◇ *I could smell gin on her ~.* | **out of ~** ◇ *I'm a little out of ~ after my run.* | **under your ~** ◇ *He was whispering rude remarks about her under his ~.* | **~ of** ◇ *It was a still day, without a ~ of wind.*
PHRASES **a ~ of fresh air** (*often figurative*) ◇ *I'm going outside for a ~ of fresh air.* ◇ *The new secretary is a ~ of fresh air.* | **an intake of ~** ◇ *When the news was announced, there was a sharp intake of ~.* | **in the same ~** ◇ *How can we trust a government that mentions community care and cutbacks in the same ~?* | **short of ~** ◇ *I felt a little short of ~ and had to sit down.* | **take sb's ~ away** (*figurative*) ◇ *The sheer audacity of the man took my ~ away.* | **with bated ~** ◇ *We waited for the decision with bated ~.*

breathe *verb*

1 air/breath

ADV. **fast, quickly, rapidly | slowly | deeply | shallowly | hard, heavily** ◇ *They were both breathing hard from the steep climb.* | **gently, softly | easily, steadily** ◇ *She was beginning to ~ more easily.* | **normally, properly** ◇ *Try to ~ normally.* | **barely, hardly** ◇ *I can barely ~ here.* | **in, out** ◇ *She ~d slowly in and out.*
VERB + BREATHE **can** ◇ *I can't ~!* | **can barely, can hardly, can**

scarcely | not dare ◇ *He hardly dared ~ in case they heard him.*
PREP. **through** ◇ *Always ~ through your nose.*

2 say quietly

ADV. **huskily, quietly, softly** ◇ *'I love you!' she ~d softly.*

breathing *noun*

ADJ. **deep, shallow | controlled, even, regular, rhythmic, steady | irregular, laboured/labored, ragged, uneven** ◇ *His ~ was uneven, and he could hardly speak.* | **quick, rapid | slow | heavy** ◇ *She picked up the phone and heard sounds of heavy ~.*
VERB + BREATHING **control, regulate**
BREATHING + VERB **quicken, slow, slow down**
BREATHING + NOUN **apparatus | difficulties, problems | exercise** ◇ *Try ~ exercises to calm your nerves.*

breathless *adj.*

VERBS **be, feel, seem, sound | become | leave sb, make sb** ◇ *The unaccustomed exercise left him ~.*
ADV. **extremely, fairly, very, etc.** ◇ *He sounded rather ~.* | **a little, slightly, etc. | almost, nearly**
PREP. **with** ◇ *The children peered through the open door, ~ with excitement.* | **from** ◇ *We had to stop, ~ from exertion.*

breathtaking *adj.*

VERBS **be**
ADV. **absolutely, quite, simply, truly**

breed *noun*

1 type of animal

ADJ. **new | rare | hardy | pure | domestic**
VERB + BREED **keep** ◇ *a farm that keeps rare ~s* | **use** ◇ *This ~ is used for both milk and meat production.* | **recognize** ◇ *Three years later the ~ was officially recognized.*
PREP. **~ of** ◇ *a new ~ of dairy cattle*

2 particular type of person

ADJ. **new | dying, rare** ◇ *Entertainers of this sort are now a dying ~.* | **special** ◇ *It takes a special ~ of person to be a surgeon.*
PREP. **~ of** ◇ *a new ~ of international criminals*
PHRASES **a ~ apart** ◇ *Health workers are a ~ apart in their commitment and dedication to duty.*

breed *verb*

ADV. **in captivity | successfully | commercially | selectively, specially, specifically** ◇ *fish that have been selectively bred for their appearance*
PREP. **for** ◇ *dogs that are bred for their fighting ability*

breeding *noun*

1 activity of producing plants/animals

ADJ. **animal, horse, livestock, plant, etc. | selective** ◇ *Certain characteristics can be developed through selective ~.* | **captive** ◇ *a campaign to save the condor by captive ~*
BREEDING + NOUN **season | stock | programme/program**

2 good manners

ADJ. **good** ◇ *Her good ~ shows in her exquisite manners.*
VERB + BREEDING **have** ◇ *The young man clearly has ~.*

breeze *noun*

ADJ. **faint, gentle, light, little, slight, soft | stiff, strong | sudden | chill, chilly, cold, cool, cooling, fresh | warm | pleasant** ◇ *pleasant sea ~s* | **evening, morning, night | spring, summer | ocean** (*esp. AmE*)**, sea | northerly, westerly, etc.**
BREEZE + VERB **blow, come, drift** ◇ *A light ~ came off the sea.* | **ruffle sth, rustle sth, stir sth** ◇ *A sudden ~ rustled the long dry grass.* | **sweep** ◇ *The cool ~ swept through the trees.* | **come up** ◇ *A ~ came up in the late afternoon.* | **drop**

VERB + BREEZE feel ◊ *I felt the* ~ *on my face.*
PREP. in a/the ~ ◊ *The curtains fluttered in the right* ~.

breezy adj.

1 windy
VERBS be
ADV. very | a little, slightly, etc. ◊ *It's a little* ~ *up here.*
2 cheerful and relaxed
VERBS be, seem, sound ◊ *She tried to sound* ~ *on the phone.*
PHRASES bright and ~ ◊ *His bright and* ~ *manner sometimes irritated people.*

bribe noun

VERB + BRIBE give sb, offer (sb), pay sb ◊ *He admitted paying* ~s *to police officers.* | accept, take
PREP. in ~s ◊ *He paid out millions of dollars in* ~s. | ~ of ◊ *a* ~ *of €200*

bribery noun

ADJ. election
VERB + BRIBERY resort to
BRIBERY + NOUN scandal | allegation (*esp. BrE*) | charge | case
PHRASES ~ and corruption ◊ *The charge in the present case is one of* ~ *and corruption.*
→ Note at CRIME (for more verbs)

brick noun

ADJ. red ◊ *a house of red* ~ | adobe, clay, concrete, glass, mud | house (*BrE*)
VERB + BRICK lay ◊ *Chuck decided to lay the* ~s *himself.* | use ◊ *We rebuilt the fireplace using salvaged* ~s. | hurl (*esp. BrE*), throw
BRICK + NOUN wall | building, house, structure | facade | works (usually **brickworks**) ◊ *He got a job at the local brickworks.*
PREP. in ~, of ~ ◊ *houses of* ~
PHRASES ~ by ~ ◊ *They moved the whole house,* ~ *by* ~. | ~s and mortar (*figurative*) ◊ *to invest in* ~s *and mortar* | a course of ~s ◊ *They put an extra course of* ~s *around the pool.*

bride noun

ADJ. beautiful, lovely, radiant | blushing | child, teenage, young | new | future, intended, prospective | jilted | mail-order (*esp. AmE*)
VERB + BRIDE give away ◊ *The bride's father traditionally walks with her to the altar to give her away.* | toast ◊ *Everyone raised their glasses to toast the* ~ *and groom.* | kiss ◊ *You may now kiss the* ~.
BRIDE + VERB wear sth | look ◊ *The* ~ *looked radiant in an ivory gown.*
PHRASES the ~ and groom

bridegroom (*also* groom) noun

ADJ. prospective | proud
PHRASES the bride and ~

bridge noun

1 structure across a river, road, etc.
ADJ. high, humpback (*BrE*), narrow | rail, railroad (*AmE*), railway (*BrE*), road | cantilever, pontoon, suspension, swing (*BrE*) ◊ *The soldiers built a pontoon* ~ *across the Euphrates.* | rope, steel, stone, wooden | toll ◊ *Charges for the toll* ~ *are set to rise.* | pedestrian (*esp. BrE*)
VERB + BRIDGE build | destroy | wash away ◊ *Floods washed away several* ~s. | cross ◊ *Cross the* ~ *and turn right into the town.* | close | design
BRIDGE + VERB cross sth, span sth ◊ *The new* ~ *will cross the river at this point.* | connect sth, link sth
PREP. across a/the ~, over a/the ~ ◊ *It was windy driving*

over the ~. | under a/the ~ ◊ *The road goes under the old* ~. | ~ across, ~ over ◊ *a* ~ *over the river*
2 card game
... OF BRIDGE game, rubber ◊ *I enjoy a game of* ~ *occasionally.*
VERB + BRIDGE play
BRIDGE + NOUN tournament | partner, player

brief noun report; instructions

ADJ. clear (*esp. BrE*), detailed, thorough (*AmE*) | daily (*AmE*) | news (*AmE*) | court, legal, planning (*BrE*) | intelligence, mission (*AmE*) | presidential (*AmE*)
VERB + BRIEF prepare, produce, write | give ◊ *We were given daily* ~s *by the commander.* (*AmE*) ◊ *I was given the* ~ *of reorganizing the department.* (*BrE*) | stick to (*BrE*) ◊ *He told me to stick to my* ~ (= do only what I was asked).
PREP. in a/the ~ ◊ *She makes all these points in her* ~. | outside sb's ~ (*BrE*) ◊ *How the new policy is to be implemented is outside his* ~. | ~ on ◊ *a technical* ~ *on food hygiene*
PHRASES be part of sb's ~ (*BrE*) ◊ *It's not part of my* ~ *to advise on financial matters.* | hold no ~ for sb/sth (*BrE*) ◊ *I hold no* ~ *for either side in this conflict.*

brief verb

ADV. fully, properly (*BrE*), well
PREP. about ◊ *The men have been fully* ~ed *about the intended mission.* | on ◊ *Each member of my crew took turns to* ~ *me on his particular duties.*

brief adj.

VERBS be ◊ *I promised to be* ~. | keep sth, make sth ◊ *Could you make it* ~? *I have a meeting in ten minutes.*
ADV. extremely, fairly, very, etc. | comparatively, relatively | necessarily ◊ *This necessarily* ~ *account concentrates on two main areas.* | mercifully ◊ *The wait was mercifully* ~, *little more than an hour.* | tantalizingly ◊ *The diary entries were tantalizingly* ~.

briefcase noun

ADJ. battered (*esp. BrE*) ◊ *He wore a torn suit and carried a battered* ~. | bulging | leather, metal, plastic
VERB + BRIEFCASE open, snap open | close, lock, shut, snap shut | carry, hold, pick up | drop, put down
BRIEFCASE + VERB be full of sth, be stuffed with sth, contain sth

briefing noun

ADJ. detailed, full, thorough | background | formal, informal | final ◊ *She returned to Washington for a final* ~. | media, news, press | daily, regular, weekly
VERB + BRIEFING give sb ◊ *All staff will be given a full* ~ *tomorrow.* | get, receive | arrange, hold ◊ *I asked him to arrange a formal* ~. | attend | tell ◊ *He told a press* ~ *that he had no plans to resign.*
BRIEFING + NOUN session | document, paper | room
PREP. at a/the ~ ◊ *Details of the plan will be announced at a press* ~ *later today.* | ~ by, ~ from ◊ *a* ~ *by the commanding officer* | ~ on ◊ *a* ~ *on security issues*

brigade noun

ADJ. airborne (*AmE*), armoured/armored, combat (*AmE*), fire (*BrE*), infantry
VERB + BRIGADE command, lead | form ◊ *A special army* ~ *is to be formed.* | join | deploy
BRIGADE + NOUN commander | headquarters
PREP. in a/the ~ ◊ *units in 1st Commando Brigade* | ~ of ◊ *a* ~ *of infantry*

brigadier noun → Note at RANK

bright adj.

1 full of light
VERBS be ◊ *The offices are going to be* ~ *and airy.* | look, seem ◊ *The factory's future now looks* ~. (= seems good) |

become, grow ◇ *Her timid eyes grew ~ and she looked ready to venture on.* | **remain** | **dawn, glow, shine** ◇ *The sun shone ~ and hot.* ◇ *The following morning dawned ~ and warm.* | **burn**
ADV. **extremely, fairly, very, etc.** | **intensely, surprisingly, unusually** ◇ *The white feathers looked surprisingly ~.* | **reasonably** ◇ *The morning was reasonably ~.* | **too, unnaturally** ◇ *Her eyes were unnaturally ~.* | **still** ◇ *The sky was still ~ in the west.*

2 intelligent

VERBS **be** ◇ *Ms Newman is ~, opinionated and decisive.*
ADV. **extremely, fairly, very, etc.** | **exceptionally, incredibly** ◇ *Thomas is an exceptionally ~ boy.*

brighten *verb*

ADV. **considerably** | **a little, slightly, etc.** | **visibly** ◇ *Their rather heavy faces ~ed visibly.* | **immediately** | **suddenly** | **up** ◇ *She ~ed up a little at the thought of the cruise.*

brilliance *noun*

ADJ. **great, sheer** | **academic, intellectual, technical**
... OF BRILLIANCE **flash** ◇ *There were flashes of ~ from several of the players.*
PREP. **with ~** ◇ *He played with great ~.*

brilliant *adj.*

VERBS **be, look**
ADV. **just, really, truly** ◇ *Her performance was truly ~.* ◇ *Winning that race was just ~. (esp. BrE)* | **absolutely, quite, totally, utterly** ◇ *an absolutely ~ idea* | **technically** ◇ *Her performance was technically ~ but lacked feeling.*
PREP. **at** ◇ *He's ~ at chess.*

brim *noun*

1 top edge of a cup, bowl, etc.

PHRASES **full to the ~** | **fill sth to the ~** ◇ *She filled the bowl to the ~.*

2 flat edge around the bottom of a hat

ADJ. **broad, deep, wide** ◇ *a straw hat with a wide ~*
PREP. **beneath a/the ~, under a/the ~** ◇ *She watched the crowd from beneath the ~ of her hat.*

bring *verb*

PHR V **bring sb up**
ADV. **badly, well** ◇ *children who have been well brought up*

brink *noun*

ADJ. **very**
VERB + BRINK **be (poised) on, hover on, stand on, teeter on** ◇ *Scientists are on the ~ of making a major new discovery.* ◇ *animals hovering on the very ~ of extinction* | **bring sb to** | **fight back from, pull back from** | **bring sb/sth back from, pull sb/sth back from** ◇ *He pulled the company back from the ~ (= saved it from disaster).*
PREP. **~ of** ◇ *the ~ of bankruptcy/death/war*

broad *adj.*

VERBS **be**
ADV. **extremely, fairly, very, etc.** | **reasonably, relatively** | **enough, sufficiently** ◇ *He questioned whether the curriculum was ~ enough in scope.* | **overly (esp. AmE)** | **unusually** ◇ *His job gave him an acquaintance with an unusually ~ spectrum of society.*

broadcast *noun*

ADJ. **radio, television** | **cable, satellite** | **digital, Web** | **live** | **outside** | **election, news, party political (BrE), religious** | **digital** | **network (esp. AmE)** ◇ *There is pressure to cancel the network ~ of the movie.*
VERB + BROADCAST **make** ◇ *The president made a radio ~ to mark the end of the war.* | **hear, see, watch** | **receive**
PREP. **in a/the ~** ◇ *More details will be given in our news ~.* | **~ by** ◇ *a ~ by the president* | **~ on** ◇ *a radio ~ on the problems of unemployment*

broadcast *verb*

ADV. **live** | **nationally** | **originally** ◇ *This interview was originally ~ last Friday.*
PREP. **from** ◇ *We will ~ live from the ship.* | **to** ◇ *a Christmas message ~ to the nation*

broadcaster *noun*

ADJ. **commercial** ◇ *Existing commercial ~s claim the new stations are illegal.* | **independent** | **public, public-service** ◇ *The country has a national public-service ~.* | **local, national** | **radio, television** | **cable, satellite** | **digital, Web** | **large, major** | **religious (esp. AmE)**

brochure *noun*

ADJ. **colour/color, full-colour/full-color, glossy** | **illustrated** ◇ *Send for our illustrated ~.* | **holiday (BrE), hotel, tourist, travel** | **informational (AmE), promotional (esp. AmE)**
... OF BROCHURE **copy**
VERB + BROCHURE **browse through, leaf through, look through, read** ◇ *I leafed through the travel ~.* | **produce, publish**

broiler *noun (AmE)*

ADJ. **hot** ◇ *Place under a hot ~ until brown.*
VERB + BROILER **preheat**
BROILER + NOUN **pan**
PREP. **under a/the ~**

broke *adj.*

VERBS **be** | **go (= go bankrupt)** ◇ *The company went ~ last year.*
ADV. **completely, flat (informal), totally (esp. AmE)** | **stone (AmE), stony (BrE) (both informal)** ◇ *I'm stony/stone ~ at the moment.* | **nearly**

broken *adj.*

VERBS **be** | **get** ◇ *How did the jug get ~?*
ADV. **badly** ◇ *One of his legs was badly ~.*

broker *noun*

ADJ. **credit, insurance, mortgage, real estate (AmE)** ◇ *Ask advice from an insurance ~.* | **honest (= an independent person or country that acts between two sides in a dispute)** | **power** ◇ *He used his position to establish himself as a power ~.*
VERB + BROKER **act as, be**
PREP. **~ between** ◇ *He acted as ~ between the two opposing sides.* | **~ for** ◇ *a ~ for the company*
→ Note at JOB

bronchitis *noun* → Special page at ILLNESS

bronze *noun*

1 metal

ADJ. **cast** | **burnished, polished**
VERB + BRONZE **be cast in, be made from/in/of/out of** ◇ *The figure was cast in ~.*
BRONZE + NOUN **sculpture, statue** | **plaque**
PREP. **in ~** ◇ *She works mainly in ~.*

2 (also bronze medal) in sports

ADJ. **Olympic**
VERB + BRONZE **earn, get, take, win** ◇ *She got a ~ in the long jump.*

brooch *(esp. BrE) noun*

ADJ. **cameo** | **diamond, pearl, etc.**
VERB + BROOCH **have on, wear** | **pin** ◇ *She pinned a large amethyst ~ to her lapel.*

broom *noun*

ADJ. **witch's** | **stiff**

VERB + BROOM **sweep sth with, use** | **grab** (*esp. AmE*) ◊ *Grab a ~ and let's clean up.*
BROOM + NOUN **closet** (*AmE*), **cupboard** (*BrE*) | **handle**
PHRASES **~ and dustpan, dustpan and ~** (*both AmE*)

brothel noun

VERB + BROTHEL **go to, visit** ◊ *He used to visit a ~ on the outskirts of town.* | **run** ◊ *His aunt ran a ~.*
BROTHEL + NOUN **keeper, owner**
PREP. **in a/the ~** ◊ *She works in a ~.*

brother noun

ADJ. **big, elder, older** ◊ *Bill idolizes his big ~, who is a professional boxer.* | **baby, kid** (*informal*), **little, small, younger** | **twin** | **full** (= sharing both parents) | **beloved, much-loved** ◊ *She wrote daily to her beloved ~, Leo.* | **long-lost** ◊ *His old teacher greeted him like a long-lost ~.* | **dead, deceased, late** ◊ *He married the wife of his late ~.* | **bachelor, unmarried**
PHRASES **blood ~s** (= close friends who have sworn to remain friends for life), **~ and sister** ◊ *Do you have any ~s and sisters?* | **like ~s** ◊ *The boys are so close, they're like ~s.*

brow noun

1 line of hair above the eye → See also EYEBROW

ADJ. **dark, heavy** | **bushy** | **delicate**
VERB + BROW **arch, lift, raise** ◊ *She arched a ~ when she saw the bill.* | **draw together, knit** ◊ *He knitted his ~s in concentration.*
BROW + VERB **lift, rise** | **twitch** | **draw together** ◊ *His ~s drew together in a worried frown when he heard the remark.*

2 forehead

ADJ. **broad, wide** | **furrowed** ◊ *He stared at the visitors beneath a furrowed ~.* | **stern** | **weary** | **damp, perspiring, sweating, sweaty** | **fevered**
VERB + BROW **mop, wipe** | **furrow, pucker** (*esp. AmE*), **wrinkle** ◊ *She wrinkled her ~ thoughtfully.*
BROW + VERB **crease, furrow, wrinkle** ◊ *His ~ furrowed as he racked his brains over the question.* | **clear** ◊ *For a while she looked puzzled; then her ~ cleared.* | **darken** ◊ *His ~ darkened in anger.*
PREP. **across your ~** ◊ *His shaggy hair fell loosely across his ~.* | **from your ~** ◊ *She brushed back a stray lock of hair from her ~.* | **over your ~** ◊ *His hair fell over his ~ as he turned his head.*

brown adj., noun

ADV. **very** ◊ *He looked very ~ after the cruise.* (*esp. BrE*) | **uniformly** ◊ *The once-green fields were now uniformly ~.*
ADJ. **dark, deep** ◊ *her dark ~ eyes* | **light, pale, soft** | **rich, warm** ◊ *lovely warm ~s and golds* | **bright** ◊ *bright ~ eyes* | **drab, dull, muddy** | **chestnut, chocolate, golden, reddish, rusty**
→ Special page at COLOUR

browser noun

ADJ. **Internet, Web** | **default** ◊ *What do you use as your default ~?*
VERB + BROWSER **update, upgrade**
BROWSER + NOUN **toolbar, window**
PREP. **on a/the ~** ◊ *Click the 'back' button on your ~.*
→ Special page at COMPUTER

bruise noun

ADJ. **black, dark, livid, purple** | **nasty, nice, ugly** | **faint, minor, slight** ◊ *Minor ~s can be treated at home.*
VERB + BRUISE **have, sport** | **leave** | **get, suffer** ◊ *She suffered only minor cuts and ~s.*
BRUISE + VERB **appear, form** ◊ *A ~ had formed below his left eye.* | **fade, heal**
PHRASES **cuts and ~s**

bruise verb

ADV. **badly** ◊ *His face was badly ~d.* | **easily** ◊ *She has delicate skin and ~s easily.*
PHRASES **be all ~d** ◊ *The side of his face was all ~d.* | **battered and ~d, ~d and battered** ◊ *When the assault was over, Jack stood up, battered and ~d.*

brush noun

ADJ. **stiff, stiff-bristled** ◊ *Scrub the wood thoroughly with water and a stiff ~.* | **fine, soft, soft-bristled** | **nylon, wire** | **clothes, hair** (usually **hairbrush**), **make-up, paint** (usually **paintbrush**), **pastry, scrub** (*AmE*), **scrubbing** (*BrE*), **shaving, toilet, tooth** (usually **toothbrush**)
VERB + BRUSH **apply sth with** ◊ *Apply the paint with a clean ~.* | **use, wield** | **run** ◊ *She ran a ~ through her hair.* | **dip** ◊ *She took a can of paint and dipped her ~ in it.* | **clean**
BRUSH + NOUN **stroke** ◊ *The artist has used tiny ~ strokes.*
PREP. **with a/the ~** ◊ *Remove all the rust with a wire ~.*
PHRASES **a ~ and comb, a comb and ~** (*AmE*) | **a dustpan and ~**

brush verb

1 clean with a brush

ADV. **carefully, quickly, slowly** | **down** ◊ *She hummed happily as she ~ed down her coat.* | **back** ◊ *Her hair was ~ed back in a pony tail.* | **out** ◊ *She ~ed out her long hair.*
PREP. **at** ◊ *Lucille ~ed at the blood on his jacket.*
PHRASES **~ sth clean**

2 touch lightly

ADV. **gently, lightly, softly** | **accidentally** | **barely**
PREP. **against** ◊ *She carefully avoided ~ing against the man sitting beside her.* | **by** ◊ *She ~ed by him and dashed up the stairs.* | **past** ◊ *I hardly noticed the man who ~ed past me in the corridor.* | **with** ◊ *He ~ed her lips with his.*

brutality noun

ADJ. **extreme, great, sheer** | **police** ◊ *There have been many complaints of police ~.*
... OF BRUTALITY **act** ◊ *This was an act of extreme ~.*
PREP. **~ against** ◊ *~ against prisoners* | **~ by** ◊ *~ by the security forces* | **~ of** ◊ *the ~ of war* | **~ to** ◊ *~ to others* | **~ towards/toward** ◊ *his ~ towards/toward opponents*

bubble noun

ADJ. **air, gas, soap** | **little, tiny** ◊ *The champagne was full of tiny ~s.*
VERB + BUBBLE **blow** ◊ *The children were blowing ~s.* | **burst, pop** ◊ *They jumped around, bursting the ~s.*
BUBBLE + VERB **form** ◊ *Soap ~s formed on the surface.* | **burst, pop** | **float, rise**

bubble verb

1 form bubbles

ADV. **furiously** ◊ *The water in the saucepan was bubbling furiously.* | **away, up** ◊ *The soup was bubbling away on the stove.*

2 feeling

ADV. **to the surface** ◊ *Emotions quickly ~ to the surface.* | **over, up** ◊ *He was bubbling over with excitement.*
PREP. **inside** ◊ *She could feel the anger bubbling up inside her.* | **with** ◊ *The business was still small but I was bubbling with ideas.*

bucket noun → See also PAIL

ADJ. **empty, full** | **galvanized, metal, plastic** | **leaky** | **champagne, ice** | **paint** (*AmE*), **water** | **slop** ◊ *a slop ~ full of scraps of food* | **mop** | **fire**
VERB + BUCKET **fill** ◊ *She filled the ~ with fresh water.* | **carry** | **dump, empty, pour, throw** ◊ *She poured the ~ of dirty water down the drain.*
BUCKET + VERB **be full of sth, contain sth, hold sth** | **overflow**
PREP. **in a/the ~** | **~ of** ◊ *big ~s of popcorn and Coke*
PHRASES **a ~ and spade** (*BrE*) ◊ *The children ran down to the*

beach with their ~s and spades. | **mop and ~** ◇ *The cleaner put down his mop and ~ and sat down.*

buckle *noun*

ADJ. **belt, shoe** | **brass, silver, etc.**
VERB + BUCKLE **do up, fasten** | **undo, unfasten**
→ Special page at CLOTHES

bud *noun*

ADJ. **flower, leaf, rose** | **developing**
BUD + VERB **appear** | **burst, open** | **develop, grow**
PHRASES **in ~** ◇ *The roses are in ~.*

budge *verb*

ADV. **barely, not even**
VERB + BUDGE **will not, would not** ◇ *He sat down and would not ~.* | **refuse to** ◇ *She absolutely refused to ~.*
PREP. **from** ◇ *He refuses to ~ from his principles.* | **on** ◇ *The union won't ~ on its demands.*
PHRASES **not ~ an inch** ◇ *He threw all his weight against the door, but it wouldn't ~ an inch.*

budget *noun*

ADJ. **fixed, limited, low, modest, shoestring, small, tight** ◇ *The film was was made on a shoestring ~.* | **big, generous, huge, large** | **annual, monthly, weekly, etc.** | **overall, total** | **entire** | **operating** ◇ *The museum's operating ~ for 2008 is just over $2 million.* | **family, household, personal** | **city** (*AmE*), **council** (*BrE*), **federal, government, municipal** (*AmE*), **national, state** ◇ *Military spending accounts for around 17% of the federal ~.* | **defence/defense, education, health, housing** (*BrE*), **intelligence, military, social-security** (*BrE*), **welfare** | **ad** (*AmE*), **advertising, marketing, research, training** | **school** | **capital** | **draft**
VERB + BUDGET **get, have** ◇ *The organization has a large annual ~.* | **allocate, draw up, plan, set** ◇ *The city has drawn up its ~ for next year.* | **present, propose, submit** | **approve, pass** (*AmE*) | **balance** ◇ *The school has a struggle to balance its ~.* | **adhere to** (*esp. AmE*), **keep to, meet, stick to** ◇ *Work out a weekly ~ and stick to it.* | **control, manage** | *The IT department manages its own ~.* | **strain, stretch** | **blow, bust** (*esp. AmE*), **exceed, go over, overspend** | **cut, reduce, slash, trim** | **boost, double, increase** | **fit** ◇ *a product to fit all ~s* | **spend** ◇ *They spent their entire ~ on a new kitchen.*
BUDGET + NOUN **expenditure** | **deficit, shortfall** ◇ *The annual ~ deficit for 2008 could run as high as $12.8 billion.* | **surplus** | **constraint, limit** | **cuts** | **plans, proposals** | **allocation** | **request** (*AmE*) | **crisis** | **Budget Day** (= when the British government announces its budget) | **director** (*AmE*)
PREP. **over ~, under ~** ◇ *The project is now well over ~.* | *Costs have been held under ~.* | **on ~, within ~** ◇ *All his projects are on time and on ~.* ◇ *to keep within ~* | **in the ~** ◇ *Is there any money left in the ~?* | **on a ~** ◇ *This hotel caters for people on a tight ~.* | **~ for** ◇ *The ~ for next year has not yet been set.* | **~ of** ◇ *a ~ of $5 000*

budget *verb*

ADV. **carefully, sensibly** ◇ *If we ~ carefully we should be able to afford a new car.*
PREP. **for** ◇ *We have ~ed $10 000 for advertising.*

buffer *noun*

VERB + BUFFER **act as** | **provide** | **use sth as**
BUFFER + NOUN **state, zone**
PREP. **~ against** ◇ *A family can provide a ~ against stress at work.* | **~ between** ◇ *The organization acts as a ~ between the management and the union.*

buffet *noun*

1 meal

ADJ. **free** | **all-you-can-eat** (*esp. AmE*) | **delicious, excellent** | **cold** (*BrE*) | **finger** (*BrE*) | **breakfast, dinner, lunch**

VERB + BUFFET **serve** ◇ *A lunch ~ will be served.* | **lay out** ◇ *A ~ was laid out for the conference delegates.*
BUFFET + NOUN **breakfast, dinner, lunch, meal, supper** (*BrE*) | **table** | **reception** (*esp. BrE*)

2 (*esp. BrE*) **on a train/in a station**

ADJ. **station**
BUFFET + NOUN **car** (*BrE*), **service**

bug *noun*

1 infectious illness

ADJ. **nasty** | **flu, stomach, tummy**
VERB + BUG **have** | **catch, come down with, get, pick up**
BUG + VERB **go around, go round** (*esp. BrE*) ◇ *A stomach ~ has been going around at school.* | **strike sb down** (*BrE*)
PREP. **with a/the ~** ◇ *He's off work with a flu ~.*
→ Special page at ILLNESS

2 sudden interest in sth

VERB + BUG **be bitten by, catch, get** ◇ *She's been bitten by the travel ~.*
BUG + VERB **bite (sb)**

3 sth wrong in a system/machine

ADJ. **minor** | **annoying** | **computer, software**
VERB + BUG **discover, find** | **fix**
PREP. **~ in** ◇ *a ~ in the software*

buggy *noun* → See also CART

ADJ. **baby** (*BrE*) | **beach, dune, golf** (*BrE*)
VERB + BUGGY **push** ◇ *parents pushing buggies* (*BrE*)
PHRASES **horse and ~** (*esp. AmE*)

build *noun*

ADJ. **average, medium** | **lean** (*esp. AmE*), **slender, slight, slim, small, thin** | **heavy, muscular, powerful, stocky, strong** | **athletic**
PREP. **in ~** ◇ *He's heavier in ~ than his brother.* | **of ~** ◇ *She is slight of ~ and very agile.* | **with a ~** ◇ *a small woman with a slim ~*

builder *noun*

ADJ. **good, master, reputable** | **self-employed** (*BrE*) | **local** ◇ *We got a local ~ to do the work for us.* | **custom** (*AmE*)
BUILDER + VERB **build sth**
PHRASES **builder's merchant, builder's yard** (*both BrE*) ◇ *The house will look like a builder's yard until we finish the work.*
→ Note at JOB

building *noun*

1 house, church, school, etc.

ADJ. **big, high-rise, huge, large, massive, tall, towering** | **low, low-rise, single-storey/single-story, small** | **attractive** (*esp. BrE*), **beautiful, fine, grand, imposing, impressive, landmark, magnificent** ◇ *The opera house is one of the city's landmark ~s.* | **condemned, crumbling, derelict, dilapidated, ramshackle, run-down, tumbledown** (*BrE*) | **abandoned, empty** | **ancient, historic, old** ◇ *Both architects specialize in the restoration of historic ~s.* | **17th-century, etc.** | **listed** (*BrE*) ◇ *They were refused planning permission for an extension because it was a Grade II listed ~.* | **modern** | **brick, concrete, stone, timber, wooden, etc.** | **green** (= good for the environment) | **commercial, industrial, residential** ◇ *The prices of commercial and residential ~s increased by 13.4%.* | **civic, municipal, public** | **federal, government** | **administration, administrative** | **apartment** (*AmE*), **tenement** ◇ *Housing is limited and most people live in high-rise apartment ~s.* | **church, factory, farm, headquarters, hospital, museum, office, parliament, prison, school** | **airport, terminal** | **campus** (*esp. AmE*) | **dorm, dormitory** (*both AmE*) | **downtown** (*AmE*) | **main** | **entire, whole** | **existing** | **new** | **original** | **adjacent, nearby, surrounding**
VERB + BUILDING **design** | **build, construct, erect, put up** ◇

Several new ~s are now being put up. | **complete** | **demolish, destroy, flatten, gut, knock down, pull down** (BrE), **raze, tear down** ◇ The ~ was gutted by fire. | **damage** | **renovate, restore** ◇ They're renovating the old farm ~s. | **convert** ◇ In 2008 the ~ was converted into a house. | **evacuate** | **occupy** | **lease**

BUILDING + VERB **collapse** | **house sth** | **sit, stand** ◇ a central square, where two ~s stand

2 process/business of building sth

ADJ. **road** | **brand** (business), **community, coalition, empire, nation, team**

BUILDING + NOUN **company, contractor, firm** (esp. BrE), **industry, sector, trade** | **programme/program, project, scheme** (BrE) | **activity, development, work** ◇ We're having some ~ work done. | **code** (AmE), **controls, regulations** | **land** (esp. BrE) | **site** (esp. BrE) (usually **construction site** in AmE) | **materials** | **method, technique** | **boom** | **costs** | **contractor, inspector, worker**

build-up noun

1 gradual increase

ADJ. **gradual, slow** | **steady** | **rapid** | **massive** | **military** | **heat** | **plaque**

VERB + BUILD-UP **cause, lead to** ◇ The leak led to a slow ~ of carbon dioxide. | **avoid, prevent** | **reduce**

PREP. **during the ~, in the ~** | **~ of**

2 period of time before an event

ADJ. **pre-match** (BrE), **pretrial, etc.**

PREP. **~ to** ◇ Tension is mounting in the ~ to the elections.

bulb noun

1 part of an electric lamp

ADJ. **electric** | **light** | **100-watt, 60-watt, etc.** | **bare, naked** | **single** | **bright, dim** ◇ A single dim light ~ lit the room. | **energy-efficient, energy-saving** (esp. BrE), **low-energy** (esp. BrE) | **fluorescent, incandescent** | **halogen** | **clear, coloured/colored**

VERB + BULB **change, replace** ◇ Switch the light off before you change the ~. | **remove, unscrew** ◇ Can you remove the ~ and replace it with an energy-efficient one?

BULB + VERB **light sth** ◇ The room was lit only by a single 40-watt light ~. | **go** ◇ I think the ~ is going to go. It's been flickering all evening. | **flicker** | **flash, go off** ◇ Red and green ~s flashed on and off. | **hang** ◇ A single electric light ~ hung from the ceiling. | **last** ◇ These new ~s last much longer than the ordinary ones.

2 round plant root

ADJ. **flower** | **spring, spring-flowering, summer, summer-flowering** | **daffodil, tulip, etc.**

VERB + BULB **place, plant** ◇ I'm planting some ~s for next year. ◇ Place the ~s close together. | **dig up, take up** | **grow** | **water** ◇ She usually waters the indoor ~s once a week.

BULB + VERB **grow** | **flower** | **sprout**

bulk noun

1 large size

ADJ. **considerable, huge, massive, sheer** ◇ I was amazed by the sheer ~ of the creature. | **extra**

VERB + BULK **ease, heave, shift** ◇ He heaved his considerable ~ into the chair. | **add**

2 large amount

ADJ. **great, large, overwhelming, vast**

BULK + NOUN **buying, order, purchasing** | **mail, mailing** (both esp. AmE) ◇ ~ mailing rates | **email**

PREP. **in ~** ◇ Sugar is imported in ~ from the mainland. ◇ It's usually cheaper to buy in ~.

PHRASES **the ~ of** (= most of) ◇ The great ~ of the work has now been done.

bullet noun

ADJ. **speeding** | **stray** | **single** | **live** | **explosive** | **lead, plastic, rubber** | **.45-calibre/.45-caliber, etc.** | **machine-gun, rifle, tracer** | **sniper, sniper's** ◇ She was shot through the head by a sniper's ~. | **magic, silver** (figurative) ◇ a technological silver ~ that will solve the global warming crisis

VERB + BULLET **dodge** | **fire, spray sth with** ◇ The embassy was sprayed with ~s. | **shoot** (used of a gun) ◇ faster than a machine gun can shoot ~s | **load** | **be riddled with** ◇ The body was riddled with ~s. | **put** ◇ They had put a ~ through his brain. | **deflect** | **remove**

BULLET + VERB **hit sb/sth, pierce sb/sth, shoot sb, strike sb/sth** ◇ The second ~ hit her in the back. | **miss sb/sth** ◇ The ~ missed his heart by less than an inch. | **graze sb/sth** | **enter sb/sth, penetrate sb/sth** | **kill sb** | **be lodged, lodge** ◇ Surgeons are trying to remove a ~ lodged near his spine. | **go, pass** | **fly across, around, etc. sb/sth, rip through sb/sth, smash into sb/sth, tear through sb/sth, thud into sb/sth** (esp. AmE), **whistle past sb/sth, whizz by, past, etc.** ◇ A stray ~ whistled past his ear. | **bounce, ricochet** ◇ The ~s ricocheted off the stones. | **come from sth**

BULLET + NOUN **hole** | **wound** | **scar**

PREP. **~ from** ◇ It is a ~ from the same gun that killed the Italian. | **in, ~ through** ◇ He got a ~ in the back. | **~ to** ◇ He was killed by a single ~ to the head.

PHRASES **a hail of ~s, a volley of ~s** ◇ They died in a hail of ~s. | **take a ~ (for sb)** (often figurative) ◇ I would have taken a ~ for Jack.

bulletin noun

1 short news report/official statement

ADJ. **official** | **news, weather** (esp. BrE) | **all-points** (usually abbreviated to **APB**) (AmE)

VERB + BULLETIN **issue, put out, release, send out** ◇ The government will issue an official ~ later this week.

PREP. **in a/the ~** ◇ More details will be given in our next news ~. | **~ on** ◇ a ~ on the president's health

2 short newspaper

ADJ. **monthly, weekly, etc.** | **church**

VERB + BULLETIN **produce, publish** | **read**

PREP. **in a/the ~** ◇ The details are in the June ~.

bully noun

ADJ. **big** ◇ Leave him alone, you big ~! | **class, playground, school, schoolyard** (AmE) | **neighbourhood/neighborhood** (esp. AmE)

BULLY + VERB **pick on sb** | **beat sb up**

bump noun

1 sudden strong blow

ADJ. **loud** | **minor, slight**

VERB + BUMP **feel, take**

PREP. **with a ~** ◇ We landed with a loud ~.

2 lump on the body

ADJ. **big, huge, large, nasty, nice** | **little, small, tiny** | **red** | **goose** (usually **goosebumps**) (esp. AmE)

VERB + BUMP **get, have**

PREP. **~ on** ◇ He got a nasty ~ on his head.

PHRASES **~s and bruises**

3 lump in a flat surface

ADJ. **speed** (= on a road) (esp. AmE)

VERB + BUMP **hit** ◇ We hit a ~ and the car swerved. | **smooth out** (often figurative) ◇ My job is to smooth out the ~s in supply and demand.

PREP. **~ in** ◇ a ~ in the road

bump verb

ADV. **accidentally** | **gently** | **almost, nearly**

PREP. **against** ◇ I ran after her, ~ing against people in my rush. | **into** ◇ I ~ed into the corner of a table as I left. | **on** ◇ I ~ed my head on the door frame.

bumper noun

ADJ. **front** | **back, rear**

BUMPER + NOUN **car** (*esp. AmE*) (usually ***dodgem*** in *BrE*) | **PHRASES** **~ to ~** ◊ *The cars crawled along ~ to ~ (= very close to each other).*

bun *noun*

1 small cake or bread roll

ADJ. **fresh** | **cinnamon** (*esp. AmE*) | **cream, currant, hot cross, iced, sticky** (*all BrE*) | **hamburger, hot-dog** | **VERB + BUN** **eat, have** | **bake, make, toast** | → Special page at FOOD

2 hair fastened in a round shape

ADJ. **neat, severe, tight** | **loose, messy** | **PREP.** **in a ~** ◊ *a woman with her hair tied back in a loose ~* | **into a ~** ◊ *She pulled her hair back into a messy ~.*

bunch *noun*

1 things fastened/growing together

ADJ. **big, huge, large** | **small** | **PREP.** **in a/the ~** ◊ *She put all the flowers together in one big ~.* | **~ of** ◊ *He gave me a huge ~ of red roses.*

2 group of people

ADJ. **diverse, eclectic, mixed, motley, ragtag** | **good, great, nice** | **lively, rowdy, wild** | **talented** | **PREP.** **~ of** ◊ *They are a ~ of amateurs.* ◊ *a ~ of idiots/morons/jerks/losers*

bundle *noun*

ADJ. **big, large, thick** ◊ *She was carrying a large ~ of clothes.* | **little, small, tiny** | **VERB + BUNDLE** **carry, hold** | **tie sth (up) in, wrap sth (up) in** ◊ *He tied his belongings up in a ~ and left.* | **PREP.** **in a/the ~** ◊ *The papers are in a ~ on my desk.* | **~ of** ◊ *a ~ of newspapers*

bungalow *noun* (*BrE*) house on one level

ADJ. **two-bedroom, two-bedroomed, etc.** | **detached, semi-detached** | **suburban** | **modern** | **holiday, retirement**

burden *noun*

1 responsibility/worry

ADJ. **enormous, great, heavy, huge, onerous, significant, substantial, terrible, tremendous** ◊ *The need to protect the nation places a heavy ~ on the shoulders of state leaders.* ◊ *The war was a huge ~ on the economy.* | **crippling, crushing, intolerable** | **undue, unfair** | **added, additional, extra** | **increased** | **administrative, debt, economic, emotional, financial, regulatory, tax** | **VERB + BURDEN** **bear, carry** ◊ *The manager carries the greatest ~ of responsibility.* | **assume, shoulder, take on** ◊ *She had to shoulder the ~ of childcare.* | **impose, place, put** ◊ *His illness placed an intolerable ~ on his family.* | **create** | **be, become** | **feel** ◊ *He was beginning to feel a ~ to his family.* | **increase** | **ease, lessen, lighten, reduce, relieve** | **lift, remove, take** ◊ *The administrative ~ must be lifted from local government.* | **shift** ◊ *plans to shift the ~ of taxation onto larger companies* | **share** ◊ *I need to share my ~ with someone.* | **BURDEN + VERB** **fall on sb/sth** ◊ *The economic ~ falls mainly on businesses.* | **PREP.** **~ for** ◊ *a ~ for the whole family* | **~ of** ◊ *the ~ of high taxation* ◊ *She carried a huge ~ of guilt for what she had done.* | **~ on, ~ upon** ◊ *Reducing taxes would ease the financial ~ on families.* | **~ to** ◊ *She felt she was a ~ to her parents.* | **PHRASES** **the ~ of proof** (= the responsibility of proving that sth is true) (*law*) ◊ *The ~ of proof falls on the prosecution: the accused is presumed innocent until proved guilty.* | **have a ~ on your shoulders** ◊ *He has the ~ of a large family on his shoulders.* | **the ~ of doing sth** | **lift the ~ from sb's shoulders** (*esp. BrE*), **take the ~ off sb's shoulders**

2 heavy load

VERB + BURDEN **carry** ◊ *The women carried their ~s on their backs.* | **pick up** | **lay down, put down** | **PHRASES** **a beast of ~**

bureau *noun*

ADJ. **federal, government** (*both AmE*) | **census** (*AmE*), **citizen's advice** (*BrE*), **credit** (*AmE*), **employment, news** | **convention, visitors** (*both AmE*) | **VERB + BUREAU** **contact, go to** | **establish** | **close** | **BUREAU + VERB** **handle sth** ◊ *The ~ handles millions of requests each year.* | **BUREAU + NOUN** **staff** | **chief** | **PREP.** **at a/the ~, in a/the ~** | **~ of** ◊ *the US Bureau of Prisons*

bureaucracy *noun*

1 administrative system

ADJ. **huge, large, massive, vast** | **bloated** | **federal, government, state**

2 official rules and procedures

ADJ. **cumbersome, excessive, unnecessary** | **administrative, corporate** | **VERB + BUREAUCRACY** **cut, eliminate, reduce** ◊ *The organization has promised to eliminate unnecessary ~.* | **create, increase**

bureaucrat *noun*

ADJ. **faceless** ◊ *He was just another faceless ~.* | **corrupt** | **unelected** | **senior** | **mid-level** (*AmE*) | **federal, government, state** | **career** ◊ *battles between political appointees and career ~s*

burglar *noun*

ADJ. **professional** (*BrE*) | **cat** | **suspected** (*BrE*) | **VERB + BURGLAR** **catch** | **hunt** (*BrE, informal*) ◊ *Police are hunting ~s who stole property worth £3 500.* | **BURGLAR + VERB** **break in** ◊ *The ~ had broken in through a window.* | **steal sth** | **strike** (*esp. BrE*) ◊ *Burglars had already struck twice that week in their street.* | **BURGLAR + NOUN** **alarm**

burglary *noun*

ADJ. **attempted** | **aggravated** (= burglary involving further violence or unpleasant behaviour) (*BrE, law*) | **house** (*BrE*), **residential** | **VERB + BURGLARY** **commit** | **BURGLARY + VERB** **happen, take place** (*both esp. BrE*) | **PREP.** **~ at** ◊ *Audio equipment was stolen in a ~ at the mall.* | → Note at CRIME (for more verbs)

burial *noun*

ADJ. **decent, proper** | **Christian, etc.** | **VERB + BURIAL** **give sb** ◊ *We want to give him a decent Christian ~.* | **attend, go to** | **BURIAL + VERB** **take place** | **BURIAL + NOUN** **chamber, ground, mound, pit, place, plot, site, vault** ◊ *An ancient ~ site had been disturbed.* | **ceremony, rites, service** | **PREP.** **for ~** ◊ *His body was returned home for ~.* | **~ in** ◊ *There were objections to the body's ~ in consecrated ground.*

burn *noun*

ADJ. **horrific** (*esp. BrE*), **nasty, serious, severe, terrible** | **minor, slight, superficial** | **first-degree, second-degree, etc.** | **chemical, cigarette** | **VERB + BURN** **get, suffer** | **cause** | **die from** | **treat, treat sb for** | **BURN + NOUN** **mark** | **wound** | **injury** | **~ victim** (*esp. AmE*), **~s victim** (*BrE*) | **~ center** (*AmE*), **~s centre** (*BrE*) | **PHRASES** **20%, 50%, etc. ~s** ◊ *He was treated in the hospital for 60% ~s.* | **PREP.** **~ on** ◊ *a slight ~ on the back of her hand*

burn *verb*

1 damage/injure by fire/heat

ADV. **badly, seriously, severely** | **completely** ◊ *The car was*

found abandoned in the woods, completely ~ed out. |
partially | **easily** ◇ *fair skin that ~s easily* | **down, out** ◇ *The factory ~ed down last year.*
PHRASES **be ~ed alive** | **be ~ed at the stake** ◇ *Joan of Arc was ~ed at the stake.* | **be ~ed to ashes, be ~ed to a cinder, be ~ed to a crisp** ◇ *The tower was struck by lightning and was ~ed to a cinder.* | **be ~ed to death, ~ to death** ◇ *Several people were ~ed to death.* | **be ~ed to the ground** ◇ *The building was ~ed to the ground.*

2 be on fire
ADV. **fiercely** ◇ *The fire was still ~ing fiercely.* | **steadily** | **slowly** ◇ *Fresh leaves will ~ slowly with billows of smoke.*
PHRASES **~ out of control**

3 produce light
ADV. **brightly** ◇ *Their torches ~ed brightly in the dark.*

4 be filled with strong feeling
ADV. **fiercely** ◇ *Her eyes ~ed fiercely.* | **slowly** ◇ *She could sense the anger ~ing slowly inside him.*
PREP. **with** ◇ *He was ~ing with indignation.*

burrow verb
ADV. **deep** | **down** ◇ *He switched off the lamp and ~ed down beneath the bedclothes.*
PREP. **beneath, under** ◇ *Rabbits had ~ed under the fence.* | **into** ◇ *Earthworms ~ deep into the soil.* | **through** ◇ *worms that ~ through dead wood*
PHRASES **~ your way** ◇ *Ivy had ~ed its way through the walls.*

bursary noun (esp. BrE)
ADJ. **sports, travel**
VERB + BURSARY **award sb, offer sb, provide sb with** | **receive, win**

burst noun
ADJ. **short** ◇ *a short ~ of energy* | **sudden** ◇ *a sudden ~ of enthusiasm* | **quick, rapid** ◇ *a rapid ~ of gunfire* | **occasional** | **initial** | **final** | **single** | **explosive, intense** ◇ *an intense ~ of anger* | **great, huge**
PREP. **in ~s** ◇ *He works in short ~s.* | **~ of**

burst verb
ADV. **suddenly** | **almost, nearly** | **finally** | **apart** (esp. BrE), **forth, out** ◇ *There was a danger that the engine would ~ apart.*
VERB + BURST **be about to, be going to, be ready to** ◇ *My whole head felt ready to ~.*
PREP. **out of** ◇ *I felt as though my heart would ~ out of my chest.* | **with** (figurative) ◇ *He felt he would ~ with anger.*

PHR V **burst into sth**
ADV. **suddenly** | **immediately, instantly, promptly** ◇ *She took one look at the mess and promptly ~ into tears.*
VERB + BURST INTO **be about to, be going to, be ready to** ◇ *He was just about to ~ into song.*

bury verb
1 dead person
PHRASES **be dead and buried** ◇ *Those people are now all dead and buried.* ◇ *Their ambitions were finally dead and buried.* (figurative) | **~ sb alive, lie buried, remain buried** (often figurative) ◇ *What secrets lie buried in the past?*
2 hide in the ground
ADV. **deep** | **underground** ◇ *The waste is buried deep underground.*
3 cover
ADV. **completely** ◇ *a fallen tree trunk almost completely buried in the long grass* | **partially**
PHRASES **be buried alive** ◇ *The miners were buried alive when the tunnel collapsed.* | **buried beneath sth, buried under sth** ◇ *The building was now buried under ten feet of soil.* ◇ *Your letter got buried under a pile of papers.* | **be buried up**

to your chin in sth, be buried up to your neck in sth, etc. ◇ *He was buried up to his neck in sand.*
4 put sth deeply into sth
ADV. **deep, deeply** ◇ *He slumped forward, the knife buried deep in his chest.* ◇ *her deeply buried pain* (figurative)

bus noun
ADJ. **regular** ◇ *There are regular ~es to the beach.* | **shuttle** | **double-decker, open-topped** (BrE) | **last** ◇ *I missed the last ~ and had to walk.* | **city** (esp. AmE), **local, public** | **sightseeing** (BrE), **tour, tourist** | **school, yellow** | **campaign** | **airport** | **crowded** | **team**
VERB + BUS **go by, go on, ride** (AmE), **take, travel by, use** | **wait for** ◇ *I waited 40 minutes for a ~.* | **run for** ◇ *I left work a little late and had to run for my ~.* | **catch, get** | **miss** | **board, get on, get onto** | **get off, leave** | **drive**
BUS + VERB **go, run** ◇ *Local ~es run regularly to and from the campus.* | **arrive, come** | **pull up, stop** ◇ *The ~ pulled up and we got on.* ◇ *The ~es stop outside the post office.* | **pick sb up** ◇ *The double-decker ~ stopped to pick up some more passengers.* | **leave sth** ◇ *The ~ left the city, heading north.* | **go from…, leave from…** ◇ *Buses leave from here every hour or so.* | **carry sb** ◇ *a ~ carrying 56 passengers* | **be full** | **be late**
BUS + NOUN **schedule** (esp. AmE), **times** (BrE), **timetable** (BrE) ◇ *Look up the ~ schedule on the Internet.* | **line** (esp. AmE), **route** | **lane** | **depot, shelter, station, stop, terminal** | **queue** (BrE) | **journey** (esp. BrE), **ride, trip** ◇ *a short ~ journey to work* (BrE) ◇ *a four-hour ~ journey over the mountains* (BrE, AmE) | **tour** | **conductor** (BrE), **driver, passenger** (esp. BrE), **rider** (AmE) | **fare** | **pass, ticket** | **company, line** (AmE) | **service, system** | **boycott**
PREP. **by ~** ◇ *It's about 15 minutes away by ~.* | **on a/the ~** ◇ *people who travel on ~es* | **~ for** ◇ *Is this the ~ for Recife?* | **~ from, ~ into** ◇ *the ~ into town* | **~ to** ◇ *the ~ from Charlottesville to Union Station*

bush noun
1 plant
ADJ. **rose, thorn, etc.** | **prickly, scrubby, thorny**
…OF BUSHES **clump** ◇ *a large clump of rose ~es*
VERB + BUSH **plant** | **prune, trim** ◇ *to prune the rose ~es*
BUSH + VERB **grow**
PREP. **among the ~es, in the ~es** ◇ *She was hiding in the ~es at the side of the lane.*
PHRASES **~es and trees, trees and ~es**
2 wild land in Africa/Australia
ADJ. **dense, thick** | **African, Australian** | **native** ◇ *hills that have become a wasteland after the removal of native ~*
BUSH + NOUN **fire** | **meat** (usually **bushmeat**)
PREP. **in the ~, into the ~** ◇ *They went out into the ~.*

business noun
1 buying and selling of goods
ADJ. **big** | **profitable** | **private** | **core** ◇ *It's time to focus on the company's core ~.* | **retail, wholesale** | **online** ◇ *Supermarkets are doing more online ~.* | **competitive, tough** ◇ *Retail is a tough ~.* | **catering, computer, consulting, insurance, investment, etc.** ◇ *He spent his whole life in the insurance ~.* | **entertainment, movie** (esp. AmE), **music, newspaper** ◇ *We're not trying to educate—we're in the entertainment ~.*
VERB + BUSINESS **carry on** (often law), **conduct, do, transact** (formal) ◇ *a company that has ceased to carry on ~* ◇ *He's someone I can do ~ with* (= that I find it easy to deal with). | **work in** ◇ *She works in the computer ~.* | **go into, set up in** | **go out of** ◇ *The company went out of ~ during the recession.* | **put sb/sth out of** ◇ *The new regulations will put many small companies out of ~.* | **help** ◇ *He argues that tax cuts will help ~.* | **understand** ◇ *Nobody understands the music ~ better than him.*
BUSINESS + NOUN **deal, transaction** | **opportunity, venture** | **meeting** | **lunch** | **travel, trip** | **person** (see also **businessman, businesswoman**) | **traveller/traveler** | **expense** ◇ *Meals are considered a ~ expense.* | **community,**

BUSINESS

Starting out …

set up		launch	
an agency	an office	an advertising	a project
a branch	an organization	campaign	a scheme (*BrE*)
a business	a project	a career	a takeover bid
a company	a scheme (*BrE*)	an initiative	a website
a firm	a venture	an operation	
in business (*esp. BrE*)	a website	a product	
a network		a programme/program	

Now we're in business …

do	make	manage	operate	run
the accounts	an appointment	a business	an airline	an airline
business	a bargain	a company	a facility (*esp. AmE*)	a bar
the catering	cutbacks	demand	a fleet (of trucks, etc.)	a business
a deal	a deal	the economy	a flight	a campaign
the marketing	an investment	a factory	a scheme (*BrE*)	a company
the paperwork	a killing	the finances	a service	the economy
some research	a loan	a firm	a store	a factory
	money	the funds	at full capacity	a restaurant
	a profit	a restaurant	at a loss	
	a transaction	a team		

Doing well …

boost		generate	
circulation	spending	business	profit
demand	takings	capital	publicity
the economy	tourism	cash	revenue
production	trade	employment	
profits	turnover	income	

… and not so well …

- **a company** goes bankrupt/goes under
- **a deal** falls apart/falls through
- **the euro** falls to a new low
- **growth** slows
- **negotiations** break down
- **profits** plummet/plunge
- **recession** looms
- **sales** are down
- **shares** plummet/plunge (*esp. BrE*)
  stocks plummet/plunge (*esp. AmE*)

sitting there, minding my own ~, when a man started shouting at me. | **no ~ of yours, none of your ~** ◇ *My private life is none of your ~ (= does not concern you).*

5 important matters

ADJ. **private** | **important, pressing, urgent** | **official** ◇ *This isn't a social call—I've come on official ~.* | **unfinished** ◇ *We have some unfinished ~ to discuss.*

VERB + BUSINESS **get down to** ◇ *OK, let's get down to ~.* | **deal with, discuss, talk** ◇ *I'm not going to talk ~ tonight.* | **finish** ◇ *Jack and I finished our ~ early, so we went to lunch.*

PHRASES **any other ~** (= items discussed at the end of a meeting) ◇ *I think we've finished item four. Now, is there any other ~?* | **mean ~** (= be serious about doing something) ◇ *He says he's going to make changes, and I think he means ~.*

6 situation/event

ADJ. **whole** ◇ *I'll be glad when the whole ~ is over and done with.* | **dirty, messy** ◇ *I'm just glad to be out of the whole dirty ~.* | **bad, sorry, terrible** (all esp. BrE) ◇ *It was a bad business—he couldn't work for months.* | **funny, strange** (esp. BrE) | **dangerous, risky, tricky** ◇ *Changing your life can be a risky ~.* | **serious** ◇ *Having fun is a serious ~.*

businessman, businesswoman noun

ADJ. **leading** (esp. BrE), **prominent, successful** | **astute, good, shrewd, smart** (esp. AmE) | **billionaire, millionaire, rich, wealthy** | **small** ◇ *an association of small businessmen (= people who own small businesses)* | **local** ◇ *charities supported by local businesswomen* | **retired**

busy adj.

VERBS **be, look, seem** | **become, get** | **keep, remain, stay** (esp. AmE) ◇ *She needed to keep ~.* | **keep sb** ◇ *I have enough work to keep me ~.*

ADV. **extremely, fairly, very, etc.** | **awfully, incredibly, terribly** | **especially, exceptionally, particularly, unusually** | **frantically, insanely** | **a little, slightly, etc.**

PREP. **with** ◇ *She was ~ with her make-up.*

butcher noun

ADJ. **local** | **halal, kosher** | **pork** (esp. BrE) | **master** (BrE)

→ Note at JOB

butter noun

ADJ. **fresh** | **creamy** | **rancid** | **melted** ◇ *Brush the pastry with a little melted ~.* | **softened** | **clarified** | **salted, unsalted** | **brandy** (esp. BrE), **garlic, herb** | **apple** (AmE) | **almond, cocoa** | **peanut**

... OF BUTTER **knob** (BrE), **pat, slab, stick** (AmE) ◇ *You can make frosting out of half a stick of ~ and two cups of powdered sugar.*

VERB + BUTTER **put on, spread (sth with)** ◇ *Put some ~ on the crackers, please.* ◇ *He spread ~ on the roll.* | **heat, melt, soften** | **add, beat, beat in, cream, mix, rub, rub in** ◇ *Cream the ~ and icing sugar together until light and fluffy.* ◇ *Rub the ~ into the flour.* | **churn, make**

BUTTER + VERB **spread** ◇ *This ~ doesn't spread very well.* | **melt** ◇ *The ~ melted in the heat.*

BUTTER + NOUN **sauce** | **dish, knife**

PREP. **in ~** ◇ *spinach sautéed in ~*

PHRASES **bread and ~**

→ Special page at FOOD

butter verb

ADV. **generously, thickly** (esp. BrE) | **lightly** ◇ *lightly ~ed toast*

butterfly noun

1 insect

VERB + BUTTERFLY **chase** | **collect** | **attract** ◇ *Sweetly scented flowers will attract butterflies to your garden.*

BUTTERFLY + VERB **flit, flutter, fly** | **emerge** ◇ *The ~ emerged from the pupa.*

BUTTERFLY + NOUN **wing**

2 swimming stroke

→ Note at STROKE

---

sector, world | executive, leader, manager ◇ *a conference of women ~ leaders* | associate, partner | contact | relationship ◇ *They developed a lasting ~ relationship.* | affairs, interests, matters | decision ◇ *It was purely a ~ decision.* | ethics | development | investment | secret ◇ *to protect ~ secrets* | model, plan, strategy ◇ *a ~ model for using electronic commerce* | practice ◇ *It's good ~ practice to listen to your customers.* | acumen | card | attire (esp. AmE), suit ◇ *He wore a ~ suit.* | hours ◇ *You can call the helpline during normal ~ hours.* | school | studies | major (AmE) | park ◇ *The company's offices are located in the new ~ park out of town.* | district ◇ *the city's main ~ district*

PREP. **in ~** ◇ *He's in ~.* ◇ *What ~ are you in?* ◇ *All we need is a car and we'll be in ~ (= we'll have everything we need to start what we want to do).* | **on ~** ◇ *I'm going to Paris on ~.*

PHRASES **~ as usual** (= things will continue as normal in spite of a difficult situation) ◇ *It's ~ as usual at the factory.* | **~ or pleasure** ◇ *Is the trip to Rome ~ or pleasure?* | **mix ~ with pleasure** ◇ *When I travel overseas I like to mix ~ with pleasure.* | **my, his, her etc. own ~** ◇ *He left the department to start his own ~.* | **a place of ~**

2 amount of trade done

ADJ. **brisk, good** ◇ *Business was brisk and they had sold out by midday.* | **bad, slack** (esp. BrE), **slow** | **new** ◇ *They've cut their rates to attract new ~.* | **repeat** ◇ *Our repeat ~ is 50% or higher.*

VERB + BUSINESS **do** ◇ *They're doing good ~ in Asia.* | **attract, drum up, generate** ◇ *She's in Europe drumming up ~ for her new company.* | **tout for** (BrE) ◇ *insurance salesmen touting for ~* | **affect, hurt** ◇ *Cheap imports are hurting ~ for domestic producers.* | **lose** ◇ *We're losing ~ to our main rivals.* | **handle** ◇ *We took on temporary staff to handle the extra ~.*

BUSINESS + VERB **boom, grow** ◇ *Business is booming for the big pharmaceutical companies.* | **pick up** ◇ *After a slack period, ~ is now picking up.* | **slow, slow down** ◇ *Business has slowed considerably in recent months.*

3 commercial organization

ADJ. **large, medium-sized, small** | **new** ◇ *loans for people to start new ~es* | **family, family-owned** | **global, international, local** | **private** | **state-owned** | **booming, lucrative, profitable, successful, thriving, viable** ◇ *The family owns a booming construction ~.* | **Internet, online, Web** ◇ *She runs a successful online ~.* | **traditional** ◇ *Traditional ~es are having to compete with the Internet.* | **mail-order, retail, wholesale** | **catering, grocery** (esp. AmE), **hairdressing, restaurant, etc.** ◇ *She had her own hairdressing ~.* | **legitimate** ◇ *These laws make life more difficult for legitimate ~es.*

VERB + BUSINESS **have, own** | **manage, operate, run** ◇ *It was always my dream to run my own ~.* | **establish, launch, set up, start** ◇ *They decided to start their own ~.* | **build, build up** ◇ *We built up the ~ from nothing.* | **expand, grow** ◇ *We are looking to grow the ~ over the next couple of years.* | **work in** ◇ *He works in the family ~.* | **enter, join** ◇ *After leaving school she entered the family ~.* | **leave** | **buy, take over** | **sell**

BUSINESS + VERB **do well, flourish, succeed, take off, thrive** ◇ *After six months the ~ really took off.* | **expand, grow** ◇ *The ~ is expanding fast.* | **collapse, fail** | **be based in** ◇ *He owns a management consulting ~ based in Santa Barbara.*

BUSINESS + NOUN **assets, premises** | **failure** | **owner**

→ Note at ORGANIZATION

4 work/responsibility

ADJ. **daily** | **real** ◇ *He needs time and space to get on with the real ~ of writing.*

VERB + BUSINESS **get on with, go about** ◇ *market traders going about their daily ~* | **make sth** ◇ *I shall make it my ~ to find out who is responsible.*

PHRASES **have no ~ doing sth, have no ~ to do sth** (esp. BrE) ◇ *You have no ~ (= no right) being here.* | **keep your nose out of sb's ~, mind your own ~** ◇ *Keep your nose out of my ~!* ◇ *'What are you reading?' 'Mind your own ~!'* ◇ *I was just*

button *noun*

1 for fastening clothes

ADJ. **bottom, top** ◊ *The top ~ of his shirt was undone.* | **coat, shirt, etc.** | **brass, pearl, etc.**
VERB + BUTTON **button** *(AmE)*, **do up** *(BrE)*, **fasten** | **unbutton** *(AmE)*, **undo** *(BrE)*, **unfasten** | **fumble with** | **lose** ◊ *My coat has lost a ~.* | **sew on**
BUTTON + VERB **be missing, come off** ◊ *There was a ~ missing from his shirt.*
→ Special page at CLOTHES

2 small switch

ADJ. **on, start** | **off, stop** | **control** | **fast-forward, pause, play, rewind** | **delete, mute, reset, snooze, etc.** | **alarm, panic** ◊ *She hit the alarm ~ as fast as she could.* | **elevator** *(AmE)*, **lift** *(BrE)* | **intercom** | **mouse** | **self-destruct** *(often figurative)*
VERB + BUTTON **click** *(computing)*, **depress, hit, hold down, press, punch, push, tap** ◊ *Click the left mouse ~ twice.* | **release**
PHRASES **at the touch of a ~** ◊ *The remote control allows you to change channel at the touch of a ~.* | **have your finger on, keep your finger on**

3 *(AmE)* object worn to show support

ADJ. **lapel** ◊ *She wore a 'Vote Yes' lapel ~.* | **campaign** ◊ *The candidates all distributed campaign ~s and bumper stickers.* | **peace** ◊ *He carries around an old backpack with peace ~s on it.*
VERB + BUTTON **wear** ◊ *They all wore ~s saying 'Stop the war'.*
→ Special page at COMPUTER

buy *verb*

ADV. **cheaply** ◊ *Old bicycles can be bought quite cheaply.* | **online** ◊ *Young people are very comfortable ~ing online.* | **locally** ◊ *Was the produce imported or bought locally?*
VERB + BUY **can afford to** ◊ *We can afford to ~ enough paint to do the whole house.* | **can't afford to** ◊ *I can't afford to ~ a new car.*
PREP. **at** ◊ *CDs can now be bought at the supermarket.* | **for** ◊ *He bought a car for his daughter.* ◊ *I bought it for $25.* | **from** ◊ *I bought some books from a friend.*
PHRASES **~ and sell** ◊ *She makes her living ~ing and selling antiques.* | **money can ~, money can't ~** ◊ *It's the best that money can ~.* ◊ *There are some things money can't ~.*

buyer *noun*

ADJ. **potential, prospective, would-be** | **first-time** ◊ *The houses are ideal for first-time ~s.* | **home, house** *(esp. BrE)* | **canny** *(esp. BrE)*, **discerning** *(esp. BrE)*, **savvy** *(AmE)*
VERB + BUYER **have** | **find, get** ◊ *They quickly found a ~ for their house.* | **attract, entice, interest, tempt** | **deter** | **sell sth to**
PREP. **~ for** ◊ *Did you find a ~ for your house?*
PHRASES **~ beware** (= the buyer is responsible for checking the quality of the goods) | **a buyer's market** (= when prices are low)

buzz *noun*

ADJ. **high, high-pitched** | **low** | **loud** | **angry** ◊ *the angry ~ of a wasp* | **annoying, incessant** | **background** ◊ *the background ~ of conversation*
VERB + BUZZ **hear** | **create, generate** *(both figurative)* ◊ *The movie, due out next summer, is already creating a ~.*
BUZZ + VERB **surround** *(figurative)* ◊ *An intense ~ surrounded the event.*
PREP. **~ of** *(figurative)* ◊ *I love the ~ (= excitement) of a big city.*
PHRASES **a ~ of conversation, a ~ of excitement** ◊ *There was a ~ of excitement all around the room.*

buzzer *noun*

VERB + BUZZER **press, punch** *(esp. AmE)*, **ring** ◊ *Press the ~ when you want to talk.*
BUZZER + VERB **go** *(esp. BrE)*, **go off, sound** ◊ *The ~ went off at eight o'clock.*

bypass *noun*

1 medical operation

ADJ. **coronary, heart** | **gastric** | **quadruple, triple**
VERB + BYPASS **perform** | **undergo**
BYPASS + NOUN **operation, surgery** ◊ *coronary ~ surgery*

2 *(esp. BrE)* road around a city

VERB + BYPASS **build**
PREP. **along a/the ~** ◊ *She was speeding along the ~, thinking about other things.* | **around a/the ~, round a/the ~** *(esp. BrE)* ◊ *We drove around the ~ to the airport.* ◊ *They're building a new ~ around the town.* | **on a/the ~** ◊ *the traffic on the ~*

C c

cab *noun*

ADJ. **taxi** | **hackney** *(BrE)*, **hansom** | **horse-drawn** *(BrE)*
VERB + CAB **go by, take** ◊ *Let's take a ~.* | **call (sb), get (sb), hire** *(esp. AmE)*, **order (sb), phone for** *(BrE)* ◊ *I'll call you a ~.* | **find** ◊ *We couldn't find a ~ anywhere near.* | **catch, flag, flag down, hail** ◊ *I tried to hail a ~ but none of them would stop.* | **get into, get out of** | **drive** | **pay for, pay off** | **share** ◊ *We decided to share a ~.*
CAB + VERB **draw up, pull up, stop** ◊ *The ~ pulled up and they got out.* | **pick sb up, take sb** ◊ *I ordered a ~ to take him home.* | **arrive** | **wait** ◊ *Outside, a ~ was waiting.*
CAB + NOUN **driver** | **rank** *(BrE)* | **fare** | **ride**
PREP. **by ~** ◊ *I came by ~.* | **in a/the ~** ◊ *The driver was sitting in his ~.*
PHRASES **the back of a ~** ◊ *I left my umbrella in the back of the ~.*

cabbage *noun*

ADJ. **green, red, white** | **Chinese, savoy, spring** | **boiled, pickled, raw, shredded, stuffed**
VERB + CABBAGE **boil, braise, cook** | **chop, shred**
CABBAGE + NOUN **leaf** | **patch**
→ Special page at FOOD

cabinet *noun*

1 (usually **the Cabinet**) in government

ADJ. **full** *(BrE)* ◊ *There was a meeting of the full Cabinet this afternoon.* | **inner** *(esp. BrE)* ◊ *The inner Cabinet is to meet again today.* | **shadow** (= the most important members of the opposition party) *(BrE)* | **war**
VERB + CABINET **appoint, choose, form, select** | **reshuffle** ◊ *The Prime Minister reshuffled* (= changed) *his Cabinet yesterday.* | **enter** *(esp. BrE)*, **join** | **leave** *(esp. BrE)*, **quit** | **consult** *(esp. BrE)* | **persuade, urge** *(both esp. BrE)*
CABINET + VERB **meet** | **discuss sth**
CABINET + NOUN **appointee** *(AmE)*, **member, minister** *(BrE)*, **secretary** | **appointment** *(AmE)* | **meeting** | **reshuffle** ◊ *The affair led to a mid-term Cabinet reshuffle.*

2 cupboard

ADJ. **glass** | **maple, oak, wooden, etc.** *(all esp. AmE)* | **bathroom, bedside, kitchen** | **medicine** | **china, curio** *(AmE)*, **display, trophy** ◊ *a glass china ~* | **cocktail, drinks** *(BrE)*, **liquor** *(AmE)* | **chill, chiller** *(both BrE)* | **file** *(AmE)*, **filing** *(esp. BrE)* | **storage** | **locked**
CABINET + NOUN **door, drawer**
PREP. **in a/the ~** ◊ *Past reports are kept in the filing/file ~ in my office.*

cable noun

1 set of wires

ADJ. **electric, telephone | overhead, underground | fibre-optic/fiber-optic | steel | analogue/analog, digital**
... OF CABLE **length** ◇ *a length of electric ~*
VERB + CABLE **lay, run** ◇ *Roads have to be dug up to lay underground ~s.* ◇ *Engineers plan to run the telephone ~s under the river.* | **attach, connect, plug, plug in** ◇ *Connect the ~ to the correct terminal.* ◇ *I plugged the ~ into the amplifier.* | **disconnect, unplug**
CABLE + VERB **go, run** ◇ *a ~ running under the road* | **connect sth** ◇ *new ~s connecting major cities in Europe* | **carry sth** ◇ *These ~s can carry computer data.*

2 system providing TV, Internet and phone

VERB + CABLE **get, have | install** ◇ *We just had ~ installed.*
CABLE + NOUN **television, TV | channel, network | company, operator, provider | subscriber | subscription | bill | connection | box | modem**

cadet noun

ADJ. **army, military, naval | aviation, flying** (*both AmE*) | **air, sea | police | officer** ◇ *The military academy trains up to 2 000 officer ~s each year.*
VERB + CADET **train**
CADET + VERB **march, train | graduate** (*AmE*)
CADET + NOUN **corps**

cafe (also café) noun

ADJ. **pavement** (*BrE*), **sidewalk** (*AmE*) | **transport** (*BrE*)
VERB + CAFE **eat at | frequent, go to | manage, run | own**
CAFE + VERB **serve sth** ◇ *a ~ serving drinks and light meals*
PREP. **in a/the ~**

cake noun

ADJ. **home-made | moist, rich, sticky** (*esp. BrE*) ◇ *a rich, moist fruit ~* | **almond, carrot, chocolate, cream** (*esp. BrE*), **fruit, lemon, etc. | angel food** (*AmE*), **pound** (*AmE*), **sponge | layer | birthday, Christmas** (*esp. BrE*), **wedding** ◇ *I blew out the candles on my birthday ~.*
... OF CAKE **piece, slice** ◇ *He cut her a slice of ~.*
VERB + CAKE **eat, have | bake, make | decorate, frost** (*esp. AmE*), **ice | cut** ◇ *The bride and groom cut the wedding ~.*
CAKE + NOUN **crumbs** ◇ *She brushed some ~ crumbs off her lap.* | **recipe | mix, mixture** (*BrE*) ◇ *a packet of ~ mix* (*BrE*) ◇ *a box of ~ mix* (*AmE*) ◇ *Pour the ~ mixture into a bowl.* | **pan** (*AmE*), **tin** (*BrE*) | **stand | shop** (*esp. BrE*), **stall** (*BrE*)
→ Special page at FOOD

calculate verb

1 work out a number, etc.

ADV. **accurately, exactly, precisely** ◇ *It's difficult to ~ precisely what we've spent.* | **mentally**
PREP. **according to** ◇ *The amount is ~d according to the number of years you have paid into the plan.* | **at** ◇ *The sum involved was ~d at $82 million.*

2 form an opinion using information available

ADV. **carefully, shrewdly | correctly** ◇ *He correctly ~d that the others would not dare fight back.* | **coldly** ◇ *The incident had been coldly ~d to humiliate him.*

calculation noun

1 act of calculating/sum calculated

ADJ. **accurate, correct, exact, precise** ◇ *an exact ~ of the amount spent so far* ◇ *Your ~s are correct.* | **incorrect, wrong** ◇ *It turned out that our ~s were incorrect.* | **approximate, rough** ◇ *Even a rough ~ shows that you have spent too much.* | **complex, complicated, detailed | simple | quick | mental | arithmetical** (*esp. BrE*), **mathematical, numerical, statistical | economic, financial**
VERB + CALCULATION **do, make, perform** ◇ *She did a rapid ~ in her head.* ◇ *We cannot make a precise ~ of the price until we*

have all the costs. | **base on sth** ◇ *The ~s are based on average annual data.*
PHRASES **a method of ~**

2 careful planning to get what you want

ADJ. **cold, cool, rational**
... OF CALCULATION **act** ◇ *an act of cold ~*

calculator noun

ADJ. **desk, hand-held, pocket | electronic, programmable**

calendar noun

ADJ. **busy, full** ◇ *The group has a busy social ~.* | **sporting** (*BrE*), **sports | golfing, racing, etc. | academic | social | Christian, Jewish, etc. | Gregorian, lunar, etc.**
VERB + CALENDAR **check, consult**
PREP. **in a/the ~, on a/the ~** ◇ *the most important event in the year's golfing ~*
PHRASES **mark sth on the ~, put sth on the ~** (*both esp. AmE*) ◇ *Mark the renewal date on the ~ so you don't forget.*

calf noun

ADJ. **bull, heifer | beef, dairy, veal | newborn | weaned**
VERB + CALF **produce** ◇ *A dairy cow needs to produce a ~ each year.* | **rear** ◇ *These calves are reared for beef.*
CALF + VERB **feed, graze**

call noun

1 on the telephone

ADJ. **phone, telephone | long | quick, short** ◇ *I'll just make a quick phone ~.* | **local | international, long-distance | collect** (*esp. AmE*) | **incoming | outgoing | conference | business, follow-up, sales, telemarketing** (*esp. AmE*) ◇ *We always make follow-up ~s to ensure customer satisfaction.* | **personal** ◇ *We're not supposed to make personal ~s from work.* | **emergency, urgent** ◇ *He received an urgent ~ and had to leave.* | **frantic** ◇ *She made a frantic phone ~ to her mother.* | **anonymous, crank, hoax** (*esp. BrE*), **nuisance** (*esp. BrE*), **prank, unsolicited | missed** ◇ *The screen display said '8 missed calls'.* | **wake-up** ◇ *I ordered a wake-up ~ for 6.30 the next morning.* ◇ *Last night's defeat should be a wake-up ~ for the team.* (*figurative*)
VERB + CALL **give sb, make, place** ◇ *Give us a ~ to say when you have arrived.* ◇ *She placed an anonymous ~ to the Dutch Embassy in Dublin.* | **get, have, receive | answer, deal with, field, handle, take** ◇ *I'll take the ~s upstairs.* ◇ *He spent the whole day fielding ~s from concerned parents.* | **return** ◇ *I left a message but he didn't return my ~.* | **expect** ◇ *Could you get off the phone? I'm expecting a ~.* | **miss** ◇ *She was out and missed an important ~.* | **end, finish** ◇ *I ended the ~ as quickly as possible.* | **put through, transfer** ◇ *Ask the receptionist to put your ~ through to my room.* | **intercept, monitor, screen, trace** ◇ *The police managed to trace the ~.*
CALL + NOUN **box** (*BrE*) | **centre/center**
PREP. **~ for** ◇ *Were there any ~s for me while I was out?* | **~ from** ◇ *You had a ~ from Fred.* | **~ to** ◇ *I made a ~ to a friend in London.*

2 sound to attract attention

ADJ. **loud | distinctive** ◇ *the distinctive ~ of the cuckoo* | **alarm, distress | bird | clarion, rallying** (*both figurative*) ◇ *This election is a clarion ~ for our country to face the challenges of the new era.*
VERB + CALL **let out, make, sound** ◇ *The mosque was sounding the ~ to prayer.* | **hear**
PREP. **~ for** ◇ *a ~ for help* | **~ to** ◇ *the morning ~ to prayer*

3 short visit

ADJ. **business, courtesy, sales, social | house** ◇ *The doctor does not usually make house ~s.*
VERB + CALL **make, pay (sb)** ◇ *The doctor has several ~s to make this morning.*
PREP. **on a** ◇ *She's out on a ~.* | **~ on** ◇ *When he went to Ethiopia, his first ~ was on the ambassador.*
PHRASES **first port of ~, last port of ~, next port of ~** ◇ *Our first port of ~* (= the first place we went) *was the bank.*

ADJ. **renewed, repeated** | **last** ◊ *This is the last ~ for PAM flight 199 to Salvador.* | **strike** (*BrE*)
VERB + ISSUE | **renew, repeat** ◊ *Campaigners have renewed their ~ for an independent inquiry.* | **answer, heed, respond to** ◊ *It is unlikely that they will heed ~s for a crackdown.* ◊ *Around 10 000 workers heeded the union's strike ~.* (*BrE*) | **ignore, reject, resist** ◊ *The government has resisted the ~s of the international community.*
CALL + NOUN **button** ◊ *He pushed the ~ button for the flight attendant.*
PREP. **~ for** ◊ *The charity issued a ~ for donations to assist victims of the earthquake.*
PHRASES **a ~ to action** ◊ *The book is a ~ to action.* | **a ~ to arms** (= a strong request for people to fight in the army) (*often figurative*) ◊ *The president's speech was a ~ to arms to restore the vitality of the American dream.*

5 (*informal*) decision
ADJ. **tough** | **close** | **judgement/judgment** | **line, strike** (*both sports*)

call verb

1 give a name to sb/sth
ADV. **commonly, frequently** ◊ *Buenos Aires is often ~ed the Paris of South America.* | **formerly, originally** ◊ *The area was formerly ~ed West Meadow.* | **affectionately** ◊ *His friends affectionately ~ him 'Bear'.* | **just, simply** ◊ *a character whom the writer ~s simply 'The Girl'* | **officially** ◊ *The system is officially ~ed the NPV System.* | **collectively** ◊ *a range of very small organisms, collectively ~ed nanoplankton* | **variously** ◊ *a tree variously ~ed 'rowan' and 'mountain ash'* | **aptly, rightly** | **tentatively** ◊ *He is writing a novel, tentatively ~ed 'My Future'.* | **euphemistically** ◊ *soldiers killed by what is euphemistically ~ed 'friendly fire'*
PREP. **by** ◊ *We usually ~ him by his nickname.*
PHRASES **you could hardly ~ sth…, you would hardly ~ sth…** ◊ *You could hardly ~ the show perfect, but it was successful.*

2 make sound to attract attention
ADV. **softly** | **loudly** | **out** ◊ *She ~ed out in pain.*
PREP. **for** ◊ *He ~ed for help, but no one could hear.* | **to** ◊ *a female penguin ~ing to her mate*

3 telephone
ADV. **back** ◊ *I'll ~ back later.* ◊ *Leave a message and I'll ~ you back.* | **ahead** ◊ *You should ~ ahead to make sure that seats are available.* | **free** (*BrE*), **toll-free** (*AmE*) ◊ *Call us free/toll-free on this number.* | **collect** (*AmE*)

calm noun

1 peaceful situation/manner/feeling
ADJ. **apparent** ◊ *Under his apparent ~ lay real anxiety.* | **inner** ◊ *the pursuit of inner ~* | **uneasy** | **forced** ◊ *With a forced ~ she said, 'How do you know?'* | **dead** ◊ *She felt not fear, but a kind of dead ~.* | **deadly, deathly, eerie, icy** ◊ *'I'm calling the police!' he stated with deadly ~.*
VERB + CALM **appeal for, call for** ◊ *The government appealed for ~ after the riots broke out.* | **restore** ◊ *Calm had been restored to the capital.* | **maintain, regain** ◊ *He struggled to maintain his ~ as they waited.* | **shatter** ◊ *The ~ was shattered by the sound of an explosion.*
CALM + VERB **descend, settle** ◊ *After the bomb, an uneasy ~ settled on the city.*
PHRASES **a period of ~**

2 at sea
ADJ. **dead, flat** (*esp. BrE*) ◊ *The water was a dead ~.*

calm adj.

VERBS **appear, be, feel, look, seem, sound** ◊ *I may have appeared ~ but I certainly didn't feel it.* | **become** | **keep, remain, stay** ◊ *The pilot urged the passengers to remain ~.* | **keep sb** ◊ *Keep the patient ~.*
ADV. **extremely, fairly, very, etc.** | **remarkably** ◊ *You seem remarkably ~.* | **completely, perfectly** ◊ *Her voice was firm*

and perfectly ~. | **outwardly** ◊ *The voice sounded outwardly ~.* | **strangely** ◊ *The pain had receded and he felt strangely ~.* | **dead** ◊ *The sea was dead ~.*
PREP. **about** ◊ *She seemed pretty ~ about it.*
PHRASES **~ and collected, cool, ~ and collected** ◊ *He remained at all times cool, ~ and collected.*

calorie noun

ADJ. **excess, extra** | **empty** ◊ *Alcohol has a lot of empty ~s.* | **daily** | **total** | **carbohydrate, fat** ◊ *Try to reduce the percentage of fat ~s* (= calories from fat) *in your diet.*
VERB + CALORIE **contain, have** | **consume, eat, ingest** | **burn, burn off, expend** ◊ *You need to exercise more to burn off the ~s.* | **cut, restrict** ◊ *a calorie-restricted diet* | **count, watch** ◊ *I don't count ~s, but I am careful about what I eat.*
CALORIE + NOUN **consumption, content, intake** ◊ *foods with a high ~ content* | **burn** (*esp. AmE*), **expenditure** ◊ *Mile per mile you get the same ~ burn from walking as from running.*
PHRASES **high in ~s, low in ~s** ◊ *Vegetables are relatively low in ~s.*

camera noun

ADJ. **automatic, disposable, electronic, high-resolution, high-speed, panoramic, Polaroid™, SLR, underwater** ◊ *I bought a disposable ~ from the gift shop.* | **analogue/analog, digital** | **six-megapixel, etc.** | **box, pinhole** | **cine** (*BrE*), **movie, television, TV, video** | **infrared, night-vision, thermal** | **compact, miniature, tiny** | **hidden, secret, spy** | **built-in** ◊ *a mobile phone with a built-in ~* (*BrE*) | **CCTV, closed-circuit, security, surveillance** | **hand-held, mobile** ◊ *The documentary was shot using a hand-held digital ~.*
VERB + CAMERA **aim, focus, point** ◊ *Simply point your ~ at the subject and press the button.* | **operate, use** ◊ *The ~ can be operated remotely.* | **pose for** ◊ *The outgoing and incoming presidents posed for the ~s.* | **face** ◊ *He couldn't bring himself to face the waiting ~s.* | **attach, mount** ◊ *The ~ was mounted on a hang-glider.* | **install, place, position** ◊ *Closed-circuit ~s have been installed throughout the building.* | **set up** ◊ *The crews have been setting up their ~s.* | **load**
CAMERA + VERB **film sth** | **capture sb/sth, catch sb/sth, record sb/sth** ◊ *A security ~ caught her shoplifting.* | **focus on sb/ sth, pan across sth, pan around sth, pan to sth, zoom in (on sth)** ◊ *The ~ zoomed in on a picture above the fireplace.* | **linger (on sth)** ◊ *The ~ lingers on a close-up of her face.* | **roll** ◊ *The director gave the signal and the ~s rolled.* | **click, flash** ◊ *She stepped onto the balcony and a thousand ~s clicked.*
CAMERA + NOUN **crew, team** | **operator** | **bag, equipment, lens, shutter** | **flash** ◊ *A ~ flash went off from behind the bushes.* | **angle, position** | **work** (usually **camerawork**) | **footage** ◊ *Police are checking security ~ footage.* | **trick** | **phone** ◊ *the highest-resolution ~ phone on the market*
PREP. **in front of the ~s** ◊ *He played his first game in front of the TV ~s.* | **off ~** ◊ *The incident occurred off ~* (= was not filmed). | **on ~** ◊ *The moment was caught on ~.*

camouflage noun

ADJ. **effective, excellent, good, perfect** | **army** ◊ *He was wearing army ~.* | **desert, jungle** ◊ *an army tank in desert ~*
VERB + CAMOUFLAGE **act as, provide** ◊ *The animal's markings provide effective ~.* | **wear**
CAMOUFLAGE + NOUN **pattern** | **gear, uniform** | **pants, shirt, etc.**

camp noun

1 in tents/huts
ADJ. **makeshift, temporary** | **day** (*AmE*), **holiday** (*BrE*), **sleepaway** (*AmE*), **summer** | **basketball, football, music, etc.** (*all esp. AmE*) ◊ *The kids were at basketball ~ most of the summer.* | **scout** | **base** ◊ *The mountaineers set up their base ~ at the foot of the mountain.* | **Gypsy, travellers'** (*BrE*) | **army, boot, military** | **training** | **rebel, terrorist** | **fishing, hunting** (*both esp. AmE*) | **mining**
VERB + CAMP **establish, make, pitch, set up** ◊ *They established*

a base ~ by the river. ◊ We pitched ~ just outside the woods. | **be located** | **break, strike** ◊ We broke ~ early the next morning. | **leave** | **attend, go to** ◊ There are opportunities for children to attend summer ~s. | **attack, destroy, raid** ◊ Militants raided an army ~.

CAMP + NOUN **fire** (usually *campfire*) ◊ We sat around the campfire. | **site** (usually *campsite*)

PREP. **at (a/the)** ~ ◊ The children are spending a week at a summer ~.

2 prison, etc.

ADJ. **concentration, detention, internment, labour/labor, POW, prison, prisoner-of-war, re-education** | **death, extermination** | **transit** | **refugee** ◊ the appalling conditions in the refugee ~s

VERB + CAMP **be sent to** | **enter** | **liberate**

CAMP + NOUN **inmate** | **guard** | **survivor** ◊ concentration ~ survivors

PREP. **in a/the** ~ ◊ She spent five years in a prison ~.

3 group with shared beliefs

ADJ. **hostile, opposing, rival** (esp. BrE), **warring** | **ideological, political** | **armed** ◊ The region split into two armed ~s.

VERB + CAMP **divide into, split into**

PREP. **in a/the** ~ ◊ people in both main political ~s

PHRASES **have a foot in both** ~s (= show loyalty to two different groups) ◊ He can unite the party because he has a foot in both ~s.

campaign noun

ADJ. **big, huge, major, massive** | **lengthy, long, long-running, ongoing, sustained** (esp. BrE) | **effective, successful** | **unsuccessful** | **aggressive, determined, intensive, strong, vigorous** | **bitter, fierce, vicious** | **concerted, orchestrated** ◊ a carefully orchestrated ~ against striking workers | **joint** | **official, public** | **international, local, national, nationwide, worldwide** | **one-man** (esp. BrE), **one-woman** (esp. BrE), **personal** ◊ She has fought a one-woman ~ for ten years about the lack of childcare provision in the town. | **grass-roots** ◊ They began a grass-roots ~ to encourage people to shop locally. | **congressional** (AmE), **election, electoral, gubernatorial** (AmE), **leadership** (esp. BrE), **political, presidential, primary** (AmE), **re-election, referendum** (esp. BrE) | **Conservative, Democratic, Labour, Republican, etc.** | **ad** (informal), **advertising, branding** (esp. AmE), **marketing, promotional, sales** | **PR, propaganda, publicity, public relations** | **media, poster, press** (esp. BrE), **print** (esp. AmE), **television, TV** | **anti-corruption, anti-drug, anti-smoking, etc.** | **protest** | **awareness** ◊ a health awareness ~ to promote a healthy lifestyle | **lobbying** | **fundraising** | **letter-writing** ◊ Local people started a petition and letter-writing ~ to keep the hospital open. | **literacy** | **recruitment** | **air, bombing, guerrilla, military** ◊ the terrorists' bombing ~ | **hate, terror, terrorist** | **dirty tricks** (esp. BrE), **disinformation, smear, whispering** ◊ Her political opponents ran a whispering ~ against her.

VERB + CAMPAIGN **begin, initiate, launch, mount, start, unveil** ◊ The company launched a huge advertising ~. | **conduct, execute, fight, run, undertake, wage** ◊ People have criticized the way in which she conducted her election ~. | **coordinate, manage, orchestrate, organize, plan** | **lead, spearhead** ◊ She led a successful ~ against the closure of the library. | **create, design** ◊ We designed an Internet marketing ~. | **join, support, take part in** | **finance, fund, sponsor** ◊ The anti-fur organization financed an ad ~ featuring celebrities. | **intensify, step up** ◊ The government has intensified the military ~ against the rebels.

CAMPAIGN + VERB **begin, get underway, start** ◊ The general election ~ gets underway today. | **unfold** | **be aimed at sb/sth, focus on sb/sth, target sb/sth** ◊ a concerted ~ aimed at educating young people about the dangers of drugs | **aim to do sth, be designed to do sth** ◊ The ~ aims to inform the public of the dangers of this disease. | **call for sth, demand sth** | **feature sb/sth** ◊ The ~ featured athletes talking about

healthy lifestyles. | **advertise sth, tout sth** (esp. AmE) | **fail, succeed** ◊ The ~ failed to achieve its objectives.

CAMPAIGN + NOUN **aide** (esp. AmE), **manager, staffer** (esp. AmE), **strategist, team** | **strategy** | **headquarters** ◊ A news conference was held at the party's ~ headquarters. | **issue** ◊ Education has become an important ~ issue. | **promise** ◊ The President kept his ~ promises. | **slogan** | **ad, commercial** (both esp. AmE) ◊ A Republican ~ ad alleged he was soft on crime. | **contributions, donations, finance, financing** ◊ regulations governing political ~ financing | **contributor** (esp. AmE) | **trail** ◊ election candidates on the ~ trail(= going around the country campaigning)

PREP. **during a/the** ~ ◊ They met regularly during the ~. | ~ **against** ◊ a fierce ~ against hunting | ~ **by** ◊ the political ~ by the Republicans | ~ **for** ◊ the ~ for racial equality

PHRASES **a** ~ **of disobedience, misinformation, vilification, etc.** ◊ A ~ of intimidation was waged against people trying to vote. | **a plan of** ~ (esp. BrE) ◊ After sliding in the opinion polls, the party had to rethink its plan of ~.

campaign verb

ADV. **actively, aggressively, hard, heavily** (esp. AmE), **strongly** (esp. BrE), **tirelessly, vigorously** ◊ We will ~ hard for an end to the ivory trade. | **effectively, successfully** ◊ Local people have successfully ~ed against the building. | **openly, publicly**

PREP. **against** ◊ Local communities are ~ing against the dumping of toxic waste. | **for** ◊ We have ~ed for better conditions. | **on** ◊ The group ~s on a range of environmental issues. | **on behalf of** ◊ We ~ on behalf of consumers.

campaigner noun

ADJ. **effective, good, great** | **active, tireless** | **experienced, seasoned, veteran** | **leading, prominent** (both esp. BrE)

PREP. ~ **against** ◊ a prominent ~ against drugs | ~ **for** ◊ an active ~ for animal rights | ~ **on behalf of** ◊ a veteran ~ on behalf of the disabled

campus noun

ADJ. **large, sprawling** | **small** | **main** ◊ The Engineering department is on the main ~. | **college, school, university** | **corporate** (AmE)

VERB + CAMPUS **have** ◊ The university has ~es in Cairns and Brisbane.

CAMPUS + NOUN **newspaper** (esp. AmE) | **bookstore** (AmE) | **novel** (esp. BrE)

PREP. **at/the** ~ ◊ Students at the Belfast ~ have access to excellent sports facilities. | **off** ~ ◊ The number of Harvard graduate students living off ~ has dropped. | **on** ~ ◊ She lives on ~.

can noun → See also TIN

ADJ. **aluminium/aluminum, metal, tin** | **empty** | **8 oz, 300 g, 250 ml, etc.** ◊ a 200 g ~ of tuna | **food** ◊ The floor was littered with empty food ~s. | **beer, Coke™, pop** (AmE), **soda** (AmE) | **soup, tuna, etc.** | **gas** (AmE), **jerry, oil, petrol** (BrE) | **paint** | **garbage, trash** (both AmE) | **watering** ◊ We keep the hoses and watering ~s in the shed at the end of the garden. | **aerosol, spray**

VERB + CAN **come in** ◊ This type of milk comes in a ~. | **open** ◊ We opened a ~ of sardines for lunch. | **drain, empty** ◊ She drained her ~ of beer and threw it away. ◊ He emptied a ~ of beans into the pan. | **drink, sip** | **drink from, sip at, sip from** ◊ She sipped from a ~ of Coke. | **fill** ◊ He filled a ~ with water from the pump. | **recycle**

CAN + NOUN **opener** (usually *can-opener*) (esp. AmE)

PREP. **in a/the** ~ | ~ **of** ◊ ~s of oil

canal noun

ADJ. **drainage, irrigation** | **ship**

VERB + CANAL **build, construct, dig**

CANAL + NOUN **barge, boat** | **bank, towpath**

PREP. **along a/the** ~ ◊ The barge moved slowly along the ~. | **on a/the** ~ ◊ boats on the ~

cancellation (AmE also cancelation) noun

ADJ. **last-minute** | **outright** ◊ They opted for rescheduling

rather than outright ~. | **flight, train** (*BrE*) ◊ *In the event of a flight ~, you will be compensated.* | **debt** ◊ *They campaigned for debt ~ for the poorest countries of the world.*
VERB + CANCELLATION **have** ◊ *We may be able to offer you some tickets if we have any ~s.* | **make** ◊ *Cancellations must be made in writing.* | **cause, force** ◊ *Heavy seas can cause ~ of ferry services.* | **announce**
CANCELLATION + NOUN **charge, fee**

cancer *noun*

ADJ. **breast, cervical, colon, lung, prostate, skin, etc.** | **early-stage** | **incurable, inoperable, terminal** | **localized** | **hereditary** | **childhood** ◊ *Childhood ~s have a very good survival rate.*
VERB + CANCER **have, suffer from** | **contract, develop, get** | **cause** | **prevent** | **screen sb for** ◊ *70% of women over 40 have been screened for breast ~.* | **detect, diagnose** | **cure, treat** | **die from, die of** | **beat, survive** | **battle, fight**
CANCER + VERB **spread** ◊ *The ~ has spread to his stomach.* | **occur, recur**
CANCER + NOUN **cell** | **patient, sufferer** (*esp. BrE*), **victim** | **survivor** | **incidence, risk** ◊ *The ~ risk among smokers was found to be higher.* | **deaths, mortality** ◊ *Prostate ~ deaths fell after screening was introduced.* | **research** | **researcher, specialist** | **prevention** | **detection, diagnosis, screening** | **drug, therapy, treatment**
PHRASES **a battle against ~, a struggle against ~** ◊ *He died after an 18-month battle against ~.* | **~ of the cervix, ~ of the pancreas, ~ of the prostate, etc.**
→ Special page at ILLNESS

candid *adj.*

VERBS **be**
ADV. **very** | **disarmingly, refreshingly** | **remarkably, surprisingly, unusually** | **quite** | **less than**
PREP. **about** ◊ *He was quite ~ about the way the case had been handled.* | **with** ◊ *I felt she was being less than ~ with me.*

candidate *noun*

ADJ. **potential, prospective** ◊ *Prospective parliamentary ~s met party leaders last week.* | **likely, possible, qualified, suitable, viable, worthy** ◊ *She's a likely ~ for promotion.* | **excellent, good, ideal, obvious, perfect, prime, promising, strong** ◊ *This is a prime ~ for best movie of the year.* | **leading, top** | **unlikely, unsuitable** | **successful** ◊ *The successful ~ will be fluent in French and German.* | **losing, unsuccessful** | **congressional, gubernatorial** (*AmE*), **mayoral, parliamentary, presidential, prime-ministerial** | **doctoral** (*AmE*), **PhD** (*esp. AmE*) ◊ *Elena is a doctoral ~ at Johns Hopkins University.* | **Conservative, Democratic, etc.**
VERB + CANDIDATE **put yourself forward as, stand as** (*esp. BrE*) ◊ *She decided to stand as a ~ in the local elections.* | **field, nominate, put up, run** ◊ *Our organization is putting up five ~s in the elections.* | **back, endorse, favour/favor, support, vote for** | **consider, interview, screen** | **choose, elect, select** ◊ *The committee will select the best ~ for the job.* | **reject** ◊ *We rejected most of the ~s as unsuitable.*
PREP. **~ for** ◊ *She was the only ~ for the post.*

candle *noun*

ADJ. **lighted, lit** | **flickering** | **aromatherapy, citronella, scented** | **wax** | **votive** | **holiday** (*AmE*)
VERB + CANDLE **light** | **blow out, extinguish** (*formal*), **snuff, snuff out**
CANDLE + VERB **burn** | **illuminate sth, light sth** | **flicker** | **glow** | **go out**
CANDLE + NOUN **flame** | **wax** | **holder**

candy *noun* (*AmE*) → See also SWEET

ADJ. **butterscotch, chocolate, licorice, peppermint, etc.** | **chewy, crunchy** | **sugar-free** | **Halloween**
VERB + CANDY **eat** | **unwrap** | **hand out** ◊ *People were celebrating in the streets and handing out ~.*
CANDY + NOUN **wrapper** | **bar** ◊ *a low-fat alternative to ~ bars* | **aisle, store** ◊ *The kids made straight for the ~ aisle.* | **jar**

PHRASES **like taking ~ from a baby** (= very easy) ◊ *Taking the money would be like taking ~ from a baby.*

cannabis *noun*

... OF CANNABIS **trace** ◊ *Traces of ~ were found in the pilot's blood.*
VERB + CANNABIS **smoke, use** | **grow**
CANNABIS + NOUN **consumption, dependence, use** | **user** | **leaf, plant, resin**

cannon *noun*

ADJ. **automatic** | **water** ◊ *Riot police used water ~ to disperse the crowd.*
VERB + CANNON **load, mount** | **aim** | **fire, shoot**
CANNON + VERB **boom, roar, thunder** ◊ *Cannons thundered to their right.* | **fire (sth), shoot (sth)** ◊ *As the king stepped ashore the ~s fired a salute.*
CANNON + NOUN **ball** (usually *cannonball*), **shell** | **blast, fire, shot** | **crew** | **fodder** (*figurative*) ◊ *The foot soldiers were just used as ~ fodder* (= considered not as people but as material to be used up in war).

canoe *noun*

ADJ. **dugout**
VERB + CANOE **paddle**
CANOE + NOUN **trip** | **paddle**
PREP. **by ~** ◊ *We crossed the lake by ~.*

canopy *noun*

ADJ. **glass** | **dense, thick** ◊ *a thick ~ of branches* | **forest, jungle, leafy, tree**
VERB + CANOPY **form** ◊ *The trees formed a leafy ~ above their heads.*
CANOPY + NOUN **bed** (*esp. AmE*)
PREP. **beneath a/the ~, under a/the ~** | **~ of** ◊ *The monkey was sitting beneath a ~ of branches.*

cap *noun*

1 soft flat hat

ADJ. **school** (*esp. BrE*), **shower, skull** (usually *skullcap*), **stocking** (*AmE*), **trucker** (*AmE*) | **ball** (*AmE*), **baseball, bathing, cricket, ski** (*esp. AmE*), **swim** (*AmE*), **swimming** (*esp. BrE*) | **cloth** (*esp. BrE*) | **flat, peaked** (*both esp. BrE*) | **dunce** (*AmE*), **dunce's** (*BrE*)
VERB + CAP **doff** (*old-fashioned*), **tip**
CAP + NOUN **badge** (*BrE*)
→ Special page at CLOTHES

2 covering for the end/top of sth

ADJ. **bottle** (*esp. AmE*), **hub, lens** | **filler** (*esp. BrE*), **gas** (*AmE*) | **screw** ◊ *The bottle has a screw ~.*
VERB + CAP **put on, screw on** ◊ *Put the ~ back on the pen.* | **remove, take off, unscrew**

capability *noun*

ADJ. **advanced, enhanced** | **limited** ◊ *The company's manufacturing ~ is limited.* | **potential** | **proven** ◊ *the proven ~ of this technology* | **human** ◊ *beyond the scope of human ~* | **intellectual, mental** | **technical, technological** | **manufacturing, operational, production** | **research** | **analytical, computing, design, graphics, management, multimedia, networking, printing, processing, sound, video** | **combat** (*esp. AmE*), **defence/defense, fighting, military, missile, nuclear, offensive, reconnaissance, strike, surveillance, weapons** ◊ *states that are trying to acquire (a) nuclear ~*
VERB + CAPABILITY **demonstrate, have, possess** ◊ *She has the ~ to become a very fine actress.* | **develop, expand, improve, increase** ◊ *The government wants to increase its military ~.* | **lack, lose**
PREP. **beyond sb's ~** ◊ *Organizing a whole department is beyond his ~.* | **within sb's ~** ◊ *I'm sure that your new job is*

well within your capabilities. | **~ for** ◇ *her ~ for making sensible decisions*

capable *adj.*

1 having a lot of skill

VERBS **be, seem** ◇ *She seems very ~.*
ADV. **extremely, fairly, very, etc.** | **highly** ◇ *He has proved himself a highly ~ manager.*

2 capable of able to do sth

VERBS **appear, be, feel, look, prove (yourself), seem** | **become** | **believe sb, consider sb** ◇ *She could hardly believe him ~ of such kindness.*
ADV. **fully, more than** (*esp. BrE*), **perfectly, quite, well** ◇ *She is more than ~ of doing it herself.* | **barely, hardly** (*esp. BrE*), **scarcely** (*BrE*) ◇ *He was barely ~ of writing his own name.* | **reasonably** (*BrE*) | **clearly, obviously** (*esp. BrE*) | **potentially, theoretically** | **physically** ◇ *He was not physically ~ of climbing out of the window.*

capacity *noun*

1 amount held/produced

ADJ. **high, large** ◇ *a high-capacity electric pump* ◇ *large-capacity disk drives* | **limited, small** | **maximum, total** ◇ *a total ~ of 10 gallons* | **additional, excess, spare** ◇ *excess ~ in the oil industry* | **carrying, production, seating, storage** | **nuclear** | **lung** | **engine, fuel** | **disk, memory** | **economic, productive** | **earning** ◇ *The qualification should increase my earning ~.*
VERB + CAPACITY **have** | **expand, increase** | **reduce**
CAPACITY + NOUN **audience, crowd**
PREP. **at ~** ◇ *The system was already at ~.*
PHRASES **be filled to ~, be packed to ~** ◇ *The stadium was filled to ~* (= *was full*). | **operate at full ~, work at full ~** (= *to produce the maximum amount possible*)

2 ability

ADJ. **amazing, enormous, great, infinite, remarkable** | **limited** | **innate, natural** ◇ *Children have an innate ~ to understand language.* | **intellectual, mental** | **human** ◇ *the human ~ for compassion*
VERB + CAPACITY **demonstrate, have, possess** | **develop** | **lack, lose** ◇ *She seems to have lost the ~ to enjoy herself.* | **enhance, increase** | **reduce, restrict**
PREP. **beyond sb's ~** ◇ *These questions are beyond the ~ of most students.* | **within sb's ~** ◇ *The mountain walk is well within the ~ of most fit people.* | **~ for** ◇ *her amazing ~ for organization*

3 official position

ADJ. **official** | **personal, private, unofficial** (*esp. BrE*) | **professional** | **voluntary** (*esp. BrE*) | **acting, caretaker** (*BrE*) | **advisory** | **judicial** (*esp. BrE*)
VERB + CAPACITY **act in, work in** ◇ *I have worked in an advisory ~ with many hospitals.*
PREP. **in your ~** ◇ *In my ~ as president, I would like to thank Jack for his hard work.*

capital *noun*

1 money used to start a business, etc.

ADJ. **risk, venture** ◇ *They are hoping to attract funding from venture-capital firms.* | **fixed** | **seed** (*esp. AmE*), **start-up** | **equity, investment, share** | **working** | **foreign, private** | **human, intellectual, knowledge, political, social** (*all figurative*)
VERB + CAPITAL **have** ◇ *We don't have enough ~ to buy new premises.* | **accumulate, acquire, amass** | **attract, borrow, generate, raise** ◇ *He had various ideas on how to raise ~ for the project.* | **invest, provide, put, put up, sink** ◇ *The company has put a lot of ~ into the project.* ◇ *We can't expect the government to put up the ~.* ◇ *He sank vast amounts of ~ in the venture.* | **allocate, expend** | **free, free up, release** (*esp. BrE*), **unlock** (*esp. BrE*) | **tie up** ◇ *Our ~ is all tied up in property.*

CAPITAL + NOUN **assets, goods, resources, stock** | **costs, expenditure, investment, outlay, repayment** (*esp. BrE*), **spending** | **accumulation, growth** | **account** | **funding, grant** ◇ *He secured $175 million in ~ funding from investors.* | **campaign** (*AmE*), **project** ◇ *We are launching a ~ campaign to renovate the historic building.* ◇ *investment in major ~ projects* | **gain, gains, loss** ◇ *~ gains tax* | **flows, inflow, mobility, movement, outflow** | **receipt** (*esp. BrE*) | **value** ◇ *the ~ value of the property* | **market**
PHRASES **~ and labour/labor** ◇ *Both ~ and labor were scarce.* | **an injection of ~** ◇ *Inner city areas require a large injection of ~.* | **a return on your ~** ◇ *Investors want an immediate return on their ~.*
→ Special page at BUSINESS

2 city

ADJ. **great, major** ◇ *The department store has branches in all major ~s.* | **British, Japanese, etc.** | **foreign** | **provincial, regional, state** | **cultural, finance, financial, etc.**
PREP. **in a/the ~** ◇ *the fast pace of life in the ~* | **~ of**
PHRASES **the … capital of the world** ◇ *Las Vegas is the gambling ~ of the world.*

capitalism *noun*

ADJ. **advanced, contemporary, late, modern** | **global, globalized, world** ◇ *a protest against global ~* | **competitive, consumer, entrepreneurial, free-market, laissez-faire, market** (*esp. AmE*) ◇ *He was one of the leading advocates of laissez-faire ~.* | **corporate, industrial** | **monopoly, popular, state, welfare** | **democratic** (*esp. AmE*), **liberal, neoliberal** (*AmE*) | **unbridled, unfettered, unregulated, unrestrained** ◇ *She deplored unbridled ~ as much as communism.*
VERB + CAPITALISM **destroy, overthrow, replace** | **embrace**
PREP. **under ~** ◇ *the development of agriculture under ~*
PHRASES **the advance of ~, the rise of ~** | **the fall of ~** ◇ *He predicted the fall of world ~.*

capsule *noun*

ADJ. **gelatin** | **cyanide, fish oil, vitamin**
VERB + CAPSULE **swallow, take** ◇ *To avoid capture, he swallowed a cyanide ~.*
CAPSULE + VERB **contain sth** ◇ *~s containing a poisonous drug*

captain *noun* → Note at RANK

captive *noun*

VERB + CAPTIVE **free, release** ◇ *The terrorists will only release their ~s if they get what they want.*

captive *adj.*

VERBS **take sb** ◇ *He was taken ~ on the border.* | **hold sb, keep sb** ◇ *She was held ~ in a castle.*

captivity *noun*

VERB + CAPTIVITY **escape, escape from**
PREP. **during (sb's) ~** ◇ *She was tortured many times during her ~.* | **in ~** ◇ *He died in ~.*
PHRASES **hold sb in ~, keep sb in ~** ◇ *The children were held in ~.* | **raise sth in ~** ◇ *tigers raised in ~* | **bring sb into ~, take sb into ~** | **free sb from ~, release sb from ~** ◇ *The prisoners were released from ~ after three months.*

capture *noun*

VERB + CAPTURE **avoid, elude, escape, evade** ◇ *The refugees evaded ~ by hiding in the forest.* | **lead to** ◇ *This information led to the ~ of the murderer.*

capture *verb* express

ADV. **accurately, perfectly** ◇ *That description ~s perfectly the feeling of being invisible.* | **beautifully, brilliantly, vividly** | **neatly, nicely, succinctly**
VERB + CAPTURE **try to** | **be able to, manage to** | **fail to** ◇ *The exhibition on India fails to ~ the great diversity of this fascinating country.*

car noun

1 road vehicle with four wheels → See also AUTOMOBILE

ADJ. **fast** | **new** | **diesel** (esp. BrE), **electric, fuel-efficient** (esp. AmE), **hybrid, hydrogen-powered, motor** (BrE, formal), **petrol** (BrE) | **compact** (esp. AmE), **estate** (BrE), **hatchback** (esp. BrE), **luxury, mid-size** (AmE), **saloon** (BrE) (sedan in AmE), **sports** | **second** | **armoured/armored, cop** (AmE, informal), **patrol, police, squad, unmarked** ◇ Police in an unmarked ~ had been following the stolen vehicle. | **race** (AmE), **racing** (BrE), **rally** (BrE), **stock** | **company, hire** (BrE), **rental** (esp. AmE) | **second-hand** (esp. BrE), **used** ◇ a used ~ salesman | **private** ◇ The government wants to reduce the use of private ~s. | **getaway, speeding, stolen** ◇ The robbers abandoned their getaway ~ and ran off. | **parked** ◇ There was a line of parked ~s in front of the building. | **classic, veteran** (BrE), **vintage**
VERB + CAR **drive** | **have, own, run** (esp. BrE) ◇ It's very expensive to run a ~ these days. | **lease** | **trade** (AmE), **trade in** | **take** (esp. BrE) ◇ It's too far to walk. I'll take the ~. | **borrow** | **get in, get into, pile into** ◇ He got in the ~ and they drove off. ◇ The kids all piled into the ~. | **exit** (AmE, formal), **get out of** | **start** | **pull over, pull up, stop** ◇ He pulled his ~ over at a small hotel. | **back, reverse** | **steer, swerve** ◇ He swerved his ~ sharply to the right. | **overtake, pass** | **lose control of** ◇ I lost control of the ~ and it spun off the road. | **leave, park** | **lock, unlock** | **abandon, dump** | **crash, wreck** (esp. AmE) | **impound** (esp. AmE), **tow, tow away, tow off** | **race** | **build, make, manufacture, produce** | **fix, repair, service, work on** | **take in** ◇ I have to take the ~ in for a service. (AmE) ◇ I have to take the ~ in for service. (AmE) | **wash** | **hire** (esp. BrE), **rent** (esp. AmE) | **break into, hot-wire** (informal), **steal**
CAR + VERB **start** ◇ Despite the cold, the ~ started first time. | **run on sth** ◇ ~s that run on diesel | **do sth** ◇ The ~ does 55 miles per gallon. ◇ The ~ was doing over 100 miles an hour. | **pull out** ◇ The red ~ suddenly pulled out in front of me. | **drive off, pull away** | **overtake sb/sth, pass sb/sth** | **screech by/past, speed by/past, whizz by/past, zoom by/past** | **accelerate, speed up** | **slow down** | **come to a halt, draw up** (esp. BrE), **pull up, stop** | **skid, spin, swerve** ◇ Her ~ skidded on a patch of ice. | **break down, stall** | **collide with sth, crash, hit sth** ◇ His ~ hit a van coming in the opposite direction.
CAR + NOUN **alarm, boot** (BrE), **door, engine, horn, key, phone, seat, trunk** (AmE), **tyre/tire, window** ◇ a ~ boot sale(= an outdoor sale where people sell things from the backs of their cars) (BrE) | **ride** | **park** (BrE) (parking lot in AmE) | **parking** ◇ There's not enough ~ parking in the city. | **driver** | **dealer, dealership, salesman, showroom** | **buyer** | **hire** (BrE), **rental** (AmE) | **accident, crash, wreck** (AmE) | **chase** | **racing** | **bomb, bombing** | **wash** | **tax** | **ferry** (esp. BrE)
PREP. **by ~** ◇ They take the children to school by ~. | **in a/the ~** ◇ I'll wait for you in the ~.
PHRASES **a brand of ~** (esp. AmE), **a make of ~, a model of ~** | **~s on the road** ◇ The number of ~s on the road is increasing all the time.

2 (esp. AmE) section of a train → See also CARRIAGE

ADJ. **rail** (usually railcar) (AmE), **railroad** (AmE), **railway** (BrE) | **subway** (AmE) | **cattle, coal, freight** | **baggage, dining** (BrE, AmE), **lounge** (AmE), **sleeping** (BrE, AmE), **smoking** | **Pullman** (AmE)
VERB + CAR **pull**

caravan noun

1 (BrE) vehicle pulled by a car

ADJ. **holiday, touring** | **motor**
VERB + CARAVAN **pull, tow** | **live in, stay in**
CARAVAN + VERB **park** ◇ The local farmer lets holiday ~s park on his land.
CARAVAN + NOUN **holiday** | **park, site**

2 covered vehicle that is pulled by a horse

ADJ. **horse-drawn** (esp. BrE) | **Gypsy**
VERB + CARAVAN **pull**

3 line of vehicles or animals

ADJ. **camel** | **bus** | **travelling/traveling**
VERBS **join** | **lead**
PREP. **~ of** ◇ a ~ of trucks/cars/vehicles

carbohydrate noun

ADJ. **simple** | **complex** ◇ complex ~s such as pasta | **refined** | **unrefined**
VERB + CARBOHYDRATE **be high in, contain** ◇ Nuts are high in ~s. | **burn, convert, digest** | **consume, eat** | **avoid, reduce, restrict**
CARBOHYDRATE + NOUN **content** | **consumption, intake**
PHRASES **a source of ~**

carbon noun

ADJ. **pure** ◇ Diamonds are crystals of pure ~. | **organic** | **radioactive** | **activated**
CARBON + NOUN **content** ◇ iron with a high ~ content | **atom, isotope** | **fibre/fiber** | **steel** | **emission** | **footprint** | **offsetting** | **tax**
PHRASES **a form of ~**

carbon dioxide noun

VERB + CARBON DIOXIDE **absorb, take in** ◇ Trees absorb ~ and produce oxygen. | **emit, give out** (BrE), **produce, release** | **convert** | **reduce, remove**
CARBON DIOXIDE + NOUN **emissions** | **concentration, levels** | **output, production**
PHRASES **a build-up of ~** | **emissions of ~**

card noun

1 giving written or electronic information

ADJ. **ID, identity, membership** | **business, calling, visiting** (esp. BrE) | **appointment, invitation** (esp. BrE) | **index, record, report** | **green** (= a document that legally allows sb to live and work in the US) | **flash** (usually flashcard) | **laminated** | **swipe** | **punch** | **smart**
VERB + CARD **hand sb, hand out** ◇ He went around the room handing out business ~s. | **scan, swipe** | **insert**
CARD + NOUN **catalogue** ◇ She searched the library's ~ catalogue. | **reader**
PREP. **on a/the ~** ◇ Write the main points of your speech on ~s.

2 used to pay/get money

ADJ. **plastic** ◇ He had a wallet full of plastic ~s. | **ATM** (esp. AmE), **cash, charge, credit, debit** | **cheque/check, cheque guarantee** (BrE) | **phone** | **prepaid** (esp. AmE) | **ration**
VERB + CARD **pay by, put sth on, use** ◇ She paid for the hotel by credit ~. ◇ I'll put the meal on my ~. | **accept, take** ◇ The restaurant accepts all major credit ~s. | **issue (sb with)** ◇ The bank hasn't issued me with a cash ~ yet. | **cancel** ◇ Contact the bank and cancel all your ~s.
CARD + NOUN **number** | **holder** | **company, issuer** | **payment, transaction**

3 in a computer

ADJ. **graphics, memory, network, PC, sound, video, wireless**
VERB + CARD **install** ◇ You need to install a new graphics ~.
CARD + NOUN **slot** ◇ The computer has three additional ~ slots.

4 with a message

ADJ. **greeting** (AmE), **greetings** (BrE) | **birthday, Christmas, get-well, holiday** (AmE), **sympathy**
VERB + CARD **give sb, send sb** | **sign, write** ◇ Everyone at work signed a ~ for her. | **get, receive**

5 used for a game

ADJ. **playing** | **winning** | **court** (BrE), **face, picture** | **tarot** | **baseball** (AmE), **trading** | **trump** (often figurative) ◇ This defender's ability to score vital goals has often proved a trump ~. | **wild** (often figurative) ◇ Bennett is something of a wild ~ (= it is difficult to predict what he will do).
...OF CARDS **deck** (AmE), **pack** (BrE) | **hand**

VERB + CARD **cut, deal, shuffle** | **play** ◇ *Each player in turn must play a ~.* | **pick** ◇ *'Pick a ~,' said the conjurer.* | **hold** *(often figurative)* ◇ *The kidnappers hold all the ~s*(= are in control of the situation).
CARD + NOUN **game** | **player** | **playing** | **trick** | **table**

6 cards game

...OF CARD **game**
VERB + CARDS **play** ◇ *We play ~s every Friday night.* | **lose at, win at** ◇ *He always wins at ~s.*

NOTE

Playing cards

two, three, etc. of... ◇ *the four of hearts*
jack of..., queen of..., king of..., ace of... ◇ *the ace of spades*
high..., low... ◇ *a low club*
black..., red... ◇ *You can't put a red five on a red six.*
pick up..., take... ◇ *Why didn't you pick up the king?*
have..., hold... ◇ *He knew his opponents held only spades and diamonds.*
lay down..., play..., put down... ◇ *She put down a joker.*
lead... ◇ *You should have led a high spade.*
draw... ◇ *Use your ace and king to draw the trumps.*
trump... ◇ *He trumped my ace!*
...are high, ...are trumps, ...are wild ◇ *Spades are trumps.* ◇ *This time twos are wild, aces high.*
...trick (in games like bridge and whist) ◇ *We needed to take three more spade tricks.*
on a/the... ◇ *You can play either a nine or a jack on a ten.*

---

cardboard *noun*

ADJ. **thick, thin** | **stiff** | **corrugated**
...OF CARDBOARD **piece, sheet** ◇ *a sheet of stiff black ~*
VERB + CARDBOARD **be made from/of/out of, make sth from/out of** | **cut**
CARDBOARD + NOUN **box, carton, container, sleeve, tube** | **cut-out** ◇ *a life-size ~ cut-out of Elvis Presley*

cardigan *noun*

ADJ. **cashmere, wool, woollen/woolen, woolly/wooly** (*esp. BrE*) | **hand-knitted**
VERB + CARDIGAN **knit**
CARDIGAN + NOUN **sweater** (*AmE*)
→ Special page at CLOTHES

care *noun*

1 caring for sb/sth

ADJ. **good, great** ◇ *He loved his books and took great ~ of them.* | **proper** ◇ *With proper ~, the plants may last for fifty years.* | **loving, tender** ◇ *She will need lots of tender loving ~.* | **private** | **voluntary** (*BrE*) | **constant, full-time** | **continuing, long-term** | **short-term, temporary** | **daily, day-to-day, routine** | **intensive** ◇ *Last night she was critically ill in intensive ~.* ◇ *an intensive ~ unit* | **clinical, emergency, health, medical, nursing** (*esp. BrE*), **patient** | **hospital, inpatient, institutional, residential** | **outpatient** | **community** | **domiciliary** (*BrE, formal*), **home, home-based** | **primary, secondary, tertiary** | **antenatal** (*BrE*), **maternity, prenatal** (*esp. AmE*) | **dental** | **psychiatric** | **palliative** (*medical*) | **preventive** (*esp. AmE*) | **parental** | **formal, informal** (*both esp. BrE*) ◇ *The couple relied on informal ~ from relatives.* | **foster** | **respite** | **public** ◇ *children in public ~* | **pastoral, spiritual** | **child** (*usually childcare*), **day** ◇ *Family members can provide child ~ with love and without charge.* | **client** (*esp. BrE*), **customer** | **hair, skin** (*usually haircare, skincare*)
VERB + CARE **take** ◇ *He left his job to take ~ of his sick wife.* ◇ *I'll take ~ of hiring the car.* | **deliver, provide (sb with)** ◇ *We*

have improved the way doctors deliver ~. | **need, require** | **receive** | **take sb into** (*BrE*) ◇ *The boys were taken into ~ when their parents died.*
CARE + NOUN **services** ◇ *access to basic health-care services* | **centre/center, facility, home, unit** (*all esp. BrE*) | **manager, worker** | **giver, provider** | **plan, policy, programme/program** ◇ *recent changes in health-care policy* | **delivery** | **needs** ◇ *sensitive to the health-care needs of underserved groups* | **package** (= a package of food, etc. that is sent to sb) (*AmE*) | **allowance** (*BrE*) | **order** (*BrE*)
PREP. **in ~** ◇ *He had been in foster ~ since he was five.* ◇ *He was in ~ for five years.* (*BrE*) | **in sb's ~** ◇ *You won't come to any harm while you're in their ~.* ◇ *Many historic sites are in the ~ of the Trust.* | **under the ~ of** ◇ *He's under the ~ of Dr Parks.*
PHRASES **~ of sb, in ~ of sb** (*AmE*) (written on letters, etc. and usually abbreviated to *c/o*) | **the quality of ~, the standard of ~**

2 attention/thought given to sth

ADJ. **extreme, good, great** ◇ *Great ~ should be taken to ensure that the equipment is clean.* | **extra, special** | **infinite, the utmost** ◇ *He takes the utmost ~ of his appearance.* | **meticulous, painstaking, scrupulous** (*esp. BrE*) ◇ *The little girl was writing her name with painstaking ~.* | **due** (*formal*), **proper, reasonable**
VERB + CARE **exercise, take** | **need, require** ◇ *Transporting the specimens requires great ~.*
PREP. **with ~** ◇ *A label on the box read: 'Glass—handle with care'.* | **without ~** (*BrE*) ◇ *He was found guilty of driving without due ~ and attention.*

care *verb*

ADV. **deeply, genuinely, a lot, passionately, really, truly** | **hardly, not greatly** (*esp. BrE*), **not much, not particularly** ◇ *He hardly ~s what he does any more.* ◇ *I don't know which she chose, nor do I greatly ~.* | **actually** ◇ *No one actually ~d what I thought.* | **enough** ◇ *The information is there for anyone who ~s enough to find it.*
PREP. **about** ◇ *He really ~s about the environment.* | **for** ◇ *You genuinely ~ for him, don't you?*
PHRASES **be past caring** ◇ *I'm past caring what he does*(= I don't care any more).

career *noun*

1 series of jobs that a person has

ADJ. **long** | **brief, short** | **brilliant, distinguished, glittering** (*esp. BrE*), **illustrious, stellar** (*esp. AmE*), **storied** (*AmE*), **successful** ◇ *He had a distinguished ~ as a diplomat.* | **promising** | **lucrative** | **prolific** ◇ *She had a long and prolific ~ as a director.* | **rewarding** | **flagging** (*esp. BrE*) ◇ *The movie revived his flagging ~.* | **chosen** ◇ *She achieved a lot in her chosen ~.* | **academic, diplomatic, journalistic, literary, medical, military, political, teaching, writing** | **coaching** (*esp. AmE*), **playing, pro** (*informal, esp. AmE*), **professional, sporting** | **basketball, football, gymnastics, etc.** | **acting, film** (*esp. BrE*), **Hollywood, movie** (*esp. AmE*), **musical, recording, singing, stage** ◇ *the album that launched his recording ~* | **solo** ◇ *All four band members went on to have successful solo ~s.*
VERB + CAREER **build, carve, carve out, forge, have, make, pursue** ◇ *He made a good ~ for himself in football.* ◇ *She pursued a successful ~ in medicine.* | **begin, choose, embark on, launch, start, start out on** ◇ *young actors just starting out on their ~s* | **devote to sth, spend** ◇ *She has spent her entire ~ in education.* | **advance, boost, further, jump-start** | **abandon, give up** | **jeopardize, risk** | **cut short, derail, end, finish, ruin, wreck** ◇ *a car crash which wrecked his ~* | **resume** | **rejuvenate, resurrect, revitalize, revive** | **change**
CAREER + VERB **last sth, span sth** ◇ *Her stage ~ spans sixty years.* | **begin, start, take off** | **be over, end**
CAREER + NOUN **break** ◇ *a ~ break to have children* | **advancement, development, ladder, path, progression** ◇ *a move higher up the ~ ladder* | **change, choice, move** ◇ *a smart ~ move* | **opportunities, prospects, structure** (*esp. BrE*) ◇ *The profession has no clear ~ structure.* | **high, highlight** (*both AmE*) ◇ *His performance as Al in the movie*

was a ~ high. | **earnings** (*esp. AmE*) ◇ *the first golfer to surpass $2 million in ~ earnings* | **civil servant** (*esp. BrE*), **diplomat, soldier** | **girl** (*old-fashioned*), **woman** | **counselor** (*AmE*) | **counseling** (*AmE*) | **~s advice, ~s guidance, ~s information** (*all BrE*) | **~s adviser, ~s officer** (*both BrE*) | **~s service** (*BrE*)

PREP. **during sb's ~, throughout sb's ~** ◇ *She won many awards during her acting ~.* | **~ in** ◇ *a ~ in computers* | **~ with** ◇ *a brilliant ~ with the San Francisco Ballet*

PHRASES **the height of your ~, the peak of your ~** ◇ *She was at the peak of her ~ when she injured herself.* | **a change of ~**

2 period of your life spent working/doing sth

ADJ. **chequered/checkered, colourful/colorful, turbulent, varied** ◇ *He has had a somewhat chequered/checkered ~.* | **college** (*esp. AmE*), **school, working** ◇ *She started her working ~ as a waitress.*

VERB + CAREER **have** | **start**

careful *adj.*

VERBS **be** | **make sb** ◇ *Bitter past experience had made her ~ of what she confided to Nadia.*

ADV. **extremely, fairly, very, etc.** | **awfully, especially, particularly, really** ◇ *Be particularly ~ when swimming in the lake.* | **scrupulously** | **a little, slightly, etc.**

PREP. **about** ◇ *She was very ~ about how she spoke to him.* | **of** ◇ *He's very ~ of his reputation.* | **with** ◇ *She's extremely ~ with money.*

careless *adj.*

VERBS **be** | **become, get, grow** ◇ *She had begun to grow ~.* | **make sb** ◇ *Boredom made him ~.*

ADV. **extremely, rather, very** ◇ *a rather ~ mistake* | **how, so, too** ◇ *Try not to be so ~ in the future.* | **a little, slightly, etc.**

PREP. **about** ◇ *She's ~ about her spelling.* | **of** ◇ *When performing his stunts he was ~ of his own safety.* | **with** ◇ *He's very ~ with money.*

caress *noun*

ADJ. **gentle, soft** ◇ *the gentle ~ of his fingers* | **tender, warm**

caress *verb*

ADV. **gently, lightly, softly** ◇ *His fingers gently ~ed her cheek.* | **lovingly, tenderly** | **slowly**

cargo *noun*

ADJ. **bulk, heavy** | **precious, valuable** ◇ *a precious ~ of antiques* | **deadly, hazardous, high-risk** ◇ *The terrorists parked the van with its deadly ~ in a dark alleyway.* | **dry** ◇ *dry ~, such as fruit* | **human** ◇ *The boats discharged their human ~ a little way from the shore.* | **military** (*esp. AmE*) ◇ *the packaging and transporting of military ~*

VERB + CARGO **carry, haul** (*AmE*), **move, transport** | **load, take on** ◇ *The ship stopped to take on a ~ of fruit.* | **discharge, offload** (*AmE*), **unload** | **deliver** | **handle** ◇ *The port handles ~ from all over Asia.*

CARGO + NOUN **aircraft, boat** (*esp. BrE*), **carrier, hauler** (*AmE*), **plane, ship, truck** (*esp. AmE*), **vessel** | **bay, hold** ◇ *The satellite was stowed in the shuttle's ~ bay for return to Earth.* ◇ *He was found hiding in the ~ hold of a plane.* | **compartment, container** | **handler, handling** | **capacity** (*esp. AmE*)

caricature *noun*

1 funny drawing of sb

VERB + CARICATURE **draw** ◇ *She draws ~s of well-known politicians.*

PREP. **~ of** ◇ *a ~ of Sherlock Holmes*

2 exaggerated description of sb/sth

ADJ. **crude, grotesque** | **mere** ◇ *Most of his characters were mere ~s.*

VERB + CARICATURE **be, become** | **create**

PREP. **~ of** ◇ *The two stars have become crude ~s of themselves.*

carpet *noun*

1 material for covering floors

ADJ. **deep-pile** (*esp. BrE*), **lush** (*esp. AmE*), **plush** (*AmE*), **shag** (*esp. AmE*), **shag-pile** (*BrE*), **soft, thick** | **stained, threadbare, worn** | **patterned, plain** | **wool** | **woven** | **oriental, Persian** | **fitted** (*BrE*), **wall-to-wall** | **flying, magic** | **red** (*often figurative*) ◇ *They rolled out the red ~ for the visitors.* ◇ *I didn't expect to get the red-carpet treatment* (= be treated like an important person).

... OF CARPET **roll**

VERB + CARPET **make, weave** | **fit** (*BrE*), **install** (*AmE*), **lay** ◇ *I'm having the ~s laid today.* | **roll back, roll up, take up** (*esp. BrE*) | **clean, vacuum** | **beat** | **replace**

CARPET + NOUN **design** | **runner, tile** | **fitter** (*esp. BrE*) | **weaver** | **industry, manufacturer** | **cleaner, sweeper** | **tack**

PREP. **on a/the ~** ◇ *The cat curled up on the ~.*

2 thick layer of sth that covers the ground

ADJ. **deep, thick** | **lush, soft**

VERB + CARPET **form** ◇ *The leaves formed a ~ under the trees.*

PREP. **~ of** ◇ *a deep ~ of snow*

carriage *noun*

1 vehicle pulled by horses

ADJ. **horse-drawn, open** | **royal**

VERB + CARRIAGE **ride in** | **drive** | **pull** | **climb into, get into** | **alight from, exit** (*AmE, formal*), **get out of, step out of**

PREP. **in a/the ~**

2 (*BrE*) part of a train → See also CAR

ADJ. **railway** | **full** | **empty** | **first-class, second-class** | **no-smoking, non-smoking, smoking**

VERB + CARRIAGE **get in, get into** | **get out of** | **pull**

CARRIAGE + NOUN **door, window**

PREP. **in a/the ~** ◇ *There's a seat in the next ~.*

carrot *noun*

1 vegetable

ADJ. **raw** | **cooked, steamed** | **baby** | **chopped, diced** (*esp. BrE*), **grated, shredded** (*AmE*), **sliced**

VERB + CARROT **eat, have** | **cook** | **peel** | **chop, dice, grate, slice**

CARROT + NOUN **top** | **cake** | **juice** | **stick**

→ Special page at FOOD

2 sth attractive offered to sb

VERB + CARROT **dangle, hold out, offer (sb)** ◇ *They dangled the ~ of a large salary in front of me.*

PHRASES **a ~ and stick** ◇ *to adopt the carrot-and-stick approach* (= to persuade sb to try harder by offering them a reward if they do, or a punishment if they do not)

cart *noun*

1 vehicle pulled by animals

ADJ. **heavy** | **horse-drawn** | **bullock, donkey, ox, etc.** | **farm** | **hay**

VERB + CART **drive** | **draw, pull** | **ride in** | **climb on, climb onto, get on, get onto** | **climb off, get off** | **load, unload**

CART + VERB **roll** | **clatter, creak, rumble** ◇ *The ~ rumbled on up the street.* | **carry sth**

CART + NOUN **driver** | **track** (*BrE*)

PREP. **by ~** ◇ *In the old days coal supplies came by ~.* | **in a/the ~** ◇ *She brought the vegetables in an ox ~.* | **on a/the ~, onto a/the ~** ◇ *They piled their furniture onto a ~.*

PHRASES **the back of a ~** | **a horse and ~, a pony and ~**

2 (*AmE*) small vehicle → See also BUGGY, TROLLEY

ADJ. **golf, ice-cream** | **grocery, shopping** | **baggage, luggage** | **beverage, serving** | **electric, hand** (usually *handcart*), **motorized, rolling, wheeled**

VERB + CART **push, trundle, wheel** ◇ *a man wheeling an ice-cream ~ along* | **drive**

carton noun

ADJ. **cardboard, plastic** | **egg** (*AmE*), **ice-cream, juice, milk,** etc. ◇ *Why are these milk ~s so difficult to open?* | **250 ml, half-gallon,** etc.
VERB + CARTON **open**
PREP. **in a/the ~** ◇ *The soup is sold in ~s.* | **~ of** ◇ *a ~ of cream* ◇ *a ~ of cigarettes* (*AmE*)

cartoon noun

ADJ. **animated, strip** (*BrE*) | **editorial** (*AmE*), **political**
VERB + CARTOON **draw** ◇ *He draws strip ~s for 'The Guardian'.* | **watch** ◇ *The kids spend their Saturdays watching ~s.*
CARTOON + NOUN **character** | **strip** (*BrE*) | **series, show** (*esp. AmE*) | **channel, network** (*esp. AmE*)

carved adj.

ADV. **beautifully, delicately, elaborately, finely, intricately, ornately, richly** ◇ *a richly ~ doorway* | **crudely, roughly** ◇ *a crudely ~ wooden figure*

case noun

1 example

ADJ. **classic, textbook, typical** | **clear, obvious, simple** ◇ *It was a simple ~ of mistaken identity.* | **borderline** ◇ *The teacher gave all borderline ~s a spoken test.* | **extreme** | **isolated, rare** ◇ *Except in a few rare ~s, bee stings are not dangerous.* | **exceptional, special, unusual** | **striking** | **documented, reported** ◇ *There have been documented ~s of officials accepting bribes.*
VERB + CASE **illustrate, show** | **cite, highlight** ◇ *He highlighted the ~ of Harry Farr, who was executed in 1916.* | **consider** ◇ *Let's consider the ~ of a dealer trying to make a sale.*
CASE + VERB **arise, occur** ◇ *The committee has full powers to deal with any ~s of malpractice that arise.*
CASE + NOUN **study** ◇ *a ~ study of an Amazonian tribe* | **example**
PREP. **in sb's/this ~** ◇ *In her ~, she failed the exam because she wasn't well.* | **~ of** ◇ *a ~ of animal cruelty*
PHRASES **~ by** ◇ *Complaints are dealt with on a case-by-case basis.* | **a ~ in point** ◇ *Many professions feel they deserve higher pay, and nurses are a ~ in point.*

2 the case true situation

VERB + THE CASE **be, remain** ◇ *It remains the ~ that not enough graduates are going into teaching.* | **overstate, understate** ◇ *I agree with him, but don't you think he slightly overstates the ~?*

3 of a disease

ADJ. **acute, chronic** | **advanced, bad, serious, severe** ◇ *He had a bad ~ of appendicitis.* | **mild** | **AIDS, flu, SARS,** etc. ◇ *About 25% of AIDS ~s are linked with the sharing of needles.* | **confirmed, reported** ◇ *There have been no confirmed ~s of BSE in the US.*
VERB + CASE **diagnose** ◇ *Two million new ~s of hypertension are diagnosed each year.* | **report** ◇ *The Department of Health reported five human ~s of bird flu.*
CASE + NOUN **history** ◇ *Medical students study the ~ histories of many patients.* | **notes, records**
PREP. **~ of** ◇ *a severe ~ of food poisoning*

4 police investigation

ADJ. **notorious** ◇ *the notorious ~ of the Botley strangler* | **tragic** | **assault, homicide** (*esp. AmE*), **molestation** (*AmE*), **murder, rape, robbery**
VERB + CASE **handle, investigate, work on** ◇ *Four officers are investigating the ~.* | **crack, solve** ◇ *They never solved the Jones murder ~.* | **close** | **reopen**
CASE + NOUN **file, report** ◇ *He was looking through some homicide ~ files.* | **officer** ◇ *Carter was the senior ~ officer on the investigation.*
PREP. **on the ~** ◇ *A detective is on the ~ at the moment.* | **~ of** ◇ *a ~ of theft*

5 in a court of law

ADJ. **court** | **criminal** | **civil** | **landmark, test** ◇ *This is a test ~ which will influence what other judges decide.* | **high-profile** ◇ *As a lawyer he was involved in high-profile divorce ~s.* | **antitrust** (*esp. AmE*), **divorce, libel, malpractice** (*esp. AmE*) | **death-penalty** (*esp. AmE*) ◇ *The jury are required to be unanimous in death-penalty ~s.*
VERB + CASE **bring** ◇ *He brought the ~ to the Supreme Court.* | **prosecute, pursue** | **handle, litigate** (*AmE*), **take** ◇ *This was the hardest ~ she had handled since becoming a lawyer.* ◇ *No lawyer would take his ~.* | **consider, hear, try** ◇ *The court will consider the ~ soon.* ◇ *The ~ will be heard in a higher court.* | **rehear, retry, review** | **adjourn** | **dismiss, throw out** ◇ *The ~ was thrown out for lack of evidence.* | **drop** ◇ *The prosecution decided to drop the ~.* | **decide, settle** ◇ *The ~ was settled out of court.* | **win** | **lose**
CASE + VERB **come before sb, come to court, go to court, go to trial** ◇ *The ~ came before Judge Hales.* ◇ *He was so clearly innocent, the ~ should never have gone to court.* | **collapse** ◇ *The ~ against her collapsed when a key witness was proved to have lied.* | **involve sth** ◇ *a compensation ~ involving thousands of workers* | **centre/center on sth, hinge on sth, rest on sth, turn on sth** ◇ *The ~ hinged on the evidence of the only witness.* | **raise sth** ◇ *The ~ raises a number of issues.* | **allege sth** ◇ *~s alleging violations of international law* | **challenge sth** ◇ *He brought a ~ challenging the legality of the war.*
PREP. **in a/the ~** ◇ *the evidence in the ~* | **~ against** ◇ *The ~ against her was very weak.* | **~ of**
PHRASES **a ~ to answer, no ~ to answer** (*both BrE*) ◇ *The judge ruled that the defendant had no ~ to answer.* | **the circumstances of a ~, the facts of a ~**

6 arguments

ADJ. **compelling, convincing, good, persuasive, powerful, strong** | **open-and-shut, unanswerable** (*BrE*) | **prima facie** (*law*) ◇ *There is a good prima facie ~ for believing what she says.* | **circumstantial, weak** | **defence/defense, prosecution**
VERB + CASE **have** ◇ *Our lawyer didn't think we had a ~ (= a good enough case).* | **prepare** ◇ *The defendant requested more time to prepare his ~.* | **outline, set out** | **make, make out, present, put, state** ◇ *You can make out a ~ for changing our teaching methods.* | **argue, plead** ◇ *I thought she argued her ~ very well.* | **take up** ◇ *The union has taken up the ~ of the suspended worker.* | **judge** ◇ *The teacher must judge each ~ according to its merits.* | **bolster, help, strengthen, support** ◇ *What evidence do you have to support your ~?* | **weaken**
CASE + VERB **exist** ◇ *A strong ~ exists for adopting a similar system in this country.*
PREP. **~ against** ◇ *a ~ against wearing business attire* | **~ for**
PHRASES **the ~ for the defence/defense, the ~ for the prosecution** | **the merits of a ~** ◇ *The disciplinary committee considered the merits of his ~ before fining him.*

7 container

ADJ. **carrying** ◇ *He put the binoculars back in their carrying ~.* | **packing** | **glass** ◇ *The room was full of stuffed animals in glass ~s.* | **CD, DVD** | **cartridge** (*esp. AmE*), **cigarette, glasses, jewel** (*AmE*), **jewellery/jewelry, pencil** | **guitar, violin,** etc. | **display, trophy** (*esp. AmE*) ◇ *She kept all her trophies in a display ~.* | **presentation** ◇ *a gold watch in a presentation ~*
PREP. **in a/the ~, inside a/the ~, out of a/the ~**

8 a case → See also SUITCASE (for other collocates with *case*)

ADJ. **attaché** | **overnight**

cash noun

1 money in the form of coins or notes

ADJ. **cold** (*AmE*), **hard, ready** ◇ *The drugs are sold for hard ~.* | **petty** ◇ *I took £10 out of petty ~.*
VERB + CASH **pay, pay in** ◇ *We'll have to pay ~ for the tickets.* ◇ *I paid the bill in ~.* | **hold** ◇ *The bank should hold enough ~ to satisfy customer demand.* | **withdraw** | **convert sth into, turn sth into**
CASH + NOUN **desk** (*BrE*), **drawer** (*esp. AmE*) (see also **cash register**) | **dispenser** (*BrE*), **machine** ◇ *He withdrew £100*

from a ~ machine. | **balance** | **book** | **transaction** | **advance**

PREP. **in ~** ◇ *The thieves stole $200 in ~.* ◇ *You can pay in ~ or by credit card.*
PHRASES **~ in hand** (*BrE, informal*) ◇ *He did the job for £300, ~ in hand.* | **~ on delivery**

2 money in any form

ADJ. **ready, spare** | **quick** ◇ *a chance to make some quick ~* | **hard-earned** ◇ *I refuse to spend my hard-earned ~ on presents!* | **campaign** (*AmE*) | **extra**
VERB + CASH **generate, raise** ◇ *They had a quiz to raise ~ for the hospital.* | **be short of, be strapped for, run out of** | **earn** | **shell out, spend** | **save**
CASH + NOUN **holdings, reserves, resources** | **flow** ◇ *The company is having ~ flow problems.* | **inflow, infusion, injection** | **outflow** | **deposit, payment, settlement** | **value** | **award, benefit, bonus, offer, prize** | **management** | **market** | **crisis** | **crop** ◇ *farmers who grow ~ crops for export* | **economy** | **cow** (= *a part of a business that always makes a profit*)
→ Special page at BUSINESS

cash register (*AmE also* **register**) *noun* → See also TILL

ADJ. **computerized, electronic**
VERB + CASH REGISTER **open** | **work** | **ring** (*AmE*) ◇ *Their success is ringing ~s.*
CASH REGISTER + VERB **ring** ◇ *an idea that has set ~s ringing all over the country*
CASH-REGISTER + NOUN **receipt, roll**
PREP. **at the ~, behind the ~, on the ~** ◇ *There weren't enough people on the ~s.* | **in a/the ~, into a/the ~** ◇ *Put the money straight into the ~.* | **from a/the ~, out of a/the ~** ◇ *He gave her $10 from the ~.*

casket *noun* (*AmE*) → See also COFFIN

ADJ. **wooden** | **closed, open** ◇ *an open-casket funeral* | **flag-draped** ◇ *the flag-draped ~s of soldiers coming home*
VERB + CASKET **carry** | **close** | **lower** ◇ *The ~ was lowered into the grave.* | **drape** ◇ *The ~ was draped with a large flag.*
PREP. **in a/the ~**

casserole *noun*

1 dish of meat/vegetables

ADJ. **beef, chicken, vegetable, etc.**
VERB + CASSEROLE **bake** (*AmE*), **cook, make, prepare**
CASSEROLE + NOUN **dish**
→ Special page at FOOD

2 dish for cooking casseroles

ADJ. **deep, large** | **shallow** | **flameproof** (*BrE*), **ovenproof**
PREP. **in a/the ~** ◇ *Put the chicken pieces in a ~.*

cast *noun*

ADJ. **huge, large** | **small** | **excellent, good, strong, talented** | **all-star, star-studded, stellar** (*esp. AmE*) | **ensemble** | **supporting** | **original**
VERB + CAST **feature, have** ◇ *The play has a large ~ of characters.* | **join** | **head** ◇ *Jane Simms heads the ~ of this brilliant production.* | **assemble**
CAST + VERB **perform sth** | **feature sb, include sb**
CAST + NOUN **member**
PREP. **in a/the ~** ◇ *Who is in the ~?*
PHRASES **a ~ of characters, a member of the ~**

caste *noun*

ADJ. **high, low** ◇ *He belongs to one of the highest ~s.* ◇ *low-caste families*
VERB + CASTE **belong to**
CASTE + NOUN **system** ◇ *the Hindu ~ system*
PHRASES **a member of a ~** | **of high ~, of low ~**

castle *noun*

ADJ. **grand, great, magnificent, splendid** (*esp. BrE*) | **turreted, walled** | **historic** | **ancient, medieval** | **royal** | **ruined** | **fairy-tale, fantasy**

catalogue

VERB + CASTLE **build, fortify** | **attack, besiege, lay siege to, storm** | **capture, seize, take** | **defend, hold** ◇ *The ~ was held by an opposing faction.*
CASTLE + VERB **perch, stand** ◇ *The ~ perches on a high rock.* | **overlook sth** ◇ *The ~ overlooks the town.*
CASTLE + NOUN **gate, grounds, keep, tower, wall** | **ruins**
PREP. **in a/the ~**

casual *adj.*

VERBS **appear, be, sound**
ADV. **extremely, fairly, very, etc.** | **almost** ◇ *She sounded almost ~.* | **apparently, seemingly** | **carefully** ◇ *There was something a little too carefully ~ in his tone.* | **deceptively**
PREP. **about** ◇ *He was very ~ about it all.*

casualty *noun*

1 person killed/injured in a war/an accident

ADJ. **heavy, high, serious** | **light, low** | **pedestrian, road** (*both BrE*) | **civilian, military** | **human**
VERB + CASUALTY **cause, inflict** ◇ *The guerrillas inflicted heavy casualties on the local population.* | **incur, suffer, sustain, take** ◇ *Our division suffered only light casualties.* | **avoid, minimize, prevent**
CASUALTY + NOUN **count, figures, list, rate**

2 (*BrE*) **part of a hospital**

VERB + CASUALTY **be admitted to** ◇ *He was admitted to ~ with head injuries.* | **rush sb to, take sb to**
CASUALTY + NOUN **department, unit, ward**
PREP. **in ~** ◇ *He works as a doctor in ~.*

cat *noun*

ADJ. **domestic, family, house** (*esp. AmE*), **household, pet** | **big** ◇ *She went to Africa to photograph big ~s.* | **feral, wild** | **alley, stray** | **pedigree** (*BrE*), **pedigreed** (*AmE*) | **long-haired, short-haired** | **calico** (*AmE*), **tabby, tortoiseshell, etc.** | **tom** (usually **tomcat**) | **playful** | **sleek** | **Cheshire** (*figurative*) ◇ *He was grinning like a Cheshire ~* (= *smiling widely*). | **fat** (*figurative*) ◇ *the fat ~s of big business*
VERB + CAT **have, keep, own** ◇ *We have a pet ~ called Archie.* | **feed** | **pet** (*AmE*), **stroke** (*esp. BrE*) | **neuter, spay** ◇ *They didn't want kittens, so they had their ~ spayed.* | **put down** ◇ *The ~ was in constant pain so they had it put down.*
CAT + VERB **hiss, mew, miaow/meow, purr, spit, yowl** ◇ *The ~ miaowed pitifully.* ◇ *There was a ~ yowling outside my window last night.* | **bite (sb)** | **scratch (sb)** | **creep, pad, prowl, slink** ◇ *A ~ padded silently past.* ◇ *The ~ slunk away into the darkness.* | **arch its back** | **crouch** | **curl up** | **catch sth, hunt (sth), stalk sth** | **jump, leap, pounce (on sth), spring** | **spray (sth)** ◇ *Cats mark their territory by spraying.*
CAT + NOUN **door** (*AmE*), **flap** (*BrE*) | **food** | **litter** | **dander** (*AmE*) | **hair** | **lover, owner** | **phobia**
PHRASES **fight like ~ and dog** (*BrE*), **fight like ~s and dogs** (*AmE*) ◇ *In our childhood Irina and I fought like ~(s) and dog(s).* | **play (a game of) ~ and mouse** ◇ *Young car thieves enjoy playing ~ and mouse with the police.*

catalogue (*AmE also* **catalog**) *noun*

1 list of books/objects

ADJ. **exhibit** (*AmE*), **exhibition, library**
VERB + CATALOGUE **produce, publish** ◇ *The gallery produced a ~ of young artists.* | **look through** ◇ *Look through the ~ and find this picture.*
CATALOGUE + NOUN **card**
PREP. **in a/the ~** ◇ *More details are given in our ~.*

2 book of goods for sale

ADJ. **colour/color, illustrated** | **mail-order** | **product, seed** | **online** | **print, printed**
VERB + CATALOGUE **produce, publish** ◇ *The gallery produced a ~ of young artists.* | **browse through, look at, look through** | **order, request, send for, send off for** ◇ *Send off for our illustrated ~ of garden plants.*
PREP. **in a/the ~**

catastrophe noun

ADJ. **absolute, big, complete, great, major, terrible, total** | **minor** | **national** | **global, international, world** | **ecological, economic, environmental, financial, human, humanitarian, natural, nuclear** ◇ *The country is on the brink of a humanitarian ~.* | **imminent, impending, potential**
VERB + CATASTROPHE **be** | **cause, lead (sth) to** ◇ *These policies could lead us to environmental ~.* | **have** ◇ *We had a few ~s with the food for the party.* | **be faced with, be heading for, face** ◇ *The area is now facing economic ~.* | **avert, avoid, head off, prevent** ◇ *moves to avert a national ~*
CATASTROPHE + VERB **happen, occur, strike, take place**

catastrophic adj.

VERBS **be, prove**
ADV. **absolutely, truly** | **potentially**
PREP. **for** ◇ *potentially ~ for the environment*
PHRASES **something ~** ◇ *I worried every day that something ~ would happen.*

catch noun

1 act of catching sth
ADJ. **awesome** (*AmE*), **brilliant, good, nice, spectacular** | **clean** (*esp. BrE*) | **difficult, tough** | **easy** | **game-winning** (*AmE*) | **acrobatic, diving, one-handed, running** | **slip** (in cricket) | **touchdown** (in American football) | **fair, legal** (*both AmE*)
VERB + CATCH **get** (*esp. AmE*), **make** (*AmE*), **take** (*BrE*) ◇ *Roger made some brilliant ~es at today's game.* | **drop, miss**
2 number of fish that sb has caught
ADJ. **big, good, huge, large, record** ◇ *Fishermen have been landing record ~es this season.* | **poor** (*BrE*), **small** | **annual, total**
VERB + CATCH **land, make**
CATCH + VERB **decline, fall** ◇ *Catches fell because of the new dam.* | **go up, increase**
PREP. **~ of** ◇ *a huge ~ of tuna*
PHRASES **the ~ of the day, the day's ~** ◇ *a restaurant where you can sample the day's ~*
3 device for fastening sth
ADJ. **door, window** | **safety** ◇ *the safety ~ on a gun*
VERB + CATCH **release, undo, unfasten** | **close**

categorize (*BrE* also **-ise**) verb

ADV. **broadly, generally**
VERB + CATEGORIZE **be difficult to, be hard to, be impossible to** ◇ *Her work is difficult to ~.*
PREP. **according to** ◇ *to ~ people according to their jobs* | **by** ◇ *We ~ voters by their choice of newspaper.* | **into** ◇ *Categorize the plants into four groups.* | **as** ◇ *The employees are ~d as support personnel.*

category noun

ADJ. **broad, general, large** | **narrow** | **basic** | **individual, one, single, special, specific** ◇ *We have created a special ~ for part-time workers.* | **different, discrete, distinct, separate** | **high, low** ◇ *Most of his ratings were in the highest ~.* | **important** | **high-risk** ◇ *Intravenous drug users are in a high-risk ~ for hepatitis C.* | **age, ethnic** (*esp. AmE*), **gender, income, job, occupational, racial** (*esp. AmE*), **social** | **price, size, weight**
VERB + CATEGORY **be included in, belong to, come into, fall into, fit, fit into** ◇ *The cities investigated fell into two broad categories.* | **constitute, form** ◇ *Flutes form a separate ~ of wind instruments.* | **create, define, develop, establish, invent** | **distinguish, identify, recognize**
CATEGORY + VERB **comprise sth, consist of sth, contain sth, cover sth, encompass sth, include sth** | **be based on sth** ◇ *categories based on ethnic origin*
PREP. **in a/the ~, within a/the ~** ◇ *He competed in the youngest age ~.* | **~ of** ◇ *a higher ~ of prison* | **~ for** ◇ *There's a separate ~ for children.*
PHRASES **be in a ~ (all) of its/your own, be in its/your own ~** (= to be unique) | **be in the same ~ (as sth)**

catering noun

ADJ. **commercial, contract, industrial** | **hotel, in-flight, school**
VERB + CATERING **do** ◇ *Who's doing the ~ for the party?*
CATERING + NOUN **business, industry, service** | **company, establishment** (*esp. BrE*), **firm** (*esp. BrE*) | **facilities** | **assistant** (*esp. BrE*), **manager, staff, team** | **college, course, student** (*all BrE*)

cathedral noun

ADJ. **great, magnificent** | **baroque, Gothic, medieval, etc.** | **Anglican, Catholic**
VERB + CATHEDRAL **build** | **see, visit**
CATHEDRAL + VERB **dominate sth** ◇ *The great Gothic ~ dominates the city.*
CATHEDRAL + NOUN **city** (*esp. BrE*) | **church** (*esp. BrE*) | **bell, spire** | **choir, organist**
PREP. **in a/the ~** ◇ *We went to mass in the ~.*

Catholic noun

ADJ. **Roman** | **devout, faithful** (*esp. AmE*) | **practising/practicing** | **good** | **lapsed** | **traditional** | **cradle** (*AmE*)
VERB + CATHOLIC **be, become** | **be brought up (as)** (*esp. BrE*), **be raised (as)** (*AmE*)

cattle noun

ADJ. **beef, dairy** | **Highland, longhorn, shorthorn** | **native** | **wild** | **domestic** | **live**
... OF CATTLE **head** ◇ *5 000 head of ~ died of the disease in one month.* | **herd**
VERB + CATTLE **keep, raise** (*AmE*), **rear** (*esp. BrE*) | **breed** | **tend** | **graze** ◇ *Villagers traditionally have the right to graze their ~ on the common land.* | **drive, herd, move, round up** ◇ *He moved his ~ farther down into the valley in winter.* | **kill, slaughter** | **rustle, steal**
CATTLE + VERB **graze** ◇ *~ grazing in the fields*
CATTLE + NOUN **auction, market** | **breeding, production, ranching, rearing** | **industry** | **drive** (*AmE*) | **baron** (*AmE, old-fashioned*), **breeder, dealer, farmer, herder** (*AmE*), **producer, rancher** (*AmE*) | **rustler** | **farm, ranch** | **herd** | **feed, food** | **grid** (*BrE*), **guard** (*AmE*) ◇ *There was a ~ grid/guard across the road.* | **prod** ◇ *Electric ~ prods were used against the demonstrators.* | **car** (*AmE*), **truck** | **country** (*AmE*)
PHRASES **a breed of ~**

cause noun

1 sb/sth that makes sth happen
ADJ. **real, root, true, underlying** ◇ *the root ~ of the problem* | **deeper** ◇ *A deeper ~ for resentment is the discrepancy in pay.* | **biggest, chief, clear, fundamental, important, leading, main, major, number-one, primary, prime, principal, significant** | **common** ◇ *Smoking is a common ~ of premature death.* | **likely, possible, probable** | **known, unknown** | **direct, indirect** | **immediate, initial** | **contributory** | **hidden**
VERB + CAUSE **determine, discover, find, identify, pinpoint, reveal** ◇ *attempts to identify the immediate ~ of the breakdown* | **examine, investigate, study** | **know, understand** | **address**
CAUSE + VERB **be, lie in sth, remain** ◇ *What are the ~s of the crisis?* ◇ *The real ~ of the problem lies in the poor construction of the bridge.*
PREP. **~ of** ◇ *the ~s of blindness*
PHRASES **~ and effect** | **the ~ of death** | **due to natural ~s, from natural ~s, of natural ~s** ◇ *He died of natural ~s.* | **the exact ~ of sth, the precise ~ of sth** ◇ *The precise ~ of the accident is not known.* | **have many ~s, have several ~s, have various ~s**

2 reason

ADJ. **good, great, real, reasonable, sufficient**
VERB + CAUSE **have** ◇ *We have good ~ to believe that he was involved in the crime.* | **find** ◇ *The experts may find ~ to disagree with the school's decision.* | **give (sb)** ◇ *Her health is giving us great ~ for concern.* | **show** ◇ *The onus is on government departments to show ~ why information cannot be disclosed.*
PREP. **~ for** ◇ *There is no ~ for alarm.*
PHRASES **~ for concern, with good ~, without good ~, without just ~**

3 aim that people believe in

ADJ. **deserving, good, just, noble, righteous** (*esp. AmE*), **worthwhile, worthy** ◇ *The money she left went to various worthy ~s.* | **favourite/favorite, pet** (*AmE*) | **bad, unjust** | **common** ◇ *The different groups support a common ~.* | **hopeless, lost** (= one that has failed or that cannot succeed) | **charitable, environmental, humanitarian, political, social** | **communist, conservative, liberal, socialist, etc.**
VERB + CAUSE **advance, champion, embrace, fight for, further, help, promote, serve, support** ◇ *young men willing to fight for the ~* ◇ *She would do anything that would further the ~.* | **be committed to, be sympathetic to** | **join, take up** ◇ *She has taken up the liberal ~.* | **plead** ◇ *He pleaded the ~ of the local fishermen.*
PREP. **for the ~ of, in the ~ of** ◇ *They were not prepared to sacrifice themselves for the ~ of the country.* ◇ *battles fought in the ~ of decentralization* | **in a/the ~** ◇ *prominent figures in the socialist ~*
PHRASES **(all) for a good ~** (*esp. AmE*), **(all) in a good ~** (*esp. BrE*) ◇ *The function took a lot of organizing, but was all for/in a good ~.*

caution *noun*

1 great care

ADJ. **considerable, extra, extreme, great, utmost** ◇ *The utmost ~ must be exercised when handling explosives.* | **excessive** | **due** ◇ *We proceeded with due ~.*
VERB + CAUTION **exercise, take** (*esp. AmE*), **use** | **advise, counsel, suggest, urge** ◇ *We urge ~ in the use of this medication.* | **require**
PREP. **with ~** ◇ *The information on the website should be treated with some ~.*
PHRASES **err on the side of ~** (= to be too cautious), **the need for ~** ◇ *I must stress the need for ~.* | **sound a note of ~** ◇ *The board sounded a note of ~ about the economy.* | **cast ~ to the wind/winds, throw ~ to the wind/winds** (= to start taking risks) | **a word of ~** ◇ *I would just like to add a word of ~.*

2 (*BrE*) **spoken warning given by a judge/policeman**

ADJ. **formal** ◇ *He received a formal ~.*
VERB + CAUTION **get off with, receive** | **give sb, issue, let sb off with** ◇ *They let her off with a ~.*

cautious *adj.*

VERBS **be** | **become, get, grow** | **remain** | **make sb** ◇ *Her experiences have made her ~.*
ADV. **extremely, fairly, very, etc.** | **excessively, overly, too, unduly** ◇ *He accused the government of being unduly ~.* | **deliberately** | **a little, slightly, etc.**
PREP. **about** ◇ *~ about spending money* | **of** ◇ *He warned us to be ~ of accepting their statements as fact.*

cave *noun*

ADJ. **deep, large** | **shallow, small** | **dark** | **damp, dank** | **mountain, rocky, underground** ◇ *We explored the rocky ~s along the beach.* | **ice, limestone**
VERB + CAVE **explore**
CAVE + VERB **collapse** ◇ *a collapsed limestone ~*
CAVE + NOUN **ceiling, entrance, floor, mouth, opening, roof, wall** | **complex, system** | **art, drawing, painting** | **dweller**
PREP. **in a/the ~** ◇ *We took shelter in a dark ~.*
PHRASES **the ceiling of a ~, the floor of a ~, the roof of a ~, the wall of a ~** | **the entrance to a ~, the mouth of a ~**

CD *noun*

ADJ. **budget, full-price, mid-price** | **double** | **compilation** | **accompanying, free** | **live** ◇ *a live ~ of the band's latest concert* | **debut, latest** | **audio, multimedia, music, photo, software** | **install, installation** | **read-only, recordable, writable** | **blank**
VERB + CD **insert** ◇ *She inserted a ~ into the machine.* | **play, put on** | **create, make, produce, record** ◇ *You can record your own ~ if you have the right equipment.* | **burn, burn sth onto, copy, duplicate, record** | **listen to** | **change** ◇ *Do you mind if I change the ~?* | **release** ◇ *The band's new ~ is released next week.*
CD + NOUN **drive** | **player** | **burner, changer, maker, recorder, rewriter, ripper, writer** | **burning** | **recording** | **box, case, cover, sleeve** | **holder, rack** | **collection** | **format, version**
PREP. **on ~** ◇ *That was the first album to come out on ~.* | **on a/the ~** ◇ *How many tracks are on the ~?*

CD-ROM *noun*

ADJ. **multimedia** | **interactive** | **educational** | **accompanying**
VERB + CD-ROM **burn (sth onto), duplicate** ◇ *Now you can burn your photos onto a ~.* | **create, produce** | **install**
CD-ROM + VERB **contain sth**
CD-ROM + NOUN **disk, drive** | **edition, version** ◇ *This is the ~ edition of the encyclopedia.* | **format** | **game**
PREP. **on ~** ◇ *This dictionary is also available on ~.*
→ Special page at COMPUTER

cease *verb*

ADV. **altogether, completely, entirely** ◇ *The noise faded, then ~d altogether.* | **all but, almost, virtually** | **largely** | **effectively** ◇ *My job had effectively ~d to exist.* | **forthwith** (*formal, esp. BrE*), **immediately** ◇ *These violations of the code must ~ forthwith.* | **abruptly, suddenly** ◇ *The bird's song ~d abruptly.* | **gradually** | **momentarily** | **eventually, finally** | **soon** | **long, long since** ◇ *The conversation had long ~d to interest me.*
PREP. **with** ◇ *Building ~d with the outbreak of war.*

ceasefire *noun*

ADJ. **complete** | **immediate** | **unilateral** | **unconditional** | **temporary**
VERB + CEASEFIRE **call for, demand, order** ◇ *The UN has passed a resolution calling for an immediate ~.* | **broker, negotiate** | **accept, agree, agree to, declare, sign** | **call** ◇ *A 24-hour ~ was called to allow the distribution of aid.* | **announce** | **achieve, secure** | **observe** | **enforce** | **break, violate**
CEASEFIRE + VERB **come into effect** (*esp. BrE*), **go into effect** (*AmE*) | **hold, last** ◇ *There are concerns that the ~ might not hold.*
CEASEFIRE + NOUN **agreement, deal, terms** | **line**
PREP. **~ between** ◇ *a ~ between the government and the rebels* | **~ with** ◇ *They agreed to a ~ with the Egyptian government.*
PHRASES **a violation of a ~**

ceiling *noun*

1 top surface inside a room

ADJ. **high, low, tall** (*AmE*) | **cathedral** (= a high ceiling with open space up to the roof) (*AmE*), **domed, sloped** (*AmE*), **sloping** (*BrE*), **vaulted** | **drop** (*AmE*), **false, suspended** | **plaster** | **painted** ◇ *The palace is famous for its painted ~s.*
VERB + CEILING **paint, plaster** | **reach, touch** | **drop** (*esp. AmE*), **lower** | **raise** | **support**
CEILING + VERB **collapse**
CEILING + NOUN **fan, light, tile** | **height**
PREP. **on the ~** ◇ *a fly on the ~*
PHRASES **from ~ to floor, from floor to ~** ◇ *The bathroom has mirrors from ~ to floor.*

2 top limit on wages, prices, etc.

ADJ. **debt, expenditure, price**

celebrated

VERB + CEILING **impose, place, put, set** ◇ *They've put a $50 ~ on their admission charge.* | **abolish** | **lift, raise** ◇ *The government has decided to lift price ~s on bread and milk.* | **lower** | **break**
PREP. **~ on** ◇ *a ~ on imports*

celebrated adj.

VERBS **be** | **become**
ADV. **justly, rightly** ◇ *his justly ~ portrait of Benjamin Franklin* | **internationally**
PREP. **as** ◇ *He has become ~ as an artist.* | **for** ◇ *The area is ~ for its food and wine.*

celebration noun

ADJ. **big, great, noisy** | **little, quiet, small** | **family** | **joyous** ◇ *a joyous ~ of life* | **double** ◇ *a double birthday ~* | **special** | **national, official, public, street** (*esp. BrE*) ◇ *Poor weather prevented the official ~s from taking place.* | **anniversary, birthday, centenary** (*BrE*), **centennial** (*esp. AmE*), **festive, holiday** (*AmE*), **victory, wedding** (usually with *celebrations*) ◇ *50th anniversary ~s* | **Christmas, Fourth of July, Independence Day, New Year, etc.** (usually with *celebrations*) | **religious**
VERB + CELEBRATION **have, hold** ◇ *They held a special ~ in his honour/honor.* | **join, join in** ◇ *I hope you'll join in the ~s.* | **attend**
CELEBRATION + NOUN **dinner, party**
PREP. **in ~ of** ◇ *They organized a dinner in ~ of the year's successes.*
PHRASES **a cause for ~** ◇ *The victory was a cause for great ~.* | **a ~ of sb's life, a ~ to mark sth** ◇ *They held a ~ to mark forty years of the service.*

celebrity noun

ADJ. **international, local, national** | **big, famous, major, well-known** | **A-list, B-list, Z-list, etc.** ◇ *A host of A-list celebrities turned out for the wedding.* | **minor** ◇ *He became a minor ~ among Manhattan's cultural élite.* | **favourite/ favorite** | **instant, overnight** | **guest, visiting** | **media, sporting** (*BrE*), **sports** (*AmE*), **television**
... OF CELEBRITIES **host** ◇ *Tonight's show features a host of celebrities.*
VERB + CELEBRITY **make sb** ◇ *The show's success made her an overnight ~.*
CELEBRITY + NOUN **profile, status** | **chef, hairstylist, stylist** | **magazine, website** | **gossip** | **client, guest** | **couple** | **culture** | **endorsement**
PHRASES **something of a ~** ◇ *He became something of a ~ in his home town.*

cell noun

1 smallest living part of an animal/a plant body

ADJ. **dead, living** | **healthy, normal** | **abnormal** | **blood, brain, nerve, skin, etc.** ◇ *red and white blood ~s* | **egg, sperm** | **stem** | **cancer, cancerous** | **animal, human, plant, etc.**
VERB + CELL **create, form, grow** | **attack, destroy, kill** | **collect, extract, remove**
CELL + VERB **divide** ◇ *Cells divide and form new cells.* | **develop, form, grow** | **die**
CELL + NOUN **division, growth, proliferation** | **membrane, wall**
PHRASES **the nucleus of a ~**
2 small room

ADJ. **monk's, nun's** | **jail, police, prison** | **holding** | **padded**
PREP. **in a/the ~**

cellar noun

ADJ. **damp, dark** | **old** | **deep, underground** | **vaulted** | **coal, root** (*AmE*), **wine** | **storm** (*AmE*), **pub** (*BrE*), **beer** (*esp. BrE*) | **disused**
CELLAR + NOUN **door, stairs** (*esp. AmE*), **steps** | **bar** (*esp. BrE*)

PREP. **in the ~, into the ~** ◇ *I went down into the ~ for more wine.*

cello noun → Special page at MUSIC

cellphone noun (*esp. AmE*)

ADJ. **prepaid** | **hand-held, hands-free**
VERB + CELLPHONE **grab, pick up, pull out, reach for, take out, whip out** | **use** ◇ *It's more expensive to use your ~ abroad.* | **turn off** ◇ *Please make sure all ~s are turned off during the performance.* | **charge, charge up, recharge**
CELLPHONE + VERB **ring**
CELLPHONE + NOUN **number** | **ringtone** | **carrier, company, network, operator, service** | **user** | **call, conversation** | **charger** | **tower**
PREP. **from your ~** ◇ *I'm calling from a friend's ~.* | **on your ~** ◇ *I was talking on my ~.*
PHRASES **the use of ~s**

cement noun

ADJ. **wet** | **cold** | **hard**
VERB + CEMENT **mix** | **pour**
CEMENT + VERB **harden, set**
CEMENT + NOUN **mixer** | **block, floor, step, wall** | **factory, plant, works**

cemetery noun

ADJ. **local** | **private, public** ◇ *He was buried in a private ~.* | **military** | **Catholic, Jewish, etc.** | **pet**
VERB + CEMETERY **be buried in** | **visit**
PREP. **in a/the ~**

censorship noun

ADJ. **strict** | **government, military, state, wartime** | **Internet, media, political, press** | **official**
VERB + CENSORSHIP **impose** ◇ *The government has imposed strict ~ on the press.* | **abolish, lift, tighten** ◇ *Political ~ has been tightened under the new regime.* | **relax**
CENSORSHIP + NOUN **law** | **board** (*esp. AmE*)

censure noun

ADJ. **public** | **moral** | **social** | **official** ◇ *It was unavoidable that some artists would face official ~.*
VERB + CENSURE **come under, face** ◇ *He could face ~ from his colleagues.* | **avoid, escape** ◇ *Costs will have to be kept down if severe public ~ is to be avoided.*
CENSURE + NOUN **motion** (*BrE*)
PHRASES **a motion of ~, a vote of ~** (both *BrE*) ◇ *Right-wing parties tabled a motion of ~ against the government.*

censure verb

ADV. **severely** ◇ *The manager was severely ~d for negligence.*
PREP. **for**

census noun

ADJ. **complete** | **federal, government, national, official, state** | **decennial** | **population**
VERB + CENSUS **carry out** (*esp. BrE*), **conduct, perform** (*esp. AmE*), **take** ◇ *A national ~ is taken every ten years.*
CENSUS + VERB **find, indicate, report, reveal, show** | **count, list**
CENSUS + NOUN **data, figures, records, report** (*esp. AmE*), **results, statistics** | **form, questionnaire, return** | **tract** (*AmE*) | **bureau** (*AmE*) | **taker** (*esp. AmE*)
PREP. **in a/the ~** ◇ *the questions asked in the ~*

centenary (*BrE*) (also centennial *AmE, BrE*) noun

VERB + CENTENARY/CENTENNIAL **celebrate, commemorate, mark** ◇ *The club will hold a party to celebrate its ~.*
CENTENARY/CENTENNIAL + NOUN **celebrations, year**

centimetre (*BrE*) (*AmE* centimeter) noun → Note at MEASURE

central adj.

1 most important

VERBS **be**
ADV. **very** | **absolutely** ◇ *This distinction is of absolutely ~ importance.* | **increasingly**
PREP. **to** ◇ *These facts are ~ to the case.*

2 easily reached

VERBS **be**
ADV. **fairly, quite, very** ◇ *Our house is very ~, so we can easily get around.*

centralized adj.

VERBS **be**
ADV. **highly** ◇ *a highly ~ bureaucracy* | **increasingly**

centre (BrE) (AmE center) noun

1 middle point/part of sth

ADJ. **dead, exact, true, very** ◇ *We've bought an apartment in the very ~ of São Paulo.* | **city, town** (*both esp. BrE*) | **soft** ◇ *chocolates with soft ~s*
PREP. **at the ~ (of)** ◇ *at the ~ of the universe* | **in the ~ (of)** ◇ *a museum in the ~ of Cairo*
PHRASES **the ~ of the city** (*esp. BrE*), **the ~ of (the) town** (*esp. BrE*)

2 important place for sth

ADJ. **important, leading, main, major, nerve** (*figurative*) ◇ *the economic nerve ~ of India* | **international, local, national, regional, world** | **commercial, cultural, economic, financial, industrial, trading, urban** ◇ *Tokyo is one of the main financial ~s of the world.* | **population, power**
PREP. **~ for** ◇ *The university is a major ~ for scientific research.*
PHRASES **a ~ of excellence** (= a place where a particular kind of work is done well) | **a ~ of government, a ~ of population, a ~ of power**

3 the centre/center moderate political position

CENTRE/CENTER + NOUN **party** | **ground** (*BrE*) ◇ *a party that occupies the ~ ground of national politics*
PHRASES **left of ~, right of ~** ◇ *Politically, she is considered to be slightly left of ~.*

century noun

ADJ. **19th, 20th, etc.** ◇ *It was built in the 20th ~.* ◇ *a 17th-century building* | **earlier, last, later, past, previous** ◇ *Later centuries saw the development of a complex agricultural system.* | **following, new, next** ◇ *a celebration to welcome the new ~* | **present**
VERB + CENTURY **begin, enter** ◇ *As we enter the 21st ~, the challenges facing our world seem overwhelming.* | **span** ◇ *a collection of paintings spanning four centuries*
CENTURY + VERB **begin, dawn** ◇ *As the 21st ~ dawned, the Internet promised to reshape society.* | **continue, pass, progress, unfold, wear on** | **end** | **see sth, witness sth** ◇ *The 19th ~ witnessed the publication of many books on the history of art.*
PREP. **during the ~** ◇ *The city's population doubled during the 19th ~.* | **for centuries** ◇ *There have been orchards in this region for centuries.* | **in the ... ~** ◇ *He lived in the 16th ~.* | **over the centuries** ◇ *a marble floor worn smooth over the centuries* | **through the centuries** ◇ *a tradition passed down through the centuries* | **throughout the ~** ◇ *America's influence on culture grew throughout the 20th ~.*
PHRASES **centuries old** ◇ *a centuries-old custom* | **the turn of the ~**

cereal noun

1 plant

CEREAL + NOUN **crop, foods, grain, products** | **production**

2 food

ADJ. **breakfast** | **bran, high-fibre/high-fiber, rice, wholegrain** | **fortified** ◇ *fortified breakfast ~s* ◇ *a wholewheat ~ fortified with vitamins* | **sugary**
... OF CEREAL **bowl** ◇ *a big bowl of ~* | **box** (*AmE*), **packet** (*BrE*)
VERB + CEREAL **eat, have** ◇ *I have ~ for breakfast.*

CEREAL + NOUN **bowl** | **box** (*AmE*), **packet** (*BrE*)

ceremonial adj.

VERBS **be**
ADV. **purely** ◇ *The monarch's role is purely ~.* | **largely**

ceremony noun

1 formal public/religious event

ADJ. **brief, short** | **quiet, simple** | **elaborate, glittering** (*BrE*), **lavish** | **moving, solemn** | **private, public** | **formal, important, official, special, traditional** ◇ *an official ~ to welcome the new director* | **inaugural** (*esp. AmE*), **opening** ◇ *the opening ~ of the Olympics* | **closing** | **awards, presentation, prize-giving** (*esp. BrE*) | **civil-partnership** (*in the UK*), **commitment** (*AmE*), **marriage, wedding** ◇ *a same-sex commitment ~* | **civil, religious** | **coming-of-age, naming, retirement** (*AmE*) | **burial** (*esp. AmE*), **funeral, memorial, wreath-laying** | **commencement** (*AmE*), **degree, graduation** | **inauguration, induction, initiation, signing, swearing-in** | **groundbreaking** (= to mark the beginning of construction of a new building) | **dedication, flag-raising** (*AmE*), **ribbon-cutting, unveiling** | **tea** ◇ *the Japanese tea ~*
VERB + CEREMONY **conduct, officiate** (*AmE*), **officiate at, perform** ◇ *The marriage ~ was performed by the bishop.* | **hold, host** | **attend, be present at, take part in**
CEREMONY + VERB **take place** | **commemorate sth, honour/honor sb/sth, mark sth** ◇ *a special ~ to mark the opening of the festival*
PREP. **at a/the ~** ◇ *Many dignitaries were present at the ~.* | **during a/the ~** ◇ *A lot of people wept during the funeral ~.* | **in a/the ~** ◇ *They were married in a simple ~.*

2 formal/traditional actions and words

VERB + CEREMONY **stand on** (*esp. BrE*) ◇ *I won't stand on ~ (= be formal).*
PREP. **without ~** ◇ *It was done quickly and without ~.*
PHRASES **pomp and ~** ◇ *the pomp and ~ of a royal wedding* | **with great ~** ◇ *She was buried with great ~ in the Abbey.*

certain adj.

VERBS **be, feel, look, seem** ◇ *Digby looked ~ to be the next president.* | **become, grow** ◇ *I grew more and more ~ that she was lying to me.* | **make** ◇ *Make ~ that you lock the door if you go out.*
ADV. **very** | **absolutely, quite** | **by no means** ◇ *It's by no means ~ that she'll get the job.* | **almost, virtually** | **fairly, pretty, reasonably**
PREP. **about, of** ◇ *Are you quite ~ about this?*
PHRASES **can't say for ~** ◇ *I think she's a teacher, but I couldn't say for ~.* | **not know for ~** ◇ *I don't know for ~ how many people are coming.*

certainty noun

ADJ. **absolute, complete** | **near, reasonable, virtual** ◇ *It's a virtual ~ that essential foodstuffs will go up in price.* | **moral**
... OF CERTAINTY **degree** ◇ *It's difficult to predict with any degree of ~ how much it will cost.*
PREP. **with ~** ◇ *I couldn't say with absolute ~ that he's here.*
PHRASES **a lack of ~** ◇ *There seems to be a lack of ~ over what we should do.* | **the one ~, the only ~** ◇ *The one ~ left in a changing world is death.*

certificate noun

ADJ. **birth, death, marriage** | **medical** | **school** | **gift** (*AmE*) | **digital**
VERB + CERTIFICATE **award (sb), issue** ◇ *The police are waiting for the doctor to issue a death ~.* | **earn, get, hold, receive**
PREP. **~ of** ◇ *a ~ of authenticity*

chain noun

1 line of rings joined together

ADJ. **heavy** | **thin** | **gold, silver** ◊ *She wore a long gold ~ around her neck.* | **rusty** | **bicycle** | **key** | **daisy, paper**
... OF CHAIN **length**
VERB + CHAIN **pull, pull at, yank, yank at**
CHAIN + VERB **clank**
CHAIN + NOUN **mail** (= protective covering made of chains)
PREP. **in** ~*s* ◊ *The prisoner was led away in ~s.* | **off sb's/the ~** ◊ *Let the dog off its ~.* | **on a/the ~** ◊ *They kept the dog on a ~ all day long.*
PHRASES **a ~ of office** (*BrE*) ◊ *The mayor was wearing his ~ of office.* | **a ~ on the door** ◊ *Put the ~ on the door before you go to bed.* | **a link in the ~** ◊ *Our suppliers are the weakest link in the ~.*

2 number of things in a line

ADJ. **island, mountain** | **human**
VERB + CHAIN **form** ◊ *The people formed a human ~ to pass the supplies up the beach.*
PREP. **~ of** ◊ *a ~ of volcanic islands*

3 group of shops/stores, etc. owned by the same company

ADJ. **big, large, major** | **small** | **fast-food, grocery** (*esp. AmE*), **hotel, restaurant, retail, supermarket, etc.**
CHAIN + NOUN **store**
PREP. **~ of** ◊ *a ~ of department stores*
PHRASES **part of a ~** ◊ *This hotel is part of a large ~.*

4 number of connected events or situations

ADJ. **long** | **complex** ◊ *the complex ~ of events that led to the war* | **unbroken** ◊ *He is the latest in an unbroken ~ of entertainers.* | **causal** | **food, supply** ◊ *efforts to ensure that dioxins do not enter the food ~*
VERB + CHAIN **break**
CHAIN + NOUN **reaction** | **letter**
PHRASES **a ~ of command** (= a system by which instructions are passed from one person to another) | **a ~ of events**

chair noun

1 piece of furniture → See also ARMCHAIR

ADJ. **comfortable, comfy** (*informal*), **cushioned, padded, plush, soft, upholstered** | **hard, uncomfortable** | **deep, low** | **high-backed, straight-backed, wing-backed, winged** | **rickety** | **reclining, rocking, swivel** ◊ *He lay back in the reclining ~ and went to sleep.* | **folding** | **matching** ◊ *a dining table and four matching ~s* | **empty** ◊ *He gestured to an empty ~.* | **antique** | **leather, metal, plastic, steel, wicker, wooden, etc.** | **dining, kitchen, lounge** (*esp. AmE*) | **computer, desk, office** | **beach** (*esp. AmE*), **garden** (*esp. BrE*), **lawn** (*esp. AmE*)
... OF CHAIRS **row** | **set** ◊ *a set of antique dining ~s*
VERB + CHAIR **draw up, pull up** ◊ *'Can I join you?' 'Yes, pull up a ~.'* | **pull out** ◊ *He pulled out a ~ for her.* | **grab, have, take** ◊ *Come in and take a ~.* | **give sb** ◊ *He gave her his ~.* | **push back** ◊ *He pushed back his ~ and got to his feet.* | **collapse into/onto, flop** (**back/down**) **in/into/on/onto, lower yourself into, settle** (**back**) **in/into/on, sink** (**back/down**) **into, sit** (**down**) **in/on, slump** (**back/down**) **in/into** ◊ *She dropped her bags and flopped down into the nearest ~.* | **lean back in, lie back in, lounge** (**back**) **in, recline** (**back**) **in, relax** (**back**) **in** ◊ *He put his feet up on the desk and lay back in his ~.* | **be sprawled in, sprawl in** | **lean forward in** | **straighten** (**up**) **in** ◊ *They straightened in their ~s when the manager burst in.* | **get out of, get up from/off, jump** (**up**) **from/out of, leap out of/from, rise from** ◊ *He got up from his ~ to address the meeting.* | **rock backwards and forwards in/on, shift about in** (*BrE*), **shift in, tip back** ◊ *He was shifting about uneasily in his ~.* ◊ *She tipped her ~ back and fixed her gaze full upon him.* | **swivel, swivel** (**around**) **in, swivel on** ◊ *She always swivels around in her ~.*
CHAIR + VERB **be placed, stand** ◊ *A ~ stood facing the window.* | **swivel** | **tip back** | **fall over, topple over** | **creak** ◊ *The ~*

creaked every time I moved. | **scrape sth, scrape against sth, scrape along sth** ◊ *Lisa heard a ~ scraping the floor.*
CHAIR + NOUN **arm, back, leg, seat** | **cover, frame**
PREP. **into a/the ~** ◊ *He sank into his ~ and opened the letter.* | **in a/the ~** ◊ *She leaned back in her ~ and lit a cigarette.* | **on a/the ~** ◊ *A cat was asleep on the ~.*
PHRASES **the arm of a ~, the back of a ~, the edge of a ~, the leg of a ~** ◊ *She gripped the arm of her ~ as she spoke.* ◊ *He sat nervously on the edge of his ~.*

2 person controlling a meeting

ADJ. **acting, deputy** | **honorary**
VERB + CHAIR **occupy, take** (*both esp. BrE*) ◊ *Anne took the ~* (= was chairperson) *in Carol's absence.* | **address** (**sth to**) ◊ *Please address your questions to the ~.* | **appoint sb** (**as**), **elect sb** (**as**)
PREP. **in the ~** (*esp. BrE*) ◊ *Paul Ryan was in the ~* (= was chairperson) *at today's meeting.*

3 position in a university

ADJ. **professorial**
VERB + CHAIR **hold, occupy** ◊ *He held the Chair of Psychology at Yale.* | **appoint sb to** | **resign** | **endow, establish** ◊ *A private benefactor endowed the new Chair of Japanese Literature.*

chairman (*also* chairperson) noun

ADJ. **board, campaign** (*AmE*), **club, commission, committee, company, party** ◊ *She is married to a company ~.* | **acting, current, former, incoming, interim, new, outgoing** ◊ *a report by the outgoing ~* | **deputy, vice** | **executive, honorary, non-executive**
VERB + CHAIRMAN **hold the post of, serve as, take over as** | **appoint** (**sb**), **elect** (**sb**), **name sb** | **step down as** ◊ *He steps down as ~ of the Federal Reserve next year.*
CHAIRMAN + VERB **resign, stand down** ◊ *The ~ resigned following the allegations.*
PREP. **~ of** ◊ *~ of the Senate Agriculture Committee*
→ Note at JOB

chalk noun

1 white rock

CHALK + NOUN **bed** | **cliff, downs, hill** (*all esp. BrE*) | **pit, quarry**
PHRASES **~ and cheese** (*BrE*) ◊ *My two horses are as different as ~ and cheese.*

2 piece of chalk

ADJ. **coloured/colored, white** ◊ *a box of white ~s* | **sidewalk** (*AmE*)
... OF CHALK **piece, stick**
CHALK + NOUN **drawing, line, mark, outline** | **dust** | **board** (usually **chalkboard**) (*esp. AmE*) | **talk** (*AmE*) ◊ *He gave a ~ talk on the techniques of making a sale.*
PREP. **in ~** ◊ *She had scrawled a note in ~ across the board.* | **with ~** ◊ *to write with ~*

challenge noun

1 sth new and difficult

ADJ. **big, considerable, enormous, great, huge, monumental, radical, real, serious, significant** | **daunting, difficult, formidable, stiff, tough** ◊ *The army faced the daunting ~ of fighting a war on two fronts.* | **fundamental, key, main, major, primary, ultimate** | **fresh, new, unprecedented** | **constant, continuing, ongoing** | **future** | **exciting, interesting** | **special, unique** | **economic, engineering, environmental, intellectual, logistical, physical, political, technical, technological** ◊ *Getting the instrument built and tested was a major technical ~.* | **global**
VERB + CHALLENGE **be, constitute, remain, represent** ◊ *The competitive market represents significant ~s for farmers.* | **create, offer, pose, present, provide, raise** | **address, confront, face, handle, meet, respond to, rise to, tackle, take on, take up** ◊ *The gallery has risen to the ~ of exhibiting the works of young artists.* ◊ *He has taken on some exciting new ~s with this job.* | **overcome, solve** | **enjoy, relish, welcome**

CHALLENGE + VERB **confront sb, face sb** ◊ *the ~s facing nurses in casualty* | **arise, exist, remain** ◊ *She could always be counted on when a ~ arose.* | **lie** ◊ *The ~ lies in creating a demand for the product.*

2 call for sb to fight, prove sth, etc.

ADJ. **effective, serious, strong** | **direct** | **constitutional, legal** | **leadership, title** ◊ *his title ~ to the heavyweight champion*
VERB + CHALLENGE **be, constitute, present, represent** ◊ *The demonstration represents a direct ~ to the new law.* | **file** (*esp. AmE*), **issue, mount, raise** ◊ *plans to mount a leadership ~ within the party* | **accept, take up** ◊ *I accepted his ~ to a game of chess.* | **answer** ◊ *He was answering ~s to the government's policy.* | **beat off, fight off** ◊ *Our team will have to fight off the ~ from better trained teams.* | **survive, withstand**
PREP. **~ from** ◊ *a ~ from the other political party* | **~ to** ◊ *a legal ~ to the President's power*

challenge *verb*

1 question whether sth is right/true

ADV. **directly, openly, publicly** ◊ *The newspaper was directly challenging the government's legitimacy.* | **seriously, vigorously** | **effectively** ◊ *She was effectively challenging the whole basis on which society was run.* | **successfully** ◊ *The story was completely untrue and was successfully ~d in court.* | **constantly, continually, repeatedly**
VERB + CHALLENGE **seek** ◊ *Harley sought to ~ the jurisdiction of the court.*
PREP. **on** ◊ *She ~d him on his old-fashioned views.*

2 invite sb to compete, argue, etc.

ADV. **seriously** ◊ *No one has seriously ~d the champion.* | **successfully, unsuccessfully**
PREP. **for** ◊ *She was poised to ~ for the party leadership.* | **to** ◊ *The count ~d him to a duel.*

challenger *noun*

ADJ. **closest, formidable, main, nearest, serious, strong, worthy** ◊ *Her nearest ~ is the vice-president.* | **presidential** | **Conservative, Democratic, Labour, Republican**
VERB + CHALLENGER **face** ◊ *The Senator faces a ~ with conservative views.* | **take on** ◊ *He took on various ~s, but refused to fight Jackson.* | **beat, defeat**
PREP. **~ for** ◊ *the main ~s for the world title* | **~ to** ◊ *a ~ to their competitors' dominance of the market*

challenging *adj.*

VERBS **be, prove** | **make sth** ◊ *We have changed the course to make it more ~.* | **find sth** ◊ *He found the course academically ~.*
ADV. **extremely, fairly, very, etc.** | **enough, sufficiently** ◊ *The tasks were not ~ enough for me and I got bored.* | **academically, intellectually, physically, politically, technically**

chamber *noun*

1 room/enclosed space

ADJ. **dark, darkened** | **private, secret** | **inner, outer** | **main** | **subterranean, underground** | **burial, tomb** ◊ *a Bronze Age burial ~* | **gas, torture** ◊ *Millions died in the gas ~s in the war.* | **combustion, decompression, echo, vacuum**
VERB + CHAMBER **enter** | **seal**
CHAMBER + NOUN **door**

2 large room, esp. used for formal meetings

ADJ. **grand, great, large, vast** | **high-ceilinged, vaulted** | **conference, council** (*esp. BrE*), **debating**
PREP. **in a/the ~**

3 part of a government

ADJ. **lower, upper** | **first, second** (*both esp. BrE*) | **elected** ◊ *She believes there should be an elected second ~ to replace the House of Lords.* | **legislative, parliamentary**
PHRASES **~ of commerce**

champagne *noun*

ADJ. **excellent, fine, good** | **French** | **expensive** | **cheap** | **vintage** | **non-vintage** | **fake** | **brut, dry, sweet** | **pink** | **chilled, iced**
... OF CHAMPAGNE **bottle, magnum** | **glass**
VERB + CHAMPAGNE **have** ◊ *I'll have some ~, please.* | **drink, quaff, sip** ◊ *Do you drink ~? ◊ They sat there sipping their ~.* | **break out, pop, uncork** | **pour (sb)** | **celebrate (sth) with** | **chill, have on ice, put on ice**
CHAMPAGNE + VERB **be on ice** | **flow** (*figurative*) ◊ *The ~ flowed like water at the wedding reception.* | **be flat, go flat** ◊ *The ~ had been left open and had gone flat.*
CHAMPAGNE + NOUN **bottle, flute** (= a kind of glass), **glass** | **cork** ◊ *We heard the sound of popping ~ corks next door.* | **breakfast, reception** ◊ *There was a ~ reception before the concert.* | **toast** ◊ *Financiers were drinking ~ toasts to the deal.* | **cocktail** | **house** (= company)

champion *noun*

ADJ. **great, supreme, true, undisputed** | **current, defending, reigning** ◊ *The reigning ~ will defend her title tonight.* | **former, past** | **undefeated** | **three-time, etc.** | **all-around** (*AmE*), **national, state, world** | **junior** | **Olympic** ◊ *the Olympic skating ~* | **boxing, chess, etc.** | **heavyweight, middleweight, welterweight**
VERB + CHAMPION **become, be crowned, be named** ◊ *He was crowned ~ after his fight in Atlanta.* | **beat, defeat** | **decide, determine** ◊ *The two winners will move onto a one-game final to determine the ~.*
CHAMPION + VERB **defend her/his title**
CHAMPION + NOUN **fighter, jockey, sprinter, etc.**

championship *noun*

1 competition

ADJ. **major** | **international, national, regional, state, world** | **British, European, US, etc.** | **club, conference, division, league, team** | **junior** | **basketball, swimming, tennis, etc.** | **back-to-back** (*AmE*)
VERB + CHAMPIONSHIP **hold, host** ◊ *The ~s are to be held in Rome.* | **compete in, take part in** ◊ *Over thirty children will compete in the swimming ~s.* | **win** ◊ *She has won four major ~s in the last five years.* | **lose**
CHAMPIONSHIP + VERB **take place**
CHAMPIONSHIP + NOUN **bout, fight, final, game, match** (*esp. BrE*), **race, round** | **competition, event, meet** (*AmE*), **tournament** | **contender** | **title, winner** | **run** (*AmE*) ◊ *During the team's ~ run last season, he played in 22 games.* | **season, series** (*both AmE*) | **squad, team** | **calibre/caliber** (*AmE*) | **belt, ring** (*AmE*), **trophy**
PREP. **at a/the ~** ◊ *I saw him play at last year's tennis ~.* | **in a/the ~** ◊ *the teams in the ~*

2 position/title of champion

VERB + CHAMPIONSHIP **hold** ◊ *Who holds the ~ at the moment?* | **capture, claim, clinch, earn, take, win** ◊ *He's won the ~ for the third time in a row.* | **lose** | **defend** | **regain** | **retain** ◊ *She managed to retain the ~.* | **celebrate** ◊ *The Red Sox celebrated their ~ with an extraordinary four-hour parade.*

chance *noun*

1 possibility

ADJ. **excellent, good, high, real, strong** ◊ *There is a very real ~ that the film will win an award.* | **decent, fair, fighting, legitimate, realistic, reasonable, solid, sporting** ◊ *There's a fair ~ that nobody will come to the talk.* | **little, the merest, million-to-one, minimal, outside, remote, slender, slight, slim** ◊ *There was only a million-to-one ~ of it happening.* ◊ *As long as there is an outside ~, we will go for it.* | **fifty-fifty, one-in-three, etc., 10%, 20%, etc.** ◊ *They have a 90% ~ of success.* | **zero** (*esp. AmE*) ◊ *He had zero ~ of survival.* | **survival** ◊ *What are his survival ~s?* | **election, electoral** (*esp. BrE*) | **play-off** (*AmE*)
VERB + CHANCE **give sb** ◊ *The doctors gave him (= said that he*

had) *little ~ of surviving the night.* | **be in with, have, stand** ◇ *After a poor start, they are now in with a ~ of winning.* ◇ *He doesn't stand a ~ of winning against such an experienced player.* | **assess, rate** ◇ *How do you rate our ~s of finding her?* | **fancy** (*BrE*) ◇ *I don't fancy our ~s of getting there on time.* | **boost, enhance, improve, increase, maximize** | **compromise, decrease, hurt, jeopardize, lessen, minimize, prejudice, reduce, ruin, scupper** (*BrE, informal*), **spoil** | **destroy, eliminate, end, kill** ◇ *It was a mistake which eliminated any ~ of an Australian victory.* | **risk** ◇ *He didn't want to risk the ~ of being discovered.*

PREP. **by any ~** ◇ *Are you by any ~ Mr Ludd?* | **~ of** ◇ *The missing climber's ~s of survival are slim.* | **~ for** ◇ *the variety with the best ~ for success*

PHRASES **fat ~** (*informal*) ◇ *Fat ~ (= there is no chance) of him helping you!* | **have every ~** ◇ *She has every ~ of passing the exam if she works hard.* | **no ~!** ◇ *'Will he lend us his car?' 'No ~!'* | **not a snowball's ~ in hell** (*informal*) ◇ *There isn't a snowball's ~ in hell (= there is no chance) that I'll wear that thing!* | **on the off ~** (= just in case) ◇ *I rang the company just on the off ~ that they might have a vacancy.*

2 opportunity

ADJ. **equal, fair, good, great, ideal, wonderful** ◇ *She played left-handed to give her opponent a fair ~.* ◇ *This is the ideal ~ for him to show his ability.* | **big** ◇ *This is your big ~, so grab it with both hands.* | **golden** ◇ *He had wasted a golden ~ to make history.* | **once-in-a-lifetime, rare, unique** | **only** ◇ *He realized that this might be his only ~ to save himself.* | **final, last, second** ◇ *The teacher gave her one last ~ to prove she could behave.* ◇ *There are no second ~s in this business.* | **educational, life** ◇ *The new college is intended to improve the life ~s of children in the inner city.* | **clear, clear-cut, save** (*AmE*), **scoring** (*all sports*) ◇ *He blew four of his seven save ~s.*

... OF CHANCE **element** ◇ *There is always an element of ~ in buying a used car.*

VERB + CHANCE **get, have** ◇ *I finally had the ~ to meet my hero.* | **deserve** ◇ *He deserves the ~ to give his side of the story.* | **enjoy, relish, welcome** ◇ *I would welcome the ~ to give my opinion.* | **afford (sb), give sb, offer (sb), provide (sb with)** | **deny sb** ◇ *No child should be denied the ~ of growing up in a family.* | **await, wait for** | **create, make** (*sports*) ◇ *The team created several clear ~s but failed to score.* | **see, spot** ◇ *She spotted her ~ of making a quick profit.* | **grab, grasp, jump at, seize, take** ◇ *Travis had left the door open—she seized her ~ and was through it like a shot.* ◇ *Take every ~ that comes your way.* | **blow** (*informal*), **forfeit, lose, miss, pass up, squander, throw away, turn down, waste** ◇ *They blew their ~ to go second in the league.* ◇ *I wouldn't pass up the ~ of working for them.*

CHANCE + VERB **arise, come, come your way** ◇ *When the ~ came to go to Paris, she jumped at it.*

PREP. **~ at** ◇ *Katie was his last real ~ at happiness.*

PHRASES **given the ~** ◇ *Given the ~, I'd retire tomorrow.* | **half a ~** ◇ *The dog always runs off when it gets half a ~.* | **let a ~ slip, let a ~ slip away** ◇ *If she let this ~ slip, she would regret it for the rest of her life.*

3 risk

VERB + CHANCE **take** ◇ *The guidebook didn't mention the hotel, but we decided to take a ~.*

PREP. **~ on** ◇ *The manager took a ~ on the young goalkeeper.* | **~ with** ◇ *The police were taking no ~s with the protesters.*

4 luck/fortune

ADJ. **mere, pure, sheer** | **random** | **happy, lucky** ◇ *By a happy ~ he bumped into an old friend on the plane.* | **unlucky**

VERB + CHANCE **leave sth to** ◇ *Leaving nothing to ~, he delivered the letter himself.*

PREP. **by ~** ◇ *The police came upon the hideout purely by ~.* | **due to ~** ◇ *The results could simply be due to ~.* | **through ~** ◇ *I got most answers right through sheer ~.*

PHRASES **a game of ~** ◇ *Chess is not a game of ~.* | **take your ~s** (= take a risk in the hope that things will turn out well) ◇ *He took his ~s and jumped into the water.*

change *noun*

1 becoming/making sb/sth different

ADJ. **big, considerable, dramatic, drastic, enormous, extensive, far-reaching, fundamental, important, major, marked, massive, momentous, noticeable, profound, radical, revolutionary, sea, significant, substantial, sweeping** ◇ *I need to make some drastic ~s in my life.* ◇ *Television has undergone a sea ~ in the last two years.* ◇ *These reforms have brought about significant ~s in the overall economy.* ◇ *The report called for sweeping ~s to the health system.* | **complete, wholesale** | **irreversible** | **systematic** | **cosmetic, marginal, minimal, minor, slight, small, subtle** | **lasting, long-term, permanent** | **short-term** | **abrupt, rapid, sudden** | **gradual** | **seasonal** | **net, overall** ◇ *net ~ in incomes* | **global** | **qualitative, quantitative** | **beneficial, desirable, effective, exciting, nice, pleasant, positive, refreshing, welcome** ◇ *The manual work made a welcome ~ from his previous job as a telephone operator.* | **unwelcome** | **unanticipated, unexpected, unforeseen** | **climate, constitutional, cultural, demographic, economic, environmental, evolutionary, legislative, organizational, political, population, social, structural, technological, temperature** ◇ *These policies are designed to combat the effects of climate ~.* | **career, culture, gear, lifestyle, name, personality, policy, regime, rule, sex** ◇ *the need for a culture ~ within the industry* ◇ *He made a rapid gear ~ as he approached the bend.*

VERB + CHANGE **make** ◇ *I made a couple of minor ~s to my opening paragraph.* ◇ *It made a pleasant ~ not having to work.* | **bring about, cause, effect, force, induce, produce, trigger** ◇ *How far does war bring about social ~?* | **implement, initiate, institute, introduce** ◇ *We are going to introduce a few ~s to the system.* | **undergo** | **show** ◇ *He needs to show a ~ in attitude if he is to succeed.* | **reflect** ◇ *Courses offered in schools reflect ~s in the job market.* | **document, measure, monitor** ◇ *The research will measure any ~s in the children's sleep patterns.* | **call for, demand** ◇ *He called for a ~ of mood in Scottish politics.* | **detect, note, notice, observe, see** ◇ *I've seen many ~s since I started farming.* | **oppose, resist** ◇ *We resist ~ because of fear of the unknown.* | **embrace** ◇ *Young people are more willing to embrace ~.* | **accommodate, adapt to** ◇ *Businesses have to adapt to ~.* | **prevent** | **be subject to** ◇ *Train times are subject to ~ without notice.*

CHANGE + VERB **come, happen, occur, take place** ◇ *Major economic ~s have occurred recently.* | **affect (sb/sth)** | **result in sth**

PREP. **for a ~** ◇ *I usually take the bus to school, but today I walked for a ~.* | **~ in** ◇ *The last few years have seen a ~ in attitudes to single parents.* | **~ of** ◇ *a ~ of government* | **~ from, ~ to** ◇ *the ~ from the old to the new system*

PHRASES **a ~ for the better, a ~ for the worse** ◇ *I reckon we've all made a big ~ for the better.* | **a ~ of clothes** (= an extra set of clothes to change into) ◇ *Take a ~ of clothes in case you get dirty.* | **a ~ of heart, a ~ of mind** ◇ *He said he's not coming, but he might have a ~ of heart.* | **a ~ of scene** (*BrE*), **a ~ of scenery** ◇ *I needed a ~ of scene/scenery after being in the job for so long.* | **a climate of ~** ◇ *In the current climate of ~, adaptability is vital.* | **the pace of ~, the rate of ~** ◇ *A successful company must keep up with the pace of technological ~.* | **a period of ~** ◇ *The eighties were a period of great ~ in publishing.* | **the tide of ~, the winds of ~** ◇ *The president realized he could not hold back the tide of ~, and resigned.*

2 coins/notes of low value

ADJ. **loose, small** ◇ *He emptied his pockets of loose ~.*

PREP. **in ~** ◇ *I had around £25 in ~.* | **~ for** ◇ *Ask the cashier if she has ~ for €20.*

PHRASES **chump ~** (*AmE, informal*) ◇ *$150 million is chump ~ (= a small amount of money) compared with the potential losses.*

3 money you get back if you pay too much

VERB + CHANGE **check, count** ◇ *I checked my ~ before leaving the store.* | **give** ◇ *This machine does not give ~.* | **get** | **take** | **keep** ◇ *I told the taxi driver to keep the ~.*

PREP. **~ from, ~ out of** ◊ *The meal left me with not much ~ from $200.*

change *verb*

ADV. **considerably, dramatically, drastically, fundamentally, greatly, a lot, markedly, profoundly, radically, significantly, substantially** ◊ *Our way of life has ~d dramatically over the last ten years.* ◊ *Jane has ~d a lot since she went to college.* | **completely, totally** | **slightly, subtly** ◊ *Her voice ~d subtly.* | **little** ◊ *The town has actually ~d very little in the last hundred years.* | **all the time, constantly, continually, forever** ◊ *The language is changing all the time.* ◊ *Technology has forever ~d the way businesses operate.* | **fast, overnight, rapidly, suddenly** ◊ *Attitudes to marriage are changing fast.* | **gradually, slowly** | **irrevocably, permanently**
PREP. **from** ◊ *Caracas ~d from a small town into a busy city.* | **into, to** ◊ *His anger ~d to sadness.*
PHRASES **~ out of all recognition** ◊ *The place had ~d out of all recognition.*

channel *noun*

1 television/radio station

ADJ. **radio, television, TV, video** | **cable, digital, satellite, terrestrial** | **commercial, independent** | **film** (*esp. BrE*), **movie, news, sports, etc.** | **pay-per-view**
VERB + CHANNEL **change, flip** (*AmE*), **flip through** (*esp. AmE*), **switch** ◊ *I changed ~s when the news came on.* | **change to, switch over to** (*esp. BrE*), **switch to, tune in to, tune to** | **watch** ◊ *He was watching the cartoon ~.* | **surf** ◊ *Lily surfed the ~s on the television.* | **launch** ◊ *Last year, the company launched its own TV ~.*
CHANNEL + VERB **broadcast** ◊ *This ~ broadcasts 24 hours a day.*
PREP. **on a/the ~** ◊ *There's an interesting documentary on Channel 9 tonight.*

2 route for sending information

ADJ. **direct, indirect** ◊ *Journalists always have indirect ~s for getting information.* | **formal, official** ◊ *She first tried to get a doctor's certificate through official ~s.* | **informal** | **appropriate, conventional, normal, proper, right, usual** | **effective** ◊ *an effective ~ for communication* | **diplomatic** | **communication, distribution** ◊ *worldwide distribution ~s*
VERB + CHANNEL **go through, use** ◊ *If you want a visa, you will have to go through the proper ~s.* | **establish, open, open up** ◊ *attempts to open up new ~s of communication*
PREP. **through a/the ~** ◊ *The government hopes to settle the dispute through diplomatic ~s.*
PHRASES **a ~ of communication** | **~s of distribution**

3 narrow area of water

ADJ. **deep** | **narrow** | **drainage, irrigation** ◊ *Irrigation ~s supply the crops with water.* | **river, water** ◊ *The garden has fountains and water ~s.* | **shipping**
VERB + CHANNEL **form** | **block**

chant *noun*

ADJ. **ritual, traditional** | **Gregorian** ◊ *a group of monks singing Gregorian ~* | **football** (*BrE*) ◊ *You could hear the football ~s a long way from the stadium.*
VERB + CHANT **sing** | **keep up** ◊ *The crowd kept up an incessant ~ of 'Out! Out! Out!'* | **hear**
PREP. **amid ~s** | **to ~s** ◊ *The band left the stage to ~s of 'We want more! We want more!'* | **~ of**

chaos *noun*

ADJ. **absolute, complete, pure** (*esp. AmE*), **total, utter** | **general, mass** | **controlled, organized** ◊ *He liked to work in organized ~.* | **ensuing, resulting** ◊ *In the ensuing ~, many works of art were destroyed.* | **administrative, domestic, economic, financial, political, social, traffic**
VERB + CHAOS **bring, cause, create, lead to** ◊ *A serious road accident caused traffic ~ yesterday.* | **end in, result in** ◊ *The game ended in ~.* | **be plunged into, be thrown into** | **descend into, slide into** ◊ *The country is sliding into economic ~.* | **face** | **avert, avoid** | **control**
CHAOS + VERB **break out, ensue, erupt** ◊ *Chaos broke out when the fire started.* | **reign, rule** ◊ *The government collapsed and ~ reigned.* | **surround sth** ◊ *the confusion and ~ surrounding the bombing raids*
PREP. **in ~** ◊ *The airport was in ~ during the strike.*
PHRASES **on the brink of ~, to the brink of ~** ◊ *We are on the brink of ~, economically speaking.* ◊ *The country was brought to the brink of ~.* | **order out of ~** ◊ *His brave leadership has created order out of ~.* | **a scene of ~** ◊ *Doctors worked day and night amid scenes of utter ~.* | **a state of ~**

chaotic *adj.*

VERBS **appear, be, look, seem** ◊ *Things often appear ~ to the outsider.* | **become, get** ◊ *Things have been getting ~ in the office recently.*
ADV. **extremely, fairly, very, etc.** ◊ *It was really ~ just before the show started.* | **increasingly** | **a little, slightly, etc.** ◊ *Things can be a little ~ in our house.*

chapel *noun*

1 part of a church; room/building used as a church

ADJ. **little, small** | **side** ◊ *The funeral was conducted in one of the smaller side ~s.* | **family, memorial, private, royal** | **college, school, university** | **hospital, prison** | **funerary** (*AmE*), **wedding** ◊ *They were married in a wedding ~ in Las Vegas.*
CHAPEL + VERB **be dedicated to sb** ◊ *The ~ is dedicated to St Michael.*
PREP. **in a/the ~**

2 (*esp. BrE*) church for some Protestant groups

ADJ. **Baptist, Methodist, etc.**
VERB + CHAPEL **attend, go to** ◊ *He goes to ~ every Sunday.*
PREP. **at ~** ◊ *They are still at ~ (= at a service).* | **at a/the ~** ◊ *They agreed to meet at the ~ after the service.*

chapter *noun*

1 part of a book

ADJ. **first, introductory, opening** | **concluding, final, last**
CHAPTER + VERB **be entitled sth, be titled sth** | **address sth, contain sth, cover sth, deal with sth, describe sth, discuss sth, examine sth, explore, present sth, provide sth** ◊ *This ~ covers money and banking.* | **detail sth, focus on sth**
VERB + CHAPTER **read** ◊ *I read the first few ~s and then got bored.* | **write** | **dedicate, devote** ◊ *The author devotes two ~s to language acquisition.*
PREP. **in a/the ~** ◊ *His influence on other writers will be discussed in the next ~.* | **~ about, ~ on** ◊ *a ~ on the city's architecture*

2 particular period

ADJ. **difficult, sad, unhappy** ◊ *Her return to Kansas ended a particularly unhappy ~ in her life.*

character *noun*

1 person's nature/person with a particular nature

ADJ. **excellent, exemplary, good, impeccable** | **generous, gentle, likeable, lovable, popular** | **colourful/colorful, larger-than-life, lively, real** ◊ *You must have come across some real ~s, working in the circus.* | **reformed** ◊ *He used to go out every night, but now he's a reformed ~.* | **complex, elusive, enigmatic, odd** | **forceful, formidable, strong** | **weak** | **volatile** | **prickly, unpleasant, unsavoury/unsavory** | **bad, evil, ruthless, violent** | **dubious, shady, suspicious** ◊ *Who's that suspicious ~ hanging around outside?* | **true** | **local** ◊ *The bar was full of interesting local ~s.* | **human** | **moral** ◊ *a woman of impeccable moral ~*
VERB + CHARACTER **be, have** | **form, shape** | **reveal** ◊ *She revealed her true ~ when anyone disagreed with her.* | **conceal, hide** | **reflect** ◊ *His scruffy appearance does not reflect his ~.*
CHARACTER + NOUN **trait** | **defect, flaw** | **change** ◊ *She's undergone a complete ~ change since her promotion.* |

reference ◇ *Applicants had to obtain ~ references before being considered for the work.* | **assassination** ◇ *The lawyer attempted a ~ assassination of the witness* (= tried to show the witness had a bad character). | **actor, actress**
PREP. **in sb's ~** ◇ *It's not in his ~ to tell lies.* | **out of ~** ◇ *The lawyer argued that his client's violent reaction was out of ~.*

2 nature of sth

ADJ. **distinctive, individual, unique** | **essential, fundamental, intrinsic** | **original** | **traditional** ◇ *The renovated buildings retain their traditional ~.* | **international, national, regional** ◇ *the features that make up the national ~* ◇ *Food in Italy has a distinct regional ~.* | **intimate** | **public** ◇ *the public ~ of material published on the Internet* | **military, political** | **rural, urban** ◇ *The development detracts from the rural ~ of the area.*
VERB + CHARACTER **have** ◇ *Each house in the street has its own distinctive ~.* | **assume, take on** ◇ *As you move north, the landscape takes on a different ~.* | **form** ◇ *factors that form the ~ of a nation* | **lose** ◇ *The town has lost much of its original ~.* | **retain** | **preserve** | **give sth** ◇ *It's the basil that gives the sauce its essential ~.*
PREP. **in ~** ◇ *The houses are Mediterranean in ~.*

3 interesting quality that sth has

ADJ. **considerable, great**
VERB + CHARACTER **have** ◇ *His face has character—I'll say that for it.* | **add, give sth** ◇ *the individual touches that give ~ to a house*
PREP. **of ~** ◇ *buildings of considerable ~*
PHRASES **full of ~** ◇ *The restaurant is cheap and full of ~.* | **have a ~ (all) of its own** ◇ *Your handwriting has a ~ of its own.*

4 person's inner strength

ADJ. **great**
VERB + CHARACTER **show** ◇ *The team showed great ~ in coming back to win.* | **build** ◇ *Adventure camps are considered to be character-building.*
PHRASES **strength of ~**

5 person in a story, film/movie, etc.

ADJ. **central, chief, lead, leading, main, principal, title** | **minor, supporting** | **fictional, fictitious** | **believable, realistic** | **sympathetic, unsympathetic** | **comic, heroic, tragic** | **animated, cartoon**
VERB + CHARACTER **play, portray** ◇ *The main ~ is played by Nicole Kidman.* | **inhabit** ◇ *The two lead actors inhabit their ~s fully.* | **build, create, develop, invent** ◇ *the artist who developed the Superman ~* | **feature** ◇ *The film also features the new ~ Mary Anna Morrison.* | **depict, draw** | **introduce** | **kill off** ◇ *The writers killed off her ~ when she wanted to leave the soap.*
CHARACTER + NOUN **development**
PREP. **in ~** ◇ *The actors remained in ~ to answer questions from the audience.*

6 letter/sign in writing/printing

ADJ. **Chinese, etc.** | **ASCII, numeric**
... OF CHARACTERS **set, string**
VERB + CHARACTER **insert** | **delete**
CHARACTER + NOUN **set, string**

characteristic noun

ADJ. **defining, distinctive, distinguishing, identifying, individual, special, striking, unique** ◇ *Mobility is the defining ~ of modern life.* | **personal** ◇ *Voters are primarily attracted by the charisma or personal ~s of a candidate.* | **common, family, national, shared** | **acquired, inherited** | **basic, general** | **chief, dominant, main, major, outstanding, principal** | **essential, fundamental, important, key, salient** | **desirable** | **behavioural/behavioral, biological, cultural, demographic, economic, genetic, physical, psychological, racial, sexual, social** | **human**
VERB + CHARACTERISTIC **display, exhibit, have, possess, share** ◇ *The two species have several ~s in common.* | **compare, describe, examine, identify**

characteristic adj.

VERBS **be** | **become**
ADV. **highly, very** ◇ *his highly ~ features* | **entirely** | **quite** | **fairly**
PREP. **of** ◇ *a problem that was fairly ~ of late 18th-century society*

charade noun

ADJ. **elaborate, ridiculous** (*esp. BrE*) | **little, whole** ◇ *We had to go through this whole ~ of holding auditions for the part.*
VERB + CHARADE **continue, go along with, go through** (*esp. AmE*), **keep up, maintain, take part in** ◇ *I refused to go along with their pathetic ~.* | **drop, end, give up, stop** ◇ *I suggest you give up this little ~ of yours.*
PREP. **~ of** ◇ *She struggled to maintain the ~ of not being afraid.*

charcoal noun

... OF CHARCOAL **lump, piece**
VERB + CHARCOAL **make, produce** | **burn, use**
CHARCOAL + NOUN **pencil, stick** | **drawing, sketch** | **black, grey/gray** | **filter, grill**

charge noun

1 price asked for sth

ADJ. **heavy, high** | **nominal, reasonable, small** | **minimum** | **fixed, standard** | **total** | **annual, daily, etc.** | **standing** (*BrE*) ◇ *There is a quarterly standing ~.* | **additional, extra** | **bank** (*esp. BrE*), **commission, handling, interest** | **maintenance, service** | **delivery, shipping** (*esp. AmE*) | **admission, call, call-out** (*BrE*), **cover, hire** (*esp. BrE*), **prescription** (*BrE*)
VERB + CHARGE **impose, introduce, levy, make** ◇ *We make a small ~ for wrapping your gift.* | **waive** ◇ *They agreed to waive the delivery ~s.* | **incur** ◇ *All changes will incur a ~.* | **pay** | **increase** | **reduce** | **reverse the ~s** (= when telephoning) (*BrE*)
PREP. **at a ~** ◇ *This service is available at a nominal ~.* | **for a ~** ◇ *The hotel operates a bus service to the beach for a small ~.* | **~ for** ◇ *There is no ~ for this service.* | **~ on** ◇ *a ~ on company profits*
PHRASES **free of ~** (= without any charge) ◇ *The company will deliver free of ~.*

2 official statement accusing sb of a crime

ADJ. **grave, heavy** (*esp. AmE*), **serious, reduced** ◇ *He was found guilty on a reduced ~ of assault.* | **lesser, reduced** ◇ *He was found guilty on a reduced ~ of assault.* | **baseless, false, trumped-up** | **civil, criminal, disciplinary, felony** (*AmE*), **misdemeanor** (*AmE*) | **assault, conspiracy, corruption, drug** (*esp. AmE*), **drugs** (*esp. BrE*), **fraud, murder, etc.**
VERB + CHARGE **bring, file, lay, level, make, pursue** ◇ *Police have brought a ~ of dangerous driving against the man.* | **drop, withdraw** | **answer, face** ◇ *She is almost certain to face criminal ~s.* | **avoid** ◇ *The company has managed to avoid criminal ~s in this case.* | **admit** ◇ *He has admitted the murder ~.* | **deny, dismiss, dispute** (*esp. AmE*), **rebut** (*esp. AmE*), **refute, reject** ◇ *The prime minister dismissed the ~ that he had misled Parliament.* | **fabricate, trump up** ◇ *He accused the government of fabricating the ~s for political reasons.* | **investigate** | **settle** (only used with ***charges***) (*AmE*) ◇ *The company agreed to pay $20 million to settle insider-trading ~s.* | **prove, substantiate** ◇ *The ~s will be difficult to prove.* | **dismiss, throw out** ◇ *The court dismissed the ~ against him.*
CHARGE + VERB **allege sth** ◇ *new ~s alleging the misuse of funds*
CHARGE + NOUN **sheet** (*BrE*) ◇ *At the police station a ~ sheet was made out.*
PREP. **on a/the ~** ◇ *She appeared in court on ~s of kidnapping and assault.* | **without ~** ◇ *to be detained/held/released without ~* | **~ against** ◇ *The ~s against you have been dropped.* | **~ of** ◇ *a ~ of armed robbery* | **~ related to, ~ relating to** ◇ *~s relating to the embezzlement of public funds*
PHRASES **bring ~s (against sb), prefer ~s (against sb)** (*BrE*), **press ~s (against sb)** ◇ *Many victims of crime are reluctant to press ~s against their attackers.*

3 control

ADJ. **overall** ◇ *The conductor has overall ~ of the train.* |

personal ◇ *She took personal ~ of the files.* | **sole** ◇ *Stephen will take sole ~ for the time being.* | **temporary** (*BrE*)
VERB + CHARGE **have** | **take** ◇ *We need somebody to take ~ of the financial side.* | **place sb in**, **put sb in** ◇ *John has been put in ~ of marketing.*
PREP. **in ~ (of sb/sth)** ◇ *I need to feel more in ~ of my life.* | **in sb's ~**, **under sb's ~** ◇ *The child is under my ~ until her mother returns.*

4 sudden attack
ADJ. **baton** (*BrE*), **cavalry** ◇ *They were driven back by a police baton ~.*
VERB + CHARGE **lead** ◇ *Young people are leading the ~ to clean up the city.*

charge *verb*

1 ask sb to pay money
ADV. **directly**
VERB + CHARGE **be entitled to**, **be free to**, **have a right to** ◇ *Companies are free to ~ whatever they like for their services.*
PREP. **against** ◇ *Research and development expenditure is ~d against profits in the year it is incurred.* | **at** ◇ *Calls will be ~d at 90 cents a minute.* | **for** ◇ *We don't ~ for delivery.* | **on** ◇ *The bank ~s a commission on all foreign currency transactions.* | **to** ◇ *The cost is ~d directly to the profit and loss account.*
PHRASES **~ sth to sb's account** ◇ *€50 will be ~d to your account.*

2 make an official accusation
ADV. **formally** | **jointly** (*BrE*) ◇ *The teenagers were jointly ~d with attempted murder.*
PREP. **in connection with** ◇ *A man has been ~d in connection with the attack.* | **with** ◇ *She has not yet been formally ~d with the crime.*

3 rush/attack
ADV. **headlong** | **blindly** | **around, round** (*esp. BrE*) ◇ *The children were all charging around outside.* | **in, out**
PREP. **at** ◇ *I was worried that the animal might ~ at us.* | **down** ◇ *I heard the sound of feet charging down the stairs.* | **forward, into** ◇ *She ~d into the room.* | **out of, through, towards/toward** ◇ *The rhino ~d headlong towards/toward us.* | **up**

charged *adj.*

1 full of electricity
VERBS **be**
ADV. **fully** ◇ *It's wise to take a fully ~ spare battery with you.* | **negatively, positively** | **oppositely** | **electrically** ◇ *electrically ~ particles*
PREP. **with**

2 full of strong feeling
VERBS **be**
ADV. **highly** ◇ *She had a highly ~ emotional life.* | **emotionally, erotically, politically, racially** (*esp. AmE*), **sexually** ◇ *an emotionally ~ atmosphere*

charity *noun*

ADJ. **international, local, national** | **registered** | **private** | **AIDS, animal** (*esp. BrE*), **cancer, conservation, educational, health, housing** (*esp. BrE*), **medical** | **Christian, faith-based** (*esp. AmE*), **Islamic, Muslim, religious** | **favourite/favorite**
VERB + CHARITY **donate (money) to, give (money) to, support** | **run** ◇ *She runs a ~ for homeless young people.* | **go to** ◇ *All the proceeds from the sale will go to ~.* | **ask for** | **accept** ◇ *They are proud people who don't accept ~.* | **depend on, live on** ◇ *They have no money and are forced to live on ~.*
CHARITY + NOUN **appeal** (*esp. BrE*), **drive** (*AmE*) | **auction, ball, benefit, concert, dinner, event, function, fund-raiser, game** (*esp. AmE*), **match, show** | **school** (*esp. BrE*) | **shop** (*BrE*) | **work** | **worker**
PREP. **for ~** ◇ *The school raised a lot of money for ~.* | **~ for** ◇ *a ~ for sick children*
PHRASES **an act of ~**

charm *noun*

ADJ. **considerable, great, immense, real** ◇ *a woman of considerable ~* | **easy, natural, quiet** ◇ *His natural ~ and wit made him very popular.* | **special, unique** | **personal** | **boyish, feminine** | **old-fashioned, old-world, period, traditional** | **folksy, small-town, southern** (*all esp. AmE*) ◇ *a politician with a folksy ~* | **rural, rustic** ◇ *The farmhouse had a certain rustic ~ about it.*
VERB + CHARM **have, hold, possess** | **keep, retain** ◇ *The town still retains a lot of its old-world ~.* | **turn on, use** ◇ *He can certainly turn on the ~ when he wants to!* ◇ *I nagged him for a week and used all my feminine ~.* | **exude, ooze** ◇ *He oozes ~, but I wouldn't trust him.* | **be immune to, resist** ◇ *He was unable to resist her ~s.* | **succumb to** ◇ *Many women had succumbed to his ~s.* | **be lacking in, lack** ◇ *The dining room was dark and gloomy, and the food was similarly lacking in ~.* | **lose** ◇ *The idea of being a farmer had lost its ~ for me by this time.*
PHRASES **part of the, its, etc. ~** ◇ *The area is a little run-down, but that's just part of its ~.*

charming *adj.*

VERBS **be, look, seem** | **find sb/sth**
ADV. **extremely, very, etc.** ◇ *an extremely ~ portrait* | **absolutely, perfectly, quite, thoroughly, utterly** ◇ *She looked small and gentle and altogether ~.*

chart *noun*

1 diagram showing information
ADJ. **accompanying** | **bar, flow, pie** | **flip, wall** (usually *wallchart*) ◇ *Each classroom has a flip ~ to write on.* | **medical, patient** (*AmE*) | **organization, organizational** | **depth** (= showing the places of players on the field in some sports) (*AmE*)
CHART + VERB **give sth, illustrate sth, indicate sth, list sth, show sth** ◇ *a bar ~ showing how sales had increased*
PREP. **in a/the ~** ◇ *the information given in the ~* | **on a/the ~** ◇ *The percentage of graduates is shown on the ~.*
PHRASES **off the ~s** ◇ *The wealth to be found in this town is off the ~s* (= very high).

2 detailed map of the sea/sky
ADJ. **nautical, navigation** | **weather** | **astrological, star**
PREP. **on a/the ~** ◇ *The islands were not marked on their ~.*

3 the charts (*esp. BrE*) **list of pop music records**
ADJ. **album, pop, singles**
VERB + THE CHARTS **enter, go into, hit** ◇ *Their single went straight into the ~s at number one.* ◇ *His latest single hit the ~s last week.* | **climb** | **be top of, top** ◇ *The song topped the ~s for three weeks.*
CHART + NOUN **hit**
PREP. **in the ~** ◇ *Is that song still in the ~s?*

charter *noun*

1 official written statement of principles, rights, etc.
ADJ. **draft** | **founding** | **social** | **national, UN** | **citizens', patients'** (*both BrE*)
VERB + CHARTER **draft, draw up** | **sign**
PREP. **~ for** ◇ *a national ~ for the protection of animals* | **~ of** ◇ *a ~ of workers' rights*

2 document giving rights to a town/an organization
ADJ. **royal** | **city, corporate, federal, state** (*all esp. AmE*)
VERB + CHARTER **give sb/sth, grant sb/sth, issue** | **draft** | **approve, sign** | **receive** | **amend, change** | **revoke**
PREP. **by ~** ◇ *They were given this right by royal ~.*

chase *noun*

ADJ. **long, short** | **high-speed** | **car** ◇ *The film ends with a long car ~.* | **police** | **wild goose** ◇ *He sent us on a wild goose ~* (= a search for sth that cannot be found).
VERB + CHASE **give** (*esp. BrE*), **take up** ◇ *The old lady shouted for help and then gave ~.* ◇ *A police officer arrived on the*

scene and took up the ~. | **give up** ◊ *Exhausted and hungry, the hunters finally gave up the ~.* | **join, join in** ◊ *Several children joined in the ~.*
CHASE + NOUN **scene, sequence** ◊ *The movie opens with an exciting ~ scene.*
PHRASES **the thrill of the ~** ◊ *What did he really want? Was it just the thrill of the ~?*

chasm noun

1 hole in the ground
ADJ. **deep, gaping, great, huge, vast, yawning**
CHASM + VERB **open, open up** ◊ *Suddenly a huge ~ opened in the earth.*

2 great difference of feelings/interests
ADJ. **great, growing, huge, unbridgeable, vast, wide, yawning**
VERB + CHASM **bridge, cross** | **create, open**
CHASM + VERB **separate sth** ◊ *A ~ separates my generation from my parents'.*
PREP. **~ between** ◊ *an attempt to bridge the ~ between the two cultures* | **~ of** ◊ *a huge ~ of hate and prejudice*

chat noun

1 (*esp. BrE*) **a friendly conversation**
ADJ. **brief, little, quick, short** | **long** | **cosy/cozy, fireside, friendly, good, nice** | **casual, informal** | **quiet** | **interesting** | **private**
VERB + CHAT **have** ◊ *We had a nice ~ over a cup of tea.*
PREP. **~ about** ◊ *a ~ about his new job* | **~ between** ◊ *a ~ between the star and a journalist* | **~ to, ~ with** ◊ *I'll have a ~ to John about it.* ◊ *a friendly ~ with a colleague*

2 talking informally
ADJ. **idle** ◊ *They say he's already married, but it's just idle ~.*
CHAT + NOUN **show** (*BrE*) | **line** (usually ***chatline***)

3 Internet communication
ADJ. **Internet, live, online** ◊ *You can take part in a live online ~ with the movie's director this afternoon.*
CHAT + NOUN **forum, group, room, session, site** ◊ *You can't believe all the stories you hear in Internet ~ rooms.*

chat verb

ADV. **briefly** | **amiably, amicably, happily** | **casually, easily, informally** (*esp. BrE*) ◊ *You will have a chance to circulate and ~ informally.* | **animatedly, excitedly** | **quietly** | **online** ◊ *I've been chatting online with my best friend.* | **away** ◊ *They chatted away to each other.*
PREP. **about** ◊ *We chatted briefly about the weather.* | **to** ◊ *George was in the kitchen chatting to some friends.* | **with** ◊ *I spent an hour chatting with a friend.*

chatter noun

ADJ. **constant, endless, incessant** ◊ *Her constant ~ was starting to annoy me.* | **excited, loud, nervous, noisy** | **idle** ◊ *I wish you'd stop wasting time in idle ~.* | **inane, mindless** | **background** | **Internet, radio** ◊ *Enemy radio ~ indicated the plane was carrying weapons.*
PREP. **~ about** ◊ *She was full of ~ about her new friends.*

chatter verb

ADV. **excitedly, happily, loudly** | **endlessly, incessantly** | **away, on** ◊ *He ~ed on happily for about half an hour.*
PREP. **about** ◊ *We ~ed about work.* | **to** ◊ *He ~ed excitedly to his friends.*

chauvinism noun

ADJ. **male** ◊ *a bastion of male ~* | **cultural, national** | **American, British, etc.**

cheap adj., adv.

1 low price
VERBS **be, be going** ◊ *a brand new radio going ~* | **buy sth, get sth, sell sth** ◊ *They're selling fabrics ~ this week.* | **not come** ◊ *Shoes like that don't come ~.*
ADV. **extremely, fairly, very, etc.** | **amazingly, incredibly, remarkably, ridiculously** ◊ *It's a good restaurant, and incredibly ~.* | **comparatively, reasonably, relatively** | **not exactly** (*esp. BrE*) ◊ *At £60 000 the car is not exactly ~ (= it is very expensive).* | **buy sth on the ~, get sth on the ~** ◊ *The school managed to get a couple of computers on the ~.*

2 poor quality
VERBS **be, look** ◊ *The glasses are plain without looking ~.*
PHRASES **~ and nasty** (*BrE*) ◊ *The bag looks ~ and nasty.*

check noun

1 close look to make sure sth is safe/correct
ADJ. **complete, extensive, full** (*esp. BrE*)**, thorough** | **careful, close, rigorous, tight** (*all esp. BrE*) | **cursory, quick** | **periodic, regular, routine** | **annual, daily, etc.** | **final, last** | **constant** (*esp. BrE*) | **random, spot** ◊ *In a series of spot ~s, police searched buses crossing the border.* | **independent** | **visual** ◊ *I did a quick visual ~ of the engine.* | **dental** (*BrE*)**, fitness** (*BrE*)**, health, medical** | **criminal, police, safety, security** | **background, credit, reference** | **ID** (*BrE*)**, identification** (*AmE*)**, identity** (*BrE*) | **baggage, customs** (*esp. BrE*)**, immigration** (*esp. BrE*)**, passport** (*esp. BrE*) | **stock** (*BrE*) | **consistency, quality** | **spell** (usually ***spellcheck***)**, spelling** (*BrE*) ◊ *I do a spellcheck on all my emails.* | **sound** (usually ***soundcheck***) ◊ *The band wants to do a soundcheck before the concert.*
VERB + CHECK **carry out** (*BrE*)**, complete, conduct, do, give sth, have, make, run** ◊ *I'll just have a quick ~ to see if the letter's arrived.* ◊ *A thorough ~ is made before the bags are put on the plane.* ◊ *We're running a police ~ on all applicants.* | **keep, maintain** ◊ *Police are keeping a close ~ on the house.* | **go for** (*esp. BrE*)**, undergo** ◊ *I have to go for a dental ~.*
PREP. **~ on** ◊ *a routine ~ on the factory*

2 control; restraint
ADJ. **natural** ◊ *Leaving some fields fallow provided a natural ~ on insect populations.*
VERB + CHECK **act as, provide** | **hold sth in, keep sth in** ◊ *You need to keep your temper in ~!*
PREP. **~ on** ◊ *The law acts as a ~ on people's actions.*

3 (*AmE*) **method of payment** → See CHEQUE

4 (*AmE*) **bill for food** → See also BILL
ADJ. **dinner**
VERB + CHECK **have** ◊ *Can I have the ~ please?* | **pay, pick up, split** ◊ *Uncle Louie picked up the dinner ~.*
PREP. **~ for** ◊ *The waiter handed me the ~ for my meal.*

check verb

1 examine/make sure
ADV. **always, daily, periodically, regularly** ◊ *Always ~ that the electricity is switched off before you start.* ◊ *Check the oil level regularly.* | **carefully, thoroughly** | **easily, simply**
VERB + CHECK **had better, must, need to, should** ◊ *We had better ~ that all the doors are locked.*
PREP. **against** ◊ *I'll need to ~ these figures against last year's.* | **for** ◊ *Check the roof for loose slates.* | **with** ◊ *I ~ed with her to see if she needed any help.*
PHRASES **be worth ~ing** ◊ *It's worth ~ing that there is no rust on the car.* | **~ to see if, ~ to see whether** ◊ *He was just ~ing to see if I was in my room.*

2 (*AmE*) **put a mark (✓) next to sth** → See also TICK
ADV. **simply** ◊ *To take advantage of this extra bonus offer, simply ~ the box on your order form.* | **mentally** ◊ *She began mentally ~ing off the things on her to-do list.* | **off** ◊ *The cartons were all ~ed off as they were unloaded.*

checklist noun

ADJ. **useful** | **mental**
VERB + CHECKLIST **have** | **use** | **draw up, produce, provide** ◊

My boss is drawing up a ~ of my duties. | **complete, go through, run through** ◆ We ran through the ~ of points to consider when buying a computer.
PREP. **~ for** ◆ a useful ~ for assessing different schools | **~ of** ◆ a ~ of questions

checkout noun

ADJ. **supermarket | express**
VERB + CHECKOUT **go through** ◆ You can't just go through the ~ without paying!
CHECKOUT + NOUN **assistant** (BrE), **clerk** (AmE), **girl, operator** (BrE) | **counter** (esp. AmE), **lane** (AmE), **line** (AmE), **queue** (BrE)
PREP. **at the ~** ◆ He hates waiting at the ~.

checkpoint noun

ADJ. **border | army, military, police, security | vehicle**
VERB + CHECKPOINT **set up** ◆ The army has set up ~s on all the major roads in the area. | **man** ◆ Guerrillas started firing on soldiers manning a ~. | **approach, pass**
PREP. **at a/the ~** ◆ We were stopped at the ~. | **through a/the ~** ◆ The police waved our car through the border ~.

check-up noun

ADJ. **thorough | regular | annual, monthly, etc. | routine | general | dental, health, medical, physical**
VERB + CHECK-UP **get, go for, have** ◆ At your age, you should have regular ~s. | **do, give (sb)** ◆ The company doctor does ~s on Wednesdays.

cheek noun

1 part of the face
ADJ. **flushed, hot, warm | cool | smooth, soft | ashen, pale, pallid | blushing, crimson, pink, red, rosy | hollow, sunken** ◆ His red-rimmed eyes and sunken ~s betrayed his lack of sleep. | **chipmunk** (AmE), **chubby, plump, puffy** (AmE) | **unshaven | bruised | tear-stained, wet** ◆ Her ~s were wet with tears.
VERB + CHEEK **brush, caress, dab, dab at, pat, rub, stroke, touch** ◆ She dabbed at her ~s with a handkerchief. | **kiss, peck | give (sb)** ◆ She proffered her ~ to kiss. | **press, rest** ◆ He rested his ~ on her shoulder.
CHEEK + VERB **blaze, blush, burn, flame, flush, grow hot, redden, warm** ◆ He felt his ~s burning with shame.
PREP. **across sb's/the ~** ◆ She gave him a sharp slap across his ~. | **against sb's ~** ◆ She laid her ~ against his. | **down sb's ~** ◆ A tear slid down her ~. | **in sb's ~s** ◆ She had a healthy bloom in her ~s. | **on sb's/the ~** ◆ He kissed her on both ~s and got on the train.
PHRASES **bring the colour/color (back) to sb's ~s | color floods (to) your ~s** (AmE), **the colour/color rises to your ~s, the colour/color rushes to your ~s** ◆ Colour/Color flooded to her ~s when she realized she was being watched. ◆ She smiled at him and the colour/color rose to his ~s. | **a kiss on the ~, a peck on the ~** ◆ She gave him a peck on the ~ and said goodbye.

2 (BrE) lack of respect
ADJ. **awful, barefaced, colossal** ◆ It's an awful ~, the way he keeps asking you to lend him money.
VERB + CHEEK **have** ◆ He's got a ~, making you wait outside his office.
PHRASES **of all the ~!, what a ~!** ◆ He asked you for money? Of all the ~!

cheekbone noun

ADJ. **high, prominent | chiselled/chiseled, perfect, sharp | broken, fractured**
PREP. **beneath sb's ~s** ◆ The hollows beneath his ~s showed his stress. | **on sb's ~s** ◆ A flush of anger appeared on her ~s. | **over sb's ~s** ◆ The skin stretched taut over his ~s.

cheer noun

ADJ. **big, deafening, great, hearty, huge, loud, rousing** ◆ The players were greeted by rousing ~s.
VERB + CHEER **give (sb)** ◆ They gave a big ~ when I finally

---

arrived. | **be greeted by, be greeted with, get, raise** ◆ She got a loud ~ when she finished speaking. | **hear**
CHEER + VERB **erupt, go up, ring out** ◆ A deafening ~ went up from the crowd.
CHEER + NOUN **leader** (usually **cheerleader**), **squad** (AmE)
PREP. **amid ~** ◆ He accepted the prize amid ~s. | **to ~s** ◆ She went off the stage to loud ~s. | **~ for** ◆ a ~ for democracy | **~ from** ◆ There were loud ~s from the crowd. | **~ of** ◆ ~s of welcome
PHRASES **three ~s for sb/sth** ◆ Three ~s for Mr Jones!

cheer verb

1 shout to encourage sb
ADV. **loudly, wildly** ◆ The crowd ~ed loudly as he came on stage.
PREP. **for** ◆ The fans ~ed for their team.

2 (also **cheer up**) make sb happy/more hopeful
ADV. **greatly, a lot** ◆ I was greatly ~ed by this news. ◆ Talking to Jane ~ed me up a lot. | **a bit**
PREP. **with** ◆ I ~ed her up with a trip to the zoo.

cheerful adj.

VERBS **appear, be, feel, look, seem, sound | become | keep, remain, stay** ◆ I'm amazed that she keeps so ~. | **keep sb** ◆ We tried to keep him ~.
ADV. **extremely, fairly, very, etc. | incredibly, remarkably | almost | relentlessly | falsely** (esp. AmE) ◆ 'The doctor is on her way,' said Mrs Morris, sounding falsely ~.

cheese noun

ADJ. **hard, soft | sharp, strong | mild | fat-free** (AmE), **full-fat, low-fat, reduced-fat | grated, shredded** (AmE) | **grilled, melted | processed, string | blue, cottage, cream, curd** (esp. BrE), **goat's, smoked | Cheddar, Parmesan, etc. | specialty** (AmE) | **Dutch, Swiss, etc.**
... OF CHEESE **chunk, hunk, lump** (esp. BrE), **piece, slice**
VERB + CHEESE **make | cut, grate, slice** ◆ Cut the ~ into cubes. | **melt | sprinkle (sth with), top (sth with)** ◆ Sprinkle the ~ over the beans. ◆ Sprinkle the potatoes with grated ~ and grill for a few minutes.
CHEESE + NOUN **fondue, omelette, roll, sandwich, sauce, soufflé | stick** (esp. AmE) | **board** (usually **cheeseboard**) | **plate, platter** (both esp. AmE) | **grater | factory**
PHRASES **bread and ~ | ~ and biscuits** (BrE), **~ and crackers | ~ on toast** (BrE) | **a selection of ~s**
→ Special page at FOOD

chef noun

ADJ. **excellent, good | cordon bleu** (esp. BrE), **gourmet** (esp. AmE) | **executive, head, master | apprentice, second** (BrE), **trainee** (BrE) ◆ He took a job as a trainee ~ in a London hotel. | **pastry, sushi | celebrity, top** ◆ a new book by celebrity ~ Jamie Oliver
→ Note at JOB

chemical noun

ADJ. **organic | inorganic, synthetic | dangerous, harmful, hazardous, poisonous, toxic, volatile | agricultural, environmental, household, industrial**
VERB + CHEMICAL **manufacture, produce | dump, release** ◆ ~s released by industry into our lakes and rivers | **contain | use** ◆ We don't use many ~s on our farm these days. | **be exposed to** ◆ Many workers are regularly exposed to dangerous ~s.
CHEMICAL + NOUN **factory, plant, works** ◆ pollution from a big ~ plant | **business, company | industry, manufacturing | weapon**

chemist noun

1 (BrE) person who prepares and sells medicines
ADJ. **local | dispensing**

chemistry

PHRASES **chemist's shop, the chemist's** ◇ *I've just got to go to the chemist's.*

2 specialist in chemistry

ADJ. **distinguished** | **government, industrial** | **analytical, research** | **inorganic, organic** | **medicinal** (*esp. AmE*), **physical**
→ Note at JOB

chemistry *noun*

1 subject of study

ADJ. **analytical, applied, theoretical** | **atmospheric, environmental, medicinal** (*esp. AmE*), **physical** | **industrial** | **inorganic, organic**
CHEMISTRY + NOUN **set** ◇ *For her twelfth birthday, she asked for a ~ set.*
→ Note at SUBJECT (for verbs and nouns)

2 chemical structure of substance

ADJ. **blood, soil, water, etc.** | **body, brain** ◇ *natural changes in body ~*

3 personal feelings/attraction

ADJ. **personal** | **sexual**
PREP. **~ between** ◇ *The personal ~ between the two stars is obvious.*

cheque (*BrE*) (*AmE* check) *noun*

ADJ. **big, fat** (*informal*), **large** | **blank** | **monthly** | **bad, bounced, dud** (*BrE*), **forged** | **crossed** (*BrE*) | **post-dated** | **personal** | **pay, royalty** | **giro** (*BrE*), **maintenance** (*AmE*), **unemployment** (*AmE*), **welfare** (*AmE*) | **traveller's/traveler's** ◇ *Traveller's ~s can be cashed at most hotels.* (*BrE*) ◇ *Traveler's checks can be cashed at most hotels.* (*AmE*)
VERB + CHEQUE/CHECK **issue, make out, sign, write, write out, write sb** ◇ *Shall I make the ~ out to you?* ◇ *Can I write you a ~?* | **draw** ◇ *He drew a large ~ on his company's account.* | **make payable** ◇ *Cheques should be made payable to Toyland.* | **give sb, hand sb, hand over, present** ◇ *They presented a ~ for $500 000 to the Red Cross.* | **receive, send** | **deposit, pay in** ◇ *She deposited the ~ in her husband's account.* ◇ *I need to go to the bank to pay this ~ in.* | **cash** ◇ *I'll cash a ~ at the bank.* | **pay by** | **accept** ◇ *Does the restaurant accept ~s?* | **clear, honour** (*BrE*), **pass** ◇ *He was fired for passing bad ~s.* | **bounce** (*informal*), **float** (*AmE, informal*) ◇ *He bounced three ~s last month.* | **cancel, stop** (*BrE*), **stop payment on** (*AmE*) ◇ *I asked the bank to stop the ~.* (*BrE*) ◇ *I asked the bank to stop payment on the check.* (*AmE*) | **endorse**
CHEQUE/CHECK + VERB **bounce** (*informal*) ◇ *The ~ will bounce if your salary doesn't reach your account today.* | **clear**
CHEQUE/CHECK + NOUN **account** (*BrE*) (**checking account** in *AmE*) | **card, guarantee card** (*both esp. BrE*) ◇ *Cheques must be supported by a ~ guarantee card.* | **book** (usually **chequebook/checkbook**), **stub** (*BrE*)
PREP. **~ for** ◇ *a ~ for $160*

cherry *noun*

ADJ. **black, red** | **glacé, maraschino, morello** | **juicy, sour, sweet**
...OF CHERRIES **bunch**
CHERRY + NOUN **pit** (*esp. AmE*), **stone** (*esp. BrE*) | **pie** | **soda** (*AmE*) | **blossom, tree, wood**
→ Special page at FRUIT

chess *noun*

ADJ. **computer** | **correspondence** | **junior** (*BrE*), **scholastic** (*AmE*)
...OF CHESS **game**
VERB + CHESS **play**
CHESS + NOUN **board** (usually **chessboard**), **piece, set, table** ◇ *the position of the ~ pieces on the board* | **move** | **position** | **champion, grand master, master, player** | **championship, game, match, tournament** | **club** | **computer, program** | **world** ◇ *a star of the ~ world*

chest *noun*

ADJ. **barrel, big, broad, huge, manly, massive, muscled, muscular, powerful, strong** | **narrow** | **flat** ◇ *She wears loose clothes to hide her flat ~.* | **bare, naked** | **hairy, hairless, smooth** | **bad** (*BrE*), **tight, weak** (*esp. BrE*) | **lower, upper**
VERB + CHEST **clutch, clutch at** ◇ *Clutching his ~ in agony, he fell to the ground.* | **beat, pound, thump** ◇ *'You need to have courage,' he said, thumping his ~.* | **puff, puff out** ◇ *He puffed out his ~ proudly.* | **shave, wax**
CHEST + VERB **expand, heave, rise and fall** | **puff, puff out, puff up, swell** ◇ *His ~ puffed out with indignation at the suggestion.* ◇ *His ~ swelled with pride as he accepted the award.* | **constrict** (*esp. AmE*), **tighten** ◇ *Her ~ tightened with fear.* | **ache, burn** ◇ *She ran until her ~ ached.*
CHEST + NOUN **discomfort, pain, tightness** | **injury, wound** | **complaint** (*BrE*), **condition** (*BrE*), **disease, infection, problems** | **radiograph, X-ray** | **clinic** | **muscles** | **hair** | **area, cavity**
PREP. **in the/your ~** ◇ *She was hit in the ~ by two of the bullets.* | **on the/your ~** ◇ *the hairs on his ~* | **to the/your ~** ◇ *He suffered burns to the ~ and neck.* ◇ *She clutched her baby tightly to her ~.*

chestnut *adj., noun*

ADJ. **bright, glossy, rich** | **dark, deep**
→ Special page at COLOUR

chew *verb*

ADV. **thoroughly, well** | **slowly, thoughtfully** | **up** ◇ *Chew your food up thoroughly before you swallow it.*
PREP. **at** ◇ *She was ~ing at her lower lip.* | **on** ◇ *The baby ~ed on a piece of bread.*

chicken *noun*

1 bird

ADJ. **battery** (*BrE*), **broiler, corn-fed, free-range** ◇ *Free-range ~s have happy lives.* | **live** ◇ *a crate of live ~s*
VERB + CHICKEN **keep, raise** | **kill** | **pluck**
CHICKEN + VERB **peck** | **scratch** ◇ *A few ~s were scratching around the yard.* | **cluck** | **wander**
CHICKEN + NOUN **farmer** | **coop, run** | **wire** (= wire made into sheets for fences)

2 meat

ADJ. **fresh, frozen** | **organic** | **juicy, succulent, tender** | **cooked, raw** | **cold**
...OF CHICKEN **piece, strip** ◇ *succulent pieces of ~*
VERB + CHICKEN **eat, have** | **cook** | **barbecue, fry, grill, roast, etc.** | **stuff**
CHICKEN + NOUN **breast, drumsticks, giblets, leg, liver, nuggets, piece, thigh, wing** | **broth, casserole, curry, salad, sandwich, soup, stock**
PHRASES **(a) breast of ~, (a) leg of ~**
→ Special page at FOOD

chief *noun*

ADJ. **tribal, village** | **army, corporate, council, fire, industry, intelligence, military, party, police, security, station, union** | **branch, division, section** | **counterterrorism, education, finance, health, marketing, etc.**
VERB + CHIEF **appoint (sb), become, name sb** ◇ *Sanger was appointed ~ of the Fire Department.*
PHRASES **~ of police, ~ of staff**

chief executive *noun*

ADJ. **current, former** | **acting** (*BrE*), **interim** (*esp. BrE*) | **joint** (*esp. BrE*) | **outgoing** (*esp. BrE*)
VERB + CHIEF EXECUTIVE **appoint, name**

child *noun*

ADJ. **little, small, young** ◇ *My father died while I was still a small ~.* | **newborn** | **teenage** ◇ *We have three teenage children.* | **preschool, school-aged** | **adult, grown** (*esp. AmE*), **grown-up** (*esp. BrE*) | **good, obedient, well-behaved** | **aggressive, delinquent, difficult, disobedient, fractious,**

mischievous, naughty, problem, sulky, unruly, wayward, wilful/willful ◊ *He's always been a problem ~.* ◊ *The children were quite unruly and ran around the house as if they owned it.* | bright, gifted, intelligent, precocious ◊ *a school for gifted children* ◊ *What a precocious child—reading Jane Austen at the age of ten!* | dull, slow ◊ *Teaching is particularly difficult when a class contains both slow and bright children.* | abandoned, abused, at-risk, maltreated, neglected ◊ *therapy for sexually abused children* | disadvantaged, needy, starving, underprivileged | spoiled | sickly | asthmatic, autistic, disabled, dyslexic, hyperactive, etc. | special-needs | innocent | loving | only ◊ *It was a little lonely being an only ~.* | eldest, first-born | fatherless, motherless, orphaned | adopted | bastard (*usually figurative*), illegitimate ◊ *the bastard ~ of romantic fiction and horror.* | unborn ◊ *the rights of the unborn ~* | dependent ◊ *tax concessions for families with dependent children* | street ◊ *There are a lot of street children in the poorer parts of the city.* | biracial (*AmE*), mixed-race | minority
VERB + CHILD have ◊ *How many children do you have?* | bear, give birth to, have ◊ *She didn't have her first ~ until she was nearly forty.* | father | conceive ◊ *We had trouble conceiving our first ~.* | expect ◊ *They are expecting a ~ in June.* | adopt, foster | lose ◊ *She couldn't imagine the pain of losing a ~ at birth.* | bring up, raise, rear ◊ *He had old-fashioned ideas on how to bring up children.* | indulge, pamper, spoil ◊ *You can't spoil a ~ by giving it all the affection it wants.* | love, nurture | maltreat, neglect | educate, home-school (*esp. AmE*), teach | discipline, punish, scold | abandon | abduct, kidnap | abuse, molest | immunize, vaccinate
CHILD + VERB be born ◊ *Their first ~ was born with a rare heart condition.* | develop, grow, grow up ◊ *Children grow up so quickly!* | good food for growing children | cry, scream, whimper, whine | misbehave
CHILD + NOUN actor, bride, soldier, star | prodigy | development ◊ *the emotional connections which ensure healthy ~ development* | custody ◊ *a ~ custody dispute between divorced parents* | support ◊ *After they divorced, he refused to pay ~ support.* | labour/labor | prostitution | pornography | abuse, molestation | abuser, killer, molester | abduction | psychiatrist, psychologist | protection, safety, services (*AmE*), welfare
PREP. with ~ (*literary*) ◊ *big with ~* (= pregnant)

childbirth noun

ADJ. natural
VERB + CHILDBIRTH die in ◊ *His wife died in ~ in 1928.*
CHILDBIRTH + NOUN educator (*AmE*) | class (*esp. AmE*)
PHRASES the pain of ~ ◊ *She dreaded the pain of ~.*

childhood noun

ADJ. carefree, good, happy | deprived, difficult, lonely, rough, traumatic, troubled, unhappy | normal | early, late, middle (*esp. AmE*) ◊ *From earliest ~ she'd had a love of dancing.* ◊ *His health remained poor into later ~.*
VERB + CHILDHOOD have ◊ *She had a very happy ~.* | spend ◊ *He spent most of his ~ in Egypt.* | recall, remember ◊ *I remembered my own ~ fondly.* | survive ◊ *Her second son didn't survive ~.* | lose ◊ *Children are losing their ~s so fast.*
CHILDHOOD + NOUN days, years | event, experience, memories | dream, fantasy | abuse, trauma | buddy (*esp. AmE*), friend, sweetheart | crush | home | nickname | disease, illness, mortality | cancer, leukaemia/leukemia, etc. | obesity
PREP. during ~ ◊ *He became diabetic during ~.* | from ~ ◊ *She still retained many friends from ~.* | in ~ ◊ *She died in ~.* | throughout ~ ◊ *He was moved from family to family throughout his ~.*
PHRASES scenes from sb's ~

chill noun

1 coldness

ADJ. biting, bitter, deep | cold, damp | slight | evening, morning, night | autumn (*esp. BrE*), autumnal, winter
VERB + CHILL feel ◊ *I could feel the ~ as soon as I went outside.* |

take off ◊ *I'll add some hot water to the milk to take the ~ off it* (= to make it slightly warmer).
CHILL + NOUN factor ◊ *With the ~ factor, it's nearly minus forty here.*
PHRASES a ~ in the air ◊ *There's a slight ~ in the air.*

2 feeling of fear

ADJ. sudden | icy
VERB + CHILL feel ◊ *She felt a sudden ~ at the thought of the dangers he faced.* | strike ◊ *Her words struck a ~ in his heart.*
CHILL + VERB run down sb's spine, run through sb, run up sb's spine ◊ *A ~ ran through me at the thought.*
PREP. ~ of ◊ *a ~ of fear*
PHRASES send a ~ down sb's spine, send a ~ through sb ◊ *The news sent a ~ down her spine.*

3 mild illness

ADJ. bad, nasty, severe | slight
VERB + CHILL catch, get ◊ *I caught a nasty ~ after my swim last week.*
→ Special page at ILLNESS

chilli (*BrE*) (*AmE* chili) noun

ADJ. fresh | dried | hot | mild | green, red
CHILLI/CHILI + NOUN pepper (*AmE*) | oil, powder, sauce | beans
→ Special page at FOOD

chilly adj.

VERBS be, feel ◊ *She was beginning to feel ~.* | get ◊ *We were starting to get a little ~.* | turn (*only used about the weather*) ◊ *It turned ~ in the afternoon.*
ADV. extremely, fairly, very, etc. | decidedly, distinctly | a little, slightly, etc.

chimney noun

ADJ. high, tall | short | narrow, wide | tapering | brick, stone, etc. | smoking ◊ *The air was black from smoking ~s.* | sooty | factory, industrial
VERB + CHIMNEY clean, sweep
CHIMNEY + VERB belch sth ◊ *factory ~s belching smoke over the town* | draw ◊ *This ~ doesn't draw very well.*
CHIMNEY + NOUN breast (*BrE*), flue, piece (*BrE*), pot (*BrE*), stack (*BrE*) | sweep | fire

chin noun

ADJ. square | chiselled/chiseled, pointed, pointy | firm, jutting, strong | non-existent, receding, weak | dimpled | determined, resolute, stubborn | smooth | bearded, stubbly, unshaven | double | cleft
VERB + CHIN jut (*esp. AmE*), jut out (*esp. AmE*), lift, raise, stick out, tilt, tip, tip up ◊ *Maria jutted her ~ defiantly.* ◊ *She tilted her ~ at him defiantly.* | tuck in | finger, rub, scratch, stroke, tap, touch ◊ *He stroked his ~ thoughtfully.* | lean, prop, prop up, rest ◊ *She sat resting her ~ on her hands.* | cup ◊ *He cupped her ~ with his hand.*
CHIN + VERB rise ◊ *His ~ rose in a proud gesture.* | rest ◊ *Her ~ was resting on his shoulder.* | quiver, tremble ◊ *His ~ quivered and a tear ran down his cheek.*
CHIN + NOUN strap ◊ *Fasten the ~ strap or the helmet will fall off.* | level ◊ *Slowly lower the bar to around ~ level.*
PREP. beneath sb's ~, under sb's ~ ◊ *He put his hand under her ~ and lifted her face to his.* | down sb's ~ ◊ *The juice dribbled down his ~.* | on sb's/the ~ ◊ *He had bits of food on his ~.* ◊ *She caught him with a hard blow on the ~.*

china noun

1 hard white substance

ADJ. fine | bone ◊ *fine bone ~ tableware*
VERB + CHINA be made of
CHINA + NOUN cup, dish, doll, plate, etc. | clay (*esp. BrE*)

2 cups/plates, made of china

ADJ. **best** ◇ *She got out the best ~ for the visitors.* | **broken, cracked**
... OF CHINA **set**
CHINA + NOUN **cabinet** ◇ *The ~ cabinet was filled with expensive dishes.* | **pattern** ◇ *She had already chosen the ~ pattern and table linen for their new house.*

chip *noun*

1 (*BrE*) (usually **chips**) long thin piece of fried potato, eaten hot → See also FRY

ADJ. **greasy** | **frozen, oven-ready**
... OF CHIPS **bag, plate**
VERB + CHIP **eat, have** ◇ *All he'll eat is ~s.* | **live on** ◇ *I never cook anything grand—we live on ~s and baked beans.* | **cook, fry**
CHIP + NOUN **pan** | **shop**
PHRASES **and ~s, with ~s** ◇ *fish and ~s*
→ Special page at FOOD

2 (usually **chips**) (*AmE*) thin round slice of fried potato, etc., dried and eaten cold → See also CRISP

ADJ. **potato, tortilla** (*BrE, AmE*)
... OF CHIPS **bag**
PHRASES **~s and dip, ~s and salsa**

3 microchip

ADJ. **computer, silicon** | **graphics, memory, microprocessor** | **embedded, integrated**
VERB + CHIP **make, manufacture, produce** | **design, develop** | **implant, install** ◇ *An electronic ~ could be implanted in his brain.* | **use** ◇ *This notebook uses a ~ designed for mobile computing.*
CHIP + VERB **contain sth** ◇ *a ~ containing the coding devices* | **run** ◇ *The computer has an integrated graphics ~ running at 333 MHz.*
CHIP + NOUN **design, technology** | **set** ◇ *a Pentium-compatible ~ set*
PREP. **on a/the ~** ◇ *Advances in technology have made it possible to pack even more circuits on a ~.*
PHRASES **~ and PIN** (*BrE*)
→ Special page at COMPUTER

chip *verb*

ADV. **badly** ◇ *She fell and chipped her tooth badly.* | **away** ◇ *He was chipping away at the stone.* ◇ *They chipped away at the power of the government.* (*figurative*)
PREP. **off** ◇ *We chipped the paint off the wood.*

chocolate *noun*

1 sweet brown food

ADJ. **dark, plain** (*BrE*), **unsweetened** (*AmE*) | **milk** | **white** | **bitter** | **cooking** | **fine** | **melted**
... OF CHOCOLATE **bar, slab** | **bit, chunk, piece, square** ◇ *He broke off a few squares of ~.*
VERB + CHOCOLATE **break, break up** ◇ *She broke a bar of dark ~ into four pieces.* | **grate** | **melt** ◇ *Melt the cooking ~ in a basin over hot water.* | **coat sth in, coat sth with, cover sth in, cover sth with, dip sth in, spread (sth with), sprinkle (sth with)** ◇ *a box of brazil nuts coated in ~*
CHOCOLATE + VERB **melt** ◇ *Stir until the ~ has melted.*
CHOCOLATE + NOUN **bar, chip, chunk, piece** ◇ *~ chip cookies* | **candy** (*AmE*) | **biscuit** (*BrE*), **brownie, cake, cookie** (*AmE*), **doughnut/donut, fudge, ice cream, milk, milkshake, mousse, muffin, pudding, sauce, syrup, etc.** | **factory**
→ Special page at FOOD

2 small sweet/candy made from chocolate

ADJ. **soft-centred** | **handmade**
... OF CHOCOLATES **box**
CHOCOLATE + NOUN **box**

3 drink made from powdered chocolate

ADJ. **hot, steaming** | **drinking** (*BrE*)

... OF CHOCOLATE **cup, mug** ◇ *a cup/mug of hot ~* (*BrE, AmE*) ◇ *a cup/mug of ~* (*BrE*)
VERB + CHOCOLATE **drink, sip**

choice *noun*

1 act of choosing

ADJ. **careful, good, informed, right, wise** ◇ *a careful ~ of words* | **bad, wrong** | **difficult, hard, stark, tough** ◇ *She faced the stark ~ of backing the new plan or losing her job.* | **easy, simple** ◇ *In the end, the ~ was quite easy.* | **conscious, deliberate** ◇ *When did you make a conscious ~ to become an artist?* | **natural** | **rational** | **moral** ◇ *Doctors have to make moral ~s every day of their lives.* | **personal** ◇ *These are personal ~s that people must make for themselves.* | **career, food, lifestyle** ◇ *Much ill health is the result of poor diet and lifestyle ~s.*
VERB + CHOICE **make** | **be faced with, face** | **dictate, guide, influence** ◇ *Your needs should dictate your ~.*
PREP. **by ~, from ~, out of ~** ◇ *I wouldn't have come to this bar by ~!* | **of ~** (= that is/should be chosen by a particular group of people for a particular purpose) ◇ *It's the software of ~ for business use.* | **of your ~** (= that you choose yourself) ◇ *First prize will be a meal for two at a restaurant of your ~.* | **~ about** ◇ *to make ~s about their future*

2 chance/ability to choose

ADJ. **clear** | **free** ◇ *Students have a free ~ from a range of subjects.* | **first** ◇ *You can have first ~ of all the rooms.* | **multiple** ◇ *a test with multiple ~ questions* | **consumer, parental, public** | **individual, personal**
VERB + CHOICE **have** ◇ *I now had a clear ~: either I accept their terms or I leave.* | **exercise** ◇ *Everyone in a democracy has the right to exercise ~.* | **give sb, offer sb, present sb with** ◇ *We gave her the ~, and she decided she'd like a bike for her birthday.* | **extend**
PREP. **~ about** ◇ *He had no ~ about that.* | **~ as to** ◇ *to extend parental ~ as to which schools children should attend* | **~ between** ◇ *She has a ~ between three different universities.* | **~ of** ◇ *a ~ of wines*
PHRASES **freedom of ~** | **have little ~ but to do sth, have no ~ but to do sth** ◇ *I had no ~ but to cancel my trip.* | **have no ~ in the matter** ◇ *The way he behaved meant that we had no ~ in the matter.* | **leave sb with little ~, leave sb with no ~** ◇ *Your decision leaves me with no ~ but to resign.*

3 things from which you can/must choose

ADJ. **good, wide** | **limited** | **available** ◇ *a range of available ~s*
VERB + CHOICE **have, offer** ◇ *We offer a ~ of ten different destinations.* | **limit, narrow** ◇ *Smoking may limit your ~ of contraception.* | **expand**
CHOICE + VERB **be available (to sb), be open to sb** ◇ *a limited range of ~s available to buyers*
PREP. **~ of** ◇ *The store has a very limited ~ of ties.*
PHRASES **be spoilt for ~** (= to have a large number of things from which to choose) (*BrE*)

4 sb/sth that is chosen

ADJ. **excellent, good, happy, ideal, inspired, perfect, smart** (*esp. AmE*) ◇ *It was a happy ~ of venue* | **bad, poor, unfortunate** ◇ *Baldwin was a poor ~ for such a role.* | **appropriate** | **odd** | **logical, obvious** ◇ *Bill is the obvious ~ for captain of the team.* | **popular** | **first, second** ◇ *Our first ~ for a site was already taken.* | **top** ◇ *People were asked about their top ~s for meeting locations.* | **preferred** ◇ *The hotel is the preferred ~ for business people.*
VERB + CHOICE **regret** ◇ *She was starting to regret her ~.* | **defend, justify** ◇ *Maria defended her ~ of name for the child.* | **question** ◇ *She questioned the ~ of Murphy for this role.*
PREP. **~ as** ◇ *Mary is a popular ~ as chair of the committee.* | **~ for** ◇ *I think she's a very good ~ for captain.* | **~ of** ◇ *I don't think much of her ~ of outfit.*

choir *noun*

ADJ. **massed** (*esp. BrE*) ◇ *a massed ~ of local schoolchildren* | **50-strong, etc.** | **ladies', male-voice, mixed, etc.** | **youth** | **college, school** | **cathedral, church, etc.** | **gospel**

VERB + CHOIR **be in, sing in** ◇ *She sings in the church* ~. | **join** | **conduct, direct** | **accompany**
CHOIR + VERB **perform, sing**
CHOIR + NOUN **practice** ◇ *Choir practice is on Wednesday evenings.* | **director** | **member** | **concert** | **loft, room, screen**
PREP. **in a/the** ~ ◇ *two of the girls in the* ~
PHRASES **be preaching to the** ~ (*AmE, figurative*) ◇ *I realize I may be preaching to the* ~ (= *telling someone who thinks the same*), *but I think he's gorgeous.*

choke *verb*

ADV. **almost, nearly**
VERB + CHOKE **make sb** ◇ *The fumes from the fire made her* ~.
PREP. **on** ◇ *My son nearly* ~*d on one of those nuts.*
PHRASES ~ **(sb) to death** ◇ *He* ~*d to death when a fish bone got stuck in his throat.*

cholesterol *noun*

ADJ. **elevated** (*esp. AmE*), **high, raised** | **low** | **blood** ◇ *raised blood* ~ *levels* | **bad, good**
... OF CHOLESTEROL **level** ◇ *a high/low level of* ~
VERB + CHOLESTEROL **have** (only used with *high* or *low*) ◇ *He has high* ~. | **contain** ◇ *Avocados contain no* ~. | **lower, reduce** ◇ *Eating garlic can significantly reduce* ~ *in the blood.* | **increase, raise** ◇ *This is the fat that won't raise your* ~.
CHOLESTEROL + NOUN **level** | **test** | **screening** | **drug, medication** (*esp. AmE*) **medicine**
PHRASES **be high in** ~, **be low in** ~ ◇ *foods that are low in* ~

choose *verb*

ADV. **carefully, wisely** ◇ *He chose his words carefully.* | **freely** ◇ *They can* ~ *freely from a wide range of courses.* | **voluntarily, willingly** | **consciously, deliberately, purposely, specifically** | **arbitrarily, randomly**
VERB + CHOOSE **be able to, be free to, can** ◇ *You are free to* ~ *whichever courses you want to take.*
PREP. **between** ◇ *She had to* ~ *between giving up her job or hiring a nanny.* | **from** ◇ *There are several different models to* ~ *from.*
PHRASES **pick and** ~ ◇ *You have to take any job you can get—you can't pick and* ~.

chop *noun*

ADJ. **lamb, mutton** (*esp. BrE*), **pork, veal** | **loin** ◇ *pork loin* ~*s*
VERB + CHOP **eat, have** | **braise, cook, fry, grill**
→ Special page at FOOD

chop *verb*

ADV. **finely** ◇ *Add finely chopped parsley.* | **coarsely, roughly** ◇ *Roughly* ~ *the cabbage.* | **up** ◇ *I spent the day chopping up vegetables.* | **down** ◇ *The trees are being chopped down.* | **off** ◇ *He chopped off the small branches before cutting down the tree.*
PREP. **into** ◇ *Chop the meat into small cubes.*
PHRASES ~ **sth to pieces** ◇ *The furniture had been chopped to pieces.*

chord *noun*

ADJ. **major, minor** | **C, D, etc.** | **guitar, piano**
VERB + CHORD **play, strum**
CHORD + NOUN **change, progression, sequence** | **structure**

chore *noun*

ADJ. **little, small** | **daily, day-to-day, regular, routine** | **morning** | **administrative, domestic, household** | **mundane, tedious** | **simple**
VERB + CHORE **carry out, do** ◇ *It'll take me an hour to do the household* ~*s.* | **handle, perform** ◇ *She let her husband manage the money while she handled other household* ~*s.*

chorus *noun*

1 part of a song that is repeated
ADJ. **catchy** (*informal*), **rousing, singalong** | **final**

VERB + CHORUS **join in, sing**
2 sth that a lot of people say together
ADJ. **general** | **growing** ◇ *There is a growing* ~ *of protest against the policy.*
VERB + CHORUS **join** ◇ *Many teachers have joined the* ~ *of angry voices.* | **be met with, bring** ◇ *His suggestions were met with a* ~ *of jeers.*
CHORUS + VERB **greet sb/sth**
PREP. **in** ~ (= *all together*) ◇ *'Hello!' they shouted in* ~. | ~ **of** ◇ *a* ~ *of boos*
PHRASES **a** ~ **of voices**
3 large group of singers/dancers
ADJ. **double** | **female, male** | **dawn** (= *of birds*) (*BrE*)
CHORUS + NOUN **girl, line, member**
PREP. **in a/the** ~ ◇ *She is singing in the* ~.
PHRASES **a member of the** ~

christening *noun*

VERB + CHRISTENING **attend, go to**
CHRISTENING + VERB **take place**
CHRISTENING + NOUN **gift, present** | **mug, spoon** | **robe** | **party**
PREP. **at a/the** ~ ◇ *We all got together at the* ~.

Christian *noun*

ADJ. **believing, committed, devout, faithful, good, practising/practicing, professing** (*AmE*) ◇ *Boyle was a devout* ~ *and an enthusiastic student of the Bible.* | **born-again, evangelical, fundamentalist** ◇ *He became a born-again* ~ *at 40 and turned his back on his misspent youth.* | **Orthodox, Protestant, etc.** | **conservative, liberal, right-wing**
VERB + CHRISTIAN **be brought up (as), be raised (as)**
CHRISTIAN + VERB **believe** | **pray, worship**

Christianity *noun*

ADJ. **evangelical, fundamentalist** | **Orthodox, Protestant, etc.** | **biblical** | **early**
→ Note at RELIGION (for verbs and phrases)

Christmas *noun*

ADJ. **good, nice** | **traditional** | **white** ◇ *The children are hoping for a white* ~ (= *with snow on the ground*).
VERB + CHRISTMAS **have, spend** ◇ *Did you have a good* ~? ◇ *We're going to spend* ~ *at home this year.* | **celebrate** ◇ *to celebrate* ~ *in the traditional way* | **get sth for** ◇ *What did you get for* ~?
CHRISTMAS + VERB **come** ◇ ~ *is coming!*
CHRISTMAS + NOUN **dinner** | **party** | **card, present** | **shopping** | **cake, pudding** | **lights, tree** ◇ *We're going up to town to see the* ~ *lights.* | **carol** | **Eve** | **Day, morning** | **holiday, holidays** | **celebrations**
PREP. **at** ~ ◇ *There are lots of parties at* ~. | **for** ~ ◇ *For* ~ *he gave her a silk blouse.* | **over** ~ ◇ *The library is closed over* ~.
PHRASES **Happy** ~!, **Merry** ~! | **wish sb a happy** ~, **wish sb a merry** ~

chronological *adj.*

VERBS **be**
ADV. **strictly** ◇ *a strictly* ~ *account of the events* | **broadly, roughly** ◇ *The anthology is broadly* ~.

chuckle *noun*

ADJ. **light, little, quiet, slight, soft** | **deep, low** | **hearty** | **good** | **amused, nervous**
VERB + CHUCKLE **give, have, let out** ◇ *She gave a little* ~. | **draw, elicit, get** ◇ *He got a* ~ *from a few members of the audience.* | **hold back, stifle, suppress** | **hear**
PREP. **with a** ~ ◇ *'I was only kidding!' he said with a low* ~. | ~ **about,** ~ **over** ◇ *We had a good* ~ *over the whole thing.*

chuckle *verb*

ADV. **lightly, quietly, slightly, softly** | **heartily** | **nervously**

PREP. **about, over** ◊ *She was still chuckling about the story the next day.* | **at** ◊ *He ~d at the thought of the two of them stuck in the snow.*
PHRASES **~ to yourself** ◊ *She ~d softly to herself as she remembered his astonished face.*

chug verb

ADV. **slowly, steadily** ◊ *The train chugged steadily along the West Highland Line.*
PREP. **along, down, in, out, past, etc.** ◊ *The boat chugged slowly down the river.*

chunk noun

ADJ. **big, great, huge, large, sizeable, substantial** ◊ *He bit a great ~ out of the apple.* ◊ *This one project has taken a substantial ~ of our budget.* | **small** | **bite-size ~s, bite-sized ~s, manageable ~s** ◊ *He cut the food up into bite-size ~s.* ◊ *The texts consist of short, bite-sized ~s. (figurative)* | **chocolate ~s** (*esp. AmE*), **pineapple ~s**
VERB + CHUNK **cut sth (up) into ~s**
PREP. **in a/the ~** ◊ *I bought the cheese in one big ~.* | **~ of** ◊ *a huge ~ of meat/rock/text*

church noun

1 building where Christians go to worship

ADJ. **local, parish, village** (*esp. BrE*)
VERB + CHURCH **build** | **consecrate, found** ◊ *The ~ was consecrated in 1250.* | **dedicate** ◊ *The ~ is dedicated to St Paul.*
CHURCH + NOUN **building** | **bells, clock, steeple, tower** | **pew** | **hall** | **fête** (*BrE*), **wedding**
PREP. **at a/the ~** ◊ *a chamber concert at our local ~* | **in a/the ~** ◊ *There's an interesting organ in the ~.*

2 meeting for public worship in a church

VERB + CHURCH **attend, go to** ◊ *Do you go to ~?*
CHURCH + NOUN **attendance** | **service** | **music** | **choir, congregation, organist** | **group, school** ◊ *a ~ youth group*
PREP. **after ~, before ~** ◊ *Come to our place for lunch after ~.* | **at ~** ◊ *They're at ~.* (*BrE*) | **in ~** ◊ *We decided not to get married in ~.* ◊ *They're in ~.* (*AmE*)

3 (often **the Church**) all Christians regarded as a group; particular group of Christians

ADJ. **high, low** ◊ *He loves all the high ~ traditions—incense and processions and vestments.* | **evangelical, fundamentalist** | **established** (= official), **mainline** (= official) (*AmE*) | **Christian, etc.** | **Catholic, Methodist, Protestant, etc.** | **early** ◊ *The early Church believed miracles were proof of who Jesus was.*
VERB + CHURCH **establish, found** | **lead** | **enter, go into** ◊ *He went into the Church* (= became a priest) *when he was 23.* | **join** ◊ *Linda joined the local Methodist ~.* | **leave** ◊ *He left the Church after a loss of faith.* | **serve** ◊ *He served the ~ for over sixty years.*
CHURCH + VERB **teach** ◊ *The Catholic ~ teaches that life begins at conception.*
CHURCH + NOUN **authorities, elder** | **leader, member** | **leadership, membership** | **community, group** ◊ *She was actively involved in ~ groups.* | **hierarchy** | **council** | **doctrine** | **historian** | **fathers**
PHRASES **a member of a ~**

chute noun

ADJ. **garbage** (*esp. AmE*), **laundry, rubbish** (*BrE*), **water** ◊ *a swimming pool with a long water ~*
PREP. **down a/the ~** ◊ *He tossed the discarded wrapping down the ~.*

cigar noun

ADJ. **fat** | **expensive** | **cheap** | **lit, unlit** | **Cuban**
... OF CIGARS **box**
VERB + CIGAR **smoke** | **draw on, pull on** ◊ *He paused and drew on his ~.* | **puff, puff on** | **light** | **extinguish, put out, stub out**
CIGAR + VERB **burn** ◊ *Her thin ~ burned quite quickly.* | **glow** ◊ *His ~ glowed in the darkened room.*
CIGAR + NOUN **ash, smoke** | **butt, end** | **box, case, holder** | **smoker** | **cutter** | **bar** (*AmE*)

cigarette noun

ADJ. **lighted, lit, unlit** ◊ *He accidentally dropped a lighted ~ on the chair.* | **half-smoked** | **illicit** ◊ *She slipped outside for an illicit ~.* | **hand-rolled, low-tar, unfiltered** | **clove** (*AmE*), **menthol** | **marijuana**
... OF CIGARETTES **pack** (*esp. AmE*), **packet** (*BrE*) ◊ *She smokes a pack/packet of ~s a day.* | **carton** | **case**
VERB + CIGARETTE **smoke** | **draw on, pull on, suck on** ◊ *He pulled on his ~ and waited for the train.* | **light** | **extinguish, put out, stub out** ◊ *Please extinguish all ~s now.* | **roll** ◊ *She rolls her own ~s.* | **flick, flick away** ◊ *The old man flicked his ~ onto the roadside.* | **bum** ◊ *He'd bummed a ~ from someone.* | **advertise** ◊ *Posters advertising ~s have to carry government health warnings.*
CIGARETTE + VERB **burn** ◊ *The ~ burned slowly in the ashtray.* | **glow** ◊ *The ~s glowed in the dark.* | **dangle, hang** ◊ *A ~ dangled from his lips.*
CIGARETTE + NOUN **ash, smoke** ◊ *the smell of stale ~ smoke* | **butt, end** (*BrE*) | **case, packet** (*BrE*), **pack** (*esp. AmE*) | **holder, lighter** | **smoker** | **consumption, smoking, use** | **burn** | **ad, advertising** | **company, maker, manufacturer** | **break** ◊ *He was sitting on the bench taking a ~ break.* | **tax**

cinder noun

ADJ. **glowing, hot, red** ◊ *a fireplace full of glowing red ~s*
CINDER + NOUN **path, track**
PHRASES **burned to a ~** (= completely burned) ◊ *By the time I got home, the cake was burned to a ~.*

cinema noun

1 (*BrE*) place where you go to see a film/movie → See also THEATRE

ADJ. **packed** ◊ *The ~ was packed, and we ended up sitting in the second row.* | **multiplex** ◊ *a new multiplex ~ on the edge of town*
VERB + CINEMA **go to** ◊ *How often do you go to the ~?* | **be on at** ◊ *What's on at the ~ tonight?*
CINEMA + NOUN **screen** | **audience** | **advertising** | **ad, advert, advertisement** | **chain**

2 (*esp. BrE*) films/movies in general

ADJ. **commercial, Hollywood, mainstream, popular** | **art, art-house, independent** | **avant-garde, classic, modernist** | **silent** ◊ *She started making films in the last years of silent ~.* | **digital**

circle noun

1 shape

ADJ. **complete, full** ◊ *The stones form a complete ~.* ◊ *How long does it take for the dial to rotate through a full ~?* | **concentric** | **widening** ◊ *The water rippled in widening ~s around the fountain.* | **overlapping** ◊ *a design of over-lapping ~s* | **tight** ◊ *He turned the car in a tight ~.* | **half** | **Antarctic, Arctic, polar**
VERB + CIRCLE **draw, trace** | **describe** (*technical*), **go around in, go round in** (*esp. BrE*) ◊ *If you follow the signs you find yourself going around in a ~.* | **form, make** | **cut out**
PREP. **in a/the ~** ◊ *The children stood in a ~.* ◊ *The planets move in ~s around the sun.* | **~ of**
PHRASES **the area of a ~, the circumference of a ~, the diameter of a ~, the radius of a ~** | **the centre/center of a ~, the middle of a ~**

2 group of people

ADJ. **wide** ◊ *She has a wide ~ of acquaintances.* | **narrow, small** | **charmed, close, closed, elite, intimate, magic, select** ◊ *He invited only a select ~ of friends to the wedding.* | **exalted, high** | **immediate** ◊ *They treat anyone outside their immediate ~ with suspicion.* | **inner** ◊ *He's joined the inner ~s of the court early in his career.* | **academic, aristocratic,**

artistic, business, court, diplomatic, government, intellectual, literary, official, political, royal, scientific, social, theatrical ~s ◇ *She moves in the highest social ~s.* | **family**
VERB + CIRCLE   **have** | **move in** ◇ *My brother and I move in completely different ~s* (= we have very different friends). | **join** | **expand, widen** ◇ *You need to widen your ~ of friends.*
PREP.   **in a/the ~** ◇ *Talk of religion was forbidden in the family ~.* ◇ *friends in government ~s*
PHRASES   **a ~ of acquaintances, a ~ of admirers, a ~ of friends**

3 (*BrE*) rows of seats in a theatre/theater
ADJ.   **dress, upper** ◇ *My seat is in the front row of the dress ~.*

circle verb

1 move in a circle
ADV.   **slowly** ◇ *The helicopter was circling slowly, very low.* | **overhead** ◇ *A buzzard was circling overhead.*
PREP.   **above** ◇ *Several planes were circling above the airport.* | **around, round** (*esp. BrE*) ◇ *The vultures were already circling around the dead animal.*

2 draw a circle around sth
PHRASES   **~ sth in black, red, etc.** ◇ *She ~d her birthday in red on the calendar.*

circuit noun

1 path for an electric current
ADJ.   **short** ◇ *The lights were not working because of a short ~.* | **closed** | **integrated, printed** | **electrical, electronic**
VERB + CIRCUIT   **build** | **break** | **complete** | **overload**
CIRCUIT + NOUN   **diagram**

2 places visited by sb in a particular job, sport, etc.
ADJ.   **amateur, professional** ◇ *Talent scouts spotted him playing on the amateur ~.* | **international, world** | **cabaret, comedy, festival, lecture, talk-show** (*AmE*), **tennis, etc.**
VERB + CIRCUIT   **hit, play, tour, travel, work** (*all esp. AmE*) ◇ *Young's film has hit the festival ~ in the US.* ◇ *Now he will be free to tour the talk-show ~.*
PREP.   **on a/the ~** ◇ *She's a well-known figure on the international lecture ~.*

3 movement around sth
ADJ.   **complete**
VERB + CIRCUIT   **do, make** ◇ *We did a complete ~ of the park in twenty minutes.*
PREP.   **~ of**

circular adj.

VERBS   **be, look**
ADV.   **perfectly** ◇ *He had round unblinking eyes and a perfectly ~ head.* | **almost, nearly, roughly** ◇ *The crater was two miles across and roughly ~.*

circulate verb

1 liquid/gas/air
ADV.   **freely** ◇ *Air can ~ freely through the tunnels.*
PREP.   **around, round** (*esp. BrE*) ◇ *The heart ~s blood around the body.* | **in** ◇ *sugar circulating in the bloodstream* | **through** ◇ *Blood ~s through the arteries and veins.*

2 story, idea, information, etc.
ADV.   **widely** ◇ *The book was ~d widely in Russia.* | **freely**
PREP.   **among** ◇ *newspapers circulating among minority communities* | **around, round** (*esp. BrE*) ◇ *There's a story circulating around the office that you are about to leave.* | **to** ◇ *The document will be ~d to all members.*

circulation noun

1 movement of blood around the body
ADJ.   **good** | **bad, poor** | **blood**
VERB + CIRCULATION   **have** ◇ *I have poor ~.* | **improve, increase, promote, stimulate** ◇ *to have a massage to stimulate your ~* | **impair, reduce**
PHRASES   **the ~ of the blood**

2 passing of sth between different people
ADJ.   **general, wide** | **restricted** ◇ *Restricted ~ of the report will reduce the risk of leaks outside the ministry.*
VERB + CIRCULATION   **go into** ◇ *The new coins will go into general ~ next year.* | **put sth into** | **take sth out of, withdraw sth from** ◇ *Copies of the magazine were withdrawn from ~.*
PREP.   **in ~, out of ~** ◇ *the amount of money in ~* ◇ *I was out of ~ for months after the baby was born.* (*figurative*)

3 of a newspaper, magazine, etc.
ADJ.   **large, mass, wide** | **limited, small** | **daily, monthly** | **national, nationwide**
VERB + CIRCULATION   **enjoy, have** ◇ *The newspaper has a daily ~ of 20 000.* | **boost, increase** | **lose**
CIRCULATION + VERB   **increase, rise** | **fall**
CIRCULATION + NOUN   **figures** | **area**
PREP.   **~ of**

circumference noun

VERB + CIRCUMFERENCE   **have** | **calculate, measure** ◇ *to measure the ~ of a circle*
PREP.   **in ~** ◇ *an area three miles in ~* | **~ of** ◇ *the ~ of a circle*

circumstance noun

1 (usually **circumstances**) facts/events that affect sth
ADJ.   **favourable/favorable** ◇ *The plan might work better with more favourable/favorable ~s.* | **adverse, difficult, dire, tragic, trying, unfavourable/unfavorable** ◇ *people facing adverse ~s* ◇ *He died in tragic ~s.* | **normal, ordinary** ◇ *In normal ~s I would let you use my car, but today I need it.* | **exceptional, extraordinary, extreme, special, unusual** ◇ *Only if the ~s are exceptional will we accept late applications.* | **mysterious, suspicious** ◇ *She died in rather suspicious ~s.* | **extenuating, mitigating** ◇ *His sentence was reduced because of the extenuating ~s.* | **changed, changing, different** | **unavoidable, unforeseen** | **economic, financial, historical, political, social** ◇ *life in the changing economic ~s of China* | **certain, particular, specific** | **current, present** | **right** | **life** (*esp. AmE*)
... OF CIRCUMSTANCES   **set** ◇ *an unfortunate set of ~s that made her life difficult*
CIRCUMSTANCE + VERB   **change** | **conspire** ◇ *I felt that ~s were conspiring against me.* | **force** | **dictate sth, require sth, warrant sth** ◇ *Circumstances dictate that I should leave this town forever.* | **allow**
PREP.   **according to ~** ◇ *The amount paid will vary according to ~s.* | **due to...~s** ◇ *Due to unforeseen ~s, we have had to reschedule the concert.* | **in...~s** ◇ *She died in suspicious ~s.* | **in the ~s, under the ~s** ◇ *In the ~s, you'd better call the police.* | **~ surrounding** ◇ *The bank will investigate the ~s surrounding the robbery.*
PHRASES   **by force of ~** ◇ *The survivors ate plants and insects by force of ~.* | **~s beyond our control** ◇ *The delays were due to ~s beyond our control.* | **the ~s of sb's life** ◇ *the tragic ~s of his early life* | **a combination of ~s** ◇ *We lost our position in the market due to a combination of ~s.* | **in no ~s, under no ~s** ◇ *Under no ~s should you leave the door unlocked.* | **a victim of ~** ◇ *He was simply a victim of ~.*

2 circumstances amount of money you have
ADJ.   **desperate, modest, reduced, straitened** (*formal*) | **comfortable** | **better** | **domestic, family, personal**
CIRCUMSTANCES + VERB   **improve** | **worsen**
PREP.   **in...~** ◇ *He was a writer living in straitened ~s.*

cite verb

ADV.   **above, already, earlier, here, previously** ◇ *This is similar to the example ~d above.* | **commonly, frequently, often, repeatedly** ◇ *The most commonly ~d reasons for stopping the treatment were side effects.* | **widely** | **approvingly** (*AmE*) | **specifically**
PREP.   **as** ◇ *He ~d the fall in unemployment as one of the government's successes.*

citizen *noun*

ADJ. **full** ◇ *They are fighting for acceptance as full ~s of the country.* | **naturalized** | **British, Thai, US, etc.** | **decent, good, honest, law-abiding, model** (*esp. AmE*), **respectable, responsible, solid, upright, upstanding** ◇ *This terrible crime has shocked all law-abiding ~s.* | **concerned** | **leading, prominent** ◇ *She is a prominent ~ of the town.* | **average, ordinary** ◇ *It's not clear how the new law will affect the ordinary ~.* | **innocent** | **armed** (*esp. AmE*) | **second-class** ◇ *Gay people have had enough of being treated as second-class ~s.* | **private** ◇ *lawsuits brought against private ~s* | **senior** ◇ *discounts for senior ~s* | **productive** (*esp. AmE*)
PHRASES **sb's fellow ~s**

citizenship *noun*

ADJ. **full** | **dual** | **birthright** (*AmE*) | **British, Chinese, US, etc.**
VERB + CITIZENSHIP **have, hold** ◇ *He has German ~.* | **confer, give sb, grant sb** ◇ *They were granted full French ~.* | **acquire, get, obtain, receive, take** ◇ *Ten years later, she chose to take Australian ~.* | **deny sb, refuse sb** | **be stripped of, lose** ◇ *He was stripped of his ~ when he criticized the government.* | **revoke** | **give up, renounce** ◇ *You will have to renounce ~ of this country if you apply to be a citizen of another.* | **apply for** | **claim**

city *noun*

ADJ. **big, huge, large, sprawling** | **main, major** | **small** | **great** ◇ *Bangkok is one of the great cities of the world.* | **bustling, busy, crowded** | **ancient, historic, old** | **holy** | **beautiful** | **industrial** | **cosmopolitan** | **coastal** | **home, native** ◇ *Her native ~ is Tokyo.* | **capital** | **second** | **provincial** | **cathedral** (*esp. BrE*), **port** (*esp. AmE*), **university** (*esp. BrE*) | **walled** ◇ *the old walled ~ of Cartagena* | **ruined** | **sister** (*AmE*), **twin** (*BrE*) ◇ *Bonn is Oxford's twin ~.* ◇ *the sister cities of Los Alamos, New Mexico, and Hiroshima, Japan* | **host** ◇ *the host ~ for the Olympic Games* | **lost** ◇ *the lost ~ of Atlantis*
VERB + CITY **build, found**
CITY + VERB **grow** ◇ *The ~ grew rapidly in the 19th century.* | **flourish**
CITY + NOUN **dweller, slicker** (*informal*) | **boy, girl** | **block** (*AmE*), **centre/center** (*esp. BrE*), **street** ◇ *The building runs the length of a ~ block.* ◇ *Parking is difficult in the ~ centre/center.* | **lights** | **council, government** (*AmE*) | **life** | **limits** (*esp. AmE*)
PREP. **in a/the ~** ◇ *We live in a big ~.* | **outside a/the ~** ◇ *There's a park just outside the ~.*
PHRASES **the centre/center of a ~, the heart of a ~, the middle of a ~** | **the edge of a ~, the outskirts of a ~**

civil *adj.*

VERBS **be, remain** | **become**
ADV. **extremely, fairly, very, etc.** | **remarkably** | **perfectly**
PREP. **to** ◇ *The teachers were all perfectly ~ to me.*

civilian *noun*

ADJ. **innocent, unarmed** ◇ *We demand an end to the killing of innocent ~s.* | **ordinary** | **local**
VERB + CIVILIAN **attack, kill, target**

civilization (*BrE also* **-isation**) *noun*

ADJ. **ancient, early, old** ◇ *the early ~s of Asia* | **modern, new** ◇ *the benefits of modern ~* | **advanced** | **primitive** | **Greek, Roman, etc.** | **Christian, European, Islamic, Western, etc.** ◇ *diseases that are common in Western ~* | **great** ◇ *the great ~s of the past* | **industrial** | **human** ◇ *Art and music are among the great products of human ~.* | **lost**
VERB + CIVILIZATION **bring** ◇ *to bring ~ to the outer reaches of the country* | **build, create** ◇ *a movement that aims to create a new ~* | **destroy** | **threaten** | **save**
CIVILIZATION + VERB **collapse** | **flourish**
PHRASES **the beginnings of ~, the dawn of ~** | **~ as we know it** ◇ *Could this be the end of ~ as we know it?* | **the collapse**

of a ~, the decline of a ~, the end of a ~ | **a level of ~** ◇ *to reach a higher level of ~*

clad *adj.*

VERBS **be**
ADV. **fully** ◇ *He returned fully ~.* | **partially, scantily** ◇ *a scantily ~ young woman*
PREP. **in** ◇ *Ed, ~ in his best suit, was waiting for her.*

claim *noun*

1 statement saying that sth is true

ADJ. **dubious, false, unfounded, unsubstantiated** | **conflicting** ◇ *There are conflicting ~s about the cause of the fire.* | **absurd, astonishing, bold, exaggerated, extraordinary, extravagant, grandiose, outrageous, ridiculous** | **central** ◇ *the central ~ of the book* | **health** (= a claim that a product has health benefits) (*AmE*)
VERB + CLAIM **make** ◇ *The company had made false ~s about its products.* ◇ *I make no ~ to understand modern art.* | **hear** ◇ *We have heard ~s like this many times before.* | **accept, believe** ◇ *They accepted her ~ that she had been ill-treated.* | **challenge** | **deny, dismiss, dispute, refute, reject** ◇ *Claims of a cover-up were dismissed.* | **debunk, disprove** | **back up, bolster, substantiate, support** ◇ *They were able to produce witnesses to support their ~.* | **prove, validate, verify** | **evaluate, investigate**
CLAIM + VERB **be true, stand up**
PREP. **~ about** ◇ *to investigate ~s about appalling prison conditions* | **~ of** ◇ *Claims of corruption within the police force were denied.*
PHRASES **base a ~ on sth**

2 demand for sth

ADJ. **large, small** | **excessive** ◇ *excessive wage ~s* | **legal, legitimate** | **bogus, fraudulent** ◇ *The police are investigating fraudulent ~s for fire damage.* | **accident, compensation, damage** (*esp. AmE*), **damages** (*BrE*), **insurance, medical** (*esp. AmE*), **pay, wage** (*esp. BrE*) | **discrimination, harassment, malpractice** (*esp. AmE*) | **civil** ◇ *to file a civil ~ for damages*
VERB + CLAIM **bring, file, lodge, make, put forward, put in, submit** ◇ *She brought a ~ for damages against the company.* | **drop, waive, withdraw** | **investigate** | **review** | **allow, uphold** ◇ *His ~ for compensation was upheld in court.* | **dismiss** | **win, meet, pay, settle** ◇ *We will need extra funds to meet all the insurance ~s.*
CLAIM + VERB **arise** ◇ *~s arising out of accidents at work* | **fail** ◇ *The ~ failed because the company had not been misled.*
CLAIM + NOUN **form** | **~s adjuster** (= sb whose job is to settle claims against an insurance company) (*AmE*) | **~s payment**
PREP. **~ against** ◇ *~s against the company for breach of contract* | **~ for** ◇ *a ~ for compensation* | **~ on** ◇ *to make a ~ on your insurance policy* ◇ *I have many ~s on my time.*

3 right to have sth

ADJ. **good, strong** | **competing, rival** ◇ *competing ~s for public money* | **prior** ◇ *She had a prior ~ on his affections.* | **moral** | **land, territorial**
VERB + CLAIM **have** ◇ *He has a good ~ to the land.* | **assert, lay, press, stake** ◇ *Four men laid ~ to leadership of the country.* ◇ *to stake a ~ to some of the prize money* | **establish, prove** ◇ *You will have to prove your ~ to the property in a court of law.* | **forfeit, relinquish, renounce, withdraw**
PREP. **~ on** ◇ *His children have a ~ on his estate.* | **~ to** ◇ *She renounced her ~ to the property.*

claim *verb*

1 say that sth is true

ADV. **justifiably, legitimately, rightfully, rightly** | **falsely, wrongly** ◇ *The company had falsely ~ed that its products were biodegradable.* | **plausibly** | **frequently, repeatedly** | **publicly**
VERB + CLAIM **attempt to, try to** ◇ *He tried to ~ that he had acted in self-defence.*

2 ask for sth you think you have a right to have

ADV. **back** ◇ *You can ~ back some of the cost of your treatment.*

VERB + CLAIM **be able to, be entitled to, can** ◇ *You might be entitled to* ~ *compensation if you are injured at work.* | **attempt to, try to**
PREP. **on** ◇ *Can't you* ~ *on your insurance?*

clamour (*BrE*) (*AmE* clamor) *noun*

ADJ. **noisy** | **growing** | **public** | **sudden**
VERB + CLAMOUR/CLAMOR **hear** | **create, make, raise**
CLAMOUR/CLAMOR + VERB **arise**
PREP. **above the** ~, **amid the** ~ ◇ *She could barely make herself heard above the* ~ *of the rain.* | ~ **for** ◇ *The* ~ *for her resignation grew louder.* | ~ **of** ◇ *Her head was filled with the* ~ *of voices calling her name.*

clamp *verb*

ADV. **firmly, tight, tightly** | **together** ◇ *Clamp the pieces of wood together while the glue sets.* | **in place** ◇ *Parts are* ~*ed in place with a special machine.*
PREP. **around, round** (*esp. BrE*) ◇ *She* ~*ed her arms around him.* | **on, onto** ◇ *He* ~*ed his hand firmly onto Jack's shoulder.* | **over** ◇ *A large hand* ~*ed over her mouth.* | **to** ◇ *The dog's jaws were* ~*ed to my leg.*
PHRASES ~**ed between your teeth** ◇ *He had a large cigar* ~*ed between his teeth.* | ~ **shut** ◇ *His mouth* ~*ed shut.*

PHR V **clamp down**
ADV. **hard**
PREP. **on** ◇ *to* ~ *down hard on bullying*

clang *noun*

ADJ. **loud** | **metallic**
VERB + CLANG **give, let out, make** | **hear**
PREP. **with a** ~ ◇ *The door shut with a loud* ~. | ~ **of**
PHRASES **the** ~ **of metal**
→ Note at SOUND

clank *noun*

ADJ. **loud**
PREP. **with a** ~ ◇ *The door opened with a* ~. | ~ **of** ◇ *the* ~ *and rattle of the trams*
PHRASES **the** ~ **of machinery**

clap *noun*

ADJ. **big** | **slow**
VERB + CLAP **get** | **give sb**
PREP. ~ **for** ◇ *A big* ~ *for our last contestant!*
PHRASES **a** ~ **of sb's hands** ◇ *With a* ~ *of his hands he ordered more food.*

clap *verb*

ADV. **enthusiastically, excitedly, loudly, wildly** ◇ *The audience clapped enthusiastically.* | **happily** | **politely** | **slowly**
PHRASES ~ **and cheer**

clarification *noun*

ADJ. **further**
VERB + CLARIFICATION **ask for, call for, seek** ◇ *Employers are seeking further* ~ *of the proposals.* | **need, require, want** | **request** | **give sb, offer sb, provide sb with** | **get** | **make**
PREP. ~ **of**

clarify *verb*

ADV. **fully** | **exactly** | **further** ◇ *Headings and sub-headings further* ~ *the structure of the article.*
VERB + CLARIFY **attempt to, seek to, try to** | **need to** | **help (to), serve to** | **should** | **be delighted to, be happy to, be pleased to** ◇ *I am happy to* ~ *any points that are still unclear.*

clarity *noun*

ADJ. **absolute, complete, perfect** | **admirable, crystal, exceptional, great** | **increasing** | **sufficient** | **chilling, painful, startling, terrible** ◇ *With painful* ~ *she remembered the day he had died.*

VERB + CLARITY **have** | **lack** | **lose** | **add, bring, give, offer, provide** | **enhance, improve, increase** | **achieve, gain**
PREP. **with** ~ ◇ *She expressed herself with great* ~. | ~ **of** ◇ ~ *of thought*
PHRASES **for the sake of** ~ ◇ *For the sake of* ~ *she went back over the key points.*

clash *noun*

ADJ. **angry, bitter, fierce, serious** | **armed, bloody, deadly, violent** | **head-on** ◇ *The leaders are preparing for a head-on* ~ *at the summit.* | **culture, personality**
VERB + CLASH **lead to, provoke** | **avoid**
CLASH + VERB **break out, erupt, occur**
PREP. **in a/the** ~ ◇ *Several people were injured in violent* ~*es with the police.* | ~ **between** ◇ *Clashes between the rebels and government forces have broken out in the north.* | ~ **of** ◇ *a* ~ *of opinions* | ~ **over** ◇ *Differences in the aims of the two unions have led to serious* ~*es over policy.* | ~ **with**
PHRASES **a** ~ **of cultures, a** ~ **of interests, a** ~ **of wills**

clash *verb*

ADV. **violently** | **frequently, repeatedly**
PREP. **on, over** ◇ *He has* ~*ed repeatedly with the team coach over training schedules.* | **with** ◇ *They often* ~ *violently with rival gangs.*

clasp *verb*

ADV. **firmly, tightly** ◇ *She* ~*ed her bag tightly as she walked through the crowd.* | **gently, lightly, loosely** | **together** ◇ *She faced Will, her hands* ~*ed together.*

class *noun*

1 lesson/group of students

ADJ. **big, large** | **small** | **advanced, beginners'** (*BrE*), **beginning** (*AmE*), **elementary, intermediate, introductory, remedial** | **master** (usually *masterclass*) | **biology, history, etc.** | **acting, creative-writing, dance** (*AmE*), **dancing** (*BrE*), **etc.** | **evening, night** (*esp. AmE*) | **college, high-school, kindergarten, undergraduate** (*all AmE*) | **entering, in-coming** (= the students starting a school or college in a particular year) (*both AmE*)
VERB + CLASS **attend, go to, take** ◇ *He's taking* ~*es in pottery.* | **enrol/enroll in, sign up for** | **cut** (*AmE*), **miss, skip** (*AmE*) | **disrupt, interrupt** | **hold** ◇ *The institute holds evening* ~*es throughout the year.* | **offer** ◇ *The college offers* ~*es in many subjects.* | **conduct, give, lead** (*AmE*), **run** (*esp. AmE*), **take, teach** ◇ *Who's taking the* ~ *today?* | **address** | **dismiss** ◇ *Class dismissed!* | **fail, flunk** (*both AmE*) | **pass** (*AmE*) | **ace** (*AmE, informal*) | **drop** | **cover** | **observe, sit in on**
CLASS + VERB **be easy, be hard** | **be available** | **graduate** (*AmE*)
CLASS + NOUN **member, teacher** | **size** | **discussion** | **work** | **reunion** | **schedule** (*AmE*) | **period** (*AmE*)
PREP. **in (a/the)** ~ ◇ *We'll start the exercise in* ~. ◇ *Which history* ~ *are you in?* | ~ **in** ◇ *She's going to evening* ~*es in Italian.*
PHRASES **the back of the** ~, **the front of the** ~ ◇ *He sat at the back of the* ~. | **be top of the** ~, **come top of the** ~ ◇ *She came top of the* ~ *in English.* | **the** ~ **of ...** (= a group of students who finish their studies in a particular year) ◇ *the* ~ *of 2008* | **the entire** ~, **the whole** ~

2 social/economic group

ADJ. **leisure** (= rich people), **lower, lower-middle, middle, upper, upper-middle, working** ◇ *sections of the working* ~ | **chattering** (*BrE*), **educated, elite, governing, political, privileged, professional, ruling, wealthy** ◇ *topics being discussed at the breakfast tables of the chattering* ~*es* | **capitalist, entrepreneurial, merchant** | **labouring/labor-ing, peasant** | **landed, landowning** | **dominant** | **social, socio-economic** ◇ *Membership of the club is drawn from all social* ~*es.*
CLASS + NOUN **structure, system** | **consciousness** | **interests** |

conflict, differences, divisions, struggle, war, warfare | issue

3 group of things

ADJ. **large, small** | **distinct** | **special** | **rare** | **age, weight** VERB + CLASS **constitute, form** ◊ *These writers form a distinct ~ in Russian literature.* PREP. **~ of** ◊ *a rare ~ of neurological diseases* PHRASES **be in a ~ of your own, be in a different ~** (= to be much better than others)

4 high quality/style

ADJ. **great, real** ◊ *a player of great ~* VERB + CLASS **have** ◊ *She has real ~.* PHRASES **a touch of ~** ◊ *The musical entertainment added a touch of ~ to the occasion.*

classic noun

1 famous book, play, etc.

ADJ. **great, true** | **minor** | **contemporary, modern** | **old** | **all-time** | **timeless** ◊ *Charles Dickens's timeless ~, 'Oliver Twist'* | **cult, popular** | **instant** ◊ *The song became an instant ~ and shot to number one.* | **film, literary, movie** (*esp. AmE*) | **comedy, horror, sci-fi, etc.** | **pop, rock, etc.** VERB + CLASSIC **be, become, remain** PHRASES **be considered a ~** PREP. **~ of** ◊ *one of the great ~s of English literature*

2 Classics study of Greek/Roman culture

→ Note at SUBJECT

classification noun

ADJ. **broad, general** | **detailed** | **simple** | **higher, lower** ◊ *The rooms are of the standard expected from a hotel in a higher ~.* | **arbitrary** | **racial, social** | **job** | **security** ◊ *a document with the security ~ 'confidential'* VERB + CLASSIFICATION **defy** ◊ *a style of dancing that defies ~* | **make** | **develop, propose** CLASSIFICATION + NOUN **scheme** (*BrE*), **system** | **error** PREP. **~ into** ◊ *the broad ~ of music into classical and pop* PHRASES **a system of ~**

clatter noun

ADJ. **loud, noisy** | **metallic** | **sudden** VERB + CLATTER **make** ◊ *The wheels of the cart made a terrible ~ on the road.* | **hear** PREP. **with a ~** ◊ *She dropped her fork with a ~.* | **~ of** ◊ *There was a ~ of hoofs and several riders drew up.*

clatter verb

ADV. **loudly, noisily** PREP. **against** ◊ *The mug ~ed against her teeth.* | **down** ◊ *Something heavy came ~ing down the stairs.* | **on** ◊ *His boots ~ed on the stairs.* | **to** ◊ *The knife ~ed noisily to the floor.* PHRASES **come ~ing, go ~ing**

clause noun

1 in a legal document

ADJ. **confidentiality, indemnity, penalty** ◊ *The penalty ~ specifies that late delivery will be fined.* | **escape, exclusion, exemption, get-out, let-out, opt-out** | **grandfather** (= allowing an old rule to continue to apply in some situations) (*AmE*), **sunset** (= ending a law after a particular date) VERB + CLAUSE **contain, have** ◊ *The contract contains a confidentiality ~.* | **add, include, insert, put in** ◊ *We added an opt-out ~ to the agreement.* | **delete, take out** | **amend** | **violate** (*esp. AmE*) | **invoke** PREP. **in a/the ~** ◊ *There is some ambiguity in this ~.* | **under a/the ~** ◊ *Under Clause 5.8, the company is responsible for the health of its employees.* | **~ on** ◊ *a ~ on pollution*

2 in grammar

ADJ. **main, subordinate** | **conditional, dependent, finite,** independent, infinitive, non-finite, relative | non-restrictive, restrictive ◊ *a restrictive relative ~* | **adverbial, nominal, noun** PREP. **in a/the ~** ◊ *The completed action is in the main ~.*

claustrophobia noun

VERB + CLAUSTROPHOBIA **get, suffer from** | **give sb** ◊ *I hate elevators—they give me ~.* PHRASES **a feeling of ~**

claustrophobic adj.

VERBS **be, feel, seem** ◊ *I felt a little ~ in the tiny room.* | **become, get** | **make sb** ◊ *Crowds make me ~.* | **find sth** ◊ *I find that building intensely ~.* ADV. **extremely, fairly, very, etc.** ◊ *The atmosphere was somewhat ~.* | **intensely** | **a little, slightly, etc.**

claw noun

ADJ. **razor-sharp, sharp** ◊ *a cat with sharp ~s* | **curved** | **large, long** | **powerful, strong** | **retractable** VERB + CLAW **sharpen** | **dig, sink** ◊ *The tiger dug its ~s into his leg.* | **bare, show** ◊ *The lion growled and showed its ~s.* | **extend, flex** | **retract** CLAW + VERB **dig into sth** | **rake** CLAW + NOUN **mark** PREP. **in sb's ~s** ◊ *The cat held a bird in its ~s.*

clay noun

ADJ. **heavy** | **fine** | **soft** | **damp, sticky, wet** | **china** (*esp. BrE*), **modelling/modeling** ... OF CLAY **lump** VERB + CLAY **mould/mold, shape** ◊ *She moulded/molded the ~ into the shape of a head.* | **bake, fire** | **be made from/in/of/out of, make sth from/in/out of, mould/mold sth from/in/out of** ◊ *a figure made of ~* | **roll, roll out** CLAY + NOUN **modelling/modeling** | **mould/mold** PREP. **in ~** ◊ *plants that grow in damp ~*

clean verb

ADV. **effectively, well** ◊ *This product ~s baths very effectively.* | **easily** ◊ *Ceramic tiles can be easily ~ed.* | **properly, thoroughly** ◊ *I ~ the house thoroughly once a week.* | **carefully, gently** ◊ *He gently ~ed the wound and dressed it.* | **out, up** ◊ *I ~ed out all the cupboards.* PREP. **away** ◊ *She wiped her foot to ~ away the blood.* | **from, off** ◊ *I ~ed the mud off the kitchen floor.* | **with** ◊ *Clean the glass with a soft cloth.* PHRASES **freshly ~ed** ◊ *The freshly ~ed windows sparkled.* | **need ~ing** ◊ *Your shoes need ~ing!*

clean adj.

VERBS **be, look, seem, smell** ◊ *The room smelled ~ and fresh.* | **stay** ◊ *The bathroom doesn't stay ~ for long.* | **brush sth, get sth, scrape sth, scrub sth, wash, wipe sth** ◊ *I scrubbed the floor to get it ~.* ◊ *She wiped all the surfaces ~.* | **leave sth** ◊ *Please leave the kitchen ~.* | **keep sth** ◊ *You're supposed to keep your room ~.* ADV. **extremely, fairly, very, etc.** | **completely, perfectly, totally** | **reasonably, relatively** | **immaculately, spotlessly** ◊ *The whole house was spotlessly ~.* | **almost, nearly** ◊ *It's almost ~. I just have to wipe the table.* PHRASES **~ and tidy** (*esp. BrE*), **neat and ~** (*AmE*) ◊ *His room is always ~ and tidy/neat and ~.* | **lovely and ~** (*BrE*), **nice and ~** ◊ *The water was lovely and ~.*

cleaner noun

1 person who cleans

ADJ. **hospital, house** (*AmE*), **office, school** (*BrE*), **street** | **window** | **professional** → Note at JOB

2 substance/instrument used for cleaning

ADJ. **bathroom, carpet, drain, floor, glass, household, oven, toilet** ◊ *chemicals that are found in all household ~s* | **all-purpose**

cleanliness *noun*

ADJ. **excessive** | **personal** ◇ *His mother gave him a lecture about personal ~.*
PHRASES **a standard of ~, a state of ~** ◇ *The bathroom was in a good state of ~.*

cleanse *verb*

ADV. **thoroughly** | **gently**
PREP. **of** ◇ *a treatment to ~ the body of toxins*

clear *verb*

1 remove sth that is not wanted/needed

ADV. **completely, totally** ◇ *The site must be completely ~ed and made safe for children.* | **partially** | **hastily, quickly** ◇ *She hastily ~ed a space for him to sit down.* | **away** ◇ *Can you ~ away all your toys now?* | **up** ◇ *I want you to ~ all this mess up.*
PREP. **from** ◇ *They ~ed the mud from the steps.* | **of** ◇ *We ~ed the path of leaves.* | **off** ◇ *Clear those papers off the desk.*

2 your head/mind

ADV. **suddenly** ◇ *His face suddenly ~ed as understanding dawned.*
VERB + CLEAR **try to** ◇ *I went for a walk to try to ~ my head.* | **help (to)** ◇ *Correct breathing helps to ~ the mind and reduce tension.*

3 prove sb innocent

ADV. **formally** ◇ *The three defendants were formally ~ed by the judge.*
PREP. **of** ◇ *Four men accused of assault have been ~ed of all charges.*

clear *adj.*

1 easy to understand

VERBS **be, seem** | **become** | **get sth, make sth** | **find sth**
ADV. **extremely, fairly, very, etc.** | **abundantly** | **absolutely, crystal, perfectly, quite** ◇ *You have to make your intentions crystal ~ to them.* | **by no means, not entirely, not exactly, not quite** ◇ *It wasn't entirely ~ whether she wanted us to help.* | **reasonably, relatively** | **painfully** | **increasingly**
PREP. **to** ◇ *It was increasingly ~ to us that there was a problem.*
PHRASES **~ and concise**

2 sure/certain

VERBS **be**
ADV. **extremely, fairly, very, etc.** | **absolutely, quite**
PREP. **about** ◇ *She was very ~ about her reasons for leaving.* | **on** ◇ *Are you ~ on that point?*

3 easy to see/hear

VERBS **be, look** | **become, grow**
ADV. **extremely, fairly, very, etc.** ◇ *The photograph wasn't very ~.* | **reasonably**
PHRASES **loud and ~**

4 easy to see through

VERBS **be** | **become**
ADV. **extremely, fairly, very, etc.** ◇ *The water was fairly ~.* | **absolutely, completely** | **reasonably**

5 free from things that are blocking the way

VERBS **be, look, seem** | **remain, stay** | **keep sth** ◇ *Make sure you keep all gutters and drainpipes ~ of leaves.*
ADV. **completely** | **fairly, pretty, reasonably**
PREP. **of** ◇ *The roads are reasonably ~ of snow.*

clearance *noun*

1 removal of sth old/unwanted

ADJ. **forest, land, site, slum**
CLEARANCE + NOUN **work** | **sale** (= when goods are sold cheaply to get rid of them quickly) | **rack** (= in a clearance sale) (*AmE*)
PREP. **on ~** (= reduced in price) ◇ *These coats are on ~.*

2 official permission

ADJ. **official, proper** | **top-secret** | **customs, diplomatic, entry, medical, security** | **take-off**

VERB + CLEARANCE **get, obtain, receive** ◇ *You'll need to get security ~ for this job.* | **have** | **apply for, request, seek** | **await** | **give sb, grant sb** ◇ *The pilot was granted ~ to land.* | **refuse sb**

3 distance between sth and sth passing under/beside it

ADJ. **ground** ◇ *We need to increase the vehicle's ground ~.*
VERB + CLEARANCE **allow (sb/sth), give sb/sth, leave** ◇ *Make sure you allow enough ~ on each side.* ◇ *Always give bikes plenty of ~.*
PREP. **~ above** ◇ *~ above the light to prevent overheating* | **~ between** ◇ *There wasn't enough ~ between the bus and the top of the bridge.*

clench *verb*

ADV. **firmly, tight, tightly** ◇ *His jaw was ~ed tight.* ◇ *His jaw was tightly ~ed.* | **involuntarily, unconsciously** ◇ *Her hands ~ed involuntarily.* | **together** ◇ *She sat with hands ~ed together in her lap.*
PHRASES **~ed between sb's teeth** ◇ *He had a pipe ~ed between his teeth.*

clerk *noun*

1 person working in an office

ADJ. **chief, senior** | **assistant, junior** | **articled** (*BrE*), **law** (*AmE*) | **bank, city** (*AmE*), **council** (*BrE*), **county** (*AmE*), **court, office, parish** (*BrE*), **solicitor's** (*BrE*), **town** (*esp. AmE*) | **accounting** (*AmE*), **accounts** (*BrE*), **booking** (*BrE*), **file** (*AmE*), **filing** (*BrE*), **supply** (*AmE*) ◇ *He started work as a railway booking ~.* | **mail** (*AmE*), **postal** (*AmE*), **post office**
PREP. **~ to** ◇ *a former ~ to Chief Justice George P. Willison*
PHRASES **the office of ~, the post of ~**

2 (*AmE*) **person working in a shop/store or hotel**

ADJ. **bookstore, grocery, sales, store** | **desk, hotel, motel**
→ Note at JOB

clever *adj.*

1 (*esp. BrE*) **having intelligence; having skill or ability**

VERBS **be, seem, sound**
ADV. **extremely, fairly, very, etc.** | **extraordinarily, incredibly**
PREP. **at** ◇ *I became quite ~ at making tasty meals out of nothing.* | **with** ◇ *~ with his hands*
PHRASES **too ~ by half** ◇ *Bob irritates me—he's too ~ by half!* | **too ~ for your own good**

2 (of a thing) **ingenious**

VERBS **be**
ADV. **extremely, fairly, very, etc.** | **fiendishly** (*esp. BrE*) ◇ *a simple yet fiendishly ~ idea*

cliché (also **cliche**) *noun*

ADJ. **old, tired, usual, well-worn, worn-out** | **popular** ◇ *a popular ~ about Californians* | **media, sports, etc.** | **film** (*esp. BrE*), **movie** (*esp. AmE*)
VERB + CLICHÉ **spout, use** ◇ *Try to avoid using ~s in your writing.* | **avoid**
PREP. **~ about**

click *noun*

ADJ. **loud, sharp** | **audible** | **faint, little, quiet, small, soft** | **metallic** | **double, left, right, single** (used about clicks on a computer mouse) ◇ *a double ~ on the filename* | **mouse**
VERB + CLICK **give, give out, make** ◇ *The answering machine gave a sharp ~.* | **hear**
PREP. **with a ~** ◇ *He closed his briefcase with a ~.* | **~ of** ◇ *She heard the ~ of shoes on the marble floor.*

client *noun*

ADJ. **big, important, large, major** ◇ *The company needs to focus on its biggest ~s.* | **new** | **potential, prospective** | **current, established, existing, regular** | **former, old** |

business, corporate | private | individual | wealthy | celebrity
VERB + CLIENT **advise, assist, help, serve, service** (*AmE*) ◊ *A new branch has been opened to serve ~s in Dallas.* | **have** | **find, get** | **act for, represent** | **take on** ◊ *She's so busy that she's not taking on any new ~s.* | **attract** ◊ *a campaign to attract new ~s*
PREP. **on behalf of ~** ◊ *On behalf of my ~, I would like to remind you of your obligations in this matter.*

clientele *noun*

ADJ. **large, narrow, small** | **broad, diverse** | **loyal** | **regular, usual** | **exclusive, fashionable, select, upscale** (*AmE*) | **international**
VERB + CLIENTELE **attract, have** ◊ *The restaurant has a large regular ~.* | **cater for, cater to, serve** ◊ *The boutique caters for a rather select ~.* | **build** (*esp. AmE*), **build up** (*esp. BrE*), **develop, establish** ◊ *It takes time to build (up) a ~.*

cliff *noun*

ADJ. **high, towering** | **low** | **dramatic, precipitous, sheer, steep, vertical** | **craggy, jagged, rocky, rugged** | **chalk, limestone, etc.** | **coastal, mountain, sea**
... OF CLIFFS **line** ◊ *a long line of ~s surrounding the bay*
VERB + CLIFF **climb, scale** | **descend** | **jump off**
CLIFF + VERB **fall, fall away, rise, rise up** ◊ *The ~s fall away to the north.* ◊ *Rugged sandstone ~s rose up from the beach.* | **overlook sth, tower** ◊ *Steep ~s towered above the river.* | **crumble** ◊ *crumbling ~s*
CLIFF + NOUN **edge, face, ledge, side, top, wall** | **path, walk**
PHRASES **be perched on a ~** ◊ *The hotel was perched high on a ~ overlooking the ocean.* | **the base of the ~, the bottom of the ~, the foot of the ~** | **the edge of the ~** | **the top of the ~**

climate *noun*

1 weather conditions of a particular region

ADJ. **hot, warm** | **cold, cool** | **mild** | **extreme, harsh, inhospitable, severe** ◊ *the severe northern ~* | **damp, humid, wet** | **arid, dry** | **desert, equatorial, Mediterranean, subtropical, temperate, tropical** | **northern, southern, etc.** | **global** ◊ *global ~ change*
VERB + CLIMATE **have** ◊ *The city has a warm ~.* | **affect**
CLIMATE + NOUN **change** | **research, study** | **conditions, patterns**
PREP. **in a/the ~** ◊ *Little grows in such a dry ~.*

2 opinions, etc. people have at a particular time

ADJ. **favourable/favorable** | **hostile, unfavourable/unfavorable** | **current, present, prevailing** ◊ *a set of ideas that challenge the prevailing ~ of pessimism* | **changed, changing** | **business, cultural, economic, emotional, financial, ideological, intellectual, investment, moral, political, social**
VERB + CLIMATE **create, foster** | **change** | **improve**
PREP. **in a/the ~** ◊ *His ideas on equality are viewed as utopian in the current political ~.* | **~ for** ◊ *a ~ for economic recovery* | **~ of** ◊ *The new policies have created a ~ of fear.*
PHRASES **a ~ of opinion**

climax *noun*

1 exciting/important event, point in time, etc.

ADJ. **big, dramatic, exciting, explosive, grand, great, powerful, stunning, thrilling** | **emotional** | **fitting** | **inevitable**
VERB + CLIMAX **come to, hit** (*AmE*), **reach** ◊ *The crisis reached its ~ in the 1970s.* | **approach, build to, build up to, near, work up to** ◊ *The story gradually builds to a powerful ~.* | **bring sth to** ◊ *The affair was brought to a ~ when the chairman resigned.* | **form, mark, represent** ◊ *Yesterday marked the ~ of the celebrations.*
CLIMAX + VERB **come** ◊ *The ~ came at the end of the second act of the play.*

PREP. **at the ~** ◊ *The hero dies at the ~ of the opera.* | **in a/the ~** ◊ *In a dramatic ~, our team lost by one goal.* | **~ to** ◊ *His promotion was a fitting ~ to a worthy career.*

2 highest point of sexual pleasure

ADJ. **sexual**
VERB + CLIMAX **achieve, reach** ◊ *She found it hard to achieve a/reach ~.*

climb *noun*

1 act of climbing

ADJ. **long, slow** | **short** | **arduous, difficult, hard, steep, tough** (*esp. AmE*) | **uphill** (*often figurative, esp. AmE*) ◊ *The airline faces an uphill ~ to compete with top air carriers.* | **easy** | **steady** | **final** ◊ *We rode to Pamba then made the final ~ on foot.*
VERB + CLIMB **do, make** ◊ *I was fitter the first time I did the ~.*
PREP. **on a/the ~** ◊ *I broke my ankle on a ~ last week.* | **~ from, ~ to** ◊ *the short ~ from the road to the summit* | **~ up** ◊ *They began the long ~ up the hill.*

2 increase in value/amount/status

ADJ. **long, slow** | **rapid** | **gradual, steady** | **upward** ◊ *the upward ~ of interest rates*
PREP. **~ against** ◊ *the dollar's ~ against the euro* | **~ in** ◊ *a steady ~ in the cost of travel* | **~ out of** ◊ *a long slow ~ out of recession* | **~ to** ◊ *her rapid ~ to stardom*

climb *verb*

1 move up to the top of sth

ADV. **high** ◊ *Don't ~ too high.* | **slowly** | **nimbly, quickly, rapidly, swiftly** | **carefully** | **wearily**
PREP. **up** ◊ *He ~ed slowly up the ladder.* | **onto** ◊ *Two boys ~ed onto the roof.* | **into** ◊ *He ~ed into the truck and drove off.* | **over** ◊ *I ~ed over the fence into the meadow.*
PHRASES **~ to the top** ◊ *We ~ed right to the top of the mountain.* | **go ~ing** (= for sport) ◊ *He goes ~ing every summer.*

2 move/lead upwards

ADV. **gradually, slowly** | **steadily** | **steeply** | **up**
VERB + CLIMB **begin to** ◊ *The path began to ~ quite steeply.*
PREP. **from** ◊ *The road gradually ~s up from the town.* | **to** ◊ *The plane took off and ~ed to 20 000 feet.* | **up** ◊ *The path ~s steeply up the mountainside.*

3 increase

ADV. **quickly, rapidly, sharply, steeply** ◊ *Prices have ~ed sharply in recent months.* | **steadily** | **slowly** ◊ *The vaccination rate began to ~ slowly.*
PREP. **above** ◊ *The temperature had ~ed above 90 degrees.* | **from, to** ◊ *Unemployment has ~ed from two million to three million.*

cling *verb*

1 hold tightly

ADV. **closely, firmly, tightly** ◊ *I clung closely to my mother's arm.* | **desperately, fiercely, helplessly** ◊ *She clung fiercely to him.* | **precariously** ◊ *houses ~ing precariously to sheer cliffs* | **together** ◊ *The children clung together in fear.*
PREP. **onto** ◊ *She clung onto my arm.* | **to** ◊ *He clung tightly to the raft to keep himself afloat.*

2 stay close

ADV. **close, closely** ◊ *The ground mist clung closely to the bushes.*
PREP. **to**
PHR V **cling (on) to sth**
ADV. **still** | **doggedly, rigidly, steadfastly, stubbornly, tenaciously** ◊ *He still ~s stubbornly to his socialist ideas.* | **desperately, fiercely** ◊ *She was desperately ~ing on to life.* | **barely** ◊ *He lay there, barely ~ing to consciousness.*

clinic *noun*

ADJ. **hospital** | **health, medical** | **private** | **special** (*esp. BrE*) | **specialized, specialty** (*both AmE*) | **free, public** (*both AmE*) | **outpatient, walk-in** | **local, rural** | **ambulatory** (*AmE*), mobile (*esp. AmE*) | **vet, veterinary** (*both AmE*) | **abortion, birth-control, family-planning** | **antenatal** (*BrE*), **maternity, prenatal** (*AmE*) | **fertility, infertility, IVF** | **breast, eye,** etc. | **diabetic, psychiatric,** etc. | **drug, methadone, rehab** (*informal*), **rehabilitation** | **golf, tennis,** etc.

VERB + CLINIC **attend, go to, visit** | **hold, operate, put on** (*AmE*), **run** ◊ *We operate free rural health ~s.* ◊ *Holmes put on a boxing ~* (= *gave a very good performance*) *and beat Shavers twelve out of twelve rounds.* | **staff** ◊ *The ~ is staffed by volunteers.* | **be treated at** ◊ *She is being treated at a diabetic ~.*

CLINIC + VERB **specialize in sth** | **offer, provide** | **cater for** (*BrE*), **cater to** (*AmE*), **serve** (*esp. AmE*) ◊ *HIV ~s serving inner-city populations*

CLINIC + NOUN **doctor, nurse, staff, worker** | **appointment** | **patient**

PREP. **at a/the ~** ◊ *He was treated at the hospital's eye ~.* | **in a/the ~** ◊ *She works in a birth-control ~.* | **~ for** ◊ *a ~ for asthma sufferers*

clip noun

1 used for holding things together

ADJ. **bicycle** (*BrE*), **hair, nose, paper, tie** | **belt, pocket** (*AmE*) | **bulldog** (*BrE*), **spring** | **alligator** (*esp. AmE*), **crocodile** (*esp. BrE*) | **butterfly** (*AmE*)

VERB + CLIP **attach, fasten, put, put in, put on** ◊ *She put a ~ in her hair.* | **take off, undo, unfasten**

CLIP + VERB **hold sth** ◊ *Paper ~s held the picture in place.*

2 small section from a film/movie

ADJ. **brief, short** | **film** (*esp. BrE*), **movie** (*esp. AmE*), **video** | **audio, music, sound** | **interview, news**

VERB + CLIP **see, view, watch** | **play, show** | **download**

PREP. **in a/the ~** ◊ *You will see in this ~ how well she acts.* | **~ from** ◊ *a ~ from a Sherlock Holmes movie*

3 (esp. AmE) container for bullets

ADJ. **ammo** (*informal*), **ammunition** | **empty** | **spare**

VERB + CLIP **empty** | **load, unload** | **check**

clipping noun

1 piece cut off sth

ADJ. **fingernail, nail, toenail** | **grass, hedge** (*BrE*), **lawn**

2 (esp. AmE) piece cut out from a newspaper → See also CUTTING

ADJ. **magazine, news, newspaper, press** ◊ *She had kept all the press ~s about the murder.* | **file** | **service**

PREP. **~ from** ◊ *a ~ from the 'Los Angeles Times'*

cloak noun

ADJ. **heavy, thick** | **hooded** | **black, dark,** etc. | **ragged, tattered** | **velvet, wool, woollen/woolen,** etc.

VERB + CLOAK **be wrapped in** | **drape, throw** ◊ *She threw a heavy ~ over her shoulders.* | **draw, pull, wrap** ◊ *He pulled his ~ tightly around himself.* | **remove, throw off**

CLOAK + VERB **billow, flow, flutter, fly, sweep, swirl** ◊ *a flowing black ~* ◊ *She stormed off, her ~ flying behind her.*

→ Special page at CLOTHES

clock noun

ADJ. **accurate** | **12-hour, 24-hour** | **digital, electric** | **atomic** | **time** | **bedside, kitchen** | **alarm, carriage, cuckoo, grandfather, pendulum, travel** (*AmE*), **travelling** (*BrE*), **wall** | **ticking** | **countdown** (*AmE*) ◊ *His countdown ~ reads forty seconds.* | **biological, body, circadian** (*biology*), **internal** ◊ *With jet lag, your biological ~ is out of synch with the actual time.*

VERB + CLOCK **reset, set, wind** ◊ *I've set my alarm ~ for six tomorrow.* | **move back** (*AmE*), **put back** (*BrE*), **set back** (*AmE*), **turn back** (*often figurative*) ◊ *Let's turn back the ~ to the last decade.* | **move ahead** (*AmE*), **put forward** (*BrE*), **set ahead** (*AmE*), **turn forward** (*often figurative*) | **calibrate, synchronize** | **stop** (*for example in a game*) ◊ *Pressing the buzzer stops the ~.* | **check, glance at, look at** | **watch** ◊ *employees who are always watching the ~* (= *wanting their day's work to end*) | **beat** (= *do something in less time*

than is allowed) ◊ *The player beat the ~ and set a new record.*

CLOCK + VERB **beep, buzz, chime (sth), ring, strike sth, tick** ◊ *The ~ struck the hour.* ◊ *I could hear a ~ ticking somewhere in the house.* | **stop** | **keep time** ◊ *This ~ doesn't keep time.* | **be fast, be slow** ◊ *That clock's fast.* | **gain time, lose time** | **be right, be wrong** | **go back, go forward** ◊ *The ~s go back tonight.* | **say sth, tell sth** ◊ *The ~ on the wall said twelve o'clock.* ◊ *Her ~ told her it was time to get up.* | **go off** ◊ *My alarm ~ didn't go off this morning.*

CLOCK + NOUN **face** | **tower** | **radio**

PREP. **against the ~** ◊ *to work against the ~* (= *to work fast in order to finish before a particular time*) | **around the ~, round the ~** (= *all day and all night*) (*esp. BrE*) ◊ *to work around the ~* | **by the ~** ◊ *It's ten o'clock by the kitchen ~.*

PHRASES **the dial of a ~, the face of a ~, the hands of a ~**

close noun

VERB + CLOSE **bring sth to** ◊ *The chairperson brought the meeting to a ~.* | **come to, draw to** ◊ *The decade drew to a ~ with the threat of war hanging over Europe.*

PREP. **at the ~ of, by the ~ of, towards/toward the ~ of** ◊ *At the ~ of trading, he had lost thousands of pounds on the stock market.*

close verb

1 door, book, eyes, etc.

ADV. **firmly, tightly** ◊ *He ~d the door firmly.* | **gently, quietly, silently, softly** ◊ *She gently ~d the door behind her.*

2 shop/store, business, road, etc.

ADV. **permanently, temporarily** | **officially** ◊ *Tomorrow college officially ~s for the vacation.* | **down, off, up** ◊ *That factory's been ~d down now.*

PREP. **to** ◊ *The museum has been temporarily ~d to the public.*

close adj., adv.

1 near

VERBS **be** | **come, draw, get, move** ◊ *She grew increasingly nervous as the audition drew closer.* | **keep, stay** ◊ *Keep ~ to me.* | **hold sb, hug sb, pull sb**

ADV. **extremely, remarkably, very** | **fairly, quite, reasonably, relatively** | **awfully** (*esp. AmE*), **dangerously, frighteningly, perilously, precariously, uncomfortably** ◊ *The car came perilously ~ to running her down.* | **tantalizingly** ◊ *Victory was tantalizingly ~.* | **geographically** | **together** ◊ *Their birthdays are very ~ together.*

PREP. **to** ◊ *Get ~ to the microphone.*

2 friendly and loving

VERBS **be, feel, seem** ◊ *The two sisters seemed very ~.* | **become, grow** ◊ *After the death of their parents the two children grew very ~.* | **bring sb** ◊ *These horrific events brought the family closer.* | **remain**

ADV. **very** | **quite**

PREP. **to** ◊ *He was very ~ to his older brother.*

closed adj.

VERBS **be** | **remain** ◊ *The library will remain ~ until next week.* | **keep sth** ◊ *Keep that door ~, will you?*

ADV. **firmly, properly, tightly** ◊ *Are the windows firmly ~?* ◊ *Her mouth was tightly ~.* | **completely, fully** ◊ *Make sure the lid is completely ~.* ◊ *The valve can be adjusted from fully open to fully ~.* | **almost, nearly** ◊ *She was squinting through almost ~ eyes.* | **half, partially, partly** ◊ *The sun streamed through the partially ~ blinds.* | **officially** | **permanently, temporarily**

PREP. **for** ◊ *The building is ~ for repairs.* | **to** ◊ *Twenty miles of beaches were officially ~ to the public.*

closet noun (esp. AmE) → See also CUPBOARD, WARDROBE

ADJ. **big, huge, large** | **small, tiny** | **built-in** | **walk-in** | **broom, coat, linen** | **bedroom, hall, hallway** | **storage, supply**

VERB + CLOSET close, open | lock | raid, rummage through, search ◇ *I raided Bob's ~ for something to wear.* ◇ *He searched his ~ for something to wear.* | clean, clean out, organize | fill
CLOSET + VERB be filled with sth, hold sth ◇ *Her ~ was filled with black clothes.*
CLOSET + NOUN door | space ◇ *Do you have much ~ space in your new house?*
PREP. in the ~ ◇ *clothes hanging in the ~* | from the ~ ◇ *I picked a shirt from the ~.* | to the ~ ◇ *He went to the ~ and pulled out a suit.*
PHRASES be in the ~, stay in the ~ (= refuse to say publicly that you are gay) (*BrE, AmE*) | come out of the ~ (= say publicly that you are gay) (*BrE, AmE*) ◇ *More public figures are finding the courage to come out of the ~.* | a skeleton in the/sb's ~ (= something shocking in your past) (*BrE, AmE*) ◇ *They were hoping to find some skeletons in his ~.*

close-up *noun*

ADJ. extreme, tight (*AmE*) ◇ *The movie opens on a tight ~ of Audrey.*
CLOSE-UP + NOUN detail ◇ *The slide gave ~ detail of petal formation.* | image, photo, photograph, picture, shot, view
PREP. in ~ ◇ *The wound was photographed in extreme ~.*

closure *noun*

1 closing of road, factory, etc.

ADJ. complete, total ◇ *The accident caused the complete ~ of the road.* | partial | immediate | eventual | permanent, temporary | planned, possible, proposed, threatened | factory, hospital, pit, plant (*AmE*), road, school, etc.
VERB + CLOSURE be earmarked for, be threatened with, face ◇ *Several schools face eventual ~.* | cause, force ◇ *Imposing higher taxes would force the ~ of many bookshops.* | prevent, save sth from, stop ◇ *The mine has been saved from ~.* | announce
CLOSURE + NOUN plan, programme/program (*esp. BrE*) | order (*esp. BrE*)
PHRASES under threat of ~ ◇ *The factory is under threat of ~.*

2 feeling of satisfactory conclusion

ADJ. final | narrative
VERB + CLOSURE be looking for, need, seek ◇ *People who lose family members need ~, not false hope.* | achieve | bring, provide (sb with) | need
PHRASES a sense of ~ ◇ *The conviction of their son's murderer gave them a sense of ~.*

3 (*AmE*) fastening

ADJ. drawstring, snap, Velcro™, zipper | resealable | tamper-evident

clot *noun*

ADJ. blood ◇ *a blood ~ on her brain*
VERB + CLOT dissolve, remove | prevent | form ◇ *patients who have a tendency to form ~s more readily*
CLOT + VERB form

cloth *noun*

1 material used for making clothes, curtains, etc.

ADJ. coarse, fine | woven | cotton, woollen/woolen ◇ *a jacket made from woollen/woolen ~*
... OF CLOTH bale, bolt, length | piece, scrap, strip
VERB + CLOTH make, produce, weave | dye
CLOTH + NOUN industry, manufacture, merchant, mill (*esp. BrE*), trade (*esp. BrE*)

2 piece of cloth used for a particular purpose

ADJ. soft | damp, wet ◇ *Wipe the table with a damp ~.* | dry | cleaning, floor (*esp. BrE*), polishing | dish (usually *dishcloth*) | face (usually *facecloth*) (*esp. AmE*) | table (usually *tablecloth*) | tea (*BrE*)
VERB + CLOTH dampen, dip in sth, moisten, soak in sth

clothed *adj.*

VERBS be
ADV. fully ◇ *Jenny was fully ~.* | barely (*AmE*), lightly, partially, scantily (*esp. AmE*) ◇ *It was warm and she was lightly ~.* ◇ *Her partially ~ body was found in woods nearby.*
PREP. in ◇ *~ in white*
PHRASES fed and ~ ◇ *the problems of keeping the family fed and ~*

clothes *noun*

ADJ. beautiful, elegant, fancy, fine, lovely, nice, pretty | cheap, expensive | new, old | dry, wet | clean, fresh | dirty, filthy, soiled | dishevelled/disheveled, ragged, ripped, shabby, tattered, torn | crumpled, rumpled (*esp. AmE*), wrinkled | skimpy, tight | baggy, ill-fitting, loose | designer, fashionable, trendy | old-fashioned | second-hand | comfortable, sensible | best, evening, formal, smart (*esp. BrE*) ◇ *He wore his best ~ to the interview.* | casual, everyday, normal, ordinary, regular (*AmE*) | outrageous, strange | warm | summer, winter | outdoor | baby, maternity, mourning, night, riding, school, sports, work, working | outer | civilian, plain ◇ *an officer in plain ~ (= not in uniform)*
... OF CLOTHES set, suit ◇ *I'm going to take a set of clean ~ with me.* ◇ *a new suit of ~ for the baby*
VERB + CLOTHES pull on, put (back) on | remove, shed, strip off, take off, tear off | change ◇ *Aren't you going to change your ~ for the party?* | make, sew (*esp. AmE*) | dry, fold, iron, mend (*esp. BrE*), put away, wash | pack, unpack | choose, pick out (*esp. AmE*) | borrow
CLOTHES + NOUN shop (*esp. BrE*), store (*AmE*) | designer | dryer, washer (*both AmE*) | hanger | line (usually *clothesline*), peg (*esp. BrE*), pin (usually *clothespin*) (*AmE*) | basket, hamper (*AmE*)
PREP. in ~ ◇ *She didn't recognize him in his everyday ~.*
PHRASES a change of ~

clothing *noun*

ADJ. light | heavy, warm | baggy, loose, loose-fitting | tailored, tight | revealing, skimpy | comfortable, sensible, suitable | casual | designer | tattered, torn | cast-off, second-hand, used, vintage | summer, winter | outdoor | outer | protective, waterproof ◇ *Workers at the factory wear protective ~.* | traditional (*esp. AmE*) ◇ *She wore traditional Chinese ~.* | civilian (*esp. AmE*) | sports
... OF CLOTHING article, item, piece | layer | set (*esp. AmE*)
CLOTHING + NOUN business, company, factory (*esp. BrE*), firm (*esp. BrE*), industry, line (*AmE*), manufacturer, shop, store (*esp. AmE*), trade (*esp. BrE*)
PHRASES a change of ~

cloud *noun*

1 mass of very small drops of water in the sky

ADJ. dense, heavy, thick | light | fluffy, puffy (*esp. AmE*), wispy (*esp. AmE*) | cirrus, cumulonimbus, cumulus, etc. | high, low | broken, scattered ◇ *skies of broken ~* | fast-moving, scudding (*literary*) | black, dark, grey/gray, white | rain, storm, thunder ◇ *Rain ~s were looming on the horizon.* | ominous, threatening
... OF CLOUD band, bank, blanket, layer, mass, wisp ◇ *a layer of high ~*
VERB + CLOUD seed (= to place a substance in a cloud to make it produce rain)
CLOUD + VERB form, gather, mass ◇ *Dark ~s were gathering in the west.* | cover sth, envelop sth, obscure sth | break, clear, disperse, lift, part ◇ *The ~s broke a little, and the sun came out.* | drift, float, hang, hover, loom, move, pass, race, roll, scud (*literary*), swirl ◇ *Thick ~ hung over the moor.* ◇ *A ~ passed over the sun.* ◇ *White ~s scudded across the sky.*
CLOUD + NOUN bank, cover, layer ◇ *The ~ cover is quite dense today.* | formation
PREP. above the ~s, below the ~s ◇ *We were flying above the ~s.* | through the ~s ◇ *She could see the sun through the ~s.*
PHRASES a break in the ~, a break in the ~s

2 mass of smoke, dust, etc.

ADJ. great, huge ◇ *a great ~ of black smoke* | dense, thick |

CLOTHES

You can **wear** clothes or you can **have** clothes **on**:

I'm going to wear my little black dress to the party.
He's got a very strange hat on.

You can **be dressed in** clothes, fabric or a particular colour/color:

She was dressed | *in jeans.*
| *all in black.*
| *in green velvet.*

You can **put on** and **take off** any sort of clothing. You can also:

pull on	pull up	slip on	slip into	shrug into/on	throw on
boots	a dress	a dressing gown	a pair of jeans	a coat	a coat
gloves	jeans	(*BrE*)/a robe	something more	a jacket	a dressing gown
a jacket	knickers (*BrE*)	(*AmE*)	comfortable		(*BrE*)/a robe
a pair of sth	pants	a jacket			(*AmE*)
pants	a skirt	a pair of sth			a jacket
socks	a sleeve	shoes			a pair of jeans
a sweater	socks				a shirt
tights	trousers				some clothes
trousers	(*esp.BrE*)				a top
(*esp. BrE*)					

She pulled on a pair of faded jeans and a sweater.
Wait while I slip into something more comfortable.
Throwing on his coat, he made for the door.

pull off	pull down	remove	drop	shrug off	kick off
boots	knickers (*BrE*)	clothes	pants	a coat	boots
a coat	pants	a coat	trousers	a jacket	sandals
gloves	a skirt	glasses	(*esp. BrE*)		shoes
a hat	trousers	gloves			
a jacket	(*esp.BrE*)	a hat			
a shirt		a helmet			
shoes		a jacket			
socks		a shirt			
		shoes			

She pulled off her gloves and held out her hand.
He removed his glasses and rubbed the bridge of his nose.
I kicked off my sandals and felt the warm sand slipping between my toes.

Fasteners

do up/undo	zip (up)/unzip	button (up)/ unbutton	lace up/ unlace	tie/untie (*esp. AmE*)	fasten/ unfasten
a belt	a coat	a blouse	boots	a belt	a belt
buttons	a dress	a coat	shoes	boots	a bra
flies (*BrE*)/a fly	flies (*BrE*)/a fly	a dress		a robe (*AmE*)	a buckle
jeans	a jacket	flies (*BrE*)/fly		a scarf	buttons
laces	jeans	a jacket		shoes	a helmet
pants (*AmE*)	pants (*AmE*)	jeans		shoelaces	a necklace
a shirt	a skirt	pants (*AmE*)			
a tie	trousers	a shirt			
trousers	(*esp. BrE*)				
(*esp. BrE*)					
a zip (*BrE*)/					
zipper (*AmE*)					

His fingers fumbled to do up the small buttons on his shirt.
My laces came undone and I nearly tripped.
Tom buttoned his overcoat up to his neck and raised his collar.

billowing, swirling | **mushroom** ◇ *the mushroom ~ from a nuclear bomb* | **dust, gas, radioactive, smoke**
VERB + CLOUD **create, form** ◇ *The wind blew across the beach, forming ~s of sand.* | **belch, release**
PREP. **~ of** ◇ *a thick ~ of steam*

cloudy *adj.*

VERBS **be** | **look** ◇ *The beer looked ~.* | **start** (*BrE*) ◇ *England and Wales will start ~.* | **become** ◇ *Later it will become ~ with rain in places.* | **remain, stay** ◇ *It stayed ~ for most of the day.*
ADV. **extremely, fairly, very, etc.** ◇ *a rather ~ sky* | **a little, slightly, etc.** ◇ *Sometimes the drinking water becomes slightly ~.* | **mostly, partly**

clout *noun*

ADJ. **considerable, enormous** ◇ *a politician with enormous ~* | **economic, financial, marketing** (*esp. AmE*), **political** ◇ *the growing political ~ of the army*
VERB + CLOUT **carry, have, wield** ◇ *He has a lot of ~ within the party.* | **exercise, use** ◇ *The companies used their ~ to influence policy.* | **gain, increase** ◇ *This movie is an opportunity to increase his ~ in Hollywood.*

club *noun*

1 group of people who meet to share an interest

ADJ. **country, exclusive, private** ◇ *members of an exclusive ~* | **local** | **social** | **youth** | **fan, sports** | **fitness, health** | **badminton, golf, etc.** ◇ *She plays at the local tennis ~.* | **chess, drama, etc.** | **book**
VERB + CLUB **belong to** ◇ *She belongs to a book ~.* | **become a member of, join** | **form, found, start** | **run** ◇ *Who runs the tennis ~?*
CLUB + NOUN **chairman** (*esp. BrE*), **manager, member, official, player, secretary** (*esp. BrE*) | **basketball, cricket, football, etc.** | **bar** (*esp. BrE*), **house** (usually **clubhouse**)
PREP. **in a/the ~** ◇ *How many people are there in the ~?*
→ Note at ORGANIZATION

2 where people go and listen to music, dance, etc.

ADJ. **comedy, dance, jazz, night** (usually **nightclub**), **strip** | **gay, lesbian**
CLUB + NOUN **circuit, DJ, scene** ◇ *a new style of music on the New York ~ scene*

3 playing card

→ Note at CARD

clue *noun*

ADJ. **good, important, useful, valuable** | **vital** | **obvious** | **subtle** | **visual** | **cryptic**
VERB + CLUE **contain, have, hold** ◇ *The picture contains subtle ~s about the site's history.* ◇ *Diet may hold the ~ to the causes of migraine.* | **give (sb), offer, yield** ◇ *The hat gives a ~ to the identity of the killer.* ◇ *The letter yielded no ~s.* | **furnish (sb with), provide (sb with), supply (sb with)** | **leave, leave behind** ◇ *The burglar left no ~s.* | **hunt for, look for, search for** | **discover, find, uncover, decipher, piece together** | **miss** ◇ *We must have missed some vital ~.* | **follow** | **follow up**
PREP. **~ about** ◇ *This research might provide an important ~ about how cancer develops.* | **~ (as) to** ◇ *a ~ as to her whereabouts*

clump *noun*

ADJ. **big, great** (*esp. BrE*), **large** | **little, small** | **dense, thick** ◇ *These plants quickly form dense ~s.*
VERB + CLUMP **form**
PREP. **in a/the ~** ◇ *situated in a ~ of trees* | **~ of** ◇ *large ~s of rhododendrons*

cluster *noun*

ADJ. **little, small** | **large** | **compact, dense**

PREP. **in a/the ~** ◇ *The church stood in a small ~ of houses.* | **~ of** ◇ *a dense ~ of buildings*

cluster *verb*

ADV. **closely, densely, tightly** | **together** ◇ *The group ~ed together closely.*
PREP. **about** (*BrE*), **around, round** (*esp. BrE*) ◇ *The children ~ed around their teacher.*

clutch *noun*

1 sb/sth's clutches sb/sth's power/control

VERB + CLUTCHES **fall into** ◇ *She fell into the ~es of the rebel forces.* | **escape, escape from**
PREP. **in sb's ~** ◇ *They had him in their ~es.* | **out of sb's ~** ◇ *Once she was out of their ~es, she fled across the border.*

2 in a car

VERB + CLUTCH **drop** (*AmE*), **engage, put your foot on** | **disengage, let out, pop** (*AmE*), **release, take your foot off** ◇ *Put it into first gear and let the ~ out slowly.*
CLUTCH + VERB **engage** | **disengage** | **slip**
CLUTCH + NOUN **pedal**

clutch *verb*

ADV. **firmly, tightly** | **desperately** | **suddenly**
PREP. **at** ◇ *He felt himself slipping and ~ed at a branch.*
PHRASES **~ sth in your hand** ◇ *She ~ed her handbag tightly in one hand.* | **~ sth to your chest** ◇ *She ~ed the letter to her chest.*

clutter *noun*

VERB + CLUTTER **clear, clear up, eliminate, get rid of, reduce**
PREP. **amid the ~, among the ~** ◇ *The cat managed to find a spot to sleep amid all the ~ of my study.* | **in a/the ~** ◇ *The tune is lost in a ~ of noise.*

coach *noun*

1 person who trains people in sports, etc.

ADJ. **good, successful, top** ◇ *a top basketball ~* | **professional** | **chief** (*esp. BrE*), **head** | **assistant** | **national** | **club** | **athletics, basketball, football, tennis, etc.** | **sports** | **batting, hitting, pitching** (*all AmE*) | **acting, drama** (*BrE*), **voice**
→ Note at JOB

2 (*BrE*) **bus for longer journeys** → See also BUS

ADJ. **express** | **private** | **luxury** | **air-conditioned**
VERB + COACH **go by, travel by** | **board, get on** | **get off** | **drive** | **hire**
COACH + NOUN **station** | **driver** | **holiday, journey, tour, trip** | **travel** | **party** | **company** | **service**
PREP. **by ~** ◇ *They are planning to tour Germany by ~.* | **in a/the ~, on a/the ~**

3 large carriage pulled by horses

ADJ. **royal**
VERB + COACH **drive** | **ride in**
COACH + VERB **drive**
COACH + NOUN **road** ◇ *This is the old ~ road.* | **house**
PHRASES **a ~ and horses**

coal *noun*

1 black mineral

ADJ. **clean, smokeless** | **hard** | **soft** | **brown** | **bituminous, coking** | **opencast** (*BrE*) ◇ *opencast ~ mining*
...OF COAL **lump, piece**
VERB + COAL **mine, produce** | **burn, use** | **shovel**
COAL + VERB **burn**
COAL + NOUN **fire** | **mine, pit** ◇ *My grandfather worked in ~ mines in England and Wales.* | **mining, production** | **merchant, miner** | **company, plant** (*esp. AmE*) | **industry** | **deposit, field** (usually **coalfield**), **seam** ◇ *There are substantial reserves of methane gas trapped in ~ seams in the area.* | **reserves** | **bucket, scuttle** (*both esp. BrE*) | **bunker, cellar** (*both esp. BrE*) | **dust, gas, tar** ◇ *These men had spent their lives breathing ~ dust.* ◇ *a dye made from ~ tar*

2 (usually **coals**) burning pieces of coal

ADJ. **burning, glowing, hot, live, red-hot**
VERB + COAL **glow** ◊ *Red-hot ~s glowed in the fireplace.*

coalition noun

ADJ. **strong | loose | broad, broad-based, international, multilateral, multiracial, rainbow** ◊ *a broad-based ~ of religious and community groups* | **majority, minority | grand** ◊ *a grand ~ of various environmental groups* | **centre-left/center-left, centre-right/center-right, conservative, left-wing, liberal, progressive, radical, right-wing | two-party, three-party, etc.** | **bipartisan | governing, government, ruling | opposition | political**
VERB + COALITION **assemble, build, create, forge, form, organize, put together** ◊ *The two parties have formed a ~.* | **join | head, lead** ◊ *a ~ led by the Socialist Party*
COALITION + VERB **break up, collapse, fall, fall apart**
COALITION + NOUN **government | member, partner, party, spokesman | forces, troops**
PREP. **in (a/the) ~** ◊ *The two parties governed in ~ for four years.* ◊ *the biggest party in the government ~* | **~ between** ◊ *a ~ between the Socialists and Communists* | **~ of** ◊ *a broad ~ of democratic and republican groups* | **~ with** ◊ *They formed a ~ with the Greens.*

coast noun

ADJ. **rocky, rugged, wild | east, eastern, etc. | Atlantic, Mediterranean, etc. | mainland | sea**
... OF COAST **stretch** ◊ *This stretch of ~ is famous for its beaches.*
VERB + COAST **hit, reach | approach, near** ◊ *The boat sank as she neared the ~ of Ireland.* | **follow, hug** ◊ *The path hugs the ~ all the way to Riomaggiore.*
COAST + VERB **stretch** ◊ *The ~ stretched far into the distance.*
COAST + NOUN **highway** (*AmE*), **road**
PREP. **along the ~** ◊ *We drove south along the ~.* | **around the ~, round the ~** (*esp. BrE*) ◊ *They sailed around the ~ to St John's.* | **at the ~** ◊ *We spent a day at the ~.* | **off the ~** ◊ *an island two miles off the ~ of Brazil* | **on the ~** ◊ *a village on the Mediterranean ~*

coastline noun

ADJ. **long | beautiful, spectacular | rocky, rugged, wild | Atlantic, Mediterranean, etc. | unspoiled**
... OF COASTLINE **stretch** ◊ *long stretches of unspoilt ~*
VERB + COASTLINE **follow** ◊ *The road follows the Pacific ~.*
COASTLINE + VERB **stretch** ◊ *The ~ stretches for miles.* | **erode**
PREP. **along a/the ~** ◊ *They sailed along the rugged ~.* | **around a/the ~, round a/the ~** (*esp. BrE*) ◊ *They're sailing around the Atlantic ~ of Florida* | **off a/the ~** ◊ *They fish off the Wanganui ~.*

coat noun

1 piece of clothing

ADJ. **long | short | three-quarter length | heavy, thick | light | winter | waterproof | fur-trimmed | fur, leather, mink, tweed, wool, etc. | double-breasted, single-breasted | duffel, pea** (*AmE*), **sport** (*AmE*), **trench | frock, morning** (*esp. BrE*), **tail** (usually ***tailcoat***) | **lab** (*informal*), **laboratory, white**
VERB + COAT **don, pull on, put on, shrug (yourself) into, shrug on, slip on, throw on | pull off, remove, shed** (*esp. AmE*), **shrug off, shrug out of, slip off | button, button up** ◊ *The ~ was buttoned up wrong.* | **unbutton, unzip | get, grab** ◊ *Get your ~, it's time to go.* | **hang, hang up | take** ◊ *Let me take your ~.*
COAT + NOUN **collar, pocket, sleeve, tail | closet** (*AmE*), **hanger, hook, rack** (*esp. AmE*)
→ Special page at CLOTHES

2 fur/hair covering an animal's body

ADJ. **long | short | thick | rough | smooth | shaggy, silky** ◊ *a dog with a long shaggy ~* | **glossy | spotted, striped | winter**
VERB + COAT **shed** ◊ *The dog sheds its winter ~ once the weather becomes warmer.*

3 layer of sth covering a surface

ADJ. **thick | light** (*AmE*), **thin | fresh, new** ◊ *The room needs a fresh ~ of paint.* | **base | final, top** (usually ***topcoat***)
VERB + COAT **apply, put on** ◊ *Make sure the base ~ has thoroughly dried before applying the topcoat.*
COAT + VERB **dry**
PREP. **~ of** ◊ *a ~ of paint/varnish*

coat verb

ADV. **completely | heavily, liberally, thickly** ◊ *Liberally ~ the fish fillets with flour.* | **lightly | specially** ◊ *The fabric has been specially ~ed to improve its water resistance.*
PREP. **in** ◊ *Coat the fish in the sauce.* | **with** ◊ *The furniture was thickly ~ed with dust.*

coating noun

ADJ. **thick | fine, light, thin | outer, surface | protective | magnetic, non-stick, reflective | chocolate, metal, plastic**
VERB + COATING **be covered in** (*esp. BrE*), **be covered with** (*esp. AmE*), **have** ◊ *The fruit is covered in/with a thick ~ of chocolate.* | **apply** ◊ *Apply a thin ~ of glue to the surface.* | **form** ◊ *Frost formed a white ~ on the windows.*

coax verb

ADV. **gently**
VERB + COAX **try to | manage to | fail to**
PREP. **from** ◊ *He could ~ tears and laughter from his audience.* | **into** ◊ *He gently ~ed life back into my frozen toes.* | **out of** ◊ *She never failed to ~ good results out of her students.*

cocaine noun

ADJ. **crack, freebase, powder** (*esp. AmE*)
... OF COCAINE **gram, kilogram, ounce | line**
VERB + COCAINE **abuse, freebase, inject, smoke, sniff, snort, use**
COCAINE + NOUN **possession | injection | baron | cartel**
→ Note at DRUG (for more verbs and nouns)

cocktail noun

1 mixed alcoholic drink

ADJ. **pre-dinner | afternoon, evening | champagne | house, special** ◊ *The house ~ is the caipirinha. Cheers!*
VERB + COCKTAIL **make, mix | serve | drink, have | sip**
COCKTAIL + NOUN **bar, lounge | cabinet, glass, napkin** (*AmE*), **shaker | list, menu** (*esp. AmE*) | **circuit** ◊ *a familiar face on the ~ circuit* | **dress | hour | party, reception | waiter, waitress**

2 dish of small pieces of food

ADJ. **prawn** (*BrE*), **seafood, shrimp** (*AmE*) | **fruit**

3 mixture of different things

ADJ. **deadly, lethal | heady, potent, powerful** ◊ *The show was a heady ~ of jazz and political satire.* | **drug**
PREP. **~ of** ◊ *a lethal ~ of vodka and drugs*

coconut noun

ADJ. **desiccated** (*esp. BrE*), **fresh, grated, shredded, toasted**
... OF COCONUT **bunch** ◊ *huge bunches of fresh ~s* | **piece**
VERB + COCONUT **eat, have | grow | harvest, pick | break open, open** ◊ *She broke open the ~ and drank its sweet milk.*
COCONUT + NOUN **cream, milk, oil | palm, tree** ◊ *a bay fringed with swaying ~ palms* | **grove, plantation | fibre/fiber, husk, matting** (*BrE*), **shell**

code noun

1 system of letters, etc. for secret information

ADJ. **secret | Morse**
VERB + CODE **break, crack, decipher** ◊ *The ~ was difficult to crack.* | **use, write in | invent, make up**
CODE + NOUN **name, phrase, word | breaker**
PREP. **in ~** ◊ *All the messages were in ~.*

2 numbers/letters for identifying sth

ADJ. **area** (esp. AmE), **dialling** (BrE) ◊ What's the area ~ for Boston? | **post** (usually **postcode**) (BrE), **postal** (BrE), **zip** (AmE) | **bar, charge** (BrE) | **security** | **three-letter, four-digit, etc.** | **DNA, genetic** | **error** (= on a computer)
VERB + CODE **generate**
CODE + NOUN **number** | **generator**

3 computer language

ADJ. **binary** (= a system of computer programming instructions), **executable, HTML, source** | **malicious**
VERB + CODE **execute** | **write** | **modify, rewrite**

4 set of rules for behaving

ADJ. **strict** | **unwritten** ◊ There is an unwritten ~ that says 'Do not date your best friend's ex'. | **ethical, moral, professional** | **civil, criminal, disciplinary, penal, tax** ◊ planned changes in the US tax ~ | **Highway** ◊ the Highway Code (= the official rules for users of public roads in Britain) | **dress**
VERB + CODE **have** | **adopt, draw up, establish, formulate, lay down** (esp. BrE) ◊ The company has drawn up a new disciplinary ~. | **enforce** | **revise, simplify** | **comply with, follow** | **break, infringe** (esp. BrE), **violate** ◊ The principal said I had violated the school's dress ~.
PHRASES **a ~ of behaviour/behavior, a ~ of conduct** | **a ~ of ethics** | **a ~ of honour/honor** | **a ~ of practice** ◊ The profession has a strict ~ of practice.

coexist verb

ADV. **peacefully** ◊ What makes it difficult for the communities to ~ peacefully?
PREP. **alongside, with** ◊ Modern farming methods ~ with more traditional practices.

coffee noun

ADJ. **strong** | **weak** | **black, dark** ◊ a mug of strong black ~ | **milky** (esp. BrE), **white** (BrE) ◊ She drinks very milky ~ with lots of sugar. | **frothy** (esp. BrE) | **sweet** | **bitter** | **hot, steaming** ◊ a pot of piping hot ~ ◊ He brought in two mugs of steaming ~. | **lukewarm** | **cold** | **iced** | **flavoured/ flavored, hazelnut** | **fresh** ◊ The others will be back soon—I'll go and make some fresh ~. | **excellent, expensive, good** | **gourmet, organic, specialty** (AmE) | **decaf, decaffeinated** | **filter** (esp. BrE), **ground, percolated, real** | **instant** | **Irish** (= with whiskey added), **Turkish** (= very strong, black and sweet) | **afternoon, morning**
... OF COFFEE **cup, mug, pot**
VERB + COFFEE **drink** ◊ Do you drink ~? | **have** ◊ I had two ~s while I waited. | **take** ◊ 'How do you take your ~?' 'Milk, no sugar, thanks.' | **sip, take a mouthful of, take a sip of** ◊ He took a sip of his ~. | **down, drain, drink up, finish** | **stir** | **pour (sb)** | **go for** (esp. BrE), **go out for** ◊ Let's go out for a ~ when you've finished work. | **brew, make** ◊ freshly brewed ~ ◊ I'll make some ~ for breakfast. | **grind** ◊ freshly ground ~
COFFEE + VERB **get cold, go cold** | **be laced with sth** ◊ ~ laced with cognac | **keep sb awake**
COFFEE + NOUN **cup, mug** | **machine, maker, percolator, pot** | **grounds** | **bean** | **break, klatch** (AmE) | **bar, shop**
PREP. **in your ~** ◊ I have milk but no sugar in my ~.
PHRASES **an aroma of ~, a smell of ~** ◊ An inviting smell of ~ wafted into the room. | **coffee-making facilities** (esp. BrE) ◊ Tea and coffee-making facilities are available in the rooms.

coffin noun (esp. BrE) → See also CASKET

ADJ. **wooden** | **flag-draped** ◊ the flag-draped ~s of soldiers coming home
VERB + COFFIN **carry, take** | **lower** ◊ The ~ was lowered into the grave.
PREP. **in a/the ~**

coherence noun

ADJ. **internal** ◊ Your essay lacks internal ~. | **narrative, structural** | **ideological, intellectual, logical, thematic, theoretical** ◊ theories which lack ideological ~ | **overall**
... OF COHERENCE **degree**
VERB + COHERENCE **have** | **achieve, create, give sth, maintain, provide** ◊ They have struggled to create ~ within the group. | **lack, lose**
PREP. **~ between** ◊ a lack of ~ between the policy and the speech | **~ in, ~ within** ◊ There's a strong sense of ~ in the school curriculum.
PHRASES **a sense of ~**

coherent adj.

VERBS **be, seem** | **become**
ADV. **remarkably, very** ◊ You're not being very ~. | **perfectly** ◊ a perfectly ~ remark | **logically** ◊ a logically ~ theory | **reasonably** | **barely** ◊ He sounded barely ~ on the phone.

coil noun

ADJ. **tight** | **thick** ◊ thick ~s of blonde hair
PREP. **in a ~** ◊ She wore her hair in a neat ~. | **~ of** ◊ a ~ of rope

coil verb

ADV. **tightly** | **loosely** | **up** ◊ He ~ed the rope up tightly and put it away.
PREP. **around, round** (esp. BrE) ◊ The snake ~ed itself around a branch. | **into** ◊ Her hair was neatly ~ed into a bun.

coin noun

ADJ. **bronze, copper, gold, silver** | **antique, rare** | **commemorative** | **counterfeit, fake** | **dollar, penny, pound, etc.**
VERB + COIN **issue** | **mint, strike** ◊ The last silver ~s were minted in 1964. | **flip** (esp. AmE), **toss** (esp. BrE) ◊ They flipped/tossed a ~ to see who should go first. | **collect**
COIN + VERB **be in circulation, circulate** ◊ Some of the ~s are still in circulation. | **clink, jingle** ◊ ~s jingling in his pockets | **land** ◊ What is the probability of the ~ landing heads?
COIN + NOUN **purse** (esp. AmE) | **collector** | **flip, toss** (both AmE)
PHRASES **the flip of a ~** (esp. AmE), **the toss of a ~** (esp. BrE)

coincide verb

1 happen at the same time

ADV. **exactly, precisely** ◊ Her visit ~d exactly with a visit by the American president. | **roughly**
VERB + COINCIDE **be planned to, be timed to**
PREP. **with** ◊ The singer's arrival was timed to ~ with the opening of the festival.

2 be the same

ADV. **closely** | **exactly, perfectly**
PREP. **with** ◊ Our views on this issue ~ closely with yours.

coincidence noun

ADJ. **complete, pure, sheer** ◊ It was pure ~ that they were both in Vegas on the same day. | **mere** | **happy, lucky** ◊ What a happy ~ to meet you at the airport just when I wanted to see you. | **unfortunate** | **amazing, bizarre, curious, extraordinary, funny, incredible, odd, remarkable, strange, weird, wonderful**
... OF COINCIDENCES **series, set, string** ◊ They met through a series of strange ~s.
COINCIDENCE + VERB **happen** ◊ Remarkable ~s do happen in real life.
PREP. **by (a) ~** ◊ By ~, we both went to the same school. ◊ By an unfortunate ~, their house was broken into on the day he lost his job.

coincidental adj.

VERBS **be**
ADV. **completely, entirely, merely, purely** ◊ These parallels cannot be merely ~. | **hardly** ◊ The timing is hardly ~.

coke noun

1 Coke™ drink

ADJ. **diet** | **large, medium, small**

... OF COKE **bottle, can, glass**
VERB + COKE **have** ◇ *I'll have a Coke, please.* | **drink, sip**
COKE + NOUN **bottle, can** | **machine**
PHRASES **rum and Coke**

2 cocaine

... OF COKE **line**
VERB + COKE **sniff, snort**
→ Note at DRUG

3 fuel

... OF COKE **lump, piece**
VERB + COKE **manufacture, produce** | **burn, use**
COKE + NOUN **works** | **boiler, fire, furnace, oven**

cold *noun*

1 lack of heat; low temperature

ADJ. **biting, bitter, extreme, freezing** | **winter**
VERB + COLD **feel** ◇ *I don't feel the ~ as badly as many people.* |
keep out ◇ *The house has extra insulation to keep out the ~.*
| **be blue with, be numb with** ◇ *My hands were blue with ~.*
PREP. **against the ~** ◇ *We were well wrapped up against the ~.*
| **out in the ~** *(often figurative)* ◇ *He stood out in the ~ and
waited.* ◇ *Millions of ordinary workers feel left out in the ~ by
the shift to digital technology.*

2 common illness

ADJ. **bad, heavy** *(BrE)*, **nasty** ◇ *She won her match despite
suffering from a heavy ~.* | **mild, slight** | **common** ◇ *When
will they find a cure for the common ~?* | **chest, head**
VERB + COLD **have, nurse, suffer from** ◇ *Jim stayed at home
because he was nursing a ~.* | **catch, go down with** *(BrE)* ◇ *I
must have caught a ~ on the bus.* ◇ *If you stay out in the rain
you'll catch ~!*
→ Special page at ILLNESS

cold *adj.*

1 not hot or warm

VERBS **be, feel, look, seem** | **become, get, go, grow, turn** ◇
As evening fell it got very ~. ◇ *The room grew ~.* ◇ *In January
it turned very ~.* | **remain, stay** | **make sb/sth** ◇ *The rain
overnight had made the water ~.* | **keep sth** ◇ *Use ice to keep
the drinks ~.*
ADV. **extremely, fairly, very, etc.** | **bitterly, freezing, terribly**
◇ *It's bitterly ~ outside.* ◇ *There was a freezing ~ wind.*

2 not cooked/having become cold after cooking

VERBS **be** | **get, go** ◇ *Your dinner's getting ~.* ◇ *The water has
gone ~.* *(BrE)* ◇ *The sight of him standing there made her
blood go ~.* *(figurative)* | **eat sth, serve sth** ◇ *Bake in the oven
for twenty minutes. Serve hot or ~.*
ADV. **stone** ◇ *This soup is stone ~!*

coldness *noun*

ADJ. **icy** ◇ *The icy ~ of the water revived her.*
VERB + COLDNESS **feel** ◇ *He felt the ~ of the wall behind him.*
PREP. **~ between** ◇ *the ~ between Jack and Martha* | **~ in** ◇
There was a ~ in her voice. | **~ towards/toward** ◇ *his ~
towards/toward his parents*

collaborate *verb*

ADV. **actively, closely**
PREP. **on, with** ◇ *We have ~d closely with the university on this
project.*

collaboration *noun*

ADJ. **active, close** | **effective, fruitful, happy, successful** |
interdisciplinary, international | **artistic, creative** |
research
... OF COLLABORATION **degree**
VERB + COLLABORATION **foster** ◇ *The project is designed to foster
~ between the university and industry.*
PREP. **in ~ with** ◇ *Rock musicians are working in ~ with an
orchestra to create a new opera.* | **~ among** ◇ *a ~ among
experts in various fields* | **~ between** ◇ *a ~ between two
writers* | **~ with** ◇ *the results of a fruitful ~ with the industry*

collapse *noun*

1 building, etc. suddenly falling

ADJ. **sudden** ◇ *the sudden ~ of the bridge*
PHRASES **be in danger of ~**

2 medical condition

ADJ. **sudden** | **mental, nervous, physical**
VERB + COLLAPSE **be close to, be on the point of, be on the
verge of** ◇ *She was on the verge of nervous ~.*
PHRASES **a state of ~** ◇ *He was in a state of mental and
physical ~.*

3 sudden/complete failure of sth

ADJ. **complete, total** | **general** | **virtual** | **sudden** |
economic, financial ◇ *the sudden economic ~ of 2001*
VERB + COLLAPSE **bring about, cause, contribute to, lead to,
result in, trigger** ◇ *The war has led to the ~ of agriculture in
the area.* | **be faced with, face** | **be on the brink of, be on
the point of, be on the verge of** | **avoid, prevent** | **predict**
| **watch, witness**
PREP. **~ into** ◇ *a ~ into anarchy*

collapse *verb*

1 of a building

ADV. **completely**
PREP. **into** ◇ *Several buildings have ~d into the ocean.* | **under**
◇ *The roof ~d under the weight of snow.*

2 of a sick person

ADV. **suddenly** | **immediately** | **almost, nearly**
PREP. **against** ◇ *The man ~d against the wall and slid down it.*
| **from** ◇ *She ~d suddenly from a heart attack.* | **with** ◇ *She
~d with shock.*
PHRASES **~ in a heap** ◇ *He ~d in a heap on the floor.*

3 fail

ADV. **eventually, finally** ◇ *In November the strike finally ~d.* |
quickly, rapidly | **suddenly** | **almost, nearly, virtually**
PHRASES **to ~ in the face of sth** ◇ *The theory ~d in the face of
the evidence.*

collar *noun*

1 on a shirt, coat, dress, etc.

ADJ. **open, undone** *(esp. BrE)* ◇ *His tie was knotted below his
open ~.* ◇ *His ~ was undone.* | **button-down** | **spread** *(esp.
AmE)* | **high, stand-up, wing** *(esp. BrE)* | **tight** | **starched,
stiff** | **detachable** | **coat, shirt, etc.** | **fur, lace** | **clerical,
dog** ◇ *The minister had his dog ~ on.*
VERB + COLLAR **have** ◇ *The shirt had a button-down ~.* | **have
on, wear** | **button, do up** *(esp. BrE)* | **adjust, fix** *(esp. AmE)*,
straighten ◇ *He was standing in front of the mirror,
adjusting the ~ of his shirt.* | **unbutton, undo** | **pull up,
turn up** ◇ *She turned up her coat ~ for extra warmth.* | **pull
down, turn down** | **loosen**
COLLAR + NOUN **button, stud** | **size**
PHRASES **~ and tie** *(BrE)* ◇ *He wore a ~ and tie for the occasion.*

2 around an animal's neck

ADJ. **dog** | **flea** | **choke** *(AmE)*, **radio, training** *(AmE)*
VERB + COLLAR **have on, wear** | **slip** *(BrE)* ◇ *The dog slipped its
~ and ran off.*

colleague *noun*

ADJ. **close, trusted** | **junior, senior** | **female, male** |
professional, work | **academic, business, faculty** *(AmE)*,
medical, scientific | **cabinet, parliamentary** *(both esp. BrE)*
| **former**

collection *noun*

1 group of objects

ADJ. **big, extensive, huge, large, major, massive, substan-
tial, vast** | **small** | **growing** | **complete, comprehensive** |
core, permanent ◇ *The permanent ~ is displayed on the first
floor.* | **reserve** ◇ *The museum has a large reserve ~ in*

collector

storage, | amazing, excellent, extraordinary, fascinating, fine, good, great, important, impressive, interesting, magnificent, outstanding, remarkable, rich, stunning, superb, unique, useful | priceless, valuable | bizarre, disparate, diverse, eclectic, heterogeneous, jumbled, miscellaneous, motley, odd, random, strange, varied ◇ *Running through the tale is a motley ~ of loners looking for love.* | **representative** ◇ *We have a small but representative ~ of Brazilian art.* | **celebrated** (*esp. BrE*), **distinguished, famous, prestigious, renowned** | **family, personal, private** ◇ *the largest private art ~ in the world* | **public** | **international, local, national** | **historic, historical** | **reference, research** ◇ *a research ~ available for study by historians* | **archival, archive, library, museum** ◇ *a historical archive ~ of 20 000 documents* | **antiques, art, book, CD, coin, DVD, manuscript, music, photographic, picture, plant, record, specimen, stamp** | **digital** | **special**
VERB + COLLECTION **boast, have, own** ◇ *The museum boasts a superb ~ of medieval weapons.* | **acquire, amass, assemble, build up, compile, create, gather, make** ◇ *He built up his ~ over a period of ten years.* ◇ *She made a ~ of Roman coins and medals.* | **start** | **add to, expand** ◇ *The ~ has been added to over the years.* | **complete** ◇ *She needed only one more stamp to complete her ~.* | **bequeath, donate** ◇ *He donated his art ~ to the Guggenheim Museum.* | **hold, house, keep** ◇ *a new building to house the national ~* | **display, exhibit, show** ◇ *A glass-fronted cabinet displayed a ~ of china.* | **feature, showcase** ◇ *The exhibition features a magnificent ~ of bronze statues.* | **see, view, visit** ◇ *I was allowed to view his family ~ of miniatures.* | **consult, examine, study** ◇ *Historians frequently ask to consult the ~.* | **catalogue, organize** ◇ *She had the task of organizing the ~ of rare manuscripts.* | **digitize**
COLLECTION + VERB **consist of sth, contain sth, include sth** ◇ *The ~ contains some 500 items.* | **cover sth, span sth** ◇ *The ~ covers all phases of Picasso's career.* ◇ *The museum's ~ spans 5 000 years of art history.* | **come from…** | **date from…** ◇ *major ~s dating from the 11th to the 19th century* | **grow** ◇ *The museum's ~ is growing all the time.* | **be available, be on display, be on show, be on view** ◇ *The ~ is rarely on view to the public.* | **go on display, go on show, go on view** ◇ *The ~ is to go on public display for the first time next month.*
PREP. **~ of** ◇ *a valuable ~ of antique porcelain*
→ Note at ART

2 taking sth away/bringing sth together

ADJ. **routine, systematic** ◇ *the systematic ~ of data* | **efficient** | **free** (*esp. BrE*) ◇ *We offer free ~ of waste.* | **weekly** | **data, intelligence** | **debt, rent, revenue, tax** ◇ *the need for more efficient tax ~* | **garbage** (*esp. AmE*), **refuse, rubbish** (*BrE*), **trash** (*AmE*), **waste**
VERB + COLLECTION **await, be ready for** (*both BrE*) ◇ *Your car is awaiting ~.* | **arrange, organize** (*both BrE*) ◇ *They will arrange ~ of the chairs.*
COLLECTION + NOUN **point, site** ◇ *a lack of ~ points for waste paper* | **service** ◇ *a refuse ~ service* | **method**
PREP. **~ of** ◇ *There are some difficulties with the ~ of reliable data.*
PHRASES **a method of ~** ◇ *different methods of data ~*

3 poems/stories/music

VERB + COLLECTION **compile, edit, produce, publish** ◇ *to publish a ~ of scholarly essays* | **release** ◇ *The band has just released a ~ of their greatest hits.*
PREP. **~ of**

4 money

ADJ. **house-to-house, street** (*both BrE*) | **charity, church**
VERB + COLLECTION **have, make, organize, take** (*esp. BrE*), **take up** (*esp. AmE*) ◇ *We will have a ~ for charity at the end of the concert.* ◇ *A ~ will be taken (up) at the end of the service.*
COLLECTION + NOUN **box, plate** ◇ *the church ~ plate*
PREP. **~ for** ◇ *a street ~ for famine relief*

5 new clothes

ADJ. **new** | **autumn** (*BrE*), **fall** (*AmE*), **spring, etc.** | **ready-to-wear**
VERB + COLLECTION **create, launch** ◇ *She has recently launched her new ready-to-wear ~.* | **show, unveil** ◇ *the first designer to unveil his ~ for the spring season*

collector noun

ADJ. **great, major** ◇ *a major ~ of Japanese art* | **avid, enthusiastic, keen** (*esp. BrE*), **passionate, serious** | **private** | **antique, art, book, coin, plant, record, stamp**
PHRASES **a collector's item** ◇ *This vase is very rare and is almost a collector's item.*

college noun

ADJ. **community, local** | **private, public** (*AmE*), **state** (*esp. AmE*) | **Christian, Ivy League, junior, liberal arts** (*all AmE*) | **City Technology College** (abbreviated to *CTC*), **further education** (abbreviated to *FE college*), **sixth-form, tertiary, tutorial** (*all BrE*) | **university** (*esp. BrE*) | **military, police, secretarial, teachers** (*AmE*), **teacher-training** (*BrE*), **technical, training** (*esp. BrE*) | **agricultural, art, music, sports, veterinary** | **Bible** (*AmE*), **theological** (*esp. BrE*)
VERB + COLLEGE **attend, go to** | **enter, start** | **forgo** (*AmE*), **skip** | **drop out of, flunk out of** (*AmE*), **quit** (*AmE*) | **finish, graduate** (*AmE*), **graduate from, leave** ◇ *After graduating (from) ~, I landed a job in marketing.*
COLLEGE + VERB **offer sth, run sth** ◇ *The ~ runs a course for would-be arts administrators.* | **attract sb** | **employ sb** | **graduate sb** (*AmE*) ◇ *The ~ graduated 50 students last year.*
COLLEGE + NOUN **administrator, faculty** (*AmE*), **lecturer** (*esp. BrE*), **professor** (*esp. AmE*), **staff, teacher** ◇ *the ~ staff* (= all the people who work there) (*BrE*) ◇ *the ~ staff* (= all the people who work there apart from those who teach) (*AmE*) | **chancellor** (*esp. AmE*), **dean, president** (*AmE*), **principal** (*BrE*) | **boy, dropout, girl** (*esp. AmE*), **graduate, kid** (*informal*), **student** | **freshman** (*esp. AmE*), **junior** (*AmE*), **senior** (*AmE*), **sophomore** (*AmE*) | **buddy** (*informal*), **mate** (*BrE, informal*), **room-mate** | **fraternity** (*AmE*) | **building, campus** | **chapel, library, room** | **accommodation** (*BrE*), **dorm** (*AmE, informal*), **dormitory** (*AmE*) | **class** (*AmE*), **course, degree, education** | **credits** (*AmE*) | **admissions, application, enrolment/enrollment** | **graduation** ◇ *~ graduation exercises* (*AmE*) | **fees** (*BrE*), **tuition** (*AmE*) | **loan** | **life** | **athletics** (*AmE*), **sports** | **basketball, football, etc.** | **bookstore** (*esp. AmE*) | **team**
PREP. **at ~** ◇ *She's away at ~ in Virginia.* ◇ *I got interested in politics when I was at ~.* (*BrE*) | **in ~** ◇ *Not all the lecturers are in ~ at any one time.* (*BrE*) ◇ *I got interested in politics when I was in ~.* (*AmE*) | **to ~** ◇ *He's hoping to go to ~ next year.* | **~ of** ◇ *a ~ of education*

collide verb

ADV. **almost, nearly** | **head-on** ◇ *Two trains ~d head-on.*
PREP. **with** ◇ *His car nearly ~d with a bus.*

collision noun

ADJ. **serious** (*esp. BrE*) | **multiple** | **head-on, mid-air** | **high-speed, violent** | **train, vehicle** (*both esp. AmE*)
VERB + COLLISION **be involved in, have** ◇ *I had a ~ with a bus.* | **avoid, prevent** | **cause**
COLLISION + VERB **happen, occur** ◇ *The ~ occurred near the hospital.*
PREP. **in a/the ~** ◇ *She was injured in a ~.* | **in ~ with** (*BrE*) ◇ *The car was in ~ with a van.* | **~ between** ◇ *a head-on ~ between two cars* | **~ with** ◇ *a ~ with a train*
PHRASES **be on a ~ course with sth** ◇ *An iceberg was on a ~ course with the ship.*

colonel noun → Note at RANK

colony noun

1 country ruled by another country

ADJ. **overseas** ◇ *Britain's overseas colonies* | **American,**

British, French, etc. | former ◇ *the former Portuguese ~ of Macao* | independent, self-governing | penal, plantation
VERB + COLONY establish ◇ *Settlers established a new ~ in the early 18th century.*
PREP. in a/the ~

2 group of animals/plants

ADJ. huge, large, thriving | small | breeding, nesting | ant, bird, seal, etc.
VERB + COLONY form ◇ *Some of the insects will leave to form a new ~.*
PREP. in a/the ~ ◇ *The birds nest in huge colonies.* | ~ of ◇ *a ~ of ants*

colour *(BrE)* *(AmE* color*)* noun

1 quality that makes sth red, etc.

ADJ. bold, bright, brilliant, glowing, iridescent, vibrant, vivid | dark, deep ◇ *Dark ~s suit you best.* | intense, lush *(esp. AmE)*, rich, saturated, strong ◇ *the intense ~ of new leaves* | faded, light, muted, pale, pastel, soft, subdued, subtle | dull | garish, gaudy, loud, lurid | autumn *(esp. BrE)*, autumnal, earthy, fall *(AmE)*, warm | cool ◇ *cool ~s like blue and gray* | sombre/somber | attractive, beautiful, lovely | good ◇ *Green is a good ~ on you.* | complementary, contrasting | matching | basic | primary, secondary | indeterminate, neutral | natural | blue, red, etc. ◇ *The curtains went a strange orange ~ when we washed them.* | bluish, reddish, etc. | pure, solid, uniform ◇ *Simple patterns and solid ~s are particularly effective.* | full ◇ *a 48-page reference section in full ~* ◇ *a 24-page full-colour booklet* | eye, hair, skin ◇ *What is her natural hair ~?*
... OF COLOUR/COLOR dash, flash, splash | mass, riot ◇ *The garden is a riot of ~ in spring.* | spot, touch
VERB + COLOUR/COLOR change ◇ *The chameleon changes ~ to match its surroundings.* | add ◇ *The silk cushions add ~ to an otherwise dull room.* | match ◇ *Your shirt matches the ~ of your eyes.* | wear ◇ *I like to wear bright ~s.*
COLOUR/COLOR + VERB match (sth) | clash | fade | run ◇ *This ~ runs, so wash the shirt separately.* | range from... ◇ *The leaf ~ ranges from dark green to almost brown.*
COLOUR/COLOR + NOUN combination, range, scheme ◇ *We have to choose a ~ scheme for the dining room.* | palette | code, coding | illustration, photograph, photography, picture, plate, printing, reproduction | monitor, printer, screen, television
PREP. in ~ ◇ *The flowers are pale blue in ~.* ◇ *Is the film in ~ or black and white?* ◇ *The book is lavishly illustrated in full ~.* | in a ~ ◇ *The scarf is available in six different ~s.*
PHRASES a combination of ~s, a range of ~s

2 of a person's skin

COLOUR/COLOR + NOUN bar *(BrE)*, barrier *(AmE)*
PREP. of ~ *(esp. AmE)* ◇ *people of ~*
PHRASES on the basis of ~, on (the) grounds of ~ ◇ *to discriminate on the basis of ~*

3 redness in the face

ADJ. heightened, high ◇ *You could tell she was excited by the heightened ~ in her cheeks.* | faint
VERB + COLOUR/COLOR have ◇ *You have a little more ~ in your cheeks now.* | bring ◇ *The walk brought ~ to her face.* | be drained of, drain of, lose ◇ *His face drained of all ~.*
COLOUR/COLOR + VERB flood sth, rise, rush ◇ *The ~ rose in his face.* ◇ *I could feel the ~ rush to my cheeks.* | drain ◇ *The ~ drained from her face when she saw him.* | come back, return ◇ *Gradually the ~ returned to his cheeks.*

4 interesting or exciting details

ADJ. local ◇ *a journalist in search of a bit of local ~*
VERB + COLOUR add, give sth, lend ◇ *His asides lent ~ to the story.*
PHRASES full of ~

colour *(BrE)* *(AmE* color*)* verb

ADV. heavily, strongly ◇ *His opinions are heavily ~ed by his own experiences.* | naturally

coloured *(BrE)* *(AmE* colored*)* adj.

VERBS be
ADV. boldly, brightly, brilliantly, gaily *(esp. BrE)*, highly, intensely, richly, strongly *(esp. BrE)*, vibrantly, vividly ◇ *She wore a richly ~ silk dress.* | beautifully | delicately | uniformly | differently, variously ◇ *variously ~ birds* | naturally | oddly

colouring *(BrE)* *(AmE* coloring*)* noun

ADJ. natural | dark | hair
VERB + COLOURING/COLORING have ◇ *He daughter has very dark ~.*

column noun

1 tall stone post

ADJ. huge, tall | fluted ◇ *colonnades of fluted Doric ~s* | classical | concrete, marble, stone, etc. | Corinthian, Doric, Ionic
COLUMN + VERB support sth ◇ *The roof is supported by four huge ~s.*

2 piece of writing in a newspaper

ADJ. regular ◇ *He has a regular ~ in a weekly newspaper.* | daily, weekly, etc. | syndicated *(esp. AmE)* | newspaper | advice *(AmE)*, agony *(BrE)*, correspondence, editorial, financial, gossip, leader *(BrE)*, letters, obituary, op-ed *(AmE)*, opinion, personal
VERB + COLUMN have, write | read | syndicate *(esp. AmE)* | publish, run
COLUMN + NOUN inches ◇ *So many ~ inches are devoted to movie stars.*
PREP. in a/the ~ ◇ *She saw his name in an obituary ~.* | ~ about, ~ on ◇ *a weekly ~ on movies showing in the capital*

3 long line of people, vehicles, etc.

ADJ. huge, long | armoured/armored, tank | marching
PREP. in ~s ◇ *to march in ~s* | ~ of ◇ *a ~ of troops*
PHRASES the head of the ~

coma noun

ADJ. deep | irreversible
VERB + COMA fall into, go into, lapse into, sink into, slip into ◇ *He fell into a ~ after suffering a stroke.* | come out of | induce
COMA + NOUN patient, victim
PREP. in a/the ~ ◇ *He has been in a ~ since the accident.*

comb noun

1 used for making your hair neat

VERB + COMB use | drag, pull, run ◇ *She ran a ~ through her tangled hair.*
PHRASES a brush and ~

2 act of combing

VERB + COMB could do with, need ◇ *Your hair could do with a ~!* | give sth ◇ *She gave her hair a ~.*

combat noun

ADJ. fierce, intense, mortal | armed, unarmed | close, hand-to-hand | open | single | active, actual | modern | ground, land, urban | aerial, air, air-to-air
VERB + COMBAT be engaged in, be locked in, engage in ◇ *The troops were locked in hand-to-hand ~.* | see ◇ *Our platoon has yet to see ~.* | send sb into
COMBAT + NOUN mission, operation | zone | force, patrol, troops, unit | veteran | aircraft, vehicle | boots, equipment, fatigues, gear, jacket *(BrE)*, suit, uniform | capability, effectiveness, power, readiness | action, experience
PREP. in ~ ◇ *He was killed in ~.* | in ~ with ◇ *The soldiers are in ~ with rebel forces.* | ~ against ◇ *in mortal ~ against dragons* | ~ between ◇ *a fierce ~ between two champions*

COLOURS/COLORS

Things can **be**, **look**, **go** or **turn** blue, green, red, etc. You can also **make sth** or **colour/color**, **dye**, **paint** or **stain sth** blue, green, red, etc.

The pages of the book have gone yellow.
I've dyed my shirt green.

bright	brilliant	light	pale	soft
blue	blue	blue	blue	blue
green	green	brown	brown	brown
orange	red	green	gold	green
pink		grey	green	grey/gray
purple		pink	grey	pink
red		purple	orange	purple
yellow		red	pink	yellow
		yellow	purple	
			yellow	

> *a bright red car*
> *The water was a brilliant blue.*
> *light blue eyes*
> *a pale yellow blouse*
> *The walls were painted a soft blue.*

dark	deep	dull	rich	vivid	warm
blue	blue	brown	blue	blue	brown
brown	brown	green	brown	green	red
green	orange	red	green	orange	yellow
grey	pink		red	pink	
pink	purple			red	
purple	red			yellow	
red	yellow				

> *She was wearing a dark green skirt.*
> *They choose deep purple for the curtains.*
> *The sky had turned deep orange.*
> *The bricks are a dull grey.*
> *The room was decorated in rich browns and greens.*
> *His eyes were a vivid green.*
> *warm brown eyes*

Other expressions:

a shade of ~
- *a beautiful shade of red*

in ~
- *She was dressed all in pink.*
- *Have you got this shirt in blue?*
- *You look good in green.*

wear ~
- *I can't wear yellow—it makes my eyes look strange.*

~ suits sb
- *Orange suits you.*

combat verb
ADV. **effectively, successfully** ◇ *She argued that the only way to ~ inflation effectively was to keep interest rates high.*
VERB + COMBAT **help (to)** | **be designed to**
PHRASES **action to ~ sth, efforts to ~ sth, measures to ~ sth, policies to ~ sth** ◇ *Measures to ~ violent crime have been proposed.*

combination noun
ADJ. **ideal, perfect, right, unbeatable, winning** ◇ *The band played with a winning ~ of gusto and precision.* | **attractive** (*esp. BrE*), **delicious, good, happy, interesting, potent, powerful** | **amazing, curious, odd, rare, strange, unique, unusual** | **dangerous, deadly, lethal** ◇ *High debt and low earnings are a lethal ~.* | **colour/color** ◇ *an unusual colour/color ~*
PREP. **in ~ (with)** ◇ *The materials can be used singly or in ~.* ◇ *Hepatitis D exists only in ~ with the hepatitis B virus.* | **~ of** ◇ *a delicious ~ of herbs and spices*

combine verb
ADV. **successfully** ◇ *She successfully ~s her career with family life.* | **well** ◇ *The illustrations ~ well with the text.*
PREP. **against** ◇ *to ~ against a common enemy* | **with** ◇ *Combine the flour with the water to make a stiff paste.*

comeback noun
ADJ. **amazing, big, dramatic, good, great, incredible, remarkable, strong, successful** | **long-awaited** (*esp. BrE*) | **political** | **fourth-quarter, second-half, etc.**
VERB + COMEBACK **make, mount, stage** ◇ *He made one of the most remarkable ~s in modern politics.* | **attempt**
COMEBACK + NOUN **trail** ◇ *The player is on the ~ trail after a serious knee injury.* | **attempt** | **victory**

comedian noun
ADJ. **great, popular** | **radio, stand-up, television, TV** ◇ *He started out as a stand-up ~.* | **alternative** (*BrE*)
→ Note at JOB

comedy noun
ADJ. **high, low** | **film** (*esp. BrE*), **movie** (*esp. AmE*), **television, TV** | **alternative, light, musical, physical, romantic, screwball, situation, sketch, slapstick, teen** (*esp. AmE*) ◇ *a popular romantic ~* ◇ *The show contains some wonderful slapstick ~.* | **black, dark**
VERB + COMEDY **do, play** ◇ *Does he play ~?*
COMEDY + NOUN **actor, actress, writer** | **film** (*esp. BrE*), **movie** (*esp. AmE*), **series, show** | **routine, sketch** | **club**
PHRASES **a ~ of errors** ◇ *The case quickly became a ~ of errors.* (*figurative*) | **a ~ of manners**
→ Note at PERFORMANCE (for more verbs)

comfort noun
1 having all your body needs/a pleasant life
ADJ. **complete, great, maximum, modest, reasonable** ◇ *They live in modest ~.* | **comparative** (*esp. BrE*), **relative** | **added** ◇ *a quilted cover for added ~* | **domestic, personal, physical**
COMFORT + NOUN **level** | **zone** ◇ *She's willing to venture outside her ~ zone* (= *try things that are more challenging*).
PREP. **for ~** ◇ *I dress for ~ rather than elegance.* | **in ~** ◇ *I like to travel in reasonable ~.* | **~ of** ◇ *He enjoys dangerous sports from the ~ of his couch.*
PHRASES **a degree of ~, a standard of ~** ◇ *The hotel offers a high standard of ~.* | **in the ~ of your own home** ◇ *Learn a new language in the ~ of your own home.* | **too close for ~** ◇ *The sound of gunfire was too close for ~.*
2 help/kindness to sb who is suffering
ADJ. **great** | **little, small** | **cold** ◇ *A drop in the unemployment rate was cold ~ for those without a job* (= *not much comfort at all*).
... OF COMFORT **crumb, word**
VERB + COMFORT **bring sb, give sb, offer sb, provide sb with** ◇ *His kind words brought some ~ to the grieving parents.* |

derive, draw, find, get, have, seek, take ◇ *They sought ~ in each other.* ◇ *We took great ~ from the fact that our savings were safe.* | **need** ◇ *I need all the ~ I can get right now.*
COMFORT + NOUN **food** ◇ *Chocolate is a great ~ food.*
PREP. **~ in** ◇ *She found ~ in music.*
PHRASES **a source of ~**
3 sb/sth that helps when you are suffering, etc.
ADJ. **great**
PREP. **~ to** ◇ *The children have been a great ~ to me through all of this.*
4 sth that makes life easier
ADJ. **modern** | **creature, home** (*BrE*), **material** ◇ *I hate camping—I miss all my creature ~s.* | **spiritual**

comfort verb
ADV. **greatly** ◇ *The idea that he was not alone ~ed him greatly.*
PHRASES **be ~ed to know** ◇ *He was ~ed to know that most people in the class knew even less than he.* | **being ~ed by family, friends, etc.** ◇ *The victim's widow was today being ~ed by family and friends.* | **feel ~ed**

comfortable adj.
1 allowing you to feel relaxed
VERBS **be, feel, look** ◇ *The bed felt ~.* | **make sth** ◇ *We must think how we can make the room more ~ for you.*
ADV. **extremely, fairly, very, etc.** | **incredibly, wonderfully** ◇ *an incredibly ~ chair* | **perfectly** | **enough, moderately, reasonably** ◇ *The hotel was ~ enough.* | **surprisingly**
PHRASES **change into something more ~, slip into something more ~** ◇ *I'll change into something more ~ when I get home.*
2 not having any pain/worry
VERBS **be, feel, look** ◇ *Did you feel ~ and relaxed at the party?* | **become, get** ◇ *This bed is lumpy—I just can't seem to get ~.* | **make sb/yourself** ◇ *Make yourself ~!* | **keep sb**
ADV. **very** | **completely, entirely, fully, perfectly, quite, totally** ◇ *I was not entirely ~ about the plans they had made.* | **increasingly**
PREP. **about** ◇ *She didn't feel ~ about going out alone.* | **with** ◇ *I don't feel ~ with him.*
PHRASES **~ in your (own) skin**
3 having/providing enough money for all your needs
VERBS **be**
ADV. **very** | **quite, relatively** ◇ *I had a relatively ~ life in Brazil.*

comforting adj.
VERBS **be, feel** | **find sth**
ADV. **extremely, fairly, very, etc.** | **wonderfully** | **hardly, not particularly** | **oddly, strangely** ◇ *She found his voice strangely ~.*
PHRASES **warm and ~**

comic adj.
VERBS **be**
ADV. **richly, truly, wonderfully** ◇ *Many of the scenes in the book are richly ~.* | **almost** | **a little, slightly, etc.** | **faintly, mildly** | **blackly, darkly, grotesquely** ◇ *a blackly ~ futuristic fantasy*

comical adj.
VERBS **be, look, seem, sound** | **become** | **make sth** ◇ *What made it so ~ was that their hats kept falling off.* | **find sth**
ADV. **extremely, fairly, very, etc.** | **almost** | **a little, slightly, etc.** ◇ *He is a slightly ~ figure.* | **faintly** (*esp. BrE*)

command noun
1 order
ADJ. **basic, simple**
VERB + COMMAND **carry out, obey** | **disobey, ignore** | **bark,**

give, issue, shout ◊ *an army officer barking ~s at his men* ◊ *He issued the ~ to retreat.*
PREP. **at sb's ~** ◊ *I am at your ~* (= ready to obey you). ◊ *At her ~ all work stopped.*
PHRASES **your wish is my ~** (= I will do whatever you want me to do) (used esp. in stories)

2 instruction to computer

ADJ. **spoken, verbal, voice | keyboard | basic, simple**
VERB + COMMAND **enter, type | use | send | execute, run | receive**
COMMAND + NOUN **line, prompt**

3 control over sb/sth

ADJ. **complete, full, total** ◊ *He was in complete ~ of the situation.* | **direct** ◊ *under the direct ~ of Lieutenant Sykes* | **overall, personal, sole** ◊ *She was in sole ~ of one million pounds.* | **integrated, joint, unified** ◊ *NATO's integrated military ~* | **central, high, supreme** ◊ *the military high ~* | **air, army, military, naval | battle, combat**
VERB + COMMAND **have** ◊ *He had ~ of 3 000 soldiers.* | **assume, take, take over | gain, get | give sb, put sb in | maintain | be relieved of, lose, relinquish** ◊ *She has lost ~ of her senses.*
COMMAND + NOUN **centre/center | chair, deck, module, post, ship | structure**
PREP. **in ~** ◊ *Who is in ~?* ◊ *She is second in ~.* | **in ~ of** ◊ *He was put in ~ of the navy.* | **under sb's ~** ◊ *The division was under the ~ of General George.* | **~ over** ◊ *his ~ over resources*
PHRASES **the chain of ~, the line of ~**

4 ability to do/use sth

ADJ. **excellent, fluent, good, impressive, perfect | poor**
VERB + COMMAND **have | demonstrate, show | improve**
PREP. **at your ~** ◊ *The vast knowledge he has at his ~ will be invaluable in the job.* | **~ of** ◊ *She has an excellent ~ of French.*

commander noun

ADJ. **senior, supreme, top | deputy, subordinate** (*AmE*) **| joint | air-force, army, military, naval, navy, police | battalion** (*BrE*), **brigade, company, corps, division** (*esp. AmE*), **group, platoon, unit | fleet, flight, squadron | Allied** ◊ *General Eisenhower was Supreme Allied Commander in Western Europe.*
PREP. **~ of** ◊ *the ~ of US forces in Iraq*
PHRASES **Commander-in-Chief**
→ Note at RANK

commend verb

PREP. **for** ◊ *He was ~ed for his brave actions.* | **to** ◊ *She said she would ~ the proposal to the Board.*
PHRASES **be highly ~ed, be widely ~ed** ◊ *His book was highly ~ed.* | **sth has little, much, nothing, etc. to ~ it** (*formal*) ◊ *The proposed site has much to ~ it.*

commendable adj.

VERBS **be, seem**
ADV. **highly, very** ◊ *The government's action here is highly ~.* | **entirely** (*esp. BrE*)

comment noun

ADJ. **brief | fair** ◊ *What she said was fair ~.* (*BrE*) ◊ *What she said was a fair ~.* (*BrE, AmE*) **| favourable/favorable, nice, positive | adverse, derogatory, disparaging, negative, unfavourable/unfavorable | critical** ◊ *Highly critical ~s have been made about the conduct of some politicians.* ◊ *a book with critical ~ on the various strands of feminism* | **hostile, snarky** (*AmE, informal*), **snide, unfair | caustic, scathing | rude, sardonic, smart-ass** (*AmE, informal*), **stupid | ironic, sarcastic, wry | witty | constructive, helpful, useful, valuable | incisive, insightful, interesting, perceptive, shrewd | cryptic | uninformed** (*esp. BrE*) **| general | detailed | casual, offhand, off-the-cuff, passing,**

throwaway ◊ *He made a few casual ~s to her about her hair and now she's chopped it all off!* ◊ *This idea deserves more than passing ~.* | **editorial, official, personal, press, public | Editorial** ~ *in the press tended to support the government in this matter.* | **written | political, social** ◊ *Her novels were a vehicle for shrewd social ~.* | **sad** ◊ *The attack is a sad ~ on the public's understanding of mental illness.*
VERB + COMMENT **have, make, pass** ◊ *If you have any ~s, please send them to the above address.* ◊ *She made a cryptic ~ about how the movie mirrored her life.* ◊ *I would prefer not to pass ~ before I have more information on the case.* | **give, offer | add, leave, post** (= on the Internet), **send, submit, write** ◊ *Feel free to post your ~s if you have any.* | **read | hear | attract, cause, draw, elicit, excite** ◊ *The article attracted much adverse ~.* | **appreciate, invite, seek, welcome** ◊ *The school has invited ~s from parents about the new curriculum.* | **get, receive** ◊ *We have received many helpful ~s from fellow-sufferers.* | **decline** (*AmE*) ◊ *KPJ officials declined ~.* | **disregard, ignore | direct** ◊ *She directed all her ~s at Steve.*
PREP. **without ~** ◊ *She accepted his diagnosis without ~.* | **~ about, ~ on** ◊ *a general ~ on the weather* | **~ from** ◊ *We welcome ~s from readers.*
PHRASES **be available for ~, be unavailable for ~** ◊ *The spokesman was not available for ~ last night.* | **no ~** ◊ *When asked about the allegations, the chairman replied 'no comment'.* | **a source of ~** ◊ *His visits were the source of much ~.* | **questions and ~s** ◊ *Viewers are encouraged to phone in questions and ~s.*

comment verb

ADV. **favourably/favorably | adversely** (*esp. BrE*), **critically, unfavourably/unfavorably | bitterly, sarcastically | drily, wryly | quietly, softly | publicly**
VERB + COMMENT **decline to, refuse to** ◊ *The president refused to ~ on the affair.*
PREP. **about** ◊ *People were ~ing about her abilities.* | **on** ◊ *He refused to ~ on the proposals.* | **to** ◊ *She ~ed to me that she liked it.*

commentary noun

1 on the radio/television

ADJ. **brief | live | running** (= continuous) ◊ *She kept up a running ~ on the festivities.* | **accompanying | radio, television, TV** ◊ *I was listening to the radio ~ on the game.* | **audio | colour/color** (= giving background information during a sports broadcast) (*AmE*)
VERB + COMMENTARY **do, give, keep up, provide | feature, include | listen to | have** ◊ *The deleted scenes have an optional ~ by the director.*
COMMENTARY + NOUN **box** (*BrE*) ◊ *the reporters in the ~ box* | **track** (= on a DVD)
PREP. **~ on** ◊ *The station provided live ~ on the African Nations Cup.*

2 criticism/discussion of sth

ADJ. **detailed | critical | political, social | good, incisive, insightful, interesting**
VERB + COMMENTARY **provide** ◊ *The novel provides a powerful social ~ on post-war Mexico.* | **offer, write**
PREP. **~ on**
PHRASES **be a sad ~ (on sth)** (= to reflect badly on sth) ◊ *The petty quarrels were a sad ~ on the state of the government.*

commentator noun

1 person who commentates on sth

ADJ. **sports | basketball, cricket, football, etc. | match, race** (*both BrE*) **| radio, television, TV**
→ Note at JOB

2 person who gives opinions on sth in the media

ADJ. **influential | independent | foreign | media | cultural, economic, legal, news** (*AmE*), **political, social** ◊ *Political ~s are predicting that the minister will have to resign.* | **conservative, liberal | left-wing, right-wing**
PREP. **~ on** ◊ *a ~ on current affairs*

commerce *noun*

ADJ. **foreign, global, international** | **domestic, interstate** (*AmE*) | **electronic, Internet, online**
VERB + COMMERCE **engage in** ◇ *The marketplace was where merchants engaged in ~.* | **regulate** | **affect** | **facilitate**
PREP. **~ between** ◇ *~ between China and Africa* | **~ with** ◇ *the development of ~ with Asia*
PHRASES **a chamber of ~** | **the world of ~** ◇ *She has little experience of the world of ~.*

commercial *noun*

ADJ. **radio, television, TV** | **beer, car, etc.** | **30-second, etc.** | **campaign** (*AmE*)
VERB + COMMERCIAL **do, make** ◇ *She ended up doing ~s, which ironically revived her acting career.* ◇ *The company has made ~s for leading sportswear manufacturers.* | **air, broadcast, run** (*esp. AmE*), **show** | **skip** (*AmE*) | **see, watch**
COMMERCIAL + VERB **air** (*esp. AmE*), **appear** | **feature sb/sth** ◇ *The ~ features a moody young man.*
COMMERCIAL + NOUN **break** ◇ *The movie was so full of ~ breaks it was impossible to enjoy.*
PREP. **in a/the ~** ◇ *She's in a ~ for cars.* | **~ for**

commission *noun*

1 asking sb to do a piece of work for you

ADJ. **private, public**
VERB + COMMISSION **accept, get, receive** ◇ *The firm will accept ~s for most types of architectural work.* ◇ *During the 1940s he received ~s for several large religious paintings.* | **give sb**

2 official group asked to report on sth

ADJ. **international, national** | **independent** | **bipartisan** (*AmE*), **joint** | **federal, government** | **judicial, official, parliamentary, presidential, royal, state** | **permanent, standing** | **special** | **roving** | **election, electoral** | **fact-finding, investigating, investigative** | **planning** | **truth** (= to find out about human rights abuses)
VERB + COMMISSION **appoint, create, establish, set up** ◇ *The government has set up a joint ~ to consider the problem.* | **chair, head, preside over**
PREP. **~ for** ◇ *the ~ for racial equality* | **~ on** ◇ *a ~ on domestic violence*
PHRASES **a ~ of inquiry** (*BrE*)

3 money for selling sth/providing a service

ADJ. **big, high** | **small** | **fixed**
VERB + COMMISSION **earn, get, receive** | **pay** | **charge** ◇ *That bank charges a high ~ for overseas withdrawals.* | **deduct**
PREP. **in ~** ◇ *She earned $2 000 in ~ last month.* | **on ~** ◇ *Most of the salespeople are on ~.* | **~ for, ~ on** ◇ *They get a 10% ~ on every encyclopedia they sell.*
PHRASES **on a ~ basis** ◇ *to work on a ~ basis*

commission *verb*

ADV. **specially** ◇ *specially ~ed works* | **newly, recently**
PREP. **from** ◇ *The report was ~ed from scientists in five countries.*

commissioner *noun*

ADJ. **high** | **assistant, deputy** | **special** | **police** (*esp. AmE*) | **city, county, state** (*all AmE*) | **insurance** (*AmE*) | **baseball** (*AmE*)
VERB + COMMISSIONER **appoint, appoint sb (as)**
PREP. **~ for** ◇ *He was appointed United Nations High Commissioner for Refugees.*

commitment *noun*

1 willingness to give time/energy to sth

ADJ. **absolute, complete, full, total** | **clear, deep, firm, genuine, great, passionate, real, serious, strong** | **continued, continuing, lifelong, long-standing, long-term, ongoing, unwavering** ◇ *The company is making a long-term ~ to breaking into the American market.* | **increased, increasing** | **general, open-ended** | **government, personal, professional, public** | **emotional, ideological, moral, political, religious**

... OF COMMITMENT **degree, level**
VERB + COMMITMENT **give, make** ◇ *The president made a firm ~ to increasing spending on health.* | **demonstrate, display, show** ◇ *to demonstrate a ~ to human rights* | **lack** | **affirm, reaffirm** | **require, take** ◇ *Learning to play the violin requires strong ~.*
PREP. **~ on** ◇ *The government avoided giving any ~s on spending.* | **~ to** ◇ *his lifelong ~ to the socialist cause*
PHRASES **a lack of ~**

2 a responsibility

ADJ. **big, considerable, major** | **binding** | **prior** | **international, overseas** | **business, domestic, family, financial, military, social, teaching, work**
VERB + COMMITMENT **have, take on** ◇ *I don't want to take on any more ~s.* | **fulfil/fulfill, honour/honor, meet** ◇ *She can't meet her financial ~s.* | **get out of, wriggle out of** ◇ *He is trying to wriggle out of his various domestic ~s.*
PREP. **~ on** ◇ *to honour/honor ~s on reduction of air pollution*

3 agreeing to use money/time/people for sth

ADJ. **heavy** ◇ *a heavy ~ of capital* | **time**
PREP. **~ of** ◇ *The war on poverty requires a ~ of resources from the developing nations.*

committed *adj.*

VERBS **be, feel** | **become** | **remain**
ADV. **extremely, fairly, very, etc.** | **deeply, fiercely, firmly, highly, seriously, strongly** | **absolutely, completely, fully, totally, wholly** | **genuinely** | **irrevocably** ◇ *The country was now irrevocably ~ to war.* | **actively** | **personally** ◇ *The president is personally ~ to this legislation.* | **emotionally, ideologically, politically** ◇ *She cared for Jem in her way but did not want to become emotionally ~.*
PREP. **to** ◇ *We are ~ to improving services.*

committee *noun*

ADJ. **central** | **joint** | **standing** | **ad hoc, special** | **select** | **congressional, senate** | **executive, management, steering** | **advisory, consultative** | **disciplinary, investigating, planning** | **strike** (*BrE*) | **appeal** (*BrE*) | **audit, finance** | **search** (= for finding the right person to do a job) (*esp. AmE*), **selection** | **ethics** | **political action** (= a group that tries to get a particular person elected) (*AmE*)
VERB + COMMITTEE **create, establish, form, organize, set up** | **chair, head** ◇ *Mr Taylor will chair the board's audit ~.* | **appoint (sb to), elect (sb to)** ◇ *He was appointed to the advisory ~ last month.* | **be on, serve on, sit on** ◇ *She serves on several ~s.* | **leave, stand down from** | **disband**
COMMITTEE + VERB **meet** ◇ *The ~ meets every Thursday.* | **approve, conclude, decide, find, recommend**
COMMITTEE + NOUN **member** | **chair, chairman** | **meeting**
PREP. **on a/the ~** ◇ *I talked to some of the people on the ~.* | **~ on** ◇ *a ~ on the safety of medicines* | **~ of** ◇ *a ~ of experts*
→ Note at ORGANIZATION

commodity *noun*

1 product/raw material

ADJ. **basic, important, primary** | **cheap** | **expensive** | **rare, scarce** ◇ *Coal is becoming a rare ~.* | **marketable, saleable** | **export** | **perishable** | **agricultural, industrial** ◇ *basic agricultural commodities* | **global**
VERB + COMMODITY **produce**
COMMODITY + NOUN **market** | **exchange** | **futures, prices** | **export, trade, trading** | **broker, trader** | **production**
PHRASES **trade in commodities**

2 sth that is useful

ADJ. **hot, precious, valuable** ◇ *Time is a very valuable ~.* | **rare, scarce** | **global**

common *adj.*

1 happening/found often

VERBS **be, seem** | **become** | **remain**

ADV. **extremely, fairly, very**, etc. ◊ *These problems now seem fairly ~.* | **increasingly**
PREP. **among, in** ◊ *Stomach pain is very ~ in children.*

2 shared

VERBS **be**
PREP. **to** ◊ *This attitude is ~ to most young men in the armed services.*
PHRASES **have sth in ~** ◊ *Jane and I have nothing in ~.* ◊ *I have nothing in ~ with Jane.* ◊ *The two cultures have a lot in ~.* | **hold sth in ~** ◊ *They hold the property as tenants in ~* (= they share it). | **in ~ with** (*esp. BrE*) ◊ *India, in ~ with* (= like) *many other countries, has experienced major changes over the last 100 years.*

3 (*BrE*) showing a lack of education

VERBS **be, seem, sound** ◊ *I wish you wouldn't use that word—it sounds so ~.*
ADV. **very** | **a bit, rather, slightly** ◊ *I don't like Sandra. She seems a little ~ to me.*

common ground *noun*

VERB + COMMON GROUND **have, share** ◊ *The people on the course all share a lot of ~.* | **establish, find** | **find yourself on**
PREP. **on ~** ◊ *We found ourselves on ~ on the question of education.* | **~ between** ◊ *to find ~ between the two sides*
PHRASES **an area of ~**

commonplace *adj.*

VERBS **be, seem** | **become** | **regard sth as** ◊ *Such actions were regarded as ~ during the war.*
ADV. **very** | **almost** | **enough, fairly, quite, rather** ◊ *Her situation sounded ~ enough.*
PREP. **among** ◊ *These ideas are ~ among teenagers.*

common sense *noun*

ADJ. **good, sound** | **plain, pure, simple** | **practical**
VERB + COMMON SENSE **have** ◊ *That child has no ~! At least he had the ~ to turn the water off before he left.* | **exercise, rely on, show, use** ◊ *Use a bit of ~!*
COMMON SENSE + VERB **prevail** ◊ *I hope that ~ will prevail.* | **dictate sth, suggest sth, tell sb sth** ◊ *Common sense should tell you that people will find out sooner or later.*
PHRASES **(not) an ounce of ~** ◊ *He doesn't have an ounce of ~.*

commotion *noun*

ADJ. **big, great, huge, loud** (*esp. AmE*), **terrible** | **sudden**
VERB + COMMOTION **cause, make** ◊ *The people upstairs were making a great ~.* | **hear** | **see** (*AmE*)
COMMOTION + VERB **break out, erupt** | **die down**
PREP. **in a/the ~** ◊ *Lots of furniture had been knocked over in the ~.* | **~ about, ~ over** ◊ *What's all the ~ about?*

commune *noun*

ADJ. **hippy**
VERB + COMMUNE **join** ◊ *He gave up his job in the city and joined a ~.* | **belong to** | **form, set up**
PREP. **in a/the ~, on a/the ~** ◊ *She lives in a ~.*

communicate *verb*

ADV. **clearly, effectively, successfully, well** | **directly** | **easily, openly** | **electronically, telepathically, verbally** ◊ *By this age most children have begun to ~ verbally.*
PREP. **by** ◊ *We usually ~ by letter.* | **through** ◊ *We ~d through an interpreter.* | **to** ◊ *She is unable to ~ her ideas to other people.* | **with** ◊ *couples who ~ well with one another*

communication *noun*

1 act of communicating

ADJ. **clear, effective, good, open** ◊ *Good ~ is important for business.* | **poor** | **direct, face-to-face** | **two-way** |

interpersonal | **regular** | **electronic, non-verbal, oral, verbal, written** | **business** | **animal, human**
VERB + COMMUNICATION **have** ◊ *I haven't had any ~ with him for several years.* | **establish** | **enhance, facilitate, improve** | **maintain** | **prevent** ◊ *measures which prevented ~ with the outside world*
COMMUNICATION + VERB **break down** ◊ *Communication between the two sides has broken down.*
COMMUNICATION + NOUN **skills** | **style** | **breakdown, problem**
PREP. **in ~ with** ◊ *We are in regular ~ with the kidnappers.* | **~ between** ◊ *to establish direct ~ between the towers* | **~ by** ◊ *~ by letter* | **~ with** ◊ *We need better ~ with clients.*
PHRASES **a breakdown in ~, a breakdown in ~s** | **channels of ~, lines of ~** ◊ *to keep open the channels of ~* | **a lack of ~** | **a means of ~, a method of ~, a system of ~** ◊ *Letters are their only means of ~.*

2 communications systems for sending information

ADJ. **good** | **global, international** | **mass** | **broadband, digital, online, radio, satellite, telephone, wireless** | **rail, road**
VERB + COMMUNICATIONS **have** | **cut off, disrupt**
COMMUNICATIONS + NOUN **centre/center** | **links, network, system** | **satellite, technology** | **equipment, tool**
PREP. **~ between** ◊ *They tried to disrupt ~s between the two offices.* | **~ with** ◊ *Paris has good rail ~s with other major cities.*

3 message

ADJ. **formal, official, personal**
VERB + COMMUNICATION **receive** | **send** | **intercept**
PREP. **~ about** ◊ *He received an official ~ about the reorganization.* | **~ from, ~ to** ◊ *a ~ from the officer to the general*

communion *noun*

1 Communion in church

ADJ. **Holy** | **First** | **open**
VERB + COMMUNION **go to** ◊ *We went to Holy Communion in the cathedral.* | **administer, celebrate, give** ◊ *Communion was celebrated by the Reverend John Harris.* | **receive, take** ◊ *Most of the people present took Communion.* | **deny sb, refuse sb**
COMMUNION + NOUN **service** | **cup, rail, table** | **wafer, wine**
PREP. **at ~** ◊ *There were only half a dozen people at Communion.*

2 sharing thoughts/feelings

ADJ. **close** | **personal** | **spiritual**
PREP. **in ~ with** ◊ *He lived in close ~ with nature.* | **~ with** ◊ *her personal ~ with God*

communiqué *noun*

ADJ. **official, unofficial** | **joint**
VERB + COMMUNIQUÉ **issue** | **receive**
PREP. **in a/the ~** ◊ *The announcement was made in a ~ issued by the Defence Minister.*

communism *noun*

ADJ. **international** | **Soviet**
VERB + COMMUNISM **embrace** | **defeat, fight, overthrow**
PREP. **under ~** ◊ *a book describing life under ~*
PHRASES **the collapse of ~, the fall of ~** | **the fight against ~, the struggle against ~** | **the rise of ~, the spread of ~**

community *noun*

ADJ. **large, small** | **close, close-knit, tight-knit** ◊ *a close-knit fishing ~* | **diverse** | **lively, thriving, vibrant** | **global, international** | **local** | **broader, wider** ◊ *the concerns of the local and wider ~* | **disadvantaged, low-income** (*AmE*), **poor, underserved** (*AmE*) | **ethnic, expatriate, immigrant, minority** | **indigenous, native** (*AmE*) | **faith, religious** | **Asian, black**, etc. ◊ *the Asian ~ in Britain* | **Christian, Muslim**, etc. | **farming, mining**, etc. | **coastal, rural, village** | **urban** | **academic, business, intelligence, medical, scientific** | **gay, lesbian** | **gated, residential, retirement** (*all AmE*) | **blogging, online, virtual**

COMMUNITY + NOUN **service, work** | **policing** | **care** (*BrE*) | **centre/center** | **college, garden, hospital, library, park** (*all AmE*) | **spirit** ◊ *The town has a strong ~ spirit.* | **relations** | **action, development, outreach** | **involvement, participation** | **activist, leader, organizer** (*AmE*) | **group, organization**
PREP. **in a/the ~, within a/the ~** ◊ *divisions within the scientific ~*
PHRASES **the ~ as a whole, the ~ at large** ◊ *an initiative that should benefit the ~ at large* | **a/the ~ of faith** (*AmE*) | **a member of the ~** | **part of a ~** | **a pillar of the ~** (= a strong supporter of the community), **a sense of ~** ◊ *There is a strong sense of ~ in this town.*

commute *verb*

ADV. **daily, every day** | **regularly** | **back and forth**
PREP. **between** ◊ *He ~d daily between London and Surrey.* | **from, to** ◊ *She ~s from Sunset Park to Manhattan each morning.*

companion *noun*

ADJ. **agreeable** (*esp. BrE*), **boon** (*literary*), **charming, delightful, entertaining, good, pleasant, wonderful** | **close, constant, faithful, inseparable, loyal** ◊ *A cute little terrier was his constant ~.* ◊ *Fear was her constant ~.* (*figurative*) | **life, long-time** | **female, male** | **canine, human** | **dining, dinner** | **drinking, travelling/traveling, walking** ◊ *He was an entertaining dinner ~.*
COMPANION + NOUN **animal**
PREP. **~ for, ~ to** ◊ *She lived in the house as a ~ to our grandmother.*

companionship *noun*

ADJ. **close** | **constant** | **female, male** | **human** | **intellectual**
VERB + COMPANIONSHIP **need** | **provide (sb with)** ◊ *A dog provides some ~.* | **seek** | **enjoy, find, have**
PREP. **for ~** ◊ *She had only her cat for ~.* | **~ with** ◊ *She had never had any close ~ with another woman.*

company *noun*

1 business organization

ADJ. **big, large, leading, major** ◊ *a major Japanese ~* | **medium-sized, mid-sized** (*esp. AmE*) | **small** | **reputable** | **profitable, successful** | **associated** (*BrE*), **holding, joint-stock, limited** (*in the UK*), **parent** ◊ *a public limited ~* | **start-up** ◊ *a small start-up software ~* | **family-owned, state-owned** | **private, public** | **international, multinational, national** | **commercial, utility** | **manufacturing, trading** ◊ *an international trading ~* | **drug, pharmaceutical** | **bus, insurance, oil, etc.** ◊ *a small insurance ~* | **dotcom, Internet, tech**
... OF COMPANIES **group**
VERB + COMPANY **create, establish, form, found, launch, set up, start, start up** | **manage, operate, run** | **build, grow** | **own** | **acquire, buy, take over** ◊ *The ~ has been taken over by a rival.* | **dissolve** | **sell** | **work for** ◊ *She's been working for the same ~ for ten years.* | **join** | **leave, resign from** | **sue**
COMPANY + VERB **make sth, manufacture sth, produce sth, sell sth, supply sth** ◊ *The ~ produces cotton goods.* | **operate** | **expand, grow** | **shrink** | **merge** | **fail, go bankrupt, go bust, go into liquidation, go out of business, go to the wall** (*informal*), **go under** ◊ *During the recession many small companies went out of business.*
COMPANY + NOUN **director, executive** | **owner, president** | **official, representative, spokesman, spokeswoman** | **policy** | **profits** | **car, pension** | **logo, name** | **headquarters** | **website** | **employee**
PREP. **in a/the ~** ◊ *He has shares in several companies.* | **within a/the ~** ◊ *the division of power within a ~*
PHRASES **a director of a ~**
→ Special page at BUSINESS

2 group of actors, dancers, etc.

ADJ. **large, small** | **touring** | **ballet, opera, repertory, stock** (*AmE*), **theatre/theater** ◊ *a small touring opera ~*
→ Note at ORGANIZATION (for verbs)

3 being with sb else

ADJ. **good, pleasant** ◊ *He's very good ~.* | **poor**
VERB + COMPANY **have** ◊ *It's nice to have a bit of ~ for a change.* | **keep sb** ◊ *I'll stay and keep you ~.* | **need, want** | **provide (sb with)** ◊ *A cat would provide her with some ~.* | **seek** | **enjoy** ◊ *I always enjoy her ~.*
PREP. **for ~** ◊ *I took my mother with me for ~.* | **in sb's ~** ◊ *He's nervous in the ~ of his colleagues.*
PHRASES **have the pleasure of sb's ~, request the pleasure of sb's ~** (*both formal*) | **like your own ~, prefer your own ~** (= to like being alone)

4 group of people together

ADJ. **mixed** (= men and women) | **assembled** ◊ *He glanced around the assembled ~.*
VERB + COMPANY **keep** (= to spend time with people) ◊ *John's mother was worried about the ~ he kept.*
PREP. **in ~** ◊ *Those children don't know how to behave in ~.* ◊ *That's not something to say in mixed ~.*
PHRASES **get into bad ~, keep bad ~** (= to be friends with people that others disapprove of) | **present ~ excepted** (= used after being rude or critical about sb to say that the people you are talking to are not included in the criticism)

5 visitor or visitors

VERB + COMPANY **expect, have** ◊ *We're expecting ~ this afternoon.*

comparable *adj.*

VERBS **be** | **become**
ADV. **closely, quite, very** ◊ *Its brain is closely ~ to the brain of a chimpanzee.* | **directly, exactly** | **broadly, generally, roughly** | **almost** | **in no way, not in any way, not remotely** ◊ *The regional variation in Australian accent is not in any way ~ to that found in the UK or US.* ◊ *There are no other scanners even remotely ~ to this in terms of quality of image produced.* | **not strictly** | **easily**
PREP. **in** ◊ *The two machines are ~ in size.* | **to** ◊ *a job ~ to mine* | **with** ◊ *The earthquake was ~ with others in recent years.*
PHRASES **something ~ (to sth)** ◊ *He was dressed in something ~ to a tribal costume.* | **there is nothing ~ (to sth)**

compare *verb*

ADV. **favourably/favorably, well** ◊ *The city ~s favourably/favorably with other parts of Brazil.* | **unfavourably/unfavorably** | **closely** | **accurately, directly, systematically** | **easily** | **constantly**
VERB + COMPARE **cannot, do not** ◊ *These mountains do not ~ with* (= are not nearly as high, impressive, etc. as) *the Himalayas.*
PREP. **with** ◊ *Few things ~ with* (= are as good as) *the joy of walking on a bright spring morning.*
PHRASES **~ and contrast** | **be nothing ~d to sb/sth** ◊ *I've had some difficulties but they were nothing ~d to yours* (= they were not nearly as bad as yours). | **nothing ~s to sb/sth** (= nothing is as good as sb/sth) | **be often ~d to sb/sth** ◊ *The golfer Tiger Woods is often ~d to Jack Nicklaus.*

comparison *noun*

ADJ. **favourable/favorable, unfavourable/unfavorable** | **fair, unfair** | **broad, crude** (*esp. BrE*), **simple** | **accurate, careful, close, detailed, direct** | **meaningful, useful, valid** | **apt, good, interesting** | **inevitable** | **performance, price, etc.** ◊ *a price-comparison site*
VERB + COMPARISON **draw, make, perform** ◊ *It's difficult to make a direct comparison—the two things are so different.* | **allow, enable, facilitate, permit** | **invite** ◊ *The similarity between the two invites ~.* | **bear, stand** ◊ *Our problems don't bear ~ with those elsewhere.*
PREP. **by ~ (with)** ◊ *Jane is still young, and Fiona seems old by ~.* | **for ~** ◊ *Let's put them side by side for ~.* | **in ~ to, in ~ with** ◊ *The glasses are small in ~ with the old ones.* | **~ between** ◊ *a ~ between figures for last year and this year* | **~**

with ◇ *a ~ with other schools* | *~ of* ◇ *a ~ of unemployment rates over the past 15 years*
PHRASES **a basis for ~** ◇ *to provide a basis for ~* | **a point of ~** | **for the purposes of ~**

compartment noun

1 section of a train
ADJ. **first-class, second-class** | **non-smoking, smoking** | **baggage** (*esp. AmE*), **luggage** (*esp. BrE*) | **driver's, passenger** | **sleeping**
PREP. **in a/the ~**

2 section of a container, etc.
ADJ. **separate** | **hidden, secret** | **battery, freezer, glove, storage** ◇ *Your sunglasses are in the glove ~.* | **overhead** | **watertight**
VERB + COMPARTMENT **be divided into** ◇ *The case is divided into four separate ~s.*
PREP. **in a/the ~**

compass noun

ADJ. **digital, magnetic**
VERB + COMPASS **use** | **check**
COMPASS + VERB **show sth** ◇ *A ~ shows you which direction is north.*
COMPASS + NOUN **needle** | **bearing, reading** | **direction, point**
PHRASES **a map and ~, the points of the ~** ◇ *People arrived from all points of the ~.*

compassion noun

ADJ. **deep, great** | **genuine, true** | **human**
VERB + COMPASSION **be filled with, feel, have** | **show (sb)** | **lack**
COMPASSION + NOUN **fatigue** ◇ *In cities where many people beg, citizens quickly develop ~ fatigue.*
PREP. **~ for** ◇ *He was filled with an overwhelming ~ for his wife.* | **~ towards/toward** ◇ *I felt no ~ towards/toward her.* | **with ~** ◇ *The old people are treated with great ~.*
PHRASES **love and ~**

compassionate adj.

VERBS **be, feel, sound**
ADV. **deeply, very** ◇ *a deeply ~ man*

compatible adj.

VERBS **be, seem**
ADV. **highly, very** | **entirely, fully, perfectly, quite, totally, wholly** ◇ *three different, yet entirely ~ programs* | **mutually** | **directly** | **hardly** | **logically, sexually, technologically**
PREP. **with** ◇ *The theory does not seem ~ with his other ideas.*

compelling adj.

1 holding your attention
VERBS **be** | **become** | **find sth**
ADV. **very** | **utterly** | **oddly, strangely** ◇ *His eyes were strangely ~.*

2 strong/convincing
VERBS **be**
ADV. **extremely, fairly, very, etc.** | **equally** ◇ *Equally ~ is data that suggests that antidepressants leave some people with no relief at all.* | **logically** ◇ *There is no logically ~ argument to support their claims.*

compensate verb

1 remove/reduce the bad effect of sth
ADV. **amply, fully** | **more than** ◇ *The advantages of the plan more than ~ for the risks associated with it.* | **partially, partly**
PREP. **for** ◇ *His strengths more than ~ for his weaknesses.* | **with** ◇ *His voice doesn't have much range but he ~s with clever lyrics.*

2 pay money for a loss/injury
ADV. **adequately, fairly, properly, well** | **fully, in full** ◇ *People whose health has suffered will be ~d in full.* | **financially** ◇ *I expect to be ~d financially.*
PREP. **for** ◇ *The company will ~ you for the losses you have suffered.*

compensation noun

ADJ. **full** | **partial, small** | **adequate, sufficient** | **appropriate, fair, just** | **cash, financial, monetary** | **deferred** | **CEO, executive** (*both AmE*) | **employee** (*AmE*) | **unemployment** (*AmE*)
...OF COMPENSATION **amount**
VERB + COMPENSATION **award (sb), give (sb), grant (sb), offer (sb), pay (sb), provide (sb with)** | **accept, gain** (*esp. BrE*), **get, obtain, receive, win** ◇ *She got some ~ for damages.* | **deny sb, refuse sb** | **claim, demand, fight for, seek** | **determine** ◇ *the rules used for determining ~* | **be eligible for, be entitled to**
COMPENSATION + VERB **be payable** ◇ *If the government is proved negligent, ~ will be payable.*
COMPENSATION + NOUN **claim** | **committee** (*esp. AmE*) | **costs** | **fund** | **insurance** (*esp. AmE*) | **order** (*esp. BrE*) | **package** | **payment** | **benefits** (*AmE*) | **plan** (*AmE*), **policy, program** (*AmE*), **scheme** (*BrE*), **system** | **law** | **consultant, handler** (*both AmE*)
PREP. **as ~ (for)** ◇ *She received £7 000 as ~ for her injuries.* | **in ~ (for)** ◇ *They will have to pay £5 000 in ~.* | **~ for** ◇ *The money was small ~ for unfair dismissal.* | **~ from** ◇ *~ from the government*

compete verb

ADV. **effectively, successfully** | **directly** ◇ *Their products ~ directly with ours.* | **head-to-head** ◇ *The company is prepared to ~ head-to-head with the market giants.* | **globally, internationally, nationally** ◇ *The price must be right in order to ~ internationally.* | **aggressively, fiercely, intensely, vigorously** ◇ *The big companies are competing fiercely on price.* | **actively** ◇ *a readiness to ~ actively in the global system* | **favourably/favorably** | **economically**
VERB + COMPETE **cannot** ◇ *Small independent retailers can't ~ with the large stores.*
PREP. **against** ◇ *He welcomed the chance to ~ against professional athletes.* | **in** ◇ *Animals in the wild have to ~ for food.* | **in** ◇ *He regularly ~s in races.* | **with** ◇ *We have to ~ with several larger companies.*

competence noun

1 ability to do sth well
ADJ. **great** | **basic** | **academic, administrative, clinical, managerial, professional, technical** | **communicative, language, linguistic** | **athletic** | **cultural, emotional, social** | **core** ◇ *The company's core ~ lay in engineering.*
VERB + COMPETENCE **have** | **demonstrate, display, prove, show** ◇ *She shows a high level of technical ~.* | **lack** | **achieve, acquire, develop, gain** ◇ *He gradually developed the ~ to deal with the more difficult cases.* | **increase, promote** | **challenge, question** | **assess, evaluate**
PREP. **beyond sb's ~** ◇ *I'm afraid the work is beyond his ~.* | **within sb's ~** ◇ *This should be well within your ~.* | **~ as** ◇ *Students had questioned her ~ as a teacher.* | **~ for** ◇ *He displayed great ~ for the job.* | **~ in** ◇ *~ in English*
PHRASES **a level of ~, a standard of ~**

2 power to deal with sth
ADJ. **formal** | **exclusive**
VERB + COMPETENCE **have** ◇ *The commission has no formal ~ in cultural matters.*
PREP. **outside sb/sth's ~** ◇ *matters that fall outside the court's ~* | **within sb/sth's ~** ◇ *The decisions come within the ~ of the committee.*
PHRASES **an area of ~**

competent adj.

VERBS **be, feel, look, seem** | **become** | **make sb** ◇ *A year of*

college had made her more socially ~. | **consider sb, regard sb as** ◇ *He was not considered ~ to teach seven-year-olds.*
ADV. **extremely, fairly, very, etc.** | **highly** ◇ *a small number of highly ~ officials* | **fully, perfectly** | **mentally** ◇ *She was mentally ~ and she had the capacity to decide for herself.* ◇ *mentally ~ to stand trial (AmE, law)* | **culturally, socially, technically**
PREP. **in** ◇ *She is ~ in five languages.*

competition *noun*

1 event in which people try to win sth
ADJ. **international, national** | **major, prestigious** ◇ *wines that won medals at major wine ~s* | **knockout** | **sporting** (*BrE*), **sports** (*AmE*) | **bodybuilding, dancing, piano, etc.**
VERB + COMPETITION **win** ◇ *She won an international dancing ~.* | **lose** | **have, hold, launch, stage** ◇ *We're going to have a ~ to see who can swim the fastest.* | **organize** | **enter, take part in** | **withdraw from** | **dominate** ◇ *The American women dominated the ~, winning all the events.* | **judge** | **sponsor**
COMPETITION + VERB **take place** | **be open to sb** ◇ *The ~ is open to all readers of the magazine.*
COMPETITION + NOUN **winner** | **entry** | **committee**
PREP. **in a/the ~** ◇ *I won the car in a ~.* | **~ between** ◇ *a ~ between the best teams in the country* | **~ for** ◇ *a ~ for the best chef*

2 trying to achieve the same thing/gain an advantage
ADJ. **cut-throat, fierce, intense, keen, serious, severe, stiff, strong, tough** ◇ *intense ~ for the contract* | **growing, heightened, increased, increasing** | **direct** ◇ *Public education is run in direct ~ with the private sector.* | **head-to-head** ◇ *There is head-to-head ~ in production and distribution.* | **fair, free, healthy, open** | **unfair** | **friendly** ◇ *Their rivalry had been one of friendly ~.* | **domestic, local** | **foreign, global, international, overseas** | **economic**
VERB + COMPETITION **be up against, face** | **go into** ◇ *to go into ~ with British Telecom* | **beat off, fight off, see off** (*BrE*) ◇ *to fight off ~ from overseas companies* | **create, encourage, foster, introduce, promote, provide, stimulate** ◇ *policies aimed at fostering greater ~ in the industry* | **increase, intensify** ◇ *This intensified the ~ for the same investors' funds.* | **limit, minimize, prevent, reduce, stifle** | **eliminate**
COMPETITION + VERB **exist** ◇ *Fierce ~ exists between schools in the area.* | **heat up, intensify** ◇ *Competition is heating up and sales are shrinking.*
COMPETITION + NOUN **laws**
PREP. **against ~** ◇ *They won the order against fierce international ~.* | **in ~ with** ◇ *We are in ~ with some very large companies.* | **in the face of ~** ◇ *The gas companies are having to lay off staff in the face of stiff ~ from oil.* | **~ among, ~ between** ◇ *There is a lot of ~ between rival airlines.* | **~ for** | **~ from** ◇ *We face strong ~ from other countries.*

3 the people who are competing against someone
VERB + COMPETITION **outperform** ◇ *This car consistently outperforms the ~.* | **blow away** (*esp. AmE*), **crush, destroy** ◇ *Bertram blew away the ~ and won the race in record time.*

competitive *adj.*

VERBS **be** | **become, remain, stay** | **make sth** ◇ *skills training to make our industries more ~ in world markets* | **keep sth**
ADV. **extremely, fairly, very, etc.** ◇ *a very ~ person* | **brutally, fiercely, highly, intensely** ◇ *a fiercely ~ sport* | **highly ~ prices** | **increasingly** | **globally, internationally** | **economically**
PREP. **with** ◇ *Investment in research is needed to keep us ~ with other countries.*

competitor *noun*

1 in business
ADJ. **biggest, chief, leading, main, major** | **fierce, formidable, serious, strong, tough** ◇ *The company has no*

serious ~s in this area. | **potential** | **closest, direct, nearest** | **domestic, local** | **foreign, global, international, overseas**
VERB + COMPETITOR **face** ◇ *The industry is facing increasingly strong foreign ~s.* | **beat, outperform**
COMPETITOR + VERB **offer sth** ◇ *Nearly all our ~s offered free Internet services.*
PREP. **~ for** ◇ *fierce ~s for the dominant position in the Asian market*

2 person who takes part in a competition
ADJ. **strong, top** ◇ *She is one of the sport's top ~s.* | **successful** | **worthy** | **fellow** | **fitness** (= who take part in fitness contests) (*AmE*)
COMPETITOR + VERB **enter sth** ◇ *Ten ~s entered the race.*

complacent *adj.*

VERBS **appear, be, seem, sound** | **become, get, grow**
ADV. **extremely, fairly, very, etc.** | **remarkably** | **far from** ◇ *Teachers are far from ~ about this problem.* | **alarmingly, dangerously** ◇ *This view seems alarmingly ~.*
PREP. **about** ◇ *It is vital that we do not get ~ about this disease.*

complain *verb*

ADV. **bitterly** ◇ *She ~ed bitterly about the lack of help she received.* | **loudly** | **constantly, frequently, repeatedly** | **openly, publicly** | **privately**
VERB + COMPLAIN **cannot** | **can hardly** ◇ *It was entirely my own idea, so I can hardly ~.* | **have cause to, have reason to, have a right to** ◇ *He really has no right to ~.* | **begin to, start to**
PREP. **about** ◇ *All the guests ~ed about the noise.* | **at** ◇ *She ~ed at the unfairness of it all.* | **to** ◇ *I'm going to ~ to the authorities about this!* | **of** ◇ *45 officers ~ed of harassment.*

complaint *noun*

1 act of complaining
ADJ. **serious** | **common, familiar, frequent** | **minor, small** | **only** ◇ *My only ~ is that the website is a little difficult to use.* | **biggest, chief, main, major, primary** ◇ *One of the chief ~s is the cost.* | **formal, official** | **legitimate, valid** | **consumer, customer** | **citizen** (*AmE*) | **civil, criminal** (*AmE*) | **discrimination, harassment** | **ethics** (*AmE*)
VERB + COMPLAINT **have** ◇ *I have a ~ about the food.* | **bring, file, lodge, make, raise, register, voice** ◇ *He brought a ~ against his former manager.* ◇ *They filed a ~ with the Commission.* | **get, have, receive** ◇ *We have had some serious ~s from parents.* | **address, deal with, handle, hear, investigate, respond to** ◇ *The tribunal heard ~s against the director.* | **resolve** | **ignore, dismiss, reject**
COMPLAINT + VERB **arise** ◇ *~s arising from late payment* | **concern sth, relate to sth** | **allege sth**
COMPLAINT + NOUN **~ procedure** (*AmE*), **~s procedure** (*BrE*), **~ system** (*AmE*) | **letter** (*esp. AmE*) (usually *letter of complaint* in *BrE* and *AmE*) | **form**
PREP. **~ about** ◇ *a ~ about working conditions* | **~ against** ◇ *a ~ against the police* | **~ from** ◇ *a ~ from a customer* | **~ of** ◇ *a ~ of unfair dismissal* | **~ to** ◇ *to make a ~ to the authorities*
PHRASES **cause for ~, grounds for ~** ◇ *The way I was treated gave me no cause for ~.* | **a chorus of ~** | **a letter of ~** | **a matter of ~** (*BrE, law*)

2 illness
ADJ. **minor** | **chronic** | **common** ◇ *Not being able to sleep at night is a very common ~.* | **back, chest, etc.** | **physical** | **medical**
VERB + COMPLAINT **have, suffer from** ◇ *He has a minor skin ~.*

complement *noun*

1 sth that goes well with sth else
ADJ. **good, ideal, natural, necessary, nice, perfect**
PREP. **~ to** ◇ *This wine is the perfect ~ to fish.*

2 total number that makes a group complete
ADJ. **full** | **large** | **normal**

VERB + COMPLEMENT **take** ◊ *We've taken our full ~ of trainees this year.*
PREP. **~ of**

complement *verb*
ADV. **nicely, well** | **perfectly** ◊ *The dishes on the menu ~ each other perfectly.*

complete *verb*
1 finish sth
ADV. **on schedule, on time** | **successfully** ◊ *The project has now been successfully ~d.* | **just, recently** ◊ *We have recently ~d a 10-year study.* | **fully, partially** ◊ *I've fully ~d my training.*
2 write information
ADV. **accurately, correctly** ◊ *Has the form been correctly ~d?*

complete *adj.*
1 having/including all the parts
VERBS **be, seem** | **survive** ◊ *The book survives ~ only in the second edition of 1533.* | **make sth** ◊ *You've made my life ~.*
ADV. **remarkably** ◊ *a remarkably ~ account of the negotiations* | **very** ◊ *A very ~ index provides easy reference to topics in the book.* | **far from, less than, not quite** | **almost, essentially, largely, nearly, virtually** | **fairly, reasonably, relatively**
2 finished
VERBS **be, seem**
ADV. **almost, nearly, substantially, virtually** ◊ *The job is almost ~.* | **far from** | **not yet**

completion *noun*
ADJ. **rapid, speedy** | **early** | **timely** | **satisfactory, successful** | **college, school** (*both AmE*) | **course, project, task, etc.**
VERB + COMPLETION **near, reach** ◊ *The renovation of the museum is now nearing ~.* | **bring sth to** ◊ *to bring the project to ~* | **delay** | **prevent** | **be due for** ◊ *The bridge is due for ~ in May.* | **celebrate, mark** ◊ *There was a party to celebrate the ~ of the project.*
COMPLETION + NOUN **date** | **time** | **rate**
PREP. **after ~, following ~** ◊ *Payment will be made following successful ~ of the job.* | **before ~, prior to ~** ◊ *The floorboards were replaced prior to ~ of the sale.* | **near ~** ◊ *The book is near ~.* | **pending ~** ◊ *Development of the site has been delayed pending ~ of the road.* | **on ~ of, upon ~ of** ◊ *The committee will report back to us on ~ of the study.*
PHRASES **the date of ~**

complex *noun*
1 set of buildings
ADJ. **huge, large, vast** | **entertainment, holiday** (*BrE*), **leisure, shopping, sports** | **apartment** (*AmE*), **factory, hospital, housing, museum, office** | **industrial, military**
VERB + COMPLEX **build**
2 mental/emotional problem
ADJ. **real, terrible** | **inferiority, superiority** | **castration, guilt, Oedipus, persecution**
VERB + COMPLEX **have, suffer from** | **develop, get** ◊ *Don't nag him about his handwriting or he'll get a ~.* | **give sb**
PREP. **~ about** ◊ *She has a ~ about her big ears.*

complex *adj.*
VERBS **be, look, seem, sound** | **become**
ADV. **extremely, fairly, very, etc.** | **enormously, exceedingly, extraordinarily, highly, hugely, immensely, incredibly, infinitely** ◊ *This is a highly ~ matter.* | **especially, exceptionally, particularly** | **increasingly** | **relatively** | **surprisingly** | **unnecessarily** | **technically** ◊ *technically ~ surgery*

complexion *noun*
1 skin/face
ADJ. **beautiful, clear, flawless, fresh, glowing, healthy, lovely, nice, perfect** | **dull, pallid, pasty, sallow** | **creamy, fair, light, milky, pale** | **dark, olive, swarthy, tan** (*AmE*), **tanned** | **florid** (*esp. BrE*), **pink, rosy, ruddy** ◊ *a young girl with a rosy ~* | **smooth**
VERB + COMPLEXION **have** | **give sb** ◊ *Years of heavy drinking had given Moira a florid ~.*
2 general nature/character of sth
ADJ. **different, new** | **political, social** ◊ *a change in the political ~ of the council*
VERB + COMPLEXION **put, take on** ◊ *What you have told us puts a different ~ on the situation.* ◊ *The joke took on a rather serious ~ when the police became involved.* | **change** ◊ *Hughes helped change the ~ of Hollywood.*

complexity *noun*
ADJ. **considerable, enormous, extraordinary, extreme, great, immense** | **full, sheer** ◊ *Only now did he understand the full ~ of the problem.* | **growing, increasing** | **bewildering** | **unnecessary** | **added** | **biological, economic, linguistic, structural, technical** ◊ *The critics failed to understand the structural complexities of the novel's language.* | **emotional, psychological**
...OF COMPLEXITY **degree, level**
VERB + COMPLEXITY **convey, demonstrate, illustrate, reflect, reveal, show** ◊ *It is difficult to convey the sheer ~ of the situation.* | **emphasize, highlight, underscore** (*AmE*) ◊ *The video emphasizes the ~ of this debate.* | **capture** ◊ *The author has managed to capture the ~ of this man.* | **create** ◊ *These programs create additional complexities to the pricing system.* | **appreciate, grasp, recognize, understand** | **underestimate** | **explore** ◊ *a love story which explores the complexities of emotional infidelity* | **explain** | **address, handle** | **increase, reduce**
COMPLEXITY + VERB **arise (from sth)**
PREP. **of... ~** ◊ *a pay system of unnecessary ~*

complicate *verb*
ADV. **enormously, greatly, seriously, significantly** ◊ *These events will greatly ~ the situation.* | **further**
PHRASES **be ~d by the fact that** ◊ *The issue is ~d by the fact that a vital document is missing.*

complicated *adj.*
VERBS **be, look, seem, sound** ◊ *It all sounds very ~.* | **become, get** ◊ *This is where the story gets ~.*
ADV. **extremely, fairly, very, etc.** | **enormously, extraordinarily, fiendishly, highly, immensely, incredibly, particularly, terribly** ◊ *The world of finance is fiendishly ~.* | **overly, unnecessarily** | **insanely** | **increasingly** | **a little, slightly, etc.**

complication *noun*
1 problem
ADJ. **major** | **added, additional, further** | **undue, unnecessary** | **political**
VERB + COMPLICATION **add, cause** ◊ *The presence of an armed gang added a major ~.* | **avoid** ◊ *We always try to avoid any unnecessary ~s.*
COMPLICATION + VERB **arise, ensue, occur** ◊ *Further ~s arose when they published an interview with his family.*
2 medical
ADJ. **acute, dangerous, life-threatening, serious, severe** | **fatal** | **chronic, long-term** | **minor** | **significant** | **common** | **rare** | **local** | **potential** | **birth, diabetic, medical, post-operative, pregnancy**
VERB + COMPLICATION **develop, have, suffer** ◊ *She developed ~s two weeks after the treatment.* | **die from, die of** | **cause** | **avoid, prevent**
COMPLICATION + VERB **arise, develop, occur** ◊ *Complications develop if the drug is not used correctly.* | **result from sth**
COMPLICATION + NOUN **rate** ◊ *~ rates from eye surgery*

PREP. **~ with** ◊ ~s with her pregnancy. | **~ from** ◊ He died of ~s from cancer surgery. | **~ of** ◊ the devastating ~s of diabetes

PHRASES **a risk of ~s** ◊ The treatment carries a high risk of ~s. | **~s related to sth** ◊ He died from ~s related to diabetes.

complicity noun

ADJ. **alleged, apparent** ◊ her alleged ~ in the bombing | **active** | **government, police**

PREP. **~ between** ◊ the ~ between the army and drug smugglers | **~ in** ◊ her ~ in a plot to kill the president | **~ with** ◊ She did not suspect him of ~ with the authorities.

PHRASES **an act of ~**
→ Note at CRIME (for verbs)

compliment noun

1 expression of praise

ADJ. **big, great, tremendous, ultimate** ◊ To listen to someone is the greatest ~ you can pay. | **biggest, highest** | **nice, wonderful** | **unexpected** | **backhanded, left-handed** (AmE) ◊ In a backhanded ~ she said he looked very good for his age.

VERB + COMPLIMENT **give, pay sb** | **mean sth as** ◊ Please don't misunderstand me—I meant it as a ~. | **get, receive** | **accept, acknowledge, take** ◊ She acknowledged their ~s with a big smile. | **appreciate** | **regard sth as, take sth as** ◊ I'll take that as a ~. | **fish for** ◊ She's always fishing for ~s about her looks. | **repay, return** ◊ He returned her ~ by saying how well she looked.

PREP. **~ on** ◊ She received several ~s on her speech. | **~ to** ◊ If Mark's wearing a suit, that'll be a ~ to you!

2 (formal) your compliments good wishes

VERB + COMPLIMENTS **give sb, present (sb with), send sb** ◊ Please give my ~s to your wife.

COMPLIMENTS + NOUN **slip** (BrE) ◊ The only enclosure was a formal ~s slip from the accounts department.

PREP. **with sb's ~** (= free) ◊ All guests will receive a bottle of champagne with our ~s. | **~ to** ◊ my ~s to the chef (= to show that you like a particular dish)

complimentary adj.

VERBS **be**

ADV. **extremely, fairly, very, etc.** | **highly** ◊ She made some highly ~ remarks about their school.

PREP. **about**

comply verb

ADV. **fully** | **reluctantly** | **happily, willingly** | **quickly**

VERB + COMPLY **fail to, refuse to** ◊ When requested to leave, they refused to ~.

PREP. **with** ◊ Candidates must ~ strictly with these instructions.

component noun

ADJ. **basic, central, core, critical, crucial, essential, fundamental, important, integral, key, main, major, necessary, primary, principal, significant, vital** | **minor** | **active** | **common** ◊ The researchers discovered a common ~ in all types of the organism. | **standard** ◊ Our software is becoming a standard ~ of many computer systems. | **individual, separate, simple** ◊ Individual ~s for the car can be very expensive. | **chemical, genetic** | **electrical, electronic** | **structural** | **aircraft, engine, etc.** | **course** | **off-the-shelf**

VERB + COMPONENT **add, include, incorporate, install, integrate** | **design** | **assemble** | **manufacture**

COMPONENT + NOUN **failure** ◊ Component failure was the cause of the accident. | **manufacturer, supplier**

PREP. **~ in** ◊ a crucial ~ in our success.

composed adj.

1 composed of made up of sth

VERBS **be**

ADV. **entirely, exclusively, solely, wholly** ◊ The committee was ~ entirely of specialists. | **chiefly, largely, mainly, mostly, overwhelmingly, predominantly, primarily** ◊ Bones are largely ~ of calcium.

2 in control of your feelings

VERBS **be, feel, look, seem**

ADV. **extremely, fairly, very, etc.** | **remarkably** | **perfectly** ◊ He was pale but perfectly ~. | **outwardly**

composer noun

ADJ. **famous, fine, great** | **established, important, leading, major, successful** | **minor** | **prolific** ◊ Verdi was a prolific ~ of operas. | **classical** | **avant-garde, modern** | **contemporary, living** | **opera** | **18th-century, 19th-century, etc.**

VERB + COMPOSER **commission**

COMPOSER + VERB **compose sth, write sth**
→ Note at JOB

composition noun

1 parts that form sth

ADJ. **overall** ◊ The overall ~ of the Senate was Democrats 57 and Republicans 43. | **internal** ◊ the character of the state and its internal ~ | **exact, precise** | **changing** ◊ the changing ~ of the workforce | **age, class, demographic, ethnic, family, gender, household, population, racial, social** ◊ the ethnic ~ of the region | **species** | **chemical, mineralogical**

VERB + COMPOSITION **determine** ◊ elections to determine the ~ of the assembly | **analyse/analyze, measure, study** | **alter, change** ◊ Irradiation changes the chemical ~ of a spice.

COMPOSITION + VERB **change, differ** ◊ Has household ~ changed in the last decade?

PHRASES **a change in the ~ of sth**

2 piece of music

ADJ. **classical, instrumental, musical** | **original** ◊ an original ~ by a popular young composer

VERB + COMPOSITION **write** | **perform, play**

PREP. **~ by** ◊ a ~ by John Cage | **~ for** ◊ a ~ for violin and piano

3 art of writing music

VERB + COMPOSITION **study** | **teach**

PHRASES **a method of ~**

4 piece of writing

ADJ. **literary, original, poetic, prose**

VERB + COMPOSITION **do, write** ◊ In the exam you will have to do a ~.

PREP. **~ on** ◊ a ~ on the effects of crime

5 work of art

ADJ. **abstract, figure, formal, pictorial** | **original** | **perfect**

VERB + COMPOSITION **create**

PREP. **~ by** ◊ a ~ by the sculptor, Bernt Notke

composure noun

ADJ. **calm, cool, perfect**

VERB + COMPOSURE **hold, keep, maintain, retain** | **lose** ◊ She totally lost her ~ and began shouting. | **gain, recover, regain** | **gather** ◊ She closed her eyes for a moment, to gather her ~. | **ruffle** ◊ Nothing could ruffle his ~.

PREP. **with ~** ◊ She answered with perfect ~.

compound noun

1 chemical

ADJ. **chemical** ◊ Scientists have produced a new chemical ~. | **inorganic, organic** | **synthetic** | **natural** | **molecular, simple** | **active, toxic, volatile** | **carbon, iron, etc.**

VERB + COMPOUND **form, make, produce** ◊ At the right temperature, the chemicals will form a ~. | **develop, synthesize** | **discover, identify** | **isolate**

COMPOUND + VERB **contain sth** | **be derived from sth, be found in sth, derive from sth, occur** ◊ ~s derived from rainforest plants

PREP. **~ of** ◊ a ~ of oxygen and hydrogen

2 area of land and buildings

ADJ. **military, palace, prison** | **secure, walled** ◇ *Police are investigating a raid on a secure ~.*
PREP. **in a/the ~, inside a/the ~** ◇ *life inside the prison ~*

comprehend verb

ADV. **fully** | **barely** ◇ *She could barely ~ what was happening to her.* | **easily**
VERB + COMPREHEND **be able to, be unable to** | **cannot, fail to** ◇ *She failed to ~ the seriousness of the situation.* | **be difficult to, be impossible to** ◇ *It is difficult to ~ how far away the stars are.*

comprehensible adj.

VERBS **be** | **become** | **make sth** ◇ *We changed the wording of the text to make it more ~.*
ADV. **easily, readily** ◇ *The instructions should be easily ~ to parents.* | **entirely, fully, perfectly** | **barely** ◇ *His French was barely ~.* | **mutually**
PREP. **to** ◇ *The system is perfectly ~ to most people.*

comprehension noun

1 understanding

ADJ. **human**
VERB + COMPREHENSION **have** ◇ *He apparently has no ~ of the suffering of others.* | **defy** ◇ *The level of violence used defies ~.* | **check** ◇ *There are exercises for checking ~.*
COMPREHENSION + NOUN **skills**
PREP. **beyond (sb's)** ~ ◇ *Why he can't do it himself is beyond my ~.* | **without** ~
PHRASES **a lack of** ~ ◇ *He showed a total lack of ~.*

2 language exercise

ADJ. **listening, reading**
VERB + COMPREHENSION **do** ◇ *We did a listening ~.*
COMPREHENSION + NOUN **test** | **question** | **skills**

comprehensive adj.

VERBS **be**
ADV. **extremely, fairly, very, etc.** ◇ *The list is fairly ~.* | **fully, totally** ◇ *fully ~ insurance* | **truly**

compromise noun

ADJ. **acceptable, fair, good, happy** (*esp. BrE*)**, possible, pragmatic, reasonable, sensible, suitable** | **ideal** | **painful, uneasy, unsatisfactory** ◇ *After months of negotiations, they have reached an uneasy ~.* | **inevitable, necessary** | **political** | **historic**
VERB + COMPROMISE **agree on, arrive at, come to, find, forge, make, reach, strike, work out** ◇ *I'm not making any more ~s.* ◇ *They're still trying to work out an acceptable ~.* | **look for, seek** ◇ *It is best to try to seek a ~ rather than a perfect solution.* | **broker, negotiate** | **offer, suggest** ◇ *After much discussion, she offered a ~.* | **accept** | **reject**
COMPROMISE + NOUN **agreement, deal, formula, position, proposal, resolution, solution** | **bill, legislation** (*both AmE*) | **candidate** ◇ *He might be an attractive ~ candidate if both sides' first choices are rejected.*
PREP. **~ between** ◇ *It was a fair ~ between the two sides.* | **~ on, ~ over** ◇ *They came to a ~ over the exact amount to be paid.* | **~ with** ◇ *There could be no ~ with the nationalists.*
→ Special page at MEETING

compromise verb

1 in order to reach agreement

VERB + COMPROMISE **be prepared to, be ready to** | **refuse to** ◇ *He wanted his own way and refused to ~.*
PREP. **on** ◇ *Unions and management seem ready to ~ on the level of the increase.* | **with** ◇ *They debated whether to ~ with the opposition parties.*

2 damage/put in danger

ADV. **fatally, seriously, severely, significantly** ◇ *The affair seriously ~d the party's prospects of success.* | **potentially**
VERB + COMPROMISE **be prepared to, be ready to** | **refuse to**
PREP. **on** ◇ *We are not prepared to ~ on safety standards.*

compulsion noun

ADJ. **strange** | **inner**
... OF COMPULSION **element** (*BrE*) ◇ *There is an element of ~ in the new plan for the unemployed.*
VERB + COMPULSION **feel, have** ◇ *He felt an inner ~ to write.*
PREP. **under** ~ ◇ *You are under no ~ to disclose this information.*
PHRASES **there is no** ~ ◇ *There is no ~ to say anything.*

computer noun

ADJ. **fast, high-speed, powerful** | **sophisticated, state-of-the-art** | **desktop, hand-held, laptop, mobile, notebook, palmtop, portable, tablet, touch-screen, wearable, wireless** | **home, personal** ◇ *the market for home ~s* | **office** | **mainframe, networked, remote** | **analogue/analog, digital, parallel** | **on-board**
VERB + COMPUTER **access, operate, run, use** | **switch off, switch on** | **log off, log onto** | **boot up, start up** | **shut down** | **reboot, restart** | **crash** ◇ *It's awful when a virus crashes your ~.* | **program** | **build** ◇ *Building a ~ has many benefits over buying one.* | **install** | **link, network** ◇ *Computers can be networked using modems and telephone lines.* | **hold sth on, store sth on** ◇ *The data is all held on ~.* | **hack, hack into** ◇ *He hacked (into) the school ~ with the principal's password.* | **fix** ◇ *technicians who fix ~s* | **upgrade**
COMPUTER + VERB **run, work** | **hold sth, store sth** ◇ *The ~ stores data in a buffer until the printer can accept it.* | **crash, freeze** | **shut down** | **be down, be up** ◇ *The ~s are all down* (= not functioning) *at the moment.* | **say** ◇ *My ~ says that the hard drive is corrupted.*
COMPUTER + NOUN **network, program, system** | **equipment, hardware, software** | **language** | **science, technology** | **industry** | **keyboard, monitor, screen, terminal, etc.** | **file** | **chip** | **animation, game, graphics, model, simulation** ◇ *A ~ model is used to predict forces affecting the aircraft in flight.* | **printout** | **virus, worm** | **crime** | **security** | **glitch** ◇ *The problem was caused by a ~ glitch.* | **literacy, skills** | **consultant, engineer, expert, hacker, programmer, scientist, technician, user** | **geek, nerd** | **whizz/whiz** | **company, industry, manufacturer** | **lab** (*informal*)**, room** | **time** ◇ *Such a large sorting operation can take up a lot of ~ time.*
PREP. **on (a/the)** ~ ◇ *It's all stored on the ~.*

computing noun

COMPUTING + NOUN **skills** | **power** ◇ *a hand-held device that has as much ~ power as many desktop PCs*
PREP. **in** ~ ◇ *He works in ~*
→ Note at SUBJECT (for verbs and nouns)

con noun (informal)

ADJ. **big** ◇ *The seance was just a big ~.*
CON + NOUN **game** (*AmE*)**, trick** (*BrE*) | **artist, man**

conceal verb

ADV. **completely** | **partially, partly** | **barely, scarcely** ◇ *He waited with barely ~ed impatience.* | **easily** ◇ *The camera is small and easily ~ed.* | **carefully, cleverly, cunningly** (*esp. BrE*) | **dishonestly** (*BrE, law*) | **effectively, successfully**
VERB + CONCEAL **be able to, be unable to** ◇ *She was unable to ~ her surprise.* | **try to** | **manage to**
PREP. **from** ◇ *He ~ed the truth from her.*

concede verb

ADV. **eventually, finally** | **readily** ◇ *She readily ~s that there is much work still to be done.* | **grudgingly, reluctantly** ◇ *He reluctantly ~d that he was not fit enough to play.* | **implicitly**

COMPUTERS

Installing software

- **boot up/start up** the **computer**
- **insert** the program **disk/CD-ROM** or **download** the **software** from a **website**
- **follow** the set up **instructions**
- **reboot/restart** the computer

Creating a document

- **select** the new document **option** from the **drop-down menu** or **click on** the new document **icon**
- **type**, **edit**, and **format** the **document**
- **print (out)** the **document**
- **save** and **close** the **document**

Cutting and pasting text

- **scroll down** the **text** to find the **block of text** you want to **move**
- **position** the **cursor** at the beginning of the block of text
- **hold down** the **left mouse button** and **drag** the **mouse** to **highlight** the block of text
- **release** the **left mouse button**
- **click on** the **right mouse button** and **select** the cut text **option** from the **pop-up menu**
- **move** the **cursor** to where you want the text to go
- **select** the paste text **option**

Looking up something on the Internet

- **go on** the **Internet**
- **type in** the **website address** or **click (on)/follow** a **link**
- **access** the **website**
- **browse/search** the **website** to find the information
- if necessary, **download** the **information**

Running several applications at the same time

- **double-click on** the different program **icons**
- **move** and **resize** the program **windows** as required
- **click on** a program's **window** to use that program
- when finished, **close** the **windows**

Backing up a file

- if saving data onto a **CD-ROM**, **insert** a **blank disk** and **format** it if necessary
- if using an old disk, **wipe** the **disk** or **delete/erase** some of the **files** to **create space**
- **compress/zip** the **file** if it is too large
- **copy/save** the **file** onto the disk
- **eject/remove/take out** the **disk**
- alternatively, **back-up** or **upload** the data onto a **server** or **save** it on a **memory stick**

(*AmE*) ◇ *The company seems to be implicitly conceding that sales have been poor.*
VERB + CONCEDE **be forced to** | **be prepared to, be willing to** ◇ *He was not prepared to ~ that he had acted illegally.* | **be reluctant to, be unwilling to** | **refuse to**
PREP. **to** ◇ *The firm should ~ a significant salary increase to its employees.*

conceivable *adj.*

VERBS **be, seem** | **become**
ADV. **entirely, perfectly** (*esp. BrE*), **quite** ◇ *It's quite ~ that she hasn't heard the news yet.* | **just** (*esp. BrE*) ◇ *I suppose it's just ~ that we've made a mistake.* | **barely, scarcely**
PHRASES **every ~ sth** ◇ *We had to draw up plans for every ~ emergency.*

conceive *verb*

1 (*formal*) think of/imagine
ADV. **brilliantly, carefully, well** ◇ *The plan was brilliantly ~d.* | **poorly** | **broadly** ◇ *The course is very broadly ~d* (= it covers a wide range of topics). | **narrowly** | **initially, originally** ◇ *The dam project was originally ~d in 1977.*
VERB + CONCEIVE **cannot** ◇ *I cannot ~ why you paid out so much money.* | **be difficult to, be impossible to** ◇ *It is difficult to ~ of a society without money.* | **be easy to, be possible to**
PREP. **of** ◇ *We ~ of ourselves as individuals.*

2 become pregnant
ADV. **naturally** ◇ *She was unable to ~ a child naturally and was offered fertility treatment.* | **immaculately** ◇ *the Christian belief in Jesus as being immaculately ~d*
VERB + CONCEIVE **be able to, be unable to**

concentrate *verb*

ADV. **hard, intensely** (*esp. AmE*), **intently** (*esp. BrE*) ◇ *She was sitting at her desk concentrating hard.* | **fully, properly** ◇ *I was tired and couldn't ~ properly.* | **mainly, mostly, predominantly, primarily** | **particularly** | **entirely, exclusively, purely, solely**
VERB + CONCENTRATE **be unable to, cannot** ◇ *I tried to work but I found I couldn't ~.* | **be difficult to, be hard to, be impossible to** | **tend to** ◇ *Banks tend to ~ on short-term lending.* | **try to**
PREP. **on** ◇ *He ~d mainly on the flying and spoke very little.*

concentrated *adj.*

1 of your attention
VERBS **be**
ADV. **fully, totally** ◇ *Kate sat up, her attention now totally ~.*
2 of a substance
VERBS **be**
ADV. **highly, very** ◇ *The liquid is found in a highly ~ form.*
3 found in one place
VERBS **be**
ADV. **heavily, highly, particularly, very** | **increasingly** | **largely, mainly, mostly, overwhelmingly, primarily** | **disproportionately** ◇ *These jobs are disproportionately ~ in the service sector.* | **geographically** ◇ *The immigrant community is strongly ~ geographically.*
PREP. **at, in** ◇ *Most of the country's industry is ~ in the north.* | **within** ◇ *Childbearing is ~ within the first decade of married life.*

concentration *noun*

1 giving all your attention/effort to sth
ADJ. **deep, great, intense** | **absolute, total** ◇ *a look of total ~ on her face* | **good** | **poor** | **exclusive**
VERB + CONCENTRATION **demand, need, require** ◇ *The game requires great ~.* | **lose** | **break, disturb** ◇ *Don's voice from outside broke my ~.*
CONCENTRATION + NOUN **lapse** (*esp. AmE*)

PREP. **~ on** ◇ *his ~ on his writing*
PHRASES **a lack of ~** | **a lapse in ~, a lapse of ~** ◇ *One momentary lapse in ~ could prove fatal.* | **powers of ~** ◇ *She has great powers of ~ for a child her age.*

2 large number/amount of sth in one place
ADJ. **elevated, great, heavy, high, large** ◇ *The greatest ~ of traffic is downtown.* | **low** | **varying** | **calcium, glucose, oxygen, salt, etc.** ◇ *Evaporation gradually increases the salt ~ of the water.* | **geographical**
VERB + CONCENTRATION **increase** | **decrease, reduce** | **calculate, determine, estimate**
CONCENTRATION + VERB **increase, rise** ◇ *The ~ of nitrates in the drinking water has risen in recent years.* | **decrease, fall**

concept *noun*

ADJ. **basic, simple** ◇ *The ~ of my book is very simple.* | **broad, general, overall** | **broader, wider** (*esp. BrE*) ◇ *'Mental handicap' should be replaced with the broader ~ of 'learning difficulties'.* | **entire, whole** ◇ *The whole ~ of responsibility was alien to him.* | **central, core, essential, fundamental, important, key** | **clear, precise** | **ambiguous, elusive, nebulous, vague** ◇ *Culture is a fairly nebulous ~.* ◇ *The ~ of 'adequate medical care' is too vague.* | **complex, difficult, sophisticated** | **abstract, intellectual, theoretical** ◇ *The book provides concrete interpretations of some rather abstract ~s.* | **alien, bizarre, strange** | **interesting** | **underlying** | **useful** | **innovative, modern, new, novel, original, revolutionary** | **old-fashioned, traditional** | **business, design, economic, historical, legal, mathematical, political, psychological, religious, scientific**
VERB + CONCEPT **have** ◇ *Teachers should have a clear ~ of what society is.* | **grasp, understand** ◇ *She finds it difficult to grasp abstract ~s.* | **define, formulate, frame** ◇ *the need to create new words to frame new ~s* | **advance, introduce, invent, popularize** | **apply** ◇ *Students must be able to apply classroom ~s to practical situations.* | **develop, refine** | **explain, illustrate** | **discuss, explore** | **embrace** ◇ *Not all companies have embraced the ~ of diversity in the workplace.* | **reinforce**
PREP. **~ of** ◇ *He formulated the ~ of imaginary time.*

conception *noun*

1 idea/understanding
ADJ. **clear, distinct** ◇ *We now have a clearer ~ of the problem.* | **broad, general** | **narrow** | **modern, new** | **alternative, different** | **traditional** | **popular** | **initial, original** | **classical, liberal** ◇ *liberal ~s of the role of the state* | **Christian, Jewish, etc.**
VERB + CONCEPTION **have** | **develop** ◇ *Saussure began developing his ~ of linguistics in 1916.* | **challenge, change** ◇ *The Internet challenges traditional ~s of copyright.*
PREP. **in ~** ◇ *His work is strikingly fresh in ~.*
PHRASES **have no ~ of sth** ◇ *You have no ~ of what her life is like.*

2 becoming/making sb pregnant
ADJ. **immaculate**
VERB + CONCEPTION **prevent**
CONCEPTION + NOUN **probability, rate**
PREP. **at ~** ◇ *Sex identity is fixed at ~.*
PHRASES **the moment of ~**

concern *noun*

1 feeling of worry
ADJ. **considerable, deep, grave, great, serious** | **growing, mounting** | **genuine** ◇ *He demonstrated genuine ~ for others.* | **general, widespread** | **national, public** ◇ *public ~ about increased taxes* | **particular** ◇ *There is particular ~ about the use of pesticides.*
VERB + CONCERN **feel** ◇ *He felt some ~ for her safety.* | **articulate, express, show, voice** | **arouse, cause, heighten** ◇ *The lack of firefighting equipment has caused ~.* | **allay, alleviate, assuage, ease** | **appreciate, understand** | **cite, echo** ◇ *He cited public ~ over airport security.* | **dismiss**
PREP. **in sb's ~** ◇ *She forgot her own worries in her ~ for him.* | **out of ~** | **~ about, ~ over** ◇ *She expressed her deep ~*

about conditions at the factory. | **~ for** ◇ *Out of ~ for her health, we suggested she take a week off work.*

PHRASES **be of (no) ~ to sb** ◇ *Increased use of drugs is of great ~ to parents.* | **(a) cause for ~** ◇ *The president's health is giving serious cause for ~.* | **a lack of ~** ◇ *I was surprised by her lack of ~.* | **a matter of ~** ◇ *Stress at work is a matter of ~ to staff and management.*

2 sth that worries/affects you

ADJ. **chief, main, major, overriding, paramount, primary** ◇ *What are your main ~s as a writer?* | **common** ◇ *a common ~ for new parents* | **pressing, serious** ◇ *I have other, more pressing ~s.* | **legitimate, valid** | **environmental, ethical, privacy, safety, security** ◇ *This new technology brings with it security ~s.*

VERB + CONCERN **outweigh, override** ◇ *Practical necessity overrides any other ~s.*

PHRASES **be none of sb's ~** ◇ *How much we paid is none of your ~.*

concern verb

1 affect/involve

ADV. **directly** | **mainly, mostly** ◇ *The letter is for both of us, but it mainly ~s you.*

PREP. **in** ◇ *Everyone who was directly ~ed in (= had some responsibility for) the incident has now resigned.*

2 worry sb

ADV. **a lot, greatly, really** ◇ *It really ~s me that he doesn't eat properly.* | **slightly**

concerned adj.

1 worried about sth

VERBS **be, feel, look, seem, sound** | **become, get, grow** | **remain**

ADV. **extremely, fairly, very, etc.** | **deeply, especially, genuinely, gravely, greatly, particularly, seriously, terribly** | **increasingly** | **a little, slightly, etc.** | **(not) overly, (not) unduly** ◇ *She was not unduly ~ by the prospect of managing on her own.* | **naturally, understandably** | **rightly** | **simply**

PREP. **about, at, by, over** ◇ *The leadership was ~ at the perceived failure to find a solution,* | **for** ◇ *We are now deeply ~ for his safety.*

2 interested in sth

VERBS **be**

ADV. **especially, particularly, specifically** | **entirely, exclusively, solely** | **centrally, chiefly, essentially, largely, mainly, mostly, predominantly, primarily, principally** ◇ *Cubist painting was not primarily ~ with lifelike representation.* | **closely** (*esp. BrE*), **directly, intimately**

PREP. **with** ◇ *Social anthropology is centrally ~ with the diversity of culture.*

concert noun

ADJ. **big** | **sell-out** (*esp. BrE*), **sold-out** (*esp. AmE*) | **evening, lunchtime** | **inaugural, opening** | **closing, farewell, final** ◇ *He will be giving his farewell ~ as Music Director.* ◇ *The orchestra performs its final ~ of the season tomorrow.* | **live, public** | **free** | **open-air, outdoor** | **prom, promenade** (*both BrE*) | **carol** (*BrE*) | **classical, jazz, pop** (*esp. BrE*), **rock** | **choral, orchestral, symphony** | **gala, subscription** ◇ *She sang at a gala ~ to celebrate the music of Stephen Sondheim.* | **benefit, charity, fund-raising** | **tribute**

... OF CONCERTS **series**

VERB + CONCERT **attend, go to, watch** | **enjoy** | **give, perform** (*esp. AmE*), **perform at** (*esp. BrE*), **perform in** (*esp. BrE*), **play, play in** | **have, hold, host, present, put on, stage** ◇ *The band is putting on its biggest ~ of the year.* | **organize** | **sponsor** | **cancel**

CONCERT + NOUN **hall, platform, venue** | **performance, programme/program** | **ticket** | **artist, pianist** | **promoter** | **series, tour**

PREP. **at a/the ~** | **~ of** ◇ *a ~ of military music* | **~ for, ~ in aid of** (*esp. BrE*) ◇ *We're organizing a ~ for charity.*

concession noun

1 sth you agree to in order to end an argument

ADJ. **important, key, major, significant, substantial** (*esp. BrE*) | **limited, minor, small** | **special** | **territorial**

VERB + CONCESSION **grant (sb/sth), make, offer (sb/sth)** | **extract, get, obtain, win, wring out of sb** (*esp. BrE*) ◇ *China can use its huge market to extract ~s out of foreign companies.* | **demand**

PREP. **~ on** ◇ *The pressure group has won a number of ~s on environmental policy.* | **~ to** ◇ *The company will be forced to make ~s to the union.*

PHRASES **make no ~s to sb/sth** ◇ *They made no ~s to his disability.*

2 special right to do sth

ADJ. **trade** | **logging, oil, timber**

VERB + CONCESSION **grant (sb/sth)** | **obtain, secure, win** ◇ *The company has just won a mining ~ in the north of the country.*

3 (*BrE*) lower charge for certain groups of people

ADJ. **tax** (*BrE, AmE*) | **travel**

CONCESSION + VERB **be available to** ◇ *Travel ~s are available to older people.*

conclusion noun

1 opinion reached after considering the facts

ADJ. **correct** | **logical, reasonable, valid** | **inescapable, inevitable, obvious** | **definite, definitive, firm** ◇ *It is difficult to draw any firm ~s at such an early stage.* | **erroneous, false, incorrect, wrong** | **main** | **hasty, startling, surprising** ◇ *How did he reach this startling ~?* | **preliminary, tentative** ◇ *Only tentative ~s can be drawn from these results.*

VERB + CONCLUSION **arrive at, come to, draw, reach** ◇ *I can't draw any ~s from what she said.* | **jump to, leap to** ◇ *We don't want to jump to the wrong ~.* ◇ *Don't go jumping to ~s before you know the facts.* | **base on, derive from** ◇ *He bases his ~s on very limited research.* | **lead to, point to** ◇ *It all points to the ~ that nobody knew what was going on.* | **confirm, justify, reinforce, strengthen, support** ◇ *The data he collected strengthened his ~s.* | **warrant** ◇ *This does not warrant the ~ that he failed.*

2 ending of sth

ADJ. **satisfactory, satisfying, successful** | **fitting** ◇ *This performance was a fitting ~ to his career.* | **foregone** ◇ *The result of the game was a foregone ~.* | **hasty** | **final, ultimate** ◇ *The story's ultimate ~ does not come as a surprise.*

VERB + CONCLUSION **bring about, bring sth to** ◇ *The meeting was brought to a hasty ~.* | **come to**

PREP. **in ~** ◇ *In ~, I would like to thank you all for your hard work.*

→ Special page at MEETING

conclusive adj.

VERBS **appear, be, seem**

ADV. **absolutely** | **fairly, pretty** ◇ *They produced some fairly ~ evidence.* | **by no means, far from, hardly, not very** ◇ *The argument was far from ~.*

concrete noun

ADJ. **solid** | **bare** ◇ *a floor made of bare ~* | **fresh, wet** | **precast, ready-mixed** | **reinforced**

... OF CONCRETE **layer, slab**

VERB + CONCRETE **mix** | **lay, pour** | **be made from/of/out of** | **set sth in** ◇ *The pathway is formed from large pebbles set in ~.* ◇ *I do not regard this plan as set in ~.* (*figurative*)

CONCRETE + VERB **set** ◇ *Before the ~ sets the surface can be given a final smoothing over.*

CONCRETE + NOUN **block, slab** | **building, floor, wall** | **jungle**

concur verb

ADV. **strongly** ◇ *I strongly ~ with that idea.* | **entirely, fully,**

wholeheartedly | generally ◊ *Scientists generally ~ that climate change is a reality.*
PREP. **in, with** ◊ *Historians have concurred with each other in this view.*

concussion *noun*

ADJ. **mild, minor, slight** | **bad, major, serious, severe**
VERB + CONCUSSION **get, have, suffer, sustain** ◊ *She suffered mild ~.* (*BrE*) ◊ *Doctors said he suffered a ~ during the football game.* (*AmE*)
PREP. **with ~** ◊ *He was carried off the field with mild ~.* (*BrE*) ◊ *He was carried off the field with a mild ~.* (*AmE*)

condemn *verb*

ADV. **roundly, strongly, vehemently, vigorously** | **unequivocally, utterly** (*esp. BrE*) | **unanimously, universally** | **explicitly, specifically** ◊ *The President specifically ~ed the ads.* | **openly, publicly** ◊ *She publicly ~ed the deal.* | **rightly** ◊ *They rightly ~ such opinions as racist.*
PREP. **for** ◊ *He was roundly ~ed for his mistake.*
PHRASES **be widely ~ed** ◊ *The action has been widely ~ed by human rights groups.*

condemnation *noun*

ADJ. **harsh, severe, strong** | **universal, widespread** | **blanket, wholesale** (*both esp. BrE*) ◊ *He issued a blanket ~ of all terrorism.* | **official, public** ◊ *There's been no official ~ of the bombing.*
VERB + CONDEMNATION **express, issue** ◊ *I can only express my strong ~ of this terrible outrage.* ◊ *The UN issued a ~ of the regime.* | **deserve** ◊ *Such treatment deserves ~.* | **draw** ◊ *The violence has drawn firm ~ from all the main political leaders.*
CONDEMNATION + VERB **come from sb/sth** ◊ *Condemnation of this policy has come from all political parties.*

condition *noun*

1 state of sth

ADJ. **excellent, good, immaculate, mint, perfect, pristine** | **reasonable** | **bad, poor, terrible** | **original** ◊ *The clock was restored to its original ~.* | **physical**
VERB + CONDITION **assess, evaluate**
PREP. **in…~** ◊ *The car is still in excellent ~.*

2 sb's state of health

ADJ. **critical, serious** | **stable** ◊ *Doctors say his ~ is now stable.* | **weakened** ◊ *In his weakened ~, it took a long time for the wound to heal.* | **peak** ◊ *a young athlete in peak ~* | **mental, physical** ◊ *There has been a marked deterioration in her mental ~.*
CONDITION + VERB **get better, improve** ◊ *Without this treatment, her ~ won't improve.* | **deteriorate, get worse, worsen** | **assess, monitor**
PREP. **in a…~** (*BrE*), **in…~** (*esp. AmE*) ◊ *He is still in (a) critical ~ in the hospital.* | **out of ~** (*esp. BrE*) ◊ *I haven't been exercising much recently, so I'm a little out of ~.*
PHRASES **be in no ~ to do sth** ◊ *You're in no ~ to tackle the stairs.*

3 illness

ADJ. **medical** | **life-threatening, serious** | **benign** | **chronic** | **incurable** | **treatable** | **rare** | **debilitating, disabling** | **degenerative** | **pathological** | **pre-existing** (*esp. AmE*) ◊ *The insurance will not cover you for a pre-existing ~.* | **mental, psychiatric** ◊ *She was unable to give informed consent because of a mental ~.* | **heart, skin, etc.**
VERB + CONDITION **have, suffer from** ◊ *He has a rare skin ~.* | **be born with** ◊ *All three babies were born with an incurable heart ~.* | **treat** ◊ *The drug is used to treat ~s such as epilepsy.* | **diagnose** | **aggravate, exacerbate, worsen** ◊ *Alcohol abuse worsened his heart ~.*

4 conditions situation/circumstances

ADJ. **favourable/favorable, good, ideal, optimal** (*esp. AmE*), **optimum** ◊ *Conditions are ideal for starting a business.* | **appalling, awful, deplorable, dreadful, harsh, inhumane,** severe, terrible | **difficult, poor, unfavourable/unfavorable** | **adverse, extreme** ◊ *adverse ~s for driving* | **freak, treacherous** (both only used about the weather) ◊ *freak weather ~s* | **stressful** ◊ *people working under stressful ~s* | **dangerous, hazardous, unsafe** | **squalid, unhygienic, unsanitary** | **normal, prevailing** | **changing** ◊ *Animals adapt to changing environmental ~s.* | **controlled** ◊ *The experiment is conducted under strictly controlled ~s.* | **experimental, laboratory** | **driving, housing, living, operating, sanitary, working** ◊ *The working ~s in the factory are dreadful.* | **economic, market, political, social** | **ambient, atmospheric, climatic, environmental, lighting, meteorological, physical, soil, weather** ◊ *Paint shades can vary under different lighting ~s.* | **dry, humid, moist, warm** ◊ *plants that can survive dry ~s*
VERB + CONDITIONS **live in, work in, work under** ◊ *An enormous number of people live in ~s of poverty.* | **alleviate, ameliorate, improve** ◊ *an effort to improve working ~s at the plant* | **create** ◊ *Warm, wet weather can create ideal ~s for plant diseases.* | **simulate** ◊ *The chamber simulates ~s found at high altitudes.*
CONDITIONS + VERB **exist, persist, prevail** ◊ *As long as these weather ~s prevail, we are unable to rescue the climbers.* | **change** | **improve** | **deteriorate, worsen**
PREP. **in ~** ◊ *in normal flight operating ~s* | **under ~** ◊ *The samples are heated under experimental ~s.*

5 rule

ADJ. **strict** | **special**
VERB + CONDITION **attach, impose, lay down, set, set out, specify** ◊ *the ~s attached to the granting of citizenship* ◊ *The UN has imposed strict ~s on the ceasefire.* | **accept, agree to** ◊ *They would not agree to our ~s.* | **abide by, comply with, fulfil/fulfill, meet, observe, satisfy** ◊ *To get a basic pension you must satisfy two conditions…* | **be subject to** ◊ *The bar was licensed subject to the ~ that no children be admitted.* | **be in breach of** (*BrE*) ◊ *He denied being in breach of bail ~s.*
CONDITION + VERB **apply** ◊ *Special ~s apply to the use of the library's rare books.*
PREP. **on ~ that** ◊ *They agreed to lend us the car on ~ that we returned it before the weekend.* | **on…~, under…~** (*AmE*) ◊ *I'll agree to the plan on one ~: my name doesn't get mentioned to the press.* | **under the ~s of** ◊ *Under the ~s of the agreement, all foreign troops will leave by May.*
PHRASES **a breach of a ~** (*BrE*) | **~s of employment, sale, etc.** | **terms and ~s** ◊ *the terms and ~s of the contract*

6 necessary situation

ADJ. **necessary, sufficient** ◊ *a necessary and sufficient ~ for the eradication of unemployment*
VERB + CONDITION **create** ◊ *We are working to create the ~s for peace.*
PREP. **~ for**

7 state of group

ADJ. **human** ◊ *Work is basic to the human ~ (= the fact of being human).*
VERB + CONDITION **improve** ◊ *We are aiming to improve the ~ of the urban poor.*

condolences *noun*

ADJ. **deep** (*esp. AmE*), **heartfelt, sincere**
VERB + CONDOLENCES **convey** (*esp. BrE*), **express, extend, give (sb), offer (sb), send (sb)** ◊ *We would like to extend our heartfelt ~ to the families of the victims.* | **accept** ◊ *Please accept our sincere ~.*

condom *noun*

ADJ. **used**
…OF CONDOMS **box, pack** (*esp. AmE*), **packet** (*esp. BrE*)
VERB + CONDOM **put on, use, wear** | **carry** | **distribute, provide** | **buy, obtain**

condominium (*also informal* condo) *noun* (*esp. AmE*)

ADJ. **high-rise**
VERB + CONDOMINIUM **buy, rent** | **stay in** ◊ *We were staying in a ~ just off of the beach.*

condone *verb*

ADV. **implicitly, tacitly**
VERB + CONDONE **cannot** ◇ *We cannot ~ violence of any sort.*

conducive *adj.*

VERBS **be** | **seem**
ADV. **especially, highly, particularly** ◇ *Daylight is highly ~ to good plant growth.* | **hardly** ◇ *The noise was hardly ~ to a good night's sleep.*
PREP. **to** ◇ *an environment ~ to learning*

conduct *noun*

1 way of behaving

ADJ. **good** ◇ *The prisoner was released early for good ~.* | **discreditable** (*BrE*), **disgraceful, immoral, improper, inappropriate, unethical, ungentlemanly** (*BrE*), **unprofessional, unseemly** (*esp. BrE*) | **aggressive** (*esp. BrE*), **violent** | **criminal, disorderly, fraudulent** (*law, esp. BrE*), **illegal, negligent, unlawful, wrongful** ◇ *He was arrested for disorderly ~.* | **unsporting** (*BrE*), **unsportsmanlike** (*esp. AmE*) | **homosexual, sexual** | **personal** | **business, professional** ◇ *The business ~ of this bank will be subject to UK rules.* ◇ *Our organization sets high standards of professional ~.* | **police** | **human, moral** ◇ *It is tempting to think of morality as a guide to human ~.*
VERB + CONDUCT **engage in** ◇ *The committee concluded that the senators had engaged in improper ~.* | **govern, regulate** ◇ *rules governing police ~* | **explain** ◇ *The police chief was asked to explain his ~.*
PREP. **~ by** ◇ *The violent ~ by the strikers was condemned.* | **~ towards/toward** ◇ *her ~ towards/toward her husband*
PHRASES **a code of ~, rules of ~, standards of ~**

2 management of sth

ADJ. **proper** ◇ *The elders were responsible for the proper ~ of community life.* | **day-to-day** ◇ *the day-to-day ~ of the business of the company*

conduct *verb*

1 organize sth/carry sth out

ADV. **independently, separately** ◇ *Education was ~ed separately for males and females.* | **jointly, simultaneously** ◇ *a survey ~ed jointly by two teams of researchers* | **personally** | **properly** | **successfully** | **regularly, routinely** ◇ *We regularly ~ safety inspections.* | **online** ◇ *Today, 50% of opinion polls are ~ed online.*

2 (*formal*) **conduct yourself behave**

ADV. **honourably/honorably, well, with dignity** ◇ *She ~s herself with great dignity.*
PREP. **as** ◇ *He always ~ed himself as a gentleman.* | **in** ◇ *They have ~ed themselves in a very professional manner.*

3 heat/electricity

ADV. **well** ◇ *a substance which ~s electricity well*

conductor *noun*

1 person who conducts an orchestra

ADJ. **great** | **famous** | **chief, principal** | **guest** | **choral, opera, orchestra, symphony** (*esp. AmE*)
PREP. **~ of, ~ with** ◇ *the principal ~ of the San Francisco Symphony*
PHRASES **the conductor's baton**
→ Note at JOB

2 substance that allows heat/electricity to pass through

ADJ. **excellent, good** | **bad, poor** | **electrical** | **lightning** (*BrE*)

confederation *noun*

ADJ. **loose** ◇ *a loose ~ of states.*
VERB + CONFEDERATION **establish, form, found** | **join**
PREP. **~ between** ◇ *a ~ between two states* | **~ of** ◇ *a ~ of employers*

conference *noun*

ADJ. **international, national, regional, world** | **one-day, etc.** | **annual, quarterly** | **inaugural, preliminary, preparatory** | **consultative** | **joint** | **private** | **phone, telephone, video** | **formal** | **full** | **successful** | **well-attended** | **high-level, summit** | **news, press** | **academic, industry, inter-governmental** (*BrE*), **management, ministerial, party, staff** (*esp. BrE*) | **parent-teacher** (*AmE*) | **constitutional, education, environment, peace, trade, etc.**
...OF CONFERENCES **series**
VERB + CONFERENCE **attend, go to** | **hold, host** | **sponsor** | **organize, plan, schedule** | **call, convene**
CONFERENCE + VERB **meet, take place** | **begin, open** | **close, end** | **bring sb together** ◇ *The ~ brought together historians working in a variety of fields.* | **be entitled sth, be titled sth** (*AmE*) ◇ *a ~ entitled 'Strategies for Epidemic Control'* | **feature sth, include sth** ◇ *The ~ featured a keynote address by one of our most eminent scientists.* | **address sth, be devoted to sth, examine sth, focus on sth, look at sth** ◇ *a ~ devoted to the topic of peace* ◇ *a ~ examining cross-border cooperation* | **hear sth** ◇ *The ~ heard an appeal from a representative from one of the more deprived areas.* | **agree sth, decide sth, vote sth** ◇ *The ~ agreed to adopt a set of compromise proposals.* | **adopt sth, approve sth, back sth, support sth** ◇ *The ~ adopted a resolution on minority rights.* | **recommend sth** | **condemn sth, reject sth**
CONFERENCE + NOUN **centre/center, facilities, venue** | **hall, room** | **table** | **platform** (*esp. BrE*) ◇ *The party leader made a morale-boosting speech from the ~ platform.* | **chair, chairman, presenter** (*esp. AmE*), **speaker** | **attendees** (*AmE*), **delegates, participants** | **committee, organizer** | **agenda, proceedings, programme/program** | **theme** | **debate, discussion, talks** | **paper, presentation, report, speech** | **resolution** | **registration** | **session** | **call** ◇ *Conference calls allow participants across the nation to meet over the telephone.* | **season**
PREP. **at a/the ~** ◇ *We met at an international ~.* | **in ~ with** ◇ *He was in ~ with (= in a meeting with) his lawyers all day.* | **~ about** ◇ *a ~ about Internet piracy* | **~ between** ◇ *a ~ between the warring parties* | **~ for** ◇ *a ~ for catering managers* | **~ on** ◇ *a ~ on economic aid* | **~ with** ◇ *Management had a joint ~ with the union.*

confess *verb*

ADV. **freely, openly, publicly, readily** | **allegedly**
VERB + CONFESS **have to, must** ◇ *I must ~ that I didn't have much faith in her ideas.*
PREP. **to** ◇ *He was arrested and ~ed to the murder.* ◇ *She ~ed to me that she had known his true identity for some time.*

confession *noun*

1 admitting guilt

ADJ. **full** | **public** | **true** ◇ *It's difficult to believe it's a true ~ after all her lies.* | **false** | **alleged** | **coerced, forced** | **signed, taped, videotaped** (*AmE*), **written** | **deathbed**
VERB + CONFESSION **make** | **sign, write** | **get, obtain, secure** | **coerce, extract, force** ◇ *He claims his ~ was extracted under torture.* | **retract** ◇ *She made a false ~ during the trial which she later retracted.* | **exclude** (*BrE*) ◇ *The court excluded the ~ wrongly obtained by the police.*
PREP. **~ by** ◇ *an alleged ~ by the defendant* | **~ from** ◇ *a ~ from the prisoner* | **~ of** ◇ *a true ~ of a terrible crime* | **~ to** ◇ *a ~ to murder*
PHRASES **force a ~ out of sb, get a ~ out of sb** ◇ *The police forced a ~ out of him.*

2 to a priest

VERB + CONFESSION **go to** ◇ *I used to go to ~ every Saturday as a child.* | **hear** ◇ *The priest heard her ~ and granted absolution.*
CONFESSION + NOUN **booth** (*esp. AmE*), **box**
PHRASES **an act of ~**

confidence noun

1 belief in others

ADJ. **absolute, complete, full, total** ◊ *The company needs the full ~ of its investors.* | **great, high, real, strong** (AmE) ◊ *Confidence is high among the team's supporters.* | **low** (AmE) ◊ *Generally there is low public ~ in government institutions.* | **reasonable** | **growing, increased, increasing** | **new, renewed** | **misplaced** ◊ *The general's ~ in his army proved misplaced.* | **public** ◊ *public ~ in the government* | **business, consumer, customer, investor, market, voter**
VERB + CONFIDENCE **enjoy, feel, have** ◊ *This government no longer enjoys the ~ of the public.* ◊ *We all have complete ~ in this product.* | **express** ◊ *He expressed ~ in the new plans.* | **be lacking in, lack** | **share** ◊ *She wished that she shared his ~.* | **maintain, retain** ◊ *to maintain public ~ in the system of justice* | **bolster, boost, build, build up, enhance, improve, increase, raise, strengthen** ◊ *Higher profits should raise business ~.* | **gain** | **breed, create, engender, generate, give (sb), inspire, instil/instill, promote** ◊ *The training is designed to give staff ~ in managing problems.* ◊ *The company's record does not really inspire ~.* | **rebuild, renew, restore, revive** ◊ *an effort to renew investor ~ in corporate America* | **lose** ◊ *This government has lost the ~ of the public.* | **damage, dent** (esp. BrE), **erode, sap, shake, undermine, weaken** ◊ *Only one bank scandal is needed to shake the ~ in the financial markets.* | **destroy, shatter**
CONFIDENCE + VERB **decline, decrease, fall, wane** | **grow, increase, rise, soar** | **return** ◊ *Confidence has returned to the market.*
PREP. **~ about** ◊ *The captain was not lacking in ~ about his team's prospects.* | **~ among** ◊ *a loss of ~ among investors* | **~ between** ◊ *efforts to build ~ between employers and unions* | **~ in** ◊ *They have no ~ in the legal system.*
PHRASES **a crisis of ~** ◊ *There is a crisis of ~ in the university about its future role.* | **have every ~, have the utmost ~** ◊ *The captain of the football team said he had every ~ in his men.* | **a lack of ~, a loss of ~** | **a ~ motion** (also *a no-confidence motion*) (esp. BrE), **a ~ vote** (also *a no-confidence vote*), **a vote of ~, a vote of no ~** ◊ *The government lost a ~ vote.* ◊ *This is a tremendous vote of ~ for the government.*

2 belief in yourself

ADJ. **considerable, enormous, great** | **supreme, tremendous, utter** | **unshakable, unwavering** | **added, extra** | **new-found, renewed** | **growing, increased, increasing** | **calm, cool, quiet** ◊ *She gave an outward appearance of quiet ~.* | **easy** ◊ *She spoke in a tone of easy ~.* | **false** ◊ *All his false ~ had drained away.* | **inner, personal**
VERB + CONFIDENCE **have** ◊ *She has very little ~ in her own abilities.* | **demonstrate, display, project** (esp. AmE), **show** | **feel** ◊ *'I can explain,' he said, with a ~ he did not feel.* | **be full of, brim with, exude, ooze, radiate** ◊ *Since she got the new job, she's been brimming with ~.* ◊ *a man who exudes ~* | **be lacking in, lack** ◊ *A lot of children are lacking in ~.* | **acquire, develop, gain, gather** ◊ *She's gained a lot of ~ over the last year.* | **grow in** ◊ *As the weeks went by he grew in ~.* | **lose** ◊ *During his illness he really lost his ~.* | **get back, rebuild, recover, regain, restore** ◊ *He's really striking the ball well and has recovered his ~.* | **bolster, boost, build, build up, develop, encourage, enhance, improve** ◊ *Winning the competition really boosted her ~.* | **give sb, instil/instill** ◊ *They are gradually instilling ~ in their staff.* | **dent** (esp. BrE), **sap, shake, undermine, weaken** ◊ *Failing his exams really dented his ~.* | **destroy, shatter**
CONFIDENCE + VERB **drain, drain away, evaporate** (esp. BrE), **go** ◊ *My ~ went completely after my first major defeat.* | **grow, increase, rise** ◊ *Their ~ grew with each success.*
CONFIDENCE + NOUN **boost, booster, builder** (AmE) ◊ *The home team badly need a ~ booster.* | **building** ◊ *Getting the certificate does a lot in terms of ~ building.*
PREP. **with ~** ◊ *She answered the question with ~.* | **~ about** ◊ *I lacked ~ about how I looked.* | **~ in** ◊ *his ~ in himself*
PHRASES **a lack of ~** | **a loss of ~**

3 trust

ADJ. **absolute, complete, full, total** | **mutual**
VERB + CONFIDENCE **enjoy, have** ◊ *Security institutions have to have the ~ of all communities.* | **keep, retain** | **earn, gain, get, win** | **build** ◊ *an environment which builds mutual ~* | **betray, break** ◊ *She promised not to break his ~.* | **place, put** ◊ *Are we to place ~ in a man who cannot remember a phone call he made last week?* | **withhold** | **take sb into** ◊ *She thought she might take Leo into her ~.*
CONFIDENCE + NOUN **game** (AmE), **trick** (BrE) | **man** (AmE) (usually **con man** in BrE and AmE), **trickster** (BrE)
PREP. **in ~** ◊ *I really can't talk about this—she told me in ~.*
PHRASES **a breach of ~** ◊ *Telling other people what I'd said was a total breach of ~.* | **in strict ~** ◊ *Questions will be dealt with in the strictest ~.*

4 secret

ADJ. **whispered**
VERB + CONFIDENCE **exchange, share** ◊ *The girls exchanged whispered ~s.* | **keep** ◊ *Can you keep a ~?* | **betray** ◊ *I could never forgive Mike for betraying a ~.* | **encourage, invite** ◊ *She didn't encourage ~s.*

confident adj.

VERBS **appear, be, feel, look, seem, sound** ◊ *We feel ~ that these results are accurate.* | **become, get, grow** ◊ *He's becoming more ~ as he gets older.* ◊ *She gradually grew more ~.* | **remain** | **make sb** ◊ *Going to college has made her more ~.*
ADV. **extremely, fairly, very, etc.** | **highly, remarkably** | **absolutely, completely, entirely, fully, supremely, totally** | **overly** ◊ *He was overly ~, perhaps to the point of arrogance.* | **increasingly** | **reasonably** | **100%, 95%, etc.** ◊ *I'm 95% ~ of success.* | **quietly, serenely** ◊ *He came out of the interview feeling quietly ~.* ◊ *She sauntered onto the set, looking serenely ~.* | **socially** ◊ *young people who appear to be socially ~, but inside are a bundle of neuroses*
PREP. **about** ◊ *We are ~ about the future.* | **in** ◊ *I'm very ~ in our ability to maintain leadership.* | **of** ◊ *I'm fully ~ of winning the title.*

confidential adj.

VERBS **be** | **remain** | **consider sth as, hold sth** (AmE), **keep sth, treat sth as** ◊ *The affair must be kept ~.* ◊ *Information about prices is to be treated as ~.*
ADV. **highly** | **absolutely, completely, strictly, totally** ◊ *The findings are strictly ~.* | **commercially** (BrE) ◊ *commercially ~ data*

confidentiality noun

ADJ. **complete, strict, total** ◊ *It is important to maintain strict ~ at all times.* | **client, patient** ◊ *To maintain patient ~, the forms were anonymous.*
VERB + CONFIDENTIALITY **assure, ensure, guarantee, maintain, preserve, promise, protect, respect** ◊ *efforts to protect the ~ of the client* | **breach, break, compromise, violate** ◊ *He breached ~ by releasing information on weapons tests.* | **sacrifice, waive** ◊ *The newspapers have agreed to waive ~.*
CONFIDENTIALITY + NOUN **agreement, clause, law, provision** ◊ *They urged lawmakers to include ~ provisions in any new system.* | **concerns, issues**

confine verb

ADV. **entirely, exclusively, solely, strictly, totally** | **increasingly** | **essentially, largely, mainly, mostly, primarily** ◊ *The discussion will be ~d largely to general principles.* | **generally, normally, typically** ◊ *Condemned prisoners are typically ~d to small cells for 23 hours a day.* | **by no means, hardly, not just, not necessarily** ◊ *Poverty and deprivation are by no means ~d to the north of the country.* | **safely** (esp. AmE) ◊ *Not all horror stories are safely ~d to the television set or movie screen.*
PREP. **to** ◊ *Let's ~ our attention to the problem of illegal drugs.* ◊ *She's been ~d to a wheelchair since having a bad fall.* ◊ *They ~d themselves to purely economic matters.*

confinement *noun*

ADJ. **close** ◊ *The animals are kept in close ~.* | **solitary** | **home** (*AmE*) ◊ *He was sentenced to six months of home ~.* | **involuntary** ◊ *involuntary ~ to a psychiatric hospital* | **physical** | **long-term, short-term**
VERB + CONFINEMENT **be held in, be kept in** | **be placed in, be put in** | **escape** ◊ *those birds that escape ~ and adapt to new environments*
PREP. **in ~** ◊ *He spent eleven years in solitary ~.* | **~ to** ◊ *their ~ to army barracks*

confines *noun*

ADJ. **close, cramped, limited, narrow, rigid, small, strict, tight** ◊ *issues that go beyond the limited ~ of the book* ◊ *within the strict ~ of the law* | **immediate** | **comfortable, comfy** (*informal*), **cosy/cozy, friendly** (*AmE*), **safe** ◊ *The dim, familiar ~ of the room grew clearer as my eyes adjusted to the indoor darkness.* ◊ *She returned to the cosy/cozy ~ of her lodgings on the second floor.* | **cool, dark, quiet** ◊ *She stepped into the cool, dark ~ of a roadside inn.* ◊ *in the quiet ~ of a Bloomington hotel room*
VERB + CONFINES **escape, leave** ◊ *Most airmen aren't allowed to leave the ~ of the base.* | **transcend** ◊ *The gay community is transcending the narrow ~ of the ghetto.* | **enter** ◊ *They left the half-lit streets and entered the ~ of a cemetery.*
PREP. **beyond the ~ of, outside the ~ of** ◊ *She wanted to experience things outside the close ~ of family life.* | **in the ~ of, within the ~ of** ◊ *He spent three years within the narrow ~ of the prison.*

confirm *verb*

ADV. **just, merely, only, simply** ◊ *This latest tragedy merely ~s my view that the law must be tightened.* | **independently** ◊ *These results were independently ~ed in a study of 48 patients.* | **officially** ◊ *The plans were officially ~ed yesterday.* | **unanimously** (*AmE*) ◊ *Clement was unanimously ~ed to serve on the District Court.* | **experimentally** (*technical*) ◊ *I wanted to find a way to experimentally ~ the results.*
VERB + CONFIRM **be able to, be unable to, can, could** | **appear to, seem to, tend to** ◊ *These new symptoms tend to ~ my original diagnosis.* | **help (to)** ◊ *Your veterinarian will suggest some tests to help ~ the diagnosis.*

confirmation *noun*

ADJ. **additional, further** ◊ *Practically every new piece of documentary evidence provides additional ~ that the charges are true.* | **independent** | **direct** | **final** | **email, verbal, visual, written** | **judicial** (*AmE*), **official** | **experimental, laboratory** (*both technical*) ◊ *Our data provide experimental ~ of these predictions.*
VERB + CONFIRMATION **ask for** | **need, require** | **seek** ◊ *The police are seeking independent ~ of certain details of the story.* | **await, wait for** | **get, have, obtain, receive** | **give sb, provide (sb with)**
CONFIRMATION + VERB **come** ◊ *Written ~ came three days later.*
CONFIRMATION + NOUN **hearing** (*AmE*)
PREP. **in ~** ◊ *She nodded in ~.*
PHRASES **~ in writing** (*BrE*) ◊ *We need ~ in writing before we can send your order out.* | **subject to ~**

conflict *noun*

1 fight/argument

ADJ. **great, major** | **bitter, brutal, serious, violent** | **escalating, increasing** | **constant, continued, continuing, ongoing** | **long-running, long-standing, prolonged, protracted** | **unresolved** ◊ *He is in constant ~ with the authorities.* | **open, overt** | **global, internal, international, interstate, regional** | **armed, military** | **domestic, family, generational, interpersonal** (*esp. AmE*), **marital** (*AmE*) | **civil, class, cultural, ethnic, industrial, political, religious, sectarian, social** | **future, impending, potential** ◊ *Our ability to mobilize large numbers of trained men in time of emergency could forestall future ~,*
VERB + CONFLICT **bring sb/sth into, cause, come into, create, lead to, provoke** ◊ *His work brought him into ~ with more conventional scientists.* ◊ *The decision led to a bitter ~*

between the management and unions. | **avert, avoid, prevent** ◊ *They hid their feelings to avoid ~.* | **handle, manage** ◊ *There is more to a successful relationship than simply managing ~.* | **end, resolve, settle, solve** ◊ *The UN are hoping to resolve the ~ quickly.*
CONFLICT + VERB **arise (from sth), occur** ◊ *The ~ arose from different ambitions within the team.* | **erupt, flare up** | **rage** | **escalate, intensify** | **revolve around sth** | **begin, end**
PREP. **during a/the ~, in a/the ~** ◊ *Thousands have been arrested in violent ethnic ~s in the region.* | **in ~** ◊ *They found themselves in ~ over the future of the company.* | **in ~ with** ◊ *in ~ with management* | **~ about, ~ over** ◊ *a ~ over ownership of the land* | **~ between** ◊ *~s between different ethnic groups* | **~ with** ◊ *to end the ~ with France* | **~ within** ◊ *serious ~s within the ruling party*
PHRASES **an area of ~, a source of ~** | **in direct ~ with sb**

2 difference between ideas, wishes, etc.

ADJ. **fundamental, irreconcilable, serious, sharp** | **direct** | **inherent** ◊ *the inherent ~ between what farmers and environmentalists want* | **inner** | **emotional, ideological, personality**
CONFLICT + NOUN **situation** | **management, resolution** ◊ *the key to successful ~ management* | **avoidance**
PREP. **in ~ with** ◊ *in direct ~ with his wishes* | **~ between** ◊ *the ~ between science and religion* | **~ of** ◊ *a serious ~ of opinion*
PHRASES **a ~ of interest, a ~ of interests** (*esp. BrE*) | **a ~ of loyalties**

conflict *verb*

ADV. **apparently, seemingly** ◊ *how to reconcile apparently ~ing goals* | **potentially** ◊ *potentially ~ing values*
PREP. **with** ◊ *His opinions ~ed with mine.*

conform *verb*

ADV. **closely, exactly, fully, perfectly**
VERB + CONFORM **be expected to, be forced to, be required to, have to, must, should** ◊ *the attempt to force science to ~ with a political or social ideology* | **fail to** | **refuse to** ◊ *The toys fail to ~ to current safety standards.* | **appear to** ◊ *The accountant's reports appear to ~ with the requirements of professional standards.*
PREP. **to** ◊ *All companies are required to ~ to these rules.* | **with** ◊ *This equipment ~s fully with the latest safety regulations.*

conformity *noun*

ADJ. **absolute, complete** | **mindless, unthinking** ◊ *They act in unthinking ~ to customs.* | **rigid, strict** ◊ *They do not observe rigid ~ to the doctrines of the church.* | **outward** ◊ *a society of outward religious ~* | **cultural, ideological, political, religious, social**
...OF CONFORMITY **degree**
VERB + CONFORMITY **achieve, bring sth into, ensure** ◊ *to bring national laws into ~ with international conventions* | **demand, enforce, impose** ◊ *Governments often invoke patriotism to enforce ~.*
PREP. **in ~ with** ◊ *The procedure is in strict ~ with standard international practices.* | **~ between** ◊ *to achieve ~ between all the plans* | **~ to** ◊ *~ to the accepted standards* | **~ with** ◊ *We work to ensure ~ with the customer's wishes.*

confront *verb*

ADV. **directly, head-on, squarely** ◊ *The new state ~ed head-on the question of national identity.* ◊ *He is willing to ~ problems directly.* | **aggressively, angrily** | **immediately, suddenly** | **constantly, continually** ◊ *These texts constantly ~ the reader with their demanding claims.*
PHRASES **be ~ed with sth** ◊ *I was suddenly ~ed by the task of rewriting the entire book.* | **find yourself ~ed by sth** ◊ *The demonstrators found themselves ~ed by a line of police, blocking the road.*

confrontation noun

ADJ. **full-scale, major, serious** ◊ *Their demands could lead to a serious ~ with management.* | **direct, face-to-face, head-on, outright** | **open** | **final** ◊ *The final ~ on a train is classic thriller material.* | **bitter, bloody, heated, ugly, violent** | **armed, military, nuclear** | **climactic, dramatic** ◊ *Their climactic ~ brings the novel to a dramatic close.* | **political** | **physical, verbal** ◊ *He hoped that a physical ~ would not ensue.*

... OF CONFRONTATIONS **series**

VERB + CONFRONTATION **get into, have** | **lead to, provoke** | **bring sb into** ◊ *His actions brought him into direct ~ with the authorities.* | **risk** ◊ *He would be very foolish to risk a ~ with Robert.* | **force** ◊ *He probably will have little choice but to force a ~ sooner or later.* | **avoid**

CONFRONTATION + VERB **arise, take place**

PREP. **~ about, ~ over** ◊ *Lewis had a ~ about money with his stepfamily.* ◊ *She had a series of heated ~s with her parents over homework.* | **~ between** ◊ *a head-on ~ between the two governments* | **~ with** ◊ *a ~ with the police*

confuse verb

1 make sb unable to think clearly; make sth unclear

ADV. **completely, really, thoroughly, totally, utterly** ◊ *Seeing the two of them together totally ~d me.* | **slightly, somewhat** | **deliberately** ◊ *They have deliberately ~d the general public with their claims.* | **further** ◊ *I will try to be brief and avoid further confusing the issue.*

2 mistake sb/sth for another person/thing

ADV. **easily** ◊ *You can easily ~ the two paintings.*

PREP. **for** (*esp. AmE*) ◊ *The condition can sometimes be ~d for influenza.* | **with** ◊ *I sometimes ~ Jane with her sister.*

confused adj.

VERBS **appear, be, feel, look, seem, sound** | **become, get** ◊ *He was beginning to get rather ~.* | **remain** | **leave sb** ◊ *He left his audience thoroughly ~.*

ADV. **extremely, fairly, very, etc.** | **highly, hopelessly** ◊ *a highly ~ picture of a complex situation* | **completely, horribly, terribly, thoroughly, totally, utterly** ◊ *'Why?' she asked, suddenly horribly ~.* | **increasingly** | **a little, slightly, etc.** | **mildly** ◊ *'So what is it we have to do?' Jake asked, looking mildly ~.* | **clearly, obviously** ◊ *Dr. Solaris turned to her, obviously ~.* | **genuinely** | **equally** ◊ *He looked at his father, who looked equally ~.* | **momentarily** ◊ *George paused, momentarily ~.*

PREP. **about** ◊ *He was very ~ about his feelings.* | **at** ◊ *The policemen looked a little ~ at her question.* | **by** ◊ *I'm ~ by the whole thing.*

confusing adj.

VERBS **appear, be, look, seem, sound** | **become, get** | **make sth** ◊ *The two new members had the same name, which made things ~.* | **find sth** ◊ *I find the policy extremely ~.*

ADV. **extremely, fairly, very, etc.** | **highly, terribly, utterly** | **a little, slightly, etc.** | **potentially**

PREP. **for** ◊ *The new signs will be very ~ for tourists.* | **to** ◊ *All this information can be ~ to the user.*

confusion noun

ADJ. **complete, total, utter** | **considerable, great** | **mild, slight** | **general, mass, widespread** | **understandable** ◊ *They are very hard to tell apart, so the ~ is understandable.* | **pure** ◊ *His expression was one of pure ~.* | **initial** | **momentary** | **unnecessary** | **mental** | **ensuing, resulting**

VERB + CONFUSION **avoid, prevent** ◊ *a few key tips to help you avoid any ~* ◊ *I kept my ex-husband's last name to prevent ~.* | **cause, create, generate, lead to, result in, sow** | **add to** ◊ *This latest decision has only added to the general ~.* | **minimize** ◊ *medication labels that minimize ~* | **clarify, clear up, dispel, eliminate** | **plunge sb/sth into, throw sb/**

sth into ◊ *The office has been thrown into total ~ by her resignation.* | **sense** ◊ *I could sense her ~ and frustration.*

CONFUSION + VERB **arise, reign** ◊ *Confusion reigns when two managers give conflicting instructions.* | **surround sth** ◊ *The government needs to clear up the ~ surrounding its policy on water.*

PREP. **in (the) ~** ◊ *She stared at them both in utter ~.* ◊ *In the ~ that followed, she managed to slip away unnoticed.* | **~ about, ~ over, ~ regarding** ◊ *There is widespread ~ about the government's health policy.* ◊ *There has been considerable ~ regarding the facts of her death.* | **~ among** ◊ *The announcement caused a lot of ~ among the students.* | **~ as to** ◊ *~ as to the whereabouts of the man* | **~ between** ◊ *~ between letters of the alphabet* | **~ with** ◊ *the ~ of this book with her last one*

PHRASES **a scene of ~, a state of ~** | **to avoid ~** ◊ *To avoid ~, label each box clearly.*

congested adj.

VERBS **be** | **become, get**

ADV. **chronically, heavily, highly, severely, very** ◊ *one of the nation's most chronically ~ airports* ◊ *The roads to Lagos were heavily ~.* | **increasingly** ◊ *controllers trying to manage increasingly ~ airports*

PREP. **with** ◊ *The city streets were ~ with vehicles.*

congestion noun

ADJ. **chronic, serious, severe** | **increased, increasing** | **highway** (*AmE*), **road, traffic** ◊ *the nation's dependence on cars and the resulting highway ~* ◊ *Parking near the school causes severe traffic ~.* | **downtown** (*AmE*), **urban** ◊ *a study of downtown traffic ~* | **Internet, network** ◊ *Engineers are hoping network ~ will become a thing of the past.* | **chest, nasal**

VERB + CONGESTION **cause, lead to** | **alleviate, avoid, ease, minimize, reduce, relieve** ◊ *measures to ease the increasing ~ in Hong Kong* | **increase, worsen**

CONGESTION + NOUN **charge, pricing** (*both BrE*)

conglomerate noun

ADJ. **big, giant, huge, large, vast** ◊ *the giant pharmaceutical ~s* | **global, international, multinational** ◊ *one of seven global media ~s that dominate the industry* | **business, financial, industrial** | **entertainment, food, media, mining, publishing, etc.**

congratulate verb

ADV. **heartily, warmly** | **personally, publicly** ◊ *The President himself is here to personally ~ the winner.*

VERB + CONGRATULATE **have to, must, want to, wish to, would like to** ◊ *I must ~ you on your excellent exam results.* ◊ *I just wanted to ~ you on your victory.*

PREP. **for** ◊ *The employees should be ~d for the part they have played in the success.* | **on** ◊ *She ~d me warmly on my performance.* ◊ *The organizers are congratulating themselves on attracting record numbers to the event.*

PHRASES **sb is to be ~d** ◊ *The company is to be ~d on its success.* | **to join sb in congratulating sb** ◊ *Please join me in congratulating Luke on an outstanding season.*

congratulations noun

ADJ. **heartfelt, hearty, sincere, warm** ◊ *May I offer my heartiest ~ on your promotion?* | **special** ◊ *Special ~ go out to Eric for a job done well.* | **belated** ◊ *Allow me to offer my belated ~ to you on becoming the first woman member.*

VERB + CONGRATULATIONS **express, extend, give (sb), offer (sb), send (sb)** ◊ *Please give your parents my ~.* | **say, shout, yell** ◊ *The crowd got to their feet, applauding and yelling ~.* | **accept, receive** ◊ *She received many ~ after the concert.* | **deserve** ◊ *They all deserve sincere ~ for giving us this latest example of courage.*

PREP. **~ on** ◊ *Please accept my warmest ~ on your engagement.* | **~ to** ◊ *Congratulations to Tony on his new job!*

PHRASES **~ are in order** ◊ *'It would seem that ~ are in order!' Kevin said.*

congregation *noun*

ADJ. **large** | **small** | **local** ◇ *members of local ~s* | **religious** ◇ *Almost every religious ~ has a social role.* | **Christian, Lutheran, Methodist, Protestant, etc.** | **conservative, Jewish, orthodox, reformed**

VERB + CONGREGATION **address** ◇ *The priest stood up to address the ~.* | **lead** ◇ *The minister led the ~ in a hymn.* | **serve** ◇ *a lay minister serving a small rural ~* | **establish, form** ◇ *He had established a small ~ in New York City.* | **join** | **attend** (*AmE*) ◇ *people attending the ~ where she and her family worship*

PREP. **in a/the ~**

PHRASES **a member of a ~**

congress *noun*

1 large formal meeting/series of meetings

ADJ. **international, national, world** | **annual** | **party** | **extraordinary** | **full**

VERB + CONGRESS **attend** ◇ *Three hundred delegates attended the party ~.* | **address | convene, hold | organize | open** ◇ *The general secretary opened the ~ on global warming.* | **close**

CONGRESS + VERB **take place** | **adopt sth, agree to sth, approve sth** ◇ *The ~ agreed to the tax-cutting package.* | **call for sth | elect sb | vote**

CONGRESS + NOUN **attendee, delegate, participant** ◇ *We wanted to offer the ~ participants a greater diversity of content.*

PREP. **at a/the ~** ◇ *We met again at the annual ~.* | **~ on** ◇ *a ~ on language in education*

2 Congress (in the US and some other countries) group of people elected to make laws

ADJ. **Democratic, Republican** ◇ *The Republican ~ applauded this news enthusiastically.*

VERB + CONGRESS **call** ◇ *The committee will call a national ~ of 1000 delegates.* | **suspend** ◇ *President Fujimori suspended Congress and the judiciary.* | **dissolve** ◇ *Within two years of coming to power, he dissolved Congress and the courts.* | **go to** ◇ *They will have to go to Congress to get the money.* | **take sth to** ◇ *Outraged, he took his case to Congress.*

CONGRESS + VERB **approve sth, authorize sth** ◇ *Congress approved most of the new powers.* ◇ *Congress authorized $18 billion to launch the program.* | **enact sth, mandate sth** (*AmE*), **pass sth** ◇ *Congress passed a series of important measures.* ◇ *Congress annually enacts legislation to fund NASA.* | **reject sth | consider sth, debate sth** ◇ *Congress debated the issue at length.* | **vote** ◇ *Congress voted to delay a decision.* | **appropriate sth** (*AmE*) ◇ *Congress appropriated $75 million for the program.* | **adjourn** ◇ *Congress adjourned for the year without approving an economic stimulus package.*

CONGRESS + NOUN **member** | **leader**

PREP. **in ~** ◇ *The liberals in Congress felt the reforms did not go far enough.*

PHRASES **a member of Congress** | **a session of Congress** ◇ *legislation for the next session of Congress*

Congressman, Congresswoman *noun*

ADJ. **Democratic, Republican | conservative, liberal | local | leading | incumbent | four-term, eight-term, etc. | freshman** (*AmE*) | **former**

VERB + CONGRESSMAN/CONGRESSWOMAN **elect (sb), re-elect (sb)** ◇ *He was elected congressman in 1997.* | **lobby | contact, write** ◇ *Many people have written their congressmen with complaints.*

CONGRESSMAN/CONGRESSWOMAN + VERB **call for sth** ◇ *a leading congressman who's calling for a crackdown on illegal aliens*

conjecture *noun*

ADJ. **pure** ◇ *Whether the business will survive another ten years is pure ~.* | **just, mere, only** ◇ *These are mere ~s on our part.*

PREP. **~ about, ~ as to** ◇ *There was a lot of ~ as to the extent of her wealth.*

PHRASES **a matter for ~** ◇ *Whether she will run for a second term in office is a matter for ~.* | **open to ~** (*esp. BrE*)

connect *verb*

1 join

ADV. **directly** ◇ *Downstairs toilets were ~ed directly to the drains.* | **physically | remotely, wirelessly** ◇ *A classroom modem allows you to ~ remotely to the server.* ◇ *laptops that ~ wirelessly to the Net*

PREP. **to** ◇ *Connect the machine to the power supply.* | **with** ◇ *A corridor ~s his office with the main building.*

2 link

ADV. **closely, inextricably, intimately, seamlessly** ◇ *Bad diet is closely ~ed with many common illnesses.* | **directly | loosely** ◇ *Those details are only loosely ~ed to the plot.* | **causally | politically | emotionally**

PREP. **to** ◇ *I was feeling alive and ~ed to nature.* ◇ *I think Seb was ~ed to the murder.* ◇ *The entire family is ~ed to the Mafia.* | **with** ◇ *The police were looking for evidence to ~ him with the crime.*

connection *noun*

1 relationship between two things

ADJ. **clear, close, direct, intimate, strong** ◇ *There is a close ~ between family background and academic achievement.* | **tenuous | obvious | causal | emotional, spiritual** ◇ *a deep physical and spiritual ~ with nature* | **deep** ◇ *His deepest ~ is with his father, Frank Sr.*

VERB + CONNECTION **have** ◇ *His death had no ~ with drugs.* | **discover, establish, find, form, make, see** ◇ *Researchers have now established a ~ between air pollution and asthma.* ◇ *She did not make the ~ between her diet and her poor health.* | **draw, trace** ◇ *Kierkegaard draws a ~ between anxiety and free will.* | **forge** ◇ *a government initiative to forge new ~s with industry* | **feel** ◇ *We need to feel a ~ to nature.* | **explore** ◇ *This essay explores the ~s between technology and nature.* | **maintain** ◇ *He maintained his southern ~ through summer visits with his relatives.* | **strengthen** ◇ *This helps companies strengthen their ~s to their customers.* | **share** ◇ *He and John seem to share a ~.* | **break, sever** ◇ *She wanted to sever all her ~s with the company.* | **re-establish** ◇ *Anna helped Rachel re-establish her ~ with her brother.* | **deny** ◇ *He denied any ~ to the scam.*

PREP. **in ~ with** ◇ *I am writing in ~ with your recent job application.* | **~ among** ◇ *They helped establish ~s among labs from Honolulu to Paris.* | **~ between** ◇ *the ~ between crime and alcohol* | **~ to, ~ with** ◇ *What is your ~ with the school?*

PHRASES **in that/this ~** (= for reasons connected with sth recently mentioned)

2 electrical connection, etc.

ADJ. **loose | electrical | phone, telephone | cellular** (*esp. AmE*), **mobile | always-on, broadband, cable, dial-up, DSL, ethernet, high-speed, Internet, wireless** ◇ *speedy, always-on Internet ~s* ◇ *A fast cable ~ is recommended.* ◇ *Each laptop has a wireless ethernet ~.* ◇ *a high-speed network ~ that makes accessing the Internet easy*

VERB + CONNECTION **break** ◇ *If you break the ~, the light won't come on.*

CONNECTION + NOUN **charge, fee**

PREP. **~ to** ◇ *We're waiting for ~ to the water mains.*

3 bus/train/plane

ADJ. **good | tight | bus, rail, train**

VERB + CONNECTION **make | miss**

PREP. **~ between** ◇ *There are good ~s between the resort and major cities.*

4 person you know

ADJ. **good | aristocratic** (*esp. BrE*), **business, family, personal, political, professional, social**

VERB + CONNECTION **have** ◇ *I have some good business ~s in New York.* ◇ *He has ~s* (= he knows people who would be able to help him). | **use** ◇ *She used her ~s to get the job.*

PREP. **through ~** ◇ *He got his job through ~s.*

connoisseur *noun*

ADJ. **great, real, true** ◊ *Only the true ~ could tell the difference between these two wines.* ◊ *This is one of those movies that will separate the casual movie-goers from the real ~s.* | **art, music, wine**
PREP. **~ of** ◊ *a great ~ of Japanese art*

connotation *noun*

ADJ. **obvious, strong** ◊ *the obvious symbolic ~s of his name* | **broad** (*esp. AmE*), **wider** (*esp. BrE*) ◊ *The term 'at-risk youth' has taken on broad ~s.* ◊ *The notion of abuse has wider ~s than the physical.* | **negative, sinister, unfortunate** | **derogatory, pejorative** ◊ *the derogatory ~ of the term 'diva'* | **positive** | **cultural, moral, political, racial, religious, sexual** ◊ *words that today have religious ~s*
VERB + CONNOTATION **acquire, carry, have** ◊ *That word has strong sexual ~s.* ◊ *The term 'native' has acquired pejorative ~s among some groups.* | **lose** | **attach, give sth** ◊ *the negative ~s attached to the word 'academic'*
PREP. **~ of** ◊ *The word carries ~s of romance.*

conquest *noun*

ADJ. **violent** ◊ *the desire of each tribe to show its superiority through violent ~* | **military** | **Muslim, Norman, Roman, Spanish, etc.** ◊ *the Roman ~ of Britain* | **colonial, imperial** | **territorial** ◊ *Trade rather than territorial ~ was held to be the route to progress.* | **sexual** | **latest** ◊ *Alicia's latest ~, Victor*
VERB + CONQUEST **make** ◊ *The army made many ~s in the east.* | **complete**
PREP. **by ~, through ~** ◊ *He continued to expand his kingdom by ~.* | **~ of** ◊ *the Spanish ~ of Mexico*

conscience *noun*

ADJ. **clean** (*esp. AmE*), **clear, easy, good** ◊ *How can you do your job with a clean ~?* ◊ *I have a clear ~.* | **bad, guilty, troubled, uneasy** ◊ *a dying man with a guilty ~* | **civic, environmental, moral, political, social** ◊ *consumers with an environmental ~* ◊ *a government with no social ~* | **religious** | **tender** ◊ *I never knew a more tender ~ on every point of duty.* | **collective** ◊ *the collective ~ of American business* | **individual** ◊ *It should be a matter of individual ~.*
VERB + CONSCIENCE **have** ◊ *He had no ~ about taking his brother's money.* | **appease, assuage, clear, ease, salve, soothe** ◊ *After the meal she spent a week dieting to salve her ~.* | **prick, trouble** | **appeal to, arouse, awaken, rouse, stir** | **shock** ◊ *a bill which has shocked the ~ of every middle-class community* | **wrestle with** ◊ *He wrestled with his ~ all night long.* | **follow** ◊ *I have only ever followed my ~.* | **examine** ◊ *At the end of each day, examine your ~.*
CONSCIENCE + VERB **guide sb/sth, tell sb sth** ◊ *He felt his ~ telling him to apologize.* ◊ *It's important to let your ~ guide your decisions.* | **bother sb, prick sb** (*esp. BrE*), **trouble sb** (*esp. BrE*) ◊ *Her ~ was bothering her a little.* ◊ *Her ~ pricked her every time she thought of how cruel she had been to Kirby.* | **dictate sth** ◊ *My ~ dictates that I resign.*
PREP. **on your ~** ◊ *I'm sure she has something on her ~.* ◊ *It was on his ~ that he hadn't called her.*
PHRASES **an act of ~** (*esp. AmE*) ◊ *His decision appears to have been an act of ~.* | **an attack of ~** ◊ *Best came forward because of an attack of ~.* | **a crisis of ~** | **freedom of ~, liberty of ~** | **in all ~, in ~, in good ~** (= honestly) ◊ *We cannot in all ~ refuse to help.* | **let ~ be your guide** | **a matter of ~** ◊ *This question is a matter of individual ~.* | **man/woman/people of ~** ◊ *How could people of ~ allow this to happen?* | **a pang of ~, a prick of ~** (*BrE*), **a twinge of ~** (*esp. BrE*) ◊ *I had a sudden pang of ~ that I really ought to tell the truth.* | **the right of ~, the rights of ~** (*both AmE*) | **the voice of ~** ◊ *She refused to listen to the voice of ~.*

conscious *adj.*

1 aware of sth

VERBS **be, seem** | **become** | **remain**

ADV. **extremely, fairly, very, etc.** | **acutely, deeply, highly, intensely, terribly** ◊ *She became acutely ~ that someone was watching her.* ◊ *We are now deeply ~ of these issues.* | **completely, fully, perfectly** ◊ *He was completely ~ of her warm body next to his.* | **increasingly** | **barely, hardly** ◊ *I was hardly ~ of my surroundings.* | **vaguely** ◊ *He fell, and was vaguely ~ of Tara standing over him.* | **painfully** ◊ *He was painfully ~ of how hard it was going to be to explain.* | **environmentally, politically, socially** ◊ *The company is extremely environmentally ~* (= aware of environmental problems and how to deal with them).
PREP. **of** ◊ *I am very ~ of the need for secrecy.*

2 able to see/hear/feel

VERBS **be** | **become** | **remain, stay** (*esp. AmE*) ◊ *She remained ~ throughout the operation.* | **keep sb** ◊ *Try to keep the patient ~.*
ADV. **completely, fully** ◊ *The patient is not yet fully ~.* | **barely, hardly** ◊ *One man was so drunk he was barely ~.* | **minimally** (*AmE*) ◊ *treatment decisions for persons in a minimally ~ state* | **half, partially** (*esp. AmE*) ◊ *I was only half ~.*

consciousness *noun*

1 being able to see/hear/feel things

ADJ. **full** | **higher** ◊ *to aspire to a higher ~* | **cosmic, divine** ◊ *powerful states of cosmic ~* | **altered** | **individual** | **animal, human** ◊ *the modern study of animal ~*
VERB + CONSCIOUSNESS **lose** ◊ *She hit her head on a rock and lost ~.* | **recover, regain** ◊ *When she regained ~ she was in a hospital bed.* | **bring sb back to** ◊ *The cold water brought me back to full ~.* | **enter** ◊ *The words slowly entered her ~.* | **alter** ◊ *In some cultures shamans use drugs to alter ~.*
PHRASES **a level of ~, a state of ~** ◊ *an altered state of ~*

2 being aware of sth

ADJ. **full** ◊ *I left the room with full ~ of the impression I would make.* | **growing** | **collective, popular, public** ◊ *Hip-hop exploded into popular ~ at the same time as the music video.* | **national** | **modern** | **historical** | **class, cultural, environmental, feminist, gay, political, religious, social, working-class** ◊ *a new political ~ among young people* | **black, ethnic** (*esp. AmE*), **racial** ◊ *African American racial ~* | **civic** | **critical** ◊ *Our role as educators is to develop a critical ~ among our students.* | **false** (*technical*) ◊ *He claims that it's a form of false ~ for working people to vote.*
VERB + CONSCIOUSNESS **develop, raise** ◊ *They have succeeded in raising ~ on many issues.* | **enter** ◊ *imagery that has entered the national ~ through the media* | **alter** ◊ *a change that altered our collective ~ forever* | **be lodged in, lodge itself in** ◊ *The idea firmly lodged itself in the public ~.*
PREP. **in (the) ~** ◊ *a key position in feminist ~* | **~ about** (*esp. AmE*) ◊ *a new ~ about the health consequences of pesticides* | **~ among** | **~ of** ◊ *a growing ~ of environmental issues among children*

conscription (*esp. BrE*) *noun* → See also DRAFT

ADJ. **universal** | **military** | **compulsory, forced** ◊ *the forced ~ of boys into the army*
VERB + CONSCRIPTION **introduce** ◊ *his decision to institute military ~* | **abolish, end** | **avoid** ◊ *He injured himself to avoid ~.*

consensus *noun*

ADJ. **broad, clear, common, general, prevailing, rough, widespread** ◊ *That seems to be the prevailing ~.* | **global, unanimous, universal** ◊ *a universal ~ about the problems of the exchange rate system* ◊ *The world's scientists have reached a nearly unanimous ~ that the surface of the Earth is warming as a result of human activities.* | **overwhelming, strong** | **emerging, growing** | **tacit, unspoken** | **inter-national, national** | **bipartisan** (*AmE*) ◊ *There is a bipartisan ~ against the legalization of drugs.* | **current** ◊ *the current ~ about AIDS in Africa* | **political, social** | **expert, scholarly, scientific** ◊ *There is no scholarly ~ on how these terms are defined.* | **critical** ◊ *A critical ~ has emerged about these poems.* | **liberal**

VERB + CONSENSUS **achieve, arrive at, reach** | **build, develop, forge, form** ◊ *a magazine attempting to build a ~ about sustainable science* ◊ *The agency helped develop a ~ on conservation.* | **reflect, represent** | **break** (*esp. BrE*), **shatter** ◊ *He was the first to shatter the ~ and criticize the proposal.*
CONSENSUS + VERB **exist** ◊ *No clear ~ exists over the next stage of the plan.* | **emerge** ◊ *A general ~ on the problem is beginning to emerge.* | **form** ◊ *Over time a ~ formed.* | **break down** ◊ *There are signs that the ~ is breaking down.*
CONSENSUS + NOUN **opinion, view** ◊ *This is not ~ opinion yet.* | **statement** ◊ *There are guidelines in a 2007 ~ statement from the Institute.*
PREP. **by ~** ◊ *They have always governed by ~.* | **~ about, ~ on, ~ over** ◊ *It is difficult to reach a ~ about electoral reform.* | **~ among, ~ between, ~ within** ◊ *no ~ among the members*
PHRASES **a ~ of opinion** ◊ *The general ~ of opinion is that a high-fat diet is bad for you.* | **a lack of ~**

consent noun

ADJ. **full** | **common, general, mutual, unanimous** ◊ *By unanimous ~, the Senate inserted a moratorium.* | **explicit, express** ◊ *The information should generally be considered private unless there is explicit ~ to disclose it.* | **implied** ◊ *Completion of the survey was taken as implied ~ to participate.* | **tacit** ◊ *Your silence implies tacit ~ to these proposals.* | **voluntary** ◊ *A contract requires the voluntary ~ of the parties entering into it.* | **informed** ◊ *Doctors must obtain the informed ~ of all patients before giving any treatment.* | **prior** ◊ *No action can be taken without the prior ~ of the owner.* | **formal, signed** (*AmE*), **written** ◊ *A record of their written ~ must be on file.* | **oral** (*AmE*), **verbal** ◊ *They provided verbal ~ for the interview to be taped.* | **presumed** (*AmE*) ◊ *the policy of presumed ~ for organ donation* | **parental, spousal** (*AmE*)
VERB + CONSENT **give (sb), grant (sb), provide** ◊ *You must give written ~ before the documents can be released.* | **refuse (sb), withdraw, withhold** ◊ *At any time during the study, parents could withdraw their ~.* | **gain, get, have, obtain, secure** ◊ *Do you have the ~ of your employer?* ◊ *The investigators secured the ~ of the suspects to take their computers away.* | **receive** ◊ *The proposal received unanimous ~.* | **require, seek | nod** ◊ *Judge Roberts nodded his ~ and she began.* | **sign** (*esp. AmE*) ◊ *Your family, in effect, signs the ~ for you.*
CONSENT + NOUN **agreement, decree, law** (*all AmE*) | **document, form** ◊ *Doctors pressed her to sign a ~ form for emergency surgery.* | **procedure** (*AmE*), **process** (*both AmE*) | **requirement** (*AmE*) ◊ *The removal of the patient ~ requirement was denounced by the opposition.*
PREP. **by ~, by ~ of** ◊ *government by ~* ◊ *The article is reprinted by ~ of the author.* | **by common ~, by general ~, by mutual ~** ◊ *The contract can only be broken by mutual ~.* | **with sb's ~, without sb's ~** ◊ *Your property cannot be sold without your ~.* | **~ for** ◊ *He gave his ~ for treatment.* | **~ from** ◊ *~ from the parents* | **~ to** ◊ *He withheld his ~ to the marriage.*
PHRASES **the age of ~** (= the age at which sb is legally old enough to agree to have a sexual relationship)

consent verb

ADV. **freely, willingly** ◊ *I asked him to provide it and he willingly ~ed.* | **graciously, kindly** ◊ *He has kindly ~ed to give us some of his valuable time.* | **reluctantly** ◊ *He reluctantly ~ed to the material being edited.*
PREP. **to** ◊ *Her father would not ~ to the marriage.*

consequence noun

ADJ. **full** | **unintended** ◊ *The Act could have certain unintended ~s.* | **far-reaching, important, profound, significant** ◊ *a debate with potentially significant legal ~s* | **adverse, bad, catastrophic, damaging, dangerous, deadly, deleterious** (*formal, esp. AmE*), **devastating, dire, disastrous, fatal, grave, harmful, negative, serious, severe, terrible, tragic, unfortunate, unpleasant** ◊ *a new sonar system that could have deadly ~s for whales* ◊ *The kidnappers threatened him with dire ~s if their demands were not met*

immediately. ◊ *There could be grave ~s for the economy.* | **beneficial, good, positive** | **main, major** | **direct, immediate** | **practical** ◊ *The practical ~s of his decision were considerable.* | **indirect** | **inevitable, necessary, unavoidable** ◊ *This is a tragic yet unavoidable ~ of war.* | **likely, possible, potential** | **predictable** | **unanticipated, unexpected, unforeseen** ◊ *better planning to ensure that there are fewer unanticipated ~s* | **logical, natural** | **long-term, short-term** | **unintended** | **ecological, economic, emotional, environmental, financial, legal, physical, physiological, political, social** ◊ *to face up to the physical ~s of ageing* | **health** ◊ *the links between dietary choices and health ~s*
VERB + CONSEQUENCE **have, lead to** ◊ *The practice had far-reaching environmental ~s.* | **accept, bear, face (up to), suffer, take** ◊ *You must accept the full ~s of your actions.* | **fear** | **assess, consider, examine, explore** | **foresee, predict** ◊ *They cannot predict the precise ~s of an increase in average temperature.*
CONSEQUENCE + VERB **arise, ensue** (*esp. BrE*), **follow, occur, result** ◊ *the important electoral ~s that will follow from this decision*
PREP. **as a ~** ◊ *Hundreds of people lost their jobs as a direct ~ of the merger.* | **in ~ (of)** (*law*) ◊ *The employer is liable for compensation payable in ~ of injury to one of its employees.* | **~ for** ◊ *This could have serious ~s for the economy.* | **~ on** ◊ *a gritty look at war and its ~s on human life*
PHRASES **of (any) ~** ◊ *I'd never done anything of ~ in my life.* ◊ *Scorsese's first feature film of any ~* | **of little ~, of no ~** ◊ *The majority of these losses are of little ~.* ◊ *Minor slips are of no ~.* | **of great ~, of serious ~** ◊ *Matters of justice are of great ~.*

conservation noun

ADJ. **biodiversity** (*esp. AmE*), **energy, environmental, forest, habitat, nature, resource, soil, water, wildlife** ◊ *a large-scale habitat ~ plan* | **bird, elephant, etc.** | **species** | **architectural, building** (*BrE*) | **art**
CONSERVATION + NOUN **body, group, movement, organization** ◊ *an avid supporter of the ~ movement* | **efforts, initiative, measure, policy, programme/program, project, scheme** (*BrE*), **strategy, work** ◊ *the pledge to develop coral reef ~ strategies* | **concern, issue, priority** | **status** ◊ *Such data can be helpful in evaluating the ~ status of plants.* | **ethic** (*AmE*) | **area** ◊ *a national park and ~ area* (*AmE*) ◊ *No new building is permitted in ~ areas.* (*BrE*) | **biologist, biology** (*both esp. AmE*)

conservatism noun

ADJ. **diehard, entrenched** (*both BrE*) | **moderate, relative** | **compassionate** ◊ *his message of compassionate ~* | **modern** | **traditional** | **inherent, innate, natural** ◊ *the innate ~ of the business community* | **cultural, economic, fiscal, ideological, political, religious, social**
PREP. **~ in** ◊ *people's ~ in musical taste*

conservative noun

ADJ. **diehard, hard-line, staunch** | **right-wing** | **political** | **compassionate** | **cultural, fiscal, social** | **Christian, religious** (*both AmE*)

conservative adj.

VERBS **be** | **become** | **remain**
ADV. **extremely, fairly, very, etc.** | **deeply, highly, profoundly, solidly, staunchly** ◊ *a staunchly ~ nominee* | **overly** ◊ *The gloomy forecasts are based on overly ~ projections of growth.* | **ideologically** ◊ *Her views are by no means ideologically ~.* | **increasingly** | **largely, predominantly** | **moderately, relatively** ◊ *moderately ~ voters* | **basically, essentially, fundamentally, generally** ◊ *She takes a basically ~ view of society.* ◊ *a fundamentally ~ political outlook* | **inherently** ◊ *the army's inherently ~ values* | **notoriously** ◊ *Banks are notoriously ~ about their dealings with clients.* | **traditionally** ◊ *a traditionally ~ profession* |

culturally, fiscally, morally, politically, religiously (*esp. AmE*), **socially** ◊ *the culturally ~ world of commerce and industry*

consider *verb*

ADV. **carefully, seriously, strongly** (*AmE*) ◊ *I'm seriously ~ing the possibility of emigrating.* ◊ *I was strongly ~ing leaving her on her own.* | **briefly** ◊ *I did briefly ~ going on my own.* | **separately** ◊ *Each case is ~ed separately.*
PREP. **for** ◊ *We are ~ing her for the job of designer.*
PHRASES **generally ~ed to be sth, widely ~ed to be sth** ◊ *He is widely ~ed to be a future star.*

consideration *noun*

1 careful thought about sth

ADJ. **careful, detailed, full, serious** ◊ *After careful ~, I have decided to resign.* ◊ *What is needed is a full ~ of the dilemma.* | **adequate, due, proper, sufficient** (*esp. BrE*) | **further** ◊ *His argument deserves further ~.* | **thoughtful** ◊ *Both options require thoughtful ~ of the costs.* | **critical** ◊ *The final issue was devoted to critical ~s of individual writers.* | **special, urgent** (*esp. BrE*) | **active**
VERB + CONSIDERATION **give sth, take sth into** ◊ *We will give your proposals serious ~.* ◊ *You must take the size of the room into ~.* | **deserve, merit, warrant** ◊ *Several limitations of this study merit ~.* | **need, require** | **receive**
PREP. **after ~** ◊ *After due ~, it was decided not to offer her the job.* | **for sb's ~** ◊ *I enclose the report for your ~.* | **in ~ of** (= as payment for sth) (*formal*), **on ~** ◊ *On ~, we have decided not to come.* | **under ~** ◊ *proposals under active ~*
2 thinking about other people's wishes and feelings

VERB + CONSIDERATION **have** ◊ *You have no ~ for me, nor for anyone else.* | **show sb, treat sb with** ◊ *She showed little ~ for the beginners.*
PREP. **out of ~** ◊ *He did it out of ~ for his daughter.* | **~ for**
3 sth you think about when deciding sth

ADJ. **important, key, main, major** ◊ *Pricing and product availability are key ~ to users.* | **overriding, paramount, primary, prime** | **minor, secondary** | **additional** ◊ *Here are a few additional ~s that may help in making the correct decision.* | **aesthetic, commercial, cost, economic, environmental, ethical, financial, health, legal, moral, personal, political, practical, pragmatic, safety, security, strategic, theoretical** ◊ *Cost is normally secondary to such issues as how effective each method will be.*
VERB + CONSIDERATION **be** ◊ *Taxes are a major ~ when thinking about selling or buying a house.* | **take account of** (*esp. BrE*), **take into account** ◊ *There are several important safety ~s that must be taken into account.*
PHRASES **to be worth ~** ◊ *The new software offers some features worth ~.*

consist *verb*

PHRV **consist of sth**
ADV. **entirely, exclusively, merely, only, simply, solely** ◊ *Their conversation ~ed almost entirely of gossip.* | **chiefly, essentially, largely, mainly, mostly, predominantly, primarily, principally** | **basically** ◊ *a gas station that basically ~s of two gas pumps and a vending machine* | **generally, often, typically, usually** ◊ *The settlements often ~ of simple huts.*

consistency *noun*

1 always having the same standard, opinions, etc.

ADJ. **absolute, complete** | **good, great, remarkable** | **internal** | **overall** ◊ *The songs on the album have an overall ~ of approach.* | **intellectual, logical** ◊ *Intellectual ~ is the hallmark of a fine legal mind.* | **stylistic, thematic**
...OF CONSISTENCY **degree, level**
VERB + CONSISTENCY **demonstrate, show** ◊ *He has shown remarkable ~ in his exam results.* | **achieve, ensure, find, maintain, provide** ◊ *The team must find ~ in its game.* |

lack | **improve** ◊ *Romero needs to improve his ~ by throwing more first-pitch strikes.*
PREP. **~ in, ~ of** ◊ *a ~ of approach* | **~ with** ◊ *to maintain ~ with past practice*
2 thickness/firmness of a liquid substance

ADJ. **thick, thin** | **soft** | **creamy, smooth** | **rubbery** | **runny** ◊ *a fudgy concoction with a rather runny ~* | **rock-like** ◊ *The soil is baked to a rock-like ~.* | **desired, right** ◊ *Knead the dough to the right ~.*
VERB + CONSISTENCY **have** ◊ *The mixture should have the ~ of thick cream.* | **give**

consistent *adj.*

1 always behaving in the same way

VERBS **be** | **become** | **remain**
ADV. **extremely, fairly, very, etc.** | **highly, remarkably** | **absolutely, completely, entirely, quite, wholly** ◊ *His attitude isn't absolutely ~.* | **largely** | **reasonably, relatively** ◊ *A writer must maintain a relatively ~ perspective or tone.*
2 in agreement with sth

VERBS **appear, be, seem** ◊ *These findings appear ~ across racial and ethnic groups.* | **remain, stay**
ADV. **completely, entirely, fully, perfectly** | **broadly, generally, largely** ◊ *Our results are generally ~ with the results of other analyses.* | **fairly, pretty, quite, reasonably, relatively** ◊ *The portrait of Powell in the book is pretty ~ with what everybody knows.* | **strikingly, surprisingly** ◊ *The pattern is strikingly ~ in the four samples.* ◊ *The results of this study are surprisingly ~ with previous estimates.* | **internally** ◊ *His argument is not even internally ~ (= different parts of the argument contradict each other).* | **logically**
PREP. **across, among** (*AmE*) ◊ *These findings are ~ across all the studies.* ◊ *These findings were statistically ~ among studies.* | **between** ◊ *These results were ~ between genders, and regardless of age and parent education level.* | **with** ◊ *The figures are fully ~ with last year's results.*

consolation *noun*

ADJ. **great** | **small**
VERB + CONSOLATION **have** ◊ *She had the ~ of coming second in her last race of the day.* | **seek** ◊ *She tends to seek ~ in food.* | **draw** (*esp. BrE*), **find, take** ◊ *He drew little ~ from this fact.* ◊ *When her mother died, she found ~ in her religious beliefs.* ◊ *Although we lost the game, we took some ~ from the fact that we played well.* | **bring (sb), offer (sb), provide (sb with)** ◊ *The next game will probably offer them the ~ of winning.*
PREP. **~ for** | **~ to** ◊ *The children were a great ~ to me at that time.*
PHRASES **be (of) little ~ to sb, be (of) small ~ to sb, be (of) some ~ to sb** ◊ *This news was of little ~ to us.* | **if it is any ~ (to sb)** ◊ *If it's any ~ to you, the weather here is also awful.* | **sb's one ~, sb's only ~** ◊ *When she lost her job, her only ~ was that she had some savings in the bank.*

conspicuous *adj.*

VERBS **be, feel, look, seem** | **become** | **make sb** ◊ *Its yellow skin makes it highly ~.*
ADV. **extremely, fairly, very, etc.** ◊ *The new building was rather ~.* | **highly**
PHRASES **~ by your absence** (= not present in a situation or place, when it is obvious that you should be there)

conspiracy *noun*

ADJ. **big, great, larger, massive, vast** | **grand** | **criminal, government, media, political** ◊ *charges of criminal ~ and corruption* | **alleged** | **global, international, worldwide**
VERB + CONSPIRACY **be involved in, join** ◊ *I suspected that he was involved in the ~.* | **be part of** ◊ *This action was part of a ~ to deceive the public.* | **organize** ◊ *Who organized the ~ against the president?* | **expose, uncover** ◊ *Officials have uncovered a ~ to discredit the government.* | **see, suspect** ◊ *He's the sort of person who sees a ~ around every corner.*
CONSPIRACY + NOUN **theory** | **charge** ◊ *All three men were convicted on ~ charges.*

PREP. **~ against** ◊ *a ~ against the king* | **~ between** ◊ *a ~ between the police and the right-wing parties*
PHRASES **a ~ of silence** ◊ *There is a ~ of silence about the killer* (= *nobody will say what they know*).
→ Note at CRIME (for more verbs)

constable noun (BrE)

ADJ. **police** | **Chief, Detective** | **beat, special, uniformed** ◊ *The force hopes to increase the number of its beat ~s.* ◊ *Special ~s provide part-time assistance for the regular police force.*
PHRASES **the rank of ~**

constant adj.

VERBS **be** | **remain, stay** ◊ *The level of unemployment remains fairly ~ at around 10%.* | **hold sth** (*technical*), **keep sth** ◊ *All variables except one must be held ~.* ◊ *The temperature must be kept ~.*
ADV. **fairly, reasonably, relatively** | **approximately, essentially, more or less, roughly** | **almost, nearly, virtually** | **remarkably** | **absolutely**
PREP. **across** ◊ *These electrical properties are virtually ~ across a wide range of temperatures.* | **over** ◊ *Prices have remained ~ over this period.*

consternation noun

ADJ. **considerable, great** | **widespread**
VERB + CONSTERNATION **cause, create, fill sb with** ◊ *The announcement created surprise and ~.* ◊ *The thought of meeting him filled me with ~.* | **express, feel, greet sth with** ◊ *His resignation was greeted with ~.*
PREP. **in ~** ◊ *She stared at me in ~.* | **~ among** ◊ *There is some ~ among business leaders.*

constipation noun

ADJ. **severe** | **chronic**
... OF CONSTIPATION **bout**
VERB + CONSTIPATION **have, suffer from** | **cause** | **prevent** | **relieve, treat**
→ Special page at ILLNESS

constituency noun

1 (*esp. BrE*) district that elects a political representative
ADJ. **important, key** | **home** (*AmE*), **local** | **marginal** (*BrE*) ◊ *The Tories are concentrating their campaign in the key marginal constituencies.* | **target** | **electoral, parliamentary** (*BrE*), **senatorial** (*AmE*) | **inner-city, urban** | **suburban** | **county, rural**
VERB + CONSTITUENCY **represent** ◊ *He represents a ~ in the north of England.*
CONSTITUENCY + NOUN **boundaries** | **MP** (*BrE*)
PREP. **in a/the ~** ◊ *the people in this ~*

2 group in society
ADJ. **broad, wider** | **core, key, natural, traditional** ◊ *These people are the party's natural ~.* | **important, powerful** (*esp. AmE*) | **domestic, political, religious** (*esp. AmE*) | **Democratic, Republican, etc.** (*AmE*) ◊ *African-American voters are a key Democratic ~.*
VERB + CONSTITUENCY **appeal to, represent** ◊ *The party needs to appeal to a broader ~.* | **build, create** (*both esp. AmE*) | **alienate** (*esp. AmE*) ◊ *This position risks alienating an important ~.*
PREP. **in a/the ~**

constitution noun

1 laws/rules of a country
ADJ. **federal, state** | **democratic** | **written** ◊ *Britain does not have a written ~.* | **unwritten** | **draft, proposed** | **new** | **interim, permanent**
VERB + CONSTITUTION **draft, draw up, prepare, write** ◊ *plans to draft a new ~* | **have** | **adopt, approve, enact, promulgate, ratify, sign** ◊ *The new ~ will be adopted next year.* | **amend, change, rewrite** ◊ *A resolution to amend the ~ gained support.* ◊ *Parliament will vote to change the ~.* | **interpret** ◊ *The president felt free to interpret the ~ as he saw*

fit. | **uphold** | **violate** ◊ *The president's actions violate the ~.* | **reject, suspend** ◊ *The ~ was suspended and the army was placed in full control.* | **be enshrined in** ◊ *These principles are enshrined in the country's ~.*
CONSTITUTION + VERB **allow sth, guarantee sth, provide sth, provide for sth, require sth, say sth, stipulate sth** ◊ *The ~ stipulated that a general election must be held within 120 days.* | **forbid sth, prohibit sth**
PREP. **according to a/the ~, under a/the ~** ◊ *Under the ~, an election must be called every five years.* | **in a/the ~** ◊ *These rights are established in the federal ~.*
PHRASES **an amendment to a ~** | **a clause in a ~** | **the principles of a ~** | **the provisions of a ~, the terms of a ~**

2 ability of the body to stay healthy
ADJ. **good, strong** | **delicate, weak** | **physical**
VERB + CONSTITUTION **have** ◊ *The child had a weak ~ and was always ill.*

constrained adj.

VERBS **be, feel**
ADV. **highly, severely, tightly** ◊ *She felt tightly ~ by her family commitments.*

constraint noun

ADJ. **important, major** | **severe, tight** ◊ *The government has placed tight ~s on spending this year.* | **budget, budgetary, financial** | **legal, space, time**
VERB + CONSTRAINT **impose, place, put** | **relax, remove** | **face**
PREP. **within a/the ~** ◊ *We have to work within severe ~s.* | **without ~** ◊ *I felt free to speak to her without ~.* | **~ on, ~ upon** ◊ *There are major financial ~s on all schools.*

construction noun → See also BUILDING

1 roads/buildings
ADJ. **large, massive** ◊ *massive ~s of bamboo and paper* | **basic, simple** ◊ *It has a basic ~ of brick under a tiled roof.* | **complex** | **heavy** ◊ *the heavy ~ industry* | **solid** ◊ *walls of solid ~* | **careful** ◊ *The drainage system needs careful ~.* | **new** | **brick, concrete, steel, timber** (*esp. BrE*), **wood, wooden** ◊ *a massive steel ~* ◊ *a schoolhouse of brick ~* | **bridge, building, canal, highway** (*AmE*), **railroad** (*AmE*), **railway** (*BrE*), **road** ◊ *Road and bridge ~ is underway.* | **home** (*esp. AmE*), **house, housing, residential** (*AmE*)
VERB + CONSTRUCTION **begin, start** | **complete** ◊ *Construction of the new road has now been completed.* | **oversee**
CONSTRUCTION + VERB **be underway**
CONSTRUCTION + NOUN **industry, market** (*esp. AmE*), **sector** | **business, company, firm** (*esp. BrE*), **group** | **programme/ program, project** | **contract** | **permit** (*AmE*) | **job** | **work** | **crew, manager, team, worker** | **site** (*esp. AmE*), **yard** | **costs** | **management, schedule** (*esp. AmE*) | **equipment** (*esp. AmE*), **materials** | **method, process, technique**
PREP. **during (the) ~** ◊ *Major engineering challenges will be faced during ~.* | **under ~** ◊ *A new factory is under ~.*

2 grammar
ADJ. **grammatical, linguistic, sentence, syntactic** | **active, passive**

consult verb

ADV. **widely** ◊ *We ~ed quite widely before deciding what to do.* | **closely** | **frequently, regularly** | **adequately, properly** ◊ *They felt they had not been adequately ~ed.*
VERB + CONSULT **need to, should** ◊ *If the pain persists you should ~ your doctor.*
PREP. **about** ◊ *I need to ~ my teacher about changing my course.* | **with** ◊ *We are ~ing closely with our partners.*

consultant noun

1 sb who gives advice
ADJ. **business, campaign** (*esp. AmE*), **computer, design, educational, financial, industry, management, marketing, media, political, public relations** (abbreviated to *PR*),

security, technical, technology | independent, outside ◇ *The review was carried out last year by independent ~s.* | senior

VERB + CONSULTANT **act as** ◇ *He was happy to act as a ~ to the company.* | **bring in, employ (sb as), engage (sb as)** (*esp. BrE*), **hire (sb as), use** ◇ *We brought in a management ~ to sort out the mess.*

PREP. **~ in** ◇ *a ~ in design, printing and advertising* | **~ on** ◇ *a ~ on business ethics* | **~ to, ~ with** ◇ *They work as ~s to a software company.*
→ Note at JOB

2 (*BrE*) hospital doctor of high rank

ADJ. **hospital, NHS** ◇ *She is now a hospital ~.*

CONSULTANT + NOUN **cardiologist, gynaecologist, obstetrician, paediatrician, pathologist, physician, psychiatrist, surgeon,** etc.

PREP. **~ in** ◇ *a ~ in psychiatry*
→ Note at DOCTOR

consultation *noun*

1 process of consulting

ADJ. **close | extensive, full, wide | proper** (*BrE*) **| joint** ◇ *a joint ~ with doctors and patients* | **public** ◇ *There will be a period of public ~ before a decision is reached.*

VERB + CONSULTATION **have, hold** ◇ *The police chiefs will hold a ~ with all the relevant groups.*

CONSULTATION + NOUN **document, paper | period | process**

PREP. **in ~ with** ◇ *The plan was developed in close ~ with the local community.* | **without ~** ◇ *They have taken this decision without any ~.* | **~ about, ~ on** ◇ *The company has promised wide ~ on its expansion plans.* | **~ between** ◇ *a ~ between teachers and parents* | **~ with** ◇ *We need more ~ with the unions.*

2 with a doctor, etc.

ADJ. **personal** (*esp. AmE*), **private | free | initial | expert** (*esp. AmE*) ◇ *You should seek expert ~.* | **legal, medical, psychiatric, surgical,** etc.

VERB + CONSULTATION **have, provide** ◇ *The practice provides medical ~s for drug addicts.* | **seek** (*esp. AmE*)

CONSULTATION + NOUN **service | fee**

PREP. **~ with** ◇ *I had a ~ with a dermatologist.* ◇ *Consultation with a rheumatologist should be sought.* (*AmE*)

consumer *noun*

ADJ. **big, great, heavy, large** ◇ *We are the biggest ~s of tropical hardwoods after Japan.* | **average, ordinary | individual | potential, target** (*esp. AmE*) **| passive** ◇ *Mass culture turns audiences into passive ~s.* | **smart** (*AmE*), **sophisticated | domestic | industrial** (*esp. AmE*) **| online | green | foreign | electricity, energy**

VERB + CONSUMER **offer, provide, supply** ◇ *We supply domestic ~s* | **reach, target | educate, persuade | exploit** ◇ *They exploit ~s by charging high prices.* | **protect** ◇ *What can be done to protect the ordinary ~ from unscrupulous operators?* | **satisfy**

CONSUMER + VERB **buy sth, pay sth, spend sth | demand sth, need sth, want sth**

CONSUMER + NOUN **applications, brands, devices, durables** (*BrE*), **electronics, goods, products, services** ◇ *the market for ~ durables* | **attitudes, awareness, behaviour/behavior, choice, confidence, demand, interest, needs, preferences, tastes, trends** ◇ *Economists forecast that falling ~ confidence will cut into household purchases.* | **education, research | credit, debt, expenditure, loan** (*esp. AmE*), **spending | protection, rights | advocate** (*AmE*), **group, organization, watchdog** ◇ *Consumer watchdogs have accused banks of 'appalling arrogance' in the way they treat customers.* | **culture, society** ◇ *We are living in a ~ society.* | **market, sector | prices** ◇ *the ~ prices index* (*BrE, AmE*) ◇ *the ~ price index* (*BrE*) **| boom** (*esp. BrE*) ◇ *Government policy encouraged a ~ boom.* | **boycott** ◇ *The country could face a ~ boycott of its exports.*

PREP. **among ~** ◇ *two years of research among ~s*

ADJ. **heavy, high** ◇ *the country with the highest fuel ~ in the world* | **low | average | overall, total | excessive, moderate | conspicuous** (= buying expensive goods in order to impress people and show how rich you are) | **annual, daily** ◇ *Reducing our annual ~ of energy is an important first step.* | **current | per capita | domestic, home, local** ◇ *Half of the small crop was kept for home ~.* | **world | household | individual, personal | mass | public | private | future** ◇ *households that save for future ~* | **alcohol, beer, cigarette, drug, food, meat, tobacco, water, wine | electricity, energy, fuel, gas, gasoline** (*AmE*), **oil, petrol** (*BrE*), **power**

... OF CONSUMPTION **level**

VERB + CONSUMPTION **boost, encourage, increase, promote, stimulate** ◇ *Doctors say that we need to increase their ~ of fruit and vegetables.* | **cut down, lower, reduce** ◇ *You need to reduce your alcohol ~.*

CONSUMPTION + VERB **go up, grow, increase, rise | decline, decrease, fall, go down**

CONSUMPTION + NOUN **expenditure | figures, levels, rate | habits, patterns | goods | tax**

PREP. **for sb's ~** (= intended to be read or heard by sb) ◇ *The documents were not for public ~.*

PHRASES **fit for human ~, unfit for human ~** (= safe/not safe to be eaten) ◇ *meat that is unfit for human ~*

contact *noun*

1 meeting/talking/writing to sb

ADJ. **close** ◇ *She is still in close ~ with Sarah.* | **constant, daily, frequent, regular | direct, personal** ◇ *Have you had any direct ~ with the director of the company?* | **face-to-face, visual | email, radio, telephone | human** ◇ *She was deprived of all human ~ for three weeks.*

VERB + CONTACT **be in, have | come into, establish, get in, initiate, make** ◇ *In his job he comes into ~ with many different people.* ◇ *We first established ~ with the organization in 2002.* ◇ *When I arrive Delhi I'll get in ~ with him.* | **put sb in** ◇ *I put my cousin in ~ with a friend who works at the company.* | **keep, maintain** ◇ *Maintaining ~ after many years can be difficult.* | **keep in, remain in, stay in** ◇ *Let's try to stay in ~!* | **break off | lose**

PREP. **~ between** ◇ *There has been no ~ between them for several years.* | **~ with** ◇ *I have very little ~ with Simon now.*

2 person you know who can help you

ADJ. **good, useful, valuable | business, personal**

VERB + CONTACT **have** ◇ *He has a lot of good ~s in the music industry.* | **build up** (*esp. BrE*), **develop, make** ◇ *It takes time to develop ~s.* ◇ *I made a lot of useful business ~s at the conference.* | **provide | use** ◇ *He used his ~s to get his son a publishing job.*

3 when people/things touch/see each other

ADJ. **physical, sexual** ◇ *The disease is transmitted through physical ~.* | **eye** ◇ *He never makes eye ~ with me.*

VERB + CONTACT **come into** ◇ *Do not let the glue come into ~ with water.* | **avoid, prevent**

PREP. **in ~** ◇ *For a brief moment their lips were in ~.* | **on ~** ◇ *The light will go out on ~ with water.* | **~ between** ◇ *There should be no ~ between the separate samples.* | **~ with**

contact *verb*

ADV. **immediately | initially | directly | personally | by email, by phone, by telephone** ◇ *He can be ~ed by phone on the number given below.*

PHRASES **do not hesitate to ~ sb** ◇ *Please do not hesitate to ~ me if you have any questions.*

contact lens (*also* lens) *noun*

ADJ. **gas-permeable, hard, soft | daily-wear, disposable | extended-wear | tinted**

VERB + CONTACT LENS **have in, wear | put in | remove, take out | clean, disinfect | rinse, soak**

contagious *adj.*

VERBS **be, become, prove** ◇ *The new disease proved ~.*

container noun

1 box, bottle, etc.

ADJ. **airtight, closed, sealed, waterproof** (*esp. AmE*), **watertight** (*esp. BrE*) | **insulated** | **empty** | **full** | **shallow** | **disposable, reusable** | **childproof** | **suitable** ◇ *Tubes are the ideal ~ for paint as air is excluded.* | **special** | **shipping** | **storage** | **aluminium/aluminum, cardboard, glass, metal, plastic, steel, Tupperware™, wooden** | **food, milk, water**
VERB + CONTAINER **fill** ◇ *Fill the ~ with water.* | **store sth in**
CONTAINER + VERB **contain sth, hold sth** ◇ *a ~ holding five gallons*
CONTAINER + NOUN **garden, plant** (*both AmE*)
PREP. **in a/the ~** ◇ *Keep the seeds in an airtight ~.* | **~ for** ◇ *childproof ~s for dangerous substances* | **~ of** ◇ *a ~ of milk*

2 large metal box for transporting goods

ADJ. **empty** | **full** | **bulk, cargo, freight, shipping**
CONTAINER + VERB **contain sth, hold sth** ◇ *~s holding shipments of bananas*
CONTAINER + NOUN **lorry** (*BrE*), **ship** | **port**

contaminated adj.

VERBS **be** | **become**
ADV. **heavily, highly** ◇ *A lot of our drinking water is now heavily ~.* | **potentially**
PREP. **with** ◇ *The meat was believed to be ~ with salmonella.*

contamination noun

ADJ. **serious, widespread** | **possible, potential** | **environmental, food, soil, water** | **bacterial, chemical, radioactive**
... OF CONTAMINATION **level** ◇ *There is already a high level of environmental ~.*
VERB + CONTAMINATION **cause** | **avoid, prevent** | **minimize** (*esp. AmE*), **reduce**
PREP. **~ by** ◇ *Always keep food covered to prevent ~ by flies.* | **~ from** ◇ *There is a danger of serious ~ from radioactive waste.* | **~ with** ◇ *Wash everything thoroughly to avoid ~ with bacteria.*
PHRASES **a risk of ~** | **a source of ~**

contemplate verb

ADV. **seriously** ◇ *She was seriously contemplating moving to Mexico.* | **even** ◇ *How could you even ~ such an idea?*
VERB + CONTEMPLATE **be prepared to** (*BrE*), **be willing to** ◇ *Are you willing to ~ retraining?* | **cannot, could not** | **refuse to**
PHRASES **too awful to ~, too horrible to ~** ◇ *The thought of war was too awful to ~.*

contemplation noun

ADJ. **quiet, silent** | **deep, serious**
VERB + CONTEMPLATION **be deep in, be lost in** ◇ *She was lost in ~ of the scene in front of her.*
PREP. **in ~ (of)** ◇ *He spent many hours in deep ~.* | **~ of** ◇ *the ~ of beauty*

contemporary adj.

1 belonging to the same time as sb/sth else

VERBS **be**
ADV. **exactly** | **nearly** | **broadly** (*BrE*), **roughly** ◇ *a period broadly ~ with the Shang dynasty*
PREP. **with** ◇ *a composer ~ with Beethoven*

2 modern

VERBS **be**
ADV. **decidedly, thoroughly, very** ◇ *His work is very ~.*

contempt noun

1 lack of respect

ADJ. **complete, deep, great, open, outright, pure, utter, withering** | **cold, icy** | **healthy** (*esp. BrE*) ◇ *She'd developed what she considered a healthy ~ for authority.* | **barely disguised** (*esp. BrE*), **thinly disguised**
VERB + CONTEMPT **feel, have, hold sb/sth in** ◇ *He felt nothing but ~ for them.* ◇ *Politicians seem to be generally held in ~ by the police.* | **betray, demonstrate, display, express, show** ◇ *His remarks betray an utter ~ for the truth* (= are completely false). | **conceal, hide** | **regard sb/sth with, treat sb/sth with** | **deserve, earn** ◇ *I shall treat that suggestion with the ~ it deserves.*
PREP. **~ for** ◇ *He has a deep ~ for racists.* | **beneath ~** ◇ *His treatment of his children is beneath ~* (= so bad it is not even worth feeling contempt for). | **with ~** ◇ *She looked at him with barely disguised ~.*

2 (*also* **contempt of court**) refusal to obey a court

ADJ. **civil, criminal**
VERB + CONTEMPT **be held in** ◇ *She was held in ~ for refusing to testify.*
PREP. **in ~**

contemptuous adj.

VERBS **be, sound** ◇ *Her voice sounded almost ~.*
ADV. **utterly** | **almost** | **openly**
PREP. **of** ◇ *He was utterly ~ of her efforts.*

contender noun

ADJ. **serious, strong** | **leading, main, major, number-one, obvious** (*esp. BrE*), **top** ◇ *Senator Clinton was considered a leading ~ for the Democratic presidential nomination.* | **genuine, legitimate** (*esp. AmE*), **likely, possible, real, worthy** | **presidential** | **Democratic, Republican** | **championship, medal, title** ◇ *He's gone from being a serious title ~ to being totally written off.* | **play-off** (in American football)
PREP. **~ for** ◇ *a strong ~ for the gold medal*

content noun

1 **contents** things inside sth

VERB + CONTENTS **dump, empty, pour, spill** ◇ *She emptied the ~s of her bag on the floor*

2 subject matter

ADJ. **original** | **quality, rich** | **digital, multimedia, online, Web** | **editorial** | **news** | **course** | **sexual**
VERB + CONTENT **create** | **deliver, provide** | **access** ◇ *The way people are accessing their Web ~ is changing.*
CONTENT + NOUN **provider** ◇ *Record companies have had to transform themselves into digital ~ providers.*

3 amount of a substance that sth contains

ADJ. **high** ◇ *foods with a high fat ~* | **low** | **alcohol, calorie, carbon, cholesterol, fat, fibre/fiber, mineral, moisture, protein, sugar, sulphur/sulfur, vitamin, etc.**

content adj.

VERBS **appear, be, feel, seem**
ADV. **extremely, fairly, very, etc.** | **perfectly, quite, utterly** ◇ *I'm perfectly ~ just to lie in the sun.* | **reasonably, relatively** | **apparently** | **strangely** ◇ *She felt strangely ~.*
PREP. **with** ◇ *She seemed quite ~ with the idea.*

contention noun

1 opinion that sb expresses

ADJ. **main** ◇ *Her main ~ is that staff should get better training.*
VERB + CONTENTION **support** ◇ *There is no evidence to support her ~.* | **dispute, reject**

2 disagreement/competition between people

ADJ. **play-off, title** (*both AmE*) ◇ *The Comets were eliminated from play-off ~.*
PREP. **~ between** ◇ *There is no ~ between the two groups.*
PHRASES **an area of ~, a bone of ~, a point of ~, a source of ~** ◇ *Where to spend Christmas is always a bone of ~ in our family.* | **in ~ (for sth)** ◇ *There were three left in serious ~ for the prize.* | **out of ~ (for sth)** ◇ *The Jaguars are now out of ~.*

contentious adj.

VERBS be, prove | become | remain
ADV. extremely, fairly, very, etc. | highly ◇ *Abortion is a highly ~ issue.* | increasingly | politically

contentment noun

ADJ. deep, quiet ◇ *He gazed out to sea, with a feeling of deep ~.* ◇ *She fell asleep in quiet ~.*
VERB + CONTENTMENT find ◇ *They finally found ~ in living a simple life.* | feel
PREP. with ~ ◇ *She sighed with ~.*
PHRASES a feeling of ~

contest noun

ADJ. close, equal (*BrE*), even, tight | closely fought (*esp. BrE*), hard-fought | one-sided, unequal (*BrE*) ◇ *The ~ was too one-sided to be exciting.* | open ◇ *This ~ is wide open: any of half a dozen teams could win it.* | fair ◇ *The other bidders for the contract complained that it had not been a fair ~.* | exciting, good, great, real, thrilling | bitter | head-to-head ◇ *The contestants are eliminated one by one until the last two compete in a head-to-head ~.* | global, international, local, national, regional | election, electoral, gubernatorial (*AmE*), leadership (*esp. BrE*), political, presidential, primary | beauty, popularity, song, talent | athletic (*esp. AmE*), sporting (*esp. BrE*), sports (*esp. AmE*)
VERB + CONTEST have, hold, run ◇ *We have three major beauty ~s a year.* ◇ *Talent ~s are held in the club.* | sponsor (*AmE*) | compete in, enter, take part in ◇ *A third candidate has entered the ~ for the Republican nomination.* | lose, win
CONTEST + VERB take place
PREP. during a/the ~ ◇ *During the election ~ newspapers are not allowed to publish public opinion polls.* | in a/the ~ ◇ *Both sides are predicting victory in this close ~.* | out of a/the ~ ◇ *Jackson has injured his knee and is now out of the ~.* | ~ against ◇ *He won his opening ~ against Costa of Argentina.* | ~ between ◇ *the ~ between these two great boxers* | ~ for ◇ *the ~ for the leadership of the party* | ~ over ◇ *In the animal kingdom intruders usually lose ~s over territories.* | ~ with ◇ *The New Zealanders are looking forward to future ~s with South Africa.*
PHRASES a ~ of skills (*esp. AmE*), a ~ of strength | be no ~ (= used when one side in a contest is much stronger than the other and is sure to win) | the winner of a ~

contest verb

1 in a competition
ADV. bitterly, fiercely, hotly, keenly (*esp. BrE*) ◇ *The election was bitterly ~ed.* | closely, tightly | successfully
2 oppose
ADV. fiercely, hotly, strongly, vigorously ◇ *His views on evolution are strongly ~ed by other scientists.* | successfully ◇ *Defence lawyers successfully ~ed the case.*

context noun

ADJ. broad, full, general, larger, overall, wider ◇ *You have to see the problem in a wider ~.* | narrow | immediate ◇ *A work which transcends its immediate historical ~ and speaks to later generations.* | correct, natural, proper, real, right | appropriate, realistic, relevant ◇ *to present examples of language in use in an appropriate ~* | certain, given, particular, specific ◇ *These actions only have meaning within certain specific ~s.* | original | changed, changing, different, new, novel | meaningful ◇ *Children need meaningful ~s for their work in science.* | neutral | contemporary, modern | current, present | everyday, normal | domestic, global, international, local, national, regional | urban | human ◇ *It is natural to find conflict in the work environment, in the family, or any other human ~.* | conversational | experimental, practical, theoretical | classroom, educational, school | clinical | business, commercial, economic, work | cultural, environmental,

family, institutional, social | geographical, historical, legal, literary, political, religious | fictional | Christian, Islamic, etc. | African, Asian, etc.
VERB + CONTEXT give (sb), offer (sb), provide (sb with) ◇ *Institutions provide a ~ in which individuals can take on different roles.* | place sth in, put sth into, set sth in ◇ *This speech needs to be set in the ~ of Britain in the 1960s.* | create, establish ◇ *How can teachers create the right ~ for kids?* | quote sth out of, take sth out of ◇ *Her reply was quoted out of ~ and seemed to mean something quite different from what she had intended.*
PREP. in (a/the) ~ ◇ *Similar problems have arisen in other ~s.* ◇ *His decision can only be understood in ~.* | within a/the ~ ◇ *You have to look at these remarks within the ~ of the recent scandals.* | ~ for ◇ *a neutral ~ for sharing and debating ideas*
PHRASES a range of ~s, a variety of ~s

continent noun

ADJ. African, Australian, North American, etc. | entire, whole
VERB + CONTINENT cross ◇ *He crossed a whole ~ to find his family.* | cover, span ◇ *The police investigation spanned three ~s.*
CONTINENT + VERB drift, move ◇ *The evidence that the ~s have drifted is overwhelming.*
PREP. across a/the ~ ◇ *He journeyed across ~s in his quest for adventure.* | on the ~ ◇ *Wolves are still found on the ~ of Europe.*

contingent noun

ADJ. large, strong, substantial | small | military, police | international, UN | Brazilian, Canadian, etc.
VERB + CONTINGENT lead ◇ *NATO agreed to send a peacekeeping ~ of 30 000 troops.* | send
PREP. ~ from ◇ *a strong ~ from Kyoto Art School* | ~ of ◇ *a large ~ of American troops*

continuation noun

ADJ. direct | logical, natural
VERB + CONTINUATION see ◇ *The years 2007–08 saw the ~ of the university's planned expansion.* | ensure | be seen as, represent ◇ *His research could be seen as a natural ~ of the work done by Professor Lang.*

continuity noun

ADJ. greater | remarkable | unbroken ◇ *After centuries of unbroken ~, the landscape was being changed out of all recognition.* | cultural, historical, narrative
VERB + CONTINUITY ensure, establish, give sb/sth, maintain, provide (sb/sth with) ◇ *More liaison between the old manager and the new one should ensure greater ~.* | emphasize, stress ◇ *She is anxious to stress the ~ with the past in this new work.* | need | lack | break ◇ *The author deliberately breaks the narrative ~ in order to confound the reader's expectations.*
PREP. ~ between ◇ *There is often a lack of ~ between one government and the next.* | ~ in ◇ *historical ~ in the feminist movement* | ~ of ◇ *To ensure ~ of care, it is better for a single doctor to treat the patient.*
PHRASES a lack of ~, a need for ~ ◇ *the need for ~ of employment* | a sense of ~ ◇ *We aim to give children a sense of ~.*

contraception noun

ADJ. effective, reliable | artificial | emergency | oral
VERB + CONTRACEPTION practise/practice, use ◇ *A lot of couples now use ~.* ◇ *They never used any ~.* | provide
PHRASES a form of ~, a method of ~ ◇ *a very reliable method of ~*

contraceptive noun

ADJ. effective | oral | emergency | prescription (*AmE*)
VERB + CONTRACEPTIVE take, use

contract *noun*

1 written agreement

ADJ. **long-term, permanent** | **guaranteed** (*esp. AmE*) | **casual** (*BrE*), **fixed-term** (*BrE*), **short-term** | **three-year, two-year,** etc. | **formal, written** | **verbal** | **standard** | **legal, valid** | **void** ◇ *The ~ was declared void.* | **enforceable, unenforceable** | **binding, non-binding** (*AmE*) | **current, existing, new, original** | **big, huge, important, large, major** | **fat, lucrative** ◇ *My advertising firm just won a lucrative ~ with a cigarette company.* | **exclusive** | **business, commercial** | **employment, maintenance, research, service** | **catering** (*BrE*), **construction, production** | **defence/defense, military** | **federal, government** | **record, recording** | **marriage**
VERB + CONTRACT **have** ◇ *Many workers do not have written ~s.* | **bid for, bid on** (*AmE*), **tender for** ◇ *Eighteen companies are bidding for the ~.* | **award (sb), give sb, offer sb, place** | **get, land, receive, secure, win** | **lose** ◇ *The firm lost the ~ to a large London company.* | **negotiate** ◇ *She managed to negotiate a permanent ~ with the company.* | **draft, draw up, prepare, write** | **conclude, enter into, make, sign** ◇ *He entered into a ~ with his former employer.* | **extend, renew** | **carry out** (*BrE*), **execute, fulfil/fulfill** ◇ *the company fulfilling the construction ~* | **honour/honor** | **cancel, end, repudiate** (*BrE, law*), **rescind** (*law, esp. BrE*), **terminate** ◇ *Either party can terminate the ~ at any time.* | **be subject to** (*esp. BrE*) ◇ *The offer has been accepted, subject to ~ (= the agreement is not legally binding before contracts are signed).* | **be in breach of, breach, break, violate** ◇ *If you go on strike you will be in breach of ~.* | **enforce** (*law*) | **exchange** (*law*) ◇ *The successful bidder must exchange ~s immediately and pay a deposit.*
CONTRACT + VERB **expire** ◇ *The ~ expires at the end of next year.* | **be worth sth** ◇ *a series of major ~s worth millions*
CONTRACT + NOUN **work, worker** (= one on a fixed-term contract) | **manufacturer** | **dispute, negotiation** | **award** | **extension** | **law**
PREP. **in a/the ~** ◇ *They put a clause in the ~ stipulating that the work should be finished by next month.* | **on a ~** ◇ *He's on a three-year fixed-term ~.* | **under ~ (to)** ◇ *At that stage of her career she was still under ~ to one of the big Hollywood studios.* | **under a/the ~** ◇ *Under her ~ of employment, Mrs Lee could not be required to work at a different site.* | **~ between** ◇ *the ~ between the employer and the employee* | **~ for** ◇ *They won a ~ for the delivery of five planes.* | **~ with** ◇ *Do you have a ~ with your employer?*
PHRASES **(a) breach of ~** ◇ *The company is being sued for breach of ~.* | **a ~ of employment, a ~ of sale** ◇ *You should make sure that you have a formal ~ of employment.* | **the terms of a ~** ◇ *By using cheaper materials, the company has broken the terms of its ~.* | **under the terms of a ~** ◇ *Under the terms of the ~ the job should have been finished yesterday.*

2 agreement to kill sb

VERB + CONTRACT **take out** | **have out** ◇ *He has a ~ out on you.*
CONTRACT + NOUN **killer, killing**
PREP. **~ on** ◇ *She took out a ~ on her ex-husband.*

contractor *noun*

ADJ. **independent, private** | **external** (*esp. BrE*), **outside** | **government** | **prime** ◇ *The prime ~ can take on several subcontractors.* | **approved** ◇ *a list of approved ~s* | **haulage** (*BrE*) | **building, concrete** (*AmE*), **demolition, electrical, engineering** (*esp. BrE*), **masonry** (*AmE*), **roofing** | **civilian, defence/defense, military**
VERB + CONTRACTOR **employ, hire, select, use** ◇ *We'll need to employ a building ~ to do the work.*

contradict *verb*

ADV. **blatantly** (*esp. AmE*), **clearly, completely, directly, flatly, totally** (*esp. AmE*) ◇ *John's account of the event directly ~s Stephen's.*
VERB + CONTRADICT **appear to, seem to**

contradiction *noun*

ADJ. **complete, direct, flat** | **blatant** (*esp. AmE*), **glaring, obvious** | **basic, fundamental** ◇ *There's a basic ~ in the*

whole idea of paying for justice.* | **inherent** | **logical** | **apparent, seeming** | **inner, internal**
PREP. **in ~ to, in ~ with** ◇ *That's in direct ~ to what he said yesterday.* | **~ between** ◇ *There is an apparent ~ between the needs of workers and those of employers.* | **~ of** ◇ *That's a ~ of what you just said.*
PHRASES **a ~ in terms** ◇ *The idea is almost a ~ in terms.*

contradictory *adj.*

VERBS **appear, be, seem, sound**
ADV. **completely** ◇ *The evidence is completely ~.* | **quite, rather, somewhat** | **apparently, seemingly** ◇ *two apparently ~ opinions* | **inherently** | **internally** ◇ *The argument is internally ~ (= contradicts itself).* | **mutually** ◇ *The evidence demonstrates how easily people can hold mutually ~ beliefs.*
PREP. **to** ◇ *He did something ~ to his orders.*

contrary *adj.*

VERBS **be, run, seem** ◇ *These results run ~ to our expectations.* ◇ *It seems ~ to common sense.*
ADV. **completely, directly, entirely** (*esp. BrE*), **quite, totally** ◇ *The new claim is directly ~ to what was originally stated.* | **clearly**
PREP. **to** ◇ *Contrary to what the public was told, weapons were still being exported.*
PHRASES **~ to expectations** ◇ *Contrary to expectations, we didn't have any hold-ups.* | **~ to popular belief** ◇ *Contrary to popular belief, the economy is doing well.*

contrast *noun*

ADJ. **clear, marked, sharp, stark, strong** ◇ *There is a stark ~ between the lives of the rich and those of the poor.* | **complete, direct** | **dramatic, startling, striking, stunning, vivid** ◇ *Her hair was black, a stunning ~ to her pale complexion.* | **interesting, refreshing, welcome** ◇ *The two cities make an interesting ~.*
VERB + CONTRAST **make, offer, present, provide, show** ◇ *The fresh fruit provides a ~ to the rich chocolate pudding.* | **draw** ◇ *He draws a sharp ~ between himself and his opponents.* | **emphasize, highlight** ◇ *The writer emphasizes the ~ between conventional and alternative medicine.* | **heighten**
PREP. **by ~** ◇ *When you look at their new system, ours seems very old-fashioned by ~.* | **in ~, in ~ to, in ~ with** ◇ *The company lost $13 million this year, in ~ with a profit of $15 million last year.* ◇ *In ~, the south suffered very little hurricane damage.* | **~ between** ◇ *The ~ between the sisters was very strong.* | **~ in** ◇ *The ~ in their appearance was striking.* | **~ to** ◇ *This busy social life was a complete ~ to his old quiet life.* | **~ with** ◇ *The flowers provide a ~ with the dark background.*
PHRASES **stand in … contrast to sb/sth** ◇ *Their attitudes to marriage stand in stark ~ to those of their parents.*

contrast *verb*

1 compare things in order to show differences

ADV. **favourably/favorably, unfavourably/unfavorably** ◇ *He ~ed her brashness unfavourably/unfavorably with his mother's gentleness.*
PREP. **with**
PHRASES **compare and ~** ◇ *Compare and ~ the two main characters in the play.*

2 be clearly different

ADV. **dramatically, greatly, markedly, sharply, starkly, strikingly, strongly, vividly** | **beautifully, nicely, perfectly** ◇ *His cream shirt ~ed beautifully with his tan skin.* | **oddly** | **favourably/favorably** ◇ *The open approach ~s favourably/favorably with the exclusivity of some universities.*
PREP. **with** ◇ *This statement ~s starkly with his previous statements.*

contravene verb

ADV. **blatantly, clearly, directly** ◇ *actions that blatantly ~ the rules of civilized warfare*

contravention noun

ADJ. **clear, direct**
PREP. **in ~ of** ◇ *He was in direct ~ of the law.* | **~ of** ◇ *This was a clear ~ of the rules.*

contribute verb

1 give

ADV. **enormously, generously, greatly, handsomely, heavily, substantially** ◇ *His research has ~d enormously to our understanding of this disease.* ◇ *Many people ~d generously to the appeal.* | **positively** ◇ *people who want to ~ positively to their communities* | **equally** ◇ *a situation where husband and wife ~ equally to the family budget* | **fully** | **financially**
VERB + CONTRIBUTE **be asked to, be encouraged to**
PREP. **to** ◇ *I would like to ~ to the church restoration fund.* | **towards/toward** ◇ *The company ~d $50 000 towards/toward training costs.*
PHRASES **have little, a lot, etc. to ~ (to sth)** ◇ *He had very little to ~ to the conversation.*

2 help cause sth

ADV. **greatly, importantly, largely, materially, mightily** (*AmE*), **significantly, substantially** ◇ *Parental involvement ~s significantly to children's learning.* | **effectively** | **disproportionately** ◇ *countries that ~ disproportionately to global warming* | **actively, directly** ◇ *Unemployment ~s directly to homelessness.* | **indirectly** | **potentially** ◇ *These images could potentially ~ to the development of eating disorders.* | **undoubtedly** | **unwittingly**
PREP. **to** ◇ *Several factors might ~ to the development of the disease.*

3 write for a newspaper, etc.

ADV. **regularly** ◇ *a talented photographer who ~d regularly to 'The Face'*
PREP. **to** ◇ *Students are encouraged to ~ articles to the university magazine.*

contribution noun

1 sth that helps cause/increase sth

ADJ. **important, meaningful, significant** | **big, enormous, great, huge, major, strong, substantial** | **minor, modest, small** | **invaluable, positive, useful, valuable** ◇ *We like to think that we are making a positive ~ to society.* | **distinguished, notable, outstanding, seminal, unique** ◇ *He was recognized for his unique ~ to the arts.* | **individual, personal** ◇ *Each of these writers has made an individual ~ to the discussion.* | **relative** ◇ *Researchers have argued over the relative ~s of nature and nurture to the human personality.*
VERB + CONTRIBUTION **make** ◇ *He made a major ~ to peace in the region.* | **acknowledge, appreciate, recognize, value** ◇ *The author acknowledges the ~s of scientist Charles Green.*
PREP. **~ to** ◇ *a valuable ~ to science*

2 money given to help pay for sth

ADJ. **generous, large** | **small** | **annual, monthly** | **charitable** (*esp. AmE*) | **voluntary** ◇ *We rely entirely on voluntary ~s.* | **campaign** (*esp. AmE*) | **insurance, pension** ◇ *employers' pension and health insurance ~s* | **tax-deductible**
VERB + CONTRIBUTION **make, offer, pay** | **ask for, solicit**
PREP. **~ to, ~ towards/toward** ◇ *Residents made a net ~ to public finances of $2.6 billion.* ◇ *We were asked to make a ~ towards the cost of the meal.* (*BrE*)

contributor noun

ADJ. **important, key, significant, valuable** | **big, large** | **leading, main, major, principal** | **frequent, regular** ◇ *The core of regular ~s is essential to the magazine.* | **occasional** | **long-time** (*AmE*) ◇ *She was a long-time ~ to Time Magazine.* | **generous, wealthy** | **net** ◇ *net ~s to the economy* |

campaign (*AmE*) ◇ *Politicians are often suspected of trying to appease campaign ~s from the oil industry.* | **corporate** (*esp. AmE*)
PREP. **~ to** ◇ *Carbon dioxide is the largest ~ to the greenhouse effect.*

control noun

1 power over sb/sth

ADJ. **absolute, complete, full, total** | **effective, proper** (*esp. BrE*) | **close, strict, tight** ◇ *Weeds should be kept under strict ~.* | **direct** | **centralized, government, political, social, state** | **civilian, military** ◇ *He defended the tradition of civilian ~ over the military.* | **parental**
VERB + CONTROL **have** | **achieve, assert, establish, gain, get** | **assume, grab, seize, take, win** ◇ *A military junta took ~ of the country.* | **wrest (from sb)** ◇ *attempts to wrest ~ of the town from government forces* | **keep, maintain, retain** ◇ *She struggled to keep ~ of her voice.* | **lose** | **cede, relinquish, surrender** ◇ *He lost ~ of the car when he swerved to avoid a bicycle.* | **hand over, transfer** ◇ *He wants to hand over ~ of social security to the private sector.* | **get out of, go out of** ◇ *The car went out of ~ on the icy road.* | **reassert, re-establish, regain, retake** ◇ *Enemy forces have now regained ~ of the area.* | **give sb/sth** ◇ *The idea is to give local authorities full ~ of their own budgets.* | **exercise, exert** ◇ *Editors do not exercise ~ over large sections of their newspapers.* | **centralize** ◇ *government plans to centralize ~ of schools* | **bring sth under, get sth under** ◇ *They soon got the situation under ~.*
CONTROL + NOUN **freak** ◇ *He's a real ~ freak.*
PREP. **beyond your ~, outside your ~** ◇ *Parking is outside my ~.* | **in ~ (of)** ◇ *The elected government is back in ~.* | **out of ~** ◇ *I had this feeling that things were out of ~.* | **under (sb's) ~** ◇ *Everything is under ~* ◇ *The department was under the ~ of Bryce Thompson.* | **~ over** ◇ *They have little ~ over that side of the business.*
PHRASES **circumstances beyond sb's ~** ◇ *The race has been called off due to circumstances beyond our ~.*

2 limiting/managing sth

ADJ. **quality** | **inventory** (*esp. AmE*), **stock** (*esp. BrE*) | **budgetary** (*esp. BrE*), **cost, rent** | **crowd** ◇ *The police are experts in crowd ~.* | **air traffic, traffic** | **birth** | **arms, gun** | **crime** | **damage** | **erosion, flood, pest, pollution, weed** | **bladder, impulse, weight** ◇ *Many teenagers have poor impulse ~.*
VERB + CONTROL **improve** | **ensure**
CONTROL + NOUN **measure, mechanism** ◇ *New crime ~ measures have failed.* | **centre/center, room, tower** ◇ *the air traffic ~ tower*

3 (usually controls) method of limiting/managing sth

ADJ. **strict, stringent, tight, tough** (*esp. BrE*) | **lax** | **border, export, price** ◇ *calls for tougher export ~s*
VERB + CONTROL **implement, impose, introduce** ◇ *The government has imposed strict ~s on new building.* | **tighten** ◇ *The country has tightened its border ~s.* | **relax** ◇ *plans to relax price ~s* | **lift, remove**
PREP. **~ on** ◇ *They have introduced ~s on public spending.*

4 for operating a machine

ADJ. **remote** | **volume** | **cruise**
VERB + CONTROL **take** ◇ *Once we were in the air, I was allowed to take the ~s.*
CONTROL + NOUN **panel** | **device, stick** (*AmE*), **unit** ◇ *a programmable ~ unit* | **circuit, valve** ◇ *the water pressure ~ valve*
PREP. **at the ~s** ◇ *Chief Air Officer Sedley was at the ~s of the Boeing 707.*

control verb

1 restrict/manage

ADV. **carefully, precisely, rigidly, strictly, tightly** ◇ *Conditions in the greenhouse are carefully controlled.* ◇ *Expenditure within the company is tightly controlled.* | **adequately, effectively, properly** | **poorly** | **centrally, directly**

ADV. **automatically, electronically, manually** ◇ *The shutters can be electronically controlled.* | **remotely** | **easily** ◇ *You can easily ~ the speed of the fan.*

controller noun

ADJ. **air traffic, flight** (*AmE*), **ground** (*esp. AmE*) | **programme** (*BrE*) ◇ *He is the new programme ~ for BBC2.* | **financial** (*esp. BrE*), **production** (*BrE*) | **game** (*AmE*), **remote, wireless** (*both esp. AmE*)

PREP. **~ for** ◇ *the company's ~ for global marketing and sales*
→ Note at JOB

controversial adj.

VERBS **be, prove** | **become** | **remain**
ADV. **extremely, fairly, very, etc.** | **highly, intensely** ◇ *a highly ~ subject* | **potentially** ◇ *He addresses such potentially ~ issues as the role of women in society.* | **politically**

controversy noun

ADJ. **considerable, great, major** | **bitter, fierce** (*esp. BrE*), **heated, intense, raging** | **growing** | **fresh, further, new, renewed** | **current, recent** | **continued, continuing, long-standing, ongoing** | **public** | **academic, critical, scholarly** (*esp. BrE*) | **ethical, legal, political, scientific** | **religious, theological**
VERB + CONTROVERSY **arouse, cause, create, engender, excite** (*esp. BrE*), **generate, give rise to** ◇ *What they are doing is bound to stir up ~.* | **fuel, ignite, provoke, spark, spark off, stir, stir up, trigger** | **be dogged by** (*esp. BrE*), **be marked by, be surrounded by** ◇ *This year's championships have been marked by ~.* | **avoid, shy away from** ◇ *The president seemed anxious to avoid ~ about these appointments.* | **end, quell, resolve, settle** ◇ *Public funding could resolve the ~ surrounding campaign finance.* | **run into** (*BrE*) ◇ *The network ran into ~ over claims of faked documentary footage.* | **be no stranger to** ◇ *Ms Benjamin, who is no stranger to ~ herself, said the scandal could have serious repercussions.* | **court** ◇ *The singer deliberately courts ~ with his lyrics.*
CONTROVERSY + VERB **arise, break out, erupt** ◇ *A fierce ~ has broken out over the issue.* | **rage** ◇ *Controversy is raging over the route of the new road.* | **exist** ◇ *Controversy exists as to how safe these drugs are.* | **continue, persist** ◇ *Today, the ~ continues over whether Shakespeare wrote all his plays.* | **centre/center on sth** ◇ *The ~ centred/centered on the issue of compensation for the victims.* | **surround sth** ◇ *Much ~ surrounds the new exam.*
PREP. **amid** ~ ◇ *He has resigned amid continuing ~ over his expense claims.* | **~ about, ~ concerning, ~ over** ◇ *There has been a lot of ~ over the use of these drugs.* | **~ among** ◇ *~ among historians* | **~ between** ◇ *~ between the two leaders* | **~ surrounding** ◇ *the bitter ~ surrounding the introduction of the new regulations* | **~ with** ◇ *her long-running ~ with fellow academics*
PHRASES **a matter of ~, a source of ~, a subject of ~** | **a firestorm of ~** (*AmE*), **a storm of ~** ◇ *The book raised a storm of ~.*

convenience noun

1 being useful/easy/suitable

ADJ. **great** | **added, additional, extra** ◇ *All our chalets include a microwave for extra ~.* | **administrative, political** ◇ *The system is based on administrative ~ rather than public benefit.*
VERB + CONVENIENCE **offer, provide**
CONVENIENCE + NOUN **food** ◇ *The children like ~ food such as pizzas.* | **store** (*esp. AmE*)
PREP. **at your ~** ◇ *Can you telephone me at your ~ (= when it is convenient for you) to arrange a further meeting?* | **for (your)** ◇ *I keep my cookbooks in the kitchen for ~.* ◇ *An order form is enclosed for your ~.*
PHRASES **a marriage of ~** (= a marriage for practical reasons, not love) (*business*), **at your earliest ~** (= as soon as possible) (*business*), **comfort and ~** ◇ *In this resort you can enjoy all the comfort and ~ of modern tourism.* | **for the**

sake of ~ ◇ *We leave the keys near the front door for the sake of ~.*

2 sth useful

ADJ. **great** ◇ *It's a great ~ living near the station.* | **modern** ◇ *They wouldn't like to live without modern ~s such as microwaves.*

convenient adj.

VERBS **be, prove, seem** | **make sth** | **find sth** ◇ *I find the new system much more ~.*
ADV. **extremely, fairly, very, etc.** | **highly** | **mutually** (*esp. BrE*) ◇ *We arranged a mutually ~ time to meet.* | **politically**
PREP. **for** ◇ *Would this be ~ for you?* ◇ *The house is very ~ for the shops.* (*BrE*) | **to** (*AmE*) ◇ *The house is ~ to downtown.*

convention noun

1 way sth is done

ADJ. **accepted, established, long-standing, old, traditional, well-established** ◇ *It's an established ~ that the part is played by a woman.* | **normal, standard, usual** | **polite** (*esp. BrE*) ◇ *Her work refuses any concession to polite ~s of 'good taste'.* | **arbitrary** | **rigid, strict** | **cultural, legal, social** ◇ *the rigid social ~s of Victorian Britain* | **artistic, cinematic, comic, dramatic, journalistic, literary, narrative, operatic, poetic** ◇ *The novel refuses to conform to the narrative ~s of 19th-century realism.* | **orthographic, rhetorical, spelling** ...OF CONVENTIONS **set**
VERB + CONVENTION **adhere to, conform to, follow, keep to, observe** ◇ *They followed the Greek ~ of pinning gifts of money to the bride's dress.* | **break, break with, buck, challenge, defy, flout, subvert** ◇ *She knew that she had broken an important social ~.* ◇ *He challenged the ~s of painting.* ◇ *No young politician can afford to flout ~ in this way.*
CONVENTION + VERB **demand sth, dictate sth** ◇ *Convention dictated that dangerous physical action is the part of heroes, not heroines.*
PREP. **according to ~, by ~** ◇ *By ~, planets are named after Roman gods.*
PHRASES **a break with ~** ◇ *In a surprising break with ~, she wore a red wedding dress.* | **a matter of ~**

2 conference

ADJ. **annual** | **international, national, state** (*AmE*) | **Democratic, Republican, etc.** | **constitutional, nominating** (*AmE*), **party, political, presidential** ◇ *A constitutional ~ was elected to try to agree on a new form of government.*
VERB + CONVENTION **have, hold, host** | **arrange, organize, plan** | **attend, go to** | **address** ◇ *He addressed the annual Republican ~.*
CONVENTION + VERB **take place**
CONVENTION + NOUN **centre/center, hall** (*AmE*) | **floor** (*AmE*) ◇ *journalists reporting from the ~ floor* | **attendee** (*AmE*), **chair, chairman, delegate, organizer, speaker** | **city, hotel** ◇ *Dallas is one of the top ~ cities in the United States.*
PREP. **at a/the ~** ◇ *She was at the Democratic ~.*
PHRASES **delegates to a ~**

3 international agreement

ADJ. **global, international** | **European, UN, etc.** | **climate, human rights, etc.** | **draft**
VERB + CONVENTION **adopt, ratify, sign** ◇ *Over 60 countries have yet to ratify the climate ~.* | **adhere to, comply with** ◇ *Most countries have adhered to the ~.* | **breach, violate** ◇ *This practice breaches the arms ~.*
CONVENTION + VERB **apply, govern sth** ◇ *a ~ governing the conditions under which mining is permitted* | **establish sth** ◇ *The ~ established procedures for the transport of toxic waste.* | **ban sth**
PREP. **under a/the ~** ◇ *This is forbidden under the Convention on Human Rights.* | **~ against** ◇ *the UN ~ against torture* | **~ between** ◇ *the 1869 ~ between Turkey and Persia* | **~ for** ◇ *the Berne Convention for the Conservation of European*

Wildlife | **~ on** ◊ *the 1951 United Nations Convention on refugees*
PHRASES **a breach of a ~**

conventional *adj.*

VERBS **be, seem**
ADV. **extremely, fairly, very, etc.** | **highly** | **entirely, utterly** (*esp. AmE*) | **largely** | **seemingly**

conversation *noun*

ADJ. **brief, short** | **lengthy, long** ◊ *We engaged in a long ~.* | **endless, pointless** ◊ *We had to listen to endless ~s about high prices and food shortages.* | **everyday, general, normal, ordinary** | **casual, idle, informal** ◊ *It's not a subject that often crops up in casual ~.* | **intimate, personal, private** | **face-to-face, one-on-one** (*AmE*) ◊ *The two of you need to have a face-to-face ~.* | **one-sided, two-way** ◊ *Think of prayer as a two-way ~.* | **phone, telephone** | **overheard, recorded, taped** | **civilized, polite** ◊ *We sat making polite ~ and feeling rather uncomfortable.* | **friendly, pleasant** | **animated, lively** | **heated** | **fascinating, good, intelligent, interesting, stimulating** ◊ *He said that television had been the death of good ~.* | **candid, honest** | **deep, in-depth, meaningful, proper, real, serious** ◊ *There was no time for a proper ~.* | **simple** ◊ *When you are struggling with an unfamiliar language, the simplest ~s can be misinterpreted.* | **strange** | **chance** ◊ *A chance ~ led to a brilliant new career for the young student.* | **awkward, desultory, halting, stilted** ◊ *We carried on a rather awkward ~.* | **hushed, murmured, quiet, whispered** | **ongoing** (*esp. AmE*) ◊ *There is an ongoing ~ in society about how we raise our children.* | **imaginary** | **after-dinner, dinner** | **adult** ◊ *Young children become quickly bored by adult ~.* | **water-cooler** (*AmE*) ◊ *The book became an instant best-seller and topic of water-cooler ~ (= a popular subject for discussion, for example between people who work together).*
... OF CONVERSATION **snatch** ◊ *I overheard snatches of a ~ between two doctors.*
VERB + CONVERSATION **carry on, have, hold, make** ◊ *You can't hold a private ~ there.* ◊ *I tried to make ~ with the three people around the table.* | **begin, initiate, open, spark, start, strike up** ◊ *He was waiting for her to open the ~.* | **draw sb into, engage sb in** ◊ *When I tried to engage him in ~, she always interrupted.* | **fall into, get into** ◊ *I got into ~ with one of the directors.* (*BrE*) ◊ *I got into a ~ with Chris about UFOs.* (*AmE*) | **be deep in, be engaged in** ◊ *They were deep in ~ and didn't notice the time.* | **continue, keep up** ◊ *Cara kept up a one-sided ~.* | **control, dominate** | **bring around, bring round** (*esp. BrE*), **steer, turn** ◊ *I managed to bring the ~ around to why they were leaving.* ◊ *He tried to steer the ~ away from the topic of money.* ◊ *She turned the ~ to her work.* | **enter, join, join in** | **break off** | **conclude, end, finish** | **avoid** ◊ *She avoided ~ with the other passengers.* | **encourage** ◊ *I was courteous but didn't encourage ~.* | **hear, listen to, overhear** | **record, tape** ◊ *Police taped the ~.* | **break into, interrupt** | **resume** | **recall, remember** ◊ *I recall a ~ in which he told me he would never leave Paris.*
CONVERSATION + VERB **occur, take place** ◊ *When did this ~ take place?* | **continue, proceed** ◊ *The ~ proceeded in French.* | **flow** ◊ *They all relaxed and ~ flowed freely.* | **come around to sth, come round to sth** (*esp. BrE*), **drift, move on (to sth), switch, turn to sth, veer back to sth, veer off sth** ◊ *The ~ drifted away from babies.* ◊ *The ~ moved on to other things.* ◊ *The ~ turned to football.* | **revolve around** | **cease, end, stop** ◊ *All ~ ceased and everyone turned around.* ◊ *The ~ ended when the vacuum cleaner started up.* | **die, die away, die down** | **dry up** (*BrE*), **run dry** (*esp. AmE*) ◊ *All too soon the stilted ~ ran dry.*
PREP. **during ~** ◊ *In the Western world it is polite to maintain eye contact during ~.* | **in ~ with** ◊ *In tonight's show we hear Chris Toole in ~ with the artist Mary Withers.* | **~ about** ◊ *We had a long ~ about old cars.* | **~ between** ◊ *a ~ between Jane and her parents* | **~ on** ◊ *a ~ on the topic of activities for children* | **~ with** ◊ *I had an interesting ~ with Dick Wortley.*
PHRASES **an attempt at ~** ◊ *She ignored all my attempts at ~.* | **be in … conversation (with sb)** ◊ *Don was in close ~ with the girl on his right.* | **a buzz of ~, a hum of ~** ◊ *She could hear him over the buzz of ~ and laughter.* | **during the course of (the) ~** ◊ *During the course of ~, it emerged that Sheila had lived in Nigeria.* | **keep the ~ going** ◊ *Our hostess did her best to keep the ~ going.* | **a lull in the ~** | **a topic of ~** ◊ *The main topic of ~ was the war.*

conversion *noun*

1 change to a new form/system/use
ADJ. **barn** (*BrE*), **loft** | **currency** ◊ *There are no charges for currency ~.* | **data, file** | **energy** ◊ *Cheap solar energy ~ has been the dream of scientists since the 1970s.*
VERB + CONVERSION **carry out, undertake**
CONVERSION + NOUN **kit** ◊ *a ~ kit that lets your vehicle run on non-polluting fuel* | **chart, table** ◊ *Consult the ~ table to figure out the weight in kilos.*
PREP. **~ from, ~ into** ◊ *A local building company will carry out the ~ of the farm buildings into business units.* | **~ to** ◊ *~ from analogue/analog to digital data*

2 religious
ADJ. **Christian, religious, spiritual** | **deathbed** | **forced** ◊ *the forced ~ of Jews during the Inquisition* | **overnight, sudden** (*both figurative*) ◊ *her overnight ~ to market economics*
VERB + CONVERSION **experience, undergo** ◊ *In the 90s he underwent a religious ~.*
CONVERSION + NOUN **experience**
PREP. **~ from, ~ to** ◊ *her ~ from Islam to Christianity*

3 in rugby
VERB + CONVERSION **kick** | **add** ◊ *The try came in the third minute and Jon Bland added the ~.*

convert *noun*

ADJ. **new, recent** | **enthusiastic** | **reluctant** | **Catholic, Jewish, etc.**
VERB + CONVERT **become** | **attract, gain, make, win** ◊ *an attempt to gain ~s to her cause* | **seek**
PREP. **~ from** ◊ *Pope Clement was a ~ from paganism.* | **~ to** ◊ *a recent ~ to Catholicism*

convey *verb*

ADV. **clearly, perfectly, powerfully, vividly** ◊ *The novel vividly ~s the experience of growing up during the war.* | **accurately, adequately** | **effectively, fully, successfully**
VERB + CONVEY **can, could** ◊ *Gestures can ~ meaning as well as words.* | **try to** | **manage to** | **fail to**
PREP. **to** ◊ *He managed to ~ his enthusiasm to her.*

convict *noun*

ADJ. **escaped**
CONVICT + NOUN **labour/labor** (*esp. AmE*)

convict *verb*

ADV. **wrongfully, wrongly** | **rightly**
PREP. **for** ◊ *She was ~ed for her part in the crime.* | **of** ◊ *He was ~ed of the murder of two teenagers.* | **on** ◊ *He was ~ed on a drug charge.* ◊ *They were ~ed on all 13 counts.*

conviction *noun*

1 for a crime
ADJ. **earlier, previous** (*esp. BrE*), **prior** (*AmE*) | **spent** (*BrE*) ◊ *You are not obliged to acknowledge spent ~s.* | **successful** (*esp. BrE*) | **unsafe** (*BrE*), **wrongful** ◊ *Keeping this information from the jury could result in a wrongful ~.* | **criminal** | **drug, murder, etc.**
VERB + CONVICTION **have** ◊ *He has three criminal ~s.* | **lead to** ◊ *A reward is offered for information leading to the ~ of the attacker.* | **obtain, secure, win** ◊ *They need strong evidence to secure a ~.* | **escape** ◊ *He believes that too many defendants are escaping ~ by claiming that they are insane.* | **appeal** (*AmE*), **appeal against** (*BrE*) ◊ *He appealed against*

his ~ for murder. ◇ Her lawyer said that she plans to appeal her ~. | **overturn, quash** (BrE), **reverse** (AmE) | **affirm** (AmE), **uphold**
CONVICTION + VERB **be based on** ◇ a ~ based on very slim evidence
CONVICTION + NOUN **rate** ◇ The ~ rate for rape is low.
PREP. **on ~** ◇ His sentence on ~ would be life imprisonment. | **~ against** ◇ The court overturned the ~ against her. | **~ for** ◇ a ~ for murder
PHRASES **the rate of ~**

2 belief/appearance of belief
ADJ. **absolute, complete, total, unshakable, utter** | **deep, deeply held, firm, fundamental, great, passionate, real, strong** ◇ It is my firm ~ that nothing will change until we address the root causes of the problem. ◇ There was no great ~ in his voice. | **growing** | **personal** | **inner** | **ideological, moral, political, religious, theological** | **Catholic, Christian, etc.**
VERB + CONVICTION **have, hold** ◇ She had this absolute ~ that what she liked others would like. | **share** ◇ They share a deep ~ that their views on world matters are still vitally important. | **express** | **carry** ◇ Her explanation failed to carry ~ (= failed to sound convincing) in the face of the facts. | **reflect** ◇ The American Constitution reflects certain religious ~s. | **shake** ◇ Nothing could shake her ~ that she could not be beaten. | **reinforce, strengthen** ◇ These experiences reinforced my ~ that music helps learning. | **lack** ◇ Her arguments lacked ~.
CONVICTION + NOUN **politics** (BrE) ◇ the demise of consensus and the rise of ~ politics
PREP. **with ~, without ~** ◇ 'Not true!' she said with ~. | **~ about** ◇ He had a strong personal ~ about the power of the printed word.
PHRASES **have the courage of your ~s** (= to be brave enough to do what you feel to be right)

convinced adj.
VERBS **appear, be, feel, seem, sound** | **become** ◇ She became ~ that something was wrong. | **remain**
ADV. **absolutely, completely, fully, quite, thoroughly, totally, utterly** | **deeply, firmly** | **increasingly** | **almost** | **by no means** (esp. BrE) | **not altogether, not entirely, not fully, not quite** | **fairly** | **half** ◇ She was still only half ~. | **apparently**
PREP. **of** ◇ He was ~ of her innocence.

convincing adj.
VERBS **be, look, seem, sound** | **find sth** ◇ I found his argument pretty ~. | **make sth** ◇ Details make your story more ~.
ADV. **extremely, fairly, very, etc.** | **completely, thoroughly, totally, utterly** | **hardly, not altogether, not entirely, not wholly** | **far from, not remotely** ◇ He was far from ~ as a leader. | **enough, sufficiently** ◇ She produced a ~ enough performance as the wronged wife.

convoy noun
ADJ. **armed, army, military, naval, troop** | **truck** (AmE), **vehicle** | **fuel, logistics, supply** (all esp. AmE) | **aid, food, humanitarian, relief** ◇ the proposal to send 500 armed soldiers to escort food ~s
VERB + CONVOY **lead** | **escort, protect** | **ambush, attack, hit, target**
CONVOY + VERB **carry sth** | **arrive** | **move, pass, travel** ◇ A roadside bomb exploded as the ~ passed.
PREP. **in ~** ◇ The trucks were driving in ~. ◇ The ships sailed in ~. | **~ of** ◇ a large ~ of trucks carrying medical supplies | **~ to** ◇ the next aid ~ to the war-torn region

convulsion noun
ADJ. **violent** | **sudden**
VERB + CONVULSION **go into, have, suffer, suffer from** ◇ The patient lost consciousness and went into ~s. | **cause**

cook noun
ADJ. **excellent, good, gourmet** (esp. AmE), **great, wonderful** ◇ He's a very good ~. | **amateur** (esp. BrE), **home** ◇ easy recipes for home ~s | **professional** ◇ She wants to become a professional ~. | **fry** (AmE), **short-order** ◇ He found work as a short-order ~ in a local diner.
→ Note at JOB

cook verb
ADV. **fully, thoroughly, well** ◇ Make sure you ~ the meat well. | **perfectly** ◇ The vegetables were ~ed perfectly. | **evenly, gently, slowly** ◇ Turn the fish over so that it ~s evenly. | **quickly**
PHRASES **be ~ed through** ◇ Ensure that the meat is ~ed through. | **freshly ~ed** ◇ the smell of freshly ~ed bacon

cooker (BrE) noun → See also RANGE, STOVE
ADJ. **electric, gas** | **pressure**
COOKER + NOUN **hob, hood**

cookery noun (esp. BrE)
ADJ. **basic** ◇ Before he leaves home, he needs to learn some basic ~. | **vegetarian** | **cordon bleu** | **microwave** | **Chinese, Eastern, French, etc.**
VERB + COOKERY **learn**
COOKERY + NOUN **demonstration** | **class, course, lesson, school** | **book** (BrE), **column, magazine, programme/ program** | **expert, writer**

cookie noun (esp. AmE)
ADJ. **chocolate, chocolate chip, gingerbread** (AmE), **oatmeal, sugar** (AmE) | **home-made** | **fortune** (= containing a message that makes a prediction about your future)
... OF COOKIES **plate** | **bag, batch, box**
VERB + COOKIE **bake, make** | **sell** ◇ Girl Scouts went around the neighborhood selling ~s.
COOKIE + NOUN **crumb, dough** | **jar** | **cutter, sheet** | **recipe**
PHRASES **~s and milk, milk and ~s**
→ Special page at FOOD

cooking noun
ADJ. **good, gourmet** (esp. AmE), **great** ◇ We enjoyed some of her gourmet ~. | **home** ◇ I miss my mother's good home ~. | **traditional** ◇ traditional southern ~ | **regional** | **Chinese, Italian, etc.** ◇ French regional ~ | **Mediterranean, southern, Tex-Mex** | **vegetarian** | **slow**
VERB + COOKING **do** ◇ Who does most of the ~ in your house?
COOKING + NOUN **oil** | **show** (= on TV) (AmE)
PREP. **during ~** ◇ Stir the mixture to prevent the beans sticking to the bottom during ~. | **in ~** ◇ I use yogurt a lot in ~.

cool verb
1 (also **cool down**) become colder
ADV. **a little, slightly, etc.** | **completely** | **quickly, rapidly** ◇ Dry soil ~s rapidly when air temperatures fall. | **gradually, slowly** ◇ Her tea was slowly ~ing in front of her.
VERB + COOL **allow sth to, let sth** ◇ Allow the cake to ~ thoroughly before removing it from the tin.
2 (also **cool down, cool off**) become calmer
ADV. **considerably** | **slightly, somewhat** ◇ He's ~ed down somewhat since this morning,

cool adj.
1 fairly cold
VERBS **be, feel, look** ◇ The forest looked ~ and shady. | **become, get** ◇ It will probably get ~ later, so bring a coat. | **keep sth** ◇ Try to keep the drinks ~.
ADV. **very** | **a little, slightly, etc.** | **fairly, quite, rather** | **relatively** ◇ It was a relatively ~ night. | **completely** ◇ Wait until the cake is completely ~ before cutting. | **deliciously, pleasantly, refreshingly, wonderfully** ◇ The cave was refreshingly ~. | **surprisingly, unseasonably, unusually** ◇ The weather that June was unseasonably ~.

2 calm

VERBS **appear, be, look** | **keep, remain, stay** ◇ *She managed to stay ~ during the meeting.* | **act, play it** (*informal*) ◇ *He forced himself to count to ten and act ~.* ◇ *For once I felt uncertain about my real feelings. I decided to play it ~.*
ADV. **very** | **pretty**
PREP. **about** ◇ *She's completely ~ about what happened.* | **with** (*AmE, informal*) ◇ *I knew I needed surgery, and I was ~ with it.*
PHRASES **~, calm and collected** ◇ *He did his best to appear ~, calm and collected.*

3 not friendly/enthusiastic

VERBS **act** (*AmE*), **appear, be, sound** | **remain**
ADV. **distinctly** (*esp. BrE*), **very** | **rather, somewhat**
PREP. **about** ◇ *She was distinctly ~ about their plans.* | **towards/toward** ◇ *He was ~ towards me.* (*BrE*) ◇ *I'm sorry I acted ~ toward you.* (*AmE*)

4 used to show approval

VERB + COOL **be** ◇ *It's so ~ you came back!* | **look, sound** ◇ *You look really ~ in those jeans.*
ADV. **extremely, fairly, very, etc.** | **so** | **totally** | **amazingly**

cooperate (*BrE also* co-operate) *verb*

ADV. **fully** ◇ *He has said he will ~ fully with the police enquiries.* | **closely**
VERB + COOPERATE **will, would** | **agree to, be prepared to** (*esp. BrE*), **be willing to** | **refuse to**
PREP. **in** ◇ *The two companies are cooperating in the development of a new engine.* | **on** ◇ *We are cooperating on a research project.* | **with** ◇ *The company has agreed to ~ with the employment survey.*

cooperation (*BrE also* co-operation) *noun*

ADJ. **close** | **complete, full** | **better, greater, increased** | **active** | **effective** | **global, international, local, regional** | **mutual** ◇ *a society founded on mutual ~ and shared prosperity* | **cultural, economic, military, political, social, technical**
VERB + COOPERATION **need, require** | **ask for, call for, demand, seek** ◇ *She called for closer ~ on drugs control.* ◇ *They are seeking the ~ of senior medical staff.* | **enlist, gain, get, secure** ◇ *We are hoping to enlist the ~ of women's groups.* | **give (sb), offer (sb)** | **encourage, enhance, facilitate, foster, improve, increase, promote** ◇ *an attempt to promote ~ between universities and industry* | **ensure**
PREP. **in ~ with** ◇ *The film was made in ~ with the Board.* | **with sb's ~, without sb's ~** ◇ *With the ~ of the public, the police may be able to catch this man.* | **~ among** ◇ *increased technical ~ among large companies* | **~ between** ◇ *political ~ between the two groups* | **~ from** ◇ *You will need some ~ from your family.* | **~ in** ◇ *We asked for their ~ in the collection of data.* | **~ on** ◇ *They offered their ~ on the project.* | **~ with** ◇ *We should like to thank you for your ~ with us.*
PHRASES **have the ~ of sb** ◇ *We have the full ~ of all the departments involved.* | **a lack of ~** | **a need for ~** ◇ *There is a need for greater economic ~.*

coordinate (*BrE also* co-ordinate) *verb*

ADV. **carefully, closely, highly, tightly, well** ◇ *a carefully ~d policy* | **loosely**
PREP. **with** ◇ *We try to ~ our activities with those of other groups.*

coordination (*BrE also* co-ordination) *noun*

1 working together

ADJ. **better, greater** | **close, effective** | **poor** | **inter-agency, internal, international** | **economic, policy** | **colour/color** ◇ *advice on colour/color ~*
VERB + COORDINATION **need, require** | **facilitate, improve** | **ensure, provide** ◇ *We must make a real effort to ensure greater ~ between the different groups.*

PREP. **in ~ with** ◇ *a leaflet produced by the government in ~ with professional bodies* | **~ among, ~ between** ◇ *to facilitate better ~ between departments* | **~ in** ◇ *a lack of ~ in government policy* | **~ of** ◇ *~ of conservation activities* | **~ with**
PHRASES **a lack of ~** | **a need for ~** ◇ *a need for ~ with the training department*

2 ability to control your movements

ADJ. **excellent, good** | **poor** | **motor, physical** | **hand-eye** ◇ *You need good hand-eye ~ to play racket sports.*
VERB + COORDINATION **have** | **lack** | **develop, improve** | **affect**
COORDINATION + NOUN **problem**
PHRASES **a lack of ~**

cope *verb*

ADV. **admirably, effectively, well** ◇ *She ~s very well under pressure.* | **adequately** (*esp. BrE*) ◇ *Will the prison system ~ adequately with the increasing numbers of prisoners?* | **easily**
VERB + COPE **be able, can** | **be unable to, cannot** ◇ *She is unable to ~ with her increasing workload.* ◇ *He felt that he couldn't ~ any longer.* | **have to** ◇ *She had to ~ without any help.* | **learn (how) to** | **struggle to, try to** ◇ *She was struggling to ~ with the demands of a new baby.* | **be difficult to**
PREP. **with** ◇ *Some people find unemployment very difficult to ~ with.*
PHRASES **sb's ability to ~, a way of coping** ◇ *a way of coping with bereavement*

copper *noun*

ADJ. **pure** | **molten** | **beaten** | **burnished** ◇ *Her hair shone like burnished ~.*
VERB + COPPER **mine** | **produce** | **contain**
COPPER + NOUN **mine** | **miner** | **mining, production, smelting** | **deposit, ore** | **alloy** | **sulphate/sulfate** | **coin** | **pipe, tube** | **cable, wire** | **plate, pot** | **colour/color**
PREP. **in ~** (= using copper) ◇ *She works mainly in ~.*
PHRASES **an alloy of ~ and sth, an alloy of ~ with sth** ◇ *Brass is an alloy of ~ and zinc.*

copy *noun*

1 document/work of art

ADJ. **accurate, faithful, good** | **cheap, crude, poor** ◇ *It was not the original painting, but a crude ~.* | **carbon, exact, facsimile** (*esp. BrE*), **identical, perfect, true** ◇ *The twins were carbon copies of each other.* ◇ *It must be certified as a true ~ of the original document.* | **draft, working** | **clean, fair** | **master, original, top** ◇ *Take a photocopy of the master ~.* | **additional, duplicate, extra, further, second, spare** | **multiple** ◇ *The copier had been set for multiple copies.* | **modern** | **certified** | **photographic, photostat, Xerox™** (*esp. AmE*) | **backup** ◇ *Remember to make backup copies of all your disks.* | **read-only** | **hard, paper, printed** ◇ *You will need to supply a hard-copy version of all files.* | **digital, electronic**
VERB + COPY **create, make, print, run off, take** ◇ *I ran off a couple of copies of the letter.* | **attach, enclose** ◇ *I attach a ~ of the report.* ◇ *Please find enclosed a ~ of the draft document.* | **email, forward, send** | **circulate, distribute, supply** ◇ *Copies of the article were circulated to members of the committee.* | **get, obtain, receive** | **keep** ◇ *Remember to keep copies of all your correspondence.*
COPY + NOUN **machine** (*AmE*) | **room** (*AmE*) | **center, shop** (*both AmE*) | **paper**
PREP. **~ of** ◇ *I don't keep copies of my own letters.*

2 book, newspaper, etc.

ADJ. **additional, extra, further, second, spare** | **only, single** | **back** (*esp. BrE*), **old** ◇ *I have a few back copies of the newspaper.* | **advance** ◇ *Advance copies of the book were sent out to reviewers.* | **evaluation, review** | **complimentary, free** ◇ *Free copies of the leaflet are available.* | **bootleg, illegal, pirate, pirated, unauthorized** ◇ *pirated copies of the latest movie releases* | **manuscript, printed, proof** | **hardback, paperback** | **digital, electronic** | **CD, DVD** |

bound, leather-bound, presentation ◇ *The candidate must submit two bound copies of his or her thesis.* | **battered, dog-eared, old, tattered, well-thumbed, worn** ◇ *my battered ~ of Shakespeare's plays* | **second-hand, used** | **perfect, pristine** | **own, personal** | **autographed, signed**
VERB + COPY **print, produce** | **circulate, distribute, sell** | **buy, order, request** | **download** | **have, own** | **borrow** | **autograph, sign** ◇ *Author Bob Woodhouse will be signing copies of his new book.*
COPY + VERB **circulate** ◇ *Even with the new legislation pirate copies will circulate.* | **be available**
PREP. **~ of** ◇ *my own ~ of 'Beowulf'*

3 written material

ADJ. **good, great** | **ad** (*informal*), **advertising, marketing, promotional** | **editorial** | **knocking** (*BrE, informal*) ◇ *Knocking ~ (= writing that just says how bad sb/sth is) is simply lazy journalism.*
VERB + COPY **edit, prepare, produce, write** ◇ *those who prepare the reporters' ~ for the paper* | **make** ◇ *This will make great ~ for the advertisement.*
COPY + NOUN **editor, writer** (usually ***copywriter***) | **deadline** ◇ *The ~ deadline for the next issue is May 1.* | **desk** (= part of a newsroom where articles are given a final edit) (*AmE*)

copy *verb*

1 make a copy

ADV. **illegally** ◇ *illegally copied software*
PREP. **from, onto** ◇ *Data can be copied from the computer onto disk.*
PHRASES **~ and paste** ◇ *Use the clipboard to ~ and paste information from websites.* | **be widely copied** ◇ *The product has been widely copied by other manufacturers.*

2 write sth down exactly

ADV. **carefully, laboriously, meticulously** | **exactly, faithfully, word for word** | **down, out** | *I copied down several phone numbers from the list.* ◇ *They laboriously copied out manuscripts.*
PREP. **from, into, onto** ◇ *She copied all the addresses from the website into her address book.* ◇ *He copied all the details from the brochure onto a piece of paper.*

3 do the same as sb else

ADV. **blindly, slavishly** ◇ *She slavishly copies the older girl's style.*
PREP. **from** ◇ *He copied that mannerism from his brother.* | **off** ◇ *She was caught ~ing off another student.*

copyright *noun*

VERB + COPYRIGHT **have, hold, own, retain** ◇ *The publisher has the ~ on all his books.* | **breach, infringe** ◇ *By publishing the book, they were guilty of infringing ~.* | **be protected by** ◇ *Databases are generally protected by ~.*
COPYRIGHT + VERB **protect sth** ◇ *Copyright protects your work from being commercially exploited by someone else without your consent.* | **expire, lapse**
COPYRIGHT + NOUN **infringement, violation** | **law, protection** | **holder, owner**
PREP. **in ~, out of ~** (both esp. *BrE*) ◇ *The songs remain in ~.* ◇ *His work is now out of ~.* | **~ on** ◇ *The family still holds the ~ on his works.*
PHRASES **breach of ~, infringement of ~** ◇ *They sued her for breach of ~.* | **ownership of ~** ◇ *Ownership of ~ can be transferred.*

cord *noun*

1 string/rope

ADJ. **thick, thin** | **long, short** | **strong** | **elastic, leather, nylon, silk** | **bungee** (*AmE*) | **gold, silver** | **dressing-gown** (*BrE*) | **nerve, spinal, umbilical, vocal**
... OF CORD **length, piece** ◇ *You need a piece of thick ~ about two feet long.*
VERB + CORD **pull** | **knot, tie (sth with)** ◇ *He knotted the ~ of his dressing gown.* (*BrE*) | **undo, untie**

2 (*esp. AmE*) **electrical cable** → See also FLEX

ADJ. **long** | **electric, electrical** | **power** | **extension** | **phone, telephone**
... OF CORD **length**
VERB + CORD **plug in** | **pull out, unplug, yank, yank out** | **cut** ◇ *Cutters are useful for cutting electric ~ to the right length.*
CORD + VERB **connect sth** ◇ *a ~ connecting two PCs*

cordon *noun*

ADJ. **tight** | **police, security**
VERB + CORDON **form, throw** (*BrE*) ◇ *The security forces have formed a ~ around the apartment.* ◇ *Police officers threw a ~ around his car to protect him.* | **break through** ◇ *The crowd managed to break through the police ~.*
CORDON + VERB **prevent sth** ◇ *A police ~ prevented the marchers from entering the main square.*
PREP. **~ around, ~ round** (*esp. BrE*) ◇ *There is a tight security ~ around the area.*

core *noun*

ADJ. **hollow** ◇ *Each fibre/fiber has a hollow ~.* | **dense, solid, strong** | **copper, iron, etc.** | **reactor** ◇ *nuclear reactor ~s* | **central, essential, inner, innermost, very** ◇ *This is seen as the central ~ of the government's policy.* ◇ *A new spirit welled up from the very ~ of the nation.* | **outer** | **common** ◇ *a common ~ of shared understanding* | **hard** ◇ *A hard ~ of supporters gathered to see the star arrive.* ◇ *hard-core party members* | **emotional** ◇ *the emotional ~ of her music*
VERB + CORE **form, make up** ◇ *These ideas formed the ~ of his philosophy.* | **surround** | **get to** ◇ *We want to get to the ~ of the problem.*
PREP. **at sth's ~** ◇ *At the ~ of our convictions is belief in individual liberty.* | **to the ~** ◇ *She was shaken to the ~ by the news.* ◇ *He's a politician to the ~ (= in all his attitudes, beliefs and actions).*
PHRASES **the earth's ~** ◇ *heat from the earth's ~*

corn *noun*

1 (*BrE*) **cereal crop (wheat, etc.)**

ADJ. **ripe** ◇ *The ~ is still green.* | **young**
... OF CORN **ear, sheaf** | **bag, sack** | **field**
VERB + CORN **grow** | **sow** | **cut, harvest** | **thresh** | **grind**
CORN + VERB **grow**
CORN + NOUN **field** | **harvest** | **mill**

2 (*AmE*) **plant producing yellow grains**

ADJ. **field, Indian, sweet** (*BrE, AmE*) (usually ***sweetcorn*** in *BrE*) | **biotech, genetically modified** (abbreviated to ***GM***), **transgenic** | **non-GM, organic** | **seed** | **canned** | **fresh, frozen** | **white, yellow** | **creamed, popped, roasted** | **caramel, kettle**
... OF CORN **ear** | **bushel** | **field**
VERB + CORN **plant** | **grow, produce, raise** | **harvest** | **grind** | **eat**
CORN + VERB **grow**
CORN + NOUN **field** | **crop, harvest, yield** | **cob** (usually ***corncob***) (*BrE, AmE*), **husk, kernel, plant, seed, stalk** | **flour** (usually ***cornflour***), **meal** (usually ***cornmeal***) (*BrE, AmE*), **oil** (*BrE, AmE*), **starch** (usually ***cornstarch***), **syrup** (*BrE, AmE*) | **bread, chips, dog, pone, tortilla** | **grower**
PHRASES **~ on the cob** (= corn cooked with all the grains still attached) (*BrE, AmE*)

3 area of hard skin on the foot

VERB + CORN **have, suffer from** | **treat**

corner *noun*

1 where two lines/edges meet

ADJ. **bottom, top** | **left, right** | **left-hand, right-hand** | **back, front** | **lower, upper** | **southern, south-western, etc.** | **outer, outside** | **inner, inside** | **opposite** | **sharp** | **rounded** ◇ *Smooth rounded ~s make cleaning easier.* | **awkward** ◇ *Make sure the staircase is well lit, with no*

awkward ~s. | **extreme, far, very** ◊ He took a seat in the far ~ of the cafe.
CORNER + NOUN **booth** (esp. AmE), **cupboard, office, seat, table** ◊ The waiter led us to a ~ table. | **cabinet** | **pocket** (= on a pool table, etc.)
PREP. **in a/the ~** ◊ Put your address in the top right-hand ~ of the page.
PHRASES **the four ~s of sth** ◊ the four ~s of his bed | **right in the ~** ◊ They chose a table right in the ~ of the restaurant.

2 of roads

ADJ. **street** ◊ There were a lot of young men hanging around on street ~s. | **sharp, tight** ◊ It's a rather sharp ~ and she took it a little too fast. | **blind** ◊ I hate coming out of that lane because it's a blind ~.
VERB + CORNER **round, take, turn** ◊ As they turned the ~ all the bags slid to one side. | **approach**
CORNER + NOUN **bar** (AmE), **shop** (BrE), **store** (AmE) ◊ the local ~ shop/store
PREP. **around a/the ~, round a/the ~** (esp. BrE) ◊ A white van came around the ~. | **at a/the ~** ◊ at the ~ of West Street and Park Street | Turn right at the first ~. | **on a/the ~** ◊ the bank on the ~ of Mount Street

3 place/region

ADJ. **empty, quiet, secluded** ◊ He found a quiet ~ and got on with his work. | **little, small, tiny** ◊ Welcome to our little ~ of Philadelphia. | **distant, far, far-flung, remote** ◊ a remote ~ of Afghanistan | **picturesque** | **dark, darkened, gloomy, shadowed, shadowy** ◊ She sat in a dark ~ of the room. | **shady, sheltered** ◊ a cool shady ~ of the park | **forgotten, hidden, obscure, odd, private, secret** ◊ The box had been tucked away in an odd ~ of the attic.
PREP. **in a/the ~** ◊ She tucked herself away in a ~ and read all day.
PHRASES **a ~ of your mind** (figurative) ◊ He pushed the thought back into the darkest ~ of his mind.

4 difficult situation

ADJ. **tight** ◊ He's used to talking his way out of tight ~s.
VERB + CORNER **back sb into, drive sb into, force sb into** | **get sb/yourself into, have sb in** ◊ They had her in a ~ and there was nothing she could do about it.

5 in football (soccer), hockey, etc.

ADJ. **penalty** | **short**
VERB + CORNER **award (sb)** ◊ The referee awarded a ~. | **take** ◊ Moore took the ~. | **force, win** ◊ He managed to force a ~. | **concede** ◊ James blocked the shot but conceded a ~. | **miss** | **clear**
CORNER + NOUN **kick**

coroner noun

ADJ. **deputy** | **county**
CORONER + VERB **issue sth** ◊ The ~ issued a burial certificate. | **order sth** ◊ The ~ ordered an investigation into the man's death. | **determine sth** | **record a verdict of sth** (BrE) ◊ The ~ recorded a verdict of accidental death.
PHRASES **a coroner's court, a coroner's inquest** | **a coroner's report, a coroner's verdict** | **the coroner's office**

corporal noun → Note at RANK

corporation noun

ADJ. **big, giant, huge, large, major** | **powerful** | **foreign** | **global, international, multinational, transnational** | **private, public** | **broadcasting, business, finance, industrial, media, oil** | **for-profit, non-profit** | **parent** (AmE)
CORPORATION + NOUN **tax** (BrE)
→ Note at ORGANIZATION (for verbs)

corps noun

ADJ. **elite** ◊ the elite ~ of the army | **multinational** ◊ a multinational ~ under US command | **cadet, officer,**

volunteer | **air, army, diplomatic, marine, medical** | **media, press** ◊ the UN press ~
CORPS + NOUN **commander**
PREP. **in a/the ~** ◊ He's a gunner in the US marine ~.

corpse noun

ADJ. **human** | **naked** | **bloody, charred, headless, mangled, mutilated** | **decaying, rotting** | **bloated** | **dead, lifeless** | **mummified** | **living, walking** ◊ For over a year he lay in his hospital bed, a living ~.
VERB + CORPSE **lay out** ◊ The ~ had been laid out on a marble slab. | **discover, find** | **embalm** | **dismember, mutilate**
CORPSE + VERB **be sprawled, lie** ◊ They saw the ~ sprawled on the steps.
PHRASES **be littered with ~s, be strewn with ~s** ◊ The ground was littered with the ~s of enemy soldiers.

correct adj.

VERBS **be, prove, seem** ◊ His first idea proved ~.
ADV. **absolutely, completely, entirely, perfectly, quite** ◊ What you say is perfectly ~, but it gives the wrong impression. | **not entirely, not strictly** ◊ He is not entirely ~ in his assumptions. | **basically, broadly, essentially, fundamentally, largely, more or less, substantially** ◊ His estimate has turned out to be more or less ~. | **clearly, undoubtedly** | **ideologically, politically** (sometimes disapproving) ◊ He was an interesting speaker, if not always politically ~ in his views. | **legally, technically** | **morally** | **anatomically, factually, grammatically** ◊ The sentence is grammatically ~, but not very idiomatic.
PREP. **in** ◊ The diagram is ~ in every detail. ◊ I think I am ~ in saying that this project is the first of its kind.

correction noun

ADJ. **minor, small** | **necessary** ◊ Make any necessary ~s before the text is printed. | **error, spelling** | **vision** | **market** ◊ These stock-market ~s were expected. | **course** (esp. AmE) ◊ in-flight course ~ ◊ Now is the time to make any course ~s. (figurative)
VERB + CORRECTION **make** | **need, require** ◊ There are some programming errors that need ~.
CORRECTION + NOUN **fluid**
PREP. **for** ◊ The work was returned to the student for ~. | **~ to** ◊ I have to make one or two ~s to the text before it's finished.

correctness noun

ADJ. **grammatical, ideological, political** (sometimes disapproving)
VERB + CORRECTNESS **doubt, question** ◊ She doubted the ~ of the information. | **be convinced of** ◊ She was convinced of the ~ of the decision. | **confirm**

correlate verb

ADV. **closely, highly, significantly, strongly, well** | **moderately, poorly, weakly** | **directly** | **positively** | **inversely, negatively**
VERB + CORRELATE **be found to, be shown to** ◊ High morale among staff was found to ~ positively with productivity.
PREP. **to** ◊ Property values are negatively ~d to the tax rate. | **with** ◊ The average speed of the vehicles ~s closely with the severity of the accident caused.

correlation noun

ADJ. **close, good, high, remarkable, significant, strong** | **clear, obvious** | **direct, simple** ◊ There is a direct ~ between exposure to sun and skin cancer. | **broad, general, overall** | **low, poor, weak** | **positive** | **inverse, negative** | **statistical**
VERB + CORRELATION **have** ◊ The second group of measurements had a high ~ with the first. | **discover, establish, find, observe, see** | **demonstrate, indicate, reveal, show** ◊ The study showed a significant ~ between smoking and heart disease. | **examine**
CORRELATION + VERB **exist** ◊ A strong ~ exists between obesity in parents and in their children.
PREP. **~ between** ◊ the ~ between speed and risk of accident | **~ with** ◊ the ~ of height with weight

correspond *verb*

1 be the same; match

ADV. **closely, well** | **directly, exactly, precisely** | **approximately, broadly, generally, roughly**
PREP. **to** ◇ *The word ~s roughly in meaning to our 'homesickness'.* | **with** ◇ *The movement of the dot on the screen ~s exactly with the movement of the control lever.*

2 write letters

ADV. **regularly**
PREP. **with** ◇ *She ~ed regularly with her former teacher.*

correspondence *noun*

1 letters exchanged

ADJ. **confidential, personal, private** | **business, diplomatic, official** | **regular** | **email, written** | **extensive, voluminous**
... OF CORRESPONDENCE **item** (*BrE*) ◇ *Numerous items of ~ have been received on this subject.* | **pile** (*esp. BrE*) ◇ *He was leafing through piles of ~.*
VERB + CORRESPONDENCE **enter into, exchange, have** ◇ *It would be foolish for a doctor to enter into ~ with a patient.* ◇ *I have had ~ with the company director on this matter.* | **carry on, keep up, maintain** ◇ *We kept up a ~ for many months.* | **address, send** ◇ *Please send ~ to 'Money Monthly'.* | **receive** | **read** | **answer, deal with, handle** ◇ *The secretary deals with all the ~.* | **catch up on** ◇ *I would spend the time reading or catching up on my ~.* | **intercept** ◇ *The department intercepted the ~ of foreign diplomats.*
CORRESPONDENCE + NOUN **course, school** (*AmE*) ◇ *I did a ~ course in economics.* | **column** (*esp. BrE*) ◇ *the ~ columns of the 'London Review of Books'*
PREP. **by ~, through ~** ◇ *All our business is conducted by ~.* | **in ~ with** ◇ *I have been in ~ with the manager of the store.* | **~ about, ~ concerning, ~ on, ~ regarding, ~ relating to** ◇ *files full of confidential ~ relating to the company's expansion plans* | **~ between** ◇ *I have seen the ~ between the company and the college.* | **~ from** ◇ *The editor welcomes ~ from readers on any subject.* | **~ with** ◇ *copies of her ~ with the composer*

2 connection

ADJ. **direct, exact, one-to-one** | **close**
PREP. **~ between** ◇ *a close ~ between theory and practice*

correspondent *noun* reporter

ADJ. **network** (*AmE*), **news, newspaper, television, TV** | **business, media, political, science, sports, war, etc.** | **congressional** (*AmE*), **parliamentary** (*BrE*) | **foreign, international, national** (*AmE*) | **chief, senior** | **special** ◇ *A report from our special ~ at the UN.* | **American, Moscow, 'New York Times', etc.**
CORRESPONDENT + VERB **cover sth** | **report (sth), write (sth)**
PREP. **~ for** ◇ *a ~ for a Canadian newspaper*

corridor *noun* → See also HALLWAY

ADJ. **endless, long** | **short** | **narrow, wide** | **central, main** | **brightly lit** | **badly lit, dark, darkened, dim, gloomy** | **dank, draughty/drafty** | **deserted, empty** | **carpeted, stone** | **hospital, hotel, school** | **access** | **labyrinthine** (*formal*) ◇ *the labyrinthine ~s of the building* | **land** ◇ *a now-submerged land ~ between northern African and southern Europe*
VERB + CORRIDOR **line** ◇ *Portraits line the ~s of the palace.* | **walk, wander** ◇ *It was interesting to walk the ~s of my old school.*
CORRIDOR + VERB **lead from sth, lead off from sth** ◇ *Narrow ~s lead off from the main hallway.* | **lead to sth** ◇ *a ~ that leads to the kitchen* | **run along sth, run down sth** ◇ *The ~ runs down the middle of the building.* | **connect sth, link sth** ◇ *The ~ links the old part of the hospital with the new.*
CORRIDOR + NOUN **wall**
PREP. **along a/the ~, down a/the ~** ◇ *The office is just down the ~ on the left.* | **in a/the ~** ◇ *I put my head down as I passed him in the ~.* | **at the end of a/the ~, to the end of a/the ~**

PHRASES **the ~s of power** (*figurative*) ◇ *She had considerable influence in the ~s of power.* | **a labyrinth of ~s, a maze of ~s** ◇ *She led us through a maze of hotel ~s to our room.*

corrosion *noun*

VERB + CORROSION **cause** | **prevent** | **suffer from** ◇ *a building whose structure is suffering from ~* | **resist**
CORROSION + NOUN **resistance**
PHRASES **signs of ~**

corrosive *adj.*

VERBS **be**
ADV. **highly, very** ◇ *Many highly ~ substances are used in the nuclear industry.*

corrupt *adj.*

VERBS **be** | **become**
ADV. **hopelessly, thoroughly, totally, very** ◇ *The whole regime is thoroughly ~.* | **inherently** | **notoriously** ◇ *one of the most notoriously ~ city councils* | **morally, politically**

corruption *noun*

ADJ. **endemic, massive, rampant, rife, widespread** ◇ *Corruption was rife before the election.* | **gross, serious** | **petty** | **alleged** | **financial, moral, political** | **high-level, official** | **corporate** (*esp. AmE*), **government, police, public** (*AmE*)
... OF CORRUPTION **case**
VERB + CORRUPTION **attack, combat, fight, tackle** ◇ *He strongly attacked ~ in the government.* ◇ *This police unit was established to fight ~.* | **eliminate, end, root out, stop** | **curb, stem** | **prevent** | **investigate** | **be involved in** (*esp. BrE*) | **expose, reveal**
CORRUPTION + NOUN **scandal** ◇ *She was brought down by a ~ scandal.* | **allegation, charge** ◇ *The ~ allegations proved false.* | **investigation, probe** | **case**
PREP. **~ among** ◇ *~ among high-ranking officials* | **~ in** ◇ *~ in government*
PHRASES **accusations of ~, allegations of ~, charges of ~** | **bribery and ~** | **a culture of ~**
→ Note at CRIME

cosmetic *noun* (usually **cosmetics**)

ADJ. **expensive** | **cheap** | **natural** | **hypo-allergenic**
... OF COSMETICS **line** ◇ *We're introducing a new line of ~s*
VERB + COSMETIC **use, wear** | **apply, put on**
COSMETIC + NOUN **company, industry**

cosmetic *adj.*

VERBS **be**
ADV. **merely, purely** ◇ *Opponents described the reforms as a purely ~ exercise.* | **largely, mostly**

cost *noun*

1 money needed to buy sth

ADJ. **considerable, high** ◇ *The high ~ of energy was a problem for consumers.* | **enormous, exorbitant, huge, prohibitive** ◇ *The ~ of repairs would be prohibitive.* | **low, minimal** | **escalating, increasing, rising, soaring, spiralling/spiraling** | **basic** | **full, overall, total** ◇ *You will have to bear the full ~ of the work.* | **added, additional, extra** ◇ *She was unwilling to pay the extra ~ to get a room to herself.* | **associated** | **hidden** | **average** ◇ *A total of 3.6 million tickets at an average ~ of $58 are available.* | **gross, net** | **budgeted, estimated, projected** | **likely, potential** | **real, true** | **annual, monthly, etc.** | **replacement** ◇ *What is the current replacement ~ of these assets?* | **marginal** (*business*) ◇ *Competition will drive the price down near to the marginal ~* (= the cost of the work and materials to produce the product). | **per-unit, unit** (= the cost of producing one item) (*business*) | **initial, upfront** | **capital, start-up** (*both*

business) ◊ *The capital ~ of these projects* (= what it costs to set them up) *is some $100 million.* | **direct, indirect**
VERB + COST **carry** (*AmE*), **have** ◊ *The entire project carries a ~ of $2 million.* | **bear, cover, meet, pay** ◊ *Contractors can now be required to carry the ~ of delays.* ◊ *Allow €100 per day to cover the ~ of meals.* ◊ *Delegates receive allowances to meet the ~ of travel.* | **drive up, increase, push up** ◊ *Inflation is pushing up the ~ of living.* | **bring down, cut, decrease, drive down, lower, reduce, slash** | **keep down** | **estimate, put** ◊ *I would put the ~ of a new employee at $80 000 a year.* | **calculate, work out** | **afford** | **spread** ◊ *You can spread the ~ of your loan repayment over 10 years.* | **reimburse** | **offset** | **share, subsidize**
COST + VERB **escalate, go up, increase, rise, soar** ◊ *The ~ of dental treatment is increasing.* | **fall, go down**
COST + NOUN **reduction, savings** ◊ *the pursuit of ~ reduction* | **increase** | **containment** (*AmE*), **control** | **overrun** ◊ *There were ~ overruns on each project.* | **estimate** | **advantage** | **structure** | **base** ◊ *It is essential that we operate with the lowest possible ~ base and most efficient facilities.* | **accounting**
PREP. **at a ~ of** ◊ *A new computer system has been installed at a ~ of £80 000.* | **~ to** ◊ *The ~ to the government will be quite high.*
PHRASES **an increase in ~, a reduction in ~** | **at great ~, at a great ~ to sth** ◊ *The victory was achieved at great ~ to the country's infrastrucure.* | **at minimal ~, at a minimal ~ to sth** ◊ *Now people can access the Internet at minimal ~.* | **at no extra ~** ◊ *The hotel offers tea and coffee at no extra ~.* | **the ~ of living** ◊ *The ~ of living has risen sharply in the last year.* | **~ per day, unit, child, etc.** ◊ *the ~ per day for an electrician*

2 costs money needed to run a business, home, etc.

ADJ. **considerable, enormous, great, high, huge** | **low** | **escalating, increasing, rising, soaring, spiralling/spiraling** ◊ *We have had to raise our prices because of rising ~s.* | **administration, administrative, borrowing, construction, development, fuel, labour/labor, maintenance, manufacturing, production, research** ◊ *research and development ~s* | **operating, running** | **shipping, transport** (*esp. BrE*), **transportation** (*esp. AmE*), **travel** | **health-care, medical** | **fixed, variable** (*business*) ◊ *Fixed ~s include rent.* | **out-of-pocket** | **overhead**
VERB + COSTS **incur** ◊ *The corporation will pay all ~s and expenses incurred.* | **pay** | **increase** | **bring down, cut, lower, reduce** ◊ *The company has to find ways of cutting ~s.* | **control, keep down, minimize** ◊ *The use of cheap materials helped to keep ~s down.* | **cover** ◊ *We're hoping that we'll at least cover ~s at the conference.* | **recoup, recover** | **defray**
COSTS + VERB **be associated, be involved** ◊ *the ~s associated with buying and selling property* | **escalate, go up, increase, rise, soar** ◊ *The company's ~s have risen over the last 5 years.*

3 effort/loss/damage to achieve sth

ADJ. **considerable, enormous, great, heavy, huge** ◊ *They advanced a few hundred yards, but at a heavy ~ in life.* | **dreadful, terrible** ◊ *the terrible ~ of the war in death and suffering* | **real, true** | **environmental, financial, human, personal, political, social** ◊ *the environmental ~ of nuclear power*
VERB + COST **outweigh** ◊ *Do the benefits outweigh the ~s?* | **suffer** (*esp. AmE*) ◊ *The country has suffered the enormous ~ of trade sanctions.* | **count** ◊ *The town is now counting the ~ of its failure to provide adequate flood protection.*
PREP. **at ~ (to), at a ~ (to)** ◊ *He worked non-stop for three months, at considerable ~ to his health.* ◊ *The raid was foiled, but at a ~: an injured officer who was lucky to survive.* | **at the ~ of** ◊ *She saved him from the fire but at the ~ of her own life.* | **~ in** ◊ *I felt a need to please people, whatever the ~ in time and energy.*
PHRASES **~s and benefits** ◊ *the ~s and benefits of this strategy* | **at all ~s, at any ~** ◊ *You must stop the press finding out at all ~s.* | **to your ~** ◊ *He's a ruthless businessman, as I know to my ~* (= I know from my own bad experience).

4 costs in a court case

ADJ. **court** (*AmE*), **legal** | **administrative**
VERB + COSTS **incur** ◊ *Both sides incurred ~s of over $50 000.* | **pay** ◊ *He was fined £200 and ordered to pay ~s.* | **be awarded** ◊ *If you win your case you will normally be awarded ~s.*

costly *adj.*

VERBS **be, become, prove**
ADV. **extremely, fairly, very, etc.** | **enormously** | **especially, particularly** | **increasingly** | **potentially** | **prohibitively** | **relatively** | **politically** ◊ *The candidate's mistake proved embarrassing and politically ~.*
PREP. **for** ◊ *The six-month delay will be ~ for the company.* | **in** ◊ *This process is ~ in computer time.* | **in terms of** ◊ *These teaching methods are too ~ in terms of staff resources.* | **to** ◊ *These measures could be ~ to employers.*

costume *noun*

ADJ. **full** ◊ *For the dress rehearsal, the cast will be in full ~.* | **colourful/colorful, elaborate, lavish** | **outlandish, outrageous, ridiculous** | **folk** (*esp. AmE*), **national, traditional** | **dance** (*esp. AmE*) | **period** ◊ *Many locals dressed in period ~ for the celebrations.* | **Halloween** (*esp. AmE*) ◊ *I have a great idea for my Halloween ~.* | **eighteenth-century, Victorian, etc.** | **bunny, clown, fairy, etc.** | **bathing** (*old-fashioned*), **swimming** (*both BrE*)
VERB + COSTUME **be dressed in, dress in, have on, wear** ◊ *He had a cowboy ~ on.* | **don, put on** ◊ *For Halloween he donned a superhero ~.* | **create, design, make, sew** ◊ *He designed the ~s for a production of 'The Firebird'.*
COSTUME + NOUN **design** | **designer** | **drama** ◊ *The movie is a ~ drama based on a 19th-century novel.* | **change** ◊ *The main character had five ~ changes.* | **ball, party** (*both esp. AmE*) ◊ *They celebrated New Year's Eve with a ~ party.* | **jewellery/jewelry**
PREP. **in ~** ◊ *The battle was re-enacted by actors in period ~.*

cottage *noun*

ADJ. **humble, little, simple, small, tiny** | **charming, cosy/cozy** (*esp. AmE*), **picturesque, quaint** | **country, rural** (*esp. BrE*) | **derelict** (*BrE*) | **half-timbered** (*esp. BrE*), **stone, thatched, wooden** | **rented** | **farm** (*esp. BrE*), **tied** (*BrE*) (= owned by a farmer and rented to a farm worker) | **holiday** (*BrE*), **summer, weekend** (*esp. BrE*) | **guest** ◊ *They put us up in a guest ~ next to their house.*
VERB + COTTAGE **have, own** ◊ *It was her dream to have a little ~ in the country* | **live in, stay in** ◊ *We stayed in a ~ on a farm.* | **rent, take** (*BrE*) ◊ *We rented a ~ for a week.* | **build** ◊ *They built a small guest ~ on their land.* | **let** (*BrE*) | **buy** | **sell**
COTTAGE + NOUN **home** | **garden** | **industry**
PREP. **in a/the ~**

cotton *noun*

ADJ. **100%, pure** ◊ *a pure ~ T-shirt* | **light, thin** ◊ *She was shivering in her thin ~ dress* | **fine** | **soft** | **raw** | **combed** (*esp. AmE*) | **natural, organic** (*both esp. AmE*) | **plain** | **printed** | **mercerized** | **sewing** (*BrE*)
...OF COTTON **bale, bolt**
VERB + COTTON **grow** | **pick** | **plant** | **wear**
COTTON + NOUN **fibre/fiber, thread, yarn** (*AmE*) | **ball** (*esp. AmE*), **bud** (*BrE*), **swab** (*AmE*) | **wool** (*BrE*) | **field, plantation** | **farmer** | **picker** | **industry** | **mill** | **gin** | **cloth, fabric** | **shirt, sock, sweater, etc.** | **reel** (*BrE*) | **candy** (= sticky threads of melted sugar) (*AmE*)

couch *noun*

ADJ. **comfortable, comfy** (*informal*), **plush** (*esp. AmE*), **soft** (*esp. AmE*) | **leather, velvet** | **overstuffed** (*esp. AmE*) ◊ *She settled down to read on the huge, overstuffed ~.* | **worn** ◊ *The room contained an old worn ~.* | **living-room** (*AmE*) ◊ *He was sprawled on the living-room ~ watching TV.* | **pull-out** (*AmE*) ◊ *You can sleep on the pull-out ~.* | **psychiatrist's** ◊ *She spends several hours a week on the psychiatrist's ~.*
VERB + COUCH **lie (down) on, recline on, sink back on, sink into, sit (down) on, sprawl on, stretch (out) on** ◊ *They sat*

down on the wide ~. | **get up from, rise from, slide off, swing your legs off, swing yourself off**
COUCH + NOUN **cushion** (*esp. AmE*), **pillow** (*AmE*) | **potato** (= sb who spends all their time sitting on a couch) ◊ *He's turned into a real ~ potato since he subscribed to the sports channel.*
PREP. **on a/the ~** ◊ *He slept on the ~.*

cough noun

ADJ. **little, polite** (*esp. BrE*), **slight** ◊ *The butler gave a little ~ to announce his presence.* | **violent** | **bad, nasty, terrible** | **mild** | **chesty** (*BrE*) | **barking, dry, hacking, racking** | **chronic, persistent** | **occasional** | **smoker's** ◊ *He had a smoker's ~ and nicotine-yellowed fingers.*
VERB + COUGH **give** ◊ *He gave a slight, apologetic ~ and said, 'Excuse me.'* | **have, suffer from** | **catch, develop, get** | **stifle, suppress** ◊ *She struggled to stifle a ~.*
COUGH + NOUN **drop** (*esp. AmE*), **medicine, mixture** (*BrE*), **remedy** (*AmE*), **suppressant, sweet** (*BrE*), **syrup**
→ Special page at ILLNESS

cough verb

ADV. **a bit, a little, lightly, slightly** | **weakly** | **discreetly, politely** (*esp. BrE*) | **awkwardly, nervously, uncomfortably** | **loudly, violently** | **harshly** | **uncontrollably** | **up** ◊ *He vomited and began ~ing up blood.*
PHRASES **~ and splutter** ◊ *The brandy made her ~ and splutter.* | **a ~ing fit** ◊ *He had a ~ing fit and couldn't speak for a few moments.*

council noun

1 local or national government

ADJ. **executive, governing, ruling, state** | **national** | **legislative** | **local** | **borough, city, community, county, district, municipal, neighbourhood/neighborhood, parish, provincial, regional, town** | **metropolitan, rural, urban** (*all esp. BrE*) | **tribal** | **elected**
VERB + COUNCIL **elect** | **control** (*esp. BrE*) ◊ *Many county ~s are now controlled by the Conservatives.* | **gain control of, retain control of, win control of** (*all BrE*)
COUNCIL + VERB **meet** | **vote** ◊ *The Spokane city ~ voted unanimously to ask for his resignation.* | **adopt sth, approve sth, decide sth, pass sth**
COUNCIL + NOUN **elections** | **member, representative** | **meeting** | **chamber** | **president** | **resolution** | **leader, seat**
PREP. **on a/the ~** ◊ *She's on the borough ~.*
PHRASES **a seat on a ~** ◊ *Our party won the majority of seats on the city ~s.*

2 (*BrE*) organization that provides local services

VERB + COUNCIL **apply to** ◊ *Students should apply to their local ~ for a grant.*
COUNCIL + VERB **provide, spend**
COUNCIL + NOUN **employee, staff, worker** | **services** | **estate, flat, house, housing** | **tax**

3 group chosen to give advice, money, etc.

ADJ. **advisory, funding, governing, research** ◊ *the governing ~ of the Mormon Church* | **arts, sports** | **student** | **ecumenical**
VERB + COUNCIL **create, establish, form, found, set up, start** | **apply to** ◊ *As a struggling young composer, she applied to the California Arts Council for grant money.*
COUNCIL + VERB **award sb sth, give sb sth** ◊ *The Arts Council gives grants for local projects.*
COUNCIL + NOUN **member**
PREP. **~ for** ◊ *They are setting up a new ~ for the arts.*
→ Note at ORGANIZATION

councillor (AmE also councilor) noun

ADJ. **borough** (*BrE*), **city, county** (*BrE*), **district** (*BrE*), **local, parish** (*BrE*), **town** (*esp. BrE*) | **Conservative, Labour, etc.** | **former** | **newly elected** (*BrE*)
VERB + COUNCILLOR **elect sb (as)**

counsel noun

1 advice

ADJ. **good, wise**
VERB + COUNSEL **give (sb), offer (sb), provide** | **seek** | **accept, follow, get, listen to, take** ◊ *Listen to the ~ of your elders.*
COUNSEL + VERB **prevail** (*esp. BrE*) ◊ *In the end, wiser ~s prevailed.*
PREP. **~ on** ◊ *He is there to give you ~ on all matters.*
PHRASES **a ~ of despair** (= advice not to try to do sth because it is too difficult) (*formal*)

2 lawyer

ADJ. **legal** ◊ *They were denied legal ~ or the right to call witnesses.* | **chief, lead** (*AmE*), **senior** | **assistant** (*AmE*), **deputy** (*AmE*), **junior** | **leading** (*BrE*) ◊ *The accused was represented by a leading ~.* | **former** | **independent, outside, special** (*all AmE*) ◊ *An independent ~ was appointed to conduct an internal investigation.* | **prosecuting, prosecution** (*both BrE*) ◊ *The witness was cross-examined by the prosecuting ~.* | **defence/defense, defending** (*BrE*) | **opposing** ◊ *Lawyers do not usually interrupt opposing ~ during closing arguments.* | **King's, Queen's** (*in the UK*) | **general** (*esp. AmE*) ◊ *She is general ~ for the American Bankers Association.* | **legislative** (*AmE*) ◊ *He worked for the committee as legislative ~ on issues of crime policy.*
VERB + COUNSEL **appoint, hire** (*AmE*), **retain** (*esp. AmE*) | **consult** (*esp. AmE*) | **brief, instruct** ◊ *He instructed his ~ to file bankruptcy proceedings.*
COUNSEL + VERB **represent sb** | **cross-examine sb, question sb** | **argue sth, claim sth, state sth, submit sth** (*esp. BrE*) ◊ *His ~ argued that he had not intended to harm the women.*
PREP. **~ for** ◊ *the ~ for the defence/defense.* ◊ *the ~ for the prosecution* ◊ *She is lead ~ for the plaintiffs in the case.*

counselling (BrE) (AmE counseling) noun

ADJ. **group, individual** | **professional** | **couples** (*esp. AmE*), **marital** (*esp. AmE*), **marriage** (*esp. AmE*), **marriage guidance** (*BrE*), **premarital** (*esp. AmE*) | **family** | **college** (*esp. AmE*), **school** (*esp. AmE*), **student, youth** (*esp. AmE*) | **peer** (*esp. AmE*) | **abortion, genetic** ◊ *We provide fertility treatment and genetic ~ for couples trying to conceive.* | **bereavement, mental-health** (*AmE*), **psychological, stress** | **career** (*AmE*), **vocational** | **business, debt** | **nutritional** (*esp. AmE*)
VERB + COUNSELLING/COUNSELING **give sb, offer (sb), provide (sb with)** ◊ *The survivors were offered ~.* | **get, have, receive** | **be in need of, need** ◊ *Many of the victims of the tragedy still need ~.* | **seek** | **recommend** ◊ *Their doctor recommended professional ~.* | **refer sb for, refer sb to** ◊ *He was suspended from school and referred for ~.*
COUNSELLING/COUNSELING + NOUN **centre/center, service** ◊ *the new student ~ and guidance service* | **session** | **skills**
PREP. **~ for** ◊ *~ for parents and children* ◊ *~ for depression*

counsellor (esp. BrE) (AmE usually counselor) noun

person trained to advise or help people

ADJ. **accredited** (*BrE*), **certified** (*AmE*), **professional, trained** | **credit** (*AmE*), **debt** (*BrE*), **family, genetic, grief, marriage** (*AmE*), **marriage guidance** (*BrE*), **mental-health** | **college** (*esp. AmE*), **school** (*esp. AmE*), **student, youth** (*esp. AmE*) | **peer** (*esp. AmE*) | **camp** (= a person in charge of young people at a summer camp) (*AmE*)
VERB + COUNSELLOR **see, talk to** ◊ *He talked to a ~ about his marriage difficulties.*
→ Note at JOB

count noun

1 act of counting

ADJ. **quick** | **daily** ◊ *Our daily ~ of Web traffic tells us many people are visiting our site.* | **vote** ◊ *The vote ~ should be repeated.*
VERB + COUNT **do, have** ◊ *We did a quick ~ of the children and there were none missing.*
PHRASES **at the last ~, at the latest ~** ◊ *At the last ~ she had*

43 cats! | **for a ~ of** ◊ *Raise your leg and hold it there for a ~ of ten.*

2 measurement/total

ADJ. **total** | **accurate** | **elevated** (*esp. AmE*), **high** ◊ *an abnormally high white blood cell ~* | **low** | **blood, calorie, cell, pollen, sperm** ◊ *The pollen ~ is very high in the spring.* | **body, head** ◊ *The movie has a high body ~ (= many people are killed).* ◊ *The company now has a head ~ of around 70 staff.*

VERB + COUNT **reduce** | **increase** | **keep** ◊ *Keep a ~ of your calorie intake for one week.* | **lose** ◊ *I've lost ~ of the times I've heard that joke.*

COUNT + VERB **go up, increase, rise** | **drop, fall, go down** ◊ *Her white cell ~ has gone down again.*

3 legal charge

ADJ. **felony** (*AmE*)

PREP. **~ of** ◊ *to be charged with two ~s of murder*

counter *noun*

1 long flat surface

ADJ. **checkout** (*AmE*), **post office** (*BrE*), **shop** (*esp. BrE*), **store** (*AmE*) ◊ *There was a line of people waiting at the checkout ~.* | **cosmetic** (*AmE*), **cosmetics, make-up** | **deli, delicatessen, meat** ◊ *He works at the meat ~.* | **bar, lunch** (*AmE*) ◊ *They sat on high stools at the bar ~.* | **check-in** (*AmE*), **reception, ticket** (*esp. AmE*) ◊ *an airline check-in ~* | **bathroom** (*AmE*), **kitchen** (*esp. AmE*), **sink** (*AmE*) ◊ *She put her bags down on the kitchen ~.* | **Formica™** (*esp. AmE*), **glass, granite, marble, wooden**

VERB + COUNTER **serve at** (*esp. AmE*), **serve behind** (*esp. BrE*), **work at** (*esp. AmE*), **work behind** ◊ *Mary worked behind the ~ at Bacon's for a few hours a week.* | **wipe, wipe down** ◊ *The bartender wiped down the ~ in silence.* | **approach** ◊ *He approached the ~ and showed his ticket.*

COUNTER + NOUN **top** (*esp. AmE*) ◊ *The kitchen had black marble ~ tops.* | **staff** (*BrE*) ◊ *post office ~ staff*

PREP. **across a/the ~** ◊ *He pushed the money across the ~ to her.* | **at a/the ~, behind a/the ~** ◊ *The assistant behind the ~ gave a curt nod.* | **on a/the ~** ◊ *all the goods on the ~* | **over the ~** (*often figurative*) ◊ *She handed me my coffee over the ~.* ◊ *This kind of medication cannot be bought over the ~ (= without a prescription).*

2 action used to prevent sth

ADJ. **effective**

PREP. **~ to** ◊ *an effective ~ to the blandness of modern culture*

counter-attack *noun*

ADJ. **effective, strong, successful**

VERB + COUNTER-ATTACK **launch, mount**

PREP. **~ against** ◊ *The soldiers mounted a strong ~ against the rebels.*

counterpart *noun*

ADJ. **direct** ◊ *the difficulty of translating terms with no direct ~ in the other language* | **modern** ◊ *the modern ~s of those medieval writers* | **female, male** ◊ *Women soldiers will join their male ~s at the army base.* | **older, younger** | **domestic, foreign** | **rural, urban** | **northern, southern, etc.** | **American, British, European, French, etc.** ◊ *The president met his French ~.* | **real-life** ◊ *The actress who played the Queen looked uncannily like her real-life ~.*

VERB + COUNTERPART **have** ◊ *European environmentalists have their ~s in the US.*

PREP. **~ in** ◊ *corporations that trade with their ~s in other countries*

country *noun*

1 area of land with its own government

ADJ. **beautiful, fascinating, great** ◊ *this great ~ of ours* | **hot, tropical** | **cold** | **landlocked** | **different, foreign, overseas, strange** ◊ *It's difficult to live in a foreign ~ when you don't*

speak the language. ◊ *students from overseas countries* | **home, native, own** | **adopted** ◊ *Many servicemen gave their lives for their adopted ~.* | **host** ◊ *The refugees do jobs that workers in the host ~ refuse to do.* | **neighbouring/ neighboring** | **distant, far, faraway** | **independent, sovereign** (*esp. AmE*) | **occupied** | **free** ◊ *'It's a free ~!' he shouted. 'I can do what I like!'* | **enemy, friendly** | **neutral, non-aligned** (*esp. BrE*) | **war-ravaged, war-torn** | **African, Arab, etc.** | **Eastern, Western, etc.** | **English-speaking, francophone, etc.** | **EU, NATO, etc.** | **member, non-member** ◊ *OECD member countries* | **developed, industrial, industrialized** | **developing, Third-World, underdeveloped** | **advanced** ◊ *economically advanced countries* | **impoverished, low-income, poor** | **middle-income** | **affluent, high-income, rich, wealthy** | **densely populated, populous** | **capitalist, communist, democratic, socialist** | **Catholic, Islamic, etc.** | **oil-exporting, oil-producing, oil-rich**

VERB + COUNTRY **govern, rule, run** ◊ *The ~ was ruled by a brutal dictatorship.* ◊ *the politicians who run the ~* | **lead** ◊ *He accused the government of leading the ~ to disaster.* | **attack, conquer, invade, occupy** | **defend, protect** ◊ *We must remember those who died defending their ~.* | **serve** ◊ *I'm proud to serve my ~.* | **liberate, save** ◊ *a commander who saved his ~ from invasion* | **divide, polarize, split** ◊ *The issue of the single currency has divided the ~.* | **unite** | **destabilize, destroy, devastate, ravage** ◊ *Years of civil war had ravaged the ~.* | **rebuild** | **democratize, modernize, pacify, stabilize** | **flee, leave** ◊ *The former president has been forced to flee the ~.* | **enter** ◊ *new restrictions on goods entering the ~* | **love** ◊ *He loved his ~ deeply.* | **betray** | **play for, represent** ◊ *She represented her ~ at the Beijing Olympics.* | **tour, travel, visit** ◊ *He plans to travel the ~ by motorcycle.*

COUNTRY + VERB **border sth** ◊ *countries bordering the Black Sea* | **produce sth** | **export sth, import sth** ◊ *The ~ exports around 80% of its output.* | **agree sth, ratify sth, sign sth** ◊ *The two countries signed a basic treaty of cooperation.* | **compete, participate** ◊ *Over 30 countries participated in the Games.* | **need sth** ◊ *Our ~ needs a leader like her.* | **face sth, struggle (with sth), suffer (from sth)** ◊ *The ~ is suffering from rising unemployment.*

PREP. **across a/the ~** ◊ *They drove across the ~.* | **all over a/ the ~** ◊ *They are holding special events all over the ~.* | **around a/the ~, round a/the ~** (*esp. BrE*) ◊ *This is just one of 33 sites around the ~.* | **in a/the ~** ◊ *people who live in this ~* | **throughout a/the ~** ◊ *New schools are being built throughout the ~.*

PHRASES **countries around the globe, countries around the world** ◊ *We operate in ten countries around the globe.* | **~ of (sb's) birth, ~ of origin** ◊ *the ~ of his birth* ◊ *He cannot be deported to his ~ of origin.* | **in this ~ and abroad** ◊ *The play has been enjoyed by audiences in this ~ and abroad for many years.* | **a part of a ~** ◊ *There will be rain in many parts of the ~ tomorrow.* | **the ~ as a whole** ◊ *The rich benefited from the reforms, not the ~ as a whole.*

2 area of land with particular features

ADJ. **desert, hill, hilly, mountain, mountainous, open** ◊ *The town is surrounded by miles and miles of open ~.* | **rough, wild** | **farming, wine** ◊ *This part of Africa is rich farming ~.* | **hunting, walking** (*both esp. BrE*) ◊ *superb walking ~*

...OF COUNTRY **stretch, tract** ◊ *a beautiful stretch of ~* ◊ *Whole tracts of ~, once fertile, have become arid.*

3 land away from towns/cities

COUNTRY + NOUN **life** | **air** | **lane, road** | **area, district** (*both esp. BrE*) | **town, village** (*esp. BrE*) | **cottage, estate, home, house** (*esp. BrE*), **manor, mansion, residence** (*esp. BrE*), **retreat, seat** (*BrE*) | **inn, pub** (*BrE*) | **park** (*BrE*) | **fair** | **walk** (*esp. BrE*) | **boy, girl** | **gentleman, squire** (*esp. BrE*) | **bumpkin, dweller, folk, people**

PREP. **across ~** ◊ *They rode across ~.* | **in the ~** ◊ *She lives in the ~.*

countryside *noun*

ADJ. **attractive** (*esp. BrE*), **beautiful, glorious** (*BrE*), **lovely, magnificent** (*esp. BrE*), **picturesque, spectacular** (*esp. BrE*),

stunning (*esp. BrE*), wonderful (*esp. BrE*) | unspoiled ◊ *miles of unspoiled ~* | open | green, lush ◊ *a walk through the lush green ~* | flat | hilly, mountainous, rolling, rugged | wild (*esp. BrE*) | peaceful, quiet, rural (*esp. AmE*) | local (*esp. BrE*), nearby, surrounding | English, French, etc.
... OF COUNTRYSIDE **area** (*esp. BrE*) | acres, miles ◊ *miles of beautiful ~*
VERB + COUNTRYSIDE **conserve, preserve, protect** (*all esp. BrE*) | ravage (*esp. BrE*) ◊ *The ~ has been ravaged by pollution.* | roam, tour, wander, wander around, wander through ◊ *In the afternoons they roamed the ~ around the house.* | scour ◊ *Police scoured the ~ in search of the missing man.* | dot ◊ *Castles and churches dot the ~.*
PREP. **in the ~** ◊ *I dream of living in the ~.* | surrounded by **~** ◊ *a small town surrounded by picturesque ~* | through (the) **~** ◊ *Soon we were driving through pleasant open ~.* | **~ around** ◊ *the ~ around Oxford*

county *noun*

ADJ. **border** (*esp. BrE*), coastal, metropolitan, rural, urban (*AmE*) ◊ *the Welsh border counties* | eastern, western, etc. | historic (*esp. BrE*) | home ◊ *He returned to his home ~ in North Carolina.* ◊ *London and the home counties* (= the counties around London) | native (*BrE*) ◊ *He was elected MP for his native ~ of Merioneth.* | adjacent, neighbouring/neighboring, surrounding ◊ *London and its surrounding counties*
VERB + COUNTY **represent** ◊ *She represents the ~ in Parliament.* (*BrE*)
COUNTY + NOUN **boundary** (*esp. BrE*), line (*AmE*) ◊ *The river forms the ~ boundary.* | resident (*AmE*) | seat (*AmE*), town (*BrE*) (= where the local government is based) ◊ *the town of Sierra Blanca, the ~ seat of Hudspeth County, Texas* ◊ *Trowbridge is the ~ town of Wiltshire.* | commission (*AmE*), council, department (*AmE*), government (*esp. AmE*) ◊ *Fairfax County Department of Family Services* | attorney, clerk, coroner, judge, official, prosecutor, sheriff (*all AmE*) | chairman (*esp. AmE*), councillor (*esp. BrE*), executive (*esp. AmE*) | court, courthouse (*AmE*), jail (*AmE*) | hospital, library, school | cricket (*BrE*) | championship, match (= in cricket)
PREP. **in a/the ~** ◊ *people who live in this ~*

coup *noun*

1 (*also* **coup d'état**) violent change of government
ADJ. **abortive, attempted, failed, unsuccessful** | successful | bloody | bloodless | army (*esp. BrE*), military | palace ◊ *He deposed his father in a palace ~ in 1970.* | communist, right-wing, etc. | boardroom ◊ *She lost her position in a boardroom ~* (= a sudden change of power in a company).
VERB + COUP **launch, mount, stage** | foil, put down ◊ *The ~ was immediately put down and the plotters were shot.* | engineer, foment, orchestrate, plan, plot | lead | come to power in, seize power in ◊ *He seized power in a military ~.*
COUP + NOUN **attempt, plot** | leader, plotter
PREP. **~ against** ◊ *a ~ against the president*

2 achievement
ADJ. **big, great, major, real, spectacular** (*esp. BrE*) ◊ *Winning that contract was her greatest ~.* | diplomatic, intelligence, marketing, propaganda, publicity
VERB + COUP **pull off, score** ◊ *He managed to pull off a major diplomatic ~.*

couple *noun*

ADJ. **adorable** (*AmE*), attractive, beautiful, cute (*AmE*), good-looking, great, handsome, lovely | happy, loving, perfect, romantic | elderly, middle-aged, old, retired, young | heterosexual | gay, homosexual, lesbian, same-sex | engaged, honeymoon, married, newly married, newly-wed ◊ *The hotel was full of honeymoon ~s.* | cohabiting, unmarried | interracial (*AmE*) | childless, infertile ◊ *childless ~s seeking to adopt*
VERB + COUPLE **make** ◊ *They make a beautiful ~.*
PHRASES **the happy ~** (= the two people getting married) ◊ *We stood and drank a toast to the happy ~.*

coupon *noun*

ADJ. **valid** ◊ *This ~ is valid until 31 January.* | discount, free, money-off (*BrE*) | entry (*BrE*) ◊ *To enter the competition, fill in the entry ~ on page 6.* | clothing, food, petrol (*BrE*), etc.
VERB + COUPON **give, offer** ◊ *They are offering 50%-off ~s.* | get, receive ◊ *New members receive ~s for complimentary services.* | collect, save ◊ *She had saved enough ~s to get a free flight.* | complete (*BrE*), fill in (*BrE*), fill out | clip (*AmE*), cut out (*esp. BrE*) | redeem, use | mail (*AmE*), post (*BrE*) | return, send, send off (*all esp. BrE*) ◊ *Cut out and return this ~ to claim your free gift.*

courage *noun*

ADJ. **considerable, extraordinary, great, immense, out-standing** (*esp. BrE*), remarkable, tremendous | personal ◊ *an act of personal ~ that moved people* | intellectual, moral, political ◊ *Caring for elderly relatives requires considerable moral ~.* ◊ *This is a chance for him to show leadership and political ~.* | physical ◊ *stories of incredible physical ~*
VERB + COURAGE **require, take** ◊ *It takes ~ to sing in public.* | have ◊ *I didn't have the ~ to tell him.* | lack ◊ *He lacked the ~ to try something new.* | demonstrate, display, show | find, gather, muster, muster up, pluck up, summon ◊ *I finally plucked up enough ~ to speak to Rachel.* | admire, applaud ◊ *I admire your ~ in saying what you think.*
PHRASES **~ under fire** (= when you are being attacked, physically or figuratively) ◊ *He showed great calmness and ~ under fire.* | have the **~** of your convictions (= to be brave enough to do what you feel to be right)

courageous *adj.*

VERBS **be, seem**
ADV. **extremely, fairly, very, etc.** | incredibly

courier *noun*

ADJ. **drug** | motorbike (*BrE*), motorcycle | bicycle, bike (*informal*), cycle (*esp. BrE*)
VERB + COURIER **act as** ◊ *He has admitted to acting as a drug ~.* | send, use ◊ *I'll send a ~ with the blueprints.* | send sth by ◊ *Urgent deliveries of medicine may be sent by motorcycle ~.*
→ Note at JOB

course *noun*

1 complete series of lessons or lectures
ADJ. **computer, psychology, Spanish, etc.** | crash, intensive | short | two-day, two-week, etc. | advanced, beginners', intermediate, introductory | college-level, graduate-level (*both AmE*) | day (*BrE*), evening (*esp. BrE*), night (*AmE*) | elective (*AmE*) ◊ *Psychology is offered as an elective ~.* | required (*AmE*) ◊ *Students take required ~s in music theory and performance.* | refresher, remedial ◊ *He enrolled in a remedial mathematics ~.* | induction (*BrE*) | training | correspondence, online, Web-based | external (*BrE*) | in-house (*esp. BrE*)
VERB + COURSE **attend, do, take** ◊ *He took a crash ~ in Spanish.* | enrol on (*BrE*), join (*esp. BrE*), sign up for | teach | offer, run ◊ *The school runs ~s all year round.* | design, develop ◊ *We have designed the ~ for students at all levels of ability.* | complete, finish ◊ *She has completed a ~ in first aid.* | pass | fail, flunk (*informal, esp. AmE*)
COURSE + VERB **run** ◊ *The ~ runs from January till March.* | consist of sth, cover sth, focus on sth, include sth ◊ *The ~ consists of both lectures and practical workshops.*
PREP. **~ in** ◊ *a ~ in art history* | **~ on** ◊ *a ~ on the development of capitalism*

2 (*esp. BrE*) period of study at a college/university
ADJ. **full-time, part-time** | one-year, two-year, etc. | access (*BrE*), foundation (*BrE*) | graduate, postgraduate, under-graduate | degree, diploma, honours/honors ◊ *a joint-honours ~ in French and Russian* (*BrE*) | mathematics, physics, psychology, etc. | academic | vocational | sandwich (*BrE*)

VERB + COURSE **offer, run** ◇ *the only university in the UK to offer ~s in computer games technology* | **complete, finish** | **drop out of**

3 route/direction

VERB + COURSE **alter, change, reverse** (*esp. AmE*) ◇ *The boat altered ~ during the storm.* | **chart, plot, set** ◇ *We set ~ for Vancouver Island.* | **navigate, steer** | **follow** ◇ *The path follows the ~ of the river.* | **resume** ◇ *The plane resumed its original ~.*
PREP. **off ~** ◇ *We're a long way off ~.* | **on ~** ◇ *We're on ~ for our destination.*
PHRASES **on a collision ~** ◇ *The two planes were on a collision ~.* | **be blown off ~** ◇ *The boat was blown off ~.*

4 way of acting

ADJ. **best, better** | **prudent** ◇ *Taking action without knowing all the facts would not be a prudent ~.*
VERB + COURSE **adopt, choose, follow, pursue, steer, take** ◇ *She shrewdly steered a middle ~ between the two factions.* ◇ *It was the best ~ of action to take in the circumstances.*
COURSE + VERB **be open to sb** ◇ *It was the only ~ open to him.*
PHRASES **a ~ of action**

5 development of sth over a period of time

ADJ. **natural, normal, usual** ◇ *It's best to let things follow their natural ~.*
VERB + COURSE **change** ◇ *an event that changed the ~ of his life* | **reverse** (*esp. AmE*) ◇ *The dollar fell sharply for two days, and then reversed ~.* | **affect, decide, determine, dictate, influence, shape** ◇ *War has determined the ~ of much of human history.* | **follow, run, take** ◇ *Her career followed a similar ~ to her sister's.* ◇ *We could do nothing but let the disease run its ~.* | **resume** ◇ *Prices resumed their upward ~.*
PREP. **during the ~ of** ◇ *during the ~ of the war* | **in the ~ of** ◇ *In the ~ of time, I began to understand.*
PHRASES **the ~ of history** ◇ *This was an event that changed the ~ of history.* | **in due ~** (= at the appropriate time; eventually) | **in the normal ~ of events, in the ordinary ~ of events** ◇ *In the normal ~ of events, you should get a reply by Monday.* | **let nature take its ~** ◇ *When the dog responded so badly to the treatment, we decided to let nature take its ~* (= stop treating it and let it die naturally).

6 part of a meal

ADJ. **main** | **first, second, etc.**
PREP. **for a/the ~** ◇ *We had chicken for our main ~.*

7 in a sport/a race

ADJ. **golf** | **nine-hole** | **obstacle, race** (usually *racecourse*) (*BrE*) (*racetrack* in *AmE*)
VERB + COURSE **complete** ◇ *Only ten yachts completed the ~.* | **build, design**

8 series of medical treatments

VERB + COURSE **give sb, put sb on** ◇ *She's been put on a ~ of injections.* | **prescribe (sb)** | **take** | **complete, finish** ◇ *If you are prescribed antibiotics, it's important to finish the ~.*
PREP. **~ of** ◇ *a ~ of antibiotics*

court noun

1 law

ADJ. **civil, criminal** ◇ *She should seek damages through the civil ~s.* ◇ *The case will be tried before a criminal ~.* | **Appeals Court, circuit, district, federal, Supreme Court, trial** (*all in the US*) ◇ *They took their case to the Appeals Court.* | **Appeal Court, Crown Court, High Court, magistrates'** (*all in England and Wales*) ◇ *They took their case to the Appeal Court.* ◇ *the High Court of Justice* | **sheriff** (*in Scotland*) | **higher, superior** ◇ *The banks may decide to appeal to a higher ~.* ◇ *The case was appealed to a higher ~.* (*AmE*) | **highest, supreme** ◇ *This is the highest ~ in the country.* | **lower** | **juvenile** | **civilian, military** | **bankruptcy, divorce, family** ◇ *They are likely to end up in the divorce ~.* (*BrE*) ◇ *They are likely to end up in divorce ~.* (*AmE*) | **traffic** (*AmE*) | **small claims** | **county** | **international** | **European, French, etc.** | **ecclesiastical, Islamic, rabbin-**

ical, sharia | **moot** (= where law students train to become lawyers) (*AmE*) | **kangaroo** (= an illegal court)
VERB + COURT **go to, take sb/sth to** ◇ *We are prepared to go to ~ to get our compensation.* ◇ *They took their employer to ~.* | **come to, get to, go to** ◇ *The case should not be allowed to go to ~.* | **bring sth to** ◇ *There wasn't enough evidence to bring the case to ~.* | **settle sth out of** ◇ *The dispute was settled out of ~.* | **appear before, appear in, attend** ◇ *She is too young to appear before the ~.* ◇ *He will appear in ~ tomorrow charged with the murder.* | **tell** ◇ *Will you please tell the ~ what happened on that morning?* | **ask, petition, urge** ◇ *The company asked the ~ to overrule the tribunal's decision.* | **convince, persuade** ◇ *We were trying to convince the ~ that the rules should be changed.* | **preside over** ◇ *The ~ was presided over by Judge Owen.* | **adjourn** ◇ *Court was adjourned for the weekend.*
COURT + VERB **hear sth** ◇ *The ~ heard how the mother had beaten the 11-year-old boy.* | **acquit sb, clear sb** ◇ *The ~ acquitted Reece of the murder of his wife.* | **convict sb, sentence sb** ◇ *The ~ sentenced him to life in prison.* | **dismiss sth, overturn sth, quash sth, reject sth** ◇ *The ~ dismissed the appeal.* ◇ *The guilty verdict was quashed by the appeal ~.* | **refuse sth** ◇ *The Supreme Court refused to allow the appeal.* | **uphold sth** ◇ *The ~ upheld the plaintiff's claim of unfair dismissal.* | **grant sth, issue sth, order sth** ◇ *The ~ issued an injunction.* | **affirm sth, conclude sth, decide sth, declare sth, find sth, hold sth, reason sth, rule sth** ◇ *The ~ held that she was entitled to receive compensation.* | **agree** ◇ *A higher ~ agreed that the trial judge had been mistaken.* | **disagree** ◇ *The company argued there was no case to answer, but the ~ disagreed.*
COURT + NOUN **bailiff, clerk, judge, official, registrar** (*BrE*), **staff, stenographer** (*esp. AmE*), **usher** (*BrE*) ◇ *She was appointed a high ~ judge in 1998.* | **action, case, proceedings** | **hearing, trial** | **injunction, order, summons** ◇ *She tried to get a ~ order to prevent him from coming near her.* ◇ *He received a ~ summons for non-payment of tax.* | **decision, ruling** | **appearance** ◇ *Divorce no longer requires a ~ appearance.* | **date** ◇ *Once a lawsuit is filed, a ~ date is set.* | **battle** ◇ *They could now face a ~ battle for compensation.* | **procedure, process** | **costs** | **document, record** ◇ *Court documents showing illegal transactions were released to the press.* | **system** | **building, house** (usually *courthouse*) (*esp. AmE*)
PREP. **at ~** ◇ *He should be tried at the International Court in the Hague.* | **before a/the ~** ◇ *The case is now before the ~.* | **in ~** ◇ *Relatives of the dead girl were in ~.*
PHRASES **contempt of ~** ◇ *He was charged with contempt of ~ after shouting at a witness.* | **a ~ of appeal** ◇ *The case may be heard by a ~ of appeal next month.* ◇ *the Court of Appeal* (*in England and Wales*) ◇ *the Court of Appeals* (*in the US*) | **~ of claims** (*in the US*), **~ of inquiry** (*BrE*), **a ~ of law** ◇ *I don't think that argument would stand up in a ~ of law.* | **a ward of ~** (*BrE*), **a ward of the ~** (*AmE*) ◇ *The child was made a ward of (the) ~ when her parents were jailed.*

2 for sports

ADJ. **basketball, squash, tennis, etc.** | **clay, grass, hard** ◇ *She is a good player on hard ~s.* ◇ *He hopes to repeat his success on the grass ~s of Wimbledon.* | **indoor** ◇ *an indoor volleyball ~*
PREP. **off (the) ~** ◇ *The players are good friends off ~ and train together.* ◇ *He was a real gentleman both on and off ~ and a delight to play.* | **on (the) ~** ◇ *The players have been on ~ for an hour.*

3 kings/queens

ADJ. **imperial, royal** ◇ *a member of the imperial ~ of Kyoto*
COURT + NOUN **circles** ◇ *Mozart quickly became well known in ~ circles.* | **jester**
PREP. **at (a/the) ~** ◇ *life at the ~ of Charles I* ◇ *life at ~*

court verb

ADV. **actively, aggressively** (*AmE*), **assiduously** ◇ *The band has actively ~ed a young audience.*

courteous adj.

VERBS **be, seem**

ADV. **extremely, fairly, very, etc.** | **unfailingly** ◇ *She was unfailingly ~ and helpful.*
PREP. **to** ◇ *He was perfectly ~ to me.*

courtesy noun

ADJ. **great, unfailing, utmost** | **common, simple** (*esp. AmE*) ◇ *It's common ~ to give up your seat for elderly people.* | **professional** ◇ *She contacts clients regularly as a professional ~.*
VERB + COURTESY **do sb, have, show, treat sb with** ◇ *She might have done me the ~ of replying to my letter.* ◇ *You could at least have had the ~ to let me know.*
PREP. **with ~** ◇ *He listened to all the complaints with great ~.* | **~ to** ◇ *her unfailing ~ to everyone*
PHRASES **a matter of ~** ◇ *It's a matter of ~ to write and thank people after a party.*

court martial noun

VERB + COURT MARTIAL **order** ◇ *The general ordered an immediate ~.* | **hold** | **be threatened with, face**
PREP. **at a/the ~** ◇ *The officer was convicted of desertion at a ~.* | **by ~** ◇ *He was tried by ~.*

courtship noun

ADJ. **long** | **brief, whirlwind** ◇ *After a whirlwind ~, they married and went to live in Bath.*
VERB + COURTSHIP **initiate**
COURTSHIP + NOUN **behaviour/behavior, display, ritual, song** ◇ *the elaborate ~ display of the pigeon*
PREP. **during a/the ~** ◇ *They often went there together during their ~.*

courtyard noun

ADJ. **central, inner, interior, internal** | **outer** | **enclosed, walled** | **open** | **main** | **castle, palace, school** ◇ *We sat on a bench in the school ~.* | **cobbled, cobblestone** (*AmE*), **grassy, paved**
VERB + COURTYARD **face, overlook** ◇ *Her bedroom overlooked the ~.* | **enclose, surround** ◇ *The ~ is surrounded on three sides by stables.*
PREP. **around a/the ~** ◇ *The hotel is built around a central ~.* | **in a/the ~** ◇ *We sat in the inner ~ of the college.*

cousin noun

ADJ. **first, second** | **distant, remote** (*BrE*) | **close, kissing** (*AmE*) (*both figurative*) ◇ *These pigs are close ~s of the wild hog.* ◇ *the popular idea that creativity and madness are kissing ~s* | **baby, little** ◇ *I have a new baby ~.* | **female, male** | **long-lost** ◇ *Completely out of the blue, she got a letter from her long-lost ~ in Ohio.* | **beloved, favourite/favorite**
PHRASES **~ once, twice, etc. removed** ◇ *She's my first ~ once removed (= of a different generation).*

cover noun

1 sth put on/over sth

ADJ. **protective** | **removable, reversible** | **leather, plastic** | **dust** ◇ *We spread dust ~s over the furniture while the builders were working.* | **cushion, duvet, mattress, pillow** (*AmE*), **seat** | **loose** (*BrE*) ◇ *a sofa with a loose ~* | **album, CD, DVD** | **manhole**
VERB + COVER **put on, replace** | **lift, open, remove, take off** ◇ *He held his nose as he lifted the ~ off the bin.*
PREP. **~ for** ◇ *a ~ for the swimming pool*

2 sth that is over sth

ADJ. **dense, thick** ◇ *a thick ~ of snow* | **cloud, ice, snow** ◇ *We descended into JFK through thick cloud ~.* | **canopy, forest, ground, tree, vegetation, vegetative** (*technical, esp. AmE*) ◇ *plants that provide good ground ~*

3 outside of a book/magazine

ADJ. **back, front** | **hard, soft** | **glossy** | **book, magazine**
VERB + COVER **adorn, grace** ◇ *Her image has graced the ~s of many glossy magazines.* | **design**
COVER + NOUN **illustration, image, photo, photograph, picture** | **art, artwork, design** | **article, feature, story** |

page | **shoot** (= the activity of taking a photograph for a magazine cover) | **boy** (*AmE*), **girl, model** (*AmE*) | **price** (= the price that a book or magazine is sold for) ◇ *The author only gets 1% of the ~ price.*
PREP. **on a/the ~** ◇ *a picture of the author on the back ~.*

4 the covers blankets, sheets, etc.

ADJ. **bed** | **thick, warm** | **thin**
VERB + THE COVERS **get under** | **pull up** | **fling off, pull back, push back, throw back** ◇ *She threw back the ~s and got out of bed.* | **pull off, rip off, yank off** (*esp. AmE*) ◇ *'Get up!' she said, yanking off the ~s.* | **tuck around sb**
PREP. **under the ~**
PHRASES **pull the ~s over your head** ◇ *He pulled the ~s over his head and tried to get back to sleep.*

5 (*BrE*) **insurance against sth** → See also COVERAGE

ADJ. **comprehensive, full** | **wide** ◇ *This company provides wider ~.* | **standard** | **additional** | **insurance** | **fire, health, indemnity, life, medical**
VERB + COVER **have** | **give sb, provide (sb with)**
PREP. **~ against** ◇ *~ against accidental damage* | **~ for** ◇ *~ for contents*

6 shelter/protection from the weather, damage, etc.

ADJ. **air** ◇ *The planes provided air ~ for the attack.*
VERB + COVER **dive for, run for, take** ◇ *We ran for ~ as it started to rain.* | **seek** | **find** | **give sb, provide (sb with)** | **break** (= leave) ◇ *The deer broke ~ as the hunters approached.*
PREP. **under ~** ◇ *All the seats are under ~.* | **under ~ of** ◇ *We attacked at night, under ~ of darkness.* | **~ from** ◇ *They sought ~ from the wind.*

7 sth that hides the real nature of sth

ADJ. **perfect** | **diplomatic, official, political** ◇ *spies operating under diplomatic ~*
VERB + COVER **blow** (= reveal) ◇ *He realized his ~ had been blown*
COVER + NOUN **story** ◇ *The guard believed her ~ story.*
PREP. **~ for** ◇ *The club is a ~ for various criminal activities.*

cover verb

1 put sth over sth to hide or protect it

ADV. **completely, entirely** | **loosely** | **partially, partly** ◇ *Her hair partially ~ed her face.* | **barely** ◇ *Her dress barely ~ed her chest.* | **up** ◇ *She used dried leaves and twigs to ~ up the hole.*
VERB + COVER **try to** ◇ *She tried to ~ her face with her hands.* ◇ *He tried to ~ his embarrassment by starting to rub his hands together.* | **use sth to**
PREP. **with** ◇ *He ~ed the body with a cloth.*

2 form a layer on sth

ADV. **completely**
PREP. **in** ◇ *The cars were all ~ed in snow.* | **with** ◇ *The children were completely ~ed with mud.*

3 include; pay for

ADV. **barely, hardly** ◇ *The payments he gets barely ~ his expenses.* ◇ *We've hardly ~ed a quarter of the course.*
VERB + COVER **help (to)** | **be intended to** | **be extended to** ◇ *The tax may be extended to ~ books.*

4 insurance

PREP. **against** ◇ *This policy should ~ you against accidental injury.* | **for** ◇ *a policy that ~s you for fire and theft*

coverage noun

1 reporting of news/sports

ADJ. **considerable, extensive, massive** ◇ *There's been massive television ~ of the World Cup.* | **around-the-clock** (*esp. AmE*), **non-stop, round-the-clock, wall-to-wall** (*esp. AmE*) | **comprehensive, full, gavel-to-gavel** (= from the beginning to the end) (*AmE*) | **detailed, in-depth** | **wide, widespread** | **international, local, national, worldwide** | **prime-time** |

limited | **saturation** | **media, news, newspaper, press, radio, television, TV** ◇ *The TV company was given a special award for its news ~.* | **live** ◇ *There's live ~ of the game on TV.* | **exclusive** | **balanced, biased** | **favourable/favorable, negative, positive** | **election, sports, war, etc.**

VERB + COVERAGE **give sth, provide (sth with)** ◇ *The resignation was given widespread ~.* | **attract, get, have, receive** ◇ *The wedding had wide press ~.* | **dominate** ◇ *The story dominated local news ~.* | **read, watch**

COVERAGE + VERB **focus on sth** ◇ *Media ~ of the march focused on the few fights that broke out.*

PREP. **~ of**

2 (*AmE*) insurance against sth → See also COVER

ADJ. **insurance** | **dental, health, health-care, medical, prescription, prescription-drug** | **liability** | **universal**

VERB + COVERAGE **offer, provide** | **buy, get, have, obtain, purchase** | **expand, extend** ◇ *the possibility of expanding health-care ~ to all* | **lose** ◇ *People fear losing ~ if they switch employers.*

PREP. **~ for** ◇ *Business liability protection will provide ~ for damages in the event of a legal claim.*

covered *adj.*

VERBS **be** | **become** | **remain** | **leave sb/sth** ◇ *The car sped past, leaving us ~ in mud.*

ADV. **well** ◇ *Make sure all cooked meat is well ~.* | **absolutely, completely, entirely, fully, totally** | **densely, thickly** ◇ *The ground is densely ~ with large trees.* | **evenly** | **sparsely, thinly** ◇ *the ground was sparsely ~ with grass.* | **permanently, temporarily** ◇ *60% of the land is permanently ~ in ice.*

PREP. **by** ◇ *Each body was ~ by a blanket.* | **in** ◇ *I was ~ in blood.* | **with** ◇ *The path was now completely ~ with thick snow.*

PHRASES **~ from head to foot, ~ from head to toe** ◇ *He crawled out, ~ from head to foot in soot.*

cover-up *noun*

ADJ. **big, massive** | **government**

VERB + COVER-UP **be engaged in, be implicated in, be involved in** ◇ *Military leaders were involved in a massive ~.* | **accuse sb of**

PREP. **~ by** ◇ *~s by the police*

PHRASES **allegations of a ~, claims of a ~**

cow *noun*

ADJ. **beef** | **dairy, milch** (*BrE, often figurative*), **milk** (*esp. AmE*) ◇ *The region is treated as a milch ~ by central government.* | **sacred** (*often figurative*) ◇ *the sacred ~ of free-market economics*

... OF COWS **herd**

VERB + COW **breed** | **milk** | **kill, slaughter**

COW + VERB **low, moo** | **chew the cud, graze** | **calve** ◇ *The ~ had difficulties calving.*

COW + NOUN **byre** (*BrE*), **shed** (usually *cowshed*) | **pasture** | **chip** (*AmE*), **dung, manure, muck, pat** (usually *cowpat*) (*BrE*), **patty** (*AmE*), **pie** (*AmE*) | **bell** (usually *cowbell*)

PHRASES **a breed of ~**

coward *noun*

VERB + COWARD **brand sb, call sb, label sb** ◇ *He was branded a ~ in some newspapers.*

cowardice *noun*

ADJ. **moral, political** ◇ *It is an act of moral ~ for a society to neglect its poor.*

VERB + COWARDICE **show** | **accuse sb of**

PHRASES **an act of ~, ~ in the face of the enemy** ◇ *Any soldier displaying ~ in the face of the enemy was shot.*

crack *noun*

1 line on the surface of sth where it has broken

ADJ. **big, deep, huge, large, long, serious** (*esp. BrE*) | **short, small** | **fine, hairline, thin**

CRACK + VERB **appear** | **develop, spread** | **run** ◇ *A fine ~ ran up the wall.*

2 narrow opening

ADJ. **narrow, small, tiny** | **wide**

VERB + CRACK **fill, seal** ◇ *We filled the ~s in the plaster before hanging the wallpaper.*

CRACK + VERB **appear** ◇ *Wide ~s appeared in the ground during the drought.* | **open up, widen**

PREP. **~ in** ◇ *There's a ~ in the fence big enough to look through.*

PHRASES **a ~ of light** ◇ *a tiny ~ of light under the door* | **open a door, window, etc. a ~** ◇ *Could you open the window just a ~?*

3 sudden loud sound

ADJ. **loud, resounding, sharp** | **sickening** | **satisfying** | **audible**

VERB + CRACK **hear**

CRACK + VERB **echo** ◇ *A loud ~ echoed off the empty walls.*

PREP. **with a ~** ◇ *The chandelier hit the floor with a ~.* | **~ of**

PHRASES **the ~ of a whip** | **a ~ of thunder**
→ Note at SOUND

crack *verb* become mentally ill

ADV. **completely** | **finally** ◇ *The stresses of her job became too great and she finally ~ed.* | **up** ◇ *He thought he'd never get through the ordeal without ~ing up.*

PHRASES **~ under the pressure, ~ under the strain, show signs of ~ing** ◇ *He is under a lot of pressure but is showing no signs of ~ing.*

PHR V **crack down**

ADV. **hard**

PREP. **on** ◇ *to ~ down hard on crime*

crackdown *noun*

ADJ. **bloody, violent** | **major, massive** | **new** | **federal, government, military, police** | **security**

VERB + CRACKDOWN **announce, promise, threaten** | **call for, demand, order** ◇ *The government has ordered a ~ on truancy.* | **have, launch, mount**

PREP. **~ on** ◇ *They're having a ~ on private phone calls from the office.*

cracked *adj.*

ADV. **badly, severely** ◇ *The dish was badly ~.* | **slightly**

cradle *verb*

ADV. **gently** ◇ *He picked the child up and gently ~d him in his arms.*

PREP. **against** ◇ *She sat with the child ~d against her.* | **in**

craft *noun*

1 activity needing skill with your hands

ADJ. **skilled** ◇ *Sheep shearing is a highly skilled ~.* | **ancient, traditional** | **country, local, rural**

VERB + CRAFT **practise/practice** ◇ *The men practised various traditional ~s.*

CRAFT + NOUN **activity, project, work** | **industry** | **worker** | **centre/center, exhibition, fair, show, workshop** | **shop** (*esp. BrE*), **store** (*esp. AmE*) | **skill** | **tradition** | **guild, union** | **foam, glue** (*AmE*), **knife**

PHRASES **art and ~** ◇ *Subjects taught include art and ~, drama, and languages.* | **arts and ~s** ◇ *The gallery has major exhibitions of arts and ~s.*

2 all the skills needed for an activity

VERB + CRAFT **hone, learn, master, perfect, study** ◇ *It took her years to perfect her ~.* | **ply** (*esp. AmE*) ◇ *comedians plying their ~ for an agency*

PHRASES **a master of your ~** ◇ *a carpenter who is a real master of his ~*

ADJ. small | assault, fishing, landing, patrol, pleasure, river, sailing

craftsman noun

ADJ. fine, good | master, skilled, trained | local

craftsmanship noun

ADJ. exquisite, fine, meticulous, quality, skilled, superb ◊ We admired the superb ~ of the furniture.
PREP. with ~ ◊ bowls made with exquisite ~
PHRASES standard of ~ ◊ a very high standard of ~

cramp noun

ADJ. agonizing, bad, painful, severe | sudden ◊ She had a sudden painful ~ in her left leg. | leg, muscle | abdominal ~s, menstrual ~s, stomach ~s
... OF CRAMP attack (BrE) ◊ I was suddenly seized by an attack of ~.
VERB + CRAMP get, have, suffer | ease, relieve | prevent
PREP. ~ in ◊ I was beginning to get ~ in my leg. (BrE) ◊ I was beginning to get a ~ in my leg. (AmE)

crash noun

1 sudden loud noise

ADJ. almighty, deafening, great, huge, loud, resounding, thunderous | sickening, terrible ◊ There was a sickening ~ as her head hit the ground.
VERB + CRASH hear | make ◊ The bike hit the street and made a loud ~.
CRASH + VERB come from ◊ A loud ~ came from the kitchen.
PREP. with a ~ ◊ The plates fell to the floor with an almighty ~. | ~ of ◊ a distant ~ of thunder ◊ the ~ of the waves

2 accident involving a car, plane, etc.

ADJ. horrific, major, serious (esp. BrE) ◊ a major air ~ | fatal | head-on | high-speed | airplane (AmE), automobile (AmE), bus, car, coach (BrE), helicopter, plane, train | air, highway (in the US), motorway (in the UK), rail, road | alcohol-related | spectacular ◊ He had survived a spectacular ~ in a truck race. | fiery (AmE) ◊ a fiery ~ which killed the pilot
VERB + CRASH cause | have ◊ In thirty years of driving she had never had a ~. | survive ◊ He had survived a plane ~. | avoid, prevent ◊ She swerved to avoid a ~.
CRASH + VERB happen, occur | involve sth ◊ a ~ involving two cars and a bus | kill sb | claim sth ◊ The ~ claimed three lives.
CRASH + NOUN victim | site | landing | barrier (BrE)
PREP. in a/the ~ ◊ He was killed in a train ~.

3 business failure

ADJ. financial | bank, dotcom, property (BrE), stock-market ◊ the stock-market ~ of 1987
PREP. ~ in ◊ a ~ in share prices

crate noun

ADJ. metal, plastic, wooden | beer, milk, orange, etc. | packing, shipping ◊ Their possessions had all been packed into shipping ~s.
... OF CRATES pile, stack
VERB + CRATE pile, stack ◊ They stacked the ~s in the corner of the yard. | pack sth in, pack sth into ◊ They packed the books into the ~s. | pack, unpack ◊ They packed the ~s with books. | load, unload | open
CRATE + VERB contain sth
PREP. ~ of ◊ a ~ of oranges

crater noun

ADJ. deep, gaping, huge, large ◊ The blast blew a gaping ~ in the road. | shallow, small | bomb, shell | meteor | impact | volcanic | lunar | smoking
VERB + CRATER create, form, leave, make
CRATER + NOUN floor, rim | lake
PREP. in a/the ~

PHRASES the edge of a ~, the lip of a ~, the side of a ~ ◊ We peered over the lip of the ~ into the volcano.

craving noun

ADJ. desperate (esp. BrE), intense, strong | food ~s | hunger ~s | carb ~s (esp. AmE), carbohydrate ~s, chocolate, sugar ~s, sweet ~s
VERB + CRAVING develop, feel, get, have ◊ He had a ~ to see the world. | satisfy ◊ She skipped meals to satisfy her ~ for chocolate. | control, curb, reduce
PREP. ~ for ◊ a desperate ~ for affection

crawl noun

1 very slow speed

ADJ. slow
PREP. at a ~ ◊ The traffic was moving at a slow ~.
VERB + CRAWL be down to ◊ Westbound traffic was down to a ~. | slow down to, slow to

2 swimming stroke

→ Note at STROKE

crawl verb

ADV. quickly, slowly | about (esp. BrE), along, around, away, back, forward, round (esp. BrE), through ◊ We spent an hour ~ing around on our hands and knees looking for the key.
VERB + CRAWL manage to ◊ As night fell, we managed to ~ back to our lines. | start to ◊ Has the baby started to ~ yet?
PREP. across, along, into, off, out of, over, under, up ◊ There's an insect ~ing up your leg!
PHRASES ~ on (your) hands and knees

crayon noun

ADJ. coloured/colored | wax
... OF CRAYONS box
VERB + CRAYON colour/color sth (in) with, draw (sth) with, use ◊ She used ~s to draw the picture.
CRAYON + NOUN drawing
PREP. in ~ ◊ The notice was written in ~.

craze noun

ADJ. current, latest, new | passing ◊ Is this interest in health foods just a passing ~? | dance, diet, fashion, fitness, etc.
VERB + CRAZE start ◊ The singer started a ~ for piercings.
CRAZE + VERB sweep sth, sweep through sth ◊ Doctors warned of the latest drug ~ to sweep America. | hit sth ◊ It's the latest ~ to hit San Francisco.
PREP. ~ among ◊ the latest ~ among children | ~ for ◊ the ~ for sports clothing

crazy adj.

1 (esp. AmE) mad/wild

VERBS be, seem, sound | go ◊ I'd go ~ if I lived here. | drive sb ◊ The group's performance always drives the audience ~.
ADV. really | absolutely, completely, totally | a little, slightly, etc. | half, pretty, quite
PREP. with ◊ We were ~ with excitement.

2 very angry

VERBS be | go | drive sb ◊ The kids would answer back, and that drove her ~.
ADV. absolutely, completely
PREP. at ◊ He went ~ at me for letting the dog out.

creak noun

ADJ. loud | slight
VERB + CREAK give ◊ The gate gave a loud ~ as he pushed it open. | hear
PREP. with a ~ ◊ The gate swung open with a ~. | ~ of
PHRASES the ~ of a floorboard, door, etc.
→ Note at SOUND

creak verb

ADV. **loudly** | **slightly** | **slowly**
PREP. **under** ◇ *The chair ~ed under his weight.*
PHRASES **~ and groan** ◇ *The ice ~ed and groaned underfoot.* | **~ open** ◇ *The door ~ed open an inch.*

cream noun

1 fatty part of milk

ADJ. **clotted, thick, whipped** | **double** (*BrE*), **heavy** (*AmE*) | **single** (*BrE*) | **fresh** | **sour, soured** | **sweet** (*AmE*) | **pouring** (*BrE*), **whipping**
... OF CREAM **dollop** ◇ *She piled great dollops of ~ onto her apple pie.*
VERB + CREAM **beat, whip, whisk** ◇ *Whisk the ~ and sugar together.* | **fill sth with, serve sth with, top sth with** ◇ *Fill the meringues with whipped ~.*
CREAM + VERB **go off** (*BrE*) ◇ *This cream's gone off!*
CREAM + NOUN **bun** (*BrE*), **cake** (*BrE*), **cheese, puff, sauce** | **tea** (= a meal of tea with scones with jam and cream) (*BrE*)
PHRASES **and ~, with ~** ◇ *We had strawberries and ~ for dessert.*
→ Special page at FOOD

2 substance that you rub into your skin

ADJ. **face, hand** | **day, night** ◇ *She was massaging night ~ into her face and neck.* | **anti-wrinkle, barrier, cleansing, moisturizing, shaving, sun** (*esp. BrE*) | **antibiotic, anti-fungal, antiseptic, steroid** | **topical** ◇ *a topical antibiotic ~* | **over-the-counter** (*esp. AmE*)
VERB + CREAM **apply, massage, put on** ◇ *Put a little antiseptic ~ on the grazed skin.*

creamy adj.

VERBS **be, look, seem, taste** ◇ *Stir the mixture until it looks ~.* ◇ *It tastes deliciously ~.*
ADV. **deliciously, very, wonderfully**
PHRASES **~ white** ◇ *~ white flowers*

crease noun

1 untidy line/fold

ADJ. **deep**
VERB + CREASE **have** ◇ *She had lots of deep ~s at the corners of her eyes.* | **iron out, remove, smooth, smooth out** ◇ *She smoothed the ~s from the tablecloth.*
PREP. **~ in** ◇ *There were a lot of ~s in her skirt.*

2 neat line that is put onto fabric/paper

ADJ. **sharp**
PREP. **~ in** ◇ *He even has ~s in his jeans.*

crease verb

ADV. **a little, slightly, etc.** ◇ *His shirt had ~d a little in the suitcase.*
PHRASES **be ~d, get ~d** ◇ *Her clothes were badly ~d.*

creation noun

ADJ. **employment, job** | **wealth**
VERB + CREATION **advocate, call for, propose, recommend, urge** ◇ *They recommended the ~ of a new government agency to be responsible for the environment.* | **encourage, facilitate, foster, support** | **approve** | **oppose** ◇ *They joined forces to oppose the ~ of wind farms.* | **announce** ◇ *Last month, they announced the ~ of a new company.* | **allow for** ◇ *The new Act allows for the ~ of vocational schools.* | **allow, enable** | **avoid, prevent** | **lead to**

creative adj.

VERBS **be, feel** ◇ *I don't always feel ~.* | **become**
ADV. **extremely, fairly, very, etc.** | **highly** ◇ *a highly ~ artist* | **genuinely, truly** ◇ *genuinely ~ thinking*

creativity noun

ADJ. **great** | **true** | **artistic, cultural, intellectual, musical, scientific** | **human** | **individual, personal**
VERB + CREATIVITY **have** ◇ *I wanted an agency that had real ~.* | **demonstrate, express, show** ◇ *It was his way of expressing his ~.* ◇ *Her approach showed great ~.* | **develop, encourage, enhance, foster, inspire, promote, stimulate** ◇ *A good teacher can encourage artistic ~.* | **inhibit, stifle** ◇ *This rigid approach stifles ~.* | **use** ◇ *Developers were forced to use their ~ and originality to develop new games.*
PREP. **~ in** ◇ *This exercise encourages ~ in the use of language.*
PHRASES **scope for ~** ◇ *My job doesn't give me much scope for ~.*

creature noun

ADJ. **living** ◇ *All living ~s need food.* | **primitive, simple** | **complex** | **intelligent** | **cold-blooded, warm-blooded** | **wild** ◇ *the wild ~s of the forest* | **social** ◇ *Dogs are more social ~s than cats.* | **solitary** | **night, nocturnal** | **aquatic, marine, sea, underwater, water** | **woodland** ◇ *Woodland ~s such as owls are increasingly common in towns.* | **ape-like, bat-like, etc.** | **little, small, tiny** ◇ *These timid little ~s exude a pungent smell when threatened.* | **giant, huge** | **helpless** ◇ *The newborn young are helpless ~s.* | **pathetic, poor** | **dangerous** | **furry** | **winged** | **four-legged** | **beautiful, magnificent** ◇ *It is awesome to see these magnificent ~s in flight.* | **exotic, strange** ◇ *a strange ~ from another planet* | **alien, humanoid** | **magical, mystical, mythical, mythological** | **demonic, evil, foul, monstrous, vile**

crèche (*BrE*) (also creche) noun

VERB + CRÈCHE **establish, set up** | **have, offer, provide, run**
CRÈCHE + NOUN **facilities** | **worker**
PREP. **in a/the ~** ◇ *Younger children can be left in the ~.*

credentials noun

1 qualities/training/experience

ADJ. **excellent, good, impeccable, impressive, solid, strong** | **right** ◇ *She always had the right ~ to make it in the world of country music.* | **academic, educational, teaching** | **diplomatic, military, political, professional, scientific, etc.** | **conservative, democratic, green, socialist, etc.** | **national-security** (*AmE*)
VERB + CREDENTIALS **have** ◇ *Actor Brent Everett has impressive ~.* | **earn** | **establish, prove** ◇ *They had already established their ~ as architects with office buildings.* | **burnish** (*esp. AmE*), **emphasize, strengthen, underline** (*esp. BrE*) | **question** ◇ *Rush questioned his ~ to lead the group.*
PREP. **~ as** ◇ *First, he had to establish his ~ as a researcher.* | **~ for** ◇ *She had excellent ~ for the job.*

2 documents

ADJ. **media, press** (*AmE*) ◇ *Nearly 200 reporters applied for press ~ to cover the case.*
VERB + CREDENTIALS **present** | **check, examine** | **issue** | **get**

credibility noun

ADJ. **great, high** | **real** | **moral, political, professional, scientific** | **personal** | **instant** ◇ *He had instant ~ with customers.* | **street**
VERB + CREDIBILITY **carry, have** ◇ *The certificate has great ~ in the US.* | **be lacking in, lack** | **gain, regain** ◇ *The government is desperate to regain ~ with the public.* | **lose** | **bring, build, establish, give, lend, provide** ◇ *Recommendations from two previous clients helped to establish her ~.* ◇ *Funding from the World Bank lends ~ to the project.* | **maintain, retain** | **restore** | **add, enhance, increase** ◇ *The use of computer models adds ~ to the forecasts.* ◇ *State backing for the plan will enhance its ~.* | **challenge, damage, destroy, diminish, erode, hurt, undermine** | **question**
CREDIBILITY + VERB **suffer** ◇ *Her ~ suffered in her handling of the crisis.*
CREDIBILITY + NOUN **gap** ◇ *Newspapers were talking of a ~ gap between her policies and her achievements.* | **issue, problem**

◇ *Anti-dope campaigners are faced with a ~ problem.* | **crisis** | ◇ *The administration was facing a ~ crisis.*
PREP. **~ among, ~ as** ◇ *her ~ as a witness* | **~ for** ◇ *He's been helping to restore market ~ for a new industrial process.*

credible *adj.*

VERBS **appear, be, seem** | **become** | **make sth** | **find sth** ◇ *I'm not sure that I find her story ~.*
ADV. **highly, very** | **completely** (*esp. BrE*), **fully** (*esp. AmE*), **quite** ◇ *You need imagination to make what you write fully ~.* | **barely** (*esp. BrE*), **hardly, scarcely** (*esp. BrE*) ◇ *It seems hardly ~ that anyone could have walked so far in a day.*

credit *noun*

1 arrangement to pay later; money borrowed
ADJ. **long-term, short-term** | **interest-free** | **foreign** | **bank** | **consumer, export, trade**
VERB + CREDIT **have, use** | **get, obtain** ◇ *If you don't have a regular income you may be unable to get ~.* | **extend, give sb, grant (sb), offer (sb), provide** ◇ *Most stores selling furniture or will offer ~.* | **deny sb, refuse sb** ◇ *The bank refused further ~ to the company.* | **arrange** | **expand** ◇ *We propose to expand ~ in order to create demand.*
CREDIT + NOUN **account** (*BrE*), **agreement, arrangement, facilities, system, terms** (see also **credit card**) | **limit** ◇ *Your ~ limit is now $2 000.* | **period** | **sale, transaction, transfer** (*BrE*) | **rating, score, scoring, standing** ◇ *He has a bad ~ rating* (= seems unlikely to pay the money back). | **history, record** ◇ *people with poor ~ histories* | **file, report** ◇ *The ~ report will show all the consumer debt a person has.* | **risk** ◇ *He's a bad ~ risk.* | **control** | **crunch, squeeze** (*esp. BrE*) | **expansion** ◇ *increases in debt created by ~ expansion* | **bureau** (*AmE*), **industry, institution, market, union** | **analyst** | **note** (*BrE*) ◇ *If damaged items have to be returned, the manufacturer may issue a ~ note.* | **insurance**
PREP. **on ~** ◇ *I bought it on ~.*
PHRASES **a letter of ~** (= a letter from one bank to another that enables you to obtain money)

2 money in a bank account or owed to you
ADJ. **direct** (*BrE*) ◇ *I'm paid by direct ~ into my bank account.*
VERB + CREDIT **have** ◇ *I have three ~s on my bank statement.*
CREDIT + NOUN **balance** ◇ *a ~ balance of €265*
PREP. **in ~** ◇ *My account is in ~.* | **~ of** ◇ *a ~ of £35*

3 praise/approval
ADJ. **great** | **extra** | **full** | **partial** | **due, proper** ◇ *We should give due ~ to all who helped make the event a success.*
VERB + CREDIT **give sb** | **claim, get, receive, take** ◇ *Why should she get all the ~?* | **do sb, reflect** ◇ *Your concern does you ~.* ◇ *The success of the venture reflects great ~ on the organizers.* | **deserve**
PREP. **to sb's ~** ◇ *To her ~, she gave them lunch.* | **~ for** ◇ *At least give him ~ for trying.*
PHRASES **give credit where credit is due** | **to sb's great ~** ◇ *To her great ~, she does not try to avoid the truth.* | **to sb's eternal ~** (*esp. BrE*), **to sb's everlasting ~** (*esp. AmE*)

4 the credits list of people who worked on a film/ movie, etc.
ADJ. **opening** | **closing, end, final** | **film** (*esp. BrE*), **movie** (*esp. AmE*)
VERB + THE CREDITS **watch**
THE CREDITS + VERB **roll** ◇ *We left before the final ~s began to roll.*

5 sb/sth that brings respect to sb/sth else
ADJ. **great**
PREP. **~ to** ◇ *He's a great ~ to the school.*

6 unit of study at a university, college or school
ADJ. **course** ◇ *Participants were given course ~ for their participation in the study.* (*AmE*) | **college** (*AmE*)
VERB + CREDIT **earn** ◇ *He took some advanced courses to earn college ~s.* | **award, grant** | **offer** ◇ *modules offering continuing education ~s* | **transfer** ◇ *Students may have difficulty transferring ~s to other institutions.*
CREDIT + NOUN **hour** (*AmE*) ◇ *Tuition costs are based on the number of ~ hours enrolled.*

credit *verb*

1 put money in the bank
PREP. **with** ◇ *The bank ~ed the oil company with $500 000.*
PHRASES **~ sth to sb's account**

2 with an achievement/quality
PREP. **with** ◇ *I ~ed you with a little more sense.*
PHRASES **be ~ed as sth, be ~ed with sth** ◇ *She is generally ~ed as having written over 50 novels.* | **be ~ed to sb** ◇ *The work has been ~ed to a 16th-century bishop.* | **be generally ~ed with sth, be widely ~ed with sth** ◇ *He is widely ~ed with having started the Middle East peace process.*

3 (*BrE*) believe
VERB + CREDIT **can hardly, can scarcely** ◇ *I could hardly ~ it when she told me she was leaving.* | **be hard to** ◇ *I find what he says rather hard to ~.*

credit card *noun*

ADJ. **valid** ◇ *Your ~ is no longer valid.*
VERB + CREDIT CARD **pay by, use** ◇ *We paid by ~.* | **accept, take** ◇ *Do you accept ~s?* | **issue** | **put sth on** ◇ *I put the bill on my ~.*
CREDIT CARD + VERB **expire** ◇ *My ~ expires at the end of June.*
CREDIT-CARD + NOUN **details, information, number** ◇ *Can you give me your credit-card number?* | **debt** ◇ *The first way to reduce credit-card debt is to pay more than the minimum payment.* | **bill** | **balance** | **statement** | **payment, transaction** | **account** | **loan** | **purchases** | **fraud** | **company, issuer**
PREP. **on your ~** ◇ *He ran up a huge bill on his ~.*

creditor *noun*

ADJ. **foreign** | **private** | **large** | **secured, unsecured**
VERB + CREDITOR **pay, pay off, repay** ◇ *They agreed to repay their ~s over a period of three years.* | **avoid, evade**
CREDITOR + NOUN **country, nation**

credulity *noun*

VERB + CREDULITY **strain, stretch** ◇ *The plot of the novel stretches ~ to the limit.*

creed *noun*

ADJ. **political, religious**
VERB + CREED **adopt, embrace** ◇ *Other countries have adopted this political ~ enthusiastically.* | **reject**

creek *noun* (*AmE*) small stream

ADJ. **tidal** | **little, small**
VERB + CREEK **cross**
CREEK + NOUN **bed, bottom** | **bank**

creep *verb*

ADV. **quietly, silently** | **slowly** | **stealthily** | **carefully, cautiously** | **about** (*esp. BrE*), **around, away, back, forward, in, out, up** ◇ *I could hear someone ~ing around downstairs.* ◇ *He crept up behind me.*
PREP. **along** ◇ *He crept stealthily along the corridor.* | **down** | **into** (*figurative*) ◇ *Suspicion crept into her voice.* | **over** (*figurative*) ◇ *A feeling of dread crept over him.* | **out of** | **up on** ◇ *The cat quietly crept up on the pigeon.* ◇ *Fatigue was ~ing up on her.* (*figurative*)

creepy *adj.* (*informal*)

VERBS **be, feel, look, seem** ◇ *It feels a little ~ in here.* | **get** ◇ *It can get pretty ~ in the cellar at night.*
ADV. **extremely, fairly, very, etc.** | **a little, slightly, etc.** | **downright, just, plain** ◇ *That guy is just ~.* | **totally** (*esp. AmE*) | **genuinely, truly**

crescendo *noun*

ADJ. **deafening**

VERB + CRESCENDO **reach, rise to** ◇ *The music reached a deafening ~.*

crest noun

VERB + CREST **reach** ◇ *We finally reached the ~ of the ridge.*
PREP. **on a/the ~** ◇ *We stood on the ~ of the hill.*
PHRASES **ride the ~ of sth** (*figurative*) ◇ *The group were riding the ~ of popularity* (= *were enjoying great popularity*). ◇ *They are riding the ~ of the wave at the moment.*

crew noun

ADJ. **experienced | inexperienced, novice | emergency, skeleton** ◇ *During the holiday period, there remains only a skeleton ~ of about 20 workers.* | **aircraft** (*esp. BrE*), **airline** (*esp. AmE*), **boat, bomber, helicopter, lifeboat, ship's, submarine, tank, train | air, bridge, cabin, deck, flight, ground, maintenance, support | camera, film, movie** (*esp. AmE*), **news, production, stage, television, TV | ambulance, fire** ◇ *Fire ~s were called to the scene.* | **cleaning, clean-up** (*esp. AmE*), **construction, demolition, maintenance, repair, rescue, road | wrecking** (*AmE*) | **command | gun | pit** (*esp. AmE*) | **one-man, two-man, etc.**
VERB + CREW **join | lead | assemble | employ** (*esp. BrE*), **hire | train**
CREW + NOUN **member**
PREP. **in a/the ~** ◇ *all the men and women in the ~*
PHRASES **cast and ~** ◇ *The cast and ~ of the movie are giving it their all.* | **a member of the ~**

cricket noun

1 sport

ADJ. **county, international, school, village | club, first-class | professional | championship, league, test, World Cup | one-day, four-day, etc. | Sunday | attacking** ◇ *The crowd loves to watch attacking ~.*
... OF CRICKET **game**
VERB + CRICKET **play | watch | follow**
CRICKET + NOUN **game, match | championship, competition | field, ground, pitch | ball, bat | pavilion | captain, manager, team | club | enthusiast, fan, lover | season | tour | scene** ◇ *This game marks his comeback to the international ~ scene.* | **commentator | memorabilia** ◇ *an auction of ~ memorabilia*
→ Special page at SPORTS

2 insect

CRICKET + VERB **chirp, sing** ◇ *The only sound was a ~ chirping.*

crime noun

1 illegal act

ADJ. **appalling** (*esp. BrE*), **awful, bloody, brutal, despicable, dreadful** (*esp. BrE*), **grave, great, heinous, horrible, horrific, serious, terrible, unspeakable, vicious** ◇ *one of the most horrific ~s of recent times* | **big, major** ◇ *the biggest ~ since the Great Train Robbery* | **lesser, minor, petty** ◇ *He was charged with the lesser ~ of possession.* | **real** ◇ *She claimed that the real ~ is that burglars and muggers usually get a light sentence.* | **non-violent, violent | perfect** ◇ *He boasted of having carried out the perfect ~.* | **notorious** ◇ *one of the most notorious ~s in history* | **capital** ◇ *After the reforms the only capital ~s were treason and murder.* | **alleged** ◇ *She never faced trial for her many alleged ~s.* | **unsolved | copycat** ◇ *the danger of copycat ~s in the wake of the shootings* | **motiveless** ◇ *an apparently motiveless ~* | **victimless** ◇ *Insider dealing has been called a victimless ~.* | **white-collar | drug, drug-related, gun | sex, sexual | hate** ◇ *a hate ~ against a young gay man* | **war | political | terrorist | federal** (*AmE*)
VERB + CRIME **carry out, commit, do, perpetrate** (*formal*) | **report** ◇ *Many ~s are never reported to the police.* | **investigate | solve** ◇ *a man who solves ~s using old-fashioned detective work* | **prosecute** (*AmE*) ◇ *a system of justice to prosecute ~s of terrorism* | **punish** ◇ *Hate ~s are*

not punished severely enough in my opinion. | **witness | confess** ◇ *He confessed his ~ to his sister.*
CRIME + VERB **involve sth** ◇ *~s involving firearms* | **happen, occur** ◇ *The ~ occurred in broad daylight.* | **be punishable by sth** ◇ *~s punishable by death*
CRIME + NOUN **scene | victim | suspect**
PREP. **~ against** ◇ *~s against humanity*
PHRASES **a ~ of passion, a ~ of violence | the scene of the ~** ◇ *No weapon was found at the scene of the ~.* | **the punishment fits the ~** ◇ *The punishment should fit the ~.*

NOTE

Crimes

be guilty of…, commit… ◇ *Two key witnesses at her trial committed perjury.*
accuse sb of…, charge sb with… ◇ *He has been accused of her murder.*
convict sb of…, find sb guilty of… ◇ *She was found guilty of high treason.*
acquit sb of… ◇ *The engineer responsible for the collapse of the bridge was acquitted of manslaughter.*
admit…, confess to…, deny… ◇ *She admitted 33 assault charges.* | *All three men have denied assault.*
plead guilty/not guilty to… ◇ *He pleaded guilty to a charge of illegal possession of explosives.*
investigate (sb for)… ◇ *She is being investigated for suspected bribery.*
be suspected for/of… ◇ *He was the least likely to be suspected of her murder.*
be/come under investigation for… ◇ *She was the second minister to come under investigation for corruption.*
be wanted for…, be wanted on charges of… ◇ *He was wanted on charges of espionage.*
solve a case/crime/murder/robbery/theft ◇ *The police and the public must work together to solve the murder.*
arrest sb for… ◇ *Jean was arrested for arson.*
be tried for…, stand trial for… ◇ *to stand trial for extortion*
… case, … trial ◇ *The nurse's murder trial continues.*
… charge ◇ *The police agreed to drop the conspiracy charges against him.*
a charge of…, a count of… ◇ *The jury convicted her on two counts of theft.*

2 illegal activity in general

ADJ. **serious | petty | non-violent, violent | recorded | unrecorded | growing, mounting, rising | rampant** ◇ *a time of great poverty and rampant ~* | **white-collar** ◇ *Identity theft is the fastest growing white-collar ~ in the country.* | **corporate | organized | juvenile, youth | international, local | rural, urban | car, property, street | drug, drug-related, gun, knife** ◇ *Gun ~ is just part of an increasingly lawless society.* | **computer** ◇ *attempts to prevent hacking and computer ~*
VERB + CRIME **carry out, commit, perpetrate** (*formal*) | **combat, fight, tackle | beat, crack** (*informal*) ◇ *Police forces will exchange ideas on cracking ~.* | **deter, prevent, stop | control, cut, reduce** ◇ *How can we reduce knife ~ in our cities?* | **detect, investigate** ◇ *The public have a crucial role to play in detecting ~.* | **solve | punish | cause | be driven to, turn to** ◇ *He says that bored youngsters turn to ~.*
CRIME + VERB **double, increase, rise**
CRIME + NOUN **figures, level, rate, statistics | control, prevention | problem, wave** ◇ *the country's ~ problem* | **spree | squad** ◇ *a senior detective with the serious ~ squad* | **investigation | lab** (*AmE, informal*) ◇ *The computers were sent to a ~ lab for analysis.* | **family** (*AmE*), **group, ring, syndicate** ◇ *leading members of an organized ~ syndicate* | **boss, lord** ◇ *one of New York's biggest ~ lords* | **drama, fiction, film** (*esp. BrE*), **movie** (*esp. AmE*), **novel, series, show** (*esp. AmE*), **story, thriller** ◇ *the latest TV ~ series* | **reporter, writer** ◇ *the newspaper's ~ reporter* ◇ *a new short story by the popular ~ writer*

PHRASES **a crackdown on ~** ◊ *a crackdown on drug-related ~* | **~ and disorder** | **~ and punishment** | **fear of ~** ◊ *Fear of ~ imprisons many elderly people in their homes.* | **an increase in ~** | **a life of ~** ◊ *Unemployed young people were likely to be tempted into a life of ~.* | **sb's partner in ~** | **a victim of ~** ◊ *Victims of ~ may be able to obtain compensation.*

criminal *noun*

ADJ. **dangerous, violent** | **real, serious** | **habitual, hardened** | **career, professional** | **master** | **petty, street** | **convicted** | **known, suspected, wanted** ◊ *He has been associating with known ~s.* | **potential** | **notorious** | **common** ◊ *She was treated like a common ~.* | **corporate, white-collar** | **war** ◊ *He was tried as a war ~.*

VERB + CRIMINAL **catch** ◊ *I told him to pass the information to the police so they could catch the ~s.* | **convict, prosecute**

crimson *adj., noun*

1 red

ADJ. **dark, deep, rich** ◊ *a beautiful deep ~*
→ Special page at COLOUR

2 red in the face

VERBS **be** | **blush, flush, go, turn** ◊ *He flushed ~ and began to shout angrily at Frank.*
ADJ. **bright, deep** ◊ *He turned bright ~.*
PREP. **with** ◊ *She was ~ with rage.*

cripple *verb*

1 injure

ADV. **for life, permanently** ◊ *As a child she contracted polio and was ~d for life.* | **emotionally**
PHRASES **be ~d with** ◊ *He's eighty and ~d with arthritis.* | **leave sb ~d** ◊ *The disease left him ~d.*

2 damage

ADV. **severely** ◊ *A strike would severely ~ the airline.* | **financially** ◊ *The industry has been financially ~d by these policies.*

crisis *noun*

ADJ. **acute, grave, major, serious, severe, terrible, worst** ◊ *the worst economic ~ for fifty years* | **deepening, growing, mounting, ongoing, unfolding** (*esp. AmE*) | **impending, looming, potential** ◊ *The plan could save the country from a looming energy ~.* | **current, present** | **global, inter-national, national** | **constitutional, ecological, economic, environmental, financial, fiscal, humanitarian, nuclear, political, social** | **budget, cash, currency, debt, liquidity** ◊ *the Third-World debt ~* | **energy, health, hostage, housing, immigration, oil, refugee** | **family, personal** | **moral, spiritual** | **identity** | **mid-life**
VERB + CRISIS **be faced with, be hit by, experience, face, go through, have** (*informal*)**, suffer, undergo** ◊ *With competition from cheap imports, the industry is facing a serious ~.* | *He's having a midlife ~.* | **cause, create, lead to, precipitate, provoke, spark off, trigger** | **address, alle-viate, deal with, defuse, ease, handle, manage, over-come, resolve, respond to, solve, tackle** ◊ *Union leaders are taking immediate steps to defuse the ~.* ◊ *attempts to ease the town's housing ~* | **survive, weather** | **avert, avoid, prevent** | **end** | **aggravate, exacerbate**
CRISIS + VERB **arise, erupt, hit, occur** ◊ *We are just waiting for the next ~ to arise.* | **deepen, unfold, worsen** | **loom** | **be over** ◊ *As soon as the ~ was over, she relaxed.*
CRISIS + NOUN **point** ◊ *The team's dismal season has reached ~ point.* | **situation** | **intervention, management** ◊ *an expert in ~ management*
PREP. **during a/the ~** ◊ *Three people died during the hostage ~.* | **in (a/the) ~** ◊ *The government is in ~.* ◊ *She's no good in a ~.* | **~ in** ◊ *the growing ~ in education* | **~ over** ◊ *a ~ over pensions*
PHRASES **a ~ of confidence** ◊ *The company is suffering a severe ~ of confidence.* | **a ~ of faith** | **a ~ of conscience** | **at/in moments of ~, at/in times of ~** ◊ *In times of ~ it's good to have someone you can rely on for advice.*

crisp *noun* (*BrE*) (usually **crisps**) → See also CHIP

ADJ. **potato** | **plain** | **cheese and onion, prawn cocktail, ready salted, salt and vinegar, smoky bacon, etc.**
... OF CRISPS **bag, packet** ◊ *a packet of smoky bacon ~s*
VERB + CRISP **eat**
CRISP + NOUN **bag, packet**
→ Special page at FOOD

criterion *noun*

ADJ. **sole** | **basic, main, primary** (*esp. AmE*) | **strict, stringent** | **objective** | **admission, eligibility, inclusion, selection**
... OF CRITERIA **range, set**
VERB + CRITERION **fit, fulfil/fulfill, meet, satisfy** ◊ *She failed to meet the stringent selection criteria.* | **define, develop, establish, lay down** (*BrE*)**, lay out** (*AmE*)**, set** | **adopt, apply, use** ◊ *The other groups agreed to adopt our criteria.*
PREP. **according to a/the ~** ◊ *Team members will be selected according to strict criteria.* | **by a/the ~** ◊ *By this ~, very few people are suitable.* | **~ for** ◊ *The report lays down criteria for disciplining staff.*

critic *noun*

1 person who says what is bad/wrong with sth

ADJ. **bitter, fierce, harsh, hostile, severe, tough, trenchant** (*esp. BrE*) ◊ *She is one of her husband's severest ~s.* | **worst** ◊ *I am my own worst ~.* | **outspoken, vocal, vociferous** | **persistent** | **chief, great, leading, major, prominent** ◊ *He is now a major ~ of the nuclear industry.*
VERB + CRITIC **answer, respond to** | **defend yourself against** | **prove wrong, silence** ◊ *She is looking for a chance to prove her ~s wrong.*
CRITIC + VERB **accuse sb** ◊ *Critics accused the government of giving in to pressure from the tobacco companies.* | **argue sth, believe sth, charge sth, claim sth, contend sth, fear sth, point sth out, say sth, suggest sth** ◊ *Critics point out that poverty still exists.* | **complain, question** | **be right, be wrong**
PREP. **~ of** ◊ *an outspoken ~ of government policy*

2 person who gives opinions about books, films/ movies, etc.

ADJ. **good, great, incisive** (*esp. AmE*) | **distinguished, influential, leading** | **art, cultural, drama, film, literary, media, movie, music, restaurant, social, television, theatre/theater, etc.**
CRITIC + VERB **hail sth, praise sth, rave** ◊ *The movie was hailed by ~s as a triumphant piece of realism.* | **attack sth, pan sth, slate sth** (*BrE*) ◊ *The play was panned by ~s.* | **call, describe sth** ◊ *Some ~s are calling him 'the new De Niro'.* ◊ *Critics described the paintings as worthless.*
→ Note at JOB

critical *adj.*

1 disapproving

VERBS **be** | **become** | **remain**
ADV. **extremely, fairly, very, etc.** | **bitterly** (*esp. BrE*)**, deeply, fiercely** (*esp. BrE*)**, harshly, highly, severely, sharply, strongly** | **increasingly** | **overly** ◊ *I think you're being overly ~.* | **equally** | **a little, slightly, etc.** | **mildly** | **openly** ◊ *She became openly ~ of party policy.*
PREP. **of** ◊ *The report was highly ~ of the company's poor safety record.*

2 important

VERBS **be** | **become**
ADV. **really** | **absolutely** | **increasingly**
PREP. **for** ◊ *Maintaining control of the the budget is absolutely ~ for success.* | **to** ◊ *This reorganization is ~ to the long-term future of the company.*

criticism *noun*

1 expressing disapproval of sb/sth

ADJ. **bitter, fierce, harsh, heavy, intense, serious, severe,**

criticize

186

sharp, strident, strong, trenchant | telling ◇ *A more telling ~ is that he reduces ethics to interpersonal relationships.* | adverse (*esp. BrE*), damaging (*BrE*), damning (*esp. BrE*), hostile (*esp. BrE*), negative, scathing | fair, just, justifiable, legitimate, valid ◇ *She made a number of valid ~s.* | unfair | constructive, helpful (*esp. AmE*) ◇ *Teachers need honest feedback and constructive ~.* | considerable, extensive, widespread | constant | common | basic, fundamental | main, major, substantial | minor | general | direct, explicit, outspoken | implicit, implied | fresh ◇ *Two successive defeats have brought fresh ~.* | growing, increasing, mounting | media, press | public
... OF CRITICISM **barrage** ◇ *The star faced a barrage of ~ for his actions.*
VERB + CRITICISM **address, direct, express, level, make, voice** ◇ *The report levels ~ at senior managers.* | **attract, be open to, be singled out for, come in for, come under, deserve, draw, face, get, invite, meet with, prompt, provoke, raise** (*esp. AmE*), **receive, spark** ◇ *The government came under fierce ~ for its policies.* ◇ *The proposal is open to several important ~s.* ◇ *Scientists have raised strong ~s of creationist ideas.* | **avoid, deflect, escape, forestall** ◇ *She sought to deflect ~ by blaming her family.* | **accept, handle, meet, reply to, respond to, take, welcome** ◇ *He finds it hard to take ~.* | **answer, counter, dismiss, reject** ◇ *She countered my ~s by saying we had no choice in the matter.* | **silence** | **imply** ◇ *None of what has been said should be taken to imply ~.* | **offer** ◇ *to offer ~ and receive it*
CRITICISM + VERB **come from sb** ◇ *The harshest ~ came from right-wingers.* | **centre/center on sth** ◇ *Criticism centred/centered on the lack of information provided.*
PREP. **~ about** ◇ *The main ~ about the information provided is that it arrives too late.* | **~ against** ◇ *~s against the Church* | **~ for** ◇ *They received ~ for continuing to supply the faulty goods.* | **~ from** ◇ *We are bound to face ~ from both sides.* | **~ of** ◇ *There has been serious ~ of the teaching methods used in the school.* | **~ over** ◇ *We came in for some sharp ~ over this decision.*

2 of a play, book, film/movie, etc.

ADJ. **practical, textual** | **academic, art, biblical, cultural, film, historical, literary, music, scientific, social** | **contemporary** | **feminist, Marxist, structuralist**, etc.

criticize (*BrE also* **-ise**) *verb*

ADV. **bitterly, fiercely** (*esp. BrE*), **harshly, heavily, roundly, severely, sharply, strongly, unfairly** | **directly, openly, publicly** ◇ *She has openly ~d the government.* | **implicitly** | **justifiably, rightly** ◇ *Their record on human rights has been justifiably ~d.* | **constantly, frequently, repeatedly**
PREP. **for** ◇ *She ~d the system for being secretive.*
PHRASES **be widely ~d (as sth)** ◇ *The law was widely ~d as racist.* | **~ sb/sth on the grounds that** ◇ *The movie was ~d on the grounds that it glorified violence.*

critique *noun*

ADJ. **detailed, effective, incisive** (*esp. AmE*), **penetrating, powerful, radical, searching, sharp, strong** (*esp. AmE*), **telling, thorough, trenchant** | **devastating, scathing** | **implicit** | **feminist, moral, political, postmodern, social** ◇ *a radical feminist ~ of gender*
VERB + CRITIQUE **give, make, offer, present, provide** | **develop**
PREP. **~ of** ◇ *The book provides a thorough ~ of current theories.*

crop *noun*

1 plants grown for food

ADJ. **agricultural** | **cash, commercial, export** ◇ *Most farmers now produce cash ~s such as coffee and tobacco for the export market.* | **fodder** (*BrE*), **food, forage** ◇ *Fodder ~s are used to feed livestock.* | **subsistence** | **staple** ◇ *Rice is a staple ~ for more than half of the world's population.* | **traditional** | **cover** (= grown to protect and improve the soil) | **spring,**

winter | growing, standing ◇ *Rivers burst their banks and flooded standing ~s.* | arable (*BrE*), cereal, fruit, grain, root, seed, vegetable | organic | biotech, genetically engineered, genetically modified (abbreviated to *GM*)
VERB + CROP **cultivate, grow, produce, raise** ◇ *Most of the farmers grow arable ~s.* | **plant, sow** | **bring in, harvest, reap** | **damage, destroy** ◇ *Summer flash floods destroyed the ~s.* | **rotate** | **spray** ◇ *Crops are sprayed with highly toxic chemicals to prevent insect damage.* | **protect** | **sell**
CROP + VERB **grow** | **fail** ◇ *Isolated communities were extremely vulnerable if ~s failed.*
CROP + NOUN **rotation** ◇ *Crop rotation helps prevent soil erosion.* | **damage, failure, loss** | **production, yield** ◇ *to boost ~ yields* | **protection** | **dusting** | **plant**
PREP. **~ of** ◇ *a ~ of carrots*

2 total amount of grain, fruit, etc. grown

ADJ. **abundant, bumper, excellent, good, heavy, record** | **poor** | **early** ◇ *Bring strawberry plants indoors for an early ~.* | **potato, rice, wheat**, etc.
VERB + CROP **get, harvest, have, reap** ◇ *a record ~ was harvested* ◇ *We had a very good ~ of apples last year.* | **bear, produce, yield** ◇ *It takes three to five years for a new plantation to bear a ~.*
PREP. **~ of**

crop *verb*

ADV. **closely** ◇ *His hair was closely cropped.*
PHRASES **~ sth short** ◇ *His hair had been cropped short and he looked different.*

cross *noun*

1 mark made by drawing one line across another

VERB + CROSS **draw, put** ◇ *I've put a ~ on the map to show where the hotel is.*

2 Christian symbol

ADJ. **gold, silver, stone, wooden** ◇ *She wore a gold ~ on a chain around her neck.* ◇ *The grave was marked with a stone ~.* | **market** (*esp. in the UK*) | **Celtic**
VERB + CROSS **wear**
PREP. **on the ~** ◇ *a painting of Christ on the ~*
PHRASES **(make) the sign of the ~** ◇ *The priest blessed her, and made the sign of the ~ over her.*

3 in football/soccer or hockey

ADJ. **deep, low, perfect**
PREP. **~ by, ~ from** ◇ *a deep ~ from Reed*

cross *verb*

ADV. **quickly, slowly** | **safely, successfully** ◇ *Children must be taught to ~ the road safely.* | **back, over** ◇ *Let's ~ over now while the road is clear.*
VERB + CROSS **try to** ◇ *They were arrested trying to ~ the border.*
PREP. **from, into** ◇ *They ~ed from the States into Canada.* | **over** ◇ *We ~ed over the river into Sweden.*

cross *adj.* (*esp. BrE*)

VERBS **be, feel, look, seem, sound** | **become, get** ◇ *I'm going to get very ~ before long.* | **make sb** ◇ *It really makes me ~ to see people dropping litter in the street.*
ADV. **extremely, fairly, very**, etc. | **a little, slightly**, etc.
PREP. **about** ◇ *Are you still ~ about me forgetting the flowers?* | **at** ◇ *She was very ~ at the way she'd been treated.* | **for** | **with** ◇ *She was very ~ with him for being late.*

cross-examination *noun*

VERB + CROSS-EXAMINATION **be subject to, face** ◇ *Evidence is given on oath and witnesses are subject to ~.* | **stand up to** (*BrE*), **withstand** ◇ *His alibi would not have withstood ~.*
PREP. **during ~, in ~** ◇ *He was found to have lied twice in ~.* | **on** (*esp. AmE*) ◇ *On ~, she sounded confused.* | **under ~** ◇ *The defendant broke down under ~.*

crossing *noun*

1 trip across a stretch of water

ADJ. **rough** | **smooth** | **ferry** (*esp. BrE*) ◇ *There are six ferry ~s*

a day. | **ocean, river, sea** (*esp. BrE*) | **Atlantic, Channel, transatlantic, etc.**
VERB + CROSSING **attempt, complete, make** ◊ *You can only make the ~ in good weather.*
PREP. **during a/the ~** ◊ *We discussed our plans during the ~.* | **~ from, ~ to** ◊ *a rough ~ from Bali to Flores*

2 place where you can cross sth

ADJ. **border** | **grade** (*AmE*), **level** (*BrE*) (= over a railway/railroad) | **railroad** (*AmE*), **railway** (*BrE*) | **road, street** | **pedestrian, pelican, zebra** (*all BrE*) (= where people can cross the road) (**crosswalk** in *AmE*)
CROSSING + NOUN **point** ◊ *the main ~ point on the border*
PREP. **at a/the ~** ◊ *They were stopped and searched at the border ~.* ◊ *We were caught at the grade ~.* (*AmE*) | **on a/the ~** ◊ *A passenger train smashed into a lorry on a level ~.* (*BrE*)

crossroads *noun*

1 place where two roads cross

VERB + CROSSROADS **come to**
PREP. **at the ~** ◊ *Turn right at the next ~.*

2 important point in your life, career, etc.

ADJ. **critical** (*esp. AmE*), **important** | **career**
VERB + CROSSROADS **face** (*esp. AmE*), **stand at** | **reach**
PREP. **at a/the ~** ◊ *We are standing at an important ~ in the history of our species.* | **~ in** ◊ *He had reached a ~ in his career.* | **~ of** ◊ *I knew I was at the ~ of my career.*

cross section *noun*

ADJ. **broad, fair, good, large, representative, wide**
VERB + CROSS SECTION **be drawn from** ◊ *The contestants are drawn from a ~ of society.* | **represent**
PREP. **~ of** ◊ *We interviewed a wide ~ of people.*

crossword (*also crossword puzzle*) *noun*

ADJ. **cryptic** (*BrE*), **quick**
VERB + CROSSWORD **do, solve**
CROSSWORD + NOUN **clue** (*esp. BrE*)

crouch *verb*

ADV. **low** ◊ *The hare ~es low on the ground.* | **down** ◊ *We ~ed down to avoid being seen.*
PREP. **behind** ◊ *She was ~ing behind the sofa.* | **over** ◊ *They ~ed over the dead animal.*

crow *noun*

ADJ. **black** | **carrion**
... OF CROWS **flock**
CROW + VERB **fly** | **perch** ◊ *The black ~ perched on the telephone pole.* | **caw**

crow *verb*

ADV. **triumphantly, with delight** ◊ *She gave the purse to Ruby, who ~ed with delight.*
PREP. **about, over** ◊ *The company hasn't much to ~ about, with sales down compared with last year.*

crowd *noun*

1 large number of people in one place

ADJ. **big, bumper** (*BrE*), **capacity, enormous, good, great, huge, large, massive, packed, record, sell-out, vast** ◊ *The show played to capacity ~s.* | **small** | **gathering, growing** | **assembled** ◊ *The president read a declaration to a vast assembled ~.* | **entire, whole** | **jostling, milling, surging** ◊ *We pushed our way through the milling ~s of guests.* | **noisy** | **admiring, adoring, appreciative, cheering, enthusiastic, excited, expectant** | **angry, hostile, partisan** | **rush-hour** (*esp. BrE*) | **diverse, motley** (*esp. BrE*) ◊ *the usual motley ~ of tourists, hawkers and pigeons* | **football, theatre/theater** | **home, hometown** (= at a sports game) (*AmE*)
VERB + CROWD **attract, bring, bring in, draw, gather, get, pull, pull in** ◊ *Boxing is a sport that always attracts large ~s.* | **break up, disperse** ◊ *Police were called to disperse the ~.* | **control** | **address, entertain, play to, work** | **join, mingle with** | **avoid** ◊ *If you want to avoid the ~s, get there early.* |

face | **scan, search, watch** | **get lost in** ◊ *She was afraid she might get lost in the ~.*
CROWD + VERB **assemble, collect, gather** ◊ *An expectant ~ gathered outside his house.* | **grow, swell** ◊ *The ~ grew to over 15 000.* | **rush** ◊ *The ~ rushed forward.* | **flock, mill, throng sth, throng around sb/sth** ◊ *Crowds have been flocking to the beaches in this hot weather.* ◊ *~s thronging the streets of Rio* ◊ *A ~ thronged around the wounded man.* | **disperse, melt away, thin out** ◊ *After the ambulance drove off, the ~ dispersed.* | **part** | **chant, cheer, erupt, roar, scream** | **boo, hiss, jeer** | **line the street** ◊ *Crowds lined the streets of the city as the president's car approached.*
CROWD + NOUN **control** | **favourite/favorite** ◊ *She didn't win but she was clearly the ~ favourite/favorite.* | **noise** | **scene**
PREP. **among a/the ~** ◊ *A bewildered child was wandering among the ~.* | **in a/the ~** ◊ *I saw some familiar faces in the ~.* | **through a/the ~** ◊ *She fought her way through the ~.* | **~ of** ◊ *a big ~ of football supporters*
PHRASES **the back of a ~, the front of a ~, the middle of a ~**

2 the crowd ordinary people

VERB + THE CROWD **be one of, follow** ◊ *She's happy to follow the ~.* | **stand out from** ◊ *We all like to think we stand out from the ~* (= are different from other people).
PHRASES **a face in the ~** ◊ *To her I'm just another face in the ~.*

crowded *adj.*

VERBS **be** | **become, get**
ADV. **extremely, fairly, very, etc.** ◊ *The station was very ~.* | **densely** ◊ *They live in densely ~ conditions.* | **increasingly** | **a little, slightly, etc.**
PREP. **with** ◊ *The store was ~ with shoppers.*

crown *noun*

1 that a king/queen wears

ADJ. **gold**
VERB + CROWN **wear** | **place, put on** ◊ *The ~ was placed upon the new monarch's head.*

2 the crown position/power of a king/queen

ADJ. **imperial, royal**
VERB + THE CROWN **offer sb** ◊ *In 1688 the ~ was offered to William and Mary.* | **accept** | **refuse**
THE CROWN + VERB **pass** ◊ *In 1553 the ~ passed from Edward VI to Mary.*

3 (usually the Crown) the state as represented by a king/queen

VERB + CROWN **serve**
CROWN + NOUN **Crown Court** (in England and Wales) | **jewels** | **colony, land** ◊ *a piece of Crown land*

4 honour of being the best in a sports competition

ADJ. **heavyweight, Olympic** (*esp. BrE*), **world, etc.**
VERB + CROWN **capture, claim, take, win** | **lose** ◊ *He lost his world ~ to the Korean champion.* | **fight for** | **defend, regain, retain**

crucial *adj.*

VERBS **be, prove, seem** | **become** | **remain** | **consider sth, deem sth, regard sth as, see sth as**
ADV. **really, very** | **absolutely** ◊ *It's absolutely ~ that we get this right.* | **fairly** (*esp. BrE*), **pretty, quite** | **clearly, obviously**
PREP. **for** ◊ *The talks are ~ for the success of the plan.* | **to** ◊ *Secrecy is ~ to this police operation.*

cruel *adj.*

VERBS **be, seem, sound** | **become**
ADV. **extremely, fairly, very, etc.** ◊ *an extremely ~ regime* | **incredibly, unspeakably** | **a little, slightly, etc.** | **deliberately** | **unnecessarily**
PREP. **to** ◊ *I can't stand people who are ~ to animals.*

cruelty noun

ADJ. **extreme, great** ◇ *an act of extreme* ~ | **deliberate** (*esp. BrE*) | **casual** | **mental** | **animal, child** (*esp. BrE*) ◇ *Cases of child ~ occur more often than they are observed.* | **human** ◇ *the depths of human ~*
VERB + CRUELTY **inflict, show (sb)** ◇ *How can you inflict such ~ on a child?* ◇ *Her stepmother showed her nothing but ~.* | **suffer** ◇ *The children suffered mental ~ and neglect.* | **see** ◇ *She was shocked to see such ~.*
PREP. **~ to, ~ towards/toward** ◇ *~ to animals*

cruise noun

ADJ. **luxury, pleasure** ◇ *a pleasure ~ around the bay* | **leisurely** | **Caribbean, Mediterranean, world, etc.** | **boat, river** | **honeymoon**
VERB + CRUISE **go on, take** ◇ *She used all her savings to go on a world ~.*
CRUISE + NOUN **boat, liner, ship** | **company, line, operator** | **holiday** (*BrE*), **vacation** (*AmE*)
PREP. **on a/the ~** ◇ *They met on a ~.* | **~ along** ◇ *a ~ along the coast* | **~ around, ~ round** (*esp. BrE*)

cruiser noun

ADJ. **battle, heavy, light, merchant** (*BrE*) | **cabin, motor** (*BrE*), **pleasure**
PREP. **on a/the ~** ◇ *He served on a battle ~.*

crumb noun

ADJ. **biscuit** (*esp. BrE*), **bread** (usually ***breadcrumbs***), **cake, cookie** (*AmE*), **cracker, food**
VERB + CRUMB **brush, sweep, wipe** ◇ *She brushed the cake ~s off the table.* ◇ *I swept away the ~s.* | **leave** ◇ *He didn't even leave any ~s on his plate.* | **drop, scatter** ◇ *She bit into the roll, scattering ~s.*
PREP. **~ of** ◇ *a few ~s of bread*

crunch verb

ADV. **loudly** | **underfoot** ◇ *Snow ~ed underfoot.*
PREP. **on** ◇ *She was ~ing loudly on an apple.*

crusade noun

ADJ. **great** | **holy, moral, personal**
VERB + CRUSADE **embark on, launch, mount, start** ◇ *The charity tonight launched its great ~ against homelessness.* | **be engaged in, join, wage** ◇ *She seems to be waging a personal ~ to stop this building work.* | **lead**
PREP. **on a ~** ◇ *He is on a ~ to take the church to the people.* | **~ against** ◇ *The book urges parents to join a ~ against crime.* | **~ for** ◇ *For 23 years he led a ~ for peace.*

crush noun

ADJ. **big, huge, major** (*esp. AmE*) | **little, small** | **silly, stupid** | **childhood, schoolgirl, teenage** | **secret**
VERB + CRUSH **have** | **develop, get**
PREP. **~ on** ◇ *She had a huge ~ on one of her teachers.*

crush verb

ADV. **slightly** | **almost, nearly** | **finely** ◇ *Crush the garlic finely before adding.* | **underfoot** ◇ *insects that had been ~ed underfoot*
PREP. **against** ◇ *She was ~ed against the wall.* | **beneath, under** ◇ *He was ~ed beneath a bus.* | **between** ◇ *She was ~ed between two cars.*
PHRASES **be ~ed, get ~ed** | **~ sb to death**

crust noun

1 on a loaf of bread, pie, etc.

ADJ. **thick, thin** | **flaky** (*esp. AmE*) | **bread, pastry, pie, pizza**
PHRASES **a ~ of bread** ◇ *We saved a few ~s of bread for the birds.*

2 hard layer on the outside of sth

ADJ. **thick, thin**
VERB + CRUST **form** ◇ *The mud had formed a thick ~ on the surface of the road.*
CRUST + VERB **form** ◇ *Put the lid on, or a ~ will form on the paints.*
PREP. **~ of** ◇ *a thin ~ of ice*
PHRASES **the earth's ~**

crutch noun

ADJ. **emotional, psychological** (*both figurative*) ◇ *He saw religion as an emotional ~.*
VERB + CRUTCH **need, use** ◇ *He needs ~es to walk.* | **use sth as** ◇ *She uses her work as a psychological ~.*
PREP. **on ~, with ~** ◇ *She can only walk with ~es.*

crux noun

ADJ. **real**
VERB + CRUX **be** ◇ *This is the real ~ of the issue to me.*
CRUX + VERB **lie** ◇ *The ~ of the matter lies in our lack of expert knowledge.*
PHRASES **the ~ of the matter, the ~ of the problem**

cry noun

1 shout/loud noise

ADJ. **great, loud** | **faint, little, low, small, soft, weak** | **choked, muffled, stifled, strangled** | **piercing, sharp, shrill** | **hoarse** ◇ *the hoarse ~ of a crow* | **agonized, anguished, desperate, mournful, plaintive, terrible** ◇ *a plaintive ~ for help* | **startled** | **triumphant** | **involuntary** | **sudden** | **battle, rallying, war, warning** | **animal, bird**
VERB + CRY **give, let out, raise, utter** ◇ *She gave an agonized ~ as they lifted the fallen branch from her leg.* ◇ *He was too weak to raise even the smallest of cries.* | **muffle, stifle** ◇ *He tried to yell out, but the hand muffled his cries.* ◇ *She stifled a small ~.* | **hear**
CRY + VERB **echo, go up, ring out** ◇ *A ~ went up when it was discovered their man had escaped.* | **come from sb/sth, escape sb/sth** ◇ *An involuntary ~ escaped her as he entered the room.*
PREP. **with a ~** ◇ *He fell to the ground with a ~.* | **~ for** (*figurative*) ◇ *Her suicide attempt was really a desperate ~ for help.* | **~ of** ◇ *a ~ of despair/delight*
→ Note at SOUND

2 act of crying

ADJ. **good** | **little**
VERB + CRY **have** ◇ *You'll feel better when you've had a good ~.*

cry verb

1 produce tears

ADV. **a lot, hard** | **a little** | **almost, nearly** | **never, rarely** | **bitterly** ◇ *He put his head on his arms and cried bitterly.* | **loudly** | **quietly, silently, softly** | **hysterically, uncontrollably** | **alone**
VERB + CRY **begin to, start to** | **want to** ◇ *I felt like I wanted to ~.* | **make sb** | **leave sb to** ◇ *children who are left to ~ alone*
PREP. **about** ◇ *What are you ~ing about?* | **for** ◇ *a child ~ing for his mother* | **over** ◇ *I wasn't going to waste time ~ing over him!* | **with** ◇ *Anna was almost ~ing with frustration.*
PHRASES **~ like a baby** ◇ *Finally he broke down and cried like a baby.* | **~ your eyes out** | **~ yourself to sleep, feel like ~ing** ◇ *I felt like ~ing when I found out what had happened.* | **a shoulder to ~ on** (*figurative*) ◇ *He was a fatherly shoulder to ~ on when things went wrong.*

2 shout

ADV. **aloud, out** | **suddenly** | **angrily, indignantly** ◇ *'Never!' he cried angrily.* | **desperately** | **excitedly, happily, triumphantly** | **passionately**
VERB + CRY **want to** ◇ *She wanted to ~ out to him not to be so stupid.* | **hear sb** ◇ *I heard her ~ out in her sleep.*
PREP. **in** ◇ *'What do you mean?' she cried in agitation.* ◇ *'Who's there?' she cried in a shrill voice.*
PHRASES **~ for help** ◇ *She cried for help as the fire spread.* | **~ out in anguish, fear, pain, etc., etc.**

crystal noun

ADJ. **single** | **small, tiny** | **large** | **ice, snow** | **quartz, rock,** etc. | **salt**
CRYSTAL + VERB **form, grow** ◇ *Ice ~s had formed on the window.*

crystal ball noun

VERB + CRYSTAL BALL **gaze into, look into** ◇ *I can't look into my ~ and tell you what will happen!* | **have** ◇ *I don't know if it will work—I don't have a ~.*

cubicle noun

ADJ. **little, small, tiny** | **separate** | **empty** | **next** ◇ *I don't even know my colleague in the next ~.* | **changing** (*BrE*), **shower, toilet** | **office** (*esp. AmE*)
CUBICLE + NOUN **curtain, door** | **wall**
CUBICLE + VERB **occupy** | **enter, leave**
PREP. **in a/the ~**

cuddle noun

ADJ. **big** (*esp. BrE*) ◇ *He gave her a big ~ and told her not to worry.*
VERB + CUDDLE **have** (*esp. BrE*) ◇ *They were having a ~ on the sofa.* | **give** ◇ *Give Daddy a big ~.*
PHRASES **a kiss and a ~** (*BrE*) ◇ *He just wants a comforting kiss and a ~ and he'll be all right.*

cue noun

ADJ. **visual**
VERB + CUE **wait for** | **follow, take** ◇ *Her husband took his ~, and said that it was time for them to leave.* | **miss** | **give sb, provide** ◇ *She had not yet been given the ~ to go on to the stage.* ◇ *This remark provided the ~ for the crowd to start jeering.*
PREP. **on ~** ◇ *I can't just cry on ~!* | **~ for** ◇ *This was the ~ for him to come into the room.*
PHRASES **right on ~** ◇ *Ella came in right on ~, just as they were being rude about her.* | **take your ~ from sb/sth** ◇ *They all took their ~ from their leader.*

cuisine noun

ADJ. **excellent, fine, superb** (*esp. BrE*) | **local, native** (*esp. AmE*), **regional** ◇ *We sampled the local ~.* ◇ *He missed his native ~.* | **authentic, traditional** ◇ *authentic Thai ~* | **gourmet** (*esp. AmE*) | **international** | **Asian, French, Italian,** etc.
VERB + CUISINE **feature, offer, serve** ◇ *The hotel has a large dining room serving superb local ~.* | **sample, try** | **eat, enjoy**

culmination noun

ADJ. **logical, natural** (*esp. AmE*) ◇ *This massive work was the logical ~ of her long career.*
VERB + CULMINATION **mark, represent** ◇ *The show marked the ~ of months of hard work.* | **reach** ◇ *The space race reached its ~ in the first moon walk.* | **see** ◇ *2008 saw the ~ of the project.*
PREP. **at the ~ of** ◇ *A decision will be taken at the ~ of the initial research.*

culpable adj.

VERBS **be** | **believe sb, hold sb** | **make sb** ◇ *His refusal to admit his mistake makes him even more ~ in my view.*
ADV. **equally** | **morally**
PREP. **in** ◇ *You are equally ~ in this affair.* | **of** ◇ *She believed him ~ of murder.*

culprit noun

ADJ. **big, chief, main, major, primary** (*esp. AmE*), **prime, real, true, worst** ◇ *In the battle to stay slim, the biggest ~ is lack of exercise.* | **likely, obvious, possible**
VERB + CULPRIT **hunt, hunt for** (*both esp. BrE*) ◇ *Police hunting the ~s have condemned the attack.* | **apprehend** (*esp. BrE*), **catch, discover, find, identify, track down**

cult noun

1 worship of a person/thing

ADJ. **personality** ◇ *the personality ~ of the president*
CULT + NOUN **figure, hero, icon** (*esp. AmE*) ◇ *He became a ~ figure during the 1960s.* | **status** ◇ *The book achieved ~ status as soon as it was published.* | **following** ◇ *The show has built up a ~ following.* | **band, book, film** (*esp. BrE*), **movie** (*esp. AmE*), **novel, show** | **classic, favourite/favorite, hit, phenomenon**
PREP. **~ of** ◇ *the ~ of youth*

2 religious group

ADJ. **religious** ◇ *the members of a religious ~* | **pagan, satanic**
CULT + NOUN **leader, member** | **image, object, statue** | **practice**

cultivate verb

1 land

ADV. **intensively** ◇ *The land here has been intensively ~d for generations.*

2 crops

ADV. **widely** | **successfully** ◇ *Olives have been ~d successfully in Australia.*

3 try to develop sth

ADV. **actively, assiduously, carefully, deliberately** ◇ *This modern image is actively ~d by the company.* | **successfully**

cultivated adj.

VERBS **be**
ADV. **highly** ◇ *a highly ~ woman* | **carefully, deliberately** ◇ *a carefully ~ image*

culture noun

1 customs, ideas, beliefs, etc.

ADJ. **ancient, primitive** | **dominant** | **modern, traditional** | **patriarchal** | **human** | **alien, foreign** | **indigenous, native** | **local, national** | **global, world** | **black, Greek, Islamic, Western,** etc. ◇ *These ideas have always been central to Western ~.* | **rural, urban** | **mainstream, underground** | **gay** | **diverse, vibrant** | **bourgeois, working-class,** etc. | **street, youth** ◇ *As young people started to have more money, a significant youth ~ developed.* | **dance, hip-hop, rock,** etc. | **computer, drug, football** (*BrE*) | **legal, political, scientific,** etc. ◇ *the political ~ of the US* | **company, corporate, organizational** | **business, professional** | **academic, intellectual** | **religious, secular** | **capitalist, commercial, consumer, enterprise, materialistic,** etc. ◇ *the development of the enterprise ~* | **celebrity** | **wider** ◇ *Prisoners are isolated from the wider ~ of society at large.*
VERB + CULTURE **assimilate** ◇ *The Romans gradually assimilated the ~ of the people they had conquered.* ◇ *Newcomers to the company are soon assimilated into the ~.* | **embrace** ◇ *immigrants who embrace American ~* | **build, create, develop, foster, produce, shape** ◇ *The new director is trying to foster a ~ of open communication within the company.* | **change, transform** ◇ *The computer has changed the ~ of the design profession.* | **understand** ◇ *Children need to learn to understand ~s other than their own.* | **maintain, preserve** | **reflect** ◇ *The paintings reflect African American ~.*
CULTURE + VERB **develop**
CULTURE + NOUN **group** ◇ *a country containing many language and ~ groups* | **shock** ◇ *She experienced great ~ shock when she first came to Europe.* | **clash, wars** (*esp. AmE*) | **change**
PREP. **in a/the ~** ◇ *In some ~s children have an important place.*
PHRASES **a clash of ~s** | **a ~ of fear, a ~ of secrecy, a ~ of violence**

2 art, literature, music, etc

ADJ. **contemporary, modern, postmodern** | **mass, pop,**

popular | folk | high | literary, musical, oral, print ◇ *Jokes are an important part of our popular oral ~.*
PHRASES **a man of ~, a woman of ~**

cunning *noun*

ADJ. **great** | **devious, low** (*esp. BrE*) | **animal** | **native** ◇ *She relied on her native ~ to survive.*
VERB + CUNNING **have** ◇ *She had great ~ and ruthlessness.* | **show** | **use** ◇ *He had used ~ to get what he wanted.*
PREP. **with ~** ◇ *She managed him with great ~.*

cup *noun*

1 container

ADJ. **empty** | **full** | **half-empty, half-full** | **broken, chipped, cracked** | **china, porcelain** | **disposable, Dixie™** (= paper cup) (*AmE*), **drinking** (*AmE*), **paper, plastic, polystyrene** (*BrE*), **Styrofoam™** (*AmE*) | **tin** | **coffee, tea** | **egg** | **yogurt** (*AmE*) | **measuring** (*AmE*) | **sippy** (= for babies) (*AmE*)
VERB + CUP **fill, refill** | **drain, empty** ◇ *She was so thirsty that she drained her ~.* | **lift, pick up, raise** ◇ *She raised her ~ to her lips.* | **place, put down, replace, set down** | **drink from, drink out of** ◇ *Customers don't like drinking out of plastic ~s.*
CUP + VERB **contain sth**
CUP + NOUN **holder**
PHRASES **a ~ and saucer**

2 drink

ADJ. **strong** ◇ *I like a good strong ~ of tea first thing in the morning.* | **fresh** ◇ *My coffee was cold, so I ordered a fresh ~.* | **hot, steaming, warm**
VERB + CUP **offer sb** | **make (sb)** | **pour (sb)** ◇ *I'm making tea. Can I pour you a ~?* | **buy, order** | **help yourself to** | **stir** ◇ *Enrique stirred his fourth ~ of coffee of the day.* | **drink, enjoy, have** ◇ *I drink about ten ~s of coffee a day.* | **sip** | **finish**
PREP. **~ of**
PHRASES **a nice ~ of tea** (*BrE*) ◇ *You sit down and I'll make you a nice ~ of tea.*

3 in a competition

ADJ. **challenge** | **knockout** | **American, European, World, etc.** | **gold, silver**
VERB + CUP **win** ◇ *Who won the ~?* | **lose** | **present (sb with)** ◇ *The ~ will be presented to the winning team by the president.* | **lift, raise** ◇ *He lifted the ~ for the sixth time this year* (= it was the sixth time he had won).
CUP + NOUN **competition** ◇ *They were the first Turkish team to win a major ~ competition.* ◇ *the Ryder Cup competition* | **clash** (*BrE*), **match** (*esp. BrE*) ◇ *The team are ready for next week's World Cup clash with Italy.* | **race** | **final, quarter-final, semi-final** (*all BrE*) | **victory, win** | **winner** | **holder** | **contender, hopeful**
PHRASES **the first, etc. round of the ~**

cupboard *noun* → See also CLOSET

ADJ. **big, deep, large** | **little, small, tiny** | **high, low** | **walk-in** (*BrE*) | **built-in, fitted** (*BrE*) | **bare, empty** | **wall** (*BrE*) | **bathroom, hall** (*BrE*), **kitchen** | **storage, store** | **airing, broom, food, linen, medicine, stationery** (*all BrE*) ◇ *There's a broom ~ under the stairs.*
VERB + CUPBOARD **close, open** | **look in** | **put sth in** ◇ *Put the glasses in the ~.* | **keep sth in**
CUPBOARD + VERB **be full of sth** ◇ *The ~ was full of old spices.*
CUPBOARD + NOUN **door** | **space** ◇ *Do you have much ~ space in your new house?*
PREP. **in a/the ~** ◇ *Put the plates in the ~.*

curb *noun*

1 control; limit

VERB + CURB **impose, introduce, put**
PREP. **~ on** ◇ *Many companies have imposed ~s on smoking in the workplace.*

2 (*AmE*) edge of pavement/sidewalk → See KERB

curb *verb*

ADV. **drastically** ◇ *This legislation will drastically ~ the power of local authorities.*
VERB + CURB **attempt to, try to** | **be designed to, be intended to** ◇ *a new law designed to ~ harmful emissions from factories*
PHRASES **aimed at ~ing sth** ◇ *a range of policies aimed at ~ing inflation* | **an attempt to ~ sth, an effort to ~ sth** | **measures to ~ sth**

cure *noun*

1 medicine/treatment that can cure an illness

ADJ. **effective, instant, miracle, wonder** ◇ *There is no instant ~ for this condition.* | **rest** ◇ *His new job was almost a rest ~ after the stresses of the army.* | **possible, potential** | **cancer** | **hangover**
VERB + CURE **have** ◇ *If the disease is detected early, it has a ~.* | **look for, seek** | **develop, discover, find**
CURE + VERB **work** ◇ *The ~ works by boosting the body's immune system.*
PREP. **~ for** ◇ *scientists seeking a ~ for AIDS* | **~ from** ◇ *He was hoping for a ~ from his debilitating illness.*
PHRASES **prevention is better than ~** ◇ *Prevention is better than ~, so start taking care of yourself.* | **the search for a ~** ◇ *the search for a ~ for the common cold* | **there is a ~ (for sth), there is no ~ (for sth)** ◇ *There is no known ~ for the disease.*

2 return to good health

ADJ. **miraculous** | **complete, permanent**
VERB + CURE **bring about, effect, provide** ◇ *These drugs can sometimes effect miraculous ~s.* ◇ *Science cannot provide a ~ for all the world's problems.* (*figurative*)

cure *verb*

ADV. **completely** | **miraculously** ◇ *She still believed that somehow she could be miraculously ~d.*
PREP. **of** ◇ *He was now completely ~d of his illness.*

curfew *noun*

ADJ. **strict** | **24-hour, dusk-to-dawn** | **night, night-time** | **7 p.m., etc.**
VERB + CURFEW **declare, impose, order, place sth under** ◇ *A five-day ~ was declared by the government.* ◇ *The whole area has been placed under ~.* | **enforce** | **lift** ◇ *The strict ~ has now been lifted.* | **break, defy** ◇ *Protesters defied the ~ and took to the streets.* | **have** (*AmE*) ◇ *Why do you have to go home now if you don't have a ~?* | **be late for, miss** (*both AmE*) ◇ *I have to get back or I'll miss my ~.*
CURFEW + VERB **be in force** ◇ *A dusk-to-dawn ~ was in force.*
CURFEW + NOUN **violation** | **law** (*AmE*)
PREP. **under ~** ◇ *The city is still under ~.* | **~ on** ◇ *Many people are in favour/favor of a ~ on young people.*

curiosity *noun*

ADJ. **great, intense** | **insatiable** ◇ *She has an insatiable ~ about life.* | **mild** | **idle, mere, pure, sheer, simple** ◇ *'Why do you ask?' 'Mere ~.'* | **genuine** | **open** ◇ *Kaylee stood staring with open ~.* | **natural** ◇ *School should awaken a child's natural ~.* | **morbid** | **intellectual, scientific** | **public**
VERB + CURIOSITY **have** | **arouse, awaken, pique** (*esp. AmE*), **spark** ◇ *Their ~ was aroused by his strange clothes.* | **satisfy**
CURIOSITY + VERB **get the better of sb, overcome sb** ◇ *Harry's ~ got the better of him and he unlocked the cupboard.* | **take over** | **grow**
PREP. **out of ~** ◇ *We went to the show out of ~ more than anything else.* | **with ~** ◇ *The children watched us with mild ~.* | **~ about** ◇ *I needed to satisfy my ~ about what it was like to make records.*
PHRASES **a sense of ~**

curious adj.

1 eager to find out about sb/sth

VERBS **be, feel, seem** | **became, get, grow** | **remain** | **make sb** ◇ *Her secretive manner had made me ~.*

ADV. **extremely, fairly, very, etc.** | **deeply, intensely** ◇ *I was intensely ~ to know more about him.* | **a little, slightly, etc.** | **mildly** | **genuinely** | **naturally** ◇ *Puppies are naturally ~.* | **just, merely, simply** ◇ *I'm just ~ to know what you think.* | **intellectually**

PREP. **about** ◇ *I was ~ about how she would react.* | **as to** ◇ *She was ~ as to why he was there.*

PHRASES **~ to find out, know, see, etc. sb/sth**

2 strange/unusual

VERBS **be, feel, look, seem** | **find sb/sth**

ADV. **extremely, fairly, very, etc.** ◇ *I find it very ~ that you did not tell anyone.* | **a little, slightly, etc.** ◇ *a slightly ~ statement.*

curl noun

1 piece of hair

ADJ. **natural** | **loose, soft, wavy** | **tight** | **little** | **thick** | **long** | **corkscrew, spiral** | **auburn, blonde, dark, etc.** | **slight** ◇ *His hair had a slight ~ to it.* | **stray** ◇ *She pushed a stray ~ away from her eyes.* | **tangled, unruly, untamed** ◇ *She smoothed down her tangled ~s.* | **damp**

VERB + CURL **have** ◇ *She has beautiful blonde ~s.* | **press back, push back, smooth back, stroke back** | **smooth down** | **ruffle, run your fingers through** | **tease** ◇ *He carefully teased his ~s into place.* | **shake** ◇ *She shook her dark ~s sadly.* | **brush**

CURL + VERB **fall, tumble** ◇ *Her auburn ~s tumbled about her face.* | **hang** | **bounce** | **frame sth** ◇ *Her face was framed by a mop of black ~s.*

PREP. **in ~s** ◇ *His hair spilled in ~s over his forehead.* | **through the/your ~s** ◇ *She raked a comb through her ~s.*

PHRASES **a cascade of ~s, a mass of ~s, a mop of ~s** ◇ *Her hair was styled into a cascade of spiral ~s.* | **lose its ~** ◇ *Her hair lost its ~ as she got older.*

2 sth with a curved round shape

ADJ. **faint** ◇ *He acknowledged her remark with a faint ~ of his lips.*

PREP. **~ of** ◇ *a ~ of smoke*

curl verb

ADV. **tightly** | **slightly** | **back, up** ◇ *She ~ed her legs up under her.*

PREP. **around, round** (*esp. BrE*) ◇ *His fingers ~ed tightly around the steering wheel.* | **from** ◇ *Smoke was ~ing up from the chimney.* | **into** ◇ *The cat ~ed into a ball and fell asleep.*

PHRASES **~ed up** ◇ *She was lying ~ed up on her bed.* | **~ (up) at the edges** ◇ *The photograph was brown and ~ing at the edges.*

curly adj.

VERBS **be** | **go**

ADV. **all** (*informal*), **very** ◇ *Your hair's gone all ~!* | **slightly** | **naturally** ◇ *She wished she had naturally ~ hair.*

currency noun

1 money used in a particular country

ADJ. **domestic** | **foreign** ◇ *They prefer to be paid in foreign currencies.* | **common, global, international** ◇ *US dollars are considered common ~ in international transactions.* | **local** ◇ *You can convert sterling into the local ~.* | **national** | **European, Japanese, etc.** | **single** ◇ *the single European ~* | **major** | **stable, strong** ◇ *A stable ~ means that your savings do not diminish in value* | **weak** | **hard** | **paper** | **official** | **convertible** | **reserve**

VERB + CURRENCY **change, convert sth into, convert sth to, exchange** | **buy, sell** | **issue** | **use** | **devalue** | **revalue** | **support** ◇ *The fund supports weak currencies.* | **peg, tie** ◇ *Argentina's ~ was pegged to the dollar.* | **float**

CURRENCY + VERB **rise** | **depreciate, fall** | **float, fluctuate** ◇

---

currency

For four months all major currencies floated. ◇ *The system allows currencies to fluctuate within certain limits.*

CURRENCY + NOUN **conversion, exchange, translation** | **markets** ◇ *They make money by speculating on the ~ markets.* | **deal, dealing, speculation, trade, trading** | **dealer, speculator, trader** | **crisis** | **fluctuation, movements** | **devaluation** | **system** | **reform** | **reserves** | **board**

PREP. **in ... ~** ◇ *She had $500 in foreign ~.*

2 being believed/accepted/used by many people

ADJ. **common, general, wide, widespread** | **new** | **cultural, political, social**

VERB + CURRENCY **enjoy, have** ◇ *This belief has general ~.* | **gain** ◇ *How did the idea gain ~?*

> **NOTE**
>
> ### Currencies
>
> **change sth into/to..., convert sth into/to...** ◇ *I want to change 100 dollars into euros.*
>
> **buy..., sell...** ◇ *The bank will sell you one Russian rouble for 4.14 Japanese yen.*
>
> **a 20-pound, 50-euro, etc. note** (*BrE*), **a 20-dollar, 50-euro, etc. bill** (*AmE*), **a 50-cent, one-pound, etc. coin** ◇ *a dollar bill* ◇ *a pound coin*
>
> **for a...** ◇ *How many dinars will I get for a dollar?*
>
> **in (the)...** ◇ *The contract is denominated in euros.* ◇ *How much is that in US dollars?* ◇ *a tax of 30p in the pound*
>
> **... for...** ◇ *The company promises to match any money the charity makes dollar for dollar.*
>
> **... worth of sth** ◇ *a million pounds' worth of books*
>
> **a high..., a rising..., a strong...** ◇ *Business should benefit from a stronger euro.*
>
> **a falling..., a low..., a weak...** ◇ *The yen gained 10 points against a weak dollar.*
>
> **... is overvalued** ◇ *Research suggests that the pound is overvalued.*
>
> **float...** ◇ *The UK floated sterling in June 1972.*
>
> **devalue...** ◇ *The Fiji dollar may have to be devalued.*
>
> **defend..., prop up..., protect..., shore up..., support...** ◇ *Will the central bank intervene to prop up the euro?*
>
> **... is worth sth** ◇ *One Saudi Arabian riyal is worth approximately 0.27 US dollars.*
>
> **... strengthens** ◇ *The peso strengthened on the foreign exchanges.*
>
> **... comes under pressure** ◇ *The pound came under pressure against the dollar.*
>
> **... closes, opens** ◇ *The pound closed yesterday at 1.9830 dollars.*
>
> **... is fixed to, ... is pegged to** ◇ *Many emerging countries have their currencies pegged to the dollar.*
>
> **... value** ◇ *The dollar value of the stock rose to $11.5 billion.*
>
> **... terms** ◇ *The rise in government spending was equivalent to only 9% in dollar terms.*
>
> **... exchange rate** ◇ *All prices are based on the South African rand exchange rate.*
>
> **... equivalent** ◇ *She was paid the dollar equivalent of £10 000.*
>
> **against the...** ◇ *The yen has strengthened against the pound.*
>
> **to the...** ◇ *How many dollars are there to the pound?*
>
> **depreciation of the..., devaluation of the..., reflation of the...** ◇ *the devaluation of the peso in 1994*
>
> **a run on the...** ◇ *The government increased interest rates to avoid a run on the rouble (= sudden large selling of the currency).*
>
> **the value of the...** ◇ *a rise in the value of the euro*
>
> → See also the note at PER CENT

current noun

1 continuous flowing movement of water

ADJ. **fast, fast-flowing, powerful, strong, swift | cold, warm | rip | tidal | dangerous, treacherous | ocean, water | prevailing** ◇ *The prevailing ~ flows from east to west.* | **offshore**

CURRENT + VERB **flow | carry sb/sth, sweep sb/sth** ◇ *The strong ~ carried the boat downstream.* ◇ *She was swept away by the treacherous ~s.*

PREP. **against a/the ~** ◇ *He was swimming against the ~.* | **in a/the ~** ◇ *The boat was carried along in the ~.* | **with a/the ~** ◇ *It's easier to go with the ~.*

2 flow of air

ADJ. **warm | air, wind** ◇ *Birds of prey use warm air ~s to lift them high in the sky.* | **convection**

PHRASES **a ~ of air**

3 flow of electricity through a wire

ADJ. **high, strong | low, weak | electric, electrical | alternating, direct | input, inward | output, outward**

VERB + CURRENT **generate, induce, produce | carry, conduct, pass, transmit | switch off, switch on** ◇ *Check all your wiring before switching on the ~.*

CURRENT + VERB **flow, pass through sth** ◇ *Measure the ~ flowing in the wire.*

curriculum noun

ADJ. **broad, broadly based, wide | narrow** ◇ *Teachers feel that the present ~ is too narrow.* | **core** ◇ *Students choose from optional subjects in addition to the core ~.* | **national, official | mainstream** ◇ *His disability does not prevent him from following the mainstream ~.* | **standard | traditional | academic, educational | college, school, university | primary, secondary** (both esp. BrE) | **elementary-school, high-school, middle-school** (all in the US) | **undergraduate | course | English, geography, mathematics, etc. | comprehensive, rigorous** (both AmE) | **hidden** ◇ *Children learn many of their attitudes to life from the hidden ~ at school.*

VERB + CURRICULUM **create, design, develop, plan | broaden | change, revise | implement | introduce sth into** ◇ *Chinese has been introduced into the ~ as an option.* | **teach | follow | offer**

CURRICULUM + NOUN **content, subjects | area | materials | design, development, planning | aims, objectives | change, reform, review | committee** (AmE) | **guide, specialist** (both AmE)

PREP. **across the ~** ◇ *Students use computers across the ~ (=* in all or most subjects). | **in a/the ~** (AmE), **on a/the ~** (BrE) ◇ *Spanish is in the ~.* ◇ *They all have to study French because it's on the ~.* | **within a/the ~** ◇ *the balance of subjects within the ~*

PHRASES **areas of the ~** ◇ *We cover all areas of the ~.*

curriculum vitae (BrE) (also CV) noun → See also RÉSUMÉ

ADJ. **current | impressive | full**

... OF CVS **pile**

VERB + CURRICULUM VITAE **update | write | submit | email, post, send | read** ◇ *We read all the CVs but only interviewed three people*

PREP. **in a ~** ◇ *There's still a glaring hole in his résumé.*

curry noun

ADJ. **hot | mild | beef, chicken, vegetable, etc. | Indian, Thai**

VERB + CURRY **go for** (BrE) ◇ *Let's go for a ~ after the film.*

CURRY + NOUN **paste, powder | sauce | house** (= a restaurant that serves curry) (BrE)

→ Special page at FOOD

curse noun

1 word used for expressing anger

ADJ. **muffled | loud**

VERB + CURSE **mutter | let out, utter | hear**

CURSE + NOUN **word** (AmE)

2 wish that sth terrible will happen to sb

ADJ. **ancient | evil, terrible | family**

VERB + CURSE **utter | place, put | break, lift, remove**

PREP. **under a ~** ◇ *She thought that she must be under a ~.* | **~ on, ~ upon** ◇ *The witch is supposed to have put a ~ on the house.*

curse verb

ADV. **roundly | loudly | aloud | quietly, softly, under your breath** ◇ *He ~d under his breath as the hammer slipped.* | **inwardly, mentally, silently | angrily**

PREP. **for** ◇ *I ~d her roundly for being late.*

PHRASES **~ and swear** (BrE) | **~ and shout, yell, scream, etc.** ◇ *She was cursing and screaming at me just because I was late.* | **~ the day** ◇ *He was now cursing the day he ever got involved.* | **~ your luck** ◇ *She ~d her luck that she had had to wait for so long.*

cursor noun

ADJ. **mouse**

VERB + CURSOR **insert, move, place, position, put**

CURSOR + NOUN **key**

→ Special page at COMPUTER

curtail verb

ADV. **drastically, seriously, severely, sharply, significantly** ◇ *His power has been severely ~ed.* | **further | abruptly**

curtain noun

1 fabric that covers a window/opening → See also DRAPE

ADJ. **shower | closed, drawn, open | lace, silk, velvet | net** (BrE) | **heavy, thick | sheer**

VERB + CURTAIN **close, draw, open, pull, shut** ◇ *They sat in the dark with the ~s drawn.* ◇ *She pulled back the ~s, and sunlight streamed in.* | **hang**

CURTAIN + VERB **hang** ◇ *Pretty ~s hung either side of the kitchen window.* | **billow, blow, flutter** ◇ *The ~s billowed as the wind caught them.*

CURTAIN + NOUN **rail, rod** (AmE)

PREP. **behind a/the ~** ◇ *He took a bag from a shelf behind some ~s.*

2 in a theatre/theater

ADJ. **final**

CURTAIN + VERB **go up, open, part, rise | close, come down, fall** ◇ *At the end of the play the ~ came down to tremendous applause.*

curve noun

1 line or surface that bends

ADJ. **gentle, graceful, slight, smooth, soft | sharp, tight | sweeping, wide | sensual, voluptuous** ◇ *the voluptuous ~ of her hips* | **feminine ~s, womanly ~s | downward, upward | natural** ◇ *the natural ~ of your spine*

VERB + CURVE **form, make** ◇ *The seats were arranged to form a ~.*

PREP. **in a ~** ◇ *The road follows the coast in a wide ~.* | **of** ◇ *the ~ of his neck*

PHRASES **hug sb's ~s** ◇ *The evening dress hugged her ~s beautifully.*

2 (AmE) bend in the road

ADJ. **sharp, tight** ◇ *The road went around in a tight ~.*

VERB + CURVE **come around, hug, negotiate, round** ◇ *He slowed down to negotiate the ~.*

PREP. **around a/the ~** ◇ *The car vanished around a ~.* | **at a/the ~** ◇ *Slow down at the ~s.* | **into a/the ~** ◇ *A good motorcyclist leans into the ~s.* | **~ in** ◇ *a ~ in the road*

3 on a graph

ADJ. **steep | bell | normal, standard | growth | grading (=**

of students' grades) (*AmE*) | **learning** (= the rate at which you learn sth new) ◊ *Start-up businesses often have a steep learning ~.*

VERB + CURVE **plot**
CURVE + VERB **flatten out** | **indicate sth, show sth**
PHRASES **grade on a ~** (= to adjust scores so that they fit a normal curve) (*AmE*)

curve *verb*

ADV. **gently, slightly** ◊ *a gently curving stream* | **gracefully** | **strongly** | **sharply** | **away, down, up** ◊ *The path ~d down to the bay.*
PREP. **around, round** (*esp. BrE*), **towards/toward, etc.** ◊ *The road ~d away around the back of the hill.*
PHRASES **~ into a smile** ◊ *His mouth ~d into a smile.*

cushion *noun*

ADJ. **plump, soft** ◊ *He sank back into the soft ~s of the sofa.* | **couch** (*esp. AmE*), **sofa** | **scatter** (*BrE*), **throw** (*AmE*) | **seat**
VERB + CUSHION **plump, plump up** ◊ *She plumped up the sofa ~s before the guests arrived.*
CUSHION + NOUN **cover**
PREP. **on a/the ~** ◊ *I rested my elbow on a ~.*

custard *noun*

ADJ. **banana, caramel** (*AmE*), **egg, vanilla** | **frozen** (*AmE*) | **creamy, thick** | **smooth** (*esp. BrE*) | **lumpy** (*esp. BrE*)
VERB + CUSTARD **make** | **pour** (*esp. BrE*)
CUSTARD + VERB **thicken** (*esp. BrE*) | **set**
CUSTARD + NOUN **powder** (*esp. BrE*) | **pie** | **sauce** (*AmE*)
PHRASES **and ~, with ~** (*both esp. BrE*) ◊ *some apple pie and ~* → Special page at FOOD

custody *noun*

1 legal right/duty to take care of sb/sth

ADJ. **child** ◊ *a bitter child ~ dispute* | **joint, sole** | **full** | **legal** | **physical** (*AmE*) | **safe** ◊ *If valuables are placed in the safe, the hotel is responsible for their safe ~.*
VERB + CUSTODY **ask for, claim, demand, fight for, seek, want** | **award sb, give sb, grant sb** ◊ *The parents were given joint ~ of the two children.* | **gain, get, win** | **take** (*AmE*) | **regain** | **have** | **share** | **lose**
CUSTODY + NOUN **battle, dispute** | **arrangement** | **case, hearing**
PREP. **~ of**

2 being guarded/kept in prison

ADJ. **military, police** ◊ *The man died while in police ~.* | **protective** ◊ *The opposition leader has been taken into protective ~.* | **federal, state** (*both in the US*)
VERB + CUSTODY **be remanded in** (*BrE*), **be taken into** ◊ *A man has been remanded in ~ charged with the murder of an eight-year-old girl.* | **be held in, be kept in** | **escape from** | **be released from**
PREP. **in ~** ◊ *She will remain in ~ while reports are prepared about her mental condition.* | **under ~** (*AmE*) ◊ *They did not have enough evidence to place her under ~.* ◊ *The children were under protective ~.* | **out of ~** ◊ *They try to keep young people out of ~.*

custom *noun*

ADJ. **accepted, age-old, ancient, established, old, traditional** | **quaint, strange** | **local, native** (*esp. AmE*) | **family** | **marriage, religious, social**
VERB + CUSTOM **follow, observe, practise/practice** (*esp. AmE*), **respect** ◊ *They still follow the ~ of pinning money to the bride's dress.* | **adopt** | **learn** | **know** | **maintain, preserve, revive**
CUSTOM + VERB **die out, disappear** ◊ *The ~ died out in the 19th century.* | **prevail, survive** ◊ *These ~s still prevail in remote areas.*
PREP. **according to a/the ~, in accordance with (a/the) ~** ◊ *They poured wine around the trees in accordance with local ~.* | **through ~** ◊ *The rules have grown up through ~ and are not laid down by law.* | **~ of**

PHRASES **as is/was the ~** ◊ *People threw coins onto the stage, as was the ~.*

customer *noun*

ADJ. **big, favoured/favored** (*esp. BrE*), **favourite/favorite** (*esp. AmE*), **good, important, key, large, major** ◊ *They are one of our biggest ~s.* ◊ *They organized an evening's entertainment for key ~s.* | **long-standing, long-time, loyal, valued** | **regular** | **current, existing, old** | **repeat** (*AmE*) | **new** | **potential, prospective, would-be** ◊ *There are a large number of potential ~s for the new product.* | **paying** | **dissatisfied, unhappy** | **angry, irate** | **happy, satisfied** ◊ *We like to think that we have satisfied ~s.* | **domestic** | **internal** | **external, outside** | **foreign, international, overseas** | **personal, private** | **business, commercial, corporate, industrial, retail**
VERB + CUSTOMER **have** | **deal with, help, serve, service** (*AmE*) | **attract, draw, entice, get, lure** ◊ *It's a special offer to attract new ~s.* | **lose** ◊ *We can't afford to lose any more ~s.* | **keep, retain** | **satisfy**
CUSTOMER + NOUN **care, relations, relationship** (*AmE*), **service, support** ◊ *If you have a complaint, contact the ~ care unit.* ◊ *Part of good ~ relations is knowing how to deal with complaints.* | **account, order** | **agreement** ◊ *The terms of the guarantee will be set out in the ~ agreement.* | **demand** ◊ *This cheaper model was produced in response to ~ demand.* | **demands, needs, requirements, specifications** | **feedback, reaction** ◊ *The questionnaire is to test ~ reaction to the new store design.* | **dissatisfaction, satisfaction** ◊ *They carried out a ~ satisfaction survey.* | **loyalty** | **complaints, enquiries** (*BrE*), **questions** (*AmE*), **requests** | **hotline** | **survey** | **data, information, profile, records** | **base, list** ◊ *They are hoping that TV advertising will increase their ~ base.*

customs *noun*

ADJ. **French, UK, US, etc.**
VERB + CUSTOMS **clear, go through** ◊ *We cleared ~ by five o'clock.* ◊ *You will have to declare these goods when you go through ~.* | **wave sb through** ◊ *We were waved through ~ without a pause.*
CUSTOMS + NOUN **controls, regulations** ◊ *the removal of European ~ controls* | **duty** ◊ *We had to pay ~ duties on the beer.* | **building, hall, office, post** (*esp. BrE*) ◊ *the ~ post on the border* | **agent, inspector, officer, official** | **authorities** | **formalities, procedures** | **declaration, document, documentation, form** ◊ *We had to fill out ~ forms on the plane.* | **clearance** ◊ *We were waiting for the goods to receive ~ clearance.*
PREP. **at ~** ◊ *We got stopped and searched at the Italian ~.* | **through ~**

cut *noun*

1 hole/opening made by cutting

ADJ. **clean, neat** | **little, small** | **long** | **straight**
VERB + CUT **make** | **give** ◊ *a high-quality blade that gives a clean ~*
PREP. **~ in** ◊ *Using sharp scissors, make a small ~ in the material.*

2 wound

ADJ. **bad, deep, nasty** | **little, small, tiny** ◊ *He has a small ~ on his finger.* | **minor, slight, superficial** | **clean** | **fresh, new** | **open** | **paper**
VERB + CUT **have** | **get, suffer** ◊ *She got a bad ~ over her right eye.* | **clean** ◊ *Clean the ~ and cover it to prevent infection.* | **bandage, cover, dress** | **heal**
CUT + VERB **heal** ◊ *A clean ~ heals quickly.*
PREP. **~ on** ◊ *a ~ on her hand* | **~ to** ◊ *One man was attacked and suffered ~s to his face.*
PHRASES **~s and bruises, ~s and scrapes**

3 act of cutting sb's hair; hairstyle

ADJ. **hair** (usually *haircut*) | **short** | **buzz** (*AmE*), **crew**

VERB + CUT **have** ◊ *I've made an appointment to have a haircut.* | **need** | **give sb**
PHRASES **~ and blow-dry**

4 reduction

ADJ. **big, deep, large, major, severe, sharp, significant, substantial** | **draconian, dramatic, drastic, huge, massive, savage** (*BrE*) | **across-the-board, swingeing** (*BrE*) | **small** | **federal, government** | **income** (*esp. AmE*), **pay, salary, wage** (*esp. BrE*) | **expenditure, financial** (*BrE*), **spending** | **benefit, budget, defence/defense, education, funding, job, service, staff** | **cost, interest-rate, price, rate** (*esp. AmE*), **tax** | **proposed**
... OF CUTS **round** ◊ *The company has announced a new round of job ~s.*
VERB + CUT **impose, make** ◊ *They are planning to make substantial ~s in the service.* | **announce, propose** ◊ *proposed tax ~s* | **face** | **accept, suffer, take** ◊ *The staff have all had to take a ~ in salary.* | **oppose, support**
CUT + VERB **come into effect** ◊ *The ~s will come into effect next May.*
PREP. **~ in** ◊ *~s in public spending*

5 piece of meat

ADJ. **choice, expensive, good, lean, prime** | **cheap** | **cold ~s** (*esp. AmE*)
PREP. **~ of** ◊ *The recipe calls for a good lean ~ of beef.*

6 share in the profits

VERB + CUT **get, have, take** ◊ *By the time the organizers have had their ~, there won't be much left.* | **want** ◊ *If there's money to be made from selling photos of her, she wants her ~.*
PREP. **~ of** ◊ *He takes a ~ of the profits.*

cut *verb*

1 with a knife, scissors, etc.

ADV. **thick** ◊ *Make sure you ~ the bread nice and thick.* | **thinly** | **cleanly, neatly** ◊ *Cut the stem cleanly, just beneath a leaf joint.* | **easily** ◊ *Sandstone ~s easily.* | **lengthways** (*esp. BrE*), **lengthwise** ◊ *Cut the carrots in half lengthwise.* | **away, back, down, off, out** ◊ *Some trees had been ~ down.*
PREP. **away** ◊ *They ~ away all the dead branches from the tree.* | **back** | **from** | **into** ◊ *She picked up the knife and ~ into the meat.* | **off** | **out** | **through** ◊ *He ~ the bread into thin slices.* | **through** ◊ *I can't ~ through this wood.*
PHRASES **~ and paste** (*computing*) ◊ *You can ~ and paste between different programs.* | **~ sb/sth free, ~ sb/sth loose** ◊ *Two survivors were ~ free after being trapped for twenty minutes.* | **~ sb's hair short** ◊ *I told the stylist I wanted my hair ~ short.* | **~ sth into pieces** ◊ *Cut the cake into six pieces.* | **~ sth in half, ~ sth in two** ◊ *She ~ the loaf in two and gave me one of the halves.* | **~ sth open** ◊ *She fell and ~ her head open.* | **freshly ~** ◊ *freshly ~ flowers*

2 reduce sth

ADV. **considerably, dramatically, drastically, sharply, significantly** | **short** ◊ *His career was ~ short by injury.*
VERB + CUT **try to** | **manage to** ◊ *We have managed to ~ our costs drastically.* | **be forced to, have to**
PREP. **by** ◊ *The department has to ~ its spending by 30%.* | **from, to** ◊ *The price has been ~ from €250 to €175.*

PHR V **cut back**

ADV. **drastically, severely, significantly** ◊ *Social work services have been ~ back drastically.*
VERB + CUT BACK **be forced to, have to**
PREP. **on** ◊ *Local authorities have been forced to ~ back on expenditure.* | **to** ◊ *We should ~ back to previous levels of spending.*

cut down

ADV. **considerably, drastically** | **gradually**
VERB + CUT DOWN **try to** | **manage to** | **advise sb to**
PREP. **on** ◊ *I'm trying to ~ down on fatty foods.*

---

cut sb/sth off

1 interrupt sb/sth

ADV. **abruptly, suddenly** ◊ *His thoughts were abruptly ~ off by a blinding flash of pain.*

2 prevent sb/sth from leaving/reaching a place

ADV. **completely, totally** | **effectively, largely, virtually**
PREP. **from** ◊ *They were completely ~ off from the outside world.*

cutback *noun*

ADJ. **drastic, major, severe, sharp** | **budget, budgetary, economic, financial** | **production** | **federal, government**
VERB + CUTBACK **impose, make** ◊ *Many schools are having to make major ~s.* | **announce**
PREP. **~ in** ◊ *a sharp ~ in military spending*

cutting *noun*

1 piece cut off from a plant

ADJ. **leaf, root, stem**
VERB + CUTTING **take**
CUTTING + VERB **root, take** ◊ *You can see whether the ~s have taken.*
PREP. **from a/the ~** ◊ *These plants are easy to propagate from leaf ~s.* | **~ from** ◊ *Take ~s from mature plants in the spring.*

2 (*BrE*) **piece cut out from a newspaper** → See also CLIPPING

ADJ. **newspaper, press** ◊ *She had kept all the press ~s about the murder.*
PREP. **~ from** ◊ *a ~ from 'The Guardian'*

CV → See CURRICULUM VITAE

cycle *noun*

1 series of events that happen repeatedly

ADJ. **annual, daily, monthly, seasonal, weekly** ◊ *the annual ~ of church festivals* | **irregular, regular** ◊ *women with irregular menstrual ~s* | **complete, entire, whole** | **continuous, endless, never-ending** ◊ *the endless ~ of birth, death and rebirth* | **natural** ◊ *Life is a natural ~, just like the changing seasons.* | **vicious** ◊ *caught up in a vicious ~ of bingeing and dieting* | **virtuous** | **lunar, solar** ◊ *the 76-year solar ~* | **carbon, water** ◊ *a diagram of the water ~* | **breeding, menstrual, reproductive** | **sleep** | **business, economic** | **boom-and-bust** | **development** | **election** (*AmE*) | **news** (*esp. AmE*) | **life** ◊ *the life ~ of the butterfly*
VERB + CYCLE **follow, go through** ◊ *The market is simply going through an economic ~.* | **complete** ◊ *To complete the ~, oxygen is necessary.* | **repeat** | **break, end, stop** | **create, start** | **continue, perpetuate**
CYCLE + VERB **begin again** ◊ *Male and female adults mate, the female lays eggs, and the ~ begins all over again.* | **continue, repeat (itself)** ◊ *This ~ of events continually repeats itself.*
CYCLE + NOUN **length, time**
PREP. **in a/the ~** ◊ *at this point in the ~* | **per ~** ◊ *The number of young produced per breeding ~ varies from species to species.*
PHRASES **a ~ of abuse, poverty, violence, etc.** | **part of the ~ (of sth)** ◊ *part of the ~ of birth and death*

2 (*esp. BrE*) **bicycle**

ADJ. **motor** (usually *motorcycle*) (*BrE, AmE*), **pedal**
VERB + CYCLE **ride**
CYCLE + NOUN **ride** ◊ *We're going for a ~ ride this afternoon.* | **helmet** | **lane, path, route, track** ◊ *Cars are not allowed in the ~ lanes.* | **race**

cyclone *noun*

ADJ. **tropical**
CYCLONE + VERB **hit sth** ◊ *Cyclone Tracy hit Darwin on Christmas Eve, 1974.* | **destroy sth, devastate sth** ◊ *The islands have been devastated by ~s in recent months.*
PREP. **in a/the ~** ◊ *trees damaged in the ~*
PHRASES **the eye of the ~** (= the central point)

cymbal *noun*

ADJ. **clashing, crashing**
VERB + CYMBAL **clash, hit**
CYMBAL + VERB **crash** ◊ *the sound of ~s crashing*
CYMBAL + NOUN **crash** ◊ *The piece ends with a ~ crash.*
PHRASES **a clash of ~s, a crash of ~s**
→ Special page at MUSIC

cynical *adj.*

VERBS **be, feel, seem, sound** ◊ *I hope I don't sound unduly ~.*
| **become, get, grow** | **remain**
ADV. **extremely, fairly, very, etc.** | **deeply** ◊ *his deeply ~ attitude* | **completely, totally, utterly** (*esp. BrE*) | **overly, unduly** | **a little, slightly, etc.**
PREP. **about** ◊ *I'm a little ~ about her motives.*

cynicism *noun*

ADJ. **bitter, jaded** (*esp. AmE*)**, weary** (*esp. BrE*) ◊ *He spoke in a tone of weary ~.* | **deep** | **widespread** | **public** | **political**
... OF CYNICISM **hint, note, touch** (*esp. BrE*) ◊ *There was a hint of ~ in his voice.*
VERB + CYNICISM **breed** ◊ *Evidence of corruption can only breed public ~.*
PREP. **with ~** ◊ *She viewed his new interest in her with ~.* | **~ about** ◊ *There is now widespread ~ about the political system.*

D d

dagger *noun*

ADJ. **curved, sharp** | **ceremonial, jewelled/jeweled**
VERB + DAGGER **draw, pull out, unsheathe** | **sheathe**

dam *noun*

ADJ. **hydroelectric**
VERB + DAM **build, construct** | **breach** ◊ *The ~ has been breached and there is a danger of flooding.*
DAM + VERB **burst** ◊ *The ~ burst and the valley was flooded.* | **break** (*figurative, esp. AmE*) ◊ *I began to cry—it was as if a ~ had broken inside me.* | **hold sth back** ◊ *The ~ holds back the water.*
PREP. **~ across, ~ on** ◊ *a large hydroelectric ~ on the Colorado River*

damage *noun*

1 harm/injury

ADJ. **considerable, enormous, great, heavy, massive, serious, severe, significant, substantial, untold** ◊ *The power plant will cause untold ~ to the local environment.* | **minimal, minor, slight** | **extensive, widespread** | **irreparable, irreversible, lasting, long-term, permanent** ◊ *The incident did permanent ~ to relations between the two countries.* | **potential** | **criminal, malicious, wilful** (*all BrE, law*) ◊ *He was prosecuted for criminal ~ to a vehicle.* | **accidental** ◊ *The insurance policy covers the building for accidental ~.* | **emotional, environmental, mechanical, physical, psychological, structural** | **brain, liver, nerve, etc.** ◊ *She suffered serious brain ~ at birth.* | **property** | **collateral**
VERB + DAMAGE **cause, do, inflict** ◊ *The earthquake caused widespread ~ to property.* ◊ *They inflicted severe psychological ~ on their opponents.* | **suffer, sustain** | **repair** | **pay for** | **assess** | **avoid, prevent** | **limit, minimize, reduce**
DAMAGE + VERB **occur, result**
DAMAGE + NOUN **assessment, report** | **control, limitation** (*esp. BrE*) ◊ *Serious ~ control was needed after the information was leaked to the papers.* ◊ *The attempt at stopping the floods turned into a damage-limitation exercise.*
PREP. **~ by** ◊ *The building suffered extensive ~ by fire in 1925.* | **~ from** ◊ *Crops are sprayed with chemicals to prevent ~ from insects.* | **~ to** ◊ *lasting ~ to the environment*

dance

PHRASES **the cost of the ~** ◊ *The cost of the ~ is estimated at around $2 billion.* | **the ~ is done** ◊ *Don't try to apologize—the ~ is done.* | **the extent of the ~** ◊ *At the moment it is difficult to assess the extent of the ~.*

2 damages money you can claim from sb

ADJ. **civil** | **substantial** | **punitive**
VERB + DAMAGES **incur, suffer** ◊ *~s incurred by the unfairly sacked workers* | **claim, seek, sue** (**sb**) **for** ◊ *He decided to sue the company for ~s.* | **assess** ◊ *The court will assess the ~s.* | **award** (**sb**) | **pay** (**sb**) | **obtain, receive, recover, win** | **be liable for, be liable in** (*BrE*) (*both law*) ◊ *If goods are lost in transit, the carrier will be liable for ~s.*
DAMAGES + NOUN **action** (*BrE*)**, claim** ◊ *A woman is to bring a civil ~s claim against the two men.* | **award**
PREP. **in ~** ◊ *They are claiming $5 million in ~s.* | **~ for** ◊ *He received ~s for personal injury.* | **~ of** ◊ *She was awarded ~s of £90 000.*
PHRASES **an action for ~s** (*BrE*)**, a claim for ~s** ◊ *The judge upheld her claim for ~s against her former employer.*

damage *verb*

ADV. **badly, heavily, seriously, severely** ◊ *The building was badly ~d by fire.* | **slightly** | **irreparably, permanently** ◊ *She may have ~d her health irreparably.*

damaging *adj.*

VERBS **be, prove** | **become**
ADV. **extremely, fairly, very, etc.** | **deeply** (*esp. BrE*)**, highly, immensely** (*esp. BrE*)**, profoundly, seriously, severely** ◊ *This scandal could prove seriously ~ to the government.* | **possibly, potentially** | **economically, environmentally, politically, psychologically** ◊ *Building the proposed new road would be environmentally ~.*
PREP. **to** ◊ *Smoking is ~ to health.*

damp *noun* (*BrE*)

ADJ. **penetrating, rising**
VERB + DAMP **have, suffer from** ◊ *The house had woodworm and rising ~.* | **check for, look for** | **find** ◊ *The surveyor found ~ in the kitchen.*

damp *adj.*

VERBS **be, feel, look, smell** ◊ *The room smelled ~.* | **become, get** | **make sth** ◊ *The rain had made the walls ~.*
ADV. **extremely, fairly, very, etc.** | **a little, slightly, etc.** ◊ *Our clothes got a little ~.* | **still**

dance *noun*

1 series of steps/movements to music

ADJ. **little** | **fast, lively** | **slow, stately** | **first, last** ◊ *Save the last ~ for me.* | **traditional** | **ritual** | **ballroom, folk, square, tap, etc.** | **rain, victory** | **mating** ◊ *pigeons performing their mating ~*
VERB + DANCE **dance, do, perform** ◊ *In her delight she got up and did a little ~.* | **have** ◊ *May I have the next ~? I felt like having a ~.* | **like** ◊ *Would you like a ~?* | **sit out** ◊ *She had to sit out the last ~ because of a twisted ankle.*
DANCE + NOUN **music, rhythm** | **performance, programme/program, routine, sequence, step** | **partner** | **class, instructor, lesson, school, teacher** | **club** | **floor, hall, studio**

2 social meeting with dancing

ADJ. **barn, square** | **school** | **homecoming, prom, Sadie Hawkins** (= when female students invite male students) (*all AmE*) | **dinner, tea**
VERB + DANCE **go to** | **hold**
DANCE + NOUN **band**
PREP. **at a/the ~** ◊ *They met at a ~.*

3 dancing as a form of art/entertainment

ADJ. **contemporary, modern** | **classical**
DANCE + NOUN **company, troupe** | **style**

PHRASES **a school of ~, a style of ~**

dance verb

ADV. **wildly** ◇ *They ~d wildly down the street.* | **slowly** | **well** | **about** (*esp. BrE*), **around, away, off** | **together**
VERB + DANCE **ask sb to** | **want to** | **feel like dancing**
PREP. **for** ◇ *He was almost dancing for joy.* | **to** ◇ *We ~d to the music.* | **with** ◇ *Will you ~ with me?*

dancer noun

ADJ. **brilliant** (*esp. BrE*), **excellent, fine, good, great, wonderful** ◇ *He's a brilliant ~!* | **professional** | **trained** | **leading, principal** ◇ *a principal ~ with the San Francisco Ballet* | **female, male** | **ballet, ballroom, belly, classical, exotic, flamenco, go-go, tap** ◇ *She's a very good flamenco ~.*
DANCER + VERB **perform (sth)** ◇ *~s performing in the street* | *classical ~s performing modern work* | **move** ◇ *The ~s moved gracefully to the music.*
→ Note at JOB

dancing noun

ADJ. **wild** | **slow** | **ballet, ballroom, belly, country, disco, flamenco, folk, line, square, traditional, etc.** ◇ *She does line ~ and yoga in the evenings.*
VERB + DANCING **do, go** ◇ *They liked to go ~ every Saturday night.*
DANCING + NOUN **class, lesson** ◇ *She's taking ~ lessons.* | **school** | **career** | **partner** | **shoes** | **display** (*esp. BrE*)
PHRASES **~ in the streets** ◇ *There was ~ in the streets when we heard that the war was over.*

danger noun

ADJ. **big, considerable, enormous, extreme, grave, great, mortal, obvious, real, serious, significant, terrible** ◇ *They are in grave ~ of losing everything.* ◇ *She knew that she was now in mortal ~.* ◇ *There is a real ~ that the bridge will collapse from the weight of traffic.* | **acute** (*esp. BrE*), **immediate, imminent, impending** ◇ *They are in imminent ~ of attack.* | **clear and present** ◇ *The hackers' actions are a clear and present ~ to our banking system.* | **constant, ever-present** ◇ *the ever-present ~ of crime* | **long-term** | **inherent** ◇ *There are inherent ~s in the system.* | **hidden** | **true** ◇ *We're only now waking up to the true ~s of pesticides.* | **possible, potential** | **perceived** | **personal** | **health, physical** | **public** ◇ *The pollution from the factory is a public ~.* | **little** ◇ *There is little ~ of another crash.*
VERB + DANGER **be exposed to, face** ◇ *On their journey across the desert they faced ~ of all sorts.* | **be fraught with, involve** ◇ *The task was fraught with ~.* | **cause, create** ◇ *He was convicted of causing ~ to other road users.* | **pose, present, represent** ◇ *the ~s posed by the possession of nuclear weapons* | **be aware of, foresee, identify, know, perceive, realize, recognize, see, sense, smell, spot, understand** ◇ *No one foresaw the ~.* ◇ *The animal seemed to sense ~.* | **highlight, illustrate** | **run** ◇ *A company must keep developing or it runs the ~ of stagnating.* | **court** ◇ *Some people take crazy risks because they get a thrill from courting ~.* | **avert** ◇ *Vigorous action is needed to avert the ~ of runaway inflation.* | **lessen, minimize, reduce | increase | avoid, escape | ignore | underestimate**
DANGER + VERB **await, exist, face sb, lie (in sth), lurk, threaten sb** ◇ *One of the biggest ~s facing us may be climate change.* ◇ *The ~ lies in becoming too complacent.* ◇ *Where would they hide if ~ threatened?* | **arise from sth, come from sb/sth** ◇ *The biggest ~ to gorillas comes from humans.* | **pass** ◇ *We waited until all ~ had passed.* | **remain**
DANGER + NOUN **area, point, spot** (*esp. BrE*), **zone** ◇ *Despite the high levels of radiation, people are now moving back into the ~ zone.* | **signals, signs** ◇ *He recognized the ~ signs and gave up smoking.* | **money** (*BrE*), **pay** (*AmE*) ◇ *They should be paid ~ money for the job they're doing.* ◇ *They should get ~ pay for the job they're doing.*
PREP. **in ~** ◇ *We weren't in any ~.* | **in ~ of** ◇ *The plant is now in ~ of extinction.* | **out of ~** ◇ *They ran until they were out*

of *~.* | **~ from** | **~ of** ◇ *We're in serious ~ of becoming a nation of worriers.* | **~ to** ◇ *There is no ~ to the public from these chemicals.*
PHRASES **be off the ~ list, be on the ~ list** (*both BrE*) ◇ *He was in a critical condition, but is now off the ~ list.*

dangerous adj.

VERBS **be, feel, look, prove, seem, sound** | **become, get** ◇ *The situation could get ~.* | **remain** | **make sth** ◇ *The ice is making the roads very ~ tonight.* | **consider sth, regard sth as** ◇ *The escapee is not considered ~.*
ADV. **extremely, fairly, very, etc.** | **exceedingly, highly, incredibly, terribly** ◇ *a highly ~ situation* | **increasingly** | **a little, slightly, etc.** | **possibly, potentially** | **downright, positively** ◇ *It's a risky idea, if not downright ~!* | **inherently** | **notoriously** ◇ *This route through the mountains is notoriously ~.* | **politically** ◇ *Raising income tax is considered politically ~.*
PREP. **for** ◇ *This treatment is extremely ~ for the mother.* | **to** ◇ *not ~ to humans*

dare verb

ADV. **barely** (*esp. AmE*), **hardly, scarcely** ◇ *I hardly ~d to breathe.*
VERB + DARE **wouldn't** ◇ *I wouldn't ~ go by myself.*

daring adj.

VERBS **be, feel** | **become, get, grow** ◇ *He had grown more ~.* | **consider sth, think sth** ◇ *Her actions was considered very ~ at the time.*
ADV. **very** | **a little, slightly** | **pretty, quite, rather**

dark noun

ADJ. **pitch** ◇ *I fumbled for the light switch in the pitch ~.* | **gathering** ◇ *We could just make out some figures in the gathering ~.*
PREP. **after ~** ◇ *The girls weren't allowed out after ~.* | **before ~** ◇ *We'd better try and finish this job before ~.* | **in the ~** ◇ *I hate getting up in the ~.*
PHRASES **afraid of the ~** ◇ *Many small children are afraid of the ~.*

dark adj.

VERBS **be, look, seem** | **become, get, go, grow, turn** ◇ *It gets ~ at about six o'clock.* ◇ *Suddenly the whole sky went ~.* ◇ *As it grew ~, they gathered around the fire.* | **remain, stay**
ADV. **extremely, fairly, very, etc.** | **completely** | **a little, slightly, etc.** | **almost, nearly** ◇ *It's only three o'clock and it's nearly ~ already.* | **already** | **still**

darkness noun

ADJ. **complete, pitch, total, utter** ◇ *The building was in pitch ~.* | **deep, inky** ◇ *the inky ~ of the tunnel* | **gathering, growing** ◇ *It was becoming impossible to see the map in the gathering ~.*
VERB + DARKNESS **be plunged into** ◇ *The electricity failed and the house was plunged into ~.* | **lie in, stand in** ◇ *The valley lay in ~.* | **penetrate, pierce**
DARKNESS + VERB **close in, come, descend, fall** ◇ *We arrived at the town just as ~ fell.* | **envelope sb/sth, surround sb/sth** | **swallow sb/sth** ◇ *The room was swallowed by ~.* | **lift** ◇ *We waited for the ~ to lift.*
PREP. **in (the) ~** ◇ *The building was in ~.* ◇ *Her eyes seemed to glow in the ~.* | **into the ~** ◇ *The car disappeared into the ~.* | **out of the ~** ◇ *A figure appeared out of the ~.*
PHRASES **the hours of ~** ◇ *The bombing took place during the hours of ~.* | **under cover of ~** ◇ *They moved from place to place under cover of ~.*

dash noun

1 sudden quick movement

ADJ. **quick, sudden** | **frantic, mad, wild** (*esp. AmE*) | **final, last-minute** (*both esp. BrE*)
VERB + DASH **make**
PREP. **~ across** ◇ *We had to make a frantic ~ across town to get*

our plane | **~ for** ◇ *He made a ~ for the door.* | **~ from** | **~ through** ◇ *a mad ~ through back alleys* ◇ *The book starts with a quick ~ through the country's history. (esp. BrE)* | **~ to** ◇ *He made a 200-mile ~ to the hospital when a kidney donor became available.*

2 small amount of sth

VERB + DASH **add** ◇ *Add a ~ of lemon juice.*
PREP. **~ of** ◇ *The food is European with a ~ of Morocco.*

dash *verb*

1 go/run quickly

ADV. **frantically** | **about** (*esp. BrE*), **around, back, forward, off, out** ◇ *I have to ~ off now.*
VERB + DASH **have to, must** (*esp. BrE*) ◇ *I have to dash—I'm late.*
PREP. **across, along, down, in, into, out of, through, to, up** ◇ *He ~ed frantically across the road.*

2 destroy sth

ADV. **quickly** | **cruelly** (*esp. BrE*) ◇ *Her hopes were cruelly ~ed when her parents refused to let her go.*

data *noun*

ADJ. **accurate, reliable** | **comprehensive, detailed, extensive** | **limited** | **preliminary, raw** ◇ *We have amassed a large amount of raw ~ for analysis.* | **factual, hard** ◇ *There is no hard ~ to support these theories.* | **available, published** | **unpublished** | **personal** | **digital, empirical, experimental, numerical, observational, quantitative, scientific, statistical** | **demographic, environmental, financial, genetic, geological, historical, technical**
... OF DATA **piece** ◇ *One vital item of ~ was missing from the table.* | **mass, set** ◇ *Special software is needed to manipulate the mass of ~.* ◇ *Although we were using the same set of ~, we obtained different results.*
VERB + DATA **acquire, amass, capture, collect, gather, generate, get, obtain** ◇ *We need to collect more ~ before we can do any more work.* | **enter, feed in** ◇ *The next step is to feed in all this ~.* | **have, hold, record, store** ◇ *They are not allowed to hold ~ on people's private finances.* | **access, retrieve** | **analyse/analyze, compare, examine, interpret, look at, study** | **use** | **handle, manage, manipulate, process** ◇ *The computer can manipulate massive amounts of ~.* | **exchange, share, transfer** | **send, transmit** | **present (sb with), show** | **provide (sb with), publish, report** ◇ *The government departments refused to provide the ~ that we required.* | **fit** ◇ *This theory seems to fit the available ~.*
DATA + VERB **be derived from sth** ◇ *The ~ derived from this project has increased our knowledge of how genes work.* | **illustrate sth, indicate sth, reflect sth, show sth, suggest sth** ◇ *Data indicates that most crime is committed by young males.* ◇ *This ~ reflects the magnitude of the problem.* | **support sth**
DATA + NOUN **acquisition, capture, collection** ◇ *Weather conditions have made accurate ~ collection difficult.* | **entry, input** | **storage** | **access, retrieval** | **analysis, handling, management, manipulation, processing** | **exchange, interchange, stream, transfer, transmission** | **protection, security** ◇ *These demands could breach EU data-protection laws.* | **loss** | **source** | **archive, bank** (usually *databank*), **base** (usually *database*), **centre/center, file, network, set** ◇ *The fuller ~ set for this period permits a much more detailed analysis.* | **service, structure, system**
PREP. **in the ~** ◇ *We have found some very interesting things in the ~.* | **~ about** ◇ *Data about patients is only released with their permission.* | **~ for** ◇ *We have no ~ for southern Mexico.* | **~ from** ◇ *My aim is to synthesize ~ from all the surveys.* | **~ on** ◇ *~ on the effects of pollution*
PHRASES **the acquisition, handling, storage, etc. of ~** | **a source of ~**

database *noun*

ADJ. **large** | **comprehensive** | **central, national, public** | **computer, computerized, electronic** | **online**
VERB + DATABASE **build, build up, create, establish, set up** ◇ *We're trying to create our own computerized ~.* | **maintain** |

add (sth) to, update ◇ *The ~ is updated monthly.* | **access, search, use**
DATABASE + VERB **contain sth** ◇ *The new ~ contains 200 000 images.*
DATABASE + NOUN **application, engine, server, software, system** | **technology** | **design, development** | **management** | **access, search** | **administrator** | **entry**
PREP. **in a/the ~** ◇ *We have over 8 000 customer names in our ~.* | **on a/the ~** ◇ *The information is stored on a large ~.* | **~ of** ◇ *a very large ~ of information*

date *noun*

1 particular day

ADJ. **earlier, earliest** ◇ *She suggested an earlier ~ for the meeting.* | **later, latest** | **exact, firm, specific** ◇ *I can't give you specific ~s.* | **target** | **provisional** (*esp. BrE*), **tentative** | **unspecified** | **effective** | **significant** ◇ *May 7, 2005 was a very significant ~ in my life.* | **closing** ◇ *The closing ~ for applications is May 22.* | **expiration** (*AmE*), **expiry** (*BrE*) ◇ *What's the expiration/expiry ~ on your credit card?* | **delivery, publication, release** | **arrival, departure** | **due** ◇ *The baby was born exactly on its due ~.* | **anniversary, birth** | **pull** (*AmE*), **sell-by** ◇ *This yogurt is past its sell-by ~.* | **cut-off, end** ◇ *Historians disagree on the cut-off ~ for the medieval period.* | **commencement** (*esp. BrE*), **start** | **completion** ◇ *The building was not finished by the completion ~.*
VERB + DATE **agree, agree on, arrange, decide, decide on, fix, set** ◇ *Can we fix ~s for the trip?* ◇ *Has a ~ been set for the meeting?* | **find** | **give sb** ◇ *Give me a couple of ~s are good for you.* | **check** | **change** | **announce**
DATE + NOUN **stamp** | **book** (usually *datebook*)
PREP. **after a/the ~** ◇ *We cannot accept applications received after this ~.* | **at a ... ~** ◇ *The election is scheduled to take place at an unspecified ~ in the spring.* | **before a/the ~** | **by a/the ~** ◇ *The building must be finished by the ~ agreed.* | **from a/the ~** ◇ *The agreement runs from that ~.* | **on a/the ~** ◇ *I have two meetings on that ~.* | **~ for** ◇ *We need to set a ~ for the wedding.* | **~ of** ◇ *the ~ of the election*
PHRASES **the big ~** ◇ *the biggest ~ in the country music calendar* | **at a future ~, at some future ~** ◇ *More money will be made available at some future ~.* | **at a later ~** ◇ *We can do that at a later ~.* | **~ of birth** ◇ *Please give your name, address and ~ of birth.* | **of recent ~** ◇ *The foundations are Roman, but the rest of the building is of more recent ~.* | **put a ~ on sth** ◇ *It's difficult to put a ~ on when the idea started.* | **today's ~** ◇ *What's today's ~?*

2 appointment to meet sb socially

ADJ. **dinner, lunch** | **blind** ◇ *She met her husband on a blind ~.* | **double** (= when two couples have a date together) | **hot** ◇ *She had a hot ~ and wanted to look her best.* | **first**
VERB + DATE **have** ◇ *I have a ~ with Camilla on Friday night.* | **find** ◇ *I need to find a ~ for Friday.* | **make** (*esp. BrE*) ◇ *We must make a ~ to have lunch.* | **keep** ◇ *She wanted to arrive in time to keep her ~.* | **break** (*AmE*), **cancel** ◇ *He really didn't want to break his ~ with Alicia.*
DATE + NOUN **movie** (*AmE*) ◇ *It's a great ~ movie.* | **rape**
PREP. **on a ~** ◇ *She's out on a ~ with her new girlfriend.* | **~ with**

date *verb*

ADV. **accurately, precisely** ◇ *It has not yet been possible to ~ the paintings accurately.*

datebook *noun* (*AmE*) → See also DIARY

VERB + DATEBOOK **note sth down in, put sth (down) in, write sth (down) in** ◇ *I wrote it down in my ~ so I wouldn't forget.*
PREP. **in a/your ~**

dated *adj.*

VERBS **appear, be, feel, look, seem, sound** | **become**
ADV. **extremely, fairly, very, etc.** | **hopelessly** (*esp. BrE*) | **a little, slightly, etc.** ◇ *These ideas seem a little ~ now.* |

curiously (*BrE*) ◊ *The movie's characters speak in a curiously ~ way.*

daughter noun

ADJ. **baby, infant, newborn** | **little, small, young** | **adolescent, teenage** | **adult** (*esp. AmE*), **grown-up** (*esp. BrE*) | **6-month-old, 2-year-old, etc.** | **only** | **twin** | **eldest, first-born, middle, oldest, youngest** | **elder, younger** | **adopted** | **illegitimate, legitimate** | **dutiful, good** | **beloved** | **long-lost** | **married, unmarried**
VERB + DAUGHTER **have** ◊ *They have three young ~s.* | **bear** (*formal*), **give birth to** ◊ *His wife recently gave birth to a ~.* | **bring up, raise** (*esp. AmE*) ◊ *Living alone and trying to bring up a small ~ is no easy task.*
DAUGHTER + VERB **grow up**

dawn noun

1 early morning

ADJ. **grey/gray** | **early**
VERB + DAWN **greet** ◊ *He always got up to greet the ~.* | **see, watch**
DAWN + VERB **break, come, come up** ◊ *Dawn was breaking over the valley.*
DAWN + NOUN **light, sky** | **chorus** ◊ *The ~ chorus (= birds singing) woke Robyn at five.* | **patrol, raid** ◊ *Ammunition was seized during a ~ raid on the house.*
PREP. **at** ◊ *That morning, she rose at ~.* | **before ~** | **by ~** | **till ~, until ~** | **towards/toward ~**
PHRASES **(at) the crack of ~** (= as soon as it begins to get light), **from ~ to dusk** ◊ *He works from ~ to dusk, and often well into the night.*

2 beginning

ADJ. **false** ◊ *This sudden success may prove to be a false ~ (= not the beginning of continued success).* | **new**
VERB + DAWN **mark, signal** ◊ *This appointment marked the ~ of a productive era in her scientific career.* | **see** ◊ *We are seeing the ~ of a new era.*
PREP. **~ of** ◊ *the ~ of civilization/history* ◊ *Let's think back to the ~ of time.*

dawn verb

1 begin

PHRASES **~ bright, clear, cold, sunny, etc.** ◊ *The day ~ed bright and sunny.*

2 become clear

ADV. **suddenly** | **gradually, slowly** ◊ *It slowly ~ed on me that he might have been mistaken.* | **eventually, finally**
VERB + DAWN **begin to** ◊ *It was beginning to ~ on her that she had been fooled.*
PREP. **on** ◊ *The dreadful truth finally ~ed on me.*

day noun

1 period of 24 hours

ADJ. **the following, (the) next** | **the previous** | **the other** ◊ *I was in your area the other ~ (= recently).* | **one, some** ◊ *I hope we meet again some ~.* | **the very** ◊ *It happened on the very ~ (= the same day) that Kemp was murdered.* ◊ *The letter arrived the very next ~.* | **auspicious, big, eventful, historic, memorable, red-letter, special** | **field** ◊ *The tabloid press had a field ~ with the latest government scandal.* | **normal, ordinary** | **fateful, sad** ◊ *those killed in the hail of bullets fired on that fateful ~* | **Christmas, Independence, Mother's, Thanksgiving, etc.** | **feast, holy** | **election, market, opening, pay, polling, visiting, wedding** | **sports** (*BrE*) | **game** (*AmE*), **match** (*esp. BrE*) | **rest, school, study, training** ◊ *the pattern of the school ~*
DAY + VERB **pass** ◊ *He thought of her less as the ~s passed.* | **come** ◊ *When that ~ comes, I plan to be far away.*
PREP. **by the ~** ◊ *He's getting stronger by the ~.* | **for a/the ~** ◊ *They stayed for ten ~s.* | **in a/the ~** ◊ *We hope to finish the*

job in a few ~s. | **on the ~ (of)** ◊ *On the ~ of his wedding he was very nervous.* | **~ of** ◊ *It was the ~ of the big game.*
PHRASES **~ by ~** ◊ *Morale was sinking ~ by ~.*

NOTE

Days of the week

last… , next… , that… , this… , this coming… ◊ *The concert is this coming Wednesday.* ◊ *Are you free next Thursday?*
the… before, the previous… ◊ *I'd been paid the previous Friday.*
the following… ◊ *She was due to start work the following Monday.*
… of last/next week, … of that/this week ◊ *He arrived on Monday of last week.*
the… before last ◊ *We came here the Tuesday before last.*
… week, a week on… ◊ *I've bought tickets for Thursday week (= for the performance that is seven days after Thursday).*
the first, second, last… in the month, the first, second, last… of the month ◊ *The museum is free on the last Sunday of every month.*
alternate… , each… , every… ◊ *The competition is held on alternate Wednesdays.*
all day… ◊ *The restaurant is closed all day Saturday.*
…afternoon, evening, morning, night, etc. ◊ *I'll see you on Friday evening.* ◊ *Saturday lunchtimes are very busy in the restaurant.*
first thing (on)… ◊ *I'll post it first thing on Monday morning.*
late (on)… ◊ *The crash occurred late on Tuesday night.*
one… ◊ *One Saturday morning, without telling anyone of my plan, I boarded a bus and headed out.*
spend… ◊ *She liked to spend Saturday afternoon shopping.*
manage… (*informal*) ◊ *I could manage (= meet you on) Tuesday, say 11.30?*
open/closed (on)… ◊ *We're open every day except Sunday.*
… arrives, … comes, … dawns (*literary*) ◊ *Monday dawned, with a promise of sunshine.*
on (a)… ◊ *A public meeting is to be held on Wednesday at the church.* ◊ *We'll meet Monday.* (*informal, esp. AmE*) ◊ *She was born on a Sunday.* ◊ *I like to just relax on Saturdays.*
between… and… , (from)… to… , through (*AmE*) ◊ *The office is open until 5 p.m. Monday to Friday.* ◊ *We'll be in Miami Tuesday through Friday.*
by, no later than… ◊ *Entries are to arrive no later than Monday, October 1.*
for… ◊ *A special meeting is arranged for Friday, May 17.*
Monday's deadline, election, game, meeting, race, etc. ◊ *He was not present at Tuesday's meeting.*

---

2 time between sunrise and sunset

ADJ. **beautiful, bright, fine, glorious, hot, nice, sunny, warm** | **cloudy, cold, grey/gray, rainy, windy** | **autumn** (*esp. BrE*), **fall** (*AmE*), **spring, summer, summer's, winter, winter's** ◊ *a fine summer's ~* | **fun, good, great, happy, lovely, perfect, wonderful** ◊ *Memories of happy ~s on the hills never fade.* | **bad, terrible** ◊ *It's been one of the worst ~s of my life.* | **full** ◊ *I knew I had a full day's driving ahead of me.*
VERB + DAY **spend** ◊ *We spent the ~ gardening.* | **start** ◊ *Be sure to start the ~ with a good breakfast.* | **see** ◊ *I never thought I would see the ~ when free elections would be held in this country.*
DAY + VERB **break, dawn** ◊ *As ~ dawned I found her already hard at work.* | **go** ◊ *How did your ~ go?*
PREP. **by ~** ◊ *We preferred to travel at night and rest by ~.* | **during the ~** | **for a/the ~** ◊ *We went to the beach for the ~.*
PHRASES **all ~ (long)** | **at the end of the ~** | **~ and night** | **one of those ~s** ◊ *It's been one of those ~s when everything's gone wrong.*

ADJ. **work** (usually *workday*) (*AmE*), **working** (*BrE*) | **bad, busy, hard, long, tiring** ◇ *a hard ~ at the office* | **good, quiet, slow** | **7-hour, 8-hour,** etc. ◇ *I do a 9-hour ~* | **half** | **sick** ◇ *I am entitled to ten paid sick ~s a year.* | **vacation** (*AmE*)

PHRASES **a good day's work**

4 (often **days**) particular period of time

ADJ. **early, former, old, olden** ◇ *in the early ~s of television* | **school, student, young** ◇ *in his younger ~s* | **glory, golden, happy, heady** ◇ *the heady ~s of the 'swinging sixties'* | **dark** ◇ *the dark ~s of recession* | **playing** ◇ *Some players go into management once their playing ~s are over.*

PREP. **in sb's ~** ◇ *Things were very different in my grandfather's ~.* | **of the ~** ◇ *the government of the ~* | **since the ~s of** ◇ *Much has changed since the ~s of my youth.*

PHRASES **gone are the ~s when…** ◇ *Gone are the ~s when you could smoke in restaurants.* | **the bad old ~s, the good old ~s** ◇ *That was in the bad old ~s of rampant inflation.* | **in this ~ and age** | **in those ~s** | **the present ~** ◇ *a study of drama from Ibsen to the present ~* | **these ~s** ◇ *Kids grow up so quickly these ~s.* | **those were the ~s** (= used to suggest that a time in the past was better than now)

daylight *noun*

ADJ. **broad, full** ◇ *He was robbed in broad ~.* | **bright** | **natural** ◇ *I prefer to work in natural ~.*

VERB + DAYLIGHT **let in** ◇ *The thin curtains let in the ~.* | **keep out, shut out** ◇ *The shutters were closed to keep out the ~.* | **emerge into** ◇ *The prisoners emerged blinking into the ~.*

DAYLIGHT + VERB **filter through sth, flood in, penetrate (sth)** ◇ *A little ~ was filtering through the curtains.* ◇ *He drew back the curtains and the ~ flooded in.* ◇ *The ~ penetrated to the far corners of the room.* | **break, come** ◇ *Around 6 a.m. ~ broke.* | **fade** ◇ *The evening turned cool as ~ faded.*

DAYLIGHT + NOUN **hours** ◇ *The public has access during ~ hours.*

PREP. **before ~** ◇ *She was up before ~.* | **by ~** ◇ *By ~ the fire was almost under control.* | **in ~** ◇ *I can see better in ~.* | **into the ~** ◇ *She went back out into the ~.*

PHRASES **the hours of ~** ◇ *The machines roar incessantly during the hours of ~.*

daytime *noun*

DAYTIME + NOUN **phone number, telephone number** | **drama, show, soap, television** | **temperature** | **hours**

PREP. **during the ~** | **in the ~** ◇ *Resist the temptation to nap in the ~.*

dazed *adj.*

VERBS **appear, be, feel, look, seem, sound** ◇ *She looked ~ and frightened.* | **leave sb** ◇ *The punch left him ~ and bleeding.*

ADV. **a little, slightly,** etc. ◇ *I still felt a little ~.* | **almost** | **half**

PREP. **by** ◇ *half ~ by shock*

PHRASES **~ and confused** ◇ *We were left feeling ~ and confused.*

dead *adj.*

VERBS **be, lie** ◇ *His wife lay ~ beside him.* | **look** | **play** ◇ *The animal will sometimes escape danger by playing ~.* | **drop, fall, fall down** ◇ *He just dropped ~ one day at work.* | **shoot sb, strike sb** ◇ *Gunmen shot ~ two unarmed police officers.* ◇ *She had been struck ~ by lightning.* | **find sb** ◇ *The woman was found ~ with a rope around her neck.* | **declare sb, pronounce sb** ◇ *She was declared ~ on arrival at the hospital.*

ADV. **quite** (*esp. BrE*) ◇ *I'm afraid he's quite ~.* | **almost, nearly** | **already** ◇ *By the time the police arrived, he was already ~.*

PHRASES **~ and buried** (*figurative*) ◇ *In ten years he'll be ~ and buried as a politician.* | **~ and gone** ◇ *That won't happen until long after I'm ~ and gone.* | **~ or alive** ◇ *A reward was offered for his capture ~ or alive.* | **more ~ than alive** ◇ *Poor child, she looks more ~ than alive.*

deadline *noun*

ADJ. **strict, tight**

VERB + DEADLINE **face, have, work to** ◇ *We're working to a very tight ~.* | **impose, set** ◇ *The ~ set by the court is Monday.* | **extend** ◇ *We're asking them to extend the ~.* | **make, meet** ◇ *It will be a struggle to meet the ~.* | **miss**

DEADLINE + VERB **approach, loom, near** ◇ *She began to panic as the ~ approached.* | **expire, pass** ◇ *The Wednesday ~ passed without any communication from the rebel leader.*

PREP. **before a/the ~, by a/the ~** ◇ *I must get this report finished by tomorrow's ~.* | **~ for** ◇ *The ~ for entries is noon Thursday.*

deadlock *noun*

ADJ. **political**

VERB + DEADLOCK **reach** (*esp. BrE*) ◇ *The strike appeared to have reached a ~.* | **break, end, resolve** (*BrE*)

PREP. **in ~** ◇ *The two were in ~.* ◇ *The two were in a ~.* (*AmE*) | **~ between** ◇ *the ~ between striking workers and their employer* | **~ in** ◇ *The summit called for an end to the ~ in the peace talks.* | **~ over** ◇ *an attempt to break the ~ over the issue of pay*

PHRASES **end in ~** (*BrE*), **end in a ~** (*AmE*) ◇ *The negotiations ended in (a) ~.*

deaf *adj.*

VERBS **be** | **be born** ◇ *Their child was born ~.* | **become, go** ◇ *He eventually went ~.* | **remain** ◇ *She remained ~ until she died.* | **leave sb, make sb** ◇ *Standing next to the machine all day left her ~ in one ear.*

ADV. **completely, profoundly** (*technical*), **stone, totally** ◇ *Many of these children are profoundly ~.* ◇ *It's no good shouting—he's stone ~.* | **legally** (*AmE*) | **a little, slightly,** etc. ◇ *She spoke loudly because her mother was a little ~.* | **partially** | **nearly**

PREP. **to** (*figurative*) ◇ *The committee remained ~ to our suggestions.*

PHRASES **~ in one ear**

deal *noun*

ADJ. **fair, good, sweet** (*AmE*) | **bad, raw, rotten, rough** ◇ *Immigrants often get a bad ~ when it comes to pay.* | **blockbuster** (*AmE, informal*), **major** ◇ *They are hoping to clinch a major ~ to supply computers to the army.* | **exclusive** ◇ *The TV station has signed an exclusive ~ to show every game of the season.* | **lucrative** | **five-year,** etc. | **long-term** | **compromise** (*esp. BrE*) | **cut-price** (*BrE*) ◇ *The company are offering cut-price ~s on many flights.* | **shady** ◇ *He has been mixed up in several shady ~s with arms dealers.* | **back-room, secret** | **sweetheart** (= unfairly treating one person or company better than another) (*AmE*) ◇ *They can't offer us a sweetheart ~ on the rental fees we pay.* | **package** ◇ *The union accepted a package ~ including higher pensions.* | **business, financial, political, trade** | **record** ◇ *The band eventually signed a record ~.* | **endorsement, financing, pay, sponsorship** | **licensing** | **arms, weapons** | **peace** | **last-minute** | **two-book, three-picture,** etc. ◇ *The band signed a two-album ~ with a record company.*

VERB + DEAL **agree** (*BrE*), **agree on, agree to, close, complete, conclude, cut** (*informal*), **do, finalize, ink** (*AmE, informal*), **make, reach, seal, sign, strike** ◇ *Management and unions have agreed a new ~ on pay and productivity.* ◇ *I'll make a ~ with you—I'll work evenings if you'll work weekends.* | **arrange, broker, hammer out, negotiate, structure** (*esp. AmE*), **work out** ◇ *The company structured a ~ to purchase the competitor out of bankruptcy.* | **clinch, get, land, secure, swing** (*informal, esp. AmE*), **win** ◇ *Nurses have taken to the streets to get a fair ~ from the government.* | **have** ◇ *She has a lucrative ~ with a cosmetics company.* | **pull out of** ◇ *We pulled out of the ~ because of rising costs.* | **nix** (*AmE, informal*), **scupper** ◇ *Any sponsorship ~ would be scuppered if Jones misses the Olympics.* | **offer (sb), propose** | **announce** | **pursue, seek** ◇ *The company hopes to pursue* similar ~s with other providers. | **accept, approve** ◊ Staff have accepted a ~ offering them a 2% share of profits. | **block, oppose, reject** | **sweeten** ◊ He even sweetened the ~ with a $5 000 signing bonus.

DEAL + VERB **go ahead, happen** ◊ The pay ~ will not now go ahead. | **fall apart, fall through** ◊ The ~ fell through when the author received a more attractive offer. | **involve sb/sth** | **allow sth** | **expire**

DEAL + NOUN **maker** ◊ business brokers and other ~ makers (esp. AmE) | **breaker, killer** (informal, both esp. AmE) ◊ Lack of accounting clarity can discourage investors and become a ~ breaker.

PREP. **in a/the ~** ◊ They took over the company in a £750 000 ~. | **under a/the ~** ◊ Under the ~, you save money if you repay the loan early. | **~ between** ◊ a ~ between Brazil and Argentina | **~ from** ◊ You may get a better ~ from another bank. | **~ on** ◊ I got a very good ~ on my new car. | **~ over** ◊ The unions are ready to do a ~ over pay. | **~ with** ◊ The company has done a ~ with the cleaning staff.

PHRASES **get a fair ~, get a square ~** ◊ The union tries to get a square ~ for all its members. | **part of the ~** ◊ An increased pay offer is part of the ~. | **the terms of the ~** ◊ Under the terms of the ~, the band has to make two albums a year.

→ Special page at BUSINESS

deal verb

ADV. **directly**

PREP. **in** ◊ The business ~s in second-hand books. | **with** ◊ Our factory ~s directly with its customers.

PHR V **deal with sth**

ADV. **quickly, speedily** | **at length, fully** ◊ This topic is dealt with at greater length in the following chapter. | **adequately, effectively** | **fairly, honestly, properly** ◊ You have not dealt fairly with me. | **harshly** | **easily** ◊ Not all complaints are so easily dealt with. | **separately** ◊ The two issues should be dealt with separately. | **together**

PHRASES **a way of ~ing with sth** ◊ We discussed different ways of ~ing with the problem.

dealer noun

ADJ. **authorized, licensed** ◊ It is always a good idea to sell through a licensed ~. | **independent, private** | **reputable** ◊ Always buy from a reputable ~. | **shady, unscrupulous** | **street** ◊ Addicts were forced to buy from street ~s. | **drug** | **cocaine, crack, heroin, etc.** | **arms, firearms, gun** | **antique, antiques** | **art** | **auto** (AmE), **boat, car, used-car** | **scrap**

DEALER + VERB **offer, sell** ◊ art ~s offering period and regional paintings

PREP. **through a/the ~** ◊ She sold the painting through a Boston art ~. | **~ in** ◊ a ~ in antiques

→ Note at JOB

dealings noun

ADJ. **extensive** | **direct, personal** | **day-to-day** ◊ The new arrangements will help the banks in their ordinary day-to-day ~. | **future** | **corrupt, illegal, shady, underhand** (esp. BrE) | **business, commercial, financial**

VERB + DEALINGS **have** ◊ They had extensive ~ with officials in Kabul.

PREP. **in your ~ with** ◊ We need to be very careful in our ~ with these distressed young people.

death noun

ADJ. **early, premature, untimely** ◊ The president's untimely ~ has thrown the country into chaos. | **sudden, unexpected** | **immediate, instant** | **quick** | **lingering, slow** | **approaching, imminent, impending** | **certain, inevitable** ◊ He had been miraculously saved from almost certain ~. | **preventable** ◊ Obesity is a leading cause of preventable ~s. | **needless, senseless, unnecessary** ◊ needless ~s in a war created by hatred | **horrible, horrific, terrible** | **grisly, gruesome** | **tragic** ◊ the tragic ~ of their son | **mysterious,**

suspicious ◊ Police are not treating the ~ as suspicious. | **unexplained** | **natural, unnatural** | **accidental** ◊ a verdict of accidental ~ | **wrongful** ◊ People can sue for wrongful ~. (AmE, law) | **brutal, violent** ◊ Police report a decrease in violent ~s. | **agonizing, painful** | **painless** | **cot** (BrE), **crib** (AmE) | **neonatal** ◊ The most common cause of neonatal ~ is birth defects. | **road** | **cancer, cancer-related** ◊ More than 30% of all cancer ~s in the country can be attributed to smoking. | **drug-related, overdose** ◊ an increase in drug overdose ~s | **shooting** | **combat** (AmE) ◊ Women accounted for 2% of all combat ~s. | **civilian** ◊ The bombing resulted in many civilian ~s. | **living** (figurative) ◊ the living ~ of captivity

VERB + DEATH **bring, cause, lead to, mean, result in** ◊ the drivers who bring ~ to our roads ◊ Poor living conditions can lead to early ~. ◊ Touching the wires means instant ~. ◊ The brutal attack resulted in the man's ~. | **die, face, meet, suffer** ◊ She died a slow and painful ~. ◊ He met his ~ two years later. | **contemplate** | **risk** | **fear** | **approach, be near, near** ◊ avoid, cheat, defy, escape** ◊ He escaped ~ by inches when a tree fell on his tent. | **hasten** ◊ drugs which will hasten the ~ of a terminally ill patient | **prevent** | **fake** ◊ She faked her own ~ so he couldn't find her. | **save sb from** | **grieve, mourn** ◊ They are still mourning the ~ of their daughter. | **avenge** ◊ How far would they go to avenge the ~ of their friend? | **order** ◊ What kind of man orders the ~ of his own sister? | **investigate** | **experience, witness** ◊ He witnessed the ~ of his mother from tuberculosis. | **celebrate, commemorate, mark** ◊ a service to commemorate the ~ of thousands of soldiers | **record** ◊ No ~s from the disease have been recorded since 1990. | **bleed to, burn to, choke to, freeze to, starve to** | **condemn sb, sentence sb to** | **batter sb to, beat sb to, burn sb to, choke sb to, club sb to, crush sb to, flog sb to, hack sb to, kick sb to, put sb to, stab sb to, stone sb to, torture sb to, trample sb to** | **be punishable by, be punished by** ◊ Incest was punishable by ~.

DEATH + VERB **come, happen, occur** ◊ Her ~ came at the age of 82. ◊ More ~s occur in winter. | **result from sth** ◊ ~s resulting from disease | **approach** ◊ It's a curious sensation, knowing that your ~ is approaching soon.

DEATH + NOUN **rate** ◊ The government's campaign aims to cut the ~ rate from heart attacks. | **count, toll** ◊ The ~ toll in the earthquake has been put at over one thousand. | **penalty, sentence** ◊ If found guilty of drug trafficking, the pair could face the ~ penalty. | **row** ◊ There are currently over 3 000 prisoners on ~ row. | **certificate** | **benefit** ◊ Your next of kin will receive ~ benefit if you die in an accident. | **duties** (BrE), **tax** (AmE) ◊ After the ~ duties had been paid, there was little money left for the family. | **threat** ◊ The actor has received ~ threats since appearing in the controversial movie. | **wish** ◊ He took drugs as if he had some kind of ~ wish. | **notice** ◊ a ~ notice in the newspaper | **record** ◊ Chicago's birth and ~ records | **date** ◊ It's easier to trace ancestors if you know their birth or ~ dates. | **agonies, throes** ◊ The snake was writhing in its ~ agonies. | **bed** (usually **deathbed**) ◊ On his deathbed, my father made me promise not to sell the house. | **squad** ◊ Paramilitary ~ squads are operating in the area. | **march** ◊ The prisoners were sent on a ~ march through the jungle. | **warrant** (often figurative) ◊ By publicly condemning the terrorists, he was signing his own ~ warrant. | **camp** ◊ He died as a prisoner of war in an enemy ~ camp. | **scene** ◊ The movie contains plenty of ~ scenes. | **cult**

PREP. **after (sb's) ~** ◊ Do you believe in life after ~? | **at ~** (formal) ◊ The average age at ~ of plague victims was 14. | **before (sb's) ~** | **in ~** ◊ His face looked more peaceful in ~ than it had during his last days. | **near (to) ~** ◊ It was clear that the dog was near ~. | **on sb's ~** ◊ On Samuel's ~, the farm passed to his sons. | **by ~** ◊ ~ by starvation | **~ from** ◊ Two ~s from cholera have been reported.

PHRASES **cause of ~** ◊ The coroner said the cause of ~ was a stroke. | **a matter of life and ~, a matter of life or ~** ◊ Delivering on time is a matter of life and ~ for a small company. | **put sb to ~** | **sentence of ~** ◊ Four prisoners were under sentence of ~.

debate noun

1 discussion

ADJ. **considerable** | **growing** ◊ *the growing ~ on school reform* | **fierce, heated, intense, lively, raging, robust, serious, spirited, vigorous** ◊ *There has been heated ~ about whether the movie should be allowed.* | **acrimonious, bitter, contentious** ◊ *The club started admitting women in 1901 after years of bitter ~.* | **rational, reasoned** ◊ *The nature of this book is to provoke reasoned ~.* | **honest, open** ◊ *Honest ~ is the foundation of democracy.* | **continuing, ongoing** ◊ *the ongoing ~ over American foreign policy* | **age-old, long-running, long-standing** | **endless** | **contemporary, current** | **broader, wider** ◊ *You cannot separate unemployment from the wider ~ about the economy.* | **public** ◊ *Television actually encourages public ~ about such issues.* | **national** | **internal** ◊ *Efforts to reduce the budget have led to a lot of internal ~ at the studio.* | **philosophical, political, scientific, theological** | **academic, intellectual, scholarly**
VERB + DEBATE **have** | **contribute to** ◊ *Many leading charities have contributed to the ~ on world poverty.* | **enter, join** ◊ *He was reluctant to enter the ~ for or against war.* | **encourage, promote** ◊ *A healthy society promotes vigorous ~.* | **fuel, generate, ignite, provoke, spark off, spur, start, stimulate, stir, trigger** ◊ *This accident has sparked off an intense ~ on road safety.* | **reignite, rekindle, renew, reopen** ◊ *The incident has reignited public ~ over the role of teachers.* | **drive, influence** | **stifle** ◊ *He accused the government of trying to stifle ~.* | **frame, shape** ◊ *The entire ~ is framed in terms of what you can do to protect yourself.* | **lose, win** ◊ *The environmentalists seem to have lost the ~ over the building of this road.* | **resolve, settle** | **dominate** ◊ *Three major issues have dominated the education ~.* | **shift** ◊ *These events shifted ~ from economic issues to social ones.* | **be a matter for, be open to** ◊ *The benefits of the new law are open to ~.*
DEBATE + VERB **occur, take place** ◊ *A ~ about safety is taking place in schools everywhere.* | **rage** | **arise, erupt** | **centre/center on sth, focus on sth, revolve around sth** ◊ *The ~ focused on who should pay for the changes.*
PREP. **under ~** ◊ *The issue is still under ~.* | **~ about, ~ on, ~ over** ◊ *the ~ on the environment* | **~ among** ◊ *the ~ among academics* | **~ between** | **~ surrounding** ◊ *the ~ surrounding contemporary art* | **~ with**
PHRASES **the subject of ~** ◊ *The proposed changes to the law have been the subject of much ~.*

2 a formal discussion

ADJ. **brief** | **lengthy, long** | **acrimonious, fierce, heated, lively, stormy** ◊ *a stormy ~ in the House of Commons* | **televised** | **congressional, legislative, presidential, vice-presidential** (*in the US*) ◊ *legislative ~s over gay marriage* | **parliamentary** (*in the UK*) ◊ *a parliamentary ~ on the fishing industry* | **policy**
VERB + DEBATE **have** ◊ *We had a brief ~ about whether or not to accept the offer.* | **hold, host** ◊ *The union holds ~s for students.* | **participate in, speak in, take part in** ◊ *Do you ever speak in ~s?* | **moderate** (*esp. AmE*) | **open** ◊ *The president will open the ~.* | **close** | **lose, win** ◊ *The government lost the ~ in the House of Commons.* ◊ *The poll showed that the Democrat won last night's presidential ~.*
DEBATE + NOUN **moderator** (*AmE*) | **coach, team** (*both AmE*) | **performance** (*esp. AmE*) ◊ *Experts pore over the President's ~ performances.*
PREP. **during a/the ~, in a/the ~** | **~ about, ~ on, ~ over** ◊ *Many of these points were raised during the ~ on prison reform.*

debate verb

ADV. **fully, properly** (*esp. BrE*), **seriously, thoroughly** | **fiercely, hotly, vigorously** ◊ *The issue is still being hotly ~d.* | **openly, publicly** ◊ *The question of security needs to be ~d publicly.* | **at length, endlessly, extensively**
PREP. **with** ◊ *a presidential candidate debating with his opponent* ◊ *He sat there debating with himself what to do.*
PHRASES **be widely ~d** ◊ *The report has been widely ~d in the industry.*

debit verb

ADV. **automatically**
PREP. **from** ◊ *The money will be ~ed from your account.* | **with** (*BrE*) ◊ *Your current account is automatically ~ed with the amount of your purchase.*

debris noun

ADJ. **falling, flying** ◊ *She was hit on the head by flying ~.* | **food, plant, rock** ◊ *These worms feed on plant ~.* | **organic, woody** | **burning** | **construction, garden, industrial** (*all esp. AmE*) | **orbital, rocky, space, volcanic**
... OF DEBRIS **piece** | **heap, pile**
VERB + DEBRIS **scatter, send** ◊ *The tank exploded, scattering ~ all over the field.* | **clear, clear away, clear sth of, clear up, remove** ◊ *Teams of people are working to clear the ~.* ◊ *Remember to clear the drain of ~ regularly.* | **search through, sift through** ◊ *Police have spent the day sifting through the ~ for clues.*
DEBRIS + VERB **accumulate** ◊ *Debris accumulates at the bottom of the bottle.* | **fly** ◊ *Debris from the explosion was flying all over the place.* | **fall, rain, rain down** ◊ *Debris rained down around them.* | **hit sb/sth** | **cover sb/sth**
PREP. **among the ~, in the ~** ◊ *She found a pair of children's shoes among the ~.*

debt noun

1 sum of money owed

ADJ. **big, crippling, enormous, heavy, high, huge, large, massive, substantial** ◊ *He was burdened with crippling ~s.* | **mounting** ◊ *a company faced with mounting ~s* | **outstanding, unpaid** ◊ *She used her lottery winnings to pay off her outstanding ~s.* | **bad** (= that cannot be repaid) ◊ *Bad ~ has hit the bank's profits this year.* | **long-term, short-term** | **overall, total** | **gross, net** | **commercial, corporate** | **federal, government** | **consumer** | **external, foreign, international** | **national, public** ◊ *The country has a national ~ of 80% of GNP.* | **personal** ◊ *He used the cash to pay off personal ~s.* | **gambling** | **credit-card, loan, mortgage** ◊ *Managing your student loan ~ is not easy.*
VERB + DEBT **be burdened with, have, owe (sb)** ◊ *the substantial ~s that the company owed to the bank* | **accumulate, incur, run up** ◊ *She ran up huge ~s on her credit card.* | **clear, eliminate, meet, pay, pay back, pay off, repay, retire** (*AmE, finance*), **settle** ◊ *Without a job, he'll never clear his ~s.* ◊ *It'll take months to pay off all your ~s.* | **reduce** | **tackle** ◊ *The new governments main aim is to tackle the country's massive ~.* | **default on** ◊ *The company defaulted on its ~ and its assets were seized.* | **cancel, erase, forgive, wipe out, write off** ◊ *After a series of meetings, the banks were forced to write off the company's ~s.* | **service** (= pay interest on) ◊ *The fall in exports has left the country unable to service its ~s.* | **refinance, reschedule, restructure** ◊ *The company has reached a deal allowing it to restructure its ~s.* | **consolidate** ◊ *He wanted to consolidate his ~s into one payment.* | **manage** ◊ *The first step in managing your ~ is to stop incurring it.* | **secure** ◊ *a ~ secured on property*
DEBT + VERB **fall due** (*BrE*) | **stand at sth, total sth** ◊ *The national ~ stands at $7 billion.* | **arise from sth** (*BrE*) ◊ *~s arising from bad investments*
DEBT + NOUN **collection, collector** | **payment, repayment** | **burden, level, load, obligation** ◊ *Data show that ~ levels at private companies are increasing.* | **problem** | **management** ◊ *We offer financial and debt-management advice.* | **cancellation, forgiveness, relief** | **reduction** | **consolidation** | **service** | **crisis** ◊ *a solution to the ~ crisis of the developing world*
PREP. **of ~** ◊ *$80 million of ~*
PHRASES **a burden of ~** ◊ *Faced with a mounting burden of ~, he sold off the company.* | **payment of a ~, repayment of a ~, settlement of a ~**

2 state of owing money

ADJ. **serious**
VERB + DEBT **get into, go into, slip into** ◊ *It is easy to get into*

serious ~ with a credit card. | **get out of** ◇ You can get out of ~ by strict economizing.
PREP. **in ~** ◇ He was heavily in ~ by the time he sought advice. | **out of ~** ◇ We're all struggling to stay out of ~.
PHRASES **deeply in ~, heavily in ~**

3 sth that you owe sb
ADJ. **great**
VERB + DEBT **owe** | **acknowledge, recognize** | **repay** ◇ She was simply repaying a ~, saving his career in return for him saving hers.
PREP. **in sb's ~** ◇ I will be forever in Ruth's ~ for the excellent advice she gave me. | **~ to** ◇ In the introduction, the author acknowledges her ~ to other writers on the subject.
PHRASES **owe a ~ of gratitude to sb** ◇ We owe a great ~ of gratitude to our families for their support.

decade noun
ADJ. **current, present** | **coming, ensuing, following, next** | **last, past, preceding, previous, recent** | **closing, early** ◇ the early ~s of the 19th century | **intervening** | **entire, full, whole** ◇ almost a full ~ of unparalleled economic growth | **post-war**
VERB + DECADE **spend** ◇ Hines has spent the last ~ in Austin, Texas. | **span** ◇ a career spanning four ~s | **enter** ◇ Now entering her fourth ~, the singer is living alone in New York.
DECADE + VERB **elapse, go by, pass** ◇ This ~ has passed uneventfully. | **begin, open, start** ◇ This ~ began badly for us. | **close, end** | **see sth, witness sth** ◇ The past ~ has seen a huge rise in the number of broadband users.
PREP. **during a/the ~, in a/the ~, over a/the ~, throughout a/the ~** | **for a/the ~** | **within a/the ~**

decay noun
ADJ. **rapid** | **slow** | **dental** (esp. BrE), **tooth** | **industrial** (esp. BrE), **urban** | **moral, physical, social**
VERB + DECAY **cause** ◇ Bacteria stick to food debris in the teeth, causing ~. | **stop** ◇ Without a lot of money, the mayor won't be able to stop urban ~. | **reverse** ◇ This government promises to reverse industrial ~. | **prevent** ◇ The wood is treated with preservative to prevent ~. | **fall into** ◇ old buildings that had fallen into ~
PREP. **in ~** ◇ The derelict buildings are the signs of a town in ~. | **~ in** ◇ Smoking accelerates ~ in the heart and arteries. | **~ of** ◇ the slow ~ of the castle and the surrounding buildings
PHRASES **the process of ~** | **signs of ~** ◇ My dentist could not find any signs of ~. | **an odour/odor of ~, a smell of ~, a stench of ~** ◇ A smell of ~ pervaded the air. | **a state of ~**

decayed adj.
VERBS **be, look** | **become**
ADV. **badly** ◇ Some of her teeth were very badly ~. | **completely** ◇ The wood was completely ~.

deceased adj.
VERBS **be**
ADV. **recently** ◇ her recently ~ husband | **now** ◇ She was named after her now ~ grandmother. | **sadly** (BrE) ◇ His mother is now sadly ~.

deceive verb
ADV. **easily** ◇ Human nature is such that we easily ~ ourselves. | **deliberately**
VERB + DECEIVE **attempt to, try to**
PREP. **into** ◇ The public should not be ~d into buying inferior goods.

December noun → Note at MONTH

decency noun
ADJ. **common, human** ◇ a lack of common ~ | **basic, simple** | **moral** | **public** ◇ Your conduct is an affront to public ~.
VERB + DECENCY **have** ◇ He might have had the ~ to let us know.

decent adj.
1 good/acceptable
VERBS **be, look** ◇ The bar looked ~ enough.
ADV. **really, very** | **perfectly** | **fairly, half, halfway, pretty, quite, reasonably, relatively** ◇ We had trouble finding a hotel that was halfway ~. | **enough**
PREP. **to** ◇ My uncle has been pretty ~ to me.
2 honest/respectable
VERBS **be**
ADV. **very** | **really** | **perfectly, thoroughly**
PHRASES **do the ~ thing** ◇ I think he should do the ~ thing and resign.

deception noun
ADJ. **cruel** | **elaborate** ◇ His elaborate ~ fooled everyone. | **deliberate, intentional** | **outright** ◇ He wasn't sure whether it was an act of carelessness or an act of outright ~.
VERB + DECEPTION **practise/practice, use** ◇ He'll use ~ to get what he wants. | **detect, see through** ◇ She failed to see through his ~. | **obtain sth by** (esp. law) ◇ She was charged with obtaining property by ~.

decide verb
ADV. **eventually, finally, ultimately** ◇ We finally ~d to stay where we were. | **sensibly, wisely** ◇ He ~d very wisely to keep his money rather than spend it. | **consciously** | **immediately, quickly, suddenly** | **arbitrarily** | **reluctantly** ◇ We've reluctantly ~d to sell the house. | **collectively, unanimously, unilaterally** ◇ They had unanimously ~d to go with the captain's plan.
VERB + DECIDE **be able to** | **be unable to, cannot** ◇ I can't ~ what to do. | **have to, must** ◇ You will have to ~ soon. | **try to** | **be difficult to**
PREP. **against** ◇ They ~d against taking legal action | **between** ◇ It was difficult to ~ between the various options. | **in favour/favor of** ◇ They ~d in favour/favor of reducing the fees. | **on, upon** ◇ We're still trying to ~ on a venue.
PHRASES **~ for yourself** ◇ She should be allowed to ~ for herself. | **the task of deciding sth** ◇ The committee will have the task of deciding whether more cash should be made available. | **to be ~d** ◇ The exact time of the meeting is still to be ~d.

decision noun
ADJ. **big, crucial, fateful, important, key, landmark** (law), **major, momentous** ◇ It was a big ~ to make. ◇ In a landmark ~, the court agreed to hear evidence from twenty years earlier. | **life-and-death, life-changing** ◇ Presidents must make momentous life-and-death ~s while in office. | **difficult, hard, tough** ◇ the difficult ~ of whether to go to college or nurse her sick mother | **easy** | **firm** ◇ We need a firm ~ by Friday. | **prompt, snap, split-second** ◇ I had to make a snap ~ about what to do with the money. | **hasty, knee-jerk, rash** | **last-minute** | **final, irreversible, irrevocable** ◇ Tomorrow the board will meet to make their final ~. ◇ The ~ is irreversible. | **informed** ◇ I need more facts before I can make an informed ~. | **arbitrary** | **good, intelligent, prudent, rational, right, sensible, smart** (esp. AmE), **wise** | **timely** | **bad, poor, unwise, wrong** | **unpopular** | **controversial, questionable** | **fateful** ◇ He died after making the fateful ~ to drive that evening. | **collective, joint, unanimous** ◇ In the end, the ~ to scrap the project was unanimous. | **majority, split** | **court, government, etc.** | **investment, policy, etc.** | **clinical, ethical, political, tactical, etc.**
VERB + DECISION **arrive at, come to, make, reach, take** (BrE) ◇ Key ~s are always taken by the editor. | **face** ◇ She now faces the toughest ~ of her life. | **affect, drive, guide, impact** (AmE), **influence, shape, sway** ◇ I didn't want to influence his ~. | **announce, give (sb), issue** ◇ The committee will give us their ~ tomorrow. | **abide by** ◇ The ~ has been made, and we must all abide by it. | **respect** ◇ Her parents respected her ~ not to marry. | **affirm, uphold** ◇ The management committee upheld her ~ to fire two of her staff. | **implement**

◇ *Failure to implement the ~ would be a great shame.* | **reconsider, rethink, review, revisit** (*esp. AmE*) | **defend, explain, justify** ◇ *She defended her ~ not to give him the job.* | **regret** | **appeal** (*AmE*), **appeal against** (*BrE*), **challenge, oppose, protest** (*AmE*), **protest against** ◇ *plans to challenge this ~ in the High Court* | **criticize** | **question** | **applaud, praise, support** | **override, overrule, overturn, quash, reverse** ◇ *Nobody has the authority to overrule his ~.* | **await** | **defer, delay, postpone**

DECISION + NOUN **process** ◇ *The most persuasive talker often dominates the ~ process.* | **time** ◇ *It's ~ time, and deciding is difficult.*

PREP. **~ about, ~ on** ◇ *a ~ on her future*
→ Special page at MEETING

decisive *adj.*

VERBS **be, prove**
ADV. **potentially** ◇ *He had one potentially ~ factor in his favour/favor: the element of surprise.* | **ultimately** (*esp. BrE*) ◇ *It is the chief executive's opinion which is ultimately ~.*

deck *noun*

1 top outside floor of a ship/boat
ADJ. **open**
VERB + DECK **go up on** ◇ *When we heard the alarm, we went up on ~.*
PREP. **below ~** ◇ *The passengers were trapped below ~.* | **on ~** ◇ *I joined the others on ~.*

2 one of the floors of a ship, etc.
ADJ. **lower, top, upper** | **aft, cargo, command, main, mess, poop, promenade, saloon, sun**
VERB + DECK **swab**
PREP. **on a/the ~** ◇ *We were sitting on the top ~ of the bus.* (*BrE*)

3 wooden area attached to building
ADJ. **wooden** | **back, front** | **roof** | **sun**

4 (*esp. AmE*) **of cards** → See PACK

declaration *noun*

ADJ. **formal, solemn** | **ringing** ◇ *The Russian leader received a ringing ~ of support yesterday.* | **bold** | **joint** | **unilateral** | **official** | **public**
VERB + DECLARATION **issue, make** ◇ *The government will issue a formal ~ tomorrow.* | **adopt, sign** ◇ *All four countries have adopted the ~ against hunting these rare animals.*
PREP. **~ about, ~ on** ◇ *the UN ~ on Human Rights* | **~ of** ◇ *a ~ of war*

declare *verb*

ADV. **virtually** ◇ *He has virtually ~d war on his own party.* | **immediately, promptly** ◇ *Martial law was immediately ~d.* | **formally, officially** | **openly, publicly** | **proudly, triumphantly** ◇ *She proudly ~d that she had once met John Wayne.* | **loudly** | **boldly, confidently, firmly** ◇ *'I'm going to win!' he ~d confidently.* | **famously** ◇ *Stravinsky famously ~d that music expressed nothing.* | **solemnly** | **flatly** | **simply** ◇ *'You're here,' she ~d simply.* | **unanimously** | **unilaterally** ◇ *The communists had unilaterally ~d a ceasefire.* | **hereby** (*law or formal*) ◇ *We, the people of Indonesia, hereby ~ Indonesia's independence.*
PREP. **to** ◇ *He ~d his true feelings to her.*

decline *noun*

ADJ. **catastrophic, considerable, dramatic, drastic, large, major, marked, massive, serious, severe, significant, substantial** | **precipitous, sharp, steep** | **rapid, sudden** | **gentle, modest, slight** | **gradual, slow** | **continuing, progressive, steady, sustained** ◇ *a steady ~ in manufacturing* | **general, long-term, overall** | **absolute, inevitable, inexorable, irreversible, terminal** ◇ *an industry in terminal ~* | **economic, industrial, moral, urban** ◇ *the moral ~ of the nation* | **mental, physical** | **population, price** | **national** | **seasonal** | **age-related**
VERB + DECLINE **experience, fall into, go into, suffer** ◇ *The*

---

cloth trade went into gradual ~. | **cause, lead to** ◇ *The increased price of gold led to the ~ of his business.* | **arrest, halt, stem, stop** ◇ *We must halt this ~ in standards.* | **slow** | **prevent** | **reverse** | **offset** | **accelerate, hasten** | **see, witness** ◇ *We have seen a sharp ~ in educational standards over recent years.* | **lament** ◇ *They lament the ~ of old-fashioned communities.*

DECLINE + VERB **occur** ◇ *Most of the ~ occurred in the 1990s.* | **begin**
PREP. **in ~** ◇ *The industry is still in ~.* | **on the ~** ◇ *His career has been on the ~ for some years now.* | **~ in** ◇ *a steep ~ in sales* | **~ of** ◇ *the ~ of small farming communities*
PHRASES **the ~ and fall of sth** ◇ *the ~ and fall of a great civilization*

decline *verb*

1 become smaller/weaker
ADV. **considerably, dramatically, drastically, markedly, sharply, significantly, steeply, substantially** ◇ *The economy has ~d sharply in recent years.* | **somewhat** | **a little, slightly, etc.** | **fast, quickly, rapidly** ◇ *The market for these products is declining fast.* | **steadily** | **gradually, slowly** | **further**
PREP. **by** ◇ *Profits ~d by 6% this year.* | **from, to** ◇ *The number of full-time staff has ~d from 300 to just 50.*
PHRASES **~ in importance, numbers, size, etc.** ◇ *This section of the market has slowly ~d in importance.*

2 refuse
ADV. **politely, respectfully**

decorate *verb*

1 make sth attractive
ADV. **elaborately, gaily** (*old-fashioned*), **heavily, intricately, lavishly, ornately, richly** ◇ *The room was lavishly ~d with tinsel.* | **beautifully, elegantly, nicely, tastefully** | **simply, sparsely** (*esp. AmE*)
PREP. **with** ◇ *Decorate the cake with raspberries and whipped cream.*

2 (*esp. BrE*) **with paint/wallpaper**
ADV. **nicely, pleasantly, tastefully** ◇ *The bedrooms are tastefully ~d.* | **simply**
PREP. **in** ◇ *The room is ~d in pale blues and greens.*

3 give sb a medal
PREP. **for** ◇ *He was ~d for bravery.*
PHRASES **highly ~d** ◇ *the most highly ~d unit in the army*

decoration *noun*

1 decorative object, pattern, etc.
ADJ. **Christmas, Halloween, etc.** | **festive, holiday** (*AmE*), **seasonal** (*esp. AmE*) | **beautiful** | **elaborate, lavish, ornate** | **colourful/colorful** | **Christmas-tree** | **table** | **mural, wall** | **architectural** | **floral** | **carved, engraved, painted**
VERB + DECORATION **hang, put up** | **put away, take down** ◇ *The ~s were taken down and put away for another year.* | **add, apply** ◇ *Decoration is applied to the plates before the final firing.*
DECORATION + VERB **hang** ◇ *Christmas ~s hung from every corner.* | **come down** (*esp. BrE*) ◇ *It's time for the ~s to come down.* | **adorn sth**

2 style in which a house, a room, etc. is decorated
ADJ. **home** (*esp. AmE*), **interior** | **set** ◇ *An Oscar was given for the art direction and set ~.*
VERB + DECORATION **design** (*esp. BrE*) ◇ *The interior ~ was designed by Pernassi.*

3 medal, etc.
ADJ. **military** | **numerous** ◇ *Sean had received numerous ~s, including the Purple Heart.*
VERB + DECORATION **award sb** | **receive**
DECORATION + NOUN **~s committee** (*AmE*)

PREP. **~ for** ◇ *the country's highest ~ for bravery* (BrE) ◇ *the country's highest ~ for valor* (AmE)

decorative adj.

VERBS **be, look**
ADV. **extremely, fairly, very, etc.** | **highly** ◇ *The style is ornate and highly ~.* | **merely, purely** ◇ *The items he makes are purely ~.*

decrease noun

ADJ. **dramatic, drastic, great, large, marked, sharp, significant, substantial** ◇ *There has been a sharp ~ in pollution since the law was introduced.* | **modest, slight, small** | **gradual, progressive, steady** | **rapid, sudden** | **corresponding, relative** ◇ *Fewer houses are available, but there is no corresponding ~ in demand.* | **general, overall** | **threefold, tenfold, etc.** | **5%, 25%, etc.**
VERB + DECREASE **demonstrate, display, exhibit, indicate, reveal, show** ◇ *This year's figures show a ~ of 30% on last year.* | **experience, have, suffer** ◇ *It is not uncommon to experience a ~ in confidence after a divorce.* | **report** ◇ *Half the companies in the survey reported a ~ in sales.* | **cause, lead to, produce, result in**
PREP. **on the ~** ◇ *Marriage is still on the ~.* | **from … to …** ◇ *a ~ from 62% to just under half* | **in** ◇ *The new treatment led to a huge ~ in the number of deaths.* | **~ of** ◇ *a ~ of 20%*

decrease verb

ADV. **considerably, dramatically, drastically, greatly, markedly, sharply, significantly, substantially** | **slightly, somewhat** ◇ *Spending has ~d slightly this year.* | **rapidly** | **progressively, steadily** | **gradually, slowly**
PREP. **by** ◇ *Crime has ~d by 20%.* | **from, to** ◇ *Average family size has ~d from five to three children.* | **with** ◇ *The number of quarrels among children ~s with age.*
PHRASES **~ in number, size, value, etc.** ◇ *The heart gradually ~s in size.*

decree noun

ADJ. **emergency** ◇ *He has been governing by emergency ~ under the provisions of the constitution.* | **divine, papal, presidential, religious, royal** | **government** | **court, judicial** (esp. AmE) | **divorce** | **consent** (AmE)
VERB + DECREE **issue, pass** ◇ *The president issued a ~ prohibiting trade unions.* | **sign** | **enforce** ◇ *Local inspectors helped enforce presidential ~s.* | **revoke** | **govern by, legislate by, rule by** ◇ *The general will rule by ~ until a general election.*
PREP. **in a/the ~** ◇ *In an emergency ~, the government banned all rallies.* | **~ on** ◇ *a ~ on property rights*

dedicated adj.

VERBS **appear, be, seem** | **remain**
ADV. **extremely, fairly, very, etc.** | **highly, truly** ◇ *The workforce is small but highly ~.* | **absolutely, totally, utterly** (esp. BrE)
PREP. **to** ◇ *She is totally ~ to her job.*

dedication noun

ADJ. **complete, total** | **great, real** | **single-minded, unwavering** | **lifelong**
VERB + DEDICATION **have** ◇ *Not everyone has the ~ and the talent to achieve this.* | **demonstrate, show** | **need, require** ◇ *You will need ~ and determination to complete the course.* ◇ *The job requires total ~.* | **take** ◇ *It takes ~ to be successful in a sport.*
PREP. **~ to** ◇ *I really admire Gina for her ~ to her family.*

deduce verb

ADV. **easily** | **logically** ◇ *The total amount can be ~d logically from the figures available.*
VERB + DEDUCE **be able to, can** | **be possible to** ◇ *Using the evidence available, it is possible to ~ a lot about how these people lived.*
PREP. **from** ◇ *We ~d from his absences that he was not happy at college.*

deduct verb

ADV. **at source** (BrE) ◇ *Tax is ~ed at source.* | **automatically** ◇ *This amount will be automatically ~ed from your salary.*
PREP. **from**

deduction noun

1 working things out from the facts

ADJ. **brilliant** | **logical** | **reasonable**
VERB + DEDUCTION **make**
PREP. **by ~** ◇ *She arrived at this conclusion by logical ~.* | **~ about** ◇ *We can make some ~s about the history of the ruins.*
PHRASES **powers of ~** ◇ *a detective with excellent powers of ~* | **a process of ~** ◇ *She arrived at the solution by a simple process of ~.*

2 taking an amount from a total; the amount taken

ADJ. **monthly, weekly** ◇ *monthly ~s for health insurance* | **tax** | **payroll** (esp. AmE) | **charitable** (AmE)
VERB + DEDUCTION **make** ◇ *The company automatically makes tax ~s from your salary.* | **itemize** | **claim** ◇ *You should claim the ~ when you file your tax return.* | **get, take** (both AmE) ◇ *A skilled accountant will make sure that you take the proper business ~s.*
PREP. **~ for** ◇ *~s for travel costs* | **~ from** ◇ *~s from his wages*

deed noun

ADJ. **brave, daring, glorious, good, great, heroic, kind, mighty, noble** ◇ *She felt that she had done her good ~ for the day.* | **bad, dark, dastardly, dirty, evil, horrible, terrible** ◇ *They paid children to do their evil ~s.* | **past** ◇ *demands that the country should apologize for its past ~s*
VERB + DEED **commit, do, perform, perpetrate** (formal) ◇ *She would not be able to relax until the ~ was done.* ◇ *warriors who performed glorious ~s* ◇ *evil ~s perpetrated by wicked people*
PREP. **in ~, in ~s** ◇ *He frequently expressed his love for her in words if not in ~s.*

deep adj.

1 a long way from top to bottom/front to back

VERBS **be, look** ◇ *The water looks very ~ there.*
ADV. **extremely, fairly, very, etc.**

2 low in tone

VERBS **be, sound** ◇ *Her voice sounded very ~ on the telephone.* | **become**
ADV. **extremely, fairly, very, etc.**

3 strongly felt

VERBS **be, go, run** ◇ *This suspicion runs very ~ among some government members.* | **become**
ADV. **extremely, fairly, very, etc.**

defeat noun

ADJ. **complete, comprehensive** (esp. BrE), **decisive, heavy, major, overwhelming, resounding, serious, stunning, total** ◇ *Their party suffered a heavy ~ in the election.* | **bitter, catastrophic, crushing, devastating, disastrous, embarrassing, humiliating, ignominious** (formal) ◇ *The battle ended in a humiliating ~.* | **narrow** ◇ *They lost 4–3 in their second narrow ~ of the week.* | **consecutive, successive** | **final, ultimate** | **election, electoral, political** | **military**
VERB + DEFEAT **accept, admit, concede** ◇ *She is very determined, and will never admit ~.* ◇ *The prime minister conceded ~ and resigned.* | **face** | **experience, suffer** | **go down to, slump to** (both BrE, sports) ◇ *The team went down to their fifth consecutive ~.* | **reverse** (BrE) ◇ *A good politician can always reverse any ~s.* | **avoid** ◇ *We just need to avoid ~ in our last two games.* | **inflict** ◇ *The army inflicted a heavy ~ on rebel forces.* | **end in** | **lead to**
PREP. **~ against** ◇ *last week's crushing ~ against their rivals* | **~ by** ◇ *their ~ by the Brazilians*

defeat *verb*

ADV. **comprehensively** (*BrE*), **convincingly** (*esp. BrE*), **decisively, easily, handily** (*AmE*), **heavily** (*BrE*), **overwhelmingly, roundly, soundly, thoroughly** ◇ *The English were decisively ~ed by the rebels in the battle that followed.* ◇ *The senator was decisively ~ed by his rivals.* | **completely, totally** | **militarily** ◇ *He said it was impossible to ~ the terrorists militarily.* | **narrowly** ◇ *Our team was narrowly ~ed in the final.* | **eventually, finally, ultimately**
PREP. **by** ◇ *The motion was ~ed by 20 votes to 18.*

defect *noun*

ADJ. **fundamental, major, obvious, serious, severe** ◇ *a fundamental ~ in the product* | **mild, minor, slight, small** ◇ *Goods with slight ~s are sold at half price.* ◇ *The child had a mild heart ~.* | **construction** (*esp. AmE*), **manufacturing, mechanical** (*esp. BrE*), **structural** | **birth, congenital, genetic** ◇ *All lambs are checked for birth ~s when they are born.* | **developmental, physical, visual** | **sight, speech** | **eye, heart** | **character**
VERB + DEFECT **contain, have, suffer from** ◇ *The book contains serious ~s.* ◇ *He has a congenital heart ~.* | **show** ◇ *The photograph shows slight ~s due to age.* | **find, identify, observe** ◇ *The inspector found ~s in the aircraft's construction.* | **cause, induce, produce** ◇ *There is evidence that air pollution can cause birth ~s.* | **prevent** | **correct, cure, remedy, repair** ◇ *This is a physical ~ that cannot be cured.* ◇ *The builders agreed to remedy the structural ~s.*
PREP. **~ in** ◇ *major ~s in the education system* | **~ of** ◇ *a ~ of her character*

defective *adj.*

VERBS **be, prove** ◇ *If the goods prove ~, the customer has the right to compensation.*
ADV. **highly, seriously** (*esp. BrE*), **severely** ◇ *Her vision is severely ~.* | **partially, slightly** | **mentally**

defence (*BrE*) (*AmE* defense) *noun*

1 action to protect sb/sth from attack

ADJ. **adequate, effective** | **immune, natural** ◇ *the body's natural ~ against viruses* | **homeland** (*AmE*), **national, territorial** | **air** | **civil** | **nuclear**
VERB + DEFENCE/DEFENSE **come to, leap to, rush to, spring to** ◇ *He always sprang to Rose's ~ when Ed tried to criticize her.*
PREP. **in ~ of** ◇ *to fight in ~ of your country* | **~ against** ◇ *~ against attacks from the north*
PHRASES **weapons of ~**

2 sth that protects sb/sth from sth

ADJ. **effective, strong** | **coastal, sea** | **perimeter** (*AmE*) ◇ *Perimeter ~s around airports and government buildings should be strengthened.* | **anti-missile, missile**
VERB + DEFENCE/DEFENSE **put up** ◇ *They put up an effective ~ against the guerrilla forces.* | **bolster, improve, strengthen** | **weaken** | **destroy, overcome, overwhelm** ◇ *With her tears she completely overwhelmed his ~s.* | **build, build up, rebuild** ◇ *They are building up ~s along the river.* | **breach, penetrate** ◇ *The sea breached the coastal ~s in a number of spots.*
DEFENCE/DEFENSE + NOUN **mechanism**
PREP. **~ against**

3 forces, etc. for protecting a country

DEFENCE/DEFENSE + NOUN **capability, establishment, force, forces, system** | **Defense Department, Defense Secretary** (*in the US*) | **minister, ministry** (*in the UK*) | **policy, strategy** | **analyst, expert, planner** | **contractor, industry** | **budget, cuts, expenditure, spending**

4 argument, esp. in court

ADJ. **good** | **robust, solid, spirited, staunch, stout** (*BrE*), **strong, vigorous** | **adequate** | **legal** | **insanity** (*esp. AmE*) ◇ *The judge rejected her insanity ~.*

VERB + DEFENCE/DEFENSE **conduct, make, mount, offer, put up, raise**
DEFENCE/DEFENSE + NOUN **attorney** (*AmE*), **counsel, lawyer, team** | **witness**
PREP. **in sb's ~** ◇ *She spoke in his ~.* | **~ of, ~ to** ◇ *a ~ to murder*
PHRASES **counsel for the ~**

5 in sports

ADJ. **good, solid, staunch** (*esp. BrE*), **stout** (*BrE*), **strong**
VERB + DEFENCE/DEFENSE **play** (*AmE*) | **put up** | **destroy, penetrate** | **improve, strengthen, upgrade** (*AmE*)
PREP. **in ~** (*BrE*), **on ~** (*AmE*) ◇ *to play in ~* ◇ *He plays on ~.*

defenceless (*BrE*) (*AmE* defenseless) *adj.*

VERBS **be, feel, lie** (*esp. BrE*) ◇ *He was kicked as he lay ~ on the ground.* | **leave sb** ◇ *They were left virtually ~ against enemy attack.*
ADV. **completely, totally, utterly** ◇ *She felt utterly ~.* | **almost, practically, virtually**
PREP. **against** ◇ *They were completely ~ against enemy attack.*
PHRASES **poor ~** ◇ *How could anyone steal from a poor ~ old lady?*

defend *verb*

1 protect against attack

ADV. **adequately, effectively, properly** (*esp. BrE*), **successfully** ◇ *Computer users need to ensure their systems are properly ~ed.* ◇ *She successfully ~ed herself against an attack from someone larger and stronger.* | **heavily** ◇ *The city was heavily ~ed against attack.* | **lightly** ◇ *They attacked the left flank, which was only lightly ~ed.*
PREP. **against**

2 support

ADV. **actively, aggressively** (*esp. AmE*), **fiercely, passionately, robustly** (*BrE*), **strongly, vehemently, vigorously** ◇ *The company has vigorously ~ed its decision to reduce the workforce.* | **staunchly, steadfastly, stoutly** (*BrE*), **valiantly** | **adequately, effectively, successfully** | **publicly**
PREP. **against** ◇ *She ~ed her department against accusations of incompetence.*

3 in sports/competitions

ADV. **successfully**
PREP. **against** ◇ *The champion successfully ~ed his title against the challenger.*

defendant *noun*

ADJ. **criminal** | **convicted, guilty**
VERB + DEFENDANT **accuse, charge** ◇ *The ~ was charged with disturbing the peace.* | **prosecute, sue** ◇ *a ~ being sued by an insurance company* | **convict, find guilty** ◇ *The ~ was convicted of murder.* ◇ *The jury found the ~ guilty on all counts.* | **sentence** ◇ *The ~ was sentenced to three years in prison.* | **acquit, find not guilty** | **release**
DEFENDANT + VERB **plead guilt, plead not guilty**
PREP. **against the ~** ◇ *the plaintiff's claim against the ~* | **for the ~** ◇ *Several witnesses gave evidence for the ~.* | **~ in** ◇ *a ~ in bankruptcy proceedings*

defensive *adj.*

1 protecting against attack

VERBS **be**
ADV. **purely** ◇ *These are purely ~ measures.* | **essentially, largely** ◇ *a largely ~ campaign*

2 showing you feel sb is criticizing you

VERBS **be, feel, look, seem, sound** | **become, get, grow** ◇ *Whenever anyone mentions women's rights, he gets rather ~.*
ADV. **extremely, fairly, very, etc.** | **fiercely** ◇ *He did not once glance at his listeners and seemed fiercely ~.* | **a little, slightly, etc.** | **overly**
PREP. **about** ◇ *He is extremely ~ about his work.*

defer verb

ADV. **indefinitely** ◇ *The decision has been deferred indefinitely.* | **endlessly**
VERB + DEFER **agree to, decide to**
PREP. **for** ◇ *Sentence was deferred for six months.* | **pending** ◇ *Diagnosis was deferred pending further assessment.* | **till, until** ◇ *We agreed to ~ discussion of these issues until the next meeting.*

deference noun

ADJ. **great**
VERB + DEFERENCE **accord, give, grant, show, treat sb with** ◇ *The actress was accorded all the ~ of a visiting celebrity.* ◇ *Why do you treat your boss with such ~?* | **owe (to) sb**
PREP. **in of ~ to, out of ~ to** ◇ *The traditional menu was changed in ~ to Western tastes.* | **with ~** ◇ *She spoke with great ~.* | **~ to, ~ towards/toward** ◇ *~ towards/toward your elders*

defiance noun

ADJ. **blatant, direct, open** ◇ *blatant ~ of the rules*
PREP. **in ~ (of)** ◇ *She held up a clenched fist in ~.* ◇ *They organized a street demonstration in complete ~ of the government ban.* | **out of ~** ◇ *I left the room messy out of sheer ~.*
PHRASES **an act of ~** | **a gesture of ~**

defiant adj.

VERBS **appear, be, feel, look, seem** | **remain** ◇ *Despite the criticisms, she remained ~.*
ADV. **openly** ◇ *Sylvia tossed back her dark hair in a gesture that was openly ~.*

deficiency noun

ADJ. **major, serious, severe** | **slight** | **dietary, nutritional** | **immune** | **enzyme, hormone, mineral, nutrient, vitamin** | **calcium, iron, etc.**
VERB + DEFICIENCY **have, suffer from** ◇ *He's suffering from a severe vitamin ~.* | **correct, make good, make up, overcome, remedy** ◇ *I've been prescribed iron to make up the ~.* ◇ *An engineer could remedy the deficiencies in the design.* | **detect, identify** | **indicate** ◇ *These symptoms indicate a protein ~.* | **cause, induce** ◇ *Lack of sunlight can cause ~ in vitamin D.*
PREP. **~ in** ◇ *serious deficiencies in the health service*

deficient adj.

VERBS **be, prove** | **become**
ADV. **gravely, sadly** (*esp. BrE*)**, seriously, severely, woefully** ◇ *An educational system which fails to teach basic arithmetic is seriously ~.* | **slightly** | **intellectually, mentally**
PREP. **in** ◇ *Their food is ~ in iron.*

deficit noun

ADJ. **enormous, huge, large, massive, serious, substantial** | **ballooning, exploding, growing, soaring** | **small** | **net, overall** | **projected** | **balance-of-payments, budget, current-account, federal, financial, fiscal, trade** | **national** | **attention, cognitive, neurological** ◇ *attention ~ disorder* ◇ *His teacher thought he had some sort of cognitive ~.*
VERB + DEFICIT **face, have, run, show** ◇ *If the government didn't run such huge ~s, the country would not have financial problems.* ◇ *The trade balance shows a ~ of two million dollars.* | **go into, move into, run up, slip into** ◇ *to prevent the country from moving into ~* ◇ *The company has run up a ~ of £30 000.* | **increase, widen** | **address, tackle** | **cut, halve, narrow, reduce, shrink** ◇ *You cannot cut a budget ~ simply by raising taxes.* | **correct, eliminate, erase, make up, wipe out** ◇ *We will find it hard to make up this ~.* | **overcome** | **overturn** (*BrE, sports*) ◇ *United are hoping to overturn a two-goal ~ from the first leg.* | **finance, fund** ◇ *The government was forced to sell state-owned companies to fund the budget ~.*

DEFICIT + VERB **run at sth** ◇ *a budget ~ running at 7% of GDP* | **grow, increase, rise, widen** | **balloon, soar** ◇ *The US trade ~ ballooned to a record $167 billion.* | **decrease, fall, narrow, shrink**
PREP. **in ~** ◇ *The UK remained in ~ with all countries outside the EU.* | **~ with** ◇ *the US trade ~ with Japan*

define verb

ADV. **accurately, carefully, correctly, exactly, explicitly, precisely, specifically** ◇ *It is important to ~ these terms accurately.* | **clearly, fully, sharply, strongly, well** | **adequately** ◇ *There may be problems if responsibilities are not adequately ~d.* | **poorly** | **broadly** ◇ *We have chosen to ~ the scope of our study quite broadly.* | **loosely, vaguely** | **closely, narrowly, rigidly, rigorously, strictly, tightly** | **succinctly** | **simply, solely** | **easily** | **formally, officially** | **objectively** | **traditionally** | **culturally, geographically, socially** ◇ *the culturally ~d role of women* | **legally**
VERB + DEFINE **be difficult to, be impossible to** | **be easy to** ◇ *Social values are not easy to ~.*
PREP. **as** ◇ *Thread count is ~d as the number of threads in one square inch of fabric.* | **by** ◇ *This type of lymphoma is ~d by the presence of specific malignant cells.* | **in terms of** ◇ *The difficulty of a problem was ~d in terms of how long it took to complete.*

definition noun

ADJ. **careful, clear, concise, exact, precise, unambiguous** ◇ *The term 'partner' requires careful ~.* ◇ *The author provides a clear ~ of cultural awareness.* | **comprehensive, exhaustive** (*BrE*)**, inclusive** | **adequate, satisfactory** | **broad, expanded, expansive** (*esp. AmE*)**, loose, wide** | **narrow, rigid, rigorous, strict** ◇ *According to a strict ~, the expenses of a self-employed person can be deducted from tax.* | **formal, official, statutory** ◇ *The firm falls within the statutory ~ of a 'small company'.* | **dictionary** | **legal, mathematical** ◇ *The mathematical ~ of an even number is one that is exactly divisible by 2.* | **accepted, conventional, standard, textbook, traditional** | **alternative** | **workable, working** ◇ *We need a good working ~ of 'pollution'.*
VERB + DEFINITION **give (sb), offer (sb), propose, provide (sb with)** | **adopt, use** ◇ *They have adopted a very narrow ~ of success.* | **fit, meet** ◇ *This unusual building barely fits the ~ of a house.* | **broaden, change, expand, stretch** ◇ *He has expanded the ~ of sculpture.* | **accept** ◇ *She refused to accept the ~ of woman as man's subordinate.*
DEFINITION + VERB **encompass sth, include sth**
PREP. **according to a/the ~** ◇ *According to a strict ~ of 'assault', she was not assaulted.* | **by ~** ◇ *A clinic for women would, by ~, deal with pregnancy and childbirth.* | **under a/the ~** ◇ *Under the broader ~ of 'poverty', thousands more people would be included.*

deformed adj.

VERBS **be** | **be born** | **become**
ADV. **badly, severely** ◇ *She had a badly ~ hand.* | **slightly** | **hideously, horribly**

deformity noun

ADJ. **severe** | **congenital, genetic** | **birth** (*esp. BrE*) | **physical** | **facial, hip, limb, etc.**
VERB + DEFORMITY **have, suffer from** | **cause** | **correct**

defunct adj.

VERBS **be** | **become** | **make sth** ◇ *The LP was made ~ by the arrival of the CD.*
ADV. **almost** | **largely** | **sadly** | **long** ◇ *the ruined buildings of a long ~ mine* | **now** ◇ *He wrote for the now ~ newspaper, the Daily Correspondent.* | **recently**

defy verb

ADV. **openly** ◇ *Journalists were openly ~ing the authorities.*
VERB + DEFY **be prepared to** (*esp. BrE*)**, be willing to** ◇ *He is willing to ~ his own party.* | **continue to** ◇ *The protesters continued to ~ a court injunction.*

degenerate verb
ADV. **quickly, rapidly | easily**
PREP. **into** ◇ *The solemn event rapidly ~d into farce.*

degrading adj.
VERBS **be, seem | find sth** ◇ *He found the work very ~.*
ADV. **very | rather, slightly** ◇ *the rather ~ conditions in the prison | morally*
PREP. **to** ◇ *pictures that are ~ to women*

degree noun
1 measurement of angles
VERB + DEGREE **rotate, spin, turn** ◇ *I turned the wheel 90 ~s,*
PREP. **through...~s** ◇ *The camera turned through 180 ~s.* ◇ *The car had spun through 180 ~s on impact.*

2 measurement of temperature
VERB + DEGREE **reach** ◇ *Temperatures inside the burning building are estimated to have reached 600 ~s centigrade.*
PREP. **at...~s** ◇ *Water boils at 100 ~s centigrade.*
PHRASES **~s Celsius, ~s centigrade, ~s Fahrenheit | ~s above zero, ~s below zero | minus 10, 20, etc. ~s**

3 amount/level
ADJ. **considerable, good, great, high, large, substantial, the utmost** ◇ *She allowed us a considerable ~ of freedom.* | **exceptional, extraordinary, remarkable, surprising, unprecedented, unusual** ◇ *Today we rely on computer technology to an unprecedented ~.* | **certain, fair, moderate, modest** ◇ *It was possible to date these remains with a fair ~ of accuracy.* | **low, minimal, slight, small** ◇ *He would try anything to make her even the smallest ~ happier.* | **lesser** ◇ *The tax changes will especially hit those on high incomes and, to a lesser ~, small businesses.* | **different, variable, various, varying** ◇ *They work hard, but with varying ~s of success.* | **same** ◇ *These products don't get the same ~ of testing as officially approved medications.* | **alarming, dangerous, extreme** ◇ *His arguments are simplistic to an extreme ~.* | **acceptable, adequate** (*esp. AmE*)**, meaningful** (*esp. AmE*)**, real, significant** ◇ *The book fails to answer the question with any acceptable ~ of certainty.* | **appropriate, necessary, proper, requisite** (*esp. BrE*)**, right | unacceptable** (*esp. BrE*)
VERB + DEGREE **assess, determine** ◇ *Psychologists examined her to assess the ~ of her illness.*
PREP. **in...~s** ◇ *The party leaders were all found to be corrupt in varying ~s.* | **of...~** ◇ *employees of various ~s of ability* | **to a...~** ◇ *The boss sometimes follows her instincts to an alarming ~.* | **with a...~ of** ◇ *We all tried to find out about the bus service, with varying ~s of success.* | **~ of** ◇ *There is a ~ of risk in any sport.*
PHRASES **by ~s** ◇ *By ~s, the company's turnover dwindled to nothing.* | **in equal ~** ◇ *I felt excitement and sadness in equal ~ as I waved goodbye to my colleagues.* | **a greater or lesser ~** ◇ *We were all disappointed to a greater or lesser ~.* | **to the nth ~** (= to an extreme degree) ◇ *The children tested her patience to the nth ~.*

4 qualification
ADJ. **college, university | associate, bachelor's** (*esp. AmE*)**, first** (*esp. BrE*)**, ordinary** (*BrE*)**, undergraduate | advanced, doctoral** (*esp. AmE*)**, graduate, higher, master's, postgraduate, research** (*esp. BrE*) **| BA, MA, PhD, etc. | honours/honors** (*esp. BrE*) **| good | first-class, second-class, third-class** (*in the UK*) ◇ *Candidates must have at least an upper second class honours ~.* | **honorary | business, history, law, medical, philosophy, etc. | professional** ◇ *Candidates must hold a professional ~ in architecture.* | **joint, joint-honours** (*BrE*) ◇ *She earned a joint ~ in Spanish and Psychology.* | **four-year, two-year, etc. | part-time** (*esp. BrE*)
VERB + DEGREE **have, hold | do, pursue, take** ◇ *He took a ~ in law then joined a law firm.* | **be awarded, complete, earn** (*esp. AmE*)**, finish, gain, get, obtain, receive | award (sb), confer (on sb), grant (sb)** ◇ *The University conferred on him the honorary ~ of Doctor of Laws.* ◇ *institutions that grant doctoral ~s*
DEGREE + NOUN **course** (*esp. BrE*)**, programme/program |**

level ◇ *people educated to ~ level or beyond* ◇ *a degree-level course* (*BrE*)
PREP. **~ in** ◇ *a ~ in economics*

dehydration noun
ADJ. **severe** ◇ *He died from severe ~.* | **mild**
VERB + DEHYDRATION **suffer from | die from, die of | cause | avoid, prevent**

deity noun
ADJ. **powerful, supreme | lesser, minor** ◇ *one of the minor Greek deities* | **benevolent | patron** ◇ *a shrine to the patron ~ of the city* | **female, male | Hindu, Roman, etc. | local, pagan**
VERB + DEITY **honour/honor, worship** ◇ *a tribe that worshipped two main deities* | **invoke**

dejected adj.
VERBS **appear, be, feel, look** ◇ *She looked sorrowful and ~.* | **become, grow**
ADV. **completely, thoroughly, totally, utterly** ◇ *They were thoroughly ~ and miserable.* | **rather | a little, slightly, etc.**
PREP. **about** ◇ *I was feeling rather ~ about the future.*

delay noun
ADJ. **considerable, enormous** (*esp. BrE*)**, lengthy, long, major, serious, significant, substantial** ◇ *After a considerable ~, the government has agreed to accept the recommendations.* | **five-minute, six-month, two-hour, etc. | excessive** (*esp. BrE*)**, inordinate** (*esp. BrE*)**, undue** (*esp. BrE*)**, unnecessary** ◇ *Undue ~s have been caused by people not doing their jobs properly.* | **inevitable, unavoidable | brief, short, slight | minimal, minimum | unexpected, unforeseen | frustrating | costly | bureaucratic** ◇ *The building project has been plagued by bureaucratic ~s.* | **further | airport, flight, traffic, travel | time** ◇ *There is a five-minute time ~ on the bank's safe.*
... OF DELAYS **series** ◇ *After a series of lengthy ~s, the case finally came to court.*
VERB + DELAY **be subject to** (*esp. BrE*) ◇ *Flights to New York may be subject to ~.* | **be plagued by, encounter, experience, face, suffer** ◇ *Passengers have experienced long ~s.* ◇ *The project has been plagued by ~s.* | **cause, lead to** ◇ *The strike has led to some ~s in train services.* | **avoid, eliminate, minimize, prevent, reduce** ◇ *Please address your letters properly so as to reduce ~s.* | **apologize for** ◇ *I apologize for the ~ in replying to you.*
DELAY + VERB **occur** ◇ *Passengers complain about lack of information when travel ~s occur.*
PREP. **without ~** ◇ *Please send him the information without ~.* | **~ in** ◇ *~s in getting to the airport* | **~ of** ◇ *a ~ of several weeks* | **~ to** ◇ *further ~s to the plan*

delay verb
ADV. **seriously, significantly, substantially** ◇ *Mellanby's arrival was seriously ~ed by a late train.* ◇ *These drugs can significantly ~ the onset of the disease.* | **indefinitely | further | unduly** (*esp. BrE*) **| temporarily | slightly, somewhat | deliberately**

delegate noun
ADJ. **conference, congress, convention | congressional, government, party, union | Democratic, Republican**
VERB + DELEGATE **choose, elect, select | send** ◇ *They decided not to send a ~ to the conference.*
DELEGATE + VERB **attend (sth)** ◇ *No fewer than 2 000 ~s attended the conference.* | **approve, vote (on sth)** ◇ *The ~s voted to support the resolution.* | **vote for sb/sth**
PREP. **~ from** ◇ *a ~ from the local party* | **~ to** ◇ *the British ~ to the United Nations*

delegation noun

1 people who represent a company, country, etc.

ADJ. **large, small** | **high-level, high-powered** (*esp. BrE*) | **international** | **all-party, joint** (*both BrE*) ◇ *The Prime Minister met with an all-party ~ from the city council.* | **government, military, official, parliamentary, state, union** (*BrE*) | **business, peace, trade**
VERB + DELEGATION **send** | **head, lead** ◇ *A well-known academic will head the ~.* | **meet**
DELEGATION + VERB **represent sth** ◇ *a ~ representing the new regime* | **include sth** ◇ *The ~ included representatives from nine nations.* | **visit sb/sth** ◇ *The ~ will visit several Middle Eastern countries for talks* | **meet sb**
PREP. **in a/the ~** ◇ *all the ministers in the ~* | **~ from** ◇ *an official ~ from Austria* | **~ of** ◇ *a high-powered ~ of Asian businessmen*
PHRASES **the head of a ~, the leader of a ~** | **a member of a ~**

2 giving a job to sb with a lower rank

ADJ. **effective, successful** ◇ *All managers should learn effective ~.*
PREP. **by ~** ◇ *Many of these tasks can be dealt with by ~.* | **~ of** ◇ *~ of responsibility*

delete verb

ADV. **accidentally, inadvertently** | **automatically** | **completely, permanently** | **partially**
PREP. **from** ◇ *His name will be ~d from the list.*
PHRASES **~ as appropriate** (*BrE*) ◇ *Mr/Mrs/Ms (~ as appropriate)*

deliberation noun

1 careful consideration/discussion of sth

ADJ. **careful, rational, thoughtful** ◇ *After careful ~, it was agreed to abandon the project.* | **lengthy** (*esp. BrE*), **long**
VERB + DELIBERATION **begin, start** ◇ *The jurors will now begin their ~s.* | **resume**
PREP. **~ about, ~ on** ◇ *your ~s on his future*

2 speaking/moving slowly and carefully

ADJ. **calm, slow** | **great**
PREP. **with ~** ◇ *With slow ~, he tore the letter into pieces.*

delicacy noun

1 rare and expensive type of food

ADJ. **great** | **exotic, rare** | **expensive** | **local** ◇ *Have you tried any of the local delicacies?*
VERB + DELICACY **be considered** ◇ *The eggs of this bird are considered a great ~.* | **sample, try**

2 care and sensitivity/requiring care and sensitivity

ADJ. **extreme, great, utmost** ◇ *He handled the situation with extreme ~.*
PREP. **with ~** ◇ *These objects are very old and should be treated with great ~.*
PHRASES **a matter of (some) ~**

3 lightness and gentleness

ADJ. **exquisite** ◇ *the exquisite ~ of the embroidery*

delicate adj.

VERBS **be, feel, look** ◇ *Her bones felt as ~ as a bird's.* ◇ *The glasses looked very ~.* | **become**
ADV. **extremely, fairly, very, etc.** ◇ *a rather ~ child* ◇ *This is a somewhat ~ subject.* | **surprisingly** ◇ *He had a surprisingly ~ touch.* | **politically** ◇ *a politically ~ situation*

delicious adj.

VERBS **be, look, smell, sound, taste** ◇ *The recipe sounds ~.* ◇ *The beef tasted ~.*
ADV. **incredibly, most, really, truly** ◇ *The meal was really ~.* | **absolutely, quite** | **rather**

delight noun

1 feeling of great pleasure

ADJ. **great** | **absolute, utter** | **pure, sheer** | **mischievous** (*esp. BrE*), **perverse** | **childish, childlike** | **girlish** (*esp. BrE*) | **evident, obvious** | **aesthetic, sensory, sensual, spiritual, visual** ◇ *Flowering trees provide shade as well as visual ~.*
VERB + DELIGHT **express** | **find, take** ◇ *She took evident ~ in frightening the children with horror stories.* | **bring, give sb** | **laugh with, scream with, squeal with** ◇ *Alice squealed with sheer ~ when she saw the monkeys.*
PREP. **in ~, with ~** ◇ *We danced around with childish ~.* | **of ~** ◇ *She gave a whoop of ~ and dived into the water.* | **to your ~** ◇ *To my great ~, they offered me the job.* | **~ at** ◇ *He expressed his ~ at seeing us all again.* | **~ in** ◇ *I find a perverse ~ in listening to traffic.*
PHRASES **a cry, gasp, squeal, etc. of ~** | **much to sb's ~** ◇ *Much to the ~ of the crowd, the band came back and did three encores.*

2 sth that gives great pleasure

ADJ. **real** | **constant** ◇ *The baby was a constant ~ and source of amazement.* | **unexpected** | **culinary, gastronomic** | **earthly** ◇ *He became deeply religious and turned away from earthly ~s.*
VERB + DELIGHT **explore, sample** | **enjoy, savour/savor** ◇ *Savour the culinary ~s of Morocco.*
PREP. **~ to** ◇ *The old lady's reminiscences were a continual ~ to Constance.*

delighted adj.

VERBS **appear, be, feel, look, seem**
ADV. **highly, only too** (*both esp. BrE*) ◇ *Mrs Cartwright said she would be only too ~ to present the prizes.* | **really** | **absolutely, quite** | **clearly, obviously** | **secretly** ◇ *'Poor Gloria,' she said, although she was secretly ~.* | **genuinely**
PREP. **at** ◇ *They were highly ~ at the court's decision.* | **by** ◇ *I'm ~ by your news.* | **with** ◇ *He's really ~ with his new MP3 player.*

delightful adj.

VERBS **be, seem, sound**
ADV. **most, really** ◇ *It has been a most ~ evening.* | **absolutely, quite, simply, truly**
PHRASES **~ little** ◇ *It was a ~ little fishing village.*

deliver verb

1 goods/letters

ADV. **free of charge** ◇ *The company will ~ free of charge.* | **by hand, personally** ◇ *The package had been ~ed by hand.* | **directly** ◇ *Online training sessions are ~ed directly to your desktop.*
PREP. **to** ◇ *The letter was ~ed to his office.* | **by, via** ◇ *messages ~ed via email*
PHRASES **have sth ~ed** ◇ *You can either pick up the goods or have them ~ed.*

2 provide a service, etc.

ADV. **consistently** | **effectively, efficiently, successfully**
PREP. **on** ◇ *products that ~ on customer expectations*

3 baby

ADV. **safely** ◇ *The baby was ~ed safely on Tuesday night.* | **by Caesarean, by Caesarean section, by C-section** (*AmE*) | **vaginally**

delivery noun

1 act of delivering sth; goods delivered

ADJ. **large, small** | **express, fast, immediate, prompt, quick** | **on-time** (*esp. AmE*) | **late** | **morning, next-day, overnight** | **recorded** (*BrE*) (*certified mail* in *AmE*), **scheduled, special** ◇ *Ensure all material is properly packed and sent by recorded ~.* | **guaranteed** ◇ *guaranteed express ~ to over 170 countries* | **efficient** ◇ *We need more efficient ~ of humanitarian aid.* | **safe** | **mail** (*esp. BrE*), **newspaper, pizza** ◇ *All mail deliveries*

were suspended during the strike. ◇ *a pizza* ~ *boy* | **home** ◇ *We offer free home* ~. | **service** ◇ *The cuts will inevitably impact on service* ~. | **health-care** | **content** ◇ *Digital content* ~, *especially music and video, is the next big business.*
VERB + DELIVERY **do, make** ◇ *We do all our deliveries in the mornings.* | **accept, take** ◇ *The government has now taken* ~ *of the new fighter planes.* | **get, receive** ◇ *We receive only one* ~ *of books per week.* | **guarantee** ◇ *We guarantee* ~ *before 9 a.m. the next day.* | **ensure** ◇ *Order by 30 November to ensure* ~ *by Christmas.* | **enhance, facilitate, improve** ◇ *We have invested to improve service* ~. | **speed, speed up** | **delay** | **await** ◇ *We are awaiting* ~ *of some new office furniture.*
DELIVERY + NOUN **truck** (*esp. AmE*), **van** | **date, schedule, time** | **route** | **boy, guy** (*AmE, informal*), **man** ◇ *He was employed at the local grocery store as a* ~ *boy.* | **charge** | **service** | **mechanism, method, system** ◇ *an electronic message* ~ *system*
PREP. **for** ~ ◇ *completed orders for* ~ | **on** ~ ◇ *Please pay the driver on* ~. | ~ **to** ◇ *The company offers free* ~ *to your home.*

2 giving birth to a baby

ADJ. **difficult, easy** | **premature, preterm** | **breech** | **vaginal** | **Caesarean, Caesarean-section, C-section** (*AmE*) | **forceps** ◇ *The figures show an increase in forceps deliveries.*
VERB + DELIVERY **have** ◇ *She had a very easy* ~ *with her second child.*
DELIVERY + NOUN **room**

delusion noun

ADJ. **dangerous** | **paranoid** | **collective, mass, popular** (*esp. AmE*) ◇ *He dismissed the so-called miracle as a collective* ~.
VERB + DELUSION **get, harbour/harbor, have, suffer, suffer from** ◇ *The psychiatrist said she was suffering from paranoid* ~*s.*
PREP. **under a/the** ~ ◇ *He seemed to be under the* ~ *that he would make his fortune within a few years.* | ~ **about** ◇ *He had no* ~*s about his feelings for Kate.* | ~ **of** ◇ *She had* ~*s of persecution.*
PHRASES ~*s of grandeur* (= a belief that you are more important than you actually are) ◇ *Don't go getting* ~*s of grandeur.*

demand noun

1 firm request

ADJ. **legitimate, realistic, reasonable** ◇ *I think your* ~ *for a higher salary is perfectly reasonable.* | **outrageous, unrealistic, unreasonable** | **non-negotiable** | **radical** | **urgent** | **central, key, main, major** | **fresh, new, renewed** ◇ *There have been new* ~*s for the government to take action to reduce crime.* | **final** ◇ *A final* ~ *for payment had been issued.* | **written** | **financial, political** | **opposition** (*esp. BrE*), **popular, public, union** ◇ *The management had no intention of meeting union* ~*s.* | **pay** (*esp. BrE*), **ransom, salary, tax** (*esp. BrE*), **wage** (*esp. BrE*) ◇ *A ransom* ~ *has been made for the kidnapped racehorse.*
VERB + DEMAND **issue, make, present, press, put forward** ◇ *Demands have been made for the immediate distribution of food to the refugees.* | **renew, repeat, step up** ◇ *Campaigners have stepped up their* ~*s for immediate government action.* | **face** | **respond to** | **accommodate, agree to, give in to, meet, satisfy, yield to** ◇ *The government cannot give in to the* ~*s of an illegal organization.* | **refuse, reject, resist** ◇ *The reporter refused their* ~ *that he reveal his sources.*
PREP. **on** ~ ◇ *Campaigners insist that abortion should be available on* ~. | ~ **for,** ~ **from** ◇ ~*s from the opposition for a recount of the votes*

2 need/desire for goods/services

ADJ. **big, buoyant** (*BrE*), **considerable, enormous, great, heavy, high, huge, insatiable, peak, strong, unprecedented** ◇ *Demand for the product is enormous.* | *There's always a great* ~ *for our soups in winter.* | **burgeoning, escalating, ever-increasing, growing, increased, increasing, rising, soaring, surging** | **excess, extra** | **constant, steady** ◇ *She is in constant* ~ *to make public appearances and give interviews.* | **changing, fluctuating, seasonal** |

current, future | **latent, likely** (*esp. BrE*), **pent-up, potential, projected** | **overall, total** ◇ *We can estimate that total market* ~ *for electrical goods will rise by 8%.* | **declining, falling, limited, low, reduced, slowing, sluggish** | **consumer, customer, market, popular, public** ◇ *By popular* ~, *the play will run for another week.* | **domestic, export, foreign, global, local, world, worldwide** ◇ *The slowdown in domestic* ~ *was offset by an increase in exports.* | **electricity, energy, housing, labour/labor, etc.**
...OF DEMAND **level** ◇ *a high level of* ~
VERB + DEMAND **accommodate, cope with, fulfil/fulfill, handle, meet, satisfy, supply** ◇ *The factories are staying open to meet the consumer* ~ *for this product.* | **create, drive, generate** ◇ *It is the job of the marketing manager to create* ~ *for the new product.* | **boost, fuel, increase, spur, stimulate** ◇ *Low interest rates are fuelling/fueling* ~ *for credit.* | **reduce** | **exceed, outstrip** ◇ *Supply normally exceeds* ~ *for the bulk of consumer goods.* | **forecast** ◇ *It can be difficult to forecast* ~ *in the construction industry.*
DEMAND + VERB **grow, increase, rise** ◇ *Demand for personal computers has risen sharply.* | **decline, fall, slow, slow down** ◇ *As* ~ *slows, the need to export will return.* | **exceed, outstrip** ◇ *In the housing market,* ~ *is outstripping supply.*
PREP. **in** ~ ◇ *These old machines are still in* ~. | ~ **among** ◇ *the potential* ~ *among children* | ~ **for** ◇ *increased* ~ *for health products* | ~ **from** ◇ *the* ~ *from consumers* | ~ **on** ◇ *This section of the population makes a high* ~ *on health-care resources.*
PHRASES **supply and** ~ ◇ *the law of supply and* ~
→ Special page at BUSINESS

3 demands difficult/tiring things you have to do

ADJ. **considerable, enormous, excessive, extra, great, heavy, high, impossible** ◇ *I think the* ~*s of this job are excessive.* | **exacting, pressing** | **growing, increasing** | **changing** ◇ *Teacher training has to evolve to meet the changing* ~*s of the profession.* | **competing, conflicting, contradictory** | **day-to-day, everyday** ◇ *the day-to-day* ~*s of the job* | **external** ◇ *The person who cannot say no to others' requests is likely to be overwhelmed by external* ~*s.* | **economic, emotional, financial, physical, practical, sexual, social, technical** ◇ *The emotional* ~*s of the job can be overwhelming.*
VERB + DEMANDS **impose, make, place** ◇ *My elderly parents make a lot of* ~*s on me.* | **fulfil/fulfill, respond to** ◇ *We must prepare children to respond to the* ~*s of work.* | **accommodate, cope with, handle** ◇ *How do they cope with the conflicting* ~*s of work and family life?* | **balance, juggle** ◇ *Juggling the daily* ~*s of career and family is rewarding, but never easy.*
PREP. ~ **on,** ~ **upon** ◇ *My work seems to make more and more* ~*s on my time.*

demand verb

ADV. **angrily, coldly, furiously, harshly, impatiently, indignantly, irritably, roughly, sharply** ◇ *'Where are the keys?' she* ~*ed angrily.* | **loudly**
PREP. **from** ◇ *He had* ~*ed money from her.* | **of** ◇ *They failed to provide the information* ~*ed of them.*

demanding adj.

VERBS **be, seem** | **become, get**
ADV. **extremely, fairly, very, etc.** | **highly** | **increasingly** | **overly** (*esp. AmE*), **too** ◇ *The role is not overly* ~. | **physically, technically** ◇ *a technically* ~ *piece of music to play*

demise noun

ADJ. **sad, tragic, unfortunate** | **rapid, sudden** ◇ *The war brought about the industry's sudden* ~. | **early, premature, untimely** ◇ *He praised the union's aims but predicted its early* ~. | **imminent, impending** | **eventual, final, ultimate** | **inevitable** | **apparent** | **political** ◇ *the events which contributed to his political* ~

VERB + DEMISE bring about, cause, contribute to, lead to | hasten | meet | predict | see
PREP. ~ of ◇ *the ~ of the USSR*

democracy *noun*

ADJ. genuine, real, true | stable | political | constitutional, parliamentary, participatory, representative | direct | industrial, liberal | multiparty | modern, new | Western
VERB + DEMOCRACY believe in, promote, support ◇ *people who believe in true ~* | defend, fight for, protect | build, create, establish | bring, spread | restore ◇ *The military regime has promised to restore ~ soon.* | undermine
PREP. in a/the ~ ◇ *We live in a multiparty ~.*
PHRASES the road to ~ ◇ *the need to overcome political apathy and advance on the road to ~* | the spread of ~

democratic *adj.*

VERBS be, seem | become | remain ◇ *There have been major changes in the constitution, but the system remains ~.*
ADV. genuinely, truly | fully, thoroughly ◇ *a fully ~ society* | fairly, reasonably ◇ *They have a fairly ~ form of government.* ◇ *I think it was a reasonably ~ decision.*

demolition *noun*

VERB + DEMOLITION be due for (*esp. BrE*), be threatened with ◇ *The church has been threatened with ~ for years.* | prevent, save sth from ◇ *They started a campaign to save the houses from ~.*

demon *noun*

ADJ. evil | inner, personal
VERB + DEMON be possessed by ◇ *The people believed the girl was possessed by ~s.* | cast out, exorcize ◇ *an ancient ritual to exorcize ~s* | face | battle, fight ◇ *She's had to battle her personal ~s throughout her adult life.*

demonstrate *verb*

1 show

ADV. amply, beyond doubt, clearly, conclusively, convincingly, effectively, powerfully, successfully, well ◇ *The study ~s beyond doubt the effectiveness of the new drug.* | consistently, repeatedly | adequately | further | easily | elegantly, neatly (*esp. BrE*) | empirically, experimentally | directly | publicly | graphically, vividly ◇ *This tragedy graphically ~s the dangers of extreme sports.*
PREP. to ◇ *The President must ~ to the country that he is really in control.*

2 protest

ADV. peacefully
PREP. against ◇ *Campaigners were demonstrating against the slaughter of dolphins.* | for ◇ *Their objective was to ~ peacefully for civil rights.*

demonstration *noun*

1 public protest/march

ADJ. big, huge, large, large-scale, major, massive | mass, popular, public ◇ *mass ~s against cuts in the health service* ◇ *The president's decision provoked public ~s.* | street | spontaneous | peaceful ◇ *Thousands gathered for a peaceful ~.* | violent | protest ◇ *a protest ~ against the war* | political | student | anti-war, civil rights, peace, pro-democracy, etc.
VERB + DEMONSTRATION hold, organize, stage ◇ *Taxi drivers staged a ~ against the new law.* | go on (*BrE*), join, participate in, take part in | lead | call off (*esp. BrE*) ◇ *The ~ was called off at the last minute.* | break up, disperse (*esp. BrE*) ◇ *Police in riot gear dispersed the ~.* | ban, suppress (*esp. BrE*) | provoke, spark ◇ *The government does not wish to provoke further ~s.*
DEMONSTRATION + VERB take place | call for sth ◇ *~s calling for an end to sanctions* | greet ◇ *The visiting president was greeted by hostile ~s.*

PREP. at a/the ~ ◇ *police intervention at ~s* | during a/the ~ ◇ *Hundreds were arrested during ~s in the capital.* | ~ against, ~ in protest at (*esp. BrE*), ~ in protest of (*AmE*) ◇ *~s in protest at the arrests* ◇ *~s in protest of the administration* | ~ in favour/favor of, ~ in support of ◇ *student ~s in support of a multiparty system*

2 showing/explaining sth

ADJ. physical, practical ◇ *physical ~s of affection* | live | successful | cookery (*esp. BrE*), cooking (*esp. AmE*), product, technology, etc.
VERB + DEMONSTRATION conduct, do, give sb, perform ◇ *I'll give a quick ~ of some first-aid techniques.* | see, watch

3 sth that shows clearly that sth is true

ADJ. clear, convincing, dramatic, impressive, perfect, vivid ◇ *The strike was a dramatic ~ of the power of the workforce.* | simple
VERB + DEMONSTRATION provide

demonstrator *noun*

ADJ. angry ◇ *Angry ~s threw stones.* | peaceful | student | anti-government, pro-democracy, etc.
... OF DEMONSTRATORS crowd, group ◇ *Police opened fire on a crowd of peaceful ~s.*
VERB + DEMONSTRATOR disperse (*esp. BrE*) ◇ *Troops were brought in to disperse the ~s.* | clash with, fire on, open fire on, use sth against ◇ *Water cannon and tear gas were used against the ~s.* | arrest | kill, shoot ◇ *Two student ~s were shot and killed.*
DEMONSTRATOR + VERB gather, take to the streets ◇ *The ~s had gathered in the cathedral square.* | march ◇ *Demonstrators marched on Washington.* | protest ◇ *~s protesting against the lack of housing* | call for sth, demand sth ◇ *~s calling for the removal of the government* | chant (sth) ◇ *~s chanting anti-war slogans* | carry sth ◇ *~s carrying placards* | disperse ◇ *The ~s refused to disperse.* | clash with sb ◇ *Demonstrators clashed with government soldiers in the country's capital yesterday.* | attack sth, storm sth ◇ *Demonstrators then tried to storm the police headquarters.*
PHRASES clashes between police and ~s

denial *noun*

ADJ. firm (*esp. BrE*), strong, vehement, vigorous ◇ *When I asked if she had cheated in the exam, she answered with a vehement ~.* | explicit, flat, outright ◇ *The document contains an explicit ~ that the company ever sold arms.* | government, official ◇ *Despite official ~s, it appears the government did make a deal with the terrorists.*
VERB + DENIAL issue, make ◇ *The chairman of the company issued a ~ of the allegations.* ◇ *Jefferson made no ~ of his actions on that night.*
PREP. ~ from ◇ *a ~ from senior officials* | in ~ ◇ *Some people are in ~ about the situation.*

denounce *verb*

ADV. angrily, bitterly, roundly, strongly | openly, publicly ◇ *He was publicly ~d as a traitor.*
PREP. for ◇ *The government was bitterly ~d for the emergency measures.* | to ◇ *Someone must have ~d them to the authorities.*
PHRASES be widely ~d ◇ *These new regulations have been widely ~d.*

density *noun*

ADJ. high, low | average ◇ *an average ~ of 2.4 people per hectare* | population, traffic ◇ *The population ~ in this city is very high.* | bone
VERB + DENSITY calculate, determine, estimate, measure | increase | reduce
DENSITY + VERB change, vary | increase, rise | decline, decrease, fall

dent *noun*

ADJ. big, great (*esp. BrE*), huge, large | real, serious, severe (*esp. BrE*), significant (*all figurative*) ◇ *The latest health scare*

has made a significant ~ in the sales of beef. | **little, slight, small, tiny**
VERB + DENT **leave, make, put** ◊ *The impact of the stones made little ~s in the metal.* | **have**
PREP. **~ in** ◊ *My side of the car had a large ~ in it.*

dent *verb*

1 make a dent in sth

ADV. **badly** ◊ *The car was quite badly ~ed on one side.* | **slightly**

2 damage sth

ADV. **badly, seriously, severely** ◊ *Being turned down for the job ~ed his pride quite badly.* ◊ *Cheap goods from overseas could severely ~ the company's sales.* | **slightly** | **barely**
VERB + DENT **fail to** (*esp. BrE*) ◊ *The experience failed to ~ her confidence.*

dentist *noun*

ADJ. **good** | **qualified, registered** (*both BrE*) | **private** (*BrE*) | **NHS** (*in the UK*) | **pediatric** (*AmE*) | **cosmetic**
VERB + DENTIST **recommend** | **register with** (*BrE*) ◊ *She wasn't registered with the ~.*
→ Note at DOCTOR (for more verbs)
DENTIST + NOUN **appointment** (*AmE*) | **office** (*AmE*) | **chair**
PHRASES **a dentist's appointment** (*BrE*) | **a/the dentist's office** (*AmE*) | **a/the dentist's chair** (*BrE*)

dentures *noun*

ADJ. **ill-fitting** | **partial**
... OF DENTURES **set** ◊ *a new set of ~*
VERB + DENTURES **have in, wear** ◊ *She doesn't wear her ~ at night.* | **put in** | **remove, take out** ◊ *Remember to clean your ~ after you take them out.*

denunciation *noun*

ADJ. **angry, bitter, fierce** (*esp. BrE*), **strong** | **public** | **ritual**
VERB + DENUNCIATION **issue, make** (*esp. BrE*) ◊ *In his speech, he issued a bitter ~ of government policy.*
PREP. **~ of** ◊ *a public ~ of the corrupt system*

deny *verb*

1 say sth is not true

ADV. **adamantly, emphatically, fiercely, firmly, hotly, steadfastly** (*esp. AmE*), **strenuously, strongly, vehemently, vigorously** ◊ *Both women vehemently ~ the charges against them.* | **angrily, indignantly** | **categorically, flatly** ◊ *He has categorically denied being involved in the fraud.* | **explicitly, expressly** | **completely, totally** | **implicitly** | **formally, officially** | **publicly** | **immediately, promptly, quickly** | **initially** | **simply** ◊ *If anyone accuses me I'll simply ~ it.* | **consistently, repeatedly** ◊ *He has consistently denied murdering his estranged wife.*
VERB + DENY **cannot** ◊ *You can't ~ that it seems a very attractive idea.* | **try to** ◊ *I know it was you I saw, so there's no use trying to ~ it.*
PHRASES **no one could ~ (that)... , no one would ~ (that)...** ◊ *No one would ~ that there is a very great need for change.* | **there is no ~ing sth** ◊ *There is no ~ing the fact that she is an excellent scholar.*

2 refuse sb sth

ADV. **cruelly** (*esp. BrE*) ◊ *They were cruelly denied victory by a header from Reece.* | **effectively** ◊ *Children could be compelled to work on the farm, effectively ~ing them schooling.* | **routinely, systematically** ◊ *The country's government systematically denies its citizens basic rights to free expression.*
PREP. **to** ◊ *You cannot ~ this opportunity to me.*

depart *verb*

VERB + DEPART **be due to** (*esp. BrE*), **be scheduled to** ◊ *The plane was scheduled to ~ later that day.* | **be waiting to** | **prepare to**
PREP. **for** ◊ *He ~s for Los Angeles tomorrow morning.* | **from** ◊ *We ~ from Heathrow at ten o'clock tonight.*

depend

department *noun*

1 of a government

ADJ. **federal, government, state** | **Education Department, Health Department, etc.** | **fire, police** (*both AmE*) ◊ *The Tokyo police ~ is clamping down on organized crime.*
DEPARTMENT + NOUN **official, spokesman, spokesperson, spokeswoman** | **personnel** (*AmE*), **staff**
PREP. **~ for** ◊ *the Department for Transport* (*in the UK*) | **~ of** ◊ *the Department of Transportation* (*in the US*)

2 of an organization

ADJ. **accident and emergency** (*BrE*), **casualty** (*BrE*), **emergency** (*AmE*), **hospital, outpatient** | **design, finance, HR, legal, marketing, personnel, planning, publicity, sales, etc.** | **biology, English, science, etc.**
VERB + DEPARTMENT **head, manage, run** ◊ *Staff criticized the way the history ~ was run.* | **join** ◊ *A new member of staff has joined the ~.* | **create, establish** | **contact** ◊ *Contact our sales ~ for more information.*
DEPARTMENT + NOUN **chair** (*esp. AmE*), **coordinator, head, manager** | **member** (*esp. AmE*), **staff**
PREP. **in a/the ~** ◊ *Complaints are dealt with in a different ~.* | **within a/the ~** ◊ *to gain promotion within the ~* | **~ of** ◊ *the Department of Planning*
PHRASES **the head of a/the ~, the head of ~** | **a member of a/the ~**

departure *noun*

1 leaving/going away from a place

ADJ. **abrupt, sudden** ◊ *Everyone was a little puzzled by her sudden ~.* | **hasty, quick** | **voluntary** | **early, late** | **imminent, impending** ◊ *The guard blew his whistle to warn of the train's imminent ~.* | **scheduled** | **flight** ◊ *The last check-in time is 45 minutes before flight ~.*
VERB + DEPARTURE **make** ◊ *He made a hasty ~.* | **hasten** ◊ *Her disagreement with the MD probably hastened her ~.* | **delay** | **announce** ◊ *Our boss sent out an email announcing her ~.*
DEPARTURE + NOUN **point** ◊ *Atocha station was the ~ point for our tour.* | **date, time** | **gate, lounge** ◊ *We sat in the ~ lounge waiting for our flight to be called.*
PREP. **before ~, prior to ~** ◊ *You should receive your flight tickets at least a week prior to ~.* | **on ~** ◊ *All visitors must sign the book on arrival and again on ~.* | **~ for** ◊ *his ~ for Naples* | **~ from** ◊ *her ~ from Toronto*
PHRASES **the day, time, etc. of ~** | **the point of ~** (*figurative*) ◊ *The author takes Freud's dream theories as the point of ~ for his essay.*

2 sth different from what is usual/expected

ADJ. **new** | **big** (*informal*), **complete, dramatic, fundamental, major, marked, radical, sharp** (*AmE*), **significant** ◊ *This project represents a big ~ for me.* | **refreshing** (*esp. AmE*), **welcome**
VERB + DEPARTURE **be, mark, represent**
PREP. **~ from** ◊ *This document marks a radical ~ from earlier recommendations.*

depend *verb*

PHR V **depend on/upon sb/sth**

1 be affected by sth

ADV. **critically, crucially, greatly, strongly, very much** ◊ *The future of the company will ~ crucially on how consumers respond.* | **entirely, solely** | **largely, mainly, primarily, really** | **partly, rather** (*esp. BrE*), **to some extent** | **ultimately** ◊ *Whether or not we can go ultimately ~s on the weather.* | **directly**
VERB + DEPEND ON/UPON **seem to** ◊ *The outcome seems to ~ on the type of soil used.*

2 need

ADV. **heavily** | **entirely, solely** | **directly**
PREP. **for** ◊ *She ~s entirely on her parents for money.*

dependable adj.

VERBS **be, seem** | **find sb** ◇ *I find him very ~.*
ADV. **extremely, fairly, very,** etc.

dependence noun

1 needing sb's help/support

ADJ. **great, heavy** ◇ *a heavy ~ on imported materials* | **absolute, complete, total** ◇ *his total ~ on his family* | **continuing, growing, increased, increasing** ◇ *The country has a growing ~ on foreign aid.* | **excessive** | **mutual** ◇ *Their relationship is based on a strong mutual ~.* | **economic, financial** | **emotional, physical, psychological**
VERB + DEPENDENCE **have** | **increase** | **reduce** ◇ *The government wants to reduce industry's ~ on coal.*
PREP. **~ on, ~ upon** ◇ *her economic ~ on her husband*

2 being addicted to sth

ADJ. **alcohol, drug, nicotine, substance,** etc.
PREP. **~ on** ◇ *~ on alcohol*

dependent adj.

1 needing sb/sth

VERBS **be, feel** | **become, grow** | **remain**
ADV. **closely, deeply, greatly, heavily, highly, very** ◇ *Many of the patients are closely ~ on staff for day-to-day emotional support.* ◇ *The country is heavily ~ on oil and gas imports.* | **critically, crucially** ◇ *Modern science is critically ~ on high-performance computing.* | **absolutely, completely, entirely, solely, totally, utterly, wholly** ◇ *Jane had never met anyone so utterly ~.* ◇ *The land is dry and wholly ~ on irrigation.* | **increasingly** | **overly** | **largely, mainly, partially, partly** ◇ *74% of people in the survey were at least partially ~ on their cars.* | **directly** | **mutually** ◇ *The various organs of the body do not function in isolation but are mutually ~.* | **economically, financially** | **emotionally**
PREP. **on, upon** ◇ *Small companies are ~ upon the local economy.*

2 dependent on/upon influenced/decided by sth

VERBS **be**
ADV. **strongly** | **entirely, fully** (*esp. AmE*), **solely, totally** ◇ *The amount of benefit you receive is entirely ~ on the amount you have paid in.* | **largely, mainly** ◇ *Your access to a good education is largely ~ on where you live.* | **partially, partly**

depict verb

ADV. **graphically, vividly** ◇ *The book vividly ~s the Hollywood of the 1950s.* | **accurately** | **clearly** ◇ *The carving clearly ~s a dragon inside a circle.*

deplete verb

ADV. **seriously, severely** ◇ *Both teams were severely ~d by injuries.* | **quickly, rapidly** | **completely**

depletion noun

ADJ. **rapid** | **severe, significant** | **resource** | **oil, oxygen, ozone,** etc.
VERB + DEPLETION **cause, lead to** ◇ *Increased consumption of water has led to the rapid ~ of reserves.* | **prevent** ◇ *Quota systems were set up to prevent ~ of fish stocks.*
PREP. **~ of** ◇ *the ~ of the ozone layer*

deploy verb

ADV. **effectively, successfully** ◇ *Tanks were ~ed effectively during the long campaign.* | **widely** | **fully** | **currently** ◇ *15 000 UN peacekeepers are currently ~ed in the country.* | **quickly, rapidly**
PREP. **against** ◇ *She rejected the arguments that had been ~ed against her.*

deployment noun

ADJ. **effective, efficient, successful** | **rapid** | **initial** | **full** ◇ *Without the full ~ of resources, we cannot achieve our aims.* | **force** (*esp. AmE*), **military, troop**
VERB + DEPLOYMENT **be available for**

deport verb

ADV. **forcibly** (*esp. BrE*)
PREP. **to** ◇ *Many refugees were forcibly ~ed back to the countries they had come from.* | **from** ◇ *He was ~ed from Britain last week.*

deportation noun

ADJ. **mass** ◇ *the mass ~ of refugees* | **forced**
VERB + DEPORTATION **be threatened with, face** | **await** | **recommend sb for** (*BrE*) ◇ *The Home Secretary has recommended the two drug dealers for ~.*
DEPORTATION + NOUN **hearing** (*esp. AmE*), **order, proceedings** ◇ *The government issued a ~ order against the four men.*
PHRASES **the threat of ~**

deposit noun

1 money paid into a bank account

ADJ. **bank, building-society** (*BrE*) ◇ *Bank ~s have increased by 2.3%.* | **cash** | **direct** (*AmE*) | **dollar, sterling,** etc.
VERB + DEPOSIT **make** ◇ *She made a ~ of £60 into her account.*
DEPOSIT + NOUN **account** (*BrE*)

2 money which is the first payment for sth

VERB + DEPOSIT **pay, put down**
PREP. **~ on** ◇ *We've put down the ~ on our new car.*

3 money paid when you rent sth

ADJ. **refundable, returnable** (*BrE*) ◇ *All ~s are refundable.* | **non-refundable, non-returnable** (*BrE*) | **security**
VERB + DEPOSIT **give (sb), leave (sb), pay (sb)** ◇ *You have to pay a ~ of $1 200 as well as two months' rent.* | **require** | **get back** ◇ *You'll get back your ~ once we've checked the bikes are all right.* | **forfeit, lose** ◇ *If furniture is damaged, you will forfeit your ~.*
PREP. **~ on** ◇ *I had to leave a €50 ~ on the bike.*

4 layer of sth

ADJ. **large** | **rich** | **thick, thin** ◇ *The floods left a thick ~ of mud over the fields.* | **gas, mineral, oil, ore,** etc. ◇ *an area with large mineral ~s* | **glacial, sedimentary** | **calcium** | **fat, fatty**
VERB + DEPOSIT **contain, have** ◇ *The region has many ~s of valuable oil.* | **form, leave** | **find** | **remove**

depot noun

ADJ. **distribution, storage, supply** | **maintenance, repair, service** | **freight** (*esp. BrE*) | **ammunition** (*AmE*), **arms, army, weapons** ◇ *an explosion at an arms ~* | **fuel, gas,** etc. | **bus, railroad** (*AmE*), **train, tram** (*BrE*) ◇ *on its way back to the bus ~*

depreciate verb

ADV. **quickly, rapidly** | **fully** (*AmE*)
VERB + DEPRECIATE **be likely to**
PREP. **against** ◇ *The US dollar is expected to ~ against the euro.* | **by** ◇ *The peso ~d by 9%.*
PHRASES **~ in value** ◇ *Cars ~ in value rapidly.*

depressed adj.

1 unhappy/mentally ill

VERBS **be, feel, look, seem, sound** | **become, get, grow** ◇ *You mustn't let yourself get ~.* | **remain, stay** | **make sb** ◇ *It makes me ~ just looking at him.*
ADV. **extremely, fairly, very,** etc. | **deeply, seriously, severely, terribly** ◇ *She became severely ~ after her mother's death.* | **thoroughly** | **increasingly** | **a little, slightly,** etc. | **mildly** | **chronically, clinically, suicidally** ◇ *At the time he was suicidal and clinically ~.*
PREP. **about** ◇ *She's terribly ~ about losing her job.* | **by** ◇ *I was ~ by our lack of progress.*

2 not economically successful

VERBS **be** | **become** | **remain, stay**

depressing *adj.*

VERBS **be** | **become, get** | **find sth**
ADV. **extremely, fairly, very,** etc. | **deeply** (*esp. BrE*), **profoundly** ◇ *We found it a deeply ~ experience.* | **a little, slightly,** etc.

depression *noun*

1 unhappiness/mental illness

ADJ. **serious, severe** | **black** (*esp. BrE*), **deep** ◇ *moments of deep ~* | **acute, chronic** | **mild, minor** | **moderate** | **clinical** | **manic** | **post-natal, post-partum** (*AmE*)
...OF DEPRESSION **bout, fit, period** ◇ *The actor says he suffers frequent bouts of ~.* ◇ *In a fit of ~, she threw away all her books.* ◇ *A period of acute ~ can sometimes follow childbirth.*
VERB + DEPRESSION **develop, fall into, go into, succumb to** ◇ *She fell into a black ~ and refused to leave her room.* | **experience, have, suffer, suffer from** ◇ *She was diagnosed as having clinical ~.* | **be treated for** ◇ *His wife had left him and he was being treated for ~.* | **come out of, get over, overcome** ◇ *She was gradually coming out of her ~.* | **cause, lead to, trigger** ◇ *Bereavement can often lead to ~.* | **alleviate, reduce, relieve, treat** ◇ *a new drug used to treat ~* | **prevent**
DEPRESSION + VERB **deepen** | **lift** ◇ *Her ~ has lifted now.* | **affect sb** ◇ *Depression affects a surprising number of people.* | **occur**
PREP. **in ~** ◇ *He may have killed himself in ~.* | **with ~** ◇ *He's been off work for months with ~.*
PHRASES **the depths of ~** ◇ *I was in the depths of ~ after receiving my exam results.* | **feelings of ~** | **the onset of ~** ◇ *The onset of ~ often follows a traumatic event.* | **a state of ~** ◇ *He was in a state of acute ~.* | **symptoms of ~** | **treatment for ~** ◇ *She had been receiving medical treatment for ~.*
→ Special page at ILLNESS

2 period of reduced economic activity

ADJ. **great, major, serious, severe** | **worldwide** | **economic** ◇ *The country is experiencing a severe economic ~.*
VERB + DEPRESSION **be in the grip of, experience** | **go into** ◇ *The market has gone into ~.*
DEPRESSION + VERB **deepen** ◇ *The ~ seems to be deepening.*
PREP. **during a/the ~, in a/the ~** ◇ *Many people lost their jobs in the great ~ of the 1930s.*
PHRASES **the depths of a ~** | **a period of ~** ◇ *periods of severe economic ~*

3 hollow part in the surface of sth

ADJ. **shallow, slight, small** | **deep**
PREP. **~ in, ~ on** ◇ *The photos show a shallow ~ on the planet's surface.*

deprivation *noun*

ADJ. **extreme, severe** | **relative** | **sensory** | **emotional** | **economic, material, social** ◇ *an area of acute social and economic ~* | **inner-city, urban** | **rural** (*esp. BrE*) | **sleep** ◇ *a study of the effects of sleep ~* | **food, oxygen**
VERB + DEPRIVATION **experience, suffer** ◇ *Many of the people suffered severe ~.*

deprived *adj.*

VERBS **be, feel**
ADV. **extremely, severely, very** | **totally** ◇ *plants that are totally ~ of light* | **relatively** | **economically, emotionally, socially** ◇ *emotionally ~ children*
PREP. **of** ◇ *children who are ~ of love*

depth *noun*

1 distance from top to bottom or from back to front; deep part of sth

ADJ. **considerable, great** ◇ *species that live at considerable ~* ◇ *They go down to great ~s below the surface.* | **maximum** | **soil, water** | **shallow** ◇ *Water normally moves more slowly at shallower ~s.* | **abyssal** (*technical*) ◇ *the abyssal ~s of the ocean* | **black, dark, murky** | **watery** ◇ *The ship's mast finally disappeared into the watery ~s.*
VERB + DEPTH **plumb, plunge into, reach**
DEPTH + NOUN **perception**
PREP. **at ~** ◇ *The camera must be strong enough to resist the immense water pressure at ~.* | **at a ~ of, from a ~ of, to a ~ of** ◇ *These fish are found at a ~ of over 300 feet.* | **at a...~, from a...~, to a...~** ◇ *The clam burrows in the sand to a considerable ~.* | **out of your ~** (*BrE*) ◇ *I don't like going out of my ~ in the sea.*
PHRASES **the ~s, the ~s of the ocean, the ~s of the sea** (*esp. BrE*) ◇ *sharks lurking in the murky ~s* | **the ocean ~s**

2 of feelings, knowledge, etc.

ADJ. **considerable, great** ◇ *Younger students cannot be expected to have great ~ of understanding.* | **black, dark** ◇ *the dark ~s of despair* | **hidden, unexpected** ◇ *I suspect she has hidden ~s.* ◇ *the unexpected ~ of his feelings for her* | **emotional** ◇ *music of great emotional ~*
VERB + DEPTH **plumb, plunge to, reach** ◇ *The story plumbed the ~s of tabloid journalism.* | **lack** ◇ *It lacks the complexity or ~ of his best movies.* | **add, give, provide** | **have** | **reveal, show** ◇ *Her paintings reveal hidden ~s.*
PREP. **in ~** ◇ *I studied phonology in ~ at college.* | **out of your ~** ◇ *The writer seems a little out of her ~ when dealing with the emotional issue involved.* | **~s of** ◇ *The rejection plunged her into the dark ~s of despair.*
PHRASES **~ of emotion, ~ of feeling** ◇ *The demonstration showed the ~ of feeling against the war.*

deputy *noun*

1 second most important person

ADJ. **acting** | **former** ◇ *a former ~ chairman of the party* | **chief**
VERB + DEPUTY **appoint (sb as)** ◇ *A new ~ has not yet been appointed.* | **act as**
DEPUTY + NOUN **chair, chairman, chief, director, editor, governor, head, leader, manager, minister, president,** etc. ◇ *He was appointed ~ head of the school.*
PREP. **~ to** ◇ *She is acting as ~ to the chairman of the board.*

2 member of a parliament

ADJ. **parliamentary** ◇ *133 of the parliamentary deputies voted against the treaty.* | **opposition** | **right-wing, socialist,** etc.
VERB + DEPUTY **elect** ◇ *Three women were among the 77 deputies elected.*

deranged *adj.*

VERBS **be, seem** | **become**
ADV. **completely** | **slightly** | **mentally** ◇ *They took her into hospital because she was mentally ~.*

derelict *adj.*

VERBS **be, lie, look, seem, stand** ◇ *The land lay ~ for ten years.* | **become**
ADV. **almost, virtually** (*esp. BrE*)

derive *verb*

ADV. **clearly** ◇ *The lions clearly ~ some benefit from living in groups.* | **largely, mainly, primarily** | **partly** | **solely** | **directly** ◇ *This income was ~d directly from his writing.* | **originally, ultimately**
PREP. **from** ◇ *We can ~ some comfort from this fact.*

descend *verb*

1 move downwards

ADV. **quickly, rapidly** | **slowly** | **carefully**

2 lead downwards

ADV. **steeply** | **gently, gradually**
PREP. **into, to** ◇ *The path ~s steeply to the town.*
PHRASES **~ into chaos, ~ into farce** (*BrE*) | **~ into madness** (*esp. BrE*) (*all figurative*)

3 be descended from sb/sth be related to sb/sth

ADV. **directly** ◇ *The breed is almost directly ~ed from the Eurasian wild boar.* | **ultimately**

VERB + DESCEND **claim to** ◇ *He claims to be ~ed from a Spanish prince.*

descendant noun

ADJ. **direct, lineal** ◇ *Quechua, the lineal ~ of the Inca language* | **immediate** | **distant** ◇ *He was an O'Conor and a distant ~ of the last High King of Ireland.* | **living, modern** | **spiritual** ◇ *He is Brecht's spiritual ~.*

descent noun

1 movement down

ADJ. **fast, rapid, swift** (*esp. BrE*) | **slow** | **steep** | **gentle, gradual** | **long** | **difficult, easy** ◇ *They began the difficult ~ of the mountain's south face.* | **final** ◇ *The plane was making its final ~.*

VERB + DESCENT **make** | **begin, start** | **continue** | **slow** ◇ *The space capsule used parachutes to slow its ~.*

PREP. **during a/the ~, on a/the ~** ◇ *The engines failed on the plane's ~ to Newark.* | **~ down** ◇ *I made a slow and painful ~ down the stairs.* | **~ from** ◇ *the ~ from the top of the mountain* | **~ into** (*figurative*) ◇ *his ~ into alcoholism* | **~ to** ◇ *The plane began its gentle ~ to Narita.*

PHRASES **a rate of ~** ◇ *We slowed the balloon's rate of ~.*

2 surface that goes downwards

ADJ. **gentle** | **steep**

3 family origins

ADJ. **direct, lineal** ◇ *She claims direct ~ from Queen Victoria.* | **common** ◇ *Most European languages have a common ~.* | **mixed** | **African, Chinese, European, Irish,** etc.

VERB + DESCENT **claim, have** | **trace** | **share** ◇ *groups sharing common ~*

PREP. **by ~** ◇ *She is Hungarian by ~.* | **~ from** ◇ *He claims to have traced ~ from Christopher Columbus.*

PHRASES **a line of ~** ◇ *Humans and other apes followed separate lines of ~ from a common ancestor.* | **of Mexican, Scottish,** etc. **~** ◇ *She is of mixed European and African ~.*

describe verb

ADV. **accurately, exactly, in detail** ◇ *Their daily lives are ~d in detail.* | **aptly, well** | **clearly, simply** | **fully** ◇ *This process is fully ~d in section three of the book.* | **adequately** | **briefly** ◇ *He ~d briefly what happened.* | **vividly** | **variously** ◇ *The shirt was variously ~d as 'pink', 'salmon' and 'rose'.*

VERB + DESCRIBE **cannot** ◇ *Words cannot ~ our feelings at that moment.* | **be difficult to, be hard to, be impossible to** | **go on to** ◇ *He goes on to ~ vividly how Lincoln was assassinated.*

description noun

ADJ. **complete, comprehensive, detailed, full** ◇ *The catalogue gives a full ~ of each product.* | **accurate, apt, clear, exact, excellent, fair, fitting, good, perfect** ◇ *'Like a fish out of water' was an apt ~ of how I felt in my new job.* | **rich, vivid** ◇ *a vivid ~ of life in the Wild West* | **graphic, lurid** ◇ *She gave us a lurid ~ of the birth.* | **lengthy, long** | **brief, short** | **basic, simple** | **general, vague** | **objective** ◇ *A report is generally an objective ~ rather than a statement of opinion.* | **formal** | **verbal, written** | **physical** | **job** ◇ *There was no mention of any cleaning in my job ~.*

VERB + DESCRIPTION **give (sb), issue** (*BrE*)**, offer (sb), provide (sb with)** ◇ *Police have issued a ~ of the gunman.* ◇ *She was able to provide a ~ of the intruder.* | **fit, match** ◇ *A man fitting your ~ was seen entering the building.* ◇ *Police have arrested two men matching the ~s of the robbers.* | **beggar, defy** ◇ *His face was so odd that it defies ~.*

DESCRIPTION + VERB **apply to sb, fit sb** ◇ *I realized to my horror that the ~ of the killer could fit me.*

descriptive adj.

VERBS **be**

ADV. **highly, very** ◇ *a highly ~ account of her journey through Africa* | **purely** ◇ *The passage is purely ~.* | **merely, simply** | **largely, mainly**

PREP. **of** ◇ *The terms are ~ of strong emotion.*

desert noun

ADJ. **arid, barren, dry, hot** ◇ *green fields surrounded by arid ~* | **vast** | **empty, open** (*esp. AmE*) | **inhospitable** | **Arctic, polar** | **high** | **flat** | **cultural** (*figurative*) ◇ *The town has become a cultural ~.*

VERB + DESERT **become, turn into, turn to** ◇ *The land loses its protective cover of vegetation and soon turns into ~.* | **cross** ◇ *He became the first person to cross the ~ on foot.*

DESERT + VERB **stretch** ◇ *The ~ stretched for endless miles on all sides of us.*

DESERT + NOUN **area, country, land, landscape, region** ◇ *vast tracts of ~ land* | **conditions** | **heat** | **sand, soil** | **floor, surface** | **plain** | **animal, plant**

PREP. **across the ~, through the ~** ◇ *their journey across the ~* | **in the ~** ◇ *cold nights in the ~* | **into the ~** ◇ *He drove off into the ~.*

deserted adj.

VERBS **appear, be, look, seem** | **become**

ADV. **completely, totally** ◇ *The streets were completely ~.* | **almost, virtually** | **largely** | **apparently**

deserve verb

ADV. **certainly, definitely, really, surely** ◇ *You really ~ a medal!* | **probably** | **justly, richly, rightfully** (*esp. AmE*)**, rightly, truly** ◇ *He finally received the recognition that he so richly ~d.* | **fully, thoroughly, totally, well** ◇ *This hotel fully ~s its four-star grading.* | **clearly** ◇ *Philip's efforts clearly ~ praise.* | **hardly, scarcely** ◇ *It's true she made a mistake but she hardly ~s to lose her job.*

PREP. **for** ◇ *She ~s some reward for all her hard work.*

PHRASES **~ better** ◇ *His work received only a tiny mention in the journal; he ~s better.* | **well ~d** ◇ *At last she managed to have a well-deserved rest.*

deserving adj.

VERBS **be, seem**

ADV. **very** | **equally** ◇ *All the causes seem equally ~.*

PREP. **of** ◇ *the areas most ~ of study*

design noun

1 making drawings of how sth should be made

ADJ. **graphic** | **computer-aided** ◇ *a specialist in computer-aided ~* | **architectural, industrial, interior** | **software, Web, website** ◇ *He set up his own software ~ company.*

DESIGN + NOUN **business, company, consultancy, firm** | **chief, consultant, director, engineer, professional, staff, team** | **centre/center, department, studio** | **work** ◇ *She's done some ~ work for us in the past.* | **process** ◇ *The new program really speeds up the ~ process.* | **phase, stage** ◇ *elements that are being included in the next ~ phase* | **goal** ◇ *One of our main ~ goals was to make the product easy to use.* | **tool** ◇ *Digital ~ tools are essential.* | **program, software** | **project** | **ability, expertise, skills** | **challenge** ◇ *Making the building accessible for disabled people was another major ~ challenge.* | **magazine** ◇ *an interior ~ magazine*

PHRASES **art and ~** ◇ *I'm doing a course in art and ~.*

2 the way sth is made/a drawing of this

ADJ. **basic, simple** | **complex, sophisticated** | **intelligent** (= the claim that life did not evolve, but was created by an intelligent being) | **excellent, good** | **poor** | **adventurous, bold, cutting-edge, experimental, innovative, original, revolutionary** | **modern** | **new** | **preliminary** | **attractive, beautiful, sleek, stylish** ◇ *a car with a sleek modern ~* | **classical, conventional, traditional** | **minimalist** | **ergonomic** | **sustainable** | **overall** ◇ *The overall ~ of the workspace is critical.* | **patented**

VERB + DESIGN **come up with, create, develop, produce** ◇

He's come up with a really good ~ for a solar-powered car. | **employ, follow, use** ◇ We followed the traditional ~. | **finalize** | **improve, modify, refine** | **simplify** | **guide, influence** | **unveil** ◇ Last week the architect unveiled his ~ for a museum on Prague's waterfront.

DESIGN + VERB **include sth, incorporate sth** ◇ The office ~s incorporate quiet rooms where employees can take a break. | **allow sth, enable sth** ◇ The clever ~ allows natural light to flood into the room. | **offer sth, provide sth** ◇ The new label ~ provides nutrition facts. | **evolve**

DESIGN + NOUN **detail, element, feature** ◇ The latest model incorporates some novel ~ features. | **concept, idea, solution** ◇ We put forward two alternative ~ concepts for the new library. | **consideration** ◇ Building security is now a major ~ consideration. | **criterion, philosophy, principle, strategy** | **brief, requirements, specifications** ◇ The chair she had sketched was far bigger than stipulated in the ~ brief. | **standards** ◇ Strict ~ standards ensure that new buildings are compatible with existing architecture. | **fault, flaw** | **award** ◇ The car wouldn't win any ~ awards, but it's very reliable. | **competition** ◇ The company won an international ~ competition for the concert hall. | **change, modification**

PREP. **in ~** ◇ The machine is very simple in ~. | **of ... ~** ◇ a vehicle of revolutionary ~ | **to a ... ~** ◇ The other houses are built to a more conventional ~. | **~ for** ◇ the architect's ~s for the cathedral

PHRASES **at the ~ stage** ◇ Their new car is still at the ~ stage.

3 pattern that decorates sth

ADJ. **elaborate, intricate** | **simple** | **abstract, circular, floral, geometric, symmetrical**

VERB + DESIGN **have** ◇ The building has intricate geometric ~s on several of the walls. | **paint, trace**

DESIGN + NOUN **theme** ◇ trendy boutique hotels with avant-garde ~ themes | **motif**

4 intention

ADJ. **evil, sinister** | **grand** ◇ His grand ~ was to connect up every academic institution in the world.

VERB + DESIGN **harbour/harbor, have** ◇ I suspected that he had some sinister ~s.

PREP. **by ~** ◇ Had it happened by accident or by ~?

design verb

ADV. **carefully, cleverly, intelligently** ◇ These shelves have been ~ed very cleverly to fit into corners. | **badly, poorly** ◇ The website was poorly ~ed. | **beautifully, elaborately, elegantly, intricately, nicely** | **especially, explicitly, expressly, specially, specifically** ◇ the first yogurt ~ed especially for babies and toddlers | They run specially ~ed courses for managers. | **exclusively, solely, uniquely** ◇ a service ~ed exclusively for women | **largely, mainly, primarily** ◇ Many new performance halls are ~ed primarily for music. | **initially, originally** ◇ The trail was originally ~ed to give our staff a quiet place to walk. | **newly** | **ergonomically**

PREP. **for** ◇ The instruments are ~ed for use in very cold conditions.

designate verb

ADV. **formally, officially** ◇ The area has now been formally ~d as a Site of Special Scientific Interest. | **specially, specifically** | **originally** | **newly** | **clearly**

PREP. **for** ◇ These areas have been specially ~d for children.

designer noun

ADJ. **good, talented** | **professional** | **chief, lead** (AmE), **principal, senior** ◇ the company's chief fashion ~ | **young** | **famous, renowned, well-known** | **leading, top** ◇ one of the country's top fashion ~s | **dress, fashion, jewellery/jewelry, textile** | **garden, landscape, urban** | **interior** ◇ They brought in an interior ~ to do the house. | **graphic** | **kitchen** | **furniture, lighting** | **architectural, industrial, technical** | **costume, set, theatre/theater** ◇ She works as a set ~ for the Metropolitan Opera. | **game, program, software, system, systems, Web**

VERB + DESIGNER **bring in, hire** (esp. AmE) | **consult, consult with** (AmE)

DESIGNER + NOUN **clothes, fashion** | **handbag, jeans, shoes, etc.** | **goods** | **brand, label, name** | **store** (esp. AmE) | **baby** (= a baby which has been chosen for its genetic characteristics) | **stubble** (= a very short beard) (BrE) | **drug, steroid** (= drugs which have been made so they are similar to an illegal drug)
→ Note at JOB

desirable adj.

1 (formal) to be wished for

VERBS **be, seem** | **become** | **consider sth, deem sth, feel sth** (esp. BrE), **regard sth as, see sth as, think sth, view sth as** ◇ A new direction was considered ~ for both parties. ◇ This kind of work is seen as ~.

ADV. **eminently, extremely, highly, very** ◇ Experience of computers is highly ~. | **particularly** | **clearly, obviously** ◇ It is clearly ~ to have a common set of principles throughout the industry. | **economically, morally, politically, socially**

PHRASES **it is ~ that ...** ◇ It is ~ that interest rates should be reduced. (BrE) ◇ It is ~ that interest rates be reduced. (AmE)

2 causing sexual desire

VERBS **be** | **become** | **find sb**

ADV. **extremely, very** ◇ He found her intensely ~. | **sexually**

desire noun

ADJ. **burning, deep, fervent, fierce, great, intense, passionate, strong, urgent** | **growing** ◇ There's a growing ~ among consumers for more organic products. | **sudden** | **insatiable, unquenchable** ◇ Most children have an insatiable ~ for knowledge. | **overwhelming, uncontrollable** | **frustrated, thwarted, unfulfilled** | **repressed** | **hidden, secret** ◇ She confessed a secret ~ to be famous. | **earnest, genuine, real, sincere** | **selfish** | **desperate** | **obsessive** | **human** ◇ The human ~ for answers is very great. | **individual, personal** | **innate, natural** | **subconscious, unconscious** | **basic** ◇ The search for a better life is one of the most basic ~s of human beings. | **conflicting** ◇ He is filled with conflicting ~s. | **carnal, erotic, sexual** | **heterosexual, homosexual, same-sex** | **mutual** ◇ a long-lasting relationship based on our mutual ~ for peace

VERB + DESIRE **feel, harbour/harbor, have** ◇ I suddenly felt an overwhelming ~ to laugh | **share** ◇ He did not share her ~ for books. | **arouse, create** ◇ His childhood had created a ~ for stability in his life. | **fuel, stimulate** ◇ This was all Liam needed to fuel his ~ for revenge. | **articulate, communicate, express, indicate, profess, reveal, signal, state, voice** ◇ The chairman expressed his ~ to expand the company. | **fulfil/fulfill, gratify, indulge, satisfy** | **control, overcome, resist, suppress** ◇ He suppressed the ~ to run from the room. | **demonstrate, reflect** ◇ His actions reflect his ~ to fit in. | **be driven by, be motivated by** ◇ They were motivated by a deep ~ for money and fame.

PREP. **~ for** ◇ Horses need to satisfy their ~ for space and freedom.

PHRASES **an object of ~** ◇ He felt he was nothing more to her than an object of ~.

desire verb

ADV. **greatly, really, truly, very much** ◇ A home of her own was something she had always very much ~d.

desk noun

1 type of table

ADJ. **big, huge, large, massive** | **executive** | **small** | **leather-topped, metal, wooden** | **mahogany, oak, etc.** | **antique** | **empty** ◇ The empty ~ suggested she had already gone home. | **cluttered, messy, untidy** (esp. BrE) | **writing** | **computer** | **office, school**

VERB + DESK **sit at** | **get up from, leave** ◇ He got up from his ~ and went to the window. | **clean, clean out, clear** ◇ My ~ gets very cluttered if I don't clear it at the end of each day. | **arrive on, cross, hit, land on** ◇ A very strange request landed

on my ~ this morning. | **cover, litter** ◊ *Papers littered the ~ and the floor.*
DESK + NOUN **drawer, top** | **calendar** (*esp. AmE*), **diary** (*BrE*) | **chair, lamp, phone** | **space** ◊ *a computer which takes up less ~ space* | **job** | **jockey** (= someone who works at a desk) (*AmE, informal*)
PREP. **at a/the ~** ◊ *He was sitting at his ~ working when we got home.* | **behind a/the ~** ◊ *The manager sat frowning behind his ~ throughout the whole interview.* | **on a/the ~** ◊ *I left the file on your ~.*
2 place in a building where a service is provided
ADJ. **front, main, reception** ◊ *Leave your valuables at the reception ~.* | **hotel** | **cash** (*BrE*), **check-in, help, information, reference, registration, security, service, support** (*esp. AmE*), **trading** ◊ *She paid for the book at the cash ~.* ◊ *Staff experiencing problems with their computers should call the help ~.* | **news** | **anchor** (= where a television presenter sits) (*AmE*), **copy** (= where news text is edited) (*AmE*)
VERB + DESK **call** ◊ *She called the front ~ to let them know that he would be arriving.* | **man, run, work** (*AmE*) ◊ *I worked the front ~ as one of my first jobs.*
DESK + NOUN **clerk** (*AmE*), **officer, staff** | **editor** | **duty** ◊ *They put me on ~ duty for a month.*
PREP. **at the … ~** ◊ *There was a long wait at the check-in ~.* | **on the … ~** ◊ *We asked the man on the information ~ for a map of the city.*

desolate *adj.*

1 empty and depressing
VERBS **be, seem, stand** ◊ *The house stands ~ and empty.* | **become** | **leave sth** ◊ *The land was left ~.*
ADV. **completely, quite** ◊ *The landscape was completely ~.* | **rather** ◊ *a rather ~ place*
2 very unhappy
VERBS **be, feel, look, sound** ◊ *He looked as ~ as Ruth felt.* | **become**
ADV. **utterly** ◊ *She was utterly ~ after losing her baby.*

despair *noun*

ADJ. **black, deep** | **complete, total, utter**
VERB + DESPAIR **feel** | **fall into** ◊ *He fell into ~ over his failure as a husband.* | **drive sb to** ◊ *a teenager driven to ~ by the hypocrisy of the adult world*
PREP. **in ~** ◊ *Robert shook his head in ~.* | **of ~** ◊ *She let out a cry of ~.* | **with ~** ◊ *He cried out with ~.* | **~ at, ~ over** ◊ *I felt ~ at being deceived.* ◊ *his ~ over the loss of his wife*
PHRASES **the depths of ~** ◊ *When he became ill he sank to the depths of ~.* | **in a moment of ~** | **a feeling of ~, a sense of ~** ◊ *I was overcome with a feeling of utter ~.*

desperate *adj.*

VERBS **be, feel, look, seem, sound** | **become, get** ◊ *I was starting to get ~.* | **make sb** ◊ *The sudden loss of his money had made him ~.*
ADV. **extremely, fairly, very, etc.** | **really, truly** | **absolutely, utterly** ◊ *She felt utterly ~.* | **increasingly** | **almost** | **a little, slightly, etc.**
PREP. **about** ◊ *I felt ~ about my future.*

desperation *noun*

ADJ. **pure, sheer** | **quiet** | **growing, increasing** ◊ *We realized with a sense of growing ~ that nobody knew we were in there.*
… OF DESPERATION **hint, note** ◊ *There was a note of ~ in her voice.*
VERB + DESPERATION **feel** | **drive sb to** ◊ *Driven to ~ by the noise, we called the police.*
PREP. **in (your)** ◊ *In ~, I decided to try acupuncture.* ◊ *In his ~ to escape, Tom had slipped and broken a leg.* | **out of ~** ◊ *She became a thief out of sheer ~.* | **~ about, ~ at** ◊ *Many of us feel a quiet ~ at the future.*
PHRASES **an act of ~** ◊ *The robbery was an act of ~.* | **courage,**

strength, etc. **born of ~** ◊ *With strength born of ~, she managed to break down the door.*

despicable *adj.*

VERBS **be, seem** | **find sth** ◊ *What I find particularly ~ is their neglect of old people.*
ADV. **absolutely, truly, utterly** ◊ *It was an absolutely ~ thing to do.* | **particularly** | **pretty**

despise *verb*

ADV. **absolutely, really, thoroughly, truly** | **clearly** | **secretly** ◊ *He secretly ~d his father.* | **openly**
PREP. **for** ◊ *She thoroughly ~d him for his weakness.*

despondent *adj.*

VERBS **be, feel** ◊ *Patients often feel ~.* | **become, get, grow** ◊ *His work was rejected again and again, and he grew more and more ~.*
ADV. **extremely, fairly, very, etc.** | **utterly** ◊ *She was feeling utterly ~.* | **a little, slightly, etc.**
PREP. **about** ◊ *He had become rather ~ about his lack of progress.* | **over** (*esp. AmE*) ◊ *He is increasingly ~ over losing his family.*

dessert *noun*

ADJ. **delicious** | **rich** | **decadent** | **frozen** | **sweet** | **chocolate, fruit**
VERB + DESSERT **eat, have** | **make** | **order** ◊ *The waiter asked us if we'd like to order a ~.* | **serve** ◊ *After ~ was served, the chef introduced himself.* | **skip**
DESSERT + NOUN **apple** | **wine** | **menu** | **table** (*esp. AmE*) | **cart** (*AmE*), **trolley** (*BrE*) | **plate**
PREP. **for ~** ◊ *We had mousse for ~.* | **~ of** ◊ *We finished off with a ~ of honey and nuts.*
→ Special page at FOOD

destination *noun*

ADJ. **eventual, final, ultimate** | **intended** ◊ *We got lost and ended up miles away from our intended ~.* | **unknown** | **desired** | **favourite/favorite, hot, popular** ◊ *Amsterdam is the hot travel ~ in the Netherlands.* ◊ *The town is a popular ~ for art lovers.* | **ideal, perfect** | **attractive** | **premier, prime, top** ◊ *This small town is the country's top mountain-biking ~.* | **major** ◊ *The restaurants are located in capital cities and major tourist ~s.* | **exotic** | **holiday** (*BrE*), **resort** (*AmE*) | **tourist, travel, vacation** (*AmE*) ◊ *The island is an ideal travel ~.* | **entertainment, golf, leisure** (*all esp. AmE*) ◊ *The casino is the largest entertainment ~ in the state.* | **international** ◊ *The airline operates flights to most international ~s.* | **online, Web** ◊ *Your website is only one potential online ~ where people can find out about your company.*
VERB + DESTINATION **arrive at, reach** ◊ *At around 1.00 p.m. we reached our final ~.* | **approach, near** ◊ *My steps slowed down as I neared my ~.* | **visit** | **become** ◊ *The city has become a popular ~ for backpackers.* | **create** ◊ *The aim was to create a ~ for ski enthusiasts.*
DESTINATION + NOUN **resort** (*AmE*) ◊ *Sun Valley Lodge was the first ~ ski resort in the US.* | **airport, city, country** | **wedding** (in a place away from home) (*esp. AmE*) ◊ *They had a ~ wedding on a beach in Brazil.*
PREP. **to a/the ~** ◊ *The deposed leader is reported to have fled the capital to an unknown ~.* | **~ for** ◊ *a popular ~ for golf enthusiasts*
PHRASES **the country, port, state, etc. of ~** ◊ *The goods are examined by customs at the port of ~.*

destiny *noun*

ADJ. **your own** ◊ *He wanted to take control of his own ~.* | **manifest** | **human** | **true** ◊ *He came to Paris and found his true ~ as a poet.* | **economic, political** | **ultimate**
VERB + DESTINY **face, meet** ◊ *The time was right for him to meet his ~.* | **fulfil/fulfill** ◊ *She felt that she had fulfilled her ~.* | **accept** ◊ *There's not much you can do but accept your ~.* | **avoid, escape** ◊ *No man can escape his ~.* | **control** ◊ *Can we control our own ~?* | **find** ◊ *She had to find her ~ on her own.* | **alter, change** ◊ *It was a decision which could have*

changed my ~. | **decide, determine, shape** ◊ *Something was about to happen that would shape her ~.*
DESTINY + VERB **await sb, lie** ◊ *the ~ that awaited him* ◊ *Her ~ lay in that city.*
PHRASES **be in control of your own ~, be master of your own ~** ◊ *She set up her own business because she wanted to be in control of her own ~.* | **a sense of ~** ◊ *He was driven on by a strong sense of ~.*

destroy verb

1 damage sth so badly that it no longer exists
ADV. **completely, entirely, totally, utterly | all but, almost, effectively, nearly, practically, virtually** ◊ *Their lives have been virtually ~ed by this tragedy.* | **largely | partially, partly | eventually, ultimately** ◊ *Our greed may ultimately ~ the planet.* | **systematically** ◊ *The rainforest is being systematically ~ed.* | **single-handedly** ◊ *That guy just single-handedly ~ed everything we've worked for.* | **easily | for ever, permanently | immediately, instantly** ◊ *The bomb hit, instantly ~ing the building.* | **quickly, rapidly | slowly** ◊ *Depression and despair slowly ~ed his life.* | **deliberately | accidentally, inadvertently | physically** ◊ *He physically ~ed the computer by smashing it to pieces.* | **literally** ◊ *The earthquake literally ~ed their villages.* | **by fire** ◊ *The building was ~ed by fire last year.*
VERB + DESTROY **can, could, etc.** ◊ *Drugs can ~ the lives of young people.* | **threaten to** ◊ *This disease threatens to ~ many of our native trees.*
PHRASES **an attempt to ~ sth** ◊ *a new attempt to ~ enemy positions* | **be capable of ~ing sth** ◊ *These weapons are capable of ~ing the entire planet.* | **be intent on ~ing sth** ◊ *She seemed intent on ~ing everything they had built up together.*

2 kill an animal
ADV. **humanely**
PHRASES **have to be ~ed** ◊ *The horse fell and had to be ~ed.*

destruction noun

ADJ. **complete, total, utter, wholesale | large-scale, mass, massive, widespread** ◊ *modern weapons of mass ~* | **rapid | imminent | final, ultimate | systematic | wanton** ◊ *the wanton ~ of public property* | **ecological, environmental, forest, habitat, ozone** ◊ *the environmental ~ caused by road building* | **property** ◊ *The earthquake caused loss of life and property ~.* | **nuclear** ◊ *the threat of nuclear ~ which haunts the post-war world* | **physical | deliberate, intentional | mutual** ◊ *a war of mutual ~*
VERB + DESTRUCTION **bring (about), cause, lead to, result in, wreak** (*formal*) ◊ *the ~ brought about by war* | **avoid, prevent, stop** ◊ *Some shopkeepers closed early to prevent the wholesale ~ of their property by the hooligans.* | **escape, survive** ◊ *Three of the paintings escaped ~.* ◊ *He had miraculously survived the ~ of the spacecraft.* | **see, watch, witness** ◊ *He witnessed the ~ of most of his work in a studio fire.* | **seek** ◊ *those who seek the ~ of our way of life*
PHRASES **leave a trail of ~** ◊ *The tornado left a trail of ~ behind it.* | **the seeds of ~** ◊ *By doubling its prices, the industry sowed the seeds of its own ~.* | **test sth to ~** (*BrE*) ◊ *Children will quickly test their toys to ~.*

destructive adj.

VERBS **be, seem | become**
ADV. **extremely, fairly, very, etc. | highly | ultimately** ◊ *It was a very short-sighted and ultimately ~ plan.* | **potentially** ◊ *potentially ~ emotions* | **environmentally, socially** ◊ *environmentally ~ policies*
PREP. **of** ◊ *Clearing trees by burning is highly ~ of the forest environment.* | **to** ◊ *These substances can be ~ to health.*

detached adj.

VERBS **be, feel, seem, sound | become | remain**
ADV. **largely, very | completely, totally, wholly | a little, slightly, etc. | curiously, oddly, strangely** ◊ *He felt curiously ~ from what was going on.* | **emotionally**
PREP. **from** ◊ *She tries to remain emotionally ~ from her patients.*

detachment noun

ADJ. **complete | clinical, professional** ◊ *She gazed at the body with almost clinical ~.* | **cool | critical | emotional**
VERB + DETACHMENT **have, show** ◊ *The judges show impartiality and ~.*
PREP. **with ~** ◊ *She watched with complete ~ as the others made all the preparations.* | **~ from** ◊ *his increasing ~ from reality*
PHRASES **an air of ~** | **a feeling of ~, a sense of ~**

detail noun

ADJ. **little, minor, minute, small, subtle, tiny** ◊ *It is important to get even the small ~s right.* | **considerable, fine, great, meticulous, painstaking** ◊ *Now let us examine this idea in greater ~.* ◊ *Every new animal or plant found was recorded in meticulous ~.* | **exact, explicit, precise** ◊ *I don't need to know the precise ~s of your quarrel.* | **excruciating** ◊ *He described the event to his friends in excruciating ~.* | **fascinating, interesting | colourful/colorful, vivid | juicy, salacious** ◊ *She was telling me all the juicy ~s of her love life.* | **gory, graphic, grisly, gruesome, lurid, sordid** ◊ *I can still remember the accident in graphic ~.* | **chilling, disturbing, shocking** ◊ *The report uncovers disturbing ~s of abuse.* | **intimate** ◊ *The diary contains intimate ~s of their life together.* | **complete, exhaustive, full** ◊ *We'll give you full ~s of how to enter our competition later.* | **bare ~s, brief ~s, sketchy ~s** ◊ *I only know the barest ~s of his plans.* ◊ *He only managed to give the police a few sketchy ~s of the robbery.* | **crucial, essential, important, nitty-gritty** (*informal, esp. AmE*), **pertinent** ◊ *The book covers the nitty-gritty ~s of starting a business.* | **insignificant, irrelevant, trivial | telling** ◊ *It was a small but telling ~.* | **practical** ◊ *I haven't sorted out the practical ~s of getting there yet.* | **complex, intricate | final** ◊ *Everyone must approve the basic plan before the final ~s are drawn up.* | **concrete** ◊ *Can you give me some concrete ~s of how you've been saving money?* | **mundane** ◊ *the mundane ~s of his daily life* | **biographical, factual, historical, operational, personal, technical**
...OF DETAIL **point** ◊ *I must correct some points of ~ in your article.* | **wealth** ◊ *The book provides a wealth of ~ on daily life in ancient China.* | **level** ◊ *Ensure that your diagrams contain the appropriate level of ~.*
VERB + DETAIL **give, go into, offer, present, provide, send, supply** ◊ *Do not give any technical ~s of the product at this stage.* ◊ *I don't want to go into any more ~ than necessary.* | **disclose, divulge, pass on, release ~s, reveal** ◊ *The committee refused to disclose ~s of the proposals.* | **share** ◊ *He had shared intimate ~s of his life with a stranger.* | **explain, lay out, lay sth out in, set out, set sth out in, spell out, spell sth out in** ◊ *Details of the pension plan are set out below.* ◊ *The rules are set out in ~ in chapter seven.* | **establish, finalize, iron out, work out, work sth out in** ◊ *We haven't yet worked out the travel ~s.* | **discuss, hammer out, negotiate** ◊ *We still need to negotiate the ~s of the contract.* | **handle** ◊ *Natalie handled the ~s of her travel.* | **uncover** ◊ *Historians claim to have uncovered ~s of the writer's secret affair.* | **hear, learn, read | fill sb in on** ◊ *I'll give you a call later and fill you in on the ~s.* | **spare sb** (*informal*) ◊ *'We had a terrible time—' 'Oh, spare me the ~s (= don't tell me any more).'* | **contain, have, include** ◊ *Tomorrow's papers will contain full ~s of the case.* | **show** ◊ *The receipt shows ~s of the item purchased.* | **find out ~s, get ~s** ◊ *You can find out more ~s of the offer from your local travel agent.* | **enter ~s** ◊ *Enter your ~s in the form below then click on 'submit'.* | **take ~s** ◊ *The secretary took my ~s and said they would get back to me.* | **check, examine, study** ◊ *Make sure you check the ~s of the policy before you sign it.* | **record** ◊ *The computer records the ~s of everyone entering the country.* | **absorb, memorize** ◊ *She had memorized every ~ of his body.* | **omit | neglect, overlook** ◊ *He had overlooked one crucial ~.* | **be lacking in, lack** ◊ *The speech was well delivered but lacking in ~.* | **sweat the ~s** (*AmE, informal*) ◊ *He leaves experts to sweat the ~s (= worry about them).* | **spill** (*informal, esp. AmE*) ◊ *Spill the gory ~s about*

your worst relationship. | **post ~s, publish** (= on the Internet) ◊ *Click here for more ~s posted by Ken.* | **confirm** ◊ *They wrote to confirm the ~s of the meeting.*

DETAIL + VERB **emerge** ◊ *New ~s are emerging on the alleged terror plot.* | **suggest sth** ◊ *This ~ suggests that the killer knew his victim.* | **reveal sth, show sth**

PREP. **for ~s** ◊ *For ~s contact Joanna Morland.* | **in ~** ◊ *I haven't looked at the proposal in ~ yet.* | **over a/the ~** ◊ *They're still arguing over the ~s of the contract.* | **~ about** ◊ *I won't go into ~ about the threats she made.* | **~ of** ◊ *She revealed the ~s of her plan.* | **~ on** ◊ *For more ~ on how to obtain a visa, see page 8.* | **~ surrounding** ◊ *The ~s surrounding his death are not known.*

PHRASES **attention to ~** ◊ *The secret of their success lies in their attention to ~.* | **down to the last ~** ◊ *an expedition planned down to the last ~* | **every last ~** ◊ *She remembered every last ~ of what I'd told her the month before.* | **an eye for ~** ◊ *He has an excellent eye for ~.* | **full of ~** ◊ *Her short stories are full of ~ and wit.* | **a lack of ~** ◊ *The report was criticized for its lack of ~.*

detailed *adj.*

VERBS **be, seem**
ADV. **extremely, fairly, very, etc.** ◊ *a very ~ account of the events* | **extraordinarily, highly, immensely** (*esp. BrE*), **incredibly** | **fully** | **increasingly** | **meticulously, minutely** | **exquisitely, finely, richly** ◊ *the exquisitely ~ carvings on the cathedral door* | **incredibly, unusually**

detain *verb*

ADV. **briefly** ◊ *He was kidnapped and briefly ~ed by a terrorist group.* | **indefinitely** ◊ *Prisoners cannot be ~ed indefinitely without charge.* | **illegally**
VERB + DETAIN **need not** (*esp. BrE*) ◊ *This issue need not ~ us long.*
PREP. **for** ◊ *She was arrested and ~ed for distributing pro-democracy leaflets.* | **in connection with** ◊ *Over 60 people have been ~ed in connection with the coup attempt.*
PHRASES **be ~ed in custody, be ~ed in hospital** (*both BrE*) ◊ *Two people were ~ed in hospital following the crash.* | **~ sb without charge, ~ sb without trial** ◊ *He has been ~ed without trial for nearly two years now.*

detect *verb*

ADV. **early, late** ◊ *Some cancers can now be cured if they are ~ed early.* | **quickly, rapidly** | **automatically** | **easily, readily** ◊ *Some substances can be ~ed fairly easily.* | **clearly** | **accurately, correctly, successfully** | **consistently, reliably** | **visually**
VERB + DETECT **be able to, be sensitive enough to, can** ◊ *a machine that is sensitive enough to ~ tiny amounts of explosives* | **be unable to** | **be designed to** | **fail to** ◊ *The test failed to ~ any illegal substances.* | **be difficult to, be hard to, be impossible to** | **be easy to, be possible to, be used to**
PHRASES **be capable of ~ing sth** | **a means of ~ing sth, a method of ~ing sth, a way of ~ing sth**

detection *noun*

ADJ. **early** ◊ *Our aim is the early ~ and treatment of all cancers.* | **crime** (*esp. BrE*), **fraud** | **error** | **radiation** | **cancer** ◊ *the quest to improve breast cancer ~*
VERB + DETECTION **avoid, escape, evade** ◊ *Their prey can sometimes escape ~ by remaining still.* | **improve**
DETECTION + NOUN **rate** ◊ *The latest figures show falling fraud ~ rates.* | **method, system, technique** | **device, equipment** ◊ *radiation ~ equipment* | **technology**

detective *noun*

ADJ. **private** ◊ *She hired a private ~ to follow her husband.* | **undercover** | **store** ◊ *The store ~ was keeping a close eye on a suspected shoplifter.* | **police** | **amateur** | **fictional** ◊ *Sherlock Holmes was Conan Doyle's fictional ~.* | **homicide**

(*AmE*) | **hard-boiled** | **lead** (*AmE*) ◊ *Thomson was the lead ~ in the Ramsay case.*
VERB + DETECTIVE **hire**
DETECTIVE + VERB **investigate sth** ◊ *~s investigating the case*
DETECTIVE + NOUN **agency** | **work** ◊ *We are going to have to do some ~ work on this.* | **fiction, novel, series, show** (*esp. AmE*), **story** | **hero**

detention *noun*

ADJ. **arbitrary** ◊ *Opponents of the regime had been subject to arbitrary ~.* | **pretrial** | **indefinite** ◊ *If found guilty, she could face indefinite ~.* | **illegal** | **incommunicado** (*esp. AmE*) | **preventive** ◊ *Suspects were placed in preventive ~.* | **military**
VERB + DETENTION **be in, remain in** ◊ *147 of the illegal immigrants remain in ~.* | **hold sb in, place sb in, sentence sb to** ◊ *He was held in ~ from 1991 to 2001.* ◊ *They were sentenced to 12 months' ~.* | **authorize** | **be subject to, face** | **receive** | **release sb from** | **challenge** ◊ *Prisoners have the right to challenge their ~s.* | **serve** ◊ *Lawyers argued that she should be allowed to serve her ~ in her home country.* | **give** ◊ *Any student caught smoking would be given ~ immediately.* | **be sent to** (*AmE*), **go to** (*AmE*), **have** ◊ *My first day of school, and I have ~.*
DETENTION + NOUN **camp, centre/center, facility** | **area, cell, hall, room** | **operations** (*esp. AmE*) | **policy**
PREP. **in ~** ◊ *She spent 18 years in ~.* | **under ~** ◊ *He made the confession while under ~.*
PHRASES **a period of ~, a term of ~** ◊ *The judge will set the period of ~.*

deter *verb*

ADV. **hardly** ◊ *Her words of warning would hardly ~ him.* | **effectively** ◊ *Will this harsher punishment effectively ~ criminals?* | **easily**
VERB + DETER **be likely to, be unlikely to** | **be enough to, be sufficient to** | **attempt to** | **be designed to** | **do little to, do nothing to** ◊ *The present system does little to ~ corporate crime.*
PREP. **from** ◊ *These new rules are likely to ~ people from coming forward for help.*

deteriorate *verb*

ADV. **badly, seriously, severely** | **dramatically, quickly, rapidly, sharply** | **slowly** | **gradually, steadily** | **significantly** | **further**
VERB + DETERIORATE **begin to** ◊ *His health began to ~ quite seriously.* | **continue to** | **be likely to**
PREP. **into** ◊ *The unrest rapidly ~d into civil war.*

deterioration *noun*

ADJ. **marked, serious, significant** ◊ *a serious ~ in relations between the two governments* | **rapid, sharp** | **gradual, progressive, steady** | **slow** | **mental, physical** ◊ *Mental and physical ~ both occur naturally with age.* | **economic, environmental**
VERB + DETERIORATION **cause, lead to, result in** ◊ *The stress led to a gradual ~ in her health.* | **prevent** ◊ *Limits on waste dumping will prevent further environmental ~.* | **arrest** (*formal*) ◊ *Steps need to be taken quickly to arrest the ~ in the countries' relations.* | **experience, see** ◊ *The period has seen a spectacular ~ of political stability.* | **show**
DETERIORATION + VERB **occur**
PREP. **~ in** ◊ *a rapid ~ in his condition* | **~ of** ◊ *a steady ~ of our economic advantage*
PHRASES **signs of ~** ◊ *The car's bodywork was already showing signs of ~.*

determination *noun*

1 will to continue

ADJ. **dogged, fierce, great, grim, gritty** (*esp. BrE*), **ruthless, single-minded, steely, strong, stubborn** | **quiet** | **absolute, sheer** ◊ *He succeeded by hard work and sheer ~.* | **clear** ◊ *She demonstrated a clear ~ to improve her performance.* | **renewed** ◊ *With a renewed ~, she stood up.*
VERB + DETERMINATION **be full of, have** ◊ *She was full of ~ to*

achieve her goals. ◇ He has the ~ to succeed. | **demonstrate, reveal, show** ◇ She has shown great ~ and skill. | **express, signal** ◇ She expressed her ~ to continue in the job. | **require** | **lack**

PREP. **with** ~ ◇ He hung on with grim ~.

PHRASES ~ **to succeed, win, etc.**

2 process of discovering the facts about sth

ADJ. **age, sex** | **accurate, precise**

determine verb

1 discover the facts about sth

ADV. **exactly, precisely** ◇ We need a detailed investigation to ~ exactly why these cancers are occurring. | **reliably** | **conclusively, definitively** | **unambiguously** | **objectively**

VERB + DETERMINE **try to** | **be used to, help to** ◇ Computer models help to ~ whether a particular area is likely to flood. | **be easy to, be possible to** | **be difficult to, be impossible to** ◇ It is difficult to ~ the exact cause of the illness. | **be necessary to** | **be able to**

2 make sth happen in a particular way

ADV. **biologically, culturally, genetically** ◇ the debate about whether such attitudes are biologically or culturally ~d | **ultimately** ◇ a decision which would ultimately ~ the fate of the project | **directly** ◇ Reproductive success is directly ~d by attractiveness to the female. | **largely, mainly, primarily** | **partly** | **solely, uniquely**

determined adj.

VERBS **appear, be, look, seem, sound** | **become** | **remain** | **make sb** ◇ The opposition to her plan made her more ~ than ever.

ADV. **extremely, fairly, very, etc.** | **absolutely, quite, utterly** ◇ They were quite ~ that he wasn't going to do it. | **clearly, obviously** | **fiercely, grimly** ◇ His voice was grimly ~. | **quietly** (esp. BrE)

deterrent noun

ADJ. **effective, good, great, powerful, real** | **credible** | **the ultimate** (esp. BrE) ◇ Defenders of the death penalty regard it as the ultimate ~. | **nuclear** ◇ They stressed the need for an independent nuclear ~. | **strategic** (esp. AmE)

VERB + DETERRENT **act as, be, provide** ◇ a punishment that will act as a ~ to other offenders

DETERRENT + NOUN **effect** ◇ They were arguing about the ~ effect of nuclear weapons.

PREP. **as a** ~ ◇ The bodies of executed criminals were hung on the city gates as a ~. | ~ **against** ◇ a ~ against cheating | ~ **for** ◇ There is no effective ~ for these young criminals. | ~ **to** ◇ a ~ to crime ◇ a ~ to all but the most determined attacker

detour noun → See also DIVERSION

ADJ. **lengthy** (esp. BrE), **long** | **brief, little, short, slight, small** | **five-mile, etc.**

VERB + DETOUR **make, take** ◇ We had to make a lengthy ~ through the backstreets. | **be worth** ◇ The monument is well worth a ~.

DETOUR + NOUN **route** (AmE) | **sign** (AmE)

PREP. ~ **around** ◇ Trucks now face a five-mile ~ around the bridge. | ~ **from** ◇ Her career took a ~ from the expected path. | ~ **through** | ~ **to** ◇ The ship made a ~ to the south.

detrimental adj.

VERBS **be, prove, seem** | **become**

ADV. **extremely, fairly, very, etc.** | **highly, seriously** | **potentially**

PREP. **to** ◇ This move could be seriously ~ to the economy.

devastation noun

ADJ. **complete, total, utter** | **widespread** | **ecological, environmental** | **economic** | **emotional**

VERB + DEVASTATION **cause, wreak** ◇ The hurricane caused widespread ~. ◇ We surveyed the ~ wrought by the fire.

PHRASES **a scene of** ~ ◇ He surveyed the scene of utter ~

beneath him. | **a trail of** ~ ◇ The tornado left a trail of ~ in its wake.

developed adj.

VERBS **be, seem**

ADV. **highly, strongly, very, well** ◇ He has a highly ~ sense of humour/humor. | **fully** | **partially** | **finely** | **poorly** ◇ She was born prematurely with poorly ~ lungs. | **newly, recently** | **economically** ◇ economically ~ countries | **overly** ◇ an overly ~ sense of his own importance

developer noun

1 person/company that develops land/buildings

ADJ. **big, major** | **local** ◇ A local ~ is planning to build a supermarket on the site. | **private** ◇ The houses are being built by a private ~. | **commercial** | **speculative** | **housing, property** (esp. BrE), **real estate** (AmE) ◇ plans by a big property ~ to build fifty new houses | **land**

DEVELOPER + VERB **build sth, develop sth**

2 person/company that creates new products

ADJ. **lead, leading** | **independent** | **product** | **game, software, Web**

DEVELOPER + VERB **create sth**

development noun

1 developing sth

ADJ. **full** ◇ School should encourage the full ~ of a student's talents. | **gradual** | **rapid** | **accelerated** | **continued, ongoing** | **arrested** | **sustainable** ◇ The agency supports and promotes sustainable economic ~. | **healthy, normal** | **abnormal** | **commercial, economic, industrial, socio-economic** | **evolutionary, historical** | **regional** | **community, rural, suburban, urban** ◇ community ~ projects | **human** | **brain, cell, etc.** | **artistic, cognitive, educational, emotional, intellectual, language, linguistic, moral, personal, physical, professional, psychological, sexual, social, spiritual** ◇ There is tremendous opportunity for personal and professional ~ at our company. | **product, software, Web, website** | **drug, vaccine** | **business** | **curriculum** | **adolescent, child** | **property** (esp. BrE), **real estate** (AmE)

VERB + DEVELOPMENT **aid, allow, assist, encourage, enhance, facilitate, favour/favor, foster, permit, promote, spur, stimulate, support** ◇ Education stimulates the ~ of rational thinking. ◇ A group of experts has been brought together to support the ~ of the project. | **accelerate, speed up** ◇ Environmental factors can accelerate the ~ of certain cancers. | **initiate, pioneer** | **guide, influence, shape** ◇ He influenced the ~ of modern dance. | **affect, impact** (esp. AmE) | **arrest, delay, discourage, halt, hamper, hinder, impede, inhibit, prevent, restrict, retard, slow** ◇ Too much emphasis on memorizing facts can inhibit the ~ of creative thinking. | **undergo** ◇ The city has undergone rapid ~. | **finance** ◇ The company went deep into debt to finance the ~ of the engine. | **lead, monitor, oversee, spearhead** ◇ A UN team is monitoring the ~ of the peace process. | **trace, track** ◇ In the opening chapter, the author traces the ~ of judo from its ancient roots.

DEVELOPMENT + VERB **occur, take place** | **continue, progress**

DEVELOPMENT + NOUN **initiative, plan, programme/program, project, scheme** (BrE), **strategy** | **aid, assistance** | **tool** | **efforts, work** ◇ The invention requires more ~ work to make it viable. | **process** ◇ the lengthy ~ process of a new model of car | **phase** | **cycle** ◇ the three-year ~ cycle of their products | **budget, capital, fund, grant** | **costs, expenditure** | **agency, company, firm, organization** | **committee, department, office** | **consultant, director, expert, manager, officer, team** | **opportunity**

PREP. **during** ~ ◇ Cell divisions during ~ occur in a fixed sequence. | **in** ~ ◇ A more powerful version of this electric bus is currently in ~. | **under** ~ ◇ A new vaccine is under ~.

PHRASES **research and** ~ ◇ I do a lot of research and ~ work in my job. | **a stage in the** ~ **of sth** ◇ an important stage in the

~ *of Sino-American relations* | **a stage of ~** ◊ *This is a perfectly normal stage of ~.*

2 new event/idea

ADJ. **exciting, important, major, radical, remarkable, significant, striking** | **the latest, new, recent** | **logical** ◊ *The move from TV to movies was a logical ~ in her career.* | **unexpected** | **welcome** | **positive** | **political, scientific, technical, technological**

DEVELOPMENT + VERB **occur, take place, unfold** ◊ *the significant ~s taking place in the health service*

PREP. **~ in** ◊ *new ~s in medicine*

3 area of new buildings

ADJ. **housing, residential** | **business, commercial** | **ribbon** (*BrE*) ◊ *Ribbon ~s (= lines of buildings) extended along the main road.* | **mixed-use** ◊ *The building plans are for a mixed-use ~.*

deviate *verb*

ADV. **considerably, significantly, substantially** (*esp. AmE*) | **slightly**

PREP. **by** ◊ *Output may ~ from the average by as much as 30%.* | **from** ◊ *We had to ~ significantly from our usual route.*

device *noun*

ADJ. **clever, ingenious** | **labour-saving/labor-saving, useful** | **complex, sophisticated** | **simple** | **hi-tech** | **hand-held, mobile, portable** | **automatic, digital, electrical, electronic, mechanical** | **USB, wireless** | **bugging, communication, contraceptive, display, measuring, medical, monitoring, optical, recording, safety, storage, timing, warning** ◊ *Police found several bugging ~s in the room.* | **explosive, incendiary** ◊ *improvised explosive ~s* ◊ *An incendiary ~ exploded in the store, setting fire to furniture.* | **nuclear**

VERB + DEVICE **be fitted with, have** ◊ *All new cars are now fitted with these safety ~s.* | **connect, install** ◊ *Now connect the ~ to your computer.* | **build, design, develop, make** | **use** ◊ *He measured the room using an ingenious new electronic ~.* | **test**

DEVICE + VERB **comprise sth** (*esp. AmE*), **consist of sth** ◊ *The ~ consists of a large wheel mounted on a metal post.* | **be designed to** ◊ *a tiny ~ designed to trace telephone calls* | **use** ◊ *The ~ uses a transmitter that connects to your computer.* | **work** ◊ *The ~ worked exactly as I'd hoped.*

PREP. **~ for** ◊ *a useful ~ for checking electrical circuits*

devil *noun*

VERB + DEVIL **believe in** | **worship** | **be possessed by** ◊ *He behaved like someone possessed by ~s.*

DEVIL + NOUN **worship** | **worshipper**

PHRASES **the ~ incarnate** (*figurative*) ◊ *His views make him the ~ incarnate to extreme conservatives.*

devoid *adj.* devoid of

VERBS **appear, be, seem** | **become** | **remain**

ADV. **completely, entirely, quite, totally, utterly** ◊ *Are you totally ~ of common sense?* | **almost, largely, nearly, practically, virtually** ◊ *The land is almost ~ of vegetation.*

devote *verb*

PHR V **devote sth/yourself to sth**

ADV. **entirely, exclusively, solely, specifically** ◊ *She ~d herself entirely to writing.* | **mainly**

devoted *adj.*

VERBS **be, seem** | **become** | **remain**

ADV. **extremely, fairly, very, etc.** | **absolutely** (*esp. BrE*), **completely, totally, utterly** | **passionately**

PREP. **to** ◊ *They were totally ~ to each other.*

devotion *noun*

ADJ. **deep, great** | **fanatical, intense, passionate, single-**

minded ◊ *Their single-minded ~ to the care of the dying was admirable.* | **absolute, complete, total** ◊ *her total ~ to her husband* | **selfless** | **blind, slavish** ◊ *He was mocked for his slavish ~ to his boss.* | **lifelong, undying** ◊ *his lifelong ~ to his work* | **personal** | **religious** ◊ *a man of deep religious ~*

VERB + DEVOTION **express, show** | **inspire**

PREP. **with ~** ◊ *He cared for his mother with great ~.* | **~ to** ◊ *They showed great ~ to each other.*

PHRASES **~ to duty** ◊ *The judge praised the firefighters for their bravery and ~ to duty.* | **~ to the cause** ◊ *She will be remembered for her selfless ~ to the cause of the poor.* | **an object of ~** ◊ *The statue of the king became an object of ~.*

devour *verb*

ADV. **eagerly, greedily, hungrily** ◊ *He ~ed the food greedily.* | **quickly** ◊ *The animal quickly ~ed its prey.*

dew *noun*

ADJ. **heavy** ◊ *There was a heavy ~ this morning.* | **morning** ◊ *The sun had dried the early morning ~.*

... OF DEW **drop** ◊ *Drops of ~ shone on the grass.*

DEW + VERB **form** | **drip, fall** | **glisten**

DEW + NOUN **drop** (usually *dewdrop*) | **point**

PHRASES **damp with ~, wet with ~** ◊ *The grass was still wet with ~.*

dexterity *noun*

ADJ. **great** | **manual**

VERB + DEXTERITY **demand** (*esp. BrE*), **require** ◊ *Video games require great manual ~.* | **have** ◊ *I don't have the ~ for juggling.*

PREP. **with ~** ◊ *She handled the discussion with ~.*

diagnose *verb*

ADV. **correctly** | **incorrectly, wrongly** ◊ *Her condition was wrongly ~d by the doctor.* | **newly** ◊ *newly ~d patients* | **clinically** ◊ *people with clinically ~d diabetes*

PREP. **with** ◊ *He was ~d with leukaemia.*

diagnosis *noun*

ADJ. **accurate, correct, right** | **incorrect, wrong** | **definite, definitive, firm, positive, specific** | **provisional, tentative** ◊ *Without the results of the test, the doctor could only make a tentative ~.* | **early** ◊ *Early ~ is critical for successful treatment.* | **initial, original** | **final** | **primary** | **clinical, medical, psychiatric** ◊ *clinical ~ of schizophrenia* | **AIDS, cancer, etc.**

VERB + DIAGNOSIS **establish, give, make, provide, reach** ◊ *The doctor cannot give a ~ without knowing the full medical history.* | **confirm, suggest, support** ◊ *Further tests have confirmed the ~.* | **receive**

PREP. **after ~, before ~** ◊ *Patients may suffer from some of the symptoms years before ~.* | **~ of** ◊ *the ~ of the disease* ◊ *a ~ of cancer*

PHRASES **a method of ~** ◊ *They are using new methods of ~.*

diagram *noun*

ADJ. **clear** | **detailed** | **simple** | **block, flow, network, schematic, tree, Venn** | **circuit, wiring**

VERB + DIAGRAM **draw** ◊ *Draw a simple ~ of the leaf structure.* | **see** ◊ *See the ~ on page 31.*

DIAGRAM + VERB **depict sth, illustrate sth, indicate sth, represent sth, show sth** ◊ *a flow ~ showing the stages in the printing process*

PREP. **in a/the ~** ◊ *Compare this system to the one shown in ~ B.* | **on a/the ~** ◊ *The trees will be planted at the points marked on the ~.* | **~ of** ◊ *a ~ of the human nervous system*

dial *noun*

VERB + DIAL **adjust, set, spin** (*esp. AmE*), **turn, twist** ◊ *Set the ~ for the number of copies required.* ◊ *I went to my locker, spun the ~, and got my books out.*

dialect *noun*

ADJ. **local, native, regional** | **rural, urban** | **non-standard** |

VERB + DIALECT **speak, speak in**
DIALECT + NOUN **form, word** | **speaker** | **group** ◇ *the two major ~ groups of Inuit* | **poetry**

dialogue (AmE also dialog) noun

ADJ. **close** ◇ *There needs to be a closer ~ between management and staff.* | **direct** ◇ *The government refused to engage in direct ~ with the terrorists.* | **healthy, honest** (*esp. AmE*), **open** ◇ *an honest and open ~ about racial identity in the US* | **public** | **constructive, meaningful, real, serious** | **ongoing** | **political** ◇ *a serious political ~*
VERB + DIALOGUE **engage in, have, hold** ◇ *Managers are willing to hold a ~ with union leaders.* | **begin, create, enter into, establish, open, start** ◇ *His movies create their own ~ with the viewer.* ◇ *The government must enter into a ~ with industry on this issue.* | **continue, resume** | **encourage** ◇ *attempts to encourage ~ between the two groups*
PREP. **~ about** ◇ *~ about concrete issues* | **~ among** ◇ *The school encourages a climate of ~ among the teachers.* | **~ between** ◇ *the need for ~ between the two sides in the dispute* | **~ on** ◇ *a constructive ~ on pay and working conditions* | **~ with** ◇ *They have agreed to resume their ~ with the teachers.*

diameter noun

ADJ. **inner, inside, internal** ◇ *The tubes have an internal ~ of 2 mm.* | **external, outer, outside** | **large, small**
VERB + DIAMETER **calculate, determine, estimate, find, measure** ◇ *a method of calculating the ~ of the earth* | **increase, reduce** | **have**
PREP. **in ~** ◇ *The mirror is ten inches in ~.*

diamond noun

1 precious stone

ADJ. **flawless, perfect** | **real** | **fake** | **synthetic** | **cut** | **uncut** | **industrial**
VERB + DIAMOND **cut** | **polish** | **set** | **be encrusted with, be studded with** ◇ *earrings encrusted with ~s* | **drip with, wear** ◇ *an old woman dripping with ~s*
DIAMOND + VERB **glitter, sparkle**
DIAMOND + NOUN **mine** | **industry, trade** | **dealer, merchant** | **earring, necklace, ring**

2 playing card
→ Note at CARD

diaper noun (AmE) → See also NAPPY

ADJ. **dry, fresh** | **wet** | **dirty, soiled** | **disposable, throwaway** | **cloth** | **adult, baby**
VERB + DIAPER **have on, wear** | **soil, wet** | **check** | **change** | **put on** | **remove, take off**
DIAPER + NOUN **change** ◇ *It was time for a ~ change.* | **bag** | **cover** | **pin** | **rash**
PREP. **in ~** ◇ *Isn't he old to be still in ~s?*

diarrhoea (AmE diarrhea) noun

ADJ. **severe** | **mild** | **acute, chronic** | **intermittent, persistent**
VERB + DIARRHOEA/DIARRHEA **experience, have, suffer from** | **develop, get** | **cause**
→ Special page at ILLNESS

diary noun

1 for writing down what happens each day

ADJ. **detailed** | **daily** | **personal, private, secret** | **food, travel** ◇ *He jotted down observations on the places he visited in his travel ~.* | **online, video**
VERB + DIARY **keep** ◇ *I starting keeping a ~ when I was thirteen.* | **note sth in, record sth in, write sth in** ◇ *'It's all over,' he wrote in his ~ for April 21.* | **read** ◇ *No one is allowed to read my ~.*
DIARY + NOUN **entry**
PREP. **in a/your ~** ◇ *I've made a note in my ~.*
PHRASES **an entry in a ~**

2 (*BrE*) for appointments → See also DATEBOOK

ADJ. **appointments, bookings, engagement, social** | **desk, pocket** | **electronic**
VERB + DIARY **have sth in** ◇ *I didn't have the meeting in my ~.* | **put sth in, write sth in** ◇ *Put it in your ~ before you forget.*
PREP. **in a/your ~**

dice (also die esp. in AmE) noun

ADJ. **loaded**
VERB + DICE **play** | **roll, throw** ◇ *You decide who's going to start by throwing the ~.* | **shake**
DICE + NOUN **game**
PREP. **on a/the ~** ◇ *You move forward according to the number on the ~.*
PHRASES **a/the roll of the ~, a/the throw of the ~** ◇ *The roll of the ~ went against them.*

dictatorship noun

ADJ. **communist, fascist** | **left-wing, right-wing** | **military** | **totalitarian** | **brutal, repressive** | **benevolent**
VERB + DICTATORSHIP **establish, set up** ◇ *The generals established a military ~.* | **support** | **overthrow** ◇ *They succeeded in overthrowing the fascist ~.*
PREP. **during a/the ~** ◇ *the atrocities that took place during his ~* | **under (a/the) ~** ◇ *These men had all lived under ~.*

dictionary noun

ADJ. **good** | **comprehensive, unabridged** | **electronic, online** | **picture** | **pocket** | **English, French, etc.** | **English-Spanish, Spanish-English, etc.** | **bilingual, monolingual** | **learner's** | **standard** | **technical** | **etymological, historical, pronunciation** | **biographical, encyclopedic, medical** ◇ *I decided to consult a medical ~.*
VERB + DICTIONARY **check, consult, look sth up in, use** ◇ *If you don't know the meaning of a word, look it up in the ~.* ◇ *a way of teaching children how to use dictionaries* | **need** ◇ *You need a ~ to understand what he's saying half the time.* | **compile, write** | **edit** | **publish**
DICTIONARY + NOUN **definition, entry**
PREP. **in a/the ~** ◇ *I couldn't find the word in the ~.*

die noun (esp. AmE) → See DICE

die verb

ADV. **peacefully** | **suddenly, unexpectedly** | **tragically** ◇ *Her father ~d tragically in a car crash.* | **in infancy, prematurely, young** ◇ *One of their children ~d in infancy.* | **in childbirth** | **nearly** ◇ *I nearly ~d when they told me the price.*
VERB + DIE **be going to** ◇ *I thought I was going to ~.* | **be allowed to** ◇ *She should be allowed to ~ peacefully.*
PREP. **for** ◇ *to ~ for your country* | **from** ◇ *The accident victim ~d from her injuries.* | **of** ◇ *He ~d of a heart attack.*
PHRASES **~ a natural, violent, etc. death**

diesel noun

VERB + DIESEL **run on, use** ◇ *These buses run on ~.*
DIESEL + NOUN **generator, power** | **fuel, oil** | **emissions, exhaust, fumes** | **car, engine, locomotive, model, train, truck** (*esp. AmE*), **vehicle** ◇ *The ~ model is slightly more expensive.*

diet noun

1 food sb/sth usually eats

ADJ. **good, healthful** (*AmE*), **healthy, nutritious, sensible** | **balanced, varied, well-balanced** | **adequate** ◇ *People can fight infection more easily if they have an adequate ~.* | **bad, poor, unhealthy** | **staple** ◇ *a staple ~ of cornmeal and vegetables* | **daily** | **vegan, vegetarian** | **American, Mediterranean, Western, etc.**
VERB + DIET **consume, eat, have** ◇ *It is important to eat a balanced ~.* | **live on, survive on** ◇ *They had to survive on a*

~ *of insects and berries.* | **feed sb, feed sb on, keep sb on** | **change** ◊ *She was told to change her ~ and quit smoking.* | **supplement**
DIET + VERB **consist of sth, contain sth** ◊ *The animal's ~ consists mainly of grasses.*
PREP. **in a/the ~** ◊ *the amount of fat in your ~* | **on a ~** ◊ *These animals live on a mainly vegetarian ~.* | **~ of** ◊ *They were fed on a ~ of rice and vegetables.*
PHRASES **a ~ high in sth, a ~ rich in sth** ◊ *a ~ rich in vitamins and minerals*

2 when you want to lose weight/are ill

ADJ. **strict** | **weight-loss, weight-reducing** | **crash, starvation** ◊ *Crash ~s are not the best way to lose weight.* | **fad** | **calorie-controlled** (*esp. BrE*)**, low-calorie** (*esp. AmE*) | **restricted, special** | **dairy-free, gluten-free, etc.** | **high-fibre/high-fiber, high-protein, etc.** | **low-carb, low-fat, etc.**
VERB + DIET **follow, have** ◊ *If you follow this ~, you're bound to lose weight.* | **go on, start** | **stick to** ◊ *I have to stick to a low-fat ~.* | **be on** ◊ *I'd love a dessert, but I'm on a ~.*
DIET + NOUN **drink, food** | **Coke™, soda** (*esp. AmE*) | **pill** | **plan** ◊ *Lose pounds with our new ~ plan!* | **book**
PREP. **on a ~** ◊ *athletes on a special high-protein ~*

differ verb

1 be different

ADV. **considerably, dramatically, enormously, fundamentally, greatly, markedly, radically, sharply, significantly, substantially, widely** ◊ *The two approaches ~ markedly* ◊ *Opinions ~ widely on this issue.* | **little** | **slightly, somewhat** | **clearly**
PREP. **according to** ◊ *Conditions of employment ~ according to the type of company you are working for.* | **among** ◊ *The rates of violent crime ~ed greatly among the four cities.* | **between** ◊ *Social organization ~s significantly between the different groups.* | **from** ◊ *His ideas ~ little from those of his father.* | **in** ◊ *The models ~ in size and shape.*

2 have a different opinion

VERB + DIFFER **agree to** (*esp. BrE*) ◊ *In the end we agreed to ~.* | **beg to** ◊ *I beg to ~* (= I disagree with you).
PREP. **about, over** ◊ *The two sides still ~ over details of the plan.* | **on** ◊ *The two parties ~ on all the major issues.* | **with** ◊ *It didn't seem right that I should ~ with him.*

difference noun

1 way in which people/things are not the same

ADJ. **big, broad, considerable, dramatic, enormous, great, huge, large, major, profound, radical, real, sharp, substantial, vast, wide** ◊ *A little extra care makes a big ~.* ◊ *I noticed a real ~ in his attitude.* | **basic, essential, fundamental** | **crucial, important, key, main, significant** ◊ *A small number of additional jobs can make a crucial ~ to economic conditions.* ◊ *We found no significant ~ between the two groups.* | **clear, distinct, marked, noticeable, observed, obvious, striking** ◊ *There is a striking ~ between eastern and western Europe.* | **apparent** | **minor, slight, small, subtle** | **potential** | **qualitative, statistical** | **national, regional** | **age, class, cultural, ethnic, gender, genetic, physical, psychological, racial, sex, social** | **historical, ideological, political** | **structural** | **temperature, time** ◊ *What's the time ~ between New York and Tokyo?*
VERB + DIFFERENCE **make** ◊ *The new central heating has made an enormous ~ to the house.* ◊ *What ~ does it make if he doesn't have a car?* | **mean** ◊ *One tiny mistake when you're climbing could mean the ~ between life and death.* | **emphasize, exaggerate, focus on, highlight, stress, underline** ◊ *We should be focusing on what we have in common rather than emphasizing our ~s.* | **appreciate, be aware of, detect, feel, find, know, note, notice, observe, perceive, recognize, see, spot, tell** ◊ *I found very little ~ in price.* ◊ *Only an expert would know the ~ between the male and the female.* ◊ *Can you spot the ~ between these two photos?* ◊ *It's difficult to tell the ~ between butterflies and*

moths. | **understand** | **explain, illustrate** | **examine, explore, look at** ◊ *The study explores the ~s between the way girls and boys talk.* | **compare** | **demonstrate, exhibit** (*formal*)**, indicate, reveal, show** ◊ *The questionnaire showed vast ~s in what kind of product people want.* | **mark, reflect** ◊ *Our different attitudes to life reflect the ~s in our backgrounds.*
DIFFERENCE + VERB **be, lie** ◊ *The ~ lies in the way the fruit is prepared.* | **arise (from sth), exist** ◊ *The ~s in size arise from the amount of sunshine each plant gets.* | **explain sth, reflect sth, suggest sth**
PREP. **~ among** ◊ *There are few important policy ~s among the main parties.* | **~ between** ◊ *There's a big ~ between reading about skiing and doing it yourself.* | **~ from** ◊ *He was very aware of his ~ from the other children.* | **~ in** ◊ *The ~ in price is not very significant.* | **~ of** ◊ *a crucial ~ of emphasis* | **~ with** ◊ *The ~ with this information service is that it's free.*
PHRASES **a... with a ~** ◊ *If you want a travel destination with a ~, come to Iceland.* | **all the ~ in the world** ◊ *There's all the ~ in the world between choosing to do something and being forced to do it.* | **a great deal of ~, a lot of ~** ◊ *The extra money will make a lot of ~ to us.* | **make all the ~** ◊ *Just five minutes' exercise a day could make all the ~.* | **no ~, not much ~** ◊ *There's not much ~ between baseball and softball.*

2 sum of money in addition to the sum expected

VERB + DIFFERENCE **pay** ◊ *If you decide on the more expensive model, you can bring this one back and pay the ~.* | **make up** ◊ *He didn't have enough money, but his aunt agreed to make up the ~.* | **pocket** ◊ *He sold the car for more than he'd paid and pocketed the ~.* | **split** (*figurative*) ◊ *I wanted to leave early and Ian wanted to leave late, so we split the ~ and left at noon.*

3 disagreement

ADJ. **irreconcilable, major, serious, sharp** | **minor, slight** | **outstanding** ◊ *These talks aim to resolve the outstanding ~s between the two sides.*
VERB + DIFFERENCE **have** ◊ *They have had some minor ~s, but in general they get on well together.* | **make up** (*BrE*)**, patch up, put aside, reconcile, resolve, settle** ◊ *We're going to get the two sides together to see if they can't settle their ~s.*
DIFFERENCE + VERB **arise, emerge, occur** ◊ *Differences may arise when the young people do not have the same expectations as their parents.* | **remain** ◊ *Although the talks were generally successful, ~s remain between the groups.*
PREP. **~ as to, ~ over** ◊ *There were some ~s as to how to deal with the crisis.*
PHRASES **a ~ of opinion** ◊ *She and Luke had a ~ of opinion over how much money they should spend.* | **have your ~s** ◊ *Like any married couple, we have our ~s.*

different adj.

VERBS **appear, be, feel, look, seem, sound, taste**
ADV. **very** | **far** ◊ *This is a far ~ movie from his previous one.* | **clearly, distinctly, markedly, significantly, strikingly, substantially, vastly** | **dramatically, drastically** (*esp. AmE*)**, fundamentally, radically** ◊ *This school is radically ~ from most others.* | **altogether, completely, entirely, quite, totally** | **whole** ◊ *That's a whole ~ matter.* | **rather, somewhat** | **slightly** | **subtly** ◊ *The tune returns in a subtly ~ guise.* | **materially, qualitatively** | **refreshingly** ◊ *a refreshingly ~ approach to language learning*
PREP. **from** ◊ *Human beings are ~ from other animals.* | **to** (*BrE*) ◊ *Their customs are very ~ to ours.* | **than** (*AmE*) ◊ *The movie's ~ than the original book.*

differentiate verb

ADV. **clearly**
VERB + DIFFERENTIATE **be important to** | **be easy to, be possible to** | **be difficult to**
PREP. **between** ◊ *It is not always possible to ~ between the two diseases.* | **from** ◊ *features which clearly ~ this product from other similar ones*

difficult adj.

VERBS **be, look, prove, remain, seem, sound** | **become, get**

◊ *It is getting more and more ~ to find a job.* | **make sth** ◊ *The fog made driving very ~.* | **find sth**
ADV. **extremely, fairly, very, etc.** | **exceedingly, extraordinarily, incredibly, particularly** | **doubly** ◊ *Her disability made taking care of the home and raising a family doubly ~.* | **increasingly** | **a little, slightly, etc.** | **notoriously** ◊ *Birth rates are notoriously ~ to predict.*

difficulty *noun*

ADJ. **considerable, enormous, extreme, grave, great, major, real, serious, severe** ◊ *We had enormous ~ in getting hold of the right equipment.* | **insurmountable** | **increasing** ◊ *questions of increasing ~* | **inherent** ◊ *the difficulties inherent in treating overdose patients* | **potential** | **particular, special** ◊ *English spelling presents special difficulties for foreign learners.* | **economic, financial** | **practical, technical** ◊ *I think we've managed to overcome most of the practical difficulties.* | **behavioural/behavioral, emotional, learning** ◊ *children with learning difficulties*
... OF DIFFICULTY **level** ◊ *The games have various levels of ~.*
VERB + DIFFICULTY **encounter, experience, face, get into, have, run into** ◊ *Anyone experiencing ~ with radio reception should call us on the new helpline.* | **Some companies are getting into ~.** ◊ *Let me know if you have any difficulties.* ◊ *I had little ~ in persuading the others to come.* ◊ *The plan has run into serious difficulties.* | **cause, create, make, pose, present** ◊ *Will it cause any difficulties if I go early?* ◊ *She is always making difficulties for herself.* | **increase** ◊ *This increases the ~ of the shot.* | **cope with, deal with, overcome, resolve, solve, surmount** | **avoid** ◊ *how to avoid technical difficulties* | **be fraught with** ◊ *The situation was fraught with ~.* | **illustrate** | **report** ◊ *Please report any difficulties to the help desk.*
DIFFICULTY + VERB **arise** ◊ *Difficulties arise when people fail to consult their colleagues.* | **lie (in sth)** ◊ *The ~ lies in identifying the precise nature of the problem.*
PREP. **despite a/the ~** ◊ *Despite all the difficulties, he still remains optimistic.* | **in ~** ◊ *Some companies are already in ~.* ◊ *We could see that the swimmer was in difficulties. (esp. BrE)* | **with ~, without ~** ◊ *We crossed the border without any ~.* ◊ *Life in the city was not without its difficulties.* | **~ in** ◊ *She had ~ in starting her car.* | **~ of** ◊ *the ~ of finding an affordable hotel* | **~ with** ◊ *I'm having ~ with the engine.*

dig *noun*

1 (esp. BrE) small push
ADJ. **sharp**
VERB + DIG **give** ◊ *She gave him a sharp ~ in the ribs.* | **feel, get**
PHRASES **a ~ in the ribs**

2 critical remark
ADJ. **little** | **sly** (esp. BrE) ◊ *I resisted the temptation to get in a sly ~ at Fred.*
VERB + DIG **get in, have, make, take** (AmE)
PREP. **~ about** | **~ at** ◊ *They were having a little ~ at her about the way she tells everybody else what to do.*

3 in the ground
ADJ. **archaeological**
VERB + DIG **go on** ◊ *I went on a ~ over the summer.*
DIG + VERB **reveal sth** ◊ *The ~ revealed the site of a Roman villa.*

dig *verb*

ADV. **deep, deeply** ◊ *We'll have to ~ deep to get at the roots.* | **down**
PREP. **for** ◊ *They were digging for buried treasure.* | **into** ◊ *I could feel the teeth ~ into my skin.* ◊ *He was unwilling to ~ into Sylvia's past. (figurative)* | **through** ◊ *We found ourselves digging through solid clay.*

digest *verb*

ADV. **easily** ◊ *Some foods are ~ed more easily than others.* | **fully** | **partially** ◊ *partially ~ed food* | **slowly**
VERB + DIGEST **can** ◊ *He has to avoid fat because his body can't*

~ it. | **be easy to** | **be difficult to, be hard to** ◊ *Cheese is very difficult to ~.* ◊ *The news was hard to ~. (figurative)*

digestion *noun*

ADJ. **good** | **poor**
VERB + DIGESTION **have** ◊ *She has very poor ~.* | **aid, help, improve** ◊ *Peppermint aids ~.* | **slow**

digit *noun*

ADJ. **binary, decimal** ◊ *the decimal ~s 0 to 9* | **double, single** ◊ *double-digit inflation*
... OF DIGITS **sequence, series, set, string** ◊ *a sequence of binary ~s*
PHRASES **three, four, etc. ~s long** ◊ *The number can be up to eight ~s long.*

dignity *noun*

ADJ. **enormous, great** | **calm, quiet** ◊ *She spoke to him with quiet ~.* | **human, personal** ◊ *the importance of human ~*
VERB + DIGNITY **have, possess** ◊ *These people have enormous ~.* | **keep, maintain, preserve, protect, retain** ◊ *We all want to maintain our ~ in old age.* | **give sb** ◊ *Being treated in the privacy of your own room gives you more ~.* | **bring** ◊ *He brings a quiet ~ to the role.* | **regain, restore** | **respect** | **lose** ◊ *The awful thing about old age is losing your ~.* | **destroy, rob sb of, strip sb of** ◊ *Slavery destroys human ~.* ◊ *Keeping prisoners in such dreadful conditions strips them of all ~.* | **muster** ◊ *With as much ~ as he could muster, he left the room.*
PREP. **below sb's ~** (esp. AmE), **beneath sb's ~** ◊ *He clearly regarded manual work as beneath his ~.* | **with ~** ◊ *the right to die with ~*
PHRASES **an air of ~** ◊ *His aristocratic voice gives him an air of ~ and power.* | **a lack of ~** | **a loss of ~** ◊ *He hoped that he could change his mind without loss of ~.* | **a sense of ~** ◊ *She had a strong sense of ~.* | **with your ~ intact** ◊ *He needed a way to retreat with his ~ intact.*

dilemma *noun*

ADJ. **acute** (esp. BrE), **appalling** (esp. BrE), **big, difficult, genuine** (esp. BrE), **great, impossible** (esp. BrE), **real, serious, terrible, thorny** (esp. AmE) | **central, essential, fundamental** ◊ *The fundamental ~ remains: in a tolerant society, should we tolerate intolerance?* | **common, familiar** | **interesting** | **human** | **personal** | **ethical, moral** | **social** | **policy, political**
VERB + DILEMMA **create, pose, present sb with** ◊ *This poses a difficult ~ for teachers.* | **be caught in, be faced with, confront, face, find yourself in, have** ◊ *They were caught in a real ~.* | **resolve, solve** ◊ *I could see no way of resolving this moral ~.*
DILEMMA + VERB **arise, occur** ◊ *the ~ that arises when a doctor has to decide whether or not to prescribe an expensive treatment* | **lie** ◊ *The ~ over human cloning lies at the heart of the ethical choices facing society.* | **confront sb, face sb** ◊ *The ~ facing the country's allies was even more serious.*
PREP. **in a/the ~** ◊ *The president is now in a ~.* | **~ about, ~ over** ◊ *She faced a ~ about whether to accept the offer or not.* | **~ between** ◊ *the perennial ~ between work and family commitments*
PHRASES **a solution to a ~, a way out of a ~** ◊ *I couldn't see any way out of the ~.*

dilute *verb*

1 liquid
ADV. **highly** ◊ *The fragrances are highly ~d.* | **slightly** ◊ *Dilute the juice slightly with water.*
PREP. **in** ◊ *The perfumes are ~d in vegetable oils.* | **with**

2 effect/quality
ADV. **significantly, somewhat** ◊ *The effect of this policy has now been considerably ~d.*

dimension

dimension *noun*

1 (often **dimensions**) measurements

ADJ. **approximate** | **exact, precise** ◊ *It is important to measure the exact ~s of the room.* | **overall** | **compact, small** ◊ *Despite the unit's compact ~s, there's still plenty of room for expansion.* | **great, large** ◊ *a structure of considerable ~s* | **horizontal, vertical** | **fourth, second, third** ◊ *The fourth ~, time, is also finite in extent.* | **physical, space, spatial, temporal, time**
VERB + DIMENSION **check, measure** ◊ *Can we just check the ~s of the bedroom again?*
PHRASES **in two ~s, in three ~s** ◊ *a model in three ~s*

2 aspect

ADJ. **added, additional, different, extra, further, new** | **distinct** ◊ *In looking at population ageing we will consider two distinct ~s.* | **wider** ◊ *There is a wider ~ to the question.* | **crucial, essential, important, key, main, major, significant** | **global, international, local, national, regional** ◊ *This gives an important international ~ to the project.* | **aesthetic, class, cultural, economic, emotional, ethical, historical, human, ideological, moral, personal, political, psychological, religious, social, spiritual, etc.** | **tragic**
VERB + DIMENSION **add, bring, give (sth), provide** ◊ *Her illness adds an extra ~ to the problem.* | **have** ◊ *The affair had a different ~ now.* | **acquire, take on** ◊ *The crisis acquired a new ~.* | **explore**
PREP. **~ to** ◊ *the spiritual ~ to our lives*

din *noun*

ADJ. **awful, deafening, raucous, terrible** | **constant**
VERB + DIN **create, make** ◊ *Who's making that awful ~?* | **hear**
PREP. **above the ~, over the ~** ◊ *Charles shouted above the ~.* ◊ *She could not be heard above the ~ of the crowd.* | **~ of**
PHRASES **the ~ of battle** (*literary*)

dine *verb*

ADV. **al fresco** ◊ *the joys of dining al fresco* | **in style** ◊ *We ~d in style in the hotel restaurant.* | **out** ◊ *Dining out in attractive surroundings is one of life's great pleasures.*
PREP. **on** ◊ *We ~d on fresh local fish.*

dinghy *noun*

ADJ. **inflatable, rubber** | **sailing** (*BrE*)
VERB + DINGHY **row, sail** (*esp. BrE*) ◊ *I sailed the ~ across the bay.*
DINGHY + NOUN **sailing, sailor** (*both BrE*)
PREP. **in a/the ~** ◊ *She rowed ashore in the ~.* | **into a/the ~**

dining room *noun*

ADJ. **large, spacious** | **cosy/cozy, small** | **elegant** | **formal** | **communal** | **executive** | **hotel**
DINING ROOM + VERB **seat sb** ◊ *The ~ seats up to 60 guests.* | **serve sth** (*esp. AmE*) ◊ *a comfortable ~ serving just-caught seafood*
DINING-ROOM + NOUN **furniture** | **chair, table** ◊ *dining-room chairs and tables* | **set** (*AmE*)

dinner *noun*

1 main meal of the day

ADJ. **delicious, excellent, good, gourmet** (*esp. AmE*), **slap-up** (*BrE, informal*), **sumptuous** ◊ *We were treated to an excellent ~ with every kind of seafood imaginable.* | **four-course, three-course, etc.** | **big** | **light** | **leisurely** | **quick** | **early, late** | **candlelight** (*esp. AmE*), **candlelit, romantic** | **intimate, private, quiet** | **family** | **birthday, Christmas, holiday** (*AmE*), **Sunday, Thanksgiving** (*in the US*) | **potluck** (= to which each guest brings some food, which is then shared) (*AmE*) | **school** (*BrE*) | **frozen** (*esp. AmE*), **TV** | **chicken, seafood, steak, turkey, etc.**
DINNER + NOUN **table** ◊ *There was never much conversation at the ~ table in my family.* | **things** ◊ *We didn't wash up the ~ things until the morning after.* | **plates, service** ◊ *a bone-china ~ service* | **menu** ◊ *The extensive ~ menu includes Russian delicacies.* ◊ *The school ~ menu always includes a balance of food types.* (*BrE*) | **bell** | **money** (*BrE*) ◊ *I always forgot to take my ~ money to school.* | **lady** (*BrE*) (**lunch lady** in *AmE*) | **time** | **date** | **reservation** | **companion**
→ Note at MEAL (for verbs)

2 formal evening occasion, with dinner

ADJ. **elegant, fancy, lavish** | **black-tie, formal, official** | **informal** | **annual** ◊ *The club's annual ~ is this week.* | **anniversary, celebratory, rehearsal** (= for the families of a couple the day before their wedding) (*AmE*), **wedding** (*AmE*) | **farewell** | **awards** | **charity, fund-raising** | **gala** ◊ *A gala ~ was held to celebrate the world premiere of the movie.* | **state** ◊ *A state ~ was held in honour/honor of the visiting Japanese premier.*
VERB + DINNER **give, hold, host, throw** ◊ *My old school is giving a fund-raising ~.* | **attend** ◊ *We attended the formal reunion ~.* | **be invited to** | **change for, dress for** ◊ *Are we expected to dress for ~?* | **speak at** ◊ *The former Olympic champion was invited to speak at a charity ~.*
DINNER + NOUN **party** ◊ *They invited three couples to a ~ party at their house.* | **engagement** | **dance** ◊ *the society's annual ~ dance* | **guests** | **jacket, suit** (*both BrE*) | **theater** (= a restaurant where you see a play after your meal) (*AmE*)

dip *noun*

1 quick swim

ADJ. **quick** | **refreshing**
VERB + DIP **take** ◊ *I took a quick ~ in the hotel pool before lunch.*

2 decrease

ADJ. **sharp** | **slight** | **sudden** | **occasional** ◊ *the occasional ~s in the market*
VERB + DIP **suffer, take** ◊ *Share prices have taken a slight ~.* | **experience, see** ◊ *The nation is experiencing an economic ~.*
PREP. **~ in** ◊ *a sharp ~ in temperature*

dip *verb*

1 in liquid

ADV. **lightly** ◊ *She dipped the brush lightly in the varnish.* | **quickly** ◊ *Quickly ~ the tomatoes in boiling water.*
PREP. **in, into** ◊ *He dipped his finger in the water*

2 go/move downwards

ADV. **gently** ◊ *hills which ~ gently to the east* | **slowly** ◊ *The sun was slowly dipping out of sight.* | **steeply** | **down** ◊ *The road dipped steeply down into the town.*
PREP. **below** ◊ *The sun dipped below the horizon.*

3 prices, support, etc.

ADV. **slightly** | **sharply** ◊ *Support dipped sharply to 51%.*
PREP. **below** ◊ *when unemployment ~s below a certain point*

diploma *noun*

1 certificate; qualification

ADJ. **college, high-school** (*in the US*), **university** | **engineering, law, medical, etc.**
VERB + DIPLOMA **accept, take** | **hand sb, hand out** | **have, hold** | **be awarded, earn, gain, get, obtain, receive** | **award (sb), confer (on sb)** ◊ *The university awards ~s in higher education.* | **lead to** ◊ *The course leads to a ~ in psychiatric nursing.* | **study for** (*esp. BrE*), **take** (*BrE*) ◊ *She was taking a diploma in business management.*
DIPLOMA + NOUN **course, programme/program** | **holder** ◊ *Diploma holders have a far better chance of employment than those with no qualification.*
PREP. **~ from** ◊ *a fake ~ from a non-existent school* | **~ in** ◊ *a ~ in hotel management* | **~ of** ◊ *~ of higher education*
PHRASES **at ~ level** ◊ *Most students here are studying for a qualification at ~ level.*

2 (*BrE*) course of study

ADJ. **graduate, postgraduate, professional** | **higher** | **national** ◊ *The college offers the Higher National Diploma in*

computer studies. | **full-time, part-time** | **one-year, two-year**, etc.
VERB + DIPLOMA **complete**

diplomacy noun

1 managing international relations

ADJ. **careful, shrewd** | **clever, deft, effective, skilful/skillful** ◇ *It will take deft ~ to sustain the fragile momentum.* | **aggressive, coercive** (*esp. AmE*), **forceful** ◇ *He also wants more aggressive unilateral ~.* | **gunboat** ◇ *What they could not take by political intrigue they took by gunboat ~ (= threatening military action).* | **checkbook** (*AmE*) ◇ *The time for checkbook ~ is over.* | **global, international, multilateral** ◇ *We will continue to seek solutions to the problems of this region through multilateral ~.* | **secret** | **personal** ◇ *Churchill's highly personal ~ in seeking a meeting with the Russians* | **public** (*esp. AmE*) ◇ *the challenge to improve public ~ and define the country's message to the world* | **cultural** ◇ *Cultural ~ between the two countries was an integral part of this development.* | **traditional** ◇ *a crisis lying outside the scope of traditional ~* | **quiet** ◇ *The understanding between the two countries came about through quiet ~.* | **failed** ◇ *The raid followed years of failed ~.* | **preventive** | **shuttle** ◇ *a round of shuttle ~ between Washington and Brussels* | **American, Anglo-French, European, Russian, US**, etc.
VERB + DIPLOMACY **use** ◇ *We prefer to use ~ rather than force to get people to move.* | **conduct, pursue** ◇ *This was no way to conduct ~.* ◇ *She urged the leaders to pursue ~.*
DIPLOMACY + VERB **fail** ◇ *if ~ fails and combat is necessary* | **work** ◇ *There's a familiar rule that ~ works best when backed by the threat of force.*
PREP. **by ~, through ~** ◇ *We must try and resolve this situation through ~ rather than conflict.*

2 skill in dealing with people

ADJ. **great** | **quiet**
VERB + DIPLOMACY **have** ◇ *We need someone who has tact and ~.* | **exercise, show, use** ◇ *I thought you showed great ~ in dealing with him.* | **try** ◇ *Kerry's willingness to try ~ holds out at least a hope of making progress.* | **need, require** ◇ *Trying to get the divorced couple to agree calls for a great deal of ~.*
PREP. **by ~, through ~** ◇ *The way forward in this situation is by ~ and negotiation.* | **with ~** ◇ *She handled the awkward situation with her usual quiet ~.*

diplomat noun

ADJ. **chief, prominent, senior, top** ◇ *Washington's top ~ in Havana* | **consummate, distinguished, experienced, good, skilled** | **former, retired** | **foreign** | **career, professional** | **American, British, US**, etc. | **Western** ◇ *a Western ~ in Islamabad*
VERB + DIPLOMAT **be, serve as, work as** ◇ *He served as a ~ in Russia before the war.*

direct verb

1 aim

ADV. **mainly, mostly, primarily, principally** ◇ *Tax cuts have been ~ed primarily at the better-off.* ◇ *His anger was mostly ~ed towards/toward Peter.* | **clearly** | **straight** ◇ *He ~ed the light straight in her face.* | **specifically** | **exclusively, solely** ◇ *The attacks were ~ed solely at military targets.*
PREP. **against** ◇ *anger ~ed specifically against ethnic minorities* | **at** ◇ *criticism clearly ~ed at upper management* | **away from** ◇ *This merely ~s attention away from the real issues.* | **into** ◇ *I found myself being ~ed into a dark room.* | **onto** ◇ *The machine ~s light onto a special film.* | **through** ◇ *a detour that ~s you through narrow, dimly lit streets* | **to** ◇ *I ~ed my question to the chairman.* | **towards/toward** ◇ *We are ~ing our efforts towards/toward helping young people.*

2 film/movie

ADV. **expertly, masterfully, skilfully/skillfully** ◇ *The film is expertly ~ed and beautifully photographed.*
PREP. **by** ◇ *It was ~ed by Luc Besson.* | **with** ◇ *He ~s with flair and sensitivity.*

direct adj.

VERBS **be**
ADV. **extremely, fairly, very**, etc. ◇ *Her manner can be rather ~.* ◇ *He asked me some very ~ questions.* | **disconcertingly** ◇ *his disconcertingly ~ gaze* | **refreshingly** ◇ *a refreshingly ~ discussion of the agency's priorities* | **emotionally** ◇ *The album is her most emotionally ~ work to date.*

NOTE

Points of the compass

due… (of) ◇ *The park is due north of Santa Cruz.*
far… ◇ *a small town in the far north of Canada* ◇ *The reserve is a little further south on the coast.*
down south, up north ◇ *They have moved down south (= to the south of the country).*
journey… (*esp. BrE*), **way…** ◇ *On our way south we passed through hostile territory.*
road…, track… ◇ *the road west out of the city*
be…of, lie…of ◇ *San Diego is south of Los Angeles.*
north-east, south-east ◇ *The farm lies 60 miles north-east of Cape Town.*
come…, go… ◇ *I thought we were going east.*
drive…, fly…, run…, travel…, walk… ◇ *From Fort William drive north for a couple of miles.*
set off… ◇ *The troops set off north.*
carry on…, continue…, proceed… ◇ *The road continues west for ten miles.*
bear…, head… ◇ *Take the N1 heading west from Bern.*
turn… ◇ *When you reach the top, turn west.*
face…, look… ◇ *The kitchen window faces south.* ◇ *The painting depicts the river looking north from the bridge.*
…bank, …coast, …shore ◇ *the south bank of the river*
…wind ◇ *a bitter east wind*
in the… (of) ◇ *I live in the north.* ◇ *There are lakes in the north-east of Poland.*
from the… (of) ◇ *The wind is coming from the west.*
to the… (of) ◇ *Oxford is to the north-west of London.*
towards/toward the… ◇ *Towards/Toward the north the woods turn into pine forests.*
which way is…? ◇ *Which way is west?*

---

direction noun

1 where to/from

ADJ. **same** ◇ *They were both going in the same ~.* | **different, opposing, opposite, reverse, separate** (*esp. AmE*) ◇ *We are pulled in opposing ~s by our emotions.* ◇ *The ride in the reverse ~ is a mere $4.* ◇ *We both walked off in separate ~s.* | **right, wrong** ◇ *Unfortunately, we were going in the wrong ~.* | **general** ◇ *I fired in the general ~ of the officer's head, and missed.* | **expected** (*esp. AmE*), **predicted** ◇ *America has not moved in the expected ~.* | **unexpected** ◇ *Support came from an unexpected ~.* | **clockwise** ◇ *Turn the dial in a clockwise ~.* | **anticlockwise** (*BrE*), **counterclockwise** (*AmE*) | **downward, upward** ◇ *These figures may have to be revised in an upward ~.* | **backward, forward** ◇ *She shoved Sarah in the general forward ~.* | **northerly, southerly**, etc. ◇ *The current flows in a south-easterly ~.* | **east-west, north-south** ◇ *The runway was constructed in a north-south ~.* | **horizontal, vertical** ◇ *A scanner deflects the laser beam in horizontal and vertical ~s.* | **random** ◇ *He started to run in a random ~.* | **cardinal, compass** (*both esp. AmE*) ◇ *a house oriented exactly to the cardinal ~s* ◇ *I measured the distance and compass ~ between successive positions.* | **wind** ◇ *When sailing, keep a constant check on changes in wind ~.*
VERB + DIRECTION **take** ◇ *Which ~ do we have to take?* | **change, reverse, switch** ◇ *The wind had changed ~.* ◇ *What happens if you reverse the ~ of the current?* ◇ *Suddenly, the wind switched ~s.* | **flow in, go in, go off in** | **follow, head**

in, move in, travel in ◇ *Dan followed the ~ the sign had pointed.* ◇ *The convoy is moving in the ~ of the capital.* | **veer in, veer off in** ◇ *While he was studying in Paris, his thinking suddenly veered off in a new ~.* | **come from, come in** ◇ *He was hit by a truck coming in the opposite ~.* | **face, face in** ◇ *I didn't see the accident because I was facing in the opposite ~.* | **glance in, look in, nod in, point in** ◇ *She glanced in his ~.* ◇ *'Look!' she said, pointing in the ~ of the coast.* | **indicate, point out** ◇ *The adults gazed in the ~ indicated.* | **nudge sb in, point sb in** ◇ *We have to nudge politicians in the right ~.* ◇ *I can't come with you, but I can point you in the general ~.* | **pull (sb/sth) in** (*often figurative*) ◇ *There are different considerations, pulling in different ~s.*

PREP. **from a/the ~** ◇ *There was shriek of laughter from the ~ of Sarah's room.* ◇ *Let's approach the subject from a different ~.* | **in a/the ~** ◇ *The aircraft was flying in a northerly ~.*

PHRASES **the ~ of flow, the ~ of movement, the ~ of travel** ◇ *I prefer to be facing the ~ of travel.* | **the ~ of sb's gaze** ◇ *She followed the ~ of his gaze.* | **from all ~s, from both ~s** ◇ *People came running from all ~s.* | **in all ~s, in both ~s** ◇ *The blast sent debris flying in all ~s.* ◇ *The road was blocked in both ~s.* | **a glance in sb/sth's ~, a nod in sb/sth's ~** ◇ *People passed by without a glance in her ~.* ◇ *The report gives a brief nod in the ~ of green issues* (= mentions them briefly). (*figurative*) | **a sense of ~** ◇ *I don't have much sense of ~.* | **in any particular ~, in no particular ~** ◇ *The story does not go in any particular ~.* ◇ *She stalked away, in no particular ~.*

2 development

ADJ. **new** ◇ *The party must take a new ~ if it is to survive.* | **right, wrong** | **desired** ◇ *These incentives should move the industry in the desired ~.* | **positive** ◇ *I felt the company was headed in a positive ~.* | **promising** ◇ *This points to a promising new ~ for cancer research.* | **clear** ◇ *No clear ~ in policy can be identified.* | **future** ◇ *the debate about the future ~ of socialism* | **policy, strategic** ◇ *His understanding of our business will further strengthen our strategic ~.*

VERB + DIRECTION **take** ◇ *It is hard to know which ~ the Church will take.* | **change, shift** (*esp. AmE*) ◇ *It's time to change ~ and find a new job.* ◇ *The company needed to shift ~ if it was going to survive.* | **go in, move in** ◇ *At least things are moving in the right ~ now.* | **influence, shape** ◇ *the critical decisions that shape the ~ of our lives* | **determine** ◇ *First determine the ~ of your expected business growth.* | **set** ◇ *The proposals aim to set a new ~ for local government.* | **indicate** ◇ *The recommendations indicate possible ~s for further studies.*

PHRASES **a change of ~** ◇ *This was a major change of ~ for Britain's foreign policy.* | **a shift in ~** ◇ *The book signals a shift in ~ from her earlier novels.* | **a step in … direction** ◇ *The first step in this ~ will be a discussion with the unions.* | **step in the right ~, a step in the wrong ~** ◇ *The new law is undoubtedly a step in the right ~, but it doesn't go far enough.* | **in one ~** ◇ *I was being pushed in one ~.* ◇ *The market is moving primarily in one ~.*

3 purpose

ADJ. **clear** ◇ *Do not let the discussion fragment into a desultory conversation with no clear ~.*

VERB + DIRECTION **be lacking in** (*esp. BrE*), **lack** ◇ *Once again her life felt lacking in ~.*

PHRASES **a sense of ~** ◇ *We are looking for somebody with a clear sense of ~.*

4 (often **directions**) instructions

ADJ. **clear, good, precise, specific** ◇ *Isabel's ~s are always very precise.* ◇ *The teacher gives specific ~s and corrects your pose.* | **step-by-step** ◇ *Each card has step-by-step ~s on one side.* | **easy-to-follow** ◇ *Each chapter includes easy-to-follow ~s for a variety of activities.* | **stage** ◇ *Shakespeare's famous stage ~, 'Exit, pursued by a bear.'* | **driving** ◇ *Internet sites that offer everything from driving ~s to subway maps* | **online** ◇ *Just follow the online ~s to take the quiz.* | **label** (*AmE*) ◇ *Follow label ~s for best results.*

VERB + DIRECTION **ask, ask for** ◇ *Let's stop and ask for ~s.* |

give sb, provide ◇ *Can you give me ~s for getting to John's?* ◇ *signs providing ~s to the new concert hall.* | **get** ◇ *We got ~s to the hall from a man in the town.* | **follow** ◇ *Just follow the ~s on the box.*

PREP. **~ for** ◇ *Are there any ~s for putting up the tent?* | **~ to** ◇ *Can you give me ~s to the post office?*

5 control/guidance

ADJ. **clear** ◇ *In effective classrooms the teacher provided clear ~.* | **strategic** ◇ *the strategic ~ of the company* | **spiritual** ◇ *The monarch looks to the archbishop for spiritual ~.* | **government** ◇ *All such research is under government ~.*

VERB + DIRECTION **give sb, provide (sb with)**

PREP. **under sb's ~** ◇ *They work under the ~ of a senior manager.* | **~ from** ◇ *The new workers need ~ from a supervisor.*

directive noun

ADJ. **clear** ◇ *Don't start anything without a clear ~ from management.* | **general** | **important, prime** | **advance, advanced, written** (*all AmE, law*) ◇ *You can spell out your preferences in an advance ~, so that your family and doctors know what you want.* | **draft, proposed** | **specific** (*esp. AmE*) ◇ *The book offers no specific ~s for what the reader should do.* | **congressional, EU, government, presidential, etc.** | **policy, political** | **environmental, security, etc.**

VERB + DIRECTIVE **give, issue** ◇ *The EU issued a new drinking water ~.* | **adopt, approve, sign** | **comply with, follow, implement, obey** ◇ *All companies must comply with the new ~.* | **receive** ◇ *They said they didn't receive any ~s from the White House or the Pentagon.* | **block, oppose** (*both esp. BrE*) | **violate** (*esp. AmE*)

DIRECTIVE + VERB **come into force** (*esp. BrE*) ◇ *A new EU ~ on maternity leave will come into force next month.* | **require sth** ◇ *The ~ requires member states to designate sites of special scientific interest.*

PREP. **in accordance with a/the ~** ◇ *They acted in accordance with the latest ~ from Brussels.* | **in a/the ~** ◇ *The proposals are contained in a European ~ on wild birds.* | **under a/the ~** ◇ *Private health services will be allowed under the ~.* | **~ for** ◇ *a new set of ~s for the security team* | **~ from** ◇ *a ~ from the European Commission* | **~ on** ◇ *a ~ on data protection*

PHRASES **the provisions of a ~, the terms of a ~** (*esp. BrE*)

director noun

1 controls a company/an organization

ADJ. **company, managing** | **executive, non-executive** | **assistant, associate, deputy** | **senior** ◇ *Alan Watt, senior ~ of marketing and strategy* | **founding** ◇ *She is the founding ~ of graduate programs.* | **acting, interim** ◇ *Ms Hidden has replaced her as acting ~.* | **art, commercial, communications, editorial, finance, marketing, medical, production, sales, technical** | **national, regional** ◇ *the company's regional ~ in North America* | **athletic** ◇ *He was athletic ~ of Mills College.* | **personnel** ◇ *the company's personnel ~* | **museum** ◇ *an eminent museum ~ and curator* | **programme/program** (*esp. AmE*) ◇ *Fred Madison, technology program ~ for the Industrial and Technology Assistance Corp.*

PHRASES **the board of ~s** | **the post of ~** (*esp. BrE*)

→ Note at JOB

2 of a film/movie, play, etc.

ADJ. **film** (*esp. BrE*), **movie** (*esp. AmE*), **theatre/theater** | **Bollywood, Hollywood, etc.** | **artistic, creative, musical** | **casting** ◇ *He became associate ~ of California Ballet in 1983.* | **programme/program** ◇ *Milberg is the station manager and programme/program ~ at WDAM Radio.* | **award-winning**

PHRASES **the role of ~** ◇ *He now felt ready to take on the role of ~.*

→ Note at JOB

directory noun

ADJ. **business, telephone, trade** (*esp. BrE*) ◇ *I found the company's name in a trade ~.* | **Internet, online, Web** ◇ *an online ~ that shows who lives at what address* | **searchable** ◇

a searchable ~ of lawyers and law firms | **city** (*esp. AmE*), **local** ◇ *the 1801 Philadelphia city ~* | **membership** (*esp. AmE*) ◇ *the association's 2009 membership ~* | **comprehensive** ◇ *a comprehensive ~ of training resources*
VERB + DIRECTORY **check, consult** ◇ *She decided to check the business ~ for the address.* | **compile, create** | **edit** | **produce, publish**
PREP. **in a/the ~** ◇ *Names are listed alphabetically in the ~.* | **~ of** ◇ *a ~ of names and numbers*

dirt noun

1 substance that makes sth dirty

ADJ. **excess, loose** ◇ *She brushed the loose ~ off her coat.* | **ingrained** | **dog** (*BrE*) | **accumulated** ◇ *Clean your face with soap to remove accumulated ~ and oil.*
... OF DIRT **speck** | **streak** ◇ *He had streaks of ~ all over his face.* | **layer**
VERB + DIRT **be covered in, be covered with** ◇ *His shoes were covered in ~.* | **brush off, clean off, dust off** (*esp. AmE*), **remove, rub, rub off, scrape, scrub off, shake, wash off, wipe** ◇ *He rubbed the ~ off his face.* (*BrE*) ◇ *He rubbed the ~ from his face.* (*AmE*) | **sweep** ◇ *He swept the ~ out onto the porch.* | **show** ◇ *The white rug really shows the ~.* | **attract** (*esp. AmE*) ◇ *This material does not attract much ~.* | **loosen** (*esp. AmE*) ◇ *Massage your scalp to loosen any ~.*
DIRT + VERB **accumulate** ◇ *Dirt had accumulated in the corners of the windows.* | **cover** ◇ *Blood and ~ covered his face.*
DIRT + NOUN **fleck** (*AmE*), **particle, speck** ◇ *Sunlight steamed through the ~ particles in the air.*

2 (*AmE*) soil/mud

ADJ. **excess, loose** ◇ *She filled the hole with loose ~.* | **soft** ◇ *Her fingernails raked the soft ~ beneath her.* | **dry, wet** ◇ *a floor of dry ~* | **hard-packed, packed** ◇ *He landed hard on the packed ~.* | **bare** (*AmE*) ◇ *The front lawn has patches of bare ~.* | **cold** ◇ *He picked himself up off the cold ~.* | **fill** ◇ *a couple of inches of fill ~* | **infield** (*AmE*) ◇ *Rose picked the ball up off the infield ~.* | **ingrained** | **fresh** ◇ *the mounds of fresh ~ over all the graves*
... OF DIRT **layer**
VERB + DIRT **be covered in, be covered with** ◇ *His shoes were covered in ~.* | **dig, move, shovel** ◇ *The men started to shovel ~ into the open grave.* | **throw** ◇ *They threw ~ into my face.*
DIRT + NOUN **course, driveway, lane, path, road, street, strip, track, trail** ◇ *the Palermo ~ course* | **floor, ground** | **wall** ◇ *The blow knocked him against the ~ wall.* | **lot, parking lot, yard** ◇ *the ~ yard in front of the barn* | **farmer** | **farm** ◇ *He grew up on a ~ farm in upstate New York.* | **clod, clump** ◇ *They throw sticks and ~ clods up into the air.* | **mound, pile** | **smudge, stain** ◇ *I tried to rub off a ~ stain on my sleeve.*
PREP. **in the ~** ◇ *children playing in the ~*

3 harmful/unpleasant information about sb

VERB + DIRT **have** | **get** (*esp. AmE*) ◇ *We need to get some ~ on her.* | **dig, dig up** ◇ *He could dig up so much ~ on her.*
PREP. **~ on** ◇ *Do you have any ~ on the new guy?*
PHRASES **dish the ~** ◇ *She just loves to dish the ~* (= tell people unkind/unpleasant things about sb).

dirty adj.

VERBS **be, feel, look** | **get** ◇ *Go and play football if you like, but don't get ~!* | **get sth, make sb/sth** ◇ *He's not frightened of getting his hands ~* (= doing physical work). (*figurative*) ◇ *The soot had made everything ~.*
ADV. **extremely, fairly, very, etc.** | **filthy** (*informal, BrE*), **horribly** (*esp. AmE*), **incredibly** ◇ *Everything in the room was incredibly ~.* | **a little, slightly, etc.**

disability noun

ADJ. **chronic, profound, serious, severe, significant** | **mild** (*esp. AmE*) ◇ *Many children with mild disabilities are integrated in general education.* | **lifelong, long-term, permanent** ◇ *8 000 babies a year develop long-term disabilities resulting from this infection.* | **cognitive, developmental, emotional** (*AmE*), **intellectual, mental, phys-**

ical, psychiatric (*esp. AmE*), **psychological** (*esp. AmE*) ◇ *children who have severe developmental disabilities* | **hearing, visual** (*both esp. AmE*) ◇ *lectures for students with hearing disabilities* | **learning, reading** (*AmE*) ◇ *Up to 20% have a learning ~.* | **hidden** ◇ *those with a visible or a hidden ~*
VERB + DISABILITY **experience, have, suffer, suffer from** ◇ *patients who have suffered ~ after stroke* | **cause** ◇ *No one knows what causes learning disabilities.* | **cope with, live with** ◇ *people who are learning to live with ~* | **diagnose, identify** ◇ *an attempt to identify learning ~ among children* | **overcome** ◇ *She has overcome her ~ to become an artist.* | **prevent** ◇ *The drug's utility in preventing long-term ~ is unproven.*
DISABILITY + NOUN **movement, organization** | **discrimination** | **rights** ◇ *an article on ~ rights* | **activist** (*esp. AmE*) ◇ *She was a vocal ~ activist.* | **issues** ◇ *Staff members have been educated in ~ issues.* | **allowance, benefit, check** (*AmE*), **claim** (*esp. AmE*), **compensation** (*esp. AmE*), **pay** (*AmE*), **payment, pension** ◇ *She saved the money from her monthly ~ payments.* | **coverage** (*AmE*), **insurance** (*esp. AmE*) | **status** (*esp. AmE*) ◇ *the criteria required for ~ status*

disabled adj.

VERBS **be** | **be born** | **become** | **leave sb** ◇ *The accident left him badly ~.*
ADV. **profoundly** (*esp. BrE*), **seriously, severely, very** ◇ *a new home for severely ~ people* | **partially** | **permanently** | **developmentally** (*esp. AmE*), **mentally, physically**

disadvantage noun

ADJ. **big, considerable, decided** (*esp. AmE*), **distinct, grave, great, huge, major, obvious, real, serious, severe, significant, substantial** ◇ *Lack of qualifications is an obvious ~.* | **main, primary** (*AmE*), **principal** | **slight** | **added, additional** | **long-term** | **competitive** ◇ *These requirements will have to be standardized if some banks are not to suffer a competitive ~.* | **strategic, tactical** (*both esp. AmE*) ◇ *The fog was giving them a tactical ~.* | **economic, educational, financial, racial, social, socio-economic** ◇ *the problems of racial ~ and poverty* | **cost** (*esp. AmE*) ◇ *This put them at a crippling cost ~.* | **possible, potential** ◇ *A potential ~ of this method is that it requires considerable expertise to perform it accurately.* | **inherent** ◇ *the inherent ~ that low-income communities face* | **unfair** ◇ *Some students were at an unfair ~.*
VERB + DISADVANTAGE **experience, face, have, suffer, suffer from** ◇ *the ~ experienced by older people in the workplace* ◇ *The present system has the ~ that nobody really understands how it works.* ◇ *Competition has its ~s.* | **offset, outweigh** ◇ *The plan's advantages outweigh the ~s.* | **overcome** | **avoid**
PREP. **at a ~** ◇ *We were at a distinct ~ compared with children from richer families.* ◇ *There was no reason for her to feel at a ~.* | **despite a/the ~** ◇ *Despite these ~s, many older people maintain an active social life.* | **to sb's ~** ◇ *This change in the law will be to the ~ of small companies.* | **~ for** ◇ *another ~ for the night-worker* | **~ in** ◇ *There are ~s in using this treatment.* | **~ to** ◇ *There are ~s to all those approaches.*
PHRASES **advantages and ~s** ◇ *Each plan has its own advantages and ~s.* | **place sb at a ~, put sb at a ~** ◇ *The fact that he didn't speak another language put him at a ~.*

disadvantaged adj.

VERBS **be** | **become**
ADV. **extremely, very** | **seriously, severely** (*esp. BrE*) | **slightly** | **economically, educationally, financially, materially, socially, socio-economically**

disagree verb

ADV. **emphatically** (*esp. AmE*), **passionately, profoundly, sharply, strenuously, strongly, vehemently, vigorously, violently, wholeheartedly** ◇ *The only time we sharply ~d was over the children's education.* | **completely, entirely, totally** ◇ *I ~ totally with this policy.* | **fundamentally** | **flatly**

◇ *I flatly ~ with that policy.* | **respectfully** ◇ *I must respectfully ~ with her on this point.* | **simply** ◇ *He and I simply ~.* | **openly, publicly** ◇ *I feel uncomfortable publicly ~ing with a colleague.* | **personally** ◇ *I personally ~d with several elements of the proposal.* | **obviously** ◇ *Victoria and I obviously ~ on this issue.* | **not necessarily**
VERB + DISAGREE **be difficult to, be hard to, can hardly** ◇ *When I pointed out that it had been her idea in the first place, she could hardly ~.*
PREP. **about** ◇ *Frank and Alison ~ about everything.* | **on** ◇ *We ~ on this matter.* | **over** ◇ *Many in the government ~ over the scale of the changes.* | **with** ◇ *I ~ strongly with this idea.* ◇ *It is difficult to ~ with the chairman on this point.*
PHRASES **to agree to ~** (= *to agree with sb that you have different opinions about sth*)

disagreement *noun*

ADJ. **bitter, considerable, deep, major, profound, serious, sharp, significant, strong, substantial, substantive** (*esp. AmE*)**, total, wide, widespread** ◇ *There is wide ~ on this issue.* | **minor, slight** | **basic, fundamental** | **continuing** | **internal** ◇ *internal ~s within the party* | **genuine, honest** ◇ *Honest ~ is often a healthy thing.* | **respectful** (*formal, esp. AmE*) ◇ *I would like to note my respectful ~ with this sentiment.* | **ideological, moral, principled** (*formal, esp. AmE*) ◇ *I'm sure you have principled ~s with several of Dean's positions.* | **legitimate, reasonable** ◇ *There are legitimate ~s about the best way to help the poor.* | **public** ◇ *the incessant public ~s among the commissioners* | **family** | **policy, political** | **inevitable** ◇ *the inevitable ~s over what tactics they should use*
VERB + DISAGREEMENT **be in, have** ◇ *They were in ~ about the move to Ohio.* ◇ *They had a ~ about the best way to get to the beach.* | **express, indicate, register, show, voice** ◇ *She expressed ~ with the government's policy.* | **resolve, settle, solve** ◇ *How is a basic ~ of this nature to be resolved?* | **address** (*esp. AmE*)**, discuss, handle** (*esp. AmE*) ◇ *a forum for both sides to address their ~s over the issues* | **cause, lead to, provoke** | **avoid** ◇ *Great care is taken to avoid overt ~s within the group.* | **reflect** ◇ *These exchanges reflected fundamental ~s about methods and goals.*
DISAGREEMENT + VERB **arise, occur** ◇ *A ~ arose over who should pay for the trip.* | **exist** ◇ *Disagreement exists over the pattern of demand for coal.* | **remain** | **centre/center around sb/sth, centre/center on sb/sth** ◇ *a ~ centring/ centering on the link between crime and unemployment*
PREP. **in ~** ◇ *He shook his head in ~.* | **~ about, ~ as to, ~ over** ◇ *They had a major ~ over who should clean the car.* | **~ among** ◇ *There is considerable ~ among art historians as to the age of the sculpture.* | **~ between** ◇ *a serious ~ between the two experts* | **~ on** ◇ *There is fundamental ~ on these matters.* | **~ with** ◇ *He had a ~ with his girlfriend.*
PHRASES **an area of ~** ◇ *There are several areas of ~ between the two governments.* | **a point of ~** ◇ *Another point of ~ was over privacy issues.* | **a source of ~** ◇ *Money was a constant source of ~.* | **room for ~, scope for ~** (*BrE*) ◇ *There is plenty of room for ~ in this controversial area.*

disappear *verb*

ADV. **altogether, completely, entirely, fully** (*esp. AmE*)**, totally** | **all but, effectively, essentially, largely, mostly, nearly, practically, virtually** ◇ *The traditional way of life has all but ~ed.* | **literally** ◇ *The woman literally ~ed on her way home from work one night.* | **gradually, slowly** | **abruptly, immediately, instantly, overnight, promptly, quickly, rapidly, soon, suddenly** ◇ *He started the treatment and his symptoms ~ed overnight.* ◇ *a rapidly ~ing way of life* | **briefly, momentarily, temporarily** ◇ *His grin momentarily ~ed from his face.* | **eventually, finally** | **forever** ◇ *A number of species could soon ~ forever.* | **subsequently** | **magically, miraculously, mysteriously** ◇ *The controversy is not going to magically ~.* | **without a trace, without trace** (*esp. BrE*) ◇ *Her father ~ed without trace when she was ten.* | **quietly** ◇ *Her personal website quietly ~ed from the Internet.* |

apparently, seemingly | **just, simply** ◇ *The plane suddenly just ~ed from the radar screen.*
PREP. **behind** ◇ *The sun ~ed behind a cloud.* | **from** ◇ *Wildlife is fast ~ing from our countryside.* | **into, through, under,** etc.
PHRASES **~ from sight, ~ from view** ◇ *She watched until he had ~ed from view.*

disappearance *noun*

ADJ. **abrupt, sudden** ◇ *How could he explain his abrupt ~ from the party?* | **rapid** ◇ *the rapid ~ of our countryside* | **gradual** | **subsequent** | **eventual** | **recent** ◇ *the recent ~ of two CIA agents* | **complete, total** | **virtual** | **apparent** | **mysterious, strange** (*esp. AmE*)**, unexplained**
VERB + DISAPPEARANCE **cause, lead to** ◇ *Modern farming practice has led to the virtual ~ of this bird.* | **investigate** ◇ *Police are investigating the mysterious ~ of two young men.* | **explain** | **solve** (*AmE*) ◇ *The police can use that information to solve her ~.* | **notice** ◇ *Luckily no one had noticed my ~.* | **report** ◇ *48 hours have passed since his ~ was reported to the police.*
PREP. **~ from** ◇ *the ~ of money from my desk*

disappointed *adj.*

VERBS **be, feel, look, seem, sound** | **leave sb** ◇ *The decision left them very ~.*
ADV. **extremely, fairly, very,** etc. | **bitterly, deeply, desperately** (*BrE*)**, greatly, hugely** (*esp. BrE*)**, sadly, sorely, terribly** ◇ *I was bitterly ~ when I didn't get into college.* ◇ *If you think I'll agree to that, then you're going to be sadly ~.* | **almost** ◇ *He seemed almost ~ when I agreed to go.* | **a little, slightly,** etc. | **mildly** | **clearly, obviously** | **visibly** | **genuinely** ◇ *Jerry sounded genuinely ~.*
PREP. **about** ◇ *I'm ~ about John not coming.* | **at** ◇ *They're ~ at the result.* | **by** ◇ *I was slightly ~ by her attitude.* | **in** ◇ *He's ~ in his daughter.* | **with** ◇ *We're ~ with the new car.*

disappointing *adj.*

VERBS **be, prove, seem** | **find sth**
ADV. **extremely, fairly, very,** etc. | **bitterly, deeply, desperately** (*BrE*)**, hugely** (*esp. BrE*)**, terribly** ◇ *The movie was terribly ~.* | **a little, slightly,** etc.
PREP. **for** ◇ *This was very ~ for all the fans watching the game.* | **to** ◇ *That was very ~ to me.*

disappointment *noun*

1 sadness because sth has not happened, etc.

ADJ. **bitter, considerable, deep, extreme, great, immense, intense, profound, sharp** | **complete, total, utter** ◇ *To their utter ~ they found nothing.* | **mild, slight** ◇ *Riley blinked to hide his mild ~.* | **obvious** | **initial** ◇ *His initial ~ at losing gave way to a new resolve.*
VERB + DISAPPOINTMENT **be aware of, feel, sense** ◇ *He was aware of sharp ~ and betrayal.* ◇ *She couldn't quite conceal the deep ~ she felt.* | **hear, see** ◇ *She must have seen the ~ in my expression.* | **express, voice** | **betray, reflect, show** ◇ *His voice betrayed his ~.* | **bite back, conceal, cover, hide, mask, swallow** ◇ *He bit back his ~.* ◇ *Her laugh covered her ~.* | **feign** ◇ *He feigned ~. Secretly, he was relieved.* | **avoid** ◇ *To avoid ~, we recommend you reserve your seat early.* | **handle, overcome** ◇ *He couldn't help Anita overcome her ~.* | **face** ◇ *I just can't face the ~ of my family and friends.* | **bring** ◇ *Every failed attempt brings ~ and discouragement.* | **be doomed to** ◇ *Their expectations were doomed to ~.* | **notice** ◇ *Ethan noticed the ~ in Lisa's eyes.* | **share** ◇ *I know you will share our ~ at the lack of progress on this issue.*
DISAPPOINTMENT + VERB **show** ◇ *He let his ~ show.* | **fill sb** ◇ *He couldn't help the feelings of ~ that filled him.* | **set in** ◇ *The problem must be rectified before ~ sets in.*
PREP. **to sb's ~** ◇ *To her ~, they didn't go through Oxford but skirted around it.* | **~ about** ◇ *Cross expressed ~ about the damage.* | **~ at** ◇ *Paul couldn't hide his ~ at not being asked to the party.* | **~ in** (*esp. AmE*) ◇ *his ~ in his son* | **~ over** ◇ *Campaigners have voiced ~ over the government's decision.* | **~ with** ◇ *He expressed to me his ~ with art in the 20th century.*

PHRASES **a feeling of ~, a sense of ~** | **tears of ~** | **imagine my ~** ◊ *You can imagine my ~ at finding all the plants damaged by caterpillars.*

2 sb/sth that is disappointing

ADJ. **big, bitter, crushing, grave, great, huge, immense, major, sad, serious, severe, terrible** ◊ *I'm afraid I was a sad ~ to my mother.* | **real** ◊ *The ending of the book is a real ~.* | **complete, total** ◊ *The Mandarin Bar is a complete ~.* | **minor, slight, small** ◊ *A small ~ for me was the poor quality of the photographs.* | **inevitable** | **personal** | **romantic** ◊ *Her past is marred by romantic ~s.* | **box-office** ◊ *The film was a box-office ~.*

VERB + DISAPPOINTMENT **have** ◊ *She's had a lot of ~s in the past.* | **experience, suffer** ◊ *Over the years they suffered one ~ after another.* | **come as** ◊ *This news has come as a ~ to local business leaders.* | **bring** ◊ *The following year brought a major ~.* | **prove** ◊ *He has proved a great ~ to those hoping for change in the region.* | **be considered** ◊ *Her 2004 season will be considered a ~.*

DISAPPOINTMENT + VERB **come, follow sth** ◊ *His second ~ came last year when he failed to get selected for the first team.*

PREP. **~ for** ◊ *The dropping of these tour dates was a great ~ for the many fans of the band.* | **~ to** ◊ *It was a big ~ to us when she left.*

disapproval *noun*

ADJ. **strong** ◊ *Several countries have expressed their strong ~ of the law.* | **faint, mild** | **widespread** | **official** | **public** ◊ *The decision met with widespread public ~.* | **parental** ◊ *parental ~ of smoking* | **moral, social** | **23%, etc.** (*esp. AmE*) ◊ *The latest poll has him at 47% approval and 49% ~.*

... OF DISAPPROVAL **note** ◊ *There was more than a note of ~ in her voice.*

VERB + DISAPPROVAL **express, indicate, mark, register, show, voice** ◊ *To mark his ~ he refused to go to the wedding.* ◊ *Her face registered her ~.* ◊ *The students are showing their ~ by refusing to attend lectures.* | **feel, sense** ◊ *Even at this distance she could sense his ~.*

DISAPPROVAL + NOUN **rating** (*esp. AmE*) ◊ *The President's ~ rating has hit 55%.*

PREP. **in ~** ◊ *Her lip curled in ~.* | **with ~** ◊ *Marcos noted the boy's earring with ~.* | **~ at** ◊ *She was stiff with ~ at the notion.* | **~ for** ◊ *There is strong social ~ for these activities.* | **~ of** ◊ *his ~ of Wallace's conduct*

PHRASES **a chorus of ~** (*esp. BrE*) ◊ *There was a chorus of ~ from the crowd.* | **an expression, a frown, a look, etc. of ~** ◊ *Seeing the look of ~ on the doctor's face, I put out my cigarette.* | **a hint of ~** ◊ *More than a hint of ~ was in the boy's voice.* | **a murmur of ~** ◊ *Early murmurs of ~ were quickly silenced.* | **a sign of ~** ◊ *Agatha took this as a sign of ~.*

disapprove *verb*

ADV. **strongly** | **thoroughly** (*esp. BrE*) | **morally, socially** (*both AmE*) ◊ *bigots who morally ~ of homosexuality*

PREP. **of** ◊ *He strongly ~d of the way his daughter was behaving.*

disapproving *adj.*

VERBS **be, look**

ADV. **very** | **mildly, slightly**

disarmament *noun*

ADJ. **nuclear** ◊ *They campaigned for nuclear ~.* | **general, global, international, multilateral** ◊ *The party supports multilateral ~.* | **unilateral** | **complete, full, total** | **peaceful**

VERB + DISARMAMENT **demand** ◊ *a UN resolution that demands the ~ of the country* | **support** | **achieve** ◊ *He believes in using limited force to achieve ~.*

DISARMAMENT + NOUN **negotiations, talks** | **agreement, treaty** | **process** | **programme/program** (*esp. AmE*) | **issue** (*esp. AmE*) ◊ *diplomatic efforts to resolve remaining ~ issues* | **obligation** ◊ *failures to comply with ~ obligations*

disarray *noun*

ADJ. **complete, total, utter** | **general** | **some** | **financial**

VERB + DISARRAY **fall into** ◊ *His personal life fell into ~ when his wife left him.* | **throw sth into** ◊ *Our plans were thrown into ~ by the strike.*

PREP. **in ~** ◊ *The meeting broke up in ~.* | **~ within** ◊ *a period of ~ within the party*

PHRASES **a state of ~**

disaster *noun*

1 bad event/situation

ADJ. **awful, big, catastrophic, devastating, enormous** (*esp. AmE*), **great, horrible, huge, large-scale** (*esp. AmE*), **major, massive, terrible, worst** ◊ *the biggest ~ in the history of the industry* | **deadly** (*AmE*) ◊ *the deadliest natural ~ in US history* | **imminent, impending, looming** ◊ *Everyone had the feeling that ~ was imminent.* ◊ *It seemed that nothing could prevent the impending ~.* | **possible, potential** | **certain** ◊ *It would spell certain economic ~ for our local community.* | **coming, future** ◊ *He called for a full investigation to help prevent future ~s.* | **unforeseen** ◊ *the unforeseen ~ that has just been thrust upon us* | **unprecedented** ◊ *This is an unprecedented natural ~.* | **global, national** | **natural** ◊ *earthquakes, floods and other natural ~s* | **man-made** | **air, ecological, environmental, flood, flooding, hurricane, military, mine** (*esp. AmE*), **mining, nuclear, rail, tsunami** ◊ *fears of a nuclear ~* | **human, humanitarian** ◊ *the world's worst humanitarian ~* | **economic, financial, social** ◊ *Their departure spells social ~ for the region.* | **personal** | **unfolding** ◊ *the unfolding storm ~ in the South* | **costly** ◊ *Hurricane Katrina was the costliest natural ~ in history.*

VERB + DISASTER **bring, cause, create, lead to** ◊ *One person's mistakes can bring ~ to someone else.* ◊ *attempts to find out what caused the ~* | **mean, spell** ◊ *Just one mistake can mean ~.* ◊ *The drought spelled economic ~ for the country.* | **avert, avoid, prevent, save sb/sth from, stave off, ward off** ◊ *A major ~ was averted only just in time.* ◊ *What can be done to ward off environmental ~?* | **anticipate, foresee, predict** ◊ *Independent analysts in the market predicted ~.* | **court, invite** ◊ *It's courting ~ to go into the mountains without proper weatherproof clothing.* | **be heading for** ◊ *his firm belief that the whole world was heading for ~* | **face** ◊ *In the last match of the series England were facing ~.* | **experience, suffer** ◊ *There are many who have suffered personal ~s but managed to rebuild their lives.* | **handle** ◊ *No government could have handled a ~ of this magnitude effectively.* | **overcome, survive** ◊ *It was a miracle any of the passengers or crew survived the ~.* | **end in, result in** ◊ *The show ended in ~ when the tent collapsed.*

DISASTER + VERB **happen, occur, strike, take place** ◊ *Will we ever find out why the ~ occurred?* ◊ *Everything was going fine. Then, without warning, ~ struck.* | **unfold** ◊ *Europe's worst environmental ~ is unfolding at this very moment.* | **befall sb/sth, hit sb/sth, strike (sb/sth)** ◊ *the economic ~ that befell the country* | **affect sb/sth** ◊ *communities affected by ~s* | **loom, threaten** ◊ *We could all see that ~ loomed for the company.* | **ensue** ◊ *His prediction was not heeded, and ~ ensued.*

DISASTER + NOUN **area, scene, site, zone** ◊ *Only rescue workers are allowed into the ~ area.* ◊ *The area has been declared a ~ zone.* | **aid** (*esp. AmE*), **assistance** (*esp. AmE*), **relief, response** ◊ *counties eligible for federal ~ assistance* ◊ *The ~ relief operation will continue over the summer.* | **recovery** (*esp. AmE*) ◊ *The majority of enterprises aren't spending very much on ~ recovery at all.* | **plan, planning** (*both esp. AmE*) ◊ *We have a ~ plan in place before every mission.* | **preparation, preparedness** (*both esp. AmE*) ◊ *the planning and implementation of ~ preparedness* | **management** ◊ *They had no real experience in ~ management.* | **declaration** (*AmE*) ◊ *This morning I signed a ~ declaration for the state.* | **fund** ◊ *the governor's ~ fund* | **victim** | **scenario** ◊ *It become a financial ~ scenario.* | **film** (*esp. BrE*), **flick** (*informal*), **movie** (*esp. AmE*) ◊ *a Hollywood ~ movie*

PREP. **in a/the ~** ◇ *In a ~ everyone needs to keep calm.*
PHRASES **a ~ waiting to happen** ◇ *Any one of these nuclear plants may be a ~ waiting to happen.* | **in the aftermath of a ~** ◇ *In the aftermath of the ~ people were too shocked to give a clear picture of what had happened.* | **a recipe for ~** ◇ *Letting her organize the party is a recipe for ~* (= sth that is likely to go badly wrong). | **a walking ~, a walking ~ area** (both figurative, esp. BrE) ◇ *I am a walking ~ when it comes to paperwork.* | **a victim of a ~** ◇ *an organization which provides help for the victims of the ~*

2 a failure

ADJ. **absolute, complete, real, total, unmitigated, utter** ◇ *The play was a complete ~ from beginning to end.* | **business, economic, electoral, fashion, financial, political, public relations** (abbreviated to *PR*), **social** ◇ *the greatest electoral ~ of the century* ◇ *The shirt was a definite fashion ~.* ◇ *Buying that house turned out to be a financial ~.*
VERB + DISASTER **prove, turn out to be** ◇ *High-rise buildings proved a social ~.* | **become, turn into** ◇ *I can already foresee the night turning into a total ~.*
PREP. **a ~ for sb/sth** ◇ *The festival ended up being a financial ~ for the promoters.*

disastrous *adj.*

VERBS **be, prove** | **become**
ADV. **absolutely, completely, quite, truly, utterly** ◇ *The policy was absolutely ~ for the economy.* | **fairly, pretty** | **potentially** | **ecologically, economically, environmentally, financially, politically** | **equally** ◇ *This could have equally ~ consequences.*

disbelief *noun*

ADJ. **absolute, complete, outright, pure, sheer, total, utter** | **widespread** | **open** | **mock** ◇ *He raised his eyebrows in mock ~.* | **suspended** ◇ *A look of suspended ~ came across his face.* | **amused, astonished, furious, horrified, shocked, stunned**
VERB + DISBELIEF **feel** ◇ *I felt ~ first of all, then outrage.* | **express** ◇ *The president publicly expressed his ~ at what had happened.* | **hear, see, sense** ◇ *I could see the ~ in her eyes.* ◇ *She could sense his ~.* | **greet sth with** ◇ *My stories were greeted with ~.* | **shake your head in, stare in, watch in** ◇ *We could only watch in ~ as the car rolled into the water.* | **suspend** ◇ *If you don't mind suspending your ~, you should enjoy this movie.*
PREP. **in ~** ◇ *My mouth dropped open in ~.* | **to sb's ~** ◇ *To my horrified ~, the animal was running in my direction.* | **~ at** ◇ *Hilary shook her head in ~ at the news.*
PHRASES **an expression of ~, a look of ~** ◇ *with looks of utter ~ on their faces* | **suspension of ~** ◇ *The movie version requires greater suspension of ~ than the book.*

disc (*also* disk *esp. in AmE*) *noun*

1 computer disk → See DISK

2 music, video → See also CD

ADJ. **compact, DVD, vinyl** ◇ *I have an old vinyl ~ of her singing.*
VERB + DISC **play** | **insert** ◇ *He inserted the ~ into the machine.* | **hear, listen to, watch** | **burn, produce, record** | **recommend** ◇ *I highly recommend this ~.* | **release** ◇ *The ~ was released in 1998.* | **eject, load** ◇ *I ejected the ~ before the end.*
PREP. **on (a/the) ~** ◇ *He is one of the greatest singers on ~.* ◇ *The Prokofiev sonata comes first on the ~.* | **~ of** ◇ *a ~ of Mozart quartets*

3 part of the body

ADJ. **herniated** (esp. AmE), **prolapsed, slipped** ◇ *He's in bed with a slipped ~.*
VERB + DISC **slip** ◇ *She's slipped a ~.*

discard *verb*

ADV. **completely, entirely** ◇ *These ideas have now been*

completely ~ed. | **largely** | **quickly** ◇ *Rose quickly ~ed the idea.* | **simply** ◇ *the parts of the animal that people may simply ~ as inedible* | **easily**
PREP. **in favour/favor of** ◇ *Older managers have been ~ed in favour/favor of younger people.*

discern *verb*

ADV. **clearly, easily, readily** (esp. AmE) ◇ *She could clearly ~ a figure walking up to the house.* | **barely** (esp. AmE), **dimly** (esp. BrE), **just, only**
VERB + DISCERN **be able to, can** | **be difficult to, be hard to** | **be possible to** | **be easy to**

discernible *adj.*

VERBS **be** | **become**
ADV. **clearly, easily, readily** ◇ *The difference between the two is readily ~.* | **just** | **barely, scarcely** ◇ *Her face was barely ~ in the gloom.* | **immediately**

discharge *noun*

1 act of discharging; thing discharged

ADJ. **thick** | **nasal, vaginal, etc.** | **industrial, sewage, waste** | **ocean, river** | **electrical, radioactive** (esp. BrE) ◇ *thunder and lightning caused by an electrical ~* | **accidental** (esp. AmE) ◇ *an accidental ~ from a dropped gun*
VERB + DISCHARGE **have**
PREP. **~ from** ◇ *a thick ~ from the nose*

2 from court

ADJ. **absolute** (BrE) | **conditional** (BrE)
VERB + DISCHARGE **give** ◇ *He was given an absolute ~ but banned from driving for twelve months.*

3 from army, navy, etc.

ADJ. **dishonourable/dishonorable, honourable/honorable** | **early**
VERB + DISCHARGE **get, receive** | **give**

discharge *verb*

1 from army, navy, etc.

ADV. **dishonourably/dishonorably, honourably/honorably**
PREP. **from** ◇ *He was found guilty and dishonourably/dishonorably ~d from the army.*

2 from prison/court

ADV. **conditionally** (BrE) ◇ *He was conditionally ~d after admitting the theft.* | **formally** ◇ *She was formally ~d by the court.*

3 gas/liquid

ADV. **directly**
PREP. **from** | **into** ◇ *Raw sewage was ~d from the treatment plant directly into the river.*

4 (formal) **duty**

ADV. **fully, properly** (esp. BrE) ◇ *He could not properly ~ his duties.* | **faithfully** (esp. AmE) ◇ *I will faithfully ~ my duties.*

5 (formal) **gun**

ADV. **accidentally** ◇ *The police officer accidentally ~d a firearm while unloading it.*

disciple *noun*

ADJ. **ardent, devoted, faithful, loyal** ◇ *She was an ardent ~ of Freud.* | **beloved** ◇ *John, the beloved ~ of Jesus*
VERB + DISCIPLE **become** | **make** ◇ *He commanded them to go out and make ~s of all nations.*

discipline *noun*

1 training people to behave; behaving well

ADJ. **effective, firm, good, rigorous** ◇ *We need better ~ in our schools.* | **harsh, iron, rigid, strict** ◇ *strict military ~* | **lax, poor** ◇ *Discipline was too lax.* | **student, team** | **church, military, party, prison, school, social, work** | **parental**
VERB + DISCIPLINE **enforce, exercise, impose** ◇ *the ~ that the party exercises over its members* | **instil/instill** ◇ *We need someone who is good at instilling ~.* | **maintain** ◇ *The*

teacher was unable to maintain ~. | **submit to** ◊ They submitted to the ~ imposed by their leaders. | **learn** ◊ Students have to learn ~. | **have** ◊ The school was criticized for having very poor ~. | **lack** ◊ Modern schools lack ~. | **need** ◊ She believes children need ~. | **restore**
DISCIPLINE + NOUN **problem**
PHRASES **a breach of ~** (esp. BrE) ◊ It's unfair to dismiss somebody for a single breach of ~. | **a breakdown in ~**, a **breakdown of ~** ◊ a breakdown of ~ in the classroom | **a lack of ~** | **order and ~** ◊ He quickly brought order and ~ to the regiment.

2 controlling yourself

ADJ. **good, great** ◊ It is good ~ to learn to delegate. | **strict** | **personal** | **mental, spiritual** | **physical** | **business, commercial, financial, fiscal, industrial, market, monetary** ◊ The government has stabilized the economy through strict fiscal ~. | **message** (= the practice of only talking about what is relevant to your aims, by a politician) (AmE)
VERB + DISCIPLINE **have** ◊ He'll never get anywhere working for himself—he has no ~. | **show** | **lack** | **apply, bring** ◊ something to help you bring ~ to your decision-making process | **demand, require, take** ◊ It takes great ~ to learn a musical instrument.
PHRASES **a lack of ~**

3 subject of study

ADJ. **core, main, major** ◊ Students are to be tested on the three core ~s: mathematics, English and science. | **different, distinct, independent, individual, separate** ◊ When did sociology emerge as a distinct ~? | **established, traditional** | **emerging, new** | **related** ◊ social work and its related ~s | **academic, intellectual, scholarly** ◊ They established psychology as an academic ~. | **professional** (esp. AmE) | **humanities, science, scientific, etc.**
PREP. **across ~s** ◊ There is a lack of communication across ~s (= between teachers and students of different subjects). | **within a/the ~** ◊ Within a ~ there may be more than one school of thought.
PHRASES **different ~s, diverse ~s** ◊ academics from diverse academic ~s | **multiple ~s** (esp. AmE) ◊ experts in multiple ~s | **a range of ~s** ◊ The university offers a wide range of ~s.

disclose verb

ADV. **fully** ◊ He had not fully ~d all his business dealings. | **publicly** | **voluntarily**
VERB + DISCLOSE **be obliged to, be required to, must** ◊ State law requires unions to ~ financial information. | **be reluctant to** | **fail to, refuse to** ◊ He failed to ~ all the information.
PREP. **to** ◊ She was accused of disclosing confidential material to a competitor.
PHRASES **previously ~d** ◊ The amounts of money were higher than previously ~d.

discomfort noun

1 slight pain

ADJ. **acute** (esp. BrE), **considerable, extreme, great, severe** | **growing** ◊ He became conscious of a growing ~. | **little, mild, minimal, minor, slight** ◊ You may experience some slight ~ after the operation. | **obvious** | **bodily, physical** | **abdominal, chest, etc.**
...OF DISCOMFORT **amount, degree**
VERB + DISCOMFORT **complain of, experience, feel, get, have, suffer** ◊ Some of the patients complained of ~. | I didn't have much ~ after the operation. | **cause** | **ease, lessen, minimize, reduce, relieve** ◊ Not eating late at night should help to relieve the ~.
PREP. **in ~** ◊ He appeared to be in great ~. | **with ~, without ~** ◊ You should be able to drive without ~ after about two weeks.
PHRASES **pain and ~, pain or ~** | **the ~ associated with sth** ◊ the ~ associated with wearing a wig

2 embarrassment

ADJ. **great** | **obvious** | **growing** | **a little, slight**
VERB + DISCOMFORT **cause** ◊ The revelations caused some ~ to the president. | **enjoy** ◊ Paula smiled, enjoying her sister's ~.

| **notice, sense** ◊ Sensing her ~, he apologized for mentioning her boyfriend. | **hide** | **show** ◊ I tried not to show my ~ with the situation.
DISCOMFORT + VERB **grow, increase**
PHRASES **a sense of ~**

disconcerting adj.

VERBS **be** | **become** | **find sth**
ADV. **extremely, fairly, very, etc.** ◊ I found all that noise rather ~. | **highly** | **a little, slightly, etc.**

discontent noun

ADJ. **general, widespread** | **growing, increasing** | **simmering** | **popular, public** ◊ Public ~ with the economy remained at a high level. | **political, social**
VERB + DISCONTENT **breed, cause, give rise to, lead to, provoke** ◊ The higher tax provoked widespread ~ among the poor. | **fuel** ◊ Overcrowded conditions will only fuel ~ among prisoners. | **feel** ◊ the ~ that many people felt | **seethe with** ◊ The country was seething with ~ and the threat of revolution was real. | **express, voice** ◊ The peasants expressed their ~.
DISCONTENT + VERB **grow, spread**
PREP. **~ among** ◊ ~ among the workforce | **~ about, ~ at, ~ over** ◊ ~ among students about the lack of funding for education | **~ with** ◊ growing ~ with the government | **~ within** ◊ There were reports of growing ~ within the army.
PHRASES **a feeling of ~, feelings of ~** | **murmurs of ~, rumbles of ~, rumblings of ~** | **a source of ~**

discord noun

ADJ. **internal** | **family, marital, relationship** (AmE) | **political, social**
...OF DISCORD **hint, note** ◊ A note of ~ surfaced during the leaders' meeting.
VERB + DISCORD **cause, create, sow** | **avoid**
PHRASES **a source of ~** ◊ The contrasts between rich and poor nations are a source of ~.

discount noun

ADJ. **big, deep** (esp. AmE), **generous, good, large, significant, steep** (esp. AmE), **substantial** | **huge, major** (esp. AmE), **massive** (esp. BrE) | **special** ◊ There is a special ~ for employees. | **employee** (AmE), **staff** (BrE), **trade** ◊ They offer a trade ~ to builders. | **group** | **cash** ◊ We offer a 5% cash ~ for prompt payment. | **bulk, volume** | **price**
VERB + DISCOUNT **allow sb, give (sb), offer (sb)** ◊ They only give you a ~ if you buy more than a certain amount. | **get, obtain, receive** | **be entitled to, qualify for** ◊ If you collect ten bonus points, you will be entitled to a ~. | **negotiate** ◊ It is important to negotiate a good ~ and obtain books on approval.
DISCOUNT + NOUN **card, coupon** (esp. AmE), **voucher** (BrE) ◊ Members are given a ~ card which entitles them to 20% off. ◊ a prescription drug ~ card (AmE) | **program** (AmE), **scheme** (BrE) | **price, rate** | **shop, store** (= that regularly sells goods at a discount) | **airline, carrier** (both AmE)
PREP. **at a ~** ◊ Tickets are available to members at a ~. | **~ of** ◊ a ~ of 30% | **~ on** ◊ Customers are allowed a ~ on orders over $500.
PHRASES **a rate of ~**

discourage verb

ADV. **actively, positively** (esp. BrE), **strongly** ◊ Smoking is actively ~d in the university. | **effectively** ◊ Our system effectively ~s investment.
VERB + DISCOURAGE **try to**
PREP. **from** ◊ We tried to ~ him from resigning.
PHRASES **(not) easily ~d** ◊ Children are easily ~d from reading. ◊ I'm not easily ~d.

discover verb

ADV. **quickly, soon** ◊ We soon ~ed we'd been mistaken. |

suddenly | subsequently | eventually, finally | accidentally | first, originally
VERB + DISCOVER **be amazed to, be astonished to, be astounded to, be surprised to** ◊ *She was surprised to ~ he was perfectly capable around the house.* | **be alarmed to, be appalled to, be dismayed to, be horrified to, be a shock to, be shocked to** ◊ *It was a terrible shock to ~ the full extent of the problem.* | **be delighted to, be fascinated to, be intrigued to** | **be fascinating to** ◊ *It would be fascinating to ~ more about the town's history.* | **be a surprise to, be surprising to** | **be difficult to** | **be possible to** | **aim to** | **attempt to, try to** ◊ *We are trying to ~ the truth about his disappearance.* | **be able to, be unable to**
PHRASES **an attempt to ~ sth** | **newly ~ed, recently ~ed** ◊ *recently ~ed evidence* | **only to ~ sth** ◊ *I arrived at the campsite, only to ~ that it was closed for the winter.* | **an opportunity to ~ sth** | **waiting to be ~ed** ◊ *There's great talent out there just waiting to be ~ed.*

discovery *noun*

ADJ. **big, great, important, major, significant** ◊ *potentially the biggest scientific ~ for fifty years* | **startling, surprising, unexpected** | **amazing, remarkable** | **exciting** | **fascinating, interesting** | **grim** (*esp. BrE*), **grisly, gruesome** ◊ *the grisly ~ of a decapitated body* | **latest, new, recent** | **accidental, chance** ◊ *All these were chance discoveries made by scientists engaged in other investigations.* | **fortuitous, serendipitous** | **archaeological, medical, scientific** | **drug** | **personal** ◊ *The story tells of a man's journey of personal ~.*
VERB + DISCOVERY **make** ◊ *New scientific discoveries are being made all the time.* | **lead to** ◊ *Their work led to some important medical discoveries.* | **await** ◊ *There may be many unexpected treasures awaiting ~.* | **announce, report**
PREP. **~ by** ◊ *a ~ by a French scientist* | **~ of** ◊ *the ~ of oil in the North Sea*
PHRASES **a process of ~** | **a journey of ~, a voyage of ~** (*both figurative*) ◊ *To tour Sri Lanka is to take a voyage of ~ through a land of endless variety.* | **share a/your ~ (with sb)**

discredit *noun*

VERB + DISCREDIT **bring, reflect** ◊ *By telling lies he brought ~ upon the Army.* ◊ *Your failure reflects no ~ upon you—you did your best.* | **bring sth into, do sb** (*both BrE*) ◊ *She brought the whole system into ~.* ◊ *It does us great ~ to treat foreigners so badly.*
PREP. **to sb's ~** ◊ *His selfish decision is greatly to his ~.* | **~ to** ◊ *They were a ~ to their country.*

discrepancy *noun*

ADJ. **big, glaring, great, huge, large, major, marked, material** (*law, esp. BrE*), **serious, significant, substantial, wide** ◊ *the glaring ~ between the crime and the punishment* | **minor, slight, small** | **apparent**
VERB + DISCREPANCY **account for, explain** ◊ *How do you explain the apparent discrepancies between the money and the receipts?* | **discover, find, note, notice, observe** ◊ *She failed to notice the ~ between the name on the letter and the name on the passport.* | **point out** | **reveal, show** | **ignore** | **reconcile, resolve**
DISCREPANCY + VERB **exist** | **arise, occur**
PREP. **~ between** ◊ *Discrepancies occurred between the written and electronic records.* | **~ in** ◊ *There were wide discrepancies in the evidence.*

discretion *noun*

1 freedom to make decisions

ADJ. **broad, considerable, full, wide** | **greater, more** | **absolute, complete, sole, unfettered** (*law*) ◊ *They give themselves complete ~ as to what information they will hand out.* | **executive, judicial, management, managerial, personal, professional** ◊ *The president used his executive ~ to pardon the two men.*
VERB + DISCRETION **have** | **exercise, use** ◊ *The courts exercise ~*

in the area of minor traffic violations. | **give sb** ◊ *They would like local bodies to be given greater ~ as to how the money is spent.*
PREP. **at sb's ~** ◊ *Bail is granted at the ~ of the court.* ◊ *There is no service charge and tipping is at your ~.* | **~ about** ◊ *We have ~ about how much to charge.* | **~ as to** ◊ *She has considerable ~ as to how the money is spent.* | **~ over** ◊ *Judges should be given more ~ over sentencing.*
PHRASES **an abuse of ~** (*esp. AmE*) | **the exercise of ~** | **leave sth to sb's (own) ~** ◊ *'Do you want me to do the job myself or hire a photographer?' 'I'll leave it to your ~.'*

2 being discreet

ADJ. **great, the utmost**
VERB + DISCRETION **call for, need, require** ◊ *This case calls for the utmost ~.* | **rely on** ◊ *This is confidential, but I know that I can rely on your ~.*
PREP. **with ~** ◊ *to act with ~*
PHRASES **a lack of ~, a need for ~**

discriminate *verb*

ADV. **positively** (*esp. BrE*) | **actively** | **unfairly, unlawfully** (*law, esp. BrE*) | **racially** ◊ *He claims he was racially ~d against when he applied for the job.*
PREP. **against** ◊ *The present law ~s unfairly against women.* | **in favour/favor of** (*esp. BrE*) ◊ *They ~ positively in favour/favor of workers from ethnic minorities.* | **on (the) grounds of** ◊ *Companies must avoid discriminating on the grounds of race or gender.*

discrimination *noun*

1 treating a person/group unfairly

ADJ. **gender, sex, sexual, sexual-orientation** (*esp. AmE*) | **age, class, race, racial** | **religious, social** | **disability** | **pregnancy** (*esp. AmE*) | **viewpoint** (*AmE*) ◊ *the First Amendment's ban on viewpoint ~* | **widespread** ◊ *There is widespread ~ against doctors of Asian origin.* | **active, blatant, direct, overt** ◊ *evidence of active ~ against black workers* | **subtle** | **intentional** | **direct, indirect** (*both BrE*) | **perceived** | **positive** (*BrE*), **reverse** (*AmE*) ◊ *positive ~ in favour of disadvantaged racial groups* ◊ *They claim to be the victims of reverse ~.* | **illegal, unlawful** ◊ *Overt sex or race ~ is illegal.* | **legal** | **employment, job, workplace** (*esp. AmE*) | **housing** (*AmE*) | **government, institutional, institutionalized** ◊ *institutionalized ~ against women in the police*
...OF DISCRIMINATION **level** ◊ *Levels of ~ against recent immigrants are high.*
VERB + DISCRIMINATION **amount to, constitute** ◊ *Racist remarks by an employer to an employee can amount to unlawful ~.* | **encounter, experience, face, suffer, suffer from** ◊ *Many disabled people suffer ~ at work.* | **practise/practice** | **allege, claim** ◊ *lawsuits alleging ~* | **be opposed to, combat, fight** | **ban, bar** (*esp. AmE*), **forbid, outlaw, prohibit** | **eliminate, end, stop**
DISCRIMINATION + VERB **occur** ◊ *The ~ occurred at the shortlisting stage, not the interviews.* | **exist** ◊ *Does racial ~ still exist in the workplace?*
PREP. **~ against** ◊ *~ against women* | **~ by** ◊ *~ by age/race* | **~ in favour/favor of** ◊ *Some companies practise ~ in favour of older people.* (*BrE*) ◊ *Some companies practice ~ in favor of older people.* (*AmE*) | **~ on the grounds of** ◊ *It's time we banned ~ on the grounds of age.*
PHRASES **an act of ~** | **~ based on sth** ◊ *~ based on sexuality* | **evidence of ~** | **a form of ~** | **racial and ethnic ~** (*AmE*) ◊ *The law now prohibits racial and ethnic ~.* | **a victim of ~**

2 ability to recognize differences

ADJ. **fine, great** | **colour/color**
VERB + DISCRIMINATION **make** ◊ *Young children find it difficult to make fine ~s.* | **show** ◊ *She showed great ~ in rejecting the poor quality teas.*
PREP. **~ between** ◊ *~ between right and wrong*

discuss *verb*

ADV. **exhaustively, fully, in detail, thoroughly** ◊ *The plan was ~ed in great detail.* | **at length, endlessly, extensively** ◊ *These ideas will be ~ed at greater length in the next chapter.* |

briefly | further | freely, openly ◊ *This problem has never been ~ed openly before.* | informally | critically, intelligently, seriously ◊ *Students should be encouraged to ~ critically the information they are given.* | publicly | explicitly (*esp. AmE*)

VERB + DISCUSS convene (sth) to, meet to ◊ *to convene a conference to ~ the country's political future* ◊ *The committee meets regularly to ~ these issues.* | want to, wish to, would like to | need to | refuse to ◊ *He refused to ~ it with me.* | be able to | be prepared to, be willing to ◊ *I'm not prepared to ~ this on the phone.*

PREP. with ◊ *I'd like to ~ this matter with you later.*

PHRASES as ~ed ◊ *We will send you an invoice as ~ed.* | a forum to ~ sth | have sth to ~ ◊ *Can you leave us alone? We have business to ~.* | an opportunity to ~ sth | widely ~ed ◊ *The proposals have been widely ~ed in the media.*

discussion *noun*

ADJ. detailed, extensive, full, in-depth, thorough (*esp. AmE*) ◊ *They had a detailed ~ of the issues.* | extended, lengthy, long | brief | considerable ◊ *After considerable ~, they decided to accept our offer.* | initial, preliminary | ongoing | further ◊ *The plan was agreed without further ~.* | broad, general, wide-ranging ◊ *a wide-ranging ~ on women's rights* | public | formal, informal ◊ *After the lecture there will be an opportunity for informal ~.* | bilateral, class, classroom, group, panel, round-table ◊ *a series of bilateral ~s with North Korea* ◊ *Women were asked to take part in small group ~s.* | one-on-one (*AmE*), one-to-one (*esp. BrE*) | face-to-face | candid, frank, honest, open | constructive, helpful, meaningful, useful | deep, insightful, serious, thoughtful | animated, heated, intense, lively ◊ *a heated ~ about politics* | fascinating, interesting | critical | rational | academic, philosophical, scholarly, technical, theoretical | political | email, online

VERB + DISCUSSION have, hold ◊ *We had a long ~ about the plans for next year.* ◊ *The two governments are to hold ~s on the border issue.* | enter into ◊ *We are hoping to enter into ~s with union leaders.* | be involved in, join in, participate in, take part in ◊ *They refused to take part in the ~s.* | generate, initiate, prompt, provoke, spark ◊ *These latest findings have generated a lot of ~ of the moral issues involved.* | encourage, facilitate, stimulate | merit, warrant | set up ◊ *ways of setting up ~s between children to explore each other's viewpoints* | begin, open, start ◊ *Who is going to start the ~?* | dominate, lead ◊ *The ~ was led by the director of marketing.* | bring sth up for, come up for, open sth up for ◊ *The issue should come up for ~ at the conference.* ◊ *The topic must be opened up for general ~.* | open up ◊ *We need to open up a ~ on the basic aspects of the theory.* | confine ◊ *I wish to confine the ~ to income taxation.* | sum up ◊ *Let us sum up the ~ so far.* | conclude, end ◊ *We decided to end the ~ before it got out of hand.* | continue ◊ *We'll continue this ~ some other time.* | defer, postpone | follow up ◊ *Discussion should be followed up by a written report.*

DISCUSSION + VERB take place ◊ *Discussions have taken place between the two leaders.* | centre/center on, focus on, revolve around ◊ *Discussion centred on the contribution different groups would make to the project.* | break out, ensue ◊ *An intense ~ broke out about the importance of intuition.* ◊ *Adam raised the issue of multimedia and much useful ~ ensued.* | continue

DISCUSSION + NOUN group | document | topic | board, forum, list ◊ *online ~ forums* ◊ *I unsubscribed from every email ~ list I was on.*

PREP. for ~ ◊ *the subject for ~* | during a/the ~, in a/the ~ ◊ *During our ~s we raised many issues that need deeper consideration.* | in ~ with ◊ *The company had been in ~ with companies in Brazil.* | under ~ ◊ *Plans for a new road are still under ~.* | ~ about, ~ on ◊ *an important forum for ~ about the arts* | ~ among ◊ *a ~ among parents, teachers, and students* | ~ as to ◊ *Discussion continues as to the relative merits of the different plans.* | ~ between ◊ *~s between the company and the unions* | ~ of ◊ *a ~ of the issues involved* | ~ with ◊ *~s with the government*

PHRASES a basis for ~ ◊ *We can use the draft document as a basis for ~.* | ~ and debate ◊ *The incident has provoked much ~ and debate.* | a forum for ~ ◊ *The group provides a forum for the ~ of ideas.* | the outcome of a ~ ◊ *The outcome of the ~s is a decision to proceed with Phase 2 of the project.* | a subject for/of ~, a topic for/of ~

→ Special page at MEETING

disdain *noun*

ADJ. great | utter | obvious | aristocratic, haughty, snobbish, snooty (*informal, esp. AmE*)

VERB + DISDAIN feel, have ◊ *She did not hesitate to express the ~ that she felt.* | express, show ◊ *Judges sometimes show great ~ for the law.* | look on sb/sth with, look upon sb/sth with, treat sb/sth with ◊ *Traditionalists look upon the changes with ~.* | hide ◊ *Marcus had trouble hiding his ~ for the man.*

PREP. in ~ ◊ *She turned her head away in ~.* | with ~ ◊ *Why does he treat his father with such ~?* | ~ for ◊ *He has an aristocratic ~ for money.*

PHRASES an expression of ~, a look of ~

disease *noun*

ADJ. common | obscure, rare | dangerous, serious | mild | acute, chronic, severe | debilitating, degenerative | deadly, fatal, incurable, killer, life-threatening, terminal ◊ *fears of a new killer ~* | curable, treatable | preventable | communicable, contagious, infectious | non-communicable | congenital, genetic, hereditary, inherited | childhood ◊ *childhood ~s such as mumps and chicken pox* | tropical | blood-borne, insect-borne, waterborne | occupational | bowel, heart, liver, etc. ◊ *He suffered from coronary heart ~* | cardiovascular, pulmonary, etc. | mental | sexually transmitted, social, venereal | autoimmune, circulatory, respiratory, etc. | bacterial, viral | Alzheimer's, Crohn's, Parkinson's, etc. | foot-and-mouth, hoof-and-mouth (*AmE*), mad cow, etc. | Dutch elm

... OF DISEASE outbreak ◊ *fears of an outbreak of the ~*

VERB + DISEASE have, suffer from ◊ *He has a serious lung ~.* | catch, contract, develop, get ◊ *You can't catch the ~ just from physical contact.* ◊ *She got a rare liver ~ when she was only twenty.* | die from, die of ◊ *Children are still dying in their millions from preventable ~s.* | cause ◊ *a ~ caused by a vitamin deficiency* | carry, pass on, spread, transmit ◊ *the ticks that carry the ~* ◊ *Such unhygienic practices spread ~.* ◊ *The ~ is transmitted by mosquitoes.* | inherit | detect, diagnose | treat | combat, fight ◊ *The government must take action to fight this deadly ~.* | control, manage ◊ *new drugs which help to control the ~* | cure | prevent ◊ *It's better to prevent ~ by ensuring a clean water supply.* | eradicate, stamp out, wipe out ◊ *The ~ has been eradicated from the world.*

DISEASE + VERB spread ◊ *They want to stop the ~ from spreading.* | affect sb, afflict sb, occur, strike sb | develop, progress | kill sb ◊ *The ~ has killed 500 people so far this year.*

PREP. with a/the ~ ◊ *the number of people with this ~* | ~ in ◊ *Avian flu can cause severe ~ in humans.* | ~ of ◊ *a ~ of the digestive system*

PHRASES a cure for a ~ | the incidence of (a) ~ ◊ *the overall incidence of ~ in the world* | a patient with a ~, sufferer from a ~ ◊ *Sufferers from Alzheimer's ~ can't cope at home.* | the progression of a ~ ◊ *Drugs can slow down the progression of the ~, but not cure it altogether.* | resistance to ~ ◊ *Tobacco lowers the body's resistance to ~.* | the risk of ~ ◊ *the risk of coronary heart ~* | the spread of (a) ~ ◊ *measures to prevent the spread of the ~* | the symptoms of a ~ | the treatment for a ~, the treatment of a ~

→ Special page at ILLNESS

disfigure *verb* be disfigured

ADV. badly, grossly, hideously, horribly, severely ◊ *He was badly ~d by the accident.* | permanently | facially

disgrace noun

1 loss of respect

VERB + DISGRACE **fall into** ◊ *Their father fell into ~ and lost his business.* | **bring** ◊ *His crime had brought ~ upon his whole family.* | **be sent home in, be sent off in** (*BrE*) ◊ *She was sent home from the Olympics in ~.*
PREP. **in ~** ◊ *He's in ~ for having left his room in a mess.*
PHRASES **there's no ~ in sth** ◊ *There's no ~ in being poor.*

2 disgraceful person/thing

ADJ. **absolute, utter** (*both esp. BrE*) ◊ *This room is an absolute ~ (= because it is very dirty/untidy)!* | **national, public** ◊ *The state of our hospitals is a national ~.*
PREP. **~ to** ◊ *The filthy streets are a ~ to the town.*

disgraceful adj.

VERBS **be**
ADV. **absolutely, quite** (*esp. BrE*), **utterly** (*esp. BrE*) ◊ *There's litter everywhere. It's absolutely ~.*

disguise noun

ADJ. **clever, good** | **thin** ◊ *State regulation often served as a thin ~ for corruption.*
VERB + DISGUISE **adopt, don, put on, wear** ◊ *She adopted an elaborate ~ to help her pass through the town unrecognized.* | **be** ◊ *His angelic look is just a ~.* | **see through** ◊ *We all saw through his ~ immediately.*
PREP. **in ~** ◊ *He preferred to travel in ~.*

disguise verb

ADV. **cleverly, cunningly** ◊ *She was cleverly ~d as a policewoman.*
VERB + DISGUISE **cannot** | **try to**
PREP. **from** ◊ *You cannot ~ what you are doing from your family.*
PHRASES **an attempt to ~ sth** ◊ *He made no attempt to ~ his liking for her.* | **~ yourself as sb/sth** ◊ *He was ~d as a police officer.* | **heavily ~d, well ~d** ◊ *He spoke in a heavily ~d voice.* | **barely ~d, poorly ~d, thinly ~d** ◊ *In her speech she made several thinly ~d attacks on the president.*

disgust noun

ADJ. **great** | **absolute, complete, pure, total, utter** | **mild, slight** | **obvious** ◊ *Mr Haynes shook his head in obvious ~ and walked off.* | **public**
VERB + DISGUST **feel** | **express, show** | **hide** ◊ *She tried to hide the ~ that she felt.* | **fill sb with** ◊ *Decent people were filled with ~ for whoever committed the crimes.* | **turn away in, walk away in** ◊ *He threw her one look, then turned away in ~.* | **shake your head in, wrinkle (up) your nose in**
PREP. **in ~** ◊ *Marion threw down the book in ~.* | **with ~** ◊ *They both looked with ~ at the men.* | **at** ◊ *I couldn't find the words to express my ~ at his actions.* | **~ over** ◊ *expressions of public ~ over the affair* | **~ with** ◊ *People are showing their ~ with the existing regime.*
PHRASES **a snort of ~** ◊ *He gave a snort of ~.* | **an expression of ~, a look of ~** | **a feeling of ~, a sense of ~** | **much to your ~** ◊ *Much to his ~, he found himself sharing a carriage with a noisy young family.*

disgusted adj.

VERBS **be, feel, look** | **become**
ADV. **really** | **absolutely, quite, thoroughly, totally** | **rather, slightly**
PREP. **at** ◊ *I'm quite ~ at the way he's treated you.* | **by** ◊ *I was absolutely ~ by the whole business.* | **with** ◊ *I was thoroughly ~ with the brutality of the system.*

disgusting adj.

VERBS **be, look, smell, sound, taste** ◊ *That soup tastes ~!* | **find sth** ◊ *I find his conduct ~.*
ADV. **particularly, really, truly** | **absolutely, quite, totally,**

dish noun

1 container

ADJ. **deep** | **flat, shallow** | **empty** | **baking, roasting, serving** | **ovenproof** (*esp. BrE*) | **china, glass, metal, plastic, silver** | **casserole, gratin** (*esp. BrE*), **pie, soufflé, soup** | **butter, candy** (*AmE*), **food, soap, vegetable** ◊ *your pet's food ~* | **culture, lab** (*informal*), **laboratory, Petri**
PREP. **in a/the ~** ◊ *Arrange the salad in a serving ~.*

2 the dishes plates, bowls, etc.

ADJ. **clean, washed** | **dirty, unwashed** ◊ *The dirty breakfast ~es were still in the sink when we got home.* | **breakfast, dinner**
VERB + THE DISHES **clean** (*AmE*), **do, wash** ◊ *It's your turn to do the ~es.* | **dry** ◊ *He dried the ~es and put them away.* | **clear, clear away, put away**

3 type of food

ADJ. **main, side** ◊ *Serve one or two main ~es with a choice of salads and nibbles.* | **favourite/favorite** ◊ *Do you have a favourite/favorite ~?* | **delicious, tasty, wonderful** | **popular** | **elaborate** | **simple** ◊ *a simple ~, beautifully prepared* | **classic, traditional** | **exotic** | **savoury/savory, sweet** | **spicy** | **cold, hot** | **international, local, national, regional** ◊ *The national ~ is 'feijoada'—pork with beans.* | **Chinese, French, etc.** | **vegetarian** | **cheese, egg, fish, meat, pasta, rice, seafood, vegetable** ◊ *Goulash is a meat ~.* | **breakfast, dinner** (*esp. AmE*), **lunch, supper** (*esp. BrE*) ◊ *Smoked salmon makes a wonderful supper ~.* | **signature** (= *a dish that identifies a particular restaurant/chef*)
VERB + DISH **cook, make, prepare** ◊ *She cooked us a delicious French ~ with pork and tomatoes.* | **serve** ◊ *a restaurant that serves traditional Indian ~es* | **eat** | **recommend** | **order** | **sample, try** ◊ *They sampled all the local ~es.*
PHRASES **the ~ of the day** ◊ *I can recommend the ~ of the day.*
→ Special page at FOOD

dishonest adj.

VERBS **be, seem** | **become** | **consider sth, regard sth as** ◊ *What they are doing is not considered ~.*
ADV. **deeply, thoroughly** (*esp. BrE*), **very** | **downright** ◊ *I think he's downright ~!* | **basically, fundamentally** | **intellectually**

dishwasher noun

VERB + DISHWASHER **load, stack** (*esp. BrE*) | **empty, unload** | **run** ◊ *It wastes energy to run the ~ half empty.*
DISHWASHER + NOUN **detergent, liquid, powder, tablet** (*esp. BrE*)

disillusioned adj.

VERBS **be, feel** | **become, get, grow**
ADV. **extremely, fairly, very, etc.** | **deeply** | **completely, thoroughly, totally, utterly** | **a little, slightly, etc.** | **increasingly**
PREP. **by** ◊ *They felt bitter and ~ by the decision.* | **with** ◊ *Later in life he grew rather ~ with communism.*

disillusionment noun

ADJ. **general, popular** (*esp. AmE*), **public, widespread** | **growing** | **political**
VERB + DISILLUSIONMENT **cause**
PREP. **~ among** ◊ *There is widespread ~ among young people.* | **~ with** ◊ *There is growing public ~ with the present system of government.*

disintegrate verb

ADV. **completely** ◊ *The plane completely ~d on impact.* | **quickly, rapidly** | **slowly** ◊ *The social fabric of this country is slowly disintegrating.*
VERB + DISINTEGRATE **begin to** ◊ *The bag had begun to ~.*
PREP. **into** ◊ *The country has ~d into separate states.*

disintegration noun

ADJ. **complete, total** | **gradual** ◊ *the gradual ~ of traditional values* | **rapid** | **slow** | **political, social** ◊ *indicators of social ~ such as divorce, suicide and petty theft*
VERB + DISINTEGRATION **lead to, result in** ◊ *This defeat led to the ~ of the empire.*

disk noun → See also DISC

ADJ. **computer** | **hard** | **CD-ROM, DVD** | **CD-R, CD-RW, DVD-R, etc.** | **floppy, zip** (*esp. AmE*) | **master** ◊ *The master ~ can be duplicated as many times as required.* | **backup** | **program** | **data** | **server, system** | **boot** | **blank** | **laser, magnetic, optical**
VERB + DISK **insert, put in** ◊ *Insert the ~ into the drive slot.* | **remove, take out** | **format** | **read** ◊ *The computer reads the ~.* | **burn, copy, duplicate** ◊ *I'll copy the ~ into a file.* | **copy (sth) to, save (sth) to, save sth on** ◊ *The program automatically saves to ~ every 15 minutes.* ◊ *Save the document to ~ before closing it.* ◊ *The information can be saved on a ~.* | **erase, wipe** ◊ *If you wipe that old ~, we can use it again.* | **hold sth on, store sth on** ◊ *The records will be stored on the computer's hard ~.*
DISK + VERB **contain sth** ◊ *The ~ contains the program you'll need.* | **hold sth** ◊ *Each ~ holds 4.7 GB.*
DISK + NOUN **capacity, space** ◊ *I'm running out of ~ space on my computer.* | **drive** | **storage**
PREP. **from ~** ◊ *The information required can then be retrieved from ~.* | **on (a/the) ~** ◊ *Do you have the file on ~?* ◊ *the data on the ~* | **onto ~** ◊ *It is safest to save your design onto ~.* | **to ~** ◊ *You simply download the pages to ~.*
→ Special page at COMPUTER

dislike noun

1 feeling of not liking sb/sth

ADJ. **deep, extreme, great, intense, real, strong, violent, visceral** ◊ *Several committee members expressed their intense ~ of the chairman.* | **growing** | **general** ◊ *Consumers show a general ~ for genetically modified food products.* | **obvious** | **immediate, instant** | **instinctive** | **active** ◊ *She threw him a look of active ~.* | **personal** | **mutual** ◊ *In spite of their mutual ~ and hostility, they often worked together.*
VERB + DISLIKE **feel, harbour/harbor** (*esp. BrE*), **have** ◊ *She felt ~ rather than sympathy as he told his story.* ◊ *My father has a great ~ of long hair on boys.* | **express, show** | **develop** ◊ *Her husband developed a strong ~ for the dog.*
PREP. **with ~** ◊ *Sonia stared at me with ~ and distrust.* | **~ for** ◊ *She had a deep ~ for Robert's wife.* | **~ of** ◊ *their ~ of central government*
PHRASES **a feeling of ~, a look of ~** | **take a ~ to sb** ◊ *I took an instant ~ to my new colleague.*

2 sth you do not like

PHRASES **sb's likes and ~s** ◊ *I've told you all my likes and ~s.*

dislike verb

ADV. **cordially, greatly, heartily, intensely, really, strongly** ◊ *She ~d her boss intensely.* | **particularly** | **simply** ◊ *He simply ~d working with committees and avoided it whenever possible.* | **instinctively** | **actively** ◊ *There are very few foods that I actively ~.*
PHRASES **be generally ~d, be universally ~d, be widely ~d** ◊ *The new teacher was universally ~d.*

disloyalty noun

VERB + DISLOYALTY **show** | **accuse sb of** ◊ *Her friends accused her of ~.*
PREP. **~ to** ◊ *He has shown ~ to the party and is not to be trusted.*

dismal adj.

VERBS **be, look** | **become**
ADV. **extremely, fairly, very, etc.** ◊ *Last year's results were fairly ~.* ◊ *It was a really ~ day.*

dismay noun

ADJ. **deep** (*esp. BrE*), **great, utter** ◊ *The government has* expressed 'deep dismay' at police violence against protesters. | **growing** | **widespread** (*esp. BrE*)
VERB + DISMAY **feel** ◊ *I felt a mounting ~ at the prospect.* | **express, voice** | **hide** ◊ *It was impossible to hide my ~ at what I had seen.* | **cause** ◊ *The laws on hunting cause ~ to many animal lovers.*
PREP. **in ~** ◊ *Louise stared at the torn letter in ~.* | **with ~** ◊ *I read of her resignation with some ~.* | **~ at** ◊ *his ~ at her reaction* | **~ over** ◊ *Brady made no secret of his ~ over his treatment.*
PHRASES **fill sb with ~** ◊ *What she heard filled her with ~.* | **(you can) imagine my ~** ◊ *Imagine my ~ when I saw his picture in the paper.* | **(much) to sb's ~** ◊ *Much to my ~, she was out when I called.*

dismiss verb

1 decide sth is not important

ADV. **quickly** | **immediately, out of hand, summarily** ◊ *He ~ed her suggestion out of hand.* | **blithely, casually, cavalierly** (*esp. AmE*), **easily, lightly, readily, simply** ◊ *Children's fears should never be ~ed lightly.* | **contemptuously** ◊ *She contemptuously ~ed their complaints.* | **completely, entirely, outright** ◊ *His plan was ~ed outright by his friends.* | **routinely** ◊ *Such reports are routinely ~ed as hysteria.*
VERB + DISMISS **be unable to, cannot** | **not be possible to** ◊ *It is no longer possible to ~ the link between climate change and carbon emissions.* | **be difficult to, be easy to** ◊ *It is easy to ~ him as nothing more than an old fool.* | **try to**
PREP. **as** ◊ *She ~ed their arguments as irrelevant.* | **from** ◊ *She tried to ~ the idea from her mind.*

2 remove sb from a job

ADV. **fairly** | **unfairly, wrongfully** (*esp. BrE*) ◊ *The court ruled that Ms Hill had been unfairly ~ed.* | **constructively** (*BrE*) | **summarily**
PREP. **from** ◊ *He was summarily ~ed from his job.*

dismissal noun

1 from a job

ADJ. **automatic, immediate, instant** (*esp. BrE*), **summary** ◊ *His attack on the manager led to his instant ~.* | **constructive** (*BrE*), **unfair, wrongful** ◊ *an employee claim for unfair ~*
VERB + DISMISSAL **lead to** | **call for** ◊ *Crash victims are calling for the ~ of the bus driver.* | **be faced with, be threatened with, face, risk** ◊ *They were warned that they risked ~ if the strike continued.* | **warrant** ◊ *These mistakes were not nearly serious enough to warrant his ~.* | **appeal** (*AmE*), **appeal against** (*BrE*), **claim** ◊ *Cooke, who was with the firm 30 years, claims unfair ~.* | **uphold** (*esp. AmE*) ◊ *The court upheld the ~.*
PREP. **~ for** ◊ *his ~ for poor performance* | **~ on the grounds of** ◊ *She is now faced with ~ on the grounds of misconduct.*
PHRASES **grounds for ~, reason for ~**

2 refusing to consider sth

ADJ. **arrogant, casual, cavalier** (*esp. AmE*), **easy** | **abrupt, curt, offhand** | **outright, wholesale** ◊ *His wholesale ~ of women composers is indefensible.*
PREP. **~ of** ◊ *his callous ~ of her father's illness*

dismissive adj.

VERBS **be, seem, sound**
ADV. **extremely, fairly, very, etc.** | **overly, very** | **completely** | **openly** | **equally** ◊ *Other critics were equally ~.* | **a little, slightly, etc.**
PREP. **of** ◊ *She was very ~ of his achievements.*

disobedience noun

ADJ. **civil** ◊ *He called for a campaign of civil ~.* ◊ *the threat of mass civil ~* | **wilful/willful**
VERB + DISOBEDIENCE **punish (sb for)** | **practise/practice** ◊ *Thoreau practiced civil ~ against an imperialist war.* |

advocate ◇ *He advocated non-violent civil ~ as a strategy to achieve civil rights.*
PREP. **~ to** ◇ *their ~ to authority*
PHRASES **an act of ~** ◇ *His outburst was seen as an act of ~.*

disorder noun

1 untidy state; lack of order

ADJ. **complete**
VERB + DISORDER **throw sth into** ◇ *The country was thrown into ~ by the strikes.*
PREP. **in ~** ◇ *He died suddenly, leaving his financial affairs in complete ~.*
PHRASES **a state of ~**

2 violent behaviour/behavior

ADJ. **serious** (*esp. BrE*) | **widespread** | **violent** (*esp. BrE*) | **alcohol-related, drink-related** (*both BrE*) ◇ *the pressures on police caused by drink-related ~* | **civil, crowd** (*BrE*), **public** (*esp. BrE*), **social** | **political** | **youth** (*BrE*) ◇ *problems of youth ~ in our cities*
... OF DISORDER **outbreak** (*esp. BrE*) ◇ *There have been outbreaks of serious public ~.*
VERB + DISORDER **create, lead to** | **quell** ◇ *Troops were sent in to quell the ~.* | **combat, curb, tackle** (*all esp. BrE*) ◇ *The initiative aims to tackle alcohol-related ~ in towns.* | **tolerate** (*esp. BrE*) ◇ *The police will not tolerate ~ of any kind on our streets.* | **prevent** ◇ *new restrictions aimed at preventing social ~*

3 illness

ADJ. **serious, severe** | **chronic** | **common, rare** | **genetic, inherited** | **blood, brain, etc.** | **circulatory, eating, etc.** ◇ *Anorexia is a common eating ~.* | **physical** | **behavioural/ behavioral, emotional, mental, nervous, neurological, personality, psychiatric, psychological** | **attention deficit, bipolar, obsessive compulsive, post-traumatic stress, seasonal affective, etc.**
VERB + DISORDER **have, suffer from** ◇ *She suffers from a rare blood ~.* | **develop** ◇ *Some people develop psychological ~s as a result of trauma.* | **cause** ◇ *the argument that thin models in magazines cause eating ~s* | **prevent** ◇ *Consumption of fatty acids may help prevent the ~.* | **treat** | **diagnose** ◇ *Her doctor diagnosed a thyroid ~.*
DISORDER + VERB **affect sth** ◇ *~s affecting the very old, such as senile dementia*
PREP. **~ of** ◇ *~s of the digestive system*
→ Special page at ILLNESS

disorganized adj.

VERBS **be, seem** | **become**
ADV. **extremely, fairly, very, etc.** | **highly, hopelessly** ◇ *He never gets anywhere on time. He's hopelessly ~.* | **completely, totally** | **a little, slightly, etc.**

disparity noun

ADJ. **considerable, enormous, great, gross, huge, vast, wide** | **growing** | **glaring, obvious** | **economic, income, pay** ◇ *the glaring economic disparities between different groups in our society* | **ethnic, gender, racial** (*all AmE*) ◇ *the issue of gender ~ in the student population*
VERB + DISPARITY **address, reduce** ◇ *America should address the racial disparities in its criminal justice system.* | **eliminate** | **increase** | **explain** | **reveal, show**
PREP. **~ between** ◇ *The great ~ between the teams did not make for an entertaining game.* | **~ in** ◇ *the ~ in their salaries* | **~ of** ◇ *a ~ of resources*

disperse verb

ADV. **quickly, rapidly** | **widely** ◇ *The population in this area is very widely ~d.* | **evenly, uniformly** ◇ *The bird-feeding system evenly ~s food and water.* | **randomly** | **geographically, spatially** ◇ *geographically ~d political and economic power*
VERB + DISPERSE **begin to** ◇ *The crowd slowly began to ~.*

PREP. **around** ◇ *Members of her family are now ~d around the world.* | **over** ◇ *The seeds are ~d over a wide area.* | **throughout** ◇ *Warm air rises and ~s throughout the building.*

display noun

1 arrangement of things

ADJ. **attractive, beautiful, colourful/colorful, dazzling, excellent, fine, good, interesting, stunning** | **eye-catching, prominent** ◇ *There was a prominent ~ of her photographs in the living room.* | **special** | **public** | **permanent, temporary** | **static** ◇ *The jewels are normally kept on static ~ in the museum.* | **audio-visual, interactive, visual** ◇ *An audio-visual ~ gives visitors an idea of what life was like aboard a sailing ship.* | **floral** (*esp. BrE*) ◇ *a beautiful floral ~ in the park* | **in-store, wall, window** | **museum, shop** (*esp. BrE*), **store** (*esp. AmE*)
VERB + DISPLAY **have** ◇ *The museum has a fine ~ of old medical instruments.* | **feature** ◇ *The show featured a ~ of some of Mack's costume designs.* | **arrange, create, mount** (*esp. BrE*) ◇ *We plan to mount a ~ of the children's work in the lobby area.* | **go on** ◇ *Examples of her work will go on permanent ~ in the new museum.* | **put sth on** ◇ *The birds were put on ~ at the zoological society.* | **see, view** ◇ *People waited for hours to see the ~.*
DISPLAY + VERB **illustrate sth, show sth** ◇ *The ~ illustrates the traditional industries of the town.* | **feature sth, include sth** ◇ *The ~ includes examples of her work in progress.*
DISPLAY + NOUN **board, cabinet** (*esp. BrE*), **case, rack, shelf, stand** ◇ *a glass-fronted ~ cabinet* | **window** (*esp. AmE*) ◇ *the ~ windows of a department store* | **area, space** ◇ *The spacious lobby also functions as a ~ area.*
PREP. **on ~** ◇ *Designs for the new museum are on public ~ in the library.* ◇ *On ~ are necklaces and bracelets made from amber.* | **~ of** ◇ *a ~ of Roman coins*
→ Note at ART

2 performing a skill

ADJ. **astonishing, awesome, breathtaking, brilliant, devastating** (*esp. BrE*), **great, impressive, magnificent, outstanding, spectacular, spirited** (*BrE*), **superb** (*esp. BrE*), **virtuoso** ◇ *a virtuoso ~ of guitar playing* | **disappointing** (*BrE*), **lacklustre** (*BrE*), **poor** (*esp. BrE*) | **firework** (*esp. BrE*), **fireworks** | **pyrotechnic** ◇ *The sun set in a pyrotechnic ~ that burned up the whole sky.* | **aerial, aerobatic, air, flying, parachute** (*BrE*) ◇ *Hundreds of people experienced the dramatic aerial ~.* ◇ *the RAF Falcon parachute ~ team* | **courtship, mating, sexual**
VERB + DISPLAY **give, perform, put on** ◇ *The male performs a magnificent courtship ~.* ◇ *They put on a spectacular fireworks ~.* | **treat sb to** ◇ *The crowd was treated to an impressive ~ of tennis.* | **see, watch**
DISPLAY + NOUN **team** ◇ *an aerobatic ~ team*
PREP. **~ of** ◇ *They gave a virtuoso ~ of disco dancing.*

3 showing a particular feeling/quality

ADJ. **rare** | **impressive, incredible, striking** ◇ *Members of the community closed ranks in an impressive ~ of unity.* | **open, public** ◇ *an open ~ of affection for her husband* | **outward** ◇ *Despite his outward ~ of friendliness, I sensed he was concealing something.* | **conspicuous, ostentatious, overt** ◇ *an ostentatious ~ of wealth* | **elaborate, extravagant** ◇ *He made an elaborate ~ of surprise.* | **aggressive** ◇ *There may be specific events which trigger aggressive ~s in your dog.*
VERB + DISPLAY **see, witness** ◇ *I witnessed a rare ~ of affection between them.*
PREP. **~ of** ◇ *She slammed the door behind her in a ~ of ill-temper.*

4 on a computer screen, etc.

ADJ. **computer, screen** | **data, graphical** (*esp. AmE*), **graphics, video, visual** | **colour/color, monochrome** | **high-resolution, low-resolution** ◇ *a high-resolution computer ~* | **LCD, LED, liquid crystal, plasma** | **flat-panel** (*esp. AmE*), **flat-screen, widescreen** | **analogue/analog, digital**
DISPLAY + VERB **indicate sth, show sth** ◇ *The LCD ~ shows the time in hours and minutes.*

DISPLAY + NOUN **device, panel, screen, unit** ◇ ~ *screen equipment* ◇ *a visual* ~ *unit* | **system**

display verb

ADV. **clearly, prominently** ◇ *His football trophies were prominently ~ed in the kitchen.* | **proudly** | **openly, publicly**
PREP. **to** ◇ *She proudly ~ed her certificate to her parents.*

displeasure noun

ADJ. **extreme, great** ◇ *The President indicated his great ~ with the media coverage.* | **divine** ◇ *the belief that eclipses are signs of divine ~*
VERB + DISPLEASURE **incur** ◇ *His tactless words had incurred his father's deep ~.* | **express, make known, register, show, voice** ◇ *The veterans made their ~ known to the senator.* ◇ *He wrote her a letter registering his ~.* | **hide** ◇ *He made no attempt to hide his ~.*
PREP. **~ at** ◇ *his ~ at being ignored* | **~ with** ◇ *her ~ with her colleagues*

disposal noun

ADJ. **safe** | **illegal** | **ultimate** ◇ *the problems of the ultimate ~ of nuclear waste* | **garbage** (*AmE*), **refuse** (*esp. BrE*), **rubbish** (*BrE*), **sewage, trash** (*AmE*), **waste** | **bomb** (*esp. BrE*), **explosive ordnance** (*military*) | **land, landfill**
DISPOSAL + NOUN **facility, site** ◇ *The waste must be taken to an approved ~ facility.* | **method** | **system, unit** (*esp. BrE*) ◇ *a kitchen waste ~ unit* | **company** ◇ *a waste ~ company* | **expert, squad** (*BrE*), **team** ◇ *The device was defused by army bomb ~ experts.*

disposed adj.

VERBS **be, feel, seem**
ADV. **favourably/favorably, kindly, well** | **naturally**
PREP. **to** ◇ *She seems well ~ to the move.* | **towards/toward** ◇ *People are naturally ~ towards/toward speculation.*

disposition noun

ADJ. **cheerful, cheery** (*AmE*), **happy, pleasant, sunny, sweet** | **friendly** | **gentle** | **nervous** | **melancholic** (*esp. AmE*), **melancholy** (*esp. BrE*) | **nasty, sour** (*both AmE*) | **genetic, natural** ◇ *Do people have a natural ~ to be good?*
VERB + DISPOSITION **have, show** ◇ *These dogs show a very sociable ~.*
PREP. **of a … ~** ◇ *This movie is not recommended for those of a nervous ~.*

disproportionate adj.

VERBS **be, seem**
ADV. **grossly, hugely, vastly, wildly** | **completely, quite, totally, wholly** (*law, esp. BrE*)
PREP. **to** ◇ *The punishment was grossly ~ to the crime.*

dispute noun

ADJ. **considerable, major, serious** ◇ *There is considerable ~ over the precise definition of 'social class' as a term.* ◇ *The incident sparked off a major ~ between the two countries.* | **minor, petty** | **acrimonious, bitter, heated** | **damaging** (*BrE*) | **continuing, lengthy, long-running, long-standing, ongoing, protracted** | **outstanding** ◇ *He proposed a negotiated settlement of the outstanding ~s between the two countries.* | **public** | **international, local** | **internal** ◇ *There were lengthy internal ~s between the two wings of the party.* | **custody** (*esp. AmE*), **domestic, family, marital** | **industrial** (*esp. BrE*), **labour/labor** (*esp. AmE*), **pay** (*esp. BrE*) | **border, boundary, land, territorial** | **jurisdictional** ◇ *a jurisdictional ~ between the Army and the CIA* | **legal** | **contract, contractual, patent** | **ideological, political** | **commercial, financial, trade** | **doctrinal, religious, theological**
VERB + DISPUTE **cause, lead to, provoke, spark** ◇ *one of the many factors that led to the ~* | **engage in, enter, enter into** | **be drawn into** ◇ *Governments are often drawn into ~s about matters of public taste and decency.* | **be embroiled in, be engaged in, be involved in** ◇ *They became embroiled in a ~ with their competitors.* | **deal with, handle** ◇ *Police*

have difficulties in dealing with domestic ~s. | **adjudicate, arbitrate, arbitrate in** (*BrE*), **decide, mediate, mediate in** (*BrE*) ◇ *The purpose of industrial tribunals is to adjudicate ~s between employers and employees.* | **end, resolve, settle, solve** | **lose, win** | **avoid, prevent** | **be open to** ◇ *His theories are open to ~* (= can be disagreed with).
DISPUTE + VERB **arise, begin, erupt, occur** ◇ *No one could remember exactly how the ~ had arisen.* | **escalate** | **concern sth** ◇ *~s concerning environmental protection* | **involve sb/sth**
PREP. **beyond ~** ◇ *The matter was settled beyond ~ by the court judgment* (= it could no longer be argued about). | **in ~ (with)** ◇ *The actual sum of compensation due is still in ~* (= being argued about). ◇ *The employees have been in ~ with management for three weeks.* | **under ~** ◇ *the matters under ~* | **~ about, ~ over** | **~ among** ◇ *The exact relationship between the two languages is a matter of ~ among scholars.* | **~ as to** ◇ *There is no ~ as to the facts.* | **~ between** ◇ *a long-standing ~ between the families over ownership of the land.* | **~ with**
PHRASES **a matter, point, subject, etc. of ~** | **the resolution of a ~, the settlement of a ~**

dispute verb

ADV. **hotly, strongly, vigorously** ◇ *The effectiveness of this treatment is still hotly ~d.*
VERB + DISPUTE **can** ◇ *No one can ~ the fact that men still hold the majority of public offices.*

disregard noun

ADJ. **complete, total, utter** | **blatant, flagrant** | **callous, cavalier, cynical** | **reckless, wanton** ◇ *their reckless ~ for human life* | **blithe, fine** (*ironic, esp. BrE*) ◇ *With a fine ~ for geography, she decided to drive to the island.* | **apparent**
VERB + DISREGARD **demonstrate, show**
PREP. **~ for** ◇ *He showed complete ~ for the feelings of his family.* | **~ of** ◇ *their flagrant ~ of the rules*

disrepair noun

VERB + DISREPAIR **fall into** ◇ *The building had fallen into ~.*
PREP. **in ~** ◇ *Much of the old building was still in ~.*
PHRASES **a state of ~**

disreputable adj.

VERBS **be, look, seem**
ADV. **thoroughly, very** | **rather, slightly, vaguely** ◇ *He had a vaguely ~ appearance.* | **intellectually** ◇ *This approach remains intellectually ~ even now.*

disrepute noun

VERB + DISREPUTE **fall into** ◇ *The old system had fallen into ~.* | **bring sth into** ◇ *Such wild claims bring science into ~.* ◇ *The players' conduct is likely to bring the game into ~.* (*BrE*)
PREP. **in ~** ◇ *This theory is now in ~.*

disrespect noun

ADJ. **complete, total, utter** | **blatant** | **healthy**
VERB + DISRESPECT **have, show, treat sb/sth with** ◇ *She felt he had total ~ for women.* | **mean no** ◇ *I mean no ~ to the team, but their performance was poor.*
PREP. **~ for** ◇ *The new manager showed a healthy ~ for formality.*
PHRASES **no ~ intended, no ~ to …** ◇ *No ~ intended sir; it was just a joke.*

disrupt verb

ADV. **badly** (*esp. BrE*), **seriously, severely, significantly** ◇ *The bad weather has seriously ~ed supplies of food.* | **completely, totally** | **partially, temporarily** | **potentially** ◇ *They warned that climate change could potentially ~ economic activity.*

VERB + DISRUPT **threaten to** | **attempt to** | **be designed to** ◇ *The attacks are designed to ~ plans for the elections.*
PHRASES **an attempt to ~ sth**

disruption *noun*

ADJ. **considerable** (*esp. BrE*), **great, major, massive, serious, severe, significant** | **minimal, minimum** ◇ *how to organize the building work so as to cause minimum ~* | **widespread** (*esp. BrE*) | **economic, family, political, social** ◇ *the effects of family ~ during childhood* | **traffic** | **supply** ◇ *The war has led to supply ~ of crude oil.*
VERB + DISRUPTION **cause, create, lead to** | **experience, suffer** ◇ *The city suffered some ~ due to a bomb scare.* | **avoid, prevent** | **minimize**
DISRUPTION + VERB **occur**
PREP. **~ to** ◇ *The bombing campaign caused massive ~ to industry.* | **~ in** ◇ *an unexpected ~ in Internet service*

disruptive *adj.*

VERBS **be, become, prove**
ADV. **extremely, fairly, very, etc.** | **highly** ◇ *a highly ~ group of students* | **potentially** ◇ *potentially ~ elements in society* | **socially**
PREP. **to** ◇ *Long working hours are very ~ to home life.*

dissatisfaction *noun*

ADJ. **deep** | **growing, increasing** | **general, widespread** | **popular, public** | **consumer, customer** | **marital, sexual** | **body** (*esp. AmE*) ◇ *We're seeing an increased trend in body ~.* | **job**
VERB + DISSATISFACTION **cause, create, lead to** ◇ *Pay cuts have led to widespread ~.* | **express, voice**
PREP. **~ about, ~ over** ◇ *~ over the slow progress of the peace process* | **~ among** ◇ *There was widespread ~ among the public.* | **~ at** ◇ *She expressed deep ~ at the way the interview had been conducted.* | **~ with** ◇ *There is growing ~ with the current style of management.*
PHRASES **a feeling of ~, a sense of ~** | **a cause of ~, a source of ~** ◇ *My salary is still a source of ~.*

dissatisfied *adj.*

VERBS **be, feel** | **become, grow** | **remain** | **leave sb** ◇ *Many people will be left ~.*
ADV. **extremely, fairly, very, etc.** | **deeply, highly, profoundly** ◇ *The decision left us feeling deeply ~.* | **increasingly** | **a little, slightly, etc.**
PREP. **with** ◇ *She's very ~ with her current job.*

dissent *noun*

ADJ. **serious, strong, vigorous** (*esp. AmE*) ◇ *The war provoked strong ~.* | **growing** | **internal** ◇ *internal party ~* | **legitimate** ◇ *efforts to suppress legitimate ~* | **political, religious** ◇ *Political ~ is not tolerated.*
VERB + DISSENT **cause** | **express, register, show** ◇ *There are many ways of expressing ~.* ◇ *It is easier to register ~ in the Internet era.* | **brook, tolerate** | **crush, quash, silence, stifle, suppress** ◇ *The regime ruthlessly suppresses all ~.*
PREP. **~ against** ◇ *popular ~ against the Church* | **~ from** ◇ *His ~ from his family's religious beliefs caused a lot of ill-feeling.*
PHRASES **a voice of ~** ◇ *In the early 1960s the voices of ~ began to rise.*

dissertation *noun*

ADJ. **research** | **doctoral, Master's, undergraduate** (*BrE*) | **MSc, PhD, etc.** | **15 000-word, etc.** | **unpublished**
VERB + DISSERTATION **do, prepare, write** ◇ *Students can either do a ~ or take part in a practical project.* | **publish** | **complete, finish** | **present, submit** ◇ *Candidates are required to present a ~ of between 8 000 and 12 000 words.* | **defend**
PREP. **~ on** ◇ *He wrote his Master's ~ on rats.*

disservice *noun*

ADJ. **grave, great, terrible, tremendous**
VERB + DISSERVICE **do sb**
PREP. **~ to** ◇ *This violence will do a grave ~ to their cause.*

dissident *noun*

ADJ. **leading, prominent** | **political, religious** | **exiled, imprisoned**
VERB + DISSIDENT **imprison, jail** ◇ *regimes that murder political opponents and imprison ~s*

dissimilar *adj.*

VERBS **appear, be, look**
ADV. **highly, markedly, radically, very** | **completely, entirely, quite, totally, wholly** | **not altogether, not entirely, not too**
PREP. **from** ◇ *His views are not ~ from ours.* | **to** ◇ *The way of life here is not altogether ~ to that in other parts of India.*

dissolve *verb*

1 become/make sth liquid
ADV. **completely** ◇ *The aspirin hasn't ~d completely yet.* | **gradually, slowly** | **instantly, quickly** | **easily, readily** | **away** ◇ *The limestone has simply ~d away.*
PREP. **in** ◇ *Dissolve the sugar in water.*

2 end sth officially
ADV. **formally, officially** ◇ *Their marriage was formally ~d last year.* | **effectively** ◇ *The civilian government was effectively ~d.*

distance *noun*

1 amount of space between two points
ADJ. **considerable, enormous, fair, good, great, huge, large, long, vast** ◇ *The town is a considerable ~ from the coast.* ◇ *It's quite a good ~ to the nearest town.* ◇ *The people travel vast ~s to find food.* | **short, small** | **reasonable** | **certain, given** | **average, mean** ◇ *the average ~ covered during pursuits by cheetahs* | **equal** | **maximum, minimum** | **optimal** (*AmE*), **optimum** | **correct, right** | **exact** | **estimated** | **full** | **extra** | **fixed** | **varying** | **infinite** | **comfortable, discreet, respectful, safe** ◇ *The cat sat and watched us from a safe ~.* | **braking** (*esp. BrE*), **stopping** ◇ *Allow for greater stopping ~s when pulling a loaded trailer.* | **geographic** (*esp. AmE*), **geographical** (*esp. BrE*), **physical** ◇ *These immigrants face problems of physical ~.*
VERB + DISTANCE **cover, cross, go, move, travel, traverse** ◇ *He moved a short ~ up the valley.* ◇ *The spacecraft has the ability to traverse great ~s.* ◇ *Nobody thought he would last 15 rounds but he went the full ~.* (*figurative*) | **drive, fly, swim, walk, etc.** ◇ *The young birds were soon flying ~s of 200 feet or more.* ◇ *She sprinted the entire ~.* | **bridge, span** ◇ *The arch spans a ~ of 285 feet.* | **keep, maintain** ◇ *I kept a comfortable ~ behind the van.* | **close, shorten** ◇ *He was gradually closing the ~ between himself and the other runners.* | **calculate, determine, measure** | **estimate, gauge, judge** ◇ *It is very difficult to judge ~s in the desert.*
DISTANCE + NOUN **runner, swimmer** ◇ *a champion ~ swimmer* | **running**
PREP. **at a ~** ◇ *She followed them at a discreet ~.* | **at a ~ from** ◇ *When launching a kick, it is essential to be at the correct ~ from your opponent.* | **at a ~ of** ◇ *The town is situated at a ~ of twenty miles from Porto.* | **from a ~ (of)** ◇ *Visitors can only view the painting from a ~ of three yards.* | **over a ~ (of)** ◇ *The sound can be heard over a ~ of more than five miles.* | **within a ~** ◇ *children living within a certain ~ of the school* | **~ away from** ◇ *The house is a short ~ away from the bus station.* | **~ between** ◇ *What's the ~ between London and Edinburgh?* | **~ from** | **~ to** ◇ *the ~ from our house to the school*
PHRASES **a ... distance ahead, away, apart, etc., some ~ ahead, away, apart, etc.** ◇ *The leaders in the race were a considerable ~ ahead.* ◇ *A bomb exploded some ~ away.* | **within commuting ~, within driving ~, within walking ~** ◇ *The bars are within walking ~.* | **within shouting ~, within spitting ~, within striking ~, within touching ~**

(*esp. BrE*) ◊ *The cat was now within striking ~ of the duck.* ◊ *We came within spitting ~ of winning the cup.* (*figurative*)

2 point a long way away/being far away

ADJ. **far, middle** ◊ *I could just see the hills in the far ~.*
VERB + DISTANCE **gaze (off) into, look (off) into, stare (off) into | stretch (off) into** ◊ *The road stretches off into the ~.*
DISTANCE + NOUN **education** (*AmE*), **learning** ◊ *The college offers a wide range of distance-learning courses.* | **vision** ◊ *to have good ~ vision*
PREP. **at a ~** ◊ *At a ~ it is difficult to make out the detail on the building.* | **from a ~** ◊ *We admired the palace from a ~.* | **in the ~** ◊ *In the ~ was a small town.*

3 not being too closely involved

ADJ. **critical, professional | emotional, psychological, social**
VERB + DISTANCE **keep, maintain** ◊ *She was warned to keep her ~ from Jay if she didn't want to get hurt.* ◊ *Sociologists must maintain critical ~ from the ideas of society at any particular time.*
PREP. **~ from** ◊ *He felt a sense of ~ from the others.*
PHRASES **a sense of ~**

distant adj.

1 far away in space

VERBS **be, sound | become, grow** ◊ *The sound of the engine was growing more and more ~.*
ADV. **extremely, fairly, very, etc. | far** (*literary*) ◊ *in far ~ lands* | **relatively | increasingly | geographically, physically** ◊ *geographically ~ areas of the world*
PREP. **from** ◊ *The stars are more ~ from the earth than the sun.*
PHRASES **two miles ~, three days ~, etc.** ◊ *These sites were often several miles ~ from each other.*

2 far away in time

VERBS **be**
ADV. **impossibly** ◊ *The medieval mind can seem impossibly ~.* | **historically**
PHRASES **in the far ~ future | in the not too ~ future, in the not too ~ past** ◊ *In the not too ~ future, we may witness the cloning of human beings.* | **the dim and ~ past** (*BrE*) ◊ *stories from the dim and ~ past*

3 not friendly/not paying attention

VERBS **be, feel, look, seem, sound** ◊ *He felt oddly ~ from her.* | **become, grow | remain | find sb**
ADV. **extremely, fairly, very, etc. | increasingly** ◊ *Their relationship has grown increasingly ~ in recent years.* | **a little, slightly, etc. | oddly, strangely** ◊ *Even his children found him strangely ~ and impersonal.* | **emotionally**
PHRASES **cold and ~** ◊ *When they met, he was very cold and ~.*

distaste noun

ADJ. **deep, extreme, great, profound, strong | general** ◊ *They are country people with a general ~ for all things urban.* | **personal | growing | obvious** ◊ *She regarded the child with evident ~.*
VERB + DISTASTE **feel, have | express, show** ◊ *She was trying not to show her ~.* | **hide** ◊ *He couldn't hide the deep ~ that he felt for many of their customs.* | **eye sb/sth with, look at sb/sth with, regard sb/sth with**
PREP. **in ~** ◊ *She wrinkled her nose in mock ~.* | **with ~** ◊ *Jim looked with ~ at the cockroach in his soup.* | **~ at** ◊ *He couldn't hide his ~ at having to sleep in such a filthy room.* | **~ for** ◊ *Joe had a profound ~ for violence.*
PHRASES **an expression of ~, a look of ~**

distasteful adj.

VERBS **be, seem | find sth**
ADV. **extremely, fairly, very, etc. | deeply** (*esp. BrE*), **highly, particularly** ◊ *I find his attitude highly ~.* | **a little, slightly, etc.**
PREP. **to** ◊ *It all seems a little ~ to me.*

distinct adj.

VERBS **be | appear | become | remain | keep sth** ◊ *It is necessary to keep these two issues ~.* | **consider sth as, regard sth as, see sth as**
ADV. **very | completely, entirely, quite, radically, totally, wholly | fairly | essentially, fundamentally | clearly | sufficiently** ◊ *Manufacturers hope their new products will be sufficiently ~ to command higher prices.* | **analytically, conceptually, formally** (= distinct in form), **qualitatively** ◊ *Political power should be regarded as analytically ~ from economic power.* | **anatomically, genetically, geographically, historically, physically, etc.** ◊ *geographically ~ regions*
PREP. **from** ◊ *The various dialects are quite ~ from one another.*
PHRASES **as ~ from** ◊ *She was studying lung cancer, as ~ from other types of cancer.*

distinction noun

1 clear difference

ADJ. **critical, crucial, important, key, main, major, vital | basic, essential, fundamental | clear, clear-cut, obvious, real, rigid, sharp, strong | fine, subtle** ◊ *It was a subtle ~ but a very important one.* | **broad, general | simple | logical | meaningful, significant, useful, valid | arbitrary, artificial, false, meaningless | absolute** ◊ *Is there always an absolute ~ between right and wrong?* | **conventional, old, traditional** ◊ *the conventional ~ between pure and applied science* | **categorical, conceptual, formal, qualitative, semantic, theoretical | legal, moral | class, cultural, gender, racial, social**
VERB + DISTINCTION **draw, make** ◊ *She draws an important ~ between the different kinds of illness.* | **note, recognize, see, understand** ◊ *We can see a sharp ~ between ambition and greed.* | **blur, collapse, erase** (*esp. AmE*), **obscure** ◊ *The ~ between amateur and professional players is being blurred.*
DISTINCTION + VERB **lie** ◊ *Cultural ~s lie at the heart of these issues.* | **exist** ◊ *No legal ~ existed between cities and other corporations.*
PREP. **without ~** ◊ *All groups are entitled to this money without ~* (= without a difference being made between them). | **~ between | ~ of** ◊ *a society without ~s of class and privilege*

2 excellence/fame

ADJ. **considerable, great | dubious | rare | unique | academic, intellectual, professional, social** ◊ *Election to the NAE is an indication of professional ~.*
VERB + DISTINCTION **have** ◊ *He has the dubious ~ of being the world's most famous gangster.* | **achieve, earn** ◊ *She achieved ~ in several fields of scholarship.*
DISTINCTION + VERB **belong** ◊ *New York does not have the nation's oldest subway system; that ~ belongs to Boston.*
PREP. **of ~** ◊ *She is a historian of great ~.* | **with ~** ◊ *He served with ~ in the First World War.*

distinctive adj.

VERBS **be**
ADV. **extremely, fairly, very, etc. | highly, particularly, truly** ◊ *The shell has a highly ~ pattern.* | **visually**

distinguish verb

ADV. **clearly, sharply | carefully | easily, readily** ◊ *The adult bird can be readily ~ed by its orange bill.* | **accurately, reliably** ◊ *Troops cannot always reliably ~ between combatants and civilians.*
VERB + DISTINGUISH **be able to, can, could, etc. | be unable to | be difficult to, be hard to, be impossible to, be possible to | be important to, be necessary to** ◊ *It is important to ~ between cause and effect.*
PREP. **between** ◊ *It is often difficult to ~ clearly between fact and fiction in this book.* | **from** ◊ *She could not ~ one child from another.*
PHRASES **have difficulty ~ing, have difficulty in ~ing, have trouble ~ing** ◊ *Small children have difficulty ~ing fiction from reality.*

distinguishable adj.

VERBS **be** | **become**
ADV. **clearly, easily, readily** | **barely, hardly, scarcely**
PREP. **by** ◊ *The animal is easily ~ by the black stripes above its eye.* | **from** ◊ *The male bird is barely ~ from the female.*

distort verb

ADV. **grossly, seriously, severely** ◊ *He was accused of grossly ~ing the facts.* | **completely** | **slightly** | **deliberately**

distortion noun

1 change in shape/sound

ADJ. **severe** | **slight** | **inevitable** | **image**
VERB + DISTORTION **cause, create, lead to** ◊ *The wrong chemical balance can cause severe ~ of the photographic image.* | **avoid** | **minimize** | **correct**

2 changing sth so that it is shown falsely

ADJ. **gross, serious** ◊ *His report was attacked as a gross ~ of the truth.* | **deliberate**
VERB + DISTORTION **correct** ◊ *Every mistake or ~ that they print must be corrected.*

distract verb

ADV. **easily** ◊ *He's easily ~ed from his work.* | **momentarily, temporarily** ◊ *A noise outside momentarily ~ed her.*
PREP. **(away) from** ◊ *an attempt to ~ attention away from the real problems in the country*

distracted adj.

VERBS **appear, be, look, seem** | **become, get** ◊ *It's easy to get ~ when you're studying.*
ADV. **somewhat, very** | **a little, slightly, etc.** ◊ *She seemed slightly ~, as if something was worrying her.* | **momentarily** ◊ *Luke looked momentarily ~.*

distraction noun

ADJ. **unwanted** | **good, nice, welcome** | **brief, momentary** | **constant** | **minor** | **big, huge, major** ◊ *Her odd appearance is a major ~ whenever she is on screen.* | **unnecessary** | **driver** (esp. AmE) ◊ *new laws to address driver ~ caused by phone conversations*
VERB + DISTRACTION **cause, create** ◊ *She caused a ~ by setting off the alarm.* | **provide** ◊ *The TV provided a ~ from his work.* | **use** ◊ *Becca used the ~ to make a run for it.* | **eliminate, minimize** | **avoid**
PREP. **without ~** ◊ *She worked hard all morning, without ~.* | **~ from** ◊ *Work was a welcome ~from her problems at home.*
PHRASES **drive sb to ~** ◊ *My kids drive me to ~ at times.* | **love sb to ~**

distraught adj.

VERBS **appear, be, look, seem, sound** ◊ *She sounded absolutely ~.* | **become** | **leave sb** ◊ *His mother's death left him utterly ~.*
ADV. **extremely, fairly, very, etc.** | **absolutely, completely, utterly** | **emotionally**
PREP. **at** ◊ *They were extremely ~ at the news of his accident.*

distress noun

ADJ. **acute, considerable, deep, extreme, great, immense** (BrE), **severe, significant** | **genuine, real** | **obvious** | **unnecessary** (esp. BrE) | **general** | **emotional, mental, moral, personal, physical, psychological** ◊ *the physical ~ of hunger* ◊ *the personal ~ associated with unemployment* | **economic, financial, social** ◊ *The causes of social ~ include inadequate housing.* | **marital, relationship** (both AmE) ◊ *an unhappy young couple in acute relationship ~*
VERB + DISTRESS **cause (sb)** | **experience, feel, suffer** ◊ *the ~ that she felt when her parents argued* ◊ *The animals suffer great pain and ~ when hunted.* | **show (signs of)** ◊ *She seemed calm and showed no signs of ~.* | **hide** ◊ *He tried to*

hide his ~, but the tremor in his voice was unmistakable. | **express** ◊ *Hall expressed his ~ at the court's failure to uphold his rights.* | **avoid** | **alleviate, ease, reduce, relieve** | **see, sense** ◊ *Sensing her ~, Luke walked over and patted her shoulder.*
DISTRESS + NOUN **call, signal** ◊ *The sinking ship sent out a ~ call.*
PREP. **in ~** ◊ *The child was clearly in ~.* ◊ *a ship in ~* | **to sb's ~** ◊ *He dropped out of college, to his family's ~.* | **~ at** ◊ *her obvious ~ at hearing such bad news* | **~ over** ◊ *The president issued a statement expressing her ~ over the affair.*
PHRASES **a damsel in ~** ◊ *medieval ballads about a knight saving a damsel in ~* | **a source of ~** ◊ *Getting old is a source of ~ to men as well as women.*

distressing adj.

VERBS **be** | **become** | **find sth** ◊ *I found the story deeply ~.*
ADV. **extremely, very** | **deeply, highly** | **quite, rather** | **emotionally**
PREP. **for** ◊ *The divorce was extremely ~ for the children.*

distribute verb

1 give sth out

ADV. **equally, fairly** | **unequally** | **widely** ◊ *The leaflets have been widely ~d.* | **free** ◊ *Copies of the book were ~d free to each school in the district.*
PREP. **among** ◊ *We ~d the money equally among the team members.* | **between** | **to** ◊ *Aid is being ~d to people in need.* | **by, via** ◊ *Viruses are often ~d via email.*

2 spread sth

ADV. **evenly, uniformly** ◊ *Wealth is not evenly ~d between age groups.* | **unevenly** | **non-randomly, randomly** (both technical) ◊ *Smokers were randomly ~d in the sample interviewed.* | **identically** | **irregularly, patchily, sparsely** | **broadly, widely** ◊ *The trend is broadly ~d and not just a big-city phenomenon.* | **well** ◊ *Generous workspaces must be well ~d throughout the library.* | **globally** ◊ *The plant is globally ~d.* | **geographically**
PREP. **across, among, between, throughout** ◊ *There are over 35 000 species of orchid ~d throughout the world.*

3 supply sth for sale

ADV. **internationally, nationally** ◊ *nationally ~d brands of fruit juice* | **exclusively** ◊ *The cheese is imported and ~d exclusively by Norland Inc.* | **illegally**

distribution noun

1 way sth is shared or exists over an area

ADJ. **egalitarian, equitable, fair** ◊ *to ensure a fair ~ of wealth* | **inequitable, unfair** | **equal** ◊ *an equal ~ of wealth between people of different age groups* | **unequal** | **even, uniform** ◊ *After applying the cream, comb through to ensure even ~.* | **uneven** ◊ *The country was noted for its uneven ~ of land resources.* | **patchy** | **optimal, optimum** | **relative** ◊ *the relative ~ of continents and oceans* | **general, overall** ◊ *the general ~ of earthquakes around the world* | **broad, wide, widespread** ◊ *the broad ~ of Bronze Age artefacts* ◊ *the wider ~ of wealth throughout society* | **local, localized** ◊ *Fish populations assume highly localized ~s within each river.* | **global, regional, worldwide** | **spatial** | **statistical** | **income, wealth** | **weight** | **age, class, geographical, population, sex, social** ◊ *the social class ~ of the male population* | **normal, skewed, smooth** (all technical) ◊ *a normal ~ with a bell-shaped frequency curve* | **non-random, random** (both technical) | **binomial, frequency, probability** (all technical)
VERB + DISTRIBUTION **achieve, ensure** ◊ *The engine is mounted in the middle to achieve a more even weight ~.* | **analyse/ analyze, examine, investigate, observe** | **determine** ◊ *Radiology was used to determine the ~ of the disease.* | **have** ◊ *These birds have a wide geographical ~.* | **exhibit, show** (both technical) ◊ *IQs within the population show a normal ~.*
DISTRIBUTION + NOUN **pattern** ◊ *Animal herds may form in response to the ~ patterns of food.* | **map** ◊ *~ maps of the most important tropical diseases* | **curve** (technical) ◊ *people at the low end of the ~ curve of intelligence*

PREP. **~ across** ◊ *the ~ of resources across society* | **~ among** ◊ *data on wealth ~ among age groups* | **~ between** ◊ *a disparity in age ~ between groups* | **~ over** ◊ *the ~ of trees over the estate* | **~ throughout** ◊ *uniform ~ of the chemical throughout the timber*
PHRASES **a change in ~** ◊ *changes in the ~ of wealth and income*

2 giving/delivering sth to people

ADJ. **free** ◊ *The document contains sensitive information and is not suitable for free (= unrestricted) ~.* ◊ *The previously free (= not paid for) ~ of textbooks will now be confined to students who are needy.* | **general** ◊ *Our catalogue lists all our books that are available for general ~.* | **selective** | **exclusive** ◊ *The publisher has signed an agreement for the exclusive ~ of the books in the US.* | **proper** | **electronic** ◊ *the electronic ~ of software to customers* | **global, international, local, national, worldwide** ◊ *Roads are used for local ~ of goods.* | **electricity, food, fuel, gas, land, water,** etc. ◊ *land ~ policies* | **retail, wholesale** ◊ *the wholesale and retail ~ of a huge variety of goods*
VERB + DISTRIBUTION **control, handle, organize** ◊ *The company is to handle the ~ of the product in Europe.* | **be available for** ◊ *2 000 copies of the booklet have been printed and are available for ~.* | **ensure** ◊ *to ensure the proper ~ of medical aid* | **allow, allow for** ◊ *to allow for the ~ of aid*
DISTRIBUTION + NOUN **agreement, arrangement, deal** ◊ *Her company has signed a non-exclusive ~ agreement.* | **list** ◊ *email ~ lists* | **rights** | **costs** | **channel** ◊ *We have many ~ channels for our software, including electronic.* | **chain, infrastructure, network, pipeline** (*AmE*) ◊ *There are more firearms in the ~ pipeline than most people realize.* | **method** | **process** | **system** | **facilities** ◊ *The company wants to invest in new ~ facilities.* | **base, centre/center, depot, outlet, point, site** ◊ *The company has decided to use Chennai as its ~ base.* | **platform** ◊ *The Internet is our ~ platform now.* | **operation** ◊ *The company has ~ operations in 33 countries worldwide.* | **business, company** | **industry**
PREP. **for ~** ◊ *free leaflets for ~ overseas* | **~ among** ◊ *food for ~ among the homeless* | **~ between** ◊ *the ~ of the health budget between various hospitals* | **~ by** ◊ *the ~ by the government of a leaflet explaining the new tax* | **~ through** ◊ *~ through department stores* | **~ to** ◊ *The food was packed up for ~ to outlying communities.*
PHRASES **a/the chain of ~** ◊ *There are savings to be made by bypassing retailers in the chain of ~.* | **a channel of ~**

3 payment

ADJ. **capital, dividend, share** | **cash**
VERB + DISTRIBUTION **make** ◊ *When are ~s likely to be made to creditors?*

distributor noun

ADJ. **global, international, overseas, worldwide** | **local, national** | **exclusive, sole** | **authorized, licensed** | **independent** | **big, large, leading, main, major, primary** ◊ *We are the primary ~ of the system in Mexico.* | **small** | **wholesale** | **food** | **film, movie** (*AmE*) | **software**
VERB + DISTRIBUTOR **appoint (sb) as** ◊ *We have been appointed sole ~ of a number of Hungarian wines.* | **act as** ◊ *We will act as the exclusive ~ for these Russian goods to the world market.*
DISTRIBUTOR + NOUN **network**
PREP. **through a/the ~** ◊ *You can get the book through your local ~.* | **~ for** ◊ *the exclusive ~ for these goods* ◊ *a ~ for the German market* ◊ *a ~ for Hewlett-Packard*

district noun

ADJ. **neighbouring/neighboring, surrounding** ◊ *Fire crews from all the surrounding ~s helped to fight the fires.* | **central, downtown** (*AmE*) ◊ *Every city has its central business ~.* ◊ *The apartment is approximately fifteen minutes from the downtown ~.* | **outlying, remote** ◊ *a new station to help people commuting from outlying ~s* | **northern, southern,** etc. | **affluent, exclusive, rich, wealthy** | **poor, working-class** ◊ *the shacks in the poorest ~s of the city* | **slum** | **historic** | **conservation** (*AmE*) | **coastal, country, local, metropolitan, rural, suburban, urban** | **business, commercial, financial** (*AmE*), **industrial, residential,**

warehouse (*esp. AmE*) | **arts, entertainment, shopping, theatre/theater** ◊ *Times Square is the entertainment ~ of New York.* | **garment, meat-packing, mining** (*all AmE*) | **administrative** | **electoral, polling, voting** (*AmE*) | **congressional, federal, judicial, legislative** (*all in the US*) ◊ *a federal ~ court in New York* | **postal** (*in the UK*) | **Democratic, Republican** ◊ *It's a heavily Democratic ~.* | **swing** (= in which people often change who they vote for) (*AmE*) | **home** (*esp. AmE*) ◊ *He hasn't yet registered to vote in his home ~.* | **health** (*esp. BrE*), **military, school** (*AmE*) ◊ *He has been transferred to a hospital in a different health ~.* | **red-light**
VERB + DISTRICT **create** ◊ *efforts to create a single business ~ in downtown Beijing* | **draw, redraw** (*both AmE, politics*) ◊ *They redrew ~s to make sure Republican candidates would win.* | **represent** ◊ *He represented his ~ in Congress.* | **win** (*AmE*) ◊ *Clinton barely won the ~ in 1996.*
DISTRICT + VERB **stretch** ◊ *Their ~ stretches from the mountains to the sea.* | **include sth** ◊ *The ~ includes much of the Ribault River.* | **offer sth, provide sth**
DISTRICT + NOUN **authority, council** ◊ *the ~ health authority* (*in the UK*) | **attorney, judge, official** (*all in the US*) | **councillor, nurse** (*both in the UK*) | **court** (*in the US*) | **hospital** (*in the UK*) | **office** | **boundary** ◊ *Redrawing ~ boundaries would change the election results.*
PREP. **in a/the ~, within a/the ~** ◊ *The hotel is located within Beijing's business ~.*

distrust noun

ADJ. **deep, deep-seated, profound** | **growing** | **widespread** | **general** ◊ *He had a general ~ of the government.* | **public** | **mutual** | **healthy** ◊ *She has a healthy ~ of door-to-door salesmen.*
VERB + DISTRUST **feel, have** | **express, show** | **create** ◊ *The many policy changes have created growing ~ among employees.* | **overcome** ◊ *Great efforts were made to overcome public ~.*
PREP. **~ between** ◊ *~ between the two governments* | **~ in** ◊ *investor ~ in the equity markets* | **~ of** ◊ *a ~ of the media*
PHRASES **a climate of ~**

disturbance noun

1 actions that upset the normal state of sb/sth

ADJ. **great, major, serious** | **minimal, minimum, minor, slight** | **environmental, physical** ◊ *environmental ~s caused by roads and traffic*
... OF DISTURBANCE **level** ◊ *an unacceptable level of ~ to our staff*
VERB + DISTURBANCE **cause, create, make** ◊ *The traffic causes serious ~ to residents.* | **experience, suffer** | **feel, sense** ◊ *Fish can sense ~s in the water.* | **minimize** | **reduce** | **prevent** ◊ *She moved the nest very carefully to prevent ~ to the birds.*
PREP. **without ~** ◊ *a place where you can work without ~* | **~ from** ◊ *from noisy traffic* | **~ of** ◊ *the ~ of marine life caused by oil spillages* | **~ to** ◊ *Buildings should create minimum ~ to the environment.*

2 (esp. BrE) violent public event

ADJ. **serious** ◊ *The decision led to serious ~s in all the country's main cities.* | **violent** | **public** | **crowd** (*BrE*) | **civil, political, racial, social** | **domestic** (*BrE, AmE*) ◊ *Police had been called to a domestic ~.*
VERB + DISTURBANCE **cause, give rise to, lead to, trigger** ◊ *He was arrested and charged with causing a ~.* ◊ *An influx of refugees has triggered ~s in the city.* | **be involved in** ◊ *Large numbers of workers involved in the ~s have been arrested.* | **deal with, put down, quell** ◊ *Troops were brought in to put down the ~.*
DISTURBANCE + VERB **occur** | **involve sb** ◊ *~s involving members of a crowd of 550 demonstrators*
PREP. **during a/the ~, in a/the ~** ◊ *Several people were injured during a ~ in the capital city.* | **~ among** ◊ *There had been violent ~s among the prisoners.* | **~ between** ◊ *~s between members of two rival factions*

PHRASES a ~ of the peace (law, esp. BrE) (usually **disturbing the peace** in AmE)

3 emotional/physical upset

ADJ. serious, severe | behavioural/behavioral, emotional, mental, psychiatric, psychological ◇ teenagers suffering from a psychological ~ | menstrual, visual | sleep | mood, personality
VERB + DISTURBANCE experience, have, suffer from ◇ 9% of children have a serious emotional ~. | report ◇ Many patients reported sleep ~s after taking the drug.
PREP. ~ in ◇ a ~ in liver function ◇ emotional ~s in children

disturbed adj.

1 mentally ill

VERBS be, seem | become
ADV. deeply, highly, seriously, severely, very ◇ Many of our patients are severely ~. | behaviourally/behaviorally, emotionally, mentally, psychologically ◇ emotionally ~ children

2 very anxious

VERBS be, feel | become
ADV. deeply, greatly, profoundly, very | quite, rather | a little, slightly, etc. | vaguely (esp. AmE)
PREP. by ◇ I felt vaguely ~ by the incident.

disturbing adj.

VERBS be | become | remain | find sth
ADV. extremely, fairly, very, etc. | deeply, highly, profoundly ◇ a profoundly ~ experience | a little, slightly, etc. | vaguely | oddly

disuse noun

VERB + DISUSE be in ◇ Much of the factory is in ~. | fall into ◇ A new bridge was built ten years ago and the old one has fallen into ~.
PREP. from ~, through ~, with ~ ◇ Her muscles had become weak through ~.
PHRASES a period of ~

ditch noun

ADJ. deep, wide | shallow, small | open | muddy | drainage, irrigation | roadside
VERB + DITCH dig
DITCH + VERB run ◇ The ~ ran parallel to the road. | surround sth ◇ The lettuce beds are surrounded by a deep ~.
PREP. in a ~, into a ~ ◇ I tripped and fell into a muddy ~.

dive noun

1 of an aircraft

ADJ. steep, vertical | gentle, shallow | spiral
VERB + DIVE go into ◇ The plane went into a steep ~. | pull out of ◇ The pilot seemed to be having difficulty in pulling out of the ~.

2 move/jump/fall

ADJ. headlong, nose (usually **nosedive**) (both often figurative) The economy is on a headlong ~ to disaster. ◇ His acting career took a nosedive. | sudden | deep | running ◇ She made a running ~ to get across the crevasse.
VERB + DIVE make, take ◇ She made a ~ for the door. ◇ He took a ~ in the penalty area and won his team a controversial penalty. ◇ The market is volatile and profits could take a ~. (figurative)
PREP. ~ for ◇ There would be a ~ for the bar as soon as the show finished.

dive verb

1 jump into water

ADV. deep, head first | down
PREP. for ◇ to ~ for pearls | from ◇ She ~d from the top diving board. | into ◇ He ~d head first into the water. | off

PHRASES go diving ◇ He went to Greece to go diving.

2 of birds/aircraft

ADV. suddenly | vertically ◇ Unlike some birds, it does not ~ vertically.
PREP. from, to ◇ The plane suddenly ~d from 10 000 feet to 5 000.

3 move/jump/fall

ADV. head first, headlong | back, down, forward
PREP. beneath | into ◇ He ~d headlong into the ditch. | through | under
PHRASES ~ for cover ◇ We heard an explosion and ~d for cover.

diverge verb

ADV. considerably, dramatically, sharply, significantly, widely | slightly | rapidly
PREP. from ◇ This country's interests ~ considerably from those of other countries.

diverse adj.

VERBS be, seem | become
ADV. extremely, fairly, very, etc. | enormously, exceptionally, highly, incredibly, remarkably, widely | richly ◇ The school is a richly ~ community. | wildly (esp. AmE) ◇ The 1970s saw wildly ~ roles for the actor. | increasingly | relatively | apparently, seemingly | culturally, demographically, economically, ethnically, geographically, linguistically, racially, religiously, socially ◇ an ethnically ~ population | biologically, genetically

diversion noun

1 change of direction

ADJ. brief, short (esp. BrE) | major (esp. BrE) | water
VERB + DIVERSION make, take ◇ From Poiso we make a short ~ to drive to the top of the mountain.
PREP. from ◇ the ~ of water from the river into the reservoir | ~ to ◇ The pilot set the aircraft up for a ~ to the nearest suitable airfield.

2 (BrE) temporary route → See also DETOUR

ADJ. temporary ◇ A temporary ~ has been set up to take traffic away from the accident site. | traffic
VERB + DIVERSION set up | signpost ◇ The road will be closed for two days; ~s have been signposted.
DIVERSION + VERB be in operation ◇ The main road is now closed and ~s are in operation.

3 distraction

ADJ. welcome
VERB + DIVERSION create, provide ◇ The fire was started to create a ~, allowing some prisoners to escape.
PREP. ~ from ◇ TV provided a welcome ~ from our routine.

4 pleasant activity

ADJ. fun, nice, pleasant | little, minor (esp. BrE)
VERB + DIVERSION make, provide ◇ The party would make a pleasant ~ in his rather dull social life.

diversity noun

ADJ. considerable, enormous, extraordinary, great, immense, remarkable, rich, tremendous, wide ◇ There is need for greater ~ and choice in education. ◇ the rich ~ of the city's cultural life | growing, increased, increasing | high, low ◇ The south-east has the highest ~ of freshwater fish in the country. | biological, ecological, gene, genetic, species ◇ the need to preserve biological ~ | cultural, ethnic, gender, intellectual (esp. AmE), linguistic, political, racial, religious | ideological | geographic (esp. AmE), geographical, regional | global
VERB + DIVERSITY achieve, create | encourage, enhance, foster, promote ◇ Our party believes in encouraging cultural ~, not division. | celebrate, embrace ◇ People are being encouraged to celebrate the ~ of their communities. | appreciate, respect, value ◇ You're lucky to work for a company which values ~. | maintain, preserve, protect ◇ The producer was under pressure to maintain a ~ in his

output. | **reflect, represent** ◇ *The teaching profession does not yet reflect the ~ of the population.* | **increase | decrease, reduce | allow, allow for** ◇ *Tyrannies do not allow ~ and disagreement.*
PREP. **~ in** ◇ *~ in the style of the reports* | **~ of** ◇ *There is a wide ~ of views on this subject.*

divide *noun*

ADJ. **big, deep, great, sharp | growing | north-south, etc. | class, cultural, economic, ethnic, gender, generational, ideological, political, racial, religious, sectarian, social | partisan** (*esp. AmE*), **party | digital** ◇ *the digital ~ between people with access to technology and those without*
VERB + DIVIDE **create | widen** ◇ *policies which have widened the ~ between rich and poor* | **close, narrow | bridge, cross, straddle** ◇ *advice on bridging cultural ~s* ◇ *a style which straddles the ~ between classic and modern* | **address** ◇ *attempts to address the racial ~ in this country*
DIVIDE + VERB **widen | narrow | open, open up | separate sth** ◇ *a ~ separating those who have access to computers and those who don't*
PREP. **~ between** ◇ *the sharp ~ between rich and poor regions* | **~ in** ◇ *The leader's speech aimed to close the embarrassing ~ in party ranks.*

divide *verb*

1 separate into parts
ADV. **broadly, roughly** ◇ *This report is ~d broadly into two parts.* | **exactly | clearly | conveniently, neatly** ◇ *Vegetarians ~ neatly into two groups.* | **evenly | arbitrarily, randomly** ◇ *They were randomly ~d into three groups.*
PREP. **into** ◇ *The children ~d into three teams.*
PHRASES **~ in two** ◇ *the point where the river ~s in two*

2 share
ADV. **equally**
PREP. **among** ◇ *The money was ~d equally among his sons.* | **between** ◇ *They ~d their time between London and Boston.*

3 cause disagreement
ADV. **bitterly, deeply, seriously, sharply** ◇ *This issue has bitterly ~d the community.* | **increasingly | closely, evenly | ethnically, politically, racially** ◇ *The fragile peace has deteriorated in this ethnically ~d city.*
PHRASES **be ~d about sth, be ~d on sth, be ~d over sth** ◇ *Board members were deeply ~d on the issue.*

dividend *noun*

1 payment on a company share
ADJ. **big, high, large | 10%, etc. | total | gross, net** (*both BrE*) **| annual, quarterly | final, interim** (*both BrE*) **| company, corporate | share** (*esp. BrE*), **stock** (*esp. AmE*) **| cash**
VERB + DIVIDEND **pay | distribute | get, receive | announce, declare** ◇ *The company has not yet declared its ~s for this year.* | **boost, increase, lift** (*BrE*), **raise | hold, maintain** ◇ *The interim ~ is maintained at 2.5 cents per share.* | **cut, reduce, slash | tax**
DIVIDEND + VERB **be up** ◇ *The ~ is up 10.6%.* | **go up, grow, rise** ◇ *The ~ should rise to 5 cents.* | **stay** ◇ *The ~ stays at 0.5p.* | **be payable** ◇ *The final ~, payable on July 1, is reduced to 1p.*
DIVIDEND + NOUN **payment, payout | distribution | growth, increase | cut | income, total, yield** ◇ *The fund has a ~ yield of 5.75%.* | **rate | tax | cheque/check | stocks** (*AmE*) **| policy**
PREP. **~ on** ◇ *They have announced the quarterly ~ on the shares.*
PHRASES **an increase in a ~**

2 benefit/reward
ADJ. **big, great, handsome, huge, large, rich | economic, political | peace**
VERB + DIVIDEND **bring, pay, produce, reap, yield** ◇ *Her hard work paid ~s when she won the school dancing competition.* ◇ *The company reaped rich ~s with its new strategy.*
PREP. **~ in** ◇ *The chain's investment in new stores is bringing ~s in new customers.*

diving *noun*

ADJ. **deep-sea, scuba, sub-aqua** (*BrE*) **| commercial** (*esp. BrE*)
VERB + DIVING **go**
DIVING + NOUN **board | equipment, gear, suit | bell** ◇ *A ~ bell is usually used for operations below 150 feet.* | **coach, instructor | expedition, trip | accident**

divisible *adj.*

VERBS **be**
ADV. **infinitely** ◇ *He argued that all matter was infinitely ~.* | **evenly** ◇ *A prime number is evenly ~ only by itself and 1.*
PREP. **by** ◇ *Twelve is ~ by four.* | **into** ◇ *Plants are ~ into three main groups.*

division *noun*

1 dividing sth into separate parts
ADJ. **clear, simple** ◇ *Sometimes there is no simple ~ between good and evil.* | **complex | rigid | broad, rough | equal, fair | unequal** ◇ *an unequal ~ of the cake* | **conventional, traditional** ◇ *the traditional ~ of language into grammar and vocabulary* | **hierarchical** ◇ *hierarchical ~ between 'workers' and 'management'* | **threefold, three-way, tripartite | cell | nuclear**
VERB + DIVISION **make** ◇ *You can make a rough ~ of his music into 'light' and 'serious'.*
PREP. **~ among** ◇ *His will detailed his assets and gave instructions for their ~ among his children.* | **~ between** ◇ *the ~ of the money between the members* | **~ into** ◇ *In selling there is a broad ~ into direct and indirect methods.*
PHRASES **the ~ of labour/labor | the ~ of wealth**

2 differences between two groups, things, etc.
ADJ. **bitter, deep, great, sharp** ◇ *There are sharp ~s within the party over the proposals.* | **fundamental | factional, internal** ◇ *factional ~s within the party* | **north-south | class, cultural, ethnic, gender, ideological, political, racial, sectarian, social**
VERB + DIVISION **cause, create, provoke | exploit | deepen, exacerbate, reinforce | heal** ◇ *The speech is intended to heal ~s within the party.* | **overcome, transcend** ◇ *faith and love which transcends every ~ and prejudice*
PREP. **~ among** ◇ *There are reports of serious ~s among senior party members.* | **~ between | ~ within** ◇ *~ within the government*

3 section of an organization
ADJ. **regional | international, multinational | manufacturing, marketing, news, retail, sales, training, wholesale | administrative** ◇ *the administrative ~s of the empire* | **airborne, armoured/armored, infantry**
VERB + DIVISION **command, head, lead, oversee, run | establish, form | launch** ◇ *The company recently launched its publishing ~.* | **deploy** (= *an army division*)
DIVISION + NOUN **chief** (*esp. AmE*), **commander** (= *in the army*), **director, head, leader, manager, president** (*esp. AmE*) **| headquarters**
PREP. **in the ... ~** ◇ *She works in the marketing ~.*

4 in sports
ADJ. **first, high, junior, low, premier, second, senior, top, etc.** ◇ *He's now playing in the higher ~s.* | **heavyweight, lightweight, middleweight, etc.** (= *in boxing, etc.*)
VERB + DIVISION **clinch, win** (*both AmE*) ◇ *The Ravens finished 10–6 and won the ~.* | **dominate**
DIVISION + NOUN **championship, crown, title** ◇ *The team won its tenth consecutive ~ title.* | **competition, game, series** (*all AmE*) **| champ** (*informal*), **champion, winner | rivals | lead** (*AmE*) ◇ *The team have a three game ~ lead.*
PREP. **in the ... ~** ◇ *They compete in the senior ~ of the chess league.*

5 dividing one number by another
ADJ. **long**
VERB + DIVISION **do** ◇ *Can you do long ~?*
PREP. **~ by** ◇ *~ by three*

divisive adj.

VERBS **be** | **become**
ADV. **extremely, fairly, very, etc.** | **deeply** | **potentially** |
politically, racially, socially ◇ *He believes that unemployment is socially ~ and is leading to the creation of an underclass.*

divorce noun

ADJ. **amicable, uncontested** | **no-fault** | **acrimonious, bitter, messy, nasty, painful, ugly** | **quick, quickie** (*informal*) | **parental** ◇ *Parental ~ can have lasting negative consequences for children.* | **civil** ◇ *The church may disapprove but Catholics can and do obtain civil ~s.*
VERB + DIVORCE **want** | **apply for, ask for, file for, petition for, seek, sue for** ◇ *She filed for ~ in 1996.* | **initiate** ◇ *The majority of ~s are initiated by women.* | **get, have, obtain** ◇ *He told her that he was married but getting a ~.* | **experience, go through** ◇ *She watched her parents go through an acrimonious ~.* | **agree to, consent to** | **contest** ◇ *These days ~ is rarely contested.* | **finalize** ◇ *Once the ~ is finalized, I plan to move to Bermuda.* | **handle** ◇ *the lawyers handling their ~* | **grant (sb)** ◇ *Over 50 000 ~s were granted last year.* | **end in** ◇ *An increasing number of marriages end in ~.* | **consider** ◇ *Neither partner had considered ~.*
DIVORCE + VERB **come through** ◇ *He is waiting for the ~ to come through before he remarries.*
DIVORCE + NOUN **court** | **case, proceedings, process** | **petition** | **papers** ◇ *He hasn't signed the ~ papers yet.* | **decree, settlement** | **figures, rate, statistics** ◇ *The ~ rate has been growing steadily since 1971.* | **law** | **attorney** (*AmE*), **lawyer** | **mediation**
PREP. **~ from** ◇ *her ~ from the star* | **~ on the grounds of** ◇ *She is seeking a ~ on the grounds of cruelty.*
PHRASES **grounds for ~** ◇ *He cited adultery as grounds for ~.*

dock noun

1 place for loading/unloading ships

ADJ. **commercial** | **coal, fish, etc.** | **boat, ferry, shipping** (*all esp. AmE*) | **fishing** (*AmE*)
VERB + DOCK **build, construct** | **arrive at, arrive in** | **enter** | **leave**
DOCK + NOUN **company** | **strike** | **worker**
PREP. **at a/the ~** ◇ *A car pulled up at the ~.* | **in ~** ◇ *The ship is in ~ for repairs.* | **on a/the ~** ◇ *the cargo stacked on the ~*

2 the dock in a court of law

VERB + THE DOCK **enter, go into, step into** | **appear in, be in** ◇ *She was in the ~ on charges of attempted fraud.*
PREP. **from the ~** ◇ *an outburst from the ~* | **in the ~** ◇ *The defendant stood in the ~.*

doctor noun

ADJ. **excellent, good** | **female, male, woman** | **qualified** | **experienced** | **trainee** (*BrE*) | **junior, senior** (*both BrE*) | **medical** | **military, prison, school, team** | **family** (*esp. BrE*), **local, primary-care** (*AmE*) ◇ *Who is your family ~?* | **hospital** | **emergency-room** (abbreviated to **ER**) (*AmE*) | **NHS** (*in the UK*) | **private** | **locum** (*BrE*) | **eye** | **flying** (*in Australia*) | **witch**
VERB + DOCTOR **register with** (*BrE*) ◇ *You should register with a ~ as soon as possible.* | **call, fetch** (*BrE*), **get, send for** ◇ *We called the ~ immediately.* (For more verbs see note.)
PHRASES **a doctor's appointment** | **a doctor's office** (*AmE*), **a doctor's surgery** (*BrE*) | **doctor's orders** ◇ *He left the hospital against doctor's orders.*

doctorate noun

ADJ. **honorary** | **engineering, music, etc.**
VERB + DOCTORATE **do, study for, take** ◇ *She's doing a ~ in ancient history.* | **complete, finish** ◇ *He's completed his ~ on bees.* | **have, hold** ◇ *The applicants all have ~s from good universities.* | **be awarded, be granted, gain, get, obtain, receive**

DOCTORATE + NOUN **degree** | **program** (*AmE*) (usually **doctoral program**)
PREP. **~ from** ◇ *a ~ from Cornell University* | **~ in** ◇ *a ~ in Business Administration* | **~ of** ◇ *a ~ of divinity* | **~ on** ◇ *a ~ on post-colonial development*

doctrine noun

ADJ. **Catholic, Christian, Islamic, etc.** | **church** | **economic, legal, military, political, religious** | **classical, conventional, established, orthodox, traditional** | **contemporary, current** | **prevailing** | **basic, central** | **false**
… OF DOCTRINE **point** ◇ *communities divided on points of ~* | **body** ◇ *an influential body of ~*
VERB + DOCTRINE **advocate, expound, preach, proclaim, teach** | **defend** | **develop, establish, formulate** | **accept, adhere to, adopt, be committed to, believe, believe in, embrace, follow, subscribe to, support, uphold** ◇ *They were all committed to the ~ of social equality.* | **abandon, oppose, reject, undermine** ◇ *She rejected the traditional Christian ~s.* | **apply, invoke**
PREP. **in ~** ◇ *The Church welcomed all who were considered sound in ~.*

document noun

1 official paper/book

ADJ. **important, key** ◇ *one of the key ~s in this case* | **relevant** | **lengthy, long** | **brief, short** | **10-page, etc.** | **complete, entire, whole** ◇ *This statement must be understood in the context of the entire ~.* | **detailed** | **draft** | **revised** | **final** | **original** ◇ *The original ~ has been lost or destroyed.* | **paper, printed, written** | **published, unpublished** | **attached, enclosed** ◇ *Please sign the enclosed ~ and return it to me.* | **single** ◇ *A constitution need not be a single ~.* | **classified, confidential, privileged** (*law*), **secret, sensitive, top-secret** | **private** | **declassified, public** | **available** ◇ *Documents will be available at the news conference.* | **internal** ◇ *details of internal UN ~s* | **signed, unsigned** | **disclosed** (*esp. BrE*), **leaked** | **incriminating** | **authentic, genuine** | **fake, false, forged, fraudulent** (*esp. AmE*), **phoney/phony** (*esp. AmE*) | **court, government, legal, official** | **policy, strategy** | **travel** ◇ *Keep your travel ~s in a secure place.* | **registration** (*esp. BrE*) ◇ *the car's registration ~* (*BrE*) | **contract, offer** (*BrE*), **tender** (*BrE*) (*all business*) ◇ *He has promised to send out a formal offer ~ to shareholders by Monday.* | **briefing, consultation** (*BrE*), **consultative** (*BrE*), **discussion, planning, working** ◇ *The Department issued a consultation ~.* ◇ *a working ~ in the discussions for a final treaty* | **basic, framework** (*esp. BrE*) | **guidance** | **supporting** | **binding, contractual** (*BrE*) ◇ *A ~ signed in another country is as legally binding as one signed at home.* | **constitutional, founding** *(esp. AmE)* ◊ *The 1840 treaty is widely regarded as New Zealand's founding ~.* | **historical**

... OF DOCUMENT **copy**

VERB + DOCUMENT **draft, draw up, prepare, produce** ◊ *The government has produced an important new policy ~.* | **type, write** | **revise** | **disclose** *(law)*, **issue, publish, release** ◊ *a consultative ~ issued by the Department* | **declassify** | **obtain, receive** | **file** ◊ *Copies of the relevant ~s must be filed at court.* | **hand sb, hand over, present, submit** ◊ *Supporting ~s must be submitted to the supervisory authority.* | **produce, show** ◊ *He was unable to produce the ~ that he claimed would prove his case.* | **circulate, send, send out** | **leak** ◊ *~s leaked from the government to the press* | **destroy** ◊ *He was trying to destroy ~s that testified to his guilt.* | **go through, read, read through** ◊ *Go through the ~ checking for errors.* | **search through** ◊ *I had to search through 4 000 ~s to find the information I needed.* | **consider, examine, study** | **review** *(esp. AmE)* | **adopt, approve, execute** *(law)*, **sign** ◊ *The conference adopted a ~ on minority rights.* | **authenticate** | **forge** | **refer to** | **attach, enclose** ◊ *The relevant ~s are enclosed for your information.* | **scan** ◊ *Existing paper ~s could be scanned into a computer.*

DOCUMENT + VERB **concern sth, deal with sth, focus on sth, relate to sth** | **contain sth, cover sth, include sth** ◊ *~s covering various points of concern* | **refer to sth** | **acknowledge sth, describe sth, detail sth, explain sth, indicate sth, list sth, note sth, outline sth, record sth, say sth, set out sth, state sth, tell sb sth** ◊ *The ~ says they are against tax rebates.* | **call for sth, propose sth, suggest sth** ◊ *a ~ calling for a ceasefire* | **reveal sth, show sth** | **summarize sth** | **confirm sth** | **be called sth, be entitled sth, be headed sth** ◊ *a ~ entitled 'Guidelines for Good Practice'* | **be written** ◊ *The ~ is written in Chinese.* | **be dated ... , date back to ... , date from ...** ◊ *~s dating back to the 1920s* ◊ *The ~ is dated 775.*

PREP. **according to a/the ~** ◊ *According to leaked cabinet ~s, no compensation would be paid.* | **in a/the ~** ◊ *He particularly criticized the terminology in the ~.* | **throughout a/the ~** ◊ *There is a disclaimer throughout the official ~s.* | **~ about, ~ concerning** ◊ *a ~ concerning arbitration procedures in Cairo* | **~ of** ◊ *a ~ of 2 000 words* ◊ *Her journal is an important ~ of 19th-century rural life* | **~ on** ◊ *a ~ government ~ on education policy*

PHRASES **a draft of a ~, a version of a ~** | **the authenticity of a ~** ◊ *There is little reason to doubt the authenticity of this ~.*

2 computer file

ADJ. **electronic** | **printed** | **HTML, XML, etc.** | **hypertext, text** | **new** ◊ *I saved my work and opened a new ~.* | **saved** | **active, current** ◊ *Highlight a passage in the active ~ and click on the print icon.*

VERB + DOCUMENT **close, open** | **display** ◊ *to display ~s on screen* | **view** | **retrieve** | **download** | **scroll through** ◊ *Scroll through the ~ using the scroll bar.* | **search** ◊ *a software tool for searching ~s* | **create, generate** ◊ *To create a new ~, select New from the File menu.* | **edit** | **save** ◊ *Save the ~ before closing.* | **format** | **spellcheck** | **receive, send** ◊ *Send and receive ~s at the click of a button.* | **print, print out** | **attach**

PREP. **in a/the ~** ◊ *Cut and paste is used to move text to a new place in the ~.*

→ Special page at COMPUTER

documentary *noun*

ADJ. **film, radio, television, TV** | **controversial** | **science, wildlife, etc.** | **forty-minute, half-hour, hour-long, etc.** | **feature** *(esp. AmE)*, **feature-length** | **fly-on-the-wall** *(esp. BrE)*

VERB + DOCUMENTARY **do, make, produce** ◊ *She has made a television ~ on poverty in our cities.* | **film** | **air** *(esp. AmE)*, **broadcast** *(esp. BrE)*, **show** | **see, watch**

DOCUMENTARY + NOUN **feature, film, programme/program, series** ◊ *a ~ film maker*

PREP. **in a/the ~** ◊ *There were some interesting interviews in the ~.* | **~ about, ~ on** ◊ *a ~ about identical twins*

dog *noun*

ADJ. **domestic, family, pet** | **stray** | **feral, wild** | **pedigree** *(esp. BrE)*, **pure-bred** *(esp. AmE)* | **mongrel** | **lap, toy** ◊ *The lady was kissing a little lap ~.* | **puppy** *(often figurative, esp. AmE)* ◊ *He looked at me with puppy-dog eyes.* | **faithful, friendly** | **good, well-behaved, well-trained** | **bad** ◊ *Bad ~! What are you doing there?* | **dangerous, fierce, savage, vicious** | **junkyard** *(AmE, figurative)* ◊ *election lawyers who are mean as junkyard ~s* | **mad, rabid** | **mangy** | **show** ◊ *Rex was a champion show ~.* | **working** | **bird** *(AmE)*, **gun, hound** *(AmE)*, **hunting** | **sled** | **guide, Seeing Eye dog™** *(AmE)* ◊ *The labrador is being trained to be a guide ~ for the blind.* | **police** | **bomb-sniffing** *(AmE)*, **cadaver** *(AmE)*, **drug-sniffing** *(AmE)*, **sniffer** *(esp. BrE)*, **tracker** ◊ *Sniffer ~s were used to find the drugs.* | **attack, fighting** | **guard** | **rescue** | **farm** | **top** *(often figurative)* ◊ *The team wanted to prove that they were top ~s in the region.*

... OF DOGS **pack**

VERB + DOG **have, keep, own** ◊ *The dog's owner was banned from keeping ~s for five years.* | **breed** ◊ *These ~s were bred to hunt small animals.* | **train** ◊ *He's trained his ~ to sit on the back of his bike.* | **feed** | **take for a walk, walk** ◊ *I'm just going to walk the ~.* | **pet** *(esp. AmE)*, **stroke** *(esp. BrE)* | **neuter, spay** *(esp. AmE)* ◊ *We didn't want puppies so we had the ~ neutered.* | **worm** ◊ *The stray ~s are wormed and treated with flea powder.* | **muzzle** | **destroy** *(esp. BrE)*, **put down, put to sleep** ◊ *A ~ that bit a five-year-old child was later destroyed.* ◊ *We recently had to put our ~ to sleep.*

DOG + VERB **bark, bay, howl, pant, whine** ◊ *The ~ barked loudly at the stranger.* | **growl, snarl** | **yap, yelp** ◊ *The little ~s were yapping at my ankles.* | **run, scamper, walk** | **bound, leap** ◊ *The ~ bounded up to me and started licking my hand.* | **roam (sth), wander (sth)** ◊ *Stray ~s roamed the streets at night.* | **attack sb/sth, go for sb/sth** ◊ *The ~ went for him and bit him twice on the leg.* | **bite sb/sth, snap** | **maul sb/sth, savage sb/sth** *(esp. BrE)* | **lick** | **chew sth, chew sth up, gnaw sth, gnaw at sth** ◊ *The ~ chewed up one of my shoes.* ◊ *A ~ was gnawing at an old bone.* | **sniff** ◊ *A ~ was sniffing around my heels.* | **prick up its ears, wag its tail** | **scratch** ◊ *The ~ was scratching at the door to be let in.* | **foul sth** *(BrE)* ◊ *Owners who allow their ~s to foul the footpath will be fined.*

DOG + NOUN **basket** | **biscuit, food** | **collar** | **lead** *(BrE)*, **leash** *(esp. AmE)* | **dirt** *(BrE)*, **excrement** *(formal)*, **faeces/feces** *(formal)*, **mess** *(BrE)*, **poo, turd** | **breeder, handler, lover, owner, trainer, walker** | **catcher, warden** ◊ *The ~ warden rounds up stray dogs and takes them to the pound until claimed.* | **fight** | **pound** | **show** | **racing** | **track** ◊ *Races have been held at this ~ track for seventy years.* | **park** *(AmE)*

dogma *noun*

ADJ. **old, traditional** | **current, prevailing** | **rigid** | **central** ◊ *the central ~ of molecular biology* | **party, political, religious** ◊ *The newspaper seeks to be independent of political ~.* | **Catholic, Christian, Marxist, etc.**

VERB + DOGMA **accept** | **challenge, question** ◊ *People are beginning to question the old ~s.* | **reject**

dole *noun (BrE)*

VERB + DOLE **claim, go on, sign on** ◊ *She lost her job and had to claim ~.* ◊ *As soon as he was made redundant, he signed on the ~.* | **draw, get** ◊ *The factory closure will mean another few hundred people drawing the ~.*

DOLE + NOUN **money** | **queue** ◊ *School-leavers were joining the ~ queue every day.* | **office**

PREP. **off the ~** ◊ *Many had come off the ~ and set up their own small businesses.* | **on the ~** ◊ *She was on the ~ for three years before she got a job.*

doll *noun*

ADJ. **little, tiny** | **china, paper, plastic, porcelain, rag, wooden** ◊ *a child playing with a rag ~* | **baby** | **mechanical** | **Russian** | **voodoo** *(often humorous)* ◊ *She'll be sticking pins in a voodoo ~ of her ex-boyfriend.* | **blow-up**

VERB + DOLL play with
DOLL + NOUN ~ house (usually *dollhouse*) (*AmE*), doll's house (*BrE*)

dollar *noun* → Note at CURRENCY

domain *noun*

ADJ. private, public | Internet
DOMAIN + NOUN name ◇ *Register a ~ name if you want people to find your website.* | registration
PREP. in a/the ~, within a/the ~ ◇ *This information is all in the public ~.* | outside a/the ~ ◇ *things that happen outside the ~ of the home*

dominance *noun*

ADJ. absolute, clear, complete, overwhelming, total | growing, increasing | cultural, economic, military, political, social, territorial | market | male | global, world ◇ *the competition for new markets and global ~*
VERB + DOMINANCE achieve, assert, assume, establish, exert, gain ◇ *The company soon achieved complete ~ in the marketplace.* | have, maintain, retain ◇ *The company is determined to maintain ~ in the market.* | demonstrate, show ◇ *He had to show his ~ by beating the other men.* | challenge, undermine ◇ *Ex-colonial countries began to challenge the cultural ~ of Europe.*
PREP. ~ in ◇ *American ~ in heavyweight boxing* | ~ over ◇ *He asserted his ~ over the other party members.*

dominant *adj.*

VERBS be, seem | become | remain
ADV. extremely, fairly, very, etc. | completely, fully, overwhelmingly, totally | increasingly | economically, politically, socially ◇ *the economically ~ class*

dominate *verb*

ADV. absolutely, completely, entirely, overwhelmingly, thoroughly, totally, utterly ◇ *She completely ~d the conversation.* | clearly | increasingly ◇ *His work increasingly ~s his life.* | largely

domination *noun*

ADJ. complete, total | cultural, economic, ideological, military, political | class, racial | male, patriarchal, white | colonial, foreign, imperial, Western | global, world | corporate | market
VERB + DOMINATION seek ◇ *countries that seek world ~* | achieve, establish ◇ *They achieved political ~ of the area.* | maintain, retain ◇ *The company has struggled to maintain its ~ in the marketplace.* | come under, fall under ◇ *The country came under foreign ~.* | be free from, be free of ◇ *The country longs to be free of colonial ~.*
PREP. under sb's ~ ◇ *The country is still under foreign ~.* | ~ over ◇ *their economic ~ over the Far East*

donation *noun*

ADJ. generous, large, sizeable, substantial | small | company, corporate | personal, private | public ◇ *The project is funded by public ~.* | anonymous | voluntary | charitable, political | campaign (*esp. AmE*) | cash, financial, monetary (*esp. AmE*) | tax-deductible | online | blood, egg, organ, sperm, etc.
VERB + DONATION give, make, send ◇ *He made a generous ~ to the charity.* | accept, get, receive, take | appeal for, ask for, solicit (*esp. AmE*) | collect | depend on, need, rely on
PREP. in ~s ◇ *The charity has received over $10 million in ~s.* | ~ to ◇ *a ~ to a charity* | ~ towards/toward ◇ *a ~ towards/toward the building of a new hospital*

donkey *noun*

VERB + DONKEY ride
DONKEY + VERB bray | graze

DONKEY + NOUN cart | ride (*esp. BrE*) | work (*figurative, esp. BrE*) ◇ *I've done all the ~ work (= the hard boring part of a job).*

donor *noun*

1 gives a part of their body

ADJ. blood, bone-marrow, egg, kidney, organ, sperm, etc. | potential, prospective | compatible, suitable ◇ *The operation will go ahead as soon as a suitable ~ can be found.* | healthy | living
DONOR + VERB donate sth, give sth ◇ *Donors give blood twice a year.*
DONOR + NOUN blood, egg, organ, sperm, etc. ◇ *Donor organs are constantly required for transplant operations.* | card ◇ *He carried a ~ card.*

2 gives money/goods

ADJ. wealthy | big, generous, large, major | anonymous ◇ *The charity received £50 000 from an anonymous ~.* | private | corporate | aid ◇ *Japan has been one of the country's biggest aid ~s.* | campaign (*esp. AmE*)
DONOR + VERB give sth, make a donation, pledge sth ◇ *Donors pledged a total of $1 000 million in relief aid.*
DONOR + NOUN country, government ◇ *loans from rich ~ countries to developing nations*

doom *noun*

ADJ. impending | certain
VERB + DOOM spell ◇ *Fuel shortages spelled the ~ of such huge gas-guzzling cars.*
PHRASES ~ and gloom ◇ *It's not all ~ and gloom and there is lots to look forward to.* | a feeling of ~, a sense of ~ ◇ *As I approached the exam room, I had a feeling of impending ~.* | meet your ~ ◇ *Prepare to meet your ~ (= die).* | seal sb's ~ ◇ *He sealed his own ~ by having an affair with another woman.*

doomed *adj.*

VERBS be, seem
ADV. inevitably | ultimately
PHRASES ~ to extinction ◇ *The species was ~ to extinction.* | ~ to failure ◇ *The project was ~ to failure from the start.*

door *noun*

ADJ. open | closed, shut | locked, unlocked | half-open ◇ *The ~ was half-open when we got there.* | back, front, rear, side ◇ *the back ~ of a house* ◇ *the rear ~ of a car* | entrance, main | inner, internal ◇ *The inner ~ leads to the safe and is always locked after 5 p.m.* | external, outer ◇ *All external ~s should be bolted top and bottom.* | big, great, heavy, huge, massive, solid, thick ◇ *She had trouble pushing the heavy ~ open.* | narrow, wide | iron, oak, steel, wooden, etc. | glazed | double, French (*esp. AmE*), patio ◇ *Go along the corridor and through the double ~s.* | screen (*esp. AmE*) | automatic, folding, revolving, sliding, swing (*BrE*), swinging (*AmE*) ◇ *He got stuck in a revolving ~.* ◇ *She pushed her way through the swing/swinging ~s.* | apartment (*esp. AmE*), bathroom, flat (*BrE*), kitchen, etc. | closet (*esp. AmE*), cupboard (*esp. BrE*), fridge, refrigerator | elevator (*AmE*), lift (*BrE*) | cubicle (*esp. BrE*), shower, stall (*AmE*) | barn, Dutch (*AmE*), stable | garage | car | driver's, passenger | stage ◇ *fire (= a heavy door used to prevent a fire from spreading in a building)* | trap (usually *trapdoor*) | magic, mysterious, secret
VERB + DOOR fling open, open, pull open, push open, throw open ◇ *He flung the ~ open and caught them stuffing a document back into a briefcase.* | try ◇ *I tried the ~ but it was locked.* | bang, close, shut, slam | pull closed, pull shut, pull to (*BrE*), push to (*BrE*), slam shut ◇ *He pulled the ~ shut.* | bar, bolt, lock ◇ *He arrived home to find the ~ barred.* ◇ *Remember to bolt the ~ before you go to bed.* | unbolt, unlatch (*esp. AmE*), unlock | keep closed, keep shut, leave closed, leave shut | leave on the latch (*BrE*) ◇ *I left the ~ on the latch so that I could sneak back in later.* | keep open, leave ajar, leave open, prop open ◇ *Someone had propped the fire ~ open with a pile of books.* | come in, go in | come out, go out, slip out of ◇ *He came in the side ~.* | approach,

head for | **bang on, knock at, knock on** ◇ *I banged on the ~ for several minutes but still couldn't wake them.* | **answer** ◇ *Go and answer the ~.* | **work** (*AmE*) ◇ *He was working the ~ at the event.* | **see sb to** | **break down, kick down, kick in** ◇ *They had to break the ~ down to get into the house.* | **block**

DOOR + VERB **creak** | **burst open, creak open, fly open, open, slide open, swing open** ◇ *The ~ burst open and a little boy ran in.* | **swing shut, swing to** (*BrE*) | **hang open** | **be ajar, stand ajar** ◇ *The ~ stood ajar so I could see a narrow section of the room.* | **be open, stand open** | **be jammed, be stuck** ◇ *The ~ was jammed shut.* | **bang, rattle, shake** ◇ *I was woken by a ~ banging in the wind.* ◇ *The ~ banged shut.* | **click shut, close, shut, slam, slam shut** | **connect sth** ◇ *The ~ connecting the two offices is kept locked.* | **lead to sth, open onto sth** ◇ *This ~ leads to my bedroom.* ◇ *The ~ opens onto a sunny terrace.* | **be set in the wall** ◇ *I stopped at a low oak ~ set in the stone wall.* | **bear sth, be marked sth** ◇ *The ~ bore a notice saying 'Private'.* ◇ *I went through the ~ marked 'Waiting Room'.*

DOOR + NOUN **handle, knob** (usually *doorknob*) | **frame, jamb** ◇ *He leaned against the ~ jamb.* | **furniture** (*BrE, technical*), **knocker** | **bell** (usually *doorbell*) | **chain** (*esp. BrE*), **latch** (*esp. AmE*), **lock** ◇ *Always put the ~ chain on.* | **key** | **mat** (usually *doormat*) | **stop** (usually *doorstop*) ◇ *This book would make a good doorstop.* | **opener** ◇ *automatic garage ~ openers* | **hinge** ◇ *a creaking ~ hinge* | **mirror** (*esp. BrE*), **panel** (on a car) ◇ *Parking is helped by wide ~ mirrors.* | **man** (usually *doorman*), **staff** | **prize** (= a prize for having the winning ticket handed out at the entrance to a social event) (*AmE*)

PREP. **around the ~, round the ~** (*esp. BrE*) ◇ *She stuck her head around the ~ to say goodbye.* | **at the ~** ◇ *There's someone at the ~.* | **in the ~** ◇ *He stood in the ~ for several minutes before deciding whether he'd stay.* | **through the ~** ◇ *He looked through the ~ to make sure the children were all right.* ◇ *She poked her head through the ~ to say goodbye.* | **~ into, ~ to** ◇ *the ~ into the backyard* | **~ between** ◇ *the ~ between the laundry room and the garage*

PHRASES **close, shut etc. the ~ behind you** ◇ *He banged the front ~ behind him as he left.* | **hold the ~ for sb, open the ~ for sb** | **blow a ~ off its hinges, pull a ~ off its hinges, take a ~ off its hinges** | **shut, slam, etc. the ~ in sb's face**

doorbell noun

VERB + DOORBELL **press, ring** | **answer** ◇ *He refused to answer the ~.* | **hear**

DOORBELL + VERB **chime, ring, sound** ◇ *I heard the ~ ring, and went to see who was there.*

PHRASES **a ring on the ~** (*esp. BrE*)

doorway noun

ADJ. **open** | **narrow** | **arched** | **shop** (*BrE*) ◇ *We sheltered in a shop ~.* | **bedroom, kitchen, etc.**

VERB + DOORWAY **block**

PREP. **in a/the ~** ◇ *A tall figure was standing in the ~.* | **through a/the ~** ◇ *We passed through the ~ and found ourselves in a walled garden.* | **~ into, ~ to** ◇ *the ~ to the living room*

dope noun

VERB + DOPE **smoke**

DOPE + NOUN **smoking** | **fiend** | **pedlar/peddler** (*esp. AmE*) | **test** (*esp. BrE*) ◇ *She was disqualified from competing for a year after failing a ~ test.*
→ Note at DRUG

dosage noun

ADJ. **high, low** | **correct, proper** (*esp. AmE*), **recommended** | **standard, usual** | **daily**

VERB + DOSAGE **give (sb), take** ◇ *Always take the correct ~.* | **increase** | **decrease, lower, reduce** | **adjust, change**

dose noun

ADJ. **high, large, massive, strong** ◇ *a strong ~ of painkillers* | **healthy, hefty** ◇ *The movie also contains a healthy ~ of comedy.* (*figurative*) | **low, small** | **correct, recommended** |

standard, usual | **double, full, single** | **maximum** | **cumulative** | **daily** | **fatal, lethal** ◇ *a lethal ~ of radiation*

VERB + DOSE **get, receive, take** ◇ *patients who receive high ~s of this drug* ◇ *I had forgotten to take my ~ of antibiotic.* | **administer, deliver, give sb** ◇ *The nurse will administer the correct ~.* ◇ *She needs to be given a daily ~ of the medicine.* | **prescribe** | **increase** | **reduce** | **adjust, change**

double verb

ADV. **more than** ◇ *Our profits have more than ~d this year.* | **almost, nearly, practically, virtually** ◇ *The price of houses has nearly ~d in the last ten years.* | **at least** | **effectively** | **approximately, roughly** | **easily** ◇ *This percentage could easily ~.*

PREP. **in** ◇ *The town has approximately ~d in size since 1960.* | **to** ◇ *The party almost ~d its share of the vote to 21%.*

double bass noun → Special page at MUSIC

doubt noun

ADJ. **considerable, grave, real, serious, severe** | **slight** ◇ *Without the slightest ~ this is a remarkable exhibition.* | **gnawing, lingering, nagging, niggling** | **growing, increasing** | **personal, private** ◇ *He made clear his own private ~s about it.* | **reasonable** ◇ *We have established beyond all reasonable ~ that the painting was indeed by Rembrandt.* ◇ *It is almost impossible to prove guilt beyond reasonable ~.* (*esp. BrE*) ◇ *It is almost impossible to prove guilt beyond a reasonable ~.* (*esp. AmE*) | **religious**

VERB + DOUBT **raise** ◇ *His failure to appear raises serious ~s as to his reliability.* | **entertain, feel, harbour/harbor, have** ◇ *She still felt the same niggling ~: was he really telling the truth?* | **express, voice** | **clear up, dispel, erase** (*esp. AmE*), **remove, resolve** ◇ *The announcement dispelled any ~s as to the prince's intentions.* | **cast, throw** ◇ *Her record of dismissals casts ~ on her ability to hold down a job.* | **call sth into, throw sth into** ◇ *The proposed development has been thrown into ~ by the decision.* | **be open to** ◇ *Their honesty is open to ~.*

DOUBT + VERB **appear, arise** ◇ *Doubts have arisen over the viability of the schedule.* | **exist** ◇ *Considerable ~ exists as to the precise origin of this custom.* | **persist, remain** | **surround sth** ◇ *From the start, ~s surrounded her claim to be the missing heiress.*

PREP. **beyond ~, beyond a ~, beyond all ~, beyond any ~** ◇ *The evidence proves beyond ~ that he is innocent.* | **in ~** ◇ *The arrangements for the event still seemed to be in ~.* ◇ *If in ~, consult your doctor.* | **without ~, without a ~** ◇ *She is without a ~ the best player I know.* | **~ about, ~ over** ◇ *Some committee members still had ~s about the plans.* | **~ in** ◇ *There is no ~ in my mind that this man is Tom.*

PHRASES **beyond a shadow of (a) ~, without a shadow of (a) ~** ◇ *This proves without a shadow of ~ that we were right.* | **have your ~s about sth** ◇ *They say they'll be here on time, but I have my ~s about that.* | **leave no, little, some, etc. ~** ◇ *She leaves no ~ as to her view of Picasso's work.* | **there is little ~ (that)** ◇ *There is little ~ the documents are fake.*

doubt verb

ADV. **highly** (*esp. AmE*), **seriously, very much** ◇ *I never seriously ~ed his story.* | **privately** ◇ *Lee privately ~ed the truth of this statement.*

PHRASES **not ~ sth for a moment, second, etc.** ◇ *I didn't ~ for a second that she was telling the truth.*

doubtful adj.

1 feeling doubt

VERBS **be, feel, look, seem, sound** ◇ *Eric was far from sure and Marion looked ~.* | **become** | **remain**

ADV. **extremely, fairly, very, etc.** | **a little, slightly, etc.**

PREP. **about** ◇ *She was rather ~ about the wisdom of eating the seafood.*

2 unlikely

VERBS **be, look, seem | remain**
ADV. **extremely, fairly, very,** etc. | **highly** ◇ *Even if we could go, which is highly ~, John wouldn't be able to come with us.* | **increasingly | a little, slightly,** etc.

dough *noun*

ADJ. **firm | soft | smooth | sticky | bread, cookie** (*esp. AmE*), **pastry** (*esp. AmE*), **pizza,** etc.
... OF DOUGH **ball, lump, piece**
VERB + DOUGH **make | knead, shape** ◇ *Knead the ~ lightly, then shape it into a round loaf.* | **roll out, turn out** ◇ *Turn the ~ out onto a lightly floured surface.*
DOUGH + VERB **rise** ◇ *Leave the ~ to rise.*

downfall *noun*

ADJ. **eventual, ultimate | dramatic, tragic**
VERB + DOWNFALL **bring about, cause, lead to** ◇ *a scandal that brought about his ~* | **contribute to, hasten** ◇ *The failure of this plan contributed to her eventual ~.* | **plot** ◇ *They were found guilty of plotting the ~ of the government.*
DOWNFALL + VERB **come** ◇ *The movement's ~ came with the failed coup d'état.*
PHRASES **be sb's ~** ◇ *His greed was eventually his ~.*

downpour *noun*

ADJ. **heavy, torrential | relentless, steady | sudden | tropical**
PREP. **in** ◇ *We got caught in a torrential ~.*
PHRASES **a ~ of rain**

downturn *noun*

ADJ. **serious, severe, sharp, significant | mild, slight | economic, market | global | cyclical**
VERB + DOWNTURN **experience, suffer, take** ◇ *The building industry is experiencing a severe ~ in its workload.* | **survive, weather | see, witness**
PREP. **~ in** ◇ *The 1990s witnessed a sharp ~ in the party's fortunes.* | **~ of** ◇ *a sharp ~ of the economy*

doze *noun*

ADJ. **light**
VERB + DOZE **have** ◇ *She had a little ~ after lunch.* | **drift into, fall into, slip into** (*esp. AmE*) ◇ *Sitting in an armchair in front of the fire, I soon fell into a ~.*

draft *noun*

1 rough/early version of a written document

ADJ. **early, first, initial, original, preliminary | rough, working | revised | final**
VERB + DRAFT **draw up, prepare, produce, write** ◇ *She produced an initial ~ of her plans.* | **complete, finish** ◇ *I finished the first ~ in late August 2007.* | **send, submit** ◇ *I sent an early ~ to an agent.* ◇ *The students were invited to submit ~s for feedback.* | **review** ◇ *He reviewed an earlier ~ of this manuscript.* | **approve** ◇ *The preliminary ~ of the agreement has been approved.* | **issue, publish, release**
DRAFT + NOUN **agreement, bill, budget, constitution, contract, document, letter, report, treaty | law, legislation | plan, proposal**
PREP. **in a/the ~** ◇ *These details were not included in the preliminary ~.*
PHRASES **in ~ form** (*esp. BrE*) ◇ *The document is still in ~ form.*

2 the draft (*esp. AmE*) **order to serve in the armed forces**
→ See also CONSCRIPTION

ADJ. **military**
VERB + THE DRAFT **avoid, dodge | oppose, support | bring back, reinstate**

3 (*AmE*) **current of air** → See DRAUGHT

draft (*also* draught *esp. in BrE*) *verb*

ADV. **carefully, properly** (*esp. BrE*), **well | badly, poorly** ◇ *Some of the clauses in the contract had been very poorly ~ed.* | **originally** ◇ *The bill as originally ~ed would have made the tobacco companies a lot more vulnerable to lawsuits.* | **hastily, quickly** ◇ *hastily ~ed pieces of legislation*

drain *noun*

1 pipe/hole that dirty water goes down

ADJ. **blocked** (*esp. BrE*), **clogged** (*AmE*) **| storm**
VERB + DRAIN **block** (*esp. BrE*), **clog** (*AmE*) **| clear, unblock** (*BrE*), **unclog** (*AmE*) **| lay** ◇ *They were busy laying the ~s for the new houses.*
DRAIN + NOUN **cleaner** ◇ *a bottle of ~ cleaner*

2 sth that uses up time/money/resources

ADJ. **heavy, major, serious | emotional, energy | cash, financial | brain** ◇ *scientists joining the brain ~ (= moving to a country where they can work in better conditions and earn more)*
PREP. **~ on** ◇ *These losses have been a major ~ on the company's resources.*

drain *verb*

1 make sth empty/dry

ADV. **thoroughly, well** ◇ *Remove the artichokes, ~ thoroughly and allow to cool.* ◇ *well-drained soil* | **poorly | quickly, slowly | away, out** ◇ *The water quickly ~ed away down the sink.* ◇ *The surgeon ~s out any excess fluid.*
PREP. **out of** ◇ *The blood ~s out of the body.*

2 make sb/sth weaker, poorer, etc.

ADV. **completely, totally, utterly | emotionally, mentally, physically | away** ◇ *The country's coal reserves are being ~ed away.*
PREP. **of** ◇ *His voice was utterly ~ed of emotion.* | **out of** ◇ *Her energy seemed to ~ out of her.*
PHRASES **be ~ed, feel ~ed** ◇ *Sue felt exhausted and emotionally ~ed.*

drama *noun*

1 play for the theatre/theater, etc.; **plays**

ADJ. **compelling, powerful | gritty, hard-hitting** ◇ *a gritty police ~* | **classical, contemporary, modern | daytime, prime-time** (*both esp. AmE*) **| hour-long, one-hour,** etc. ◇ *She stars in a new one-hour ~ about a woman judge.* | **two-part, four-part,** etc. (*all esp. BrE*) **| comedy** (*esp. BrE*), **musical | radio, television, TV | costume, historical, period | epic, tragic | Greek, Jacobean,** etc. **| courtroom, crime, hospital, medical, police** ◇ *Millions follow this hospital ~ twice a week.* | **psychological | domestic, family** ◇ *The movie is a heart-warming family ~.* | **ensemble | romantic | teen**
VERB + DRAMA **write** ◇ *It is very difficult to write good ~.* | **create, produce, stage** ◇ *the first episode of a new police ~ produced for television* | **watch**
DRAMA + NOUN **production | serial** (*BrE*), **series | festival | critic** ◇ *the ~ critic for the Times* | **class, club, department, school, training | teacher | major** (*AmE*), **student** ◇ *He's a ~ major at Howard University.*
PREP. **in a/the ~** ◇ *the actors in a ~* | **~ about** ◇ *a powerful television ~ about city life*
→ Note at SUBJECT

2 exciting event

ADJ. **human | real-life** ◇ *The actor was involved in a real-life ~ when he was held up at gunpoint last night.*
DRAMA + VERB **play out, unfold** ◇ *a collection of people watching the ~ unfold outside the nightclub*

3 excitement

ADJ. **high | human** ◇ *Art should deal with the human ~ and tragedy of everyday life.*
... OF DRAMA **touch** ◇ *The argument added a touch of ~ to an otherwise dull day.*

VERB + DRAMA **be full of** ◊ *The afternoon was full of ~ and excitement.* | **add, heighten** ◊ *The arrival of the police heightened the ~ further.*
DRAMA + VERB **surround sth** ◊ *The media loved all the ~ surrounding their divorce.*
DRAMA + NOUN **queen** (= someone who makes situations seem more serious than they really are)
PHRASES **a moment of ~**

dramatic *adj.*

VERBS **be, sound**
ADV. **extremely, fairly, very, etc.** | **highly, intensely** | **especially, particularly** | **overly** ◊ *I don't want to sound overly ~, but it changed my life.* | **suitably** ◊ *Her entrance was accompanied by suitably ~ music.*

drape (AmE also drapery) *noun (esp. AmE)* → See also CURTAIN

ADJ. **heavy, thick** | **floral** | **silk, velvet, etc.** | **hanging**
VERB + DRAPE **close, draw, pull** ◊ *The heavy ~s were drawn shut.* | **open, pull back**
DRAPE + VERB **hang** | **cover**

drape *verb*

ADV. **casually, loosely** | **elegantly**
PREP. **across, over** | **around, round** (*esp. BrE*) ◊ *He sat with his arm ~d casually around her shoulders.*
PHRASES **be ~d in sth, be ~d with sth** ◊ *The body was ~d in a blanket.*

draught (BrE) (AmE draft) *noun*

ADJ. **cold, icy** ◊ *A cold ~ of air blew in from the open window.*
VERB + DRAUGHT/DRAFT **create** | **prevent**
DRAUGHT/DRAFT + VERB **blow, come, whistle** ◊ *a ~ coming under the door*
DRAUGHT + NOUN **excluder** (*BrE*) ◊ *Fit ~ excluders to the bottoms of doors.*
PREP. **~ from** ◊ *the ~ from the window*
PHRASES **a ~ of air**

draught *verb (esp. BrE)* → See DRAFT

draw *noun (esp. BrE)*

ADJ. **goalless, scoreless** | **one-all, three-three, etc.** | **creditable, honorable** | **disappointing** | **consecutive, successive** ◊ *Hull City were held to a second successive ~.*
VERB + DRAW **end in** ◊ *The game ended in a two-all ~.* | **earn, get, secure, snatch** | **force, hold sb to** ◊ *San Marino held them to a goalless ~.*
PREP. **~ against, ~ with** ◊ *their 1–1 ~ with United*

draw *verb*

1 make pictures

ADV. **accurately, beautifully, carefully, clearly, well** ◊ *a beautifully drawn picture* ◊ *He ~s very well.* | **badly, crudely, quickly, roughly** ◊ *a crudely drawn child's face*

2 pull

ADV. **half, partly** ◊ *The blinds were partly drawn.* | **back** ◊ *She drew back the curtains and let the sunlight in.* | **aside, to one side** ◊ *I tried to ~ him aside so I could talk to him in private.* | **away** ◊ *He approached her but she drew away.* | **up** ◊ *She sat with her legs drawn up on the sofa.* | **out** ◊ *The ducts ~ out stale air.* | **together** (*figurative*) ◊ *The project enables students to ~ together their skills and experience.* | **randomly** ◊ *We drew names randomly out of a hat.*
PREP. **onto** ◊ *She drew me onto the balcony* | **out of** ◊ *He drew the cork out of the bottle.* | **to** ◊ *I drew my chair up to the fire.* | **towards/toward**

3 attract

ADV. **immediately** | **inevitably, inexorably, irresistibly** ◊ *Her gaze was drawn irresistibly to the scene outside.* | **instinctively** ◊ *Animals are instinctively drawn to those who like them.* | **increasingly** ◊ *He was increasingly drawn to the idea of making short films.*

PREP. **from** ◊ *The plan has drawn interest from local businessmen.* | **to** ◊ *We asked the surfing champion what first drew him to the sport.*
PHR V **draw on/upon sth**
ADV. **heavily** ◊ *The novelist ~s heavily on her personal experiences.*
draw sth up
ADV. **professionally, properly** ◊ *Make sure the contract is properly drawn up.*

drawback *noun*

ADJ. **big, main, major, real, serious, significant** | **minor, slight** | **obvious** | **possible, potential**
VERB + DRAWBACK **have (its, their, etc.), suffer from** ◊ *This strategy has its ~s.* ◊ *The system suffers from two major ~s.* | **overcome** ◊ *We have to find ways of overcoming these ~s.* | **outweigh** ◊ *The benefits of this system far outweigh the ~s.*
PREP. **~ of** ◊ *The ~s of this method are obvious.* | **~ to** ◊ *Bad weather was the main ~ to camping in the north.* | **~ with** ◊ *The one big ~ with the plan was its high cost.*

drawer *noun*

ADJ. **deep, shallow** ◊ *a desk with two deep ~s on either side* | **open** | **locked** | **bottom, middle, top** | **kitchen** | **bedside table, bureau** (*esp. AmE*), **desk, dresser** (*esp. AmE*), **night-stand** (*AmE*) | **file-cabinet** (*AmE*), **filing-cabinet** (*esp. BrE*) | **cutlery** (*BrE*), **silverware** (*AmE*) | **cash, file** (*AmE*), **junk** (*esp. AmE*) | **sock, underwear** | **secret**
VERB + DRAWER **open, pull open, pull out, slide open** ◊ *She pulled open the second ~ down to find the money had gone.* | **close, push in, push shut, shut, slam shut** ◊ *He pushed the ~ shut with a bang.* | **lock, unlock** | **reach into** ◊ *She reached into the ~ and found the key to the safe.* | **go through, look through, rummage in, rummage through, search** ◊ *What do you think you are doing, rummaging through my ~s?* | **empty** | **clean out** (*esp. AmE*), **organize**
PREP. **from a/the ~, out of a/the ~** ◊ *She took the gun from the ~.* | **in a/the ~** ◊ *He put the letters in the ~.*

drawing *noun*

ADJ. **chalk, charcoal, ink, line, pastel, pencil** ◊ *a set of charcoal ~s by a local artist* | **black-and-white** | **original, preliminary, preparatory** ◊ *The bridge looked quite different from the architect's original ~s.* | **scale** ◊ *a scale ~ of a jet* | **architectural, engineering, technical, working** ◊ *a working ~ of the proposed power station* | **life** ◊ *He earned money as a model for life-drawing classes.*
VERB + DRAWING **create, do, execute, make** ◊ *He made a ~ of how the Roman villa must have looked.*
DRAWING + VERB **depict sth, show sth** ◊ *The ~ shows the Market Square.* | **accompany sth, illustrate sth** ◊ *Beautiful line ~s accompany the text.*
DRAWING + NOUN **board** ◊ *These days, designers spend more time at the computer than at the ~ board.*
PREP. **in a/the ~** ◊ *The door opened onto a courtyard, as shown in the ~.* | **~ by** ◊ *a pencil ~ by Picasso*
→ Note at ART

drawl *noun*

ADJ. **deep, soft** | **languorous, lazy, slow** | **slight** | **nasal** | **Southern, Texan, etc.**
VERB + DRAWL **have** ◊ *He had a slow, Southern ~.*
PHRASES **in a ~** ◊ *'Howdy, pardner,' he said in his slow Texan ~.* | **with a ~** ◊ *She spoke with a soft Southern ~.*

drawl *verb*

ADV. **lazily, slowly, softly** ◊ *'Come in!' he ~ed softly.* | **sarcastically, sardonically**

dread *noun*

ADJ. **great, mortal** ◊ *Her greatest ~ was that she would lose*

her job. | existential, nameless (both esp. AmE) | constant | creeping, growing, mounting
VERB + DREAD feel, have ◇ the ~ she felt at the thought of meeting him again ◇ He had a ~ of hospitals. | live in ◇ He lived in constant ~ that one day he might be found out. | fill sb with ◇ Does the thought of flying fill you with ~?
PREP. in ~ of ◇ After her shoplifting spree she lived in mortal ~ of being found out. | ~ of ◇ her ~ of discovery
PHRASES a feeling of ~, a sense of ~

dread verb

ADV. absolutely ◇ I have to go to the dentist tomorrow and I'm absolutely ~ing it! | rather | always ◇ He had always ~ed being singled out.

dreadful adj.

VERBS be, feel, look, smell, sound, taste ◇ Poor thing! You look absolutely ~! (= very ill)
ADV. really ◇ I feel really ~ about letting you down. | absolutely, quite (BrE), truly ◇ a truly ~ hat | pretty, rather | just, simply
PREP. for ◇ It must have been ~ for you!

dream noun

1 while you are asleep

ADJ. awful, bad, disturbing, horrible, terrible ◇ a child frightened by a bad ~ | bizarre, odd, strange, weird | fevered | pleasant | lucid, vivid, erotic, wet | recurrent, recurring | prophetic ◇ He had a prophetic ~ about a train crash the night before the disaster. | day (usually day-dream), waking ◇ His waking ~ was rudely interrupted by the telephone.
VERB + DREAM dream, have ◇ She fell asleep and dreamed strange ~s. ◇ I had a very disturbing ~ last night. | awake from, wake from | be awoken from, be woken from ◇ I was awoken from my ~ by a knock at the door. | remember ◇ I hardly ever remember my ~s. | interpret | haunt, invade, plague ◇ Images of the crash still haunted his ~s years later.
DREAM + VERB come true ◇ I hope my ~ about prison won't come true! | haunt sb, plague sb ◇ vivid ~s that regularly haunted him ◇ She is plagued by strange ~s. | fade, fade away ◇ She opened her eyes and the ~ faded.
DREAM + NOUN interpretation
PREP. in a/the ~ ◇ In her ~, she was on board a ship heading for America. | ~ about ◇ a recurrent ~ about being late for an exam
PHRASES as (if) in a ~ ◇ She found herself standing in front of the crowded hall and making her speech, as if in a ~. | sweet ~s ◇ 'Sweet ~s!' she said, turning off the light.

2 sth that you want very much to happen

ADJ. big, great ◇ Her biggest ~ was to become a singer. | lifelong, long-held ◇ her lifelong ~ of swimming with dolphins | boyhood, childhood | distant ◇ His plans to travel the world now seemed like a distant ~. | crazy, impossible ◇ Peace no longer seemed an impossible ~. | pipe ◇ He spent his life chasing pipe ~s (= fantasies that are unlikely to come true). | unfulfilled, unrealized | broken, shattered | utopian | romantic ◇ She had this romantic ~ of living in a windmill.
VERB + DREAM cherish, have ◇ the great utopian ~ that they have cherished for so long | achieve, fulfil/fulfill, live, live out, realize ◇ At last his ~s were fulfilled. | chase, follow, pursue ◇ He left his job to pursue his ~ of opening a restaurant. | abandon ◇ He never abandoned his ~ of finding his real mother. | crush, shatter ◇ The injury shattered her ~ of running in the Olympics. | keep alive ◇ The victory keeps San Marino's ~ of a World Cup place alive.
DREAM + VERB come true ◇ He put all his efforts into making his ~ of a united country come true. | turn into a nightmare, turn sour (esp. BrE) ◇ Their ~ turned into a nightmare as the ship began to sink.
DREAM + NOUN holiday (BrE), home, house, job, vacation

(AmE) ◇ After Betty retired, she designed and built her ~ house. | land (usually dreamland) (esp. BrE), world ◇ The government is living in a ~ world if they think voters will agree to higher taxes.
PREP. ~ of ◇ their ~ of a fairer world
PHRASES the American ~ ◇ Born a poor boy in Kansas, he lived the American ~ as a successful inventor. | the ... of sb's ~s ◇ the house of her ~s ◇ the girl of his ~s | beyond sb's wildest ~s ◇ They achieved a success beyond their wildest ~s. | a ~ come true ◇ Their cruise in the Bahamas was a ~ come true. | hopes and ~s ◇ She confided in him all her hopes and ~s. | live the ~ ◇ At last I feel I'm living the ~.

dream verb

ADV. always ◇ As a child she always ~ed of working with animals. | often ◇ He often ~ed of owning a house right on the beach. | never ◇ I never ~ed I'd actually get the job. | still | long ◇ People have long ~ed of an egalitarian society. | just, only ◇ It was the kind of trip most of us can only ~ about.
VERB + DREAM wouldn't ◇ I wouldn't ~ of going without you (= I would never go without you).
PREP. about, of

dress noun

1 piece of clothing

ADJ. beautiful, elegant, gorgeous | plain, simple ◇ She looked elegant in a simple black ~. | ankle-length, floor-length, full-length, knee-length, long | short | skimpy | clinging, figure-hugging (esp. BrE), skintight, tight, tight-fitting | loose-fitting, shapeless | backless, halter (AmE), low-cut, off-the-shoulder, revealing, sleeveless, strapless | flowing, silky, slinky | floral, flowered (esp. AmE), flowery, frilly, sequinned/sequined, sparkly | cotton, silk, etc. | designer, fancy (AmE) | ball, cocktail, evening, party, prom (AmE) | bridesmaid (AmE), bridesmaid's (esp. BrE), wedding | communion | Easter | maternity
VERB + DRESS unzip, zip, zip up | hitch up, lift, pull up ◇ She hitched up her long ~ so it wouldn't drag in the mud. | pull down | smooth, straighten ◇ She sat down and smoothed her ~ over her legs. | go with, match ◇ The hat went with her new ~ wonderfully. | rip, ruin, tear
DRESS + NOUN shop | designer | size
PREP. in a/the ~ ◇ She appeared in a slinky satin ~.
→ Special page at CLOTHES

2 clothes for either men or women

ADJ. ceremonial, formal | casual, informal | evening | modern | period | national, traditional ◇ He was wearing traditional Scottish ~. | fancy (= clothes that make you appear to be a different character) (BrE) ◇ the costumes worn at the fancy-dress ball | battle, military | civilian
DRESS + NOUN code ◇ The club has a strict ~ code. | sense ◇ He has poor ~ sense. | coat (AmE), pants (AmE), shirt, shoes (AmE), suit | uniform ◇ in full ~ uniform
PREP. in ... ~ ◇ a performance of 'Hamlet' in modern ~

dress verb

1 put on clothes

ADV. hurriedly, quickly | slowly | carefully
PREP. in ◇ He ~ed carefully in the brown suit he had been married in.
PHRASES be fully ~ed ◇ She lay down on her bed, fully ~ed. | get ~ed ◇ She got ~ed quickly.

2 wear clothes

ADV. beautifully, elegantly, fashionably, immaculately, impeccably, nattily (old-fashioned), neatly, nicely, smartly (esp. BrE), stylishly, well ◇ Susan always ~es very elegantly. ◇ She was determined to be the best ~ed woman at the wedding. | badly, poorly, shabbily | appropriately, suitably | inappropriately | decently, modestly, properly | conservatively, plainly, simply, soberly | professionally (esp. AmE) ◇ She was ~ed professionally in a business suit. | formally | casually | expensively | flamboyantly, osten-tatiously, richly | provocatively, scantily | alike, identically, similarly ◇ The twins were ~ed identically. | differently ◇ She began to act and ~ differently.

PREP. **as** ◊ *The waiters were ~ed as clowns.* | **for** ◊ *I have to ~ smartly for work.* | **in** ◊ *The women were all ~ed in blue skirts and white blouses.* | **like** ◊ *Why does she always ~ like a boy?*
PHRASES **~ to the nines** (*esp. AmE*), **~ up to the nines** (*BrE*) ◊ *She always ~es (up) to the nines.*

dressing *noun*

1 covering put on a wound

ADJ. **clean, fresh, sterile** | **surgical, wound** | **gauze**
VERB + DRESSING **apply, put on** ◊ *Clean the wound and put on a fresh ~.* | **change** | **remove**

2 sauce for food, esp. salads

ADJ. **creamy** | **home-made** | **fat-free, low-fat** (*both esp. AmE*) | **French, salad, vinaigrette** | **blue cheese, Ranch™** (*AmE*), **Thousand Island, etc.**
PREP. **in a ~, with a ~** ◊ *salad with a vinaigrette ~* | **~ for** ◊ *a herb ~ for fish*

drift *verb*

1 be carried along by the wind/water

ADV. **slowly** | **helplessly** ◊ *Cold and hungry, they ~ed helplessly closer to the Arctic.* | **downstream** ◊ *The boat ~ed slowly downstream.* | **along, back, down, out, up, etc.** ◊ *Smoke ~ed up from the campfire.*
PREP. **from, to, towards/toward, etc.** ◊ *They were ~ing out to sea.* | **with** ◊ *We ~ed with the current.*

2 move slowly/without purpose

ADV. **aimlessly** | **gradually, slowly** ◊ *Her gaze gradually ~ed to the bookshelf.* | **quietly, silently** | **eventually, finally** ◊ *He finally ~ed back to his home town.* | **about** (*esp. BrE*), **around, back, down, round** (*esp. BrE*), **up, etc.** ◊ *Voices ~ed up through the floorboards.* | **apart, away, off** ◊ *Over the years the two friends ~ed apart.*
VERB + DRIFT **begin to** | **seem to** | **allow sth to, let sth to** ◊ *He allowed his thoughts to ~ back to his conversation with Carrie.*
PREP. **about** (*BrE*), **around, round** (*esp. BrE*) ◊ *He spent the day ~ing aimlessly around the house.* | **across** ◊ *She ~ed across the room to where we were standing.* | **between** ◊ *She began to ~ between sleep and wakefulness.* | **from** ◊ *We seem to be ~ing away from the point.* | **into** ◊ *He ~ed into teaching, but never really enjoyed it.* | **out of** ◊ *He ~ed in and out of consciousness.*

PHR V **drift off**
ADV. **gradually, slowly**
PREP. **into** ◊ *He ~ed off into a deep slumber.*
PHRASES **~ off to sleep** ◊ *She closed her eyes and slowly ~ed off to sleep.*

drift *noun*

1 slow movement

ADJ. **gradual, slow** | **leftward, rightward** ◊ *He criticized the rightward ~ of the party.* | **continental**
PREP. **~ (away) from** ◊ *the ~ of people away from rural areas into urban slums* | **~ (back) to** ◊ *As the strike went on, there was a gradual ~ back to work.* | **~ into** ◊ *his ~ into crime* | **~ towards/toward**

2 general meaning of sth

ADJ. **general, main**
VERB + DRIFT **catch, follow, get** ◊ *I didn't follow the speech exactly, but I caught the main ~ of what was being said.*

3 pile of snow/sand made by the wind

ADJ. **deep** | **sand, snow** (usually ***snowdrift***)

drink *noun*

ADJ. **cold, cool, iced, refreshing** ◊ *I could do with a nice cool ~.* | **hot, warm** | **milky** (*BrE*) | **sugary, sweet** | **fruit, fruity** (*AmE*) | **carbonated, fizzy** (*BrE*) | **non-alcoholic, soft** | **alcoholic** | **stiff, strong** (= with a lot of alcohol in it) | **mixed** (*AmE*) | **diet, low-calorie** | **energy, sports** (*esp. AmE*) | **caffeinated** | **long** ◊ *She took a long ~ of cold water.* | **quiet** (*esp. BrE*) | **quick** | **after-dinner, pre-dinner** ◊ *They*

invited us for pre-dinner ~s. | **early-evening, lunchtime** (*esp. BrE*) | **celebratory** | **farewell** (*esp. BrE*) | **welcome** (*esp. BrE*) ◊ *You will be offered a welcome ~ on arrival at the hotel.* | **free** ◊ *The entrance charge includes a free ~.*
... OF DRINKS **round** ◊ *We ordered a round of ~s while waiting for a table.*
VERB + DRINK **consume** (*formal*), **drink, have** ◊ *I'll just drink my ~ then we can go.* ◊ *She had a hot ~ and went to bed.* | **enjoy** ◊ *They were enjoying a ~ by the pool.* | **want** ◊ *Do you want a ~?* | **need** ◊ *I really need a cold ~.* | **sip** | **down, finish, knock back** ◊ *He knocked back his ~ in one go and ordered another one.* | **take** ◊ *He took a ~ of his beer and sat down.* | **go for** (*BrE*), **go out for** ◊ *Would you like to go out for a ~ after work?* | **buy (sb), get (sb), grab, offer (sb), order (sb)** ◊ *Can I buy you a ~?* ◊ *Let's go grab a ~.* | **pour (sb), serve (sb)** ◊ *He poured himself a stiff ~ to calm his nerves.* | **make, mix** ◊ *He taught her how to mix ~s.* | **refill** ◊ *She went around refilling everyone's ~s.* | **spill** ◊ *Some idiot spilled my ~.* | **spike** ◊ *The robbers spiked his ~ before taking his wallet and passport.* | **drive sb to** ◊ *Her money problems drove her to ~* (= made her start drinking a lot of alcohol). | **turn to** (*esp. BrE*) ◊ *After his wife died, he turned to ~.*
DRINK + NOUN **~s party** ◊ *We've been invited to a ~s party.* | **~s cabinet** (*esp. BrE*) ◊ *She took a bottle from the ~s cabinet.* | **problem** (*BrE*) (***drinking problem*** in *AmE*) ◊ *She suspected her boss had a ~ problem.* | **bottle** ◊ *Plastic ~ bottles can be recycled.*
PREP. **in a/the ~** ◊ *Do you want ice in your ~?* | **~ of** ◊ *I'll have a ~ of milk, please.*
PHRASES **food and ~** (*esp. BrE*), **food and ~s** ◊ *a stand serving food and ~s*

drink *verb*

1 take liquid into the body

ADV. **greedily, thirstily** ◊ *I opened the can and drank thirstily.* | **deeply** | **down, up** ◊ *He filled a cup with water and drank it down in one gulp.* ◊ *Drink up, and let's go home.*
VERB + DRINK **find sth to, get yourself sth to, have sth to** ◊ *Go and get yourself something to eat and ~.*
PREP. **from** ◊ *He drank from a tumbler.* | **through** ◊ *She was ~ing soda through a straw.*
PHRASES **eat and ~, eat or ~** ◊ *Do you want something to eat or ~?*

2 drink alcohol

ADV. **excessively, heavily, to excess, too much** ◊ *He's been ~ing heavily since he lost his job.* | **in moderation, moderately, responsibly, sensibly** (*esp. BrE*) ◊ *ads that tell people to ~ responsibly* | **steadily** ◊ *She had been ~ing steadily since the early morning.* | **regularly** ◊ *She had never been someone who drank regularly.* | **alone** ◊ *I never ~ alone.* | **legally** ◊ *At that age they can legally ~ alcohol.*
PHRASES **~ and drive** ◊ *The campaign aims to persuade people not to ~ and drive.* | **~ like a fish** (= drink a lot) ◊ *Simon was ~ing like a fish that evening.* | **~ yourself to death** ◊ *He knew that he was probably ~ing himself to death.*

drinker *noun*

ADJ. **binge, hard, heavy** ◊ *This liver condition is common in heavy ~s.* | **light, moderate** | **habitual, regular** | **problem** ◊ *help for the families and friends of problem ~s* | **underage** ◊ *She claimed advertisers were targeting underage ~s.* | **social** ◊ *She is a social ~ only—she never drinks at home.* | **beer, coffee, tea, etc.** ◊ *I'm not a big tea ~.*

drinking *noun*

ADJ. **binge, excessive, heavy** ◊ *the health problems associated with heavy ~* | **moderate** | **teen** (*AmE*), **underage** ◊ *new measures aimed at preventing underage ~*
VERB + DRINKING **control, cut down on, limit, reduce** ◊ *His doctor had advised him to limit his ~.* | **stop**
DRINKING + NOUN **bout, session** | **buddy, companion**

drip noun

1 water dripping

ADJ. **slow, steady**
PREP. **~ of** ◇ *the steady ~ of water from the tap*

2 drop of water that falls down from sb/sth

VERB + DRIP **catch** ◇ *There were buckets to catch the ~s from the ceiling.*
DRIP + VERB **fall** ◇ *Drips fell from the roof of the cave.*
PREP. **~ from** ◇ *~s from the tap*

3 medical equipment

ADJ. **intravenous** (abbreviated to *IV*) | **morphine, saline**
VERB + DRIP **fix up, set up** | **be attached to, be on** ◇ *He is on a saline ~.* | **attach sb to, put sb on** | **take sb off** ◇ *He was taken off his ~ last night.*

drive noun

1 trip by car

ADJ. **long** | **easy, short** | **eight-hour, sixty-mile, etc.** | **leisurely** | **scenic** ◇ *It's one of the most scenic ~s in Europe.* | **test**
VERB + DRIVE **go for, take** ◇ *Let's go for a ~.*
DRIVE + NOUN **time** ◇ *The spots will run during ~ time radio.* ◇ *a housing development within a 30-minute ~ time from the airport*
PREP. **within a ~** ◇ *All my family live within an hour's ~.*
PHRASES **a … drive away** ◇ *The lakes are only a short ~ away.*

2 way a vehicle is moved

ADJ. **all-wheel** (*esp. AmE*), **four-wheel, front-wheel, rear-wheel** | **left-hand, right-hand** ◇ *Left-hand ~ cars make driving in Britain difficult.*

3 (*esp. BrE*) path/road outside a house → See also DRIVEWAY

ADJ. **winding** | **gravel** | **tree-lined** | **private** | **front**
DRIVE + VERB **lead to, lead up to** ◇ *He pulled into a long ~ leading up to a large villa.*
DRIVE + NOUN **block** ◇ *A number of police cars blocked the ~.*
PREP. **down the ~, in the ~, on the ~** ◇ *There was a car parked on the ~.* | **up the ~** ◇ *He walked up the front ~ of the vicarage.*

4 energy/determination

ADJ. **competitive** | **personal** | **narrative** ◇ *You need to inject more narrative ~ into the story.*
VERB + DRIVE **have** | **lack** ◇ *He lacks the competitive ~ needed to succeed.*

5 desire/need

ADJ. **basic, innate, inner, instinctive** (*esp. BrE*), **instinctual** (*esp. AmE*) | **human** | **creative** | **emotional, sex, sexual**

6 effort

ADJ. **big** | **relentless** | **national, nationwide** | **export, marketing, sales** | **cost-cutting, efficiency** (*both esp. BrE*) | **membership, organizing** (*AmE*), **petition** (*AmE*), **recruitment, voter-registration** (*esp. AmE*) | **fund** (*AmE*), **fundraising, pledge** (*AmE*) | **blood, clothing, food** (*all AmE*) ◇ *We organized a food ~ for the city's homeless shelters.* | **anti-corruption, anti-drug, etc.**
VERB + DRIVE **launch, organize** ◇ *We're going to launch a big recruitment ~ in the spring.* | **spearhead** ◇ *The Popular Front spearheaded the ~ for independence.*
PREP. **~ against** ◇ *a ~ against corruption* | **~ by** ◇ *the recent recruitment ~ by the police* | **~ for** ◇ *the country's ~ for modernization* | **~ towards/toward** ◇ *a ~ towards/toward higher safety standards*

7 computing

ADJ. **CD-ROM, disk, DVD, flash, floppy, hard, optical, zip** (*esp. AmE*) | **external, removable** | **built-in, internal**
VERB + DRIVE **format, reformat** | **defrag** (*informal*), **defragment** | **install** | **install sth on, install sth onto**
DRIVE + NOUN **bay**

8 in sports

ADJ. **powerful, strong, thunderous** (*BrE*) | **angled, crisp** (*both BrE*) | **scoring, touchdown** (*both AmE*) | **line** (in baseball) ◇ *He hit a line ~ straight at me.* | **left-foot, right-foot** (in football/soccer) ◇ *Cole scored with a thunderous left-foot ~.* | **backhand, forehand** (in tennis) ◇ *a forehand ~ down the line*
VERB + DRIVE **hit** | **hook, slice** (in golf)
→ Special page at SPORTS

drive verb

ADV. **fast, quickly** ◇ *You shouldn't ~ so fast!* ◇ *She drove quickly back to the office.* | **slowly** | **carefully, safely** | **recklessly** ◇ *He was arrested for driving recklessly.* | **around, away, back, off, on** ◇ *She got into the car and drove away.* | **home** ◇ *I'll ~ you home.*
PREP. **down, from, to** ◇ *We drove from Quebec to Ottawa.*
PHRASES **drink and ~**

driver noun

ADJ. **careful, good, safe** | **bad, dangerous, reckless** | **drunk, drunken, hit-and-run** (*esp. BrE*) ◇ *He was killed by a drunken ~.* | **experienced, inexperienced** | **learner** (*BrE*), **student** (*AmE*) | **designated** ◇ *I didn't drink because I was the designated ~.* | **car** ◇ *a campaign aimed at car ~s to promote walking and cycling* | **ambulance, bus, cab, coach** (*BrE*), **engine** (*BrE*), **limo** (*informal*), **lorry** (*BrE*), **tanker** (*esp. BrE*), **taxi, train, truck** (*esp. AmE*), **van** (*BrE*) | **F1** (*esp. BrE*), **race-car** (*AmE*), **racing, rally** (*esp. BrE*) | **back-seat** ◇ *I can't stand back-seat ~s.*
→ Note at JOB

driveway noun → See also DRIVE

ADJ. **winding** | **concrete, dirt** (*AmE*), **gravel** | **circular** (*esp. AmE*) | **large, long, steep**
VERB + DRIVEWAY **shovel** (*AmE*) ◇ *When it snows I have to shovel the ~.* | **line** ◇ *huge evergreens lining the ~* | **block** ◇ *A number of police cars blocked the ~.*
DRIVEWAY + VERB **lead to, lead up to** ◇ *a long ~ leading up to the winery*
PREP. **down the ~, in the ~, on the ~** ◇ *There was a car parked on the ~.* | **up the ~** ◇ *He walked up the ~ to the house.*

driving noun

ADJ. **good, safe** ◇ *a new campaign to promote safe ~* | **aggressive, bad, careless, dangerous, erratic, reckless** ◇ *She was charged with reckless ~.* | **drink** (*BrE*), **drunk** (*esp. AmE*), **drunken, impaired** (*AmE*) ◇ *Police stopped 30 motorists for drink ~ on New Year's Eve.* | **off-road** ◇ *Most people who own a Jeep never use it for off-road ~.*
VERB + DRIVING **do the** ◇ *I usually do the ~ and he navigates.* | **be banned from** (*esp. BrE*), **be disqualified from** (*BrE*) ◇ *He was banned from ~ for six months after failing a breath test.*
DRIVING + NOUN **conditions** | **seat** (*esp. BrE*) | **test** (see also *driving license*) | **instructor, lesson, school** | **experience, skill** | **offence/offense** (*esp. BrE*) | **charge** ◇ *There wasn't enough evidence for a dangerous ~ charge.* | **ban** (*esp. BrE*) ◇ *She was given a large fine and a two-year ~ ban.*
PHRASES **~ under the influence** (abbreviated to *DUI*), **~ while intoxicated** (abbreviated to *DWI*) (*both AmE*)

driving licence (*BrE*) (*AmE* driver's license) noun

ADJ. **valid** | **current** | **clean** (*esp. BrE*) | **full** (*BrE*) | **commercial** (*AmE*) | **provisional** (*BrE*)
VERB + DRIVING LICENCE/DRIVER'S LICENSE **have, hold** | **get, obtain** | **lose** | **issue**

drizzle noun

ADJ. **fine, light, slight** | **persistent, steady**
DRIZZLE + VERB **fall** ◇ *Light ~ fell all afternoon.*
PREP. **in a/the ~, through a/the ~** ◇ *We walked home through the ~.*

drone noun

ADJ. **low** | **distant** | **constant, continuous, steady** | **monotonous**

VERB + DRONE **hear**

PREP. **with a ~** ◇ *The planes flew overhead with a low ~.* | **~ of** ◇ *the continuous ~ of the engine*

drop noun

1 reduction

ADJ. **big, considerable, huge, large, massive** | **marked, noticeable, significant, substantial** | **dramatic, drastic, precipitous, rapid, severe, sharp, sudden** | **slight, small** | **steady** | **pressure, price, temperature** ◇ *A sudden temperature ~ could lead to a new ice age.*

VERB + DROP **experience, suffer** ◇ *The restaurant has suffered a big ~ in trade.* | **cause, lead to**

PREP. **~ in** ◇ *The glut of coffee led to a sharp ~ in prices.*

2 vertical distance down from a place

ADJ. **precipitous, sheer, steep, vertical** ◇ *The cliff plunged in a sheer ~ down to the beach.* | **long**

3 small round mass of liquid

ADJ. **single** ◇ *We mustn't waste a single ~.* | **tiny** ◇ *Tiny ~s of sweat appeared on her forehead.* | **tear** (usually **teardrop**) | **dew, rain** (usually **dewdrop, raindrop**)

VERB + DROP **wipe, wipe off** ◇ *She wiped a ~ of water from her chin.*

DROP + VERB **fall** ◇ *Great ~s of rain started to fall.* | **roll down sth**

PREP. **~ of** ◇ *Large ~s of sweat rolled down her face.*

drop verb

1 allow sth to fall

ADV. **accidentally** | **carelessly, casually** ◇ *He casually ~s the latest buzzwords into the conversation.* | **almost, nearly** | **instantly, promptly** ◇ *He saw Emma and promptly dropped his tray of drinks.*

PREP. **in, into, on, onto** ◇ *I accidentally dropped my glasses into the water.*

2 jump/move downwards

ADV. **heavily** | **gently, lightly** | **immediately, instantly, quickly** | **slowly** ◇ *He slowly dropped to the floor.* | **down, open** ◇ *Her mouth dropped open in disbelief.*

VERB + DROP **let sth** ◇ *She smiled and let her eyes ~ again.* | **be ready to** ◇ *I'm ready to ~* (= because I am so tired).

PREP. **into, onto, to** ◇ *The cheese ~s onto a conveyor underneath.*

PHRASES **~ like a stone** (*figurative*) ◇ *Her heart dropped like a stone at this news.*

3 become lower

ADV. **considerably, dramatically, drastically, significantly, substantially** ◇ *The price of oil has dropped significantly.* | **fast, rapidly** | **abruptly, precipitously, sharply, suddenly** | **steadily** | **slightly** | **further**

VERB + DROP **be likely to, be unlikely to** ◇ *Sales are likely to ~ further.*

PREP. **below** ◇ *The temperature rarely ~s below 40°.* | **by** ◇ *The price has dropped by 15%.* | **from, to** ◇ *The number of children in the class has dropped from 25 to 18.*

4 slope downwards

ADV. **sharply, steeply** | **away**

PREP. **into, to, towards/toward** ◇ *The land dropped steeply away into a small valley.*

5 no longer include sb in sth

ADV. **quietly** | **unceremoniously** ◇ *She was unceremoniously dropped by her record label.*

PREP. **from** ◇ *He has been quietly dropped from the England team.* | **in favour/favor of**

6 stop doing sth/be stopped

ADV. **quietly** ◇ *The subject was quietly dropped.* | **immediately, quickly, suddenly** ◇ *He suddenly dropped his habitual*

banter. | **eventually, finally** | **altogether** ◇ *When nobody volunteered, the idea was finally dropped altogether.*

VERB + DROP **let sth** ◇ *Can't we just let the matter ~?* | **agree to, decide to** ◇ *Both countries have agreed to ~ border controls.*

PREP. **in favour/favor of** ◇ *The formal grade of Geologist was dropped in favour/favor of Scientific Officer.*

drought noun

ADJ. **devastating, extreme, severe, terrible, worst** ◇ *It has been the worst ~ in the country's history.* | **long, prolonged** | **summer**

VERB + DROUGHT **have** ◇ *England has had several summer ~s in recent years.* | **cause** | **break, end** ◇ *A week of good rains has broken the ~.* | **survive, tolerate, withstand** ◇ *plants that can withstand ~*

DROUGHT + VERB **affect sth** ◇ *Large areas of Africa are affected by severe ~.*

DROUGHT + NOUN **conditions** | **resistance, tolerance** ◇ *crops that are chosen for their ~ tolerance*

PREP. **during a/the ~, in a/the ~** ◇ *Some of the newer plants in the garden died during the ~.*

PHRASES **in times of ~** | **months, years, etc. of ~**

NOTE

Illegal drugs

do… (*informal*), **experiment with…, take…, try…, use…** ◇ *She confessed to having experimented with drugs in her youth.*

be/get high on… ◇ *They committed the crime while high on drugs.*

be addicted to…, be dependent on…, be/get hooked on… (*informal*) ◇ *bodybuilders who are addicted to steroids*

be on… (*informal*) ◇ *He seemed to be on acid most of the time.*

be off…, come off… ◇ *He's tried several times to come off cocaine.*

possess… ◇ *She was arrested on charges of possessing narcotics.*

deal…, deal in…, sell…, smuggle…, supply…, traffic…, traffic in… ◇ *The country imposes the death penalty for trafficking in marijuana.*

seize… ◇ *The heroin seized has an estimated street value of £600 000.*

…abuse, …addiction, …consumption, …use ◇ *Heroin abuse has increased sharply.*

…habit (*informal*), **…problem** ◇ *She allegedly has a $500-a-day coke habit.*

…overdose ◇ *Heroin overdose is a major cause of death among users.*

…addict, …user ◇ *heroin users*

…dealer, …trafficker, …smuggler ◇ *a cocaine dealer*

…production, …smuggling, …trade, …trafficking ◇ *The authorities have been accused of active involvement in the narcotics trade.*

abuse of…, addiction to…, dependence on…, use of… ◇ *the use of cocaine*

trade in… ◇ *measures to combat the trade in narcotics*

---

drug noun

1 substance used as a medicine

ADJ. **powerful, strong** | **effective** | **safe** | **modern, new** | **wonder** ◇ *They're hailing it as the new wonder ~.* | **anti-cancer, anti-inflammatory, anti-malarial, antiviral, etc.** | **sedative** | **psychoactive** | **prescription** ◇ *You used to be able to buy this medicine over the counter, but it is now a prescription ~.* | **non-prescription, over-the-counter** | **generic** ◇ *We want to make it possible for African companies*

to produce cheaper generic ~s. | **brand-name** (*esp. AmE*) |
performance-enhancing ◇ *an athlete who tested positive for performance-enhancing ~s*
... OF DRUG **course, dose**
VERB + DRUG **be on, take** ◇ *Are you taking any other ~s at present?* | **prescribe (sb), put sb on** ◇ *The doctor put me on anti-inflammatory ~s.* | **give sb, treat sb with** | **administer, give sb** ◇ *The nurses came around to give the patients their ~s.* | **develop, manufacture, produce** ◇ *new ~s that have been developed recently* | **market** | **test** | **approve** ◇ *Some veterinary ~s are not approved for use in food-producing animals.* | **be resistant to, not respond to** ◇ *Some infections are now resistant to ~s.*
DRUG + VERB **cure sth, help sth, treat sth** ◇ *~s that help the growth of skin tissue*
DRUG + NOUN **company** | **prices** ◇ *Prescription ~ prices rose.*
PREP. **~ against** ◇ *a powerful ~ against tuberculosis* | **~ for** ◇ *He's taking ~s for depression.*

2 illegal substance

ADJ. **illegal, illicit** | **addictive** | **hallucinogenic, mood-altering, psychoactive, psychotropic** | **class A, dangerous, hard** ◇ *heroin and other hard ~s* | **soft** ◇ *Some addicts start on soft ~s.* | **designer** (= artificially produced) | **recreational** ◇ *They had a liberal attitude to recreational ~s.*
VERB + DRUG **inject** (See note for more verbs.)
DRUG + NOUN **baron, kingpin** (*esp. AmE*), **lord** | **pusher** | **cartel** | **misuse** | **screening, testing** ◇ *Some workplaces have introduced mandatory ~ screening.* | **~ offense** (*AmE*), **~s offence** (*BrE*) | **~ charge** (*esp. AmE*), **~s charge** (*BrE*) | **sentencing** (*esp. AmE*) ◇ *a review of the ~ sentencing laws to make penalties harsher* | **~ squad, ~s squad** (*both BrE*) | **~ czar** (*AmE*), **~s tsar** (*BrE*) ◇ *The new federal ~ czar claimed the nation was winning the war on drugs.* ◇ *the government's former ~s tsar* | **war** ◇ *the latest moves in the ~ war* (See note for more nouns.)
PHRASES **drink and ~s** (*BrE*), **~s and alcohol** (*esp. AmE*) ◇ *the dangers of ~s and alcohol*

drum noun

ADJ. **bass, bongo, electronic, kettle** (usually *kettledrum*), **kick, side, snare, steel** | **tribal** | **war** | **jungle**
VERB + DRUM **bang, beat, hit, pound** | **play**
DRUM + NOUN **kit, set** (*esp. AmE*) | **stick** (usually *drumstick*) | **machine, pad** | **beat** (usually *drumbeat*), **pattern, rhythm, roll, sound** | **music** | **work** | **solo** | **track** ◇ *He showed us how to program a ~ track.* | **loop** (= repeated pattern of sounds made by an electronic drum) | **circle** (= a group of people playing drums together) (*esp. AmE*) | **major, majorette** (*esp. BrE*)
PHRASES **a roll of ~s**
→ Special page at MUSIC

drunk adj.

VERBS **be, feel, look, sound** ◇ *I was beginning to feel very ~.* | **get** ◇ *Harry went out and got ~ last night.* | **get sb, make sb** ◇ *Andrew decided to try and get Sharon ~. ◇ The wine had made him ~.*
ADV. **extremely, fairly, very, etc.** | **blind, completely, roaring** ◇ *He came home blind ~, as usual.* | **almost** (*often figurative*) ◇ *She was almost ~ with all these new impressions.* | **half** ◇ *He was still half ~.* | **a little, slightly, etc.**
PREP. **with** (*figurative*) ◇ *~ with fatigue*
PHRASES **~ driver, ~ driving** (*both esp. AmE*) ◇ *She was arrested for ~ driving.*

dry verb

ADV. **carefully, completely, properly, thoroughly** ◇ *Wait until the paint has completely dried.* ◇ *Always ~ clothes thoroughly before you wear them again.* | **partially** | **quickly, rapidly** | **slowly** | **naturally** | **off, out** ◇ *We left the wood in the shed to ~ out.* | **overnight** ◇ *Allow the paper to ~ overnight.*

VERB + DRY **allow sth to, leave sth to, let sth** ◇ *It's best to let your hair ~ naturally.*
PHR V **dry up**

1 become empty of water
ADV. **completely** ◇ *It's been so hot this year that the pond has dried up completely.*

2 be no longer available
ADV. **completely** ◇ *Funds have completely dried up.* | **virtually**

dry adj.

VERBS **be, feel, look, seem** | **become, get, go, run** ◇ *Come into the warm and get ~, both of you.* ◇ *Ruth felt her mouth go ~.* ◇ *The wells in most villages in the region have run ~.* ◇ *Vaccine supplies started to run ~ as the flu outbreak reached epidemic proportions.* (*figurative*) | **keep, remain, stay** ◇ *We managed to keep ~ by huddling in a doorway.* ◇ *There is every prospect of the weather remaining ~ this week.* | **pat sb/sth, rub sb/sth, towel sb** ◇ *Rinse the mushrooms and pat ~. ◇ Towel yourself ~ before getting dressed.* | **bleed sb, milk sb, squeeze sb, suck sb** (*all figurative*) ◇ *The big corporations are bleeding some of these small countries ~* (= taking all their money). | **keep sth** ◇ *This type of wound is best kept ~ without a dressing.*
ADV. **extremely, fairly, very, etc.** | **bone, completely, perfectly, quite, thoroughly, totally** ◇ *The river was bone ~. ◇ Make sure the paint is thoroughly ~.* | **almost, nearly** | **barely, hardly, scarcely** (*often figurative*) ◇ *The ink was scarcely ~ on the agreement before fighting broke out again.* | **mainly, mostly** ◇ *The day will start bright and mainly ~.* | **little, slightly, etc.** | **reasonably** (*esp. BrE*), **relatively**

dubious adj.

VERBS **be, seem, sound** | **become**
ADV. **extremely, fairly, very, etc.** | **highly** ◇ *some highly ~ information* | **increasingly** | **a little, slightly, etc.** | **ethically, morally** ◇ *It sounds a morally ~ proposition.* | **constitutionally** (*esp. AmE*), **legally, politically**

duck noun

ADJ. **wild** | **long-tailed, mallard, etc.** | **plastic, rubber** ◇ *A rubber ~ floated in the bath.* | **roast, roasted** (*esp. AmE*)
... OF DUCKS **flock** ◇ *A flock of ~s bobbed near the shore.*
VERB + DUCK **feed** ◇ *Every afternoon they went to the park to feed the ~s.* | **hunt**
DUCK + VERB **quack** | **paddle, swim** ◇ *The ~s paddled furiously to grab the bread.* | **bob** | **dive** | **dabble** | **waddle** ◇ *A family of ~s waddled along the river bank.* | **nest** | **fly** | **migrate**
DUCK + NOUN **breast** ◇ *Slice the ~ breast and serve.* | **confit** | **egg** | **fat** ◇ *In a large saucepan, melt the ~ fat.* | **pond** | **blind** (= a small shelter from where you can watch ducks) (*AmE*) | **hunter, hunting** (*both AmE*) | **season** (= the time when ducks are hunted) (*AmE*)

duke noun → Note at PEER

dull adj.

VERBS **appear, be, look, seem, sound** | **become, get** ◇ *The work gets a little ~ at times.* | **make sth** ◇ *The long lectures made the afternoon ~.* | **find sth**
ADV. **extremely, fairly, very, etc.** | **deadly, dreadfully** (*esp. BrE*), **incredibly, mind-numbingly** ◇ *The movie was long and deadly ~.* | **a little, slightly, etc.** | **disappointingly**

dumb adj.

1 unable to speak
VERBS **be** | **become, be struck** ◇ *They were struck ~ with amazement.*
PREP. **with** ◇ *She sat there, ~ with rage.*
PHRASES **deaf and ~**

2 (*esp. AmE, informal*) **stupid**
VERBS **be, feel, look, seem, sound** ◇ *I'm sure my question sounded really ~.* | **act, play** ◇ *I decided to act ~.*

ADV. **extremely, fairly, very**, etc. | **incredibly** | **plain** (*informal*)

dump *verb*

ADV. **illegally, legally** ◊ *The company had illegally ~ed toxic waste.* | **unceremoniously** ◊ *They carried him down to the beach and ~ed him unceremoniously in the freezing water.* | **quickly** | **simply** ◊ *The waste is often simply ~ed overboard.* | **at sea** (*esp. BrE*), **in the ocean** (*esp. AmE*), **overboard** | **down** ◊ *He ~ed the boxes down in the kitchen.*

dump *noun*

ADJ. **garbage** (*esp. AmE*), **refuse, rubbish** (*BrE*), **trash** (*AmE*), **waste** ◊ *the cleaning up of a toxic waste ~.* | **nuclear** | **city, town**
DUMP + NOUN **site** ◊ *Local residents have organized a protest against the planned ~ site.* | **truck** (*AmE*)
PREP. **at a/the ~** ◊ *Radioactive waste has been found at the ~.* | **to a/the ~** ◊ *They took the mattress to the ~.* | **~ for** ◊ *a new ~ for nuclear waste*

duplicate *noun*

ADJ. **exact** ◊ *The ring was an exact ~ of her mother's ring.*
VERB + DUPLICATE **create, make** ◊ *We made a ~ of the key.*
PREP. **in ~** ◊ *The contract is prepared in ~, so that both parties can sign it.*

duplicate *verb*

ADV. **exactly** ◊ *The original experiment cannot be exactly ~d.* | **simply** ◊ *I wanted to avoid simply duplicating work that had already been done.* | **easily** (*esp. AmE*) ◊ *This is a natural look which you can easily ~ at home.*

duplication *noun*

ADJ. **unnecessary, wasteful** ◊ *Duties have been reassigned to avoid wasteful ~ of work.*
VERB + DUPLICATION **avoid, eliminate, prevent, reduce** ◊ *The new procedures should reduce ~ of medical care and treatment.*

duration *noun*

ADJ. **brief, short** | **limited** ◊ *Jobs were of limited ~ and usually paid low wages.* | **long, prolonged** | **indefinite** | **maximum, minimum** | **overall, total** ◊ *The overall ~ of the flight was 11 hours.* | **average, mean** | **expected, likely** ◊ *the expected ~ of the disease* | **desired, ideal**
VERB + DURATION **decrease, reduce, shorten** ◊ *Taking antibiotics will shorten the ~ of the illness.* | **limit** | **extend, increase** | **calculate, determine, estimate, measure**
PREP. **for the ~ (of)** ◊ *She stayed there for the ~ of the trip.* | **of ... ~** ◊ *The next contract will be of shorter ~.* | **throughout the ~ of** ◊ *This continued throughout the ~ of their marriage.*

dusk *noun*

ADJ. **gathering**
DUSK + VERB **approach, fall, settle, settle in** (*AmE*) ◊ *Dusk was falling as we drove home.*
PREP. **after ~** | **at ~** | **before ~** | **in the ~** ◊ *The lamps twinkled in the gathering ~.*
PHRASES **from dawn to ~**

dust *noun*

ADJ. **fine** | **airborne** | **radioactive** | **house, household** | **desert** (*esp. AmE*) | **cosmic, moon** | **brick** (*esp. BrE*), **chalk, coal, gold**, etc. | **fairy, magic, pixie** (*esp. AmE*)
... OF DUST **cloud, layer** ◊ *The tractor came up the track in a cloud of ~.* ◊ *There was a layer of fine ~ on the table.* | **particle, speck** ◊ *Remove any particles of ~ on the surface of the paint.* ◊ *microscopic specks of ~*
VERB + DUST **collect, gather** ◊ *Her chess set lay on a shelf gathering ~.* | **be covered in, be covered with** | **brush, remove, shake, sweep, sweep up, wipe** ◊ *He brushed the ~ off his clothes.* ◊ *She shook the ~ from her hair.* | **blow** ◊ *The wind was blowing ~ through the streets of the city.*

DUST + VERB **lie** ◊ *The ~ now lay in a thick layer on her piano.* | **coat sth, cover sth** ◊ *Dust covered the whole shelf.* | **settle** ◊ *The ~ settled on everything in the kitchen.* ◊ *I waited for the ~ to settle from her resignation before talking to her about it.* (*figurative*) | **blow, float, fly, swirl** ◊ *Dust swirled around them like a misty cloud.* | **fall, rise** | **fill sth** ◊ *He started coughing as ~ filled his lungs.* | **clear** ◊ *The ~ cleared and Hari could see a tiger.*
DUST + NOUN **cloud** | **grain, mote** (*old-fashioned*), **particle** | **storm** | **ball, bunny** (= a mass of dust and small pieces of hair, thread, etc.) (*informal*) (*both AmE*) | **devil** (= a small column of dust over land, caused by the wind) | **bowl** | **mite** ◊ *a house ~ mite* | **cover** (*esp. AmE*), **sheet** (*BrE*) (= for furniture, etc.) | **cover** (*esp. AmE*), **jacket** (= of a book) | **mask**

dustbin (*BrE*) *noun*

VERB + DUSTBIN **chuck sth in, dump sth in, throw sth in** ◊ *She chucked the potatoes in the ~.* | **go in** ◊ *These old shoes can go in the ~ now.* | **be consigned to, be destined for** (*figurative*) ◊ *The politicians who lost the elections will be consigned to the ~ of history.* | **empty** ◊ *How regularly are the ~s emptied?* | **put out** ◊ *We put out the ~s on a Wednesday morning before the van comes.*
DUSTBIN + NOUN **bag, liner** | **lid** | **man** ◊ *The ~ men forgot to empty our bin this morning.*
PREP. **~ of** (*figurative*) ◊ *The pollution in this country makes it the ~ of Europe.*

duty *noun*

1 sth that you have to do because it is right or expected

ADJ. **contractual, legal, statutory** (*esp. BrE*) ◊ *Retailers have a statutory ~ to provide goods suitable for their purpose.* | **fiduciary** ◊ *the company's fiduciary ~ to its shareholders* | **constitutional** (*esp. AmE*) | **general, primary** ◊ *the general ~ of the police to preserve the peace* | **professional** | **civic, public** ◊ *I feel it is my civic ~ to vote.* | **patriotic** | **Christian, religious** | **family, filial, parental** | **ethical, moral** ◊ *He felt it was his moral ~ to help others.* | **absolute, bounden** (*formal*), **sacred, solemn, sworn** ◊ *I feel it's my bounden ~ to try and help her.*
VERB + DUTY **have, owe** (*law*) ◊ *You have a legal ~ to take reasonable care.* ◊ *The company owes a ~ of care to all its customers.* | **carry out, do, fulfil/fulfill, meet, perform** ◊ *I suppose we'd better do our ~ and report the accident.* ◊ *She felt she had fulfilled her ~ by providing him with a son.* | **fail in** ◊ *He had failed in his ~ to his daughter.* | **breach, violate** ◊ *She had violated her legal ~ of confidentiality.* | **avoid, neglect, shirk** ◊ *I'd be shirking my ~ if I didn't warn him.* | **abandon** ◊ *I can't abandon my ~.* | **assign, charge sb with, impose** ◊ *It was a ~ imposed by her father.* | **assume, take on** ◊ *He took on the ~ of maintaining the family home.*
DUTY + VERB **call** ◊ *I wanted to stop and chat, but ~ called and I went back to the office.*
PREP. **under a/the ~** ◊ *You are under a statutory ~ to keep accurate records.* | **~ of** ◊ *It's the ~ of each and every one of us to do their best for the team.* ◊ *They have a ~ of confidentiality.* | **~ to, ~ towards/toward** ◊ *They have a ~ to their parents to work hard.*
PHRASES **a breach of ~** ◊ *It was a clear breach of professional ~.* | **do your ~ by sb** ◊ *You feel that you have to do your ~ by your children.* | **be ~ bound to do sth** ◊ *An employer is not ~ bound to provide a reference when an employee leaves.* | **(above and) beyond the call of ~** ◊ *The time he put in helping new recruits went beyond the call of ~.* | **~ done** ◊ *She put down the phone and went out, her ~ done.* | **feel it your ~ to do sth** ◊ *I felt it my ~ to go to the police.* | **in breach of a ~** (*formal, esp. BrE*) ◊ *It was ruled that the injured man was in breach of his ~ by not wearing the safety equipment provided.* | **a sense of ~** ◊ *I did it out of a sense of ~.*

2 tasks that you do when you are at work

ADJ. **light** ◊ *When I returned to work after my illness I was put on light duties.* | **onerous** (*esp. BrE*) | **day, night** ◊ *At 10.45 p.m. she reported for night ~.* | **combat** (*esp. AmE*), **escort, guard, occupation** (*esp. AmE*), **patrol, peacekeeping, point** (*BrE*), **sentry** ◊ *The troops are here to perform peacekeeping duties.* | **active, inactive** (in the military) ◊ *He's been suspended from active ~.* | **daily, regular, routine** | **temporary** | **full-time, part-time** | **official** | **administrative, operational, professional, teaching** | **domestic, household** ◊ *My household duties were not particularly onerous.* | **kitchen** ◊ *He was was on kitchen ~.* | **assigned** ◊ *He was unable to perform his assigned duties because of ill health.* | **military** | **jury** (*esp. AmE*) ◊ *Several years ago I was called for jury ~.* | **double** (*esp. AmE*) ◊ *The regular presenter does double ~ as a staff writer.*

VERB + DUTY **have** ◊ *The members of staff each have their own duties.* | **pull** (*AmE, informal*) ◊ *Sergeant Wilson had pulled parking-lot ~.* | **see** (*military*) ◊ *veterans who saw combat ~ in Vietnam* | **carry out, complete, discharge, do, execute, perform, undertake** ◊ *She was unable to carry out her duties because she was too ill.* | **handle** (*esp. AmE*) ◊ *The company prefers to handle translation duties in-house.* | **come on, go on, report for** ◊ *Colleagues became suspicious when he failed to report for ~.* | **come off, go off** ◊ *What time do you go off ~?* | **avoid, neglect, shirk** ◊ *He was accused of neglecting his professional duties.* | **resume, return to** ◊ *He leaves the hospital tomorrow and is expected to resume his duties at the beginning of next month.* | **relinquish** | **be released from** ◊ *Her son was released from ~ in the army to visit her in hospital.* | **be relieved of, be suspended from** ◊ *When he failed to turn up for training, he was relieved of his duties as captain.* | **share, split** (*esp. AmE*) ◊ *I share the cooking duties with Bell.*

DUTY + VERB **fall to sb** ◊ *The cleaning duties now fell to Rachel.*
DUTY + NOUN **manager** (*BrE*), **officer** ◊ *the supermarket's senior ~ manager* ◊ *He went to the police station and spoke to the ~ officer.* | **doctor, nurse** (*both esp. BrE*) | **station** (*AmE*) ◊ *The soldier was sent to his new ~ station.* | **assignment** (*AmE*) ◊ *He has volunteered for temporary ~ assignments in counterterrorism activities.*

PREP. **off ~** ◊ *I'm off ~ tomorrow night.* | **on ~** ◊ *You're not allowed to drink alcohol on ~.*

PHRASES **the execution of your duties, the performance of your duties** ◊ *The company is liable if you are injured during the execution of your ~.*

3 tax

ADJ. **heavy, high** ◊ *the heavy ~ on cigarettes* | **low** | **customs** (*esp. BrE*), **excise** (*BrE*), **export, import** ◊ *excise ~ on spirits* | **alcohol, fuel, tobacco, etc.** (*all BrE*) ◊ *Tobacco ~ is a major source of revenue for the government.* | **stamp** (*BrE, old-fashioned*) (= a tax in the UK on some legal documents) ◊ *The bank will urge ministers to raise the 1% stamp ~ threshold.*

... OF DUTY **amount** ◊ *We tried to estimate the amount of ~ we would have to pay.*

VERB + DUTY **impose, slap on sb/sth** ◊ *They are going to slap ~ on foreign cars.* | **increase, put up, raise** ◊ *They're going to put up the ~ on tobacco.* | **cut, lower, reduce** | **pay** | **avoid, evade** ◊ *They claim that the wine is for personal use and so evade the ~.* | **be liable to** ◊ *Perfume is liable to import ~.* | **be exempt from** ◊ *Beer for personal use is exempt from ~.*

DUTY + VERB **be payable** (*BrE*) ◊ *There will also be stamp ~ payable at the applicable rate.*

PREP. **in ~** ◊ *By changing its supplier, the company saved thousands of pounds in import ~.* | **~ on** ◊ *You have to pay ~ on all electrical goods.*

duvet noun (*BrE*) → See also QUILT

ADJ. **double, king-size, single** | **light, lightweight, thick, thin** | **warm**
VERB + DUVET **pull** ◊ *She climbed into bed and pulled the ~ over*

her. | **fling back, kick off, throw back** ◊ *He flung back the ~ and got out of bed.*
DUVET + NOUN **cover**
PREP. **beneath a/the ~, under a/the ~** ◊ *He snuggled down under the warm ~.*

DVD noun

ADJ. **blank** | **recordable, rewritable** | **bonus, special-edition** ◊ *The first edition of the album comes with a bonus ~.* | **bootleg, pirate** (*esp. BrE*), **pirated**
VERB + DVD **see, view, watch** ◊ *I haven't seen the first ~ so I can't compare them.* | **play** ◊ *I want a system that will play ~s.* | **rent** | **create, make, produce** | **release** | **burn, copy, rip** | **pop in** ◊ *Pop this ~ in and sit back and relax.*
DVD + NOUN **player, recorder** ◊ *a multi-region ~ player* | **drive** ◊ *the ~ drive in my PC* | **burner, ripper** (*AmE*), **writer** | **disk** | **case** | **package, set** | **collection** | **format, version** ◊ *The movie is available in ~ format.* | **technology** | **playback** ◊ *Consumers are demanding high-quality ~ playback.* | **release** | **movie** | **rental, sales**
PREP. **on ~** ◊ *The movie is now available on ~.* | **~ of** ◊ *~s of his movies are distributed by this company.*

dweller noun

ADJ. **city, town, urban** | **country, rural** | **slum** ◊ *the poor slum ~s of the capital city* | **cave, cliff, forest** | **apartment** (*esp. AmE*) ◊ *Apartment ~s are still primarily couples and singles.*

dwelling noun (*formal*)

ADJ. **makeshift, temporary** | **permanent** | **humble, modest** | **private** | **family, single** | **human** ◊ *The building looked more like a doll's house than a human ~.* | **cliff** ◊ *the ancient Native American cliff ~s*
VERB + DWELLING **build** ◊ *an application to convert the old barn into a ~* | **occupy**
DWELLING + NOUN **house** (*BrE, law*), **place** (*old-fashioned*), **unit** (*technical, esp. AmE*)

dwindle verb

ADV. **fast, quickly, rapidly** ◊ *Supplies of coal are dwindling fast.* | **gradually, slowly** | **steadily** | **away, down** (*esp. AmE*) ◊ *Membership of the club had ~d away to nothing.*
PREP. **into** ◊ *The group's support ~d into insignificance.* | **to** ◊ *Profits slowly ~d to nothing.*

dye noun

ADJ. **fabric, food, hair, etc.** | **chemical, synthetic** | **natural, organic, plant, vegetable** | **blue, red, etc.** | **fluorescent**
VERB + DYE **use** | **inject** ◊ *The researchers injected a fluorescent ~ into an area of a rat's brain.*
PREP. **in (a/the) ~** ◊ *The cloth is then soaked in blue ~.*

dynamic adj.

VERBS **be, seem** | **become** | **remain** ◊ *The business has managed to change and remain ~.*
ADV. **extremely, fairly, very, etc.** | **highly, truly** ◊ *These countries are characterized by highly ~ economies.* | **inherently** | **visually** ◊ *It is important that a poster be visually ~.*

dynamite noun

1 explosive

... OF DYNAMITE **stick**
VERB + DYNAMITE **blow sth up with, use** ◊ *They used five tons of ~ to blow up the rock.*
DYNAMITE + VERB **explode**

2 sb/sth that causes great excitement, shock, etc.

ADJ. **absolute, pure** | **political** ◊ *Don't mention the war—it's political ~.*

dynasty noun

ADJ. **ancient** ◊ *the last surviving heir of an ancient ~* | **great** |

political, royal | family | ruling ◇ *the ruling dynasties of the Visigoths*
VERB + DYNASTY **build, establish, found | overthrow**
DYNASTY + VERB **begin | come to an end, end | reign, rule**
PREP. **during a/the ~** ◇ *a porcelain figure made during the Tang ~* | **from a/the ~** ◇ *bowls and pots from the twelfth ~* | **under a/the ~** ◇ *The civil service was established under the previous ~.*
PHRASES **the end of a ~, the fall of a ~, the rise of a ~** ◇ *the rise and fall of the Habsburg ~* | **the founder of a ~** | **a member of a ~**

eager adj.

VERBS **appear, be, look, seem, sound | become**
ADV. **extremely, only too, really, very** ◇ *They were only too ~ to help us.* | **overly** (*esp. AmE*) ◇ *He wasn't overly ~ to give us any information.* | **especially, particularly** ◇ *Muir's friends were especially ~ for him to write the book.* | **quite**
PREP. **for** ◇ *We were ~ for news.*

eagle noun

ADJ. **bald, golden, etc.**
EAGLE + VERB **circle, fly, soar | swoop | nest | breed**
EAGLE + NOUN **feather | nest | population | eye** (*figurative*) ◇ *The tiny error didn't escape the ~ eye of her boss.*

ear noun

1 part of the body

ADJ. **left, right | inner, middle | external, outer | big, large | long** ◇ *a rabbit with long floppy ~s* | **pointed, pointy | floppy | pierced | torn** ◇ *Blood from his torn ~ was soaking his collar.* | **listening** ◇ *In the silence everyone seemed to be aware of listening ~s.* | **sensitive | human** ◇ *Dogs can hear things that human ~s can't hear.* | **attentive, open** (*BrE*), **receptive, sympathetic** ◇ *Even if my fears were silly, he always had an open ~.* ◇ *She did not like the plan, as she made clear every time she found a receptive ~* (= sb willing to listen). ◇ *She always provided a sympathetic ~ for students with problems.* | **modern** ◇ *Some of the words used in 18th-century writing sound strange to modern ~s.* | **Western** ◇ *Chinese music uses a scale that is unfamiliar to Western ~s.*
VERB + EAR **plug, stop** ◇ *He plugged his ~s to drown out the music.* ◇ *At first I stopped my ~s to what I did not want to hear.* | **block, close, cover, shut** ◇ *The music was so loud I had to cover my ~s.* | **strain** ◇ *I strained my ~s to catch the conversation in the other room.* | **cock, prick up** ◇ *The dog pricked up its ~s.* | **flatten, lay back, pin back, put back** ◇ *A horse may show annoyance by putting its ~s back.* | **flick, twitch** ◇ *The horse lifted its head and flicked its ~s.* | **nibble, nibble on, nuzzle** ◇ *She nibbled on his ~.* | **pierce** ◇ *I've just had my ~s pierced.* | **clean, clean out, syringe** (*BrE*) ◇ *He could hear much better after having his ~s cleaned out.* | **echo in, pound in, ring in** ◇ *The voices buzzing all around echoed in her ~s.* ◇ *My heart was pounding in my ~s.* ◇ *He went home with the teacher's warning ringing in his ~s.* | **fill, flood** ◇ *The sound of the blast filled my ~s.* | **assault, greet, hit, meet, strike** ◇ *A blast of punk rock music assaulted her ~s.* | **reach** ◇ *If news of the break-in reaches the boss's ~s, we're in trouble.* | **hurt** ◇ *The music was so loud that it hurt my ~s.* | **hiss in, whisper (sth) in | shout in, yell in | press** ◇ *He pressed his ~ to the door, but heard nothing.*
EAR + VERB **catch sth, detect sth, hear sth, pick sth up** ◇ *When the notes are played so close together the ~ hears no space between them.* | **prick, prick up, twitch** ◇ *His ~s pricked up when he heard his name mentioned.* | **tell sb sth** ◇ *She couldn't see, but her ~s told her that the guards had arrived.* | **be alert, listen** ◇ *He waited in the darkness, his ~s alert for the slightest sound.* ◇ *Her ~s listened expectantly.* | **strain** ◇ *She stood outside the room, her ~s straining to hear what they were saying.* | **pop** ◇ *If you swallow as the plane*

---

takes off, it stops your ~s from popping. | **ring** ◇ *The explosion set my ~s ringing.* | **ache, hurt, pound | redden** ◇ *Christopher felt his ~s reddening.* | **stick out** ◇ *He has really big ~s that stick out.*
EAR + NOUN **canal, drum, lobe | infection, problem | wax** (usually *earwax*) | **drops | plug** (usually *earplug*), **protector | protection | flap, muffs** (usually *earmuffs*) ◇ *She put on her earmuffs and went out into the snow.* | **buds** (*esp. AmE*), **phones, piece, set** (usually *earbuds, earphones*, etc.) ◇ *I love my portable music player, but I hate earbuds.* | **tag** ◇ *Each animal receives an individual ~ tag.* | **piercing** ◇ *He had three ~ piercings.* | **cuff**
→ See also EARRING
PREP. **in your ~** ◇ *'Taxi?' said a voice in my ~.*
PHRASES **be all ~s** ◇ *Come on, tell me, I'm all ~s* (= I want to hear). | **beam, grin, smile, etc. from ear to ear** ◇ *He was beaming from ear to ear.* | **bend sb's ~** (= talk a lot to someone about something) ◇ *She bent my ~ about it for three days.* | **can't believe your ~s** ◇ *She actually apologized. I couldn't believe my ~s!* | **catch sb's ~** ◇ *A small noise caught his ~.* | **clap, hold, put, etc. your hands over your ~s** ◇ *She put her hands over her ~s to block out what he was saying.* | **(have) a word in sb's ~** (*esp. BrE*) ◇ *Have a quiet word in her ~ about it before it's too late.* | **sb's ~s are burning** (= a person thinks that someone is talking about them) ◇ *'We were talking about you last night.' 'I thought my ~s were burning.'* | **fall on deaf ~s** ◇ *Their complaints about the poor service fell on deaf ~s* (= were ignored). | **for sb's ~s alone** ◇ *I have a few words for your ~s alone.* | **keep an ~ open, keep your ~s open** ◇ *I'll keep my eyes and ~s open for a second-hand bike for you.* | **lend an ~** (= listen to what someone is saying) ◇ *He was always willing to lend an ~.* | **music to sb's ~s** ◇ *He arrived home hungry, and the noise from the kitchen was music to his ~s.* | **go in one ~ and out the other** ◇ *I knew that my words were going in one ~ and out the other* (= the person wasn't listening to what I was saying). | **have sb's ~** ◇ *This was the woman who had the ~ of the President.* (= was trusted by him/her) | **talk sb's ~ off** ◇ *I'm sorry for talking your ~ off.* (= talking a lot) | **turn a deaf ~ to sth** ◇ *The teacher turned a deaf ~ to the boy's requests* (= ignored them). | **with half an ~** ◇ *He listened to her with only half an ~ as he watched TV.*

2 ability to recognize sounds

ADJ. **fine, good, keen, sharp** ◇ *He has a keen ~ for dialogue.* ◇ *His sharp ~s had picked up the uncertainty in her voice.* | **trained, untrained** ◇ *To the trained ~ the calls of these birds sound quite different.*
VERB + EAR **have | attune** ◇ *It takes time to attune your ~ to the local accent.*
PREP. **by ~** ◇ *She usually plays the guitar by ~, rather than reading the music.* | **~ for** ◇ *He has a good ~ for accents and can usually tell where a speaker comes from.*
PHRASES **have a tin ~ for sth** (*esp. AmE*) ◇ *She has a tin ~ for melody* (= does not appreciate it).

earl noun → Note at PEER

early adj.

VERBS **be, feel, seem**
ADV. **extremely, fairly, very, etc. | awfully** ◇ *You're here awfully ~, aren't you?* | **a little, slightly, etc.** ◇ *I'm sorry I'm a little ~.* | **relatively | surprisingly, unusually** ◇ *These discoveries were made at a surprisingly ~ date.* | **ridiculously** ◇ *I have to get up ridiculously ~.*
PREP. **for** ◇ *It's a little ~ for lunch.* | **in** ◇ *He discovered these pleasures ~ in life.*

earn verb

1 to get money for work, etc.

ADV. **consistently | reportedly, reputedly** (*esp. BrE*) ◇ *She reportedly ~s more than $475 000 a year*
VERB + EARN **have to, need to | expect to** ◇ *The company expects to ~ €600 million on sales.*

PREP. **from** ◊ *profits ~ed from real estate sales*
PHRASES **a/the chance to ~ sth, a/the opportunity to ~ sth** ◊ *the opportunity to ~ more money* | **~ a living as sth** ◊ *the difficulty of ~ing a living as an artist* | **~ enough to do sth** ◊ *The workers barely ~ enough to live on.* | **sb's/the ability to ~ sth** ◊ *his ability to ~ a living lecturing*

2 to get sth you deserve

ADV. **really** ◊ *'I feel I've really ~ed this!' she said, picking up her cup of coffee.* | **richly, rightfully** (*esp. AmE*), **rightly** (*esp. BrE*), **truly** ◊ *He has truly ~ed the admiration of his colleagues.* | **quickly** ◊ *He quickly ~ed the respect of his colleagues.*
VERB + EARN **have to, need to** ◊ *First you have to ~ their respect.* | **seek to, try to** | **be likely to** | **go on to** ◊ *He went on to ~ a PhD in astronomy from the University of Maryland.*

earnings noun

ADJ. **high, record, strong** | **low, meagre/meager** | **average** | **annual, hourly, quarterly, weekly** | **first-quarter, second-quarter, etc.** | **expected, future, projected** ◊ *the company's projected ~ for the next twelve months* | **reported** | **total** | **average** | **gross, pre-tax, taxable** | **after-tax, net** ◊ *Her net ~ last year were $15 000.* | **real** ◊ *Blue-collar workers saw their real ~ diminish.* | **export, investment** | **company, corporate** | **career, lifetime** ◊ *Her win in Australia has taken her career ~ through the million-dollar barrier.* | **lost** (*law*) ◊ *damages awarded for lost ~* | **immoral** (= by working as a prostitute) (*BrE, law*) ◊ *He was jailed for six months in June for living off immoral ~.*
... OF EARNINGS **level** ◊ *Levels of ~ are still rising.*
VERB + EARNINGS **have** ◊ *People with a university education tend to have higher ~.* | **generate** ◊ *~ generated by investing your income* | **calculate, estimate** | **declare** ◊ *You must declare all ~ to authorities.* | **tax** | **boost, increase, lift** (*esp. AmE*), **push** (*esp. AmE*), **raise** ◊ *The show has pushed her ~ past $2 million a year.* | **announce, post, report** (*all business*) ◊ *The company reported ~ of $2.9 million.*
EARNINGS + NOUN **estimate, forecast, projection** ◊ *his 2008 ~ estimate of 73 cents a share* | **target** | **announcement** ◊ *the second-quarter ~ announcement* | **growth** | **shortfall** ◊ *An ~ shortfall might point to problems with our forecasting abilities.*
PREP. **~ from** ◊ *Chile's ~ from exports rose by 2%.* | **~ of** ◊ *annual ~ of £20 000*
PHRASES **ten times, twenty times, etc. ~** ◊ *The stock trades at about 40 times ~.* | **growth in ~** ◊ *the growth in average ~ over the last ten years* | **loss of ~** ◊ *She is also claiming compensation for loss of ~.* | **revenue and ~, revenues and ~** ◊ *long-term increases in corporate revenues and ~*
→ Note at PER CENT (for more verbs)
→ Special page at BUSINESS

earphones noun

ADJ. **stereo** | **MP3 player**
... OF EARPHONES **pair, set**
VERB + EARPHONES **have on, wear** | **put on, take off**
PREP. **through ~** ◊ *She was listening to her MP3 player through ~.*

earring noun

ADJ. **drop, hoop, stud** | **clip-on** | **chandelier** (*AmE*), **dangly** | **diamond, pearl, etc.** | **gold, silver, etc.** | **matching** ◊ *She was wearing a diamond necklace with matching ~s.*
... OF EARRINGS **pair, set** ◊ *She wore a pair of dangly ~s.*
VERB + EARRING **have on, wear** | **put in, put on** | **take off, take out**

earth noun

1 the world

ADJ. **the entire, the whole**
VERB + EARTH **circle, orbit** ◊ *satellites orbiting the ~* | **create** | **destroy** | **protect, save** | **inhabit** ◊ *humans and other species that inhabit the ~* | **roam, walk, wander** ◊ *when*

dinosaurs roamed the ~ ◊ *a lost spirit, wandering the ~* | **rule** ◊ *Dinosaurs ruled the ~ for hundreds of millions of years.* | **hit, reach** ◊ *the last asteroid that hit the ~* | **leave** ◊ *No one knows what happens to us after we leave this ~.*
EARTH + VERB **orbit sth, revolve, rotate, spin** ◊ *The ~ orbits the sun.* ◊ *The ~ revolves on its axis.*
EARTH + NOUN **history, sciences** | **scientist** | **orbit**
PREP. **above the ~** ◊ *We are flying at 30 000 feet above the ~.* | **around the ~, round the ~** (*esp. BrE*) ◊ *the moon's orbit around the ~* | **on (the) ~** ◊ *The island was there before there was life on ~.* | **to ~** ◊ *The astronauts were able to send the information back to ~.*
PHRASES **inherit the ~** ◊ *The Bible says the meek will inherit the ~.* | **(the) planet ~** ◊ *the future of life on planet Earth* | **the centre/center of the ~, the surface of the ~** | **the earth's atmosphere, core, surface, etc.**

2 the ground; soil

ADJ. **bare** ◊ *There was nothing but bare ~ to be seen.* | **fertile** | **barren, infertile** | **rich** | **soft** | **hard, solid** | **dry, parched** | **damp, moist, wet** | **cold, frozen** | **warm** | **fresh, freshly dug** | **loose** ◊ *I filled the pot with a handful of loose ~.* | **baked** (*esp. BrE*) ◊ *The sun beat down on the baked ~.* | **scorched** ◊ *The wreckage of the plane was scattered across the scorched ~.* ◊ *the retreating army's scorched ~ policy* (= to set fire to crops, buildings, etc.). | **chalky, sandy** | **dark**
... OF EARTH **clod, clump, lump** ◊ *My boots were caked in big clods of wet ~.*
EARTH + VERB **shake, tremble**
EARTH + NOUN **bank, mound** ◊ *I scrambled to the top of the steep ~ bank.* | **tremor** ◊ *Furniture fell over as the room was shaken by an ~ tremor.*
PREP. **in the ~** ◊ *The plants must have their roots in the ~.* | **under the ~** ◊ *in mines deep under the ~*

earthquake noun

ADJ. **big, great, huge, large, major, massive, powerful, severe, strong** | **devastating** | **minor, small** | **undersea, underwater** ◊ *the tsunami caused by an undersea ~*
VERB + EARTHQUAKE **cause, trigger** | **experience** ◊ *The area has not experienced a major ~ in more than 700 years.* | **feel** ◊ *I don't understand why we felt the ~ and you didn't.* | **survive, withstand** ◊ *The school was built to withstand ~s.* | **predict** ◊ *You can't accurately predict ~s.* | **record** ◊ *It was the biggest ~ ever recorded in the US.*
EARTHQUAKE + VERB **happen, hit (sth), occur, strike (sth)** ◊ *The ~ hit the city at two in the morning.* | **rock sth, shake sth** ◊ *The ~ shook buildings throughout the business district.* | **destroy sth, devastate sth, kill sb, leave sb homeless** | **cause sth** | **measure sth** ◊ *an ~ measuring 5.8 on the Richter scale*
EARTHQUAKE + NOUN **activity** ◊ *an organization which monitors ~ activity* | **zone** | **survivor, victim** | **damage** | **prediction** | **hazard, risk**
PREP. **in a/the ~** ◊ *The building was destroyed in an ~.*
PHRASES **the epicentre/epicenter of an ~** ◊ *the evacuation of coastlines within 600 miles of the earthquake's epicentre/epicenter* | **the magnitude of an ~**

ease noun

ADJ. **consummate** (*esp. BrE*), **great** | **astonishing, incredible, remarkable, surprising** | **alarming** (*esp. BrE*) ◊ *I obtained the drugs with alarming ~.* | **comparative, equal, relative** ◊ *All questions were handled with equal ~ and mastery.* | **apparent, seeming** ◊ *I was surprised at the apparent ~ with which he got into the building.* | **contemptuous** (*esp. BrE*) ◊ *She returned her opponent's serve with contemptuous ~.* | **practised/practiced**
PREP. **for ~ in** ◊ *The back of the garment is split for ~ in walking.* | **for ~ of** ◊ *The whole machine is designed for ~ of use.* | **with ~** ◊ *They passed the exam with ~.* | **~ of** ◊ *The car brings ~ of access to the countryside.*

ease verb

1 make sth less painful/serious/difficult

ADV. **considerably, greatly** ◊ *The situation would be considerably ~d if more money were made available.* |

slightly, somewhat | gradually | away ◇ *The pain in my leg gradually ~d away.*
VERB + EASE help (to) ◇ *The new road should help ~ traffic problems.* | begin to ◇ *Tensions between the two countries are beginning to ~.* | try to

2 move carefully

ADV. carefully, gently | slowly ◇ *I ~d myself slowly out of bed.* | away, back, down, forward, etc. ◇ *Jean ~d back on the pillows and relaxed.*
PREP. away from | into ◇ *He ~d himself into the driving seat.* | out of ◇ *She carefully ~d the car out of the garage*

east *noun, adj.* → Note at DIRECTION

Easter *noun*

ADJ. early, late ◇ *~ is early this year.*
VERB + EASTER have, spend ◇ *Have a good ~.* ◇ *I prefer to spend ~ at home.* | celebrate
EASTER + NOUN egg | celebrations, festival, holiday, season (*AmE*) | Day, Monday (*esp. BrE*), morning, Saturday (*esp. BrE*), Sunday, week, weekend | dinner (*AmE*) | service ◇ *Many people attend an ~ service at their local church.* | story ◇ *the ~ story in the Bible* | break (*esp. BrE*), holidays (*BrE*), vacation | bunny | basket (*esp. AmE*)
PREP. at ~ ◇ *The house opens to the public at ~.* | for ~ ◇ *We usually go away for ~.* | over ~ ◇ *The library is closed over ~.*
PHRASES Happy ~!, wish sb a happy ~

easy *adj.*

VERBS be, look, seem, sound | become, get ◇ *Life is getting easier for us.* | remain | make sth ◇ *These changes should make your job easier.* | find sth ◇ *I found the exam quite ~.*
ADV. extremely, fairly, very, etc. | awfully, exceptionally | especially, particularly | enough, reasonably ◇ *It is ~ enough to see how it happened.* | comparatively, relatively | amazingly, incredibly, remarkably, ridiculously, surprisingly ◇ *The written test was ridiculously ~.* | apparently, seemingly (*esp. AmE*) | not exactly ◇ *Doing all that while injured isn't exactly ~.* | increasingly | deceptively ◇ *It looks deceptively ~ to hit the ball into the hole.*
PREP. for ◇ *Writing is not ~ for her.*
PHRASES all too ~ ◇ *It was all too ~ to forget why we had been sent there.* | as ~ as 1, 2, 3, as ~ as ABC, as ~ as pie (= very easy) | the easiest thing in the world ◇ *It is the easiest thing in the world to blame your parents.* | be no ~ task ◇ *Contacting everyone was no ~ task.* | make sth as ~ as possible ◇ *We want to make it as ~ as possible for members to participate.* | not as ~ as it looks, seems, sounds, etc. ◇ *Playing tennis is not as ~ as it looks.* | quick and ~ ◇ *a book designed for quick and ~ reference*

eat *verb*

ADV. well ◇ *We ate very well most of the time* (= had lots of nice food). | a lot, enough, too much ◇ *He's not ~ing enough.* | healthfully (*AmE*), healthily, properly, sensibly ◇ *I'm trying to ~ more healthily.* ◇ *She doesn't ~ sensibly* (= doesn't eat food that is good for her). | poorly | hungrily, ravenously | heartily | sparingly ◇ *Barton did not feel very hungry and ate sparingly.* | barely, hardly ◇ *He'd barely eaten any breakfast.* | quickly, slowly | in silence, quietly, silently | happily ◇ *Everyone happily ate the huge meal.* | alone, together
VERB + EAT find sth to, get (yourself) sth to, grab sth to, have sth to ◇ *Do you have anything to ~?* | have enough to | and, try to ◇ *Try and ~ something. It will do you good.*
PHRASES a bite to ~ (= some food) ◇ *Do you want to grab a bite to ~?* | ~ and drink ◇ *Go and get yourself something to ~ and drink.* | ~ like a horse (= eat a lot) ◇ *She's very thin but she ~s like a horse!* | ~ sb out of house and home ◇ *He's ~ing us out of house and home* (= eating a lot of our food). | go ~ (*esp. AmE*) ◇ *Let's go ~.* | good enough to ~ (*figurative*) ◇ *You look good enough to ~!* | go out to ~ ◇ *We went out to ~ for a Chinese New Year celebration.* | a place to ~ (= a cafe or restaurant) ◇ *Are you looking for a place to ~?* | sit down to ~ ◇ *We eventually sat down to ~ at 8.30 p.m.*

eater *noun*

ADJ. fish, fruit, meat, plant ◇ *The bats live in the tropics and are fruit ~s.* ◇ *I am a meat ~ but I am also an animal lover.* | big, good, hearty (*esp. BrE*), voracious ◇ *All my children are big ~s.* | finicky (*AmE*), fussy, picky ◇ *He eats anything—he's not a fussy ~.* | healthy | binge, compulsive | messy

ebb *noun*

EBB + NOUN tide ◇ *They left port on the ~ tide.*
PREP. against an/the ~ ◇ *It was difficult sailing upstream against a strong ~.* | on an/the ~ ◇ *By this time, the tide was on the ~.* ◇ *We floated away from the beach on the ~.* | with an/the ~ ◇ *They went out to sea with the ~.*
PHRASES the ~ and flow of sth ◇ *the natural ~ and flow of water* ◇ *We see a constant ~ and flow of jobs.* (*figurative*)

ebb *verb*

ADV. away ◇ *He knew that his life was ~ing away.* | slowly ◇ *Calla felt her fear slowly ~ing away.*
VERB + EBB begin to ◇ *Her strength began to ~.* | seem to

eccentric *adj.*

VERBS be, look, seem | become, get ◇ *The old lady was getting very ~.* | consider sb, find sb, regard sb as ◇ *We were definitely regarded as ~.*
ADV. extremely, fairly, very, etc. | highly, wildly (*esp. BrE*) | a little, slightly, etc. | mildly | endearingly (*esp. BrE*) ◇ *his endearingly ~ nature spilling into his speech* | increasingly ◇ *In his last years, he became increasingly ~.*

echo *noun*

ADJ. distant, faint | clear, distinct, loud, strong (*often figurative*) ◇ *There are clear ~es of Elvis Presley in his vocal style.* | hollow | eerie, ghostly ◇ *The initial reports had an eerie ~ of the attacks two weeks earlier.* ◇ *ghostly ~es of Virginia's past* | returning ◇ *The bat compares the sound of its cry with the sound of the returning ~.*
VERB + ECHO hear, listen for, listen to ◇ *We could just hear a faint ~.* | make, produce, send back, send out ◇ *Their footsteps on the bare boards sent out hollow ~es.* | contain, have (*both figurative*) ◇ *The story has ~es of Alice in Wonderland.* | find (*figurative*) ◇ *The political upheavals find an ~ in the art of the time.*
ECHO + VERB bounce back, bounce off sth, rebound, reverberate ◇ *The ~es reverberated through the auditorium.* | come back, return ◇ *An ~ came back from the walls of the building.* | die, die away ◇ *The ~ slowly died away.*
PREP. ~ from ◇ *the ~ from a brick wall*

echo *verb*

1 come back as an echo

ADV. faintly, slightly, softly | loudly | eerily, strangely | ominously | hollowly ◇ *The sound ~ed hollowly through the tall empty house.* | still | back ◇ *Their voices ~ed back across the water.*
VERB + ECHO seem to
PREP. across ◇ *The protest seemed to ~ across the room.* | around, round (*esp. BrE*) ◇ *His voice ~ed around the room.* | down ◇ *Her footsteps ~ed down the corridor.* | in ◇ *Her screams still ~ed in his ears.* | off ◇ *The call ~ed off the walls of the cave.* | through ◇ *Laughter ~ed through the house.* | with ◇ *The great hall ~ed with laughter.*

2 repeat/agree with sb/sth

ADV. exactly | widely ◇ *an opinion that is widely ~ed in the tabloid press* | clearly | merely, only, simply ◇ *In his statement, the police chief merely ~ed the views of his deputy.* | incredulously ◇ *'He's gone!' Viv ~ed incredulously.*
VERB + ECHO seem to ◇ *Their ideas seem to ~ our own.*

eclipse *noun*

ADJ. lunar, solar | partial, total ◇ *a total lunar ~*
PHRASES an ~ of the moon, an ~ of the sun

ecology noun

ADJ. **fragile** | **natural** ◇ *Non-native plants have colonized the area and altered the natural ~.* | **animal, human, plant, wildlife** (*AmE*) | **forest, marine** | **behavioural/behavioral, evolutionary, physiological** | **landscape** (*AmE*) | **global, local**
VERB + ECOLOGY **damage, disrupt** | **study**
ECOLOGY + NOUN **movement** | **research**

economical adj.

VERBS **be, seem** ◇ *Solid fuel would be more ~.*
ADV. **extremely, fairly, very, etc.** | **highly, remarkably** ◇ *This new oven is highly ~.*
PREP. **in** ◇ *This arrangement is more ~ in its use of staff.* | **of** ◇ *more ~ of time and resources* | **with** ◇ *This arrangement is more ~ with space.*
PHRASES **~ with the truth** ◇ *She accused him of being ~ with the truth* (= not telling the truth).

economics noun

ADJ. **applied, theoretical** | **classical, conventional, mainstream, orthodox** | **free-market, Keynesian, laissez-faire, liberal, market, Marxist, monetary, neoclassical, supply-side, trickle-down** | **contemporary, modern** ◇ *trends in modern ~* | **global, international** | **basic, simple** ◇ *He shows an understanding of basic ~ here.* | **agricultural, behavioural/behavioral** (*esp. AmE*), **business, development, environmental, health, industrial, labour/labor, welfare**
PHRASES **a school of ~**
→ Note at SUBJECT (for verbs and nouns)

economist noun

ADJ. **chief, leading, prominent, senior, top** | **distinguished, eminent, influential, respected** | **prize-winning** | **academic, government, professional** | **classical, free-market, Keynesian, liberal, neoclassical, etc.** | **conservative, mainstream, progressive** | **contemporary, modern** | **agricultural, business, development, environmental, health, labour/labor, political** | **global, international, regional**
→ Note at JOB

economy noun

1 operation of a country's money supply

ADJ. **booming, buoyant** (*esp. BrE*), **dynamic, healthy, prosperous, robust, sound, stable, strong, thriving, vibrant** | **expanding, growing** | **improving, recovering, strengthening** | **ailing, bad** (*esp. AmE*), **declining, depressed, failing, faltering, flagging, moribund, sagging** (*esp. AmE*), **slowing, sluggish, slumping** (*esp. AmE*), **sputtering** (*esp. AmE*), **stagnant, struggling, troubled, weakening** ◇ *The government devalued the currency to try to revive the flagging ~.* | **fragile, vulnerable, weak** | **overheated** | **bubble** ◇ *In order for our bubble ~ to continue expanding, Americans must continue spending.* | **competitive** | **sustainable** | **advanced, developed, modern** | **developing, emerging, new, third-world** | **agrarian, agricultural, capitalist, free-market, industrial, industrialized, knowledge-based, liberal, market, mixed, monetary, planned, political, rural, socialist** ◇ *a modern industrial ~* | **domestic, global, globalized, internal, international, local, national, world** ◇ *the increasingly competitive global ~* | **black, illicit** (*AmE*), **informal, underground** ◇ *The black ~ booms when there is high unemployment.*
VERB + ECONOMY **build, create, rebuild** ◇ *Each party has its own strategy for building a strong ~.* | **control, handle, manage, regulate, run** ◇ *The government was accused of failing to run the ~ competently.* | **bolster, boost, develop, expand, grow** (*esp. AmE*), **improve, jump-start, kick-start, rescue, revitalize, revive, spur, stimulate, strengthen** | **cripple, damage, destabilize, destroy, devastate, disrupt, harm, hurt, ruin, undermine, weaken, wreck** | **drive, fuel**

◇ *Income from this exported crop drove the ~ of Mali.* | **slow** ◇ *Government measures to slow the ~ failed to curb fuel demand growth.* | **shape, transform** ◇ *This massive retailer has been shaping the ~ for a decade.* | **benefit, help, support, sustain** ◇ *We want to support the local ~.* | **threaten** ◇ *Should we be worried that a dollar crisis threatens the ~?* | **fix** (*esp. AmE*), **stabilize** | **reform, restructure** | **liberalize, modernize** ◇ *Japan has successfully modernized its ~.* | **diversify** ◇ *Cuba should have been able to diversify its ~.* | **dominate** ◇ *Tourism clearly dominates the local ~.*
ECONOMY + VERB **boom, develop, expand, flourish, grow, improve** | **be in recession, go into recession** | **collapse, contract, decline, fail, falter, shrink, slow, stagnate, struggle, suffer** | **pick up, rebound, recover, stabilize, turn around, turn round** (*esp. BrE*) | **be based on sth** ◇ *The region has an ~ based on services and finance.* | **emerge from sth** ◇ *The South African ~ emerged from decades of international isolation.* | **experience sth** ◇ *It has been a while since the ~ experienced a deep economic downturn.* | **function, operate, perform** ◇ *The ~ is functioning very poorly.* | **move** ◇ *It's the industry which keeps our national ~ moving.* | **hum** (*AmE*), **hum along** (*esp. AmE*) ◇ *The ~ is humming along at a healthy 4% pace.* | **create sth, generate sth, produce sth**
PHRASES **an area of the ~, a sector of the ~** ◇ *Drivers are needed in all sectors of the ~.* | **the backbone of the ~, the mainstay of the ~** ◇ *Agriculture was the backbone of the ~.* | **a downturn in the ~, a downturn of the ~** ◇ *A downturn in the ~ is affecting many small businesses.* | **growth in the ~, growth of the ~** ◇ *A small manufacturing sector inhibits growth in the ~.* | **control, handling, management, etc. of the ~** ◇ *37% approved the president's handling of the ~.* | **the size of the ~, the state of the ~** ◇ *The government has been criticized over the state of the ~.*
→ Special page at BUSINESS

2 careful use of money/time/resources

ADJ. **significant** | **false** ◇ *Buying cheap shoes is a false ~.* | **fuel** ◇ *The company has improved the fuel ~ of all its vehicles.*
VERB + ECONOMY **achieve, make** ◇ *We could achieve major economies in time with this new machinery.*
ECONOMY + NOUN **drive** (*BrE*) ◇ *Savings are being planned as part of a huge ~ drive.*
PREP. **~ in** ◇ *possible economies in telephone costs*
PHRASES **~ of effort, ~ of movement** ◇ *It was impressive to see her ~ of movement as she worked the machine.* | **~ of scale** ◇ *Bigger markets can provide significant economies of scale.*

ecstasy noun

1 feeling

ADJ. **pure, sheer** | **religious, sexual**
VERB + ECSTASY **feel** ◇ *He had never felt such ~ as he did that night.*
PREP. **in ~** | **~ at** ◇ *Kate closed her eyes in ~ at the thought of a cold drink.* | **~ over** ◇ *I was in sheer ~ over the prospect of meeting my idol.*

2 Ecstasy drug

ECSTASY + NOUN **pill, tablet** (*esp. BrE*)
→ Note at DRUG (for more verbs and nouns)

ecstatic adj.

VERBS **be, feel, look** | **become**
ADV. **absolutely, positively** | **not exactly**
PREP. **about** ◇ *Annie was ~ about the idea.* | **at** ◇ *Martin was not exactly ~ at the news.*

edge noun

1 place where sth ends

ADJ. **top, upper** ◇ *the top ~ of the picture frame* | **bottom, lower** | **inner, inside** | **outer, outermost, outside** | **front, rear** | **left, right** ◇ *the left ~ of the image* | **northern, southern, etc.** | **far, near, opposite** ◇ *She could see rocky cliffs on the opposite ~ of the lake.* | **bevelled/beveled, curved, raised, rounded, scalloped, smooth, straight** ◇ *the* rounded ~s of her collarbone | **exposed** | **cut, frayed** ◇ *Flip the fabric over so the cut ~ is now to your left.* ◇ *My fingers played with the frayed ~s of my jeans.* | **very** ◇ *Erosion has left the house perched on the very ~ of the cliff.* | **cliff, forest, water's** ◇ *A row of boats was beached at the water's ~.*

VERB + EDGE **reach** ◇ *We had reached the ~ of the map and didn't know which way to go.* | **skirt** ◇ *The road skirts the western ~ of the forest.* | **clutch, grab, grasp, grip** ◇ *I gripped the ~ of my desk to steady myself.* | **catch** ◇ *My foot caught the ~ of the table.* | **border, line** ◇ *Trees lined the ~s of the path.* | **define, mark** ◇ *A trellis provided shade and defined the ~s of the courtyard.* | **form** ◇ *The building forms the northern ~ of the courtyard.* | **align** | **sand, seal, trim**

PREP. **along the ~, around the ~, round the ~** (*esp. BrE*) ◇ *Smoke was making its way around the ~s of the door.* | **at the ~** ◇ *Soon we were at the ~ of the woods.* | **on the ~** ◇ *She sat on the ~ of her bed.* | **over the ~** ◇ *The car rolled over the ~ of the cliff.*

PHRASES **right on the ~** ◇ *They live right on the ~ of town.*

2 sharp side of sth

ADJ. **razor-sharp, sharp** | **cutting** | **serrated** ◇ *a knife with a serrated ~* | **jagged, ragged, rough** | **smooth** | **blunt**
VERB + EDGE **sharpen**

3 advantage

ADJ. **competitive** | **slight** | **big** (*informal, esp. AmE*), **decided, decisive, definite** | **winning** | **extra** ◇ *Their training gave them an extra ~.* | **technological**
VERB + EDGE **give sb/sth** | **gain, have, hold** ◇ *to gain a competitive ~ over rival suppliers* | **keep, maintain, retain** ◇ *Taiwan still retained a decisive ~ in many industries.* | **lose**
PREP. **~ over** ◇ *The intensive training she had done gave her the ~ over the other runners.*

edge *verb*

ADV. **carefully, cautiously, nervously** | **slowly** | **backward, forward** | **ahead** ◇ *The Italian ~d ahead to win the race.*
PREP. **ahead of** ◇ *He drew level and for a moment ~d ahead of his rival.* | **along** ◇ *He ~d carefully along the narrow ledge.* | **away from** ◇ *Heaton began to ~ away from Jed and headed for the stairs.* | **towards/toward** ◇ *We slowly ~d our way towards/toward the exit.*
PHRASES **~ your way**

edgy *adj.*

VERBS **appear, be, feel, seem, sound** | **become, get** ◇ *He began to get very ~.* | **make sb** ◇ *She made Jeff ~ with her constant demands.*
ADV. **all, very** ◇ *She was all ~ that evening.* | **a little, slightly,** etc. ◇ *She had been a little ~ all day.*
PREP. **about** ◇ *Hester seemed ~ about something.* | **with** ◇ *He was rather ~ with her.*

edition *noun*

ADJ. **first, second,** etc. ◇ *a dealer that specializes in rare first ~s* | **early** ◇ *The passionate collector will go for early ~s.* | **later** ◇ *Later ~s had a glossary.* | **the latest, new, recent** | **current, the original** | **forthcoming, future, upcoming** (*esp. AmE*) | **limited, special** ◇ *The book appeared in a limited ~ of 3 000.* | **10th-anniversary, 50th-anniversary,** etc. | **de luxe** | **hardback, hardcover** (*esp. AmE*), **leather-bound, paperback** | **pocket** | **abridged** ◇ *They have brought out an abridged ~ of the encyclopedia.* | **expanded** | **illustrated** | **revised, updated** | **critical** ◇ *a critical ~ of Shakespeare's plays* | **scholarly** | **facsimile** ◇ *a facsimile ~ of Dr Johnson's Dictionary of 1755* | **electronic, online** | **print, printed** | **live** ◇ *There will be a live ~ of the show tomorrow night.* | **evening, morning** ◇ *The story made it into the evening ~ of the newspaper.*
VERB + EDITION **bring out, issue, print, produce, publish, release** | **edit, illustrate** | **read, watch** | **review**
EDITION + VERB **appear, be out, come out** ◇ *The first ~ of the newspaper appeared in 1859.* | **contain sth, feature sth, offer sth** ◇ *This ~ features a new section on Chinese cooking.*
PREP. **in a … ~** ◇ *The encyclopedia will shortly be out in a revised ~.* | **~ of** ◇ *the November ~ of 'Vogue'*

editor *noun*

1 prepares text, video, etc. for publication

ADJ. **general** | **assistant, senior** | **commissioning** (*esp. BrE*) | **copy** | **freelance** | **book, film, movie** (*esp. AmE*), **programme/program** | **art, fiction, medical, music, picture**

2 of a newspaper/magazine

ADJ. **chief, executive** (*esp. AmE*), **managing, top** (*esp. AmE*) | **deputy** | **assistant, associate** | **contributing** (*esp. AmE*) | **consulting** (*AmE*) | **joint** (*esp. BrE*) | **founding** | **guest** | **journal, magazine, newsletter, newspaper, tabloid** (*esp. BrE*) | **editorial page** (*AmE*), **features, news, op-ed** (*AmE*), **review** ◇ *Russell did a terrific job as book review ~.* | **photo, picture** | **specialist** | **City** (*BrE*), **economics, fashion, financial, foreign, literary, medical, political, sports, technical, travel** ◇ *On page 12, our economics ~ comments on the takeover bid.* | **online**
PHRASES **a letter to the ~**
→ Note at JOB

editorial *noun*

ADJ. **newspaper** | **front-page** | **lead** (*esp. AmE*) ◇ *The lead ~ in today's New York Times criticized the policy.* | **full-page** | **lengthy** | **guest** (*esp. AmE*) | **anonymous, unsigned** (*AmE*)
VERB + EDITORIAL **write** | **carry, publish, run** ◇ *The paper only occasionally carries ~s.* ◇ *The newspaper ran a hard-hitting ~ criticizing the government's economic policies.*
PREP. **in an/the ~** ◇ *He declared his support for the president in an ~.* | **~ on** ◇ *an ~ on the problem of crime*

educated *adj.*

VERBS **be, seem, sound**
ADV. **highly, very, well** ◇ *She seemed intelligent and well ~.* | **poorly** | **reasonably** (*esp. BrE*) | **properly** | **fully** | **broadly** ◇ *the need for a broadly ~ workforce* | **classically, formally** ◇ *Less formally ~ people can acquire professional competence.* | **liberally** | **expensively** (*esp. BrE*), **privately**

education *noun*

ADJ. **decent, excellent, first-class, good, high-quality, quality, well-rounded** | **poor** | **compulsory** | **formal** ◇ *Although he had had little formal ~, he could read and write well.* | **classical** ◇ *He received a classical ~.* | **liberal** | **all-round** (*BrE*), **basic, general** ◇ *He'd received an excellent general ~ in Poland.* | **comprehensive** (*esp. BrE*), **public-school** (= provided by the government) (*AmE*), **universal** ◇ *the party's policy on comprehensive ~* ◇ *Nigeria committed itself to universal primary ~.* | **early-childhood** (*esp. AmE*), **preschool** | **elementary, primary** (*esp. AmE*) | **secondary** (*esp. BrE*) | **adult, continuing, further** (*BrE*), **higher, tertiary** ◇ *a college of further ~* ◇ *41% had some post-secondary ~.* | **college** (*esp. AmE*), **high-school** (*in the US*), **public-school** (= private) (*in the UK*), **university** | **graduate, undergraduate** (*both esp. AmE*) | **remedial** (*AmE*), **special** | **in-service, professional, vocational** | **military, teacher** | **maternal, parental** ◇ *How well a child does at school is influenced by the level of parental ~.* | **distance, online** (*both esp. AmE*) ◇ *Technology allows distance ~ to occur at all levels.* | **AIDS, health** | **sex, sexuality** (*AmE*) | **arts, music, science,** etc. | **religious, theological** | **full-time, part-time** | **public, state** | **private** ◇ *parents who choose private ~ for their children* | **Catholic, Christian,** etc. | **single-sex** ◇ *Researchers have found that single-sex ~ may benefit girls.* | **bilingual, multicultural**
VERB + EDUCATION **acquire, get, have, obtain, receive** ◇ *He was at a disadvantage because of the poor ~ he had received.* | **pursue** ◇ *She brought up two children while pursuing a college ~.* | **deliver, give sb, offer, provide (sb with)** ◇ *The school provides an excellent general ~.* | **deny sb** ◇ *No one is denied an ~ because they are poor in this country.* | **lack** ◇ *Many people lack the ~ and training that is needed for these jobs.* | **enter** ◇ *students entering higher ~* | **continue, extend** ◇ *She went to college to continue her ~.* | **leave** ◇

young people who are just leaving full-time ~ | **complete**, **finish** ◇ *He went to America to complete his ~.* | **improve**, **reform** ◇ *The project seeks to improve ~ for students.* | **promote** | **finance sb's**, **fund sb's** ◇ *They set up an account to fund their daughter's ~.*
EDUCATION + NOUN **authority** (*in the UK*), **committee**, **department**, **ministry** (*in the UK*), **sector**, **service**, **system** ◇ *funds provided by the local ~ authority* ◇ *We need to invest in the higher ~ sector.* | **officer** (*esp. BrE*), **official** | **minister**, **secretary** (*both in the UK*) | **policy** | **reform** | **reformer** | **bill** | **campaign**, **initiative**, **programme/program**, **project**, **scheme** (*BrE*) ◇ *The department has launched a new health ~ campaign.* | **activities** ◇ *They want to broaden their research and ~ activities.* | **facilities**, **materials**, **resources** | **budget**, **funding** | **spending** | **class**, **course**, **session** ◇ *adult ~ courses* | **process** | **centre/center**, **college**, **establishment**, **institution**, **provider** | **setting** ◇ *children in early ~ settings* | **community** (*esp. AmE*), **world** ◇ *a policy that has been adopted by the entire ~ community* | **expert**, **leader**, **specialist** | **requirement** (*AmE*) ◇ *There are additional ~ requirements for nurses on this course.* | **levels**, **standards** ◇ *efforts to improve ~ standards* | **loan** (*AmE*) (***student loan*** in *BrE*)
PREP. **in ~** ◇ *students in full-time ~* | **through ~** ◇ *We acquire much of our world knowledge through ~.* | **~ about** ◇ *~ about danger on the roads*

eerie *adj.*

VERBS **be**, **feel**, **look**, **sound**
ADV. **extremely**, **fairly**, **very**, etc. | **distinctly** (*esp. BrE*), **downright** ◇ *This place has a distinctly ~ atmosphere.* | **almost** ◇ *a silence so long that it was almost ~* | **a little**, **slightly**, etc.

effect *noun*

1 change that is caused by sth

ADJ. **decisive**, **dramatic**, **far-reaching**, **important**, **marked**, **powerful**, **profound**, **pronounced**, **significant**, **strong** | **marginal**, **minimal**, **modest**, **negligible** | **main**, **major**, **principal** | **full** ◇ *The full ~s of the new tax have not yet been felt.* | **no apparent**, **no appreciable**, **no detectable**, **no discernible**, **no measurable**, **no noticeable**, **no visible** ◇ *There was no discernible ~ on cell growth.* | **likely**, **possible**, **potential**, **predictable**, **probable** | **subtle** | **disproportionate** | **residual** | **adverse**, **catastrophic**, **crippling**, **damaging**, **debilitating**, **deleterious**, **destructive**, **detrimental**, **devastating**, **disastrous**, **harmful**, **ill**, **negative**, **serious**, **traumatic**, **undesirable**, **unfortunate** ◇ *the crippling ~ of sanctions on the economy* ◇ *He didn't seem to have suffered any ill ~s from his fall.* | **chilling** ◇ *It's a policy that will have a chilling ~ on free speech.* | **destabilizing**, **stabilizing** | **the opposite** ◇ *His comment was intended to calm the situation but it had the opposite ~.* | **unintended** | **beneficial**, **positive**, **salutary** | **the desired** ◇ *We had problems with mosquitoes, but this spray had the desired ~.* | **moderating** (*esp. AmE*) | **magical**, **remarkable** ◇ *Giving up smoking had a magical ~ on his stamina.* | **immediate** | **direct**, **indirect** | **short-term** | **lasting**, **long-term**, **permanent** | **domino**, **knock-on**, **ripple**, **spillover** (*esp. AmE*), **trickle-down** ◇ *Any delay in delivery of materials will have a knock-on ~ throughout the production process.* (see also ***side effect***) | **practical** | **aggregate**, **combined**, **cumulative**, **net**, **overall** | **deterrent** ◇ *The deterrent ~ of the death penalty has long been questioned.* | **inhibitory** ◇ *The drug has well-documented inhibitory ~s on sexual function.* | **calming**, **hypnotic**, **sedative**, **soothing**, **soporific** | **therapeutic** | **protective** | **placebo** | **toxic** | **inflationary** | **corrosive** | **greenhouse** ◇ *policies to reduce emissions of gases which cause the greenhouse ~*
VERB + EFFECT **bring about**, **exert**, **have**, **produce** ◇ *The drug exerts a powerful ~ on the brain.* | **take** ◇ *The medicine started to take ~ after a few minutes.* | **experience**, **feel**, **suffer**, **suffer from** ◇ *Women feel the ~s of alcohol more quickly than men.* | **recover from** | **note**, **observe** | **detect** | **demonstrate**, **exhibit**, **illustrate**, **reveal**, **show** | **analyse/analyze**, **assess**, **determine**, **estimate**, **evaluate**, **examine**, **explore**, **investigate**, **measure**, **monitor**, **quantify**, **study**, **test** | **document** ◇ *I am interested in documenting the ~s of international events on ordinary people.* | **compare** | **blunt**, **buffer** (*esp. AmE*), **cushion**, **diminish**, **lessen**, **limit**, **minimize**, **mitigate**, **reduce**, **soften** ◇ *to minimize the ~s of economic change* | **ameliorate** | **cancel out**, **eliminate**, **negate**, **nullify** | **counter**, **counteract**, **counterbalance**, **moderate**, **neutralize**, **offset** | **block**, **combat**, **suppress** ◇ *a face cream designed to combat the ~s of age* | **overcome** | **reverse** | **amplify**, **compound**, **enhance**, **exacerbate**, **magnify**, **maximize** | **mimic**, **simulate** ◇ *drugs which mimic the ~s of hormones* | **aim at** ◇ *That is precisely the ~ I was aiming at.* | **be worried about**, **fear** | **overestimate**, **underestimate** | **ignore**, **neglect** | **predict** | **describe**, **explain**
EFFECT + VERB **exist**, **occur** | **spread** | **last** | **arise from sth**, **result from sth** ◇ *the serious health ~s which result from obesity* | **disappear**, **wear off** ◇ *How soon will the ~s of the drug wear off?* | **differ**, **vary**
PREP. **in ~** ◇ *The border closure meant, in ~, that no trade took place between the countries.* | **to this ~**, **to that ~** ◇ *They told us to go away, or words to that ~.* | **with…~** ◇ *The plague struck again with devastating ~.* | **~ on**, **~ upon** ◇ *The dry weather had an adverse ~ on the potato crops.*
PHRASES **cause and ~** ◇ *key historical concepts such as cause and ~* | **to little ~**, **to no ~** ◇ *The air conditioning came on, to little ~.*

2 use of an official rule, plan, etc.

ADJ. **immediate**
VERB + EFFECT **come into** ◇ *The new regulations come into ~ next month.* | **bring sth into**, **put sth into** ◇ *The recommendations will soon be put into ~.*
PREP. **in ~** ◇ *Some laws from the 18th century are still in ~.* | **with ~** ◇ *The bank has cut interest rates with immediate ~.*

3 impression that a speaker, book, performance, etc. gives

ADJ. **dramatic**, **startling**, **striking**, **stunning** | **maximum**, **optimum** | **the desired** ◇ *I found that by adding white I could achieve the desired ~.* | **overall** ◇ *The overall ~ of the painting is overwhelming.*
VERB + EFFECT **give (sth)**, **have** ◇ *The stage lighting gives the ~ of a moonlit scene.* | **achieve**, **create** | **enhance**, **heighten** ◇ *The dramatic ~ was heightened by her black dress and dead white face.* | **spoil**
PREP. **for…~** ◇ *'You know why I'm here?' Doug paused for maximum ~.* | **to…~** ◇ *She uses animal sounds to startling ~ in her music.*

4 techniques used when making sth

ADJ. **special** | **cinematic** | **audio**, **sound** | **optical**, **visual** | **lighting** | **elaborate** | **digital**

effective *adj.*

1 producing the result you want

VERBS **be**, **look**, **prove**, **seem** | **make sth** | **find sth** ◇ *We find advertising on the radio very ~.*
ADV. **extremely**, **fairly**, **very**, etc. | **enormously**, **especially**, **extraordinarily**, **highly**, **incredibly**, **remarkably**, **tremendously** ◇ *a highly ~ technique* | **completely**, **fully**, **totally**, **truly** | **especially**, **particularly** | **moderately**, **partially**, **reasonably** | **equally** | **generally** ◇ *The drug is generally ~ in reducing pain.* | **increasingly** | **surprisingly** | **consistently** | **enough** ◇ *This method is ~ enough with greenfly.* | **not sufficiently** | **immediately** | **potentially** | **devastatingly**, **powerfully** ◇ *Sneezes are devastatingly ~ at spreading infection.* | **politically** ◇ *What makes a speech politically ~?*
PREP. **at** ◇ *~ at keeping out the wind* | **in** ◇ *~ in helping people to stop smoking*

2 of laws/rules

VERBS **be** | **become** | **remain**
ADV. **fully** | **partially** | **directly**, **immediately** ◇ *directly ~ treaty provisions* | **legally**

effectiveness *noun*

ADJ. **overall** | **great, high** (*esp. AmE*), **increased** | **maximum** | **limited** | **relative** | **potential** | **long-term** ◇ *The drug's long-term ~ has yet to be established.* | **operational, organizational** | **political** | **combat** (*esp. AmE*), **military** | **teacher** ◇ *Exam results are sometimes used as a measure of teacher ~.* | **clinical, therapeutic, treatment**

VERB + EFFECTIVENESS **analyse/analyze, assess, check, determine, estimate, evaluate, examine, gauge, investigate, judge, measure, monitor, study, test** | **compare** | **demonstrate, indicate, prove, show** ◇ *The exam results demonstrated the ~ of the teaching.* | **achieve, ensure** ◇ *You may need to increase the dose to achieve maximum ~.* | **maintain** | **affect, impact, influence** | **boost, enhance, improve, increase, maximize** | **decrease, destroy, diminish, hamper, impair, limit, reduce, undermine** | **lose** ◇ *The drugs work well at first but gradually lose their ~.* | **question** ◇ *Many people questioned the ~ of economic sanctions.*

PREP. **~ as** ◇ *They're doing tests to evaluate the ~ of this herb as an antiseptic.* | **~ in** ◇ *the ~ of penicillin in controlling bacterial infection*

efficiency *noun*

ADJ. **ruthless** | **great, high** ◇ *attempts to achieve greater ~ in the production process* | **improved, increased** | **increasing** | **maximum, peak** (*esp. AmE*) ◇ *The optimum design allows bartenders to work at peak ~.* | **low** | **reduced** | **overall** | **relative** | **cost** | **energy, fuel, thermal** | **mental, physical** | **administrative, business, economic, industrial, management, mechanical, operational, organizational, production, technical**

VERB + EFFICIENCY **achieve** | **maintain** | **demonstrate, show** | **bring, create, deliver, offer, provide** ◇ *The Internet's promise to bring more ~ to the distribution chain is still materializing.* | **boost, enhance, gain, improve, increase, promote** | **maximize** | **decrease, reduce** | **lose** | **assess, calculate, determine, estimate, evaluate, examine, measure, test**

EFFICIENCY + NOUN **drive** (*esp. BrE*), **measures** ◇ *New procedures had been introduced as part of an ~ drive.* | **benefits, gains, improvements, increases, savings** ◇ *the ~ gains resulting from improved technology* | **losses** | **levels, standards** ◇ *We have failed to improve fuel ~ standards.* | **rating, score** | **expert** (*esp. AmE*)

PREP. **with ~** ◇ *The uprising was put down with ruthless ~.* | **~ in** ◇ *greater ~ in energy use*

efficient *adj.*

VERBS **appear, be, look, seem, sound** | **become** | **make sth**
ADV. **extremely, fairly, very, etc.** | **highly, incredibly, remarkably** | **perfectly** ◇ *We already have a perfectly ~ system—why change it?* | **brutally, ruthlessly** ◇ *He was ruthlessly ~ in acquiring estates.* | **increasingly** | **reasonably, relatively** | **economically, environmentally, technically**

PREP. **at** ◇ *Their equipment was not as ~ at finding gold as today's machinery.* | **in** ◇ *The heating system is very ~ in its use of fuel.*

effort *noun*

1 physical/mental energy needed to do sth

ADJ. **considerable** | **hard** ◇ *It took a whole day of hard ~ to knock down the wall.* | **constant, sustained** | **extra** | **minimal** ◇ *an outfit which enables you to look good with minimal ~* | **wasted** | **physical** | **intellectual, mental**
...OF EFFORT **amount** ◇ *the amount of ~ required*
VERB + EFFORT **demand, need, require, take** ◇ *It takes constant ~ to become fluent in a language.* | **devote, exert, expend, invest, put in** ◇ *All the team members have put in a great deal of ~.* | **waste** | **spare no** ◇ *No ~ has been spared to make this hotel a welcoming, comfortable place.* | **be worth** ◇ *The walk is difficult but well worth the ~.*
EFFORT + VERB **go into** ◇ *A lot of ~ went into making the costumes.*

PREP. **with ~, without ~** ◇ *This can be done quickly and with very little ~.*
PHRASES **a great deal of ~** | **time and ~** ◇ *Senior leaders are investing time and ~ in studying the issue.*

2 attempt to do sth

ADJ. **ambitious, big, enormous, great, Herculean, huge, major, massive, remarkable, special, tremendous** ◇ *I can see you have made a big ~ to clean up.* | **brave, heroic, superhuman, valiant** | **all-out, concentrated, determined, strenuous, tireless** | **painstaking** | **desperate, frantic** ◇ *their frantic ~s to put out the fire* | **final, last, last-ditch** ◇ *The UN General Secretary flew in a last-ditch ~ to save the talks.* | **continuing, ongoing, sustained** ◇ *the continuing ~ to find the missing girls* | **renewed** | **pioneering** ◇ *pioneering ~s to restructure the industry* | **genuine, good-faith** (*AmE*), **positive, real, serious, sincere** ◇ *Districts have not made a good-faith ~ to implement public school choice.* | **feeble, half-hearted** ◇ *She made a feeble ~ to smile, then started crying again.* | **successful** | **worthwhile** | **failed, fruitless, futile, unsuccessful, vain** | **misguided** | **collaborative, collective, combined, concerted, cooperative, coordinated, joint, team** ◇ *Students, teachers and families got together in a team ~ to decorate the school.* | **international** | **conscious, deliberate** ◇ *I have to make a conscious ~ to be polite so early in the morning.* | **voluntary** ◇ *The museum relies on the voluntary ~s of enthusiasts.* | **diplomatic** ◇ *Diplomatic ~s to end the crisis failed.* | **grassroots** ◇ *a grass-roots ~ by workers to transform their country* | **get-out-the-vote** (*AmE*) ◇ *The Democratic get-out-the-vote ~ placed heavy emphasis on the youth vote.* | **fund-raising, marketing, outreach** (*esp. AmE*), **humanitarian, recovery, relief, rescue** | **anti-terrorism, counter-terrorism** | **clean-up, conservation, rebuilding, reconstruction, restoration**

VERB + EFFORT **make** | **initiate, launch** ◇ *They launched an AIDS education ~.* | **mount, undertake** ◇ *The report outlines the ~s undertaken by the industry.* | **fund** | **accelerate, expand, increase, intensify, redouble, renew, step up** ◇ *The police have renewed their ~s to find the murderer.* | **continue** | **channel, concentrate, focus** ◇ *The police tried to channel their ~s into searching the forest.* | **redirect, refocus** | **coordinate, orchestrate, organize** | **combine, pool** ◇ *Governments are pooling their ~s to stem international terrorism.* | **duplicate** ◇ *We tried to ensure that ~s were not duplicated.* | **lead, spearhead** ◇ *He spearheaded ~s to raise money for the school.* | **target** ◇ *We're targeting our ~s at making our website appealing to younger people.* | **fail in** ◇ *He failed in his ~s to give up smoking.* | **resist** ◇ *The wound resisted all my ~s to stop it from bleeding.* | **abandon** | **complicate** | **derail, frustrate, hamper, hinder, impede, sabotage, stymie** (*informal, esp. AmE*), **thwart, undermine** ◇ *Critics said the plan would undermine ~s to address the current crisis.* | **be rewarded for, reward** ◇ *Her ~s were rewarded when she won an Oscar.* | **applaud, praise** ◇ *The gallery owner applauded the ~s of firefighters to save the exhibits.* | **appreciate** ◇ *We all appreciate your ~s.* | **oppose, support**

EFFORT + VERB **come to nothing, fail, fall flat, fall short** | **pay off, succeed, work** | **culminate in sth, produce sth, result in sth** | **be aimed at sth, be targeted at sth, focus on sth** ◇ *educational ~s targeted at children from ethnic minorities* | **earn sb sth** ◇ *Her ~s earned her a Nobel Prize.*

PREP. **in an/your ~** ◇ *The club has changed the rules in an ~ to make them fairer.* | **through sb's ~** ◇ *Through their ~s, enough money was raised to buy the equipment.*

PHRASES **your best ~s** ◇ *Despite our best ~s, we didn't manage to win the game.* | **a reward for your ~s** ◇ *Second prize was a fair reward for his ~s.* | **make every ~** ◇ *We are making every ~ to obtain the release of the hostages.*

effortless *adj.*

VERBS **appear, be, look, seem** ◇ *Tom made the jump look ~.*
ADV. **apparently, seemingly** ◇ *her apparently ~ performance* | **almost**

egg *noun*

1 of birds/as food

ADJ. **fresh** | **bad, rotten** | **free-range, organic** | **chicken, duck, hen's, quail's, etc.** | **unhatched** | **boiled, devilled/ deviled, fried, hard-boiled, poached, scrambled, soft-boiled** | **raw** | **beaten** | **Scotch** (*BrE*) | **chocolate, Easter**
... OF EGGS **clutch** ◊ *She lays a clutch of four ~s on average.* | **box** (*BrE*), **carton** (*AmE*)
VERB + EGG **lay, produce** | **deposit** (of insects, reptiles, etc.) | **hatch** | **incubate** | **emerge from, hatch from** | **guard, protect** ◊ *The males stay and guard the ~s.* | **bury** ◊ *Many reptiles bury their ~s.* | **collect** | **boil, cook, fry, poach, scramble** | **break, crack** ◊ *Crack two ~s into the mixture.* | **separate** ◊ *Separate the ~s, putting the whites to one side.* | **beat, whisk** | **brush sth with** ◊ *Brush the pastry with a little beaten ~.*
EGG + VERB **hatch** | **break, crack**
EGG + NOUN **shell** (usually **eggshell**) | **white, yolk** | **box** (*BrE*), **carton** (*AmE*) | **laying, production** | **cup** | **mayonnaise, noodles, pasta, roll** (= a type of Chinese food consisting of a thin tube of pastry filled with vegetables and/or meat and fried) (*AmE*), **salad, sandwich** | **wash** ◊ *Brush the dough with ~ wash.* | **timer** | **beater** (*esp. AmE*) (**whisk** in *BrE*) | **hunt** ◊ *We're just decorating eggs for the ~ hunt.*
PHRASES **the white of an ~, the yolk of an ~** | **bacon and ~s, ham and ~s** ◊ *a breakfast of bacon and ~s*
→ Special page at FOOD

2 cell from which a new young creature is formed

ADJ. **fertilized** | **unfertilized** | **donor** ◊ *Many women conceive through the use of a donor ~.*
VERB + EGG **fertilize** ◊ *Only one sperm fertilizes an ~.* | **produce, release** | **donate**
EGG + NOUN **donor** | **donation** | **removal** | **formation** | **cell** | **sac**
PHRASES **the nucleus of an ~**

ego *noun*

ADJ. **big, bloated, enormous, huge, inflated, large, massive, strong** ◊ *a conceited man with a very big ~* | **fragile, weak** | **bruised, wounded** ◊ *He was lucky to escape with just a bruised ~ when he fell off his bike.* | **healthy** | **human, male**
VERB + EGO **have** ◊ *He has a huge ~.* | **boost, feed, flatter, inflate, massage, stroke** ◊ *She likes to mix with people who flatter her ~.* | **satisfy** | **protect** | **bruise, crush, damage, deflate, dent, hurt, wound**
EGO + NOUN **boost** | **gratification** (*esp. AmE*) | **trip**
PHRASES **a blow to sb's ~** ◊ *It was a huge blow to his ~ to find out he was so unpopular.* | **a boost to sb's ~** | **check your ~ (at the door)** (*AmE, informal*) ◊ *Professionals need to check their ~s* (= be less egoistic) *and change their techniques.*

eject *verb*

1 push/send sth out

ADV. **forcibly** | **physically** | **summarily** (*esp. BrE*) ◊ *They were summarily ~ed by the security guard.*
PREP. **from** ◊ *He was forcibly ~ed from the restaurant.*

2 make an emergency exit

ADV. **safely**
PREP. **from** ◊ *All the crew members ~ed safely from the plane.*

elaborate *verb*

ADV. **further** ◊ *This point will be ~d further in the next chapter.* | **at length** | **briefly** ◊ *Let me briefly ~ on this.*
VERB + ELABORATE **attempt to, try to** | **refuse to**
PREP. **on, upon** ◊ *They refused to ~ on the reasons for their decision.*

elaborate *adj.*

VERBS **be, look, seem, sound** ◊ *The plans looked very ~.* | **become**

ADV. **extremely, fairly, very, etc.** | **highly** ◊ *highly ~ carvings* | **increasingly**

elastic *noun*

ADJ. **loose, tight** ◊ *an old skirt with loose ~* | **hair** (*AmE*) | **knicker** (*BrE*)
... OF ELASTIC **length, piece** ◊ *The skirt is held up by a length of ~ around the waist.*
ELASTIC + VERB **break, go** (*esp. BrE*), **snap** ◊ *The ~ in these socks has gone.*

elated *adj.*

VERBS **be, feel, look, seem, sound**
ADV. **very** | **absolutely** | **strangely**
PREP. **at** ◊ *I felt strangely ~ at the news.* | **by** ◊ *~ by our victory* | **with** ◊ *~ with his success*

elation *noun*

ADJ. **great, pure, sheer** | **unbelievable** | **mild** | **curious** | **momentary**
VERB + ELATION **experience, feel**
PREP. **~ at** ◊ *She showed her ~ at having finally achieved her ambition.*
PHRASES **a feeling of ~, a mood of ~, a sense of ~** ◊ *I felt a strange sense of ~.* | **tears of ~**

elbow *noun*

ADJ. **left, right** | **sharp** | **dislocated, fractured** | **sore** | **pitching, throwing** (both in baseball)
VERB + ELBOW **lean, place, rest** ◊ *He rested one ~ on the wall as he spoke.* | **lean on, prop yourself up on, raise yourself up on** ◊ *She opened her eyes and propped herself up on one ~ to look at him.* | **catch, grasp, take** ◊ *He caught her ~ to steady her.* | **jab, slam** (*esp. AmE*), **thrust** ◊ *She thrust her ~ into her attacker's face.* | **bend, flex** | **extend, straighten** | **bang, hit** ◊ *I banged my ~ on the table as I got up.* | **dislocate, fracture, injure** | **lock** ◊ *Extend your arms without locking your ~s.*
ELBOW + NOUN **joint, ligament** | **injury** | **pain, problem** | **surgery** | **pad** | **room** ◊ *The office cubicles give you hardly any ~ room.*
PREP. **above the ~** | **at your ~** ◊ *A voice at my ~ said, 'Please sit down!'* | **below the ~** ◊ *The whole of his arm below the ~ was badly burned.* | **beneath your ~, under your ~** ◊ *She slid a hand under his ~ to guide him.* | **by the ~** ◊ *He took his guest by the ~ and steered him in the direction of the bar.* | **on one ~** ◊ *He raised himself on one ~ and looked at the bedside clock.*
PHRASES **be up to your ~s in sth** ◊ *He was up to his ~s in hot water.* | **the crook of your ~** ◊ *She was cradling a small bundle in the crook of her ~.* | **dig your ~ into sb's ribs** ◊ *She dug her ~ into Jim's ribs to remind him not to give the secret away.* | **rub ~s with sb** (*figurative, AmE*) ◊ *He had been rubbing ~s with celebrities.*

elect *verb*

ADV. **annually** ◊ *Members of the council are ~ed annually.* | **locally, nationally** | **democratically, freely, popularly** | **unanimously** | **directly, indirectly** ◊ *It was decided that the president should be ~ed directly in free elections.* | **duly, formally** | **legally, legitimately**
PREP. **to** ◊ *She was the first black woman ~ed to Congress.* ◊ *He was ~ed to Parliament in 1997.*
PHRASES **be ~ed, get ~ed** ◊ *What changes will he make if he gets ~ed?* | **be declared ~ed** ◊ *Any candidate with more than half the votes shall be declared ~ed.* | **be ~ed unopposed** ◊ *Five were successful, three being ~ed un-opposed.* | **newly ~ed, recently ~ed** ◊ *the newly ~ed chairman*

election *noun*

ADJ. **clean** (*esp. AmE*), **fair, free, open** | **fraudulent, rigged, stolen** | **close** ◊ *Predicting the result of close ~s is a perilous game.* | **landslide** ◊ *The party won a landslide ~.* | **contested, disputed** ◊ *They demanded a rerun of the disputed presidential ~.* | **historic** | **competitive** | **popular** ◊

the democratic concept of popular ~s | **democratic, multi-party, non-partisan** | **direct, indirect** | **fresh, new** | **last** | **recent** | **early** ◇ *The prime minister may decide to call an early ~.* | **scheduled** ◇ *the scheduled Lebanese ~s in May* | **forthcoming, upcoming** (*esp. AmE*) | **special** | **primary** (*in the US*), **run-off** (*esp. AmE*) | **midterm, off-year** (*AmE*) | **recall** (= an election to remove an elected official from office) (*AmE*) ◇ *The Governor faces an unprecedented recall ~.* | **county, federal, local, municipal, national, nationwide, provincial, regional, state, statewide** (*AmE*) | **congressional, council** (*esp. BrE*), **general, gubernatorial** (*AmE*), **judicial, leadership, legislative, local-government, mayoral, papal, parliamentary, party, presidential, Senate** | **school board** | **student council** (*AmE*), **student government** (*AmE*), **student union** (*BrE*)

VERB + ELECTION **conduct, have, hold, run** | **call** | **contest, fight** | **run for** (*esp. AmE*), **stand for** (*esp. BrE*) | **dispute** ◇ *a bitterly disputed ~* | **lose, win** | **concede** | **sweep** (*AmE*) ◇ *The party swept Turkish ~s in November.* | **affect, influence** | **sway** (*esp. AmE*), **swing, tip** (*esp. AmE*) ◇ *votes which could swing the entire national ~* | **decide, determine** ◇ *The people will decide this ~ and they will prove all the polls wrong.* | **organize, schedule** (*esp. AmE*) | **monitor, oversee, supervise** | **cancel, delay, postpone** | **derail** ◇ *The violence in the country will not derail the ~s.* | **fix, manipulate, rig, steal** ◇ *claims that voter fraud had stolen the ~ for the Republicans* | **boycott**

ELECTION + VERB **take place** | **be due, be scheduled for** ◇ *Elections are scheduled for November.* | **approach, loom**

ELECTION + NOUN **campaign** | **manifesto** (*esp. BrE*), **pledge** (*esp. BrE*), **promise** | **statement** | **issue** ◇ *Education is a key ~ issue.* | **debate** | **strategy** | **battle, contest** | **turnout** ◇ *The ~ turnout in 2008 was high.* | **ballot, poll** | **outcome, result, returns** (*esp. AmE*) ◇ *A lot hangs on the ~ result.* ◇ *All counties have now certified their ~ returns.* | **defeat, victory** | **broadcast** (*esp. BrE*), **coverage, news** | **procedure, process, system** | **candidate** | **administrator** (*AmE*), **commissioner, judge** (*AmE*), **monitor, observer, official** (*AmE*), **worker** | **board** (*esp. AmE*), **commission** | **office** | **date, day, eve, night, period, season, time, year** ◇ *It was successful in rallying voters at ~ time.* | **cycle** ◇ *The US is reaching the end of its latest presidential ~ cycle.* | **fraud** | **reform**

PREP. **at a/the ~, in a/the ~** ◇ *in the 2001 general ~* | **by ~** ◇ *Membership of the committee is by ~.* | **~ to** ◇ *her ~ to the Senate*

PHRASES **the outcome of an ~** | **the run-up to an ~** ◇ *opinion poll results in the run-up to ~s*

electorate *noun*

ADJ. **educated, informed** | **apathetic, sceptical/skeptical** | **divided, polarized** | **general** ◇ *His statements are likely to cost him dearly among the general ~.* | **total** ◇ *Catholics make up over a quarter of the total ~.* | **local** (*esp. BrE*), **national** | **mass** ◇ *The rise of a mass ~ forced politicians to broaden their appeal.* | **middle-class, working-class, etc.** | **American, British, etc.** | **Democratic, Republican, etc.**

VERB + ELECTORATE **divide** ◇ *issues which have divided the ~*

ELECTORATE + VERB **go to the polls, vote** ◇ *the representative chosen by the ~*

PHRASES **the ~ as a whole, the ~ at large** ◇ *the need to appeal to the ~ at large*

electrician *noun*

ADJ. **licensed** (*AmE*), **qualified, trained** | **apprentice** (*esp. BrE*) | **self-employed**

VERB + ELECTRICIAN **call in, hire** (*esp. AmE*) ◇ *We need to call in an ~ to sort out the wiring.*

ELECTRICIAN + VERB **rewire sth, wire sth** ◇ *You'll need a qualified ~ to rewire your house.* | **install sth** | **check sth, fix sth, repair sth**

→ Note at JOB

electricity *noun*

ADJ. **high-voltage, low-voltage** | **mains** (*BrE*) | **static** | **cheap, low-cost** | **free** | **wholesale** | **clean, green** (*esp. BrE*), **renewable** (*esp. BrE*) | **solar, wind-generated**

VERB + ELECTRICITY **create, generate, make, produce** | **deliver, provide, supply** ◇ *The hydroelectric plant provides ~ for half the island's population.* | **have** ◇ *All the houses now have ~.* | **conduct** ◇ *Metals conduct ~ well.* | **be powered by, consume, use** | **cut off, disconnect** ◇ *Her ~ was cut off when she didn't pay her bill.* | **lose** ◇ *More than a million customers lost ~ following the flooding.* | **restore** ◇ *Crews did their best to restore ~ after the storm.* | **save** ◇ *I switched the light off to save ~.* | **sell** | **buy, purchase**

ELECTRICITY + VERB **flow, run** ◇ *Electricity flows through the wires in the circuit.* | **surge through sth**

ELECTRICITY + NOUN **bill** ◇ *Insulating your house could cut your ~ bill by half.* | **charges, costs, prices, rates** (*esp. AmE*) ◇ *a 10% drop in ~ prices* | **meter** (*esp. BrE*) | **board** (*esp. BrE*), **company, industry, sector, supplier** | **supply** | **grid, network, system** ◇ *The town will soon be connected to the national ~ grid.* | **market** | **consumption, demand, usage, use** | **shortage** | **crisis** ◇ *the company's role in California's ~ crisis* | **blackout** ◇ *A high-voltage fault sparked an ~ blackout.* | **generation, production** | **deregulation** | **generator, plant, substation** (*esp. BrE*) | **pylon** (*esp. BrE*) | **cable, line, wire**

electric shock *noun*

ADJ. **massive** (*esp. BrE*), **powerful, severe, strong** | **mild, small**

... OF ELECTRIC SHOCKS **series** ◇ *a series of ~s to her brain*

VERB + ELECTRIC SHOCK **get, receive, suffer** | **administer, deliver** | **give sb/sth** | **be tortured with**

ELECTRIC-SHOCK + NOUN **therapy, treatment**

PREP. **~ on** ◇ *He felt a strong ~ on his back.* | **~ to** ◇ *They administer ~s to the heart.*

electronics *noun*

ADJ. **high-tech, sophisticated, state-of-the-art** | **digital** | **automotive** (*esp. AmE*), **consumer, defence/defense, home** (*esp. AmE*), **medical**

ELECTRONICS + NOUN **business, company, firm** (*esp. BrE*), **giant, group** ◇ *Their company merged with a Japanese ~ giant.* | **industry, maker** (*esp. AmE*), **manufacturer** | **market, sector** (*esp. BrE*) | **retailer, supplier** | **store** (*esp. AmE*) | **device, equipment, product** | **engineer, specialist, technician** (*esp. AmE*)

→ Note at SUBJECT (for more verbs and nouns)

elegance *noun*

ADJ. **great** | **classical** | **casual, simple, understated** | **a certain** ◇ *The original poem has a certain ~ that is lost in the translation.* | **sartorial** (*esp. BrE*) ◇ *John has never been known for his sartorial ~.*

... OF ELEGANCE **air, touch** ◇ *The ironwork lends a touch of ~ to the house.*

VERB + ELEGANCE **display, have** ◇ *The building has great ~ and charm.* | **lack** | **add, give sth, lend sth** ◇ *The pillars give a classical ~ to the room.*

elegant *adj.*

VERBS **be, feel, look**

ADV. **extremely, fairly, very, etc.** | **particularly** | **beautifully** ◇ *the beautifully ~ spire of the church* | **casually, quietly** ◇ *the quietly ~ wives of the directors* | **classically** ◇ *a classically ~ hotel* | **surprisingly** | **supremely** (*esp. BrE*) ◇ *the artist's supremely ~ portraits of society beauties*

element *noun*

1 one part of sth

ADJ. **basic, core, critical, crucial, decisive, distinctive, essential, fundamental, important, key, main, major, necessary, principal, significant, vital** | **considerable, large** ◇ *There is a considerable ~ of danger in her job.* | **dominant** ◇ *The promise of tax cuts became the dominant ~ in the campaign.* | **fringe** ◇ *These ideas are not just the province of a fringe ~ in the party.* | **competitive** ◇ *There is*

too much of a competitive ~ in the sales department. |
disparate, diverse ◊ *the disparate ~s brought together in
these paintings* | **racial, sexual** ◊ *Police say there may have
been a racial ~ to the attacks.* | **human** ◊ *He emphasizes the
human ~ of the story.* | **constituent, constitutive** (*esp. AmE*)
◊ *the constituent ~s of the universe* | **functional, structural** |
architectural, decorative, design, musical, visual ◊ *the
narrative and decorative ~s in Pop art*
VERB + ELEMENT **be, comprise, constitute, form** | **contain,
have, include, involve** ◊ *These stories do contain an ~ of
truth.* | **blend, combine, fuse, incorporate, integrate, mix**
◊ *an offbeat theatrical production that combines ~s of
fantasy and satire* | **add, introduce**
PREP. **~ in** ◊ *This constitutes one of the key ~s in their reform
package.* | **~ of** ◊ *Practical work will form a major ~ of the
syllabus.* ◊ *There may have been an ~ of jealousy in her
response.*

2 the elements bad weather
VERB + THE ELEMENTS **brave** ◊ *I put on my thick coat ready to
brave the ~s.* | **battle, battle against** ◊ *He told us stories of
how he had battled the ~s on his mountaineering trips.* | **be
exposed to, be open to** ◊ *The place was completely exposed
to the ~s.* | **be protected from, be sheltered from**
PHRASES **protection from the ~s, shelter from the ~s**

elephant noun
ADJ. **African** | **Asian, Indian** | **bull, cow** | **female, male** |
baby | **trained** | **wild** | **rogue** | **orphaned** ◊ *a conserva-
tionist who cares for orphaned ~s*
... OF ELEPHANTS **herd**
VERB + ELEPHANT **hunt, poach, shoot** ◊ *It's been about five
years since the last ~ was poached for its ivory.* | **cull, kill**
ELEPHANT + VERB **trumpet** | **charge, stampede** | **trample sb**
ELEPHANT + NOUN **herd** | **population** | **tusk** | **ivory** | **dung** |
conservation | **gun**

elevator noun (AmE) → See also LIFT
ADJ. **glass** | **express, high-speed** | **creaky** ◊ *We took a creaky
old ~ up to the third floor.* | **freight, grain, service** ◊ *The
agents in the station sent the checked baggage down stairs on
a freight ~.* | **hotel**
VERB + ELEVATOR **ride, take** ◊ *He rode the ~ to the 43rd floor.* |
use | **board, enter** | **exit, leave** | **call** ◊ *York pressed the
button to call the ~.* | **install**
ELEVATOR + VERB **go up** | **descend, go down** | **arrive, reach
sth** | **stop** | **close, open** | **ding** ◊ *The ~ dinged and the door
opened.*
ELEVATOR + NOUN **shaft** ◊ *One guy fell down the ~ shaft.* | **door**
◊ *The ~ doors closed behind her.* | **button** | **lobby** | **music** |
man, operator | **ride** | **system**

eliminate verb
ADV. **altogether, completely, entirely, totally** ◊ *The risk
cannot be ~d altogether.* ◊ *This procedure does not completely
~ the possibility of an accident.* | **almost, nearly, practically,
virtually** | **largely** | **effectively, essentially** ◊ *Getting this
job has effectively ~d his financial worries.* | **successfully** |
possibly, potentially | **eventually, ultimately** ◊ *a policy
that they claim will eventually ~ corruption in the industry* |
gradually | **quickly, rapidly** | **immediately**
VERB + ELIMINATE **seek to, take steps to, try to** | **help (to)** | **be
designed to** ◊ *The single market is designed to ~ barriers to
free movement.* | **be impossible to**
PREP. **from** ◊ *Try to ~ fatty foods from your diet.*

elite noun
ADJ. **governing, power** (*esp. AmE*), **ruling** ◊ *He was an
influential member of the ruling ~.* | **powerful, privileged** |
corrupt | **educated** | **landed, moneyed** (*esp. AmE*), **wealthy**
| **metropolitan, urban** | **local, national** | **foreign** |
Western | **black, white** | **conservative, liberal** | **techno-
cratic** ◊ *the European Union's technocratic ~s* | **business,**

**corporate, cultural, economic, intellectual, media, mili-
tary, political, professional, secular, social**
VERB + ELITE **create, form** ◊ *These people form an ~ who have
the power to make decisions.* | **join**
PHRASES **a member of an ~** ◊ *a club for members of the
business ~*

eloquent adj.
VERBS **be** | **wax** ◊ *He waxed ~ about her talents as an actress.*
ADV. **extremely, fairly, very, etc.** ◊ *a very ~ speaker* |
remarkably | **especially, particularly**
PREP. **about, on** ◊ *He grew very ~ on the subject.*

elusive adj.
VERBS **be, prove** ◊ *Further movie roles have proved somewhat
~ for the young actor.* | **become** | **remain**
ADV. **extremely, fairly, very, etc.** ◊ *a very eloquent speaker* |
highly | **ever** ◊ *He was searching for the ever ~ 'perfect job'.* |
strangely ◊ *A cure has proved strangely ~.* | **notoriously** ◊
Truth is a notoriously ~ quality. | **frustratingly, madden-
ingly** ◊ *The murderer remained frustratingly ~.*

email (also e-mail) noun
ADJ. **junk, spam, unsolicited, unwanted** | **abusive** (*esp. BrE*),
angry (*esp. AmE*), **nasty** (*esp. AmE*) | **incoming, outgoing**
VERB + EMAIL **compose, type, write** | **fire off, send** ◊ *When I
saw what he'd written I fired off an angry ~.* | **get, receive** |
exchange ~s | **use** ◊ *Some members used ~ to renew their
membership.* | **have** ◊ *If a member does not have ~, a letter is
sent.* | **access, check, open, read** ◊ *software which allows
you to access your ~s from any computer* ◊ *Most people check
their ~ several times a day.* | **answer, reply to, return** ◊ *He
never returns my ~s.* | **forward** | **delete** | **archive, store** |
retrieve | **download** | **print** | **scan** | **monitor** ◊ *Some
companies monitor all employee ~.* | **post** ◊ *You cannot post
private ~s to the website.* | **block, filter** ◊ *filtering devices
that block unwanted ~*
EMAIL + VERB **arrive** ◊ *An ~ arrives in your inbox.* | **announce
sth, claim sth, say sth, state sth, tell sb sth** ◊ *an ~
announcing his promotion* | **ask sth, request sth** ◊ *I sent an
~ asking about their products.* | **contain sth** ◊ *The ~ contains
a link to the retailer's website.*
EMAIL + NOUN **address** | **message** | **attachment** | **service,
system** ◊ *a free ~ service* | **server** | **provider** ◊ *Web-based ~
providers* | **subscriber, user** | **account** | **box** (*esp. AmE*),
inbox | **program, software** | **access** ◊ *Each of the rooms has
Internet and ~ access.* | **link** | **reply, response** ◊ *The next
day I got 400 ~ responses.* | **list** ◊ *Add your name to the ~ list.*
| **alert, reminder, update, warning** ◊ *You can sign up to
receive ~ alerts.* | **confirmation, enquiry** (*esp. BrE*),
invitation, notification, query, request ◊ *Users receive ~
notification of special offers.* | **campaign, survey** |
**communication, conversation, correspondence, discus-
sion, exchange, interview** | **contact** ◊ *She is in constant ~
contact with a number of college staff.* | **newsletter** | **traffic**
◊ *the rise in corporate ~ traffic* | **spam** | **hoax** (*esp. AmE*),
scam | **virus, worm**
→ Special page at COMPUTER

embargo noun
ADJ. **complete, strict, total** | **partial** | **mandatory** | **crippling**
◊ *the crippling economic ~ against Haiti* | **international** |
economic | **arms, oil, trade**
VERB + EMBARGO **impose, place, put, put in place** ◊ *Congress
put an ~ on trade with these countries.* | **enforce, tighten** |
end, lift ◊ *The government has agreed to lift the ~ imposed
ten years ago.* | **break, violate** ◊ *We knew the arms ~ was
being broken.*
PREP. **~ against** ◊ *the international ~ against the country* | **~
on** ◊ *a strict ~ on oil imports*

embark verb
PHR V **embark on/upon sth**
ADV. **immediately** | **reluctantly** | **recently** ◊ *The company
has recently ~ed on a new venture.* | **already** ◊ *She has
already ~ed on her studies.*

embarrassed *adj.*

1 shy/awkward/ashamed

VERBS **be, feel, look, seem, sound** | **become**
ADV. **extremely, fairly, very, etc.** | **acutely, deeply, terribly** | **almost** | **a little, slightly, etc.** | **faintly** ◊ *He looked faintly ~.* | **clearly, obviously, visibly**
PREP. **about** ◊ *She's ~ about her height.* | **at** ◊ *He felt acutely ~ at being the focus of attention.* | **by** ◊ *She seemed almost ~ by her own outburst.* | **for** ◊ *Amy felt ~ for him.*

2 not having any money

VERBS **be**
ADV. **financially**

embarrassing *adj.*

VERBS **be, prove, sound** | **become, get** | **make sth** ◊ *My mother's presence made the situation even more ~.* | **find sb/ sth** ◊ *I found the whole evening deeply ~.*
ADV. **extremely, fairly, very, etc.** | **acutely** (*esp. BrE*), **deeply, excruciatingly, highly, particularly, terribly, toe-curlingly** (*BrE*) ◊ *a deeply ~ moment* | **increasingly** | **almost** | **a little, slightly, etc.** | **potentially** | **politically**
PREP. **for** ◊ *It was acutely ~ for us all.* | **to** ◊ *This latest incident could be ~ to the government.*

embarrassment *noun*

1 feeling of being embarrassed

ADJ. **acute, considerable, great** | **total, utter** | **slight** ◊ *She smiled to hide her slight ~.* | **further** | **obvious** | **personal** | **public** ◊ *The agreement was made in secret to avoid public ~.*
VERB + EMBARRASSMENT **feel** ◊ *I felt some ~ as we shook hands.* | **suffer** ◊ *He suffered great personal ~ after failing the tests.* | **cover, hide** | **cause** | **risk** ◊ *Pender decided to risk ~ and seek help.* | **avoid, prevent** ◊ *The government wishes to avoid further ~ over the affair.* | **blush with, flush with, squirm with** (*esp. BrE*) ◊ *I still squirm with ~ at the thought of it.* | **die from, die of** (*figurative*) ◊ *I could have died of ~ when I saw her standing behind me.* | **ease, relieve** | **save sb, spare sb** ◊ *Helen changed the subject to save me the ~ of replying.*
PREP. **in** ◊ *We all watched in silent ~ as Mr Rogers started to cry.* | **with ~, without ~** ◊ *I could finally talk about my problem without ~.* | **~ at** ◊ *her ~ at being found out* | **~ over** ◊ *the government's ~ over the affair*
PHRASES **(much) to sb's ~** ◊ *Much to his ~, Mike realized that a small crowd was watching him.* | **feelings of ~** | **a flush of ~** ◊ *A flush of ~ came to her cheeks.* | **a source of ~**

2 sb/sth that makes you embarrassed

ADJ. **great, huge, major, serious, severe** (*esp. BrE*) | **potential** | **financial, political, social** | **national** ◊ *The president became a national ~.*
VERB + EMBARRASSMENT **be, become, prove** ◊ *The protests were becoming something of an ~ to the government.* | **consider sb/sth**
PREP. **~ for** ◊ *The episode was a huge ~ for all concerned.* | **~ to** ◊ *The poor child was considered an ~ to his family.*

embassy *noun*

ADJ. **foreign** | **American, British, Chinese, etc.**
VERB + EMBASSY **close, open** ◊ *They broke off diplomatic relations and closed the embassies in each other's country.* | **reopen** | **attack, bomb, storm** | **guard**
EMBASSY + NOUN **building, compound** | **official, personnel, staff** | **spokesman, spokeswoman** | **bombing**
PREP. **at a/the ~** ◊ *She works at the Malaysian ~ in Buenos Aires.* | **in a/the ~** ◊ *a fire in the Spanish ~* | **outside a/the ~** ◊ *a protest outside the American ~*

embedded *adj.*

VERBS **be** | **become**
ADV. **deeply, firmly** | **culturally** ◊ *societies where tattooing is culturally ~*

PREP. **in, within** ◊ *These ideas are deeply ~ in our culture.*

embrace *noun*

ADJ. **close, strong, tight, warm** ◊ *the comfort of her warm ~* | **comforting, gentle, loving, sweet, tender** | **passionate** | **friendly, protective** | **long, quick**
VERB + EMBRACE **be locked in, hold sb in** ◊ *They were locked in a passionate ~ on the station platform.* | **tighten** ◊ *He closed his eyes and tightened his ~.* | **feel** ◊ *She would give anything just to feel his warm ~ again.* | **share** ◊ *The two friends shared one last ~.* | **accept** ◊ *She accepted his warm ~.* | **return** (*esp. AmE*) ◊ *He returned the ~ for a moment.* | **escape, escape from, free yourself from** ◊ *He managed to free himself from her ~.* | **release sb from** ◊ *He released her from his ~.*
PREP. **in an ~** ◊ *two lovers in a tight ~* | **into an ~** ◊ *He drew her into his ~.*

embrace *verb*

1 put your arms around sb

ADV. **tightly, warmly** ◊ *He rose from his chair and ~d her warmly.* | **gently, passionately**

2 accept sth

ADV. **genuinely, really, truly** ◊ *the only party which fully ~s the concept of democracy* | **completely, fully** | **widely** (*esp. AmE*) ◊ *Soccer has become more widely ~d by Americans.* | **eagerly, enthusiastically, happily, passionately, readily, warmly, wholeheartedly, with enthusiasm** ◊ *She ~d the feminist cause with enthusiasm.* | **increasingly** | **openly, publicly**

embroider *verb*

ADV. **beautifully, delicately, exquisitely, finely** | **elaborately** | **heavily, richly** ◊ *a robe of richly ~ed silk*
PREP. **on** ◊ *She ~ed flowers on the front of the dress.* | **with** ◊ *She ~ed the dress with flowers.*

embryo *noun*

ADJ. **developing** | **fertilized** | **early** ◊ *the cells of an early ~* | **frog, human, etc.** | **frozen** ◊ *frozen ~s stored at a fertility clinic* | **cloned**
VERB + EMBRYO **create, produce** ◊ *The couple has produced three ~s for implantation.* | **implant** ◊ *Two or three ~s are implanted into the woman's body.* | **transfer** | **donate** | **clone** ◊ *the current debate over cloning human ~s* | **freeze** | **destroy, discard, kill** ◊ *Some people believe that destroying an ~ is murder.*
EMBRYO + VERB **develop**
EMBRYO + NOUN **development, growth** | **cell** | **research**

emerge *verb*

1 come out

ADV. **slowly** | **suddenly** | **eventually, finally** | **fully** ◊ *The plant has fully ~d from the soil.*
PREP. **from** ◊ *The world is only slowly emerging from recession.* | **into** ◊ *They suddenly ~d into brilliant sunshine.* | **out of** ◊ *the musical forms that ~d out of the American black experience*
PHRASES **~ fully formed** ◊ *His enormous talent had ~d fully formed.*

2 become known

ADV. **clearly, strongly** ◊ *One thing ~s very clearly from this study.* | **gradually** | **quickly, soon** ◊ *The answer to the problem quickly ~d.* | **recently** | **later, subsequently** ◊ *It subsequently ~d that he had known about the deal all along.* | **eventually, ultimately** ◊ *What eventually ~d from the election disaster was a realization that it was time for change.*
VERB + EMERGE **begin to, start to** ◊ *Problems with this drug are now beginning to ~.*
PREP. **from** ◊ *Several facts started to ~ from my investigation.*

3 start to exist
ADV. **rapidly** ◇ *The Pacific region has rapidly ~d as a leading force on the world stage.* | **gradually, slowly** | **naturally**
PHRASES **newly ~d, newly emerging** ◇ *newly emerging areas of science*

emergence *noun*

ADJ. **gradual** | **rapid, sudden** | **recent** | **early, late**
VERB + EMERGENCE **lead to** ◇ *Conditions after the war led to the ~ of a new type of political party.* | **herald, mark, signal** | **trace** | **see, witness** ◇ *The last decade saw the ~ of a dynamic economy.* | **encourage, facilitate, promote** ◇ *The annual competition has encouraged the ~ of several talented young musicians.* | **prevent**
PREP. **~ as** ◇ *his ~ as the party's leader* | **~ from** ◇ *the island's ~ from the sea*

emergency *noun*

ADJ. **dire, extreme, major, real, serious, true** ◇ *Don't call me unless its a real ~.* | **life-threatening** | **sudden, unexpected, unforeseen** | **complex** | **international, national, state** ◇ *in times of national ~* | **health, medical, surgical** ◇ *It's a disaster and a public-health ~ in the making.* | **Make sure your policy covers you in case of medical ~.** | **family** ◇ *He missed the meeting because of a family ~.* | **military** | **humanitarian** | **in-flight** (*esp. AmE*) | **fire, snow** (*both AmE*)
VERB + EMERGENCY **have** ◇ *When a member of staff has a family ~, a project can get delayed.* | **cope with, deal with, handle, respond to** ◇ *firefighters on call to respond to emergencies* | **declare** ◇ *The assembly declared a national ~.* | **be, constitute** ◇ *Complete retention of urine constitutes a medical ~.*
EMERGENCY + VERB **arise, happen, occur** ◇ *Call this number if any unforeseen ~ should arise.*
EMERGENCY + NOUN **situation** ◇ *Would you know what to do in an ~ situation?* | **action, measures, plan, procedures, response** | **preparedness** (*esp. AmE*) | **management** | **laws, legislation, regulations** | **powers** ◇ *The police have been given ~ powers to deal with the crisis.* | **rule** ◇ *The government imposed ~ rule and suspended civil rights.* | **meeting, session, summit, talks** ◇ *an ~ session of the United Nations* | **cover** (*esp. BrE*) ◇ *The army provided ~ cover when the ambulance service went on strike.* | **checklist** | **services** ◇ *The ~ services are struggling to cope with the number of call-outs.* | **crew, official, personnel** (*esp. AmE*), **responders** (*AmE*), **worker** ◇ *An ~ crew was called out.* ◇ *the New York police and fire and ~ responders* | **aid, assistance, funds, help, relief, supply** ◇ *Emergency supplies of food have been flown to the area.* | **fund** | **leave** (*AmE*) ◇ *He got ~ leave when his Dad died.* | **call** ◇ *The ambulance crashed while answering an ~ call.* | **backup** (*esp. AmE*), **rescue** | **shutdown** ◇ *an ~ shutdown of the nuclear reactor* | **centre/center, department, room** (*esp. AmE*), **ward** ◇ *one of the busiest accident and ~ departments in Scotland* (*BrE*) | **doctor** (*esp. BrE*), **physician** (*esp. AmE*), **vet** | **admission, case** ◇ *Emergency admissions to the hospital are given top priority.* | **care, medicine, operation, surgery, treatment** | **contraception** | **appendectomy, Caesarean, etc.** | **kit** | **repairs** | **exit** | **landing** | **evacuation** ◇ *the ~ evacuation of more than 300 passengers* | **brake** | **shelter** | **button, equipment, vehicle** | **lights** | **generator**
PREP. **for ~** ◇ *She told me to keep the money for emergencies.* | **in an ~** ◇ *I need to know what to do in an ~.*
PHRASES **in case of ~, in case of emergencies** ◇ *There's a fire blanket on the kitchen wall in case of emergencies.* | **a state of ~** ◇ *The president immediately declared a state of ~.*

emigration *noun*

ADJ. **large-scale, mass**
... OF EMIGRATION **wave** ◇ *He called for a halt to the recent wave of ~.*
PREP. **~ from** ◇ *~ from Europe to America* | **~ to**

emission *noun*

ADJ. **harmful, noxious, toxic** | **gaseous** | **automobile** (*esp. AmE*), **exhaust, tailpipe** (*AmE*), **vehicle** | **industrial** | **atmospheric** | **greenhouse gas** ◇ *the Kyoto protocol on cutting greenhouse gas ~s* | **acid, carbon, carbon dioxide, lead, mercury, methane, sulphur/sulfur, etc.** | **global** ◇ *global ~s of carbon dioxide*
VERB + EMISSION **generate, produce** | **curb, cut, lower, minimize, reduce** ◇ *We must take action to cut vehicle ~s.* | **eliminate** | **control, limit, regulate** | **offset** ◇ *New power plants must offset ~s by funding climate-change projects.* | **measure, monitor**
EMISSION + VERB **increase** | **decrease, fall**
EMISSION + NOUN **levels, rates**
PREP. **~s from** ◇ *measures to reduce harmful ~s from traffic*

emotion *noun*

ADJ. **deep, extreme, intense, overwhelming, powerful, profound, strong, violent** | **genuine, heartfelt, real, true** | **complex** | **conflicting, contradictory, mixed, tangled** ◇ *She felt torn by conflicting ~s.* | **strange** | **dark, destructive, negative, violent** ◇ *We teach people to handle negative ~s such as fear and anger.* | **positive** | **inner, innermost** | **basic, primary** | **pure, raw** ◇ *a moving performance full of raw ~* | **painful** | **heightened** ◇ *the heightened ~s which resulted from the terrorist attack* | **pent-up, suppressed** ◇ *Years of pent-up ~ came out as he sobbed.* | **human** ◇ *Fear is a normal human ~.*
... OF EMOTION **flicker, hint, trace** ◇ *There wasn't a hint of ~ in his eyes.* | **flood, rush, surge, wave** ◇ *She felt a sudden rush of ~ at the thought of seeing him again.* | **display** ◇ *She could not cope with such public displays of ~.*
VERB + EMOTION **experience, feel** ◇ *the ~s that we experience as children* ◇ *He felt no ~ as she left.* | **be choked with, be filled with, be overcome with** ◇ *Her voice was choked with ~.* | **be devoid of, be drained of, lack** | **communicate, convey, display, express, show** ◇ *Drama can help children to express their ~s.* ◇ *The woman's face showed no ~.* | **capture** ◇ *The film captures the real ~ of this terrible event.* | **release** ◇ *Releasing these ~s is part of the healing process.* | **channel** | **share** ◇ *Boys often find it difficult to share their ~s.* | **betray, reveal** | **shake with, tremble with** ◇ *She realized she was shaking all over with ~.* | **bottle up, conceal, hide, hold back, mask, repress, stifle, suppress** | **control, regulate** | **cope with, deal with, fight, handle, manage** | **confront** ◇ *Victims of crime are encouraged to confront their ~s.* | **arouse, elicit, evoke, provoke, stir, stir up, trigger** ◇ *an incident that has aroused strong ~s locally* | **be charged with, be full of** ◇ *a speech that was charged with ~* | **read, sense** ◇ *You could read his ~s by looking into his eyes.*
PREP. **with ~, without ~** ◇ *She spoke with deep ~.*
PHRASES **depth of ~, intensity of ~** ◇ *The movie has a surprising depth of ~ for a comedy.* | **~s run high** (= people feel very angry, nervous, excited, etc.) ◇ *Emotions are running high on the issue.* | **a gamut of ~s, a range of ~s** ◇ *Her performance in the play covered the whole gamut of ~s.*

emotional *adj.*

VERBS **be, feel, look, sound** | **become, get, grow** ◇ *He got very ~ during the speech.* | **make sb** ◇ *Having all her friends around her made her very ~.*
ADV. **extremely, fairly, very, etc.** | **deeply, highly, intensely** | **overly**
PREP. **about** ◇ *Don't be so ~ about everything!*
PHRASES **in an ~ state** ◇ *He was in a very ~ state.*

emotive *adj.*

VERBS **be, seem** | **become**
ADV. **highly, powerfully, very** ◇ *He raised the highly ~ issue of bullfighting.*

empathy *noun*

ADJ. **deep, great** | **genuine, real** | **human**
VERB + EMPATHY **feel, have** | **demonstrate, express, show** | **develop** | **lack**

PREP. **~ between** ◊ *The nurse should try to develop ~ between herself and the patient.* | **~ for** ◊ *I felt real ~ for my mother and what she had been through.* | **~ with** ◊ *She had a deep ~ with animals.*
PHRASES **a feeling of ~** | **a lack of ~**

emperor *noun*

ADJ. **reigning** | **future** | **late**
VERB + EMPEROR **be, become** | **crown sb** ◊ *Charlemagne was crowned Emperor on Christmas Day, 800 AD.*
PREP. **under an/the ~** ◊ *It was under the ~ Justinian that these advances were made.* | **~ of** ◊ *the ~ of Japan*
PHRASES **the reign of an ~** ◊ *during the reign of the last ~*

emphasis *noun*

1 special importance/attention

ADJ. **big** (*informal*), **considerable, great, heavy, huge** ◊ *schools that put a heavy ~ on sporting achievement* | **strong** | **little** ◊ *Little ~ was placed on educating people about the dangers.* | **growing, increasing** | **continued** | **renewed** | **current, new, recent** ◊ *with the new ~ on individuality and creative expression* | **traditional** | **main, major, primary** ◊ *We discussed where the main ~ should be placed.* | **particular, special, specific** ◊ *Examine the events leading to the war, with particular ~ on France's role in them.* | **exclusive** | **equal** ◊ *Both subjects should be given equal ~.* | **added, extra, increased** | **excessive, undue** ◊ *I believe the education system places undue ~ on exam results.* | **cultural** ◊ *a cultural ~ on educational achievement*
VERB + EMPHASIS **give, lay, place, put** ◊ *The company lays great ~ on customer care.* | **have, receive** ◊ *Education received special ~.* | **change, shift** ◊ *The Democrats shifted the ~ away from direct taxation.* | **add**
EMPHASIS + VERB **move, shift** ◊ *In recent years, the ~ has moved away from punishing drug addicts towards/toward helping them.* | **fall on sth**
PREP. **~ on, ~ upon** ◊ *The ~ is on keeping fit rather than developing lots of muscles.*
PHRASES **a change of ~, a shift of ~**

2 stress on a word/phrase

ADJ. **great** ◊ *'I', he said with great ~, 'was the one.'* | **slight** ◊ *His slight ~ on the word 'lady' was definitely mocking.* | **extra** ◊ *He put extra ~ on the word 'never'.*
VERB + EMPHASIS **put**
PREP. **with ~** ◊ *She repeated the question with ~.* | **~ on** ◊ *Put the ~ on the second syllable.*

emphasize (*BrE also* **-ise**) *verb*

ADV. **clearly, heavily, strongly** | **rightly** ◊ *The new law rightly ~s parental responsibility.* | **consistently, continually, repeatedly** | **increasingly** | **especially, particularly**
VERB + EMPHASIZE **must, should** ◊ *I must ~ that this is only a summary.* | **be important to** ◊ *It is important to ~ this point.* | **seem to, serve to, tend to** ◊ *All the arguments serve to ~ the controversy surrounding this disease.* | **fail to** | **be at pains to, be keen to** (*esp. BrE*) ◊ *I have been at pains to ~ the positive aspects of discipline.*

empire *noun*

1 group of countries

ADJ. **big, great, large, mighty, vast** | **powerful** | **far-flung** | **colonial, overseas** ◊ *the decline of the old colonial ~s* | **world** | **ancient** | **Ottoman, Roman**, etc.
VERB + EMPIRE **establish, found** | **destroy, dismantle** ◊ *The Japanese ~ was quickly dismantled.* | **expand, extend** | **rule** | **lose** ◊ *By now Britain had lost its ~.*
EMPIRE + VERB **grow** | **collapse, crumble, fall, fall apart** ◊ *The mighty ~ finally crumbled.*
EMPIRE + NOUN **building** | **builder**
PHRASES **the break-up of an ~, the decline of an ~, the fall of an ~** | **part of an ~** ◊ *a country that is still part of the ~*

2 group of companies/organizations

ADJ. **big, huge, large, vast** | **little** (*figurative*) ◊ *All the bureaucrats jealously guarded their own little ~s.* | **business, commercial, financial, industrial, media** | **global**

VERB + EMPIRE **build, build up, create** ◊ *He has built a huge business ~ from humble beginnings.* | **expand** | **run** ◊ *the staff who help run his hotel ~*
EMPIRE + VERB **collapse, crumble**
PHRASES **the collapse of an ~**

employ *verb*

1 pay sb to work

ADV. **actively, directly** ◊ *By 1960 the arms industry directly ~ed 3.5 million people.* | **indirectly** | **currently** ◊ *Mark is currently ~ed as a Professor of Linguistics.*
PREP. **in** ◊ *A large part of the workforce is ~ed in agriculture.*
PHRASES **be fully ~ed** | **be gainfully ~ed** ◊ *Those not gainfully ~ed are dependent on their savings.* | **be permanently ~ed, be temporarily ~ed** | **be irregularly ~ed, be regularly ~ed**

2 use

ADV. **commonly, extensively, frequently, often, regularly, widely** ◊ *The safety net is an image commonly ~ed in everyday life.* | **generally, primarily, routinely, typically, usually** | **increasingly** ◊ *Self-checkout terminals are increasingly ~ed by retailers.* | **effectively, successfully, usefully** | **properly** ◊ *When properly ~ed, non-lethal weapons will save lives.*

3 be employed be busy doing sth

ADV. **better** ◊ *Your time would be better ~ed doing something else.* | **busily, usefully**
PREP. **in** ◊ *Will and Joe were busily ~ed in clearing out all the furniture.*

employee *noun*

ADJ. **paid, salaried** | **full-time, part-time** ◊ *We have around 100 full-time ~s.* | **hourly** (= paid per hour of work) (*AmE*) | **permanent** | **seasonal** (*AmE*), **temporary** | **retired** | **entry-level** (*AmE*), **junior, low-level** (*esp. AmE*) | **senior** | **graduate** | **key** | **front-line** (*esp. AmE*) | **rank-and-file** (*AmE*) | **long-serving** (*BrE*), **long-time** (*AmE*), **loyal** | **dedicated, hard-working** | **potential, prospective** | **new** | **former** | **fellow** | **female, male** | **manual** | **skilled, unskilled** | **blue-collar, white-collar** | **non-union, union, unionized** (*all esp. AmE*) | **at-will** (= a worker who does not have a lot of legal rights) (*AmE*) | **civilian** ◊ *a civilian ~ of the Army* | **city** (*esp. AmE*), **council** (*BrE*), **federal, government, municipal** (*esp. AmE*), **public, public-sector, state** | **airline** (*esp. AmE*), **bank, factory, hotel, postal** (*esp. AmE*), **store** (*esp. AmE*), etc. | **disgruntled** ◊ *a disgruntled ~ seeking revenge* | **valuable**
VERB + EMPLOYEE **employ, have** ◊ *The company has only 60 ~s.* | **hire** (*esp. AmE*), **recruit** ◊ *the company's battle to recruit and retain ~s* | **dismiss, fire, lay off, make redundant** (*BrE*), **sack** (*esp. BrE*), **terminate** (*esp. AmE*) ◊ *a fair reason for dismissing an ~* ◊ *The company made hundreds of ~s redundant.* | **evaluate, screen** | **attract** ◊ *The company has worked to attract older ~s.* | **retain** | **manage** | **motivate** | **educate, train** | **compensate** (*esp. AmE*), **reward** | **pay**
EMPLOYEE + VERB **join sth, participate in sth** | **work** ◊ *~s who work more than 20 hours per week* | **perform (sth)** ◊ *~s who can perform comfortably in a highly diverse work environment* | **leave, quit** (*esp. AmE*) ◊ *Why do my ~s keep quitting?* | **retire** | **earn sth, get sth, receive sth** | **complain (about sth)** | **sue (sb)** ◊ *an ~ who sued for unpaid overtime*
EMPLOYEE + NOUN **benefits** ◊ *In addition to a competitive salary, the company offers attractive ~ benefits.* | **status** (*esp. BrE*) ◊ *Freelance workers do not enjoy the benefits of ~ status.* | **relations** | **retention, turnover** (*both esp. AmE*) | **morale, satisfaction** (*both esp. AmE*) | **performance, productivity** (*both esp. AmE*) | **development, training** | **incentive** (*esp. AmE*) | **handbook** (*esp. AmE*) | **base** (*esp. AmE*) ◊ *Maintaining a diverse ~ base requires ongoing commitment.* | **salaries** | **pension** (*esp. AmE*) ◊ *The value of state ~ pension plans has plunged over the past three years.* | **discount** (*esp. AmE*) | **theft** (*AmE*) ◊ *The retail industry loses $13 billion annually to ~ theft.* | **involvement, participation**

employer noun

ADJ. **big, large, major, top** ◇ *one of the region's major ~s* | **small** | **local** | **corporate, private** | **government, public** | **civilian** | **good** ◇ *The hotel prides itself on being a good ~ that treats its staff well.* | **unscrupulous** (*esp. BrE*) ◇ *the use of illegal workers by unscrupulous ~s* | **equal-opportunities** (*BrE*), **equal-opportunity** (*AmE*) | **future, potential, prospective** | **current** | **former, previous**

VERB + EMPLOYER **have, work for** | **sue** ◇ *He sued his ~ for personal injuries.* | **force, require** ◇ *The action forced the ~s to improve their pay offer.*

EMPLOYER + NOUN **sanctions** (*AmE*) ◇ *~ sanctions that penalize employers who hired unauthorized workers* | **contributions** ◇ *~ contributions to pension plans*

employment noun

ADJ. **paid, salaried** | **full-time, part-time** | **lifelong, lifetime, long-term, permanent, stable, steady** | **continued** | **short-term, temporary** | **regular** | **casual** | **formal** | **seasonal** | **gainful, meaningful** ◇ *The company was one of the first to offer meaningful ~ to the blind.* | **full, total** ◇ *The government aims to achieve full ~ within three years.* | **high, low** ◇ *an area of very low ~* | **skilled, unskilled** | **blue-collar, white-collar** | **factory, office** | **federal, public** | **female, male** | **youth**

... OF EMPLOYMENT **level** ◇ *policies aimed at maintaining a high level of ~*

VERB + EMPLOYMENT **look for, seek** ◇ *recent graduates seeking ~* | **find, gain, get, obtain, secure** ◇ *He finally secured ~ in a local factory.* | **accept, take up** (*formal*) ◇ *He took up ~ with the company in May 2002.* | **give up, leave, lose** ◇ *She lost her ~ when the company closed.* | **terminate** ◇ *One company terminated his ~ after 30 days.* | **give sb, offer sb** | **create, generate, provide** ◇ *This investment will certainly create ~ in the area.* ◇ *The steelworks provided ~ for thousands of people.* | **ensure, guarantee** | **boost, increase, raise, stimulate** ◇ *policies designed to stimulate ~*

EMPLOYMENT + VERB **grow, increase, rise** | **decline, fall**

EMPLOYMENT + NOUN **opportunities, options, possibilities, prospects** ◇ *There are few ~ prospects in the town for unqualified young people.* | **rights** | **discrimination** (*esp. AmE*) ◇ *laws prohibiting ~ discrimination* | **training** | **programme/program** (*esp. AmE*) ◇ *a state-subsidized ~ programme/program* | **agency, service** | **status** ◇ *The survey studied the ~ status of people within the community.* | **history** ◇ *Interviewers will look carefully at a candidate's ~ history.* | **agreement, contract** | **conditions, terms** | **data, figures, records, statistics** | **levels, rate** | **picture, situation** ◇ *The ~ picture is not good.* | **patterns, trends** | **growth** | **market** ◇ *graduates entering the ~ market* | **policy** ◇ *the government's full-employment policy* | **law, legislation** | **lawyer** | **tax** (*AmE*) | **practices** ◇ *The company's ~ practices have been widely criticized.*

PREP. **in ~** ◇ *Most of last year's graduates are now in ~.* | **out of ~** ◇ *She had been out of ~ for three years.*

PHRASES **conditions of ~, terms of ~** ◇ *Union negotiate conditions of ~.* | **a contract of ~** | **patterns of ~, trends of ~** ◇ *significant changes in patterns of ~*

→ Special page at BUSINESS

empty verb

1 make sth empty

ADV. **completely** ◇ *The cupboards had all been completely emptied.* | **out** ◇ *We emptied out the tank.*

PREP. **of** ◇ *He emptied the bottle of its contents.*

2 become empty

ADV. **completely** | **quickly, rapidly** | **slowly** | **directly** ◇ *Water from the underground pipes empties directly into nearby streams.* | **out** ◇ *The room gradually emptied out.*

PREP. **into** ◇ *The castle had a deep moat which emptied into the lake.* | **of** ◇ *The streets soon emptied of shoppers.*

empty adj.

VERBS **appear, be, feel, lie, look, seem** ◇ *The box lay ~ on the bed.* | **become** | **remain, stand, stay** ◇ *The city is letting useful housing stand ~.* | **leave sth** ◇ *The house had been left ~ for several weeks.*

ADV. **completely, entirely, quite, totally, utterly** ◇ *There was a vast expanse of totally ~ sky to look at.* | **almost, nearly, practically, virtually** | **largely, mostly** | **half** ◇ *a half-empty box of chocolates* | **fairly, quite, rather, relatively** ◇ *Some parts of the city are desperately overcrowded while others are relatively ~.* | **very** ◇ *We all feel very ~ now she's gone.* | **apparently, seemingly** | **eerily, strangely, surprisingly** ◇ *The house felt strangely ~ without the children.* | **otherwise** ◇ *There were a few chairs, but the room was otherwise ~.*

PREP. **of** ◇ *The streets were ~ of people.*

enclose verb

ADV. **completely, fully, totally** ◇ *The non-smoking section was completely ~d in glass.* | **partially**

PREP. **in, within** ◇ *The ring is ~d in a plastic case.*

encore noun

VERB + ENCORE **do, give, play** ◇ *The singer gave four ~s.* | **get** ◇ *You'll never get an ~ if you perform like that!* | **call for, demand** ◇ *The audience called for an ~.*

PHRASES **as an ~, for an ~** ◇ *For an ~ he sang an unaccompanied folk song.*

encounter noun

ADJ. **brief** ◇ *I did not see him again, except for a brief ~ on a train.* | **first, initial, last, previous** | **early** ◇ *her early ~s with contemporary art* | **recent** | **final** | **casual, chance, random, unexpected** ◇ *It was a chance ~ that led to the setting up of the new political party.* | **close, intimate** ◇ *I decided not to risk a second close ~ with the snakes.* | **face-to-face, personal** | **direct** ◇ *The press conference was her first direct ~ with the media.* | **fateful, strange** | **aggressive, armed, dangerous, unpleasant, violent** | **cultural, social** ◇ *the language we use in everyday social ~s* | **colonial** ◇ *the colonial ~ of indigenous craftsmen with Europeans* | **erotic, sexual** | **romantic** | **homosexual** | **alien** ◇ *examination of UFO sightings and alien ~s*

VERB + ENCOUNTER **have** ◇ *I had my first ~ with him two years ago.* | **survive** ◇ *Few men survive an ~ with her!* | **win** | **avoid** | **recall, remember** | **describe**

ENCOUNTER + VERB **occur, take place** | **result in sth**

PREP. **~ between** ◇ *violent ~s between police and protesters* | **~ with** ◇ *my first ~ with my new boss*

encounter verb

ADV. **commonly, frequently, often, regularly** ◇ *Walruses were commonly ~ed in the Shetland Islands until recently.* | **normally** | **occasionally** | **rarely** | **never** | **first** ◇ *an idea I first ~ed when I was in the army* | **previously**

VERB + ENCOUNTER **be likely to** ◇ *What are the difficulties you are most likely to ~?*

encourage verb

ADV. **greatly, highly** (*AmE*), **strongly** ◇ *We were greatly ~d by the support we received.* ◇ *Speaking your mind is highly ~d at these sessions.* | **especially, particularly** ◇ *She especially ~d young scientists.* | **actively, positively** ◇ *The government must actively ~ investment in these areas.* | **deliberately, explicitly, openly** | **inadvertently, unwittingly**

VERB + ENCOURAGE **aim to, try to, want to** | **be designed to** ◇ *These questions are designed to ~ debate.* | **be likely to** ◇ *Newspapers should not publish material that is likely to ~ discrimination.*

PREP. **in** ◇ *Her head of department ~d her in her research work.*

PHRASES **an attempt to ~ sth, an effort to ~ sth**

encouragement noun

ADJ. **considerable, great, strong** | **a little, gentle** | **the slightest** ◇ *Given the slightest ~, he'd leave his job.* | **extra,**

further ◇ *We needed no further ~ to stop work.* | **constant** | **active, positive** | **tacit** | **verbal**
VERB + ENCOURAGEMENT **give sb, offer (sb), provide (sb with)** ◇ *Mick was always ready to offer advice and ~.* | **shout, yell** | **use** ◇ *Instead of criticism, use ~.* | **need** | **draw, find, get, have, receive, take** ◇ *I draw great ~ from the fact that the library is always full.*
PREP. **with ~** ◇ *With a little ~, she could do really well.* | **~ by, ~ from** ◇ *You need ~ from people who understand what you are trying to do.* | **~ to** ◇ *Getting the boss's support was a great ~ to those involved.*
PHRASES **support and ~** ◇ *We are grateful to all our friends for their support and ~.* | **words of ~** ◇ *Perhaps I can offer a few words of ~ to those who did not win any prizes this time.*

encouraging *adj.*

VERBS **be, look, seem, sound** | **remain**
ADV. **extremely, highly, immensely, most** (*esp. BrE*), **really, tremendously, very** ◇ *This news is most ~.* | **mildly, quite, reasonably** | **hardly**

encyclopedia (*BrE also* -paedia) *noun*

ADJ. **online** | **illustrated** | **medical** | **baseball, football, etc.** (*esp. AmE*)
VERB + ENCYCLOPEDIA **consult, find sth in, look sth up in, use** | **compile, write** | **edit** | **publish**
ENCYCLOPEDIA + NOUN **article, entry**
PREP. **in an/the ~** ◇ *I looked the Civil War up in my ~.*
PHRASES **an entry in an ~** ◇ *There are over 20 000 entries in the ~.*

end *noun*

1 furthest part of sth
ADJ. **bottom, lower** | **top, upper** | **back, hind** (*esp. AmE*), **rear, tail** (*figurative*) ◇ *I just caught the tail ~ of the movie.* | **front** | **extreme, far, very** ◇ *That's his wife sitting at the far ~ of the table.* | **opposite, other** | **round, square** | **pointed, sharp** | **cheap, low** ◇ *housebuyers at the cheap ~ of the market* | **expensive, high** | **deep, shallow** (*of a swimming pool*) ◇ *The company believes in throwing new employees in at the deep ~ with no training.* (*figurative*) | **free, loose** ◇ *Take the free ~ of the rope and pass it through the hole.* ◇ *The author tied up all the loose ~s of the story in the final chapter.* (*figurative*) | **west, western, etc.** ◇ *the southern ~ of the lake*
VERB + END **come to, get to, reach** ◇ *Continue until you reach the ~ of the street.* | **block** | **grab, grasp, take hold of** | **join, tie** ◇ *Tie both ~s of the string together.* | **attach, connect** | **cut, trim**
END + NOUN **part, piece, portion, section** | **table** | **panel, wall** | **zone** (*in American football*)
PREP. **at the ~** ◇ *Turn into Hope Street and our house is right at the ~.* | **on ~** ◇ *Stand it on ~ (= upright).*
PHRASES **at one ~** ◇ *The rope was unfastened at one ~.* | **change ~s** ◇ *The teams changed ~s at half time.* | **close to the ~, near the ~** | **end over end** (*AmE*) ◇ *The car was lifted up by the winds and tumbled end over end along the ground.* | **~ of the spectrum** ◇ *The two parties represent opposite ~s of the political spectrum.* | **end to end** ◇ *They arranged the tables end to end.* | **from end to end** ◇ *The famous Las Vegas Strip is about three miles from ~ to ~.* | **right at the ~** ◇ *The bank is right at the ~ of the street.* | **split ~s** ◇ *You should have your hair trimmed every few weeks to get rid of split ~s.*

2 last part of sth
ADJ. **abrupt, sudden** | **early, premature, untimely** ◇ *The injury brought her career to an early ~.* | **dramatic, tragic** | **inevitable** | **fitting** ◇ *The award was a fitting ~ to a distinguished career.*
VERB + END **come to, get to, reach** ◇ *The meeting finally came to an ~ at six.* ◇ *I'll never get to the ~ of this book!* | **approach, draw to, near** ◇ *As the evening was drawing to an ~, the firework display took place.* | **bring (sth to), put** ◇ *Talks were in progress to bring an ~ to the fighting.* | **call for, demand** ◇ *call for an ~ to the violence* | **announce, declare** | **celebrate** | **mark, mean, signal, signify, spell** | **catch, see, watch** ◇ *I only caught the ~ of the game.*

END + VERB **be in sight** ◇ *There's no ~ in sight to the present crisis.*
END + NOUN **user** | **point** | **product, result** ◇ *The movie's backers were delighted with the ~ product.* | **credits** (= of a film/movie, etc.)
PREP. **at an ~** ◇ *The proceedings are expected to be at an ~ by 6 p.m.* | **at the ~** ◇ *They get married at the ~ of the movie.* | **by the ~** ◇ *He wants the reports by the ~ of the month.* | **in the ~** ◇ *In the ~, they decided to spend Christmas at home.* | **to the ~** ◇ *He won't win, but he'll keep fighting to the ~.* | **towards/toward the ~** ◇ *I was getting bored towards/ toward the ~ of the talk.* | **till the ~, until the ~** ◇ *I'm staying until the ~ of this week.* | **up to the ~** ◇ *It stayed hot right up to the ~ of September.* | **~ to** ◇ *What the business community wants is an ~ to the recession.*
PHRASES **at the very ~, right at the ~** ◇ *You don't know who the murderer is until right at the ~ of the book.* | **from beginning to ~** ◇ *His story was one big lie from beginning to ~.* | **the beginning of the ~** ◇ *It wasn't the end of their marriage, but it was the beginning of the ~.* | **the ~ of an era** ◇ *Her death marks the ~ of an era.* | **the ~ of the line, the ~ of the road** (*both figurative*) ◇ *The loss of this contract could signal the ~ of the line for the shipyard.* | **to the bitter ~, until the bitter ~** ◇ *We will fight this case to the bitter ~.*

3 aim/purpose
ADJ. **noble, worthwhile, worthy** | **desirable, desired** | **ultimate** | **destructive** | **practical, pragmatic** | **common** ◇ *Despite our differences, we were working to a common ~.* | **selfish** | **commercial, economic, ideological, political, social, utilitarian**
VERB + END **accomplish, achieve, attain** ◇ *She was prepared to lie in order to achieve her ~s.* | **further, pursue, work to** | **serve** | **become**
PREP. **to…~s** ◇ *The money might have been used to more worthy ~s.* | **to this ~** ◇ *She wished to have a house built, and to this ~ she hired a local architect.*
PHRASES **an ~ in itself** ◇ *For her, shopping had become an ~ in itself.* | **a means to an ~** ◇ *I don't enjoy studying computing—it's just a means to an ~.* | **the ~ justifies the means** ◇ *He defended a morality in which the ~ justifies the means.* | **for your own ~s, to your own ~s** ◇ *She is exploiting the current situation for her own ~s.* | **with this ~ in view** (= in order to achieve this)

4 death
ADJ. **sad, tragic** | **bad, horrible, sticky** (*informal, esp. BrE*), **violent** ◇ *to come to a sticky (= unpleasant, but deserved) ~* ◇ *He was bound to meet a violent ~ one day.* | **untimely**
VERB + END **come to, meet** (*literary*) ◇ *He met his ~ at the Battle of Little Big Horn.*
END + VERB **come** ◇ *The ~ came when he collapsed after playing golf.*

end *verb*

ADV. **abruptly, suddenly** ◇ *The meeting ~ed abruptly when the chairman was called away.* | **prematurely** | **at last, eventually, finally** ◇ *At last the war ~ed.* | **all but, effectively, virtually** ◇ *A back injury effectively ~ed her career.* | **inconclusively** ◇ *The peace talks have ~ed inconclusively.* | **never** ◇ *We thought they'd never ~.* | **happily, peacefully, well** | **badly, disappointingly, unhappily** | **disastrously, tragically** | **quickly**
PREP. **in** ◇ *The attempt finally ~ed in failure.* | **with** ◇ *The show ~ed with a song.*
PHRASES **~ in disaster** ◇ *The military action could ~ in disaster.* | **~ in tears** (*figurative*) ◇ *After all that excitement the day was bound to ~ in tears (= unhappily).* | **~ on a … note** ◇ *His speech ~ed on a positive note.*

endanger *verb*

ADV. **greatly, seriously** ◇ *Taking these drugs could seriously ~ your health.* | **recklessly**
VERB + ENDANGER **be likely to** ◇ *They are accused of causing an explosion likely to ~ life.*

trials to test their physical and mental ~ in space. | **build**,
build up, enhance, improve, increase ◇ *Swimming a little*
farther each session will build ~.
ENDURANCE + NOUN **test** | **exercise, training** | **athlete, runner**
| **race**
PREP. **beyond** ~ ◇ *He felt he had been provoked beyond* ~.
PHRASES **a feat of** ~ ◇ *They are capable of amazing feats of* ~.
| **the limit of your** ~, **the limits of your** ~ ◇ *She was almost*
at the limits of her ~. | **powers of** ~ ◇ *The task was a test of*
their powers of ~. | **strength and** ~ ◇ *Heavy manual work*
calls for strength and ~. | **a test of** ~ ◇ *Running a marathon*
is seen by many as the ultimate test of ~.

endeavour (BrE) (AmE endeavor) noun

ADJ. **collaborative, collective, cooperative, joint** | **brave,**
heroic | **honest** ◇ *the government's honest* ~s *to improve the*
lives of the poor | **noble, worthwhile, worthy** | **lifelong** ◇
Learning a foreign language well can be a lifelong ~. | **future**
| **fruitless, futile, unsuccessful** | **successful** | **human** ◇
Enthusiasm is a vital ingredient in all human ~. | **artistic,**
creative ◇ *She always encourages her children in their*
artistic ~s. | **commercial, educational, entrepreneurial**
(esp. AmE), **intellectual, political, scientific**
VERB + ENDEAVOUR/ENDEAVOR **make, pursue, undertake** ◇ *You*
must make an ~ *to work harder.*
PREP. **in an** ~ ◇ *We wish her every success in this* ~. ◇ *In an* ~
to improve the service, they introduced free parking.
PHRASES **your best** ~s (BrE) ◇ *Despite her best* ~s, *she couldn't*
persuade anyone to volunteer. | **a field of** ~ ◇ *He has the*
ability to achieve success in whatever field of ~ *he should*
choose. | **make every** ~ ◇ *We will make every* ~ *to obtain*
sufficient supplies.

ending noun

ADJ. **happy** | **sad, tragic, unhappy** | **bad, good** | **dramatic** |
fairy-tale ◇ *The crowd cheered on the unknown Tunisian,*
hoping for a fairy-tale ~ *to the race.* | **perfect** ◇ *The meal*
was the perfect ~ *to a great weekend.* | **abrupt** ◇ *I was*
surprised by the abrupt ~ *to the conversation.* | **original** |
alternate (AmE), **alternative, different**
VERB + ENDING **have** ◇ *The book has a sad* ~. | **ruin, spoil** ◇ *I*
don't want to ruin the ~ *for you.* | **write** | **change, rewrite**
PREP. ~ **to** ◇ *This is a happy* ~ *to a rather sad story.*

endless adj.

VERBS **be, seem** ◇ *The long walk back seemed* ~.
ADV. **almost, nearly** (esp. AmE) | **practically, virtually** |
apparently, seemingly ◇ *a seemingly* ~ *list of repairs to be*
carried out | **potentially** ◇ *a potentially* ~ *sequence of*
repeated shapes

endorse verb

ADV. **enthusiastically, heartily, strongly, warmly, whole-**
heartedly | **entirely, fully** | **overwhelmingly, unanimously**
| **broadly** ◇ *The government has broadly* ~d *the research*
paper. | **explicitly, openly** ◇ *The plan does not explicitly* ~
the private ownership of land. | **implicitly, tacitly** (esp. AmE)
| **formally, officially** ◇ *The newspaper has formally* ~d *the*
Democratic candidate. | **publicly** | **effectively**
VERB + ENDORSE **fail to, refuse to**

endorsement noun

ADJ. **enthusiastic, full, overwhelming, ringing, strong,**
unanimous | **lukewarm** ◇ *The new design only received a*
lukewarm ~ *from head office.* | **official** | **implicit, tacit** |
celebrity, government (esp. AmE) | **product**
VERB + ENDORSEMENT **be, constitute** | **imply** | **give sth, make**
(AmE), **offer sth** ◇ *We are happy to give the product our full*
~. | **withdraw, withhold** | **require** | **seek** ◇ *They are now*
seeking ~ *for their ideas.* | **get, receive, win** | **have** ◇ *These*
measures have the strong ~ *of the party.*
ENDORSEMENT + NOUN **contract, deal** (both esp. AmE) ◇ *He*
signed a four-year ~ *deal.*
PREP. ~ **as** ◇ *her* ~ *as leader of the delegation* | ~ **by** ◇ ~ *of the*
product by the appropriate body | ~ **for** ◇ ~ *for the plan* | ~
from ◇ *His presidential campaign won* ~ *from several*
celebrities.

endurance noun

ADJ. **great, long** (esp. AmE), **remarkable** | **sheer** | **mental,**
physical | **human**
VERB + ENDURANCE **have, show** ◇ *She showed great* ~ *in the*
face of pain. | **test** ◇ *The astronauts will undergo a series of*

enemy noun

ADJ. **bitter, deadly, great, implacable, mortal, sworn** |
biggest, worst | **dangerous, formidable, powerful** | **chief,**
main, principal ◇ *The lion is the zebra's chief* ~. | **ancient,**
old, traditional ◇ *Iraq's traditional* ~, *Iran* | **real, true** |
common ◇ *They united in the face of a common* ~. | **natural**
◇ *The Church and the Communist Party were natural*
enemies. | **perceived** | **invisible, unseen** | **potential** |
external, foreign | **political**
VERB + ENEMY **have** ◇ *She didn't have an* ~ *in the world.* |
make ◇ *He made many enemies during his brief reign.* ◇ *I*
didn't want to make an ~ *of Mr Evans.* | **attack, fight, fight**
against ◇ *He was prepared to use any weapon to fight*
against his enemies. | **defeat, destroy, eliminate, kill** |
confront, engage, face, meet ◇ *He turned to face his* ~. |
know ◇ *It is important to know your* ~. | **defend sth**
against, protect sb/sth against, protect sb/sth from ◇ *The*
cat uses its claws to protect itself against enemies. | **deter** ◇
The skunk releases a pungent smell to deter the ~.
ENEMY + VERB **attack sb/sth**
ENEMY + NOUN **army, forces, soldiers, troops, unit** |
defences, lines, positions, ranks ◇ *The spies managed to*
penetrate behind ~ *lines.* | **camp** | **action, attack, bombing,**
fire ◇ *the first casualty from* ~ *action* ◇ *The men came under*
~ *fire.* | **activity** ◇ *Intelligence reported* ~ *activity just off the*
coast. | **country, territory** | **aircraft, fighter, plane, ship,**
tank | **missile, weapon** | **propaganda** | **prisoner** | **target**
PREP. **against an/the** ~ ◇ *They decided to use the weapon*
against the ~. | ~ **of** ◇ *an* ~ *of God*
PHRASES **your own worst** ~ ◇ *Some dancers become their own*
worst enemies, criticizing themselves for every imperfection. |
fall into ~ **hands** ◇ *The document must not at any price fall*
into ~ *hands.* | **in the face of the** ~ ◇ *He was shot for*
desertion in the face of the ~. | **an** ~ **of the State** ◇
Thousands of perceived enemies of the State were imprisoned.
| **public** ~ ◇ *Since the scandal he has become public* ~
number one (= very unpopular).

energetic adj.

VERBS **be, feel, seem**
ADV. **extremely, fairly, very, etc.** | **highly, remarkably** ◇ *She*
seems remarkably ~ *for a woman her age.* | **quite** ◇ *I'm*
feeling quite ~ *today.*

energy noun

1 ability to be active/work hard

ADJ. **boundless, endless, inexhaustible, limitless, unflag-**
ging, unlimited ◇ *I admire her boundless* ~. | **pure, raw,**
sheer | **excess, surplus** | **nervous, restless** | **manic** |
youthful | **creative** ◇ *There is a lack of creative* ~ *in the*
industry. | **emotional, mental, physical, sexual** | **pent-up** |
negative, positive
... OF ENERGY **amount, level** ◇ *You can judge how healthy you*
are by the amount of ~ *you have.* | **great deal** ◇ *Bringing up*
twins requires a great deal of ~. | **burst** ◇ *With a sudden*
burst of ~, *he ran to the top of the hill.*
VERB + ENERGY **be bursting with, be full of, have** ◇ *The*
children are always full of ~. ◇ *I don't seem to have any* ~
these days. | **exude, radiate** | **feel** ◇ *You could feel the* ~
coming back to you from the audience. | **lack** ◇ *He never*
seems to lack ~. | **put** ◇ *She put all her* ~ *into her work.* ◇ *I*
will put all my energies into improving the situation. (esp.
BrE) | **expend** (formal), **spend, use** | **channel, concentrate,**
devote, direct, focus, turn ◇ *Prisoners are encouraged to*

channel their ~ into exercise. | **add, bring, give** | **boost** | **conserve, save** | **work off** ◇ *The kids were running around, working off their surplus ~.* | **waste** ◇ *We don't want to waste our ~ trying to persuade people who are just not interested.* | **drain, sap** ◇ *The hills sapped his ~ and he got off his bike for frequent rests.* | **muster, muster up, summon, summon up** ◇ *She eventually summoned up the ~ to cook dinner.* | **invest** ◇ *We must invest our time and ~ in the development of our craft.*

ENERGY + VERB **flag** ◇ *It was late and my ~ was beginning to flag.* | **dissipate, drain away**

ENERGY + NOUN **level, reserves** ◇ *My ~ levels are still low.* | **bar, drink** | **boost** ◇ *Sugar provides an ~ boost.*

PHRASES **~ and enthusiasm** ◇ *She always works with ~ and enthusiasm.* | **an outlet for your ~** ◇ *Football gives them an outlet for their ~.* | **time or ~** ◇ *I don't have the time or ~ to argue with you.* | **a waste of ~** ◇ *It's a waste of ~ cutting this grass—nobody's going to see it.*

2 source of power

ADJ. **alternative, clean, green, renewable** ◇ *the change from fossil fuels to renewable ~* | **atomic, nuclear, solar, wave, wind** | **cheap**

... OF ENERGY **amount** ◇ *The new power station produces vast amounts of ~.*

VERB + ENERGY **generate, produce** | **harness** ◇ *attempts to harness solar ~* | **release** | **provide, supply** | **consume, use** | **store** ◇ *No battery could store enough ~ to turn over a car's engine.* | **conserve, save** | **waste** | **need, require**

ENERGY + NOUN **production** | **consumption, use** | **demand, needs, requirements** ◇ *total ~ requirements for the coming year* | **supply** ◇ *The nuclear plant provides a fifth of the nation's ~ supplies.* | **resources, sources** | **reserves, stores** | **conservation** | **savings** ◇ *equipment that offers long-term ~ savings* | **efficiency** | **bill, costs, prices** | **crisis, problem, shortage** ◇ *The country could face an ~ crisis if demand continues to rise.* | **company, industry, sector** ◇ *state control of the ~ industries* | **market** ◇ *The cost of solar power needs to fall before it makes an impact on the ~ market.* | **plan, policy, programme/program, project, strategy** ◇ *a government-sponsored renewable ~ project* | **management** | **independence** (*esp. AmE*)

PHRASES **a demand for ~** ◇ *The demand for ~ is expected to increase dramatically.* | **a form of ~** | **a source of ~**

enforce *verb*

ADV. **fully, rigidly, rigorously, strictly, stringently, vigorously** ◇ *The rules were strictly ~d.* | **consistently** | **selectively** | **effectively, properly** | **legally**

VERB + ENFORCE **can** ◇ *The ban cannot be legally ~d.* | **be difficult to, be hard to, be impossible to** | **help (to)** ◇ *a system of local inspectors to help ~ presidential decrees* | **seek to, take steps to** ◇ *The government may take steps to ~ compliance with the new measures.* | **decline to, refuse to**

enforcement *noun*

ADJ. **law** | **peace** ◇ *soldiers involved in peace ~ operations overseas* | **civil rights** (*AmE*), **drug** (*esp. AmE*) | **border, immigration** (*both AmE*) | **effective, proper** | **rigorous, strict, stringent, strong, vigorous** | **better, tighter, tougher** ◇ *Newspapers called for tougher ~ of the existing laws on drugs.* | **lax** | **selective** (*esp. AmE*) ◇ *the selective ~ of immigration laws* | **judicial, legal, police**

ENFORCEMENT + NOUN **agent, officer, official** | **personnel** | **agency, authority, body** ◇ *federal law ~ agencies* | **law ~ bodies** | **machinery, mechanism, system** ◇ *The court is ineffective because it lacks the necessary ~ machinery.* | **powers** | **action, efforts, measures, methods, operations, practices, procedures, proceedings**

engage *verb*

ADV. **actively, directly** ◇ *Our contributors are actively engaging with tradition.* | **fully, seriously** | **constructively, effectively, successfully** | **critically, emotionally, intellectually, politically** ◇ *The party is attempting to ~ young voters politically.*

VERB + ENGAGE **fail to, refuse to**

PREP. **with** ◇ *We acknowledge the need to ~ directly with these problems.*

PHR V **engage (sb) in sth**

ADV. **actively** ◇ *people who actively ~ in shaping the world they live in* | **constructively** ◇ *They constructively ~ critics in debates.* | **openly** | **regularly, routinely** (*esp. AmE*) ◇ *The army was regularly ~d in combat.*

VERB + ENGAGE IN **attempt to, seek to, try to** ◇ *He tried to ~ me in conversation.* | **be eager to, be willing to** | **be reluctant to, be unwilling to**

engaged *adj.*

1 doing sth

VERBS **be**

ADV. **deeply, heavily** ◇ *those who are deeply ~ in party politics* | **fully, totally** | **largely, mainly, primarily** | **actively, directly** ◇ *He is actively ~ in strategic discussions.* | **busily** | **constantly** | **currently** | **intellectually, politically, socially** | **otherwise** (*formal*) ◇ *I'm afraid Mr Wilson cannot see you now as he is otherwise ~.*

PREP. **in** ◇ *She was ~ in conversation with a client.* | **on** ◇ *He is actively ~ on several projects.* | **with** ◇ *We need to become more ~ with our history as a nation.* ◇ *Mrs Scott is ~ with a customer at the moment.* (*BrE*)

2 having promised to marry sb

VERBS **be** | **become, get** ◇ *The couple got ~ last month.*

ADV. **happily** | **newly, recently**

PREP. **to** ◇ *She's ~ to an actor.*

PHRASES **~ to be married**

engagement *noun*

1 appointment

ADJ. **previous, prior** ◇ *Mrs Meyer regrets that she is unable to attend owing to a previous ~.* | **important** | **business, official, public, social** | **royal** | **dinner, lunch** | **speaking**

VERB + ENGAGEMENT **have** | **keep** ◇ *It is important that I keep this ~.* | **carry out** (*formal, esp. BrE*) ◇ *The chairman will carry out no official public ~s during the month of August.* | **cancel** ◇ *The president was forced to cancel all public ~s.*

PREP. **~ with** ◇ *He had an important ~ with his financial adviser.*

2 agreement to get married

ADJ. **long** | **broken**

VERB + ENGAGEMENT **announce** | **celebrate** | **break** (*esp. AmE*), **break off, cancel, end**

ENGAGEMENT + NOUN **ring** | **party**

PREP. **~ to** ◇ *He announced his ~ to his long-time girlfriend.*

3 being involved

ADJ. **constructive, effective** | **active** | **intense, passionate, serious** ◇ *his serious intellectual ~ with this issue* | **creative, emotional, imaginative, intellectual** | **civic** (*AmE*), **political** ◇ *Higher education can contribute to civic ~.* ◇ *the decline in political ~*

VERB + ENGAGEMENT **encourage, promote** (*esp. AmE*) ◇ *Her church promoted civic ~.* (*AmE*) | **facilitate** (*esp. AmE*) | **increase**

PREP. **~ in** ◇ *the lack of ~ in politics* | **~ with** ◇ *Feminist criticism is a starting point for a deeper ~ with the text.*

engine *noun*

1 part of a vehicle that produces power

ADJ. **big, powerful** | **small** | **twin ~s** ◇ *a large plane with twin ~s* | **2-litre/2-liter, 1200 cc, 20-valve, four-cylinder, two-stroke, etc.** | **300-hp** (*esp. AmE*), **200-bhp** (= brake horsepower) (*BrE*), **etc.** ◇ *a 580-horsepower ~* | **diesel, gas** (*AmE*), **gasoline** (*AmE*), **petrol** (*BrE*) | **internal-combustion, jet, outboard, piston, turbine, turbo, turbocharged** | **aircraft, airplane** (*AmE*), **rocket** | **car**

VERB + ENGINE **crank, crank up, fire, ignite, start, switch on, turn on** ◇ *The rocket ~ is ignited.* | **cut** (*informal*), **kill** (*informal*), **shut down, shut off, switch off, turn off** ◇ *He* pulled up under some trees and cut the ~. | **gun** (*AmE*), **rev, rev up, run** ◇ *She sat at the traffic lights revving the* ~. | **power** ◇ *Its* ~ *is powered by both gasoline and electricity.* | **repair, service, tune** | **lubricate** | **build** | **fit (sth with), install** ◇ *The new model is fitted with a more powerful* ~.

ENGINE + VERB **run** ◇ *She waited with the* ~ *running while he bought a paper.* ◇ *The* ~ *runs on diesel.* | **idle, tick over** (*BrE*) ◇ *I kept the* ~ *ticking over.* | **catch** ◇ *I pressed the starter and the* ~ *caught first time.* | **fire, fire up, start** ◇ *The engine's firing on all four cylinders now.* | **shut down, shut off, stop** | **break down, die, fail, quit** (*AmE*), **seize** (*AmE*), **seize up, stall** | **misfire** | **overheat** | **cough, splutter** ◇ *The* ~ *coughed and died.* | **roar, scream** ◇ *The plane's* ~ *roared as it prepared for take-off.* | **hum, purr** | **race, rev, rev up** ◇ *He heard a car* ~ *racing behind him.*

ENGINE + NOUN **capacity, power, speed** | **compartment, room** ◇ *the ship's* ~ *room* | **component, part** | **oil** | **failure, problems, trouble** ◇ *It looks as if we've got some* ~ *trouble.* | **builder, maker, manufacturer** | **plant** | **noise**

PREP. **in an/the** ~ ◇ *You need more oil in the* ~.

PHRASES **be powered by a … engine** ◇ *This model is powered by a diesel* ~. | **the noise, roar, sound, etc. of the** ~

2 vehicle that pulls a train

ADJ. **large, powerful** | **diesel, electric, steam** | **railroad** (*AmE*), **railway** (*BrE*)

VERB + ENGINE **build**

ENGINE + NOUN **driver** (*esp. BrE*) | **shed** (*BrE*)

engineer *noun*

1 designs/builds engines, roads, etc.

ADJ. **chief** | **chartered** (*BrE*), **qualified, skilled, trained** ◇ *You need the advice of a qualified* ~. | **consultant, consulting** | **aeronautical, aerospace, aircraft, flight** | **automotive** (*esp. AmE*) | **electrical, electronics** | **computer, software** | **recording, sound** | **manufacturing** (*esp. AmE*) | **civil, highway, mining, railway** (*BrE*), **structural** | **city** | **design, production** | **project** | **agricultural, chemical, marine, mechanical**

ENGINEER + VERB **build sth, design sth, develop sth** ◇ ~*s who designed and built advanced military aircraft*

→ Note at PROFESSIONAL (for more verbs)

2 repairs machines/equipment

ADJ. **qualified, skilled, trained** | **maintenance** (*esp. BrE*), **service, support** ◇ *We were on the phone with a technical support* ~. | **heating, lighting, telephone** (*all BrE*)

VERB + ENGINEER **call in, call out** (*both BrE*)

→ Note at JOB (for more verbs)

engineer *verb*

1 manage to arrange sth

ADV. **brilliantly, carefully, deliberately** ◇ *She carefully* ~*ed a meeting with the chairman.*

VERB + ENGINEER **seek to, try to**

2 design and build sth

ADV. **carefully, finely, precisely** | **superbly, well** ◇ *The car is superbly* ~*ed and a pleasure to drive.* | **specially, specifically** (*esp. AmE*) ◇ *This heavier-weight paper is specifically* ~*ed for inkjet printing.* | **socially** | **genetically** ◇ *genetically* ~*ed plants*

engineering *noun*

ADJ. **heavy, light** | **precision** | **advanced** | **aeronautical, aerospace** | **civil, structural** | **agricultural, industrial** | **electrical, electronic** | **process, systems** | **chemical, design, ecological, genetic, mechanical, software, etc.** | **social** | **reverse**

… OF ENGINEERING **piece** ◇ *The bridge is a fine piece of* ~.

ENGINEERING + NOUN **company, firm, group** | **industry** | **project** | **services** | **work, works** (*esp. BrE*) ◇ *Train services on Sunday will be restricted because of* ~ *works.* (*BrE*)

PHRASES **a feat of** ~ ◇ *The building is a remarkable feat of* ~.

→ Note at SUBJECT (for more verbs and nouns)

English *noun*

ADJ. **plain** ◇ *You'd have no trouble understanding his point if he'd written the article in plain* ~! | **spoken, written** | **conversational** ◇ *They taught conversational* ~ *to a group of Japanese students.* | **accented** (*esp. AmE*) ◇ *He spoke in heavily accented* ~. | **American, British, Indian, etc.** | **China** | **African American Vernacular, Black** | **BBC, the Queen's** | **proper** | **pidgin** | **Early, Middle, Modern, Old**

→ Note at LANGUAGE (for more collocates)

engrossed *adj.*

VERBS **appear, be, look, seem** | **become, get**

ADV. **deeply, very** | **completely, thoroughly, totally** | **apparently**

PREP. **in** ◇ *He seemed completely* ~ *in his book.*

enhance *verb*

ADV. **considerably, dramatically, greatly, much, significantly, substantially** ◇ *The attractiveness of the book is much* ~*d by Mark Stevens's drawings.* | **directly** | **further** | **undoubtedly**

VERB + ENHANCE **can, could, may, might** ◇ *things that can significantly* ~ *the quality of your life* | **help (to), serve to** | **be designed to, seek to** ◇ *reforms designed to* ~ *market efficiency*

PHRASES **digitally** ~*d* ◇ *The images have been digitally* ~*d.* | **surgically** ~*d* ◇ *Has he had his nose surgically* ~*d?*

enigmatic *adj.*

VERBS **be** | **remain**

ADV. **extremely, fairly, very, etc.** | **highly** ◇ *His reply was highly* ~. | **a little, slightly, etc.** | **equally**

enjoy *verb*

ADV. **enormously, greatly, hugely, immensely, really, thoroughly, tremendously, truly** ◇ *She greatly* ~*s her work.* ◇ *We* ~*ed the game immensely.* | **especially, particularly** | **quite, rather** | **simply** ◇ *I simply* ~ *the feeling of power.* | **clearly, obviously** | **always**

VERB + ENJOY **be able to** | **seem to** ◇ *The kids all seemed to* ~ *themselves.* | **begin to** ◇ *I was just beginning to* ~ *it when the rain came down.*

PHRASES ~ **yourself** ◇ *Everyone seemed to be* ~*ing themselves.* | **just** ~ **it/sth** ◇ *Don't feel guilty about it—just* ~ *it!*

enjoyable *adj.*

VERBS **be, look, sound** | **become** | **make sth** ◇ *I always try to make my lessons* ~. | **find sth**

ADV. **extremely, fairly, very, etc.** | **highly, hugely** (*esp. BrE*), **immensely, most, thoroughly** ◇ *We had a most* ~ *evening.* | **especially, particularly**

enjoyment *noun*

ADJ. **great, huge, real** | **full, maximum** ◇ *A large income is not necessary for the full* ~ *of life.* | **pure, sheer** ◇ *For sheer* ~*, you can't beat this game.* | **evident, obvious** | **quiet, simple**

VERB + ENJOYMENT **derive, find, get, have, take** ◇ *They found real* ~ *just in being together.* | **bring (sb), give sb, provide (sb with)** ◇ *The show brought* ~ *to millions of viewers.* | **add to, enhance, increase** ◇ *Food is there to keep you healthy and enhance your* ~ *of life.* | **spoil**

PREP. **for (sb's)** ~ ◇ *I play tennis purely for* ~. | **with** ~ ◇ *Mackie was smiling with* ~. | ~ **in** ◇ *I still find* ~ *in the job.* | ~ **of** ◇ *Your* ~ *of the movie depends on being able to overlook the terrible acting.*

PHRASES **a source of** ~ ◇ *Her little grandson has been a source of great* ~ *to her.* | **for your own (personal)** ~ ◇ *I did this work for my own* ~, *not for money.*

enlarge *verb*

ADV. **considerably, dramatically, greatly, vastly** ◇ *The castle was* ~*d considerably in the 15th century.* | **slightly** | **gradually**

holdings of Danish art.
PREP. **to** ◇ *The images were ~d to the size of a wall of a room.*

enmity *noun*

ADJ. **bitter** | **age-old, lasting, long-standing, old, trad-itional, undying** ◇ *He had earned their lasting ~.* | **personal**
VERB + ENMITY **earn (sb), incur** | **put aside**
PREP. **~ between** ◇ *the fierce ~ between the two groups* | **~ towards/toward** ◇ *his ~ towards/toward the Church*

enormity *noun*

ADJ. **full** (*esp. BrE*)**, sheer** ◇ *It took time for the full ~ of the attack to sink in.*
VERB + ENORMITY **appreciate, grasp, realize, recognize, understand** ◇ *It's difficult to grasp the sheer ~ of the tragedy.* | **bring home** ◇ *Her words brought home the ~ of what was happening.*

enquire (*also* inquire *esp. in AmE*) *verb*

ADV. **further** | **pleasantly, politely** ◇ *Adam ~d politely whether they had enjoyed the show.* | **anxiously** | **eagerly, hopefully** | **curiously** | **casually, innocently** | **evenly | gently, mildly** | **quietly, softly** | **coldly, coolly** ◇ *'You wish to speak with me?' he ~d coldly.* | **sarcastically, sweetly** (*ironic*) ◇ *'Do you mean blackmail?' she ~d sweetly.*
PREP. **about** ◇ *To ~ about tickets, call the number below.* | **after** (*esp. BrE*) ◇ *Rose was enquiring after you* (= asking how you were)*.* ◇ *She ~d after my mother's health.* | **as to** ◇ *He didn't ~ as to my identity.* | **into** (*esp. BrE*) ◇ *A commission has been set up to ~ into alleged malpractice.*

enquiry (*also* inquiry *esp. in AmE*) *noun*

1 (*esp. BrE*) official investigation

ADJ. **detailed, thorough** | **full, full-scale, major** | **initial, preliminary** | **immediate** | **ongoing** | **open, public** | **confidential** | **internal** | **independent** | **joint** ◇ *a joint ~ undertaken by the two departments* | **formal, official** | **informal** | **congressional, government, judicial, parlia-mentary** (*in the UK*)**, police** | **disciplinary** (*BrE*) | **criminal** | **fatal-accident, fraud, murder, etc.** (*all BrE*)
VERB + ENQUIRY **carry out** (*esp. BrE*)**, conduct, have, hold, undertake** | **announce** ◇ *The governor announced an ~ into the events.* | **begin, establish, initiate, launch, open, set up, start** ◇ *Police have launched a murder ~.* | **complete** | **adjourn** (*BrE*) | **reopen** | **call for, demand** ◇ *Newspapers are calling for a full independent ~ into the affair.* | **order** ◇ *The government has ordered a public ~ into the affair.* | **be subjected to, face** ◇ *You may be subjected to a disciplinary ~.* | **attend** (*BrE*) | **be involved in** | **chair, head, lead** ◇ *The ~ will be chaired by a judge.*
ENQUIRY + VERB **be underway, take place** ◇ *A major ~ is underway after the death of a union official.* ◇ *The ~ will take place behind closed doors.* | **begin, commence, start** | **hear sth** ◇ *The ~ heard this week that the crash was unavoidable.* | **consider sth, examine sth, investigate sth** | **reveal sth** | **conclude sth, establish sth, find sth** ◇ *An ~ found that the vintage plane was in good working order.* | **rule sth** ◇ *The ~ ruled that the cars should be fitted with bigger bumpers.* | **blame sb/sth**
ENQUIRY + NOUN **report** | **team** | **process**
PREP. **at an/the ~** ◇ *At the ~ they maintained that nothing illegal had been done.* | **during an/the ~, in an/the ~** ◇ *arguments during the ~* | **pending an ~** ◇ *The director has been suspended, pending an internal ~.* | **by** ◇ *the outcome of enquiries by the police* | **~ into** ◇ *an ~ into the environmental effects of the proposed new road*
PHRASES **a steward's ~** (in horse racing) | **the outcome of an ~, the result of an ~** | **the subject of an ~** ◇ *He now finds himself the subject of an ~ after reports of financial irregularities.*

2 (*esp. BrE*) request for information

ADJ. **exhaustive, extensive, thorough** ◇ *I've made exhaustive enquiries, but haven't been able to find what I want.* | **detailed** | **general, specific** ◇ *Our office is open every day and can help you with all your general enquiries.* | **discreet** |

informal | **routine** | **initial, preliminary** | **customer, media** | **door-to-door, house-to-house** (*both BrE*) ◇ *Police officers carried out house-to-house enquiries.* | **email, phone, telephone, written**
... OF ENQUIRIES **flood, stream** ◇ *After the disaster, the police had a flood of enquiries about missing relatives.*
VERB + ENQUIRY **make, pursue** ◇ *The police are still pursuing their enquiries.* (*BrE*) | **send** | **welcome** ◇ *The faculty welcomes enquiries from prospective entrants.* | **get, have, receive** ◇ *We've had many enquiries from concerned customers.* | **be inundated with** | **answer, deal with, handle, respond to** | **assist (sb) in/with, help (sb) in/with** ◇ *Police believe he can help them with their enquiries into a robbery.*
ENQUIRY + NOUN **desk, office** (*both BrE*) | **service** (*BrE*) | **form** ◇ *You are requested to complete an ~ form.*
PREP. **pending ~** ◇ *She has been released on bail pending further enquiries.* | **~ about, ~ as to, ~ concerning, ~ regarding, ~ relating to** ◇ *enquiries as to the whereabouts of Eve Smith* | **~ by** ◇ *enquiries by police* | **~ from** ◇ *enquiries from the public* | **~ into** ◇ *I'm making enquiries into the possibility of going by train.*
PHRASES **direct an ~ to sb** ◇ *The committee directed its enquiries to Mrs Taylor.*

3 asking questions/collecting information

ADJ. **careful, systematic** | **further** | **academic, intellectual, scholarly** | **critical, empirical, rational, serious** | **free, open** ◇ *We should proceed in a spirit of open ~.* | **historical, philosophical, scientific, sociological, theological** ◇ *The purpose is one of scientific ~.*
VERB + ENQUIRY **encourage** ◇ *The subjects on the curriculum encourage intellectual ~.*
PREP. **~ concerning, ~ into** ◇ *~ into the origins of the universe*
PHRASES **an area of ~** ◇ *The purpose of the research is to open up this area of ~.* | **a board of ~, a commission of ~, a committee of ~** | **a line of ~** ◇ *The police have assured us that all possible lines of ~ are being pursued.* | **a method of ~** ◇ *Methods of ~ vary from subject to subject.* | **a spirit of ~** ◇ *Children are born with a spirit of ~.*

enrolment (*BrE*) (*AmE* enrollment) *noun*

ADJ. **high, low** | **large** (*esp. AmE*) | **total** ◇ *Total ~ fell between 1991 and 1997.* | **open** (= not restricted) | **college, school, university** ◇ *an explosion in public school enrollments* | **student** | **freshman** (*AmE*)**, graduate, undergraduate** | **black, hispanic, minority, etc.**
VERB + ENROLMENT/ENROLLMENT **boost, increase**
ENROLMENT/ENROLLMENT + VERB **be up, go up, grow, increase, rise** | **be down, decline, go down, fall**
PREP. **on ~** ◇ *The full fee is payable on ~.* | **~ for** ◇ *Enrolment for engineering courses is low this year.* | **~ in** ◇ *~s in evening classes* | **~ on** (*esp. BrE*) ◇ *~ on a computer course*

ensure (*also* insure *esp. in AmE*) *verb*

ADV. **practically, virtually** | **effectively** | **(not) only, simply** ◇ *The system not only ~s maximum discounts, but also helps the company track usage.* ◇ *The alternative simply ~s that the problem will get worse.*
VERB + ENSURE **must** | **aim to, try to** | **take action to, take care to, take steps to** ◇ *We must take steps now to ~ the survival of these animals.* | **be designed to** ◇ *provisions designed to ~ safe conditions of work* | **help (to)** | **be important to, be necessary to, be sufficient to** ◇ *It is important to ~ that delegates have been properly briefed.*
PHRASES **an attempt to ~ sth** | **efforts to ~ sth, measures to ~ sth** | **thereby ensuring sth** ◇ *The therapist must treat the cause of the problem, thereby ensuring the symptoms do not return.*

entangled *adj.*

VERBS **be** | **become, get** ◇ *The fishing lines had become*

hopelessly ~. | **find yourself** ◇ *Carlos finds himself deeply ~ in police corruption.*
ADV. **hopelessly, inextricably** | **deeply** | **increasingly** | **romantically** ◇ *Molly became romantically ~ with her boss.*
PREP. **in** ◇ *He became ~ in legal disputes.* | **with** ◇ *Sara got ~ with some political group.*

enter *verb*

1 come/go into a place

ADV. **illegally** ◇ *people who ~ the country illegally* | **cautiously** | **quickly, slowly** | **quietly, silently** | **suddenly**
VERB + ENTER **allow sb/sth to, permit sb/sth to** ◇ *He stood back to allow us to ~.* | **forbid sb to**
PREP. **by, through** ◇ *We ~ed through a large iron gate.* | **from** ◇ *The dancers ~ed from the side of the stage.*
PHRASES **~ and exit, ~ and leave** ◇ *They pass each other as they ~ and exit the building.*

2 add information to sth

ADV. **manually** ◇ *You may need to ~ this information manually.* | **automatically**
PREP. **in** ◇ *Your details have been ~ed in our database.* | **into, on, onto** ◇ *Please ~ all your personal details on the form provided.* ◇ *Enter the data onto the computer.*

PHR V **enter into sth**
ADV. **freely, voluntarily** ◇ *Staying married is a choice that is freely ~ed into.*

enterprise *noun*

1 plan/project

ADJ. **great** | **exciting** | **ambitious, difficult, hazardous** | **successful** | **collaborative** (*esp. AmE*), **collective, common, cooperative, joint** (*esp. BrE*) ◇ *The project is a joint ~ with the Business School.* | **criminal** | **academic, research, scientific**
VERB + ENTERPRISE **embark on, start, undertake** ◇ *They are willing to undertake a new ~.* | **abandon**
ENTERPRISE + VERB **fail, succeed**
PREP. **in an/the ~** ◇ *The team leader will be the most important factor in this difficult ~.*

2 a business

ADJ. **large, large-scale** | **small, small-scale** | **profitable, successful** | **family, private** | **government-sponsored** (*AmE*), **public, social** (*esp. BrE*), **state, state-owned** | **global, multinational** | **business, commercial, for-profit** (*esp. AmE*) ◇ *the complex organization of a business ~* | **agricultural, economic, farming, industrial, manufacturing**
VERB + ENTERPRISE **build, create** | **control, manage, run** ◇ *He runs a successful small ~.* | **invest in** | **privatize**
ENTERPRISE + VERB **operate** | **expand, grow, succeed** | **fail**
PREP. **in an ~, within an ~** ◇ *something that affects all the workers in the ~*

3 development of businesses

ADJ. **free, private** ◇ *The Act will encourage private ~.* | **local** | **corporate, individual**
VERB + ENTERPRISE **encourage, promote**
ENTERPRISE + NOUN **culture** (*esp. BrE*) ◇ *The government has promoted the ~ culture.*

4 abilities/imagination

ADJ. **great** ◇ *I thought she showed great ~.*
VERB + ENTERPRISE **show**
PHRASES **a spirit of ~**

entertain *verb*

1 invite sb to eat/drink with you

ADV. **lavishly** ◇ *The Bradfords always ~ed lavishly at Christmas.*
PREP. **to** (*BrE*) ◇ *They ~ed us to lunch in their new house.*

2 interest/amuse sb

ADV. **thoroughly** ◇ *Everyone was thoroughly ~ed.*

PREP. **with** ◇ *She ~ed us with stories of her travels.*
PHRASES **~ and educate, ~ and enlighten, ~ and inform** ◇ *Films can ~ and educate, make you laugh or cry.* | **keep sb ~ed** ◇ *We hired a magician to keep the children ~ed.*

3 think about an idea/hope/feeling

ADV. **seriously** ◇ *I am amazed that such a crazy idea could be seriously ~ed.* | **briefly** ◇ *briefly ~ing hopes that he might keep the affair a secret*
VERB + ENTERTAIN **be prepared to, be willing to** ◇ *She would make no promises, but was willing to ~ the idea.* | **refuse to**

entertaining *adj.*

VERBS **be, sound** | **become** | **make sth** ◇ *He tried to make his speech more ~.* | **find sth** ◇ *The others seemed to find my discomfort hugely ~.*
ADV. **extremely, fairly, very, etc.** | **highly, hugely, immensely, incredibly, marvellously/marvelously** (*esp. BrE*), **vastly, wildly** (*esp. AmE*), **wonderfully** ◇ *It was highly ~ for the people around them.* | **thoroughly** | **mildly, moderately** (*esp. AmE*)
PHRASES **~ and informative** ◇ *The book is an ~ and informative read.*

entertainment *noun*

ADJ. **lavish** | **pure** ◇ *It's pure ~ and there's nothing wrong with that.* | **good** | **escapist, mindless** | **free** | **live** | **evening, nightly** ◇ *Passengers can enjoy free nightly ~.* | **half-time, pre-game** (*AmE*), **pre-match** (*BrE*) ◇ *the half-time ~ at football games* | **home, in-flight, public, street** | **mass, popular** ◇ *Movies were the new mass ~.* | **family, light, wholesome** ◇ *Vote for your top light ~ show.* | **adult** | **digital, video** | **interactive** | **musical, sports**
VERB + ENTERTAINMENT **lay on** (*BrE*), **offer, provide, put on** ◇ *They provided lavish ~ for their guests.* | **enjoy**
ENTERTAINMENT + NOUN **business, company, industry, media, world** | **centre/center, complex, venue** | **district** (*esp. AmE*) ◇ *Tokyo's ~ district* | **programme/program** | **show** | **news** ◇ *The leading piece of ~ news in the US is the Oscars.* | **value** ◇ *The movies were bought for their ~ value.* | **licence** (*BrE*)
PREP. **for sb's ~** ◇ *Ladies and gentlemen, for your ~, we present Magic Man.*
PHRASES **a form of ~** | **a place of ~** ◇ *places of ~ such as bars* | **a source of ~** ◇ *The television was his only source of ~.* | **the world of ~** ◇ *stars from the world of ~*

enthral (*BrE*) (*AmE* enthrall) *verb*

PHRASES **be enthralled by sth, be enthralled with sth** ◇ *They were enthralled with the play.* | **hold sb enthralled, keep sb enthralled** ◇ *She kept her audience enthralled throughout her twenty-minute performance.* | **listen enthralled, watch enthralled** ◇ *The children listened enthralled as the storyteller unfolded her tale.*

enthusiasm *noun*

ADJ. **burning, enormous, extraordinary, immense, passionate, tremendous** | **considerable, great** | **little** | **genuine, real** | **obvious** | **growing** | **boundless, unbounded, unbridled** ◇ *The cruise director demonstrated boundless ~ and energy.* | **undiminished** | **excessive** | **spontaneous, sudden** | **new, new-found, renewed** ◇ *We went about our task with renewed ~.* | **early, initial** | **general, widespread** | **popular, public** | **personal** | **infectious** | **boyish, youthful** | **innocent** | **natural** | **religious**
... OF ENTHUSIASM **burst, surge** ◇ *After an initial burst of ~ for jogging, I gradually lost interest.*
VERB + ENTHUSIASM **be full of, feel, have** ◇ *Her voice was full of ~.* | **convey, express, show** ◇ *She managed to convey an ~ she did not feel.* ◇ *The team have shown ~ and commitment.* | **muster, summon up** | **feign** ◇ *He accepted the invitation with feigned ~.* | **conceal, hide** | **share** | **maintain** | **lose** | **lack** | **arouse, engender, fire (sb with), generate** ◇ *The trip has fired his ~ for all things French.* | **curb, dampen, dent** (*esp. BrE*), **temper** (*esp. AmE*) ◇ *This weather would dampen anyone's ~ for swimming.*
ENTHUSIASM + VERB **bubble over, bubble up** ◇ *He tried to hide*

the boyish ~ bubbling up inside him. | **grow** | **fade, wane, wear off**
PREP. **with ~, without ~** ◇ *I look forward to the challenge ahead with great ~.* | **~ about** ◇ *Few people expressed ~ about the current leaders.* | **~ among** ◇ *The idea aroused immense ~ among party workers.* | **~ for** ◇ *The initial ~ for the project was wearing off.*
PHRASES **sb can't contain their ~** ◇ *She grinned, unable to contain her ~.* | **energy and ~** ◇ *Cruise brings a lot of energy and ~ to his roles.* | **a lack of ~** ◇ *Both sides have shown a distinct lack of ~ for discussion.*

enthusiastic *adj.*

VERBS **be, feel, look, seem, sound** | **become, get**
ADV. **extremely, fairly, very, etc.** | **all, highly, immensely, incredibly, wildly** ◇ *She's all ~ about China now that she's been there.* ◇ *The audience was wildly ~.* | **less than, not overly, not particularly, not too** ◇ *Neil did not seem particularly ~ about his job.* | **largely** ◇ *Film critics are largely ~ about the thriller.* | **fairly, quite** | **genuinely**
PREP. **about** ◇ *He was very ~ about the idea.* | **in** ◇ *We were ~ in our support of him.*

entity *noun*

ADJ. **discrete, distinct, independent, separate, single** ◇ *Church and empire were fused in a single ~.* | **basic** | **abstract** | **artificial** | **biological, physical** | **living** | **business** (*esp. AmE*), **commercial** (*esp. AmE*), **corporate** | **for-profit, non-profit** (*both AmE*), **federal** (*esp. AmE*), **government** (*esp. AmE*), **governmental** | **national, sovereign** | **private, public** | **economic, legal, political, religious, social** ◇ *A company is a separate legal ~.*
VERB + ENTITY **create, form** ◇ *The two companies will combine to form a new ~.* | **become**

entrance *noun*

1 door/place through which you enter sth
ADJ. **narrow, wide** | **main** | **back, front, rear, side** | **separate** | **north, west, etc.** | **secret** | **service** (*AmE*), **tradesman's** (*esp. BrE*) | **cave, church, harbour/harbor, school, subway** (*AmE*), **tunnel, etc.**
VERB + ENTRANCE **use** ◇ *While the front door is being repaired, please use the side ~.* | **mark** ◇ *The little porch marked the ~ to a churchyard.* | **have** ◇ *The building has only one ~.* | **block** ◇ *She stood firm, blocking the ~.* | **guard**
ENTRANCE + NOUN **area, foyer, hall** (*esp. BrE*), **hallway** (*esp. AmE*), **lobby** | **door, doorway, gate, porch** | **passage, way** | **ramp**
PREP. **at the ~, by a/the ~** ◇ *The band left by the rear ~ to escape photographers.* | **in the ~** ◇ *She stood in the ~ to the ward.* | **through the ~** ◇ *Go through the main ~ into the yard.* | **~ from** ◇ *There is a back ~ from West Street.* | **~ to** ◇ *He was waiting at the ~ to the cave.*

2 act of coming in
ADJ. **big, dramatic, grand**
VERB + ENTRANCE **make** ◇ *She made a grand ~ once all the guests were assembled.* | **gain** ◇ *Some of the protesters tried to gain ~ to the meeting.*
PREP. **~ into** ◇ *her ~ into politics*

3 right to enter a place
VERB + ENTRANCE **gain** ◇ *students hoping to gain ~ to college* | **deny sb**
ENTRANCE + NOUN **charge, fee** | **ticket** ◇ *an ~ ticket to the zoo* | **requirements** | **exam, examination**

entrant *noun*

ADJ. **new** | **early, late** | **college, school, university** (*esp. BrE*) ◇ *the entry requirements for medical school ~s* | **competition** | **winning** ◇ *The winning ~ received tickets to the movie.*
VERB + ENTRANT **attract** ◇ *The competition attracted 46 ~s.*
PREP. **~ for** ◇ *the ~s for the award* | **~ in** ◇ *You will automatically be registered as an ~ in the prize draw.* | **~ into** ◇ *another new ~ into the multimedia market* | **~ to** ◇ *the number of ~s to higher education*

entrepreneur *noun*

ADJ. **good, great, successful** | **creative, innovative** | **ambitious, dynamic** | **large-scale, small, small-scale** | **individual, private** | **budding, potential, would-be** ◇ *a recent MBA graduate and budding ~* | **experienced, veteran** | **serial** ◇ *a serial ~ who had founded four companies* | **business** | **dotcom, Internet, music, property** (*BrE*), **real estate** (*esp. AmE*), **retail, etc.**

entry *noun*

1 right to enter sth
ADJ. **free** ◇ *The club offers free ~ to women on Thursdays.* | **college, school, university** (*esp. BrE*)
VERB + ENTRY **apply for** | **gain** | **allow sb, grant sb** ◇ *They were later allowed ~ into the country.* | **deny sb, refuse sb, restrict** ◇ *It has been necessary to restrict ~ into the club.* | **guarantee sb** | **delay**
ENTRY + NOUN **criteria, qualifications, requirements, standard** | **barrier** (*business*) ◇ *The state should reduce ~ barriers for developing countries.* | **visa** | **pass, ticket** ◇ *Entry tickets to most attractions are included in the price.* | **fee**
PREP. **~ into** ◇ *The course will ease students' ~ into a career.* ◇ *These qualifications will not guarantee you ~ into the police.* (*BrE*) | **~ to** ◇ *undocumented workers seeking ~ to the US* ◇ *Entry to university should be based on academic potential.* (*BrE*)
PHRASES **right of ~** ◇ *The landlord had the right of ~ to the building with due warning.*

2 act of coming in
ADJ. **forced, forcible** ◇ *The house was quiet, and there were no signs of a forced ~.* | **unauthorized** ◇ *The sign on the gates read 'No Unauthorized Entry'.* | **illegal** | **dramatic** | **triumphal** ◇ *Caesar's triumphal ~ into Rome*
VERB + ENTRY **force, gain** ◇ *He found the door locked, but he forced an ~.* | **bar, block, prevent** ◇ *Fire marshals barred ~ to the hall.* ◇ *A branch blocked their ~.* | **make** ◇ *The champion made his usual dramatic ~ into the arena.*
ENTRY + NOUN **point** ◇ *Drugs are believed to come into the country through five main ~ points.* | **code** (*esp. AmE*)
PREP. **~ into** ◇ *Hungary's ~ into the EU* | **~ to** ◇ *She wondered how she could gain ~ to the building.*
PHRASES **a/the point of ~** ◇ *New York was the point of ~ for most immigrants arriving in the US.*

3 sb/sth that enters a competition
ADJ. **winning** ◇ *The winning ~ will be published in next month's issue.* | **late**
VERB + ENTRY **mail** (*AmE*), **post** (*BrE*), **send, send in, submit** ◇ *Send in your ~ as soon as possible!* | **attract, get, have, receive** ◇ *The show attracted entries from all over the country.* ◇ *We have had a lot of entries this year.* | **judge**
ENTRY + NOUN **coupon** (*BrE*), **form** | **fee** | **deadline**
PREP. **~ for** ◇ *We had too many entries for this event.* | **~ in** ◇ *There were a record 2 000 entries in the under-17 section.* | **~ to** ◇ *one of the best entries to our competition*

4 one item in a list/book
ADJ. **diary, journal** (*esp. AmE*) | **dictionary, encyclopedia** | **blog, weblog** | **catalogue, database**
VERB + ENTRY **make, write** | **post** ◇ *I post the occasional blog ~.* | **read** | **contain**
PREP. **in an/the ~** ◇ *Very little information is given in the diary entries.* | **~ for** ◇ *Look at the dictionary ~ for 'welcome'.* | **~ in** ◇ *the last ~ she made in her diary* | **~ on** ◇ *First examine the entries on the marriage register.*

5 (*AmE*) **entrance to a building, room, etc.**
ENTRY + NOUN **way** (usually *entryway*) | **hall** | **door, gate**
PREP. **~ to** ◇ *the dramatic ~ to the gallery*

envelope *noun*

ADJ. **bulky, fat, thick** | **large, small** | **sealed** | **return** (*AmE*), **self-addressed, stamped addressed** (*BrE*) ◇ *Please enclose a* self-addressed ~ *if you would like a reply.* ◊ *a self-addressed stamped ~* (*AmE*) | **postage-paid, prepaid, reply-paid** (*BrE*) ◊ *To apply, use the enclosed reply-paid ~ (no stamp needed).* | **padded** | **airmail** | **brown, buff, manila, plain, white** ◊ *an official-looking manila ~*

VERB + ENVELOPE **open, rip open, slit open, steam open, tear open** ◊ *The letter was suspicious, and I considered steaming open the ~.* | **address, mark** ◊ *an ~ addressed in my mother's round handwriting* ◊ *The ~ was marked 'Personal'.* | **seal** | **mail** (*AmE*), **post** (*BrE*), **send** | **stuff** ◊ *You don't earn much stuffing ~s.*

ENVELOPE + VERB **contain sth, enclose sth**

PREP. **in an/the ~** ◊ *I had put the letter in the wrong ~.* | **into an/the ~** ◊ *He quickly stuffed the money back into the ~.* | **on an/the ~** ◊ *I couldn't read the address on the ~.* | **~ of** ◊ *He gave her the ~ of certificates.*

PHRASES **the back of an ~** ◊ *I scribbled his phone number on the back of an ~.*

envious *adj.*

VERBS **appear, be, feel, look, seem, sound** ◊ *She tried not to appear ~.* | **become** | **make sb** ◊ *Don't tell me any more—you're making me ~!*

ADV. **extremely, fairly, very, etc.** | **almost** | **a little, slightly, etc.**

PREP. **of** ◊ *He had always felt ~ of his brother.*

environment *noun*

1 conditions of the place where you are

ADJ. **immediate** ◊ *Cold-blooded animals depend on the temperature of their immediate ~.* | **external** | **alien, new, unfamiliar** | **natural** ◊ *marine life in its natural ~* | **changing, ever-changing** (*esp. AmE*) | **comfortable, protected, safe, secure, stable** | **friendly, supportive** | **hospitable, pleasant** | **clean, healthy** | **stimulating** | **favourable/favorable, ideal** ◊ *This period provided an ideal ~ for the spread of communism.* | **uncertain, unstable** | **dangerous** | **noisy** | **competitive** | **stressful** | **extreme, harsh, hostile** | **fragile** ◊ *Walkers can unwittingly damage the fragile ~ in which the birds live.* | **built, urban** ◊ *the quality of our natural and built ~s* | **rural** | **cold, warm** | **aquatic, coastal, forest, marine, mountain** | **domestic, family, home** ◊ *Children learn best in their home ~.* | **physical** | **cultural, emotional, social** | **office, work, working, workplace** ◊ *A comfortable working ~ will increase productivity.* | **online** | **classroom, educational, learning, school, teaching, training** | **economic, financial** ◊ *Investors are showing more caution in the current economic ~.* | **political** | **business, commercial, corporate** ◊ *She now had to transfer her design skills to a commercial ~.* | **professional**

VERB + ENVIRONMENT **create, foster, provide** ◊ *parents who strive to provide a stimulating ~ for their children to grow up in* | **adapt to** ◊ *creatures that have adapted to hostile desert ~s* | **alter, change** | **shape** | **improve** | **explore** ◊ *The cat walked around, exploring its new ~.* | **control**

PREP. **in an/the ~** ◊ *people working in increasingly competitive ~s* | **~ for** ◊ *an ~ for economic growth* | **~ of** ◊ *an ~ of fear*

PHRASES **an ~ conducive to sth** ◊ *The hospital architect tries to create an ~ conducive to healing.* | **today's ~** ◊ *In today's competitive business ~, companies focus on minimizing costs.*

2 the environment the natural world

ADJ. **natural** | **global, world** | **local**

VERB + THE ENVIRONMENT **preserve, protect, safeguard, save** ◊ *The government should do more to protect the ~.* | **clean up, improve** | **affect, have an impact on, impact** (*AmE*) ◊ *factors that have a huge impact on the ~* | **damage, harm, pollute** ◊ *industries which damage the ~* | **threaten**

ENVIRONMENT + NOUN **agency, committee, department, group** (*all esp. BrE*) | **chief** (*BrE*), **minister** (*esp. BrE*) | **spokesman, spokeswoman** (*both BrE*) | **correspondent,**

editor (*both BrE*) | **policy** (*esp. BrE*) | **protection** (*esp. BrE*) | **issues**

PREP. **in the ~** ◊ *the amount of carbon in the ~*

PHRASES **conservation of the ~, protection of the ~** | **damage to the ~** ◊ *farming methods that minimize damage to the ~* | **harmful to the ~** ◊ *The label identifies the products that are least harmful to the ~.* | **pollution of the ~**

envisage (*esp. BrE*) *verb*

ADV. **initially, originally** ◊ *It was originally ~d that the talks would take place in the spring.* | **currently** | **always, never** ◊ *It was never ~d that this would be a long-term solution.* | **clearly**

VERB + ENVISAGE **can** ◊ *I can ~ difficulties if we continue with this policy.* | **be difficult to, be hard to, be impossible to** | **be easy to, be possible to**

PHRASES **~ yourself doing sth** ◊ *I cannot ~ myself playing again next season*

envision (*esp. AmE*) *verb*

ADV. **initially, originally** ◊ *The work took longer than initially ~ed.* | **easily** ◊ *I can easily ~ them working together.* | **currently** | **always, never** | **clearly**

VERB + ENVISION **can** ◊ *Can you ~ such a scenario?* | **be difficult to, be hard to, be impossible to** | **be easy to, be possible to**

PHRASES **~ yourself doing sth** ◊ *He ~ed himself dying in a pool of his own blood.*

envoy *noun*

ADJ. **personal, special** | **senior, top** | **diplomatic, peace** | **papal, presidential, royal** | **UN** | **American, British, etc.**

VERB + ENVOY **be, serve as** | **appoint (sb as)** ◊ *The government has not yet appointed an ~ to the area.* | **dispatch, send** ◊ *A special peace ~ was sent to the area.*

PREP. **~ from** ◊ *a special ~ from the American president* | **~ to** ◊ *He served as ~ to the French government.*

envy *noun*

ADJ. **extreme** | **unconscious** | **class, social** | **penis** ◊ *the Freudian concept of penis ~*

... OF ENVY **tinge, touch** ◊ *I detected a tinge of ~ in her tone.* | **pang, stab, twinge** ◊ *I felt a twinge of ~ for the people who lived there.*

VERB + ENVY **be consumed with, be green with, feel, have** ◊ *I had no ~ of his success.* | **express, show** | **arouse, excite, fill sb with, inspire** ◊ *Her youth and looks aroused extreme ~ in her rivals.*

PREP. **with ~** ◊ *I look with ~ on those lucky people with big families.* | **~ at** ◊ *I was filled with ~ at their adventurous lifestyle.* | **~ for** ◊ *the ~ she felt for her sister*

PHRASES **be the ~ of sb/sth** ◊ *British television is the ~ of the world (= is admired by everyone).* | **an object of ~** ◊ *Her car was an object of ~ among her friends.*

envy *verb*

ADV. **greatly, really** | **secretly** | **almost**

PREP. **for** ◊ *I secretly envied her for her good looks.*

epidemic *noun*

ADJ. **major** | **global, national, worldwide** | **growing** | **deadly, devastating** | **cholera, flu, foot-and-mouth, typhoid, etc.** | **crack, heroin, etc.** | **silent**

VERB + EPIDEMIC **become** | **combat, fight** | **cause**

EPIDEMIC + VERB **break out, occur, strike (sth)** ◊ *A typhus ~ struck in the winter of 1919–20.* | **spread, sweep (sth)** ◊ *the flu ~ sweeping the country*

PREP. **during an/the ~, in an/the ~** ◊ *Over fifty people died during the flu ~ last winter.* | **~ of** ◊ *an ~ of cholera*

PHRASES **reach ~ proportions** ◊ *Marriage breakdown in the West has reached ~ proportions.*

episode *noun*

1 one separate event in sb's life/a story

ADJ. **dramatic, exciting** | **bizarre, extraordinary** | **sad, tragic**

| **shameful, unfortunate, unpleasant** | **latest** ◇ *She has only told you about the latest ~ in a long history of mental illness.* | **brief** | **major** | **acute, severe** (*medical*) ◇ *an acute ~ of pneumonia* | **recurrent** (*medical*) | **depressive, manic, psychotic** (*all medical*)

VERB + EPISODE **remember** | **forget** | **experience**

PREP. **during an** ~ ◇ *during a brief ~ of socialist rule* | **~ from** ◇ *I still remember that ~ from my childhood.* | **~ in** ◇ *an extraordinary ~ in American history*

PHRASES **the entire ~, the whole ~** ◇ *He says he just wants to forget the whole unfortunate ~.*

2 one part of a TV/radio drama

ADJ. **exciting, thrilling** ◇ *Don't miss next week's exciting ~!* | **classic** | **next, upcoming** (*esp. AmE*) | **previous** | **first, second, etc.** | **pilot** | **premiere** (*AmE*) | **final, last** | **two-part** | **half-hour, hour-long, one-hour, etc.**

VERB + EPISODE **catch, see, watch** ◇ *I caught a few ~s of seasons one and two.* | **miss** | **do, film, make, record, shoot** ◇ *The next ~ has not yet been filmed.* | **direct** | **air** (*esp. AmE*), **broadcast** | **repeat, rerun** (*AmE*)

PREP. **during an/the ~, in an/the ~** ◇ *It happened in the final ~ of 'Star Trek'.*

epitaph *noun*

ADJ. **fitting**

VERB + EPITAPH **write** | **make, stand as** ◇ *These movies stand as an ~ to the great director.*

PREP. **as an ~** ◇ *He wanted these lines as his ~.* | **~ for** ◇ *She wrote the perfect ~ for the poet.* | **~ on** (*esp. BrE*) ◇ *Joyce's ~ on King Edward VIII* | **~ to** ◇ *It makes a fitting ~ to a great career.*

PHRASES **be sb's ~**

epoch *noun*

ADJ. **new** | **modern, present** | **early, past** | **historical**

VERB + EPOCH **mark** ◇ *The dropping of the first atom bomb marked a new ~ in warfare.*

PREP. **during an/the ~, in an/the ~** ◇ *the importance of the computer in the present ~* | **~ of** ◇ *an ~ of great social change* | **~ in** ◇ *Welfare reform was an ~ in the history of US social policy.*

PHRASES **the beginning of an ~, the end of an ~**

equal *noun*

ADJ. **intellectual, social**

VERB + EQUAL **consider sb (as), regard sb as, treat sb as** ◇ *He did not regard himself as her intellectual ~.*

PREP. **as an ~** ◇ *He talks even to small children as ~s.* | **between ~s** ◇ *An interview should be a conversation between ~s.* | **without ~** ◇ *His guitar playing is without ~.*

PHRASES **be sb's ~** ◇ *I shall never be his ~ at chess.* | **first among ~s** ◇ *He was regarded as the 'first among equals' by the other office clerks.* | **have few ~s** ◇ *When it comes to plain speaking, she has few ~s.* | **have no ~ ~s** ◇ *In fighting, they had no ~s.*

equal *adj.*

1 same in size, quantity, value, etc.

VERBS **be** | **become** | **make sth** ◇ *We moved some of the better players to make the two sides ~.*

ADV. **absolutely, exactly, in every way, precisely** ◇ *Their test results were ~ in every way.* | **almost, essentially** (*esp. AmE*), **nearly, virtually** | **about, approximately, more or less, relatively** (*esp. AmE*), **roughly** ◇ *The EU nations together have an economy about ~ in size to that of the US.* | **just** | **at least** ◇ *Fitness is important in soccer, but of at least ~ importance are skills.*

PREP. **in** ◇ *The two books are more or less ~ in length.* | **to** ◇ *One pound is roughly ~ to two dollars.*

2 having the same rights

VERBS **be** | **be born** ◇ *I believe everyone is born ~.*

ADV. **genuinely, truly**

3 equal to sth able to do sth

VERBS **be, feel, prove, seem** ◇ *I hope that he proves ~ to the*

challenge. | **become** | **make sb** ◇ *I felt that nothing could make me ~ to the demands being made of me.*

ADV. **more than** ◇ *I felt more than ~ to the task.*

equality *noun*

ADJ. **complete, full, perfect** | **greater** | **genuine, true** | **formal** ◇ *the goal of formal ~ before the law* | **economic, legal, political, social** | **gender, race, racial, sexual** | **human**

VERB + EQUALITY **have** ◇ *Women do not yet have true ~ in the company.* | **achieve** | **demand, fight for, seek, strive for, want** | **promote, support** | **establish** | **ensure, guarantee** | **deny**

PHRASES **~ before the law** ◇ *The State shall not deny anyone ~ before the law.* | **~ of opportunity** ◇ *People from these minority groups must have ~ of opportunity.*

PREP. **~ between** ◇ *They fought for greater ~ between the sexes.* | **~ for** ◇ *the task of achieving ~ for gay men* | **~ in** ◇ *These women are demanding fairness and ~ in their pay.* | **~ with** ◇ *The women are demanding full ~ with the men of their tribe.*

equate *verb*

ADV. **directly** ◇ *The constellations in the night sky cannot be directly ~d with the heroes of Greek mythology.* | **roughly** | **simply** | **automatically** | **often** ◇ *Education is often ~d with intelligence.* | **not necessarily** ◇ *Invention and progress do not necessarily ~ with improvement.* | **mistakenly**

VERB + EQUATE **can** ◇ *Money cannot be ~d with happiness.* | **be difficult to, be hard to** ◇ *It's hard to ~ this gentle woman with the monster portrayed in the newspapers.*

PREP. **with** ◇ *We are taught to ~ beauty with success.*

equation *noun*

1 mathematical statement

ADJ. **basic, simple** ◇ *This can be shown by a simple ~.* | **complex, complicated** | **algebraic, math** (*AmE*), **mathematical** | **differential, quadratic, simultaneous, etc.**

VERB + EQUATION **solve, work out** ◇ *I could not find a way of solving the ~.* | **derive, obtain** ◇ *The ideal gas ~ is derived from this model.* | **satisfy** ◇ *the range of values of x which would satisfy this ~* | **balance** | **write**

PREP. **~ for** ◇ *the ~ for a straight line*

PHRASES **a side of the ~** ◇ *the numbers on the right-hand side of the ~*

2 situation

VERB + EQUATION **be a part of, come into, enter, enter into** ◇ *The availability of water is also part of the ~.* ◇ *Money also comes into the ~.*

equator *noun*

VERB + EQUATOR **cross** | **straddle**

PREP. **around the ~** ◇ *Rainforests occur around the ~.* | **at the ~** ◇ *The sun heats the sea more at the ~ than at the poles.* | **close to the ~, near the ~** ◇ *in an area near the ~* | **on the ~** ◇ *The lake lies exactly on the ~.*

PHRASES **north of the ~, south of the ~** ◇ *The island is just 80 miles north of the ~.*

equip *verb*

ADV. **lavishly, splendidly** (*esp. BrE*), **superbly** (*esp. BrE*), **well** ◇ *The resort is well equipped for sailing.* | **badly, poorly** | **comprehensively, fully, properly** | **adequately, suitably** | **specially**

VERB + EQUIP **seek to, try to**

PREP. **for** ◇ *The hostel is specially equipped for wheelchair access.* | **with** ◇ *The car is fully equipped with all the latest gadgets.*

PHRASES **be equipped to deal with, be equipped to handle sth** ◇ *People have to be emotionally equipped to handle their success.* | **come equipped with** ◇ *Rooms vary in size and come equipped with television and telephone.*

equipment noun

ADJ. **the latest, modern, state-of-the-art, up-to-date** | **high-tech, sophisticated, technical** | **expensive** | **sensitive** | **heavy** | **portable** | **basic, standard** | **essential, necessary, vital** ◊ *Hospitals are increasingly depending on charity for vital ~.* | **special, specialist** (*esp. BrE*)**, specialized** | **defective, faulty** | **outdated** | **kitchen** | **school** | **exercise** (*esp. AmE*)**, gym, sports** | **play, playground** ◊ *The local council is supplying new play ~ for the playground.* | **business, office** | **laboratory, scientific** | **computer, electrical, electronic** | **medical** | **military** | **communication, navigation, radar, radio, telecom, telecommunications** | **camera, digital, photographic, video** | **life-saving, protective, safety, security** | **rescue** | **garden, gardening** | **construction** (*esp. AmE*) | **mental, physical** (*both figurative*) ◊ *He lacks the mental ~ to succeed in politics.*
... OF EQUIPMENT **item, piece**
VERB + EQUIPMENT **buy, purchase** | **sell** | **provide, supply** | **use** ◊ *The plane uses state-of-the-art navigation ~.* | **install** | **upgrade** | **operate** | **test** | **need, require** ◊ *No special ~ is needed.*
EQUIPMENT + VERB **consist of sth** ◊ *The basic ~ consists of a plastic mask and a length of rope.* | **work** | **malfunction**
EQUIPMENT + NOUN **maker, manufacturer** | **supplier, vendor** | **hire** (*BrE*)**, rental** (*esp. AmE*)
PREP. **~ for** ◊ *high-tech ~ for keeping the temperature steady*
PHRASES **the proper ~, the right ~** ◊ *Never go climbing without the proper ~.*

equivalent noun

ADJ. **direct, exact** | **approximate, closest** (*esp. AmE*)**, nearest** (*esp. BrE*)**, rough** ◊ *the nearest ~ we have to a carnival* | **contemporary, modern, modern-day** ◊ *the modern ~ of the Roman baths* | **moral** ◊ *The campaign says that hunters are the moral ~ of murderers.* | **aural, visual** ◊ *These drawings are the visual ~s of stage whispers.* | **verbal** | **architectural, cinematic, journalistic, literary, musical, sporting** (*esp. BrE*)**, etc.** | **digital, electronic, online** ◊ *the online ~ of the telephone* | **female, male** | **American, British, etc.** | **cash** (*business*) ◊ *The company has $43.8 million in cash and cash ~s.*
VERB + EQUIVALENT **be, be considered, represent** | **become** | **have** ◊ *a word which has no direct ~ in English* | **produce, provide** | **earn, receive** ◊ *each sponsor received the ~ of £1 million worth of advertising.* | **pay (sb)** ◊ *He's only paid the ~ of $200.*
PREP. **~ for** ◊ *There is no exact male ~ for witches.* | **~ in** ◊ *It is the approximate ~ in height to the Matterhorn.* | **~ of** ◊ *This qualification is the ~ of a degree.* | **~ to** ◊ *This concert hall is the American ~ to London's Albert Hall.*

equivalent adj.

VERBS **be, seem** | **become**
ADV. **exactly, precisely** | **almost, essentially, practically** | **approximately, broadly, more or less, roughly** ◊ *the price we would pay elsewhere for a broadly ~ house* | **logically, mathematically** | **morally**
PREP. **in, to** ◊ *These first computers were ~ in power to a modern calculator.*

era noun

ADJ. **golden, great** ◊ *the golden ~ of radio* | **new** | **different** | **present** | **modern** | **bygone, earlier, past, previous** ◊ *The room had the elegance of a bygone ~.* | **antebellum** (*AmE*) | **pre-war** | **post-war** | **apartheid, civil rights, colonial, post-imperial** | **Communist, Nazi, Soviet, etc.** | **dotcom** | **Clinton, Thatcher, etc.** | **Edwardian, Napoleonic, Victorian, etc.** | **Baroque, Classical, Romantic, etc.** | **Christian, Common** ◊ *the early centuries of the Christian Era* | **silent** ◊ *movies of the silent ~*
VERB + ERA **herald, mark, usher in** ◊ *The fall of the Berlin Wall ushered in a whole new ~.* | **enter, move into** ◊ *The country has entered an ~ of high unemployment.* | **characterize, define**

ERA + VERB **begin** | **end**
PREP. **during an/the ~, in an/the ~** ◊ *We live in an ~ of religious uncertainty.* | **into ~** ◊ *a practice that has survived into the present ~* | **~ in** ◊ *a new ~ in the history of art*
PHRASES **the beginning of an ~, the dawn of an ~, the dawning of an ~** ◊ *It feels like the dawning of a new ~* | **be on the threshold of a new ~** | **the end of an ~**

eradicate verb

ADV. **completely, entirely, totally** | **successfully**
VERB + ERADICATE **try to** | **help (to)** | **be difficult to, be hard to** | **be impossible to** ◊ *These insects are very difficult to ~.*
PREP. **from** ◊ *The disease has now been successfully ~d from the world.*
PHRASES **an attempt to ~ sth, an effort to ~ sth**

erase verb

ADV. **completely, entirely, fully** | **partially** | **virtually** | **effectively** ◊ *This event has been effectively ~d from written records.* | **accidentally** | **digitally**
VERB + ERASE **attempt to, seek to, try to** | **want to** ◊ *She wanted to ~ the message before her parents heard it.* | **be determined to** ◊ *They are determined to ~ the bad memories of last year's defeats.*
PREP. **from** ◊ *These people have been virtually ~d from the history book.*

erect verb

ADV. **hastily, quickly** | **specially** ◊ *The event will take place in a specially ~ed marquee.*
PREP. **around** ◊ *An electric fence was ~ed around the campus.* | **on** ◊ *A large monument was ~ed on the battlefield.*
PHRASES **newly ~ed, recently ~ed** ◊ *the newly ~ed station buildings*

erect adj.

1 standing/sitting straight up

VERBS **be** | **sit, stand, walk** ◊ *He sat very ~, listening intently.* | **hold sth** ◊ *She held her head ~ as she walked proudly up to the platform.* | **keep sth/oneself** ◊ *Keep your trunk ~ throughout the exercise.*
ADV. **very** | **perfectly** ◊ *Janice was standing perfectly ~.*

2 stiff

VERBS **be** | **become**
ADV. **completely, fully**

erection noun

VERB + ERECTION **achieve, get, have** | **maintain, prolong, sustain** | **lose** | **give sb**

erode verb

ADV. **badly, seriously, severely, significantly, substantially** ◊ *Walkers should stick to obvious paths, even if they are badly ~d.* ◊ *The experience had seriously ~d his confidence in himself.* | **completely** | **further** | **eventually, gradually, slowly** ◊ *The distinction between social classes is slowly being ~d.* | **steadily** ◊ *The river bank had been steadily ~d over the years.* | **quickly, rapidly** | **easily** | **away** ◊ *The rocks have ~d away over time.*
VERB + ERODE **begin to, start to** ◊ *Without adequate protection from plants, the river banks began to ~.* | **continue to** ◊ *Our trade position continues to ~.* | **threaten to** ◊ *the commercial pressures that threaten to ~ local traditions* | **tend to**

erosion noun

ADJ. **serious, severe, significant** ◊ *Acid rain has caused severe ~ on the hillside.* | **further** ◊ *He risks further ~ of his support among voters.* | **rapid** | **gradual, slow, steady** ◊ *the steady ~ of their civil liberties* | **beach, coastal, shoreline, soil** | **glacial, water, wind** | **price** ◊ *the steady price ~ that has occurred in Japan*
VERB + EROSION **cause, contribute to, lead to, result in** | **control, minimize** (*esp. AmE*)**, prevent, protect sth from, reduce** | **experience, suffer, suffer from** ◊ *The area suffers badly from coastal ~.* | **increase** ◊ *This damages soil*

structure, which increases ~. | **see, witness** ◇ *The country has seen a progressive ~ of constitutional freedoms.*
EROSION + VERB **affect sth** ◇ *the areas worst affected by soil ~* | **occur**
EROSION + NOUN **rate**
PHRASES **the ~ of sth** ◇ *the ~ of civil liberties* | **the rate of ~**

erotic adj.
VERBS **be** | **become** | **find sth**
ADV. **extremely, fairly, very, etc.** | **highly, powerfully, strangely** | **mildly, vaguely** | **blatantly, overtly** ◇ *There were some overtly ~ scenes in the movie.*

errand noun
ADJ. **little, small** | **simple** | **daily** (esp. AmE) | **last-minute**
VERB + ERRAND **do, go on, run** ◇ *She made her brother run some little ~s for her.* | **complete, finish** (both esp. AmE) | **send sb on** ◇ *My boss kept sending me out on ~s.*
PREP. **on an ~** ◇ *She's gone on an ~ for her mother.*

erratic adj.
VERBS **be, seem** | **become** | **remain**
ADV. **extremely, fairly, very, etc.** | **highly, wildly** | **completely** | **increasingly** ◇ *their increasingly ~ policy decisions* | **a little, slightly, etc.**

error noun
ADJ. **egregious** (esp. AmE), **fundamental, glaring, grave, great, grievous, major, serious** ◇ *The report contained some glaring ~s.* | **fatal** ◇ *He made the fatal ~ of borrowing more than he could pay back.* | **minor, small** | **careless** | **embarrassing, unfortunate** | **past** ◇ *The ability to learn from past ~s is vital in business.* | **common** | **grammar** (esp. AmE), **grammatical, spelling, typing, typographical** | **factual** | **experimental, statistical** | **standard** (statistics) | **random, systematic** | **measurement** (esp. AmE), **sampling** ◇ *His research interests include measurement ~ in survey research.* | **rounding** (esp. AmE) ◇ *The difference is due to a rounding ~ in the first calculation.* | **unforced** (sports) ◇ *The American produced five double faults and 35 unforced ~s.* | **tactical** ◇ *The Kenyan athlete made a tactical ~ in starting too fast.* | **administrative, clerical, medical** | **human, pilot** ◇ *The plane crash was caused by human ~, not mechanical failure.*
VERB + ERROR **commit, make** ◇ *He had committed a grave ~ in letting them see the document.* ◇ *She made several serious ~s during the race.* | **cause** ◇ *~s caused by illegibly written orders* | **contain** ◇ *The document contained a lot of typing ~s.* | **introduce** ◇ *An editorial ~ was introduced into the copy.* | **catch** (esp. AmE), **detect, discover, find, identify, spot** ◇ *Thank you for catching that silly ~ on my part.* ◇ *I found several factual ~s in the report.* | **point out** ◇ *The ~ was pointed out to her by one of her colleagues.* | **report** | **realize, recognize** ◇ *I only realized my ~ when it was too late.* | **acknowledge, admit** ◇ *Have the courage to admit your ~.* | **avoid** ◇ *She has avoided the common ~ of writing too much.* | **prevent** | **repeat** ◇ *Do not repeat the ~s of your parents and grandparents.* | **correct, eliminate, fix** (esp. AmE), **rectify** ◇ *Glasses can correct most ~s in your vision.* | **minimize** (esp. AmE), **reduce** ◇ *the use of computer systems to reduce hospital ~s* | **regret** (esp. AmE) ◇ *We regret the clerical ~ made in the letter sent to Mr Finlay.* | **compound** ◇ *The paper accidentally printed the victim's address, then compounded their ~ by printing her name the next day.*
ERROR + VERB **arise (from sth), occur, result (from sth)** ◇ *~s arising from inadequate information*
ERROR + NOUN **detection** | **correction** | **message** ◇ *An ~ message comes up when I try to open the program.* | **rate** ◇ *machines with relatively high ~ rates*
PREP. **in ~** (= by mistake) ◇ *The machine had been switched off in ~.* | **~ in** ◇ *He checked his letter for ~s in spelling.* ◇ *He realized his ~ in not attending the funeral.*
PHRASES **a comedy of ~s** ◇ *His attempts to arrange a party ended up as a comedy of ~s.* | **an ~ in judgement/judgment** (esp. AmE), **an ~ of judgement/judgment** (esp. BrE) ◇ *The president had made an amazing ~ of judgement.* | **an ~ of fact** ◇ *The speech contained many ~s of fact.* | **a margin of ~**

◇ *The margin of ~ for a racing driver is tiny.* | **the ~ of one's ways** ◇ *Will they realize the ~ of their ways before it is too late?*

erupt verb
ADV. **violently** ◇ *the volcano which ~ed violently last month* | **suddenly** ◇ *His anger suddenly ~ed into furious shouting.* | **periodically** ◇ *Epidemics periodically ~ed throughout the 19th century.* | **occasionally** ◇ *Violence occasionally ~s between the opposing factions.* | **spontaneously** ◇ *The audience spontaneously ~ed into a standing ovation.* | **finally** ◇ *Michael finally ~ed, jumping up from his seat.*
VERB + ERUPT **threaten to**
PREP. **in** ◇ *The crowd ~ed in cheers and sobs of joy.* | **into** ◇ *violence that threatened to ~ into a full-scale war* | **with** ◇ *The room ~ed with laughter.*

eruption noun
1 explosion of a volcano
ADJ. **big, great, major, massive, violent** ◇ *It was the biggest ~ of Vesuvius for some years.* | **explosive** ◇ *volcanic clouds from explosive ~s* | **minor** | **volcanic, volcano** (AmE)
VERB + ERUPTION **predict**
ERUPTION + VERB **happen, occur, take place**
PREP. **in an/the ~** ◇ *The temple was destroyed in a violent ~.*
2 sudden start of sth loud/violent
ADJ. **sudden** ◇ *a sudden ~ of fighting*
VERB + ERUPTION **cause, trigger** ◇ *The news could trigger an ~ of violence.*
PREP. **~ of**

escalate verb
1 become/make sth worse
ADV. **quickly, rapidly** | **gradually, steadily** ◇ *Violence between the two sides has been steadily escalating.* | **suddenly**
PREP. **into** ◇ *The conflict could ~ rapidly into a full-scale war.* | **to** ◇ *a small local disagreement that ~s to civil war*
2 increase
ADV. **dramatically** ◇ *Prices had recently ~d dramatically.* | **sharply** ◇ *The cost of raw materials has ~d sharply.*
PREP. **to** ◇ *The budget ~d to £32 million.*

escalation noun
ADJ. **dramatic, major, serious** | **rapid** | **gradual** | **further** | **military, nuclear** ◇ *the threat of nuclear ~*
VERB + ESCALATION **lead to** ◇ *The reorganization has led to a dramatic ~ in costs.* | **prevent** | **represent** ◇ *This bill represents another ~ in the war on drugs.* | **see, witness** ◇ *This week witnessed a significant ~ in the global financial crisis.*
PREP. **~ in** ◇ *a serious ~ in the fighting* | **~ into** ◇ *the ~ of the conflict into an all-out war* | **~ of** ◇ *an ~ of the level of violence in video games* | **~ to** (esp. AmE) ◇ *It could result in ~ to major ground action.*

escalator noun
ADJ. **down, up** ◇ *kids running up a down ~*
VERB + ESCALATOR **ride** (AmE), **take, use** ◇ *We rode the ~ up toward our restaurant.* ◇ *Take the ~ down to the lower level.* | **ascend, go up** | **descend, go down**
ESCALATOR + VERB **carry sb** ◇ *Passengers are carried by ~ to the first floor.* | **lead to sth** ◇ *the ~ leading down to the lower level*

escape noun
1 getting away from a place
ADJ. **attempted** | **successful** | **great** ◇ *one of the greatest ~s of all time* | **daring** ◇ *the daring ~ of a Resistance fighter from prison* | **hasty, quick** ◇ *I made a hasty ~.*
VERB + ESCAPE **make, make good** ◇ *He made his ~ through the window.* ◇ *I found an open door and made good my ~.* | **plan**

| **attempt** ◊ *a group of slaves that attempted an ~* | **block**, **prevent** ◊ *He stepped in front of me, blocking my ~.* | **allow** ◊ *The ground became swamped, allowing no ~.*
ESCAPE + NOUN **attempt, bid** (*esp. BrE*) | **route** | **vehicle** | **hatch, ladder, tunnel** | **plan** ◊ *Together they formulated an ~ plan.*
PREP. **~ from** ◊ *his ~ from the prison camp*
PHRASES **a means of ~, a way of ~** ◊ *She looked around for a means of ~.* | **a possibility of ~** ◊ *There was clearly no possibility of ~.*

2 avoiding sth unpleasant or boring

ADJ. **close, narrow, near** | **lucky, miraculous, remarkable** ◊ *A driver had a lucky ~ after a brick was dropped on his car from a bridge.* | **temporary** ◊ *young people's need for temporary ~ from the demanding journey into adulthood* | **perfect, ultimate, welcome** ◊ *For many, the ultimate ~ is a tranquil beach filled with white sand.*
VERB + ESCAPE **have** | **plan, plot** ◊ *Celine has been plotting her ~ for months.* | **need, seek** ◊ *city dwellers seeking ~ from stress* | **find** ◊ *Craig finds ~ in dreams.* | **offer, provide** ◊ *This play offered an ~ from the everyday.*
PREP. **~ from** ◊ *He had a narrow ~ from gunfire.*

escape *verb*

ADV. **barely, just, narrowly** ◊ *They narrowly ~d being killed in the fire.* | **not completely, not entirely, not fully** ◊ *The head of department cannot entirely ~ responsibility for this situation.* | **somehow** ◊ *Apparently, they had ~d somehow and gotten home.* | **largely** ◊ *The city largely ~d bombing in the campaign.* | **eventually, finally** ◊ *She eventually ~d to the US.* | **never** ◊ *Tony may never ~ his emotional struggle.* | **easily** ◊ *They're so small they can easily ~ notice.* | **safely, successfully** ◊ *pilots who successfully ~d while their aircraft was being shot down*
VERB + ESCAPE **cannot** | **be impossible to** | **be easy to** ◊ *It was easy to ~ in the confusion of the besieged city.* | **attempt to, seek to, try to** | **struggle to** ◊ *He got hurt while struggling to ~.* | **hope to, want to, wish to** ◊ *a lonely man who wants to ~ his lifestyle* | **need to** ◊ *I need to ~. I want to go away from here.* | **manage to** | **let sb** ◊ *It was stupid of Lee to let them ~.* | **help sb (to)**
PREP. **from** ◊ *to ~ from danger* | **into** ◊ *They ~d into the forest.* | **to** ◊ *The family ~d to the West.* | **with** ◊ *Thieves ~d with property worth over $5000.* | **without** ◊ *The driver ~d without injury.*
PHRASES **~ alive** ◊ *Only two of the men ~d alive.* | **~ sb's clutches** ◊ *He had managed to ~ the clutches of the police yet again.* | **~ from it all** ◊ *We would always go there to ~ from it all.* | **~ (sb's) notice** ◊ *errors that had ~d my notice* | **~ unharmed, ~ unhurt, ~ uninjured, ~ unscathed** | **~ with your life** ◊ *She was very lucky to ~ with her life.*

escort *noun*

ADJ. **armed, military, motorcycle, police, security** | **convoy, destroyer, fighter** (*esp. AmE*) (*all military*) | **female, male**
VERB + ESCORT **be accompanied by, have** ◊ *She had a police ~ to the hospital.* | **give sb, provide (sb with), send** ◊ *Can you give us an ~?* ◊ *The army provided a small armed ~ for the delegation.* | **need, require** ◊ *The referee needed a police ~ as he left the stadium.*
ESCORT + NOUN **vehicle, vessel** | **duty, mission** (*esp. AmE*) ◊ *Get your planes ready for ~ duties.* | **service**
PREP. **under ~** ◊ *The opposition leader was arrested and taken to the capital under ~.* | **with an ~, without an ~** ◊ *They left with a small ~.* | **~ for** ◊ *an ~ for the Queen's car* | **~ of** ◊ *an ~ of ten soldiers*

espionage *noun*

ADJ. **corporate, economic, industrial** ◊ *The big computer companies are very worried about industrial ~.* | **international** | **American, British, etc.**
VERB + ESPIONAGE **be engaged in, be involved in, conduct** (*esp. AmE*), **engage in** | **be executed for, be imprisoned for**

ESPIONAGE + NOUN **activity, operations** (*esp. AmE*) ◊ *evidence of ~ activities in Australia* | **case** (*esp. AmE*) ◊ *one of the most important ~ cases of the 20th century* | **investigation** | **agent** (*esp. AmE*) | **network** (*esp. AmE*) | **thriller** (*esp. AmE*) ◊ *She has written eight ~ thrillers.*
PREP. **~ against** ◊ *She was found guilty of ~ against the United States.* | **~ on behalf of** ◊ *~ on behalf of foreign states*
PHRASES **the world of ~** ◊ *the shadowy world of ~*
→ Note at CRIME (for more verbs)

essay *noun*

... OF ESSAYS **anthology, collection, selection, series, set, volume** ◊ *In 2001 she published a collection of ~s.*
VERB + ESSAY **do, write** ◊ *Have you done your ~ yet?* | **finish** ◊ *I finished my ~ about 10 o'clock last night!* | **conclude** ◊ *He concludes the ~ by calling for a corrective.* | **publish** | **hand in, turn in** (*esp. AmE*) ◊ *Essays handed in late will not be accepted.* | **contribute, submit** | **present** ◊ *A version of this ~ was presented at the Astronomical Society.* | **read** | **collect** ◊ *The fifteen ~s collected in this volume.*
ESSAY + VERB **be entitled sth, be titled sth** (*esp. AmE*) ◊ *an ~ entitled 'Memory'* | **address sth, discuss sth, examine sth, explore sth** ◊ *The ~s explore Einstein's personal development.* | **provide sth** ◊ *This ~ provides a comprehensive overview of the subject.* | **argue sth, suggest sth**
ESSAY + NOUN **question, title, topic** ◊ *You have to answer three out of eight ~ questions in the exam.* | **assignment** ◊ *Lunch was the only time she could finish her ~ assignment.* | **competition** (*esp. BrE*), **contest** (*AmE*) ◊ *the teenage winner of an ~ contest* | **collection** (*esp. AmE*)
PREP. **in an/the ~** ◊ *He made some very good points in his ~.* | **~ about, ~ on** ◊ *We have to write an ~ on the environment.* | **~ by** ◊ *an ~ by Montaigne*

essence *noun*

1 basic/most important quality of sth

ADJ. **real, true, very** | **divine, inner, spiritual** ◊ *The girl has her own spiritual ~.* | **human** | **pure**
VERB + ESSENCE **capture, distil, embody, encapsulate** ◊ *They distilled the ~ of their message into three principles.* ◊ *His paintings embody the very ~ of the post-war years.* | **define** | **grasp, understand** | **convey, express, represent, reveal** | **preserve** | **miss** ◊ *His work misses the ~ of what Eastern religion is about.* | **destroy, lose**
PREP. **in ~** ◊ *His theory was not new in ~.* | **~ of** ◊ *The freedom to pick your leaders is the ~ of a democracy.*
PHRASES **of the ~** ◊ *Time is of the ~.*

2 (*BrE*) concentrated substance → See also EXTRACT

ADJ. **almond, coffee, vanilla, etc.** | **flower, herbal, plant**
... OF ESSENCE **drop** ◊ *Add a few drops of vanilla ~.*
VERB + ESSENCE **add, use**

essential *adj.*

VERBS **appear, be, seem** | **become** ◊ *It is becoming almost ~ for students to have a second language.* | **remain** | **make sth** ◊ *Increased competition makes it ~ for the business to innovate.* | **consider sth, deem sth, find sth, regard sth as, see sth as, think sth** ◊ *Do you consider these textbooks ~ for the course?*
ADV. **really, truly, very** (*AmE*) | **absolutely** | **almost, virtually** | **fairly** | **clearly** ◊ *A printer is clearly ~ to such a task.* | **equally** ◊ *Diet is crucial; exercise is equally ~.* | **by no means** ◊ *Although useful, the accessories are by no means ~.*
PREP. **for** ◊ *the skills ~ for success* | **to** ◊ *He believed that some form of religion was ~ to human life.*

essentials *noun*

ADJ. **bare, basic** ◊ *the bare ~ for existence*
VERB + ESSENTIALS **grasp, learn** ◊ *Just try and grasp the ~ of the argument.* ◊ *You need to learn the ~ of HTML.* | **provide** ◊ *The relief agencies are trying to provide food and other basic ~.* | **concentrate on** ◊ *Don't let's worry about the details at this stage. Let's concentrate on the ~.* | **cover** ◊ *The basic course covers the ~ of setting up your own company.* | **lack** | **take** ◊ *I tried to take the bare ~.*

establish *verb*

1 start/create sth

ADV. **initially, originally** ◇ *The Internet was originally ~ed by scientists to share information.* | **formally** ◇ *The League was formally ~ed in 1920.*
VERB + ESTABLISH **attempt to, seek to, try to** ◇ *We try to ~ links with schools.* | **help (to), help sb (to)** | **agree to** ◇ *The two countries agreed to ~ full diplomatic relations.* | **be able to** | **be important to**
PHRASES **an attempt to ~ sth, an effort to ~ sth** | **newly ~ed, recently ~ed** ◇ *He was appointed to the newly ~ed Department for Safety.*

2 make sth known and accepted

ADV. **firmly, securely** ◇ *His position in the organization is now firmly ~ed.* | **fully** ◇ *By the 7th century Buddhism was fully ~ed in Japan.* | **effectively** | **clearly** ◇ *We have now clearly ~ed ourselves as the leader in the market.* | **successfully** ◇ *We have successfully ~ed clear rules that most students accept.*
VERB + ESTABLISH **attempt to, seek to, try to** | **help (to), help sb (to)** ◇ *The exhibition helped her ~ herself as an artist.*
PREP. **as** ◇ *He has now ~ed his reputation as a popular musician.*
PHRASES **become ~ed, get ~ed** ◇ *The festival has become ~ed as an annual event.* | **previously ~ed** ◇ *a previously ~ed formula*

3 make certain of sth

ADV. **conclusively, definitely, definitively, unequivocally** | **empirically, scientifically** ◇ *The effectiveness of the new drug has not yet been scientifically ~ed.*
VERB + ESTABLISH **attempt to, seek to, try to** ◇ *Police are still trying to ~ the identity of the dead man.* | **help (to)** | **be able to** | **be possible to** | **be difficult to** | **be important to**
PHRASES **an attempt to ~ sth, an effort to ~ sth**

establishment *noun*

1 act of starting sth

ADJ. **formal** ◇ *the formal ~ of the republic in 1948* | **gradual, rapid** | **successful**
VERB + ESTABLISHMENT **advocate, call for, propose, recommend, support** ◇ *The commission is calling for the ~ of a national holiday.* | **agree to** | **lead to** ◇ *This report led to the ~ of a special committee to investigate the matter.* | **allow, allow for, enable, encourage, facilitate, provide for** ◇ *We would like to encourage the ~ of new farm businesses.* | **prevent** | **announce** | **see** ◇ *The months that followed saw the ~ of a strong military presence in the region.*
PREP. **with the ~ of** ◇ *With the ~ of major new markets, the economy is thriving.*

2 business, organization, etc.

ADJ. **drinking, eating** | **licensed** (*esp. BrE*) ◇ *the supply of alcohol in licensed ~s* | **commercial, retail** (*both esp. AmE*) | **educational, military, religious, etc.** | **research, training** ◇ *She's now running a small government research ~.*
→ Note at ORGANIZATION (for verbs)

3 the establishment people in positions of power

ADJ. **mainstream** ◇ *the mainstream political ~* | **academic, art, literary, media, medical, military, musical, political, scientific** ◇ *the Washington media ~* | **clerical, ecclesiastical, religious** | **British, French, etc.** ◇ *The British Establishment is very slow to accept change.* | **conservative, liberal** ◇ *a pillar of the liberal ~* | **Democratic, Republican, etc.**
VERB + THE ESTABLISHMENT **offend** ◇ *His abstract paintings offended the art ~.* | **challenge** ◇ *O'Connor challenged the liberal ~ on many things.*

estate *noun*

1 land owned by a person/family/organization

ADJ. **big, great, huge, large, substantial, vast** | **sprawling** ◇ *the family mansion and sprawling country ~* | **small** | **country, rural** ◇ *the family's country ~* | **grand, palatial** ◇ *He owned a palatial ~ in California.* | **royal** | **family** ◇ *the family ~ at Kostroma* | **landed** (*esp. BrE*) ◇ *Gilbert was heir to*
an extensive landed ~. | **sugar, wine** ◇ *Bordeaux's most famous wine ~* | **freehold, leasehold** (*both BrE, law*)
VERB + ESTATE **have, own** ◇ *The family owns a large ~ in the north.* | **buy** ◇ *Queen Victoria bought the ~ in 1848.* | **manage, run**
ESTATE + NOUN **manager, owner, worker** (*BrE*) | **management** | **agency, agent** (*both BrE*) (*real estate agency, real estate agent* in *AmE*)
PREP. **on an/the ~** ◇ *the number of people living on the ~* | **~ of** ◇ *an ~ of 20 000 acres*
PHRASES **an heir to an ~** ◇ *The young prince is the heir to a vast ~ in the west of the country.*

2 (*BrE*) land with a lot of buildings of the same type

ADJ. **large, massive** | **small** | **deprived, run-down** ◇ *youngsters living on deprived housing ~s* | **council, housing** | **private** | **industrial, trading** ◇ *The factory is on a large industrial ~ on the outskirts of town.*
VERB + ESTATE **build**
PREP. **on an/the ~** ◇ *She lives on a council ~ in Leeds.*

3 (*law*) property that sb leaves when they die

ADJ. **personal** | **taxable** ◇ *assets from your taxable ~*
VERB + ESTATE **bequeath** (*formal*), **leave** ◇ *The bulk of his ~ was bequeathed to his son Jacob.* ◇ *She left her whole ~ to her niece.* | **inherit** ◇ *She inherited her father's ~.* | **own** ◇ *His personal ~ is worth $30 million.* | **settle** ◇ *It took seven years to settle the ~.*
ESTATE + VERB **be valued at sth, be worth sth**
ESTATE + NOUN **tax** (*AmE*) ◇ *to transfer ~ taxes to the next generation* | **sale**

esteem *noun*

ADJ. **great, high** | **low** | **personal** ◇ *I needed to do it for my own personal ~.* | **mutual** ◇ *We parted with expressions of mutual ~.* | **critical, popular, public, social** ◇ *Her work has been steadily gaining critical ~ in recent years.*
VERB + ESTEEM **earn** ◇ *She had earned the ~ of everyone in the town.* | **enjoy, have** ◇ *the high public ~ now enjoyed by the armed forces* | **lose** ◇ *He had lost all of his personal ~.* | **accord sb** ◇ *the level of social ~ accorded to doctors* | **boost, build, build up, raise** ◇ *Recent reviews of her work have raised her ~.*
PREP. **in ... ~** ◇ *the status of teachers in the public ~* | **~ for** ◇ *the public's ~ for the president* ◇ *I have great ~ for you.* | **~ of** ◇ *The school's aim is to build the self-esteem of the children.*
PHRASES **hold sb/sth in great, high, low, etc. ~** ◇ *He is held in the highest ~ by all who know him.* | **a mark of ~, a token of ~** ◇ *We would like to offer you this gift as a mark of our ~.*

estimate *noun*

ADJ. **official, unofficial** | **current, recent** ◇ *Current ~s suggest that supplies will run out within six months.* | **early, initial, original, preliminary** | **latest** ◇ *Inflation could rise by 15% according to the latest ~.* | **accurate, inaccurate** ◇ *Inaccurate ~s can lead to overproduction.* | **fair, good, realistic, reasonable, reliable** | **best** ◇ *Flight times in the brochure are based on our best ~, and will be confirmed as soon as possible.* | **approximate, rough** | **precise** ◇ *The manufacturers will not make precise ~s.* | **conservative, low** ◇ *I think 15 000 will turn out to be a very low ~.* | **high, inflated** ◇ *According to the highest ~, over 100 000 men died in the battle.* | **optimistic, pessimistic** | **overall** ◇ *an overall ~ of test performance* | **annual** ◇ *annual ~s of total cost* | **cost, earnings** ◇ *The slump is causing analysts to revise earnings ~s for next year.* | **population** ◇ *annual population ~s for small geographic areas* | **casualty** ◇ *Casualty ~s vary considerably.*
VERB + ESTIMATE **calculate, make** ◇ *Can you make an ~ of the numbers involved?* | **generate, give (sb), produce, provide (sb with), submit** ◇ *Three companies submitted ~s for the work.* | **obtain** ◇ *How can one obtain the revised ~s?* | **adjust, refine, revise** | **compare** ◇ *We compared ~s for various materials.* | **exceed** ◇ *It appears that the total will exceed the ~.*

estimate + VERB **be based on sth** | **indicate sth, predict sth, reflect sth, say sth, show sth, suggest sth** ◇ *One ~ suggests that 30 000 jobs may be lost.* | **put sth at** ◇ *Some ~s put the figure as high as 50%.* | **differ, range, vary** ◇ *Cost ~s vary from $50 000 to $200 000.*
PREP. **according to an/the ~** ◇ *According to the revised ~, four million people will be without homes.* | **at an ~** ◇ *Even at a conservative ~, there is a lot of work to be done.* | **in an/the ~** ◇ *In his first ~, he suggested a figure of £5 000.* | **~ by, ~ from** ◇ *By one ~ she earns $80 million a year.* | **~ for** ◇ *We will send you an ~ for the repairs.* | **~ of** ◇ *an ~ of profits* | *an ~ of £300*

estimate *verb*

ADV. **currently** | **initially, originally** | **previously** ◇ *substantially more than previously ~d* | **accurately, correctly, precisely, reliably** | **roughly** ◇ *how to roughly ~ your caloric intake* | **conservatively** ◇ *It is conservatively ~d that not less than half a million people died in the famine.*
VERB + ESTIMATE **be difficult to, be hard to, be impossible to** | **be easy to, be possible to** ◇ *This made it possible to ~ the effect of workplace ventilation.* | **be used to** ◇ *The results of the survey were used to ~ the preferences of the population at large.*
PREP. **at** ◇ *We ~d the cost at €50 000.*

estimation *noun*

VERB + ESTIMATION **go up in** (*esp. BrE*), **rise in** ◇ *He went up in my ~ when I heard about his charity work.* | **go down in** (*esp. BrE*)
PREP. **in sb's ~** ◇ *In my ~, you've done a good job.*

estranged *adj.*

VERBS **be, feel** | **become**
ADV. **deeply** | **completely** | **increasingly**
PREP. **from** ◇ *He felt deeply ~ from the society he lived in.*

ethics *noun*

ADJ. **personal** ◇ *She resigned over an issue of personal ~.* | **social** ◇ *He teaches a class on social ~.* | **Christian, Jewish, etc.** | **business, corporate, environmental, journalism** (*AmE*), **journalistic, media, medical, professional, etc.** ◇ *The study was approved by the medical ~ committee.*
PHRASES **a code of ~** ◇ *There should be a code of business ~ which indicates how clients are to be served.* | **a matter of ~, a question of ~.** ◇ *It's the committee's job to decide on matters of ~.*

etiquette *noun*

ADJ. **professional, social** ◇ *He showed his contempt for social ~ by not wearing a tie.* | **correct, proper** ◇ *He did not know the proper ~ for greeting people of such high rank.* | **strict** ◇ *the strict ~ of palace life* | **bad, poor** ◇ *She considered it poor ~ to invite people over and then cancel just the day before.* | **email, phone** ◇ *How good is your email ~?* | **business** ◇ *a business ~ expert* | **court** ◇ *a breach of court ~*
VERB + ETIQUETTE **know** ◇ *I don't know the ~ required here.*
ETIQUETTE + VERB **demand sth, dictate sth, require sth** ◇ *Etiquette requires that winners make a speech.*
PHRASES **a breach of ~** ◇ *The lawyer was accused of a breach of professional ~.* | **matters of ~, questions of ~** ◇ *He is an expert on matters of ~.* | **the rules of ~** ◇ *She knew how to address bishops according to the rules of ~.*

euphoria *noun*

ADJ. **early, initial** ◇ *after the initial ~* | **general** | **intense, pure** | **mild** | **patriotic, post-war**
...OF EUPHORIA **wave** ◇ *The news sparked a wave of ~ across the country.*
VERB + EUPHORIA **feel** ◇ *the ~ we all felt when they were finally defeated* | **induce, produce** ◇ *These substances produce ~ when taken in small doses.*
EUPHORIA + VERB **evaporate, fade**

PREP. **~ about** ◇ *All the ~ about the 'new methods' soon faded.* | **~ of** ◇ *the ~ of victory* | **~ over** ◇ *By then, the ~ over the fall of the Berlin Wall had evaporated.*
PHRASES **a feeling of ~, a state of ~**

euro *noun* → Note at CURRENCY

euthanasia *noun*

ADJ. **voluntary** | **involuntary, non-voluntary** | **active, passive**
VERB + EUTHANASIA **perform, practise/practice** | **legalize**

evacuate *verb*

ADV. **immediately** | **safely, successfully** | **medically** (*esp. AmE*) ◇ *6 000 soldiers have been medically ~d since the war began.*
VERB + EVACUATE **help (to)** ◇ *to provide aircraft to help ~ refugees* | **need to** | **order sb to** ◇ *Every police unit has been ordered to ~ all civilians.*
PREP. **from** ◇ *Helicopters were used to ~ people from their homes.* | **to** ◇ *The man has now been safely ~d to the mainland.*

evacuation *noun*

ADJ. **large-scale, mass, massive** | **emergency, immediate** | **forced, mandatory** (*AmE*) ◇ *Officials called for a mandatory ~.* | **voluntary** (*esp. AmE*) | **medical** (*esp. AmE*) ◇ *an airborne medical ~* | **casualty** | **wartime** | **fire** ◇ *a fire ~ drill*
EVACUATION + NOUN **area, zone** | **route** (*esp. AmE*) ◇ *Make sure children know the emergency ~ routes.* | **centre/center** (*esp. AmE*) ◇ *The high school was used as an ~ center.* | **order** | **plan, scheme** (*BrE*) | **drill** ◇ *tsunami ~ drills* | **efforts** | **procedures, process**
PREP. **~ from** ◇ *the ~ of civilians from the area* | **under ~** (*esp. AmE*) ◇ *The county was under a mandatory ~.*

evade *verb*

1 escape
ADV. **narrowly** ◇ *They narrowly ~d a police car which was approaching.* | **successfully**
VERB + EVADE **attempt to, try to** | **manage to** ◇ *He managed to ~ capture and escaped over the border.* | **help (to)**

2 avoid dealing with sth
ADV. **simply** ◇ *Her response was simply to ~ the problem altogether.* | **carefully, neatly, skilfully/skillfully** | **easily** ◇ *Responsibility could not be so easily ~d.* | **altogether, completely**
VERB + EVADE **attempt to, seek to, try to** | **help (to)** | **continue to**

evaluate *verb*

ADV. **effectively** (*esp. AmE*), **fully, properly, thoroughly** | **carefully, rigorously, systematically** ◇ *The evidence should be carefully ~d.* | **accurately** (*esp. AmE*) | **constantly, continually, continuously, regularly** (*all esp. AmE*) | **critically** | **positively** ◇ *The role of stay-at-home mother is more positively ~d in working-class communities.* | **honestly** (*esp. AmE*) | **independently, objectively** (*esp. AmE*) | **empirically, scientifically, statistically** ◇ *These probabilities can be ~d empirically.*
VERB + EVALUATE **aim to, attempt to, be designed to** | **help (to)** ◇ *to help ~ the success of the campaign* | **begin to** | **continue to** | **be used to** ◇ *criteria used to ~ employees' performance* | **be difficult to, be hard to** | **be impossible to** ◇ *It was impossible to ~ the safety of the new drug.* | **be possible to** ◇ *How is it possible to ~ a company?*

evaluation *noun*

ADJ. **comprehensive, rigorous, systematic, thorough** | **careful, detailed** | **independent, objective** (*esp. AmE*) | **subjective** (*esp. AmE*) ◇ *subjective ~s of the costs* | **critical, empirical, statistical** ◇ *a critical ~ of the film* | **initial, preliminary** ◇ *We'll revisit our initial ~.* | **negative, positive** (*both esp. AmE*) ◇ *She generally gets positive ~s from her managers.* | **formal** | **job** (*esp. BrE*), **performance** (*esp. AmE*)

◇ *a new pay structure based on job* ~*s* | **student** (*AmE*) ◇ *the end-of-course student* ~*s* | **annual** (*esp. AmE*) ◇ *his employees' annual* ~*s* | **clinical, medical, psychiatric, psychological** (*all esp. AmE*) (usually *clinical, etc. assessment* in *BrE*) ◇ *the results of clinical* ~*s*
VERB + EVALUATION **carry out, conduct, do, make, perform** ◇ *We still have to carry out an* ~ *of the results.* | **receive, undergo** ◇ *He is undergoing psychiatric* ~. | **complete** ◇ *a recently completed* ~ *of primary health care* | **require** ◇ *symptoms that require medical* ~
EVALUATION + NOUN **procedure, process** | **study** | **form** (*esp. AmE*) ◇ *During dinner, guests fill out a wine* ~ *form.* | **criteria** ◇ *The project developed a set of* ~ *criteria.*
PREP. **in an/the ~** ◇ *In their* ~ *of the project, they considered only certain aspects of it.* | **under ~** ◇ *The new system is still under* ~.

eve *noun*

ADJ. **Christmas, Midsummer's, New Year's** | **election** (*AmE*) ◇ *a special election* ~ *show*
PREP. **on the ~ of** ◇ *opinion polls published on the* ~ *of the election*

even *adj.*

1 level/smooth
VERBS **be, look** ◇ *The floor isn't completely* ~.
ADV. **very** | **absolutely, completely**

2 same size/level
VERBS **be** | **become** | **keep sth** ◇ *Try to keep your stitches absolutely* ~.
ADV. **very** | **absolutely, completely** | **fairly** ◇ *Try to keep the room at a fairly* ~ *temperature.*

3 equal
VERBS **be, seem** | **remain**
ADV. **very** | **fairly, more or less, relatively** ◇ *The scores remained more or less* ~ *throughout the competition.* | **dead** ◇ *Analysts say the race is dead* ~.

evening *noun*

1 part of the day
ADJ. **this, tomorrow, yesterday** | **Friday, Saturday, etc.** | **weekday** (*esp. BrE*) ◇ *a popular place to hang out on weekday* ~*s* | **April, May, etc.** | **spring, summer, etc.** | **long** ◇ *the long winter* ~*s* | **dark** | **quiet** | **balmy, beautiful, fine** (*esp. BrE*), **golden, warm** | **romantic** ◇ *The two spent a romantic* ~ *together.* | **cold, cool, dry** | **early, late** ◇ *It was early* ~ *and very still.* | **previous** ◇ *8 o'clock the previous* ~ | **following, next** ◇ *The ball would take place the following* ~. | **entire, whole** ◇ *He spent the entire* ~ *chatting with friends.*
VERB + EVENING **spend** ◇ *We spent the* ~ *walking around the town.* | **begin, start** ◇ *We started our* ~ *by watching TV.* | **end** ◇ *What a way to end an* ~! | **enjoy** ◇ *thoroughly enjoying a quiet* ~ *at home* | **ruin, spoil** ◇ *I don't want to ruin your* ~.
EVENING + VERB **progress, wear on** ◇ *As the* ~ *wore on, Phil became very drunk.*
EVENING + NOUN **light, sky, star, sun** | **air, breeze** ◇ *the cool* ~ *air* | **meal** (*esp. BrE*) | **stroll, walk** | **shift** | **class, course** | **entertainment, event, performance, reception, show** | **prayer, service** | **rush hour** | **news, newscast** (*AmE*), **newspaper, paper**
PREP. **during the ~** | **for an/the ~** ◇ *Her parents were out for the* ~. | **in the ~** | **(on) Friday, etc. ~, on the ~ of** ◇ *on the* ~ *of May 15*
PHRASES **an ~ off, an ~ out** ◇ *You deserve an occasional* ~ *out.* | **good ~**

2 event happening in the evening
ADJ. **gala, musical, social** | **open** (*BrE*), **parents'** (*esp. BrE*) ◇ *Prospective students were invited to the school's open* ~. | **enjoyable, fun, lovely, memorable, nice, perfect, pleasant, successful, wonderful**
VERB + EVENING **hold** ◇ *The club will hold a social* ~ *to welcome new members.* | **host** ◇ *He hosted the* ~ *in front of a celebrity*

audience. | **open** ◇ *The orchestra opened the* ~ *with an overture.*
EVENING + NOUN **clothes, dress, gown, wear**
PREP. **during the ~, for the ~**

event *noun*

1 sth that happens
ADJ. **big, great, important, major, significant** | **historic, key, landmark, life-changing, momentous, pivotal, seminal, watershed** (*esp. AmE*) ◇ *Tonight's show looks back at the key* ~*s of the year.* | **dramatic, remarkable** | **main** | **happy** | **cataclysmic, catastrophic, sad, stressful, tragic, traumatic** | **rare** ◇ *Outside big cities, murder is a rare* ~. | **current, recent** ◇ *in-depth articles related to current* ~*s* ◇ *recent* ~*s in Saudi Arabia* | **future** ◇ *our inability to forecast future* ~*s* | **subsequent** ◇ *Subsequent* ~*s proved him wrong.* | **historical, political**
VERB + EVENT **witness** ◇ *When the ship finally reached land, only a few of the crew were left to witness the* ~. | **record** ◇ *We had a huge party, and hired a photographer to record the* ~. | **describe, recount, relate** ◇ *Carter related the* ~*s of the past hour to him.* | **recall, remember** ◇ *She tried to recall the* ~*s of the previous night.* | **celebrate, commemorate, mark** ◇ *Today is the hospital's fiftieth anniversary, and there will be a party to mark the* ~.
EVENT + VERB **happen, occur, take place, unfold** ◇ *TV viewers watched in horror as* ~*s unfolded.* | **lead to sth** ◇ *These* ~*s quickly led to confusion.* | **lead up to sth** ◇ *The police are trying to establish a picture of* ~*s leading up to the killing.*
PHRASES **a chain of ~s, a sequence of ~s, a series of ~s** | **the course of ~s** ◇ *Would it have been possible to change the course of* ~*s?* | **in any ~** ◇ *I think the economy will recover in any* ~. | **in the ~** ◇ *In the* ~ *though, the dinner was a very entertaining affair.* | **in the ~ of sth, in the ~ that…** ◇ *In the unlikely* ~ *of a crash, please remain calm.*

2 planned social occasion
ADJ. **big, important, landmark, main, major, special** ◇ *Their 1981 production was a landmark* ~. | **popular** | **prestigious** ◇ *The Birmingham meeting is one of the most prestigious* ~*s in the racing calendar.* | **inaugural** | **international, national** ◇ *a new international art* ~ | **annual, regular** | **charity** ◇ *They host frequent charity* ~*s in their home.* | **gala** ◇ *a special opening-night gala* ~ | **forthcoming** (*esp. BrE*), **upcoming** (*esp. AmE*) ◇ *Forthcoming* ~*s are listed on the back page of the local newspaper.* | **fund-raising, musical, social, sporting** | **black-tie, formal** ◇ *a black-tie* ~ *at the Waldorf Astoria*
VERB + EVENT **hold, organize, stage** ◇ *The* ~ *will be held in the grounds of the house.* | **host** ◇ *We hosted a charitable* ~ *for a local organization.* | **plan, schedule** ◇ *Forty such* ~*s are scheduled this year.* | **publicize** | **attend, support** ◇ *I would like to thank everyone who attended our charity evening for supporting the* ~. | **sponsor** ◇ *They sponsored various community* ~*s.* | **boycott** ◇ *Several leading players boycotted the* ~ *in protest.*
EVENT + VERB **take place**

3 race/competition
ADJ. **big, main** ◇ *This race will be the main* ~ *of the afternoon.* | **international, national** ◇ *Local winners compete in a national* ~ *in September.* | **individual, team** | **men's, women's** | **field, track** | **distance, long-distance, middle-distance, sprint** | **backstroke, breaststroke, freestyle** (all in swimming) | **Olympic** | **one-day, two-day, etc.**
VERB + EVENT **enter, enter for, take part in** ◇ *A record number of teams have entered the* ~. | **win** | **host** ◇ *The Association hosted a special three-day sailing* ~.
EVENT + VERB **take place** ◇ *The team* ~*s will take place later this week.*
PREP. **in an/the ~** ◇ *African runners swept the medals in the distance* ~*s.*

evict *verb*

ADV. **forcibly** | **unlawfully** (*esp. BrE*)
VERB + EVICT **attempt to, seek to, try to, want to**

PREP. **from** ◊ *They were forcibly ~ed from their home.*

eviction noun

ADJ. **illegal, unlawful** (*esp. BrE*) ◊ *He claimed damages for unlawful ~.* | **forced**
VERB + EVICTION **be threatened with, face** | **resist**
EVICTION + NOUN **notice, order** (*esp. BrE*), **warrant** (*BrE*) | **proceedings**
PREP. **~ from** ◊ *They are facing ~ from their home.*

evidence noun

ADJ. **abundant, ample, considerable, extensive, plentiful, significant, substantial, sufficient, widespread** ◊ *There is ample ~ that the world is getting hotter.* | **growing, increasing, mounting** | **clear, compelling, conclusive, convincing, decisive, definitive, good, hard, incontrovertible, irrefutable, overwhelming, persuasive, positive, powerful, solid, striking, strong, unambiguous, unequivocal** | **adequate** | **flimsy, inadequate, insufficient, limited, little, scant** | **concrete, direct, firm, first-hand, objective, physical, tangible** ◊ *The figures provide concrete ~ of the bank's claim.* | **credible** ◊ *We found no credible ~ to support this allegation.* | **indirect** | **available, current, present** ◊ *Available ~ points to pilot error as the cause of the crash.* | **additional, fresh, further, more, new** | **crucial, important, valuable, vital** ◊ *They accused the prosecution of withholding crucial ~.* | **prima facie** (*law*) ◊ *I'll accept this as prima facie ~ that there might be a problem.* | **corroborating, corroborative, supporting** ◊ *They convicted the wrong man on the basis of a signed confession with no corroborative ~.* | **conflicting** ◊ *Another team of scientists has come up with conflicting ~.* | **damning, incriminating** ◊ *The scandal is damning ~ of the government's contempt for democracy.* | **anecdotal, circumstantial, material** ◊ *There is plenty of anecdotal ~ to suggest that crime is beginning to rise.* ◊ *There was a mass of circumstantial ~ linking Watson to the murder.* | **documentary, observational, photographic, statistical, textual, video** (*esp. BrE*), **visible, visual** ◊ *The court was shown photographic ~.* | **archaeological, empirical, factual, formal, historical** | **clinical, DNA, experimental, forensic, medical, scientific** | **false** ◊ *She admitted giving false ~ to the court.*
... OF EVIDENCE **piece** | **scrap** ◊ *She mulled over these scraps of ~.* | **body, mass** ◊ *A body of ~ emerged suggesting that smoking tobacco caused serious diseases.*
VERB + EVIDENCE **have** ◊ *We do not have the ~ to prove these claims.* | **look for, search for** | **accumulate, collect, come across, come up with, discover, find, gather, obtain, produce, uncover** ◊ *Scientists have found fresh ~ to suggest that a huge explosion led to the extinction.* | **offer (sb), provide (sb with), show (sb)** ◊ *The tapes provided ~ of her intentions.* | **give, present (sb with), reveal** ◊ *She was hoping she would not have to give ~ in court.* | **see** ◊ *He says he's been working hard, but I haven't seen any ~ of it.* | **consider, examine, study** | **evaluate, weigh** ◊ *They will weigh this ~ and come to a rational conclusion.* | **review** | **cite (sth as)** ◊ *The team cited ~ from a recent earthquake to back up their idea.* ◊ *The rise in crime is often cited as ~ of a general breakdown of authority.* | **submit, use sth in** ◊ *The police officer took a statement which was later used in ~.* | **hear** ◊ *We must wait to hear his ~ before we make any judgement.* | **admit, allow** ◊ *The judge can decide whether to admit or exclude ~.* | **exclude** | **destroy** ◊ *Prosecutors say they destroyed ~ related to the case.*
EVIDENCE + VERB **exist** | **come to light, emerge** | **accumulate, grow, mount** ◊ *Evidence is accumulating that a defective gene may be responsible for this disease.* | **confirm sth, demonstrate sth, establish sth, indicate sth, point to sth, prove sth, reveal sth, show sth, suggest sth, support sth** ◊ *The ~ pointed to the existence of an international smuggling network.* | **be based on sth, be derived from sth, come from sth** ◊ *~ of growing poverty based on extensive surveys* | **contradict sth** ◊ *No new ~ has contradicted this research.* | **implicate sb/sth, link sb/sth** ◊ *~ linking her to the crime*

PREP. **as ~** ◊ *He cited Australia's success as ~ for his theory.* | **in ~** ◊ *A photo of the victim's injuries was produced in ~.* | **on ... ~** ◊ *On present ~ the team will be lucky to make the final.* | **on the ~ of** ◊ *On the ~ of his latest exhibition, Miller is an artist who is past his best.* | **~ about, ~ concerning, ~ regarding, ~ relating to** ◊ *The team have been collecting ~ about war crimes.* | **~ against** ◊ *The woman went to court to give ~ against her attacker.* | **~ for** ◊ *What ~ do you have for that claim?* | **~ from** ◊ *~ from historical documents* | **~ of** ◊ *Scientists are looking for ~ of life on other planets.* | **~ on** ◊ *The first chapter reviews the ~ on how children learn language.*
PHRASES **to be in ~** ◊ *a trend that has been much in ~ in recent years* | **in the face of ~, in the teeth of ~** ◊ *The company denies, in the face of overwhelming ~, that smoking causes cancer.* | **in the light of ~** ◊ *In the light of new ~, a new enquiry into the crash is likely to take place.* | **lack of ~** ◊ *The kidnapping charge was dropped because of lack of ~.* | **not a scrap of ~, not a shred of ~** ◊ *He made the accusations without a shred of ~ to back them up.*

evident adj.

VERBS **appear, be, seem** | **become** | **remain** | **make sth** ◊ *The silence of the forest was made ~ by the occasional snap of a twig.*
ADV. **extremely, fairly, very, etc.** | **abundantly** (*esp. AmE*), **clearly, plainly, readily** (*esp. AmE*), **strongly** ◊ *Those characteristics are abundantly ~ in Webster's essay.* | **fully** (*esp. AmE*), **perfectly, quite** (*esp. BrE*) | **especially, particularly** | **increasingly, more** | **less** ◊ *Their symptoms may be less ~ to their caregivers.* | **equally** ◊ *The commitment to local products is equally ~ on the restaurant's wine list.* | **immediately** | **already** ◊ *It is already ~ that new roads only generate new traffic.* | **painfully** ◊ *The strain of her work schedule was becoming painfully ~.*
PREP. **from** ◊ *It was fairly ~ from her tone of voice that she disapproved.* | **in** ◊ *His anger was ~ in his attitude to the others.* | **to** ◊ *It was ~ to me that the mission would fail.*

evil noun

ADJ. **great** | **absolute, pure** ◊ *the pure ~ in his soul* | **intrinsic** ◊ *the intrinsic ~ of taking a human life* | **lesser** ◊ *This sort of job is a lesser ~ than unemployment.* | **moral, social** ◊ *to combat the social ~s of poverty, disease and ignorance*
VERB + EVIL **commit, do** ◊ *His simple message was that God will punish those that do ~.* | **combat, fight, resist** ◊ *You can always choose to resist ~.* | **defeat, destroy, overcome** ◊ *a duty to defeat the ~ of terrorism*
PHRASES **the forces of ~** ◊ *a perpetual struggle between the forces of good and the forces of ~* | **good and ~** ◊ *not a simple choice between good and ~* | **a necessary ~** ◊ *He calls war 'a necessary evil'.* | **the root of all ~** ◊ *He sees money as the root of all ~.*

evil adj.

VERBS **be, look, seem** | **become**
ADV. **particularly, really, truly, very** ◊ *Kristin smiled a particularly ~ smile.* | **completely, totally, wholly** | **basically, inherently, intrinsically** ◊ *He believes that all people are basically ~.*

evoke verb

ADV. **beautifully, clearly, effectively, nicely, powerfully, successfully, vividly** ◊ *The novel vividly ~s the life of the Irish in Australia.* | **immediately** | **still** ◊ *Her face, though sad, still ~d a feeling of serenity.*
VERB + EVOKE **attempt to, seek to, try to, want to** | **help (to)** ◊ *products that help ~ an old-fashioned mood* | **be able to, manage to, seem to** | **be designed to, be intended to, be meant to** ◊ *narrative techniques that are intended to ~ sympathy from the reader* | **use sth to** ◊ *Music can be used to ~ childhood.*
EVOKE + NOUN **the ability to ~ sth, the power to ~ sth** ◊ *the actor's ability to ~ a variety of emotions*

evolution noun

ADJ. **gradual, slow** | **rapid** | **continued, continuous, ongoing** | **long-term** ◊ *the long-term ~ of ecosystems* | **early** ◊ *during the early ~ of animals* | **natural, organic** ◊ *organic ~ by natural selection* | **peaceful** ◊ *the peaceful ~ to democracy* | **biological, cultural, historical, political, social, spiritual, technological** | **parallel** ◊ *the parallel ~ of science and art* | **animal, human, mammalian** | **Darwinian, naturalistic** (*AmE*)
VERB + EVOLUTION **trace** ◊ *a book tracing the ~ of the English language* | **drive, influence, shape** ◊ *the forces that drove the ~ of the European financial system* | **undergo** ◊ *The movement is undergoing an ideological ~.*
EVOLUTION + VERB **happen, occur, proceed, take place** ◊ *Evolution proceeds by a series of small changes.* | **work** ◊ *competing theories as to how ~ works* | **require** ◊ *Evolution requires intermediate forms between species.*
PREP. **~ from … to …** ◊ *his ~ from comedian to serious actor* | **~ of** ◊ *the ~ of the human species* | **~ towards/toward** ◊ *the country's gradual ~ towards/toward democracy*
PHRASES **the theory of ~** ◊ *people who reject the theory of ~*

evolve verb

ADV. **gradually, slowly** | **quickly, rapidly** | **eventually** ◊ *the theory which eventually ~d from this study* | **constantly, continually, continuously** | **steadily** ◊ *Veterinary medicine is steadily evolving to meet the demands of pet owners.* | **considerably, dramatically, significantly** ◊ *The market has ~d considerably in recent years.* | **naturally, differently, independently, separately** ◊ *Monkeys in the New World ~d separately from those in the Old World.* | **together** ◊ *Africa and its wildlife ~d together.*
VERB + EVOLVE **continue to** | **tend to** ◊ *Online games tend to ~ over time.*
PREP. **according to** ◊ *Our products have been evolving according to the requirements of the times.* | **from** ◊ *More complex animals gradually ~d from these very simple creatures.* | **into** ◊ *The protest movement ~d into a well-organized political party.* | **out of** ◊ *A lot of Michael's work has ~d out of his experience with travel.* | **towards/toward** ◊ *the idea that society ~s towards/toward greater complexity*
PHRASES **fully ~d, highly ~d** ◊ *These are very highly ~d animals.*

exaggerate verb

ADV. **greatly, grossly, vastly, wildly** ◊ *These figures have been greatly ~d.* | **a little, slightly, etc.** | **rather, somewhat** | **further** | **easily** ◊ *The historical significance of these events can be easily ~d* (= it is easy to think they are more significant than they are). | **deliberately**
VERB + EXAGGERATE **tend to** ◊ *John does tend to ~ slightly.* | **be easy to** | **be difficult to, be hard to, be impossible to** ◊ *It is difficult to ~ the importance of developing good study habits.*
PHRASES **highly ~d** ◊ *The allegations were highly ~d.*

exaggeration noun

ADJ. **great, gross, huge, wild** | **mild, slight**
… OF EXAGGERATION **degree** ◊ *There was a degree of ~ in his description of events.*
VERB + EXAGGERATION **be given to, be prone to** ◊ *John is not usually given to ~.* | **allow for** ◊ *Their results, even allowing for ~, are impressive.*
PREP. **without ~** ◊ *There were, without ~, hundreds of applications for the job.*
PHRASES **a bit of an ~** ◊ *It would be a bit of an ~ to say that I'm desperate to leave.* | **it is no ~ to say sth** ◊ *It is no ~ to say that having a baby changes your life.*

exam noun

1 formal test → See also EXAMINATION

ADJ. **difficult** | **easy** | **entrance, placement** (*AmE*) (*placement test* in *BrE*) | **exit** (*AmE*), **final, graduation** (*AmE*) ◊ *the California high-school exit ~* | **end-of-semester** (*esp. AmE*), **end-of-term** (*esp. BrE*), **end-of-year** | **semester** (*AmE*) | **midterm** (*esp. AmE*) | **college** (*AmE*) | **school** ◊ *Girls are doing better than boys in every school ~.* (*BrE*) | *I just finished my*

last law school ~. (*AmE*) | **professional** | **external** (*esp. BrE*) | **A level, GCSE** (*in the UK*) | **SAT** (*in the US*) | **certification, licensing, qualifying** (*all AmE*) ◊ *students who passed the national teacher certification ~* | **bar** (*AmE*) ◊ *the New York state bar ~* | **chemistry, French, geography, etc.** | **comprehensive** (*AmE*) ◊ *a Master's program's comprehensive ~* | **mock** (*BrE*) ◊ *I did badly in the mock ~ but passed the real thing.* | **multiple-choice, oral, practical, written**
VERB + EXAM **cram for** (*esp. AmE*), **prepare for, review for** (*AmE*), **revise for** (*BrE*), **study for** ◊ *I can't go out because I'm revising for end of year ~s.* | **do** (*BrE*), **sit** (*BrE, formal*), **sit for** (*AmE, formal*), **take** ◊ *When do you sit your final ~s?* | **resit** (*BrE*), **retake** | **pass** ◊ *In spite of her worries, she passed the ~.* | **fail, flunk** (*informal, esp. AmE*), **ace** (*AmE, informal*), **do well in** (*BrE*), **do well on** (*AmE*) ◊ *I want to do well in my ~s.* | **do badly in** (*BrE*), **do badly on** (*AmE*) | **cheat in** (*BrE*), **cheat on** (*AmE*) ◊ *Candidates found cheating in/on any ~ will be disqualified.* | **set** ◊ *The final ~ is set by an external board.* | **administer, invigilate** (*esp. BrE*), **proctor** (*AmE*) | **grade** (*AmE*), **mark** (*BrE*)
EXAM + VERB **begin, start** | **be coming up** ◊ *The midterm ~s are coming up.* | **be over, end** (*esp. AmE*), **finish** (*esp. BrE*) ◊ *As soon as the ~s are over I'm off to Mexico.*
EXAM + NOUN **practice, preparation, revision** (*BrE*) | **paper, question** | **grade, marks** (*BrE*), **results** (*esp. BrE*), **score** (*esp. AmE*) | **pass** (*esp. BrE*) | **technique** (*BrE*) | **nerves** (*BrE*) ◊ *Most students suffer from ~ nerves to some extent.* | **period, time, week** (*esp. AmE*) ◊ *There is a subdued atmosphere in the school at ~ time.* | **board** (*BrE*) ◊ *The regional ~ boards try to ensure equal standards.* | **room**
PREP. **in an/the ~** (*BrE*) ◊ *He did badly in his history ~.* | **on an/the ~** (*AmE*) ◊ *We had to study to do well on the ~.* | **~ for** ◊ *an ~ for nurses* | **~ in** ◊ *an ~ in chemistry* | **~ on** ◊ *We had an English ~ on this play.*

2 (*AmE*) medical test

ADJ. **thorough** ◊ *She performed a thorough ~ and didn't find anything unusual.* | **routine** | **follow-up** ◊ *The follow-up ~s showed the baby was healthy.* | **physical** | **gynecological, neurological, etc.** | **abdominal, pelvic, rectal, etc.** (*all medical*) | **breast, chest, eye, etc.** ◊ *You should have a clinical breast ~ every year.* | **ultrasound, X-ray, etc.**
VERB + EXAM **do, perform** | **have** ◊ *I had an eye ~.*
EXAM + VERB **reveal sth, show sth** ◊ *A cardiac ~ revealed a regular rate and rhythm.*
EXAM + NOUN **room, table**
PREP. **~ of** ◊ *an ultrasound ~ of the baby* | **~ on** ◊ *The doctor will then perform a physical ~ on the child.*

examination noun

1 (*formal*) formal test → See also EXAM

ADJ. **certification** (*AmE*), **entrance** | **final** ◊ *He has just completed his final ~s at São Paulo University.* | **school** (*esp. BrE*) | **formal** | **competitive** ◊ *Entrance was by competitive ~.* | **external** (*esp. BrE*), **public** ◊ *One of the teacher's principal duties is to prepare students for external ~s.* | **A level, GCSE** (*in the UK*) | **multiple-choice, oral, practical, written**
VERB + EXAMINATION **prepare for, study for** | **do** (*BrE*), **sit** (*BrE*), **sit for** (*AmE*), **take** ◊ *She will take her ~s later this year.* | **fail, pass** | **set** ◊ *The ~s are set by individual teachers.* | **administer**
EXAMINATION + NOUN **paper, question** (*both esp. BrE*) ◊ *He was marking school ~ papers during the summer vacation.* (*BrE*) | **results** (*esp. BrE*), **scores** (*esp. AmE*) | **hall, room** | **process, system** ◊ *the faults in the ~ system* | **board** (*BrE*)
PREP. **~ in** ◊ *He failed his ~ in history.* | **~ on** ◊ *an ~ on human anatomy*

2 looking at sth carefully

ADJ. **careful, close, complete, comprehensive, detailed, full, in-depth, lengthy, rigorous, systematic, thorough** ◊ *Each of the proposals deserves careful ~.* | **brief, cursory, superficial** | **initial, preliminary** | **further** ◊ *Most of them don't really bear further ~.* | **critical** ◊ *The school curriculum*

has undergone critical ~ in recent years. | **microscopic** ◇ a microscopic ~ of the cell structure | **clinical, forensic, medical, physical, post-mortem, psychiatric, scientific** | **breast, oral, pelvic, rectal, etc.** | **ultrasound, X-ray, etc.** | **annual, follow-up** (esp. AmE), **periodic, routine** ◇ a periodic health ~ ◇ a routine breast ~ | **intimate** (BrE) ◇ genital checks and other intimate ~s | **visual** ◇ A visual ~ corroborated this.
VERB + EXAMINATION **carry out, conduct, do, make, perform, undertake** ◇ He carried out a post-mortem ~. ◇ We will make a more thorough ~ of the area later. | **come under, be subjected to, be subject to, have, undergo** ◇ I was advised to have a full eyesight ~. | **require** ◇ This argument requires ~ from several angles. | **allow, permit** ◇ Constraints of space do not permit a thorough ~ of all of these points. | **deserve, warrant** ◇ These figures warrant closer ~. | **stand up to** ◇ His ideas do not stand up to close ~.
EXAMINATION + VERB **confirm sth, demonstrate sth, reveal sth, show sth** ◇ A medical ~ showed no signs of hypertension. | **indicate sth, suggest sth**
EXAMINATION + NOUN **couch** (BrE), **table** ◇ Patients were asked to lie on the ~ table. | **room** (esp. AmE) ◇ They rushed her into the ~ room.
PREP. **on** ~ ◇ On closer ~ the wood was found to be rotten. | **under** ~ ◇ Several items of clothing are still under ~. | **~ on** ◇ We did ~s on the bodies.

examine verb

ADV. **carefully, closely, in detail, minutely** ◇ Each case must be carefully ~d. ◇ We shall now proceed to ~ these two aspects of the problem in detail. | **exhaustively, fully, properly, really, thoroughly** | **meticulously, rigorously, systematically** ◇ This survey systematically ~d their claims. | **briefly, quickly** | **individually, separately** ◇ This claim needs to be ~d separately. | **directly, explicitly, specifically** ◇ the few studies that have specifically ~d the effectiveness of the drug | **further** | **critically** ◇ Critically ~ your work as if you were looking at someone else's efforts. | **empirically** (esp. AmE) ◇ one of the very few studies to empirically ~ this problem | **medically**
VERB + EXAMINE **aim to, attempt to, be designed to, propose to, seek to, set out to** ◇ This study sets out to ~ the possible effects of climate change. | **proceed to** | **stop to** ◇ Anna stopped to ~ a plant growing by the stream. | **begin to** ◇ Only recently have historians begun to ~ its impact and influence. | **continue to** ◇ We continue to ~ new ways of doing business. | **be necessary to, need to** | **be helpful to, be instructive to, be useful to, be worthwhile to** ◇ It is instructive to ~ the data we have so far. | **want to, wish to** | **not bother to** ◇ He didn't even bother to ~ the note. | **fail to** ◇ He fails to ~ the implications of such a development.
PREP. **for** ◇ The room was ~d minutely for clues.
PHRASES **let us examine …** ◇ Let us ~ the implications of this theory.

example noun

1 sth that is typical/demonstrates a point

ADJ. **characteristic, classic, prime, quintessential, stellar** (AmE), **supreme, textbook, typical, ultimate** ◇ This is a classic ~ of a badly designed building. | **excellent, fine, good, great, impressive, magnificent, outstanding, perfect, stunning, superb, wonderful** ◇ a magnificent ~ of 18th-century architecture | **fascinating, interesting, intriguing** | **notable, prominent, remarkable, striking, telling** ◇ a telling ~ of how difficult it can be to succeed in business | **isolated** ◇ This is far from an isolated ~. | **graphic, vivid, dramatic, extreme, spectacular** | **clear, obvious, simple, straightforward** | **blatant, flagrant, glaring** ◇ His treatment of his secretary was a blatant ~ of managerial arrogance. | **egregious** (AmE), **worst** ◇ the most egregious ~ of his mishandling of the situation ◇ This is among the worst ~s of corporate greed. | **poor** ◇ This film is a poor ~ of the genre. | **notorious** | **familiar, famous, well-known** | **common** | **rare** | **illustrative, representative** | **helpful, illuminating, instructive, salient, useful** | **practical** ◇ The book is full of

practical ~s of classroom activities. | **concrete, particular, specific** ◇ Let me give a concrete ~ of what I mean. | **real-life, real-world** ◇ a book filled with real-life ~s that anyone can relate to | **hypothetical** | **contemporary, historical** ◇ He uses a number of historical ~s to support his thesis.
VERB + EXAMPLE **give sb, offer, provide (sb with)** ◇ Let me give you a few ~s of what I mean. | **contain, illustrate, include, present, represent, show** ◇ The leaflet includes several ~s of bad grammar. ◇ the ~ shown in Figure 2 | **cite, draw, take (sth as)** ◇ She illustrates her point with ~s drawn from contemporary newspaper accounts. ◇ To take an obvious ~, if there is a good harvest the price of grain will fall. | **use** ◇ Fisher used a hypothetical ~ to illustrate his point. | **consider** ◇ Consider the following example… | **see** ◇ We've seen other ~s of this same problem recently. | **find**
EXAMPLE + VERB **demonstrate sth, highlight sth, illustrate sth, show sth** | **indicate sth, suggest sth** ◇ These ~s suggest that there is a connection between the two processes.
PREP. **for** ~ ◇ An athlete, for ~, might turn the pedals 80 times a minute. | **in an/the** ~ ◇ The teacher in our ~ is clearly wrong. | **~ of** ◇ We can still find ~s of discrimination today.

2 person thought to be a good model

ADJ. **good, great, inspiring, shining, sterling** (esp. AmE) ◇ She is a shining ~ of how to organize your time. | **bad, poor**
VERB + EXAMPLE **set, show** ◇ You must set a good ~ to the children. | **follow** ◇ I think all schools should follow the ~ of this one. | **hold sb/sth up as** ◇ The film was held up as an ~ of good cinema. | **be inspired by** ◇ I was inspired by the ~ of the athletes who trained so hard.
PREP. **by** ~ ◇ Children learn by ~. | **~ to** ◇ His generosity is an ~ to us all.
PHRASES **make an** ~ **of sb** ◇ The teacher made an ~ of him by suspending him from school.

exasperation noun

ADJ. **sheer, utter** | **mild**
… OF EXASPERATION **hint**
VERB + EXASPERATION **feel** | **express, vent** ◇ The organization has expressed its ~ with the government. | **hide**
PREP. **in** ~ ◇ She rolled her eyes in sheer ~. ◇ He groaned in ~. | **with** ~ ◇ He snorted with ~. | **~ at** ◇ the ~ he felt at his failure | **~ with** ◇ their ~ with the government rules
PHRASES **a groan, grunt, sigh, etc. of** ~ ◇ With a groan of ~, he picked up the bags himself.

excavate verb

ADV. **completely, fully** ◇ The area has not yet been fully ~d. | **extensively** | **partially, partly** | **carefully**
PREP. **from** ◇ Pottery has been ~d from the site.

excavation noun

ADJ. **archaeological** | **recent** ◇ recent ~s of underground burial chambers | **extensive**
VERB + EXCAVATION **carry out, conduct, do** ◇ Further ~s at the site are now being carried out.
EXCAVATION + VERB **reveal sth, uncover sth, unearth sth** ◇ Excavations of the site have revealed an Iron Age settlement. | **take place** ◇ The ~s took place between 1925 and 1939.

exceed verb

ADV. **considerably, far, greatly, significantly, substantially, vastly** | **clearly, comfortably** (esp. BrE), **easily** ◇ The House voted by 327 votes to 93, comfortably ~ing the required two-thirds majority. | **slightly** | **barely** ◇ Their numbers barely ~ 100 in the wild. | **consistently, frequently, often, regularly, routinely, typically** | **rarely, seldom** ◇ Summer temperatures rarely ~ 27°C. | **generally, normally, usually**
VERB + EXCEED **be expected to, be likely to** ◇ Income is expected to ~ expenditure. | **be unlikely to**

excellence noun

ADJ. **academic, artistic, athletic** (AmE), **culinary** (esp. BrE), **design, educational, journalistic, literary, manufacturing, musical, operational** (AmE), **professional** (esp. AmE), **scientific, sporting** (BrE), **technical** | **human** | **continued** ◇ our pursuit of continued ~

degree, level, standard ◇ *The restaurant's standards of ~ have won it several awards.*
VERB + EXCELLENCE **pursue, strive for** ◇ *The school strives for academic ~.* | **demand** ◇ *We demand ~ here at Trinity Hill School.* | **achieve, attain** | **maintain, sustain** | **demonstrate** ◇ *She had to demonstrate ~ as a dancer, singer, and comedienne.* | **recognize, reward** ◇ *This award recognizes ~ in urban design.* | **promote** ◇ *The mission of the festival is to promote ~ in children's films.*
PREP. **~ in** ◇ *The Business School has a reputation for ~ in research.*
PHRASES **a centre/center of ~** ◇ *The college aims to be a world centre/center of ~ in the field of marine biology.* | **the pursuit of ~** ◇ *her relentless pursuit of professional ~*

excellent *adj.*

VERBS **appear, be, look, prove, remain, seem, sound** | **consider sth** ◇ *The school is considered ~.*
ADV. **most, really, truly** | **absolutely, quite** | **rather** | **generally** ◇ *The meals are generally ~.* | **consistently, uniformly** ◇ *The performances and recordings are uniformly ~.* | **apparently** | **potentially** | **otherwise** ◇ *In an otherwise ~ issue, I found Creed's article very unconvincing.*
PREP. **at** ◇ *Clancey was ~ at keeping the kids under control.* | **for** ◇ *These potatoes are ~ for baking.*

exception *noun*

ADJ. **big, great, important, main, major** ◇ *the one great ~ to that* | **clear, conspicuous, glaring, notable, noteworthy** (*esp. AmE*), **noticeable, obvious, significant, striking** ◇ *Most industries have suffered badly in the recession, but there have been a few notable ~s.* | **minor, rare** | **lone** (*esp. AmE*), **only, single, sole** ◇ *all American presidents, with the sole ~ of Carter* | **occasional** ◇ *There are occasional ~s to my generalization.* | **limited, partial** ◇ *all of them – with the partial ~ of Ireland* | **certain, specific** ◇ *There should be specific ~s written into the plan.* | **special** ◇ *We are making a special ~ for Emma because of her condition.* | **possible** ◇ *With the possible ~ of the US, no other nation experienced a more severe depression.* | **interesting** ◇ *There was an interesting ~ to this general pattern.* | **honourable/honorable** (*esp. BrE*) ◇ *With a few honourable/honorable ~s, politicians kept quiet about the corruption.*
VERB + EXCEPTION **make** ◇ *No parking is allowed, but an ~ is made for disabled drivers.* | **carve, carve out** (*both AmE*) ◇ *The reform bill carves out several specific ~s for treatment of health expenses.* | **allow, grant** ◇ *She asked the state Supreme Court to grant an ~.* | **remain** ◇ *Such initiatives remain the ~, rather than the rule.* | **represent** ◇ *They represent an ~ to the rule.*
PREP. **with the ~ of** ◇ *The whole of the island was flooded with the ~ of a small area in the north.* | **without ~** ◇ *Without ~, all employees must carry their identity card with them at all times.* | **~ to** ◇ *Guide dogs are the one ~ to the store's ban on dogs.*
PHRASES **be no ~** ◇ *The weather had been rainy for days, and the day of the race was no ~.* | **be the ~ rather than the rule** ◇ *Nowadays a job for life is very much the ~ rather than the rule.* | **the ~ to the rule** ◇ *Most of his family are sports enthusiasts, but he's the ~ to the rule.* | **with a few ~s** ◇ *With a few ~s, the songwriting is very good.*

exceptional *adj.*

VERBS **be** | **remain** | **consider sb/sth** ◇ *The teacher considers Jamie's performance truly ~.* | **do sth**
ADV. **highly, pretty, really, very** | **quite, truly, wholly** (*esp. BrE*)
PHRASES **nothing ~** ◇ *There is nothing ~ about east London* | **something ~** ◇ *We will have to do something ~ to win.*

excerpt *noun*

ADJ. **brief, little, short** | **lengthy, long** ◇ *Here is a rather lengthy ~ from the essay.* | **5-minute, 10-minute, etc.** ◇ *This DVD contains a 10-minute ~ from the stage show.* | **exclusive** (*esp. AmE*) ◇ *an exclusive ~ from his new book* | **following** ◇ *The following ~s all come from the 'Spring Symphony'.* |

book, video (*both esp. AmE*) ◇ *She compiled dozens of book ~s about the country.*
VERB + EXCERPT **contain, feature, include, play, present, print, provide, publish, quote, read, run** (*esp. AmE*), **show** ◇ *The article included ~s from various interviews.* ◇ *Let's run a little ~ of what Governor Dixon had to say.*
PREP. **~ from** ◇ *The paper published some short ~s from Mandela's memoirs.* | **~ of** (*esp. AmE*) ◇ *a short ~ of a poem by Keats*

excess *noun*

1 too much of sth
ADJ. **rhetorical, stylistic, verbal** ◇ *His statements cannot be simply dismissed as rhetorical ~.* | **financial** | **scandalous, wretched** (*AmE*) ◇ *Washington has always been a city of wretched ~es.* | **alcoholic** (*BrE*) | **worst ~es** ◇ *the worst ~es of the 1980s*
VERB + EXCESS **avoid, contain, curb** ◇ *'Avoid excess' is the golden rule for a healthy life.* | **commit ~es, perpetrate ~es** ◇ *the worst ~es committed by the occupying army*
PREP. **in ~** ◇ *The drug can be harmful if taken in ~.* | **to ~** ◇ *They never smoked or drank to ~.*

2 an amount by which sth is larger than sth else
ADJ. **large** | **slight**
PREP. **in ~ of** ◇ *The car can travel at speeds in ~ of 150 miles per hour.* | **~ of** ◇ *a large ~ of gas*

excessive *adj.*

VERBS **appear, be, seem** | **become** | **consider sth, regard sth as, see sth as** ◇ *He considered the level of tax ~.*
ADV. **grossly, wildly** | **rather, somewhat** | **a little, slightly, etc.** | **perhaps** ◇ *The influence of her ideas was perhaps ~.* | **clearly, manifestly** (*BrE, law*) ◇ *The sentence which was imposed was manifestly ~.*

exchange *noun*

1 giving/receiving sth in return for sth else
ADJ. **fair** | **mutual, reciprocal, two-way** ◇ *We get together once a month for a mutual ~ of ideas.*
PREP. **in ~ (for)** ◇ *Wool and timber were sent to Egypt in ~ for linen or papyrus.* | **~ between** ◇ *There were ~s of goods between the two regions.* | **~ for** ◇ *She considered free language lessons a fair ~ for a place to stay.*

2 angry conversation/argument
ADJ. **brief** | **acrimonious** (*esp. BrE*), **angry, bitter, heated, sharp** | **spirited** ◇ *They've had many spirited ~s.* | **frank** ◇ *a full and frank ~ of views* | **free** ◇ *a free ~ of ideas and opinions* | **verbal** ◇ *a bitter verbal ~*
PREP. **~ about** ◇ *angry ~s about the problem of unemployment* | **~ between** ◇ *There were many acrimonious ~s between the two men.* | **~ over** ◇ *an ~ over the question of Joe Hill's guilt* | **~ with** ◇ *Members got into heated ~s with the chairperson.*
PHRASES **an ~ of views** ◇ *She had a full and frank ~ of views with her boss before resigning.*

3 of foreign currencies
EXCHANGE + NOUN **rate** (also *rate of exchange* esp. in *BrE*)

4 visit
ADJ. **academic, cross-cultural** (*esp. AmE*), **cultural, intercultural** (*esp. AmE*) ◇ *a constant cultural ~ by young people on the Internet* | **student, youth** | **official**
VERB + EXCHANGE **go on**
PREP. **on an/the ~** ◇ *She is in France on a student ~.* | **~ with** ◇ *an ~ with a German student*

excitable *adj.*

VERBS **be, seem** | **become**
ADV. **extremely, fairly, very, etc.** | **highly, overly** (*esp. AmE*) ◇ *He isn't overly ~.* | **easily** ◇ *The horses have easily ~ nervous systems.*

excited *adj.*

VERBS **be, feel, look, seem, sound** | **become, get, grow** | **get sb, make sb** ◇ *Don't get the children too ~.*
ADV. **extremely, fairly, very, etc.** | **all, highly, terribly, tremendously, wildly** ◇ *He was all ~ about his new car.* ◇ *By now the crowd was wildly ~.* | **overly** (*esp. AmE*) ◇ *Maura tried not to look overly ~.* | **increasingly** | **a little, slightly, etc.** | **strangely** | **sexually**
PREP. **about** ◇ *The kids seem pretty ~ about the holidays.* | **at** ◇ *~ at the news* | **by** ◇ *He was puzzled but strangely ~ by the commotion.*

excitement *noun*

ADJ. **considerable, extreme, great, high, intense, tremendous** | **breathless, feverish, giddy** (*esp. AmE*), **heady, wild** | **genuine, pure, real, sheer** ◇ *For sheer ~, white-water rafting is hard to beat.* | **initial** | **sudden** | **growing, heightened, mounting** | **added, further** | **suppressed** | **nervous** | **pleasurable** | **strange** | **childlike** ◇ *I step lightly, with childlike ~.* | **youthful** | **intellectual, physical, political, sexual**
... OF EXCITEMENT **buzz, flurry, flush, frisson** (*esp. BrE*), **ripple, rush, surge** ◇ *She felt a surge of ~ when she heard the song.* | **element** | **level**
VERB + EXCITEMENT **be bubbling with, be filled with, be flushed with, be giddy with, be tingling with, be trembling with, feel** ◇ *She was filled with ~ and apprehension.* ◇ *Her face was flushed with ~.* | **cause, create, generate** ◇ *The news caused tremendous ~ among scientists.* | **bring** ◇ *My visits always brought great ~ to my family.* | **conceal, contain, control, hide, suppress** ◇ *He couldn't suppress the ~ in his voice.* | **add** ◇ *The element of risk just adds ~.*
EXCITEMENT + VERB **build up, grow, mount, rise** ◇ *The tension and ~ built up gradually all day.* | **bubble, bubble up** ◇ *Excitement was bubbling up inside her.* | **course through sb/ sth, run through sb/sth** ◇ *She could feel the ~ coursing through her veins.* | **fill sb/sth** ◇ *Both fear and ~ filled her mind.* | **die down, wear off**
PREP. **in ~** ◇ *She clapped her hands in ~.* | **with ~** ◇ *You'll jump up from your seat with ~.* | **~ among** ◇ *The news has caused great ~ among scientists.* | **~ at** ◇ *her ~ at the prospect of a new job* | **~ of** ◇ *the ~ of meeting new people*
PHRASES **an air of ~** ◇ *There was an air of ~ about the place.* | **a feeling of ~, a sense of ~** | **a state of ~** | **a lack of ~**

exciting *adj.*

VERBS **be, look, seem, sound** | **become, get** ◇ *The movie was just getting ~ when we had to leave.* | **make sth** ◇ *to make the race more ~ for spectators* | **find sth** ◇ *She found the idea terrifically ~.* | **keep sth** ◇ *It keeps my life ~ and challenging.*
ADV. **extremely, fairly, very, etc.** | **enormously, especially, extraordinarily, immensely, incredibly, particularly, terribly, terrifically, tremendously, unbelievably, wildly, wonderfully** | **equally** | **not overly** (*esp. AmE*) ◇ *It wasn't an overly ~ moment.* | **potentially** ◇ *the germ of a potentially ~ innovation* | **genuinely, truly** ◇ *a genuinely ~ time to be studying computing* | **visually** ◇ *a book that is attractive and visually ~* | **sexually**
PHRASES **~ new** ◇ *an ~ new magazine*

exclaim *verb*

ADV. **loudly, softly** | **angrily, indignantly** | **excitedly, happily** | **triumphantly** | **suddenly**
PREP. **at, over** ◇ *They all ~ed over her beautiful clothes.* | **in, with** ◇ *They ~ed in horror at the price.* ◇ *She ~ed with delight at the sight of the presents.* | **to** ◇ *'Listen to this child!' he ~ed to his companions.*

exclamation *noun*

ADJ. **sharp, sudden** | **loud** | **muffled, small**
VERB + EXCLAMATION **give, let out, utter** ◇ *She gave a loud ~ of*

delight. | **make** ◇ *She took his hand and made an ~ of shock.* | **stifle, suppress**

exclude *verb*

ADV. **altogether, completely, entirely, totally** | **not absolutely, not wholly** ◇ *The possibility of error cannot be absolutely ~d.* | **virtually** | **generally, largely** | **permanently** | **previously** | **apparently** | **clearly** | **automatically** ◇ *Unlawfully obtained evidence is not automatically ~d from a criminal trial.* | **necessarily** | **actively, deliberately** | **explicitly, expressly, specifically** | **effectively** ◇ *Women in such societies are effectively ~d from public affairs.* | **rigorously, systematically** | **unfairly** | **historically, traditionally** ◇ *a club that has traditionally ~d minorities and women*
VERB + EXCLUDE **be designed to** | **attempt to, try to** | **seek to, want to, wish to** ◇ *a clause that seeks to ~ liability for death or serious injury* | **tend to** ◇ *Certain groups tend to be ~d from full participation in society.* | **serve to** ◇ *The measure would serve to ~ certain voters.* | **appear to, seem to**
PREP. **from** ◇ *Women were ~d from the club.*
PHRASES **feel ~d** ◇ *Many local people felt ~d from decisions that affected their own community.* | **socially ~d** (*esp. BrE*) ◇ *services designed to assist the socially ~d*

exclusion *noun*

ADJ. **complete, systematic, total** | **virtual** | **permanent** | **continued** ◇ *women's continued ~ from political life* | **economic, political, social** ◇ *the problem of social ~* | **racial** (*esp. AmE*)
EXCLUSION + NOUN **zone** ◇ *A 20-mile ~ zone was set up around the power station to guard against further explosions.* | **order** (*BrE*) ◇ *an ~ order to keep your partner out of your home*
PREP. **to the ~ of** ◇ *Don't study a few topics to the ~ of all others.* | **~ from** ◇ *disciplinary measures including ~ from school*

exclusive *adj.*

1 belonging to/used by only one person/group
VERBS **be**
ADV. **almost** ◇ *the course's almost ~ concentration on grammar* | **not necessarily** ◇ *The recording deal is not necessarily ~. The band can record material for other companies as well.*
PREP. **to** ◇ *These products are ~ to our outlets.*

2 not welcoming to everyone
VERBS **be** | **become** | **remain** | **keep sth** ◇ *The owners of the golf club are determined to keep it ~.*
ADV. **extremely, fairly, very, etc.** ◇ *a somewhat ~ venue* | **racially, socially**

3 not able to exist/be true at the same time
VERBS **be**
ADV. **mutually** ◇ *The two options are not mutually ~ (= you can have them both).*

excursion *noun*

ADJ. **brief, little, short** | **day, evening, full-day, half-day, weekend, week-long** | **three-day, two-day, etc.** | **annual** | **outdoor** | **boat, coach** (*BrE*), **train** | **shopping, sightseeing** | **shore** ◇ *We signed up for a shore ~ to New Orleans.*
VERB + EXCURSION **go on, make, take (sb on)** ◇ *We decided to make an all-day ~ to the island.* | **arrange, organize, plan** | **offer, run** ◇ *Our ship offers 13 different ~s.*
PREP. **~ into** (*figurative*) ◇ *her first ~ into business* | **~ to** ◇ *He took us on an ~ to the ruined city.*

excuse *noun*

1 reason given
ADJ. **perfect, wonderful** | **excellent, good, great, legitimate, valid** | **convincing, decent, plausible, reasonable** | **acceptable** ◇ *an acceptable ~ for missing school* | **bad, feeble, flimsy, lame, lousy** (*esp. AmE*), **pathetic, poor, weak** (*esp. AmE*) | **convenient, easy, handy** ◇ *The children*

provided a convenient ~ for missing the party. | **dumb** (*AmE*), **ridiculous, stupid** ◊ *He made up some stupid ~ to the teachers.* | **standard, usual** | **built-in** (*AmE*) ◊ *a built-in ~ for failure* | **possible** ◊ *What possible ~ could he have?* | **every** ◊ *She seized on every ~ to avoid doing the work.* | **the slightest** ◊ *He became moody and unreasonable, flailing out at Katherine at the slightest ~.*

VERB + EXCUSE **have** ◊ *He had no ~ for being so late.* | **give, make, offer** ◊ *She made some feeble ~ about the car having broken down.* ◊ *You don't have to make ~s for her* (= try to think of reasons for her actions). ◊ *It's late. I'm afraid I'll have to make my ~s* (= say I'm sorry, give my reasons and leave). | **give sb, offer sb, provide (sb with)** ◊ *Delivering the stuff for George gave me an ~ to take the car.* ◊ *Her mother's illness provided her with an ~ to stay at home.* | **need** | **look for** | **create, find, invent, make up, think of, think up** ◊ *She had to find a valid ~ for leaving the room.* ◊ *He made up a rather lame ~ for the work being late.* | **use sth as** ◊ *The political crisis is being used as an ~ to dock people's pay.* | **run out of** ◊ *He's run out of ~s for not cleaning his room.* | **become** ◊ *Don't let perfectionism become an ~ for never getting started.* | **mumble** ◊ *Justin mumbled some ~ and left.* | **accept, believe, buy** (*informal, esp. AmE*) | **hear** ◊ *I don't want to hear any more ~s.* | **reject**

PREP. **~ about** ◊ *He invented a pathetic ~ about losing his watch.* | **~ for** ◊ *It's just an ~ for a party.*

PHRASES **there is no ~ for...** ◊ *There's no ~ for such conduct.*

2 bad example of sth

ADJ. **lousy** (*esp. AmE*), **miserable, pathetic, pitiful, poor, sad, sorry** (*esp. AmE*) ◊ *She's a pitiful ~ for an actress.* ◊ *a sorry ~ for a man*

PREP. **~ for** ◊ *Why get involved with that pathetic ~ for a human being?*

execute *verb*

1 kill sb as an official punishment

ADV. **summarily** | **illegally** | **publicly** | **wrongly** ◊ *innocent people who are wrongly ~d*

PREP. **as** ◊ *He was ~d as a martyr to his Catholic faith.* | **for** ◊ *He was ~d for treason.*

2 perform/carry out sth

ADV. **beautifully, boldly, brilliantly, cleanly, flawlessly, neatly, perfectly, properly, skilfully/skillfully, successfully, superbly** (*esp. BrE*), **well** ◊ *The movement was beautifully ~d.* ◊ *The second goal was superbly ~d.* | **carefully, meticulously** ◊ *a carefully ~d and well-presented study* | **faithfully** (*law, esp. AmE*) ◊ *I swear that I will faithfully ~ the office of President of the United States.* | **badly, poorly**

PHRASES **duly ~d** (*law, BrE*) ◊ *The agreement had been duly ~d.*

execution *noun*

1 killing sb as an official punishment

ADJ. **public** | **mass** | **judicial** | **extrajudicial** | **federal, state** (*both esp. AmE*) ◊ *a senator's request to suspend federal ~s* | **state-sponsored** (*esp. AmE*) | **arbitrary, summary** ◊ *Human rights organizations have accused the army of summary ~s.* | **political** | **mock** | **scheduled** ◊ *the hours before his scheduled ~* | **imminent, impending** | **juvenile** (*AmE*) ◊ *the Supreme Court decision to ban juvenile ~s*

VERB + EXECUTION **order** ◊ *The tribunal ordered the ~ of 42 coup plotters.* | **face** ◊ *If caught, the men could face ~.* | **await** ◊ *prisoners who are on death row awaiting ~* | **suffer** (*formal*) ◊ *She was taken prisoner and suffered eventual ~.* | **escape** | **delay, postpone, stay, suspend** ◊ *The US Supreme Court refused to stay the ~.* | **halt, stop** | **oversee** ◊ *The army oversaw the trial and ~ of the king.* | **carry out** ◊ *Executions were carried out in the prison yard.* | **attend, watch, witness**

EXECUTION + VERB **go ahead, take place** ◊ *A bell was tolled when ~s took place.*

PREP. **~ by** ◊ *~ by hanging*

PHRASES **a stay of ~** ◊ *The judge had granted a stay of ~.*

2 carrying out a plan/order

ADJ. **effective** (*esp. AmE*), **successful** ◊ *the successful ~ of the plan* | **proper** ◊ *proper ~ of the exercise* | **flawless, good,**

perfect, precise ◊ *great ideas and flawless ~* | **poor** ◊ *the poor ~ of the film*

VERB + EXECUTION **delay, stay** (*law*), **suspend** (*law*) ◊ *The court has discretion to stay or suspend ~ of the order.* (*BrE*)

PHRASES **the ~ of your duty** ◊ *She was charged with obstruction of a police officer in the ~ of his duties.*

executive *noun*

1 person with an important job in business

ADJ. **chief, senior** | **high-flying** (*esp. BrE*), **high-level** (*esp. AmE*), **high-powered, high-ranking** (*esp. AmE*), **top, top-level** (*AmE*) ◊ *a top ~ in a large corporation* | **junior** | **key** ◊ *contracts to prevent the loss of key ~s* | **busy** | **successful** ◊ *one of the most successful TV ~s around* | **former, retired** | **female, woman** ◊ *The contract gives a female ~ maternity leave rights.* | **business, company, corporate, industry** ◊ *oil company ~s* | **account, advertising, finance, legal** (*BrE*), **marketing, public relations** (abbreviated to *PR*), **sales** | **media, network** (*esp. AmE*), **news** (*AmE*), **record** (*AmE*), **studio, television, TV** ◊ *One TV network ~ has already called for more deregulation.* | **airline, auto** (*AmE*), **oil** (*esp. AmE*), **technology** (*AmE*)

2 part of a government/organization

ADJ. **central, national** ◊ *She is a member of the party's national ~.* | **political** | **government, party, union** (*esp. BrE*) | **strong** ◊ *Conservatives are believers in a strong ~.* | **elected** | **ruling** (*BrE*)

VERB + EXECUTIVE **control** (*esp. BrE*) ◊ *Parliament's ability to control the ~*

EXECUTIVE + VERB **decide sth**

EXECUTIVE + NOUN **member** (*esp. BrE*) ◊ *the council's ~ member for education* (*BrE*) | **meeting** (*esp. BrE*) | **board, committee**

PHRASES **a member of an ~**

exempt *adj.*

VERBS **be** | **become** | **remain** | **consider sth** ◊ *Research might be considered ~ from regulation.*

ADV. **completely, entirely, fully, totally, wholly** | **largely** | **partially** | **previously**

PREP. **from** ◊ *This income is totally ~ from taxation.*

exemption *noun*

ADJ. **complete, full, total** | **blanket** ◊ *The bill gives sensitive police files a blanket ~.* | **partial** | **temporary** | **special** | **personal** (*esp. AmE*) ◊ *taxpayers seeking to claim a personal ~* | **religious** (*esp. AmE*) ◊ *religious ~s from statutes and administrative rules* | **medical** | **tax** | **antitrust** (*AmE*)

VERB + EXEMPTION **be entitled to, be subject to, enjoy, qualify for, receive** ◊ *These goods are subject to ~ from tax.* ◊ *They enjoyed ~ from customs duties on goods to be used by themselves.* | **apply for, claim, request, seek** | **gain, get, obtain** | **give (sb), grant (sb)** | **allow, provide** (*esp. AmE*) ◊ *The regulations provide an ~ from this law.* | **refuse** | **eliminate** (*esp. AmE*) | **lose**

EXEMPTION + VERB **apply (to sb/sth), cover sb/sth, relate to sb/sth** (*esp. BrE*) ◊ *The ~ applies to home buyers.*

EXEMPTION + NOUN **clause**

PREP. **~ for** ◊ *There are parking restrictions with ~s for disabled drivers.* | **~ from** ◊ *You may be able to apply for ~ from local taxes.* | **~ on** ◊ *tax ~s on gifts to spouses*

exercise *noun*

1 use of the body to keep healthy

ADJ. **good, healthy** | **hard, heavy, high-intensity** (*esp. AmE*), **intense, strenuous, vigorous** | **gentle, light, moderate** ◊ *Try to do fifteen minutes of gentle ~ every day.* | **regular** | **daily, morning** | **adequate** | **aerobic, cardiovascular, weight-bearing** ◊ *Weight-bearing ~ increases the health of bones.* | **endurance** | **mental, physical** | **outdoor**

VERB + EXERCISE **do, get, take** (*BrE*) ◊ *John never does any ~.* ◊ *Do you take enough ~?* | **need** | **recommend** ◊ *The doctor recommended regular ~.*

EXERCISE + NOUN **programme/program**, **regime**, **regimen** (*esp. AmE*), **routine** | **session** | **class** | **ball**, **bike**, **equipment**, **machine** | **mat** | **room** (*esp. AmE*) | **video**
PREP. **during ~** ◇ *Stop frequently to rest during ~ until you are fitter.*
PHRASES **a form of ~**, **a kind of ~**, **a type of ~** | **lack of ~** ◇ *Lack of ~ is a risk factor in heart disease.*

2 set of movements/activities

ADJ. **great** ◇ *This is a great ~ for the upper back.* | **basic**, **simple** | **warm-up** | **breathing**, **relaxation**, **strengthening**, **stretching** | **chest**, **leg**, etc. | **daily**, **morning** ◇ *He began his daily ~s.* | **mental**, **physical** ◇ *Mental ~s can help older people to sustain their mental abilities.* | **floor** ◇ *Combine yoga with stretching and floor ~s.* | **group**
... OF EXERCISES **series**, **set**
VERB + EXERCISE **do**, **execute** (*AmE*), **perform** ◇ *Remember to do your breathing ~s every day.* | *You may find it helpful to perform this ~ in front of the mirror.* | **try** ◇ *I did try some basic relaxation ~s.* | **repeat** | **recommend** ◇ *She recommends the following ~s to increase circulation.*

3 set of questions

ADJ. **easy**, **simple** | **difficult**, **hard** | **practical**, **written** | **interactive** | **practice** | **comprehension**, **grammar**, **listening**, **translation**, **writing**
... OF EXERCISES **series**, **set**
VERB + EXERCISE **do** | **try** ◇ *Ask your students to try this ~ before the next class.* | **complete** ◇ *You will complete these ~s for homework.* | **practise/practice** ◇ *Practise/Practice the following ~ at least twice a day.* | **give sb** | **create**
PREP. **~ in** ◇ *an ~ in translation*

4 use of a power/a right/a quality

ADJ. **effective** ◇ *the effective ~ of power by the government* | **free** ◇ *the free ~ of informed choice* | **legitimate**, **proper** | **improper** (*law, esp. BrE*) ◇ *an improper ~ of a discretionary power*
VERB + EXERCISE **limit**, **regulate** (*law*) | **justify**
PHRASES **the ~ of authority**, **the ~ of power** ◇ *to limit the ~ of political power* | **the ~ of discretion**

5 for a particular result

ADJ. **simple**, **straightforward** | **major**, **massive** (*esp. BrE*) ◇ *The Government instituted a massive ~ in social control.* | **successful** | **fascinating**, **interesting**, **useful**, **valuable**, **worthwhile** | **arbitrary**, **cosmetic**, **cynical**, **empty**, **fruitless**, **futile**, **pointless** ◇ *In the end it proved a pointless ~.* | **academic**, **intellectual**, **mental**, **paper** (*esp. BrE*), **practical**, **technical**, **theoretical** ◇ *This is not a purely academic ~: it should have a real impact on the way we work.* | **costly**, **expensive** | **political** ◇ *The whole consultation process was just a cynical political ~.* | **consultation** (*BrE*) | **cost-cutting**, **damage-limitation**, **marketing**, **propaganda**, **public relations** (abbreviated to **PR**) (*all esp. BrE*) | **evaluation** | **role-playing**, **team-building** ◇ *We run team-building ~s with employees at each office.*
VERB + EXERCISE **carry out**, **conduct**, **perform** ◇ *The company has just carried out a major cost-cutting ~.* | **embark on**, **mount** (*both BrE*) ◇ *Before embarking on any ~, you should conduct a cost-benefit analysis.*
PREP. **~ in** ◇ *The seminar was a valuable ~ in information exchange.*
PHRASES **the aim of the ~**, **the object of the ~** ◇ *The object of the ~ is to increase public awareness of environmental issues.*

6 for soldiers/police

ADJ. **major** | **field**, **field-training** (*AmE*), **training** ◇ *We were out on a field ~.* | **live-fire** (*AmE*) | **tactical** | **joint** ◇ *US forces took part in joint ~s with the British Navy.* | **military**, **naval**
VERB + EXERCISE **conduct**, **do**, **execute** (*AmE*), **take part in** ◇ *We have conducted training ~s in seven separate states.* | **complete** ◇ *They recently completed a four-week ~ in Poland.*
PREP. **on ~** ◇ *Half the regiment was away on ~.*

exercise verb

ADV. **effectively**, **properly** (*esp. BrE*) | **fully** ◇ *the conditions*

necessary to fully ~ these rights* | **lawfully** | **freely** ◇ *the right to freely ~ your religion*
VERB + EXERCISE **be able to**, **be unable to** ◇ *They found themselves unable to ~ influence and maintain independence.* | **be free to** ◇ *Managers are free to ~ their discretion in these cases.* | **have the right to** ◇ *They have the right to ~ self-determination.* | **choose to** ◇ *Each of us has a vote—if we choose to ~ it.* | **be necessary to**, **need to** ◇ *It is necessary to ~ caution when making recommendations.* | **continue to** ◇ *The all-powerful steering committee continued to ~ control.* | **fail to** ◇ *The company's representative failed to ~ due care.*

exertion noun

ADJ. **considerable**, **extreme**, **great**, **strenuous**, **vigorous** | **mental**, **physical** ◇ *Try to avoid physical ~.*
PREP. **from ~** ◇ *She was hot and breathless from the ~ of cycling uphill.* | **with ~** ◇ *flushed and sweating with ~ after digging*

exhaust noun

ADJ. **auto** (*AmE*), **automobile** (*AmE*), **car**, **engine**, **vehicle** | **diesel** ◇ *Diesel ~ contains a lot of soot.*
EXHAUST + NOUN **emission**, **fumes**, **gas**, **pollution**, **smoke** ◇ *a plan to reduce ~ emissions* | **air** ◇ *ducts which draw out ~ air and replace it with fresh* | **fan**, **manifold**, **pipe**, **system**
PREP. **from an/the ~** ◇ *pollution from car ~s*

exhaust verb

1 make sb very tired

ADV. **completely**, **totally**, **utterly** ◇ *The swimming had completely ~ed him.* | **emotionally**, **mentally**, **physically** ◇ *The experience had ~ed her physically and emotionally.*

2 use sth up completely

ADV. **completely** | **almost**, **nearly** ◇ *The funds are nearly ~ed.* | **quickly**, **rapidly** ◇ *Their limited resources were quickly ~ed.*

exhausted adj.

VERBS **be**, **feel**, **look**, **seem**, **sound** ◇ *She found herself ~ most of the time.* | **become**, **get** | **find yourself** | **leave sb** ◇ *The row had left him physically ~.*
ADV. **really** | **absolutely**, **completely**, **quite**, **thoroughly**, **totally**, **utterly** ◇ *He fell into bed utterly ~.* | **pretty**, **rather** | **emotionally**, **mentally**, **physically** ◇ *She felt emotionally ~.*
PREP. **from** ◇ *I was ~ from the day's work.* | **with** ◇ *She was ~ with fear and the constant tension.*

exhausting adj.

VERBS **be** | **become** | **find sth**
ADV. **extremely**, **fairly**, **very**, etc. ◇ *a really ~ day* | **utterly** | **emotionally**, **mentally**, **physically**

exhaustion noun

ADJ. **complete**, **pure**, **sheer**, **total**, **utter** | **extreme** | **emotional**, **mental**, **nervous**, **physical** | **heat**
VERB + EXHAUSTION **suffer from** ◇ *She was taken to the hospital suffering from ~.* | **feel** ◇ *Never had she felt such utter ~.* | **be close to**, **be near to**, **near** ◇ *He was hollow-eyed and seemed very close to ~.* ◇ *The rowers were nearing ~.* | **be overcome by**, **be overcome with**, **collapse from**, **collapse with**, **drop from** (*esp. AmE*) ◇ *Two of the horses collapsed with ~.* | **drive sb to**, **lead to** ◇ *Don't work too hard and drive yourself to ~.* | **be dead from**, **be dead with** | **die from**, **die of**
PREP. **in ~** ◇ *He fell silent, with his head bowed in ~.* | **with ~** ◇ *She was faint with ~.*
PHRASES **at the point of ~**, **to the point of ~** ◇ *driven to the point of complete ~* | **a state of ~** | **a wave of ~** ◇ *Suddenly a wave of ~ hit him.* | **on the brink of ~**, **to the brink of ~** ◇ *They have been pushed to the brink of ~.*

exhaustive adj.

VERBS **be**
ADV. **by no means**, **hardly**, **not necessarily** (*esp. BrE*) ◇ *This list is by no means ~.* | **fairly**, **nearly** (*esp. AmE*), **pretty** ◇ *After a fairly ~ investigation, they were able to put things*

right. | **seemingly** ◇ *The report includes a seemingly ~ list of 160 benefits.*

exhibit *noun*

1 (*AmE*) collection of things shown to the public → See also EXHIBITION

ADJ. **art** | **photo, photographic, photography** | **interactive, multimedia, online, virtual** | **hands-on** | **touring, traveling** ◇ *a traveling ~ of antiques* | **changing, rotating** ◇ *The library has a policy of mounting changing ~s.* | **permanent, temporary** | **big, small** | **major** ◇ *a major ~ of the painter's work* | **educational** | **public** | **special** ◇ *The library is celebrating its tenth anniversary with a special ~.* | **solo** ◇ *The artist is now having her first solo ~ in New York.*
VERB + EXHIBIT **see, tour, view** | **create, curate, design, mount, organize, plan** | **feature, have, host, house** ◇ *The museum features rotating ~s.*
EXHIBIT + VERB **open** ◇ *The ~ opened to the public on July 1.* | **run** ◇ *The ~ runs through February 1.* | **be called sth, be entitled sth, be titled sth** | **explore sth, feature sth, highlight sth, include sth, present sth, show sth** ◇ *The ~ features unique photographs of San Francisco in the 1900s.*
EXHIBIT + NOUN **gallery, hall** | **area, floor, space** ◇ *the museum's new ~ space* | **booth** ◇ *Hundreds of companies had ~ booths.* | **coordinator, curator**
PREP. **on** ◇ *There are forty gigantic works on ~.* | **~ of** ◇ *an ~ of video art* | **~ on** ◇ *an ~ on local history*
→ Note at ART
2 single object in a museum, etc.
VERB + EXHIBIT **see, view** | **touch** | **display, house**

exhibition *noun* (*esp. BrE*) → See also EXHIBIT

ADJ. **big, large** | **small** | **important, major** ◇ *a major ~ of the painter's work* | **annual, summer** (*BrE*) | **international** | **public** | **permanent** | **changing, loan, special, temporary** ◇ *The library has a policy of mounting changing ~s.* ◇ *There is a series of special ~s throughout the year.* | **touring, travelling/traveling** ◇ *a touring ~ of Impressionist drawings* | **gallery, museum** | **online, virtual** | **art, craft** (*BrE*) | **photo, photography, photographic** | **collaborative** (*BrE*), **group, joint** | **one-man, one-woman, solo** ◇ *By 1914 Picasso had held solo ~s in England, Germany and Spain.* | **retrospective** | **trade** ◇ *the international food trade ~ in Cologne*
VERB + EXHIBITION **have, hold, host** ◇ *The museum hosted a big ~ of her work last year.* | **house** ◇ *The old factory has been converted to house an ~.* | **attend, go to, see, visit** | **arrange, curate, organize, plan** | **display** (*BrE*), **install, mount, present, put on, put together, show** (*BrE*), **stage** ◇ *They plan to stage an art ~ in the library.* | **launch, open** ◇ *The mayor will open the ~ next week.* | **sponsor** | **go on** (*BrE*) ◇ *The portrait is going on public ~ for the first time.* | **accompany** ◇ *the catalogue that accompanies the ~*
EXHIBITION + VERB **open** ◇ *The ~ opens at the Metropolitan Museum of Art in July.* | **close, end** | **appear** (*AmE*), **be on** (*BrE*), **be on view, continue, run, take place** ◇ *The ~ is on view from 11 April to 5 July.* | **be called sth, be entitled sth** | **bring sth together, comprise sth, contain, feature sth, include sth, show sth** ◇ *The ~ includes drawings by Rembrandt.* | **chart sth, cover sth, illustrate sth, trace sth** ◇ *an ~ illustrating the history and development of the university* | **be dedicated to sb/sth, be devoted to sb/sth** ◇ *an ~ devoted to female painters*
EXHIBITION + NOUN **area, centre/center, floor, gallery, hall, room, space, venue** (*BrE*) ◇ *The new wing will provide a new ~ space.* | **stand** (*BrE*) ◇ *Hundreds of companies had ~ stands.* | **catalogue** | **programme/program, schedule** (*esp. AmE*) ◇ *the gallery's ~ schedule for next year*
PREP. **on** ~ ◇ *A selection of her paintings is on ~ at the Whitechapel Art Gallery.* | **~ of** ◇ *an ~ of contemporary art* | **~ on** ◇ *an ~ on local history*
→ Note at ART

exile *noun*

1 being sent to live in another country
ADJ. **long** | **permanent** | **enforced** (*esp. BrE*), **forced** | **self-**

imposed, voluntary | internal** ◇ *Many spent decades in prison or in internal ~.* | **tax** (*BrE*) ◇ *They are in tax ~ from the UK.*
VERB + EXILE **be driven into, be forced into, be sent into** | **flee into, go into** ◇ *He went into ~ after the overthrow of the government.* | **live in** ◇ *They joined the many other Armenians living in ~.* | **die in** | **recall sb from** | **return from** ◇ *He still hopes to return from ~ one day.*
PREP. **in** ~ ◇ *She had spent 40 years in ~.* | **~ from** ◇ *Dante died in ~ from Florence.* | **~ to** ◇ *his ~ to America*
PHRASES **a place of ~, sb's return from** ~ ◇ *the story of the emperor's return from ~*
2 person forced to live in another country
ADJ. **political** | **tax** (*esp. BrE*) | **returning**
EXILE + VERB **live** ◇ *a political ~ living in London* | **return** ◇ *A general amnesty was granted, allowing political ~s to return freely.*

exile *verb*

ADV. **permanently, temporarily** | **effectively** ◇ *He was effectively ~d after a failed bid for power.* | **forcibly**
PREP. **for** ◇ *He was ~d for his beliefs.* | **from** ◇ *The family was ~d from France.* | **to** ◇ *He was ~d to Siberia.*

exist *verb*

ADV. **actually, really** ◇ *Do these creatures really ~?* | **already, still** ◇ *Few of these monkeys still ~ in the wild.* | **previously** | **no longer, not any more** ◇ *I didn't think people like that ~ed any more.* | **not yet** ◇ *The technology did not yet ~.* | **currently** | **only, solely** ◇ *companies that ~ solely for the purpose of mortgage lending* | **primarily** | **independently** ◇ *He argued that ideas do not ~ independently of the language that expresses them.*
VERB + EXIST **be known to** ◇ *the enormous volcanoes now known to ~ on Mars* | **appear to, be believed to, be supposed to** ◇ *They appear to ~ in significant numbers.* ◇ *a species with only about a thousand believed to ~ in the wild* | **continue to** | **cease to**

existence *noun*

1 state of existing
ADJ. **actual, real** ◇ *El Cid's actual ~ is not in doubt.* | **possible** ◇ *the possible ~ of life beyond Earth* | **brief** | **continued, continuing, future** | **10-year, 50-year, etc.** ◇ *over the course of his company's 20-year ~* | **very** ◇ *The peasants depend on a good harvest for their very ~ (= in order to continue to live).* | **mere** ◇ *The mere ~ of these strange creatures fascinated him.* | **entire, whole** ◇ *Throughout its entire ~, it has been a deeply contested concept.* | **autonomous, independent, separate** ◇ *any organism capable of independent ~* | **human** ◇ *the mystery of human ~* | **material, physical** | **social** | **earthly, mortal** ◇ *Christianity taught that our earthly ~ was merely a preparation for life after death.*
VERB + EXISTENCE **be in** ◇ *The idea has been in ~ for centuries.* | **have** ◇ *a virtual world that has no real ~* | **come into, pop into** (*AmE, informal*), **spring into** ◇ *The organization came into ~ ten years ago.* | **fade from, fade out of, go out of** ◇ *There was a fear that the club might go out of ~ for lack of support.* | **bring sth into, call sth into** ◇ *They are striving to bring into ~ a new kind of society.* | **be aware of, know of** | **be unaware of** | **affirm, assert** | **assume, posit, postulate, presuppose** ◇ *The theory assumes the ~ of a 'meritoc-racy'—that there is equal opportunity for all.* | **accept, acknowledge, admit, admit to, believe in, recognize** ◇ *He didn't believe in the ~ of God.* | **deny** | **doubt** | **question** ◇ *She questioned the ~ of God.* | **imply, indicate, suggest, support** ◇ *There is research that strongly supports the ~ of repressed memories.* | **discover, reveal** | **confirm, demon-strate, establish, prove, validate, verify** ◇ *Scientists were able to verify the ~ of this particle.* | **disprove** | **explain** ◇ *How do you explain the ~ of closely related species in widely separated locations?* | **justify** | **forget, ignore** ◇ *The girl's parents continued to ignore her very ~.* | **endanger,**

jeopardize, threaten ◇ *Climate changes threaten the continued ~ of the species.* | **end** ◇ *He wanted to end his ~ once and for all.* | **owe** ◇ *The school owed its ~ to the generosity of one man.* | **ensure, guarantee** | **maintain** ◇ *Let's battle on to maintain our ~.* | **be vital to** ◇ *A super-efficient sense of smell is no longer vital to our ~.*
EXISTENCE + VERB **depend on sth, depend upon sth** ◇ *The company's ~ depends on continued growth.*
PREP. **in ~** ◇ *the only instrument of its kind in ~*
PHRASES **the struggle for ~** ◇ *Darwin viewed the struggle for ~ as being the major promoter of evolution.*

2 way of living

ADJ. **bare, hand-to-mouth, meagre/meager, miserable, precarious** ◇ *He lived a hand-to-mouth ~ in the less attractive areas of London.* | **comfortable, peaceful, quiet** | **sheltered** ◇ *She had lived such a sheltered ~.* | **middle-class** ◇ *a comfortable middle-class ~* | **meaningful** ◇ *his yearning for a more meaningful ~* | **boring, dull, humdrum, mundane** | **pathetic, pitiful, wretched** | **meaningless** | **empty, isolated, lonely, solitary** | **nomadic** | **rural, suburban, urban** | **daily, day-to-day, everyday** | **previous, prior** ◇ *He claimed to be able to remember a previous ~.*
VERB + EXISTENCE **enjoy, have, lead, live** | **eke out, endure** ◇ *They eke out a precarious ~ foraging in the forest.*
PHRASES **a mode of ~** ◇ *the transition from one mode of ~ to another*

exit noun

1 way out

ADJ. **back, rear** | **side** | **east, south, etc.** ◇ *He left through the south ~.* | **main** ◇ *I walked through the school's main ~.* | **airport, school, etc.** | **emergency, fire** | **the nearest** ◇ *She headed for the nearest ~.* | **secret** ◇ *I remember that there's a secret ~ here.*
VERB + EXIT **head for, make for** | **bolt for, make a beeline for, make a dash for, run for, rush for** | **reach** | **bar, block** ◇ *Do not leave bags lying around which could block the emergency ~s.* | **guard, watch** | **seal, seal off**
EXIT + NOUN **sign** | **door, gate, point** | **route**
PREP. **to the ~, towards/toward the ~** ◇ *They moved towards/toward the ~s.* | **~ from** ◇ *the ~ from the hall* | **~ to** ◇ *an ~ to the street*

2 act of leaving

ADJ. **fast, hasty, quick, rapid, speedy, swift** | **abrupt, sudden** ◇ *Carole's abrupt ~ from their lives* | **easy** ◇ *emergency doors providing for easy ~ in the event of a fire* | **dignified** | **graceful** ◇ *She was trying to make a graceful ~ from public life.* | **grand** ◇ *Then we made our grand ~.* | **dramatic** ◇ *The students made a dramatic ~ toward the end of his speech.* | **early, premature** ◇ *her early ~ from the tournament, in only the second round* | **mass** | **play-off** *(AmE, sports)* ◇ *The team is likely to make a quick play-off ~.* | **first-round, second-round, etc.** *(sports)*
VERB + EXIT **make** ◇ *She turned on her heel and made what she hoped was a dignified ~.*
EXIT + NOUN **visa** | **poll** ◇ *Exit polls showed that more than 70% of voters opposed the proposal.* | **plan, strategy** ◇ *He was searching for an ~ strategy.* | **exam** *(AmE)* ◇ *You have to pass the ~ exam in order to graduate.* | **interview** *(esp. AmE)* ◇ *We go back and look at our ~ interviews as to why people leave.*
PREP. **~ from** ◇ *a mass ~ of members from the party*

3 for traffic → See also JUNCTION

ADJ. **freeway, highway, interstate** *(all in the US)* | **motorway** *(in the UK)* | **northbound, southbound, etc.** *(BrE)* | **the next** ◇ *I pulled off the road at the next ~.*
VERB + EXIT **get off at** *(AmE)*, **take** ◇ *You need to get off at the next ~.* ◇ *Take the first ~ over the bridge.*
EXIT + NOUN **ramp** *(esp. AmE)* | **point** ◇ *the number of entry and ~ points on the main road network*
PREP. **~ for** ◇ *The driver took the ~ for LaGuardia.* | **~ to** ◇ *They took the ~ to the hospital.*

expand verb

ADV. **considerably, dramatically, enormously, exponentially, greatly, massively, radically, significantly, vastly** ◇ *The business has ~ed greatly over the last year.* | **further** | **globally, internationally, nationally, nationwide, worldwide** ◇ *A number of the rental companies are ~ing globally.* | **abroad, overseas** ◇ *Internet companies ~ing abroad* | **fast, quickly, rapidly** | **aggressively** ◇ *Both companies are aggressively ~ing their business models in Europe.* | **successfully** ◇ *Several brands have successfully ~ed their market presence.* | **gradually, slowly** | **constantly, continually, continuously** | **suddenly** | **steadily** | **outwards/outward**
VERB + EXPAND **aim to, be eager to, be keen to, hope to, intend to, look to, plan to, seek to, want to, work to** ◇ *The company is looking to ~ its operations overseas.* | **attempt to, try to** ◇ *American publishers attempted to ~ their markets overseas.* | **need to** ◇ *I needed to ~ my possibilities of making a living.* | **help (to)** ◇ *The store has helped ~ the British cheese market by encouraging small dairy farmers.* | **begin to, start to** | **continue to** | **seem to**
PREP. **beyond** ◇ *He has plans to ~ beyond computer consulting to include engineer training.* | **from** ◇ *The number of managers has ~ed from 700 to 1300.* | **into** ◇ *The town has ~ed into a city.* | **to**

expanse noun

ADJ. **broad, endless, great, huge, infinite, large, limitless, long, vast, wide** ◇ *a vast ~ of sand* | **unbroken** | **barren, bleak, desolate, empty** ◇ *a bleak ~ of concrete* | **flat** ◇ *She stood looking out over the flat ~ of fields.* | **open** | **grassy, treeless** | **blue, green, grey/gray, white** ◇ *the white ~s of the frozen north* | **shining** ◇ *the desk's shining ~ of polished wood*
PREP. **~ of**

expansion noun

ADJ. **big, considerable, enormous, great, huge, major, massive, significant, substantial, vast** ◇ *The company was now set for major ~.* | **maximum** | **dramatic, marked, remarkable, unprecedented** ◇ *an unprecedented ~ in linguistic studies at universities* | **rapid** | **sudden** | **gradual** | **continuing, further, ongoing** | **continued, steady, sustained** | **relentless** | **current** | **future** ◇ *This is land being held for future ~.* | **million-dollar, 5 million-dollar, etc.** ◇ *an $80 million ~ of its Madras factory* | **eastward, westward, etc.** | **global, international, overseas, worldwide** | **successful** | **aggressive** ◇ *The board decided to embark on aggressive overseas ~.* | **healthy** | **planned, proposed** | **reckless, uncontrolled** | **business, commercial, corporate** *(esp. AmE)* ◇ *economic, industrial, market* | **monetary** ◇ *This will slow the rate of monetary ~.* | **capitalist, imperialist** | **colonial, imperial, territorial** | **military** ◇ *an unprecedented military ~ around the globe* | **geographic** *(esp. AmE)*, **geographical** ◇ *the geographical ~ of industry in the late 19th century* | **population** | **urban** | **airport, prison** *(esp. AmE)*, **etc.** ◇ *the largest prison ~ in American history*
VERB + EXPANSION **show** ◇ *The economy is still showing healthy ~.* | **experience, undergo** ◇ *The museum is undergoing a major ~.* | **accommodate, allow, allow for, permit, provide for** ◇ *The design of the front pockets allows for ~.* | **be set for** *(esp. BrE)* ◇ *The company is set for further ~ into niche areas.* | **call for** | **propose** ◇ *She proposed a modest ~ of unemployment benefits.* | **plan** ◇ *They are planning a major ~ in research and development.* | **approve, favour/favor** ◇ *The executive board has approved this ~.* | **encourage, facilitate, promote, support** | **drive, fuel** ◇ *Foreign investment fuelled/fueled this ~.* | **limit, restrict** | **slow, slow down** | **oppose** ◇ *He opposed ~ of the army and navy.* | **block, halt, stop** | **prevent** | **embark on** | **finance, fund** ◇ *In order to finance ~ on this scale, the government has relied heavily on borrowing.*
EXPANSION + VERB **occur, take place**
EXPANSION + NOUN **plan, programme/program**
PREP. **~ into** ◇ *~ into the luxury car market* | **~ in** ◇ *a great*

PHRASES **a period of ~** ◇ a period of rapid economic ~ | **the rate of ~** ◇ The rate of ~ of our overseas trade has been spectacular. | **potential, room, scope, etc. for ~** ◇ The company believes there is scope for ~ in this sector.

expect verb

ADV. **confidently** ◇ She confidently ~s to win. | **fully** ◇ My parents fully ~ us to get married. | **rightly** ◇ They rightly ~ to be obeyed. | **not necessarily** ◇ I do not necessarily ~ an easy answer to this question. | **not really** ◇ I didn't really ~ them to come. | **half** ◇ I was half ~ing to see Jim at the concert. | **initially, originally** | **honestly** ◇ Did you honestly ~ me to believe that? | **seriously** ◇ You can't seriously ~ me to sympathize with you.

VERB + EXPECT **be fair to, be natural to, be reasonable to, can, can realistically, can reasonably** ◇ We can ~ to see an improvement in the weather over the next few days. | **be unfair to, be unrealistic to, be unreasonable to, can hardly** ◇ It would be unreasonable to ~ them to do all that work for free. | ◇ You can hardly ~ to learn a foreign language in a few months. | **be foolish to** ◇ It would be foolish to ~ this at his age. | **be naive** ◇ Was she really naive enough to ~ that he had changed? | **would, would normally** ◇ I would ~ the factory to be working again as normal by next week. | **be entitled to, have a right to** ◇ You are entitled to ~ certain minimum standards of hygiene.

PREP. **from** ◇ We ~ good results from our employees.

PHRASES **as ~ed** ◇ As ~ed, they lost the election. | **(only) to be ~ed** ◇ The wine list is excellent, as is to be ~ed from such a high-class restaurant. | **be widely ~ed** ◇ The economy is widely ~ed to pick up in the first half of next year. | **~ a lot, too much, etc. of sb** ◇ I think my parents always ~ed too much of me. | **when you least ~ sth** ◇ An accident can happen anywhere, at any time, just when you least ~ it.

expectation noun (usually **expectations**)

ADJ. **big, great, high, lofty** (esp. AmE) | **modest** ◇ I have modest ~s about what my research can accomplish. | **low** ◇ Many children start with low ~s. | **growing, rising** | **heightened, increased, raised** ◇ Heightened ~s for educational progress had not been realized. | **diminished, lowered** | **optimistic, positive** | **negative, pessimistic** | **normal** ◇ It doesn't conform to people's normal ~s of what a zoo is. | **clear, confident** | **legitimate** (law), **rational, realistic, reasonable** | **false, inflated, naive, unrealistic, unreasonable** | **disappointed, unfulfilled, unmet** (esp. AmE) ◇ Low growth is likely to bring unfulfilled ~s. | **wild** ◇ This realization of our dreams surpassed even our wildest ~s. | **initial, original** ◇ They've found success far beyond their initial ~s. | **prior** ◇ This result is contrary to our prior ~s. | **future** | **common, general, widespread** ◇ There is still a general ~ that married couples will have children. | **popular, public** | **conventional, traditional** | **family, parental** | **cultural, social, societal** (esp. AmE) | **gender** (esp. AmE) ◇ Religion reinforces traditional gender ~s to varying extents. | **consumer, customer** | **market** | **economic, financial, inflation, inflationary** | **earnings** | **career, life**

VERB + EXPECTATION **have, hold** ◇ You have unrealistic ~s. ◇ differences in the ~s held by different social groups | **establish, form** ◇ the way in which ~s are formed | **base** ◇ These high ~s are based on the fast pace of technological developments. | **arouse, build, build up, create, generate, raise, set, set up** ◇ the high ~s aroused by civil rights legislation | **change, revise** ◇ Users have changed their ~s of library services. | **heighten** | **lower, reduce, temper** (esp. AmE) ◇ Her approach sought to lower people's ~s. | **manage** ◇ Here are some tips to help you manage your ~s for yourself. | **influence, shape** | **come up to** (esp. BrE), **confirm, conform to, fit** (esp. AmE), **fit in with** (esp. AmE), **fulfil/fulfill, live up to, match, meet, reach, realize, satisfy** ◇ Her new car has not lived up to her ~s. | **beat, exceed, go beyond, surpass** | **disappoint, fall short of** ◇ The reality of the cruise fell short of our ~s. | **confound, contradict** (esp. AmE), **defy, violate** (esp. AmE) ◇ The rise in share price confounded ~s. ◇ She has defied all ~s with her career.

EXPECTATION + VERB **grow, rise** | **change** ◇ In later years his ~s changed.

PREP. **above ~** ◇ Sales came in above ~s this week. | **against ~** ◇ Against all ~s, she was enjoying herself. | **contrary to ~** ◇ The building work was completed on time, contrary to ~. | **below ~** ◇ What should you do when an employee's performance is below ~? | **beyond ~** ◇ The course has produced results way beyond ~. ◇ He had been successful beyond his ~s. | **in the ~ of, in the ~ that** ◇ They bought real estate in the ~ of a rise in prices. | **~ about ~** the government's ~s about the economy | **~ for** ◇ We have high ~s for her future. | **~ of** ◇ We certainly had a reasonable ~ of success. | **~ regarding, ~ with regard to** ◇ She has high ~s regarding the deal. | **~ surrounding** ◇ the tensions and ~s surrounding the show

PHRASES **have every ~** ◇ I have every ~ of cheering the team on to victory in the final. | **in line with ~s** ◇ Profits are broadly in line with ~s.

expedient adj.

VERBS **be, prove** | **appear, seem** ◇ It seems ~ to clarify the concept. | **become** | **make sth** | **consider sth, deem sth, judge sth, think sth** | **find sth** ◇ The government found it ~ to relax censorship a little.

ADV. **politically**

expedition noun

ADJ. **major** ◇ a major ~ to climb Mount Everest | **little, small** | **international, joint** ◇ The Canadians agreed to a joint ~ with the French. | **foreign** | **successful** | **ill-fated** ◇ John Franklin's ill-fated ~ to the Arctic | **climbing, diving, fishing, hunting, scouting, shopping, etc.** | **archaeological, research, scientific** | **military, naval** | **punitive** ◇ The army sent a punitive ~ into Mexico. | **Antarctic, Everest, etc.** | **British, Spanish, etc.** ◇ Spanish exploratory ~s in the 16th century

VERB + EXPEDITION **go on, make** ◇ He had made two ~s to Spain to study wild plants. | **embark on, set off on, set out on, undertake** ◇ She was about to embark on a major ~. | **head, lead** | **join** | **accompany** ◇ Every scientific ~ was accompanied by a photographer. | **organize, plan** | **launch, mount** ◇ They plan to launch an ~ into the mountains. | **finance, fund, sponsor** | **send**

EXPEDITION + VERB **leave, set off, set out, start** | **return** ◇ The ~ returned only two weeks after it had left. | **arrive, reach sth** ◇ On January 21 the ~ reached the South Pole.

EXPEDITION + NOUN **leader, member** | **party, team**

PREP. **on an/the ~** ◇ She was out on a shopping ~. | **~ against** ◇ He led a military ~ against the rebels. | **~ into** ◇ an ~ into the interior of Australia | **~ to** ◇ a naval ~ to West Africa

PHRASES **the leader of an ~, a member of an ~**

expel verb

ADV. **forcibly** ◇ They were forcibly expelled from their farm by the occupying authorities. | **immediately** | **permanently** ◇ Any student may be permanently expelled for coming to school with a weapon.

PREP. **for** | **from** ◇ Expel all the air from your chest.

PHRASES **be expelled from school** (esp. BrE), **get expelled from school** (esp. AmE) ◇ He was/got expelled from school for taking drugs.

expenditure noun

ADJ. **considerable, great, heavy, high, huge, large, major, massive, significant** ◇ The group is calling for higher ~ on education. | **low, minimum, modest** | **average** ◇ the family's average ~ on food | **aggregate, overall, total** | **gross, net** (both esp. BrE) | **additional, extra, further** | **decreased, increased** | **excessive** | **necessary, unnecessary** | **estimated, planned, projected, proposed** | **actual** ◇ The next two items refer to actual ~s incurred, rather than estimates. | **current, future** ◇ Pay constitutes two thirds of all current ~. | **annual** | **general** | **per capita** ◇ the country with the highest per capita ~ on health care in the EU | **direct**

◇ the total direct ~ on training | **operating** | **budget** | **capital** ◇ The company reduced capital ~ on plant and machinery. | **financial** (esp. AmE) | **energy** | **local, national** | **federal, government, public, state** ◇ Public ~ was running at 44.6% of GNP. | **business, corporate** (esp. AmE) | **household, independent** (AmE, politics), **personal, personal-consumption** (AmE), **private** | **consumer** | **advertising, marketing, research, research and development** (abbreviated to **R & D**) | **defence/defense, education, health, health-care, medical, military, security, social, tax, welfare,** etc.

... OF EXPENDITURE **item** ◇ You may wish to take out a loan for a major item of ~. | **amount** | **level**

VERB + EXPENDITURE **make** (esp. AmE) ◇ They intended to make capital ~s for equipment and expansion. | **increase** | **control, cut, limit, minimize, reduce** ◇ plans to cut health ~ | **estimate** | **approve, authorize** | **monitor** | **justify** ◇ The results justified the ~. | **incur** (esp. BrE) | **involve, require** ◇ Malls require huge ~s on air conditioning. | **have** ◇ Both brands had heavy advertising ~. | **finance, fund, meet** ◇ Make sure you have enough in the current account to meet ~.

EXPENDITURE + VERB **go up, grow, increase, rise** | **fall, go down** | **amount to sth** ◇ Total ~ amounted to approximately £1 million. | **exceed sth** ◇ people whose annual ~ exceeds their income | **arise from sth, arise out of sth** (esp. BrE) ◇ extra ~ arising from the commission's report into health and safety

EXPENDITURE + NOUN **cut** ◇ public ~ cuts | **limit** | **level** | **pattern**

PREP. **~ for** ◇ They incurred enormous ~s for publicity during the launch years. | **~ of** ◇ government ~ of more than £500 million | **~ on** ◇ increased ~ on the rail network

PHRASES **a cut in ~, a reduction in ~** | **an increase in ~, a rise in ~**

expense noun

1 cost/money spent on sth

ADJ. **considerable, enormous, great, huge, significant, vast** | **added, additional, extra** | **annual, monthly** ◇ Your monthly housing ~ should not be greater than 28% of your income. | **unexpected, unforeseen** | **unnecessary** | **public** ◇ The bridge was built at public ~. | **personal**

VERB + EXPENSE **go to, incur** ◇ They went to all the ~ of redecorating the house and then they moved. | **involve, put sb to** (esp. BrE) ◇ Their visit put us to a lot of ~. | **bear, cover, meet** ◇ She had to meet the ~ herself. | **spare no** ◇ No ~ was spared (= they spent as much money as was needed) to make the party a success. | **avoid, save** ◇ Save the ~ of calling out a plumber by learning some of the basics yourself. | **cut, minimize** (esp. AmE), **reduce** ◇ You can reduce your ~s by selling your old car at a good price. | **be worth** ◇ The results are well worth the ~. | **justify** ◇ a claim large enough to justify the ~ of insurance policy premiums

EXPENSE + VERB **rise** ◇ My ~s are constantly rising and my income stays the same.

PREP. **at sb/sth's ~** ◇ They had to repair the damage at their own ~. ◇ He built up the business at the ~ of his health. | **at ... ~** ◇ The house was transformed at great ~. ◇ The package includes admission to the park at no extra ~.

PHRASES **at taxpayer ~** (AmE), **at taxpayers' ~, at the taxpayer's ~** ◇ It emerged that they had received free first-class travel at the taxpayer's ~.

2 sth that makes you spend money

ADJ. **big, considerable, major, significant** | **incidental** ◇ Relocated employees received grants towards/toward incidental ~s like buying carpets. | **ongoing** ◇ Insurance is an ongoing ~. | **business, management** ◇ Meetings, and the time for them, are a considerable management ~. | **capital** ◇ The process turned out to be a significant capital ~. | **depreciation, interest** (both esp. AmE) ◇ Net interest ~ increased to $5.9 million from $4.1 million.

3 expenses money spent for a particular purpose

ADJ. **high, low** ◇ Medical ~s can be quite high if you are not

---

insured. | **allowable, eligible** (esp. AmE), **legitimate, reasonable** ◇ You can claim back the tax on legitimate business ~s. | **deductible, tax-deductible** ◇ Start keeping track of deductible ~s such as charitable contributions. | **basic** ◇ The guides are unpaid except for basic ~s. | **miscellaneous** | **ongoing** ◇ your ongoing ~s such as your employees' salaries | **out-of-pocket** (= paid for by an employee, to be claimed back later from the employer) ◇ Any out-of-pocket ~s incurred on the firm's business will be reimbursed. | **total** ◇ Total employee ~s were up about 6%. | **personal** | **living** | **household** | **administrative, maintenance, operating, operational, overhead** (all esp. AmE) | **business, work-related** | **marketing** (esp. AmE) | **travel, travelling/traveling** (esp. BrE) | **moving** (esp. AmE), **relocation, removal** (BrE) | **childcare, college, educational** (esp. AmE), **health-care, legal, medical** | **funeral**

VERB + EXPENSES **meet** | **cover, defray, meet, offset, pay, reimburse** ◇ He was given a sum of money to cover his travel ~s. | **claim, claim back** (BrE), **claim for** ◇ They are claiming ~s for travel and meals. | **recoup** ◇ We will recoup our ~s within 24 months. | **deduct** ◇ You will have to pay income tax on the rent you receive, although you can deduct ~s such as insurance. | **cut, lower** (esp. AmE), **minimize** (esp. AmE), **reduce** ◇ in an effort to reduce ~s and boost profits

EXPENSES + VERB **arise from sth, arise out of sth** (both esp. BrE) ◇ You can expect to receive compensation for all ~s arising out of the accident. | **increase, rise** ◇ Operating ~s rose by more than 23% last year.

EXPENSE + NOUN **~ account** ◇ Put the cost of the meal on your ~ account. | **~s claim** (esp. BrE), **~ report** (AmE) | **~ reimbursement** (AmE) ◇ You will receive ~ reimbursement for up to $5 000 for legal representation.

PREP. **on ~s** (BrE) ◇ I think we deserve a night out on ~s.

PHRASES **all ~s paid** ◇ a two-day, all-expenses-paid trip to New York City | **spare no ~** ◇ When it came to the wedding, no ~ was spared (= a lot of money was spent).

expensive adj.

VERBS **be, look, prove, seem, sound** ◇ Her suit looked extremely ~. | **become, get** ◇ Food in this country is getting very ~. | **make sth** ◇ Adding these safety features would make the cars too ~. | **find sth** ◇ I found the food very ~.

ADV. **extremely, fairly, very,** etc. | **amazingly, astronomically, enormously, exceedingly, extortionately, extremely, hideously, highly, horrendously, horribly, hugely, incredibly, insanely, ludicrously** (esp. BrE), **massively, outrageously, prohibitively, ridiculously, ruinously** (esp. BrE), **terribly** ◇ Some of these legal cases are enormously ~. ◇ Giving every patient an annual flu shot would be prohibitively ~. | **moderately** | **a little, slightly,** etc. | **increasingly** | **comparatively, relatively** | **notoriously** | **obviously**

experience noun

1 knowledge/skill obtained by seeing/doing sth

ADJ. **considerable, extensive, great, long, vast, wide** | **limited, little** ◇ companies with limited ~ in the field | **good, invaluable, valuable** ◇ She didn't get paid much but it was all good ~. | **relevant** ◇ Both candidates for the presidency were short of relevant ~. | **previous, prior** ◇ Do you have any previous ~ of this type of work? | **direct, first-hand, hands-on, practical, real, real-world** ◇ the importance of hands-on ~ as well as academic training | **professional, work** | **clinical, teaching** | **field** (esp. AmE) ◇ Students require field ~ rather than just observation. | **combat**

VERB + EXPERIENCE **have** | **lack** | **gain, get** | **offer, provide** | **bring** ◇ The returning soldiers bring valuable ~ to the Army. | **broaden** ◇ She wanted to broaden her ~ in international affairs. |

PREP. **~ of** ◇ She has considerable professional ~ of translation.

PHRASES **a lack of ~, a wealth of ~** ◇ The new player will bring a wealth of ~ to the team.

2 the things that have happened to you

ADJ. **past** ◇ We're in for a difficult couple of weeks, if past ~ is anything to go by. | **recent** | **historical** | **direct, first-hand, hands-on, lived, personal** ◇ She has brought personal ~ to

expertise

bear on her analyses of business history. | **vicarious** ◇ *I love reading: I have an insatiable appetite for vicarious ~.* | **subjective** ◇ *Experience is subjective and very hard to measure.* | **common, shared** ◇ *his peers, with whom he shares the common ~ of being black in a white society* | **common** ◇ *It is a matter of common ~ that disorder will increase if things are left to themselves.* | **daily, everyday** ◇ *Choose illustrative examples from the children's everyday ~.* | **human** ◇ *There are few areas of human ~ that have not been written about.* | **sensory**

VERB + EXPERIENCE **have** | **share** | **learn by, learn from** ◇ *We all learn from ~.* | **be based on, draw on** ◇ *The book is based on personal ~.* ◇ *In her book, she draws on her first-hand ~ of mental illness.* | **reflect** ◇ *These views reflect my own personal ~.*

EXPERIENCE + VERB **suggest sth, teach (sb) sth** ◇ *Experience has taught me that life can be very unfair.* | **show sth** ◇ *Experience shows that this strategy does not always work.*

PREP. **by ~, from ~** ◇ *We know from ~ that hot objects are painful to touch.* | **in sb's ~** ◇ *In my ~, very few people really understand the problem.* | **~ of** ◇ *He has direct ~ of poverty.*

3 event/activity that affects you

ADJ. **enjoyable, exhilarating, good, great, interesting, memorable, pleasant, positive, rewarding, rich, unforgettable, valuable, wonderful** | **bad, harrowing, negative, painful, traumatic, unnerving, unsettling** ◇ *I had a bad ~ with fireworks once.* | **hair-raising, nerve-racking** ◇ *a hair-raising ~ of white-water rafting* | **emotional, humbling, salutary** (*BrE*), **sobering** | **personal, subjective** | **collective, common, shared** ◇ *The use of drama can motivate students by allowing them to share a common ~.* | **common** ◇ *It is a common ~ to feel that an author writes well, without being able to say why.* | **unique** | **overall, whole** ◇ *He found the whole ~ traumatic.* | **real-life** | **past** | **childhood, early, formative** ◇ *Early ~s shape the way we deal with crises in later life.* | **educational, learning** | **sensory** | **listening, viewing, user** ◇ *The goal is to enhance the user ~ on computing devices.* | **mystical, religious, spiritual, visionary** | **psychic** | **sexual** | **cultural** | **near-death** | **out-of-body**

VERB + EXPERIENCE **enjoy, go through, have, undergo** ◇ *I think you will enjoy the ~ of taking part in the show.* ◇ *She has been through a very traumatic ~.* | **come through, get over** ◇ *It could take him years to get over this ~.* | **describe, discuss, recount, relate, report, talk about** | **share** ◇ *Does anyone have any experiences—good or bad—that they would like to share with the group?* | **relive** ◇ *Reliving past ~s can release powerful feelings that have been pent up too long.* | **be based on** ◇ *The novel is based on his ~ in the war.* | **create, offer** ◇ *We aim to create an ~ the consumer will remember.* | **enhance** ◇ *The sound system greatly enhances the ~ of the movie.*

PHRASES **quite an ~** ◇ *It was quite an ~ being involved in running the festival.*

experience verb

ADV. **actually** | **directly, first-hand, personally** ◇ *He hadn't directly ~d the fighting in the city.* ◇ *people who have actually ~d these problems first-hand* | **vicariously** | **subjectively** | **fully**

experienced adj.

VERBS **be, seem, sound** | **become**
ADV. **extremely, highly, really, vastly** (*esp. BrE*), **very** ◇ *The staff are all highly ~.* | **quite** | **suitably** (*esp. BrE*) ◇ *The task needs the skills of a suitably ~ engineer.* | **widely** ◇ *a widely ~ and articulate politician* | **sexually**
PREP. **in** ◇ *She's very ~ in caring for children.*

experiment noun

ADJ. **animal** ◇ *a few hippies protesting against animal ~s* | **field, laboratory** | **educational, medical, psychological, scientific** | **practical** | **simple** | **brief** | **further** ◇ *Further ~s will be carried out to verify this result.* | **careful, control** (*science*), **controlled** | **independent** (*science*) | **successful** | **failed, unsuccessful** ◇ *the USSR's failed ~ in social planning* | **pilot, preliminary** | **early, pioneering** | **classic, classical,**

famous, well-known ◇ *Pavlov's famous ~ with the dog and the dinner bell* | **unique** ◇ *Brazil's unique ~ with alcohol-powered cars* | **bold** ◇ *the country's bold ~ with economic reform* | **interesting** | **ingenious**

VERB + EXPERIMENT **carry out, conduct, do, perform, run** | **try** ◇ *The school decided to try an ~ in single-sex teaching.* | **repeat** | **design** | **set up** | **describe, report** ◇ *a classic ~ reported in 1964*

EXPERIMENT + VERB **confirm sth, demonstrate sth, find sth, illustrate sth, prove sth, reveal sth, show sth, support sth** | **indicate sth, suggest sth** | **be aimed at sth, be designed to do sth** ◇ *an ~ aimed at cutting road deaths resulting from excessive speeding* | **involve sth, use sth** | **be successful, work** ◇ *If the conditions are not right, the ~ will not work.* | **fail**

PREP. **by ~** ◇ *The appropriate concentration of the drug is best determined by ~.* | **during an/the ~** ◇ *The animals seemed healthy during the ~.* | **in an/the ~** ◇ *In these ~s, chilling is necessary.* | **~ in** ◇ *the country's brief ~ in multiparty democracy* | **~ on** ◇ *The team carried out ~s on cancer tissue.* | **~ with** ◇ *an ~ with zinc chips and hydrochloric acid*

experiment verb

ADV. **successfully** | **freely** ◇ *The students freely ~ed with paints.* | **sexually**
VERB + EXPERIMENT **begin to** | **continue to**
PREP. **on** ◇ *They ~ed successfully on the plants to discover disease-resistant varieties.* | **with** ◇ *We have ~ed with various different designs of kite.*

expert noun

ADJ. **real** | **leading** | **acknowledged, recognized** | **professional, qualified** | **self-proclaimed, self-styled** | **so-called** | **international, world** ◇ *She is a world ~ on butterflies.* | **local** | **independent, outside** | **computer, financial, gardening, health, industry, legal, marketing, medical, military, scientific, security, technical, etc.**

... OF EXPERTS **committee, panel, team** ◇ *A panel of ~s will answer questions from the television audience.*

VERB + EXPERT **ask, consult, talk to** | **seek advice from, take advice from** (*both esp. BrE*) | **hire**

EXPERT + VERB **advise sb/sth, agree sth, argue sth, believe sth, claim sth, fear sth, predict sth, reckon sth** (*esp. BrE*), **recommend sth, say sth, suggest sth, tell sb, think sth, warn (sb)** ◇ *Experts agree that a balanced diet is the key to great health.*

PREP. **~ at** ◇ *He's an ~ at getting his own way.* | **~ in** ◇ *an ~ in skin care* | **~ on** ◇ *an ~ on European art*

expertise noun

ADJ. **considerable, extensive, great** | **limited** | **appropriate, relevant** ◇ *Each area of the curriculum should be led by a staff member with appropriate ~.* | **necessary** ◇ *An outsider will lack the necessary ~ to run the company.* | **existing** | **particular, special, specialist** (*esp. BrE*) | **specific** ◇ *areas of special ~* | **collective, combined** ◇ *They met regularly to develop their collective ~.* | **in-house, local, outside** ◇ *We sometimes have to call on outside ~.* | **staff** | **subject** | **academic, business, clinical, engineering, financial, legal, management, managerial, marketing, medical, professional, scientific, technical, technological**

... OF EXPERTISE **degree, level** ◇ *A high degree of ~ is required for this work.*

VERB + EXPERTISE **have** ◇ *She has great ~ in these matters.* | **lack** | **need, require** | **acquire, develop, gain** | **build on** ◇ *This project builds on the existing ~ of our staff.* | **lend, provide** ◇ *Professor Simpson provided ~ in engineering.* | **apply, bring, bring to bear, use** ◇ *How could he apply his academic ~ to practical matters?* ◇ *He will bring a great deal of ~ to bear on this issue.* | **bring together, call on, draw on** ◇ *The project brings together ~ in teaching and library provision.* ◇ *We need to draw on the professional ~ of a large number of teachers.* | **rely on** | **offer, pass on** (*esp. BrE*),

share ◇ *The teachers would be available to share ~ and offer advice.*
EXPERTISE + VERB **be available** ◇ *We need to discover what relevant ~ is available to us.*
PREP. **~ in** ◇ *I have gained ~ in specialist financial areas.* | **~ on** ◇ *She brings ~ on general financial and technical matters.*
PHRASES **an area of ~, a field of ~** | **a range of ~** ◇ *The variety of technology requires a wide range of ~.*

explain *verb*

ADV. **in detail** ◇ *I ~ed the issues in great detail.* | **fully** ◇ *The reasons for the accident have not been fully ~ed.* | **adequately, properly, really, satisfactorily, well** | **partially, partly** ◇ *This partly ~s why he was so late.* | **exactly** | **briefly** | **quickly** | **easily, readily, simply** ◇ *This phenomenon can be easily ~ed.* | **clearly** | **carefully** | **calmly** | **helpfully, patiently** ◇ *The doctor ~ed patiently what the treatment would be.* | **concisely, succinctly** ◇ *The general principles behind the method used are ~ed clearly and concisely.* | **excitedly**
VERB + EXPLAIN **be able to, be unable to, can** ◇ *I know I'm late, but I can ~ why.* | **attempt to, seek to, try to** | **help (to)** | **purport to** ◇ *Many theories purport to ~ growth in terms of a single cause.* | **be difficult to, be hard to** ◇ *It's difficult to ~ exactly how the system works.* | **hasten to** ◇ *She saw his quick frown and hastened to ~.* | **let sb** ◇ *Let me ~ what I mean.*
PREP. **about** ◇ *She tried to ~ about her fears and anxieties.* | **to** ◇ *She ~ed the plan to me very carefully.*
PHRASES **~ everything** ◇ *I have a letter here which ~s everything.* | **go a long way, some way, etc. towards/toward ~ing sth** ◇ *This goes some way towards/toward ~ing the hostility between the two groups.*

explanation *noun*

ADJ. **convincing, credible, good, likely, logical, natural, obvious, plausible, probable, rational** ◇ *The most likely ~ is that his plane was delayed.* | **implausible, inadequate, unlikely** | **acceptable, adequate, reasonable, satisfactory, sufficient** | **further** ◇ *No further ~ is necessary.* | **no apparent** ◇ *There was no apparent ~ for the attack.* | **clear, coherent** | **complete, comprehensive, detailed, full** | **partial** | **complex, complicated, easy, simple** | **innocent, prosaic** ◇ *There's sure to be a perfectly innocent ~ for all this—though I admit it looks bizarre.* | **convenient** | **accepted, traditional** ◇ *There is no generally accepted ~ of this practice.* | **official** | **possible** | **alternative** | **correct, real, true** | **brief** | **lengthy, long** | **verbal** | **general** | **common** ◇ *the common ~s for cancer* | **only, sole** ◇ *It's the only ~ that makes any kind of sense.* | **causal** ◇ *The causal ~ must be that old age causes poverty, not that poverty causes people to be old.* | **ad hoc** | **cultural, historical, political, psychological, scientific, sociological, technical, theoretical**
VERB + EXPLANATION **have** ◇ *I had no ~ for her strange mood.* | **give (sb), offer (sb), provide (sb with)** ◇ *He only offered a partial ~ for his lateness.* | **go into, launch into** ◇ *She launched into a detailed ~ of every aspect of her work.* | **advance, propose, put forward** ◇ *one ~ advanced by Marxist historians* | **call for, need, require, want** ◇ *An ~ is clearly called for.* | **look for, seek** | **find, think of** ◇ *I can think of one possible ~ for her reaction.* | **ask for, demand** ◇ *She wrote to the company demanding an ~.* | **wait for** | **deserve, merit** ◇ *I suppose you deserve an ~.* | **owe sb** ◇ *I think you owe me an ~.* | **receive** | **accept** | **defy** ◇ *Her success has been so remarkable as to defy ~.*
EXPLANATION + VERB **lie** ◇ *The simplest ~ for his achievements lies in his greater ability and superiority over his contemporaries at college.* | **emerge, occur to sb** ◇ *No single clear ~ emerged from the experiments.* ◇ *A more credible ~ now occurred to her.* | **exist** ◇ *Several possible ~s exist.* | **suggest sth**
PREP. **in ~** ◇ *'I've worked with them before, you see,' he added, in ~.* | **without ~** ◇ *She left suddenly and without ~.* | **~ about** ◇ *He entered into a technical ~ about software and programming.* | **~ as to** ◇ *He provided no ~ as to why he was late.* | **~ for** ◇ *There is probably some perfectly logical ~ for their absence.* | **~ from** ◇ *We are still waiting for a full ~ from the teacher concerned.*
PHRASES **an attempt at ~** ◇ *The men left quickly with no attempt at ~.* | **by way of ~** ◇ *'I had to see you,' he said, by way of ~.*

explicable *adj.*

VERBS **be, seem** | **become**
ADV. **easily, readily** (both esp. BrE) ◇ *These atrocities are not readily ~ by any of the usual analyses of politics.* | **entirely, perfectly, wholly** ◇ *His actions are entirely ~.* | **largely** | **partly**
PREP. **by** ◇ *The delay is partly ~ by the roadworks.* | **in terms of** ◇ *The differences in the children's achievements were not wholly ~ in terms of their social backgrounds.*

explicit *adj.*

VERBS **be** | **become** | **make sth, render sth** ◇ *We think such information should be made ~ and not left vague.*
ADV. **extremely, fairly, very, etc.** | **highly** ◇ *a highly ~ description of torture* | **absolutely, fully, quite** ◇ *Our orders were quite ~.* | **increasingly** | **sexually**
PREP. **about** ◇ *The government has been quite ~ about its intentions.* | **as to** ◇ *She told him he needed to improve, without being ~ as to how.*

explode *verb*

1 blow up

ADV. **simultaneously** ◇ *20 bombs ~d almost simultaneously.* | **accidentally, prematurely** ◇ *A bomb might ~ prematurely.* | **spectacularly, violently** | **outwards/outward, upwards/upward**
VERB + EXPLODE **fail to** ◇ *A blast bomb was thrown but the device failed to ~.*

2 get angry/dangerous/moving

ADV. **literally** | **nearly, practically** ◇ *My heart was nearly exploding in fright.* ◇ *Jessie practically ~d with laughter.* | **suddenly** | **finally**
VERB + EXPLODE **be about to, be ready to, be set to** ◇ *A disagreement over public spending is set to ~.* | **be liable to, be likely to** | **seem to**
PREP. **into** ◇ *He suddenly ~d into action.* | **with** ◇ *She literally ~d with anger.*

exploit *noun*

ADJ. **daring, heroic** | **legendary** ◇ *His courage and ~s were legendary.* | **wartime** | **military, sexual** ◇ *He was always bragging about his sexual ~s.* | **goal-scoring, record-breaking** (both esp. BrE)

exploit *verb*

1 treat sb unfairly for your own advantage

ADV. **mercilessly, ruthlessly** ◇ *The workers are ruthlessly ~ed by their employers.* | **cynically** ◇ *He pursued his own interests, cynically ~ing his privileged position as trustee.* | **shamelessly** | **deliberately** | **sexually**

2 make the best use of sth

ADV. **extensively, heavily** | **fully, to the full** (esp. BrE), **to the fullest** (esp. AmE) ◇ *The company has been successful in ~ing new technology to the full.* ◇ *Birds ~ these wind patterns to the fullest.* | **further** | **widely** | **effectively, profitably, successfully** | **properly** | **quickly** | **easily** | **cleverly, skilfully/skillfully** ◇ *The architect has cleverly ~ed new materials and building techniques.* | **commercially** ◇ *She was eager to ~ her discovery commercially.*
VERB + EXPLOIT **be determined to, be keen to** (esp. BrE), **hope to, seek to** | **be quick to** ◇ *The team were quick to ~ their competitive advantage.* | **attempt to** | **fail to**

exploitation noun

1 unfair use of sb

ADJ. **brutal, ruthless** ◊ *her ruthless ~ of popular fear* | **cynical, shameless** | **blatant** | **capitalist, class, economic, industrial, sexual** | **labour/labor** (*esp. AmE*)
VERB + EXPLOITATION **prevent** | **struggle against** ◊ *The party's avowed aim was to struggle against capitalist ~.* | **be open to, be vulnerable to** ◊ *Migrant workers are vulnerable to ~.* | **be based on** ◊ *societies based on the ~ of slaves*

2 use of sth

ADJ. **effective, efficient, full, successful** | **direct** ◊ *the direct ~ of natural forests* | **large-scale** | **sustainable** | **commercial** | **mineral, resource** | **human** ◊ *Turtles are increasingly threatened by human ~.*
VERB + EXPLOITATION **be ripe for** ◊ *Emergent democracies created markets that were ripe for ~.*

exploration noun

1 of a place

ADJ. **energy** (*esp. AmE*), **gas, mineral, oil, petroleum** | **polar** | **space** | **offshore** ◊ *the heavy cost of offshore oil ~* | **archaeological, scientific** | **extensive** | **detailed** | **future** | **human**
VERB + EXPLORATION **carry out** ◊ *Extensive ~ was carried out using the latest drilling technology.* | **begin** | **continue**
EXPLORATION + VERB **take place** ◊ *areas where mineral ~ is taking place*
EXPLORATION + NOUN **activity** ◊ *Exploration activity slowed during the 1970s.* | **programme/program** | **company** ◊ *an oil ~ company*
PREP. **~ for** ◊ *speculative ~ for oil*

2 of an idea/subject

ADJ. **brief** | **extensive** | **deep, full, in-depth, thorough** | **careful, detailed** ◊ *My ideas needed more careful ~.* | **further** ◊ *These findings merit further ~.* | **creative, critical** ◊ *creative ~ of music as a medium in education* | **intellectual** | **personal** ◊ *her personal ~ of spirituality*
VERB + EXPLORATION **need, require** | **begin** | **continue**

explore verb

1 travel around an area

VERB + EXPLORE **be keen to** (*esp. BrE*), **want to, wish to** | **be free to** ◊ *In the afternoon you'll be free to ~ a little on your own.*
PREP. **for** ◊ *companies exploring for oil*

2 think about sth in detail

ADV. **extensively** | **briefly** | **fully, thoroughly** ◊ *These questions have not been fully ~d yet.* | **properly, systematically** | **carefully, deeply** (*esp. AmE*), **in detail** ◊ *This idea is worth exploring in some detail.* | **further** | **usefully** ◊ *The movie usefully ~s some of the issues surrounding adoption.*
VERB + EXPLORE **need to** | **be keen to** (*esp. BrE*), **want to, wish to** | **aim to, seek to** | **begin to, continue to**

explorer noun

ADJ. **great** ◊ *the great Portuguese ~s of the 15th century* | **intrepid** | **early** | **Antarctic, Arctic, polar** | **deep-sea, underwater** | **space**
EXPLORER + VERB **discover sth** ◊ *The waterfall is named after the ~ who discovered it.*

explosion noun

1 sudden loud bursting/exploding

ADJ. **almighty** (*esp. BrE*), **big, deafening, enormous, great, huge, large, loud, major, massive, powerful, tremendous, violent** | **minor, small** | **muffled** ◊ *There was a muffled ~ somewhere on their right.* | **distant** ◊ *The floor shook with a distant ~.* | **controlled** | **test** ◊ *a nuclear test ~* | **accidental** | **bomb, chemical, gas, mine, volcanic** | **atomic, nuclear** | **terrorist** | **social** (*figurative*) ◊ *If no action is taken, the country runs the risk of a social ~.*
VERB + EXPLOSION **cause, create, set off, trigger** ◊ *The build-up of gas caused a small ~.* | **carry out** (*esp. BrE*) ◊ *Bomb*

disposal experts carried out a controlled ~ on the suspect package.* | **hear** | **prevent** | **survive**
EXPLOSION + VERB **come, happen, occur, take place** ◊ *The ~ came 20 minutes after a coded warning to the police.* ◊ *The ~ occurred just after noon.* | **erupt, go off** ◊ *A massive ~ erupted behind him.* | **rock sth, shake sth** ◊ *A huge ~ rocked the entire building.* ◊ *The ~ shook nearby homes.* | **blow sth out, destroy sth, rip through sth** ◊ *An ~ blew out the front windows.* ◊ *A massive ~ ripped through the chemical works.* | **injure sb, kill sb** | **cause sth** ◊ *The ~ caused major structural damage.* | **echo, sound** ◊ *A loud ~ echoed around the valley.*
PREP. **in an/the ~** ◊ *Three people were injured in the ~.*

2 sudden large increase

ADJ. **sudden** | **great** ◊ *a great ~ of creativity* | **veritable** ◊ *In the 1860s a veritable ~ of major scientific publications took place.* | **population** | **information** ◊ *How can we keep up with the information ~?* | **price, wage** (*BrE*)
VERB + EXPLOSION **see, witness** ◊ *I believe we will see an ~ in lawsuits of this kind.*
EXPLOSION + VERB **occur, take place**
PREP. **~ in** ◊ *a sudden ~ in the number of students* | **~ of** ◊ *an ~ of interest in learning Japanese*

explosive noun

ADJ. **high** ◊ *a bomb containing 200 lb of high ~* | **powerful** | **home-made, improvised** | **conventional** | **chemical, liquid, plastic**
VERB + EXPLOSIVE **make, manufacture** | **use** | **carry** | **plant** ◊ *They planted ~s in the tunnel.* | **find** ◊ *Explosives were found near the scene.* | **detonate, set off**
EXPLOSIVE + NOUN **~s expert**

explosive adj.

1 capable of exploding

VERBS **be**
ADV. **highly** ◊ *a highly ~ mixture of gases*

2 causing strong feelings

VERBS **be** | **become**
ADV. **extremely, fairly, very, etc.** | **highly** ◊ *Race is a highly ~ issue.* | **potentially** ◊ *The political situation is potentially ~.* | **politically**

exponent noun

ADJ. **chief, foremost, leading, main, principal, prominent** | **great, outstanding** | **best-known, famous** | **early** ◊ *He was an early ~ of multimedia in the classroom.*
PREP. **~ of** ◊ *a leading ~ of the flute*

export noun

ADJ. **chief, important, main, major, principal** | **biggest, largest** ◊ *Coffee is the country's biggest ~.* | **record** ◊ *The industry has achieved record ~s in the past year.* | **total** ◊ *In 2001 total ~s were valued at $2 billion.* | **net** | **British, US, etc.** | **world** ◊ *The US share of world ~s has declined.* | **illegal** ◊ *We must stop the illegal ~ of live animals.* | **live** ◊ *lambs for live ~* | **capital, commodity** | **agricultural, farm, industrial, manufactured, manufacturing** | **arms, banana, beef, coal, coffee, food, grain, oil, timber, etc.**
... OF EXPORTS **level, value, volume**
VERB + EXPORT **boost, encourage, expand, increase, promote** | **limit, reduce, restrict** ◊ *plans to restrict the ~ of arms to certain countries* | **control** | **allow** | **ban, prohibit** | **prevent, stop**
EXPORT + VERB **grow, increase, rise** ◊ *Oil ~s have risen steadily.* | **drop, fall** | **be valued at sth, total sth** ◊ *Exports will total $30 billion by 2036.* | **account for sth** ◊ *Oil ~s account for nearly 80% of the country's foreign earnings.* | **go to** ◊ *89% of Mexican ~s go to the US.*
EXPORT + NOUN **crop, goods** | **business, industry, trade** | **market, sector** | **earnings, revenue, sales, value** | **figures, performance** ◊ *a strong ~ performance* | **growth** | **controls, licence/license, quota, restrictions, subsidy, tax** ◊ *a call for*

tougher art ~ controls | **ban** ◇ *an ~ ban on live cattle* | **drive** ◇ *the ~ drive by Japanese industry* | **order** ◇ *how to win more ~ orders*
PREP. **for** ~ ◇ *This is where the fruit is packaged for ~.* | **~ from** ◇ *~s from the EU to Canada* | **~ of** ◇ *the ~ of cattle* ◇ *~s of beef* | **~ to**
PHRASES **a ban on ~s** ◇ *to place a ban on ~s of toxic waste* | **a decline in ~s, a fall in ~s** | **an increase in ~s, a rise in ~s** → Note at PER CENT (for more verbs)

export *verb*

ADV. **widely** ◇ *The local wine was widely ~ed.* | **abroad** (*esp. BrE*), **overseas** (*esp. AmE*) | **illegally, legally** ◇ *illegally ~ed works of art*
PREP. **from** ◇ *Last year 2 000 birds were ~ed from the island.* | **to** ◇ *The country ~s sugar to Europe.*

exporter *noun*

ADJ. **big, large, major** | **leading, top** ◇ *China is the top ~ of telecommunications equipment.* | **second-largest, third-largest, etc.** | **second-biggest, etc.** (*esp. BrE*) | **food, grain, oil, etc.** ◇ *the biggest oil ~ in the world* | **net** ◇ *The country is a net ~ of food.*
PREP. **~ of** ◇ *~s of wine*

expose *verb*

1 uncover sth

ADV. **completely, fully** | **briefly** | **suddenly** | **deliberately** ◇ *a gesture that deliberately ~d the line of her throat*
PREP. **to** ◇ *These drawings must not be ~d to the air.*

2 show the truth

ADV. **fully** | **clearly** ◇ *a report which clearly ~s the weakness of the government's economic policy* | **publicly** ◇ *He was publicly ~d as a liar and a cheat.* | **cruelly** (*esp. BrE*) ◇ *He was outclassed by a team that cruelly ~d his lack of pace.*
VERB + EXPOSE **threaten to** | **seek to, try to**
PREP. **as** ◇ *She has been ~d as a fraud.*

3 to sth harmful

ADV. **directly** | **constantly, repeatedly** ◇ *The general public is constantly ~d to radiation.* | **regularly**
PREP. **to**

exposed *adj.*

VERBS **be, feel** | **become** | **leave sb/sth** ◇ *Depletion of the ozone layer leaves the earth's surface increasingly ~ to harmful radiation from the sun.*
ADV. **extremely, fairly, very, etc.** | **heavily** (*business*), **highly** ◇ *The country became highly ~ to the vagaries of international markets.* | **completely, fully, totally** | **partially** | **increasingly** | **relatively** | **dangerously, painfully** ◇ *The postponement of difficult decisions left the government dangerously ~ to American influence.*
PREP. **to** ◇ *The house is very ~ to westerly winds.*

exposure *noun*

1 to sth harmful

ADJ. **high, massive** | **maximum** | **excessive** | **increased** | **low-level** | **chronic** (*medical*), **long, long-term, prolonged** | **brief, short-term** | **constant, continued, continuous, regular, repeated** | **cumulative** | **chemical, radiation, sun** | **asbestos, pesticide** | **human** ◇ *long-term human ~ to mercury* | **occupational** ◇ *80% of patients with this form of cancer have had some occupational ~ to asbestos.* | **prenatal** (*medical*) ◇ *prenatal ~ to cigarette smoke*
VERB + EXPOSURE **receive, suffer, suffer from** ◇ *She suffered a massive ~ to toxic chemicals.* | **increase** | **limit, minimize, reduce** ◇ *Banks will seek to minimize their ~ to risk.* | **avoid**
PREP. **~ to** ◇ *The report recommends people to avoid prolonged ~ to sunlight.*

2 to experience

ADJ. **brief** | **greater** | **limited**

VERB + EXPOSURE **give sb, provide** | **get, have** | **increase**
PREP. **~ to** ◇ *We try to give our children ~ to other cultures.*

3 showing the truth

ADJ. **full** ◇ *full ~ of the links between government officials and the arms trade* | **public**

4 on TV, in newspapers, etc.

ADJ. **media, press, television** | **regular** (*esp. BrE*) ◇ *He receives regular ~ in the papers.*
VERB + EXPOSURE **give sb/sth, provide** ◇ *The magazine aims to give ~ to the work of women artists.* | **gain, get, have, receive** ◇ *a would-be television personality who is constantly trying to get media ~*

express *verb*

ADV. **well** ◇ *Perhaps I have not ~ed myself very well.* | **fully** ◇ *She ~es herself most fully in her paintings.* | **forcefully, strongly** | **repeatedly** | **explicitly, openly, publicly** ◇ *He ~ed his anger openly.* | **privately** | **freely** ◇ *Differences of opinion were freely ~ed in public debate.* | **clearly** | **simply** | **cogently** ◇ *Students must learn to ~ a point of view cogently and with clarity.* | **exactly, precisely** | **concisely, succinctly** | **eloquently** ◇ *The poet eloquently ~es the sense of lost innocence.*
VERB + EXPRESS **be able to, feel able to** | **be unable to, feel unable to** ◇ *Many patients feel unable to ~ their fears.* | **find it difficult to**
PHRASES **a chance to ~ sth, an opportunity to ~ sth**

expression *noun*

1 on sb's face

ADJ. **neutral** | **blank, dazed, glazed, vacant** ◇ *They all just looked at me with blank ~s.* | **deadpan** ◇ *He cracks jokes with a deadpan ~ on his face.* | **curious, enigmatic, inscrutable, odd, strange, unreadable** | **calm** | **guarded** | **thoughtful** | **dreamy, wistful** | **doubtful, wary** | **anxious, concerned, troubled, worried** | **bleak, grim, serious** | **annoyed** | **angry, fierce, furious, stern** | **hangdog, hurt, melancholy, mournful, pained, sad** ◇ *He hung around with this pathetic hangdog ~ on his face.* | **intense, rapt** | **horrified, shocked, stunned, surprised** | **baffled, bemused, bewildered, confused, puzzled, quizzical** | **alert** | **bored** | **amused, wry** | **benign, sympathetic** | **satisfied, smug** | **innocent** | **fleeting** | **facial** ◇ *The actors's gestures and facial ~s are perfect.*
VERB + EXPRESSION **have, hold, wear** ◇ *She had a very bewildered ~ on her face.* ◇ *The children's faces all wore the same rapt ~.* | **assume, put on** ◇ *She carefully put on her most innocent ~.* | **take on** ◇ *Rose's face took on the fierce ~ of a schoolgirl talking about her most hated teacher.* | **show** ◇ *His face showed no ~.* | **catch, notice, see** ◇ *Catching a fleeting ~ on Lucy's face, she persisted with her question.* | **examine, observe, watch** | **gauge, read** ◇ *I looked at her, trying to read the ~ on her face.* | **change** ◇ *His face never changed ~.*
EXPRESSION + VERB **alter, change** ◇ *His ~ changed to embarrassment.* | **grow…, turn…** ◇ *His ~ grew thoughtful.* ◇ *Her ~ suddenly turned serious.* | **remain sth** | **relax, soften** ◇ *His ~ softened when he saw her.* | **darken, harden** ◇ *Her ~ hardened into one of strong dislike.* | **freeze** | **betray sth, reveal sth, show sth, suggest sth, tell sb sth** ◇ *Her ~ betrayed nothing of her thoughts.* ◇ *His grim ~ told her it would be useless.* | **cross sth, flit across sth** ◇ *She had been watching the ~ that crossed his face.* | **appear on sth** ◇ *A surprised ~ appeared on her face.*
PREP. **without ~** ◇ *'Go on,' she said, without ~.* | **~ of** ◇ *He wore an ~ of anxiety on his face.*
PHRASES **the ~ in sb's eyes, the ~ on sb's face** ◇ *He looked at her with a very strange ~ in his eyes.*

2 showing feelings/ideas

ADJ. **clear** ◇ *Her statement was a clear ~ of her views on this subject.* | **concrete, material, practical, tangible** ◇ *The report gave concrete ~ to the fears of many immigrants.* | **direct** ◇ *Just because there is no direct ~ of prejudice, that does not mean the prejudice does not exist.* | **full** ◇ *The new concept of form reached its fullest ~ in the work of Picasso.* |

highest, perfect, ultimate ◊ *His highest ~ of praise was 'Not bad!'* ◊ *the highest ~ of human creativity* | **effective, powerful** | **simple** | **natural** ◊ *He wanted to write a verse drama in which the verse would seem a natural ~ of modern life.* | **spontaneous** | **free** ◊ *the right of free ~* | **open, overt, public** ◊ *the open ~ of emotion* | **outward** ◊ *the outward ~ of inner emotional feelings* | **formal** | **characteristic, classic** ◊ *Modernism was the characteristic ~ of the experience of modernity.* | **unique** | **collective** ◊ *The harvest festival was the occasion for the collective ~ of a community's religious values.* | **individual, personal** ◊ *to allow scope for individual ~* | **visible, visual** | **emotional, physical, sexual** | **oral** (*esp. AmE*), **verbal, written** ◊ *the verbal ~ of one's feelings* ◊ *A constitution is the written ~ of the people's will.* | **artistic, creative, cultural, linguistic, literary, musical, poetic, political, religious** | **human**

VERB + EXPRESSION **achieve, find, reach, receive** ◊ *an anger and frustration that finds ~ in* (= is shown in) *violence* | **give sth** ◊ *Only in his dreams does he give ~ to his fears.*

PREP. **beyond ~** ◊ *She suddenly felt happy beyond ~* (= so happy that she could not express it).

PHRASES **freedom of ~** ◊ *Freedom of ~* (= freedom to say what you think) *is a basic human right.* | **a means of ~** ◊ *Words, as a means of ~, can be limiting.*

3 words

ADJ. **common** | **colloquial, slang, vernacular** | **vulgar** | **strange, unusual** | **favourite/favorite** | **figurative, idiomatic, metaphorical** | **American, English, etc.** | **geographical** ◊ *Until the mid-nineteenth century, 'Italy' was just a geographical ~.*

VERB + EXPRESSION **use** ◊ *He tends to use strange ~s like 'It's enough to make a cat laugh'.* | **hear** ◊ *I've not heard that ~ before.*

EXPRESSION + VERB **mean sth**

expressive *adj.*

VERBS **be** | **become**

ADV. **extremely, fairly, very, etc.** | **deeply, highly, wonderfully** ◊ *She has a wonderfully ~ voice.* | **emotionally**

PREP. **of** ◊ *His art is deeply ~ of emotions.*

expulsion *noun*

ADJ. **automatic** | **immediate** | **mass** | **forced, forcible**

VERB + EXPULSION **lead to, result in** ◊ *Copying from another candidate results in automatic ~.* | **call for, demand** | **order** ◊ *The government ordered the immediate ~ of the two men.* | **be threatened with, face** ◊ *Several students now face ~.* | **appeal against** (*BrE*) ◊ *an ex-party member who intends to appeal against his ~*

PREP. **~ from** ◊ *her ~ from the society*

PHRASES **grounds for ~** ◊ *His disruptive conduct was felt to be sufficient grounds for his ~.*

extend *verb*

ADV. **greatly, significantly** ◊ *Next year we will greatly ~ the range of goods that we sell.*

PREP. **beyond** ◊ *The country's power ~s far beyond its military capabilities.* | **from, to** ◊ *The repayment period will be ~ed from 20 years to 25 years.*

extension *noun*

1 (*BrE*) part added to a building → See also ADDITION

ADJ. **planned, proposed** | **home, kitchen** | **one-storey, two-storey, etc.**

VERB + EXTENSION **add, build**

PREP. **~ to** ◊ *They're building an ~ to their house.*

2 extra time

ADJ. **one-week, two-year, etc.** | **contract** ◊ *The player has signed a five-year contract ~.*

VERB + EXTENSION **apply for, ask for, request** ◊ *He's applied for an ~ of his visa.* | **negotiate** | **get, receive** ◊ *She got an ~ for writing her essay.* | **give sb, grant sb** | **sign**

3 making sth larger/taking sth further

ADJ. **considerable, great, major, massive** (*esp. BrE*),

significant | **modest** | **further** ◊ *This new job is a further ~ of his role as a manager.* | **gradual** ◊ *a gradual ~ of the powers of central government* | **hair** ◊ *Hair ~s make your hair look longer.* | **brand** (*business*) ◊ *The company sees brand ~s as a means of tempting back customers.*

4 taking an argument/a situation further

ADJ. **logical, natural, obvious** ◊ *The team appraisal is a logical ~ of the individual appraisal interview.*

PREP. **by ~** ◊ *The blame lies with the teachers and, by ~, with the politicians.*

extent *noun*

ADJ. **full, greatest, maximum, overall** ◊ *The overall ~ of civilian casualties remained unclear.* | **actual, exact, precise, true** | **geographical, territorial**

VERB + EXTENT **reach** ◊ *The network had reached its greatest ~ in route mileage.* | **see** | **consider, examine, explore, investigate** | **assess, calculate, estimate, evaluate, gauge, judge, measure** | **define, determine, establish, identify** ◊ *a statement defining the ~ of Latvia's territory* | **discover** | **acknowledge, appreciate, realize, recognize** | **know, understand** ◊ *We do not yet know the ~ of her injuries.* | **demonstrate, illustrate, indicate, make clear, reflect, reveal, show** ◊ *The operation revealed the ~ of the cancer.* | **discuss** | **clarify, explain** | **emphasize, highlight, underline** (*esp. BrE*), **underscore** (*esp. AmE*) ◊ *The victory underlined the ~ to which Prussia had become a major power.* | **increase** | **exaggerate, overstate** ◊ *She was exaggerating the true ~ of the problem.* | **downplay, understate** ◊ *Those figures actually understate the ~ of the problem.* | **overestimate, underestimate** | **ignore** | **conceal, obscure** | **limit, reduce, restrict** ◊ *to reduce the ~ of deforestation* | **affect**

PREP. **in ~** ◊ *The park is about 20 acres in ~.* | **to an ~** ◊ *To an ~* (= to some degree) *East-West distrust continued throughout the war.* | **to a …~** ◊ *He had withdrawn from the company of his friends to an alarming ~.*

PHRASES **at sth's greatest ~** (*esp. BrE*) ◊ *At its greatest ~ the empire comprised most of western France.* | **to a considerable ~, to a great ~, to a large ~, to a significant ~** | **to a certain ~, to some ~** ◊ *To some ~, we are all responsible for this tragic situation.* | **to a lesser ~, to a limited ~, to a small ~** ◊ *The pollution of the forest has seriously affected plant life and, to a lesser ~, wildlife.* | **to the ~ possible** (*esp. AmE*), **to the fullest, greatest, maximum, etc. ~ possible** ◊ *I will answer your questions about this case to the ~ possible.* | **to the same ~** ◊ *People no longer live in small communities to the same ~ as they used to.*

exterior *noun*

1 outside of a building

ADJ. **elegant**

VERB + EXTERIOR **clean, decorate, paint**

PREP. **~ of** ◊ *the ~ of the building* | **behind an/the ~** ◊ *Hidden behind a plain ~ is a wonderful hotel.* | **on the ~** ◊ *There is an abundance of fine sculpture, both on the ~ and inside.*

2 way sb appears or behaves

ADJ. **calm, placid** ◊ *Her calm ~ hides very passionate feelings.* | **cool, icy** | **bluff** (*BrE*), **gruff, rough, tough**

EXTERIOR + VERB **belie, conceal, hide** ◊ *His bluff ~ belied a connoisseur of antiques.*

PREP. **behind sb's ~** ◊ *Behind his cool ~ lurks a reckless and frustrated person.* | **beneath sb's ~, underneath sb's ~** ◊ *Beneath her charming ~ lies a very determined woman.*

extinct *adj.*

VERBS **be** | **become, go** | **make sth** | **presume sth, think sth** ◊ *The species was presumed ~.*

ADV. **completely, totally** | **long** ◊ *Dinosaurs are, of course, long ~.* | **all but, almost, nearly, practically, virtually** ◊ *The numbers of these animals have been falling steadily and they are now almost ~.*

extinction noun

ADJ. **global, mass, total, widespread** ◇ *the mass ~ of the dinosaurs* | **near, virtual** | **imminent** | **eventual** | **local** | **species**
VERB + EXTINCTION **cause, lead to** ◇ *Modern farming methods have led to the total ~ of many species of wild flowers.* | **be doomed to, be in danger of, be on the brink of, be on the edge of, be on the verge of, be threatened with, face** ◇ *The island's way of life is doomed to ~.* ◇ *These animals are now on the verge of ~.* | **prevent** | **be saved from, survive**

extortion noun

ADJ. **attempted** | **alleged**
EXTORTION + NOUN **racket** ◇ *He was known for running a brutal ~ racket.*
→ Note at CRIME (for verbs)

extra noun

ADJ. **little** ◇ *There was no money left over for luxuries or little ~s.* | **optional** (*BrE*) | **hidden** (*esp. BrE*) ◇ *£400 is a lot to pay, but there are no hidden ~s.* | **added** ◇ *Regular guests also get added ~s like free room service.* | **DVD** ◇ *The DVD ~s include trailers and a behind-the-scenes feature.*
VERB + EXTRA **have, include** ◇ *The DVD has a couple of interesting ~s.* ◇ *No ~s are included.*
EXTRA + VERB **include sth** ◇ *Optional ~s include anti-lock brakes and an electric sunroof.*

extract noun

1 passage from a book/piece of music

ADJ. **brief, short** | **long**
VERB + EXTRACT **read** (*esp. BrE*) | **publish** (*esp. BrE*)
EXTRACT + VERB **be from, be taken from** ◇ *The ~ is taken from a long essay.*
PREP. **~ from** ◇ *He read out a brief ~ from his book.*

2 substance taken from another substance

ADJ. **natural** ◇ *conditioners made from natural plant ~s* | **herbal** | **green tea, malt, meat, plant, root, yeast, etc.** | **almond, vanilla** (*both AmE*) (*almond, etc. essence* in *BrE*)
PREP. **~ of** ◇ *~ of apricot*

extradition noun

VERB + EXTRADITION **avoid, escape** ◇ *It won't be easy for them to escape ~.* | **ask for, demand, request, seek** ◇ *The new government will seek the ~ of the suspected terrorists.* | **allow, order** (*esp. BrE*) ◇ *A judge ordered her ~ to Britain.* | **waive** (*esp. AmE*) | **await, face** (*esp. BrE*) ◇ *The man is in prison tonight, awaiting ~ to Syria.* | **fight** ◇ *His lawyer announced that he will fight ~.*
EXTRADITION + NOUN **hearing, proceedings** (*esp. BrE*) | **agreement, treaty** ◇ *There is no ~ agreement between the two countries.* | **request**
PREP. **~ from, ~ to**

extraordinary adj.

VERBS **appear, be, feel, look, seem, sound** | **make sth** ◇ *What makes it so ~ is that the experts had all dismissed her theories as nonsense.* | **find sth** ◇ *I find her attitude quite ~.* | **regard sth as, see sth as**
ADV. **most, really, truly** | **absolutely, quite, simply** ◇ *It seems absolutely ~.* | **rather**

extravagant adj.

VERBS **be, feel, seem** ◇ *I go to that restaurant for lunch if I'm feeling ~.* | **become**
ADV. **particularly, very, wildly** ◇ *He had a wildly ~ lifestyle.* | **rather, somewhat** | **a little, slightly, etc.**
PREP. **with** ◇ *You mustn't be so ~ with other people's money.*

extreme noun

ADJ. **opposite, polar** ◇ *Their views are at opposite ~s from each other.* | **logical** | **new** ◇ *She has taken cleanliness to a new ~.* | **climatic, political, temperature** ◇ *It's a difficult place to live because of its climatic ~s.*
VERB + EXTREME **avoid** ◇ *Avoid any ~s of temperature.* | **go to, reach** ◇ *There is no need to go to such ~s.* | **carry sth to, take sth to** ◇ *It's foolish to take any dieting to ~s.* | **represent**
PREP. **at an/the ~** ◇ *At the ~, some nuclear waste is so radioactive it has to be kept isolated for thousands of years.* | **between ~s** ◇ *There has to be a solution between these ~s.* | **in the ~** ◇ *His voice was scornful in the ~.* | **to the ~** ◇ *She was always generous to the ~.* | **~s of** ◇ *These photographs show ~s of obesity and emaciation.*
PHRASES **at one ~, at the other ~** ◇ *At the other ~, women still childless at 32 were more likely to be from a professional background.* | **go from one ~ to the other** ◇ *She goes from one ~ to the other, and either works very hard or does absolutely nothing.* | **go to the opposite ~, go to the other ~** ◇ *After always putting too much salt in her cooking, she went to the opposite ~ and banished it completely.*

extreme adj.

VERBS **be** | **appear, seem, sound** | **become** | **consider sth**
ADV. **particularly, really, very** | **a bit, fairly, a little, quite, rather, somewhat** ◇ *Some of his views seem rather ~.*
PHRASES **at its most ~** ◇ *This is hero-worship at its most ~.*

extremist noun

ADJ. **left-wing, right-wing** ◇ *an attack by right-wing ~s* | **radical** | **political, religious** | **anti-abortion** | **Christian, Hindu, Islamic, Jewish, etc.**
EXTREMIST + NOUN **element, group, movement, organization, party**

exuberance noun

ADJ. **sheer** ◇ *She was laughing from the sheer ~ of the performance.* | **youthful** ◇ *The band displays a youthful ~ and sense of fun.* | **natural**
VERB + EXUBERANCE **display, exhibit, express** (*esp. AmE*) | **curb** ◇ *He has to learn to curb his natural ~.*

eye noun

1 part of the body

ADJ. **left, right** | **amber, blue, brown, dark, golden, green, grey/gray, hazel, pale, etc.** | **big, enormous, huge, large, wide** ◇ *She just looked at me with those big blue ~s of hers.* ◇ *His ~s were wide with horror.* | **narrow** | **close-set, wide-set** | **deep, deep-set, heavy-lidded, hollow, hooded, sunken** | **beady, piggy** | **baggy, puffy, swollen** | **bleary, bloodshot, exhausted, red, red-rimmed, sleepy, tired, weary** ◇ *Her bleary ~s showed that she hadn't slept.* | **bright, brilliant, glowing, luminous, lustrous, sparkling, starry, twinkling** | **clear, limpid, liquid** | **soft, warm** | **cloudy, misty, moist, rheumy, tear-filled, tearful, teary** (*esp. AmE*), **watery** | **dry** | **sightless, unseeing** | **half-closed, narrowed** | **unblinking** | **dazed, unfocused** | **mad, staring, wild** | **angry, cruel, fierce** | **anxious** | **greedy, hungry** ◇ *The dog's hungry ~s were on my sandwich.* | **curious, prying** ◇ *He drew the curtains to make sure no prying ~s saw what he was doing.* | **intelligent, keen, sharp, shrewd** | **penetrating, piercing** | **intense** | **cold, dull, expressionless, glassy, glazed, lifeless, steely, vacant** | **downcast, sad, solemn, soulful**
VERB + EYE **open** | **close, shut** | **lift, raise** | **lower** | **avert** ◇ *She averted her ~s from his face.* | **cast, turn** ◇ *I cast my ~s around the room but couldn't see any familiar faces.* ◇ *He turned his ~s to the door when he heard the handle turning.* | **roll** ◇ *She rolled her ~s in disgust.* | **blink** | **narrow, screw up, squeeze shut** ◇ *He screwed up his ~s against the glare of the sun.* ◇ *Tina squeezed her ~s shut and bit her lip.* | **widen** | **focus** | **strain** ◇ *I didn't want to strain my ~s to read, so I turned on the light.* | **protect** ◇ *Skiers wear goggles to protect their ~s from the sun.* | **shade, shield** ◇ *He held up the newspaper to shield his ~s from the sun.* | **cover** | **test** | **gouge** ◇ *She reached up and tried to gouge her attacker's ~s.* | **rub, wipe** | **catch** ◇ *A movement in the reeds caught my ~* (= attracted my attention). | **look sb in, meet** ◇ *She looked*

her father straight in the ~ and answered his question truthfully. ◊ He seemed unwilling to meet my ~s.

EYE + VERB **dilate, fly open, grow wide, open, round, shoot open, snap open, widen** ◊ Her ~s dilated with horror at what she had done. ◊ Her ~s flew open in surprise. ◊ His ~s rounded in mock amazement. | **close, shut | flutter open, flutter shut | stream, water** ◊ My ~s stream when I chop onions. | **hold sth** ◊ His ~s held a mischievous gleam. | **be alight with sth, blaze, brighten, flare, flash, gleam, glint, glisten, glitter, glow, light up, shine, smoulder/smolder, spark, sparkle, twinkle** ◊ She laughed, her ~s alight with excitement. ◊ His ~s blazed with menace. | **mirror sth, reflect sth** ◊ His ~s reflected his anguish. | **blur, brim with tears, cloud, fill with tears, mist, well, well up | darken, dim, dull, glaze, glaze over** ◊ Her ~s glazed over when I said I worked in dictionaries. | **harden, soften** ◊ His ~s hardened as he remembered how they had laughed at him. | **narrow, sharpen | burn, hurt, prick, prickle, smart, sting** ◊ Her ~s prickled with unshed tears. | **be drawn to sb/sth, follow sb/ sth, turn to sb/sth** ◊ His ~s were drawn to a bundle of papers in the corner. ◊ My ~s followed his every move. | **fall on sb/ sth, land on sb/sth, settle on sb/sth | catch sth** ◊ Her ~ caught mine. | **gaze at sb/sth, stare at sb/sth, watch sb/sth | fasten on sb/sth, fix on sb/sth, focus on sb/sth, lock on sb/sth** ◊ She tried to sit up, her ~s fixed on Jean's face. | **be fixed on sb/sth, be glued to sb/sth, be intent on sb/sth, be riveted on/to sb/sth, be trained on sb/sth | linger on sb/ sth, rest on sb/sth | not leave sb/sth** ◊ His ~s never left mine. | **look at sb/sth, peer at sb/sth, regard sb/sth | glare at sb/sth | lock, lock together, meet** ◊ Their ~s locked together in a battle of wills. | **dart, flick, flicker, flit, glance, go, leap, move, run, shift, shoot, travel** ◊ His ~s darted from face to face. | **roll, swivel** ◊ She tried the door, her ~s rolling in panic. | **dance** ◊ Her ~s danced with amusement. | **roam, rove** ◊ He let his ~s roam around the scene. | **drift, slide, slip, stray, wander** ◊ His ~s drifted over to Helen's chair. | **probe sth, rake sth, scan sth, scour sth, search sth, sweep sth** ◊ His ~s scanned the room as he entered. | **drop, fall, lower** ◊ Her ~s dropped to her lap as she answered. | **lift | bore into sb, pierce sb** ◊ She could feel the old lady's ~s bore into her. | **accustom to sth, adjust to sth, become accustomed to sth, grow accustomed to sth** ◊ As my ~s accustomed to the darkness, I could make out a shape by the window. | **blink | twitch | crinkle, crinkle up, squint, wrinkle** ◊ His ~s crinkled up at the corners as he smiled. ◊ Her ~s squinted against the brightness. | **strain** ◊ My ~s strained to make anything out in the darkness. | **slant | bulge, pop** ◊ His ~s bulged in fury. | **betray sth, give sb/ sth away, show sth** ◊ His narrow ~s betrayed his impatience. ◊ She responded softly, her ~s showing concern. | **tell (sb) sth** ◊ Her ~s told me nothing. | **question (sb) | laugh, smile | plead | mock sb | appraise sb/sth, examine sb/sth, scrutinize sth, study sb/sth, survey sb/sth | take sth in** ◊ My ~s took in every detail as I entered the house for the first time in twenty years.

EYE + NOUN **muscles, socket | contact** ◊ I knew he was lying because he wouldn't make ~ contact with me. | **movement** ◊ Rapid ~ movements frequently accompany dreaming. | **doctor, specialist, surgeon | hospital | operation, surgery, treatment | exam, examination, test | damage, defect, disease, disorder, infection, injury, strain | drops** ◊ The doctor gave me ~ drops to put in three times a day. | **protection** ◊ It is essential to wear some form of ~ protection. | **liner** (usually **eyeliner**), **make-up, shadow** (usually **eyeshadow**) **| colour/color | level** ◊ Your computer screen should be at ~ level. | **candy** (informal, figurative) ◊ The series has plenty of ~ candy (= people that are pleasant to look at).

PREP. **in your ~s** ◊ There were tears in his ~s as he spoke. ◊ The sun was in my ~s and I couldn't see the road. | **under sb's ~** ◊ I want you under my ~ (= where I can see you).

PHRASES **as far as the ~ can see** ◊ The tide was out, leaving nothing but mud as far as the ~ could see. | **before your very ~s** ◊ Before our very ~s, the bird snatched the fish from the plate and flew off. | **can't keep your ~s off sb/sth, can't take your ~s off sb/sth** ◊ He couldn't keep his ~s off the girl sitting opposite him. | **roll your ~s heavenward** (= to show that you are annoyed or impatient) ◊ She rolled her ~s

heavenward when she saw what her husband was wearing. | **a gleam in sb's ~, a glint in sb's ~, a twinkle in sb's ~** ◊ He looked at me with a twinkle in his ~. | **have an ~ on sb/sth** (= be watching) ◊ The store detective had his ~ on a group of boys who were acting suspiciously. | **keep an ~ on sb/sth** (= watch) ◊ Could you keep an ~ on my bag for a moment? | **keep an ~ out for sb/sth, keep your ~s open for sb/sth** (= watch out for) ◊ I walked around the store, keeping an ~ out for bargains. | **lay ~s on/upon sb/sth, set ~s on/upon sb/sth** ◊ Tom fell in love the moment he laid ~s on her. ◊ From the moment he set ~s on her he knew that he wanted to marry her. | **out of the corner of your ~** ◊ Out of the corner of her ~, she saw Harry start forward. | **tears fill sb's ~s | to/with the naked ~, to/with the unaided ~** ◊ The planet should be visible to the naked ~ (= without a telescope). | **under sb's watchful ~** ◊ A boy was playing outside under the watchful ~ of his mother. | **with your own ~s** ◊ If I hadn't seen his jump with my own ~s, I would never have believed it possible.

2 ability to see

ADJ. **eagle, good, keen, quick, sharp** ◊ The children's eagle ~s spotted an ice-cream seller half a mile away. ◊ A surgeon needs a good ~ and a steady hand.

PREP. **~ for** ◊ Her skill at working with wood is coupled to a keen ~ for design.

3 way of seeing

ADJ. **careful, cautious, close, suspicious, wary, watchful** ◊ The government is keeping a close ~ on the economy. | **critical, stern | jaundiced | fresh, new** ◊ He saw his students with new ~s now that he had a child of his own. | **kindly, sympathetic | discerning | experienced, expert, practised/practiced** ◊ To an expert ~, the painting is an obvious fake. | **inexperienced, untrained | artistic**

PREP. **in sb/sth's ~** ◊ She can do no wrong in his ~s. ◊ In the ~s of the law his knife was an offensive weapon. | **through sb's ~s** ◊ You need to look at your website through the user's ~s. | **to sb's ~** ◊ To my ~, the windows seem out of proportion. | **with a …~** ◊ She viewed the findings with a critical ~. | **with the ~ of** ◊ He looked at the design with the ~ of an engineer.

PHRASES **in your mind's ~** (= your imagination) ◊ He pictured the scene in his mind's ~.

eye verb

ADV. **keenly** (esp. BrE)**, narrowly, sharply, shrewdly | curiously, speculatively, thoughtfully | carefully, cautiously, suspiciously, warily | nervously | doubtfully, uncertainly | coldly, coolly | greedily, hungrily** ◊ The children ~d the cakes greedily.

eyebrow noun → See also BROW

ADJ. **heavy, thick | thin | bushy, shaggy | plucked, shaped | dark | arched, cocked** (esp. AmE)**, lifted, raised** ◊ Ellen looked at me with a raised ~. | **amused | mocking, sardonic | cynical, sceptical/skeptical | enquiring, questioning, quizzical**

VERB + EYEBROW **arch, cock, lift, quirk, raise** ◊ 'Really?' she said, raising a cynical ~. | **furrow** ◊ He furrowed his ~s in confusion. | **pluck** ◊ She spent hours in front of the mirror, plucking her ~s.

EYEBROW + VERB **arch, lift, rise, shoot up** ◊ Her ~s arched quizzically. ◊ His dark ~s lifted in surprise. | **furrow**

EYEBROW + NOUN **pencil | ring** ◊ She had short blonde hair and an ~ ring.

eyelash (also **lash**) noun

ADJ. **thick | long | black, dark | false**

VERB + EYELASH **bat, flutter** ◊ She smiled and fluttered her ~es at the ticket inspector. | **curl** ◊ Curl your ~es and add a couple of coats of mascara.

EYELASH + VERB **flutter**

eyelid noun → See also EYELID

ADJ. **lower, upper** | **closed, half-closed** | **drooping, heavy, hooded**
VERB + EYELID **lift** ◇ *She lifted one ~ to see what he was doing.* | **close, open**
EYELID + VERB **droop** | **flutter**
PREP. **behind (your)** ~ ◇ *She watched him from behind half-closed ~s.*

eyesight noun

ADJ. **excellent, good, keen** | **bad, failing, poor** ◇ *Failing ~ finally forced her into an old people's home.*
VERB + EYESIGHT **have** ◇ *Owls have good ~.* | **lose** ◇ *She has started to lose her ~.*
EYESIGHT + VERB **deteriorate, fail**

F f

fabric noun

1 cloth

ADJ. **beautiful, luxurious, rich** ◇ *rich ~ wall coverings* | **delicate, fine, light, lightweight, sheer, soft, thin** | **coarse, durable, heavy, thick** | **stretch, stretchy** (*informal*) | **breathable** | **waterproof** | **floral, patterned, plain, printed** | **cotton, nylon, woollen/woolen, etc.** | **knit** (*esp. AmE*), **knitted** (*esp. BrE*), **woven** | **non-woven** | **synthetic** | **curtain, dress, upholstery**
... OF FABRIC **length, piece, strip** | **swatch**
VERB + FABRIC **make, produce, weave** ◇ *The ~ is woven on these machines.* | **cut, tear**
FABRIC + NOUN **conditioner** (*esp. BrE*), **softener** ◇ *My clothes smell of ~ softener.* | **swatch** ◇ *~ swatches of the different types of mattress covering*

2 basic structure of a society/way of life

ADJ. **basic** ◇ *the basic ~ of family life* | **economic, moral, political, social** | **historic** ◇ *The city retains much of its historic ~.* | **urban**
VERB + FABRIC **destroy** ◇ *The government's policies have destroyed the social ~.* | **threaten** ◇ *He believes that such legislation would threaten the ~ of our society.*
PHRASES **the very ~ of sth, the whole ~ of sth** ◇ *a threat to the very ~ of society*

face noun

1 front part of the head

ADJ. **angelic, beautiful, cute, handsome, lovely, perfect, pleasant, pretty, sweet** | **plain, terrible, ugly** | **colourless/colorless, grey/gray, pale, pallid, white** | **flushed, pink, red, ruddy** ◇ *Her ~ was flushed after her run.* | **tanned** | **dark** | **sallow** | **heart-shaped, oval, round, square** | **bearded, freckled, unshaven** | **smooth, lined, wrinkled** | **pock-marked** | **fat, plump** ◇ *She had a plump, pretty ~.* | **gaunt, haggard, lean, pinched, thin, wizened** | **craggy, rugged** ◇ *a craggy ~ with deep-set eyes and bushy brows* | **delicate** | **elfin** ◇ *Her short hair suited her elfin ~.* | **baby** | **painted** | **happy, smiling** | **tear-stained, tear-streaked** (*esp. AmE*) | **human**
VERB + FACE **have** ◇ *She has a beautiful, oval ~.* | **tilt, turn** ◇ *She turned her ~ away.* ◇ *He tilted her ~ up to his.* | **bury, cover, hide**
FACE + VERB **look, peer, stare** ◇ *A ~ peered around the door at him.* | **appear**
PREP. **in the/sb's** ~ ◇ *The ball hit him in the ~.* ◇ *His eyes were sunken in his gaunt ~.* | **on the/sb's** ~ ◇ *She put some powder on her ~.*
PHRASES **a sea of ~s** (= many faces) ◇ *From the stage, he looked down at a sea of ~s.*

2 expression on sb's face

ADJ. **animated, cheerful, friendly, grinning, happy, radiant, smiling** ◇ *the sight of Sarah's smiling ~ beaming up at him* | **smiley** ◇ *She drew a little yellow smiley ~.* | **anxious, concerned, troubled, worried** | **frightened, shocked, surprised** | **disgusted** ◇ *She made a disgusted ~ at that and walked away.* | **angry, furious** | **hard, set, stern** ◇ *His ~ was set and hard.* | **grave, grim, serious, solemn** | **long, sad** ◇ *The news for the company isn't good, judging from the long ~s in the boardroom.* | **tired** | **funny** ◇ *She made a funny ~ and gave a snorting sort of laugh.* | **honest, innocent, kind** | **expectant** | **rapt** | **expressive, open** ◇ *She looked at the honest, open ~ of her husband.* | **blank, expressionless, impassive, poker** ◇ *His ~ remained impassive, so strong was his self-control.*
VERB + FACE **make, pull** ◇ *What are you pulling a ~ at now?* | **search** ◇ *He searched her ~ for some clue as to what she meant.* | **appear on, cross, spread across** ◇ *A wry smile crossed his ~.*
FACE + VERB **look, seem** ◇ *His ~ looked a little confused.* | **grow, turn** ◇ *Her ~ suddenly grew serious.* | **brighten, glow, light up** ◇ *Her little ~ lit up when I gave her the present.* | **beam, smile** ◇ *The ~ smiled benignly at him.* | **break into a smile** ◇ *Her ~ broke into a wide smile.* | **cloud, crumple, drop, fall** ◇ *Her ~ crumpled and she started crying.* '*I can't come,' she said. His ~ fell.* | **clear** ◇ *His ~ cleared and she smiled back.* | **darken, harden, set** ◇ *Her ~ darkened with anger.* ◇ *His ~ set in grim lines.* | **soften** ◇ *The father's ~ softened as he hugged his little boy.* | **burn, flame, flush, go red, redden** ◇ *Jack's ~ flushed with embarrassment.* | **go white, pale** ◇ *Her ~ paled with fright.* | **contort, crease, pucker, tighten, twist** ◇ *Her ~ contorted in pain.* | **betray sth, reveal sth, show sth** ◇ *Her ~ betrayed no emotion at all.*
PREP. **on sb's** ~ ◇ *She had a big smile on her ~.*
PHRASES **a ~ like thunder** (= a very angry face) (*BrE*) ◇ *Mr Hibbs came in with a ~ like thunder.* | **keep a straight** ~ (= not laugh or smile, although you find sth funny) | **an/the expression on sb's** ~, **a/the look on sb's** ~ ◇ *The look on his ~ was priceless.* | **a grin on sb's** ~, **a smile on sb's** ~, **a smirk on sb's** ~ | **a frown on sb's** ~

3 front part/side of sth

ADJ. **front, rear** | **North, South, etc.** | **steep** ◇ *We slowly climbed the steep ~ of the crag.* | **cliff, rock** | **clock**
PHRASES **~ down, ~ downwards/downward** ◇ *She placed the cards ~ down on the table.* | **~ up, ~ upwards/upward**

4 person

ADJ. **familiar, old** ◇ *I looked around for a familiar ~.* ◇ *I'm so bored with seeing the same old ~s!* | **different, fresh, new, strange, unfamiliar** | **famous, well-known** ◇ *a restaurant where you often see famous ~s*
VERB + FACE **see**

5 particular character/aspect of sth

ADJ. **human** ◇ *bureaucracy with a human ~* | **acceptable, unacceptable** (*both esp. BrE*) ◇ *Social deprivation is the unacceptable ~ of capitalism.* | **public** ◇ *He has become the public ~ of the company.* | **true** | **changing** ◇ *the changing ~ of Britain* | **entire, whole** ◇ *This discovery changed the whole ~ of science.*

facet noun

ADJ. **important** | **interesting** | **distinct, particular** | **different, many, multiple, various** ◇ *My job has many different ~s and is never the same from day to day.* | **new**
VERB + FACET **have** ◇ *She has another important ~ to her personality.*

facilitate verb

ADV. **greatly** ◇ *The use of computers has greatly ~d the company's ability to keep accurate records.* | **further**
VERB + FACILITATE **be designed to, help (to)**

facility noun

1 (usually **facilities**) buildings/services/equipment

ADJ. **excellent, first-class, good** | **adequate, appropriate,**

proper, suitable | inadequate, poor (*esp. BrE*) | basic,
limited ◇ *a hotel with only basic facilities* | modern, state-
of-the-art, up-to-date | extensive | extra (*esp. BrE*) |
available, existing ◇ *We are looking to upgrade the existing
facilities.* | essential, necessary ◇ *to improve access to
essential facilities* | community (*esp. BrE*), local ◇ *hospitals,
schools and other major community facilities* | communal,
shared ◇ *The communal facilities were in a bad state.* |
public | disabled (*BrE*) ◇ *The stadium was criticized for its
lack of disabled facilities.* | conference | airport, hotel |
bar (*BrE*) | leisure (*esp. BrE*), recreational, social (*esp. BrE*) |
sporting (*esp. BrE*), sports | play (*esp. BrE*) | transport (*esp.
BrE*), transportation (*esp. AmE*), travel (*esp. BrE*) | parking |
shopping (*esp. BrE*) | dining | catering (*BrE*), cooking (*esp.
BrE*), kitchen (*esp. BrE*) | baby-changing (*BrE*), bathroom,
laundry, sanitary, shower, toilet (*BrE*), washing (*esp. BrE*) |
en suite (*esp. BrE*), private ◇ *All bedrooms offer private
facilities* (= a private bathroom). | health, health-care,
hospital, medical | childcare, crèche (*BrE*), day-care,
nursery (*esp. BrE*) | educational, training | library,
research | laboratory
VERB + FACILITY have, offer, provide | improve, upgrade |
make use of, use ◇ *I made full use of the computing
facilities.*
FACILITY + VERB be available, exist | include sth ◇ *Facilities
include a large indoor pool, jacuzzi and sauna.*
FACILITY + NOUN management, manager
PREP. ~ for ◇ *The school has no facilities for the teaching of
music.* ◇ *The hotel provides excellent facilities for children.*
PHRASES a range of facilities

2 (*esp. AmE*) a building used for a particular activity
ADJ. large | 50 000-square-foot, etc. | modern, state-of-the-
art | purpose-built (*BrE*) | new | existing ◇ *plans to
renovate an existing* ~ | permanent, temporary ◇ *a
temporary storage* ~ *for blood samples* | long-term ◇
residents of long-term care facilities | federal, local, state ◇
prisoners in state and federal facilities | community, public
| private | commercial, industrial | maintenance,
manufacturing, processing, production, storage, testing,
transport, … treatment ◇ *a water treatment* ~ | correc-
tional, detention ◇ *He spent 90 days at the county's local
correctional* ~. | military | weapons | chemical, nuclear |
health, health-care, hospital, medical ◇ *a mental health* ~
| dining | childcare, day-care | educational, training |
fitness, sports | practice ◇ *She trains with the team at their
practice* ~. | research | lab (*informal*), laboratory |
communication, communications
VERB + FACILITY design | build, construct | expand | open ◇
The company expects to open its ~ *by late September.* | use ◇
The old ~ *is now used for storage of dry products.* | manage,
operate | maintain | lease, rent | tour, visit ◇ *A doctor
visited the* ~ *and found deplorable conditions.*
FACILITY + VERB be located ◇ *a production* ~ *located in New
Mexico* | house ◇ *The 100 000 square-foot* ~ *houses labs for
NASA's research.*
PREP. ~ for ◇ *a new* ~ *for military training*

3 special feature of a machine/service
ADJ. central ◇ *The archive offers a central* ~ *for cataloguing
and indexing data.* | backup ◇ *The report warns that there
are no backup facilities if the reprocessing plant breaks down.*
| support ◇ *training and other support facilities* | special |
useful | technical | credit, loan, overdraft (*BrE*) ◇ *a bank
account with an overdraft* ~ | editing, help, mail, search (*all
computing*)
VERB + FACILITY have, offer, provide | use
FACILITY + VERB allow sth, allow for sth ◇ *The software's 'list'*
~ *allows users to compile their own list.*
PREP. ~ for ◇ *The device has a* ~ *for storing any sound you
like.*

4 natural ability
ADJ. amazing, great
VERB + FACILITY have | show
PREP. with ~ ◇ *He played with great* ~. | ~ for ◇ *She showed
an amazing* ~ *for mind-reading.*

fact *noun*

ADJ. important, interesting, relevant, salient ◇ *You must
look at all the relevant* ~*s.* | basic, simple | cold, concrete,
hard, incontrovertible, inescapable, observable, obvious,
plain, straightforward, true, undeniable ◇ *The police have
to support their case with hard* ~*s.* ◇ *These are all
incontrovertible* ~*s.* | bare, disturbing, harsh, sad, stark,
unpalatable (*esp. BrE*), unpleasant ◇ *the bare* ~*s of war* ◇ *a
rather harsh* ~ *of life* | known ◇ *The known* ~*s of the case are
as follows.* | little-known, well-known ◇ *It is a well-known* ~
that girls do better than boys at school. | proven | historical,
scientific | mere ◇ *The mere* ~ *of your being there will
arouse their suspicions.*
VERB + FACT be aware of, have, know ◇ *We don't have all the*
~*s yet.* ◇ *She already knew the* ~*s she needed.* | ascertain,
establish, find out ◇ *the best way of establishing the* ~*s* |
check, consider, examine, look at ◇ *I think you need to
check your* ~*s.* ◇ *For God's sake, look at the* ~*s!* | prove ◇
These ~*s have not yet been proved.* | collect, gather | select
◇ *Historians must first select the* ~*s that they present.* | give,
present, report, state ◇ *The job of the teacher is not simply
to impart* ~*s.* ◇ *I'm not making excuses—I'm just stating a* ~. |
interpret ◇ *different ways of interpreting the* ~*s* | account
for, explain ◇ *How do you account for the* ~ *that
unemployment is still rising?* | accept, acknowledge,
appreciate, face, recognize ◇ *She wouldn't accept the* ~ *that
she had lost.* ◇ *I appreciate the* ~ *that you're under a lot of
pressure at the moment.* ◇ *I'm afraid you'll have to face* ~*s.
She'll never marry you.* | grasp ◇ *He doesn't seem able to
grasp this basic* ~. | learn | deny, dispute ◇ *No one can deny
this* ~. | forget, ignore, overlook ◇ *This approach ignores
the* ~ *that people, not computers, commit crimes.* | be
oblivious to | conceal, disguise, hide ◇ *If he was bored, he
managed to hide the* ~ *very well.* | obscure ◇ *The recent
improvements should not obscure the* ~ *that general
standards are still far too low.* | change ◇ *This does not
change the* ~ *that a crime has been committed.* | draw
attention to ◇ *The report draws attention to the* ~ *that the
country is now a net exporter of the product.* | emphasize,
highlight, underline (*esp. BrE*), underscore (*esp. AmE*) |
confine sb/yourself to (*esp. BrE*), stick to ◇ *Just stick to the*
~*s.* | be based on ◇ *a novel based on historical* ~ | reflect ◇
Prices reflect the ~ *that the company is aiming at the luxury
market.* | stem from ◇ *He knew their bitterness stemmed
from the* ~ *that he was in charge.* | be explained by, be
supported by | be complicated by, be compounded by, be
exacerbated by ◇ *The problem was compounded by the* ~
that I had no idea what I was looking for. | hate, lament,
regret, resent ◇ *We waited miserably, lamenting the* ~ *that
our suitcases had been put on the wrong plane.* ◇ *She
resented the* ~ *that I had more freedom than her.*
FACT + VERB remain ◇ *The* ~ *remains that we are still two
teachers short.*
PREP. after the ~ ◇ *On some vital decisions employees were
only informed after the* ~ (= *when it was too late to change
them*). | apart from the ~ ◇ *She was happy, apart from the*
~ *that she could not return home.* | despite the ~, in spite
of the ~, notwithstanding the ~ ◇ *He got the job, despite
the* ~ *that he has no experience.* | due to the ~ ◇ *Due to the*
~ *that they did not read English, the prisoners were unaware
of what they were signing.* | given the ~ ◇ *The findings are
not surprising, given the* ~*s:* … | in ~ ◇ *I used to live in
France; in* ~, *not far from where you're going.* | ~ about ◇
We learned several interesting ~*s about elephants.*
PHRASES (as) a matter of ~ ◇ *It's not wild speculation! It's a
plain matter of* ~. ◇ *'I suppose you'll be leaving soon, then?'
'No, as a matter of* ~ *I'll be staying for another two years.'* |
~s and figures ◇ *All the* ~*s and figures were presented at the
meeting.* | the ~ of the matter ◇ *A new car would be
wonderful but the* ~ *of the matter is that we can't afford one.*
| the ~s of the case ◇ *The* ~*s of the case are quite
straightforward.* | a ~ of life (= *a situation that cannot be
changed*) ◇ *It is an sad* ~ *of life that the most deserving
people do not often achieve the most success.* | the ~s of life
(= *the details about sex and how babies are born, esp. as*

told to children) | **~ or fiction?** ◊ *The Loch Ness Monster: ~ or fiction?* | **the ~s speak for themselves** (= further explanation about sth is unnecessary because the facts prove it is true) | **get your ~s right, get your ~s straight, get your ~s wrong** ◊ *If you're going to make accusations, you'd better get your ~s right.* | **have the ~s at your fingertips** ◊ *When making your presentation, it is important to have all the ~s at your fingertips* (= to have the information you need and be able to find it and use it quickly). | **in actual ~, in point of ~** ◊ *I thought the work would be difficult. In actual ~, it's very easy.* | **in view of the ~ that ...** ◊ *Voluntary work was particularly important in view of the ~ that women were often forced to give up paid work on marriage.* | **know for a ~** ◊ *Do you know for a ~ that he is in London?* | **not to mention the ~ that ...** ◊ *It's very hard to do this on a home computer. Not to mention the ~ that it's actually illegal.* | **a question of ~, a statement of ~** ◊ *It's a simple statement of ~.* | **a recognition of the ~ that ...** ◊ *a growing recognition of the ~ that learning may take different forms*

faction *noun*

ADJ. **dominant, main, major** | **internal** | **competing, opposing, rival, warring** ◊ *He brokered a ceasefire agreement between the warring ~s.* | **breakaway** | **dissident, rebel** | **armed** | **military, parliamentary, political** | **ethnic, religious** | **conservative, hard-line, left-wing, liberal, moderate, radical, right-wing** | **anti-government, anti-war, etc.**
VERB + FACTION **lead**
PREP. **~ in** ◊ *the largest ~ in the civil war* | **~ within** ◊ *the dominant ~ within the government*

factor *noun*

ADJ. **big, important, main, major, relevant, significant** ◊ *one of the most significant ~s* | **critical, crucial, deciding, decisive, determining, key, vital** ◊ *This is regarded as the crucial ~ in deciding who should get priority.* ◊ *Money proved to be the deciding ~.* | **contributing, contributory** ◊ *Poor organization was certainly a contributory ~ to the crisis.* | **complicating** ◊ *A complicating ~ is her parents' refusal to cooperate with the police.* | **limiting** | **mitigating** ◊ *The appeal judges spoke of strong mitigating ~s in the case.* | **aggravating** | **additional** | **single** ◊ *The closure of the mine was the single most important ~ in the town's decline.* | **common** ◊ *Look for the common ~ in all these cases.* | **external, extraneous, extrinsic** ◊ *External ~s in the production of disease include pollution of the environment.* | **internal, intrinsic** | **causal, causative** | **risk** ◊ *Studies have established that smoking is a risk ~ for cancer.* | **contextual, demographic, economic, environmental, genetic, political, psychological, situational, social** | **human** ◊ *The human ~ is crucial to success in team management.*
VERB + FACTOR **consider, take into account** ◊ *A variety of other ~s will be taken into account.* | **identify** | **depend on**
FACTOR + VERB **be involved, operate** ◊ *the contextual ~s which operate to hinder understanding* | **affect sth, be responsible for sth, cause sth, contribute to sth, determine sth, influence sth, predispose sb/sth to sth** ◊ *environmental ~s which predispose children to middle-ear infections* | **explain sth, constrain sth, inhibit sth, militate against sth** ◊ *one of the ~s that influenced his decision* | **interact** ◊ *We examine how economic and social ~s interact.* | **include sth** | **be at play** ◊ *There are several ~s at play here.*
PREP. **~ behind** ◊ *the main ~s behind the dollar's weakness* | **~ in** ◊ *a key ~ in the decision*
PHRASES **a combination, number, variety, etc. of ~s** ◊ *The outcome will depend on a number of ~s.*

factory *noun*

ADJ. **large** | **small** | **modern** | **abandoned** (*esp. AmE*), **disused** (*esp. BrE*) | **aircraft, auto** (*esp. AmE*), **automobile** (*esp. AmE*), **car** | **clothing, garment, textile** | **chemical, munitions, etc.**
VERB + FACTORY **build, open, set up** ◊ *capital to set up a ceramics ~* | **close, close down, shut, shut down** ◊ *They had to close the ~ down in the recession.* | **manage, own, run**
FACTORY + VERB **make sth, produce sth** | **open** | **close, close down, shut, shut down** ◊ *The ~ closed down ten years ago.*
FACTORY + NOUN **manager, owner, worker** | **job, production, work** | **buildings** | **closure** | **floor** ◊ *a worker on the ~ floor* | **farm, farming** ◊ *the ~ farming of beef, pork and chicken*
PREP. **at ~, in ~** ◊ *He works in a shoe ~.*

factual *adj.*

VERBS **be**
ADV. **entirely, purely, strictly** | **basically, largely** | **supposedly** ◊ *the speculative nature of the supposedly ~ information conveyed through the media*

faculty *noun*

1 natural ability of the body/mind

ADJ. **higher** ◊ *the evolution of man's higher faculties* | **cognitive, intellectual, mental, rational** ◊ *He is not in full possession of all his mental faculties.* | **creative, critical, imaginative, moral** | **human**
VERB + FACULTY **be in possession of, have** ◊ *She is over eighty but still has all her faculties.* | **lose** | **develop** ◊ *We try to develop the student's critical faculties.*
PREP. **~ for** ◊ *our ~ for picking up speech even in noisy environments*

2 university department

ADJ. **Arts, English, law, medical, etc.**
FACULTY + NOUN **member**
PREP. **in a/the ~** ◊ *students who are doing degrees in the Arts Faculty* | **~ of** ◊ *the Faculty of Arts*
PHRASES **a member of the ~** | **the dean of (the) ~, the head of (the) ~**

3 (*AmE*) the teachers at a university

ADJ. **college, departmental, university** | **full-time, part-time** | **adjunct** ◊ *Teachers are typically part-timers and adjunct ~.* | **junior, senior** | **tenured, untenured** ◊ *The degree of job security for tenured ~ is high relative to most other jobs.* | **non-tenure-track, tenure-track**
VERB + FACULTY **hire, recruit** | **retain** | **join** ◊ *She joined the ~ of the University of Maryland.* | **be on** ◊ *He is currently on the ~ at the University of Texas.*
FACULTY + NOUN **appointment, position** ◊ *I was fortunate to receive a ~ appointment at Ohio State.* | **development, recruitment** ◊ *Larger grants may ensure more funding for ~ development.* | **research** | **governance** | **committee, senate** ◊ *a hearing before a ~ committee* | **union** | **adviser, mentor** ◊ *My ~ adviser made an effort to contact me.*
PREP. **on the ~** ◊ *her colleagues on the ~* | **~ at** ◊ *the ~ at public institutions* | **~ of** ◊ *the ~ of the University of Iowa*

fad *noun*

ADJ. **current, latest, new** | **passing** | **management** | **food** (*esp. BrE*) ◊ *Most children have food ~s at some time.*
PREP. **~ for** ◊ *the ~ for cosmetic surgery*

fade *verb*

ADV. **fast, quickly, rapidly** ◊ *Hopes of a peace settlement were fading fast.* | **soon** | **gradually, slowly** | **quietly** ◊ *It was impossible for her to ~ quietly into the background.* | **away**
VERB + FADE **begin to** | **seem to** ◊ *All else seemed to ~ into insignificance.*
PREP. **from** ◊ *The smile ~d from his face.* | **into** ◊ *Their voices ~d into the distance.*

fail *verb*

1 not succeed

ADV. **dismally, miserably** ◊ *I tried to cheer her up, but ~ed miserably.* | **spectacularly** ◊ *She came up with several plans that ~ed spectacularly before finally achieving success.* | **never** ◊ *That joke never ~s.*
VERB + FAIL **cannot** ◊ *The song can't ~ to be a hit* (= will definitely be a hit). | **can hardly** | **be bound to, be**

destined to, be doomed to ◊ *an enterprise that was doomed to ~ from the start*
PREP. **in** ◊ *Doctors are ~ing in their duty if they do not warn their patients of the dangers.*
PHRASES **try and ~** ◊ *Others have tried and ~ed.*

2 fail to do sth not do sth

ADV. **completely, totally** ◊ *The authorities have totally ~ed to address this problem.*

failing noun

ADJ. **great, major, serious** (*esp. BrE*), **worst** ◊ *Vanity is her worst ~.* | **common, human** ◊ *the very human ~ of wanting to tell other people what to do* | **moral** | **personal** | **intelligence** ◊ *an official report into intelligence ~s*
VERB + FAILING **have** ◊ *We all have our ~s.* | **expose, highlight, identify** ◊ *The investigation exposed huge ~s in the system of medicines regulation.* | **acknowledge, recognize** | **address** ◊ *The committee is being urged to address ~s in the law.*

failure noun

1 lack of success

ADJ. **complete, total** | **abject, humiliating** ◊ *The attempt ended in abject ~.* | **inevitable** | **costly** | **alleged, apparent, perceived** | **relative** | **initial** ◊ *Initial ~ was followed by unexpected, if modest, success.* | **ultimate** ◊ *War is the ultimate ~ of public communication.* | **personal** | **moral** | **academic** | **economic, financial** | **military**
VERB + FAILURE **be doomed to, end in, result in** ◊ *All her efforts were doomed to ~.* | **admit, tolerate** ◊ *He was too proud to admit ~.* ◊ *I will not tolerate ~.* | **lament** ◊ *He lamented his ~ to formulate a satisfactory theory.* | **explain** | **attribute, blame** ◊ *He attributes the ~ of the project to lack of government support.* ◊ *I blame the ~ of our relationship on my husband.* | **expect** ◊ *Children who are doing badly tend to expect ~ and criticism.* | **fear** | **avoid**
FAILURE + NOUN **rate** ◊ *There is a high ~ rate with this treatment.*
PHRASES **fear of ~** ◊ *Fear of ~ should not deter you from trying.* | **a history of ~** ◊ *John had a long history of academic ~.* | **a possibility of ~, a risk of ~** | **a sense of ~**

2 unsuccessful person/thing

ADJ. **big, great, serious** | **complete, total, utter** | **catastrophic, disastrous** | **abject, conspicuous, dismal, humiliating, lamentable** (*esp. BrE*), **miserable** | **costly** | **heroic** (*BrE*) ◊ *If she could not succeed, she would at least be a heroic ~.* | **alleged, apparent, perceived** | **relative** | **past** ◊ *to learn from past ~s* | **rare** (*esp. BrE*) ◊ *The movie was one of the rare ~s in his career.* | **unexpected** | **personal** | **collective** | **moral** | **academic** | **economic, financial** ◊ *economic ~ and increasing unemployment* | **military**
VERB + FAILURE **be, represent** | **prove** ◊ *The venture proved a costly ~.* | **experience, have** | **feel** (*BrE*), **feel like** (*esp. AmE*) ◊ *I felt (like) a complete ~.* | **consider sb/sth, regard sb/sth as** | **brand sb/sth** (*esp. BrE*) ◊ *Her parents had long since branded her a ~.*
FAILURE + VERB **arise from sth** ◊ *~s arising from circumstances beyond your control*
PREP. **~ of** ◊ *The decision to withdraw funding represents a ~ of imagination.*

3 not doing sth

ADJ. **fundamental** | **general** | **manifest** | **consistent, constant, continued, continuing, persistent, repeated** | **government, management** ◊ *government ~ to listen to the voice of the electorate*
VERB + FAILURE **excuse, justify** ◊ *Nothing can excuse your ~ to ask my permission.* | **constitute** ◊ *This breach constitutes a serious ~ in performance.*

4 of a machine, system, part of the body, etc.

ADJ. **mechanical, structural, technical** | **battery, brake, component, computer, engine, equipment, power, system** | **hardware, software** (*both computing*) | **bank, business, commercial, company, corporate, institutional, market** ◊ *Business ~s rose by 30% in 2001.* | **heart, kidney, liver, organ** ◊ *the commonest cause of acute liver ~* | **cardiac, hepatic, renal, respiratory** (*all medical*) ◊ *patients with chronic renal ~* | **crop, harvest** | **communication** | **intelligence, policy**
VERB + FAILURE **cause, lead to, result in** ◊ *a rare viral infection that can lead to heart ~* | **experience, suffer** ◊ *The aircraft seems to have experienced an engine ~.* | **prevent**
FAILURE + VERB **occur** ◊ *A power ~ occurred between 4 and 5 p.m.*
PREP. **~ in** ◊ *a ~ in the computer system*

faint verb

ADV. **almost, nearly**
VERB + FAINT **be about to, be going to** ◊ *He was so pale she thought he was going to ~.*
PREP. **at** ◊ *He would ~ at the sight of blood.* | **from** ◊ *She ~ed from lack of air.* | **with** ◊ *She almost ~ed with shock.*

faint adj.

1 not strong or clear

VERBS **be, sound** ◊ *His voice sounded ~ and far away.* | **become, grow** ◊ *The whispers grew fainter and fainter, then stopped altogether.*
ADV. **extremely, very** ◊ *I can't make out the number—it's very ~.* | **rather**

2 near to losing consciousness

VERBS **be, feel, look**
ADV. **extremely, very** | **almost** | **a bit, a little, quite** ◊ *I was beginning to feel a little ~.*
PREP. **with** ◊ *I was ~ with hunger.*

fair noun

ADJ. **annual** | **antiques, art, book, craft, horse** (*BrE*), **school** (*both esp. AmE*), **steam** (*BrE*) | **career, job, science, trade** | **fun** (*usually funfair*) (*BrE*) | **local, street** | **county, state** (*both AmE*)
VERB + FAIR **attend, go to, visit** | **have, hold, host** ◊ *The city is holding its annual trade ~ in May this year.* | **organize** ◊ *She is organizing next year's book ~.*
FAIR + VERB **take place**
PREP. **at a/the ~** ◊ *I bought it at a local craft ~.*

fair adj.

VERBS **be, seem** | **make sth** ◊ *I'll give you ten pounds each to make it ~.* | **consider sth, think sth** ◊ *I didn't think it ~ that the others should be allowed to go but not me.*
ADV. **scrupulously, very** ◊ *It's important to be scrupulously ~ when grading the final exam paper.* | **absolutely, completely, entirely, perfectly, quite, totally** ◊ *I don't care what he thinks. It seems perfectly ~ to me.* ◊ *That doesn't seem quite ~.* | **hardly, not really** ◊ *It's hardly ~ that I should be working while everyone else is enjoying themselves!* | **pretty, reasonably**
PHRASES **to be ~** ◊ *To be ~, we hadn't really spent enough time on the job.*
PREP. **to** ◊ *That seems ~ to all sides.*

fairness noun

ADJ. **basic, elementary, simple** ◊ *This is a matter of basic ~.* | **scrupulous** (*esp. BrE*) ◊ *Dr Jones was treated with scrupulous ~ by his employers.* | **procedural** (*law*) | **economic** ◊ *issues of economic ~ and personal equality*
VERB + FAIRNESS **achieve, ensure, guarantee** ◊ *a way of achieving ~ to the accused* | **question** ◊ *Many people questioned the ~ of the election.*
FAIRNESS + VERB **demand sth, require sth** ◊ *Fairness demanded an equal division of the winnings.*
PREP. **in (all) ~** ◊ *In all ~ to him, I should say that most of his story is true.* | **with ~** ◊ *They were all treated with strict ~.* | **~ in** ◊ *the need for ~ in applying these rules* | **~ to** ◊ *The new system of waiting lists should guarantee ~ to all patients.*
PHRASES **a sense of ~** ◊ *Children have a very strong sense of ~.*

faith noun

1 trust in sb/sth

ADJ. **enormous, great, tremendous** | **absolute, complete, implicit, total, unshakable, unwavering** | **little** ◊ *I have little ~ in doctors these days.* | **blind** ◊ *He seems to have a blind ~ in his boss.* | **abiding** ◊ *an artist whose work reflects his abiding ~ in humanity* | **renewed** | **touching** ◊ *She showed a touching ~ in my ability to resolve any and every difficulty.* | **public** ◊ *Business crime undermines public ~ in the business system.*

VERB + FAITH **have** | **pin** (*esp. BrE*), **place, put** ◊ *He distrusted political systems and placed his ~ in the genius of individuals.* ◊ *She did not pin much ~ on their chances of success.* | **show** | **share** ◊ *I wish I shared your ~ in the jury system.* | **lack, lose** ◊ *people who lose ~ in themselves* | **shake, undermine** | **destroy** | **renew, restore** ◊ *They are trying to restore ~ in the political system.* | **regain** | **retain** ◊ *If the company can retain its customers' ~ it could become the market leader.* | **affirm, express, proclaim**

PREP. **~ in** ◊ *Her ~ in human nature had been badly shaken.*

PHRASES **an act of ~** | **a lack of ~** | **a leap of ~** ◊ *These reforms are totally untested and will require a leap of ~ on the part of teachers.* | **have every ~ in sb**

2 strong religious belief

ADJ. **religious** | **deep, genuine, strong, true** | **simple** | **unquestioning** | **new-found** ◊ *her new-found ~ in Jesus* | **active** ◊ *a large decline in the number of people who have an active ~ of any sort* | **personal**

VERB + FAITH **have** | **come to, find** ◊ *He found ~ gradually, rather than in a sudden conversion.* | **lack, lose** | **shake, undermine** | **regain** | **strengthen** | **proclaim**

FAITH + NOUN **healer, healing**

PREP. **through ~** ◊ *They believe that people can come to salvation through ~.* | **~ in** ◊ *After her son's death she lost her ~ in God.*

PHRASES **an article of ~** (*often figurative*) ◊ *the team's greatness was an article of ~ for him* (= a belief that could not be questioned).

3 religion

ADJ. **living** ◊ *Christianity is a living ~ which has shaped their history.* | **world** ◊ *The study of other world ~s is an important part of religious education.* | **Catholic, Jewish, Muslim, Sikh, etc.**

VERB + FAITH **profess** | **practise/practice** ◊ *Christians were allowed to practise/practice their ~ unmolested by the authorities.* | **keep alive, uphold** ◊ *Their aim was to keep alive the traditional Jewish ~.* | **pass on, preach, spread, teach** ◊ *the role of parents in passing on the ~ to their children* ◊ *He felt the call to preach the ~ to others.*

FAITH + NOUN **tradition** | **community, group** ◊ *a committee which is made up of members of different ~ groups* | **school** (*BrE*) ◊ *the debate on ~ schools*

PHRASES **people of different ~s**

4 intention to do right

ADJ. **bad, good** ◊ *The judge did not find any bad ~* (= intention to do wrong) *on the part of the defendants.*

VERB + FAITH **break** (= break a promise to sb)

PHRASES **in bad ~** ◊ *Thet had entered into the contract in bad ~.* | **in good ~** ◊ *We printed the report in good ~, but have now learned that it was incorrect.* | **keep ~ with sb** ◊ *As manager, he was not prepared to keep ~ with* (= keep a promise to) *the players who had failed him.* | **keep the ~** ◊ *They kept the ~* (= remained faithful) *in the face of ridicule.*

faithful adj.

1 loyal

VERBS **be** | **remain, stay** ◊ *soldiers who stayed ~ to the king*

ADV. **extremely, very** ◊ *He has been a very ~ friend to me.* | **absolutely, completely, utterly**

PREP. **to** ◊ *He had remained completely ~ to his wife.*

2 accurate

VERBS **be**

ADV. **extremely, fairly, very, etc.** | **remarkably** | **completely, entirely**

PREP. **to** ◊ *The movie is ~ to the original novel.*

fall noun

1 accident

ADJ. **bad, nasty, terrible** ◊ *She took a bad ~ while out riding.* | **accidental**

VERB + FALL **have, suffer, take** ◊ *The doctor says she's had a very nasty ~.* | **break, cushion** ◊ *Luckily a bush broke his ~.* | **survive** ◊ *The chances of surviving a ~ under a train are almost nil.* | **prevent**

PREP. **in a/the ~** ◊ *He was hurt in a ~ at his home yesterday.* | **~ from** ◊ *She broke her neck in a ~ from a horse.*

2 of snow/rocks

ADJ. **heavy** | **light** | **fresh** ◊ *a fresh ~ of snow* | **rock, snow** (usually **snowfall**)

PREP. **~ of** ◊ *covered by a light ~ of volcanic ash*

3 decrease

ADJ. **big, dramatic, great, large, marked, massive, significant, substantial** ◊ *a big ~ in house prices* ◊ *This triggered the recent dramatic ~s on the Tokyo stock exchange.* | **modest, slight, small** | **steady** | **rapid, sharp, steep, sudden** | **unexpected** | **continuing, further** | **overall** (*esp. BrE*) | **catastrophic**

VERB + FALL **bring, cause, contribute to, lead to, trigger** | **see, suffer** ◊ *Share prices suffered a slight ~ yesterday.* | **record, reveal** (*esp. BrE*), **show** ◊ *The opinion polls show a significant ~ in her popularity.* | **report** ◊ *Both companies reported a ~ in profits in the first quarter of this year.* | **represent** (*esp. BrE*) ◊ *This figure represents a ~ of 21% on the same period last year.*

FALL + VERB **occur** ◊ *The ~ in age at first marriage occurred during the second half of the 18th century.*

PREP. **~ in** ◊ *a large ~ in share prices*

4 defeat

VERB + FALL **bring about, cause, contribute to, lead to** ◊ *the actions that led to his eventual ~ from power*

PREP. **~ from**

PHRASES **the rise and ~ of sth** ◊ *a book charting the rise and ~ of the Habsburg Empire*

5 (*AmE*) **autumn**

ADJ. **last, this past** | **the following, next, this, this coming** | **early, late**

FALL + NOUN **weather** | **color** ◊ *The trees were on fire with vibrant ~ colors.* | **foliage** ◊ *New England's gorgeous ~ foliage* | **harvest** | **equinox** | **semester, term** ◊ *He returned to school a month into the ~ semester.*

→ Note at SEASON (for more collocates)

fall verb

1 drop to the ground

ADV. **heavily** ◊ *She fell heavily to the ground.* | **steadily** ◊ *The rain was ~ing steadily.* | **freely** ◊ *Tears fell freely from her eyes.* | **limply** ◊ *Her hands fell limply to her sides.* | **down, off, overboard** ◊ *A tile fell off the roof.* ◊ *He fell overboard in heavy seas.*

VERB + FALL **be about to** | **let sb/sth** ◊ *She lifted her arm, but then let it ~.*

PREP. **from** ◊ *He fell from the fourth floor.* | **into** ◊ *One of the kids fell into the river.* | **on** ◊ *the snow ~ing on the fields* | **onto** ◊ *Loose bricks were ~ing down onto the ground.* | **to** ◊ *The plate fell to the floor.*

2 suddenly stop standing

ADV. **almost, nearly** ◊ *He stumbled and almost fell.* | **headlong** ◊ *She fell headlong, with a cry of alarm.* | **down, over** ◊ *One of the children fell over.* | **backwards/backward, forward**

VERB + FALL **be about to** ◊ *The house looked as if it was about to ~ down.*

PHRASES **stumble and ~, trip and ~**

3 decrease

ADV. **dramatically, rapidly, sharply, significantly, steeply** ◊ *The price of coal fell sharply.* | **slightly** | **steadily**
VERB + FALL **be expected to, be likely to** ◊ *Demand is likely to ~ by some 15%.* | **continue to**
PREP. **below** ◊ *Winter temperatures never ~ below 10°C.* | **by** ◊ *Expenditure on education fell by 10% last year.* | **from** ◊ *The number of people unemployed has fallen from two million to just over one and a half million.* | **to** ◊ *Her voice fell to a whisper.*

4 belong to a group

ADV. **squarely**
PREP. **into** ◊ *Out of over 400 staff there are just 14 that ~ into this category.* | **outside** ◊ *That topic ~s outside the scope of this thesis.* | **under** ◊ *This ~s under the heading of scientific research.* | **within** ◊ *This case ~s squarely within the committee's jurisdiction.*

false adj.

1 not true, genuine or real

VERBS **be, look, prove, sound**
ADV. **absolutely, completely, entirely, quite, totally, utterly** ◊ *The gossip about her later proved to be entirely ~.* | **simply** ◊ *This claim is simply ~.* | **certainly** | **blatantly, clearly, demonstrably, obviously, patently** ◊ *Their claim was patently ~.* | **knowingly** ◊ *The law can punish knowingly ~ statements.*
PHRASES **true or ~** ◊ *Lagos is the capital of Nigeria. True or ~?*

2 not showing your true feelings

VERBS **be, ring, sound** ◊ *Ella's enthusiasm rang ~.*
ADV. **very** | **slightly** ◊ *Helen's voice sounded slightly ~.*

falter verb

ADV. **slightly** | **never** ◊ *His courage never ~ed.* | **momentarily** | **badly** ◊ *The team's performance ~ed badly after the break.*
VERB + FALTER **begin to** ◊ *The economy is beginning to ~.*

fame noun

ADJ. **considerable, great** ◊ *the years of his greatest ~* | **local** | **national** | **international, world, worldwide** ◊ *She gained international ~ as a dancer.* | **lasting** | **fleeting, momentary, temporary** | **instant, sudden** | **new-found** | **posthumous** ◊ *Largely unknown in his lifetime, Mendel's discoveries earned him posthumous ~.*
VERB + FAME **enjoy** ◊ *He was enjoying his new-found ~.* | **achieve, come to, find, gain, rise to, shoot to, win** ◊ *She found ~ on the stage.* ◊ *He shot to ~ in 1997 when he won the US Open.* | **bring sb, earn sb** ◊ *HIs adventure brought him both ~ and notoriety.* | **seek**
FAME + VERB **rest on sth** ◊ *Her ~ rests on a single book.* | **come to sb** ◊ *a man to whom ~ came very late* | **grow, spread** ◊ *The restaurant's ~ spread quickly.*
PHRASES **at the height of sb/sth's ~** ◊ *In 1934, when at the height of his ~, he disappeared.* | **sb/sth's biggest, chief, greatest, main, etc. claim to ~** ◊ *The town's main claim to ~ is being the home of one of the strangest buildings in the world.* | **~ and fortune** ◊ *After this concert she was firmly on the road to ~ and fortune.* | **a/sb's rise to ~**

familiar adj.

1 well-known

VERBS **be, feel, look, seem, smell, sound** ◊ *The place felt faintly ~ to me.* | **become** | **make sth**
ADV. **extremely, fairly, very, etc.** | **awfully** ◊ *His face looked awfully ~.* | **entirely** | **increasingly** | **faintly, reasonably, vaguely** | **enough** ◊ *The report's conclusions were already ~ enough to the government.* | **already** | **immediately, instantly** ◊ *His face was instantly ~, even after all those years.* | **somehow** ◊ *a name that was somehow ~* | **curiously, eerily, oddly, strangely** ◊ *Her face looked strangely ~.* | **comfortingly** ◊ *The kitchen smelled warm and inviting and comfortingly ~.* | **all too, depressingly, hauntingly** (*esp. AmE*), **horribly** (*esp. BrE*), **painfully,**

sickeningly ◊ *a situation which has become all too ~ to most teachers*
PREP. **to** ◊ *The name sounded vaguely ~ to her.*

2 familiar with sth having a good knowledge of sth

VERBS **be, seem** | **become, get, grow** ◊ *I was now getting much more ~ with the local area.*
ADV. **extremely, fairly, very, etc.** | **intimately** | **completely, fully, thoroughly** ◊ *You will need to be thoroughly ~ with our procedures.* | **overly** ◊ *I'm not overly ~ with these issues.* | **increasingly** | **reasonably** | **remotely** ◊ *Anyone even remotely ~ with Germany knows that beer plays a significant role in its culture.* | **already**

familiarity noun

1 knowing sb/sth well

ADJ. **greater, intimate** | **basic, passing** (*esp. AmE*)
VERB + FAMILIARITY **have** ◊ *I had only a basic ~ with computers.* | **acquire, gain** ◊ *Over the years, he gained greater ~ with the culture and way of life in the country.* | **assume** ◊ *The article assumes a basic ~ with the main issues.* | **require** ◊ *60–70% of jobs now require some ~ with IT.*
PREP. **~ with** ◊ *her detailed ~ with her subject*
PHRASES **a lack of ~**

2 friendly informal manner

ADJ. **comfortable** (*esp. AmE*), **easy** ◊ *He treated her with the easy ~ of an equal.*

family noun

1 group of people related to each other

ADJ. **big, large** | **entire, whole** ◊ *a summer movie for the whole ~* | **close, close-knit** ◊ *We are a very close-knit ~ and support each other through any crises.* | **happy, loving, supportive** | **dysfunctional** ◊ *The movie is a portrait of a dysfunctional ~.* | **nuclear, traditional** ◊ *the nuclear ~ of parents and children* | **average** | **immediate** ◊ *We've only told the immediate ~ (= the closest relations).* | **extended** ◊ *It was difficult to maintain contact with members of his extended ~.* | **lone-parent** (*BrE*), **one-parent, single-parent** ◊ *the difficulties faced by one-parent families* | **two-parent** | **adoptive** ◊ *They help find emotionally damaged children placements with adoptive families.* | **real** | **patriarchal** | **military** ◊ *She grew up in a military ~.* | **working** | **middle-class, working-class, etc.** | **low-income, middle-income** | **old** | **aristocratic, imperial, noble, royal** | **powerful, prominent** | **affluent, landowning, rich, wealthy, well-to-do** | **poor** ◊ *tax incentives for low-income families* | **homeless** | **bereaved** ◊ *a helpline set up to counsel bereaved families* | **human** ◊ *the rights of all members of the human ~*
VERB + FAMILY **belong to, be one of, be part of, come from** ◊ *He belonged to an aristocratic ~.* ◊ *We all knew her so well that we felt she was almost part of the ~.* ◊ *Many of our students come from poor families.* | **marry into** ◊ *She married into a wealthy ~.* | **run in** ◊ *a medical condition which runs in the ~* | **be in** ◊ *This painting has been in our ~ for generations.*
FAMILY + NOUN **background, history** ◊ *Do you know anything about her ~ background?* ◊ *a ~ history of heart disease* | **tradition** ◊ *In 1941 he carried on the ~ tradition and enlisted in the army.* | **connections, relationships, ties** ◊ *They prefer to stay in their home country because of ~ ties.* | **group, member** | **friend** | **life** | **business** | **home** | **commitments** ◊ *The job wouldn't really fit in with my ~ commitments.* | **income** | **doctor** (*esp. BrE*), **physician** (*AmE*) | **holiday** (*BrE*), **vacation** (*AmE*) | **feud** | **heirloom** | **motto** | **name** (= surname) | **planning**
PREP. **in a/the ~** ◊ *These problems occur in all families.* | **within a/the ~** ◊ *issues which create conflict within the ~*
PHRASES **~ and friends** ◊ *The support of ~ and friends is vital.* | **a member of a ~**

2 children

ADJ. **large, small** | **young** ◊ *parents with young families*
VERB + FAMILY **have** ◊ *I always wanted to have a large ~.* | **start**

◇ *They got married last year and plan to start a ~ (= have children) soon.* | **bring up, raise** ◇ *It's a struggle to bring up a ~ on a low income.* | **feed, support** ◇ *It is difficult for them to earn enough to feed their families.*
FAMILY + NOUN **size** ◇ *Average ~ size has decreased since the 19th century.* | **man** ◇ *a good ~ man, completely devoted to his wife and kids*

famine *noun*

ADJ. **devastating, great, severe, terrible** | **widespread** | **man-made**
VERB + FAMINE **face, suffer** ◇ *Four million people are now facing ~.* ◇ *countries that regularly suffer ~s* | **survive** | **cause** | **prevent**
FAMINE + VERB **strike** ◇ *When ~ strikes, it is often women and children who suffer the most.*
FAMINE + NOUN **relief** | **victim**
PREP. **during a/the ~** ◇ *Thousands of people died during the terrible ~ of that year.*
PHRASES **a threat of ~**

famous *adj.*

VERBS **be** | **become** | **make sb/sth** ◇ *The school was made ~ by its association with Charles Dickens.*
ADV. **extremely, fairly, very, etc.** | **equally** | **internationally** (also **world-famous**) ◇ *internationally ~ rock stars* | **locally** | **justly, rightly** ◇ *The city is justly ~ for its nightclubs.*
PREP. **as** ◇ *He was ~ as both a teacher and a scientist.* | **for** ◇ *The town became ~ for its lace.*
PHRASES **rich and ~** ◇ *One day I'll be rich and ~, you'll see!*

fan *noun*

1 enjoys watching/listening to sb/sth very much
ADJ. **adoring, ardent, avid, big, dedicated, devoted, great, huge, keen** (*esp. BrE*), **loyal, number-one, real, true** ◇ *I'm a big ~ of Italian food.* ◇ *one of the team's biggest ~s* ◇ *The singer says her dad is her number one ~.* | **lifelong, long-time** | **diehard, hard-core** ◇ *Only diehard Tolkien ~s will enjoy this book.* | **obsessive, rabid** (*humorous, esp. AmE*) ◇ *a film that millions of rabid ~s have waited years to see* ◇ *The actress is asking the court to protect her from an obsessive ~.* | **casual** (*esp. AmE*) | **armchair** (*BrE*) ◇ *For armchair ~s back home, it was one of the highlights of the Olympics.* | **baseball, basketball, cricket, football, racing, rugby, soccer, sports, etc.** | **jazz, music, rock, etc.** | **film** (*esp. BrE*), **movie** (*esp. AmE*) | **home** (*esp. BrE*) ◇ *The goal was greeted by jubilation from the home ~s.* | **away** (*BrE*), **travelling** (*BrE*), **visiting** (*esp. BrE*) | **opposing, opposition** (*BrE*), **rival** (*esp. BrE*) ◇ *There were clashes between opposing ~s after the game.*
VERB + FAN **be, become** ◇ *I'm a big ~ of her music.* | **delight, please, satisfy** ◇ *The big band sound of Syd Lawrence and his Orchestra will delight ~s.* | **attract** | **alienate** | **disappoint, let down** ◇ *Fans will not be disappointed.*
FAN + VERB **flock, gather, turn out, turn up** ◇ *Tennis ~s flocked to Wimbledon.* ◇ *More than 40 000 ~s turned up for the 12-hour event.* | **pack sth, pack into sth** ◇ *Over 120 000 ~s packed into the stadium.* | **line up** (*esp. AmE*), **queue** (*BrE*), **queue up** (*BrE*), **wait** | **watch sth** | **applaud (sb/sth), boo (sb/sth), chant sth, cheer (sb/sth)** ◇ *Over 25 000 ~s applauded both teams off the field.* | **clamour/clamor (for sth)** ◇ *Hundreds of ~s clamoured/clamored to catch a glimpse of the star.*
FAN + NOUN **club, site, website** | **letter, mail** | **fiction** ◇ *I have a piece of ~ fiction on their website.* | **base** ◇ *The show has an extensive and loyal ~ base.*

2 machine that creates a current of air
ADJ. **electric** | **cooling** | **extractor** | **ceiling, overhead**
FAN + VERB **blow** ◇ *a ~ blowing cold air*
FAN + NOUN **belt, blade, heater** (*esp. BrE*)

fanatic *noun*

1 (*informal*) **person who is enthusiastic about sth**
ADJ. **baseball, cricket, football, sports, etc.** ◇ *He's a real football ~.* | **fitness, keep-fit** (*BrE*) | **self-confessed** (*esp. BrE*) ◇ *a self-confessed football ~*
2 person with extreme views
ADJ. **religious** | **right-wing** | **crazed, murderous**
FANATIC + VERB **attack, kill, murder**

fancy dress *noun* (*BrE*) → See also COSTUME

VERB + FANCY DRESS **don, wear** ◇ *Several of the managers donned ~ for the office party.*
FANCY-DRESS + NOUN **ball, party** ◇ *We've been invited to a fancy-dress party.* | **costume** | **shop**
PREP. **in ~** ◇ *Many of the marathon runners compete in ~.*

fanfare *noun*

ADJ. **great** (*often figurative*) ◇ *The new building was opened with great ~ in January 1895.* | **little** (*figurative*) ◇ *The movie was released with little ~ in 2006.* | **trumpet**
VERB + FANFARE **give, play, sound**
FANFARE + VERB **surround sth** (*figurative*) ◇ *It was a bold law but there was a distinct lack of ~ surrounding its passage.*
PHRASES **a ~ of trumpets**

fang *noun*

ADJ. **long** | **sharp** | **white**
VERB + FANG **bare, reveal, show** ◇ *The wolf growled and bared its sharp ~s.* | **sink** ◇ *The snake sank its ~s into its victim.*

fantastic *adj.*

1 very good
VERBS **be, feel, look, smell, sound, taste** ◇ *I felt ~ after my swim.* ◇ *This cake tastes ~.*
ADV. **really, truly, utterly** ◇ *We had really ~ weather in Rio.* | **absolutely, just, pretty, quite** ◇ *The sense of freedom was absolutely ~.*
2 strange
VERBS **be, look, seem, sound**
ADV. **rather** ◇ *It may sound rather ~, but it's the truth.*

fantasy *noun*

ADJ. **mere, pure, sheer, total** ◇ *Most of what they told us was pure ~.* | **ultimate** ◇ *the ultimate human ~: being able to fly* | **utopian** | **wild** ◇ *She dismissed the idea as a wild ~.* | **escapist** | **paranoid** | **violent** | **revenge** ◇ *She was seething with anger and filled with revenge fantasies.* | **personal, private, secret** | **childhood, childish** | **adolescent** | **erotic, romantic, sexual** | **male**
VERB + FANTASY **enjoy, entertain, have, indulge in** ◇ *She didn't entertain silly fantasies about love at first sight.* | **build, create, weave** ◇ *She had woven a whole ~ about living near the coast.* | **feed, feed off, fuel** | **act out** ◇ *Children can act out their fantasies in a secure environment.* | **fulfil/fulfill, indulge, live, live out, play out, satisfy** ◇ *My childhood fantasies were finally fulfilled.* ◇ *He was willing to indulge her wildest fantasies.* ◇ *He was able to play out his ~ of rock stardom.*
FANTASY + NOUN **life** | **land, realm, world** ◇ *You're living in a ~ world.* | **figure** ◇ *children that project their own identities onto ~ figures* | **adventure, book, film, game, genre, movie, novel, story, writer** | **baseball, basketball, football, sports** (*esp. AmE*) | **league, team**
PREP. **~ about** ◇ *She had a ~ about going to live on a South Pacific island.* | **~ of** ◇ *adolescent fantasies of power, glory and recognition*
PHRASES **the realm of ~** (*esp. AmE*), **the realms of ~** (*BrE*) ◇ *The idea belonged in the realms of ~.* | **a world of ~** ◇ *She felt she had entered a world of ~.*

farce *noun* ridiculous situation

ADJ. **complete, total** ◇ *The whole procedure has become a complete ~.*
VERB + FARCE **become, degenerate into, end in, turn into** ◇

The debate degenerated into ~ when opposing speakers started shouting at each other.

fare noun

1 money paid to travel by bus, taxi, etc.

ADJ. **expensive, high | cheap, low | adult** (*esp. BrE*), **full, normal, standard** (*BrE*) **| child's** (*esp. BrE*), **concessionary** (*BrE*), **discounted, half** (*esp. BrE*), **reduced | last-minute, sale, walk-up** (*all AmE*) **| one-way** (*esp. AmE*), **single** (*BrE*) **| return** (*BrE*), **round-trip** (*AmE*) **| first-class, second-class | coach** (= cheapest seats on a plane) (*AmE*) **| air, bus, cab, coach** (= bus) (*BrE*), **ferry** (*esp. BrE*), **rail** (*esp. BrE*), **subway** (*AmE*), **taxi, train, tube** (*BrE*)
VERB + FARE **pay** ◊ *I'm afraid you will have to pay the full ~.* **| charge** ◊ *Buses charged a standard ~ of about 20 pence per mile.* **| increase, put up** (*BrE*), **raise | cut, lower, reduce, slash** ◊ *air ~s slashed by a massive 30%* **| introduce, offer** ◊ *The airline has introduced a cheap ~ to New York.* **| dodge** (*BrE*) ◊ *They caught him trying to dodge bus ~s.*
FARE + VERB **cost (sb) sth** ◊ *The ~ will cost you less if you travel midweek.* **| start at sth, start from sth** ◊ *Last-minute ~s start at $219 each way.* **| range from sth to sth** ◊ *Round-trip ~s range from $118 to $258.* **| go up, increase, rise**
FARE + NOUN **hike** (*esp. AmE*), **increase, rise** (*BrE*) **| structure** ◊ *a simplified ~ structure*
PREP. **at ... ~** ◊ *Children travel at half ~.* (*esp. BrE*)
PHRASES **an increase in ~s, a rise in ~s** (*esp. BrE*) **| a reduction in ~s** ◊ *The company promised reductions in ~s.*

2 passenger in a taxi

VERB + FARE **pick up** ◊ *The taxi driver picked up a ~ outside the opera house.*

3 food; material for listening to, reading, etc.

ADJ. **gourmet, rich | plain, simple | hearty, light** (*esp. AmE*) **| healthy, wholesome** (*esp. AmE*) **| local | vegetarian | English, Italian, Mexican, etc. | Christmas | average, daily, normal, regular** (*esp. AmE*), **standard, staple, traditional, typical, usual** ◊ *Trials involving celebrities are the daily ~ of newspapers.* ◊ *The band's music was standard rock ~.* **| family** ◊ *This movie is perfect family ~.* **| television, TV**
VERB + FARE **offer, serve** ◊ *a restaurant serving traditional Scottish ~* **| sample** ◊ *tourists seeing the sights and sampling the local Mexican ~*

fare verb

ADV. **badly, poorly, well** ◊ *She should ~ better in this competition.* ◊ *This movie ~d poorly at the British box office.* ◊ *He ~d well against his main rival.*

farewell noun

ADJ. **fond | emotional, tearful | sad | silent** ◊ *I said a silent ~ to my home as I left for the city.* **| final, last**
VERB + FAREWELL **bid sb/sth, say, wish sb** ◊ *We bade them a final ~.* **| wave** ◊ *I waved ~ to my friends from the deck of the ship.* **| make** ◊ *The families made their ~s to each other.* **| give sb** ◊ *The team was given an emotional ~ by a crowd of 500 000.* **| exchange** ◊ *They exchanged fond ~s at the station.* **| be** ◊ *Is this ~ or will we see each other again?*
FAREWELL + NOUN **appearance** ◊ *This famous warplane is about to make its ~ appearance.* **| address, speech | ceremony, concert, performance, tour** ◊ *the band's ~ tour* **| dinner, party | gift, present | letter, note** ◊ *a ~ letter to my family* **| kiss** ◊ *Let me give her a ~ kiss.*
PREP. **in ~** ◊ *He raised his hand in ~.* **| ~ to** ◊ *She was sorry to bid ~ to Portugal.*

farm noun

ADJ. **big, large | little, small | 100-acre, 200-hectare, etc. | local, nearby, neighbouring/neighboring, surrounding | isolated, outlying, remote | hill** (*BrE*) **| family, home | conventional, traditional | private | collective, cooperative | commercial, corporate** (*AmE*) **| state | factory, industrial** (*esp. AmE*), **intensive** (*esp. BrE*) **| experimental, research** (*esp. AmE*) **| model** ◊ *Ten model ~s have been set up to showcase modern production methods.* **| working** ◊ *The area combines a working ~ and a farming museum.* **|**

organic | arable (*BrE*), **livestock, mixed | breeding** (*esp. AmE*), **horse** (*esp. AmE*), **stud** (*esp. BrE*) **| chicken, coffee** (*esp. AmE*), **dairy, fish, fruit, hog** (*AmE*), **pig, poultry, sheep, shrimp** (*esp. AmE*), **tree** (*esp. AmE*), **trout, turkey, etc. | truck** (*AmE*) **| wind** ◊ *controversial plans to build a wind ~ on the island*
VERB + FARM **have, own | manage, operate, run | work, work at, work on** ◊ *During the war, few men were left to work the ~.* ◊ *The children had to work on the family ~.* **| build, establish, set up, start | live on | be raised on** (*esp. AmE*), **be reared on** ◊ *I was raised on a country ~.* ◊ *The pigs are raised on factory ~s.* (*esp. AmE*) **| inherit | visit**
FARM + VERB **be located, lie** ◊ *The ~ lies on the hills above the lake.* **| grow sth, produce sth** ◊ *a ~ growing tobacco* ◊ *a dairy ~ producing gourmet cheeses* **| operate** ◊ *The 80-acre ~ now operates around the clock.*
FARM + NOUN **produce, product** ◊ *Farm produce, including fruit and corn, was their principal export.* ◊ *~ products such as eggs and vegetables* **| animal | labourer/laborer, worker | labour/labor | chore** (*esp. AmE*), **work | manager, owner | management | field** (*esp. AmE*), **land** (usually **farmland**) **| building | equipment, implements, machinery, tractor | policy** (*esp. AmE*) **| bill** ◊ *Republicans hope to pass the ~ bill in the current fiscal year.* **| program** (*AmE*) ◊ *the US ~ program for wheat* **| subsidies** ◊ *The EU has decided to cut ~ subsidies.* **| exports, production** (both *esp. AmE*) ◊ *We anticipate our overall ~ production next year to be lower.* **| income** ◊ *Farm incomes rose 11% last year.* **| economy** (*AmE*), **sector** (*esp. AmE*) ◊ *The ~ economy was stable.* ◊ *Today, the ~ sector employs about 3% of our workforce.* **| life** ◊ *village and ~ life* **| boy, girl, kid** (*informal, esp. AmE*) **| family, household** (both *esp. AmE*) ◊ *a poor ~ family* **| cottage** (*BrE*), **house** (usually **farmhouse**) **| shop** (*BrE*), **stand** (*AmE*), **store** (*AmE*) ◊ *The farmer's wife runs the ~ shop.* ◊ *Bo was working the ~ stand.* **| supply store** (*AmE*) ◊ *Local ~ supply stores are expected to lose business.* **| community, country, state, town** (*all AmE*) ◊ *the rolling ~ country of central Kentucky* ◊ *an Illinois ~ town* **| belt** (*AmE*) ◊ *the Kansas ~ belt* **| road, track** (*esp. BrE*)
PREP. **at a/the ~** ◊ *The police are investigating a fire at a nearby ~.* **| down on the ~** ◊ *The myth of happy animals down on the ~ is now far from the truth.* **| on a/the ~** ◊ *He had lived on that ~ all his life.*

farm verb

ADV. **heavily, intensively** ◊ *The land has been intensively ~ed.* **| organically** ◊ *They ~ organically now.*

farmer noun

ADJ. **big, large, large-scale | small, small-scale** ◊ *a new plan to help the small ~* **| peasant, tenant | poor, subsistence** ◊ *Settlers were primarily subsistence ~s.* **| rich, successful, wealthy | gentleman, yeoman** ◊ *Jefferson's ideal of a nation of yeoman ~s* **| family** (*esp. AmE*) **| independent | commercial | hill** (*BrE*) **| rural | local, neighbouring/ neighboring | organic | conventional** ◊ *A lot of conventional ~s have converted to organic.* **| arable** (*BrE*), **grain** (*AmE*) **| livestock | dairy | cattle, chicken, fish, hog** (*AmE*), **pig, poultry, sheep, etc. | coffee, corn, cotton, peanut, potato, rice, soya bean** (*BrE*), **soybean** (*AmE*), **tobacco, wheat, etc. | truck** (*AmE*)

farming noun

ADJ. **small-scale** ◊ *They lived by fishing and by basic small-scale ~.* **| family** ◊ *the decline of traditional family ~ | subsistence | hill** (*BrE*) **| conventional, traditional | modern | commercial, corporate** (*AmE*) **| battery** (*BrE*), **factory, industrial** (*esp. AmE*), **intensive | organic, sustainable | arable** (*BrE*), **livestock, mixed | dairy | fish, poultry, sheep, etc.**
VERB + FARMING **be engaged in, work in**
FARMING + NOUN **community | industry, sector | business, operation** (*esp. AmE*) ◊ *a ~ operation where sheep are raised*

| method, practice, system, technique | land | area, town, village | family

fascinating adj.

VERBS **be, look, prove, sound** ◇ *His testimony in court could prove ~.* | **become** | **seem** ◇ *It just seemed really ~ to me.* | **make sth** | **find sth**

ADV. **deeply, especially, incredibly, most** (*esp. BrE*), **particularly, really, terribly** (*esp. BrE*), **truly, very** ◇ *a most ~ book* ◇ *'This is all very ~,' said Wilcox, 'but I have a meeting in five minutes.'* | **absolutely, quite, utterly** | **pretty, rather** ◇ *I find him rather ~.* | **endlessly** ◇ *I find the natural world endlessly ~.* | **oddly, strangely** | **equally** ◇ *Renoir's later life is equally ~.*

PREP. **to** ◇ *What was ~ to me was the way the creatures moved.*

fascination noun

ADJ. **deep, great** | **particular, peculiar, special** | **certain** ◇ *These two artists share a certain ~ with the female body.* | **growing** | **continuing, endless, enduring, lifelong, long-standing, ongoing, perennial** | **current** ◇ *our current ~ with nationalism* | **horrified** ◇ *I watched in horrified ~.* | **morbid, strange, unhealthy** ◇ *a morbid ~ with death* | **public** ◇ *the public ~ with crime*

VERB + FASCINATION **have, hold** ◇ *The sea holds a ~ for all children.* | **develop, feel, find, have** ◇ *He had a deep ~ with all types of train.* | **exert** ◇ *These exotic plants exert a ~ all of their own.* | **share** ◇ *She shared his ~ for motorcycles.*

PREP. **in ~, with ~** ◇ *She watched in ~ as the cat pounced on the mouse.* ◇ *He looked on in horrified ~ as the ship drew nearer to the rocks.* | **~ for** ◇ *She developed a ~ for these creatures.* | **~ in** ◇ *He found great ~ in her quiet, frank manner.* | **~ with** ◇ *a lifelong ~ with music*

PHRASES **part of the ~** ◇ *Seeing over a thousand species of fish is part of the ~ of the reef.* | **a source of ~ for sb, a source of ~ to sb** ◇ *His letters have been a source of ~ to a wide audience.*

fashion noun

1 style of dressing, etc. popular at a particular time

ADJ. **contemporary, current, latest, modern, new** | **changing, passing** ◇ *changing ~s in education* ◇ *This theory, though recent, is more than a passing ~.* | **high** ◇ *The store sells everything from casual clothes to high ~.* | **classic** ◇ *classic ~s for your wardrobe* | **designer** ◇ *the influence of Italian designer ~ on the industry* | **popular** ◇ *the popular ~s of the day* | **autumn** (*esp. BrE*), **fall** (*AmE*), **spring, summer, winter** ◇ *The new summer ~s have arrived.* | **French, Italian** ◇ *a passion for French ~s and goods* | **female, male, street, youth** | **architectural, cultural, intellectual, literary**

VERB + FASHION **be, be in** ◇ *She wore a wig, as was the ~ of the day.* ◇ *Black is always in ~.* | **become, come into** ◇ *Pessimism has become the ~.* ◇ *When did flares first come into ~?* | **fall out of, go out of** ◇ *Careful spending has gone out of ~ in our consumer society.* | **be out of** | **come back into** | **be back in** | **set, start** ◇ *He set a ~ for large hats.* | **follow, keep up with** ◇ *I've given up trying to keep up with the latest ~s.* | **wear** ◇ *She always wore the latest ~s.* | **love** ◇ *She loves ~ and make-up.*

FASHION + VERB **change** ◇ *The book traces how ~s have changed over the years.*

FASHION + NOUN **statement** ◇ *Flares were a ~ statement of the seventies.* | **trend** ◇ *the latest ~ trend* | **model** ◇ *She started her career as a ~ model.* | **show** | **shoot** ◇ *photographers at ~ shoots* | **magazine** | **plate** (*esp. AmE*), **spread** ◇ *She looked like a ~ plate.* ◇ *a magazine ~ spread* | **scene** ◇ *fresh interest in the New York ~ scene* | **capital** ◇ *Paris, the world's ~ capital* | **runway** (*AmE*) ◇ *the ~ runways of Italy and France* | **business, industry, market, trade, world** ◇ *Her summer collection took the ~ world by storm.* | **brand, company, house, label, line** ◇ *one of the most successful ~ houses in Milan* ◇ *I've started my own ~ line.* | **retailer, shop** (*BrE*), **store** | **design, photography** | **designer, director, editor, photographer, stylist, writer** | **consultant, expert, guru,**

maven (*AmE*) ◇ *the world's top ~ experts* | **icon** ◇ *She was respected as a ~ icon.* | **sense** ◇ *She had no ~ sense whatsoever.* | **advice, tip** ◇ *I need your expert ~ advice.* | **accessory, item** | **victim** ◇ *this season's must-have accessories that no ~ victim will be seen without* | **disaster** ◇ *What were your worst ~ disasters?* | **police** (*humorous*) ◇ *Somebody call the ~ police, please!*

PREP. **after the ~ of** ◇ *She spoke in French after (= copying) the ~ of the court.* | **~ for** ◇ *the ~ for long dresses* | **~ in** ◇ *Fashions in art come and go.*

PHRASES **changes in ~** | **the ~ of the day** | **the height of ~** ◇ *The palazzo represents the height of architectural ~ for the mid-17th century.* | **the world of ~** ◇ *household names in the world of ~ and design*

2 way you do sth

ADJ. **true ...** ◇ *He insisted the meeting be held, in true spy novel ~, in the open air.* | **normal, standard, usual** ◇ *Application for the course can be made in the normal ~.* | **conventional, time-honoured/time-honored, traditional** ◇ *They celebrated their win in traditional ~ by spraying champagne everywhere.* | **proper** ◇ *Address me in a proper ~.* | **characteristic, classic, typical** ◇ *He delivered his speech in classic ~.* ◇ *We had just gone out when, in typical ~, the rain came down.* | **identical, same, similar** ◇ *Each chapter is structured in a similar ~.* | **different** ◇ *Light and sound are recorded in such different ~s.* | **limited** ◇ *He has a small vocabulary and is only able to express himself in a limited ~.* | **negative, positive** ◇ *when people confront you in a negative ~* | **no uncertain** (*esp. BrE*) ◇ *Karpov struck back in no uncertain ~ to win the seventh game.* | **meaningful** | **best** (*often ironic*), **exemplary, fine, impressive** ◇ *'Like hell they are!' he replies in best John Wayne ~.* ◇ *She has corrected that oversight in fine ~.* | **appropriate** | **cavalier** | **coherent, consistent, controlled, orderly, organized, regular, systematic** ◇ *We need to tackle this problem in a coordinated ~.* | **ad hoc, desultory, haphazard, piecemeal, random, roundabout** | **arbitrary** | **direct, honest, straightforward** ◇ *He asked questions in a direct ~.* | **serious** ◇ *She writes in a serious ~ about the future* | **deliberate** ◇ *They act in a purposeful and deliberate ~.* | **leisurely, relaxed** ◇ *She was strolling in a leisurely ~ in the opposite direction.* | **logical, predictable** | **convincing** ◇ *She laid out her argument in a convincing ~.* | **circular, linear** ◇ *The story moves in circular ~.* ◇ *Costs and revenues are assumed to behave in a linear ~.* | **timely** ◇ *I strive to get my work done in a timely ~.* | **dramatic, spectacular** | **grand** ◇ *slowly descending the stairs in a grand ~* | **bizarre, curious, odd, peculiar, strange** | **mysterious** | **friendly** | **entertaining** ◇ *He presents it in an entertaining ~.* | **businesslike** | **democratic**

VERB + FASHION **act in, behave in** | **proceed in** ◇ *Please proceed in an orderly ~ to the promenade deck.* ◇ *The convention proceeded in the normal ~.*

PREP. **after a ~** ◇ *So they became friends, after a ~ (= to some extent).* | **in a ~** ◇ *Why are they behaving in such a ridiculous ~?* ◇ *The troops embarked in an orderly ~.*

fashionable adj.

VERBS **be, look** | **become** | **remain** | **make sth** | **consider sth**

ADV. **extremely, highly, very** ◇ *Furnishings of this sort are now highly ~.* | **increasingly** | **quite, rather** | **currently** | **newly** | **suddenly** ◇ *a young and suddenly ~ actor* | **no longer**

PREP. **among** ◇ *These cars are no longer ~ among the young.*

fast noun

ADJ. **long**

VERB + FAST **go on, keep, observe** ◇ *All members of the religious community keep these ~s.* | **break** ◇ *In the evening the people break their ~.*

fast adj., adv.

VERBS **be, seem** ◇ *Her pulse seemed very ~.*

ADV. **extremely, fairly, very, etc.** ◇ *I suppose delivery in two days is pretty ~, really.* ◇ *I should make a very ~ profit on these.* | **awfully, exceptionally, particularly, remarkably,** surprisingly | reasonably, relatively | a little, slightly, etc. | amazingly, blazingly, blindingly, impossibly, incredibly, unbelievably, unusually ◊ *He came around the corner blindingly ~.* | **dangerously**

fasten *verb*

ADV. **firmly, properly, securely, tightly** ◊ *We ~ed all the windows securely.* | **up** | **together** ◊ *She ~ed the papers together with a paper clip.*

PREP. **to** ◊ *She ~ed the rope to a tree.*

fat *noun*

1 substance directly under your skin

ADJ. **excess, extra, stored** ◊ *Are you carrying extra ~ around your middle?* | **body** | **baby** (*AmE*), **puppy** (*BrE*) ◊ *He had lost all his baby ~/puppy ~.*

VERB + FAT **gain, put on** ◊ *If you eat too much you will put on ~.* | **go to, run to** ◊ *She was middle-aged and running to ~.* | **burn, burn off, lose, shed** ◊ *Exercise helps you burn off excess ~.* | **store** ◊ *the amount of ~ stored in the body* | **break down** ◊ *Claims that anti-cellulite creams can break down ~ are controversial.*

FAT + VERB **accumulate** ◊ *The waistline is usually the first area where ~ accumulates.*

PHRASES **not an ounce of ~** ◊ *His body was all muscle, with not an ounce of ~.* | **a roll of ~** ◊ *He had great rolls of ~ around his middle.*

2 in your diet/used in cooking

ADJ. **dietary** | **added, excess, extra** | **reduced** ◊ *a reduced-fat diet* | **high** | **visible** | **total** ◊ *Eat a diet low in total ~.* | **healthful** (*AmE*), **healthy, unhealthy** ◊ *the best wholefood sources of healthy ~s* | **animal, vegetable** | **hydrogenated, monounsaturated, polyunsaturated, saturated, trans, unsaturated** ◊ *margarines that contain polyunsaturated ~s* | **cooking** | **bacon, beef, duck, pork, etc.** | **rendered** ◊ *rendered bacon ~* | **hot** ◊ *Put the chicken in hot ~ and braise thoroughly.*

VERB + FAT **contain, have** ◊ *This cheese has a lot of ~ in it.* | **be high in ~, be low in ~** ◊ *Ice cream is high in ~ and sugar.* | **consume, eat** ◊ *The amount of ~ you eat can affect the health of your heart.* | **cut down on, reduce** ◊ *It's easy to cut down on ~ without changing your diet too much.* ◊ *Reduce saturated ~s in your diet.* | **avoid, cut out, eliminate** ◊ *Avoid excess saturated ~s as found in meat, poultry, and eggs.* ◊ *She has cut out ~ altogether in an effort to lose weight.* | **cut, remove, trim** ◊ *Trim any visible ~ off the meat before cooking.* | **drain, drain off, pour off, skim off** ◊ *Remove the turkey from the pan and drain off the excess ~.* | **add** ◊ *Add the remaining duck ~ and chicken stock and bring to a boil.*

FAT + VERB **contain sth** ◊ *Fats contain more calories than carbohydrates.*

FAT + NOUN **intake** ◊ *the relationship between ~ intake and cholesterol levels* | **content** ◊ *Despite its very low ~ content, it is deliciously creamy.*

fat *adj.*

VERBS **be, feel, look** | **become, get, grow** | **make sb** ◊ *Try to cut out the foods that are making you ~.* | **call sb** ◊ *Are you calling me ~?*

ADV. **enormously, hugely, immensely, really, very** | **quite, rather**

PHRASES **big ~** ◊ *I was sitting next to a big ~ man.* ◊ *a big ~ envelope stuffed with money*

fatal *adj.*

1 causing death

VERBS **be, prove**

ADV. **nearly** (*esp. AmE*) ◊ *He has not driven since his nearly ~ accident earlier this year.* (**near-fatal** in *BrE*) | **always, invariably** | **often, sometimes, usually** | **rarely** | **possibly, potentially** ◊ *a possibly ~ setback to his plans* ◊ *The disease is potentially ~.*

PREP. **for** ◊ *This kind of accident is almost always ~ for the pilot.* | **to** ◊ *a chemical which is invariably ~ to small mammals*

2 causing serious trouble

VERBS **be, prove**

ADV. **absolutely** | **ultimately** ◊ *Her disregard of this advice was ultimately ~.*

PREP. **to** ◊ *Tax increases have proved ~ to the nation's business community.*

fate *noun*

1 sb/sth's future

ADJ. **awful, grim, horrible, terrible** | **cruel, unhappy** ◊ *What an unfortunate ~ the gods had condemned her to.* | **sad, tragic** | **better, worse** ◊ *Jackson deserves a better ~ than this.* ◊ *They decided to kill themselves rather than suffer a worse ~ at the hands of their enemy.* | **common, usual** | **likely** ◊ *Under-representation is the likely ~ of small parties.* | **eventual, final, ultimate** | **inevitable** ◊ *the almost inevitable ~ awaiting gorillas and tigers* | **uncertain, unknown** ◊ *She faces an uncertain ~.* ◊ *The ultimate ~ of the captured troops is unknown.* | **the same, similar** ◊ *She broke her ankle before the big game, then suffered the same ~ a month later.* | **different** ◊ *His brother met an altogether different ~.* | **economic, political** ◊ *They're worried about their political ~.*

VERB + FATE **face** ◊ *He faces a grim ~ if he is sent back to his own country.* | **meet, suffer, undergo** | **share** ◊ *He had no desire to share the ~ of his executed comrades.* | **avoid, be spared, escape** ◊ *Fortunately, Robert was spared this cruel ~.* ◊ *She managed to escape the ~ of the other rebels.* | **deserve** ◊ *What had he done to deserve such a terrible ~?* | **accept, be resigned to** ◊ *The condemned men were resigned to their ~.* | **bemoan, curse, lament** ◊ *Instead of just bemoaning your ~, why not do something to change it?* | **contemplate, ponder** | **control** ◊ *She has taken steps to control her own ~.* | **choose** ◊ *the rights of a woman to choose the ~ of her body* | **seal** ◊ *He had signed his confession and sealed his own ~.* | **decide, determine** ◊ *An extraordinary general meeting to decide the company's ~ will be held on Thursday.* | **affect, alter, change, influence** ◊ *Will it change the ~ of the company?* | **abandon sb/sth to, leave sb/sth to** ◊ *The generals abandoned the men to their ~.* | **rescue sb/sth from, save sb/sth from** | **discover, hear, hear of, know, know of, learn, learn of** ◊ *He will learn his ~ in court tomorrow.* | **predict** ◊ *the prophet who predicts ~ and can see the future* | **await** ◊ *The convicts awaited their ~ in prison.*

FATE + VERB **await sb/sth, be in store for sb/sth, lie in store for sb/sth** ◊ *They were warned of the dreadful ~ that awaited them if ever they returned to their homes.* | **befall sb/sth** ◊ *Worst of all was the ~ that befell the captured rebel general.* | **be in the balance, hang in the balance** ◊ *The ~ of the African wild dog hangs in the balance* (= is uncertain). | **be tied to sth** ◊ *Our ~ is tied to yours.* | **depend on sth** ◊ *This team's ~ depends on how it performs today.*

PHRASES **leave your ~ in sb's hands, place your ~ in sb's hands, put your ~ in sb's hands** | **have sb/sth's ~ in your hands, hold sb/sth's ~ in your hands** ◊ *The jury held the ~ of the accused in their hands.* | **a ~ worse than death** (*often humorous*) ◊ *Getting married seemed a ~ worse than death.* | **sb's ~ rests in sb's hands** ◊ *His ~ rests in the hands of the judges.*

2 power controlling everything

ADJ. **cruel** ◊ *He believed that the universe was controlled by the whims of a cruel ~.* | **kind** ◊ *Fate was kind to me.*

VERB + FATE **believe in** ◊ *Such coincidences are almost enough to make one believe in ~.* | **tempt** ◊ *It would be tempting ~ to say that we will definitely win the game.* | **leave sth to** ◊ *I have a great deal of trust and I leave everything to ~.*

FATE + VERB **decide sth, decree sth** ◊ *Fate decreed that she would never reach America.* | **intervene** ◊ *He secretly hoped that ~ would intervene and save him having to meet her.* | **strike** ◊ *Only weeks later ~ struck again, leaving her unable to compete.* | **deal a/its hand, deal sb a hand** ◊ *Anne accepted the cruel hand that ~ had dealt her.* | **take a hand** ◊

Fate took a hand in (= influenced) *the outcome of the championship.* | **have in store for sb/sth, hold in store for sb/sth** ◇ *Little did she know what ~ had in store for her.* | **conspire against sb** ◇ *For some reason ~ conspired against them and everything they did was problematic.* | **smile on sb, smile upon sb** ◇ *Fate was not smiling upon her today.*
PHRASES **an accident of ~, a turn of ~, a twist of ~** ◇ *It seemed a cruel twist of ~ that the composer should have died so young.* | **let ~ take its course** ◇ *He was content standing aside, letting ~ take its course.* | **the hand of ~** ◇ *The new job had come at just the right time for him. Was it the hand of ~?*

father noun

ADJ. **lone** (*esp. BrE*), **single** ◇ *As a single ~, he found it a struggle bringing up three children.* | **married, unmarried** | *a married ~ of two* | **divorced** | **widowed** | **absent, absentee, estranged** | **long-lost** ◇ *Ryan has gone looking for his long-lost ~.* | **biological, natural, real, true** | **adoptive, foster** | **second, surrogate** ◇ *I always thought of you as a second ~.* ◇ *Elena's brother was a surrogate ~ to her kids after her husband died.* | **expectant** ◇ *He paced like an expectant ~.* | **new** ◇ *Meet your new ~.* ◇ *The new ~ took his son into his arms.* | **doting, proud** ◇ *He has just become the proud ~ of a baby girl.* | **young** | **ageing/aging, elderly, old** | **ailing, dying, sick** ◇ *He has an ailing ~ and two younger brothers to support.* | **dead, deceased, late** | **grieving** ◇ *the grieving ~ of two children lost at sea* | **caring, devoted, good, great, loving, responsible, wonderful** ◇ *He is very good with children and would make a devoted ~.* ◇ *He was a wonderful ~ to her.* | **beloved, dear** ◇ *She kept the books that had belonged to her beloved ~.* | **bad** ◇ *He was both a bad husband and a bad ~.* | **distant** ◇ *He had a domineering mother and a cold, distant ~.* | **domineering, overbearing, overprotective, strict** | **abusive, alcoholic, drunken, violent** | **famous** ◇ *He followed the footsteps of his famous ~ into the film industry.* | **doctor, engineer, immigrant, etc.** ◇ *Their musician ~ encouraged their love of music.*
VERB + FATHER **resemble, take after** ◇ *The two boys were like their mother in character, but Louise took after her ~.* | **follow, succeed** ◇ *She followed her ~ into the legal profession.* ◇ *He succeeded his ~ as Professor of Botany.* | **inherit sth from** ◇ *She inherited the urge to travel from her ~.* | **honour/honor, love, obey, respect** ◇ *Try your best to honour your ~.* | **lose** ◇ *I lost my ~ when I was nine.* | **bury** ◇ *I buried my ~, and mourned his death.*
FATHER + NOUN **figure** ◇ *Some of his students regard him as a ~ figure.*
PHRASES **a ~ of two, etc.** ◇ *Smith, a ~ of two, was arrested on charges of theft.* | **~ to sb** ◇ *Jesse is now married and ~ to a young son.* | **follow in your father's footsteps** ◇ *He followed in his father's footsteps and became a motor mechanic.* | **from ~ to son** ◇ *The land passes on from ~ to son.* | **the death of your ~, the loss of your ~**

fatigue noun

1 great tiredness

ADJ. **extreme, severe** ◇ *swimmers who are in a state of extreme ~* | **growing** | **chronic** ◇ *conditions such as chronic ~, insomnia and depression* | **general** | **mental, physical** | **muscle** ◇ *Correcting your posture prevents muscle ~ and injury.* | **battle** ◇ *soldiers suffering from battle ~* | **compassion** ◇ *Compassion ~ among donor countries means there is less money for worthy causes.* | **driver** ◇ *car accidents caused by driver ~*
VERB + FATIGUE **experience, feel, suffer from** ◇ *Tom began to feel ~ and weakness once more.* | **combat, fight, fight off, reduce** ◇ *The right vitamins help you combat ~.* | **avoid, prevent** ◇ *simple lifestyle strategies to prevent ~* | **cause**
FATIGUE + VERB **set in** ◇ *She had to stop work when ~ set in.* | **overcome sb**
PREP. **from ~** ◇ *He was crying from cold and ~.* | **with ~** ◇ *The man was shivering with ~.*
PHRASES **a feeling of ~** | **signs of ~**

2 fatigues clothes worn by soldiers

ADJ. **army, battle, combat, military** | **camouflage**
PHRASES **in ~** ◇ *soldiers in combat ~s*
→ Special page at CLOTHES

faucet noun (AmE) → See also TAP

ADJ. **water** | **cold-water, hot-water** | **dripping, leaky** ◇ *She repaired a leaky ~.* | **bathtub, sink** | **bathroom, kitchen, outdoor** | **brass, chrome, etc.**
VERB + FAUCET **open, turn on** ◇ *She turned the sink ~ on.* | **turn off** | **fix, repair** | **install**
FAUCET + VERB **drip, leak** ◇ *Is the ~ dripping again?*
FAUCET + NOUN **handle, spout**
PREP. **from ~** ◇ *the water from a ~* | **under ~** ◇ *He stuck his head under the ~.*

fault noun

1 responsibility for sth wrong

ADJ. **stupid** ◇ *It's his own stupid ~ his car was stolen—he should have kept it locked.* | **entire** ◇ *It was my entire ~. I ruined everything.*
FAULT + VERB **lie with sb** ◇ *The ~ lay not with her but with her manager.*
PREP. **at ~** ◇ *The party at ~ in a court case usually pays the other party's legal costs.* | **through sb's ~** ◇ *Many of the soldiers died through his ~.* | **without ~** ◇ *Having made an error of judgement she was not without ~ in the matter.*
PHRASES **be all sb's ~, be entirely sb's ~** ◇ *It's all your own ~, you know.* | **be largely sb's ~, be partly sb's ~** | **~ on sb's part** (*law*) ◇ *the absence of ~ on the part of the prosecution* | **through no ~ of your own** ◇ *people who, through no ~ of their own, have lost their homes*

2 weakness in sb's character

ADJ. **big, great** ◇ *Her great ~ was that she thought too much of herself.* ◇ *My biggest ~ was my laziness.* | **moral** | **personal**
VERB + FAULT **have** ◇ *We all have our ~s.* | **be blind to, overlook** ◇ *He is blind to his son's ~s.* ◇ *She was prepared to overlook his ~s.* | **point out** ◇ *No one had ever pointed out my ~s to my face before.* | **accept, acknowledge, admit, admit to, realize, see** ◇ *At least he admits to his ~s.* ◇ *I have to accept and realize my ~s.*
PREP. **~ in** ◇ *Incorrectness in speech was considered a great ~ in a gentleman.*
PHRASES **for all sb's ~s** ◇ *For all her ~s (= in spite of her faults) she was a great woman.* | **to a ~** ◇ *He is generous to a ~ (= perhaps too generous).*

3 sth wrong or not perfect with sth

ADJ. **major, minor** | **dangerous, serious** | **common** ◇ *a common ~ with this type of machine* | **glaring, obvious** ◇ *These are just a few of the glaring ~s that ruined the movie for me.* | **real** ◇ *The only real ~ of the book is its looseness of structure.* | **possible** | **design, electrical, mechanical, structural, technical** (*all esp. BrE*) ◇ *Of course, minor mechanical ~s sometimes occur.*
VERB + FAULT **have** ◇ *The engine has a serious ~.* | **develop** ◇ *The car soon developed another ~.* | **look for** | **detect, diagnose, discover, find, identify, locate** ◇ *They've found a major ~ with the electrical system.* ◇ *When she tested the recorder she could find no ~ with it.* | **find, pick** (*BrE*) ◇ *My mother did nothing but find ~ with my manners.* ◇ *He's deliberately picking ~ with the meal to get a reduction on the bill.* | **correct, fix, rectify** (*esp. BrE*), **repair** ◇ *We're trying to correct the ~s in the program.* | **report** (*esp. BrE*) ◇ *You should report any ~ directly to the phone company.*
FAULT + VERB **occur** | **lie in sth** ◇ *The ~ lay in the structure of the economy.*
PREP. **~ in** ◇ *Diabetes is caused by a ~ in the insulin production of the body.* | **~ with** ◇ *She was always finding ~ with his manners.*
PHRASES **for all its ~s** ◇ *For all its ~s (= in spite of the faults), we love this city.*

4 in tennis

ADJ. **double** | **foot**
VERB + FAULT **serve** ◇ *Even tennis champions sometimes serve double ~s.*

ADJ. **earthquake, geological**
FAULT + NOUN **line** | **scarp** | **system, zone**

favour (BrE) (AmE favor) noun

1 sth that helps sb

ADJ. **big, great, huge** | **little, small** | **special** | **personal** ◇ *As a personal ~ to me, please don't release my story to the press.* | **last** ◇ *She had one last ~ to ask her brother.* | **political, sexual**
VERB + FAVOUR/FAVOR **ask** ◇ *I came here to ask you a big ~.* | **expect** ◇ *I don't expect any ~s from my friends on the tennis court.* | **bestow, do, grant sb** ◇ *Rodrigo accepted the ~s bestowed on him by the new king.* | *Do yourself a ~ and cut your credit cards in half.* | **owe sb** ◇ *I'll ask Jane. She owes me a ~.* | **repay, return** ◇ *Thanks very much. I'll return the ~ one day.* | **seek** | **need** ◇ *He needed another ~ from her.* | **get, obtain** | **accept, receive**

2 approval or support for sb/sth

ADJ. **good, great, high, particular** ◇ *Traditionally, vigilante groups have found greater ~ on the political right.* | **divine, government, political, royal** | **public** ◇ *This did not meet with public ~.*
VERB + FAVOUR/FAVOR **be in, enjoy, have** | **find, gain, win** ◇ *Her political views have not found ~ in recent years.* | **court, curry, seek** ◇ *He tried to curry ~ with the teachers.* ◇ *Artists sought the ~ of wealthy patrons.* | **show** ◇ *As an examiner, she showed no ~ to any candidate.* | **be out of** | **fall from, fall out of, lose** ◇ *The senior officials were punished and rapidly fell from ~.* ◇ *This idea has long since fallen out of ~.* | **be back in, bring sth back into, come back into** ◇ *A style of art can go out of fashion and then come back into ~ fifty years later.* | **argue in, speak in** ◇ *She argued in ~ of this policy.* | **speak out in** ◇ *No one was willing to speak out in ~ of their colleague.* | **come down in, come out in, decide in, find in, resolve in, rule in, vote in** ◇ *The committee came down in ~ of setting up a national body.* ◇ *The court found in ~ of the plaintiffs.* | **work in** ◇ *Environmental conservation generally works in ~ of maintaining the status quo.* | **go in** ◇ *The golf tournament went in the Americans' ~* (= they won).
PREP. **in ~ of** ◇ *He is strongly in ~ of capital punishment.* ◇ *Early in his musical career he abandoned blues in ~ of jazz.* | **in sb's/sth's ~** ◇ *This piece of software has two points in its ~: it's fast and inexpensive.* | **~ among** ◇ *This argument found ~ among advocates of multiculturalism.* | **~ with** ◇ *She is too popular with the public to find much ~ with the critics.*
PHRASES **an argument in sb's/sth's ~** ◇ *an argument in ~ of censorship* | **a bias in sb/sth's ~** | **look with ~ on sb/sth, look with ~ upon sb/sth** ◇ *Depth of training is looked upon with ~ by many employers.* | **without fear or ~** (= in a fair way)

favour (BrE) (AmE favor) verb

ADV. **greatly, heavily, overwhelmingly, strongly** ◇ *We strongly ~ reform of the system.* | **especially, particularly** ◇ *Haitians especially ~ seafoods.* | **clearly** | **increasingly** ◇ *Pot plants are increasingly ~ed as gifts by guests.* | **slightly** ◇ *The polls slightly ~ the Republicans.* | **consistently** | **personally** ◇ *I personally ~ this last option.* | **traditionally**
VERB + FAVOUR/FAVOR **appear to, be known to, be likely to, be thought to, seem to, tend to** ◇ *The prime minister is thought to ~ an early referendum on the issue.* | **continue to** ◇ *She continues to ~ large-scale developments.*
PREP. **at the expense of** ◇ *He ~ed some individuals at the expense of others.* | **for** ◇ *The Democrat candidate is ~ed for re-election.* | **over** ◇ *News coverage should not ~ one party over another.*

favourable (BrE) (AmE favorable) adj.

VERBS **be, look, seem** | **become** | **remain** | **consider sth** ◇ *terms that could hardly be considered ~*
ADV. **extremely, fairly, very, etc.** | **exceptionally, highly** ◇ *She gained a highly ~ impression of the company.* | **overwhelmingly** | **especially, particularly** | **mostly, rela-**

tively | **broadly** (BrE), **generally, largely** ◇ *His proposals met with a largely ~ response.* | **consistently**
PREP. **for** ◇ *Conditions are now ~ for skiing.* | **to** ◇ *The court's verdict was ~ to their client.*

favourite (BrE) (AmE favorite) noun

1 sb/sth that you like more than others

ADJ. **absolute, big, firm** (BrE), **great, hands-down** (AmE), **huge** (esp. BrE), **particular, special** ◇ *This painting is a particular ~ of mine.* | **all-time, established, long-time, old, perennial, traditional** ◇ *This movie is my all-time ~.* ◇ *You will find all your old ~s in this book of poems.* | **new** ◇ *They perform their greatest hit and a new ~.* | **family, personal, popular** | **cult** ◇ *The movie has become a cult ~.* | **sentimental** ◇ *He began recording sentimental ~s.* | **fan** (esp. AmE) ◇ *a theme song that remains a fan ~* | **audience, crowd** ◇ *The band started with a crowd ~.* | **holiday** (esp. AmE) ◇ *It may become a holiday ~ on video.* | **childhood** ◇ *They were singing their childhood ~, 'Waterloo'.*
VERB + FAVOURITE/FAVORITE **become** | **remain** | **choose, pick** ◇ *If I had to choose a ~, it would be Monet's 'Water Lilies'.*
PREP. **~ among** ◇ *He is a ~ among his teammates.* | **~ for** ◇ *The forest was a ~ for family walks.* | **~ of** ◇ *This song is an old ~ of mine.* | **~ with** ◇ *The song is a firm ~ with their fans.*

2 competitor expected to win

ADJ. **big, clear, clear-cut, firm** (BrE), **heavy** (esp. AmE), **hot, odds-on, overwhelming, red-hot** (BrE), **solid** (esp. AmE), **strong** ◇ *She is odds-on ~ to win an award.* | **second** | **joint** (BrE) | **slight** | **early** ◇ *China was the early ~ to win the bidding.* | **even-money** ◇ *The horse is an even-money ~.* | **2–1, etc.** ◇ *Tiger Woods is 3–2 ~ to win the Challenge.* | **3-point, 6-point, 12-point, etc.** (all AmE) ◇ *The Colts are 5.5-point ~s at San Francisco this week* | **home** (esp. BrE), **hometown** (esp. AmE), **local** | **race, title** (BrE) | **pre-season** | **prohibitive** (AmE) ◇ *Gunn and Moran are prohibitive ~s.*
VERB + FAVOURITE/FAVORITE **look** (BrE), **look like, start (as)** ◇ *On paper, Stanford looks like the ~.* ◇ *The Brazilians still look firm ~s to take the title.* | **emerge as**
PREP. **~ for** ◇ *Jopanini is second ~ for Saturday's race.*
PHRASES **~ to win** ◇ *The Spanish are the ~s to win.*

favouritism (BrE) (AmE favoritism) noun

VERB + FAVOURITISM/FAVORITISM **show** | **accuse sb of**
PREP. **~ to, ~ towards/toward** ◇ *She denied showing ~ to any of her students.*
PHRASES **accusations of ~** ◇ *He resigned over accusations of ~.*

fax noun

ADJ. **incoming** | **junk**
VERB + FAX **send (sb)** | **get, receive**
FAX + NOUN **machine** | **number** | **line** | **message** | **modem, software** | **paper** | **service**
PREP. **by ~** ◇ *There was still time to receive copies by ~.* | **~ from, ~ to**

fear noun

ADJ. **big, deep, deep-seated, genuine, great, intense, overwhelming, pure, real, terrible, utter** ◇ *My biggest ~ was that my children would get sick.* ◇ *It was the first time she had experienced real ~.* | **worst** | **growing, general, widespread** | **constant, nagging** ◇ *the constant ~ of discovery* | **irrational, unfounded, unreasonable** ◇ *Our ~s proved unfounded.* | **legitimate, well-founded** | **primal** ◇ *the most primal ~, that of death* | **mortal, paralysing/paralyzing** | **public** ◇ *Public ~s about the disease increased.* | **childhood** ◇ *the girl's childhood ~ of being eaten by monsters*
VERB + FEAR **experience, feel, have** ◇ *She did not know why she should feel such ~.* | **be filled with, be gripped by, be paralysed/paralyzed by, be paralysed/paralyzed with, tremble with** | **express, show, voice** ◇ *The boy showed no ~.* ◇ *Doctors have voiced ~s that we may be facing an epidemic.* | **confront, face** | **cause, inspire, instil/instill** ◇ *the ~ that her mother had instilled in her* | **fuel, heighten, raise, stoke** ◇

This incident will fuel ~s of a full-scale war. ◇ *This stoked ~s of financial difficulties.* | **exploit** | **confirm** ◇ *My worst ~s were confirmed.* | **allay, alleviate, assuage, calm, conquer, dispel, ease, overcome, quell** ◇ *The government is anxious to allay the public's ~s.* ◇ *She managed to overcome her ~.* | **hide, mask**

FEAR + VERB **abate, subside** ◇ *When she heard the news, some of her ~ subsided.* | **grow** (*esp. BrE*) ◇ *Fears are growing of a new oil embargo.* | **grip sb, haunt sb, overcome sb** ◇ *A sudden ~ gripped him.* | **course through sb, wash over sb, wash through sb** | **strike sb**

PREP. **for ~ of** ◇ *Nobody refused for ~ of being fired.* | **in ~** ◇ *He ran away in ~.* | **in ~ of** ◇ *The men hesitated in ~ of whatever was to come next.* | **out of ~** ◇ *He lied out of ~.* | **through ~** ◇ *The students obeyed through ~ of punishment.* | **with ~** ◇ *His face was white with ~.* | **without ~** ◇ *She stared at him without ~.* | **~ about** ◇ *his ~ about what might happen* | **~ for** ◇ *my ~ for her safety.* | **~ of** ◇ *They have a terrible ~ of failure.* | **~ over** ◇ *new ~s over terrorism*

PHRASES **~ and loathing** | **~ and trembling, ~ and trepidation** ◇ *The men set off in ~ and trepidation.* | **live in** ◇ *The people live in ~ of attack by the bandits.* | **strike ~ into (the heart of) sb** ◇ *The sound of gunfire struck ~ into the hearts of the villagers.*

fear *verb*

ADV. **genuinely, greatly, really** ◇ *This disease is greatly ~ed.* ◇ *I really ~ed that this might be the end.* | **rightly** ◇ *Everyone rightly ~ed the coming war.*

VERB + FEAR **seem to** | **begin to** | **learn to** ◇ *He learned to ~ and respect this force of nature.*

PREP. **for** ◇ *We ~ed for their safety.*

PHRASES **have little to ~, have nothing to ~** ◇ *You have nothing to ~ from him.* | **have reason to ~ sth** | **have no reason to ~ sth**

fearful *adj.*

VERBS **appear, be, feel, look, seem, sound** | **become, grow** | **remain** | **leave sb, make sb** ◇ *The experience had left her ~ and uncertain.*

ADV. **extremely, fairly, very, etc.** | **deeply** | **almost** | **a little, slightly, etc.**

PREP. **about** ◇ *understandably ~ about the future* | **for** ◇ *I felt ~ for my life.* | **of** ◇ *He was ~ of every shadow.*

fearless *adj.*

VERBS **be, seem** | **make sb**

ADV. **absolutely, completely, quite, totally, utterly**

PREP. **in** ◇ *She was ~ in her attacks on public figures.*

feasibility *noun*

ADJ. **economic, technical**

VERB + FEASIBILITY **consider, discuss, examine, explore, investigate, look at, look into, study** | **assess, determine, establish, evaluate, test** ◇ *a drilling project to assess the ~ of bringing the water four miles into the town* | **demonstrate** | **confirm, prove** | **doubt, question** ◇ *Some of them doubted the ~ of the proposal.*

FEASIBILITY + NOUN **study** ◇ *They have launched a ~ study for the construction of a new road.*

feasible *adj.*

VERBS **appear, be, look, seem** | **become** | **consider sth** ◇ *A tunnel was not considered economically ~.* | **prove sth** ◇ *The treatment has not proved ~.*

ADV. **entirely, perfectly, quite** ◇ *It's perfectly ~ to produce electricity without creating pollution.* | **barely, hardly, not really** | **administratively, commercially, economically, financially, politically, technically, technologically** (*esp. AmE*)

feast *noun*

1 special meal

ADJ. **delicious** | **veritable** (*often figurative*) ◇ *a veritable ~ of music* | **big, grand, great, huge, lavish, sumptuous** ◇ *Villagers used to hold a great ~ at harvest time.* | **celebratory, family, holiday** (*AmE*), **village** (*esp. BrE*), **wedding** | **Christmas, Thanksgiving**

VERB + FEAST **give, have, hold, host** | **make, prepare** ◇ *The women were busy preparing the wedding ~.* | **provide** (**sb with**) ◇ *The salmon provide a delicious ~ for the brown bear.* | **attend** | **eat** ◇ *First everyone ate a grand ~.* | **enjoy**

PREP. **at a/the ~** | **~ of** ◇ *a ~ of Spanish food and wine*

2 religious festival

ADJ. **movable**

VERB + FEAST **celebrate**

FEAST + NOUN **day**

PREP. **on the ~ of** ◇ *on the ~ of St John* | **~ of** ◇ *the ~ of Passover*

feat *noun*

ADJ. **amazing, astonishing, brilliant, extraordinary, impressive, incredible, remarkable, spectacular** | **considerable, great** | **major** | **heroic, superhuman** ◇ *superhuman ~s of strength* | **difficult, no mean, no small** ◇ *Dragging the fully laden boat across the sand was no mean ~.* | **rare** | **unprecedented** ◇ *an unprecedented ~ in the history of the industry* | **easy** | **impossible** | **acrobatic, athletic, intellectual, physical** ◇ *physical ~s of strength and skill* | **engineering, technical, technological** ◇ *The tunnel was one of the greatest engineering ~s of the 19th century.*

VERB + FEAT **accomplish, achieve, do, manage, perform, pull off** ◇ *people doing unbelievable ~s* ◇ *He has pulled off an extraordinary ~ in completing the voyage single-handedly.* | **be capable of** ◇ *She was capable of remarkable ~s of endurance.* | **duplicate** (*esp. AmE*), **repeat** | **match** | **emulate** (*esp. BrE*) ◇ *He emulated the ~ of the legendary athlete Jesse Owens.* | **attempt**

PREP. **~ of** ◇ *a remarkable ~ of strength*

feather *noun*

ADJ. **breast, neck, tail, wing** | **ostrich, peacock, etc.** | **flight** ◇ *a fledgling with new flight ~s* | **primary** | **downy, fluffy** ◇ *the downy ~s on the duck's breast*

VERB + FEATHER **preen** ◇ *a swan preening its ~s* | **fluff, fluff out, fluff up** ◇ *The owl fluffed out its ~s.* | **ruffle** ◇ *Its ~s were ruffled by the chill breeze.* | **pluck** ◇ *I had to pluck the dead hen's ~s.* | **grow** ◇ *The chicks have grown their adult ~s.*

FEATHER + NOUN **bed, mattress, pillow** | **duster** | **boa, headdress**

PHRASES **as light as a ~**

feature *noun*

1 important part of sth

ADJ. **basic, central, critical, crucial, essential, fundamental, important, key, main, major, principal, significant** | **conspicuous, distinct, distinctive, distinguishing, dominant, notable, noteworthy, noticeable, predominant, prominent** ◇ *a distinctive ~ of his poems* | **outstanding, remarkable, striking** | **appealing, attractive, endearing, eye-catching, nice** | **interesting, peculiar, special, specific, unusual** | **salient** ◇ *He took me around our new offices, pointing out all the salient ~s.* | **handy, useful** | **cool, neat, nifty** (*all informal*) | **characteristic, classic, defining, identifying, particular, typical** | **unique** | **common, shared** ◇ *the common ~ in all these cases* | **permanent, regular** ◇ *These walks became a regular ~ of his day.* | **recurring** ◇ *Self-deprecation is a recurring ~ as Stevenson talks.* | **redeeming** ◇ *The one redeeming ~ of the plan was its low cost.* | **desirable, favourite/favorite** | **original** ◇ *The house retains most of its original ~s.* | **built-in** | **standard** | **added, additional, extra** | **optional** | **advanced, enhanced, innovative, new, novel** ◇ *some of the more advanced ~s of the software* | **architectural, constructional, design, physical, structural** | **geographical, geological, landscape, topographical** | **stylistic** | **energy-saving,**

safety, security ◆ *a car with new built-in safety ~s |*
interactive ◆ *The site brims with interactive ~s.*
VERB + FEATURE **brim with, have, include, incorporate** ◆ *The
site had a number of interesting ~s. |* **retain | add** ◆ *We're
adding new ~s and functionality every month. |* **offer** ◆ *The
network offers interactive ~s. |* **share** ◆ *Their life histories
shared many common ~s. |* **lack | point out**
FEATURE + VERB **distinguish sth** ◆ *the essential ~ that
distinguishes anorexia nervosa from other eating disorders |*
characterize sth ◆ *A ~ that characterizes all anteaters is a
slow metabolic rate. |* **include sth** ◆ *Special ~s include
passenger airbags. |* **allow sth, enable sth** ◆ *A touch-screen ~
allows visitors to call up relevant information.*

2 features sb's face
ADJ. **attractive, beautiful, handsome, nice | delicate, fine,
soft** ◆ *a slim figure with delicate ~s |* **pale | neat** ◆ *a woman
with small, neat ~s |* **striking** ◆ *her striking, dark-eyed ~s |*
rugged ◆ *I admired his rugged ~s. |* **angular, chiselled/
chiseled | sharp** ◆ *He had sharp ~s, with high cheekbones. |*
**aquiline, hawk-like | boyish | masculine | facial |
physical** ◆ *He has the right physical ~s for the role.*
VERB + FEATURES **have** ◆ *She has very delicate ~s. |* **contort |
soften**
PREP. **with ~** ◆ *a young woman with fine ~s*

3 newspaper article/television item
ADJ. **big, major, special | regular** ◆ *The magazine runs a
regular ~ on ethnic cooking. |* **daily, monthly, weekly | in-
depth**
VERB + FEATURE **do, have, publish, run, write** ◆ *Next month
they will publish a special ~ on computer books.*
FEATURE + NOUN **writer | ~s editor | ~s section | story**
PREP. **~ on** ◆ *an in-depth ~ on the Italian fashion scene*

feature *verb*

1 include sth as an important part
ADV. **regularly** ◆ *Women's magazines regularly ~ diets and
exercise regimes. |* **rarely | frequently, often | typically** ◆
His movies typically ~d torrid romances.
PHRASES **be ~d in sth, be ~d on sth** ◆ *His work is ~d in a
special documentary tonight.* ◆ *The school has been ~d on
television.*

2 have a part in sth
ADV. **heavily, highly, largely** (*esp. BrE*), **prominently, strongly**
◆ *Reading over his past speeches, you'll see that housing,
public health and education ~ strongly.*
PREP. **in** ◆ *Garlic ~s prominently in her recipes.*

February *noun* → Note at MONTH

federation *noun*

ADJ. **loose** ◆ *He proposed a loose ~ of local groups. |* **national,
regional, state** (*AmE*) **| international, world** ◆ *the Inter-
national Judo Federation |* **athletics, soccer, etc.** ◆ *the
British Athletics Federation |* **employers', labour/labor,
police** (*BrE*), **trade-union**
VERB + FEDERATION **create, establish, form**
FEDERATION + VERB **break up** ◆ *The ~ broke up in 1989.*
PREP. **in a/the ~** ◆ *the six republics in the ~ |* **within a/the ~**
◆ *He urged them to remain within the ~. |* **~ of** ◆ *a ~ of over
3000 organizations*
PHRASES **a member of a ~**

fed up *adj.*

VERBS **be, feel, look, seem, sound | become, get, grow** ◆
The children were starting to get a little ~.
ADV. **really, very** ◆ *You look really ~! |* **absolutely** (*esp. BrE*),
completely, quite (*esp. BrE*), **thoroughly, totally** (*esp. BrE*) **|
pretty, rather** (*esp. BrE*) **| a little, slightly, etc.**
PREP. **about** (*esp. BrE*) ◆ *He still sounds pretty ~ about
everything. |* **of** (not considered correct in standard
English) **| with** ◆ *I'm absolutely ~ with the whole thing.*

fee *noun*

ADJ. **exorbitant, fat** (*informal*), **hefty, high, huge, large,**

substantial ◆ *I expect you had to pay a fat ~ to your divorce
lawyers. |* **low, modest, nominal, reasonable, small** ◆ *We
had to pay a nominal ~ to join the club. |* **Their ~s are
reasonable. | fixed, flat, set** ◆ *Many tax advisers now offer
fixed-fee interviews. |* **full | reduced | normal, standard,
usual | appropriate** ◆ *Send the form, together with the
appropriate ~, to this address. |* **additional, extra, top-up**
(*BrE*) ◆ *There is no additional ~ for this insurance cover.* ◆
university top-up ~s | **late** (*esp. AmE*), **outstanding** (*esp. BrE*),
unpaid (*esp. BrE*) ◆ *We will be taking active steps to collect the
outstanding ~s. |* **upfront | annual, hourly, monthly,
yearly | one-off** (*BrE*), **one-time** (*AmE*) **| enrolment/
enrollment, initiation** (*AmE*) ◆ *a $1200 initiation ~ |*
attorney (*AmE*), **court, filing** (*AmE*), **legal | consultancy** (*esp.
BrE*), **consulting** (*esp. AmE*), **contingency, management,
professional** ◆ *the professional ~s of the lawyers and
accountants involved |* **admission, entrance, entry, joining**
(*esp. BrE*), **membership, subscription** ◆ *a £30 membership ~
|* **user | administration** (*esp. AmE*), **administrative** (*esp.
AmE*), **application, arrangement** (*BrE*), **booking** (*BrE*),
cancellation, franchise (*esp. AmE*), **handling, licence/
license, licensing, processing, referral, registration, roy-
alty, service** (*esp. AmE*), **set-up, transaction | college** (*BrE*),
course (*BrE*), **school** (*BrE*), **student, tuition | rental |
maintenance** (*esp. AmE*) **| parking | transfer** (= charges
paid by a sports team buying a player from another team)
(*BrE*) **| green** (*BrE*), **greens** (= a charge to use a golf course)
(*AmE*)
VERB + FEE **charge, impose** ◆ *They charge higher ~s to overseas
students. |* **incur** ◆ *Employees are reimbursed for any legal ~s
incurred when they relocate. |* **pay | collect, command,
earn, generate, receive** ◆ *The company will earn a ~ for
every barrel of oil produced. |* **waive** ◆ *He agreed to waive his
usual ~. |* **refund, reimburse | increase, raise | lower,
reduce | agree** (*BrE*) **| negotiate** ◆ *She negotiated a ~ of
$1800 a week. |* **set** ◆ *Freelance writers often set their own
~s. |* **cover** ◆ *You'll need money to cover ~s and expenses. |*
afford
FEE + VERB **be due, be payable** ◆ *All ~s are payable when the
invoice is issued. |* **apply** ◆ *Additional security ~s apply. |*
cover sth, include sth ◆ *The ~ includes the cost of testing the
electric wiring. |* **go up, increase, rise** ◆ *The admission ~ has
gone up.*
FEE + NOUN **income, revenue** ◆ *The company's consultancy ~
income rose by 3% last year. |* **payment | schedule** (*AmE*) **|
structure | increase**
PREP. **for a ~** ◆ *For a small ~, anyone can use these facilities. |*
~ for ◆ *We now charge a ~ for museum entrance. |* **~ on** ◆
the administrative ~s on the pension scheme

feed *verb*

1 give food to a person/animal/plant
ADV. **properly, well** ◆ *Have they been ~ing you well? |* **poorly**
◆ *The children were poorly fed. |* **barely** ◆ *She could barely ~
and clothe herself. |* **regularly**
VERB + FEED **help (to)** ◆ *How can we ~ a hungry world? |*
afford to ◆ *He could no longer afford to ~ his family.*
PREP. **on** ◆ *She fed the children on junk food. |* **to** ◆ *Most of the
crop is fed to the cattle. |* **with** ◆ *The animals are fed with hay
and grass.*
PHRASES **a mouth to ~** ◆ *He saw the new baby as just another
mouth to ~.*

2 eat
ADV. **voraciously** ◆ *The bears ~ voraciously in summer and
store energy as fat. |* **mainly, mostly, predominantly,
primarily | exclusively**
PREP. **on** ◆ *The seals ~ mainly on fish and squid.*

3 supply sth
ADV. **directly | constantly** ◆ *Receptors constantly ~
information into the system.*
PREP. **into** ◆ *The data is fed directly into a computer. |*

through ◇ *This ~s the paper through to the printer.* | **to, with** ◇ *The media were being fed with accusations and lies.*

feedback noun

ADJ. **constructive, favourable/favorable, good, great, helpful, positive, useful, valuable** | **negative** | **appropriate, relevant** | **honest** | **critical** | **direct** | **accurate** | **immediate, instant** ◇ *The writer gets no immediate ~ and simply has to imagine the reader's reaction.* | **regular** | **informal** | **email, verbal, written** ◇ *The the facilitator offers verbal ~ to each student.* | **consumer, customer, reader, student, user** ◇ *The Internet can be a useful source of customer ~.*
VERB + FEEDBACK **give sb, provide (sb with), send** ◇ *I invite you to send your ~ to our editors.* | **offer** | **get, have, obtain, receive** | **collect, gather** | **ask for, seek, solicit** (*esp. AmE*) | **appreciate, welcome**
PREP. **~ about, ~ on** ◇ *They will be given ~ on their performance.* | **~ from** ◇ *I've had a lot of very constructive ~ from the students about this.* | **~ to** ◇ *We provide advice and support to members.*

feel verb

ADV. **deeply, strongly** ◇ *She felt her mother's death very deeply.* | **really** ◇ *I really felt bad about what I had done.* | **keenly** ◇ *Her loss has been keenly felt.*
PREP. **about** ◇ *He ~s very strongly about a lot of issues.* | **for** ◇ *I really ~ for you in your position.*

feeling noun

1 sth that you feel/sense

ADJ. **strong** | **overwhelming** ◇ *Rielle had an overwhelming ~ of guilt.* | **definite, distinct** | **nagging, sneaking, sneaky, vague** ◇ *I had a nagging ~ that I had forgotten something.* | **amazing, awesome** (*informal, esp. AmE*), **glorious, good, great, incredible, marvellous/marvelous, nice, pleasant, warm, wonderful** ◇ *It was a good ~ to be arriving home again.* | **fuzzy** ◇ *It gave me a warm fuzzy ~ to hear him say that.* | **awful, bad, horrible, nasty, queasy, sick, sickening, sinking, terrible, tight** ◇ *He suddenly had a terrible sinking ~ in the pit of his stomach.* ◇ *I have a tight ~ in my stomach.* | **painful** ◇ *the painful ~ in his gut* | **creepy** (*informal*), **uncomfortable, uneasy** ◇ *She gives me this creepy ~.* | **empty, hollow** | **guilty** | **curious, eerie, funny, odd, peculiar, strange, weird** | **familiar** ◇ *I started to get a familiar ~ in my stomach.* | **gut, instinctive** ◇ *My gut ~ was that we couldn't trust her.* | **general, popular, public, widespread** ◇ *The general ~ of the meeting was against the decision.* | **nationalist, patriotic** ◇ *There's a great patriotic ~ in the country.*
VERB + FEELING **experience, feel, get, have** ◇ *He felt a wonderful warm ~ come over him.* ◇ *Do you get the ~ that we're not welcome here?* | **give sb, leave sb with** ◇ *She was left with the ~ that he did not care.* | **shake** ◇ *I couldn't shake the ~ that something was wrong with him.* | **know** (*informal*) ◇ *'I really resent the way he treated me.' 'I know the ~ (= I know how you feel).'* | **arouse, evoke, inspire** ◇ *a case that has aroused strong public ~* | **ignore** ◇ *She ignored the queasy ~ in her stomach.* | **enjoy, like, love** ◇ *She loved the ~ of being close to him.* | **hate** ◇ *I hated the ~ of uncertainty.*
FEELING + VERB **come over sb, creep over sb** | **be mutual** ◇ *'I'm going to miss you.' 'The feeling's mutual (= I feel exactly the same).'*
PREP. **~ about** ◇ *I had a ~ about that place.* | **~ of** ◇ *a ~ of excitement*

2 feelings opinions/emotions/love

ADJ. **deep, intense, strong** | **ambivalent, mixed** ◇ *I had mixed ~s about meeting them again.* | **genuine** ◇ *a sweet old man with genuine ~s for Virginia* | **positive, tender, warm** | **bad, hostile, ill, negative** | **hurt, injured** (*esp. BrE*) | **guilt** ◇ *I don't have those guilt ~s any more.* | **inner, innermost, real, true** | **pent-up** ◇ *She could finally release her pent-up*

~s. | **personal** | **human** | **religious** | **sexual** | **romantic** ◇ *I can bring out Aminta's romantic ~s.*
VERB + FEELINGS **experience, harbour/harbor, have, suffer** ◇ *She experienced a whole range of ~s.* ◇ *He still harboured/harbored ~s of resentment.* ◇ *She was lucky that she had suffered no more than hurt ~s.* | **develop** ◇ *They begin to develop ~s for one another.* | **admit, confess, express, give vent to, let out, release, reveal, show, vent, voice** ◇ *Heather is slowly admitting her ~s.* ◇ *He finds it difficult to express his ~s.* ◇ *I finally gave vent to my ~s and started yelling at him.* | **articulate, convey, describe, discuss, explain, talk about** ◇ *We discussed our innermost ~s.* | **capture, reflect** ◇ *Her poems reflected her personal ~s.* | **bottle up, bury, deny, fight, fight back, hide, hold back, keep to yourself, mask, repress, suppress** ◇ *I fought back my ~s of jealousy.* ◇ *I kept my ~s to myself.* ◇ *She tried to hide her true ~s.* | **ignore** ◇ *I tried to ignore my irrational ~s of jealousy.* | **hurt** ◇ *I'm sorry if I've hurt your ~s.* | **spare** ◇ *We didn't tell Jane because we wanted to spare her ~s.* | **arouse, engender, evoke, inspire** ◇ *The debate aroused strong ~s on both sides.* | **heighten** ◇ *It was the practical aspect of life that heightened her ~s of loneliness and loss.* | **sort out, understand** | **reciprocate, return** ◇ *Although she did not reciprocate his ~s, she did not discourage him.* | **share** ◇ *He had never been one to share his ~s.*
FEELINGS + VERB **sweep over sb, wash over sb, well up inside sb** | **run high** (*esp. BrE*) ◇ *Feelings were running high as the meeting continued.*
PREP. **~ about** ◇ *I don't have any strong ~s about it one way or the other.* | **~ for** ◇ *She still had a lot of ~s for David.* | **~ of** ◇ *his ~s of grief* | **~ on** ◇ *I have mixed ~s on that.* | **~ towards/toward** ◇ *her ~s of anger towards/toward him*
PHRASES **no hard ~s** (*informal*) ◇ *Someone has to lose. No hard ~s, eh?*

3 understanding/sensitivity/sympathy

ADJ. **great, wonderful** | **genuine** ◇ *What I love about this book is its genuine ~ for people.*
VERB + FEELING **have** ◇ *You have no ~ for the sufferings of others.* | **develop** ◇ *He had developed a ~ for when not to disturb her.*
PREP. **with ~** ◇ *She spoke with ~ about the plight of the homeless.* | **~ for** ◇ *She has a wonderful ~ for texture.*

4 (*also* **feelings** *esp. in AmE*) **anger**

ADJ. **bad, ill**
VERB + FEELING **cause, create, lead to** | **stir up**
PREP. **~ against** ◇ *Their aim was to stir up ~/~s against the war.* | **~ between** ◇ *I don't want any bad ~/~s between us.*

5 ability to feel physically

VERB + FEELING **lose** | **regain**
PREP. **~ in** ◇ *After the accident he lost all ~ in his legs.*

6 atmosphere

VERB + FEELING **create, recreate** ◇ *They have managed to recreate the ~ of the original building.*
PREP. **~ of** ◇ *The drink gave me a ~ of confidence.*

fellow noun

1 man

ADJ. **old, young** | **big, little, tall** | **good-looking, handsome** | **clever, smart** (*esp. AmE*) | **charming, decent, fine, good, jolly** (*esp. BrE*), **nice, splendid** (*esp. BrE*) | **interesting** | **strange** | **lucky** | **poor** (= unlucky) ◇ *The poor ~ had his wallet stolen.*

2 in a college, university, etc.

ADJ. **junior, senior** | **honorary** (*esp. BrE*), **research, teaching** | **postdoctoral** (*esp. AmE*) | **resident** (*AmE*), **visiting** (*esp. AmE*) | **distinguished** (*AmE*)
VERB + FELLOW **elect sb, name sb** (*AmE*)
PREP. **~ of** ◇ *She was elected a ~ of the Academy.*

felon noun (*esp. AmE*)

ADJ. **convicted** | **former** | **violent**
FELON + VERB **serve sth** ◇ *~s who have served their sentence*

felony noun (AmE)

ADJ. **federal | serious | first-degree, second-degree, third-degree | aggravated | non-violent, violent | drug, drug-related**
VERB + FELONY **commit | be punishable by** ◇ *a ~ punishable by up to six years in prison* | **be charged with**
FELONY + NOUN **charge | conviction | offense | assault, murder, etc.** ◇ *He was charged with ~ assault.*

feminine adj.

VERBS **be, feel** ◇ *He made her feel ~.* | **look** ◇ *She looked very ~ with her hair like that.*
ADV. **extremely, fairly, very, etc. | decidedly, distinctly | almost | traditionally** ◇ *Her name fits in with a traditionally ~ image.* | **stereotypically** ◇ *stereotypically ~ qualities like compassion*

feminism noun

ADJ. **contemporary, modern | liberal, socialist | militant, radical | pioneering | mainstream | lesbian | black | second-wave, third-wave | Western**

feminist noun

ADJ. **active, committed | modern | early, pioneering | militant, radical | liberal | lesbian | black, white | Western**

fence noun

ADJ. **high, tall | low | barbed-wire, chain-link, iron, mesh, metal, picket, rail** (*esp. AmE*)**, steel, stone** (*AmE*)**, wire, wood** (*AmE*)**, wooden, wrought-iron** ◇ *The house was surrounded by a white picket ~.* | **electric, electrified** (*AmE*) | **back, backyard** (*AmE*)**, garden | border** (*esp. AmE*)**, boundary, perimeter, security** ◇ *the airport perimeter ~* | **invisible** (= to keep pets in) (*AmE*) | **left-field, outfield, right-field** (all in baseball) | **privacy** (*AmE*) ◇ *She walked over to the tall wooden privacy ~.* | **political** (*figurative*) ◇ *a proposal approved by people on both sides of the political ~*
VERB + FENCE **build, erect, put up | climb, climb over, hop** (*AmE*)**, hop over** (*esp. AmE*)**, jump, jump over, scale | mend** (*figurative*) ◇ *The White House already is struggling to mend ~s with Europe.*
FENCE + NOUN **post | line** (*esp. AmE*) ◇ *the ~ line separating the United States from Mexico*
PREP. **over a/the ~** ◇ *She leaned over the ~.* | **~ around, ~ round** (*esp. BrE*) ◇ *a ~ around the site*

fend verb

PHR V **fend for yourself**
VERB + FEND FOR **be able to | be left to, have to** ◇ *The children were left to ~ for themselves.* | **learn to** ◇ *Clara learned to ~ for herself.* | **let sb** ◇ *We can let our guests ~ for themselves.*

fender noun (AmE) → See also WING

ADJ. **front, rear**
VERB + FENDER **dent**
FENDER + NOUN **bender** (= a minor accident) (*informal*) ◇ *I had a ~ bender on my first day.*

ferment noun

ADJ. **great, intense | artistic, creative, cultural, intellectual | technological | social | political, revolutionary** ◇ *a period of intense political ~*
PREP. **in (a) ~** ◇ *The country was in ~.*

ferocity noun

ADJ. **great, sheer**
PREP. **with ~** ◇ *It attacks its prey with great ~.*

ferry noun

ADJ. **car, passenger | cross-Channel** (*BrE*)
VERB + FERRY **get, ride** (*AmE*)**, take, use | wait for | catch | board | drive off, get off | operate**
FERRY + VERB **carry sb, take sb** ◇ *a ~ carrying more than a*

thousand people | **arrive, come in** (*esp. BrE*)**, dock** ◇ *We watched the ~ dock.* | **depart, go, leave, sail** (*BrE*) ◇ *The ~ departs at 8 p.m.* | **cross sth** ◇ *the ferries that cross the Mekong River* | **run** ◇ *Ferries run every hour or so.*
FERRY + NOUN **crossing, journey** (*BrE*)**, ride, trip | route | boat | passenger | pilot** (*AmE*) | **dock, port, terminal | line, operator, service**
PREP. **aboard a/the ~, on a/the ~, on board a/the ~** ◇ *the people on the ~* | **by ~** ◇ *We went by night ~.* | **~ across, ~ over** ◇ *We caught the ~ across the river.* | **~ between** ◇ *the ~ between Cape Cod and the islands* | **~ for** (*esp. BrE*)**, ~ to** ◇ *We caught the ~ to Fire Island.* ◇ *the ~ for Italy* | **~ from** ◇ *the ~ from Toronto to Rochester*

fertile adj.

VERBS **be, look | become | prove** ◇ *women who proved particularly ~* | **remain, stay**
ADV. **extremely, fairly, very, etc. | highly, particularly** ◇ *a highly ~ soil*

fertilizer (BrE also -iser) noun

ADJ. **natural, organic | artificial, chemical, inorganic, synthetic** (*esp. AmE*) | **nitrogen, phosphate | liquid**
VERB + FERTILIZER **apply, spray, spread, use** ◇ *He spread ~ on the field with a rake.*

fervour (BrE) (AmE fervor) noun

ADJ. **great | evangelical, moral, religious | nationalist, nationalistic, patriotic, political, revolutionary**
VERB + FERVOUR/FERVOR **arouse** ◇ *The speech aroused nationalist ~.* | **lose** ◇ *Its followers have lost their religious ~.*
PREP. **with ~** ◇ *He took up the cause with evangelical ~.* | **~ for** ◇ *their ~ for the cause*

festival noun

1 series of performances/events

ADJ. **big, huge, major | annual | spring, summer, etc. | three-day, five-day, etc. | international, local, national, regional, village | outdoor, street | arts, cultural | art, film, literary** (*esp. BrE*)**, music, poetry | dance, drama** (*BrE*)**, opera, theatre/theater | folk, jazz, rock, etc. | beer, wine | gay pride, pride | Christian, Hindu, Jewish, Muslim, etc. | flower** (*BrE*)
VERB + FESTIVAL **have, hold | host | attend, go to, visit | organize, run | sponsor | participate in** (*esp. AmE*)**, take part in** (*esp. BrE*) | **appear at, play, play at** ◇ *I like to play any big ~s.* | **open** ◇ *The dance troupe will open the ~ on June 13.*
FESTIVAL + VERB **take place | begin, open, start | attract sb** ◇ *The ~ attracts thousands of visitors every year.* | **feature sb/sth** ◇ *a ~ featuring five local bands* | **commemorate sth, mark sth**
FESTIVAL + NOUN **director, organizer | events, programme/program | performance | audience | circuit** ◇ *the film ~ circuit* | **grounds**
PREP. **at a/the ~** ◇ *He's appearing at a local folk ~ tonight.* | **during a/the ~** ◇ *the movies shown during the eight-day ~* | **in a/the ~** ◇ *the events in this year's ~*

2 religious celebration

ADJ. **great, important, major | annual | pagan, religious | traditional | ancient | Christian, Hindu, etc. | harvest**
VERB + FESTIVAL **celebrate, observe** ◇ *The family always celebrates the Jewish ~s.*
PREP. **at/on a/the ~** ◇ *the pilgrims who arrived on major ~s*

festivities noun

ADJ. **Christmas, holiday** (*AmE*)**, seasonal** (*esp. BrE*) | **anniversary, wedding | evening, weekend | inaugural** (*esp. AmE*)
VERB + FESTIVITIES **join, join in, take part in | attend | enjoy**
PREP. **during the ~**

feud noun

ADJ. **long, long-running, long-standing, old** | **ongoing** | **bitter** | **bloody** | **petty** | **blood** ◇ *Blood ~s added to the local crime rate.* | **family, internecine, personal, private** ◇ *a long-standing family ~* | **public**
VERB + FEUD **have** | **start** ◇ *The incident started a family ~.* | **settle** ◇ *a time to settle old ~s* | **end**
PREP. **~ between** ◇ *the ~s between rival companies* | **~ over** ◇ *They had a long-running ~ over money.* | **~ with** ◇ *his personal ~ with the city authorities*

fever noun

1 high temperature

ADJ. **high, raging** ◇ *She had a very high ~.* | **mild, slight** | **persistent** | **glandular** (*BrE*) (**mononucleosis** in *AmE*), **rheumatic, scarlet, etc.**
... OF FEVER **bout** ◇ *He suffered from recurrent bouts of ~.*
VERB + FEVER **have, run, suffer from** ◇ *He put his hand to my forehead as if I was running a ~.* | **catch, come down with, contract, develop, get** ◇ *James has come down with a ~.* | **cause** | **die of** | **bring down, reduce** ◇ *drugs which can help to bring down the ~* | **be accompanied by** ◇ *Inflammation is frequently accompanied by ~.*
PREP. **with a ~** ◇ *He was in bed with a ~.*
→ Special page at ILLNESS

2 nervous excitement

ADJ. **baseball, election, gold, war, World Cup**
FEVER + VERB **grip sb** ◇ *Election ~ suddenly gripped the nation.*
PREP. **in a ~ of** ◇ *She was in a ~ of anxiety about him.*

fibre (*BrE*) (*AmE* fiber) noun

1 in food

ADJ. **dietary** ◇ *your total daily intake of dietary ~* | **vegetable**
VERB + FIBRE/FIBER **be high in, be rich in** ◇ *foods that are rich in ~*
FIBRE/FIBER + NOUN **content** ◇ *foods that have a high ~ content* | **intake** | **supplement**
PHRASES **an intake of ~, a source of ~** ◇ *Peaches are a good source of ~.*

2 material/body tissue

ADJ. **coarse** | **hollow** | **strong** | **natural** | **artificial, man-made, synthetic** | **cotton, nylon, polyester, silk, textile, wool** | **asbestos, carbon, coconut, paper, wood** | **carpet** | **glass, optical** | **muscle, nerve** | **moral** (*figurative*) ◇ *It isn't just a lack of moral ~ that leads to a rising divorce rate.*
VERB + FIBRE/FIBER **be made from, be made of** ◇ *Wear underwear that is made from natural ~s.*
FIBRE/FIBER + NOUN **optics**

fiction noun

1 stories that are not true

ADJ. **contemporary, modern** | **classic** | **popular, pulp** | **literary, serious** | **short** ◇ *She has written novels and short ~.* | **experimental** | **mainstream** | **adult, children's** | **crime, detective, domestic, erotic, fan, genre, Gothic, historical, horror, romantic, science, speculative**
VERB + FICTION **publish, write** | **create** | **read**
PHRASES **a work of ~** ◇ *He has written over 20 works of ~.* | **a writer of ~** ◇ *a well-known writer of crime ~*

2 sth that is not true

ADJ. **pure** ◇ *Don't believe what she says—it's pure ~!* | **legal**
VERB + FICTION **keep up, maintain** ◇ *She still tries to maintain the ~ that she is happily married.* | **create**
PHRASES **fact and ~** ◇ *Fact and ~ became all jumbled up in his report of the robbery.*

fictional adj.

VERBS **be** ◇ *The names of the characters are entirely ~.*
ADV. **completely, entirely, purely, wholly**

fictitious adj.

VERBS **be** ◇ *His story is wholly ~.*
ADV. **completely, entirely, purely, totally, wholly** | **largely**

fidelity noun

ADJ. **great** | **absolute** | **marital, sexual**
VERB + FIDELITY **maintain**
PREP. **with** ◇ *The story is told with great ~ to the original.* | **~ to** ◇ *They still maintain ~ to their religious tradition.*

fidget verb

ADV. **nervously, uncomfortably** | **slightly** | **constantly**
PREP. **with** ◇ *She was ~ing nervously with her pen.*

field noun

1 on a farm

ADJ. **cultivated, ploughed/plowed** | **grass, grassy, green** ◇ *the green ~s of my homeland* | **muddy, snowy** | **enclosed** | **open** | **neighbouring/neighboring, surrounding** | **fertile** | **arable** | **fallow** | **irrigated** | **paddy, rice** | **corn, wheat, etc.**
VERB + FIELD **work in** ◇ *People were working in the ~s.* | **cultivate, work** ◇ *Despite the war, they continued to work the ~s.* | **plough/plow, till** | **plant, sow** ◇ *He planted ~s full of sunflowers.* | **irrigate** | **fertilize** | **clear** | **graze in**
PREP. **across a/the ~, through a/the ~** ◇ *We walked across the ~.* | **(out) in a/the ~** ◇ *tractors working out in the ~* | **~ of** ◇ *a ~ of wheat*

2 subject/activity

ADJ. **chosen, specialist** ◇ *All of them are experts in their chosen ~.* | **specialized** | **research** | **career** (*AmE*) | **burgeoning, emerging** | **evolving, growing** | **related** | **medical** | **academic**
VERB + FIELD **work in** ◇ *people who work in this ~* | **open up** ◇ *This discovery has opened up a whole new ~ of research.*
PREP. **in a/the ~** ◇ *There has been no solid research in this ~.* | **outside a/sb's ~** ◇ *I can't answer that—I'm afraid it's outside my ~.* | **~ of** ◇ *I work in the ~ of computer science.*
PHRASES **an expert in the ~, a leader in the ~** | **a ~ of research, a ~ of study** | **in their respective ~s** ◇ *These academics are world leaders in their respective ~s.*

3 practical work

VERB + FIELD **work in**
FIELD + NOUN **experiment, investigation, research, study, trial** | **methods** | **trip** ◇ *We went on a geology ~ trip.*
PREP. **in the ~** ◇ *essential reading for those working in the ~*

4 for playing a sport → See also PITCH

ADJ. **playing** | **sports** | **football, rugby, soccer, etc.**
VERB + FIELD **take** (*BrE*) ◇ *Today they take the ~ (= go on to the field to play a match) against county champions Essex.*
PREP. **on a/the ~** ◇ *people walking their dogs on the school's playing ~* | **off the ~** ◇ *Players need discipline both on and off the ~ (= when playing and in other areas of their lives).*

5 the field competitors in a sport/business

ADJ. **strong** | **crowded** | **male-dominated**
VERB + THE FIELD **dominate, head, lead** ◇ *She managed to head the ~ across the finishing line of the marathon.* ◇ *They lead the ~ in home entertainment systems.* | **enter** | **leave**
THE FIELD + VERB **include sb** ◇ *The strong ~ includes three world record holders.*
PREP. **ahead of the ~** ◇ *His superb technique puts him head and shoulders ahead of the ~.*

6 in science

ADJ. **energy, force** | **electric, electrical, electromagnetic, gravitational, magnetic** ◇ *the earth's magnetic ~*
FIELD + NOUN **strength**

7 computing

ADJ. **data, display, input**
VERB + FIELD **create** ◇ *You will need to create separate ~s for first name, last name and address.* | **move between** ◇ *the use of keys to move between ~s*
→ Special page at COMPUTER

fieldwork noun

ADJ. **extensive, intensive** | **ethnographic**
VERB + FIELDWORK **be engaged in, carry out, conduct, do, participate in, undertake**
PREP. **during ~, in the course of ~** ◇ *evidence obtained during ~* | **~ on** ◇ *extensive ~ on chimpanzees*

fifty-fifty adj., adv.

VERBS **be** | **divide sth, go, split sth** ◇ *We'll divide the profit ~.* ◇ *We went ~ on the meal.*
ADV. **about, around, roughly** ◇ *The chances of reaching the survivors in time are about ~.*

fight noun

1 struggle using physical force

ADJ. **big** | **fierce** | **brutal, nasty, vicious** | **real** ◇ *Suddenly the argument developed into a real ~.* | **good** ◇ *There's nothing he likes so much as a good ~.* | **clean, fair** ◇ *It was a fair ~ and Stephen won.* | **close** | **running** ◇ *He was killed during a series of running ~s outside a disco.* | **stand-up, straight** ◇ *In a straight ~ the army usually won.* | **bar** (*AmE*), **pub** (*BrE*), **street** | **gang** | **fist, knife, sword** | **food, pillow, snowball, water** | **championship, title** ◇ *the world title ~ between Tyson and Lewis* | **professional** | **heavyweight, etc.** | **bull** (usually *bullfight*), **cock, dog** | **boss** (in computer games)
VERB + FIGHT **pick, start** ◇ *He tried to pick a ~ with me.* ◇ *I don't know who started the ~.* | **be asking for** (*esp. AmE*), **be looking for, be spoiling for, want** ◇ *Andy was drunk and spoiling for a ~.* | **be in, get into, get involved in, have** ◇ *Don't get into any more ~s!* | **break up, stop** ◇ *The ~ was broken up by a teacher.* | **win** | **lose** | **see, watch**
FIGHT + VERB **take place** ◇ *The dog ~s took place every Sunday morning.* | **break out, erupt, start** | **ensue** ◇ *A ~ ensued which left one man dead.*
FIGHT + NOUN **scene, sequence** | **club** (*esp. AmE*) | **fan**
PREP. **in a/the ~** ◇ *He killed a man in a ~.* | **~ about, ~ over** ◇ *They nearly had a ~ over who should move first.* | **~ between** ◇ *~s between hostile clans* | **~ with** ◇ *They got involved in a ~ with some older boys.*

2 trying to get/do sth

ADJ. **brave, good, strong** ◇ *She died at the age of 43 after a brave ~ against cancer.* | **hard, long, real, tough, uphill** (*AmE*) ◇ *a long ~ to beat inflation* | **bitter, desperate** | **legal** | **custody** (*esp. AmE*)
VERB + FIGHT **put up** ◇ *Coal workers are determined to put up a ~ to save their jobs.* | **lead, spearhead** (*esp. BrE*) ◇ *lawyers leading the ~ for compensation for the injured workers* | **join, join in** ◇ *Doctors have now joined in the ~ to make this treatment available to all.* | **face** ◇ *Now he is facing his toughest ~ yet—back to fitness after a series of injuries.* | **be engaged in** ◇ *He is still engaged in a bitter ~ with his old company.* | **carry on, continue, keep up** ◇ *She said they would continue their ~ to find a cure for AIDS.* | **step up** ◇ *The government has vowed to step up the ~ against crime.* | **take** ◇ *She vowed to take her ~ to the High Court.* | **win** | **lose** ◇ *Are we losing the ~ against illegal drugs?* | **give up** ◇ *She just gave up her ~ for life.*
FIGHT + VERB **be on** ◇ *The ~ is on to have this brutal practice stamped out.* | **continue, go on** ◇ *The ~ for justice goes on.*
PREP. **without a ~** ◇ *I'm not giving up without a ~!* | **~ against, ~ with** (*AmE*) ◇ *a new weapon in the ~ against car crime* ◇ *his ~ with cancer* | **~ for** ◇ *their ~ for a fair deal*
PHRASES **a ~ for life, a ~ for survival** ◇ *the company's desperate ~ for survival in a cut-throat market* | **have a ~ on your hands** ◇ *Union leaders know that they have a real ~ on their hands.*

3 competition

ADJ. **brave, good, great, strong, tremendous** | **straight**
VERB + FIGHT **put up** ◇ *The team put up a good ~ (= they played well) but were finally beaten.*
FIGHT + VERB **be on**
PREP. **~ between** ◇ *This will be a straight ~ between the two parties.* | **~ for** ◇ *The ~ for supremacy in the sport is on.*
PHRASES **a ~ to the death** (*figurative*) ◇ *By 1807 politics had become a ~ to the death between the two factions.* | **a ~ to**

the finish ◇ *If the polls are wrong and it's a ~ to the finish, the result may not be known until all the votes have been counted.* | **have a ~ on your hands** ◇ *She now has a ~ on her hands* (= will have to play very well) *to make it through to the next round.* | **make a ~ of it** ◇ *No doubt Ferguson wants his team to make a ~ of it.*

4 (*esp. AmE*) **argument**

ADJ. **big, huge, terrible** | **petty, stupid** | **little**
VERB + FIGHT **have** | **cause** | **get into, pick, provoke, start**

fight verb

1 in a war/battle

ADV. **bravely, gallantly, valiantly** | **bitterly, fiercely, hard** | **effectively** | **back, off**
VERB + FIGHT **be prepared to, be ready to** ◇ *He did not believe that the enemy was ready to ~.* | **continue to**
PREP. **against** ◇ *They fought bravely against the enemy.* | **alongside** ◇ *He fought alongside his comrades.* | **for** ◇ *They fought for control of the island.* | **over** ◇ *They were ~ing over disputed land.* | **with** ◇ *He taught me how to ~ with a sword.*
PHRASES **~ to the death** ◇ *The soldiers were prepared to ~ to the death if they had to.*

2 struggle against/hit sb

ADV. **bitterly, hard** | **dirty** | **back, off** ◇ *He was stabbed as he tried to ~ the robbers off.*
VERB + FIGHT **be prepared to**
PREP. **against** ◇ *She fought hard against his strong grip.* | **with** ◇ *Riot police fought with militants demonstrating in support of the uprising.*

3 in a contest

ADV. **bitterly, hard** | **successfully**
VERB + FIGHT **be determined to, be prepared to, be ready to** ◇ *We need a good manager who is prepared to ~ for a fair share of the funds.* | **continue to**
PREP. **for** ◇ *Regional monopolies were bitterly fought for.*
PHRASES **fiercely fought** ◇ *The second half was fiercely fought, but neither side managed to score.*

4 try to stop/achieve sth

ADV. **hard, like a tiger, tooth and nail** (= in a very determined way) ◇ *He fought hard to overcome his disability.* ◇ *The residents are ~ing tooth and nail to stop the new development.* | **doggedly, stubbornly, tenaciously** | **desperately** | **successfully** | **back** ◇ *It is time to ~ back against street crime.*
VERB + FIGHT **be determined to, be prepared to, be ready to, vow to** | **continue to** | **help (to)**
PREP. **against** ◇ *They are committed to ~ing against racism.* | **for** ◇ *We are ~ing for equal rights.*

5 argue

ADV. **bitterly** | **constantly**
PREP. **about** ◇ *It's a trivial matter and not worth ~ing about.* | **over** ◇ *Children will ~ even over small things.* | **with** ◇ *He's always ~ing with his brother.*
PHRASES **~ like cat and dog** (*BrE*), **~ like cats and dogs** (*AmE*)

fighting noun

ADJ. **bitter, fierce, hard, heavy, intense, serious** | **bloody** | **continued, continuing** | **fresh** (*esp. BrE*), **renewed** | **sporadic** | **constant** | **hand-to-hand** ◇ *The sword and mace were the preferred weapons for hand-to-hand ~.* | **house-to-house, street, urban** | **factional**
VERB + FIGHTING **end, halt, stop** ◇ *The talks are intended to end the ~.* | **take part in** ◇ *The conspirators took no part in the ~ which ensued.* | **be killed in, die in** | **escape, flee** ◇ *refugees fleeing the ~*
FIGHTING + VERB **take place** | **begin, break out, erupt, flare, start** ◇ *Fierce ~ broke out among the refugees.* | **ensue, follow** | **continue, go on** | **rage** ◇ *For nearly two months the ~ raged.* | **intensify** | **die away, die down, diminish** ◇ *Even if the ~ dies down, no answer is in sight to the political crisis.* | **cease, end, stop** | **resume**

figure

PREP. **during the ~, in the ~** ◇ *He was badly wounded during the ~.* | **~ between** ◇ *There has been renewed ~ between the government forces and the rebels.*
PHRASES **do the/sb's ~** ◇ *He prefers others to do the ~ for him.* | **a lull in the ~**

figure *noun*

1 amount/price

ADJ. **high** | **low** | **double** ◇ *Four players reached double ~s in the scoring column.* | **accurate, exact** | **approximate** (*esp. BrE*), **ballpark, rough, round** | **dollar** (*AmE*) ◇ *You can't put a dollar ~ on the lives ruined by the hurricane.* | **real, reliable, true** | **official** | **latest** | **inflated** | **target** | **attendance, census, sales, trade, unemployment** | **audience, viewing** (*both esp. BrE*)
VERB + FIGURE **reach** ◇ *The rate of inflation has now reached double ~s.* | **exceed** | **add, add together, add up, calculate** | **compile** | **disclose, release** ◇ *The government has just released new unemployment ~s.* | **cite, give, quote** | **inflate**
FIGURE + VERB **add up** ◇ *These ~s don't add up.* | **be bandied about** ◇ *Lots of different ~s were being bandied about.* | **indicate sth, suggest sth** | **reflect sth**
PHRASES **according to (the) ~s** ◇ *The industry remains in the doldrums, according to official ~s out today.* | **in round ~s**

2 person

ADJ. **great** | **central, key, pivotal** | **important, influential, leading, major, powerful, prominent** ◇ *a key ~ on the committee* | **famous, well-known** | **larger-than-life** | **popular, respected** | **controversial** | **public** | **national** | **senior** | **familiar** ◇ *He was a familiar ~ in the town.* | **unlikely** ◇ *They were visited by the unlikely ~ of Bill Clinton.* | **authority, dominant** | **father, mother, parental** | **tragic** | **comic, ridiculous** | **cult, heroic, iconic, legendary, mythical, mythological** | **historical** | **literary, political, religious** | **government, opposition**
PREP. **~ of** ◇ *a ~ of authority/fun*

3 shape of a person

ADJ. **cloaked, hooded, masked, robed** | **life-size** | **dark, shadowy** | **ghostly** | **seated, standing, etc.** ◇ *The seated ~ in the corner beckoned me over.* | **approaching, retreating** | **sleeping** | **central** ◇ *the central ~ in the photo* | **lone, single, solitary** | **human**
FIGURE + NOUN **painter** | **drawing, painting**

4 shape of sb's body

ADJ. **beautiful, fine, good, handsome, lovely, stunning** ◇ *She still had a lovely ~.* | **curvy, hourglass** | **sexy** | **lean, slender, slim** | **bulky, full, large, stocky** | **lanky, tall, towering** | **dashing, imposing, striking** | **slight, small, tiny, trim** | **lithe**
VERB + FIGURE **cut, have** ◇ *He cut a dashing ~ in his uniform.* | **keep** ◇ *She's kept her ~ after all these years.* | **watch** ◇ *You need to watch your ~.* | **lose**
PHRASES **a fine ~ of a man, a fine ~ of a woman**

5 picture/diagram

VERB + FIGURE **refer to, see** ◇ *See Figure 8.*
FIGURE + VERB **illustrate sth, show sth**

figure *verb*

ADV. **largely, prominently, significantly, strongly** (*esp. BrE*) | **hardly** (*esp. BrE*) ◇ *Vegetables hardly ~ at all in their diet.*
PREP. **among** ◇ *This man did not ~ among the suspects.* | **in** ◇ *The issue ~d prominently in our discussion.*

file *noun*

1 collection of papers

ADJ. **bulging, bulky** (*BrE*), **thick** | **box** (*BrE*), **card, lever-arch** (*BrE*), **Manila, paper** ◇ *six box ~s bulging with notes* | **official** | **confidential, personal, secret** | **detailed** | **case** ◇ *The work involves preparing case ~s and attending court.* | **information** | **client, customer, personnel** | **court, newspaper, office, police, security** | **medical**

... OF FILES **box, stack** ◇ *A stack of ~s awaited me on my desk.*
VERB + FILE **have, keep, maintain** ◇ *The company keeps secret ~s on all its employees.* ◇ *Personnel ~s are kept in secure storage.* | **keep sth on** ◇ *Your application will be kept on ~* (= kept for possible future use). | **collate, compile, prepare** ◇ *He had compiled a ~ of largely circumstantial evidence.* | **enter sth into** (*esp. BrE*) ◇ *The details of the incident will be entered into the ~.* | **open** ◇ *The police have opened a ~ on the case.* | **close** ◇ *The ~ on the murder was closed five years ago.* ◇ *She closed the ~ and put it aside.* | **reopen** ◇ *Police have reopened the ~ on the missing girl.* | **review** | **update** ◇ *It is important to update customer ~s.* | **pull, pull out, remove, take out** ◇ *She went to the filing cabinet and took out a ~.* | **check, examine, go through, look at, read, scan** ◇ *I'll check the ~s for any information on the case.* | **burn, destroy**
FILE + VERB **contain sth**
FILE + NOUN **cabinet, drawer** (*both AmE*) (*filing cabinet* in *BrE*) | **folder** | **clerk** (*AmE*)
PREP. **in a/the ~** ◇ *the information contained in the police ~s* | **on ~** ◇ *All the details of the transaction are on ~.* | **~ on** ◇ *The police already have a thick ~ on that family.*

2 on a computer/disk

ADJ. **large** | **computer, digital, electronic** | **data, database, document, spreadsheet, text** | **executable, program** | **system** | **audio, music, sound** | **graphics, image** | **multimedia** | **video** | **master** | **backup** ◇ *to make/take a backup ~* | **log** | **HTML, PDF, etc.** | **compressed, ZIP** | **infected** | **help**
... OF FILES **directory, list, set**
VERB + FILE **create** | **download, upload** | **hold sth in, store sth in** ◇ *the information held in this ~* | **close, open** | **save** | **load** | **install** | **access, read, view** ◇ *You need a special password to access this ~.* | **back up, copy** | **edit, modify** | **delete, erase** | **delete sth from** ◇ *Data has been deleted from this ~.* | **name, rename** | **recover, retrieve** ◇ *how to recover deleted ~s* | **hold, store** ◇ *The ~s are stored in Mac format.* | **compress** | **send, transfer** ◇ *Files are transferred between workstations.* | **export, import** | **share** | **attach** | **overwrite** | **encrypt**
FILE + VERB **contain sth**
FILE + NOUN **name** | **format, size** | **server** | **sharing** | **system** | **transfer** | **extension** | **manager**
PREP. **in a/the ~** ◇ *The names and addresses are all kept in computer ~s.*
→ Special page at COMPUTER

file *verb*

1 put sth in a file

ADV. **alphabetically** | **electronically** | **mentally** ◇ *She mentally ~d the name away for later.* | **away** ◇ *These notes should be carefully ~d away for future reference.*
PREP. **under** ◇ *The card is ~d alphabetically under the name of the editor.*

2 record sth officially

ADV. **formally, officially** ◇ *He has now formally ~d a complaint against the police.* | **jointly**
PREP. **for** ◇ *to ~ for bankruptcy/divorce* | **with** ◇ *A copy of the notice must be ~d with the court.*

3 walk in line

ADV. **silently** | **out, past** ◇ *The long line of mourners ~d silently past.*
PREP. **in, into, out of, past, through**

fill *verb*

ADV. **fast, quickly, rapidly** ◇ *At the moment, most reservoirs are ~ing fast.* | **suddenly** | **gradually, slowly** | **partially** | **immediately, instantly** | **completely, entirely** | **up**
VERB + FILL **begin to** ◇ *The sails began to ~.* | **seem to** ◇ *He seemed to ~ the room with his presence.*
PREP. **with** ◇ *Fill the bucket with water.*
PHRASES **be ~ed to capacity** ◇ *The school is ~ed to capacity—we simply can't take any more students.* | **be ~ed to the brim (with sth)** ◇ *The drawers were all ~ed to the brim.*

fillet (*AmE also* filet) *noun*

ADJ. **fish** | anchovy, cod, haddock, salmon, etc. | beef, pork
FILLET + NOUN **steak** (*esp. BrE*) | **knife**
PREP. **~ of** ◇ *~ of beef with a red wine sauce*
→ Special page at FOOD

filling *noun* in a tooth

ADJ. **dental** | amalgam, gold, white
VERB + FILLING **have** ◇ *She's only eight years old and she already has five ~s.* ◇ *I went to the dentist yesterday and had two ~s.* | **do, give sb** ◇ *The dentist said she would do the ~ immediately.* | **replace**
FILLING + VERB **come out, fall out**

film *noun*

1 (*esp. BrE*) moving pictures → See also MOVIE

ADJ. **long** | short | feature-length | entertaining, exciting, good, great, interesting | blockbuster, successful | awful, bad, boring | epic | violent ◇ *She thought the ~ far too violent to show to children.* | **R-rated** (*AmE*), **X-rated** | animated | silent | black-and-white | big-budget, low-budget | Bollywood, Hollywood | independent, indie | television, video | action, adventure, children's, comedy, documentary, gangster, sci-fi | feature | porn, pornographic | horror, slasher, snuff | classic | cult | mainstream | foreign, foreign-language | upcoming (*esp. AmE*)
VERB + FILM **see, view, watch** | enjoy, like, love | go to (see), take sb to (see) | direct, make, produce, shoot ◇ *She makes children's ~s.* ◇ *The ~ was shot on location in Kenya.* | **be in, do** ◇ *Cruise does around four ~s a year.* | **take** ◇ *~ taken by security cameras* | **cut, edit** ◇ *The ~ was heavily edited for screening on television.* | **distribute, release, screen, show** ◇ *The ~ was finally released after weeks of protest by religious groups.* | **promote** | ban, censor
FILM + VERB **be on, show** ◇ *There's an interesting ~ on at the multiplex.* | **come out, open, premiere** ◇ *The ~ came out last week.* | **be based on sth** ◇ *a ~ based on the novel by Charles Potter* | **be called sth, be entitled sth** ◇ *a ~ entitled 'Bitter Moon'* | **capture sth** ◇ *The ~ manages to capture the mood of the times.* | **contain sth, include sth** ◇ *The ~ contains explicit scenes of violence.* | **depict sth, portray sth, present sth, represent sth, show sth** ◇ *The ~ depicts immense courage amid the horrors of war.* | **tell sth** ◇ *This ~ tells the remarkable story of a disabled actor.* | **feature sb, star sb** ◇ *The ~ stars Nicole Kidman as a nightclub singer.* | **record sth** ◇ *a ~ recording the first powered flight* | **deal with sth** ◇ *a ~ dealing with old age* | **open** ◇ *The ~ opens with a bird's-eye shot of London.* | **end** | be a hit, be a success | be nominated for sth
FILM + NOUN **director, editor, maker, people, producer, writer** ◇ *The script has plenty of what ~ people call 'bankability'.* | **crew, team, unit | world | actor, actress, legend, star** | part, role | career, debut, work | credits ◇ *We stayed for the ~ credits* ◇ *His ~ credits* (= the films he has made) *as director include 'Mood Music' and 'Lies'.* | **critic, reviewer | review | buff, fan, lover | premiere | censor, censorship | screenplay, script | music, score, soundtrack | narrative | scene | stunt** ◇ *He was killed when a ~ stunt went wrong.* | **poster | studio | set** ◇ *They built a massive ~ set of an airport.* | **adaptation, version** ◇ *the ~ version of the best-selling novel* | **classic** ◇ *the ~ classic 'Fantasia'* | **documentary, drama | genre | clip, footage, sequence | report** ◇ *The news always contains several ~ reports.* | **series** ◇ *the 'Star Wars' ~ series* | **archives, library | business, company, industry | mogul | distributor | making, production | festival | show | awards | camera, equipment, projector, recorder | rights** ◇ *The scramble for the ~ rights to her next novel has already begun.* | **school, student**
PREP. **in a/the ~** ◇ *There is a great car chase in the ~.* | **on ~** ◇ *They captured the incident on ~.* | **~ about** ◇ *a ~ about Nelson Mandela* | **~ from** ◇ *a ~ from Spanish director Luis Eduardo Aute* | **~ of** ◇ *They've just started shooting a ~ of the novel.* | **~ with** ◇ *a ~ with an all-star cast*
PHRASES **the beginning of the ~, the end of the ~** | be in ~s (= work in the film industry) | **the climax of a ~** | the plot

of a ~ | a ~ with subtitles | the screening of a ~, the showing of a ~

2 used for taking photographs

ADJ. **black-and-white, colour/color | fast** ◇ *Fast ~ is best for action shots.* | **35 mm, etc.**
... OF FILM **reel, roll** ◇ *a roll of 35 mm ~*
VERB + FILM **load, put in | remove, take out | rewind | develop, process** ◇ *I get my ~ developed locally.* | **expose** ◇ *In the darkroom they found that only half the ~ had been exposed.* | **splice** ◇ *He spliced the two lengths of ~ together.*

3 thin layer of a substance/material

ADJ. **fine, thin | surface | plastic**
VERB + FILM **be covered with, be covered with** ◇ *The books were covered in a thin ~ of dust.*
PREP. **~ of** ◇ *There was a fine ~ of sweat on her forehead.*

film *verb*

ADV. **secretly** ◇ *The controversial experiment involved secretly ~ing a group of children.* | **on location** ◇ *The serial was ~ed on location in Italy.*
PHRASES **beautifully ~ed** ◇ *fast-paced, well acted and beautifully ~ed in the Blue Ridge Mountains*

filthy *adj.*

VERBS **be, feel, look, smell | get | leave sth, make sth** ◇ *He always leaves the bath absolutely ~!*
ADV. **really | absolutely**

final *noun*

1 last game/match in a competition

ADJ. **grand** ◇ *He got through to the grand ~ of the competition.* | **area** (*esp. BrE*), **national, regional, state, world | men's, women's | championship, cup** (*BrE*), **tournament**
VERB + FINAL **hold, host, stage** (*BrE*) ◇ *Never before have two countries hosted the ~s.* | **be through to, enter, get through to, go through to, make, make it to, qualify for, reach** ◇ *If we play well, we hope to make it to the ~.* | **compete in, contest, meet sb in, play in** ◇ *Russia met Canada in the ~.* | **win**
FINAL + VERB **be played, take place**
PREP. **in the ~** ◇ *Who is in the men's ~?*

2 finals exams

ADJ. **college** (*AmE*), **school** (*AmE*), **university** (*BrE*)
VERB + FINALS **revise for** (*BrE*), **study for | do** (*esp. BrE*), **have, sit** (*BrE*), **take | fail, pass**

finale *noun*

ADJ. **dramatic, exciting, rousing, thrilling** (*esp. BrE*) ◇ *The evening ended with a grand ~ of fireworks and music.* | **climactic, grand | fitting | season, series** (*both AmE*)
VERB + FINALE **end in, end with, have, reach** ◇ *The reality show had a thrilling ~ last night.* | **provide** (*esp. BrE*) ◇ *This victory provided a fitting ~ to a brilliant season for the club.*
PREP. **~ to** ◇ *a rousing ~ to an evening of enthralling music*

finance *noun*

1 (*AmE usually* **financing**) money needed to fund sth

ADJ. **cheap** (= borrowed at low interest) | **necessary | additional, extra** (*BrE*), **further** (*BrE*) ◇ *the need to obtain additional ~* | **long-term, medium-term, short-term | joint | external | international | private, public | private-sector, public-sector | bridging** (*BrE*) ◇ *You may require bridging ~ until the sale of your own property is completed.* | **debt, loan** (*esp. BrE*) | **equity | bank** ◇ *the availability of bank ~ for small businesses* | **housing, mortgage, real estate** (*AmE*) | **structured**
VERB + FINANCE **allocate, provide | need, require**
FINANCE + VERB **be available** ◇ *the ~ available to local government* | **arrange, get, obtain, raise** ◇ *She struggled to get the necessary ~ for her training.*

FINANCE + NOUN **company, house** (*BrE*) | **industry, sector** ◇ *The banking and ~ sector was booming.*
PREP. **~ for** (*esp. BrE*) ◇ *Several banks are providing ~ for the project.*
PHRASES **a source of ~**

2 managing money

ADJ. **high** ◇ *the world of high ~* (= finance involving large companies or countries) | **company, corporate** | **government, local-government, public, state** | **consumer, personal** ◇ *that most emotive of personal ~ issues—taxation* | **global, international**
FINANCE + NOUN **director, minister, officer** ◇ *Local government ~ officers found the tax very difficult to administer.* | **committee, department**

3 finances money available

ADJ. **healthy, sound** (*both esp. BrE*) ◇ *Our family ~s are not very healthy at the moment.* | **tight** | **precarious** ◇ *The company's ~s are looking a little precarious.* | **company** | **government, public, state** | **family, household, personal, private** | **campaign** (*AmE*)
VERB + FINANCES **have** ◇ *We don't have the ~s to throw a big party.* | **lack** | **control, deal with, handle, manage, plan, run** ◇ *how to plan your ~s for a comfortable retirement* | **get in order, keep in order, sort out** (*esp. BrE*) ◇ *The company was under pressure to get its ~s in order.* | **bolster** (*esp. AmE*), **boost** (*esp. BrE*), **improve** | **be a drain on, put a strain on, strain, stretch** (*esp. BrE*) ◇ *Buying a new car need not put a strain on your ~s.*
FINANCES + VERB **be a mess** (*esp. AmE*), **be in a mess** (*esp. BrE*) ◇ *Their ~s are (in) a mess.*
PHRASES **the state of sb's ~s**
→ Special page at BUSINESS

finance verb

ADV. **entirely, wholly** | **largely, mainly** | **partially, partly** | **privately, publicly** ◇ *The new roads will be ~d privately.* | **jointly** ◇ *The project was ~d jointly by the British and French governments.* | **directly** | **properly** (*esp. BrE*), **well** ◇ *the introduction of a properly ~d system*
VERB + FINANCE **help (to)** | **be needed to, be required to** ◇ *the money needed to ~ the redevelopment* | **be used to**

find noun

ADJ. **good, great, real** | **exciting, interesting, remarkable, spectacular** ◇ *The letters were a real ~.* | **big, important, major, significant** | **rare** | **new, recent** | **lucky** ◇ *A lucky ~ is telling us a lot about life 10 000 years ago.* | **unexpected** | **archaeological, fossil** | **medieval, prehistoric**
VERB + FIND **discover, make, unearth** (*esp. BrE*) ◇ *prehistoric ~s made in an unexplored cave* | **yield** ◇ *To date the site has yielded many interesting ~s.* | **report** ◇ *I reported my ~ to the landowner.*

finding noun

1 (usually findings) result of research into sth

ADJ. **important, key, significant** ◇ *I'll now summarize the key ~s from these studies.* | **main** | **general** | **interesting** | **striking, surprising, unexpected** | **novel** | **positive** | **conflicting** | **early, initial, original** | **interim, preliminary** ◇ *He will present his preliminary ~s at the conference.* | **new, recent** ◇ *The original results conflict with more recent ~s.* | **scientific** | **laboratory** | **clinical** | **empirical, experimental** | **research, study, survey**
VERB + FINDING **record, write up** ◇ *Students were asked to write up their ~s in the form of a report.* | **summarize** | **announce, give, present, publish, report** ◇ *The ~s of the commission have not yet been made public.* ◇ *They will present their ~s to senior police officers.* | **make public, release, reveal** | **explain, interpret** | **examine** | **comment on, discuss** | **confirm, corroborate, support** ◇ *UN official reports supported the preliminary ~s.* | **contradict** |

challenge ◇ *Scientists have challenged the ~s of the researchers.* | **replicate**
FINDING + VERB **be based on sth** ◇ *The ~s are based on interviews with more than 2 000 people.* | **relate to sth** ◇ *Our ~s relate to physically rather than visually handicapped students.* | **apply to sth** ◇ *The ~s from the case study school may apply to schools elsewhere.* | **demonstrate sth, reveal sth, show sth** ◇ *Our ~s point to a lack of training among social services staff.* | **imply sth, indicate sth, point to sth, point towards/toward sth, suggest sth** | **agree with sth, be consistent with sth, be in agreement with sth, be in line with sth, confirm sth, support sth** ◇ *Our recent ~s are in line with those of an earlier study.* | **conflict (with sth), contradict sth** | **lead to sth** ◇ *The ~s led to the conclusion that…* | **provide sth** ◇ *The research ~s will provide practical assistance for teachers.* | **be made** ◇ *Similar ~s were made in Spain.* | **emerge** ◇ *Similar ~s emerged from a later experiment.*
PREP. **~ about** ◇ *recent scientific ~s about sleep patterns* | **~ for** ◇ *The ~s for one group can be applied to the others.* | **~ from** ◇ *~s from a recent research project* | **~ on** ◇ *newly published ~s on the depopulation of the countryside*

2 decision by a court

VERB + FINDING **make** | **justify** ◇ *The facts of this case do not justify a ~ of negligence.* | **uphold** ◇ *The appeal court upheld a ~ that the agreement was unlawful.*
PREP. **~ against** ◇ *a ~ against him by the commission* | **~ in favour/favor of** ◇ *The court made a ~ in favour/favor of the defendant.*

fine noun

ADJ. **big, heavy, hefty, huge, large, massive, stiff, substantial** ◇ *He was forced to pay a hefty ~.* | **small** | **maximum** | **two-hundred-dollar, five-hundred-pound, etc.** | **parking, speeding** | **civil** (*esp. AmE*), **criminal**
VERB + FINE **get** (*esp. BrE*), **receive** ◇ *I got a ~ for parking illegally.* | **pay** | **give (sb)** (*esp. BrE*), **impose, levy** ◇ *Heavy ~s were levied on offenders.* | **be liable for, be liable to, face, risk** ◇ *Drivers risk heavy ~s for driving without insurance.* | **be punishable by, carry, lead to** ◇ *Violations carry a maximum ~ of $1000.* | **increase**
PREP. **in** ◇ *They face up to five years in prison and more than $1 million in ~s.* | **~ for** ◇ *a ~ for water pollution*

fine verb

ADV. **heavily** ◇ *Any company found to be breaking these rules will be heavily ~d.*
PREP. **for** ◇ *He got ~d £200 for parking illegally.*
PHRASES **get ~d**

fine adj.

1 good enough/suitable

VERBS **be, look, seem, smell, sound, taste** | **turn out** ◇ *I knew that everything would turn out ~ in the end.*
ADV. **absolutely, completely, just, perfectly, totally, truly** (*esp. AmE*) ◇ *Don't worry. Your voice sounds absolutely ~.* | **exceptionally, particularly** ◇ *He has done an exceptionally ~ job of reorganizing things.*
PREP. **for** ◇ *This paper's not very good quality, but it's ~ for rough work.*

2 in good health/happy and comfortable

VERBS **be, feel, look, seem** ◇ *George looks ~ now.*
ADV. **absolutely, completely** ◇ *I feel absolutely ~.* | **physically**

3 (esp. BrE) bright and sunny/not raining

VERBS **be** | **turn out** ◇ *It's turned out ~ again today.* | **keep, remain, stay** ◇ *Let's hope it stays ~ for the wedding.*

4 thin/small

VERBS **be**
ADV. **extremely, fairly, very, etc.** ◇ *Her hair is very ~.* ◇ *a very ~ distinction* | **exceptionally**

finger noun

ADJ. **first, index, pointer** (*AmE*) | **middle** | **ring, third, wedding** ◇ *I noticed the ring on the third ~ of her left hand.* |

little, **pinky** (*AmE*) | broken, dislocated, injured, severed | pointing | accusatory, accusing, warning ◊ *The teacher raised a warning ~ and we stopped talking.* | delicate, elegant, graceful, slender, slim | long | bony, lean, skeletal, skinny, thin | chubby, fat, plump, podgy (*BrE*), pudgy, stubby | calloused/callused, clawed, gnarled | gentle ◊ *She took off his bandages with gentle ~s.* | capable, deft, nimble, skilful/skillful, skilled ◊ *Her nimble ~s undid the knot in seconds.* | nervous, numb | shaking, shaky, trembling | clumsy ◊ *His clumsy ~s struggled with the buttons.* | limp | cold, frozen, icy | extended, out-stretched | intertwined | dirty, filthy, grubby, sticky | gloved | manicured | trigger
VERB + FINGER **point** ◊ '*It was them!' she cried, pointing an accusing ~ at the boys.* ◊ *The investigators pointed the ~ of blame at the driver of the crashed bus.* (*figurative*) | draw ◊ *The man drew a ~ across his throat in a threatening gesture.* | insert, jam, poke, put, shove, stick, thrust ◊ *Everyone put their ~s in their ears when the shooting started.* | jab, stab ◊ *The protester was jabbing a ~ aggressively at a policeman.* | entwine, interlace, intertwine, lace, thread ◊ *He gently laced his ~s between mine.* | hook ◊ *She hooked her ~s in the belt loop of his jeans.* | hold up, raise ◊ *She raised a ~ to her lips to ask for silence.* | wag, waggle, wave, wiggle ◊ '*None of that!' cried the teacher, wagging her ~.* | twiddle ◊ *Dad started twiddling his ~s nervously.* | dip ◊ *I dipped my ~ in the sauce and licked it.* | lick | run, trace, trail ◊ *She ran her ~ along the dusty shelf.* ◊ *Sally trailed her ~s in the water idly.* | drum, tap ◊ *He was drumming his ~s nervously on the arm of the chair.* | click, snap ◊ *We were swaying and clicking our ~s in time to the music.* ◊ *He snapped his ~s and the waiter came running.* | shut, trap ◊ *The child needed treatment after trapping her ~ in the car door.* | cut, slice | break, dislocate | crook ◊ *He crooked a ~ to tell us to go over to him.* | clench, close, curl ◊ *Tina curled her slender ~s into a fist.* | extend, spread, stretch, stretch out ◊ *He held up his hand with the ~s extended.* | flex | prick ◊ *The nurse pricked my ~ to get some blood.*
FINGER + NOUN **bones, joints | movement | injury | puppet**
PREP. **with your ~s** ◊ *It's easiest to eat corn with your ~s.*
PHRASES **the ~ of blame, the ~ of fate, the ~ of suspicion** (*all figurative*) ◊ *The ~ of suspicion was pointed at the construction company.* | **the tips of the ~s**

fingernail *noun*

ADJ. **long | sharp | black, dirty | broken | manicured | painted, red**
VERB + FINGERNAIL **clip** (*esp. AmE*), **cut | paint | bite, chew | break | dig in** ◊ *She dug her ~s into my neck.* | **run | tap** ◊ *She tapped her ~s against the table impatiently.* | **examine, inspect** ◊ '*Actually, I'm leaving,' she said, examining her ~s.*
FINGERNAIL + VERB **dig in | scrape** ◊ *the horrible sound of ~s scraping across a blackboard* | **grow**
FINGERNAIL + NOUN **polish** (*esp. AmE*) | **clippers**
PREP. **under the/your ~s** ◊ *I noticed I had dirt under my ~s.*

fingerprint *noun*

... OF FINGERPRINTS **set** ◊ *The police were able to obtain a set of ~s from the suspect.*
VERB + FINGERPRINT **leave** ◊ *She was careful not to leave any ~s.* | **check (sth) for, dust sth for, examine sth for, look for** ◊ *The car is being examined for ~s.* | **find | take** ◊ *The investigator questioned him and took his ~s.* | **match** ◊ *The suspect's ~s have been matched with those found at the scene of the crime.*
FINGERPRINT + NOUN **reader, scanner | analysis, identification, recognition | database** ◊ *Many states have their own ~ databases.*

finish *noun*

1 last part/end of sth

ADJ. **exciting, fantastic, good, great, thrilling, tremendous** (*esp. BrE*) ◊ *His best ~ was 11th in the Hungarian Grand Prix.* | **perfect** ◊ *It was the perfect ~ to a wonderful day.* | **disappointing | sprint, storming** (*BrE*) | **strong** ◊ *The runners came around the bend for a sprint ~ in the home straight.* | **close, dramatic, nail-biting, photo, tight** ◊ *It*

was a photo ~, *with three horses neck and neck at the finishing line.* | **second-place, etc. | last-place** (*AmE*), **runner-up** ◊ *The team had another last-place ~.* | **podium** ◊ *The pair just missed out on a podium ~ when they took fourth place.* | **uphill** ◊ *He won a hard uphill ~ at the recent Tour de Suisse.*
VERB + FINISH **be in at** (*BrE*) ◊ *Her car suffered from gearbox trouble, but she was still in at the ~.*
FINISH + NOUN **line** (*AmE*)
PREP. **at the ~** ◊ *Several runners needed medical attention at the ~.* | **to a/the ~** ◊ *They fought bravely right to the ~.* | **~ to** ◊ *a dramatic ~ to the game*
PHRASES **from start to ~** ◊ *He was in the lead from start to ~.*

2 look/feel of sth

ADJ. **good, neat** (*BrE*), **perfect | professional** (*esp. BrE*) | **decorative | fine, smooth | textured | natural | faux** (*AmE*) ◊ *The walls have a faux ~ that mimics old plaster walls.* | **paint, painted | polished | gloss, glossy, matt/matte, mirror, satin, shiny | chrome, metallic, nickel, stainless-steel, wood** ◊ *a guitar with a natural wood ~* | **surface | durable | protective | floor, wall, etc.** ◊ *The wall and floor ~es are all of the the highest standard.* | **exterior, interior**
VERB + FINISH **have** ◊ *This paint has a gloss ~.* | **achieve, get** ◊ *With our new tool you get a perfect ~ every time.* | **create, give (sth), produce, provide** ◊ *This trim really does give the garment a professional ~.* | **match** ◊ *The wall has been painted to match the ~ of the original.* | **apply** ◊ *Make sure the surface is clean and smooth before the ~ is applied.*
FINISH + NOUN **coat** (*AmE*)
PREP. **to a ~** ◊ *Sand the wood to a fine ~ using steel wool.* | **with a ~** ◊ *a door handle with a metallic ~* | **~ on** ◊ *How did you achieve that ~ on the wood?*

finish *verb*

ADV. **almost, nearly | barely, just** ◊ *She had just ~ed dressing when the telephone rang.* | **recently | soon | eventually, finally | quickly** ◊ *I quickly ~ed my tea.* | **lamely, quietly, softly** ◊ '*I had no idea... ' I ~ed lamely.* | **off** ◊ *He ~ed off by welcoming the new arrivals.*
VERB + FINISH **let sb** ◊ *Let me just ~ what I'm doing.*
PREP. **by** ◊ *He ~ed by telling us about his trip to Spain.* | **with** ◊ *The evening ~ed with a few songs.* ◊ *Have you ~ed with the vacuum cleaner yet?*

fire *noun*

1 destructive flames

ADJ. **big, huge | fierce, raging | serious | catastrophic, devastating, disastrous | house, kitchen | bush, forest, wild-land** (*AmE*) | **electrical**
VERB + FIRE **be on** ◊ *The house is on ~!* | **catch** ◊ *A lantern was knocked over and the barn caught ~.* | **cause, set sth on, start** ◊ *Groups of rioters attacked and set the police headquarters on ~.* | **ignite, spark** ◊ *A missile ignited a ~ that burned for three days.* | **fan** ◊ *Strong winds fanned the ~.* | **add fuel to, fuel** (*both figurative*) ◊ *Frustrated ambitions can fuel the ~ of anger and resentment.* | **extinguish, put out | douse, smother** ◊ *The sprinkler system came on and doused the ~.* | **fight** ◊ *He joined the crowds of men and women fighting the ~.* | **contain, control** ◊ *Firefighters struggled to control the ~.* | **prevent | be damaged by, be damaged in, be destroyed by, be destroyed in | be killed by, be killed in, die in | survive**
FIRE + VERB **occur | break out, erupt, start** ◊ *A ~ broke out in the mail room.* | **go out | blaze, burn, rage** ◊ *The ~ burned for three days before it was finally contained.* | **engulf sb/ sth, spread, sweep through sth** ◊ *In 1925 a disastrous ~ swept through the museum.* | **lick sth, lick at sth** ◊ *The ~ licked the roof of the house.* | **damage sth | consume sth, destroy sth, gut sth** ◊ *The ~ gutted the building, leaving just a charred shell.*
FIRE + NOUN **safety** ◊ *legislation related to ~ safety* | **hazard, risk** ◊ *Foam-filled couches are a serious ~ hazard.* | **drill, practice** (*BrE*) ◊ *We have regular ~ drills.* (see also **fire**

alarm) | **brigade** (*BrE*), **department** (*AmE*), **service** (*BrE*) ◇ *Call the ~ brigade/department!* | **crew** ◇ *Fire crews arrived and began to fight the flames.* | **chief, commissioner, marshal, officer, official** | **station** | **engine, truck** (*AmE*) | **hydrant** | **hose, sprinkler** | **extinguisher** | **escape** ◇ *The thief got away down the ~ escape.* | **door** | **damage** ◇ *The building suffered extensive ~ damage.* | **code** (*AmE*) ◇ *~ code violations* | **prevention** | **season** (*esp. AmE*) ◇ *In 2008, the ~ season started with a huge fire in New Mexico.*

PHRASES **bring a ~ under control** ◇ *Firefighters have now managed to bring the ~ under control.* | **set ~ to sth** ◇ *Someone had set ~ to her car.*

2 burning fuel for cooking/heating

ADJ. **blazing, crackling, hot, roaring, warm** | **dying, smouldering/smoldering** | **flickering** | **little** | **open** | **charcoal, coal, log, oil, wood** | **camp** (usually *campfire*) | **cooking**

VERB + FIRE **build, make** | **kindle, light** ◇ *Kim had managed to kindle a little ~ of dry grass.* | **feed, poke, stir, stoke, stoke up, tend** ◇ *She fed the ~ with the branches next to her.* | **On** *cold nights we stoked up the ~ to a blaze.* | **put sth on** ◇ *Put some more wood on the ~.* | **cook on, cook over** ◇ *When we go on safari we like to cook on an open ~.*

FIRE + VERB **burn** ◇ *Although it was summer a ~ burned in the hearth.* | **roar** ◇ *A ~ roaring in the hearth added warmth to the room.* | **kindle, light** ◇ *We had plenty of dry wood, so the ~ lit easily.* | **die, die down** ◇ *The ~ was beginning to die down.* | **burn itself out, burn out, go out** | **crackle** | **glow** | **flicker** | **smoke** ◇ *The ~ smoked instead of burning properly.*

PHRASES **the glow from a ~, the glow of a ~** ◇ *The interior was only lit by the golden glow of the ~.*

3 (*esp. BrE*) apparatus for heating rooms

ADJ. **electric, gas**

VERB + FIRE **light, put on, switch on, turn on** ◇ *Use a match to light the gas ~.* | **switch off, turn off**

FIRE + VERB **be off, be on** ◇ *Is the ~ still on?*

4 shots from guns

ADJ. **heavy, withering** (*esp. AmE*) | **anti-aircraft, covering, friendly** ◇ *Several soldiers were killed in friendly ~ due a mistake by allied forces.* | **enemy, hostile** | **direct, indirect** | **incoming** | **automatic, rapid** | **artillery, sniper** | **cannon, machine-gun, mortar, rifle**

... OF FIRE **burst** ◇ *a burst of machine-gun ~*

VERB + FIRE **open** ◇ *The troops opened ~ on the crowd.* | **return** ◇ *She returned ~ from behind the low wall.* | **exchange** | **cease, hold** ◇ *'Cease ~!' He yelled.* ◇ *They were told to hold their ~ until the enemy came closer.* | **be under, come under** ◇ *We were under constant ~ from enemy snipers.* ◇ *The EU came under ~ from the US over its biotech policy.* (*figurative*) | **draw** ◇ *A few soldiers were sent out to draw* (= attract) *the enemy's ~.* | **avoid, dodge**

FIRE + VERB **rain down** ◇ *Enemy ~ continued to rain down.* | **hit sb/sth**

PHRASES **be in the line of ~** ◇ *Unfortunately he was in the line of ~* (= between the people shooting and what they were shooting at) *and got shot.*

fire *verb*

ADV. **blindly, indiscriminately, randomly, wildly** ◇ *She ~d blindly into the mass of shadows.* | **directly** ◇ *A dense volley of missiles was ~d directly at the ship.* | **rapidly** | **continuously, repeatedly** | **accidentally** | **accurately** | **wide** ◇ *Whitlock purposely ~d wide.* | **back** | **off** ◇ *They ~d off a volley of shots.*

VERB + FIRE **be ready to** ◇ *He grabbed the shotgun, ready to ~ if anyone entered.* | **order sb to** ◇ *He ordered the troops to ~ over the heads of the crowd.*

PREP. **at** ◇ *She ~d a revolver at her attacker.* | **into** ◇ *He ~d the gun into the air.* | **on, upon** ◇ *The police ~d on protesters in the square.*

fire alarm *noun*

VERB + FIRE ALARM **set off** ◇ *It was thought that the ~ had been*

set off as a prank. | **install** ◇ *Fire alarms have been installed in the building.*

FIRE ALARM + VERB **go** (*esp. BrE*), **go off, sound** ◇ *The ~ went off when I was making a coffee.*

FIRE-ALARM + NOUN **system**

firearm *noun*

ADJ. **imitation** (*BrE*), **replica** | **unlicensed** | **loaded** | **concealed** | **defensive** (*AmE*)

VERB + FIREARM **be in possession of, own, possess** ◇ *The police charged her with possessing an illegal ~.* | **carry** | **lock up, store** | **handle, use** ◇ *new army recruits learning how to handle ~s* | **discharge**

FIREARMS + NOUN **training** | **enthusiast, expert, instructor** | **dealer, retailer** | **sales** | **business, industry** | **company, manufacturer** | **owner** | **ownership, possession** | **certificate** (*BrE*), **licence/license** | **safety** | **law** | **offence/offense** (*esp. BrE*) ◇ *He is wanted for robbery and ~s offences/offenses.* | **accident** | **death**

firefighter *noun*

ADJ. **full-time, part-time** | **volunteer**

VERB + FIREFIGHTER **call, call out** ◇ *Firefighters were called to a house in Summertown.* | **kill** ◇ *A wildfire near Sydney killed three ~s.*

FIREFIGHTER + VERB **battle sth** (*AmE*), **fight sth, tackle sth** (*BrE*) ◇ *Firefighters tackled a warehouse blaze.* | **battle** ◇ *Firefighters battled to save a historic building after arsonists set it alight.* | **put sth out** | **rescue sb, save sb** ◇ *Firefighters rescued a driver trapped in the wreckage of his car.* | **die** → Note at JOB

fireplace *noun*

ADJ. **big, enormous, great, huge, large, massive** | **small** | **open** | **outdoor** (*esp. AmE*) | **brick, cast-iron, marble, stone**, etc. | **gas, wood-burning** (*both AmE*) | **working**

VERB + FIREPLACE **have** ◇ *Every room in the house has a ~.* | **build, install**

PREP. **in a/the ~** ◇ *A log fire crackled in the ~.*

firework *noun*

VERB + FIREWORK **light** ◇ *Be very careful when lighting ~s.* | **let off, set off, shoot** (*AmE*), **shoot off** (*AmE*) ◇ *They set off ~s in their backyard.* | **watch** ◇ *Thousands of people jammed into People's Square to watch the ~s.*

FIREWORK + VERB **explode, go off** | **light up sth**

FIREWORKS + NOUN **display, show**

firing squad *noun*

VERB + FIRING SQUAD **face** ◇ *He could face a ~ if found guilty of the charges.* | **be executed by, be shot by** ◇ *She was executed by ~.*

PREP. **before a/the ~, in front of a/the ~** ◇ *Many died in front of the ~.*

firm *noun*

ADJ. **big, large, major** | **medium-sized** | **small** | **well-known** | **successful** | **prestigious** | **established** | **start-up** (*esp. BrE*) ◇ *start-up ~s in the booming computer market* | **private** | **family** | **international, multinational** | **foreign** | **local** | **Boston-based, Tokyo-based**, etc. | **accountancy** (*esp. BrE*), **accounting** (*esp. AmE*), **audit, auditing, consulting, engineering, law, manufacturing, marketing, PR, software** (*esp. AmE*), etc. | **mail-order** (*esp. BrE*)

VERB + FIRM **establish, found, launch, set up, start, start up** (*esp. BrE*) ◇ *She set up her own software ~.* | **head, head up, manage, run** | **merge with** ◇ *They are likely to merge with a bigger ~.* | **acquire, buy, buy out, take over** ◇ *The ~ was taken over by a multinational consultancy.* | **close, close down** ◇ *the decision to close down the ~* | **own** | **work for** | **join, leave** | **employ, hire** ◇ *She hired a ~ of private detectives to follow him.*

FIRM + VERB **be based in sth** ◇ *a ~ called Data Inc., based in Chicago* | **expand, grow** | **merge** | **compete** ◇ *Local ~s are finding it difficult to compete in the international market.* | **operate** ◇ *US ~s operating in China* | **close, close down,**

collapse, fail, go bust (*esp. BrE*), go into liquidation (*esp. BrE*) ◇ *The well-established ~ closed down with the loss of 600 jobs.* | develop sth, make sth, manufacture sth, produce sth, sell sth | specialize in sth ◇ *a ~ specializing in high-tech products* | employ sb, hire sb (*esp. AmE*) ◇ *The ~ employs 85 000 people around the world.*
PREP. in a/the ~, within a/the ~ ◇ *the different departments within the ~*
PHRASES a client of a ~ | a ~ of accountants, consultants, solicitors, etc. (*BrE*) | a partner in a ~
→ Note at ORGANIZATION
→ Special page at BUSINESS

firm adj.

1 solid/strong

VERBS be, feel, look, seem | remain, stay ◇ *Exercise is important if you want your muscles to stay ~.* | make sth ◇ *Use extra stuffing to make the cushions firmer.* | keep sth ~ ◇ *exercises to keep your muscles ~*
ADV. extremely, fairly, very, etc.

2 not likely to change

VERBS be, sound | hold, remain, stand ◇ *Jo held ~: nothing else would do.* ◇ *We stand ~ on these principles.*
ADV. extremely, fairly, very, etc.
PREP. with ◇ *I have always been quite ~ with my children.*

first aid noun

ADJ. emergency
VERB + FIRST AID administer, give ◇ *While one of you gives ~, the other should call an ambulance.* | receive (*BrE*) | be trained in ◇ *One member of staff should be trained in ~.*
FIRST-AID + NOUN box, kit | course, training ◇ *those who've had first-aid training* | post (*BrE*)

fish noun

1 animal that lives and breathes in water

ADJ. freshwater, marine, saltwater, sea | cold-water, tropical | aquarium | predatory | farmed | wild
... OF FISH school, shoal
VERB + FISH catch, land ◇ *He landed a big ~.* | breed, farm, have, keep ◇ *~ farmed in Canada* ◇ *He keeps tropical ~.*
FISH + VERB swim | hatch | bite ◇ *The ~ aren't biting (= taking the bait) today.*
FISH + NOUN species | eggs | bowl, pond, tank | food | population, stocks ◇ *the depletion of ~ stocks* | hook | farm | farming | farmer

2 fish as food

ADJ. fresh | dried, frozen, salted, smoked | fatty, oily | white | raw | fried, grilled
... OF FISH bit, piece | fillet/filet
VERB + FISH eat, have | clean, fillet, gut, prepare, skin ◇ *I cleaned and filleted the ~.* | marinate | bake, cook, fry, grill, poach, steam
FISH + VERB taste ◇ *This ~ tastes funny.*
FISH + NOUN bone | fillet/filet | dish | cake (*usually fishcake*) (*esp. BrE*), finger (*BrE*), paste, pie (*BrE*), sauce, soup, stew, stick (*AmE*), stock | oil | market, shop (*BrE*) | knife, slice (*BrE*)
PHRASES ~ and chips (*esp. BrE*)
→ Special page at FOOD

fisherman noun

ADJ. avid (*esp. AmE*), keen (*esp. BrE*) | good | local ◇ *Local fishermen are protesting about the latest government regulations.* | commercial | recreational, sport, sports (*AmE*) | deep-sea
FISHERMAN + VERB catch sth
→ Note at JOB

fishing noun

ADJ. good ◇ *This stretch of the river is renowned for its good ~.* | coarse (*BrE*), deep-sea, drift-net, saltwater, sea | game, salmon, shark, trout, etc. | commercial, industrial | recreational | illegal

VERB + FISHING go ◇ *He goes ~ every weekend.*
FISHING + NOUN equipment, gear, line, rod, tackle | boat, craft, fleet, trawler, vessel | harbour/harbor (*esp. BrE*), port, town, village | area, grounds, spot, zone ◇ *the rich ~ grounds off the coast of Namibia* ◇ *Just below that bridge is a good ~ spot.* | dock, pier (*both AmE*) | activity ◇ *controls on ~ activity* | quotas | agreement ◇ *The two countries have signed a new ~ agreement.* | ban | rights ◇ *Fishing rights are held by the local angling club.* | licence/license | expedition, holiday (*BrE*), trip | club | lodge | business, industry | methods, techniques
PREP. ~ for ◇ *Ecuador announced a ban on ~ for shrimp.*

fist noun

ADJ. balled (*esp. AmE*), clenched, closed, tight | loose | little, small, tiny | giant, huge, large, massive | gloved | bare ◇ *He was punching the man with his bare ~s.* | left, right | flying ◇ *I managed to duck his flying ~s.* | angry ◇ *Diago pounded an angry ~ against the wall.*
VERB + FIST form, make ◇ *He closed his fingers to form a ~.* | ball (*esp. AmE*), clench, close, tighten | unclench, uncurl | bang, beat, hit, plant, pound, punch, slam, smack, smash, strike, thump ◇ *He banged his ~ loudly on the table.* ◇ *He punched his ~ in the air.* | drive, ram, shove, throw, thrust ◇ *He thrust his ~ forward and smashed her face.* | shake, wave ◇ *The man was shaking his ~ at us through the window.* | pump ◇ *'Yeah, you did it!' Sally said, pumping her ~ in the air.* | lift, raise ◇ *She raised her ~ in a gesture of defiance.* | swing ◇ *He swung his ~s wildly at his attacker's head.* | bring back, draw back, pull back ◇ *She drew back her ~ and threw a punch at his nose.* | use ◇ *Cailean was tired of using his ~s to get everything he wanted.*
FIST + VERB ball, clench, curl, tighten ◇ *She saw Joe's ~s clench.* | collide with sth, connect with sth, hit sth, strike sth ◇ *He felt Michelle's ~ connect with his jaw.* | pound (sth), slam (sth), smash (sth) ◇ *A ~ slammed on the table in front of her.* | land ◇ *His ~ landed forcefully against Mike's jaw.* | fly ◇ *She ran at him, her ~s flying.*
FIST + NOUN fight
PREP. in your ~ ◇ *She was holding a hammer in her ~.*
PHRASES clench your hand into a ~

fit noun

1 way sth fits/way two things match

ADJ. excellent, good, nice ◇ *We need to achieve the best ~ between the staff required and the staff available.* | correct, exact, ideal, perfect, proper, right | bad, poor ◇ *The door was a poor ~ and didn't open properly.* | close, snug, tight | loose | comfortable ◇ *The sweater is a comfortable fit—not too tight and not too loose.* | natural | custom (*esp. AmE*) ◇ *The cap is made of 92% polyester with 8% Spandex for a custom ~.*
VERB + FIT achieve, get, produce ◇ *File away any excess metal until a snug ~ is achieved.* | ensure ◇ *The shoe has a special strap to ensure a good ~.*
PREP. ~ between ◇ *a good ~ between the recruit and the job*
PHRASES a lack of ~ ◇ *He argues that there is a lack of ~ between our system of values and capitalism.*

2 sudden attack of illness

ADJ. convulsive, epileptic, fainting
VERB + FIT have, suffer ◇ *She suffered a major ~ last year.* | suffer from ◇ *He suffers from ~s of depression.* | bring on, cause, trigger ◇ *He suffers from a brain disorder that can trigger convulsive ~s.* | control ◇ *new drugs that can control ~s* | prevent
FIT + VERB happen, occur
PREP. during a ~ ◇ *She hurt her arm during one of her ~s.*

3 short period of coughing/laughter/strong feeling

ADJ. coughing, sneezing | crying, giggling, laughing, screaming | hysterical | sudden ◇ *In a sudden ~ of anger, he snatched the book from her hand.* | uncontrollable ◇ *He burst into an uncontrollable ~ of laughter.* | major
VERB + FIT have, pitch (*AmE*), throw ◇ *My dad will throw a*

major ~ *if he finds out!* | **burst into, collapse in, collapse into, erupt in, erupt into, fall into** ◊ *She collapsed in a* ~ *of laughter.* | **bring on** ◊ *The cold air brought on one of his coughing* ~*s.*
FIT + VERB **be over, pass** ◊ *When her coughing* ~ *was over she continued to speak.*
PREP. **in a** ~ **of** ◊ *He pushed the referee in a* ~ *of temper.* | ~ **of** ◊ *a* ~ *of anger/giggles*
PHRASES **in** ~**s** (*BrE*), **in** ~**s of laughter** ◊ *The comedian had them all in* ~*s of laughter.*

fit *verb*

1 right size/type

ADV. **closely, neatly, nicely, securely, snugly, tightly, well** ◊ *The pencils* ~ *neatly into this box.* | **loosely** | **exactly, perfectly** ◊ *The screws* ~ *the holes exactly.* | **properly** ◊ *The shoes don't* ~ *properly.* | **badly, poorly** ◊ *If the top of the box* ~*s badly, the contents will spill out.* | **barely, hardly** ◊ *jeans which barely* ~ *his stout body* | **easily** ◊ *That chair should* ~ *into the room easily.* | **comfortably** ◊ *PDAs are designed to* ~ *comfortably in a jacket pocket.* | **together** ◊ *These two pieces of wood* ~ *together to make the base.*
VERB + FIT **be designed to** ◊ *The waste unit is designed to* ~ *under the sink.*
PREP. **in, into, onto, over, under, etc.** ◊ *Will this box* ~ *into the cupboard?*

2 agree/match; make sth suitable

ADV. **perfectly** | **seamlessly** ◊ *The haunting melody* ~*s seamlessly within the song.*
PREP. **for** (*esp. BrE*) ◊ *Your experience* ~*s you perfectly for the job.* | **with** ◊ *The words* ~ *perfectly with the music.*

fit *adj.*

1 healthy

VERBS **be, feel, look, seem** | **become, get** ◊ *the struggle to get* ~ *and stay* ~ | **keep, stay** ◊ *Go for a little jog to keep* ~. | **make sb** ◊ *Exercising once a week is not enough to make you* ~. | **keep sb** ◊ *gentle exercises designed to keep you* ~
ADV. **extremely, fairly, very, etc.** | **fighting** (*esp. BrE*) ◊ *He seemed fighting* ~ *and ready for action.* | **fully** (*BrE*) ◊ *John isn't fully* ~ *yet after his operation.* | **physically** ◊ *She felt physically fitter and more alive than she could ever remember.*
PREP. **for** (*BrE*) ◊ *The doctor said she was now* ~ *for work.*
PHRASES **as** ~ **as a fiddle** (= very healthy) | ~ **and healthy,** ~ **and well** (*esp. BrE*) ◊ *She looks really* ~ *and healthy.* | ~ **and ready** | **lean and** ~

2 suitable

VERBS **consider sth, see, think** ◊ *The newspaper did not see* ~ *to publish my letter.* ◊ *You must do as you think* ~.
PREP. **for** ◊ *The food was not* ~ *for human consumption.*
PHRASES ~ **and proper** (*law, esp. BrE*) ◊ *circumstances in which someone is not considered a* ~ *and proper person to run a bank* | ~ **for a king** ◊ *It was a meal* ~ *for a king.* | **in no** ~ **state** ◊ *He's so angry he's in no* ~ *state to see anyone.*

fitness *noun*

ADJ. **full, peak** | **low** | **general, overall** | **individual, personal** | **aerobic, physical** | **cardiorespiratory, cardiovascular** | **mental** | **match** (*BrE*) ◊ *Tomkins is back to match* ~ *and is expected to play in the final.*
... OF FITNESS **degree, level** ◊ *You need a good level of physical* ~ *for this sport.*
VERB + FITNESS **attain** ◊ *He has attained peak* ~ *this season.* | **maintain** ◊ *Regular exercise helps to maintain physical* ~. | **be back to, get (sb) back to, regain, return to** | **build, build up, enhance, improve, increase, work on** ◊ *A special trainer has been brought in to work on her* ~. | **measure** | **prove** ◊ *The coach has given him a week to prove his* ~.
FITNESS + NOUN **level** ◊ *First, determine your present* ~ *level.* | **training** | **plan, programme/program, regime, regimen** (*AmE*), **routine** | **class** | **equipment** | **video** | **assessment,**

check (*BrE*), **test** | **goal** | **centre/center, club, facility** ◊ *a* ~ *club with gym and squash courts* | **buff, enthusiast, fanatic, freak** ◊ *She's a bit of a* ~ *freak. She goes running every night.* | **consultant, expert, guru** | **coach, instructor, trainer** | **industry** | **benefits** ◊ *Skiing offers many* ~ *benefits.*
PHRASES **health and** ~ ◊ *Walking is good for health and* ~.

fitting *adj.*

VERBS **be, seem** ◊ *It seemed entirely* ~ *that she should be wearing black.* | **consider sth, think sth** ◊ *I did not think it* ~ *to ask James about his daughter's death.*
ADV. **very** | **entirely, perfectly**

fix *noun*

1 solution to a problem

ADJ. **quick** ◊ *There is no quick* ~ *to the breakdown in negotiations between the two companies.* | **easy, simple** ◊ *There are no quick or easy* ~*es.* | **short-term, temporary** | **long-term, permanent** | **technical, technological** | **bug** ◊ *The new software incorporates many bug* ~*es and product improvements.*
VERB + FIX **find** | **make** ◊ *They made a quick* ~ *of part of the problem.*

2 amount of sth, esp. a drug

ADJ. **daily, regular** ◊ *my daily* ~ *of coffee* | **next** ◊ *He was like a heroin junkie needing his next* ~. | **caffeine** ◊ *I need my caffeine* ~!
VERB + FIX **have** ◊ *He gets withdrawal symptoms if he hasn't had his regular* ~. | **need** | **get**

3 difficult situation

VERB + FIX **be in** ◊ *I was in a* ~. | **get in, get into** ◊ *How did you get into such a* ~? | **get (sb) out of** ◊ *I lent her the money to get her out of a* ~.

fix *verb*

1 (*esp. BrE*) attach sth firmly

ADV. **firmly, securely** | **directly**
PREP. **onto, to** ◊ *The handrail can be* ~*ed directly to the wall.*
PHRASES ~ **sth in place,** ~ **sth in position** ◊ *Fix the bars in position with the screws provided.*

2 repair/correct sth

ADV. **easily** | **quickly** ◊ *a problem which can be* ~*ed quickly*
PHRASES **get sth** ~**ed** ◊ *We need to get the TV* ~*ed.*

fixed *adj.*

VERBS **be, seem** | **become** | **remain, stay**
ADV. **very** | **firmly, securely** (both *esp. BrE*) ◊ *Check that the boards are all securely* ~. | **rigidly** ◊ *His gaze was rigidly* ~ *ahead.* | **relatively** | **permanently**

fixture *noun*

1 sth fixed in a house

ADJ. **original** ◊ *an exceptional example of Victorian architecture with the original* ~*s intact* | **light** ◊ *The apartment still has the original light* ~*s.* | **permanent** (often figurative) ◊ *The new conductor is now a permanent* ~ *in the orchestra.*
PHRASES ~**s and fittings** (*BrE*)

2 (*BrE*) sporting event

ADJ. **important, major** | **difficult** | **away, home** | **annual, regular** | **opening** | **final** | **international, friendly** | **league** | **sporting**
VERB + FIXTURE **play** ◊ *The team is playing an important* ~ *this evening.* | **fulfil** ◊ *The club was fined for not fulfilling its* ~*s at the weekend.* | **make sth** ◊ *There are plans to make the race an annual* ~. | **arrange, schedule** | **stage** ◊ *The golf club has staged many international* ~*s.* | **postpone**
FIXTURE + NOUN **list** ◊ *a full* ~ *list of friendly matches*
PREP. ~ **against** ◊ *a home* ~ *against Leeds*

flag noun

ADJ. national | battle | burning | tattered ◇ *A tattered ~ hung from the roof of the burned-out building.* | **chequered/ checkered** ◇ *Hamilton took the chequered/checkered ~ to win his fourth Grand Prix of the season.* | **white** | **offside** (in football/soccer, hockey, etc.) | **warning** (*usually figurative*) ◇ *The fact that it was so cheap should have been a warning ~ for me.*
VERB + FLAG fly, hang, hang out, hoist, raise, run up ◇ *a ship flying a Russian ~* | **plant** | **lower** | **wave** ◇ *The crowd all waved ~s as the president came past.* | **unfurl** | **carry** | **salute** | **capture** | **burn**
FLAG + VERB hang | flap, flutter, fly, wave ◇ *a ~ fluttering in the breeze* | **be at half mast, fly at half mast**
FLAG + NOUN pole (*usually* **flagpole**)
PREP. under a/the **~** ◇ *a ship sailing under the Liberian ~* | **~ of** ◇ *a ~ of truce*
PHRASES **~ of convenience** | **~ of surrender**

flail verb

ADV. desperately, helplessly, wildly ◇ *She ran along, her arms ~ing wildly.*

flair noun

ADJ. considerable, great | a certain | real | natural | artistic, creative, design, dramatic, entrepreneurial (*esp. BrE*), imaginative (*esp. BrE*), theatrical, visual
VERB + FLAIR have ◇ *She has a natural ~ for languages.* | **show** | **lack** ◇ *His designs are all right, but he lacks artistic ~.* | **develop** | **add**
PREP. with **~** ◇ *jazz guitarists who improvise with ~* | **~ for** ◇ *an activist with a ~ for publicity*

flame noun

1 hot bright stream of fire

ADJ. hot | small | bright | dancing, flickering, leaping | naked (*BrE*), open (*AmE*) ◇ *pork cooked over an open ~* ◇ *Never smoke near a naked ~.* | **candle, gas** | **Olympic**
... OF FLAME ball, sheet, tongue ◇ *The plane crashed in a ball of ~s.* ◇ *Sheets of ~ shot into the air.*
VERB + FLAME ignite, light, spark (*often figurative*) ◇ *His childhood interest in the game had ignited a ~ of passion for football.* | **rekindle** (*often figurative*) ◇ *They tried to rekindle the ~s of romance.* | **blow out, extinguish, snuff, snuff out** | **feel** (*often figurative*) ◇ *She felt a ~ of anger flicker and grow.*
FLAME + VERB burn, crackle ◇ *The ~ burned brightly.* | **grow** | **die, go out** ◇ *The candle ~ flickered and went out.* | **leap, rise, shoot** ◇ *Flames leaped from the burning house.* ◇ *Flames shot high into the air.* | **lick (sth)** ◇ *Orange ~s were already licking around the foot of the stairs.* | **dance, flicker** ◇ *Flames danced in the gas lantern.*
PHRASES **the crackle of ~s**

2 flames fire

ADJ. blazing, burning, crackling, roaring | intense
VERB + FLAMES be engulfed in | go up in ◇ *All the historical records have gone up in ~s* (= *have been destroyed by fire*). | **burst into, erupt in, explode in, explode into** ◇ *The helicopter burst into ~s.* | **fuel** (*often figurative*) ◇ *Ethnic tensions helped fuel the ~s of civil war.* | **fan, feed, stoke** ◇ *Winds fanned the ~s.* | **fight** ◇ *He fought the ~s for two hours.* | **control** ◇ *Firefighters have been trying to control the ~s.* | **douse, extinguish, put out, quench, smother** ◇ *Men came with buckets of water and began to douse the ~s.* | **be beaten back by** ◇ *They tried to get into to the house but were beaten back by the ~s.*
FLAMES + VERB roar | die down | spread, sweep through sth ◇ *They watched the ~s sweep through the old wooden barn.* | **burst from sth, erupt from sth** | **consume sth, engulf sth** ◇ *The ~s quickly spread and engulfed their home.* | **light sth, light sth up** ◇ *The ~s lit up the skyline.*
PREP. in **~s** ◇ *A large part of the building was in ~s.* ◇ *The aircraft was shot down in ~s.*

flammable (*also* inflammable *esp. in BrE*) adj.

VERBS be

flank noun

ADJ. left, right | north, northern, etc. | lower ◇ *the lower ~s of Vesuvius*
VERB + FLANK attack ◇ *They decided to attack their enemy's southern ~.* | **cover, defend, guard, protect** (*all often figurative*) | **expose** (*often figurative*) ◇ *This meant exposing his ~s to his political enemies.*
PREP. along a/the **~** ◇ *along the eastern ~ of Greenland* | **down the ~** ◇ *a beautiful pass down the right ~* | **on a/the ~** ◇ *The army was attacked on the left ~.*

flap noun

ADJ. small | loose ◇ *a loose ~ of skin* | **tent** | **pocket** ◇ *a stylish jacket with leather cuffs and pocket ~s* | **cat** (*BrE*)
VERB + FLAP lift, lift back, lift up, open, pull back, push aside ◇ *He pulled back the tent ~.* | **close** | **lower** ◇ *The pilot lowered the ~s as the aircraft came into land.*

flare noun

1 bright unsteady light/flame; sudden feeling

ADJ. brief, sudden ◇ *There was a sudden ~ as a fuel tank exploded.* | **bright** | **solar** ◇ *Radiation comes from the sun during solar ~s.*
VERB + FLARE feel ◇ *She felt a sudden ~ of anger.*

2 device producing a bright flame

ADJ. distress (*BrE*), signal (*AmE*)
VERB + FLARE see ◇ *If they did not see a green ~ in ten minutes, they were to launch the attack.* | **fire, send** ◇ *The ship's crew sent up a distress ~.* | **drop** ◇ *The bomber dropped a ~ to illuminate the target.*
FLARE + VERB burn ◇ *They could see orange ~s burning in the distance.* | **illuminate sth, light sth, light sth up** ◇ *Flares lit up the night sky.*
FLARE + NOUN gun

flash noun

1 sudden bright light; sudden idea/emotion/action

ADJ. great | blinding, bright, brilliant | sudden | brief, momentary, quick | occasional | rare ◇ *a rare ~ of wit* | **lightning** | **laser** | **news** (*usually* **newsflash**) | **hot** (*AmE*) (**hot flush** *in BrE*) ◇ *She was experiencing hot ~es as part of menopause.*
VERB + FLASH experience, feel, have ◇ *He felt a brief ~ of jealousy.* ◇ *She had a sudden ~ of inspiration.* | **emit** | **catch, detect, notice, see** ◇ *We caught a ~ of white in the bushes.*
FLASH + VERB erupt | illuminate sth, light sth, light sth up ◇ *A bright ~ of lightning lit up the sky.* | **blind** ◇ *We were blinded by the ~.*
PREP. **~ from** ◇ *The ~es from the guns illuminated the sky.* | **~ of** ◇ *a sudden ~ of light*

2 bright light for a camera

ADJ. built-in | camera
VERB + FLASH use ◇ *I don't think the picture will come out in this light. Try using the ~.*
FLASH + VERB go off, work ◇ *The ~ didn't go off.*
FLASH + NOUN photography
PREP. with (a) **~** ◇ *I took it with ~.*

flash verb

1 shine

ADV. briefly ◇ *It was only the sun, ~ing briefly on her hair.* | **brightly**
PREP. at ◇ *A car ~ed its headlights at me.*

2 show emotion

ADV. suddenly | angrily, dangerously, menacingly ◇ *Her eyes ~ed angrily.*
PREP. with ◇ *Her eyes suddenly ~ed with anger.*

flashback *noun*

ADJ. **sudden**
VERB + FLASHBACK **get, have**
PREP. **in (a) ~** ◇ *The story is told in ~.* | **~ to** ◇ *I had a sudden ~ to the time immediately after the war.*

flashlight *noun* (*esp. AmE*) → See also TORCH

ADJ. **pocket, small**
VERB + FLASHLIGHT **point, shine** ◇ *Neesha pointed her ~ at the floor.* ◇ *Don't shine the ~ in my face!*
FLASHLIGHT + NOUN **beam** ◇ *The ~ beam revealed a pile of sacks.*

flask *noun*

ADJ. **metal, silver | water | hip** (*BrE*) **| conical, culture, glass, round-bottom** (*all science*) **| Thermos™, vacuum** (*both BrE*)
VERB + FLASK **fill | carry** ◇ *When he climbed in the snow he always carried a silver ~ of brandy for emergencies.* | **pull out** ◇ *She pulled out her ~ and drank from it.* | **open, unscrew | drink (sth) from, take a swallow from, take a swig from**
FLASK + VERB **contain sth** ◇ *a culture ~ containing 4 ml of the medium*
PREP. **~ of** ◇ *He had a ~ of Scotch in his pocket.*

flat *noun*

1 (*BrE*) set of rooms → See also APARTMENT

ADJ. **big, spacious | modest | cramped, little, poky, small, tiny | comfortable, cosy | beautiful, nice | luxury, posh | shabby | modern | self-contained | purpose-built | furnished, unfurnished | one-room, studio | one-bedroomed, two-room, etc. | bachelor, granny** ◇ *Even the prices of small bachelor ~s are unbelievable.* ◇ *They converted two rooms of their house into a granny ~ for Tony's elderly mother.* | **attic, basement, bottom, downstairs, first-floor, ground-floor, penthouse, top, top-floor, upstairs** ◇ *the people who live in the downstairs ~* | **high-rise** ◇ *a block of high-rise ~s* | **empty, unoccupied | rented | council | holiday | next** ◇ *They live in the next ~.*
...OF FLATS **block** ◇ *The tall blocks of ~s dominated the skyline.*
VERB + FLAT **have, own** ◇ *They have a ~ in Paris and a house in Normandy.* | **rent** ◇ *The musician rented a ~ in a fashionable area of London.* | **let, sublet** ◇ *The landlady found they had been illegally subletting the ~.* | **buy, sell | find (sb), look for** ◇ *Do you think that the council could find me another ~?* | **get (sb)** ◇ *We got her a ~ in the same block as ours.* | **live in, occupy, stay in** ◇ *Our ~ is one of the two occupied in the block.* | **share | move into | move from, move out from, move out of | build | decorate, refurbish** ◇ *a contract to refurbish 18 council ~s* | **lock, lock up | let sb/yourself into** ◇ *She let herself into the ~ with the spare key.* | **leave, let sb/yourself out of | break into | evict sb from**
FLAT + VERB **be located** ◇ *The ~ is located in a modern development.* | **face sth, overlook sth** ◇ *a luxury block of ~s overlooking the marina*
PREP. **at a/the ~** ◇ *I'll meet you back at your ~.* | **in a/the ~** ◇ *She lives in the top ~.*
PHRASES **convert sth into ~s, divide sth into ~s, make sth into ~s, turn sth into ~s** ◇ *The house has now been converted into ~s.*

2 flats low-lying land

ADJ. **coastal** (*esp. BrE*), **tidal | mud** (usually **mudflat**), **salt, sand** ◇ *mud and sand ~s rich in animal life*
PREP. **on the ~** ◇ *These birds live on the tidal ~s.*

flat *adj.*

VERBS **be, look | become | lie, stay** ◇ *I can't get this material to lie ~.* ◇ *She lay ~ on the ground.* | **remain, stay** ◇ *Interest rates have remained ~.* | **fold sth, get sth, make sth, press sth** ◇ *Shall I fold the paper ~ or roll it up?* | **knock sb** ◇ *He knocked me ~ on my back.*

ADV. **extremely, fairly, very, etc. | absolutely, completely, perfectly** ◇ *The sea was almost completely ~.* | **almost, nearly**

flattered *adj.*

VERBS **be, feel**
ADV. **extremely, fairly, very, etc. | immensely | a little, slightly, etc.**
PREP. **at** ◇ *She felt vaguely ~ at the suggestion.*

flattering *adj.*

VERBS **be | find sth**
ADV. **extremely, fairly, very, etc. | hardly, less than** ◇ *The descriptions of her were less than ~.*
PREP. **to** ◇ *This style of dress is ~ to most women.*

flaunt *verb*

ADV. **openly, proudly** ◇ *openly ~ing their wealth*
PREP. **in front of** ◇ *She ~ed her success in front of the others.*

flavour (*BrE*) (*AmE* flavor) *noun*

1 taste of food

ADJ. **delicious, fine** (*esp. BrE*), **good, lovely** (*esp. BrE*), **pleasant** (*esp. BrE*), **wonderful | characteristic** (*esp. BrE*), **distinctive, particular, unique | full, pronounced** (*esp. BrE*), **rich, strong | complex, intense | delicate, mild, subtle | extra | fresh | sweet | bitter, sharp, sour, tangy | salty | spicy | smoky | exotic | cheese, chocolate, fruit, lemon, mint, nutty, etc. | ice-cream | natural | artificial** (*AmE*) (usually **artificial flavouring** in *BrE*)
VERB + FLAVOUR/FLAVOR **have** ◇ *It has a very mild ~.* | **keep, retain** ◇ *Delicate herbs keep their ~ better when frozen.* | **lose | add, give sth, impart, lend (sth), provide** ◇ *a spice that gives a characteristic ~ to a range of dishes* | **bring out, enhance, improve, release** ◇ *The lemon juice brings out the natural fruit ~s.* ◇ *Bay leaves should be broken to release their ~.* | **spoil | destroy** ◇ *Cooking the vegetable destroys its wonderful delicate ~.* | **appreciate, enjoy, savour/savor, taste** ◇ *Enjoy the ~ of fresh fish.*
FLAVOUR/FLAVOR + NOUN **enhancer** ◇ *Salt is a common ~ enhancer.*
PREP. **for ~** ◇ *Cream may be added to the sauce for extra ~.* | **in ~** ◇ *It is stronger in ~ than other Dutch cheeses.* | **with a ~** ◇ *a dish with a strong spicy ~*
PHRASES **full of ~** ◇ *vegetables that are fresh and full of ~*

2 particular quality/atmosphere

ADJ. **distinctive, particular, unique | strong** ◇ *The festival has a strong international ~.* | **international, local, regional** ◇ *The festival has a strong international ~.* | **American, Scandinavian, etc. | political**
VERB + FLAVOUR/FLAVOR **have** ◇ *The college has a truly international ~.* | **acquire, take on** ◇ *The music festival has taken on a distinctly German ~.* | **lose | add, give sth, impart, provide** ◇ *The intervention of the authorities gave union struggles a decidedly political ~.* | **experience, get** ◇ *The children experienced the ~ of medieval life.* ◇ *She rotated around the departments to get a ~ of all aspects of the business.* | **appreciate, enjoy | capture** ◇ *The movie captures the ~ of rural life in this area.* | **convey**
PREP. **with a ... ~** ◇ *a TV show with a Mexican ~*

flavoured (*BrE*) (*AmE* flavored) *adj.*

VERBS **be** ◇ *The food they eat is very highly ~.*
ADV. **highly, intensely, richly, strongly, well** (*BrE*) **| delicately** ◇ *a delicately ~ clear soup*
PREP. **with** ◇ *This dish is ~ with basil and garlic.*

flavouring (*BrE*) (*AmE* flavoring) *noun*

ADJ. **artificial** (*esp. BrE*), **natural** ◇ *This product contains only natural ~s.* | **food | vanilla** (*esp. BrE*)
...OF FLAVOURING/FLAVORING **drop** ◇ *Add a few drops of vanilla ~.*
VERB + FLAVOURING/FLAVORING **contain | use** ◇ *We don't use any artificial ~s in our products.* | **add**

flaw noun

ADJ. **big, main, major, serious** | **basic, critical, fatal, fundamental** | **inherent** | **minor, small** | **obvious** | **design** | **security** | **character**
VERB + FLAW **contain, have** ◊ *Unfortunately, this plate has a small ~ in it.* | **look for** | **discover, find, identify, see, spot** ◊ *It took me a long time to find the ~ in her logic.* ◊ *Engineers have identified serious design ~s in the proposed nuclear waste dump.* | **expose, highlight, point out, point to, reveal** ◊ *The markets have exposed the fatal ~ in the government's economic policy.* | **correct, fix**
FLAW + VERB **appear, become apparent** ◊ *Flaws have appeared in the new version of the software.*
PREP. **~ in** ◊ *one of the major ~s in his character*

flawed adj.

VERBS **be, seem** | **remain**
ADV. **badly, deeply, highly** (AmE)**, hopelessly, seriously** | **fatally** ◊ *a series of fatally ~ judgements* | **fundamentally** | **inherently** | **slightly, somewhat** | **conceptually, methodologically** ◊ *The study was methodologically ~.*

flea noun

VERB + FLEA **get, have** | **be infested with** | **control, kill** ◊ *This drug is given to dogs to control ~s.*
FLEA + VERB **bite** | **carry disease, spread disease**
FLEA + NOUN **bite** | **collar, powder**

flee verb

ADV. **abroad** (esp. BrE)**, across the border, into exile** ◊ *Hundreds of refugees fled across the border to escape the fighting.* | **north, south, etc.** | **in panic, in terror** ◊ *The children fled in terror as the hay caught fire.*
VERB + FLEE **be forced to, have to** ◊ *They were forced to ~ the country.* | **try to** | **manage to** | **turn and ~** ◊ *They turned and fled when they saw the gang approaching.*
PREP. **from** ◊ *She dropped the phone and fled from the office.* | **into, to** ◊ *They fled to Britain when the war started.*
PHRASES **~ empty-handed** ◊ *When the police arrived the burglars fled empty-handed.* | **~ for your life** ◊ *She had to ~ for her life when soldiers attacked her town.* | **~ like the wind** ◊ *When danger threatens, collect your possessions and ~ like the wind.* | **~ to safety** ◊ *The family managed to ~ to safety.*

fleet noun

ADJ. **entire** ◊ *The entire ~ was sunk.* | **great, huge, large** ◊ *a large ~ of warships* | **small** | **fishing, whaling** | **merchant** | **naval** | **battle, invasion** | **enemy** | **submarine, tanker** | **car, vehicle** ◊ *the company car ~*
VERB + FLEET **operate** ◊ *He operated a small fishing ~.* | **command** | **send, send in** ◊ *The ~ was sent in and the country prepared for war.* | **ground** | **defeat, destroy** | **join** ◊ *The ship sailed to join the ~ at Barbados.* | **maintain** ◊ *To maintain a submarine ~ is a major commitment.*
PREP. **in a/the ~** ◊ *There were over 500 ships in the enemy ~.* | **~ of** ◊ *a ~ of taxis*

flesh noun

1 soft part of sb's body
ADJ. **firm, smooth, soft, tender** | **pale, pink, white** | **bare, exposed, naked** | **raw** | **torn** | **burned, burning** | **decaying, rotting** | **dead, living** | **animal, human**
VERB + FLESH **touch** | **cut, cut into** ◊ *The chain cut into his tender ~.* | **strip, tear at, tear off** ◊ *Falcons usually strip the ~ off their prey.* ◊ *African hunting dogs will tear at the ~ of their victim until it is weak.* | **dig into, pierce, pierce into, tear, tear into** ◊ *The weapon tore into his ~.* | **eat** | **become, make sth** (literary) ◊ *In the Christian tradition, God is made ~ (= becomes human).*
FLESH + VERB **crawl, creep** (both figurative) ◊ *The story made his ~ creep (= made him feel afraid).*
FLESH + NOUN **wound** ◊ *The injury was only a ~ wound.* | **tone** ◊ *The tights come in various ~ tones.*
PREP. **in the ~** ◊ *Thousands of fans gathered to see the band in the ~ (= see the band in reality and not just in a picture).*

PHRASES **~ and blood** ◊ *a man of ~ and blood (= not a ghost)* | **~ and bone** ◊ *The knife cut through ~ and bone.* | **the pleasures of the ~, the sins of the ~, the temptations of the ~** | **the smell of ~** ◊ *the smell of rotting ~*

2 soft part of fruit/vegetables
ADJ. **soft** | **sweet** | **juicy**
VERB + FLESH **chop, cut** | **scoop, scoop out** ◊ *Cut the melon in half and scoop out the ~.*

flex noun (BrE) → See also CORD

ADJ. **long** | **trailing** ◊ *Long trailing ~es are a serious trip hazard.* | **electric, electrical** | **kettle, telephone, etc.**
... OF FLEX **length**
VERB + FLEX **cut** ◊ *Side cutters are useful for cutting electrical ~ to length.*

flexibility noun

ADJ. **considerable, great** ◊ *German workers accept the need for greater ~ in the face of global competition.* | **added, additional, extra, increased, more** | **maximum** | **enough, sufficient** | **financial** | **operational** ◊ *Management systems can be built that increase operational ~.* | **labour/labor, market**
... OF FLEXIBILITY **degree** ◊ *The work involves a considerable degree of ~.*
VERB + FLEXIBILITY **have** ◊ *You have considerable ~ in this job and can choose how to do things.* | **lack** | **demonstrate, show** | **maintain, retain** | **bring (sb/sth), give (sb/sth), introduce, provide (sb/sth with)** ◊ *The new range of machines will bring ~ to your business computing.* | **allow (sb/sth), offer (sb/sth), permit** ◊ *The courses are designed to allow maximum ~.* | **improve, increase** ◊ *The treatment increased the ~ of her muscles.* | **encourage** ◊ *an initiative to encourage greater ~ in teaching and learning* | **reduce** | **need, require**
PREP. **~ in** ◊ *This will give schools greater ~ in their use of resources.* | **~ over** ◊ *~ over the deadline*
PHRASES **a need for ~** ◊ *There is a need for greater ~ in the way the network is managed.*

flexible adj.

VERBS **be, seem** | **become** | **remain, stay** | **make sth** ◊ *We need to make the working day more ~.* | **keep sth**
ADV. **extremely, fairly, very, etc.** | **completely, highly** | **infinitely** ◊ *Human beings are infinitely ~ and able to adjust when survival depends on it.* | **enough, sufficiently**
PHRASES **about** ◊ *My mother is fairly ~ about what time I need to be home.*

flick noun

ADJ. **quick** | **deft**
VERB + FLICK **give (sth)** ◊ *The fish gave a quick ~ of its tail.*
PREP. **with a ~** | **~ of** ◊ *With a ~ of his wrist he removed the ash from the end of his cigarette.*
PHRASES **at the ~ of a switch** ◊ *Heat is available at the ~ of a switch (= instantly).*

flick verb

ADV. **casually** | **nervously** | **quickly** | **away, back**
PREP. **across** ◊ *His tongue ~ed nervously across dry lips.* | **from** ◊ *He casually ~ed away some dust from his jacket.* | **off** ◊ *She ~ed the ash off her cigarette.* | **over** ◊ *His eyes ~ed quickly over the screen.*
PHRASES **~ sth open** ◊ *She snatched up her briefcase and ~ed it open.*

PHR V **flick through sth**
ADV. **absent-mindedly, casually, idly** ◊ *She ~ed idly through a magazine.* | **quickly**

flicker noun

ADJ. **faint, slight, small, tiny** ◊ *She caught the faintest ~ of amusement on his face.* | **brief** | **sudden** | **last** (often *figurative*) ◇ *The police stamped out the last ~s of freedom.* | **candle**

VERB + FLICKER **show** | **catch, notice, see** | **detect, feel** ◇ *She felt a brief ~ of jealousy.*

FLICKER + VERB **cross sth** ◇ *A ~ of guilt crossed his face.* | **catch sb's eye** ◇ *A ~ of movement caught her eye.*

PREP. **~ of** ◇ *'He'll soon be here,' she thought, with a ~ of excitement.* ◇ *She spoke without a ~ of fear.*

PHRASES **the ~ of a candle, the ~ of a flame** ◇ *The brief ~ of a candle flame caught our eyes.* | **a ~ of sb's/the eyes** ◇ *Her only reaction was a slight ~ of her eyes.* | **a ~ of hope, a ~ of interest** ◇ *Stock markets showed barely a ~ of interest in the election result.* | **a ~ of light, a ~ of movement** ◇ *He saw a ~ of light in the darkness.* | **a ~ of recognition** ◇ *The witness stared at the accused but she showed not a ~ of recognition.* | **a ~ of a smile** ◇ *I noticed a ~ of a smile on her face.*

flicker *verb*

ADV. **briefly, for a moment, momentarily** | **slightly** | **nervously** ◇ *Her eyes ~ed nervously in anticipation.* | **rapidly** | **off, out** | **on and off** ◇ *The lights ~ed on and off.*

PREP. **across, over** ◇ *His gaze ~ed over her.*

PHRASES **~ into life, ~ to life** ◇ *The television screen ~ed into life.* | **~ open** ◇ *Kate's eyes ~ed open.*

flight *noun*

1 trip by air; plane making a flight

ADJ. **round-trip** (*AmE*) ◇ *The first prize is a round-trip ~ to Rio.* | **inbound, return** ◇ *The return ~ was held up by six hours.* ◇ *The first prize is a return ~ to Rio.* (*BrE*) | **outbound** ◇ *The outbound ~ was smooth.* | **connecting** | **shuttle** | **commercial** | **regular, scheduled** | **charter** | **daily, weekly** | **direct, non-stop** | **delayed** | **two-hour, three-hour, etc.** | **short** | **long, long-distance, long-haul, red-eye** (*esp. AmE*) | **cross-country** (*esp. AmE*), **domestic, internal** (*esp. BrE*) | **international, transatlantic** | **maiden** ◇ *The aircraft made its maiden ~ in January 2000.* | **early** | **day, evening, morning, night** | **bumpy, smooth** ◇ *The bumpy ~ brought on a bout of airsickness.* | **mercy** (*BrE*), **relief** | **military** | **reconnaissance, surveillance** | **routine** | **training** ◇ *a routine training ~* | **solo** | **air, space** | **airline, balloon, helicopter, plane, rocket** ◇ *a hot-air balloon ~* | **cargo, passenger** | **budget** (*BrE*), **cheap, discounted**

VERB + FLIGHT **catch, take, travel on** ◇ *They caught an early ~ back to Boston.* | **miss** ◇ *We arrived at the airport just in time to make our ~.* | **have** ◇ *Did you have a good ~?* | **enjoy** ◇ *I hope you enjoy the ~.* | **make** ◇ *The plane made its maiden ~ in 1976.* | **be booked on, be booked onto, be on** ◇ *I'm on the first ~ to Milan in the morning.* | **book (sb), book sb/yourself on, book sb/yourself onto, get** ◇ *He asked her to book him on the next available ~ to Geneva.* ◇ *We managed to get a non-stop ~ to New York.* | **charter** ◇ *The team has chartered a special ~ for their fans.* | **confirm** | **cancel, suspend** ◇ *The UN has suspended relief ~s because of shelling around the airport.* | **change** ◇ *If you need to change a ~, the fee is $100.* | **board** | **operate** ◇ *The airline operates regular ~s to Greece.* | **delay, hold up** | **divert** ◇ *The ~ was diverted to Delhi because of a bomb scare.* | **ground** ◇ *All ~s have been grounded for security reasons.* | **blow up**

FLIGHT + VERB **be bound for sth** ◇ *a ~ bound for Antigua* | **leave, take off** | **originate** ◇ *a ~ originating from Tokyo* | **arrive** | **land** | **be full** ◇ *I'm afraid I can't book you onto that ~ as it's full.*

FLIGHT + NOUN **number** ◇ *We need your time of arrival and ~ number.* | **schedule** | **operations** ◇ *The snow was severe enough to disrupt ~ operations.* | **time** ◇ *The ~ time from Heathrow to Marseilles is less than two hours.* | **delay** ◇ *Your travel insurance compensates you for ~ delays.* | **cancellation** | **attendant, crew** | **commander, engineer** (*both military*) | **school** | **deck** | **controller** | **instruments** | **recorder** ◇ *The ~ recorder should help to establish why the plane suddenly crashed.* | **simulator** | **path** ◇ *They have persuaded the authorities to divert the ~ path of the military jets away from their town.*

PREP. **aboard a/the ~, on a/the ~, on board a/the ~** ◇ *passengers aboard a ~ bound for Johannesburg* | **during a/ the ~** ◇ *Please refrain from smoking during the ~.* | **~ for** ◇ *She took a ~ for Los Angeles.* | **~ from, ~ out of** ◇ *They waited for the first ~ out of Lisbon.* | **~ to** ◇ *a ~ from Sydney to Tokyo*

2 action of flying

ADJ. **soaring, sustained** | **low-level** | **horizontal, level** | **high-speed, supersonic** | **space** | **manned** ◇ *the enormous costs of manned space ~*

VERB + FLIGHT **be capable of** ◇ *Barn owls are capable of ~ at 56 days.* | **achieve** ◇ *Bats are the only mammals to have achieved sustained ~.* | **take** ◇ *They watched the young eagles take ~.*

PREP. **during ~** ◇ *The wings vibrate during ~.* | **in ~** ◇ *a flock of geese in ~*

PHRASES **the line of ~** ◇ *the line of ~ of a golf ball*

3 number of stairs/steps

ADJ. **long, short** | **narrow, wide** | **steep**

VERB + FLIGHT **climb, climb up, go up, run up, walk up** | **descend, go down, run down, walk down** | **fall down**

FLIGHT + VERB **lead ...** ◇ *a ~ of steps leading to the foyer* | **go down sth, go up sth** ◇ *A ~ of steps goes up the left-hand side of the room.*

PREP. **down a/the ~, up a/the ~** ◇ *My office is just up that ~ of stairs.*

PHRASES **a ~ of stairs, a ~ of steps** ◇ *The villa is fronted by a ~ of stairs.*

4 running away

ADJ. **headlong** | **urban, white** (= the movement of white people from cities) (*both AmE*)

VERB + FLIGHT **put (sb/sth) to** (*literary*) ◇ *The army was defeated and the king put to ~.* | **take** ◇ *As soon as they detected the cheetah it took ~.*

PREP. **in ~** ◇ *Left-wing opposition leaders, in ~ from persecution, went across the border.* | **~ from** ◇ *a headlong ~ from danger* | **~ into** ◇ *a ~ into the unknown* | **~ to** ◇ *The story tells of his ~ to safety.*

flinch *verb*

ADV. **barely, hardly** ◇ *He hardly ~ed when he was hit.* | **almost** | **never, not** | **a little, slightly, etc.** | **visibly** | **inwardly** ◇ *She ~ed inwardly as he took her hand.* | **away, back** (*AmE*)

VERB + FLINCH **make sb** ◇ *Her finger touched the scar on his forehead, making him ~.*

PREP. **at** ◇ *She ~ed visibly at the sight of the body.* | **from** ◇ *She ~ed away from him.* ◇ *She won't ~ from speaking her mind.* (*figurative*) | **with** ◇ *He ~ed with the force of the blow.*

float *verb*

1 on water/in air

ADV. **gently** | **slowly** | **downstream** | **downwards/down- ward** | **upwards/upward** | **about** (*esp. BrE*), **around, away, back, down, off, out, up**

VERB + FLOAT **seem to** ◇ *Her voice seemed to ~ gently on the water.*

PREP. **across** ◇ *A few small clouds ~ed across the sky.* | **down** ◇ *chunks of ice ~ing down the river* | **in** ◇ *pieces of wood ~ing in the water* | **on** ◇ *A few leaves ~ed on the surface of the water.*

2 currency

ADV. **freely** ◇ *The government decided to allow the peso to ~ freely.*

VERB + FLOAT **allow sth to**

flood *noun*

1 large amount of water

ADJ. **catastrophic, devastating, great, severe** | **flash** | **spring, summer, etc.**

VERB + FLOOD **cause** ◇ *Heavy rainfall in the mountains caused the ~s.*

FLOOD + VERB **come** ◇ *No one knew that the ~ was coming.* | **hit sth, strike sth** ◇ *This summer the region was struck by*

devastating ~s. | **inundate sth** ◊ *The fields were inundated by heavy ~s.* | **cause sth** ◊ *The ~ caused widespread destruction.* | **subside** ◊ *The ~s are slowly subsiding.*
FLOOD + NOUN **water** (usually *floodwater* or *floodwaters*) ◊ *The floodwaters did not begin to recede until September.* | **plain** | **damage** | **alert** (*BrE*), **warning** | **victim** | **control, defence/defense, prevention, protection, relief** | **insurance**
PHRASES **be in (full) ~** (*esp. BrE*) ◊ *The river was in full ~ (= had flooded its banks).*
2 large number/amount
ADJ. **great** | **constant** | **sudden**
FLOOD + VERB **inundate sb/sth** ◊ *She was inundated by ~s of fan mail.*
VERB + FLOOD **bring, cause** | **release, unleash**
PREP. **~ of** ◊ *a great ~ of refugees*
PHRASES **a ~ of memories** (*esp. AmE*) ◊ *Writing about St. John's brings back a ~ of nostalgic memories.* | **in ~s of tears** (= crying a lot) ◊ *The little girl was in ~s of tears.*

floor *noun*

1 lower surface of a room
ADJ. **bare, cold, hard** ◊ *I can't sleep on the bare ~!* | **dirty, dusty** | **wet** | **clean, polished, smooth** | **cement, concrete, stone** | **dirt** (*esp. AmE*) | **hardwood, parquet, wood, wooden** | **carpeted, linoleum, marble, tiled** | **bathroom, kitchen, etc.** | **raised** | **dance**
VERB + FLOOR **clean, mop, polish, scrub, sweep, wash, wax, wipe** | **drop to, fall to** ◊ *His glass fell to the ~ and broke.* | **hit** | **reach, touch** | **pace, walk** | **cover, litter**
FLOOR + NOUN **covering, mat, tile** | **lamp** (*esp. AmE*) | **space** | **exercises** | **plan**
PREP. **on the ~** ◊ *Do you mind sitting on the ~?*
PHRASES **from ~ to ceiling** ◊ *Bookcases lined the walls from ~ to ceiling.*
2 bottom of the sea, a forest, etc.
ADJ. **canyon, cave, desert, forest, ocean, sea, valley**
3 level in a building
ADJ. **bottom, first** (= at entrance level) (*AmE*), **ground** (*BrE*) | **top** | **first, second, third, etc.** (In *BrE*, the first floor is the floor above the entrance level. This is called the *second floor* in *AmE*.) | **mezzanine** | **lower, upper**
VERB + FLOOR **occupy** ◊ *The offices occupy the top ~ of the building.*
PREP. **on the ~** ◊ *a cafe on the mezzanine ~*

floorboard *noun*

ADJ. **wooden** | **bare** | **polished** | **loose** | **creaky, squeaky**
VERB + FLOORBOARD **lift, lift up** ◊ *Lift some loose ~s to get at the pipes.*
FLOORBOARD + VERB **creak** ◊ *The wooden ~s creaked as he walked down the corridor.*
PREP. **beneath the ~s, under the ~s, underneath the ~s** ◊ *They said that he kept his money under the ~s.*
PHRASES **a gap between the ~s, a gap in the ~s** (both *esp. BrE*) ◊ *She could hear voices through the gaps in the ~s.*

flop *noun*

ADJ. **big, resounding, spectacular** ◊ *The show was the biggest ~ in TV history.* | **complete, total** | **expensive** ◊ *The concert may prove an expensive ~ unless more people decide to go.* | **box-office, commercial**

flour *noun*

ADJ. **bread, cake** | **all-purpose** (*AmE*), **baking** (*AmE*), **plain** (*BrE*), **self-raising** (*BrE*), **self-rising** (*AmE*) | **strong** (*BrE*) | **refined, white, wholemeal** (*BrE*), **wholewheat** | **unbleached** | **rice, rye, wheat, etc.**
...OF FLOUR **bag, cup** (*AmE*), **sack**
VERB + FLOUR **use** | **add, blend, combine, fold in, mix, mix in, rub sth in, rub sth into, stir, stir in** ◊ *Blend the ~ with a little milk to make a smooth paste.* ◊ *Rub the butter into the ~.* | **sieve, sift** ◊ *Sift the ~ and salt into a bowl.*

FLOUR + NOUN **mill**
→ Special page at FOOD

flourish *noun*

ADJ. **final** | **dramatic, rhetorical, theatrical** ◊ *a speech full of rhetorical ~es*
VERB + FLOURISH **add** | **end in, end with, finish with**
PREP. **with a ~** ◊ *With a final ~ she laid down her pen.* ◊ *Bill signed on the bottom line with a ~.*

flow *noun*

ADJ. **heavy, large, massive** | **good** | **adequate** | **poor** ◊ *Our shower doesn't work very well because of the poor water ~.* | **main** | **increased, increasing** | **decreased, reduced** | **ceaseless, constant, continuous, endless** | **free, uninterrupted** ◊ *the uninterrupted ~ of traffic* | **even, smooth, steady** ◊ *to maintain an even ~ of work through the department* | **easy, natural** ◊ *I liked the concerto for its natural ~.* | **outward** ◊ *the outward ~ of investment from the country* | **annual, daily, seasonal** | **data, information** | **air, gas, heat** | **blood, menstrual** | **lava, river, water** | **traffic** | **capital, cash, financial, investment, production, trade, work** | **narrative**
VERB + FLOW **have** ◊ *Big pension funds have a constant ~ of cash.* | **get, obtain** ◊ *Squeeze the tube slowly to obtain an even ~.* | **allow** ◊ *We like to allow a free ~ of ideas in our company.* | **create, generate, produce, provide** ◊ *The system provides a continuous ~ of information to the market.* | **keep, maintain** ◊ *He kept up a ~ of chatter.* | **ensure** ◊ *Use a wide pipe to ensure an adequate ~ of water.* | **control, manage, regulate** | **follow** | **encourage, facilitate, stimulate** ◊ *to encourage the ~ of revenue into the country* | **enhance, improve, increase, restore** ◊ *The company is trying to enhance its cash ~.* | **affect** | **disrupt, impede, reduce, restrict, slow, slow down** ◊ *The continual bombing disrupted the ~ of supplies to the ground troops.* | **block, break, break up, cut, cut off, halt, interrupt, staunch, stem, stop** ◊ *They tried to staunch the ~ of blood.* | **direct** | **divert** ◊ *The main ~ of water has been diverted to a new course.* | **join** | **measure**
FLOW + NOUN **rate** ◊ *The ~ rate was measured at 9.5 gallons per second.* | **chart, diagram**
PREP. **against the ~** ◊ *They have to swim against the ~ of the river.* | **~ among** ◊ *information ~ among all the different groups* | **~ from** ◊ *First cut off the water ~ from the boiler.* | **~ into** ◊ *She joined the ~ of immigrants to the country.* | **~ of** ◊ *a constant ~ of information* | **~ through** ◊ *the ~ of data through the system*
PHRASES **the ebb and ~** ◊ *the ebb and ~ of the tide* ◊ *He was at the mercy of the ebb and ~ of public opinion.* (*figurative*) | **in full ~** ◊ *She tried to interrupt his speech, but he was already in full ~ (= talking continuously).* | **the rate of ~** ◊ *the rate of ~ of water through the pipe*

flow *verb*

ADV. **easily, effortlessly, freely, smoothly** ◊ *We talked, and the conversation ~ed freely.* ◊ *Wine and beer ~ed freely.* | **seamlessly** ◊ *The songs ~ seamlessly into one another.* | **gently, gracefully** | **fast, quickly, rapidly, swiftly** ◊ *The river ~s very fast here.* | **slowly, steadily** | **naturally, nicely, well** ◊ *In a good production of the play, the action and the words ~ naturally.* | **directly** ◊ *Some of these changes will ~ directly from the legislation.* | **constantly, continuously** | **away, back, in, out, past** | **together**
VERB + FLOW **seem to** | **begin to, start to** | **continue to** ◊ *Imported food aid continued to ~ in.*
PREP. **across, along, between, down** ◊ *a small stream that ~ed down the hillside* | **from** ◊ *Blood was still ~ing from the wound.* | **into** ◊ *One day seemed to ~ into the next.* | **out of, over, through** ◊ *Information ~s continuously through the network.* | **to** ◊ *to get blood ~ing to the brain*
PHRASES **ebb and ~** ◊ *The sea ebbed and ~ed.* ◊ *The number of buyers has ebbed and ~ed.* (*figurative*) | **~ in a … direction** ◊ *The best thing is when ideas ~ in both directions.* | **~ in the**

breeze, ~ **in the wind** ◇ *Her long hair ~ed in the wind as she ran.*

NOTE

Flowers

grow... ◇ *Tulips are grown everywhere.*

breed... ◇ *She breeds orchids in her greenhouse.*

plant..., **put in**... ◇ *Spring is the best time to plant chrysanthemums.*

dig out..., **dig up**..., **take out**... ◇ *Dig up your geraniums before the first frosts.*

spray..., **water**... ◇ *It's a good idea to spray your roses against greenfly.*

prune roses, **deadhead**... ◇ *Don't forget to deadhead the pansies.*

pick (sb)... ◇ *I picked some daffodils for you.*

smell... ◇ *He stopped to smell the flowers.*

arrange... ◇ *She arranged the tulips in a vase.*

bring (sb)..., **give (sb)**..., **send (sb)**..., **take (sb)**... ◇ *I sent him flowers to apologize.*

deliver..., **order**... ◇ *I ordered flowers online for her birthday.*

... **grows** ◇ *Daffodils grow wild in the mountains.*

... **blooms**, ... **is in bloom**, ... **comes into flower**, ... **comes out**, ... **is in flower**, ... **is out**, ... **flowers** ◇ *The spring flowers were just coming out.* ◇ *What time of year do daffodils flower?*

... **smells** ◇ *Some of these roses smell absolutely wonderful.*

... **closes**, ... **closes up**, ... **opens**, ... **opens up** ◇ *You know it's summer when the first daisies open.*

... **droops**, ... **wilts**, ... **withers** ◇ *The petunias were already wilting in the hot sun.*

... **is over** ◇ *It was April and the snowdrops were long over.*

a bouquet of..., **a bunch of**..., **a garland of**..., **a posy of**..., **a spray of**..., **a vase of**... ◇ *a spray of mixed violets and primroses*

---

flower *noun*

ADJ. **bright**, **brightly coloured/colored**, **brilliantly coloured/ colored**, **colourful/colorful**, **fragrant**, **scented** | **delicate** | **little**, **small**, **tiny** | **big**, **huge**, **large** | **bell-shaped**, **star- shaped**, etc. | **exotic**, **rare** | **garden**, **tropical**, **wild** | **spring**, **summer**, etc. | **seasonal** | **beautiful**, **lovely**, **pretty** ◇ *What beautiful ~s!* | **fresh** | **cut** | **dried**, **pressed** | **dead**, **wilted** | **artificial** | **plastic**, **silk** | **closed**, **open** ◇ *The ~s were still tightly closed.* | **blooming** | **hibiscus**, **lotus**, etc.
... OF FLOWERS **bouquet**, **bunch**
VERB + FLOWER **bear**, **have**, **produce** ◇ *It was the first year that the cactus had produced ~s.* | **pollinate** ◇ *The ~s are pollinated by insects.* | **get**, **receive**
FLOWER + VERB **appear** | **go to seed**
FLOWER + NOUN **bud**, **head**, **petal**, **seed**, **spike**, **stalk**, **stem** | **bed**, **border** | **arrangement**, **arranger**, **arranging** ◇ *I'm learning ~ arranging.* | **display** | **basket**, **container**, **pot** (usually *flowerpot*), **vase** | **garden**, **festival** (*BrE*), **show** | **market**, **seller**, **shop**, **stall** (*esp. BrE*), **stand** | **power** (= hippy culture)
PREP. **in ~** ◇ *It was June and the roses were in ~.*
PHRASES **a bank of ~s**, **a carpet of ~s**, **a mass of ~s** ◇ *The alleys were adorned with banks of ~s.* ◇ *The forest floor was a carpet of wild ~s.* | **covered in ~s** ◇ *The bush was absolutely covered in ~s.* | **come into** ◇ *If the winter weather is mild, plants may come into ~ too early.* | **in full ~** ◇ *The park will have cherries in full ~ this month.*

flu *noun*

ADJ. **mild** | **bad** | **gastric** (*BrE*), **stomach** (*AmE*) | **avian**, **bird** | **pandemic**

... OF FLU **bout** (*esp. BrE*), **case**, **dose** ◇ *She's had a nasty dose of ~.* (*BrE*) ◇ *She's had a nasty dose of the ~.* (*AmE*) | **strain**
VERB + FLU **be in bed with** (*esp. BrE*), **have**, **suffer from** | **catch**, **come down with**, **contract**, **get**, **go down with** (*BrE*)
FLU + NOUN **bug**, **virus** | **epidemic**, **outbreak**, **pandemic** | **symptoms** | **victim** | **vaccine** | **jab** (*BrE*), **shot** (*AmE*), **vaccination** | **strain** | **season** (= time when a lot of people suffer from flu)
PHRASES **a bout with the ~** (*AmE*) ◇ *She was off work for four days because of a bout with the ~.*
→ Special page at ILLNESS

fluctuate *verb*

ADV. **considerably**, **greatly** | **dramatically**, **widely**, **wildly** ◇ *Prices have ~d wildly in recent years.* | **constantly** ◇ *constantly fluctuating patterns*
PREP. **according to** ◇ *Traffic congestion ~s according to the time of day.* | **around** ◇ *The number of students ~s around 100.* | **between** ◇ *The number of unemployed ~s between two and three million.*

fluctuation *noun*

ADJ. **considerable**, **large**, **wide**, **wild** | **local**, **minor**, **small** | **rapid** | **short-term** | **cyclical**, **periodic**, **seasonal** ◇ *seasonal ~s in the demand for fuel* | **annual**, **daily** | **random** | **climatic**, **hormonal**, **temperature** | **currency**, **economic**, **exchange-rate**, **market**, **price**
VERB + FLUCTUATION **cause**, **produce** ◇ *factors which cause these exchange-rate ~s* | **be subject to**, **experience** ◇ *The number of students can be subject to considerable ~.*
FLUCTUATION + VERB **occur** ◇ *the climatic ~s that have occurred over the last ten years* | **cause sth**
PREP. **~ in** ◇ *There have been wide ~s in oil prices in recent years.*

fluency *noun*

ADJ. **oral**, **verbal** | **reading**
VERB + FLUENCY **achieve**, **acquire**, **develop** ◇ *Some young children achieve great ~ in their reading.*
PREP. **~ in** ◇ *Fluency in spoken English is essential.*

fluid *noun*

ADJ. **excess** | **amniotic**, **bodily**, **body**, **intravenous** | **brake**, **cleaning**, **correction**, **lighter** | **windshield**, **wiper** (*both AmE*)
VERB + FLUID **drain** ◇ *They drained a lot of ~ from his lungs.* | **drink** ◇ *Change your diet and drink plenty of ~s.* | **lose** | **replace** ◇ *It's important to replace ~s and salts that are lost during exercise.* | **retain** ◇ *Retaining excess ~ could be a problem.*

fluid *adj.*

VERBS **be** | **become** | **remain** | **keep sth** ◇ *I think we should try and keep our arrangements ~ at this stage.*
ADV. **extremely**, **fairly**, **very**, etc. | **highly** ◇ *It's a highly ~ situation.*

flurry *noun*

1 small amount of rain/snow

ADJ. **snow**
PHRASES **a ~ of snow**

2 short sudden burst of sth

ADJ. **brief**, **sudden** ◇ *There was a sudden ~ of interest in the book.* | **initial** | **recent**
PREP. **~ of**
PHRASES **a ~ of activity**, **a ~ of excitement**

flush *noun*

ADJ. **faint**, **slight** | **deep**, **pink**, **red** | **sudden** ◇ *a sudden ~ of rising excitement* | **hot** (*BrE*) (*hot flash* in *AmE*) ◇ *Hot drinks can cause hot ~es.*
VERB + FLUSH **feel** ◇ *She felt a ~ of anger creeping into her face.* | **bring** ◇ *The promise in his voice brought a deep ~ to her cheeks.*

FLUSH + VERB **creep, rise, spread, suffuse sth** ◇ *A ~ of embarrassment rose to her cheeks.*
PREP. **~ in** ◇ *She had a slight pink ~ in her cheeks.* | **~ of** ◇ *There was a faint ~ of red on those pale cheeks.*
PHRASES **the first ~ of enthusiasm, passion, youth, etc.** (= a time when enthusiasm, etc. is new, exciting and strong) ◇ *I'm no longer in the first ~ of youth.*

flush *verb*
ADV. **deeply | a little, slightly, etc. | angrily, guiltily** ◇ *He made his excuses, ~ing guiltily.*
PREP. **in** ◇ *Her face ~ed in anger.* | **with** ◇ *He ~ed scarlet with embarrassment.*
PHRASES **~ red, scarlet, etc.**

flute *noun* → Special page at MUSIC

flutter *noun*
1 quick, light movement
ADJ. **little**
VERB + FLUTTER **give** ◇ *His heart gave a little ~ as the ladder slipped a couple of inches.*
PREP. **~ of** ◇ *a ~ of her eyelashes*
2 state of nervous excitement
VERB + FLUTTER **feel** ◇ *She felt a ~ of excitement.* | **cause**
PREP. **in a ~** ◇ *They arrived in a ~.* | **~ of**

fly *noun*
1 insect
VERB + FLY **shoo** (*AmE*), **shoo away** (*esp. AmE*), **swat** ◇ *I swatted the ~ with a newspaper.* | **attract | catch**
FLY + VERB **buzz** ◇ *A ~ was buzzing against the window.* | **crawl | land (on sth)** ◇ *A ~ landed on the butter.*
FLY + NOUN **larva | spray**
2 (*BrE also* **flies**) on trousers/pants
ADJ. **button**
VERB + FLY/FLIES **button, button up, do up, zip up | undo, unzip** ◇ *Do you know your ~ is undone?* ◇ *Your flies are undone!* (*BrE*)
FLY + NOUN **button**
→ Special page at CLOTHES

fly *verb*
ADV. **high, low | fast, slowly | about** (*esp. BrE*), **around, back, down, out, past | away, off**
PREP. **above** ◇ *We watched the birds ~ing high above us.* | **over** ◇ *a plane ~ing low over the sea*

focus *noun*
1 special interest/attention
ADJ. **central, main, major, primary, prime, principal, real | important, special | particular, specific | greater, increased | new, renewed | clear, intense, sharp, strong** ◇ *The restructuring is designed to give a sharper ~ on key markets.* | **narrow, tight** ◇ *I found the ~ of the debate too narrow.* | **broad | exclusive, single, sole | single-minded | media** ◇ *The media ~ has now shifted onto something else.* | **mental**
VERB + FOCUS **act as, become, remain, serve as** ◇ *Cities have always acted as the principal ~ of political life.* | **give sb/sth, provide (sb/sth with) | have** ◇ *The problem with your plan is that it doesn't have a clear ~.* | **keep, maintain | change, move, shift, switch** ◇ *The legal team tried to shift the ~ onto the victim.* | **narrow, sharpen | broaden, expand | lose | lack | bring sth into** ◇ *This case has brought the problem of drug abuse in schools into sharp ~.* | **come into** ◇ *The question of compensation comes into ~.* | **direct, place, put, turn** ◇ *I've directed my ~ towards/toward developing my skills.*
FOCUS + VERB **be on sb/sth, remain on sb/sth** ◇ *Our primary ~ this term will be on group work.* | **shift, turn to sth** ◇ *The ~ has now shifted towards/toward the problem of long-term unemployment.*

PREP. **~ for** ◇ *She became a ~ for all his anger.* | **~ of** ◇ *the ~ of my research* | **~ on** ◇ *an increased ~ on younger people*
PHRASES **a change of ~, a shift of ~ | the ~ of attention** ◇ *He found he was now their main ~ of attention.*
2 point/distance at which sth is clearly seen
ADJ. **sharp | soft** ◇ *soft-focus shots of baby animals*
VERB + FOCUS **come into** ◇ *When I got glasses suddenly the whole world came into ~.*
PREP. **in** ◇ *The binoculars were not in ~.* | **out of ~** ◇ *The children's faces are out of ~ in the photograph.*

focus *verb*
1 give attention to sth
ADV. **especially, heavily, largely, mainly, mostly, particularly, primarily, principally | completely, entirely, exclusively, only, solely, totally** ◇ *The study ~es exclusively on schools.* | **increasingly | fully | firmly** ◇ *The attention of the news media was firmly ~ed on the elections.* | **specifically | clearly | directly | closely, intensely, sharply | narrowly | initially**
VERB + FOCUS **need to | try to | decide to | tend to | help (to)** ◇ *Think of some questions that will help ~ the discussion.*
PREP. **on, upon** ◇ *We need to ~ upon the main issues.*
PHRASES **highly ~ed, tightly ~ed** ◇ *The department undertakes highly ~ed research.* | **narrowly ~ed** ◇ *The study was criticized for being too narrowly ~ed.*
2 adjust your eyes
ADV. **hard, intently | automatically**
VERB + FOCUS **try to** ◇ *She blinked and tried to ~.*
PREP. **on, upon** ◇ *The eye will automatically ~ on the small group in the foreground.*

foe *noun*
ADJ. **bitter, dangerous, deadly, formidable, implacable** ◇ *He knew that Carlton could be an implacable ~.* | **common | old** ◇ *In the final the play against their old ~s, Italy.* | **former | political**
VERB + FOE **defeat, vanquish** (*figurative*) ◇ *She had fought many battles, vanquished many ~s.* | **fight**
PREP. **against a ~** ◇ *to join forces against a common ~*
PHRASES **friend and ~** ◇ *His newspaper articles criticized friend and ~ alike.* | **friend or ~** ◇ *She was unsure as yet whether he was friend or ~.*

fog *noun*
ADJ. **dense, heavy, thick | freezing** (*BrE*) | **patchy** ◇ *Drizzle and patchy ~ are forecast.* | **swirling | morning**
... OF FOG **bank, blanket, layer, patch** ◇ *The town was shrouded in a thick blanket of ~.*
VERB + FOG **be shrouded in, be covered with**
FOG + VERB **cover sth, envelop sth, lie, shroud sth, surround sth** ◇ *A freezing ~ lay over the valley.* | **close in, come down** (*esp. BrE*), **descend, roll in** ◇ *A dense ~ came down in the afternoon.* ◇ *A heavy ~ rolled in from the coast.* | **thicken | clear, disperse, lift** ◇ *The ~ had lifted by late morning.* | **drift, swirl** ◇ *~ drifting over the water* | **obscure sth** ◇ *A bank of ~ obscured the farmhouse.*
FOG + NOUN **patches** (*esp. BrE*) | **bank** (*esp. AmE*) | **lamp** (*BrE*), **light** (= on cars) | **horn** (usually **foghorn**)
PREP. **in (a/the) ~, into (a/the) ~** ◇ *We got lost in the ~.* | **through (a/the) ~** ◇ *We drove slowly through the ~.*

foil *noun*
1 metal in a thin sheet
ADJ. **aluminium** (*BrE*), **aluminum** (*AmE*), **gold, silver, tin | kitchen** (*BrE*)
... OF FOIL **piece, sheet | roll**
VERB + FOIL **cover sth with, wrap sth in** ◇ *I wrapped the sandwiches in ~.*
2 sth that shows off the qualities of sth else
ADJ. **good, ideal** (*esp. BrE*), **perfect**

VERB + FOIL be, provide
PREP. as a ~ ◇ *She has used mosses as a ~ for the bright red flowers in the bed.* | **~ for, ~ to** ◇ *The couple provided the perfect ~ for one another.*

fold noun

1 part of sth folded

ADJ. loose, soft | deep, heavy | neat | vertical
VERB + FOLD be hidden behind, be hidden by, be hidden in ◇ *The troops were hidden by the deep ~s of the ground.* | fall in ~s, hang in ~s ◇ *The fabric fell in soft ~s.* ◇ *the heavy ~s of his cloak*
PREP. in a/the ~ ◇ *She hid the note in a ~ in her robe.* | ~ in ◇ *a ~ in the land*
PHRASES ~s of flesh, ~s of skin ◇ *the loose ~s of flesh under her chin*

2 the fold group of people who feel they belong

ADJ. international (*BrE*)
VERB + THE FOLD join | leave | come back into, come back to, return to | be back in ◇ *The country is now firmly back in the international ~.* | bring sb (back) into, bring sb (back) to ◇ *The indigenous people were brought into the Catholic ~.* | welcome sb (back) into, welcome sb (back) to ◇ *His father finally accepted him back into the family ~.*
PREP. within a/the ~ ◇ *opposing viewpoints within the international ~*

fold verb

ADV. carefully, neatly ◇ *He carefully ~ed the typed sheets and replaced them in the envelope.* | gently ◇ *Her hands lay gently ~ed in her lap.* | loosely, tightly | in half, in two ◇ *She ~ed the piece of paper in half.* | back, down, over | up ◇ *I ~ed up the clothes and put them away.*
PREP. into ◇ *She ~ed the clothes into a neat bundle.*

foliage noun

ADJ. green | bright, dark | dense, heavy, lush, luxuriant, thick | dead | evergreen | spring, summer, etc. | tropical | variegated

folk noun

ADJ. decent, fine (*esp. AmE*), good, honest, law-abiding | common, everyday, normal, ordinary, plain (*AmE*), regular (*esp. AmE*) ◇ *It's the ordinary everyday ~ who come to shop at this market.* | humble, simple | friendly | rich | poor | working, working-class | elderly, old | young | black, white | men (usually *menfolk*) ◇ *He described the customs of the menfolk of his family.* | city, country ◇ *places that appeal to city ~* | local
PHRASES sb's ~s (= someone's parents) ◇ *I am going to visit my ~s during the holidays.* | the ~s back home

folklore noun

ADJ. popular | local | baseball, cricket, sporting, etc.
VERB + FOLKLORE be part of | become part of, enter (*esp. BrE*), enter into (*esp. BrE*), pass into (*esp. BrE*) ◇ *The victory became part of sporting ~.*
FOLKLORE + VERB have it that… ◇ *Local ~ has it that prehistoric men drove cattle over these cliffs.*
PREP. according to ◇ *According to popular ~, anyone who owns such a picture will have bad luck.* | in…~ ◇ *a character in American ~*

follow verb

1 go after sb/sth

ADV. closely ◇ *Johnson finished first, closely ~ed by Stevens and Higgins.* | reluctantly | dutifully, obediently ◇ *The dog ~ed obediently at her heels.* | blindly ◇ *She ~ed blindly, stumbling over stones in her path.* | quietly, silently | slowly | on ◇ *You go ahead and we'll ~ on later.*
VERB + FOLLOW beckon sb to, beckon to sb to ◇ *She beckoned him to ~ her.*

PHRASES being ~ed ◇ *As she walked home, she had the feeling she was being ~ed.* | ~ close behind (sb), ~ right behind (sb) ◇ *Ray came out of the bedroom, Mary ~ing close behind.*

2 happen after sth

ADV. closely, quickly, shortly, soon, swiftly ◇ *More information will ~ shortly.* | directly, immediately, instantly ◇ *in the period immediately ~ing the election*
PHRASES (be) ~ed by sth ◇ *Any argument was always ~ed by a few days of silence.* | ~ in the wake of sth ◇ *the workers' revolts that ~ed in the wake of the student uprising*

3 happen/be true as a result of sth

ADV. not necessarily ◇ *It does not necessarily ~ that sleep loss would cause these symptoms.* | logically | naturally | automatically
PREP. (on) from ◇ *Several conclusions ~ on from his statement.*

4 accept advice/instructions

ADV. carefully, to the letter ◇ *Follow my instructions very carefully.* | dutifully, obediently

5 copy

ADV. faithfully ◇ *The movie ~s the book faithfully.* | blindly, slavishly ◇ *It wasn't in his nature to ~ blindly.* ◇ *slavishly ~ing the views of his teachers*
VERB + FOLLOW be expected to, be likely to ◇ *Other companies are likely to ~ Z-Quest in applying for an exemption.*
PHRASES ~ in sb's footsteps ◇ *He wanted to ~ in his mother's footsteps and be a ballroom dancer.* | ~ in the tradition of sb/sth ◇ *How do your feel your writing ~s in the tradition of the South?* | ~ suit (= act or behave in the way that sb else has just done)

6 understand sth

ADV. not quite ◇ *I'm sorry, but I don't quite ~ you (= understand what you are saying).*
VERB + FOLLOW be easy to | be difficult to, be hard to, be impossible to ◇ *His argument was difficult to ~.*

follower noun

ADJ. ardent, close, enthusiastic, keen (*esp. BrE*) ◇ *an ardent ~ of the sport* | dedicated, devoted, devout, faithful, loyal, true ◇ *a true ~ of Islam* | camp
…**OF FOLLOWERS** band
VERB + FOLLOWER be, become | have ◇ *She still has many loyal ~s.* | attract | lead ◇ *He led a small band of ~s to form their own community.*
PREP. among sb's ~ ◇ *He was not powerful enough to command respect among his ~s.* | ~ of ◇ *~s of Christ*

following noun

ADJ. big, considerable, great, huge, large, mass, strong | small | local | dedicated, devoted, faithful, fanatical, loyal | enthusiastic | personal (*esp. BrE*) | cult ◇ *They enjoy a cult ~ in Japan.* | international
VERB + FOLLOWING command, enjoy, have | acquire, attract, build up, create, gain, gather
PREP. among ◇ *Top Burgundies attract a fanatical ~ among wine buffs.*

follow-up noun

ADJ. long-term | immediate, quick | six-month, two-year, etc. | regular | proper
VERB + FOLLOW-UP need, require | plan | write ◇ *She is writing a ~ to her best-selling novel.*
FOLLOW-UP + NOUN period | action, work ◇ *After the report, advisers are expected to carry out ~ work.* | discussion, interview, meeting, session | questionnaire | assessment, evaluation | appointment | visit ◇ *You will receive a ~ visit from the person conducting the assessment.* | care, treatment ◇ *They were attending hospital for ~ treatment.* | report, study, survey ◇ *a long-term ~ study of all children born in Great Britain in one week* | article, story | data, information | question | call, email, letter ◇ *Always make a ~ telephone call.*
PREP. ~ to ◇ *We are planning a ~ to today's event.*

folly noun

ADJ. **pure, sheer** | **ultimate** | **youthful** | **human** | **economic, political**
VERB + FOLLY **realize, recognize, see** ◇ *Suddenly she saw the ~ of it all.* | **demonstrate, expose, show** ◇ *These facts demonstrate the ~ of the policy.* | **underline**
PHRASES **an act of ~** ◇ *That would be an act of sheer ~!* | **the ~ of your ways** ◇ *They have finally seen the ~ of their ways.* | **the height of ~** ◇ *To sign away his rights to the book would have been the height of ~.* | **your own ~** ◇ *She laughed bitterly at her own ~.*

fond adj. fond of sb/sth

VERBS **be, seem** | **become, grow** | **remain**
ADV. **extremely, fairly, very, etc.** | **especially, genuinely, immensely** (*esp. BrE*), **particularly** ◇ *She seems genuinely ~ of the children.*

fondness noun

ADJ. **great** | **certain, particular, special**
VERB + FONDNESS **feel, have** | **develop**
PREP. **~ for** ◇ *I've always had a certain ~ for her.*

food noun

ADJ. **delicious, excellent, good, great, superb, tasty, wonderful** | **favourite/favorite** | **decent** | **real** | **adequate, enough, sufficient** ◇ *Everyone has the right to adequate ~ and clean water.* | **ample** | **basic, everyday, staple** ◇ *lower fat alternatives to everyday ~s* ◇ *Retail prices of staple ~s remain unchanged.* | **traditional** | **plain, simple** | **exotic, speciality** (*BrE*), **specialty** (*AmE*) | **fine, gourmet, quality** ◇ *Our restaurant serves the finest ~s.* | **cheap** | **bad, poor, unhealthy** | **healthful** (*esp. AmE*), **healthy, nourishing, nutritious, proper, the right, wholesome** ◇ *Healthy ~ can and should be delicious* ◇ *Lack of proper ~ led to much illness among seamen.* ◇ *It's is important to get plenty of exercise and to eat the right ~s.* | **diet, health** ◇ *Essential oils can be bought from most good health ~ stores* | **rabbit** (*informal, disapproving*) *My father preferred to eat meat and hated rabbit ~* (= salad vegetables). | **fast, junk, snack** | **carry-out** (*AmE*), **takeaway** (*BrE*), **takeout** (*AmE*) | **hot** | **cold** | **raw, uncooked** | **leftover** | **rotten** | **fresh** | **natural** | **whole** (usually **wholefood**) | **organic** | **frozen** | **dry** | **canned, tinned** (*BrE*) | **processed** | **convenience** | **fatty, fried, high-fat, starchy, stodgy** (*esp. BrE*) ◇ *She is trying to cut down on fatty ~s.* | **high-calorie, rich** ◇ *Avoid rich ~s like pastries.* | **sugary, sweet** | **savoury/savory** (*esp. BrE*) **spicy** | **Chinese, Indian, Mexican, etc.** | **vegetarian** | **dairy** | **genetically engineered, genetically modified** (abbreviated to **GM**) | **animal, plant, vegetable** (= food that comes from animals/plants) ◇ *Omnivores are able to eat animal or vegetable ~.* | **solid** ◇ *The baby refuses to swallow any solid ~.* | **baby** | **cat, dog, fish, pet** | **animal, plant** (= food for animals/plants) | **diner** (*AmE*), **hospital, party, prison, pub** (*BrE*), **restaurant** | **imported** | **comfort** ◇ *Ice cream is my comfort ~ of choice* (= food that makes me feel happier).
...OF FOOD **plate, portion** | **morsel, scrap** ◇ *They moved from town to town begging scraps of ~.*
VERB + FOOD **consume, eat, have** ◇ *the amount of ~ that an average family consumes in a week* ◇ *You should eat more fresh ~s.* ◇ *She had had no ~ for two days.* | **enjoy, like, love** ◇ *He obviously enjoys good ~.* | *people who live on junk ~* | **be off, go off** (*BrE*) ◇ *The dog is off its ~.* | **avoid, cut back on** (*esp. AmE*), **cut down on** (*esp. BrE*), **cut out** | **be short of, go short of, run short of** ◇ *The city was under siege and began to run short of ~.* | **be without, go without, live without, survive without** ◇ *We had been days without ~.* | **offer (sb)** ◇ *Fast-food companies are starting to offer their customers healthier ~.* | **give sb, provide (sb with), serve (sb), supply (sb with)** ◇ *a restaurant that serves good healthy ~* | **feed sb/sth, feed sb/sth on** ◇ *He always fed Whiskers the best cat ~.* ◇ *She fed her baby on wholesome ~.* | **handle** ◇ *Always take great care when handling ~.* | **cook, do, make, prepare** ◇ *A lot of people can't be bothered to cook good ~.* ◇ *Who's doing the ~ for the party?* | **smell, taste** ◇ *Taste the ~*

and tell me what you think. | **cut, cut up** | **pick at** ◇ *He had lost his appetite and picked at his ~.* | **play with** ◇ *Stop playing with your ~ like a baby!* | **chew** | **swallow** | **gulp, gulp down** ◇ *She told the kids not to gulp down their ~.* | **digest** | **order** ◇ *They sat down at the restaurant table and immediately ordered their ~.* | **grow, produce** ◇ *Farmers are not producing enough ~ for the country's growing population.* | **import** | **buy, sell** | **beg, beg for, hunt for, look for, scavenge for, search for** ◇ *The male eagle hunts for ~.* | **find** ◇ *Most mammals use their sense of smell to find ~.* | **keep, store** ◇ *Keep ~ fresher for longer with our new sealable containers.* ◇ *Bears store ~ for the winter.* | **contaminate** | **put out** ◇ *He put out ~ for the birds.* | **share**
FOOD + VERB **smell, taste** ◇ *Does the ~ taste good?* | **be in short supply, be short** ◇ *Food is short here, and people go hungry.* | **run out** | **arrive, come** ◇ *When their ~ arrived they ate in silence.* | **contain** ◇ *Try to eat a variety of ~s that contain protein.*
FOOD + NOUN **resource, source, supply** ◇ *Fruit is an important ~ source for bats.* ◇ *The fish market is a ready ~ supply for seabirds.* | **supplies** ◇ *The UN has been issuing emergency ~ supplies to the refugees.* | **stuff** (usually **foodstuff**) ◇ *Many basic foodstuffs, such as bread and milk, are tax-free.* | **crop, plant** ◇ *basic ~ crops such as beans and corn* | **group** | **item, product** ◇ *The labels on ~ products give information about their nutritional content.* | **consumption, intake** ◇ *His doctor warned him to reduce his daily ~ intake.* | **quality** | **preparation** | **hygiene** (*esp. BrE*), **safety, security** | **scare** (*esp. BrE*) ◇ *There has been a ~ scare over salmonella in eggs.* | **allergy** | **distribution** | **crisis, shortage** | **rationing, rations** | **stamp** (*AmE*) | **industry, market, service** ◇ *We intend to increase our share of the ~ market.* | **manufacturing, production, system** | **company, manufacturer, producer** | **court** (*AmE*), **market, outlet, retailer, shop, store, supplier** ◇ *the ~ court at the shopping mall* ◇ *Britain's first organic ~ market* ◇ *a fast ~ outlet* | **prices** | **bill** ◇ *I am trying to cut my weekly ~ bill by one third.* | **policy, programme/program** ◇ *US ~ policy* | **poisoning** | **additives** | **colouring/coloring** | **label** | **processor** ◇ *Blend the egg yolks, lemon juice and herbs in a ~ processor.* | **chain, web** ◇ *Plankton is at the bottom of the marine ~ chain.*
PREP. **for ~** ◇ *animals that are killed for ~* | **without ~** ◇ *After three days without ~, the men were close to starvation.*
PHRASES **~ and drink** (*BrE*), **~ and drinks** (*AmE*) ◇ *Gina had prepared ~ and drink/drinks for the party.* | **~ and water** ◇ *Food and water were running out.* | **~ and wine** ◇ *The Dordogne region is famous for its ~ and wine.* | **a smell of ~** ◇ *There was a smell of ~ from the kitchen* | **a supply of ~** ◇ *The ocean provides the people with an endless supply of ~.* | **the taste of ~** ◇ *the characteristic taste of our ~*

fool noun

ADJ. **big, great, silly, stupid** ◇ *You're an even bigger ~ than I thought.* | **absolute, complete, total, utter** | **poor** (= unfortunate) | **old** (= used to show sympathy, affection or a lack of respect) ◇ *The poor old ~ was imprisoned on my account.* | **young** | **little** ◇ *You silly little ~!*
VERB + FOOL **feel** (*esp. BrE*), **feel like** ◇ *I felt such a ~ when I realized what I'd done.* (*BrE*) ◇ *I felt like a ~ when I realized what I'd done.* | **look** (*esp. BrE*), **look like** ◇ *They had left me looking like a ~.* | **act like, behave like** ◇ *Stop behaving like a ~!* | **suffer** ◇ *She doesn't suffer ~s gladly.* | **call sb** | **take sb for** ◇ *He had taken me for a complete ~.*
PREP. **like a ~** ◇ *Like a ~, I told her everything.* | **~ of a sth** ◇ *That ~ of a doctor has prescribed me the wrong medicine!*
PHRASES **act the ~, play the ~** ◇ *Stop acting the ~ and be serious!* | **be no ~, be nobody's ~** (= be too clever to be deceived by sb/sth) ◇ *She's nobody's ~. She had the car checked by a mechanic before buying it.* | **make a ~ of sb/ yourself, make a ~ out of sb** ◇ *She was angry at having been made a ~ of.* | **more ~ (sb)** (*BrE*) ◇ *I thought it was safe to leave my suitcase there. More ~ me* (= I was stupid to think so).

FOOD AND COOKING

Describing food

- delicious, home-made, moist, rich **cake**
- a creamy, delicious, rich **dessert**
- a delicious, savoury, tasty, traditional **dish**
- a balanced, decent, delicious, gourmet, healthy, hearty, home-cooked, light, nutritious, proper, tasty **meal**
- crisp, crunchy, fresh, green, light **salad**
- creamy, rich, spicy, sweet-and-sour, tangy, thick **sauce**
- a healthy, light, quick, salty, savoury/savory (*esp. BrE*), tasty **snack**
- clear, creamy, hearty, home-made, thick, thin **soup**

Quantifiers

- a **clove** of garlic
- a **fillet/filet** of fish
- a **head** of lettuce
- a **knob** of butter (*BrE*)
- a **pat/stick** (*AmE*) of butter
- a **pinch** of salt
- a **rasher** (*esp. BrE*)/ **slice** of bacon
- a **sprig** of parsley
- a **stalk** of celery (*AmE*)
  a **stick** of celery (*BrE*)

Preparation

- sprinkle, top with grated **cheese**
- beat, whisk **eggs**
- clean, fillet, gut, skin **fish**
- chop, grind (*AmE*), marinate, mince (*BrE*), slice, tenderize **meat**
- add, blend, combine, mix, pour in, stir in **ingredients**
- chop, peel, wash **vegetables**

Cooking

- melt, soften **butter**
- boil, fry, poach, scramble **eggs**
- bake, fry, grill, poach, steam **fish**
- fry, grill, roast **meat**
- brown, soften **onions**
- heat (up), stir **soup**; bring **soup** to the boil
- boil, roast, sauté, stir-fry, steam **vegetables**
- preheat **the oven** to 350°
- lower, remove the pan from, take the pan off, turn down/up **the heat**

Serving

- garnish with **herbs**
- sprinkle with **lemon juice**
- drizzle, pour **oil**
- drain **pasta**
- ladle **soup**
- carve **meat**
- dress, toss a **salad**
- season (with **salt** and **pepper**) to taste

fool *verb*

ADV. **completely** | **easily** ◊ *She's not easily ~ed.*
VERB + FOOL **cannot** | **try to**
PREP. **into** ◊ *He ~ed them into thinking he was a detective.* | **with** ◊ *You can't ~ me with all that nonsense!*
PHRASES **have sb ~ed** ◊ *She had me completely ~ed for a moment.*

foolish *adj.*

VERBS **appear, be, feel, look, seem, sound**
ADV. **extremely, fairly, very,** etc. | **incredibly** | **completely, utterly** | **a little, slightly,** etc.

foolproof *adj.*

VERBS **be, seem** | **make sth** ◊ *We're trying to work out a way to make the system ~.*
ADV. **absolutely** | **nearly, virtually** ◊ *The system is virtually ~.*

foot *noun*

1 part of the body

ADJ. **left, right** | **back, front** ◊ *He shifted his weight onto his back ~.* | **dainty, little, small, tiny** | **big, enormous** | **narrow, wide** | **flat** ◊ *He was excused military service because of his flat feet.* | **bare** ◊ *It's dangerous to walk on the beach in/with bare feet.* | **blistered, swollen** | **broken** | **dirty, smelly** | **booted, stockinged** ◊ *He padded across the room in his stockinged feet* (= wearing socks but no shoes). | **webbed** ◊ *Ducks' webbed feet help them to swim.* | **silent** ◊ *He slipped across the corridor on silent feet.* | **quick** ◊ *a player with quick feet and a great turn of pace* | **leaden** ◊ *He walked to the examination room with leaden feet.* | **winged** (*often figurative*) ◊ *She flew on winged feet* (= ran fast) *up the narrow stairway.*
VERB + FOOT **get to, jump to, leap to, rise to, scramble to** ◊ *He got shakily to his feet.* | **be on** ◊ *I've been on my feet all day and I need to sit down for a rest.* | **place, plant, put** ◊ *I planted my feet firmly on the chair and reached up to the top window.* ◊ *She put her ~ down on the accelerator and the car lurched forward.* | **lift, raise** ◊ *He raised his ~ off the brake.* | **stamp, stomp** | **tap** ◊ *She was tapping her ~ impatiently.* | **swing** ◊ *He swung a ~ at the ball but missed completely.* | **kick** | **shuffle** | **drag** ◊ *She dragged her feet as she reluctantly followed her parents.* | **wipe** ◊ *Wipe your feet when you come in from the street.* | **tread on** (*esp. BrE*)
FOOT + VERB **catch** ◊ *His ~ caught in the cable and he fell under the train.* | **slip** ◊ *My ~ slipped as I was about to shoot and I missed the ball.* | **crunch, pound, shuffle** ◊ *I heard feet crunching over the gravel outside the house.* | **dangle** ◊ *I sat by the river with my feet dangling in the water.* | **kick** ◊ *They carried him out of the room with his feet kicking.* | **sink** ◊ *My feet sank deep into the mud.* | **hit sth, touch sth** ◊ *He shivered as his feet touched the cold floor.*
FOOT + NOUN **massage** | **injury** | **passenger** (*BrE*), **soldier** ◊ *Foot passengers were allowed to leave the ferry before the vehicles.* | **traffic** | **patrol** ◊ *soldiers on ~ patrol* | **pedal**
PREP. **beneath your ~, under your ~** ◊ *The snow crunched beneath her feet.* | **from ~ to ~** ◊ *They looked unsure and shifted uneasily from ~ to ~.* | **on ~** ◊ *The city is best explored on ~.* | **in the/your ~** ◊ *He's broken several bones in his left ~.* | **with the/your ~** ◊ *She kicked the ball with her right ~.*
PHRASES **the ball of the/your ~** ◊ *I squatted down to speak to the boy, balancing on the balls of my feet.* | **from head to ~** ◊ *She was dressed from head to ~ in green velvet.* | **put your feet up** ◊ *He likes to put his feet up and watch TV when he gets home.* | **set ~ in sth, set ~ on sth** ◊ *the first European to set ~ in Australia* | **the sole of the/your ~** ◊ *The soles of my feet were covered in blisters.*

2 measurement

→ Note at MEASURE

football *noun* → See also SOCCER

1 game

ADJ. **attractive, good** | **entertaining, exciting, great** | **fine, fluent, neat** (*all BrE*) | **one-touch** (*BrE*) ◊ *The Dutch team impressed the fans with their classy one-touch ~.* | **amateur,** **pro** (*esp. AmE*), **professional** | **boys', girls', men's, women's** | **junior, senior** (*both BrE*) | **first-team** (*BrE*) | **college, high-school** (*AmE*), **varsity** (*AmE*) | **club, league, non-league** (*all BrE*) | **domestic** (*BrE*), **international, world** | **live** (*esp. BrE*) | **American** (*BrE*), **Australian rules, Canadian, Gaelic** | **rugby** | **flag, tackle, touch** (*all AmE*) | **five-a-side** (*BrE*) | **fantasy** ... OF FOOTBALL **game**
VERB + FOOTBALL **play** | **watch** | **follow** ◊ *Even people who don't follow ~ closely take great pride in their team.* | **coach**
FOOTBALL + NOUN **club, league** | **squad, team** | **hero, legend, player, star** | **field, ground** (*BrE*), **pitch** (*BrE*), **stadium** | **terraces** (*BrE*) ◊ *The government is trying to tackle violence on the ~ terraces.* | **boots** (*BrE*), **cleats** (*AmE*), **jersey, kit** (*BrE*), **shirt, shoes** (*AmE*), **shorts** (*BrE*), **strip** (*BrE*), **uniform** (*AmE*) | **helmet, pads** (both in American football) | **captain, coach, referee** | **agent, management, manager** | **fan, follower** (*BrE*), **jock** (*AmE*), **supporter** (*BrE*) | **crowd** | **championship, game, match** (*BrE*), **play-off** (*esp. AmE*), **tournament** | **draft** (*AmE*) | **season** | **practice, training** | **career** | **hooliganism, violence** (*both esp. AmE*) | **hooligan** (*esp. BrE*) | **chant** (*BrE*) | **coverage, news** | **commentator, pundit** (*esp. BrE*), **writer** | **world** ◊ *The ~ world was rocked by the scandal.* | **scholarship** (*esp. AmE*) | **trial** (*BrE*), **tryout** (*AmE*)

2 ball

ADJ. **leather** | **political** (*figurative*) ◊ *Children's education should not be treated as a political ~.*
VERB + FOOTBALL **catch, kick, kick around** (*BrE*), **punt** (*AmE*), **throw, toss** (*esp. AmE*)
→ Special page at SPORTS

footballer *noun* (*BrE*)

ADJ. **brilliant, good, skilful, talented, top, top-class** | **famous** | **keen** | **amateur, professional** | **international** | **premiership**
FOOTBALLER + VERB **play**

foothold *noun*

1 place to put your foot when climbing

ADJ. **firm, secure**
VERB + FOOTHOLD **have** | **find, get, scrabble for** ◊ *He found a secure ~ and pulled himself up.* ◊ *She scrabbled for a ~ on the steep grassy bank.*

2 strong position for making further progress

ADJ. **firm, secure, strong** | **permanent**
VERB + FOOTHOLD **have** | **establish, gain, get, secure** ◊ *The company is trying to gain a ~ in the European market.* | **maintain** | **lose** | **regain** | **give (sb/sth), provide (sb with)** ◊ *I hope the book will provide a ~ for students of the subject.*
PREP. **~ in** ◊ *The company has a firm ~ in this market.*

footing *noun*

1 secure grip with your feet

ADJ. **firm, sure**
VERB + FOOTING **keep** ◊ *He struggled to keep his ~ on the slippery floor.* | **regain** | **be sure of** ◊ *She looked over her shoulder to be sure of her ~.* | **lose, miss** | **provide (sb with)** ◊ *The sole of this shoe will provide a firm ~ even on slippery surfaces.*

2 basis on which sth exists/operates

ADJ. **firm, good, proper, secure, solid, sound, strong, sure** | **equal, the same** ◊ *All claimants stand on an equal legal ~.* | **new** | **permanent** ◊ *The arrangement was put on a permanent ~ earlier this year.* | **commercial** (*esp. BrE*), **financial, legal** | **war** ◊ *The army was placed on a war ~* (= prepared for war).
VERB + FOOTING **be on, stand on** ◊ *The two teams stand on an equal ~.* | **be back on** | **gain, get, have** ◊ *Planning procedures gained a ~ in local government.* | **find** | **regain** (*esp. AmE*) ◊ *His career never quite regained its ~.* | **get (sth) on, place sth on, put sth on** ◊ *We need to get the business on a sound ~.* | **get (sth) back on**
PREP. **on a ... ~** ◊ *an attempt to put the economy on a more secure ~*

---

footpath noun (esp. BrE)

ADJ. public | long-distance
VERB + FOOTPATH follow, take, use | keep to
FOOTPATH + VERB follow sth, lead, run ◇ The ~ runs along the canal. | cross sth ◇ a ~ crossing farmland | link sth ◇ the ~ linking Sprotton and Lumm
FOOTPATH + NOUN network, system
PREP. along a/the ~ ◇ We walked along the ~. | by (a/the) ~ ◇ The monastery is an hour away by ~. | down a/the ~, on the ~ ◇ We stood on the ~ and waited for a gap in the traffic. | up a/the ~ | ~ across, ~ along, ~ alongside, ~ from, ~ over, ~ through, ~ to ◇ the ~ through the woods

footprint noun

1 mark left by a foot

ADJ. fresh | muddy, wet
...OF FOOTPRINTS set ◇ a set of ~s in the sand
VERB + FOOTPRINT leave, make ◇ The intruder had left some ~s in the snow. | find, see ◇ The detective found fresh ~s in the mud next to the victim. | follow ◇ They had fled through the snow, and police had followed their ~s.
FOOTPRINT + VERB lead ◇ The wet ~s led back to the pool.

2 impact on the environment

ADJ. carbon | ecological
VERB + FOOTPRINT reduce ◇ Steps must be taken to reduce our carbon ~.

footstep noun (usually footsteps)

ADJ. heavy | light | dragging ◇ He heard the sound of heavy, dragging ~s in the corridor. | measured, slow | brisk, hurried, quick, rapid, running | loud | soft | approaching | receding, retreating
VERB + FOOTSTEP hear, listen to | listen for ◇ She listened for her mother's ~s. | follow, retrace ◇ I am retracing the ~s of the lost expedition.
FOOTSTEP + VERB run, walk | halt, stop ◇ The ~s halted in the doorway. | approach, come, draw, head ◇ The ~s came closer as she listened. | recede | pass, pass on ◇ The ~s passed on, receding down the corridor. | descend the stairs | die away, fade, fade away ◇ Her ~s died away as she walked down the path. | crunch, echo, pound, sound ◇ Hurried ~s sounded on the stairs.
PHRASES the sound of (sb's) ~s

forbid verb

ADV. strictly ◇ Smoking is strictly forbidden. | absolutely, totally ◇ You cannot do that. I absolutely ~ it. | explicitly, expressly, specifically
PREP. from ◇ He was forbidden from leaving the country.
PHRASES be forbidden by law

force noun

1 physical strength, power or violence

ADJ. considerable, great, terrible, tremendous | full, maximum | brute, sheer | reasonable (esp. BrE) | sufficient | excessive | unlawful (BrE) | deadly, lethal | explosive | physical | gale, hurricane ◇ The wind was increasing to gale ~. ◇ hurricane-force winds
VERB + FORCE employ, resort to, use ◇ In the end, we had to resort to brute ~ to get the door open. | take sth by ◇ The troops marched in and took the city by ~. | feel ◇ Everyone felt the ~ of his argument.
PREP. by ~ ◇ The king made laws and imposed them by ~.
PHRASES catch the full ~ of sth, feel the full ~ of sth, take the full ~ of sth ◇ Our house took the full ~ of the bomb blast. ◇ I felt the full ~ of her criticism. | ~ of personality, ~ of will ◇ She used her sheer ~ of personality to keep the family together. | meet ~ with ~ (esp. AmE) ◇ The country's

attempts to meet ~ with ~ (= resist an attack using force) led to the outbreak of war. | the use of ~ ◇ The regulations allow the use of ~ if necessary.

2 effect that causes sth to move

ADJ. powerful, strong | weak | attractive | repulsive | external, internal ◇ Deep internal ~s cause movements of the earth's crust. | lateral | centrifugal, centripetal, electromagnetic, electromotive, gravitational, mechanical, nuclear, physical, tidal
VERB + FORCE apply, exert, generate, produce ◇ The sun exerts a ~ on the earth. | increase | decrease, reduce | balance ◇ The ~s of expansion are balanced by forces of contraction.
FORCE + VERB act on sth ◇ lateral ~s acting on the car's suspension | balance sth
FORCE + NOUN field ◇ the ~ field of a magnet
PREP. ~ between ◇ the attractive and repulsive ~s between individual particles
PHRASES a balance of ~s ◇ the balance of nuclear ~s in atoms | the ~ of gravity

3 legal authority of sth

ADJ. binding, legal, statutory (BrE) ◇ The contract was not signed and has no binding ~.
VERB + FORCE come into ◇ The new law comes into ~ as from midnight tomorrow. | bring sth into (esp. BrE)
PREP. in ~ ◇ Some archaic laws are still in ~.
PHRASES the ~ of law ◇ Professional standards often do not have the ~ of law (= cannot be enforced).

4 sb/sth with power/influence

ADJ. considerable, formidable, great, irresistible, major, overwhelming, potent, powerful, significant, strong, unstoppable | active, controlling, dominant, driving, main, moving | motivating | persuasive | constructive, creative, dynamic, positive, progressive | destructive, disruptive, negative ◇ She was seen as a potentially disruptive ~ within the party. | cohesive, unifying | competitive, conflicting, countervailing, opposing, reactionary | internal | external, international, outside ◇ The play portrays a marriage torn apart by external ~s. | invisible, unseen | natural ◇ powerful natural ~s such as earthquakes and drought | spiritual, supernatural | dark, demonic, evil, malevolent | cultural, economic, intellectual, market, moral, political, productive, revolutionary, social ◇ powerful social and economic ~s
VERB + FORCE remain ◇ Though officially retired, she remains the creative ~ behind the design business. | balance ◇ This is a politician who does not like to balance market ~s. | fight ◇ to fight the ~s of evil
PREP. ~ behind ◇ Local parents were the driving ~ behind the project. | ~ for ◇ Competition is a ~ for change in industry.
PHRASES a balance of ~s ◇ shifts in the balance of political ~s in Europe | a ~ to be reckoned with ◇ With its new players, the team is now very much a ~ to be reckoned with. | the ~s of nature

5 group of people trained for a particular purpose

ADJ. large | small, token ◇ a token ~ of only 300 men | 100-strong, etc. | superior | crack, elite, special ◇ These elite ~s are the best equipped and trained in the world. | combined, joint ◇ the combined ~s of MI5 and Scotland Yard ◇ a joint task ~ | allied, coalition, multinational | strategic | labour/labor, sales, work (usually workforce) ◇ the US labour/labor ~ | armed, armoured/armored, military, paramilitary | government, loyal | enemy, guerrilla, hostile, occupation, occupying, opposition, rebel ◇ He called on the local population to rise up against the occupying ~s. | friendly | regular | reserve | all-volunteer, volunteer | conventional | nuclear | assault, combat, defence/defense, expeditionary, fighting, invasion, peace, peacekeeping, police, security, strike (See also task force.) | air, airborne, amphibious, ground, land, naval
VERB + FORCE assemble, create, form, mobilize, set up ◇ A large expeditionary ~ is now being assembled. | send ◇ the decision to send armed ~s over the border | provide |

deploy, employ, use ◇ *A small peacekeeping ~ will be deployed in the area.* | **withdraw** | **command, head, head up, lead** | **join** ◇ *She decided to join the armed ~s.* | **train** | **support** ◇ *More troops have been called in to support the coalition ~s there.* | **combine, join** ◇ *The two companies have joined ~s to form a new consortium.*
FORCE + VERB **control sth** ◇ *Rebel ~s now control most of the capital.* | **operate** ◇ *UN ~s operating in the region*
PREP. **in a/the ~** ◇ *people in the security ~s*
PHRASES **a member of a ~, the withdrawal of a ~** ◇ *a deadline for the withdrawal of ~s*

foreboding noun

ADJ. **dark, deep**
VERB + FOREBODING **feel, have** ◇ *I felt a gloomy ~ that something was going to go wrong.* | **be full of** ◇ *He returned, full of ~, to the scene of the accident.* | **fill sb with**
PREP. **~ of** ◇ *She had a ~ of danger.*
PHRASES **a feeling of ~, a sense of ~**

forecast noun

ADJ. **good, optimistic** | **gloomy, pessimistic** | **conservative** | **accurate, correct** | **detailed** | **revised** | **annual** | **early** | **long-range, long-term** ◇ *a long-range weather ~* | **short-term** ◇ *a short-term ~ of the economy* | **local** | **official** | **economic, financial, market, shipping** (*BrE*) (*shipping news* in *AmE*), **weather** | **cash-flow** (*esp. BrE*), **earnings, growth, inflation, profit, revenue, sales**
VERB + FORECAST **prepare, produce** | **give, issue, make, provide** ◇ *The government has issued a pessimistic economic ~.* | **revise, update** | **lower, raise** ◇ *This week the company is expected to raise its revenue ~.* | **rely on** | **check** ◇ *Check the weather ~ before you set out.* | **be in line with** ◇ *The interest rate is in line with the ~.*
FORECAST + VERB **call for sth** (*AmE*), **predict sth, say sth, suggest sth** ◇ *This morning's weather ~ called for snow.* ◇ *Some ~s suggest that the increase in heart disease will continue for some time.* | **assume sth** | **be based on sth** ◇ *~s based on a complicated procedure*
PREP. **~ about** ◇ *Forecasts about the economy are often misleading.* | **~ for** ◇ *~s for earnings in 2015* | **~ of** ◇ *~s of population growth*

forecast verb

ADV. **accurately, correctly** | **originally, previously** ◇ *higher costs than those originally ~*
VERB + FORECAST **be difficult to, be hard to**

forefront noun the forefront

VERB + THE FOREFRONT **remain at, remain in** ◇ *Education remains at the ~ of the state's planning.* | **keep sb/sth at, keep sb/sth in, keep sb/sth to** (*BrE*) | **come into** (*AmE*), **come to** ◇ *She came to the ~ as governor after the political change.* | **push sb/sth into, push sb/sth to, thrust sb/sth into, thrust sb/sth to** ◇ *His new job thrust him to the ~.* | **bring sb/sth to, place sb/sth at, place sb/sth in, put sb/sth (back) at, put sb/sth (back) in** ◇ *The new factory could put the town back at the ~ of steel manufacture.*
PREP. **at the ~ (of), in the ~ (of)** ◇ *issues at the ~ of government policy*
PHRASES **at the ~ of sb's mind, in the ~ of sb's mind, to the ~ of sb's mind** ◇ *This question remained at the ~ of her mind.*

foreground noun

VERB + FOREGROUND **occupy** ◇ *A happy family occupies the ~ of the painting.*
PREP. **in the ~** ◇ *This issue is very much in the ~.*

forehead noun

ADJ. **broad, high, wide** | **sloping** | **furrowed, wrinkled** | **smooth** | **sweaty**
VERB + FOREHEAD **crease, wrinkle** | **mop, wipe** | **hit, rub, slap, smack, tap** ◇ *He groaned and slapped his ~, as if suddenly remembering something obvious.* | **kiss**

PREP. **across your ~** ◇ *He rubbed a hand across his ~ as though he were tired.* | **from your ~** ◇ *He wiped the sweat from his ~.* | **in the ~** ◇ *He had a gash in the ~.* | **off your ~** ◇ *She pushed her wet hair off her ~.* | **over your ~** ◇ *His hair fell over his ~.*

foreign adj.

1 not coming from your own country
VERBS **be, look, sound** ◇ *The name sounded ~.*
ADV. **slightly** ◇ *a slightly ~ accent* | **distinctly** ◇ *He was a small man, distinctly ~ in appearance.*

2 foreign to sb not typical of sb/not known to sb
VERBS **be, feel, seem**
ADV. **very** | **completely, entirely, quite, totally, utterly** ◇ *This kind of attitude is completely ~ to her.*

foresee verb

ADV. **clearly** | **reasonably** (*esp. BrE*) ◇ *He could not reasonably have foreseen the consequences.*
VERB + FORESEE **can** ◇ *We could ~ no difficulties with these proposals.* | **be difficult to, be impossible to** ◇ *It is impossible to ~ the future.*

foresight noun

ADJ. **considerable, great** | **perfect** (*esp. AmE*)
VERB + FORESIGHT **have** ◇ *He had the ~ to bring in the chairs before the rain started.* | **show** ◇ *The plans showed great ~.* | **lack**
PHRASES **a lack of ~**

forest noun

ADJ. **dense, thick** | **impenetrable** | **deep** | **dark** | **native, natural** | **national** | **ancient, old, primeval, virgin** | **mature, old-growth** | **rain** (usually **rainforest**), **tropical** | **coniferous, deciduous** | **hardwood** | **beech, birch, pine,** etc.
...OF FOREST **stretch, tract** ◇ *a large stretch of virgin ~*
VERB + FOREST **plant** | **clear, cut down, destroy** ◇ *Forest is being cleared to make way for new farming land.* | **conserve, protect** | **manage** | **be covered by, be covered in** ◇ *Much of Europe was once covered in ~.* | **enter** ◇ *He warned her never to enter the ~ at night.*
FOREST + VERB **stretch** ◇ *Thick ~ stretched as far as the eye could see.* | **surround** ◇ *the ~ surrounding the village*
FOREST + NOUN **tree** | **floor** | **canopy** | **land** | **fire** | **ranger** | **management**
PREP. **in a/the ~** ◇ *They got lost in the ~.* | **through a/the ~** ◇ *We slashed our way through the dense ~.*
PHRASES **the edge of the ~, the heart of the ~, the middle of the ~**

forestry noun

ADJ. **commercial** | **community** (*AmE*) | **sustainable**
FORESTRY + NOUN **plantation** (*BrE*) | **practice** | **track** (*BrE*) | **worker** | **industry, management** | **policy, programme/ program, project** | **department**

forethought noun

VERB + FORETHOUGHT **have** ◇ *We had had the ~ to book places in advance.*
PREP. **with ~, without ~** ◇ *He had made the remark completely without ~.*
PHRASES **a lack of ~**

forgery noun → Note at CRIME

forget verb

ADV. **completely, quite** (*esp. BrE*), **totally** ◇ *I completely forgot you were coming today.* | **clean** (*old-fashioned, informal*) ◇ *I clean forgot to give your brother the message.* | **almost, nearly** | **never** ◇ *I'll never ~ the expression on his face.* |

quickly, soon | instantly, promptly ◊ *'I will,' she promised, and promptly forgot about it.* | momentarily, temporarily ◊ *Her joy was so infectious that he momentarily forgot his own fears for the future.* | easily ◊ *The experience of nearly getting killed is not easily forgotten.* | conveniently (*ironic*) ◊ *He conveniently forgot to tell me he was married.*

VERB + FORGET seem to ◊ *You seem to ~ that it was your idea in the first place.* | tend to | want to | try to | be easy to ◊ *It is easy to ~ that not all countries have these advantages.* | let sb ◊ *Let's ~ last night, shall we?* | make sb

PREP. about ◊ *Oh yes! I almost forgot about the party.*

PHRASES ~ all about sth ◊ *In the excitement I forgot all about my little brother.* | keep forgetting ◊ *She keeps forgetting where she's put her glasses.* | largely forgotten ◊ *His pioneering work in the field was largely forgotten until the late 1940s.*

forgive *verb*

ADV. quite ◊ *I suspect that Rodney has never quite forgiven either of them.* | ever, never ◊ *Can you ever ~ me?* | easily ◊ *Donna would not easily ~ Beth's silly attempt to trick her.*

VERB + FORGIVE be able to, be unable to, can ◊ *I couldn't ~ him.* | be easy to ◊ *An insult like that isn't easy to ~.* | ask sb to, beg sb to ◊ *He fell to his knees and begged God to ~ him.* | try to

PREP. for ◊ *She never forgave him for losing her ring.*

PHRASES ~ and forget ◊ *He was not the sort of man to ~ and forget.*

forgiveness *noun*

ADJ. complete | divine

VERB + FORGIVENESS find, have, receive ◊ *Do I have your ~?* | ask, ask for, beg, beg for, pray for, seek | need, want | deserve | find ◊ *victims of violence who can nevertheless find ~ in their hearts* | offer (sb), show (sb)

PREP. ~ for ◊ *He begged her ~ for his mistake.*

fork *noun*

1 tool for eating

ADJ. toasting | salad (*AmE*) | plastic

VERB + FORK pick up | put down | use

PREP. on a/the ~ ◊ *She impaled a piece of meat on her ~.* | with a ~ ◊ *Mash the mixture with a ~.*

PHRASES a knife and ~ ◊ *He put the knives and ~s on the table.*

2 place where sth divides into two parts

ADJ. left, right

VERB + FORK take ◊ *As you pass the farm, take the right ~ of the track up the hill.*

PREP. at a/the ~ ◊ *Bear left at the ~ in the road.* | in ~ ◊ *a monkey sitting in the ~ of the tree* | ~ in ◊ *a ~ in the road*

form *noun*

1 type of sth/way of doing sth

ADJ. common ◊ *Strikes are the most common ~ of industrial protest.* | different, various ◊ *various ~s of surveillance* | extreme ◊ *an extreme ~ of socialism* | pure ◊ *In its purest ~, the substance is highly explosive.* | basic, simple | complex | mild | severe, virulent ◊ *a virulent ~ of the flu* | early, original, traditional ◊ *an early ~ of bicycle* | final ◊ *The document was edited before being circulated in its final ~.* | new | art, literary, musical ◊ *Storytelling has acquired the status of an art ~.* | life ◊ *primitive life ~s at the bottom of the sea* | digital, electronic ◊ *The data is stored in digital ~.* | graphic, tabular ◊ *The results of the survey are shown below in tabular ~.* | liquid | physical

VERB + FORM take ◊ *Bullying can take many ~s.* | give ◊ *A film gives physical ~ to a novel's characters.*

PREP. in…~ ◊ *The gas is stored in liquid ~.* | in the ~ of ◊ *These costs were passed on in the ~ of higher rents.* | ~ of ◊ *Swimming is one of the best ~s of exercise.*

PHRASES in any shape or ~ ◊ *The company will not tolerate discrimination in any shape or ~.* | in some ~ or other ◊ *We spend most of our time communicating in some ~ or other.*

2 shape

ADJ. human ◊ *paintings of the human ~* | adult | sleeping

VERB + FORM alter, change ◊ *a mythical creature that could change its ~* | assume, take on ◊ *a god who could take on human ~*

PREP. in a/the ~ ◊ *Two weeks later the moth will emerge in its adult ~.*

3 piece of paper with questions on it

ADJ. application, booking (*BrE*), consent, entry, order, registration, reservation (*AmE*) | online ◊ *Please fill out the online ~ on our website.*

VERB + FORM complete, fill in (*BrE*), fill out ◊ *Please complete the application ~ and return it to us.* | sign | return

4 how well sb/sth is performing

ADJ. fine, good, great, top ◊ *The team entered the tournament in top ~.* | poor | current, present

VERB + FORM maintain ◊ *The team is hoping that it can maintain its current ~.* | find ◊ *She urgently needs to find her ~.* | regain

PREP. in ~ ◊ *She was in fine ~ for the tournament.* ◊ *Ben was in great ~ at the wedding.* ◊ *Barcelona are the team in ~.* (*BrE*) | off ~ (*BrE*) ◊ *Her recent illness possibly explains why she was off ~ in this race.* | on ~ (*esp. BrE*) ◊ *He'll be a difficult opponent to beat; he's really on ~ today.* ◊ *Yesterday's game saw him back on ~.* | on sb's ~ (*esp. BrE*) ◊ *On his present ~ it seems likely that he will win.* | out of ~ (*BrE*) ◊ *The team was out of ~ and did not play as well as expected.*

PHRASES a return to ~ ◊ *His recent performances mark a welcome return to ~.*

form *verb*

1 make/organize sth

VERB + FORM attempt to, try to | agree to, decide to | ask sb to, invite sb to (*both esp. BrE*) ◊ *The leader of the party with the most seats is invited to ~ a government.* | help (to)

PHRASES newly ~ed, recently ~ed ◊ *a newly ~ed political party*

2 make sth into a shape

PREP. into ◊ *She ~ed the clay into a ball.*

PHRASES fully ~ed ◊ *The plan came in a flash of inspiration, fully ~ed.* | perfectly ~ed ◊ *a perfectly ~ed body*

formal *adj.*

1 very correct/official

VERBS be, seem, sound | become

ADV. extremely, fairly, very, etc. | strictly ◊ *Learning was by rote and strictly ~.*

2 concerned with the way sth is done

VERBS be

ADV. merely, purely ◊ *Getting approval for the plan is a purely ~ matter: nobody will seriously oppose it.* | largely ◊ *The monarch retains largely ~ duties.*

formality *noun*

1 action that is necessary according to custom/law

ADJ. mere ◊ *Your acceptance into the club will be a mere ~.* | customs, legal (*both esp. BrE*)

VERB + FORMALITY complete (*esp. BrE*), deal with, go through ◊ *It only took a few minutes to complete the legal formalities.* | dispense with, drop (*esp. AmE*) ◊ *Let's dispense with the formalities and get down to work.*

PHRASES just a ~, merely a ~, only a ~ ◊ *She was clearly the best candidate for the job, so her interview was just a ~.*

2 polite/formal way of behaving

ADJ. stiff

…OF FORMALITY degree, level ◊ *It is important to be aware of the level of ~ required at any social function.*

format noun

ADJ. **large, small** | **standard** | **digital** | **file** | **DVD, PDF, etc.**
VERB + FORMAT **follow, use** ◊ *All the lectures follow the same basic ~.* | **change** ◊ *For this year, we have decided to change the ~ of the conference slightly.* | **support** ◊ *The drive supports the following DVD ~s.*
PREP. **in a/the ~** ◊ *The book is now available in a slightly smaller ~.*

formation noun

1 making/developing sth

ADJ. **policy** ◊ *the top civil servants who are responsible for policy ~*
VERB + FORMATION **lead to, result in** ◊ *This dispute led to the ~ of a new breakaway group.* | **prevent**

2 arrangement/group/pattern

ADJ. **close, tight** | **battle** ◊ *The troops advanced in battle ~.* | **family, household, social** ◊ *changing patterns of marriage and family ~*
FORMATION + NOUN **flying**
PREP. **in a … ~** ◊ *The men were grouped in a close ~.* | **in ~** ◊ *a squadron of planes flying in ~*

3 sth that has been formed

ADJ. **cloud, geological, rock** | **military, political**

formidable adj.

VERBS **be, look, seem** ◊ *The task looks ~.* | **remain** | **find sth** ◊ *Men found her ~.* | **make sth**
ADV. **extremely, fairly, very, etc.** ◊ *a very ~ opponent* | **a little, slightly, etc.**

formula noun

1 group of signs/letters/numbers

ADJ. **complex, complicated** | **simple** | **secret** | **algebraic, chemical, mathematical, scientific**
VERB + FORMULA **devise, work out** ◊ *A simple mathematical ~ has been devised to allow you to calculate the interest due.* | **apply, use**
PREP. **~ for** ◊ *the ~ for finding the area of a circle*

2 method of solving a problem

ADJ. **good, magic, successful, winning** | **standard, traditional** | **basic** | **face-saving** (*esp. BrE*) ◊ *The government was forced to find a face-saving ~ to cover its misjudgement.* | **political**
VERB + FORMULA **have** ◊ *No one has a magic ~ for keeping youngsters away from crime.* | **follow** ◊ *Each of his novels follows the same successful ~.* | **come up with, devise, find, hit on, provide, work out** ◊ *We think we might have hit on a winning ~.* | **change** ◊ *Why change a winning ~?*
PREP. **~ for** ◊ *What is their ~ for success?*

formulate verb

ADV. **fully** | **carefully, properly** ◊ *His ideas are always very carefully ~d.* | **clearly, explicitly** | **specially, specifically** ◊ *products that are specially ~d for safe use on leather*
VERB + FORMULATE **try to** | **help (to)**

fort noun

ADJ. **hill** | **border** (*esp. AmE*) | **Iron Age, Roman, Saxon, etc.** ◊ *an Iron Age hill ~* | **snow** (*AmE*)
VERB + FORT **attack** | **hold** ◊ *Government forces managed to hold the ~.* | **build**
FORT + VERB **fall** ◊ *The ~ finally fell after a week of intense fighting.*
PREP. **at a/the ~, in a/the ~** ◊ *All was calm at the ~ that night.*

forthcoming adj.

1 available

VERBS **be** ◊ *Help was immediately ~.*

ADV. **readily** (*esp. BrE*) | **immediately**

2 willing to give information

VERBS **be**
ADV. **not very**
PREP. **about** ◊ *She wasn't very ~ about where she'd been.*

forthright adj.

VERBS **be, seem**
ADV. **extremely, fairly, very, etc.** | **characteristically** ◊ *He was characteristically ~ in his reply.*
PREP. **about** ◊ *She's always been very ~ about her preferences.*

fortnight noun (*BrE*)

ADJ. **next** | **last, past, previous** | **whole**
VERB + FORTNIGHT **spend** ◊ *We've spent the last ~ in Spain.*
FORTNIGHT + VERB **elapse, go by, pass** ◊ *A ~ passed and we still hadn't heard from them.*
PREP. **after a/the ~, during a/the ~, for a/the ~, in a/the ~** ◊ *We hope to leave in the next ~.* | **over a/the ~, within a/the ~**

fortress noun

ADJ. **great** | **impenetrable, impregnable, strong** | **grim** | **stone**
VERB + FORTRESS **attack, besiege, lay siege to** | **take** ◊ *Greek warriors took the ~ with little effort.* | **hold, occupy** | **build**
FORTRESS + VERB **fall** ◊ *The ~ fell after a nine-day siege.*
FORTRESS + NOUN **city, town** | **walls**
PREP. **in a/the ~** ◊ *They took refuge in the ~.*

fortunate adj.

VERBS **be, feel, seem** | **consider sb, count yourself, think sb** ◊ *We consider ourselves extremely ~.*
ADV. **extremely, fairly, very, etc.** | **indeed** (*esp. BrE*) ◊ *He was indeed ~ in his friends.*
PREP. **for** ◊ *It was ~ for us that the rain stopped.* | **in** ◊ *We are ~ in having a lot of land.*

fortune noun

1 luck

ADJ. **good** | **bad, ill**
… OF FORTUNE **piece, stroke** ◊ *By a stroke of good ~, Steven was still in his office.*
VERB + FORTUNE **have** | **bring (sb)** ◊ *A horseshoe nailed to your door is supposed to bring good ~.*
FORTUNE + VERB **be on sb's side, favour/favor sb, smile on sb** ◊ *For once, ~ was on our side: the weather improved in time for the game.* ◊ *Fortune smiled on me that day* (= I had good fortune).
PHRASES **as good ~ would have it** ◊ *As good ~ would have it, a bus came along just when I needed it.* | **a change in ~, a change of ~** ◊ *All we can do is hope for a change in ~.* | **have the good ~ to do sth** ◊ *I had the good ~ to work with people I liked.*

2 fortunes what happens to sb/sth

ADJ. **declining, flagging** | **changing, fluctuating, mixed** ◊ *a year of mixed ~s for the company* | **economic, electoral, political**
VERB + FORTUNES **boost, improve, revive** ◊ *The party still hopes to revive its flagging electoral ~s.* | **reverse** | **follow** ◊ *fans who follow the ~s of their chosen team*
FORTUNES + VERB **change, fluctuate** (*esp. BrE*) ◊ *A company's ~s can change overnight.* | **improve, rise** | **decline, fall** ◊ *as the country's ~s rose and fell*
PHRASES **a reversal of ~, a reversal of ~s** (*esp. BrE*) ◊ *The company suffered a reversal of ~ when public taste changed.*

3 what is going to happen to sb in the future

VERB + FORTUNE **read, tell** ◊ *They went to have their ~s read.*
FORTUNE + NOUN **teller, telling**

4 very large amount of money

ADJ. **considerable, enormous, great, immense, large,**

substantial (*esp. BrE*), **vast** | **small** (= quite large) ◇ *Rebuilding the house must have cost a small ~.* | **family, personal**
VERB + FORTUNE **accumulate, acquire, amass, build, build up, earn, make, win** | **inherit** | **leave (sb)** ◇ *Her aunt died and left her a ~.* | **lose, squander** ◇ *He lost his ~ in the crash of 1929.* ◇ *She squandered the family ~.* | **find, seek** ◇ *They went to seek their ~ in the city.* | **be worth** ◇ *Some of those old toys are worth a ~ now.* | **cost** | **pay, spend** ◇ *She spends a ~ on clothes!*
FORTUNE + NOUN **hunter** (= a person who tries to become rich by marrying sb with a lot of money)
PREP. **~ from** ◇ *He built his ~ from breeding horses.* | **~ in** ◇ *She made a ~ in the property boom.* | **~ on** ◇ *They sold their house at the right time and made a ~ on it.* | **~ out** ◇ *He has amassed a considerable ~ out of trading shares.*
PHRASES **fame and ~** ◇ *They went to America in search of fame and ~.* | **heir to a ~, heiress to a ~** ◇ *He was sole heir to the family ~.*

forum *noun*

1 way people can exchange ideas
ADJ. **important, useful** | **public**
VERB + FORUM **create, offer, provide (sb with)** | **have** | **act as** (*esp. BrE*), **be used as, serve as** | **become**
PREP. **~ for** ◇ *The conference provides a useful ~ for the exchange of views and ideas.*

2 meeting at which people can exchange ideas
ADJ. **open, public** ◇ *The movie show was followed by an open ~ on editing techniques.* | **international, national** | **community** | **economic, political, social** | **discussion** | **Internet, online, web** ◇ *Check out our online discussion ~.*
VERB + FORUM **hold, host** ◇ *We will be hosting a two-day ~ on childcare.* | **attend, go to**
FORUM + VERB **take place**
PREP. **~ on** ◇ *An international ~ on economic development took place in Brussels.*

foul *noun*

ADJ. **blatant** (*esp. BrE*), **clear** (*BrE*), **deliberate, flagrant** (*AmE*), **nasty** (*esp. BrE*) | **hard, offensive, personal, technical** (all in basketball)
VERB + FOUL **commit** | **draw** (in basketball) | **call** (in basketball) ◇ *The referee did not call a ~ on the player.*
PREP. **~ on** ◇ *He was sent off for a clear ~ on Leonard.* (*BrE*) ◇ *He drew a fourth ~ on Camby.* (*AmE*)

foul play *noun*

1 criminal activity
VERB + FOUL PLAY **suspect** | **rule out** (*esp. BrE*) ◇ *The police have ruled out ~ in their investigation of his death.*
PHRASES **evidence of ~** ◇ *The police found no evidence of ~.*

2 (*BrE*) **play that is against the rules**
ADJ. **deliberate, serious**
VERB + FOUL PLAY **be guilty of** ◇ *He was clearly guilty of ~ and deserved to be sent off.*

foundation *noun*

1 organization that provides money for sth
ADJ. **charitable, private** | **research**
VERB + FOUNDATION **establish, set up, start** ◇ *a charitable ~ established in 1983*
PREP. **~ for** ◇ *a private ~ for the arts*

2 foundations parts of a building below the ground
ADJ. **deep** | **concrete**
VERB + FOUNDATIONS **dig, lay** ◇ *Concrete ~s have been laid.* | **shake, undermine** ◇ *The thunder seemed to shake the very ~s of the building.* ◇ *They had dug too deep and undermined the ~s of the house.*
FOUNDATION + NOUN **stone** ◇ *The ~ stone was laid in 1911.* | **wall** (*AmE*)

3 basis for sth
ADJ. **excellent, firm, good, secure, solid, sound, strong** | **shaky, weak** | **ideological, intellectual, moral, philosophical, political, scientific, theoretical** | **economic**
VERB + FOUNDATION **build, create, form, lay, provide (sth with), set** ◇ *This agreement laid a sound ~ for future cooperation between the two countries.* | **build on** ◇ *We now have a firm ~ to build on.* | **rest on** ◇ *The peace treaty rests on shaky ~s.* | **rock, shake, strike at, threaten, undermine** ◇ *an event which rocked the ~s of British politics* | **destroy**
FOUNDATION + NOUN **course, year** (*both BrE*) ◇ *The Fine Arts degree starts with a ~ year.*
PREP. **~ for** ◇ *to provide a solid ~ for democracy*
PHRASES **rock sth to its ~s, shake sth to its ~s** ◇ *The scandal rocked the legal establishment to its ~s.* | **the very ~** ◇ *He believes terrorism undermines the very ~s of our society.*

4 facts that show that sth is true
VERB + FOUNDATION **have no** ◇ *malicious gossip which has no ~*
PREP. **without ~** ◇ *The rumours/rumors of his resignation are entirely without ~.*

founder *noun*

ADJ. **original** | **company**
FOUNDER + NOUN **member** (*BrE*) (***founding member*** in *AmE*) ◇ *a ~ member of the band*

fountain *noun*

ADJ. **drinking** (*esp. BrE*), **water** (*AmE*) | **ornamental**
FOUNTAIN + VERB **play** (*esp. BrE*), **splash** ◇ *A white marble ~ played in the middle of the square.*

fourth *noun* (*esp. AmE*) → See also QUARTER

VERB + FOURTH **cut sth into ~s, divide sth into ~s, fold sth into ~s**
PREP. **~ of** ◇ *one ~ of total sales* ◇ *a ~ of the city population*

foyer *noun*

ADJ. **entrance, front** (*esp. AmE*) | **grand** (*esp. AmE*), **main** | **cinema** (*BrE*), **hotel, school, station, theatre/theater** | **crowded**
VERB + FOYER **enter**
PREP. **across the ~, in the ~** ◇ *We arranged to meet up in the ~ of the Hyatt hotel.*

fraction *noun*

1 part/amount
ADJ. **large, significant, sizeable, substantial** | **mere, small, tiny** ◇ *A mere ~ of available wind energy is currently utilized.*
PREP. **~ of** ◇ *Why not grow your own fruit at a ~ of the price?*
PHRASES **just a ~, only a ~** ◇ *The average income is high, though many people earn just a ~ of that average.*

2 exact part of a number
ADJ. **vulgar** (*BrE*) | **decimal** | **improper**
VERB + FRACTION **express sth as** ◇ *Express 25% as a ~.*

fracture *noun*

ADJ. **stress** ◇ *He suffered a stress ~ of the right foot.* | **hairline** | **compound, multiple, simple** | **hip, leg, skull, spinal, etc.**
VERB + FRACTURE **suffer, sustain**

fragrance *noun*

ADJ. **fresh, pleasant, sweet** | **delicate, light, subtle** | **floral** | **spicy**
VERB + FRAGRANCE **have** ◇ *This perfume has a light, fresh ~.* | **smell**
FRAGRANCE + VERB **fill sth** ◇ *The ~ of lavender filled the room.*
PHRASES **full of ~** (*esp. BrE*) ◇ *fruits full of exquisite ~ and sweetness*

frail *adj.*

VERBS **be, look, seem** | **become, get, grow**
ADV. **extremely, fairly, very, etc.** | **physically** ◇ *Some old people become physically ~.*

frailty noun

ADJ. **increasing** ◇ *Despite increasing physical ~, he continued to write stories.* | **human** ◇ *a figure of authority, but one all too prone to human frailties* | **physical**

frame noun

1 of a door/picture/window

ADJ. **door, window** | **photo, photograph, picture** | **metal, steel, wire, wood, wooden**
PREP. **in a/the ~** ◇ *pictures in gold ~s*

2 shape of sb's body

ADJ. **athletic, big, bony, lanky, large, lean, muscular, petite, powerful, skinny, slender, slight, small, tall, thin, wiry**
VERB + FRAME **have** ◇ *She has a small ~.*
PREP. **with a … ~** ◇ *a man with a lean, athletic ~*

framework noun

ADJ. **basic, broad, general** | **wider** ◇ *The needs of individual schools need to be considered in a wider ~.* | **existing** | **flexible** | **comprehensive** | **coherent** | **common** | **useful** | **analytical, conceptual, intellectual, theoretical** | **legal, political, social** | **regulatory** | **administrative, institutional, management, policy** | **economic, financial** (*esp. BrE*) | **chronological, historical** ◇ *Carbon dating provides us with a basic chronological ~.*
VERB + FRAMEWORK **build, create, develop, establish, have, set** ◇ *They established a basic ~ of ground rules for discussions.* | **offer (sb), provide (sb with)**
PREP. **outside a/the ~** ◇ *Negotiations were conducted outside the ~ of the treaty talks.* | **within a/the ~** ◇ *The committee will work within the ~ of certain broad objectives.* | **~ for** ◇ *a legal ~ for the regulation of public access to databases*

franchise noun

1 permission to sell sth

ADJ. **fast-food, rail** (*BrE*), **sports** (*AmE*), **television** (*BrE*), etc. | **film** (*BrE*), **movie** (*esp. AmE*) | **successful**
VERB + FRANCHISE **have, hold** (*esp. BrE*), **own** ◇ *the company that holds the ~ for the south-east of the country* | **acquire, buy, get, win** ◇ *The company has just won a television ~.* | **operate, run** ◇ *He runs a local pizza ~.* | **build, expand** (*both esp. AmE*) | **award (sb), give sb, grant sb** ◇ *The ~ was awarded to a French company.* | **sell** ◇ *TV ~s will be sold to the highest bidder.* | **lose** ◇ *The licensee lost its ~ to Carlton TV.*
FRANCHISE + NOUN **system** | **business, company, operation** | **holder** (*esp. BrE*), **owner** | **agreement** | **auction, bid** (*both BrE*) | **fee**
PREP. **~ for** ◇ *The diving school has acquired a ~ for scuba equipment.*
PHRASES **on a ~ basis** (*BrE*) ◇ *Catering in the schools is run on a ~ basis.*

2 (*formal*) right to vote in elections

ADJ. **democratic** | **universal** ◇ *the fight for a universal ~* | **limited, restricted** | **parliamentary**
VERB + FRANCHISE **qualify for** ◇ *It was decided that all men in the armed forces should qualify for the ~.* | **exercise** ◇ *He had to exercise the ~ on behalf of other council members.* | **extend, widen** ◇ *The ~ was later extended to all adults over eighteen.*

frank adj.

VERBS **be**
ADV. **extremely, fairly, very, etc.** | **remarkably** | **absolutely, perfectly, quite** ◇ *Let me be perfectly ~ with you.* | **disarmingly, refreshingly** (*esp. BrE*) ◇ *She surveyed Sophie from top to toe in a disarmingly ~ way.* | **brutally** ◇ *She was brutally ~ in her assessment of our chances.* | **surprisingly**
PREP. **about** ◇ *Macmillan was quite ~ about his concerns.* | **with** ◇ *To be ~ with you, I don't really think you have a chance.*

PHRASES **full and ~** ◇ *a full and ~ exchange of views* | **to be ~ (with you) …** ◇ *To be ~, I don't care who wins.*

frantic adj.

VERBS **be, seem** | **look, sound** | **become, get, go, grow** | **drive sb** (*esp. BrE*) ◇ *The children have been driving me ~ all day!*
ADV. **really** | **absolutely** ◇ *He was absolutely ~ by the time we got home.* | **increasingly** | **a little, slightly, etc.** | **almost**
PREP. **with** ◇ *We were starting to get ~ with worry.*

fraud noun

ADJ. **massive** | **serious** (*esp. BrE*) | **complex, sophisticated** (*both esp. BrE*) | **attempted** (*esp. BrE*) | **alleged** | **computer, mail** (*AmE*), **wire** (*AmE*) ◇ *A bank lost several million pounds through a sophisticated computer ~.* | **election, electoral, vote, voter** | **corporate, credit-card, financial, insurance, securities, tax, etc.**
FRAUD + NOUN **squad** (*BrE*) ◇ *detectives from the ~ squad* | **case, charge**
→ Note at CRIME (for verbs)

freak noun

1 (*informal*) person with a very strong interest in sth

ADJ. **computer, fitness, health, speed** ◇ *For the real speed ~, there is a fuel-injection version of the car.* | **control** ◇ *Her dad is a total control ~.* | **neat** (*AmE*) ◇ *I'm such a neat ~ that I clean up after other people.*
PHRASES **a bit of a ~**

2 strange/unusual event

PREP. **~ of** ◇ *This was no more than a ~ of history.*
PHRASES **a ~ of nature**

3 sb who is considered to be strange

ADJ. **total** | **sick** (*esp. AmE*) ◇ *What kind of sick ~ is this guy?*
VERB + FREAK **feel like** | **regard sb as, see sb as** ◇ *Other students regarded him as a ~.*
PHRASES **a bit of a ~** ◇ *I felt like a bit of a ~ in my strange clothes.*

free verb

VERB + FREE **struggle to, try to** ◇ *She struggled to ~ herself from his grip.* | **manage to**
PREP. **from** ◇ *They succeeded in ~ing their friends from prison.* | **of** ◇ *He had finally been ~d of his responsibilities.*
PHRASES **be ~d on bail** ◇ *The court ruled that he should be ~d on bail of $50 000.*

free adj., adv.

1 not controlled by rules

VERBS **be, feel, seem** | **become** | **remain** | **leave sb** ◇ *The government wants to leave companies ~ to make their own decisions.*
ADV. **completely, entirely, quite, totally** ◇ *The students are entirely ~ to choose their own courses.* | **truly** | **fairly, reasonably, relatively**
PREP. **from** ◇ *The organization wants to remain ~ from government control.*

2 not in prison; not restricted/trapped

VERBS **be, roam, run** ◇ *animals roaming ~ across the plains* | **break, get, pull** ◇ *The ship broke ~ from its moorings.* ◇ *They tied him up but he managed to get ~.* ◇ *She managed to pull ~ of her attacker.* | **go, walk** ◇ *He said he would let the prisoners go ~.* ◇ *She walked ~ from jail.* | **remain** | **cut sb/sth, let sb/sth, pull sb/sth, set sb/sth** ◇ *He was trapped by his leg, but his rescuers cut him ~.* ◇ *They let their prisoner ~.* ◇ *The birds were set ~.*
ADV. **completely, entirely, totally** | **truly**

3 costing nothing

VERBS **be, come** ◇ *This attractive poster comes ~ with the magazine.*

ADV. **absolutely, completely, entirely, totally** | **virtually**
PHRASES **for ~** ◊ *We might be able to get some plants for ~.* | **~ of charge** ◊ *We will send you our booklet ~ of charge.*
PREP. **for** ◊ *The exhibition is ~ for children under ten.*

4 free from/of sth *without sth*

VERBS **be** | **become** | **remain, stay** | **keep sth** ◊ *We've managed to keep the garden ~ of weeds this year.*
ADV. **completely, entirely, totally** ◊ *At last he's totally ~ from pain.* | **relatively** | **virtually**

5 not being used

VERBS **be, seem** | **become** | **keep sth** ◊ *The hospital needs to keep some beds ~ for emergencies.*
ADV. **completely**

6 not busy

VERBS **be** ◊ *Are you ~ this afternoon?* | **keep sth** ◊ *We try and keep Sundays ~.*
ADV. **completely, entirely, totally** | **fairly, pretty, reasonably**

freedom *noun*

ADJ. **complete, full, maximum, perfect, real, total, true** | **considerable, great** ◊ *The new syllabus allows students greater ~ of choice.* | **relative** | **basic, fundamental** ◊ *Living without war is a fundamental ~.* | **human** | **individual, personal** ◊ *Individual ~ should be balanced against the rights of the community.* | **new, new-found** ◊ *When she lost her job, she at first relished her new-found ~.* | **academic, artistic, creative, economic, intellectual, political, press, religious, sexual** ◊ *Without academic ~, we cannot do any research.*
... OF FREEDOM **measure** ◊ *Teachers can exercise a measure of ~ in their choice of materials.*
VERB + FREEDOM **enjoy** (= *have*), **have** ◊ *Publishers here enjoy comparative ~ to publish what they want.* | **enjoy, relish** (*esp. BrE*), **value** ◊ *I was enjoying the ~ of not having to go to work.* ◊ *As a society we value ~ and privacy.* | **seek, want** | **find** | **exercise** | **achieve, gain, obtain, secure, win** ◊ *The women have won many new ~s for themselves.* | **maintain, preserve, retain** | **defend, protect** ◊ *This newspaper defends ~ of speech.* | **promote** | **give up, lose, surrender** ◊ *As Mike saw it, marriage would mean giving up his ~.* | **cost sb** ◊ *His inability to resist temptation would eventually cost him his ~.* | **allow sb, give sb, grant sb, offer sb, permit sb** | **bring (sb), provide** ◊ *The party claims it can bring ~ and democracy to the country.* | **guarantee** ◊ *The constitution guarantees ~ of the press.* | **deny sb** ◊ *He was denied ~ of movement for a month.* | **curtail, inhibit, limit, reduce, restrict, threaten** ◊ *I don't want to curtail my daughter's ~.* ◊ *Our ~ was threatened by press censorship.* | **take, take away** | **violate**
PREP. **~ from** ◊ *~ from fear and pain* | **~ in** ◊ *Managers have considerable ~ in running their offices.* | **~ of** ◊ *to allow greater ~ of information*
PHRASES **~ of choice** | **~ of expression, ~ of speech** | **~ of movement** | **~ of the press**

freelance *adj., adv.*

VERBS **be, work** (*esp. BrE*) ◊ *He's been ~ for several years.* ◊ *She works ~ from home.* | **go** (*esp. BrE*) ◊ *She decided to give in her notice and go ~.*
PHRASES **on a ~ basis** ◊ *She continued to work for the company on a ~ basis.*

freeway *noun* (*in the US*) → See also HIGHWAY, INTERSTATE, MOTORWAY

ADJ. **major** | **six-lane, eight-lane, etc.** | **busy**
VERB + FREEWAY **get on** | **get off, pull off** | **cross**
FREEWAY + NOUN **exit** | **overpass** | **chase**
PREP. **along a/the ~, down a/the ~** ◊ *We were driving down the ~.* | **on a/the ~** ◊ *an accident on the ~*

freeze *noun*

1 putting a particular level on sth

ADJ. **immediate** | **complete, total** (*esp. BrE*) ◊ *a complete ~ on emissions* | **hiring** (*esp. AmE*), **pay, price, wage** (*esp. BrE*)
VERB + FREEZE **impose** ◊ *The government has imposed a price ~ on bread.* | **announce**
PREP. **~ on** ◊ *a ~ on fares*

2 cold weather with a temperature below 0°

ADJ. **big** (*esp. BrE*), **deep** (*AmE*), **hard** (*AmE*) ◊ *The weather report advised us to prepare for a big ~.* ◊ *Internet advertising is still in a deep ~.* (*AmE, figurative*) | **autumn, spring, etc.** (*esp. BrE*)
FREEZE + NOUN **warning** (*AmE*) ◊ *A hard ~ warning is in effect from midnight Sunday.*

freeze *verb*

1 become ice/extremely cold

ADV. **solid** ◊ *The pond had frozen solid.* | **over, up** ◊ *The lake has frozen over.* ◊ *The pipes have frozen up.* | **quickly**
PREP. **into** ◊ *like water freezing into ice*
PHRASES **~ to death** ◊ *Hundreds of homeless people could ~ to death this winter.* ◊ *Turn up the heat—I'm freezing to death!* (*figurative*)

2 preserve food

ADV. **well** ◊ *Many vegetables ~ very well.*

3 stop moving

ADV. **suddenly** | **for a moment, for a second, momentarily** ◊ *His smile froze for a moment.* | **immediately, instantly** | **completely**
VERB + FREEZE **seem to** ◊ *Suddenly, Ronny seemed to ~.*
PREP. **in, with** ◊ *She froze with horror when she saw the body.* | **into** ◊ *Maggie's face had frozen into a cold mask.*
PHRASES **~ to the spot** ◊ *He was so surprised he froze to the spot.* | **~ on the spot** (*AmE*)

4 wages/prices

ADV. **effectively** ◊ *Salaries were effectively frozen for six months.*
PREP. **at** ◊ *Prices have been frozen at this level for over a year now.*

freezer *noun*

ADJ. **domestic** (*BrE*) | **chest** | **deep** (*AmE*) | **walk-in** (*esp. AmE*)
VERB + FREEZER **fill, stock** | **defrost**
FREEZER + NOUN **compartment** | **cabinet** (*BrE*), **case** (*AmE*) ◊ *the products in your supermarket's ~ cabinet/case* | **section** (*esp. AmE*) | **bag, container** | **space**

freezing *noun*

VERB + FREEZING **reach**
FREEZING + NOUN **point**
PREP. **above ~** ◊ *In the Antarctic, the temperature rarely rises above ~.* | **around ~** ◊ *Temperatures were around ~.* | **below ~** ◊ *The temperature dropped below ~ this afternoon.*

freezing *adj.*

VERBS **be, feel, look** ◊ *The water was ~.*
ADV. **absolutely** ◊ *It's absolutely ~ out there!*
PHRASES **~ cold** ◊ *It was a ~ cold day.*

freight *noun*

ADJ. **heavy** | **air, ocean** (*AmE*), **rail, railroad** (*AmE*), **road, sea** (*esp. BrE*)
VERB + FREIGHT **carry, handle, haul, move, transport** ◊ *All vehicles carrying ~ need a special permit.* ◊ *an agent handling ~ and passengers*
FREIGHT + NOUN **car** (*AmE*), **train, transport** (*esp. BrE*), **transportation** (*AmE*), **truck** (*esp. AmE*), **wagon** | **container** | **traffic** | **depot** (*esp. BrE*), **terminal** (*esp. BrE*), **yard** | **carrier, company, forwarder, hauler** (*AmE*) | **business** (*esp. BrE*), **industry** | **service** | **charges, costs, rate** | **elevator** (*AmE*)

frenzy noun

ADJ. **feeding** ◊ *The smell of blood sent the sharks into a feeding ~.* | **media** | **buying** | **mad, wild**
VERB + FRENZY **drive sb/sth into, send sb/sth into, throw sb/sth into, whip sb/sth (up) into, work sb/sth into** ◊ *He was so angry that he worked himself into a ~.* | **cause, create** | **feed, fuel**
PREP. **in a/your ~** ◊ *She tore the letter open in a ~.*
PHRASES **a ~ of activity** | **in a ~ of excitement, in a ~ of rage, in a ~ of violence**

frequency noun

1 rate at which sth happens

ADJ. **great** | **increased, increasing** | **reduced** | **estimated, expected** | **different, same, similar** | **relative** ◊ *The relative ~ of this illness in the area is of concern to all doctors.* | **alarming** ◊ *Bullets bounced off the rock with alarming ~.*
VERB + FREQUENCY **decrease in, increase in** ◊ *These incidents have increased in ~.* | **decrease, increase, reduce** ◊ *The drug can reduce the ~ and severity of attacks.* | **assess, calculate, compare, determine, estimate, measure, observe** | **affect, change**
PREP. **with** ◊ *Accidents of this sort are happening with increasing ~.*

2 of a wave

ADJ. **high, low** | **microwave, radio, vibration, wave** | **signal**
FREQUENCY + NOUN **range, spectrum** | **band** | **modulation**

frequent adj.

VERBS **be, seem** | **become** ◊ *The attacks have become increasing ~.*
ADV. **extremely, fairly, very, etc.** | **increasingly** | **relatively** ◊ *She was a relatively ~ visitor to the house.*
PREP. **among, in** ◊ *Coughs and colds are ~ among young children.*
PHRASES **at ~ intervals** ◊ *She called her family at ~ intervals.*

fresh adj.

VERBS **be, look, smell, taste** | **stay** ◊ *Mushrooms don't stay ~ for long.* | **eat sth, have sth** ◊ *It's best to eat them ~.* | **keep sth** ◊ *Put it in the refrigerator to keep it ~.*
ADV. **extremely, fairly, very, etc.** | **still**
PHRASES **lovely (and) ~** (*esp. BrE*), **nice (and) ~** ◊ *There's some ham and nice ~ bread.* ◊ *The croissants are nice and ~.*

friction noun

1 disagreement between people/groups

ADJ. **considerable** | **increasing** | **constant** ◊ *I'm exhausted from the constant ~ between my boss and my colleagues.* | **internal**
VERB + FRICTION **cause, create, generate, lead to, produce** ◊ *His decision led to considerable ~ in his family.* | **prevent**
PREP. **~ between** ◊ *~ between the two ethnic groups* | **~ with** ◊ *Her requests for time off created ~ with her boss.*
PHRASES **a cause of ~, a source of ~**

2 rubbing of one thing against another

VERB + FRICTION **cause, generate, produce** ◊ *Rubbing the stones together produces ~.* | **minimize, reduce**

Friday noun → Note at DAY

fridge (*BrE*) noun → See also REFRIGERATOR

ADJ. **domestic** | **walk-in** | **empty, full**
VERB + FRIDGE **raid** ◊ *The kids raid the ~ when they get home.* | **fill, stock** ◊ *The ~ was stocked with food and drink.* | **defrost**
FRIDGE + NOUN **door** | **magnet**
PREP. **in the ~** ◊ *Place the dough in the ~ overnight.*

friend noun

ADJ. **best, bosom, close, dear, fast** (*AmE*), **good, great, intimate, real, special** ◊ *Her best ~ at school was called Anna.* ◊ *I'm inviting only my closest ~s to the party.* | **faithful, loyal, real, true, trusted** | **lifelong, long-standing**

(*esp. BrE*), **long-time, old** ◊ *It was so relaxing to be among old ~s.* | **long-lost** | **new, new-found** | **female, guy** (*AmE, informal*), **male, woman** ◊ *He was last seen leaving a restaurant with a female ~.* | **gay, straight** | **single** ◊ *Does your sister have any single ~s?* | **fair-weather** ◊ *People he had trusted turned out to be only fair-weather ~s.* | **so-called, supposed** ◊ *My so-called ~s are making fun of me because of my weight.* | **mutual** ◊ *We met each other through a mutual ~.* | **family, personal** | **childhood, college, school** ◊ *Do you keep in touch with any school ~s?* | **imaginary** | **online**
VERB + FRIEND **become** ◊ *They became ~s after meeting at college.* | **remain, stay** ◊ *We stayed ~s even after we grew up and left home.* | **find, make** ◊ *He finds it difficult to make ~s.* ◊ *She's made ~s with the little girl who lives next door.* | **win** ◊ *He won't win any ~s if he carries on talking like that.* | **have** ◊ *She doesn't have many good ~s.* | **lose**
PREP. **~ from** ◊ *a ~ from high school*
PHRASES **a circle of ~s, a group of ~s** ◊ *He introduced me to his circle of ~s.* | **a ~ of a ~** | **a ~ of mine, yours, etc.** ◊ *I was given this necklace by a good ~ of mine.* | **be just ~s (with sb)** (= not having a romantic relationship with someone) | **be more than just ~s (with sb)** (= be having a romantic relationship with someone) | **~s and family, ~s and neighbours/neighbors** | **make ~s (with sb)** | **need a ~** ◊ *If you need a ~, just call me.* | **sb's only ~** | **sb's own ~s** ◊ *Even his own ~s don't believe him.*

friendly adj.

1 behaving in a kind/pleasant way

VERBS **appear, be, look, seem, sound** | **become**
ADV. **extremely, fairly, very, etc.** | **exceptionally, genuinely** ◊ *Frank was a genuinely ~ guy.* | **perfectly** ◊ *He seemed detached, but perfectly ~.* | **overly, too** ◊ *He was starting to get too ~ (= in a sexual way).* | **almost** ◊ *For once he seemed almost ~.* | **not exactly, not particularly** ◊ *Her manner was not exactly ~* | **naturally**
PREP. **to, towards/toward** ◊ *He was always ~ towards/toward me.*

2 being friends

VERBS **be, seem** | **become, get** | **remain**
ADV. **extremely, fairly, very, etc.** ◊ *They were pretty ~ when they worked together.*
PREP. **with** ◊ *She's very ~ with Maureen.*
PHRASES **be on ~ terms (with sb)** ◊ *We have managed to remain on ~ terms.*

3 easy to use/helpful/not harmful

VERBS **be**
ADV. **environmentally** ◊ *environmentally ~ cleaning products*

friendship noun

ADJ. **deep, firm, good, great, strong** ◊ *Their quarrel meant the end of a beautiful ~.* ◊ *They formed a close ~ at college.* | **close, intimate** | **beautiful, warm** | **real, true** | **innocent, platonic** ◊ *Their affair had started out as an innocent ~.* | **eternal, lasting, lifelong, long, long-standing** ◊ *They made vows of eternal ~ to each other.* ◊ *It was a period of her life when she made some lifelong ~s.* | **new, old** | **personal**
VERB + FRIENDSHIP **build, develop, establish, forge, form, make, start up, strike up** ◊ *He finds it difficult to make lasting ~s.* ◊ *Jo struck up a ~ with a girl in her class.* | **maintain** | **cement** ◊ *We cemented our ~ with a beer.* | **cultivate** ◊ *He's trying to cultivate his ~ with the Edwards family.* | **promote** ◊ *The aim of the festival is to promote ~ between the two countries.* | **rekindle, renew** ◊ *It will be a pleasure to renew our ~.* | **destroy, ruin, spoil, wreck** ◊ *How can you let such a silly incident ruin your ~?* | **end** | **lose** | **risk** | **betray** ◊ *He betrayed our ~ by revealing my secret to his cousin.* | **value**
FRIENDSHIP + VERB **develop, grow** ◊ *Friendships need time to develop.* | **begin, start** | **end**
PREP. **~ between** ◊ *He was jealous of the ~ between his wife*

and daughters. | **~ with** ◊ *Her mother did not approve of her ~ with Ahmed.*
PHRASES **bonds of ~**, **ties of ~** ◊ *The ties of ~ between us will never be broken.* | **the hand of ~** ◊ *He extended the hand of ~ towards/toward his former enemy.* | **a gesture of ~** ◊ *In a gesture of ~ she invited them to her wedding.* | **an offer of ~** ◊ *She offended them by turning down their offer of ~.* | **a spirit of ~** ◊ *We hope the spirit of ~ between our countries will remain.* | **a token of your ~** ◊ *Please accept this gift as a token of our ~.*

fright noun

1 fear

ADJ. **stage**
VERB + FRIGHT **take** | **be shaking with, be trembling with** | **die of** (*informal*) ◊ *He almost died of ~ when the fish jumped out of the water.*
PREP. **in ~** ◊ *She cried out in ~.* | **with ~** ◊ *They stood there, frozen with ~.* | **~ at** ◊ *The birds took ~ at the sight of the cat and flew off.*

2 sudden feeling of fear

ADJ. **terrible**
VERB + FRIGHT **get, have** ◊ *Leah got such a ~ that she dropped the tray.* ◊ *I had a terrible ~ this morning when I saw you there.* | **give sb**
PHRASES **a bit of a ~** (*esp. BrE*), **the ~ of sb's life** ◊ *You gave me the ~ of my life, jumping out like that!* | **quite a ~**

frighten verb

ADV. **really** ◊ *The prospect of war really ~s me.* | **almost** | **easily** ◊ *a man who doesn't ~ easily* (= become frightened easily)
VERB + FRIGHTEN **want to** | **not mean to** ◊ *I didn't mean to ~ you.* | **try to**
PHRASES **~ sb to death, ~ the life out of sb** (*BrE*) (*all informal*) ◊ *Don't creep around like that! You ~ed me to death!*

frightened adj.

VERBS **be, feel, look, seem, sound** | **become, get** ◊ *I got ~ when he lost his temper.*
ADV. **extremely, fairly, very, etc.** | **badly, genuinely, terribly** | **almost** | **a little, slightly, etc.** | **suddenly**
PREP. **about** ◊ *I was nervous and ~ about the future.* | **by** ◊ *Most of us are ~ by our emotions.* | **of** ◊ *I'm rather ~ of dogs.*
PHRASES **~ out of your wits, ~ to death** (*both informal*) ◊ *She was ~ to death when she saw her small daughter on the edge of the cliff.* | **too ~ (of sb/sth) to do sth** ◊ *My friend is too ~ of my father to come to our house.*

frightening adj.

VERBS **be, feel, look, seem, sound** | **become, get** ◊ *The situation was getting ~.* | **make sth** ◊ *What can we do to make the experience less ~?* | **find sth** ◊ *He found the responsibility rather ~.*
ADV. **extremely, fairly, very, etc.** | **genuinely, positively, truly** | **almost** | **a little, slightly, etc.**
PREP. **for** ◊ *This is extremely ~ for elderly people.* | **to** ◊ *It was all very ~ to a small boy.*

fringe noun

1 (*BrE*) hair → See also BANGS

ADJ. **heavy, thick** | **floppy** | **long**
VERB + FRINGE **grow out** | **cut, trim** ◊ *My ~ needs cutting.* | **push** ◊ *She kept pushing her ~ off her forehead.*
PREP. **from beneath your ~, from under your ~** ◊ *She stared at us from beneath her ~.*

2 (*esp. BrE*) outer edge of a place, group, society, etc.

ADJ. **outer** | **radical** | **eastern, western, etc.** | **coastal, urban** | **lunatic** (*BrE*) ◊ *the lunatic ~ of the nationalist parties*
VERB + FRINGE **remain on** ◊ *He has always remained on the ~s of mainstream politics.*

FRINGE + NOUN **area** | **group** | **meeting** | **theatre/theater, venue** ◊ *He moved from ~ theatre/theater to the West End.*
PREP. **along the ~** ◊ *the forests along the eastern ~ of the Andes* | **around the ~** ◊ *new housing around the urban ~* | **beyond the ~** ◊ *Beyond this ~ no agriculture is possible.* | **on the ~, on the ~s** ◊ *These people live on the ~s of society.*

frog noun

FROG + VERB **hop, jump** ◊ *The ~ jumped into the pond.* | **croak**
FROG + NOUN **spawn** (usually *frogspawn*)
PHRASES **frogs' legs** (= eaten as food)

front noun

1 area where fighting takes place in a war

ADJ. **eastern, western, etc.** ◊ *Thousands were killed on the eastern ~.* | **battle, war**
VERB + FRONT **send sb to** ◊ *Even young teenagers were sent to the ~.*
PREP. **at the ~** ◊ *A new battalion arrived at the ~.* | **on the ~** ◊ *They had to fight on two ~s.*

2 way of behaving that hides your true feelings

ADJ. **common, unified, united** | **bold, brave, strong** | **false** (*esp. AmE*) ◊ *Without that false ~, I wouldn't be able to face the world.*
VERB + FRONT **put on** ◊ *She put on a brave ~, but I knew how miserable she was.* | **keep, present, show** | **form**
PREP. **~ for** ◊ *Her aggressive outbursts are just a ~ for her shyness.*

frontier noun

1 (*BrE*) border between countries

ADJ. **common** ◊ *Neither country would guarantee the integrity of their common ~.* | **eastern, northern, etc.** ◊ *There were very few border controls on the south-western ~.* | **Franco-Spanish, French-Spanish, etc.**
VERB + FRONTIER **cross** ◊ *The army crossed the ~ in the middle of the night.* | **reach** | **control, defend, guard** ◊ *The rebels control the ~ and the surrounding area.*
FRONTIER + NOUN **controls, post** | **guard** | **zone**
PREP. **across the ~** ◊ *The weapons were smuggled across the ~.* | **along the ~** ◊ *an army grouping along the ~* | **at the ~** ◊ *There was an army checkpoint at the ~.* | **on the ~** ◊ *people living on the German ~* | **over the ~** ◊ *They were forced to retreat back over the ~.* | **~ between** ◊ *the ~ between India and Pakistan* | **~ with** ◊ *France's ~ with Germany*

2 the frontier the edge of land that is known

ADJ. **wild** ◊ *America's wild ~* | **western**
VERB + FRONTIER **explore** | **tame** | **settle**
FRONTIER + NOUN **province, settlement, town** | **mentality, spirit**

3 border between what we know and do not know

ADJ. **final, last** | **new** | **next** | **technological**
VERB + FRONTIER **explore** ◊ *Space is the final ~ for us to explore.* | **advance, expand, extend, open, push back** ◊ *The scientists' work will push back the ~s of physics.*

frost noun

ADJ. **hard, heavy, killing** (*AmE*), **severe** (*BrE*), **sharp** (*BrE*) | **white** | **hoar** | **light** | **early, late** ◊ *The young plants all died in the late ~.* | **first, last** | **spring, winter, etc.** | **ground** (*BrE*) ◊ *a heavy ground ~* | **night** (*BrE*)
... OF FROST **touch** (*esp. BrE*) ◊ *There was just a touch of ~ in the air.* | **degree** (*BrE*) ◊ *There were ten degrees of ~ last night.*
VERB + FROST **be covered in, be covered with** ◊ *The windows were covered in ~.*
FROST + NOUN **damage** | **date** (*AmE*) | **line** (*AmE*)
FROST + VERB **arrive, come, set in** (*esp. BrE*) ◊ *The winter ~s have arrived.* | **melt** ◊ *The car was wet with melting ~.*
PHRASES **a danger of ~** (*esp. AmE*), **a risk of ~** (*esp. BrE*)

frosting noun (*AmE*) → See also ICING

ADJ. **buttercream, vanilla** | **colored**
VERB + FROSTING **cover sth with, pipe, spread** ◊ *Spread a little ~ on the cupcakes.*

frown noun

ADJ. **deep, heavy** | **faint, little, slight, small, tiny** | **confused, puzzled, thoughtful, worried** | **disapproving** | **angry, fierce**

VERB + FROWN **give** ◊ *The boy gave a small ~.* | **wear** ◊ *She wore a worried ~.* | **crease into, form** ◊ *Her face creased into a ~.* | **be drawn together in, draw together in** ◊ *His brows drew together in a ~.*

FROWN + VERB **appear, disappear** | **darken, deepen** | **grow darker, grow deeper** ◊ *Her ~ grew deeper at the memory.* | **crease sth** ◊ *A ~ of concern creased her forehead.* | **mar sth** ◊ *A ~ marred his handsome features.* | **cross sth** ◊ *A ~ crossed her brow.* | **turn into sth**

FROWN + NOUN **line**

PREP. **with a ~** | **~ of** ◊ *a ~ of concentration/disapproval*

PHRASES **a ~ on your face**

frown verb

ADV. **darkly, deeply, heavily** | **slightly** | **disapprovingly** | **impatiently** | **thoughtfully** ◊ *She studied the letter, ~ing thoughtfully.*

PREP. **at** ◊ *She turned and ~ed at him.* | **in** ◊ *He looked at the coded message, ~ing in concentration.* | **with** ◊ *He ~ed with annoyance.*

fruit noun

1 part of a plant

ADJ. **fresh** | **overripe, ripe, unripe** | **rotten** | **candied, dried** | **fleshy, juicy, soft** | **bitter, sweet** | **canned, tinned** (*BrE*) | **exotic, tropical** | **wild** | **citrus** ◊ *citrus ~s such as limes and lemons*

...OF FRUIT **piece** ◊ *Finish the meal with a piece of fresh ~.*

VERB + FRUIT **eat, have** | **bear, produce, yield** ◊ *The crab apple bears a small, bitter ~.* | **pick** | **peel, prepare**

FRUIT + VERB **grow** | **ripen**

PHRASES **~ and vegetables** ◊ *five daily portions of ~ and vegetables*

FRUIT + NOUN **tree** | **juice, punch, smoothie** | **cocktail, cup, salad** | **basket** | **bowl** | **flavour/flavor**

2 the fruits good result/reward

VERB + THE FRUITS **enjoy** ◊ *Their work left them enough time to enjoy the ~s of their success.* | **reap** ◊ *He was now reaping the ~s of all his hard work.*

PHRASES **the first ~s of sth** ◊ *the first ~s of the government's health campaign*

fruitful adj.

VERBS **be, prove**

ADV. **extremely, fairly, very, etc.** | **particularly** | **potentially**

PREP. **in** ◊ *This research has been particularly ~ in helping our understanding of the disease.*

fruitless adj.

VERBS **be, prove, seem**

ADV. **completely, utterly** | **largely** | **apparently** | **ultimately**

frustrated adj.

VERBS **appear, be, feel, look, seem, sound** | **become, get, grow** ◊ *I'm starting to get ~.* | **leave sb, make sb** ◊ *This failure leaves the child depressed and ~.*

ADV. **extremely, fairly, very, etc.** ◊ *She sounded rather ~ to me.* | **deeply** | **completely, totally** (*esp. AmE*) | **increasingly** | **a little, slightly, etc.** | **clearly, obviously** | **sexually**

PREP. **at** ◊ *Both sides in the dispute appeared very ~ at the lack of progress.* | **by** ◊ *We were ~ by the long delays.* | **with** ◊ *Sometimes he gets really ~ with his violin playing.*

frustrating adj.

VERBS **be, prove** | **become, get** | **make sth** | **find sth** ◊ *I found the delays intensely ~.*

ADV. **extremely, fairly, very, etc.** | **deeply** (*esp. BrE*), **incredibly, intensely, particularly, terribly** | **increasingly** | **a little, slightly, etc.** | **ultimately** ◊ *It was an ultimately ~ experience.*

PREP. **for** ◊ *It was rather ~ for all of us.*

frustration noun

ADJ. **big, considerable, great** ◊ *My biggest ~ was not having enough time.* | **pure, sheer, utter** ◊ *I shouted at him in sheer ~.* | **angry** | **pent-up** | **growing, mounting, rising** | **sexual**

VERB + FRUSTRATION **experience, feel, seethe with** ◊ *He was still seething with angry ~.* | **express, show, take out, vent, voice** ◊ *He took his pent-up ~ out on his family.* | **hide** | **cause, create, lead to** ◊ *These petty rules can lead to ~ and anger.* | **understand** | **sense** ◊ *I sensed ~ in her voice.*

PREP. **in** ◊ *He clenched his fists in ~.* | **out of** ◊ *I was crying out of ~.* | **through ~** ◊ *Several people resigned through ~.* | **with ~** ◊ *I could have wept with ~.* | **~ at** ◊ *Many have expressed ~ at the delays.* | **~ over** ◊ *They're showing ~ over the lack of progress.* | **~ with** ◊ *their ~ with bureaucracy*

PHRASES **anger and ~, ~ and anger** | **a feeling of ~, a sense of ~** | **share sb's ~** ◊ *I agree that we are accomplishing nothing at the moment, and I share your ~.* | **tears of ~** ◊ *There were tears of ~ in her eyes.*

fry verb

ADV. **gently, lightly**

PREP. **in** ◊ *Fry the vegetables gently in oil.*

fry noun (usually **fries**) (*esp. AmE*) → See also CHIP

ADJ. **French** | **curly** | **frozen** | **large, medium, small** ◊ *two double cheeseburgers with medium fries* | **crispy** | **greasy, soggy**

...OF FRIES **order** | **basket, plate** | **side** ◊ *He ordered a side (= side order) of fries.*

VERB + FRY **dip** ◊ *Noah dipped his fries in the ketchup.* | **supersize** ◊ *Don't supersize your fries if you want to look good on the beach.*

PHRASES **and fries, with fries**

→ Special page at FOOD

fuel noun

ADJ. **clean, smokeless** (*BrE*), **unleaded** | **fossil, nuclear** | **diesel, hydrogen** | **liquid, solid** | **domestic** (*esp. BrE*), **household** | **aviation, jet, rocket** | **spent** ◊ *The plant reprocesses spent ~ from nuclear power stations.* | **renewable** | **alternative, conventional**

VERB + FUEL **burn, consume, run on, use** ◊ *power stations which burn fossil ~s* ◊ *What sort of ~ does the car run on?* | **ignite** | **burn sth as, use sth as** ◊ *The power plant burns sugar cane as ~.* | **conserve, save** | **waste** | **produce, provide** | **process, reprocess** | **dump** (= of an aircraft)

FUEL + NOUN **bill, costs, prices** | **consumption** ◊ *a car with high ~ consumption* | **economy, efficiency** ◊ *The engine gives good ~ economy.* | **supply** | **gauge, pump, tank** | **cell** | **tanker, truck** | **oil**

fugitive noun

ADJ. **wanted** ◊ *one of the most wanted ~s sought by the Italian police* | **dangerous**

VERB + FUGITIVE **be, become, remain** | **harbour/harbor** | **capture, catch**

PREP. **~ from** ◊ *~s from justice*

fulfil (*BrE*) (*AmE* **fulfill**) verb

ADV. **really** | **completely** | **not quite** ◊ *The movie doesn't quite ~ its promise.* | **adequately** | **properly** | **effectively** | **successfully** | **admirably** ◊ *The building is still fulfilling its original purpose admirably.* | **finally, ultimately**

VERB + FULFIL/FULFILL **be able to, be unable to, can** ◊ *Alan was finally able to ~ his promise to Sarah.* | **must** ◊ *Students must ~ the following entry criteria.* | **seek to, try to** | **fail to**

fulfilment (*BrE*) (*AmE* **fulfillment**) noun

1 doing sth to the required standard

ADJ. **ultimate** | **order** (*AmE*)

PREP. **~ of** ◊ *the ~ of a promise*

FRUIT

Growing

*Pineapples **grow** in tropical climates.*
*We've been **growing** raspberries for years.*
*Blackberries **ripen** in the autumn/fall.*
*We haven't **had** any pears yet this year.*
*This tree **produces** very sweet plums.*
*She **picked** a ripe apricot and started to eat it.*
*Growers are expecting a bumper apple **harvest**.*
*a bumper apple **crop/crop of** apples*
*He's a peach **grower**.*

Plantations

- apple, cherry **orchards**
- citrus, lemon, olive, orange **groves**
- banana, pineapple **plantations**

Plants

- apple, banana, cherry, lemon, lime, mango, olive, orange, peach, pear, plum **trees**
- apple, cherry, lemon, orange **blossom**
- blackberry, blueberry, gooseberry **bushes**
- banana, strawberry **plants**
- grape **vines**

Seeds

- apple, grape, orange **pips** (*esp. BrE*)
  apple, grape, orange **seeds** (*AmE*)
- apricot, cherry, peach, plum **stones**
  apricot, cherry, peach, plum **pits** (*AmE*)
- apple **cores**

Skin

- apple, banana, grapefruit, lemon, orange **peel**
- banana, grape **skin**
- lemon, melon, orange **rind**
- lemon, lime, orange **zest**
- the **grated rind/zest** of a lemon

Pieces of fruit

- apple, banana, lemon, orange **slices**
- a **slice** of apple, lemon, lime, melon, orange
- a **wedge** of lemon, lime
- pineapple **chunks**

Preparing and preserving

- **peel** an apple, a banana, a grape, an orange
- **slice** an apple, a banana, an orange, a strawberry
- **squeeze** a lemon, a lime, an orange
- **fried/mashed** banana
- **baked** apple
- **dried** apricots
- **canned/tinned** (*BrE*) peaches, pineapple

Taste

- **sweet/sour** apples, cherries, grapes, oranges
- **juicy** apples, grapes, mangoes, melons, peaches, plums, oranges
- **fresh** berries, lemons, limes, oranges, pineapple, strawberries
- **ripe** bananas, berries, melons, peaches, pears, plums
- **overripe** bananas, melons, plums

2 feeling of satisfaction

ADJ. **great** ◊ *She needed greater ~ in her job.* | **complete** | **partial** | **personal** ◊ *her search for personal ~* | **human** | **emotional, intellectual, professional, religious, sexual, spiritual** | **wish** ◊ *Most computer games provide some kind of wish ~.*

VERB + FULFILMENT/FULFILLMENT **find, gain, get** | **provide (sb with)** | **seek**

PREP. **~ from** ◊ *He gets a lot of ~ from his charity work.* | **~ in** ◊ *I can't find ~ in doing housework.*

PHRASES **a sense of ~** ◊ *They gain a sense of ~ from their work.*

full adj.

1 holding/containing as much as it will hold

VERBS **be, look, seem** | **become, get** ◊ *The garage is getting ~ of junk again.*

ADV. **absolutely, completely** ◊ *The kitchen was absolutely ~ of flies!* | **almost, nearly, virtually** (*esp. BrE*) ◊ *The reservoirs are all virtually ~.* | **half, two-thirds, etc.** | **too**

PREP. **of** ◊ *The bottle was half ~ of water.*

2 containing a lot of sth

VERBS **be, look, seem**

ADV. **extremely, fairly, very, etc.** ◊ *Her wine glass was still fairly ~.*

3 having had enough to eat or drink

VERBS **be, feel**

ADV. **absolutely, completely** | **rather**

PHRASES **~ up** (*BrE*) ◊ *I'm ~ up. I can't eat another thing.*

fume verb

ADV. **inwardly, quietly, silently**

PREP. **about, over** ◊ *She was still quietly fuming about Peter's remarks.* | **at** ◊ *We were all fuming at the delay.* | **with** ◊ *She was fuming with rage.*

PHRASES **fuming mad** (*AmE*) ◊ *Hurry up or else he'll be fuming mad.* | **be left fuming** (*BrE*) ◊ *Motorists were left fuming as police closed the road for six hours.* | **be positively fuming** ◊ *Tracy was positively fuming over the loss of her phone.* | **sit (there) fuming, stand (there) fuming** ◊ *He sat fuming over what he had just learned.*

fumes noun

ADJ. **acrid, noxious, poisonous, toxic** | **diesel, exhaust, gas** (*AmE*), **petrol** (*BrE*), **traffic** | **paint** | **carbon monoxide, etc.**

... OF FUMES **cloud** ◊ *Clouds of toxic ~ escaped from the chemical plant.*

VERB + FUMES **emit, give off, produce** ◊ *The fire gave off choking ~.* ◊ *an industrial process which produces toxic ~* | **breathe, breathe in, inhale** | **smell**

FUMES + VERB **kill sb, overcome sb** ◊ *A firefighter was overcome by ~ at a blaze in a plastics factory.* | **escape** ◊ *Sometimes exhaust ~ escape into the vehicle.*

fun noun

ADJ. **enormous, excellent** (*BrE*), **good, great, terrific, tremendous** | **pure, sheer** | **clean, good clean, harmless, innocent, plain** (*esp. AmE*) ◊ *The boys' game started as harmless ~ but ended in tragedy.* ◊ *It was just plain ~.* | **family**

VERB + FUN **be, become, get** | **look, seem, sound** | **have** ◊ *We had a lot of ~ at Mick's party.* ◊ *He decided to have a little ~ at his friend's expense.* | **ruin, spoil** ◊ *We won't let the rain spoil our ~.* | **want** | **find**

FUN + NOUN **day** ◊ *She organized an annual ~ day for local children.*

PREP. **for ~** ◊ *I write for ~, not because I expect to make money.* | **in ~** ◊ *I only said it in fun—don't take it seriously!* | **~ for** ◊ *a game that's ~ for kids*

PHRASES **be no ~** ◊ *It's no ~ getting up at 4 a.m. on a cold, rainy morning.* | **a bit of ~** ◊ *I was only having a bit of ~.* | **full of ~** ◊ *This movie is full of ~.* | **~ and games** ◊ *School isn't all ~ and games.* | **just for ~, just for the ~ of it** ◊ *They took up motor racing just for the ~ of it.* | **miss the ~ ◊**

You're missing all the ~! | **the real ~** ◊ *That's when the real ~ started!* | **a sense of ~** ◊ *You have to have a sense of ~ to be a good teacher.* | **suck (all) the ~ out of sth** (*AmE*), **take the ~ away from sth, take the ~ out of sth** ◊ *Must you take all the ~ out of everything?*

function noun

1 purpose/special duty of sb/sth

ADJ. **important, useful, valuable** | **critical, crucial, essential, key, vital** | **chief, main, major, primary, prime** | **basic** | **particular, specific** | **proper** | **original** | **dual** ◊ *The committee has a dual ~, both advisory and regulatory.* | **bodily, brain, liver, mental, etc.** ◊ *Fortunately, his head injuries left his bodily ~s unimpaired.*

VERB + FUNCTION **have** | **carry out, fulfil/fulfill, perform, serve** ◊ *All members carry out their own particular ~s.* ◊ *The club serves a useful ~ as a meeting place.*

2 important social event

ADJ. **charity, official, social** ◊ *The couple attended a charity ~ in aid of cancer research.*

VERB + FUNCTION **hold** | **attend, go to**

FUNCTION + NOUN **room** ◊ *The reception will be held in the hotel's ~ room.*

function verb

ADV. **effectively, efficiently, smoothly, successfully, well** | **optimally** | **flawlessly, perfectly** | **correctly, normally, properly** ◊ *All the instruments were ~ing normally.* ◊ *I can't ~ properly without a coffee.* | **adequately, satisfactorily** ◊ *Problems arise when the body's immune system is not ~ing adequately.* | **poorly** | **barely** ◊ *My brain could barely ~ through the pain.* | **autonomously, independently** ◊ *a system in which judges ~ independently of politics* | **largely, mainly, primarily** ◊ *The organization ~s primarily through volunteer efforts.* | **actually** ◊ *This model does not describe accurately the way a market economy actually ~s.* | **still** ◊ *The bombs continued to fall, but somehow the city still ~ed.*

VERB + FUNCTION **be able to, be unable to, can** ◊ *When nutrients are in short supply the body cannot ~ normally.* | **begin to** | **continue to** | **cease to**

PHRASES **fully ~ing** ◊ *The group has now become a fully ~ing political organization.*

fund noun

1 sum of money collected for a particular purpose

ADJ. **large** | **special** | **appeal** (*BrE*), **charitable, charity, disaster, relief** ◊ *The newspaper launched an appeal ~ for victims of the disaster.* | **international** | **contingency, emergency, reserve** | **hardship** (*BrE*) | **benevolent** (*esp. BrE*), **campaign, compensation, insurance, investment, memorial, prize, social, trust** ◊ *It will be a challenge to raise campaign ~s for the election.* | **pension, retirement** | **equity, hedge, managed, mutual** | **foreign, offshore** | **global** | **central**

VERB + FUND **create, establish, launch, set up, start** ◊ *They set up an investment ~ to provide money for their retirement.* | **administer, manage, run** | **draw on, raid** ◊ *They don't want to draw on the ~ unless they have to.* | **invest** ◊ *The ~ was invested in a range of state bonds.*

FUND + NOUN **holder, investor, manager, provider, trustee** | **account, management** | **performance** | **value**

PREP. **in a/the ~** ◊ *There is currently over $200 000 in the ~.* | **into a/the ~** ◊ *The money received is paid directly into a pension ~.*

2 funds money that is available and can be spent

ADJ. **adequate, sufficient** | **insufficient** | **limited** ◊ *There are only limited ~s available.* | **unlimited** | **substantial** | **surplus** | **additional, extra** | **available** | **much-needed, vital** (*both esp. BrE*) | **federal, government, private, public, state** | **church, school** | **lottery** (*esp. BrE*)

VERB + FUNDS **have** ◊ *We have insufficient ~s to pay for the building work.* | **spend** ◊ *Most of the ~s are spent on*

fund

software. | **be short of, run out of** ◇ *We're short of ~s at the moment.* | **appeal for** (*esp. BrE*), **solicit** (*esp. AmE*) ◇ *The school is appealing for ~s to invest in new equipment.* | **boost** (*esp. BrE*), **borrow, build** (*esp. AmE*), **build up, collect, generate, get, obtain, raise, receive, secure** | **allocate, distribute, lend, make available, provide, release** ◇ *Funds will be made available to ensure the provision of hospital services.* | **withhold** ◇ *They voted to withhold ~s from any organization which didn't sign the agreement.* | **deposit, withdraw** ◇ *Clients can withdraw ~s without any notice.* | **channel, direct, use** ◇ *The government is to channel more ~s into local projects.* | **earmark** ◇ *The ~s are earmarked for the health sector.* | **invest** | **transfer** | **embezzle, misappropriate** (*esp. BrE*), **misuse** (*AmE*)

PREP. **~ for** ◇ *a charity event to raise ~s for local schools* | **~ from** ◇ *Funds from the event will support the work of the hospice.*

PHRASES **access to ~s** ◇ *The current account offers savers instant access to ~s.* | **a flow of ~s** ◇ *the flow of ~s between various economic sectors* | **a lack of ~s, a shortage of ~s** ◇ *The project was hampered by lack of ~s.*

→ Special page at BUSINESS

fund *verb*

ADV. **largely, mainly, primarily** | **entirely, wholly** ◇ *The venture is ~ed entirely by its board of directors.* | **partially, partly** | **generously, heavily, lavishly, properly, well** | **fully** ◇ *fully ~ed day care for our children* | **adequately** | **inadequately, poorly** | **centrally, directly** ◇ *Infrastructure projects are centrally ~ed.* ◇ *The GDPC is not directly ~ed by the taxpayer.* | **federally, publicly** | **externally, independently, privately** | **jointly** ◇ *a plan jointly ~ed by central and local government* | **solely** ◇ *The museum is ~ed solely from voluntary contributions.*

VERB + FUND **be used to, help (to)** ◇ *This money will help to ~ administration costs.* | **agree to** | **refuse to**

fundamental *adj.*

VERBS **be, seem** | **remain** | **consider sth, regard sth as** ◇ *We consider these rights ~ to democracy.*

ADV. **really, truly, very** ◇ *I think they made a very ~ mistake.* | **absolutely, quite** (*esp. BrE*) ◇ *This principle is absolutely ~.* | **fairly** (*esp. BrE*), **rather** (*esp. AmE*)

PREP. **to** ◇ *Improved funding is ~ to the success of the project.* | **for** ◇ *Low interest rates are ~ for growth.*

fundamentals *noun*

ADJ. **basic, underlying** | **good** (*AmE*), **solid** (*esp. AmE*), **sound, strong** (*esp. AmE*) ◇ *The figures confirm that Brazil's sound economic ~ remain in place.* | **very** ◇ *The new law strikes at the very ~ of a free press.* | **business, economic**

VERB + FUNDAMENTALS **teach** | **grasp, learn, master, understand** ◇ *We quickly mastered the basic ~ of navigation.* | **go back to, return to** (*both esp. AmE*) ◇ *The government went back to ~, concentrating on avoiding food shortages.* | **change, improve**

funding *noun*

ADJ. **adequate, proper, sufficient** | **generous, significant, substantial** | **full** ◇ *The President has promised full ~ for the plans.* | **inadequate, insufficient** | **additional, extra, increased** | **limited** | **direct** | **initial** | **long-term** | **annual, three-year, etc.** ◇ *the industry's annual ~ requirement* | **emergency, short-term** | **official** | **core** | **central** (*esp. BrE*) | **internal** | **external, outside** ◇ *Half of the research posts depend on outside ~.* | **international, local, national** | **foreign** | **federal, government, public, public-sector** (*esp. BrE*), **state** | **private, private-sector** (*esp. BrE*) | **corporate** | **grant, lottery** (*esp. BrE*) | **development, education, research, science** | **start-up, venture** | **library, school, university, etc.**

VERB + FUNDING **award sb/sth, give sb/sth, provide (sb/sth with)** ◇ *The refusal to provide extra ~ for schools caused a storm.* | **allocate** | **request, seek** | **raise** ◇ *It gave us more*

time to raise the necessary ~. | **attract, get, obtain, receive, secure, win** | **lose** | **boost, increase** | **cut, reduce, slash** | **freeze** | **cut off, stop, withdraw, withhold** | **deny sb/sth, refuse (sb/sth)** | **restore** | **approve, authorize**

FUNDING + VERB **come from sb/sth** ◇ *Most of our ~ comes from private sources.* | **go** ◇ *We need to make sure that the ~ goes to areas where its most needed.* ◇ *About 70% of current ~ has gone on schools.* | **increase, rise** | **fall** | **dry up, run out** ◇ *Much of the ~ dried up in the 1980s.*

FUNDING + NOUN **shortfall** | **crisis** | **cut** | **increase** | **levels** | **package** (*esp. BrE*) | **arrangement, formula** ◇ *We're hoping they will change the ~ formula.* | **agency, body** | **bill** (*AmE*)

PREP. **... in ~, ... of ~** ◇ *£25 million in ~* | **~ from** ◇ *The school has attracted ~ from a number of sources.* | **~ to** ◇ *an increase in ~ to drug rehabilitation clinics*

PHRASES **a cut in ~, an increase in ~** | **a lack of ~** | **a level of ~** ◇ *Present levels of ~ have forced the school to close.* | **a source of ~**

funeral *noun*

ADJ. **family** | **private** ◇ *The family held a private ~.* | **public** | **church** | **closed-casket, open-casket** (*both AmE*) | **simple** | **elaborate, large** | **Catholic, Jewish, etc.** | **state** | **military** | **decent, proper, respectable** ◇ *His savings were just enough to pay for a respectable ~.* | **traditional** | **mass** ◇ *a mass ~ of the victims of the fire*

VERB + FUNERAL **attend, come to, go to** | **arrange, plan** ◇ *The dead man's son arranged the ~.* | **conduct** ◇ *A clergyman friend of the family conducted the ~.* | **have** ◇ *She had a simple ~, as she had requested.*

FUNERAL + VERB **be held, take place** ◇ *The ~ was held in St Mary's Church.*

FUNERAL + NOUN **ceremony, mass, obsequies** (*formal*), **rites, service** | **oration, sermon, speech** | **prayer** | **dirge, march, music** | **wreath** | **cortège, procession** | **party** (= the people going to a funeral) (*BrE*) | **car** | **director** | **chapel, home, parlour/parlor** | **costs, expenses** | **arrangements, plans** | **business, industry** | **pyre** ◇ *the flames of the ~ pyre*

PREP. **at a/the ~** ◇ *He read out a poem at her ~.*

funny *adj.*

1 making you laugh

VERBS **be, look, seem** | **become, get** ◇ *The movie gets funnier nearer the end.* | **find sth**

ADV. **extremely, fairly, very, etc.** | **brilliantly** (*esp. BrE*), **genuinely, hilariously, hysterically, incredibly, laugh-out-loud, outrageously, painfully** (*esp. BrE*), **riotously** (*esp. BrE*), **screamingly, side-splittingly, terribly, uproariously, wickedly, wildly, wonderfully** ◇ *His performance was hilariously ~.* ◇ *You should have seen it—it was terribly ~!* | **surprisingly** | **almost** | **mildly** | **not remotely** ◇ *He's not even remotely ~.* | **unintentionally** | **inherently** | **darkly**

2 strange

VERBS **be, feel, look, seem, smell, sound, strike sb as, taste** ◇ *Didn't it strike you as ~ that Adam wasn't there?* ◇ *This wine tastes ~.* | **find sth** ◇ *Don't you find it a little ~ that she never mentions her husband?*

ADV. **rather, very** ◇ *Helen gave me a rather ~ look.* | **a little, slightly, etc.**

PHRASES **~ little** ◇ *He's a ~ little man.* | **~ old** ◇ *It's a ~ old world, isn't it?*

fur *noun*

ADJ. **thick** | **matted** ◇ *The cat's ~ was matted with blood.* | **silky, soft** | **shaggy** | **warm** | **real** | **fake, faux, fun** (*esp. AmE*), **synthetic** | **animal** | **fox, rabbit, etc.**

VERB + FUR **be wrapped in, wear** ◇ *She was wearing her ~.* | **be lined with, be trimmed with** ◇ *a cloak lined with ~*

FUR + NOUN **industry, trade** | **trader, trapper** | **farm** | **farming** | **product** | **coat, hat, jacket, stole** | **collar, trim** ◇ *The coat was orange with a ~ trim.*

PREP. **in a/your ~** (= wearing a fur coat, etc.) ◇ *elegant women in ~s* | **of ~** ◇ *a collar of ~*

furious *adj.*

VERBS **be, feel, look, seem, sound** | **become, get** | **make sb** ◇ *Their incompetence made me ~.*
ADV. **absolutely** | **still** | **I'm still ~ with him.** | **reportedly** ◇ *The President was reportedly ~ at the comment.*
PREP. **about** ◇ *He was simply ~ about what had happened to his mother.* | **at** ◇ *The president is said to be ~ at the newspaper report.* ◇ *You must be ~ at me for not telling you sooner.* | **over** ◇ *She was still ~ over suggestions that she had lied to the public.* | **with** ◇ *I got absolutely ~ with him.*

furnace *noun*

1 space where glass or metal is heated

ADJ. **blazing, fiery, hot, red-hot** | **glass, steel** | **arc, blast**
VERB + FURNACE **stoke** | **fire** (*esp. BrE*) ◇ *There was enough coal to fire the ~s.*
FURNACE + VERB **burn** ◇ *The ~s burned fiercely.*

2 (*AmE*) device to provide heating and hot water in a building → See also BOILER

ADJ. **coal, electric, gas, oil**
VERB + FURNACE **install, replace**
FURNACE + NOUN **room**

furnished *adj.*

ADV. **fully** ◇ *The apartment is fully ~.* | **partially, partly** | **beautifully, comfortably, elegantly, expensively, luxuriously, nicely, richly, tastefully, well** ◇ *His rooms were comfortably ~.* ◇ *The villa was expensively ~ throughout.* | **modestly, simply** ◇ *a simply ~ room* | **barely** (*esp. AmE*), **sparsely**

furniture *noun*

ADJ. **antique, period** ◇ *an 18th-century town house, complete with period ~* | **contemporary, modern** | **fine, quality** ◇ *The wood is used for making fine ~.* | **cheap, second-hand** | **flat-pack** (*esp. BrE*) | **rustic** | **ornate** | **elegant** | **handmade** | **designer** | **upholstered** | **broken** | **bedroom, dining-room, living-room, office** | **garden, lawn** (*AmE*), **outdoor, patio** | **household** | **leather, pine, plastic, wooden, etc.**
...OF FURNITURE **item, piece**
VERB + FURNITURE **arrange, move, move around, rearrange** ◇ *The room would look bigger if we rearranged the ~.* | **dust** | **design** | **manufacture** | **assemble**
FURNITURE + NOUN **item, piece** (*both esp. AmE*) | **dealer, designer, maker, manufacturer, mover** (*AmE*), **restorer** (*esp. BrE*) | **retailer** | **business, industry** | **shop** (*esp. BrE*), **showroom, store, warehouse** | **removal** | **design** | **polish**
PHRASES **~ and fittings** (*esp. BrE*) ◇ *All the original ~ and fittings will be reinstated.*

furore (*also* **furor** *esp. in AmE*) *noun*

ADJ. **current, recent** | **media, public** | **international** | **political**
VERB + FURORE **cause, create, provoke, spark** ◇ *His choice of words created quite a ~.*
FURORE + VERB **surround sth** ◇ *the ~ surrounding her appointment* | **erupt** ◇ *A political ~ erupted following his appointment as director.* | **follow, result from sth** | **die down**
PREP. **amid a/the ~** (**of**) ◇ *His resignation passed almost unnoticed amid the ~ of the elections.* | **~ about, ~ over** ◇ *the ~ over the proposed introduction of tax on fuel* | **~ among** ◇ *The sale of the two players caused a ~ among the fans.*

fury *noun*

ADJ. **blind, cold, intense, pure, raw** | **controlled, pent-up** ◇ *He growled with barely controlled ~.* | **unbridled** | **full** ◇ *He would have to face the full ~ of his father.* | **impotent** | **silent** | **public**
VERB + FURY **be beside yourself with, be shaking with, feel** ◇ *He was beside himself with ~.* ◇ *I had never felt such ~ before.* | **express** | **unleash, vent** ◇ *He vented his ~ on the cat.* | **direct** ◇ *She directed her ~ at her father.* | **contain, control** | **arouse, cause, ignite** (*esp. AmE*), **provoke** (*esp. BrE*), **spark**

(*esp. BrE*) ◇ *That kind of treatment would drive anyone to ~.* ◇ *The decision to close the factory has provoked ~.*
FURY + VERB **erupt** ◇ *Fury erupted over a speech made by the Prime Minister.* | **grow, mount, rise** | **burn** ◇ *Fury burned inside me.* | **fade, subside** ◇ *His face and body sagged as his ~ fadeed.*
PREP. **in** (**a**) **~** ◇ *She turned on him in a ~.* | **with ~** ◇ *He reacted with cold ~* | **~ against** ◇ *Her ~ against him rose.* | **~ at** ◇ *He kicked the tree in ~ at his own stupidity.*
PHRASES **turn your ~ on sb** ◇ *I hoped she wouldn't turn her ~ on me.*

fuse *noun*

1 (*AmE also* **fuze**) device that makes a bomb explode

ADJ. **short** | **long, slow**
VERB + FUSE **set** ◇ *He set the ~ to thirty minutes.* | **light**

2 in an electric circuit

ADJ. **5-amp, 10-amp, 13-amp, etc.** | **blown**
VERB + FUSE **change, replace** | **blow** ◇ *When the machine was switched on it blew a ~.*
FUSE + VERB **blow** ◇ *Fuses blow if they are overloaded.*
FUSE + NOUN **wire** (*BrE*) | **box** ◇ *The fire started in the ~ box downstairs.*

fuss *noun*

ADJ. **awful** (*esp. BrE*), **big, great, huge, terrible** (*esp. BrE*)
VERB + FUSS **cause, create, kick up, make, raise** (*AmE*) ◇ *She kicked up a huge ~ when she heard about it.*
FUSS + VERB **surround sth** ◇ *the ~ surrounding the controversial movie* | **blow over** (*esp. BrE*), **die down** ◇ *Once the ~ has blown over, we'll be able to get on with work as usual.*
PREP. **without ~, without a ~** ◇ *They left quietly, without a ~.* | **~ about** ◇ *She made a big ~ about not having a window seat on the plane.* | **~ over** ◇ *I think it's all a lot of ~ over nothing.*
PHRASES **make a ~ of sb** ◇ *The children were all making a great ~ of the new baby.* | **with the minimum of ~** ◇ *The job was done with the minimum of ~.*

futile *adj.*

VERBS **be, prove, seem** | **consider sth, describe sth as** ◇ *The president described these activities as ~.*
ADV. **completely, entirely** (*esp. BrE*), **quite, totally, utterly** ◇ *an utterly ~ struggle for justice* | **largely, rather** | **increasingly** | **apparently, seemingly** (*esp. AmE*) | **ultimately** ◇ *Their attempts were impressive but ultimately ~.*

futility *noun*

ADJ. **utter** | **ultimate**
VERB + FUTILITY **know, realize, recognize, see** ◇ *She could see the utter ~ of trying to protest.* | **demonstrate, show** ◇ *This demonstrates the ~ of resisting temptation.*
PHRASES **a feeling of ~, a sense of ~**

future *noun*

1 time that will come after the present

ADJ. **foreseeable, immediate, near, not-too-distant, short-term** ◇ *Things will continue as they are for the foreseeable ~.* ◇ *A new branch of the store will be opening in the near ~.* | **distant, far, remote** ◇ *Trying to forecast the far ~ is a problematic exercise.* | **indefinite** ◇ *Nothing will change for the indefinite ~.*
VERB + FUTURE **look to, plan for** ◇ *Don't think too much about past troubles—look to the ~.* | **foretell, look into, predict** | **embrace** ◇ *All of us need to embrace the ~.*
FUTURE + VERB **bring** (**sb**), **hold** ◇ *whatever the ~ may bring you* ◇ *Who can tell what the ~ holds?*
PREP. **for the ~** ◇ *What are your plans for the ~?* | **in** (**the**) **~** ◇ *In ~, please contact me first.* (*BrE*) ◇ *In the ~, please contact me first.* (*AmE*) ◇ *The possibility of travel to other solar*

systems still lies in the distant ~. | **of the ~** ◊ *The stars of the ~ are competing this month.*
PHRASES **a vision for the ~, a vision of the ~** ◊ *In her speech, the director outlined her vision for the ~.*

2 what will happen to sb/sth

ADJ. **bright, brilliant, exciting, glorious, golden** (*esp. BrE*) **great, healthy, promising, prosperous, rosy, successful** ◊ *He has a great ~ as a designer.* | **better** | **hopeful, peaceful** | **secure, stable** | **sustainable, viable** | **bleak, gloomy** (*esp. BrE*), **grim, uncertain** ◊ *He forecasts an uncertain ~ for the industry.* | **long-term** | **economic, financial, political** | **shared** ◊ *united by our common history and our shared ~* | **entire, whole** ◊ *He felt his entire ~ was at risk.* | **utopian**
VERB + FUTURE **face, have** ◊ *The company faces a very uncertain ~.* | **create** ◊ *We want to create a better ~ for everyone.* | **determine, influence, shape** ◊ *the right to determine their own ~ in a democratic fashion* | **assure, guarantee, secure** ◊ *The sale secured his financial ~.* | **jeopardize, threaten** | **envisage** (*esp. BrE*), **envision** (*esp. AmE*), **forecast, predict** | **consider, contemplate, ponder, ponder on** ◊ *After being dropped from the team the young defender is considering his ~.* | **discuss** | **plan** ◊ *You need to take time to plan your ~.* | **invest in** ◊ *She decided to invest in her ~ by taking a course.*
FUTURE + VERB **await (sb)** ◊ *A great ~ awaits you.*
PREP. **~ as** ◊ *She has a very promising ~ as a musician.* | **~ in** ◊ *He could see no ~ in his job.*
PHRASES **a question mark over the ~ of sb/sth** (*esp. BrE*) ◊ *A question mark hangs over the ~ of the company.*

fuze *noun* (*AmE*) → See FUSE

G g

gadget *noun*

ADJ. **little, small** | **mobile, portable** | **clever, cool** (*informal*), **handy, neat, nifty** (*informal*), **useful** | **must-have** | **latest, modern, new** | **high-tech** ◊ *We live in a world filled with high-tech ~s.* | **digital, electrical, electronic** ◊ *kids that hassle their parents to buy the latest electronic ~* | **wireless** | **expensive** | **consumer** (*esp. AmE*) | **household** (*esp. BrE*), **kitchen**
VERB + GADGET **use** | **design, develop, invent**
GADGET + NOUN **lover** | **freak, geek** (*esp. BrE*) (*both informal*)
PREP. **~ for** ◊ *She has invented a nifty little ~ for undoing stubborn nuts and bolts.*

gag *noun*

1 piece of cloth

VERB + GAG **put on** ◊ *They tied him up and put a ~ on him.* | **remove, take off**

2 joke

ADJ. **funny, good, great** ◊ *the movie's best ~s* | **cheap, lame** | **old** | **obvious** | **gross-out** (*AmE, informal*) | **sight, visual** ◊ *a mixture of wit and instant visual ~s* | **running**
VERB + GAG **crack** (*BrE*), **tell** | **write**
PREP. **~ about**

gage *noun* (*AmE*) → See GAUGE

gain *noun*

ADJ. **big, considerable, dramatic, enormous, huge, impressive, major, real, significant, spectacular, substantial, tremendous** ◊ *This change in the tax system will mean big ~s for some companies.* | **solid, strong** ◊ *The party has made solid ~s in all areas of the country.* | **tangible** | **minimal, modest, small** | **double-digit** (*business, esp. AmE*) | **rapid,**

steady | **immediate** | **future** | **potential** | **long-term, short-term** | **annual, daily, monthly, etc.** | **windfall** | **net, overall** ◊ *The party made an overall ~ of 39 seats.* | **ill-gotten** ~s ◊ *She tucked her ill-gotten ~s into her purse and left.* | **hard-won** | **personal, private** ◊ *They were found to have used the investments for their private ~.* | **commercial, economic, financial, material, monetary** ◊ *There will be no financial ~ for mothers from this new system.* | **electoral** (*esp. BrE*), **political** ◊ *the right made huge electoral ~s* | **military, territorial** | **fat** (*AmE*), **weight** ◊ *She was upset by her recent weight ~.* | **efficiency, productivity** ◊ *There is still scope for efficiency ~s.* | **fitness**
VERB + GAIN **achieve, make, reap** ◊ *He is already reaping political ~s.* | **maximize, minimize** | **increase, reduce** | **consolidate** ◊ *There needs to be joint political action to consolidate the ~s of the elections.* | **bring (sb), produce, yield** ◊ *Better workplace design can bring real ~s in productivity.* | **seek** ◊ *Volunteers give their time without seeking any monetary ~.* | **show** ◊ *August showed a ~ of 144 000 jobs.* | **offset** ◊ *The party has an uphill battle to offset the ~s made by other parties.* | **outweigh** ◊ *The costs far outweigh any efficiency ~s.* | **reverse, wipe out** ◊ *War and poverty have reversed previous ~s in children's health.*
PREP. **for** ◊ *It's amazing what some people will do for ~.* | **~ from** ◊ *€3.9 million ~s from the sale of stock* | **~ in** ◊ *Last year there was only a modest ~ in earnings.*

gain *verb*

ADV. **quickly, rapidly** | **gradually, slowly, steadily** ◊ *His ideas gradually ~ed acceptance.* | **immediately, suddenly** | **eventually, finally, ultimately** | **successfully** | **enormously, immensely, significantly** ◊ *The industry will ~ enormously from the new proposals.* | **financially**
VERB + GAIN **stand to** ◊ *The company stands to ~ a lot from this government plan.* | **expect to, hope to** ◊ *What do you hope to ~ by this action?* | **attempt to, seek to, strive to, try to** ◊ *Protesters tried to ~ access to the palace.* | **fail to**
PREP. **from** ◊ *We all ~ed a lot from the experience.*
PHRASES **have everything, little, a lot, nothing, etc. to ~, have everything, little, a lot, nothing, etc. to be ~ed** ◊ *Why not give it a go? You have nothing to lose and everything to ~.* ◊ *I don't think there's anything to be ~ed from this course of action.*

gait *noun*

ADJ. **rolling, shuffling** | **unsteady** | **awkward** | **slow**
PREP. **with a ~** ◊ *He walked with a rolling ~.*

gala *noun*

ADJ. **charity, royal** | **fund-raising** | **opening-night** | **annual** | **black-tie** | **swimming** (*BrE*) (*swim meet* in *AmE*)
VERB + GALA **have, hold, host** | **attend, go to**
GALA + NOUN **celebration, concert, dinner, fund-raiser, performance, premiere, reception** | **event, function** | **day, evening, night**

galaxy *noun*

ADJ. **distant, remote** | **nearby, nearest, neighbouring/ neighboring** | **known** | **young** | **large, massive** | **elliptical, spiral**
VERB + GALAXY **create, form** | **discover, find** | **observe, study** | **explore**
PREP. **in a/the ~** ◊ *scientists observing phenomena in nearby galaxies*

gale *noun*

ADJ. **howling, severe, strong** | **force-8, etc.** | **northerly, westerly, etc.** (*esp. BrE*) | **autumn** (*esp. BrE*), **fall** (*AmE*), **winter, etc.** | **Atlantic, North Sea, etc.**
VERB + GALE **get caught in** ◊ *We got caught in a howling ~.*
GALE + VERB **blow, sweep** (*esp. BrE*) ◊ *A strong ~ was blowing along the coast.*
GALE + NOUN **warning**
PREP. **in ~** ◊ *The tree had come down in a ~ the night before.*
PHRASES **be blowing a ~** (*esp. BrE*) ◊ *It's blowing a ~ out there!* | **~s of laughter**

gallantry noun

ADJ. **outstanding** | **conspicuous**
VERB + GALLANTRY **demonstrate, show** ◇ *a soldier who had demonstrated outstanding ~*
GALLANTRY + NOUN **award, medal**

gallery noun

1 for art

ADJ. **art, exhibition, fine-art** (*AmE*), **picture, portrait, sculpture** | **museum** | **commercial, private, public** | **national** ◇ *He offered ten major paintings to start a national ~ of modern art.* | **prestigious**
VERB + GALLERY **go to, visit**
GALLERY + VERB **display sth, exhibit sth, feature sth, show sth, showcase sth** ◇ *Some of his work has been exhibited by local art galleries.* | **carry sth, contain sth, house sth** ◇ *a fabulous ~ housing the work of major artists* | **specialize in sth** ◇ *a ~ specializing in ceramics* | **close, open**
GALLERY + NOUN **space** ◇ *The building will provide plenty of new ~ space.* | **exhibit** (*AmE*), **exhibition, show** | **curator, director, manager, owner, staff** | **visitor** | **opening** | **scene** | **guide** (= book)
PREP. **at a/the ~** ◇ *The painting is now on display at the National Gallery.* | **in a/the ~** ◇ *There were very few people in the ~.*

2 on the Internet

ADJ. **interactive, online, virtual** | **photo** | **extensive** ◇ *There is also an extensive ~ of photos.*

3 in a hall

ADJ. **long, wide** | **first-floor, upper, upstairs** | **press, public** | **packed** | **viewing**
PREP. **in a/the ~** ◇ *I found myself in a wide ~ looking down on the floor below.*

gallon noun → Note at MEASURE

gallop noun

ADJ. **fast, good** | **steady**
VERB + GALLOP **break into** ◇ *The horses broke into a ~ when they heard the gunshot.*
PREP. **at a ~** ◇ *They reached the farm at a ~.* | **into a ~** ◇ *The noise startled the horse into a ~.* | **~ through** (*figurative*) ◇ *The documentary starts with a ~ through the history of television.*
PHRASES **at full ~** ◇ *riders coming at full ~*

gamble noun

ADJ. **big, enormous, great, huge, major, massive** | **calculated** | **high-risk, risky** (*esp. AmE*) | **dangerous, reckless** | **desperate** ◇ *It was time for a last desperate ~.* | **bold** | **financial** (*esp. BrE*) | **political**
VERB + GAMBLE **take** | **lose**
GAMBLE + VERB **pay off** ◇ *I took a calculated ~ and it paid off.* | **fail**
PREP. **~ on** ◇ *Backpackers with a heavy load should resist taking a ~ on the weather.*
PHRASES **a bit of a ~, something of a ~** ◇ *Trying to find the right pension can be a bit of a ~.*

gambler noun

ADJ. **compulsive, heavy, inveterate, pathological** (*esp. AmE*), **problem** ◇ *Most compulsive ~s are not successful.* | **professional**

gambling noun

ADJ. **compulsive, pathological** (*esp. AmE*), **problem** ◇ *He went to a psychiatrist about his compulsive ~.* | **illegal** ◇ *The police are trying to stop all illegal ~.* | **legal, legalized** | **interactive, Internet, online** | **casino, casino-style**
VERB + GAMBLING **legalize** | **ban**
GAMBLING + NOUN **casino, club** (*esp. BrE*), **den** | **table** | **site, website** ◇ *Internet ~ sites* | **business, operation** ◇ *online ~ operations* | **industry** | **debt** ◇ *She ran up ~ debts worth thousands.* | **revenue** | **laws, legislation** | **man** ◇ *If I were a*

~ man, I'd put my money on him resigning soon. | **addict** | **addiction, habit, problem**

game noun

1 activity/sport

ADJ. **ball, board, card** | **computer, online, PC, video** | **adventure, role-playing, war** | **guessing** | **good, great** ◇ *This is a good ~ for getting people to mix.* | **entertaining, fun** | **competitive** ◇ *competitive ~s in which there is always a winner and a loser* | **team** ◇ *How I hated team ~s at school!* | **party** | **children's** ◇ *children's party ~s like Musical Chairs* | **indoor, outdoor** ◇ *It's hard to find indoor ~s for children.*
VERB + GAME **learn** ◇ *Children love learning new ~s.* | **create, design, develop, invent** ◇ *The company is developing ~s to play on mobile phones.* | **release**
GAME + NOUN **player** | **designer, developer** | **~s company, ~s industry** | **~ room** (*AmE*), **~s room** (*BrE*)

2 competition

ADJ. **big** (= important) ◇ *The guys are in training for their big ~.* | **close, tight, tough** ◇ *It's going to be a close ~.* | **evenly contested, keenly contested** (*both esp. BrE*) | **play-off** | **away, home** | **championship, league** ◇ *their first league ~ of the season* | **title** | **exhibition** | **baseball, basketball, football, soccer** (*AmE*), etc.
VERB + GAME **have, play** ◇ *Last night he played the final ~ of his career.* | **have, play** ◇ *Shall we have a ~ of chess?* | **lose, win** ◇ *We won the first ~ and lost the second.* | **draw** (*esp. BrE*), **tie** (*esp. AmE*) | **level** (*BrE*) ◇ *The team fought back to level the ~.* | **attend** | **see, watch** | **dominate** ◇ *The early stages of the ~ were dominated by the home team.* | **decide, seal** | **abandon, postpone**
PREP. **~ against, ~ with** (*BrE*) ◇ *this week's ~ against the Titans* | *next week's ~ with Liverpool* | **~ of** ◇ *To pass the time, we played a ~ of cards.* ◇ *a ~ of tennis*

3 how sb plays

ADJ. **fine, good, great, perfect** ◇ *That girl plays a great ~ of bridge.*
VERB + GAME **have, play** ◇ *Trevor had a good ~.* | **pitch, throw** (*both AmE*) ◇ *He pitched a perfect ~ at Atlanta.* | **improve, lift, raise** ◇ *Hendry raised his ~ to become the champion.*
GAME + NOUN **winner** (*esp. AmE*)

4 games sports competition

ADJ. **Commonwealth, Olympic**, etc.
VERB + GAMES **compete in, participate in, take part in** (*esp. BrE*) ◇ *She's hoping to participate in the next Olympic Games.* | **host** ◇ *Chicago's bid to host the Olympic Games* | **hold** ◇ *The Olympic Games are held every four years.*

5 business/activity

VERB + GAME **be in** ◇ *How long have you been in this ~?* | **enter** ◇ *Lufthansa entered the ~ with a 25% stake in the company.*
PREP. **~ of** ◇ *the ~ of life/politics*
PHRASES **all part of the ~** ◇ *Getting dirty was all part of the ~ to the kids.* | **new to this ~** ◇ *I'm new to this ~ myself.*

6 secret plan

ADJ. **little, silly, stupid** | **dangerous** ◇ *He was unwittingly caught up in a dangerous ~ of lies and betrayals.*
VERB + GAME **play** ◇ *I realized that he had been playing a stupid ~ with me.* | **put an end to** ◇ *I'll soon put an end to her silly little ~s.* | **give away** ◇ *Don't let him talk to anybody or he'll give the ~ away.*

gamut noun

ADJ. **complete, entire, full, whole** | **wide**
VERB + GAMUT **cover, run, run through, span** ◇ *The course covers a wide ~ of subjects.*
PREP. **~ of** ◇ *The exhibition runs the whole ~ of artistic styles.*

gang noun

1 group of criminals

ADJ. **street** ◇ *a street ~ known as the Hooligans* | **local** |

armed, **masked** ◇ *The robbery was carried out by an armed ~.* | **criminal**, **organized**, **organized-crime** | **drug** | **mafia**, **paramilitary** | **terror** (*esp. BrE*) | **teenage**, **youth** | **biker**, **motorcycle** | **rival** ◇ *Fights had ensued between rival ~s of football fans.* | **notorious** | **vicious**, **violent**
VERB + GANG **belong to**, **join** ◇ *A lot of the boys belong to ~s.* ◇ *He forced me to join his ~.*
GANG + NOUN **attack**, **fight**, **violence**, **war**, **warfare** ◇ *Her cousin was killed in a ~ fight when he was only 16.* | **crime** | **member** | **leader** | **activity** | **life** ◇ *a tale of LA ~ life* | **culture**, **mentality** | **rape**
PREP. **in a/the ~** ◇ *We were in the same ~.* | **~ of** ◇ *a ~ of thugs*
PHRASES **a member of a ~**

2 group of friends

ADJ. **usual**
PREP. **~ of** ◇ *I go out with a ~ of friends most Saturdays.*
PHRASES **one of the ~** ◇ *Her friends made me feel welcome and treated me as one of the ~.*

gaol *noun* (*BrE*) → See JAIL

gap *noun*

1 space between things

ADJ. **big**, **huge**, **large**, **wide** | **narrow**, **small**, **tiny**
VERB + GAP **leave** | **fill**, **seal**, **span** ◇ *Seal the ~s around the windows with a sealant.*
GAP + VERB **appear**, **open up** ◇ *He flashed his headlights and changed lanes whenever a ~ opened up.*
PREP. **through a/the ~** ◇ *A rabbit darted through a ~ in the fence.* | **~ between** ◇ *Position the tiles, leaving a narrow ~ between the edges.* | **~ in** ◇ *A huge ~ had appeared in the hedge.*

2 period of time

ADJ. **long**, **short** | **two-year**, **etc.** | **awkward** (*esp. BrE*)
VERB + GAP **fill** ◇ *Ads are just there to fill the ~s between quiz shows.*
GAP + NOUN **year** (*BrE*) ◇ *I'm planning to travel in my ~ year* (= the year between school and university).
PREP. **after a/the ~** ◇ *She returned to teaching after a twelve-year ~.* | **~ between** ◇ *a job to fill the ~ between high school and college* | **~ in** ◇ *a ~ in his career*

3 difference

ADJ. **big**, **enormous**, **huge**, **large**, **significant**, **substantial**, **vast**, **wide**, **yawning** | **unbridgeable** ◇ *the unbridgeable ~ between the two cultures* | **ever-widening**, **growing**, **widening** | **narrow** | **age**, **generation** ◇ *Despite the age ~, romance blossomed.* | **cultural**, **culture** | **gender** ◇ *the gender ~ in earnings* | **black-white**, **racial** | **wealth** | **credibility** ◇ *Newspapers were talking of a credibility ~ between what he said and what he did.* | **achievement**, **information**, **knowledge**, **skills** ◇ *the knowledge ~ between doctor and patient* | **trade** | **income**, **pay**, **wage** (*esp. AmE*)
VERB + GAP **address**, **bridge**, **close**, **eliminate**, **narrow**, **reduce**, **span** ◇ *an attempt to bridge the ~ between the academic world and industry* | **widen** | **highlight**
GAP + VERB **open up** ◇ *A huge ~ has opened up between expectations and what is deliverable.* | **grow**, **widen** | **close**, **narrow** | **separate sb/sth** ◇ *He realized how narrow the ~ was that separated him from his pagan ancestors.*
PREP. **~ between** ◇ *The ~ between rich and poor widened.*

4 where sth is missing

ADJ. **big**, **enormous**, **great**, **huge**, **important**, **large**, **serious**, **significant**, **yawning** ◇ *serious ~s in their knowledge* | **glaring**, **obvious**
VERB + GAP **create**, **leave** ◇ *His death left a huge ~ in my life.* | **identify**, **see**, **spot** (*esp. BrE*) | **close**, **fill**, **fill in**, **plug** ◇ *Her appointment will fill the ~ created when the marketing manager left.* | **exploit** ◇ *The company has exploited a lucrative ~ in the market.*
PREP. **~ in** ◇ *legislation to close a ~ in the law*

garage *noun*

1 for keeping cars in

ADJ. **double**, **single**, **triple** | **four-car**, **two-car**, **etc.** | **attached** (*esp. AmE*), **detached**, **lock-up** (*BrE*) | **integral** (*BrE*), **integrated** (*AmE*) | **disused** (*BrE*) | **converted** | **underground** | **bus** (*esp. BrE*) | **parking** (*AmE*)
VERB + GARAGE **build**, **construct**, **erect** | **demolish**
GARAGE + NOUN **door** | **space** | **sale**
PREP. **in a/the ~** ◇ *Don't forget to put the car in the ~.*

2 for repairing cars

ADJ. **local**
VERB + GARAGE **own**, **run** | **take sth to** ◇ *I took the car to the local ~ to get it fixed.*
GARAGE + NOUN **mechanic**, **owner** | **business** | **forecourt** (*BrE*)
PREP. **at a/the ~** ◇ *The car's still at the ~.*

garbage *noun* → See also RUBBISH, TRASH

1 (*esp. AmE*) **waste material**

ADJ. **household**, **kitchen** (*AmE*) | **rotting**
...OF GARBAGE **bag**, **pile** | **tons**
VERB + GARBAGE **take out** (*AmE*) ◇ *Don't forget to take out the ~.* | **collect**, **remove** ◇ *During the crisis, ~ was not collected.* | **dispose of**, **dump**, **throw**, **throw away**, **throw out** ◇ *Someone just dumped their ~ into my backyard.* | **leave** | **strew**, **strew around** (both usually passive) ◇ *There was ~ strewn around everywhere.* | **pick up** ◇ *We picked up all the ~ we could find.*
GARBAGE + NOUN **bag**, **can** ◇ *I put the broken glass in the ~ can.* | **truck** | **dump**, **heap** | **collection**, **disposal** | **chute**
PHRASES **throw sth in the ~**

2 sth that is stupid or not true (*informal*)

ADJ. **absolute**, **complete**, **pure**, **utter** ◇ *This movie is pure ~.* | **worthless** ◇ *His ideas were discarded like worthless ~.* | **old** ◇ *It's mostly the same old ~.*
PHRASES **~ in**, **~ out** | **a piece of ~**, **a pile of ~** (both *informal*) ◇ *The second series was a piece of ~.*

garden *noun* → See also YARD

ADJ. **beautiful**, **lovely**, **pretty** | **lush** | **landscaped**, **manicured** ◇ *a large country house with beautiful land-scaped ~s* | **big**, **large** | **small**, **tiny** | **back**, **front** (both esp. BrE) ◇ *They hang out washing in their back ~s.* (*BrE*) | **backyard** (*AmE*) ◇ *These flowers brighten up backyard ~s all over the country.* | **flower**, **herb**, **kitchen**, **rose**, **vegetable** ◇ *Most of the hotel's salads are grown in its own kitchen ~.* | **rock**, **water** ◇ *a rock ~ with an astonishing variety of alpine plants* | **cottage**, **country** (*esp. BrE*), **formal**, **town** (*BrE*), **walled** ◇ *plants suitable for a small town ~* | **community**, **private**, **public** | **botanic**, **botanical** | **beer**
VERB + GARDEN **create**, **design**, **lay out** (*esp. BrE*), **plan** ◇ *She has created a ~ out of a wilderness.* ◇ *We got someone to design the ~ for us.* ◇ *The ~ is laid out in 18th-century style.* | **plant** ◇ *We planted the ~ with wild flowers.* | **dig**, **do** (*esp. BrE*), **tend**, **tidy** (*esp. BrE*), **tidy up** (*esp. BrE*), **weed** ◇ *Weekends were spent tending the ~.* | **cultivate**, **grow** (*AmE*), **keep** (*esp. AmE*), **maintain** ◇ *Old Mr Kenyon still keeps a ~.* | **water** ◇ *Maggie unwound the hose and watered the ~.* | **overlook** ◇ *The house overlooks the ~.*
GARDEN + NOUN **flower**, **plant** | **soil** | **pest** ◇ *aphids, one of the commonest ~ pests* | **hose**, **tools** | **gate**, **path**, **shed**, **wall** | **gnome** (= for decoration) | **furniture**, **seat** | **centre/ center** (*esp. BrE*), **store** (*AmE*) ◇ *We got the gravel at our local ~ store.* | **party**
PREP. **in a/the ~**, **into a/the ~** ◇ *Mary's out in the ~.*
PHRASES **the bottom of the ~** (*esp. BrE*), **the end of the ~**

gardener *noun*

ADJ. **avid** (*esp. AmE*), **enthusiastic**, **keen** (*esp. BrE*) | **expert**, **good**, **master** (*AmE*) | **amateur** (*BrE*), **home** (*AmE*) | **assistant**, **head** | **organic** ◇ *The organic ~ avoids the use of pesticides.* | **landscape**, **market**
→ Note at JOB

gardening noun

ADJ. **organic** | **landscape, market**
VERB + GARDENING **do** ◇ *It's my husband who does the ~.*
GARDENING + NOUN **business** ◇ *She started up her own market ~ business two years ago.* | **book, magazine** | **programme/ program, show** ◇ *a TV ~ show* | **equipment, gloves, tools** | **expert**

garlic noun

ADJ. **fresh** | **raw** | **wild** | **roasted**
... OF GARLIC **clove**
VERB + GARLIC **peel** | **chop, crush, mince** (*AmE*)
GARLIC + NOUN **bulb, clove** | **bread, butter** | **sausage** (*esp. BrE*) | **powder** (*AmE*)
→ Special page at FOOD

garment noun

ADJ. **outer** | **finished** | **foundation** | **heavy** | **knitted, silk, woollen/woolen**
VERB + GARMENT **have on, wear** ◇ *She wore a heavy knitted ~.*
GARMENT + NOUN **industry** | **factory**

gas noun

1 substance like air

ADJ. **deadly, noxious, poisonous, toxic** | **explosive, flammable, inflammable** (*esp. BrE*), **radioactive** | **compressed, hot** | **colourless/colorless, odourless/odorless** | **inert, noble** | **exhaust, greenhouse** ◇ *pollution from greenhouse ~es* | **hydrogen, methane** | **mustard, nerve, sarin, tear** ◇ *Police used water cannon and tear ~ against demonstrators.* | **laughing** (= nitrous oxide) (*informal*)
VERB + GAS **emit, give off, produce, release** ◇ *It gives off a poisonous ~ as it decomposes.*
GAS + VERB **build up** ◇ *Noxious ~es had built up in the sewer.*
GAS + NOUN **escape, leak** ◇ *Toxic ~es can escape through one of the pipes.* | **emissions** ◇ *greenhouse ~ emissions* | **chamber** ◇ *Millions of Jews were sent to the ~ chambers by the Nazis.* | **mask**

2 for heating/cooking

ADJ. **butane** (*esp. BrE*), **coal, natural, propane** (*esp. BrE*) | **bottled, Calor™** (*BrE*), **cooking** (*AmE*)
VERB + GAS **cook with** ◇ *I prefer to cook with ~.* | **light, turn on** ◇ *I lit the ~ and put the soup on to warm.*
GAS + NOUN **appliance, boiler** (*esp. BrE*), **central heating** (*BrE*), **cooker, fire, furnace** (*AmE*), **heater, lamp, oven, range** (*AmE*), **stove** | **bottle** (*BrE*), **canister, cylinder, pipeline** | **board** (*BrE*) | **exploration, industry** | **field, reserves** ◇ *Chinese ~ reserves are now being tapped.* | **supply** | **leak** ◇ *All ~ leaks should be reported as soon as possible.*
PHRASES **~ mark 2, 3, etc.** (*BrE*) ◇ *Set the oven at ~ mark 4.*

3 (*AmE*) fuel for cars, etc. → See also GASOLINE

GAS + NOUN **pedal** ◇ *He hit the ~ pedal and headed off.* | **station** ◇ *We stopped at a ~ station to fill up.*

gash noun

ADJ. **big, deep, great, long** ◇ *The bulldozers carved a great ~ through the forest.* | **small** | **bloody, nasty, terrible** ◇ *He had a nasty ~ on his shoulder.*
VERB + GASH **get, have** | **cut, tear** ◇ *The rocks tore a long ~ in the ship's hull.* | **leave** ◇ *The accident left a deep ~ in his leg.*

gasoline (*also* gas) noun (*AmE*) → See also PETROL

ADJ. **leaded, unleaded** | **high-octane** | **regular**
... OF GASOLINE **gallon, tank**
VERB + GASOLINE **run on, use** ◇ *My car runs on unleaded ~.* | **guzzle** ◇ *Smaller cars don't guzzle so much ~.* | **run out of** ◇ *We ran out of ~ and had to walk.* | **pump** ◇ *During high school he pumped ~ to make some money.* | **douse sb/sth with, pour** ◇ *They can't resist pouring ~ on a raging fire.* (*figurative*) | **smell** ◇ *Can you smell ~?* | **smell of**
GASOLINE + NOUN **engine, tank** | **pump** | **station** | **tanker** | **fumes, vapor** | **prices** | **tax** | **shortage** | **additive**

gathering noun

gasp noun

ADJ. **big, great** | **little, short, small** | **quick, sharp, sudden** | **ragged** (*esp. AmE*) | **audible, loud** | **shocked, startled, surprised** | **strangled** | **involuntary** | **collective** ◇ *You could hear a collective ~ from the audience.*
VERB + GASP **give, let out** | **stifle** | **bring** ◇ *The stunt brought shocked ~s from the audience.* | **hear** | **take, take in** ◇ *He was taking in great ~s of air.*
GASP + VERB **escape sb**
PREP. **between ~s** ◇ *'Listen carefully,' he said, between ~s of breath.* | **in ~s** ◇ *He leaned against the railing, his breath coming in short ~s.* | **with a ~** ◇ *She gave a little ~ of delight.* | **~ of**
→ Note at SOUND

gasp verb

ADV. **almost** | **suddenly** | **aloud, audibly, loudly** | **breathlessly, softly**
VERB + GASP **make sb** ◇ *The cold made her ~.* | **manage to** ◇ *'No!' she managed to ~.*
PREP. **at** ◇ *She ~ed at his boldness.* | **in** ◇ *Denise almost ~ed aloud in astonishment.* | **with** ◇ *She was ~ing with pain.*
PHRASES **~ for air, ~ for breath** | **leave sb ~ing** ◇ *Her breath went and left her ~ing for air.*

gate noun

ADJ. **front, main** | **entrance, exit** | **back, side** | **inner, outer** | **double, five-bar** (*BrE*), **five-barred** (*BrE*) ◇ *a wide driveway with double ~s* | **big, great, large** ◇ *The great ~s of the abbey were shut fast.* | **heavy** | **high** | **narrow** | **open** | **closed, locked** | **iron, metal, steel, wooden, wrought-iron** | **city, factory, farm, garden, park, prison, school, etc.** | **security** | **departure** ◇ *A flight attendant was stationed at the departure ~ to check tickets.* | **starting** ◇ *The horses began entering the starting ~.* | **lock** (*esp. BrE*), **sluice**
... OF GATES **set** ◇ *a set of ornamental ~s*
VERB + GATE **open** | **bar, close, lock, shut** ◇ *Don't forget to shut the ~ when you leave.* ◇ *The defenders had closed and barred all the city ~s.* | **go through** ◇ *Go through the ~ and continue down the track.*
GATE + VERB **open, swing open** ◇ *The heavy ~ swung open.* | **close, shut, slam, slam shut** ◇ *The ~ shut behind him.* | **lead to sth**
PREP. **through a/the ~** ◇ *He led us through a ~ into a little garden.*

gather verb

1 come together in a group

ADV. **quickly** | **about** (*BrE*), **around, round** (*esp. BrE*), **together**
PREP. **around, round** (*esp. BrE*) ◇ *The boys ~ed around the car.* | **for** ◇ *They are all ~ing for a major conference.*

2 bring people/things together

ADV. **hastily, hurriedly, quickly** ◇ *She hastily ~ed all her belongings together.* | **carefully** | **together, up**

3 increase

ADV. **quickly, rapidly** ◇ *The movement for reform rapidly ~ed momentum.* | **slowly**
VERB + GATHER **begin to, start to** ◇ *As the weeks passed, Charlie began to ~ strength.* | **continue to**

gathering noun

1 meeting

ADJ. **big, large** | **small** | **private, public** | **informal, intimate** | **formal** | **family, political, religious, social** | **international, national** | **annual** | **holiday** (*AmE*)
VERB + GATHERING **attend, go to** ◇ *In some cultures, women are not allowed to attend public ~s.* | **have, hold, host, organize** ◇ *We're having a small family ~ to mark our wedding anniversary.* | **address**
GATHERING + VERB **take place**

PREP. **~ of** ◊ *The president addressed a ~ of local government officials.*
PHRASES **a ~ of the clan/clans** (*humorous, esp. BrE*) ◊ *We all go to my parents' at Christmas for the annual ~ of the clan.*

2 collecting

ADJ. **information, intelligence**

gauge (*AmE also* gage) *noun*

1 measuring instrument

ADJ. **accurate** | **fuel, gas** (*AmE*)**, oil, petrol** (*BrE*) | **depth, pressure, rain, temperature**
VERB + GAUGE **check, glance at, look at, read** ◊ *The pilot checked the fuel ~ frequently.*
GAUGE + VERB **indicate sth, read sth, show sth, tell sb sth** ◊ *The fuel ~ was reading 'empty'.* ◊ *The depth ~ tells you how deep you have dived.* | **measure sth**

2 distance between rails

ADJ. **broad, narrow, standard**

3 fact for judging sth

ADJ. **accurate, good, reliable, useful**
VERB + GAUGE **be seen as, serve as** ◊ *This company is seen as a ~ of our industrial well-being.*
PREP. **~ of**

gauge (*AmE also* gage) *verb*

ADV. **accurately, correctly, precisely, properly** | **carefully**
VERB + GAUGE **be able to, can** | **try to** | **be difficult to, be hard to, be impossible to** ◊ *It is difficult to ~ accurately how much fuel is needed*

gay *adj.*

VERBS **be, look, sound** | **act** | **become, turn**
ADV. **openly** ◊ *He is openly ~.*
PHRASES **~ and lesbian** ◊ *the ~ and lesbian section in the bookstore*

gaze *noun*

ADJ. **direct, fixed, level, steady, watchful** ◊ *She felt embarrassed under his steady ~.* | **intense, intent, penetrating, piercing, searching** | **clear** | **cold, cool, hard, icy, steely** | **angry, critical, stern, withering** | **curious, questioning** | **blue, dark, grey/gray, etc.** ◊ *His deep blue ~ held hers.* | **public** (*figurative*) ◊ *Rock stars are constantly exposed to the public ~.*
VERB + GAZE **direct, fix (sb with), focus, turn** ◊ *They fixed their ~ on the dark line of the coast ahead.* ◊ *She fixed him with a level ~.* ◊ *He turned his ~ on me.* | **catch, meet, return** ◊ *She refused to meet my ~.* | **hold** | **follow** ◊ *I followed her ~ and spotted a lion on the horizon.* | **avert, drop, lower, shift, tear** ◊ *She deliberately averted her ~ when he came in.* ◊ *Carla tore her ~ from the sea.* | **avoid** ◊ *She avoided his ~.*
GAZE + VERB **drift, flick, flicker, move, roam (sth), shift, sweep (sth), travel, wander** ◊ *His ~ flickered over the room.* | **follow sth** ◊ *Her ~ followed Simon's through the archway.* | **fix on sth, lock (with sth), meet sth** ◊ *Her ~ fixed on his and held it unblinkingly.* ◊ *His ~ locked with hers.* | **hold sth** | **linger, rest** ◊ *Rebecca's ~ rested on the child thoughtfully.* | **fall** ◊ *Her ~ fell on Kate's tousled hair.* | **narrow** ◊ *The dark ~ narrowed.*
PREP. **under sb's ~** ◊ *He blushed under her angry ~.*

gaze *verb*

ADV. **intently, steadily** ◊ *He ~d steadily into the distance.* | **absently, blankly** ◊ *He ~d absently at the passing crowd.* | **dreamily, thoughtfully, wistfully** | **admiringly, adoringly, fondly, longingly, lovingly** ◊ *She ~d admiringly up at him.* | **down, out, up** ◊ *He ~d out over the lake.*
PREP. **at** ◊ *Every one ~d at her beautiful jewels.* | **in** ◊ *They ~d in wonder at the mighty peaks.* | **into** ◊ *She ~d steadily into his face.*

gear *noun*

1 in a vehicle

ADJ. **bottom, top** (*both BrE*) ◊ *She was driving along in top ~.* | **high, low** | **first, second, etc.** | **reverse**
VERB + GEAR **engage, select** ◊ *Engage first ~ and move off.* | **change** (*esp. BrE*)**, shift** (*AmE*)**, switch** (*usually figurative*) ◊ *It's difficult to steer and change/shift ~ at the same time.* ◊ *He found it hard to switch ~s when he retired.* | **change into** (*BrE*)**, move into, put sth into, shift into** (*AmE*)**, slam into, slip sth into** ◊ *She put the car into first ~ and drove off.* | **move up, step up** (*often figurative*) ◊ *Coming out of the final bend, the runner stepped up a ~ to overtake the rest of the pack.* | **crash** (*BrE*)**, grind** ◊ *He was crashing the ~s because he was so nervous.*
GEAR + NOUN **change** ◊ *She made a smooth ~ change.* | **lever, shift** (*AmE*)**, stick** (*usually* **gearstick**) (*BrE*)
PREP. **in (a/the) ~** ◊ *I was driving along in third ~.* ◊ *Some drivers leave the car in ~ when parking on hills.* | **out of ~** ◊ *Leave the car out of ~.*

2 equipment/clothes

ADJ. **camping, climbing, fishing, hiking, riding, running, sports, swimming** | **breathing** (*esp. BrE*) ◊ *firemen in breathing ~* | **protective** ◊ *The hot weather makes it hard for soldiers in protective ~.* | **landing** ◊ *the plane's landing ~* | **battle, combat, riot** | **outdoor** | **designer** ◊ *She was the only one wearing expensive designer ~.*
VERB + GEAR **be dressed in, have on, wear** ◊ *She had her running ~ on.* | **put on, take off**
PREP. **in…~** ◊ *a group of men in combat ~*

gear *verb* **be geared to sth; be geared towards/toward sth**

ADV. **primarily** | **specifically** ◊ *Our training sessions are ~ed specifically to the needs of older workers.* | **clearly** | **entirely, exclusively** ◊ *an economy exclusively ~ed towards/toward tourism*

gem *noun*

1 jewel

ADJ. **precious, priceless**
PHRASES **encrusted with ~s, studded with ~s** ◊ *a belt studded with priceless ~s*

2 person/thing

ADJ. **little** | **absolute, real, true** ◊ *The second side of their new album contains some real ~s.* | **rare** | **forgotten, hidden, undiscovered** ◊ *She worked in the antiques trade, searching out hidden ~s in the most unlikely places.* | **architectural** ◊ *architectural ~s like the Taj Mahal*
PHRASES **a ~ of a sth** ◊ *This is a ~ of a show.*

gender *noun*

ADJ. **female, male** | **same** | **opposite**
GENDER + NOUN **relations** | **differences, divisions, gap** ◊ *She examines the interplay between changing ~ divisions and urban change.* | **equality, equity** (*esp. AmE*) | **bias, discrimination, imbalance, inequality** ◊ *The government is working on tackling ~ inequalities in employment.* | **identity, norm, role, stereotype** ◊ *Managers may value different qualities in men than in women, reinforcing ~ stereotypes.* | **issues, politics**

gene *noun*

ADJ. **dominant, recessive** | **abnormal, defective, mutant** | **human**
VERB + GENE **carry, have** ◊ *people who carry the ~ that causes this disease* | **pass on** ◊ *The ~ is passed on to their children.* | **inherit** | **identify, map** ◊ *We may be able to identify the ~s responsible for disease resistance.*
GENE + VERB **affect sth, be responsible for sth, cause sth, control sth, influence sth** ◊ *Genes control the development of an embryo.* | **evolve, mutate**
GENE + NOUN **pool** ◊ *A ~ pool of at least 300 animals is necessary to maintain a healthy tiger population.* | **defect,**

mutation ◇ *Gene mutations are alterations in the DNA code.* | **sequence** | **therapy**
PREP. **~ for** ◇ *An individual may pass on to future generations its ~s for tallness.*

general *noun*

ADJ. **one-star, two-star, three-star, etc.** (*all AmE*)
GENERAL + VERB **command sth, lead sth** ◇ *Both ~s had commanded units in that area.*
→ Note at RANK

generalization (*BrE also* -isation) *noun*

ADJ. **broad, gross** (*esp. AmE*), **hasty, sweeping** | **abstract, vague** | **useful, valid**
VERB + GENERALIZATION **make**
PREP. **~ about** ◇ *The author makes several sweeping ~s about the causes of the crisis.*

generalize (*BrE also* -ise) *verb*

VERB + GENERALIZE **can** | **be easy to, be possible to** | **be difficult to, be hard to, be impossible to** | **be dangerous to**
PREP. **about** ◇ *It is impossible to ~ about such a complicated subject.* | **from** ◇ *We cannot ~ from these few examples.*

generate *verb*

ADV. **quickly** | **automatically, spontaneously** ◇ *People used to believe that dirt spontaneously ~d disease.* | **randomly** ◇ *a sequence of randomly ~d numbers* | **locally**
VERB + GENERATE **help (to)** ◇ *the opportunity to help ~ ideas* | **be used to** ◇ *The wind turbines are used to ~ electricity.* | **be expected to, be likely to** ◇ *The lottery is expected to ~ substantial funds for charities.*
PREP. **from** ◇ *Living cells ~ energy from food.* ◇ *profits ~d from the company's activities*

generation *noun*

1 people/period of time

ADJ. **current, present** | **new, younger** | **older** ◇ *The older ~ preferred the traditional kind of ceremony.* | **coming, future, later, next, rising** ◇ *The forest will be preserved for future ~s.* | **earlier, former, last, past, preceding, previous** ◇ *These children seem to have a stronger sense of purpose than the previous ~.* | **the wisdom of past ~s** | **first, second, etc.** ◇ *The second ~ of immigrants often adopted British names.* ◇ *a second-generation Korean-American artist* | **subsequent, succeeding, successive** ◇ *Succeeding ~s have added to the stock of stories and legends.* | **whole** ◇ *The First World War slaughtered a whole ~.* | **baby-boom, baby-boomer** (= people born after the Second World War), **post-war** | **~ X** (= people born between the early 1960s and the middle of the 1970s who seem to lack a sense of direction in life) | **lost** ◇ *a lost ~ of dropouts*
VERB + GENERATION **belong to** ◇ *people who belong to a younger ~* | **date back, go back, stretch back** ◇ *a family history stretching back ~s*
GENERATION + VERB **grow up** ◇ *a ~ who grew up on fast food*
GENERATION + NOUN **gap** ◇ *I was aware of a real ~ gap between us.*
PREP. **for a ~** ◇ *The consequences of the leak may not become apparent for a ~ or more.* | **for ~s** ◇ *This kind of apple has been grown for ~s.*
PHRASES **from ~ to ~** ◇ *The recipe has been handed down from ~ to ~.* | **from one ~ to the next**

2 production of sth

ADJ. **electricity, power** ◇ *different methods of power ~* | **income, revenue**

generator *noun*

ADJ. **diesel, gas, petrol** (*BrE*), **steam, wind** | **electrical, electricity, power** | **portable** | **emergency**
VERB + GENERATOR **drive, power** ◇ *A water turbine drives the ~.*
GENERATOR + VERB **produce sth, supply sth** ◇ *The wind ~ supplies 120 watts in a strong breeze.* | **run**

generosity *noun*

ADJ. **extraordinary, great, incredible** | **boundless, selfless**
VERB + GENEROSITY **extend, show (sb)** ◇ *He thanked them for the extraordinary ~ they had shown.* | **appreciate** | **take advantage of** ◇ *Their guests took advantage of their ~, overstaying their welcome by several days.* | **repay** ◇ *How can I repay your ~?*
PREP. **~ to, ~ towards/toward** ◇ *their great ~ to the school*
PHRASES **an act of ~** | **~ of spirit** ◇ *She showed an unusual ~ of spirit to those who had opposed her.* | **thanks to the ~ of sb** ◇ *The hospital has now bought a new body scanner, thanks to the ~ of local fund-raisers.*

generous *adj.*

VERBS **appear, be, feel, seem, sound** | **become**
ADV. **extremely, fairly, very, etc.** | **exceedingly, extraordinarily, incredibly, most** ◇ *You have been most ~.* | **overly** ◇ *The review panel criticized the payments as overly ~.* | **reasonably, relatively**
PREP. **of** ◇ *Thank you for your donation. It was very ~ of you.* | **to** ◇ *They have been extremely ~ to the church.* | **with** ◇ *She's very ~ with her praise.*

genetics *noun*

ADJ. **evolutionary** | **molecular** | **medical** | **human, plant** | **population** | **Mendelian**
PHRASES **the science of ~**
→ Note at SUBJECT (for verbs and nouns)

genitals *noun*

ADJ. **female, male**
VERB + GENITALS **cover** | **touch** | **display, exhibit, expose**

genius *noun*

1 very great and unusual ability

ADJ. **great, pure, real, sheer, true** | **natural** | **wayward** (*esp. BrE*)
... OF GENIUS **flash, spark, stroke, touch** ◇ *In a flash of pure ~, she realized the answer to the problem.* ◇ *It was a stroke of ~ on my part to avoid such awkward questions.*
VERB + GENIUS **have** ◇ *She has a ~ for sorting things out.* | **show** ◇ *a work which shows real ~*
GENIUS + VERB **lie in sth** ◇ *His ~ lies in his ability to convey pure terror in his work.*
PREP. **of** ◇ *a writer of ~* | **~ for** ◇ *his ~ for pinpointing the absurd*

2 person with great and unusual ability

ADJ. **great** | **natural** | **eccentric, mad** | **creative** | **boy** | **evil** | **artistic, comedic** (*esp. AmE*), **comedy, comic, computer, literary, math** (*AmE*), **mathematical, maths** (*BrE*), **military, musical, scientific, etc.**

genocide *noun*

ADJ. **mass** ◇ *Refugees gave accounts of the mass ~.* | **cultural**
PREP. **~ against** ◇ *~ against ethnic minorities*
→ Note at CRIME (for verbs)

gentle *adj.*

VERBS **appear, be, look, seem** | **become**
ADV. **extremely, fairly, very, etc.** | **almost** | **surprisingly** | **deceptively** ◇ *His mouth looked deceptively ~.*
PREP. **on** ◇ *The new treatments are ~ on your hair.* | **with** ◇ *She was very ~ with the children.*

gentleman *noun*

1 man who is polite to others

ADJ. **perfect, real, true** ◇ *He's a real ~, always kind and considerate.*
PHRASES **be no ~** ◇ *He may be famous, but he's no ~.* | **too much of a ~** ◇ *He was too much of a ~ to ask them for any money.*

2 way of referring to a man

ADJ. **elderly | distinguished | handsome**

3 rich man with a high social position

ADJ. **country** ◇ *He retired to his estate and lived the life of a country ~.*

GENTLEMAN + NOUN **farmer**

genuine *adj.*

1 real

VERBS **be, look, prove | consider sth** ◇ *The document is not considered ~.*

ADV. **absolutely, completely, entirely, perfectly, quite, totally** ◇ *Her happiness was perfectly ~.* | **apparently, seemingly**

2 sincere

VERBS **appear, be, look, seem, sound**

ADV. **really, truly, very | absolutely, completely, perfectly, quite** ◇ *I'm convinced she is absolutely ~.* | **enough** ◇ *His offer sounded ~ enough.* | **apparently, seemingly**

geography *noun*

ADJ. **economic, historical, human, physical, political | cultural, social** ◇ *the cultural ~ of the South*

→ Note at SUBJECT (for verbs and nouns)

geology *noun*

ADJ. **applied, engineering | physical, structural | environmental, marine | petroleum | Pleistocene, Quaternary, etc.**

PHRASES **the science of ~**

→ Note at SUBJECT (for verbs and nouns)

geometry *noun*

ADJ. **algebraic, coordinate, differential, fractal, solid, three-dimensional | Euclidean, non-Euclidean | basic | internal, local | sacred** ◇ *Pre-Christian sacred ~ was incorporated into church architecture.*

→ Note at SUBJECT (for verbs and nouns)

germ *noun*

ADJ. **deadly** ◇ *The epidemic was caused by a deadly ~.* | **drug-resistant, resistant | flu, strep** (*AmE*), **typhoid, etc.**

VERB + GERM **carry, spread** ◇ *Children carry all kinds of ~s home from school.* | **destroy, kill** ◇ *They used bleach to kill any ~s in the sink and drain.*

GERM + NOUN **warfare**

gesticulate *verb*

ADV. **wildly** ◇ *He ~d wildly as he tried to make her understand.*

PREP. **at** ◇ *The other woman was gesticulating at the ambulance.* | **to** ◇ *She was gesticulating to me with her hands.* | **towards/toward** ◇ *The officer ~d towards/toward the refugees.*

gesture *noun*

1 movement that expresses sth

ADJ. **dramatic, expansive, expressive, extravagant, flamboyant, melodramatic, rhetorical, sweeping, theatrical** ◇ *She made an expansive ~ with her arms.* | **abrupt | subtle, vague** ◇ *He responded with a vague ~ in the direction of the beach.* | **crude** (*esp. AmE*), **obscene, rude | angry, defiant, dismissive, threatening | helpless**

VERB + GESTURE **make** ◇ *The children made rude ~s at them.*

PREP. **by ~** ◇ *They communicate entirely by ~.* | **in a ~** ◇ *He waved his arms in a melodramatic ~.* | **with a ~** ◇ *She waved us away with an impatient ~.* | **~ of** ◇ *a ~ of despair*

2 sth that shows other people what you think/feel

ADJ. **kind, nice, sweet, thoughtful** ◇ *I thought it was a nice ~ to send everyone a card.* | **bold** ◇ *a bold ~ of reconciliation* | **simple | dramatic, extravagant, grand** ◇ *He had the respect*

of his people without the need for grand ~s. | **noble | conciliatory, friendly, goodwill | romantic | empty, small, symbolic, token** ◇ *Words and empty ~s are not enough—we demand action!* ◇ *a token ~ of their good intentions* | **futile | political**

PREP. **as a ~** ◇ *Several hostages were released as a goodwill ~.* | **in a ~** ◇ *In a dramatic ~, he threw the money on the table.* | **~ against** ◇ *The invasion attempt was intended as a political ~ against his opponents.* | **~ of** ◇ *His gift was a ~ of friendship.* | **~ towards/toward** ◇ *The president's speech was seen as a conciliatory ~ towards/toward former enemies.*

gesture *verb*

ADV. **vaguely | frantically, wildly | expansively, grandly | impatiently | helplessly**

PREP. **at** ◇ *She ~d at him to step back.* | **about** (*BrE*), **around** ◇ *He ~d around the room, lost for words.* | **for** ◇ *He ~d abruptly for Virginia to get in the car.* | **to** ◇ *Davis ~d to the waiter.* | **towards/toward** ◇ *He ~d vaguely towards/toward the house.*

ghost *noun*

VERB + GHOST **see** ◇ *You look as if you've seen a ~!* | **believe in** ◇ *I don't believe in ~s.* | **conjure, invoke, summon | exorcize, lay to rest** ◇ *A priest was called in to exorcize the ~.*

GHOST + VERB **appear, haunt sth, walk, wander** ◇ *dark, cold nights when ~s walk*

GHOST + NOUN **story**

PREP. **~ of** ◇ *The ~ of a hanged man is said to haunt the house.*

PHRASES **as pale as a ~, as white as a ~** ◇ *He looked as pale as a ~.*

giant *noun*

1 very large man

PHRASES **a gentle ~** ◇ *Some people are intimidated by his size, but in fact he's a gentle ~.* | **a ~ of a man** ◇ *He was a ~ of a man, standing nearly seven feet tall.*

2 sth that is very large/important

ADJ. **corporate, multinational | industrial, oil, pharmaceutical, retail, software, telecom, etc.** ◇ *The oil ~ Esso is planning to set up a new refinery in the port.* | **literary** ◇ *Camus is considered to be one of the twentieth century's literary ~s.*

PREP. **~ among** ◇ *The Amazon is a ~ among rivers.* | **~ of** ◇ *The company is now one of the ~s of the computer industry.*

giddy *adj.*

VERBS **be, feel | become, come over all** (*BrE, informal*), **get** ◇ *My mum came over all ~ and had to sit down.* | **leave sb, make sb** ◇ *Steep stairs may leave you ~ and faint.*

ADV. **positively | a little, slightly, etc.**

PREP. **from** ◇ *He felt ~ from the sleeping pill.* | **with** ◇ *I was ~ with the heat.* ◇ *She was ~ with anticipation about spending two months with her father.* (*figurative, esp. AmE*)

gift *noun*

1 sth that you give to sb

ADJ. **generous, kind, thoughtful** (*esp. AmE*) ◇ *Thank you all for your kind ~s.* | **expensive, lavish, precious, valuable** ◇ *She received lavish ~s of clothes and perfume.* | **lovely, special, wonderful | perfect | small | free** ◇ *When you place your first order with us, we will send you a free ~.* | **birthday, Christmas, Hanukkah, holiday** (*AmE*) | **anniversary, Christening, graduation** (*AmE*), **parting, shower** (*AmE*), **wedding** ◇ *an outfit that Aunt Marilyn gave as a baby shower ~.* | **hostess** ◇ *These little boxes make perfect hostess ~s* (= for the hostess of a party, etc.). | **monetary** (*esp. AmE*) | **gag** (*AmE*) | **unwanted** ◇ *the problem of what to do with unwanted ~s*

VERB + GIFT **bear, bestow, bring (sb), buy (sb), exchange, give sb, make sb, offer sb, present, send (sb)** ◇ *He arrived home bearing ~s for everyone.* ◇ *They gave each other ~s at Christmas.* ◇ *She wanted to make a ~ to her grandchildren.* | **accept, get, receive** ◇ *Please accept this small ~.* ◇ *The children all received ~s.* | **wrap | open, unwrap**

GIFT + NOUN **shop** | **wrap** | **card**, **tag** | **bag**, **basket**, **box**, **pack**, **set** ◇ *New customers will receive a free ~ pack containing a selection of our products.* ◇ *a ~ set of shampoo, soap and hand cream* | **certificate** (*AmE*), **token** (*BrE*), **voucher** (*BrE*) | **idea** ◇ *Here are ten great ~ ideas for your friends.* | **tax**

PREP. **as a ~** ◇ *Her parents brought a set of spoons as a ~.* | **~ for** ◇ *There were ~s for all the children.* | **~ from** ◇ *This vase was a ~ from my mother.* | **~ to** ◇ *The golf clubs were her ~ to her husband.*

PHRASES **shower ~s on sb** (*esp. BrE*), **shower sb with ~s**

2 natural ability

ADJ. **amazing**, **extraordinary**, **great**, **outstanding**, **remarkable**, **special**, **unique**, **wonderful** ◇ *his great ~s as a teacher* | **rare** | **God-given**, **innate**, **natural**, **special** | **artistic**, **musical**

VERB + GIFT **have**, **possess**

PREP. **~ for** ◇ *She has a natural ~ for music.*

gifted *adj.*

VERBS **be**

ADV. **extremely**, **very** | **exceptionally**, **extraordinarily**, **highly**, **immensely**, **incredibly**, **prodigiously**, **supremely** | **naturally** ◇ *a naturally ~ athlete* | **uniquely** | **academically**, **athletically**, **genetically** (*AmE*), **intellectually**, **musically**, **physically** (*esp. AmE*) ◇ *academically ~ children*

PREP. **at** ◇ *He's very ~ at languages.* | **in** ◇ *~ in the art of healing* | **with** ◇ *Their helpers are ~ with amazing powers of patience.*

gig *noun* performance; job

ADJ. **live** | **paid**, **paying** | **benefit**, **charity** (*both BrE*) | **free** (*BrE*) | **acting**, **consulting**, **modeling**, **speaking** (*all AmE*) | **pub** (*BrE*)

VERB + GIG **do**, **play** ◇ *They're doing a ~ in Boston tonight.* | **get**, **land** ◇ *She landed her first ~ on Sesame Street.* | **go to**

PREP. **at a/the ~** ◇ *He played with the band at a recent ~.*

giggle *noun*

ADJ. **little**, **slight**, **small** | **high-pitched** | **hysterical**, **nervous** | **girlish**

VERB + GIGGLE **give**, **let out** | **stifle**, **suppress** ◇ *I just managed to stifle a ~ at the absurd idea.* | **hear**

PREP. **with a ~** ◇ *'Age before beauty!' she said with a ~.* | **~ about**, **~ at** ◇ *We shared a ~ about the new office romance.*

PHRASES **collapse into ~s**, **dissolve into ~s** ◇ *We all collapsed into ~s.* | **a fit of (the) ~s** | **get the ~s** (*esp. BrE*), **have the ~s** (*esp. AmE*) ◇ *Alison tends to get the ~s at the most inappropriate moments.* ◇ *She still has the ~s about the experience.* | **have a ~** (*esp. BrE*), **share a ~** (*esp. AmE*) ◇ *They all had a ~ at my expense.* ◇ *We shared a ~ at their predicament.*

giggle *verb*

ADV. **helplessly**, **hysterically**, **nervously**, **uncontrollably** ◇ *The children ~d hysterically.*

PREP. **about** ◇ *They ~d about their teacher's accident.* | **at** ◇ *We ~d at the picture.* | **over** ◇ *We were giggling over some old photos.* | **with** ◇ *The children ~d with delight.*

PHRASES **a fit of giggling** ◇ *They collapsed in a fit of giggling.*

gimmick *noun*

ADJ. **latest**, **new** ◇ *a new ~ to encourage people to spend more* | **election**, **marketing**, **publicity**, **sales** ◇ *The promise of lower taxation may have been just an election ~ to gain votes.*

PHRASES **just a ~**, **nothing more than a ~**, **only a ~** ◇ *He dismissed the event as just a publicity ~.*

gin *noun*

ADJ. **stiff** | **double**, **large** | **small** | **pink**, **sloe**

VERB + GIN **drink**, **have** ◇ *'What are you drinking?' 'I'll have a ~ and tonic, please.'* | **sip** | **pour** (**sb**) ◇ *She poured herself a large ~.*

PHRASES **a ~ and tonic**

girl *noun*

ADJ. **baby** ◇ *They've had a baby ~.* | **little**, **small**, **young** ◇ *When she was a little ~, she dreamed of becoming a ballerina.* | **five-year-old**, **etc.** | **adolescent**, **teenage**, **teenaged** (*esp. AmE*) | **great** | **bubbly**, **happy**, **lively** | **lovely**, **nice**, **sweet** | **attractive**, **beautiful**, **good-looking**, **gorgeous**, **handsome**, **pretty**, **stunning** | **single**, **unmarried** | **party** ◇ *Tracey is known for being a party ~.*

girlfriend *noun*

ADJ. **current**, **latest**, **new** | **first**, **last** | **former**, **old** (also **ex-girlfriend**) | **long-term**, **serious**, **steady** | **live-in** | **pregnant** | **jealous**

... OF GIRLFRIENDS **string**, **succession**

VERB + GIRLFRIEND **have** | **find**, **get** | **meet** | **live with** | **sleep with** | **propose to** | **marry** | **kiss**

gist *noun* the gist

ADJ. **general**

VERB + THE GIST **convey**, **give** (**sb**) ◇ *It is difficult to convey the ~ of Reich's ideas simply.* | **catch** (*esp. AmE*), **get**, **understand**

PREP. **~ of** ◇ *I could follow the general ~ of their conversation.*

glad *adj.*

VERBS **be**, **feel**, **look**, **seem**, **sound** | **make sb** ◇ *The smell of the sea air makes you ~ to be alive!*

ADV. **extremely**, **fairly**, **very**, **etc.** | **awfully**, **only too**, **really** ◇ *She was only too ~ to escape them all.* | **just** ◇ *I'm just ~ it's all over.* | **almost** ◇ *Danny looked almost ~ to be going.* | **secretly** ◇ *She was secretly ~ of his company.*

PREP. **about** ◇ *What have I got to be ~ about?* | **for** ◇ *We're ~ for you both.* | **of** ◇ *I was very ~ of his help.*

glamorous *adj.*

VERBS **be**, **feel**, **look**, **seem**, **sound** | **become** | **consider sth**, **regard sth as**, **see sth as** ◇ *Canoeing is not seen as ~ in the way that skiing is.*

ADV. **extremely**, **fairly**, **very**, **etc.** | **less than** (*esp. BrE*), **not exactly** (*esp. AmE*) ◇ *Working in publishing turned out to be less than ~.*

glamour (*BrE*) (*AmE* **glamor**) *noun*

... OF GLAMOUR **touch** ◇ *Several movie stars were invited to add a touch of ~ to the occasion.*

VERB + GLAMOUR/GLAMOR **have** ◇ *He had a ~ about him that she found very attractive.* | **lack** ◇ *Jumbo jets somehow lack the ~ of the transatlantic liner.* | **add**, **give sb/sth**, **lend sb/sth** ◇ *Her long dark hair lent her a certain ~.*

PHRASES **a certain ~**

glance *noun*

ADJ. **backward**, **sidelong**, **sideways** ◇ *She cast a sidelong ~ at Fern.* | **brief**, **cursory**, **fleeting**, **quick**, **swift** ◇ *After a cursory ~ at the report he frowned.* | **casual** | **covert**, **furtive**, **nervous**, **surreptitious** ◇ *The man walked slowly along, casting furtive ~s behind him.* | **accusing**, **angry**, **baleful**, **disapproving**, **reproachful**, **scornful**, **sharp**, **suspicious**, **withering** ◇ *Meena threw him an angry ~.* | **curious**, **puzzled**, **questioning**, **quizzical** | **admiring**, **approving** | **knowing** | **meaningful** ◇ *The couple exchanged meaningful ~s but said nothing.* | **amused**, **wry** | **anxious**, **nervous**, **worried**

VERB + GLANCE **cast** (**sb**), **dart**, **give** (**sb/sth**), **have**, **shoot** (**sb**), **steal**, **take**, **throw** (**sb**) ◇ *He gave her a mocking ~.* ◇ *I had a quick ~ at the article, but I haven't read it yet.* ◇ *He stole a sidelong ~ at the young woman sitting next to him on the train.* ◇ *She took one last ~ in the mirror and then left.* | **exchange** ◇ *They exchanged knowing ~s.* | **catch** ◇ *I caught the teacher's ~ and nearly burst into nervous laughter.* | **attract**, **draw** ◇ *Their car attracted admiring ~s wherever they went.*

GLANCE + VERB **move** ◇ *Her ~ flickered briefly across to the group standing at the other side of the street.* | **meet** ◇ *Their*

~s met, then they both looked away. | **fall on sb/sth, rest on sb/sth** ◇ *His ~ fell on a pile of papers at one side of the desk.*
PREP. **at a ~** ◇ *The software allows you to see at a ~ what fonts you have on the computer.* | **with a ~** ◇ *With a quick ~ at the time, she stood up and prepared to leave.* | **without a ~** ◇ *He left without a backward ~.* | **~ at** ◇ *A ~ at my watch told me it was already past six o'clock.* | **~ of** ◇ *He ignored my ~ of disapproval.* | **~ over** ◇ *He kept throwing nervous ~s over his shoulder.*
PHRASES **at first ~** ◇ *At first ~ the contract seemed to be fine.*

glance *verb*

ADV. **briefly, quickly, sharply** ◇ *Norton ~d sharply at him.* | **anxiously, fearfully, nervously** ◇ *She ~d nervously over her shoulder.* | **curiously** ◇ *He ~d curiously around him.* | **covertly** ◇ *He ~d covertly at his watch.* | **barely, hardly** ◇ *She barely ~d at him.* | **down, up** ◇ *She ~d up at him.*
VERB + GLANCE **pause to, turn to** ◇ *He turned to ~ in our direction.* | **happen to** ◇ *At that moment she happened to ~ up.*
PREP. **about** (*esp. BrE*), **around, round** (*esp. BrE*) ◇ *She ~d around the room.* | **across, over** ◇ *She ~d across to where the others were standing chatting.* | **at** ◇ *She ~d briefly at his lapel badge.* | **towards/toward** ◇ *He ~d towards/toward the kitchen.*

gland *noun*

ADJ. **enlarged, swollen** ◇ *She's gone to bed with swollen ~s and a temperature.* | **adrenal, pineal, pituitary, thyroid, etc.** | **lymph, salivary, sweat, etc.** ◇ *Female ants release pheromones from their scent ~s.*
GLAND + VERB **release sth, secrete sth**

glare *noun*

1 strong light

ADJ. **blinding, full, harsh, hot** | **sudden** ◇ *A sudden ~ of headlights lit the driveway.*
VERB + GLARE **reflect** ◇ *The walls were whitewashed to reflect the ~ of the sun.* | **reduce** ◇ *We wore sunglasses to reduce the ~ from the road.* | **be blinded by, be dazzled by** ◇ *For a moment she was blinded by the harsh ~ of the sun.* | **be caught in** ◇ *The rabbit was caught in the ~ of the car's headlights.*
PREP. **against the ~** ◇ *We screwed up our eyes against the blinding ~ from the searchlights.* | **in the ~ of, under the ~ of** ◇ *Under the ~ of the street lights, visibility was good.* | **~ from**
PHRASES **the ~ of publicity** (*figurative*) ◇ *The divorce was conducted in the full ~ of media publicity.*

2 angry look

ADJ. **angry, baleful, defiant, furious, hostile, malevolent, menacing, withering** | **icy, steely, stony** | **warning**
VERB + GLARE **fix sb with, give sb, send sb, shoot (sb), turn on sb** ◇ *She fixed her questioner with an icy ~.* | *He sent her a ~ that was full of suspicion.* ◇ *She shot a warning ~ at her companion.* ◇ *He turned his baleful ~ on the cowering suspect.*

glare *verb*

ADV. **angrily, balefully, fiercely, furiously** | **back** ◇ *I looked at her and she ~d angrily back.*
PREP. **at, down at, up at** ◇ *He stood at the bottom of the stairs, glaring up at us.*

glass *noun*

1 transparent substance

ADJ. **clear, coloured/colored, opaque, plain, smoked, tinted** | **broken** | **flying** ◇ *A bomb went off, and many people were injured by flying ~.* | **bulletproof, cut, frosted, plate, safety, stained, toughened**
... OF GLASS **piece** | **pane, sheet** | **fragment, shard, sliver, splinter** ◇ *The floor was littered with fragments of broken ~.*

VERB + GLASS **blow, make** ◇ *We watched the craftsmen blowing ~.* ◇ *The factory makes safety ~.* | **break, crack, shatter, smash**
GLASS + VERB **break, crack, shatter, smash, splinter** ◇ *the sound of ~ breaking*
GLASS + NOUN **beads, bottle, bowl, eye, jar, vase, vial** | **cabinet, case** | **door, panel, partition, roof, wall, window** | **table** | **fibre/fiber** ◇ *a boat made of ~ fibre/fiber*
PREP. **behind ~** ◇ *The books were all behind ~ (= in glass cases).* | **on ~** ◇ *She cut her foot on some ~.* | **under ~** ◇ *We grow fruit under ~ (= in a glasshouse).* | **through ~** ◇ *He could see the light through the frosted ~.*

2 for drinking

ADJ. **brimming** (*esp. BrE*), **full** | **half-empty, half-full** | **empty** | **beer, brandy, champagne, sherry, whisky/whiskey, wine** | **crystal** ◇ *a set of crystal ~es* | **tall** ◇ *a tall ~ of milk* | **fresh** (*esp. AmE*) ◇ *He poured her a fresh ~ of sherry.* | **pint** ◇ *beer in a pint ~*
VERB + GLASS **have** ◇ *He had a small ~ of lager with his meal.* | **drink, sip** ◇ *She sat sipping a ~ of champagne.* | **drain, empty** | **fill, pour, refill, top up** ◇ *The waiter filled their ~es.* | **clean, polish, wash** ◇ *The butler was polishing the brandy ~es.* | **lift, raise** ◇ *She raised the ~ to her lips.* | **hand sb** ◇ *I handed her a ~ of wine.* | **put down, set down** ◇ *I put my ~ down on the table.* | **clink** ◇ *They clinked ~es, still laughing.*
GLASS + VERB **clink** ◇ *He heard ~es clinking in the other room.*
PREP. **in a/the/sb's ~** ◇ *the red liquid in his ~* | **~ of** ◇ *She had had three ~es of wine already.*
PHRASES **(a) ~ in (your) hand** ◇ *He sat back, ~ in hand.*

glasses *noun*

ADJ. **dark, tinted** ◇ *I wear blue-tinted ~ on sunny days.* | **reading** | **half-moon, round** | **thick** ◇ *a short, fat man with greasy black hair and thick ~* | **granny** | **owlish** | **heavy** | **gold-rimmed, horn-rimmed, steel-rimmed, wire-framed, wire-rimmed** | **rimless** | **field, opera**
... OF GLASSES **pair**
VERB + GLASSES **have on, wear** | **put on** | **remove, take off** | **look over, peer over** ◇ *Her father lowered his paper and peered over his ~ at her.* | **adjust, push up** ◇ *She pushed her ~ up and rubbed the bridge of her nose.* | **clean, polish, wipe**
GLASSES + VERB **steam up** ◇ *His ~ steamed up as soon as he came indoors.* | **be perched on sth, perch on sth** ◇ *Horn-rimmed ~ perched on the bridge of her nose.*
PREP. **behind (your) ~** ◇ *She blinked behind her ~.* ◇ *Their anxious faces were hidden behind dark ~.*

gleam *noun*

1 soft light

ADJ. **dull, faint** | **distant**
PREP. **~ of** ◇ *the distant ~ of the sea*
PHRASES **a ~ of light** ◇ *a faint ~ of light from under the door*

2 in sb's eyes

ADJ. **cold, dark, strange** | **predatory, speculative** | **mischievous, sardonic, wicked** | **sudden**
VERB + GLEAM **have** ◇ *He had a speculative ~ in his eyes.*
GLEAM + VERB **come into sb's eye/eyes, enter sb's eye/eyes, light sb's eye/eyes** ◇ *A sudden ~ came into her eye as she remembered that tomorrow was her day off.*
PREP. **~ of** ◇ *A ~ of laughter lit his eyes.*
PHRASES **a ~ in sb's eye/eyes**

gleam *verb*

ADV. **dully, faintly, softly** ◇ *The knife's blade ~ed dully in the dark.*
PREP. **with** ◇ *The long oak table ~ed with polish.*
PHRASES **~ golden, white, etc.** ◇ *The pebble beach ~ed white in the moonlight.*

glimmer *noun*

ADJ. **faint, tiny** ◇ *In the east we could see the first faint ~ of dawn.* ◇ *The faint ~ of an idea had crept into his mind.* (*figurative*)
PREP. **~ of**

glimpse noun

1 brief sight of sb/sth

ADJ. **brief, fleeting, the merest, momentary, quick** | **occasional, rare** ◇ *They caught occasional ~s of great birds circling.* | **tantalizing** ◇ *This was my first tantalizing ~ of the islands.* | **first, last** ◇ *Later we caught our first ~ of the sea.*
VERB + GLIMPSE **catch, get, have, take** ◇ *Thousands of people had gathered, hoping to catch a ~ of the star.* ◇ *We only had a fleeting ~ of the sun all day.* | **afford sb**
PREP. **~ at** ◇ *He took a quick ~ at the map.* | **~ of** ◇ *We got just a brief ~ of the car as it rushed by.*

2 brief experience of sth

ADJ. **brief** | **fascinating, intriguing** | **rare** ◇ *This scene may give a rare ~ of Charles's personal style as king.*
VERB + GLIMPSE **get, have, take** | **afford sb, allow sb, give sb, offer (sb), provide** ◇ *That smile afforded her a brief ~ of the other side of Adam.*
PREP. **~ at** ◇ *The exhibition offers a fascinating ~ at life beneath the waves.* | **~ into** ◇ *Take a ~ into the future of space travel.* | **~ of** ◇ *She got a ~ of a very different way of life.*

glint noun

1 flash of light

ADJ. **metallic**
VERB + GLINT **catch, see** ◇ *Among the trees I caught a ~ of blue.*
PREP. **~ of**

2 in sb's eye

ADJ. **dangerous, determined** | **mischievous, playful, teasing**
VERB + GLINT **have** ◇ *He had a dangerous ~ in his eyes.*
GLINT + VERB **appear in sb's eye/eyes, come into sb's eye/eyes** ◇ *A determined ~ appeared in her eye.*
PREP. **~ in** | **~ of** ◇ *There was a ~ of amusement in her eyes.*

glint verb

ADV. **angrily** ◇ *His eyes ~ed angrily.*
PREP. **with** ◇ *Her eyes ~ed with amusement.*

glitter verb

1 shine brightly

ADV. **brightly** ◇ *Crystal chandeliers ~ed brightly above them.*
PREP. **in** ◇ *His metal buttons ~ed in the sunlight.* | **with** ◇ *Trees and grass ~ed with dew.*

2 show emotion

ADV. **coldly, dangerously, darkly, fiercely, strangely** ◇ *His deep-set eyes ~ed coldly.*
PREP. **with** ◇ *Her eyes ~ed with delight.*

globe noun the globe

ADJ. **entire**
VERB + THE GLOBE **span** ◇ *a commercial service that will soon span the ~* | **circle, circumnavigate, travel** ◇ *one of the first boats to circumnavigate the ~* ◇ *She travels the ~ in search of good writers of children's stories.*
PREP. **across the ~** ◇ *The news soon spread across the ~.* | **all over the ~** ◇ *Motor vehicles are found all over the ~.* | **around the ~, round the ~** (*esp. BrE*) ◇ *Chess fans around the ~ watched the match with breathless interest.*
PHRASES **all parts of the ~, every corner of the ~** ◇ *Athletes from every corner of the ~ competed in the Games.*

gloom noun

1 sadness

ADJ. **deep** ◇ *She was in a deep ~ because not even a postcard had arrived from Ricky.* | **general** (*esp. BrE*) | **economic** ◇ *the general economic ~*
VERB + GLOOM **be filled with, be sunk in, sink into** ◇ *He was sunk in deep ~ at the prospect of being alone.* ◇ *I sank into ~ and depression.* | **fill sb with** ◇ *The news filled me with ~.* | **cast** ◇ *Talk of his ill health cast ~ over the celebrations.* | **dispel, lift** (*esp. BrE*) ◇ *efforts to dispel their ~*
GLOOM + VERB **deepen, descend** (*both esp. BrE*) ◇ *Their ~ deepened as the election results came in.* ◇ *She felt ~ descend*

on her shoulders. | **lift** ◇ *When the ~ finally lifts, the pessimists will be surprised at how much has been going right.*
PREP. **in ~** ◇ *The nation was deep in ~.* | **~ about** ◇ *There is a general ~ about the farming industry.*
PHRASES **doom and ~, ~ and despondency** (*BrE*) ◇ *Despite falling demand, the year has not been all doom and ~.* ◇ *the darkest feelings of ~ and despondency*

2 darkness

ADJ. **deep** | **deepening, descending, gathering** ◇ *He peered into the gathering ~.* | **cold, damp** | **evening** ◇ *The fog looked ominous in the evening ~.*
VERB + GLOOM **penetrate, pierce** ◇ *The sound of distant police whistles pierced the ~.* | **adjust to, become accustomed to, get accustomed to** ◇ *Slowly, my eyes became accustomed to the ~.* | **peer into, peer through**
GLOOM + VERB **deepen** (*BrE*), **descend** ◇ *We sat and watched as the ~ descended.*
PREP. **in the ~** ◇ *We lost sight of them in the ~.* | **into the ~** ◇ *She watched him disappear into the ~.* | **out of the ~** ◇ *Two figures materialized out of the ~.* | **through the ~** ◇ *She could see the house faintly through the ~.*

gloomy adj.

VERBS **be, feel, look, seem, sound** | **become, get** ◇ *Now, don't start to get ~.* | **remain**
ADV. **very** ◇ *The future looked very ~.* | **far from** (*esp. BrE*) ◇ *The committee's view was in fact far from ~.* | **pretty, rather**
PREP. **about** ◇ *Many businesses remain ~ about the prospects for the economy.*

glory noun

1 fame/honour

ADJ. **personal** ◇ *They are driven by a craving for personal ~.* | **reflected** ◇ *She basked in the reflected ~ of her daughter's success.* | **greater** ◇ *The force behind all his reforms was the greater ~ of the state.* | **military** ◇ *young soldiers eager to win military ~*
VERB + GLORY **cover yourself in, cover yourself with, get, win** ◇ *He covered himself in ~ and came home a rich man.* ◇ *Typical! I do all the work and she gets all the ~.* (*informal*) | **bring (sb)** ◇ *Victory brought them ~, fame and riches.* | **bask in** | **steal, take** ◇ *I didn't want to steal her ~, so I stayed in the background.*
GLORY + NOUN **days** ◇ *Quarterman's ~ days are long behind him.*
PREP. **for the ~ of, to the ~ of** ◇ *They built many churches, great and small, to the ~ of God.*
PHRASES **a blaze of ~** ◇ *It's my last ever tournament and I hope to go out in a blaze of ~!* | **sb's moment of ~** ◇ *His moment of ~ came when he won the Olympic downhill skiing event.*

2 beauty/beautiful feature

ADJ. **full** ◇ *You cannot appreciate the bridge's full ~ by going over it; it is best viewed from below.* | **crowning** ◇ *The city's crowning ~ is its Gothic cathedral.*
PHRASES **in all her, his, etc. ~** ◇ *Seeing the Rockies in all their ~ was an awesome experience.* | **restore sth to its former ~** ◇ *The 18th-century building has been restored to its former ~.*

gloss noun

ADJ. **clear, high** ◇ *Use a high ~ paint.* | **lip** (usually *lipgloss*)
VERB + GLOSS **add** ◇ *We used a gel to add ~ to her hair.* | **lose** (*esp. BrE*)
GLOSS + NOUN **finish, paint** ◇ *furniture with a dark ~ finish*

glove noun

ADJ. **long** | **fingerless** | **protective** | **cotton, kid** (*often figurative*), **latex, leather, plastic, rubber, woollen/woolen** ◇ *Treat her with kid gloves—she's very sensitive.* | **baseball, boxing, driving, evening, gardening, oven** (*BrE*), **surgical**
... OF GLOVES **pair**

VERB + GLOVE **pull on** | **peel off** (*esp. AmE*), **pull off** ◇ *She pulled off her ~ to reveal a wedding ring.*
GLOVE + NOUN **box, compartment** ◇ *Don't keep important documents in the ~ compartment of your car.*
→ Special page at CLOTHES

glow *noun*

1 steady light

ADJ. **cosy/cozy, rich, soft, warm** | **dim, dull, faint, pale** | **steady** | **eerie** (*esp. AmE*), **ghostly**
VERB + GLOW **cast, give sth, throw** ◇ *The lamplight gave a cosy/cozy ~ to the room.* ◇ *The sunset threw an orange ~ on the cliffs.* | **be bathed in** ◇ *The whole town was bathed in the ~ of the setting sun.*
GLOW + VERB **light sth** ◇ *Our faces were lit by the faint green ~ of the dashboard lights.* | **surround sth**
PREP. **~ from** ◇ *the soft ~ from the lamp* | **~ of**

2 in sb's face

ADJ. **healthy, pink, rosy, warm**
VERB + GLOW **have** ◇ *Her cheeks had a healthy ~.*
PHRASES **bring a ~ to sb's face** ◇ *The wine had brought a warm ~ to her face.*

3 feeling

ADJ. **rosy, warm**
VERB + GLOW **bask in, bathe in, feel** ◇ *She bathed in the warm ~ of first love.*
PREP. **~ of** ◇ *He felt a ~ of pride as he watched them.*

glow *verb*

1 give out light/heat

ADV. **faintly, softly** ◇ *Two lamps ~ed softly in the lounge.*
PHRASES **~ orange, red, etc.** ◇ *The stones around the bonfire ~ed red with the heat.*

2 look healthy, happy, angry, etc.

ADV. **positively**
PREP. **with** ◇ *She was positively ~ing with happiness.*

glue *noun*

... OF GLUE **bottle** (*esp. AmE*), **pot** (*esp. BrE*), **tube** ◇ *All you will need is a sharp knife and a tube of ~.*
VERB + GLUE **apply, put on** ◇ *Put ~ on both the surfaces.* | **sniff** ◇ *He took to sniffing ~.*
GLUE + VERB **dry, set** ◇ *It takes about an hour for the ~ to set.*

glue *verb*

ADV. **firmly** ◇ *Her eyes were ~d firmly to the computer screen.* (*figurative*) | **down, together** ◇ *Glue the pieces firmly together.* | **in place, into place** ◇ *The shells were ~d in place.*
PREP. **onto, to** ◇ *Someone's ~d this coin to the table!*

go *verb*

1 happen

ADV. **smoothly, well** ◇ *Everything went very smoothly.* | **badly**

2 pass

ADV. **quickly, slowly** ◇ *The cruise went very quickly.* | **by** ◇ *The days seemed to ~ by very slowly.*

3 look/taste good with sth

ADV. **well** | **together** ◇ *Leeks and potatoes ~ well together in a soup.*
PREP. **with** ◇ *That tie ~es well with that shirt.*

PHR V **go down**
ADV. **badly, well**
PREP. **with** ◇ *The novel went down well with the public.*

go on
ADV. **endlessly**
PREP. **about** ◇ *He ~es on endlessly about his health problems.* | **at** (*esp. BrE*) ◇ *Stop ~ing on at me about that money.* | **with** ◇ *We'll ~ on with the presentations after lunch.*
PHRASES **~ on and on** ◇ *The flight just seemed to ~ on and on.*

goal *noun*

1 (in sports) frame into which a ball is kicked/hit

ADJ. **open** ◇ *He kicked the ball into an open ~.*
VERB + GOAL **go in, play in** ◇ *The goalkeeper was injured so a defender had to go in ~.*
PREP. **in** ◇ *Who's in ~ for Arsenal?*

2 point scored in a game

ADJ. **brilliant** (*esp. BrE*), **excellent, good, great, spectacular** (*esp. BrE*), **stunning** (*esp. BrE*), **superb** (*esp. BrE*), **well-taken** (*BrE*) | **scrappy** (*BrE*), **soft** ◇ *The fans were annoyed that the team gave away such a soft ~.* | **decisive** (*esp. BrE*), **winning** | **equalizing** | **important, useful** (*BrE*), **vital** (*BrE*) | **own** (*BrE*) ◇ *Vega scored an unfortunate own ~ when he slipped as he tried to clear the ball.* | **field** (in rugby and American football) ◇ *Two field ~s gave the Tigers an early lead.* | **penalty** (in football/soccer)
VERB + GOAL **get, score** | **kick** (in rugby and American football) | **head, head in** (both in football/soccer) | **make** ◇ *Bahr made his fifth field ~ of the day.* (in American football) ◇ *Visconti scored one ~ himself and made two for Lupo.* (in football/soccer) | **concede, give away** (*BrE*), **let in** | **allow, disallow** ◇ *The referee disallowed the ~.*
GOAL + VERB **come from sb/sth** ◇ *The equalizing ~ came from Cole.* ◇ *The second ~ came from a penalty.* (in football/soccer)
PREP. **~ against** ◇ *They scored three ~s against the home team.* | **~ for** ◇ *his first ~ for Spain* | **~ from** ◇ *A late ~ from Owen won the game for Liverpool.*
→ Special page at SPORTS

3 aim

ADJ. **immediate, short-term** ◇ *Our immediate ~ is to earn enough money to keep the business going.* | **long-term, ultimate** | **main, major, primary, prime** | **clear, explicit, specific, stated** | **ambitious** ◇ *They have set themselves some ambitious ~s.* | **modest** | **desirable** | **achievable, attainable, realistic** | **unattainable, unrealistic** | **elusive** | **personal** | **common** ◇ *We are all working towards/toward a common ~.* | **twin** ◇ *The prison service pursues the twin ~s of the punishment and rehabilitation of offenders.* | **strategic** | **political**
VERB + GOAL **have** ◇ *It is important to have explicit ~s.* | **share** | **define, establish, set (sb)** | **pursue, strive for, work towards/toward** | **achieve, attain, reach**
PREP. **~ of** ◇ *their ~ of providing free university education for everyone*

goalkeeper (*AmE also* goaltender) *noun*

ADJ. **brilliant** (*esp. BrE*), **excellent, good, top** | **Canadian, England, Liverpool, Sharks, etc.** ◇ *The England ~ played brilliantly.* | **international** | **backup** (*AmE*), **reserve, substitute** | **rookie** (*AmE*), **young** | **veteran**
PREP. **~ for** ◇ *He now plays as ~ for Liverpool.*

goat *noun*

ADJ. **billy, male** | **female, nanny** | **wild** | **mountain**
... OF GOATS **flock, herd**
VERB + GOAT **keep** | **milk** | **tether** ◇ *Tethered ~s grazed among the apple trees.*
GOAT + VERB **bleat** | **graze** | **wander**
PHRASES **goat's cheese, goat's milk**

god (*also* God) *noun*

ADJ. **pagan** | **Christian, Greek, Roman, etc.** | **Christian, Jewish, etc.** ◇ *the Jewish God* | **false, heathen** ◇ *those who follow false ~s* | **fertility** | **sun**
VERB + GOD **believe in, follow, have** ◇ *Do you believe in God?* ◇ *The Romans had many ~s.* | **praise, pray to, thank, worship** ◇ *The people worshipped pagan ~s.* | **obey, serve** | **find** ◇ *He has given up drinking and found God.*
GOD + VERB **exist** ◇ *Can we prove that God exists?*
PREP. **~ of** ◇ *the Roman ~ of war*
PHRASES **faith in God** ◇ *Nothing ever shook her faith in God.* | **God's will, the will of God** ◇ *He saw the accident as the will of God.*

goddess noun

ADJ. **pagan** | **Egyptian, Roman, etc.** | **ancient** | **fertility, mother** | **moon, sun** | **screen** (*figurative*) ◇ *She dreamed of becoming a Hollywood screen ~.* | **domestic** (*figurative*) ◇ *She has a reputation for being a domestic ~.*
VERB + GODDESS **pray to, worship**
PREP. **~ of** ◇ *Aphrodite, the ~ of love*

goggles noun

ADJ. **protective, safety** | **driving, flying, motorcycle, ski, snow, swimming** | **night-vision**
... OF GOGGLES **pair**
VERB + GOGGLES **have on, wear** | **put on, take off**
GOGGLES + VERB **steam up** ◇ *My swimming ~ keep steaming up so I can't see.*

gold noun

1 yellow metal

ADJ. **pure** | **real** | **solid** | **fool's** | **9-carat, 18-carat, etc.** | **molten** | **beaten, rolled** | **burnished** | **tarnished** | **white**
VERB + GOLD **extract, mine, produce** | **look for, pan for, prospect for** ◇ *He spent weeks panning for ~ in the river.* | **discover, find, strike** | **be set in** ◇ *The rubies were set in 18-carat ~.*
GOLD + NOUN **mine, miner, mining, prospecting, prospector** | **rush** ◇ *a gold-rush town* | **deposit, dust, nugget** | **bar, bullion, ingot** | **bracelet, chain, coin, earring, jewellery/ jewelry, necklace, ring, etc.** | **leaf, plate** | **market, reserves, stocks** ◇ *falling government ~ stocks* | **standard** ◇ *The currency was tied to the ~ standard.* ◇ *Disney remains the ~ standard of family entertainment.* (*figurative*)
PHRASES **a vein of ~** ◇ *The next day he struck a rich vein of ~.*

2 gold medal

ADJ. **Olympic**
VERB + GOLD **get, take, win** ◇ *She got a ~ in the long jump.* | **go for** ◇ *She's going for ~ this time.*

golden adj.

VERBS **be, gleam, look** ◇ *The walls gleamed ~ in the light of the setting sun.* | **turn** ◇ *The whole sky turned ~ and red.*
ADV. **faintly, softly** ◇ *the faintly ~ afternoon light*

golf noun

ADJ. **amateur, championship, pro** (*informal, esp. AmE*), **professional** ◇ *Amateur ~ is very competitive.* | **crazy, mini** (usually *minigolf*), **miniature** (*AmE*) ◇ *The hotel offers miniature ~ and other activities for children.*
... OF GOLF **game, round**
VERB + GOLF **play** | **take up** | **watch**
GOLF + NOUN **course, links** | **hole** ◇ *The eighth at Banff is one of the world's great ~ holes.* | **club** ◇ *She decided to join a ~ club.* | **bag, ball, buggy, cart, club, equipment, glove, shoes, tee, umbrella** ◇ *You can borrow ~ clubs if you want a game.* | **swing** ◇ *His coach says his ~ swing needs improving.* | **championship, game, match, tournament** | **title** | **handicap** ◇ *She has a ~ handicap of 18.* | **professional, star** | **fan** | **season** | **circuit, scene, tour** | **clinic, lesson** ◇ *The club is holding a ~ clinic next week, where golfers can get advice from the pros.* | **correspondent, journalist, reporter, writer** | **magazine** | **holiday** (*BrE*), **package, trip** (*esp. AmE*), **vacation** (*AmE*) ◇ *Choose from over 100 ~ packages in our brochure.* | **widow** ◇ *She's been a ~ widow since she gave her husband his first set of clubs.*
→ Special page at SPORTS

golfer noun

ADJ. **brilliant, good, great** | **experienced** | **high-handicap, low-handicap** | **6-handicap, 12-handicap, etc.** | **champion, top** | **keen** (*esp. BrE*) | **amateur, professional** | **club**
GOLFER + VERB **play**

good noun

ADJ. **common** ◇ *The results of the research should be used for the common ~.*
VERB + GOOD **do (sb)** ◇ *You can try talking to her, but I don't think it will do much ~.* ◇ *It will do you ~ to get out of the house more often.*
PREP. **for sb/sth's ~** ◇ *When the his health problems continued, he resigned for the ~ of the party.*
PHRASES **a force for ~** ◇ *In disadvantaged areas, schools can be a force for ~.* | **for sb's (own) ~** ◇ *I know you don't want to go into the hospital, but it's for your own ~.* | **for the ~ of sth, ~ and evil** ◇ *the struggle between ~ and evil* | **a power of ~** ◇ *That break has done me a power of ~.*

good adj.

VERBS **be, feel, look, seem, smell, sound, taste** | **become, get** ◇ *She's getting very ~ at reading now.*
ADV. **dead** (*BrE*), **extremely, really, very** ◇ *a really ~ movie* | **especially, particularly** | **perfectly** ◇ *Why ruin a perfectly ~ story?* | **fairly, pretty, quite, reasonably** ◇ *You've done a pretty ~ job.* | **surprisingly** ◇ *The food was surprisingly ~.*
PREP. **at** ◇ *He's very ~ at music.* | **for** ◇ *Vegetables are ~ for you.* | **to** ◇ *She was very ~ to me when my husband died.* | **with** ◇ *She's ~ with figures.*

good-looking adj.

VERBS **be**
ADV. **extremely, fairly, very, etc.** ◇ *He was tall and fairly ~.* | **incredibly, strikingly**

goods noun

ADJ. **consumer, electrical** (*esp. BrE*), **electronic, household, luxury** ◇ *a store selling electrical ~* | **durable, perishable** ◇ *A 'use by' date must be stamped on all perishable ~.* | **baked, canned** (*both esp. AmE*) | **manufactured, mass-produced** | **trade** | **capital** | **material** | **cheap, low-priced** | **branded** | **second-hand** | **defective** (*esp. BrE*), **faulty** (*esp. BrE*), **shoddy** | **stolen** ◇ *He was accused of handling stolen ~.* | **counterfeit, fake** (*esp. BrE*)
VERB + GOODS **make, manufacture, produce** ◇ *factories which produce luxury ~ for the export market* | **buy, purchase** | **export, import** | **provide, sell, supply** | **deliver** ◇ *The ~ will be delivered within ten days.* | **transport**
GOODS + NOUN **lorry, train, vehicle, wagon** (*all BrE*) | **yard** (*BrE*)
PHRASES **~ and services**

goodwill noun

VERB + GOODWILL **enjoy** (*esp. BrE*), **have** | **create, generate** ◇ *Addressing customers in their own language helps create ~.* | **win** | **lose, squander** ◇ *They are in danger of losing the government's ~.* | **depend on, rely on** | **show**
GOODWILL + NOUN **gesture**
PREP. **~ to, ~ towards/toward** ◇ *He expressed ~ towards/ toward his former colleagues.*
PHRASES **a gesture of ~** ◇ *The government released him as a gesture of ~.* | **in a spirit of ~** ◇ *They made the offer in a spirit of ~.*

goose noun

ADJ. **wild** | **roast**
... OF GEESE **flock** | **gaggle** (only used for geese on the ground)
GOOSE + VERB **waddle** | **hiss, honk** | **feed, graze** | **fly** ◇ *geese flying south for the winter* | **migrate**

gorgeous adj.

VERBS **be, look, sound** ◇ *Doesn't Kate look ~?*
ADV. **really** | **absolutely, drop-dead, simply, utterly** ◇ *a drop-dead ~ Hollywood icon* | **rather** (*esp. BrE*)

gospel noun

ADJ. **Christian** | **apocryphal, canonical** | **Synoptic** (= the Gospels of Matthew, Mark and Luke in the Bible)
VERB + GOSPEL **bring, preach, proclaim, spread, take** ◊ *She preached the Christian ~ to the poor and destitute.* | **hear** ◊ *Thousands came to hear the ~.*
GOSPEL + NOUN **message, story**

gossip noun

1 unkind talk about other people

ADJ. **latest** | **idle, juicy, malicious, salacious** | **celebrity** | **tabloid**
...OF GOSSIP **bit, piece, tidbit** (*AmE*), **titbit** (*BrE*) ◊ *I heard an interesting bit of ~ yesterday.*
VERB + GOSSIP **spread** ◊ *Someone has been spreading malicious ~ about me.* | **exchange, swap** | **hear, listen to** ◊ *You shouldn't listen to idle ~.* | **get** | **know** ◊ *He knows all the juicy ~.*
GOSSIP + VERB **circulate, go around, go round** (*esp. BrE*) ◊ *A piece of silly ~ was going around the school.*
GOSSIP + NOUN **column, columnist** ◊ *I saw it in the ~ column of the local newspaper.*
PREP. **~ about** ◊ *a magazine full of ~ about famous people*

2 conversation about other people

ADJ. **good**
VERB + GOSSIP **have**
PREP. **~ about** ◊ *We had a good ~ about the boss.* | **~ with** ◊ *She's having a ~ with Maria.* (*BrE*)

govern verb

ADV. **effectively, well** | **directly** ◊ *The colony was ~ed directly from Paris.*
VERB + GOVERN **be fit to, be unfit to** ◊ *He accused the opposition party of being unfit to ~.*

government noun

1 people in control of a country

ADJ. **central, federal, local, national, provincial, regional, state** | **Conservative, Democratic, Labour, Republican, etc.** ◊ *the country's new Communist ~* | **left-wing, right-wing** | **coalition** | **minority** ◊ *The socialists won 42% of the seats and formed a minority ~.* | **caretaker, interim, provisional, transitional** ◊ *The president dissolved the assembly and swore in an interim ~.* | **military** | **puppet** | **foreign** | **French, Western, etc.** ◊ *The report on world poverty calls for urgent action from Western ~s.* | **current, future, new**
VERB + GOVERNMENT **elect** ◊ *The present ~ was elected last year.* | **establish, form** ◊ *A new ~ was formed in September of that year.* | **install** ◊ *A puppet ~ was installed as the occupying forces withdrew.* | **swear in** | **head, run** ◊ *a new ~ headed by a former military leader* | **bring down, destabilize, oust, overthrow, topple** ◊ *This crisis could bring down the British ~.* ◊ *The group aims to overthrow the military ~.* | **support**
GOVERNMENT + VERB **come to power** | **take office** ◊ *On May 23 a coalition ~ took office.* | **fall, resign** ◊ *a national emergency that could cause the ~ to fall* | **announce sth** ◊ *The ~ announced the cancellation of the dam project.* | **introduce sth, launch sth**
GOVERNMENT + NOUN **agency, body, department** | **building, offices** | **funds, money** | **aid, assistance, backing, funding, grant, subsidy, support** | **expenditure, spending** | **cuts** ◊ *The hospital has been hit by ~ cuts.* | **control, regulation** | **intervention, involvement** ◊ *calls for ~ intervention in the dispute* | **employee, minister, official, representative, spokesman, spokesperson** | **sources** ◊ *According to ~ sources, two people died in the incident.* | **figures, statistics** | **post** | **reshuffle** (*esp. BrE*) ◊ *The former minister was relieved of his post in last month's extensive ~ reshuffle.* | **decisions, legislation, measures, plans, policy, programme/program, proposals** | **service** | **report** | **propaganda**

PREP. **in ~** ◊ *a problem facing whichever party is in ~* | **under a/the ~** ◊ *measures that were introduced under the last ~*
PHRASES **a change in ~, a change of ~** ◊ *It is time we had a change of ~.* | **the ~ of the day** ◊ *This was a decision taken by the ~ of the day.* | **a member of a ~** ◊ *The president has been meeting members of the French ~.*

2 act of governing

ADJ. **democratic, representative** | **firm** (*esp. BrE*), **good, strong** ◊ *We need strong ~ to take the country through this crisis.* | **weak** | **big, small** ◊ *We believe in low taxation and small ~.*

governor noun

ADJ. **deputy, lieutenant** | **acting, interim** ◊ *She was appointed as acting ~ until an election could be held.* | **incumbent, sitting** (*both esp. AmE*) | **former** | **colonial, district, provincial, regional, state** | **Fed** (= the Federal Reserve in the US) | **Democratic, Republican** | **military** | **prison, school** (*both BrE*) | **parent** (*BrE*) ◊ *She served as a parent ~ at her children's school.*
VERB + GOVERNOR **appoint, appoint sb (as), elect, elect sb (as)** | **recall** (*AmE*) ◊ *They voted to recall the sitting ~.* | **become** | **serve as**
PHRASES **a board of ~s**

gown noun

1 woman's long dress

ADJ. **long** | **floor-length** | **elegant** | **flowing** ◊ *She was dressed in a long flowing ~.* | **strapless** | **ball, bridal, evening, wedding**
GOWN + VERB **be trimmed with sth** ◊ *She wore a white satin ~ trimmed with lace.*
PREP. **in a/the ~**

2 worn by judges, surgeons, etc.

ADJ. **academic** | **hospital, surgical**
PREP. **in a/the ~**
PHRASES **town and ~** (= the residents of a university town and the members of its university) (*esp. BrE*)
→ Special page at CLOTHES

GP noun (*BrE*)

ADJ. **excellent, good** | **qualified** | **experienced** | **family, local** ◊ *Who is your local ~?* | **on-call** ◊ *They arranged for the local on-call ~ to make a house call to the patient.* | **locum**
VERB + GP **register with** ◊ *You should register with a ~ as soon as possible.*
GP + VERB **refer sb** ◊ *The ~ referred her to a specialist.*
→ Note at DOCTOR (for more verbs)

grab verb

ADV. **suddenly** | **quickly**
VERB + GRAB **try to** | **manage to** ◊ *He managed to ~ a couple of hours' sleep.*
PREP. **at** ◊ *I grabbed at his arm as he ran past.* | **by** ◊ *As he walked past the boys, one of them grabbed him by the arm.* | **from** ◊ *Somebody tried to ~ her handbag from her.*
PHRASES **~ hold of sth** ◊ *He grabbed hold of a handrail to save himself from falling.*

grace noun

1 attractive movement

ADJ. **easy, effortless, fluid, lithe** | **natural** | **uncommon** ◊ *a debut album of uncommon ~ and beauty* | **feline**
VERB + GRACE **have, move with**
PREP. **with ~** ◊ *Ann moved with easy ~.*

2 kindness of God

ADJ. **divine, heavenly, sublime, supernatural** ◊ *the power of divine ~ operating in their souls* | **sovereign** | **sacramental**
VERB + GRACE **bestow, confer, pour, pour out** ◊ *The mantra bestows Siva's ~ upon the devotee.*

grade noun

1 level/quality

ADJ. **high, top** ◇ *a piece of high-grade building land* ◇ *He still wants to play top-grade football.* | **low, poor** ◇ *low-grade steel*

2 mark given for a piece of work/an exam

ADJ. **final** ◇ *The oral exam constitutes 10% of the final ~.* | **A, B, etc.** ◇ *an A-grade essay* | **excellent, good, high** | **bad, low, poor** | **failing, passing** (both AmE) ◇ *She got a failing ~ for that assignment.* | **course** (AmE)
VERB + GRADE **achieve, attain, earn, get, have, receive** ◇ *She got good ~s in her exams.* (BrE) ◇ *She got good ~s on her exams.* (AmE) | **bring up** (esp. AmE), **improve, raise** (esp. AmE) ◇ *I need to improve my ~s.* | **award (sb), give sb**
PHRASES **~ point average** (AmE) ◇ *You've maintained a 3.9 ~ point average.*

3 level of importance/level of pay at work

ADJ. **high, senior** ◇ *He has asked to be put onto a higher ~.* ◇ *large pay increases for senior ~s* | **junior, low** | **pay**
PREP. **at a/the … ~** ◇ *She was offered a job at a lower ~.* | **on a/the … ~** ◇ *The majority of staff are on the same ~.*

4 (AmE) **level at school**

ADJ. **sixth, third, etc.** ◇ *Sam is in (the) second ~.*
VERB + GRADE **enter, start** ◇ *My son will be starting third ~ this fall.* | **complete, finish** | **skip** ◇ *He skipped a ~ so he finished high school early.* | **reach** | **teach**
GRADE + NOUN **level** | **school**
PREP. **in … ~** ◇ *My daughter is in (the) fifth ~.*

5 (esp. AmE) → See GRADIENT

grade verb

1 arrange in groups

ADV. **carefully** ◇ *a series of stories carefully ~d for beginner to intermediate students* (esp. BrE) | **finely** ◇ *finely ~d nuances of language*
PREP. **according to** ◇ *The timber is ~d according to its thickness.* | **by** ◇ *The containers are ~d by size.* | **from … to …** ◇ *Eggs are ~d from small to extra large.*

2 (esp. AmE) **give grade for a piece of work/an exam**

ADV. **fairly, objectively** ◇ *I don't think he ~d our essays fairly.*

gradient (also grade esp. in AmE) noun

ADJ. **steep** | **gentle, slight** | **downhill, uphill**
VERB + GRADIENT/GRADE **have** ◇ *The road has a fairly steep ~.*
PREP. **on a ~** ◇ *The field was on a slight ~.*

graduate noun

ADJ. **business-school, law-school, college, high-school** (in the US), **medical-school, university** ◇ *job opportunities for university ~s* | **arts, engineering, history, law, medical, science, etc.** | **doctoral** (AmE) | **cum laude, magna cum laude, summa cum laude** (all in the US) | **Oxbridge** (= from Oxford or Cambridge) (BrE) | **new, recent**
GRADUATE + NOUN **course, degree, program** (AmE) | **education** (AmE), **studies, work** | **level** ◇ *She has taught at both the undergraduate and ~ levels.* | **school** (AmE) | **student** | **assistant** (esp. AmE) | **recruit, trainee** (both BrE) ◇ *He joined the company as a ~ trainee.* | **recruitment** (BrE) ◇ *The company places great importance on ~ recruitment and training.*
PREP. **~ in** ◇ *a ~ in sociology*

graduation noun

ADJ. **college, high-school** (esp. AmE), **university**
GRADUATION + NOUN **ceremony, day** ◇ *Mark's whole family attended his ~ ceremony.* | **speech** (esp. AmE) | **speaker** (esp. AmE) | **party** (esp. AmE) | **gift** (AmE), **present** (esp. AmE) | **gown** ◇ *She was wearing a mortar board and ~ gown.* | **rate** (esp. AmE)
PREP. **after ~** ◇ *She managed to find a job immediately after ~.* | **on ~, upon ~** ◇ *On ~, he plans to travel around Asia.*

grant noun

---

graffiti noun

ADJ. **obscene, offensive** | **racist**
… OF GRAFFITI **piece**
VERB + GRAFFITI **daub** (BrE), **scrawl, spray, spray-paint, write** ◇ *Racist ~ was sprayed on the walls.* | **be covered in, be covered with, be daubed with** (BrE), **be sprayed with** ◇ *The buildings were covered with ~.* | **clean, remove**
GRAFFITI + NOUN **artist** ◇ *a fashionable ~ artist* | **vandal**

graft noun

1 on part of the body

ADJ. **bone, skin**
VERB + GRAFT **do** ◇ *Doctors are hoping to do a bone ~ to repair the damaged bone.* | **undergo** ◇ *Linda had to undergo four skin ~s.*
GRAFT + VERB **take** ◇ *If the skin ~ takes, surgeons will do another operation a few weeks later.*

2 (BrE) **hard work**

ADJ. **hard** ◇ *Starting a new business involves a lot of hard ~.*
VERB + GRAFT **do** ◇ *Most of the ~ was done for them by their assistants.*

grain noun

1 seeds of wheat, etc.

ADJ. **large, small** | **whole** ◇ *The journal reports that eating whole ~s protects against diabetes.* | **cereal, rice, wheat, etc.** | **pollen**
VERB + GRAIN **grow, produce** | **store**
GRAIN + NOUN **harvest, production, yield** | **crop** | **exports, imports** | **elevator** (= a building used for storing grain) (AmE)

2 natural pattern of lines in wood

ADJ. **fine, smooth** | **coarse** | **natural** ◇ *This wood has a beautiful natural ~.* | **wood**
PREP. **across the ~, against the ~** | **along the ~, with the ~** ◇ *Cut the wood along the ~.*

gram noun → Note at MEASURE

grammar noun

ADJ. **correct, good** ◇ *Spelling and good ~ are both very important.* | **bad, incorrect, poor** | **Arabic, French, Latin, etc.** ◇ *the complexities of English ~*
VERB + GRAMMAR **correct, teach** ◇ *People were too polite to correct my ~ when I spoke German.* | **learn**
GRAMMAR + NOUN **rules**
PHRASES **the rules of ~**

grandeur noun

ADJ. **majestic, sheer** ◇ *the majestic ~ of the Grand Canyon* | **rugged** (BrE) ◇ *the rugged ~ of the mountains* | **epic, scenic** (esp. AmE) | **faded, former**

grandparent noun

ADJ. **maternal, paternal** | **doting, proud** ◇ *a present from his doting ~s*
… OF GRANDPARENTS **set** ◇ *I've sent photos of the children to both sets of ~s.*

grant noun

ADJ. **large, substantial** | **small** | **full** (esp. BrE) ◇ *Full student maintenance ~s are a thing of the past.* (BrE) | **annual** | **block, capital** (esp. BrE) ◇ *The school has received a large capital ~ to improve its buildings.* | **maintenance** (BrE) ◇ *Poorer students would get maintenance ~s of up to £1 500 a year.* | **emergency** (esp. BrE) ◇ *emergency ~s for special needs for items such as clothing* | **discretionary** | **mandatory** (BrE) | **educational, student** | **project, research** ◇ *There is a lot of competition for research ~s.* | **improvement, land, renovation** (esp. BrE), **training, etc.** ◇ *home improvement ~s*

grant

grant

for householders (*BrE*) | **federal, government, local-authority** (*BrE*), **state,** etc.
VERB + GRANT **apply for** | **be eligible for, qualify for** ◇ *You may be eligible for a student* ~. | **get, obtain, receive** ◇ *You can get a* ~ *if you've lived in the area for three years.* | **award (sb), give sb, make (sb), offer (sb), provide (sb with)** ◇ *The government has awarded a* ~ *for the restoration of the building.* | **be funded by, be funded with** ◇ *The report was funded by a* ~ *from the Department.* | **cut** ◇ *The group's annual* ~ *from the Arts Council has been cut.*
PREP. **~ for** ◇ *a* ~ *for a youth project* | **~ from** ◇ *a* ~ *from the funding authority* | **~ to** ◇ *The program offers* ~*s to small businesses.*

grant *verb*

ADV. **expressly, specifically** ◇ *the rights expressly* ~*ed by the terms of the lease* | **automatically** | **finally** ◇ *Planning permission was finally* ~*ed in October.* | **rarely** | **hereby** (*law*) ◇ *Permission is hereby* ~*ed to reproduce this material.*
VERB + GRANT **agree to, decide to** | **refuse to** ◇ *The judge refused to* ~ *him bail.* | **be willing to**

grape *noun*

ADJ. **sweet** | **black, green, purple** | **red, white** | **wine** | **seedless**
... OF GRAPES **bunch**
VERB + GRAPE **eat, have** | **grow** | **harvest, pick** ◇ *The first* ~*s are harvested in mid-August.* | **crush, tread** ◇ *The peasants used to tread the* ~*s in huge vats.*
GRAPE + NOUN **harvest** | **juice**
→ Special page at FRUIT

graph *noun*

ADJ. **bar, line**
VERB + GRAPH **construct** (*esp. AmE*), **create** (*esp. AmE*), **draw, produce** | **plot (sth on)** ◇ *The figures are all plotted on a* ~.
GRAPH + VERB **indicate sth, represent sth, show sth** ◇ *She drew a* ~ *showing the relationship between costs and sales.*
GRAPH + NOUN **paper** ◇ *The small squares on the* ~ *paper are 1 mm wide.*
PREP. **in a/the ~** ◇ *I decided to show the results in a bar* ~. | **on a/the ~** ◇ *We can see on this* ~ *how the company has grown over the last year.*

graphics *noun*

ADJ. **computer, computer-generated** | **basic, simple** ◇ *The screen can display simple* ~ *as well as text.* | **high-end, state-of-the-art** | **fancy, flashy** (*disapproving, informal*) | **colour/color** | **high-resolution** | **three-dimensional, two-dimensional** | **2-D, 3-D**
VERB + GRAPHICS **create, produce** | **display** | **support** ◇ *The editor's PC should support desktop publishing and* ~.
GRAPHICS + NOUN **application, package, program, software, system** | **capability, performance** | **card, file** | **design, designer**
→ Special page at COMPUTER

grasp *noun*

1 holding sth

ADJ. **firm, tight** (*esp. AmE*) ◇ *She felt a firm* ~ *on her hand.*
VERB + GRASP **slip from** ◇ *As she jumped forward, the ball slipped from her* ~. | **escape, slip out of** (*usually figurative*) ◇ *He slipped out of our* ~ (= *he escaped*). | **prise sth from** (*BrE*), **pry sth from** (*esp. AmE*), **rip sth from, snatch sth from, wrench sth from, wrest sth from** ◇ *She wrenched the bottle from his* ~. | **tighten** (*esp. AmE*)
PREP. **beyond your ~** ◇ *The key was on a high shelf, just beyond her* ~. | **in your ~** ◇ *He kept the letter firmly in his* ~. | **from sb's ~** ◇ *The robber tried to free the case from her* ~. | **out of sb's ~** ◇ *She kicked the gun out of his* ~. | **within (your) ~** (*often figurative*) ◇ *Just when victory seemed within* ~, *the referee blew his whistle.*

2 understanding

ADJ. **firm, good, impressive, solid, strong** | **feeble, limited, poor, shaky, tenuous** | **intellectual** ◇ *The task was beyond the intellectual* ~ *of some of the students.* | **intuitive** ◇ *We have no intuitive* ~ *of the immensity of time.*
VERB + GRASP **have** | **get** ◇ *Working with native speakers helped me get a good* ~ *of the language.*
PREP. **beyond sb's ~** ◇ *These ideas are all beyond his* ~. | **within sb's ~** | **~ of** ◇ *a poor* ~ *of mathematics*

grasp *verb*

1 take hold of sb/sth suddenly and firmly

ADV. **firmly, tightly**
PREP. **at** ◇ *Her hands were* ~*ing at his coat.* | **by** ◇ *She* ~*ed him tightly by the wrist.*
PHRASES **~ hold of sb/sth** ◇ *She* ~*ed hold of the banister to support herself.*

2 understand sth

ADV. **fully** ◇ *He had not fully* ~*ed the fact that he was the one who would pay for all this.* | **not quite, not really** ◇ *I hadn't really* ~*ed what they were talking about.* | **quickly, easily, readily** ◇ *a means by which students can more easily* ~ *the basics of science*
VERB + GRASP **try to** | **be unable to, fail to** ◇ *She failed to* ~ *the significance of these facts.* | **quick to** ◇ *He was quick to* ~ *the basic principles.* | **be difficult to, be hard to** ◇ *Some of these concepts are very difficult to* ~.

grass *noun*

ADJ. **green** | **coarse, rough, thick** | **soft** | **lush** | **long, tall** | **short** | **fresh-cut, freshly cut, freshly mowed** (*AmE*), **freshly mown** | **damp, wet** | **dry** | **wild**
... OF GRASS **blade** ◇ *I've walked along that path for so many years I know every blade of* ~. | **clump, tuft** ◇ *There were only a few clumps of coarse* ~ *for the animals to eat.*
VERB + GRASS **eat** | **cut, mow**
GRASS + VERB **grow**
GRASS + NOUN **clippings** (*esp. AmE*), **cuttings** (*esp. BrE*) | **seed** ◇ *I sowed a little bag of* ~ *seed.* | **verge** (*BrE*) ◇ *We parked on the* ~ *verge by the side of the road.*
PREP. **across the ~** ◇ *They all set off across the* ~. | **in the ~** ◇ *I found the wallet lying in the* ~. | **on the ~** ◇ *You're not allowed to walk on the* ~. | **through the ~** ◇ *The dog came running through the long* ~.

grate *verb* rub sth into small pieces

ADV. **coarsely** | **finely** ◇ *Sprinkle the top of the dish with some finely* ~*d cheese.*
PHRASES **freshly ~d** ◇ *a teaspoon of freshly* ~*d nutmeg*

grateful *adj.*

VERBS **be, feel, look, seem, sound** | **remain**
ADV. **extremely, really, very** | **genuinely, truly** ◇ *We are truly* ~ *to you and your family.* | **especially, particularly** | **deeply, enormously, immensely, more than, most, profoundly** ◇ *I am more than* ~ *for their generous response.* ◇ *Thank you for your help. I really am most* ~. | **almost** ◇ *His father looked almost* ~ *for once.* | **quite, rather** | **just** ◇ *I'm just* ~ *the injury is not as bad as we'd feared.* | **always** | **eternally, forever** ◇ *I'm eternally* ~ *that we managed to go there before the war.* ◇ *I'll be forever* ~ *for your help.*
PREP. **for** ◇ *I'm really* ~ *for your help.* | **to** ◇ *I'm immensely* ~ *to you for your support.*

gratifying *adj.*

VERBS **be** | **find sth**
ADV. **extremely, immensely, incredibly, most, really, very** | **especially, particularly** | **personally** (*esp. AmE*)
PREP. **for** ◇ *It is most* ~ *for me to know that my work has been useful.*

gratitude *noun*

ADJ. **deep, profound** | **heartfelt, sincere** | **eternal, undying**
VERB + GRATITUDE **feel** ◇ *the very deep* ~ *I felt towards/toward*

her | **express, extend, show** | **have** ◇ *You have our undying ~.* | **deserve, earn (sb)** ◇ *They deserve our ~ for all the work they do.* ◇ *His kindness earned him her eternal ~.*
PREP. **in** ◇ *He almost wept in ~ when he saw the money.* | **with ~** ◇ *I remember them with ~.* | **~ at** ◇ *my ~ at her thoughtfulness* | **~ for** | **~ to, ~ towards/toward** ◇ *I would like to express my deep sense of ~ to the staff for their patience.*
PHRASES **as a token of your ~** ◇ *I sent him some money as a token of my ~.* | **owe a debt of ~ to sb** ◇ *We owe her a deep debt of ~ for her services.* | **a feeling of ~, a sense of ~**

grave *noun*

ADJ. **deep, shallow** ◇ *The body was found in a shallow ~.* | **open** ◇ *The mourners threw flowers into the open ~.* | **fresh, freshly dug** | **unmarked** ◇ *His body is buried in an unmarked ~.* | **common, communal** (*esp. BrE*), **mass** ◇ *A mass ~ has been discovered outside the town.* | **watery** ◇ *He rescued her from a watery ~* (= *saved her from drowning*). | **early** ◇ *She smoked herself into an early ~* (= *died young as a result of smoking*).
VERB + GRAVE **dig** | **mark** ◇ *The ~ was marked by a simple headstone.* | **desecrate** ◇ *Some of the ~s have been desecrated by vandals.* | **visit** ◇ *Whenever he goes home he visits his mother's ~.*
PREP. **beyond the ~** ◇ *The old lady still influences the family from beyond the ~.* | **in a/the ~** ◇ *I'll be in my ~ by the time that happens!* | **on a/the ~** ◇ *She puts fresh flowers on her husband's ~ every Sunday.*

gravity *noun*

1 natural force

ADJ. **low, weak, zero** ◇ *the weak ~ on the moon* | **strong**
VERB + GRAVITY **defy** ◇ *The building leans so much that it seems to defy ~.*
GRAVITY + VERB **pull sth** ◇ *Gravity pulls objects together.* | **bend sth** ◇ *Gravity bends light like a lens.*
PREP. **by ~** ◇ *The water flows from the tank by ~ to the houses below.*
PHRASES **centre/center of ~** (*often figurative*) ◇ *a low centre/ center of ~* ◇ *The world's economic centre/center of ~ is shifting east.* | **the force of ~** | **the law of ~, the laws of ~**

2 seriousness

ADJ. **extreme** ◇ *I don't think you realize the extreme ~ of the situation.*
VERB + GRAVITY **appreciate, realize, understand**
PREP. **with ~** ◇ *The threat is not being treated with the ~ it deserves.*

graze *noun*

ADJ. **minor, slight, small**
VERB + GRAZE **have, suffer** ◇ *She suffered only minor ~s in the crash.*
PREP. **~ on** ◇ *I had a ~ on my leg.*
PHRASES **be just a ~** | **cuts and ~s** (*esp. BrE*)

graze *verb*

1 of animals

ADV. **contentedly, peacefully, quietly** ◇ *Sheep were grazing peacefully in the fields.*
VERB + GRAZE **allow sth to, turn sth out to** ◇ *The cattle were turned out to ~.*
PREP. **on, upon** ◇ *lambs grazing on the rough moorland pasture*

2 break the surface of your skin

ADV. **badly** ◇ *She had ~d her elbow quite badly.* | **just, only** ◇ *The bullet only ~d his shoulder.*
PREP. **on** ◇ *He fell and ~d his knees on a rock*

grease *noun*

ADJ. **bacon** (*AmE*)
VERB + GREASE **be covered in, be covered with, be smeared with** ◇ *The kitchen surfaces were all smeared with ~.* |

dissolve, remove | **wipe, wipe off** ◇ *I wiped the ~ off my hands.*
GREASE + NOUN **mark, spot** (*esp. AmE*), **stain**

grease *verb*

ADV. **well** | **lightly** ◇ *Place the cakes on a lightly ~d baking tray.*

great *adj.*

1 large in amount, degree, size, etc.

VERBS **be** | **become**
ADV. **very** ◇ *The play was a very ~ success.*
PHRASES **~ big** ◇ *There's a ~ big hole in this sleeve.* | **no** ◇ *Don't worry. It's no ~ loss.*

2 admired

VERBS **be**
ADV. **really, truly, very** ◇ *He was a truly ~ man.*

3 very good/pleasant

VERBS **be, feel, look, seem, smell, sound, taste** ◇ *You're looking ~. Marriage must suit you!*
ADV. **just, really** ◇ *That's really ~ news!* | **absolutely** ◇ *The food smells absolutely ~.*

greatness *noun*

ADJ. **true** ◇ *This book tells you nothing about the true ~ of his paintings.* | **future, potential** ◇ *The Puerto Rican was tipped for future ~.* | **former** | **artistic, literary** | **national** ◇ *He was made into a symbol of national ~.* | **presidential** (*esp. AmE*)
VERB + GREATNESS **achieve** ◇ *those people who have achieved ~* | **be destined for** ◇ *a woman who was destined for ~*
GREATNESS + VERB **lie** ◇ *Her ~ lies in her deep understanding of human nature.*

greed *noun*

ADJ. **pure, sheer, simple** | **human, personal** | **corporate** ◇ *the evils of corporate ~*
VERB + GREED **satisfy** ◇ *She killed him to satisfy her ~.* | **be consumed by, be driven by**
PREP. **~ for** ◇ *He was driven by ~ for money and power.*

green *adj., noun*

ADJ. **cool** | **apple, aqua** (*esp. AmE*), **bottle, emerald, forest, kelly** (*AmE*), **leafy, lime, lush, mint, olive, sage** ◇ *the lush ~ grass* ◇ *an olive ~ carpet*
→ Special page at COLOUR

greet *verb*

1 say hello to sb

ADV. **cheerfully, enthusiastically, warmly** ◇ *The two men ~ed one another warmly.* | **politely** | **coolly** ◇ *Stella ~ed her mother coolly.*
VERB + GREET **be there to, be waiting to** ◇ *You must be there to ~ your guests.* ◇ *My parents were waiting to ~ us at the door.* | **come to, rise to, turn to** ◇ *The president rose to ~ his guests.*
PREP. **with** ◇ *She ~ed him with a quick kiss.*
PHRASES **~ sb by name** ◇ *The head teacher ~ed all the students by name.*

2 react to sth in particular way

ADV. **enthusiastically** | **coolly**
PREP. **with** ◇ *The news was ~ed with astonishment.*

greeting *noun*

1 first words you say when you meet sb

ADJ. **formal, friendly, polite** | **traditional** ◇ *The traditional Muslim ~ is 'Salaam'.*
VERB + GREETING **call, call out, nod, shout, smile, wave** ◇ *He jumped to his feet and called out a ~.* ◇ *They said nothing, but nodded a polite ~.* | **exchange** ◇ *The delegates shook hands and exchanged ~s.* | **give (sb), offer (sb)** ◇ *He offered*

me a warm ~ and invited me in. | **acknowledge, respond to, return** ◊ *I said 'Good morning!', but she didn't return the ~.* | **ignore**
PREP. **in ~** ◊ *He held out his hand in ~.*

2 greetings good wishes

ADJ. **personal, warm** | **birthday, Christmas, festive** (*esp. BrE*), **holiday** (*AmE*), **New Year, seasonal**
VERB + GREETINGS **bring, extend, send (sb)** ◊ *He brought Christmas ~s from the whole family.* ◊ *We extend our ~s to you and thank you for listening to us.*
GREETINGS/GREETING + NOUN **~ card** (*AmE*), **~s card** (*BrE*) ◊ *Millions of ~s/~ cards are sent at Christmas.*

grenade noun

ADJ. **hand, smoke, stun** | **rocket-propelled** | **fragmentation** (*esp. AmE*) | **live**
VERB + GRENADE **be armed with, carry, have** ◊ *The hijackers were armed with hand ~s.* | **hold** ◊ *She was holding the ~ above her head, ready to throw.* | **hurl, lob, throw, toss** ◊ *I tossed the ~ through the open door.* | **fire** | **pull the pin from, pull the pin out of**
GRENADE + VERB **land** | **explode, go off**
GRENADE + NOUN **attack** | **launcher**

grey (esp. BrE) (AmE usually gray) adj., noun

1 colour/color

ADV. **uniformly** | **very** ◊ *The sky looks very ~. I think it's going to rain.* | **quite** (*esp. BrE*), **rather, slightly**
ADJ. **dark** | **light, pale** ◊ *a light ~ suit* | **charcoal, silvery, slate, steel** ◊ *His steel gray hair was clipped short as usual.*
→ Special page at COLOUR

2 with grey hair

VERBS **be** | **go, turn** ◊ *He went ~ before he was forty.*
ADV. **very** | **quite, slightly** ◊ *He'd turned quite ~.* | **mostly** ◊ *The old man's beard was mostly ~.* | **completely** ◊ *She was completely ~ by the age of thirty.* | **prematurely**

grid noun

1 pattern of lines that cross each other

ADJ. **rectangular, square** | **regular** | **street** (*esp. AmE*) ◊ *the Manhattan street ~*
VERB + GRID **superimpose** ◊ *We superimposed a ~ over the image.*
GRID + NOUN **line, pattern, square, system** ◊ *The artist drew a set of ~ lines over the area to be painted.*

2 system of squares drawn on a map

GRID + NOUN **line, reference** (*BrE*), **square** ◊ *The ~ lines on the map run north-south.* ◊ *A ~ reference gives the position of a place to within 100 m.*

3 (*esp. BrE*) system of electric cables

ADJ. **electric** (*esp. AmE*), **electrical** (*esp. AmE*), **electricity, power, utility** (*AmE*) | **national** (*esp. BrE*)
GRID + NOUN **system** ◊ *Power can be fed from wind generators into the electricity ~ system.*

grief noun

ADJ. **deep, great, inconsolable, intense, overwhelming, real** | **personal, private** ◊ *I felt awkward at intruding on their private ~.* | **public** | **unresolved** (*esp. AmE*)
VERB + GRIEF **be consumed by, be consumed with, be overcome by, be overcome with, be stricken with, experience, feel** ◊ *Her parents were stricken with ~.* | **express, show** | **cause** | **die from, die of** | **come to terms with, cope with, deal with, overcome** ◊ *They are still struggling to come to terms with their ~.* | **understand** ◊ *She understood my ~ because she too had lost a child.* | **share** ◊ *He feels that he can't share his ~ with anyone.*
GRIEF + NOUN **counselling/counseling, counsellor/counselor** (*both esp. AmE*) | **process** (*esp. AmE*) | **reaction**
PREP. **~ at** ◊ *Children can feel real ~ at the loss of a pet.* | **~ for**

◊ *her ~ for her dead husband* | **~ over** ◊ *~ over the loss of a friend's life*
PHRASES **a feeling of ~, a sense of ~**

grievance noun

ADJ. **genuine, legitimate, real** ◊ *Some people will complain even if they have no genuine ~.* | **historical** (*esp. AmE*), **long-standing, old** | **individual, personal** | **specific** | **economic, political, social** ◊ *By the 1950s, political ~s were again being voiced.*
VERB + GRIEVANCE **harbour/harbor, have, nurse** ◊ *She still nursed her old ~.* | **air, express, voice** | **file** (*AmE*) | **hear** (*formal*), **listen to** ◊ *No one would listen to their ~s.* | **address, redress, remedy** (*esp. BrE*), **settle** ◊ *Managers would make every effort to address individual ~s.*
GRIEVANCE + NOUN **procedure, process** | **committee** (*AmE*)
PREP. **~ about, ~ over** ◊ *The meeting will be a chance to air your ~s about the organization.* | **~ against** ◊ *He had a personal ~ against the professor.*
PHRASES **a sense of ~**

grieve verb

ADV. **deeply** ◊ *She had ~d deeply for her father.* | **privately, silently** | **still**
PREP. **for** ◊ *They are still grieving for their child.* | **over** ◊ *He is still grieving over the loss of his daughter.*

grill noun

1 (*BrE*) part of a cooker → See also BROILER

ADJ. **hot** ◊ *Cook under a hot ~ for 7 minutes.* | **electric, gas**
VERB + GRILL **heat, preheat** ◊ *Preheat the ~ to medium.*
GRILL + NOUN **pan**
PREP. **under a/the ~** ◊ *Place the chops in the grill pan, and put it under the ~.*

2 framework of metal bars that you cook food on

ADJ. **charcoal, gas** (*AmE*) | **barbecue** (*esp. AmE*) | **backyard** (*AmE*)
VERB + GRILL **preheat, prepare**
PREP. **on a/the ~** ◊ *Once the charcoal is glowing, place the food on the ~.*

grimace noun

ADJ. **little, slight, small** | **pained, painful** (*esp. AmE*) | **wry** | **facial**
VERB + GRIMACE **give (sb), make** ◊ *She made a wry ~.* | **twist into** ◊ *His face twisted into a ~.*
GRIMACE + VERB **twist sth** ◊ *An ugly ~ twisted her face.*
PREP. **with a ~** ◊ *He acknowledged his mistake with a wry ~.* | **~ of** ◊ *a ~ of disgust/pain*

grimace verb

ADV. **slightly** | **inwardly**
PREP. **at** ◊ *He ~d slightly at the pain.* ◊ *She ~d at him.* | **in, with** ◊ *She ~d in disgust.*

grime noun

VERB + GRIME **be covered in, be covered with** | **wash away, wash off, wipe away, wipe off**
PHRASES **a layer of ~** ◊ *Over the years, the painting has become covered in a thick layer of ~* | **dirt and ~** ◊ *Dirt and ~ hung to their clothes.*

grin noun

ADJ. **big, broad, Cheshire** (*AmE*), **Cheshire-cat, huge, large, wide** | **faint, feeble, slight, small** | **friendly, sympathetic** | **happy** | **infectious** | **lazy** | **cheesy, foolish, goofy, silly, stupid** | **boyish, cheeky** (*BrE*), **devilish, devious, impish, mischievous, playful, sly, teasing** ◊ *Edmund looked up with an impish ~.* | **mocking, teasing** | **cocky, smug** | **satisfied** | **sheepish, shy** | **rueful, sardonic, wry** | **knowing** | **insane, manic** | **amused** | **evil, feral** (*esp. AmE*), **hideous, malicious, sinister, wicked, wolfish** | **crooked, lopsided** | **gap-toothed, toothless, toothy**
VERB + GRIN **have** ◊ *He had a cheeky ~.* ◊ *I wondered why Dad had a ~ on his face.* | **crack, flash (sb), give (sb), let out**

(*AmE*) ◇ *He gave the photographer a big ~.* | **grin, smile** ◇ *He grinned his adorable ~.* | **force, manage** ◇ *He forced a ~ despite feeling angry.* | **break into, curl into** (*AmE*), **form, split into** ◇ *The old man's face broke into a ~.* ◇ *Her lips started to form a slight ~.* | **fight, fight back, hide, hold back, stifle, suppress** ◇ *She tried to stifle a ~.* | **wear** | **return**

GRIN + VERB **broaden, grow, grow broader, grow wider, widen** | **appear, break out** (**across sb's face**), **come across sb's face, come over sb's face, creep across sb's face, creep onto sb's face, cross sb's face, form on sb's face, spread across sb's face, spread over sb's face** ◇ *A mischievous ~ spread across the little girl's face.* | **be plastered across sb's face, be plastered on sb's face, light sb's face, light up sb's face, play on sb's face, split sb's face, tug at sb's lips** ◇ *a ~ tugging at the corners of his lips* | **disappear, fade** ◇ *His wry ~ faded.* | **turn into sth** ◇ *Her ~ turned into a frown.*

PREP. **with a ~** ◇ *'Fooled you!' he said, with a cheeky ~.* | **~ at** ◇ *a ~ at his wife* | **~ of** ◇ *a ~ of triumph*

PHRASES **take the ~ off your face, wipe the ~ off your face** ◇ *Take that ~ off your face!* | **wipe the ~ off sb's face** ◇ *I'll soon wipe that silly ~ off her face.*

grin *verb*

ADV. **broadly, widely** ◇ *He appeared in the doorway grinning broadly.* | **slightly, weakly** | **crookedly** | **brightly, cheerfully, happily** | **amiably** | **boyishly, cheekily** (*BrE*), **devilishly, impishly, mischievously, playfully** | **madly, wildly** | **triumphantly** | **proudly** | **inanely, stupidly** | **nervously, sheepishly** ◇ *He just stood there, tongue-tied and grinning sheepishly.* | **apologetically, ruefully, wryly** ◇ *She grinned apologetically when she saw him.* | **evilly, maliciously, slyly, wolfishly** | **knowingly** | **smugly** | **back, down at, up at** ◇ *She relaxed and grinned wickedly back at him.* ◇ *He lay grinning impishly up at me.*

PREP. **at** ◇ *He stopped eating to ~ at me.* | **like** ◇ *He just stood there, grinning like an idiot.* | **to** ◇ *She grinned to herself at the thought.* | **with** ◇ *They grinned with pleasure.*

PHRASES **~ ear to ear** (*AmE*), **~ from ear to ear** ◇ *She looked at us, grinning from ear to ear.*

grind *verb*

ADV. **coarsely** | **finely** ◇ *The cement need not be finely ground.* | **down, up** ◇ *Grind the seeds down to a powder.*

PREP. **into** ◇ *machinery for ~ing wheat into flour* | **to** ◇ *The coffee is ground to a fine powder.*

PHRASES **freshly ground** ◇ *freshly ground black pepper*

grip *noun*

1 hold on sth

ADJ. **firm, good, secure, solid** (*esp. AmE*), **strong, tight** | **crushing, death, iron, painful, vice-like/vise-like** ◇ *Her upper arms were seized in an iron ~.* | **gentle, loose, weak** | **comfortable**

VERB + GRIP **have** ◇ *He still had a firm ~ on my arm.* | **get, take** ◇ *Taking a tight ~ on the hook, he began to pull it closer.* | **keep** ◇ *Keep a secure ~ on the rope at all times.* | **lose** ◇ *She slipped and lost her ~ of the rope.* | **strengthen, tighten** ◇ *Robert tightened his ~ on her shoulder.* | **loose, loosen, relax, release, slacken** | **adjust, change, shift**

GRIP + VERB **tighten** ◇ *She felt his ~ tighten painfully on her wrist.* | **loosen, relax, slacken** ◇ *His ~ slackened and she tore herself away.*

PREP. **in a/sb's ~** ◇ *Hold the microphone in a firm ~.* ◇ *She was powerless in his iron ~.* | **~ on** ◇ *She relaxed her ~ on the door frame.*

PHRASES **break sb's ~** ◇ *He finally broke her ~ and escaped.*

2 power/control

ADJ. **firm, iron, powerful, strong, tight, vice-like/vise-like** | **tenuous** ◇ *She has a tenuous ~ on reality.* | **death, icy**

VERB + GRIP **have** ◇ *The Church does not have a strong ~ on the population.* | **get, take** ◇ *The government needs to get a ~ on this problem.* ◇ *Get a ~!* (= take control of yourself, your life, etc.) (*informal*) | **keep, maintain** ◇ *We need to keep a tight ~ on costs.* | **strengthen, tighten** ◇ *They managed to*

strengthen their ~ on the southern part of the country. | **loosen** | **lose** (*informal*) ◇ *Sometimes I feel I'm losing my ~ (= losing control of my life, etc.).*

PREP. **in sth's ~** ◇ *Winter still held them in its iron ~.* ◇ *a country in the ~ of recession* | **~ on** ◇ *The government does not seem to have a very firm ~ on the economy.*

PHRASES **come to ~s with sth, get to ~s with sth** (= to begin to take control of sth or understand sth difficult) ◇ *I'm slowly getting to ~s with the language.*

grip *verb*

ADV. **firmly, hard, tightly** | **gently, lightly, loosely**

PREP. **at** ◇ *She gripped hard at the arms of her chair.* | **by** ◇ *He gripped her gently by the shoulders.*

grit *noun*

1 small pieces of stone

... OF GRIT **bit, piece** ◇ *A bit of ~ got into my eye.*

2 courage/determination

ADJ. **sheer, true**

VERB + GRIT **have** ◇ *Don't give in yet. You have more ~ than that.* | **display** (*esp. BrE*), **show** ◇ *The team showed their true ~ and played a magnificent game.*

groan *noun*

ADJ. **loud** ◇ *He let out a loud ~ of frustration.* | **little, slight, small, soft** | **deep, low** | **long** | **muffled, quiet** | **audible** | **annoyed, exasperated, frustrated** | **collective**

VERB + GROAN **emit, give, let out, utter** | **bite back** (*AmE*), **hold back, stifle, suppress** | **hear**

PREP. **with a ~** ◇ *He stood up slowly with a ~ of pain.* | **~ of** ◇ *a ~ of annoyance*

PHRASES **moans and ~s** ◇ *The doctors all ignored her moans and ~s.*

→ Note at SOUND

groan *verb*

ADV. **loudly** | **quietly, softly** | **slightly** | **aloud, out loud** | **inwardly, mentally, silently** ◇ *He ~ed inwardly at the thought of spending another day in that place.*

PREP. **in, with** ◇ *Some of the patients were ~ing in/with pain.* | **at, from** ◇ *He ~ed at/from the pain.*

PHRASES **moan and ~** ◇ *There's no point in moaning and ~ing about not having any money.*

grocery *noun*

1 groceries food, etc. → See also SHOPPING

ADJ. **weekly** ◇ *my weekly groceries*

... OF GROCERIES **bag** ◇ *He walked in and set the bag of groceries down on the floor.*

VERB + GROCERIES **buy, get** (*esp. AmE*) ◇ *Mom wanted me to get the groceries.* | **deliver** ◇ *We have our groceries delivered.* | **bag** (*AmE*), **pack** | **put away, unload, unpack** (*all esp. AmE*)

GROCERY + NOUN **bag**

2 (*esp. AmE*) used before a noun

GROCERY + NOUN **list** | **bill** | **bag, sack** (*AmE*) | **items** (*BrE, AmE*) | **cart** (*AmE*) | **shopping** (*BrE, AmE*) ◇ *I have to do some ~ shopping.* | **store** (*BrE, AmE*)

3 (*esp. BrE*) (*AmE usually* **grocery store**) shop/store → See also SUPERMARKET

ADJ. **corner, local, neighbourhood/neighborhood** ◇ *the corner ~* (*esp. BrE*) ◇ *the corner ~ store* (*esp. AmE*)

GROCERY/GROCERY STORE + NOUN **checkout** (*AmE*) ◇ *a ~ checkout* ◇ *a ~ store checkout* (*both AmE*) | **aisle, shelves** (*both esp. AmE*) | **clerk** (*AmE*) ◇ *a ~ clerk* ◇ *a ~ store clerk* (*both AmE*) | **business, chain** ◇ *a ~ business/chain* (*BrE, AmE*) ◇ *a ~ store business/chain* (*AmE*)

groomed *adj.*

VERBS **be, look** ◇ *She is always perfectly ~.*

ADV. **well** | **immaculately, impeccably, perfectly** | **beautifully**

groove noun

ADJ. **deep, shallow** | **narrow, wide**
VERB + GROOVE **carve, cut, make** ◊ *Running water had carved a ~ down the face of the wall.* | **form**
PREP. **~ in** ◊ *a deep ~ in the surface of the rock*

grope verb

ADV. **blindly** | **about** (*BrE*), **around, round** (*esp. BrE*)
PREP. **for** ◊ *She ~d blindly for the door handle.*
PHRASES **~ your way** ◊ *I ~d my way across the pitch-black stage.*

ground noun

1 solid surface of the earth

ADJ. **firm, hard, solid** | **muddy, soft** | **damp, wet** | **dry, dusty** | **cold, frozen** | **dirt** (*AmE*) | **concrete, stone** (*both esp. AmE*) | **snow-covered, snowy** | **sandy** | **fertile** (*often figurative*) ◊ *The fall of the old regime provided fertile ~ for opportunism.*
VERB + GROUND **fall to, hit, strike, touch** ◊ *The helicopter burst into flames when it hit the ~.* | **reach** ◊ *Her feet don't reach the ~ when she sits down.* | **get off, leave** ◊ *The plane was so overloaded it couldn't leave the ~.* ◊ *His plan is too costly to ever get off the ~.* (*figurative*) | **cover, litter** ◊ *the broken branches which littered the ~* | **kick, paw, pound** ◊ *The horse pawed the ~ impatiently.* | **scan, search** ◊ *Her eyes searched the ~.* | **shake** ◊ *Thunder shook the ~.*
GROUND + NOUN **level** ◊ *The window is just above ~ level.* | **forces, troops**
PHRASES **the ~ beneath sb's feet**
PREP. **above ~, below ~** ◊ *The roots may spread as far below ~ as does the foliage above ~.* | **in the ~** ◊ *a hole in the ~* | **on the ~** ◊ *He sat down on the ~.* | **under the ~** ◊ *The tunnel goes deep under the ~.*

2 area of land

ADJ. **high, low** ◊ *The town stands on high ~ and is not prone to flooding.* | **open** | **difficult, rocky, rough, stony, uneven** | **bare, barren** | **flat, level** | **marshy** | **hallowed, holy, sacred** ◊ *He stood on the hallowed ~ of Yankee Stadium.* (*figurative*)
... OF GROUND) **patch, piece** ◊ *We found a patch of open ~ in the middle of the woods.*

3 piece of land used for a particular purpose

ADJ. **burial** | **dumping** ◊ *The river has become a dumping ~ for industrial waste.* | **camp** (*AmE*), **parade** | **battle** | **breeding, feeding, nesting, spawning, wintering** ◊ *The estuary is a breeding ~ for birds and marine life.* ◊ *Poverty is a breeding ~ for terrorism.* (*figurative*) | **fishing, hunting** | **staging** (*esp. AmE*) | **meeting**
PREP. **at a/the ~, in a/the ~** ◊ *all the graves in the burial ~*

4 (BrE) stadium

ADJ. **cricket, football, rugby, etc.** | **practice, recreation, sports, training** | **away, home**
PREP. **at a/the ~** ◊ *I'll meet you at the football ~.* | **inside a/ the ~** ◊ *The atmosphere inside the ~ was electric.*

5 grounds land surrounding a large building

ADJ. **extensive, large** | **castle, hospital, palace, school, etc.** | **surrounding**
VERB + GROUNDS **be set in, have** ◊ *The palace is set in extensive ~s.* | **cross, enter, walk**
PREP. **in the ~s (of)** (*esp. BrE*) ◊ *She lived in the ~s of the castle.* | **on the ~s (of)** (*AmE*) ◊ *The doctor's office is on the ~s of the hospital.*

6 area of interest/study/discussion

ADJ. **familiar, home, old** ◊ *I was on more familiar ~ now that we were talking about our own system.* ◊ *I apologize if I'm going over old ~.* | **firm, solid** | **dangerous, rocky, shaky** ◊ *Legally, we're on very shaky ~ (= our actions may not be legal).* ◊ *Both relationships hit rocky ~.* | **safe** | **common** ◊ *Both parties in the debate shared some common ~.* | **middle** ◊ *a search for middle ~ between the two sides* | **neutral**
VERB + GROUND **cover, go over, tread** ◊ *Several researchers have published articles covering this ~.* ◊ *We just seem to be going over the same ~ that we covered last year.*
PREP. **on ... ~** ◊ *He knew he was on dangerous ~ talking about money.*
PHRASES **break new ~** ◊ *Her architectural designs have broken new ~.* | **hold your ~, stand your ~** ◊ *She held her ~ in the debate.* | **the moral high ~** ◊ *I was angry with his blatant attempt to take the moral high ~.* | **shift your ~** ◊ *Each time he seemed to be losing the argument, he just shifted his ~.*

7 grounds reason for sth

ADJ. **good, reasonable, strong, sufficient** | **legitimate, valid** | **ethical, humanitarian, moral** | **economic, legal, political, etc.**
VERB + GROUNDS **have** ◊ *The police had reasonable ~s for arresting her.* | **be, give (sb)** ◊ *His evasiveness gave ~s for suspicion.*
PREP. **on ... ~s** ◊ *Permission to open a mine was denied on environmental ~s.* | **on the ~s of** ◊ *He resigned on the ~s of ill health.* | **~ for** ◊ *Drunkenness at work was sufficient ~s for instant dismissal.*

ground verb be grounded in/on sth

ADV. **firmly, solidly, thoroughly, well** ◊ *His book is firmly ~ed in memories of his own childhood.* | **historically, religiously, scientifically, etc.**

grounding noun

ADJ. **firm, good, solid, thorough** | **basic** | **moral, theoretical, etc.**
VERB + GROUNDING **have** ◊ *All applicants for the job should have a basic ~ in computer skills.* | **get** | **give (sb), provide (sb with)** ◊ *The course should give you a thorough ~ in financial matters.*
PREP. **~ in** ◊ *to get a good ~ in science*

groundless adj.

VERBS **be, prove, seem**
ADV. **completely, totally** ◊ *Our fears proved totally ~.*

groundwork noun

ADJ. **basic** | **legal, theoretical, etc.**
VERB + GROUNDWORK **do, lay, prepare, provide (sb with), set** ◊ *The first meeting laid the ~ for the final agreement.* ◊ *The first year provides the basic ~ for the study of science.*
PREP. **~ for** ◊ *We are already doing the ~ for the introduction of the plan next year.*

group noun

ADJ. **big, large, wide** ◊ *She has a very wide ~ of friends.* | **little, select, small** ◊ *The president met with a select ~ of senior negotiators.* | **coherent, cohesive, homogeneous, tight, tight-knit, tightly knit** ◊ *The strangers who came together for the course soon became a cohesive ~.* | **diverse, heterogeneous** | **organized** | **minority** ◊ *Disabled drivers are an ever-growing minority ~.* | **dominant, powerful** | **cultural, demographic, ethnic, racial, social** | **family** ◊ *The animals live in family ~s of 10–20 individuals.* | **age, peer** ◊ *He started smoking because of peer-group pressure.* | **discussion** ◊ *a discussion ~ that meets once a month* | **research, study** | **self-help, support** | **focus** | **business, consumer, student** | **action, advocacy** (*esp. AmE*), **interest, pressure, special-interest** ◊ *Local parents have formed an action ~ to campaign for better road safety.* | **working** | **rebel, splinter** ◊ *A few members of the party broke away to form a splinter ~.* | **extremist** | **hate** (*esp. AmE*) | **terror, terrorist** | **church, religious** | **conservation, environmental** | **theatre/theater** | **book, reading** | **youth** | **pop, rock** | **blood** ◊ *What blood ~ are you?* (*BrE*) | **comparison, control** | **muscle** | **user**
VERB + GROUP **create, form, found, organize, set up, start** | **constitute** | **head, lead, manage, run** | **represent** |

become a member of, join | leave ◇ *He left the ~ last year to pursue a solo career.*
GROUP + VERB **form** ◇ *The ~ formed back in 1992.* | **split up** ◇ *The ~ has split up and re-formed several times with different musicians.* | **comprise, consist of, include**
GROUP + NOUN **leader, member** | **activity, discussion, work** | **photo** | **hug**
PREP. **as a ~** ◇ *The gorillas go foraging for food as a ~.* | **in a/the ~** ◇ *There are fifteen of us in the ~.* | **within a/the ~** ◇ *Within a ~, each individual had a definite status.* | **~ of** ◇ *a ~ of young mothers*
PHRASES **divide sb/sth into ~s** ◇ *We divided the class into small ~s.*
→ Note at ORGANIZATION

group verb

1 increase
ADV. **closely** | **broadly, loosely** | **thematically** ◇ *Works in the exhibition are ~ed thematically.* | **together**
PREP. **according to, by** ◇ *Eggs were ~ed according to size.* ◇ *The children were ~ed by age.* | **around, round** (*esp. BrE*) ◇ *They sat ~ed around the fire.* | **in, into** ◇ *These stories can be loosely ~ed into three types.* | **with** ◇ *The England team was ~ed with Uruguay and Holland.*
PHRASES **~ sth under a heading** ◇ *The names were ~ed under four different headings.*

grow verb

1 increase
ADV. **fast, quickly, rapidly** | **considerably, dramatically, significantly, substantially** | **slowly** | **slightly** | **exponentially** ◇ *The business has grown exponentially over the past ten years.* | **steadily** | **constantly, continuously**
VERB + GROW **seem to** | **begin to, start to** | **continue to** | **be expected to**
PREP. **at** ◇ *The Chinese economy has grown at a record pace.* | **by** ◇ *Profits are expected to ~ by 10% next year.* | **from** ◇ *Her media empire grew from small beginnings.* | **in** ◇ *She continued to ~ in confidence* | **into** ◇ *The town grew into a city.*

2 of a person, animal, etc.
ADV. **fast, quickly, rapidly** | **slowly** | **normally**
PREP. **into** ◇ *The small puppy quickly grew into a very large dog.* | **to** ◇ *to ~ to maturity*

3 of plants, hair, etc.
ADV. **well** ◇ *Tomatoes ~ best in direct sunlight.* | **poorly** | **fast, quickly, rapidly** | **slowly** | **slightly** | **thickly, vigorously** ◇ *the nettles that grew thickly around the house* | **outwards/outward, upwards/upward** ◇ *As the island subsided, the reef grew upward and outward.*
VERB + GROW **allow sth to, let sth** ◇ *I want to let my hair ~.*
PREP. **from** ◇ *The tree grew from a small acorn.* | **into** ◇ *Small acorns ~ into great oak trees.* | **to** ◇ *These plants can ~ to a height of six feet.*
PHRASES **~ unchecked** ◇ *A rose had been allowed to ~ unchecked up one of the walls.*

4 make plants grow
ADV. **organically** ◇ *organically grown produce* | **commercially** | **locally** | **successfully**
VERB + GROW **be easy to** ◇ *a plant which is easy to ~*
PHRASES **~ sth from seed**

growl noun

ADJ. **deep, low** | **guttural, soft, throaty** | **loud** | **angry, frustrated, threatening** ◇ *The dog gave a threatening ~.* | **small**
VERB + GROWL **give, let out** | **hear**
PREP. **with a ~** ◇ *He spoke with a deep soft ~ in his throat.* | **~ of** ◇ *The ~ of the engine.*
→ Note at SOUND

growl verb

ADV. **angrily, ferociously, fiercely, menacingly** ◇ *'I'm a desperate man,' he ~ed menacingly.* | **playfully** | **deeply, loudly, lowly** (*AmE*), **softly** | **slightly**

PHRASES **~ sth under your breath** ◇ *'Mosquitos!' she ~ed under her breath.*
PREP. **at** ◇ *The dog ~ed softly at me.* | **in** ◇ *to ~ in annoyance* | **with** ◇ *Her stomach was ~ing with hunger.*

growth noun

1 increase in sth
ADJ. **considerable, exponential, significant, strong** ◇ *the exponential ~ in world population* | **high** ◇ *The country is experiencing a period of high ~.* | **real** ◇ *real GDP ~* | **dramatic, enormous, impressive, phenomenal, spectacular, tremendous** | **explosive, fast, rapid** ◇ *the explosive ~ of personal computers in the 1990s* | **modest, slow, sluggish** ◇ *The factory has achieved a steady ~ in output.* | **steady, sustainable** | **low** ◇ *a vicious circle of low ~ and low productivity* | **long-term** | **future** | **economic, industrial** | **job, productivity, revenue, etc.** | **population**
VERB + GROWTH **achieve, experience** | **maintain, sustain** | **accelerate, boost, encourage, foster, fuel, promote, spur, stimulate** | **control, limit** ◇ *new measures to control the ~ of traffic on the roads* | **slow**
GROWTH + NOUN **rate** ◇ *The economy enjoyed the highest ~ rate in Asia.* | **potential, prospects** | **pattern** | **area, industry, market** ◇ *Communications technology has proved to be a ~ area.* | **curve**
PREP. **~ in** ◇ *There was a rapid ~ in the numbers of private cars.*
PHRASES **a rate of ~**
→ Special page at BUSINESS

2 growing
ADJ. **healthy, normal** ◇ *A good diet is vital for healthy ~.* | **abnormal** | **vigorous** | **excessive** ◇ *the excessive ~ of algae in rivers* | **new** | **bacterial, cell, hair, muscle, plant, tumour/tumor, etc.** | **intellectual, personal, spiritual**
VERB + GROWTH **encourage, stimulate** ◇ *Give the plants a good pruning to encourage ~.* | **inhibit, retard** (*esp. AmE*), **stunt, suppress** ◇ *Lack of food had stunted his ~.* | **affect**
GROWTH + NOUN **hormone** | **defect** | **spurt** | **chart**

3 abnormal lump in the body
ADJ. **cancerous, malignant** | **benign**
VERB + GROWTH **have**
PREP. **~ on** ◇ *He had a cancerous ~ on his lung.*

grudge noun

ADJ. **long-standing, old** ◇ *It's time to forget old ~s.* | **personal**
VERB + GRUDGE **bear, harbour/harbor, have, hold, nurse** ◇ *I don't hold ~s for very long.*
GRUDGE + NOUN **match** ◇ *It's a ~ match between the two teams.*
PREP. **~ against** ◇ *Do you know anyone who might have a ~ against you?*

grunt noun

ADJ. **little, slight, small, soft** | **low** | **non-committal** ◇ *He gave a non-committal ~ in reply.* | **loud** | **angry, annoyed, frustrated, etc.**
VERB + GRUNT **give, let out** | **hear**
PREP. **with a ~** ◇ *He lifted the heavy box with a ~.* | **~ of** ◇ *a ~ of pain*
→ Note at SOUND

grunt verb

ADV. **loudly** | **softly** | **angrily** | **merely, only** ◇ *He merely ~ed at her and nodded his head.*
PREP. **at** ◇ *His father ~ed at him as he left the room.* | **in** ◇ *She asked him a question and he ~ed in reply.* ◇ *He ~ed in pain.* | **with** ◇ *She stirred the soup, ~ing with satisfaction.*
PHRASES **~ and groan** ◇ *Grunting and groaning, they heaved the wardrobe up the stairs.*

guarantee noun

1 written promise by a company

ADJ. **full** ◊ *The company offers a full money-back ~.* | **lifetime, three-year, two-year, etc.** | **money-back**
VERB + GUARANTEE **carry, come with, have** ◊ *All our products come with a two-year ~.* | **give (sb), offer (sb)**
PREP. **under ~** (*BrE*) (**under warranty** in *AmE*) ◊ *The car is still under ~, so you should be able to get it repaired free of charge.* | **~ against** ◊ *The window frames carry a 20-year ~ against rot or decay.* | **~ for** ◊ *The garage gives a year's ~ for all repair work.* | **~ on** ◊ *The contractors offer a full money-back ~ on all their work.*

2 promise that sth will be done/will happen

ADJ. **absolute, firm** (*esp. BrE*) | **cast-iron** (*BrE*), **ironclad** (*esp. AmE*) | **long-term** | **constitutional, federal** (*esp. AmE*), **government, legal** ◊ *The country gives a constitutional ~ of the rights of minorities.* | **personal** | **loan** | **security**
VERB + GUARANTEE **give (sb), offer (sb), provide (sb with)** | **demand, want** | **get, receive** ◊ *We didn't get any firm ~ of a loan.* | **violate** (*esp. AmE*)
PREP. **~ against** ◊ *There was no ~ against misuse of the political power.* | **~ for** ◊ *The demonstrators were demanding ~s for fair elections.* | **~ of** ◊ *Arriving early is no longer a ~ of getting a place.*

guarantee verb

1 promise to do sth/promise sth will happen

ADV. **absolutely** ◊ *I can absolutely ~ that you will enjoy the show.* | **personally** ◊ *I personally ~ total and immediate support in all measures undertaken.* | **constitutionally, federally** (*both esp. AmE*)
VERB + GUARANTEE **be able to, can**
PHRASES **be fully ~d** ◊ *All our electrical goods are fully ~d.*

2 make sth certain to happen

ADV. **absolutely** | **almost, practically, virtually** | **effectively** ◊ *The complicated electoral system effectively ~s the president's re-election.* | **automatically** ◊ *A degree does not automatically ~ you a job.* | **by no means, not necessarily** ◊ *The outcome is by no means ~d.*

guard noun

1 person who guards sb/sth

ADJ. **armed, uniformed** ◊ *The building is protected by armed ~s.* | **border, gate** (*AmE*), **prison, security** | **head** | **personal, private** | **military**
VERB + GUARD **post, station** ◊ *Guards had been posted all around the TV studio.*
GUARD + VERB **patrol sth** ◊ *Guards patrolled the perimeter fence.* | **protect sth** | **escort sb** | **be on duty**
GUARD + NOUN **duty** | **dog**

2 being ready to prevent attack or danger

ADJ. **close** | **24-hour, constant, round-the-clock** | **armed** ◊ *The accused was taken to court under armed ~.* | **heavy** ◊ *He arrived under heavy ~.* | **military, police**
PREP. **off (your) ~** ◊ *The question seemed to catch him off his ~.* ◊ *He caught me completely off ~.* | **on (your) ~** ◊ *Several police officers were on ~ outside the factory.* ◊ *He was always on his ~ against moneymaking schemes.* | **under ~** ◊ *The prisoners were under close ~.* | **~ against, ~ over** ◊ *Two police officers kept ~ over the burned-out building.*
PHRASES **drop your ~** ◊ *Matt relaxed a little, dropping his ~.* | **keep ~ of sth** ◊ *Would you like me to keep ~ of your room?* | **keep your ~ up, keep up your ~** ◊ *No one can keep their ~ up all the time.* | **stand ~** ◊ *A solider stood ~ outside the palace.*

3 group of soldiers/policemen who guard sb/sth

ADJ. **civil, national, palace, presidential, royal** | **honour/ honor** | **advance** | **elite**
VERB + GUARD **change** ◊ *The ~ was changed every two hours.* | **call out** ◊ *It would only be a matter of minutes before the alarm was raised and the ~ called out.*

PHRASES **~ of honour/honor** ◊ *Fellow soldiers formed a ~ of honour/honor at his wedding.*

4 cover that prevents injury

ADJ. **trigger** | **fire** | **shin, shoulder, wrist**

guard verb

ADV. **well** ◊ *The mountain pass is well ~ed.* | **carefully** ◊ *a bird carefully ~ing its eggs* | **fiercely, jealously** ◊ *She jealously ~ed her position of power.*
PREP. **against** ◊ *They ~ the city against attack.* | **from** ◊ *pop stars who need to be ~ed from their fans*
PHRASES **closely ~ed, heavily ~ed** ◊ *The military base is closely ~ed.* | **~ sb/sth with your life** ◊ *He was under instructions to ~ the key with his life.* | **tightly ~ed** ◊ *tightly ~ed privacy*

guardian noun

1 person/institution that guards/protects sth

ADJ. **self-appointed** ◊ *She has become the self-appointed ~ of the nation's conscience.* | **moral**
VERB + GUARDIAN **act as** ◊ *The people act as ~s of the land.*

2 person who is responsible for a child

ADJ. **legal**
VERB + GUARDIAN **be, become** | **appoint, appoint sb (as), name sb (as)** ◊ *The court appoints a legal ~ for the child.* | **act as**
PHRASES **parents or ~s**

guerrilla noun

ADJ. **armed** | **urban** ◊ *Urban ~s detonated a car bomb in front of the company's headquarters.* | **communist, right-wing, separatist**
GUERRILLA + NOUN **army, band, force, group, movement, organization, unit** | **commander, fighter, leader** | **activity, attack, campaign, offensive, raid, resistance, struggle, war, warfare** ◊ *Ten years of ~ resistance followed the occupation.* | **tactics**

guess noun

ADJ. **fair, good, reasonable, safe** ◊ *April is a safe ~ for first deliveries.* | **educated, informed** ◊ *She could make an educated ~ as to what was wrong with him.* | **rough, wild** ◊ *At a rough ~, I'd say we're about twenty miles from home.* | **correct, lucky** ◊ *'How did you know?' 'It was just a lucky ~.'* | **first, initial**
VERB + GUESS **have** (*BrE*), **hazard, make** (*BrE*), **take** (*AmE*), **venture** (*esp. AmE*) ◊ *If you don't know the answer, have/take a ~.* ◊ *If I might hazard a guess…* | **give sb** ◊ *'Where's Tom?' 'I'll give you three ~es!'* (= the answer is obvious and you should guess it easily)
GUESS + VERB **be correct, be right**
PREP. **at a ~** ◊ *At a ~, I'd say there's a problem with the fuel pump.* | **~ about, ~ as to, ~ at** ◊ *He made a wild ~ as to how much the piano might cost.*
PHRASES **sb's best ~** ◊ *What's your best ~ on what's going to happen?* | **a ~ based on sth** ◊ *a ~ based on your experience*

guess verb

ADV. **correctly, right** | **incorrectly, wrong** ◊ *Jane had ~ed wrong about who was responsible for the fire.* | **easily** ◊ *an easily ~ed password*
VERB + GUESS **can** ◊ *Can you ~ his age?* | **can only** ◊ *We can only ~ how fast a dinosaur might have run.* | **try to** | **be easy to, not be difficult to, not be hard to** ◊ *It's not hard to ~ where they went.*
PREP. **at** ◊ *I was only ~ing at her age.* | **from** ◊ *She ~ed from his expression that he had not won.*
PHRASES **could have ~ed, might have ~ed, should have ~ed** ◊ *So it was Rob who broke the window? I might have ~ed!* | **~ again** ◊ *That's not the answer. Guess again.* ◊ *If you think I'm lying, well ~ again.* | **if you haven't already ~ed** ◊ *If you haven't already ~ed, I'm going out with Steve.* | **I ~ so, I ~ not** | **let me ~** ◊ *What star sign are you? No, let me ~.* | **you can probably ~, you have probably ~ed** ◊ *You can*

guesswork *noun*

ADJ. **pure** | **educated** ◇ *Their results owe more to educated ~ than to actual knowledge.*
VERB + GUESSWORK **be based on** ◇ *Their price estimates are based on pure ~.* | **involve** | **eliminate**
PHRASES **a matter of ~** ◇ *Long-term forecasts were largely a matter of ~.* | **take the ~ out of sth** ◇ *weekly shopping lists that take the ~ out of meal planning*

guest *noun*

1 person that you invite to your home

ADJ. **house** | **honoured/honored, welcome** ◇ *She was treated as an honoured/honored ~.* ◇ *You are always a welcome ~ in our house.* | **surprise, unexpected, uninvited** ◇ *She tactfully discouraged their uninvited ~s from staying longer.* | **unwanted, unwelcome** ◇ *The refugees were made to feel like unwanted ~s in the country.* | **invited** | **overnight**
VERB + GUEST **be** ◇ *You're the guest—you can choose what we watch.* | **have** ◇ *When we have ~s, they usually sleep in the study.* | **invite** ◇ *She had invited six ~s.* | **entertain** ◇ *She felt that she had to entertain her ~s.* | **receive**
GUEST + NOUN **bathroom, bed, bedroom, house** (= a building where guests stay) (*AmE*), **room, suite**

2 person invited to an event

ADJ. **distinguished, important** | **chief** (*esp. BrE*) ◇ *The athlete was chief ~ at the schools sports day.* | **dinner, party, wedding** ◇ *The best man welcomed the wedding ~s as they arrived.*
VERB + GUEST **greet, welcome** | **accommodate, seat** | **have, host** | **serve** | **bring**
GUEST + VERB **arrive** | **attend sth** ◇ *The banquet was attended by 200 ~s.*
GUEST + NOUN **book, list**
PHRASES **a ~ of honour/honor, sb's personal ~**

3 person who is staying at a hotel

ADJ. **hotel** | **frequent, regular** | **occasional** | **new** | **out-of-town** (*AmE*)

4 at a public event/on a radio or television show

ADJ. **special** ◇ *Movie star Matt Damon is one of the special ~s on tonight's show.* | **featured** | **mystery** | **musical**
GUEST + NOUN **star** | **artist, conductor, vocalist** ◇ *Guest artists from all over Europe will take part in the concert.* | **lecturer, speaker** | **appearance, shot** (*AmE*) ◇ *She made a rare ~ appearance on the show.* | **spot**
PHRASES **our next ~** ◇ *Our next ~ is a bona fide television star.*

guidance *noun*

ADJ. **clear, detailed, proper, specific** | **careful** | **firm** ◇ *Parents need to provide their children with firm ~.* | **gentle** | **helpful, useful, valuable** ◇ *The handbook gives helpful ~ on writing articles.* | **practical** | **general** ◇ *These notes are for general ~ only.* | **additional, further** | **divine, spiritual** ◇ *She prayed for divine ~.* | **expert, legal, parental, professional, technical** | **marriage** (*BrE*) ◇ *a marriage ~ counsellor* | **career, vocational** | **ethical, moral**
VERB + GUIDANCE **give (sb), offer (sb), provide (sb with)** ◇ *We can give ~ to students on which courses to choose.* | **issue** | **could use** (*AmE*), **need** | **ask for, look (to sb) for, seek, want** ◇ *Children look to their parents for ~.* ◇ *I think you should seek ~ from your lawyer on this matter.* | **receive** | **follow**
GUIDANCE + NOUN **counselor** (= at a school) (*AmE*)
PREP. **under...~, under the ~ of** ◇ *Volunteers are restoring the building under expert ~.* | **~ about** ◇ *~ about university degrees* | **~ as to** ◇ *Guidance must be given as to what tasks the learner should attempt.* | **~ on** ◇ *The Safety Officer provides ~ on firefighting and office safety.*

guide *noun*

1 sth that helps you plan what you are going to do

ADJ. **approximate, general, rough** | **accurate**

VERB + GUIDE **give (sb), provide (sb with)** | **use sth as** ◇ *Use the table below as a ~ to how much detergent to use.*
PHRASES **be just a ~, be only a ~** ◇ *Remember, this chart is only a ~.*
PREP. **~ as to** ◇ *These figures give a rough ~ as to the sales we can expect.* | **~ to**

2 book that gives information about a subject

ADJ. **excellent, good** | **essential, handy, helpful, informative, invaluable, practical, reliable, useful, valuable** | **basic, brief, quick, short, simple** | **complete, comprehensive, definitive, in-depth** ◇ *This book is the definitive ~ to world cuisine.* | **step-by-step** ◇ *a step-by-step ~ to creating your own website* | **illustrated** | **pocket** | **how-to, study, survival** ◇ *a survival ~ for business managers* | **media** (*AmE*) | **pronunciation, reference** ◇ *The book contains a quick reference ~ to essential grammar at the back.* | **resource** (*AmE*) | **curriculum** (*AmE*) | **voter** (*AmE*) | **TV** | **field** | **electronic, interactive, online**
PREP. **~ to** ◇ *a ~ to British birds*

3 person

ADJ. **tour, tourist** ◇ *Our tour ~ showed us around the old town.* | **experienced, professional** | **local, native** | **mountain, river** | **spiritual**
VERB + GUIDE **act as, be** ◇ *He agreed to go with them and act as their ~.*

4 book for tourists

ADJ. **holiday** (*BrE*), **travel** | **hotel, restaurant** | **city, street**
VERB + GUIDE **consult** ◇ *I consulted my ~ as I walked around the cathedral.* | **write** | **publish**

guide *verb*

1 influence sb's actions

VERB + GUIDE **help (to)** ◇ *the information and data which help ~ the affairs of the business* | **serve to** ◇ *This book will serve to ~ you in the fulfilment of a successful relationship.* | **try to**
PREP. **into** ◇ *the ways in which young people are ~d into employment* | **on** ◇ *Schools were firmly ~d on the details of the curriculum*

2 explain sth/help sb

ADV. **carefully** ◇ *Their teacher carefully ~s them through rehearsals.* | **expertly** ◇ *They ~ you expertly through the whole process.*
VERB + GUIDE **help (to)**
PREP. **in** ◇ *He ~d me in my research.* | **on** ◇ *a document guiding teachers on how to maintain discipline* | **through** ◇ *He ~d us through the intricacies of the divorce law.*

3 help sb move

ADV. **carefully, gently** ◇ *He took her arm, gently guiding her.*
PREP. **across, along, etc.** ◇ *She ~d him across the busy road.* | **to, towards/toward** ◇ *He ~d her hand to his face.*

guideline *noun*

ADJ. **clear, good, helpful, practical, useful** | **basic** (*esp. AmE*), **broad, general, simple** | **comprehensive, detailed, explicit, specific** | **strict, stringent** | **draft, proposed** | **new, revised, updated** | **voluntary** ◇ *A task force has formed to develop voluntary ~s.* | **recommended** | **formal, official** | **federal, government** | **international, national, state** | **planning** (*esp. BrE*), **safety, security** | **clinical, ethical, legal** | **sentencing** ◇ *The US Supreme Court is reviewing sentencing ~s.*
... OF GUIDELINES **set** ◇ *The organization has issued a set of ~s for builders to follow.*
VERB + GUIDELINE **develop** | **propose, recommend, suggest** | **draw up, establish, formulate, lay down** (*esp. BrE*), **lay out** (*esp. AmE*), **set out** | **accept, adopt, approve** ◇ *The following ~s were approved in October 1995.* | **give (sb), issue, offer (sb), provide (sb with), release** ◇ *The document gives clear ~s on the use of pesticides.* | **adhere to, apply, enforce, follow, implement, meet, stick to** ◇ *We have to follow the safety ~s laid down by the government.* ◇ *A number of deals*

have not met the ~s. | **breach** (esp. BrE), **ignore**, **violate** ◇ The minister is accused of allowing the company to breach ~s on arms sales.
GUIDELINE + VERB **apply** ◇ The same general ~s on when to dress formally apply to both men and women. | **state sth** | **require sth** ◇ The ~s require this information to be made available to the public. | **recommend sth, suggest sth** ◇ The ~s recommend that children under 12 avoid these foods.
PREP. **under ~** ◇ Under federal ~s, they must serve at least five years in prison. | **within ~** ◇ Within clear ~s, managers can use their budget to entertain clients. | **~ about** ◇ detailed ~s for doctors about how to deal with difficult patients | **~ for** ◇ The article suggests some ~s for healthy eating. | **~ from** ◇ ~s from the Department of Education | **~ on** ◇ new EU ~s on food hygiene

guilt noun

1 feeling

ADJ. **intense, overwhelming, terrible, tremendous** | **lingering** | **sexual** | **Catholic, Jewish, etc.** | **liberal, middle-class** (esp. BrE), **white** (all disapproving) ◇ These actions are merely intended to assuage white liberal ~. | **collective, personal** ◇ They feel a sense of collective ~ for the Holocaust. | **survivor**
...OF GUILT **pang, twinge**
VERB + GUILT **bear, carry** ◇ It helped him bear the ~ he felt. | **be consumed with, be driven by, be haunted by, be overwhelmed with, be racked with, experience, feel, suffer** ◇ I knew that the next day I would be consumed with ~. ◇ You needn't feel any ~ about me. | **alleviate, assuage, ease** ◇ Talking to her helped to assuage my ~.
GUILT + VERB **overwhelm sb, wash over sb** | **consume sb, weigh down on sb, weigh on sb**
GUILT + NOUN **complex** | **feelings** | **trip** (= things you say in order to make sb feel guilty about sth) ◇ She was trying to lay a ~ trip on me.
PREP. **~ about, ~ at, ~ over** ◇ He had no feelings of ~ over what he had done.
PHRASES **a burden of ~** ◇ the burden of ~ that she carried with her | **a feeling of ~, a sense of ~**

2 fact of having broken a law/done sth wrong

VERB + GUILT **admit, confess** | **deny** ◇ Many of the accused would deny their ~ to the magistrates. | **determine, establish, prove** ◇ It might be difficult to prove his ~.
GUILT + VERB **lie** ◇ There is no doubt as to where the ~ lies.
PHRASES **an admission of ~** ◇ I took his silence as an admission of ~. | **proof of ~**

guilty adj.

1 feeling/showing guilt

VERBS **feel, look**
ADV. **extremely, really, very** | **horribly, incredibly, terribly** ◇ She has a terribly ~ conscience about it. | **almost** ◇ I feel almost ~ that so many good things are happening to us. | **rather, somewhat** ◇ She was looking rather ~ when I came into the room. | **a little, slightly, etc.** | **vaguely** | **equally** ◇ Matt and Chrissy both looked equally ~.
PREP. **about** ◇ I feel very ~ about leaving her.

2 having broken the law/done sth wrong

VERBS **be, plead** ◇ He pleaded ~ to starting the fire. | **believe sb, presume sb** ◇ No one believed him ~ of this terrible crime. ◇ A person should never be presumed ~. | **deem sb, find sb, hold sb, prove sb** ◇ Company directors may be deemed ~ of a crime if their company causes pollution. ◇ He was found ~ of murder. | **declare sb, pronounce sb** ◇ He was pronounced ~. | **vote** ◇ The jury voted not ~ on all counts.
ADV. **certainly, clearly, obviously** ◇ She was certainly ~, but the police couldn't prove it. | **equally** ◇ Anyone who supports terrorists is equally ~ of terrorist crimes.
PREP. **of** ◇ She was ~ of fraud.

guinea pig noun person used in experiments

ADJ. **human** ◇ The company used my client as a human ~.
VERB + GUINEA PIG **act as, be** ◇ Twenty students volunteered to act as ~s. | **use sb as**
PREP. **~ for** ◇ Dealers used their clients as ~s for their untried techniques.

guitar noun

ADJ. **acoustic, bass, electric, steel** | **lead, rhythm** | **blues, classical, jazz, rock, etc.** | **slide** | **six-string, twelve-string, etc.** | **air** ◇ He would stand in front of the mirror, playing air ~ (= playing an imaginary electric guitar) to Van Halen songs.
VERB + GUITAR **strum, strum on** ◇ As she sang, she strummed her ~. | **pluck** ◇ He gently plucked his ~. | **tune**
GUITAR + NOUN **string** | **pick, plectrum** (esp. BrE) | **amp** (informal), **amplifier** | **case, strap** | **lick, riff** | **accompaniment** | **chord**
→ Special page at MUSIC

gulf noun

ADJ. **big, deep, enormous, great, huge, unbridgeable, vast, wide, yawning** | **growing, widening** ◇ a growing ~ between the prosperous south and the declining towns of the north | **cultural, ideological** ◇ the ideological ~ that separated the two branches of the movement
VERB + GULF **create** ◇ This atrocity has created a huge ~ between the two groups. | **widen** ◇ Other factors widened the ~ that separated rich from poor. | **emphasize, illustrate** ◇ The documentary illustrated the ~ between industrialized and developing countries. | **bridge** ◇ The new degree course aims to bridge the ~ between education and industry.
GULF + VERB **exist** | **divide sb/sth, separate sb/sth** ◇ the yawning ~ that separates the two cultures | **open, open up** ◇ A ~ had opened up between the former friends.
PREP. **~ between** ◇ an unbridgeable ~ between home and school life | **~ in** ◇ the huge ~ in level between professional and amateur teams | **~ of** ◇ A ~ of mistrust still exists between them.

gull (also seagull) noun → See SEAGULL

gulp noun

1 amount you swallow when you gulp

ADJ. **big, deep, great, huge, large, long**
VERB + GULP **take** ◇ She took a large ~ of wine from the bottle. | **down sth in** (informal), **drink sth in, swallow sth in** ◇ I downed it in one ~.
PREP. **in ~s** ◇ She drank the tea in great ~s. | **~ of**

2 act of gulping

ADJ. **loud, noisy** | **quick** ◇ She drained half the mug in one quick ~.
VERB + GULP **give** ◇ He gave a loud ~ and stopped mid-sentence.
PREP. **with a ~** ◇ 'I'm afraid I've broken it,' she said with a ~.
PHRASES **in one ~, in a single ~** ◇ He downed half the contents of the glass in one loud ~.

gulp verb

1 eat/drink sth quickly

ADV. **greedily** | **quickly** ◇ She quickly ~ed down the rest of her coffee. | **noisily** | **down** ◇ She ~ed down her coffee and left.

2 make a swallowing movement

ADV. **nervously** ◇ The man ~ed nervously and nodded.
PHRASES **~ for air, ~ for breath** ◇ Keith swam to the surface and ~ed for air.

gum noun

ADJ. **lower, upper** | **toothless** ◇ The old man smiled to reveal toothless ~s. | **bleeding, swollen**
GUM + NOUN **disease**

gun noun

ADJ. **big, heavy** | **loaded** | **enemy** ◇ They succeeded in

silencing the enemy ~s. | **anti-aircraft, anti-tank, artillery, field, hand** (usually *handgun*), **machine, semi-automatic** ◇ *a.50-calibre/.50-caliber machine ~* | **.45-calibre/.45-caliber, .50-calibre/.50-caliber, etc.** | **stun, taser, tranquillizer/tranquilizer** | **laser, radar** (= used by the police to check the speed of cars) | **harpoon, spear** (usually *speargun*) | **glue** (*AmE*), **nail, pellet, spray, staple** | **fake, replica, toy** | **air** | **squirt, water** (*both AmE*) (*water pistol* in *BrE*) | **paintball**
VERB + GUN **be armed with, carry, have, tote** (*informal, esp. AmE*) ◇ *Look out! He has a ~!* | **load, reload** ◇ *I loaded the ~ with my last two bullets.* | **draw, produce, pull, pull out** ◇ *He pulled a ~ from his pocket.* | **brandish, wave, wave around, wield** ◇ *She brandished the ~ menacingly.* | **aim, hold, point, raise** ◇ *He raised his ~, aimed and fired.* | **cock** ◇ *He grinned and cocked the ~ with his thumb.* | **man** ◇ *Enemy ship approaching! Man the ~s!* | **handle, use** | **fire, shoot** | **drop, lay down, lower, put down** | **holster** (*esp. AmE*) ◇ *Jorge quickly holstered his ~.* | **silence**
GUN + VERB **blaze, fire, go off** ◇ *Guns were firing and grenades going off all around.* | **aim at sb/sth, point at sb/sth** | **shoot sth** ◇ *This new ~ shoots a laser beam at the target.* | **jam** | **be mounted** ◇ *There was a machine ~ mounted on the back of the Jeep.*
GUN + NOUN **control** (*esp. AmE*), **law** ◇ *a state that has strict ~ control laws* ◇ *a ~ control advocate* | **crime, violence** ◇ *Anyone can be affected by ~ violence.* | **culture** ◇ *These kids have grown up in a drugs and ~ culture.* | **safety** (*esp. AmE*) ◇ *My big brother taught me about ~ safety.* | **ban** (*esp. AmE*) | **amnesty** (*BrE*) ◇ *The police pointed to the success of a ~ amnesty earlier this year.* | **lobby** ◇ *the powerful ~ lobby in the US* | **shop, store** (*both esp. AmE*) | **dealer, maker, manufacturer** | **owner** | **ownership, possession** | **enthusiast, nut** (*esp. AmE*) | **club** | **show** (*AmE*) | **attack, battle** | **crew** | **emplacement, position** | **turret** | **carriage** (*esp. BrE*) | **barrel** | **rack** | **belt** ◇ *They grudgingly took off their ~ belts and holsters.*
PHRASES **the barrel of a ~** ◇ *I found myself looking down the barrel of a ~.* | **~s and ammunition** ◇ *We're very short of ~s and ammunition.* | **hold a ~ on sb, hold a ~ to sb's head** ◇ *Two armed men held a ~ to his head and made him empty the safe.* | **a/the smoking ~** (= something that shows that sb has done sth wrong or illegal) ◇ *There's no smoking ~ that they have found to date.* | **turn a ~ on yourself** ◇ *The gunman turned the ~ on himself.*

gunfire *noun*

ADJ. **heavy, intense** | **scattered, sporadic** | **enemy** | **celebratory** ◇ *Bursts of celebratory ~ could be heard on the streets.* | **distant** | **automatic** ◇ *We heard the rapid crackle of automatic ~.*
... OF GUNFIRE **burst** ◇ *A burst of ~ echoed across the square.*
VERB + GUNFIRE **hear** | **spray, spray sb/sth with** ◇ *The terrorists boarded the bus and sprayed the passengers with ~.* ◇ *They sprayed ~ into the crowd.* | **exchange** ◇ *Youths exchanged ~ with police.s* | **be hit by, be wounded by** ◇ *A convoy was hit by ~.*
GUNFIRE + VERB **break out, erupt** ◇ *Heavy ~ broke out in the capital last night.* | **echo, ring out**
PHRASES **the crackle, rattle, sound, etc. of ~** | **an exchange of ~** ◇ *They were killed in an exchange of ~ between riot police and demonstrators.*

gunshot *noun*

VERB + GUNSHOT **hear** ◇ *We heard ~s just before midnight.*
GUNSHOT + NOUN **wound** ◇ *He died of ~ wounds to the chest.* | **victim**
PHRASES **the noise of a ~, the sound of a ~**

gurgle *noun*

ADJ. **little** | **low**
VERB + GURGLE **emit, give, let out** | **hear**
PREP. **with a ~** ◇ *The water emptied with a ~.* | **~ of** ◇ *He gave a low ~ of laughter.*
→ Note at SOUND

gust *noun*

ADJ. **great** | **little, small** | **huge, powerful, strong** | **sudden** | **freak** (*BrE*) ◇ *A car was blown off the road by a freak ~ of wind.* | **occasional** | **cold** | **wind** (*esp. AmE*) ◇ *The hurricane's wind ~s topped 110 miles an hour.*
PREP. **~ of** ◇ *a sudden ~ of wind*
PHRASES **blow in ~s, come in ~s** ◇ *The wind came in great ~s off the Pacific.*

gut *noun*

1 tube in the lower part of the body
ADJ. **healthy**
VERB + GUT **pass through**
GUT + NOUN **flora** (*technical*), **wall**
PREP. **in the/your ~**

2 guts organs inside the body
PHRASES **blood and ~s** (*figurative*) ◇ *I don't like movies that are full of blood and ~s.* | **a pain in your ~** (*AmE*), **a pain in your ~s** (*BrE*) ◇ *I had a terrible pain in my ~s after eating too many plums.*

3 guts courage/determination
VERB + GUTS **have** ◇ *She had the ~s to stand up to the school bully.* | **take** ◇ *It takes ~s to keep on running even though you have blistered feet.*

gut *verb*

ADV. **completely, totally** ◇ *The hotel was completely gutted by fire last year.*

guy *noun* (*informal*)

ADJ. **decent, friendly, funny, good, great, nice, sweet, wonderful** | **cute** (*esp. AmE*), **gorgeous, hot** (*esp. AmE*) | **smart, wise** (*disapproving, both esp. AmE*) | **bad** | **normal, ordinary, regular** ◇ *Colleagues described the killer as 'just a regular guy'.* | **poor** ◇ *The poor ~ is worn out.* | **big, little** | **middle-aged, old, young** | **black, white** | **gay** | **tough** | **crazy**

gym *noun*

ADJ. **fully equipped, well-equipped** (*both esp. BrE*) | **high-school** (*esp. AmE*), **school** | **home** (*esp. AmE*) | **local** | **indoor** | **climbing, jungle** (*both AmE*)
VERB + GYM **join** ◇ *I joined the local ~.* | **go to, hit** (*esp. AmE*) ◇ *I hit the ~ at 6.00 again this morning.*
GYM + NOUN **session** (*esp. BrE*), **workout** | **membership** | **floor** (*esp. AmE*) | **locker** | **equipment** | **bag, clothes, shoes** (= shoes for the gym), **socks, shorts** (*all esp. AmE*) | **shoes** (= light canvas shoes) (*BrE*) | **class** (*esp. AmE*) ◇ *I played basketball in ~ class.* | **teacher** (*esp. AmE*) ◇ *a high-school ~ teacher* | **rat** (*AmE, slang*) ◇ *He's a bit of a ~ rat* (= spends all his time in the gym).
PREP. **at the ~** ◇ *You can tell he works out at the ~.* | **in the ~** ◇ *She spends all her time in the ~.*

gymnast *noun*

ADJ. **brilliant, elite, good, talented, top** | **Olympic**
GYMNAST + VERB **train** ◇ *young ~s who have to train for up to five hours a day* | **compete, perform** | **win sth** ◇ *the Olympic ~ who won a gold medal on a sprained ankle*

gymnastics *noun*

ADJ. **rhythmic** | **artistic** | **competitive**
VERB + GYMNASTICS **do** ◇ *She does ~ at school.*
GYMNASTICS + NOUN **exhibition** | **championships, competition** | **coach** | **team** | **club**
→ Special page at SPORTS

H h

habit noun

ADJ. **annoying, antisocial** (*BrE*), **bad, dangerous, destructive, dirty, disconcerting** (*BrE*), **disgusting, filthy, horrible, irritating, nasty, poor, terrible, unfortunate** ◇ *Life has a nasty ~ of repeating itself.* ◇ *poor eating ~s* | **charming** (*often ironic*), **endearing, good** ◇ *one of his more endearing ~s* ◇ *her charming ~ of setting fire to cats* | **curious, eccentric, odd, peculiar, strange, unusual, weird** | **unhealthy** ◇ *The children are developing unhealthy eating ~s.* | **healthful** (*AmE*), **healthy** | **lifelong, old** | **daily, normal, regular, usual** | **ingrained** ◇ *deeply ingrained ~s of thought* | **nervous** ◇ *It was a nervous ~ she'd had for years.* | **expensive** | **personal, sexual, social** ◇ *I found some of his personal ~s rather disconcerting.* | **lifestyle** ◇ *Healthy lifestyle ~s begin when you're young.* | **mental** ◇ *Mental ~s are not easily changed.* | **buying, shopping, spending** ◇ *an effort to change the buying ~s of the British public* | **dietary, drinking, eating, feeding, food** | **exercise, sleeping, work** ◇ *The pills affected your sleeping ~s.* ◇ *Ellington's work ~s were a marvel to all.* | **reading, viewing** ◇ *women's television viewing ~s* | **cocaine, crack, drug, gambling, heroin, smoking** ◇ *I'm trying to kick the smoking ~.*

VERB + HABIT **be in, have** ◇ *She had been in the ~ of drinking five or six cups of coffee a day.* ◇ *She has some very annoying ~s.* ◇ *He had an irritating ~ of singing tunelessly around the house.* | **acquire, adopt, cultivate, develop, establish, fall into, form, get in, get into, make** ◇ *I had fallen into my old bad ~ of leaving everything until the last minute.* ◇ *Try to get into good ~s and eat regular healthy meals.* ◇ *Make a ~ of noting down any telephone messages.* | **become** ◇ *Don't let eating between meals become a ~.* | **break (yourself of), get out of, give up, kick** ◇ *a difficult ~ to break* ◇ *You must break yourself of the ~.* ◇ *I got out of the ~ of getting up early.* | **change** | **support** ◇ *He turned to crime to support his ~.*

HABIT + VERB **change** ◇ *The nation's eating ~s have changed significantly.*

PREP. **by ~** ◇ *Much of what we do in daily life is done by ~.* | **from ~** ◇ *I just did it from ~.* | **out of ~** ◇ *I sat in my old seat purely out of ~.*

PHRASES **a creature of ~** ◇ *Horses are creatures of ~ and like to have a daily routine.* | **force of ~** ◇ *Mr Norris woke up early from force of ~.* | **the ~ of a lifetime** ◇ *It's hard to change the ~ of a lifetime.* | **a hard ~ to break** ◇ *Caffeine can be a hard ~ to break.* | **old ~s die hard**

habitable adj.

VERBS **be** | **remain** | **make sth, render sth** ◇ *They've done their best to make the house ~.*

ADV. **barely** ◇ *The room was barely ~.*

habitat noun

ADJ. **native, natural** ◇ *her observations of wild chimps in their natural ~* | **suitable** ◇ *a decline in the amount of suitable ~* | **preferred** ◇ *The bird's preferred ~ is grassy prairie.* | **important** | **endangered, fragile, threatened** ◇ *Peat bogs are one of Europe's most threatened ~s.* | **coastal, forest, marine, wetland, wildlife, woodland** | **bear, tiger, etc.** ◇ *an agreement that preserved 2 500 acres of prime bear ~*

VERB + HABITAT **provide** ◇ *The forest provides a ~ for hundreds of species of plants and animals.* | **inhabit, occupy** ◇ *bird species that occupy forest ~s* | **conserve, preserve, protect** ◇ *new measures to protect wildlife ~s* | **restore** ◇ *One of our objectives is to restore ~s for native species.* | **damage, destroy, disrupt, threaten** ◇ *Development is destroying the animal's native ~.* | **lose** ◇ *These animals will lose their ~s by the flooding of the area.*

HABITAT + VERB **support sth** ◇ *The many different ~s support a wide variety of birds.* | **disappear** ◇ *Their preferred ~ is disappearing rapidly.*

HABITAT + NOUN **destruction, loss** ◇ *Many species are threatened in the wild due to ~ destruction by man.* | **restoration**

PREP. **in a/the ~** ◇ *the animals and plants in this woodland ~* | **for ~** ◇ *The moorland is an important ~ for many rare bird species.*

PHRASES **loss of ~** ◇ *The greatest danger to tigers now is through loss of ~.*

hack verb

ADV. **away, off** ◇ *They ~ed away at the dense vegetation.* ◇ *We ~ed off the dead branches.*

PREP. **at** ◇ *She ~ed at the hedge with the shears.*

PHRASES **~ sth to bits, ~ sth to pieces** ◇ *The body had been ~ed to pieces.* | **~ sb to death** ◇ *He was ~ed to death by the mob.* | **~ your way** ◇ *The explorers had to ~ their way through dense jungle.*

haemorrhage (*BrE*) (*AmE* hemorrhage) noun

ADJ. **massive, severe** | **fatal** | **recurrent** | **acute** ◇ *The patient died from acute cerebral ~.* | **brain, cerebral** | **internal**

VERB + HAEMORRHAGE/HEMORRHAGE **have, suffer** ◇ *Twelve hours later she suffered a massive brain ~.* | **die from, die of** | **stem, stop** (*both usually figurative*) ◇ *The newspaper sold its websites in a bid to stem the ~ of cash from the business.*

hail noun

HAIL + VERB **fall** ◇ *Hail fell shortly after lunch.* | **melt** ◇ *The ~ melted once the sun came out.*

HAIL + NOUN **stone** (usually *hailstone*) | **storm** (usually *hailstorm*)

PREP. **in (the) ~** ◇ *We got caught in the ~.* | **through (the) ~** ◇ *It was terrible driving through the ~.*

hair noun

ADJ. **auburn, black, blond, brown, chestnut, dark, fair, ginger** (*BrE*), **golden, grey/gray, grizzled, jet-black, light, raven** (*literary*), **red, sandy, silver, silvery, white, yellow** | **bushy, coarse, curly, fine, flyaway** (*esp. AmE*), **frizzy, kinky** (*AmE*), **nappy** (*AmE*), **shaggy, spiky, straight, thick, wavy, wiry, wispy** | **beautiful, glossy, shiny, silky, sleek** | **dishevelled/disheveled, dry, dull, fuzzy, greasy, matted, messy, scruffy, tangled, tousled, unkempt, unruly, untidy** (*esp. BrE*), **windswept** ◇ *a new shampoo for dull or dry ~* ◇ *His ~ was tousled and he looked as if he'd just woken up.* | **cropped, long, short, shoulder-length, waist-length** ◇ *She had shoulder-length black ~.* | **stray** ◇ *She pushed a stray ~ behind her ear.* | **thinning** | **body, chest, facial, pubic** | **cat, dog, etc.** ◇ *The rug was covered with cat ~s.*

... OF HAIR **lock, wisp**

VERB + HAIR **have** ◇ *She had beautiful auburn ~.* | **lose** ◇ *He had turned forty and was beginning to lose his ~.* | **wear** ◇ *She wore her long ~ loose on her shoulders.* | **arrange, do, fix, tidy** (*esp. BrE*) ◇ *I don't like the way she's arranged her ~, do you?* ◇ *I'll be down in a minute, I'm just doing my ~.* ◇ *She showered, fixed her ~, and applied make up.* | **braid** (*esp. AmE*), **plait** (*BrE*), **put up, tie back** ◇ *Why don't you put your ~ up for this evening?* | **brush, comb** | **shampoo, wash** | **cut, trim** ◇ *He went to the barber's to have his ~ cut.* | **blow-dry, dry** | **style** ◇ *They had styled my ~ by blowing it out straight.* | **curl, gel, perm, relax, straighten** ◇ *I've decided to have my ~ permed.* | **bleach, colour/color, dye** | **grow** ◇ *I'm trying to grow my ~.* | **shave** ◇ *His ~ was shaved close to his head.* | **mess up, muss** (*AmE*), **ruffle** | **smooth, stroke** ◇ *Kyle reached out to stroke her ~.* | **flick, toss** ◇ *She tossed her long ~ out of her eyes.*

HAIR + VERB **grow** ◇ *Why don't you let your ~ grow?* | **curl** ◇ *His ~ curls naturally.* | **fall, flow, hang, lie, tumble** ◇ *Her blond ~ fell over her eyes.* | **gleam, glint, glisten, shine**

HAIR + NOUN **loss** ◇ *how to cope with ~ loss* | **salon, stylist** | **colour/color** | **accessory** ◇ *Her only ~ accessory was a headband.* | **extension** ◇ *a stylist specializing in ~ extensions* | **removal** ◇ *waxing, and the other ~ removal methods available for men*

haircut _noun_

ADJ. **decent, good** | **bad** | **boyish** | **new** | **stylish, trendy** | **short** | **high and tight, military** | **spiky** | **mullet, pageboy, skinhead** (_esp. BrE_), etc.
VERB + HAIRCUT **get, have** ◇ _You ought to have a ~ before the interview._ | **need** ◇ _He was unshaven, and badly needed a ~._

half _noun_

ADJ. **first, second** | **last, latter** ◇ _in the latter ~ of the 19th century_ | **top, upper** | **bottom, lower** ◇ _the lower ~ of the window_ | **front** | **back, rear** ◇ _the rear ~ of the car_ | **left, right** ◇ _the left ~ of the brain_ | **northern, western, etc.** ◇ _the northern ~ of the country_ | **remaining** ◇ _Cut the remaining ~ into large chunks._
PREP. **by ~** ◇ _Costs rose by ~._ | **in ~** ◇ _We divided the money in ~._ | **in the…~** ◇ _He played well in the second ~._ | **~ of** ◇ _the first ~ of the concert_ ◇ _Over a ~ of all accidents happen in the home._
PHRASES **about ~, almost ~, around ~, at least ~, over ~** ◇ _Over ~ of all the people interviewed said they were disappointed in the government._ | **~ and ~** ◇ _We split the work ~ and ~._ | **one, two, three, etc. and a ~** ◇ _She's four and a ~ years old now._ | **sb's other ~** (= husband/wife/ partner) ◇ _You'll have to ask my other ~._

hall _noun_

1 inside the front entrance of a house/building → See also ENTRY
ADJ. **entrance, entry** | **front** ◇ _Her brother was standing in the front ~._ | **reception** | **narrow** | **dark, darkened** ◇ _He hurried them along the narrow, dark ~._
VERB + HALL **lead to** ◇ _The ~ led to a locked door._
PREP. **across the ~** ◇ _the room across the ~_ | **along the ~** | **at the end of the ~, to the end of the ~** | **down the ~** ◇ _There were strange noises coming from the room down the ~._ | **in the ~**

2 building/large room
ADJ. **cavernous, huge, spacious, vast** | **magnificent** | **empty** | **crowded, packed** | **main** ◇ _More than 200 members of the public packed the main ~ at the conference building._ | **grand, great** | **assembly, conference, convention, meeting** | **booking** (_BrE_), **ticket** (_esp. BrE_) | **banquet, banqueting** (_esp. BrE_), **dining** | **chow** (_AmE, informal_), **mess** ◇ _at dinner in the mess ~_ | **concert, dance, exhibit** (_AmE_), **exhibition, lecture, market, prayer, sports, wedding** (_AmE_) | **exam, examination** (_both esp. BrE_) | **church, city, communal, community, council, county** (_BrE_), **parish** (_esp. BrE_), **public, school, town, union, village** (_BrE_) | **study** (_AmE_) | **beer** | **bingo, pool, snooker** (_BrE_) | **residence** (_AmE_)
VERB + HALL **crowd, crowd into, fill, pack** ◇ _The strains of the national anthem filled the ~._
PREP. **in the ~, into the ~, through the ~** ◇ _His voice echoed through the ~._
PHRASES **~ of residence** (_BrE_) ◇ _Most first-year students live in the ~s of residence._

hallucination _noun_

ADJ. **mild** | **vivid** | **auditory, visual** | **drug-induced**
VERB + HALLUCINATION **experience, have, suffer** ◇ _For a moment I thought I was having ~s._ | **cause, induce**

hallway _noun_ → See also CORRIDOR

ADJ. **long** | **narrow, wide** | **crowded** ◇ _She walked through the crowded ~s to the locker room._ | **deserted, empty** | **dark, dimly lit** | **bright, brightly lit** | **carpeted** | **communal** (_BrE_) | **main** | **downstairs, upstairs** | **school** (_esp. AmE_)
VERB + HALLWAY **enter** | **fill, line** ◇ _Lockers lined the ~s._ | **roam, walk down, wander** ◇ _I walked down the ~, not knowing where I was heading._
HALLWAY + VERB **connect, lead to**

halt _noun_

ADJ. **abrupt, sudden** ◇ _The bus came to an abrupt ~ outside the school._ | **crashing, grinding, screeching, shuddering** ◇

The strike brought the capital city to a grinding ~. ◇ _The plan suddenly came to a screeching ~._ | **complete, dead** | **immediate** | **temporary** | **virtual**
VERB + HALT **come to, draw to, grind to, lurch to, screech to, shudder to, skid to, slide to** ◇ _The economy seems to be grinding to a ~._ ◇ _The car skidded to a ~ just inches from the river._ | **bring sth to, put** ◇ _Production was brought to a temporary ~ when power supplies failed._ ◇ _enough jobs to put a ~ to emigration_ | **call** ◇ _Scientists have decided to call a ~ to the tests._ | **call for, demand** | **order** ◇ _They have ordered a ~ to local elections._
PREP. **~ in** ◇ _a ~ in nuclear testing_ | **~ to** ◇ _The protesters are calling for a ~ to the export of live animals._

halt _verb_

ADV. **virtually** | **effectively** ◇ _The strike effectively ~ed production at the factory._ | **abruptly, immediately, suddenly** ◇ _All these ideas for expansion were abruptly ~ed by the outbreak of war._ | **briefly, temporarily** | **finally**
VERB + HALT **attempt to, try to** | **threaten to** | **fail to** ◇ _We are failing to ~ the destruction of the rainforest._
PHRASES **~ in your tracks** ◇ _A sudden shout made them ~ in their tracks and look around._ | **~ sth in its tracks** ◇ _The project has been ~ed in its tracks by this intervention._

halve _verb_

ADV. **more than** | **almost, nearly, virtually** | **approximately, roughly** | **effectively**
PREP. **in** ◇ _The shares have more than ~d in value since the summer high of 572p._ | **to** ◇ _Overall operating profits ~d to $24 million._

ham _noun_

ADJ. **lean** | **baked, boiled** (_esp. BrE_), **cooked, cured, smoked** | **country** (_AmE_), **honey-baked** (_AmE_), **honey-roast** (_BrE_), **Parma** | **canned** (_AmE_), **tinned** (_BrE_) | **cold** ◇ _cold ~ and salad_ | **sliced**
... OF HAM **piece, slice**
VERB + HAM **eat, have** | **bake, cook, roast** | **carve, slice**
HAM + NOUN **roll** (_esp. BrE_), **salad** (_esp. BrE_), **sandwich** | **hock** ◇ _Cut the meat from the ~ hock._
→ Special page at FOOD

hammer _noun_

VERB + HAMMER **hit sth with, tap sth with, use, wield** | **swing** ◇ _He swung it with all his strength._
HAMMER + NOUN **blow** (_often figurative_) ◇ _The decision is a ~ blow for the coal industry._
PHRASES **a ~ and chisel, a ~ and nails** | **~ and sickle** ◇ _the ~ and sickle of the Soviet flag_

hamper _verb_

ADV. **badly, greatly, seriously, severely** ◇ _Rescue efforts were severely ~ed by the bad weather._ | **further**

hand _noun_

1 part of the body
ADJ. **left, right** | **beautiful, delicate, long-fingered, pretty, slender** | **manicured, well-manicured** | **calloused/cal-lused, rough** | **soft** | **firm, strong** | **limp** ◇ _He offered a limp ~ to shake._ | **frail** | **arthritic** | **gnarled** | **clawed, claw-like** | **bony** ◇ _He holds out a bony ~ for her to shake._ | **hairy** | **cool** ◇ _His ~, when she shook it, was cool and firm._ | **clammy, sweaty** ◇ _He clutched the cane in his clammy ~._ | **dirty, filthy, greasy, grimy, grubby, sticky, unwashed** ◇ _He wiped his greasy ~s on the front of his overalls._ | **clean** | **gloved** | **open** ◇ _She gestured to the window with an open ~._ | **outstretched** ◇ _She walked up to him with her ~ outstretched to take his._ | **free** ◇ _With his free ~ he took hold of the knife._ | **cupped** ◇ _She rested her chin in her cupped ~._ | **busy, deft** ◇ _Her busy ~s had transformed the tiny room into a work of art._ | **willing** ◇ _There's plenty of work for willing ~s_ | **eager** ◇ _Eager ~s reached out to help him._ | **nervous, shaking, shaky,**

trembling, unsteady | steady ◇ *A surgeon needs a good eye and a steady ~.* | **comforting, friendly, gentle, sympathetic** ◇ *He put a friendly ~ on his friend's knee.* ◇ *He laid a gentle ~ on his brother's shoulder.* | **generous, liberal** (*both figurative*) ◇ *She filled our glasses with a generous ~.* | **capable, expert, guiding, practised/practiced, reassuring, skilful/skillful, skilled** ◇ *With a practised ~ he motioned a waiter to bring a fresh pot of coffee.* | **careless, clumsy | invisible** (*figurative*) ◇ *the invisible ~ of the market*

VERB + HAND **take** ◇ *She took the child's ~ and helped him climb the steps.* | **grab** ◇ *He grabbed my ~ and motioned for me to follow him.* | **reach for** ◇ *He reached for her ~ and held it tightly.* | **hold, hold on to** ◇ *They walked along, holding ~s.* ◇ *She held on to my ~ as I tried to leave.* | **clutch, grasp** ◇ *Hannah grasped her ~.* | **clutch sth in, clutch sth with, grasp sth in, grasp sth with, hold sth in** ◇ *He held the key in his ~.* ◇ *Beth grasped the rope with both ~s.* | **press, squeeze, touch** ◇ *She pressed his ~. 'I know,' she said softly.* | **shake** ◇ *He shook Blake's ~ as if they were long lost friends.* ◇ *He shook ~s with all of us before leaving.* | **feel** ◇ *I felt a ~ on my shoulder.* | **extend, hold out, put out, reach out** ◇ *She smiled and extended a ~ in welcome.* ◇ *He put out a ~ as if to touch her.* | **lay, place, press, put, rest** ◇ *He laid a ~ on her arm.* ◇ *She put her ~s to her cheeks in embarrassment.* ◇ *She rested her ~ on my shoulder.* | **slap** ◇ *Jimmy slapped his ~ over his mouth.* | **slide** ◇ *He slid his ~s into his pockets.* | **run** ◇ *Clive ran a ~ through his hair.* | **withdraw** ◇ *Slowly Ruth withdrew her ~ from his.* | **hold up, lift, put up** (*esp. BrE*) **raise, throw up** ◇ *He lifted his ~ to her face.* ◇ *Several students raised their ~s to answer the question.* ◇ *She held up her ~ in farewell.* ◇ *He threw up his ~s in despair when he saw the damage.* | **spread** ◇ *She shrugged and spread her ~s. 'That's all I can tell you.'* | **wave | clap** ◇ *We were all clapping our ~s in time to the music.* | **clasp, clench, wring** ◇ *He had his ~s clasped behind his head.* ◇ *She clenched her ~s in her lap to hide their trembling.* ◇ *He was sobbing and wringing his ~s by the grave.* | **beat** ◇ *He beat his ~s on the steering wheel in frustration.* | **cup** ◇ *I cupped my ~ over the mouthpiece of the phone so they couldn't hear me.* | **fold** ◇ *She folds her ~s in prayer.* | **rub** ◇ *She shivered, rubbing her ~s together fiercely.* | **wash | wipe**

HAND + VERB **shake, tremble** ◇ *Her ~ shook as she lifted the glass to her lips.* | **be outstretched, reach out, shoot out** ◇ *She stood up and went over to him, her ~s outstretched.* ◇ *A strong ~ reached out and caught hold of her arm.* | **grope for sth, reach for sth, seek sth** ◇ *My ~ groped for the door handle.* ◇ *His ~ sought hers.* | **find sth** ◇ *His ~ eventually found the light switch.* | **catch sth, clamp, clasp sth, grab sth, grasp sth, seize sth** ◇ *The policeman kept a firm ~ clamped on his shoulder.* | **clutch sth, grip sth, hold sth | clamp, clench, close around sth, close on sth** ◇ *A heavy ~ clamped over her mouth.* ◇ *My ~s clenched together tightly.* ◇ *A ~ closed around her wrist.* | **claw sth, claw at sth, pull sth, tug sth** ◇ *His ~s clawed at the muddy earth.* | **cup sth** ◇ *His ~s cupped her face.* | **push sth | squeeze sth, tighten sth | brush sth, brush across sth, brush against sth, caress sth, stroke sth, touch sth** ◇ *His ~ brushed against hers.* | **creep, go, move, slide, slip, steal, stray** ◇ *Muriel's ~ crept to her neck to hold her pearls.* | **fly** ◇ *Her ~ flew to her mouth. 'Oh no!'* | **jerk, twitch | run over sth, run through sth, trail** ◇ *Her ~ ran over the surface, feeling the different textures.* | **freeze, still** ◇ *His ~ froze in mid-gesture.* | **hover, roam** ◇ *My ~ hovered over the switch for a moment.* ◇ *His ~ roamed over her shoulders.* | **fumble** ◇ *My ~s fumbled with the key.* | **lie, rest** ◇ *His ~ rested on her shoulder.* | **go up, shoot up | come down, descend, drop** ◇ *A large ~ descended on his shoulder.* ◇ *His ~s dropped to his sides and he fell to the floor.* | **withdraw | lift, rise** ◇ *Her ~ lifted to place a cigarette in her mouth.* | **cover sth** ◇ *Her ~ moved to cover his.*

HAND + NOUN **gesture, movement, position, signal | dryer, towel | axe/ax, drill, saw** (*usually* **handsaw**) **| tools | pump | blender, mixer** ◇ *Purée with a ~ blender or food processor.* | **puppet | drum | mirror | baggage, luggage** (*both esp. BrE*) (**carry-on baggage** *in AmE*) ◇ *You can take your laptop on the plane as ~ luggage.* | **cream, lotion, sanitizer** (*AmE*),

soap | grenade, gun (*usually* **handgun**) **| injury | count, recount** (*both esp. AmE*) ◇ *a ~ recount of the vote for governor*

PREP. **by** ◇ *Delicate clothes should be washed by ~.* | **by… ~s** ◇ *The rocks looked like they had been shaped by human ~s.* | **in your ~** ◇ *She had a piece of paper in her ~.* ◇ *Can I leave these queries in your capable ~s?* (*figurative*) | **on your ~** ◇ *She had large rings on both ~s.* | **with your ~** ◇ *Operate the gears with your left ~.*

PHRASES **ball your ~s into fists | fall into the wrong ~s** (*figurative*) ◇ *Guards made sure that the food supplies didn't fall into the wrong ~s.* | **get your ~s off sb/sth, keep your ~s off sb/sth, take your ~s off sb/sth** ◇ *She warned her brother to keep his ~s off her bag.* | **get your ~s on sth, lay your ~s on sth** ◇ *I desperately need to lay my ~s on some money by Monday.* | **~ in ~** ◇ *They walked ~ in ~ along the path.* | **~s on hips** ◇ *She stood in the doorway, ~s on hips.* | **head in your ~s** ◇ *He sat with his head in his ~s.* | **in safe ~s** (*figurative*) ◇ *He retired feeling confident that his company was in safe ~s.* | **a safe pair of ~s** (*figurative*) ◇ *She gained a reputation as a safe pair of ~s.* | **a show of ~s** ◇ *She asked for a show of ~s* (= asked people to vote). | **on (your) ~s and knees** ◇ *He was on his ~s and knees, looking for a contact lens.* | **out of sb's ~s** (*figurative*) ◇ *I don't work in that department any more, so the problem is out of my ~s.* | **the palm of your ~** ◇ *She studied the object in the palm of her ~.* | **with your bare ~s** ◇ *He killed the lion with his bare ~s.*

2 a hand help

VERB + A HAND **give sb, lend (sb)** ◇ *Can you give me a ~ with loading the van?* ◇ *At harvest time all the locals lend a ~.* | **need** ◇ *Do you need a ~ with those invoices?* | **want** ◇ *Do you want a ~ with that?*

3 role in a situation

VERB + HAND **have | strengthen** ◇ *The strategic alliance served to strengthen the country's ~ in the region.*

PREP. **~ in** ◇ *Several of his colleagues had a ~ in his downfall.*

4 in card games

ADJ. **bad, good**

VERB + HAND **deal (sb)** ◇ *Who dealt the last ~?* ◇ *She felt that life had dealt her a bad ~.* (*figurative*) | **get, have | play | overplay** (*usually figurative*) ◇ *The party leadership overplayed its ~.* | **reveal, show** (*usually figurative*) ◇ *Now the EU has revealed its ~.*

hand verb

ADV. **effectively, practically | formally, officially** ◇ *formally ~ing over power to the new government* | **personally** ◇ *She wanted to ~ the petition to the president personally.* | **just, merely, simply** ◇ *They would simply ~ her over to the magistrate as a thief.* | **quickly | immediately, promptly | grudgingly, reluctantly** ◇ *He grudgingly ~ed me the money.* | **carefully, gently** ◇ *Keith gently ~ed me the little baby girl.* | **silently, wordlessly | back, down, in, out, over** ◇ *She ~ed out the exam papers.*

VERB + HAND **agree to, be happy to, be prepared to, be ready to, be willing to | be reluctant to, refuse to | force sb to | get ready to, prepare to** ◇ *The court is getting ready to ~ down a potentially historic decision.*

PREP. **to** ◇ *He ~ed the book to Sally.*

handbag noun → See also PURSE

ADJ. **big, capacious** (*formal*), **large | designer**

VERB + HANDBAG **clutch, hold | carry | swing | reach into | fumble in, rummage around in, rummage in** ◇ *She was rummaging in her ~ for her keys.* | **search, search in, search through** ◇ *She was rummaging in her ~ for her keys.* | **snatch** ◇ *She had her ~ snatched as she sat having a coffee.*

PREP. **from a/the ~, out of a/the ~** ◇ *She took a pen out of her large leather ~.* | **in a/the ~, into a/the ~** ◇ *She put her wallet into her ~.*

PHRASES **the contents of a ~**

handcuffs *noun*

... OF HANDCUFFS **pair, set** ◇ *The policeman slipped a pair of ~ on his wrists.*
VERB + HANDCUFFS **have on, wear** | **put on, slip on** ◇ *The other policeman put the ~ on him.* | **remove, take off, undo, unfasten, unlock**
PREP. **in ~** ◇ *He was taken away in ~.*

handful *noun*

1 amount that can be held in one hand

ADJ. **good** | **double** ◇ *She bent and pulled up a double ~ of weeds.*
PREP. **~ of** ◇ *She grabbed ~s of the dirty snow.*

2 small number of people/things

ADJ. **small, tiny** | **mere** ◇ *Having to cope with a mere ~ of staff was too much for her.* | **good, large** ◇ *She has a good ~ of Hollywood roles under her belt.*
PREP. **~ of** ◇ *Only a ~ of people know the true situation.*
PHRASES **just a ~ of sth, only a ~ of sth** ◇ *We have received only a small ~ of letters on this subject.*

handicap *noun*

1 physical/mental disability

ADJ. **serious, severe** | **mild** | **mental, physical, visual** ◇ *She can't drive because of her visual ~.*
VERB + HANDICAP **be born with, have, suffer, suffer from** ◇ *Over a million people in this country suffer from mental ~.* | **cause** | **cope with, overcome** ◇ *She has managed to overcome her physical ~s.*
PREP. **despite a/the ~** ◇ *Despite her ~, Jane is able to hold down a full-time job.*

2 disadvantage

ADJ. **big, considerable** (*esp. BrE*), **great, major, real, serious, severe** ◇ *Lack of books was a major ~.*
VERB + HANDICAP **have, suffer** ◇ *If you don't speak the language, you'll have a real ~.* | **prove** ◇ *His lack of height can prove a ~ against tall players.*
PREP. **despite a/the ~** | **~ to** ◇ *This could be a serious ~ to her education.*

handicapped *adj.*

VERBS **be, be born** ◇ *Steven was born severely ~.* | **leave sb** ◇ *An accident at birth left him badly ~.*
ADV. **badly, seriously, severely** | **mildly, slightly** | **permanently** | **mentally, physically, visually** ◇ *special equipment for visually ~ children*

handkerchief *noun*

ADJ. **clean** | **crumpled, dirty** | **pocket** | **lace, linen, paper, silk** | **embroidered**
VERB + HANDKERCHIEF **blow your nose on, use** ◇ *He blew his nose on a dirty ~.* | **wave**

handle *noun*

ADJ. **long, short** | **carrying** ◇ *The table folds up and comes complete with a carrying ~.* | **door** | **broom, fork, knife, pickaxe/pickax, etc.** | **brass, metal, wooden, etc.**
VERB + HANDLE **have** | **pull, push, try, turn** ◇ *You have to turn the ~ and then pull it.* ◇ *He tried the ~ but the door was locked.* | **grasp, grip**
PREP. **on a/the ~** ◇ *His initials were on the knife ~.*

handle *verb*

1 touch sth with your hands

ADV. **carefully, with care** ◇ *A label on the crate read: 'Handle with care'.* | **carelessly** ◇ *Gardening tools can be hazardous if carelessly ~d.* | **roughly** ◇ *Many of the prisoners were roughly ~d; some were killed.*

2 deal with sb/sth

ADV. **competently, efficiently, properly, skilfully/skillfully, successfully, well** ◇ *I think you ~d that situation very well.* | **badly** | **carefully, delicately** ◇ *This issue may need to be ~d*

carefully. | **easily** ◇ *Her next question was not so easily ~d.* | **routinely** ◇ *The library routinely ~s a wide variety of queries.*
VERB + HANDLE **be able to, be unable to, can, know how to** ◇ *This was a problem that I just couldn't ~.* ◇ *She knew how to ~ publicity.* | **be designed to, be equipped to** ◇ *He wasn't mentally equipped to ~ this situation.* | **learn how to** | **be easy to** | **be difficult to, be hard to** ◇ *Large meetings are more difficult to ~.*
PREP. **with** ◇ *She ~d the crisis with total assurance.*

handling *noun*

ADJ. **careful, delicate, gentle** ◇ *Timid children need gentle ~ to build up their confidence.* | **careless, clumsy, rough** | **sensitive, sympathetic** ◇ *Issues such as drug addiction require sensitive ~ on TV.* | **insensitive** | **competent** ◇ *She was praised for her competent ~ of the crisis.* | **baggage, cargo, freight** | **food** ◇ *hygienic food-handling practice* | **data, information**
VERB + HANDLING **need, require** | **improve**
PHRASES **shipping and ~** ◇ *The cost is $11 plus $5 for shipping and ~.*

handout *noun*

1 food/money given to people who need it badly

ADJ. **free** | **government, state** (*esp. BrE*) | **cash**
VERB + HANDOUT **give (sb)** | **get, receive** ◇ *All those eligible will receive a cash ~.*
PREP. **~ from** ◇ *a ~ from the government* | **~ to** ◇ *state ~s to the poor*

2 sheet/leaflet

VERB + HANDOUT **distribute, give sb, give out** (*esp. BrE*)
PREP. **in a/the ~** ◇ *More information can be found in the ~.* | **~ on** ◇ *We were given a ~ on job hunting.*

handshake *noun*

ADJ. **firm, hearty** (*esp. AmE*) | **limp** ◇ *She wasn't impressed by his limp ~.* | **secret** | **golden** (= money given to sb when they leave their job) ◇ *He received a $150 000 golden ~ when he lost his job.*
VERB + HANDSHAKE **have** ◇ *He had a firm ~.* | **give sb** ◇ *Fawcett gave me a hearty ~.*
PREP. **with a ~** ◇ *They sealed the agreement with a ~.* | **~ from** ◇ *a ~ from the chairman*

handsome *adj.*

VERBS **be, look** | **become, grow**
ADV. **extremely, fairly, very, etc.** | **devastatingly, exceedingly, extraordinarily, incredibly, strikingly** ◇ *He was young and devastatingly ~.* | **almost** | **classically, darkly, ruggedly** ◇ *his ruggedly ~ features*
PHRASES **tall, dark (and) ~** ◇ *a tall, dark, ~ stranger*

handwriting *noun*

ADJ. **clear, good, legible, neat** ◇ *Her ~ was neat and legible.* | **bad** (*esp. AmE*), **illegible, messy** (*esp. AmE*), **poor** (*esp. BrE*), **sloppy** (*esp. AmE*), **terrible** ◇ *Why do doctors have such terrible ~?* | **spidery**
VERB + HANDWRITING **have** | **read** ◇ *Her ~ is very difficult to read.* | **recognize** ◇ *I didn't recognize the ~ on the envelope.*
PREP. **in your ~** ◇ *She copied out the lines in her best ~.*

handy *adj.* (*informal*)

1 useful

VERBS **be** | **come in** ◇ *I advise you to buy one—it may come in ~ one day.*
ADV. **extremely, really, very** | **quite**
PREP. **for** ◇ *The arrangement was ~ for both of us.*

2 nearby

VERBS **be** | **have sth** | **keep sth** ◇ *Always keep a cloth ~ to wipe up any mess.*
ADV. **quite, very** (*both BrE*)

PREP. **for** (*BrE*) ◇ *My new house is very ~ for the station.*

3 good at using sth

VERBS **be**

ADV. **extremely, fairly, very, etc.**

PREP. **at** ◇ *'I'm pretty ~ at giving out advice,' claimed Mark.* | **with** ◇ *Lucy is very ~ with a drill.*

hang *verb*

ADV. **limply, loosely** ◇ *He had lost weight and the suit hung loosely on him.* | **uselessly** ◇ *Her injured arm hung uselessly at her side.* | **upside down** ◇ *The sloth spends most of its time ~ing upside down from the branches.* | **down** ◇ *Large leaves hung down from the branches of the trees.*

PREP. **by** ◇ *The monkey was ~ing by its tail from the beams overhead.* | **from** ◇ *Banners hung from every window.*

PHR V hang on

1 keep hold of sth

ADV. **tight** ◇ *Hang on tight—we're off.*

VERB + HANG ON **try to**

PREP. **for** ◇ *She hung on for dear life.* | **to** ◇ *Hang on to (= keep) those old photographs—they may be valuable.* | **with** ◇ *Martin tried to ~ on with one hand.*

2 wait

ADV. **a minute, a second** ◇ *Hang on a minute—I'll just see if he's here.*

hanker *verb*

ADV. **secretly** | **always** | **still**

PREP. **after** ◇ *She's always ~ing after excitement.* | **for** ◇ *I still ~ed for the farm life.*

haphazard *adj.*

VERBS **be, seem** | **become**

ADV. **extremely, fairly, very, etc.** | **apparently, seemingly**

PHRASES **in a ~ fashion, in a ~ manner, in a ~ way** ◇ *The town had grown in a somewhat ~ way.*

happen *verb*

ADV. **actually, really** ◇ *She couldn't quite believe that all this was actually ~ing to her.* | **just** ◇ *I don't remember learning to swim, it just ~ed.* | **never** | **spontaneously** ◇ *Sometimes fun activities just ~ spontaneously; at other times they take careful planning.* | **overnight, quickly** ◇ *Change doesn't ~ overnight.* | **again**

VERB + HAPPEN **be going to** ◇ *They could only wait and see what was going to ~.* | **be likely to** | **be bound to** ◇ *Mistakes are bound to ~ sometimes.* | **tend to** ◇ *What tends to ~ is that students spend the first week of the course in a blind panic, but settle down by the second or third week.* | **want sth to** | **make sth** ◇ *You have to make things ~ if you want them to happen.* | **let sth** ◇ *Don't just sit back and let it ~.*

PREP. **to** ◇ *She didn't know what was ~ing to her.*

happiness *noun*

ADJ. **deep** (*esp. AmE*), **great** | **perfect, pure, sheer, true** | **eternal, lasting** | **future** ◇ *Living together before you marry is no guarantee of future ~.* | **earthly** | **human** | **personal** | **domestic, family, marital**

VERB + HAPPINESS **be filled with, feel** | **glow with** ◇ *Her face was glowing with ~.* | **cry with, sigh with** | **achieve, find** ◇ *She seems to have found ~ with her new husband.* | **bring (sb)** ◇ *It is easy to believe that money brings ~.* | **buy (sb)** ◇ *You cannot buy ~.* | **wish sb**

PREP. **with ~** | **~ at** ◇ *He was weeping with ~ at being free.*

PHRASES **a feeling of ~** | **wish sb every ~** ◇ *We wish them every ~ in their new life.*

happy *adj.*

1 feeling pleasure

VERBS **appear, be, feel, look, seem, sound** ◇ *Outwardly the couple appeared ~.* ◇ *Andrew felt happier than he had been*

for a long time. | **become** | **make sb** ◇ *Money won't make you ~.* | **keep sb** ◇ *He went home from time to time, to keep his mother ~.* | **die** ◇ *I can die ~ knowing that I have achieved this.*

ADV. **extremely, fairly, very, etc.** | **only too, particularly** ◇ *We'd be only too ~ to accept your invitation.* | **completely, perfectly** ◇ *Dad seemed perfectly ~ with my explanation.* | **genuinely, truly** ◇ *For the first time in her life, she felt truly ~.* | **far from, not altogether, not at all, not entirely, not exactly, not particularly, not too, not totally** ◇ *Her boss was not entirely ~ about the situation.* | **relatively** | **just** ◇ *I'm just ~ to be back home.* | **amazingly, blissfully, deliriously, ecstatically, ridiculously, strangely, surprisingly** | **clearly, obviously**

PREP. **about** ◇ *I'm not too ~ about her attitude.* | **for** ◇ *So you're getting married, I hear. I'm really ~ for you!* | **with** ◇ *I was quite ~ with the way things went.*

2 giving pleasure

VERBS **be, seem**

ADV. **extremely, fairly, very, etc.** | **gloriously** (*esp. BrE*), **particularly, wonderfully** ◇ *It had been a wonderfully ~ time.* | **quite**

harassment *noun*

ADJ. **racial, sexual** | **police** | **constant, continual**

VERB + HARASSMENT **be subject to, be subjected to, suffer** ◇ *She had been subjected to continual sexual ~.*

PREP. **~ by** ◇ *They are complaining about ~ by the police*

PHRASES **a victim of ~**

→ Note at CRIME (for more verbs)

harbour (*BrE*) (*AmE* harbor) *noun*

ADJ. **deep, deep-water** | **good, safe, sheltered** | **natural** | **busy** | **picturesque, pretty** | **fishing**

VERB + HARBOUR/HARBOR **have** ◇ *The town has a small natural ~.* | **come into, enter, go into** ◇ *They entered the ~ with flags flying.* | **go out of, leave**

HARBOUR/HARBOR + NOUN **defences/defenses, wall** | **town** | **area** | **entrance, mouth** (*BrE*) | **authority** (*BrE*), **master**

PREP. **in (a/the) ~** ◇ *The fishing fleet is in ~.* ◇ *the activity in the ~* | **into (a/the) ~** ◇ *The damaged vessel was towed into ~.* | **out of a/the ~** ◇ *We sailed out of the ~ at daybreak.*

PHRASES **the entrance to a ~, the mouth of a ~**

hard *adj.*

1 solid/stiff

VERBS **be, feel, look, seem** ◇ *The chairs felt ~ and uncomfortable.* | **become, go** ◇ *Don't leave the cake uncovered or the icing will go ~.* | **stay**

ADV. **extremely, fairly, very, etc.** | **a little, slightly, etc.**

PHRASES **rock ~** ◇ *The toffee was rock ~.*

2 difficult

VERBS **be, look, seem** | **become, get** ◇ *Life got very ~.* | **make sth** ◇ *If you tell the children the answers, it only makes it harder for them to do the work on their own.* | **find sth** ◇ *I found the exam quite ~.*

ADV. **extremely, fairly, very, etc.** | **a little, slightly, etc.**

hardback (*also* hardcover *esp. in AmE*) *noun*

VERB + HARDBACK/HARDCOVER **publish** | **come out in** ◇ *His second book came out in ~ last month.*

HARDBACK/HARDCOVER + NOUN **book, edition**

PREP. **in ~** ◇ *It's only available in ~.*

hardship *noun*

ADJ. **appalling** (*BrE*), **considerable, extreme, genuine** (*esp. BrE*), **great, real, severe** | **undue, unnecessary** (*esp. BrE*) | **economic, financial, material** (*esp. AmE*), **personal, physical**

VERB + HARDSHIP **cause** | **impose** | **bear, endure, experience, face, suffer, survive** ◇ *a close community which makes these ~s easier to bear* ◇ *Students may suffer severe financial ~ as a result of the government's decision.* ◇ *They have already survived considerable ~.*

HARDSHIP + NOUN **fund** (*BrE*) | **payment** (*BrE*) ◇ *The union made ~ payments to some of the sacked workers.*
PREP. **in ~** ◇ *They are living in genuine ~.* | **without ~** ◇ *They could improve our conditions without undue ~ for themselves.* | **~ among** ◇ *widespread ~ among students* | **~ to** ◇ *The cold was no real ~ to me.*
PHRASES **times of ~** ◇ *In times of economic ~, companies cut back on training.*

hardware *noun*

ADJ. **computer** | **military** ◇ *companies selling military ~* | **new**
... OF HARDWARE **piece** ◇ *The laptop drawing tablet is a very useful piece of ~.*
VERB + HARDWARE **design, develop** | **provide, supply** ◇ *We supply computer ~ to businesses.* | **use**
HARDWARE + NOUN **component, device, product** | **environment, platform, system** ◇ *This application runs on a wide variety of ~ platforms.* | **configuration** | **design, development** | **company, maker, manufacturer, supplier, vendor**
→ Special page at COMPUTER

harm *noun*

ADJ. **considerable, great, serious, untold** (*esp. BrE*) ◇ *He was clearly intent on inflicting serious ~ on someone.* | **irreparable, lasting, permanent** | **emotional, mental, physical, psychological** ◇ *elderly people in danger of physical or emotional ~* | **economic, environmental**
VERB + HARM **cause, do, inflict** ◇ *The huge fall in exports has done a great deal of ~ to the economy.* | **mean (sb), wish sb** ◇ *I'm sorry if I upset you—I didn't mean any ~.* ◇ *No one wishes you ~.* | **come to, suffer** ◇ *I don't think he'll come to any ~ if his mother is with him.* | **keep sb from, prevent, protect sb from, shield sb from** ◇ *The children were removed from their parents to prevent ~ to them.* ◇ *She tried to shield her child from ~.*
HARM + VERB **come to sb/sth** ◇ *I don't want any ~ to come to these pictures.*
PREP. **~ from** ◇ *babies at risk of serious ~ from their parents* | **~ to** ◇ *the ~ done to the environment*
PHRASES **more ~ than good** ◇ *The drugs he was prescribed did him more ~ than good.* | **out of harm's way** ◇ *The younger children were kept out of harm's way.*

harm *verb*

ADV. **seriously** ◇ *Misusing drugs in pregnancy can seriously ~ your baby.* | **deliberately** | **physically**
VERB + HARM **intend to, want to** ◇ *He claimed that he had not intended to ~ the girl.* | **try to**

harmful *adj.*

VERBS **be, prove** ◇ *The spraying could prove ~ to humans.* | **become** | **consider sth** ◇ *She actually considered fresh air ~.*
ADV. **extremely, very** | **particularly, positively** ◇ *These products are often positively ~.* | **quite** | **possibly, potentially** ◇ *A lot of these chemicals are potentially very ~.* | **(not) necessarily** ◇ *Not all virus infections are necessarily ~ to vines.* | **intrinsically** | **environmentally, socially** ◇ *These pesticides are environmentally ~.*
PREP. **to** ◇ *pesticides that are ~ to the environment*

harmless *adj.*

VERBS **appear, be, look, seem, sound** | **make sth, render sth** ◇ *chemical wastes which have to be rendered ~* | **consider sth**
ADV. **absolutely, completely, perfectly, quite, totally** | **almost, virtually** | **enough** ◇ *He looks ~ enough.* | **comparatively, fairly, mostly, pretty, reasonably, relatively** | **apparently, seemingly** ◇ *a small and seemingly ~ creature* | **environmentally**
PREP. **to** ◇ *The substance is ~ to people.*

harmony *noun*

1 state of agreement

ADJ. **complete, perfect** | **relative** ◇ *They've lived together in reasonable ~ for many years.* | **domestic, political, racial, social** ◇ *On the surface their life was a model of domestic ~.*
VERB + HARMONY **achieve** | **bring, create** | **maintain, preserve** ◇ *They try to maintain ~ between the two communities.* | **restore** | **foster, promote** ◇ *The Church tries to promote racial ~.* | **live in**
PREP. **in ~** ◇ *They work together in ~.* | **~ between** ◇ *They try to foster ~ between different groups of people.* | **~ with** ◇ *people living in perfect ~ with nature*
PHRASES **a sense of ~** ◇ *A new sense of ~ developed in the community.*

2 pleasant combination of different musical notes

ADJ. **musical** | **vocal** | **beautiful** | **five-part, four-part, etc.** ◇ *an arrangement with four-part ~*
PREP. **in ~** ◇ *to sing in ~*

harness *noun*

1 for a horse

ADJ. **leather**
VERB + HARNESS **put on** | **remove, take off**
PREP. **in (a) ~** ◇ *a horse in ~*

2 for a person

ADJ. **child** | **safety** | **climbing, parachute** | **shoulder** | **four-point, five-point, etc.**
VERB + HARNESS **have on, wear** | **do up, fasten** ◇ *She fastened the safety ~ tightly around her waist before starting the descent.* | **undo, unfasten**
PREP. **in a/the ~** ◇ *Another man in a ~ was being lowered from the helicopter.*

harness *verb*

ADV. **effectively, successfully** | **fully**
VERB + HARNESS **attempt to, seek to, try to** ◇ *They are attempting to ~ the power of the sun.* | **manage to**
PREP. **for** ◇ *How can this energy be ~ed effectively for the good of humankind?*

harp *verb*

PHR V **harp on**
ADV. **always, constantly** ◇ *He is always ~ing on about the war.* | **still**
PREP. **about**
PHRASES **keep ~ing on** ◇ *Don't keep ~ing on about my age!*

harsh *adj.*

VERBS **appear, be, prove, seem, sound** ◇ *It may seem ~ to criticize him after his death.* | **become**
ADV. **extremely, fairly, very, etc.** | **exceptionally, particularly** | **increasingly** | **a little, slightly, etc.** | **overly, unduly, unnecessarily** ◇ *He accused her of being unduly ~.* | **surprisingly**

harvest *noun*

ADJ. **abundant** (*esp. AmE*), **bountiful, bumper, good, large, rich** ◇ *We've had a bumper ~ of apples this year.* ◇ *She returned from the conference with a rich ~ of knowledge.* (*figurative*) | **bad, disastrous, poor** ◇ *a series of poor ~s in the 1830s* | **cereal, corn, grain, potato, wheat, etc.** | **final**
VERB + HARVEST **bring in, gather, gather in, get in, reap** ◇ *They were busy getting the ~ in.* ◇ *We are now reaping the ~ of our hard work last year.* (*figurative*)
HARVEST + VERB **fail** ◇ *The strawberry ~ failed because of the drought.*
HARVEST + NOUN **season** (*esp. AmE*), **time** | **festival**
PREP. **after (the) ~** ◇ *Potatoes are normally sprayed after ~.* | **during ~, during the ~** ◇ *Potatoes often sustain damage during ~.* ◇ *During the ~ they work from dawn to dusk.* | **~ of** ◇ *a good ~ of potatoes*

hassle *noun*

ADJ. **legal** ◇ *They faced interminable legal ~s if they wanted to claim compensation.*
VERB + HASSLE **get, have** ◇ *I started to get all this ~ from my boss about increasing productivity.* | **give sb** ◇ *He gave me so*

much ~ I decided it wasn't worth it. | **eliminate** (esp. AmE), **save** ◊ It saves a lot of ~ if you buy them on the Internet. | **be worth** ◊ Camping isn't really worth all the ~. | **not want** ◊ I don't want the ~ of opening a new bank account.
PREP. **with no ~, without ~** ◊ She got the computer set up with no ~ at all. | **~ about, ~ over** ◊ I've had so much ~ over this business.
PHRASES **take the ~ out of sth** ◊ Package tours take all the ~ out of travel arrangements.

haste noun

ADJ. **great** ◊ She worked with great ~. | **indecent** (esp. BrE), **undue, unseemly** (esp. BrE) ◊ He accused the government of undue ~ in bringing in the new law.
VERB + HASTE **make** ◊ I had to make ~ if I wasn't to be late.
PREP. **in ~, in your ~** ◊ They obviously left in great ~. ◊ In his ~ to get home, he forgot to go to the library. | **with ~** ◊ He married again with almost indecent ~. | **without ~** ◊ They approached without ~.
PHRASES **with all ~** (esp. BrE) ◊ The ships were ordered to sea with all ~.

hat noun

ADJ. **broad-brimmed, wide-brimmed** | **floppy** | **battered** | **pointed** | **tall** | **fur, straw, wool** (esp. AmE), **woollen/woolen, woolly/wooly** (esp. BrE) | **baseball, bobble** (BrE), **bowler, cocked, cowboy, hard, panama, party, peaked, riding, sun, ten-gallon, three-cornered, top, trucker** (esp. AmE) | **silly, stupid**
VERB + HAT **don, place** ◊ He placed a battered felt ~ on his head. | **doff, remove** | **raise, tip, touch** ◊ The doorman tipped his ~ as we entered. | **pull down** ◊ He pulled his ~ down over his face.
HAT + VERB **be trimmed with sth** ◊ The governor wore a cocked ~ trimmed with white feathers.
HAT + NOUN **box** (usually **hatbox**) | **shop, store** (AmE) | **stand** (usually **hatstand**) | **band, pin** (usually **hatband, hatpin**) → Special page at CLOTHES

hatch noun

ADJ. **closed, open** ◊ Leave the ~ open. | **access, escape** | **serving** (esp. BrE) ◊ She opened the serving ~ and put the soup on the counter. | **kitchen, loft** (both BrE)
VERB + HATCH **lift, open, raise** ◊ She lifted the ~ and slid it away from the opening. | **batten down, close, shut** ◊ They battened down the ~es and prepared for the storm. ◊ He ordered the ~es to be closed.
PREP. **through a/the ~** ◊ They got out through the escape ~. | **~ between** ◊ a ~ between the kitchen and the dining room | **~ to** ◊ a ~ to the dining room

hate noun

1 strong feeling of dislike

ADJ. **absolute, pure** ◊ In her eyes he could see naked ~.
VERB + HATE **be filled with, be full of, burn with** ◊ He burned with ~ for everyone and everything.
HATE + NOUN **campaign, figure** (esp. BrE), **mail** ◊ victim of a vicious ~ campaign ◊ She became a ~ figure for politicians on the left. | **crime, speech**
PREP. **~ for** ◊ full of ~ for the people who had betrayed her

2 sb/sth you hate

ADJ. **pet** (BrE) ◊ Jazz has always been a pet ~ of mine.

hate verb

ADV. **particularly, really** | **absolutely** ◊ I absolutely ~ cooking. | **almost** ◊ For a moment she almost ~d him. | **just** ◊ Don't you just ~ people who are always right? | **always** ◊ I always ~d school. | **still**
VERB + HATE **begin to, come to, grow to** ◊ He came to ~ the town, with its narrow prejudices. | **love to** ◊ the media baron all the liberals love to ~
PREP. **for** ◊ He ~d me for standing up to him.

~ it when ◊ I ~ it when you lose your temper like that. | **~ to say, see, think, etc.** ◊ I'd ~ to say how many hours I've spent trying to fix my computer.

hatred noun

ADJ. **bitter, deep, intense, passionate, pure, violent** ◊ She shot him a look of pure ~. | **absolute, implacable** | **blind, irrational** | **class, ethnic, race, racial, religious** | **mutual**
VERB + HATRED **be filled with, be full of, feel, have** ◊ She was full of ~ and bitterness. ◊ He has a deep ~ of the police. | **incite, preach, stir up** ◊ He is accused of stirring up racial ~. | **breed, fuel** ◊ Ignorance can breed ~. | **express**
HATRED + VERB **flare** (esp. AmE) ◊ Hatred flared inside her.
PREP. **in ~, with ~** ◊ She stared at it in ~. | **~ against** ◊ They were blamed for inciting ~ against religious minorities. | **~ between** ◊ the intense ~ between the two communities | **~ for** ◊ I felt no ~ for him. | **~ of** ◊ his ~ of women | **~ towards/toward** ◊ their ~ towards/toward the oppressors
PHRASES **a feeling of ~**

haul noun

1 act of hauling

VERB + HAUL **give sth**
PREP. **~ on** ◊ When I shout, give a ~ on the rope.

2 distance

ADJ. **long, short** ◊ the long ~ back to Cape Town ◊ a short-haul passenger plane | **final, last** ◊ the final ~ up the hill to the finishing line
PREP. **~ from, ~ to**

3 (esp. BrE) of fish, stolen goods, etc.

ADJ. **big, large, record** ◊ The thieves got away with a record ~ of £25 million. | **drugs**
VERB + HAUL **get, get away with** ◊ The gang did not expect to get such a large ~.
HAUL + VERB **be worth sth** ◊ a ~ worth £30 000
PREP. **~ of** ◊ the biggest ever ~ of illegal drugs

haunt noun

ADJ. **favourite/favorite, old, popular** (esp. BrE), **regular, usual** | **tourist** (esp. BrE) ◊ The area was a popular tourist ~.
VERB + HAUNT **go back to, return to, revisit** (all esp. BrE) ◊ We've been back to some of our old ~s.

haunt verb

1 appear as a ghost in a place

ADV. **reputedly** (esp. BrE), **supposedly** ◊ a castle which is reputedly ~ed
VERB + HAUNT **come back to, return to** ◊ He said he would come back to ~ her. ◊ That decision came back to ~ him in later life. (figurative)

2 be always in your mind

ADV. **still** ◊ the great fear that still ~s her | **forever** ◊ He will be ~ed forever by his failed attempt to rescue the children.
VERB + HAUNT **continue to** ◊ These visions continued to ~ her for many years.

haven noun

ADJ. **safe** ◊ The aim is to create a safe ~ for the thousands of refugees. | **tax** | **wildlife**
VERB + HAVEN **create, offer (sb), provide (sb with)** | **become** | **find**
PREP. **in a/the ~** ◊ They were living in a safe ~ away from the fighting. | **~ for** ◊ The woods are a ~ for wildlife. | **~ of** ◊ This house is a ~ of peace compared with ours.

havoc noun

VERB + HAVOC **cause, create, play, wreak**
PREP. **~ among** ◊ The new tax could wreak ~ among smaller companies. | **~ for** ◊ High winds have been creating ~ for farmers. | **~ in** ◊ The disease can cause ~ in commercial orchards. | **~ on** ◊ The flood wrought ~ on the countryside. | **~ to** ◊ The storm caused ~ to wildlife. | **~ with** ◊ The fog played ~ with flight schedules.

hawk *noun*

HAWK + VERB **hover** | **swoop, swoop down** ◊ *The ~ swooped low over the field.*

PHRASES **watch (sb) like a ~** ◊ *He waited, watching his prisoner like a ~.*

hay *noun*

... OF HAY **bale**

VERB + HAY **cut, harvest, make** ◊ *The freshly harvested ~ was taken into the hayloft.* ◊ *They make ~ to feed the cattle in winter.*

HAY + NOUN **field** (*esp. AmE*), **meadow** (*esp. BrE*) | **bale** | **barn, loft** (usually *hayloft*) | **rick** (*esp. BrE*), **stack** (usually *hayrick, haystack*) | **ride** (usually *hayride*) (= a ride in a tractor) (*AmE*)

PREP. **in the ~** ◊ *The children were playing in the ~.*

hazard *noun*

ADJ. **big, great, major, real, serious** | **constant** | **possible, potential** | **hidden, unexpected, unseen** | **environmental, industrial, natural, occupational** ◊ *industrial ~s such as excessive noise and pollution* ◊ *Loneliness is one of the occupational ~s of being a writer.* | **health** ◊ *Other people's smoke is now seen as a health ~.* | **fire** ◊ *Those piles of newspapers are a serious fire ~.*

VERB + HAZARD **cause, create, pose, present** ◊ *Production of these chemicals poses serious environmental ~s.* | **be exposed to, encounter, face** ◊ *The worst ~ we faced was having our money stolen.* | **avoid** ◊ *Go in September if you want to avoid the ~ of extreme heat.* | **eliminate, minimize** | **cope with, deal with, negotiate** (*esp. BrE*) ◊ *Companies should have systems for dealing with work ~s.*

PREP. **~ for** ◊ *Stairs are a ~ for young children.* | **~ to** ◊ *The burning of industrial waste is a major ~ to human health.*

PHRASES **exposure to a ~** ◊ *Try and reduce your exposure to ~s such as poor quality air.*

hazardous *adj.*

VERBS **be, prove** | **become** | **consider sth**

ADV. **extremely, fairly, very, etc.** | **particularly** | **potentially** ◊ *the burning of potentially ~ medical waste* | **environmentally** ◊ *environmentally ~ substances*

PREP. **for** ◊ *These conditions are very ~ for shipping.* | **to** ◊ *chemicals that are ~ to human beings*

haze *noun*

ADJ. **thick** ◊ *a thick ~ of smoke* | **faint, thin** ◊ *The sun now had a faint golden ~ around it.* | **shimmering** | **smoky** | **heat** ◊ *A heat ~ shimmered above the fields.*

HAZE + VERB **hang, shimmer** ◊ *In the evenings a blue ~ hung in the valleys.* | **surround sth** ◊ *The locomotive was surrounded by a ~ of smoke.*

PREP. **in a/the ~** ◊ *Meetings are always conducted in a ~ of cigarette smoke.* | **through a/the ~** | **~ of** ◊ *He watched the world through a ~ of tobacco smoke.*

hazy *adj.*

1 not clear because the air is difficult to see through

VERBS **be, look** ◊ *The distant mountains looked ~ and mysterious.* | **become** | **remain**

ADV. **very** | **a little, rather, slightly** ◊ *Generally, it will be rather ~ today, with some hill fog.*

PREP. **with** ◊ *The summers were ~ with pollution.*

2 confused

VERBS **be** | **become, get** | **remain**

ADV. **extremely, fairly, very, etc.** ◊ *I have only a very ~ idea about how the economy works.* | **a little, slightly, etc.** ◊ *My memory of that day is a little ~ now.* | **still** ◊ *I'm still slightly ~ about the details of what happened.*

PREP. **about** ◊ *I'm a little ~ about my family history.*

head *noun*

1 part of the body

ADJ. **bare** | **bald** | **shaved** | **blonde, dark, fair, grey/gray,**
greying/graying | **bent, bowed** ◊ *She sat with bowed ~.* | **throbbing** | **severed** ◊ *The city gates were adorned with severed ~s.* | **crowned** (*figurative*) ◊ *The message was sent to all the crowned ~s* (= kings and queens) *of Europe.*

VERB + HEAD **poke, pop, put, stick** ◊ *He put his ~ around the door.* | **bob, cock, crane, incline, jerk, tilt, turn** ◊ *She jerked her ~ in the direction of the door.* | **lift, raise** | **bend, bow, drop, duck, hang, lower** ◊ *He hung his ~ in shame.* | **swing, throw back, toss** ◊ *He threw his ~ back and laughed out loud.* | **nod, shake** ◊ *They nodded their ~s in agreement.* ◊ *She shook her ~ in disbelief.* | **scratch** ◊ *He scratched his ~, not understanding a word.* ◊ *Detectives have been left scratching their ~s over the stolen painting.* (*figurative*) | **bang, hit** | **pat, rub** | **clutch, hold** ◊ *He lay writhing on the ground, clutching his ~ in pain.* | **bury** ◊ *She buried her ~ in the pillow.* | **cover** | **lay, lean, rest** ◊ *She rested her ~ on his shoulder.* | **shave** ◊ *He shaved his ~ and became a monk.*

HEAD + VERB **ache, pound, throb** | **bob, jerk, nod, tilt, turn** ◊ *Her ~ tilted to one side as she considered the question.* | **droop, drop, fall, hang down, hang low** ◊ *His ~ drooped and tears fell into his lap.* | **rest** | **hit sth** ◊ *I'm normally asleep as soon as my ~ hits the pillow.*

HEAD + NOUN **injury** | **cold**

PREP. **above your ~** ◊ *The thunder burst with a grand crash above our ~s.* | **over your ~** ◊ *The soldiers were ordered to fire over the ~s of the crowd.*

PHRASES **from ~ to foot, from ~ to toe** ◊ *We were covered from ~ to foot in mud.* | **a fine, full, good, thick, etc. ~ of hair** (= a lot of hair) ◊ *a woman with a beautiful ~ of chestnut hair* | **have, hold, put, etc. your ~ in your hands** ◊ *He put his ~ in his hands, exasperated.* | **~ first** ◊ *He dived ~ first into the water.* ◊ *She got divorced and rushed ~ first into another marriage.* (*figurative*) | **a nod of the ~** ◊ *The ambassador dismissed him with a curt nod of the ~.* | **a shake of the ~** ◊ *She declined with a brief shake of the ~.*

2 mind

ADJ. **clear, cool, level** ◊ *She needed to keep a clear ~ if she was to remain in control.* | **good** ◊ *I have a good ~ for figures.*

VERB + HEAD **use** ◊ *I wish you'd use your ~* (= think carefully before doing or saying something). | **enter** ◊ *It never entered my ~ that he might be lying.* | **pop into** ◊ *It was the first name that popped into my ~.* | **get it into** ◊ *When will you get it into your ~* (= understand) *that I don't want to discuss this any more!* ◊ *For some reason she got it into her ~* (= started to believe) *that the others don't like her.* | **put sth into** ◊ *Who's been putting such weird ideas into your ~?* | **get sth out of, put sth out of** ◊ *I can't get that tune out of my ~.* ◊ *Try to put the exams out of your ~ for tonight.* | **bother** ◊ *Don't bother your pretty little ~ with things like that!* | **clear** ◊ *I decided to go for a walk to clear my ~.*

HEAD + VERB **spin** ◊ *He could feel his ~ spinning after only one drink.*

PREP. **in your ~** ◊ *I can't work it out in my head—I need a calculator.* | **inside your ~** ◊ *It was an accident, said a voice inside his ~.*

PHRASES **can't get your ~ round sth** (= can't understand sth) (*BrE, informal*) ◊ *She's dead. I can't get my ~ round it yet.* | **need your ~ examined** ◊ *He looked at me as if I needed my ~ examined* (= as if I were crazy). | **your thick ~** (= used to show that you are annoyed that sb does not understand sth) (*informal*) ◊ *When will you get it into your thick ~ that I don't want to see you again!*

3 heads side of a coin

VERB + HEADS **call** ◊ *I called ~s and it came down tails.* | **come down, come up** (*esp. AmE*)

PHRASES **~s or tails?**

4 of a group, organization, school, etc.

ADJ. **assistant, deputy** | **department, departmental** | **nominal, titular** ◊ *He is only the nominal ~ of the company.* | **former**

HEAD + NOUN **coach, gardener, teacher** (*BrE*), **waiter** | **boy, girl** (= in a school) (*both BrE*)

PHRASES **a ~ of department** | **the ~ of the family, the ~ of**

the household | a ~ of government, a ~ of state ◇ *a summit meeting of ~s of state* | **the ~ of the group**
→ Note at JOB

head *verb*

1 go

ADV. **north, northwards, etc.** ◇ *We ~ed west for two days.* | **down, off, out, up, etc.** | **back** ◇ *Let's ~ back home.* | **home**
PREP. **back to** ◇ *We ~ed straight back to school.* | **for** ◇ *He turned and ~ed for the door.* | **towards/toward** ◇ *She stood up and ~ed towards/toward the exit.*

2 (*also* **head up**) be in charge of sth

VERB + HEAD **appoint sb to** ◇ *She has been appointed to ~ up the research team.*

headache *noun*

1 pain in the head

ADJ. **bad, chronic, severe, terrible | mild, slight | dull | pounding, splitting, throbbing | blinding | migraine, tension** ◇ *He developed a severe migraine ~.*
VERB + HEADACHE **experience, have, suffer from** ◇ *I have a splitting ~.* | **develop, get** ◇ *We all get ~s from time to time.* | **complain of** ◇ *The workers had complained of ~s and nausea.* | **bring on, cause, give sb** ◇ *Exhaust fumes made him drowsy and brought on a ~.* ◇ *Red wine gives me a ~.* | **relieve | plead** ◇ *She had left the party early, pleading a ~.*
HEADACHE + NOUN **medicine** (*esp. AmE*), **pill, tablet** (*esp. BrE*) | **pain** (*esp. AmE*)
→ Special page at ILLNESS

2 sb/sth that causes worry/difficulty

ADJ. **big, huge, major, real | constant**
VERB + HEADACHE **create** ◇ *These regulations have created major ~s for many businesses.*
PREP. **~ for** ◇ *Uneven cash flow proved to be a major ~ for the company.*

heading *noun*

ADJ. **broad, general** ◇ *Books should be listed under a broader ~ such as 'engineering'.* | **main, major | chapter, section | subject, topic | letter** (*esp. BrE*) ◇ *With the computer, we can print our own letter ~s.*
VERB + HEADING **come under, fall under** ◇ *These drugs come under the ~ of non-medical substances.*
PREP. **under a/the ~** ◇ *I've organized what I have to say about unemployment under three main ~s.*

headlights *noun*

ADJ. **dipped** (*BrE*) | **bright | oncoming | car**
VERB + HEADLIGHTS **switch on, turn on | dip** (*BrE*) | **flash** ◇ *He flashed his ~ at the oncoming car.* | **see** ◇ *She saw ~ coming from around the corner.*
HEADLIGHTS + VERB **flash, shine** ◇ *The ~ shone on empty streets as we drove through the town.* | **illuminate sth** ◇ *My ~ finally picked out a road sign.*
PHRASES **the glare of ~**

headline *noun*

1 title of an article in a newspaper

ADJ. **newspaper, tabloid** ◇ *'Carnage at Airport!' screamed the tabloid ~.* | **banner, front-page | lurid** (*esp. BrE*), **screaming, sensational** ◇ *lurid ~s about the sex lives of the stars* | **sporting** (*BrE*), **sports**
VERB + HEADLINE **carry, have, run** ◇ *The paper carried the front-page ~ 'Drugs Company Shamed'.* | **read, scan, see** ◇ *I just had time to scan the ~s before leaving for work.* | **capture, dominate, generate, get, grab, hit, hog** (*esp. BrE*), **make ~s** ◇ *She's always in the ~s.* ◇ *He always manages to grab the ~s.* ◇ *The hospital hit the ~s when a number of suspicious deaths occurred.* ◇ *The story has been hogging the ~s for weeks.* ◇ *The story was important enough to make the*

~s. | **write** ◇ *Journalists don't usually write the ~s for their stories.*
HEADLINE + VERB **announce sth, blare sth** (*esp. AmE*), **declare sth, proclaim sth, read sth, say sth, scream sth** ◇ *The ~ said 'Star Arrested'.*
HEADLINE + NOUN **news** ◇ *'Dog bites man' is hardly ~ news!*
PREP. **in a/the ~** ◇ *The most unusual fact in the story is often used in the ~.* | **under a/the ~** ◇ *The Daily Gazette ran a story under the ~ 'Pope's Last Words'.* | **with a/the ~** ◇ *a story in the newspaper with the ~ 'Woman Gives Birth on Train'* | **~ about** ◇ *There was a banner ~ about drugs in schools.*
PHRASES **make ~ news** ◇ *The engagement of the two tennis stars made ~ news.*

2 the headlines main news stories on TV/radio

ADJ. **news | national**
VERB + THE HEADLINES **hear** ◇ *Let's just hear the news ~s.* | **look at, see, watch**

headquarters *noun*

ADJ. **international, local, national, regional, world | main | permanent | temporary | field | administrative, campaign, operational** ◇ *He chose Chicago as the site of the Republican national campaign ~.* | **army, military | brigade, command, division | police | company, corporate, group | party**
VERB + HEADQUARTERS **have** ◇ *The organization has its ~ in Brussels.* | **build, establish, locate, set up** ◇ *The company has set up its European ~ in the UK.* | **close, open** ◇ *They're planning to close their ~ in Washington.* | **move**
HEADQUARTERS + VERB **be located** ◇ *The company's ~ are located in Rome.*
PREP. **at (the) ~** ◇ *They're very worried about this at ~.* ◇ *She works at the company's ~.*

heal *verb*

ADV. **completely, fully, properly** ◇ *The wound hasn't ~ed properly yet.* | **partially | nicely, well | slowly | quickly | eventually, finally | up** ◇ *The wound ~ed up very nicely.*

health *noun*

ADJ. **excellent, full, good, perfect | bad, declining, delicate, failing, fragile, frail, ill, poor** ◇ *He had to retire due to ill ~.* | **general, overall | long-term | mental, physical, sexual | environmental, occupational** ◇ *environmental ~ officers* | **public** ◇ *There is no threat to public ~ from this paint.* | **personal | human**
VERB + HEALTH **enjoy, have** ◇ *She's never really enjoyed good ~.* | **ensure, look after** (*esp. BrE*), **maintain, protect** ◇ *You need to maintain your physical and mental ~.* | **enhance, improve** ◇ *ways to improve the nation's general ~* | **promote** ◇ *a campaign to promote better ~ in the workplace* | **recover, regain, restore | nurse sb back to, restore sb to** ◇ *She was nursed back to full ~.* ◇ *Doctors worked for weeks to restore him to ~.* | **damage, harm, ruin, undermine | endanger, risk, threaten** ◇ *Some athletes are prepared to risk their ~ to win a medal.* | **affect | monitor**
HEALTH + VERB **improve** ◇ *Her ~ gradually improved.* | **deteriorate, fail, worsen** ◇ *His ~ began to fail under the heavy pressures of the job.*
HEALTH + NOUN **care** ◇ *How is primary ~ care best delivered?* ◇ *community ~ care* (see also ***health service***) | **system | authority** (*esp. BrE*), **board** (*esp. BrE*), **department** ◇ *the local ~ authority* (*BrE*) | **issue, needs, problem | hazard, risk | benefit** ◇ *the ~ benefits of physical activity* | **education | centre/center, clinic, facilities** ◇ *a community ~ centre/center* | **insurance, plan** ◇ *private ~ insurance* | **food** ◇ *~ food stores* | **official, professional, visitor** (*in the UK*), **worker** ◇ *Health visitors give families support for infant care and development.* | **provider | warning** ◇ *The air quality was so bad that the government issued a ~ warning.* | **minister** (*BrE*)
PHRASES **bad for your ~, good for your ~** ◇ *Smoking is bad for your ~.* | **~ and safety** ◇ *~ and safety at work* | **(not) in the best of ~, in good ~, in poor ~** ◇ *He was in much better*

~. | **sb's state of** ~ (esp. BrE) ◇ *He is unable to travel far because of his state of* ~.

387   **heart**

healthy adj.

1 not ill; producing good health

VERBS **appear, be, be born, feel, look, seem** | **become** | **keep, remain, stay** | **make sb** ◇ *Working in the open air has made him very* ~. | **keep sb** ◇ *Her good diet had kept her* ~. | **consider sth** ◇ *a new diet which is considered much healthier than previous ones*
ADV. **extremely, fairly, very, etc.** ◇ *We have a very* ~ *diet.* | **completely** (esp. AmE), **perfectly** ◇ *He's a perfectly* ~ *child.* | **reasonably** | **generally** | **apparently** ◇ *The rare disorder strikes apparently* ~ *boys between the ages of five and twelve.* | **otherwise** ◇ *She looked pale, but otherwise* ~. | **mentally, physically**
PHRASES **fit and** ~

2 working well

VERBS **be** | **remain**
ADV. **extremely, fairly, very, etc.** ◇ *The economy is extremely* ~ *at the moment.* | **reasonably, relatively** | **basically, fundamentally, generally** | **financially**

heap noun

ADJ. **big, great, large** | **little, small** | **crumpled** | **ash** (AmE, usually figurative), **rubbish** (BrE), **scrap, slag, spoil** (esp. BrE), **trash** (AmE) ◇ *the ash* ~ *of history* ◇ *colliery spoil* ~*s* | **compost, manure** (esp. BrE)
VERB + HEAP **be piled in** ◇ *Papers were piled in great* ~*s on the desk.* | **collapse in, fall down in, fall in** (all figurative) ◇ *He collapsed in an exhausted* ~ *on the floor.*
PREP. **in a/the** ~ ◇ *His clothes lay in a crumpled* ~ *on the floor.* | **on a/the** ~, **onto a/the** ~ ◇ *Throw the potato peelings on the compost* ~. | ~ **of** ◇ *a great* ~ *of stones*
PHRASES **the bottom of the** ~, **the top of the** ~ (figurative) ◇ *These workers are at the bottom of the economic* ~.

hear verb

1 be aware of sounds

ADV. **clearly, well** ◇ *He's getting old and he can't* ~ *very well.* | **barely, just** ◇ *I could just* ~ *the music in the distance.* | **distantly** ◇ *Distantly he* ~*d the report of another gun.* | **correctly** ◇ *'Sheep?' It sounded so unlikely that Sally did not think she could have* ~*d correctly.*
VERB + HEAR **can** ◇ *Can you* ~ *me clearly at the back?* | **pretend not to** | **strain to**

2 be told about sth

VERB + HEAR **be delighted to, be glad to, be gratified to, be pleased to** ◇ *I was delighted to* ~ *about your promotion.* | **be sorry to** ◇ *I was sorry to* ~ *of your father's death.* | **be interested to, be surprised to** ◇ *I was surprised to* ~ *that she was married.* | **want to** ◇ *I told Michael what he wanted to* ~. | **let sb** ◇ *Let's* ~ *you sing.* ◇ *You'd better not let Dad* ~ *you say that.*
PREP. **about** ◇ *I've* ~*d about this sort of thing before.* | **of** ◇ *On* ~*ing of his plight, a businessman offered him a job.*
PHRASES ~ **little, a lot, nothing, etc. about sth** ◇ *We* ~ *very little about these issues nowadays.*

hearing noun

1 ability to hear

ADJ. **acute, excellent, good, normal, sharp** | **bad** (esp. AmE), **impaired, poor**
VERB + HEARING **have** ◇ *Whales have acute* ~. | **lose** ◇ *She lost her* ~ *when she was a child.* | **get back, regain** (esp. AmE) ◇ *Is there any chance that he'll get his* ~ *back?* | **affect, impair**
HEARING + VERB **deteriorate, go** ◇ *His* ~ *began to deteriorate.* ◇ *Her* ~ *was already going.* | **come back, improve** ◇ *Two months after the accident her* ~ *came back.*
HEARING + NOUN **impairment, loss, problems** | **aid** ◇ *to have/ wear a* ~ *aid* | **protection** (esp. AmE) | **person** ◇ *a course in sign language for both deaf and* ~ *people*
PHRASES **hard of** ~ ◇ *You'll have to speak more loudly. I'm afraid she's a little hard of* ~.

2 trial in a court, etc.

ADJ. **final, preliminary** | **fair** | **formal, full** | **open, public** | **private, secret** | **oral** (BrE) | **appeal, confirmation, custody, disciplinary, pretrial** | **committee, congressional, court, tribunal** (BrE)
VERB + HEARING **conduct, hold** ◇ *The committee has decided to hold the* ~ *in public.* | **schedule** ◇ *An appeal* ~ *is scheduled for later this month.* | **ask for, call for, demand, request** ◇ *Protesters are calling for a public* ~. | **get, have** ◇ *She said that she had had a very fair* ~ *from the disciplinary tribunal.* | **open** (esp. BrE) | **tell** ◇ *The* ~ *was told that the child had been left with a 14-year-old babysitter.*
HEARING + VERB **take place** | **begin, open**
PREP. **at a/the** ~ ◇ *At a preliminary* ~ *the judge announced that the trial would begin on March 21.* | **in a/the** ~ ◇ *She was granted a divorce in a five-minute* ~. | **pending a/the** ~ ◇ *Pending the* ~ *of the case by the court, the business will be allowed to continue operating.* | **without a** ~ ◇ *The judge dismissed the case without a* ~.

3 chance for an opinion to be considered

ADJ. **fair, sympathetic**
VERB + HEARING **give sb/sth** ◇ *At least give our ideas a fair* ~ *before you reject them.* | **get** ◇ *You haven't much chance of your plan getting a sympathetic* ~. | **deserve** ◇ *Their views deserve a* ~.
PREP. ~ **for** ◇ *All I'm asking is a fair* ~ *for my ideas.*

hearsay noun

VERB + HEARSAY **be based on, rely on** ◇ *Her judgements are based on* ~ *rather than evidence.*
HEARSAY + NOUN **evidence**
PREP. **by** ~ ◇ *She discovered a world of parties and pleasure she had hitherto only known by* ~. | **from** ~ ◇ *They started to piece the story together from* ~.

heart noun

1 part of the body

ADJ. **healthy, strong** | **bad, weak** | **beating, pounding, racing** | **artificial** | **human**
HEART + VERB **beat** | **pump sth** ◇ *The* ~ *pumps blood through the body.* | **fail, stop** | **flutter, hammer, palpitate, pound, race, throb, thud, thump**
HEART + NOUN **rate, rhythm** | **complaint** (esp. BrE), **condition, defect, disease, failure, murmur, problem, trouble** (see also **heart attack**) ◇ *a triple* ~ *bypass operation* | **bypass, operation, surgery, transplant** | **patient** | **monitor** | **muscle**

2 feelings/emotions

ADJ. **big, good, kind, pure, soft, tender, true, warm** | **cold, dark, hard** | **broken** | **heavy, sinking** ◇ *With a heavy* ~, *she watched him go.* | **light** ◇ *He set off with a light* ~.
VERB + HEART **have** ◇ *She has a kind* ~. ◇ *Have you no* ~? | **break** ◇ *He broke her* ~. | **pierce** ◇ *Her words pierced my* ~. | **touch** ◇ *His sad story touched her* ~. | **gladden, melt, warm** | **capture, steal, win** | **follow** ◇ *Just follow your* ~ *and you'll be happy.* | **harden** | **open, pour out** ◇ *Finally, he broke down in tears and poured out his* ~ *to her.* | **fill** ◇ *Relief filled his* ~.
HEART + VERB **jump, leap, lurch, miss a beat, skip a beat** ◇ *Her* ~ *leaped with joy.* | **ache** ◇ *My* ~ *aches when I think of their sorrow.* | **break** ◇ *Inside, his* ~ *was slowly breaking.* | **melt** ◇ *He smiled and her* ~ *melted.* | **desire sth** ◇ *everything your* ~ *could desire* | **sink** | **go out** ◇ *Our* ~*s go out to (= we sympathize deeply with) the families of the victims.*
PREP. **at** ~ ◇ *At* ~ *he is a republican.* | **from the** ~ ◇ *I could tell he spoke from the* ~. | **in your** ~ ◇ *In my* ~, *I knew it wasn't true.*
PHRASES **an affair of the** ~ (= a romance) ◇ *Her novels tend to deal with affairs of the* ~ | **a change of** ~ (= a change of attitude) ◇ *He could have a change of* ~ *and settle down to family life.* | **from the bottom of your** ~ ◇ *I beg you, from the bottom of my* ~, *to spare his life.* | ~ **and soul** ◇ *He committed himself* ~ *and soul to the cause.* | **have a** ~ **of**

gold (= to be a very kind person), **have a ~ of stone** (= to be a person who does not show others sympathy or pity), the **~s and minds of sb** ◇ *to win the ~s and minds of the nation's youth* | **in good ~** (= cheerful and well) (*BrE*), **put (your) ~ into sth** ◇ *He really puts his ~ into his singing.* | **sick at ~** (= very unhappy), **with all your ~**, **with your whole ~** (*esp. AmE*) ◇ *I wish you well with all my ~.*

3 important/central part

ADJ. **very** | **real, true** ◇ *This brings us to the real ~ of the matter.*
VERB + HEART **lie at** ◇ *The distinction between right and wrong lies at the ~ of all questions of morality.* | **go to** ◇ *The committee's report went to the ~ of the government's dilemma.*
PREP. **at the ~** ◇ *the issue at the ~ of modern government* | **~ of** ◇ *We live in the very ~ of the city.*
PHRASES **the ~ of the matter, the ~ of the problem**

4 playing card

→ Note at CARD

heart attack noun

ADJ. **fatal** | **massive, serious** ◇ *She died of a massive ~.* | **mild, minor** | **apparent** (*esp. AmE*), **suspected** (*esp. BrE*)
VERB + HEART ATTACK **have, suffer** ◇ *He suffered a fatal ~ while jogging.* | **die of** | **give sb** ◇ *You're going to give me a ~ one of these days!*
→ Special page at ILLNESS

heartbeat noun

ADJ. **steady** | **irregular** | **racing, rapid** ◇ *She was suddenly aware of her racing ~.*
VERB + HEARTBEAT **monitor** | **feel** | **hear**
HEARTBEAT + VERB **quicken**
PHRASES **the sound of a ~** ◇ *The first track on the album begins with the sound of a ~.*

heartland noun

ADJ. **agricultural, industrial** ◇ *the industrial ~ of Germany* | **Conservative, Labour, etc.** | **traditional** (*esp. BrE*)
PREP. **in a/the ~** ◇ *The party has lost seats in its traditional ~ of southern Thailand.*

heat noun

1 being hot/level of temperature

ADJ. **burning, fierce** (*esp. BrE*), **great, intense, searing, terrible, tremendous** ◇ *The soil is baked dry by the fierce ~ of the sun.* | **gentle** | **excess, excessive** ◇ *If circulation is impaired, the body cannot lose excess ~.* | **red, white** (*often figurative*) ◇ *Everything he did was at white ~ and lightning speed.* | **radiant** | **body**
VERB + HEAT **feel** ◇ *We could feel the tremendous ~ coming from the fire.* | **disperse, dissipate, give out, lose** ◇ *Even after the sun had set, the stones continued to give out ~.* | **conserve, retain** ◇ *The thick walls retain the ~.* | **absorb** ◇ *Darker surfaces absorb ~.* | **conduct** ◇ *Being a metal, copper readily conducts ~.* | **create, generate, give off, produce, provide, radiate** ◇ *Computers and photocopiers all generate ~ of their own.* | **withstand** ◇ *a material which can withstand ~s of up to 2 000°C*
HEAT + VERB **build up, increase** ◇ *He tried to ignore the ~ building up in the confined space.* | **come from sth, come off sth** (*esp. AmE*), **radiate from sth, radiate off sth** (*esp. AmE*) ◇ *I could feel the ~ coming from the fire.*
HEAT + NOUN **loss** | **exhaustion, stress, stroke** (usually **heatstroke**) ◇ *She slumped to the ground suffering from ~ exhaustion.*
PREP. **~ from** ◇ *the ~ from the fire*

2 hot weather/conditions

ADJ. **baking** (*esp. BrE*), **blazing, blistering, boiling, extreme, great, intense, oppressive, scorching, searing, shimmering, stifling, suffocating, sweltering, unbearable** ◇ *We walked more than ten miles in the blistering ~.* | **dry** |

humid, steamy, sultry ◇ *the steamy ~ of New York in summer* | **40-degree, 90-degree, etc.** | **afternoon, midday, morning** | **summer** | **desert, tropical**
HEAT + VERB **grow** ◇ *Daily the ~ grew.* | **get to sb** ◇ *I think the ~ is getting to all of us.*
HEAT + NOUN **haze** ◇ *A ~ haze shimmered above the fields.* | **wave** (usually **heatwave**) | **source**
PREP. **in the ~** ◇ *I can't work in this ~.*
PHRASES **the ~ of the day** ◇ *To avoid the ~ of the day we went out in the mornings.*

3 source of heat

ADJ. **high** | **gentle, low** | **medium, moderate** | **direct** ◇ *Chocolate should never be melted over direct ~.* | **dry**
VERB + HEAT **turn up** ◇ *Turn up the ~ to caramelize the sugar.* | **lower, reduce, turn down** | **remove sth from, take sth off** ◇ *Bring to the boil slowly, then remove from the ~.* | **return sth to** ◇ *Return the pan to the ~ and stir.*
PREP. **off the ~** ◇ *Make sure the pan is off the ~.* | **on a ... ~** ◇ *Cook on a low ~ for five minutes.* | **over a ... ~** ◇ *Simmer the sauce over a gentle ~.*

4 (*AmE*) in a building/room → See also HEATING

ADJ. **electric, radiant**
VERB + HEAT **have** ◇ *The house has electric ~.* | **have on, use** ◇ *Andy had the ~ on full blast in the car.* | **turn on** ◇ *They are afraid to turn the ~ on because it's so expensive.* | **turn off** ◇ *They have their ~ turned off during the morning.* | **turn down, turn up** ◇ *I turned the ~ down several notches.* | **provide** ◇ *These industries provide ~ for our homes and fuel for our cars.*
HEAT + VERB **be on, be on high, be on low** ◇ *The ~ was on but the window was open.* ◇ *The heat's on low.* | **be off** | **come on** | **go off** ◇ *Our ~ goes off at ten o'clock and comes on again at six.*

5 strong feelings

ADJ. **sudden** ◇ *He stared at her, sudden ~ in his eyes.*
HEAT + VERB **flare, flood sth, rise** ◇ *Heat flooded her cheeks.*
PREP. **in the ~ of** ◇ *in the ~ of battle/passion* | **with ~** ◇ *'It was your idea,' Henry said with ~.*
PHRASES **in the ~ of the moment** ◇ *Michael bitterly regretted those angry words, spoken in the ~ of the moment.*

6 race/competition

ADJ. **qualifying, regional** (*BrE*) | **dead** ◇ *Competition was fierce, with a dead ~ in one of the races* (= with two competitors finishing in exactly the same time).
VERB + HEAT **win** ◇ *She won her ~.*
PREP. **in a/the ~** ◇ *He fell in the first ~.*

heat verb

ADV. **gently, slowly** ◇ *Heat the sauce gently for a few minutes.* | **well** ◇ *Make sure the soup is well ~ed.* | **through, up** ◇ *Allow the food enough time to ~ through.* ◇ *They ~ up the food in a microwave oven.*

heater noun

ADJ. **convector** (*BrE*), **fan** (*esp. BrE*), **storage** (*BrE*) | **portable** | **electric, gas, kerosene** (*esp. AmE*), **oil, paraffin** (*BrE*) | **greenhouse, pool, room, space** (*AmE*), **water** | **hot-water** (*esp. AmE*), **immersion** (*BrE*)
VERB + HEATER **have off, have on** | **turn off, turn on** | **turn down, turn up** | **install**
HEATER + VERB **be off, be on** ◇ *Even with the ~ full on, the room felt cold.*

heating noun (*esp. BrE*) → See also HEAT

ADJ. **electric, gas-fired** (*BrE*), **radiant** (*AmE*), **solar** ◇ *gas-fired central ~* | **central, domestic, home, space** (*AmE*), **underfloor** | **water**
VERB + HEATING **have** ◇ *The house has central ~.* | **have on, keep on, leave on, use** ◇ *We haven't had the ~ on this evening.* | **put on, switch on** (*esp. BrE*), **turn on** ◇ *They are afraid to put the ~ on because it's so expensive.* | **switch off** (*esp. BrE*), **turn off** ◇ *They have their ~ turned off during the morning.* | **turn down, turn up** | **fit, install, provide, put in** ◇ *We're having central ~ installed.*
HEATING + VERB **be on, be on high, be on low** ◇ *The ~ was on*

but the window was open. ◇ *The heating's on low.* | **be off** | **come on** | **go off** ◇ *Our ~ goes off at eleven o'clock and comes on again at seven.* | **work** ◇ *The ~ doesn't work.* | **break down** ◇ *The house was very cold because the ~ had broken down.*

HEATING + NOUN **bill** (*BrE*, *AmE*) | **system** (*BrE*, *AmE*) ◇ *What sort of ~ system does your new place have?* | **oil** (*BrE*, *AmE*)

heaven *noun*

1 believed to be the home of God

VERB + HEAVEN **ascend to, go to** ◇ *I feel like I've died and gone to ~.*

PREP. **from ~** ◇ *Our child seemed a gift from ~.* | **in ~** ◇ *It was a marriage made in ~.* (*figurative*)

PHRASES **the kingdom of ~**

2 place/situation in which you are very happy

ADJ. **absolute, pure** (*esp. AmE*), **sheer** ◇ *It was sheer ~ being alone at last.*

PREP. **in ~** ◇ *The kids were in absolute ~ at the fair.*

PHRASES **a ~ on earth** ◇ *The island is truly a ~ on earth.* | **sb's idea of ~** ◇ *Building up a tan by the pool with a good book is my idea of ~.*

heavy *adj.*

1 weighing a lot

VERBS **be, feel, look, seem** ◇ *My suitcase was beginning to feel very ~.* | **become, get, grow** ◇ *You're getting too ~ to carry!* ◇ *She felt her eyelids growing ~* (= she was getting sleepy). | **make sth** ◇ *The bottles of wine made the bag even heavier.* | **find sth** ◇ *I didn't find it too ~ to carry.*

ADV. **extremely, fairly, very, etc.** ◇ *Be careful. That box is rather ~.*

2 worse than usual

VERBS **be** | **become, get** ◇ *The rain was getting very ~.*

ADV. **extremely, fairly, very, etc.** ◇ *The traffic's really ~ on the roads today.*

hedge *noun*

ADJ. **high** (*esp. BrE*), **low, tall, thick** ◇ *A tall ~ separates the two properties.* | **boundary, garden** (*both esp. BrE*) | **privet, yew, etc.** ◇ *a thick privet ~*

VERB + HEDGE **plant** | **clip** (*esp. BrE*), **trim** ◇ *Trim the ~ and collect the trimmings.*

HEDGE + NOUN **clippings** (*BrE*), **trimmings** (*esp. BrE*) | **trimmer** | **maze**

heel *noun*

1 back part of the foot

VERB + HEEL **lean back on, sit back on, squat on** ◇ *She took a potato from the fire and sat back on her ~s.* | **rock (back) on** ◇ *The punch rocked him back on his ~s.* ◇ *He rocked back and forth on his ~s as he laughed.* | **pivot on, spin on, turn on** ◇ *He turned on his ~ and marched away angrily.* | **click, click together** ◇ *The officer clicked his ~s together and saluted.*

HEEL + VERB **click**

HEEL + NOUN **injury**

PREP. **at your ~s** ◇ *She came up the path with two little dogs at her ~s.* | **under the ~** (*figurative*) ◇ *For years the nation had been under the ~ of a dictatorial regime.*

PHRASES **close on sb's ~s, hard on sb's ~s, hot on sb's ~s** (*all figurative*) ◇ *They reached the border with the police hot on their ~s.*

2 part of a shoe/sock

ADJ. **low** | **high, spike, spiked** (*esp. AmE*), **stiletto, wedge** | **three-inch, etc.** | **boot**

VERB + HEEL **catch** ◇ *She caught her ~ and tripped on the step.*

HEEL + NOUN **bar** (*BrE*) ◇ *I took my shoes to a ~ bar to have them repaired.*

height *noun*

1 how tall sb/sth is

ADJ. **full, maximum** ◇ *He drew himself up to his full ~ and glared at us.* | **considerable, great, towering** ◇ *Her great ~*

was rather a handicap. | **average, medium, middle** ◇ *a man of middle ~* | **low**

VERB + HEIGHT **determine, measure** | **have** | **grow to, reach** ◇ *The plants grow to a maximum ~ of 24 inches.* | **adjust** ◇ *You can adjust the ~ of the chair.* | **increase, reduce**

PREP. **in ~** ◇ *The wall is nine feet in ~.*

2 distance above the ground/sea level

ADJ. **considerable, great** ◇ *The object had clearly fallen from a considerable ~.* | **ceiling, chest, head, shoulder, waist, etc.** ◇ *Bring your hands to shoulder ~.*

VERB + HEIGHT **gain** | **lose** ◇ *The plane was beginning to lose ~.* | **maintain** ◇ *The pilot was unable to maintain ~.* | **attain, climb to, reach, rise to** ◇ *The balloon reached a ~ of 20 000 feet.*

PREP. **at a ~ of** ◇ *The animal lives in lakes at a ~ of 6 000 feet above sea level.*

3 (*usually* **heights**) high place

ADJ. **mountain, rocky** ◇ *The condor soars effortlessly above the mountain ~s.*

VERB + HEIGHTS **scale** ◇ *They were the first expedition to scale the ~s of Everest.* | **be afraid of** | **have a head for** (*esp. BrE*) ◇ *A steeplejack has to have a good head for ~s.*

PREP. **from a ~** ◇ *The pattern of the ancient fields is clearly visible from a ~.*

PHRASES **a fear of ~s**

4 **heights** high level of achievement

ADJ. **commanding, dizzy** (*esp. BrE*), **dizzying, giddy** (*esp. BrE*), **lofty** ◇ *They have risen to the dizzy ~s of the semi-finals.* | **new** ◇ *The group's popularity reached new ~s when they released their second album.*

VERB + HEIGHTS **achieve, climb to, reach, rise to, scale** ◇ *She rose to undreamed-of ~s of power and fame.*

heighten *verb*

ADV. **dramatically, greatly** ◇ *This latest attack has greatly ~ed fears of an all-out war.* | **further**

VERB + HEIGHTEN **serve to** ◇ *Seeing others enjoying themselves only served to ~ his sense of loneliness.*

heir *noun*

ADJ. **legal, legitimate, rightful** ◇ *the rightful ~ to the throne* | **natural, real, true** ◇ *The socialists saw themselves as true ~s of the Enlightenment.* | **worthy** | **direct** ◇ *When the Earl of Surrey died in 1347 he left no direct ~.* | **immediate** | **chosen, designated** | **apparent, presumptive** (*both only after* **heir**) ◇ *On his brother's death he became ~ apparent to the title.* | **future** ◇ *He's the future ~ to the throne.* | **sole** | **female, male** | **royal** | **political, spiritual**

VERB + HEIR **have** ◇ *He has no ~ to leave his fortune to.* | **beget** (*formal*), **produce** ◇ *He planned to marry and produce an ~ for his estate.* | **name** ◇ *On his deathbed he named his second son as his ~.* | **become, fall** (*esp. BrE*) ◇ *At the age of twenty he fell ~ to a large estate.*

PREP. **~ to** ◇ *He is the sole ~ to a large mining fortune.*

PHRASES **the ~ to the throne** | **sb's son and ~** ◇ *He left most of his property to his eldest son and ~.*

heirloom *noun*

ADJ. **family** | **precious**

HEIRLOOM + VERB **be passed down, come down** ◇ *The brooch is a family ~ which came down to her from her grandmother.*

HEIRLOOM + NOUN **seed, tomato, variety, vegetable** (*all AmE*)

helicopter *noun*

ADJ. **air-force, army, coastguard** (*BrE*), **Coast Guard** (*in the US*), **military, naval, police** | **civilian, private** | **presidential** | **rescue** | **ambulance** (*BrE*) ◇ *An air ambulance ~ came to the rescue.* | **assault, attack, combat** | **armed** | **reconnaissance** | **transport** | **cargo** | **twin-engine** | **hovering, low-flying** | **downed** ◇ *Troops rescued the crew of a downed ~.* | **waiting** ◇ *They crowded onto a roof to board a waiting ~.* | **model** (*BrE*)

VERB + HELICOPTER fly, pilot ◇ *He flew ~s during the Gulf War.* | board | land | deploy, dispatch, launch, scramble *(BrE)* ◇ *The police ~ was scrambled to search for the missing man.* | charter, hire *(esp. BrE)*, rent *(AmE)* | down, shoot down ◇ *The ~ was downed by a missile.* | ground ◇ *The ~s were grounded by bad weather.*
HELICOPTER + VERB fly | circle, hover ◇ *The ~ hovered above the airstrip.* | buzz ◇ *Helicopters buzzed overhead.* | take off | land | swoop down, swoop in | crash | carry sb, ferry sb, transport sb ◇ *a ~ carrying troops* | airlift sb, rescue sb ◇ *A rescue ~ airlifted the injured man to hospital.* | be equipped with sth | fire (sth) | drop sth ◇ *Helicopters dropped supplies.* | patrol sth
HELICOPTER + NOUN flight, ride, trip *(esp. BrE)* | tour ◇ *We're going to take a ~ tour of the island.* | assault, attack, strike | rescue, search | deck, pad | crew, pilot | fleet | carrier, gunship | accident, crash | blade
PREP. by ◇ *The victims were flown to the hospital by ~.* | in a/the ~ ◇ *There were three people in the ~ when it crashed.*

hell *noun*

1 place bad people are said to go to when they die

ADJ. eternal
VERB + HELL go to ◇ *He was terrified of going to ~ when he died.*
HELL + NOUN fire (usually ***hellfire***)
PREP. in ~ ◇ *tormented souls in ~*
PHRASES the fires of ~, the flames of ~ ◇ *Lava poured out of the volcano, glowing like the fires of ~.*

2 very unpleasant place/situation

ADJ. absolute, pure, sheer, total *(esp. AmE)*, utter ◇ *It was sheer ~ having to sit through hours of boring lectures!* | living ◇ *The last few weeks have been a living ~ for the refugees.* | personal, private ◇ *She'd been going through her own personal ~ over the last month.* | suburban, urban
VERB + HELL endure, go through ◇ *She's been going through ~ with that bad tooth.* | give sb, make sb's life ◇ *Her boss is making her life ~.* | escape ◇ *I'm never going to escape this ~.*
PREP. in ~ ◇ *'We're living in ~!' said one of the refugees.*
PHRASES the... from ~ ◇ *She's the girlfriend from hell—I don't know know why he puts up with her.* | ~ on earth ◇ *For someone who doesn't like heat, Florida would be ~ on earth.*

helmet *noun*

ADJ. leather, metal, plastic, steel, tin *(esp. BrE)* | protective | full-face, visored | combat, riot ◇ *Police in riot ~s lined the streets.* | bicycle, bike, crash, cycle *(BrE)*, motorbike *(BrE)*, motorcycle, safety | football, hockey *(both AmE)* | fireman's, policeman's *(both esp. BrE)* | horned, Viking | Kevlar™, pith
VERB + HELMET have on, wear | don, put on | pull off, remove, take off
HELMET + NOUN visor

help *noun*

ADJ. big, considerable, enormous, great, huge, immense, invaluable, real, substantial, tremendous, valuable ◇ *You've been a big help—thanks.* ◇ *It's a great ~ having you around.* ◇ *This plan offers real ~ to working mothers.* | generous | much-needed | direct ◇ *The careers officer gives direct ~ as well as advice.* | additional, extra ◇ *Is there any extra ~ for disabled students?* | mutual ◇ *The system is based on mutual ~ rather than on payment for services.* | voluntary *(BrE)*, volunteer ◇ *The homeless shelter relies entirely on volunteer ~.* | federal, international | immediate | emergency ◇ *The organization provides emergency ~ for refugees.* | online ◇ *The software comes with excellent online ~.* | individual ◇ *Teachers have little time to give individual ~ to students.* | expert, skilled, specialist *(BrE)*, technical | practical | outside ◇ *They can usually manage by themselves, but occasionally need outside ~.* | domestic, household *(esp. AmE)*, kitchen | financial, legal, medical,

professional, psychiatric ◇ *When the symptoms persisted, I decided to seek medical ~.*
VERB + HELP get, have, receive ◇ *They had substantial ~ from farmers.* | appeal for *(esp. BrE)*, ask for, beg for, call for, request, scream for, seek, send for, shout for, solicit *(esp. AmE)* ◇ *Police are appealing for ~ in catching the killers.* ◇ *I opened the window and called for ~.* | bring, enlist, fetch *(BrE)*, find, get, obtain, recruit, summon ◇ *He enlisted the ~ of a private detective in his search for the truth.* ◇ *He ran to get ~.* | could use *(AmE)*, need, require, want ◇ *Do you need any ~ unloading the car?* | accept ◇ *He's too proud to accept ~.* | refuse | come to, give sb, offer (sb), provide (sb with) ◇ *Passers-by came to the woman's ~ when she was mugged.* | appreciate, welcome ◇ *I really appreciate your ~.* | acknowledge
HELP + VERB arrive, come ◇ *He lay injured for four hours before ~ arrived.* | be at hand *(informal)* ◇ *Don't panic—help is at hand.*
HELP + NOUN desk, line (usually ***helpdesk***, ***helpline***) ◇ *For further information, call our helpline.* | menu ◇ *The program has a ~ menu.*
PREP. beyond ~ ◇ *Some of the injured animals were beyond ~ and had to be destroyed.* | of ~ ◇ *The manual is too technical to be of ~ to the user.* | with ~ ◇ *With a little ~, I think I could fix the computer myself.* ◇ *We broke open the lock with the ~ of a hammer.* | ~ for ◇ *They provide special ~ for the long-term unemployed.* | ~ from ◇ *With ~ from a parent, a child can do simple cooking.* | ~ in ◇ *Local teachers provided invaluable ~ in developing the material.* | ~ to ◇ *She's been a big ~ to her father.* | ~ with ◇ *He'll need ~ with this homework.*
PHRASES an appeal, a plea, a request, etc. for ~ ◇ *The family's request for ~ went unanswered.* | a cry for ~ ◇ *I heard a cry for ~ from inside the building.* | in need of ~ ◇ *The man was clearly in need of urgent medical ~.* | an offer of ~ ◇ *He rudely rejected her kind offer of ~.*

help *verb*

1 do sth for sb

ADV. a lot ◇ *My mother ~s me a lot.* | a bit *(esp. BrE)*, a little | gently ◇ *He gently ~ed her back into the chair.* | actively ◇ *He had actively ~ed many Jews to escape.*
VERB + HELP be able to, can ◇ *Can you ~ me with my homework?* | be unable to, cannot ◇ *I'm afraid I can't ~ you.* | try to ◇ *I was only trying to ~.*
PREP. across ◇ *I ~ed her across the road.* | into | out of ◇ *She ~ed the old man out of the car.* | with ◇ *We all ~ with the housework.*
PHRASES ~ sb to their feet ◇ *Mike ~ed the old lady to her feet.* | a way of ~ing ◇ *the best way of ~ing your child*

2 make sth easier/better

ADV. considerably, dramatically, enormously, greatly, immeasurably, a lot, really, significantly, tremendously ◇ *Talking to a counsellor/counselor ~ed her enormously.* ◇ *The whole process was greatly ~ed by the widespread availability of computers.* | a bit *(esp. BrE)*, a little | certainly, definitely, undoubtedly ◇ *It certainly ~ed that her father is a millionaire!* | surely | supposedly ◇ *Lavender oil supposedly ~s you sleep.* | hardly ◇ *His statement hardly ~ed his case.* | not necessarily ◇ *Intense guilt won't necessarily ~ here.* | in some way, somehow ◇ *I thought a walk would ~ somehow.* | financially | directly | generally | inadvertently, unwittingly ◇ *Many people inadvertently ~ thieves by leaving keys in full view.*
VERB + HELP be designed to ◇ *The minimum wage is designed to ~ people in low-pay service industries.*
PREP. in ◇ *Iron ~s in the formation of red blood cells.*

helper *noun*

ADJ. willing | voluntary, volunteer *(both BrE)* | little ◇ *He became Dad's little ~.* | domestic, kitchen *(both esp. AmE)* (usually ***domestic help***, ***kitchen help***)
... OF HELPERS band ◇ *He recruited a band of willing ~s.*

helpful *adj.*

VERBS be, prove | consider sth, find sb/sth

ADV. extremely, fairly, very, etc. | enormously, especially, immensely, incredibly, most (*esp. BrE*), particularly ◊ *Thank you, you have been most ~.* | not at all, not particularly, not terribly | overly (*esp. AmE*) | genuinely | potentially
PREP. for ◊ *This information would be extremely ~ for teenagers.* | in ◊ *Graphs are ~ in presenting the information.* | on ◊ *He was very ~ on how to do the accounts.* | to ◊ *The stairlift will be ~ to the older patients.*
PHRASES friendly and ~ ◊ *I found all the staff friendly and ~.*

helping noun

ADJ. big, generous, heaping (*AmE*), huge, large ◊ *a generous ~ of potatoes* | small | double, extra, second | healthy ◊ *The steak came with a healthy (= large) ~ of fries.*
VERB + HELPING eat, have
PREP. ~ of ◊ *I had an extra ~ of meat.*

helpless adj.

VERBS appear, be, feel, lie, look, seem, stand, watch ◊ *John felt completely ~.* ◊ *He lay ~ in the hospital ward.* | become | leave sb, render sb ◊ *He was left ~ and alone.* ◊ *She was rendered ~ by panic.*
ADV. absolutely, completely, quite, totally, utterly | apparently, seemingly | almost, virtually | physically
PREP. against ◊ *She was ~ against his strength.* | before ◊ *Kirk stood ~ before this giant of a man.* | in the face of ◊ *I felt ~ in the face of all these rules and regulations.* | with ◊ *She was ~ with anger.*

helplessness noun

ADJ. complete, utter | learned (*esp. AmE*)
PHRASES a feeling of ~, a sense of ~ ◊ *A feeling of utter ~ washed over him.*

hemorrhage noun (AmE) → See HAEMORRHAGE

hen noun

ADJ. battery, free-range (*esp. BrE*) | mother ◊ *She fussed around like a mother ~.* | broody | laying | game (*AmE*)
VERB + HEN keep
HEN + VERB lay, lay eggs ◊ *My ~s have stopped laying.* ◊ *The ~ laid three beautiful speckled eggs.* | cluck, squawk ◊ *I could hear the ~s clucking in the farmyard.* | roost | peck, scratch ◊ *The ~s pecked hopefully at the dusty floor.*
HEN + NOUN coop (*BrE*), house

hepatitis noun

ADJ. severe | acute, chronic | active | viral | infectious | drug-induced
VERB + HEPATITIS have, suffer from | be infected with, contract, get
HEPATITIS + NOUN infection, virus | patient | vaccine | jab (*BrE, informal*), shot (*informal, esp. AmE*), vaccination ◊ *Have you had your ~ B vaccination?*
PHRASES ~ A, ~ B, ~ C
→ Special page at ILLNESS

herb noun

ADJ. dried, fresh | wild | mixed ◊ *Add a teaspoonful of mixed ~s.* | chopped | aromatic, fragrant | bitter, pungent | culinary | healing (*esp. AmE*), medicinal, tonic (*esp. AmE*), traditional
... OF HERBS bunch
VERB + HERB garnish sth with ◊ *Serve cold, garnished with fresh ~s.* | add | use | take ◊ *Ali recommends taking ~s to facilitate recovery.* | grow, plant | gather, pick
HERB + NOUN bed, garden | species | butter, oil, salad (*esp. BrE*), sauce, tea (usually *herbal tea*) | extract
PHRASES ~s and spices ◊ *The shop sells a large range of ~s and spices.*
→ Special page at FOOD

herd noun

1 group of animals

ADJ. great, huge, large, vast | small | entire, whole | national (= all the animals of a particular type in a country) (*BrE*) ◊ *Bad weather has decimated the national ~.* | beef, breeding, dairy ◊ *The farm has only a small dairy ~.* | pedigree (*BrE*) | wild | cattle, cow, elephant, etc.
HERD + NOUN instinct
PREP. in a/the ~ ◊ *The animals tend to graze in a ~.* | ~ of ◊ *a large ~ of cows*
PHRASES a member of a ~

2 group of people

ADJ. common | thundering (*esp. AmE*) ◊ *They hired a thundering ~ of corporate executives.*
VERB + HERD follow ◊ *If you feel so strongly, why follow the ~ (= do the same as everybody else)?* | stand apart from (*AmE*), stand out from ◊ *She prided herself on standing out from the common ~.*
HERD + NOUN instinct, mentality

heritage noun

ADJ. glorious, precious, proud, rich ◊ *The country has a long and proud ~.* | unique | natural | common, national, shared ◊ *Folk songs are part of our common ~.* | ancient | architectural, artistic, cultural, historic, historical, industrial, literary, maritime, musical, religious, spiritual | ethnic, racial | diverse, mixed ◊ *A third of the country's population is of mixed racial ~.* | African, Jewish, etc. | biological, family, genetic
VERB + HERITAGE have ◊ *The city has an exceptionally rich ~ of historic buildings.* | claim ◊ *the 40 million or so Americans who claim an Irish ~* | conserve (*esp. BrE*), preserve, protect, safeguard (*esp. BrE*) ◊ *an organization whose aim is to protect our ~ of wild plants* | abandon, destroy, lose ◊ *I will not abandon my religious ~.* | celebrate, embrace, reclaim ◊ *The performance shows how African Americans celebrate their ~.* | explore ◊ *She made a conscious attempt to explore her Jewish ~.* | trace ◊ *It's a family-run business that traces its ~ back to 1884.* | share ◊ *They share a common ethnic ~.*
HERITAGE + NOUN attraction (*BrE*), building (*esp. BrE*), centre/center, museum, park, site | trail, walk (*BrE*) | tourism | industry | language | conservation, preservation (*esp. AmE*), protection | status ◊ *The site has UNESCO World Heritage status.*

hernia noun

ADJ. hiatus | sports (*AmE*)
VERB + HERNIA have, suffer from | repair
HERNIA + NOUN operation, repair, surgery | problem (*esp. BrE*)
→ Special page at ILLNESS

hero noun

ADJ. big, great ◊ *He was one of the great football ~es of his day.* | genuine, real, true | all-time ◊ *Einstein is the all-time ~ of many scientists.* | unsung ◊ *She was an unsung ~ of the British film industry.* | forgotten | reluctant, unlikely | brave, intrepid ◊ *The song remembers the brave ~es who died for their country.* | romantic, tragic ◊ *Being short and overweight, he was an unlikely romantic ~.* | action, swashbuckling ◊ *Tired of playing the swashbuckling ~, he sought out more challenging roles.* | conquering ◊ *He returned home from the tournament a conquering ~.* | all-American (*BrE*) | have-a-go (= sb who is not in the police, etc. who tries to prevent a crime) (*BrE*) | fallen ◊ *a fallen ~ trying to regain his position* | cult ◊ *James Dean was a cult ~ of the fifties.* | folk, hometown (*BrE*), local, national, popular | fictional, legendary, mythical | real-life | eponymous, titular ◊ *Don Quixote, the eponymous ~ of the novel by Cervantes* | boyhood, childhood ◊ *Bugs Bunny was one of my childhood ~es.* | working-class | war | military, naval | decorated | film (*esp. BrE*), movie (*esp. AmE*) |

comic, football, guitar, musical, **sporting** (*BrE*), **sports** (*AmE*) ◇ *In this album she pays tribute to her musical ~es.* | **Olympic** | **cultural**

VERB + HERO **be hailed (as)** ◇ *He was hailed as a ~ after the rescue.* | **become, make sb into, turn sb into** ◇ *The fight to save the forest turned him into a local ~.* | **die** ◇ *He died a national ~.* | **celebrate, commemorate, honour/honor, salute** | **cheer** | **emulate** | **play, portray** ◇ *Tom Cruise played the ~.* | **meet** ◇ *a chance to meet his ~*

HERO + VERB **battle, fight** | **rescue sb, save sb/sth** | **inspire sb**

HERO + NOUN **status** ◇ *O'Reilly enjoyed ~ status based on his ability with a ball.* | **figure** ◇ *His father was a ~ figure to him.* | **worship**

PREP. **~ to** ◇ *He was a ~ to all his friends.*

PHRASES **be no ~** ◇ *John was no hero—he was willing to let others fight.* | **give sb a hero's welcome, receive a hero's welcome** | **~ of the hour** ◇ *Everyone played brilliantly, but Jones was the ~ of the hour.* | **(die) a hero's death**

heroin *noun*

ADJ. **pure** | **cheap** | **street**

...OF HEROIN **dose, gram, ounce, shot, wrap**

VERB + HEROIN **inject, shoot, smoke** | **prescribe**

HEROIN + NOUN **possession** | **overdose** ◇ *a fatal ~ overdose* | **dealing**

→ Note at DRUG (for more verbs and nouns)

heroine *noun*

ADJ. **great** ◇ *Violetta is one of the great tragic ~s of opera.* | **real** ◇ *Cassandra is the real ~ of the story.* | **national** (*esp. BrE*) | **romantic, tragic, feisty** (*esp. BrE*), **plucky** | **feminist** | **unsung** ◇ *She remains one of the unsung ~s of the war.* | **eponymous, titular** ◇ *Jane Eyre, the eponymous ~ of the novel by Charlotte Brontë* | **fictional** | **action** | **sporting** (*BrE*)

heroism *noun*

ADJ. **extraordinary, real, true** | **individual**

VERB + HEROISM **display, show** ◇ *The firefighters displayed both ~ and staunchness.* | **celebrate**

PHRASES **an act of ~**

herring *noun*

ADJ. **fresh** | **pickled, salted, smoked**

VERB + HERRING **catch**

HERRING + NOUN **fillet/filet** | **fishery**

→ Special page at FOOD

hesitate *verb*

ADV. **a little, slightly** | **briefly, momentarily** | **(for) a minute, (for) a moment, (for) a second, etc.** ◇ *Alison ~d a moment, as if she were waiting for him.* | **barely** ◇ *I barely ~d before saying yes.*

VERB + HESITATE **appear to, seem to** | **make sb** ◇ *Something about his smile made her ~.*

PREP. **about** ◇ *I didn't ~ about working with Craig.* | **between** ◇ *He was hesitating between a glass of wine and an orange juice.* | **over** ◇ *He stood hesitating over whether to join the fight.*

hesitation *noun*

ADJ. **brief, momentary, slight** ◇ *There was a momentary ~ before he replied.* | **considerable** | **little** ◇ *He answered them with little ~.* | **initial** ◇ *After some initial ~, teachers seem to have accepted the new system.*

VERB + HESITATION **hear, notice, see, sense** ◇ *She could sense the ~ in Katelyn's voice.*

PREP. **after...~** ◇ *After much ~, they decided to leave.* | **without ~** ◇ *She answered immediately, without any ~.*

PHRASES **have no ~** ◇ *I have no ~ in recommending him for the job.* | **a moment of ~, a moment's ~** ◇ *After a moment's ~, he nodded.* | **without**

further **~** ◇ *Now without further ~, let me introduce you to tonight's main speaker.*

hibernation *noun*

ADJ. **long** | **deep** | **winter**

VERB + HIBERNATION **go into** ◇ *At the first sign of colder weather many insects go into ~.* | **emerge from**

PREP. **in ~** ◇ *The tortoise spends the winter months in ~.*

hiccup (*also* hiccough) *noun*

1 sound made in the throat

ADJ. **small** | **loud**

VERB + HICCUP **give, let out** ◇ *She gave a loud ~.*

2 hiccups series of hiccups

VERB + HICCUPS **get** ◇ *I ate too quickly and got ~s.* (*BrE*) ◇ *I ate too quickly and got the ~s.* (*AmE*) | **have** ◇ *He had ~s.* (*BrE*) ◇ *He had the ~s.* (*AmE*)

3 small problem

ADJ. **little, minor, slight** | **occasional** | **initial** | **temporary**

PREP. **~ in** ◇ *This one defeat was the only ~ in the team's steady progress.*

hide *noun*

ADJ. **thick, tough** ◇ *Elephants have a very tough ~.* | **leathery, scaly** | **raw** | **tanned** | **animal** | **buffalo, cow, elephant, etc.**

VERB + HIDE **tan** ◇ *The ~ is tanned for leather.*

hide *verb*

1 go/put sth where you/it cannot be seen

ADV. **away** ◇ *She hid the documents away in a drawer.* | **quickly** ◇ *He quickly hid behind a large plant.* | **easily** ◇ *He could easily ~ in the woods.* | **secretly**

VERB + HIDE **prefer to, want to** ◇ *She wanted to run away and ~.* ◇ *He accused the president of preferring to ~ from the truth.* (*figurative*)

PREP. **among** ◇ *They were hiding among the bushes.* | **behind** ◇ *He hid behind a false identity.* (*figurative*) | **beneath** ◇ *He had a weak mouth which he hid beneath a beard.* | **from** ◇ *They tried to ~ from their enemies.* | **in** ◇ *figures hiding in the shadows* | **under** ◇ *He hid the book under his bed.*

PHRASES **carefully hidden, completely hidden, well hidden** ◇ *The letters were well hidden in a drawer.* | **cleverly hidden** ◇ *It had been cleverly hidden under furniture.* | **discreetly hidden** ◇ *The TV was discreetly hidden in a corner.* | **half hidden** ◇ *The buildings were half hidden by the trees.* | **hidden deep in sth** ◇ *tiny villages hidden deep in the softly rolling hills* | **hidden from sight, hidden from view** ◇ *The house was hidden from view by a large fence.* | **lie hidden, remain hidden** ◇ *treasures which have lain hidden in bank vaults since the war* | **partially hidden, partly hidden** ◇ *The house was partially hidden behind some trees.* | **a place to ~ (sth)** ◇ *I'll find a better place to ~ it.*

2 keep sth secret

ADV. **well** | **completely** | **barely** ◇ *She could barely ~ her distaste.* | **deliberately** ◇ *He had deliberately hidden the illness from his boss.*

VERB + HIDE **be able to, be unable to** ◇ *She was unable to ~ her delight at his failure.* | **try to** | **make no attempt to** ◇ *He made no attempt to ~ his anger* | **manage to**

PREP. **from** ◇ *The government tried to ~ the evidence from the public.*

PHRASES **keep sth hidden** ◇ *feelings that she had kept completely hidden all these years* | **previously hidden** ◇ *Hypnotherapy can bring out previously hidden emotions.* | **remain hidden, stay hidden** ◇ *The truth may well remain hidden for ever.*

hiding *noun*

VERB + HIDING **go into** ◇ *He had gone into ~ just after war broke out.* | **come out of** ◇ *After the car had passed by they came out of ~.*

PREP. **in ~** ◇ *The fugitive had spent five weeks in ~.*

hierarchical *adj.*

VERBS **be** ◇ *The company's structure is rigidly ~.* | **become**
ADV. **extremely, fairly, very, etc.** | **rigidly, strictly, strongly**

hierarchy *noun*

ADJ. **complex** | **rigid, strict** ◇ *the rigid class ~ of rural society* | **traditional** | **existing** | **administrative, bureaucratic, corporate, management, managerial, organizational** | **caste, class, racial, social** | **gender** | **dominance** | **Catholic, church, ecclesiastical, religious** | **party, political** ◇ *high up in the party ~* | **judicial, military**
VERB + HIERARCHY **create, develop, establish, form** ◇ *A new management ~ was created within the company.* | **maintain, reinforce** | **move up, rise in, rise through** ◇ *He joined the party in 1966 and quickly moved up the ~.* | **challenge**
HIERARCHY + VERB **be based on sth**
PREP. **in a/the ~** ◇ *She is above me in the ~.* | **within a/the ~** ◇ *There was a range of opinion within the political ~ on the issue.* | **~ of** ◇ *There was a clear ~ of power in the company.*
PHRASES **sb's level, position, status, etc. in a ~**

high *noun*

1 high level or point

ADJ. **all-time, historic, new, record** ◇ *The number of prisoners has reached a historic ~.* | **previous** | **five-year, ten-year, etc.** | **career** ◇ *He hit a career ~ with his performance as Al.*
VERB + HIGH **hit, reach** ◇ *Share prices reached an all-time ~ yesterday.*

2 feeling of great pleasure or happiness

ADJ. **real, tremendous** | **emotional** | **natural** ◇ *He was still on a natural ~ after cheating death.* | **adrenalin, caffeine**
VERB + HIGH **experience, get** ◇ *the ~ she got from her job* | **give sb** ◇ *The drug gives you a tremendous ~.*
PREP. **on a ~** ◇ *She's been on a real ~ since she got her exam results.* ◇ *We want to finish on a ~.*
PHRASES **the ~s and lows** ◇ *the emotional ~s and lows of an actor's life*

highlight *noun*

ADJ. **absolute, definite, main, major, real, undisputed** (*esp. BrE*), **undoubted** (*esp. BrE*) ◇ *The real ~ of the trip for me was the visit to the Tower of London.* | **notable** (*esp. BrE*) | **obvious** | **personal** | **comic, football, musical, sporting** (*BrE*), **sports** (*AmE*) | **career** | **edited ~s** (*BrE*), **recorded ~s** (*BrE*), **video ~s** ◇ *Recorded ~s of the game will be shown later tonight.* ◇ *streamed video ~s from today's news*
PHRASES **the ~ of the day, week, year, etc.** ◇ *The ~ of the week was Saturday's fireworks.*

highlight *verb*

ADV. **clearly** ◇ *These figures clearly ~ the difference in world living standards.* | **dramatically, graphically, starkly** ◇ *The needs of these children were dramatically ~ed by the Action Group.* | **merely, only, simply** ◇ *The talks merely ~ed the great gulf between the two sides.* | **particularly, specifically** | **rightly** | **repeatedly** | **recently**
VERB + HIGHLIGHT **serve to** ◇ *The incident has sadly only served to ~ the differences within the party.*

high school *noun* (*in the US*) → See also SCHOOL

ADJ. **junior, senior** | **local, private, public** | **Catholic**
VERB + HIGH SCHOOL **enter, start** | **go to** ◇ *I went to ~ in Ohio.* | **complete, finish, graduate from** | **drop out of** ◇ *He dropped out of ~ when he was seventeen.*
HIGH-SCHOOL + NOUN **class** ◇ *Jessica went to Yale after graduating at the top of her high-school class.* | **freshman, junior, senior, sophomore** | **grad** (*AmE, informal*), **graduate** | **dropout** | **buddy** (*informal*), **classmate, friend, sweetheart** ◇ *He married his high-school sweetheart.* | **dance, graduation, prom** | **degree, diploma** | **education** | **career** ◇ *During her high-school career in Virginia she won ten state titles.* | **days, years** ◇ *Mitsuka was almost at the end of her high-school years.* | **yearbook** | **reunion** | **athlete, cheerleader, coach, player** | **athletics, ball** (*AmE*), **basket-**

ball, football, etc. ◇ *He played high-school ball at St. Peters.* | **gym** | **biology, chemistry, etc.** | **level** ◇ *physics classes at the high-school level*
PREP. **after ~** ◇ *What do you plan to do after ~?* | **during ~** ◇ *Janine dated many boys during ~.* | **from ~** ◇ *an old friend from ~* | **in ~** ◇ *I was a senior in ~.* ◇ *We knew each other back in ~.* ◇ *I'd known her since my sophomore year in ~.* | **through ~** ◇ *She had good grades all the way through ~.*
PHRASES **fresh out of ~, right out of ~, straight out of ~** ◇ *an 18-year-old kid who is fresh out of ~*

highway *noun* (*esp. AmE*)

ADJ. **wide** | **three-lane, two-lane, etc.** ◇ *a four-lane ~* | **divided** (*AmE*) | **elevated** | **toll** (*AmE*) | **public** (*formal in BrE*) ◇ *He was fined for obstructing the public ~.* (*BrE*) | **federal** | **interstate, main, major, national** | **county, provincial, rural** | **coastal, desert, mountain** | **east-west, north-south** | **deserted, empty, lonely** | **busy** | **information** (*figurative*) ◇ *I'm still learning how to navigate the information ~.*
VERB + HIGHWAY **drive, travel, use** ◇ *I used to travel that ~ with my family.* | **take** ◇ *He took ~ 314 heading north.* | **hit, reach** ◇ *Once you hit the ~, the only services are at Eagle Plains.* | **leave, pull off** ◇ *We pulled off the ~ and stopped for a break.* | **block, clog** (*AmE*), **obstruct** | **close** | **build** | **maintain**
HIGHWAY + NOUN **traffic** | **bridge, exit, interchange, overpass, sign** | **rest area, rest stop** (*both AmE*) | **infrastructure, network, system** | **construction, improvement, maintenance** | **regulation** | **authority, department** | **boss, chief, official** | **robber, robbery** | **contractor, engineer, officer, patrolman** (*AmE*) | **patrol** (*AmE*) | **safety** | **speed** ◇ *A blowout at ~ speeds can be dangerous.* | **accident**
PREP. **along the ~, down the ~, up the ~** ◇ *They tore along the ~.* | **off the ~** | **on the ~, onto the ~**
PHRASES **~s and byways** ◇ *He travels the ~s and byways of Texas.*

hike *noun*

ADJ. **long** | **strenuous** | **ten-mile, two-day, etc.**
VERB + HIKE **go on** ◇ *The boys have gone on a ~ with the Scouts.*
PREP. **on a ~** ◇ *They met on a ~.* | **~ from, ~ to** ◇ *It's a long ~ from Sydney to Perth.*

hill *noun*

ADJ. **big, high, long, tall** ◇ *The bus sped down the long ~.* | **little, low, small** ◇ *The town is set on a small ~.* | **sloping** | **steep** | **gentle, slight** | **rolling ~s, undulating ~s** ◇ *The landscape is made up of low, rolling ~s.* | **rounded** | **dark, blue, green, etc.** | **bare, barren, forested, grassy, open, rocky, rugged, sandy** (*esp. AmE*), **wooded** | **snow-covered, snowy** | **lush, verdant** | **distant, far** ◇ *the distant blue ~s* | **isolated** (*esp. BrE*) | **remote** | **surrounding ~s** ◇ *Troops forced villagers to flee to the surrounding ~s.* | **coastal** | **chalk, limestone, etc.** ◇ *the limestone ~s of Kentucky* | **ski** (*AmE*)
VERB + HILL **ascend** (*formal*), **climb, climb up, go up, scale** ◇ *They climbed a steep ~ and came to the town.* | **crest, top** (*both esp. AmE*) ◇ *They crested a small ~ and then the path curved.* | **come down, descend** (*formal*) | **take to the ~s** (*literary*) ◇ *We took to the ~s in a variety of four-wheel-drive vehicles.* | **roam the ~s, walk the ~s** | **cover, dot** ◇ *Olive groves cover the ~s.* ◇ *the houses which dotted the ~*
HILL + VERB **overlook sth, rise** ◇ *a ~ overlooking the wide valley below* ◇ *Wooded ~s rise behind the town.* | **surround sth**
HILL + NOUN **climbing, walking** (*usually hillwalking*) | **climb, race** (*esp. BrE*) | **walker** (*usually hillwalker*) | **sheep** (*BrE*) | **farm, farmer, farming** (*all esp. BrE*) | **station** (= a small town in the hills, esp. in India), **town, village** (*BrE*) ◇ *In the heat of summer the rich fled to the ~ stations.* | **country** | **tribe** | **fort** | **top** (*usually hilltop*) | **slope** | **start** (= starting a vehicle on a slope) (*BrE*)

PREP. **down a/the ~** ◇ *A grassy path led down the ~.* | **in the ~s** ◇ *There are several lead mines in the ~s above the town.* | **on a/the ~** ◇ *The church is perched on a ~.* | **over a/the ~** ◇ *Over the ~ lies another town.* | **up a/the ~** ◇ *A few yards up the ~, on the left, was a turning.* | **~ above** ◇ *the ~s above the town*

PHRASES **the bottom of a/the ~, the foot of a/the ~** ◇ *A spring emerges at the bottom of the ~.* | **the crest of a/the ~, the top of a/the ~**

hillside *noun*

ADJ. **steep** | **rocky** | **bare, exposed, open** (*all esp. BrE*) | **grassy, green, wooded** ◇ *On our left was a wooded ~.* | **terraced** | **distant**
VERB + HILLSIDE **be set on** ◇ *Many of the chalets are set on a ~ reached by steps.* | **cover, dot** ◇ *Tiny flowers dotted the ~.*
HILLSIDE + NOUN **vineyard** | **town, village**
PREP. **down a/the ~** ◇ *A stream tumbles down the steep ~.* | **on a/the ~** ◇ *The house was on a ~ outside the town.* | **up a/the ~** ◇ *We clambered up the ~ to the ridge above.* | **above** ◇ *the ~ above the town*

hinder *verb*

ADV. **greatly, seriously, severely** ◇ *These killings have seriously ~ed progress towards/toward peace.*
VERB + HINDER **be likely to, tend to** ◇ *Bulky clothes tend to ~ movement.*
PHRASES **help or ~ sth** ◇ *factors which might help or ~ a child's progress at school* | **~ rather than help sth** ◇ *These laws will ~ rather than help progress.*

hindrance *noun*

ADJ. **big** (*esp. AmE*), **great** (*esp. AmE*), **major, serious**
VERB + HINDRANCE **be, prove** ◇ *Having a car in the city might prove a ~.*
PREP. **without ~** (*formal*) ◇ *We were allowed to travel around the country without ~.* | **~ to** ◇ *The new regulations are actually a great ~ to teachers.*
PHRASES **without let or ~** (*BrE, law*)

hindsight *noun*

PREP. **in ~** ◇ *Their first idea was deemed, in ~, a mistake.* | **with ~** ◇ *This all seems obvious with ~.*
PHRASES **~ is a wonderful thing** ◇ *I should have guessed... but ~ is a wonderful thing.* | **(with) the advantage of ~, (with) the benefit of ~** ◇ *It is easy to criticize others when you have the benefit of ~.*

Hinduism *noun* → Note at RELIGION

hint *noun*

1 suggestion
ADJ. **big, broad, clear** (*esp. BrE*), **heavy, not-so-subtle** (*esp. AmE*), **obvious, strong** ◇ *He gave a broad ~ that he was on the verge of leaving.* | **gentle, little, subtle, vague** | **tantalizing** | **dark** (*esp. BrE*) | **early** ◇ *There were early ~s that their marriage might be in trouble.*
VERB + HINT **drop, give (sb)** ◇ *I dropped a few subtle ~s about the payment being due.* | **catch** (*AmE*), **get, take** ◇ *OK, I get the ~!* ◇ *Can't you take a ~ and leave me alone?*
PREP. **~ about** | **~ from** ◇ *a ~ from my boss about my absences from the office* | **~ to** ◇ *Is that a ~ to me to leave?*

2 small amount of sth
ADJ. **strong** ◇ *a dish with a strong ~ of garlic* | **barest, faint, little, merest, slightest, small, tiny** ◇ *The slightest ~ of gossip upset her.* | **occasional** | **first** ◇ *She felt the first ~ of panic as the train pulled into the station.*
VERB + HINT **detect, notice, sense** ◇ *Do I detect a ~ of jealousy in your voice?* | **show** ◇ *He showed not a ~ of remorse.* | **betray, reveal** ◇ *Her voice betrayed a ~ of uneasiness.*
PREP. **~ of** ◇ *There was a ~ of amusement in his voice.*

PHRASES **at the first ~ of sth** ◇ *At the first ~ of trouble I'll call the police.*

3 piece of advice
ADJ. **handy, helpful, practical, useful** | **household**
VERB + HINT **give (sb), offer (sb)**
PREP. **~ about** ◇ *The book gives some useful ~s about how to plan your garden.* | **~ on** ◇ *a book full of handy ~s on painting*

hint *verb*

ADV. **broadly, heavily** (*esp. BrE*), **strongly** ◇ *He ~ed strongly that he would be resigning soon.* | **subtly** | **darkly** ◇ *She ~ed darkly that all was not well.* | **even** ◇ *She even ~ed that she might resign.* | **merely, only**
PREP. **at** ◇ *The problems are only ~ed at in the report.*

hip *noun*

ADJ. **lean** (*esp. AmE*), **narrow, slender, slim, small** ◇ *Her ~s were still narrow like a girl's.* | **ample, wide** | **curvy, shapely** | **childbearing** | **broken, dislocated, fractured** | **bad, bruised, sore** | **arthritic** | **artificial, replacement**
VERB + HIP **have your hands on, put your hands on** ◇ *He put his hands on his ~s and sighed.* | **gyrate, move, roll, shake, sway, swing, wiggle** ◇ *She wiggled her ~s seductively as she walked.* | **rotate, swivel, turn, twist** ◇ *Twist your ~s in your opponent's direction as you punch.* | **lift, raise** | **thrust** | **break, dislocate, fracture** | **replace**
HIP + VERB **move, sway, swing** ◇ *Her ~s were swaying seductively in time to the music.*
HIP + NOUN **fracture, injury** | **pain** | **operation** (*esp. BrE*), **surgery** (*esp. AmE*) | **replacement** ◇ *My grandmother's having a ~ replacement.* | **bone, joint, socket** | **measurement** | **flask** (*BrE*) ◇ *He took a swig of whisky from his ~ flask.* | **pocket** ◇ *Don't carry money or documents in your ~ pocket.*
PREP. **across the ~s** ◇ *She was wearing a short blue dress, belted across the ~s.* | **at the ~** ◇ *He had his leg amputated at the ~.* | **from the ~** ◇ *The gun could be fired from the shoulder or from the ~.* | **on the ~** ◇ *She was carrying a baby on her ~.* | **to the ~** ◇ *The skirt is slit to the ~ on one side.*
PHRASES **hands on (your) ~s** ◇ *He leaned casually against the door, hands on ~s.*

hire *noun*

1 (*esp. BrE*) **use of a car, etc. for payment**
ADJ. **bicycle, car, equipment, etc.**
HIRE + NOUN **car** ◇ *Our ~ car broke down after only an hour.* | **charge, cost** | **company, firm, shop** (*BrE*) ◇ *a car ~ firm* ◇ *a costume ~ shop*
PREP. **for ~** (*BrE, AmE*) ◇ *There are boats for ~ on the lake.* | **on ~** ◇ *vehicles currently on ~* | **on ~ from, on ~ to** ◇ *The equipment is on ~ from a local company.* | **~ of** ◇ *The main expense was the ~ of a car.*

2 (*esp. AmE*) **new person in a job**
ADJ. **new, recent** | **potential, prospective**

hire *verb*

1 (*esp. BrE*) **borrow a car, etc. for payment**
ADV. **by the day, week, etc.** ◇ *What's the cost of hiring by the day?* | **locally** ◇ *Ski equipment can be ~d locally.*
PREP. **from** ◇ *Bicycles can be ~d from several local shops.*

2 (*esp. AmE*) **give sb a job**
ADV. **by the day** ◇ *Workers were ~d by the day.*
VERB + HIRE **can/can't afford to** ◇ *The television studio couldn't afford to ~ a top-notch cast.*
PHRASES **~ and fire** ◇ *Who is responsible for hiring and firing around here?*

hiss *noun*

ADJ. **loud, sharp** | **faint, low, slight, soft** ◇ *There was a low ~ on the tape.* | **audible, noticeable**
VERB + HISS **give, let out** ◇ *The snake gave a ~.* | **hear**
PREP. **with a ~** ◇ *She drew in her breath with a ~.* | **~ of** ◇ *We could hear the faint ~ of escaping gas.*

PHRASES **boos and ~es** | **a ~ of air** | **a ~ of pain** ◇ *She let out a ~ of pain.*
→ Note at SOUND

hiss *verb* say sth in an angry, hissing voice

ADV. **angrily, furiously** ◇ *'Don't be stupid!' she ~ed furiously.* | **quietly, softly** | **loudly** | **menacingly, venomously** | **urgently**
PREP. **at** ◇ *She ~ed at me to be quiet.*
PHRASES **~ (sth) through your teeth** ◇ *'Go away!' he ~ed through clenched teeth.*

historian *noun*

ADJ. **distinguished, eminent, great, leading, noted, respected** ◇ *a talk given by an eminent social ~* | **serious** ◇ *No serious ~ today accepts this theory.* | **academic, professional** | **amateur** | **official** ◇ *the official ~ of the United States Army* | **presidential** (*esp. AmE*) | **contemporary, future** ◇ *The oldest tradition goes back to the contemporary ~ John Foxe.* ◇ *What will future ~s make of the late 20th century?* | **ancient, medieval, modern** ◇ *She is a writer as well as a distinguished modern ~.* | **local** | **architectural, art, church, cultural, economic, film, legal, literary, military, political, social, etc.** | **revisionist** ◇ *Revisionist ~s have questioned the accepted version of events.*

history *noun*

1 the past, esp. as a subject of study

ADJ. **contemporary, early, recent** ◇ *the early ~ of the trade union movement* ◇ *things that happened in recent ~* | **ancient, medieval, modern** | **human** | **local** | **family** | **American, British, world, etc.** | **official** ◇ *the official ~ of the university* | **revisionist** | **recorded** ◇ *The debate about the origins of the universe has been going on throughout recorded ~.* | **oral** ◇ *Oral ~ provides an account of those aspects of people's experience that are not recorded in documents.* | **intellectual** | **art, church, cultural, economic, literary, military, political, social, etc.** | **environmental** (*esp. AmE*), **evolutionary, geologic** (*AmE*), **geological** | **past** ◇ *They had an affair once, but that's past ~ now* (= no longer important or relevant).
... OF HISTORY **piece** ◇ *She created a piece of ~ by winning her fourth title.*
VERB + HISTORY **be steeped in** ◇ *a building that is steeped in ~* | **go down in, make, pass into** ◇ *He will go down in ~ as a wise adviser and a kind man.* | **fade into** ◇ *He made ~ by being the first man to walk on the moon.* | **fade into** ◇ *The war has now faded into ~.* | **trace** ◇ *The regiment traces its ~ back to 1803.* | **chronicle, document, write** | **recount, relate, tell** | **distort, rewrite** ◇ *her attempt to rewrite ~ with herself in the role of heroine* | **reconstruct**
HISTORY + VERB **go back to sth** ◇ *The town's ~ goes back to colonial times.* | **go back ...** ◇ *The ~ of this organization goes back many years.* | **reveal sth, show sth, suggest sth, teach sth, tell sth** ◇ *History shows that high approval ratings are no guarantee of re-election.* | **repeat itself** ◇ *Years later, family ~ repeated itself with Eve's daughters.*
HISTORY + NOUN **book** (*figurative*) ◇ *She has earned her place in the ~ books.*
PREP. **during sth's ~** ◇ *The country has suffered several invasions during its ~.* | **in (sth's) ~** ◇ *the most extraordinary meeting in ~* ◇ *the best player in the sport's ~* | **~ of** ◇ *the ~ of the world* ◇ *She studies ~ of art.* | **throughout ~** ◇ *There have been conflicts such as this throughout ~.*
PHRASES **change the course of ~** ◇ *events that could change the course of ~* | **a period of ~** ◇ *This is a fascinating period of ~.* | **the lessons of ~** (*figurative*) | **the rest is ~** (= the rest of the story does not need to be told because it is well known) | **a sense of ~** ◇ *a people with no sense of ~* | **a slice of ~** ◇ *The team grabbed a slice of ~ here today* (= achieved sth that will be remembered).
→ Note at SUBJECT (for more verbs and nouns)

2 facts about sb/sth's life/existence in the past

ADJ. **chequered/checkered, colourful/colorful, fascinating, interesting, rich, turbulent** ◇ *The city has a rich and fascinating ~.* | **long** ◇ *She has a long ~ of mental illness.* |
previous, subsequent | **shared** | **case** ◇ *She familiarized herself with the case ~ of her new patient.* | **credit, employment, family, life, medical, personal, sexual** ◇ *The doctor will need some details of your medical ~.* ◇ *I know nothing about his personal ~.*
VERB + HISTORY **have** ◇ *They have a ~ of trying to interfere.*
PREP. **~ of** ◇ *a ~ of heart disease in the family*

hit *noun*

1 act of hitting sth/sb

ADJ. **direct**
VERB + HIT **deliver, give sth, land, make, score** ◇ *Give it a good ~.* ◇ *At last he managed to score a ~.* | **receive, suffer, take** ◇ *One of the tanks took a direct ~.*
HIT + NOUN **list** ◇ *She was at the top of the terrorists' ~ list* (= list of people they intended to kill). ◇ *Which services are on the government's ~ list?* (*figurative*) | **man, squad** ◇ *He claimed that a ~ man had been paid $20 000 to kill him.*

2 sb/sth that is very popular

ADJ. **big, greatest, huge, massive, real, runaway, smash** ◇ *The show has been a smash ~.* | **surprise** | **breakout** (*AmE*) | **immediate, instant** | **box-office, chart** (*esp. BrE*), **pop** (*esp. BrE*) ◇ *She is here to promote her latest chart ~.*
HIT + NOUN **album, film** (*esp. BrE*), **movie** (*esp. AmE*), **record, show, single, song**
PREP. **~ with** ◇ *The series has been a big ~ with children.*

hit *verb*

1 strike

ADV. **hard** ◇ *She didn't ~ me very hard.* | **repeatedly** | **directly** ◇ *He was ~ directly in the back.* | **almost, nearly** ◇ *A taxi almost ~ him as he was crossing the street.* | **accidentally** ◇ *I accidentally ~ my knee on the desk.*
VERB + HIT **want to** ◇ *I was so angry, I wanted to ~ him.* | **be going to** ◇ *I was afraid he was going to ~ me.*
PREP. **in** ◇ *She ~ him in the face.* | **on** ◇ *I ~ my head on the low doorway.* | **with** ◇ *He ~ her with a stick.*
PHRASES **~ sb over the head** ◇ *He was ~ over the head with a broken bottle.*

2 have a bad effect on sb/sth

ADV. **badly, hard, heavily, severely** ◇ *Our department has been badly ~ by the cutbacks.* ◇ *Some businesses have been ~ very hard by the rise in interest rates.*

hitch *noun*

ADJ. **slight** | **last-minute** (*esp. BrE*) ◇ *There are always a few last-minute ~es at the dress rehearsal.* | **legal** (*BrE*), **technical** ◇ *There was a slight technical ~ which delayed the plane's take-off.*
PREP. **without a ~** ◇ *Everything went without a ~.* | **~ in** ◇ *There's been a ~ in the plans.*

HIV *noun*

VERB + HIV **acquire, contract, get** | **have, suffer from** ◇ *people suffering from ~ and AIDS* | **be affected by, be infected with** | **spread, transmit** | **test negative for, test positive for** | **screen sth for, test sb/sth for** ◇ *Blood is screened for ~.* | **prevent** | **treat** | **combat, fight**
HIV + NOUN **infection, transmission** | **prevention** | **antibody, virus** | **carrier, sufferer** | **status** ◇ *If you are unsure of your ~ status, consider having a test.* | **test**
PHRASES **HIV-negative, HIV-positive**
→ Special page at ILLNESS

hoard *noun*

ADJ. **big, large, major, vast** ◇ *one of the biggest ~s of Roman coins ever found* | **small** | **cash** ◇ *He controls a cash ~ of some $1 billion.*
PREP. **in ~s** (*esp. BrE*) ◇ *Gold coins have been found in ~s in many parts of the country.* | **~ of** ◇ *a vast ~ of treasure*

hoarse adj.

VERBS **be, sound** | **become, get, go** | **make sb/sth, scream yourself, shout yourself** ◊ *All the shouting had left her rather ~.* ◊ *Excitement made her voice ~.* ◊ *He shouted himself ~, but still no one came.*
ADV. **extremely, fairly, very, etc.** | **a little, slightly, etc.**
PREP. **from** ◊ *Her voice was ~ from shouting.* | **with** ◊ *His voice was ~ with anxiety.*

hoax noun

ADJ. **elaborate** ◊ *It turned out to be an elaborate ~.* | **cruel** ◊ *He described the deception as a cruel ~.* | **bomb** (*BrE*) | **email, Internet, virus** ◊ *He had been the victim of a computer virus ~.*
VERB + HOAX **perpetrate** ◊ *a ~ perpetrated by the government* | **fall for** | **expose**
HOAX + NOUN **email, letter** | **call, caller** (*both BrE*)

hobby noun

ADJ. **enjoyable, fun, interesting, relaxing** | **favourite/favorite** | **expensive** ◊ *Photography can be an expensive ~.*
VERB + HOBBY **have** ◊ *Do you have any hobbies?* | **enjoy, indulge, indulge in, pursue** ◊ *She never had any time to pursue her hobbies.* | **start, take up** ◊ *Why don't you take up a new ~?*
PREP. **among your ~s** ◊ *Music and karate are among her hobbies.* | **as a ~** ◊ *He collects postcards as a ~.*

hockey noun

ADJ. **field** (*AmE*), **ice** (*BrE*) | **air, floor** (*AmE*), **roller, street** | **men's, women's** | **college** (*esp. AmE*), **collegiate** (*AmE*), **high-school** (*AmE*), **varsity** (*AmE*) | **junior, senior** | **major-league, minor-league** (*both AmE*) | **Olympic, pro** (*esp. AmE*), **professional**
VERB + HOCKEY **play, watch** ◊ *She plays ~ in the winter.*
HOCKEY + NOUN **ball, mask, pads, puck, skates, stick** | **arena** (*esp. AmE*), **field, pitch** (*BrE*), **rink, stadium** | **championship, game, match, tournament** | **coach, goalie, player** | **star** | **fan** | **club, squad** (*BrE*), **team** ◊ *He plays in the college ~ team.* (*BrE*) ◊ *He plays on the college ~ team.* (*AmE*) | **league, season, tournament**
→ Special page at SPORTS

hold noun

1 act/way of holding sth

ADJ. **firm, tight** ◊ *He still had me in a tight ~.*
VERB + HOLD **catch, get, grab, grasp, seize, take** ◊ *Take ~ of the handle and give it a hard pull.* | **have, keep** ◊ *He kept a firm ~ on my hand.* | **lose** ◊ *He lost his ~ on the rock and was swept away by the tide.* | **tighten** | **loosen, relax, release** ◊ *She finally released her ~ on me.*
PREP. **~ on** ◊ *He tightened his ~ on her.*

2 influence/control over sb

ADJ. **firm, powerful, secure, strong, tight** ◊ *He still has a firm ~ on the party.* | **fragile, precarious, tenuous, weak** ◊ *Her ~ on power was now quite tenuous.*
VERB + HOLD **have** | **maintain** | **lose** ◊ *The allies lost their ~ on the south of the country.* | **consolidate, increase, strengthen, tighten** ◊ *Enemy forces have consolidated their ~ on the northern province.* | **break, loosen, weaken** ◊ *an attempt to break the ~ of the Church*
PREP. **~ on** ◊ *This had weakened his ~ on power.* | **over** ◊ *He no longer had any ~ over her.*

hold verb

1 in your hands/arms

ADV. **firmly, securely, tightly** | **carefully** | **gently, loosely**

2 opinion, etc.

ADV. **commonly, widely** ◊ *This view is not widely held.* | **deeply, firmly, strongly** ◊ *deeply held religious beliefs* | **privately, publicly** ◊ *privately held views*

holder noun

ADJ. **licence/license, passport, ticket, visa** ◊ *Only ticket ~s will be allowed in.* | **account, credit-card, policy** ◊ *Account ~s with the bank qualify for a discount on loans.* | **cup** (*BrE*), **record, title** ◊ *the current record ~* | **job** (*esp. BrE*), **office, post** (*BrE*) ◊ *She wondered why the previous job ~ had left.* ◊ *a coup d'état against an elected presidential office ~.* | **copyright, patent**

hold-up noun

1 robbery

ADJ. **armed** | **bank**
VERB + HOLD-UP **carry out** (*BrE*)

2 delay

ADJ. **lengthy** | **traffic**

hole noun

ADJ. **big, deep, gaping, great, huge, large, massive, yawning** | **small, tiny** | **circular, round** | **jagged, ragged** ◊ *The missile had torn a jagged ~ in the side of the ship.* | **bullet, drill, screw** ◊ *The wall was full of bullet ~s.* | **drainage** | **mouse, rabbit, etc.**
VERB + HOLE **bore, create, cut, dig, drill, make, punch, wear** ◊ *We dug a deep ~ to bury the animals in.* ◊ *She punched two ~s in each sheet of paper.* ◊ *He had worn a ~ in the knees of his jeans.* | **blast, blow, break, burn, rip, tear** | **fill, fill in, patch, plug** ◊ *I uprooted the tree and filled the ~ with earth.* ◊ *We used cement to plug the ~s.*
PREP. **down a/the ~** ◊ *The snake disappeared down a ~.* | **in a/the ~** ◊ *There was water in the ~.* | **through a/the ~** ◊ *We climbed through the ~.* | **~ in** ◊ *I made an extra ~ in my belt.*
PHRASES **full of ~s** ◊ *The old blankets were now full of ~s.* | **riddled with ~s** ◊ *The car was riddled with bullet ~s.*

holiday noun

1 (BrE) period of time away from home for pleasure
→ See also VACATION

ADJ. **enjoyable, exciting, fun-filled, good, lovely, wonderful** | **disastrous** ◊ *We had a disastrous camping ~.* | **dream** ◊ *What would be your dream ~?* | **foreign, overseas** | **summer, winter** | **7-night, two-week, etc.** | **package** | **family** | **activity, adventure, camping, skiing** ◊ *I learned to windsurf on an activity ~.*
VERB + HOLIDAY **go on, have, take** ◊ *We're going on ~ to France this summer.* ◊ *Are you having a ~ this year?* | **book** ◊ *Have you booked your summer ~ yet?* | **cancel** ◊ *I got ill and had to cancel my ~.*
HOLIDAY + NOUN **destination, resort, venue** ◊ *a popular seaside ~ resort* | **accommodation, cottage, home** ◊ *They also have a ~ home at the seaside.* | **camp, complex, village** | **period, season** ◊ *The pool is open throughout the ~ season.* | **brochure** | **business, company, firm** ◊ *The recession hit the package ~ business hard.* | **insurance** ◊ *You should take out ~ insurance before you leave.* | **arrangements, plans** | **romance** ◊ *Their ~ romance turned into a lasting relationship.* | **photos, snaps**
PREP. **on (a) ~** ◊ *They met while on ~ in Spain.*
PHRASES **a ~ of a lifetime** ◊ *This is your chance to win the ~ of a lifetime.*

2 (BrE) period of rest from work/school → See also VACATION

ADJ. **annual, Christmas, Easter, summer** ◊ *The school is now closed for the Christmas ~s.* | **school** | **paid**
VERB + HOLIDAY **be entitled to, get, have** ◊ *You are entitled to 24 days' paid ~ per year.* ◊ *I have three weeks' a year.* | **take** ◊ *I'm taking the rest of my ~ in October.* | **spend** ◊ *She spent her ~ decorating the house.* | **need** ◊ *I really need a ~!*
HOLIDAY + NOUN **time** | **entitlement** | **pay** | **job** ◊ *She had a ~ job as a gardener when she was a student.*
PREP. **during the ~s** ◊ *It can be difficult to keep children occupied during the long summer ~s.* | **in the ~s** ◊ *My aunt's coming to stay in the ~s.* | **on ~** ◊ *I'm afraid Mr Adamek is on ~ this week.*

ADJ. **bank** (*in the UK*), **federal** (*in the US*), **national, public, religious** | **Christian, Jewish,** etc. | **Christmas, Easter, Labor Day** (*in the US*), **Memorial Day** (*in the US*), **Thanksgiving** (*in the US*) | **winter, year-end** (*both AmE*)
VERB + HOLIDAY **celebrate** (*esp. AmE*) ◊ *I go back a couple of times a year to celebrate the ~s with my family.* | **spend** ◊ *We always spend the ~s together.*
HOLIDAY + NOUN **break, weekend** ◊ *The roads will be busy on Monday as it's a ~ weekend.* | **season** (*esp. AmE*) ◊ *This ~ season was the worst in 25 years for retailers.* | **cheer, spirit** (*both esp. AmE*) ◊ *I'm just trying to spread a little ~ cheer.* | **celebrations, concert, meal, party** (*all esp. AmE*) | **decorations, gift** (*both AmE*) | **card** (*AmE*)

hollow *noun*

ADJ. **deep** | **little, shallow, slight** | **damp, dark, grassy** | **sheltered** | **natural**
PREP. **in a/the ~** ◊ *Snow lay in dark ~s.* | **~ in** ◊ *a ~ in the ground* | **~ of** ◊ *the ~ of her throat*

home *noun*

1 where sb lives; where sb/sth comes from

ADJ. **family, marital** (*BrE*), **matrimonial** (*BrE*), **parental** (*BrE*) ◊ *It's unusual for young people over 25 to still live in the family ~.* | **boyhood, childhood** | **adopted** | **permanent, temporary** ◊ *a shelter for people with no permanent ~* ◊ *a temporary ~ for the paintings* | **current, former** | **new, old** | **good, happy, loving, safe, secure** (*BrE*), **stable** ◊ *These children badly need a stable ~ life.* | **broken** ◊ *children from a broken ~* (= whose parents are no longer together) | **single-parent, two-parent** ◊ *More and more children in the school are from single-parent ~s.* | **middle-class, working-class,** etc. | **winter** ◊ *The mudflats offer a winter ~ to thousands of migrating swans.* | **natural, spiritual** ◊ *The first time he visited New Orleans he knew he had found his spiritual ~.*
VERB + HOME **be away from, get away from, leave** ◊ *He didn't leave ~ until he was 24.* | **abandon, flee** ◊ *The people abandoned their ~s and headed for the hills.* | **find (sb/sth), give sb/sth** ◊ *Perhaps we could find a ~ for the kitten.*
HOME + NOUN **address, number** ◊ *Try calling me on my ~ number after six o'clock.* | **background, conditions, environment, life, situation** ◊ *He came from an appalling ~ background.* ◊ *She had never had a stable ~ life.* | **comforts** (*esp. BrE*) ◊ *She desperately missed her ~ comforts while camping.* | **appliance** | **cinema** (*BrE*), **entertainment, theater** (*AmE*) ◊ *the market for ~ entertainment systems* | **movie, video** ◊ *We have a ~ movie of my dad teaching me to swim.* | **use** ◊ *This computer is marketed for ~ use.* | **computer** | **user** ◊ *a laser printer aimed at the ~ user* | **study** ◊ *The course is suitable for classroom or ~ study.* | **work, worker, working** (*all esp. BrE*) ◊ *He supplements his income with part-time or ~ work.* | **office** | **care, nursing, visit** ◊ *The doctor was assaulted on a ~ visit.* | **remedy, treatment** ◊ *I've tried all the ~ remedies for headaches without success.* | **leave** ◊ *He went missing while on ~ leave from prison.* | **consumption** ◊ *He claimed he had bought the cigarettes for ~ consumption.*
PREP. **at ~, away from ~** ◊ *Her job means she's away from ~ for weeks at a time.* | **back ~, in your own ~** | **~ of** ◊ *Andalusia, the ~ of flamenco*
PHRASES **a ~ away from ~** (*AmE*), **a ~ from ~** (*BrE*) ◊ *The hotel's friendly atmosphere makes it a real ~ (away) from ~.* | **~ sweet ~** (= used to say how pleasant your home is), **on the ~ front** (= used to introduce domestic news) ◊ *On the ~ front, the fuel crisis continues to worsen.* | **welcome ~** ◊ *The banner said 'Welcome ~, Dad!'*

2 house, flat/apartment, etc.

ADJ. **beautiful, comfortable, nice** | **luxurious, luxury, magnificent, palatial** | **private** | **new, new-build** (*BrE*) | **custom** (*AmE*) | **existing, old** | **affordable, humble, modest** | **dream** ◊ *They found their dream ~ on the shore of a lake.* | **detached, semi-detached** | **terrace, terraced** (*both BrE*) | **modern, traditional, Victorian** | **own** ◊ *They designed and built their own ~.* | **rental** (*AmE*), **rented** | **council** (*BrE*) |

ranch, tract (*both AmE*) | **country, seaside** (*esp. BrE*), **suburban, village** (*esp. BrE*) ◊ *He used to spend the summer painting at his country ~.* | **holiday** (*BrE*), **second, summer, vacation** (*AmE*), **weekend, winter** ◊ *They also have a weekend ~ in the Catskills.* | **caravan** (*BrE*), **mobile** (*esp. AmE*), **motor** (usually ***motorhome***), **trailer** ◊ *The storm wrecked the family's motorhome.* | **ancestral, historic, stately** (*BrE*) ◊ *Priceless antique furniture was destroyed in the fire at the stately ~.*
VERB + HOME **own** ◊ *He'd always dreamed of owning his own ~.* | **buy, purchase** | **build** | **decorate, furnish** | **destroy**
HOME + NOUN **buyer, owner** | **ownership** | **builder** | **building, construction** | **sales** | **improvement, maintenance, repairs** | **extension** (*BrE*) | **loan** | **furnishings** | **contents** (*BrE*) ◊ *Make sure you insure your ~ contents for an adequate amount.* | **insurance** | **security** ◊ *Fitting a burglar alarm is the most effective way to increase ~ security.*

3 place that provides care for sb/sth

ADJ. **care** (*esp. BrE*), **children's, convalescent, foster, nursing, old people's** (*esp. BrE*), **residential** (*BrE*), **rest, retirement** | **funeral** | **purpose-built** (*BrE*) ◊ *Work begins this week on a purpose-built ~ for the city's homeless.*
VERB + HOME **run** ◊ *They run a retirement ~ for the elderly.*

homeland *noun*

ADJ. **beloved** ◊ *They were devastated that they had to leave their beloved ~.* | **ancestral, ancient, original, traditional** ◊ *the struggle to defend their ancient ~* | **former** | **national, tribal** | **independent** | **adopted** ◊ *He wants his children to grow up in his adopted ~.* | **American, Jewish, Palestinian,** etc.
VERB + HOMELAND **defend, protect, secure** ◊ *It is is the role of the army to protect the ~.* | **flee, leave** ◊ *During the war, they were forced to flee their ~.* | **go back to, return to, visit** ◊ *He longs to return to his ~.*
HOMELAND + NOUN **defence/defense, security** (*both esp. AmE*)
PREP. **in a/sb's ~** ◊ *They hope to remain in their ~.*

homeless *adj.*

VERBS **be** | **become, end up, find yourself** ◊ *He found himself ~ after his marriage broke up.* | **leave sb, make sb, render sb** ◊ *Three hundred people were left ~ by the earthquake.*
ADV. **intentionally, unintentionally** (*both esp. BrE*) | **chronically** (*AmE*)

homesick *adj.*

VERBS **be, feel** | **become, get** | **make sb** ◊ *Seeing other families together made him terribly ~.*
ADV. **desperately, terribly** (*esp. BrE*), **very** | **a little, slightly,** etc.
PREP. **for** ◊ *She felt ~ for her country.*

homework *noun*

ADJ. **English, science,** etc.
...OF HOMEWORK **piece**
VERB + HOMEWORK **do** ◊ *Have you done your physics ~ yet?* | **finish** | **hand in** ◊ *I want you to hand in this ~ on Friday.* | **get, have** ◊ *They get a lot of ~ in English.* | **assign** (*esp. AmE*), **give (sb), set (sb)** ◊ *The science teacher always gives a lot of ~.* | **grade** (*esp. AmE*), **mark** (*esp. BrE*)
PREP. **for** ◊ *We had to write out one of the exercises for ~.* | **~ on** ◊ *I have some ~ to do on the Civil War.*

homicide *noun* (*esp. AmE*)

ADJ. **criminal, culpable** (*esp. BrE*), **negligent, unlawful** (*esp. BrE*) | **vehicular** (*AmE*) | **justifiable** ◊ *The jury reached a verdict of justifiable ~.* | **multiple** | **double, triple,** etc.
HOMICIDE + NOUN **detective** | **unit** | **investigation** | **rate** | **victim** | **case**
→ Note at CRIME (for verbs)

homogeneous adj.

VERBS **be** | **become**
ADV. **remarkably, very** | **fairly, relatively** | **culturally, ethnically, racially** ◇ *a culturally ~ society*

homosexual noun

ADJ. **practising/practicing** | **closet, closeted, repressed** | **female, male**

honest adj.

VERBS **be, seem, sound**
ADV. **extremely, fairly, very,** etc. | **scrupulously, truly** | **absolutely, completely, perfectly, quite, totally** | **less than, not entirely** ◇ *I don't think you've been entirely ~ with me.* | **refreshingly** | **brutally, painfully** ◇ *Let's be brutally ~ about this: you don't have a hope of succeeding.* | **intellectually**
PREP. **about** ◇ *Try to be ~ about how you feel.* | **in** ◇ *He is always scrupulously ~ in his business activities.* | **with** ◇ *My parents were always completely ~ with me.*
PHRASES **~ enough** ◇ *She seems ~ enough.* | **to be ~ (with you)** ◇ *To be quite ~ with you, I don't think he's the right person for the job.* | **open and ~** ◇ *She was totally open and ~ about her feelings.*

honesty noun

ADJ. **absolute, complete, total** ◇ *I always expect total ~ from my employees.* | **blunt** (esp. AmE)**, brutal, raw, unflinching** ◇ *'Don't you love me?' 'I don't know,' she said with brutal ~.* | **emotional, intellectual** ◇ *You need ruthless intellectual ~ about your own skills, weaknesses and motives.* | **refreshing**
VERB + HONESTY **admire, appreciate, value** | **question** ◇ *Are you questioning my ~?* | **have** ◇ *She had the ~ to admit her mother was right.* | **expect, require**
PREP. **with ~** ◇ *She answered the questions with complete ~.* | **~ about** ◇ *I appreciate your ~ about this.*
PHRASES **~ and integrity** ◇ *He has the ~ and integrity to be chairman.* | **in all ~, in ~** ◇ *In all ~, the book was not as good as I expected.* ◇ *Who in ~ can blame her?*

honey noun

ADJ. **clear** | **runny** | **wild**
... OF HONEY **jar, pot**
VERB + HONEY **make, produce** ◇ *How do bees make ~?* ◇ *a jar of locally produced ~* | **gather** ◇ *to gather ~ from the hive* | **spread (sth with)** ◇ *He spread some ~ on his bread.*
HONEY + NOUN **bee**
PHRASES **as sweet as ~**
→ Special page at FOOD

honeymoon noun

ADJ. **brief, short** ◇ *We had a brief ~ in Paris.* | **long** | **second** ◇ *After so many years of marriage, we're planning a second ~.*
VERB + HONEYMOON **go on, have, leave for, spend** ◇ *They go on ~ the day after the wedding.* (BrE) ◇ *They go on their ~ the day after the wedding.* (AmE)
HONEYMOON + VERB **be over** (usually figurative) ◇ *The ~ was over and the reality of what she had taken on began to dawn.*
HONEYMOON + NOUN **couple** | **suite** | **cruise** | **period, phase** (AmE) (both figurative) ◇ *There was always a ~ period when my father started a new job.*
PREP. **for a ~** ◇ *They can't decide where to go for their ~.* | **on ~** ◇ *While on ~ in Bali, she learned to scuba dive.*

honour (BrE) (AmE honor) noun

1 sth that makes you feel proud

ADJ. **great, rare, special, tremendous** ◇ *Eastlake Studio received top ~s in the interior design category.* | **dubious** ◇ *Max was given the dubious ~ of organizing the children's party.*
VERB + HONOUR/HONOR **have** ◇ *I had the rare ~ of being allowed into the artist's studio.* | **do sb** (formal)**, give sb** ◇ *Will you do me the ~ of dining with me?* | **share** ◇ *He shared the ~ of being the season's top scorer with Andy Cole.*

2 great respect

PREP. **in sb's ~** ◇ *They organized a party in his ~.*
PHRASES **a guard of ~** (esp. BrE) ◇ *The coffin was accompanied by a guard of ~.* | **(the) guest of ~** ◇ *The president was guest of ~ at the society's banquet.* | **a lap of ~** (esp. BrE) ◇ *The crowd cheered while the athletes ran their lap of ~.* | **a mark of ~** ◇ *They stood in silence as a mark of ~ to the drowned sailors.* | **the place of ~, the seat of ~** | **a roll of ~** (BrE) (**honor roll** in AmE) ◇ *The school's roll of ~ lists everyone killed in the war.* ◇ *She was on the ~ roll every semester of high school.* ◇ *I never made the ~ roll.*

3 good reputation

ADJ. **family, national, personal** ◇ *He was now satisfied that the family ~ had been restored.*
VERB + HONOUR/HONOR **defend, fight for, preserve, save, uphold** ◇ *She felt she had to defend the ~ of her profession.* | **restore** | **bring, do** ◇ *This biography does great ~ to the poet's achievements.* ◇ *She brought ~ to her country as an Olympic medal-winner.*
HONOUR/HONOR + VERB **be at stake** ◇ *National ~ is at stake in this game.*
HONOUR/HONOR + NOUN **code, system** ◇ *~ code violations*
PREP. **on your ~** (old-fashioned) ◇ *I swear on my ~ (= very seriously) that I knew nothing about this.* | **with ~** | **without ~** ◇ *a man without ~*
PHRASES **a badge of ~** ◇ *He saw his injuries as a badge of ~.* | **a code of ~** ◇ *The secret society had a strong code of ~.* | **a man of ~** | **a matter of ~, a point of ~** ◇ *It is a matter of ~ to keep our standards as high as possible.* | **a sense of ~** | **sb's word of ~** ◇ *I give you my word of ~ I will not forget what I owe you.*

4 award, official title, etc.

ADJ. **full ~s, high, major, top** ◇ *the stars who took top ~s at the MTV Awards* ◇ *television's highest ~* | **academic, battle, civilian, military, political**
VERB + HONOUR/HONOR **award (sb), bestow, confer, give sb** ◇ *The Order of Merit is the highest civilian ~ that can be conferred on someone.* | **accept, pick up, receive, scoop** (BrE)**, take, win** ◇ *It was the British who took the ~s at last night's Oscars.* | **earn**
HONOUR/HONOR + NOUN **list, system** (both in the UK) ◇ *He was made a life peer in the New Year's ~s list.*
PHRASES **with full military ~s** ◇ *He was buried with full military ~s.*

5 honours/honors in education

ADJ. **combined, joint** (both BrE) | **first-class, second-class** (both BrE)
HONOURS/HONORS + NOUN **class** (AmE)**, course** (BrE)**, degree, program** (AmE) ◇ *He's in the third year of his ~s course.* ◇ *I took an ~s class in English.* | **graduate, student**
PREP. **~ in** ◇ *She earned a bachelor's degree with ~s in English.* | **with ~** ◇ *She holds an MBA with ~s from the University of California, Los Angeles.* ◇ *He passed with second-class ~s.*

honourable (BrE) (AmE honorable) adj.

VERBS **be**
ADV. **very** ◇ *a very ~ man* | **completely, entirely, perfectly** (esp. BrE) ◇ *My intentions were entirely ~.*

honoured (BrE) (AmE honored) adj.

VERBS **be, feel**
ADV. **deeply, extremely, greatly, highly, truly, very** ◇ *I am deeply ~ to be invited to this momentous occasion.*

hood noun

1 part of a coat, etc. that covers the head

VERB + HOOD **pull up, put up** ◇ *She put up her ~ when it started to rain.* | **lower, pull back, pull off, remove** ◇ *He walked into the room and pulled off his ~.*
PHRASES **with the ~ down, with the ~ up** ◇ *He was wearing a jacket with the ~ up.*
→ Special page at CLOTHES

2 (*AmE*) part of a vehicle covering the engine → See also
BONNET

ADJ. **car** | **crumpled, dented**
VERB + HOOD **open, pop** | **close** | **hit** ◇ *The sound of a bird hitting the ~ of the car*
PHRASES **the ~ of a/the car**

hooked *adj.*

VERBS **be** | **become, get** ◇ *I first got ~ on scuba diving when I was twelve.* | **get sb** | **keep sb** ◇ *a master storyteller who knows how to keep his readers ~*
ADV. **completely, totally, well and truly** (*esp. BrE*)
PREP. **on** ◇ *She's completely ~ on TV.*

hope *noun*

1 belief that sth you want will happen

ADJ. **deep** (*esp. AmE*), **fervent, great** ◇ *a feeling of considerable ~* ◇ *It is my fervent ~ that you will be able to take this project forward.* | **high** (only used with *hopes*) ◇ *We have high ~s for the project.* ◇ *Hopes are high that a resolution to the conflict can be found.* | **best, main** ◇ *Privatization seems to offer the best ~ for the industry.* | **faint, slight, vague** ◇ *There was still a faint ~ that they would accept the offer.* | **real, sincere** ◇ *without any real ~ of success* ◇ *It is my sincere ~ that she will find happiness at last.* | **realistic, reasonable** | **desperate, wild** | **false, forlorn, vain** ◇ *He wasn't trying to give her false ~.* ◇ *It seemed a forlorn ~ that we would find a taxi.* | **dashed** | **early** ◇ *His early ~s of freedom were now gone.* | **last, only** ◇ *He had one last ~ to cling to.* | **fresh, new, renewed** ◇ *the treatment gave him renewed ~* | **sudden** ◇ *Her dark eyes lit with sudden ~.* | **lingering** (*esp. BrE*), **remaining** ◇ *These figures kill off any lingering ~s of an early economic recovery.* | **personal**
... OF HOPE **flicker, glimmer, ray, spark** ◇ *I looked at her and felt a glimmer of ~.*
VERB + HOPE **be full of, cherish, entertain, feel, harbour/harbor, have, hold, see** ◇ *He secretly cherished ~s that George would marry his daughter.* ◇ *Political leaders do now entertain the ~ that a settlement can be found.* ◇ *She saw little ~ of meeting the targets.* | **express, voice** ◇ *The Mexican president expressed ~ for cooperation on trade.* | **share** | **pin, place, put** ◇ *He pinned all his ~s on getting that job.* | **find** ◇ *Maybe we can find some ~ for humanity after all.* | **cling to, keep alive, live in** ◇ *It is important to keep alive the ~ that a peace settlement might be found.* ◇ *I haven't yet found a place to rent, but I live in ~.* | **not hold out** ◇ *I don't hold out much ~ of finding a buyer.* | **abandon, give up, lose** ◇ *I didn't give up ~ of being released.* | **bring sb, give sb, offer (sb), provide, raise** ◇ *The use of fish oil to treat cancer has brought fresh ~ to millions of sufferers.* ◇ *This announcement has raised ~s that the crisis may be coming to an end.* | **boost** (*esp. BrE*) ◇ *The latest job figures have boosted ~s for the economy.* | **crush, dash, destroy, end, kill, kill off, shatter, wreck** (*esp. BrE*) ◇ *Her ~s of going to college have now been dashed.*
HOPE + VERB **lie, rest** ◇ *Her only ~ lay in escape.* ◇ *Their main ~s rest on their new striker.* | **grow, rise** ◇ *Hopes of a peaceful end to the strike are now growing.* | **flare** (*esp. AmE*), **flare** (*AmE*), **spring, spring up, surge** ◇ *Hope flared up inside her.* | **remain** ◇ *Hope remains that survivors will be found.* | **die, disappear, fade** ◇ *Hope faded after wrecked remains of the ship were washed onto the shore.*
PREP. **beyond ~** ◇ *damaged beyond ~ of repair* | **in ~ of, in the ~ that, in ~s that** (*AmE*) ◇ *I am writing to you in the ~ that you can help me obtain some information.* ◇ *I am writing this letter in ~s that it will be forwarded to the editor.* | **without ~** ◇ *She felt weak and without ~.* | **~ for** ◇ *young people who are full of ~ for the future* | **~ of** ◇ *I have no ~ of winning.*
PHRASES **every ~ of sth, little ~ of sth, no ~ of sth, some ~ of sth** ◇ *We have every ~ of completing the project this year.* ◇ *There is little ~ that they will be found alive.* | **grounds for ~, reason for ~** ◇ *We now have good grounds for ~.* | **keep your ~s up** ◇ *We're trying to keep our ~s up.* | **not a ~ in hell** (*informal*) ◇ *You don't have a ~ in hell of finding a job.* |

a sign of ~, a symbol of ~ | **not get your ~s up** ◇ *I'll see what I can do, but don't get your ~s up too much.*

2 sth you wish for

ADJ. **big ~s, high ~s** ◇ *They have high ~s for their children.* | **future** | **distant** ◇ *Peace is a distant ~ in this war-torn region.* | **personal** | **unfulfilled** ◇ *a bitter tale of unfulfilled ~s* | **championship, medal, Olympic, play-off, title, etc.** ◇ *the team's championship ~s*
VERB + HOPE **carry** ◇ *Every time he plays he carries the ~s of the entire nation.*
PREP. **~ for, ~ of**
PHRASES **your ~s and dreams, expectations, fears, etc.** ◇ *She told me all her ~s and dreams.*

3 sb/sth that will help you get what you want

ADJ. **big, bright** | **last, one, only** ◇ *He turned to her in despair and said, 'You're my last ~.'* ◇ *Our one ~ was that the hurricane would change direction.* | **medal**
VERB + HOPE **represent** ◇ *He represents our best ~ for a swimming medal.*
PREP. **~ for** ◇ *She is Britain's brightest ~ for a medal.* | **~ of** ◇ *The operation was Kelly's only ~ of survival.*

hope *verb*

ADV. **certainly, desperately, fervently, really, sincerely, very much** ◇ *They ~d desperately that their missing son would come home.* ◇ *I sincerely ~ that you will be successful.* | **only** ◇ *I only ~ you're right.* | **secretly** ◇ *He secretly ~d that she wouldn't be home.*
VERB + HOPE **(not) dare (to)** | **hardly dare, scarcely dare** (*esp. BrE*) ◇ *I hardly dared to ~ the plan would succeed.* | **begin to** | **continue to**
PREP. **for** ◇ *We are hoping for good weather.*
PHRASES **~ against ~** (= to continue to hope for sth even though it is very unlikely) | **~ for the best** (= to hope that sth will happen successfully, esp. where it seems likely that it will not)

hopeful *adj.*

1 thinking that sth good will happen

VERBS **be, feel, seem, sound** ◇ *I feel ~ that a peaceful solution will be found.* | **become, get** ◇ *Don't get too ~. We may not be able to go.* | **remain** ◇ *The police remained ~ that she would be found alive.*
ADV. **extremely, fairly, very, etc.** | **almost**
PREP. **about** ◇ *She was not very ~ about her situation.* | **of** (*BrE*) ◇ *The police are ~ of catching the thieves.*

2 making you think that sth good will happen

VERBS **be, look, seem** ◇ *Things aren't looking very ~ at the moment.*
ADV. **extremely, fairly, very, etc.** ◇ *There are some fairly ~ signs of recovery in the US market.*

hopeless *adj.*

VERBS **be, look, seem** | **feel** ◇ *She felt lonely and completely ~.*
ADV. **absolutely, completely, pretty, quite, totally, utterly** ◇ *The situation seemed completely ~.* ◇ *He's a pretty ~ dancer* (= very bad). (*BrE*) | **apparently, seemingly** | **rather**
PREP. **at** (*esp. BrE*) ◇ *I'm absolutely ~ at languages.* | **with** (*esp. BrE*) ◇ *I've always been ~ with machinery.*

horizon *noun*

1 line where earth and sky meet

ADJ. **northern, southern, etc.** | **distant, far** ◇ *The sea stretched away to the distant ~.*
VERB + HORIZON **scan** ◇ *The captain scanned the ~ for any sign of other vessels.*
PREP. **above the ~** ◇ *I watched the pale sun climb over the ~.* | **below the ~** ◇ *The sun was sinking rapidly below the western ~.* | **beyond the ~** ◇ *Land was still out of sight beyond the ~.* | **on the ~** ◇ *A cloud of dust on the ~*

announced the arrival of the cavalry. | **over the ~** ◇ *The moon was rising over the ~.*

2 horizons limits to knowledge/experience

ADJ. **limited, narrow | new | cultural, intellectual, musical, political** ◇ *Her trips to Asia have broadened her cultural ~s.*
VERB + HORIZONS **broaden, expand, open up, widen** ◇ *It is hoped that the course will open up new ~s for students.* | **limit, narrow** ◇ *Their ~s were limited to events within the town community.*
HORIZONS + VERB **stretch** ◇ *His ~s didn't stretch beyond his next game.*
PREP. **beyond your ~** ◇ *They had become aware of possibilities beyond their own limited ~s.*

hormone noun

ADJ. **female, male | growth, sex** ◇ *children who do not produce enough growth ~*
VERB + HORMONE **produce, release, secrete** ◇ *Hormones are secreted into the bloodstream.* | **take**
HORMONE + NOUN **production | therapy, treatment | replacement** ◇ *women taking ~ replacement therapy* | **deficiency, imbalance | balance, level**

horn noun

1 part of an animal

ADJ. **buffalo, bull's, cow's, rhino, etc.** ◇ *ornaments made of rhino ~* | **curled, curved** ◇ *a large bull with curved ~s* | **sharp**

2 warning device on a vehicle

ADJ. **car**
VERB + HORN **beep, blare, blow, honk, sound** (*BrE*), **toot** (*BrE*) ◇ *Passing motorists honked their ~s.*
HORN + VERB **beep, blare, honk, hoot, sound** ◇ *Another ~ blared behind me.*
HORN + NOUN **blast** ◇ *Impatient ~ blasts began to sound behind him.*
PREP. **on a/the ~** ◇ *He gave a furious blast on his ~.*

3 musical instrument

VERB + HORN **blow**
HORN + NOUN **section**
→ Special page at MUSIC

horoscope noun

VERB + HOROSCOPE **cast** ◇ *To cast someone's ~, you need to know their date and exact time of birth.* | **read**
HOROSCOPE + VERB **say sth** ◇ *What does your ~ say?*

horrible adj.

VERBS **be, feel, look, seem, smell, sound, taste**
ADV. **really** ◇ *That was a really ~ thing to say!* | **absolutely, quite, truly** ◇ *a truly ~ sight* | **just** ◇ *It's just ~ thinking about it.* | **pretty** ◇ *a pretty ~ experience*
PREP. **to** ◇ *My sister has always been ~ to me.*

horrific adj.

VERBS **be, look**
ADV. **really | absolutely, quite, truly** ◇ *Some of the scenes we witnessed were quite ~.* | **fairly** (*BrE*), **pretty**

horror noun

1 feeling of fear/shock

ADJ. **abject, absolute, pure, sheer, utter** ◇ *The thought of working nights fills me with abject ~.* | **mock** ◇ *She raised her hands in mock ~ when she saw my new haircut.*
VERB + HORROR **feel, have** ◇ *She felt ~ and pity at seeing Marcus so ill.* ◇ *She had a ~ of snakes.* | **fill sb with** ◇ *The possibility of meeting him again filled me with ~.* | **imagine** ◇ *Imagine my ~ when I discovered I'd be working for my ex-wife.* | **overcome | recoil in** ◇ *Anna recoiled in ~ as the spider approached.* | **express**
HORROR + NOUN **film** (*esp. BrE*), **movie, story** ◇ *They were*

trying to scare each other with ~ stories about going to the dentist.
PREP. **in ~** ◇ *They watched in ~ as the aircraft crashed to the ground.* | **to your ~** ◇ *To his ~, he saw a dead body lying beside the road.* | **with ~** ◇ *He realized with absolute ~ that he no longer had the money.* | **~ of** ◇ *I'm trying to overcome my ~ of insects.*
PHRASES **a look of ~**

2 sth frightening/shocking

ADJ. **full, real, true** ◇ *He never experienced the full ~s of trench warfare.* | **ultimate** ◇ *I used to regard public speaking as the ultimate ~.* | **unspeakable**
VERB + HORROR **commit, inflict, perpetrate** ◇ *He had witnessed ~s committed by the enemy.* | **experience, know, suffer | see, witness | describe**

horse noun

ADJ. **beautiful, fine, good, great, lovely, magnificent** ◇ *He was mounted on the finest ~ you could ever see.* | **bay, black, chestnut, grey/gray | thoroughbred | wild | unbroken | nervous, restless | frightened, startled | fancied** (*BrE*) ◇ *The two most fancied ~s finished last.* | **loose, riderless, runaway** ◇ *Three jockeys were injured when a loose ~ ran across the track.* | **fresh** ◇ *They would need fresh ~s if they were to reach the border the next day.* | **fast | lame | heavy, shire** (*esp. BrE*) ◇ *Heavy ~s were used for delivering beer.* | **riding, saddle | carriage, cart** (usually ***carthorse***), **draught/draft, dray | pack | cavalry, police | race** (usually ***racehorse***) | **quarter** (*esp. AmE*) | **champion | pantomime** (*BrE*) ◇ *He got a part as the rear end of a pantomime ~.* | **rocking**
VERB + HORSE **breed | own, train | get ready** ◇ *Get my ~ ready and wait for me.* | **saddle | be mounted on, mount | dismount** (*esp. AmE*), **dismount from | ride | spur, spur on, urge** ◇ *He urged his ~ into a gallop.* | **lead | brush, brush down, groom | shoe | stable | handle** ◇ *She has a knack for handling ~s.* | **frighten | hobble, tether, tie**
HORSE + VERB **canter, gallop, trot, walk** ◇ *Several ~s trotted past us.* | **prance** ◇ *There are ten ~s running in the next race.* | **plod** ◇ *The weary ~ plodded up the hill.* | **neigh, snort, whinny | bolt | rear, rear up, shy | plunge** ◇ *The cart overturned, the ~ plunging and rearing in its traces.* | **fall, slip, stumble** ◇ *The ~ stumbled and threw its rider.* | **throw sb | jump | pull sth** ◇ *They passed an old ~ pulling a cart full of apples.* | **graze | stand**
HORSE + NOUN **box** (usually ***horsebox***) (*BrE*), **trailer** (*AmE*) ◇ *The car in front was pulling a horsebox.* | **breeder, dealer** (*esp. BrE*), **lover, owner, rider, trainer | hooves | droppings, dung, manure, shit** (*slang*) | **flesh** (usually ***horseflesh***) | **fair** (*BrE*) ◇ *Hundreds of animals are bought and sold at the annual ~ fair.* | **race | racing, riding** (*BrE*) (***horseback riding*** in *AmE*) | **show, trials** ◇ *He won second prize in a ~ show.* | **trough** ◇ *The ~ trough was full of stagnant water.* | **whip** (usually ***horsewhip***) | **trading** (usually ***horse-trading***) (*figurative*) *political horse-trading*
PREP. **on a/the ~**
PHRASES **a ~ and carriage, a ~ and cart**

hospital noun

ADJ. **community, district** (*esp. BrE*), **local | NHS** (*in the UK*), **private, public, state | day, long-stay** (*BrE*) | **general | children's, maternity, mental, psychiatric, etc. | teaching, university | field, military**
VERB + HOSPITAL **go into, go to** ◇ *He had to go to ~ for treatment.* (*BrE*) ◇ *He had to go to the ~ for treatment.* (*AmE*) | **rush sb to, take sb to** ◇ *She was rushed to ~.* (*BrE*) ◇ *She was rushed to the ~.* (*AmE*) | **admit sb to, readmit sb to** ◇ *He has been readmitted to ~.* (*BrE*) ◇ *He has been readmitted to the ~.* (*AmE*) | **stay in** ◇ *How long will I have to stay in ~?* (*BrE*) ◇ *How long will I have to stay in the ~?* (*AmE*) | **come out of, leave** ◇ *She came out of ~ this morning.* (*BrE*) ◇ *She came out of the ~ this morning.* (*AmE*) | **discharge sb from**
HOSPITAL + NOUN **administrator, doctor, staff, worker | inpatient, outpatient, patient | care, services, treatment | clinic, unit, ward | bed, room | admission, stay | records | system**
PREP. **at a/the ~** ◇ *She works at the John Radcliffe Hospital.* |

in (a/the) ~ ◇ *He is in ~ recovering from surgery.* (*BrE*) ◇ *He is in the ~ recovering from surgery.* (*AmE*) ◇ *I used to work as a cleaner in a ~.* | **to (a/the) ~** ◇ *He was taken to ~ as a precaution.* (*BrE*) ◇ *He was taken to the ~ as a precaution.* (*AmE*) ◇ *We went to the ~ to visit my grandmother.*
PHRASES **admission to ~** (*BrE*), **admission to the ~** (*AmE*) | **a stay in ~** (*BrE*), **a stay in the ~** (*AmE*)

hospitality *noun*

ADJ. **generous, gracious** (*esp. AmE*), **lavish** (*esp. BrE*), **warm** | **Scottish, Southern, etc.** | **corporate** ◇ *the company's corporate ~ budget*
VERB + HOSPITALITY **extend** (*formal*), **offer (sb), provide (sb with), show sb** ◇ *We would like to thank you for the warm ~ extended to us during our recent visit.* | **accept** ◇ *We were glad to accept their generous ~.* | **enjoy** | **repay, return** ◇ *You must allow me to repay your ~.* | **abuse** (*esp. BrE*)
PREP. **~ to** ◇ *a duty to offer ~ to strangers*

host *noun*

1 person who receives and entertains visitors

ADJ. **charming** (*esp. BrE*), **generous, genial, good, gracious, perfect** ◇ *George was a perfect ~.*
VERB + HOST **act as, play** ◇ *The town is playing ~ to a film crew.*
HOST + NOUN **city, club** (*esp. BrE*), **community, country, family, government, nation, society, state** ◇ *The ~ club is to be congratulated on its organization of the tournament.*
PREP. **~ to** ◇ *The park is ~ to a beautiful ornamental lake.*

2 person who introduces a television or radio show

ADJ. **chat-show** (*BrE*), **game-show, radio, talk-show, television, TV** ◇ *The event will be opened by television ~ Bill Punter.* | **guest**

host *verb*

ADV. **jointly** ◇ *The tournament is to be jointly ~ed by India, Pakistan and Sri Lanka.*
VERB + HOST **agree to, offer to** | **be keen to** (*BrE*) ◇ *The country is very keen to ~ the Winter Olympics in six years' time.*
PHRASES **a bid to ~ sth** ◇ *the city's bid to ~ the Olympic Games in the year 2008*

hostage *noun*

VERB + HOSTAGE **hold (sb), keep (sb)** ◇ *Eight people were held ~ for four months.* | **seize, take (sb)** ◇ *The gunmen took 24 ~s.* | **free, release, rescue** ◇ *diplomatic efforts to get the ~s released* | **execute, kill**

hostel *noun*

1 place for students, etc. to stay

ADJ. **student** (*esp. BrE*), **youth**
VERB + HOSTEL **stay at** ◇ *We stayed at a youth ~ in Perugia.*
HOSTEL + NOUN **accommodation** (*BrE*), **accommodations** (*AmE*)
PREP. **at a/the ~** ◇ *We stayed at a student ~ during the conference.*

2 (*BrE*) place for homeless people to stay

ADJ. **refugee** | **bed-and-breakfast** | **bail, probation** ◇ *a probation ~ for young offenders*
VERB + HOSTEL **stay at, stay in** ◇ *homeless families staying in bed and breakfast ~s*
PREP. **in a/the ~** ◇ *He lives in a ~ for the homeless.*

hostile *adj.*

VERBS **appear, be, feel, seem** | **become, turn** | **remain** | **make sb** ◇ *The experience has made him generally ~ to women.* | **consider sth, deem sth, perceive sth as, regard sth as, see sth as** ◇ *They were reluctant to take any step that might be regarded as ~.*
ADV. **bitterly, decidedly, deeply, downright, extremely, positively** (*esp. BrE*), **unremittingly, very** ◇ *He was deeply ~ to the idea of psychotherapy.* ◇ *The audience gave him a downright ~ reception.* | **entirely, totally** | **increasingly** | **apparently** | **potentially** | **generally** | **actively, openly,**

overtly (*esp. AmE*) | **mutually** | **uniformly** ◇ *The press became uniformly ~ to the new administration.*
PREP. **to** ◇ *Many people were openly ~ to the idea.* | **towards/ toward** ◇ *He was extremely ~ towards/toward her.*

hostility *noun*

1 opposition/aggressive feelings or actions

ADJ. **bitter** (*esp. BrE*), **considerable, deep, extreme, great, implacable** | **downright, open, outright, overt** ◇ *Mixed-race couples faced open ~.* | **veiled** ◇ *There was a barely veiled ~ in her tone.* | **general, widespread** | **popular** (*esp. BrE*), **public** ◇ *the widespread popular ~ to the war* | **personal** | **continuing, growing** | **mutual** | **racial**
VERB + HOSTILITY **feel, sense** ◇ *the deep ~ felt by many teenagers against the police* | **express, show** | **arouse, attract** (*esp. BrE*), **provoke** ◇ *Such a move might arouse public ~.* | **be greeted with, be met with, encounter, face, meet with** ◇ *The proposal was met with outright ~.*
PREP. **~ between** ◇ *You could almost feel the ~ between her and her mother.* | **~ against, ~ to, ~ towards/toward** ◇ *the bitter ~ towards/toward the occupying forces*

2 hostilities fighting in a war

ADJ. **major** | **active** (*esp. AmE*)
VERB + HOSTILITIES **cease, end** ◇ *Both sides finally agreed to suspend hostilities.* | **resume** (*esp. BrE*) ◇ *Hostilities were resumed later that year.*
HOSTILITIES + VERB **begin, break out, commence** | **cease, end** ◇ *On the November 11, 1918, hostilities ceased.* | **continue, resume** (*esp. BrE*)
PREP. **~ against** ◇ *the official cessation of hostilities against Japan* | **~ between** ◇ *Hostilities broke out between the two provinces later that year.*
PHRASES **the cessation of hostilities** | **an outbreak of hostilities**

hot *adj.*

1 of the weather

VERBS **be** | **become, get, grow, turn** ◇ *The sun shone fiercely down and it grew hotter and hotter.*
ADV. **extremely, fairly, very, etc.** | **baking** (*esp. BrE*), **blazing, boiling, exceptionally, extremely, incredibly, intensely, oppressively, really, scorching, stiflingly, swelteringly, unbearably, uncomfortably, unusually** ◇ *a boiling ~ summer day* ◇ *It was unbearably ~ in the car.* | **a little, slightly, etc.** ◇ *This weather's a little ~ for me.*

2 of a person

VERBS **be, feel, look** ◇ *Don't you feel ~ so close to the fire?* | **get, grow, turn** ◇ *She was beginning to get uncomfortably ~.* ◇ *His face grew ~ at the memory of his embarrassment.*
ADV. **extremely, fairly, very, etc.** | **boiling, burning, uncomfortably** ◇ *I was boiling ~ and sweaty.* ◇ *His forehead was burning ~.* | **a little, slightly, etc.**

3 of a thing

VERBS **be, feel, look, seem** | **get** | **keep, stay** ◇ *The food should stay ~ until we're ready to eat.* | **keep sth** ◇ *The containers keep the food ~ for five hours.* | **eat sth, serve sth** ◇ *Serve ~ or cold accompanied by bread and a salad.*
ADV. **extremely, fairly, very, etc.** ◇ *Wash the tablecloth in fairly ~ soapy water.* | **scalding** | **piping, sizzling, steaming** (all used about food) ◇ *a bowl of piping ~ soup* ◇ *Make sure the fat is sizzling ~.* | **a little, slightly, etc.** | **moderately** ◇ *Bake in a moderately ~ oven.* | **enough** ◇ *The ground was ~ enough to fry an egg.*

4 spicy

VERBS **be, taste**
ADV. **extremely, fairly, very, etc.** ◇ *I love really ~ food.* ◇ *That was a pretty ~ curry!* | **a little, slightly, etc.**

hotel *noun*

ADJ. **big, large** | **little, small** | **250-room, etc.** | **cheap, expensive** | **five-star, four-star, etc.** | **beautiful, com-**

ten minutes past the ~ | **to the ~** (*esp. BrE*) ◊ *ten minutes to the ~*

3 time when you do a particular activity

ADJ. **lunch** | **peak, rush** ◊ *rush-hour traffic* | **happy** (= time in the early evening when a bar sells alcoholic drinks at lower prices than usual)
VERB + HOUR **spend** ◊ *I spent my lunch ~ shopping.*
PREP. **~ of** ◊ *an ~ of rest*

4 hours time when sb is working/a business is open

ADJ. **office, opening, visiting, working** ◊ *the hospital's visiting ~s* | **flexible** | **long** | **regular** | **licensing** (*BrE*) ◊ *Britain's licensing ~s* (= when pubs are allowed to open)
VERB + HOURS **work** ◊ *She works very long ~s.* | **keep** ◊ *He keeps regular ~s.*
PREP. **after ~** ◊ *He spends a lot of time in his office after ~s.* | **out of ~** (*esp. BrE*) ◊ *Doctors often have to work out of ~s.*

5 time when sth happens

ADJ. **darkest, finest** ◊ *The war years were often thought of as the country's finest ~.* | **antisocial** (*esp. BrE*), **unearthly** (*esp. BrE*), **ungodly, unsocial** (*esp. BrE*) ◊ *I apologize for calling you at this ungodly ~.* ◊ *Bakers have to work unsocial ~s.* | **early, early-morning** (*esp. AmE*), **small, wee small ~s** (= the hours after midnight) ◊ *The party continued well into the early ~s.* | **late** | **waking** ◊ *She spends every waking ~ at the gym.*
HOUR + VERB **come** ◊ *The ~ had come for us to leave.*
PREP. **between the ~s of** ◊ *The office is closed between the ~s of twelve and two.* | **~ of** ◊ *the ~s of darkness*
PHRASES **your ~ of need** ◊ *She helped me in my ~ of need.*

house noun

1 building that is made for one family to live in

ADJ. **beautiful, comfortable, elegant, fancy** (*esp. AmE*), **fine, grand, handsome, lovely, luxurious, magnificent, posh** (*esp. BrE*), **pretty** | **dream** ◊ *They built their own dream ~ overlooking the river.* | **dingy, gloomy, ugly** | **derelict, dilapidated, ramshackle, shabby, untidy** (*BrE*) | **abandoned** | **detached, semi-detached** | **row** (*AmE*), **terrace** (*BrE*), **terraced** (*BrE*) | **big, enormous, gigantic, huge, large, palatial, spacious** | **rambling** ◊ *It was easy to get lost in the rambling ~.* | **little, modest, small, tiny** ◊ *They lived in a modest semi-detached ~ in the suburbs.* | **single-storey/ single-story, single-storeyed/single-storied, two-storey/ two-story, etc.** | **four-bedroom, four-bedroomed, eight-room, eight-roomed, etc.** | **brick, gabled** (*esp. BrE*), **half-timbered** (*esp. BrE*), **red-brick, thatched** | **expensive** | **private** | **council** (*BrE*) | **rented** | **empty, unoccupied, vacant** | **country, suburban, town** (usually ***townhouse*** in *AmE*) | **great, manor** (*BrE*), **mansion** (*esp. BrE*) ◊ *The great ~ stood on the edge of the town.* | **farm** (usually ***farmhouse***) | **ranch** (*AmE*) | **tract** (*AmE*) | **ancestral** | **communal, group** (*AmE*), **shared** (*BrE*) ◊ *I live in a group/shared ~* (= with people who are not my family). | **summer** | **beach** | **tree** | **halfway, safe** ◊ *a halfway ~ for prisoners returning to society* ◊ *The police provided a safe ~ for the informer.* | **haunted**
VERB + HOUSE **live in, occupy** ◊ *a ~ occupied by students* | **share** ◊ *She shares a ~ with three other nurses.* | **buy, rent** | **sell** | **have, own** | **let** (*esp. BrE*), **let out** (*esp. BrE*), **rent out** ◊ *We let out our ~ when we moved to America.* ◊ *We're only planning on renting the ~ out for a few years.* | **repossess** (*esp. BrE*) ◊ *Their ~ was repossessed when they couldn't keep up their mortgage payments.* | **move** (*BrE*), **move into, move out of** ◊ *It's stressful moving ~.* ◊ *We had to move out of our ~.* | **set up** ◊ *They want to set up ~ together.* | **keep** ◊ *She kept ~* (= cooked, cleaned, etc.) *for her elderly parents.* | **play** ◊ *The children were playing ~, giving dinner to their dolls.* | **build** | **demolish, knock down, tear down** | **maintain** | **decorate** (*esp. BrE*), **do up** (*BrE*), **redecorate, refurbish, renovate** ◊ *They bought an old ~ and are gradually renovating it.* | **furnish** | **clean** | **insulate, rewire** | **add onto, extend** ◊ *We're hoping to extend the ~.* ◊ *Our challenge was to add onto the ~ in a respectful way.* | **search** ◊ *Police officers have been searching the ~ for clues.* | **wake up** ◊ *You'll wake up the whole ~* (= all the people in the house) *with that noise.*

---

fortable, **de luxe, elegant, excellent, fancy** (*esp. AmE*), **fine, first-class, good, grand, luxurious, luxury, nice, pleasant** (*esp. BrE*), **posh** (*esp. BrE*), **quality** (*esp. BrE*), **smart** (*esp. AmE*), **top** ◊ *all the style and comfort that only the best ~s can provide* ◊ *It was a luxury ~ with its own swimming pool and restaurant.* | **boutique** | **seedy** | **modern** | **old, traditional** | **friendly** (*BrE*) | **family-friendly, gay-friendly, pet-friendly, etc.** | **family, family-run** (*esp. AmE*) ◊ *a family ~ with a playground for small children* ◊ *a friendly family-run ~* | **independent, private** | **international** | **airport** | **country** (*esp. BrE*), **country-house** (*BrE*) ◊ *a small country ~* | **holiday** (*BrE*), **resort, tourist** | **beachfront** (*esp. AmE*), **seafront** (*BrE*), **seaside** (*esp. BrE*) | **local, nearby**
VERB + HOTEL **stay at, stay in** ◊ *We're staying at a cheap ~ near the train station.* | **book in at** (*BrE*), **book into** (*esp. BrE*), **check in at, check in into** ◊ *We checked into the ~, then went for a walk along the beachfront.* | **check out of** | **book** | **find** | **own** | **manage, run** | **build**
HOTEL + VERB **be located, be situated** ◊ *The ~ is situated in the heart of the city.* | **boast sth, feature sth, have sth, offer sth, provide sth** ◊ *The ~ features a beautiful dining room overlooking the lake.* ◊ *The ~ offers excellent facilities.*
HOTEL + NOUN **accommodation** (*BrE*), **accommodations** (*AmE*), **bedroom, room, suite** | **reservation** | **bed** | **bar, restaurant** | **foyer, lobby** | **manager, owner, worker** | **management, staff** | **guest** | **industry** | **chain, group**
PREP. **at a/the ~** ◊ *We met at the ~.* | **in a/the ~** ◊ *We're staying in a ~ near the beach.*

hotline noun

ADJ. **telephone** | **24-hour** | **free, toll-free** (*AmE*) | **customer-service, information, ticket** | **national** | **credit-card** (*BrE*) | **suicide** (*esp. AmE*)
VERB + HOTLINE **call, phone, ring** (*BrE*) ◊ *Call our 24-hour ~ to find out if you have won a prize.* | **establish, set up** ◊ *A telephone ~ has been set up to give information about schedules.* | **have, run** ◊ *The company has an information ~ that customers can call if they are worried about products.*

hound noun

ADJ. **hunting**
... OF HOUNDS **pack**
HOUND + VERB **bark, bay** ◊ *We could hear the ~s barking at the fox.* | **pick up the scent** ◊ *The ~s picked up the scent of the fox.* | **chase sth, follow sth, pursue sth** ◊ *In this sport, ~s chase an artificial scent.* | **run**
PHRASES **ride to ~s** (*BrE*) ◊ *Days off were spent riding to ~s* (= hunting with horses and dogs).

hour noun

1 period of sixty minutes

ADJ. **full, solid** ◊ *I slept for eight solid ~s.* | **contact, credit** (*AmE*) (both education) ◊ *the number of contact ~s per week*
VERB + HOUR **take** ◊ *It takes two ~s to get to Vancouver.* | **spend** | **waste** | **last** ◊ *The performance lasted three ~s.* | **gain, lose** ◊ *You lose five ~s when you fly from New York to London.*
HOUR + VERB **go by, pass** ◊ *An ~ passed and she still hadn't arrived.*
PREP. **by the ~** ◊ *They're paid by the ~.* | **for an ~** ◊ *She worked for three ~s.* | **in an ~, within an ~** ◊ *I should be back within a couple of ~s.* | **over an ~, under an ~** ◊ *He's been gone for over an ~.* | **per ~** ◊ *Top speed is 120 miles per ~.* | **within the ~** ◊ *We hope to be there within the ~* (= in less than an hour). | **~ of** ◊ *There are still two ~s of daylight left.*
PHRASES **half an ~** | **~ after ~** | **in an hour's time** (*esp. BrE*) | **with every passing ~** ◊ *She grew more worried with every passing ~.*
→ Note at MEASURE

2 the hour time when a new hour starts

VERB + THE HOUR **chime, strike** ◊ *The clock struck the ~.*
PREP. **on the ~** ◊ *Buses leave every ~ on the ~.* | **past the ~** ◊

HOUSE + VERB **be situated, lie, stand** ◇ *The ~ stood a short distance from the woods.* | **face sth, overlook sth** ◇ *The ~ faces south, making the most of the sun.* ◇ *~s overlooking the park* | **loom** ◇ *The ~ loomed over him as he waited at the front door.* | **be worth sth** | **collapse, fall down** | **burn down, catch fire, catch on fire** (AmE) | **come into view**
HOUSE + NOUN **agent** (BrE) | **buyer, owner** ◇ *The bank offers attractive rates to first-time ~ buyers.* | **tenant** (BrE) | **building, construction** | **decoration** (BrE), **improvement** (esp. BrE), **renovation, repairs** | **builder, painter** | **contents** (esp. BrE) | **design, plan, planning** | **hunting** | **move** (esp. BrE) ◇ *They helped us with our ~ move.* | **prices, rents** (esp. BrE), **values** (esp. BrE) | **purchase** | **sales** | **insurance** (esp. BrE) (usually **home insurance** in AmE) | **front, interior** | **number** | **keys** | **guest** | **call** ◇ *In the morning, the doctor makes ~ calls.* | **arrest** ◇ *The former dictator is under ~ arrest in his country mansion.* | **dust** | **blaze** (BrE), **fire** | **party** | **husband** ◇ *He's happy being a ~ husband while his wife goes out to work.* | **plant** | **fly, mouse, sparrow, etc.**
PREP. **at sb's/the ~** ◇ *I finally tracked him down at his ~ in Denver.* | **from ~ to ~** ◇ *She went from ~ to ~ collecting signatures for her campaign.* | **in a/the ~** ◇ *It was so hot outside we stayed in the ~.*

2 in a theatre/theater

ADJ. **empty** | **full, packed**
VERB + HOUSE **play to** ◇ *They played to a packed ~.*
HOUSE + NOUN **lights** | **manager**
PHRASES **bring the ~ down** (= please the audience very much) | **front of ~** (= the area used by the audience) ◇ *I work front of ~.* ◇ *the front-of-house staff*

house *verb*

ADV. **permanently, temporarily** ◇ *The fish can be temporarily ~d in a smaller aquarium.* | **individually, separately** ◇ *The rabbits were ~d individually.* | **adequately** (esp. BrE) ◇ *At no time in the 19th century were the working classes adequately ~d.* | **badly** (esp. BrE) ◇ *The losers in this society are the homeless and badly ~d.*

household *noun*

ADJ. **average** ◇ *The average ~ spends more on housing than on food.* | **domestic, private, etc.** | **rural, urban** | **poor, wealthy** | **royal** ◇ *He was a member of the royal ~.* | **middle-class, working-class** | **high-income, low-income, poor, etc.** | **family, married-couple, single-parent, single-person, etc.**
VERB + HOUSEHOLD **maintain, manage, run** | **head** ◇ *~s headed by a single parent* | **set up** ◇ *Becoming an adult and setting up a ~ no longer mean the same thing.*
HOUSEHOLD + NOUN **appliance, contents** (esp. BrE), **furniture, goods, item, product** ◇ *The ~ contents are covered by a separate insurance policy.* | **cleaner** | **bills, budget, debt, expenditure, expenses, income, savings** | **chore, duties, task** | **garbage** (AmE), **rubbish** (BrE), **trash** (AmE), **waste**
PHRASES **the head of the ~** ◇ *The head of the ~ is responsible for completing the form.*

housekeeping *noun*

ADJ. **good** ◇ *The company has made considerable savings through good ~, such as avoiding wastage.* | **bad, poor** ◇ *My financial problems were made worse by my bad ~.*
HOUSEKEEPING + NOUN **allowance** (BrE), **money** (esp. BrE) ◇ *Her husband spent the ~ money on gambling.*

housework *noun*

ADJ. **heavy, light** ◇ *The doctor said I could do a little light ~.*
VERB + HOUSEWORK **do** ◇ *I spent all morning doing ~.* | **help with** ◇ *Her husband never helps with the ~.*
PHRASES **do your share of the ~** ◇ *He does his fair share of ~.*

housing *noun*

ADJ. **affordable, cheap, good, low-cost, low-income** (esp. AmE) ◇ *They provide good low-cost ~ for workers.* | **subsidized** (esp. AmE), **supported** (BrE) | **decent, good** | **adequate** | **bad** (esp. BrE), **inadequate, poor** (esp. BrE), **substandard** (esp. AmE) ◇ *Many health problems are made worse by inadequate ~.* | **permanent, temporary** | **council** (BrE), **local-authority** (BrE), **public** (esp. AmE), **public-sector** (BrE), **social** (esp. BrE) ◇ *Public expenditure on social ~ provision has doubled in the last five years.* | **private** | **rental** (AmE), **rented** (BrE) | **student** | **sheltered** (BrE) ◇ *sheltered ~ for old people* | **high-rise, terraced** (BrE) ◇ *The area is dominated by terraced ~.* | **rural, urban**
VERB + HOUSING **build, provide**
HOUSING + NOUN **association** (BrE), **authority, committee** (BrE), **department, office** | **conditions** | **complex, development, estate** (BrE), **programme/program, project** (AmE), **scheme** (BrE), **unit** ◇ *Many new ~ developments had sprung up around the city.* | **construction** | **provision** (esp. BrE) | **stock** | **market** | **prices** | **crisis, shortage** | **boom, bubble** ◇ *What happens when the ~ boom finally slows?* | **allowance, assistance, benefit** (BrE), **subsidy** (esp. AmE), **voucher** (AmE) ◇ *She receives a substantial ~ allowance on top of her salary.* ◇ *I received ~ benefit when I was unemployed.*
PREP. **in…~** ◇ *Too many families are still living in substandard ~.*

hover *verb*

ADV. **nearby** | **anxiously** ◇ *He was ~ing anxiously outside.* | **uncertainly** ◇ *She ~ed uncertainly near the front door.* | **menacingly** ◇ *Black clouds were ~ing menacingly on the horizon.*
PREP. **about** (esp. BrE), **around, behind, by, near** ◇ *She couldn't bear him ~ing around her.*
PHRASES **~ in the background** ◇ *Susan was ~ing in the background, uncertain what to do.* | **~ in the doorway**

howl *noun*

ADJ. **long** | **loud** | **eerie, unearthly** ◇ *He broke down and let out an unearthly ~.*
VERB + HOWL **give, let out** | **hear**
PREP. **with a ~** ◇ *With a ~ he leaped at his foe.* | **~ of** ◇ *a ~ of pain* ◇ *~s of laughter/protest*
PHRASES **be greeted with ~s of sth, be met with ~s of sth** (both esp. BrE) ◇ *His comments were met with ~s of outrage.* → Note at SOUND

huddle *noun*

ADJ. **little, small, tight**
VERB + HUDDLE **get into, go into** ◇ *The team went into a ~ at half-time to discuss their tactics.* | **break** (in American football)
PREP. **in a ~** ◇ *They stood in a tight ~, whispering.* | **~ of** ◇ *A little ~ of men stood in one corner.*

huddled *adj.*

VERBS **be, lie, sit, stand** ◇ *Felipe sat ~ in his chair.* | **find sb** ◇ *She found him ~ in a corner, shaking violently.*
PREP. **against** ◇ *Karen was ~ against the wall.* | **beneath, under** ◇ *She lay ~ under the blankets.* | **in** ◇ *He slept, ~ in an armchair.*

huff *noun*

VERB + HUFF **be in, get in, go off in**
PREP. **in a ~** ◇ *He's in a ~ because he wasn't invited.* ◇ *She went off in a ~ after losing the game.* | **~ over** ◇ *Alison's in a ~ over the joke they played on her.*

hug *noun*

ADJ. **big, huge** | **affectionate, comforting, friendly, loving, reassuring, warm** | **tight** | **quick** | **group** ◇ *Come on, everyone—time for a group ~.*
VERB + HUG **give sb** ◇ *He gave the children a quick ~, then got into the car.* | **get** ◇ *It was always nice to get a ~ from Evan.*
PHRASES **~s and kisses**

hug *verb*

ADV. **close, tight, tightly** ◇ *George went to his daughter and*

hugged her tightly. | **gently** | **back** ◇ *She gave him a big hug and he hugged her back.*
PREP. **to** ◇ *He reached out and hugged her to him.*
PHRASES **~ and kiss sb**

huge *adj.*

VERBS **be, look** | **become, grow** ◇ *Her eyes grew ~ in astonishment.*
ADV. **pretty, really** ◇ *This is a really ~ amount of money.* | **absolutely** ◇ *Their house is absolutely ~!* | **potentially** ◇ *There's a potentially ~ demand for this product.*

hum *noun*

ADJ. **faint, gentle, soft** | **low** | **high-pitched** | **constant, steady** ◇ *I could hear the constant ~ of distant traffic.* | **background**
VERB + HUM **hear**
PREP. **~ of** ◇ *the background ~ of the air-conditioning*

hum *verb*

ADV. **quietly, softly** | **loudly** | **happily** | **tunelessly** | **along** ◇ *I was humming along with the music.*
VERB + HUM **begin to** ◇ *He began to ~, somewhat tunelessly.*
PHRASES **~ to yourself** ◇ *She was humming softly to herself.*

humanity *noun*

ADJ. **great, true** | **common, shared** ◇ *Guilt and a sense of common ~ make people less harsh.*

humidity *noun*

ADJ. **high, low** | **ambient** (*technical*), **relative** ◇ *in dry weather, when the ambient ~ is low*
...OF HUMIDITY **level**
VERB + HUMIDITY **control** ◇ *The air con controls the temperature and ~ in all the rooms.* | **maintain** | **increase, reduce**
HUMIDITY + VERB **increase, rise** | **drop**
HUMIDITY + NOUN **level** | **control** ◇ *The museum is equipped with sophisticated ~ controls.*

humiliate *verb*

ADV. **deeply** | **completely, totally, utterly** ◇ *She felt completely ~d.* | **publicly** ◇ *Lowe was publicly ~d by his colleagues.*
PREP. **in front of** ◇ *I had been assaulted and deeply ~d in front of all my friends.*
PHRASES **feel ~d** ◇ *I have never felt so ~d in all my life.*

humiliating *adj.*

VERBS **be** | **find sth**
ADV. **deeply, very** | **totally, utterly** ◇ *He found the experience utterly ~.* | **pretty, rather**
PREP. **for** ◇ *It was pretty ~ for him to lose in that way.* | **to** ◇ *a settlement that was deeply ~ to their country*

humiliation *noun*

ADJ. **great, painful** | **total, utter** | **further** | **daily** ◇ *These people endure daily ~.* | **public** | **national** | **final, ultimate** ◇ *He was forced to face the ultimate ~ the next morning.* | **sexual**
VERB + HUMILIATION **be subjected to, endure, face, suffer** ◇ *She suffered the ~ of having her house searched.* | **feel** ◇ *They felt the intense ~ of having failed.*
PHRASES **a feeling of ~, a sense of ~**

humorous *adj.*

VERBS **be** | **become** | **find sth**
ADV. **extremely, fairly, very, etc.** | **gently, mildly, slightly** ◇ *She has written her description of him in a mildly ~ vein.* | **unintentionally** | **blackly, darkly, wryly** ◇ *The stories range from the darkly ~ to the despairing.*

humour *(BrE)* *(AmE* **humor**) *noun*

1 amusing quality/ability to find things funny

ADJ. **wry** ◇ *With wry ~, they laugh at their misfortunes.* | **ironic, tongue-in-cheek** | **self-deprecating** | **deadpan, dry** | **gentle, subtle** | **sly** | **irreverent** | **black, dark, gallows, grim** | **caustic, sardonic** | **slapstick, visual** | **unintentional** | **schoolboy** (*BrE*) ◇ *His colleagues soon got fed up with his schoolboy ~.* | **lavatorial, toilet** (*both esp. BrE*) | **gross-out** (*informal, esp. AmE*) ◇ *This movie takes crude gross-out ~ to a new low.*
...OF HUMOUR/HUMOR **touch** ◇ *Her speech was serious, but not without the occasional touch of ~.*
VERB + HUMOUR/HUMOR **be full of, contain** ◇ *The stories are full of ~.* | **use** ◇ *The movie uses ~ to make its points.* | **appreciate, see** ◇ *The man who lost his shoes failed to see the ~ of the situation.*
PHRASES **a brand of ~** ◇ *a television sitcom with its own peculiar brand of ~* | **sense of ~** ◇ *to have a dry/good/great/warped/weird/wicked sense of ~*

2 mood

ADJ. **good** ◇ *Her good ~ was restored by the excellent meal.*
PHRASES **in (a) good ~** ◇ *The remarks were made in good ~.* ◇ *He was obviously in a good ~ this evening.*

hunch *noun*

ADJ. **strong** (*esp. AmE*)
VERB + HUNCH **have** ◇ *I had a ~ that she was not telling the truth.* | **act on, follow, play** ◇ *Acting on a ~, I waited outside her house to see if she went out.* ◇ *I decided to follow my ~ and come and see you.* | **confirm** ◇ *Her ~es were confirmed the next day.* | **back** (*esp. BrE*) ◇ *He decided to back his ~es with serious money.*
PREP. **on a ~** ◇ *I called on a ~ to ask if he had any work for me.*

hunger *noun*

1 feeling of wanting to eat

ADJ. **extreme** ◇ *Any good weight loss regime should not lead to extreme ~.* | **constant** | **global, world**
VERB + HUNGER **feel** ◇ *It is usual to feel ~ during exercise.* | **be weak from, be weak with** | **die from, die of** ◇ *Thousands of people have died of ~.* | **alleviate, relieve, satisfy** ◇ *ways to alleviate world ~* ◇ *Perhaps the cat was killing to satisfy its ~.* | **end** ◇ *the campaign to end world ~*
HUNGER + NOUN **pangs** ◇ *mid-morning, when those ~ pangs strike* | **strike** ◇ *About 60 prisoners have gone on ~ strike.*
PHRASES **pangs of ~**

2 strong desire for sth

ADJ. **deep, great, insatiable** | **real** ◇ *There is a real ~ and passion for football in China.* | **spiritual**
VERB + HUNGER **feel, have** | **satisfy**
HUNGER + VERB **grow**
PREP. **~ for** ◇ *She has an insatiable ~ for knowledge.*

hungry *adj.*

VERBS **be, feel, go, look** ◇ *the number of children who have to go ~* | **become, get** | **make sb** ◇ *Seeing everyone eating had made him extremely ~.*
ADV. **extremely, fairly, very, etc.** | **desperately, ravenously, terribly** ◇ *We were all ravenously ~ after the walk.* | **a little, slightly, etc.** | **always** | **still**

hunt *noun*

1 hunting wild animals

ADJ. **bear, fox, seal, tiger, etc.**
VERB + HUNT **go on, take part in** ◇ *She had never taken part in a fox ~ before.*
HUNT + NOUN **follower, supporter** (*both BrE*) ◇ *Hunt followers deny the sport is cruel.* | **saboteur** (*BrE*) ◇ *clashes between hunt supporters and ~ saboteurs* | **meeting** (*BrE*)

2 searching for sb/sth

ADJ. **massive, nationwide** (*both esp. BrE*) ◇ *Police launched a nationwide ~ for the woman.* | **police** (*BrE*) | **murder** (*BrE*) ◇ *Police forces in five counties are now involved in the murder*

~. | **scavenger** (*esp. AmE*), **treasure** | **job** | **witch** (usually *witch-hunt*) (*often figurative*) *The investigation turned into a full-scale Communist witch-hunt.*
VERB + HUNT **begin, launch** (*esp. BrE*) ◇ *A massive police ~ was launched for the missing child.* | **continue** ◇ *Police are continuing their ~ for the arsonist.* | **lead** (*esp. BrE*) ◇ *Detectives leading the ~ for the killer believe he may be in hiding.* | **join** | **step up** (*esp. BrE*) ◇ *The mountain rescue team is stepping up its ~ for the missing climbers.* | **call off** (*esp. BrE*) ◇ *The ~ for survivors has now been called off.*
HUNT + VERB **begin, be on** ◇ *The ~ is on for potential employees with experience of electronic publishing.* | **continue**
PREP. **~ for**

hunting noun
ADJ. **big-game, deer, fox** (usually *fox-hunting*), **etc.** ◇ *He was killed by a lion while big-game ~ in Africa.* | **commercial** ◇ *commercial ~ of minke whales* | **illegal**
VERB + HUNTING **go** ◇ *Local people go ~ in the woods.* ◇ *We went ~ for bargains at the antique market.* (*figurative*) | **ban** ◇ *Should fox-hunting be banned?*
HUNTING + NOUN **knife, rifle** | **ground** ◇ *These waters are a ~ ground for sharks.* | **lodge** ◇ *The king built a large ~ lodge in the mountains.* | **trip** | **season**
PREP. **~ of** ◇ *the ~ of deer*
PHRASES **happy ~ ground** (*figurative*) ◇ *Crowded markets are a happy ~ ground for pickpockets.*

hurdle noun
1 in a race
VERB + HURDLE **clear, jump, jump over** ◇ *She cleared the first few ~s easily.* | **fall at** (*esp. BrE*), **hit** (*esp. BrE*) ◇ *His horse fell at the final ~.*
2 problem/difficulty
ADJ. **big, difficult, high** | **main, major, significant** | **final, first, last, next** ◇ *The first big ~ in putting your car on the road is getting insurance.* | **legal, regulatory, technical**
VERB + HURDLE **face** ◇ *This is perhaps the most difficult ~ that we face.* | **clear, jump, overcome, pass** ◇ *We'll jump each ~ as we come to it.* ◇ *You have already overcome the first major ~ by passing the entrance exam.* | **fall at** (*esp. BrE*), **hit** (*esp. BrE*) ◇ *The plan fell at the first ~.*

hurricane noun
ADJ. **major, powerful**
HURRICANE + VERB **hit sth, strike (sth)** ◇ *A ~ hit the city yesterday at 5 p.m.* | **come** ◇ *We had been warned there was a ~ coming.* | **damage sth, destroy sth, devastate sth** ◇ *The fields were devastated by the ~.* | **blow** ◇ *The ~ blew ashore near San Fernando.*
HURRICANE + NOUN **force** ◇ *hurricane-force winds* | **warning** | **damage, victim** | **relief** | **season**
PREP. **in a/the ~** ◇ *The roof blew off in a ~.*
PHRASES **the eye of the ~** (= the central point)

hurry noun
ADJ. **big, great, real, tearing** (*esp. BrE*), **terrible** (*esp. BrE*) ◇ *I was late for work and in a big ~.*
PREP. **in a ~** ◇ *They were in a ~ to set off.* | **in no ~** ◇ *She's in no ~ to find out how much her phone bill comes to.* | **in your ~** ◇ *In his ~ to leave, he forgot his laptop.*

hurt noun
ADJ. **deep, great**
VERB + HURT **feel** ◇ *the deep ~ that he felt when Jane left him* | **cause** ◇ *He knew that he had caused his boyfriend a lot of ~.* | **see** ◇ *I could see the ~ in her eyes.*

hurt verb
1 cause pain/injury
ADV. **badly, seriously** ◇ *She fell and ~ her leg quite badly.* ◇ *No one was seriously ~ in the accident.* | **actually, physically** ◇ *I was shaken, but not actually ~.* | **slightly**

2 be/feel painful
ADV. **badly, a lot, really** ◇ *My ankle still ~s quite badly.* ◇ *Does it ~ a lot?* ◇ *Ouch! It really ~s.* | **slightly**
VERB + HURT **be going to** ◇ *I knew it was going to hurt—but not that much!* | **begin to**
3 upset sb
ADV. **badly, deeply, really, terribly** ◇ *Her remarks ~ him deeply.* ◇ *They never told me why and that really ~.*
VERB + HURT **attempt to, try to** ◇ *Are you deliberately trying to ~ me?* | **want to** ◇ *Why would I want to ~ her?* | **not mean to** ◇ *I never meant to ~ anyone.*

hurt adj.
1 injured
VERBS **be, look** | **get** ◇ *Stop that or you'll get ~!*
ADV. **badly, seriously** ◇ *Steve didn't look seriously ~.* | **physically** | **slightly**
2 upset
VERBS **be, feel, look, seem, sound** | **get**
ADV. **deeply, extremely, really, terribly, very** | **a bit, quite, rather, slightly**
PREP. **by** ◇ *Roy seemed deeply ~ by this remark.*

hurtful adj.
VERBS **be** | **find sth** ◇ *I found some of his comments rather ~.*
ADV. **deeply, very** ◇ *She made some very ~ remarks.* | **particularly**
PREP. **to** ◇ *What he said was deeply ~ to me.*

husband noun
ADJ. **future, prospective** | **suitable** | **former** (also *ex-husband*) | **dead, deceased, late** | **first, second, etc.** | **new** | **devoted, good, loving, wonderful** | **beloved** | **faithful** | **cheating, errant** (*esp. BrE*), **unfaithful** | **absent, estranged** | **jealous** | **abusive, violent** | **house** (= a man who stays at home to care for children, cook, clean, etc. while his partner works)
VERB + HUSBAND **find, meet** ◇ *That was the day she met her future ~.* | **marry** | **be divorced from, be separated from, divorce, leave, walk out on** ◇ *She suddenly walked out on her ~, leaving him to bring up the children.* | **betray, cheat on** | **lose** ◇ *She lost her ~ to cancer a year ago.*
PHRASES **~ and wife** ◇ *They lived together as ~ and wife for over thirty years.*

hush noun
ADJ. **sudden** | **deathly, eerie** ◇ *A deathly ~ settled around the stadium.* | **expectant**
HUSH + VERB **descend, fall** ◇ *A sudden ~ fell over the room as the head teacher entered.*

hut noun
ADJ. **makeshift** | **bamboo, mud, stone, straw, wooden** | **thatched** ◇ *the thatched ~s of local villagers* | **round** | **little, small** | **ramshackle** ◇ *They live in ramshackle ~s constructed of discarded building materials.* | **beach, mountain** | **fisherman's, fishing, shepherd's, etc.** | **Nissen** (*BrE*), **Quonset™** (*AmE*) | **site** (*BrE*) ◇ *The builders were collecting their wages from the site ~.*
VERB + HUT **build, make** ◇ *~s built with mud bricks*
PREP. **in a/the ~** ◇ *The refugees spent the winter in tents or makeshift ~s.*

hygiene noun
ADJ. **good** | **poor** ◇ *infections that are the result of poor food ~* | **dental, food** (*BrE*), **oral, personal, public** ◇ *Many skin diseases can be prevented by good personal ~.* | **hand** ◇ *Good hand ~ by hospital staff is vital in preventing infection.*
HYGIENE + NOUN **regulations, standards** (both *esp. BrE*) ◇ *The restaurant was in breach of food ~ regulations.* (*BrE*) | **habits**

(*esp. AmE*), **practices** ◊ *children with poor ~ habits* | **item** (*AmE*), **product** ◊ *feminine/personal ~ products*
PHRASES **standards of ~**

hymn *noun*

ADJ. **rousing** ◊ *The service began with a rousing ~.* | **old, traditional** | **modern** | **gospel** (*esp. AmE*)
VERB + HYMN **play, sing**
HYMN + NOUN **book** | **tune**

hype *noun* (*informal*)

ADJ. **media** | **marketing** | **pre-fight, pre-game** (*esp. AmE*), **pre-match** (*esp. BrE*), **pre-season, etc.**
VERB + HYPE **live up to** ◊ *The movie failed to live up to all the ~.* | **get** ◊ *This new game is getting plenty of ~.*
HYPE + VERB **surround sth** ◊ *the ~ surrounding her latest book*
PREP. **~ about** ◊ *I don't believe all the ~ about how good the French team will be this season.*

hypnosis *noun*

VERB + HYPNOSIS **have, undergo** | **use** | **put sb under** ◊ *I decided to put him under ~ and ask him again.* | **induce** | **be susceptible to**
HYPNOSIS + NOUN **session**
PREP. **during ~** ◊ *changes in breathing observed during ~* | **under ~** ◊ *the things that people remember under ~*

hypothesis *noun*

ADJ. **plausible** | **bold** ◊ *Scientists have proposed a bold ~.* | **speculative** | **alternative, competing** | **testable** | **working** ◊ *These observations appear to support our working ~.* | **scientific**
VERB + HYPOTHESIS **construct, develop, form, formulate, have, make, present, propose, put forward, suggest** ◊ *It is possible to make a ~ on the basis of this graph.* ◊ *A number of hypotheses have been put forward.* | **consider, discuss, evaluate, examine, test, test out** ◊ *She used this data to test her ~* | **confirm, prove, support** | **accept** | **reject** ◊ *None of the hypotheses can be rejected at this stage.*
HYPOTHESIS + VERB **concern sth** ◊ *Her ~ concerns the role of electromagnetic radiation.* | **be based on sth** | **predict sth** ◊ *The ~ predicts that children will perform better on task A than on task B.* | **propose sth, suggest sth**
PREP. **on a/the ~** ◊ *Her study is based on the ~ that language simplification is possible.* | **~ about** ◊ *an interesting ~ about the development of language* | **~ concerning** ◊ *a speculative ~ concerning the nature of matter* | **~ on** ◊ *The results confirmed his ~ on the use of modal verbs.*

hypothetical *adj.*

VERBS **be** ◊ *This is a purely ~ situation.*
ADV. **entirely, purely** | **merely**

hysteria *noun*

ADJ. **mass, public** | **mild** (*esp. BrE*), **near** | **media, tabloid** (*BrE*) ◊ *Unnecessary anxiety has been caused by media ~ and misinformation.* | **religious** | **anti-communist, war**
... OF HYSTERIA **fit** ◊ *She sometimes flew into fits of ~.* ◊ *There was a note of ~ in his voice.*
VERB + HYSTERIA **border on** ◊ *Sam arrived in a state of excitement bordering on ~.* | **cause, create, fuel, generate, whip up** ◊ *Some parts of the media are creating ~ and exaggerating an important issue.* ◊ *the ~ whipped up by some newspapers*
HYSTERIA + VERB **sweep sth, sweep across sth, sweep through sth** ◊ *the ~ that swept through the country* | **surround sth** ◊ *There is still so much ~ surrounding the issue.*
PREP. **~ about** ◊ *public ~ about the bombings* | **~ over** ◊ *~ over AIDS*
PHRASES **on the point of ~, on the verge of ~** ◊ *She was babbling, on the verge of ~.*

hysterical *adj.*

1 suffering from/caused by hysteria

VERBS **act, be, sound** ◊ *Susan realized that she sounded ~.* | **become, get, go** ◊ *Calm down, you're getting ~.*
ADV. **completely** | **almost, nearly** ◊ *Now Mary was almost ~.* | **a little, slightly, etc.** | **mildly, rather** | **increasingly** (*esp. BrE*) ◊ *The political rhetoric is increasingly ~.*
PREP. **with** ◊ *Her parents were ~ with panic.* (*figurative*) ◊ *The audience was almost ~ with laughter.*

2 very funny

VERBS **be**
ADV. **absolutely, totally** (*esp. AmE*) ◊ *The whole episode was absolutely ~!*

ice *noun*

ADJ. **thick** ◊ *Is the ~ thick enough to walk on?* | **thin** (*often figurative*) ◊ *You're skating on thin ~* (= you're taking a risk). | **melting** | **crushed** ◊ *The glass was filled with green liquid and crushed ~.* | **black** ◊ *Motorists have been warned about black ~ on the roads.* | **pack, sea** (*esp. BrE*)
... OF ICE **block, slab** ◊ *The spray froze and formed great blocks of ~ on the front of the ship.*
VERB + ICE **form**
ICE + VERB **form** ◊ *Ice had formed on the pond.* | **crack, melt** ◊ *The ~ was beginning to melt.*
ICE + NOUN **cube** | **bucket** | **water** (*AmE*) (*iced water* in *BrE*) | **skate** | **dancing, skating** | **show** (= performed by skaters) | **rink** | **hockey** (usually just *hockey* in *AmE*) | **time** (in ice hockey) ◊ *He averaged more than ten minutes of ~ time* (= playing) *per game.* | **sculpture** | **axe/ax, pick** | **cap, field, floe, sheet, shelf**
PREP. **on (the) ~** ◊ *People were skating on the ~.*

ice cream *noun*

ADJ. **chocolate, strawberry, vanilla, etc.**
... OF ICE CREAM **scoop** | **carton, tub**
VERB + ICE CREAM **eat, have**
ICE CREAM + VERB **melt**
ICE-CREAM + NOUN **carton, cone, sundae** | **scoop** | **parlour/ parlor, shop** | **truck** (*AmE*), **van** (*BrE*) | **man**
PHRASES **and ~, with ~** ◊ *apple pie with ~*
→ Special page at FOOD

icing (*esp. BrE*) *noun* → See also FROSTING

ADJ. **fondant, royal** | **chocolate, lemon, etc.**
VERB + ICING **cover sth with, pipe, spread** ◊ *Pipe a little green ~ around the strawberries.*
ICING + NOUN **sugar** (*BrE*) | **bag**

icon *noun*

1 small symbol on a computer screen

ADJ. **desktop, folder, network, program, etc.**
VERB + ICON **click on, double-click on, right-click on** ◊ *Did you click on the ~ next to the name of the file?* | **click, double-click, right-click** ◊ *Click the 'modems' ~.* | **drag** ◊ *I dragged the ~ into the recycle bin.*
→ Special page at COMPUTER

2 person considered to be a symbol

ADJ. **national** | **popular** | **cultural** | **gay, lesbian** | **feminist** | **fashion, pop, sporting** (*BrE*), **sports** (*AmE*), **style**

idea *noun*

1 plan/suggestion

ADJ. **bright, brilliant, clever, excellent, good, great, marvellous/marvelous, nice, wonderful** | **valuable, worthwhile** | **exciting, interesting, stimulating** | **constructive, positive** | **creative, imaginative, innovative,** novel, original | wacky | big ◇ *The latest big ~ is to get women more interested in soccer.* | **alternative** ◇ *Family therapy is used as an alternative ~ to medication.* | **fresh, new** | **old** | **absurd, bad, mistaken, ridiculous, stupid** | **crackpot, crazy, mad, outlandish, wild** | **half-baked** | **ambitious, big, grand** ◇ *He joined the company as an office assistant with big ~s.* | **grandiose** | **basic** ◇ *The basic ~ is that we all meet up in London.* | **whole** ◇ *I think the whole ~ is ridiculous.*

VERB + IDEA **have** ◇ *Do you have any ~s for a present for Lara?* | **come up with, dream up, hit on, hit upon, produce, think up** | **draw, get** ◇ *Her ~s are drawn mainly from Chinese art.* | **contribute, offer** | **moot** (*formal, esp. BrE*) | **propose, put forward, suggest** | **promote, push, push forward, sell** ◇ *They managed to push the ~ of expanding through the committee.* | **welcome** ◇ *Most employees welcome the ~ of a ban on smoking.* | **consider, entertain, flirt with, toy with** ◇ *I'm toying with the ~ of leaving my job.* | **mull over, turn over** ◇ *He kept turning the ~ of resigning over in his mind.* | **encourage, generate** ◇ *Brainstorming is a good way of generating ~s.* | **reject, scoff at, veto** | **test, try, try out** | **bounce around, bounce off sb, brainstorm, discuss, explore, talk about** ◇ *I met up with a designer to bounce a few ~s around.* ◇ *It's useful to have someone to bounce ~s off.* | **exchange, pool, share** | **give sb** ◇ *What gave you the ~ to go freelance?* | **apply, implement, put into action, put into practice, take up** ◇ *The ~ had long been mooted but nothing had been done to put it into practice.* | **transform, translate** ◇ *How could we translate the ~ into business reality?* | **steal** ◇ *She accused the company of stealing her ~.* | **impose** ◇ *She always tries to impose her own ~s on the rest of the team.*

IDEA + VERB **come into sb's brain, come into sb's head, come into sb's mind, come to sb, flash through sb's brain, flash through sb's mind, hit sb, occur to sb, pop into sb's head, strike sb** ◇ *The ~ for the invention came to him in the bath.* | **emerge, evolve, form, grow** ◇ *An ~ began to form in his mind.* | **flow** ◇ *His ~s flowed faster than he could express them.* | **come from sb/sth, date back from sth, date back to sth, originate, start, stem from sth** ◇ *The ~ for the Olympics originated with Pierre de Coubertin.* | **work, work out** ◇ *That ~ didn't work out so well.* | **lead** ◇ *The ~ eventually led to the invention of the telephone.* | **come to nothing**

PREP. **~ about** ◇ *I have an ~ about how to tackle the problem.* | **~ for** ◇ *We were asked to suggest ~s for improving efficiency.* | **~ of** ◇ *She had the ~ of advertising on the Internet.*

PHRASES **be open to ~s** ◇ *I don't know what to do, but I'm open to ~s.* | **the germ of an ~** ◇ *The germ of his ~ came from watching a bird make a nest.* | **have other ~s** ◇ *I wanted to take the week off, but my boss had other ~s.* | **have the right ~** ◇ *The party had the right ~, but failed to win over the voters.* | **it might be an ~** ◇ *It might be an ~ to leave a note on the door for Marcos.*

2 thought/impression

ADJ. **clear, concrete, precise** | **abstract** | **theoretical** | **basic, general, rough, vague** ◇ *He gave me a rough ~ of what was wanted.* | **central, key, main** ◇ *The book introduces the key ~s of sociology.* | **dominant** | **fixed** | **preconceived** | **definite, firm, strong** ◇ *She has very definite ~s about what kind of a job she wants.* | **complex, difficult** | **simple, simplistic** ◇ *The movie is based on a simple ~, but a powerful one.* | **conventional** | **traditional** | **radical, revolutionary** | **contradictory** | **erroneous, false, wrong** ◇ *I don't want anyone getting the wrong ~ about me.* | **funny, strange** | **utopian** | **romantic** ◇ *People have a romantic ~ of the police force.* | **newfangled** | **outdated** | **not the faintest, not the foggiest, not the slightest** (*all informal*) ◇ *I haven't the faintest ~ what she meant.* | **artistic, economic, intellectual, moral, musical, philosophical, political, scientific** | **feminist, nationalist, socialist, etc.**

VERB + IDEA **get** ◇ *You'll soon get the ~* (= understand). | **espouse, have, hold** ◇ *He holds very different ~s to mine about discipline.* | **develop, form, shape** ◇ *the experiences that shaped her ~s* | **introduce** | **express** | **communicate, convey, get across, get over, present, promote, put out**

there (*AmE*) ◇ *It was a struggle to get our ~s across.* ◇ *I wanted to put the ~ out there.* | **demonstrate, explain, expound, illustrate** | **clarify, formalize, formulate, organize, structure** ◇ *Give careful thought to how to structure your ~s in the essay.* | **reinforce, support** | **change, reconsider, revise** ◇ *They had to reconsider their ~s in the light of new evidence.* | **accept, embrace, take up** | **dismiss, reject** | **challenge** ◇ *These photographs challenge conventional ~s of beauty.* | **harbour/harbor** ◇ *I hope he's not still harbouring/harboring ~s about asking me out.* | **be obsessed with** ◇ *He's obsessed with the ~ of getting a motorcycle.* | **relish** ◇ *I don't relish the ~ of sharing an office with Tony.*

IDEA + VERB **amuse sb, appeal to sb, please sb** ◇ *The ~ of going to his rescue amused her.* | **catch on, take hold, take off** ◇ *Some people started recycling, and the ~ caught on.*

PREP. **~ about** ◇ *She has some funny ~s about how to motivate staff.* | **~ behind** ◇ *The ~ behind the ceremony is to keep the gods happy to ensure a good crop.* | **~ of** ◇ *Swimming in an icy river is not my ~ of fun.*

ideal *noun*

ADJ. **high, lofty, noble** ◇ *Sam was a real leader who had high moral ~s.* | **unattainable** ◇ *This is not an unattainable ~.* | **romantic** ◇ *romantic ~s of motherhood* | **traditional** | **aesthetic, artistic, cultural, ethical, moral, political, social** | **democratic, liberal, revolutionary, socialist** | **Platonic** ◇ *Platonic ~s of beauty*

VERB + IDEAL **be committed to, believe in, cling to, embrace, espouse, have, support** ◇ *They still clung to the old ~s.* | **share** ◇ *We obviously share the same ~s.* | **pursue, strive for** | **achieve, attain, be true to, conform to, live up to, uphold** ◇ *A journalist should always live up to the ~s of truth, decency, and justice.* | **fall short of** ◇ *This agreement falls far short of the ~.* | **abandon, betray** ◇ *She was accused of betraying her political ~s.* | **embody, reflect, represent** ◇ *the democratic ~s embodied in the charter* | **promote**

ideal *adj.*

VERBS **be, look, prove, seem, sound** | **make sth** ◇ *The hotel's size makes it ~ for large conferences.*

ADV. **absolutely** | **almost, nearly** (*esp. AmE*) | **hardly, less than** ◇ *Language learning often takes place in a less than ~ environment.*

PREP. **for** ◇ *The houses are absolutely ~ for families with young children.*

identical *adj.*

VERBS **appear, be, look, seem, sound** | **remain**

ADV. **absolutely, completely, exactly** | **not necessarily** ◇ *Different spreadsheet packages tend to be similar, though not necessarily ~.* | **almost, largely, more or less, nearly, practically, pretty much, substantially, virtually** ◇ *The two houses were more or less ~.* | **apparently, seemingly** (*esp. AmE*) | **basically, essentially** | **otherwise** ◇ *They're shaded differently but are otherwise ~.* | **chemically, functionally, genetically**

PREP. **in** ◇ *These two models are absolutely ~ in appearance.* | **to** ◇ *This knife is ~ to the one used in the attack.* | **with** ◇ *offspring that are genetically ~ with the parents*

identification *noun*

1 act of identifying sb/sth

ADJ. **accurate, correct, precise** | **positive** | **mistaken** ◇ *There is virtually no risk of mistaken ~ in cases of date rape.* | **quick, rapid** | **early** ◇ *Early ~ of adolescents at risk for violence is needed.* | **easy** | **eyewitness** (*esp. AmE*) ◇ *Eyewitness ~ is not as reliable as we tend to believe.* | **biometric, fingerprint, radio frequency, visual** ◇ *the science of biometric ~*

VERB + IDENTIFICATION **make** ◇ *She was unable to make a positive ~ of the suspect.* | **allow, enable, permit** ◇ *Red and black wires are used to enable ~ of specific circuits.* |

facilitate ◇ *The examination facilitates the early ~ of any health problems.*
IDENTIFICATION + NOUN **parade** (*BrE*) ◇ *He stood on an ~ parade at the police station.* | **procedure, process, technique**

2 proof of identity

VERB + IDENTIFICATION **carry, have** ◇ *Always carry some ~.* ◇ *Do you have any ~?* | **produce, provide, show** ◇ *One passenger couldn't provide ~.* | **ask for, check** ◇ *The police checked their ~.* | **need, require** ◇ *To vote, Florida law requires a photo ~ with a signature.*
IDENTIFICATION + NOUN **card, document, papers** | **badge, bracelet, device, label, tag, technology** | **code, number** ◇ *The vehicle's ~ number is stamped on the engine.*
PHRASES **a means of ~** ◇ *My only means of ~ was my credit card.* | **for ~ purposes** ◇ *having their picture taken for ~ purposes*

identify *verb*

ADV. **accurately, correctly, rightly** ◇ *The new test will enable us to ~ more accurately patients who are most at risk.* ◇ *Did you ~ all the pictures correctly?* | **falsely, incorrectly, mistakenly, wrongly** | **positively** | **clearly, unambiguously, unequivocally, uniquely** ◇ *We have not yet clearly identified the source of the pollution.* ◇ *a serial number that uniquely identifies the disk* | **formally** ◇ *Someone has to formally ~ the body.* | **easily, readily** ◇ *I could ~ him easily if I saw him again.* | **quickly, rapidly** ◇ *Business trends are rapidly identified by this system.* | **tentatively** ◇ *All three structures dated to the third century and were tentatively identified as shrines.* | **reliably** | **properly** | **successfully** ◇ *Jaime successfully identified all 45 different species.* | **automatically** ◇ *a computer program to automatically ~ any query ending with a question mark* | **explicitly, specifically** ◇ *The pressbook did not specifically ~ the film's setting.* | **publicly** ◇ *Ms. Wilson was publicly identified as a CIA operative.* | **initially, originally** | **visually** ◇ *The surgeon visually identifies and cuts out the cancerous tissue.*
VERB + IDENTIFY **be able to, be unable to, can, manage to** ◇ *tests that can ~ people at risk of cancer* | **be easy to, be possible to** | **be difficult to, struggle to** | **be necessary to, need to** | **attempt to, endeavour/endeavor to, seek to, strive to, try to** | **hope to** ◇ *The researchers hope to ~ ways to improve the treatment.* | **learn to** ◇ *Participants learn to ~ different species by their calls.* | **allow sb to, be used to, enable sb to, help to, serve to** | **decline to, refuse to** ◇ *The newspaper declined to ~ the source of the allegations.* | **fail to** ◇ *Most students failed to ~ the quotation.*
PHRASES **efforts to ~ sb/sth** ◇ *He has stepped up efforts to ~ and acquire other small companies.* | **a means of ~ing sb/ sth, a way of ~ing sb/sth, a way to ~ sb/sth** ◇ *one means of ~ing the disease in its early stages*

PHR V **identify with sb**
ADV. **closely, completely, fully, strongly** ◇ *She identified strongly with the main character in the play.* | **readily**
VERB + IDENTIFY WITH **can** ◇ *I can't ~ with men like him.*

identify sb with sth
ADV. **closely** ◇ *The policy is closely identified with the President himself.* | **clearly** | **increasingly** ◇ *Great orchestras came to be identified increasingly with German conductors.*

identity *noun*

ADJ. **true** | **assumed, false** ◇ *He was discovered living under an assumed ~ in South America.* | **mistaken** ◇ *This is obviously a case of mistaken ~.* | **new** | **secret** ◇ *They didn't reveal her secret ~ to her family members.* | **stolen** ◇ *the use of a stolen ~ in the commission of a crime* | **strong** | **distinct, distinctive, individual, personal, separate, unique** ◇ *These populations have managed to maintain distinct identities.* | **collective, common, communal, shared** | **dual, multiple** ◇ *Shanghai itself has multiple identities.* | **civic, class, corporate, cultural, national, political, professional, regional, religious, sexual, social** | **Catholic, Islamic, Jewish, etc.** | **black, ethnic, racial** ◇ *the struggle for black ~*

| **American, Asian, etc.** | **female, feminine, gender, male, masculine** | **gay, homosexual, lesbian** | **genetic** ◇ *the shared genetic ~ of identical twins* | **brand** ◇ *the ability to maintain a strong brand ~*
VERB + IDENTITY **build, construct, create, define, determine, develop, establish, find, forge, form, shape** ◇ *They are still struggling to establish their ~ as a political party.* ◇ *The company forged its own ~ by producing specialist vehicles.* | **give sb/sth** ◇ *He felt that having a job gave him an ~.* | **affirm, assert, express** ◇ *the way in which African American writers have asserted their ~* | **reclaim** ◇ *It is crucial that she reclaim her ~ and confirm where she belongs.* | **base** ◇ *an ethnic ~ based on their common national ancestry* | **share** ◇ *They share a collective ~, united by an independent spirit.* | **keep, maintain, preserve, retain** ◇ *Many minority groups are struggling to maintain their cultural ~.* | **lose** | **change** ◇ *He changed his ~ on his release from prison.* | **adopt, assume, take on** ◇ *The company adopted a new corporate ~, including a new logo.* ◇ *She was given a false passport and assumed a new ~.* | **disclose, expose, leak, reveal** ◇ *Someone in the administration leaked the ~ of an undercover CIA agent.* ◇ *He refused to reveal the ~ of his client.* | **determine, discover, find out, learn, uncover** ◇ *Determining the ~ of the killer will take all his considerable skills.* | **guess** ◇ *It was easy to guess the ~ of the thief.* | **know** ◇ *It is important to know the ~ and nature of the enemy.* | **confirm, verify** ◇ *The system will verify the ~ of incoming visitors.* | **conceal, disguise, hide, keep secret, mask, protect** ◇ *Her voice was disguised to conceal her ~.* | **steal** ◇ *His ~ was stolen and used to purchase goods from a catalogue.*
IDENTITY + NOUN **bracelet, tag** | **card, documents, papers** | **parade** (*BrE*) ◇ *The victim picked out her attacker in an ~ parade.* | **fraud, theft** ◇ *credit-card ~ theft* | **thief** | **verification** ◇ *The technology is typically used for ~ verification.* | **confusion, crisis, issue** ◇ *The country suffered from an ~ crisis for years after the civil war.* | **politics** (*esp. AmE*) ◇ *the ~ politics of gender or race* | **development, formation** (*both esp. AmE*) ◇ *the importance of family history within ~ formation*
PREP. **~ as** ◇ *Scotland has never lost its ~ as a separate nation.* | **~ between** ◇ *the stylistic ~ between the first text and the others*
PHRASES **proof of ~** ◇ *The police officer asked him for proof of ~.* | **a search for ~** ◇ *His search for his cultural ~ took him to where his parents were born.* | **a sense of ~**

ideology *noun*

ADJ. **dominant, prevailing** | **official** | **competing, opposing** ◇ *They are divided by opposing ideologies.* | **shared** ◇ *They're rooted in a shared ~.* | **underlying** ◇ *the underlying ~ of neoliberalism* | **core** ◇ *These businesses have a core ~ of which profit is but one ideal.* | **coherent** ◇ *The party's policies were based on prejudice rather than on any coherent ~.* | **powerful, strong** | **narrow** ◇ *the narrow ~ of the extreme right* | **radical** ◇ *the radical ~ of the French Revolution* | **evil, hateful** (*esp. AmE*) ◇ *They share a hateful ~ that rejects tolerance.* | **cultural, economic, gender** (*esp. AmE*)**, political, racial, religious** ◇ *Gender ~ still has an important role in determining how couples allocate household tasks.* | **bourgeois, capitalist, communist, extremist, feminist, fundamentalist, liberal, Marxist, nationalist, revolutionary, socialist, etc.**
VERB + IDEOLOGY **have** ◇ *The party had a Marxist ~.* | **adopt, embrace, espouse, support** ◇ *They distanced themselves from the upper class and adopted a communist ~.* | **promote, spread** ◇ *They want to spread their ~ of hope.* | **impose** ◇ *an ~ imposed by an elite group* | **share** ◇ *They share a common political ~.* | **base** ◇ *a unique ~ based on the concept of service* | **challenge** ◇ *This ~ was challenged in the early twentieth century.* | **reject**

idiot *noun*

ADJ. **babbling** (*esp. AmE*)**, big, blithering, brainless, bumbling, gibbering, little, mindless, right** (*BrE, informal*)**, stupid** ◇ *What stupid ~ left their shoes on the stairs?* | **absolute, complete, real, total, utter** | **drunken** ◇ *He was*

giggling like a drunken ~. | **village** ◇ *He looked like the village ~.*
VERB + IDIOT **be, feel** (*BrE*), **feel like, look like, sound like** ◇ *I felt (like) a complete ~, standing there in front of all those people!* | **act like, behave like** ◇ *She knew she was acting like an ~.* | **call sb** ◇ *She called me an ~.*
PHRASES **make an ~ of yourself** ◇ *He's made a complete ~ of himself over this woman!*

idle *adj.*

1 lazy

VERBS **be** | **become** | **remain, stay** ◇ *He never stayed ~ for long.*
ADV. **bone** (*BrE, informal*) ◇ *She never lifts a finger to help. She's bone ~.*

2 not in use

VERBS **be, lie, sit, stand** ◇ *Half of their machines are lying ~.* | **become** ◇ *He did not let the factory become ~.* | **remain** | **leave sth** ◇ *The land was left ~ for years.*

idol *noun*

ADJ. **pop** (*esp. BrE*), **rock, sports, etc.** | **film** (*esp. BrE*), **movie** (*esp. AmE*), **screen** ◇ *her screen ~, Marilyn Monroe* | **matinee** ◇ *a matinee ~ of a bygone era* | **teen, teenage** ◇ *By this time Pitt had become a teenage ~.* | **boyhood, childhood** | **big, great, huge** ◇ *She is still my biggest ~.* | **false** ◇ *Superheroes are false ~s.* | **fallen** ◇ *Many fallen ~s blame anyone but themselves for their downfall.*
VERB + IDOL **make (sb)** ◇ *Teenagers made Dean their ~.* ◇ *The movie made an ~ of her.* | **emulate, imitate** ◇ *kids trying to emulate their ~s* | **meet** ◇ *She'd always wanted to meet her ~.*

ignite *verb*

ADV. **spontaneously** ◇ *The burning foam generates such heat that other items ~ spontaneously.* | **instantly, suddenly** | **easily** ◇ *an explosive that is easily ~d*
VERB + IGNITE **fail to** ◇ *The gunpowder sometimes fails to ~.*

ignition *noun*

VERB + IGNITION **start, turn, turn on** ◇ *Josh turned the ~ and the car sputtered to life.* | **switch off, turn off**
IGNITION + NOUN **key, switch** ◇ *He turned the ~ key.* | **system**
PREP. **in the ~** ◇ *I must have left the key in the ~.*

ignorance *noun*

ADJ. **complete, total, utter** | **profound, sheer** ◇ *This showed a profound ~ of local customs.* | **appalling, gross** ◇ *our appalling ~ of international events* | **general, widespread** | **blissful** | **wilful/willful** ◇ *a policy based on wilful ~ of history*
VERB + IGNORANCE **betray, demonstrate, display, expose, reveal, show** ◇ *I tried not to betray my ~.* ◇ *He showed a remarkable ~ of the facts.* | **feign** ◇ *'Where?' he asked, feigning ~.* | **admit, confess, plead, profess** ◇ *I had to confess my ~.* ◇ *He pleaded ~ of any wrongdoing.* | **live in, remain in** ◇ *The sisters lived in total ~ of each other.* | **keep sb in** ◇ *He was kept in ~ of his true identity.* | **be based on** ◇ *These attitudes are based on ~ and fear.*
PREP. **due to ~** ◇ *mistakes due to ~* | **in ~ (of)** ◇ *She remained in blissful ~ of these events.* | **in your ~** ◇ *Outsiders, in their ~, fail to understand this.* | **through ~** ◇ *Many lives are lost through ~.* | **~ about** ◇ *There is still widespread ~ about this disease.* | **~ as to, ~ of** ◇ *widespread ~ of the causes of the Civil War*

ignorant *adj.*

VERBS **appear, be, feel, seem, sound** | **act** ◇ *I decided to continue acting ~, just to make fun of her.* | **remain, stay** (*AmE*) ◇ *The general public remained totally ~ of the danger.* ◇ *I wanted to stay ~ of my fate for a few more precious hours.* | **keep sb** ◇ *We were kept ~ of the facts.*
ADV. **extremely, fairly, very, etc.** | **completely, entirely, incredibly, plain, profoundly, totally, utterly, wholly** ◇ *Don't ask Paul. He's completely ~.* | **largely** | **simply** ◇ *They are simply ~, I'm afraid to say.* | **blissfully** ◇ *We went to bed*

that night blissfully ~ of the storm to come. | **wilfully/willfully** | **woefully**
PREP. **about** ◇ *He was completely ~ about the country's political system.* | **of** ◇ *We are still woefully ~ of the causes of this disease.*

ignore *verb*

ADV. **altogether, completely, entirely, totally, utterly** | **almost, practically, virtually** | **effectively, essentially, largely** | **basically** ◇ *Shona basically ~d her.* | **promptly** ◇ *a look of disapproval which he promptly ~d* | **generally** | **typically** ◇ *The press typically ~s a problem until it causes a crisis.* | **just, merely, simply** ◇ *The government has simply ~d the problem altogether.* | **consistently** | **routinely, systematically** ◇ *Social services routinely ~ the problems facing at-risk young women.* | **frequently, repeatedly** | **apparently** | **easily** ◇ *The diesel fumes from the buses are not easily ~d.* | **conveniently** (*ironic*) ◇ *The managers conveniently ~d these statistics.* | **blatantly** ◇ *Safety guidelines had been blatantly ~d.* | **carefully, deliberately, determinedly, intentionally, pointedly, purposely, resolutely, steadfastly, studiously** ◇ *She sat at her desk and studiously ~d me.* | **wilfully/willfully** ◇ *Hill wilfully ~d the conventions of the banking world.* | **blithely, cheerfully, happily** ◇ *He blithely ~d her protests and went on talking.* | **politely** ◇ *The group politely ~d her remark.*
VERB + IGNORE **cannot, cannot afford to** ◇ *a warning the president cannot afford to ~* | **be difficult to, be hard to, be impossible to** | **be foolish to, be stupid to, be wrong to** ◇ *It would be foolish to ~ them completely.* | **tend to** ◇ *Scientists have tended to ~ these findings.* | **be willing to** ◇ *People seem very willing to ~ the risks.* | **choose to, decide to, prefer to** ◇ *The judge chose to ~ the views of the doctors.* ◇ *He preferred to ~ these comments.* | **attempt to, try to** | **pretend to** ◇ *I shrugged, pretending to ~ him.* | **learn to** ◇ *I've learned to ~ all of my sister's hurtful comments.* | **manage to** ◇ *Jason had managed to ~ a lot of the pressure for most of his career.* | **continue to**
PHRASES **be widely ~d** ◇ *Safety standards are widely ~d in the industry.* | **~ sth at your peril** ◇ *The pernicious effect of this advertising on children is a problem that we ~ at our peril.* | **~ the fact that…** ◇ *Did you think I'd ~ the fact that you were suffering from shock?* | **sth can be safely ~d** (*ironic*) ◇ *These people occupy such a marginal position in society that the authorities think they can be safely ~d.*

ill (*esp. BrE*) *adj.* → See also SICK

VERBS **appear, be, feel, look, seem** | **lie** ◇ *He was lying ~ in bed.* | **become, be taken** (*BrE*), **fall, get, grow** | **remain** | **make sb** ◇ *I can't eat bananas. They make me ~.* (*esp. BrE*) ◇ *That type of government corruption makes me ~.* (*figurative, esp. AmE*)
ADV. **critically, dangerously, desperately, extremely, gravely, really, seriously, severely, terribly, very** ◇ *His mother is seriously ~ in the hospital.* | **almost** ◇ *Robyn was almost ~ with excitement and outrage.* | **pretty, quite, rather, slightly** | **genuinely** | **violently** ◇ *She was taken violently ~ and had to be put to bed.* | **acutely** | **chronically** ◇ *chronically ~ patients* | **fatally, incurably, mortally, terminally** ◇ *a hospice for the terminally ~* | **mentally, physically** ◇ *the problems faced by mentally ~ people*
PREP. **with** ◇ *He fell ~ with cholera in 1849.* | **from** ◇ *They arrive at the hospital ~ from malnutrition.*

illegal *adj.*

VERBS **be** | **become** | **remain** | **declare sth, deem sth, make sth, rule sth** ◇ *Their action was ruled ~ by the International Court.* ◇ *The sale of these knives should be made ~.*
ADV. **highly** | **blatantly** ◇ *blatantly ~ counter-intelligence methods* | **clearly** ◇ *Such acts are clearly ~.* | **strictly** (*esp. BrE*), **totally** | **possibly, potentially** | **allegedly** | **technically** ◇ *Prize-fighting remained popular, though technically ~.*

illiteracy noun

ADJ. **widespread** ◇ *Illiteracy was widespread at that time.* | **adult** ◇ *poverty and high rates of adult ~* | **functional** ◇ *Functional ~ affects as many as one in five Americans.* | **scientific** ◇ *the public's scientific ~*
... OF ILLITERACY **level, rate**
ILLITERACY + NOUN **rate** ◇ *Illiteracy rates have fallen in recent years.*

illiterate adj.

VERBS **be**
ADV. **completely, totally** | **almost, largely, virtually** | **mostly** ◇ *These soldiers are mostly ~.* | **functionally** ◇ *People judged to be functionally ~ lack the basic reading and writing skills required in everyday life.* | **economically, scientifically** ◇ *Is it surprising that young people who are politically ~ do not bother to vote?*

illness noun

ADJ. **deadly, fatal, incurable, terminal** | **catastrophic** (*AmE, law*), **critical, dangerous, debilitating, devastating, life-threatening, major, serious, severe, terrible** ◇ *He suffered from a debilitating ~ which made everyday life a struggle.* | **mild, minor** | **treatable** ◇ *Clinical depression is a treatable ~.* | **preventable** ◇ *TB is a major cause of preventable ~ and death.* | **lengthy, lingering, long, long-standing, long-term, prolonged** | **degenerative, progressive** | **brief, short** | **final, last** | **acute, chronic** | **sudden** ◇ *Kerry died of a sudden ~.* | **infectious** | **family, genetic** ◇ *We assess the applicant's history of family ~.* | **painful** | **mysterious, mystery, unexplained** ◇ *They had failed to find the cause of his mystery ~.* | **common** ◇ *Diabetes is a common ~.* | **rare** ◇ *He became blind after contracting a rare ~.* | **depressive, mental, psychiatric, psychological, psychotic, stress-related** | **psychosomatic** | **medical** ◇ *Depression is a treatable medical ~.* | **AIDS-related, flu-like, food-borne** (*esp. AmE*), **physical, respiratory, smoking-related, viral** | **childhood**
... OF ILLNESS **bout, episode** ◇ *an acute episode of mental ~*
VERB + ILLNESS **experience, have, suffer, suffer from** ◇ *those who experience mental ~* ◇ *Badly fed children suffer a lot of minor ~es.* ◇ *people who suffer from mental ~* | **catch, contract, develop, get** ◇ *people who never seem to catch the ~es their friends get* ◇ *He contracted a serious ~ and died a month later.* | **diagnose** | **treat** ◇ *The drug is used to treat a wide range of ~es.* | **cure, heal** (*esp. AmE*) ◇ *The only thing that could cure her ~ was a special herb.* | **control, manage** ◇ *ways to help arthritis sufferers manage their ~* | **survive** ◇ *She survived a life-threatening ~.* | **beat** ◇ *Claire is optimistic she can beat her ~.* | **cause** ◇ *~es caused by poverty* | **prevent** ◇ *a drug that may be helpful in preventing ~es such as cancer* | **battle, combat** | **fight, fight off, overcome, recover from** ◇ *The immune system enables the body to fight off ~.* | **fake, feign** ◇ *She feigned ~ so that she wouldn't have to go to school.* | **nurse sb through** ◇ *She nursed her father through his final ~.* | **bear** ◇ *She bore her final ~ with great courage.*
ILLNESS + VERB **affect sb, afflict** (*formal*) ◇ *The mystery ~ affected hundreds of people.* ◇ *Mental ~ afflicts one in four people.* | **plague sb** ◇ *Her childhood was plagued by ~.* | **hit (sb), strike (sb)** ◇ *The ~ struck while he was touring.* | **arise, occur** ◇ *Some ~es occur more frequently following puberty.* | **cause sth** ◇ *the pain and distress caused by your ~* | **progress** ◇ *As his ~ progressed, Neil began to have difficulty speaking.* | **result (from sth)** ◇ *Sometimes it's hard to tell whether ~es result from bacteria or viruses.* | **require sth** ◇ *Both ~es require treatment.*
PREP. **after ~** ◇ *He's just returned to work after ~.* | **because of ~, due to ~, through ~** ◇ *earnings lost through ~* | **with ~** ◇ *people with serious psychological ~es* | **~ among** ◇ *a high rate of ~ among the workers* | **~ associated with** ◇ *the ~es associated with HIV infection* | **~ from** ◇ *the first case of ~ from the Ebola virus* | **~ in** ◇ *episodes of ~ in children*
PHRASES **the onset of an ~** ◇ *the sudden onset of ~ in a parent*

illogical adj.

VERBS **be, seem, sound**
ADV. **completely, entirely, quite, totally** | **highly** | **rather** | **a little, slightly, etc.**

ill-treatment noun

VERB + ILL-TREATMENT **suffer**
PHRASES **~ at sb's hands** ◇ *They suffered ~ at the hands of the guards.*

illuminate verb

1 give light to sth

ADV. **brightly, brilliantly, clearly** | **fully** ◇ *With the room fully ~d, they students were able to see what they were doing.* | **beautifully** ◇ *The red glow of the sun beautifully ~d the sky.* | **barely, dimly, faintly, partially, slightly, softly** ◇ *The room was dimly ~d by the soft glow of the lamp.* | **briefly** | **instantly, suddenly**

2 make sth clear

ADV. **greatly** ◇ *an incident which greatly ~d the problems we faced*
VERB + ILLUMINATE **help (to)** ◇ *The study of the present also helps to ~ the past.* | **serve to** ◇ *These confessions serve to ~ his argument.*

illuminating adj.

VERBS **be, prove** | **find sth**
ADV. **extremely, fairly, very, etc.** | **especially, highly, most** (*esp. BrE*), **particularly** ◇ *I found his talk most ~.* | **not particularly** ◇ *The information he'd gathered wasn't particularly ~.*

illumination noun

ADJ. **bright, good, strong** | **dim** ◇ *Imaginative stage lighting provided dim ~.* | **artificial** ◇ *the artificial ~ of the studio* | **natural** ◇ *The skylights are designed to optimize natural ~.*
... OF ILLUMINATION **level** ◇ *lights providing a good level of ~*
VERB + ILLUMINATION **provide** ◇ *The skylight will provide good ~ from above.*
ILLUMINATION + VERB **come from sth** ◇ *Most of the ~ came from candles.*
PHRASES **a source of ~** ◇ *The only source of ~ was a single small window.*

illusion noun

ADJ. **dangerous** ◇ *To believe you have nothing more to learn is a dangerous ~.* | **optical, visual** ◇ *The road ahead looks wet, but in fact this is an optical ~.* | **false** ◇ *I don't want to give him any false ~s.* | **comforting** ◇ *The slogan provides the comforting ~ that something is being done.* | **grand** ◇ *I never had any grand ~s of winning.* | **romantic** ◇ *I abandoned my romantic ~s a long time ago.* | **mere, pure, simple** ◇ *The figure was only a trick of light, a mere ~.*
VERB + ILLUSION **be under, entertain, have** ◇ *They are under no ~s about the difficulties ahead of them.* | **create, give (sb), produce, provide** ◇ *The huge size of the vehicle gives the ~ of safety.* | **foster, harbour/harbor, maintain, perpetuate, preserve, sustain** ◇ *They are trying to maintain the ~ that the company is in good shape.* | **break, destroy, dispel, shatter** ◇ *Within the first week at college all my ~s were shattered.* | **lose** ◇ *I think I have lost all the ~s I had left.*
PREP. **~ about, ~ as to** ◇ *She had no ~s about her attractiveness.*
PHRASES **be all an ~** ◇ *It turned out that their happy marriage was all an ~.*

illustrate verb

1 put pictures in sth

ADV. **copiously** (*esp. AmE*), **generously, heavily, lavishly, profusely** (*esp. AmE*), **richly** | **fully** | **attractively, beautifully, handsomely, superbly** | **photographically** (*esp. AmE*) ◇ *a collection of photographically ~d magazines*
PREP. **by** ◇ *Most items are ~d by a photograph.* | **with** ◇ *The new edition is heavily ~d with photographs of aircraft.*

ILLNESSES

You can **have** any illness or disease:
I'm warning you—I have a bad cold.
Have the kids had chickenpox?

Get can be used with diseases or illnesses that you often have:
He gets really bad hay fever every summer.

Suffer from is used in more formal contexts and with more serious diseases:
This medicine is often recommended for patients who suffer from arthritis.

You can also:

catch	develop	come/go down with	contract	suffer
chickenpox	AIDS	appendicitis	AIDS	a breakdown
a cold	an allergy (to sth)	bronchitis	hepatitis	a concussion
a cough	arthritis	chickenpox	HIV	a heart attack
flu (*BrE*)/the flu	asthma	a cold	measles (*BrE*)/	an injury
German measles	cancer	diarrhoea/diarrhea	the measles	a miscarriage
measles (*BrE*)/	cataracts	flu (*BrE*)/the flu	meningitis	a stroke
the measles	diabetes	food poisoning	pneumonia	
a stomach bug	a fever	measles	polio	
	high blood pressure	mono (*AmE*)	tuberculosis	
	an infection	mumps (*BrE*)/		
	pneumonia	the mumps		
	a tumour/tumor			
	an ulcer			

*an **attack of** (the) flu, nerves, shingles; an asthma **attack***
*a **bout of** bronchitis, coughing, the flu, pneumonia, sickness*
*a **bout with** cancer, colic, depression, the flu (all AmE)*
*a coughing, an epileptic **fit***

Is it serious?

no	yes
a bit of a cold, a cough (*both esp. BrE*)	a **bad/heavy/nasty** cold
mild asthma, depression	a **bad/nasty/severe** attack of sth, bout of sth
a **mild** attack of sth, bout of sth, case of sth	a **bad/hacking/racking** cough
a **mild** heart attack, infection	a **bad/splitting** headache
a **slight** cold, headache	a **massive/serious** heart attack, stroke

What's the treatment?

take	be given/ be on/take	have/undergo	have/be given	have/be given/ receive /undergo
medicine	antibiotics	an examination	acupuncture	chemotherapy
pills	drugs	an operation	an anaesthetic/	therapy
tablets	medication	surgery	anesthetic	treatment
(*esp. BrE*)	painkillers	a transplant	a blood transfusion	
			an injection	
			a jab (*esp. BrE*)	
			a scan	
			a shot (*esp. AmE*)	
			an X-ray	

illustration

412

2 make sth clear using examples/pictures

ADV. **amply** | **aptly, brilliantly, neatly, nicely, superbly** (*esp. BrE*), **well** ◊ *The dire consequences of chronic underfunding are nowhere better ~d than in the nation's schools.* | **perfectly** | **effectively** | **merely, simply** ◊ *His question merely ~s his ignorance of the subject.* | **clearly, dramatically, graphically, powerfully, strikingly, vividly** | **brutally, starkly, tragically** ◊ *The case tragically ~s the dangers of fireworks.*

VERB + ILLUSTRATE **serve to** ◊ *Two examples serve to ~ this point.* | **attempt to, seek to, try to** ◊ *What she attempts to ~ is the difference between her company and her competitors.* | **help (to)** ◊ *He is showing these silent films to help ~ his story of survival.* | **be enough to, suffice to** ◊ *Two more examples will suffice to ~ this point.* | **be chosen to, be designed to, be intended to**

PREP. **by** ◊ *This consequence can be ~d by a simple example.* | **to** ◊ *a way of illustrating to the chairman the folly of his decision*

illustration noun

1 picture in a book, etc.

ADJ. **black-and-white, colour/color, coloured/colored, full-colour/full-color** | **cartoon, photographic, watercolour/watercolor, etc.** | **botanical, medical, etc.** | **full-page** ◊ *a wonderful book with full-page ~s* | **beautiful, fine, wonderful** | **colourful/colorful** | **detailed** ◊ *the new Inca map, with a detailed ~ of ancient Machu Picchu* | **book, cover** | **accompanying**

ILLUSTRATION + VERB **depict sth, show sth** | **accompany sth** ◊ *the ~s accompanying the text* | **appear** ◊ *His ~s have appeared in the pages of numerous publications.*

PREP. **in an/the ~** ◊ *The kite is assembled as shown in the ~.* | **with an/the ~** | **~ by** ◊ *'The Black Cat' by Alan Ahlberg, with ~s by Arthur Robins*

2 example

ADJ. **excellent, good, perfect** | **clear, dramatic, graphic, striking, vivid** ◊ *These events are a graphic ~ of the fact that their promises cannot be trusted.* | **simple** ◊ *Let us take a very simple ~.* | **classic, textbook** ◊ *It was a textbook ~ of the way the UN works.*

VERB + ILLUSTRATION **serve as** ◊ *Chicago serves as an ~ of the problems faced by such cities.* | **give (sb), offer, present, provide** ◊ *We then present an empirical ~ of these points.* ◊ *Explain the policy of détente and provide some ~s of how it worked in practice.* | **take, use sth as, use sth for** ◊ *I will use one recent example as an ~.*

ILLUSTRATION + NOUN **purposes** (*AmE*) ◊ *These figures are for ~ purposes only.* (**illustrative purposes** in *BrE*)

PREP. **as an ~** ◊ *As an ~ of this point, I'm going to tell you a true story.* | **by way of ~** ◊ *He quoted several famous writers by way of ~.*

image noun

1 impression of sb/sth given to the public

ADJ. **good, positive** | **negative** | **tarnished** ◊ *The party needs to clean up its somewhat tarnished ~.* | **poor** ◊ *The industry had a poor ~.* | **false** ◊ *The history books built up a false ~ of an unpopular president.* | **clean, clean-cut** (*esp. BrE*), **perfect, squeaky-clean, wholesome** ◊ *He's a good player with a clean ~.* ◊ *He represents the perfect ~ of a clean-living college boy.* | **macho** | **hackneyed** ◊ *the hackneyed ~ of the poor student* | **traditional** ◊ *traditional ~s of motherhood* | **media, public, screen** ◊ *In real life she looks nothing like her screen ~.* | **brand, corporate** ◊ *Champagne houses owe their success to brand ~s.*

VERB + IMAGE **create** ◊ *The company needs to create a new ~ for itself.* | **convey, cultivate, present, project, promote** ◊ *a book which presents positive ~s of older people* | **change, transform** | **bolster, boost, burnish** (*esp. AmE*), **clean up, enhance, improve, polish, revive** ◊ *an effort to improve the organization's public ~* | **soften** ◊ *She is now seeking to*

soften her ~ for voters. | **keep up, live up to, maintain** ◊ *The group has failed to live up to its macho ~.* ◊ *Eastwood has maintained an ~ as a tough guy.* | **shed** ◊ *The industry is trying to shed its negative ~.* | **mar** (*esp. AmE*), **ruin, tarnish**

2 mental picture of sb/sth

ADJ. **powerful, vivid** | **sudden** ◊ *She had a sudden mental ~ of herself in a wedding dress.* | **positive** | **negative** | **distorted** ◊ *the distorted ~s in his dreams* | **enduring, indelible** ◊ *It leaves indelible ~s imprinted on your mind.* | **unrealistic** | **unrealistic ~s of the ideal body** | **popular** | **ideal** ◊ *the ideal ~ of American citizenship* | **stereotyped, stereotypical** | **mental** | **body** ◊ *help with eating disorders and body ~* | **literary, poetic** | **dream**

VERB + IMAGE **have** | **bring to mind, call to mind, conjure, conjure up, evoke, recall, summon, summon up** ◊ *Samba always seems to conjure up ~s of Brazil.* ◊ *the ability to summon up ~s in the mind* | **build, build up, form** ◊ *I like to build up ~s of the characters and setting before I start to write.* | **fit** ◊ *He didn't fit my ~ of the boss.* | **use** | **reinforce** ◊ *Treating disabled people like children only reinforces negative ~s of disability.*

PREP. **~ from** ◊ *He started to recall ~s from his past.*

3 copy

ADJ. **living, spitting** ◊ *He's the spitting ~ of his father!* | **mirror** ◊ *Charity was a mirror ~ of her twin.*

4 picture

ADJ. **compelling, dramatic, graphic, memorable, poignant, powerful, spectacular, striking, stunning, unforgettable** | **disturbing, gruesome, horrible, horrific, violent** ◊ *powerful and disturbing ~s of the war* | **familiar, iconic** | **visual** ◊ *The visual ~ is steadily replacing the written word.* | **flickering, moving** ◊ *flickering ~s on a screen* | **blurred, blurry, fuzzy** | **faint** ◊ *After exposure a faint ~ is visible.* | **still** ◊ *the use of still and moving video ~s* | **live** ◊ *Visitors can view live radar ~s and listen in to the control tower.* | **recorded** | **close-up** ◊ *a live close-up ~ of her face* | **colour/color** | **black-and-white, monochrome** | **high-resolution** | **clear, crisp, sharp** ◊ *realistic 3D graphics with sharp ~s* | **three-dimensional** ◊ *The machine can capture a three-dimensional ~ of a patient's heart.* | **photographic, TV, video** | **screen** ◊ *Each illustration is displayed as a complete screen ~.* | **computer, digital, radar, satellite, X-ray** | **thumbnail** ◊ *Under each thumbnail ~ is a link to a larger illustration.* | **holographic** | **graven** (*literary*) ◊ *It was forbidden to worship graven* (= carved) *~s.* | **painted** ◊ *the painted ~ of a human being* | **religious** | **pornographic**

VERB + IMAGE **generate, produce, reproduce** ◊ *the ~s produced on laser printers* | **capture, download, record, scan, upload** ◊ *She longed to capture the ~ on film.* | **edit** | **distort** | **bear** ◊ *humorous posters bearing an ~ of a squatting dog* | **display, post, show** ◊ *the pixel information used to display a digital ~* ◊ *Advertisers have given permission to post these digital ~s.* | **print** | **process** | **enlarge** ◊ *The devices are capable of enlarging the ~.* | **acquire, obtain** | **view** | **store** ◊ *You can store these ~s in a separate computer file.* | **juxtapose** ◊ *The display juxtaposed ~s from serious and popular art.* | **use** ◊ *These ~s are used for marketing purposes.*

IMAGE + VERB **depict sth, reflect sth, represent sth, reveal sth, show sth** ◊ *heat ~s that show where most of the activity in the brain is* | **suggest sth** | **flicker** | **fade**

IMAGE + NOUN **capture, processing** | **analysis** ◊ *~ analysis and feature recognition* | **distortion, manipulation** | **compression** | **processor** | **database, file** ◊ *They can connect directly to the ~ files and allow the customer to view them.* | **transfer** ◊ *a standard video output for ~ transfer or remote viewing*

→ Special page at COMPUTER

imagery noun

ADJ. **evocative, graphic, powerful, stark, violent, vivid** ◊ *the vivid visual ~ of dreams* | **negative** ◊ *the negative ~ of gays and lesbians on TV* | **positive** | **popular** ◊ *The novels draw on popular ~ from newspapers.* | **traditional** ◊ *the traditional Christian ~ of crucifixion* | **visual** | **mental** ◊ *Illustrations may come between the text and the reader's own mental ~.* | **dream** ◊ *his continuing quest to explore dream ~*

| biblical, erotic, poetic, religious, sexual | abstract, surreal, symbolic | natural, representational | photographic, radar, satellite, video | high-resolution | computer-generated, digital | 3-D, three-dimensional | aerial, overhead (*esp. AmE*) ◊ *The Pentagon is searching for overhead ~ from satellites or spy planes.*
VERB + IMAGERY **draw on, employ, use** | **create, produce, provide** ◊ *The equipment provides intelligence ~ for tactical commanders.* | **evoke** ◊ *He evokes complex ~ with a single well-placed word.*

imaginable *adj.*

VERBS **be**
ADV. **barely, hardly, scarcely** (*esp. BrE*) ◊ *To such poor people, the idea of having a choice of food is barely ~.*
PHRASES **the best … imaginable, the most … imaginable, the worst … imaginable** ◊ *It was the most boring movie ~!* | *They live in the worst conditions ~.* | **every ~ sth** ◊ *They had every ~ shade of green.* ◊ *They had every shade of green ~.*

imaginary *adj.*

VERBS **be**
ADV. **completely, entirely, purely, wholly** ◊ *The characters in this book are purely ~.* | **largely** ◊ *a largely ~ threat*

imagination *noun*

ADJ. **great** | **active, creative, fertile, lively, rich, strong, vivid** | **fevered, overactive, overheated, wild** ◊ *It's just a product of your fevered ~!* | **limited** ◊ *a movie of such limited ~* | **collective, popular, public** ◊ *a popular hero who inspired the collective ~* | **visual** ◊ *I was no good at art—I have a very poor visual ~.* | **artistic, cultural, historical, literary, musical, poetic, political, romantic** ◊ *It requires a strong effort of historical ~ to understand the Roman attitude to death.* | **moral** (*esp. AmE*) | **religious** ◊ *an education that stimulates the moral ~* | **human** ◊ *the powers of the human ~* | **pure**
VERB + IMAGINATION **have** | **show** | **lack** ◊ *Today's music lacks ~.* | **require, take** ◊ *It does not take great ~ to guess what happened next.* | **use** ◊ *I don't have a picture of this, so you'll just have to use your ~.* | **captivate, capture, catch, excite, feed, fire, fuel, grab** (*esp. BrE*), **ignite, inspire, seize, spark, stimulate, stir** ◊ *19th-century writers fired the popular ~ with their tales of adventure.* | **engage, grip** | **haunt** ◊ *The film haunted the ~s of viewers.* | **exercise, stretch** | **defy** ◊ *The scale of the disaster defied ~ (= was greater than you could imagine).* | **leave sth to** ◊ *As for their reaction, I'll leave that to your ~!*
IMAGINATION + VERB **conjure sth up** ◊ *His ~ conjured up a vision of the normal family life he had never had.* | **play tricks on you, run away with you, run riot** (*esp. BrE*), **run wild, work** ◊ *Was it only her ~ playing tricks on her?*
PREP. **beyond (your) ~** ◊ *misery that is beyond most people's ~* | **in the/your ~** ◊ *Nobody hates you—it's all in your ~!* | **with ~, without ~** ◊ *He was totally without ~.*
PHRASES **a lack of ~** | **a figment of sb's ~, a product of sb's ~** ◊ *The figure vanished as silently as if it had simply been a figment of her ~.* | **by no stretch of the ~, not by any stretch of the ~** ◊ *Not by any stretch of the ~ could she be called beautiful (= she was definitely not beautiful in any way).* | **with a little ~** ◊ *With a little ~ you can create a delicious meal from yesterday's leftovers.* | **a hold on the/sb's ~** ◊ *the Pyramids retain a remarkable hold on the human ~.*

imaginative *adj.*

VERBS **be, seem**
ADV. **extremely, fairly, very, etc.** | **brilliantly, highly, most** (*esp. BrE*), **particularly, richly, wildly, wonderfully** ◊ *a wonderfully ~ story*

imagine *verb*

1 form a picture of sth in your mind
ADV. **clearly, easily, readily** ◊ *I could clearly ~ the scene in the office.* | **barely, hardly, scarcely** (*esp. BrE*) ◊ *I could hardly ~ living in such a remote and desolate spot.* | **just** ◊ *She could just ~ her mother's look of horror.* | **quite** ◊ *The sight was disturbing as you can quite ~.* | **almost** ◊ *When I think about this story I can almost ~ the look on his face.* | **ever, possibly** ◊ *the best guitarist you could possibly ~* | **fully** (*esp. AmE*) ◊ *I couldn't fully ~ what it could be.* | **actually** ◊ *I can't actually ~ her falling for that trick.* | **always** ◊ *I always ~d him following in his father's footsteps.* | **vividly** ◊ *She had so vividly ~d it time and time again.*
VERB + IMAGINE **can** ◊ *I can well ~ the atmosphere at home at this moment.* ◊ *There's more at stake here than you can possibly ~.* | **try to** | **begin to, start to** ◊ *I can't even begin to ~ the horrors that they have been through.* ◊ *I started to ~ what he might say.* | **dare to** ◊ *He hardly dared to ~ what else was going to be divulged.* | **love to** ◊ *He loved to ~ himself as the hero.* | **be difficult to, be hard to, be impossible to, be tough to** ◊ *It is difficult to ~ a world without money.* | **be absurd to, be far-fetched to** | **be easy to** | **be free to** ◊ *The artist is free to ~ anything she pleases.*
PHRASES **let us ~** ◊ *Let us ~ what really might have happened.*
2 see/hear/think sth that is not true/does not exist
ADV. **really, seriously** ◊ *You don't seriously ~ I'll agree to that?* | **almost** ◊ *I could almost ~ you were jealous.* | **actually** | **just, merely, simply** ◊ *She knew she was simply imagining things.* | **fondly, naively** (*both esp. BrE*) ◊ *I had fondly ~d that riding a mule would be easy.*
VERB + IMAGINE **be easy to**
PHRASES **be imagining things** ◊ *Had I really heard a noise, or was I just imagining things?* | **real and ~d, real or ~d** ◊ *He was always quick to avenge insults, real or ~d.*

imbalance *noun*

ADJ. **growing** | **dangerous, extreme, huge, massive, serious, severe** ◊ *dangerous ~s in potassium and other body chemicals* | **global, regional** (*esp. BrE*) | **economic, financial, fiscal, gender, power, racial, trade** | **chemical, hormonal, hormone, thyroid** | **mental** ◊ *The patient had long shown signs of mental ~.* | **structural** ◊ *Can he resolve the structural ~ of the deficit?*
VERB + IMBALANCE **cause, create** | **exacerbate** ◊ *A higher dollar will only exacerbate the trade ~.* | **address** ◊ *Vigorous action is needed to address global ~s.* | **correct, rectify, redress, reduce** ◊ *Increased recruitment of women engineers will help correct the gender ~ in the profession.*
IMBALANCE + VERB **occur** | **exist** ◊ *the large trade ~s now existing between Europe and the US* | **cause sth** ◊ *Chemical ~s actually cause the sleep disturbances.*
PREP. **~ between** ◊ *an ~ between imports and exports* | **~ in** ◊ *An ~ in certain chemicals leads to disturbances in the brain's function.* | **~ of** ◊ *an ~ of power or authority*

imitation *noun*

1 copy of a thing
ADJ. **accurate, good, passable** | **exact, perfect** | **cheap, crude, pale, poor** ◊ *Accept no cheap ~s of our product!* ◊ *Their version of jazz funk is a pale ~ of the real thing.* | **mere** ◊ *They are mere ~s of existing products.*
2 act of copying sth
ADJ. **slavish** | **direct** ◊ *Children are seen as learning to write by direct ~ of adult models.*
PREP. **in ~ of** ◊ *The poems, some in ~ of Whitman, are unremarkable.*
3 copy of the way sb speaks, behaves, etc.
ADJ. **accurate, fair, good, passable** | **perfect** ◊ *He does a perfect ~ of a turkey.* | **close, convincing** ◊ *a voice that's a close ~ of a snake hiss* | **bad, lame, poor**
VERB + IMITATION **do, give, perform** ◊ *He does a very good ~ of Liza Minelli.*

immaculate *adj.*

VERBS **be, look** | **keep sth**
ADV. **absolutely**

immaterial adj.
VERBS **be, prove, seem** | **become**
ADV. **completely, entirely, quite, wholly** ◇ *The condition of the car is quite ~ as long as it works.* | **almost** | **relatively**
PREP. **to** ◇ *These facts are ~ to the problem.*

immature adj.
VERBS **be, seem, sound**
ADV. **extremely, fairly, very, etc.** | **a little, slightly, etc.** | **developmentally, emotionally, physically, politically, sexually**

immediacy noun
VERB + IMMEDIACY **lack** | **convey** ◇ *The drawings convey both ~ and a sense of violence.*
PHRASES **a lack of ~** ◇ *The book had a lack of ~ for most people.*

immediate adj.
VERBS **be, seem** ◇ *The effect seems ~.*
ADV. **almost** ◇ *The painkillers brought almost ~ relief.*

immerse verb
1 put sth in liquid
ADV. **completely, fully, totally** | **partially**
PREP. **in** ◇ *The seeds need to be completely ~d in water.*
2 concentrate completely on sth
ADV. **deeply** ◇ *Clare and Phil were deeply ~d in conversation.* | **completely, fully, thoroughly, totally** | **immediately** ◇ *I immediately ~d myself in the task.* | **in** ◇ *For six months I totally ~d myself in my work.*

immigrant noun
ADJ. **illegal** | **undocumented** (*esp. AmE*) ◇ *the 11 million undocumented ~s living in California* | **legal** ◇ *the number of legal ~s to the US* | **foreign** | **Hispanic, Irish, Italian, Jewish, Mexican, etc.** | **newly arrived, recent, recently arrived** | **would-be** | **first-generation, second-generation** ◇ *Like many first-generation ~s, they worked hard and saved most of their earnings.* | **working-class** | **poor** | **skilled** ◇ *The government is eager to attract skilled ~s.* | **unskilled**
... OF IMMIGRANTS **flood, influx, tide, wave**
VERB + IMMIGRANT **accept, welcome** | **attract, draw, encourage** ◇ *These factors attracted new ~s.* | **bring, smuggle** ◇ *boats bringing illegal ~s over from North Africa* | **assimilate** (*esp. AmE*) ◇ *a careful mechanism for assimilating ~s* | **employ, hire** ◇ *Businesses may want to hire skilled ~s.* | **assist, help** | **detain** ◇ *the circumstances under which ~s were detained* | **target** ◇ *anti-terrorist legislation that targeted ~s* | **deport, return** ◇ *ships laden with would-be ~s who were forcibly returned* | **exclude** ◇ *a law designed to exclude Chinese ~s*
IMMIGRANT + VERB **arrive, enter sth, move to sth, pour into sth, settle sth** ◇ *~s seeking to enter the country* ◇ *the ~s who poured into America* | **come from sth** | **flee sth** ◇ *European ~s fleeing Nazism in the 1930s* | **live in sth, settle in sth** ◇ *a family of Turkish ~s living in California* ◇ *European ~s settled much of Australia.* | **work** ◇ *a young Afghan ~ who has worked at the store for years* | **found sth** ◇ *The company was founded by two ~s from Bangladesh.* | **speak sth** ◇ *recent ~s who do not speak English* | **seek sth** ◇ *Mexican ~s seeking farm work* | **experience sth** | **face sth** ◇ *the issues faced by Dominican ~s* | **assimilate** ◇ *Italian ~s assimilated easily into Brazilian society.*
IMMIGRANT + NOUN **community, family, generation, group, minority, population** | **labourer/laborer, student, worker** | **labour/labor** | **neighbourhood/neighborhood** | **status** ◇ *They are trying to secure ~ status for their families.* | **experience** ◇ *different aspects of the ~ experience* | **rights** | **culture, identity**
PREP. **~ from** | **~ to** ◇ *She was the daughter of Chinese ~s to America.*

immigration noun
1 coming to live in a country
ADJ. **illegal** | **undocumented** (*AmE*) | **legal** | **large-scale, mass, massive** | **increased** | **uncontrolled** ◇ *the impact of uncontrolled ~* | **continued, continuing** ◇ *the immense and continuing ~ from Latin America* | **Hispanic, Jewish, Mexican, etc.**
VERB + IMMIGRATION **control, curb, curtail, limit, prevent, reduce, restrict, stop** ◇ *laws restricting ~ into the US* | **discourage, increase** ◇ *I think we need to discourage illegal ~.* | **encourage** ◇ *The authorities quickly encouraged ~.*
IMMIGRATION + NOUN **bill, control, crisis, debate, enforcement, law, legislation, policy, proposal, reform, restrictions, rules** | **agent** (*AmE*), **authority, court** (*esp. AmE*), **office, officer, official, service** | **attorney** (*AmE*), **judge** (*AmE*), **lawyer** | **case, hearing, proceedings** | **violation** ◇ *They were arrested for ~ violations.* | **quota** ◇ *a Senate debate on ~ quotas* | **rate** ◇ *the ~ rate for the US* | **status** ◇ *the ~ status of the worker* | **records** ◇ *US attorneys match ~ records to voting rolls.* | **papers** ◇ *His wife finally received her ~ papers.*
PREP. **~ from** ◇ *There was a sudden increase in ~ from Europe.*
2 (*also* **immigration control**) at a port/airport
VERB + IMMIGRATION **go through, pass through** ◇ *We landed at Heathrow and went through customs and ~.*
IMMIGRATION + NOUN **checks, procedures** ◇ *calls for tighter ~ procedures*

immobile adj.
VERBS **lie, remain, sit, stand, stay** ◇ *She seemed scarcely to breathe as she lay ~.* | **become** | **hold sb, leave sb, render sb** ◇ *For a moment shock held her ~.* ◇ *The accident left him totally ~.*
ADV. **completely, perfectly, totally, utterly** | **almost, largely, practically, virtually** | **relatively**

immoral adj.
VERBS **be, seem** | **condemn sb/sth as, consider sb/sth, deem sth, denounce sb/sth as, find sth, regard sb/sth as, think sb/sth, view sb/sth as** ◇ *He condemned the government's action as ~.*
ADV. **extremely, fairly, very, etc.** | **completely, deeply, downright, highly, profoundly, totally, utterly** | **inherently, intrinsically**

immortality noun
ADJ. **personal** (*technical*) ◇ *Some religions include a doctrine of personal ~.* | **baseball, cinematic, literary, sporting** (*BrE*), **etc.** (*all figurative*)
VERB + IMMORTALITY **achieve, attain** | **bestow, confer, give sb, grant** ◇ *It was in the power of the gods to confer ~ upon mortals.*
PHRASES **the ~ of the soul** ◇ *They believe in the ~ of the soul.*

immune adj.
1 protected against a disease
VERBS **be, seem** | **become** | **remain, stay** | **make sb** ◇ *The vaccination doesn't necessarily make you completely ~.*
ADV. **completely, totally**
PREP. **to** ◇ *Many people are ~ to this disease.*
2 not affected by sth
VERBS **appear, be, prove, seem** | **become** | **remain**
ADV. **completely, entirely, totally, wholly** | **by no means, far from** ◇ *Children are far from ~ to the cruelty that is latent in all humans.* | **almost, largely, virtually, seemingly** | **relatively** | **somehow** ◇ *He seems to believe that the president is somehow ~ from criticism.*
PREP. **from** ◇ *He is ~ from prosecution as long as he is in office.* | **to** ◇ *She's quite ~ to criticism.*

immunity noun
1 protection against disease
ADJ. **strong** | **acquired, natural** | **impaired** | **lifelong** ◇

Infection usually confers lifelong ~ to the disease. | **herd** ◊ *Polio has been eradicated due to vaccination and herd ~.* |
VERB + IMMUNITY **have** ◊ *The island's inhabitants had no ~ to the diseases carried by the explorers and quickly succumbed.* | **lack** | **acquire**, **build up**, **develop** ◊ *Once you have had a cold you build up ~ to that particular virus.* | **confer** ◊ *The vaccine only confers ~ for a few months.* | **stimulate** ◊ *the use of vaccines to stimulate ~* | **boost** | **impair**, **lower** ◊ *High levels of stress may lower your ~ to common illnesses.*
IMMUNITY + VERB **develop** ◊ *A strong ~ to reinfection develops after one year.*
PREP. **~ against**, **~ to** ◊ *The newcomers lacked ~ against local strains of the disease.*

2 protection from danger/punishment
ADJ. **complete**, **total** | **diplomatic**, **legal**, **parliamentary** ◊ *Several ministers were stripped of parliamentary ~ as a prelude to facing corruption charges.*
VERB + IMMUNITY **enjoy** | **claim**, **seek** | **confer**, **give sb**, **grant (sb)**, **guarantee (sb)**, **provide** | **abolish**, **lift**, **strip sb of** ◊ *The Supreme Court lifted the company's ~ from criminal prosecution.* | **waive** ◊ *He has agreed to waive his diplomatic ~ and face prosecution.* | **lose**
PREP. **~ from** ◊ *Unions were granted ~ from prosecution for non-violent acts.*

immunize (BrE also **-ise**) verb
ADV. **fully** | **routinely**
PREP. **against** ◊ *Children have been routinely ~d against polio since 1958.* | **with** ◊ *They ~d some mice with a dose of the live vaccine.*

impact noun
1 effect/impression
ADJ. **big**, **considerable**, **dramatic**, **enormous**, **great**, **high**, **huge**, **important**, **main**, **major**, **massive**, **powerful**, **profound**, **strong**, **tremendous** ◊ *a high-impact message aimed at changing people's attitudes* | **discernible**, **measurable**, **noticeable**, **real**, **significant**, **substantial** ◊ *A 1% rise is enough to have a measurable ~ on economic growth.* | **limited**, **little**, **marginal**, **minimal**, **minimum**, **negligible** | **full** ◊ *The industrial north of the country felt the full ~ of the recession.* | **maximum** ◊ *We'll show you how to dress for maximum ~ at the all-important audition.* | **overall**, **total** | **growing**, **increasing** | **added** | **disproportionate** | **combined**, **cumulative** ◊ *the cumulative ~ of a series of damaging events* | **decisive** | **direct** ◊ *Agriculture made a direct physical ~ on the landscape.* | **immediate**, **instant**, **sudden** | **initial**, **short-term** | **lasting**, **long-term** | **broader**, **far-reaching**, **wider** ◊ *It is important to appreciate the wider ~ and implications of this proposal.* | **future**, **likely**, **possible**, **potential** | **beneficial**, **favourable/favorable**, **positive** | **adverse**, **catastrophic**, **damaging**, **destructive**, **detrimental**, **devastating**, **disastrous**, **heavy**, **negative**, **serious**, **severe** | **human** ◊ *The severest human ~ on the dolphins has been the loss of habitat.* | **personal** ◊ *The personal ~ of party leaders has been very important.* | **physical**, **visual** ◊ *an attempt to reduce the visual ~ of wind farms on the landscape* | **visceral** ◊ *The film lacks the visceral ~ of her previous work.* | **cultural**, **ecological**, **economic**, **emotional**, **environmental**, **financial**, **health**, **political**, **psychological**, **social** ◊ *The environmental ~ of power generation is being assessed.*
VERB + IMPACT **achieve**, **create**, **exert**, **have**, **make** ◊ *Variations in the interest rate will have an ~ on the whole housing market.* ◊ *You certainly made a big ~ on Carter.* | **feel** ◊ *The initial ~ of the reforms will be felt most keenly in primary schools.* | **analyse/analyze**, **consider**, **examine**, **explore**, **investigate**, **monitor**, **study** ◊ *We investigated the ~ of new technologies on teaching methods.* | **assess**, **determine**, **estimate**, **evaluate**, **gauge**, **judge**, **measure**, **quantify** ◊ *It is difficult to judge the likely ~ of the changes on employment patterns.* | **underestimate** | **enhance**, **increase**, **maximize** | **alleviate**, **cushion**, **lessen**, **minimize**, **mitigate**, **offset**, **reduce**, **soften** ◊ *We are trying to minimize the ~ of price rises on our customers.* | **diminish**, **lessen**, **reduce**, **weaken** ◊ *Listening to the speech through an*

interpreter lessened its ~ somewhat. | **lose** ◊ *When peace returned, the hard-line message lost much of its ~.* | **resist**, **withstand** ◊ *This section explores how mothers resist the ~ of poverty on the health of their children.* | **be concerned about** | **appreciate**, **realize**, **recognize**, **understand** | **highlight** | **address** | **predict** | **reflect** ◊ *Architecturally, these churches reflected the ~ of the Renaissance.*
PREP. **under the ~ of** ◊ *Manufacturing fell sharply under the ~ of the recession.* | **~ on**, **~ upon** ◊ *to highlight the ~ of technology on working practices*

2 act/force of one object hitting another
ADJ. **full** | **initial** | **asteroid**, **meteorite** ◊ *the consequences of an asteroid ~*
VERB + IMPACT **take** ◊ *The front of the bus took the full ~ of the crash.* | **feel** | **absorb** ◊ *A well-designed sports shoe should absorb the ~ on the 28 bones in each foot.* | **cushion**, **lessen**, **soften** ◊ *Air bags are designed to soften the ~ for crash victims.* | **survive**, **withstand** ◊ *The crew of six may have survived the initial ~, but the whole plane went up in flames seconds later.*
IMPACT + VERB **occur** ◊ *Impact occurred seconds after the pilot radioed for help.* | **knock sb/sth ...** ◊ *The ~ knocked him off balance.*
IMPACT + NOUN **speed**, **velocity** | **crater** ◊ *Small meteorites have left ~ craters all over the planet's surface.*
PREP. **on ~** ◊ *The front of the car had crumpled on ~.*
PHRASES **the moment**, **point**, **time**, **etc. of ~**

impair verb
ADV. **dramatically**, **greatly**, **markedly**, **seriously**, **severely**, **significantly**, **substantially** ◊ *a defect that significantly ~s the safety of a car* | **mildly** | **permanently**
PHRASES **severely ~ed** ◊ *Her liver function was severely ~ed.*

impartial adj.
VERBS **be** | **remain** ◊ *The judge must remain ~.*
ADV. **completely**, **entirely**, **totally**, **truly** | **reasonably** | **supposedly**

impartiality noun
ADJ. **absolute** (esp. BrE), **complete** | **due** (BrE) ◊ *The BBC must ensure that due ~ is preserved in its news programmes.* | **journalistic**, **judicial**
VERB + IMPARTIALITY **guarantee**, **maintain**, **preserve** | **compromise** ◊ *The newspaper sought to present a range of opinions without compromising its ~.* | **question** ◊ *The judge's ~ in this case might reasonably be questioned.*

impassable adj.
VERBS **be** | **become** | **remain** | **make sth** ◊ *The mud made the roads ~.*
ADV. **completely**, **totally** | **almost**, **nearly**, **virtually**

impasse noun
ADJ. **current**, **present** | **diplomatic**, **political** | **budget** (esp. AmE) ◊ *The Governor attempted to resolve Minnesota's current budget ~.*
VERB + IMPASSE **reach** ◊ *Negotiations seemed to have reached an ~.* | **break**, **end**, **overcome**, **resolve**
PHRASES **a way out of an ~** ◊ *The proposal offered both sides a way out of the diplomatic ~.*

impassive adj.
VERBS **be**, **sit**, **stand** | **become** | **remain**
ADV. **completely**, **quite**, **totally** | **almost** ◊ *Her expression was cool, almost ~.*

impatience noun
ADJ. **growing** | **slight** | **barely concealed** | **barely controlled**
... OF IMPATIENCE **hint**, **touch**, **trace**
VERB + IMPATIENCE **feel** ◊ *She felt a growing ~.* | **sense** ◊ *Sensing her ~, I spoke quickly.* | **express**, **show** ◊ *He was*

trying hard not to show his ~. | **contain, curb, restrain** ◇ *She was unable to contain her ~.* | **conceal, hide, mask**
IMPATIENCE + VERB **grow**
PREP. **with ~** ◇ *He stamped his feet as he waited with barely concealed ~ for the telephone.* | **~ at** ◇ *He expressed ~ at the slow rate of progress.* | **~ for** ◇ *his ~ for her to return* | **~ with** ◇ *~ with the slowness of change*
PHRASES **a gesture of ~, a look of ~** ◇ *He shook his head in a gesture of ~.* | **a sigh of ~** ◇ *He bit back a sigh of ~.* | **signs of ~** ◇ *The children were beginning to show signs of ~.*

impatient *adj.*

VERBS **appear, be, feel, seem, sound** | **become, get, grow** ◇ *The children were growing ~.*
ADV. **extremely, fairly, very, etc.** ◇ *He spoke in a somewhat ~ tone.* | **increasingly** | **a little, slightly, etc.**
PREP. **about** ◇ *She's getting ~ about the delays.* | **at** ◇ *Sean was a little ~ at the time Valerie devoted to her mother.* | **for** ◇ *~ for change* | **with** ◇ *Sometimes he is very ~ with his wife.*

impede *verb*

ADV. **greatly, seriously, severely, significantly** ◇ *The bad weather seriously ~d our progress.*

impediment *noun*

ADJ. **great, major, serious** | **chief, main** | **lawful** (*BrE*), **legal** ◇ *There are no legal ~s to their appealing against the decision.*
VERB + IMPEDIMENT **be, constitute, provide** | **overcome** | **remove** ◇ *The agreement is designed to remove ~s to trade between the two countries.*
PREP. **~ to** ◇ *Their boycott of the talks constitutes a serious ~ to peace negotiations.*

impenetrable *adj.*

VERBS **be, seem** | **become** | **remain** | **find sth** ◇ *They found the jungle virtually ~.*
ADV. **almost, nearly, virtually** ◇ *His reports were virtually ~ without an explanation.* | **seemingly**
PREP. **to** ◇ *The language of this document would be ~ to anyone except a specialist.*

imperative *adj.*

VERBS **be, seem** | **become** | **remain** ◇ *It remains ~ that all sides should be involved in the talks.* | **make sth** ◇ *The collapse of the wall made it ~ to keep the water out by some other means.* | **consider sth** ◇ *We consider it absolutely ~ to start work immediately.*
ADV. **absolutely**

imperceptible *adj.*

VERBS **be**
ADV. **almost, nearly, virtually** ◇ *His head moved in an almost ~ nod.*
PREP. **to** ◇ *The slight change in the taste was ~ to most people.*

imperfect *adj.*

VERBS **be** | **remain** ◇ *Our understanding of cancer remains ~.*
ADV. **highly, very** ◇ *He spoke in very ~ English.* | **slightly** ◇ *These goods are slightly ~.* | **admittedly** ◇ *What follows is an admittedly ~ analogy…*

imperfection *noun*

ADJ. **minor, slight** | **physical**
VERB + IMPERFECTION **cover, cover up, hide** | **reveal, show, show up**
PREP. **in** ◇ *Careful inspection in daylight revealed ~s in the paintwork.*

imperialism *noun*

ADJ. **American, British, Roman, Western, etc.** | **capitalist, cultural, economic**

impersonal *adj.*

VERBS **be, seem** | **become** | **find sth** ◇ *I find the atmosphere there rather ~.* | **keep sth** ◇ *I think we should keep things entirely ~.*
ADV. **extremely, fairly, very, etc.** | **totally** | **a little, slightly, etc.** | **coldly** ◇ *The law is abstract and coldly ~.* | **seemingly**

impertinence *noun*

ADJ. **gross** ◇ *I consider his remark a gross ~.*
VERB + IMPERTINENCE **have** ◇ *She had the ~ to suggest I needed a rest.*
PHRASES **the height of ~**

impertinent *adj.*

VERBS **be, seem** | **deem sth, find sth** ◇ *She found the question highly ~.*
ADV. **extremely, fairly, very, etc.**

impervious *adj.*

VERBS **appear, be, seem** | **become** | **remain**
ADV. **completely, quite, totally** ◇ *He was completely ~ to criticism.* | **almost, largely, practically, virtually** | **apparently, seemingly**
PREP. **to** ◇ *She was ~ to his charms.*

impetus *noun*

ADJ. **considerable, great, powerful, strong, tremendous** | **main, major** | **immediate, initial, original** | **fresh, new, renewed** ◇ *Each new revelation added fresh ~ to the campaign.* | **added, extra, further** | **necessary** ◇ *His disappointment in the championships provided the necessary ~ to give everything for this final race.*
VERB + IMPETUS **add, give sb/sth, lend sth, provide (sb/sth with)** ◇ *The riots lent ~ to attempts to improve conditions for prisoners.* | **gain, receive** ◇ *The movement is steadily gaining ~.* | **lose** ◇ *With the death of its founder, the campaign lost much of its ~.*
IMPETUS + VERB **come from sth** ◇ *Much of the ~ for change came from customers' opinions.*
PREP. **~ behind sb/sth** ◇ *The main ~ behind the move west was to find gold and other minerals.* | **~ for** ◇ *the ~ for arms control agreements* | **~ towards/toward** ◇ *the ~ towards/toward urban development*

impinge *verb*

ADV. **seriously** ◇ *actions which seriously ~ on other people's personal freedoms* | **hardly** (*esp. BrE*) | **rarely** ◇ *The music industry rarely ~s on my life.* | **directly**
PREP. **on, upon** ◇ *measures which directly or indirectly ~ upon women's lives*

implausible *adj.*

VERBS **be, seem, sound** | **consider sth, deem sth** ◇ *These results might be considered ~.*
ADV. **extremely, fairly, very, etc.** | **highly** | **totally, utterly, wholly, wildly** ◇ *This idea is totally ~.* | **increasingly** ◇ *He gave a series of increasingly ~ excuses.* | **not entirely** | **inherently** | **biologically, psychologically, scientifically, etc.**

implement *noun*

ADJ. **agricultural, farm, farming, garden, gardening, kitchen, surgical** | **cooking, digging, writing, etc.** | **sharp** ◇ *Make sure that all sharp ~s have covers.* | **flint, metal, stone, wooden**

implement *verb*

ADV. **correctly, fully, properly** ◇ *These policies have never been fully ~ed.* | **partially** | **consistently, systematically** | **actually** ◇ *The proposed changes were never actually ~ed.* | **widely** ◇ *These reforms have now been widely ~ed in schools.* | **globally, locally, nationally** | **effectively, successfully** | **immediately, quickly**
VERB + IMPLEMENT **agree to, decide to, intend to, promise to** | **attempt to, seek to, try to** | **fail to** ◇ *The government*

failed to ~ the plan. | **refuse to** | **be forced to, be obliged to** | **be difficult to, be hard to** ◊ *The decision was hard to ~.*
PHRASES **easily ~ed** ◊ *It's a simple, easily ~ed system.* | **poorly ~ed** ◊ *a poorly ~ed strategy*

implementation noun

ADJ. **effective, successful** | **full** | **large-scale, widespread** ◊ *We believe that widespread ~ of this approach will result in improvements.* | **detailed** ◊ *Detailed ~ of the plans was left to the regional offices.* | **smooth** ◊ *We will consult widely to ensure smooth ~.* | **actual, practical** ◊ *The practical ~ of the regulations proved difficult.* | **early, immediate** | **gradual** | **policy**
VERB + IMPLEMENTATION **achieve, ensure** ◊ *To achieve ~ of the policy is a long, slow task.* | **accelerate, expedite, facilitate, simplify** ◊ *Hospitals have been given extra funds to facilitate the ~ of the changes.* | **delay, hinder** ◊ *They have lobbied to delay ~ of the new tax package.* | **monitor, oversee, supervise** ◊ *The UN is to supervise the ~ of the peace treaty.* | **consider, discuss**
IMPLEMENTATION + NOUN **plan, strategy** | **process** ◊ *The restructuring will take place in phases, to simplify the ~ process.* | **phase** ◊ *The new regulations are still in the early ~ phase.* | **problem**

implicate verb be implicated in sth

ADV. **deeply, heavily, strongly** ◊ *These groups are very strongly ~d in the violence.* | **directly** | **falsely** ◊ *He was falsely ~d in an attempted murder case.*

implication noun

1 possible effect/result

ADJ. **considerable, crucial, enormous, important, major, massive, significant, strong** | **main** | **deeper, profound** | **broad, far-reaching, wider, wide-ranging** ◊ *The broader ~s of the plan were discussed.* | **full** ◊ *Now they realized the full ~s of the new system.* | **direct** | **clear, obvious** | **general** | **further** | **possible, potential** | **future, long-term** | **dire, grave, serious** | **disturbing, ominous, sinister** | **adverse, negative** | **interesting** | **radical, revolutionary** | **practical** ◊ *These results have important practical ~s.* | **theoretical** | **commercial, economic, financial** | **environmental** | **educational, psychological, social, societal** | **constitutional, legal, political** ◊ *the constitutional ~s of a royal divorce* | **ethical, ideological, metaphysical, moral, philosophical, theological** | **clinical, therapeutic** | **cost, health, policy, resource** (esp. BrE), **safety, security, tax**
VERB + IMPLICATION **carry, have** ◊ *The emphasis on testing leads to greater stress among students and carries ~s of failure.* | **appreciate, grasp, realize, understand** | **assess, consider, examine, explore, ponder, study** ◊ *You need to consider the legal ~s before you publish anything.* | **digest** | **discuss** | **explain** | **draw, draw out** ◊ *Her article attempts to draw out the ~s of this argument.* | **address** ◊ *Their work addresses the ~s of new technology.* | **accept** ◊ *a society that fully accepts the ~s of disability* | **reject** | **ignore**
IMPLICATION + VERB **arise** ◊ *Several interesting ~s arise from these developments.* | **be involved** ◊ *Given the resource ~s involved, the plan will have to be scaled down.*
PREP. **~ about** ◊ *disturbing ~s about the company's future* | **~ for** ◊ *The research has far-reaching ~s for medicine as a whole.*

2 sth suggested but not said openly

ADJ. **clear, obvious** ◊ *The ~ is clear: young females do better if they mate with a new male.* | **possible** ◊ *His remark seemed to have various possible ~s.* | **unspoken**
VERB + IMPLICATION **carry, have** | **understand** | **digest** ◊ *Brian paused for a moment while he digested the ~s of this statement.* | **resent** ◊ *I resent the ~ that I don't care about my father.*
PREP. **by ~** ◊ *In refusing to believe our story, he is saying by ~ that we are lying.*

imply verb

ADV. **clearly, heavily, strongly** | **subtly** ◊ *He subtly implied that race was an issue in the case.* | **logically** ◊ *The statement logically implies a certain conclusion.* | **simply** | **generally, normally, usually** | **automatically** | **not necessarily** ◊ *This does not necessarily ~ that children achieve better results in private schools.* | **in no way** ◊ *They believe that submission in no way implies inferiority.* | **falsely, wrongly** ◊ *The article falsely implied that he was responsible for the accident.*
VERB + IMPLY **seem to** ◊ *The letter seems to ~ that the president knew about the business deals.* | **intend to, mean to** ◊ *I never meant to ~ any criticism.* | **take sth to** ◊ *This statement should not be taken to ~ that the government is exonerated of all blame.*
PHRASES **express or implied** (law), **real or implied** ◊ *the express or implied terms of the contract*

import noun

ADJ. **main, major** | **foreign, overseas** | **Australian, Japanese, etc.** | **cheap, low-priced** (esp. AmE) | **expensive** | **annual** ◊ *The value of annual ~s rose rapidly.* | **net** ◊ *the UK's net ~s of food* | **total** | **increased** | **illegal** | **parallel** (esp. BrE) ◊ *parallel ~s of brand name drugs from Spain into other countries* | **agricultural, beef, car, coal, energy, food, grain, oil, steel, textile, etc.**
VERB + IMPORT **boost** ◊ *pressure on the government to stimulate the faltering economy and boost ~s* | **cut, limit, reduce, restrict** | **discourage** | **control** | **block, halt, prevent, stop** | **ban, prohibit** ◊ *The government decided to prohibit the ~ of toxic waste.* | **allow, permit** | **finance** ◊ *Most of their oil revenues are used to finance ~s of consumer goods.* | **replace** ◊ *The industry aims both to increase exports and replace ~s.*
IMPORT + VERB **grow, increase, rise** | **drop, fall** | **be valued at sth, total sth** ◊ *Imports were valued at £516 million last month.* | **account for sth** ◊ *Imports of foodstuffs accounted for a small proportion of total ~s.*
IMPORT + NOUN **ban, control** (esp. BrE), **restrictions** | **duty, tariff** | **price** ◊ *rising ~ prices* | **licence/license** | **quota** ◊ *A restricted ~ quota was set for meat products.* | **penetration** ◊ *greater ~ penetration of the domestic market*
PREP. **~ from** ◊ *America has cut its oil ~s from the Middle East by 73%.* | **~ into** ◊ *Special duties were imposed on ~s into the republic.*
PHRASES **a ban on ~s, a restriction on ~s** | **the demand for ~s** | **a fall in ~s, a rise in ~s** | **~s and exports**
→ Note at PER CENT (for more verbs)

import verb

ADV. **directly** | **illegally, legally** | **specially**
PREP. **from** ◊ *The store's croissants are ~ed directly from France.* | **into** ◊ *These dogs are illegally ~ed into the country.* | **to** ◊ *goods that are ~ed to Britain*

importance noun

ADJ. **cardinal, central, considerable, critical, crucial, enormous, extreme, fundamental, great, high, immense, key, major, outstanding** (esp. BrE), **overriding, overwhelming, paramount, particular, profound, real, special, supreme, tremendous, vital** | **first, greatest, highest, primary, prime, utmost** ◊ *This information is of the first ~. ◊ It is of the utmost ~ that you arrive on time.* | **growing, increased, increasing** | **declining** ◊ *the declining ~ of manufacturing industry* | **lesser, limited, marginal, minor, secondary** | **general** | **added** | **immediate, continued, continuing, lasting** | **equal** | **relative** | **intrinsic** | **obvious** | **perceived** ◊ *differences in the perceived ~ of the different subjects in the curriculum* | **potential** | **public** | **international, national** | **practical** | **theoretical** | **symbolic** ◊ *the symbolic ~ of iron in German culture* | **archaeological, commercial, constitutional, cultural, ecological, economic, environmental, historic, historical, legal, military, political, social, strategic**
VERB + IMPORTANCE **have** ◊ *These finds have considerable scientific ~.* | **assume, take on** ◊ *Education takes on an added ~ at a time of economic uncertainty.* | **grow in, increase in, rise in** | **decline in, diminish in, fall in** ◊ *The*

overseas markets have now declined in ~. | **attach**, **give sth**, **place** ◊ To what objectives do you attach most ~? ◊ the ~ placed on cleanliness | **accept**, **acknowledge**, **appreciate**, **be aware of**, **grasp**, **learn**, **note**, **realize**, **recognize**, **see**, **understand** ◊ People were aware of the ~ of working with nature. | **demonstrate**, **illustrate**, **indicate**, **point to**, **reflect**, **show**, **suggest** ◊ Figure 2.2 shows the relative ~ of the different service industries. | **affirm**, **assert**, **reaffirm**, **reiterate** | **deny**, **discount**, **dismiss** ◊ I don't discount the ~ of theory, but I am really concerned with practice. | **confirm**, **reinforce** | **draw attention to**, **emphasize**, **highlight**, **point out**, **promote**, **stress**, **underline**, **underscore** (esp. AmE) ◊ The manual stresses the ~ of regular maintenance. | **diminish**, **downplay**, **minimize**, **play down** (esp. BrE) ◊ She was inclined to downplay the ~ of her own role in the affair. | **exaggerate**, **overemphasize**, **overestimate**, **overstate** | **underestimate** ◊ Don't underestimate the ~ of good presentation. | **increase** | **reduce** | **assess**, **consider**, **discuss**, **evaluate** | **explain** | **doubt**, **cast doubt on**, **question**, **throw doubt on** ◊ No one can seriously question the political ~ of the environment. | **forget**, **ignore**, **overlook**
IMPORTANCE + VERB **lie in sth** ◊ The town's ~ lies in the richness and quality of its architecture.
PREP. **of ... ~** ◊ a figure of crucial ~ in the history of design | **~ for** ◊ an area of enormous ~ for wildlife | **~ to** ◊ the ~ to the country of a healthy economy
PHRASES **in order of ~** ◊ Deal with the issues in order of ~. | **a matter of grave ~**, **a matter of great ~**, **a matter of ~**

important adj.

VERBS **be**, **seem**, **sound** ◊ Someone left a message for you—it sounded ~. | **become** | **remain** | **feel** ◊ He made me feel ~ by asking me lots of questions about myself. | **make sth** ◊ This is what makes our work so ~. | **believe sth**, **consider sth**, **deem sth**, **regard sth as**, **see sth as**, **think sth** ◊ These ideas are considered enormously ~.
ADV. **extremely**, **fairly**, **very**, **etc.** | **enormously**, **extraordinarily**, **highly**, **hugely**, **immensely**, **incredibly**, **profoundly**, **terribly**, **tremendously**, **truly** | **critically**, **crucially**, **fundamentally**, **most** (esp. BrE), **supremely**, **vitally** ◊ This is most ~: you must deliver the letter yourself. | **especially**, **particularly** | **uniquely** ◊ Several factors make this painting uniquely ~. | **increasingly** | **doubly** | **equally** ◊ These two factors are equally ~. | **fairly**, **pretty**, **quite** | **obviously** | **sufficiently** ◊ He considered the matter sufficiently ~ to call her at home. | **internationally** (esp. BrE) ◊ an internationally ~ site for these rare birds | **economically**, **functionally**, **historically**, **politically**, **strategically** ◊ historically ~ buildings
PREP. **for** ◊ It's ~ for you to understand this. | **to** ◊ Spending time with my children is ~ to me. ◊ The work of the intelligence services was crucially ~ to victory in the war.

impose verb

ADV. **effectively** ◊ The terms of the contract were effectively ~d rather than agreed. | **simply** ◊ New technology cannot be used successfully if it is simply ~d on an unwilling workforce. | **centrally** (esp. BrE) ◊ a centrally ~d school curriculum | **externally** ◊ the pressure of having to meet externally ~d targets | **artificially** ◊ Motivation to learn must come from the child; it cannot be artificially ~d. | **forcibly** ◊ The will of the majority should not be forcibly ~d on the minority. | **arbitrarily** ◊ People did not accept these national borders which had been arbitrarily ~d. | **unilaterally** ◊ One side in the conflict cannot unilaterally ~ a settlement.
VERB + IMPOSE **seek to**, **try to**
PREP. **on**, **upon** ◊ The government has ~d a ban on the sale of handguns.

imposition noun

ADJ. **unilateral** ◊ the unilateral ~ of import quotas | **unwanted**
VERB + IMPOSITION **justify** ◊ Several reasons were put forward to justify the ~ of censorship. | **oppose**, **resist**

PREP. **~ on** ◊ the ~ of tax on books

impossible adj.

1 not possible
VERBS **appear**, **be**, **look**, **prove**, **seem**, **sound** | **become** | **remain** | **make sth**, **render sth** ◊ Darkness made it ~ to continue. | **believe sth**, **consider sth**, **deem sth**, **find sth**, **regard sth as**, **see sth as**, **think sth** ◊ I found his offer ~ to resist.
ADV. **absolutely**, **completely**, **downright**, **quite** (esp. BrE), **totally**, **utterly** | **humanly** ◊ They are setting a standard that it is humanly ~ to meet. | **just**, **simply** ◊ I'm really sorry. It's just ~. | **by no means** (esp. BrE), **far from** ◊ a desirable and far from ~ objective to achieve | **almost**, **more or less** (esp. BrE), **near**, **nearly**, **next to**, **nigh**, **nigh on** (esp. BrE), **practically**, **virtually**, **well-nigh** (esp. BrE) ◊ It was well-nigh ~ for him to convince her that he was right. | **pretty** | **effectively** | **literally** | **apparently** (esp. BrE), **seemingly** | **theoretically** | **clearly**, **obviously** | **equally** ◊ Both options are equally ~. | **hitherto**, **previously** ◊ With the new equipment we will be able to accomplish hitherto ~ tasks. | **ultimately** | **economically**, **financially**, **logically**, **logistically**, **mathematically**, **physically**, **politically**, **scientifically**, **technically** ◊ The high cost of childcare made returning to work economically ~.
PREP. **for** ◊ The situation is just ~ for us. ◊ It's ~ for me to say.

2 bad-tempered; difficult to talk to/deal with
VERBS **be** | **become** | **find sb** ◊ I find her ~.
ADV. **really** | **absolutely**, **completely**, **quite**, **totally** ◊ You can be absolutely ~ at times! | **just**

impotence noun

ADJ. **relative** (esp. BrE) ◊ the relative ~ of individual governments in the face of global forces | **male** | **political**, **sexual**
VERB + IMPOTENCE **cure**, **treat** ◊ drugs which have been used to treat male ~ | **cause**
PHRASES **a feeling of ~**, **a sense of ~** ◊ Violence may result from a sense of ~.

impotent adj.

1 without enough power/influence
VERBS **be**, **feel**, **prove** | **remain** | **leave sb**, **make sb**, **render sb** ◊ Companies are rendered ~ by all the rules and regulations.
ADV. **completely**, **utterly** | **virtually** | **politically**
PREP. **against** ◊ They were virtually ~ against the power of the large companies.

2 not capable of having sex
VERBS **be** | **become** | **leave sb**, **make sb** ◊ The operation left him ~.
ADV. **sexually**

impractical adj.

VERBS **be**, **prove**, **seem** ◊ Such a solution proved ~. | **become** | **make sth**, **render sth** ◊ The weight of the machine makes lifting it ~. | **consider sth**, **deem sth**, **find sth**, **regard sth as** ◊ They found his ideas ~.
ADV. **extremely**, **fairly**, **very**, **etc.** | **highly**, **hopelessly**, **wildly** ◊ The long flowing dress was highly ~. | **completely**, **entirely**, **quite** (esp. BrE), **totally**, **utterly**, **wholly** (esp. BrE) | **often** ◊ This approach is often ~ given the size of the area. | **economically**, **financially** (both esp. AmE) | **hopelessly** ◊ He was hopelessly ~ when it came to planning new projects.

imprecise adj.

VERBS **be**, **seem**
ADV. **extremely**, **fairly**, **very**, **etc.** | **notoriously** ◊ Intelligence tests are notoriously ~.
PREP. **about** ◊ She was rather ~ about the cost of the trip.

impress verb

ADV. **really** ◊ His work really ~ed me.
VERB + IMPRESS **be determined to**, **be keen to**, **hope to**, **want**

to | **attempt to, seek to, try to** | **be designed to** | **fail to** ◇ *The results failed to ~ us.*
PREP. **with** ◇ *She ~ed us with both the depth and range of her knowledge.*
PHRASES **an attempt to ~ sb, an effort to ~ sb** | **be easily ~ed** ◇ *I was young and easily ~ed.*

impressed *adj.*
VERBS **be, look, seem, sound**
ADV. **extremely, fairly, very, etc.** | **deeply, enormously, greatly, highly, hugely** (*esp. BrE*), **incredibly, mightily** (*esp. BrE*), **much, really, terribly, thoroughly** (*esp. AmE*), **totally** (*esp. AmE*), **tremendously** | **especially, particularly** | **less than, not overly** ◇ *I was not overly ~ by the proposals.* | **mildly, slightly** (*both esp. AmE*) | **enough, sufficiently** ◇ *My wife was ~ enough to commission a portrait from the artist.* | **equally** ◇ *Others seemed equally ~ with his work.* | **genuinely** | **immediately** | **favourably/favorably** | **duly, suitably** ◇ *He mentioned a few famous acquaintances, and we were suitably ~.* | **clearly, obviously**
PREP. **at** ◇ *She was ~ at how well Stephen could dance.* | **by** ◇ *The manager was clearly ~ by Jo's work.* | **with** ◇ *He was very ~ with her house.*

impression *noun*
1 idea/feeling/opinion about sth
ADJ. **distinct, firm** (*esp. BrE*), **strong** | **main, overriding, overwhelming** | **clear, vivid** | **fleeting, vague** | **accurate** | **distorted, erroneous, false, misleading, mistaken, wrong** | **good** ◇ *The model gives a good ~ of what the building will look like.* | **favourable/favorable** | **bad** | **negative, positive** | **opposite** | **early, first, immediate, initial** ◇ *First ~s can be misleading.* | **final** | **general, overall** | **widespread** ◇ *There is a widespread ~ that schooling needs to be improved.* | **visual** | **public** | **personal, subjective**
VERB + IMPRESSION **form, gain, get, have, receive** ◇ *I got the distinct ~ that you disliked her.* | **convey, create, give (sb)**, **leave sb with, provide (sb with)** ◇ *The book leaves you with a distorted ~ of politics.* | **maintain** ◇ *She was trying to maintain the ~ that she was in control.* | **confirm** | **heighten, reinforce, strengthen, support** | **avoid** ◇ *It was difficult to avoid the ~ that he was assisting them for selfish reasons.* | **correct** ◇ *I must correct a false ~ that I gave you just now.* | **change** ◇ *Her performance did little to change my ~ of her.* | **record** ◇ *She recorded her ~s of the city in her diary.* | **share** ◇ *He shared his ~s of a recent visit to Japan.*
IMPRESSION + VERB **count** ◇ *When it comes to finding a partner, first ~s do count.*
PREP. **under a/the ~** ◇ *I was under the ~ that you weren't coming until tomorrow.* | **~ about** ◇ *I had the wrong ~ about him.* | **~ as to** ◇ *mistaken ~s as to the strength of the market*

2 effect that an experience/person has on sb/sth
ADJ. **big, deep, great, huge, powerful, profound, strong, tremendous** | **superficial** | **abiding** (*BrE*), **indelible, lasting** | **excellent, favourable/favorable, good, great** | **bad, poor, unfavourable/unfavorable** | **false, misleading, wrong** | **right** ◇ *If you want to create the right ~, I suggest you wear a suit.* | **first, immediate** ◇ *The new player failed to make an immediate ~ on the team.*
VERB + IMPRESSION **create, leave, make**
PREP. **~ on, ~ upon** ◇ *The day's events left a lasting ~ on them.*

3 drawing
ADJ. **artist's**
VERB + IMPRESSION **issue** (*BrE*) ◇ *The police have issued an artist's ~ of the attacker.*

4 amusing copy of sb
ADJ. **good** | **funny**
VERB + IMPRESSION **do** ◇ *He does some very good ~s of movie stars.*

5 mark left on an object
VERB + IMPRESSION **bear** ◇ *The wax bore the ~ of a sailing ship.*

impressionable *adj.*
VERBS **be, seem**
ADV. **extremely, fairly, very, etc.** | **highly** ◇ *He is in a highly ~ state.*

impressive *adj.*
VERBS **be, look, seem, sound** | **become** | **remain** | **make sth** ◇ *The fact that he is so young makes his achievements even more ~.* | **find sth**
ADV. **extremely, fairly, very, etc.** | **enormously** (*esp. BrE*), **highly, hugely** (*esp. BrE*), **immensely** (*esp. BrE*), **incredibly, mightily** (*esp. BrE*), **most** (*esp. BrE*), **truly** ◇ *The new building looks most ~.* | **especially, particularly** | **far from, hardly, not overly** ◇ *He was far from ~ in his semi-final against Federer.* | **undeniably, undoubtedly** (*both esp. BrE*) | **suitably** (*esp. BrE*) ◇ *A large portico provides a suitably ~ entrance to the chapel.* | **equally, similarly** ◇ *The scenery to the north of the lake is equally ~.* | **consistently** | **technically, visually** ◇ *The movie is technically ~, but lacks real excitement.*

imprint *noun*
ADJ. **indelible, lasting, permanent** (*esp. AmE*)
VERB + IMPRINT **bear** ◇ *Their products bear the ~ of Japanese design.* | **leave, make** ◇ *Glaciation has left a permanent ~ on the landscape.* ◇ *The sinister atmosphere of the place left an indelible ~ on my memory.* (*figurative*)
PREP. **~ on, ~ upon**

imprison *verb*
ADV. **falsely, unjustly, wrongfully, wrongly** ◇ *We work on behalf of people who have been wrongly ~ed.* | **briefly** | **indefinitely** | **virtually** ◇ *Her fear virtually ~ed her in her home.*
PREP. **for** ◇ *He was ~ed for debt.* | **in** ◇ *He was ~ed in a dungeon.*

imprisonment *noun*
ADJ. **six months', ten years', etc.** | **life** | **indefinite** | **false, unlawful** (*esp. BrE*), **wrongful**
VERB + IMPRISONMENT **be liable to** (*BrE*), **face** ◇ *Anyone committing the offence is liable to ~.* ◇ *The coup leaders could face life ~.* | **receive** (*esp. BrE*), **suffer** ◇ *Those who were captured suffered ~.* | **be released from** | **sentence sb to**
IMPRISONMENT + VERB **be suspended for sth** (*AmE*) ◇ *a term of ~, suspended for 15 months*
PREP. **~ for** ◇ *~ for illegal possession of weapons*
PHRASES **~ without trial** | **a period of ~, a sentence of ~, a term of ~** | **punishable by ~** ◇ *a felony punishable by ~*

improbable *adj.*
VERBS **appear, be, look, seem, sound** | **become** | **make sth** ◇ *These new facts make the theory ~.*
ADV. **extremely, fairly, very, etc.** | **highly, wildly** ◇ *a wildly ~ idea* | **inherently** (*esp. BrE*) ◇ *There is nothing inherently ~ in the idea.*

improper *adj.*
VERBS **be, seem** | **consider sth, regard sth as, think sth** (*esp. BrE*) ◇ *places where it is considered ~ for men and women to kiss in public*
ADV. **highly, most** (*esp. BrE*) | **quite** (*esp. BrE*)

impropriety *noun*
ADJ. **financial, procedural** (*BrE, law*), **sexual** | **alleged**
VERB + IMPROPRIETY **commit** ◇ *It was alleged that financial improprieties had been committed.* | **accuse sb of** ◇ *a company accused of financial improprieties and fraud*
PHRASES **a suggestion of ~** (*esp. BrE*) ◇ *There is no suggestion of ~ by the president.*

improve verb

ADV. **considerably, dramatically, drastically, greatly, im-measurably, immensely, materially, radically, really, remarkably, significantly, substantially, tremendously, vastly** ◇ *The situation has ~d dramatically during the last few months.* ◇ *This legislation will vastly ~ the quality of life of New Zealanders.* | **markedly, noticeably** ◇ *My ability to read French has ~d markedly.* | **measurably** | **certainly, definitely** | **potentially** | **marginally, modestly, slightly, somewhat** | **ultimately** | **quickly, rapidly** | **gradually, slowly, steadily** | **consistently, constantly, continually, continuously** | **generally** ◇ *Working and living conditions have generally ~d.*
VERB + IMPROVE **continue to** ◇ *The weather should continue to ~ over the weekend.* | **strive to, try to** ◇ *They are trying to ~ the working conditions in their factories.* | **help to** | **be designed to**
PHRASES **aimed at improving sth** ◇ *measures aimed at improving government efficiency* | **an attempt to ~ sth, an effort to ~ sth** | **an incentive to ~ sth** ◇ *Workers need to be given an incentive to ~ their performance.* | **much ~d** ◇ *We now offer a much ~d service to our customers.* | **new and ~d** ◇ *the new and ~d version of the website*

improvement noun

ADJ. **big, considerable, enormous, great, huge, major, marked, massive, material, radical, remarkable, significant, substantial, tremendous, vast** ◇ *The players have shown a marked ~ in recent weeks.* ◇ *We expect to see a significant ~ in the near future.* | **marginal, minor, modest, slight, small** ◇ *The latest figures are a slight ~ over last year's results.* | **notable, noticeable, obvious, visible** | **actual, definite, distinct, genuine, real, tangible** | **measurable** | **dramatic, drastic, rapid, sharp** | **gradual, incremental, steady** | **constant, continual, continued, continuing, continuous, ongoing, progressive, sustained** | **long-term** | **short-term** | **temporary** | **further** | **all-round** (BrE), **general, overall** | **important, notable** | **much-needed, necessary** | **welcome** (esp. BrE) | **useful** (esp. BrE) | **positive** | **recent** | **immediate** | **desired** (esp. AmE), **expected** | **suggested** ◇ *The suggested ~s were not carried out.* | **possible, potential** | **moral** | **economic, educational, environmental, health, safety, social** | **efficiency, organizational** (esp. AmE), **performance, productivity, quality, service** (esp. BrE), **technical, technological** | **agricultural, land** | **ground** (= stadium) (BrE), **housing** (esp. BrE), **school** ◇ *The club will spend £300 000 on ground ~s.* | **infrastructure, rail** (BrE), **road, transport** (BrE), **transportation** (AmE) | **home**
VERB + IMPROVEMENT **be, constitute, reflect, represent** ◇ *The country's economic record since 1945 represents an ~ on the period between the world wars.* | **demonstrate, exhibit, indicate, show** ◇ *Exports have showed some ~.* | **maintain** ◇ *Will the team be able to maintain its ~ of last season?* | **need, require** | **carry out, effect, make** ◇ *He made a steady ~ and was released within 10 days of admission.* | **deliver, lead to, offer, produce, provide, result in, yield** ◇ *The drug produced an ~ in all but one case.* | **achieve, bring (about), secure** (esp. BrE) ◇ *steps taken to secure ~ in students' attendance* | **seek** | **call for, demand** | **recommend, suggest** | **encourage, promote** | **announce** (esp. BrE), **report** ◇ *Wholesalers reported an ~ in sales for the third quarter.* | **note, notice, observe, see, witness** ◇ *With this exercise plan you will notice an enormous ~ in your stamina.* | **experience** ◇ *The economy has experienced steady ~.* | **find** ◇ *No ~ was found after the tenth day of treatment.*
IMPROVEMENT + VERB **occur, take place** | **result from sth** | **include sth**
IMPROVEMENT + NOUN **initiative, plan, programme/program, project, scheme** (BrE), **strategy** ◇ *We have an ambitious ~ plan for the property.* | **efforts, work** (esp. BrE) ◇ *The ~ work to houses will create jobs.* | **rate**
PREP. **~ in** ◇ *The new factory brought a huge ~ in working conditions.* | **~ on, ~ over, ~ upon** ◇ *These results are a distinct ~ on last year's.* | **~ to** ◇ *Several ~s were made to the design during its production run.*
PHRASES **an area for ~, an area of ~** ◇ *The new assessment system could pinpoint areas for ~ within the company.* | **room for ~, scope for ~** ◇ *Their average grades have risen, but there is still room for ~.* | **signs of ~** ◇ *The economy is showing signs of ~.*

improvisation noun

ADJ. **free** | **spontaneous** ◇ *Most of their music was spontaneous ~.* | **musical** | **jazz** | **guitar, piano, etc.**

improvise verb

ADV. **freely** | **hastily** (esp. BrE), **quickly** (esp. AmE) ◇ *We hastily ~d a screen out of an old blanket.* ◇ *You can quickly ~ a shield to protect your arm.*
VERB + IMPROVISE **have to** ◇ *There isn't much equipment. We're going to have to ~.*

impulse noun

1 sudden strong wish
ADJ. **strong** | **irresistible** | **first, initial, original** ◇ *My first ~ was to run away.* | **sudden** | **human** | **basic** | **instinctual, natural** | **repressed** | **conflicting, contradictory, contrary** | **aggressive, murderous, violent** | **suicidal** | **destructive** | **creative** | **sexual**
VERB + IMPULSE **feel, have** ◇ *She felt a sudden ~ to look to her left.* | **be subject to** ◇ *We are all subject to aggressive ~s.* | **be driven by** | **check, control, deny, fight, resist, restrain, stifle, suppress** ◇ *He fought down an ~ to scream.* | **give in to, obey, yield to** ◇ *She gave in to an ~ and took the money.* | **act on, follow** ◇ *Acting on ~, he picked up the keys and slipped them into his pocket.*
IMPULSE + NOUN **buy, purchase** ◇ *The little black designer dress had been an ~ buy.* | **item** (esp. AmE) ◇ *Supermarkets sell candy as ~ items at the checkout counter.* | **buying** | **buyer** | **control**
PREP. **on (an) ~** ◇ *Some people will buy a pet on ~ without any idea of what is involved.* ◇ *On an ~, I went in and bought a box of chocolates.* | **~ towards/toward** ◇ *basic ~s towards/ toward things such as food and drink*

2 movement of energy
ADJ. **electrical, nerve, neural**
VERB + IMPULSE **generate** ◇ *A neuron generates an electrical ~.* | **send, transmit** ◇ *Nerve ~s are transmitted to the brain.* | **convert sth into, transform sth into** ◇ *Radio waves are converted into electrical ~s.*

3 sth that causes sb/sth to do sth
ADJ. **democratic, political, religious**
IMPULSE + VERB **lead (sb/sth) to sth, prompt sb/sth (to do sth)** ◇ *the ~ that prompted economic change*
PREP. **~ behind** ◇ *the ~ behind a concept* | **~ for** ◇ *the ~ for social reform* | **~ towards/toward** ◇ *the political ~s towards/toward joining a trade union*

inability noun

ADJ. **apparent, seeming** | **complete, total** | **chronic** ◇ *the government's chronic ~ to face facts* | **physical**
VERB + INABILITY **have** ◇ *She has an ~ to control her rage.* | **be frustrated by** ◇ *She felt increasingly frustrated by her ~ to demonstrate her ideas.* | **demonstrate, indicate, reflect, show** ◇ *Her outbursts reflected her ~ to cope with the loss of her brother.* | **explain** ◇ *His experiences as a child explain his ~ to sustain relationships.*

inaccessible adj.

VERBS **be, prove, seem** ◇ *The mouth of the river proved ~.* | **become** | **remain** | **make sth, render sth** ◇ *A high wall made the building ~.*
ADV. **completely, totally** | **almost, virtually** | **relatively** | **largely** | **otherwise**
PREP. **by** ◇ *areas ~ by road* | **to** ◇ *The hall is ~ to wheelchair users.*

inaccuracy *noun*

ADJ. **factual, historical** | **material** (*BrE*), **significant**
VERB + INACCURACY **contain** | **be full of** ◇ *Reference works on that country, when available, are full of inaccuracies.* | **find** | **point out** | **correct** ◇ *I am writing to correct factual inaccuracies contained in your article.*
PREP. **~ in** ◇ *inaccuracies in reporting*

inaccurate *adj.*

VERBS **be, prove** | **become**
ADV. **extremely, fairly, very, etc.** ◇ *These figures are somewhat ~.* | **grossly, highly, hopelessly** (*esp. BrE*), **wildly** ◇ *a wildly ~ account of events* | **completely, entirely, quite, totally, wholly** | **a little, slightly, etc.** | **simply** ◇ *The polls he cites are simply ~.* | **notoriously** ◇ *Maps of the region are notoriously ~.* | **factually, historically** ◇ *It was good drama, but historically ~.*

inactive *adj.*

VERBS **be** | **become** | **remain**
ADV. **completely, totally** ◇ *He had been totally ~ for two weeks.* | **fairly, relatively** | **physically, sexually** | **economically, politically** (*both esp. BrE*)

inactivity *noun*

ADJ. **relative** ◇ *Her most brilliant work was done during several months of relative ~.* | **physical** | **economic, political** (*both esp. BrE*) | **enforced** (*esp. BrE*), **forced** (*esp. AmE*) ◇ *It was good to be home again after the enforced/forced ~ of the hospital bed.*
PHRASES **a period of ~** ◇ *The job entailed long periods of ~.*

inadequacy *noun*

ADJ. **personal** | **sexual, social** | **fundamental** | **total** (*esp. BrE*) | **glaring, obvious** | **perceived** ◇ *Elliott was tormented by his own perceived inadequacies.*
VERB + INADEQUACY **demonstrate, expose, highlight, point out, point to, reveal, show** ◇ *She rightly points to the ~ of the argument.* ◇ *The test soon revealed several inadequacies in the equipment.* | **realize, recognize** ◇ *I now see the ~ of the explanation.* | **cover up, hide** (*both esp. BrE*) ◇ *They possibly falsified the results to cover up the inadequacies of their theory.* | **overcome** ◇ *Clear legislative reform is needed to overcome the inadequacies of the current situation.*
PREP. **~ in** ◇ *inadequacies in educational facilities*
PHRASES **a feeling of ~, a sense of ~**

inadequate *adj.*

1 not good enough

VERBS **appear, be, look, prove, seem** | **become** | **remain** | **consider sth, find sth, judge sth, regard sth as, think sth** (*esp. BrE*) ◇ *These precautions have been judged ~.*
ADV. **deeply, grossly, hopelessly, pitifully, seriously, woefully** ◇ *His salary was pitifully ~ for the needs of his growing family.* | **completely, entirely, quite** (*esp. BrE*), **totally, utterly, wholly** (*esp. BrE*) | **simply** | **increasingly** | **clearly, manifestly** (*esp. BrE*), **obviously** | **notoriously**
PREP. **at** ◇ *People, despite their intelligence, are curiously ~ at communicating with horses.* | **for** ◇ *This computer is clearly ~ for my needs.*

2 not able to deal with a situation

VERBS **be, feel, seem** ◇ *I felt dreadfully ~.*
ADV. **extremely, fairly, very, etc.** ◇ *I suddenly felt extremely ~ as I compared myself to him.* | **deeply, hopelessly** | **totally, wholly** (*esp. BrE*) | **generally** | **sexually**
PREP. **to** ◇ *The helicopters are ~ to the demands of modern combat.*

inappropriate *adj.*

VERBS **be, seem** | **become** | **make sth** ◇ *The size of the machines makes them ~ for domestic use.* | **consider sth, feel sth, judge sth, regard sth as, see sth as, think sth** ◇ *It was felt ~ by some that such a serious occasion should include dancing.*
ADV. **extremely, fairly, very, etc.** | **highly, particularly,**

singularly (*esp. BrE*), **wildly** ◇ *This treatment was highly ~ in her case.* | **completely, entirely, quite** (*esp. BrE*), **totally, utterly** (*esp. BrE*), **wholly** (*esp. BrE*) | **increasingly** | **clearly** | **culturally, sexually, socially**
PREP. **for** ◇ *Your bright red coat would be quite ~ for a funeral.* | **to** ◇ *The existing library is totally ~ to our needs.*

inaudible *adj.*

VERBS **be** | **become**
ADV. **totally** | **almost, nearly, virtually** ◇ *His voice faded until it was almost ~.*
PREP. **to** ◇ *The sound is ~ to the human ear.*

inaugurate *verb*

ADV. **formally** (*esp. BrE*), **officially** (*esp. AmE*) ◇ *The assembly was formally ~d on in December.*

inauguration *noun*

ADJ. **formal, official** | **presidential**
VERB + INAUGURATION **attend, go to** | **mark** ◇ *a ceremony to mark the ~ of the president's third term in office*
INAUGURATION + VERB **take place**
INAUGURATION + NOUN **ceremony** ◇ *The ~ ceremony will be held on Saturday.* | **day** | **speech** | **party**

incapable *adj.*

VERBS **appear, be, feel, prove, seem** | **become** | **make sb, render sb** ◇ *The wine had made him ~ of thinking clearly.* | **deem sb**
ADV. **absolutely, completely, quite, simply, totally, utterly** | **almost** | **largely** | **clearly** | **inherently** | **constitutionally, temperamentally** ◇ *She was constitutionally ~ of bad temper.* | **physically** ◇ *He was apparently physically ~ of lowering his voice.* | **mentally** (*esp. BrE*) ◇ *This type of arrangement remains valid even if you become mentally ~.*
PREP. **of** ◇ *Computers are ~ of creative thought.*

incapacitate *verb* **be incapacitated**

ADV. **severely** | **totally** ◇ *By this time my father was totally ~d by his illness.* | **temporarily** | **mentally, physically**

incarnation *noun*

ADJ. **current, latest, modern, new, present, recent** (*figurative*) ◇ *In its new ~, the car has a more rounded body shape.* | **last** | **next** | **earlier, previous** | **original** | **future**
PREP. **~ as** ◇ *her previous ~ as a marketing executive*

incense *noun*

VERB + INCENSE **burn** | **light** ◇ *He lit some ~ and a candle.*
INCENSE + VERB **burn** ◇ *Incense burned in a corner of the room.*
INCENSE + NOUN **stick** | **burner**
PHRASES **a scent of ~, a smell of ~**

incentive *noun*

ADJ. **big, generous, good, great, huge, massive** (*esp. BrE*) | **powerful, strong** | **adequate, sufficient** | **main, major** | **added, additional, extra, more** | **less** | **little** ◇ *There was little ~ to conduct research.* | **real** | **clear** ◇ *US companies faced a clear ~ to downsize.* | **direct** ◇ *direct financial ~s to have smaller families* | **important** | **positive** | **special** | **attractive** | **perverse** | **long-term** | **political, commercial, economic, financial, fiscal, monetary** | **cash** | **material** | **price, tax** | **sales** | **investment** | **performance, work** | **employee** ◇ *employee ~s such as bonuses and commission* | **federal, government**
VERB + INCENTIVE **act as, be** ◇ *It was thought that this would act as an ~ for couples to adopt older children.* | **have** ◇ *She had the added ~ of being within reach of the world record.* | **need** | **give (sb/sth), offer (sb/sth), provide (sb/sth with)** | **create** ◇ *The government has created tax ~s to encourage investment.* | **receive** ◇ *companies that receive government*

~s | **increase** | **reduce** | **undermine** ◊ *High taxation rates have undermined work ~s.* | **eliminate, remove, take away**
INCENTIVE + NOUN **plan, programme/program, scheme** (*BrE*), **structure, system** ◊ *an ~ system based on supervisors' evaluations* | **policy** | **award, bonus, fee, package, pay, payment**
PREP. **~ to** ◊ *an ~ to investment*
PHRASES **have every ~** ◊ *Companies have every ~ to put up prices.* | **a lack of ~** ◊ *There is a lack of ~ to undertake new investment.*

incest *noun*

ADJ. **brother-sister, father-daughter, etc.** | **adult** | **consensual**
VERB + INCEST **commit** | **forbid, prohibit** ◊ *taboos forbidding ~*
INCEST + NOUN **survivor, victim** | **taboo**
PREP. **~ between** ◊ *between brother and sister*
→ Note at CRIME (for more verbs)

inch *noun* → Note at MEASURE

incidence *noun*

ADJ. **great, high** ◊ *There is a greater ~ of cancer in the families of radiation workers.* | **peak** | **low** | **growing, increased, increasing, rising** | **decreased, reduced** | **actual** | **overall** | **annual** | **recorded** (*esp. BrE*), **reported** ◊ *the highest reported ~ of air pollution*
VERB + INCIDENCE **have, show** ◊ *The country had the lowest ~ of AIDS cases proportional to its population.* ◊ *The medical histories of our patients show a high ~ of past diseases.* | **increase** | **decrease, reduce** | **find** ◊ *They found an increased ~ of childhood leukaemia in some areas.* | **measure** | **compare** ◊ *We compared the ~ of coronary heart disease and total mortality.* | **analyse/analyze, assess, determine, examine, investigate** | **explain** ◊ *The lack of vitamins may explain the higher ~ of heart disease.*
INCIDENCE + VERB **increase** | **decrease, fall**
INCIDENCE + NOUN **rate** ◊ *an ~ rate of 4 or 5 per 10 000 of the population*
PREP. **~ among** ◊ *the ~ of cancer among people* | **~ in** ◊ *The study noted an increased ~ of heart disease in women.*
PHRASES **a decrease in the ~ of sth, an increase in the ~ of sth, a variation in the ~ of sth**

incident *noun*

ADJ. **major, serious** | **little, minor, small, trivial** (*esp. BrE*) | **further** ◊ *After nearly falling twice, she managed to make it to the top of the cliff without further ~.* | **entire, whole** ◊ *He came to regret the whole ~.* | **actual, real, real-life** ◊ *The story is based on an actual ~.* | **alleged** | **recorded** (*esp. BrE*), **reported** | **latest, recent** | **past** | **bad, horrible, horrific, nasty, terrible, ugly, unsavoury** (*BrE*) ◊ *some of the worst ~s of urban violence* | **traumatic** | **violent** | **deadly, fatal, tragic** | **dramatic** | **controversial** (*esp. BrE*) | **famous, high-profile** | **infamous** | **regrettable** (*esp. BrE*) | **unfortunate** | **embarrassing** | **bizarre, curious, mysterious, strange, unusual** | **amusing** | **separate, unrelated** ◊ *The police said that two men had been arrested in unrelated ~s.* | **isolated** ◊ *It is feared that the attack may not have been an isolated ~.* | **domestic** | **racial** | **border** ◊ *Talks were called off following a border ~.* | **diplomatic, international** ◊ *An error in the translation nearly caused a diplomatic ~.* | **security** ◊ *No major security ~s happened at the Olympic Games that year.* | **terrorist** | **nuclear** | **bombing, shooting, stabbing** | **pollution** (*BrE*) | **friendly-fire** | **alcohol-related** | **off-the-ball** (*BrE, sports*) ◊ *She received a serious jaw injury in an off-the-ball ~.*
VERB + INCIDENT **cause, create, provoke** | **be responsible for** ◊ *The group is believed to have been responsible for several terrorist ~s.* | **be involved in** ◊ *The tennis star became involved in an ~ with the umpire.* | **experience** ◊ *He was asked whether he had ever experienced any ~s of discrimination.* | **deal with** (*esp. BrE*), **handle** ◊ *The ~ was extremely*

well handled. | **avoid, prevent** | **regret** | **see, witness** | **recall, remember** ◊ *He recalled a similar ~ 14 months earlier.* | **forget** | **describe, recount, relate** ◊ *She described the ~ as outrageous.* ◊ *They all laughed as he recounted the amusing ~.* | **discuss, talk about** | **cite** | **explain** | **downplay** (*esp. AmE*), **play down** (*esp. BrE*) ◊ *the government's desire to play down the ~* | **report** ◊ *The pedestrian who had nearly been run over reported the ~ to the police.* | **investigate** | **be hurt in, be injured in, be killed in** | **survive** | **pass off without** (*BrE*), **pass without, proceed without** (*esp. AmE*) ◊ *The demonstration passed without ~.*
INCIDENT + VERB **happen, occur, take place** | **arise, arise from sth, arise out of sth** ◊ *~s arising out of an industrial dispute* | **involve sb/sth** ◊ *a minor ~ involving a bus* | **cause sth, lead to sth, prompt sth, result in sth, spark sth** ◊ *The ~ sparked a riot which lasted three days.* | **demonstrate sth, illustrate sth, prove sth, show sth** ◊ *Saturday's ~ illustrates the fragility of the peace in the country.*
INCIDENT + NOUN **room** (*BrE*) ◊ *An ~ room was set up at a police station near the site of the crash.*
PREP. **~ with** (*often humorous*) ◊ *His back still hurts from an ~ with a vacuum cleaner.* | **following an/the ~** ◊ *He was asked to leave the club following an ~ with a knife.* | **in an/the ~** ◊ *Three soldiers were wounded in the ~.* | **over an/the ~** ◊ *She was never disciplined over the ~.* | **without ~** ◊ *The patrol had covered 200 miles without ~.*

incision *noun*

ADJ. **deep** | **large** | **small, tiny** | **vertical** | **surgical** | **abdominal, etc.**
VERB + INCISION **make** ◊ *The surgeon made a small ~ in the patient's cornea.*

inclination *noun*

ADJ. **strong** | **slight** ◊ *I did not feel the slightest ~ to hurry.* | **little** ◊ *He has shown little ~ to resolve the conflict.* | **natural, own, personal** ◊ *My own ~ is to be more direct in approach.* | **first** ◊ *Your first ~ may be to panic.* | **homosexual, sexual** | **artistic, political, religious**
VERB + INCLINATION **feel, have** | **show** | **lack** | **resist** ◊ *You should resist any ~ to meddle.* | **follow** ◊ *In matters of dress she followed her personal ~s rather than fashion.*
PREP. **by ~** ◊ *He is a teacher by occupation but a philosopher by ~.* | **~ for** ◊ *an ~ for war* | **~ towards/toward** ◊ *She has no ~ towards/toward mysticism.*
PHRASES **neither the time nor the ~, the time or the ~** ◊ *I have neither the time nor the ~ to play stupid games!*

incline *verb*

1 bend forward
ADV. **slightly** ◊ *Luke ~d his head slightly in acknowledgement.*
2 lean/slope
ADV. **gently, steeply**
PREP. **towards/toward** ◊ *The land ~d gently towards/toward the shore.*

inclined *adj.*

1 wanting to do sth
VERBS **be, feel, seem** ◊ *I only write when I feel ~ to.* ◊ *There's time for a swim if you feel so ~.*
ADV. **strongly, very** | **rather** ◊ *I'm rather ~ to wait a few days before deciding.* | **half** ◊ *I'm half ~ to agree with you.* | **favourably/favorably**
PREP. **towards/toward** ◊ *Advertising aims to make people feel favourably ~ towards products.* (*BrE*) ◊ *Advertising aims to make people feel favorably ~ toward products.* (*AmE*)
2 tending/likely to do sth
VERBS **appear, be, seem** | **become, grow**
ADV. **strongly, very** | **increasingly** | **rather, slightly** ◊ *She's rather ~ to become impatient.* | **less, little** (*esp. BrE*) ◊ *They are less ~ to ask questions.* | **naturally** | **criminally, mystically, romantically** ◊ *The club was a notorious hang-out for the criminally ~.*
PREP. **to** (*formal*) ◊ *people who are naturally ~ to melancholy*

3 having a natural ability for sth
VERBS **appear, be, seem**
ADV. **academically, artistically, mathematically, musically, etc.** ◇ *children who are academically ~*

inclusion *noun*

ADJ. **possible** ◇ *We welcome readers' letters for possible ~ on this page.* | **social** ◇ *The Internet promotes the social ~ of groups such as the elderly and disabled.* ◇ *the government's social ~ policy*
VERB + INCLUSION **be worthy of, deserve, justify, merit, warrant** ◇ *Some words are too infrequent to be worthy of ~ in the dictionary.* | **be eligible for, be suitable for, qualify for** ◇ *All work by current students is eligible for ~ in the journal.* | **consider sth for** | **accept** ◇ *The rebels refused to accept the ~ of representatives of the existing regime in the negotiations.* | **preclude, prevent, prohibit** ◇ *Legal issues precluded the interview's ~ on the DVD.* ◇ *They tried to prevent the ~ of any offensive material.*
PREP. **for** ◇ *an article for ~ in the newsletter*
PHRASES **criteria for ~** ◇ *There are strict criteria for ~ in the competition.*

inclusive *adj.*

1 total cost
VERBS **be**
ADV. **fully** ◇ *a fully ~ price*
PREP. **of** ◇ *The charge is ~ of food.*

2 including a wide range of people, ideas, etc.
VERBS **be** | **become** ◇ *The system has become more ~.* | **make sth**
ADV. **genuinely, truly** ◇ *We need to reach out as much as possible to make this a truly ~ organization.* | **fully, totally** | **broadly** | **culturally, racially, socially** ◇ *The government wants communities which are socially ~.*

income *noun*

ADJ. **high, large** | **six-figure** *(esp. AmE)* ◇ *The business provided him with a six-figure ~.* | **sufficient** | **average, median** ◇ *Average ~s are rising more slowly.* | **low, meagre/meager, modest, small** | **rising** | **additional, extra** ◇ *They hope that the lottery will provide additional ~ for charities.* | **total** | **future** | **guaranteed, permanent, secure** | **regular, steady** | **fixed** ◇ *She was living on a small, fixed ~ and having trouble paying her bills.* | **annual, monthly, weekly, yearly** | **national** | **per capita** ◇ *the average per capita ~* | **personal, private** *(esp. BrE)* ◇ *He has a large private ~ on top of what he earns as a teacher.* | **combined, family, household, joint** ◇ *a young couple with a combined ~ of $69 000* | **gross, pre-tax** | **taxable** | **after-tax, net, post-tax** | **discretionary** *(esp. AmE)*, **disposable** | **real** | **earned** | **unearned** | **ordinary** *(AmE)* ◇ *Tax rates are 40% on ordinary ~.* | **reported** *(esp. AmE)* ◇ *Profit figures are based on reported ~.* | **operating** ◇ *Operating ~ rose 14% to £36.5 million.* | **cash, money** *(AmE)* ◇ *the money ~s of individuals* | **retirement** | **capital, dividend, fee, foreign, investment, rental** ◇ *He planned to buy two more properties so he could live off the rental ~.* | **lost** ◇ *The industry claims the regulations have cost them $184 million in lost ~.*
VERB + INCOME **have** | **receive** ◇ *She received an ~ for life as a result of her father's will.* | **earn, generate, provide (sb with)** ◇ *Financial assets have the advantage of earning ~.* ◇ *The return on your investment can provide you with regular ~.* | **guarantee** ◇ *Social security guarantees an ~ to retired and disabled workers.* | **derive from** ◇ *The area could derive lucrative tourist ~ from the park.* | **boost, double, increase, maximize, supplement** ◇ *ways of boosting your retirement ~* ◇ *She supplements her ~ by working nights.* | **reduce** | **exceed** ◇ *For 2001, expenditure exceeded ~ by £10 000.* | **depend on** | **live on** ◇ *A large number of families in the area are living on below-average ~s.* | **redistribute** ◇ *They aim to redistribute ~ from the rich to the poor.* | **treat sth as** ◇ *Interest is treated as ~ for tax purposes.*

INCOME + VERB **arise (from sth)** *(esp. BrE)*, **come from sth, derive from sth** ◇ *If a person's ~ arises in the UK, it is subject to UK income tax.* ◇ *A lot of our ~ comes from bank interest.* | **grow, increase, rise** | **decline, drop, fall** | **stagnate** | **exceed sth**
INCOME + NOUN **bracket, group, level** ◇ *Elderly people often belong to a low ~ group.* | **earner** ◇ *people in the lowest 25% of ~ earners* | **distribution, redistribution** | **disparity, gap, inequality** ◇ *The ~ gap between rich and poor grew.* | **stream** ◇ *Customer subscriptions provide a reliable ~ stream.* | **growth** ◇ *Lower ~ growth reduces demand.* | **~s policy** *(BrE)* ◇ *There are internal disputes over the party's ~s policy.* | **support** *(esp. BrE)* ◇ *A single mother of three, she relies on ~ support.* | **statement** ◇ *a company's ~ statement* | **tax**
PREP. **on an ~** ◇ *Many families on a low ~ are dependent on state support.* | **~ from** ◇ *~ from tourism*
PHRASES **the distribution of ~, the redistribution of ~** | **a drop in ~** | **~ and expenditure** ◇ *Every company must keep control of its ~ and expenditure.* | **~ per capita, ~ per head** ◇ *Real ~ per head of population was at a low point five years ago.* | **a source of ~**
→ Note at PER CENT (for more verbs)
→ Special page at BUSINESS

incompatibility *noun*

ADJ. **fundamental** | **inherent** | **apparent** ◇ *We can explain the apparent ~ of these results.*
VERB + INCOMPATIBILITY **demonstrate** ◇ *The disastrous merger demonstrated the ~ of the two companies.*
PREP. **~ between** ◇ *Incompatibility between systems has been a major problem for computer users.* | **~ with** ◇ *Critics of the new machine point to its ~ with other products on the market.*

incompatible *adj.*

VERBS **appear, be, prove, seem** | **become** | **consider sth, see sth as**
ADV. **completely, entirely, totally, utterly, wholly** | **increasingly** | **by no means, in no way** | **not entirely** *(esp. BrE)*, **not necessarily** ◇ *Love and hate are not necessarily ~.* | **largely** | **somewhat** | **apparently, seemingly** | **potentially** | **simply** | **fundamentally, inherently** | **clearly** | **logically** | **mutually** ◇ *The two systems are mutually ~.*
PREP. **with** ◇ *This conduct is completely ~ with his role as a teacher.*

incompetence *noun*

ADJ. **gross, rank** | **sheer, utter** | **incredible, unbelievable** | **alleged** | **administrative, bureaucratic, government, managerial, police** | **economic, professional, technical**
VERB + INCOMPETENCE **demonstrate** | **tolerate** ◇ *I will not tolerate your ~ any longer!* | **accuse sb/sth of**
PREP. **~ at, ~ in** ◇ *~ in writing* | **~ on the part of** ◇ *Several officers had alleged ~ on the part of the general.*

incompetent *adj.*

VERBS **appear, be** | **consider sb/sth, deem sb/sth** *(formal)* ◇ *I know my boss considers me ~.*
ADV. **criminally, grossly** ◇ *a grossly ~ piece of reporting* | **hopelessly** | **completely, totally, utterly** | **socially, technically** | **mentally** | **legally** ◇ *the medical treatment of legally ~ patients (= those who are not able to give legal consent)*
PREP. **at** ◇ *He is utterly ~ at his job.*

incomplete *adj.*

VERBS **be** | **remain** ◇ *Her collection remained ~.* | **leave sth** ◇ *The building was left ~.*
ADV. **seriously, very, woefully** ◇ *Any view of Shostakovich is seriously ~ without knowledge of these recordings.* | **somewhat** | **inevitably, necessarily** ◇ *We begin with a brief and necessarily ~ review of UK statistics.*

incomprehensible *adj.*

VERBS **be, seem** | **remain** | **find sth** ◇ *She found his accent virtually ~.*
ADV. **completely, totally, utterly** | **almost, nearly, virtually** | **largely** | **mutually** ◇ *The language has widely differing and often mutually ~ regional dialects.*
PREP. **to** ◇ *Latin verse remained completely ~ to me.*

inconceivable *adj.*

VERBS **appear, be, seem** | **become** | **find sth** ◇ *She found the idea quite ~.*
ADV. **totally, utterly** | **almost, practically, virtually**
PREP. **to** ◇ *The thought of leaving her family was ~ to her.*

inconclusive *adj.*

VERBS **be, prove** | **remain**
ADV. **largely** ◇ *The results have been largely ~.* | **rather, somewhat** ◇ *The volume ends on a somewhat ~ note.* | **ultimately**

incongruous *adj.*

VERBS **be, look, seem** | **find sth**
ADV. **completely, totally, utterly** (*esp. BrE*) | **rather, somewhat** ◇ *I found the scene somewhat ~.* | **a little, slightly, etc.** | **seemingly** ◇ *a collage of seemingly ~ images*

inconsistency *noun*

ADJ. **serious** | **glaring** | **apparent** | **internal** ◇ *Researchers have found that internal inconsistencies in hospital case notes are common.* | **factual, logical, statistical**
VERB + INCONSISTENCY **contain** | **lead to, result in** ◇ *The lack of clear rules resulted in ~ in the awarding of prizes.* | **detect, find, notice, see, spot** ◇ *The program has found an ~ in the database files.* ◇ *She was quick to spot the inconsistencies between his two reports.* | **highlight, point out, reveal** ◇ *Commentators have pointed out the inconsistencies in the government's financial policy.* | **correct, reconcile, remove, resolve** ◇ *The amendment will remove the ~ between the two laws.*
INCONSISTENCY + VERB **arise, emerge**
PREP. **~ in** ◇ *inconsistencies in the evidence*

inconsistent *adj.*

VERBS **appear, be, seem**
ADV. **highly, very, wildly** (*esp. AmE*) | **maddeningly** (*esp. AmE*) ◇ *The team's offense has been maddeningly ~.* | **totally, wholly** (*esp. BrE*) | **not necessarily** | **somewhat** | **apparently** | **clearly** | **fundamentally** | **internally, logically** ◇ *Her argument is internally ~.* | **mutually** ◇ *The two accounts are mutually ~.*
PREP. **in** ◇ *The company is ~ in the way it disciplines staff.* | **with** ◇ *His statement was ~ with other accounts of the events.*

incontinence *noun*

ADJ. **faecal/fecal, urinary** (*both medical*) | **stress, urge** (*both medical*)
VERB + INCONTINENCE **suffer from** | **treat**
INCONTINENCE + NOUN **products** | **pad**

inconvenience *noun*

ADJ. **considerable, great, major, serious** | **mere, mild, minor, slight** ◇ *This isn't a mere ~; it's dangerous.* | **short-term, temporary** | **public** ◇ *The rail strike is likely to cause considerable public ~.*
VERB + INCONVENIENCE **endure, have, suffer** | **avoid** ◇ *I chose a different route to avoid the ~ of going through the town.* | **outweigh** ◇ *The benefits of doing this usually outweigh the ~.* | **cause (sb), put sb to** ◇ *I don't want to put you to any ~.* | **minimize, save (sb)** ◇ *You could have picked me up at the airport and saved me the ~ of having to take the bus!* | **apologize for, regret** ◇ *This store is closed today for staff training. We regret any ~ caused.*

inconvenience *verb*

ADV. **greatly, seriously** ◇ *The general public has been greatly ~d by this strike.*

inconvenient *adj.*

VERBS **be, prove** | **become** | **find sth**
ADV. **extremely, fairly, very, etc.** | **highly, most** (*esp. BrE*), **terribly** ◇ *She called at a most ~ time.* | **a little, slightly, etc.** | **politically** ◇ *Further environmental legislation could be politically ~ for the government.*
PREP. **for** ◇ *Would this afternoon be ~ for you?* | **to** ◇ *This is a time of the evening that is ~ to many viewers.*

incorporate *verb*

ADV. **fully** | **explicitly, expressly** (*BrE*) ◇ *These conditions must be expressly ~d into the contract of employment.* | **formally** ◇ *The territory was formally ~d into the Russian Empire in 1876.* | **gradually, quickly** | **eventually, finally** | **easily, readily** ◇ *These new features can easily be ~d.* | **seamlessly** ◇ *The computer components are ~d seamlessly.* | **effectively** | **typically** (*esp. AmE*) ◇ *The life cycle typically ~s the following stages…* | **successfully** | **directly** | **forcibly** ◇ *the countries which Stalin forcibly ~d into the Soviet empire*
PREP. **as** ◇ *In 1940 the area was ~d as part of the city of London.* | **in** ◇ *The data is now ~d in the total figures.* | **into** ◇ *We can ~ this information into our report.* | **within** ◇ *Results are ~d within personalized medical records.*

incorrect *adj.*

VERBS **be, prove** | **consider sth**
ADV. **absolutely** (*esp. AmE*), **completely, entirely** (*esp. AmE*), **quite** (*esp. BrE*), **totally** | **wildly** (*esp. AmE*) | **clearly, obviously, patently** | **simply** ◇ *That statement is simply ~.* | **factually, grammatically, politically, technically, etc.** ◇ *a factually ~ statement*

increase *noun*

ADJ. **big, considerable, dramatic, drastic, enormous, exponential, huge, large, major, marked, massive, significant, substantial, vast** | **moderate, modest, slight, small** | **apparent** | **rapid, sharp, steep, sudden** | **gradual, incremental, progressive, steady** | **fivefold, tenfold, etc.** | **10%, etc.** | **double-digit** (*esp. AmE*) ◇ *Sales of beef have experienced double-digit ~s.* | **concomitant** (*formal*), **corresponding, proportional, resulting** ◇ *Their reputation has improved, bringing a corresponding ~ in revenues.* | **average, mean** ◇ *The average ~ in value last year was 4.3%.* | **net, overall, total** | **across-the-board** ◇ *The pay rise represented an across-the-board ~ of between 9% for the highest paid and 32% for the lowest paid worker.* | **annual, monthly, etc.** | **projected, proposed** ◇ *Retirement planning often starts with projected cost-of-living ~s.* | **pay, salary, wage** | **budget, dividend, fare, price, rent, spending, tax, tuition** (*AmE*) | **population, productivity, temperature**
VERB + INCREASE **demonstrate, experience, see, show** ◇ *Many parts of the country have experienced an ~ in unemployment.* ◇ *This year saw an ~ in the number of job applicants.* ◇ *Profits show a steady ~.* | **enjoy** ◇ *The country is enjoying the biggest ~ in business confidence for years.* | **achieve** ◇ *We achieved a small ~ in profits of £3 257.* | **bring, bring about, cause, lead to, produce, result in** ◇ *Intensive farming has brought about an ~ in outbreaks of food poisoning.* ◇ *The war resulted in a massive ~ in government spending.* | **observe** ◇ *You would expect to observe an ~ in births during peacetime.* | **predict** ◇ *Some companies are predicting price ~s of 30% or more.* | **propose, suggest** ◇ *He proposed a large tax ~.* | **indicate, reflect, represent** ◇ *Improved profitability may indicate an ~ in competitiveness.* | **be accompanied by, involve, mean** ◇ *The measures to improve the health service will involve an ~ in government spending.* | **announce, post, report** ◇ *The company reported a 9.5% ~ in third quarter losses.*
INCREASE + VERB **occur**

PREP. **on the** ~ ◇ *Burglaries in the area are on the* ~. | **~ in** ◇ *There has been an* ~ *in demand for two-bedroom houses.* | **~ on**, **~ over** ◇ *The figures show a sharp* ~ *on last year's turnover.* | **~ to** ◇ *a dividend* ~ *to 11.4 pence*
PHRASES **a rate of ~**

increase *verb*

ADV. **considerably, dramatically, drastically, enormously, exponentially, greatly, markedly, significantly, substantially, tremendously, vastly** | **slightly** | **gradually, progressively** ◇ *Progressively* ~ *the intensity of the exercise over three weeks.* | **rapidly, sharply, steeply** | **steadily** | **slowly** | **twofold, threefold, etc.** ◇ *Sales* ~d *almost fourfold in this period.*
VERB + INCREASE **be expected to, be likely to** ◇ *Demand is expected to* ~ *over the next decade.*
PREP. **by** ◇ *The budget has* ~d *by more than a third in the last year.* | **from** | **in** ◇ *to* ~ *in amount/number/price/size* | **to** ◇ *Last month the reward was* ~d *from $20 000 to $40 000.* | **with** ◇ *Disability* ~s *with age.*

incredible *adj.*

VERBS **be, seem, sound** | **find sth** ◇ *I find this quite* ~!
ADV. **really, truly** | **absolutely, quite, totally, utterly** ◇ *Most people find this claim utterly* ~. | **just, simply** | **pretty** ◇ *You're pretty* ~, *Barbara.* | **almost** (*esp. BrE*)
PREP. **to** ◇ *It seems* ~ *to me that we didn't think of this before.*

indebted *adj.*

1 feeling grateful to sb
VERBS **be, feel** | **remain**
ADV. **deeply, greatly, much, profoundly** | **eternally, forever** ◇ *Thank you—I am forever* ~ *to you.*
PREP. **to** ◇ *I am deeply* ~ *to all the doctors and nurses who treated me.*

2 owing money to sb
VERBS **be** | **remain**
ADV. **heavily, highly, severely** ◇ *The company is heavily* ~. | **highly** ~ *countries* | **financially** ◇ *I did not want to be financially* ~ *to him.*
PREP. **to** ◇ ~ *to the bank*

indecency *noun*

ADJ. **gross** | **public** | **broadcast** (*AmE*) ◇ *legislation to multiply broadcast* ~ *fines*
PHRASES **an act of ~**
→ Note at CRIME (for verbs)

indecent *adj.*

VERBS **be, seem** | **consider sth, regard sth as** (*BrE*), **think sth** (*esp. BrE*) ◇ *photographs that are considered* ~
ADV. **grossly, positively** ◇ *conduct which is grossly* ~ ◇ *That skirt of hers is positively* ~. | **almost** ◇ *She started a new relationship with almost* ~ *haste.*

indefensible *adj.*

VERBS **be** | **find sth** ◇ *I find such actions* ~.
ADV. **totally** | **ethically, morally, politically, etc.** ◇ *It would be morally* ~ *for her to desert her father now.*

independence *noun*

ADJ. **great** | **fierce** ◇ *She had a fierce* ~ *of spirit.* | **complete, full, total** | **relative** ◇ *The council's relative* ~ *of the government means it can negotiate its own agreements.* | **genuine, real, true** | **new-found** ◇ *I didn't appreciate my new-found* ~, *but instead felt lonely.* | **growing** | **local, national** | **economic, editorial, financial, intellectual, journalistic, judicial, operational** (*esp. BrE*), **personal, political, professional** ◇ *the operational* ~ *of the Bank of England*
... OF INDEPENDENCE **degree, measure**
VERB + INDEPENDENCE **have** ◇ *Young people have more* ~ *these days.* | **lack** | **enjoy, value** ◇ *I value my* ~ *too much to get married.* | **display, show** ◇ *She displayed* ~ *in choosing a career different from that of her parents.* | **assert** ◇ *Edward*

III *tried to assert his* ~ *of the regime at court.* | **achieve, attain, gain, win** ◇ *Mexico achieved* ~ *from Spain in 1821.* | **bring (about)** ◇ *the need to bring* ~ *to the country* ◇ *a colonial crisis which brought about* ~ | **declare, proclaim** | **celebrate** ◇ *a holiday celebrating the* ~ *of Nigeria from colonial rule* | **ensure, maintain, preserve, retain** ◇ *The army is committed to ensuring the* ~ *of the country.* | **compromise** ◇ *Conflicts of interest might compromise the auditor's* ~. | **give up, lose** ◇ *She doesn't want to lose her hard-won* ~. | **regain, restore** | **encourage, foster, promote** ◇ *Parents should encourage* ~ *in their children.* | **undermine** ◇ *Economic aid tends to undermine the national* ~ *of Third-World countries.* | **seek** | **call for, demand** | **vote for** | **give sb/sth, grant sb/sth** | **recognize** ◇ *They have agreed to recognize the breakaway republic's* ~.
INDEPENDENCE + VERB **come** ◇ *Independence came to the British colonial territories in Africa in the late fifties and early sixties.*
INDEPENDENCE + NOUN **day** | **celebrations** | **movement** | **struggle**
PREP. **at** ~ ◇ *Namibia became a full member of the UN at* ~. | **~ from** ◇ ~ *from Spain* | **~ of** ◇ *the church's* ~ *of the state* ◇ ~ *of mind*
PHRASES **a call for ~** ◇ *his party's call for Scottish* ~ | **a declaration of ~** | **a lack of ~** | **a sense of ~** ◇ *Doing work experience gave me a sense of* ~. | **the struggle for ~** | **the time of ~** ◇ *The drama is set in India at the time of* ~. | **a war for ~, a war of ~** ◇ *the American War of Independence*

independent *adj.*

1 not needing other people
VERBS **be, feel, seem** | **become** | **remain** | **make sb** ◇ *Her travels in Asia have made her a lot more* ~.
ADV. **fiercely, very** ◇ *Many disabled people are fiercely* ~. | **completely** | **fairly, pretty, quite** | **economically, financially**
PREP. **of** ◇ *By the age of eighteen he was completely* ~ *of his parents.*

2 not influenced or controlled by anyone else
VERBS **be** | **become** | **remain, stay** ◇ *His company is a target for takeovers, but plans to stay* ~. | **make sth** | **declare sth** ◇ *In 1961 the country was declared* ~.
ADV. **completely, entirely, fully, genuinely, quite** (*esp. BrE*), **totally, truly, wholly** | **almost, fairly, largely, relatively, virtually** ◇ *Many local clans remain relatively* ~. | **increasingly** | **essentially** ◇ *This figure is essentially* ~ *of population size.* | **nominally, supposedly** | **newly** ◇ *newly* ~ *countries* | **politically** | **logically, statistically** ◇ *His system rests upon two logically* ~ *arguments.* | **mutually** ◇ *They are two separate, mutually* ~ *entities.*
PREP. **from** ◇ *The country became fully* ~ *from France in 1960.* | **of** ◇ *an organization that is* ~ *of the government*

indestructible *adj.*

VERBS **be, prove, seem**
ADV. **almost, nearly, practically, virtually** ◇ *Their shells are so hard they are virtually* ~. | **seemingly**

index *noun*

1 list of names/topics
ADJ. **complete, comprehensive** | **detailed** | **general** | **alphabetical** | **card** (*BrE*), **subject**
VERB + INDEX **appear in, be in** ◇ *The topic I was interested in didn't appear in the* ~. | **consult, look (sth up) in, search** ◇ *Why don't you look up her name in the* ~? ◇ *Search the* ~ *to find the address of the data file.* | **compile, create, update**
INDEX + VERB **give sth, list sth** ◇ *The* ~ *only gives the main towns.*
INDEX + NOUN **card**
PREP. **in a/the** ~ ◇ *Is there any reference to it in the* ~? | **~ to** ◇ *It's a general* ~ *to the whole work.*

2 system showing the level of sth; measure of sth

ADJ. **good, reliable, sensitive, useful** | **high, low** | **weighted** | **official** | **general** ◇ *a general ~ calculated from death and population information* | **cost-of-living, market, price** ◇ *the consumer price ~ (esp. AmE)* ◇ *the retail price ~ (BrE)* | **commodity, futures, share, stock, stock-market** | **Dow Jones, FTSE 100, etc.** | **dollar, sterling, etc.** | **body mass** (abbreviated to *BMI*), **glycaemic/glycemic** (abbreviated to *GI*), **refractive, etc.**

VERB + INDEX **have** ◇ *Those who lived in the inner cities had a high ~ of deprivation.* | **use (sth as)** ◇ *The test results were used as an ~ of language proficiency.* | **compile, construct, create** | **calculate, compute, derive** | **provide, publish** ◇ *The price ~ is published monthly.* | **drag, drive, push, take** ◇ *A wave of frenzied buying pushed the ~ up 136.2 points.* | **measure** | **track** ◇ *Most commodity funds track a specific commodity ~.*

INDEX + VERB **add sth** (esp. BrE), **gain sth, increase, jump, rise, surge** ◇ *The NYSE Financial ~ gained 20%.* | **decline, dip, drop, fall, sink** ◇ *The commodities ~ fell 3.1%.* | **measure sth** ◇ *an ~ designed to measure changes in the volume of industrial production* | **post sth** ◇ *The Morgan Stanley Cyclical ~ posted a small advance.* | **be based on sth** ◇ *an ~ based on incidents causing a loss of production* | **be linked to sth** ◇ *The increase in our standard rates will be linked to the consumer price ~.* | **index-linked pensions** (BrE) | **cover sth** ◇ *an ~ covering some 1700 companies* | **open, close, end** ◇ *The hundred shares ~ closed down 15 points.*

PREP. **in an/the ~** ◇ *dividends on shares in the ~* | **on an/the ~** ◇ *The company is listed on the Nasdaq technology stocks ~.*

PHRASES **a drop in an ~, a fall in an ~** ◇ *a 28.2 point drop in the FTSE 100 ~* | **changes in an ~** | **an increase in an ~** | **as measured by an ~** ◇ *Inflation, as measured by the consumer price ~, is expected to drop.*
→ Note at PER CENT (for more verbs)

indicate verb

ADV. **clearly, strongly** | **not necessarily** ◇ *Expense does not necessarily ~ worth.* | **usually** ◇ *This sign usually ~s a pedestrian zone.* | **previously** ◇ *Growth will be at a lower rate than previously ~d.*

VERB + INDICATE **appear to, seem to** ◇ *These facts would seem to ~ that the family was wealthy.* | **be used to** ◇ *Symbols are used to ~ the facilities available at each hotel.*

PREP. **to** ◇ *These figures ~ to me that the company is in serious trouble.*

PHRASES **~ otherwise** ◇ *He has declared support for women, but his actions have ~d otherwise.*

indication noun

ADJ. **firm** (BrE), **good, strong** | **fair** (esp. BrE) ◇ *It was a fair ~ of what was to come.* | **accurate, reliable, true** | **clear, definite, sure** ◇ *He gave his clearest ~ yet that he will keep racing.* | **important** | **useful** | **ample, sufficient** ◇ *He has given ample ~s of his intentions.* | **broad, general, rough** | **positive** | **early, initial, preliminary** | **outward, visible, visual** ◇ *Rising interest rates were an outward ~ of the change in government attitude to economic controls.* | *Some car alarms have no visual ~ that they are in operation.* | **clinical** ◇ *There was no clinical ~ for such a test.*

VERB + INDICATION **be, serve as** ◇ *The popularity of the government building project served as an ~ of public support.* | **have** ◇ *A government spokesperson said they had no ~ who was responsible for the attack.* | **give (sb), provide (sb with)** ◇ *His early successes gave some ~ of his ability.* | **get, receive** | **find, see** ◇ *The researchers say they can find no ~ that television has harmful physical effects on children.* | **regard sth as, see sth as, take sth as** ◇ *The comments made by management may be taken as an ~ of how they felt about their workers.*

INDICATION + VERB **point to sth, show sth, suggest sth** ◇ *Indications show that at least 2 000 more businesses will go bankrupt before the end of the year.*

PREP. **amid ~s of, amid ~s that...** (both esp. BrE) ◇ *He was last night locked in talks over his future amid ~s that he plans to resign.* | **~ as to** ◇ *He gave us no ~ as to what was the matter.* | **~ to** ◇ *This is an ~ to drivers who break the law that they will be punished*

PHRASES **(all) the ~s are that...** ◇ *All the ~s are that she will make a full recovery.* | **early ~s are that..., preliminary ~s are that...** ◇ *Preliminary ~s are that the tape is authentic.* | **not the slightest ~** ◇ *She smiled, not giving the slightest ~ of what had just happened.* | **there is every ~ that...** ◇ *There's every ~ that the operation has been a success.*

indicative adj.

VERBS **be** | **consider sth, interpret sth as, regard sth as, see sth as, take sth as** ◇ *The rise in unemployment is seen as ~ of a new economic recession.*

ADV. **strongly** | **(not) necessarily** ◇ *Recurrent dreams are not necessarily ~ of psychological problems.*

PREP. **of**

indicator noun sign showing what sth is like

ADJ. **accurate, good, reliable, sure** | **poor, unreliable** ◇ *Level of education is actually a poor ~ of ability to run a business well.* | **sensitive** | **crude, rough** | **simple** | **key, main, major** | **important, significant** | **useful, valuable** | **lagging, leading** (both economics, both esp. AmE) ◇ *The stock market is seen as a leading ~ of economic growth.* | **economic, financial, macroeconomic, performance, social, socio-economic** ◇ *performance ~s such as language and numeracy skills* | **prognostic** (medical)

VERB + INDICATOR **be, serve as** ◇ *These warts can serve as an ~ of other infections.* | **provide (sb with)** | **regard sth as, see sth as, take sth as** ◇ *Gold prices are often seen as an ~ of inflation.* | **use (sth as)** | **develop** ◇ *It is still difficult to develop ~s for many concepts used in social science.*

INDICATOR + VERB **point to sth, show sth, suggest sth** ◇ *Economic ~s suggest that a recovery is on the way.*

PREP. **~ for** ◇ *an ~ for the presence of minerals*

indictment noun

1 sign that sth is bad/wrong

ADJ. **devastating, powerful** | **damning, scathing, searing, stinging, terrible** (esp. BrE) ◇ *Her speech was a scathing ~ of the government's record on crime.* | **blanket, sweeping** (both esp. AmE) ◇ *This is a rather too sweeping ~ of the field of evolutionary psychology.* | **sad** (esp. BrE)

2 (law, esp. AmE) accusing sb of a crime

ADJ. **criminal, felony** (AmE) | **federal, grand jury** (both AmE) | **fresh**

VERB + INDICTMENT **bring, file, issue** ◇ *A New York jury brought criminal ~s against the founder of the organization.* | **hand down, hand out, return** (all AmE) ◇ *War crimes ~s were handed down by a UN-backed court.* | **announce** ◇ *The government announced a federal ~ against him.* | **face** ◇ *He faces ~ for perjury.* | **be charged in, be charged on** (BrE) | **be convicted on, be tried on** (both BrE) | **dismiss** ◇ *The federal district court dismissed the ~.* | **plead guilty to, plead not guilty to** (both BrE)

INDICTMENT + VERB **accuse sb of sth, allege sth, charge (sb/sth with sth)** ◇ *an ~ charging theft*

PREP. **in a/the ~** ◇ *Two men were named in the ~.* | **on ~** (BrE) ◇ *a trial on ~* | **~ against** ◇ *They issued an ~ against them.* | **~ for** ◇ *She was convicted on an ~ for conspiracy.*

indifference noun

ADJ. **complete, supreme** (esp. BrE), **total, utter** | **growing** | **deliberate, studied** | **apparent, feigned, seeming** | **benign, blithe, casual** ◇ *Try to treat such comments with benign ~.* | **callous, cold, cool** | **reckless** ◇ *Attacks have been successful because of a reckless ~ to security standards.* | **public**

VERB + INDIFFERENCE **feel** | **demonstrate, display, express, show** ◇ *She showed total ~ to his fate.* | **cultivate, feign** ◇ *He feigned ~ to criticism of his work.* | **regard sb/sth with** ◇ *They regard the change in corporate culture with a certain ~.* | **treat sb/sth with** | **be met with** ◇ *Constable's landscapes met with ~ when they were first exhibited.*

PREP. **with an ~** ◇ *Ellis spoke with a casual ~ that he did not feel.* | **~ to, ~ towards/toward** ◇ *his ~ towards/toward art*
PHRASES **an air of ~, an attitude of ~** ◇ *They have an air of studied ~ to the problem.* ◇ *She adopted an attitude of supreme ~.* | **a matter of ~** ◇ *It's a matter of ~ to me whether he goes or not.*

indifferent *adj.*

1 not interested

VERBS **appear, be, feel, seem, sound** ◇ *He appeared ~ to her suffering.* | **act** (*esp. AmE*) ◇ *Alice tried to act ~ about the incident.* | **become** | **remain**
ADV. **completely, quite, supremely, totally, utterly** | **almost** ◇ *Pat sounded almost ~.* | **largely, relatively** | **apparently, seemingly**
PREP. **about** ◇ *Most staff were ~ about the plans.* | **to** ◇ *He was coldly ~ to other people.*

2 of low quality

VERBS **be**
ADV. **very** (*esp. BrE*) ◇ *We enjoyed the day, in spite of very ~ weather.* | **rather** ◇ *a rather ~ performance*
PHRASES **good, bad and/or ~** ◇ *The festival has the usual mix of movies—good, bad and ~.*

indigestion *noun*

ADJ. **serious, severe** | **chronic** | **slight**
VERB + INDIGESTION **get, have, suffer from** | **give sb** ◇ *Rich food always gives me ~.* | **relieve, treat**
INDIGESTION + NOUN **problems** | **tablet** (*esp. BrE*)
→ Special page at ILLNESS

indignant *adj.*

VERBS **be, feel, look, sound** | **become, get, grow, wax** ◇ *She waxes ~ if anyone tries to contradict her.* | **make sb**
ADV. **extremely, fairly, very, etc.** | **a little, slightly, etc.** | **righteously** ◇ *'He deserves to be punished,' she protested, righteously ~.*
PREP. **about, over** ◇ *She became rather ~ over suggestions that she had lied.* | **at** ◇ *They were quite ~ at his remarks.*

indignation *noun*

ADJ. **great, high** (*AmE*) ◇ *His response was one of high ~.* | **public** | **moral, righteous** | **mock**
VERB + INDIGNATION **be filled with, be full of, feel** ◇ *They were full of righteous ~ at the thought of being cheated.* | **express, show** | **express** | **blush with, burn with, flush with** ◇ *His plump face flushed with ~.* | **bristle with, shudder with, tremble with** ◇ *Susan's voice shuddered with ~.* | **arouse, provoke**
PREP. **in ~** ◇ *She turned to him in ~.* | **with ~** ◇ *He refused it with some ~.* | **~ about, ~ at, ~ over** ◇ *The government expressed its ~ over the way the incident had been handled.* | **~ against** ◇ *public ~ against the government*

indiscretion *noun*

ADJ. **serious** | **minor, slight** | **personal** | **youthful** | **dietary, sexual**
VERB + INDISCRETION **commit** ◇ *He had committed a minor sexual ~.* | **regret** ◇ *I instantly regretted my ~ and asked her to keep the news to herself.*

indispensable *adj.*

VERBS **be, prove** | **become** | **make sb/sth** ◇ *He had soon made himself ~.* | **consider sb/sth**
ADV. **absolutely**
PREP. **for** ◇ *Written sources are considered absolutely ~ for today's history teaching.* | **in** ◇ *These drugs are almost ~ in the fight against the disease.* | **to** ◇ *skills which turned out to be ~ to her career*

individual *noun*

ADJ. **outstanding, talented** | **key** | **powerful** | **creative** | **average, normal, ordinary** ◇ *The average ~ watches around three hours of television per day.* | **private** ◇ *He was carrying out his functions as a trustee in the course of his business,*

rather than as a private ~. | **single** | **certain, particular** ◇ *The motives influencing a particular ~ may change from time to time.* | **autonomous, independent** | **isolated** ◇ *Society does not consist of isolated ~s, but people in a network of relationships.* | **rare, unique** ◇ *She saw the artist as a unique ~, possessing a heightened awareness of reality.* | **like-minded** ◇ *a group of like-minded ~s* | **named** ◇ *accusations of racism against named ~s* | **qualified** ◇ *We welcome applications from suitably qualified ~s.* | **healthy, infected** | **wealthy** ◇ *donations from wealthy ~s* | **human** ◇ *We know that all human ~s are unique.*
... OF INDIVIDUALS **class, group** ◇ *She had taken a group of ~s and made them into a superb team.*
VERB + INDIVIDUAL **treat sb as** ◇ *The teacher should treat each student as an ~.*
INDIVIDUAL + VERB **differ, vary** ◇ *Although ~s vary widely, the bones of the average female skeleton are smaller and lighter than the male.*
PHRASES **no one ~, no single ~** ◇ *No single ~ had done so much for the development of the motor vehicle.* | **any one ~, any single ~** ◇ *The needs of the community outweigh those of any single ~.* | **the freedom of the ~, the rights of the ~** ◇ *the issue of the freedom of the ~ versus the intervention of the state* | **the ~ concerned** ◇ *It's up to the ~ concerned to contact the police.* | **the needs of the ~** ◇ *Each course has to be tailored to the needs of the ~.* | **respect for the ~** | **vary from ~ to ~** ◇ *Eating habits are bound to vary from ~ to ~.*

individuality *noun*

ADJ. **human**
VERB + INDIVIDUALITY **have** ◇ *Each song has its own ~.* | **assert, express, show** ◇ *clothes that reflect your ~* | **give sth** ◇ *The pictures give ~ to the room.* | **maintain, retain** | **give up, lose**
PHRASES **a feeling of ~, a sense of ~** ◇ *Becoming part of a team should not mean losing your sense of ~.*

inducement *noun*

ADJ. **powerful** | **positive** | **cash, financial**
VERB + INDUCEMENT **give, offer** (sb/sth as), **provide** (sb/sth as) ◇ *The higher payments were offered as an ~.* | **receive**
PREP. **~ for** ◇ *The reduced tax is a major ~ for first-time buyers.* | **~ to** ◇ *an ~ to crime and violence* ◇ *~s to employees*

indulge *verb*

ADV. **occasionally** | **freely**
VERB + INDULGE **be able to, be free to, can**
PREP. **in** ◇ *She was free to ~ in a little romantic daydreaming.* | **with** ◇ *For a special treat, ~ yourself with one of these luxury desserts.*

indulgence *noun*

1 having whatever you want

ADJ. **excessive** | **pure, sheer** ◇ *guilty of sheer ~* | **personal** | **sexual**
PREP. **~ in** ◇ *She allowed herself only a few moments' ~ in self-pity.*
PHRASES **a life of ~**

2 sth you allow yourself

ADJ. **private** | **small** | **occasional**
VERB + INDULGENCE **allow yourself** ◇ *As a relief from work she allowed herself a few small ~s.*

3 acceptance of change to the normal way of doing sth

VERB + INDULGENCE **ask, beg, crave, request, seek** ◇ *He begged the audience's ~ to read some passages from his latest book.* | **grant** ◇ *He attacked the ~ granted to religious dissenters.*

industrial action *noun* (*esp. BrE*)

ADJ. **continuing** | **unlawful**
VERB + INDUSTRIAL ACTION **take** | **threaten** | **call for** | **vote for** | **start** | **step up** ◇ *The union is considering stepping up its ~.*

| suspend | stop | become involved in, be involved in, take part in ◇ *His research indicates an increase in the number of women involved in ~.* | support
PREP. **~ against** ◇ *The union is threatening ~ against the company.* | **~ by** ◇ *~ by air traffic controllers* | **~ in support of** ◇ *~ in support of demands for a 10% salary adjustment* | **~ over** ◇ *to take ~ over pay*

industrialist noun

ADJ. **leading, prominent, top** | **local** | **rich, wealthy**

industry noun

ADJ. **booming, growing, thriving** ◇ *one of the fastest-growing industries in the world* | **important, key, major** | **declining** | **high-tech, modern, sunrise** (*BrE*) | **sunset** (*BrE*), **traditional** | **cottage** ◇ *Weaving and knitting are traditional cottage industries.* | **domestic, local** | **global** ◇ *the global textile ~* | **private, privatized** | **nationalized, state-owned, state-run** | **heavy** | **light** | **strategic** ◇ *strategic industries such as the extraction of oil and natural gas* | **manufacturing, service** ◇ *the shift away from manufacturing to service ~* | **primary, secondary, tertiary** | **labour-intensive/labor-intensive** | **building, construction** | **engineering** (*esp. BrE*) | **shipbuilding** | **chemical, coal, electrical** (*esp. AmE*), **electricity** (*esp. BrE*), **energy, gas, mining, nuclear, oil, steel** | **agricultural, fishing, food, timber** | **pharmaceutical** | **health-care, medical** (*esp. AmE*) | **biotech** | **auto** (*AmE*), **automobile** (*AmE*), **automotive, car** (*esp. BrE*), **motor** | **computer, electronics** | **telecom** (*esp. AmE*), **telecommunications, telecoms** (*esp. BrE*) | **fashion, textile** | **advertising** | **insurance** | **entertainment, film** (*esp. BrE*), **movie** (*esp. AmE*), **music, record, recording** | **tourism, tourist** | **catering, hospitality, leisure** (*all esp. BrE*) | **hotel** | **banking, financial** | **aerospace, airline, aviation** | **publishing** | **tobacco**
VERB + INDUSTRY **benefit, develop, encourage, help, stimulate, support** ◇ *The government decided to encourage industries based on biotechnology.* ◇ *government measures to stimulate new ~* | **run down** (*BrE*) ◇ *Running down the nuclear ~ will result in heavy job losses.* | **damage, hurt** ◇ *They claim that a commercial port would damage the local tourist ~.* | **cripple, destroy, devastate** | **nationalize** | **privatize** | **deregulate, regulate** | **protect** ◇ *trade barriers erected to protect domestic ~* | **subsidize** ◇ *The state's timber ~ is heavily subsidized.* | **interfere in, interfere with** ◇ *The government has interfered in ~, with disastrous results, by attempting to alter economic trends.* | **be involved in, be involved with** ◇ *More than 140 000 people are directly involved in the ~.* | **revolutionize, transform** | **enter, go into** ◇ *students training to enter the banking ~* ◇ *She decided to leave teaching and go into ~.*
INDUSTRY + VERB **boom, develop, expand, grow, grow up, spring up** ◇ *New light industries are constantly springing up.* ◇ *The tourist ~ is still expanding rapidly.* | **decline, struggle** ◇ *When the oil ran out, other industries associated with it closed down.* | **experience sth, face sth** ◇ *industries which are experiencing substantial growth* ◇ *The ~ is facing major challenges.* | **produce sth**
INDUSTRY + NOUN **executive, leader** | **expert, insider** | **analyst, observer** | **standard** ◇ *They hope that the disk drive will become an ~ standard.*
PREP. **in ~, within ~** ◇ *In the computer ~, change comes about very rapidly.*
PHRASES **a captain of ~, commerce and ~** ◇ *The banks lend money to commerce and ~.* | **regulation of (an) ~** ◇ *proposals for regulation of the water ~* | **the revival of (an) ~** ◇ *the revival of the British film ~* | **a sector of ~** | **~ and trade** (*esp. AmE*), **trade and ~** ◇ *the Department of Trade and Industry* (*in the UK*)

inedible adj.

VERBS **be**
ADV. **totally** ◇ *The food was totally ~.* | **almost, nearly**

ineffective adj.

VERBS **be, prove, seem** ◇ *These policies have proved ~.* | **become** | **make sth, render sth** ◇ *The contract was rendered ~ by this careless wording.*
ADV. **extremely, fairly, very, etc.** | **highly** | **completely, entirely, totally** | **largely** | **politically**
PREP. **against** ◇ *These weapons are totally ~ against tanks.* | **in** ◇ *chemicals that are very ~ in killing weeds*

inefficiency noun

ADJ. **gross** | **inherent** | **bureaucratic, government** | **economic, market**
VERB + INEFFICIENCY **cause, create, lead to** ◇ *Conflict between management and workers leads to ~ in the workplace.* | **reduce** | **eliminate** ◇ *We need to eliminate inefficiencies in the production process.*

inefficient adj.

VERBS **be, seem** | **become**
ADV. **extremely, fairly, very, etc.** | **grossly, highly, hopelessly, incredibly, terribly** | **relatively** | **potentially** | **inherently** | **notoriously** | **economically** ◇ *an economically ~ system*

ineligible adj.

VERBS **be** | **become** | **make sb/sth, render sb/sth** | **consider sb/sth, declare sb/sth, deem sb/sth, rule sb/sth** ◇ *The country had been declared ~ for World Bank lending.*
PREP. **for** ◇ *The new rules have made thousands more people ~ for legal aid.*

inept adj.

VERBS **be, prove** | **seem**
ADV. **rather** | **completely** | **intellectually, politically, socially** ◇ *It would be politically ~ to make these cutbacks now.* | **comically, hopelessly, woefully**
PREP. **at** ◇ *He was rather ~ at word games.*

inequality noun

ADJ. **great, gross, substantial** ◇ *the gross social inequalities of the past* ◇ *Inequalities of income would lead to even greater inequalities in access to health care.* | **real** | **growing, increased, increasing, rising** | **global, regional** | **class, economic, educational, racial, social, socio-economic, structural** | **gender, sex** (*BrE*), **sexual** ◇ *efforts to address class and gender inequalities and to rebalance power* | **income, pay, wage** (*esp. BrE*)
VERB + INEQUALITY **cause, create, lead to** ◇ *The introduction of tuition fees would create ~ between universities.* | **maintain, perpetuate** ◇ *Some believe that education perpetuates ~.* | **reinforce** ◇ *The law merely serves to reinforce social inequalities.* | **increase** | **reduce** | **remove** ◇ *They can build a more harmonious society once ~ and exploitation are removed.* | **address, redress** ◇ *The country has had some success in redressing racial inequalities.*
INEQUALITY + VERB **exist** ◇ *inequalities that exist in wealth and income* | **arise from sth, be based on sth** ◇ *inequalities based on racism and social class* | **persist, remain** ◇ *Even in the age of compulsory school, inequalities in education have remained.* | **increase** | **decline**
PREP. **~ between** ◇ *economic ~ between men and women* | **~ in** ◇ *gender ~ in education*
PHRASES **inequalities of power, wealth, etc.** | **a pattern of ~** (*esp. BrE*)

inert adj.

VERBS **be, remain** | **become**
ADV. **completely** ◇ *She lay completely ~ on her bed.* | **relatively** | **biologically, chemically** ◇ *chemically ~ radio-active waste*

inertia noun

ADJ. **sheer** | **bureaucratic, political**
VERB + INERTIA **overcome** ◇ *The forces for change are not sufficient to overcome bureaucratic ~.*

PREP. **out of** ~ ◇ *He stayed where he was, not because he really wanted to, but out of* ~. | **through** ~ ◇ *Projects were frequently abandoned through sheer* ~.
PHRASES **a state of** ~

inevitability *noun*

ADJ. **tragic** | **a certain** | **historical**
VERB + INEVITABILITY **have** | **accept, recognize** ◇ *She was learning to accept the* ~ *of death.*
PREP. ~ **about** ◇ *The tragedy had a certain* ~ *about it.*
PHRASES **a feeling of** ~, **a sense of** ~

inevitable *adj.*

VERBS **appear, be, look, seem** | **become** | **make sth** ◇ *The scandal made her resignation* ~. | **consider sth, regard sth as, see sth as** ◇ *They came to see defeat as* ~.
ADV. **almost, virtually** | **apparently, seemingly** | **historically**
PHRASES **bow to the** ~ ◇ *She bowed to the* ~ (= accepted a situation in which she had no choice) *and resigned.*

inexhaustible *adj.*

VERBS **be, seem** ◇ *Her energy seemed* ~.
ADV. **virtually** | **apparently, seemingly**

inexpensive *adj.*

VERBS **be** | **make sth** ◇ *Their currency is undervalued, making their goods* ~ *for foreigners.*
ADV. **extremely, fairly, very, etc.** | **comparatively, relatively** ◇ *Paper is relatively* ~ *here.*

inexperience *noun*

ADJ. **relative** | **youthful** | **sexual**
VERB + INEXPERIENCE **show** ◇ *She showed her* ~ *by asking lots of trivial questions.* | **be down to** (*BrE*) ◇ *The team's defensive errors were down to* (= a result of their) ~. | **put sth down to** (*BrE*) ◇ *He put his mistakes down to* (= believed they were caused by his) ~.
INEXPERIENCE + VERB **show** ◇ *Her* ~ *in politics did not show.*
PREP. **because of** ~, **through** ~ (*esp. BrE*) ◇ *They made mistakes because of their* ~. | ~ **in** ◇ ~ *in teaching*

inexperienced *adj.*

VERBS **be, feel, seem**
ADV. **extremely, fairly, very, etc.** | **hopelessly** | **totally** ◇ *He was unqualified and totally* ~. | **relatively** ◇ *She was still a relatively* ~ *pilot.* | **politically, sexually**
PREP. **in** ◇ *She was* ~ *in teaching art.* | **with** ◇ *men who are* ~ *with children*
PHRASES **young and** ~

inexplicable *adj.*

VERBS **be, seem** | **remain** | **find sth**
ADV. **completely, quite, totally** ◇ *Their actions are completely* ~. | **apparently, seemingly** | **otherwise** ◇ *This theory makes sense of an otherwise* ~ *phenomenon.*

infancy *noun*

ADJ. **early** ◇ *The vaccination is given in early* ~.
VERB + INFANCY **survive, survive beyond** ◇ *Their first child did not survive* ~.
PREP. **during** ~, **in** ~ ◇ *Deaths during* ~ *fell dramatically in the last century.* ◇ *The new company is still in its* ~. (*figurative*) | **from** ~ ◇ *from* ~ *to late childhood* | **since** (sb's) ~ ◇ *Since her* ~ *she has been a healthy baby.* | **throughout** (sb's) ~ ◇ *He was ill many times throughout his* ~.
PHRASES **die in** ~ ◇ *She died in* ~.

infant *noun*

ADJ. **young** ◇ *He is studying hearing in very young* ~s. | **month-old, two-month-old, etc.** | **newborn** | **premature, preterm** ◇ *jaundice in premature* ~s | **full-term** | **healthy, normal** | **low-birthweight** | **human** ◇ *a book on intellectual development in the human* ~ | **female, male** | **sleeping** ◇ *Marjorie looked down at the sleeping* ~ *in her arms.*
VERB + INFANT **breastfeed, feed, nurse**

INFANT + NOUN **death, mortality** ◇ *countries with high* ~ *mortality* | **child, daughter, son** | **formula**
PHRASES **sudden** ~ **death syndrome**

infection *noun*

ADJ. **nasty, serious, severe** | **mild, minor, moderate** | **acute, chronic** | **recurrent** | **primary, secondary** ◇ *If the primary* ~ *is not treated further outbreaks may occur.* | **new** ◇ *Over 90% of all new* ~s *occur in the developing world.* | **rare** | **bacterial, fungal, viral** | **chest, ear, etc.** | **pulmonary, respiratory, urinary tract, etc.** | **herpes, HIV, yeast** (*AmE*), **etc.** | **opportunistic**
VERB + INFECTION **have, suffer, suffer from** ◇ *He's suffering from an acute lung* ~. | **be at risk from, be at risk of, be prone to, be susceptible to, be vulnerable to** ◇ *Goats appear to be more susceptible to the* ~ *than sheep.* | **be exposed to** ◇ *Vaccination is essential to protect people exposed to hepatitis B* ~. | **acquire, catch, contract, develop, get** ◇ *She's always getting chest* ~s. | **cause** | **pass, pass on, spread, transmit** ◇ *The* ~ *is passed on through the horse feed.* | **carry** ◇ *Almost all the sheep on the farm carried the* ~. | **guard against, protect sb/sth from** ◇ *to protect the body from* ~ | **avoid, prevent** | **combat, fight** ◇ *The virus affects the body's immune system so that it cannot fight* ~. | **fight off, kill** ◇ *Normally, white blood cells fight off and kill* ~s. | **recover from** | **leave/make sb susceptible to, leave/make sb vulnerable to** | **die from, die of** | **diagnose, diagnose sb with** | **treat, treat sb for**
INFECTION + VERB **develop, occur** ◇ *an* ~ *that occurs in swans* | **spread** ◇ *They want to prevent the* ~ *spreading to other parts of the body.* | **cause sth, result in sth, trigger sth** ◇ *Heavy lung* ~s *may result in pneumonia.*
PREP. **in** ~ ◇ *In acute* ~s *of the urinary tract the patient may suffer severe pain.* | ~ **from** ◇ ~ *from sewage water* | ~ **through** ◇ ~ *through unsafe sex* | ~ **with** ◇ ~ *with bacteria*
PHRASES **a cause of** ~, **the onset of** ~ ◇ *The drug must be taken from the onset of the* ~. | **resistance to** ~ ◇ *Taking vitamin C builds up your resistance to* ~. | **a risk of** ~, **a site of** ~ (*medical*) ◇ *The urethra was the primary site of* ~. | **a source of** ~ ◇ *We are trying to trace the source of* ~. | **the spread of** ~
→ Special page at ILLNESS

infectious *adj.*

VERBS **be**
ADV. **highly, very** | **potentially**

infer *verb*

ADV. **reasonably** | **correctly, incorrectly** | **directly, indirectly**
VERB + INFER **can** | **be possible to** | **be difficult to, be hard to** ◇ *It is difficult to* ~ *anything from such evidence.* | **be reasonable to** | **be wrong to**
PREP. **from** ◇ *From this study we can reasonably* ~ *that this characteristic is inherited.*

inference *noun*

ADJ. **fair, logical, reasonable, valid** | **obvious**
VERB + INFERENCE **draw, make** | **allow, support**
INFERENCE + VERB **be based on sth** ◇ ~s *based on their answers to a number of set questions*
PREP. ~ **about** ◇ *In the absence of detailed documentary evidence, we can only make* ~s *about Minoan religion.* | ~ **from** ◇ *The value of data depends on our skill in drawing* ~s *from it.*

inferior *noun*

ADJ. **intellectual, social**
VERB + INFERIOR **consider sb** ◇ *She considered everyone her intellectual* ~.

inferior *adj.*

VERBS **be, feel, seem** ◇ *Her obvious popularity made me feel*

~. | **consider sb/sth, regard sb/sth as, see sb/sth as** ◇ *He regarded women as* ~.
ADV. **decidedly, greatly** (*esp. BrE*), **markedly, significantly, vastly, very** | **slightly, somewhat** | **inherently** | **intellectually, morally, socially, technically**
PREP. **in** ◇ *These later paintings are slightly* ~ *in value.* | **to** ◇ *His later work was vastly* ~ *to his early work.*

inferiority noun

ADJ. **moral, racial, social** ◇ *the myth of racial* ~ | **intellectual**
INFERIORITY + NOUN **complex** ◇ *He had an* ~ *complex about his looks.*
PREP. ~ **to** ◇ *She accepted her* ~ *to her rivals.*
PHRASES **a feeling of** ~, **a sense of** ~

infertility noun

ADJ. **female, male**
VERB + INFERTILITY **cause, lead to** | **treat**
INFERTILITY + NOUN **clinic, treatment**

infested adj.

VERBS **be** | **become**
ADV. **heavily** ◇ *The building was heavily* ~ *with cockroaches.*
PREP. **with**

infiltration noun

ADJ. **communist, terrorist**
VERB + INFILTRATION **reduce** | **prevent, stop**
PREP. ~ **by** ◇ *The police tried to prevent* ~ *by drug traffickers.* | ~ **into** ◇ *the* ~ *of rain into the soil*

infinite adj.

VERBS **be** | **become**
ADV. **almost, nearly, practically, virtually** ◇ *an almost* ~ *variety of shades* | **apparently, seemingly** | **effectively** | **potentially**

infinity noun

1 endless space/time
VERB + INFINITY **extend into, extend to, stretch into, stretch to** ◇ *Theoretically, a line can extend into* ~.
PREP. **at** ~ ◇ *Parallel lines appear to meet at* ~. | **into** ~ ◇ *He could have jumped off the cliff into* ~.
2 number larger than any other
VERB + INFINITY **approach, tend to, tend towards/toward** ◇ *As x approaches* ~, *y approaches zero.*
PREP. **at** ~ ◇ *The usual convention is to choose the reference point at* ~.

infirm adj.

VERBS **be** | **become**
ADV. **mentally, physically**

infirmity noun

ADJ. **mental, physical**
PHRASES **age and** ~ (*literary, esp. BrE*) ◇ *those incapable of supporting themselves by reason of age and* ~

inflamed adj.

VERBS **be** | **become, get**
ADV. **severely** ◇ *Her joints are severely* ~. | **acutely, chronically**

inflammable adj. (*esp. BrE*) → See FLAMMABLE

inflammation noun

ADJ. **painful, severe** | **mild** | **acute, chronic** | **intestinal, joint, etc.**
VERB + INFLAMMATION **reduce** ◇ *Steroids often help reduce the* ~ *and itching in the skin.* | **cause**
PREP. ~ **of** ◇ ~ *of the stomach*

inflated adj.

1 expanded
ADV. **fully** | **partially**
PREP. **with** ◇ *The balloon was kept fully* ~ *with hydrogen.*
2 exaggerated
VERBS **be**
ADV. **greatly, grossly, hugely** (*esp. BrE*), **vastly, wildly** | **artificially, falsely** (*esp. BrE*) ◇ *The prices of meals are often artificially* ~.

inflation noun

ADJ. **high, massive** | **low, moderate** | **zero** | **galloping** (*esp. BrE*), **raging** (*esp. BrE*), **rampant, rising, runaway, spiralling/spiraling** (*esp. BrE*) | **double-digit** (= 10% or more) | **consumer-price, price, wage** (*esp. BrE*) | **domestic** | **grade** (= the apparent increase in students' grades over time due to the fact that exams are becoming easier)
VERB + INFLATION **cause** | **fuel, push up** | **bring down, bring under control, combat, control, curb, fight, get down, get under control, keep down, keep in check, keep under control, reduce** ◇ *policies to beat* ~ ◇ *It is vital that* ~ *is kept in check.* | **keep pace with, keep up with** ◇ *Wages are not keeping pace with* ~. | **outpace**
INFLATION + VERB **be up** | **be down** ◇ *Inflation is down to its lowest level in three years.* | **exceed sth, reach sth** ◇ *Inflation reached a monthly rate of 5%.* | **average sth, be at sth, run at sth, stand at sth** ◇ *Inflation is running at 4%.* | **edge up** (*esp. BrE*), **go up, increase, rise** | **fall, go down, slow** ◇ *Inflation has slowed to 7%.* | **erode sth** ◇ *savings eroded by* ~
INFLATION + NOUN **figures, rate** ◇ *an* ~ *rate of 2%* | **expectations, forecast, target**
PHRASES **the battle against** ~, **the fight against** ~ | **a drop in** ~, **a fall in** ~ ◇ *an drop in* ~ *to 2.4%* | **an increase in** ~, **a rise in** ~ ◇ *an increase in* ~ *to 3.5%* | **the rate of** ~

inflexible adj.

VERBS **be, seem** ◇ *The rules seemed arbitrary and* ~. | **become**
ADV. **extremely, fairly, very, etc.** ◇ *She's a good teacher, but she can be fairly* ~. | **completely, totally** ◇ *The seven-year period is not totally* ~. | **relatively**

inflict verb

ADV. **deliberately, intentionally** ◇ *When someone deliberately* ~*s damage, it is a matter for the police.*
PREP. **on, upon** ◇ *They* ~*ed a humiliating defeat on their rivals.*

influence noun

1 effect sb/sth has; power to control sb/sth
ADJ. **big, considerable, enormous, great, marked, significant, substantial, tremendous** | **growing, increasing** | **chief, dominant, major, overwhelming** | **powerful, profound, strong** ◇ *He had a profound* ~ *on modern poets.* | **subtle** | **important** | **crucial, decisive** | **potential** | **continuing, enduring, lasting** | **improper, undue** (*law*) ◇ *The court found that the bank exerted undue* ~ *over Mrs Black in getting her to sign the contract.* | **disproportionate** | **beneficial, positive** | **adverse, corrosive, corrupting, destructive, disruptive, evil, malign** (*formal*), **negative, pernicious** | **moderating, stabilizing, steadying** | **calming, restraining** | **civilizing** | **direct, indirect** | **causal, mutual** | **relative** ◇ *This paper evaluates the relative* ~ *of religions.* | **far-reaching, pervasive, wide** | **external, outside** ◇ *The religious community wished to be independent of outside* ~. | **peer** ◇ *the effects of peer* ~ *on crime* | **parental** | **foreign** | **cultural, economic, genetic, political, social, sociocultural**
VERB + INFLUENCE **have** | **gain** | **give sb** ◇ *Her wealth gave her* ~ *over affairs of state.* | **assert, exercise, exert, use, wield** ◇ *Can you use your* ~ *with the director to get me a part in the movie?* ◇ *Drug cartels wielded enormous* ~ *in the city.* | **retain** | **lose** | **expand, extend, increase, spread** ◇ *The*

unions have been able to extend their ~ over all industries. | **minimize** | **eliminate, remove** | **limit** | **diminish, reduce** | **counter, counteract** | **avoid, escape, resist** | **be under** ◇ *The court was told that he was under the ~ of alcohol when he was stopped by the police.* | **come under, fall under** ◇ *She came under the ~ of Sartre at this period.* | **be independent of** | **demonstrate, reflect, reveal, show** ◇ *Spanish architecture shows Moorish ~.* | **acknowledge, recognize, understand** | **analyse/analyze, assess, determine, evaluate, examine, explore, investigate, study** ◇ *They examined the ~ of farm size on technology adoption.* | **attribute sth to** ◇ *Much of his writing can be attributed to the ~ of Freud.* | **trace** ◇ *It's easy to trace the ~ she's exerted on contemporary artists.*

INFLUENCE + VERB **extend** ◇ *Their ~ extended as far as China.* | **grow** ◇ *The Internet's ~ is growing every day.* | **wane** ◇ *His political ~ was waning.*

PREP. **under the ~** ◇ *The town grew under the ~ of colonialism.* | **~ from** ◇ *There was no ~ from outside.* | **~ in** ◇ *She has a certain amount of ~ in the way things are organized.* | **~ on, ~ upon** ◇ *They were a major ~ upon the development of the sport.* | **~ over** ◇ *I have absolutely no ~ over him.* | **~ with** ◇ *He used his ~ with local officials to gain commercial advantages.*

PHRASES **a sphere of ~** ◇ *Rome's sphere of ~ extended as far as Scotland.* | **bring your ~ to bear on sb/sth** ◇ *She tried to bring her ~ to bear on her husband.* | **under the ~, under the ~ of alcohol, under the ~ of drink** (*BrE*) ◇ *He was arrested for driving under the ~ (= drunk).*

2 sb/sth that affects the way sb behaves/thinks

ADJ. **big, considerable, great, significant, tremendous** | **dominant, major, overwhelming** | **powerful, profound, strong** | **important** | **obvious** | **lasting** | **early** ◇ *Who were your early ~s?* | **formative** ◇ *His uncle had been a formative ~ from his earliest years.* | **diverse** ◇ *He is a writer who draws upon diverse cultural ~s.* | **outside** ◇ *Parents often seek to shelter their children from outside ~s* | **good** | **adverse, bad, corrupting, destructive, disruptive, harmful, malign** (*formal*), **negative, pernicious** | **moderating, stabilizing, steadying** | **calming, restraining** | **civilizing** | **environmental, genetic** | **artistic, cultural, intellectual, literary, musical**

VERB + INFLUENCE **be** | **have** ◇ *The band had many ~s.* | **be exposed to** ◇ *a study of children exposed to different cultural ~s* | **draw from, draw on, draw upon**

INFLUENCE + VERB **be at work** ◇ *There were a number of ~s at work in Wright's architecture.* | **affect sth, shape sth**

PREP. **~ on** ◇ *She's by far the biggest ~ on my writing.*

influence *verb*

ADV. **considerably, deeply, dramatically, enormously, greatly, heavily, highly, markedly, powerfully, profoundly, strongly, substantially** ◇ *This book ~d her profoundly.* ◇ *Attitudes are highly ~d by cultural background.* | **increasingly** | **largely, mainly, primarily** | **partly, slightly** | **potentially** | **directly, indirectly** ◇ *Pressure from industry bosses has directly ~d government policy.* | **clearly, obviously, undoubtedly** | **actively** | **critically, crucially, decisively, significantly** | **inevitably** | **favourably/favorably, positively** ◇ *actions that positively ~ health* | **adversely, negatively** | **overly, unduly** ◇ *Be aware of external factors which may unduly ~ your judgement.* | **genetically**

VERB + INFLUENCE **seem to** | **attempt to, seek to, try to** ◇ *We do not seek to ~ the decision-making process.*

PREP. **in** ◇ *Her parents tried to ~ her in her choice of university.*

PHRASES **be easily ~d** ◇ *He was naive and easily ~d by his friends.*

influential *adj.*

VERBS **be, prove** | **become**

ADV. **extremely, fairly, very, etc.** | **deeply, enormously, especially, highly, hugely, immensely, particularly** ◇ *This was a highly ~ work.* ◇ *As a writer she was hugely ~.* | **increasingly** | **potentially** | **widely** | **politically**

PREP. **in** ◇ *The group was ~ in setting up the new schools.*

influenza *noun* (*formal*)

ADJ. **avian, human**

... OF INFLUENZA **attack, bout** (*esp. BrE*)

VERB + INFLUENZA **have, suffer from** | **catch, contract** | **prevent**

INFLUENZA + NOUN **epidemic, outbreak, pandemic** | **season** (*esp. AmE*) | **virus** | **infection** | **symptoms** | **strain** ◇ *the ~ strain known as H7* | **vaccine** | **immunization, vaccination**

→ Special page at ILLNESS

influx *noun*

ADJ. **great, huge, large, massive** | **new, recent** | **sudden** | **rapid** | **constant, steady** | **daily** ◇ *the daily ~ of sightseers to the city*

VERB + INFLUX **experience** (*esp. AmE*), **have, receive** (*esp. BrE*), **see** ◇ *The hotel has received a large ~ of guests.* ◇ *Many cities saw a large ~ of migrant workers.* | **prevent** ◇ *The country sealed its borders to prevent the ~ of illegal immigrants.* | **cope with, handle** ◇ *They didn't know how they were going to cope with the sudden ~ of refugees.*

PREP. **~ of** ◇ *an ~ of immigrants* | **~ into, ~ to** ◇ *a massive ~ of foreign tourists to the coast*

inform *verb*

ADV. **merely, simply** ◇ *I am not advising you. I am merely ~ing you of the situation.* | **regularly** (*esp. BrE*) | **immediately, quickly** | **officially** (*esp. BrE*) | **personally** | **kindly, politely** ◇ *Next time you decide to take some action, kindly ~ me.* | **bluntly** ◇ *'I won't do it!' she ~ed him bluntly.* | **calmly, coldly, coolly** | **adequately, properly** ◇ *Many people questioned whether patients were ~ed adequately of the risks.* | **accurately** | **clearly** ◇ *Students are clearly ~ed that drugs will not be tolerated.* | **recently**

VERB + INFORM **be pleased to** | **regret to** ◇ *I regret to ~ you that you have been unsuccessful in your application.* | **be required to** ◇ *The clinic is required to ~ the patient about possible alternative treatments.*

PREP. **about** ◇ *efforts to ~ young people about the dangers of drugs* | **of** ◇ *We will immediately ~ you of any changes to the schedule.*

informal *adj.*

VERBS **be** | **become** | **remain**

ADV. **extremely, fairly, very, etc.** | **relatively** ◇ *Our meetings are relatively ~.*

information *noun*

ADJ. **accurate, correct, precise** | **authoritative, credible, reliable** | **erroneous, false, inaccurate, incorrect** ◇ *It is alleged that he gave false ~ to the tax authorities.* | **misleading** | **conflicting** | **complete** | **incomplete, insufficient** | **limited** | **unbiased** | **helpful, invaluable, pertinent** (*esp. AmE*), **relevant, useful, valuable** | **critical, crucial, important, vital** | **useless** | **necessary** | **timely** | **available** ◇ *Further ~ is available on request.* | **missing** | **fresh, new, latest, up-to-date, up-to-the-minute** ◇ *the latest ~ on the situation in the Middle East* | **updated** | **real-time** | **additional, extra, further, supplementary** | **general** ◇ *general ~ about the company as a whole* | **basic** ◇ *basic ~ like date of birth and phone number* | **background** | **anecdotal** | **detailed, in-depth** | **specific** | **factual** | **classified, confidential, non-public** (*esp. AmE*), **secret, sensitive** | **unclassified** | **price-sensitive** ◇ *There are legal constraints on the use of price-sensitive ~.* | **actionable** (*AmE*) | **personal** | **bibliographic, biographical, economic, educational, financial, social, technical, technological** (*AmE*), etc. | **contact** ◇ *The leaflet provides contact ~ for your local branch.* | **intelligence** | **health** | **medical, patient** | **genetic**

... OF INFORMATION **item, piece** ◇ *an interesting piece of ~* | **bit, fragment, nugget, scrap, snippet** ◇ *She let slip a few nuggets of ~ about herself.* | **mine, wealth** ◇ *This book is a mine of ~ on the Romans.*

VERB + INFORMATION contain | have ◊ *Do you have the ~ I need?* | retain, store ◊ *James is able to retain an enormous amount of factual ~ in his head.* ◊ *database systems that process and store ~.* | absorb, digest | process | incorporate, integrate (*esp. AmE*) | need, require | ask for, request, solicit | look for, seek | acquire, derive, find, gain, get, glean, obtain ◊ *~ gained from research* | collect, compile, gather ◊ *The police are still questioning witnesses and gathering ~.* | receive | dig up, uncover ◊ *Have you dug up any further ~ on the suspect?* | elicit, extract, retrieve ◊ *the difficulties of extracting ~ from government officials* ◊ *software that retrieves ~ from a variety of different sources* | access ◊ *Portable computers are good for accessing ~ while on the move.* | download, upload | post ◊ *New ~ will be posted on the Internet twice a month.* | add | submit | disclose, divulge, give, impart, make available, provide (sb with), release, reveal, supply (sb with) ◊ *a court order preventing an ex-employee from disclosing confidential ~* | leak ◊ *Someone leaked ~ to the press.* | communicate, convey, pass on, relate, relay ◊ *They passed on the ~ about the crime to the police.* | transfer, transmit | deliver | forward | yield ◊ *The research has yielded a lot of ~.* | share ◊ *The Internet allows us to share ~ with our distributors.* | circulate, disseminate, distribute ◊ *an organization that disseminates ~ about women in science* | exchange ◊ *The two countries exchange ~ on wanted criminals.* | offer, volunteer ◊ *She didn't volunteer that ~, and I didn't ask.* | withhold ◊ *It was improper of the broker to withhold the ~ from the stock exchange.* | cover up, suppress | assimilate, collate, organize | check, verify | analyse/analyze, interpret | review | record | protect, safeguard | display, present ◊ *The way you present the ~ is important.* | publish | use, utilize | act on, go on ◊ *At the moment we have very little ~ to go on.*
INFORMATION + VERB pertain to sth, relate to sth ◊ *~ relating to the social background of the child* | lead to sth ◊ *a reward for ~ leading to an arrest* | contain sth, include sth | flow ◊ *The ~ flows in both directions.*
INFORMATION + NOUN provider, service | booth (*esp. AmE*), bureau, desk, centre/center, kiosk, office | manager, officer, professional, specialist | source | content | resources | pack (*esp. BrE*), packet (*esp. AmE*), sheet | database | network, system | technology (usually *IT*) | processing | management | provision | dissemination | flow | exchange, sharing | retrieval | request | needs, requirements | overload | gap | warfare | security | age ◊ *This is the ~ age and there's an insatiable appetite for data and speed.* | revolution
PREP. according to ◊ *According to ~ received by the police, the terrorists have left the country.* | for sb's ~ ◊ *This leaflet is produced for the ~ of our customers.* | ~ about, ~ concerning, ~ on, ~ regarding ◊ *financial ~ concerning a company*
PHRASES access to ~ | the exchange of ~ | the flow of ~ ◊ *to improve the flow of ~ within the company* | a lack of ~ | a request for ~ | a source of ~

informative *adj.*

VERBS be, prove | find sth
ADV. extremely, fairly, very, etc. | highly, wonderfully (*esp. AmE*) ◊ *The survey proved highly ~.* | especially, particularly | potentially
PREP. about ◊ *The book is extremely ~ about life in Roman times.*

informed *adj.*

VERBS be | keep, stay | keep sb
ADV. closely, well ◊ *The kids are much better ~ than I was at their age.* | fully, properly, truly ◊ *Consumers must be fully ~ of the services available.* | adequately, reasonably ◊ *I offer my observations as those of an interested and reasonably ~ member of the general public.* | badly, ill, poorly | reliably ◊ *I am reliably ~ that there are plans to close this school.* |

politically ◊ *a politically ~ public* | historically, theoretically ◊ *theoretically ~ research*
PREP. about ◊ *They were poorly ~ about their rights.* | of ◊ *We will keep you ~ of any developments.* | on ◊ *Keep me ~ on progress.*

informer *noun*

ADJ. police (*esp. BrE*) ◊ *He later became a police ~.*
VERB + INFORMER become, turn (*esp. BrE*) ◊ *One of the gang members had turned ~.*
PHRASES a network of ~s

infringement *noun*

ADJ. alleged | possible | copyright, patent, trademark | serious | minor | unconstitutional (*esp. AmE*)
VERB + INFRINGEMENT be, constitute ◊ *The committee ruled that the US ban constituted an ~ of free trade.* | commit (*esp. BrE*) ◊ *sympathy for people who commit minor ~s*
PHRASES an ~ of copyright, an ~ of the law

ingenuity *noun*

ADJ. considerable, great | a little | technical | human | American, Yankee (*both AmE*)
... OF INGENUITY amount, degree ◊ *Getting out of this mess was going to require a fair degree of ~.*
VERB + INGENUITY have ◊ *someone who has the ~ to solve problems* | use ◊ *There is always a solution, so long as you are prepared to use your ~.* | demonstrate, display, show ◊ *The children showed a lot of ~.* | admire | require, take ◊ *Considerable ~ is needed to minimize costs.* ◊ *It didn't take much ~ to transform the door into a table.*
PREP. with ◊ *They adapted the available materials with great ~.* | ~ in ◊ *We have to admire his ~ in redesigning the machinery.*

ingredient *noun*

1 thing from which sth is made
ADJ. excellent, good, high-quality, quality ◊ *It always pays to use the best ~s when cooking.* | main, major, primary (*esp. AmE*), principal ◊ *the principal ~ of smog* | essential, important, vital | secret, special | basic | added, additional | individual ◊ *the chemical composition of the individual ~s* | common | active, functional (*AmE*) ◊ *salicylic acid, the active ~ in aspirin* | inert | remaining ◊ *Add all the remaining ~s and bring to the boil.* | fresh | all-natural (*esp. AmE*), natural | organic | toxic | artificial, synthetic | genetically engineered, genetically modified | exotic | local | herbal (*esp. AmE*) | dry, wet ◊ *Use a spoon to mix the dry ~s.* | raw | food | dietary (*AmE*) | salad | chemical
VERB + INGREDIENT use ◊ *I only use natural ~s.* | contain, include ◊ *The two drugs contain the same active ~s.* | add, pour ◊ *Pour all of the ~s into a blender.* | blend, combine, mix, stir, stir in ◊ *Blend all the ~s together in a bowl.* | assemble | prepare | list
INGREDIENT + NOUN list | label (*AmE*)
PHRASES a list of ~s ◊ *All food products carry a list of ~s.*
→ Special page at FOOD

2 thing/quality necessary to make sth successful
ADJ. critical, crucial, essential, fundamental, important, key, vital ◊ *Hard work is a vital ~ for success.* | main, major, primary (*esp. AmE*), principal | basic, fundamental, necessary ◊ *Forecasting is a basic ~ of business planning.* | right ◊ *The town has all the right ~s for a murder mystery.* | magic, secret, special | added, additional, extra | missing
VERB + INGREDIENT have ◊ *The Australian team had the added ~ of perseverance.* | become | provide, supply ◊ *She hopes the change of career will supply the missing ~ in her life—excitement.* | incorporate ◊ *a style which incorporated ~s from the music of many different countries*
PREP. for ◊ *Tolerance is an essential ~ for a happy marriage.* | ~ in ◊ *Individualism has been the secret ~ in developing his chain of fashion stores.*
PHRASES an ~ for success

inhabitant noun

ADJ. **local** | **early, first, original** ◊ *The island's earliest ~s came from India.* | **aboriginal, indigenous, native** | **human** | **current, present** | **former** | **permanent** | **rural**
VERB + INHABITANT **have** ◊ *São Paulo has nearly 20 million ~s.*
INHABITANT + VERB **live** ◊ *77% of the ~s lived in the countryside.*
PREP. **of … ~, with … ~** ◊ *towns of about 10 000 ~s*

inhale verb

ADV. **deeply** | **sharply** ◊ *Janet ~d sharply when she saw him.* | **quickly, slowly**

inherit verb

VERB + INHERIT **stand to** ◊ *He stood to ~ (= was likely to inherit) property worth over five million.*
PREP. **from** ◊ *She ~ed some money from her mother.*
PHRASES **be genetically ~ed** ◊ *How many of these traits are genetically ~ed?*

inheritance noun

1 money/property
ADJ. **large** | **small** | **rightful** *(literary)* ◊ *He accused his younger brother of trying to steal his rightful ~.*
VERB + INHERITANCE **leave sb** ◊ *She left him an ~ of £100 000.* | **come into, get, receive** ◊ *When he was 21 he came into a large ~.* | **have** ◊ *He had a large ~ from his parents.* | **enter, enter into, enter on, enter upon** *(all formal, often figurative)* | **claim** ◊ *When his father died, he returned to England to claim his ~.* | **lose**
INHERITANCE + NOUN **tax** | **law** | **rights**
PREP. **~ by** ◊ *The system involved ~ by the eldest son.* | **~ through** ◊ *~ through marriage*
2 sth from the past/your family
ADJ. **common** ◊ *The inhabitants share a common ~ of language and culture.* | **cultural** | **genetic**

inhibit verb

ADV. **greatly, markedly, seriously, severely, significantly, strongly** ◊ *Alcohol significantly ~s the action of the drug.* | **directly** | **completely** | **selectively, specifically** | **partially, slightly** | **effectively**
VERB + INHIBIT **tend to** ◊ *A small manufacturing sector would tend to ~ growth.*
PREP. **from** ◊ *The fear of dismissal ~ed employees from raising problems.*

inhibited adj.

VERBS **be, feel** | **become**
ADV. **extremely, fairly, very, etc.** | **a little, slightly, etc.** | **emotionally**
PREP. **about** ◊ *He was rather ~ about discussing politics.* | **by** ◊ *She felt very ~ by her own lack of experience.* | **from** ◊ *No one should feel ~ from taking part in the show.*

inhibition noun

VERB + INHIBITION **have (no)** | **show (no)** | **lose, overcome, shed** ◊ *The children, at first shy, soon lost their ~s.*
PREP. **without ~** ◊ *Young children will participate in a drama class without ~.* | **~ about** ◊ *They had no ~s about voicing their feelings.*

inhuman adj.

VERBS **be** | **consider sth, regard sth as** ◊ *We regard their treatment of the prisoners as ~.*
ADV. **totally, utterly** | **almost**

initial noun (usually initials)

VERB + INITIAL **have** ◊ *The two authors have the same ~s.* | **be known by, become known by** ◊ *She's always been known by her ~s.* | **use** | **bear, carry** *(esp. BrE)* ◊ *A stone bears the ~s 'R.P.', which stand for 'Ralph Piggot'.* | **carve, embroider, engrave (sth with), mark sth with, put, sign, write** ◊ *He carved his ~s in the rock.* ◊ *Now that she was chief executive officer, she could put the ~s CEO after her name.*
INITIAL + VERB **stand for sth**
PREP. **~ for** ◊ *SC are the ~s for Santa Catarina.*

initiation noun

INITIATION + NOUN **ceremony, rite, ritual** ◊ *an ~ ceremony for new members of the organization* | **process** | **phase, stage** | **fee** *(AmE)* ◊ *The gym charges an ~ fee of $125.*
PREP. **~ into** ◊ *It was my ~ into the world of high fashion.*
PHRASES **a rite of ~**

initiative noun

1 new plan
ADJ. **fresh, new** ◊ *fresh ~s to find a peaceful end to the conflict* | **innovative, pioneering** ◊ *pioneering ~s in bioengineering* | **current, latest, recent** | **proposed** | **ongoing** | **important, major** | **welcome** | **successful** | **practical** | **bold, exciting** | **private** | **collaborative, cooperative, joint** | **grass-roots** | **global, international, local, national, regional, statewide** *(AmE)* | **federal** *(AmE)*, **government, presidential** *(AmE)* | **strategic** | **business, e-business, e-commerce, marketing** | **diplomatic, economic, legislative, peace, policy, political** | **safety, training** | **development, research** | **education, educational, health** | **conservation, environmental** | **faith-based** *(esp. AmE)* | **community-based** *(esp. AmE)* | **outreach** | **reform** | **ballot** *(AmE)*
... OF INITIATIVES **range, series**
VERB + INITIATIVE **undertake** ◊ *The research ~ is being undertaken by a group of environmentalists.* | **plan** | **develop** | **announce, unveil** | **create, implement, introduce, launch, set up, start** ◊ *The government has launched a new policy ~.* | **be involved in** ◊ *Ten schools have been involved in the ~.* | **become involved in, get involved in** | **pursue** | **expand** | **lead, spearhead** | **approve, pass** | **oppose** | **defeat, reject** ◊ *The peace ~ was rejected out of hand.* | **fund, sponsor** ◊ *a peace ~ sponsored by the Organization of African Unity* | **back, endorse, support** ◊ *The committee endorsed an ~ by the chairman to enter discussion about a possible merger.* | **promote, push** | **welcome** ◊ *We welcome the government's ~ to help the homeless.* | **encourage**
INITIATIVE + VERB **be aimed at sth, be designed to** ◊ *a local ~ aimed at economic regeneration* ◊ *an ~ designed to promote collaborative research* | **seek to do sth** | **focus on sth** | **include sth, involve sth, relate to sth** | **fail, founder** ◊ *The ~ foundered because there was no market interest in redevelopment.*
PREP. **~ against** ◊ *a new ~ against car theft* | **~ by** ◊ *the latest ~ by the UN Secretary General* | **~ for** ◊ *an ~ for peace and human rights* | **~ on** ◊ *the government's major new ~ on crime*
→ Special page at BUSINESS
2 ability to decide/act independently
ADJ. **great, real** | **individual, personal, private** ◊ *It is a very hierarchical company and there's little place for individual ~.*
VERB + INITIATIVE **have** ◊ *He had the ~ to ask what time the last train left.* | **display, show** | **act on your own, use, work on your own** ◊ *He acted on his own ~ and wasn't following orders.* ◊ *Don't ask me what you should do all the time. Use your ~!* | **encourage, promote** | **stifle** ◊ *Raising taxes on small businesses will stifle ~.*
PREP. **on sb's ~** ◊ *The project was set up on the ~ of a local landowner.* | **~ in** ◊ *Some scientists show little ~ in applying their knowledge.*
PHRASES **a lack of ~, on your own ~** ◊ *In an unprecedented action, the army, on its own ~, arrested seven civilians.*
3 the initiative opportunity to gain an advantage
VERB + THE INITIATIVE **have, hold** ◊ *After their latest setback, the rebel forces no longer hold the ~.* | **gain, seize, take** | **maintain, retain** | **regain** ◊ *She then regained the ~ in winning the third game.* | **lose**

injection

~ ankle ◇ *Several people were seriously ~.* | **slightly** ◇ *a slightly ~ arm* | **fatally** | **physically** | **permanently**

THE INITIATIVE + VERB **come from sb/sth, lie with sb** ◇ *The ~ to reopen negotiations came from Moscow.*
PREP. **~ in** ◇ *She took the ~ in asking the board to conduct an enquiry.*

injection *noun*

1 act of injecting sb

ADJ. **intramuscular, intravenous** | **painkilling** | **tetanus** (*esp. BrE*) (usually ***tetanus shot*** *in AmE*) | **insulin, penicillin,** etc. | **Botox™, collagen** | **booster** (*esp. BrE*) (usually ***booster shot*** in *AmE*) ◇ *Can I bring my dog in for his booster ~?* | **lethal** ◇ *In some states execution is by lethal ~.* | **regular** | **daily, weekly**
VERB + INJECTION **have** ◇ *He had to have a tetanus ~ after injuring himself.* (*esp. BrE*) | **administer, give sb, perform** ◇ *They gave her an ~ to stop the pain.* (*esp. BrE*) | **get, receive** ◇ *The rats received a daily ~ of the drug.*
PREP. **by ~** ◇ *The best treatment is antibiotics, preferably by ~.* | **~ against** ◇ *an ~ against whooping cough* | **~ for** ◇ *~s for diabetes* | **~ in, ~ into** ◇ *an ~ into the vein* | **~ with** ◇ *Both groups received a second ~ with the same solution.*

2 money

ADJ. **massive, substantial** (*BrE*) ◇ *The infrastrucure requires a massive cash ~.* | **much-needed** | **capital, cash** ◇ *An undisclosed buyer will provide a much-needed cash ~ for the fragile balance sheet.*
VERB + INJECTION **need, require** | **give sth, provide (sth with)** | **get, receive**
PREP. **~ from** ◇ *a cash ~ from the state* | **~ into** ◇ *an ~ of cash into the economy*
PHRASES **an ~ of capital, cash, resources,** etc. ◇ *The company had reached the size where it needed an ~ of capital.*

injunction *noun*

1 court order

ADJ. **interim, preliminary** | **temporary** | **permanent** | **court** | **federal**
VERB + INJUNCTION **apply for, seek** | **file** (*esp. AmE*), **get, obtain, take out** (*BrE*), **win** ◇ *She took out an ~ to prevent the press publishing the information.* | **grant (sb), impose, issue** | **refuse (sb/sth)** (*esp. BrE*) | **lift** ◇ *It was agreed that the temporary ~ should be lifted.* | **uphold** | **overturn**
INJUNCTION + VERB **order sth, require sth** | **ban sth, prevent sth, prohibit sth, restrain sb/sth** (*esp. BrE*) ◇ *The court upheld an ~ barring protesters from blocking access to the company.* ◇ *an ~ restraining the disclosure of company secrets*
PREP. **~ against, ~ on** ◇ *They got an interim ~ against the union.*
PHRASES **a breach of an ~**

2 warning/order from sb in authority

ADJ. **stern**
VERB + INJUNCTION **follow, obey** ◇ *The rank and file members will follow the ~ of the party leadership.* | **ignore**

injure *verb*

1 harm yourself/sb physically

ADV. **badly, seriously, severely** | **slightly** | **physically** | **accidentally** ◇ *insurance to cover you in case one of your employees accidentally ~s someone* | **deliberately** | **permanently**

2 damage sb's reputation, pride, etc.

ADV. **seriously, severely** ◇ *This incident could seriously ~ the company's reputation.*
VERB + INJURE **be likely to** ◇ *espionage activity which was likely to ~ the national interest*

injured *adj.*

VERBS **be, lie** ◇ *He could have been lying ~ on the moors after a fall from his horse.* | **get**
ADV. **badly, critically, gravely, seriously, severely** ◇ *her badly*

~ ankle ◇ *Several people were seriously ~.* | **slightly** ◇ *a slightly ~ arm* | **fatally** | **physically** | **permanently**

injury *noun*

ADJ. **appalling** (*esp. BrE*), **bad, catastrophic, devastating, horrendous, major, nasty, serious, severe, terrible** | **crippling** | **fatal** | **multiple** | **extensive** | **minor, slight, superficial** | **traumatic** | **acute** | **old** | **lingering** (*esp. AmE*), **nagging, niggling** (*esp. BrE*), **recurring** | **long-term** | **permanent** ◇ *Researchers have determined that heading a football can cause permanent ~.* | **career-ending** (*esp. AmE*), **career-threatening, season-ending** (*esp. AmE*) (*all sports*) | **accidental** | **internal** | **visible** | **facial, head, knee, leg, spinal,** etc. | **burn, whiplash** | **sports, sports-related** | **industrial, work-related** | **overuse** (*esp. AmE*), **repetitive strain** (abbreviated to ***RSI***) | **bodily, emotional, personal** (*all law*)
... OF INJURIES **run, series, spate** ◇ *He missed most of the season with a spate of injuries.*
VERB + INJURY **do yourself** (*BrE, informal*), **incur** (*formal*), **pick up, receive, suffer, sustain** ◇ *You'll do yourself an ~ riding that old bike.* ◇ *She picked up an ~ during the quarter-final.* | **risk** ◇ *The doctor said he would risk serious ~ if he were to fall again.* | **cause (sb/sth), induce** (*formal*), **inflict** ◇ *The car turned right over, causing severe ~ to the driver.* ◇ *Please help me before our dogs inflict serious ~ on each other!* | **carry, experience, have, nurse, suffer from** ◇ *She has replaced him in the team while he nurses a shoulder ~.* | **be prone to** | **fake, feign** ◇ *He was accused of feigning ~.* | **aggravate, exacerbate** ◇ *He aggravated a neck ~ while playing for Derby County.* | **die from, die of** ◇ *The inquest heard that he died from multiple injuries.* | **avoid, escape, prevent** ◇ *Stretching exercises can help avoid ~.* ◇ *Fortunately, the passengers escaped serious ~.* | **minimize, reduce** (*esp. AmE*) | **overcome, shake off** ◇ *She has failed to shake off her stomach ~.* | **recover from, survive** | **be treated for, deal with, treat** ◇ *Finger injuries should be dealt with immediately.* ◇ *He is still being treated for injuries to his legs.* | **rehabilitate** | **heal** | **come, go,** etc. **off with** (*BrE*) ◇ *He went off (= off the playing field) with an ~ in the second half.* | **be out with** ◇ *She is out (= out of the competition/team) for six weeks with a hamstring ~.* | **be back after, be back from, come back from, return after, return from** ◇ *She should be back from ~.* | **assess** ◇ *He underwent tests to assess his injuries.* | **report**
INJURY + VERB **happen (to sb), occur** ◇ *This type of ~ could happen to any player at any time.* | **result from sth** ◇ *injuries resulting from exposure to harmful substances* | **arise from sth, arise out of sth** (*both law*) ◇ *personal injuries arising from negligence* | **cause sth** | **heal** | **affect sb/sth, bother sb, dog sb/sth, hamper sb/sth, plague sb/sth, trouble sb** ◇ *Her athletics career has been dogged by ~.* | **rob sb of sth** ◇ *an ~ which robbed him of his speed* | **decimate sb/sth** | **end sth, prevent sth** ◇ *These injuries ended her hopes of becoming a doctor.* | **slow sb down** | **limit sb to sth** | **sideline sb** ◇ *Both defenders have been sidelined by ~.* | **force sb to do sth** ◇ *The knee ~ forced him to give up playing at the age of 23.*
INJURY + NOUN **problems** ◇ *The team has a lot of ~ problems.* | **site** (*esp. AmE*) ◇ *Apply the gel to the ~ site.* | **time** (*BrE*) ◇ *They scored two goals in ~ time.* | **replacement** ◇ *He was an ~ replacement for another player.* | **list** ◇ *a player on the ~ list* | **risk** | **prevention** | **history** | **rate** | **report** | **case, claim, lawsuit** (*esp. AmE*), **suit** (*AmE*)
PREP. **because of ~** ◇ *She's unable to play because of ~.* | **through ~** ◇ *McNair continues to play through ~* (= despite having an injury). | **with ~** ◇ *He pulled out with an ~ at the last moment.* | **without ~** ◇ *a guide to lifting without ~* | **~ from** ◇ *injuries from the fire* | **~ to**
PHRASES **a claim for ~** (*law*) ◇ *a claim for personal ~* | **a risk of ~** ◇ *There is a real risk of ~ in sports such as climbing.*

injustice *noun*

ADJ. **grave, great, gross, terrible** | **perceived** | **economic, environmental, historical, political, racial, social**
VERB + INJUSTICE **experience, suffer** ◇ *He suffered the ~ of being punished for a crime which he did not commit.* |

regard sth as ◇ *The trial was regarded as the greatest ~ of the post-war criminal justice system.* | **cause** (*law*), **commit, do** (**sb/yourself**) ◇ *She remains adamant that an ~ was done.* ◇ *We may have been doing him an ~. This work is good.* | **expose** ◇ *a novel that sets out to expose social ~* | **see** ◇ *They see the ~ and want to help.* | **fight, fight against, protest** (*AmE*), **protest against, speak out against, struggle against** ◇ *She was acclaimed for speaking out against ~.* | **correct, rectify, redress, remedy** ◇ *people who work hard to correct society's ~s* | **stop**
PREP. **~ by** ◇ *a terrible ~ by the police* | **~ to** ◇ *It would be an ~ to the man to imprison him for life.*
PHRASES **the ~ of it all** ◇ *She was overwhelmed by the ~ of it all* (= of the situation). | **a sense of ~, a victim of ~**

ink *noun*
ADJ. **wet** ◇ *Be careful. The ~ is still wet.* | **coloured/colored** | **black, red, etc.** | **dark** | **India** (*esp. AmE*), **Indian** (*esp. BrE*) | **squid** | **indelible, permanent** | **invisible** | **printing** | **printer** | **pigment** (*AmE*) | **tattoo**
VERB + INK **use** ◇ *Most people now use ballpoints rather than ~.* | **write in** ◇ *He wrote very neatly in blue ~.* | **apply** | **spill** | **smear, smudge**
INK + VERB **dry** ◇ *Allow the ~ to dry.*
INK + NOUN **blot, spot, stain** | **pen** | **cartridge** ◇ *We need to replace the ~ cartridge in the printer.* | **bottle** | **pad** (usually **ink-pad**) | **drawing**
PREP. **in ~** ◇ *There were several alterations in ~.*
PHRASES **pen and ~** ◇ *a pen-and-ink drawing*

inkling *noun*
ADJ. **first** ◇ *The first ~ we had of Cliff's problem was when he didn't come to work.* | **faintest, slightest** ◇ *We didn't have the slightest ~ of the dramatic news we were about to hear.*
VERB + INKLING **have (no)** | **get** | **give (sb)** ◇ *She never gave us any ~ of what she was planning.*
PREP. **~ of**

inmate *noun*
ADJ. **fellow** | **former** ◇ *a former ~ of an Ohio prison* | **new** | **young** | **female, male** | **camp, jail** (*esp. AmE*), **prison** | **federal, state** (*both AmE*) | **death-row** | **asylum**
VERB + INMATE **transfer** (*esp. AmE*) ◇ *The ~s were transferred to an undisclosed location.* | **free, release** | **house** ◇ *a camp where more than 4 000 ~s are housed*
INMATE + VERB **escape** (*esp. AmE*) | **serve sth** ◇ *~s serving lengthy terms*
INMATE + NOUN **population** (*esp. AmE*)
PREP. **among ~** ◇ *drug and alcohol misuse among ~s*

inn *noun*
ADJ. **local** | **country** | **old, quaint** | **roadside** | **bed-and-breakfast** (*AmE*)
VERB + INN **stay at, stay in** | **own, run**

innocence *noun*
1 being not guilty of a crime, etc.
ADJ. **total**
VERB + INNOCENCE **declare, proclaim, profess** ◇ *The prisoners passionately proclaimed their ~ in front of the jury.* | **claim, plead** ◇ *She claimed total ~ of all charges.* | **maintain** ◇ *He has maintained his ~ throughout the trial.* | **protest** ◇ *Hayes has protested his ~ throughout the case.* | **demonstrate, establish, prove** | **be convinced of** ◇ *She was convinced of her son's ~.*
PHRASES **in all ~** ◇ *I asked her the question in all ~. I didn't know it was going to upset her.* | **the presumption of ~** (*law*)
2 lack of knowledge/experience
ADJ. **childish, childlike, wide-eyed, youthful** | **childhood** | **lost** | **complete, pure** | **sweet** | **injured** ◇ *She replied to her father's accusations in tones of injured ~.* | **apparent** | **false, feigned, mock**
VERB + INNOCENCE **lose** ◇ *He had lost the ~ of childhood.* | **retain** | **take advantage of** ◇ *She had taken advantage of his ~.* | **feign**

PREP. **in your ~** ◇ *In her ~, she had allowed the man into her house.* | **with … ~** ◇ *He grinned with apparent ~.* | **~ about** ◇ *There is an ~ about the story.*
PHRASES **an air of ~** ◇ *There was a touching air of ~ about the boy.* | **a look of ~, the picture of ~** ◇ *'You cheated!' 'I what?' asked David, the picture of ~* (= pretending to look innocent). | **a state of ~**

innocent *adj.*
1 not guilty
VERBS **be, plead** ◇ *He pleaded ~ to the charges.* | **believe sb, presume sb** ◇ *I had always believed her ~.* ◇ *The accused person should always be presumed ~ until proved guilty.* | **declare sb, find sb, prove sb** ◇ *The court found her ~ of the crime.*
ADV. **completely, entirely, totally, wholly** (*esp. BrE*)
PREP. **of** ◇ *I am totally ~ of this crime.*
2 not intended/intending to cause harm
VERBS **act** (*esp. AmE*), **appear, be, look, play, seem, sound** ◇ *Stop playing ~ and answer my questions, please.*
ADV. **very** | **all, perfectly** ◇ *She tried to sound all ~ as she asked the question.* ◇ *The circumstance could be perfectly ~, but suspicions have been raised.* | **relatively** | **apparently, seemingly**
3 with no experience of the world
VERBS **act, appear, be, seem** ◇ *She was sixteen and sweetly ~.*
ADV. **very** | **sweetly** | **deceptively** ◇ *He came across as deceptively ~ and childlike.* | **sexually**
PHRASES **sweet and ~** ◇ *Don't be fooled by them acting all sweet and ~.*

innocuous *adj.*
VERBS **appear, be, look, seem**
ADV. **perfectly, totally** ◇ *His comment seemed perfectly ~.* | **fairly, pretty, quite, relatively** ◇ *The liquid looked fairly ~.* | **enough** ◇ *The question appeared ~ enough, but I still did not trust her.* | **apparently, seemingly**

innovation *noun*
1 introduction of new ideas
ADJ. **constant, continuous** | **successful** | **architectural, artistic, cultural, educational, industrial, musical, organizational, scientific, stylistic, technical, technological** | **design, policy, product** ◇ *industries where constant product ~ is a criterion for survival*
VERB + INNOVATION **accelerate, encourage, facilitate, foster, promote, spur, stimulate** | **discourage, stifle** ◇ *Too strict a regulatory system will stifle ~.*
INNOVATION + VERB **happen, occur** ◇ *Technical ~ may occur directly in the factory.*
INNOVATION + NOUN **process**
PREP. **~ in** ◇ *~ in engineering*
2 new idea
ADJ. **great, important, major, significant** | **breakthrough, radical, revolutionary** | **successful** | **welcome** | **interesting** | **latest, new** | **recent** | **scientific, technical, technological, etc.** | **methodological, stylistic** ◇ *His last novel pays tribute to Joyce's stylistic ~s.*
VERB + INNOVATION **come up with** ◇ *She believed she had come up with one of the greatest ~s of modern times.* | **introduce** ◇ *Many ~s were introduced by the 1919 Act.* | **design, develop** ◇ *technological ~s designed to save energy*
INNOVATION + VERB **occur**
PREP. **~ in** ◇ *~s in machinery and instruments*

input *noun*
1 of time/knowledge/ideas
ADJ. **great, important, major, significant, substantial** | **additional** | **direct** | **local** | **specialist** (*BrE*), **technical** | **customer, user** ◇ *We have made some adjustments based on user ~.*

VERB + INPUT **have | need, require** ◊ *Once running, the system requires very little ~.* | **appreciate, value, welcome** ◊ *If you have ideas for improvements, your ~ is always appreciated.* | **seek, solicit** ◊ *We actively solicit ~ from our users.* | **get, receive | provide** ◊ *constructive criticism which provided an ~ into the school's decision-making process*
PREP. **~ by** ◊ *The report contains substantial ~ by the police.* | **~ from** ◊ *~ from various interested parties* | **~ in** ◊ *They all had some ~ in the discussion.* | **~ into** ◊ *her ~ into the survey* | **~ on** ◊ *The union would like more ~ on working conditions.* | **~ to** ◊ *I have no creative ~ to the projects I work on.*

2 for a computer

ADJ. **data | user | keyboard | analogue/analog, digital | audio, video** ◊ *There's the socket for audio ~.*
VERB + INPUT **require** ◊ *Early computers required ~ in the form of punched cards.* | **accept** ◊ *The software will accept ~ from a variety of other programs.* | **process** ◊ *It may be beyond the capability of the hardware to process the ~.* | **be used as, be used for** ◊ *Decision tables can be used as computer ~.* | **check** ◊ *Check your ~ and make sure you have selected only one item.*
INPUT + NOUN **data | file | field, form** ◊ *The cursor is positioned on the first ~ field of the page.* | **device** ◊ *an ~ device such as a keyboard*
PREP. **~ for** ◊ *~s for the printers* | **~ from** ◊ *~ from a mouse* | **~ to** ◊ *~ to a computer database*
PHRASES **~ and output**

inquest *noun (esp. BrE)* investigation into cause of death

ADJ. **full | fresh | coroner's**
VERB + INQUEST **conduct, hold | order** ◊ *The court ordered a fresh ~ into the tragedy.* | **open, reopen | adjourn** *(BrE)* | **attend**
INQUEST + VERB **open | hear sth** ◊ *An elderly woman froze to death, an ~ heard yesterday.* | **decide sth, find sth** ◊ *An ~ found that the deceased had died of a drugs overdose.* | **return a verdict** ◊ *The ~ returned a verdict of accidental death.*
INQUEST + NOUN **jury | verdict**
PREP. **at a/the ~** ◊ *A verdict of suicide was recorded at the ~.* | **~ into** ◊ *an ~ into the team's poor performance* | **~ on** ◊ *an ~ on three fishermen*

inquire, inquiry *(esp. AmE)* → See ENQUIRE, ENQUIRY

inquisitive *adj.*

VERBS **appear, be, seem | become**
ADV. **highly, very** ◊ *a highly ~ mind* | **overly** *(esp. AmE)* | **naturally** ◊ *Children are naturally ~.*
PREP. **about** ◊ *We try not to be too ~ about what he's doing.*

insane *adj.*

VERBS **be, look, seem, sound** ◊ *It seems ~ to cut the budget now.* | **become, go** ◊ *He later became ~ and was confined to an asylum.* ◊ *He went almost ~ when he heard that his daughter had died.* | **drive sb** ◊ *You're driving me nearly ~ with that noise.* | **certify sb (as)** *(BrE)*, **declare sb** ◊ *In 1975 she was certified clinically ~ and sent to a mental hospital.*
ADV. **absolutely, completely, quite** *(esp. BrE)*, **seriously** *(esp. AmE)*, **totally, utterly** ◊ *The whole idea is totally ~.* | **literally, truly | almost, nearly | a little, slightly, etc.** | **temporarily** ◊ *She claimed she was temporarily ~ during the attack.* | **clearly, obviously** ◊ *He was clearly ~.* | **mentally** *(esp. AmE)* ◊ *He displays a fearlessness that borders on the mentally ~.* | **certifiably, clinically, legally | criminally** ◊ *He is criminally ~, unable to stop himself from attacking women.*

insanity *noun*

ADJ. **total | temporary**
VERB + INSANITY **plead** ◊ *At the murder trial, he pleaded ~.* | **feign** ◊ *Hamlet feigns ~ to disguise his bloody motive.* | **stop** *(AmE, figurative)* ◊ *Congress has one option to stop this ~.*

INSANITY + NOUN **defence/defense, plea** *(both esp. AmE)* ◊ *His lawyer got him off on an ~ plea.*
PHRASES **by reason of ~** *(law)* ◊ *He was found not guilty by reason of ~.*

inscribe *verb*

ADV. **personally** ◊ *The volume had been personally ~d by the author.* | **deeply** *(figurative, esp. AmE)* ◊ *These notions were deeply ~d in American law.*
PREP. **on** ◊ *Her name was ~d on the watch.* | **with** ◊ *The watch was ~d with her name.*

inscription *noun*

ADJ. **famous | dedicatory, funerary, memorial, monumental | Greek, Latin, etc.**
VERB + INSCRIPTION **bear, carry, have** ◊ *The monument carries the ~: 'To the fallen'.* | **carve, engrave** ◊ *an ~ carved in the stone* | **read** ◊ *I wasn't able to read the ~.*
INSCRIPTION + VERB **bear sth, read sth, record sth, say sth, show sth, tell sb sth** ◊ *The ~ bears the date 1855.* ◊ *The simple ~ on her grave reads: 'She sleeps in peace.'*

insect *noun*

ADJ. **flying, winged | aquatic | beneficial** ◊ *Unfortunately, pesticides kill off beneficial ~s as well as harmful ones.* | **harmful, poisonous | biting, bloodsucking, stinging | social** ◊ *Social ~s, such as ants, live in large colonies.*
...OF INSECTS **swarm**
VERB + INSECT **repel | control, kill, trap | attract**
INSECT + VERB **buzz** ◊ *An ~ was buzzing around the room.* | **fly | crawl | swarm | bore** ◊ *Insects had bored deep into the wood.* | **bite, sting**
INSECT + NOUN **attack, infestation** ◊ *The wood should be treated against ~ attack.* | **bite, sting | eggs, larva | pests** ◊ *Birds control ~ pests.* | **repellent, spray | species | world** ◊ *Wasps are the master builders of the ~ world.*

insecure *adj.*

VERBS **appear, be, feel, look, seem | become, grow | remain**
ADV. **extremely, fairly, very, etc. | deeply, totally** *(esp. AmE)* | **increasingly | a little, slightly, etc. | economically, financially** ◊ *men who are worried about losing their jobs and becoming financially ~* | **notoriously** ◊ *a star who is notoriously ~ about her looks*
PREP. **about** ◊ *He felt a little ~ about being left alone.*

insecurity *noun*

ADJ. **deep, deep-seated, great, profound | growing | general** ◊ *the general ~ in the country* | **economic, financial | emotional | job**
VERB + INSECURITY **hide, mask** ◊ *Perhaps he is just trying to mask his own ~.*
PREP. **~ about** ◊ *her insecurities about her abilities*
PHRASES **a feeling of ~, a sense of ~**

insensitive *adj.*

1 not knowing or caring how sb else feels

VERBS **appear, be, seem, sound** ◊ *It may sound ~, but I don't understand why he's so upset.* | **become, grow | make sb | think sb** ◊ *I don't want to be thought ~, but I do think we should go ahead despite the accident.*
ADV. **extremely, fairly, very, etc. | highly, incredibly, remarkably | crassly** *(BrE)*, **grossly** *(esp. BrE)* | **totally | a little, slightly, etc. | culturally, racially** *(esp. AmE)* ◊ *The decision to serve pork was culturally ~.*
PREP. **to** ◊ *Years of abuse had made him ~ to others' suffering.*

2 not able to feel/be influenced by sth

VERBS **be | remain | make sth/sb, render sth/sb** ◊ *The device renders the system ~ to vibration.*
ADV. **extremely, fairly, very, etc. | completely, totally | almost | largely | relatively** ◊ *Its physical properties are relatively ~ to pressure changes.*
PREP. **to** ◊ *The machine is relatively ~ to changes in the atmosphere.*

insensitivity noun

ADJ. **crass** (BrE), **gross** | **cultural, racial** (esp. AmE) ◇ This was a shocking demonstration of racial ~.
VERB + INSENSITIVITY **display, show**
PREP. **~ to, ~ towards/toward** ◇ The government has shown gross ~ to the refugees.

inseparable adj.

VERBS **be, seem**
ADV. **absolutely, completely, quite** (esp. BrE), **totally** (esp. AmE) | **almost, nearly, practically, virtually** ◇ The two brothers are almost ~. | **effectively**
PREP. **from** ◇ Religion is ~ from politics.

insert verb

ADV. **carefully, gently** | **digitally** ◇ The artist digitally ~ed himself into the picture. | **automatically** ◇ The program will automatically ~ the replacement text.
PREP. **between** ◇ The English translation is ~ed between the lines of text. | **in, into** ◇ Fine needles are gently ~ed into the patient's skin. | **through** ◇ A probe was ~ed through his mouth.

insight noun

ADJ. **considerable, great, real, significant** | **deep, profound** | **detailed** | **brief** | **brilliant, good, remarkable** ◇ The objective of the research is to gain a better ~ into market forces. | **keen, illuminating, penetrating, perceptive, revealing** | **crucial, important, invaluable, valuable** | **helpful, useful** | **fascinating, interesting** | **startling** | **fresh, new, novel** | **original, unique** ◇ Freud's original ~s into the working of the mind | **rare** | **clear** | **basic, fundamental** | **direct, instant** ◇ The research will provide direct ~ into molecular mechanisms. | **additional, further** | **personal** | **critical, historical, psychological, spiritual, theoretical**
... OF INSIGHT **flash** ◇ With a flash of ~, she found the solution to the problem. | **degree, level**
VERB + INSIGHT **have** ◇ The experienced specialist has professional skills and ~. | **lack** | **show** | **afford (sb), allow (sb), give (sb), lend, offer (sb), produce, provide (sb with), yield** ◇ The letters lend some ~ into her writing process. | **gain, garner** (esp. AmE), **get, glean, obtain** | **apply** ◇ Teachers have to apply in the classroom the ~s that they gain in educational courses. | **share** ◇ We meet regularly to discuss working methods and share ~s.
PREP. **~ about** ◇ Schopenhauer's ~ about music | **~ into** ◇ a fresh ~ into Picasso's mind | **~ as to, ~ to** ◇ an ~ as to how the gene works
PHRASES **a lack of ~**

insignificance noun

ADJ. **relative**
VERB + INSIGNIFICANCE **fade into, pale into** ◇ Her achievements fade into ~ beside those of her sisters.

insignificant adj.

VERBS **appear, be, feel, look, seem** ◇ He made her feel ~. | **become** | **remain** | **consider sth, deem sth** ◇ an event that was considered ~
ADV. **very** | **completely, quite, utterly** | **almost** | **fairly, rather, relatively** | **apparently, seemingly** | **clinically, statistically** ◇ These results are statistically ~.

insinuation noun

ADJ. **veiled**
VERB + INSINUATION **make** | **resent** ◇ I deeply resent the ~ that I'm only interested in the money.
PREP. **~ about** ◇ Why did you make those veiled ~s about me? | **~ against** ◇ ~s against the unsuccessful candidate

insist verb

ADV. **firmly, strongly, vehemently** | **adamantly** (esp. AmE), **doggedly, steadfastly, stubbornly** ◇ He stubbornly ~ed on doing it all himself. | **absolutely** ◇ I'm paying for this—no, I

absolutely ~. | **loudly, quietly** ◇ She loudly ~ed that she had a right to stay. ◇ He quietly but firmly ~ed. | **always** | **repeatedly** | **still** ◇ She still ~s her critics are wrong. | **rightly** ◇ People rightly ~ on being treated as individuals.
VERB + INSIST **continue to** | **try to**
PREP. **on, upon** ◇ He ~s on speaking to you personally.

insistence noun

ADJ. **dogged, dogmatic, stubborn** | **constant, continued, repeated** ◇ their repeated ~ that the trial be held in a US court | **earlier**
VERB + INSISTENCE **abandon, drop** ◇ The union has dropped its earlier ~ that workers should receive bonus payments.
PREP. **at sb's ~, on sb's ~** ◇ At the ~ of his father, he bought himself a new suit. | **~ by** ◇ the ~ by the government that 25% of all household waste be recycled | **~ on, ~ upon** ◇ an ~ upon the highest standards of grammatical correctness

insistent adj.

VERBS **be** | **become, grow** | **remain**
ADV. **most, quite, very** ◇ She was most ~ that we shouldn't leave the door unlocked.
PREP. **about** ◇ She was ~ about inviting him. | **on, upon** ◇ He was ~ on a formal written agreement.

insoluble adj.

1 (esp. BrE) (AmE usually **insolvable**) that cannot be solved/explained
VERBS **be, seem** ◇ The problem seemed ~. | **remain**
ADV. **almost** | **apparently, seemingly**
2 impossible to dissolve in a liquid
VERBS **be**
ADV. **highly** | **relatively** | **almost, practically, virtually**
PREP. **in** ◇ These chemicals are practically ~ in water.

inspect verb

ADV. **carefully, closely, thoroughly** | **manually, physically, visually** ◇ The first step is to visually ~ the ground, looking for rocks and lumps. | **annually, periodically, regularly**
VERB + INSPECT **allow sb to, be entitled to** (BrE) ◇ Each party in the case is entitled to ~ the documents held by the other.
PREP. **for** ◇ He ~ed the water tank carefully for cracks.

inspection noun

ADJ. **careful, close, detailed, rigorous, thorough** | **full** | **brief, casual, cursory** | **routine** | **periodic** (esp. AmE), **regular** | **annual, daily, etc.** | **surprise** ◇ a surprise ~ of the premises by the health inspector | **preliminary** | **public** ◇ The records are open to public ~. | **independent** | **international** ◇ They have refused to allow international ~ of their nuclear facilities. | **manual, physical, visual** | **safety** | **medical** | **school** (esp. BrE) | **home** (AmE) (= done before buying a house) ◇ The problem was not discovered during the home ~. ◇ A standard home-inspection report summarizes the condition of the house. | **weapons** ◇ the UN weapons ~ team | **on-site, site** ◇ Following an on-site ~, the surveyor prepared a written report on the property.
VERB + INSPECTION **be available for, be open for, be open to, be subject to** ◇ A company's accounting records must be open for ~ at all times. ◇ Nursing agencies are subject to ~ by the health authority. | **undergo** ◇ All packages arriving at the building undergo an ~. | **carry out, complete, conduct, make, perform** ◇ The architect is carrying out a thorough ~ of the building. | **allow, permit** | **prepare for** | **pass** ◇ The hotel passed its annual ~. | **fail** | **require** ◇ The artwork requires close ~ by the viewer.
INSPECTION + VERB **confirm sth, determine sth, reveal sth, show sth** ◇ A brief ~ revealed it to be a fake. | **suggest sth** | **take place**
INSPECTION + NOUN **tour, visit** | **report** | **procedure, process, regime** (esp. BrE) | **team** | **panel**
PREP. **for ~** ◇ He held out the saucepan for ~. | **on ~, upon ~**

◇ *The report seemed impressive at first, but on closer ~ there were several inaccuracies.* | **~ by** ◇ *an ~ of the troops by the commander-in-chief*
PHRASES **bear close ~, bear ~** ◇ *He knew that his motives would not bear close ~ (= would be revealed as bad if someone inspected them).* | **closer ~ reveals sth, closer ~ shows sth** ◇ *a creature which closer ~ revealed to be a bat* | **a tour of ~** (*esp. BrE*)

inspector *noun*

1 official who inspects sth

ADJ. **chief** | **deputy** | **local** | **international** | **qualified** | **independent** (*esp. BrE*) | **federal** (*esp. AmE*), **government** (*esp. BrE*), **etc.** | **building, customs** (*esp. AmE*), **factory** (*esp. BrE*), **health** (*esp. BrE*), **health and safety** (*BrE*), **home** (*AmE*), **nuclear, planning** (*BrE*), **postal** (*AmE*), **safety** (*esp. BrE*), **school** (*esp. BrE*), **schools** (*BrE*), **tax** (*esp. BrE*), **ticket** (*BrE*), **weapons** ◇ *UN weapons ~s*
VERB + INSPECTOR **call, call in, send, send in** ◇ *Independent ~s were called in.* ◇ *An ~ was sent to the scene of the incident.* | **allow in, let in** ◇ *He agreed to allow weapons ~s in his country.* | **hire** (*AmE*) ◇ *You should hire a professional home ~ before buying.*
INSPECTOR + VERB **arrive, visit** | **be in charge of sth** (*esp. BrE*) ◇ *the ~ in charge of producing the report* | **check sth, look at sth, look for sth** | **report sth, report on sth**
PREP. **~ of** ◇ *an ~ of prisons* (*BrE*)
→ Note at JOB

2 police officer

ADJ. **police** | **Chief, detective** (*both BrE*)
PHRASES **the rank of ~** (*esp. BrE*) ◇ *He reached the rank of ~.*

inspiration *noun*

ADJ. **great, true** ◇ *Then I had a moment of true ~.* | **direct** ◇ *His wife was the direct ~ for the main character in the book.* | **sudden** | **fresh** | **artistic, creative, musical, poetic** | **divine**
... OF INSPIRATION **flash, moment** ◇ *In a flash of ~, I decided to paint the whole house white.*
VERB + INSPIRATION **derive, draw, find, gain, get, owe, take** ◇ *The movement draws much of its ~ from the Greek philosophers.* ◇ *Many of us found ~ in her teaching.* ◇ *Where did you get the ~ for the book?* ◇ *Her latest book owes its ~ to childhood memories.* | **give sb, provide (sb with)** | **look for, seek** ◇ *He peered into his glass, as if seeking ~ there.* | **be lacking in, lack, need**
INSPIRATION + VERB **come (from sth)** ◇ *One day the ~ just came.* | *Her ~ comes from Asia.* | **hit, strike** ◇ *I had to wait until ~ struck.*
PREP. **~ behind** ◇ *He was the ~ behind last week's victory.* | **~ for** ◇ *The sea has provided an ~ for many of his paintings.* | **~ to** ◇ *She's been a great ~ to me.*
PHRASES **a source of ~**

inspired *adj.*

VERBS **be, feel, seem** | **become**
ADV. **divinely** ◇ *divinely ~ wisdom* | **classically** ◇ *the classically ~ buildings of this period* | **politically, religiously** ◇ *politically ~ violence* | **truly** ◇ *He has some truly ~ ideas about life.*

inspiring *adj.*

VERBS **be, seem** ◇ *None of the leaders seems very ~.* | **find sth/sb** ◇ *People find her ~.*
ADV. **particularly, really, truly, very** ◇ *a very ~ sight* | **far from, hardly** (*both esp. BrE*), **less than, not particularly** ◇ *A pile of ironing is hardly ~.*

instability *noun*

ADJ. **increased** | **growing, increasing** | **inherent, internal** ◇ *the inherent ~ of financial markets* | **economic, financial, monetary** | **political, social** | **global, internal, regional** |

emotional, mental ◇ *He showed increasing signs of mental ~.*
... OF INSTABILITY **degree** ◇ *The increased inflation will inject a degree of ~ into the economy.*
VERB + INSTABILITY **cause, create, foster** ◇ *Racism causes political ~ and violence.*
INSTABILITY + VERB **arise, occur** ◇ *Instability may arise at times of change.* | **result from** ◇ *economic ~ resulting from climate change*
PHRASES **a period of ~** ◇ *a long period of economic ~* | **a source of ~**

install *verb*

ADV. **correctly, properly, safely** (*esp. BrE*) ◇ *Make sure the equipment is properly ~ed.* ◇ *She saw her guests safely ~ed in their rooms and then went downstairs.* (*BrE, figurative*) | **improperly, incorrectly** ◇ *They estimate that four out of five child car seats are ~ed improperly.* | **easily** ◇ *The loft ladder is easily ~ed.* | **successfully** | **professionally** ◇ *A professionally ~ed alarm will cost from about £500.* | **permanently** ◇ *Water softening units can be permanently ~ed into the plumbing system.* | **secretly** ◇ *A Trojan horse, secretly ~ed on your computer, can change your Internet settings.*
VERB + INSTALL **be easy to, be simple to** ◇ *The switches are cheap to buy and easy to ~.*
PREP. **in** ◇ *An anti-theft device is ~ed in the vehicle.* | **on** ◇ *Linux can be ~ed on most PCs or Macs.*
PHRASES **be ~ed as CEO, leader, president etc.** ◇ *He was recently ~ed as president of the National Medical Association.* | **newly ~ed, recently ~ed** ◇ *a recently ~ed swimming pool*

instalment (*esp. BrE*) (*AmE usually* **installment**) *noun*

1 regular payment

ADJ. **fixed** | **equal** ◇ *a loan repaid in equal annual ~s* | **first, initial** | **second, third, etc.** | **final, last** | **next** | **annual, monthly, quarterly, weekly**
VERB + INSTALMENT **pay, repay** ◇ *She sold the car before she had paid the ~s.*
INSTALMENT + VERB **become due, be due, be payable** ◇ *The next ~ is not due until July.*
INSTALMENT + NOUN **payment** | **loan** (*AmE*), **plan** ◇ *We offer an installment plan.*
PREP. **by ~** (*esp. BrE*) ◇ *The amounts are repayable by ~.* | **in ~** ◇ *Repayment is in ten ~s.* ◇ *You can pay it in ~s.*

2 part of a story

ADJ. **first, second, etc.** | **final, last** | **previous** ◇ *The last part of the trilogy is a distinct improvement on the previous installment.* | **daily, weekly** | **next**
VERB + INSTALMENT **appear in, publish (sth in)** ◇ *The 'Screwtape Letters' were published in ~s from May to November 1941.*
PREP. **~ in** ◇ *the final ~ in the trilogy*

instance *noun*

ADJ. **countless, innumerable, many, multiple, numerous, several** | **few, occasional, rare** ◇ *This is one of the few ~s where the director does not succeed.* | **isolated** | **certain, given, particular, specific** ◇ *Further information is required to determine the correct answer in any given ~.* | **documented, recorded, reported** ◇ *There are many documented ~s of mass hysteria.* | **extreme** | **notable, striking** | **classic** ◇ *This is a classic ~ of Dostoevsky's writing operating on two levels.*
VERB + INSTANCE **give, provide, represent** ◇ *North America provides the most striking ~ of European settlement on a grand scale.* | **describe, document, record, recount, report** ◇ *Students described many ~s in which they had felt uncomfortable speaking in class.* | **cite (sth as), take** ◇ *Experts cite the country as an ~ where human rights violations could lead to international intervention.* ◇ *To take a particular ~ of this problem:...* | **recall, remember** ◇ *I cannot recall any other ~ in modern times in which a huge and mighty state crumbled to dust.*
INSTANCE + VERB **occur** ◇ *An ~ of this controversy occurred last*

year. | **show sth** ◇ *This ~ shows how important it is to check that the machine is working properly before you use it.*
PREP. **for ~** (= for example) ◇ *Murder, theft and tax evasion, for ~, all have different motives and consequences.* | **in … ~** ◇ *In one ~, several people had their phones stolen.* ◇ *It is not always helpful to draw analogies, but in this ~ it is useful.* | **~ of** ◇ *This is an ~ of his general attitude to his employees.*
PHRASES **in the first ~** (*formal*) ◇ *In the first ~, a letter from your employer may be all you need.*

instant noun

ADJ. **brief, fleeting** ◇ *For a brief ~, I thought she was going to fall.* | **given, one, single** ◇ *His news was too important to be contained for a single ~ longer.* ◇ *At any given ~ the distribution of molecular speeds is always constant under the same conditions.* | **very** ◇ *He took out his keys to lock the door. At that very ~ the door flew open and a man ran into the room.*
VERB + INSTANT **hesitate for, pause for** ◇ *He paused for an ~ before continuing.*
PREP. **at … ~** ◇ *The bomb could go off at any ~.* | **for an ~** ◇ *Just for an ~ I thought he was going to refuse.* | **in an ~** ◇ *It was all over in an ~.* | **the next ~** ◇ *The next ~ she was flying through the air.* | **~ after, ~ before** ◇ *She woke up in the ~ before the phone rang.*

instantaneous adj.

VERBS **be** ◇ *Her death was almost ~.*
ADV. **almost, nearly, virtually**

instinct noun

ADJ. **deep, powerful, strong** | **gut** | **pure, sheer** ◇ *Out of pure ~, he moved back a little.* | **first, initial** ◇ *His first ~ was to run away from danger.* | **excellent, good, unerring** ◇ *Against her better ~s, she ran back into the burning house to save her paintings.* ◇ *He had an unerring ~ for when people were lying to him.* | **base** | **basic, natural, primitive** | **creative** | **aggressive, competitive** | **maternal, mothering, motherly, paternal, protective** | **fighting, hunting, killer, predatory** ◇ *He plays well but lacks that killer ~.* (*figurative*) | **self-preservation, survival** | **herd** ◇ *What makes all these people come to the club? In my view it's the herd ~.* | **sexual** | **business, commercial, political** | **animal, human**
VERB + INSTINCT **have, possess** | **lack** | **develop, hone** ◇ *In negotiating you have to develop an ~ for when to be tough and when to make a deal.* | **follow, go on, go with, obey, rely on, trust** ◇ *Why don't you just follow your natural ~s?* | **control, fight, ignore, overcome, suppress** | **satisfy** | **appeal to** ◇ *They accused the campaign of appealing to the electorate's baser ~s.* | **share** ◇ *Both superpowers shared the same ~ for self-preservation.*
INSTINCT + VERB **tell sb sth** ◇ *Her ~ told her that she was being followed.* | **drive sb, guide sb** ◇ *Artists have to learn to be guided by their ~s.* | **kick in, take over** ◇ *Her ~s took over and she dived on the escaping thief.* | **be right, be wrong** ◇ *I've trusted my ~s in the past and they've usually been right.*
PREP. **by ~** ◇ *Babies know by ~ who their mother is.* | **on ~** ◇ *I acted purely on ~.* | **~ for** ◇ *He has an ~ for survival in a tough job.*

institute noun

ADJ. **professional** | **independent** | **non-profit** (*AmE*) ◇ *a non-profit research ~ dedicated to research in the public interest* | **federal** | **international, national** | **education, educational, research, scientific, technical** | **biotechnology, economic, medical, zoological, etc.**
VERB + INSTITUTE **establish, found, set up** | **open** | **belong to** ◇ *She belongs to the Chartered Institute of Management.* | **join**
INSTITUTE + VERB **be dedicated to** ◇ *a national ~ dedicated to treating people with eating disorders* | **fund sth, support sth** ◇ *The research was funded by the National Cancer Institute.* | **say sth** ◇ *The Institute says that an unidentified virus is to blame for the syndrome.* | **publish sth** | **provide sth** ◇ *an ~ providing opportunities to graduates*
PREP. **at an/the ~** ◇ *She used to give lectures at the Mechanics' Institute.* | **in an/the ~, within an/the ~** ◇ *He is a key figure in the Institute of Mathematics.* | **~ for** ◇ *the International Institute for Economic Development* | **~ of**
PHRASES **a founder of an ~, a member of an ~**
→ Note at ORGANIZATION

institution noun

1 large organization

ADJ. **central, large, major** ◇ *the central ~s of the nation's constitution* | **powerful** | **established** | **existing** ◇ *They argue for the reform of existing political ~s.* | **traditional** | **elite, prestigious, venerable** ◇ *The College is one of the most prestigious medical ~s in the country.* | **public** | **private** | **government, governmental, state** | **international, national** | **local** | **democratic** | **for-profit, non-profit** | **academic, education, educational, higher-education, higher educational, research** ◇ *cultural ~s such as the Danish Institute* | **banking, economic, financial, lending** | **administrative, charitable, cultural, legal, military, political, religious**
VERB + INSTITUTION **build, create, found** ◇ *We need to create ~s that benefit our community.* | **reform** ◇ *They are studying ways to reform government ~s.* | **attend** ◇ *young people who attend higher-education ~s*
PREP. **at a/the ~** ◇ *a course at an ~ of higher education* | **in ~, within ~** ◇ *examination procedures within educational ~s*
→ Note at ORGANIZATION (for verbs)

2 building for people with special needs

ADJ. **mental** | **correctional** (*AmE*), **penal** | **state** (*AmE*) ◇ *He was released from the state ~ where he had been confined for four years.*
VERB + INSTITUTION **build** ◇ *The state built ~s for those who were considered insane.* | **be admitted to, be placed in** ◇ *Many people with dementia would rather remain at home than be placed in an ~.* | **be kept in**
PREP. **at ~, in ~** ◇ *patients in mental ~s* | **~ for** ◇ *an ~ for mentally ill offenders*

3 custom

ADJ. **national** ◇ *Football is a national ~ in this country.* | **cultural, economic, legal, political, religious, social** ◇ *cultural ~s such as religious and legal codes* | **mainstream** ◇ *These values are embedded in mainstream social ~s.* | **sacred** ◇ *He claimed this threatened 'the sacred ~ of marriage'.*
VERB + INSTITUTION **threaten, undermine, weaken** ◇ *These changes threaten some of our most cherished ~s.* | **strengthen** | **preserve, protect** ◇ *American laws once protected the ~ of slavery.*

instruct verb

ADV. **carefully** | **explicitly, specifically** ◇ *You were explicitly ~ed to wait here.*
PHRASES **as ~ed** ◇ *I took the antibiotics as ~ed.*

instruction noun

1 instructions information on how to do sth

ADJ. **comprehensive, full** | **adequate** | **clear, explicit** | **detailed, precise, specific, step-by-step** | **complex** | **basic, simple** | **general** | **special** | **careful** | **verbal, written** | **packet** (*BrE*) | **technical** | **safety** | **cooking, operating, washing** | **installation** | **manufacturer's**
… OF INSTRUCTIONS **list, series, set**
VERB + INSTRUCTIONS **read** ◇ *You should always read the ~s on medicines thoroughly.* | **understand** | **follow** ◇ *Just follow our simple step-by-step ~s.* | **give (sb), include, leave (sb)** ◇ *He gave her detailed ~s on the procedure to be followed.* ◇ *Step-by-step ~s are included.* | **repeat** | **come with** ◇ *Did it come with any ~s about assembling it?*
INSTRUCTIONS + VERB **tell sb sth** ◇ *There are ~s that tell you where everything goes.*
INSTRUCTION + NOUN **book, booklet, leaflet** (*esp. BrE*), **manual, sheet** (*esp. AmE*) ◇ *I had to refer to the ~ booklet.*
PREP. **according to the ~** ◇ *Microwave ovens should be serviced according to the manufacturer's ~s.* | **in accordance with the ~, in the ~** ◇ *It tells you in the ~s not to let the*

machine get too hot. | **~ about, ~ as to** ◇ *The organizer will give ~s as to what to do.* | **~ for** ◇ *follow the manufacturer's ~s for use* | **~ on** ◇ *~s on how to use the photocopier*

2 (usually **instructions**) sth that sb tells/permits you to do

ADJ. **clear, explicit, express** (*esp. BrE*), **specific** | **firm, strict** ◇ *I have strict ~s not to let anyone else in.* | **direct** | **special** | **fresh** (*BrE*), **new** | **further** | **final** | **written**
VERB + INSTRUCTION **be under, have** | **act on, act under** ◇ *She is acting under direct ~s from the president.* | **carry out, comply with, follow, obey, take** ◇ *He was disqualified for failing to comply with the referee's ~s.* | **disobey** | **ignore** | **await, wait for** ◇ *He remained under cover and waited for further ~s from headquarters.* | **accept** ◇ *Lawyers may not accept ~s in cases where they would have a conflict of interests.* | **receive** | **give (sb), issue, leave (sb), send (sb)** ◇ *The government has issued specific ~s on reducing waste disposal.* | **bark, bark out, shout, yell** ◇ *The director sat in his chair barking ~s at the cast.* | **repeat**
PREP. **according to the ~, in accordance with the ~** ◇ *We acted according to the ~s we received.* | **on (sb's) ~** ◇ *She was released on ~s from the Foreign Ministry.* | **under (sb/sth's) ~** ◇ *Under Charlemagne's ~s, many classical texts were recopied.* | **with ~, without ~** ◇ *They were not empowered to negotiate without ~s.* | **~ from, ~ to** ◇ *an ~ to Lieutenant-General Gough from General Clark*
PHRASES **carry out, follow, etc sb's ~s to the letter** (= follow them in every detail) ◇ *The jockey followed his trainer's ~s to the letter.*

3 in a computer
...OF INSTRUCTIONS **series, set**
VERB + INSTRUCTION **carry out, execute, process** ◇ *CPUs are designed to process ~s in a predictable order.*
INSTRUCTION + NOUN **set**

4 teaching
ADJ. **proper** | **formal, informal** | **advanced, basic** | **further** | **free** (*esp. AmE*) ◇ *You can often get free ~ at your local community college.* | **individual, individualized** | **practical, professional, technical** | **classroom** | **moral, religious** | **English** (*esp. AmE*), **language** ◇ *the benefits of native language ~* | **reading, writing** (*both AmE*)
...OF INSTRUCTION **course**
VERB + INSTRUCTION **get, have, receive, take** ◇ *She had no formal ~ in music.* | **He takes ~ very well.* | **need** | **offer (sb)** ◇ *The experts were on hand to offer ~ on the important steps.* | **give (sb), provide (sb with)**
PREP. **for the ~ of** ◇ *The information is for the ~ of passengers.* | **under ~** (*esp. BrE*) ◇ *drivers under ~* | **~ by** ◇ *The two-day course features ~ by leading professionals and academics.* | **~ in** ◇ *He claimed that he was not capable of giving ~ in poetry.* | **~ on** ◇ *basic ~ on using the Internet*
PHRASES **a medium of ~** ◇ *The medium of ~ throughout the course is English.*

instructive *adj.*

VERBS **be**
ADV. **extremely, fairly, very, etc.** | **highly, most** ◇ *It was a most ~ day.* | **especially, particularly**

instructor *noun*

ADJ. **certified** (*AmE*), **qualified, trained** | **experienced** | **chief, senior** | **driving, fitness, flight** (*esp. AmE*), **flying** (*BrE*), **riding, ski, swimming, yoga, etc.**
INSTRUCTOR + VERB **teach sb/sth**
→ Note at JOB

instrument *noun*

1 tool for a particular task
ADJ. **precision, sensitive** | **sophisticated** | **reliable** | **crude** | **blunt** ◇ *The autopsy revealed that the deceased had been hit with a blunt ~.* ◇ *Even though it was a somewhat blunt ~ (= not very precise), our questionnaire provided us with*

some interesting ideas. | **sharp** | **small** | **delicate** | **appropriate** | **drawing, measuring, writing** | **astronomical, mathematical, medical, navigation, navigational, optical, scientific, surgical** | **cockpit, flight**
...OF INSTRUMENTS **set** ◇ *a set of mathematical ~s*
VERB + INSTRUMENT **use** ◇ *All students should learn to use drawing ~s.* | **check, read** ◇ *to read the ~s and make a note of the wind speed and direction* | **design, develop, devise, invent** | **build, make** ◇ *All the ~s are made from glass capillary tubing.*
INSTRUMENT + VERB **measure sth** ◇ *an ~ that measures light intensity*
INSTRUMENT + NOUN **check** ◇ *The pilot did his ~ checks in preparation for take-off.* | **maker** | **panel** ◇ *There was a warning light flashing on the ~ panel.*
PHRASES **an ~ of torture** ◇ *medieval ~s of torture such as the rack and the wheel*

2 for playing music
ADJ. **musical** | **beautiful, fine** | **classical** | **modern** | **traditional** | **period** ◇ *baroque music played on period ~s* | **solo** | **orchestral** | **brass, keyboard, percussion, string, stringed, wind, woodwind** | **acoustic, electric, electronic**
VERB + INSTRUMENT **play** ◇ *She plays three musical ~s.* | **learn, learn to play** | **tune** | **make** ◇ *an ~ made by a violin maker in Canada*
INSTRUMENT + VERB **sound** ◇ *The ~ sounds like a cello.*
INSTRUMENT + NOUN **maker**
PREP. **on an/the ~** ◇ *The piece can be played on a keyboard ~.*
→ Special page at MUSIC

3 sb/sth used to make sth happen
ADJ. **chief, key, main, major, primary, principal** | **good, great** ◇ *Internet polls are considered to be better ~s than telephone polls.* | **ideal** | **important, valuable** | **powerful** | **useful** | **effective** ◇ *More effective ~s of oversight are needed.* | **flexible** | **mere** ◇ *Some cynics say that popular music is a mere ~ of capitalist domination.* | **chosen** ◇ *The despot claimed to be the chosen ~ of divine providence.* | **political** | **financial, legal**
VERB + INSTRUMENT **regard sb/sth as, see sb/sth as, view sb/sth as** ◇ *They saw criminal law as an ~ for improving public morals.* | **use sb/sth as** | **make sb/sth**
PREP. **~ for** ◇ *Criminal law is not the best ~ for dealing with family matters.* | **~ of** ◇ *the use of language as an ~ of power and social control*

instrumental *adj.*

1 important in making sth happen
VERBS **be, prove** | **become**
ADV. **highly, very** | **essentially, largely** | **merely** | **purely**
PREP. **in** ◇ *They were highly ~ in bringing the business to Newtown.*

2 made by or for musical instruments
VERBS **be**
ADV. **largely, mostly** ◇ *The songs are largely ~.* | **entirely, purely** ◇ *He's created a purely ~ score.*

insufficient *adj.*

VERBS **be, prove**
ADV. **quite, wholly** | **simply** | **clearly** | **woefully**
PREP. **for** ◇ *The resources available are quite ~ for the task.*

insulated *adj.*

1 protected against the cold, sound, etc.
VERBS **be**
ADV. **well** | **badly** (*BrE*), **poorly** | **heavily** | **properly**
PREP. **against** ◇ *The laboratory was well ~ against all outside noise.* | **with** ◇ *The hot water tank should be ~ with proper insulating materials.*

2 protected from unpleasant experiences
ADV. **completely** | **largely** ◇ *We are largely ~ from significantly higher costs.*
PREP. **from** ◇ *The wealthy feel completely ~ from an economic downturn.* | **against** ◇ *Many financial institutions are now ~ against higher interest rates.*

insult *noun*

ADJ. **bad, grave, great, terrible** ◊ *one of the worst ~s you can throw at somebody* | **final, ultimate** ◊ *To call a woman a girl is the ultimate ~.* | **calculated, deliberate** (*esp. BrE*) | **direct** (*esp. AmE*) | **personal**
VERB + INSULT **hurl, shout, throw** ◊ *They were hurling ~s at the police.* | **mean sth as** ◊ *I don't mean this as an ~, but I think the team would play better without you.* | **take sth as** ◊ *I meant it as a bit of constructive advice, but he took it as a personal ~* | **endure, suffer** ◊ *Foreigners have to suffer constant ~s from the local population.* | **exchange, trade** ◊ *The two groups of fans exchanged ~s.*
INSULT + VERB **fly** ◊ *Insults were flying back and forth.*
PREP. **~ to** ◊ *It was an ~ to his wife.*
PHRASES **add ~ to injury** ◊ *Then, to add ~ to injury* (= to make things worse)*, they told me I couldn't get on the flight.* | **an ~ to your intelligence** ◊ *The questions were a real ~ to our intelligence* (= because they were too easy).

insult *verb*

ADV. **publicly** ◊ *He was dismissed for publicly ~ing prominent politicians.*
PHRASES **be ~ed, feel ~ed** ◊ *I felt deeply ~ed that she hadn't asked me to the meeting.*

insulting *adj.*

VERBS **be, seem, sound** | **become** | **find sth** ◊ *I find it ~ to be spoken to in that way.*
ADV. **extremely, fairly, very, etc.** | **highly** | **almost** ◊ *He made the question sound almost ~.* | **a little, slightly, etc.** | **vaguely**
PREP. **to** ◊ *His opinions are highly ~ to women.*

insurance *noun*

ADJ. **comprehensive** ◊ *fully comprehensive car ~* | **adequate** | **additional** | **long-term, short-term** | **national, social, state** | **employer-provided** (*AmE*) ◊ *Many people are covered by employer-provided health ~.* | **personal, private** | **commercial** | **compulsory** | **life** | **disability, health, health-care, medical** | **home, homeowner** (*AmE*), **house** (*esp. BrE*), **household** (*BrE*) | **auto** (*AmE*), **car, motor** (*BrE*) | **travel** | **accident, fire, flood** (*esp. AmE*) | **legal-expenses** (*BrE*), **unemployment** (*esp. AmE*), **workers' compensation** (*AmE*) | **credit** (*esp. AmE*) | **liability, malpractice** (*AmE*), **professional-indemnity** (*BrE*), **public-liability** (*BrE*), **third-party** | **general, universal** (*esp. AmE*) ◊ *universal health ~* | **marine** | **special**
VERB + INSURANCE **have, maintain** ◊ *Do you have fully comprehensive ~?* ◊ *The company maintains liability ~ for its directors and officers.* (*formal*) | **lack** (*esp. AmE*) ◊ *Millions of Americans lack adequate health ~.* | **apply for** | **arrange** (*esp. BrE*), **buy, get, obtain, purchase, take out** ◊ *The contract requires me to arrange my own ~.* ◊ *The travel agent recommended that I take out travel ~.* | **afford** | **need** | **sell** | **pay** ◊ *I haven't paid the ~ yet this month.* | **claim, claim on** (*both esp. BrE*) ◊ *She set fire to her house and then claimed ~.* ◊ *We claimed for the car repairs on the ~.* | **offer (sb)** | **provide (sb with)**
INSURANCE + VERB **cover sb/sth, pay for sth** ◊ *Does your personal accident ~ cover mountain rescue?* ◊ *Millions of people in the US are not covered by health ~.* ◊ *The ~ will pay for the damage.*
INSURANCE + NOUN **cover** (*BrE*), **coverage** ◊ *~ cover for bodily injury to third parties* | **policy** ◊ *a personal ~ policy* | **plan, programme/program, scheme** (*BrE*), **system** ◊ *a compulsory health ~ system* | **contribution** (*esp. BrE*), **payment, premium** ◊ *a monthly ~ premium* ◊ *Labour has increased national ~ contributions to pay for public services.* (*BrE*) | **costs, rates** ◊ *rising ~ costs* | **claim** | **benefits, money, payout** ◊ *He bought a new suit out of the ~ money.* | **services** | **business, industry, market, sector** | **carrier** (*AmE*), **company, firm, fund, group, provider** (*esp. AmE*) | **adjuster** (*AmE*) | **agent, broker, salesman, underwriter** | **certificate** (*esp. BrE*)
PREP. **~ against** ◊ *More people are taking out ~ against the high cost of dental care.* | **~ for** ◊ *compulsory ~ for personal injury to employees* | **~ on** ◊ *The court heard that he stood to*

gain millions in ~ on his wife.* | **~ with** ◊ *Her ~ is with General Accident.*
PHRASES **a certificate of ~** (*esp. BrE*) | **a contract of ~** (*BrE*) | **a period of ~** (*BrE*) ◊ *If you make more than two claims in any period of ~ you may lose your no-claims bonus.*

insured *adj.*

VERBS **be**
ADV. **fully** | **adequately** (*esp. BrE*) | **privately** ◊ *There is evidence that privately ~ patients are offered a higher level of care.*
PREP. **against** ◊ *Your DVD player is not ~ against accidental damage.* | **for** ◊ *I was not adequately ~ for the damage my tenants caused.*

insurmountable *adj.*

VERBS **appear, be, prove, seem** ◊ *The age barrier appeared ~.* | **become**
ADV. **almost, nearly, virtually** | **apparently, seemingly** ◊ *They were now faced with seemingly ~ technical problems.*

insurrection *noun*

ADJ. **armed** ◊ *Years of discontent turned into armed ~.* | **popular** ◊ *There was a popular ~ against the police.* | **slave** (*esp. AmE*)
VERB + INSURRECTION **plan** ◊ *In 1822 he planned a slave ~ in South Carolina.* | **lead** | **launch** | **crush, put down, suppress** (*esp. AmE*)
PREP. **~ against** ◊ *~ against the monarchy*

intact *adj.*

VERBS **appear, be** | **remain, stay, survive** ◊ *The building survived almost ~.* | **emerge, return** ◊ *The team returns largely ~ to defend its title.* (*esp. AmE*) | **find sth** ◊ *We found the tomb perfectly ~.* | **keep sth, maintain sth, preserve sth** ◊ *The collection should be kept completely ~.* | **leave sth** ◊ *a group of old army buildings that had been left largely ~*
ADV. **remarkably, substantially, very much** ◊ *The character of the original house is very much ~.* | **completely, entirely, fully, perfectly** | **almost, nearly, virtually** | **basically, essentially, largely, more or less, mostly** | **fairly, reasonably, relatively** | **apparently** | **still** ◊ *The mill machinery is still ~.* | **miraculously**

intake *noun*

1 amount of food/drink taken into the body

ADJ. **high** | **moderate** | **low** | **increased** | **total** | **excessive** | **adequate** | **normal** | **average** | **recommended** | **daily** ◊ *your recommended daily ~ of vitamin C* | **regular** | **dietary, nutritional** | **caloric** (*esp. AmE*), **calorie** | **alcohol, calcium, carbohydrate, energy, fat, fibre/fiber, fluid, food, nutrient** (*esp. AmE*), **oxygen, protein, salt, sugar, vitamin, water**
VERB + INTAKE **have** ◊ *Make sure you have a balanced ~ of vitamins A, B, C and D.* | **maintain** ◊ *You should maintain a low ~ of fat.* | **boost, increase, raise** | **control, watch** ◊ *You need to watch your alcohol ~.* | **cut, cut down, cut down on, decrease, limit, lower, reduce, restrict** ◊ *One of the best ways to get to your ideal size is to cut fat ~ right down.*

2 number of students in a year

ADJ. **high** | **low** | **balanced** (*BrE*) ◊ *The government should be promoting a balanced ~ of students for every school.* | **new** | **annual** (*esp. BrE*) | **graduate** (*BrE*), **student**
VERB + INTAKE **have** ◊ *The school has an annual ~ of 20 to 30.*

3 where liquid/air enters a machine

ADJ. **air, water**
VERB + INTAKE **block, clog, clog up** ◊ *Algae has clogged the ~ to the water turbine.*

4 of breath

ADJ. **quick, sharp** ◊ *She gave a sharp ~ of breath.*
VERB + INTAKE **give** | **hear**
PHRASES **an ~ of breath**

integrate verb

1 combine two things

ADV. **closely, tightly, well** ◇ *They called for the defence system to be more closely ~d.* | **completely, fully, seamlessly, thoroughly** | **properly** | **easily** | **effectively, successfully** ◇ *The department has successfully ~d new ideas into the traditional course structure.*
PREP. **into** ◇ *The results should be ~d into the final report.* | **with** ◇ *This computer program can be ~d with existing programs.*
PHRASES **highly ~d** (= with many different parts working successfully together) ◇ *a highly ~d approach to planning* | **poorly ~d**

2 mix with other people

ADV. **well** ◇ *Immigrants here are well ~d on the whole.* | **completely, fully** | **quickly** | **racially** (*esp. AmE*)
PREP. **into** ◇ *They soon became fully ~d into the local community.* | **with** ◇ *They didn't ~ with the other children.*

integration noun

ADJ. **true** | **complete, full** | **close, seamless** | **further, greater, increased** | **rapid** | **successful** | **economic, monetary, political, racial, social** ◇ *We are working to bring about closer political ~ in the EU.* | **market** | **European** ◇ *a milestone in the process of European ~* | **global** ◇ *policies designed to promote global economic ~* | **internal** | **systems** (*computing*)
... OF INTEGRATION **degree, level**
VERB + INTEGRATION **achieve, bring about** | **accelerate, encourage, facilitate, promote, speed up** ◇ *measures to promote the social ~ of mentally handicapped people* | **require** | **lead to**
PREP. **~ between** ◇ *~ between research and higher education* | **~ into** ◇ *the ~ of disabled students into the general education system* | **~ with** ◇ *He called for greater ~ with Europe.* | **~ within** ◇ *economic ~ within the three communities*
PHRASES **a move towards/toward ~** ◇ *a move towards/ toward greater internal ~ in Europe* | **a need for ~, a process of ~**

integrity noun

1 quality of being honest and firm in your moral principles

ADJ. **great, high** | **absolute, complete** (*both esp. BrE*) | **personal** | **academic, artistic, financial, intellectual, journalistic, moral, political, professional, scientific** ◇ *She refused to compromise her artistic ~.* ◇ *The article is indicative of his contempt for the basic standards of journalistic ~.*
VERB + INTEGRITY **have** ◇ *She has great personal ~.* | **lack** | **lose** | **restore** ◇ *The minister promised to restore the honesty and ~ of the government.* | **retain** | **defend, compromise, undermine** ◇ *I would never do anything to compromise the ~ of the company.* | **impugn** (*formal*), **question** ◇ *She questioned his ~ as an artist.*
PREP. **with ~** ◇ *The code calls on members to behave with ~ at all times.*
PHRASES **an attack on sb/sth's ~**

2 state of being whole and not divided

ADJ. **physical, structural, territorial** ◇ *The country is fighting to preserve its territorial ~.* | **data** (*computing*)
VERB + INTEGRITY **have** | **lose** | **restore** | **ensure** ◇ *It's up to the user to ensure the ~ of the data they enter.* | **maintain, retain** ◇ *We all have an interest in maintaining the ~ of the ecosystem.* | **preserve, protect, safeguard** | **threaten** ◇ *The project threatens the ~ of one of the world's most important wetlands.* | **compromise, undermine** ◇ *concerns that data ~ has been compromised* | **destroy** ◇ *Nuclear weapons have the capability to destroy the physical ~ of the planet.*
PHRASES **a challenge to sth's ~, a threat to sth's ~**

intellect noun

ADJ. **brilliant, formidable, great, keen, powerful, sharp, superior, towering** | **limited, low** | **creative** | **human**
VERB + INTELLECT **have** ◇ *She has a formidable ~.* | **use** ◇ *She uses her powerful ~ to examine the relationship between human society and nature.*

intelligence noun

1 ability to understand

ADJ. **considerable, great, high** ◇ *This essay shows considerable ~.* | **acute, quick** ◇ *a writer with an acute ~* | **average, normal** | **limited, low** | **innate, native** | **human** | **emotional** ◇ *The consultancy focused on leadership and emotional ~.* | **artificial** ◇ *computer scientists who study artificial ~*
VERB + INTELLIGENCE **have** ◇ *At least he had the ~ to turn off the gas.* | **demonstrate, show** | **use** | **insult** ◇ *Please don't insult my ~ by lying to me.*
INTELLIGENCE + NOUN **test**

2 information

ADJ. **secret** ◇ *We've obtained secret ~ about enemy plans.* | **good, reliable** | **bad, faulty** | **army, military** ◇ *Military ~ is gathered using sophisticated technology.* | **business** | **criminal** | **national**
VERB + INTELLIGENCE **collect, gather, get** | **provide** | **share** ◇ *The FBI and the CIA need to share ~ on terrorism.*
INTELLIGENCE + NOUN **agency, community, service** ◇ *He works for the French ~ service.* | **officer, official** | **collection** (*esp. AmE*), **gathering** ◇ *His unit was responsible for ~ gathering in North Africa.* | **failure** | **information, report** | **operation** | **source**

intelligent adj.

VERBS **be, look, seem, sound**
ADV. **extremely, fairly, very, etc.** | **highly, incredibly, most** ◇ *a highly ~ woman* | **reasonably** ◇ *He should be able to solve the problem. He's reasonably ~.* | **obviously** | **seemingly** | **otherwise** ◇ *Why do otherwise ~ people take this event so seriously?*

intelligible adj.

VERBS **be** | **become** | **make sth, render sth** ◇ *They do their best to make science ~ to young children.*
ADV. **fully, perfectly** | **easily, readily** | **barely** ◇ *His reply was barely ~.* | **mutually** ◇ *Czech and Slovak are separate languages but they are mutually ~.*
PREP. **to** ◇ *We need an explanation that is readily ~ to ordinary people.*

intend verb

ADV. **fully** ◇ *She fully ~s to continue her sporting career once she has recovered from her injuries.* | **clearly** | **originally** ◇ *He had originally ~ed to stay in the country for only a year or two.* | **never** ◇ *I never ~ed to hurt you.*
PREP. **for** ◇ *The bomb was probably ~ed for a well-known human rights campaigner.*

intense adj.

VERBS **be** | **become, get, grow** | **remain**
ADV. **extremely, fairly, very, etc.** | **incredibly** | **especially, particularly**

intensify verb

ADV. **greatly** | **dramatically, rapidly, sharply** ◇ *The fighting in the area has intensified sharply.* | **gradually** | **further**
VERB + INTENSIFY **seem to** ◇ *The extreme cold seemed, if anything, to ~.* | **tend to** | **be likely to** | **serve to** ◇ *The reforms served only to ~ the misery of the poorer peasants.*

intensity noun

ADJ. **high, low** ◇ *a band of light with high ~* | **maximum** | **fierce, great** ◇ *The sun beat down with fierce ~.* ◇ *He studied the report with great ~.* | **emotional** | **passionate** | **same** ◇ *He was unable to play the final set with the same ~.* | **light**

VERB + INTENSITY **decrease, reduce** | **increase** ◊ *They decided to increase the ~ of the attacks.* | **decrease in, reduce in** | **grow in** ◊ *Her headaches started to increase in ~.* | **vary in** | **bring, show** ◊ *She brought passionate ~ to the role.* | **measure**
PREP. **in ~** ◊ *The pain was growing in ~.*

intensive *adj.*

VERBS **be**
ADV. **highly, very** ◊ *highly ~ courses for business and professional people* | **increasingly**

intent *adj.*

VERBS **appear, be, seem**
ADV. **apparently, seemingly** | **clearly, obviously** ◊ *They are clearly ~ on maintaining standards.* | **fully** | **still**
PREP. **on, upon** ◊ *He was ~ on murder.*

intention *noun*

ADJ. **original** ◊ *My original ~ was to study all morning, but this turned out to be impractical.* | **declared, stated** | **real, true** ◊ *She may never reveal her true ~s.* | **firm** (*esp. BrE*) | **general** | **deliberate** | **honourable/honorable, noble** | **bad, evil** | **authorial** ◊ *A text sometimes transcends authorial ~.*
VERB + INTENTION **have** ◊ *I have no ~ of changing jobs.* | **announce, declare, state** ◊ *The senator has announced his ~ to run for the presidency.* | **know**
PREP. **with a/the ~ of** ◊ *I went to the bank with the ~ of getting some cash.* | **~ behind** ◊ *The general ~ behind the project is a good one.* | **~ by** ◊ *The ~ by the local authority to build 2 000 new houses is unrealistic.* | **~ in** ◊ *His ~ in inviting us to dinner was to persuade us to back his project.*
PHRASES **the best ~s, good ~s** ◊ *It was done with the best ~s, I assure you.* | **have every ~ of doing sth, have no ~ of doing sth** ◊ *We have every ~ of winning the next election.* | **make your ~s clear** ◊ *He didn't make his ~s clear in his letter.*

interact *verb*

1 have an effect on each other

ADV. **closely** | **directly** ◊ *Cells may ~ directly with each other.* | **physically** ◊ *These devices allow the robot to physically ~ with its environment.*
PREP. **with** ◊ *This hormone ~s closely with other hormones in the body.*

2 mix with other people

ADV. **well** | **socially**
PREP. **with** ◊ *He ~s very well with other children.*

interaction *noun*

ADJ. **complex** | **direct** | **strong** | **informal** | **social** | **physical** | **human** | **face-to-face, group, two-way** | **classroom**
INTERACTION + NOUN **processes** ◊ *the ~ processes of chimpanzees*
PREP. **~ among** ◊ *Informal ~ among employees is seen as part of the ongoing training process.* | **~ between** ◊ *the complex ~ between animals and their environment* | **~ with** ◊ *What is her ~ with her boss like?* | **~ within** ◊ *~ within the group*
PHRASES **patterns of ~** ◊ *Specific patterns of ~ in the family have been observed.*

interactive *adj.*

VERBS **be** | **become**
ADV. **highly, very** (*esp. AmE*) ◊ *The gaming world is very ~.* | **truly** | **fully** ◊ *The program is fully ~.*

interchangeable *adj.*

VERBS **be, seem** | **become**
ADV. **fully** | **almost, virtually**
PREP. **with** ◊ *These parts are fully ~ with those in other machines.*

intercom *noun*

INTERCOM + VERB **buzz, crackle** | **sound**
INTERCOM + NOUN **system** | **button**
PREP. **on the ~** ◊ *I spoke to her on the ~.* | **over the ~** ◊ *Mr Jack's arrival was announced over the ~.*

intercourse *noun*

1 sex

ADJ. **sexual** | **heterosexual, homosexual** | **anal, vaginal** | **consensual, non-consensual** | **unlawful** (*esp. BrE*) | **unprotected**
VERB + INTERCOURSE **engage in, have, indulge in** (*BrE*) ◊ *She never had sexual ~ before she was married.* | **consent to** ◊ *The judge asked if she had consented to ~.*
INTERCOURSE + VERB **occur, take place** ◊ *He admitted that ~ had taken place.*
PREP. **during ~** | **~ between** ◊ *~ between consenting adults* | **~ with** ◊ *She denied having had sexual ~ with him.*

2 exchange of ideas, feelings, etc.

ADJ. **social** ◊ *Life is a pleasant blend of work and social ~.*

interest *noun*

1 desire to learn/hear more about sb/sth

ADJ. **avid, close, considerable, consuming, deep, great, intense, keen, lively, passionate, real, strong** ◊ *The police were starting to take a close ~ in the company's activities.* ◊ *She always had a great ~ in the supernatural.* | **particular, special** | **growing, increased, increasing** | **slightest** ◊ *He's never shown the slightest ~ in football.* | **little** | **general, widespread** | **current** | **worldwide** | **shared** | **serious** | **genuine** | **abiding, lifelong, long-standing** | **passing** | **sudden** ◊ *Why the sudden ~?* | **renewed** | **added** ◊ *The CD-ROM gives the book added ~.* | **active** | **polite** ◊ *He showed a polite ~ in her story.* | **personal** | **professional** | **media** ◊ *The event attracted a lot of media ~.* | **sexual**
VERB + INTEREST **have** | **evince, express, show, take** ◊ *My cousin expressed an ~ in seeing where I work.* | **feign** ◊ *She feigned ~ in a magazine article to avoid meeting the man's stare.* | **lose** | **arouse, attract, awaken, catch, create, draw, drum up, excite, generate, kindle, pique, spark, stimulate, stir up** ◊ *A sticker on a bag caught my ~.* ◊ *The government failed to drum up any public ~ in the referendum.* ◊ *A childhood trip to Europe sparked his lifelong ~ in history.* | **develop** ◊ *While in prison he developed an ~ in art.* | **increase** | **keep, maintain, sustain** ◊ *The film kept my ~ throughout.* ◊ *The channel has failed to maintain ~ in its expensive new show.* | **revive**
INTEREST + VERB **grow** | **flag, wane** ◊ *The children's ~ began to flag after half an hour of the lesson.*
PREP. **for ~, out of ~** ◊ *I'm asking purely out of ~.* | **with ~** ◊ *They listened with ~.* | **~ among** ◊ *to stimulate ~ among teachers* | **~ from** ◊ *growing ~ from younger members* | **~ in** ◊ *She took an active ~ in their welfare.*

2 quality that attracts attention

ADJ. **great** | **particular, special** ◊ *Her comments are of particular ~ to me.* | **little** | **immediate** ◊ *This information was of no immediate ~ to me.* | **broad, general, wide** | **architectural, artistic, historic, historical, scientific** | **academic** ◊ *Since the championship has already been decided, this game is of purely academic ~.* | **human** ◊ *a plot devoid of human ~* | **love** ◊ *Angelina Jolie supplies the love ~ in the movie.*
VERB + INTEREST **be of** ◊ *His books are of no ~ to me at all.* | **hold no** ◊ *Their conversation held no ~ for me.* | **add** ◊ *Bushes that flower in winter will add ~ to your garden.*
INTEREST + VERB **lie in** ◊ *The ~ of the painting lies in its unusual use of light.*
PREP. **of ~** ◊ *a building of great architectural ~*

3 sth you enjoy doing/learning about

ADJ. **diverse, varied, wide, wide-ranging** | **private** | **shared** | **outside** ◊ *He has many hobbies and outside ~s.* | **main,**

primary ◊ *My main research ~ is herbal medicine.* | **artistic, musical, etc.** | **research**
VERB + INTEREST **have** | **share** | **pursue** ◊ *He wanted time to pursue his many and varied musical ~s.*

4 money earned from investments
ADJ. **annual, monthly, etc.** | **compound, simple** | **mortgage**
VERB + INTEREST **earn, receive** | **pay** | **charge**
INTEREST + VERB **accrue, bear**
INTEREST + NOUN **rate** | **payment** | **charge**
PREP. **~ on** ◊ *to pay ~ on a loan*
PHRASES **a rate of ~** ◊ *a mortgage with a fixed rate of ~*

5 benefits that sth has for sb
ADJ. **best ~** (*esp. AmE*), **best ~s** ◊ *It's not in your best ~s to let your boss know you're looking for a new job.* ◊ *I feel it is in everyone's best ~ if I step aside now.* | **own, selfish** ◊ *You can't blame them for looking after their own ~s.* (*esp. BrE*) | **common, mutual, shared** | **competing, conflicting, contradictory** | **long-term, short-term** | **narrow** ◊ *Protectionism often simply supports narrow vested ~s.* | **direct** ◊ *Lawyers have a direct financial ~ in the outcome of the debate.* | **paramount, vital** | **powerful** | **legitimate** | **vested** | **special** (*esp. AmE*) ◊ *The views of special-interest groups are represented.* | **national, public** | **class, sectarian, sectional** | **foreign, outside** | **corporate, economic, financial, political, security, strategic, etc.** ◊ *issues of compelling strategic ~*
VERB + INTEREST **defend, guard, look after** (*esp. BrE*), **protect, safeguard** | **act in, advance, champion, further, promote, serve** ◊ *He claimed to be acting in the public ~.* | **represent** | **act against, jeopardize, threaten**
INTEREST + VERB **lie in sth** | **be at stake**
INTEREST + NOUN **group** ◊ *Various ~ groups have expressed their opposition to the policy.*
PREP. **against sb/sth's ~** ◊ *The lawyer refused to act against his client's ~s.* | **contrary to sb/sth's ~** ◊ *The union refused to support proposals that it saw as contrary to the ~s of its members.* | **in sb/sth's ~** (*esp. AmE*), **in sb/sth's ~s** (*esp. BrE*) ◊ *Continuing such a policy is short-sighted and not in the ~ of consumers.* ◊ *New work practices were introduced in the ~s of efficiency.* | **of ~** ◊ *We met to discuss matters of common ~.* | **out of ~** ◊ *He was obviously acting purely out of selfish ~.*
PHRASES **a conflict of ~, a conflict of ~s** (*esp. BrE*) ◊ *One member of the planning committee had a conflict of ~ as he lived near the proposed road.* | **have sb's ~s at heart** ◊ *Although he was sometimes too strict with his children, he had their best ~s at heart.*

6 legal right to share in profits
ADJ. **powerful** | **controlling, majority** | **minority** | **joint** | **banking, business, commercial, shipping**
VERB + INTEREST **have** ◊ *He has controlling ~s in several ventures.* | **sell**
PREP. **~ in**

interest verb
ADV. **greatly, particularly, really, very much** ◊ *It is this aspect of the work that really ~s me.*
VERB + INTEREST **try to** ◊ *She tried to ~ the director in her plan.*

interested adj.
VERBS **appear, be, feel, look, seem, sound** | **become, get** ◊ *She got very ~ in politics.* | **remain** | **get sb** ◊ *We need to get more young people ~ in the sport.* | **keep sb** ◊ *You need to keep your audience ~.*
ADV. **extremely, fairly, very, etc.** | **deeply, especially, greatly, intensely, keenly, most, particularly, passionately, seriously, terribly** ◊ *If he's seriously ~ in applying for the job, he'll do it.* | **genuinely, truly** | **increasingly** | **not at all, not in the least, not the least bit, not remotely** ◊ *He's not in the least ~ in girls.* | **not much, not very, only half** ◊ *Carrie was only half ~ in the conversation.* | **fairly, mildly, quite, vaguely** | **just** ◊ *'Why do you ask?' 'I'm just ~, that's all.'* | **enough, sufficiently** (*esp. BrE*) ◊ *I wasn't ~ enough in the argument to take sides one way or the other.* | **chiefly,**

mainly, primarily | **long** ◊ *Michael had long been ~ in architecture.* | **always** ◊ *I am always ~ in how differently people can look at the same event.* | **still** | **no longer** | **potentially** | **apparently, reportedly** | **clearly, obviously** | **actively** ◊ *As a landowner, he was actively ~ in agricultural improvements.*
PREP. **in** ◊ *She's always been ~ in other people.*

interesting adj.
VERBS **appear, be, look, seem, sound** | **become, get** | **prove** ◊ *So far, my trip has proved ~.* | **make sth** | **find sb/sth** ◊ *I find her ideas really ~.*
ADV. **extremely, fairly, very, etc.** | **certainly, deeply, especially, extraordinarily, highly, immensely, incredibly, intensely, most, particularly, terribly, truly** | **equally** | **doubly** | **mildly, moderately, vaguely** | **not remotely** ◊ *None of them had anything remotely ~ to say.* | **enough, sufficiently** ◊ *Some topics appeared ~ enough to require more detailed information.* | **potentially** | **genuinely** ◊ *This is a genuinely ~ article.* | **inherently, in itself, intrinsically** ◊ *This subject is intrinsically ~ and worthy of study in its own right.* | **always, consistently** ◊ *It was always ~ to hear his stories.* | **architecturally, geologically, historically, sociologically, visually, etc.** ◊ *architecturally ~ buildings*
PREP. **for** ◊ *It's not very ~ for visitors.* | **to** ◊ *How can we make the subject more ~ to young people?*

interfere verb
ADV. **seriously** ◊ *Emotional problems can seriously ~ with a student's work.* | **directly** ◊ *The judge cannot ~ directly in these proceedings.* | **constantly** ◊ *Why was he constantly interfering in her life?*
VERB + INTERFERE **be allowed to, have a right to** ◊ *They have no right to ~ in the internal affairs of other countries.* | **attempt to, try and, try to** ◊ *If you try and ~ in my life, I'll leave.* | **be reluctant to** ◊ *The courts are reluctant to ~ in these matters.*
PREP. **in** ◊ *outsiders interfering in local politics* | **with** ◊ *You mustn't ~ with her work.*

interference noun
ADJ. **undue, unwarranted** | **bureaucratic, federal** (*AmE*), **government, governmental, political, state** | **external, outside**
VERB + INTERFERENCE **avoid, eliminate, minimize, prevent** ◊ *The law is designed to prevent ~ by local police.* | **encounter** | **tolerate** | **resent** ◊ *They deeply resent foreign ~ in their affairs.*
PREP. **without ~** ◊ *I told her I wanted to make decisions without ~ from her.* | **~ in** ◊ *political ~ in the legal process* | **~ with** ◊ *~ with proper medical procedures*

interior noun
ADJ. **original** ◊ *The original ~ of the hotel has been replaced.* | **dark, dim, gloomy, shadowy** | **roomy, spacious** | **luxurious, plush**
VERB + INTERIOR **decorate, design** | **redecorate, renovate**
INTERIOR + NOUN **decorator, designer**
PREP. **in the ~** ◊ *There is ample space in the ~ of the car.*

interlude noun
ADJ. **brief** | **romantic** | **peaceful, pleasant** | **instrumental, musical, orchestral** ◊ *a musical ~ between two the acts of the play*
PREP. **~ between** ◊ *a peaceful ~ between periods of intense activity* | **~ in** ◊ *He'd had two romantic ~s in a rather lonely life.* | **~ of** ◊ *~s of calm*

intermediary noun
ADJ. **financial**
VERB + INTERMEDIARY **act as**
PREP. **through an ~, via an ~** (*esp. BrE*) ◊ *They were approached indirectly through an ~.* ◊ *The product is then sold to the end-user via an ~.* | **~ between** ◊ *She agreed to act as ~ between the two tribes.*

interminable *adj.*

VERBS **be, seem** ◇ *The flight seemed* ~.
ADV. **seemingly** ◇ *For several seemingly* ~ *seconds no one spoke.*

intern *noun* (*AmE*)

ADJ. **unpaid** ◇ *He began work at the White House as an unpaid* ~. | **summer** ◇ *Microsoft came to Harvard Business School to recruit summer* ~s. | **psychology, surgery, etc.** | **architectural, congressional, editorial, etc.** | **pre-doctoral, undergraduate** | **lowly** ◇ *At that time I was a lowly* ~ *at the magazine.*
VERB + INTERN **hire** ◇ *She hired an* ~ *when she had too much work to handle herself.*

Internet *noun*

ADJ. **wireless** | **broadband, high-speed** | **cable**
VERB + INTERNET **access, go on, navigate, use** ◇ *She went on the* ~ *to check air fares.* | **browse, surf** ◇ *He likes watching movies, reading, and surfing the* ~. | **comb, scan, scour, search** ◇ *They began scouring the* ~ *for information about his condition.* | **censor, regulate** ◇ *Attempts to regulate the* ~ *are usually doomed to failure.*
INTERNET + NOUN **site, website** | **gateway, portal** | **bulletin board, chat room** | **ad, magazine, radio** | **auction, broadcast, link** ◇ *Thousands logged on to view the live* ~ *broadcast of the concert.* ◇ *The auction was held in Paris with an* ~ *link to New York.* | **chat** ◇ *She often talks to fans via live* ~ *chats.* | **cafe** ◇ *You can check your email at the* ~ *cafe in the town.* | **address, domain** ◇ *Registering an* ~ *domain name is now an essential part of setting up a company.* | **access, usage, use** ◇ *unlimited/unmetered* ~ *access* | **search** ◇ *A quick* ~ *search will give you dozens of possible destinations.* | **connection** ◇ *a broadband/high-speed* ~ *connection* | **connectivity** ◇ *the challenges of providing* ~ *connectivity to rural communities* | **browser, search engine** | **provider, service provider** (abbreviated to *ISP*) | **customer, surfer, user** | **traffic** ◇ *the laying of fast networks to carry* ~ *traffic* | **brand, group** | **services** | **arm** (*esp. BrE*), **division, operation** (*BrE*) ◇ *the bank's* ~ *arm* | **entrepreneur** | **analyst, expert** | **banking, betting, dating, gambling, porn** (*informal*), **pornography, shopping, telephony** | **advertising, commerce, marketing** | **bank, business, company, firm, retailer, start-up, venture** | **industry, sector** | **fraud** | **security** | **economy** | **file** ◇ *software for downloading* ~ *files* | **image** | **software** | **appliance, infrastructure, server** | **protocol, technology** | **age** ◇ *issues facing the music industry in the* ~ *age* | **boom, bubble, revolution** ◇ *Many of the sites launched at the peak of the* ~ *boom have now disappeared.*
PREP. **on the** ~ ◇ *More and more people are shopping on the* ~. | **over the** ~ ◇ *It is possible to earn a degree over the* ~.
→ *Special page at* COMPUTER

interpret *verb*

ADV. **accurately, correctly, properly, rightly** | **erroneously, incorrectly, mistakenly, wrongly** | **differently** ◇ *Different people might* ~ *events differently.* | **clearly** | **broadly, liberally** ◇ *The term 'business' is here* ~ed *broadly to include all types of organization in the public and private sectors.* | **narrowly, restrictively** (*BrE*), **strictly** | **literally** | **faithfully** (*esp. AmE*) ◇ *judges who will faithfully* ~ *the Constitution* | **easily, readily** ◇ *These figures cannot be easily* ~ed. | **cautiously** ◇ *These results must be* ~ed *cautiously.*
VERB + INTERPRET **be difficult to, be hard to** | **be able to, be unable to** | **attempt to, seek to, try to** ◇ *We all seek to* ~ *what we hear and what we read.*
PREP. **as** ◇ *Her message was* ~ed *as a warning to the general.*
PHRASES **be** ~ed **to mean sth** ◇ *The title could be* ~ed *to mean 'human intelligence'.* | **be variously** ~ed **(as sth)** ◇ *The figure of the Ancient Mariner has been variously* ~ed (= *interpreted in various ways*). | **be widely** ~ed **as sth** ◇ *Her resignation has been widely* ~ed *as an admission of her guilt.*

interpretation *noun*

ADJ. **correct, right, true, valid** | **erroneous, false, wrong** |

plausible, possible, reasonable | **straightforward** ◇ *The film lends itself to a fairly straightforward* ~. | **simplistic** | **literal, narrow, strict** | **broad, free, generous, liberal, loose, wide** | **subjective** ◇ *The meaning of the incident is open to subjective* ~. | **alternative, competing, conflicting, different, diverse, multiple** | **artistic** | **historical, textual, theological** ◇ *feminist historical* ~s *of marriage customs* | **Biblical, scriptural** (*esp. AmE*) ◇ *His writings reflect his conservative views on Biblical* ~. | **constitutional** (*esp. AmE*), **judicial, statutory** ◇ *In any system of law, there is an inevitable element of judicial* ~.
VERB + INTERPRETATION **give sth, make, offer** ◇ *In practice, this law is often given a wide* ~ *by the police.* ◇ *Scientists made an* ~ *based on the data available.* | **be open to** ◇ *The wording of this section of the contract is open to* ~. | **favour/favor, support** ◇ *Most modern historians support this* ~. | **challenge, refute, reject** ◇ *She challenges many orthodox* ~s *of religious texts.* | **defy, preclude, resist** ◇ *His work defies simplistic* ~.
PHRASES **put an** ~ **on sth** ◇ *It is possible to put an entirely different* ~ *on her comments.*

interpreter *noun*

VERB + INTERPRETER **act as** | **speak through** ◇ *Speaking through an* ~, *a Japanese fisherman gave his account of the tidal wave.*
PREP. ~ **for** ◇ *Susan acted as* ~ *for us.*
→ *Note at* JOB

interrogation *noun*

ADJ. **police** | **further** | **coercive** (*esp. AmE*) ◇ *They have been subject to coercive* ~s *without access to lawyers.* | **lengthy** ◇ *She had to undergo a lengthy* ~.
VERB + INTERROGATION **conduct** ◇ *The* ~ *was conducted by senior police officers.* | **undergo** ◇ *He had been captured and was undergoing* ~.
INTERROGATION + NOUN **cell, room** | **methods, procedures, tactics, techniques**
PREP. **during** ~ ◇ *She revealed the name of her accomplice during* ~. | **under** ~ ◇ *Under* ~, *he refused to say anything at first.*

interrupt *verb*

ADV. **impatiently** | **rudely** ◇ *What was I saying, before we were so rudely* ~ed? | **angrily, harshly, sharply** ◇ *'Don't talk like that!' he* ~ed *harshly.* | **violently** ◇ *Their luncheon was violently* ~ed *by gunfire.* | **hastily, quickly** ◇ *'He's kidding,' I* ~ed *hastily.* | **abruptly, suddenly** | **temporarily** | **constantly, frequently, repeatedly** ◇ *The morning's work was constantly* ~ed *by phone calls.* | **occasionally, periodically**
VERB + INTERRUPT **be sorry to** ◇ *I'm sorry to* ~, *but there's a telephone call for you.* | **(not) dare (to)** ◇ *It was all irrelevant, but I didn't dare* ~ *him in mid-flow.*
PREP. **with** ◇ *I thought it better not to* ~ *her with any comment.*
PHRASES **get** ~ed ◇ *I didn't manage to finish the report. I kept getting* ~ed.

interruption *noun*

ADJ. **unwelcome** | **rude** ◇ *He began again, obviously annoyed at this rude* ~. | **sudden** | **brief, short, temporary** ◇ *The game continued after a short* ~ *because of rain.* | **constant, frequent, repeated** ◇ *I found it hard to work with all the noise and constant* ~s. | **occasional**
VERB + INTERRUPTION **ignore** ◇ *He ignored her* ~ *and carried on talking.*
PREP. **without** ~ ◇ *Can I please have this conversation on the phone without* ~s? ◇ *I managed to work for two hours without* ~. | ~ **from** ◇ *He continued speaking despite regular* ~s *from the audience.* | ~ **to** ◇ *The birth of her son was a minor* ~ *to her career.*
PHRASES **excuse the** ~, **pardon the** ~ ◇ *Excuse the* ~, *but can I borrow Jenny for a moment?*

necessary to exercise her ministerial powers of ~ in order to protect the public.

interstate noun (in the US) → See also FREEWAY, HIGHWAY, MOTORWAY

ADJ. **major** | **busy**
VERB + INTERSTATE **take** ◊ *You can take Interstate 10 all the way into Baton Rouge.* | **get on** | **get off, pull off**
PREP. **along a/the ~, down a/the ~** ◊ *We were driving down the ~.* | **on a/the ~** ◊ *an eleven-car pile-up on the ~*

interval noun

ADJ. **brief, short** ◊ *She ruled for ten years, except for a brief ~.* | **long, wide** ◊ *You are advised to leave a wide ~ before you have your next child.* | **10-minute, six month, three-year, etc.** ◊ *Try setting your automatic email checker to 30-minute ~s.* | **fixed, specified** ◊ *the amount of oxygen used by the muscles during a specified ~* | **decent** ◊ *After a decent ~ she made her new relationship public.* | **time** ◊ *They will be interviewed again after an appropriate time ~ has elapsed.*
PREP. **at ~s** ◊ *At ~s a bell rings and workers stop for a drink.* | **in the ~** ◊ *Polling day was a week away and Baldwin made two speeches in the ~.* | **~ between** ◊ *The ~s between his various illnesses grew shorter and shorter.*
PHRASES **at fixed, periodic, regular, etc. ~s** ◊ *Trains run at fixed ~s.* ◊ *He returned home during the day at regular ~s.* | **at irregular ~s, at random ~s** ◊ *The accounts were updated at irregular ~s.* | **at hourly, weekly, monthly, etc. ~s** ◊ *Meetings are held at monthly ~s.*

intervene verb

ADV. **actively, directly** | **personally** ◊ *The President ~d personally in the crisis.* | **decisively** ◊ *Government often ~s decisively in major professional issues in medicine.* | **effectively, successfully** | **forcefully, militarily** ◊ *Intervening militarily will not bring peace.* | **tactfully**
VERB + INTERVENE **be forced to, have to** ◊ *Eventually, the army was forced to ~.* | **be powerless to** (esp. BrE) ◊ *Local people feel strongly about the proposed development but are virtually powerless to ~.* | **be able to, have the ability to, have the power to, have the right to** ◊ *Our government has no right to ~.* | **be prepared to, be ready to** ◊ *Nurses should be ready to ~ on behalf of their patients.* | **be reluctant to** | **refuse to** ◊ *The UN refused to ~.*
PREP. **against** ◊ *They would not ~ against the rebels themselves.* | **between** ◊ *She went over to ~ between the two men.* | **in** ◊ *She was reluctant to ~ in what was essentially a private dispute.* | **on behalf of** ◊ *The ambassador ~d personally on behalf of the children.* | **with** ◊ *attempts to ~ with the authorities on the prisoners' behalf*

intervention noun

ADJ. **active, direct** ◊ *direct ~ to stop abuses of the environment* | **decisive** | **early, immediate, timely** ◊ *A full-scale riot was prevented by the timely ~ of the police.* | **effective, successful** | **limited** | **personal** ◊ *the Emperor's personal ~* | **federal, government, governmental, state** ◊ *He has made repeated calls for government ~ to save the steel industry.* | **external, foreign, outside** | **armed, military** ◊ *We would resist any armed ~ from outside in our country's affairs.* | **humanitarian** ◊ *This is not a humanitarian ~, it is a brutal invasion.* | **police** | **judicial, legal** | **clinical, medical, surgical** | **behavioural/behavioral, psychological** | **educational** | **economic, political, social** | **divine, supernatural** ◊ *The victory was seen as the direct result of divine ~.* | **human, manual** ◊ *The automatic process can be completed with very little manual ~.*
VERB + INTERVENTION **make** ◊ *to make a forceful ~ in a dispute* | **call for, demand, favour/favor** ◊ *The public demanded active ~.* | **oppose, resist** ◊ *We will always resist foreign ~ in our country.* | **justify, require, warrant** ◊ *The threat does not justify government ~.*
PREP. **~ against** ◊ *armed ~ against the rebels* | **~ by** ◊ *~ by a senior judge* | **~ from** ◊ *He was furious at this ~ from the press.* | **~ in** ◊ *the government's ~ in the dispute* | **~ on behalf of** ◊ *state ~ on behalf of the industry*
PHRASES **powers of ~, the right of ~** (both esp. BrE) ◊ *It was*

interview noun

ADJ. **face-to-face, in-person** (AmE), **one-on-one** (esp. AmE), **one-to-one** (BrE), **personal** | **phone** (esp. BrE), **telephone** ◊ *Telephone ~s with over 400 businesses picked up high rates of satisfaction.* | **group** | **extensive, in-depth, lengthy** | **brief** | **follow-up, second** | **police** ◊ *a police ~ with suspected terrorists* | **magazine, media, newspaper, press, radio, television** | **exclusive** ◊ *We have an exclusive ~ with the director of the movie.* | **live** ◊ *He did a live ~ on the CBC News Morning show.* | **job** ◊ *I have a job ~ tomorrow.*
VERB + INTERVIEW **carry out, conduct, do, hold** ◊ *The survey team carried out over 200 ~s with retired people.* | **arrange, schedule** ◊ *The company contacted her to arrange an ~.* | **request** ◊ *A journalist called requesting an ~.* | **schedule** | **room** | **do, give (sb), grant (sb)** ◊ *He's a very private man and rarely does ~s.* | **attend, be called for, have** ◊ *She's been called for an ~ for the manager's job.* | **air, broadcast, publish** ◊ *The ~ was published in all the papers.* | **feature** ◊ *This month we feature an ~ with Nicole Kidman.* | **audiotape, record, tape, videotape** (esp. AmE) ◊ *She taped an ~ to appear the following day on 'CBS Sunday Morning'.* | **All police ~s are recorded and transcribed.**
INTERVIEW + NOUN **panel** (esp. BrE) | **techniques** | **procedure, process** ◊ *The questions are the central point of the whole ~ procedure.* | **question** ◊ *Prepare answers to possible ~ questions.* | **footage** ◊ *The documentary combines ~ footage and clips from his films.* | **clip, segment, snippet** (all esp. AmE) | **transcript** | **request** ◊ *I get a lot of ~ requests from journalists.*
PREP. **in an/the ~** ◊ *He said in an ~ that he wanted to get married.* | **~ about** ◊ *He gave the paper an ~ about his musical tastes.* | **~ between** ◊ *an ~ between the French Foreign Minister and the President of Egypt* | **~ for** ◊ *an ~ for the post of sales manager* | **~ with** ◊ *He had an ~ with IBM.* ◊ *an ~ with the Vietnamese leader*
PHRASES **a round of ~s** ◊ *We're about to start the second round of ~s for the post.*

interviewer noun

ADJ. **experienced, good, skilled, trained** ◊ *A skilled ~ will help candidates feel relaxed.* | **radio, television, TV**
VERB + INTERVIEWER **tell** ◊ *She once told an ~, 'A dancer's life is very hard'.*
INTERVIEWER + VERB **ask (sth)** ◊ *Interviewers rarely ask about his personal life.*

intestine noun

ADJ. **large, small** | **lower, upper**
PREP. **along the ~, in the ~, through the ~** ◊ *bacteria in the small ~*
PHRASES **the wall of the ~**

intimacy noun

ADJ. **genuine, real, true** | **close, deep, great** | **emotional, physical, sexual**
VERB + INTIMACY **be capable of** ◊ *She isn't capable of real ~.* | **achieve, experience** ◊ *the artist's ability to achieve ~ with his subjects* | **enjoy** (formal) ◊ *He enjoys an ~ with the president.* | **create, foster, promote** | **develop** ◊ *Gradually, a deep emotional ~ developed between them.*
INTIMACY + VERB **develop**
PREP. **~ between** ◊ *the ~ created between student and teacher* | **~ with** ◊ *A writer must develop an ~ with the subject at hand.*
PHRASES **fear of ~** ◊ *He was prevented from declaring his love by his fear of ~.* | **a feeling of ~, a sense of ~** ◊ *The room had a peaceful sense of ~ about it.*

intimidate verb

ADV. **physically, psychologically** ◊ *Dissidents were physically ~d, threatened, and harshly interrogated.*
VERB + INTIMIDATE **try to**

PREP. **into** ◊ *The police had tried to ~ him into signing a confession.*
PHRASES **an attempt to ~ sb, an effort to ~ sb** | **be easily ~d** ◊ *He was not a man to be easily ~d.* | **feel ~d** ◊ *She did not feel ~d by him.*

intimidation *noun*

ADJ. **physical, psychological, verbal** | **voter** ◊ *There were signs of voting fraud and voter ~.*
VERB + INTIMIDATION **be subject(ed) to** (*esp. BrE*), **face, suffer** (*BrE*) ◊ *Workers were subjected to ~ as they crossed the picket line.*
PREP. **~ against** ◊ *~ against trade unions* | **~ by** ◊ *Workers continue to enter the plant despite ~ by mass pickets.* | **~ from** ◊ *fear of ~ from paramilitary organizations*
PHRASES **an act of ~** | **a campaign of ~**

intolerable *adj.*

VERBS **be, prove, seem** | **become** | **make sth** ◊ *The constant pain made her life ~.* | **consider sth, find sth** ◊ *I find his rudeness ~.*
ADV. **absolutely, quite** (*both esp. BrE*) | **increasingly** (*esp. BrE*) | **almost** ◊ *The job placed almost ~ pressure on her.*
PREP. **to** ◊ *The situation had become ~ to him.*

intolerance *noun*

1 lack of tolerance

ADJ. **racial, religious**
VERB + INTOLERANCE **display, show** | **preach** ◊ *We need to root out those who preach ~ and hate.*
PREP. **~ of** ◊ *The town began to show increasing ~ of immigrants.* | **~ to** ◊ *the professor's ~ to any views other than his own* | **~ towards/toward** ◊ *the ~ of local residents towards/toward refugees*

2 inability to digest certain substances

ADJ. **food** | **glucose, lactose, etc.**
PREP. **~ of** ◊ *theologians who wish to justify ~ of homosexuality* | **~ to** ◊ *an ~ to milk products*

intolerant *adj.*

VERBS **be** | **become**
ADV. **extremely, fairly, very, etc.** | **highly**
PREP. **of** ◊ *They are deeply ~ of all opposition.*

intonation *noun*

ADJ. **falling, flat, rising** ◊ *the rising ~ at the end of spoken questions*
INTONATION + NOUN **pattern**

intricacy *noun*

VERB + INTRICACY **comprehend, grasp, learn, master, understand, unravel** ◊ *I've never mastered the intricacies of ballroom dancing.*
PHRASES **guide, lead, steer, etc. sb through the intricacies of sth** ◊ *We can guide investors through the intricacies of the cable industry.*

intricate *adj.*

VERBS **be**
ADV. **extremely, fairly, very, etc.** | **amazingly, highly, incredibly, wonderfully** ◊ *an amazingly ~ structure* | **quite**

intrigue *noun*

ADJ. **international, political** | **court** ◊ *a tale of treachery and court ~*
VERB + INTRIGUE **engage in**
INTRIGUE + VERB **surround sb/sth** ◊ *Intrigue surrounds a woman who walked into a police station having lost her memory.*
PREP. **~ against** ◊ *The prime minister engaged in political ~s against the king.*
PHRASES **a web of ~**

intriguing *adj.*

VERBS **be, sound** ◊ *It all sounds very ~.* | **find sth** ◊ *I found the story rather ~.*
ADV. **extremely, fairly, very, etc.** | **highly, most, particularly**

introduce *verb*

1 tell people sb's name

ADV. **formally, properly** ◊ *We have met before, but we haven't been formally ~d.* | **briefly** ◊ *I briefly ~d him to my parents.*
VERB + INTRODUCE **allow me to, can, let me, may** ◊ *Let me ~ myself.* ◊ *May I ~ my wife, Sarah?*
PREP. **as** ◊ *He ~d me as a new member of the company.* | **to** ◊ *She ~d me to her friends.*

2 start using/doing sth for the first time

ADV. **recently** ◊ *They recently ~d a yogurt drink into the market.* | **first, initially, originally** ◊ *Psychologists first ~d the term in the early 1990s.* | **gradually, slowly** | **quickly, rapidly** ◊ *After coming to power, he quickly ~d land reform.* | **accidentally, inadvertently** ◊ *diseases inadvertently ~d to the area by settlers*
VERB + INTRODUCE **intend to, plan to, want to** ◊ *The local authority plans to ~ new regulations on parking.* | **attempt to, try to** ◊ *She attempted in vain to ~ some order into the classroom.*
PREP. **into** ◊ *New technology is rapidly being ~d into factories.*
PHRASES **newly ~d, recently ~d** ◊ *These measures have only been recently ~d.*

introduction *noun*

1 first use

ADJ. **early, gradual, recent, widespread** | **accidental** ◊ *the accidental ~ of species into new environments*
VERB + INTRODUCTION **delay** ◊ *The testing process delayed the ~ of the drug by at least a year.* | **accelerate, facilitate** ◊ *More liberal policies have facilitated the ~ of new technologies.* | **announce** ◊ *That year, IBM announced the ~ of its first personal computer.*
PREP. **~ into** ◊ *the gradual ~ of modern farming methods into traditional societies*

2 first part of a book/talk/performance

ADJ. **brief, short** ◊ *He began with a brief ~.* | **lengthy** ◊ *After a lengthy musical ~, the dancers finally appear.*
VERB + INTRODUCTION **write** ◊ *She wrote the ~ to his collected letters.* | **feature, include** ◊ *Her book features an ~ by French actress Catherine Deneuve.* | **skip** ◊ *Let's skip the ~ and get straight down to the facts.*
PREP. **in an/the ~** ◊ *His mother is mentioned in the ~.* | **~ to** ◊ *the ~ to her latest book*

3 book for studying a subject

ADJ. **excellent, helpful, informative, useful** ◊ *It serves as an excellent ~ to 19th-century painting.* | **thorough** ◊ *This collection provides a comprehensive ~ to his ideas.* | **general** ◊ *If you are looking for a general ~, this volume will be sufficient.* | **concise** ◊ *The book can be used as a concise ~ by developers new to the field.* | **accessible, readable**
VERB + INTRODUCTION **offer, provide** ◊ *Together, these two books offer the best possible ~ to the sport.* | **write** ◊ *He has written the best available ~ to Stravinsky's music.*
PREP. **~ to** ◊ *an ~ to computer programming*

4 telling people each other's names

ADJ. **formal, proper** ◊ *I never gave you a proper ~ to my friends.*
VERB + INTRODUCTION **do, give sb, make** ◊ *I can never remember names, so I don't like to make the ~s.*
PHRASES **a letter of ~** ◊ *He gave me a letter of ~ to the manager.* | **need no ~** ◊ *For those of us in our forties, McNamara needs no ~.*

intruder *noun*

ADJ. **unwanted, unwelcome** | **masked**

intrusion

VERB + INTRUDER **apprehend, catch** | **detect, disturb** (*BrE*), **find** ◊ *He found a masked ~ in the kitchen.* | **chase away, deter, discourage, keep away, keep out** ◊ *Dogs can deter unwelcome ~s.* | **tackle** (*BrE*) ◊ *He was stabbed when he tackled an ~ armed with a knife.* | **repel** ◊ *Staff were instructed to repel ~s with physical force, if need be.*
INTRUDER + VERB **break into, force their way into** (*esp. BrE*) ◊ *Intruders had forced their way into the house.*
INTRUDER + NOUN **alarm, alert**
PREP. **against ~s** ◊ *security measures against ~s*

intrusion noun

ADJ. **government, governmental, media, press** ◊ *This is a governmental ~ on the freedom of the press.* | **unnecessary, unwanted, unwarranted, unwelcome** | **sudden** ◊ *He leapt back in shock at this sudden ~.*
VERB + INTRUSION **resent**
PREP. **~ in** ◊ *I really resented his ~ in a family matter.* | **into** ◊ *media ~ into the lives of celebrities* | **~ on, ~ upon** ◊ *an unwarranted ~ upon the singer's privacy*
PHRASES **forgive my/the ~, pardon my/the ~** ◊ *Forgive my ~, but I need to speak with you urgently.*

intrusive adj.

VERBS **be, prove, seem** | **become** | **find sth**
ADV. **extremely, fairly, very, etc.** | **excessively, overly** (*esp. AmE*), **unnecessarily** ◊ *Many feel that advertising on the Internet has become overly ~.* | **increasingly** | **visually** (*BrE*) ◊ *The proposed building would be visually ~.*

intuition noun

ADJ. **female, feminine, woman's, women's** ◊ *Her feminine ~ told her that he was unhappy.* | **moral** (*philosophy*) ◊ *There is a moral ~ that the better-off should give to the worse-off.* | **pure** ◊ *Most business decisions are guided by pure ~.*
... OF INTUITION **flash** ◊ *It came upon him in a flash of ~.*
VERB + INTUITION **have** ◊ *She had an ~ that her mother wasn't very well.* | **rely on, trust, use** ◊ *She learned to trust her ~s about other people's motives.*
INTUITION + VERB **suggest sth, tell sb sth** ◊ *Intuition told me we were going in the wrong direction.*
PREP. **by ~** ◊ *By ~, he sensed what was wrong.* | **~ about** ◊ *an ~ about where to find wild strawberries* | **~ behind** ◊ *the ~ behind her theory*

intuitive adj.

VERBS **be**
ADV. **extremely, fairly, very, etc.** | **highly** ◊ *a highly ~ thinker* | **purely**

invalid adj.

ADV. **scientifically, statistically, technically**
VERBS **be** | **become** | **make sth, render sth** ◊ *This action would render the agreement ~.* | **consider sth, declare sth, deem sth** ◊ *The contract was declared ~.*

invaluable adj.

VERBS **be, prove** | **become** | **remain** | **make sb/sth** ◊ *His knowledge of the area made him ~.* | **find sth** ◊ *You will find their help absolutely ~.*
ADV. **absolutely**
PREP. **for** ◊ *This technology is ~ for students with poor sight.* | **to** ◊ *Your support has been ~ to us.*

invasion noun

ADJ. **full-scale** | **military** ◊ *Latest reports are of a full-scale military ~.* | **amphibious, ground, land** | **imminent, impending, planned** ◊ *Forces were massing on the border for an imminent ~.* | **unilateral, unprovoked** ◊ *We cannot accept the unprovoked ~ of a sovereign nation.* | **home** (*AmE*) ◊ *Robberies and home ~s are grim facts of daily life.*
VERB + INVASION **carry out, launch, mount** | **repel, repulse** | **counter, oppose, resist** | **justify, support**
INVASION + NOUN **fleet, force**
PHRASES **an ~ of privacy** ◊ *Having those photographers in the house was a terrible ~ of privacy.* | **fear of ~, a threat of ~**

invent verb

ADV. **practically, virtually** ◊ *He practically ~ed the modern stand-up comedy act.* | **single-handedly** ◊ *Pepys single-handedly ~ed the diary as a literary form.*
PHRASES **newly ~ed** ◊ *the newly ~ed automatic rifle*

invention noun

1 new thing

ADJ. **latest, new** | **modern, newfangled** | **brilliant, ingenious, wonderful** | **patented** | **culinary, linguistic, technological, etc.** ◊ *He dedicated many of his culinary ~s to famous people.*
VERB + INVENTION **come up with, design** | **license, patent, register** ◊ *He failed to patent his ~ and never made any money from it.* | **commercialize, market** ◊ *The two friends started a company to market their ~.*

2 untrue story

ADJ. **pure** ◊ *Most of what he says is pure ~!*
PHRASES **power of ~, powers of ~** ◊ *His powers of ~ are somewhat limited.*

inventive adj.

VERBS **be**
ADV. **extremely, fairly, very, etc.** | **brilliantly, endlessly, highly, wildly, wonderfully**

inventory noun

1 written list

ADJ. **complete, comprehensive, detailed, full**
VERB + INVENTORY **compile, complete, conduct, draw up, make, produce, take** ◊ *Disaster response teams are completing an ~ of damaged facilities.* ◊ *The manager is compiling an ~ of all the hotel furniture.* | **list sth in, list sth on** ◊ *The painting is listed in an ~ of his complete works.*
INVENTORY + VERB **list sth** ◊ *The ~ lists many rare items.*
PREP. **in an/the ~** ◊ *There were no forks in the ~.* | **on an/the ~** ◊ *That lamp isn't listed on the ~.*

2 (*AmE*) available stock

ADJ. **excess, surplus, unsold** ◊ *Hotel chains often cut prices in order to sell excess ~.*
VERB + INVENTORY **stock** ◊ *The store wanted to offer more items but stock less ~.* | **replenish** | **liquidate, sell** | **deplete, pare, reduce, slash** ◊ *Companies have slashed inventories and cut back investment.* | **be low on, run low on** ◊ *a business that is low on ~* | **manage**
INVENTORY + NOUN **control, management**

invest verb

ADV. **aggressively, heavily** ◊ *The company ~ed heavily in new technology.* | **directly** ◊ *If you ~ directly in the stock market potential profits are greater, but so are potential losses.* | **personally** ◊ *He personally ~ed $980 000 in the company.* | **safely, wisely** | **abroad, overseas**
VERB + INVEST **be willing to** ◊ *Are you willing to ~ the time and effort necessary to make the plan work?* | **look to, plan to, seek to** ◊ *investors looking to ~ in US companies* | **decide to** | **rush to** ◊ *When exchange controls were lifted, Swedes rushed to ~ overseas.* | **fail to** ◊ *The industry has failed to ~ in new product development.*
PREP. **for** ◊ *You need to think about ~ing for your retirement.* | **in** ◊ *encouragement to ~ in pension plans*

investigate verb

ADV. **carefully, closely, in detail** | **extensively** | **adequately, fully, properly, thoroughly** ◊ *The allegations have not yet been properly ~d.* | **actively, vigorously** ◊ *He claimed the Army had failed to vigorously ~ the case.* | **empirically, experimentally, rigorously, scientifically** | **further**
VERB + INVESTIGATE **ask sb to, be called in to** ◊ *Police have been called in to ~ the complaints.* | **decide to** | **agree to,**

    invite

pledge to (*esp. BrE*), **promise to** ◇ *The company has promised to* ~ *claims that its products are unsafe.* | **aim to, be designed to, seek to**
PREP. **for** ◇ *He is being ~d for illegal business dealings.*

investigation noun

ADJ. **careful, close, detailed** | **extensive** ◇ *The authorities conducted an extensive* ~ *into his tax affairs.* | **full, in-depth, thorough** | **preliminary** ◇ *After conducting preliminary ~s, government lawyers will set out areas of concern.* | **ongoing** ◇ *The ongoing* ~ *has led to numerous intelligence leads.* | **criminal, homicide** (*AmE*), **murder, police** | **congressional, federal, government** | **internal** ◇ *The board of directors commissioned its own internal* ~. | **independent** | **empirical, scientific**
VERB + INVESTIGATION **carry out, conduct, pursue, undertake** ◇ *Police are still pursuing their ~s.* | **initiate, launch, order** | **call for, demand** ◇ *He called for* ~ *into the hospital's management.* | **head, lead, oversee** | **complete** | **deserve, merit, require, warrant** ◇ *These claims certainly warrant further* ~. | **impede, obstruct** ◇ *He was on trial for allegedly obstructing an* ~ *into the bank's dealings.*
INVESTIGATION + VERB **demonstrate sth, reveal sth, show sth, uncover sth** ◇ *Closer* ~ *showed a flaw in this theory.* | **conclude, show, suggest** ◇ *An official* ~ *concluded that 9 000 people were killed or went missing during that period.*
PREP. **on** ~ ◇ *On* ~, *the noise turned out to be only a door banging.* | **under** ~ ◇ *The singer is currently under* ~ *for possessing illegal drugs.* | ~ **into** ◇ *Police have launched an* ~ *into the allegations.*
PHRASES **the subject of an** ~ ◇ *The matter is the subject of a police* ~, *and we cannot comment.*

investment noun

ADJ. **excellent, good, productive, profitable, sound, successful, wise, worthwhile** | **bad, poor** ◇ *He lost a lot of money through poor ~s.* | **high-risk, risky, speculative** | **safe** | **considerable, enormous, great, heavy, hefty** (*esp. AmE*), **high, huge, large, large-scale, major, massive, significant, sizeable, substantial** ◇ *The president has called for massive* ~ *to rebuild the country's economy.* | **low, minimal, modest, small** | **inadequate** ◇ *The country's infrastructure is crumbling because of inadequate* ~. | **maximum, minimum** | **additional, extra, further** | **gross, net** | **overall** | **new** | **necessary** | **strategic** | **direct** | **domestic, local** | **cross-border, foreign, international, inward** (*esp. BrE*), **offshore, outside, overseas** | **long-term, short-term** | **initial, original, upfront** ◇ *an initial* ~ *of $5 million* | **property** (*esp. BrE*), **real estate** (*AmE*), **share** (*esp. BrE*), **stock** (*esp. AmE*), **stock-market** ◇ *He was making a living from his real estate ~s.* | **capital, equity, financial** | **business, industrial, infrastructural, infrastructure, manufacturing** | **federal, government, public, public-sector** (*esp. BrE*), **state** | **corporate, institutional, private, private-sector** ◇ *private* ~ *in the health service* | **personal** ◇ *I had made a personal* ~ *in time and energy.* | **emotional, parental** ◇ *parents' emotional* ~ *in their children*
... OF INVESTMENT **flow, level, rate**
VERB + INVESTMENT **make** | **attract, boost, encourage, promote, spur, stimulate** ◇ *a business plan to encourage new* ~ | **discourage** | **increase** | **cut** | **recoup, recover** ◇ *It took two years before I recouped my* ~. | **realize** ◇ *She felt the time was right to realize her* ~, *and sold all her shares.* | **spread** ◇ *When buying shares, it's wise to spread your* ~ *over several companies.* | **protect**
INVESTMENT + VERB **increase, rise, soar, surge** | **decline, fall** | **return, yield** ◇ *My* ~ *yielded almost 20% annually.*
INVESTMENT + NOUN **account, fund, trust** | **portfolio** ◇ *Bonds should be part of your* ~ *portfolio.* | **levels, rates** ◇ *inadequate* ~ *levels* | **flow** ◇ *Investment flows dropped sharply and the region's growth halted.* | **plan, scheme** (*BrE*) | **strategy** ◇ *She sees art as a long-term* ~ *strategy.* | **opportunity** ◇ *We can help you identify* ~ *opportunities.* | **decision** | **income** ◇ *Investment income is subject to different tax rules.* | **bank, company, firm, trust** | **adviser, analyst, banker, manager, professional**
PREP. **as an** ~ ◇ *I don't really like modern art but I bought it as an* ~. | ~ **from** ◇ ~ *from American pension funds* | ~ **in** ◇ ~ *in local industry*
PHRASES **a loss on an** ~ ◇ *losses made on ~s in stocks and bonds* | **a profit on an** ~, **a return on an** ~ ◇ *I'm hoping for a good return on my* ~.
→ Special page at BUSINESS

investor noun

ADJ. **big, large, major** | **long-term** | **average, ordinary, small** ◇ *Many ordinary ~s stand to lose money in this affair.* | **potential, prospective, would-be** (*esp. BrE*) | **business, institutional** | **angel** (= a private individual who invests money in a new business), **individual, private, retail** | **canny** (*BrE*), **savvy** (*esp. AmE*), **sophisticated** | **cautious, risk-averse** | **novice** | **wealthy** | **domestic, local** | **foreign, international, inward** (*BrE*), **outside, overseas** | **bond, equity, mutual-fund** (*AmE*), **stock**
VERB + INVESTOR **attract, encourage, lure** ◇ *A stable company is more likely to attract potential ~s.* | **advise, warn** ◇ *They advise ~s where to put their money.* | **convince, reassure** ◇ *They announced budget cuts which they hoped would reassure ~s.* | **deter, scare, scare away, scare off, worry** ◇ *Current government policies may worry overseas ~s.* | **defraud** | **protect**
INVESTOR + VERB **buy sth, invest in sth** ◇ *Investors will be able to buy the shares from next week.* | **flock to sth** (*esp. AmE*), **pile into sth** (*esp. BrE*), **rush into sth, rush to sth** ◇ *Investors have been flocking to the region because of high bank rates.* | **sell sth** | **be interested in sth** ◇ *This is an excellent deal for ~s who are interested in smaller companies.* | **react** ◇ *In this battle for brand leadership, how ~s react is important.*
INVESTOR + NOUN **confidence** ◇ *the need to restore* ~ *confidence* | **sentiment** ◇ *Investor sentiment was running against corporate America.* | **protection**
PREP. ~ **in** ◇ ~*s in plantation forestry*

invincible adj.

VERBS **be, feel, look, seem** | **become** | **make sb** ◇ *It is a secret weapon that will make us* ~.
ADV. **almost, nearly, practically, virtually** | **seemingly**

invisible adj.

VERBS **be** | **become** | **remain** | **make sb/sth, render sb/sth** ◇ *He wished that he could make himself* ~. ◇ *It's interesting how women are rendered* ~ *in these statistics.*
ADV. **completely, totally** | **almost, nearly, practically, virtually** | **largely** | **effectively**
PREP. **to** ◇ *Infrared light is* ~ *to the human eye.*

invitation noun

ADJ. **kind** | **formal** | **open, standing** ◇ *We have an open* ~ *to use their weekend home whenever we like.* ◇ *An unlocked door is an open* ~ *to any burglar.* (*figurative*) | **personal** | **special** | **dinner, party, shower** (*AmE*), **wedding** ◇ *I got a baby shower* ~ *from a friend.*
VERB + INVITATION **get, have, receive** | **accept, take sb up on, take up** ◇ *We'd love to to take up your* ~ *to visit you some time.* | **decline** (*formal*), **refuse, turn down** ◇ *I must sadly decline your generous* ~. | **extend** (*formal*), **give (sb), issue, send, send out**
INVITATION + NOUN **list** (*esp. AmE*) ◇ *I'm on the* ~ *list.* | **card**
PREP. **at sb's** ~ ◇ *He is here to give a concert at the* ~ *of the association.* | **by** ◇ *Membership of the club is by* ~ *only.* | ~ **from** ◇ *We got a wedding* ~ *from Laura and Jennifer.* | ~ **to** ◇ *Have you received your* ~ *to the exhibition?* ◇ *The head extended an* ~ *to all parents to come and see the school.*

invite verb

1 ask sb to do sth

ADV. **formally, officially** | **cordially, graciously** (*esp. AmE*), **kindly, warmly** ◇ *You are cordially ~d to attend the annual parish meeting.* ◇ *She very kindly ~d me to lunch.* |

personally | **along, around, back, in, out, over, round** (*esp. BrE*) ◇ *They've ~d us over for a drink.*
PREP. **into** ◇ *I was never ~d into the house.* | **for** ◇ *Let's ~ them all for dinner.* | **to** ◇ *Thank you for inviting me to the meeting.*

2 encourage sth

ADV. **positively** (*esp. BrE*) ◇ *The hype surrounding the event positively ~d criticism.* | **practically** (*esp. AmE*)
VERB + INVITE **seem to** ◇ *The movie seems to ~ comparison with 'The Italian Job'.*

inviting *adj.*

VERBS **be, look, sound**
ADV. **very** ◇ *It was hot and the sea looked very ~.* | **especially** (*esp. AmE*), **particularly** | **quite** | **not particularly** ◇ *The house, with its boarded-up windows, was not particularly ~.*

invoice *noun*

ADJ. **outstanding, unpaid** ◇ *Immediate payment of the outstanding ~s was requested in a letter.* | **paid** | **original** (*esp. BrE*) | **final** (*esp. BrE*) ◇ *Please pay the final ~ within two weeks.* | **VAT** (*BrE*) ◇ *Payment will be made within 28 days after receipt of the appropriate VAT ~.* | **monthly** | **bogus** (*esp. BrE*), **fake** (*esp. AmE*), **false** (*esp. BrE*) ◇ *He submitted fake ~s totalling $278 000.* | **handwritten** ◇ *a handwritten ~ for £1352*
VERB + INVOICE **issue** (*esp. BrE*), **raise** (*BrE*), **render** (*BrE*), **send, submit** (*esp. BrE*) | **get, receive** | **pay**
INVOICE + NOUN **price, value** (*BrE*) ◇ *The shipping costs can be as high as 50% of the ~ value of the goods.*

involve *verb*

1 make sth necessary

ADV. **generally, typically, usually** ◇ *Inventions typically ~ minor improvements in technology.* | **inevitably, necessarily** ◇ *The reforms will inevitably ~ a lot of new paperwork for teachers.*

2 include sb

ADV. **actively, directly** ◇ *methods that actively ~ students in learning*
PREP. **in** ◇ *I didn't mean to ~ you in all this.*

involved *adj.*

1 taking part in sth

VERBS **be** | **become, get**
ADV. **closely, deeply, heavily, intimately, very** ◇ *She became heavily ~ in politics.* | **actively** ◇ *He wanted to be actively ~ in school life.* | **directly, primarily** ◇ *Drugs were not directly ~ in her death.* | **personally**
PREP. **in** ◇ *He was ~ in a road accident.* | **with** ◇ *She first became ~ with the organization in 1998.*

2 emotionally connected with sb

VERBS **be** | **become, get**
ADV. **deeply, heavily, very** | **personally** | **emotionally, romantically, sexually**
PREP. **with** ◇ *I never wanted to get emotionally ~ with him.*

3 complicated

VERBS **be, seem** | **become, get**
ADV. **extremely, fairly, very, etc.** ◇ *It all seems extremely ~ and complicated.*

involvement *noun*

ADJ. **active, direct** | **close, deep, intense** | **full** | **greater, increased, increasing** ◇ *Employees are demanding greater ~ in decision-making.* | **day-to-day** ◇ *When she was promoted, she missed the day-to-day ~ with customers.* | **personal** | **emotional** ◇ *Nurses usually try to avoid emotional ~ with patients.* | **parental** ◇ *He encourages parental ~ in the running of school.* | **political** | **military** ◇ *The government has ruled out military ~ in the region.* | **criminal** |

community | **alleged** ◇ *He is serving a 15-year sentence for his alleged ~ in a plot to overthrow the government.*
VERB + INVOLVEMENT **accuse sb of** | **suspect sb of** | **admit, deny** ◇ *Winters denies any ~ in the robbery.* | **suggest** ◇ *There is no evidence to suggest criminal ~.*
PREP. **~ by** ◇ *The success of the venture may lead to ~ by other foreign companies.* | **~ from** ◇ *The project needs full ~ from all members of the group.* | **~ in** ◇ *He was found to have a deep ~ in drug dealing.* | **~ of** ◇ *the ~ of parents in their children's education* | **~ with** ◇ *Her husband's ~ with another woman led to their divorce.*

iron *noun*

1 metal

ADJ. **rusty** | **cast, corrugated, galvanized, wrought** ◇ *a hut with a corrugated ~ roof* | **pig** | **scrap**
VERB + IRON **make, produce, smelt** ◇ *Germany produced enormous quantities of coal, ~ and steel.* | **be rich in, contain** ◇ *foods that are rich in ~* | **be cast in, be made from/of/out of** ◇ *a bridge made of wrought ~*
IRON + VERB **rust**
IRON + NOUN **ore** ◇ *They mine ~ ore locally.* | **bar** | **gate** | **filings** | **industry** | **foundry, works** | **deficiency** ◇ *patients with ~ deficiency* | **pill** (*esp. AmE*), **tablets** (*esp. BrE*) ◇ *I was put on ~ tablets for my anaemia.*

2 tool

ADJ. **hot, warm** | **electric, steam** | **travel** (*BrE*) | **curling** (= for making hair curly), **flat** (= for making hair straight) (*both AmE*) ◇ *You can use a curling ~ to create soft curls.*
VERB + IRON **use** ◇ *Use a cool ~ on synthetics.*

ironic (*also less frequent* **ironical**) *adj.*

VERBS **be, seem** | **find sth**
ADV. **extremely, fairly, very, etc.** | **deeply, highly, particularly** | **a little, slightly, etc.** | **doubly** | **deliciously** | **bitterly, sadly, tragically**

ironing *noun*

... OF IRONING **pile** (*esp. BrE*) ◇ *There's a pile of ~ waiting to be done.*
VERB + IRONING **do** ◇ *Who does the ~ in your house?*
IRONING + NOUN **board**

irony *noun*

ADJ. **great, heavy** ◇ *She tried to ignore the heavy ~ in his voice.* | **gentle** ◇ *She congratulated him with gentle ~.* | **bitter, cruel, sad, tragic** | **delicious** | **nice** ◇ *It is a nice ~ that the rivalry among popes was solved by their ancient rival, the Holy Roman Emperor.* | **final, supreme, ultimate** ◇ *The ultimate ~ is that the revolution, rather than bringing freedom, actually ended it completely.* | **dramatic** (= in a play, when a character's words carry an extra meaning that the character is not aware of)
... OF IRONY **hint, touch, trace** ◇ *He thanked us all without a touch of ~.*
PREP. **by a ... ~** ◇ *By a cruel ~, he died in a crash while returning home from the war.*
PHRASES **a certain ~** ◇ *There is a certain ~ in the situation.*

irrational *adj.*

VERBS **appear, be, seem** | **become** | **consider sth, regard sth as, see sth as** | **dismiss sth as** ◇ *He dismissed her fears as ~.*
ADV. **completely, quite, totally, wholly** | **increasingly** | **somewhat** | **apparently** (*esp. BrE*), **seemingly** | **inherently** ◇ *There was nothing inherently ~ in such a decision.*

irreconcilable *adj.*

VERBS **appear, be, seem** | **become**
ADV. **apparently, seemingly** ◇ *a seemingly ~ conflict* | **ultimately** (*esp. AmE*) ◇ *A one-party system is ultimately ~ with popular debate.*
PREP. **with** ◇ *These practices are ~ with the law of the Church.*

irregular adj.

1 not regular in size/shape/frequency

VERBS **be** | **become**
ADV. **highly, very** | **rather, slightly, somewhat** ◇ *The cells are slightly ~ in shape.*

2 not allowed according to the rules

VERBS **be, seem**
ADV. **highly, most, very** ◇ *It would be highly ~ for a police officer to accept money in this way.* | **slightly, somewhat** ◇ *some somewhat ~ business practices*

irregularity noun

ADJ. **serious** | **minor, slight** ◇ *a slight ~ in the surface of the wood* | **widespread** ◇ *The newspaper claimed there were widespread irregularities in the election.* | **accounting, election, electoral, financial, procedural, voting** ◇ *Investigators found no evidence of financial ~.*
VERB + IRREGULARITY **investigate** | **detect, report, uncover**
IRREGULARITY + VERB **occur** ◇ *Irregularities occur when there is no central control.*
PREP. **~ in** ◇ *Auditors have uncovered serious irregularities in the accounts.*

irrelevant adj.

VERBS **appear, be, seem** | **become** | **make sth, render sth** | **consider sth, deem sth, regard sth as, see sth as, view sth as** | **dismiss sth as** ◇ *These arguments were dismissed as ~.*
ADV. **completely, entirely, quite, totally, utterly, wholly** ◇ *This argument is entirely ~ to the question of who is right.* | **increasingly** ◇ *The UN is becoming increasingly ~.* | **almost, more or less, virtually** | **essentially, largely** ◇ *These issues are largely ~ and distract us from attending to the real questions.* | **rather, somewhat** | **simply** | **apparently, seemingly** | **politically**
PREP. **to** ◇ *Her statement is ~ to this case.* ◇ *It's all ~ to me.*

irresistible adj.

VERBS **be, prove, seem** | **become** | **make sb/sth** ◇ *The very high salary made the job ~.* | **find sb/sth** ◇ *You'll find our offer ~.*
ADV. **quite** (esp. BrE), **utterly** | **almost** | **simply** | **apparently** (esp. BrE), **seemingly** ◇ *Public spending has a seemingly ~ momentum.*
PREP. **to** ◇ *His rugged good looks made him ~ to women.*

irresponsible adj.

VERBS **be, seem** | **become** | **consider sb/sth**
ADV. **extremely, fairly, very, etc.** | **deeply, grossly, highly** ◇ *Their actions were highly ~.* | **criminally** ◇ *these extreme and criminally ~ policies* | **completely, totally, utterly** (esp. BrE), **wholly** (BrE) ◇ *He's fun, but totally ~.* | **a little, slightly, etc.** | **socially** ◇ *It is socially ~ to refuse young people advice on sexual matters.* | **fiscally** (AmE)

irrigation noun

ADJ. **large-scale** | **drip** ◇ *I could put in a drip ~ system in the rose beds.*
IRRIGATION + NOUN **project, scheme** (BrE), **system** | **canal, channel, ditch** | **pump** | **water**
PREP. **under ~** ◇ *two million acres under ~*

irritate verb

ADV. **really** ◇ *That man really ~s me!* | **slightly** | **easily** ◇ *She was moody at times and easily ~d.*

irritated adj.

VERBS **be, feel, look, sound** | **become, get**
ADV. **extremely, fairly, very, etc.** | **deeply, seriously** (esp. AmE) | **thoroughly** | **increasingly** | **a little, slightly, etc.** | **mildly** | **visibly**
PREP. **at** ◇ *She was deeply ~ at being thwarted.* | **by** ◇ *He was slightly ~ by her forgetfulness.*

irritating adj.

VERBS **be** ◇ *The sheer number of tourists can be ~.* | **become, get** ◇ *The song gets a bit ~ after a while.* | **find sth**
ADV. **extremely, fairly, very, etc.** | **highly, intensely** (esp. BrE) ◇ *I find all this highly ~* | **a little, slightly, etc.** | **mildly** ◇ *I have always found her mildly ~.* | **downright** (informal) ◇ *His voice is downright ~.*

irritation noun

1 feeling/cause of being irritated

ADJ. **considerable** (esp. BrE), **great, intense, major, some** (esp. BrE) ◇ *'I'm not American, I'm Canadian,' he replied with some ~.* | **mild, minor, slight** ◇ *the minor ~ of having to wait* | **constant**
VERB + IRRITATION **feel** ◇ *He felt slight ~ at being kept waiting.* | **express, show** ◇ *He showed no ~ at the delay.* | **conceal, hide, suppress** ◇ *She made no attempt to conceal her ~.* ◇ *He was unable to hide his ~ any longer.* | **cause** ◇ *Such delays can cause considerable ~.*
IRRITATION + VERB **grow** ◇ *She felt ~ growing in her.* | **show** ◇ *She didn't let her ~ show.*
PREP. **in ~** ◇ *Gary shook his head in ~.* | **to your ~** ◇ *I found to my great ~ that I'd forgotten the movie.* | **with ~** ◇ *'Of course not' she said with some ~.* | **~ at** ◇ *our ~ at the delay* | **~ to** ◇ *This is a major ~ to commuters.* | **~ with** ◇ *her ~ with people who were slow*
PHRASES **a sense of ~** | **a source of ~** ◇ *Traffic noise is a source of constant ~.*

2 slight pain in part of the body

ADJ. **intense, severe** | **mild** | **eye, skin** ◇ *a new cream to treat skin ~*
VERB + IRRITATION **cause, lead to** ◇ *The infection can cause intense ~ of the throat.* | **experience, get** ◇ *Stop using the cream if you get any ~.* | **prevent**

island noun

ADJ. **outlying, remote** ◇ *a ferry service to the outlying ~s* | **coral, tropical, volcanic** | **desert, deserted, uninhabited** | **offshore** ◇ *Puerto Rico and its offshore ~s*
... OF ISLANDS **chain, group** ◇ *a group of tropical ~s*
ISLAND + NOUN **chain, group** ◇ *the ~ chain of the Bahamas* | **home** ◇ *They were forced to leave their ~ home and start a new life on the mainland.* | **paradise** ◇ *the ~ paradise of Phuket* | **nation** ◇ *Fiji is a small South Pacific ~ nation.*
PREP. **on an/the ~** ◇ *He owns a house on the ~.*
PHRASES **the ... coast, side, tip, etc. of an ~** ◇ *The best beaches are on the southern tip of the ~.*

isolated adj.

VERBS **appear, be, feel** | **become, get** | **remain** | **leave sb/sth** ◇ *Without help, many elderly people would be left ~.* | **keep sb/sth** ◇ *She kept herself almost ~ from her colleagues.*
ADV. **extremely, fairly, very, etc.** | **completely, entirely, totally** | **increasingly** ◇ *The President is looking increasingly ~ from the whole agenda.* | **largely** | **effectively, essentially** | **diplomatically, economically, geographically, physically, socially** ◇ *Unless a compromise could be reached the country would be diplomatically ~ on this issue.*
PREP. **from** ◇ *a child who is ~ from other children*

isolation noun

ADJ. **complete, total** | **relative** | **enforced** (esp. BrE) ◇ *the enforced ~ of life in an Arctic weather station* | **self-imposed** ◇ *He lived in a state of self-imposed ~.* | **cultural, diplomatic, geographic** (AmE), **geographical** (esp. BrE), **political** | **international** ◇ *The country could face international ~ if it does not withdraw its troops.* | **emotional, social** ◇ *the social ~ of single mothers at home with their babies*
VERB + ISOLATION **experience, suffer, suffer from** ◇ *Many immigrants experience ~.* | **end**
ISOLATION + NOUN **hospital** (BrE), **room, ward** (esp. BrE)

PREP. **in ~** ◊ *The figures should not be looked at in ~ but as part of a pattern.*
PHRASES **in splendid ~** (*esp. BrE*) ◊ *The tower stands in splendid ~ on the cliff edge.*

issue *noun*

1 problem

ADJ. **big, burning, central, critical, crucial, important, key, main, major, serious, vital** ◊ *The economy remains the burning ~ within the party.* | **larger, wider** ◊ *The problem raises wider ~s of gender and identity.* | **minor, side** | **related** | **basic, fundamental** | **whole** | **real** ◊ *The real ~ is where the power lies.* | **contentious, controversial, difficult, thorny** ◊ *the controversial ~ of censorship* | **complex** | **live, unresolved** ◊ *The strike of ten years ago is still very much a live ~ in the town.* | **domestic, global, international, local, national, regional** | **commercial, constitutional, economic, educational, environmental, ethical, health, legal, moral, policy, political, safety, security, social, technical, theoretical**
... OF ISSUES **number, range, series**
VERB + ISSUE **raise** | **debate, discuss** ◊ *This evening we're debating the ~ of the legalization of soft drugs.* | **decide, resolve, settle** ◊ *A referendum was held to settle the ~.* | **address, consider, cover, deal with, examine, explore, face, look at, tackle** | **clarify** | **see, understand** | **focus on** ◊ *We really need to focus on this one ~ and not get sidetracked.* | **touch on** ◊ *The ~ of birth control was touched on, but we need to examine it in more detail.* | **highlight** ◊ *The report highlights three ~s.* | **confuse** ◊ *This argument should not be allowed to confuse the ~.* | **avoid, evade** | **become** ◊ *Security has become a real ~.*
ISSUE + VERB **arise** ◊ *~s arising from the survey* | **surround sth, underlie sth** ◊ *A more important ~ underlies this debate.* | **affect sb/sth, face sb/sth** ◊ *A number of ~s are affecting the dairy industry.*
PREP. **at ~** ◊ *What you say is interesting, but it does not affect the point at ~ here.* | **on an/the ~** ◊ *She spoke on the ~ of private health care.* | **~ about** ◊ *fundamental ~s about working conditions* | **~ concerning** ◊ *~s concerning the environment* | **~ relating to** ◊ *The conference examined key ~s relating to the reform.*
PHRASES **make an ~ of sth** ◊ *I'm not worried about the cost—you're the one who's making an ~ of it.*

2 one in a series of publications

ADJ. **current** | **back** | **special** ◊ *a special ~ of stamps*
VERB + ISSUE **bring out, publish**
ISSUE + VERB **come out, go on sale** | **be out**
PREP. **in an/the ~** ◊ *an article in the current ~ of 'Newsweek'*

issue *verb*

ADV. **directly** ◊ *In a statement ~d directly to the public on Thursday…* | **jointly** ◊ *a document ~d jointly by the two departments* | **immediately, promptly** ◊ *He left the company and promptly ~d a writ claiming $45 million in damages.* | **formally** ◊ *the bank which formally ~s and handles these credit cards*
PREP. **on behalf of** ◊ *a statement ~d on behalf of the UN Secretary-General* | **to** ◊ *The new guidelines have been ~d to all doctors.* | **with** ◊ *Some of the police were ~d with rifles.*
PHRASES **newly ~d** ◊ *newly ~d stamps*

itch *noun*

ADJ. **slight** | **jock** (*AmE, informal*) ◊ *The fungi that cause jock ~ thrive in warm, moist places.* | **seven-year** (*informal, humorous*) (= the desire to find a new partner after seven years in a relationship)
VERB + ITCH **feel** | **relieve, scratch, scratch at** ◊ *The dog was scratching at an ~ behind its left ear.*

itch *verb*

ADV. **terribly** ◊ *My arms were covered with a rash that ~ed terribly.* | **constantly** | **positively**

VERB + ITCH **make sb** ◊ *The heat made me ~ all over.*
PREP. **for** ◊ *He was ~ing for a chance to show how good he was.* | **with** ◊ *Her fingers positively ~ed with the desire to slap his face.*

item *noun*

ADJ. **individual, particular, single, specific** ◊ *Each individual ~ has a number.* | **essential, important** ◊ *I keep essential ~s to hand when I fly.* | **main, major** ◊ *the main ~ on the agenda* ◊ *a major ~ of expenditure* | **expensive, valuable** ◊ *Several valuable ~s were stolen.* | **personal** | **commodity, consumer** ◊ *Computers became a consumer ~ in the early 1990s.* | **luxury** ◊ *There is a higher tax on luxury ~s.* | **food** | **household** ◊ *household ~s such as plates and glasses* | **collector's** ◊ *The 1970s model has become something of a collector's ~.* | **agenda** | **menu** | **data** | **news**
PREP. **~ of** ◊ *Several ~s of clothing were found near the scene of the crime.* | **~ about, ~ on** ◊ *a news ~ about drugs in the workplace*
PHRASES **~ by ~** ◊ *Check the list carefully, ~ by ~.* | **an ~ on the agenda, list, menu, etc.**

itinerary *noun*

ADJ. **detailed, full** | **tour, travel**
VERB + ITINERARY **plan** | **follow** ◊ *We had to follow a very detailed ~.* | **change**
ITINERARY + VERB **include sth** ◊ *Your ~ includes a visit to Stonehenge.*
PREP. **in an/the ~** ◊ *Historic sites are featured prominently in their itineraries.* | **on an/the ~** ◊ *The National Gallery is on most tourists' ~.*

ivory *noun*

ADJ. **carved, polished** | **raw** ◊ *the export and import of raw ~* | **illegal** ◊ *There is still a high price for illegal ~.* | **imitation** | **elephant, walrus**
VERB + IVORY **be made from, be made of** | **carve sth from, carve sth in** ◊ *a figure delicately carved in ~* | **be inlaid with** ◊ *a table made of polished wood, inlaid with ~*
IVORY + NOUN **trade**
PREP. **in ~** ◊ *a statuette in ~ and gold*
PHRASES **the trade in ~**

ivy *noun*

ADJ. **thick** | **poison, variegated** (*esp. BrE*)
VERB + IVY **be covered in** ◊ *The walls were covered in ~.*
IVY + VERB **grow** ◊ *Ivy grew up the side of the house.* | **climb, cling, crawl, creep, trail, twine** ◊ *There was ~ clinging to the wall.*
IVY + NOUN **leaves** | **plant, vine** (*both AmE*)

J j

jab *noun*

1 sudden hit/push

ADJ. **hard, sharp** | **quick** | **elbow** | **left, right** (in boxing)
VERB + JAB **give sb** | **feel** | **land, throw** (in boxing)
PREP. **~ in, ~ to** ◊ *Scott gave him a sharp left ~ to the ribs.*

2 (*BrE, informal*) injection

ADJ. **flu, tetanus, typhoid, etc.**
VERB + JAB **have** ◊ *Did you have a flu ~ this year?* | **give sb**

jack *noun* → Note at CARD

jacket *noun*

ADJ. **fitted, tailored** | **baggy, loose** | **heavy, thick** | **light, lightweight, thin** | **double-breasted, single-breasted** | **belted, zip-up** | **padded** (*esp. BrE*), **quilted** | **bolero** | **waterproof, waxed** (*BrE*) | **check, checked, striped** | **corduroy, cotton, denim, fleece, jean** (*AmE*), **leather,** linen, sheepskin (*esp. BrE*), suede, tweed, wool | bullet-proof | camouflage | pyjama (*BrE*) (*pajama top* in *AmE*), suit, uniform | dinner (*esp. BrE*) | tuxedo (*AmE*) | smoking, sport (*AmE*), sports | shooting, ski | flight (*AmE*), flying (*BrE*) | bomber | biker, motorcycle (*esp. AmE*) | donkey (*BrE*), pea (*AmE*) | combat, flak (*both BrE*) | life

VERB + JACKET get, grab (*esp. AmE*) | pull on, shrug into, shrug on, slip on, throw on ◇ *She shrugged into her ~.* | pull off, remove, shrug off, shrug out of, slip off | button, button up, do up, zip up | unbutton, undo, unzip | hang up | drape, sling ◇ *A light cotton ~ was draped over her shoulders.*

JACKET + VERB hang ◇ *His ~ hung over the back of his chair.*

JACKET + NOUN pocket, sleeve ◇ *He pulled his passport from his inside ~ pocket.*

PHRASES a ~ and tie ◇ *Men should wear a ~ and tie for dinner.*
→ Special page at CLOTHES

jackpot noun

ADJ. £1 million, $10 million, etc. | lottery

VERB + JACKPOT get, hit (*often figurative*), scoop (*BrE*), win (*often figurative*) ◇ *The company hopes to hit the ~ with its new range of clothing.*

JACKPOT + NOUN prize (*BrE*) | winner

PREP. ~ in ◇ *They scooped the ~ in yesterday's lottery.* | ~ of ◇ *a prize ~ of £100 000*

jail (*BrE also* gaol) noun

ADJ. city (*esp. AmE*), county, local | high-security, maximum-security, top-security (*all esp. BrE*) | private | overcrowded

VERB + JAIL go to ◇ *He's gone to ~ for fraud.* | put sb in, send sb to, throw sb into | keep sb in | keep sb out of ◇ *His lawyer worked hard to keep him out of ~.* | be freed from, be out of, be released from, get out of ◇ *She could be out of ~ in two years.* | escape from | threaten sb with ◇ *He was threatened with ~ if evidence of a hoax was discovered.* | face | avoid, escape ◇ *She avoided ~ by pleading insanity.*

JAIL + NOUN sentence, term, time | cell

PREP. at a/the ~ ◇ *riots at Strangeways ~* | in (a/the) ~ ◇ *How long has she been in ~?* ◇ *There was a fire in the ~ last night.*

jam noun → See also JELLY

ADJ. home-made | apricot, raspberry, strawberry, etc.

... OF JAM dollop (*BrE*) | jar, pot (*BrE*)

VERB + JAM make | spread (sth with) ◇ *She spread the toast thinly with raspberry ~.*

JAM + NOUN jar (*BrE*) | doughnut (*BrE*), sandwich (*esp. BrE*), tart (*BrE*)

PHRASES bread and ~
→ Special page at FOOD

jam verb

ADV. constantly ◇ *People constantly jammed the street.* | up ◇ *The traffic will just ~ up our village.*

PHRASES be jammed full (of sth) ◇ *The cupboards were jammed full of old newspapers.* | be jammed solid (*esp. BrE*) ◇ *The traffic was jammed solid on the bridge.* | be jammed tight with sth ◇ *The room is jammed tight with furniture.* | be jammed together ◇ *We were jammed together shoulder to shoulder.* | be jammed with ◇ *The airport was jammed with people trying to arrange flights.*

January noun → Note at MONTH

jar noun

ADJ. storage | airtight, sealed | mason (*AmE*), screw-top (*esp. BrE*) | sterilized (*esp. BrE*) | earthenware, glass, stone (*esp. BrE*), stoneware (*esp. AmE*) | candy (*AmE*), coffee (*esp. BrE*), cookie (*AmE*), jam (*BrE*), marmalade (*BrE*), pickle, sweet (*BrE*) | tip

VERB + JAR fill ◇ *She filled the ~s with the tomato sauce.* | seal | open | preserve sth in, store sth in

JAR + VERB be filled with sth, be full of sth, contain sth ◇ *a ~ full of pickled onions*

PREP. in a/the ~, into a/the ~ | ~ of ◇ *a ~ of mayonnaise*

jargon noun

ADJ. current | impenetrable, incomprehensible, meaningless, obscure | unnecessary | academic, legal, medical, military, scientific, technical, etc.

... OF JARGON piece

VERB + JARGON speak, speak in, use ◇ *He always speaks in obscure legal ~.* | be couched in ◇ *Her emails are always couched in ~.*

PREP. in ~ ◇ *The report seemed to be written in computer ~.* | ~ for ◇ *'All necessary means' is diplomatic ~ for 'war'.*

jaw noun

1 bone that contains teeth

ADJ. bottom, lower | top, upper | firm, strong | clenched, set | slack | jutting, lantern (= in which the lower part sticks out) | square | broken, dislocated, fractured

VERB + JAW clench, set, tighten (*AmE*) | work (*AmE*) ◇ *She worked her lower ~ back and forth.* | drop ◇ *She dropped her ~ in astonishment.* | rub ◇ *He rubbed his sore ~.* | break, dislocate, fracture

JAW + VERB drop, hang, hang open ◇ *My ~ dropped in astonishment when I saw the size of the audience.* | be set, clench, set, tighten ◇ *Her ~ was set, ready for a fight.* | jut ◇ *His ~ jutted stubbornly forward; he would not be denied.*

JAW + NOUN bone, muscle

PREP. in your ~ ◇ *A muscle in his ~ pulsed angrily.* | on your ~ ◇ *He had two days' growth of stubble on his ~.* | to the ~ ◇ *a punch to the ~* | under your ~ ◇ *She had a fold of flesh under her ~.*

PHRASES the line of your ~, the set of your ~ ◇ *The stern set of the officer's ~ made Tony realize he was in trouble.*

2 jaws mouth

ADJ. gaping, open | massive, powerful ◇ *A shark can crush a boat with its massive ~s.*

VERB + JAWS clamp, close, lock, sink ◇ *The dog locked its ~s on her leg and wouldn't let go.* ◇ *A spider sank its ~s into my ankle.* | open ◇ *Pythons open their ~s wide to swallow their prey whole.* | snap ◇ *The animal's ~s snapped shut.* | escape, escape from ◇ *The antelope could not escape the crocodile's gaping ~s.*

PREP. between its ~s ◇ *The dog had his arm clamped between its ~s.*

jazz noun

ADJ. live | cool, free, free-form, modern, trad (*BrE*), traditional

VERB + JAZZ play | listen to

JAZZ + NOUN music | clarinettist, guitarist, musician, pianist, player, singer, etc. | guitar, piano, vocals, etc. | band, combo, group, quartet, trio | improvisation, standard | chords, rhythms | club, venue | concert, festival | age | scene ◇ *the rising stars of the New York ~ scene* | fan

PREP. in ~ ◇ *harmonies and rhythms common in ~*

jealous adj.

VERBS be, feel, sound | become, get, grow | make sb ◇ *Ignore her—she's only trying to make you ~.*

ADV. extremely, fairly, very, etc. | insanely, madly ◇ *I can remember feeling madly ~ when he was with other women.* | a little, slightly, etc.

PREP. about ◇ *There's nothing for you to feel ~ about.* | of ◇ *She was rather ~ of me.* ◇ *He had started to get ~ of her success.*

jealousy noun

ADJ. extreme, intense, pure | insane, irrational, obsessive, pathological | petty | professional, sexual

... OF JEALOUSY fit ◇ *He broke off the engagement in a fit of ~.* | pang, stab, twinge ◇ *I felt a pang of ~.*

VERB + JEALOUSY feel ◇ *She'd never felt ~ before.* | arouse, cause, create, provoke ◇ *Her promotion aroused intense ~ among her colleagues.*

PREP. **~ of** ◊ *his obsessive ~ of his ex-wife*
PHRASES **feelings of ~**

jeans *noun*

ADJ. **skintight, stretch, tight** | **baggy, flared, loose** | **bell-bottom, boot-cut, drainpipe, flare** (*AmE*), **flared** | **cut-off, low-rise** | **denim** | **black, blue** | **faded, stonewashed** | **ripped, scruffy** (*informal, esp. BrE*), **torn, worn, worn-in, worn-out** | **designer**
... OF JEANS **pair** ◊ *She pulled on a pair of faded blue ~.*
VERB + JEANS **pull on, pull up** | **pull off, strip off** | **zip up** | **unzip**
JEANS + NOUN **pocket**
→ Special page at CLOTHES

jelly *noun*

1 (*BrE*) (*AmE* **jello, Jell-O**™) dessert

ADJ. **lemon, raspberry, strawberry, etc.**
VERB + JELLY/JELLO **eat, have** | **make** ◊ *Shall I make a ~ for pudding?*
JELLY/JELLO + VERB **set** ◊ *Leave the ~ to set for at least four hours.* | **jiggle** (*AmE*), **wiggle** (*AmE*), **wobble** (*esp. BrE*)
JELLY/JELLO + NOUN **mould/mold**
PREP. **in ~** ◊ *fruit in ~*

2 type of jam → See also JAM

ADJ. **currant, grape, strawberry, etc.**
VERB + JELLY **make** | **spread** ◊ *I spread grape ~ on my toast.*
JELLY + NOUN **doughnut** (*esp. AmE*), **roll** (*AmE*) (**Swiss roll** in *BrE*), **sandwich** (*esp. AmE*) ◊ *peanut butter and ~ sandwiches* | **jar** (*esp. AmE*)
→ Special page at FOOD

jeopardize (*BrE also* **-ise**) *verb*

ADV. **seriously, severely** ◊ *This scandal could seriously ~ his chances of being re-elected.* | **potentially** ◊ *Any delays could potentially ~ the company's ability to do business.*

jerk *noun*

1 sudden movement

ADJ. **quick, sharp, sudden, violent**
VERB + JERK **give** ◊ *His thigh muscle gave a sudden ~.*
PREP. **with a ~ of** ◊ *She answered with a ~ of her head.*

2 (*informal*) stupid person

ADJ. **complete, real, total** | **stupid** | **arrogant, conceited, egotistical, pompous, self-centred/self-centered, selfish** | **insensitive, macho**

jerk *verb*

ADV. **abruptly, suddenly** | **sharply, violently** | **convulsively, spasmodically** | **instinctively** ◊ *She ~ed her hand back instinctively.* | **away, back, backwards/backward, down-wards/downward, forward, sideways, up, upright, up-wards/upward** ◊ *She suddenly ~ed her hand away.* ◊ *His head ~ed up.*
PHRASES **~ awake** ◊ *The train stopped and she ~ed awake.* | **~ sth open** ◊ *He ~ed the door open.* | **~ to a halt, ~ to a stop** ◊ *The bus ~ed to a stop.*

jersey *noun*

ADJ. **baseball, basketball, football, hockey, rugby, soccer** | **replica** ◊ *Where can I find replica Iranian soccer ~s?*
VERB + JERSEY **wear** | **don, pull on**
→ Special page at CLOTHES

jet *noun*

1 plane with a jet engine

ADJ. **jumbo** | **supersonic** | **regional** (*esp. AmE*) | **commercial, passenger** | **private** | **business, corporate, executive** | **charter, chartered** | **holiday** (*BrE*) | **cargo** | **air-force, fighter, military** | **low-flying** (*esp. BrE*)
VERB + JET **fly, pilot** | **charter** | **hijack** | **scramble** | **board** ◊

He was photographed boarding his private ~. | **land** ◊ *The pilot had to land the ~ in a field.*
JET + VERB **fly** | **take off** | **land** | **crash, explode**
JET + NOUN **aircraft, airliner, airplane** (*AmE*), **bomber, fighter, liner, plane** | **engine** | **fuel** | **pilot**
PREP. **by ~** ◊ *Australia was a mere couple of hours away by ~.* ◊ *She was flown by private ~ to the capital.* | **in a/the ~** ◊ *He flew to Bermuda in his private ~.*

2 stream of gas, water, etc.

ADJ. **air, gas, water**
PREP. **~ of** ◊ *Little ~s of steam spurted from the engine.*

Jew *noun*

ADJ. **devout, observant, pious, practising/practicing, religious** ◊ *His family are all observant ~s.* | **secular** | **conservative, Hasidic, orthodox** | **Ashkenazi, Sephardic** | **Progressive, Reform**
VERB + JEW **marry** | **be born** ◊ *He was born a ~ in 1st-century Palestine.* | **become**

jewel *noun*

ADJ. **precious, priceless, prized** | **bright, shining, sparkling**
VERB + JEWEL **wear** | **steal**
JEWEL + VERB **glitter, sparkle**
JEWEL + NOUN **thief** | **heist** (*esp. AmE*) | **box, case**

jewellery (*BrE*) (*AmE* **jewelry**) *noun*

ADJ. **expensive** | **cheap** | **beautiful, fine** | **flashy, gaudy** (*esp. AmE*) | **costume** | **designer** | **handmade** | **antique** | **diamond, gold, etc.**
... OF JEWELLERY **item, piece**
VERB + JEWELLERY/JEWELRY **wear** | **make** | **design** | **remove** ◊ *The nurse asked her to remove all her ~.* | **steal**
JEWELLERY/JEWELRY + NOUN **box, case** | **shop** (*esp. BrE*), **store** (*AmE*) | **design** | **designer** | **heist, robbery**
→ Special page at CLOTHES

jigsaw *noun* (*BrE*) → See also PUZZLE

ADJ. **giant, huge** | **200-piece, etc.**
... OF JIGSAW **bit, piece** ◊ *One piece of the ~ is still missing.*
VERB + JIGSAW **do** ◊ *I used to enjoy doing ~s.* | **piece together** (*figurative*) ◊ *The police managed to piece together the ~ and reconstruct the victim's last hours.* | **finish**
JIGSAW + NOUN **puzzle** | **piece**
PHRASES **a piece in a ~** (*figurative*) ◊ *This is another piece in the ~ that will help us understand the disease.*

job *noun*

1 employment

ADJ. **decent, good, great, worthwhile** | **interesting** | **high-powered, top** ◊ *It's one of the top ~s in management.* | **plum** ◊ *The plum ~s all went to friends of the prime minister.* | **cushy** ◊ *His father found him a cushy ~ in the office, with almost nothing to do and a big salary.* | **dream, ideal** ◊ *What would be your dream ~?* | **boring, dead-end, lousy** (*informal, esp. AmE*), **menial, routine, undemanding** ◊ *He was forced to take a series of menial ~s.* | **rewarding** | **challenging, demanding, difficult, taxing** | **dangerous** ◊ *It's often immigrants who do the dangerous ~s.* | **highly paid, high-paying, well-paid, well-paying** (*esp. AmE*) | **badly paid, low-paid, low-paying** (*esp. AmE*), **poorly paid** (*esp. BrE*) | **new** ◊ *The plant will provide almost 300 new ~s.* | **current, first, previous** ◊ *Three years ago she moved into her current ~.* | **full-time, part-time** | **9-to-5** | **regular, steady** ◊ *He was tempted to give up freelancing and get a regular ~.* | **permanent, temporary** | **holiday** (*BrE*), **summer** | **evening, Saturday, weekend** | **paid, unpaid** | **manual** (*esp. BrE*) | **semi-skilled, skilled, unskilled** | **blue-collar, white-collar** | **desk** ◊ *a desk ~ in the police housing department* | **factory, office** | **coaching, construction, manufacturing, teaching, etc.** | **proper, real** ◊ *He'd done lots of part-time work, but this was his first proper ~.*
VERB + JOB **have** ◊ *She has a very good ~ with a local law firm.* | **carry out, do, perform, work** (*AmE*) ◊ *I'm only doing my ~* (= doing what I am paid to do). ◊ *They are paid according to*

how well they perform their ~. | **look for, want** | **apply for, go for** | **be offered** | **accept, take** | **find, get, land, win** ◇ *She got a temporary ~ stacking shelves.* ◇ *He's just landed himself a highly paid ~ in banking.* | **lose** ◇ *He's frightened of losing his ~.* | **give up, leave, pack in** (*BrE*) **quit** (*esp. AmE*), **resign from** | **hold down, keep** ◇ *He's always had difficulty holding down a ~.* | **start** ◇ *She's starting a new ~ on Monday.* | **like, love** | **advertise** ◇ *I saw the ~ advertised on the Internet.* | **interview (sb) for** ◇ *We're interviewing for the ~ in the Sales Department.* | **give sb, offer sb** | **create, generate, provide (sb with)** ◇ *It is hoped that the development will create new ~s in the region.* | **axe** (*BrE*), **cut, eliminate, shed** ◇ *The company is hoping to shed 200 ~s.* | **export, outsource** ◇ *Companies export ~s because it is cheaper to pay foreign workers.* | **protect, safeguard** (*esp. BrE*) ◇ *The deal between the union and management should safeguard 6 000 ~s.* | **know** ◇ *He certainly knows his ~* (= *is very good at his job*).

JOB + VERB **pay** ◇ *The ~ doesn't pay very well.* | **disappear, go** ◇ *250 ~s are to go at the local steel plant.* | **entail, require** | *The ~ requires honesty, intelligence, and vision.*

JOB + NOUN **search** ◇ *It's important to devise a ~ search strategy when looking for work.* | **ad, advertisement, listings** (*esp. AmE*) ◇ *Check our website for the latest ~ listings.* | **vacancy** | **application** | **applicant** | **interview** | **offer** ◇ *Within weeks of graduation she had several ~ offers.* | **title** ◇ *His ~ title is Chief Hygiene Operative.* | **description, specifications** (*esp. BrE*) ◇ *Cleaning the office is not in my ~ description.* | **market** ◇ *There is an enormous ~ market for teachers at the moment.* | **cuts, losses** | **growth** (*AmE*) ◇ *We have seen ~ growth in a number of areas.* | **creation** | **openings** (*esp. AmE*), **opportunities, prospects** | **satisfaction** ◇ *How would you rate your ~ satisfaction?* | **security** ◇ *Workers questioned rated ~ security as being more important than high salary.* | **hunter, seeker** (*esp. BrE*) ◇ *Local companies are holding an open day for ~ seekers.* | **share, sharing** ◇ *Their boss agreed to a ~ share.* ◇ *The introduction of ~ sharing could prevent the need for ~ losses.*

PREP. **in a/the ~** ◇ *There's not much chance of promotion in a ~ like that.* | **on the ~** ◇ *You will receive training on the ~.* | **out of a ~** ◇ *She found herself out of a ~ when her boss died.* | **~ as** ◇ *She has a ~ as a waitress.* | **~ at** ◇ *She got a teaching ~ at the university.* | **~ for** ◇ *~s for women* | **~ in** ◇ *a ~ in food retailing* ◇ *a ~ in a large company* | **~ with** ◇ *He moved to a better-paid ~ with another employer.*

PHRASES **change ~s, move ~s** ◇ *Nowadays many people change ~s every few years.* | **a loss of ~s** ◇ *The closure of the cement factory will mean the loss of over 800 ~s.* | **the right person for the ~** ◇ *Despite the small number of applicants, they managed to find the right person for the ~.*

2 task

ADJ. **adequate, decent, good, nice, professional, thorough** | **admirable, amazing, awesome** (*informal, esp. AmE*), **brilliant** (*esp. BrE*), **excellent, fantastic, fine, grand** (*esp. BrE*), **great, incredible, magnificent, marvellous/marvelous, masterful** (*esp. AmE*), **outstanding, remarkable, superb, terrific, tremendous, wonderful** | **bad, lousy** (*informal, esp. AmE*), **poor, terrible** ◇ *They've done a poor ~ of managing their finances.* | **difficult, hard, tough** ◇ *They gave me the tough ~ of telling applicants that they'd been rejected.* | **easy** | **important** | **big, long** | **little, small** | **fiddly** (*BrE*), **tedious** ◇ *fiddly little ~s like wiring plugs* | **dirty** | **unenviable** ◇ *Cooper had the unenviable ~ of announcing the bad new.* | **thankless** ◇ *Keeping the house clean can be a thankless ~.*

VERB + JOB **carry out, do** ◇ *You've done a great ~ with that decorating.* ◇ *Try wedging it open—that should do the ~* (= *be effective*). | **handle** ◇ *I was very pleased with the way she handled the ~.* | **have, have on** ◇ *You'll have a hard ~ convincing them that you're right.* ◇ *The builder has a couple of ~s on at the moment.* | **give sb** | **take on** ◇ *She's taken on the ~ of organizing the Christmas party.* | **get on with** ◇ *I want to get on with the ~ of painting my room today.* | **complete, finish** ◇ *We finished the ~ in five hours.*

PREP. **~ in** ◇ *The author has done an admirable ~ in compiling all this material.* | **~ on** ◇ *You've done a good ~ on the car.*

PHRASES **get the ~ done** ◇ *We're hoping to get the ~ done this weekend.* ◇ *You can count on him—he gets the ~ done* (= *he is reliable*). | **make a good, poor, etc. ~ of sth** (*esp. BrE*) ◇ *She made a very good ~ of covering up the damage.* ◇ *He made a very professional ~ of replacing the windows.* | **odd ~s** (= *small, practical jobs*) ◇ *I spend most Saturdays doing odd ~s around the house.*

3 crime

ADJ. **bank** | **inside** (= *done by sb in the organization where the crime happens*)

VERB + JOB **do** ◇ *He got six months for that last ~ he did.* | **bungle** ◇ *The gang bungled the ~ and got caught.*

NOTE

Jobs

be …, work as … ◇ *She's a well-known writer.* ◇ *Her father, a trained chef, now works as a bus driver.*

study to be …, train as …, train to be … ◇ *She trained as a painter and sculptor.*

start as …, start work as … ◇ *He started work as a trainee chef.*

become … ◇ *I'm interested in becoming a dentist.*

be/become/get certified as … (*esp. AmE*), **qualify as …** (*esp. BrE*) ◇ *He got certified as a teacher.* ◇ *She qualified as a nurse last year.*

employ (sb as) …, have … ◇ *The company employs more than 1500 engineers.*

engage (sb as) …, get …, hire (sb as) …, recruit …, take on … ◇ *They have recruited a new designer.*

appoint (sb as) …, make sb … ◇ *He was appointed Professor of Law at Yale.* ◇ *At 39 she was made chairman of the board.*

dismiss …, fire …, sack … (*BrE*) ◇ *She was dismissed from her job after only six months.* ◇ *You're fired!* ◇ *The team sacked the coach.*

→ See also the note at PROFESSIONAL

---

jockey *noun*

ADJ. **champion, leading, top** | **winning** | **apprentice** | **amateur** (*esp. BrE*) | **jump** (= *who rides in races that involve jumping*) (*esp. BrE*), **steeplechase** (*esp. AmE*) | **stable** (= *who rides the horses of a particular trainer or training stable*)

JOCKEY + VERB **ride (sth)** ◇ *Which ~ will be riding tomorrow?* | **win (sth)** ◇ *The race was won by top ~ Eddie Andrews.*

jog *noun*

ADJ. **brisk, quick** | **slow** | **light** (*esp. AmE*) | **daily, morning**

VERB + JOG **go for** ◇ *He goes for a brisk ~ before work each morning.*

PREP. **at a ~** ◇ *I began at a slow ~ and gradually increased my pace.*

jog *verb*

ADV. **slowly, steadily** | **briskly, quickly** | **lightly**

PREP. **along, down, up** ◇ *They jogged steadily up the hill.*

PHRASES **go jogging** ◇ *She decided to go jogging each morning.* | **~ in place** (*AmE*), **~ on the spot** (*esp. BrE*) ◇ *She was jogging on the spot to keep warm.*

join *verb*

1 become a member of sth

ADV. **formally, officially** ◇ *Although a sympathizer, he never officially ~ed the party.* | **voluntarily, willingly** ◇ *Some were conscripted into the army and others ~ed voluntarily.* | **recently** ◇ *This is Nicole, who recently ~ed the company.*

VERB + JOIN **want to, wish to** | **flock to** (*esp. BrE*) ◇ *By this time people were flocking to ~ the cult.* | **decide to** | **persuade sb to** | **be allowed to** | **refuse to**

PHRASES **an invitation to ~ sth**

joint

2 do sth with sb else

ADV. **together** ◊ *Farmers can ~ together to get better prices.* | **eagerly, gladly** ◊ *I would gladly ~ you in whatever plans you have for this evening.*

VERB + JOIN **wish to** | **invite sb to** ◊ *They've invited us to ~ them on their yacht.* | **be allowed to** ◊ *She was now old enough to be allowed to ~ the adults.* | **be expected to** ◊ *Thousands of people are expected to ~ the sponsored walk.* | **decide to** | **refuse to**

PREP. **for** ◊ *Will you ~ me for a drink in the bar?* | **in** ◊ *I'm sure you will all wish to ~ me in thanking our speaker tonight.* | **with** ◊ *Please will you all ~ with me in singing the national anthem.*

PHRASES **come and ~ sb** ◊ *He waved a fork in greeting. 'Come and ~ us!'* | **an invitation to ~ sb/sth**

PHR V **join in**

ADV. **enthusiastically** ◊ *They all ~ed enthusiastically in the dancing.*

VERB + JOIN IN **want to** | **refuse to**

PREP. **with** ◊ *Everyone ~ed in with the singing.* ◊ *I wish he would ~ in with the other children.*

joint *noun*

1 in the body

ADJ. **elbow, hip, knee, etc.** | **aching, achy** (*esp. AmE*), **inflamed, painful, sore, stiff, swollen** | **artificial**

VERB + JOINT **replace** ◊ *He's going to have his hip ~ replaced.* | **dislocate** ◊ *He dislocated his elbow ~.* | **lubricate** ◊ *Synovial fluid lubricates the ~s.* | **affect** ◊ *It is an inflammatory condition affecting the ~s.*

JOINT + VERB **ache** | **creak** ◊ *He slowly stood up, ~s creaking in protest.* | **move** ◊ *The ~ should be able to move freely.*

PREP. **in a/the ~** ◊ *You have fluid in the ~.* | **~ between** ◊ *the ~ between the lower and upper parts of the arm*

PHRASES **put sth out of ~** (*BrE*) ◊ *She fell and put her knee out of ~.*

2 connecting point

ADJ. **watertight**

VERB + JOINT **make, seal**

PREP. **~ between** ◊ *a ~ between two lengths of copper*

3 bar, restaurant, etc.

ADJ. **barbecue, burger, fast-food, hamburger, pizza** (*all esp. AmE*) | **juke** (*AmE*), **strip**

4 (*BrE*) piece of meat

ADJ. **bacon**

VERB + JOINT **cook, roast** | **carve**

PREP. **~ of** ◊ *a ~ of beef/lamb/pork*

joke *noun*

ADJ. **amusing, funny, good, hilarious** ◊ *She didn't seem to find my ~s amusing.* | **old** ◊ *That's an old joke—I've heard it lots of times.* | **bad, corny, dumb** (*AmE*), **lame, silly, stupid, unfunny** (*esp. BrE*) | **cruel, sick** | **racist, sexist** | **crude, dirty, off-colour/off-color** (*esp. AmE*) | **inside** (*esp. AmE*), **private** ◊ *They kept telling inside ~s about people I didn't know.* | **running** ◊ *The show features a running ~ about a nosy dog.* | **practical** ◊ *His brothers were always playing practical ~s.* | **huge** ◊ *It's all just a huge ~ to you, isn't it?*

VERB + JOKE **crack, make, tell** ◊ *He's excellent at telling ~s.* | **play** ◊ *He's always playing ~s on people.* | **exchange, have** (*esp. BrE*), **share** ◊ *She likes to share a ~ with her employees.* | **hear** | **appreciate, enjoy, get, laugh at, like, understand** ◊ *We all fell about laughing, but he didn't get the ~.* ◊ *She doesn't like ~s about her height.* | **remember** | **spoil** ◊ *He told us the ending, completely spoiling the ~.* | **miss** ◊ *Am I missing the ~ here?* | **take** ◊ *The trouble is she can't take a ~.* | **treat sth as** ◊ *He treated his exams as a huge ~.*

JOKE + VERB **fall flat** ◊ *The audience wasn't very responsive and the ~s fell flat.* | **be on sb** ◊ *I thought I'd play a trick on them, but in the end the ~ was on me.*

PREP. **as a ~** ◊ *It was only said as a ~.* | **~ about** ◊ *Have you heard the ~ about the elephant and the mouse?*

PHRASES **make a ~ of sth** ◊ *We tried to make a ~ of our situation, but it wasn't really funny.*

joke *verb*

ADV. **half** ◊ *She was only half joking about being president one day.* | **around** ◊ *Everyone just ~d around and enjoyed themselves.* | **lamely, weakly** | **good-naturedly, playfully**

PREP. **about** ◊ *We ~d about the amount of equipment we had to carry.* | **with** ◊ *She's always joking with her friends.*

PHRASES **be only joking** ◊ *Don't worry, I'm only joking!* | **joking apart** (*BrE*), **joking aside** (= used to show you are now being serious after you have said sth funny) | **laugh and ~** ◊ *They laughed and ~d as they walked along.* | **you must be joking, you've got to be joking** (*esp. AmE*) ◊ *No way am I doing that. You must be joking!*

joker *noun* → Note at CARD

jolt *noun*

ADJ. **nasty, severe, sharp, sickening, sudden, violent** | **little, slight**

VERB + JOLT **feel** | **give** ◊ *My mother's death gave me a severe ~.* | **send** | **receive** ◊ *She received such a ~ that she nearly dropped her cup.*

PHRASES **with a ~** ◊ *The train started with a ~.* | **~ of** ◊ *The blow sent a ~ of pain through his body.* | **~ to** ◊ *His dismissal was a severe ~ to his pride.*

journal *noun*

1 serious magazine

ADJ. **academic, learned** (*esp. BrE*), **scholarly** | **professional, technical, trade** | **peer-reviewed, refereed** (*esp. AmE*) ◊ *The results of the study were published in a respected peer-reviewed ~.* | **house, in-house** (*both esp. BrE*) ◊ *the house ~ of Southern Gas* | **specialist** (*esp. BrE*), **specialized** (*esp. AmE*) | **research** | **business, literary, medical, nursing, science, scientific** | **august, leading, major, prestigious, reputable, respected** ◊ *'Nature' was the highest-ranked ~ in the survey.* | **obscure** ◊ *The paper was published in an obscure medical ~.* | **official** ◊ *It's the official ~ of the Medical Foundation.* | **international, national** | **monthly, quarterly, weekly** | **electronic, online**

...OF JOURNAL **copy** ◊ *Please send me two copies of your new ~.* | **edition, issue, volume**

VERB + JOURNAL **read** | **edit, write for** ◊ *an academic who writes for specialist ~s* | **produce, publish** | **found** ◊ *He founded a new literary ~ in 1831.* | **buy, get, subscribe to** ◊ *She subscribes to quite a few academic ~s.*

JOURNAL + VERB **come out** ◊ *The ~ comes out five times a year.* | **be dedicated to, be devoted to** ◊ *an academic ~ devoted to military history*

JOURNAL + NOUN **article, editorial** | **editor, publisher** | **subscription**

PREP. **in a/the ~** ◊ *an article in a medical ~* | **~ of** ◊ *the British Journal of Geology*

2 diary

ADJ. **personal, private** | **daily**

VERB + JOURNAL **keep, write** ◊ *She kept a daily ~ of the voyage.* | **read** | **publish** ◊ *The Captain later published his ~s.*

JOURNAL + NOUN **entry** ◊ *Her ~ entry for that day describes a thunder storm.*

PREP. **in a/the ~** ◊ *The events are all recorded in her ~.* | **~ of** ◊ *He wrote a ~ of his travels.*

journalism *noun*

ADJ. **good** | **professional** | **hard-hitting** (*esp. AmE*), **investigative, watchdog** (*AmE*) | **popular, tabloid** ◊ *The newspaper's editorial standards have sunk to the level of tabloid ~.* | **mainstream** | **yellow** (*AmE*) | **gonzo** (= reporting in newspapers that tries to shock or excite rather than give true information) (*AmE*) | **chequebook/checkbook** (*disapproving*) | **lazy, shoddy** (*esp. AmE*), **sloppy** | **online** | **magazine, newspaper, print** | **broadcast, radio,** television | fashion (*esp. BrE*), literary, medical, music, science, sports

... OF JOURNALISM **piece** ◊ *a fine piece of investigative ~*

PHRASES **a career in ~** ◊ *I'd like to have a career in ~.* | **the world of ~**

→ Note at SUBJECT (for verbs and nouns)

journalist noun

ADJ. **brilliant, good** | **experienced, veteran** | **leading, prominent, respected, top, well-known** | **award-winning, prizewinning** | **professional** | **mainstream** | **freelance** | **independent** | **investigative** | **embedded** ◊ *Embedded ~s travel and live with the forces, and are more or less under their control.* | **foreign, western** | **magazine, newspaper, print, tabloid** | **broadcast, radio, television** | **business, environmental, financial, political, sports,** etc.

VERB + JOURNALIST **speak to, talk to, tell** ◊ *She was warned against speaking to ~s about the affair.*

JOURNALIST + VERB **investigate sth** | **interview sb** | **write (sth)** ◊ *a ~ writing for a current affairs publication* | **cover sth, report sth, report on sth** | **specialize in sth** ◊ *a ~ specializing in legal issues*

PREP. **~ on, ~ with** ◊ *an investigative ~ with a French newspaper*

→ Note at JOB

journey noun → See also TRIP

ADJ. **long, marathon** (*esp. BrE*) | **short** (*esp. BrE*) | **outward** (*esp. BrE*) | **homeward, return, round-trip** (*AmE*) | **onward** (*esp. BrE*) ◊ *The bus driver told us where to change buses for our onward ~.* | **bus, car, rail, train,** etc. (*all esp. BrE*) | **five-mile, four-hour,** etc. | **comfortable, easy, good, pleasant, safe** (*all esp. BrE*) ◊ *Did you have a good ~? ◊ Bye! Safe ~!* | **arduous, difficult, gruelling/grueling** (*esp. BrE*), **hard, harrowing, tedious, terrible, tiring, tortuous** (*BrE*) | **dangerous, hazardous, perilous, treacherous** | **overland** | **cross-country** | **daily** (*esp. BrE*) | **overnight** | **epic** ◊ *an epic ~ across Africa on foot* | **amazing, fantastic, incredible** ◊ *Her search took her on an incredible ~ across the world.* | **wasted** (*BrE*) ◊ *He wasn't there and we had a wasted ~.* | **emotional, inner, intellectual, personal, sentimental, spiritual** ◊ *He made the emotional ~ back to the house he grew up in.* ◊ *The development of her poetry reflects her inner spiritual ~.*

VERB + JOURNEY **go on, have, make, undertake** ◊ *Few people have made this ~ and lived to tell the tale.* | **break** (*BrE*) ◊ *We broke our return ~ in Bangkok.* | **begin, set out on** | **continue, resume** ◊ *They continued their ~ on foot.* | **complete, finish** | **survive** ◊ *They doubted that he would survive the ~ to the nearest hospital.* | **chart, chronicle, describe, recount** ◊ *He wrote a column chronicling his ~s around the Americas.*

JOURNEY + VERB **take (sb)** ◊ *His ~ took him across central Asia.* ◊ *The ~ takes about five hours.* (*BrE*) | **begin** | **end** | **continue** ◊ *The ~ continued in silence.*

JOURNEY + NOUN **time** (*esp. BrE*)

PREP. **on ~** ◊ *They were on a ~ to the Far East.* | **~ by** ◊ *a ~ by air, bus, land, sea,* etc. | **~ of** ◊ *a ~ of 300 miles or of five days* | **~ across, ~ between, ~ through** | **~ from, ~ to** ◊ *The ~ from London to Athens took 60 hours.* | **~ down, ~ up** ◊ *the ~ down the Rhine*

PHRASES **be tired after a ~, be tired from a ~** | **a leg of a ~, a stage of a ~** ◊ *Dawn was breaking as we set out on the last leg of our ~.* | **a ~ into the unknown** ◊ *This is the story of the first astronauts and their ~ into the unknown.*

joy noun

ADJ. **pure, real, sheer, true, unadulterated, unalloyed, utter** | **ecstatic, great, overwhelming, wild** | **unbridled, unfettered, unrestrained** | **indescribable, inexpressible** | **simple** | **childlike** ◊ *His childlike ~ was infectious.* | **sudden** | **inner** (*AmE*)

VERB + JOY **bring sb** ◊ *Her books have brought great ~ to millions of people.* | **experience, feel** ◊ *the pure ~ I felt at being free again* | **share, spread** ◊ *We want children to share the ~ of music-making.* | **be filled with, be full of** | **convey, express** | **imagine** ◊ *Imagine our ~ when we saw each other*

again. | **discover, find, get, rediscover, take** ◊ *I find ~ in many kinds of music.* ◊ *She got no ~ out of working.* ◊ *I took a real ~ in telling them the truth.*

JOY + VERB **go** ◊ *All the ~ had gone out of his life.*

PREP. **to your ~** ◊ *She found to her ~ that the house had a large patio.* | **with ~** ◊ *I could have shouted with ~.* | **~ at** ◊ *Protesters expressed ~ at the government's decision.*

PHRASES **dance, jump, sing, weep,** etc. **for ~** ◊ *I literally jumped for ~ when I heard the news.* | **~ and sorrow, ~s and sorrows** ◊ *Over the years we have shared our ~s and sorrows.* | **a ~ to behold, see, watch,** etc. ◊ *The children's expressions were a ~ to behold.* | **your pride and ~** (= a person or thing that makes you feel great pride or satisfaction) ◊ *Pablo was the couple's pride and ~.* | **tears of ~**

judge noun

1 applies the law

ADJ. **experienced** (*esp. BrE*) | **learned** (*esp. BrE*) | **senior** | **presiding, trial** | **deputy** (*BrE*) | **appeal, appellate, circuit, county, district, federal** | **appeal-court, circuit-court, county-court, district-court** | **High Court** (*in the UK*), **Supreme Court** (*in the US*) | **bankruptcy, immigration** (*both AmE*) | **unelected** (*esp. AmE*) | **activist, conservative, liberal** (*all AmE*) ◊ *She has a reputation as a liberal, activist ~.*

VERB + JUDGE **be, sit as** ◊ *By next year you could be sitting as a High Court ~.* | **appoint (sb as), elect, nominate** (*both esp. AmE*) | **convince, impress, persuade, satisfy** ◊ *They must persuade the ~ that a particular juror is likely to be biased.* | **ask, tell**

JUDGE + VERB **oversee sth, preside, sit** ◊ *Which ~ will be sitting next week?* ◊ *The ~ overseeing the case ordered the documents to be produced.* | **call sb** ◊ *The ~ called the remaining witness.* | **ask sth, say sth, tell (sb) sth** ◊ *A federal ~ told the FBI they could not access the computers.* | **direct sb** (*esp. BrE*) ◊ *The ~ must direct the jury on points of law.* | **consider sth** | **accept sth, admit sth, agree (sth), allow sth, approve sth, uphold sth** ◊ *The ~ admitted the notes of the interview as evidence.* | **deny sth, disagree, dismiss sth, overrule sb/sth, overturn sth, refuse sth, reject sth** ◊ *The trial ~ dismissed her compensation claim.* ◊ *Appeals court ~s overturned the previous ruling.* | **conclude sth, decide sth, declare sth, find sth, hold sth, rule sth** ◊ *The ~ held that the company had been negligent.* | **sum up** ◊ *The ~ summed up and the jury retired to consider its verdict.* | **sentence sb** | **impose sth, order sth** ◊ *The ~ ordered the company to pay compensation to the claimant.* ◊ *A ~ could impose a substantial penalty.* | **award (sb) sth, grant (sb) sth** ◊ *The ~ awarded him damages of £20 000.*

2 decides who has won a competition

ADJ. **competition** | **independent**

... OF JUDGES **panel** ◊ *a panel of independent ~s*

JUDGE + VERB **choose sb/sth, pick sb/sth, vote for sb/sth** | **decide sth, vote on sth**

PHRASES **the judges' decision** ◊ *The judges' decision on the entries is final.*

3 has the ability/knowledge to give an opinion

ADJ. **astute, good, great, shrewd** ◊ *You are the best ~ of what your body needs.* ◊ *a shrewd ~ of character* | **bad, poor** | **impartial**

PREP. **~ of** ◊ *He is a good ~ of musical talent.*

PHRASES **a good, bad** etc. **~ of character** ◊ *She's usually a pretty shrewd ~ of character.*

judge verb

ADV. **accurately, correctly, rightly** | **wrongly** (*esp. BrE*) ◊ *I think I ~d the distance wrongly.* | **fairly, properly** (*esp. BrE*) | **harshly, unfairly** ◊ *I think you're judging her rather harshly.* | **objectively** | **subjectively** | **beautifully** (*esp. BrE*), **carefully, finely, nicely, perfectly** (*both esp. BrE*), **well** ◊ *Their performance of the concerto was beautifully ~d.* ◊ 'There's something I haven't told you.' *She ~d her words carefully.* | **accordingly** ◊ *Those who preach intolerance should be ~d*

accordingly. | **purely, solely** ◇ *He was often ~d solely on his looks.*
VERB + JUDGE **be difficult to, be hard to, be impossible to** | **be able to, be in a position to** ◇ *I am in no position to ~ whether what she is doing is right or wrong.* | **learn to** ◇ *You soon learn to ~ distances when driving.*
PREP. **according to** ◇ *He believed that schools should be ~d according to strictly academic criteria.* | **against** ◇ *You always ~ your own performance against that of others.* | **by** ◇ *You will be ~d by the work you have produced over the year.* | **from** ◇ *The age of the furniture can be ~d from the type of wood used.* | **on** ◇ *Your slogan will be ~d on its originality and style.*
PHRASES **criteria for judging** ◇ *People use different criteria for judging success at school.* | **~ by appearances** | **don't ~ a book by its cover** (= don't judge sth by how it looks) | **judging by sth, judging from sth** ◇ *He seems to have been a popular person, judging by the number of people at his funeral.* | **to ~ by, to ~ from** ◇ *To ~ from what she said, she was very disappointed.* | **~ for yourself** ◇ *Readers are left to ~ for themselves whether McCrombie is hero or villain.* | **~ sth on its merits** ◇ *Each painting must be ~d on its own merits.* | **not for me, us etc. to ~** ◇ *It's not for me to ~ whether he made the right decision.*

judgement (*also* judgment *esp. in AmE*) *noun*

1 decision/opinion

ADJ. **accurate** | **balanced** (*esp. BrE*) | **impartial, independent, objective** | **personal, subjective** | **considered, informed** ◇ *I don't have enough knowledge of the subject to make an informed judgment.* | **intuitive** | **qualitative** | **harsh** | **snap** ◇ *I hate having to make snap ~s.* | **definitive, final** ◇ *I'll reserve final judgment until I've seen all six episodes.*
VERB + JUDGEMENT **form, make** ◇ *It's difficult to form a ~ when you don't have all the facts.* | **express** ◇ *Remember to be tactful when expressing a personal ~.* | **confirm** ◇ *This latest case confirms my earlier ~.* | **come to, reach** ◇ *It is too soon to reach any definitive ~.* | **deliver, give, pass, pronounce, render** ◇ *The inspector's function is not merely to pronounce ~, but also to suggest improvements.* ◇ *It's hard to render a ~ on what happened.* | **reserve, suspend, withhold** ◇ *The court reserved ~ on the two appeals.* ◇ *We'll withhold judgment until we know all the facts.* | **obtain, win** ◇ *They obtained a ~ in their favour/favor.* | **reverse** ◇ *They are trying to get the ~ reversed.* | **abide by**
JUDGEMENT + VERB **be based on** ◇ *Our ~s must be based on our knowledge and experience.*
PREP. **in sb's ~** ◇ *What, in your ~, would be the best way to deal with the problem?* | **~ about** ◇ *She must make her own ~ about when to go.* | **~ against** ◇ *The sacked workers won a ~ against the company.* | **~ as to** ◇ *Experience helps us to form ~s as to the best course of action in given circumstances.* | **~ on** ◇ *I'm not equipped to pass ~ on such matters.*
PHRASES **~ in sb's favour/favor** ◇ *The court delivered a judgment in favour/favor of the defendant.* | **value ~** ◇ *These are not facts, they are value judgments.*

2 decision making

ADJ. **fine** (*esp. BrE*), **good, shrewd, sound** ◇ *Landing a plane requires fine ~.* | **impartial, independent** | **impaired, poor** | **aesthetic, artistic, clinical, critical, editorial, ethical, moral, political, professional** ◇ *She has a reputation for sound professional ~.*
VERB + JUDGEMENT **display, show** | **rely on** | **respect, trust** ◇ *He trusted his wife's ~.* | **doubt, question** ◇ *I don't think he's dishonest, but I question his ~.* | **back** (*esp. BrE*) ◇ *The company backed her ~ and implemented all her recommendations.* | **exercise, use** | **cloud, impair** ◇ *His emotions may have clouded his editorial ~.* | **colour/color, influence** ◇ *He never allows any prejudices to influence his ~.* | **sit in** ◇ *He felt he had no right to sit in ~ on someone he had only just met.*
JUDGEMENT + NOUN **call** (= a situation where different people will reach different decisions according to their personal

judgement) ◇ *Whether or not to prescribe an antibiotic in this case is a ~ call.*
PREP. **~ about** ◇ *You will need to exercise your own ~ about what clothes to wear.* | **~ in** ◇ *The speaker showed good ~ in his choice of topic.*
PHRASES **an error of ~** ◇ *Accepting the gift was an error of ~ on the part of the party chairman.* | **a lack of ~** | **a matter of ~** ◇ *How much money you should invest is a matter of ~.*

judo *noun*

VERB + JUDO **do, practise/practice** | **learn, study** | **teach**
JUDO + NOUN **hold, move, throw** ◇ *She managed to get the man in a ~ hold.* | **mat** | **dojo** | **instructor**
PHRASES **a black, etc. belt in ~** ◇ *He's a black belt in ~.* ◇ *He has a brown belt in ~.*
→ Special page at SPORTS

jug *noun* → See also PITCHER

ADJ. **earthenware, glass, plastic** | **cream, milk, water, wine** | **gallon, half-gallon, three-litre/three-liter, etc.** | **measuring** (*BrE*)
VERB + JUG **fill, fill up, pour sth into** ◇ *I filled up my water ~.* ◇ *He filled a ~ with juice.* (*esp. BrE*) | **pour, tip** ◇ *She poured a ~ of water over his head.* | **empty, pour sth from, pour sth out of**
PREP. **~ of** ◇ *a ~ of milk*

juice *noun*

ADJ. **fruit, lemon, tomato, etc.** | **fresh, freshly squeezed** (*esp. BrE*), **fresh-squeezed** (*AmE*) | **concentrated** | **unsweetened** | **fortified** (*AmE*)
VERB + JUICE **extract, squeeze** | **drink, sip** | **suck** ◇ *He was sucking the ~ out of a slice of orange.* | **strain** (*esp. BrE*) | **sprinkle (sth with)** ◇ *Sprinkle the avocado slices with lemon ~.* | **spill**
PREP. **~ from** ◇ *The ~ from the meat is used to make the sauce.* | **~ of** ◇ *the grated rind and ~ of two lemons*
→ Special page at FOOD

July *noun* → Note at MONTH

jump *noun*

1 movement

ADJ. **little** | **running, standing** ◇ *Cats can clear six feet with a standing ~.* | **broad** (*AmE*), **high, long, triple** | **bungee, parachute, ski**
VERB + JUMP **make** ◇ *She made a ~ for the river bank.* | **take** ◇ *He took a running ~ and just managed to clear the stream.* | **do** ◇ *He's going to do a parachute ~ for charity.* | **give** ◇ *Her heart gave a little ~ at his smile.*
PREP. **in the ... ~** ◇ *Allen won silver in the high ~.* | **with a ~** ◇ *I sat up with a ~* (= suddenly.). | **~ into** (*figurative*) ◇ *The new law is a ~ into the unknown.* | **~ onto**

2 increase

ADJ. **big, quantum** | **sharp, sudden** ◇ *There's been no sudden ~, but a steady increase year on year.* | **small**
VERB + JUMP **make** ◇ *Is he good enough to make the ~ into Formula One?*
PREP. **in** ◇ *The sportswear company reports a ~ in sales since the Olympics.*

jump *verb*

1 move off the ground

ADV. **suddenly** | **almost, nearly, practically** ◇ *She practically ~ed out of bed.* | **about** (*esp. BrE*), **around, back, down, in, off, out, up, up and down** ◇ *He was ~ing up and down with excitement.* | **overboard**
VERB + JUMP **try to** ◇ *He tried to ~ back on board.*
PREP. **from** ◇ *He had to ~ from a first floor window.* | **into, off, on** ◇ *Stop ~ing on the furniture!* | **onto** ◇ *She ~ed up onto the table.* | **out of, over** ◇ *Can you ~ over that fence?* | **through**
PHRASES **~ for joy** ◇ *They all ~ed for joy and hugged each other.*

2 move quickly or suddenly

ADV. **slightly** ◇ *She ~ed slightly at the sound of the bell.* | **immediately, instantly, quickly, suddenly** ◇ *When she heard the news she immediately ~ed on a plane to France.* | **ahead, back, backwards/backward, forward** (*all figurative*) ◇ *The movie then ~s ahead to twenty years in the future.*
VERB + JUMP **make sb** ◇ *He ~ed out and made me ~.*
PREP. **in** ◇ *He ~ed in surprise.*
PHRASES **~ out of your skin** (*figurative*) ◇ *I nearly ~ed out of my skin when he told me.*

jumper *noun* (*BrE*) knitted piece of clothing → See also SWEATER

ADJ. **baggy, loose, sloppy** | **tight** | **heavy, thick** | **light, thin** | **cashmere, cotton, woollen, woolly, etc.** | **knitted** | **crew-neck, polo-neck, turtleneck** | **Fair Isle** ◇ *a Fair Isle ~ in navy and red*
VERB + JUMPER **pull on** | **knit, make**
→ Special page at CLOTHES

junction *noun* (*esp. BrE*) → See also EXIT

ADJ. **busy** | **dangerous** | **motorway** (*in the UK*), **road** | **railway** (*BrE*)
PREP. **at a/the ~** ◇ *Turn off at ~ 6.* | **~ with** ◇ *The college is on the Manchester road, by the ~ with the A5.*

June *noun* → Note at MONTH

jungle *noun*

ADJ. **dense, impenetrable, thick** | **lush** ◇ *the lush ~s of the Yucatan Peninsula* | **tropical** | **concrete, urban** (*both figurative*) ◇ *This outback area is a far cry from the city's concrete ~.*
JUNGLE + NOUN **canopy** | **warfare** | **gym** (= climbing frame for children) (*AmE*)
PREP. **in ~** ◇ *a temple deep in the ~* | **through ~** ◇ *They hacked their way through dense ~.*

junk *noun*

ADJ. **old** ◇ *sculptures made from old ~ and scrap metal* | **useless**
... OF JUNK **bit, piece** ◇ *There were bits of ~ lying around.* | **heap, pile**
JUNK + VERB **lie about** (*esp. BrE*), **lie around**
JUNK + NOUN **shop** | **room** ◇ *They cleared out the ~ room to make a tiny bedroom.* | **heap, pile** | **material** ◇ *He made the boat out of ~ materials.* | **food** ◇ *He sits around eating ~ food all day.* | **email, mail** | **bond** (= high-risk investment) | **science** (= invalid) ◇ *The company described the report as 'junk science'.*

jurisdiction *noun*

ADJ. **limited** | **universal** ◇ *The British courts have universal ~ over torture cases.* | **exclusive** ◇ *The commissioners had exclusive ~ to decide.* | **appellate** | **civil, criminal, ecclesiastical** | **federal, local**
VERB + JURISDICTION **have, retain** ◇ *The court has no ~ in this case.* | **exercise** ◇ *The court may exercise its ~ to compel the husband to make a settlement upon his wife.* | **claim** ◇ *The offshore government claims ~ over the mainland.* | **give, grant** | **extend** | **lack** | **be subject to, come under** ◇ *He is subject to the ~ of the Indian courts.*
PREP. **beyond your ~** ◇ *She acted beyond the ~ of any teacher.* | **outside your ~** ◇ *The matter is outside the ~ of UK administrative agencies.* | **under ~** ◇ *The territory is still under Russian ~.* | **within your ~** ◇ *The matter was not within the ~ of the court.* | **~ over** ◇ *The Senate committees have exclusive ~ over the FBI.*

juror *noun*

VERB + JUROR **swear in** ◇ *The ~s were sworn in.* | **dismiss** (*AmE*) ◇ *The judge dismissed another ~.* | **instruct, tell** ◇ *The judge instructed ~s to disregard this information.*

jury *noun*

1 in a court of law

ADJ. **inquest** (*BrE*), **trial** (*esp. BrE*) | **grand** ◇ *He was indicted by a federal grand ~ on charges of distributing illegal steroids.* | **civil, criminal** (*both esp. AmE*) | **hung** ◇ *A retrial was necessary after the original trial ended with a hung ~.* | **12-member** ◇ *The 12-member ~ deliberated for five days before returning a verdict.*
VERB + JURY **serve on, sit on** | **tell** ◇ *Tell the ~ what happened, in your own words.* | **convince, impress, persuade, sway** ◇ *Her evidence finally swayed the ~.* | **direct** (*BrE*), **instruct** ◇ *The judge directed the ~ to return a verdict of not guilty.* | **convene** (*AmE*), **impanel** (*AmE*), **pick, select** | **strike** (= remove) (*AmE*) ◇ *The attorney has the right to strike jurors for any reason.* | **swear in** (*esp. BrE*) ◇ *The new ~ were sworn in.* | **sequester** (*AmE*) ◇ *Judge Ito sequestered the ~ for the entire trial.*
JURY + VERB **hear sth** ◇ *The ~ heard how the boy had obtained a knife from a friend's house.* | **investigate sth** ◇ *He will appear before a grand ~ investigating the case.* | **retire** (*esp. BrE*) | **consider its verdict** (*esp. BrE*), **deliberate** ◇ *The ~ has retired to consider its verdict.* | **be out** ◇ *The ~ is still out* (= still deciding). ◇ *The ~ is still out on this new policy.* (*figurative*) | **decide sth, deliver a/its verdict, give a verdict, reach a verdict, return a verdict** ◇ *The ~ delivered a unanimous verdict.* | **indict sb** (*esp. AmE*) ◇ *A Los Angeles grand ~ indicted him for perjury.* | **convict sb, find sb guilty** ◇ *The ~ convicted Menzies of assaulting Smith.* | **acquit sb, clear sb** (*esp. BrE*), **find sb not guilty** | **award sb** ◇ *The ~ awarded her damages of £30 000.*
JURY + NOUN **duty** (*esp. AmE*), **service** (*esp. BrE*) ◇ *It was the second time he had been called up for ~ duty/service.* | **trial** | **member** | **selection** (*esp. AmE*) | **system** ◇ *a review of the ~ system* | **indictment, investigation, subpoena** (*all esp. AmE*) ◇ *The company has been slapped with a grand ~ subpoena.* | **testimony** (*esp. AmE*) ◇ *the President's grand ~ testimony*
PREP. **before a ~** ◇ *The trial will take place before a ~.* | **on a/the ~** ◇ *There were only three women on the ~.* | **~ of** ◇ *the ~ of seven women and five men*
PHRASES **the foreman of the ~, members of the ~** | **trial by ~** ◇ *You have a right to trial by ~.*

2 of a competition

VERB + JURY **choose, select** ◇ *The ~ is selected from the winners in previous years.*
JURY + VERB **judge sth** | **consist of sb** ◇ *The ~ consisted of an architect, a photographer and an artist.* | **award (sb) sth, give sb sth** ◇ *The ~ has awarded the prize for best exhibit in the show to Harry Pearson.*
PREP. **on a/the ~** ◇ *He was on a ~ judging a songwriting competition.* | **~ for** ◇ *the ~ for the design awards*

justice *noun*

1 fairness

ADJ. **distributive, economic, environmental, natural, racial** (*esp. AmE*), **social** | **rough** ◇ *He saw it as rough ~ when he got food poisoning from the stolen meat.* | **vigilante** ◇ *the deadliest episode of vigilante ~ in American history* | **divine** ◇ *Some people saw the epidemic as divine ~.* | **poetic** ◇ *Maybe there's a sort of poetic ~ to it.*
VERB + JUSTICE **ask for, demand, pursue, seek, want** ◇ *All I'm asking for is ~.* | **achieve, get, obtain** | **promote** ◇ *They saw the reform proposals as a way to promote social ~.* | **serve** ◇ *Somebody out there needs to make sure ~ is served.* | **deny sb** ◇ *We have been denied ~ for too long.*
PHRASES **a sense of ~** ◇ *The teacher's system of punishments appealed to the children's sense of ~.*

2 law

ADJ. **civil, criminal, juvenile** | **restorative** ◇ *Restorative ~ can only work when all parties agree.* | **retributive** (*esp. AmE*) ◇ *victims seeking retributive ~* | **summary** ◇ *Civilians were not subject to summary ~.*
VERB + JUSTICE **do** ◇ *Justice must be done in every case.* |

administer, deliver, dispense, mete out ◇ *those who are ultimately responsible for dispensing* ~ | **bring sb to** | **face** ◇ *the battle for Taylor to face* ~ *before the High Court* | **escape** ◇ *So far the robbers have escaped* ~. | **obstruct** ◇ *They were accused of attempting to obstruct* ~.

JUSTICE + NOUN **department** | **system**

PHRASES **a miscarriage of** ~ ◇ *He spent twenty years in prison as a result of a miscarriage of* ~. | **pervert the course of** ~ (*BrE*) ◇ *They were accused of attempting to pervert the course of* ~.

justifiable *adj.*

VERBS **be, seem** | **become** | **consider sth, think sth** ◇ *We consider this action* ~.

ADV. **completely, entirely, perfectly** | **commercially, economically** | **ethically, morally**

PREP. **on the grounds of sth, on the grounds that …** , **on … grounds** ◇ *The cutbacks are* ~ *on the grounds of cost.* | *The rule is* ~ *on safety grounds.*

justification *noun*

ADJ. **considerable, every, some** ◇ *You have every* ~ *for feeling angry.* | **compelling** ◇ *There was no compelling* ~ *for the invasion.* | **the slightest** ◇ *She had not given him the slightest* ~ *for thinking she was interested in him.* | **adequate, ample, sufficient** | **ethical, ideological, moral** | **intellectual, philosophical, rational, scientific, theological, theoretical** | **economic, legal, political**

VERB + JUSTIFICATION **give (sb), offer (sb), provide (sb with)** ◇ *She's unable to provide any* ~ *for her actions.* | **see** | **find** ◇ *I could find no real* ~ *for the proposed reorganization.* | **need, require** ◇ *Such a step requires substantial* ~ *to be accepted by the public.*

PREP. **in** ~ ◇ *the argument which he put forward in* ~ | **with** ~ ◇ *He felt, with some* ~, *that he had been unfairly treated.* | **without** ~ ◇ *She was arrested entirely without* ~. | ~ **for** ◇ *I can see some* ~ *for her remarks.* | ~ **of** ◇ *She never presents an ideological* ~ *of her work.*

justified *adj.*

VERBS **be, feel, prove, seem**

ADV. **amply** ◇ *The suspicion proved amply* ~. | **completely, entirely, fully, perfectly, quite, totally** | **hardly, partially, partly** | **clearly** | **easily** ◇ *a logical and easily* ~ *decision* | **economically, ethically, financially, legally, morally, rationally, scientifically, theoretically** ◇ *Can her actions be morally* ~?

PREP. **in** ◇ *She felt fully* ~ *in asking for a refund.*

justify *verb*

ADV. **really, truly** ◇ *Can you really* ~ *the destruction of such a fine old building?* | **easily** ◇ *The university could not easily* ~ *spending the money on this.* | **hardly** ◇ *The result hardly justified the risks they took to get it.*

VERB + JUSTIFY **can** | **serve to** ◇ *The events that followed served to* ~ *our earlier decision.* | **appear to, seem to** ◇ *In 1865 a letter arrived that appeared to* ~ *her faith.* | **help to** ◇ *The extra effort involved would go a long way in helping to* ~ *their high price tags.* | **be easy to** ◇ *the many issues that make it easy to* ~ *the purchase* | **attempt to, seek to, try to** | **be necessary to, have to, need to** | **be difficult to, be hard to, be tough to, struggle to** ◇ *He found it very difficult to* ~ *his decision.* | **be impossible to**

PREP. **on the grounds of sth, on the grounds that …** ◇ *The decision is justified on the grounds that there is no realistic alternative.* | **to** ◇ *How will you* ~ *this pay cut to your employees?*

K k

karate *noun*

ADJ. **full-contact, Shotokan**

VERB + KARATE **do, practise/practice, study** | **teach** | **learn**

KARATE + NOUN **suit** | **chop, kick, punch** | **technique** | **competition, tournament** | **class, lesson, practice, training** | **champion, expert, master, practitioner** | **black belt** ◇ *a 34-year-old* ~ *black belt* | **instructor, teacher**

PHRASES **a black, etc. belt in** ~ ◇ *She has a brown belt in* ~. → Special page at SPORTS

keen *adj.* (*esp. BrE*) eager/enthusiastic

VERBS **appear, be, look, seem, sound** | **remain**

ADV. **extremely, fairly, very, etc.** ◇ *She's a very* ~ *gardener.* | **desperately, especially, more than, particularly, terribly** ◇ *He's particularly* ~ *on football.* | **not at all, not exactly, not overly, not too** ◇ *The banks were not at all* ~ *to lend to somebody who actually seemed to need money.* | **equally** ◇ *She is extremely keen to remain with the police and they are equally* ~ *to retain her.* | **always** ◇ *She was always* ~ *to hear the local gossip.* | **obviously** | **naturally, understandably** ◇ *She was naturally* ~ *to make a good impression.*

PREP. **for** ◇ *They were desperately* ~ *for information.* | **on** ◇ *Sally's quite* ~ *on the idea.*

PHRASES **as** ~ **as mustard** (= very keen) (*BrE, informal*)

kerb (*BrE*) (*AmE* curb) *noun*

ADJ. **dropped** (*BrE*) ◇ *Dropped* ~*s make wheelchair access easier.*

VERB + KERB/CURB **pull away from** ◇ *The car pulled away from the* ~. | **pull in to** (*esp. BrE*), **pull over to, pull up to** (*esp. AmE*) | **step off** ◇ *He stepped off the* ~ *without looking and was hit by a bike.* | **clip, hit, strike** | **jump** (*AmE*), **mount** (*BrE*) ◇ *The car mounted the* ~ *and knocked over a pedestrian.*

PREP. **at the** ~ ◇ *I parked at the* ~ *and waited.* | **on the** ~ ◇ *They stood on the* ~ *waiting to cross the road.*

kettle *noun*

ADJ. **electric**

VERB + KETTLE **fill** | **plug in** (*BrE*) | **put on** (*esp. BrE*) ◇ *I've just put the* ~ *on.* | **boil** ◇ *I'll just boil the* ~.

KETTLE + VERB **boil** ◇ *She made herself a sandwich while she waited for the* ~ *to boil.* | **sing, whistle** ◇ *The* ~ *started to sing.* | **switch itself off** (*esp. BrE*)

key *noun*

1 for a door

ADJ. **master, skeleton** | **duplicate, spare** | **apartment** (*esp. AmE*), **car, door, house, ignition, room, etc.** ◇ *She hides a front door* ~ *in a flowerpot.*

… OF KEYS **bunch, ring** (*esp. AmE*), **set** ◇ *a large bunch of* ~*s* ◇ *He fished a ring of* ~*s out of his pocket.* ◇ *a set of car* ~*s*

VERB + KEY **turn** ◇ *She turned the* ~ *in the lock.* | **insert, put in, slide in** ◇ *I slid the* ~ *into the lock and went in.* | **remove, take out** | **use** ◇ *She must have used a* ~ *to get in.* | **leave** ◇ *She left a* ~ *with the neighbours/neighbors.* | **lock in** ◇ *I'd accidentally locked the* ~*s in my car.*

KEY + VERB **open, unlock** ◇ *You need a* ~ *to open the garage.* | **lock** | **turn** ◇ *They heard a* ~ *turn in the lock.* | **jangle, jingle** ◇ *The sound of* ~*s jangling caught her attention.*

PREP. **with a/the** ~ ◇ *You have to close it with the* ~. | ~ **for** ◇ *Robbie didn't have a* ~ *for these doors.* | ~ **to** ◇ *the* ~ *to the front door*

PHRASES **get a** ~ **cut** (*BrE*) ◇ *I'll get another* ~ *cut so that you can have one.*

2 on a computer

ADJ. **Alt, arrow, backspace, control, delete, enter, escape, function, return, shift, etc.** | **hot** (= a key that you can

press to perform a set of operations quickly), **short-cut** ◊ *F1 is the short-cut ~ for calling up help.*
... OF KEYS **row** ◊ *the top row of ~s*
VERB + KEY **hit, hold down, press, punch, tap** ◊ *Hold down the Alt ~ while pressing the arrow ~s.* | **release**
→ Special page at COMPUTER

3 decisive factor

VERB + KEY **have, hold** ◊ *First-time voters could hold the ~ to the election result.*
PREP. **~ to** ◊ *Language is the ~ to understanding those around you.*

4 in music

ADJ. **major, minor** | **high, low**
VERB + KEY **change** ◊ *The piece changes ~ in the middle.*
KEY + VERB **change** ◊ *The ~ changes from C major to A minor.*
KEY + NOUN **change** | **signature**
PREP. **in a/the ~** ◊ *What ~ is it in?* ◊ *Can we try it in a lower ~?* | **~ of** ◊ *the ~ of G major*
PHRASES **a change of ~**

5 on a musical instrument

ADJ. **organ, piano, etc.** | **black, white**
VERB + KEY **caress, stroke, touch** | **depress**

keyboard *noun*

1 set of keys on a computer, etc.

ADJ. **qwerty** | **standard** | **computer, laptop, PC, typewriter** | **Bluetooth™, cordless, USB, wireless** | **on-screen** ◊ *You can access web pages by using an on-screen ~.* | **built-in** ◊ *the first pocket PC to include a built-in ~* | **full-size, miniature** | **ergonomic**
VERB + KEYBOARD **tap, tap at, tap on** ◊ *Arianne was tapping away at her ~.* | **pound, pound at, pound on** ◊ *Filled with inspiration, he started pounding his ~.*
KEYBOARD + NOUN **command, short cut** ◊ *Users can now customize ~ short cuts.* | **port** ◊ *the mouse and ~ ports on the back of your computer*
PREP. **on the ~** ◊ *Using the mouse is quicker than typing it on the ~.*
→ Special page at COMPUTER

2 set of keys on a piano, etc.

ADJ. **organ, piano, etc.**
KEYBOARD + NOUN **instrument**

3 electrical musical instrument

ADJ. **digital, electric, electronic**
PREP. **at the ~** ◊ *Ed Duke was at the ~.* | **on (a/the) ~** ◊ *He played the song on his ~.* ◊ *The recording features Herbie Hancock on ~.*
→ Special page at MUSIC

kick *noun*

1 act of kicking

ADJ. **good, hard, hefty, powerful, sharp, swift, vicious** ◊ *She gave him a hard ~ to the stomach.* ◊ *This city could use a good ~ in the pants. (AmE, figurative)* | **karate, roundhouse** *(AmE)*, **scissor** ◊ *Olivia leapt forward with a high karate ~.* | **high, leg** ◊ *an energetic performer using dance routines and high ~s* | **corner, free, goal, overhead, penalty, spot** (all in football/soccer) | **drop** (in rugby and American football) | **onside** (in American football)
VERB + KICK **give sb/sth** ◊ *Give the door a good ~ if it won't open.* | **aim** | **deliver, land, plant** ◊ *Roy landed a ~ to the man's head.* | **get, receive** ◊ *He had received a painful ~ on the knee.*
PREP. **~ at** ◊ *a ~ at goal* | **~ by, ~ from** ◊ *a ~ from Maynard in the last minute of the game* | **~ in** ◊ *a ~ in the stomach* | **~ on** ◊ *a ~ on the ankle* | **~ to** ◊ *a ~ to the ribs*

2 feeling of great pleasure/excitement

ADJ. **big, great, huge, real**
VERB + KICK **get** ◊ *He gets a real ~ out of fixing something so that it can be used again.* | **give sb** ◊ *It gave the youngsters a ~ to see their own play on television.*
PREP. **for ~s** ◊ *They don't really want the things they steal. They just do it for ~s.*

kick *verb*

1 hit sb/sth with your foot

ADV. **hard, savagely, viciously, violently** ◊ *Don't ~ the ball too hard.* | **gently** ◊ *Marcia gently ~ed the horse again to make it trot.* | **accidentally, deliberately** *(esp. BrE)* ◊ *He was sent off for deliberately ~ing an Italian player.* | **repeatedly** ◊ *Foster admitted punching and ~ing the man repeatedly.* | **around, over** ◊ *The boys were ~ing a ball around in the yard.* ◊ *Abe roared and ~ed over a table.*
PREP. **against** ◊ *She could feel the baby ~ing against her stomach wall.* ◊ *Young people often ~ against convention. (figurative)* | **at** ◊ *She ~ed at the loose pebbles by the roadside.* | **in** ◊ *They threw him to the ground and ~ed him hard in the stomach.* | **on** ◊ *She ~ed me on the knee.*
PHRASES **~ a door down** | **~ a door open, ~ a door shut** ◊ *Suddenly the far door was ~ed open.* | **~ sb to death**

2 move your feet in the air

ADV. **frantically, furiously, wildly** ◊ *He rolled over in the sand, ~ing wildly.* | **off** ◊ *They dropped their bags in the front hall and ~ed off their shoes.*
PREP. **out at** ◊ *The horse ~ed out at the dog.* | **with** ◊ *I tried to dive back under, ~ing with my legs.*
PHRASES **drag sb ~ing and screaming** ◊ *The police had to drag her ~ing and screaming out of the house.* | **~ your legs, your legs ~** ◊ *The little boy was now lying on his back ~ing his legs in the air.* ◊ *I was carried upstairs, arms waving and legs ~ing.*

kid *noun (informal)*

ADJ. **little, young** | **big, older** ◊ *The older ~s had lessons in the afternoon as well.* ◊ *He's like a big ~ with all this enthusiasm.* | **cute, good, lovely** *(esp. BrE)*, **nice** | **cool, smart** *(esp. AmE)* | **dumb** *(esp. AmE)*, **stupid** | **normal** ◊ *She was just a normal ~.* | **crazy, weird** ◊ *Now what are you two crazy ~s doing?* | **poor** ◊ *I feel desperately sorry for the poor ~.* | **rich** ◊ *a spoiled little rich ~* | **fat** ◊ *I was the fat ~ through most of my teenage years.* | **scrawny, skinny** ◊ *a skinny little ~ who looked to be no older than fourteen* | **local, neighbourhood/ neighborhood** *(esp. AmE)* ◊ *a gang of local ~s* | **street** ◊ *street ~s who rely on their ingenuity to keep alive* | **foster** ◊ *They had sixteen foster ~s and two of their own.* | **college** *(esp. AmE)*, **high-school** *(AmE)*, **school** (usually *schoolkid*)
... OF KIDS **bunch, couple, crowd, gang, group** ◊ *They're just a bunch of ~s.*
VERB + KID **have** ◊ *We both wanted to have ~s.* | **want** ◊ *She had wanted more ~s.* | **adopt, foster** ◊ *They had adopted three ~s.* | **bring up, raise** *(esp. AmE)* ◊ *I've tried to bring my ~s up to respect other people.* | **educate, teach** ◊ *Here are some fun ways to teach your ~s about healthy eating.* | **look after** *(esp. BrE)*, **take care of, watch** *(esp. AmE)* ◊ *She had offered to watch the ~s many times so Toby could go out.* | **protect** ◊ *legislation to protect ~s from violence and harassment in their schools*
PHRASES **just a ~, only a ~** ◊ *He's only a ~. You can't expect him to understand what's going on.* | **like a ~** ◊ *She was crying like a ~.* | **kids' stuff** ◊ *The movie is pure kids' stuff from beginning to end.* ◊ *That was kids' stuff compared with what lies ahead.*

kill *noun*

ADJ. **clean, easy, quick** | **fresh** ◊ *vultures sensing a fresh ~* | **fish** *(AmE)* ◊ *the worst fish ~ in recorded history*
VERB + KILL **make** ◊ *The lion made a quick ~.* | **be in at** *(BrE)* ◊ *I didn't even see the fox, let alone be in at the ~.* | **close in for, go in for, move in for** ◊ *The hunters moved in for the ~.*
PREP. **at the ~** *(BrE)* ◊ *The meat is divided up among all those present at the ~.* | **for the ~** ◊ *The animal crouched down, getting ready for the ~.*

kill *verb*

ADV. **outright** ◊ *He has fought more than fifty bulls, ~ing three outright.* | **almost, nearly** | **instantly** | **quickly** ◊ *The animals are ~ed quickly and humanely.* | **slowly** ◊ *The poison* *was slowly ~ing her.* | **eventually, finally** ◊ *the camp guards who tortured and eventually ~ed her* | **accidentally, inadvertently** | **deliberately, intentionally** ◊ *I don't believe that he intentionally ~ed her.* | **allegedly** ◊ *his trial for allegedly ~ing his wife* | **unlawfully** (*BrE, law*) ◊ *The inquest concluded that he was unlawfully ~ed.* | **needlessly** ◊ *the number of people needlessly ~ed by hospital infections* | **indiscriminately** ◊ *The terrorists had shown their willingness to ~ indiscriminately.* | **systematically** ◊ *The militias are systematically ~ing and raping civilians.* | **brutally** ◊ *There were reports of people brutally ~ed.*

VERB + KILL **want to** | **be prepared to** ◊ *They are quite prepared to ~ to achieve their ends.* | **threaten to** | **be going to, intend to, mean to, plan to** ◊ *He knew they meant to ~ him.* ◊ *Dad's going to ~ me when he finds out.* (*figurative*) | **plot to** ◊ *They plotted to ~ the dictator.* | **attempt to, seek to, try to** | **help (to)** | **make sb** ◊ *The situation must have been really awful to make her ~ herself.*

PHRASES **admit ~ing sb, admit to ~ing sb, deny ~ing sb** ◊ *He admitted ~ing her but said it was unintentional.* | **be accused of ~ing sb, be charged with ~ing sb** | **be ~ed in sth** ◊ *soldiers ~ed in battle* | **be tragically ~ed** ◊ *Their daughter was tragically ~ed in a road accident.*

killer *noun*

1 a person that kills

ADJ. **real** ◊ *I don't care what they ask me if it helps them find the real ~.* | **accused, alleged, suspected** ◊ *the trial of her daughter's accused ~s* | **would-be** ◊ *He turned to face his would-be ~.* | **convicted** | **notorious** | **bloodthirsty, brutal, cold-blooded, ruthless, vicious** ◊ *Matthew's reputation as a cold-blooded ~* | **crazed, psychopathic, psychotic** | **mass, serial, spree** (*AmE*) | **contract, hired, professional, trained** | **baby, child, cop, etc.** ◊ *a convicted child ~*

VERB + KILLER **hunt, track down** | **catch, find, stop** ◊ *I want to stop the ~ before he strikes again.* | **identify** ◊ *FBI agents identified his ~s.* | **bring to justice** ◊ *I cannot rest until this ~ is brought to justice.*

KILLER + VERB **strike** ◊ *The ~ has struck again.* | **stalk sb/sth** ◊ *For years the ~ stalked Detroit and its suburbs undetected.* | **kill sb, murder sb** ◊ *a serial ~ who murders newlyweds on their honeymoon*

KILLER + NOUN **instinct** (*figurative*) ◊ *He plays well but still lacks the ~ instinct.* | **blow** (*figurative, esp. BrE*) ◊ *Owen delivered the ~ blow soon after half-time.*

2 a disease, etc. that kills

ADJ. **big, great, leading, major** ◊ *Overdoses were the single biggest ~ among the city's young.* ◊ *Diphtheria emerged as the leading ~ of children in the 1880s.* | **deadly** ◊ *In the 19th century, cholera was one of Britain's deadliest ~s.* | **silent** ◊ *High blood pressure is known as a silent ~.* | **potential** ◊ *There is still no vaccine against this potential ~.*

KILLER + NOUN **bug** (*BrE*), **disease, strain, virus** ◊ *Heart attacks have become our number one ~ disease.* | **storm** (*esp. AmE*), **wave** ◊ *The ~ wave struck a tiny atoll in the Maldives.*

killing *noun*

1 killing sb deliberately

ADJ. **brutal, cold-blooded** ◊ *the cold-blooded ~ of a young woman* | **deliberate, intentional, targeted** | **indiscriminate, random, senseless, wanton** | **mass, serial, spree** (*AmE*) ◊ *This was the fourth mass ~ in Australia in four years.* | **contract, gangland** (*esp. BrE*), **honour/honor, political, revenge** ◊ *a brutal revenge ~* | **mercy** ◊ *Should the law allow mercy ~?* | **extrajudicial, unlawful** (*esp. BrE*) (*both law*) ◊ *a verdict of unlawful ~*

VERB + KILLING **be responsible for, carry out** | **order** ◊ *The Mafia ordered the ~.* | **justify** ◊ *How can they justify the ~ of innocent people?* | **prevent, stop** ◊ *It is difficult to prevent such ~s.* | **condemn** ◊ *a resolution condemning the ~ of Palestinian civilians* | **confess to**

KILLING + VERB **happen, occur, take place** | **continue** ◊ *the ~s that continued unchecked for days*

PHRASES **a motive for the ~** ◊ *No motive for the ~ has yet been established.*

2 making a lot of money quickly

VERB + KILLING **make** ◊ *Investors are set to make a ~ from the sell-off.*

kilo, kilogram, etc. → Note at MEASURE

kin *noun*

ADJ. **close, near** ◊ *Marriage between close ~ is prohibited.* | **blood** (*esp. AmE*) ◊ *loyalty to blood ~* | **extended** ◊ *Ties with extended ~ vary from family to family.* | **distant** | **female, male**

KIN + NOUN **group** (usually ***kin-group***), **network** (*both technical*) | **relationships**

PREP. **between ~**

PHRASES **next of ~** ◊ *One of the drivers was fatally injured; his next of ~ has been informed.*

kind *noun*

ADJ. **different, same, similar** ◊ *She does the same ~ of work as me.* | **all, another, any, some, various** ◊ *You need some ~ of cover over it to protect it from the rain.* ◊ *We stock various ~s of lawnmower.* | **each, every** | **certain, distinct, exact, particular, special, specific** ◊ *Certain ~s of food are unsuitable for small children.* | **best, good** | **bad, worst** | **right, wrong** ◊ *Be sure to eat enough of the right ~ of food.* ◊ *This is the exact ~ of thing I want.* | **common, normal, typical, usual** ◊ *I'm a fairly normal ~ of guy.* ◊ *Prostate cancer is the most common ~ of cancer in men.* | **new** ◊ *the need for a new ~ of leadership* | **favourite/favorite** ◊ *Musicals were her favourite/favorite ~ of movie.* | **funny, odd, peculiar, strange, weird** | **rare, unique** ◊ *They played a truly unique ~ of punk rock.*

PREP. **in ~** ◊ *The regions differ in size, but not in ~.* | **of a ~** ◊ *You're making progress of a ~ (= some progress, but not very much, or not of the best type). ◊ They're two of a ~ (= very like each other)—both workaholics!* | **of … ~** ◊ *books of every ~* ◊ *music of different ~s* | **of its ~** ◊ *The new school was the first of its ~.* | **~ of** ◊ *a special ~ of oil*

PHRASES **a/the ~ of thing** ◊ *Do you know the ~ of thing I mean? ◊ They sell all ~s of things.* | **a … kind of way** ◊ *I missed him, in a funny ~ of way.* | **nothing of the ~** ◊ *'I was terrible!' 'You were nothing of the ~!'* | **nothing of that ~, something of that ~, something of the ~** ◊ *'He's resigning.' 'I'd suspected something of the ~.'*

kind *adj.*

VERBS **be** ◊ *She was endlessly ~ and sympathetic.*

ADV. **extremely, fairly, very, etc.** | **especially, genuinely, most, particularly**

PREP. **of** ◊ *It really was most ~ of you to help.* | **to** ◊ *My boss has been extremely ~ to me.*

kindergarten *noun* (*esp. AmE*) → See also NURSERY

ADJ. **all-day, full-day, half-day** ◊ *their plans for Hannah to start all-day ~*

VERB + KINDERGARTEN **enter, start** | **attend, be in** ◊ *She was still attending ~ at Assumption School. ◊ My father died while I was still in ~.* | **teach** (*AmE*) ◊ *She has been teaching ~ for 13 years.*

KINDERGARTEN + NOUN **classroom** | **class** | **children, students** (*AmE*) | **teacher**

PREP. **at ~** ◊ *his first day at ~* | **in ~** ◊ *She teaches reading to students in ~.*

kindness *noun*

ADJ. **great** | **loving** | **simple** | **genuine, natural** | **unexpected** ◊ *This unexpected ~ touched her deeply.* | **small** ◊ *Small ~es meant a lot to her.* | **human**

VERB + KINDNESS **show sb, treat sb with** ◊ *They had shown him great ~. ◊ They treated us with ~ and courtesy.* | **meet with, receive** ◊ *We met with much ~ and help.* | **(not) deserve** ◊ *I don't deserve your ~.* | **appreciate** ◊ *I really* appreciate your ~. | **repay** ◇ *I tried to think of a way to repay his ~.* | **not forget**

PREP. **out of ~** ◇ *I went with her out of ~.* | **~ to, ~ towards/ toward** ◇ *I'll never forget your ~ to me.*

PHRASES **an act of ~** ◇ *Show your appreciation by little acts of ~.* | **~ itself** ◇ *She has always been ~ itself to me.* | **out of the ~ of your heart** ◇ *They volunteer out of the ~ of their hearts.*

king noun

1 male ruler

ADJ. **rightful** | **anointed, crowned, reigning** | **uncrowned** (*figurative*) ◇ *the uncrowned ~ of hip-hop* | **undisputed** (*figurative*) ◇ *He is the undisputed ~ of talk shows.* | **great, mighty** | **future** ◇ *the future ~ of England* | **deposed, exiled** | **homecoming, prom** (*both AmE*) ◇ *He was nominated for prom ~ in high school.*

VERB + KING **become** | **anoint sb, crown (sb), make sb, proclaim sb** ◇ *He was crowned ~ at the age of fifteen.* ◇ *The new ~ was crowned immediately.* | **serve** ◇ *He died bravely, serving his ~.* | **depose, overthrow**

KING + VERB **reign, rule (sb/sth), rule over sb/sth** ◇ *The ~s of Sicily also ruled over the southern part of Italy.* | **abdicate** ◇ *the king's decision to abdicate*

PREP. **under a/the ~** ◇ *Life under the new ~ was very different.* | **~ of** ◇ *the King of Spain*

2 playing card

→ Note at CARD

kingdom noun

ADJ. **independent** | **ancient, medieval** ◇ *the ancient ~ of Laos* | **heavenly** ◇ *Christ in his heavenly ~* | **animal, plant** ◇ *members of the animal ~*

VERB + KINGDOM **rule** | **inherit**

PREP. **in a/the ~** ◇ *It was one of the richest towns in the ~.* | **throughout a/the ~** ◇ *changes that were taking place throughout the ~* | **~ of** ◇ *He ruled the ancient ~ of Kaffa.*

kiss noun

ADJ. **brief, quick, swift** | **lingering, long, slow** ◇ *She leaned forward and placed a slow ~ on his forehead.* | **deep, hungry, passionate** | **big** | **hard** | **sloppy, wet** ◇ *Tom planted a wet ~ on her cheek.* | **French** ◇ *She gave him a French ~.* | **gentle, light, soft** | **affectionate, loving, sweet, tender, warm** | **little** | **chaste, friendly, innocent** | **stolen** ◇ *He contented himself with a stolen ~ as he leaned forward.* | **first** ◇ *the girl who gave him his first ~* | **final, last** ◇ *Sarah left him with a final ~ on the cheek.* | **farewell, goodbye, goodnight**

VERB + KISS **give sb** ◇ *He gave his daughter a gentle ~ on the forehead.* | **drop, lay, place, plant, press** ◇ *He touched her cheek once more and laid a ~ on her forehead.* ◇ *She planted a big ~ on his cheek.* | **steal** ◇ *The children hid behind the bike shed to steal a ~.* | **exchange, share** ◇ *Brad and Sue exchanged a ~.* | **return** ◇ *She returned his ~ with passion.* | **accept, get, receive** ◇ *Don't I get a ~?* ◇ *Mrs Davis received a ~ on the cheek from Jesse and said goodbye.* | **blow (sb)** ◇ *As the train drew away he blew her a ~.* | **shower sb with** ◇ *I wanted to take him in my arms and shower him with ~es.* | **deepen**

KISS + VERB **deepen** ◇ *His ~ deepened and became hungrier.* | **last** ◇ *The ~ only lasted for a few moments.*

PREP. **with a ~** | **~ on** ◇ *He greeted her with a ~ on the cheek.* | **~ to** ◇ *She pressed a soft ~ to his cheek.*

PHRASES **hugs and ~es** ◇ *We were greeted with hugs and ~es.*

kiss verb

ADV. **gently, lightly** | **lovingly, softly, tenderly** | **deeply, fiercely, firmly, hard, hungrily, passionately, soundly** | **briefly, quickly** | **lingeringly, long, slowly** ◇ *She ~ed her long and hard on the mouth.* ◇ *Brandon slowly ~ed her lips.*

VERB + KISS **bend to, lean over to, stoop to** ◇ *He bent to ~ her again.* | **try to** | **let sb**

PREP. **on** ◇ *She let him ~ her lightly on the cheek.*

PHRASES **~ and cuddle** (*esp. BrE*) ◇ *The love-struck pair have been spotted ~ing and cuddling at parties.* | **~ sb full on the lips, ~ sb full on the mouth** | **~ sb goodbye, ~ sb**

goodnight | **~ goodbye to sth** (*figurative*) ◇ *Well, you can ~ goodbye to your chances of promotion.*

kit noun

1 set of equipment

ADJ. **emergency, first-aid, make-up, medical, mess, repair, sewing, shaving, survival, test, tool** ◇ *She keeps an emergency medical ~ in her car.* ◇ *Check the acidity of the soil with a test ~.* | **drum** ◇ *In the middle of the stage was a drum ~.* | **media** (*AmE*), **press** (*esp. AmE*) ◇ *an electronic press ~ that features brief interviews with the movie's actors*

PREP. **in a/the ~** ◇ *There should be a needle and thread in the sewing ~.*

2 (*BrE*) **clothes for sport**

ADJ. **gym, PE, sports** | **diving, football, rugby** | **team** ◇ *the official supplier of the England team ~* | **replica** ◇ *a teddy bear dressed in a replica Real Madrid ~* | **Chelsea, England, Liverpool, etc.**

KIT + NOUN **bag**

→ Special page at CLOTHES

3 set of parts

ADJ. **construction** | **starter** ◇ *Adams paid $500 for the initial starter ~.*

VERB + KIT **assemble, install** ◇ *I spent Sunday assembling emergency ~s for the expedition.*

KIT + VERB **come with sth, consist of sth, contain sth, include sth** ◇ *Each ~ comes with a sealable bag.* ◇ *The ~ contains everything you need to make six candles.*

PREP. **from a ~** ◇ *They built the garage from a ~.* | **for** ◇ *a ~ for making candles*

PHRASES **in ~ form** ◇ *The doll's house comes in ~ form.*

kitchen noun

ADJ. **clean, spotless** | **modern** | **dirty** | **little, small, tiny** | **big, huge, large, spacious** | **open, open-plan** (*esp. BrE*) | **galley** | **fitted, fully fitted** (*both BrE*) | **communal, shared** | **domestic** (*esp. BrE*), **home** (*AmE*) | **professional, restaurant** | **mobile** | **kosher**

KITCHEN + NOUN **area** | **door, floor, window** | **cabinet, chair, cupboard, drawers, sink, stool, table, unit** (*esp. BrE*) | **counter** (*AmE*), **countertop** (*AmE*), **surface** (*esp. BrE*), **work-top** (*BrE*) | **faucet** (*AmE*), **tap** (*esp. BrE*) | **clock, equipment, gadgets, implements, knife, scale** (*AmE*), **scales** (*esp. BrE*), **scissors, timer, tools** (*esp. AmE*), **utensils** | **foil** (*BrE*) | **paper, roll, towels** (*all BrE*) (**paper towels** in *AmE*) | **island** ◇ *I sat at the ~ island eating a bowl of cereal.* | **appliance, fire, range, stove** | **facilities** ◇ *All our chalets have ~ facilities.* | **scraps, waste** | **police** (*AmE, informal*), **staff** | **maid, porter** (*BrE*), **worker** | **garden** (= for growing food for the kitchen) (*BrE*)

PREP. **in a/the ~**

knack noun

ADJ. **real** | **amazing, incredible, uncanny** | **happy, unfortunate** (*both BrE*) ◇ *He had the unfortunate ~ of making enemies in the party.*

VERB + KNACK **have** | **demonstrate, display, show** | **acquire, develop, get** ◇ *Once you get the ~, it's easy.* | **lose** ◇ *I don't cook much these days and I think I may have lost the ~.*

PREP. **~ for** ◇ *a woman with a real ~ for handling horses* | **~ of** ◇ *He has the ~ of scoring just when it's most needed.* | **~ to** ◇ *Making omelettes isn't difficult, but there's a ~ to it.*

knee noun

ADJ. **left, right** | **bony, knobbly, knobby** (*esp. AmE*) | **bare** | **bent** | **drawn-up** ◇ *I rested my chin on my drawn-up ~s.* | **arthritic, bad, bum** (*AmE, informal*), **dodgy** (*BrE, informal*), **troublesome, weak** | **sore, stiff** | **injured, scraped, skinned** (*esp. AmE*), **twisted** | **artificial** ◇ *An artificial ~ was later inserted.*

VERB + KNEE **bend, flex** | **straighten** | **draw up, pull, pull up, tuck, tuck up** ◇ *I tucked my ~s under my chin.* ◇ *She sat up* and pulled her ~s to her chest. | **hug** ◇ He hugged his ~s to keep warm. | **drop down on, drop on, drop to, fall on, fall to, get down on, go down on, sink to** ◇ He went down on his ~s and begged for forgiveness. | **sit on** ◇ She sat on her father's ~ (= lap) while he read her a story. | **blow** (AmE, informal), **blow out** (AmE, informal), **hurt, injure, sprain, twist** ◇ I injured my ~ and had to have surgery. | **graze, scrape, skin** | **slap** ◇ He slapped his ~ as he rocked with laughter. | **pat** ◇ He patted her ~ reassuringly.

KNEE + VERB **buckle, give way, weaken** ◇ Suddenly her ~s buckled and she fell to the floor. | Rita felt her ~s weakening. | **knock, shake, tremble, wobble** | **ache, hurt**

KNEE + NOUN **injury, problem, sprain, trouble** | **operation, replacement, surgery** | **brace** ◇ He refuses to wear a ~ brace. | **joint, ligament** | **socks** | **pad**

PREP. **above the ~** | **across your ~s** ◇ She had a blanket draped across her ~s. | **at sb's ~** ◇ The children had learned these stories at their mother's ~. | **below the ~** ◇ His leg was missing below the ~. | **between your ~s** ◇ If you hear the crash-landing warning, put your head between your ~s. | **in your ~** ◇ He's snapped a ligament in his ~. | **on one ~** ◇ I went down on one ~ to plug in the vacuum cleaner. | **on your ~** ◇ I balanced the pile of books on my ~s. ◇ He was on his ~s, searching for the missing spring. | **to one ~** ◇ He dropped to one ~. | **to your ~s** ◇ The blow knocked him to his ~s.

PHRASES **bring sth to its ~s** (figurative) ◇ The fuel shortage brought the country to its ~s within weeks. | **on your hands and ~s** ◇ I was on my hands and ~s, looking for my key. | **on bended ~** (figurative) ◇ She would ask for help, but would not beg for it on bended ~.

knickers noun (BrE) short underwear for women
→ See also PANTIES

ADJ. **French** | **frilly, lacy** | **skimpy**
... OF KNICKERS **pair**
VERB + KNICKERS **pull down, pull up**
PHRASES **bra and ~**
→ Special page at CLOTHES

knife noun

1 tool for cutting

ADJ. **blunt, dull** (esp. AmE) | **sharp** | **serrated** | **long** | **small** | **four-inch, six-inch, etc.** | **rusty** | **electric** | **plastic, silver, steel** | **kitchen, table** | **bread, butter, fish, steak** | **butcher** (esp. AmE), **butcher's** (esp. BrE), **chef's** | **carving, paring** (esp. AmE) | **pocket, Swiss army™** | **bowie** (esp. AmE), **hunting, sheath** (esp. BrE) | **butterfly, flick** (BrE) | **Stanley™** (BrE), **utility** (AmE) | **craft** (BrE), **X-acto™** (AmE) | **palette** | **putty** (AmE)
... OF KNIVES **set** ◇ a set of kitchen knives
VERB + KNIFE **pick up** ◇ She picked up her ~ and fork and started to eat. | **lay down, put down** | **use** ◇ Use a sharp ~ to cut away the spare dough. | **sharpen** | **hold**
KNIFE + VERB **cut, slice** ◇ That ~ doesn't cut very well—it needs sharpening. | **clatter**
KNIFE + NOUN **blade, handle** | **block, holder** | **sharpener**
PREP. **with a/the ~** ◇ The lines can be cut with a craft ~.
PHRASES **the blade of a ~, the handle of a ~** | **go under the surgeon's ~** (esp. BrE) ◇ He is to go under the surgeon's ~ (= have surgery) again on Thursday. | **a ~ and fork**

2 used as a weapon

ADJ. **long, sharp** | **combat** (esp. AmE)
VERB + KNIFE **be armed with, carry, have** ◇ She carries a ~ in her bag now. | **brandish, point, wave, wield** ◇ She pointed her ~ at Richard. ◇ He waved his ~ in her face threateningly. | **draw, draw out, produce, pull, pull out, take out, whip out** ◇ He suddenly pulled a ~ on me. | **come at sb with, stab sb with, threaten sb with** ◇ She stabbed him in the back with a 12-inch ~. | **plunge, press, push, put, stick, thrust, twist** (often figurative) ◇ He plunged the ~ deep into her heart. ◇ Just to twist the ~ (= cause additional suffering, tension, etc.), the filmmakers have provided a surprise ending. | **sharpen, whet**

KNIFE + VERB **cut sth, pierce sth, slash sth, slice sth, slice through sth** ◇ She felt a ~ slice her wrist open. | **protrude** ◇ He was slumped over his desk with a ~ protruding from his back.
KNIFE + NOUN **attack, fight** ◇ a frenzied ~ attack ◇ He and his gang had a ~ fight one night. | **cut, wound** | **blade**
PREP. **with a/the ~**
PHRASES **the blade of a ~, the hilt of a ~** | **hold a ~ against sb's throat, hold a ~ at sb's throat, hold a ~ to sb's throat, put a ~ to sb's throat** ◇ She put the ~ to his throat to frighten him into silence. | **a ~ in sb's heart** (figurative) ◇ Each word he uttered was a ~ in her heart.

knight noun

1 in the Middle Ages

ADJ. **medieval** | **chivalrous, noble** | **brave, valiant** | **armoured/armored** | **mounted**
PHRASES **a ~ errant** ◇ tales of medieval ~s errant, wandering in search of chivalrous adventures | **a ~ in armour/armor, a ~ in shining armour/armor** (figurative, humorous) ◇ She's still waiting for a ~ in shining armour/armor to come and rescue her.

2 (in the UK) man with the title 'Sir'

→ Note at PEER

knighthood noun (in the UK)

ADJ. **honorary**
VERB + KNIGHTHOOD **get, receive** | **refuse** | **award sb, bestow on sb, confer on sb, give sb, offer sb, reward sb with** ◇ He was rewarded with a ~ for his services to the government.

knitting noun

VERB + KNITTING **do** ◇ She sat doing her ~ while she watched television.
KNITTING + NOUN **machine, needle** | **pattern** | **bag** | **group**

knob noun

ADJ. **door** | **control, volume** ◇ Adjust the control ~s by pressing lightly. | **brass**
VERB + KNOB **adjust, fiddle with, touch, turn, twiddle** (BrE), **twist** ◇ I've tried fiddling with the ~s, but nothing seems to happen. | **try** ◇ I tried the ~, and this time the door opened.
PREP. **~ on** ◇ the ~s on the radio

knock noun

1 firm sharp sound

ADJ. **loud, sharp** | **gentle, light, quiet, soft** | **timid** | **sudden**
VERB + KNOCK **hear** | **answer** ◇ She hurried to answer the ~ at the door.
PHRASES **a ~ at the door, a ~ on the door** ◇ There was a loud ~ at the door.

2 sharp blow from sth

ADJ. **hard, nasty** (esp. BrE) ◇ the hard ~s of life (figurative) | **minor** (esp. BrE)
VERB + KNOCK **get, have, take** ◇ You've had a nasty ~ on the head. ◇ Their pride took quite a ~ when they lost 5–0. (figurative) | **give sb/sth**
PREP. **~ on**

knock verb

1 hit/bump

ADV. **accidentally** ◇ I accidentally ~ed the vase over.
PREP. **against** ◇ The stick ~ed against the wall. | **off** ◇ He had ~ed one of the pictures off the wall. | **on** ◇ I ~ed my head on one of the beams.
PHRASES **~ sb/sth flying** ◇ He was ~ed flying as two policemen came crashing through the door. | **~ sb off balance, ~ sb off their feet** ◇ The explosion ~ed him off his feet. | **~ sb senseless, ~ sb unconscious** ◇ The blow ~ed him unconscious. | **~ sb to the ground**

2 bang on a door

ADV. **loudly** | **gently, lightly, quietly, softly** | **politely, timidly**

PREP. **at** ◊ *Someone ~ed loudly at the door.* | **on** ◊ *She ~ed timidly on the study door and entered.*
PHRASES **without ~ing** ◊ *Dobson walked straight into her office without ~ing.*

knot noun

ADJ. **loose, tight** | **tangled** ◊ *a tangled ~ of arms and legs* | **double, overhand** | **granny, reef** (*esp. BrE*), **slip, square** (*AmE*), **etc.**
VERB + KNOT **do, tie** | **undo, untie** | **loosen, tighten**
PREP. **in** ◊ *Tie a ~ in the rope.*
PHRASES **a ~ in your stomach** (*figurative*) ◊ *She felt a ~ in her stomach which prevented her from speaking.*

knot verb

ADV. **securely, tightly** | **loosely**
PREP. **around, round** (*esp. BrE*) ◊ *She knotted the scarf loosely around her neck.*

know verb

1 have information about sth

ADV. **full well, perfectly well, very well** ◊ *I don't ~ for certain, but I think she lives in the next town.* ◊ *You ~ very well what I'm talking about!* | **for certain, for sure** ◊ *I don't ~ for certain, but I think she lives in the next town.* | **just** ◊ *I just knew there would be problems.* | **honestly not** ◊ *I honestly don't ~ what they mean to do.* | **beforehand** ◊ *If I'd known beforehand how bad it would be, I wouldn't have gone.*
VERB + KNOW **let sb** ◊ *Please let me ~ (= tell me) if there's anything I can do to help.*
PREP. **about** ◊ *He ~s a lot about music.* | **of** ◊ *I don't ~ of anyone who might be interested in the job.*
PHRASES **be widely known** ◊ *It is widely known that CFCs can damage the ozone layer.* | **~ a lot, nothing, very little, etc.** | **you never ~** ◊ *Be prepared for rain–you never ~ what the weather will be like.*

2 realize

ADV. **exactly, precisely** ◊ *I ~ exactly how you feel.* | **immediately, instantly** ◊ *I instantly knew what the call was about.* | **instinctively** ◊ *He knew instinctively where he would find her.*
PHRASES **the next thing I, he, etc. knew** ◊ *The next thing I knew, I was waking up in hospital.*

3 be familiar with sb/sth

ADV. **well** ◊ *I don't ~ John very well.* | **poorly** ◊ *The properties of this substance are poorly known.* | **barely, hardly** ◊ *But I hardly ~ the woman!* | **personally** ◊ *I don't ~ them personally.* | **internationally, nationally**
VERB + KNOW **get to** ◊ *She's very nice when you get to ~ her*
PREP. **for** ◊ *He is internationally known for his work with vaccines.*
PHRASES **be known to sb** ◊ *This man is known to the police (= as a criminal).* | **be widely known**

4 be known as have a particular name

ADV. **commonly, popularly** | **affectionately** | **collectively** ◊ *parts of the body known collectively as the sensory system* | **variously** ◊ *The drug is variously known as crack or freebase.* | **locally** | **formerly, previously** ◊ *Iran was formerly known as Persia.*
PREP. **to** ◊ *He was known as Bonzo to his friends.*

know-how noun

ADJ. **practical, scientific, technical, technological**
VERB + KNOW-HOW **have, possess** | **acquire, get**
PREP. **~ about** ◊ *to acquire a little ~ about the job* | **~ for** ◊ *He doesn't have the technical ~ for this kind of job.* | **~ in** ◊ *~ in various high-tech fields*

knowledge noun

ADJ. **new** | **basic** | **considerable, great, vast** | **complete, comprehensive, sound** (*esp. BrE*), **thorough** | **deep, detailed, in-depth, intimate, profound** ◊ *She has an intimate ~ of the Asian market.* | **broad, encyclopedic, extensive, wide** | **expert, special, specialist, specialized** |

inside ◊ *He managed to find contacts who had inside ~ of the organization.* | **local** | **direct, first-hand** | **current, up-to-date** (*esp. BrE*) | **limited, rudimentary, superficial** ◊ *I have a limited ~ of French.* | **general** ◊ *I don't like quizzes because my general ~ is so poor.* | **factual** | **practical, useful** | **working** ◊ *He has a good working ~ of the subject.* | **professional** | **medical, scientific, technical, etc.** | **trad-itional** | **human** | **common, public** ◊ *It's common ~ that he's left his wife.* | **personal** | **full** ◊ *She had acted with her parents' full ~ and consent.* | **previous, prior**
... OF KNOWLEDGE **body** ◊ *This approach reveals gaps in the current body of ~.*
VERB + KNOWLEDGE **acquire, gain** | **have, possess** ◊ *I have no ~ of his whereabouts.* | **demonstrate, show, show off** | **test** | **require** ◊ *No previous ~ is required for the job.* | **apply, use** ◊ *The job gave her the chance to apply the ~ she had acquired at college.* | **transfer** ◊ *She cannot transfer this ~ to a new situation.* | **impart, share, spread** ◊ *The bartender was happy to share his ~ of wine with us.* ◊ *The volunteers' task is to spread ~ of how to prevent the disease.* | **advance, enhance, expand, extend, improve, increase** ◊ *Research is important to advance scientific ~.* | **deny** ◊ *He denied all ~ of what had happened.*
PREP. **in the ~** ◊ *They put the car on the market in the full ~ that it had design faults.* | **to sb's ~** ◊ *He's never worked here to my ~.* | **with sb's ~** ◊ *The letter was sent with the full ~ of the head of department.* | **without sb's ~** ◊ *She borrowed my car without my ~.* | **~ of** ◊ *a wide ~ of antiques*
PHRASES **a wealth of ~** ◊ *Martin brings a wealth of ~ to the job.* | **a gap in your ~** ◊ *I did some research to fill in the gaps in my ~.* | **the pursuit of ~** | **secure in the ~** ◊ *We invested in gold, secure in the ~ that the metal would retain its value.* | **to the best of your ~** ◊ *She still lives in San Francisco to the best of my ~.*

knowledgeable adj.

VERBS **be, seem, sound** ◊ *Her lawyer seemed very ~ and experienced.* | **become**
ADV. **extremely, fairly, very, etc.** | **highly**
PREP. **about** ◊ *He's very ~ about Latin American culture.*

knuckle noun

ADJ. **bare** | **bleeding, bloodied, bruised, swollen** | **white** ◊ *She clenched the phone till her ~s were white.* | **brass**
VERB + KNUCKLE **crack** ◊ *He rubbed his hands together, cracking his ~s as he tried to control his anger.* | **bruise, graze, scrape**
KNUCKLE + NOUN **bone** (usually **knucklebone** in *AmE*)
PHRASES **rap sb on the ~s, rap sb over the ~s** (*both figurative*) ◊ *She was rapped over the ~s by her boss for criticizing the company in the press.*

kudos noun

ADJ. **considerable** (*BrE*), **special** (*AmE*)
VERB + KUDOS **acquire, gain, receive, win** | **deserve** | **give sb** (*AmE*) ◊ *You have to give her ~ for keeping it secret.* | **lose** | **bring** ◊ *Employees enjoy the ~ that the job brings as much as the financial rewards.*
KUDOS + VERB **be attached to sth** ◊ *There was considerable ~ attached to being on the advisory board.* | **go to sb** ◊ *Special ~ goes to Patrick Stewart for his role as the captain.*

L l

label noun

1 paper, etc. attached to sth

ADJ. **adhesive, sticky** | **package** | **product** | **clothing, food, nutrition** (*esp. AmE*) | **address, mailing** (*AmE*) | **luggage**

label

(*esp. BrE*) | **price** | **warning** | **care** ◇ *The care ~ says 'dry-clean only'.* | **designer** ◇ *clothes with a designer ~*
VERB + LABEL **bear, carry, have** ◇ *It doesn't have a price ~ on it.* | **attach, put on, stick on** ◇ *She stuck ~s on all the jars.* | **remove, take off** | **check, consult, read** ◇ *Always read the ~ before taking any medicine.*
PREP. **on a/the ~** ◇ *What does it say on the ~?* | **~ on** ◇ *the ~ on the bottle*

2 description
ADJ. **ideological, party**
VERB + LABEL **apply, assign, attach, slap on, use** ◇ *Why do we need to attach a ~ to these feelings?* | **reject**

3 company; brand
ADJ. **music, record** | **major** | **independent, indie** | **brand-name** (*esp. AmE*), **private** | **designer** ◇ *Designer ~s grew by nearly 4% in 2007.*
VERB + LABEL **launch** | **sign to, sign with** ◇ *The band is hoping to sign with a major ~.*
PREP. **under a/the ~** ◇ *The record was produced under the Virgin ~.*

label verb

1 put a label on sth
ADV. **appropriately, correctly, properly** | **incorrectly, wrongly** ◇ *Some of the plants were wrongly labelled/labeled.* | **carefully, clearly, neatly** ◇ *a pile of small plastic bags, each carefully labelled/labeled.*
PREP. **with** ◇ *The samples were all labelled/~ed with a date and place of origin.*

2 describe sb/sth as a particular thing
ADV. **falsely** ◇ *She was falsely labelled/labeled a liar.* | **automatically**
PREP. **as** ◇ *It would be easy to ~ the boys as troublemakers.*

laboratory noun

ADJ. **commercial, industrial** | **school, university** | **secret, underground** | **independent** | **government** | **biology, chemistry, physics, science** | **biological, chemical** | **clinical, forensic** (*esp. BrE*), **medical, nuclear, pathology** (*esp. BrE*), **public-health, research, testing**
LABORATORY + NOUN **assistant, scientist, technician, worker** | **bench, equipment, facilities** | **animal, mouse, rat** | **analysis, experiment, investigation, measurement, procedures, research, study, test, testing, work** ◇ *~ tests on animals* | **science** | **procedures** | **data, evaluation, evidence, findings, report, results** | **conditions, environment, setting** ◇ *The athletes' reflexes were tested under ~ conditions.* | **culture, strain**
PREP. **in a/the ~** ◇ *The effects of weathering can be simulated in the ~.*

labor union noun (AmE) → See UNION

labour (BrE) (AmE labor) noun

1 work
ADJ. **manual, physical** | **back-breaking, forced, hard** ◇ *He was sentenced to four years hard ~ for his crime.* | **productive, unproductive** | **unpaid**
VERB + LABOUR/LABOR **withdraw** ◇ *The miners are threatening to withdraw their ~.*
LABOUR/LABOR + NOUN **productivity** | **camp** ◇ *Dissidents were forced to work in ~ camps.*

2 workers
ADJ. **free, organized** | **wage** | **cheap, low-cost** | **casual, day** (*AmE*) | **skilled, unskilled** | **illegal** | **foreign, immigrant, migrant** | **child, slave** ◇ *It is now thought that the Pyramids were not built using slave ~.* | **prison** | **farm** | **sweatshop**
LABOUR/LABOR + NOUN **force** ◇ *the size of the ~ force* | **market, pool, supply** ◇ *an increasingly competitive ~ market* | **shortage** | **cost, costs** | **movement** ◇ *tensions between the ~*

movement and government | **organization** | **activist, leader** | **relations** | **dispute** | **law**

3 giving birth
ADJ. **difficult, easy** | **long, short** ◇ *The baby was born after a long ~.* | **preterm** ◇ *women at risk of preterm ~*
VERB + LABOUR/LABOR **go into** ◇ *She went into ~ two weeks early.* | **induce** ◇ *Labour was induced when the baby was ten days overdue.*
LABOUR/LABOR + NOUN **room, ward** (*BrE*) | **pains**
PREP. **in ~** ◇ *She was in ~ for ten hours.*

labourer (BrE) (AmE laborer) noun

ADJ. **casual** (*esp. BrE*), **day, wage** | **immigrant** (*esp. AmE*), **migrant** | **manual** | **skilled, unskilled** | **general** | **agricultural, farm, rural** (*esp. BrE*) | **forced, indentured, slave** | **builder's** (*BrE*) ◇ *He got a job as a builder's ~.*
VERB + LABOURER/LABORER **employ, hire** (*esp. AmE*)
LABOURER/LABORER + VERB **toil, work**
→ Note at JOB

lace noun

1 for a shoe → See SHOELACE

2 decorative cloth
ADJ. **delicate, fine**
VERB + LACE **make**
PHRASES **trimmed with ~** ◇ *a silk dress trimmed with ~*

lack noun

ADJ. **profound, serious, severe** | **conspicuous, distinct, notable, noticeable, obvious, remarkable** ◇ *There was a distinct ~ of urgency in his manner.* | **apparent, perceived, seeming** | **complete, sheer, total, utter** ◇ *a complete ~ of confidence* | **general, overall** ◇ *a general ~ of knowledge among the young* | **relative**
PREP. **by ~ of** ◇ *The situation was worsened by ~ of communication.* | **for ~ of** ◇ *They lost the game, but not for ~ of trying.* | **from ~ of** ◇ *She thought she would collapse from ~ of sleep.* | **through ~ of** ◇ *I've lost those skills through ~ of practice.* | **~ of** ◇ *I couldn't hide my ~ of enthusiasm.*
PHRASES **no ~ of sth** ◇ *There is certainly no ~ of interest in the subject.*

lack verb

ADV. **really** | **completely, entirely** ◇ *She completely ~s confidence.* | **apparently** ◇ *He apparently ~ed the desire to learn.* | **clearly, obviously** ◇ *His claim clearly ~ed conviction.* | **simply** ◇ *Perhaps you simply ~ the intelligence to realize just how serious this is?* | **otherwise** ◇ *Her high-heeled shoes gave her the height she otherwise ~ed.*
VERB + LACK **appear to, seem to** ◇ *His life seemed to ~ direction.*
PREP. **in** ◇ *What they ~ in talent, they make up for in conviction.*

lacking adj.

VERBS **be, feel, seem** ◇ *Her life felt ~ in direction and purpose.* | **find sth** ◇ *an area of policy where the government has been found seriously ~*
ADV. **seriously, severely** | **altogether, completely, entirely, totally, wholly** ◇ *The book is altogether ~ in originality.* | **rather, somewhat** | **a little, slightly, etc.** | **apparently** | **clearly, conspicuously, distinctly, notably, noticeably, obviously** ◇ *Tom was conspicuously ~ in enthusiasm for the idea.* | **curiously, singularly** (*esp. BrE*), **strangely** | **sadly, sorely, woefully**
PREP. **from** ◇ *the passion sadly ~ from his performance* | **in** ◇ *Her remarks were curiously ~ in perception.*

lad noun (BrE, informal)

ADJ. **little, young** | **big, strapping** ◇ *He's a strapping lad—already bigger than his father.* | **handsome** | **decent, fine, good, great, lovely, nice, smashing** | **bright, sensible**
... OF LADS **bunch, group** ◇ *They're a nice bunch of ~s.*

ladder *noun*

1 piece of equipment for climbing up sth

ADJ. **rickety** | **metal, wooden** | **long, tall** | **loft** (*esp. BrE*), **rope** | **fire-escape**

VERB + LADDER **ascend, clamber up, climb, climb up, go up, mount, scale** ◇ *He went up the ~ onto the deck.* | **come down, descend, go down** | **put up** ◇ *We put up the ~ against the wall.* | **fall off**

PREP. **on a/the ~, up a/the ~** ◇ *She was up a ~ fixing the roof.* | **down a/the ~** ◇ *I was standing lower down the ~.* | **~ to** ◇ *the ~ to the gallery*

PHRASES **the bottom of a ~, the foot of a ~, the top of a ~** | **a rung of a ~, a step of a ~** ◇ *Several of the ladder's rungs were broken.*

2 levels in a system

ADJ. **economic, evolutionary, social** ◇ *the people at the top of the social ~* | **career, corporate, promotion** | **housing, property** (*both BrE*)

VERB + LADDER **ascend, climb, move up** ◇ *She was anxious to move up the promotion ~.* | **get onto**

PREP. **higher up the ~** ◇ *creatures higher up the evolutionary ~* | **lower down the ~** | **~ of** ◇ *the ~ of fame* | **~ to** ◇ *His good looks helped him on the ~ to success.*

PHRASES **get one foot on the ~, have one foot on the ~** (*both esp. BrE*) ◇ *He finally managed to get one foot on the career ~.* | **a rung on the ~, a step on the ~** ◇ *the old problem of how to get onto the first step on the ~*

laden *adj.*

VERBS **be**

ADV. **heavily** ◇ *He took the heavily ~ tray from her.* | **fully** ◇ *a fully ~ basket* | **emotionally** (*esp. AmE*) ◇ *Try to avoid discussing emotionally ~ subjects.*

PREP. **with** ◇ *They arrived ~ with gifts.*

lady *noun*

ADJ. **elderly, middle-aged, old, young** ◇ *A little old ~ opened the door.* | **attractive, beautiful, lovely, pretty, sexy** | **charming, fine, kind, lovely, nice, sweet, wonderful** ◇ *a sweet old ~* | **proper** ◇ *I was never taught how to be a proper ~.* | **cleaning, dinner** (*BrE*), **lunch** (*AmE*), **tea** (*BrE*) ◇ *a school dinner ~* ◇ *a high-school lunch ~* | **leading** ◇ *Leading ~ Uma Thurman does a great job in this picture.* | **first** ◇ *the former first ~ of the United States* | **church** (*esp. AmE*) | **society** | **lollipop** (*BrE*) | **bag**

LADY + NOUN **friend** ◇ *We teased my uncle about his new ~ friend.*

PHRASES **a ~ of leisure** (*esp. BrE*) ◇ *She's a ~ of leisure now that she's retired.* | **ladies who lunch** (*humorous*) | **the ~ of the house**

→ Note at PEER

lag *verb*

ADV. **badly, seriously, well** | **behind** ◇ *She did well in her first year but then started to ~ behind.*

PREP. **behind** ◇ *Catering salaries ~ far behind those of other sectors.*

PHRASES **~ far behind (sb/sth), ~ way behind (sb/sth), ~ well behind (sb/sth)** ◇ *The party is still lagging way behind in the opinion polls.*

lake *noun*

ADJ. **big, huge, large** | **little, small** | **deep, shallow** | **beautiful** | **blue** | **clear** | **freshwater, salt** | **frozen** | **artificial, man-made, ornamental** (*BrE*) | **inland, mountain** | **boating** (*BrE*)

VERB + LAKE **cross** ◇ *You should cross the ~ before nightfall.* | **overlook** ◇ *a hill overlooking the ~*

LAKE + NOUN **shore** | **bed, bottom** | **water** | **house** (*esp. AmE*)

PREP. **across a/the ~** ◇ *A ferry takes people across the ~.* | **around a/the ~, round a/the ~** (*esp. BrE*) ◇ *We walked around the ~.* | **at a/the ~** ◇ *We spent a weekend at Lake Crystal.* | **in a/the ~** ◇ *Trout live in the ~.* | **into a/the ~** ◇ *She fell into the ~.* | **on a/the ~** ◇ *We went boating on the ~* ◇ *a house on the ~*

PHRASES **the edge of the ~, the middle of the ~, the shores of the ~, the side of the ~, the surface of the ~** ◇ *There is a cafe on the other side of the ~.*

lamb *noun*

1 young sheep

ADJ. **newborn** | **little** | **sacrificial** (*usually figurative*) ◇ *I am not going to be a sacrificial ~ on the altar of political correctness.*

VERB + LAMB **kill, slaughter** ◇ *the traffic in illegally slaughtered ~* | **sacrifice**

LAMB + VERB **bleat** | **frolic, gambol** (*both esp. BrE*)

2 meat

ADJ. **spring** (*esp. BrE*) | **ground** (*AmE*), **minced** (*esp. BrE*) | **grilled, roast**

LAMB + NOUN **chop, cutlet** (*esp. BrE*), **shank** | **casserole** (*esp. BrE*), **curry, stew**

PHRASES **leg of ~, rack of ~, shoulder of ~**

→ Special page at FOOD

lame *adj.*

1 unable to walk well

VERBS **be, look** | **go** ◇ *His horse had gone ~.* | **leave sb, make sb** ◇ *an accident which had left him ~*

ADV. **completely**

2 difficult to believe or accept as real

VERBS **be, seem, sound** ◇ *His excuse sounded totally ~.* ◇ *The special effects are incredibly ~.*

ADV. **extremely, fairly, very, etc.** | **incredibly, totally** | **a little, slightly, etc.**

lamp *noun*

ADJ. **bedside, desk, floor, overhead** (*AmE*), **reading, standard** (*BrE*), **standing** (*AmE*), **table** | **electric, gas, halogen, kerosene, oil, paraffin** (*BrE*) | **hurricane** | **street** (*BrE*) | **fluorescent, incandescent** | **heat** | **lava** | **magic** | **dim**

VERB + LAMP **light, switch on, turn on** | **switch off, turn off**

LAMP + VERB **illuminate sth, light sth** ◇ *The study was lit only by a small ~.* | **burn, glow, shine** ◇ *An oil ~ burned in the darkness.* | **flicker, go out**

LAMP + NOUN **shade** (usually *lampshade*)

land *noun*

1 surface of the earth

ADJ. **dry** ◇ *It was good to be on dry ~ again after months at sea.*

VERB + LAND **reach** ◇ *The explorers reached ~ after a long voyage.* | **sight** ◇ *In the distance the crew sighted ~.* | **reclaim** ◇ *The new project will reclaim the ~ from the sea.*

LAND + NOUN **mass** ◇ *chains of volcanoes running along the edge of continental ~ masses* | **surface** | **animal, mammal** | **battle, war** | **forces** ◇ *With the ~ forces defeated, everything now rested on the navy.*

PREP. **by ~** ◇ *It's impossible to reach this beach by ~ because of the high cliffs.* | **on ~** ◇ *Some animals can live both on ~ and in water.*

2 piece of ground

ADJ. **good, prime** (*esp. BrE*) ◇ *Good agricultural ~ is scarce.* | **fertile, rich** ◇ *rich agricultural ~* ◇ *~ that is rich in mineral deposits* | **marginal, poor** ◇ *animals grazing on marginal ~* | **arid, desert, dry, parched** ◇ *The ~ was very dry after the long, hot summer.* | **barren** | **derelict** (*BrE*), **waste** (usually *wasteland*) | **contaminated** | **empty, unused, vacant** | **uncultivated, undeveloped, virgin, wild** | **agricultural, arable, cultivated, farm** (usually *farmland*), **farming, pasture, ranch** (*esp. AmE*) ◇ *the clearing of forested areas to create pastures and arable ~* | **grazing** | **industrial** (*esp. BrE*) | **building, housing** (*both BrE*) | **green-belt** (*esp. BrE*), **greenfield** (*BrE*), **park** (usually *parkland*) | **rural, urban** | **private** | **public** | **federal, state** (*both esp. AmE*) | **crown**

land

(BrE), **government** | **reservation, tribal** | **common** (BrE),
communal ◇ *Everyone had the right to graze animals on
communal ~.* | **open** ◇ *They finally got out of the town and
reached open ~.* | **flat, low-lying** (esp. BrE) | **coastal, forest,
forested** (esp. AmE)
... OF LAND **area, parcel, patch, piece, plot, scrap** (esp. BrE),
strip, tract ◇ *The state owns vast tracts of ~.*
VERB + LAND **have, hold, own** ◇ *The inhabitants of a village
held ~ in common.* | **acquire, buy, purchase** | **sell** | **lease,
rent** | **reclaim** | **protect** | **cultivate, farm, plough/plow,
work** | **irrigate** | **clear** ◇ *The ~ has been cleared ready for
building.* | **develop** ◇ *They were refused permission to
develop the ~.* | **expropriate** (formal), **seize** | **distribute,
redistribute** | **grant sb** ◇ *He was granted ~ by the state.*
LAND + VERB **adjoin sth** ◇ *a piece of ~ adjoining the airport*
LAND + NOUN **agent** (esp. BrE) | **office** (AmE), **registry** (BrE) |
acquisition, purchase | **grab** ◇ *The rush for fuel and food
will lead to a global ~ grab.* | **tenure** | **management** |
reclamation (esp. BrE) | **development** | **use** | **reform** |
prices, values | **claim** | **dispute**

3 the land farming land

VERB + THE LAND **live off** ◇ *It's very fertile countryside where
you can just live off the ~.* | **farm, work, work on** ◇ *His
family had always worked the ~.* | **leave** (BrE) ◇ *Many people leave
the ~ to find work in towns.* | **get back to, go back to** ◇ *He's
tired of living in cities, and wants to get back to the ~.*

4 country

ADJ. **ancestral, native** ◇ *the tribe's ancestral ~s* | **distant,
faraway, far-off** ◇ *He journeyed to many distant ~s.* | **alien,
foreign, strange** ◇ *She was all alone in a strange ~.* |
Promised Land (often figurative) ◇ *the Promised Land of
progressive education* | **cloud cuckoo** (BrE), **fantasy, la-la**
(AmE), **never-never** ◇ *Anyone who thinks this legislation will
be effective is living in cloud cuckoo ~.*
VERB + LAND **conquer, occupy** | **rule**

land verb

1 of an aircraft

ADV. **safely** ◇ *The pilot managed to ~ the plane safely.*
VERB + LAND **be about to, be due to, be scheduled to** | **come
down to** ◇ *The plane slowly came down to ~.* | **be forced to**
◇ *The plane was forced to ~ in a nearby field.* | **be able to,
manage to**
PREP. **at** ◇ *We are due to ~ at Newark at 12.15.*

2 fall to the ground

ADV. **awkwardly, badly, painfully** ◇ *I ~ed awkwardly and
twisted my ankle.* | **expertly, gracefully, neatly** ◇ *He tensed
himself for the jump and ~ed expertly on the other side.* |
heavily | **gently, lightly, softly** | **squarely** ◇ *The coin ~ed
squarely between his feet.*
PREP. **on** ◇ *She fell and ~ed heavily on her back.*

landing noun

1 of an aircraft

ADJ. **bumpy, hard, rough** | **crash, emergency, forced** | **safe,
smooth, soft** | **successful** | **lunar, moon** ◇ *the first
successful lunar ~*
VERB + LANDING **make** ◇ *The pilot had to make an emergency ~
in a field.*
LANDING + NOUN **area, site, strip**

2 top of a staircase

ADJ. **first-floor** (BrE), **second-floor**, etc.
PREP. **off the ~** ◇ *The room opens off the ~.* | **on the ~** ◇
There's a phone on the ~ outside your room.

landlord noun

1 sb who lets a house/room

ADJ. **private** | **local** (esp. AmE) | **unscrupulous** (esp. BrE) |
absentee ◇ *The house has an absentee ~, who visits the
property once a year.*

2 (BrE) man who owns/runs a pub

ADJ. **pub**
LANDLORD + VERB **serve sb**

landmark noun

1 feature of the landscape

ADJ. **distinctive** (esp. BrE), **prominent** | **famous, well-known**
| **familiar** ◇ *After twenty years, all the familiar ~s had
disappeared.* | **city, local** | **national** | **historic, historical** |
architectural
VERB + LANDMARK **recognize** | **designate sth** ◇ *The building
has been designated a historical ~ by the Commission.*
LANDMARK + NOUN **building** | **status** (esp. AmE) ◇ *The residents
are seeking ~ status for the building.*
PREP. **~ for** ◇ *The tower was once a ~ for ships.*

2 important stage in the development of sth

ADJ. **great, important, major, significant**
VERB + LANDMARK **be, represent** ◇ *The Russian Revolution
represents a ~ in world history.*
LANDMARK + NOUN **decision, legislation** (AmE), **ruling** ◇ *a ~
decision on gay marriage* | **case** | **event** | **achievement** |
study
PREP. **~ in** ◇ *The piece is an important ~ in the history of
music.*

landscape noun

ADJ. **barren, bleak, desolate, dramatic, rocky, rugged, wild**
◇ *the dramatic ~ of the desert* | **beautiful** | **rural, urban** ◇
an urban ~ of factories and skyscrapers | **desert, mountain**
| **winter** | **industrial** | **lunar** | **cultural, economic,
political, social** (all figurative) ◇ *The political ~ of the country
has changed since unemployment rose.* | **changing** ◇ *We need
to adapt more rapidly to the changing economic ~ overseas.*
VERB + LANDSCAPE **conserve, preserve, protect** ◇ *the need to
preserve the rural ~* | **dot, litter** ◇ *Rocks of all sizes dotted the
~.* | **dominate** ◇ *The power station dominates the ~.* |
create, shape (both often figurative) | **alter, change,
transform** (all often figurative) ◇ *Their songs altered the ~ of
popular music.*
LANDSCAPE + NOUN **architect, gardener** | **architecture,
design, gardening** | **painter, photographer** | **painting,
photography**

landslide noun

1 fall of earth or rocks

VERB + LANDSLIDE **cause, trigger** ◇ *The floods caused a ~.*
LANDSLIDE + VERB **destroy sth** ◇ *The town was destroyed by
a ~.*

2 election victory

ADJ. **electoral** ◇ *Nobody predicted such an electoral ~.* |
massive | **Conservative, Labour,** etc. | **Democratic,
Republican,** etc.
VERB + LANDSLIDE **win by** ◇ *The party won by a ~.*
LANDSLIDE + NOUN **victory**

lane noun

1 (esp. BrE) narrow road

ADJ. **narrow** | **little, small** | **single-track** (BrE) | **quiet** |
dusty, muddy | **bumpy, twisting, winding** ◇ *There is plenty
to explore in the narrow winding ~s behind the cathedral.* |
leafy | **cobbled** | **country** ◇ *We drove down winding country
~s on the journey to York.* | **back** (BrE) ◇ *Lighting is poor in
the back ~s of the old town.*
VERB + LANE **turn down, turn into**
LANE + VERB **go, lead, run** ◇ *the ~ leading to the village* ◇ *The ~
runs past the lake.*
PREP. **along a/the ~** ◇ *We cycled for miles along winding
country ~s.* | **down a/the ~, in a/the ~, up a/the ~**

2 part of a wide road for one line of traffic

ADJ. **fast, slow** | **left, left-hand, right, right-hand** |
breakdown (AmE), **inside, middle, outside** (BrE), **over-
taking** (BrE), **passing** (AmE) | **northbound, southbound,**

etc. | **traffic** | **bus, express** (*AmE*), **HOV** (= high-occupancy vehicle) | **bicycle** (*AmE*), **cycle** (*BrE*)
VERB + LANE **change, get in** (*BrE*), **switch** (*esp. AmE*) ◇ *I hate changing ~s when the traffic is heavy.* ◇ *Get in ~ early when turning off.* | **keep in, stay in** (*both BrE*)
LANE + NOUN **closures** (*esp. BrE*), **restrictions** (*BrE*) ◇ *Commuters can expect ~ closures for a while longer.*
PREP. **in (the) ~** ◇ *The bus was crawling along in the slow ~.*

NOTE

Languages

excellent…, fluent…, good…, perfect… ◇ *He speaks fluent Japanese.*
bad…, broken…, poor… ◇ *I got by with broken Chinese and sign language.*
colloquial…, idiomatic…, non-standard…, pidgin…, standard… ◇ *The inhabitants speak a kind of pidgin Spanish.*
spoken…, written… ◇ *My spoken Polish is better than my written Polish.*
business… ◇ *She is doing a course in business English.*
original… ◇ *The fable is translated from the original French.*
know…, read…, speak…, understand…, use… ◇ *I am more comfortable using Spanish, if you don't mind.*
be fluent in… ◇ *She was fluent in German, Urdu and Swahili.*
do… (*esp. BrE*), **learn…, study…** ◇ *I did German at school but I've forgotten most of it.* ◇ *I've been learning Arabic for four years.*
improve…, practise/practice… ◇ *I spent a month in Rome to improve my Italian.*
master… ◇ *I never really mastered Latin.*
translate sth into… ◇ *He has translated her latest book into Korean.*
…class, …course, …lesson ◇ *I'm late for my Russian class.*
…interpreter ◇ *the need for Gujarati interpreters*
…speaker, a speaker of… ◇ *the number of Portuguese speakers in the world*
a command of…, a knowledge of… ◇ *He has a poor command of English.*
in… ◇ *What is 'apple' in French?* ◇ *He addressed me in his best Portuguese.*
→ See also the note at SUBJECT

language noun

1 system of communication

ADJ. **first, native** ◇ *She grew up in Mexico, so her first ~ is Spanish.* | **foreign, second** ◇ *How many foreign ~s does she speak?* ◇ *the teaching of English as a second ~* | **original** ◇ *Most local cinemas show films in the original ~, with German subtitles.* | **source, target** (*both technical*) | **ancient, classical, dead** ◇ *Latin is a dead ~.* | **modern** | **common, shared** | **indigenous, local** | **official** ◇ *Belgium has two official ~s.* | **national** ◇ *Portuguese is the national ~ of Brazil.* | **dominant** | **international, universal** | **minority** ◇ *Some minority ~s are dying out.* | **natural** ◇ *Computers will never be able to understand natural ~.* | **strange, unknown** ◇ *manuscripts written in an unknown ~* | **computer, programming**
VERB + LANGUAGE **speak** | **know, understand** | **use** | **learn, study** | **teach** | **master**
LANGUAGE + NOUN **acquisition, development, learning** ◇ *new methods of ~ learning* | **course, lesson** | **skill** | **barrier**
PHRASES **command of (a) ~, knowledge of (a) ~, mastery of (a) ~** ◇ *Her command of ~ is very advanced for a six-year-old.*

2 way of using language

ADJ. **spoken, written** ◇ *She could speak some Chinese, but never studied the written ~.* | **colloquial, everyday, informal** | **formal** | **expressive, flowery, literary, poetic** | **figurative,**

symbolic | **everyday, plain, simple** ◇ *His strength is that he addresses his readers in plain ~.* | **vague** | **racist, sexist** | **sign** ◇ *Not all deaf people use sign ~.* | **body** ◇ *You could tell from his body ~ that he was very embarrassed.* | **legal, technical** | **biblical** | **harsh** ◇ *She reserved her harshest ~ for those she believed had betrayed her.* | **bad, colourful/ colorful, crude, foul, obscene, offensive, strong, vulgar** ◇ *people using foul ~*
VERB + LANGUAGE **use** | **be couched in, be expressed in** | **mind, watch** ◇ *The referee told the players to mind their ~.*
PREP. **in…~** ◇ *His letter was couched in very formal ~.*
PHRASES **use of ~** ◇ *The writer's use of ~ reflects the personality of each character.*

lantern noun

VERB + LANTERN **light, shine** ◇ *He shone his ~ into the dark room.* | **hang** ◇ *They saw people hanging paper ~s from their windows.* | **carry, hold** ◇ *She carried a ~ to light her way.*
LANTERN + VERB **burn, glow, light sth, shine** ◇ *A ~ lit the small room.* | **hang** ◇ *The ~ hung from the roof.*

lap noun circuit

ADJ. **first, opening** (*BrE*) | **final, last** | **victory** ◇ *I skated a victory ~ around the rink.* | **fast** (*esp. BrE*) ◇ *The fastest ~ was completed at 208 mph.*
VERB + LAP **complete, do, finish, take** ◇ *He took a quick ~ around the empty rink.* | **race, run, swim** (*AmE*) ◇ *He was swimming ~s in the pool.*
LAP + NOUN **record** (*BrE*) ◇ *He set a new ~ record.* | **pool** (*AmE*) ◇ *an indoor heated ~ pool*
PREP. **on the…~** ◇ *He tripped and fell on the final ~.*
PHRASES **a ~ of honour/honor** ◇ *The winner did a ~ of honour/honor.*

lap verb

ADV. **gently, softly**
PREP. **against** ◇ *The waves lapped gently against the side of the ship.* | **around** ◇ *The water lapped around his ankles.* | **at** ◇ *The waves lapped at his feet.* | **over** ◇ *The freezing water lapped over her boots.*

lapel noun

ADJ. **narrow, wide** ◇ *a coat with wide ~s*
VERB + LAPEL **be pinned to** ◇ *A brooch was pinned to her ~.*
LAPEL + NOUN **badge** (*BrE*), **button** (*AmE*), **pin** (*esp. BrE*)
PREP. **in the/your ~** ◇ *He was wearing a carnation in his ~.* | **on the/your ~** ◇ *a jacket with a pin on the ~*
PHRASES **grab sb by the ~s** ◇ *He grabbed her by the ~s and shook her violently.*

lapse noun

1 small error; bad manners

ADJ. **minor** | **major, serious** ◇ *a serious ~ in judgment* | **unfortunate** | **brief, momentary, temporary** | **sudden** | **occasional, rare** ◇ *Dawson's occasional ~s of concentration* | **memory, mental** ◇ *I keep suffering these mental ~s.* | **intelligence, security** ◇ *the investigation into security ~s at the laboratory* | **odd** (*BrE*) ◇ *It was an odd ~ for one who is normally so polite.* | **ethical, moral** (*both esp. AmE*) ◇ *allegations of ethical ~s*
VERB + LAPSE **have, suffer** ◇ *I had a momentary ~ when I couldn't remember his name.*
PREP. **~ in** ◇ *a ~ in attention* | **~ of** ◇ *sudden ~s of concentration*

2 passing of time

ADJ. **brief** | **long** ◇ *I'm sorry for the long ~ of time between updates.* | **time**
PHRASES **~ of** ◇ *after a considerable ~ of time* ◇ *a time ~ of three months*

larder noun (*esp. BrE*)

ADJ. **full, well-stocked** | **bare, empty** | **walk-in**

large

VERB + LARDER **fill, stock** | **empty, raid** ◊ *He comes home from school and raids the ~.*
LARDER + NOUN **door, shelf**
PREP. **in the ~** ◊ *There wasn't much food left in the ~.*

large *adj.*

VERBS **be** | **appear, feel, look, seem** ◊ *Some of the clothes looked very ~.* | **become, get, grow** ◊ *By this time his debt had become extremely ~.* ◊ *The plant had grown quite ~.* | **remain** | **loom** ◊ *The issue looms ~ in political campaigns nationwide.*
ADV. **extremely, fairly, very, etc.** ◊ *Isn't that sweater rather ~?* | **especially, exceedingly, exceptionally, incredibly, particularly** | **comparatively, moderately, reasonably, relatively** | **enough, sufficiently** ◊ *Are you sure the hall will be ~ enough?* | **correspondingly, equally, similarly** ◊ *a huge chair behind an equally ~ desk* | **increasingly** ◊ *the increasingly ~ numbers of senior citizens* | **infinitely** ◊ *The universe is infinitely ~.* | **abnormally, disproportionately, impossibly, overly, ridiculously, surprisingly, unexpectedly, unusually** ◊ *His eyes were abnormally ~.* ◊ *Our house was not overly ~.*

laser *noun*

ADJ. **powerful** | **infrared**
VERB + LASER **use** | **aim, fire, shoot**
LASER + NOUN **beam, blast, light, ray** | **printer, scanner** | **gun** | **pointer** | **surgery, therapy, treatment**

lash *noun* → See EYELASH

last *verb*

ADV. **long** ◊ *Your car will ~ longer if you take care of it.* | **well** ◊ *Even when cut, the flowers ~ very well.* | **forever, indefinitely** ◊ *Nothing ~s forever.* ◊ *With care, the vines will ~ indefinitely.* | **rarely** ◊ *This type of happiness rarely ~s.* | **never** ◊ *Happiness never ~s.*
VERB + LAST **can** ◊ *The storm could ~ quite a long time.* ◊ *The good weather couldn't ~.* | **will** ◊ *The kids are all very enthusiastic, but it won't ~.* | **be likely to, be sure to** ◊ *a bruise that was sure to ~ for days* | **be unlikely to** ◊ *I always thought his popularity was unlikely to ~.* | **be expected to, seem to** ◊ *The flight seemed to ~ forever.* | **be built to, be made to** ◊ *This house was built to ~.*
PREP. **for** ◊ *The war ~ed for three years.* | **into** ◊ *The celebrations ~ed well into the next week.* | **through** ◊ *The effort began in November and ~ed through February.* (*AmE*) ◊ *She hoped they had enough firewood to ~ through the night.* (*BrE*) | **until** ◊ *The trial is expected to ~ until the end of the week.*
PHRASES **while sth ~s** ◊ *Make the most of this mood while it ~s.*

late *adj.*

VERBS **be, feel, seem** ◊ *I don't know what the time is, but it feels quite ~.* | **get, grow** ◊ *It's getting too ~ to do anything today.* | **make sb**
ADV. **extremely, fairly, very, etc.** | **relatively** | **a little, slightly, etc.** | **fashionably** ◊ *Kevin was fashionably ~ as always.*
PREP. **for** ◊ *I'm ~ for work.* | **in** ◊ *He took up music ~ in life.* | **into** ◊ *It was now ~ into the night.* | **with** ◊ *He was now three weeks ~ with his rent.*
PHRASES **an hour, ten minutes, etc. ~** ◊ *The train was 45 minutes ~.* | **leave it rather, very, etc. ~** ◊ *You've left it rather ~ to start your homework, haven't you?*

latitude *noun*

1 geographical position

ADJ. **high, low** | **northern, southern** | **polar, temperate, tropical** ◊ *These birds only survive in temperate ~s.*
VERB + LATITUDE **calculate, determine**
PHRASES **a line of ~**

2 freedom

ADJ. **considerable, great** | **broad** (*esp. AmE*), **wide** (*both esp. AmE*) ◊ *Their managers enjoy wide ~ to make hiring decisions.*
... OF LATITUDE **degree** ◊ *Some degree of ~ is required in interpreting the law on this point.*
VERB + LATITUDE **allow (sb), give sb, permit** (*esp. AmE*) | **enjoy**
PREP. **~ for** ◊ *This method allows very little ~ for error.* | **~ in** ◊ *Nowadays, newspapers are allowed considerable ~ in criticizing the government.*

laugh *noun*

1 sound/act of laughing

ADJ. **loud** | **light, little, short, slight, small, soft** | **deep, low, rich** | **big, good, great** ◊ *The last joke got the biggest ~.* | **belly, booming, hearty** | **harsh, shrill** | **barking, husky, throaty** | **sexy** ◊ *He laughed that warm, sexy ~.* | **tinkling** | **amused, delighted** | **embarrassed, nervous, shaky** | **bitter, cynical, derisive, dry, fake** (*esp. AmE*), **forced, hollow, humourless/humorless, mirthless, mocking, rueful, sarcastic, scornful, wry** ◊ *She forced a bitter ~.* | **genuine** ◊ *Nick responded with a genuine ~.* | **cruel, evil, sinister** ◊ *The man laughed, a harsh, evil ~.* | **cheap** ◊ *This movie is too intent upon getting cheap ~s.* | **infectious**
VERB + LAUGH **give, laugh, let out** ◊ *He gave a short, amused ~.* ◊ *She laughed a hollow ~ then fell silent.* | **have** | **share** ◊ *We all shared a good ~.* | **force, manage** | **bite back** (*esp. AmE*), **choke back, hold back, smother** (*esp. AmE*), **stifle, suppress** ◊ *She tried to suppress a ~, but ended up giggling anyway.* | **enjoy, like** ◊ *He enjoys a good ~.* | **draw, earn** (*AmE*), **get, raise** (*BrE*) ◊ *That earned a ~ from everyone.* ◊ *Few of his jokes got a ~.* ◊ *She got a ~ out of Jack.* | **hear**
LAUGH + VERB **escape sb** ◊ *A small ~ escaped her.* | **ring out** ◊ *A ~ rang out behind me.*
PREP. **for a ~** ◊ *She dyed her hair green just for a ~.* | **with a ~** ◊ *He left the room with a cynical ~.* | **~ about, ~ at** ◊ *We all had a great ~ about it when we got home.* | **~ over** ◊ *I had a good ~ over that one.*
PHRASES **be good for a ~** ◊ *Paula's always good for a ~* (= always amusing). | **have the last ~** ◊ *We'll have the last ~ if she finds out that you're the one who played the trick.* | **a ~ at sb's expense** ◊ *Oh yes, very funny—have your ~ at my expense!* | **the ~ is on sb** (= sb looks ridiculous after they have tried to make fun of sb else) | **play sb/sth for ~s** ◊ *She seemed unsure of whether to play her role seriously or for ~s.*

2 sb/sth that is amusing

ADJ. **good, great, real**
PHRASES **a barrel of ~s, a bit of a ~, a ~ a minute** (= very funny)

laugh *verb*

ADV. **aloud, loudly, out loud** ◊ *It looked so funny that I almost ~ed out loud.* | **gently, inwardly, lightly, quietly, silently, softly, under your breath** | **deeply, hard, heartily, a lot, really, uproariously** ◊ *I have not heard an audience ~ so hard for a long time.* ◊ *He ~ed heartily at his own joke.* | **just, merely, simply** ◊ *I thought she would be angry but she just ~ed.* | **almost** | **briefly, a little, shakily, sheepishly, shortly, slightly, weakly** ◊ *She ~ed slightly as she saw my expression.* | **suddenly** | **easily, freely** ◊ *She smiles and ~s easily.* | **openly, outright** | **helplessly, uncontrollably** | **cheerfully, delightedly** (*esp. AmE*), **happily, merrily** | **hysterically** | **nervously, uneasily** ◊ *I ~ed uneasily, trying to make light of the moment.* | **politely** | **good-naturedly** ◊ *Emilio tilted his head back and ~ed good-naturedly.* | **incredulously, in disbelief** | **triumphantly** | **bitterly, coldly, cynically, derisively, drily, evilly, grimly, harshly, hollowly, humourlessly/humorlessly, mirthlessly, mockingly, ruefully, sarcastically, scornfully, wickedly, wryly** ◊ *He realized how he had been fooled, and ~ed bitterly.* | **insanely, madly, maniacally, manically** | **together** ◊ *They were talking and ~ing together.*
VERB + LAUGH **have to, want to** ◊ *He looked so funny I just had to ~.* | **begin to, start to** | **try not to** ◊ *I was watching them and trying not to ~.* | **learn to** ◊ *Don't take life too seriously.*

Learn to ~ at yourself. | **make sb** ◇ *He pulled a funny face to make us ~.* | **hear sb** ◇ *I heard him suddenly ~ aloud.*
PREP. **about** ◇ *Tomorrow you'll be able to ~ about this.* | **at** ◇ *The audience ~ed at her jokes.* | **in** ◇ *Sam shook her head, ~ing in amusement.* | **over** ◇ *We were ~ing over some joke Bentley had told.* | **with** ◇ *She spent time talking and ~ing with the children.* ◇ *Trent almost ~ed with relief.*
PHRASES **burst out ~ing, bust out ~ing** (*AmE*) | **can't help ~ing, can't stop ~ing** ◇ *She was fooling around and we couldn't stop ~ing.* | **fall about ~ing** (*BrE*) ◇ *It was so funny we just fell about ~ing.* | **find yourself ~ing** ◇ *He laughed, and she found herself ~ing with him.* | **start ~ing** ◇ *Vivian started ~ing hysterically.* | **stop ~ing**

laughter noun

ADJ. **hearty, helpless, hysterical, insane, loud, maniacal** (*esp. AmE*), **raucous, uncontrollable, uproarious, wild** ◇ *I heard sounds of raucous ~ upstairs.* | **happy** | **infectious** ◇ *Her infectious ~ had everyone smiling.* | **nervous** | **muffled, quiet, silent, soft, suppressed** ◇ *She was bent over with suppressed ~.* | **derisive, mocking** | **cruel, evil, sinister** ◇ *Andrea burst into cruel ~.* | **drunken** ◇ *Gerry exploded into more drunken ~.* | **canned** ◇ *the canned ~ of a sitcom*
... OF LAUGHTER **bark, hoot, howl, roar, shout, shriek, snort** ◇ *He gave a sudden bellow of ~.* | **fit** ◇ *Everyone dissolved into fits of ~ when they saw my haircut.* | **bout** (*AmE*), **burst, chorus, gale, guffaw, peal, ripple, round, wave** ◇ *His suggestion was greeted with peals of ~.* ◇ *A ripple of ~ ran around the room.*
VERB + LAUGHTER **burst into, dissolve into, explode with** | **bellow with, cackle with, hoot with, howl with, roar with, scream with, shriek with, snort with, squeal with** | **rock with, shake with** | **draw, elicit, provoke** ◇ *Hunter's statement drew ~ from the crowd.* ◇ *The joke provoked ~ from all of them.* | **choke back** (*esp. AmE*), **contain, control, hide, hold back, muffle, smother** (*esp. AmE*), **stifle, suppress** ◇ *Will was no longer able to contain his ~.*

launch noun

ADJ. **commercial, official, press** (*esp. BrE*), **public** ◇ *The commercial ~ was the end of 2007.* ◇ *She is signing copies of her book at the official ~.* | **successful** | **imminent** (*esp. BrE*), **upcoming** | **planned, scheduled** ◇ *the postponement of the scheduled ~ on July 7* | **soft** (= in stages) ◇ *A couple of days ago we opened up the website for a soft ~.* | **book, campaign** (*esp. BrE*), **product** | **balloon, missile, rocket, satellite, shuttle**
VERB + LAUNCH **get (sth) ready for, prepare (sth) for** ◇ *They are preparing for the ~ of the new campaign next month.* | **announce** | **celebrate, mark** ◇ *a big Hollywood event to mark the ~ of the movie* | **go ahead with** | **coincide with** (*esp. BrE*) ◇ *The show is timed to coincide with the ~ of a new book on the subject.* | **attend** (*esp. BrE*), **go to, speak at** (*esp. BrE*) | **plan, schedule** ◇ *The official product ~ was scheduled for 2009.* | **delay, postpone**
LAUNCH + NOUN **date** | **party** (= for a product or book) | **facility** (*esp. AmE*), **pad, platform, site** ◇ *one of the world's largest ocean-going ~ platforms*
PREP. **after the ~, following the ~, since the ~** ◇ *In the six months since its ~ the car has sold extremely well.* | **at a/the ~** ◇ *I met her at the ~ of her new book.* | **~ for** ◇ *a spring ~ for the new TV system*

laundry noun

ADJ. **clean, dirty**
... OF LAUNDRY **pile** ◇ *There was a pile of clean ~ on her bed.*
VERB + LAUNDRY **do, wash** ◇ *The housekeeper cooks, does the ~ and cleans.* | **fold, put away**
LAUNDRY + NOUN **bag, basket, hamper** (*AmE*) | **room** ◇ *He began working in the ~ room of the hotel last May.* | **chute** | **detergent, soap** (*both AmE*) | **service** ◇ *The hotel offers a free ~ service.* | **list** (*informal, figurative, esp. AmE*) ◇ *Here's a brief ~ list of what needs fixing.*

lavatory noun (*esp. BrE*)

ADJ. **public** (*BrE*) | **gents'** (*BrE*), **ladies', men's** | **outside** | **flushing**
VERB + LAVATORY **go to, use, visit** | **need** | **flush, flush sth down**
LAVATORY + NOUN **bowl, chain, cistern, seat** | **paper** | **brush** | **cubicle** | **attendant** | **facilities**
PREP. **in the ~, on the ~** (*BrE*)

law noun

1 official rule/rules → See also MARTIAL LAW
ADJ. **administrative, case, civil, common, constitutional, criminal, statute, etc.** | **abortion, bankruptcy, business, contract, divorce, employment, family, immigration, labour/labor, libel, tax, etc.** | **federal, international, state** | **clear** ◇ *The ~ is clear: bribery is wrong.* | **unclear, vague** | **harsh, strict, stringent, tough** ◇ *Environmental ~s are strict about polluting precious water.* | **discriminatory, unconstitutional, unjust** ◇ *We believe this ~ is unconstitutional.* | **liberal** | **restrictive** ◇ *the passage of a restrictive immigration ~ in 1924* | **Jewish, Talmudic** | **Islamic, sharia**
VERB + LAW **become** ◇ *A presidential veto prevented the bill from becoming ~.* | **apply, enforce, implement, uphold** ◇ *It's the job of the police to enforce the ~.* | **follow, obey, observe, respect** | **break, flout, violate** | **adopt, create, enact, introduce, pass** | **overturn, repeal** | **amend, change, reform, revise** ◇ *Congress amended the ~ in 1998.* | **draft, write** ◇ *the legislators who drafted the ~* | **interpret** ◇ *Judges interpret this ~ in different ways.*
LAW + VERB **allow sth, authorize sth, permit sth** | **recognize sth** ◇ *a ~ recognizing civil unions for same-sex couples* | **ban sth, forbid sth, prohibit sth** ◇ *The ~ forbids gambling of any kind.* | **limit sth, restrict sth** ◇ *a ~ limiting the hours of work to ten hours per day* | **criminalize sth** ◇ *Laws criminalizing same-sex relationships were ruled unconstitutional.* | **mandate sth** (*esp. AmE*), **require sth** ◇ *The wearing of a crash helmet is required by ~.* | **govern sth, regulate sth** ◇ *the ~ governing school attendance* ◇ *the ~s regulating firearms* | **apply to sb/sth, cover sb/sth** ◇ *The ~ applies equally to businesses large and small.*
LAW + NOUN **court** (*BrE*) (also **court of law** (*BrE, AmE*)) | **case, suit** (usually **lawsuit**) ◇ *lawsuits filed by women against employers* | **enforcement** ◇ *The building was raided by ~ enforcement agents.* | **violation** (*AmE*) | **reform** ◇ *the broader implications of copyright ~ reform* | **clerk, partner** (*both AmE*) | **office, practice** (*both AmE*) ◇ *She lost her job at a Boston ~ office.* | **license** (*AmE*) | **book, journal, review** ◇ *a room filled with ~ books* | **library**
PREP. **above the ~** ◇ *No one is above the ~.* | **against the ~** ◇ *What you did was clearly against the ~.* | **beyond the ~** ◇ *individuals who are acting beyond the ~* | **by ~** ◇ *By ~, you are obliged to install smoke alarms in the factory.* | **outside the ~** ◇ *rebels who live outside the ~* | **within the ~** ◇ *The company is operating entirely within the ~.* | **~ against** ◇ *a local ~ against keeping horses* | **~ concerning, ~ on, ~ regarding, ~ relating to** ◇ *the ~s regarding child actors* ◇ *the ~ relating to the sale of goods*
PHRASES **as the ~ stands** (*BrE*) ◇ *As the ~ stands, you can get married at sixteen.* | **~ and order** ◇ *Martial law was imposed to prevent the breakdown of ~ and order.* | **the ~ of the land** ◇ *the Civil Rights Act of 1964 became the ~ of the land on July 2, 1964.* | **the letter of the ~** ◇ *In spite of the difficulties it would cause her family, the judge stuck to the letter of the ~ and jailed her.* | **take the ~ into your own hands** ◇ *When police failed to arrest the suspect, local people took the ~ into their own hands.*

2 subject of study/profession
VERB + LAW **practise/practice**
LAW + NOUN **firm** | **school** ◇ *She's in ~ school.* (*AmE*) ◇ *She's at ~ school.* (*BrE*)
→ Note at SUBJECT (for more verbs and nouns)

lawn noun

ADJ. **manicured, neat, well-tended** ◇ *a well-tended ~* | **overgrown** | **back, front**
VERB + LAWN **cut, mow, trim** ◇ *The ~ really needs mowing.* |

water ◇ *I was out watering the ~.* | **maintain, take care of** ◇ *the correct way to maintain a ~*

lawsuit noun → See SUIT

lawyer noun

ADJ. **brilliant, clever, competent, excellent, good, smart** (*esp. AmE*) | **high-powered, hotshot** (*AmE*), **leading, prominent, senior, successful, top** ◇ *A leading human rights ~ took on his case.* | **greedy, rich, wealthy** | **experienced, qualified** (*esp. BrE*) | **practising/practicing** | **academic** (*esp. BrE*) | **trial** (*AmE*) ◇ *He was a trial ~ for many years.* | **defence/defense, prosecuting, prosecution** (*esp. BrE*) ◇ *a top criminal defence ~* (*BrE*) ◇ *He brought in a hot-shot criminal defense ~ who secured a not guilty verdict.* (*AmE*) | **court-appointed** (*esp. AmE*) | **government, private** (*esp. AmE*) | **civilian, military** | **appellate** (*AmE*) | **international, local** | **antitrust** (*AmE*), **bankruptcy** (*AmE*), **civil, civil rights, commercial** (*esp. BrE*), **constitutional, corporate, criminal, divorce, employment, family, human rights, immigration, labor** (*AmE*), **libel** (*esp. BrE*), **malpractice** (*AmE*), **patent, personal-injury, tax, tort** (*AmE*) → Note at PROFESSIONAL (for verbs)

lay verb

ADV. **carefully, gently** | **neatly** ◇ *He laid the clothes neatly on his bed.* | **aside, down** ◇ *With a resigned sigh she laid aside her book.* ◇ *He laid the plates down on the table.*
PREP. **on** ◇ *She laid the child tenderly on the bed.* | **over** ◇ *They carefully laid a blanket over the body.*

PHR V **lay sth out**
ADV. **nicely, well** ◇ *Each chapter is nicely laid out with clear diagrams.* ◇ *The owners have a tastefully laid out garden.* | **clearly** ◇ *The information is there; it just isn't laid out clearly.*

lay-by noun (BrE)

VERB + LAY-BY **pull into**
PREP. **in a/the ~** ◇ *I was parked in a ~, having a nap.*

layer noun

ADJ. **fine, thin** ◇ *Everything was covered with a fine ~ of dust.* | **deep, dense, heavy, thick** ◇ *Mulch with a generous ~ of peat or compost.* | **bottom, inner, innermost, lower, middle, outer, outermost, surface, top, upper, uppermost** ◇ *the upper ~s of the earth's atmosphere* | **double, single** ◇ *The product is made from a single ~ of plastic.* | **added, additional, extra** ◇ *They put on thick hats and extra ~s of clothing.* | **alternating** ◇ *The recipe calls for alternating ~s of meat sauce and pasta.* | **protective** ◇ *a protective ~ of black plastic* | **ozone** ◇ *holes in the ozone ~* | **cloud** ◇ *We're flying just below a cloud ~ at 33 000 feet.*
VERB + LAYER **form** ◇ *Use enough gravel to form a ~ about 50mm thick.* | **add, apply** ◇ *He paints a base coat, allows it to dry, and then adds ~s of paint.* | **be covered by, be covered with** ◇ *The body had been covered with a thin ~ of soil.* | **peel away, peel back, remove** ◇ *I decided to peel back the ~s of this story.* (*figurative*)
LAYER + NOUN **cake** (*esp. AmE*)
PREP. **beneath a/the ~, under a/the ~** ◇ *Beneath the surface ~ of the skin are several further layers.* | **in ~s** ◇ *The building is constructed in ~s.* | **~ of** ◇ *an extra ~ of clothing* ◇ *a ~ of bureaucracy* ◇ *multiple ~s of meaning* (*figurative*)
PHRASES **~ after ~, ~ upon ~** ◇ *The remains lay buried under ~ upon ~ of black earth.*

layout noun

ADJ. **basic, general** ◇ *Before designing the house we planned the basic ~ of the rooms.* | **physical, visual** | **interior, internal** | **page, text** ◇ *page ~ software* | **magazine, newspaper** | **road** (*BrE*), **street**

layover noun (AmE) → See also STOPOVER

ADJ. **four-hour, etc.** | **brief, short**

lazy adj.

VERBS **be, feel** | **become, get, grow** ◇ *He had grown ~ and fat.* ◇ *We thought we were winning, so we got ~.*
ADV. **extremely, fairly, very, etc.** | **incredibly** | **plain** (*informal*) ◇ *He's just plain ~.* | **almost** ◇ *His smile was slow, almost ~.* | **a little, slightly, etc.** | **intellectually** ◇ *Most of us are intellectually ~ about large areas of the world around us.*

lead¹ noun

1 example set by sb
ADJ. **moral** (*esp. BrE*)
VERB + LEAD **give, take** ◇ *The government should give a ~ in tackling racism.* | **follow**
PREP. **~ in** ◇ *We should follow their ~ in banning chemical weapons.* | **~ on** ◇ *corporations that have chosen to take the ~ on the privacy issue*

2 position ahead of other people
ADJ. **big, clear, comfortable, commanding, good, healthy, huge, significant, sizeable, solid, strong, substantial** ◇ *For the time being, China has a solid ~ over India.* | **narrow, slight, slim, small** | **two-game, three-length, ten-point, etc.** | **overall** | **early**
VERB + LEAD **be in, gain, have** ◇ *She has a narrow ~ over the other runners.* | **go into, move into, take** ◇ *They took an early ~.* | **build** (*esp. AmE*), **build up, establish** ◇ *The team has now built up a commanding ~.* | **hold, keep, maintain, retain** | **lose** | **regain, retake** ◇ *They regained the ~ with only a few minutes left to play.* | **put sb/sth (back) into** ◇ *That game puts her back into the ~.* | **extend, increase, open** (*esp. AmE*), **open up, widen** ◇ *Houston increased their ~ to 13–7* ◇ *He had opened up a small ~ over his opponent.* | **give**
PREP. **in the ~, into the ~** ◇ *We were struggling to stay in the ~.* | **~ over** ◇ *This win gives the team a two-point ~ over their closest rival.*

3 main part in a play, show, etc.
ADJ. **romantic** | **female, male**
VERB + LEAD **play** ◇ *Her big break came when she was chosen to play the ~ in a Broadway musical.* | **sing** ◇ *She sings ~ on four tracks.*
LEAD + NOUN **character, role** | **actor, actress, dancer, singer, vocalist, vocals** | **guitar, guitarist**

4 clue
ADJ. **good, promising, solid** ◇ *Some promising ~s are already emerging.* ◇ *They have several solid ~s in their investigation.* | **new** | **possible** ◇ *The police are following every possible ~.* | **false** ◇ *It turned out to be a false ~.*
VERB + LEAD **have** | **find, get** ◇ *Did you find any ~s when you searched it?* ◇ *At last we got a ~ on the McCreary case.* | **follow, pursue** | **give**
PREP. **~ as to** ◇ *He said that he has a ~ as to where Dylan may be.* | **~ on** ◇ *~s on the murderer's identity*

lead² verb

1 show the way
ADV. **away, back, on, out** ◇ *'Lead on!' said Casey.*
VERB + LEAD **help (to)** ◇ *Five people helping to ~ a convoy of aid are feared dead.* | **allow sb to, let sb** ◇ *Let me ~ the way.*
PREP. **along, down, into, out of, through, to, etc.** ◇ *She led them along a dark corridor to a small room.*
PHRASES **~ the way** ◇ *You ~ the way and we'll follow.*

2 go to a place
ADV. **directly** | **back, down, up** ◇ *An old track led back through the woods.* | **nowhere, somewhere** (*often figurative*) ◇ *Often there are discoveries which ~ nowhere.*
PREP. **from** | **onto** ◇ *The glass doors ~ out onto a rooftop garden.* | **to** ◇ *a path ~ing from the village to the old church*

3 cause
ADV. **normally, usually** | **inevitably, inexorably, invariably** ◇ *Industrialization inevitably led to the expansion of the urban*

working class. | **certainly, likely, undoubtedly** ◇ *It will almost certainly be a disaster.* ◇ *Such actions would most likely ~ to the decline of rural communities.* | **not necessarily** ◇ *The use of soft drugs does not necessarily ~ to a progression to hard drugs.* | **automatically** ◇ *Business success does not automatically ~ to financial success.* | **naturally** ◇ *Discussion of a client's tax affairs will ~ naturally into consideration of investment options.* | **in turn** ◇ *These measures in turn led to an increased opportunity for independent music production.* | **directly** | **indirectly** | **eventually, finally, ultimately**
VERB + LEAD **can, may, might, must** | **can easily, can only** ◇ *Sugar and fat can easily ~ to obesity.* | **may well, might well** ◇ *The carbon tax might well ~ to a doubling of prices for fossil fuels.* | **appear to, seem to** | **be expected to, be likely to, tend to** ◇ *Worrying about your weight is more likely to ~ to low self-esteem.* | **be bound to**
PREP. **to** ◇ *the events that led eventually to war*

lead³ *noun*

ADJ. **molten**
VERB + LEAD **be made of**
LEAD + NOUN **pipe, piping** | **paint** | **shot** | **pencil** | **contamination, exposure, poisoning** ◇ *Lead exposure can be harmful to everyone, especially young children and babies.* | **content, levels** | **industry, mine, mining**

leader *noun*

1 person who is in charge of sth

ADJ. **born, natural, true** | **charismatic, effective, good, great, inspirational, inspired, inspiring, visionary** | **accountable** ◇ *We need to make our political ~s accountable.* | **undisputed** | **influential, key, powerful, prominent, strong, top** | **corrupt, weak** | **deputy** (*esp. AmE*) | **senior** ◇ *Some of our senior ~s have been with the company all of their careers.* | **former** | **future** ◇ *These young people will be the future ~s of our nation.* | **joint** (*esp. BrE*) | **majority, minority** (*both esp. AmE*) ◇ *a former US Senate majority ~* | **elected** ◇ *She is the elected ~ of the group.* | **local, national, world** ◇ *a meeting with world ~s at the G8 summit* | **congressional, opposition, parliamentary, party, Senate** | **Conservative, Democratic, Labour, Republican, etc.** | **military, political, religious, spiritual** | **Christian, Jewish, Muslim, etc.** | **gang, guerrilla, nationalist, rebel** | **group, project, squadron, team** ◇ *Discuss any problems with your team ~.* | **business, church, civic, community, corporate, council** (*esp. BrE*)**, government, industry, strike, student, tribal, union, youth** ◇ *Business ~s have been in talks with the government.* | **miners', teachers', etc.** (*BrE*) | **civil rights** ◇ *civil rights ~ Martin Luther King*
VERB + LEADER **be appointed, become, be elected** | **appoint (sb), appoint sb as, choose (sb as), elect (sb), elect sb as**
PHRASES **the ~ of the Opposition** (*in the UK*) | **the ~ of the pack** ◇ *They are trying to figure out who will emerge as the ~ of this pack.*

2 person/team that is best or in first place

ADJ. **undisputed** | **brand, global, market, world, worldwide** ◇ *The company is a world ~ in electrical goods.* | **championship** (*BrE*)**, league, tournament** | **joint** (*esp. BrE*) ◇ *Milner and Whyte remain joint ~s in the Player of the Year event.* | **early** ◇ *The company was an early ~ in global manufacturing.*
VERB + LEADER **overtake** ◇ *We aim to overtake the market ~s within two years.*
PREP. **behind the ~** ◇ *ten points behind league ~s* | **~ in** ◇ *the undisputed ~ in her field*

leadership *noun*

ADJ. **clear, effective, firm, good, great, outstanding, real, strong, true** ◇ *He was praised for his firm ~.* | **poor, weak** | **charismatic, dynamic, transformational** (*esp. AmE*)**, visionary** | **executive, senior, top** ◇ *the army's senior ~* | **traditional** | **personal** | **deputy** (*BrE*) ◇ *He is standing in the deputy ~ election.* | **collective, joint** | **global, local, national, world** | **transitional** | **Conservative, Democratic, Labour, Republican, etc.** | **civilian, cultural, educational** (*AmE*)**, intellectual, military, moral, political, religious,**

spiritual ◇ *Political ~ needs a particular combination of skills.* | **Christian, Jewish, Muslim, etc.** | **business, church, community, congressional, government, industry, parliamentary, party, presidential, Senate, union** | **market** ◇ *the opportunity to strengthen our market ~*
VERB + LEADERSHIP **assume, take** (*AmE*)**, take over** ◇ *When Smith died, Blair took over the ~ of the party.* | **assert** ◇ *her method of asserting personal ~* | **demonstrate, exercise, provide, show** ◇ *In the crisis he showed real ~.* | **need, require** ◇ *It's a crisis that requires strong ~.* | **lack** ◇ *The movement is deeply divided and lacks clear ~.*
LEADERSHIP + NOUN **bid** (*BrE*)**, campaign** (*esp. BrE*)**, challenge** | **ballot, battle, contest, election, race, struggle** (*all esp. BrE*) | **position, role** | **team** ◇ *the hard work of staff and the ~ team* | **structure** | **style** | **abilities, qualities, skills** ◇ *He lacks ~ qualities.* | **development, programme/program** (*both esp. AmE*) ◇ *The philosophy of the company is that ~ development cannot start early enough.* | **vacuum** ◇ *There is a ~ vacuum in the party.*
PREP. **under sb's ~** ◇ *The school has flourished under the ~ of Mr Levi.* | **~ from** ◇ *What is really needed is clear ~ from the president.* | **~ in** ◇ *Leadership in science is moving east.*
PHRASES **a challenge to sb's ~** ◇ *She withstood several challenges to her ~.* | **a lack of ~** | **sb's style of ~**

leaf *noun*

ADJ. **new, young** | **autumn, fall** (*AmE*) | **dead, dry, fallen, falling, rotting** ◇ *The ground was thick with dead leaves.* | **broad** (*esp. technical*)**, heart-shaped, oval** ◇ *broad-leaf plants* | **green, yellow, etc.** | **glossy, hairy, leathery, shiny, variegated** | **bay, lettuce, maple, oak, tea, etc.** ◇ *Stop trying to read tea leaves* (= predict the future)*.*
VERB + LEAF **have** ◇ *This plant has beautifully variegated leaves.* | **come into** (*esp. BrE*)**, grow, produce, sprout** ◇ *It was spring and the trees were coming into ~.* ◇ *In the spring the plant began to put out new leaves.* | **shed** ◇ *Deciduous trees shed their leaves annually.* | **pick, pluck** ◇ *He picked a ~ from the basil plant and started to chew it.* | **rake** ◇ *The boys helped by raking the leaves in the yard.*
LEAF + VERB **appear, emerge** ◇ *Spring arrived and the first green leaves began to appear.* | **grow** | **turn, yellow** ◇ *The summer was over and the leaves were beginning to turn.* | **drop, fall** | **blow** ◇ *dry leaves blowing in the wind* | **rustle** ◇ *The leaves rustled in the light breeze.*
LEAF + NOUN **litter, mould/mold** ◇ *the ~ litter on the forest floor*
PHRASES **in full ~** ◇ *The corn was already ripening and the trees in full ~.*

leaflet *noun*

ADJ. **free** ◇ *a free ~ explaining your tax return* | **helpful** | **explanatory** (*BrE*)**, information, instruction** | **promotional, publicity** | **campaign, election, party** (*BrE*)
... OF LEAFLET **copy**
VERB + LEAFLET **issue, produce, publish** ◇ *The Health Zone issued hundreds of ~s.* | **deliver, distribute, drop, give out, hand out, pass out, send out** ◇ *Campaigners handed out ~s to passers by.*
LEAFLET + VERB **advertise sth, explain sth**
PREP. **in a/the ~** ◇ *Details are given in our promotional ~.*

league *noun*

1 group of sports clubs that compete with each other

ADJ. **basketball, cricket, football, soccer, etc.** ◇ *They want to start a new football ~.* | **sports** (*esp. AmE*) ◇ *the standard for professional sports ~s in this country* | **local, national** | **summer** (*esp. AmE*)**, winter** (*esp. AmE*) | **Premier** (*in the UK*) | **major, minor** ◇ *major ~ baseball* | **big** ◇ *Hopefully he'll get called up to the big ~s soon.* | **junior, youth** | **Little League** (*in the US*) ◇ *a baseball field with a Little League game going on* | **professional** ◇ *the first women's professional athletic ~ in the US* | **fantasy** ◇ *players for a team in a fantasy ~*
VERB + LEAGUE **create, form, set up, start** | **enter, join** ◇ *The*

team joined the Northern League last year. | **dominate, lead** ◇ The Yankees dominated the ~ in 1998. | **win**
LEAGUE + NOUN **champions, leaders** | **championship** (esp. BrE), **cup** (BrE), **title** | **club, side** (BrE), **team** | **player** | **game, match** (esp. BrE) | **final** | **table** (BrE) ◇ The team slipped to the foot of the Northern League table. ◇ school ~ tables (= showing how well schools are performing) | **record** ◇ He set a ~ record for the longest touchdown run. | **baseball, cricket, football, etc.**
PREP. **in a/the** ~ ◇ The team is now in the Premier League.
PHRASES **at the bottom of the ~, at the top of the ~** | **come bottom of the ~, come top of the ~** | **a position in the ~** ◇ They're hoping to improve their position in the ~.

2 level of quality, ability, etc.

ADJ. **big, super, top, world** (BrE) ◇ This move propelled him into the political big ~. (BrE) ◇ This move propelled him into the political big ~s. (AmE)
PHRASES **in a different ~** ◇ Today's technology is in a different ~ (= much better). | **in a ~ of your own** ◇ As a painter he is in a ~ of his own (= much better than others). | **not in the same ~ (as…)** (= not as good as) | **out of sb's ~** ◇ A house like that is way out of our ~ (= too expensive for us).

leak noun

1 small hole/crack

VERB + LEAK **have** ◇ The boat had a small ~. | **develop, spring** ◇ The pipe has sprung a ~. | **plug, stop** ◇ I managed to plug the ~.
PREP. **~ in** ◇ a ~ in the roof

2 when gas/liquid escapes

ADJ. **major, serious** | **minor, small** | **slow** | **air, fuel, gas, oil, radiation, water** | **plumbing** (AmE)
VERB + LEAK **cause** ◇ The dismantling of a nuclear reprocessing plant caused a ~ of radioactivity yesterday. | **detect, discover, find, locate, notice** ◇ Fortunately, we discovered the ~ in time. | **fix, repair, stop** ◇ The plumber fixed the ~. | **prevent** ◇ steps that can be taken to prevent gas ~s in the future
LEAK + VERB **happen, occur** | **come from sth** ◇ If you have no idea where the gas ~ is coming from, it is always best to turn the complete system off.
PREP. **~ from** ◇ Pollution inspectors were called to a ~ from a chemical factory. | **~ of** ◇ a ~ of dangerous chemicals

3 giving away information

ADJ. **security** | **serious** ◇ serious ~s of US intelligence | **alleged** ◇ an alleged ~ of a CIA employee's name to the media
LEAK + VERB **come from sth** ◇ The ~ could only have come from one source.
PREP. **~ about** ◇ a security ~ about a number of suspicious deaths among civil servants | **~ from** ◇ a ~ from the prime minister's office | **~ of** ◇ a ~ of confidential material | **~ to** ◇ a ~ to the American authorities
PHRASES **the source of a ~** ◇ The organization's press secretary is thought to be the source of the ~.

leak verb

1 allow sth to get out through a hole

ADV. **badly** ◇ The house was old and the roof ~ed badly. | **slightly**

2 tell sb about sth

ADV. **carefully, deliberately** | **widely** ◇ The document had been widely ~ed. | **allegedly** | **illegally**
PREP. **from** ◇ confidential information that has been ~ed from the BBC | **to** ◇ The report was ~ed to the press.

lean verb

ADV. **heavily** | **lightly** | **slightly** | **casually, comfortably, lazily, nonchalantly** ◇ Kate ~ed comfortably against the wall. | **eagerly** | **confidentially, conspiratorially** | **weakly, wearily** | **precariously** | **close, near** ◇ He ~ed closer, lowering his voice. | **across, down, forward, out, over** ◇ She

~ed forward eagerly to listen to him. | **away, back, backwards/backward** ◇ He ~ed back in his chair. | **sideways**
PREP. **across** ◇ She was ~ing confidentially across the table. | **against** ◇ She ~ed her head against his shoulder. | **from** ◇ Women and children ~ed from the windows of the surrounding tenements. | **into** ◇ He ~ed into the open doorway. | **on** ◇ The old man was ~ing heavily on a stick. | **out of** ◇ She ~ed precariously out of the window. | **over** ◇ She ~ed casually over the railings. | **through** ◇ The taxi driver ~ed through his window. | **to** ◇ She ~ed to one side. | **towards/toward** ◇ He ~ed towards/toward her.

PHR V **lean on sb/sth**
ADV. **heavily** ◇ Britain ~s heavily on Europe for trade.

leap noun

1 big jump

ADJ. **big, giant** | **little** | **flying, running** ◇ He made a flying ~ at the ball.
VERB + LEAP **make, take**
PREP. **~ from, ~ into, ~ to** ◇ a ~ into the air

2 great change/increase in sth

ADJ. **big, enormous, giant, great, huge, quantum** ◇ There has been a quantum ~ in profits since 1995. | **small** | **bold, dramatic, sudden** ◇ a dramatic ~ in the number of people out of work | **conceptual, imaginative, intuitive** | **logical** | **technological**
VERB + LEAP **make, take** ◇ They've made a great ~ forward with their building in the last few years. ◇ Eight years ago, he took the ~ and formed his own company.
PREP. **~ from, ~ to** ◇ a ~ from $632 to $735 | **~ in** ◇ a ~ in prices | **~ into** ◇ a great ~ into the unknown | **~ of** ◇ a ~ of 750%
PHRASES **a ~ forward** | **a ~ of faith** ◇ I chose to take a ~ of faith and do the movie. | **by ~s and bounds, in ~s and bounds** ◇ His technique has come on in ~s and bounds this season.

leap verb

ADV. **almost, nearly, practically** ◇ He almost ~ed down the stairs when he heard who it was. | **immediately** | **suddenly** | **quickly, clear, high** ◇ She ~ed clear of the water. | **about, around, away, back, down, forward, out, up (and down)** ◇ children ~ing about with excitement
VERB + LEAP **seem to** (figurative) ◇ The photograph seemed to ~ off the page at her. | **be about to, be ready to** ◇ Don't be so nervous—anyone would think I was about to ~ on you.
PREP. **across** ◇ She ~ed across the puddles. | **from** ◇ He ~ed down from the ladder and ran over to her. | **into, off, on, onto** ◇ He ~ed onto his horse and rode off. | **out of** ◇ He ~ed out of bed when he heard the telephone. | **over** ◇ The horse ~ed over high fences.
PHRASES **~ to your feet** ◇ Rose immediately ~ed to her feet.

learn verb

1 gain knowledge/skill

ADV. **a lot** ◇ I ~ed a lot from my father. | **quickly, soon** ◇ Children ~ very quickly. ◇ They soon ~ that crying is a good way of getting attention. | **ever, never** ◇ Some people never ~, do they?
VERB + LEARN **need to** | **be eager to, want to** ◇ He was eager to ~ all she could teach him. | **have a lot to** ◇ You still have a lot to ~.
PREP. **about** ◇ The children ~ about art by painting. | **from** ◇ She ~ed from watching others. | **through** ◇ Children ~ through play.

2 become aware

VERB + LEARN **be astonished to, be astounded to, be intrigued to, be surprised to** ◇ I was surprised to ~ that he was only 23. | **be dismayed to, be saddened to**
PREP. **of** ◇ We first ~ed of the problem from her school.

learner noun

ADJ. **fast, quick, slow** ◇ She was a quick ~, and her German got better by the day. | **lifelong** (esp. AmE) | **adult, older** |

young ◇ *The book has been written with the interests of young ~s in mind.* | **language** | **foreign** (*BrE*)
LEARNER + NOUN **driver** (*BrE*)

learning *noun*

1 process of learning sth

ADJ. **effective, successful** ◇ *a model for effective ~* | **independent** | **distance** (= by correspondence course) | **early** (= of very young children) | **higher** ◇ *institutions of higher ~* | **lifelong** | **active, passive** | **formal, informal** | **rote** | **computer-assisted, online** | **language**
VERB + LEARNING **facilitate, promote** ◇ *The college is dedicated to promoting lifelong ~.*
LEARNING + NOUN **curve** ◇ *The whole team has been on a steep ~ curve since the project began.* | **environment** ◇ *The school aims to provide a supportive ~ environment.* | **experience, process** | **programme/program** | **support** | **centre/center** ◇ *The dance department's multimedia ~ centre/center is equipped with laptops.* | **differences** (*esp. AmE*) | **difficulty, disability** ◇ *a child with severe ~ difficulties*
PHRASES **a seat of ~**

2 knowledge obtained by reading and studying

ADJ. **great** | **book** (*old-fashioned*)

lease *noun*

ADJ. **long, long-term** | **short, short-term** | **ten-year, etc.** | **commercial** | **operating** (*esp. AmE*) | **land** | **mining**
VERB + LEASE **have, hold** ◇ *They have a ~ with five years to run.* | **acquire** (*esp. BrE*), **buy, enter into, get, negotiate, obtain, sign, take, take out, take out, take up** ◇ *She has taken out a new ten-year ~ on the building.* | **grant (sb), sell (sb)** ◇ *A freeholder may grant a ~ of any duration.* | **renew** | **forfeit, surrender** (*both BrE*) ◇ *They moved out and the ~ was surrendered.* | **break, terminate** | **take over** | **transfer** (*esp. BrE*)
LEASE + VERB **run** ◇ *The ~ runs from April 19.* | **take effect** (*esp. BrE*) | **come up for renewal, expire, run out**
LEASE + NOUN **agreement** | **payment**
PREP. **in a/the ~** ◇ *a new clause in the ~* | **on a ~** ◇ *The company holds the building on a long ~.* | **under a/the ~** ◇ *Under the new ~, the rent would go up.* | **~ of** ◇ *He took a ~ of the premises.* (*esp. BrE*) | **~ on** ◇ *The club has a 20-year ~ on the property.*
PHRASES **a clause in a ~, a condition of a ~, the provisions of a ~** (*esp. BrE*), **the terms of the ~** | **the length, period, term, etc. of a ~**

leather *noun*

ADJ. **thick, thin** | **soft** | **shiny** | **worn** | **black** | **genuine** (*esp. AmE*), **real** | **imitation, synthetic** | **patent** | **shoe**
VERB + LEATHER **tan** | **treat** ◇ *The ~ has been treated with wax.* | **polish** | **be made from/of/out of** ◇ *a coat made from buffalo ~* | **bind sth in** ◇ *Each volume is bound in genuine ~.* | **wear**
LEATHER + VERB **crack** ◇ *a cracked ~ belt*
LEATHER + NOUN **belt, boots, chaps, jacket, etc.** | **chair, furniture, sofa, etc.** | **bar**
PREP. **in ~** (= made of leather) ◇ *I'm looking for a pair of boots in dark brown ~.* | **in ~s** (*BrE*) (= wearing leather) ◇ *a biker in black ~s*

leave *noun*

1 period of time when you do not go to work

ADJ. **annual** | **paid, unpaid** | **extended, indefinite, weekend** | **compassionate** (*BrE*) | **family** (*AmE*), **maternity, medical** (*AmE*), **parental, paternity, sabbatical, sick, study** | **administrative** (*AmE*) | **gardening** (= period during which a person does not work but remains employed by a company in order to prevent them working for another company) (*BrE*) ◇ *She handed in her resignation and was put on three months' gardening ~.* | **home, shore**
VERB + LEAVE **be entitled to, get, have** ◇ *How much annual ~ do you get?* ◇ *I still have some ~ left this year.* | **go on, spend, take, use, use up** ◇ *She spent most of her ~ with her family.* ◇ *I still have some ~ to use up.* | **cancel** (*BrE*) ◇ *When*

the war broke out all ~ was cancelled.* | **give sb, grant sb** | **apply for**
LEAVE + NOUN **entitlement** (*esp. BrE*)
PREP. **on ~** ◇ *She's on ~ until the end of the month.*

2 official permission to do sth

ADJ. **special** (*BrE*)
VERB + LEAVE **request** ◇ *He asked ~ to absent himself for four days.* | **give sb, grant sb** | **obtain** (*esp. BrE*) | **refuse sb** (*BrE*)
PREP. **by sb's ~** (*esp. BrE*) ◇ *The appeal can only be brought by ~ of the trial judge.* | **with sb's ~, without sb's ~** ◇ *No application may be made without the ~ of the court.*
PHRASES **absent without ~** | **~ of absence**

leave *verb*

VERB + LEAVE **decide to** | **intend to, plan to, want to** | **be ready to** ◇ *We were all packed and ready to ~.* | **be about to, be going to** ◇ *Did you want something? I was just about to ~.* | **threaten to** ◇ *My secretary has threatened to ~.* | **attempt to, try to** ◇ *They were caught trying to ~ the country.* | **refuse to** | **be compelled to, be forced to, be obliged to** | **ask sb to, order sb to** ◇ *They were being extremely rowdy and the manager had to ask them to ~.* | **allow sb to, let sb** ◇ *I wanted to ~ but they wouldn't let me.* | **enable sb to**
PREP. **for** ◇ *They left for Scotland this morning.*

lecture *noun*

1 talk given to a group of people

ADJ. **fascinating, interesting** | **boring** | **formal** | **illustrated** | **impromptu** | **guest** ◇ *A two-day event of guest ~s, seminars and workshops.* | **public** | **annual** | **inaugural, introductory** ◇ *Professor Pearson gave the inaugural ~.* | **keynote, plenary** | **memorial** | **class, classroom** (*both AmE*)
...OF LECTURES **course, programme/program, series**
VERB + LECTURE **deliver, give, present** | **hold** ◇ *The society is putting on a series of ~s on the subject next term.* | **attend, go to, hear, listen to** | **miss, skip** | **prepare, write** | **have** ◇ *I have a ~ at nine tomorrow.*
LECTURE + NOUN **course, programme/program, series** | **hall, room, theatre/theater** | **notes** | **format** (*esp. AmE*) | **tour** | **circuit** ◇ *a familiar figure on the international ~ circuit*
PREP. **at/the ~** ◇ *She wasn't at the ~.* | **during a/the ~** ◇ *The fire alarm went during his ~.* | **in a/the ~** ◇ *She referred to Professor Jones's work in her ~ on Shakespeare's imagery.* | **~ by** ◇ *a ~ by Professor Snow* | **~ about, ~ on** ◇ *a ~ to the Darwin Society*
PHRASES **a ~ entitled sth, a ~ titled sth** (*AmE*) ◇ *a ~ entitled 'How to Prevent Food Poisoning'* | **a ~ on the subject of sth**

2 serious talk to sb about what they have done wrong

ADJ. **little, long** | **stern**
VERB + LECTURE **give sb** ◇ *She gave me a stern ~ on ingratitude.* | **get** ◇ *I got a ~ from Dad about coming home on time.* | **need** ◇ *I don't need any ~s from you on responsibility.*
PREP. **~ about, ~ on** ◇ *I don't take ~s from anyone on how to behave.* | **~ from**

lecturer *noun*

ADJ. **English, physics, etc.** | **guest, visiting** | **principal, senior** (*both in the UK*) | **assistant, junior** (*both in the UK*) | **college, university** (*both in the UK*)
PREP. **~ in** (*BrE*) ◇ *a ~ in design at the School of Architecture* | **~ on** ◇ *She is a frequent ~ on contemporary art and cultural theory.*
→ Note at JOB

ledge *noun*

ADJ. **high** | **wide** | **narrow, small** | **window** | **cliff, mountain, rock, rocky**
VERB + LEDGE **cling to** | **be perched on**
LEDGE + VERB **run** ◇ *A narrow ~ runs across the northern face of the cliff.*
PREP. **along a/the ~** ◇ *I felt along the ~ at the top of the door.*

| on a/the ~ ◊ *The phone was perched precariously on the window ~.*

left *noun*

1 side

ADJ. **extreme, far** ◊ *My dad's in the front row, on the extreme ~ of the picture.* | **bottom, top**
VERB + LEFT **turn to** ◊ *If you turn to your ~ you will see the site of the fort.*
PREP. **from the ~** ◊ *The car came from the ~.* | **on the/your ~** ◊ *The bank is on the ~, just after the post office.* ◊ *As you go in the door, you'll see it on your ~.* | **on the ~ of** ◊ *The icon is on the ~ of the screen.* | **to the/your ~** ◊ *He looked to the ~ and then crossed.* | **to the ~ of** ◊ *My office is just to the ~ of the main door.*
PHRASES **from ~ to right, from right to ~** ◊ *Arabic script reads from right to ~.*

2 the left political groups

ADJ. **extreme, far**
PREP. **of the ~** ◊ *In recent years the country has been ruled only by governments of the ~.* | **on the ~** ◊ *They're both on the extreme ~ of the party.* | **to the ~** ◊ *The party has moved further to the ~.* ◊ *He is somewhat to the ~ of the previous leader.*

leg *noun*

1 part of the body

ADJ. **left, right** | **front** | **back, hind, rear** | **lower, upper** ◊ *an injury to his upper ~* | **long** | **short, stumpy** | **beautiful, good, shapely** | **muscled, muscular, powerful, strong** | **skinny, slender, spindly, thin** | **fat** | **bandy** | **hairy** | **bare** | **artificial, prosthetic, wooden** | **bad, stiff** | **good** ◊ *I was able to stand on my good ~.* | **hurt** (*esp. AmE*), **injured** | **broken, fractured** | **lame** ◊ *He sat down with his lame ~ outstretched.* | **tired, weak** ◊ *She crossed the finish line on tired ~s.* | **shaky, wobbly** ◊ *He rose to his feet on shaky ~s.* | **outstretched**
... OF LEGS **pair** ◊ *a fine pair of ~s*
VERB + LEG **bend** | **brace** ◊ *He put his back against the car, braced his ~s and pushed.* | **straighten** | **cross** ◊ *I moved the chair away from the table so I could cross my ~s.* | **splay, spread** ◊ *They made him put his hands on the police car and spread his ~s.* | **extend, stretch, stretch out** ◊ *She stretched her ~s under the table.* ◊ *It was good to get out of the car and stretch our ~s (= walk around).* | **lift** ◊ *The dog lifted its ~ against the lamp post.* | **move** | **draw up, tuck under** ◊ *She sat with her ~s drawn up underneath her.* | **kick, swing, throw** ◊ *She swung her ~s over the side of the bed and reached for her crutches.* | **entwine, tangle, wrap** ◊ *They gazed at each other, their ~s entwined under the table.* | **break, injure** | **lose** ◊ *He lost a ~ in a motorcycle accident.* | **amputate** ◊ *She had her ~ amputated below the knee.* | **shave, wax** ◊ *I'm getting my ~s waxed tomorrow.*
LEG + VERB **move** ◊ *They ran together, their ~s moving in unison.* | **flail, kick** ◊ *He jumped to avoid the flailing ~ of the defender.* | **pump** ◊ *She started running, fat ~s pumping.* | **bend** | **buckle, give way** ◊ *His ~s buckled and he collapsed on the floor.* | **shake, tremble** | **dangle, hang, swing** ◊ *He sat with his ~s dangling off the bridge.* | **ache**
LEG + NOUN **exercise** | **muscle** | **cramp, injury, pains, ulcer, wound** | **room** (usually *legroom*) ◊ *You don't get much legroom on economy class.* | **extensions** ◊ *Leg extensions use the quadriceps muscles to extend the knee.*
PREP. **between the/your ~s** ◊ *The dog sloped off, its tail between its ~s.* | **in the ~** ◊ *He was shot in the ~ by a sniper.* | **on the/your ~** ◊ *I had a big bruise on my ~.* | **on one ~** ◊ *Many birds are able to stand on one ~ for hours at a time.*
PHRASES **your ~ in a cast** (*esp. AmE*), **your ~ in plaster** (*BrE*) ◊ *He was wheeled out of the hospital with his ~ in a cast/in plaster.*

2 of trousers/pants

ADJ. **pant** (*AmE*), **trouser** (*BrE*)

VERB + LEG **pull up, roll up** ◊ *He rolled up the ~s of his jeans.* | **roll down**
PHRASES **long in the ~, short in the ~** ◊ *These jeans are too long in the ~.*

3 of a journey/race

ADJ. **first, second, etc.** | **final, last** | **anchor** ◊ *The fastest runner often runs the anchor ~ (= the last part) of a relay race.* | **outbound**
PREP. **on the ... ~** ◊ *We were on the last ~ of our journey.*

legacy *noun*

1 money/property

VERB + LEGACY **bequeath (sb), leave (sb)** | **get, receive** ◊ *He received a large ~ from his uncle.*
PREP. **in a/the ~** ◊ *She left her the money in a ~.* | **~ from** ◊ *a ~ from my old teacher*
PHRASES **heir to a ~** ◊ *She is the heir to a ~ of £1 million.*

2 result of previous events

ADJ. **enduring, lasting** | **great, rich** ◊ *His influence on younger musicians is perhaps his greatest ~.* | **cultural, historical** ◊ *These problems have arisen as a result of historical legacies.* | **bitter**
VERB + LEGACY **bequeath (sb), leave (sb), leave behind** ◊ *the enduring ~ bequeathed by the war years* | **create** | **continue, preserve** ◊ *She said she would continue her father's ~.*
PREP. **~ from** ◊ *Such attitudes are a ~ from colonial times.* | **~ of** ◊ *a great ~ of technical innovation*

legal *adj.*

VERBS **be** | **become** | **make sth** ◊ *Should the use of this drug be made ~?*
ADV. **completely, perfectly** ◊ *It is perfectly ~ to charge extra for these services.*

legality *noun*

ADJ. **doubtful** (*BrE*), **dubious, questionable**
VERB + LEGALITY **challenge, question** ◊ *Her lawyer is challenging the ~ of the court order.* | **uphold** ◊ *The court ruling today upheld the ~ of military tribunals.*
PHRASES **doubt about the ~ of sth, doubts about the ~ of sth**

legend *noun*

1 well-known story

ADJ. **ancient, old** | **Greek, Inuit, Roman, etc.** | **local** | **urban**
VERB + LEGEND **become, pass into** ◊ *The story of how she was rescued has already passed into ~.* | **tell (sb)** ◊ *He told us the ~ of the ghostly horseman.*
LEGEND + VERB **live on** ◊ *The ~ of his supernatural origins lives on.* | **say sth** ◊ *Legend says that the forest is cursed.*
PREP. **according to ~** ◊ *According to ancient ~, the river is a goddess.* | **in (a/the) ~** ◊ *There have always been stories of human giants in Celtic ~ and mythology.* | **~ about** ◊ *~s about the Vikings* | **~ of** ◊ *The story is part of the ancient ~ of King Arthur.*
PHRASES **~ has it that ...** ◊ *Legend has it that the Bridge of Sighs got its name from the cries of prisoners being led across it.* | **myths and ~s** ◊ *the myths and ~s of Mexico* | **the subject of ~** ◊ *The island has long been the subject of ~.*

2 famous person/event

ADJ. **living** ◊ *movie stars who become living ~s* | **basketball, music, racing, rock, screen, sporting** (*BrE*), **sports** (*AmE*), **etc.** | **Broadway, Hollywood, etc.**

legible *adj.*

VERBS **be**
ADV. **clearly** ◊ *Her handwriting was clearly ~.* | **still** ◊ *The inscription is still ~.* | **barely**
PREP. **to** ◊ *The price must be ~ to a purchaser.*

legislation *noun*

ADJ. **federal, national, parliamentary, state** | **draft, proposed** | **fresh** (*esp. BrE*), **further, new** | **effective, tough** | **complex** | **controversial** | **unworkable** (*BrE*) ◊ *The police*

think that such ~ would be unworkable. | **anti-abortion, anti-discrimination, civil rights, employment, energy** (*esp. AmE*), **environmental, gun-control, health, housing, human rights** (*esp. BrE*), **reform, social, etc.**
... OF LEGISLATION **piece** ◊ *a major piece of ~*
VERB + LEGISLATION **need, require** | **call for, propose, push** (*esp. AmE*) ◊ *They are calling for tough ~ to tackle this problem.* | **draft, draw up** | **bring forward** (*BrE*), **initiate, put forward** (*esp. AmE*) ◊ *Anyone has the right to initiate ~.* | **sponsor** (*esp. AmE*), **support** | **push through** ◊ *The government is pushing through ~ to ban smoking in all public places.* | **approve, enact, introduce, pass, sign** (*esp. AmE*) ◊ *Congress approved ~ which outlawed the sale of the drug.* ◊ *Governor Bradbery signed ~ for $20 million in municipal relief.* | **adopt** ◊ *Member states may not adopt ~ contrary to EU law.* | **block, delay, oppose, veto** ◊ *Religious interests may try to block this ~.* | **amend** | **repeal** | **comply with** ◊ *Companies have until December 31 to comply with the new ~.*
LEGISLATION + VERB **come into effect, come into force** (*both esp. BrE*) ◊ *New ~ on adoption comes into effect at the end of the year.* | **allow sth, require sth**
PREP. **under ~** ◊ *There is no requirement to register a claim under the new ~.* | **~ against** ◊ *They are planning the introduction of ~ against sex discrimination.* | **~ on** ◊ *Legislation on this issue is urgently needed.*

legislature *noun*

ADJ. **bicameral, unicameral** | **109-member, etc.** | **elected** | **federal, national, provincial, state** | **Democratic, Republican-controlled, etc.**
VERB + LEGISLATURE **be elected to** ◊ *She is the youngest woman to be elected to the national ~.*
LEGISLATURE + VERB **approve sth, enact sth, pass sth** ◊ *The ~ passed a law to prohibit the dumping of nuclear waste.* | **vote** ◊ *The ~ voted narrowly to table a motion of no-confidence in the government.*

legitimate *adj.*

VERBS **be, seem** | **consider sth, deem sth, regard sth as, see sth as** | **make sth**
ADV. **completely** (*esp. AmE*), **entirely, perfectly, quite, totally** (*esp. AmE*), **very** (*esp. AmE*)

leisure *noun*

VERB + LEISURE **have** ◊ *We have more ~ than our parents had.*
LEISURE + NOUN **hours, time** | **activities, interests, pursuits** | **centre** (*BrE*), **complex** (*esp. BrE*) | **facilities** | **industry** | **travel, traveller/traveler**

lemon *noun*

ADJ. **fresh**
... OF LEMON **slice, wedge** ◊ *Garnish the fish with wedges of ~.* | **cake, tart, etc.**
VERB + LEMON **squeeze** ◊ *Squeeze a quarter of a ~ over the fish.* | **slice** | **garnish sth with**
LEMON + NOUN **tree** | **pip** (*BrE*), **seed** (*esp. AmE*) | **peel, rind, zest** | **juice** | **slice, wedge**
→ Special page at FRUIT

lend *verb*

ADV. **kindly** ◊ *She very kindly lent me her bicycle.*
VERB + LEND **be prepared to** (*esp. BrE*), **be ready to** (*esp. AmE*), **be willing to** | **be unwilling to, refuse to** ◊ *The bank was unwilling to ~ him the money.* | **persuade sb to** (*esp. BrE*)
PREP. **to** ◊ *I've lent my car to George for the weekend.*

lender *noun*

ADJ. **big, large, leading, major** ◊ *The bank is the largest mortgage ~ in the country.* | **money, mortgage** | **private**
PREP. **~ to** ◊ *The bank was an important ~ to the government.*

length *noun*

1 distance from one end to the other
ADJ. **entire, full, maximum, whole** ◊ *There is a maximum ~ of 2 500 words.* ◊ *A long veranda runs the whole ~ of the*
building. | **great** ◊ *a ditch of great ~ and width* | **medium** | **overall, total** | **average**
VERB + LENGTH **estimate, measure** ◊ *He measured the ~ and width of the table.* | **have** ◊ *The vehicle has an overall ~ of 12 feet.* | **grow to, reach** ◊ *These fish can reach a ~ of over five feet.* | **double in, increase in** | **cut sth to** ◊ *Measure the size of the window and cut the cloth to ~.* | **drive, extend, run, swim, travel, walk, etc.** ◊ *The fence runs the ~ of the footpath.*
PREP. **along the ~ of** ◊ *There were lights along the whole ~ of the street.* | **in ~** ◊ *The pipe was six feet in ~.*
PHRASES **at arm's ~** ◊ *He has to hold newspapers at arm's ~ to focus on the print.* ◊ *She kept him at arm's ~ until he stopped smoking.* (*figurative*) | **double, twice, three times, half, etc. the ~ of sth** ◊ *The queen bee is twice the ~ of a worker bee.*

2 amount of time that sth lasts
ADJ. **considerable, great, inordinate** | **reasonable**
VERB + LENGTH **cut, reduce, shorten** | **increase**
LENGTH + VERB **increase** | **decrease**
PREP. **at** ◊ *He told me at ~ about his new job.* | **in ~** ◊ *Each lesson was an hour in ~.*
PHRASES **~ of time** ◊ *They complained about the inordinate ~ of time they had to wait.*

3 length of a swimming pool
VERB + LENGTH **do** (*esp. BrE*), **swim** ◊ *I did 20 ~s today.*

lengthy *adj.*

VERBS **be**
ADV. **extremely, fairly, very, etc.** ◊ *Agreement was finally reached after very ~ discussions.* | **relatively**

leniency *noun*

VERB + LENIENCY **show** | **appeal for** (*BrE*)
PREP. **~ for** ◊ *She begged for ~ for her son.* | **~ of** ◊ *the undue ~ of the sentence* | **~ to** ◊ *Police offer ~ to criminals in return for information.* | **~ towards/toward** ◊ *Let's hope the judge shows ~ towards/toward her.*
PHRASES **a plea for ~** (*esp. BrE*) ◊ *Even the victim's family made a plea for ~ on behalf of the accused.*

lenient *adj.*

VERBS **be** | **become**
ADV. **extremely, fairly, very, etc.** | **unduly** (*BrE*) ◊ *The appeal judge agreed that the original sentence was unduly ~.*
PREP. **with** ◊ *The police are sometimes more ~ with female offenders.*

lens *noun*

1 curved piece of glass
ADJ. **strong, thick** ◊ *She wears glasses with very thick ~es.* | **coloured/colored, tinted** | **optical, spectacle** (*formal, BrE*) | **camera** | **fish-eye, long, magnifying, telephoto, telescopic** (*esp. BrE*), **wide-angle, zoom** ◊ *a long-lens shot of a rare bird* ◊ *The photo was taken using a zoom ~.*
LENS + NOUN **cap, cover** ◊ *I took the ~ cap off my camera and waited for a good shot.*
PREP. **through a/the ~** ◊ *a view of Mount Kilimanjaro as seen through Eddie's camera ~*
2 → See CONTACT LENS

lesbian *noun*

ADJ. **butch** | **femme, lipstick** | **out** ◊ *She's an out ~.* | **closet, closeted**
VERB + LESBIAN **come out as** ◊ *She came out as a ~ in her teens.*

lessen *verb*

ADV. **considerably, greatly, significantly** ◊ *Eating a good diet significantly ~s the risk of heart disease.* | **somewhat** | **gradually** ◊ *Time had gradually ~ed the pain of her grief.*
VERB + LESSEN **begin to** ◊ *The noise began to ~.* | **try to** | **tend**

to ◇ *Too much background detail tends to ~ the impact of the central image.* | **help (to)** ◇ *Regular exercise can help ~ the pain.*

lesson *noun*

1 period of teaching or learning

ADJ. **good, interesting** | **boring** | **individual** | **private** | **driving, English, geography, history, music, piano, swimming, etc.**
VERB + LESSON **attend, go to, have, take** ◇ *I go to Italian ~s at the local college.* ◇ *I'm taking driving ~s at the moment.* | **begin, start** ◇ *She started guitar ~s at the age of 38.* | **give (sb), offer (sb), provide, take, teach** ◇ *She gives singing ~s.* ◇ *They're offering free ~s in computing.* ◇ *I had to take a biology ~ this afternoon because the biology teacher was away.* (*BrE*) ◇ *He doesn't teach very many ~s these days.* | **get** ◇ *Students get ~s on how to organize their study time.* | **prepare** ◇ *The trouble is that teachers don't prepare their ~s carefully enough.* | **miss, skip** ◇ *He got into trouble for skipping ~s.*
LESSON + NOUN **plan** ◇ *She was preparing a ~ plan for a class she was teaching.*
PREP. **during a/the ~** ◇ *No talking was allowed during the ~.* | **in a/the ~** ◇ *You can't expect to learn all there is to know about the subject in a 45-minute ~.* | **~ about** ◇ *a ~ about the Civil War* | **~ in** ◇ *He took ~s in Thai cookery.* | **~ on** ◇ *a ~ on the Roman Empire* | **~ with** ◇ *They have a ~ with Mrs Evans at two o'clock.*

2 sth learned through experience

ADJ. **basic, big, good, great, important, salutary, useful, valuable** | **bitter, hard, painful** ◇ *It's a hard ~ to learn.* | **clear** | **real** | **life, moral** | **object** (= a practical example of what you should or should not do in a particular situation)
VERB + LESSON **draw, learn** ◇ *What ~s can we draw from this unfortunate experience?* | **teach sb** ◇ *It taught me some valuable ~s about working with other people.* | **apply** | **forget, remember** ◇ *We need to remember the ~s of history.*
PREP. **~ from** ◇ *There are important ~s to be learned from this mistake.* | **~ in** ◇ *I had learned a ~ in respecting the privacy of others.* | **~ of** ◇ *It is dangerous to ignore the ~s of the past.*

lethal *adj.*

VERBS **be, prove**
ADV. **absolutely, highly** (*esp. AmE*) ◇ *All these drugs are highly ~.* | **potentially** ◇ *It was a potentially ~ mixture of drugs.*
PREP. **to** ◇ *The pesticide is ~ to all insect life.*

lethargy *noun*

VERB + LETHARGY **shake off** ◇ *They will need to shake off their ~ if they want to win the game.*
PHRASES **a feeling of ~**

letter *noun*

1 written/printed message

ADJ. **lengthy, long** | **brief, short** | **ten-page, etc.** | **rambling** | **countless, numerous** ◇ *She received countless ~s of support while in jail.* | **occasional** ◇ *Apart from the occasional ~, they had not been in touch for years.* | **airmail** | **registered** | **handwritten** | **anonymous** | **formal, official** | **business** | **personal** | **confidential, private** | **open, public** ◇ *The editor published an open ~ to the president.* | **circular** | **chain** | **form, standard** | **sample** | **accompanying, cover** (*AmE*), **covering** (*BrE*), **explanatory** (*esp. BrE*) ◇ *The conditions are explained in the accompanying ~.* ◇ *Send your résumé with a cover ~.* (*AmE*) ◇ *Send your CV with a covering ~.* (*BrE*) | **thank-you** ◇ *I wrote my uncle a thank-you ~ as soon as I opened the present.* | **congratulatory** | **warning** | **acceptance, rejection** ◇ *I've had ten job interviews and received ten rejection ~s.* | **resignation** | **suicide** | **fan** | **love** | **intimate** | **nice** | **friendly** | **heartfelt, impassioned** ◇ *She wrote an impassioned ~ to her local newspaper to complain about the new road.* | **polite** |

apologetic | **angry, strong, strongly worded, threatening** | **indignant** | **critical** | **poison pen** ◇ *He had been sending poison pen ~s to people at work.*
VERB + LETTER **draft, write** ◇ *She drafted an angry ~ to the newspaper.* | **read** | **get, have, receive** ◇ *I haven't had a ~ from her for months.* | **mail** (*AmE*), **post** (*BrE*), **send** | **email** | **fax** | **deliver** | **forward** ◇ *The ~ was forwarded from my old address.* | **seal** | **open** | **acknowledge, answer, reply to, respond to** ◇ *I was angry that they didn't even acknowledge my ~.* | **address** ◇ *The ~ was addressed to me.* | **sign** | **publish** ◇ *The newspaper refused to publish the ~.* | **edit** ◇ *We reserve the right to cut or edit ~s.*
LETTER + VERB **arrive, come, reach sb** ◇ *I hope my last ~ has reached you.* | **be dated …** ◇ *The ~ is dated July 7.* | **cross** ◇ *Our ~s crossed.* | **be lost** | **announce sth, ask (sb) sth, explain sth, say sth, state sth, tell sb sth** ◇ *She wrote him a ~ saying that she was not coming back.* | **begin, start, start off** ◇ *The ~ started off by thanking us for our offer.* | **continue, go on** ◇ *His ~ went on to give reasons for his refusal to take part.* | **conclude, end** ◇ *The ~ concluded with a threat of possible legal action.* | **contain sth** ◇ *The ~ contained information that only the killer could know.* | **enclose sth** ◇ *The charity received an anonymous ~ enclosing a large donation.* | **appear** ◇ *A ~ headed 'Advertising Mania' appeared in the paper.*
LETTER + NOUN **writer, writing** ◇ *George Bernard Shaw was a prolific ~ writer.* | **carrier** (*AmE*) | (**postman/postwoman** in *BrE*) | **box** (*BrE*) ◇ *A card dropped through the ~ box.* (**mail slot** in *AmE*) ◇ *There's a ~ box on the corner of the street.* (**mailbox** in *AmE*) | **opener** (*esp. AmE*) | **bomb** (**mail bomb** in *AmE*)
PREP. **by ~** ◇ *Please reply by ~.* | **in a/the ~** ◇ *In your ~ of June 5…* | **~ about, ~ concerning, ~ regarding** | **~ from, ~ to** ◇ *a ~ to the editor* | **~ of** ◇ *a ~ of application/apology*

2 sign that represents a sound in a language

ADJ. **big, large** | **block, capital, upper-case** ◇ *Fill in the form in block ~s.* | **lower-case, small** | **bold** | **initial** ◇ *The company's name is made from the initial ~s of his children's names.* | **double** ◇ *Words with double ~s, such as 'accommodate', are commonly misspelled.* | **silent** ◇ *words such as 'debt' and 'half', which contain silent ~s*
PREP. **in … ~s** ◇ *His name was written in large white ~s over the doorway.*
PHRASES **the ~s of the alphabet**

lettuce *noun*

ADJ. **crisp, crunchy** | **limp** | **chopped, shredded** | **cos** (*BrE*), **iceberg, romaine** (*AmE*), **etc.**
… OF LETTUCE **head** ◇ *You need one whole head of ~ for this salad.*
VERB + LETTUCE **wash** | **grow** | **pick**
LETTUCE + NOUN **leaf**
PHRASES **on a bed of ~**
→ Special page at FOOD

level *noun*

1 amount/size/number

ADJ. **elevated, high, significant, substantial** | **record** ◇ *Industrial output has reached record ~s.* | **increasing, rising** | **excessive** ◇ *Excessive ~s of lead were found in the water.* | **low** | **decreased, reduced** | **decreasing, falling** | **moderate** | **varying** ◇ *They work hard, but with varying ~s of success.* | **detectable, undetectable** | **generous** (*esp. BrE*) ◇ *a generous ~ of financial support for the arts* | **permitted, recommended, required** ◇ *permitted ~s of chemical pollutants* | **acceptable, adequate, necessary, safe** ◇ *an acceptable ~ of risk* | **normal** ◇ *Her blood pressure has returned to its normal ~.* | **realistic, reasonable** | **dangerous, unacceptable** | **worst** ◇ *the worst ~ of business failure since 1997* | **unprecedented** | **maximum, minimum** | **desired, optimal** | **baseline** | **noise, ozone, pollution, radiation** | **crime, poverty** | **funding, staffing** | **blood-sugar, cholesterol, hormone, etc.** | **confidence, energy, stress**
VERB + LEVEL **achieve, attain, reach** ◇ *They have achieved higher ~s of efficiency.* ◇ *Crime has reached its highest ~ ever.* | **remain at** ◇ *She predicts that fuel prices will remain at*

current ~s. | **boost, elevate, improve, increase, raise** | **maintain** | **bring down, decrease, keep down, lower, reduce** | **control, regulate** | **adjust, alter, change** | **set** ◇ *Emissions are well below the ~s set by the WHO.* | **exceed** ◇ *There will be stiff penalties if companies exceed these ~s of pollution.* | **assess, determine, measure, record** | **check, monitor**
LEVEL + VERB **go up, rise, soar** | **decrease, drop, fall, go down, plummet** | **change, differ, vary** | **exceed sth**
PREP. **above a/the ~** ◇ *Mortgage rates were 10% above their current ~.* | **at a/the ~** ◇ *Rents will be kept at this ~ for another year.* | **below a/the ~** ◇ *Radiation is well below the permitted ~.* | **~ of** ◇ *They were asked to indicate the ~ of distress they experienced as a result of their experiences.*

2 stage of progress/standard

ADJ. **basic, elementary, low** ◇ *The teaching is at quite a basic ~.* | **entry** ◇ *They have a good range of entry-level computers for beginners.* | **intermediate** | **advanced, high** ◇ *Her illness has reached an advanced ~.* | **degree** | **3rd-grade, 11th-grade, etc.** (AmE) | **grade** (AmE) ◇ *He's reading at grade ~* (= at the average level for his grade). | **difficulty** ◇ *The difficulty ~ of the exercises in the book varies widely.* | **fitness** ◇ *a sport suitable for people of all fitness ~s* | **educational**
VERB + LEVEL **attain, reach** ◇ *students who have reached the intermediate ~* | **complete, do, take** ◇ *You need to do all three ~s to qualify as a chef.*
PREP. **above a/the ~** ◇ *His English is way above the ~ of the other students.* | **at a/the ~** ◇ *students at intermediate ~ ◇ She has played tennis at a high ~.* | **below a/the ~** ◇ *The book is not suitable for students below degree ~.* | **~ of** ◇ *language students at different ~s of proficiency*
PHRASES **sb's comfort ~** (= the level at which someone feels safe and comfortable) | **take sb/sth to the next ~** ◇ *It's time to take my career to the next ~.*

3 grade in an organization or structure

ADJ. **high, upper** ◇ *the upper ~s of the civil service* | **low** | **senior** | **global, international, local, national, regional** | **grass-roots** ◇ *The party needs to win support at grass-roots ~.* | **board** ◇ *These decisions are made at board ~.* | **federal, ministerial** (BrE)
VERB + LEVEL **reach, rise to** ◇ *He rose to the ~ of general manager.*
PREP. **at a/the ~** ◇ *At the local ~ there's a lot to be said for the plan.* | **on a/the ~** ◇ *The thing has to be organized on an international ~.*

4 way of considering sth

ADJ. **conscious, subconscious, unconscious** ◇ *At a conscious ~, I was satisfied with my life.* | **deep** | **superficial** | **detailed** ◇ *We probably need to look at this problem at a more detailed ~.* | **general** | **practical** | **theoretical** | **political** | **tactical** | **macro, micro**
PREP. **at a/the ~, on a/the ~** ◇ *On a superficial ~ everything appears to be in order, but at a deeper ~ you an see that there's a lot wrong.*

5 height

ADJ. **high, low** | **ground, sea, water** ◇ *the problem of rising sea ~s* | **eye, knee** ◇ *a shelf at eye ~*
VERB + LEVEL **adjust, change, lower, raise** ◇ *They are going to raise the ~ of the banks to prevent flooding.*
PREP. **above a/the ~** ◇ *200 m above sea ~* | **at a/the ~** ◇ *The plane was flying at a very low ~.* | **below a/the ~** ◇ *below the ~ of the clouds* | **on a ~ with** ◇ *On the second floor you are on a ~ with the treetops.* | **to a/the ~** ◇ *The water rose to the ~ of the ground floor windows.*
PHRASES **a change in ~, a change of ~**

6 floor in a building

ADJ. **ground, lower** | **higher, top, upper**
PREP. **on a/the ~** ◇ *Are we on the right ~ for the restaurant?* | **to a/the ~** ◇ *Take the elevator to Level Four.*

level adj.

1 with no part higher than any other

VERBS **be, look, seem** | **get sth, keep sth** ◇ *Make sure you get*

the shelf ~ before screwing it in. ◇ *Keep the pot ~, or you'll spill the coffee.*
ADV. **absolutely, completely** ◇ *The floor has to be absolutely ~.* | **approximately, more or less, nearly**

2 at the same height/position as sth

VERBS **be** | **come, draw** ◇ *As they reached the final bend, Graham drew ~ and threatened too overtake him.*
ADV. **almost, nearly**
PREP. **with** ◇ *The top of the water came ~ with her chin.*

lever noun

1 handle for operating a machine

ADJ. **brake, control, gear, shift** (AmE) | **safety**
VERB + LEVER **move, press, pull, push, release, set** ◇ *To release the brake, pull the ~.* ◇ *Push the gear ~ into first.* ◇ *The machine will stop immediately once the ~ is released.* ◇ *Set all three ~s to the 0 position.*
PREP. **by a ~, by means of a ~** ◇ *The machine is operated by means of a ~.*
PHRASES **the position of the ~**

2 means of achieving sth

ADJ. **powerful, useful**
VERB + LEVER **act as, be, give sb, provide (sb with), serve as** | **use sth as**
PREP. **~ against** ◇ *If this allegation is true, it will give us a useful ~ against him.* | **~ for** ◇ *This could serve as a powerful ~ for peace.*

leverage noun

1 force

ADJ. **enough, sufficient** | **good** | **extra** | **maximum**
VERB + LEVERAGE **have** ◇ *He tried to push the door open, but he didn't have sufficient ~.* | **gain, get, obtain** | **apply, exert** ◇ *Position the piece of wood so that maximum ~ can be applied.* | **provide** | **increase**

2 influence

ADJ. **economic, financial, political** | **bargaining, negotiating** | **enormous, good, great**
VERB + LEVERAGE **have** | **gain** ◇ *They are determined to gain more political ~.* | **give sb**
LEVERAGE + NOUN **point**
PREP. **~ in** ◇ *They suddenly had more ~ in negotiations.*
PHRASES **use sth as ~**

liability noun

1 responsibility

ADJ. **full** | **legal** | **strict** | **criminal**
VERB + LIABILITY **have** ◇ *They have no legal ~ for damage to customers' possessions.* | **accept, acknowledge, admit, assume** | **deny** | **limit** | **avoid**
PREP. **~ for** ◇ *They have denied ~ for the accident.*

2 liabilities money owed

ADJ. **substantial** | **financial, tax** ◇ *an assessment of the company's financial liabilities*
VERB + LIABILITIES **have** | **take on, take over** ◇ *He wants to know the precise amount of the liabilities he is taking over.* | **cover, discharge, meet** ◇ *There is enough money to cover existing liabilities.* | **reduce**
PREP. **~ to** ◇ *The company has liabilities to its employees.*

liable adj.

VERBS **be** | **become** | **remain** | **make sb, render sb** ◇ *Failure to provide insurance rendered him ~ to prosecution.* | **find sb, hold sb** ◇ *They could be found ~ for the entire amount.*
ADV. **strictly** | **fully** | **potentially** | **personally** | **jointly, severally** (law) ◇ *Partners are jointly and severally* (= together and individually) *~ for a partnership's debts.* | **criminally, financially, legally** | **automatically**
PREP. **for** ◇ *She's fully ~ for the company's debts.*

liaise verb (esp. BrE)

ADV. **closely, directly**
PREP. **between** ◇ *Her job is to ~ between the school and the home.* | **with** ◇ *The tax office ~s closely with our department on such matters.*

liaison noun

1 communication

ADJ. **close, effective, good** | **poor** | **community** ◇ *a community ~ officer (= for example in the police)* | **customer** ◇ *We hired someone as customer ~. (AmE)* ◇ *a customer ~ manager (BrE)* | **military**
VERB + LIAISON **maintain** ◇ *We maintained a close ~ with the union.* | **establish** (esp. AmE) ◇ *We are hoping to establish good ~s with these groups.* | **improve**
LIAISON + NOUN **committee, group, team, unit** | **officer** | **work**
PREP. **in ~ with** ◇ *It's important that we work in close ~ with other charities in this field.* | **~ between** ◇ *good ~ between management and staff* | **~ with** ◇ *She is responsible for the ~ with researchers at other universities.*

2 sexual relationship

ADJ. **romantic, sexual** | **adulterous**
VERB + LIAISON **have** ◇ *She was having a romantic ~ with her husband's best friend.*
PREP. **~ with**

liar noun

ADJ. **accomplished, good** ◇ *She's an accomplished liar—they believed every word she said.* | **bad, poor** | **big, terrible** ◇ *He's the biggest ~ I've ever known.* | **compulsive, habitual, pathological**
VERB + LIAR **call sb** ◇ *Are you calling me a ~?*
PHRASES **you little ~!** ◇ *You little liar—I never said that!*

libel noun

ADJ. **alleged** | **criminal, seditious**
VERB + LIBEL **sue (sb) for** | **claim** | **deny**
LIBEL + NOUN **action, case, lawsuit, proceedings, suit** | **writ** (BrE) | **law, lawyer** | **damages** (BrE)
PREP. **~ against** ◇ *He has issued a writ for ~ against the radio star Michael Clery.*
→ Note at CRIME (for more verbs)

liberal noun

ADJ. **leading** | **bourgeois, middle-class** | **classical, old-fashioned, traditional** | **radical** | **market** | **economic, political, religious, social** | **white** | **bleeding-heart** | **limousine** (= a rich person who expresses concern for poor people, but does nothing to help them) (AmE)

liberal adj.

1 respecting other opinions

VERBS **be**
ADV. **extremely, fairly, very, etc.** ◇ *His attitudes are fairly ~.* | **remarkably** | **relatively** | **socially**

2 in politics

VERBS **be**
ADV. **comparatively, relatively** ◇ *comparatively ~ in trade matters* | **broadly, essentially** ◇ *a broadly ~ set of policies* | **politically**
PREP. **on** ◇ *He is relatively ~ on social issues.*

3 generous

VERBS **be** | **become**
ADV. **fairly, very** ◇ *Add a fairly ~ amount of olive oil to the pasta.*
PREP. **with** ◇ *She's very ~ with her advice!*

liberalism noun

ADJ. **radical** | **bourgeois** | **laissez-faire** | **classical, traditional** | **modern** | **economic, political, social, theological**

liberation noun

ADJ. **animal, gay, national, personal, sexual, women's** (often **women's lib**, old-fashioned) | **true**
VERB + LIBERATION **achieve, attain** | **seek, want** | **celebrate**
LIBERATION + NOUN **movement**
PREP. **~ by** ◇ *the ~ of the capital by allied forces* | **~ from** ◇ *the struggle for ~ from colonial rule*
PHRASES **a feeling of ~, a sense of ~** ◇ *Up in the mountains we had the most wonderful sense of ~.* | **a fight for ~, a struggle for ~** | **a war of ~**

liberty noun

ADJ. **great** | **complete** | **basic, fundamental** ◇ *a citizens' charter which gives people basic civil liberties* | **civil** | **human, individual, personal** | **economic, political, religious** | **constitutional** (esp. AmE)
VERB + LIBERTY **enjoy, have** | **demand, fight for** | **secure, win** ◇ *The city won its ~ in the 16th century.* | **lose** ◇ *If found guilty, she is in danger of losing her ~.* | **defend, guarantee, preserve, protect, safeguard** ◇ *The law should protect the ~ of the individual.* | **threaten** ◇ *The new legislation threatens individual ~.* | **curtail, erode, restrict, violate** ◇ *Our personal ~ is being eroded.* | **deny, deprive sb of, destroy, take** | **allow sb, give sb** ◇ *The system allows us complete ~ to do the task as we like.* | **sacrifice**
PREP. **at ~** ◇ *I'm not at ~ to reveal the names of the victims.* ◇ *The escaped prisoner has been at ~ for five days. (formal)* | **~ for** ◇ *Women are demanding greater ~ for themselves.* | **~ from** ◇ *~ from the abuse of police power*
PHRASES **an infringement of ~** | **loss of ~** | **a threat to ~**

librarian noun

ADJ. **professional, qualified** | **chief, head, senior** | **assistant** | **academic, public, reference** | **college, school, university** | **corporate** (AmE)
→ Note at JOB (for verbs)

library noun

1 building

ADJ. **large, small** | **excellent, good** | **public** | **private** | **local, national, regional** | **city, county, state, town** | **branch** | **central** | **mobile** ◇ *a plan to provide mobile ~ services in rural environments* | **well-stocked** | **circulating** (historical), **lending** ◇ *In 1784 he established his first circulating ~.* | **reference** | **general** | **special, specialist** | **academic, research** | **campus** (esp. AmE), **college, departmental, school, university** | **hospital, prison** | **copyright** (in the UK) ◇ *It is a copyright ~ and receives three copies of all books published in Britain.* | **presidential** (= containing documents from a particular former president) (in the US) ◇ *the Herbert Hoover presidential ~ in West Branch, Iowa*
VERB + LIBRARY **have** ◇ *The school has an excellent ~.* | **go to, use, visit** ◇ *How often do you go to the ~?* | **borrow sth from, get sth out of, take sth out of** ◇ *I got this very interesting book out of the ~.* | **return sth to, take sth back to** ◇ *Do you have any books to take back to the ~?* | **be available at, be available from** ◇ *Do you know about the other services available at your local ~?* | **have access to** ◇ *Everyone in the country should have access to a ~.*
LIBRARY + VERB **have sth, hold sth** ◇ *The ~ has an extensive collection of books on Chinese history.*
LIBRARY + NOUN **book** | **record** | **shelf, stack** | **catalogue** | **card, ticket** (BrE) | **assistant, staff** | **patron** (esp. AmE), **user** | **facilities, provision, resources, service** ◇ *the need to improve ~ provision* | **skills** ◇ *Students are taught ~ skills in the first week of their course.* | **research**
PREP. **at a/the ~** ◇ *a poetry reading at the local ~* | **in a/the ~** ◇ *I've been reading newspapers in the ~.*

2 collection of books, etc.

ADJ. **considerable, extensive, huge, vast** | **fine, impressive,**

magnificent, valuable | personal | film, music, photo-graphic, picture, tape, video | digital, electronic, online, virtual
VERB + LIBRARY **have, possess** ◇ *The family possessed an extensive ~.* | **amass, build, build up, construct** ◇ *She had built up an impressive ~ of art books.* | **add to**
PREP. **~ of** ◇ *a personal ~ of over 1000 volumes*

licence (*BrE*) (*AmE* license) *noun*

ADJ. **valid | full | special | compulsory** (*esp. AmE*) | **driver's** (*AmE*), **driving** (*BrE*), **pilot** (*AmE*), **pilot's** (*esp. BrE*) | **car | marriage | business, commercial, export, import, oper-ating, trade, trading** ◇ *The government is currently granting no operating ~s to foreign companies.* | **casino, gaming | fishing, hunting | television, TV** (*both in the UK*) | **gun | software | entertainment, music** ◇ *The bar was refused a music ~.* | **hotel, liquor** (*AmE*), **refreshment, restaurant | medical, teaching | exclusive**
VERB + LICENCE/LICENSE **have, hold** ◇ *You have to have a ~ to sell beer.* ◇ *Applicants must hold a valid driving/driver's ~.* | **buy, gain** (*formal*), **get, obtain, receive, win** ◇ *She gained her private pilot's ~.* ◇ *I got my ~ when I was eighteen.* | **apply for, make an application for | award (sb), grant (sb), issue sb | deny sb, refuse sb | revoke, suspend, take away** ◇ *He's had his ~ taken away.* | **renew | lose** ◇ *She lost her driving ~ when she was caught over the limit.*
LICENCE/LICENSE + VERB **expire, run out** ◇ *The ~ expires at the end of the year.*
LICENCE/LICENSE + NOUN **fee | holder | number, plate** (*both AmE*) | **agreement | application**
PREP. **in a/the ~** ◇ *All these details are specified in the ~.* | **under a/the ~** ◇ *The weapons were exported under a special export ~.* | **under ~** ◇ *They are Italian trains, but they will be built in Germany under ~.* | **~ for** ◇ *a ~ for software manufacture* | **~ from** ◇ *a ~ from the Performing Rights Society*
PHRASES **the holder of a ~**

lid *noun*

1 removable top

ADJ. **airtight, close-fitting, tight, tight-fitting** ◇ *Choose a dish with a tight-fitting ~.* | **closed, sealed | hinged | box, coffin, piano, saucepan, trunk** (on a car) (*AmE*), **etc.** | **dustbin** (*BrE*), **garbage-can** (*AmE*), **trash-can** (*AmE*) | **metal, plastic, etc.**
VERB + LID **lift, open, raise** ◇ *She lifted the ~ of the box.* | **pop** (*AmE*), **pop off, prise off** (*BrE*), **pry off** (*AmE*), **remove, take off, unscrew** ◇ *We managed to remove the ~ with a lever.* | **close, replace, shut | put down, slam shut | put on, screw down, screw on** ◇ *I poured some water and screwed the ~ back on the bottle.* ◇ *The coffin ~ had been screwed down.* | **keep on** ◇ *Keep the ~ on the pan until the liquid comes to the boil.*
PREP. **on the ~** ◇ *His name was on the ~.*

2 lids of the eyes → See also EYELID

ADJ. **eye | closed, drooping, half-closed, half-open, heavy, lowered, narrowed** ◇ *She felt the tears burning against her closed ~s.* | **top, upper**
VERB + LIDS **close, lower** ◇ *She saw James walk in and hastily lowered her ~s.* | **lift, open** ◇ *She lifted her ~s and found him looking at her.*
LIDS + VERB **droop** ◇ *Heavy ~s drooped over her eyes.*
PREP. **behind ... ~** ◇ *She could still see the light flickering behind her closed ~s.* | **beneath ... ~** ◇ *She glanced at him occasionally from beneath lowered ~s.* | **through ... ~** ◇ *He was watching her through half-closed ~s.*

lie *noun*

ADJ. **big, big fat** (*informal*), **great, monstrous** ◇ *He told a big fat ~!* | **little | absolute, complete, downright, flat-out** (*AmE*), **outright, total** ◇ *That's a downright ~!* | **little white, white** ◇ *A little white ~ is surely excusable.* | **deliberate | bald-faced** (*AmE*), **barefaced, blatant, obvious, transpar-ent | elaborate** ◇ *a web of elaborate ~s* | **outrageous | vicious**
VERB + LIE **be** ◇ *That's a lie—I never said that!* | **tell (sb) |**

believe, swallow ◇ *How could she swallow such a blatant ~?* | **expose | live** ◇ *He lived a ~ for thirty years, 'married' to two women.*
LIE + NOUN **detector**
PHRASES **a pack of ~s, a tissue of ~s, a web of ~s | give the ~ to sth, put the ~ to sth** (= prove that something is not true) | **spread ~s (about sb)**

lie *verb*

1 be in a flat position

ADV. **down** ◇ *He was lying down on the bed.* | **there** ◇ *He just lay there smiling.* | **comfortably, helplessly, limply, peacefully, quietly**
PREP. **on** ◇ *She lay on her stomach.* | **in** ◇ *She likes to ~ in bed all day.*
PHRASES **~ asleep, ~ awake** ◇ *I used to ~ awake at night worrying about it.* | **~ dead, ~ unconscious** ◇ *A man lay dead in the middle of the road.* | **~ face down, ~ prone** (*formal*), **~ prostrate** (*formal*) ◇ *He was lying face down in the mud.* | **~ face up, supine** (*formal*) ◇ *Lie face up with your feet on the floor.* | **~ flat** ◇ *I was lying flat on the floor.* | **~ motionless, ~ still** ◇ *Lie still while I put the bandage on.* | **~ naked** ◇ *She was still lying naked on the bed.* | **~ sprawled** ◇ *She lay sprawled on the sofa.*

2 say sth that is not true

ADV. **convincingly** ◇ *He was unable to ~ convincingly.* | **easily | constantly, repeatedly | blatantly | deliberately, intentionally | completely, outright, totally** (*all AmE*)
PREP. **about** ◇ *She ~d about her age.* | **to** ◇ *Don't ~ to me.*
PHRASES **~ through your teeth | ~ under oath**

lieutenant *noun* → Note at RANK

life *noun*

1 living things

ADJ. **intelligent** ◇ *Is there intelligent ~ on other planets?* | **animal, bird, human, insect, plant | aquatic, marine | extraterrestrial**
LIFE + NOUN **form | cycle | sciences**

2 existence

ADJ. **eternal, everlasting | past, previous**
VERB + LIFE **lose** ◇ *He lost his ~ in an air crash.* | **bring sb back to, restore sb to | cling to, fight for** ◇ *She clung to ~ for several weeks.* | **jeopardize, risk** ◇ *She risked her ~ for the sake of the children.* | **endanger, threaten | protect, save** ◇ *a drug that will save lives* | **spare** ◇ *She begged the soldiers to spare her son's ~.* | **give, lay down, sacrifice | claim, cost** ◇ *The crash claimed 43 lives.* ◇ *His foolishness almost cost him his ~.* | **end, take** ◇ *She took her own ~.* | **value | start** (*figurative*) ◇ *The hotel started ~ as a prison.*
LIFE + VERB **be lost** ◇ *No lives were lost in the accident.*
LIFE + NOUN **assurance** (*BrE*), **insurance | jacket, preserver** (*AmE*), **vest** (*AmE*) | **boat, raft | saver | support** ◇ *She's critically ill, on ~ support.* ◇ *a life-support machine* ◇ *a life-support system*
PHRASES **an attempt on sb's ~** ◇ *There have been three attempts on the president's ~.* | **in fear for your ~, in fear of your ~** ◇ *Witnesses are living in fear for their ~ after giving evidence against the gang.* | **~ after death** ◇ *Do you believe in ~ after death?* | **loss of ~** ◇ *The plane crashed with heavy loss of ~.* | **a matter of ~ and death** ◇ *These talks are a matter of ~ and death for the factory.* (*figurative*) | **owe sb your ~** ◇ *I owe my ~ to the doctors at the hospital.* | **the right to ~ | signs of ~** ◇ *The driver showed no signs of ~.*

3 period between birth and death

ADJ. **long, short | entire, whole | early | adult | later** ◇ *In later ~ he took up writing.* | **past, previous** ◇ *He never discussed the unhappiness of his past ~.* ◇ *I think I may have been an animal in a previous ~.* | **future, next | working** ◇ *He was a miner all his working ~.*
VERB + LIFE **go through, live, spend** ◇ *She went through ~ always wanting what she couldn't get.* ◇ *He spent his whole ~*

in Rhode Island. | **end** ◊ He ended his ~ a happy man. |
shorten | **prolong** | **dedicate**, **devote** ◊ He devoted his ~ to
the education of deaf children.
LIFE + NOUN **history**, **story** | **membership** | **imprisonment**,
sentence | **expectancy**, **span** (usually *lifespan*) ◊ Japanese
people have a very high ~ expectancy. ◊ the lifespan of a
mouse | **mate** (*AmE*), **partner**
PREP. **for ~** ◊ She thought marriage should be for ~. | **in your
~** ◊ for the first time in her ~ | **throughout your ~** ◊
Throughout her ~ she was dogged by loneliness.
PHRASES **all your ~** ◊ I've known her all my ~. | **at sb's time of
~** ◊ At his time of ~ he should be starting to take things easy.
| **the end of your ~** ◊ Her paintings became more obscure
towards/toward the end of her ~. | **late in ~** ◊ She discovered
jazz quite late in ~. | **the ... of your ~** ◊ I had the fright of
my ~ when I saw the snake in my bed. ◊ He met the love of his
~ at college. | **a phase in (sb's) ~, a phase of (sb's) ~, a
stage in (sb's) ~, a stage of (sb's) ~** ◊ She sensed she was
entering a new phase in her ~. | **the prime of ~** ◊ You're still
in the prime of ~. | **the remainder of your ~, the rest of
your ~** ◊ He'll be haunted by the crash for the rest of his ~.

4 activity in the world

ADJ. **daily**, **day-to-day**, **everyday**, **ordinary** | **real** ◊ a real-life
drama | **modern** | **personal**, **private** ◊ She did not tolerate
press intrusion into her private ~. | **inner** ◊ Only his wife had
access to his inner ~. | **family**, **married** | **domestic**, **home** |
social | **love**, **sex** | **public** ◊ His fame was so sudden that he
was unprepared for public ~. | **academic**, **business**,
cultural, **economic**, **intellectual**, **political**, **professional**,
school, **spiritual** | **civic** | **night** (usually *nightlife*) ◊ What's
the nightlife like in the town? | **city**, **village**, **etc.** | **rural**,
urban
VERB + LIFE **build**, **rebuild** ◊ He built his whole ~ around his
children. ◊ She is still rebuilding her ~ after the accident.
LIFE + VERB **be complicated**, **be unfair** | **be precious**, **be
sacred**
PHRASES **an attitude to ~, an outlook on ~, a philosophy of
~, a view of ~** ◊ I've always had a fairly optimistic outlook
on ~. | **a love of ~** ◊ He always had a great love of ~. | **a
man in your ~, a woman in your ~** ◊ There has only been
one woman in her ~. | **see sth of ~** ◊ I wanted to see
something of ~ before I settled down. | **the ... side of ~** ◊ His
time in London was his first glimpse of the seamier side of ~. |
want sth from of ~, want sth out of ~ ◊ They both seem to
want the same things out of ~.

5 way of living

ADJ. **fulfilling**, **good**, **great**, **happy**, **perfect**, **wonderful** |
lonely, **miserable**, **sad**, **unhappy** | **boring** | **difficult**, **hard**
| **easy** | **charmed** | **active**, **busy**, **hectic** | **exciting** | **full** |
peaceful, **quiet** | **simple** | **normal**, **ordinary** | **healthy** |
sheltered | **double** ◊ He had been leading a double ~,
married to two women. | **secret**
VERB + LIFE **have**, **lead**, **live** ◊ She leads a busy social ~. |
enjoy | **change** ◊ Learning meditation changed her ~. |
dominate, **take over** ◊ He never let his work dominate his ~.
| **ruin** ◊ He ruined his ~ through drinking. | **enrich**
PHRASES **build a new ~, make a new ~, start a new ~** ◊ They
went to Australia to start a new ~. | **enjoy ~ to the full, live
~ to the full** ◊ He always believed in living ~ to the full. | **the
high ~** ◊ They were enjoying the high ~ in the smartest hotels
of New York. | **live a ~ of ...** ◊ They're living a ~ of luxury in
the Bahamas. | **a/the pace of ~** ◊ The pace of ~ is much
gentler on the island. | **the quality of ~** ◊ He gave up his
high-flying job and now enjoys a better quality of ~. | **a way
of ~** ◊ She loved the Spanish way of ~ and immediately felt at
home there.

6 liveliness

VERB + LIFE **come to** ◊ The city only comes to ~ at night. |
breathe, **bring sth to**, **inject** ◊ They need some new, younger
staff to breathe some ~ into the company. | **burst with**, **hum
with**, **teem with** ◊ a child bursting with ~
PHRASES **breathe new ~ into sb/sth** ◊ He hopes the

development will breathe new ~ into the community. | **full of
~** ◊ It's nice to see an old man still so full of ~.

lifeless *adj.*

1 dead

VERBS **appear**, **be**, **look** ◊ She lay ~ in the snow. | **lie**
ADV. **completely** | **almost**, **nearly** ◊ His body was limp and
almost ~. | **apparently**, **seemingly** ◊ She lay there,
apparently ~.
PHRASES **cold and ~, limp and ~**

2 without living things

VERBS **be**
ADV. **completely** ◊ a time when they earth was completely ~

3 dull/without interest

VERBS **be**, **seem** | **become**
ADV. **completely** | **rather** ◊ The acting was dull and rather ~.
PHRASES **dull and ~**

lifeline *noun*

1 rope

VERB + LIFELINE **throw sb** | **catch**, **cling to** ◊ He clung to the ~
and the woman pulled him to the bank.

2 important help

ADJ. **real**, **vital** ◊ Visits from loved ones are a vital ~ for
prisoners. | **economic**, **financial** ◊ The state pension is their
financial ~.
VERB + LIFELINE **be**, **become** ◊ While my mother was ill,
talking to Sheila became a ~ for me. | **give sb**, **hold out** |
offer (sb), **provide (sb with)**, **throw sb** ◊ The organization
provides a real ~ for many women in poverty. ◊ He threw me
a ~ when he offered me a job. | **have** ◊ With this one
unexpected victory, the team now has a ~.

lifestyle *noun*

ADJ. **healthy**, **unhealthy** | **active** | **sedentary** ◊ The increase
in obesity is a result of poor diet and a sedentary ~. | **busy**,
hectic | **stressful** | **affluent**, **comfortable**, **expensive**,
extravagant, **glamorous**, **lavish** | **modern** | **gay** | **nomadic**
| **alternative** (*esp. AmE*) ◊ She's trying to balance an
alternative ~ with her desire for a career.
VERB + LIFESTYLE **change** ◊ She had to change her ~ and eating
habits. | **enjoy**, **have**, **lead**, **live** ◊ They enjoy a very
comfortable ~. | **maintain**, **support** | **adopt** ◊ We want them
to adopt a healthier ~. | **fit**, **suit** | **promote**
LIFESTYLE + NOUN **change**, **modification** | **choice** | **habit** |
factor | **magazine**
PHRASES **a change in ~**

lifetime *noun*

ADJ. **long** ◊ wisdom gained in the course of a long ~ | **short** ◊
A ~ is too short for all the great books there are! | **entire**,
whole
VERB + LIFETIME **devote**, **spend** ◊ He devoted a ~ to working
with disabled children. | **take (sb)** ◊ It took a whole ~ to solve
the mystery of her father's disappearance. | **last (sb)** ◊ This
watch should last you a ~. | **seem**, **seem like** ◊ It seems a ~
since we first met. | **live** ◊ You can live a whole ~ and not
witness such an event.
LIFETIME + NOUN **achievement** ◊ The veteran director won a ~
achievement award. | **appointment** (*AmE*), **employment** |
membership (*AmE*) | **earnings**, **income** ◊ Payments are
based on expected ~ income. | **guarantee**, **warranty** | **ban** |
commitment
PREP. **after a ~** ◊ After a ~ as a journalist in the trouble spots
of the world, he retired to the country. | **during sb's ~** ◊ I've
seen many changes during my ~. | **in your ~** ◊ The artist was
little known in his ~. | **of a ~** ◊ She gave the performance of
a ~. | **~ in** ◊ She spent a ~ in politics. | **~ of** ◊ a ~ of
problems
PHRASES **the habits of a ~** ◊ It's hard to break the habits of a
~. | **a legend in your own ~** ◊ Callas was a legend in her
own ~. | **half a ~** | **a ~ ago**, **a ~ away** ◊ College seems a half
a ~ away. | **a lifetime's experience**, **a lifetime's work** | **a
lifetime's worth of sth** ◊ The images are part of a lifetime's

worth of photographs from Cohen's long career. | **once in a** ~ ◊ *That sort of thing happens only once in a* ~.

483

light

lift *noun*

1 (*BrE*) for taking people/goods between floors → See also ELEVATOR

ADJ. **private, service** ◊ *The hotel has a private* ~ *linking it to the beach.* | **baggage, goods, passenger, wheelchair** | **electric, hydraulic**
VERB + LIFT **go down in, go up in, take** ◊ *We took the* ~ *down to the ground floor.* | **operate**
LIFT + VERB **serve sth** ◊ *The* ~ *serves the top four floors of the building.* | **arrive**
LIFT + NOUN **button** | **doors** | **shaft** | **attendant, operator**

2 for taking people up mountains, etc.

ADJ. **ski** | **chair** (usually *chairlift*), **gondola** (*BrE*)
VERB + LIFT **take** | **operate**
LIFT + NOUN **car** | **operator** | **pass** ◊ *You'll need your* ~ *pass for the ski lifts.*

3 (*BrE*) free ride in a car, etc. → See also RIDE

ADJ. **free**
VERB + LIFT **ask for, hitch, thumb** ◊ *We stood by the roadside and thumbed a* ~. | **give sb, offer sb** | **accept** ◊ *Don't accept* ~*s from strangers.*
PHRASES **a** ~ **back, a** ~ **home** ◊ *He offered us a* ~ *home.*

4 feeling of increased happiness/excitement

ADJ. **big, great, huge, real** ◊ *Winning the semi-final gave the team a huge* ~. | **emotional**
VERB + LIFT **give sb** | **get**

lift *verb*

1 raise/move sb/sth

ADV. **almost, half** ◊ *He hugged her, almost* ~*ing her off the ground.* | **fractionally, a little, slightly** | **slowly** | **sharply** ◊ *Her head* ~*ed sharply.* | **carefully, gently, gingerly** ◊ *Carefully* ~ *the cake off the tray and cool on a wire rack.* | **easily, effortlessly** | **bodily** ◊ *She was* ~*ed bodily aboard by two sailors.* | **back, down, out, up** ◊ *She* ~*ed back the sheet.*
VERB + LIFT **can barely, can hardly** ◊ *The box was so heavy I could barely* ~ *it.* | **try to** | **manage to** | **be too heavy to**
PREP. **above** ◊ *He stood, legs apart, arms* ~*ed above his head.* | **down** ◊ *She leaned on him and he half* ~*ed her down the stairs.* | **from** ◊ *He felt as if an enormous weight had been* ~*ed from his shoulders.* | **into** ◊ *The heavy beams were* ~*ed into place.* | **off** ◊ *She* ~*ed the book up off the table.* | **out of** ◊ *He* ~*ed the baby out of its cradle.* | **over** ◊ *She* ~*ed the child over the fence.* | **to** ◊ *Juliet nodded,* ~*ing her face to David's.*

2 remove a law/rule

ADV. **completely** | **partially** ◊ *The police managed to restore calm and the curfew was partially* ~*ed.*
VERB + LIFT **agree to, decide to, vote to** ◊ *The government decided to* ~ *the ban on arms exports.* | **refuse to**

ligament *noun*

ADJ. **ankle, elbow, knee**
VERB + LIGAMENT **injure, pull, rupture, sprain, strain, tear** | **repair**
LIGAMENT + NOUN **damage, injury, problem** (*esp. BrE*), **tear** | **surgery**

light *noun*

1 brightness

ADJ. **clear, good** | **bright, brilliant, harsh, intense, strong** | **blinding** | **full** ◊ *In full* ~, *you could see Alison was well over forty.* | **bad, dim, faint, feeble, murky, poor, weak** | **subdued** | **failing** ◊ *We could hardly see the ball in the failing* ~. | **gentle, pale, soft, watery** | **mellow, warm** | **cold, cool** ◊ *in the cold* ~ *of morning* | **early, morning** | **artificial** | **natural** | **infrared, ultraviolet, UV** ◊ *film that is sensitive to ultraviolet* ~ | **white, yellow, etc.** | **visible** | **candle** (usually *candlelight*)
... OF LIGHT **beam, ray** | **burst, flash, gleam, glimmer** ◊ *There was a flash of* ~ *followed by an explosion.* | **patch, pool**

VERB + LIGHT **have** ◊ *Do you have enough* ~ *for reading?* | **generate, produce** | **cast, emit, give, give out, provide, shed, shine** ◊ ~ *emitted by a star* | **absorb** | **reflect** | **block out** | **be bathed in** | **be sensitive to**
LIGHT + VERB **gleam, glow, shine** | **come, fall, pour, stream** ◊ *Light from a tall lamp fell in a pool on the desk.* | **fill sth, flood sth** | **reflect** ◊ *The* ~ *reflecting off the snow was dazzling.* | **grow stronger, increase** | **fade, fail, thicken** | **blind sb, dazzle sb** ◊ *We were momentarily blinded by the* ~ *of the sun.* | **catch sth** ◊ *You could see the imperfections in the repair when the* ~ *caught it.* | **illuminate sth, light sth, light sth up**
LIGHT + NOUN **level** | **source** | **beam** | **therapy**
PREP. **against the** ~ ◊ *She held up the letter against the* ~. | **by the** ~ **of** ◊ *They managed to see where the door was by the* ~ *of the moon.* | **into the** ~ ◊ *Bring it into the* ~ *and we'll have a look at it.* | **in the** ~ ◊ *The place looked calm in the golden evening* ~. | ~ **from** ◊ *the* ~ *from the kitchen window*
PHRASES **(the)** ~ **at the end of the tunnel** (*figurative*) ◊ *For the first time since the start of his treatment, we can now see* ~ *at the end of the tunnel.* | **the** ~ **of day** (*figurative*) ◊ *Some of his paintings never even saw the* ~ *of day.* | **(at) the speed of** ~ ◊ *Nothing can travel faster than the speed of* ~. | **a point of** ~, **a source of** ~ ◊ *The lamp was the only source of* ~ *in the room.*

2 sth that produces light

ADJ. **bright** ◊ *the bright* ~*s of the city* | **blinking, flashing, flickering, twinkling** | **electric, fluorescent, gas, halogen, low-energy, neon, strip, strobe** | **bedside, ceiling, outside, overhead, wall** | **bathroom, landing, porch, etc.** | **street** | **security, warning** ◊ *A warning* ~ *goes on when the battery is running low.* | **brake, fog, hazard, tail** ◊ *The car was stopped at the side of the road with its hazard* ~*s flashing.* | **landing** ◊ *The pilot could just make out the runway landing* ~*s.* | **disco**
VERB + LIGHT **flick on, flip on** (*AmE*), **put on, switch on, turn on** | **have on** ◊ *Some cars already had their* ~*s on.* | **keep on, leave on** | **extinguish, flick off, flip off** (*AmE*), **put off, put out, shut off** (*AmE*), **switch off, turn off, turn out** | **turn up** | **dim, turn down** | **shine** ◊ *Someone shone a* ~ *in my face.* | **flash** ◊ *He flashed his* ~*s to warn the oncoming cars.*
LIGHT + VERB **be off, be on** | **come on, go on** ◊ *The warning* ~ *came on.* | **go off, go out** | **dim** | **fuse** | **gleam, glimmer, glow, shine** | **flash** ◊ *The blue* ~ *was flashing.* | **blink, flicker** ◊ *The* ~ *flickered a couple of times then went out.* | **blind sb, dazzle sb**
LIGHT + NOUN **switch** | **fitting** (*BrE*), **fixture** (*AmE*) (see also *light bulb*) → See also TRAFFIC LIGHT

light *verb*

1 make sth begin to burn

VERB + LIGHT **attempt to, try to** | **pause to, stop to** ◊ *She paused to* ~ *another cigarette.*

2 (often **be lit**) give light to sth

ADV. **well** ◊ *a well-lit room* | **badly, barely, dimly, faintly, poorly** ◊ *a dimly lit street* | **brightly, brilliantly** | **softly** | **briefly** ◊ *A gleam of pleasure briefly lit his face.* (*figurative*) | **immediately, instantly** ◊ *Stacey's face immediately lit up.* | **suddenly** | **up** ◊ *There was an explosion and the whole sky lit up.*
PREP. **by** ◊ *The room was dark now, lit only by a single candle.* | **with** (*figurative*) ◊ *Her face lit up with pleasure.*

light *adj.*

1 not dark

VERBS **be** | **become, get, grow, turn** ◊ *It was starting to get* ~. ◊ *As soon as it grew* ~, *we got up and dressed.* ◊ *The sky turned* ~ *once more.* | **remain, stay** ◊ *It stays* ~ *for so long on these summer evenings.* | **appear** ◊ *Remember that paint shades appear lighter in full sunlight.*
ADV. **very** ◊ *All our galleries are very* ~. | **almost** ◊ *It was*

almost ~ outside. | **barely** ◇ *It was barely ~ yet.* | **fairly** | **enough** ◇ *It was not ~ enough to see things clearly.* | **still**

2 not weighing much

VERBS **be, feel, seem** | **become, get**
ADV. **extremely, fairly, very, etc.** | **reasonably, relatively** | **enough** ◇ *The tent is ~ enough for backpacking and touring.* | **amazingly, remarkably, surprisingly** | **strangely, unusually** ◇ *The bottle felt strangely ~ between my fingers.* | **deliciously** ◇ *a deliciously ~ alternative to cake*

3 not great in amount/degree

VERBS **be** | **remain** ◇ *Trading volume remains ~.*
ADV. **very** | **remarkably** ◇ *The punishment can be remarkably ~.* | **comparatively, fairly, quite, relatively** ◇ *The traffic is usually fairly ~ in the afternoons.*

light bulb *noun* → See BULB

lighter *noun*

ADJ. **cigarette** | **butane, gas, petrol** (*BrE*) | **gold, silver** | **disposable**
VERB + LIGHTER **flick** ◇ *He flicked his ~ but it didn't catch.* | **pull out** ◇ *She pulled out a small silver ~ from her bag.*

lighting *noun*

ADJ. **bright, good, harsh, strong** | **bad, low, poor** | **dim, soft, subdued, subtle** | **ambient, moody** ◇ *the moody ~ and chilled-out atmosphere of the bar* | **dramatic, theatrical** ◇ *dramatic ~ effects* | **coloured/colored** | **adequate, proper** | **artificial, natural** | **electric, fluorescent, gas, incandescent** (*AmE*) | **street** | **exterior, outdoor** ◇ *exterior ~ and alarm systems* | **indoor, interior** | **stage** | **emergency** ◇ *The generator supplies emergency ~.* | **background** | **concealed** (*esp. BrE*), **indirect, overhead, recessed** (*esp. AmE*), **track** (*esp. AmE*) | **security**
... OF LIGHTING **level**
VERB + LIGHTING **have** ◇ *The kitchen has adequate ~.* | **use** ◇ *No special ~ was used when making the video.* | **provide** ◇ *The only ~ was provided by panels on the floor.* | **install** | **adjust, control** ◇ *Patients can adjust the ~ using a dimmer.* ◇ *a touch pad to control the ~*
LIGHTING + NOUN **level** | **arrangement, scheme, system** ◇ *a typical ~ scheme for a house* | **effects** | **designer, engineer** | **fixture** (*esp. AmE*)

lightning *noun*

ADJ. **ball, forked, sheet** ◇ *Forked ~ flickered across the sky.* | **heat** (*esp. AmE*) | **greased** (*figurative*) ◇ *He jumped out of the car like greased ~ (= very fast).*
... OF LIGHTNING **bolt, flash, streak** ◇ *A bolt of ~ struck the roof of the building.*
LIGHTNING + VERB **flash** ◇ *Lightning flashed outside.* | **illuminate sth, light sth, light sth up** ◇ *Lightning lit up the night sky.* | **hit sb/sth, strike sb/sth** ◇ *Lightning hit the tree.* ◇ *He was struck by ~.*
LIGHTNING + NOUN **bolt, flash** | **storm** | **conductor** (*BrE*), **rod** (*AmE*) | **strike** (*AmE*) ◇ *Lightning strikes caused scores of fires across the state.*
PHRASES **thunder and ~**

like *verb*

ADV. **enormously** (*esp. BrE*), **especially, genuinely, a lot, particularly, really, truly, very much** ◇ *I ~d him enormously and was sorry when he left.* ◇ *I really ~ that restaurant.* | **best, better** ◇ *Which story do you ~ best?* | **quite, rather** (*esp. BrE*) | **always, never, still** ◇ *I have always ~d Sue and I don't intend to stop now.* | **instantly** ◇ *Everyone he met instantly ~d him and wanted to be friends.* | **personally** ◇ *I personally ~d this song a lot.* | **secretly** ◇ *She guessed that he secretly ~d wearing skirts.*
VERB + LIKE **appear to, seem to** | **begin to, start to** | **come to, get to, grow to** ◇ *I hope you will get to ~ our town.* | **learn to** ◇ *I'm learning to ~ spinach.* | **want to** ◇ *I wanted to*

~ *the movie because of its message.* | **try to** ◇ *I tried to ~ her because it would be for the best.* | **pretend to** ◇ *He pretended to ~ her for Tony's sake.*
PHRASES **be universally ~d** ◇ *a man who was universally ~d* | **be well ~d** ◇ *He works hard and is well ~d by his colleagues.*

likeable (*esp. BrE*) (*also* likable *AmE, BrE*) *adj.*

VERBS **be, seem**
ADV. **extremely, fairly, very, etc.** | **genuinely, immensely, most** | **immediately, instantly** ◇ *He had a certain rakish air that made him immediately ~.*

likelihood *noun*

ADJ. **every** (*esp. BrE*) ◇ *There's every ~ that she'll be able to help us.* | **greater, increased** | **high, real, strong, substantial** | **decreased, lower, reduced** | **little** ◇ *Without a guide, there seemed little ~ of reaching our goal.*
VERB + LIKELIHOOD **decrease, diminish** (*esp. AmE*), **lessen** (*esp. AmE*), **minimize, reduce** ◇ *Taking regular exercise reduces the ~ of a heart attack.* | **enhance** (*esp. AmE*), **improve, increase, maximize, raise** | **affect, determine, influence** ◇ *This shouldn't affect the ~ of you getting the job.* | **assess, calculate, estimate, evaluate, predict** ◇ *Staff have to calculate continuously the ~ of danger.*
LIKELIHOOD + VERB **grow** | **diminish**
PREP. **~ for** (*esp. AmE*) ◇ *skills that will improve their ~ for success in college* | **~ of** ◇ *Is their any ~ of our getting our money back?*
PHRASES **in all ~** ◇ *In all ~, he'll be fit to play on Saturday.*

likely *adj.*

VERBS **appear, be, look, seem, sound** | **become** | **make sth** ◇ *a development they believed would make nuclear war more ~* | **consider sth, deem sth, think sth** ◇ *The doctors didn't think it ~ that she would ever heal completely.*
ADV. **extremely, fairly, very, etc.** ◇ *This match was never ~ to be a classic.* ◇ *It seems very ~ that he will be forced to resign.* | **entirely, especially, highly, overwhelmingly, particularly** ◇ *It is entirely ~ that the company will make another offer.* ◇ *It is highly ~ that the factory will have to close.* | **increasingly** ◇ *Juries became increasingly ~ to acquit.* | **hardly** ◇ *They're hardly ~ to get home before ten.* | **reasonably** | **equally** | **disproportionately** ◇ *Are black defendants disproportionately ~ to be wrongfully convicted?* | **ever** ◇ *the best deal they are ever ~ to get*

likeness *noun*

ADJ. **strong** ◇ *The children all share a strong family ~.* | **exact** ◇ *That is an exact ~ to the man I saw.* | **good** | **remarkable, uncanny** | **superficial** ◇ *There's a superficial ~, but they're really very different.* | **physical** | **family**
VERB + LIKENESS **see** | **bear** ◇ *She bears a remarkable ~ to her aunt.* | **capture** ◇ *a quick caricature that captured her ~* | **create, draw, paint** ◇ *She paid an artist to create his ~.*
PREP. **~ between** ◇ *I can't see any ~ between her children.* | **~ of, ~ to** ◇ *That's a good ~ of my grandfather.*

liking *noun*

ADJ. **great** | **particular, special, strong** ◇ *Brian had taken a strong ~ to him.* | **immediate, instant** ◇ *I took an instant ~ to her.*
VERB + LIKING **have** ◇ *They have little ~ for each other.* | **develop, take** | **share**
PREP. **for sb's ~** ◇ *The weather's too hot for my ~.* | **to sb's ~** ◇ *The food wasn't really to my ~.* | **~ for** ◇ *We share a ~ for Italian cooking.*

limb *noun*

ADJ. **long** | **short** | **slender, thin** | **flailing** ◇ *Two arms reached around her flailing ~s.* | **powerful, strong** | **bare, naked** | **broken, injured** | **sore** | **stiff** ◇ *I eased my stiff ~s into the hot bath.* | **tired, weary** (*esp. BrE*) | **amputated, severed** | **missing** ◇ *The missing ~ did not lessen the quality of the cat's life.* | **artificial, prosthetic** | **phantom** ◇ *sensations felt in phantom ~s after amputation* | **lower, upper** | **hind** ◇ *The animal is able to stand up on its hind ~s.*

VERB + LIMB **amputate, sever** | **lose** ◇ *people who have lost ~s in battle* | **stretch** ◇ *I stretched my ~s lazily as I sat up.*
LIMB + NOUN **development, growth** | **amputation**

lime *noun*

ADJ. **fresh**
... OF LIME **slice, wedge** ◇ *Serve the dish garnished with wedges of ~.*
VERB + LIME **squeeze** | **slice** | **garnish sth with**
LIME + NOUN **tree** | **juice**
→ Special page at FRUIT

limelight *noun*

VERB + LIMELIGHT **grab, hog, steal** ◇ *She accused her co-star of trying to hog the ~.* | **enjoy** | **seek** ◇ *He was never a man to seek the ~.* | **avoid, shun** | **share**
PREP. **into the ~** ◇ *an ordinary person who was suddenly thrust into the ~* | **in the ~** ◇ *She likes being in the ~.* | **out of the ~** ◇ *The band started touring again after two years out of the ~.*

limit *noun*

ADJ. **outer** | **northern, southern, etc.** | **three-mile, etc.** | **city, town** (*both esp. AmE*) ◇ *a few miles outside of the city ~s* | **annual, daily, etc.** ◇ *Four cups of coffee is my daily ~.* | **term** (*esp. AmE*) ◇ *term ~s for members of Congress* | **lifetime** ◇ *a lifetime ~ of five years for welfare support* | **absolute, extreme, ultimate** ◇ *I can offer you $50 but that's my absolute ~.* ◇ *The vessel is operating at the extreme ~s of the acceptable ranges.* | **higher, maximum, upper** | **lower, minimum** | **severe, strict, stringent, tight** ◇ *The application must be made within a strict time ~.* | **narrow** ◇ *We are forced to operate within relatively narrow ~s.* | **arbitrary** ◇ *the EU's arbitrary ~s on fiscal policy* | **finite** ◇ *the idea that the planet has finite ~s* | **age, height, size, speed, temperature, time, weight** ◇ *There's a weight ~ on the bridge.* | **physical** | **practical** ◇ *There's a practical ~ to how small a portable computer can be.* | **inherent** ◇ *the inherent ~s of the hardware* | **safe, safety** ◇ *The temperature is within safe operating ~s.* | **exposure** ◇ *the exposure ~s to this group of chemicals* | **emission** ◇ *The same emission ~s apply to all engines.* | **budget, contribution** (*esp. AmE*), **credit, financial** (*esp. BrE*), **income, overdraft** (*BrE*), **spending** ◇ *the IRS contribution ~s* ◇ *I don't want to go over my overdraft ~.* | **constitutional, legal, prescribed, statutory** | **acceptable, allowable, appropriate, permissible, reasonable, recommended** | **clear, specific** ◇ *Establish clear ~s, but keep rules to a minimum.* | **established, fixed, set, specified** ◇ *Most credit card issuers have set ~s on how low rates can go.* | **posted** (*AmE*) ◇ *The posted speed ~ is 35 mph.* | **normal** ◇ *The engine was still reading well above normal ~s.* | **theoretical** ◇ *the theoretical ~s of human knowledge*
VERB + LIMIT **have** ◇ *The new law has its ~s.* | **approach, near, reach** ◇ *The industry was approaching the ~s of expansion.* | **cross** | **define, determine** ◇ *the narrow ~s defined by the emperor* | **explore** ◇ *She wants Zack to be free to explore his ~s, experiment and try new things.* | **establish, impose, place, put, set** ◇ *The government has set a ~ on spending on the arts.* | **enforce** ◇ *There's a strict time ~ enforced by a penalty.* | **respect** ◇ *We want to respect the ~s that our elders have imposed on us.* | **accept, acknowledge, recognize** ◇ *They recognize the ~s of their conventional strategies.* | **expand, extend, increase, raise** | **break** ◇ *She must have broken every speed ~ in Los Angeles getting here.* | **challenge, push, stretch, test** ◇ *Their designers have pushed the ~s of technology in order to create something new.* | **lower, reduce** ◇ *This led them to reduce the upper age ~ from age 65 to age 59.* | **exceed** ◇ *You were exceeding the speed ~.* | **overcome, transcend** | **overstep, violate** | **push sb to** ◇ *She pushed me to the ~ of my abilities.*
PREP. **above a/the ~** ◇ *The level of radioactivity in the soil was found to be above recommended ~s.* | **at a/the ~** ◇ *I was almost at the ~s of my patience.* | **below a/the ~** ◇ *The price fell below the lower ~.* ◇ *The trees are found only below a ~ of 1500 feet.* | **beyond a/the ~** ◇ *Heat levels rose beyond the recommended ~s.* ◇ *Fishing beyond the twelve-mile ~ is not permitted.* | **off ~s** ◇ *The building is off ~s to the public.* ◇

She explained it was her room and it was off ~s. | **on a/the ~** ◇ *islands on the outer ~ of the continent* | **outside a/the ~s** ◇ *lonely stretch of highway outside the city ~s* | **over a/the ~** ◇ *He'd been drinking and was well over the legal ~.* | **up to a/the ~** ◇ *You can buy cigarettes up to a ~ of 200 per person.* | **within a/the ~** ◇ *They did well within the ~s of their knowledge.* ◇ *There was no school within a ~ of ten miles.* | **within ~s** ◇ *The children can do what they like, within ~s.* | **without ~** ◇ *Banks may import currency without ~.* | **~ on** ◇ *There's a ~ on the number of tickets you can buy.* | **~ to** ◇ *There's a ~ to what we can do to help.*

limit *verb*

ADV. **drastically, greatly, seriously, severely, sharply, significantly, strictly, substantially** | **effectively** ◇ *These regulations effectively ~ our available strategic choices.*
VERB + LIMIT **attempt to, seek to, take steps to, try to, work to** ◇ *They are working to ~ oil drilling in the Arctic National Wildlife Refuge.* | **be designed to** ◇ *The change in the law was designed to ~ the scope for corruption.* | **agree to** | **serve to, tend to** ◇ *Rigid job descriptions can serve to ~ productivity.* | **refuse to** ◇ *As a scientist I refuse to ~ myself to these barriers.*
PREP. **to** ◇ *The teaching of history should not be ~ed to dates and figures.*

limitation *noun*

1 limiting of sth

ADJ. **fundamental, important, major, serious, severe, significant, strict** | **damage** (*esp. BrE*) ◇ *an exercise in damage ~* | **arms** ◇ *talks on arms ~* | **budget, budgetary, financial, payment, resource** (*esp. AmE*) | **distance, space** ◇ *Because of space ~s, I can only discuss the first and second points here.* | **self-imposed** ◇ *This is a deliberate self-imposed ~.* | **potential** ◇ *another potential ~ of the study*
VERB + LIMITATION **impose, place, put on** ◇ *We've put some ~s on who and where they can purchase these.* | **remove** | **accept** ◇ *a ~ of your personal freedom*
PREP. **~ on** ◇ *~s on one's freedom of action* | **~ to** ◇ *There should be no ~s to progress in the talks.*

2 limitations sth that sb cannot do

ADJ. **fundamental, important, major, serious, severe, significant, strict** | **inherent, intrinsic, natural** ◇ *Our rational thinking has natural ~s.* | **human** ◇ *human potential and human ~s* | **obvious** ◇ *the obvious ~s of the technology* | **computational, design, physical, practical, technical, technological** | **methodological** ◇ *the methodological ~s of his research*
VERB + LIMITATIONS **have** ◇ *She has serious ~s as a mother.* | **circumvent, exceed, overcome, transcend** ◇ *At times his technique seems to transcend the ~s of the piano.* | **acknowledge, know, realize, recognize, understand** ◇ *Please don't ask me to sing—I know my ~s!* | **expose, highlight, point out, reflect, reveal, show** ◇ *The team's technical ~s were exposed by the Italians.* | **demonstrate, illustrate** ◇ *Our findings illustrate the ~s of this treatment.* | **identify** ◇ *Several ~s were identified in this study.* | **accept** ◇ *You just have to accept your ~s.* | **address** ◇ *Further research should address these ~s.* | **face** ◇ *We face considerable ~s on our capacity to assess and analyze this.*
PREP. **despite sb's/sth's ~** ◇ *It's a useful book despite its ~s.*

limited *adj.*

VERBS **appear, be, seem** | **become** | **remain** | **keep sth** ◇ *She kept the plans carefully ~ to a circle of a few trusted friends.*
ADV. **extremely, fairly, very, etc.** | **decidedly, distinctly, highly, seriously, severely, sharply, strictly** ◇ *Places are strictly ~, so you should apply as soon as possible.* | **increasingly** | **a little, slightly, etc.** | **comparatively, relatively** | **apparently** | **inevitably, necessarily** | **inherently** ◇ *This research is inherently ~ in its scope.* | **admittedly** ◇ *the books in this admittedly ~ sample* |

geographically, socially ◇ *The role that women could play was socially ~.*
PREP. **in** ◇ *We're really ~ in what we can do these days.* | **to** ◇ *The number of passengers is ~ to fifteen.*

limousine (*also informal* limo) *noun*

ADJ. **big, long** | **black, white** | **gleaming** | **stretch** | **chauffeur-driven** (*esp. BrE*), **chauffeured** (*esp. AmE*) | **waiting** ◇ *They walked back to the waiting ~.* | **airport** (*esp. AmE*) | **presidential**

limp *noun*

ADJ. **noticeable, pronounced** | **slight**
VERB + LIMP **have, walk with** | **give sb, leave sb with** ◇ *The accident had left him with a slight ~.*

limp *verb*

ADV. **badly** ◇ *He had hurt his leg and was ~ing badly.* | **a little, slightly, etc.** | **along, away, back, off, out** ◇ *He ~ed away from his car.* | **slowly** ◇ *She ~ed slowly to the door.*

limp *adj.*

VERBS **be, fall, feel, hang, lie, look** ◇ *His arm hung ~ at his side.* ◇ *Her hair looked ~ and lifeless.* | **become, go, grow** ◇ *Her body suddenly went ~.*
ADV. **very** | **completely** | **rather**

line *noun*

1 long thin mark on the surface of sth

ADJ. **long** | **short** | **thick** | **fine, thin** | **faint** ◇ *a faint white ~* | **direct, straight** | **curved, jagged, wavy, zigzag** | **diagonal, horizontal, parallel, perpendicular, vertical** | **continuous, solid, unbroken** | **broken, dashed** (*AmE*), **dotted** ◇ *Sign on the dotted ~.* | **finish** (*AmE*), **finishing** (*BrE*), **starting** (*all sports*) | **free-throw** (*AmE*), **goal** (*both sports*) ◇ *The ball bounced off the crossbar and fell behind the goal ~.* | **contour** | **boundary, state** (*AmE*) ◇ *the boundary ~ between two countries* ◇ *His family lived across the state ~ in West Virginia.* | **centre/center** ◇ *She crossed the centre/center ~ and hit an oncoming truck.*
VERB + LINE **draw, mark**
LINE + VERB **run** | **divide sth, separate sth** | **connect sth** ◇ *The pencil ~ connects one box to another.* | **correspond to sth, denote sth, depict sth, indicate sth, mark sth, represent sth, show sth** ◇ *Horizontal ~s indicate the time spent executing the program.*
PREP. **in a ~** ◇ *Walk in a straight ~.*
PHRASES **a ~ of latitude, a ~ of longitude**

2 row of people, things, words on a page, etc.

ADJ. **long, short** | **new** | **continuous**
VERB + LINE **form**
PREP. **in a/the ~** ◇ *The soldiers stood in a ~.* | **on a/the ~** ◇ *Start each paragraph on a new ~.*

3 (*AmE*) **people, etc. waiting to do sth** → See also QUEUE

ADJ. **long, short** | **checkout, lunch** ◇ *supermarket checkout ~s* ◇ *The lunch ~ was long as usual.*
VERB + LINE **form**
PREP. **in ~** ◇ *You'll have to wait in ~ like everybody else.*

4 telephone, electricity, gas, etc.

ADJ. **direct, trunk** | **power, transmission, utility** (*AmE*) | **sewer** (*AmE*) | **fuel, gas** (*both AmE*) ◇ *There were two fuel ~s coming into the engine.* | **phone, telephone** | **DSL** | **fax** | **outside, party, private** ◇ *What do I dial for an outside ~?*
VERB + LINE **hold** ◇ *Hold the ~ (= Don't put the receiver down), please.*
LINE + VERB **be busy** (*AmE*), **be engaged** (*BrE*) | **be dead, go dead**
PREP. **down the ~** ◇ *He kept shouting down the ~ at me.* | **on the ~** ◇ *It's your mother on the ~ (= on the telephone).* | **on ~** (*usually **online***) (= connected to a computer system)

5 transport/transportation

ADJ. **rail** (*AmE*), **railway** (*BrE*), **train** | **subway** (*AmE*), **underground** (*esp. BrE*) | **main** | **branch** (*esp. BrE*), **commuter, trunk** ◇ *The branch ~ is threatened with closure.*
VERB + LINE **take** ◇ *Take the green ~ and change at the first stop.*
PREP. **on a/the ~** ◇ *We live on the Northern Line.* (*BrE*)
PHRASES **the end of the ~**

6 (*usually* **lines**) **words spoken by an actor in a play**

VERB + LINES **learn, practise/practice** | **recite, say** | **forget** | **flub** (*AmE*), **fluff** (*esp. BrE*), **mess up** (*esp. AmE*) | **miss**

7 on the skin

ADJ. **worry** | **deep** ◇ *Deep ~s ran from her nose to her mouth.* | **faint** ◇ *I saw the faint ~s of concern etched into her brow.*
VERB + LINE **have** ◇ *He has ~s on his forehead.*
LINE + VERB **run** | **appear** ◇ *Deep worry ~s had appeared on her forehead.*

8 way of doing or thinking about sth

ADJ. **broad** ◇ *The broad ~s of company policy are already laid down.* | **firm, hard, strong, tough** | **official, party, political**
VERB + LINE **adopt, follow, pursue, take** | **fall into** ◇ *The actions of investors do not always fall into ~ with financial theory.* | **bring sb/sth into** ◇ *The other members of the board must be brought into ~.*
PREP. **in ~ with** (= in agreement with), **out of ~ with** (= not in agreement with) ◇ *out of ~ with party policies* | **~ on** ◇ *the official ~ on food safety*
PHRASES **a ~ of argument, a ~ of reasoning** ◇ *There's a problem with this ~ of reasoning.* | **a ~ of attack** ◇ *Our approach involves two main ~s of attack.* | **a ~ of enquiry/inquiry, a ~ of investigation, a ~ of questioning** | **a ~ of thought** ◇ *This ~ of thought perturbs me.* | **a ~ of evidence** (*esp. AmE*) ◇ *multiple ~s of evidence all leading to the same conclusion*

9 place where an army is fighting

ADJ. **battle, defensive, firing, front, offensive** (*AmE*) ◇ *The middle managers were in the firing ~ of job cuts.* (*figurative*)
PHRASES **behind enemy ~s** | **in the front ~, on the front ~** | **~ of defence/defense** ◇ *We know that intelligence is our first ~ of defence/defense against terrorism.*

lined *adj.*

1 of skin

VERBS **be**
ADV. **deeply, heavily** ◇ *Her deeply ~ face was creased into a smile.*

2 of clothes, etc.

VERBS **be**
ADV. **fully** ◇ *The coat is fully ~.*
PREP. **with** ◇ *The case was ~ with black velvet.*

linen *noun*

1 fabric

ADJ. **fine, pure** ◇ *a fine ~ shirt* | **coarse** | **soft** | **embroidered** | **plain**
VERB + LINEN **weave (sth from)**

2 sheets, tablecloths, underwear, etc.

ADJ. **clean, fresh** | **dirty, soiled** | **crisp, starched** | **bed, table** | **household**
VERB + LINEN **change** ◇ *We change the bed ~ once a week.* | **wash**
LINEN + NOUN **basket** (*BrE*), **closet** (*AmE*), **cupboard** (*BrE*)

liner *noun*

ADJ. **luxury** | **ocean, ocean-going** (*esp. BrE*), **transatlantic** | **cruise, passenger** ◇ *a job aboard a luxury cruise ~*

linger *verb*

ADV. **long** | **still** | **forever** ◇ *It will ~ forever in the minds of many people.* | **on** ◇ *The feelings of hurt and resentment ~ed on for years.*

linguistics *noun*

ADJ. **contemporary, modern** | **applied, theoretical** | **cognitive, computational, contrastive, descriptive, generative, historical, structural**
→ Note at SUBJECT (for verbs and nouns)

link *noun*

1 connection

ADJ. **close, tight** | **inextricable, strong** | **tenuous, weak** | **clear, definite, obvious** | **possible, potential** ◇ *Scientists have established possible ~s between cancer and diet.* | **alleged** ◇ *her alleged ~s to a violent separatist group.* | **critical, crucial, essential, important, key, significant, vital** ◇ *Social workers provide a vital ~ between hospital and community.* | **common** ◇ *The common ~ between the three artists is their age.* | **formal, informal** | **direct, indirect** | **historical, long-standing** (*esp. BrE*) | **connecting** | **causal** ◇ *The report failed to prove a causal ~ between violence on screen and in real life.* | **conceptual** ◇ *This provided a key conceptual ~ with earlier theory.* | **symbolic** | **missing** ◇ *the missing ~ in the search for the causes of cancer* | **tangible** ◇ *a tangible ~ with the past* | **psychic, telepathic** ◇ *They share a telepathic ~.* | **business** (*esp. BrE*), **commercial, communication, cultural, diplomatic** (*esp. BrE*) (usually *diplomatic ties* in *BrE* and *AmE*), **economic, financial, military, political, professional, sporting** (*esp. BrE*), **trade** (*esp. BrE*), **etc.** | **family, genetic** | **air** (*esp. BrE*), **rail, railway** (*BrE*), **road** (*esp. BrE*), **transport** (*BrE*), **transportation** (*AmE*)
VERB + LINK **have** | **build, create, develop, establish, forge, form, foster** (*esp. BrE*), **make** ◇ *The college is anxious to build ~s with local industries.* | **provide** | **maintain, preserve** | **strengthen** | **demonstrate, highlight, show** ◇ *research demonstrating the ~s between teaching standards and student performance* | **discover, find, identify, reveal, uncover** ◇ *No ~s have been found between the two cases.* | **examine, explore, investigate** ◇ *Her work explores the ~s between violence and gender relations.* | **indicate, suggest** ◇ *The study suggests a strong ~ between workplace culture and a business's financial performance.* | **prove** ◇ *Studies haven't proven a ~ between sugar and hyperactivity.* | **recognize** | **deny** ◇ *The author denies the ~ between capitalism and fascism.* | **weaken** | **break, cut, sever** ◇ *She has severed her last ~s with her family.*
LINK + VERB **connect sth** | **exist** ◇ *A strong ~ exists between music and the visual arts.*
LINK + NOUN **road** (*BrE*)
PREP. **~ across** ◇ *trade ~s across the border* | **~ between** ◇ *The statistics show a clear ~ between social class and crime.* | **~ in** ◇ *The sales manager is regarded as the weakest ~ in the chain.* | **~ into** (*esp. AmE*) ◇ *ER & C has strong ~s into our company and into the industry.* | **~ to** ◇ *There is no ~ to an increase in cases of the disease.* | **~ with** ◇ *the city's traditional ~ with opera*

2 electrical connection

ADJ. **audio, video** | **radio, satellite, telephone** | **Internet, network** | **modem, wireless** | **fast, high-speed** | **data, digital, email**
VERB + LINK **have** | **establish** | **lose** | **provide**
PREP. **via a/the ~** ◇ *a race transmitted via a satellite ~* | **~ to** ◇ *The driver has a radio ~ to base.* | **~ via** ◇ *We're trying to establish a ~ via satellite.*

3 to a web page

ADJ. **embedded, hypertext, Internet, navigation, text, Web, website** | **bad, broken** | **related, relevant, useful** ◇ *You'll find some useful ~s on the first couple of pages.*
VERB + LINK **have** ◇ *The page has ~s to relevant websites.* | **add, build, create** | **click, click on** | **follow** | **post, send** ◇ *I'll send you the ~ by email.* | **check, update** ◇ *The program checks ~s to all pages on this and external sites.* | **remove** | **fix**
LINK + VERB **lead to sth, point to sth** | **work**
PREP. **~ to** ◇ *a ~ to my website*

link *verb* (often **be linked**)

ADV. **closely, intimately** | **firmly, strongly, tightly** | **indirectly, loosely** | **directly, explicitly, specifically** ◇ *Diseases that can be directly ~ed to pollution.* | **indissolubly** (*formal*), **inextricably, inseparably, integrally** ◇ *Poverty and crime are inextricably ~ed.* | **clearly, obviously** | **necessarily** | **intrinsically** | **intricately** ◇ *The problems of the economy are intricately ~ed to other social issues.* | **causally** | **consistently** ◇ *Unemployment is consistently ~ed with a variety of negative health effects.* | **physically** | **genetically, historically, thematically** ◇ *diseases that might be genetically ~ed* ◇ *The stories are ~ed thematically by a number of recurring images.* | **electronically** ◇ *They started electronically ~ing these systems via high-speed networks.* | **romantically** ◇ *She has never been romantically ~ed with anyone.* | **in some way, somehow** ◇ *I could not help feeling that these factors were somehow ~ed.* | **forever** ◇ *Christmas will be forever ~ed to memories of Sam's death.* | **together, up** ◇ *The two spacecraft will ~ up in orbit.*
PREP. **into** ◇ *The computers are ~ed into a network.* | **to** ◇ *Scientists have ~ed the illness to the use of pesticides.* | **with** ◇ *the road that ~s Cairo with Alexandria*

lion *noun*

... OF LIONS **pride**
LION + VERB **growl, roar** | **attack sb, maul sb** | **catch sth, chase sth, hunt sth, stalk sth** | **kill sb/sth** | **eat sb/sth** | **prowl, roam**
LION + NOUN **cub** | **tamer** | **hunt**

lip *noun*

ADJ. **top, upper** | **bottom, lower** | **chapped, cracked, dry, parched** ◇ *She licked her parched ~s.* | **moist** | **fleshy, full, thick** | **thin** | **kissable, luscious, pouty** ◇ *She has full, pouty ~s.* | **fat** (= swollen) ◇ *She had a fat ~ and a black eye.* | **split** ◇ *He has a split ~ and his eye is swelling.* | **cleft** ◇ *babies born with a cleft ~*
VERB + LIP **bite, chew** ◇ *He bit his ~ nervously, trying not to cry.* | **press together, purse** ◇ *She pursed her ~s in disapproval.* | **part** ◇ *He parted his ~s to say something.* | **pout, pucker** | **curl** ◇ *Dan curled his ~ in disgust.* | **lick, smack** ◇ *He licked his ~s hungrily.* | **moisten, wet** ◇ *He nervously moistened his ~s with his tongue.* | **wipe** ◇ *She wiped her ~s with the back of her hand.* | **kiss** ◇ *She smiled and then kissed his ~s.*
LIP + VERB **move, part** ◇ *Her ~s parted with a cry of fear.* | **meet** ◇ *Their ~s met and the kiss was soft.* | **quiver, tremble** | **quirk** (*AmE*), **twitch** ◇ *He raised his eyebrow, and his ~s quirked.* ◇ *Renée's ~s twitched with amusement.* | **curl, curve** ◇ *His ~s curled contemptuously.* ◇ *His ~s curved into a smile.* | **pout** ◇ *The firm ~s pouted in a sulk.* | **purse, tighten** ◇ *Her ~s pursed in amusement.* | **protrude** | **brush sth, graze sth** ◇ *His ~s brushed her cheek.*
PREP. **around your ~, round your ~** (*esp. BrE*) ◇ *He ran his tongue around his ~s.* | **between your ~** ◇ *a cigarette between his ~s* | **on your ~** ◇ *There was a smile on her ~s.*

lipstick *noun*

... OF LIPSTICK **dab** ◇ *She put on a quick dab of ~ and rushed out.*
VERB + LIPSTICK **have on, wear** | **apply, put on** | **reapply, touch up** ◇ *She touched up her ~ in the mirror.* | **remove, take off, wipe off** | **smear, smudge**
LIPSTICK + VERB **smear, smudge** ◇ *Her ~ had smudged and she looked terrible.*

liquid *noun*

ADJ. **thick, viscous** | **thin** | **clear** | **colourless/colorless** | **cloudy** | **flammable** | **volatile**
... OF LIQUID **drop, pool, puddle** | **bottle, cup, glass**
VERB + LIQUID **empty, pour** ◇ *Empty the ~ into a large bowl.* | **spill** | **drain, drain off** (*esp. BrE*), **strain, strain off** (*esp. BrE*) ◇ *Drain (off) the ~ from the meat into a cup.* | **discard** ◇

Strain the fruit through a sieve, discarding the ~. | **reserve** ◇ *Drain the octopus and reserve the cooking ~.* | **bring to the boil** | **reduce** ◇ *Reduce the ~ by boiling for two minutes.* | **absorb, soak up** | **drink, sip, swallow**
LIQUID + VERB **drip, flow, ooze, pour, seep, trickle** ◇ *The cold ~ trickled down her face.*

liquidation *noun*

ADJ. **compulsory** (*BrE*), **forced** (*AmE*), **voluntary**
VERB + LIQUIDATION **be forced into, be placed in** (*BrE*), **be put into** (*BrE*), **go into** (*esp. BrE*) ◇ *The company may be forced into ~.*
PREP. **in ~** ◇ *a company in ~*

liquor *noun* (*esp. AmE*)

ADJ. **alcoholic** (*BrE*), **hard, intoxicating** (*BrE*), **strong** ◇ *I don't drink hard ~ any more.* ◇ *It is an offence to sell intoxicating ~ to anyone under the age of 18.* | **corn, malt** (*both AmE*)
VERB + LIQUOR **consume, drink** | **pour** (*AmE*) | **sell, serve** | **handle, hold** (= drink without getting drunk) (*both AmE*) ◇ *He can't hold his ~.*
LIQUOR + NOUN **bottle** (*AmE*) | **cabinet** (*AmE*) | **company, distributor, merchant, store, wholesaler** (*all AmE*) | **laws, license** (*AmE*)

list *noun*

ADJ. **long, short** | **complete, comprehensive, detailed, exhaustive, extensive, full** ◇ *We are compiling a full ~ of all local businesses.* | **endless** ◇ *the endless ~ of excuses of why he could never make his appointments* | **impressive** ◇ *The show always featured an impressive ~ of guest stars.* | **alphabetical** | **waiting** ◇ *We're on the waiting ~ for membership of the golf club.* | **membership** ◇ *the membership ~ of the Sierra Club* | **grocery** (*AmE*), **shopping** | **wine** ◇ *a restaurant with excellent food and an outstanding wine ~* | **mailing** | **reading** ◇ *For further information, see the reading ~ at the end of the chapter.* | **best-seller** ◇ *It was on the New York Times best-seller ~ for 25 weeks.* | **priority** | **task** (*AmE*), **to-do** ◇ *It's high on her to-do ~.* | **wish** ◇ *I created a wish ~ of what I wanted in a new job.* | **guest** | **cast** ◇ *The play has an impressive cast ~.*
VERB + LIST **assemble, compile, create, draw up, make, put together** | **update** | **narrow** (*esp. BrE*), **narrow down** ◇ *They have narrowed their ~ of suspects to six.* | **publish, release** | **post** ◇ *The restaurant is required to post a ~ of all the prices.* | **put sth on** ◇ *Did you put bread on the shopping ~?* | **join** ◇ *His name will likely join the ~ of other boardroom casualties.* | **scan** ◇ *Her teacher scanned the ~ of students' names.* | **head, top** ◇ *Job troubles top the ~ of stress factors for Americans today.*
LIST + VERB **comprise sth, consist of sth, contain sth, include sth** ◇ *a ~ comprising all the paintings in the gallery* | **grow** ◇ *By July the ~ had grown to approximately 350 contributors.* | **continue, go on** ◇ *Inadequate space, lack of privacy, unpleasant lighting… the ~ goes on.*
PREP. **in a/the ~** ◇ *Names of past members are not included in the ~.* | **on a/the ~** ◇ *I can't see your name on the ~.* | **~ for** ◇ *We acquired a waiting ~ for works by these artists.* | **~ of** ◇ *a ~ of 200 names*
PHRASES **the bottom of a ~, the top of a ~** ◇ *Variety is near the top of many people's ~ of job requirements.* | **high on a ~** ◇ *Safety is high on our ~ of priorities.* | **a ~ of priorities** ◇ *Going to the bank is top of my ~ of priorities today.*

listen *verb*

ADV. **actively, attentively, carefully, closely, hard, intently** ◇ *Now, ~ very carefully to what she says.* | **half-heartedly, idly, passively** ◇ *He ~ed idly to the radio chatter.* | **half** ◇ *Lucy was only half ~ing to their conversation.* | **barely, hardly** ◇ *He was hardly ~ing, for he had too much on his mind.* | **calmly, patiently** | **politely, respectfully** ◇ *The others ~ed respectfully to her words.* | **sympathetically** ◇ *We ~ed politely to his stories.* | **avidly, eagerly, raptly, with interest** ◇ *The guests were ~ing with great interest.* | **in silence, quietly, silently** ◇

They ~ed to the announcement in silence. | **anxiously** | **in awe**
VERB + LISTEN **will, would** ◇ *Nobody will ~ to me!* ◇ *I tried to warn her, but she wouldn't ~.* | **not bother to** ◇ *I didn't even bother to ~ to his reply.* | **need to, should** ◇ *You need to ~ to me!* | **be prepared to, be willing to** | **refuse to** ◇ *He refused to ~ to her explanation.*
PREP. **for** ◇ *We ~ed anxiously for the sound of footsteps.* | **to** ◇ *I was ~ing to the radio.*
PHRASES **~ with one ear** (*AmE*) ◇ *I ~ed with one ear to the conversation at the next table.*

listener *noun*

ADJ. **attentive, good, great, sympathetic** | **avid, eager** | **casual** | **music, radio**
PREP. **~ of** ◇ *~s of classical music* | **~ to** ◇ *He was an avid ~ to the radio.*

liter (*AmE*) (*BrE* litre) *noun* → Note at MEASURE

literacy *noun*

ADJ. **basic** ◇ *All the children are tested in basic ~.* | **adult** | **mass, universal** | **computer, information** (*AmE*) | **cultural, financial, media, science, technological** (*all esp. AmE*) ◇ *a movement to promote financial ~ among women* | **critical** (*AmE*) ◇ *Critical ~ questions the basic assumptions of our society.*
VERB + LITERACY **achieve, acquire** ◇ *different methods for acquiring ~* | **develop, improve, increase, promote, teach**
LITERACY + NOUN **campaign, initiative** (*AmE*), **programme/program** | **curriculum** (*AmE*) | **education, instruction** (*both esp. AmE*) | **class, course** | **test** | **acquisition, development** (*both esp. AmE*) | **skills** | **level, rate**

literate *adj.*

VERBS **be** | **become**
ADV. **extremely, fairly, very, etc.** | **highly** ◇ *Only highly ~ people are capable of discussing these subjects.* | **fully** ◇ *They are the first fully ~ generation in the country.* | **barely** ◇ *He was uneducated and barely ~.* | **economically, musically, politically, scientifically, technologically, etc.**
PREP. **in** ◇ *Both parents were ~ in English.*

literature *noun*

1 written works of art

ADJ. **classical, contemporary, modern** | **popular** | **great** | **African American, Russian, etc.** ◇ *He has a degree in English Literature.* | **19th-century, 20th-century, etc.** | **feminist, gay, lesbian**
…OF LITERATURE **piece, work**
VERB + LITERATURE **read, study, teach** | **publish** | **write** ◇ *Canadian ~ written over the past thirty years*

2 writing on a particular subject

ADJ. **extensive, vast, voluminous** | **current, existing, recent** ◇ *the current ~ in science and natural history* | **published** ◇ *the published ~ on the subject* | **growing** ◇ *There is a growing ~ on technological changes in developing countries.* | **historical, medical, scientific, etc.** | **professional** (*esp. AmE*), **scholarly** ◇ *the scholarly ~ on the rise of the environmental movement* | **promotional, sales**
…OF LITERATURE **body** ◇ *the growing body of ~ on development issues*
PREP. **~ about** ◇ *I picked up some ~ about pensions.* | **~ concerning** ◇ *the ~ concerning the modernization of trade unions* | **~ on** ◇ *There's an extensive ~ on the subject.* | **~ regarding** ◇ *the ~ regarding effectiveness and cost*

litigation *noun*

ADJ. **costly, expensive** | **endless, lengthy, protracted** | **complex** | **potential, threatened** | **pending, ongoing** | **subsequent** | **civil, commercial, criminal** | **federal** | **private** | **class-action** (*AmE*) ◇ *the class-action ~ brought by the families of the victims* | **liability** (*esp. AmE*), **malpractice, tort** (*AmE*) ◇ *the fear of medical malpractice ~* | **employment, medical**

VERB + LITIGATION **bring, conduct** (*BrE*), **file** (*esp. AmE*), **initiate, pursue** ◊ *the right to conduct ~* ◊ *The alleged victims have elected to pursue ~.* | **engage in** | **become involved in, get involved in** | **be engaged in, be involved in** | **threaten** | **end, settle** | **avoid** ◊ *The payment was made to avoid threatened ~.*

LITIGATION + NOUN **costs, expenses** | **settlement** (*esp. AmE*) | **finance** (*AmE*)

PREP. **~ against** ◊ *He engaged in endless ~ against the media.* | **~ between** ◊ *~ between private parties* | **~ over** ◊ *~ over water rights*

PHRASES **the conduct of ~** (*esp. BrE*) ◊ *the defendant's conduct of the ~* | **the cost of ~** | **the risk of ~, the threat of ~**

litre (*BrE*) (*AmE* **liter**) *noun* → Note at MEASURE

litter *noun*

... OF LITTER **pile**

VERB + LITTER **drop, leave** ◊ *Please do not leave ~ after your picnic.* | **clean up, clear up, pick up**

LITTER + VERB **be strewn** ◊ *Litter was strewn all over the field.*

LITTER + NOUN **basket, bin** (*BrE*) | **lout** (*BrE*) (**litterbug** in *AmE*) ◊ *The local council has pledged to clamp down on ~ louts.*

live *verb*

1 in a place

ADV. **alone** | **together** ◊ *She disapproves of unmarried couples living together.* | **apart, separately** ◊ *The two sisters have ~d apart for two years.* ◊ *children living separately from their parents* | **independently** ◊ *older people still living independently* | **communally** | **abroad** | **permanently** ◊ *I'm not going to ~ here permanently.*

VERB + LIVE **come to, go to** ◊ *We went to ~ in Canada when I was three.*

PREP. **among** ◊ *They ~d among the people of this remote island.* | **at** ◊ *She's ~d at this same address for four years.* | **in** ◊ *He ~s in Cape Town.* | **near** ◊ *She ~s quite near here.* | **with** ◊ *I still ~ with my parents.*

PHRASES **~ at home** ◊ *He's still living at home (= with his parents).* | **a place to ~** ◊ *young couples looking for a place to ~*

2 be alive

ADV. **longer** ◊ *Women ~ longer than men in general.* | **forever** ◊ *Who wants to ~ forever? I don't.* | **happily (ever after)** ◊ *All she wanted was to get married and ~ happily ever after.* | **comfortably, well** ◊ *Most of the people ~ very well, with nice houses and plenty to eat.* ◊ *They'll have enough money to ~ comfortably.* | **fully** ◊ *I did want to ~ more fully.* | **dangerously** ◊ *Tonight she felt like living dangerously.* | **amicably, harmoniously, peaceably, peacefully** ◊ *the need to ~ as harmoniously as possible with everyone else* | **quietly** ◊ *He was living quietly with his family.* | **cheaply** ◊ *You can ~ there quite cheaply.* | **frugally, modestly** ◊ *They ~d frugally off a diet of beans and lentils.* | **vicariously** ◊ *She tried to ~ vicariously through her children.*

PREP. **in** ◊ *Many of the people ~ in poverty and misery.* | **through** ◊ *She ~d through two world wars.* | **with** ◊ *people living with AIDS* | **without** ◊ *I absolutely could not ~ without my cell phone!*

PHRASES **(for) as long as you ~** ◊ *I shall remember this day for as long as I ~.* | **learn to ~ with sth** ◊ *people who are learning to ~ with disability* | **~ a life of sth** ◊ *He's now living a life of luxury in Australia.* | **~ to (be) 80, 90, etc., ~ to the age of 80, 90, etc.** ◊ *She ~d to the age of 95.* | **the world we ~ in** ◊ *teaching children about the world we ~ in*

live *adj., adv.*

VERBS **appear, be, perform, play, sing** ◊ *He appeared ~ on the Song and Dance Show.* ◊ *Is the show ~ or recorded?* ◊ *The band have never played this song ~ before.* | **film** ◊ *The show was filmed ~ at the Arena.* | **report, speak, talk** ◊ *We'll be reporting ~ from Beijing.* ◊ *Later we'll talk ~ with the former New York police commissioner.* | **watch (sth)** ◊ *I can watch the games ~ on TV.* | **come to sb, go out** ◊ *This concert comes to you ~ from Carnegie Hall.* ◊ *In those days the broadcasts all went out ~.* | **air** ◊ *The show will air ~ on June*

10. | **be broadcast, be carried** (*AmE*), **be screened** (*BrE*), **be shown, be televised, be transmitted** ◊ *The trial was carried ~ on a Chicago radio station.* ◊ *The game will be televised ~ this evening.* | **be recorded** ◊ *The CD was recorded ~ at a concert given last year.*

PHRASES **go ~** ◊ *The new website is expected to go ~ in October.*

livelihood *noun*

VERB + LIVELIHOOD **earn, gain** | **provide** ◊ *Fishing provides a ~ for many people.* | **protect, secure** ◊ *an insurance policy to secure your ~ in old age* | **affect, threaten** ◊ *The new law threatens the ~ of thousands of farmers.* | **destroy, take away** | **lose**

LIVELIHOOD + VERB **depend on sth** ◊ *people whose ~ depends on the forest*

PHRASES **a means of ~, a source of ~** ◊ *The boat was his main source of ~.*

liver *noun*

1 organ in the body

ADJ. **diseased, enlarged, fatty** | **healthy, normal** | **donor** ◊ *a nationwide appeal for a donor ~*

LIVER + NOUN **cancer, cirrhosis, damage, disease, dysfunction, failure, injury** | **cell, enzyme, tissue** | **function** | **biopsy, transplant, transplantation**

PREP. **in the ~** ◊ *enzymes in the ~* | **of the ~** ◊ *cirrhosis of the ~* | **to the ~** ◊ *bile acids returning to the ~*

2 liver of an animal as food

ADJ. **chopped** | **chicken, goose, pork, etc.** | **calf's, lamb's, etc.**

LIVER + NOUN **pâté**
→ Special page at FOOD

living *noun*

ADJ. **comfortable, decent, good, honest** ◊ *He makes a good ~ as a builder.* | **meagre/meager** ◊ *She eked out a meagre/meager ~ as an artist's model.*

VERB + LIVING **earn, make** ◊ *Her dream was to earn her ~ as a singer.* | **eke out, scrape** (*esp. BrE*), **scrape together** (*esp. BrE*), **scratch** ◊ *They were forced to scratch a ~ by selling things on the streets.* | **do sth for** ◊ *He asked what I did for a ~.* | **provide** ◊ *Ten acres provides a decent ~ for a rural family.*

load *noun*

ADJ. **heavy, light** ◊ *He has a heavy teaching ~ this year.* | **full** ◊ *The plane took off with a full ~.* | **maximum, peak** (*AmE*) ◊ *Maximum ~, including passengers, is 800 pounds.* ◊ *a peak ~ of about 11.5 GW* | **high** ◊ *Many companies are burdened by high debt ~s.*

VERB + LOAD **bear, carry, shoulder** | **haul** ◊ *They haul ~s of produce to market.* | **handle** ◊ *The airline simply couldn't handle the passenger ~.* | **lessen, lighten, reduce, share, spread** ◊ *We're trying to spread the ~ by employing more staff.* | **drop, dump, shed** (*BrE*) ◊ *A lorry has shed its ~ on the the A77 near Ballantrae.*

PREP. **under its, etc. ~** ◊ *The table creaked under its heavy ~.*

loaded *adj.*

1 carrying a load

VERBS **be**

ADV. **heavily** ◊ *a convoy of heavily ~ trucks* | **fully** ◊ *a fully ~ truck* | **lightly**

PREP. **with** ◊ *The van was ~ with crates of beer.*

2 biased

ADV. **heavily, very** ◊ *For me both were very ~ questions.* | **rather, slightly** | **culturally, emotionally, ideologically, politically, symbolically** ◊ *Try to avoid politically ~ terms like 'nation'.*

PREP. **against** ◊ *The odds were slightly ~ against us.* | **in favour/favor of** (*esp. BrE*) ◊ *The legislation is heavily ~ in favour/favor of employers.*

loaf noun

ADJ. **large, small** | **sliced** | **fresh, stale** | **crusty** (*esp. BrE*) | **brown, white, wholemeal** (*BrE*), etc. | **French**
VERB + LOAF **bake** | **cut, slice**
LOAF + NOUN **pan** (*AmE*), **tin** (*BrE*)
PHRASES **a ~ of bread**

loan noun

ADJ. **large, massive** | **small** | **long-term, short-term** | **high-interest, interest-free, low-interest, no-interest** (*AmE*) | **adjustable-rate** (*AmE*), **fixed-rate, variable-rate** | **guaranteed** (*AmE*), **secured, unsecured** ◇ *As it was an unsecured ~, their property was not at risk.* | **home-equity** (= in which your house is given as security for the money borrowed) (*AmE*) | **outstanding** ◇ *They used the inheritance to pay off their outstanding ~.* | **bad, non-performing** ◇ *a banking system riddled with bad ~s* | **business, consumer, personal** | **bank** | **bridge** (*AmE*), **bridging** (*BrE*), **temporary** | **home, mortgage** | **auto** (*AmE*), **car** | **student**
VERB + LOAN **apply for, ask for, request** | **arrange, get, obtain, raise** (*esp. BrE*), **take out** ◇ *She had to take out a ~ until she could sell her house.* | **give sb, grant sb, make sb, offer, provide** ◇ *My bank offered to make me a ~.* | **receive** | **pay back, pay off, repay** | **guarantee, secure, underwrite** ◇ *The banks will not agree to emergency funding unless the government will underwrite the ~.* | **consolidate** ◇ *If you have several student ~s, you can consolidate them into one lump sum.*
LOAN + VERB **total sth** ◇ *~s totalling/totaling a million euros*
LOAN + NOUN **application** | **agreement, arrangement** (*BrE*), **deal** (*BrE, sports*) ◇ *the terms of the ~ agreement with the bank* ◇ *The striker comes to the Premiership on an 18-month ~ deal from Roma.* | **interest, rate** | **guarantee** | **payment, repayment** ◇ *They were struggling to meet their monthly ~ repayments.* | **facility** (*esp. BrE*) ◇ *The bank provides personal ~ facilities at competitive rates.* | **period** (*esp. BrE*) ◇ *The book must be returned by the end of the ~ period.* | **officer** (*AmE*) ◇ *a ~ officer at a local mortgage company* | **shark** ◇ *He ran up massive debts borrowing from ~ sharks.*
PREP. **on ~** (**from**) ◇ *The paintings are on ~ from the Wallace Collection.* | **~ from** ◇ *a ~ from my brother*
PHRASES **security for a ~** ◇ *He had to use his house as security for the ~.*
→ Special page at BUSINESS

loathing noun

ADJ. **absolute, deep, intense** | **undisguised** | **mutual**
VERB + LOATHING **be filled with** ◇ *His face was filled with ~.* | **develop, feel, have**
PREP. **~ for** ◇ *She felt an intense ~ for her boss.* | **~ of** ◇ *a deep ~ of war*
PHRASES **fear and ~** ◇ *The incident has created an atmosphere of fear and ~ among the people.*

lobby noun group of people who try to influence politicians

ADJ. **powerful, strong** ◇ *a powerful anti-smoking ~* | **anti-abortion, anti-hunt, environmental, gun, industrial, nuclear, political,** etc.
VERB + LOBBY **form, organize**
LOBBY + NOUN **group, organization**
PREP. **~ against** ◇ *Many groups have together formed a ~ against cuts in education.* | **~ for** ◇ *Residents have organized a ~ for improved local facilities.*

lobby verb

ADV. **actively, aggressively, hard, heavily** | **successfully, unsuccessfully**
PREP. **against** ◇ *Head teachers have been ~ing hard against education cuts.* | **for** ◇ *The group successfully lobbied for changes in the law.* | **on behalf of** ◇ *The organization has been set up to ~ the government on behalf of all the people who have lost their pensions.*

locate verb

1 find the position of sb/sth

ADV. **accurately, correctly, precisely** ◇ *The machine can accurately ~ radioactive material.* | **quickly** | **easily**
VERB + LOCATE **be able to, be unable to, can** ◇ *We haven't yet been able to ~ a suitable site.* | **try to** | **fail to** | **be easy to** ◇ *Some stars are very easy to ~ with a telescope.* | **be difficult to** | **help (to)** ◇ *She took time to help me ~ research materials.*

2 be located be in a place

ADV. **centrally** ◇ *The hotel is centrally ~d between Dam Square and Central Station.* | **conveniently, ideally, strategically** | **primarily, typically** ◇ *Courtrooms are typically ~d in the interior of the building.* ◇ *Tribal lands are primarily ~d in remote rural regions.* | **physically** ◇ *Two people can meet in virtual reality even if physically ~d in different continents.* | **geographically** ◇ *The Web connects members regardless of where they are ~d geographically.* | **overseas** ◇ *The company has increased the share of jobs ~d overseas.*
PREP. **at, between, close to, in, near, on, outside, within,** etc. ◇ *The hotel is conveniently ~d within walking distance of the beach.*

location noun

ADJ. **exact, precise, specific** ◇ *We still do not know the precise ~ of the crash.* | **given** ◇ *The equipment allows sailors to read their geographical coordinates for any given ~.* | **geographic** (*esp. AmE*), **geographical** (*esp. BrE*), **physical** ◇ *Fees vary depending on geographic ~.* | **secret, undisclosed, unknown** | **convenient, ideal, suitable** | **central** | **remote** | **exotic** ◇ *the exotic ~s they filmed in*
VERB + LOCATION **show** ◇ *The map shows the exact ~ of the mine.* | **find, identify, pinpoint** ◇ *He couldn't pinpoint her exact ~ because of some kind of interference.* | **choose, select** ◇ *We selected these two ~s because they offer a range of services.*
PREP. **at/the ... ~** ◇ *The meeting is taking place at a secret ~.* | **on** ◇ *The movie is being made on ~ in India.*

lock noun

1 fastening device

ADJ. **combination, cylinder, deadbolt** (*esp. AmE*), **mortise, Yale™** (*BrE*) ◇ *The hotels replaced their mortise ~s on guest rooms with magnetic card readers.* | **electronic** | **safety** ◇ *Most cars are now fitted with child safety ~s on the back doors.* ◇ *safety ~s for handguns* | **gun** (*AmE*), **trigger** ◇ *trigger ~s for guns* | **bicycle, bike** (*informal*) | **door, window**
VERB + LOCK **fit** ◇ *We had new ~s fitted after the burglary.* | **break, force, pick** | **open, turn** ◇ *He turned the ~ and pushed the door open.* | **check** ◇ *She ran around the house, checking all the ~s*
PHRASES **insert the key in the ~, turn the key in the ~** | **under ~ and key** ◇ *Prisoners are kept under ~ and key 24 hours a day.*

2 small bunch of hair

ADJ. **stray** ◇ *She flicked a stray ~ of hair off her face.* | **flowing** ◇ *She had long flowing ~s and blue eyes.* | **blonde, chestnut, golden,** etc. | **curly** ◇ *He ran a hand through his curly brown ~s.*

lock verb

1 close with a lock

ADV. **carefully** ◇ *He carefully ~ed the door behind him.* | **automatically, electronically** ◇ *The door ~s automatically.*
VERB + LOCK **forget to**
PHRASES **be firmly ~ed, be securely ~ed** | **keep sth ~ed** ◇ *Keep your garage securely ~ed.*

2 put sb/sth inside sth that is locked

ADV. **away, in** ◇ *I was terrified they would ~ me in again.*
PREP. **in** ◇ *I ~ed myself in the bathroom.*
PHRASES **be safely ~ed, be securely ~ed** ◇ *All the valuables were safely ~ed away.*

STUDY PAGES

IDEAS INTO WORDS

Look at the entry for **idea**, sense 1 (plan/suggestion).

1   Look at the adjectives section (marked ADJ). Find adjectives you might
    use to express the following ideas. Sometimes more than one adjective
    is possible. You may want to use the pop-up definitions on the *Oxford
    Collocations Dictionary* CD-ROM to check the meaning of any words you
    don't know.

a   an idea that is helpful, rather than being negative or critical
b   an idea that is slightly crazy, in a good way
c   an idea that is completely crazy, in a bad way
d   an idea that has not been carefully thought out
e   an idea that seems very impressive but is not really very practical

2   Now look at the section marked VERB + IDEA. Find verbs that you might
    use to express the following ideas. Usually more than one verb is possible.

a   to find an idea
b   to suggest an idea
c   to suggest an idea in a very forceful way because you really want people to accept it
d   to think about an idea for a while before you decide whether or not it is a good idea
e   to talk about a number of different ideas before you decide which ideas are the best

3   Look at the section marked IDEA + VERB. Find verbs that you might use to
    express the following:

a   when you suddenly think of an idea
b   when ideas slowly develop in your mind
c   when ideas go through your mind
d   when an idea succeeds
e   when an idea does not develop into anything

4   Finally, look at the PHRASES section and find the expression that means
    the beginning of an idea.

USING A NOUN ENTRY

Adjectives

1 Match each of the adjectives on the left with a suitable noun from the facing column. Look at the entries for the **bold** nouns for help.

a bewildering	**ambition**
a biting	**array of** goods
a burning	**chance**
a convincing	**chasm**
driving	**rain**
a fighting	**sum** of money
a gaping	**win**
a staggering	**wind**

a shining	**defeat**
a crushing	**battle**
a haunting	**pain**
a nagging	**example**
a piercing	**scream**
a running	**statement**
a sprawling	**suburb**
a sweeping	**melody**

Quantifiers

Quantifiers are words used to talk about the amount of something, such as *a **drop** of water* or *a **piece** of information*.

2 Complete each sentence with a suitable quantifier. Look at the **bold** noun entries for help.

a There were just a few w_*isps*_ of **cloud** in the sky.

b The recent s_____ of **attacks** has made residents afraid to leave their homes.

c He is on medication to ease his frequent b_____ of **depression**.

d I just caught a brief s_____ of their **conversation** as I walked by their table.

e The constant s_____ of **traffic** past our house makes it difficult to cross the road.

f A p_____ of stray **dogs** was wandering around the abandoned plant.

g The statement was greeted with h_____ of **laughter**.

h A couple of c_____ of **garlic** will improve the taste of the sauce.

i He felt a p_____ of **guilt** for the way he had treated her.

j The new policy offers a g_____ of **hope** to small farmers.

Verb + ...

3 Cross out any verbs which do not normally collocate with the **bold** noun.

a He *got into/had/made* an **argument** with the waiter and was thrown out of the restaurant.

b He had to do two jobs to *clear/pay off/pay up* his **debts**.

c Someone *came up with/presented/put forward* the **suggestion** that we should have an auction.

d The scientists failed to *arrive at/decide/draw* any firm **conclusions** from the study.

e The company *agreed on/came to/struck* a **deal** with the union after lengthy negotiations.

f A **meeting** has been *arranged/programmed/scheduled* for next week.

g The supervisor refused to *accept/receive/shoulder* the **blame** for the accident.

h He *drummed/rattled/tapped* his **fingers** nervously on the desk as he spoke.

i We *set/took/went on* a **trip** to a nearby island on a fishing boat.

j I put up my hand to *shade/shelter/shield* my **eyes** from the sun.

... + verb

4   Complete the story with a suitable verb in each gap. Look at the **bold** noun entries for help.

I lay in bed, unable to sleep. The **wine** had f_____ freely at the party, and now my **head** was t_____ and my **stomach** was c_____ . Outside the **wind** h_____ and the **rain** l_____ against the window. My **nerve**s were o_____ e_____ as I remembered all the horror films I'd ever seen. Suddenly I heard the **key** t_____ in the front door. My **heart** began to h_____ in my chest as heavy **footsteps** e_____ on the stairs. My **mind** was ra_____, trying to think how I could save myself. The bedroom **door** c_____ open slowly, and as my **eyes** a_____ to the darkness I could make out a figure at the end of the bed. The man's **mouth** f_____ open when he saw me. It was the man who lives next door. I was in the wrong house!

... + noun

5   Choose a suitable word from the box on the right to complete each sentence. Look at the **bold** noun entry for help.

a   The hotel is located in a popular **beach** _resort_ .
b   In economy class you don't get enough **leg** _____.
c   The traffic was held up by a massive **protest** _____.
d   He was seriously injured in a **traffic** _____.
e   They're collecting money for **famine** _____.
f   The specimens were arranged in a **display** _____.
g   It's a small office with very little **shelf** _____.
h   She went through her in box deleting the **junk** _____.
i   The financial crisis was blamed for the recent **crime** _____.
j   He was working at the hospital on the **night** _____.

chances	room
boom	shift
accident	space
case	box
mail	gathering
stall	relief
aid	~~resort~~
rally	crash
hour	wave

Prepositions

6   The sentences below can be completed using just three different prepositions.
    Look at the **bold** noun entries to help you.

a   He was lying on the floor ____*in*____ **agony**.
b   Students who do not have a computer are _____ a **disadvantage**.
c   There is still **confusion** _____ the result of the vote.
d   I couldn't hear what she was saying _____ the **noise** of the crowd.
e   Please submit your requests _____ **writing** before Friday.
f   He died instantly when his bike hit a wall _____ **speed**.
g   She claims she killed him _____ **self-defence/self-defense**.
h   I'm not going out _____ this **rain**!
i   I saw him a couple of times _____ **the weekend**.
j   Her **skill** _____ negotiating makes her a valuable asset.

Phrases

7   Look at the phrases section in the entries for the **bold** nouns below to help
    you complete and match the heads and tails of the sentences.

a   Your tutor can give advice and __*lend*__ a sympathetic...
b   It was hilarious! I just couldn't _____ a straight...
c   As he looked out of the window, he _____ his...
d   I fell in love the first time I _____...
e   The kids worked so hard. They really _____ their...
f   If this report _____ into the wrong...
g   When I heard the news, I _____ sick to my...
h   They were so rude to me that I vowed never to _____...
i   You offended him! You must learn to _____ your...
j   She was so upset that she just _____ her...

stomach.

ear.

eyes on her.

face.

foot in the place again.

hands, we're in trouble.

head in her hands and cried.

hearts into the task.

mouth shut.

nose up against the glass.

USING A VERB ENTRY

Adverbs

1   In each of the following sentences one of the adverbs in *italics* is not a
common collocate of the verb in **bold**. Decide which it is and cross it out.
Use the entry for the **bold** verb to help you.

a   She **argued** *fiercely/heatedly/~~hotly~~* about her right to compensation.

b   They will *fiercely/heatedly/passionately* **defend** their rights.

c   He **grinned** *owlishly/sheepishly/wolfishly* at her.

d   He *blankly/categorically/flatly* **denies** that he has committed a crime.

e   His frugal lifestyle **contrasted** *brutally/markedly/starkly* with his wife's extravagance.

f   Her tragic story *brutally/markedly/starkly* **illustrates** how vulnerable children can be.

Verb + …

2   Complete each of these sentences with a verb phrase from the box. You may
need to change the form of the verb. Use the entries for the **bold** verbs to
help you.

be determined to   ~~be happy to~~   can afford to   fail to   hasten to   offer to   serve to   take steps to

a   I _was happy to_ **accept** the invitation to become patron of the charity.

b   The company was fined when it _____ **comply** with the regulations.

c   These unanswered questions _____ **highlight** the potential problems.

d   I _____ **add** that my knowledge of computers is pretty basic.

e   We must _____ **ensure** that such a disaster can never happen again.

f   The governor _____ **resign** when the affair became public.

g   She _____ **fight** for her rights.

h   Few patients _____ **pay** the full cost of treatment.

Prepositions

3   The following sentences can be completed using just three different prepositions.
Use the entries for the **bold** verbs to help you.

a   Unfortunately, the plan **backfired** ___ _on_ ___ me.

b   He had to **testify** _____ a colleague suspected of fraud.

c   I don't feel I can **comment** _____ their decision.

d   I think you must be **mistaking** me _____ someone else.

e   She was **treated** _____ sunstroke.

f   The prosecution lawyers have been trying to **prejudice** the jury _____ him.

g   He accused them of **plotting** _____ him.

h   We have **collaborated** _____ many projects over the years.

i   I would **advise** _____ drinking alcohol while taking this medicine.

j   National leaders **appealed** _____ calm.

Phrases

4 Match the two halves of these verb phrases. Then use the phrases to complete the sentences below. You may need to change the forms of the verbs. Use the entries for the **bold** verbs to help you.

~~drink~~	and pray
hire	and forget
forgive	~~and drive~~
hope	and turn
mix	and match
toss	and groan

a The message to drivers is simple: don't ____*drink and drive*____ .

b Managers have the power to _____workers.

c I spent all night _____, unable to sleep.

d You can _____ different patterns to create your own design.

e I was _____that she was safe and unhurt.

f After all he had done to her, she wasn't about to _____.

crack	for breath
grin	to a halt
dawn	from ear to ear
pause	bright and cold
brake	under the strain

g The car _____ outside the station.

h You need to get some rest before you _____.

i The next morning _____ .

j Katy was clearly pleased about something: she was _____ .

k Jack went on arguing, barely _____ .

Collocations of phrasal verbs

5 Complete the following story with words and phrases from the boxes. For each gap you will need to decide whether the missing word/phrase is an adverb, a verb or a preposition. You may need to change the forms of the verbs. Use the phrasal verbs sections of the **bold** verb entries to help you.

adverbs	verbs	prepositions
by chance	be forced to	from
completely	~~be left to~~	for
completely	try to	to
desperately		to
instantly		with
slowly		with

I had _*been left to*_ **fend for myself** in the desert, completely **cut off** _____ the rest of the world. The sun beat down and I was terribly thirsty. The water holes had **dried up** _____ and I _____ to **rely on** cacti _____ water. I _____ **hang on** _____ my sanity, **clinging** _____ to the hope that I would find my way out alive. I **pressed on** _____ my attempt to find water but was becoming weary. I kept walking and then _____ **stumbled across** an oasis. I _____ **burst into** loud cries of joy. There was water and trees that **blocked out** the sun _____ . I lay down in the shade and _____ **drifted off** _____ sleep. I **woke up** _____ a start and looked around me. The oasis was gone – it had been an illusion! All around me was desert and the sun was beginning to rise…

USING AN ADJECTIVE ENTRY

Verbs

1   Match each of the **bold** adjectives with a verb that can go before it, then match the combination with a suitable subject. Use the adjective entries to help you.

His mistake	emerged	**asleep.**	*I nearly fell asleep.*
His mistake	~~fell~~	**costly.**	_____
~~I nearly~~	grew	**damp.**	_____
The crowd	passed	**empty.**	_____
The driver	proved	**impatient.**	_____
The house	run	**parallel.**	_____
The house	smells	**unnoticed.**	_____
The roads	stood	**unscathed.**	_____

2   Complete each sentence with a suitable verb. Look at the entry for the **bold** adjective for help.

a   He d _rove_ me **crazy** with his constant talking.

b   She was h_____ **captive** by rebels for six months.

c   Several cars were s_____ **ablaze** by the rioters.

d   The unions were r_____ **powerless** by the new laws.

e   These shows are d_____ **unsuitable** for screening before 10 p.m.

f   The robbers b_____ the security guard **senseless.**

g   His classmates mostly r_____ him as **eccentric.**

h   The sound of a door banging j_____ me **awake.**

Adverbs

3   For each group, find an adverb in the box that collocates with all the adjectives in the group.

mutually	distinctly	fiercely	grossly	~~painfully~~	wildly

a _painfully_	b _____	c _____	d _____	e _____	f _____
aware	advantageous	competitive	different	enthusiastic	inaccurate
honest	beneficial	independent	odd	inaccurate	inadequate
shy	contradictory	loyal	uncomfortable	optimistic	offensive
slow	incompatible	protective	uneasy	popular	unfair

4   Match each **bold** adjective with a suitable adverb. Then use each combination to complete one of the sentences on the right.

blissfully	**absent**	a I'm not _unduly concerned_ by the latest figures.
conspicuously	**composed**	b She is _____ of her achievements.
eerily	**concerned**	c He seems _____ of the trouble he's caused.
justly	**familiar**	d The former chairman was _____ from the guest list.
downright	**dangerous**	e This violence has become _____ to local people.
depressingly	**proud**	f She seemed _____ , despite the pressure.
outwardly	**silent**	g The street was _____ after the explosion.
~~unduly~~	**unaware**	h These actions are _____ and should be banned.

Prepositions

5   Complete these sentences by adding a preposition and matching the two halves, using the entries for the **bold** adjectives to help you.

a The scandal was **damaging** _to_   the new software.

b I always used to be **late** ____   economic growth.

c I need some time to get **acquainted** ____   the latest crime statistics.

d She was **insistent** ____   women.

e His good looks made him **irresistible** ____   maintaining her privacy.

f Tickets are **limited** ____   school.

g We need an environment that is **conducive** ____   two per person.

h I was **alarmed** ____   the government.

Phrases

6   Complete each of the following sentences with a suitable word or phrase. Look in the 'phrases' section of the **bold** adjective entries for help.

a The missing climbers have been found **alive** and _well_ .

b I was so relieved when they got home **safe** and _____ .

c I'll show you a dish that's really **quick** and _____ .

d The whole event left me **dazed** and _____ .

e If you need any help, I'm **ready** and _____ .

f His hair is always so **neat** and _____ .

g By midnight I was **worried** _____ .

h I forgot my umbrella and I got **wet** _____ .

i When he told me the news I was **thrilled** _____ .

j If a dog comes anywhere near me I'm **scared** _____ .

k The speaker went on and on until we were **bored** _____ .

COLLOCATIONS with COMMON VERBS

do	make	have	take	give
the accounts	an appointment	an accident	action	advice to sb
business	an argument for sth	an argument	a bath/shower *(both*	sb an answer
a crossword	an attempt	a bath/shower *(both*	*esp. AmE)*	birth
a course in Spanish	the bed	*esp. BrE)*	a bite	sb a chance
damage	a cake	a break	a break	sb a choice
a deal	a case for sth	breakfast	the bus	credit to sb
a degree	changes	cancer	a (phone) call	a cry of pain
the dishes	a choice	a chance	a chance	an example
your duty	a connection	a chat *(esp. BrE)*	a class	sb a headache
an exam *(esp. BrE)*	a contribution	a cold	control	sb help
exercise	a decision	difficulty	a course in Spanish	sb a hug
an experiment	dinner	a drink	a decision *(BrE)*	sb an idea
the food for a party	an effort	a feeling	a deep breath	the impression that…
French at school	a face	fun	a dislike to sb	instructions
(esp. BrE)	a film/movie	a guess *(BrE)*	an exam	an insight into sth
good	friends	a heart attack	French at school	sb a kiss
your hair	a guess	a holiday *(BrE)/*	a guess *(AmE)*	a lecture
'Hamlet'	an impact	vacation *(AmE)*	a holiday *(BrE)/*	sb lessons
your homework	an impression (= a	an idea	vacation *(AmE)*	sb a lift *(BrE)/*
an impression (= an	strong effect)	an impact	an interest in sth	ride *(AmE)*
imitation of sb)	a mark	an interest	the lead	your opinion
your job	a mess	a look	a look	sb an order
judo	a mistake	a meeting	medicine	a party
lunch (= meet for	money	a party	a nap	a performance
lunch)	a noise	a plan	notes	sth a polish *(esp. BrE)*
60 miles per hour	a note/notes	a nap	notice	sb a present
an operation	peace	an operation	a photo/picture	priority to sth
Paris (= visit the	a photocopy	an opportunity	a pill	sth a pull
sights)	your point	patience	a risk	sb a push
research	progress	problems	a sip	sb a shock
the shopping *(BrE)/*	a promise	a shock	size 14	a sigh
some shopping	a sketch	a snack	a swim *(esp. AmE)*	a smile
a sketch	a speech	a swim	sb's temperature	a speech
a test	a statement	time	a walk	some thought to sth
a tour	a suggestion	trouble	an X-ray	sb time (to do sth)
a translation	a trip			a welcome to sb
the washing *(BrE)/*	your will			
the laundry				
some work				

1   Find the nouns in the lists for tasks and duties (for example *do the dishes*). Which verb is the most often used? Which tasks are exceptions?

2   Find expressions in each column that can be substituted by a single verb.
(For example you can *do damage* to something or just *damage* something.) Which column has the most?

3   Find expressions connected with the following:

speaking	experiencing something	producing something using your hands, your mind or your skill	physical actions
make/give a speech	*have an accident*	*make dinner*	*have/take a bath*

Can you see any patterns emerging? Are there any exceptions?

4 How many items can you find that collocate with more than one of the verbs
   (for example you can *have* or *take* a break)?
5 Complete each of the following sentences using *do, make, have, take* or *give* (more than
   one answer may be possible). If the noun in the example is not in the table above, look
   for a similar noun. For example, *fortune* is not in the list but *money* is. You can check your
   answers by looking up the entries for the nouns, but try to predict what the verbs will be
   before you do this.

a Make sure you ___*have/take*___ a look at the engine
   before you buy the car.
b After the interview I had to _____
   a test.
c They always _____ us a welcome when
   we go there.
d I sometimes _____ a nap in the afternoon
e Saturday's my day for _____ jobs around
   the house.
f The housing committee will _____
   priority to the elderly.
g Let's _____ one more swim before we go
   back to the hotel.
h He _____ a short laugh when he realized
   his mistake.
i The moment we met we _____ a dislike
   to each other.

j I told her I'd run in the marathon—I'm not going
   to _____ any promises like that again.
k She's always _____ an interest in current
   affairs.
l She _____ her fortune on the stock
   market.
m _____ a picture of me and your dad
   together.
n The kids are _____ a terrible racket.
o Her singing _____ an impression on me.
p _____ the handle a twist and the door
   should open.
q I don't know the answer, so I'll _____ a guess.
r How often do you have to _____ the
   medicine?
s Everyone else was _____ notes in the
   lecture, but I had forgotten my pen.
t A TV company is visiting our school to _____ a
   documentary about teaching!

6 Put each of the following adjectives into one of the sentences in exercise 5, before a noun
   that it collocates with. If you want to check in the dictionary you will need to look up the
   entries for the nouns.

   ~~close~~   copious   instant   keen   lasting   odd   rash   sharp   top   warm   wild

For example: Make sure you have a <u>close</u> look at the engine before you buy the car.

NATURAL DISASTERS

In each case, only one of the pair of words in *italics* forms a common collocation with the word in **bold**. Use the dictionary (looking up the bold word) to decide which is the correct collocation.

a   The famine has already *claimed/starved* thousands of **victims**.
b   The president visited the affected region in the *direct/immediate* **aftermath** of the hurricane.
c   **Rescue** *staff/workers* are still looking for survivors.
d   A massive **relief** *attempt/effort* is underway.

Sentences **e-h** each contain two pairs of *italic* words. You need to choose one from each pair. Again, look up the **bold** words.

e   Several villages have been *inundated/soaked* by the *deepest/severest* **floods** in decades.
f   The city was *affected/struck* by *an enormous/a massive* **earthquake** shortly after midnight.
g   The forest **fires**, *blown/fanned* by warm winds, *flared/raged* out of control for weeks.
h   The **volcano**, which has been *dormant/inactive* for 50 years, began *erupting/exploding* late last night.

CRIMINAL JUSTICE

In each of the sentences, there is an example of incorrect collocation in one of the two <u>underlined</u> sections. Look at the entries for the **bold** words to help you, then write a word that could be used in place of the incorrect one in the space on the right.

a   The accused men have been <u>~~sent to~~ **custody**</u> to <u>await **trial**</u>.   *remanded in (BrE)/ taken into* _____
b   Police <u>carried out a **raid**</u> on the premises early this morning and <u>did two **arrests**</u>.   _____
c   The man <u>was judged **guilty**</u> of assault and <u>sent to **prison**</u> for ten years.   _____
d   The woman will <u>stand **trial**</u>, <u>**accused** with</u> murdering her husband.   _____
e   The woman was <u>**charged** with assault</u>, a crime which <u>holds a **sentence**</u> of up to two years in jail.   _____
f   The <u>**judge** summarized</u> and the <u>**jury** deliberated</u> for eight hours before reaching a verdict.   _____
g   The jury <u>reported a **verdict**</u> of guilty and then the judge <u>passed **sentence**</u>.   _____
h   New <u>**evidence** came to light</u> and the original **verdict** was <u>squashed</u> on appeal.   _____

EDUCATION

Using the entry for the word in **bold** to help you, cross out any of the words in *italics* that do not form common collocations.

a He got *full/~~maximum~~/top* **marks** in the listening test. (*esp. BrE*)
b I got a *failing/passing/winning* **grade** in math. (*AmE*)
c We have to *do/make/write* a vocabulary **test** every Friday.
d How many students have *joined/signed up for/undertaken* the **course**?
e She was always *losing/missing out/skipping* **classes** – no wonder she *crashed/failed/flunked* the **exam**.
f He suffers badly from **exam** *nerves/stress/worries*.
g The teacher *made up/set/wrote* a difficult **exam** but *checked/graded/marked* it leniently.
h We were supposed to *do/compose/write* the **essay** by Friday but I *delivered it/handed it in/turned it in* late.
i I *attended/visited/went to* a **lecture** on Japanese cinema.
j He went to Oxford where he *did/made/took* a **degree** *in/of/on* chemistry.

DRIVING

In each case, only one or two of the words in *italics* form(s) a common collocation with the word in **bold**. Use the dictionary (looking up the bold word) to decide which combinations are possible.

a We drove down a narrow *curving/windy/winding* **road** and got stuck behind a **truck** *carrying/dragging/hauling* timber.
b I *finished/ran out of/used up* the **petrol** (*BrE*)/**gas** (*AmE*) and had to *hitch/hitch-hike/thumb* a **lift** (*BrE*)/**ride** (*AmE*) to the nearest garage.
c There's always *busy/heavy/strong* **traffic** on the highway, so I usually take the *back/minor/small* **roads**.
d The **car** *pulled down/pulled over/pulled up* by the side of the road where there was a free **parking** *room/place/slot*.
e I realized it was a *one-direction/one-way/single-way* **street**, so I had to *carry out/do/make* a **U-turn**.
f She *began/started/switched* on the **engine** to warm up the car and then started *rubbing/scraping/scratching* the ice off the **windscreen** (*BrE*)/**windshield** (*AmE*).
g The demonstration *brought/reduced/slowed* traffic to a **standstill**, and some drivers began to *beep/bonk/honk* their **horns** in frustration.
h The **car** in front *cut down/slowed down/sped down* in order to let a police **car** *overtake/pass/take over*.
i I called a breakdown company to *haul/pull away/tow away* my **car** as I had two *dead/empty/flat* **tyres/tires**.
j A **car** suddenly *pulled out/started out/ran out* in front of me and I had to *hit/slam on/tread on* the **brakes**.

POLITICS

Complete each sentence with a verb from the left and a noun from the right.
You may need to change the form of the verb. You can check your answers in
the dictionary by looking up the entries for the nouns.

elections

launch
lead
rig
run

a   The opposition has accused the government of _____*rigging*_____ the
    _____*election*_____ .
b   A week before the election, the Christian Democrats _____
    in the opinion _____ by 12%.
c   He will officially _____ his presidential _____ on Friday.
d   Castorri _____ for _____ five times, but was never
    elected.

campaign
election
office
polls

government

announce
commission
impose
hold
pass
rule out

e   Congress has finally _____ the new energy _____.
f   The government is under pressure to _____ a _____
    on tobacco advertising.
g   The administration yesterday _____ new
    _____ to reform the prison system.
h   The Prime Minister has _____ any _____ of an
    early election.
i   The President confirmed that he intends to _____ a
    _____ on the main clauses of the new constitution.
j   The Education Secretary is to _____ a _____ on the
    state of our universities.

ban
bill
plans
possibility
referendum
report

opposition

face
launch
renew

k   The opposition leader _____ a scathing _____ on
    government policy.
l   Animal rights campaigners have _____ their _____
    for a referendum on hunting.
m   The government is _____ a _____ over its decision
    to raise the basic rate of tax.

attack
backlash
call

international issues

call
deploy
honour/honor
issue

n   An international delegation urged the government to _____
    its _____ on human rights.
o   The UN will decide today whether to _____ peacekeeping
    _____ in the area.
p   The government _____ an _____ to the rebels for
    all arms to be handed over by the 15th.
q   The warring factions have agreed to _____ a _____
    while negotiations take place.

ceasefire
forces
promise
ultimatum

JOBS

1   Complete each of these sentences with an adjective from the box. Use the entries for the words in **bold** to help you.

> team   flexible   proven   short-term   skeleton   in-house
> repetitive   heavy   ~~high-powered~~   competitive

a   He didn't want the stress of a ___high-powered___ **job**.

b   He couldn't stand the _____ **work** of the production line.

c   The company offers a _____ **salary**.

d   Does your job allow you to work _____ **hours**?

e   She's hired an assistant to help with her _____ **workload**.

f   She joined the company on a _____ **contract**.

g   We gathered in my boss's office for a _____ **meeting**.

h   Applicants should have a _____ **track record** in project management.

i   All staff receive _____ **training** in IT skills.

j   They only have a _____ **staff** on duty during the holidays.

2   Fill in each gap with an appropriate verb or phrasal verb. Use the entries for the words in **bold** to help you.

a   I saw an interesting ad in the newspaper and decided to ___apply for___ the **job**.

b   The company missed his wealth of experience when he chose to _____ early **retirement**.

c   The whole union _____ **strike** in protest against the proposed job cuts.

d   Extra skills training could _____ your job **prospects**.

e   She felt she wasn't _____ her full **potential** in her current job so she _____ her notice.

f   The company had no choice but to _____ her **contract** when she _____ several important **deadlines**.

g   She had always wanted to _____ her **living** as a musician, and she finally _____ her **ambition** when she was 42.

h   I _____ a brief **stint** as a waitress when I was a student, but I wouldn't like to _____ it _____ a **living**.

3   Now find collocations in the sentences from Exercise 2 that match up with the definitions below:

a   a short time spent doing sth   ___brief stint___

b   all that you might possibly achieve   _____

c   your chances of getting a good job   _____

d   the valuable knowledge and skills that you have gained in your life and work   _____

MONEY

1 Fill in the gaps in these sentences with an appropriate word or phrase. Use the entries for the words in **bold** to help you. Sometimes more than one answer is possible.

a Private health insurance might cost an ____awful____ **lot** of money, but it's worth every penny.

b The shares have almost doubled _____ **value** since I bought them.

c Cigarettes are set to _____ **price** for the fifth successive year.

d The failure of the business left him _____ financial **ruin**.

e An oil spill would _____ economic **ruin** for the local fishing industry.

f The _____ **salary** for new employees is quite generous.

g The company _____ **bankrupt** during the recent credit crisis.

Sentences **h-m** have no words in **bold**. Read the sentences carefully to decide for yourself which word(s) you need to look up.

h We've been living _____ a/an _____ budget since the baby was born.

i It cost me more to make the chairs than I could sell them for, so I actually _____ a loss _____ the deal.

j She _____ a large bank loan and then had great difficulty _____ it _____ .

k After a surge _____ demand, the company's stock has _____ a/an _____ high.

l She _____ a fortune _____ the stock market in the 80s.

m The rising cost of fuel is _____ a strain _____ the company's finances.

2 Choose an adjective from the left-hand box and a noun from the right-hand box and match them up with the definitions below. You can look up the entries for the nouns to help you.

| small   healthy   false |
| small   take-home |

| pay   fortune   change |
| bank balance*   economy |

a coins of low value _____small change_____

b a lot of money _____

c a fair amount of money in the bank _____

d the amount of money that you have left after you have paid tax on your salary _____

e an attempt to save money by buying something cheap that does not really save money at all because the goods are of poor quality and do not last very long _____

* look up *balance*

locust *noun*

... OF LOCUSTS **plague, swarm**
LOCUST + VERB **descend on** ◊ *A swarm of ~s descended on the countryside.* | **destroy** ◊ *The ~s have destroyed a lot of the crops.*
LOCUST + NOUN **swarm**

log *noun*

1 wood

ADJ. **cut, sawn** ◊ *a pile of sawn ~s* | **fallen** ◊ *The road was blocked by fallen ~s.* | **rotting** | **blazing, burning** | **floating** | **cedar, oak, pine, etc.**
VERB + LOG **chop** (*BrE*), **saw, split** | **haul** ◊ *They haul the ~s into the sawmill.* | **add, throw, throw on** ◊ *I added another ~ to the fire.* ◊ *The fire is dying down—would you throw on another ~?*
LOG + VERB **blaze, burn, crackle** ◊ *~s crackling in the fireplace* | **float**
LOG + NOUN **cabin, house** (*esp. AmE*) | **fire**

2 written record

ADJ. **detailed** | **daily** | **captain's, ship's** | **Web** (usually **weblog** or **blog**) ◊ *He maintains two weblogs on economic topics.* | **phone** (*esp. AmE*), **server** (*computing*) ◊ *The lawyers will review phone ~s and other records.* | **error** (*computing*) ◊ *I checked the server's error ~s.*
VERB + LOG **keep, maintain** ◊ *She kept a ~ of their voyage.* | **update** ◊ *This feature continuously updates the ~ as data is written.* | **check, examine**
LOG + NOUN **book, sheet** | **entry**

logic *noun*

1 system of reasoning

ADJ. **formal** | **mathematical** | **deductive, inductive** | **Aristotelian, classical** | **fuzzy**
VERB + LOGIC **apply, use** ◊ *Philosophers use ~ to prove their arguments.*

2 use of reason

ADJ. **compelling, impeccable, inexorable** ◊ *There is a compelling ~ to his main theory.* | **faulty, flawed** ◊ *In their faulty ~, this is a great injustice.* | **perverse, strange, twisted** ◊ *What kind of twisted ~ is that?* | **circular** ◊ *This is clearly a case of circular ~.* | **basic, simple** ◊ *The plan had a simple ~ to it.* ◊ *He understood the basic ~ of deterrence.* | **cold, pure, strict** | **inherent, inner, internal, underlying** ◊ *The music has its own inner ~.* | **business, commercial, economic, political, scientific** ◊ *There is sound commercial ~ in never giving credit to retailers.*
VERB + LOGIC **accept, follow, see, understand** ◊ *I can't follow the ~ of what you are saying.* | **defy** ◊ *It's a stupid decision that completely defies ~.* | **apply, use** ◊ *You can't use the same ~ in dealing with children.* | **challenge, question** ◊ *They questioned the ~ underlying his actions.*
PREP. **~ behind** ◊ *What's the ~ behind this decision?* | **~ in** ◊ *There doesn't seem to be any ~ in the move.* | **~ of** ◊ *The ~ of this argument is very obscure.*

logical *adj.*

VERBS **appear, be, seem, sound** ◊ *It all sounds quite ~.*
ADV. **extremely, fairly, very, etc.** | **eminently, highly** | **absolutely, completely, entirely, perfectly** ◊ *His arguments seemed perfectly ~.* | **purely** ◊ *The issue here is purely ~: it has nothing to do with ethics.* | **hardly**

logo *noun*

ADJ. **distinctive** ◊ *The company has a distinctive ~ that makes it well known.* | **official** | **brand** ◊ *Children as young as three can recognize brand ~s.* | **team** (*esp. AmE*) ◊ *a red shirt with the team ~ on it* | **company, corporate**
VERB + LOGO **bear, carry, display, feature, sport** ◊ *The diary features the organization's distinctive new ~.* ◊ *His jacket sports the ~ of the Giants.* | **wear** ◊ *She wore the ~ of the sponsoring company.* | **create, design** | **unveil** ◊ *The new ~ was unveiled in a blaze of publicity.*

PREP. **~ for** ◊ *the ~ for the World Cup* | **~ of** ◊ *the ~ of the New York Police Department*

loneliness *noun*

ADJ. **aching, desperate, great, intense, terrible, utter** | **personal**
VERB + LONELINESS **experience, feel, suffer** ◊ *He experienced terrible ~ after the loss of his wife* | **ease** ◊ *To ease her ~, she spent a lot of time with her dogs.*
PHRASES **a feeling of ~, a sense of ~**

lonely *adj.*

VERBS **be, feel, look, seem** | **become, get**
ADV. **extremely, fairly, very, etc.** ◊ *It gets pretty ~ here in winter.* | **awfully, desperately, incredibly, terribly, unbearably** ◊ *She was desperately ~ at school.* | **a little, slightly, etc.**

long *verb*

ADV. **desperately** ◊ *He ~ed desperately to be back at home.* | **secretly** ◊ *They were the words she had secretly ~ed to hear.* | **always** ◊ *She had always ~ed to travel to other countries.*
PREP. **for** ◊ *He hated the city and ~ed for the mountains.*

long *adj.*

VERBS **be, look, seem** ◊ *That dress looks a little ~ to me.* | **grow** ◊ *My hair had grown ~.*
ADV. **extremely, fairly, very, etc.** ◊ *His drive to work is fairly ~.* | **awfully, exceptionally, incredibly** | **excessively, overly** (*esp. AmE*) ◊ *At 900 pages, the book is overly ~.* | **unusually** ◊ *an unusually ~ pause* | **impossibly** (*esp. AmE*), **ridiculously** ◊ *a pair of impossibly ~ legs* | **relatively** | **a little, slightly, etc.** | **enough** ◊ *Are you sure two hours will be ~ enough?*

longing *noun*

ADJ. **deep, desperate, great, intense, overwhelming, passionate, terrible, wild** ◊ *She had a desperate ~ to go back.* | **sudden** | **hopeless** | **nostalgic, wistful** ◊ *a wistful ~ for the past* | **secret** | **physical, sexual** | **human** ◊ *human ~ for truth and meaning*
VERB + LONGING **be filled with, be full of, feel, have** ◊ *He felt an overwhelming ~ to hear her voice again.* | **satisfy**
PREP. **~ for** ◊ *his intense ~ for privacy*

longitude *noun*

VERB + LONGITUDE **calculate, determine** ◊ *He tried to find out how a ship at sea could determine its ~.*
PREP. **at (a) ~** ◊ *The town is at ~ 28° west.*
PHRASES **a line of ~** ◊ *This line of ~ cuts through the jungle.*

long-lived *adj.*

VERBS **be**
ADV. **extremely, fairly, very, etc.** | **particularly, remarkably, unusually** ◊ *Some of these creatures are remarkably ~.*

look *noun*

1 act of looking at/considering sth

ADJ. **little** | **brief, cursory, quick** | **careful, close, close-up** (*esp. AmE*), **detailed, in-depth** ◊ *Take a closer ~ at it.* ◊ *The authors take an in-depth ~ at topical money issues.* | **first-hand** (*esp. AmE*) ◊ *The jury is expected to get a first-hand ~ at the murder scene today.* | **nostalgic** ◊ *The book takes a nostalgic ~ at the golden age of steam trains.* | **critical, hard, honest, realistic, serious, uncompromising** ◊ *You should take a long, hard ~ at your reasons for wanting to join the army.* | **humorous, light-hearted** ◊ *The book takes a humorous ~ at parenthood.* | **interesting** ◊ *This is an interesting ~ at Soviet foreign policy.* | **revealing** ◊ *Tonight, a revealing ~ at the King of Pop's thrilling rise to stardom.* | **behind-the-scenes, inside** ◊ *The documentary provides an inside ~ at life in the army.* | **fresh** ◊ *I think it's time to take a fresh ~ at our sales techniques.*

VERB + LOOK have, take | get ◇ *Did you get a ~ at his new car?* | sneak, steal | offer, provide ◇ *These tours offer a behind-the-scenes ~ at the making of the TV show.* | warrant ◇ *She decided the property warranted a second ~.*

PREP. ~ at ◇ *I managed to steal a ~ at the exam paper.* | ~ in, ~ into ◇ *She couldn't resist a quick ~ in the mirror.* | ~ out of ◇ *Have a ~ out of the window and see who's at the door.* | ~ over ◇ *If you take a ~ over the past few years, it's not unusual.* | ~ through ◇ *I had a brief ~ through the report before the meeting.* | ~ towards/toward ◇ *The book concludes with a ~ towards/toward the future.*

2 exploring/looking for sth

ADJ. good | little, quick | furtive ◇ *I had a furtive ~ in her bag when her back was turned.*

VERB + LOOK have | chance ◇ *She chanced a ~ behind her.*

PREP. ~ around, ~ round *(esp. BrE)* ◇ *We had a good ~ around the old town.* | ~ for ◇ *I had a ~ for websites on Egyptian music, but didn't find anything.*

3 expression on sb's face

ADJ. angry, black, dark, dirty, nasty, severe, sharp, stern ◇ *She threw him a dirty ~.* ◇ *I was given a stern ~ by a plainclothes policeman.* | scathing, scornful, withering | fierce, furious, murderous | annoyed, disapproving, exasperated | cold, cool, steely | disappointed, hurt, pained, reproachful | disgusted, horrified, shocked | incredulous, startled, stunned, surprised | desperate, frantic, panicked, scared, terrified ◇ *A panicked ~ crossed his face.* | anxious, apprehensive, concerned, doubtful, worried ◇ *They had worried ~s on their faces.* | glum, sad | grim, haunted | sideways, suspicious, wary | cautious | blank, dazed, distant, dreamy, faraway, glazed, vacant | wild ◇ *The man had a wild ~ in his eyes.* | funny, odd, strange, weird ◇ *He gave me a funny ~.* | baffled, bemused, bewildered, confused, puzzled ◇ *His comment was greeted by a puzzled ~.* | curious, inquiring, meaningful, questioning, quizzical, sceptical/skeptical, searching ◇ *My relatives gave me quizzical ~s when I told them the news.* | thoughtful | knowing, shrewd ◇ *The two girls exchanged knowing ~s.* | penetrating, piercing | earnest, intense, intent, steady | hungry | bold, challenging, determined | smug, triumphant | mischievous, sly, wicked | amused, wry | innocent, wide-eyed | coy, shy | loving, sympathetic | grateful | pleading | apologetic, guilty, hangdog, sheepish ◇ *The guilty ~ on his face told us all we needed to know.*

VERB + LOOK have | cast (sb), dart (sb), flash (sb), give (sb), shoot (sb), throw (sb) | get ◇ *I got a black ~ from Amy.* | catch ◇ *He caught her ~, and shrugged.* | exchange ◇ *They exchanged meaningful ~s.* | return ◇ *Sara returned his ~ with one of her own.* | fake, feign ◇ *Jessica feigned a stern ~.*

PREP. ~ from ◇ *A withering ~ from his wife silenced him.* | ~ of ◇ *He darted her a ~ of contempt.*

PHRASES a…look in sb's eyes, a…look on sb's face ◇ *She had a puzzled ~ in her eyes.* ◇ *He opened the door with a scornful ~ on his face.* | take that ~ off your face *(esp. BrE)*, wipe that ~ off your face *(esp. AmE)* ◇ *Wipe that smug ~ off your face before I slap you!*

4 sb/sth's appearance

ADJ. overall ◇ *the overall ~ of the house* | finished ◇ *The finished ~ is perfect for any special party.* | professional ◇ *Use high-quality paper to give your job application a more professional ~.* | classic, modern ◇ *a classic ~ that is easy to update* | clean, minimalist ◇ *She wanted a modern clean ~ for the apartment.* | distinctive ◇ *The products have a distinctive ~.* | youthful

VERB + LOOK have | like ◇ *I didn't like the ~ of the salad so I didn't touch it.* | achieve ◇ *We used a computer to help us achieve this three-dimensional ~.*

PREP. by the ~ of sb/sth, from the ~ of sb/sth ◇ *Joe isn't getting much sleep from the ~ of him.* ◇ *By the ~s of it, someone's already staying in this room.* | ~ about ◇ *He still had a youthful ~ about him.* | ~ of ◇ *a fabric with the ~ of silk*

5 looks sb's attractiveness

ADJ. good | striking | classic ◇ *He had classic good ~s.* | boyish, clean-cut, youthful ◇ *his clean-cut, boyish good ~s*

VERB + LOOKS have | lose ◇ *She's lost her ~s.*

6 fashion/style

ADJ. latest, new | casual, dressy | classic | sophisticated | individual, signature ◇ *In this issue we show you how to create a signature ~ for yourself.*

VERB + LOOK have | sport, wear ◇ *All the men sport rock star ~s.* | give sb/sth ◇ *They've given the place a completely new ~ this year.* | create, recreate | complete ◇ *You can complete that sophisticated ~ with make-up and accessories.*

LOOK + VERB be back in, be back in fashion ◇ *Big hair is back in fashion.* | come back in, come back in fashion | go out, go out of fashion ◇ *The classic ~ never goes out of fashion.*

look verb

1 turn your eyes in a particular direction

ADV. carefully, closely ◇ *Look at the machine very carefully before you buy it.* | briefly, quickly | impatiently | angrily, sharply ◇ *I ~ed up angrily at my brother.* ◇ *She ~ed up at me sharply when I said that.* | intently, searchingly | expectantly | curiously, enquiringly, questioningly, quizzically, speculatively | doubtfully, dubiously, sceptically/skeptically, suspiciously | anxiously, apprehensively, nervously | enviously, longingly ◇ *He ~ed longingly at the food on the table.* | beseechingly, imploringly, pleadingly | disapprovingly, reproachfully | pityingly | sadly | calmly, impassively | blankly | helplessly ◇ *She ~ed around helplessly.* | again ◇ *Now is the time to ~ again at these arguments.* | across, around, away, back, down, out, over, round *(esp. BrE)*, up ◇ *She ~ed over to where the others were chatting.*

VERB + LOOK turn to ◇ *He turned to ~ as she came down the stairs.* | let sb ◇ *'It's beautiful!' 'Oh! Let me ~!'*

PREP. at ◇ *What are you ~ing at?* | towards/toward ◇ *She ~ed towards/toward the door.*

PHRASES ~ and see ◇ *I'll ~ and see if I've got any sugar in the cupboard.*

2 seem/appear

VERB + LOOK make sb/sth ◇ *You made me ~ like a complete fool! You made me ~ a complete fool! (BrE)*

PREP. like ◇ *an animal that ~ed like a large hedgehog* | to ◇ *It ~s to me as if the company is in real trouble.*

PHRASES ~ as if, ~ as though

loop noun

ADJ. continuous, endless | closed, feedback *(both technical)* ◇ *positive and negative feedback ~s*

VERB + LOOP form, make ◇ *Lay the two ends of string so they make a ~ over each other.*

PREP. in a/the ~ ◇ *The tape runs in a continuous ~ lasting thirty minutes.* | through a/the ~ ◇ *Put the other end of the string through the ~.*

loophole noun

ADJ. legal, security, tax | big, gaping, glaring, huge ◇ *gaping ~s in our gun laws*

VERB + LOOPHOLE create, open ◇ *This created a ~ that people might exploit to escape conviction.* | find | exploit, use ◇ *People who don't want to pay tax will exploit any ~.* | close, plug, tighten ◇ *a law designed to close any ~s in the tax system*

LOOPHOLE + VERB allow sb/sth, enable sb/sth, let sb/sth ◇ *a ~ enabling workers to take unnecessary sick leave*

PREP. ~ in ◇ *a ~ in the regulations*

loose adj.

1 not firmly fixed

VERBS be, feel, seem ◇ *One of the bricks feels slightly ~.* | become, come, shake (sth), work (sth) ◇ *The top of the tap has come ~.* ◇ *A screw had worked ~ from the door handle.* | get sth, prise sth *(BrE)*, pry sth *(esp. AmE)*, pull sth, tear sth

ADV. rather | a little, slightly, etc.

2 not tied back

VERBS **be, fall, hang** ◇ *I let my hair fall ~ down my back.* ◇ *Her hair hung ~ about her shoulders.* | **leave sth, wear sth** ◇ *Shall I wear my hair ~?*

3 not shut in or tied up

VERBS **be** | **break, cut** (*figurative*), **get** ◇ *The animals had broken ~ from their pens.* ◇ *The organization broke ~ from its sponsors.* ◇ *He felt he had to cut ~ from his family.* | **let sth, set sth, turn sth** ◇ *I'm going to let the dogs ~.*

lord noun

ADJ. **great, noble** | **feudal** | **crime, drug, war** ◇ *He was the most notorious drug ~ in Northern Europe.* | **law** (*BrE*) ◇ *The law ~s ruled against the government last year.*

VERB + LORD **serve**

LORD + VERB **rule sb/sth**

→ Note at PEER

lorry noun (BrE) → See also TRUCK

ADJ. **big, heavy, huge, large** | **ten-ton, 12-tonne, etc.** | **army** | **articulated, container, delivery, flatbed, gritting, HGV, refrigerated, refuse, skip, tipper** | **jackknifed, overturned** ◇ *The motorway was closed by an overturned ~.*

...OF LORRIES **convoy**

VERB + LORRY **drive**

LORRY + VERB **be laden with sth, carry sth** ◇ *a ~ laden with hay* ◇ *a refrigerated ~ carrying beer* | **travel** ◇ *lorries travelling to and from local quarries* | **jackknife, overturn** ◇ *A dozen people suffered minor injuries after a ~ jackknifed on an icy M62.*

LORRY + NOUN **driver** ◇ *Her husband was a long-distance ~ driver.* | **load**

PHRASES **a ~ sheds its load** ◇ *The ~ had shed its load under the bridge.*

lose verb

1 not keep

ADV. **forever**

VERB + LOSE **be about to, be going to, be likely to, stand to** ◇ *The company stands to ~ if this deal falls through.* | **have little to, have nothing to** ◇ *You have nothing to ~ by telling the truth.* | **hate to, not bear to, not like to, not want to** | **cannot afford to** ◇ *We could not afford to ~ any more senior members of staff.* | **begin to**

2 be defeated

VERB + LOSE **hate to, not bear to, not like to, not want to** | **cannot afford to** ◇ *This was a game that Lazio could not afford to ~.* | **not intend to** | **(not) deserve to** | **be expected to**

PREP. **against** ◇ *We lost against Albyn College.* | **by** ◇ *We lost by five goals to two.* | **to** ◇ *There was really no shame in losing to Norton at that stage of his career.*

PHRASES **win or ~** ◇ *Win or ~, the important thing is to remain calm.*

PHR V lose out

ADV. **financially**

PREP. **on** ◇ *Many of the canal children were constantly on the move, and lost out on regular schooling.* | **to** ◇ *Our company lost out to one that could offer a lower price.*

loser noun

ADJ. **good** | **bad, poor, sore** (*AmE*) ◇ *He's extremely competitive and a bad ~.* | **born** ◇ *He was a born ~.* | **perennial** (*esp. AmE*) ◇ *The team has been transformed from perennial ~s into real contenders.* | **clear, obvious** | **sure** (*AmE*) ◇ *He looked like a sure ~ at the beginning of the year.* | **big, main** ◇ *The main ~ was the Unity Party, which lost eight seats.* | **real, ultimate** ◇ *If the teachers go on strike, the children are the ultimate ~s.* | **pathetic, sad** ◇ *He's just a pathetic ~ (= a stupid unsuccessful person).* | **complete, total** ◇ *She made me feel like a complete ~.*

VERB + LOSER **back** ◇ *The movie company thought they'd backed a ~ until the film won an Oscar.*

loss noun

1 losing of sth

ADJ. **appreciable, considerable, significant, substantial** | **dramatic, great, huge, major, serious** ◇ *the dramatic ~ of farmland to urban growth* ◇ *Reductions in spending would have led to a much greater ~ of jobs.* ◇ *She suffered a significant ~ of hearing after the operation.* | **slight** | **partial, total** ◇ *partial ~ of eyesight* | **permanent, temporary** | **gradual, progressive** ◇ *a gradual ~ of hope* | **rapid** ◇ *rapid weight ~* | **blood, fat, hair, hearing, heat, memory, water, weight** ◇ *Weight ~ can be a sign of a serious illness.* | **job** ◇ *The company is expected to announce 200 job ~es.*

VERB + LOSS **suffer** ◇ *He suffered a ~ of confidence.* | **cause** ◇ *The knife hit an artery, causing significant blood ~.* | **prevent** ◇ *They form a barrier to prevent water ~.*

PREP. **~ of** ◇ *~ of appetite* ◇ *~ of confidence*

PHRASES **no great ~** ◇ *She wouldn't be able to attend the lecture, which was no great ~.* | **be at a ~** ◇ *We are at a ~ to understand his actions (= we cannot understand them).*

2 amount of money lost

ADJ. **catastrophic, enormous, heavy, huge, massive, serious, significant, substantial** | **slight, small** | **net** | **pre-tax** | **overall, total** | **annual, quarterly** | **economic, financial** | **trading** | **long-term, short-term** ◇ *long-term tax revenue ~es*

VERB + LOSS **incur, make, suffer, sustain, take** ◇ *There's no way you can make a ~ on this deal.* ◇ *The business sustained ~es of €20 million.* ◇ *The company took a big ~ of 28%.* | **cut, minimize, reduce** ◇ *He decided to cut his ~es and sell the shares before they sank further.* | **recoup, recover** ◇ *It took the company five years to recoup its ~es.* | **absorb** ◇ *The fund may not be large enough to absorb these ~es.* | **offset** ◇ *We can offset the ~ against next year's budget.* | **underwrite** ◇ *No bank would be willing to underwrite such a ~.*

PREP. **at a ~** ◇ *The store was operating at a ~.* | **~ on** ◇ *We made a net ~ on the transaction.*

3 the death of a person

ADJ. **enormous, great, terrible, tremendous** ◇ *The family has suffered a terrible ~.* ◇ *The ship sank with great ~ of life.* ◇ *His passing is a tremendous ~ for all of us.* | **sad** (*esp. BrE*), **tragic** ◇ *the tragic ~ of her husband* ◇ *His death is a sad ~ to all who knew him.* | **big, catastrophic, devastating, great, heavy, severe** ◇ *the devastating ~es of the war* ◇ *The enemy suffered heavy ~es.*

VERB + LOSS **suffer, sustain, take** ◇ *Our country had sustained a tremendous ~ of innocent life.* | **inflict** ◇ *Fighter planes inflicted heavy ~es on the enemy.* | **grieve, lament, mourn, regret** ◇ *China mourned the ~ of a great leader.*

PREP. **~ to** ◇ *Her suicide was a terrible ~ to the music world.*

PHRASES **a sense of ~** ◇ *She was filled with an overwhelming sense of ~.*

lost adj.

1 unable to find the way

VERBS **be** | **get** ◇ *We got ~ in the woods.*

ADV. **completely, hopelessly** ◇ *By this time we were completely ~.*

2 not knowing what to do

VERBS **be, feel, look, seem** ◇ *I felt ~ without my watch.*

ADV. **completely, totally** ◇ *Alina was looking totally ~.* | **very** | **a bit, a little, rather** ◇ *She looked rather ~ and lonely, standing in a corner by herself.*

lot noun

1 whole amount

ADJ. **whole** ◇ *She bought the whole ~.*

2 large amount

ADJ. **awful** ◇ *I had an awful ~ of work to do.* | **whole** (*informal*) ◇ *There's not a whole ~ of difference between them.*

3 empty ground

ADJ. **empty, vacant** ◇ *He parked his caravan on a vacant ~.* | **abandoned** ◇ *abandoned ~s converted into baseball fields* | **large, small** (*both esp. AmE*) ◇ *the market for homes on smaller ~s* | **parking** (*AmE*)
VERB + LOT **build on** (*esp. AmE*) ◇ *Our house is built on a ~ that's somewhat below street level.*

lotion *noun*

ADJ. **sun, sunscreen** (*esp. AmE*), **suntan, tanning** | **cleansing, moisturizing, setting** | **body, face, foot, hand, skin** | **aftershave** | **calamine**
VERB + LOTION **apply, dab on, put on, rub in, smooth on, use** ◇ *She dabbed calamine ~ on her mosquito bites.*

lottery *noun*

ADJ. **national, state**
VERB + LOTTERY **have, hold** ◇ *We're having a ~ to raise money for homeless families.* | **run** ◇ *the company that ran the state ~* | **play** | **hit** (*AmE*), **win**
LOTTERY + VERB **fund sth, raise sth** ◇ *These programs use state lotteries to fund the student awards.* ◇ *The ~ has raised millions of pounds.*
LOTTERY + NOUN **ticket** | **winner** | **jackpot, prize** ◇ *a $3 million ~ jackpot* | **win** | **funds** | **machine** ◇ *The second ball rolled from the ~ machine.*
PREP. **in a/the ~** ◇ *I won my car in a ~* | **on the ~** ◇ *A couple scooped £10 million on the national ~.*

loud *adj.*

VERBS **be, sound** | **turn sth up** ◇ *She turned the radio up ~.*
ADV. **extremely, fairly, very, etc.** | **deafeningly, incredibly, unbearably** | **annoyingly** | **unnaturally** ◇ *Her voice sounded unnaturally ~.*
PHRASES **~ and clear** ◇ *Tommy's voice came ~ and clear from the back row.*

loudspeaker *noun*

LOUDSPEAKER + VERB **announce sth, broadcast sth** ◇ *Loudspeakers broadcast the football results.* | **blare (sth)** ◇ *Loudspeakers blared militant songs.*
LOUDSPEAKER + NOUN **announcement** | **system**
PREP. **from a/the ~** ◇ *Christmas songs blared from ~s.* | **over a/the ~** ◇ *We heard the news over the ~.* | **through a/the ~** ◇ *A woman was addressing the crowd through a ~.*

lounge *noun*

1 room in a house/hotel

ADJ. **cocktail, coffee** (*esp. BrE*), **karaoke, lobby** (*AmE*), **smoking, sun** (*BrE*), **television, TV** | **comfortable, cosy/cozy, elegant, pleasant, spacious** | **communal** (*esp. BrE*) | **faculty** (*AmE*) | **hotel** | **dorm** (*AmE*) | **executive**
LOUNGE + NOUN **area, bar** (*BrE*), **room, space** | **act, music, singer** | **chair**
PREP. **in a/the ~**

2 room at an airport

ADJ. **airport** | **arrivals** (*esp. BrE*), **departure** | **waiting** | **executive, first-class, VIP**
PREP. **in a/the ~**

love *noun*

ADJ. **all-consuming, burning, deep, great, immense, intense, overwhelming, passionate, profound** ◇ *her deep ~ for him* | **tender** | **genuine, perfect, pure, real, sheer, sincere, true** | **boundless, unconditional** | **altruistic, selfless** | **abiding, enduring, eternal, everlasting, lasting, lifelong, undying** ◇ *He had an abiding ~ of the natural world.* ◇ *You have my undying ~.* | **steadfast, unfailing** | **new-found** | **secret** | **hopeless, unrequited** ◇ *a sad tale of unrequited ~* | **doomed** | **forbidden** | **lost** ◇ *Soul Survivors is a story of lost ~.* | **mutual, shared** | **free** ◇ *They were into free ~ and avoided commitment.* | **first** ◇ *I like most sports*

but tennis is my first ~.* | **brotherly, familial, fatherly, maternal, parental, paternal, sisterly** | **puppy, teenage** | **marital, married** ◇ *The poem is a celebration of married ~.* | **courtly, platonic, romantic** ◇ *the cult of courtly ~ in the 12th century* | **erotic, physical, sexual** | **obsessive** | **heterosexual, homosexual, lesbian, same-sex** | **redemptive** | **Christian, divine, human** | **universal**
VERB + LOVE **feel, have** ◇ *She felt no ~ for him.* ◇ *He had a great ~ of life.* | **experience, know** ◇ *He had never known true ~ until now.* | **search for, seek** | **discover, find** ◇ *At last she had found true ~.* | **rediscover, rekindle** | **receive** ◇ *From John, she received the ~ she had never received from her father.* | **earn** ◇ *She has earned the ~ and respect of many people.* | **develop** ◇ *He developed a lifelong ~ of music.* | **demonstrate, express, show** | **prove** ◇ *He would do almost anything to prove his ~ for her.* | **hide** ◇ *I couldn't hide my ~ for her any longer.* | **confess, declare, pledge, proclaim, profess** ◇ *They publicly declared their ~ for each other.* | **deserve** ◇ *I don't deserve his ~.* | **doubt** ◇ *Does she doubt my ~ for her?* | **inspire, instil/instill** | **cultivate, foster, nurture** ◇ *We want to foster a ~ of learning in all children.* | **celebrate** ◇ *a party with family and friends to celebrate their ~* | **reciprocate, return** ◇ *He didn't return her ~.* | **share** ◇ *They share a ~ of music.* | **indulge** ◇ *His wealth enabled him to indulge his ~ of fast cars.* | **pursue** ◇ *It gave me the opportunity to pursue my ~ of music.* | **give sb, send (sb)** ◇ *Bob sends his ~.* | **lavish, pour** ◇ *They lavish ~ on Selah, their cat.* | **be in, fall in** ◇ *He fell in ~ with one of his students.* | **fall out of** | **make** (= have sex) ◇ *It was the first time they had made ~.* ◇ *He wanted to make ~ to her.* | **consummate**
LOVE + VERB **bloom, blossom, grow** ◇ *Love blossomed between the two of them* | **die, fade** | **prevail** ◇ *Can true ~ prevail?*
LOVE + NOUN **affair** | **triangle** | **life** | **interest, object** ◇ *She plays his ~ interest in the film.* | **rival** (*esp. BrE*) | **rat** (*BrE, informal*) | **slave** | **letter, note** | **token** | **ballad, poem, poetry, scene, song, story** | **potion, spell** | **nest**
PREP. **for ~, out of ~** ◇ *I did it for ~!* | **in ~** ◇ *We are very much in ~.* | **~ between** ◇ *the ~ between parent and child* | **~ for** ◇ *He did not know how to express his ~ for her.* | **~ of** ◇ *She had a great ~ of painting.*
PHRASES **an act of ~** | **deeply in ~, madly in ~, passionately in ~** ◇ *I was madly in ~ with her.* | **desperately in ~, head over heels in ~, hopelessly in ~** ◇ *They fell head over heels in ~.* | **~ at first sight** ◇ *Do you believe in ~ at first sight?* | **~ conquers all** ◇ *In his music dramas, ~ conquers all.* | **the ~ of sb's life** ◇ *She was the ~ of his life.*

love *verb*

ADV. **dearly, deeply, passionately, really, very much** ◇ *He ~d his wife dearly.* | **absolutely, totally** (*informal, esp. AmE*) ◇ *I absolutely ~ your shoes!* | **genuinely, really, truly** | **simply** ◇ *She simply ~d being involved.* | **unconditionally** ◇ *He wanted to be unconditionally ~d.* | **secretly** | **universally** ◇ *Flowers are universally ~d.* | **personally** ◇ *I personally ~ the song.*

lovely *adj.*

VERBS **be, feel, look, sound** ◇ *The cool water felt ~ after being in the hot sun.* ◇ *Your idea of a day on the beach sounds ~.*
ADV. **particularly, really, truly, very** ◇ *She looked really ~ in the blue dress.* | **absolutely, perfectly, quite, simply** ◇ *She has an absolutely ~ face.* | **rather** (*esp. BrE*)

lover *noun*

ADJ. **ardent, good, great, passionate** | **jilted, rejected** (*esp. BrE*), **spurned** ◇ *She was shot by her jilted ~.* | **jealous** | **doomed, star-crossed** | **former, one-time** | **lost** | **long-time** ◇ *He got married to his long-time ~.* | **potential, would-be** | **live-in** | **secret** | **married** | **gay, homosexual, lesbian** | **female, male** | **teenage, young** | **toy-boy** (*BrE, informal*) | **wealthy** (*esp. BrE*)
VERB + LOVER **be, become** ◇ *They became ~s when they worked in the same office.* | **find, have, take** ◇ *It was common for women to take ~s.* | **marry** | **leave** | **kill, murder**

low noun

ADJ. **all-time, new, record** ◇ *The pound has hit a new ~ against the dollar.*
VERB + LOW **fall to, hit, reach, sink to**
PREP. **at a ~** ◇ *Morale is at an all-time ~.*
PHRASES **highs and ~s** ◇ *He had experienced all the highs and ~s of an actor's life.*

low adj.

1 not far above the ground
VERBS **be, look, seem** ◇ *The windows look very ~ to me.*
ADV. **extremely, fairly, very, etc.** ◇ *The river was extremely ~ for winter.* | **a little, slightly, etc.**

2 small in degree/amount
VERBS **be, look, seem** | **become, get, run** ◇ *Our stocks of food were getting ~.* | **Supplies ran ~.** | **remain, stay** | **keep sth** ◇ *The government wants to keep taxes ~.*
ADV. **extremely, fairly, very, etc.** ◇ *The failure rate is extremely ~.* | **comparatively, moderately, reasonably, relatively** | **a little, slightly, etc.** | **dangerously** ◇ *His blood pressure was dangerously ~.* | **abnormally, unusually** | **artificially** | **naturally** | **ridiculously** | **historically** ◇ *historically ~ marriage statistics*
PREP. **in** ◇ *This dish is very ~ in fat.*

lower verb

ADV. **carefully, gently** | **gradually, slowly** | **quickly** ◇ *Cristina blushed and quickly ~ed her eyes.* | **down**
PREP. **into** ◇ *She ~ed herself into the driver's seat.* | **onto** ◇ *He carefully ~ed the sleeping child onto the bed.* | **to** ◇ *She ~ed herself down to the floor.*

low-key adj.

VERBS **be, seem** | **keep sth** ◇ *We want to keep the whole affair as ~ as possible.*
ADV. **very** ◇ *The wedding was a very ~ affair.* | **fairly, pretty, rather, relatively** ◇ *We have a fairly ~ approach to discipline.* | **decidedly** | **deliberately** (*esp. BrE*)

loyal adj.

VERBS **be, remain, stay**
ADV. **extremely, fiercely, intensely, very** ◇ *a fiercely ~ friend* | **absolutely, completely, totally, truly** | **steadfastly** ◇ *his steadfastly ~ friend, Annie* | **incredibly**
PREP. **to** ◇ *The troops remained ~ to the president.*

loyalty noun

ADJ. **absolute, complete, total, undivided, undying, unswerving, unwavering** ◇ *He showed unswerving ~ to his friends.* | **long-term** | **fierce, great, intense, strong, tremendous** | **unquestioning** | **blind** | **conflicting, divided, dual** ◇ *Disagreements with one's in-laws often create divided loyalties.* | **primary** ◇ *His primary ~ was to his family.* | **family, personal, tribal** | **local, regional, ethnic, religious** | **party, political** | **brand, consumer, customer**
VERB + LOYALTY **command, earn, engender, inspire, win** ◇ *He inspires great ~ from all his employees.* | **build, create** ◇ *attempts to build customer ~* | **retain** | **feel, have** | **demonstrate, display, express, prove, show** | **declare, pledge, swear** ◇ *They pledged their ~ to the king.* | **shift, switch, transfer** (*esp. BrE*) ◇ *Some party members found it hard to switch their ~ to the new leader.* | **demand, expect** | **buy** ◇ *It was a blatant attempt to buy their ~.* | **reward** ◇ *The company rewards customer ~ by offering discounts.* | **owe** ◇ *She owed no ~ to him.* | **doubt, question** | **test**
LOYALTY + VERB **be, lie, remain** ◇ *His loyalties lay with people from the same background as himself.*
LOYALTY + NOUN **oath** | **test** | **card** (= that gives benefits to regular customers of a shop/store, etc.) (*BrE*) | **points** (*BrE*) ◇ *Customers earn ~ points every time they shop in the store.* | **programme/program, scheme** (*BrE*) | **bonus** (*BrE*)
PREP. **out of ~** ◇ *She stayed on at the school out of ~ to her students.* | **~ among** ◇ *The town is the object of fierce ~ among its inhabitants.* | **~ for** ◇ *Mass advertising creates brand ~ for a product.* | **~ from** ◇ *The company expects ~ from its employees.* | **~ to** ◇ *men whose ~ is to their political careers* | **~ towards/toward** ◇ *The team members felt tremendous ~ towards/toward one another.*
PHRASES **a conflict of loyalties** | **an oath of ~, a pledge of ~** | **a sense of ~**

luck noun

ADJ. **better, good, great** | **blind, dumb** (*AmE*), **plain, pure, sheer** ◇ *It was sheer ~ that we met like that.* | **random** | **amazing, extraordinary, incredible** | **bad, cruel** (*BrE*), **hard, ill, poor** (*esp. BrE*), **rotten, terrible, tough, unfortunate** ◇ *It was rotten ~ to be sick on the day of the interview.*
... OF LUCK **piece, stroke** ◇ *By a stroke of ~ I came across it in a local bookshop.*
VERB + LUCK **have** ◇ *I haven't had much ~ recently.* | **bring (sb), give sb** ◇ *This ring has always brought me good ~.* | **wish sb** ◇ *I wished her ~ for the future.* | **need** | **chance, try** ◇ *I decided to try my ~ at the roulette wheel.* | **ride** (*BrE*) ◇ *We rode our ~ (= our luck continued) towards the end of the game.* | **press** (*AmE*), **push** ◇ *Don't push your ~!* | **bemoan** (*esp. BrE*)
LUCK + VERB **desert sb** (*esp. BrE*), **run out** ◇ *It looks as though our luck's finally run out.* | **continue, hold** ◇ *If our ~ holds, we should win.* | **change, turn** ◇ *He went on gambling, sure his ~ was about to change.* | **strike** ◇ *More bad ~ struck last week.*
PREP. **by...~** ◇ *By sheer ~ we managed to get out in time.* | **for ~** ◇ *I always carry it with me, just for ~.* | **in ~** ◇ *You're in luck—there are just two tickets left.* | **out of ~** ◇ *I had hoped there would be another train, but I was out of ~.* | **with ~** ◇ *With ~, we'll get there before it closes.*
PHRASES **as ~ would have it** ◇ *As ~ would have it, my brother offered me his apartment.* | **beginner's ~** ◇ *I don't know why I did so well—it must be beginner's ~.* | **better ~ next time** ◇ *If you didn't win a prize, better ~ next time.* | **can't believe your ~** ◇ *He couldn't believe his ~ when the other candidate for the job withdrew.* | **just my ~** ◇ *Just my ~ to get the broken chair!* | **~ is on your side** ◇ *I thought I was going to miss the train but ~ was on my side.* | **make your own ~** ◇ *You make your own ~ in business.*

lucky adj.

VERBS **be** | **get, strike, strike it** (all *informal*) ◇ *She hopes that some day she'll get ~ and win the jackpot.* | **consider yourself, count yourself, think yourself** ◇ *He considered himself ~ to have had the opportunity.*
ADV. **extremely, fairly, very, etc.** ◇ *We've been very ~ so far.* | **dead** (*BrE, informal*), **exceptionally** (*esp. BrE*), **extraordinarily, incredibly, remarkably, terribly** ◇ *She is incredibly ~ to be alive.* | **plain** ◇ *That was just plain ~.*
PREP. **for** ◇ *It was ~ for you that no one saw you.* | **with** ◇ *We certainly struck it ~ with the weather.*

lucrative adj.

VERBS **be, prove**
ADV. **extremely, fairly, very, etc.** | **highly, hugely** (*esp. BrE*), **incredibly** | **increasingly** | **potentially** | **financially** ◇ *a financially ~ venture*

ludicrous adj.

VERBS **appear, be, look, seem, sound** | **become**
ADV. **absolutely, completely, just, quite** (*esp. BrE*), **simply, totally, utterly** (*esp. BrE*) ◇ *The whole idea is absolutely ~!* | **frankly** (*BrE*) | **almost** ◇ *The plot was so simple, it was almost ~.* | **faintly** (*BrE*)

luggage (esp. BrE) noun → See also BAGGAGE

ADJ. **heavy** | **carry-on, hand** | **checked, checked-in** | **lost**
... OF LUGGAGE **item, piece** ◇ *You are only allowed one piece of hand ~.* | **set** (*AmE*) ◇ *a new set of ~*
VERB + LUGGAGE **carry** | **drag, haul** | **claim, collect, retrieve** | **check** (*esp. AmE*), **check in** ◇ *They like you to check your ~ in*

an hour before the flight. | **load**, **pack**, **unload** ◇ *She packed all the ~ into the back of the car.* | **screen**, **search** | **lose**
LUGGAGE + NOUN **area**, **capacity**, **room**, **space** ◇ *The car has a lot of ~ space.* | **compartment**, **locker** (*BrE*) | **rack** (*BrE, AmE*) | **belt**, **carousel** | **cart** (*AmE*), **trolley** | **label**, **tag**
PREP. **in your ~** ◇ *I always carry a first-aid kit in my ~.*

lukewarm *adj.*

VERBS **be**, **feel**, **seem**
ADV. **rather** | **only** ◇ *His reaction was only ~.* | **decidedly**, **distinctly** (*both esp. BrE*)
PREP. **about** ◇ *She was distinctly ~ about my idea.*

lull *noun*

ADJ. **brief**, **temporary** | **long** (*esp. AmE*)
VERB + LULL **hit** (*AmE*) ◇ *Has your fitness routine hit a ~?*
PREP. **during a/the ~** ◇ *They crossed the road during a ~ in the traffic.* | **~ in** ◇ *a brief ~ in the fighting*

lumber *noun* (*esp. AmE*) → See also TIMBER

ADJ. **softwood** | **pressure-treated**, **treated** | **scrap**
LUMBER + NOUN **mill** | **yard** | **camp** | **company**, **industry**

lump *noun*

ADJ. **big**, **giant**, **great** (*esp. BrE*), **huge**, **large** ◇ *a huge ~ of cheese* | **hard**, **heavy**, **solid** ◇ *a heavy ~ of clay* | **little**, **small** ◇ *Stir the sauce to remove any small ~s.* | **strange** ◇ *Check your breasts for strange ~s.* | **painful** ◇ *He's developed a painful ~ on his neck.* | **breast** ◇ *She's just had a breast ~ removed.* | **cancerous**, **malignant** ◇ *Tests confirmed the ~ was cancerous.* | **benign**
VERB + LUMP **have** | **detect**, **discover**, **feel**, **find**, **notice** ◇ *She felt a ~ in her breast.* | **remove** ◇ *Surgeons operated to remove the ~.* | **form**
LUMP + VERB **form** | **grow**

lunatic *noun*

ADJ. **complete**, **raving** | **crazed**, **crazy** (*both esp. AmE*) | **dangerous**
LUNATIC + NOUN **asylum** (*old-fashioned, esp. BrE*)

lunch *noun*

ADJ. **cold**, **hot** | **delicious**, **lovely** (*esp. BrE*), **nice**, **tasty** | **gourmet** (*esp. AmE*), **hearty**, **slap-up** (*BrE*) | **four-course**, **three-course**, **etc.** | **leisurely**, **long** | **quick** | **informal** (*esp. BrE*) | **heavy** | **healthy**, **light** | **sandwich** (*BrE*) ◇ *We went for a sandwich ~ at the local bar.* | **boxed** (*AmE*), **brown-bag** (*AmE*), **packed**, **sack** (*AmE*) | **picnic** | **barbecue** (*esp. BrE*), **buffet**, **carvery** (*BrE*) | **pub** (*BrE*) | **early**, **late** | **Sunday** (*esp. BrE*) | **annual** (*esp. BrE*) ◇ *The society's annual ~ will be held next Wednesday.* | **business**, **working** | **school** | **literary** (*BrE*) | **birthday**, **celebratory** (*esp. BrE*) | **fund-raising** (*esp. BrE*) | **boozy** (*BrE*), **liquid** (= consisting only of alcoholic drinks) | **set** (*esp. BrE*) ◇ *The restaurant offers a £20 set ~.*
VERB + LUNCH **eat**, **get**, **grab**, **have** ◇ *Do you want to grab some ~?* | **do** (*informal*) ◇ *Let's do ~ sometime.* | **cook**, **fix** (*esp. AmE*), **make**, **prepare** ◇ *She fixed ~ for the whole family.* | **order** | **buy** (*esp. AmE*) ◇ *Can I buy you ~?* | **bring**, **serve** | **skip**
LUNCH + NOUN **appointment**, **date**, **meeting**, **party** (*esp. BrE*) | **break**, **hour**, **interval** (*BrE*), **period**, **recess** (*AmE*) | **stop** ◇ *The tour includes a ~ stop.* | **bag**, **box**, **bucket** (*AmE*), **pail** (*AmE*), **sack** (*AmE*) | **tray** | **counter**, **table** | **buffet** | **hall**, **room** (*esp. AmE*) | **lady** (*AmE*) (*dinner lady* in *BrE*) | **things** (*BrE*) ◇ *I helped wash up the ~ things.* | **rush** (*AmE*) | **crowd** ◇ *The ~ crowd was filtering in slowly.* | **line** (*AmE*), **queue** (*BrE*) | **guest** | **money** | **menu** | **club** (*esp. BrE*) | **spot** | **bell**
PHRASES **a spot of ~** (*BrE*) ◇ *Come and have a spot of ~ with me.*
→ Note at MEAL (for verbs)

lung *noun*

ADJ. **collapsed**, **diseased**, **injured**, **punctured** | **healthy** | **transplanted**
VERB + LUNG **fill** ◇ *I opened the window and filled my ~s with cool fresh air.* | **clear**, **empty** ◇ *Coughing clears the ~s of mucus.* | **block**, **choke**, **clog** ◇ *The smoke was beginning to choke her ~s.* | **damage** | **enter** ◇ *Water had entered his ~s and he was choking.* | **penetrate**, **pierce**, **puncture** | **infect** | **burn** ◇ *The smoke was burning his ~s.* | **remove**
LUNG + VERB **work** ◇ *Your heart and ~s have to work harder if you're overweight.* | **heave** | **fill** ◇ *I let my ~s fill with the scented air.* | **collapse** | **burst** (*figurative*) ◇ *Lungs bursting, she flew across the finish line.* | **ache**, **hurt** ◇ *Her ~s ached from the exertion.* | **burn**
LUNG + NOUN **capacity**, **power** | **ailment**, **cancer**, **condition**, **disease**, **infection**, **inflammation**, **injury**, **problems**, **tumour/tumor** | **cell**, **surface**, **tissue** | **function** | **volume** | **transplant**, **transplantation** | **surgery** | **biopsy**, **scan**
PREP. **in the ~** ◇ *levels of carbon dioxide in the ~s* | **into the ~** ◇ *These particles are breathed into the ~s.* | **on the ~** ◇ *He had blood clots on the ~.*

lunge *noun*

ADJ. **sudden** | **wild** (*esp. BrE*) | **desperate** ◇ *He skipped past the defender's desperate ~.*
VERB + LUNGE **make**
PHRASES **~ at** ◇ *The burglar made a ~ at him with a knife.* | **~ for** ◇ *The boy made a sudden ~ for his wallet.* | **~ to** ◇ *a ~ to one side* | **~ towards/toward** ◇ *He made a ~ towards/toward the door.*

lurch *noun*

ADJ. **sickening**, **sudden**, **violent**
VERB + LURCH **give** ◇ *Her heart gave a ~ when she saw him.* | **feel** ◇ *John felt a ~ of fear in his stomach.*
PREP. **with a ~** ◇ *The train stopped with a ~.* | **~ into** ◇ *Starting her own business was a ~ into the unknown.*

lurch *verb*

ADV. **violently** ◇ *Suddenly the train ~ed violently.* | **slightly** | **suddenly** | **backwards/backward**, **forward**, **sideways** ◇ *She gave a little cry and ~ed forward.*
PREP. **along** ◇ *The bus ~ed along the mountain road.* | **into** ◇ *A man ~ed into her office.* | **towards/toward** ◇ *He ~ed towards/toward the door.*
PHRASES **~ to your feet** ◇ *The drunk ~ed to his feet and tried to follow us.*

lure *noun*

ADJ. **big**, **irresistible**, **powerful**, **strong**
VERB + LURE **resist** ◇ *She can't resist the ~ of the bright lights.* | **feel** ◇ *He felt the ~ of distant places.*

lust *noun*

1 sexual desire

ADJ. **pure** ◇ *a relationship based on pure ~* | **carnal**, **physical**, **sexual** | **insatiable**, **unbridled**, **uncontrollable** | **animal**, **male**, **teenage**
VERB + LUST **feel** ◇ *She felt no ~ whatsoever for him.* | **satisfy** ◇ *He used her just to satisfy his ~.*

2 strong desire for sth

ADJ. **insatiable** | **blood**
VERB + LUST **be driven by**, **have** | **satisfy**
PREP. **~ for** ◇ *She was driven by a ~ for power.* ◇ *He had his father's ~ for life.*

luxury *noun*

1 comfort and pleasure

ADJ. **great**, **pure**, **sheer** ◇ *It was sheer ~ to step into a hot bath.* | **ultimate** ◇ *the ultimate ~ of a sauna in your own home* | **relative** ◇ *We lived in relative ~.* | **real** | **modern**
...OF LUXURY **touch** ◇ *Silk sheets added the final touch of ~.*
VERB + LUXURY **enjoy** ◇ *We enjoyed the ~ of an expensive bottle*

of wine. | **afford** ◇ *We can't afford such ~.* | **live in** | **offer** ◇ *The resort offers ~ on a grand scale.*

LUXURY + NOUN **hotel** | **car, coach** (*BrE*), **liner** (*BrE*), **sedan** (*AmE*), **yacht** | **cruise** | **apartment, flat** (*BrE*), **home** | **goods, items** | **brand** ◇ *people who can afford to buy ~ brands*

PREP. **in ~** ◇ *brought up in ~*

PHRASES **have the ~ of (doing) sth** ◇ *He had the ~ of spending time at his family's summer home.* | **a life of ~** ◇ *He wasn't dead, but living a life of ~ in Australia.* | **the lap of ~** ◇ *You're certainly living in the lap of ~!*

2 sth expensive and unnecessary

ADJ. **expensive, unaffordable** | **affordable** | **little, simple, small** | *one of life's little luxuries* | **unnecessary** | **rare** ◇ *Bathrooms were a rare ~ at that time.* | **modern**

VERB + LUXURY **afford** ◇ *We can't afford luxuries.* | **enjoy, have, indulge in** | **do without** | **miss** ◇ *He missed the simple luxuries of life, like regular meals.*

LUXURY + NOUN **tax**

PHRASES **have every ~** ◇ *She's had every ~ in life.*

lyrical *adj.*

VERBS **be, feel** | **become, wax** ◇ *He waxed ~ about the variety of fish in the river.*

ADV. **intensely, very** ◇ *There are some intensely ~ passages in his first symphony.* | **almost** ◇ *She wrote an almost ~ account of her childhood.*

lyrics *noun*

ADJ. **hip-hop, pop, rap, song** | **poetic** | **confessional, heartfelt, insightful, introspective, poignant, thoughtful** | **clever, witty** | **cryptic** | **catchy** (*informal*), **memorable** | **explicit** | **banal, cheesy, inane, nonsensical** | **homophobic, misogynistic**

VERB + LYRICS **compose, pen, write** | **translate** | **set** ◇ *Strauss set several of Mackay's ~ to music.* | **read** | **belt out, deliver, scream, sing** | **mouth** | **quote, recite**

PREP. **~ about** ◇ *~ about death and misery* | **~ by** ◇ *a song with ~ by Lorenz Hart* | **~ for** ◇ *the ~ for a new tune* | **~ to** ◇ *He wrote the ~ to our first song.*

M m

machine *noun*

1 piece of equipment

ADJ. **giant, great, huge, large, powerful** | **portable** | **automated, automatic, electronic** | **sophisticated** | **efficient** | **knitting, sewing, video, washing** | **answering, fax** | **ATM, cash** | **exercise, rowing** | **arcade, gaming, karaoke, pinball** | **coffee, espresso, ice, soda** | **vending** | **dialysis, kidney, life-support, MRI, ultrasound, X-ray** ◇ *The crash victim is now on a life-support ~.* | **voting**

VERB + MACHINE **operate, run, use, work** | **install, set up** ◇ *We've had a new washing ~ installed.* | **start, stop** | **plug in, unplug** | **power** | **create, invent** | **build, make** | **service** | **fix, repair** | **design** ◇ *The ~ is designed to fit under a counter.*

MACHINE + VERB **go, work** ◇ *Is the ~ working again?* | **break down, malfunction** | **run** ◇ *The ~ runs on solar power.* | **beep, hum, whirr**

MACHINE + NOUN **operator** | **parts** | **tool** ◇ *~ tools for making weapons*

PREP. **by ~** ◇ *The potatoes are planted by ~.* | **in a/the ~** ◇ *Just put those clothes in the ~ (= the washing machine).* | **on a/the ~** ◇ *I make my own dresses on my sewing ~.* | **~ for** ◇ *a ~ for making coffee*

PHRASES **a make of ~** ◇ *What make of ~ are they using?*

2 system/organization

ADJ. **party, political** ◇ *The independent candidates did not have the support of a party ~.* | **marketing, propaganda, publicity** | **military, war** ◇ *the president's propaganda ~* | **administrative, government, state** (*all esp. BrE*)

MACHINE + NOUN **politician, politics**

PHRASES **a cog in the ~** (*figurative*) ◇ *Tired of being a tiny cog in a vast ~, he handed in his resignation.* | **a well-oiled ~** (*figurative*) ◇ *The department ran like a well-oiled ~ after the reorganization.*

machinery *noun*

ADJ. **heavy** | **complex, complicated, sophisticated** | **modern, state-of-the-art** | **electrical** | **agricultural, construction, farm, industrial**

... OF MACHINERY **piece** ◇ *large and complex pieces of ~*

VERB + MACHINERY **maintain, repair** | **manufacture** | **install, set up** | **control, drive** | **operate, use** | **replace** | **house** ◇ *The ~ is housed in a special building.*

PREP. **~ for** ◇ *~ for grinding wheat*

PHRASES **the hum of ~**

mad *adj.*

1 (*esp. BrE*) not sane → See also CRAZY

VERBS **be, look, seem** | **go** ◇ *He went ~ and spent the rest of his life locked up in a mental hospital.* ◇ *The world had gone completely ~.* | **drive sb** ◇ *His experiences in the First World War drove him ~.* ◇ *The children are driving me ~!* | **consider sb, think sb** ◇ *Her colleagues thought her quite ~.* | **pronounce sb**

ADV. **absolutely, completely, quite, totally, utterly** | **barking** (*BrE*), **raving, stark raving** (*all informal*) ◇ *What a barking ~ idea!* ◇ *You must be stark raving ~ to risk your money like that!* | **almost** | **a little, slightly, etc.** | **half**

PREP. **with** ◇ *I went ~ with joy and danced a little jig.*

2 (*informal, esp. AmE*) angry

VERBS **be, feel, look** | **get** ◇ *I get so ~ when people don't take me seriously.* | **make sb** ◇ *It makes me really ~ when people waste food.*

ADV. **extremely, fairly, very, etc.** | **hopping** | **absolutely**

PREP. **at, with** ◇ *Please don't be ~ with me!*

madness *noun*

ADJ. **absolute, complete, pure, sheer, total, utter** ◇ *It's sheer ~ to go sailing in weather like this.* | **apparent** | **collective** ◇ *The real victim in this collective ~ is our society.* | **March** (*AmE*)

PHRASES **the first sign of ~** ◇ *They say that talking to yourself is the first sign of ~!* | **a moment of ~** ◇ *In a moment of ~, I said I'd help him.*

magazine *noun*

ADJ. **new, old** | **full-colour/full-color, glossy** | **illustrated** | **bimonthly, monthly, quarterly, weekly** | **online** | **local, national, parish** (*BrE*) | **school, student** | **house** (*BrE*), **in-house, official** ◇ *the company's in-house ~* | **in-flight** | **leading, major, popular** | **prestigious, quality** | **pulp** | **defunct** | **special-interest, specialist** (*BrE*) | **general-interest, mainstream** | **gay, lesbian, teen, teenage** (*esp. BrE*), **women's** | **business, trade** | **listings** (*BrE*) ◇ *Check a listings ~ for what's on this weekend.* | **bridal, car, celebrity, computer, consumer, fashion, fitness, gardening** (*esp. BrE*), **gossip, home** (*esp. AmE*), **lifestyle, literary, motoring** (*esp. BrE*), **music, news, satirical, science, style, travel** | **dirty, girlie, porn** (*informal*), **porno** (*informal*), **pornographic, sex**

... OF MAGAZINE **copy** ◇ *Why did you buy three copies of the same ~?* | **edition, issue**

VERB + MAGAZINE **leaf through, look at, read** ◇ *I leafed through some ~s in the waiting room.* ◇ *I never read ~s.* | **edit, write for** | **print, produce, publish** ◇ *a company that publishes fashion ~s* | **found, launch, start** ◇ *Launching a ~ is a risky venture.* | **distribute** | **buy, get, subscribe to** ◇ *Which ~s do you get regularly?*

MAGAZINE + VERB **come out** ◇ *The ~ comes out once a month.* | **hit sth** ◇ *The ~ hits the newsstands this week.* | **be aimed at sb** ◇ *a ~ aimed at mothers with young children* | **be devoted to sth** ◇ *a ~ devoted to country life* | **describe sth** | **cover sth**

◇ *a trade ~ covering the furnishings industry* | **carry sth, contain sth, feature sth, offer sth, print sth, publish sth, report sth, run sth** ◇ *The ~ carried an interview with the actor considered Hollywood's hottest property.* | **quote sb** | **list sth** ◇ *The ~ lists the latest films showing in cinemas.* (*BrE*) ◇ *The ~ lists the latest movies showing in theaters.* (*AmE*) | **claim sth, say sth** ◇ *The ~ claimed that he was having an affair.* | **reveal sth**
MAGAZINE + NOUN **article, column, feature, interview, piece, report, story** | **ad, advert** (*BrE*), **advertisement** | **poll, survey** | **cover** | **page** | **clipping, cutting** (*BrE*) | **format, layout** | **columnist, editor, journalist, photographer, publisher, reporter, writer** | **reader** | **shoot** ◇ *The hotel is regularly the location for glossy ~ shoots,* | **launch** | **award** | **subscription** | **circulation** | **section** ◇ *the ~ section at the bookstore* | **rack**
PREP. **in a/the ~** ◇ *an article in a women's ~*

magic noun

1 secret power

ADJ. **black** | **white** | **ritual** | **folk** | **powerful** | **ancient**
VERB + MAGIC **cast, do, perform, practise/practice** ◇ *He earns extra money doing ~ at children's parties.* ◇ *People found guilty of practising/practicing black ~ were hanged.* | **believe in** ◇ *I don't believe in ~.* | **channel, use** ◇ *Prospero uses his ~ to attack them.* | **work** | **conjure** (*esp. AmE*), **conjure up** (*esp. BrE*), **summon** (*esp. AmE*)
MAGIC + VERB **work** ◇ *The ~ slowly begins to work, and the princess starts to come to life again.*
PREP. **by ~** ◇ *The rabbit disappeared by ~.*
PHRASES **as if by ~** ◇ *The money had reappeared as if by ~.*

2 special quality

ADJ. **absolute, pure, sheer** ◇ *The show is three hours of pure ~.* | **real** | **movie, musical** ◇ *Fans agree the musical ~ is still there.*
... OF MAGIC **element** (*esp. AmE*), **touch** ◇ *The fireworks brought a touch of ~ to the occasion.*
VERB + MAGIC **conjure, weave, work** ◇ *A hot bath and a good night's sleep worked their usual ~.* | **create, recapture, recreate** ◇ *The film fails to recapture the ~ of his earlier films.* | **experience, feel** ◇ *Visitors can experience the ~ of age-old traditions and historical sites.* | **sense** | **lose** ◇ *Many people think he has lost his ~ as a player.*
MAGIC + VERB **happen** ◇ *It's the director's job to make the ~ happen.*

magical adj.

VERBS **be** | **find sth**
ADV. **absolutely, simply, truly, very** ◇ *a truly ~ experience* | **quite** | **almost** ◇ *Her beauty had an almost ~ quality.* | **seemingly**

magistrate noun

ADJ. **examining** (*BrE*), **investigating, licensing** (*BrE*) | **chief, senior** (*BrE*) | **presiding** (*BrE*) | **city** (*esp. BrE*), **county, district** (*esp. BrE*), **federal, local, town** (*esp. BrE*) | **stipendiary** (*BrE*)
VERB + MAGISTRATE **appoint sb, appoint sb as** (*both BrE*) | **appear before, come up before** (*both BrE*) ◇ *He is due to appear before ~s on a charge of assault.*
MAGISTRATE + VERB **hear sth** (*BrE*) ◇ *The man had a history of violence, ~s heard yesterday.* | **decide sth, rule sth** ◇ *The ~ ruled that there wasn't enough evidence.* | **ban sb, convict sb, fine sb, remand sb in custody, sentence sb** (*all BrE*) ◇ *Magistrates banned him from driving for thirty days.* | **impose sth, order sth** (*both BrE*) ◇ *Magistrates imposed an Anti-Social Behaviour Order.* ◇ *A ~ ordered that they return to the UK.* | **grant sth** (*BrE*) ◇ *Magistrates granted the application for a drinks licence.* | **adjourn sth** (*BrE*) ◇ *Magistrates adjourned the case until June 9.* | **sit** (*BrE*) ◇ *Magistrates sitting in Andover imposed a three-year sentence.*
MAGISTRATE + NOUN **judge** (*AmE*)
PHRASES **magistrates' court** (*in the UK*)

magnet noun

ADJ. **powerful, strong** | **bar** | **fridge, refrigerator** (*esp. AmE*) | **babe** (*informal*), **chick** (*informal*), **tourist** (*all figurative*)
VERB + MAGNET **act as, act like** ◇ *The scent of flowers acts as a ~ to bees.*
MAGNET + VERB **attract sth**
PREP. **~ for** ◇ *The place is a ~ for tourists.*

magnetism noun

ADJ. **sheer** | **animal, personal, sexual** | **the earth's** ◇ *changes in the earth's ~*

magnificent adj.

VERBS **be, look**
ADV. **really, truly** | **absolutely, simply** ◇ *an absolutely ~ performance* | **quite** (*esp. BrE*) | **rather** | **equally**

magnify verb

ADV. **greatly, highly** ◇ *The daring of his exploits had been greatly magnified by constant telling.*
PHRASES **~ sth 50, 100, etc. times** ◇ *The picture shows the insect's head magnified ten times.*

magnitude noun

ADJ. **considerable, great** | **unprecedented** | **sheer** | **relative** | **sufficient** ◇ *a fall in costs of sufficient ~ to enable us to reduce prices* | **small**
VERB + MAGNITUDE **appreciate, comprehend, grasp, realize, understand** ◇ *They failed to comprehend the ~ of the problem.* | **assess, determine, estimate, measure, quantify** | **underestimate** ◇ *They appear to underestimate the ~ of such influences.*
PREP. **in ~** ◇ *The effects were substantial in ~.*
PHRASES **of the first ~** ◇ *Stars of the first ~ are visible to the naked eye.* (*astronomy*) ◇ *a disaster of the first ~* | **of comparable ~, of similar ~** ◇ *We will face challenges of a similar ~.* | **(by) an order of ~** ◇ *Her calculation was out by several orders of ~.*

maid noun

ADJ. **hotel, kitchen, laundry** | **lady's, parlour/parlor** (*usually parlourmaid/parlormaid*), **scullery, serving** (*all old-fashioned*) | **personal** | **live-in**
→ Note at JOB

mail noun → See also POST

ADJ. **certified** (*AmE*) (*recorded delivery in BrE*), **registered** | **express** | **first-class, second-class** (*both in the UK*) | **internal** (*esp. BrE*) ◇ *If we want to send something to another department, we use the internal ~.* | **incoming, outgoing** | **unopened** | **postal** (*AmE*), **regular** (*esp. AmE*), **snail** (*informal, humorous*) | **air** (*usually airmail*), **surface** | **electronic** (*usually email*), **video, voice** | **direct** ◇ *direct-mail advertising* | **bulk** | **junk, unsolicited, unwanted** ◇ *I throw away junk ~ without reading it.* | **fan** | **hate** ◇ *He has received death threats and hate ~ from angry fans.*
... OF MAIL **item, piece** ◇ *the strange piece of fan ~ she'd received two days earlier* | **sackful**
VERB + MAIL **post** (*BrE*), **send** | **get, receive** | **deliver** | **forward, redirect** (*BrE*) ◇ *We had our ~ redirected when we moved out.* | **intercept, steal** | **collect** ◇ *The ~ is collected twice a day.* | **sort** ◇ *The postcode allows the ~ to be sorted automatically.* | **handle** ◇ *Some people let their assistants handle the ~.* | **check** ◇ *She checked her ~ before leaving the hotel.* | **pick up** | **open** | **read** | **answer, deal with**
MAIL + VERB **come, go** ◇ *Has the ~ come yet?*
MAIL + NOUN **delivery** | **order** ◇ *All our products are available by ~ order.* | **message** | **item** | **ballot, questionnaire, survey** | **list** | **program** | **system** | **centre/center, room** | **carrier, man** (*usually mailman*) (*both AmE*) (*postman in BrE*) ◇ *The ~ carrier didn't deliver the ~ on Friday.* | **drop** (*AmE*) | **box** (*usually mailbox*), **slot** (*both AmE*) (*both letter box in BrE*) | **coach** (*BrE*), **train** (*esp. BrE*), **truck** (*AmE*) | **fraud** | **bomb** (*letter bomb in BrE*)
PREP. **by ~** ◇ *Send it by registered ~.* | **in the ~** ◇ *My reply is in the ~.* ◇ *Is there anything interesting in the ~?*

mail *verb* *(esp. AmE)*

ADV. **direct**, **directly** | **back**, **out** ◇ *Mailing out information can be very expensive.*
PREP. **to** ◇ *The brochures are ~ed direct to members.*

mailing list *noun*

ADJ. **free** ◇ *Why not join our free ~?*
VERB + MAILING LIST **go on**, **join**, **subscribe to** | **add sb to**, **put sb on** | **come off**, **unsubscribe from** | **remove sb from**, **take sb off**
PREP. **on a/the ~** ◇ *We're on the charity's ~.* | **~ for** ◇ *a ~ for teachers*

main *noun*

1

ADJ. **gas**, **water** | **broken** *(AmE)*, **burst** *(BrE)* ◇ *water damage from broken ~s* ◇ *There's a burst water ~ in Quarry Road.* | **rising** *(BrE)* | **cast-iron** *(esp. BrE)*
VERB + MAIN **lay** ◇ *They're laying a new gas ~ through the town.* | **replace** | **repair**
MAIN + VERB **serve sth** ◇ *The ~ serves four towns.*

2 mains *(BrE)*

MAINS + NOUN **electricity**, **gas**, **water** ◇ *an island without ~s electricity*
PREP. **at the ~s** ◇ *Turn the water off at the ~s.* | **on the ~s** ◇ *Some of the remoter houses in the town are not on the ~s.*
PHRASES **connected to the ~s** ◇ *The house is not yet connected to the ~s.*

mainstream *noun*

ADJ. **cultural**, **political**, **etc.**
VERB + MAINSTREAM **enter**, **hit**, **join**, **reach** | **cut sb/sth off from**, **exclude sb/sth from** ◇ *These teachers have been cut off from the ~ of educational activity.*
PREP. **in the ~**, **within the ~** ◇ *He was in the ~ of British contemporary music.* | **into the ~** ◇ *This technology was designed for specialists but is now starting to move into the ~.* | **out of the ~**, **outside the ~** ◇ *He drifted out of the ~ of society.*
PHRASES **part of the ~** ◇ *This style of drama is not part of the cultural ~.*

maintain *verb*

1 keep sth at the same level

VERB + MAINTAIN **be anxious to**, **want to** ◇ *We are anxious to ~ our close links with the police.* | **have to**, **need to** | **strive to**, **try to** | **help (to)** | **be able to** | **be difficult to** ◇ *The government's position became increasingly difficult to ~.*
ADV. **indefinitely** ◇ *This pace cannot be ~ed indefinitely.* | **simultaneously** ◇ *They are looking to cut costs while simultaneously ~ing the existing levels of service.* | **successfully** ◇ *He successfully ~ed the financial health of the company.* | **easily** ◇ *The company has easily ~ed its position as the leading brand in the money-transfer business.* | **generally**, **largely**, **normally**, **typically**, **usually** ◇ *Commercial aircraft generally ~ cabin altitudes between 6000 and 8000 feet.* | **actively**
PHRASES **the duty to ~ sth**, **the need to ~ sth** ◇ *He emphasized the need to ~ the status quo.*

2 keep sth in good condition

ADV. **carefully**, **properly**, **well** | **poorly** ◇ *a poorly ~ed central heating system*
VERB + MAINTAIN **be difficult to** | **be easy to**
PHRASES **be responsible for ~ing sth**

maintenance *noun*

1 keeping sth in good condition

ADJ. **annual**, **daily**, **regular**, **routine** | **periodic** ◇ *These fences are fairly rugged but they require periodic ~.* | **scheduled** | **long-term**, **ongoing** | **proper** | **poor** | **essential** *(esp. BrE)* ◇ *The power station has been shut down for essential ~.* | **preventative**, **preventive** *(esp. AmE)* | **careful** | **easy** ◇ *The engine is designed for easy ~.* | **low**, **minimal** ◇ *The house requires minimal ~.* | **high** ◇ *The system is expensive and requires high ~.* ◇ *his high-maintenance girlfriend* | **basic**, **general** ◇ *She was working in the garden, doing weeding and general ~.* | **aircraft**, **car**, **equipment**, **machine**, **etc.** | **road** | **building**, **home** | **software** | **health** | **lawn**
VERB + MAINTENANCE **carry out** *(esp. BrE)*, **do**, **perform** ◇ *We carry out routine ~ of the equipment.* | **provide** ◇ *a company that provides mechanical ~* | **need**, **require** | **receive** ◇ *The building has received no regular ~ since it was vacated in 1998.* | **reduce** ◇ *The use of hard surfaces in the garden is intended to reduce ~.*
MAINTENANCE + NOUN **engineer**, **man**, **technician**, **worker** | **crew**, **personnel**, **staff**, **team** | **manager**, **officer** *(AmE)*, **supervisor** | **department**, **unit** *(military)* | **management** *(AmE)* | **bill**, **costs**, **expenses**, **fee** | **budget** | **contract** | **plan**, **programme/program**, **schedule** | **facility** *(esp. AmE)*, **service**, **support** ◇ *We provide a ~ service on all our products.* | **depot**, **shop** *(AmE)* | **requirements** | **issue**, **problem** | **check** | **procedure**, **system** | **activities**, **operation**, **task**, **work** | **record** ◇ *Keep warranty papers and ~ records for any vehicle you own.* | **guide**, **manual**

2 *(BrE, law)* **money paid to support sb** → See also SUPPORT

ADJ. **child**
VERB + MAINTENANCE **pay** | **claim**
MAINTENANCE + NOUN **payments** | **arrears** ◇ *He was jailed for failing to pay ~ arrears.*
PREP. **in ~** ◇ *He pays £1000 a month in child ~.*

major *noun* → Note at RANK

majority *noun*

1 most

ADJ. **big**, **great**, **huge**, **large**, **overwhelming**, **significant**, **sizeable**, **solid**, **strong**, **substantial**, **vast** | **silent** ◇ *The march was by the silent ~ who oppose terrorism.* | **moral** | **black**, **white** ◇ *countries which have an English-speaking white ~* | **ethnic**
VERB + MAJORITY **compose**, **constitute**, **form**, **make up** ◇ *English speakers form the ~ of the population.* | **join** ◇ *He joined the ~ in criticizing the government's reforms.*
MAJORITY + NOUN **community**, **culture**, **group**, **population** | **language**, **religion** | **opinion**, **view** | **decision** | **owner**, **shareholder** | **ownership** | **interest**, **share**, **stake** ◇ *The French company holds a ~ stake in the retail chain.*
PREP. **in the ~** ◇ *In the general population, right-handed people are in the ~.*
PHRASES **in the ~ of cases** ◇ *In the vast ~ of cases, customers get their money back.*

2 in an election

ADJ. **big**, **huge**, **large**, **massive** *(esp. BrE)*, **overwhelming**, **solid**, **strong**, **substantial** | **clear**, **comfortable**, **decisive** *(esp. BrE)* | **bare**, **narrow**, **slender** *(esp. BrE)* | **slight**, **slim**, **small**, **tiny** *(esp. BrE)* | **razor-thin** *(AmE)*, **wafer-thin** *(BrE)* | **160-seat**, **etc.** | **two-to-one** *(BrE)*, **two-thirds**, **etc.** | **absolute**, **outright**, **overall** ◇ *Although they are the biggest single party, they don't have an outright ~.* | **popular** | **simple** | **working** *(esp. BrE)* ◇ *To govern effectively, he will need a working ~ in Congress.* | **electoral** | **legislative** *(esp. AmE)* | **parliamentary** | **government** *(BrE)* | **Labour**, **Republican**, **etc.** | **necessary**
VERB + MAJORITY **carry**, **command**, **have**, **hold** | **achieve**, **capture**, **gain**, **garner**, **get**, **obtain**, **secure**, **win** ◇ *They failed to win the requisite two-thirds ~.* | **build** ◇ *If the Republicans want to build a ~, they need the north-east.* | **increase** ◇ *Republicans increased their ~ in both the House and the Senate.* | **defend** *(BrE)*, **maintain**, **retain** | **lose** | **overturn** *(esp. BrE)* | **indicate**, **show**
MAJORITY + NOUN **government**, **rule** | **leader**, **whip** | **party** | **decision** | **vote**, **voting** *(esp. BrE)* | **support** | **position**, **status** | **control**
PREP. **by a ~** ◇ *They won by a huge ~.* | **~ against** ◇ *Latest opinion polls have a comfortable ~ against the reform.* | **~ in** ◇ *a ~ in the Senate* | **~ in favour/favor of** ◇ *Opinion polls*

indicated a two-thirds ~ in favour/favor of ratification of the treaty. | **~ over** ◇ *He has a decisive ~ over his main rivals.*

make-up *noun*

1 cosmetics

ADJ. **heavy, thick** | **full** ◇ *You don't wear full ~ to go swimming.* | **light** | **black, dark** | **eye** | **clown, pancake, stage**
VERB + MAKE-UP **use, wear** ◇ *I never wear ~.* | **apply, do, put on** | **remove, take off, wash off** (*esp. AmE*) | **reapply** | **check** ◇ *She was checking her ~ in the mirror.* | **fix** (*esp. AmE*) ◇ *Give me a minute to fix my ~ and I'll drop you off at the mall.* | **touch up** | **smear, smudge**
MAKE-UP + VERB **run, smear** ◇ *a tearful girl with ~ running down her face*
MAKE-UP + NOUN **artist, girl, man, person** | **application** | **brush, sponge** | **remover** | **kit** | **bag, case** | **mirror** | **chair, room** | **effects** ◇ *the ~ effects for the film* | **job, work** ◇ *He was given an Oscar for his ~ work on the film.*

2 sb's character

ADJ. **biological, emotional, genetic, mental, physical, psychological** | **unique** ◇ *the unique ~ of each person*
PHRASES **part of sb's ~** ◇ *Jealousy is not part of his ~.*

malaria *noun*

ADJ. **severe**
VERB + MALARIA **have, suffer from** | **catch, contract** | **carry, transmit** ◇ *Malaria is transmitted by mosquitoes.* | **treat** | **prevent** | **control, eradicate**
MALARIA + NOUN **case** ◇ *An increasing number of ~ cases are reported each year.* | **mosquito, parasite** | **vaccine** | **transmission** | **control**
→ Special page at ILLNESS

male *noun*

ADJ. **adult, mature** | **adolescent, immature, juvenile, young** | **old** | **alpha, dominant** ◇ *the dominant ~ in the herd* | **gay, heterosexual, homosexual** | **red-blooded** | **African American, black, Caucasian** (*esp. AmE*), **white** | **large, powerful, strong** (*all biology*) | **courting, monogamous, unmated** (*all biology*)
PHRASES **the ~ of the species** ◇ *The ~ of the species has darker feathers.*

male *adj.*

VERBS **be**
ADV. **entirely, exclusively** ◇ *The club is exclusively ~.* | **largely, mainly, mostly, overwhelmingly, predominantly, primarily** ◇ *The workforce is predominantly ~.* | **very** ◇ *I had grown up in a very ~ environment.* ◇ *That was a very ~ way of dealing with things.* | **typically** | **traditionally** ◇ *traditionally ~ interests*

malice *noun*

ADJ. **pure** | **actual** (*law*)
VERB + MALICE **bear (sb)** (*esp. BrE*) | **hold** ◇ *He bore me no ~.*
PREP. **out of ~** ◇ *She fired him out of sheer ~.* | **with ~, without ~** ◇ *'You're lying,' he said, without ~.* | **~ towards/toward** ◇ *I bear no ~ towards/toward anybody.*

mall *noun* (*esp. AmE*)

ADJ. **shopping** | **strip** (*AmE*) | **outlet** | **suburban** | **local, regional** | **indoor, outdoor** | **pedestrian** (*AmE*) | **crowded** | **big, giant, huge, large** | **virtual** ◇ *The website is a virtual shopping ~.*
VERB + MALL **hit, visit** ◇ *They hit the ~ for a wild shopping spree.* | **hang out at** ◇ *teenagers hanging out at the ~* | **enter, leave** | **build**
MALL + NOUN **store** | **parking lot** (*AmE*) | **food court** | **rat** (= a young person who spends a lot of time in malls with their friends) (*AmE, informal*) | **security, security guard** ◇ *They reported him to ~ security.*

PREP. **at the ~** ◇ *They spend a lot of time at the ~.*

malnutrition *noun*

ADJ. **severe** | **acute, chronic** | **child**
VERB + MALNUTRITION **suffer, suffer from** | **die from, die of**

mammal *noun*

ADJ. **large, small** | **higher, lower** | **endangered, rare** | **extinct** | **living** | **early, primitive** | **modern** | **wild** | **aquatic, marine, sea** | **land, terrestrial** | **carnivorous, herbivorous** | **nocturnal**
MAMMAL + NOUN **species** | **population**
PREP. **among ~s** ◇ *deaths among marine ~s*

man *noun*

1 male person

ADJ. **elderly, middle-aged, old, older, young** ◇ *a little old ~* ◇ *a middle-aged, balding ~* | **grown** ◇ *Although he is a grown ~, everyone treats him like a boy.* | **40-year-old, etc.** | **attractive, good-looking, handsome** | **ugly** | **short, tall** | **lanky, thin, wiry** | **fat, portly, stocky, stout** | **big, burly, heavy-set** (*esp. AmE*), **muscular, well-built** ◇ *I was helped by two burly men with tattoos.* | **little** ◇ *a nice little ~* | **black, white** | **dark, dark-haired, fair-haired, light-haired** (*esp. AmE*) | **bearded** | **bald, balding** | **blind** | **cloaked, hooded, masked, suited, uniformed** | **well-dressed** | **naked** | **armed, unarmed** | **able-bodied** | **sick, wounded** | **dead, drowning, dying** | **homeless** | **intelligent, wise** | **educated** | **great** ◇ *Several people made speeches in honour/honor of the great ~.* | **brave** | **charming, fine, good, kind, nice** | **honest** | **honourable/honorable** | **proud** | **quiet, soft-spoken** (*esp. AmE*) | **macho, manly** | **bad, horrible** ◇ *What a horrible ~!* | **arrogant** | **mysterious, strange** | **hard, violent** | **drunken** | **married, single** | **family** ◇ *He's a family ~ who rarely goes out with his friends.* | **bisexual, gay, heterosexual, homosexual, straight** | **professional** | **lucky** ◇ *He was a lucky ~ to have found such a partner.* | **poor** | **rich, wealthy** | **betting, gambling** ◇ *I've never been a gambling ~.* | **self-made** ◇ *He was a self-made ~ who raised himself from poverty to success.* | **right-hand** ◇ *He found success hard to come by after losing his right-hand ~.* | **leading** (= the most important male part) ◇ *George Clooney's first role as leading ~* | **innocent** | **free** ◇ *He walked out of court a free ~.* | **wanted** (= sought by the police) ◇ *Vincente is a wanted ~ back in his own country.* | **condemned**

2 human beings

ADJ. **early, prehistoric, primitive** | **Stone Age, etc.** | **Neanderthal, etc.** | **fellow** ◇ *How could a human torture his fellow ~?*
PREP. **in ~** ◇ *In ~ the brain is highly developed.*
PHRASES **known to ~** ◇ *the most poisonous substance known to ~* | **man's inhumanity to ~** ◇ *It's a powerful indictment of the horrors of war and man's inhumanity to ~.*

manage *verb*

1 succeed in doing sth

ADV. **nicely, perfectly well** (*esp. BrE*), **very well** ◇ *I can ~ perfectly well on my own, thank you.* | **successfully** | **skilfully/skillfully** ◇ *He skilfully/skillfully ~d to keep the aircraft on the runway.* | **eventually, finally** | **miraculously** | **somehow** | **barely** ◇ *Paul barely ~d to stifle a chuckle.* | **easily** ◇ *He easily ~d to disarm his attacker.* | **financially** (*BrE*) ◇ *She was finding it difficult to ~ financially.*
VERB + MANAGE **be able to, can** ◇ *Can you ~?* | **have to** ◇ *We'll just have to ~ somehow.* | **be difficult to** | **be easy to**
PREP. **on** ◇ *I don't know how they ~ on only £100 a week.* | **without** ◇ *I can ~ without a dishwasher.*
PHRASES **~ on your own**

2 control/direct sb/sth

ADV. **effectively, efficiently, properly, successfully, well** | **carefully** | **closely, tightly** ◇ *an exchange rate system that will be tightly ~d by the central bank* | **professionally** | **badly** | **easily** ◇ *The condition can be easily ~d by simple dietary adjustments.* | **actively** ◇ *We will actively ~ your*

portfolio to maximize the return on your investment. | **sustainably** ◇ *All our tropical timber products come from sustainably ~d sources.* | **centrally, remotely** | **jointly** | **privately**
VERB + MANAGE **be difficult to** ◇ *The children were very difficult to ~.* | **be easy to** | **learn (how) to** ◇ *You need to learn how to ~ your time effectively.*

manageable *adj.*

VERBS **be, seem** | **become**
ADV. **easily** ◇ *The trip is easily ~ in half an hour.* | **very** | **quite**

management *noun*

1 managing sth
ADJ. **careful, competent, effective, efficient, good, proper, prudent, sound** | **bad, poor** | **day-to-day, routine** | **general, overall** | **centralized** | **business, corporate** | **personnel, staff** | **production** | **quality** | **project** | **farm, hotel** | **hospital, school** (both esp. BrE) (usually *hospital administration, school administration* in AmE) | **classroom** | **database, network, systems** | **ecosystem** | **asset, economic, financial, investment, money, portfolio, re-source** | **brand** | **clinical, medical** ◇ *the medical ~ of obesity* | **facilities** | **data, information, knowledge** | **crisis, emergency** | **risk** | **household** | **traffic** | **waste** | **pest, weed** | **forest, land** | **storm-water** (esp. AmE) | **wildlife** | **anger, anxiety, stress** ◇ *He's been sent on an anger ~ course to help him control his temper.* | **weight** | **pain** | **change** | **time**
VERB + MANAGEMENT **need** ◇ *The project needs stronger ~.* | **perform, provide** ◇ *The company provides facility ~ and base operations support for the army.* | **handle** ◇ *Day-to-day ~ is handled by his sons.* | **be responsible for, oversee** ◇ *She is responsible for the day-to-day ~ of the company.* | **enhance, improve** | **facilitate** | **simplify** | **streamline** | **outsource**
MANAGEMENT + NOUN **agency, company, consultancy, firm** (esp. BrE) | **services** | **consultant, expert, guru, specialist** | **class, course, studies, training** | **plan, policy, programme/ program, strategy, system** | **process** | **expertise, skills** | **guidelines** | **approach, method, philosophy, practice, style, technique** | **tool** | **solution** | **fee**
PREP. **in ~** ◇ *She is now celebrating ten years in ~.* | **under sb's ~** ◇ *The club prospered under Ferguson's ~.*
PHRASES **a board of ~** | **under new ~** ◇ *The restaurant is under new ~.*

2 managers
ADJ. **junior** (BrE), **lower** | **middle** | **senior, top, upper**
VERB + MANAGEMENT **criticize** ◇ *The unions have criticized ~ over their handling of the dispute.*
MANAGEMENT + NOUN **board, committee, personnel, staff, team** | **meeting** | **decision** | **job, position, post** (esp. BrE) | **role** | **hierarchy, structure** | **shake-up** | **buyout** | **level** ◇ *This decision should be taken at a higher ~ level.*
PREP. **in … ~** ◇ *young people in middle ~*
PHRASES **a layer, level, tier, etc. of ~** ◇

manager *noun*

1 controls an organization/part of an organization
ADJ. **assistant, deputy** | **junior** (esp. BrE), **middle, mid-level** (AmE) | **senior, top** | **experienced** | **professional** | **general** | **bank, farm, hotel, store** | **facility** | **business, commercial, corporate** | **area** (esp. BrE) | **branch, department, departmental** (esp. BrE), **district, divisional** (esp. BrE), **national, office, regional** | **account, functional** (esp. AmE), **operations, personnel, product, public relations** | **campaign, programme/program, project** | **advertising, brand, catering** (esp. BrE), **construction, development, fund, marketing, money, portfolio, production, sales, technical** | **nurse** | **successful** | **long-time** | **full-time**
VERB + MANAGER **appoint, hire** (esp. AmE) ◇ *They hired a new campaign ~.* | **be named** ◇ *Last month he was named ~ of the new unit.* | **promote sb to** ◇ *He has been promoted to business development ~.* | **fire** | **replace** ◇ *Companies replace ~s who underperform relative to their rivals.* | **assist** ◇ *Your job will be to assist the production ~.* | **train**

PREP. **~ for** ◇ *the marketing ~ for a large company*
2 is in charge of a sports team
ADJ. **Brazilian, England, Yankees, etc.** | **team** | **caretaker** (BrE), **interim** ◇ *He will be the club's caretaker ~ until a new manager is appointed.* | **top** | **beleaguered** (BrE) ◇ *another disappointing day for the beleaguered England ~*
→ Note at JOB

mandate *noun*

ADJ. **popular** | **clear, strong** | **broad** | **new** | **legal, legislative, regulatory** | **constitutional** | **congressional, federal, government, state** | **electoral** ◇ *It is undemocratic to govern an area without an electoral ~.* | **political** | **divine**
VERB + MANDATE **have** | **give sb, issue** | **seek** ◇ *The party sought a ~ to reform the constitution.* | **get, obtain, receive, win** | **extend**
PREP. **in your ~** ◇ *He failed in his ~.* | **under a/the ~** ◇ *They ruled the country under a United Nations ~.* | **with a/the ~** ◇ *The party was elected with a ~ to reduce the size of government.* | **without a ~** ◇ *They accused him of acting without a ~.* | **~ for** ◇ *She has received a clear ~ for educational reform.* | **~ from** ◇ *a ~ from the United Nations to govern the territory*
PHRASES **an extension of a ~, a renewal of a ~**

mane *noun*

ADJ. **flowing** | **shaggy, tangled** | **thick** | **long** | **silky** | **black, silver, white, etc.**
VERB + MANE **have** | **shake, toss** ◇ *She shook her ~ of auburn hair.* ◇ *The horse tossed its flowing ~ behind it.* | **pat** (esp. AmE), **stroke** (esp. BrE)
PREP. **~ of** ◇ *He has a ~ of white hair.*
PHRASES **a horse's ~, a lion's ~**

maneuver *noun, verb* (AmE) → See MANOEUVRE

manhood *noun*

ADJ. **early, young**
VERB + MANHOOD **grow to** ◇ *He grew from adolescence to young ~.* | **prove** ◇ *It seemed they were fighting to prove their ~.* | **question** ◇ *I'll fight with anyone who questions my ~.*
PREP. **in ~** ◇ *He began to go bald in early ~.*

mania *noun*

1 extreme enthusiasm for sth
ADJ. **dotcom, financial, merger, etc.** | **current**
VERB + MANIA **have**
PREP. **~ for** ◇ *She had a ~ for fast cars.*
2 serious mental illness
ADJ. **acute** | **religious**
PHRASES **a state of ~**

maniac *noun*

ADJ. **sex** | **genocidal, homicidal, suicidal** | **religious**
PREP. **like a ~** ◇ *He was driving like a ~.*

manifestation *noun*

ADJ. **concrete, outward, physical, visible** | **clinical** | **behavioural/behavioral, cultural** | **clear, obvious, overt** | **extreme** | **early, first, initial** | **contemporary** | **public** ◇ *the public ~ of private grief*
PREP. **~ in** ◇ *The ~ of the disease in adults is less dramatic.*
PHRASES **in all its ~s** ◇ *the desire to combat racism in all its ~s*

manifesto *noun*

ADJ. **political** | **Conservative, Labour, etc.** (esp. BrE) | **party** (esp. BrE) ◇ *We must all support the party ~.* | **election** (esp. BrE)
VERB + MANIFESTO **draw up** (BrE), **write** | **sign** | **issue, launch** (BrE), **publish**
MANIFESTO + VERB **pledge sth** (BrE), **promise sth** (esp. BrE) ◇

The ~ promised reform of the social security system. | **call for sth, demand sth** (*esp. BrE*) | **contain sth** | **say sth**
MANIFESTO + NOUN **commitment, pledge, promise** (*all BrE*)
PREP. **in a/the ~** ◇ *The policy is outlined in the party's election ~.* | **~ for** ◇ *a ~ for reform*

manipulate *verb*

ADV. **easily** ◇ *They believe that voters can be easily ~d.* | **successfully** | **deftly, skilfully/skillfully** | **deliberately** | **genetically** ◇ *genetically ~d organisms* | **digitally** ◇ *digitally ~d images*
VERB + MANIPULATE **be able to, can** | **attempt to, try to** ◇ *Children try to ~ you.* | **be easy to** | **know how to, learn (how) to** ◇ *She knows how to ~ the audience.*
PHRASES **the ability to ~ sb/sth**

manipulation *noun*

ADJ. **careful, clever, skilful/skillful** | **cynical, deliberate** | **direct** | **political** ◇ *People think that the investigation was independent, but in fact a lot of political ~ went on.* | **statistical** | **emotional, mental** (*esp. AmE*), **psychological** | **genetic** | **digital, electronic** | **data, image** | **manual, physical**
VERB + MANIPULATION **use**
PREP. **by ~** ◇ *The government has disguised the true situation by clever ~ of the figures.*

mankind *noun*

VERB + MANKIND **save** ◇ *to save ~ from misery and destruction* | **destroy** | **benefit, help, serve** | **face** ◇ *I believe that war is one of the major evils facing ~.*
PHRASES **all ~, the whole of ~** ◇ *According to the Bible, the whole of ~ is descended from Adam.* | **benefit to ~** ◇ *It is doubtful whether this research is of any benefit to ~.* | **the dawn of ~** ◇ *objects dating back to the dawn of ~* | **the fate of ~, the future of ~** ◇ *politicians who do not care about the future of ~* | **for the benefit of ~** ◇ *The results of the research were made freely available for the benefit of all ~.* | **the history of ~** | **known to ~** ◇ *one of the most toxic substances known to ~*

manner *noun*

1 way of doing sth/behaving

ADJ. **conventional, normal, standard, traditional, usual** | **correct, proper** ◇ *You are not approaching the problem in the correct ~.* | **appropriate, satisfactory** ◇ *I did my best to behave in the appropriate ~.* | **reasonable, responsible, safe, sensible** (*esp. BrE*) ◇ *Chemical waste must be disposed of in an environmentally responsible ~.* | **efficient, productive** | **logical, methodical, orderly, rational, systematic** | **coordinated** | **consistent, uniform** | **precise** | **objective** | **controlled** | **ad hoc, arbitrary** (*esp. BrE*), **haphazard** ◇ *Files have been stored in such a haphazard ~ that they are impossible to find.* | **professional** | **constructive, positive** ◇ *The dispute could have been handled in a more constructive ~.* | **peaceful** | **straightforward** | **suspicious** ◇ *He was behaving in a highly suspicious ~.* | **joking, light-hearted, playful** | **casual, easy, informal, relaxed** | **formal** | **calm** | **offhand** ◇ *He answered in such an offhand ~ that I wondered if he'd misheard me.* | **confident, decisive** | **dignified** | **mild, quiet** | **cheerful, friendly, kind** (*esp. AmE*), **kindly** (*esp. BrE*), **pleasant, sympathetic** | **civilized, polite, respectful** | **thoughtful** | **rude** | **abrasive, aggressive, arrogant, threatening, unpleasant** (*esp. BrE*) | **forthright** | **brusque, cold** (*esp. AmE*) | **businesslike, no-nonsense** ◇ *His no-nonsense ~ gave him the reputation of being a good doctor.* | **condescending** | **authoritative** ◇ *The authoritative ~ in which he talked concealed his ignorance.* | **unladylike** | **bedside** ◇ *He's a good doctor with a sympathetic bedside ~.*
VERB + MANNER **have** | **adopt** ◇ *He tends to adopt a condescending ~ when talking to young women.* | **act in** ◇ *She accused the teacher of not acting in a professional ~.*
MANNER + VERB **change** ◇ *His ~ changed abruptly when he*

heard how much gold I wanted.* | **suggest sth** ◇ *He was not as rude as his ~ suggested.*
PREP. **in a/the ~** ◇ *The inspection was conducted in a thoroughly professional ~.* | **in the ~ of** ◇ *He lectured us in the ~ of a headmaster.* | **in your ~** ◇ *There was something in his ~ that I found very irritating.*
PHRASES **in a timely ~** ◇ *All claims must be settled in a professional and timely ~.* | **in no uncertain ~** ◇ *He told her in no uncertain ~ that her actions were unacceptable.*

2 manners polite behaviour/behavior

ADJ. **good, impeccable, perfect** ◇ *It's not good ~s to stare at people.* | **bad** | **table** ◇ *His children have no table ~s.*
VERB + MANNERS **have** ◇ *He had very bad table ~s.* | **show** ◇ *I got into trouble if I didn't show good ~s towards/toward other people.* | **teach sb** ◇ *Didn't your parents teach you any ~s?* | **learn** | **forget** ◇ *I'm sorry, I was forgetting my ~s. Can I offer you a drink?* | **remember** ◇ *After a few minutes Eve remembered her ~s and invited them all in.* | **forgive** ◇ *Forgive my ~s. I forgot to introduce myself.* | **know** ◇ *I disliked him but I knew my ~s so I answered his question.*
PHRASES **have the good ~s to do sth, have the ~s to do sth** ◇ *He could at least have had the ~s to answer my letter.* | **a lack of ~s** ◇ *Her lack of ~s is appalling.* | **mind your ~s** ◇ *Now sit down and eat and mind your ~s!*

mannerism *noun*

ADJ. **odd** | **irritating**
VERB + MANNERISM **have** | **acquire, adopt, pick up**
PREP. **~ of** ◇ *He has this irritating ~ of constantly scratching his nose.*

manoeuvre (*BrE*) (*AmE* maneuver) *noun*

1 movement performed with care and skill

ADJ. **complex, complicated** | **difficult** | **dangerous** | **clever** | **defensive, offensive** | **evasive** | **aerial**
... OF MANOEUVRES/MANEUVERS **series**
VERB + MANOEUVRE/MANEUVER **carry out, do, execute, make, perform** ◇ *The pilot has to carry out a series of complex ~s.* | **attempt, try** | **practise/practice** | **complete**

2 clever plan

ADJ. **brilliant** | **strategic, tactical** ◇ *Her withdrawal from the contest was a tactical ~.* | **diplomatic, legal, political**
VERB + MANOEUVRE/MANEUVER **use** ◇ *He used cutting-edge ~s to outsmart other bidders.* | **carry out, execute** | **pull** (*informal*)
MANOEUVRE/MANEUVER + VERB **fail**
PREP. **by a/the ~** ◇ *By this ~, he hopes to gain an advantage at a later stage.*
PHRASES **freedom of ~** ◇ *The economic conditions are restricting he bank's freedom of ~.* | **room for ~** ◇ *The government has very little room for ~ on this issue.*

3 military operation

ADJ. **military, strategic, tactical** | **operational** | **combat** | **defensive, offensive**
VERB + MANOEUVRE/MANEUVER **carry out, conduct, execute, perform**
MANOEUVRE/MANEUVER + NOUN **battalion, brigade, force, unit** | **operation** | **commander**
PHRASES **be on ~s, go on ~s** ◇ *The unit is on ~s in southern Italy.*

manoeuvre (*BrE*) (*AmE* maneuver) *verb*

ADV. **carefully** | **quickly, easily** | **deftly, expertly, skilfully/skillfully**
VERB + MANOEUVRE/MANEUVER **be difficult to, be easy to**
PREP. **around, past, through, etc.** ◇ *He carefully ~d the boat past the rocks.*
PHRASES **~ (sth) into position** | **~ your way** (*figurative*) ◇ *He had ~d his way into a position of strength in the party.* | **room to ~** ◇ *The ship had little room to ~.*

manpower *noun*

ADJ. **skilled** ◇ *a shortage of skilled ~* | **military, police** (*esp. BrE*), **etc.** | **additional**

VERB + MANPOWER **have** ◇ *They did not have the ~ to comply with every regulation.* | **need, require** | **provide** | **reduce** ◇ *Manpower will be reduced to an average of 20%.* | **increase**
MANPOWER + NOUN **shortage** | **needs, requirements** | **resources** | **acquisition** (*military*)
PREP. **in ~** ◇ *a reduction in ~* | **~ for** ◇ *a pool of ~ for the new industries*
PHRASES **the availability of ~** ◇ *The factory's opening hours over the holiday period will depend on the availability of ~.* | **a reduction in ~** | **a shortage of ~**

mansion *noun*

ADJ. **big, great, huge, large** | **30-room, etc.** | **grand, stately** | **lavish, luxurious, luxury** (*esp. BrE*) | **palatial** | **beautiful** | **country** (*esp. BrE*) | **old** | **stone** | **17th-century** (*esp. BrE*), **etc.** | **Elizabethan, Victorian, etc.** | **Beverly Hills, Hollywood, etc.** | **family** | **executive** ◇ *The rebels besieged the heavily fortified executive ~.* | **haunted**
VERB + MANSION **live in** | **have, own** | **buy** | **build** | **enter, leave**
MANSION + VERB **stand** ◇ *The historic ~ stands in 160 acres of parkland.*
MANSION + NOUN **house** | **block, flat** (*both BrE*)

manslaughter *noun* (*law*)

ADJ. **attempted** | **involuntary, voluntary** | **reckless** | **vehicular** (*AmE*) | **corporate** (*BrE*) ◇ *The directors of the company could be charged with corporate ~.*
→ Note at CRIME (for verbs)

manual *noun*

ADJ. **how-to** (*esp. AmE*), **instruction, instructional** (*esp. AmE*), **training** | **advice, self-help** | **operator's** (*AmE*), **owner's, teacher's** (*AmE*), **user, user's** | **computer, software** | **car** (*esp. BrE*), **driver's** (*esp. AmE*) | **diagnostic, maintenance, operating, operations, reference, repair, technical** | **sex** | **comprehensive, detailed** | **online, printed**
VERB + MANUAL **come with** ◇ *The computer comes with a comprehensive owner's ~.* | **check, consult, look at, read, study** ◇ *Check your ~ for details.* | **use** | **write** | **produce, publish**
MANUAL + VERB **contain sth, include sth, provide sth** | **say sth** ◇ *The ~ said not to use the fryer on wooden decks.* | **recommend sth** | **describe sth**
PREP. **according to the ~** ◇ *According to the ~, the wires should be the other way around.* | **in a/the ~** ◇ *What does it say in the ~?* | **~ for** ◇ *an instruction ~ for a knitting machine* | **~ on** ◇ *a ~ on teaching drama*

manufacture *noun*

ADJ. **local** ◇ *cotton ropes of local ~* | **metal, steel, etc.** | **cloth, cotton, textile, etc.** | **car, vehicle, etc.** | **drug, food, etc.** | (usually ***metal manufacturing***, etc.)
PHRASES **costs of ~, date of ~** ◇ *The date of ~ of the clock has been authenticated.* | **the method of ~, the process of ~**

manufacturer *noun*

ADJ. **big, large, leading, major, top** ◇ *the world's largest computer ~* | **small** | **well-known** | **reputable** | **commercial** | **independent** | **foreign, overseas** | **domestic** | **auto** (*esp. AmE*), **car, chemical, computer, food, motor** (*BrE*), **textile, etc.**
PHRASES **the manufacturer's instructions** ◇ *The guarantee may be rendered invalid if the manufacturer's instructions are not followed.*

manufacturing *noun*

ADJ. **large-scale, small-scale** | **industrial** | **heavy** | **labour-intensive/labor-intensive** (*esp. AmE*) | **computer-aided, computer-integrated, high-tech** | **metal, steel, etc.** | **cloth, cotton, textile, etc.** | **auto** (*esp. AmE*), **automotive** (*AmE*), **car** (*esp. BrE*), **motor** (*BrE*), **vehicle, etc.** | **chemical, drug, food, etc.** | **component, computer, etc.**
MANUFACTURING + NOUN **business, company, enterprise, firm** (*esp. BrE*), **organization** | **division, facility, operation, plant, site, unit** ◇ *The company set up a ~ operation in*

Lisbon. | **side** ◇ *He now works on the ~ side of the business.* | **base, industry, sector** ◇ *the decline in the country's ~ base* | **area, centre/center, town** (*esp. BrE*) | **capability, capacity** | **output, production, productivity** | **costs** | **worker, workforce** | **employment, jobs** | **methods, process, system, techniques** | **technology** | **expertise**

manure *noun*

ADJ. **animal, chicken, cow, horse, pig** | **livestock, poultry** | **farmyard** (*esp. AmE*) | **composted** | **aged, well-rotted** | **fresh** | **liquid**
VERB + MANURE **apply, spread** ◇ *the best time to spread ~ on the fields*
MANURE + NOUN **production** | **application** | **disposal, storage** | **spreader** | **heap** (*esp. BrE*), **pile** (*esp. AmE*) | **nutrient**

manuscript *noun*

1 copy of a book that has not yet been printed

ADJ. **original** | **autograph, handwritten** ◇ *the original autograph ~ of the poem* | **unpublished** | **unsolicited** | **draft** | **unfinished** | **completed** | **book** | **literary, music, musical**
... OF MANUSCRIPT **copy** ◇ *I only have one copy of the ~.*
VERB + MANUSCRIPT **write** | **prepare** | **type** | **edit, improve, revise** | **complete, finish** | **send, submit** ◇ *He submitted the ~ for publication.* | **review** | **accept, reject** ◇ *He was delighted when the ~ was accepted for publication.* | **publish**
MANUSCRIPT + NOUN **page** | **form** ◇ *The text ran to dozens of pages in ~ form.* | **submission** | **reviewer**
PREP. **in ~** ◇ *Her autobiography remained in ~ (= was not published).*

2 very old book/document, written by hand

ADJ. **ancient, early, medieval, old** | **rare** | **surviving** ◇ *the surviving ~ of 'Beowulf'* | **illuminated, illustrated**
MANUSCRIPT + VERB **survive** ◇ *earlier ~s which no longer survive*
MANUSCRIPT + NOUN **illumination** | **collection**

map *noun*

ADJ. **large-scale, small-scale** | **accurate** | **detailed** | **hand-drawn, rough, simple, sketch** | **colour-coded/color-coded** | **holographic** | **local** | **road, street** ◇ *a street ~ of Havana* ◇ *a road ~ of Florida* | **world** | **bus, subway** (*AmE*), **tube** (*BrE*), **underground** (*BrE*) | **treasure** | **contour, outline, relief, topographic, topographical** | **three-dimensional, two-dimensional** | **geological** | **weather** | **electoral, political** | **Ordnance Survey** (*in the UK*) | **tourist** | **route** | **wall** | **digital, interactive, online** | **paper**
VERB + MAP **read** ◇ *Are you good at reading ~s?* | **use** | **check, consult, examine, look at, study** | **view** ◇ *Click here to view a ~ of the area.* | **follow** ◇ *He followed the ~ to Red Square.* | **draw, make** | **redraw** (*figurative*) ◇ *In 1924 the Soviet Union redrew the ~ of Central Asia.* | **print, print out, produce, publish** | **be marked on** ◇ *The museum is clearly marked on the ~.* | **lay out, spread out, unfold** ◇ *We spread the ~ out on the floor.* | **fold, fold up** | **download** | **display** ◇ *Large ~s were displayed around the meeting room.* | **update**
MAP + VERB **indicate sth, show sth** | **depict sth, represent sth** ◇ *~s depicting details such as mountain ranges and shorelines* | **reveal sth** ◇ *Maps can reveal the history of a place.*
MAP + NOUN **projection**
PREP. **according to ~** ◇ *According to the ~, we need to head north-east.* | **off the ~** ◇ *Our town is just off the ~.* | **on a/the ~** ◇ *The road isn't on the ~.* | **~ of** ◇ *a ~ of the area* | **~ to** (*esp. AmE*) ◇ *I printed out a ~ to the party.*

marathon *noun*

1 long race

ADJ. **full, half**
VERB + MARATHON **prepare for, train for** | **compete in, run, take part in** | **complete, finish** | **win**

MARATHON + NOUN **champion** (*esp. BrE*), **runner** | **running** ◇ *He says that he keeps fit by ~ running.*

2 long activity

ADJ. **12-hour, 700-mile, all-night, etc.** | **car, cycling** (*esp. BrE*), **etc.**
MARATHON + NOUN **journey, walk** | **effort** (*esp. BrE*) | **session** ◇ *The painting would be completed in one ~ session.* | **match, race** ◇ *a ~ five-set tennis match*

marble *noun*

ADJ. **cold, cool** ◇ *The hotel is traditionally furnished, with cool ~ floors.* | **coloured/colored, grey/gray, white, etc.** | **veined** | **polished** | **gleaming** | **smooth** | **carved**
... OF MARBLE **block, slab**
VERB + MARBLE **carve** | **carve sth from/in, make sth from/in/of/out of** ◇ *a statue of Cupid carved in black ~* | **quarry**
MARBLE + NOUN **quarry** | **floor, pillar, sculpture, statue, etc.**
PREP. **in ~** ◇ *sculptures in polished white ~*

March *noun* → Note at MONTH

march *noun*

1 movement/journey

ADJ. **long** | **steady** | **slow** | **forced** | **approach** ◇ *They reached the enemy position after an arduous approach ~.* | **fifty-mile, four-day, etc.** | **half a day's, two hours', etc.** ◇ *The camp was half a day's ~ away.* | **northward, southward, etc.** | **forward, onward** (*figurative*) ◇ *the forward ~ of technology* | **inevitable, inexorable** (*formal*), **relentless, unstoppable** (*all figurative*) ◇ *the inexorable ~ of time*
VERB + MARCH **begin, set off on** ◇ *The army set off on a forced ~ north.*
PREP. **on the ~** ◇ *The army has been on the ~ for two weeks.* | **~ from** ◇ *the ~ from Selma to Montgomery* | **~ of** ◇ *a ~ of over 30 miles* | **the ~ of history/progress/science** (*often figurative*) | **~ to, ~ towards/toward** (*figurative*) ◇ *the steady ~ towards/toward equality*
PHRASES **line of ~** ◇ *Villages in the army's line of ~ were burned to the ground.* | **a ... march away** ◇ *The border was still a day's ~ away.* | **the ~ eastward, westward, etc.**

2 demonstration/parade

ADJ. **hunger, peace, pride, protest, victory** | **triumphal, triumphant** | **anti-racism, pro-democracy, etc.** | **gay pride, pride** | **peaceful**
VERB + MARCH **hold, organize, stage** | **lead** | **be on, go on, join in, take part in** | **halt, stop** ◇ *The farmers halted the ~ outside the presidential palace.* | **break up** ◇ *The ~ was broken up by police in riot gear.*
MARCH + VERB **mark sth** ◇ *a ~ marking the thirtieth anniversary of the shootings*
PREP. **at a/the ~, on a/the ~** ◇ *There were in excess of 100 000 people at the ~.* | **~ against** ◇ *a ~ against racism* | **~ for** ◇ *a ~ for the victims of the war* | **~ of** ◇ *a ~ of over 6 000 people* | **~ from, ~ to**
PHRASES **a ~ past** (*BrE*) ◇ *There will be a special ~ past of competitors.*

3 music

ADJ. **military** | **funeral, wedding** | **quick, slow**
VERB + MARCH **compose** | **play**

march *verb*

1 walk with regular steps

ADV. **briskly, swiftly** | **boldly** | **determinedly, purposefully** | **proudly** ◇ *They ~ed proudly onto the football field.* | **stiffly** | **inexorably** (*figurative*) ◇ *Time ~es inexorably on and we still have not made a decision.* | **north, south, etc.** | **ahead, forward, on, onward** ◇ *The clock ~ed onward to the year 2005.* (*figurative*) | **away, back, off, out, over, past, up (and down)** ◇ *Craig ~ed up to the door and rang the bell.* ◇ *Soldiers were ~ing up and down outside the government buildings.*

PREP. **on** ◇ *The invading army ~ed on Rome.* | **out of** ◇ *So saying, she ~ed boldly out of the house.* | **through** | **from, into, to, towards/toward** ◇ *They ~ed all the way from London to Edinburgh.*
PHRASES **~ in step** ◇ *conscripts learning to ~ in step* (= in time with each other)

2 walk in a large group to protest about sth

ADV. **peacefully** | **triumphantly**
PREP. **against** ◇ *Millions of people ~ed against the war.* | **for** ◇ *They were ~ing for peace.* | **in support of** ◇ *protesters ~ing in support of the students' demands* | **on** ◇ *The demonstrators ~ed on the British embassy.* | **through** ◇ *We ~ed peacefully through the streets.* | **to, towards/toward**

margarine *noun*

ADJ. **hard** | **soft** | **stick** (*AmE*) | **polyunsaturated**
... OF MARGARINE **tub** | **stick** (*AmE*) ◇ *Melt the stick of ~ and put it in the bottom of baking pan.*
VERB + MARGARINE **put on, spread (sth with)** ◇ *She put some ~ on her roll.* ◇ *Spread some ~ on the toast, please.* | **heat, melt, soften** | **beat, beat in, cream, mix, rub in** ◇ *Cream the ~ and sugar together.* ◇ *Rub the ~ into the flour.*
→ Special page at FOOD

margin *noun*

1 empty space at the side of a page in a book, etc.

ADJ. **generous, wide** ◇ *Leave a generous ~ on the left.* | **narrow** | **left, right** | **left-hand, right-hand**
VERB + MARGIN **adjust, leave, set**
PREP. **at the ~** ◇ *Start writing at the left-hand ~.* | **in the ~** ◇ *She scribbled notes in the ~.*

2 space, time, votes, etc. by which sth is won

ADJ. **winning** ◇ *The winning ~ was only 8 seconds.* | **comfortable, considerable, greater, large, substantial, wide** ◇ *She was not daunted by this substantial ~ of defeat.* | **huge, overwhelming** ◇ *The amendment passed by an overwhelming ~.* | **narrow, razor-thin** (*esp. AmE*), **slim, small** ◇ *The election is likely to be decided by razor-thin ~s.* | **clear, safe** | **three-to-one, two-to-one** ◇ *Her book outsold his by almost a two-to-one ~.* | **1 000-vote, 20-second, etc.** ◇ *He claimed the title with a slim 134 000-vote ~.*
VERB + MARGIN **have**
PREP. **by a ~** ◇ *She won by a clear ~.* | **~ over** ◇ *He had an 18-second ~ over his nearest rival.*
PHRASES **by the largest, narrowest, etc. of ~s** ◇ *He won by the narrowest of ~s.* | **a ~ of victory**

3 amount of extra space, time, etc.

ADJ. **good, greater, wide** ◇ *Sales predictions are open to wide ~s of error.* | **narrow** | **adequate** | **generous** | **safety**
VERB + MARGIN **allow (sb/sth), give (sb/sth), leave, provide** ◇ *The device gives a greater ~ of safety.*
PREP. **~ for** ◇ *We have substantial reserves, which provide a good ~ for uncertainties.*
PHRASES **a ~ for error, a ~ of error** ◇ *The schedule left no ~ for error.* | **a ~ of safety**

4 profit

ADJ. **fat** (*esp. AmE*), **high, large** ◇ *The company relies on fat ~s from luxury models.* | **low, narrow, razor-thin** (*esp. AmE*), **small, thin, tight** ◇ *We're working to rather tight profit ~s.* ◇ *How does the company get by with such razor-thin ~s?* | **negative** (*esp. AmE*) | **gross, net** | **profit** | **operating, pre-tax, retail** (*esp. BrE*) | **average** ◇ *Today, average ~s have slipped to just 4%.*
VERB + MARGIN **achieve, have** ◇ *These manufacturers have high gross ~s.* | **operate at, operate on** | **improve, increase** ◇ *Higher productivity has enabled them to increase their profit ~s.* | **cut, cut into, erode, reduce, squeeze** ◇ *Price rises have eroded profit ~s.*
MARGIN + VERB **increase, widen** | **narrow, shrink**
PREP. **at a ~** ◇ *They are operating at very low ~s.* | **~ on** ◇ *They hope to improve their ~s on computers.*
→ Note at PER CENT (for more verbs)

marijuana noun

ADJ. **home-grown** | **medical, medicinal**
... OF MARIJUANA **joint**
VERB + MARIJUANA **smoke** | **decriminalize, legalize, reclassify**
MARIJUANA + NOUN **cigarette, joint** | **plant**
→ Note at DRUG (for more verbs and nouns)

mark noun

1 spot/line

ADJ. **dirty, grubby** | **visible** | **distinguishing, identifying** ◇
Does he have any distinguishing ~s? | **chalk, pencil** | **finger**
(usually *fingermark*), **scuff, skid, tyre/tire** | **bite, burn,**
claw, puncture, scorch, scratch, slash, stretch, tooth ◇
There were two small puncture ~s on her arm.
VERB + MARK **get** ◇ *How did you get that ~ on your shirt?* |
leave, make ◇ *The dirty water left a ~ around the side of the*
bathtub. | **get off, get out, remove** ◇ *I can't get the*
children's dirty fingermarks off the wall.
MARK + VERB **come off, come out** ◇ *These greasy ~s just won't*
come out.
PREP. **~ on** ◇ *There were grubby ~s on the wall.*

2 sign of a quality/feeling

ADJ. **deep, indelible, permanent** ◇ *The experience left a deep*
~ on her memory. | **real** ◇ *the real ~ of a master craftsman*
VERB + MARK **bear, have** | **leave**
PREP. **~ of** ◇ *Such thoughtfulness is the ~ of a true gentleman.*
PHRASES **as a ~ of respect, make your ~** (= have an impact)
◇ *Women are continuing to make their ~ in business.*

3 (esp. BrE) used to show the standard of sb's work

ADJ. **good, high** | **bad, low, poor** | **full** ◇ *I got full ~s for my*
homework. | **top** | **pass** (BrE) ◇ *What's the pass ~ in*
chemistry? | **total** | **average**
VERB + MARK **get, receive** | **deserve** ◇ *The festival organizers*
deserve high ~s. (figurative) | **give sb** | **deduct** ◇ *Marks are*
deducted for incorrect spelling. | **gain** | **lose**
PREP. **~ for** ◇ *You get two ~s for each correct answer.* ◇ *a good*
~ for geography | **~ out of** ◇ *How many ~s out of ten would*
you give it?

4 level of sth

ADJ. **halfway** ◇ *We've reached the halfway ~ in the show.* | **tide**
(usually *tidemark*) | **high-tide, low-tide** | **high-water, low-**
water | **$10 million, £2 billion, 30-minute, etc.** ◇ *Spending*
has now reached the $1 million ~. ◇ *By the film's 30-minute*
~, most of the audience have lost the plot.
VERB + MARK **set** ◇ *Their relationship was*
approaching the two-year ~. | **reach** | **break, pass, surpass**
◇ *This year's sales figures have already passed the ~ set last*
year. | **fall short of**
PREP. **above the ~, below the ~** | **around the ~** ◇ *around*
the $500 ~ | **at a/the ~** ◇ *The river was at its low-water ~.* |
up to the ~ (= as good as sb/sth should be) ◇ *Your*
grammar is not quite up to the ~.

5 target

ADJ. **easy**
VERB + MARK **find, hit** ◇ *The shot found its ~.* | **miss,**
overshoot
PHRASES **wide of the ~** (figurative) ◇ *Shock tactics often fall*
wide of their ~.

mark verb

1 write/draw sth

ADV. **clearly** ◇ *My room was clearly ~ed on the plan.* |
carefully ◇ *She carefully ~ed where the screws were to go.* |
indelibly, permanently
PREP. **as** ◇ *Certain words were ~ed as important.* | **for** ◇ *Some*
of the crates were ~ed for export. | **in** ◇ *Mark the position of*
all the building sites in black. | **on** ◇ *All buildings are ~ed on*
the map. | **with** ◇ *The boundary was ~ed with a dotted line.*

2 affect sb/sth

ADV. **indelibly, permanently** ◇ *Christianity has indelibly ~ed*
the culture and consciousness of Europe. | **deeply** ◇ *The town*
is still deeply ~ed by the memory of the Depression.

3 be a sign of sth

ADV. **effectively** | **officially** ◇ *Members of the club officially*
~ed the occasion with a ribbon cutting ceremony. | **publicly**
◇ *The wedding ceremony publicly ~s the beginning of*
commitment to another through marriage.
VERB + MARK **appear to, seem to** ◇ *This speech appears to ~ a*
change in government policy.

marked adj.

1 easy to see

VERBS **be** | **become**
ADV. **extremely, fairly, very, etc.** | **especially, particularly,**
strongly ◇ *There is a strongly ~ difference between the two*
creatures.

2 with markings

VERBS **be**
ADV. **clearly** ◇ *The animal's tail has clearly ~ stripes.* | **heavily**
◇ *Most cranes lay two heavily ~ eggs.* | **beautifully, brightly**
PREP. **with** ◇ *These trout are beautifully ~ with bright red*
spots.

market noun

1 place where people go to buy and sell things

ADJ. **open-air, outdoor, street** | **covered, indoor** (both esp.
BrE) | **cattle, fruit and vegetable, etc.** | **antique, antiques**
| **farmers'** ◇ *She buys her vegetables from the local farmers'*
~. | **flea** (= that sells old or used goods at low prices)
VERB + MARKET **hold** ◇ *The ~ is held on Wednesdays.* | **go to** |
take sth to ◇ *They took the pigs to ~.*
MARKET + NOUN **square** | **town** (esp. BrE) | **day** | **trader** (esp.
BrE) | **stall**
PREP. **at a/the ~, in a/the ~** ◇ *I want to buy some fresh fish at*
the ~.

2 business/trade

ADJ. **competitive** | **active, booming, bullish, lively, strong,**
thriving | **bull** (finance), **rising** | **depressed, sluggish, weak**
| **bear** (finance), **falling** | **steady** | **buyer's, seller's** |
foreign, global, international, overseas, world | **domestic,**
home, internal, local | **consumer, retail** ◇ *The disks are*
designed for professional applications, rather than the
consumer ~. | **single** ◇ *the completion of the European single*
~ in 1992 | **common** | **economic** | **free** | **open** | **black**
(= illegal) | **bond, capital, commodity, credit, currency,**
equity, financial, foreign-exchange, futures, money,
securities, stock | **export** | **housing, property** (esp. BrE),
real estate (AmE) | **art, car, computer, etc.** | **job, labour/**
labor
VERB + MARKET **put sth on** | **come on, come onto, hit** ◇ *A new*
model has come on the ~. | **develop, expand** | **break into,**
enter, get into, penetrate ◇ *They're hoping to get into the*
Far Eastern ~. | **capture, corner, dominate, monopolize** |
control, drive ◇ *A relatively small group of collectors drives*
the art ~. | **distort, manipulate** ◇ *Government attempts to*
manipulate currency ~s tend to backfire. | **supply** | **flood,**
saturate ◇ *Lenders have flooded the ~ with easy credit.* | **lose**
| **depress** | **play** ◇ *an investor who knows how to play the*
market—and win | **outperform** ◇ *He believes oil stocks will*
outperform the ~ over the next 12 months.
MARKET + VERB **open up** ◇ *The Chinese ~ has opened up*
recently. | **boom, grow** ◇ *The organic food ~ is growing at*
10% a year. | **develop, evolve, mature** ◇ *Markets evolve in*
response to consumer demands. | **pick up, rally** | **decline** |
collapse, crash, slump, tank (informal, esp. AmE) | **bottom**
(esp. AmE), **bottom out** | **be down, be up** ◇ *The ~ was down*
15%. | **react, respond** ◇ *The ~s reacted quickly to the*
negative publicity. | **close** ◇ *The stock ~ closed weaker.* |
open
MARKET + NOUN **price, value** | **conditions** | **volatility** | **leader**
| **position, share** | **penetration** | **sector** | **trends**
PREP. **in a/the ~, into a/the ~** ◇ *changes in the UK ~* | **on the**
~ ◇ *one of the best car deals on the ~* | **~ in** ◇ *a thriving ~ in*
second-hand cars

PHRASES be in the ~ for sth (= be interested in buying sth) | the bottom drops out of the ~, the bottom falls out of the ~ (= the market collapses) | a gap in the ~ (*esp. BrE*) ◇ *They seem to have identified a gap in the ~.* | the bottom, lower, top, upper, etc. end of the ~ | price sb/yourself out of the ~ ◇ *Rising mortgage rates will price some people out of the ~.*

3 people who want to buy sth

ADJ. big, broad, good, huge, large | mass ◇ *Their books were geared to a mass ~.* | commercial ◇ *There is not a broad commercial ~ for these prints.* | poor, small | emerging ◇ *Emerging ~s in Asia and Latin America represent the best export opportunities for us.* | expanding, growing | shrinking | ready | niche | target ◇ *The young, health-conscious female consumer is our target ~.* | lucrative ◇ *Single professionals with no children are a lucrative ~.*
VERB + MARKET create ◇ *The company has created a niche ~ for itself.* | target ◇ *Both products are targeting the same ~.* | reach, tap, tap into ◇ *Giving away free toys is a popular way to tap the family ~.* | serve ◇ *Organic product lines have expanded from serving a small niche ~.*
MARKET + VERB expand, grow | shrink | collapse | bear sth ◇ *We will charge whatever the ~ will bear (= as much as people can be persuaded to pay).*
MARKET + NOUN segment | niche | research | researcher | demand ◇ *The ~ demand for greener housing is growing.*
PREP. ~ for ◇ *the ~ for new cars*

4 the free market

VERB + MARKET leave sth to ◇ *Some services cannot be left to the ~.* | regulate ◇ *He believes that regulating the ~ is a good thing.* | deregulate
MARKET + NOUN forces | economy | economics | reforms ◇ *The government embraced Anglo-American style ~ reforms.*

market verb

ADV. commercially ◇ *the first commercially ~ed rice harvester* | heavily | effectively, successfully | cleverly | aggressively | actively | directly ◇ *Many farmers have taken steps to directly ~ their meat to consumers.* | exclusively, specifically ◇ *The low-alcohol wine is being ~ed exclusively to women.* | online ◇ *All her products are ~ed online on her website.*
PREP. as ◇ *It will be ~ed as a tonic for the elderly.* | through ◇ *The product is being ~ed through the existing sales force.* | to ◇ *The company is not actively ~ing its products to schools.*

marketable *adj.*

VERBS be | become
ADV. extremely, fairly, very, etc. | easily, highly, readily

marketing *noun*

ADJ. clever, effective, good | poor | aggressive | online | mass | niche | direct, one-to-one (*AmE*), targeted | guerrilla (*esp. AmE*), interactive, viral, word-of-mouth | global, international, worldwide
VERB + MARKETING do ◇ *The company has done some effective ~ of the new model.* | improve
MARKETING + NOUN campaign, exercise (*esp. BrE*), strategy | blitz, effort, push ◇ *The film was a flop, despite a big ~ blitz.* | gimmick, ploy, tool | hype ◇ *Everyone will tell you their product is best but this is just ~ hype.* | director, executive, manager | consultant, guru, specialist | agency, company, department, firm (*esp. BrE*) | budget ◇ *We don't have a huge ~ budget and rely on word-of-mouth.*
PREP. in ~ ◇ *She works in ~.* | through ~, with ~ ◇ *We could get more sales through better ~.*
PHRASES sales and ~
→ Special page at BUSINESS

marketplace *noun* (often the marketplace)

ADJ. competitive, crowded | commercial, financial | global, international | online | changing, ever-changing

VERB + MARKETPLACE enter ◇ *We are working hard to enter the global ~.* | crowd, flood, saturate ◇ *New low-carb foods have flooded the ~.*
PREP. in a/the ~ ◇ *The company found it hard to survive in a changing ~.*

marquee *noun*

1 large tent

ADJ. giant, huge, large
VERB + MARQUEE erect
PREP. in a/the ~ ◇ *The wedding reception was held in a ~.* | under a/the ~ ◇ *The guests sat under a large ~.*

2 (*AmE*) covered entrance

ADJ. theater ◇ *We drove past a theater ~ with his name on it.* | lighted | showbiz

marquess (*also marquis*) *noun* → Note at PEER

marriage *noun*

1 state of being married

ADJ. good, happy, successful | broken, disastrous, failed, unhappy ◇ *She was the child of a broken ~.* | first, second, etc. | previous | early, late | modern | conventional, traditional | interfaith, interracial, mixed | gay, homosexual, lesbian, same-sex | heterosexual, straight | open | common-law | monogamous, polygamous | morganatic (*esp. BrE*) | loveless | childless | arranged, forced
VERB + MARRIAGE have ◇ *He had an unhappy ~ with an older woman.* | propose | enter into | consummate | annul, dissolve | save ◇ *They are struggling to save their ~ for the children's sake.* | legalize, recognize ◇ *Same-sex ~s are recognized in some countries already.* | ban, forbid, prohibit
MARRIAGE + VERB last | be over, break down, break up, end, fail, fall apart ◇ *Their ~ ended in divorce.*
MARRIAGE + NOUN vows | plans, proposal | partner | relationship | break-up, breakdown, problems | counselling/counseling, guidance (*BrE*) | counsellor/counselor | market ◇ *More divorced people have joined the ~ market.* | bed
PREP. by a ~, from a ~ ◇ *She's his daughter by a previous ~.* | by ~ ◇ *They are related by ~.* | in a/the ~ ◇ *She was the dominant partner in the ~.* | outside ~ ◇ *sex outside ~* | within ~ | ~ between ◇ *the ~ between John and Elizabeth* | ~ into ◇ *his ~ into a wealthy family* | ~ to, ~ with ◇ *her ~ to Jim*
PHRASES ask for sb's hand in ~, win sb's hand in ~ (*both old-fashioned*) | the break-up of a ~, the breakdown of a ~ | give sb in ~ (*old-fashioned*) | the institution of ~ | a ~ of convenience | a proposal of ~

2 wedding ceremony

ADJ. Christian, Jewish, etc. | civil | shotgun (= arranged quickly because the bride is pregnant) (usually *shotgun wedding*)
VERB + MARRIAGE celebrate ◇ *The ~ was celebrated in the cathedral.*
MARRIAGE + VERB be held, take place
MARRIAGE + NOUN ceremony | certificate (*BrE*), contract, licence/license
PREP. at a/the ~ ◇ *She wanted to be present at the ~ of her grandson.* | ~ to ◇ *Mr and Mrs Wall invite you to the ~ of their daughter Ann to Mr Thomas Lea.*

married *adj.*

VERBS be, feel ◇ *I wouldn't have felt properly ~ if it hadn't been a church wedding.* | get ◇ *When did you get ~?* | remain
ADV. newly, recently ◇ *The newly ~ couple left for their honeymoon in Spain.* | previously | happily | unhappily | lawfully, legally | properly
PREP. to ◇ *She's ~ to an actor.*
PHRASES ~ with children ◇ *All her friends are now ~ with children.*

marry *verb*

ADV. **well** ◇ *To keep his wealthy lifestyle, he had to ~ well.*
VERB + MARRY **hope to, want to** ◇ *I don't want to ~ Robert.* |
agree to, promise to ◇ *He promised to ~ her when he
returned.* | **choose to** ◇ *This was the woman he chose to ~.* |
be going to, plan to ◇ *Matt told me he was going to ~ again.*
◇ *They plan to ~ next year.* | **be able to, be allowed to, be
free to** ◇ *He believes same-sex couples should be able to ~.* |
forbid sb to ◇ *Duty forbade them to ~.* | **ask sb to** ◇ *He asked
me to ~ him but I said no.*
PREP. **for** ◇ *He married her for love, not for money.* | **into** ◇
the difficulties of ~ing into the royal family
PHRASES **get married** ◇ *They are hoping to get married next
year.* | **~ late, ~ young** ◇ *People are ~ing later these days.* |
not be the ~ing kind (= not be the kind of person who
wants to get married)

marsh *noun*

ADJ. **coastal, salt, saltwater, tidal** | **freshwater** | **grazing**
(*BrE*)
VERB + MARSH **drain**
MARSH + NOUN **grass, plant** | **bird**
PREP. **in a/the ~, on a/the ~** ◇ *He keeps his cattle on the ~es.*

marshal *noun*

1 in the army/air force
→ Note at RANK
2 security officer
ADJ. **grand** (*AmE*) | **federal** | **air, sky** (*AmE*) | **armed**

martial law *noun*

VERB + MARTIAL LAW **declare, impose, place sth under** | **lift**
PREP. **under ~** ◇ *The city remains under ~.*

martyr *noun*

1 sb who is killed/suffers for what they believe
ADJ. **early** | **glorious, holy** | **Christian, Islamic, Protestant,
etc.**
VERB + MARTYR **make sb** ◇ *Putting him to death would only
make him a ~.*
PREP. **~ to** ◇ *a ~ to the cause*
PHRASES **die a ~** | **a martyr's death**
2 sb who tries to gain sympathy
VERB + MARTYR **play** ◇ *Stop playing the ~.*
PHRASES **make a ~ of yourself**

marvel *verb*

VERB + MARVEL **can only** ◇ *One can only ~ at the way the
building has been constructed.* | **never cease to** ◇ *I never
cease to ~ at his stupidity.* | **inwardly, secretly, silently** ◇ *We
all secretly ~ at his skill.*
PREP. **at** ◇ *Aiden couldn't help but ~ at the simplicity of the
plan.*

marvellous (*BrE*) (*AmE* **marvelous**) *adj.*

VERBS **be, feel, look, sound**
ADV. **really** ◇ *This is really ~ news!* | **absolutely, quite, simply**
◇ *The food looks absolutely ~!*

mascara *noun*

ADJ. **heavy, thick** | **waterproof** | **black**
VERB + MASCARA **wear** | **apply, put on** | **remove, wipe, wipe
away, wipe off** (*esp. BrE*) ◇ *I wiped most of the ~ from under
my eyes.* | **smear, smudge** ◇ *Her tears had smudged her ~.*
MASCARA + VERB **run, smear, smudge**
MASCARA + NOUN **brush, wand**

masculine *adj.*

VERBS **be**
ADV. **extremely, fairly, very, etc.** ◇ *She has a very ~ face.* |
decidedly, distinctly | **exclusively** ◇ *The ceremony is
exclusively ~.* | **predominantly** | **essentially** | **typically** ◇
That's a typically ~ attitude! | **stereotypically** ◇ *We assume
that stereotypically ~ traits are more suited to the military.* |

traditionally ◇ *women entering traditionally ~ domains such
as construction* | **inherently** | **aggressively** ◇ *He has an
aggressively ~ approach to these questions.*

mask *noun*

1 cover for sb's face
ADJ. **face, facial, full-face** | **gas** | **breathing, oxygen** | **dust** |
protective | **surgical** | **hockey** (*AmE*), **ski** | **Halloween**
VERB + MASK **have on, wear** | **don, put on** | **pull off, remove,
strip off, take off, tear off** ◇ *In the second part of the play,
the actors take off their ~s.*
MASK + VERB **conceal sth, cover sth, hide sth** ◇ *The man's face
was hidden by a ~.*
PREP. **behind a/the ~, beneath a/the ~** ◇ *Two eyes glared at
him from beneath the ~.* | **in a/the ~** ◇ *two men in black ~s* |
~ over ◇ *She wore a ~ over her face.*
2 sth that hides sb's real feelings
ADJ. **blank, cold, emotionless, expressionless, impassive,
stony** ◇ *Her face was a blank ~ as she answered my question.*
MASK + VERB **slip** ◇ *For a moment her ~ slipped, and I saw how
scared she really was.*
PREP. **behind a/the ~** ◇ *Behind the ~ of friendliness, I know he
really dislikes me.* | **~ for** ◇ *His fooling around is a ~ for his
lack of confidence.*
PHRASES **a ~ of indifference** ◇ *He was hiding behind a ~ of
indifference but she wasn't fooled.*

mask *verb*

ADV. **completely** | **not quite, partially, partly** | **barely** |
effectively
VERB + MASK **tend to** ◇ *Varnish tends to ~ the natural grain of
the wood.*
PREP. **with** ◇ *She ~ed her anger with a smile.*

mass *noun*

1 large amount/number of sth
VERBS **enormous, great, huge, large, vast** | **broad** ◇ *Their
policies appeal to the broad ~ of the population.* | **shapeless**
◇ *When I washed the sweater, it just turned into a shapeless ~.*
| **compact, dense, solid** | **land** ◇ *the first women to cross
Antarctica's land ~ on foot* | **chaotic** ◇ *a chaotic ~ of ideas* |
swirling ◇ *a swirling ~ of shadows* | **tangled** ◇ *a tangled ~ of
hair*
PREP. **~ of** ◇ *a dense ~ of smoke* | **~es of** (*informal*) ◇ *There
were ~es of people at the concert.*
PHRASES **the huddled ~es, the unwashed ~es** (= large
numbers of poor people) ◇ *the image of America with arms
open wide to the world's huddled ~es*
2 Mass Christian ceremony
ADJ. **Catholic, requiem** | **midnight, Sunday**
VERB + MASS **attend, go to, hear** ◇ *She never failed to attend
Sunday Mass.* | **celebrate, offer, say**
PREP. **~ for** ◇ *a requiem ~ for the sailors who drowned*
3 (*technical*) quantity of material
ADJ. **atomic, molecular** | **body, bone, muscle** ◇ *Calcium
deficiency can lead to low bone ~ in adolescent girls.* | **critical**
◇ *The product has to be good enough to achieve a critical ~ of
customers.* (*figurative*)
VERB + MASS **measure** | **add, gain** ◇ *Bodybuilders trying to
gain muscle ~ eat a lot of protein.*

massacre *noun*

ADJ. **appalling** (*esp. BrE*), **bloody, brutal, terrible** ◇ *an
appalling ~ of women and children* | **genocidal** | **indis-
criminate, wholesale** ◇ *He accused the troops of the
indiscriminate ~ of civilians.*
VERB + MASSACRE **be responsible for, carry out, commit,
perpetrate, take part in** ◇ *The ~ was carried out by enemy
troops.* ◇ *As many as fifty men took part in the ~.* | **be killed
in** | **escape, survive** | **condemn, denounce**
MASSACRE + VERB **take place**

PREP. **~ by** ◊ *a ~ by rebel soldiers*
PHRASES **the victims of a ~**

massage *noun*

ADJ. **gentle, relaxing, soothing | back, body, foot, full-body, neck, scalp | deep-tissue, shiatsu, Swedish, etc. | therapeutic | cardiac, heart** ◊ *They managed to revive the injured driver with cardiac ~.*
VERB + MASSAGE **enjoy, have, receive | give sb** ◊ *The therapist gave me a ~ to ease the pain.*
MASSAGE + NOUN **parlour/parlor** (= usually a place where men pay to have sex with women) **| chair, table | oil | therapist, therapy**

massage *verb*

ADV. **firmly, vigorously | gently, lightly, softly**
PREP. **into** ◊ *Gently ~ the cream into your skin.* **| with** ◊ *He ~d her back with scented oil.* ◊ *Massage it lightly with your fingertips.*

master *noun*

1 person in charge

ADJ. **political** ◊ *His political ~s are all old right-wing politicians.* **| colonial** ◊ *This was a time when many nations were trying to shake off their colonial ~s.* **| slave** ◊ *His father was a wealthy, prominent Virginia slave ~.* **| puppet** ◊ *The director is an unseen puppet ~, operating behind the scenes.* **| cruel** ◊ *Fate can be a cruel ~.* (*figurative*)
VERB + MASTER **obey, please, serve** ◊ *corrupt people who would serve any ~* **| disobey**
PREP. **~ of** ◊ *He wants to be ~ of his own destiny.*

2 person with skill

ADJ. **acknowledged, great, undisputed** ◊ *This portrait is the work of an acknowledged ~.* **| grand** ◊ *Chaplin, the grand ~ of physical comedy* **| chess, fencing, karate, etc.**
MASTER + NOUN **builder, craftsman, painter** (*esp. BrE*)
PREP. **~ of** ◊ *a ~ of disguise*
PHRASES **be a past ~ at sth, be a past ~ of sth** (= to be very good at sth) ◊ *He's a past ~ at delaying meetings.*

3 Master's university degree

VERB + MASTER'S **do, study for, take** ◊ *He did a Master's at Hull University.* **| earn, get** ◊ *She got her Master's last year.* **| complete, finish** ◊ *In May I completed my Master's in business administration.* **| have** ◊ *Lorenzo has a Master's in communications from Boston University.*
MASTER'S + NOUN **degree, thesis**
PREP. **~ in** ◊ *a Master's in politics*

master *verb*

ADV. **completely, fully, thoroughly | not quite | quickly | easily**
VERB + MASTER **be difficult to** ◊ *a technique that was surprisingly difficult to ~* **| struggle to, try to** ◊ *the challenge of trying to ~ a new language* **| fail to**
PHRASES **~ the art of sth** ◊ *He never completely ~ed the art of lip-reading.* **| ~ the basics** ◊ *Once you've ~ed the basics, try learning more difficult chords.*

masterpiece *noun*

ADJ. **great** ◊ *It's one of the greatest ~s of Western art.* **| acknowledged** ◊ *The piece ranks with such acknowledged ~s as the Mass in G.* **| minor | forgotten, lost** ◊ *a forgotten ~ from one of America's most underrated directors* **| architectural, cinematic, culinary, literary, musical, etc.**
VERB + MASTERPIECE **compose, create, paint, produce | be considered, be hailed as, be recognized as** ◊ *Within a week of publication, the novel was hailed as a ~.*
PREP. **~ by** ◊ *a ~ by Picasso* **| ~ of** ◊ *a ~ of classical architecture*
→ Note at ART

mastery *noun*

ADJ. **absolute, complete, total | technical** ◊ *He plays the violin with technical ~, but little feeling.*
VERB + MASTERY **have** ◊ *The allied bombers had total ~ of the skies.* **| demonstrate, display, show** ◊ *He shows complete ~ of the instrument.* **| achieve, acquire, attain, gain**
PREP. **~ of** ◊ *He acquired ~ of four languages.* **| ~ over** ◊ *The king had absolute ~ over the country.*

mat *noun*

ADJ. **rubber, straw, woven | judo, wrestling, yoga, etc. | prayer, sleeping | bath | mouse** (*BrE*) (**mouse pad** in *AmE*) ◊ *Every computer user should have a good mouse ~.* **| beer** (*BrE*) **| dense, thick** ◊ *a thick ~ of hair*
VERB + MAT **lay, lay out, roll out, unroll** ◊ *The man unrolled his prayer ~.*
PREP. **~ of** ◊ *the dense ~ of roots at the bottom of the tree*
PHRASES **put out the welcome ~, roll out the welcome ~** (both figurative, esp. *AmE*) ◊ *They hoped the country would put out a welcome ~ for Western investment.*

match *noun*

1 (*esp. BrE*) in sports

ADJ. **boxing** (*BrE, AmE*)**, chess** (*BrE, AmE*)**, football** (*BrE*)**, rugby** (*BrE*)**, soccer** (usually **football match** in *BrE* and **soccer game** in *AmE*)**, tennis** (*BrE, AmE*)**, wrestling** (*BrE, AmE*)**, etc. | final, quarter-final, semi-final** ◊ *He almost made it to the final ~.* **| friendly** (= not part of a competition) (*BrE*) **| away, home** (both *BrE*) ◊ *Some fans travel miles to go to away ~es.* **| grudge** ◊ *a grudge ~ between two of the best teams in the league* **| big, crucial, important | exciting, thrilling | title | championship, competitive, cup** (*BrE*)**, league** (*BrE*) **| sparring** ◊ *We were just having a little verbal sparring ~.* (*figurative*) **| screaming, shouting** (*figurative*) ◊ *The two of them then got into a shouting ~* (= an argument with a lot of shouting).
VERB + MATCH **play** ◊ *The ~ will be played in the new stadium.* **| have** ◊ *The team had an excellent ~.* **| go to, see, watch | be defeated in, lose | clinch, win** ◊ *A late goal clinched the ~ for Porto.* **| draw** (*BrE*)**, tie** (*AmE*) ◊ *We drew our first ~ of the season 1–1.* ◊ *Lubov fought back to tie the ~.* **| level** (*esp. BrE*) ◊ *They managed to level the ~, then went 2–1 ahead.*
MATCH + VERB **take place**
PREP. **during a/the ~** ◊ *an incident which took place during Saturday's ~* **| in a/the ~** ◊ *She was injured in last week's ~.* **| against** ◊ *the ~ against Wales* **| ~ between** ◊ *the ~ between Japan and Brazil* **| ~ with** ◊ *They lost their ~ with Estonia.*

2 for lighting a fire

ADJ. **lighted, lit** (*esp. AmE*)
...OF MATCHES **book, box**
VERB + MATCH **light, strike** ◊ *He lit a ~ so they could see in the cave.* **| blow out**
PHRASES **put a ~ to sth** ◊ *Someone had put a ~ to the pile of papers.*

3 good combination

ADJ. **excellent, good, perfect** ◊ *The blouse and skirt are a perfect ~.* ◊ *Freddie and Kate are a perfect ~.*
VERB + MATCH **find, make** ◊ *Our job is to find the right ~ for our clients.* ◊ *This fabric makes a good ~ for the wallpaper.*
PREP. **~ between** ◊ *an excellent ~ between our goals and what your company offers* **| ~ for** ◊ *That sweater should be a good ~ for your skirt.*
PHRASES **meet your ~** (= meet someone equally good, strong, etc.) ◊ *I think he's finally met his ~ in Lisa.* **| the right ~** ◊ *You need to feel confident that the candidate is the right ~.*

4 sth the same

ADJ. **exact**
VERB + MATCH **find** ◊ *She has a rare blood type, and finding a ~ could take years.*
PREP. **~ for** ◊ *To forge the certificate, she needed an exact ~ for the paper and the fonts.*

match verb

1 combine well with sb/sth

ADV. **well** ◇ As a couple they are not very well ~ed (= they are not very suitable for each other). | **nicely, perfectly** ◇ The music perfectly ~es the tone of the movie. | **exactly, precisely** ◇ They found a paint that exactly ~ed the existing paint on the walls. | **closely** ◇ He chose wine that closely ~ed each dish. | **not quite** ◇ The room was full of old furniture that didn't quite ~.

PHRASES **to ~** ◇ I bought a duvet cover and some curtains to ~.

2 find sth similar/connected

ADV. **carefully** | **correctly** | **up** ◇ We have to ~ up the right pet with the right owner.

VERB + MATCH **seek to, try to**

PREP. **for** ◇ The control group in the experiment was ~ed for age and sex. | **to** ◇ The aim of the competition is to ~ the quote to the person who said it. ◇ The available organs are carefully ~ed to people in need of transplants. | **with** ◇ The agency tries to ~ single people with suitable partners.

3 be/make sth equal/better

ADV. **almost, nearly** ◇ She found that his determination almost ~ed her own. | **not quite** ◇ Nothing quite ~es the fine, subtle taste of this cheese. | **rarely** ◇ Her lovers rarely ~ her wit and intelligence.

VERB + MATCH **be able to, be unable to** ◇ The company was unable to ~ his current salary. | **try to** | **fail to** ◇ Children can be made to suffer when they fail to ~ their parents' expectations.

PREP. **for** ◇ No other rock band comes even close to ~ing their talent.

PHRASES **come close to ~ing** | **be equally ~ed, be evenly ~ed, be well ~ed** ◇ The teams were very evenly ~ed. | **be unevenly ~ed**

mate noun

1 sexual partner

ADJ. **potential, prospective** ◇ Many matchmaking sites compile lists of potential ~s using basic information. | **ideal, suitable** ◇ He's a cheat and a gambler; hardly an ideal ~.

VERB + MATE **attract, find** ◇ These birds have bright plumage to attract a ~. | **choose, select**

2 (BrE, informal) friend

ADJ. **best, good** ◇ They've been good ~s ever since they were at school together.

VERB + MATE **have** ◇ He's got loads of ~s at school.

material noun

1 cloth

ADJ. **coarse, rough, thick** | **fine, silky, soft, thin** | **woven**
... OF MATERIAL **piece, scrap, strip** ◇ A patchwork quilt is a good way of using up scraps of ~.

2 substance

ADJ. **combustible, flammable, hazardous, inflammable** (esp. BrE), **nuclear, radioactive, toxic** | **primary, raw** ◇ Higher raw ~ costs have pushed up the price of many manufactured goods. | **natural, organic, plant** ◇ the decomposition of dead organic ~ such as vegetation | **recyclable, recycled** | **artificial, man-made, synthetic** | **composite** ◇ The artificial turf is laid onto a rubber composite ~. | **biological, genetic** ◇ We have 98% of the same genetic ~ as chimpanzees. | **industrial** | **building, construction** ◇ a storeroom full of building ~s | **original** ◇ Many of the original ~s were reused in the restoration of the building. | **art, drawing, writing** ◇ Prisoners were not allowed writing ~s.

VERB + MATERIAL **contain, incorporate, use** ◇ The corn contains genetically modified ~.

3 written, printed, or recorded matter

ADJ. **fascinating, good, relevant, useful** | **source** ◇ The letters were used as source ~ in this new biography. | **original** ◇ The magazine contains not one bit of original ~. | **classified, confidential, sensitive** | **copyright, copyrighted** | **printed** ◇ The collection includes objects and printed ~. |

unpublished | **reading** ◇ This is not really suitable reading ~ for a young child. | **educational, instructional, reference, teaching** | **marketing, promotional** | **additional, bonus, extra, supplemental** (esp. AmE), **supplementary** ◇ The DVD includes some great supplementary ~. | **archival, biographical, historical** ◇ The library has a wealth of old photographs and other archival ~. | **explicit, indecent, obscene, pornographic** ◇ He was convicted of importing indecent ~.

VERB + MATERIAL **collect, find, gather, get hold of** ◇ He's collecting ~ for a new book on space travel. ◇ I can't find any relevant ~ on him in the library. | **contain, include** ◇ This new biography contains a wealth of previously unpublished ~. | **produce, publish**

PREP. **~ for** ◇ useful ~ for a documentary | **~ on** ◇ original ~ on the First World War

materialize (BrE also -ise) verb

ADV. **never** ◇ The hoped-for boom never ~d. | **suddenly** ◇ A waiter suddenly ~d at her elbow. | **fully** ◇ We learned we must take threats seriously before they fully ~.

VERB + MATERIALIZE **fail to** ◇ The rise in share prices failed to ~.

mathematician noun

ADJ. **brilliant** | **distinguished, eminent, great, noted** ◇ one of the greatest ~s of all time | **applied, pure**

mathematics noun

ADJ. **applied, pure** | **school** | **elementary, higher**
PHRASES **a branch of ~**
→ Note at SUBJECT (for verbs and nouns)

maths (BrE) (AmE math) noun

ADJ. **applied, pure** | **basic, elementary, simple** | **advanced, complicated** ◇ Working out the quantities of the ingredients involved some complicated ~. | **college, high-school** (both esp. AmE) | **fifth-grade, etc.** (in the US) | **mental** (esp. AmE) ◇ I did some quick mental ~ to work out the difference.

MATHS/MATH + NOUN **problem** ◇ The class was struggling to find the solution to a ~ problem. | **class** (esp. AmE), **lesson** (esp. BrE) | **exam, test**
→ Note at SUBJECT

matter noun

1 subject/situation that must be dealt with

ADJ. **important, pressing, serious, urgent, weighty** ◇ He left, saying he had pressing ~s to attend to. ◇ The question of his innocence is a weighty ~ for this court. | **complex, complicated, controversial, delicate, difficult, sensitive** ◇ I wasn't sure how to approach the delicate ~ of pay. | **simple, trifling** (esp. BrE), **trivial** ◇ It is then a simple ~ to print off the data you have collected. | **no easy, no simple** ◇ It is no simple ~ starting a new business. | **practical** ◇ They've agreed in theory, but now we need to discuss practical ~s. | **family, personal, private** | **subject** ◇ His articles deal with a wide range of subject ~. | **economic, environmental, financial, legal, political, procedural, religious, spiritual, technical** | **routine** ◇ The rest of the meeting was taken up by routine ~s. | **related** ◇ They talk mostly about work and related ~s. | **different, other** ◇ I don't mind lizards, but snakes are a different ~.

VERB + MATTER **bring up, broach, raise** ◇ I thought I'd better broach the ~ with my boss. ◇ The ~ will be raised at our next meeting. | **address, debate, discuss, go into, take up** ◇ I don't really want to go into this ~ now. | **press, pursue, take further** ◇ After legal advice I chose to take the ~ further. | **drop** ◇ His lawyer advised him to drop the ~. | **consider, examine, investigate, look at, look into, tackle** | **clarify, clear up, decide, resolve, settle** ◇ It's a relief to have the ~ settled. | **approach, deal with, handle, treat** ◇ Police are treating the ~ as a murder investigation.

MATTER + VERB **be related to, pertain to** (formal), **relate to** ◇

latest paintings show how the artist has really grown in ~. | **lack**

2 full growth

ADJ. **full** ◊ *It can take years for these plants to reach full ~.* | **physical, psychological, sexual**

VERB + MATURITY **attain, come to, grow to, reach** | **approach, near** ◊ *The insects lay eggs when they approach ~.*

maul *verb*

ADV. **badly, brutally, severely** ◊ *She was badly ~ed by a lion.* | **fatally**

maxim *noun*

ADJ. **general, simple** | **famous** | **old** ◊ *As the old ~ goes, 'A picture is worth a thousand words'.*

VERB + MAXIM **apply, follow, heed** ◊ *If you follow a few simple ~s, your business should be a success.* | **quote**

MAXIM + VERB **apply, hold** ◊ *The golden rule is to pay attention. The same ~ applies to parenting.*

maximum *noun*

ADJ. **absolute** | **agreed, recommended** ◊ *Do not exceed the recommended ~ of twelve drops a day.* | **legal, statutory**

VERB + MAXIMUM **achieve, reach, rise to** ◊ *The temperature reached a ~ of 35°C yesterday.* | **exceed** | **allow (sb/sth), permit (sb/sth)** ◊ *In the exam, allow yourself a ~ of 30 minutes per question.* ◊ *the ~ permitted speeds* | **limit sth to, restrict sth to** ◊ *The amount you have to pay will be limited to a ~ of £500.*

PREP. **above (the) ~, below (the) ~** | **at (the) ~** ◊ *a drive of four hours at the ~* | **to (the) ~** ◊ *He is using his talents to the ~.* | **(up) to a/the ~** | **~ of** ◊ *You can claim the allowance for a ~ of six months.*

PHRASES **~ possible** ◊ *Everyone should contribute the ~ possible.*

May *noun* → Note at MONTH

mayor *noun*

ADJ. **local** | **deputy** | **lord** (*in the UK*) ◊ *In 1662–3 he served as Lord Mayor of London.* | **Democratic, Republican, right-wing, socialist, etc.** | **current, incumbent** (*AmE*) | **former** | **big-city, small-town** (*both AmE*)

VERB + MAYOR **run for** ◊ *He is running for ~ of Bogotá.* | **elect (sb), elect sb as** | **serve as**

PREP. **~ of** ◊ *the ~ of Moscow*

maze *noun*

ADJ. **complex, complicated, confusing, intricate** | **hedge** ◊ *the famous hedge ~ at Hampton Court* | **bureaucratic** (*figurative*) ◊ *They did not have the expertise to navigate the bureaucratic ~ required for certification.*

VERB + MAZE **be lost in, get lost in** | **find your way through, navigate, negotiate** ◊ *He found his way through the complex ~ of corridors.*

PREP. **in a/the ~, through a/the ~** ◊ *I followed him through a ~ of narrow alleys.* | **~ of** ◊ *I was lost in a ~ of passages.*

meal *noun*

ADJ. **big, filling, heavy** ◊ *I always want to go to sleep after a heavy ~.* | **hearty, slap-up** (*BrE*) | **gourmet** (*esp. AmE*), **lavish, sumptuous** | **decent, proper, square, substantial** ◊ *She hadn't had a square ~ for days.* | **light, simple** ◊ *The bar serves light ~s.* | **meagre/meager** ◊ *a meagre/meager ~ of bread and cheese* | **four-course, three-course, etc.** | **appetizing, delicious, excellent, lovely** (*esp. BrE*), **tasty** ◊ *Thanks for a delicious ~.* | **home-cooked** ◊ *She has very little time to prepare home-cooked ~s.* | **balanced, healthful** (*AmE*), **healthy, nourishing, nutritious, wholesome** | **main** ◊ *When do you have your main ~ of the day?* | **evening** (*esp. BrE*), **midday** (*esp. BrE*), **noon** (*AmE*) | **hot** ◊ *Hot ~s are not available after 10 o'clock.* | **favourite/favorite** ◊ *That night he made her favourite/favorite ~.* | **vegetarian** | **festive** (*esp. AmE*) | **Christmas, Passover, Thanksgiving, etc.**

→ Special page at FOOD

She was a great source of knowledge on ~s relating to nutrition.

PREP. **in a/the ~** ◊ *I don't have much experience in these ~s.* ◊ *Do I have any choice in the ~?* | **on a/the ~** ◊ *Speak to your manager if you need help on this ~.* | **~ for** ◊ *The incident is definitely a ~ for the police.* | **~ of** ◊ *It's a ~ of concern to all of us.* ◊ *We discussed the ~ of whether or not to hire a bus.* ◊ *Getting the effect you want is a ~ of trial and error.*

PHRASES **the crux of the ~, the heart of the ~** (= the most important part of a subject/situation) | **let the ~ drop, let the ~ go, let the ~ rest** ◊ *She refused to let the ~ rest.* | **the ~ in hand** ◊ *Let's concentrate on the ~ in hand for now, and leave other issues till later.* | **be no laughing ~** ◊ *The safety of his family was no laughing ~.*

2 matters situation you are in

VERB + MATTERS **complicate, confuse, make worse, not help** ◊ *It didn't help ~s that I had a terrible cold.* ◊ *To make ~s worse, my friend then lost her keys.* | **simplify** ◊ *Let me simplify ~s by giving you my answer now.* | **arrange** ◊ *She always arranges ~s to suit herself.*

3 substance

ADJ. **solid** | **organic, vegetable** ◊ *composed entirely of organic ~* | **inanimate, inorganic** | **decaying** | **dark** (*science*) | **printed, reading**

matter *verb*

ADV. **a great deal, a lot, greatly, really** ◊ *These things ~ a lot to young children.* | **hardly, little** (*formal*), **not much, scarcely** (*esp. BrE*) ◊ *She could find a job. It hardly ~ed what.* | **no longer, not any more**

VERB + MATTER **not seem to** ◊ *Somehow it didn't seem to ~ much any more.*

PREP. **about** ◊ *It doesn't ~ about the mess.* | **to** ◊ *It didn't ~ to her that he was blind.*

PHRASES **not ~ a/one bit, not ~ a/one jot** (*BrE*), **not ~ a/one whit** (*esp. AmE*) ◊ *It doesn't ~ one whit what their ethnic background is.*

mattress *noun*

ADJ. **double, king-size, queen-size** (*AmE*), **single** | **comfortable, cushy** (*AmE*) | **firm, hard** | **soft, springy, lumpy** ◊ *an old bed with a lumpy ~* | **thin** | **air, blow-up, inflatable** | **foam** | **cot** (*BrE*), **crib** (*AmE*)

PREP. **on a/the ~** ◊ *The children slept on ~es on the floor.* | **under a/the ~** ◊ *My grandmother keeps her money under the ~.*

mature *verb*

ADV. **fully** ◊ *a fully ~d cheese* | **early** ◊ *This variety is easy to grow and ~s early.* | **quickly, rapidly** | **slowly** | **emotionally, physically** ◊ *The teenage years cover a period in which people ~ physically and emotionally.* | **nicely** ◊ *The little garden was maturing nicely.*

VERB + MATURE **allow sth to, leave sth to** ◊ *The cheese is smoked and then left to ~.*

PREP. **into** ◊ *She had ~d into a beautiful young woman.* | **to** ◊ *a young man who is maturing to adulthood*

mature *adj.*

VERBS **be** | **become** | **look** ◊ *She tries to look ~ and sophisticated.*

ADV. **extremely, fairly, very, etc.** | **fully** | **emotionally, physically, sexually** | **remarkably** ◊ *He was remarkably ~ for his age.*

maturity *noun*

1 adult behaviour/behavior

ADJ. **great, growing, increasing, new-found** ◊ *I can see an increasing ~ in how she understands the world.* | **artistic, emotional, intellectual**

VERB + MATURITY **have** | **demonstrate, display, show** ◊ *She has shown great ~ in her life choices.* | **gain, grow in** ◊ *These*

NOTE

Meals

eat…, have… ◊ *Have you had breakfast?*

take… (*formal*) ◊ *I often take lunch in the hotel bar.*

grab…, snatch… (*BrE*) ◊ *Let's grab lunch.* ◊ *I'm so busy I have to snatch meals when I can.*

come for/to…, go for/to ~ (These verbs are often used with *around* (*esp. AmE*), *out*, *over* and *round* (*esp. BrE*).) ◊ *We went to Fargo's for lunch.* ◊ *We're going out for dinner.* ◊ *We're going out for a meal.* (*BrE*) ◊ *You should come over for dinner sometime.*

ask sb to…, have sb for/to…, invite sb for/to…, take sb for/to… (These verbs are often used with *around* (*esp. AmE*), *out*, *over* and *round* (*esp. BrE*).) ◊ *He wouldn't have asked me to supper if he didn't like me.* ◊ *We must have you over for dinner sometime.* ◊ *Let me take you out for lunch.*

be out to lunch ◊ *He's out to lunch with a client.*

stop for… ◊ *We stopped for tea at the Ritz.*

join sb for…, stay for/to… ◊ *You're sure you won't stay for dinner?*

sit down to…, start…, finish… ◊ *We had just sat down to breakfast when the phone rang.*

skip… ◊ *I sometimes skip lunch if we're very busy.*

cook (sb)…, fix (sb)… (*esp. AmE*), get… ready, make (sb)…, prepare… ◊ *She hurried downstairs to fix herself some breakfast.*

have… ready ◊ *We'll have supper ready for you.*

serve… ◊ *Lunch is served from 12.30 till 2.30.*

keep… warm, warm… up ◊ *I'll be home late, so keep my dinner warm.*

provide (sb with)… ◊ *Dinner is provided in the superb hotel restaurant.*

… is available ◊ *A four-course dinner is available by prior arrangement.*

… is ready ◊ *'Breakfast's ready!' shouted Christine.*

… time (usually written as one word) ◊ *The family was always noisy at mealtimes.* ◊ *It was lunchtime.*

at…, during…, over… ◊ *Nobody spoke during supper.*

for… ◊ *What did you have for lunch?*

… of ◊ *a breakfast of pancakes and maple syrup*

mean *adj.*

1 unkind

VERBS be, feel, seem | become

ADV. extremely, fairly, very, etc. ◊ *That was a pretty ~ trick.*

PREP. to ◊ *He's so ~ to his mother!*

2 (*BrE*) not generous

VERBS be, seem | become

ADV. extremely, fairly, very, etc. ◊ *I thought it was really ~ of him not to pay for the meal.* | a little, slightly, etc. ◊ *He's a little ~ when it comes to spending money on the children.*

PREP. with ◊ *She's very ~ with her money.*

meaning *noun*

1 what sth means

ADJ. clear, exact, precise ◊ *The context makes the ~ clear.* ◊ *What is the exact ~ of this phrase?* | intended, true, underlying | correct | original | double, hidden ◊ *There's often a double ~ in jokes and riddles.* ◊ *I'm sure there's no hidden ~ in what he says.* | figurative, metaphorical, symbolic | cultural ◊ *He explores the deeper cultural ~ of 'home'.* | literal

VERB + MEANING comprehend, get, grasp, understand ◊ *I can't grasp the ~ of this quotation.* | decipher, interpret, work out ◊ *Historians are trying to decipher the ~ of the documents.* | explore, ponder ◊ *The movie ends with scenes that are supposed to leave us pondering its ~.* | assign, attach, attribute, discern ◊ *She assigns a ~ to his words they just didn't have.* | clarify, explain ◊ *The copy editor uses her*

skill to clarify the ~. | redefine ◊ *That night redefined the ~ of the word 'love' to him.* | alter, change, distort ◊ *These translation errors alter the ~ of the sentence.* | misinterpret, misunderstand ◊ *I think you misunderstood my ~.* | determine ◊ *The context largely determines the ~.* | bear, carry, have ◊ *Some of the symbols carry ~ and some just represent sounds.* ◊ *a word that has more than one ~* | acquire, take on ◊ *The word 'gay' took on its modern ~ in the 1960s.* | communicate, convey, express

PREP. in a/the ~ ◊ *ambiguity in the ~ of a phrase* | with a/the ~ ◊ *I am using the word with its original ~.* | ~ behind ◊ *the ~ behind an event*

PHRASES a nuance of ~, a shade of ~ ◊ *It is difficult for a non-Italian to grasp all the nuances of ~.*

2 purpose/importance

ADJ. deep, real, true ◊ *She's searching for the deeper ~ of life.* | spiritual ◊ *He found spiritual ~ through religion.* | intrinsic ◊ *For him, art held little intrinsic ~.*

VERB + MEANING have ◊ *Her work no longer had any ~ for her.* | acquire ◊ *As parents, our lives acquired new ~.* | find | lose ◊ *After his death, she felt life had lost all ~.* | give ◊ *Falling in love gave ~ to his life.* | contemplate, explore, ponder ◊ *You can't sit around contemplating the ~ of life all day.*

PREP. without ~ ◊ *Young people can feel that life is without ~.*

meaningless *adj.*

VERBS be | become | render sth

ADV. absolutely, quite, totally, utterly | increasingly | almost, virtually ◊ *The phrase has become almost ~.* | basically, essentially, largely | fairly, pretty | apparently, seemingly ◊ *apparently ~ jargon* | scientifically, statistically

means *noun*

1 method of doing sth

ADJ. appropriate, convenient, effective, efficient, reliable, useful ◊ *an effective ~ of mass communication* | best, preferred ◊ *Gold has been the preferred ~ of exchange for centuries.* | necessary, possible, practicable (*BrE*) ◊ *We will use every possible ~ to achieve our objective.* | alternate (*AmE*), alternative, other ◊ *War is famously 'the continuation of policy by other means'.* | primary, principal ◊ *Painting had become his primary ~ of self-expression.* | only, sole ◊ *Oil lamps were the sole ~ of illumination.* | conventional, traditional | legal, legitimate | non-violent, peaceful | military | electronic, technical ◊ *Infringement of copyright includes distribution by electronic ~.*

VERB + MEANS have ◊ *We have no ~ of knowing how they will react.* | use | offer (sb), provide (sb with) ◊ *My English teacher provided me with the ~ to enjoy reading poetry.* | develop, devise ◊ *Can you devise a ~ of overcoming the problem?*

PREP. by ~ (of) ◊ *The stone was lifted by ~ of a rope and pulley.* | through ~ ◊ *They cannot achieve their goal through legal ~.* | ~ for ◊ *the ~ for achieving happiness* | ~ of ◊ *a ~ of access/communication/transport* ◊ *a ~ of getting what you want*

PHRASES the end justifies the ~ ◊ *In the case of torture, the end can never justify the ~.* | a ~ to an end ◊ *He saw his education merely as a ~ to an end.* | by any ~ necessary, by fair ~ or foul | by no ~/not by any ~ (= not at all), ways and ~ ◊ *There are ways and ~ of raising money.*

2 money/wealth

ADJ. independent, private ◊ *She must have independent ~ to live in such style.* | limited, little, moderate, modest, slender | visible ◊ *people who lack visible ~ of support*

VERB + MEANS have | lack

MEANS + NOUN test ◊ *Eligibility for the benefit was determined by a ~ test.*

PREP. according to your ~ (= according to what you can afford) | beyond your ~ ◊ *Private school fees are beyond the ~ of most people* (= more than they can afford). | within

your ~ (= according to what you can afford) ◇ *She finds it difficult to live within her ~.*
PHRASES **a man/woman of ~** (= a rich man/woman)

measles noun

VERB + MEASLES **have** ◇ *All our children have had the ~.* | **catch, contract** | **immunize sb against, vaccinate sb against**
MEASLES + NOUN **virus** | **immunization, vaccination, vaccine** | **jab** (*BrE*), **shot** (*esp. AmE*)
→ Special page at ILLNESS

measure noun

1 official action to deal with a problem

ADJ. **appropriate, effective, necessary, practical** ◇ *We urge you to adopt all necessary ~s to guarantee people's safety.* | **key** | **extraordinary, special** ◇ *We had to resort to extraordinary ~s to find employees.* | **simple** | **desperate, draconian, drastic, extreme, harsh, radical, repressive, strong, tough** | **emergency, urgent** (*esp. BrE*) | **interim, short-term, stopgap, temporary** | **additional** | **defensive, precautionary, preventative, preventive** | **disciplinary, punitive** | **corrective, remedial** | **protective, safety, security** ◇ *New security ~s were implemented to prevent further violence.* | **conservation, control** ◇ *Development of new water sources needs to be combined with conservation ~s.* | **austerity, cost-cutting, economy** (*esp. BrE*), **efficiency** | **economic, policy** | **government**
... OF MEASURES **package** (*esp. BrE*), **raft** (*BrE*), **range** (*esp. BrE*), **series, set** (*esp. AmE*) ◇ *a package of ~s aimed at cutting pollution*
VERB + MEASURE **employ, implement, impose, institute, introduce, take, use** ◇ *Special ~s are being taken to protect the local water supplies.* ◇ *The authorities are using increasingly repressive ~s.* | **adopt, approve, enact, pass** ◇ *The Committee unanimously approved the ~.* | **defeat, oppose, veto** ◇ *The mayor threatened to veto a ~ passed by the city council.* | **propose, suggest**
MEASURE + VERB **be aimed at sth, be designed to, be intended to**
PREP. **~ against** ◇ *tougher ~s against racism* | **~ for** ◇ *~s for reducing delays*

2 amount/quantity of sth

ADJ. **broad, considerable, fair, generous, great, significant, substantial, wide**
PREP. **~ of** ◇ *He poured me a generous ~ of gin.*
PHRASES **in considerable, large, some, etc. ~** ◇ *His success was due in large ~ to your help.* | **in equal ~** ◇ *He's been praised and condemned in equal ~.* | **in no small ~**

3 unit of size/quantity

ADJ. **accurate, direct, fair, objective, precise** ◇ *This figure alone is not a fair ~ of our success.* | **broad** ◇ *GDP is considered the broadest ~ of a country's economic activity.* | **indirect** | **important** ◇ *The price of housing relative to income is an important ~ of real income.* | **quantitative, statistical** ◇ *They tried to formulate a quantitative ~ of well-being.* | **standard, standardized** ◇ *Higher scores on this standardized ~ indicate greater creativity.* | **imperial, metric** | **behavioural/behavioral** (*esp. AmE*), **performance** ◇ *Companies can use their stock price as a performance ~.*
VERB + MEASURE **calculate, derive, obtain** ◇ *This ~ is obtained by dividing corporate profits by corporate bond yields.* | **provide** ◇ *This figure provides an objective ~ of risk.*
PREP. **~ of** ◇ *an accurate ~ of length*
PHRASES **weights and ~s**

4 sign of sth

ADJ. **crude, reliable, simple, true, useful, valid** ◇ *A reliable ~ of progress is whether your children can do something they couldn't do before.* | **important** ◇ *Accepting the lower salary was seen as an important ~ of commitment.*
PREP. **~ of** ◇ *Landed income was the true ~ of the gentry.*

5 (*AmE*) in music → See also BAR

ADJ. **first, opening** ◇ *The band began playing the opening ~s.*
VERB + MEASURE **hear, play, sing** ◇ *He placed his fingers on the keys and played a few ~s.*
PREP. **~ of** ◇ *the first few ~s of Mozart's third violin concerto* | **per ~, to a/the ~** ◇ *a steady rhythm of four beats to a ~*

NOTE

Weights and measures

... of ◇ *I always drink gallons of water.*
half a..., a quarter of a... ◇ *half a pound of ham*
a half/quarter hour, inch, mile, ounce, pint, pound ◇ *a quarter pound of cheese*
cubic..., square... ◇ *a maximum flow of 3 300 cubic feet a second*
...square ◇ *The room is about 25 feet square.*
...broad, deep, high, long, tall, thick, wide ◇ *The new dock was 230 m long and 92 m wide.*
...bigger, cooler, faster, heavier, lighter, slower ◇ *The climate was several degrees warmer than it is now.*
about..., approximately..., around... ◇ *1 kilogram = approx. 2.2 pounds*
be..., cover..., measure..., span..., stretch (for)... (used with measures of distance and area) ◇ *The National Park covers 3 000 acres.* ◇ *The sandy beach stretches for over four miles.*
be..., weigh... (used with measures of weight) ◇ *She weighed over 200 pounds.*
be..., last..., take... (used with measures of time) ◇ *It takes approximately 365 and a quarter days for the earth to revolve around the sun.*
in a... ◇ *How many inches are there in a foot?*
in... ◇ *We were asked to estimate the temperature of the room in degrees centigrade.*
to a/the... ◇ *My car does 25 miles to the gallon.*
a..., per... ◇ *They're $4.50 a dozen.* ◇ *ten ounces of platinum per ton of ore*
by the... ◇ *Apples are sold by the kilogram.*
of... ◇ *The path will be built to a width of two and a half feet.*
...in area, length, size, volume, weight ◇ *Killer whales are up to 30 feet in length.*
...by... ◇ *a huge room measuring 50 m by 18 m*
to the nearest... ◇ *Give your answer to the nearest mile.*

---

measure verb

1 find the size of sth

ADV. **accurately, exactly, precisely, reliably** | **empirically, objectively, quantitatively** ◇ *Education policy places too much emphasis on things that can be quantitatively ~d.* | **carefully** | **directly** ◇ *Any type of data that could not be directly ~d was rejected.* | **indirectly** | **easily** | **experimentally** | **up** ◇ *We need to ~ up the room for a new carpet.*
VERB + MEASURE **be able to, can** ◇ *You can now ~ its length more accurately.* | **be easy to, be possible to** | **be difficult to, be hard to, be impossible to**
PREP. **for** ◇ *She's being ~d for her wedding outfit.* | **in** ◇ *Cloth is ~d in yards.*

2 judge the importance/value/effect of sth

ADV. **easily** ◇ *The policy's impact cannot be easily ~d.* | **effectively** | **objectively**
VERB + MEASURE **can** | **be easy to, be possible to** | **be difficult to, be hard to, be impossible to** ◇ *It is hard to ~ the benefits to society of the system.* | **be used to** ◇ *the criteria that are used to ~ performance*
PREP. **according to** ◇ *Is it really possible to ~ the skills of such jobs according to objective standards?* | **against** ◇ *The school's performance is ~d against a strict set of criteria.* | **by** ◇ *The policy's effectiveness cannot be ~d by numbers alone.* | **in terms of** ◇ *Success cannot be ~d merely in terms of the size of your salary.*

measurement *noun*

ADJ. **accurate, careful, exact, objective, precise** ◊ *It is important to take precise ~s of the structure.* ◊ *Objective ~ is difficult with such poor equipment.* | **quantitative** | **lab** (*informal*), **laboratory, scientific** | **standard, standardized** | **metric** | **length, pressure, temperature, etc.** | **body, bust, chest, hip, waist** | **performance**
VERB + MEASUREMENT **calculate, carry out, get, make, obtain, perform, record, take** | **convert**
MEASUREMENT + NOUN **instrument, system, technique, tool** | **scale, unit** | **error**
PHRASES **a scale of ~, a unit of ~**

meat *noun*

ADJ. **fresh** | **bad, rancid, rotten, rotting** ◊ *That ~ smells rotten.* | **tender** ◊ *Simmer the ~ for 30 minutes until tender.* | **tough** | **lean, fatty** | **dark, red, white** | **raw, uncooked** | **rare, undercooked** | **cooked, cured, dried, grilled, processed, roast, salted, smoked** | **cold** ◊ *a plate of cold ~s* | **frozen** | **ground** (*AmE*), **mince** (usually **mincemeat**) (*esp. BrE*), **minced** | **canned, lunch** (usually **lunchmeat**) (*AmE*), **luncheon, potted, tinned** (*BrE*) | **hamburger** (*esp. AmE*), **sausage** (*esp. BrE*) | **organic** | **halal, kosher** | **crab, goat, horse, etc.**
... OF MEAT **bit, chunk, lump, piece, slab, slice** | **cut, joint** (*BrE*) ◊ *She always buys the cheaper cuts of ~.*
VERB + MEAT **consume, eat** ◊ *The animals do not hunt and rarely consume ~.* ◊ *Do you eat ~?* | **chew, chew on** | **barbecue, cook, fry, grill, roast, stew** ◊ *Fry the ~ in a little olive oil.* | **marinate** | **tenderize** | **brown, seal** (*BrE*) ◊ *Turn the ~ frequently to brown it.* | **chop, cube** (*esp. BrE*), **cut, dice, grind** (*AmE*), **mince** | **bone** | **carve, slice**
MEAT + VERB **be off** (*esp. BrE*), **go off, rot, spoil** (*esp. AmE*) ◊ *The ~ has gone off.*
MEAT + NOUN **ball** (usually **meatballs**), **broth** (*esp. AmE*), **dish, loaf, patty** (*esp. AmE*), **pie** (*esp. BrE*), **stew** ◊ *recipes for simple ~ dishes* | **products** | **market** | **cleaver, grinder** (*AmE*) (**mincer** in *BrE*), **slicer, tenderizer** | **hook** | **locker** (*esp. AmE*) ◊ *It was so cold, it was like a ~ locker.* | **cutter, packer** (*both AmE*) ◊ *He eventually found employment as a ~ cutter.* | **eater** ◊ *I'm not a great ~ eater.* | **content** (*esp. BrE*) ◊ *These pies have a low ~ content.* | **packing** (*AmE*), **production** | **consumption** ◊ *Canada's ~ consumption*
→ Special page at FOOD

mechanic *noun*

ADJ. **good, skilled** | **chief** | **auto** (*AmE*), **car** (*esp. BrE*), **garage, motor** (*esp. BrE*)
→ Note at JOB

mechanics *noun*

1 how sth works/is done

ADJ. **actual, basic** ◊ *We need to discuss the actual ~ of the operation.* | **simple** ◊ *The ~ of creating a link are relatively simple.* | **complex, complicated** ◊ *Only he understood the complicated ~ of his business.*

2 science of movement and force

ADJ. **celestial, classical, fluid, Newtonian, quantum, statistical**

mechanism *noun*

1 part of a machine

ADJ. **firing, locking, steering, trigger, winding**
VERB + MECHANISM **activate** ◊ *This activates the train's tilt ~.* | **jam** ◊ *The gun froze, jamming the ~.*
MECHANISM + VERB **operate, work** ◊ *The door locking ~ doesn't work.*

2 system/method

ADJ. **effective** ◊ *an effective ~ for enforcing the rules* | **exact, precise** ◊ *Scientists have been unable to explain the exact ~ behind this effect.* | **underlying** | **complex, complicated** | **simple** | **alternative** ◊ *He suggested an alternative ~ for providing public services.* | **social** | **avoidance, control, coping, defence/defense, escape, feedback, protective, repair, survival** ◊ *The body has defence ~s against many diseases.* | **cellular, genetic, immunological, molecular, neural, physiological, psychological, etc.**
VERB + MECHANISM **provide** ◊ *The system provides a ~ whereby information is fed back into the market.* | **propose, suggest** | **investigate** | **activate, trigger** ◊ *This activates the body's thirst ~.* | **control, govern, regulate** ◊ *physiological ~s regulating the release of hormones*
MECHANISM + VERB **operate, work** | **allow sth, ensure sth**
PREP. **by the ~ of, through the ~ of** ◊ *The government is held accountable through the ~ of regular general elections.* | **~ for** ◊ *a ~ for dealing with complaints*

medal *noun*

ADJ. **bronze, gold, silver** ◊ *He won a gold ~ in the 100 metres/meters.* | **gymnastics, weightlifting, etc.** | **championship** (*esp. BrE*), **Olympic** | **commemorative** ◊ *A commemorative ~ was struck for the event.*
VERB + MEDAL **be awarded, collect, earn, get, receive, win** | **deserve** (*often figurative*) ◊ *She deserves a ~ for putting up with him.* | **award (sb), give sb, present (sb with)** | **strike**
MEDAL + NOUN **winner** | **hope, hopes** ◊ *He is a major ~ hope for Kenya.* ◊ *Her ~ hopes were dashed by injury.*
PREP. **~ for** ◊ *a ~ for bravery*
PHRASES **a ~ of honour/honor**

media *noun*

ADJ. **mass** ◊ *The event was widely covered by the mass ~.* | **audio-visual, broadcast** (*esp. BrE*), **news, print, visual** ◊ *Their PR officer handles TV, radio, and print ~ interviews.* | **digital, electronic, interactive, streaming** ◊ *They broadcast streaming ~ to PCs.* | **foreign, international, local, national, Western** | **corporate, mainstream, official, popular** | **left-wing, right-wing** | **conservative, liberal** (*both esp. AmE*)
VERB + MEDIA **accuse, blame, criticize** ◊ *Some blame the ~ for propagating negative stereotypes.* | **control, manipulate** ◊ *There is a perception that the government controls the ~.* | **dominate** ◊ *One story has dominated the ~ this week.*
MEDIA + VERB **cover sth, report sth** ◊ *The local ~ reported rioting across the country.* | **portray sb/sth (as sth)** | **focus on sth, pick sth up** (*esp. AmE*), **pick up on sth** ◊ *I think the ~ picked up on the story because she's a woman.* | **ignore sth** | **be biased** ◊ *They believe that the ~ is biased against them.*
MEDIA + NOUN **attention, coverage, interest, publicity, reporting** ◊ *There was a lot of ~ coverage of the wedding.* | **campaign** | **report** | **event** ◊ *Music has been turned into a series of ~ events.* | **blitz, circus, frenzy, hype** ◊ *The company is anxious to play down the ~ hype.* | **spotlight** | **image** ◊ *She's very different from her ~ image.* | **darling** ◊ *The two gangsters were ~ darlings in the 60s.* | **bias** | **blackout, censorship** | **freedom** | **relations** | **critic, person, pundit** | **baron, magnate, mogul, tycoon** | **ownership** | **company, conglomerate, empire, giant, group, interests, organization, outlet** | **awareness, literacy, studies**
PREP. **through the ~, via the ~** ◊ *propaganda through the ~*
PHRASES **access to the ~** | **the role of the ~**

mediation *noun*

ADJ. **international, UN, etc.** | **multiparty** | **divorce**
VERB + MEDIATION **accept** ◊ *Unless management accepts ~, the strike will never be resolved.*
MEDIATION + NOUN **efforts, process**
PREP. **through sb's ~** ◊ *The conflict ended through the ~ of the United Nations.* | **under sb's ~** ◊ *under international ~* | **~ between, ~ by** ◊ *~ by the prime minister between the two sides*

medical *noun* (*esp. BrE*) → See also PHYSICAL

ADJ. **full, regular** ◊ *Pilots undergo regular ~s.*

VERB + MEDICAL **have, undergo** | **pass** ◇ *He was accepted onto the course after passing the ~.*

medication *noun*

ADJ. **prescribed, prescription** | **non-prescription** (*esp. AmE*), **over-the-counter** | **regular** | **antidepressant, anti-inflammatory, antiviral, etc.** | **allergy, asthma, diabetes, etc.** | **oral, topical** | **herbal** (*AmE*)
VERB + MEDICATION **be on, receive, take** | **prescribe (sb)** | **administer, give sb** | **dispense** | **stop** ◇ *She stopped the ~ because of side effects.* | **adjust, change, switch** ◇ *He talked with his doctor about changing his ~.* | **need, require**
PREP. **~ for** ◇ *He is on regular ~ for his fits.*

medicine *noun*

1 science of treating/preventing illness

ADJ. **modern** ◇ *advances in modern ~* | **traditional** ◇ *qualified in traditional Chinese ~* | **folk** ◇ *Garlic was widely used in folk ~.* | **conventional, orthodox** | **alternative, complementary, holistic, homeopathic, naturopathic, etc.** | **preventative, preventive** | **academic, clinical, forensic, scientific** | **family, general** ◇ *She gave up general ~ to specialize in geriatrics.* | **geriatric, internal, obstetric, paediatric/pediatric, veterinary, etc.** | **Ayurvedic, Chinese, Oriental, Western** | **private** (*esp. BrE*), **public-health** (*BrE*), **socialized** (*esp. AmE*) ◇ *She believed private ~ was a threat to the existence of the National Health Service.*
VERB + MEDICINE **train in** | **qualify in** | **practise/practice** ◇ *people practising alternative ~*
PHRASES **a branch of ~**
→ Note at SUBJECT (for more verbs and nouns)

2 substance taken to treat an illness

ADJ. **powerful, strong** | **allergy, cough, etc.** ◇ *a bottle of cough ~* | **anti-inflammatory, antiviral, etc.** | **botanical, herbal** | **prescription** | **non-prescription** (*esp. AmE*), **over-the-counter**
... OF MEDICINE **dose**
VERB + MEDICINE **take** | **swallow** | **prescribe (sb)** | **administer, give sb** | **dispense** | **treat sb with**
MEDICINE + NOUN **cabinet, chest** | **bottle, dropper**
PREP. **~ for** ◇ *~ for a chest infection*

meditation *noun*

ADJ. **deep, profound** ◇ *Techniques of deep ~ help people under stress.* | **quiet, silent** ◇ *He stared out of the window in silent ~.* | **guided** ◇ *She uses music and guided ~ to relax and inspire.* | **Buddhist, Christian, etc.** | **religious, transcendental**
VERB + MEDITATION **do, practise/practice**
PREP. **in ~** ◇ *Adherents spend hours in ~.* | **~ on** ◇ *The novel is an extended ~ on art, love and loss.*

medium *noun*

1 means of expressing/communicating sth

ADJ. **advertising, broadcast, communication** ◇ *Radio is an important communication ~ in many countries.* | **mass** | **digital, electronic, interactive, print, printed, visual, written** | **recording, storage** ◇ *He believes tape will eventually be eliminated as a recording ~.* ◇ *An optical disk is just another kind of electronic storage ~.*
PREP. **through the ~ of** ◇ *The government communicates through the ~ of television.* | **~ for** ◇ *She used her novels as a ~ for encouraging political debate.* ◇ *She experimented with the blog as a new ~ for exploring issues.*
PHRASES **a ~ of communication** | **a ~ of instruction** (= a language used for teaching) ◇ *English is the ~ of instruction in many African countries.*

2 material/form that an artist, etc. uses

ADJ. **artistic** ◇ *Oil paint is her preferred artistic ~.* | **photographic** ◇ *The gallery has been committed to the photographic ~ for 25 years.* | **mixed media** ◇ *mixed-media artwork*

meet *noun* (*esp. AmE*)

ADJ. **gymnastics, race, swim, track** | **hunt** (*BrE*) | **championship** | **big, major** | **dual** ◇ *a dual ~ against Canada* | **spring, summer, etc.** | **swap** ◇ *a swap ~ for collectors of Star Trek memorabilia*
VERB + MEET **hold** ◇ *This year's ~ was held in Anchorage, Alaska.* | **attend, go to** ◇ *I can't go to your track ~ after school tomorrow.* | **miss** ◇ *Brooke missed the ~ due to illness.* | **win** ◇ *Sam's team won the track ~.*
MEET + NOUN **record** ◇ *Both scores were ~ records.*
PREP. **at a/the ~** ◇ *I swam faster at the last ~.* ◇ *Did you buy it at the swap ~?*

meet *verb*

1 come together

ADV. **first** ◇ *the place where they had first met* | **regularly** | **once** | **never** | **eventually, finally** ◇ *When these two finally met, the connection was electric.* | **briefly** | **privately, secretly** | **face-to-face, in person, personally** ◇ *The three sisters rarely ~ in person, but spend hours on the phone.* | **online** ◇ *an interactive site where people can ~ online*
VERB + MEET **arrange to** | **chance to, happen to** ◇ *A year or so later I happened to ~ him again.*
PREP. **at** ◇ *We met the next day at a local bar.* | **for** ◇ *I arranged to ~ her for lunch.* | **with** ◇ *Management will ~ with union representatives next week.* ◇ *I met up with my friends in town.*
PHRASES **look forward to ~ing sb** ◇ *I look forward to ~ing you next week.* | **nice to ~ you** (*esp. AmE*), **pleased to ~ you** (*esp. BrE*) (= a greeting used when you meet sb for the first time)

2 satisfy sth

ADV. **head-on** ◇ *They were determined to ~ the challenge head-on.*
VERB + MEET **be able to, can** | **be unable to, fail to** ◇ *He had failed to ~ his performance targets.* | **be designed to, be tailored to** ◇ *The course is designed to ~ the needs of young learners.*

3 sb's eyes/gaze/look

ADV. **squarely, unflinchingly, without flinching** ◇ *Leonora met his gaze without flinching.* | **briefly**
PREP. **across** ◇ *Their eyes met across the crowded room.*

meeting *noun*

1 when people come together to discuss/decide sth

ADJ. **frequent, regular** | **annual, biannual, biennial, daily, monthly, quarterly, weekly** | **all-day, day-long, hour-long** | **two-hour, etc.** | **afternoon, breakfast, lunch** (*esp. AmE*), **lunchtime** (*BrE*), **weekend, etc.** | **spring, winter, etc.** | **full** (*esp. BrE*), **plenary** | **formal, official** | **informal** | **first, founding, inaugural** | **mass** | **open-air** (*esp. BrE*) | **town** (*esp. AmE*), **town-hall** (*AmE*) | **international, local, national, regional** ◇ *The organization holds various regional ~s.* | **open, public** | **closed, closed-door** (*esp. AmE*), **private** | **secret** | **joint** ◇ *Management have called a joint ~ with staff and unions.* | **general** ◇ *The society is holding its Annual General Meeting in the conference room next Monday.* | **face-to-face, one-on-one, personal** | **bilateral, trilateral** | **high-level, summit, top-level** | **exploratory, initial, introductory, preliminary, preparatory** | **interim, follow-up** | **final** | **extraordinary, special** | **crisis** (*esp. BrE*), **emergency, urgent** | **crucial, historic, important, key, vital** (*esp. BrE*) | **impromptu** | **scheduled** | **mandatory** ◇ *We called a mandatory ~ of our department heads this morning.* | **board, cabinet, committee, corporate, council, departmental, executive, faculty** (*esp. AmE*), **family, management, ministerial, shareholder, shareholders'** (*BrE*), **staff, team, union** | **AA, PTA, etc.** | **organizational** (*esp. AmE*) | **business, sales** | **political** | **professional** (*esp. AmE*) ◇ *She was a frequent invited speaker at professional ~s.* | **editorial** ◇ *We had an editorial ~ about it.* | **scientific** | **discussion** | **protest** (*esp. BrE*) | **planning** ◇ *It was decided at a planning ~.* | **budget** ◇ *She headed off to her budget ~.* | **informational** (*AmE*) | **prayer, revival** (*esp. AmE*) | **camp** (= religious meeting held outside or in a large tent) (*AmE*) |

MEETINGS

Before the meeting

- **call/convene** the meeting, or **invite** people to **attend** the meeting
- **draw up** and **circulate** an **agenda**
- If some people are unable to attend, you may need to **postpone** or **call off/cancel** the meeting.

At the meeting

You usually appoint somebody to:
- **chair** the **meeting**
- **keep/take minutes**

After the chair has **opened** the meeting, the first **points/items** on the **agenda** are often to:
- **approve** the **minutes** of the previous meeting
- **agree on** the **agenda** for the current meeting

It may be necessary to:
- **add** an **item** to the **agenda**
- **remove** sth **from/take** sth **off** the **agenda**

In a meeting you can:

consider discuss examine	an issue **in depth/detail** a matter
debate discuss	an issue **at length**
address identity tackle	a **problem**
have	an **in-depth discussion** about/on the issue
have take	an **in-depth look** at the issue

As well as making decisions at meetings, you can also:

make	raise	give/state	agree on	reach
a proposal recommendation a suggestion	an issue an objection a point	your opinion your view	a compromise further action	(an) agreement a compromise a conclusion a consensus a decision

take	adopt	
a decision a vote	a resolution	*The commission made a proposal for a new park in the city.* *May I make a suggestion to the chairman of the board?* *The workers raised an objection to longer working hours.* *He invited the committee members to give their opinion.* *After hours of negotiation, the two sides reached a compromise.* *The shareholders took a vote on the proposed merger.*

Ending the meeting

You can:
- **adjourn** the **meeting** until a later date
- **close** the **meeting**
- **bring** the meeting to **a close**
  The chairman brought the meeting to a close by thanking all those who had attended.

After the meeting

It is usual to:
- **write up** the **minutes**
- **circulate** the **minutes**

class (*AmE*) ◊ *The students had a class ~ about cheating.* | **group** ◊ *Our group ~s take place on Saturdays.* | **chapter** (*AmE*) ◊ *both national and local chapter ~s* | **community** ◊ *Opposition has been expressed at community ~s.* | **virtual** | *They now have virtual ~s over the Internet.* | **brief, short** | **endless, interminable, long** ◊ *We had endless ~s about the problem.* ◊ *The ~ seemed interminable.* | **boring** | **angry** (*esp. BrE*), **contentious, difficult, stormy, tense** | **productive, successful**

... OF MEETINGS **series**

VERB + MEETING **have, hold** | **arrange, call, convene, organize, schedule, set** (*AmE*), **set up** ◊ *The committee has called a ~ to discuss the president's death.* | **attend, join** | **summon sb to** ◊ *He was summoned to a ~ with the head of the department.* | **observe** (*esp. AmE*) | **begin, open, start** ◊ *The chairperson opened the ~.* | **close, conclude, dismiss, end, finish** | **adjourn, break up** | **call off, cancel** | **postpone** | **host** | **chair, conduct, facilitate, preside at** (*esp. AmE*), **preside over** ◊ *I have to chair a ~ tomorrow.* | **run** ◊ *The employees who run the ~s stick to a strict agenda.* | **call to order** ◊ *The chairman called the ~ to order.* | **participate in** | **address** ◊ *He always spoke as if he were addressing a public ~.* | **sponsor** ◊ *a ~ sponsored by the Council on Foreign Relations* | **demand, request** | **get** ◊ *One phone call was enough to get an initial ~.* | **ban** (*esp. BrE*) | **boycott** | **disrupt**

MEETING + VERB **go ahead** (*esp. BrE*), **happen, occur, take place** ◊ *The ~ never happened.* ◊ *It is unclear whether the ~ will take place as planned.* | **be aimed at sth** ◊ *a ~ aimed at restoring peace in the region* | **begin, open, proceed, start** | **adjourn** ◊ *The ~ adjourned for coffee at eleven.* | **break up** ◊ *The ~ broke up after a row over whether to allow cameras in.* | **close, conclude, end** ◊ *The ~ closed on a sour note.* | **vote** (*esp. BrE*) ◊ *The ~ voted 423–133 for a strike.* | **discuss sth** | **focus on sth** ◊ *The ~s focused on ways of cutting costs.* | **approve sth** (*esp. BrE*) | **hear sth** (*esp. BrE*) ◊ *The ~ heard that two workers had been fired with no official reason given.* | **decide sth, resolve sth** (*both BrE*) | **produce sth, result in sth** ◊ *These ~s produced a settlement agreement.* | **drag, drag on** ◊ *The ~ dragged into the early hours of the next day.*

MEETING + NOUN **facilities, hall, house, place, room, space** (*esp. AmE*) | **ground** (*esp. AmE*), **point, site** (*AmE*), **spot** (*esp. AmE*) ◊ *The arts space serves as a ~ ground for professional artists.* ◊ *Jay drove to the ~ spot.* | **planner** (*AmE*) ◊ *his job as corporate ~ planner* | **agenda** (*esp. AmE*) | **schedule** (*esp. AmE*)

PREP. **in a/the ~** ◊ *I'm afraid Mrs Haley is in a ~ at the moment.* | **~ about** ◊ *a ~ about the plans for a new road* | **~ among** (*esp. AmE*) ◊ *an informal ~ among the members of the Press Agents Association* | **~ between** ◊ *a ~ between tutors and students* | **~ for** ◊ *a ~ for parents* | **~ on** ◊ *We hold public ~s on this topic.* | **~ over** (*BrE*) ◊ *Directors called a crisis ~ over the future of the company.* | **~ with** ◊ *a ~ with French officials*

PHRASES **the purpose of a ~** | **the minutes of a ~** ◊ *The secretary circulated the minutes of the previous week's ~ to all committee members.* | **the chair of a ~, the chairman of a ~**

2 coming together of two or more people

ADJ. **accidental, chance, unexpected** | **fateful** | **clandestine, secret** | **historic, unprecedented** | **emotional** (*esp. BrE*) | **romantic**

VERB + MEETING **have**

PREP. **~ with** ◊ *I had a chance ~ with an old friend last week.*

melody *noun*

ADJ. **beautiful, flowing, gentle, gorgeous, lovely, soft, sweet** | **slow** | **simple, strong** | **complex** | **haunting, memorable** | **melancholy, mournful, plaintive, sad** | **catchy** (*informal*), **familiar, popular, traditional** | **vocal** | **guitar, piano, etc.** | **folk, pop** ◊ *Irish folk melodies* | **acoustic**

VERB + MELODY **hum, play, sing** | **carry** ◊ *The clarinet carries the ~.* | **hear** | **have** ◊ *Most of her songs have a strong ~.* | **compose, create, write**

member *noun*

ADJ. **elite, high-ranking, influential, key, leading, powerful, prominent** | **ranking** (*AmE*), **senior** | **junior, rank-and-file** | **long-serving, long-standing, long-time** | **gang, group, team** | **band, orchestra** | **crew, faculty** (*esp. AmE*), **staff** | **club, fraternity** (*AmE*), **sorority** (*AmE*) | **cabinet** (*esp. BrE*), **council, party** | **audience, cast** ◊ *Biographies are available for the cast ~s.* | **class** | **guild, union** | **board, commission, committee, jury, panel** | **church, cult** | **family, household** | **clan, community, tribal** | **military, service** (= member of the armed services) (*both AmE*) | **individual** ◊ *Subscriptions are cheaper for individual ~s.* | **charter** (*AmE*), **founder, founding, original** | **fellow** ◊ *my good friend and fellow ~ of the council* | **active, enthusiastic** ◊ *She's an active ~ of her local church.* | **loyal, respected, valued** | **honorary** | **elected** | **full** | **associate** | **life** ◊ *a life ~ of the Red Cross* | **permanent** ◊ *the five permanent ~s of the UN Security Council* | **regular** ◊ *She had now become a regular ~ of the cast of singers.* | **former, retired** | **potential, prospective** | **remaining, surviving** ◊ *the surviving ~s of the band* | **card-carrying, dues-paying** (*AmE*), **paid-up** ◊ *They were card-carrying ~s of the Party.* ◊ *He was a paid-up ~ of the Communist Party.* | **full-time, part-time** | **female, male** | **minority** (*AmE*) ◊ *a minority ~ of the Senate Judiciary Committee*

VERB + MEMBER **become** | **recruit** ◊ *We must recruit new ~s to survive.* | **nominate** | **elect** | **appoint**

MEMBER + VERB **join sth** | **resign** | **attend sth, participate in sth** ◊ *10% of club ~s participated in this year's election.* | **vote** ◊ *Audience ~s voted on their favorite presentations.* | **approve sth** ◊ *WTO ~s approved the plan.*

MEMBER + NOUN **country, nation, state** | **company, institution, organization** | **church** (*esp. AmE*) ◊ *the ~ churches of the Baptist Union* | **participation** ◊ *Future plans will depend on ~ participation and input in the coming months.*

PREP. **~ of** ◊ *I've become a ~ of our local sports club.*

PHRASES **a ~ of staff** ◊ *All ~s of staff will receive a bonus.*

membership *noun*

ADJ. **associate, corporate, full, group, honorary** | **annual, lifetime, trial** ◊ *one-week trial ~s* | **association, board, church, class, club, community, family, gang, gym, party, union** ◊ *to apply for union ~* | **free** | **active** ◊ *She eventually stopped active ~ in the group.* | **individual** | **general** ◊ *The general ~ had called for her to step down.* | **student** ◊ *Individual student ~s cost about as much as the average movie.*

VERB + MEMBERSHIP **apply for, seek** | **claim** ◊ *people who claim ~ in such groups* | **gain, get** | **renew** | **maintain** ◊ *He maintains an active ~ in the association.* | **hold** (*esp. AmE*) ◊ *She has held ~ in the club since the late 1950s.* | **buy, purchase** | **give sb, grant sb** | **offer** ◊ *Gyms often offer family ~s.* | **deny sb** ◊ *She was denied ~ in the fine arts club.* | **cancel, resign** ◊ *He has resigned his ~ of the club.* | **expand, increase** ◊ *He hopes to increase ~ and attract new funding.* | **limit, restrict** ◊ *They restricted their ~ to those of direct German descent.*

MEMBERSHIP + NOUN **dues, fee** | **card** | **association, organization** (*both esp. AmE*) | **list, roster** (*AmE*) | **base** ◊ *Our ~ base spanned every age.* | **application** | **requirements** | **drive** (*esp. AmE*)

membrane *noun*

ADJ. **thin** | **permeable, semi-permeable** | **cell** | **cellular** | **mucous**

MEMBRANE + VERB **surround sth**

MEMBRANE + NOUN **wall**

PREP. **through a/the ~** ◊ *The virus passes through the cell ~.*

memento *noun*

ADJ. **family, personal** | **precious, special, treasured** | **permanent**

VERB + MEMENTO **be presented with, receive** | **keep** | **collect**

PREP. **as a ~** ◊ *They gave him a watch as a ~ of his time with the company.* | **~ for** ◊ *The director will be presented with a ~ for his long years of service.* | **~ from** ◊ *a ~ from his dear*

memo noun

ADJ. **internal** | **classified, confidential, secret** | **leaked** ◊ *the contents of a leaked ~*
... OF MEMO **copy**
VERB + MEMO **draft, prepare, type, write** | **circulate, distribute** (*esp. AmE*), **issue, post, put out, release** (*esp. AmE*), **send, send out** ◊ *I just posted this ~ onto my blog.* | **get, receive** | **obtain** ◊ *a government ~ obtained by the Associated Press* | **read, see** | **sign** | **leak**
MEMO + NOUN **pad** | **line** (*AmE*)
PREP. **in a/the ~** | **~ about** ◊ *An internal ~ about his departure had already circulated.* | **~ from, ~ of** ◊ *my ~ of June 28* | **~ on** ◊ *A ~ on the curriculum changes from the Head of Education.* | **~ to** ◊ *She circulated a ~ to the staff.*

memoir noun (sometimes memoirs)

ADJ. **personal** ◊ *a personal ~ of these important events* | **childhood** ◊ *O'Connor published a childhood ~.* | **political** ◊ *the market for political ~s* | **best-selling** | **unpublished** ◊ *an excerpt from an unpublished ~*
VERB + MEMOIR **publish, write** | **read**
PREP. **in your ~** ◊ *She describes in her ~s how she coped with her mother's death.* | **~ about** ◊ *He has published a long ~ about those years.* | **~ of** ◊ *his brief ~ of his father's life*

memorable adj.

VERBS **be** ◊ *It was a truly ~ experience.* | **make sth** ◊ *I'd like to thank everyone for helping to make this day ~ for us.* | **do sth** ◊ *For our anniversary, we wanted to do something ~.*
ADV. **extremely, fairly, very, etc.** ◊ *The title track is pretty ~.* | **especially, most, particularly, truly** ◊ *one particularly ~ evening last year* | **instantly** ◊ *Peart's lyrics are instantly ~.*
PREP. **for** ◊ *The cruise was ~ for the food.*

memorandum noun

ADJ. **internal** | **confidential, private, secret** | **leaked** | **detailed** | **explanatory** (*BrE*) | **legal** (*AmE*)
... OF MEMORANDUM **copy**
VERB + MEMORANDUM **draft, draw up, prepare, write** | **issue, send, submit** | **sign** | **date** ◊ *The ~ was dated August 23, 2001.*
MEMORANDUM + VERB **set sth out** (*BrE*) | **direct sth** (*esp. AmE*) ◊ *a ~ directing that the Army take action*
PREP. **in a/the ~** ◊ *Refer to the terms set out in the company's ~.* | **~ from, ~ to** ◊ *a ~ from the Attorney General to the President* | **~ of** ◊ *your ~ of February 14* | **~ on** ◊ *Memoranda on this topic were regularly sent to all offices.*

memorial noun

ADJ. **lasting, permanent** ◊ *The statue is a lasting ~ to those who died in the war.* | **living** | **makeshift** ◊ *a makeshift ~ marked by posters and flowers* | **fitting** | **war** | **national** | **public** (*esp. AmE*)
VERB + MEMORIAL **build, erect, establish, put up** | **create** | **become** ◊ *This ruin became a ~ for the victims of the bombing.* | **unveil** | **dedicate** ◊ *the many ~s dedicated to the Korean War* | **hold** (*AmE*) ◊ *They are holding a ~ for it.*
MEMORIAL + VERB **commemorate sb/sth, honour/honor sb** | **stand** ◊ *The ~ stands where the two roads meet.*
MEMORIAL + NOUN **ceremony, service** ◊ *A ~ service was held for him in Los Angeles last year.* ◊ *a ~ service for sailors drowned at sea*
PREP. **~ for** ◊ *a ~ for victims of the air crash* | **~ of** ◊ *a ~ of my husband* | *the national ~ of the Algerian War* | **~ to** ◊ *The president today unveiled a ~ to those who died in the disaster.*

memory noun

1 ability to remember

ADJ. **excellent, good, long, prodigious, retentive** | **awful, bad, faulty, poor, short, terrible** | **long-term, short-term** ◊ *His short-term ~ was damaged in the accident.* | **working** ◊ *the limitations of working ~* | **collective** ◊ *the nation's collective ~* | **public** ◊ *The incident faded from public ~.* |

cultural, historical, institutional (*esp. AmE*) ◊ *the historical ~ of a culture* ◊ *the Army's institutional ~* | **visual** ◊ *Bad spellers have a weak visual ~.* | **photographic** | **human**
VERB + MEMORY **jog, refresh** ◊ *Seeing your name in the paper jogged my ~.* | **lose** ◊ *Most people start to lose their ~ as they get older.* | **recover, regain** | **haunt** ◊ *one of those films that haunts the ~ long after it has been watched* | **commit sth to** ◊ *I committed the number to ~ and threw the letter away.* | **search** ◊ *She searched her ~ for their names.*
PREP. **from** ◊ *He recited the whole poem from ~.* | **~ for** ◊ *I have a good ~ for faces.*
PHRASES **in living ~, in recent ~** ◊ *the coldest winter in living ~* | **if ~ serves** (*BrE*), **if ~ serves me, if ~ serves me correctly, if ~ serves me right** ◊ *If ~ served her, his name was Stan.*

2 thought of the past

ADJ. **childhood, early** ◊ *My earliest childhood ~ is of falling in a lake.* | **dim, distant, faded, fading, faint, fuzzy** (*esp. AmE*), **hazy, vague** | **clear, vivid** | **affectionate** (*esp. BrE*), **cherished, fond, good, great, happy, lovely** (*esp. BrE*), **nostalgic, pleasant, positive, precious, special, sweet, treasured, warm, wonderful** | **favourite/favorite** | **bitter-sweet** | **haunting** ◊ *the haunting memories of lost love* | **awful, bad, bitter, disturbing, embarrassing, horrible, horrific, painful, sad, terrible, traumatic, unhappy, unpleasant, unwanted** | **powerful, strong** | **abiding** (*esp. BrE*), **enduring, lasting, lingering** ◊ *My abiding ~ of our first meeting is of a girl too shy to talk.* | **fleeting** | **forgotten, lost** ◊ *all the forgotten memories from when he was younger* | **old** ◊ *the pain of old memories* | **fresh, recent** ◊ *the fresh ~ of my momentous news this morning* | **first** ◊ *one of my first memories* | **shared** ◊ *They exchanged grins at the shared ~.* | **repressed, suppressed** ◊ *a repressed ~ of trauma* | **false** ◊ *false memories of abuse* | **false ~ syndrome** | **selective** | **recovered** ◊ *recovered memories of abusive and violent incidents* | **associative**
VERB + MEMORY **have** ◊ *I have memories of sitting on the back of the school bus.* | **bring back, evoke, recall, rekindle, revive, spark, stir, stir up, trigger** | **conjure, conjure up, retrieve** ◊ *Most young adults can retrieve memories of very early events.* | **relive** ◊ *forced to relive painful memories* | **remember** ◊ *I began to remember happy memories from my childhood.* | **retain** | **invoke** | **cherish, treasure** ◊ *I will always treasure these memories.* | **keep alive, preserve** | **share** ◊ *The actors share fond memories of what Gene meant to them.* | **block** (*esp. AmE*), **block out, blot out, bury, erase, push aside, push away, repress, suppress** ◊ *He tried to blot out his memories of the ordeal.* | **record** ◊ *Keeping a journal is a great way to record your memories.* | **hold** ◊ *a place that holds so many memories of Ellen* | **be haunted by** ◊ *still haunted by memories of his father's death*
MEMORY + VERB **come flooding back, flood back, flood sb's mind** (*esp. AmE*), **rush back to sb** ◊ *When we visited my old family home, memories came flooding back.* | **stir** ◊ *Memories stirred in Josie's mind.* | **fade**
PREP. **at the ~** ◊ *Her eyes gleamed at the ~.* | **in ~ of** ◊ *He planted some apple trees in ~ of his wife.* | **~ from** ◊ *Smells and tastes often evoke memories from the past.* | **~ of** ◊ *fond memories of her childhood*
PHRASES **in loving ~** ◊ *in loving ~ of our beloved father*

3 of a computer

ADJ. **computer, system** | **cache, working** | **flash**
VERB + MEMORY **expand** | **take up** ◊ *Photographs take up a lot of ~.*
MEMORY + NOUN **stick** | **drive** | **slot**

menace noun

1 danger

ADJ. **growing, increasing** ◊ *the growing ~ of drugs* | **great, real, serious** | **alien** ◊ *a new and alien ~ to our agriculture* | **evil** | **public** ◊ *They have become a public ~.*
VERB + MENACE **pose** ◊ *the ~ posed by car fumes* | **combat, counter, fight** ◊ *Local traders are struggling to combat the ~*

of armed robbery. | **defeat** | **become** ◇ *If paroled he will become a ~ to society.*
PREP. **~ to** ◇ *He's a ~ to society.*
2 threatening quality
ADJ. **hidden, quiet, silent** *'Where do you think you're going?' he said with quiet ~.*
PREP. **with ~** ◇ *eyes glittering with ~*
PHRASES **an air of ~** ◇ *The scar down his face added to his air of ~.*

menacing *adj.*

VERBS **be, look, seem** | **become**
ADV. **extremely, fairly, very, etc.** | **a little, slightly, etc.** | **faintly, vaguely** ◇ *She had a faintly ~ manner.* | **almost** ◇ *His voice was quiet and almost ~.* | **quietly**

menopause *noun*

ADJ. **early, premature** | **male** ◇ *The male ~ affects men who are approaching middle age.* (BrE) ◇ *Male ~ affects men who are approaching middle age.* (AmE)
VERB + MENOPAUSE **approach** | **enter, reach** | **experience, go through**
PREP. **at ~, at the ~** (BrE) | **after ~, after the ~** (BrE), **past ~, past the ~** (BrE) ◇ *a disease that can afflict women past the ~* | **during ~, during the ~** (BrE)

mention *noun*

ADJ. **brief, passing** | **special** | **earliest, first** ◇ *The earliest ~ of the town is in a 16th-century manuscript.* | **particular, specific** | **explicit** ◇ *No explicit ~ of a sexual relationship is made.* | **little, scant** ◇ *There is scant ~ of her in the literature.* | **mere** ◇ *The mere ~ of his name brings a smile to my face.* | **honourable/honorable** | **media** (esp. AmE) ◇ *The company racked up two billion media ~s in 2002.*
VERB + MENTION **deserve, merit, rate, warrant** ◇ *My cousin deserves a ~ for all his hard work.* ◇ *The war barely rates a ~ in this book.* | **earn** | **get, receive** ◇ *His professor gets a ~ in the acknowledgements.* | **make** ◇ *Special ~ must be made of Watson's wonderful performance as the doctor.* | **give sb** ◇ *Andrew Divoff is given special ~.* | **avoid, omit** ◇ *The author omitted any ~ of the report.* | **hear** ◇ *I've heard no ~ of a salary increase this year.*
PREP. **at the ~ of** ◇ *At the very ~ of his name, Kate started shaking with fright.*

mention *verb*

ADV. **already, earlier, just, previously, so far** ◇ *As already ~ed, the legislation does not consider low pay as an acceptable reason for turning down a job.* ◇ *This aspect is discussed further by Crane, whom I ~ed earlier.* ◇ *All the approaches ~ed so far are fairly conventional.* | **commonly, frequently** | **rarely, seldom** | **never** ◇ *He's never ~ed you before.* | **briefly, in passing** ◇ *He only ~ed his work in passing.* | **casually** ◇ *I casually ~ed that I might be interested in working in Florida.* | **directly, explicitly, expressly, specifically** ◇ *She did not specifically ~ your name.* | **publicly** ◇ *He was the first to publicly ~ this.* | **repeatedly** ◇ *The same places are repeatedly ~ed in the data.* | **barely, hardly, scarcely** (esp. BrE) | **not actually, not at all** ◇ *Although she didn't actually ~ the move, I am sure that was in her mind.* ◇ *My name wasn't ~ed at all.*
VERB + MENTION **not bother to, fail to, forget to, neglect to, omit to** | **hesitate to** ◇ *I hesitate to ~ it, but…* | **care to** ◇ *more hours than I care to ~* | **happen to** ◇ *Did he happen to ~ putting you in his will?* | **remember to, think to** ◇ *I just never thought to ~ it to you.*
PREP. **as** ◇ *Next spring has been ~ed as a possible time for the event.* | **in** ◇ *She didn't ~ the economy in her speech.* | **in connection with** ◇ *His name had been ~ed in connection with the murder of a local man.* | **to** ◇ *Please don't ~ this to Sally.*
PHRASES **avoid ~ing sb/sth** ◇ *He avoided ~ing his family.* | **be worth ~ing sth** ◇ *At this point, it is worth ~ing that many*

people who were adopted as babies have no desire to meet their biological parents. | **~ed above, ~ed below** ◇ *In the example ~ed above, either method of construction could have been used.* | **~ed in dispatches** (esp. BrE) ◇ *Wounded in action, he was twice ~ed in dispatches.* | **~ the fact that…** ◇ *Did I ~ the fact that I'm now single?* | **not to ~** (= used to add extra information) ◇ *He has two big houses, not to ~ his city apartment.* | **come to ~ it, now you come to ~ it, now you ~ it** (all esp. BrE) ◇ *Now that you come to ~ it, he did say something about a ghost.* | **to ~ but a few, to ~ just a few** ◇ *plumbers, printers and potters, to ~ but a few*

menu *noun*

1 list of dishes
ADJ. **extensive** | **limited** | **full** | **regular** (esp. AmE), **standard** | **special** | **simple** | **varied** | **daily** | **fixed-price, set** | **à la carte** | **three-course, etc.** | **traditional** | **seasonal** ◇ *She completely changes her seasonal ~s every few months.* | **food** (esp. AmE) | **breakfast, dinner, lunch** | **dessert** | **beverage** (AmE), **cocktail, drink** (AmE), **drinks** | **bar, café, cafeteria** (esp. AmE), **pub** (BrE) | **restaurant** | **tasting** ◇ *a ten-course tasting ~* | **takeaway** (BrE), **takeout** (AmE) | **vegetarian** | **Chinese, Italian, etc.**
VERB + MENU **consult, have, look at, peruse** (formal), **read, scan, see, study** ◇ *May we have the ~?* | **do, have, offer, serve** ◇ *Many restaurants do a very reasonable set ~ at lunchtime.* | **choose (sth) from, order (sth) from** | **plan** | **create** | **change** ◇ *The restaurant changes its ~ every six months.* | **expand** ◇ *Chef Nigel Crowther will expand the ~ to include several vegetarian options.*
MENU + VERB **feature sth, include sth, offer sth** ◇ *a ~ offering many vegetarian dishes* | **list sth** ◇ *Many ~s now list ingredients.* | **change** ◇ *The ~ changes daily.*
MENU + NOUN **board** ◇ *The chef was chalking the daily specials on the ~ board.* | **choice, selection**
PREP. **on the ~** ◇ *What's on the ~ this evening?*
PHRASES **a choice of ~** ◇ *Passengers are offered a daily choice of ~.*

2 on a computer
ADJ. **drop-down, pop-up, pull-down** | **main** | **on-screen** | **application, configuration, context, edit, file, help, main, navigation, options, service, start, tools, etc.** | **topic** ◇ *You'll find it in the topic ~.*
VERB + MENU **select sth from** | **go to** ◇ *Go to the topic ~ in the upper right hand corner.* | **access** | **look at, look in** | **open** | **navigate** ◇ *buttons that make it easy to navigate the on-screen ~* | **create, design**
MENU + NOUN **bar** | **item** | **choice, option, selection** | **page, screen** | **interface** | **button**
→ Special page at COMPUTER

mercenary *noun*

ADJ. **foreign** | **hired**
… OF MERCENARIES **army, band, group** ◇ *a small army of mercenaries*
VERB + MERCENARY **employ, hire, recruit** | **pay** | **become**
MERCENARY + NOUN **army, group**

merchandise *noun*

ADJ. **general** | **branded** | **licensed** (esp. AmE) | **quality** ◇ *excellent deals on quality ~* | **free**
… OF MERCHANDISE **piece** ◇ *a substandard piece of ~*
VERB + MERCHANDISE **buy, purchase** | **get, receive** | **carry, offer, sell, stock** ◇ *The company carries a wide range of ~.* | **move, ship**
PHRASES **a range, selection, variety, etc. of ~**

merchant *noun*

ADJ. **prosperous, rich, wealthy** | **powerful, prominent, successful** | **foreign, local** | **builders'** (BrE), **coal** (esp. BrE), **timber, wine, wool, etc.** ◇ *We bought a ton of sand from the builders' ~.*
MERCHANT + NOUN **fleet, marine** (AmE), **navy** (BrE), **seaman, ship, shipping, vessel**

mercy *noun*

ADJ. **divine, infinite** ◊ *God's infinite ~* | **great** | **tender** ◊ *I left him to the tender mercies of his mother.*
VERB + MERCY **ask for, beg for, plead for, scream for** | **deserve** | **obtain, receive** | **extend, give (sb), grant (sb), have, show (sb)** ◊ *God have ~ on us!* ◊ *They showed no ~ to their captives.*
MERCY + NOUN **dash** (*BrE*), **mission** ◊ *a ~ mission to deliver medical supplies and equipment* | **killing**
PREP. **at the ~ of** ◊ *We're at the ~ of the weather.* | **without ~** ◊ *The terrorists are completely without ~.* | **~ for** ◊ *There shall be no ~ for my enemies.* ◊ *He asked for ~ for the crimes he had committed.*
PHRASES **be grateful for small mercies, be thankful for small mercies** ◊ *I suppose we should be grateful for small mercies.*

merger *noun*

ADJ. **planned, possible, potential, proposed** | **pending** (*esp. AmE*) ◊ *talk of a pending ~ between the two companies* | **successful** | **failed** | **company, corporate** ◊ *There has been a flurry of corporate ~s and acquisitions.* | **airline, bank, media, etc.** | **big, large, major, massive**
VERB + MERGER **plan** | **agree, agree to, approve** | **block, oppose** ◊ *They threatened legal action to block the ~.* | **announce** | **complete**
MERGER + VERB **go through, happen, take place** ◊ *If the ~ goes through, thousands of jobs will be lost.* | **fail**
MERGER + NOUN **activity** | **plan, proposal** | **discussions, negotiations, talks** | **agreement, deal** | **announcement** | **partner**
PREP. **~ between** ◊ *a ~ between Dynron and Energee* | **~ with** ◊ *They completed a ~ with Monsanto.*

merit *noun*

ADJ. **considerable, exceptional, great, outstanding** | **actual, real, true** ◊ *a lawsuit that lacked any real ~* | **intrinsic** | **obvious** | **comparative, relative** ◊ *We need to consider the relative ~s of both makes of dishwasher.* | **dubious, questionable** | **individual** ◊ *Each case should be judged on its individual ~s.* | **personal** ◊ *She was elected on personal ~.* | **academic, aesthetic, architectural, artistic, intellectual, legal, literary, musical, scientific, technical** ◊ *The movie has no artistic ~ whatsoever.*
VERB + MERIT **have** | **argue, assess, compare, consider, debate, determine, discuss, evaluate, examine, judge, weigh** (*esp. BrE*), **weigh up** (*esp. BrE*) ◊ *We need to assess the ~s of both proposals before making our decision.* | **question** ◊ *I began to question the ~s of these new technologies.* | **lack** ◊ *The play lacked artistic ~.* | **prove** ◊ *She proved her ~ as a serious actress.* | **acknowledge, appreciate, recognize, see** ◊ *She saw the ~ in this arrangement.* | **find** ◊ *I find no ~ at all in any of the arguments.*
MERIT + NOUN **award** ◊ *She received a ~ award for outstanding work.* | **badge** | **pay** (*AmE*) | **increase, raise** (*both AmE*) ◊ *decisions on ~ raises and promotions* | **scholarship** (*AmE*) | **system** (*esp. AmE*) ◊ *Other schools already have ~ systems in place that reward good work.*
PREP. **according to ~** ◊ *Movies are given a rating of one to five stars according to ~.* | **on ~** ◊ *Prizes are awarded entirely on ~.* | **~ in** ◊ *There is some ~ in his argument.* | **~ to** ◊ *There is lots of ~ to the idea.*
PHRASES **no ~ in sth/doing sth** ◊ *I can see no ~ in excluding the child from school.* | **order of ~** (*BrE*) ◊ *The winners are ranked in order of ~.*

mess *noun*

ADJ. **absolute, complete, fine** (*esp. AmE*), **hopeless, real, royal** (*esp. AmE*), **total, utter** ◊ *I got myself into a complete ~.* | **entire, whole** ◊ *You started this entire ~!* | **appalling** (*BrE*), **awful, horrible, nasty, stupid, terrible, ugly, unholy** | **big, giant, huge** ◊ *The whole situation is a giant ~.* ◊ *I'm in a huge ~. I don't know what to do.* | **complicated, confusing, incoherent** ◊ *The plot is an incoherent ~.* | **chaotic, jumbled, muddled** (*esp. AmE*), **tangled, untidy** (*BrE*) ◊ *Her hair was a tangled ~.* | **bloody, disgusting, gooey, muddy, slimy, sloppy, soggy, sticky** ◊ *Soon both fighters were a bloody ~ of flying punches.* ◊ *Why don't you clean up this*

disgusting ~? | **emotional** ◊ *He's been an emotional ~ since his girlfriend left him.* | **economic, financial**
VERB + MESS **leave, make** ◊ *Must you always leave such a ~?* ◊ *She felt she was making a terrible ~ of her life.* | **clean up, clear up, tidy up** (*esp. BrE*), **wipe up** | **look** (*BrE*), **look like** (*esp. AmE*) | **become** ◊ *My life's becoming a big ~.* | **get (sb) into, get (sb) out of** ◊ *Who got us into this ~ in the first place?* | **cause, create, start** ◊ *That was what caused this whole ~ in the first place.* | **deal with, fix** (*AmE*), **resolve, sort out, straighten out** ◊ *I have to try to fix the ~ you caused.*
PREP. **in a ~** ◊ *The kitchen's in an awful ~.* ◊ *We found ourselves in a real ~.* | **~ of** ◊ *She searched through the ~ of papers on her desk.* (*esp. AmE*)
PHRASES **make a ~ of things** ◊ *I've really made a ~ of things!*

message *noun*

1 from one person to another

ADJ. **important, urgent, vital** | **brief, short** | **incoming, outgoing** | **coded, cryptic, encrypted, secret** | **electronic, email, instant, mail, SMS, text** ◊ *He has sent me a dozen instant ~s today.* | **radio** ◊ *A radio ~ was sent out to all ships in the area.* | **answering-machine, answerphone** (*BrE*), **phone, recorded, taped, voice, voicemail** ◊ *When I dial the number I'm greeted by a recorded ~.* | **error, warning** ◊ *I keep getting an error ~ when I try to connect to the Internet.* | **spam, unsolicited** ◊ *spam ~s sent to your email address* | **heartfelt** ◊ *The family sent a heartfelt ~ of thanks to everyone who helped.* | **personal** | **anonymous** ◊ *I got an anonymous text ~.*
VERB + MESSAGE **convey, give sb, pass sb, pass on, relay** ◊ *He's not here—I'll pass on the ~.* | **take** ◊ *She's out—can I take a ~?* | **bring (sb), carry, deliver, take sb** ◊ *He comes looking for Roxane, bringing a ~ from De Guiche.* | **write** | **read** | **broadcast, email, fax, send, transmit** | **forward, post** ◊ *if you want to post a ~ in an online guest book* | **record** ◊ *I recorded a new ~ for my phone.* | **encrypt** | **decode, decrypt** | **check** ◊ *I turned on my cell phone to check ~s.* | **delete** | **intercept** | **leave (sb)** ◊ *I left a ~ for her at reception.* | **get, receive** ◊ *I never got your ~.*
MESSAGE + VERB **come** | **say sth, state sth, tell sb sth** | **reach sb** ◊ *A radio ~ reached the pilot.* | **appear, arrive, flash, flash up, pop up** ◊ *Who wants spam ~s appearing on their website?* ◊ *A ~ pops up on the screen.* | **contain sth** ◊ *The email ~ contains an attachment.* | **be waiting** ◊ *I had 127 voice mail ~s waiting for me.*
PREP. **~ about** ◊ *There was a ~ about the meeting.* | **~ for** ◊ *Are there any ~s for me?* | **~ from** ◊ *an urgent ~ from your mother* ◊ *They sent ~s of hope to prisoners of war.* | **~ to** ◊ *The ~ was to your sister, not you.*

2 main idea of a book, speech, etc.

ADJ. **central, core, important, key** | **basic, fundamental, main, overall** | **clear, coherent, consistent, simple, unambiguous, unmistakable** | **ambiguous, conflicting, contradictory, mixed** | **compelling, overriding, persuasive, powerful, strong** | **inspirational, positive, upbeat** | **negative** ◊ *the negative ~s we send out* | **serious** ◊ *a novel with a serious ~* | **hidden, implicit, implied, subliminal, subtle, underlying, unspoken** ◊ *stories with hidden moral ~s* | **anti-drug** (*AmE*), **anti-drugs** (*BrE*), **anti-war, etc.** ◊ *a party with an anti-immigrant ~* | **advertising, commercial, marketing, promotional** ◊ *They found a way to transform their ideas into a marketing ~ that everyone relates to.* | **biblical, Christian, gospel** | **environmental, ideological, moral, political, religious, social** | **radical** | **subversive** ◊ *the subversive ~s their films carry* | **wrong** ◊ *I think this movie sends the wrong ~ to her young fans.* | **right** ◊ *Does this send the right ~ to our target audience?* | **chilling** ◊ *He presents a truly chilling ~ in this article.* | **take-home** (*AmE*) ◊ *The take-home ~ is: be willing to negotiate.* | **universal** ◊ *This song has a universal ~ that everybody can relate to.*
VERB + MESSAGE **broadcast, disseminate, spread** ◊ *He tries to spread the ~ of safe sex.* | **bring, communicate, drive home, get across, put across, send** ◊ *This allowed us to bring our ~*

to a different, younger audience. ◇ *We need to get this important ~ across to teenage smokers.* | **preach** | **carry, convey** ◇ *This statement carries a crucial ~ for other workers.* | **reinforce** | **tailor** ◇ *We tailor the ~ to fit the specific audience.*
MESSAGE + VERB **emerge** ◇ *A clear ~ is emerging from these government statements.* | **reach sb, resonate with sb** ◇ *Her ~ is resonating with many evangelicals.*
PREP. **~ about** ◇ *This is sending a strong ~ about the importance of climate change.* | **~ of** ◇ *The president toured the country spreading the ~ of national unity.* | **~ to** ◇ *His choices are sending mixed ~s to voters.*

metal *noun*

ADJ. **soft** | **pure** | **ferrous, non-ferrous** | **base, heavy, noble, precious, rare, trace, transition** | **cold, hot** ◇ *the sudden pressure of cold ~ against her cheek* | **bare** | **solid** | **gleaming, polished, shining, shiny, silver, silvery** | **dull** | **rusted, rusty** | **scrap** ◇ *to recycle scrap ~* | **twisted** ◇ *The bomb left a pile of jagged glass and twisted ~.* | **ductile** | **liquid, molten** | **sheet** | **corrugated** | **galvanized** | **toxic**
... OF METAL **chunk, hunk, lump, piece, shard, sheet, slab, strip** | **heap, pile** ◇ *a heap of scrap ~*
VERB + METAL **be cast in, be made from/of/out of** ◇ *a statue cast in ~* ◇ *The doors are made of ~.* | **melt, melt down** | **weld** | **recycle**
METAL + VERB **contract, expand** | **rust** | **clang, clash** ◇ *the sound of ~ clanging against ~*
METAL + NOUN **alloy** | **hydride, oxide** | **band, bar, frame, mesh, plate, pole, rod, sheet, tube** | **object** | **box, door, fence, gate, railing, roof, etc.** | **fatigue** | **detector**
PREP. **in ~** ◇ *a sculptor who works in ~*
PHRASES **the clang of ~, the clash of ~**

metaphor *noun*

ADJ. **appropriate, apt, good, perfect** | **powerful, striking** | **useful** | **central** ◇ *one of the central ~s in the book* | **extended** ◇ *an extended ~ for human existence* | **musical, spatial, visual** | **mixed**
VERB + METAPHOR **employ, invoke, use** ◇ *He uses the ~ of fire to represent hatred.* | **mix** | **develop, extend**
METAPHOR + VERB **describe sth, represent sth** | **imply sth, suggest sth** | **work** ◇ *The ladder ~ works in several ways.*
PREP. **~ for** ◇ *'This vale of tears' is a ~ for the human condition.* | **~ of** ◇ *the ~ of life as a journey*

meter *noun*

1 device for measuring gas, electricity, etc.

ADJ. **electric** (*esp. AmE*), **electricity** (*esp. BrE*), **gas, light, moisture, parking, power, pressure-level, sound-level, water**
VERB + METER **read** ◇ *The electricity company will send an employee to read your ~.* | **check** ◇ *a man in uniform checking the parking ~s* | **feed, fill** (*esp. BrE*) ◇ *I forgot to feed the ~.* | **fit, install**
METER + VERB **run, tick** ◇ *The taxi driver kept the ~ running.* ◇ *The taxi waited, the ~ ticking away.*
METER + NOUN **reader, reading** | **maid** (*esp. AmE*)

2 (*AmE*) (*BrE* **metre**) → Note at MEASURE

method *noun*

ADJ. **accurate, effective, efficient, good, practical, reliable, tried-and-tested** (*esp. BrE*), **tried-and-true** (*esp. AmE*) ◇ *Which ~ is the most effective?* | **preferred** ◇ *the preferred ~ of testing for each nutrient* | **simple** | **direct** | **indirect** ◇ *an indirect ~ of estimating a taxpayer's income* | **comparative** | **common, conventional, principal, standard, traditional, usual, well-established** | **innovative, new, novel** | **improved** ◇ *improved teaching ~s and better interaction with students* | **alternative, other** | **different, various** | **ingenious, unconventional, unorthodox, unusual** | **accounting, farming, instructional** (*AmE*), **research, scientific, teaching, training, working ~s** ◇ *modern farm-*

ing ~s | **analytic** (*esp. AmE*), **analytical, computational, experimental, heuristic, mathematical, quantitative, statistical** ◇ *This illustrates how experimental ~s can be used to explore these issues.* | **contraceptive** ◇ *a range of contraceptive ~s*
VERB + METHOD **adopt, apply, employ, follow, implement, use, utilize** ◇ *the ~ adopted by the party for the selection of its candidates* ◇ *We can apply these ~s to a wide range of problems.* | **develop, devise, invent, pioneer, work out** ◇ *New production ~s have been invented.* | **change, improve**
METHOD + VERB **involve sth** ◇ *This ~ involves cutting a very thin slice from the object.* | **work** ◇ *How does this ~ work?* | **employ sth, rely on sth, use sth** ◇ *This ~ employs computer software to guide the interviewers through the questionnaire.*
PREP. **~ for** ◇ *an alternative ~ for resolving disputes* | **~ of** ◇ *This is the best ~ of settling such arguments.*

metre (*BrE*) (*AmE* meter) *noun* → Note at MEASURE

microphone *noun*

ADJ. **boom, cordless, headset, radio, underwater, wireless** | **condenser** | **external** ◇ *There's a place to plug in an external ~.* | **built-in** | **directional, omnidirectional** | **concealed, hidden** | **live, open** ◇ *Unfortunately we were near an open ~ and all his colleagues heard what we said.*
VERB + MICROPHONE **speak into, use** | **check, test** | **wear** ◇ *He was wearing a hidden ~.*
MICROPHONE + VERB **pick sth up, record sth** ◇ *The ~ picks up the surrounding sounds.* | **amplify sth**
MICROPHONE + NOUN **input** (*esp. AmE*), **jack** | **stand** | **headset**
PREP. **behind a/the ~** ◇ *Alex Jones is back behind the ~ for a new series.* | **in front of a/the ~** ◇ *Interviewees are placed in front of the ~ and grilled.*

microscope *noun*

ADJ. **binocular, electron, high-powered, optical** | **powerful**
MICROSCOPE + NOUN **slide** ◇ *Place the specimen on a ~ slide.*
PREP. **through a/the ~** ◇ *a section of a potato as seen through a ~* | **under a/the ~** ◇ *bacteria examined under the ~*

middle age *noun*

ADJ. **early** | **late** ◇ *a woman of late ~*
VERB + MIDDLE AGE **approach** ◇ *a bald man approaching ~* | **enter, hit, reach**
MIDDLE-AGE + NOUN **spread** (*humorous*)
PREP. **during ~** ◇ *possible causes of weight gain during ~* | **in ~** ◇ *He mellowed in ~.* | **through ~** (*AmE*) ◇ *from early adulthood through ~ to retirement*
PHRASES **well into ~** ◇ *She had her first child well into ~.*

middle-aged *adj.*

VERBS **be, feel, look** ◇ *She felt ~ and dull.* | **become**
ADV. **prematurely**

middleman *noun*

VERB + MIDDLEMAN **act as, be** | **bypass** (*AmE*), **cut out, eliminate** ◇ *Some factories have cut out the ~ and sell their products directly to customers.*
PREP. **through a ~** ◇ *The company sells through a ~ because it does not have its own sales force.* | **~ between** ◇ *advisers who operate as middlemen between savers and borrowers.* | **~ for** ◇ *He acts as a ~ for companies seeking contracts overseas.*

midnight *noun*

VERB + MIDNIGHT **chime, strike** ◇ *The church clock struck ~.*
MIDNIGHT + VERB **strike** ◇ *Downstairs in the hall, ~ struck.* | **approach, come**
MIDNIGHT + NOUN **feast** (*BrE*), **snack** | **black, blue** | **sun** ◇ *the land of the ~ sun*
PREP. **approaching ~, around ~, near ~** ◇ *It was approaching ~ when I finally reached home.* | **at ~, by ~**
PHRASES **at the stroke of ~** ◇ *At the stroke of ~, Prince Charming turned back into a rat.*

midwife *noun*

ADJ. **certified nurse** (*AmE*), **qualified** (*esp. BrE*), **registered** (*BrE*) | **community** (*BrE*), **local**
MIDWIFE + VERB **deliver a baby** | **attend a birth**
→ Note at JOB

migraine *noun*

ADJ. **severe** | **acute** | **chronic**
VERB + MIGRAINE **experience, get, have, suffer from** | **bring on, cause, trigger** ◊ *Even the smell of oranges can trigger his ~.* | **prevent** | **treat**
MIGRAINE + NOUN **headache** | **attack** | **sufferer** | **medication** ◊ *I forgot to take my ~ medication.*
→ Special page at ILLNESS

migrant *noun*

ADJ. **economic** | **illegal, undocumented** (*esp. AmE*) | **rural** | **first-generation, second-generation**
MIGRANT + NOUN **labourer/laborer, worker** ◊ *They entered the country as ~ workers.* | **population** | **bird**
PREP. **~ from** ◊ *~s from rural areas* | **~ into, ~ to** ◊ *Migrants to the city send money home to their relatives.*
PHRASES **a flow of ~s, an influx of ~s**

migrate *verb*

ADV. **north, northwards, etc.** ◊ *birds that ~ south in the winter* | **seasonally**
PREP. **from, into, to, towards/toward** ◊ *birds migrating from Europe to Africa*

migration *noun*

ADJ. **seasonal** ◊ *the seasonal ~ of birds* | **autumn** (*esp. BrE*), **fall** (*AmE*), **spring** | **annual** | **internal, inward** (*esp. BrE*) | **urban** ◊ *The decline of the rural economy has caused urban ~.* | **international** | **large-scale, mass** | **bird** | **northward, southward, etc.** | **forced** ◊ *the forced ~ of African slaves* | **illegal**
... OF MIGRATION **wave** ◊ *the great waves of ~ that took Europeans to the New World*
MIGRATION + VERB **occur, take place** | **increase, begin**
MIGRATION + NOUN **path, pattern, route** ◊ *changes in the ~ routes of reindeer*
PREP. **~ from, ~ to** ◊ *~ from rural to urban areas*

mild *adj.*

1 not very cold
VERBS **be** | **become, turn** (*esp. BrE*) ◊ *Later in the week the weather turned very ~.* | **remain**
ADV. **extremely, fairly, very, etc.** | **relatively** ◊ *It's relatively ~ for the time of year.* | **generally** ◊ *The climate in Japan is generally ~.* | **surprisingly, unseasonably, unusually** ◊ *The late summer air was surprisingly ~.*

2 not severe or strong
VERBS **be, seem** ◊ *The infection seems quite ~, so she should be better soon.*
ADV. **extremely, fairly, very, etc.** | **comparatively, relatively** ◊ *The pain is comparatively ~ at the moment.* | **reasonably**

3 gentle and kind
VERBS **be, sound** ◊ *His voice was deceptively ~.*
ADV. **seemingly** | **deceptively**
PHRASES **meek and ~** ◊ *She's not so meek and ~ as she seems.*

mile *noun*

ADJ. **nautical** | **square**
VERB + MILE **cover, cycle** (*BrE*), **do, drive, fly, go, hike, ride, run, swim, travel, trudge, walk** ◊ *Good runners can cover the three ~s in just over 15 minutes.* | **clock** (*esp. AmE*), **clock up, log** ◊ *Altogether on the trip we clocked up over 1800 ~s.* | **span, stretch** ◊ *The country's Red Sea coast stretches some 500 ~s.*
PHRASES **~s an hour, ~s per hour** ◊ *The police stopped them doing 100 ~s per hour.* | **a ~ a minute** (= very fast) (*esp. AmE*) ◊ *She was talking a ~ a minute.* | **go the extra ~** ◊ *a*

willingness to go the extra ~ (= make an extra effort) *to make a project work*
→ Note at MEASURE

mileage (*also* **milage**) *noun*

ADJ. **annual, weekly** | **good, high, low** ◊ *cars that get better ~* ◊ *Car for sale: one careful owner, low ~.* | **average** | **unlimited** ◊ *Your car rental costs include unlimited ~.* | **fuel, gas** (*AmE*) ◊ *a car that gets decent gas ~*
VERB + MILEAGE **cover, do** ◊ *There was no record of the ~ the car had done.* | **get** ◊ *Just don't expect to get much ~ out of it.*
MILEAGE + NOUN **allowance** (*esp. BrE*) ◊ *The company gives a generous ~ allowance.* | **rate** | **standard** (*AmE*) ◊ *legislation raising the ~ standards for all cars*

milestone *noun*

ADJ. **critical, historic, important, key, major, significant** | **grim** ◊ *another grim ~ in the war* | **personal** | **career, development**
VERB + MILESTONE **achieve, hit, meet, pass, reach** ◊ *The company passed the £6 million ~ this year.* | **celebrate, mark** | **be, represent** ◊ *It represents a major medical ~.*
PREP. **~ in** ◊ *The movie proved to be a ~ in the history of cinema.* | **~ for** ◊ *a ~ for Chinese technology*

militant *adj.*

VERBS **be** | **become**
ADV. **extremely, fairly, very, etc.** ◊ *The women on the march were extremely ~.* | **increasingly**

military *noun*

ADJ. **foreign** ◊ *The country has twice been occupied by foreign militaries.* | **national** | **all-volunteer, professional, regular, volunteer** | **powerful, strong** | **large** | **modern** | **uniformed** | **active, active-duty**
VERB + MILITARY **serve in** ◊ *I wasn't surprised to learn that he'd served in the ~.* | **enter, join** ◊ *Coghlan joined the ~ and served in the war.* | **leave** ◊ *He left the ~ in 1993 and became a security guard.* | **call in** ◊ *The government called in the ~ to deal with the riots.* | **train** | **deploy** | **build** | **maintain** ◊ *The country maintains a strong ~ purely for defence/defense.* | **modernize, reform, transform** ◊ *efforts to transform the ~ into a 21st-century fighting force* | **strengthen** | **defeat**
MILITARY + VERB **fight** | **operate** | **seize power, take power** | **kill sb**
PREP. **among the ~, in the ~, within the ~** ◊ *reports of growing discontent among the ~*
PHRASES **a member of the ~**

militia *noun*

ADJ. **armed** ◊ *a highly armed ~* | **volunteer** | **local** | **colonial** | **government, state** | **private** | **well-regulated**
VERB + MILITIA **join, serve in** | **organize** | **form, set up** ◊ *The anarchists started to form volunteer ~s.* | **train** | **disarm, disband** | **call out** ◊ *He said he would call out the state ~ if the rebels did not surrender.*
MILITIA + NOUN **company, forces, group, unit** | **movement** (*esp. AmE*) | **fighter, man, member** | **commander, leader**

milk *noun*

ADJ. **fresh** | **curdled, sour, spoiled** (*esp. AmE*) | **full-cream** (*BrE*), **full-fat, whole** (*esp. AmE*) | **low-fat, semi-skimmed** (*BrE*) **fat-free** (*AmE*), **non-fat, skim** (*AmE*), **skimmed** (*BrE*) | **1%, 2%, etc.** (*AmE*) | **creamy** | **regular** (*AmE*) ◊ *a calcium-fortified milk which provides more calcium than regular ~* | **cold, hot, warm** | **cow's, goat's, etc.** | **breast, human** | **baby, formula** (*esp. BrE*) | **coconut, soy** (*AmE*), **soya** (*BrE*) | **lactose-free** | **condensed, evaporated** ◊ *a tin of condensed ~* (*BrE*) ◊ *a can of condensed ~* (*AmE*) | **dried, dry** (*AmE*), **powdered** | **fluid** (*AmE*) ◊ *Dried ~ keeps better than fluid ~.* | **pasteurized, unpasteurized** | **homogenized** | **long-life, UHT** (*BrE*) | **raw** | **fortified** (*AmE*) | **organic** | **flavoured/flavored** | **chocolate, strawberry** | **school**

... OF MILK litre/liter, pint | bottle, carton, cup, glass, jug, pitcher (*AmE*)

VERB + MILK drink, have, take ◇ *Do you take ~ in your coffee?* | consume | add | pour | spill | deliver ◇ *They've stopped delivering ~ in our area.* | boil, heat | produce | express ◇ *She expressed some ~ so her husband could do the night feeding.*

MILK + VERB be off (*esp. BrE*) ◇ *Don't drink the milk—it's off.* | go bad (*esp. AmE*), go off (*esp. BrE*), go sour ◇ *The ~ has gone sour.*

MILK + NOUN powder (*BrE*) | beverage, drink | pudding (*BrE*), shake (usually *milkshake*) | chocolate | product | bottle, carton, churn (*BrE*), container, jug | crate | production, supply, yield | producer | float, round (*both BrE*) | moustache/mustache | allergy | cow

mill noun

1 for making flour, etc.

ADJ. corn (*BrE*), flour, grain | water (usually *watermill*)

VERB + MILL operate | convert, restore (*both esp. BrE*) ◇ *The ~ has been converted into apartments.* | power ◇ *The river was harnessed to power the ~.*

MILL + VERB grind sth ◇ *The ~ can be seen grinding wheat.*

MILL + NOUN stone (usually *millstone*), wheel

2 factory

ADJ. cotton, feed, jute, lumber (*esp. AmE*), paper, pulp, steel, sugar, textile, woollen/woolen

VERB + MILL operate, own, run | work in

MILL + VERB produce sth

MILL + NOUN town | buildings | hand, worker | owner

mimic verb

ADV. accurately, closely ◇ *The computer model is able to ~ very closely the actions of a golfer.* | exactly, perfectly ◇ *She could ~ her father perfectly.*

VERB + MIMIC try to

mind noun

ADJ. human ◇ *the complex nature of the human ~* | conscious, subconscious, unconscious ◇ *Our subconscious ~ tries to protect us.* | logical, rational | best, brilliant, finest, great ◇ *a problem that has defeated the world's finest ~s* | agile, curious, enquiring, inquisitive, keen, lively, sharp | analytical, clear ◇ *I need a clear ~ if I want to continue with my work.* | thinking | creative, fertile, imaginative | enlightened | closed, open ◇ *Try to keep an open ~ until you've heard all the facts.* | impressionable ◇ *impressionable young ~s that are easily influenced* | dirty, one-track, perverted, sick, twisted, warped ◇ *Honestly, all you ever talk about is sex—you have a one-track ~!* | feeble, little | tired, weary | tortured, troubled | deranged, fevered, wandering | individual | collective, public ◇ *a subject which was on the nation's collective ~*

VERB + MIND come into, come to, cross, enter, flash across, flash into, go through, spring to ◇ *The thought never crossed my ~!* ◇ *I'm sure someone can help you, but no one immediately springs to ~.* | fill, flood, invade ◇ *Serious doubts began to flood my ~.* | bear in, keep in ◇ *Bear in ~ the age of the vehicle when assessing its value.* ◇ *Here are some important points to keep in mind…* | escape, slip ◇ *I'm sorry I forgot your birthday—it completely slipped my ~.* | be imprinted on, stick in ◇ *terrible images that will be imprinted on our ~s for ever* | haunt, plague, prey on ◇ *It's been preying on my ~ ever since it happened.* | occupy ◇ *He occupied his ~ by playing cards against himself.* | search ◇ *Kate desperately searched her ~ for some excuse.* | concentrate, focus ◇ *He wanted us to focus our ~s on unsolved problems.* | train ◇ *You have to train your ~ to think positively.* | clear, empty ◇ *Try meditating to clear your ~ of negative thoughts.* | free ◇ *Just free your ~ and write whatever comes.* | cloud, dull ◇ *Exhaustion clouded her ~.* | corrupt, poison, warp ◇ *She was poisoning his ~ and turning him against his family.* | control | close, open

◇ *He had closed his ~ to anything new.* | calm, ease, quiet, refresh, relax, soothe ◇ *His comments did nothing to ease my ~.* | numb | blow, boggle ◇ *a collection of photographs that will blow your ~* | read ◇ *Tell me what you want—I can't read your ~!* | probe | understand ◇ *She was the only person who understood his ~.* | engage, stimulate | exercise, stretch | lose ◇ *He feared he was losing his ~.*

MIND + VERB work ◇ *I'll never understand how his ~ works.* | drift, stray, wander ◇ *Her ~ began to wander.* | buzz, race, whirl ◇ *His ~ raced, trying to think of a way out of the situation.* | be in a turmoil (*esp. BrE*), reel, spin ◇ *Her ~ was still reeling from the shock.* | turn to sth ◇ *My ~ turned to more practical matters.*

PREP. in your ~ ◇ *You've been in my ~ a lot lately.* | in ~ ◇ *I'll keep what you say in ~.* | on your ~ ◇ *I have a lot on my ~ at the moment.*

PHRASES at the back of your ~, in the back of your ~ ◇ *The problem was always at the back of my ~.* | at the forefront of your ~, in the forefront of your ~ ◇ *Try to keep safety in the forefront of your ~ at all times.* | a frame of ~, a state of ~ ◇ *He's in rather a negative frame of ~.* | get your ~ around sth, wrap your ~ around sth (*AmE*) ◇ *I couldn't get my ~ around the concept.* | have sth in ~ ◇ *What kind of party do you have in ~?* | in the recesses of your ~ ◇ *something she had never imagined, not even in the deepest recesses of her ~.* | in your right ~ ◇ *Who in their right ~ would want to marry a murderer?* | ~ and body ◇ *refreshed in ~ and body* | no doubt in your ~ ◇ *There was absolutely no doubt in my ~ that he was guilty.* | set your ~ to sth ◇ *You can do whatever you set your ~ to.* | uppermost in your ~ ◇ *Their own problems of course remained uppermost in their ~s.*

mind verb

ADV. terribly, very much ◇ *They had thought the boys wouldn't ~ sharing; as it turned out, they ~ed very much.* ◇ *Would you ~ terribly if I went on my own?* | not a bit, not at all ◇ *I don't ~ at all telling people my age.* | not much, not really ◇ *Nobody really ~ed much about what happened to them.*

VERB + MIND not seem to ◇ *His parents didn't seem to ~ that he dropped out of college.*

PREP. about ◇ *I didn't ~ about the money.*

mine noun

1 for coal, etc.

ADJ. coal, copper, diamond, salt, tin, etc. | deep, drift, opencast (*BrE*), open-pit (*AmE*), strip (*AmE*), underground | abandoned, disused

VERB + MINE operate, run, work

MINE + VERB produce sth ◇ *At its peak, the ~ produced 5 000 tons of coal a day.*

MINE + NOUN shaft (usually *mineshaft*), workings ◇ *flooded ~ workings* | owner

PREP. at a/the ~, down a/the ~ (*BrE*), in a/the ~ ◇ *At 14, he went down the ~s.* ◇ *poor working conditions in the ~s*

2 explosive device

ADJ. anti-personnel, anti-tank, land, limpet (*esp. BrE*)

VERB + MINE bury, lay, plant ◇ *Soldiers laid anti-personnel ~s in the fields.* | detect, locate | clear, dispose of, remove ◇ *The troops are slowly clearing the ~s.* | detonate, hit, set off, strike

MINE + VERB blow up, explode, go off

minefield noun

1 area where there are mines

VERB + MINEFIELD enter | clear

2 situation full of difficulties

ADJ. ethical, legal, political ◇ *Suggesting changes to the benefits system would be a political ~.*

VERB + MINEFIELD navigate, negotiate, pick your way through ◇ *You will first have to pick your way through the ~ of professional advice.*

PREP. ~ for ◇ *Tax is a ~ for the unwary.*

miner *noun*

ADJ. **coal, copper, gold, lead, tin, uranium, etc.**
→ Note at JOB

mineral *noun*

ADJ. **essential, important, vital | trace | rare | abundant, common | industrial | ore | clay, copper, uranium, etc.**
VERB + MINERAL **be rich in, contain** ◊ *foods that are rich in essential ~s* | **collect, extract** ◊ *to extract ~s from ores* | **deposit** | **absorb**
MINERAL + VERB **be found in sth, be present in sth, occur** ◊ *calcium and other ~s found in your bones*
MINERAL + NOUN **deposits, resources, wealth | exploitation, exploration, extraction, working | content | supplement** ◊ *Many people take vitamin and ~ supplements.*
PHRASES **vitamins and ~s**

mingle *verb*

ADV. **freely** ◊ *The star ~d freely with the crowd.* | **together** ◊ *a lot of emotions all ~d together*
PREP. **with** ◊ *She felt fear ~d with excitement.*

minimum *noun*

ADJ. **absolute, bare, very | agreed, guaranteed | recommended | federal, legal, mandatory, required, statutory | age** (*AmE*) ◊ *Many states impose an age ~ of eighteen for the death penalty.*
VERB + MINIMUM **keep sth to, reduce sth to** ◊ *Two fire crews managed to keep damage to a ~.* | **reach** ◊ *The sun's temperature reached a ~ in the summer of 1981.* | **exceed** | **regard sth as** ◊ *A temperature of 121°C is regarded as the ~ necessary to achieve sterility.* | **pay** ◊ *Many people pay the ~ on their credit cards.*
PREP. **above (the) ~, at (a/the) ~** ◊ *Candidates must have a degree at a ~.* | **below (the) ~, down to a ~** ◊ *We tried to keep costs down to a ~.* | **~ of** ◊ *a ~ of $20* ◊ *a ~ of fuss*
PHRASES **the ~ necessary, the ~ needed | the ~ possible** ◊ *He's always done the ~ possible to pass his exams.* | **with the ~ of delay, with the ~ of disruption, with the ~ of fuss | with the ~ of effort** ◊ *The tent can be put up with the ~ of effort.* | **with the ~ of risk**

minister *noun*

1 (*BrE*) member of the government

ADJ. **prime | chief, principal** (*both historical*) **| deputy | junior, senior | cabinet, departmental, EU, Foreign Office, government, Home Office | defence, education, environment, finance, foreign, health, interior, justice, transport, etc. | former, outgoing**
VERB + MINISTER **appoint (sb), appoint sb as, be named, nominate (sb), nominate sb as | elect (sb), elect sb as | dismiss (sb as) | serve as** ◊ *He served briefly as prime ~ from 1920 to 1921.* | **lobby, persuade, urge** ◊ *Groups are lobbying the Transport Minister over the issue.* | **advise, consult, instruct | accuse, criticize**
MINISTER + VERB **resign, retire | be accountable to sb, be responsible for sth** ◊ *Ministers are accountable to Parliament.* ◊ *the ~ responsible for the health service* | **announce sth, declare sth, unveil sth | agree sth, agree to sth, approve sth, decide sth, endorse sth | intervene (in sth)** ◊ *The foreign ~ intervened with disastrous results.*
PREP. **~ for** ◊ *the new ~ for the Arts* | **~ of** ◊ *A new ~ of defence had been appointed.* → See also PRIME MINISTER

2 priest

ADJ. **Christian, Presbyterian, Protestant, etc. | evangelical | ordained**
VERB + MINISTER **ordain (sb), ordain sb as** ◊ *He was ordained ~ of a small rural congregation.* | **preach (sth)**
PHRASES **a ~ of religion**

ministry *noun*

1 (*BrE*) government department

ADJ. **government | Agriculture, Defence, Education, Environment, Finance, Foreign, Foreign Affairs, Health,**

Interior, Justice, Transport, etc. | key ◊ *He assumed direct control of key ministries.*
VERB + MINISTRY **run | take over | create**
MINISTRY + VERB **approve sth, support sth** ◊ *The plan was approved by the Ministry of Housing.* | **control sth | own sth** ◊ *on ministry-owned land*
MINISTRY + NOUN **official, spokesman, spokesperson**
PREP. **at the ~** ◊ *staff at the Greek Foreign Ministry* | **in the ~, within the ~** ◊ *a senior man in the Ministry of Health* | **~ of** ◊ *a spokesman for the Ministry of Culture*
PHRASES **a department at the ~, a department in the ~**

2 ministers of religion

ADJ. **church | Christian, evangelical, lay | pastoral | ordained | campus** (*AmE*)**, prison**
VERB + MINISTRY **begin, enter | leave | provide** ◊ *The church provides a valuable ~ to a growing population.*

minor *adj.*

VERBS **be, seem**
ADV. **extremely, fairly, very, etc.** ◊ *This is a very ~ operation and there is very little risk involved.* | **comparatively, relatively** ◊ *That's a relatively ~ matter—we can leave it till later.* | **apparently, seemingly**

minority *noun*

ADJ. **large, significant, sizeable, substantial | small, tiny | growing | distinct | visible | vocal, vociferous** ◊ *the view of a small but vociferous ~* | **cultural, ethnic, linguistic, national, racial, religious, sexual | Arab, Christian, etc. | black, white | oppressed, persecuted | poor | under-represented**
VERB + MINORITY **belong to | discriminate against | target**
MINORITY + NOUN **opinion, view | rights | issues | community, group, neighborhood** (*AmE*) **| population | culture | applicant, children, family, student, etc.** ◊ *Qualified ~ applicants are highly sought after.* | **language | government, party**
PREP. **among a/the ~** ◊ *You are definitely among the ~.* | **from a/the ~** ◊ *people from ethnic minorities* | **in a/the ~** ◊ *We are in the ~ on this issue.* | **~ of** ◊ *a sizeable ~ of the population*
PHRASES **only a ~** ◊ *Only a tiny ~ of products are affected.*

minute *noun*

1 one sixtieth of an hour

ADJ. **closing, final, opening** ◊ *He scored in the final ~s of the game.* | **passing** ◊ *With each passing ~, the tension mounts.* | **full, whole** ◊ *The noise lasted almost a full ~.* | **long** ◊ *Ten long ~s later, he finally had the results.* | **precious** ◊ *Gina wasted ten precious ~s on her final test question.* | **agonizing, tense** ◊ *For ten agonizing ~s she couldn't find her son.*
VERB + MINUTE **spend** ◊ *I spent ten ~s dealing with emails.* | **last, take | waste | count** ◊ *Tracey was already counting the ~s until the weekend.*
MINUTE + VERB **elapse, pass, tick by** ◊ *The ~s ticked by and still nothing happened.* | **fly by | turn into sth** ◊ *Fifteen ~s turned into thirty, and still no one called.*
MINUTE + NOUN **hand** ◊ *the ~ hand on the clock*
PREP. **after…~s** ◊ *After twenty ~s I started to get worried.* | **for…~s** ◊ *We waited for ten ~s and then left.* | **in…~s** ◊ *The movie starts in ten ~s.* | **~s after** (*AmE*)**, ~s past** (*esp. BrE*) ◊ *four ~s after/past two* | **~s of** (*AmE*)**, ~s to** ◊ *ten ~s to three*
→ Note at MEASURE

2 moment

ADJ. **last** ◊ *Don't leave everything till the last ~.* | **next** ◊ *One ~ he was fine and the next ~ he collapsed on the floor.* | **spare** ◊ *If you have a few spare ~s, you could clean the kitchen.*
VERB + MINUTE **hang on, hold on, wait** ◊ *Could you wait a ~, please?* | **have, spare** ◊ *Do you have a ~, Miss Brown?* ◊ *Can you spare a ~?* | **take** ◊ *This will only take a ~.*

PREP. **in a ~** ◇ *I'll be with you in a ~.* | **within ~s** ◇ *The ship sank within ~s.*
PHRASES **every waking ~** ◇ *They spend every waking ~ together.* | **just a ~** | **the ~ sth happens** ◇ *Tell him I want to see him the ~ he arrives.* | **not for a ~** ◇ *I never thought for a ~ he'd refuse.* | **this ~** ◇ *Come here this ~!*

3 minutes written record of what is said at a meeting

VERB + MINUTES **keep, take** ◇ *Who's going to take ~s? (esp. AmE)* ◇ *Who's going to take the ~s? (esp. BrE)* | **circulate** | **read** | **agree** *(BrE)*, **approve, sign** *(BrE)* | **write up** ◇ *I wrote up the ~s of the meeting and circulated them by email.*
PHRASES **the ~s of a meeting**
→ Special page at MEETING

miracle *noun*

ADJ. **great** | **real, true** | **little, minor, small** ◇ *The letter's survival is something of a minor ~.* | **modern** | **economic, medical**
VERB + MIRACLE **create, do, make, perform, produce, work** ◇ *Don't expect this medicine to work ~s.* | **believe in** | **ask for, expect, hope for, pray for** | **need, take** ◇ *It would take a ~ to get the old car going again.* | **see, witness**
MIRACLE + VERB **happen, occur**
MIRACLE + NOUN **worker** | **story** | **cure, drug, pill** *(esp. AmE)*
PREP. **by a ~** ◇ *By a ~ she escaped serious injury.*

miraculous *adj.*

VERBS **be, seem**
ADV. **quite, truly** ◇ *Something truly ~ happened.* | **almost** ◇ *an almost ~ escape* | **apparently, seemingly**
PHRASES **little short of ~** *(esp. BrE)*, **nothing short of ~** ◇ *a transformation that was little short of ~*

mirror *noun*

ADJ. **bathroom, bedroom** | **compact, dresser** *(AmE)*, **make-up, pocket, shaving** | **hand** *(BrE)*, **hand-held** *(AmE)* | **full-length, tall** | **framed, ornate** | **antique** | **two-way** ◇ *He watched them through a two-way ~.* | **concave, convex** | **oval, round** | **rear, rear-view, side-view** *(AmE)*, **wing** *(BrE)* ◇ *Always check your ~ before pulling out to overtake.* | **funhouse** *(AmE)* | **broken, cracked**
VERB + MIRROR **use** | **glance in, look in, look into** | **admire yourself in, examine yourself in, look at yourself/your face in** ◇ *He was busy admiring himself in the ~.* | **face, sit at, stand in front of** | **check** | **catch sight of sb/sth in, see sb/sth in** | **hang** ◇ *We hung a ~ over the fireplace.* | **break, crack, smash**
MIRROR + VERB **reflect sth, reveal sth, show sth** | **hang** ◇ *a large ~ hanging on the wall behind him*
MIRROR + NOUN **image, reflection** *(esp. AmE)* ◇ *Art can be seen as a ~ image of society.*
PREP. **in a/the ~** ◇ *She stared at her face in the ~.*

mirror *verb*

ADV. **closely** ◇ *The trends here closely ~ those in America.* | **exactly, faithfully, perfectly** | **almost**
VERB + MIRROR **seem to**
PHRASES **be ~ed by sth, be ~ed in sth** ◇ *The jump in business confidence has been ~ed by the increase in employment.* | **be ~ed in sb's face, be ~ed on sb's face** ◇ *The shock was ~ed on her face.*

miscalculate *verb*

ADV. **badly, grossly, seriously** ◇ *The government has seriously ~d the economic effect of this policy.*

miscalculation *noun*

ADJ. **grave, gross, huge, serious** | **slight** | **political**
VERB + MISCALCULATION **make**

miscarriage *noun*

ADJ. **early** | **threatened** | **spontaneous** | **recurrent**

VERB + MISCARRIAGE **have, suffer** | **cause, induce** | **end in** ◇ *Her first pregnancy ended in ~.*
PHRASES **a risk of ~** ◇ *Smoking during pregnancy increases the risk of ~.*

mischief *noun*

ADJ. **criminal** *(law)*
...OF MISCHIEF **glint, hint** ◇ *There was a glint of ~ in her eyes.*
VERB + MISCHIEF **cause, do, make** ◇ *Such people will do anything they can to make ~.* | **get into, get up to** ◇ *Don't get up to any ~ while we're out.* | **keep (sb) out of, stay out of** *(both esp. BrE)* ◇ *Try to stay out of ~, will you?*

misconception *noun*

ADJ. **common, popular, widespread** | **fundamental** | **big, great, major** *(esp. AmE)*
VERB + MISCONCEPTION **have, hold** | **give rise to, lead to** | **address** | **correct, dispel** ◇ *We hope the documentary will dispel certain ~s about the disease.*
MISCONCEPTION + VERB **be based on sth** | **arise**
PREP. **~ about** ◇ *popular ~s about AIDS*

misconduct *noun*

ADJ. **alleged** | **gross, serious** ◇ *She was fired last year for gross ~.* | **criminal** | **financial, professional, scientific, sexual** | **research** | **police, prosecutorial** *(AmE)*
VERB + MISCONDUCT **dismiss sb for, fire sb for, sack sb for** *(BrE)* | **deny** ◇ *The directors all deny financial ~.*
PREP. **~ by** ◇ *allegations of ~ by the security forces* | **~ on the part of** ◇ *There was no ~ on the part of the police.*
PHRASES **on (the) grounds of ~** *(esp. BrE)* ◇ *Staff can lose their jobs only on grounds of professional ~.*
→ Note at CRIME (for more verbs)

miserable *adj.*

VERBS **be, feel, look, sound** ◇ *We got home feeling tired and ~.* | **become** | **make sb/sth**
ADV. **extremely, fairly, very, etc.** | **absolutely, completely, thoroughly**
PREP. **about** ◇ *He felt absolutely ~ about his exams.*

misery *noun*

ADJ. **abject, great, real, sheer, untold** ◇ *This phobia can cause untold ~ for the sufferer.* | **complete** ◇ *Her ~ was made complete when she was separated from her children.* | **personal** | **human** | **economic** ◇ *the country's economic ~*
VERB + MISERY **be full of, endure, feel, live in, suffer** ◇ *people who suffer the ~ of unemployment* | **bring (sb), cause (sb), create, inflict** ◇ *The money brought him nothing but ~.* | **add to, heap** *(esp. BrE)*, **prolong** ◇ *War has now added to the ~ of these starving people.* ◇ *This financial blow heaps more ~ on the community.* | **alleviate, ease, relieve** ◇ *ways to alleviate human ~* | **end** | **put sb/sth out of** ◇ *In the end we asked the vet to put the creature out of its ~ (= kill it humanely).* ◇ *Oh, put her out of her misery—tell her who won. (humorous)* | **spare sb** ◇ *At least we were spared the ~ of having to do it all again.* | **share** *(esp. AmE)* | **forget**
PREP. **~ of** ◇ *the sheer ~ of homelessness*
PHRASES **make sb's life a ~** ◇ *His constant criticism made her life a ~.*

misfortune *noun*

ADJ. **great** | **personal**
VERB + MISFORTUNE **be dogged by** *(BrE)*, **have, suffer** ◇ *The expedition was dogged by ~.* ◇ *I had the ~ to share a room with someone who snored loudly.*
MISFORTUNE + VERB **befall sb, strike** ◇ *Misfortune struck before they had even left port.*
PHRASES **be sb's ~** ◇ *He is the rudest man it has ever been my ~ to meet.*

misgivings *noun*

ADJ. **considerable, deep, grave, great, serious**
VERB + MISGIVINGS **harbour/harbor, have** | **express, voice** ◇ *I felt I had to express my ~ about her decision.* | **share** ◇ *She shared my ~ about the planned weekend.*

PREP. **despite sb's ~, in spite of sb's ~** ◇ *He agreed, despite his ~.* | **with ~** ◇ *I viewed the process with grave ~.* | **~ about** ◇ *She had serious ~ about the whole affair, but they proved unfounded.* | **~ at** ◇ *He had considerable ~ at the prospect of moving jobs.* | **~ over** ◇ *The local people still had considerable ~ over the flood of workers into their town.*

misguided adj.

VERBS **be, seem**
ADV. **deeply, entirely, totally** | **sadly, woefully** | **rather, somewhat** | **fundamentally** ◇ *Their approach to the problem is fundamentally ~.*

mishap noun

ADJ. **major, serious** | **fatal** | **little, minor, slight**
... OF MISHAPS **series** ◇ *The group suffered an extraordinary series of minor ~s.*
VERB + MISHAP **have, suffer** ◇ *I'm afraid your son had a slight ~ in the playground.* | **cause** | **avoid, prevent**
PREP. **without ~** ◇ *We reached home without ~.*

misinterpret verb

ADV. **completely** | **easily** | **deliberately, wilfully/willfully**
VERB + MISINTERPRET **be easy to** ◇ *It would be easy to ~ results from such a small sample.*
PREP. **as** ◇ *I realized that what I'd said could be ~ed as criticism.*

misjudge verb

ADV. **badly, seriously** | **completely**

mislead verb

ADV. **seriously** | **completely, totally** | **actively** (*esp. BrE*), **deliberately, intentionally** ◇ *She was accused of deliberately ~ing the commission.* | **allegedly** | **easily** ◇ *They were naive and easily misled.*
VERB + MISLEAD **attempt to, try to** | **be liable to** (*esp. BrE*) ◇ *Statistics taken on their own are liable to ~.*
PREP. **about** ◇ *The House has been totally misled about this affair.* | **into** ◇ *The company misled hundreds of people into investing their money unwisely.*

misleading adj.

VERBS **be**
ADV. **extremely, fairly, very, etc.** | **grossly, highly, positively, profoundly** (*formal*), **seriously** | **completely, entirely** (*esp. BrE*), **totally, wholly** (*esp. BrE*) | **a little, slightly, etc.** | **potentially** | **deliberately** ◇ *Her statement was deliberately ~.* | **dangerously** ◇ *Some of the information on the website was dangerously ~.*
PREP. **about** ◇ *The brochure was extremely ~ about the cost of the surgery.*

mismanage verb

ADV. **badly, grossly** ◇ *The prison service has been badly ~d in recent years.* | **completely**

mismanagement noun

ADJ. **economic, financial, fiscal** | **gross**
VERB + MISMANAGEMENT **uncover** ◇ *An investigation uncovered ~ and a lack of proper financial controls.*
PREP. **through ~** ◇ *The project collapsed through financial ~.*

misplaced adj.

VERBS **be, prove, seem**
ADV. **entirely, totally, wholly** (*esp. BrE*) ◇ *Her confidence in him was entirely ~.* | **largely** | **rather, somewhat** | **sadly** ◇ *His optimism proved sadly ~.*

misread verb

ADV. **completely, totally** ◇ *I had completely ~ his intentions.* | **badly**
PREP. **as** ◇ *I ~ 'Mrs' as 'Mr'.*

misrepresent verb

ADV. **grossly, seriously** | **completely** | **deliberately**
PREP. **as** ◇ *Ecstasy is widely ~ed as a soft drug.*
PHRASES **be widely ~ed**

miss verb

1 not hit/catch/reach sth
ADV. **completely** | **barely, just, narrowly, nearly** ◇ *The plane crashed, narrowly ~ing a hotel.* | **somehow** ◇ *The bullet somehow ~ed his heart.* | **badly** ◇ *She attempted to hit the ball but ~ed badly.*
PREP. **by** ◇ *The bullet ~ed his head by only a few inches.*

2 not hear/see/understand
ADV. **completely** ◇ *He completely ~ed the point of what I was saying.* | **easily**
VERB + MISS **cannot** ◇ *The station is just down this road on the left. You can't ~ it.*

3 feel sad because sb is not with you
ADV. **badly, dearly, desperately, dreadfully** (*esp. BrE*), **a lot, really, terribly, truly, very much** ◇ *Your father ~es you terribly.* ◇ *I still ~ her a lot.*
PHRASES **be greatly ~ed, be sadly ~ed, be sorely ~ed** ◇ *Anne will be sadly ~ed by all who knew her.*

missile noun

1 explosive weapon
ADJ. **long-range, medium-range, short-range** | **ballistic, cruise, guided, heat-seeking, laser-guided** | **land-based** | **air-launched, shoulder-fired** | **mobile** | **intercontinental** | **strategic, tactical** | **anti-aircraft, anti-ballistic, anti-tank, etc.** | **air-to-air, air-to-ground, air-to-surface, surface-to-air, surface-to-surface** | **conventional, nuclear** | **incoming** | **enemy** | **interceptor**
VERB + MISSILE **be armed with, carry** | **aim** | **fire, launch, send** | **lob** | **destroy, intercept, shoot down** | **deploy, use** ◇ *strategic ~s deployed in sparsely populated desert areas* | **detect** | **track** | **test**
MISSILE + VERB **fly** | **destroy sth, hit sth, strike (sth)** | **kill sb** | **fall** ◇ *Missiles fell on the city.* | **target sth** ◇ *~s targeting the capital* | **miss sth** ◇ *All of the ~s missed their target.*
MISSILE + NOUN **base, site** | **attack, strike** | **launch** | **defence/defense** | **programme/program, system** | **launcher** | **warhead, weapon** | **test** | **capability, technology** | **threat**

2 object fired or thrown
VERB + MISSILE **hurl, pelt sb with, throw** ◇ *They pelted her with eggs and various other ~s.* | **fly** ◇ *Another ~ flew through the air.* | **dodge**
MISSILE + VERB **hit sb/sth, strike sb/sth**

missing adj.

VERBS **be** | **go** ◇ *a woman who went ~ three months ago* | **discover sb** ◇ *It was six hours before the seamen were discovered ~.* | **list sb (as), report sb (as)** ◇ *A leading businessman has been reported ~ from his home.*
ADV. **completely, entirely, totally** ◇ *The study of housework as work is a topic entirely ~ from sociology.* | **altogether** ◇ *The eighth rung of the ladder was ~ altogether.* | **largely** ◇ *a quality that's largely ~ in young people today* | **conspicuously, noticeably** | **sadly** ◇ *The spirit of fair play is sadly ~ from the sport these days.*
PREP. **from** ◇ *The file was ~ from its place.*
PHRASES **~ in action** ◇ *the search for US soldiers listed as ~ in action* | **~, presumed dead**

mission noun

1 important task
ADJ. **joint** ◇ *a joint Anglo-American ~* | **covert, secret, stealth, undercover** | **dangerous** | **suicide** | **historic** | **routine** | **fact-finding, training** | **tactical** | **escort** | **reconnaissance** | **bombing, combat, military, wartime** |

search-and-destroy | mercy, rescue | peacekeeping | diplomatic | humanitarian | failed, successful | special
VERB + MISSION **carry out, conduct, execute, go on, perform, undertake | accomplish, complete** ◊ *Our ~ accomplished, we headed for home.* | **dispatch sb on, give, send sb on** ◊ *An aid team will be sent on a ~ to the earthquake zone.* | **launch** ◊ *It was too late to launch a rescue ~.* | **fly, fly on** (used of military planes) ◊ *He flew a total of 41 ~s over the country.* | **abandon, abort, cancel** (esp. of military missions) ◊ *The captain instructed them to abort the ~.*
MISSION + VERB **end in failure, fail** ◊ *Their ~ ended in failure.* | **be a success, succeed**
MISSION + NOUN **objective | accomplishment** (AmE)
PREP. **on a/the ~** ◊ *He was sent on a secret ~ approved by the Pentagon.*
PHRASES **~ impossible** ◊ *Many regard his task as ~ impossible.*

2 team sent to perform a task
ADJ. **diplomatic, military, trade**
VERB + MISSION **establish, set up | send**
PREP. **~ to** ◊ *The US is sending a trade ~ to China.*

3 into space
ADJ. **shuttle, space, spacecraft | lunar, planetary | manned, unmanned | robotic**
VERB + MISSION **go on, make** ◊ *He's been on several shuttle ~s over the last decade.* | **abort**
MISSION + NOUN **control** ◊ *The spacecraft lost contact with ~ control.*
PREP. **on a/the ~** ◊ *experiments conducted on a space ~* | **~ to** ◊ *a successful spacecraft ~ to Venus*

4 special aim
ADJ. **main, primary | stated**
VERB + MISSION **have** ◊ *He now has a ~ in life: to expand the horizons of those around him.* | **pursue | fulfil/fulfill, meet**
MISSION + NOUN **statement**
PHRASES **a man with a ~, a woman with a ~** ◊ *You can tell by the determined way he talks that he is a man with a ~.* | **a sense of ~** ◊ *A powerful sense of ~ underpins everything he does.*

5 place where people work to help others
ADJ. **Christian | educational**
VERB + MISSION **establish, found | run**
MISSION + NOUN **work | hospital, school**

missionary noun

ADJ. **foreign | pioneer | evangelical, medical | Catholic, Protestant, etc.**
VERB + MISSIONARY **work as | send (sb as)** ◊ *clergy sent as missionaries to Latin America*
MISSIONARY + NOUN **work | zeal** ◊ *He argued the case for reorganization with ~ zeal.*
PREP. **as a ~** ◊ *He spent 15 years as a ~ in Africa.*

mist noun

ADJ. **dense, heavy, thick** ◊ *A heavy ~ rolled over the fields.* | **faint, fine, light, slight, thin | swirling | hazy | cold, cool | grey/gray, red, white** ◊ *There was a red ~ in front of his eyes.* | **dawn, evening, morning** ◊ *an early morning ~* | **autumn** (esp. BrE) | **sea**
VERB + MIST **be covered in, be shrouded in** ◊ *The mountain was covered in a thick ~.* | **disappear into, vanish in, vanish into** ◊ *The little town had vanished in the ~.* | **emerge from, loom out of** (esp. BrE) ◊ *A figure emerged from the ~.* | **break through, shine through** ◊ *Soon the sun would break through the ~.* | **peer into, peer through | be lost in** (figurative) ◊ *The origins of language are lost in the ~s of time.*
MIST + VERB **cover sth, hang, hover, lie, surround sb/sth** ◊ *A faint ~ hung over the valley.* | **come down** (esp. BrE), **descend** ◊ *When the ~ descends it comes quickly and covers everything.* | **clear, lift** ◊ *The ~ had cleared by mid-morning.* | **drift, float, rise, roll, swirl** ◊ *A fine ~ floated over the fields.* ◊ *a swirling ~* ◊ *a thin ~ rising from the river* | **cling to sth** ◊ *Early morning ~ still clung to the hollows.* | **fill sth | cover sth, hide sth, obscure sth, shroud sth** ◊ *A white ~ obscured the top of the hill.*
PREP. **in the ~, into the ~** ◊ *It was hard to make out the path in the ~.* | **through the ~** ◊ *The house was scarcely visible through the ~.* | **~ over** ◊ *the ~ over the lake*
PHRASES **a curtain of ~, a veil of ~**

mistake noun

ADJ. **big, colossal** (esp. AmE), **great, huge** ◊ *It is a great ~ to assume that your children will agree with you.* | **bad, dreadful, fundamental, ghastly** (esp. BrE), **grave, horrible** (esp. AmE), **serious, terrible | costly, expensive** ◊ *This dress was an expensive ~.* | **disastrous, fatal, tragic | embarrassing | elementary, little, simple** ◊ *All those problems because of one little ~!* | **common | genuine, honest | deliberate | past** ◊ *The company has learned from its past ~s.* | **careless, dumb** (AmE), **foolish, stupid | grammar, grammatical, spelling**
VERB + MISTAKE **make** ◊ *I'm sorry, I made a ~.* | **commit** ◊ *They all commit similar ~s.* | **repeat | learn from | pay for** ◊ *Ordinary people are paying for the government's ~s.* | **discover, realize** ◊ *Too late, she realized her ~.* | **avoid** ◊ *We can help you avoid costly ~s.* | **acknowledge, admit, admit to, recognize | correct, erase, fix** (AmE), **put right, rectify, undo | regret | forgive | point out** ◊ *The teacher kindly pointed out the ~.* | **eliminate** ◊ *It isn't possible to eliminate all ~s.*
MISTAKE + VERB **happen, occur** ◊ *Mistakes are bound to happen sometimes.*
PREP. **by ~** ◊ *I picked up the wrong bag by ~.* | **~ about** ◊ *I made a ~ about her.*
PHRASES **all a ~** ◊ *I kept telling myself that it was all a terrible ~.* | **an easy ~ to make** ◊ *Don't worry about it—it's an easy ~ to make!* | **make the ~ of doing sth** ◊ *A lot of people make the ~ of thinking that getting results is all that matters.* | **make the same ~** ◊ *Don't make the same ~ as I did.*

mistake verb

ADV. **easily** ◊ *An unwary observer could easily ~ this constellation for a comet.*
VERB + MISTAKE **cannot** ◊ *You can't ~ him. He has long red hair.*
PREP. **for** ◊ *I'm sorry. I mistook you for George.*
PHRASES **there is no mistaking sth** ◊ *There was no mistaking the admiration in his eyes.*

mistaken adj.

VERBS **be, prove, seem** ◊ *That view seems ~.*
ADV. **badly, fundamentally, gravely, profoundly, sadly, seriously, sorely, very (much)** ◊ *You are very much ~ if you think that people will agree to these changes.* | **completely, entirely, quite, utterly | somehow**
PREP. **about** ◊ *I think you're ~ about the time.*

mistrust noun

ADJ. **deep, profound | growing | general, widespread** (esp. BrE) | **mutual** ◊ *They will never overcome their mutual distrust.*
VERB + MISTRUST **create, foster, fuel | overcome**
PREP. **~ between** ◊ *There is suspicion and ~ between immigrants and the police.* | **~ in** ◊ *The incident has increased workers' ~ in the management.* | **~ of** ◊ *His experience left him with a ~ of banks.* | **~ towards/toward**
PHRASES **an atmosphere of ~, a climate of ~, a sense of ~** ◊ *Corruption creates a climate of ~ towards/toward authority.*

misunderstand verb

ADV. **badly | completely, fundamentally, grossly** (formal, esp. AmE), **profoundly**
PREP. **as** ◊ *My concern for their well-being was misunderstood as interference.*
PHRASES **be frequently misunderstood, be often misunderstood, be widely misunderstood | much misunderstood** ◊ *a charming and much misunderstood man*

misunderstanding *noun*

ADJ. **big, serious, terrible** | **complete, total** | **common, widespread** | **simple, slight** | **basic, fundamental, profound** | **genuine** | **possible** | **mutual**
VERB + MISUNDERSTANDING **cause, give rise to, lead to** | **avoid, prevent** ◇ *I am anxious to avoid any possible ~.* | **clarify, clear up, correct** | **betray, reflect, reveal** ◇ *His comments betrayed a complete ~ of the situation.*
MISUNDERSTANDING + VERB **arise, occur, result** ◇ *Somehow a ~ arose.* | **be based on sth, stem from sth**
PREP. **~ about** ◇ *There was widespread ~ about the aim of the project.* | **~ between** ◇ *There must have been some ~ between them.* | **~ by, ~ on the part of** ◇ *The over-simplification results in the possibility of ~ by the reader.* ◇ *I think there was some ~ on his part.* | **~ over** ◇ *a slight ~ over the terms of the contract*
PHRASES **a possibility of ~, a risk of ~** | **room for ~, scope for ~** ◇ *Leave no scope for ~s of any type.*

misuse *noun*

ADJ. **alleged, possible** | **deliberate** | **gross, serious** | **criminal** (*AmE*) ◇ *Can manufacturers be held liable for the criminal ~ of their products?* | **alcohol, drug, substance** ◇ *alcohol ~ among teenagers* | **computer** (*esp. BrE*) ◇ *He was fired for computer ~.*
VERB + MISUSE **prevent, stop** | **investigate**
PREP. **through ~** ◇ *pollution caused through ~ of pesticides* | **~ of** ◇ *He was accused of the ~ of public funds.* (*esp. BrE*)

mix *noun*

ADJ. **good, perfect, right, wonderful** ◇ *a party with just the right ~ of people* | **healthy, judicious** | **curious, odd, peculiar, strange** | **fascinating, interesting, intriguing** | **broad, rich** | **diverse, eclectic, vibrant** ◇ *an eclectic ~ of theatrical styles* | **cosmopolitan** | **complex** | **combustible, heady, potent, powerful, volatile** ◇ *His art features a volatile ~ of sexuality and violence.* | **cultural, ethnic, racial** | **marketing, product** | **brownie** (*esp. AmE*), **cake, muffin** (*esp. AmE*), **pancake** ◇ *a packet of cake ~* (*BrE*) ◇ *a box of cake ~* (*AmE*) | **concrete, mortar** | **potting, soil, soil-less** (*AmE*) ◇ *Plant the seedlings in well-drained potting ~.* | **audio, mono, sound, stereo** ◇ *The movie's sound ~ is excellent.*
VERB + MIX **contain, feature, have, include** | **offer** ◇ *The new Oak Hill development offers a ~ of housing.* | **create** ◇ *They have created a unique ~ of sounds.*
MIX + VERB **vary** ◇ *The precise ~ will vary.* | **contain** ◇ *The ~ contains soil, peat, and sand.*
PREP. **~ of** ◇ *The college has a broad ~ of students.*

mix *verb*

1 combine things
ADV. **thoroughly, well** ◇ *Mix all the ingredients together thoroughly.* | **gently** ◇ *When the rice is cooked, gently ~ in all the other ingredients.* | **in, together**
PREP. **with** ◇ *Mix yellow with blue to make green.*
PHRASES **~ and match, pick and ~** (*BrE*) (= combine things in different ways for different purposes) ◇ *You can ~ and match courses to suit your requirements.*

2 meet people
ADV. **easily, well** ◇ *a child who ~es well at school* | **freely** ◇ *Different races ~ed freely at dance halls and clubs.* | **happily** | **socially** ◇ *They worked together and often ~ed socially.*
PREP. **with** ◇ *She ~ed happily with the other children.*

mixed *adj.*

VERBS **be**
ADV. **decidedly, extremely, very** | **fairly, rather, somewhat** | **randomly** | **inextricably** ◇ *In his world view, art and religion were inextricably ~.* | **evenly** ◇ *Her background is evenly ~ between newspaper and Web journalism.* | **ethnically, racially, socially** ◇ *an ethnically ~ community*

mixture *noun*

ADJ. **fascinating, good, interesting, intriguing** | **bizarre, curious, extraordinary, odd, peculiar, strange** | **eclectic** ◇

an eclectic ~ of architectural styles | **judicious** (*esp. BrE*) ◇ *a judicious ~ of young and experienced players* | **rich** | **chaotic, confusing** | **complex** | **explosive, volatile** | **heady, potent** ◇ *Lust and revenge are a heady ~.* | **cement, concrete** | **cake** (*esp. BrE*) (usually **cake batter** in *AmE*) | **egg, flour, vegetable, etc.** ◇ *Gradually beat the flour into the egg ~.* | **cough** (*BrE*)
VERB + MIXTURE **add sth to** ◇ *Add the flour to the egg ~.* | **pour, purée, spoon, spread, stir, strain, whisk** ◇ *Pour the cake ~ into the bowl.*
MIXTURE + VERB **consist of sth, contain sth, have sth** ◇ *The ~ contains some ingredients that are difficult to find.*
PREP. **with a ~** ◇ *He looked at me with a ~ of amazement and horror.* | **~ of** ◇ *The pond contains a ~ of goldfish and carp.*

moan *noun*

ADJ. **faint, little, low, quiet, small, soft** | **deep** | **muffled** | **loud**
VERB + MOAN **emit, give, let out, make, utter** | **stifle, suppress** | **hear**
MOAN + VERB **come from sb/sb's mouth, escape sb/sb's mouth** ◇ *A low ~ of despair escaped her as she realized what had gone wrong.*
PREP. **with a ~** ◇ *He staggered about ten yards and fell down with a ~.* | **~ of** ◇ *a ~ of pleasure/pain/despair*
PHRASES **the ~ of the wind**
→ Note at SOUND

moan *verb*

1 make a low sound of pain/pleasure
ADV. **loudly** | **lightly, quietly, slightly, softly**
PREP. **in** ◇ *He ~ed in despair.* | **with** ◇ *She was still conscious and was ~ing loudly with pain.*

2 (*esp. BrE*) **complain**
ADV. **on** ◇ *They kept ~ing on about their illnesses.*
PREP. **about** ◇ *What are you ~ing about now?* | **at** ◇ *My parents ~ at me if I'm home late.* | **to** ◇ *She's always ~ing to me that she doesn't have enough money.*
PHRASES **~ and groan** ◇ *The children climbed into the bus, ~ing and groaning.*

mob *noun*

ADJ. **angry, hostile, unruly** | **baying** (*BrE*), **bloodthirsty, frenzied, howling, rioting, violent** | **heavy** (*BrE*) | **lynch**
VERB + MOB **form** | **join** | **lead** | **break up, disperse** | **incite**
MOB + VERB **attack sb/sth, chase sb, descend on sb/sth, set upon sb, surround sb/sth, torch sth** | **burn sth, burn sth down, torch sth** | **kill sb, lynch sb, murder sb** | **chant (sth), shout (sth)** ◇ *a ~ of chanting fans*
MOB + NOUN **mentality** | **justice, rule** ◇ *the lawless days of ~ rule and anarchy* | **violence**

mobile *adj.*

VERBS **be** | **become, get** ◇ *Babies start to get ~ around the age of eight months.* | **remain**
ADV. **extremely, fairly, very, etc.** ◇ *She remained fairly ~ despite her disabilities.* | **exceptionally, extraordinarily, highly** | **fully** ◇ *The barbecue is fully ~.* | **increasingly** | **geographically, socially** ◇ *a geographically ~ population* | **downwardly, upwardly** ◇ *downwardly ~ members of society*

mobile phone (*also* mobile) *noun* (*BrE*) → See also CELLPHONE

ADJ. **pay-as-you-go, prepaid** | **hand-held, hands-free** | **3G, third-generation** | **next-generation** | **GPRS, GSM, WAP**
VERB + MOBILE PHONE **use** ◇ *It's more expensive to use your mobile abroad.* | **switch off** ◇ *Please make sure all ~s are switched off during the performance.* | **top up** | **charge, charge up, recharge** | **leave a message on** ◇ *I left a message on your mobile.*
MOBILE PHONE + VERB **ring**
MOBILE-PHONE/MOBILE + NOUN **number** | **ringtone** ◇ *down-*

loadable mobile-phone ringtones | **company, network, operator** | **user** | **call** | **charger** | **mast**
PREP. **from your ~** ◇ *I'm calling from my mobile.* | **on your ~** ◇ *Call me on my mobile.*
PHRASES **the use of ~s**

mobility *noun*

ADJ. **decreased, limited, reduced, restricted** | **full** | **greater, increased** | **downward, upward** | **personal** | **class** (*esp. AmE*), **social** ◇ *Education was the key to upward social ~.* | **career, job, labour/labor, occupational** | **capital, economic** | **geographical**
VERB + MOBILITY **have** ◇ *She has limited ~ in her arms.* | **impair, limit, reduce** ◇ *a disease that impairs the ~ of many older people* | **enhance, increase** ◇ *Better education increases social ~.* | **regain** ◇ *The patient should be able to regain full ~.*
PHRASES **~ of labour/labor** ◇ *The high cost of living acts as an obstacle to ~ of labor.*

mobilize (*BrE also* -ise) *verb*

ADV. **effectively, successfully** | **quickly, rapidly** | **politically** (*esp. AmE*)
VERB + MOBILIZE **be able to, can be ~d** ◇ *The military is able to ~ rapidly.*
PREP. **against** ◇ *They successfully ~d public opinion against him.* | **for** ◇ *The country was mobilizing for war.*

mock *verb*

ADV. **bitterly, cruelly, mercilessly, ruthlessly, scornfully** | **gently, playfully** ◇ *'Too scary for you?' he ~ed gently.* | **openly** ◇ *He openly ~ed his parents.* | **subtly** ◇ *The play subtly ~s the conventions of romance.*
PREP. **at** ◇ *He ~ed at her hopes of stardom.* | **for** ◇ *She ~ed him for his failure.* | **with** ◇ *She ~ed him with her smile.*

mode *noun*

ADJ. **normal, traditional, usual** | **preferred** ◇ *Walking was his preferred ~ of travel.* | **default** | **effective** | **automatic, manual** ◇ *Most digital cameras have an automatic ~.* | **sleep, standby** ◇ *The phone displays a clock when in standby ~.* | **crisis, panic** ◇ *They're in crisis ~ at the moment.* ◇ *Everyone went into panic ~ trying to get the job finished.*
VERB + MODE **adopt, use** ◇ *Try using some other ~ of organization.* | **enter, select, switch to** ◇ *Switch from 'receive' ~ to 'transmit' ~.* | **change** ◇ *He had no intention of changing his ~ of dress.*
PREP. **in . . . ~** ◇ *The machine is in sleep ~.* | **~ of** ◇ *Their main ~ of subsistence is hunting.*
PHRASES **a ~ of address, a ~ of communication, a ~ of expression** | **a ~ of transport** (*esp. BrE*), **a ~ of transportation** (*AmE*)

model *noun*

1 copy of sth

ADJ. **full-scale, scale** | **three-dimensional** | **detailed** | **working** | **clay, plastic, wooden, etc.**
VERB + MODEL **assemble, build, construct, make**
MODEL + NOUN **aeroplane** (*BrE*), **airplane** (*AmE*), **car, railroad** (*AmE*), **railway** (*BrE*), **train**
PREP. **~ of** ◇ *She made a fantastic clay ~ of her dog.*

2 type of product

ADJ. **de luxe, luxury, popular** | **basic, standard** | **latest, new**
VERB + MODEL **do, make, produce, release** ◇ *They do several other ~s of washing machine.* ◇ *Later that year, IBM released a similar ~ at a lower price.* | **sell** | **design, develop** | **recall** ◇ *They're recalling their new ~ for modifications to the engine.*

3 example

ADJ. **excellent, good** | **role** | **simple** ◇ *We follow a simple accounting ~.* | **classical, standard, traditional** ◇ *the standard economic ~ of supply and demand* | **alternative** ◇

They offer an alternative ~ of married life. | **conceptual, experimental, statistical, theoretical** | **explanatory** | **business, clinical, economic, mathematical, medical, political, scientific** | **computer**
VERB + MODEL **give sb, present, propose, provide (sb with)** ◇ *The tape provides a ~ for students to copy.* | **construct, develop** ◇ *She developed a computer ~ to help farmers with pest control.* | **adapt, refine, simplify** | **copy** | **adopt, use** | **fit** ◇ *The book fits the classic ~ of a postmodern narrative.* | **be based on**
MODEL + NOUN **citizen, pupil** (*BrE*), **student** (*esp. AmE*) ◇ *In school, he works hard and is a ~ student.* | **home** (*AmE*)
PREP. **~ of** ◇ *She was a ~ of restraint.* | **~ for** ◇ *Successful schools must be used as ~s for the rest.*

4 person who models

ADJ. **artist's, glamour/glamor** (*esp. BrE*), **photographic** | **female, male** | **top** | **catwalk** (*BrE*), **fashion, runway** (*AmE*)
VERB + MODEL **photograph, pose, shoot**
MODEL + VERB **pose for sb/sth, sit for sb/sth** ◇ *The ~ sits for me for three hours every day.*
→ Note at JOB

model *verb*

ADV. **closely** | **loosely** | **accurately, realistically** ◇ *We can accurately ~ the development process.* | **consciously, explicitly**
PREP. **on, upon** ◇ *We aim to ~ the system on one used in French hospitals.*

modem *noun*

ADJ. **broadband, cable, dial-up, wireless** | **fast, high-speed** | **data, fax** | **built-in, external, internal**
VERB + MODEM **connect, plug in** | **unplug** | **configure, install**
MODEM + NOUN **connection, link** ◇ *Data is transmitted via a ~ link to the central office.*
PREP. **via (a/the) ~** ◇ *You can send the files to us via ~.*
→ Special page at COMPUTER

moderate *adj.*

VERBS **be**
ADV. **very** | **fairly, relatively** ◇ *a fairly ~ increase in the rate of inflation* | **politically**

moderation *noun*

ADJ. **great**
VERB + MODERATION **call for, preach** ◇ *The government called for greater ~ on the part of the unions.* | **practise/practice, show**
MODERATION + VERB **be the key to sth** ◇ *Moderation is the key to good health.*
PREP. **in ~** ◇ *Drinking alcohol is fine in ~.* | **with ~** ◇ *Always act with ~.*

modest *adj.*

1 not having a high opinion of your own abilities

VERBS **be, look, remain, seem**
ADV. **extremely, fairly, very, etc.** | **genuinely** | **falsely** ◇ *She would be falsely ~ not to acknowledge that she had come a very long way since those early days.*
PREP. **about** ◇ *He is ~ about his achievements.*

2 not very large, expensive, important, etc.

VERBS **be, seem** ◇ *Our requirements seem fairly ~.*
ADV. **extremely, fairly, very, etc.** | **comparatively, relatively** ◇ *He is looking to improve on his relatively ~ achievements so far.* | **apparently** | **surprisingly**
PREP. **in** ◇ *The new homes are ~ in scale, but very comfortable.*

modesty *noun*

ADJ. **characteristic, natural** (*esp. BrE*), **typical** ◇ *She accepted their congratulations with typical ~.* | **false** | **feminine** ◇ *Her strong will was hidden behind apparent feminine ~.*
VERB + MODESTY **display, show** | **preserve** ◇ *I wore a towel to preserve my ~.*

MODESTY + VERB **forbid sb** ◊ *Modesty forbade me from mentioning that my novel had been published.*
PREP. **with ~** ◊ *She spoke with characteristic ~.* | **~ about** ◊ *his ~ about his achievements*

modification *noun*

ADJ. **considerable, extensive, major** | **minor, slight** | **further** | **important, necessary, significant** | **behaviour/ behavior, behavioural/behavioral, dietary, lifestyle** ◊ *A diagnosis of diabetes necessitates some dietary ~s.* | **chemical, genetic** ◊ *people opposed to the genetic ~ of plants* | **structural**
VERB + MODIFICATION **involve, need, require** ◊ *The design requires considerable ~.* | **propose, recommend, suggest** | **carry out, introduce, make, undertake** (*esp. AmE*) | **receive, undergo** ◊ *The original plan had undergone fairly extensive ~s.*
PREP. **with ~, without ~** ◊ *These bikes are designed for racing and cannot be used on the road without ~.* | **~ in** ◊ *A ~ in the law has not led to an increase in prosecutions.* | **~ to** ◊ *We need to make a few ~s to the proposals.*

modify *verb*

ADV. **considerably, drastically, extensively, greatly, heavily, profoundly, radically, significantly, substantially** ◊ *The original text has been modified so radically that it is barely recognizable.* | **a bit, a little, slightly, somewhat** | **gradually** | **constantly** | **specially** | **appropriately, suitably** | **accordingly** | **chemically, genetically** ◊ *genetically modified organisms* | **structurally**
VERB + MODIFY **have to, need to** ◊ *You may need to ~ your plans a little.*
PREP. **for** ◊ *We can ~ the service for local conditions.*
PHRASES **highly modified** | **in a modified form** ◊ *These ideas are still used today, though in a slightly modified form.* | **modified to fit sth, modified to suit sth** ◊ *Stories and characters had to be modified to fit a 21st-century audience.* | **a modified version** ◊ *A highly modified version of the program is being used.*

module *noun*

1 part of machine, computer, etc.

ADJ. **command, lunar** ◊ *the tiny command ~ of the spaceship* | **memory, RAM, software** ◊ *You can buy memory ~s to increase storage capacity.* | **add-on, plug-in**
VERB + MODULE **add, configure, install, load**

2 (*esp. BrE*) unit of study

ADJ. **individual** | **compulsory, optional** | **online** ◊ *Participants who complete 10 online ~s will receive their certificates in June.*
VERB + MODULE **do, study** ◊ *I'm doing two optional ~s.* | **complete** | **divide sth into** ◊ *The course material is divided into four ~s.*

moist *adj.*

VERBS **be, feel, look** ◊ *Her skin felt ~ and feverish.* | **become, grow** ◊ *Beth's dark eyes grew ~ as she kissed her son.* | **remain, stay** | **keep sth** ◊ *Keep the atmosphere in your greenhouse slightly ~ throughout the spring.*
ADV. **very** | **a little, slightly, etc.** | **evenly** ◊ *Try to keep the soil evenly ~.*
PREP. **with** ◊ *His fingers were becoming ~ with sweat.*

moisture *noun*

ADJ. **excess** | **soil** | **body** | **surface**
...OF MOISTURE **bead, drop**
VERB + MOISTURE **absorb, draw, draw in, draw up, wick** (*esp. AmE*), **wick away** (*esp. AmE*) ◊ *Wind is caused by the sun drawing up ~ from the earth.* | **conserve, hold, hold in, retain, trap** | **lose**
MOISTURE + VERB **get in, penetrate sth** ◊ *Tiles stop ~ from penetrating your walls.* | **evaporate**
MOISTURE + NOUN **content, level** | **loss** | **build-up** ◊ *Ventilation helps prevent ~ build-up.*
PREP. **~ in** ◊ *the ~ in the soil*

mold *noun* (*AmE*) → See MOULD

mole *noun*

1 animal

MOLE + VERB **burrow, dig, tunnel**

2 person

VERB + MOLE **plant** ◊ *They suspected that a ~ had been planted in the organization.*

3 mark on the skin

ADJ. **hairy** | **raised**
VERB + MOLE **remove**

molecule *noun*

ADJ. **complex** | **simple** | **individual, single** ◊ *There may be several hundred amino acids in a single protein ~.* | **stable** | **CO_2, DNA, hydrogen, water, etc.**
VERB + MOLECULE **form** | **attach, bind**
MOLECULE + VERB **combine** | **be composed of sth, contain sth** | **interact**
PREP. **~ of** ◊ *two ~s of hydrogen*

mom *noun* (*AmE*) → See MUM

moment *noun*

ADJ. **brief, fleeting, passing** | **long** | **precious, rare** ◊ *They were making the most of those last precious ~s together.* | **intimate, quiet** | **anxious, awful, awkward, embarrassing, heart-stopping, tense, terrifying** ◊ *For one heart-stopping ~, we thought she was going to fall.* | **bad, difficult** ◊ *That was a bad ~ in my life.* | **odd, spare** ◊ *Could you look through this report when you have a spare ~?* | **exact, particular, precise, very** ◊ *I felt at home here from the very ~ I arrived.* | **good, opportune, perfect, right** ◊ *I don't think this is the right ~ to ask for a bonus.* | **inopportune, wrong** | **big, critical, crucial, decisive, defining, important, key, pivotal, seminal, watershed** ◊ *I didn't want to screw up my big ~.* ◊ *We have reached a critical ~ in the negotiations.* | **historic, historical** | **climactic, dramatic** | **blissful, glorious, magic, magical, marvellous/marvelous, memorable, unforgettable, wonderful** | **emotional, poignant, tender, touching** | **funny, humorous** ◊ *This is one of the book's funniest ~s.* | **crowning, finest, great, happiest, proudest, shining** (*esp. AmE*) ◊ *Her finest ~ came when she won the Nobel Prize.* | **unguarded** ◊ *She let the news slip in an unguarded ~.* | **senior** (*humorous*) (= a forgetful occasion) ◊ *It was a bad time to have a senior ~.* | **final, last** ◊ *Why do you leave it until the last possible ~ before getting ready?*
VERB + MOMENT **last, take** ◊ *The feeling only lasted a ~.* ◊ *This won't take a ~.* | **hesitate (for), pause (for), wait (for)** ◊ *She paused a ~ to reflect.* | **spend** ◊ *I spent a few ~s thinking what I was going to say.* | **give sb, spare** ◊ *I can only spare you a ~, I'm afraid.* | **enjoy, relish, savour/savor** ◊ *Victory was sweet, and she relished every ~.* | **cherish, treasure** ◊ *I treasure the ~s we spent together.* | **recall, relive, remember** ◊ *Afterwards she relived every ~ in her head.* | **dread** ◊ *I dread the ~ when she finds out.* | **choose, pick, seize** ◊ *He's in a bad mood today—you need to choose your ~ carefully.* | **capture** ◊ *I managed to capture the ~ on film.*
MOMENT + VERB **arrive, come, occur** ◊ *The ~ had finally come to make a move.* | **pass** ◊ *He opened his mouth to say he loved her, but the ~ passed.*
PREP. **after a/the ~** ◊ *After a ~ we followed him.* | **at a/the ~** ◊ *At that very ~ the phone rang.* ◊ *He might wake up at any ~.* | **for a/the ~** ◊ *She paused for a ~.* | **from a/the ~** ◊ *I loved her from the first ~ I met her.* | **in a/the ~** ◊ *I'll be back in a ~.* ◊ *in her rare ~s of leisure* | **~ in** ◊ *a great ~ in the country's history* | **~ of** ◊ *at the ~ of death* ◊ *It was the proudest ~ of my entire life.* ◊ *There was a ~ of silence.*
PHRASES **at a given ~, at any given ~** ◊ *You need to be aware of what you are doing at any given ~.* | **every waking ~** ◊ *I*

don't expect to spend every waking ~ at work. | **a few ~s** ◇ *Could you wait a few ~s?* | **in the heat of the ~** ◇ *In the heat of the ~ she forgot what she wanted to say.* | **a ~ ago** ◇ *He was here just a ~ ago.* | **a ~ later** ◇ *A ~ later, the ceiling fell in.* | **a ~ longer, a ~ more** ◇ *I couldn't stand it a ~ longer.* | **a ~ or two** ◇ *I stood there for a ~ or two.* | **never a dull ~** ◇ *There's never a dull ~ in this job.* | **not a ~ too soon** ◇ | **the present ~** ◇ *At the present ~, we do not have a choice.*

momentum *noun*

ADJ. **considerable, great, tremendous** | **irresistible, irreversible, unstoppable** | **initial** | **fresh** (*esp. BrE*) ◇ *She gave fresh ~ to the campaign.* | **downward, forward, upward** ◇ *There's no forward ~ in the movie.* | **political** ◇ *There is plenty of political ~ behind the proposed changes.*
VERB + MOMENTUM **have** ◇ *The campaign for change now has considerable ~.* | **build up, gain, gather, increase** ◇ *The car gathered ~ as it rolled down the hill.* | **create, generate, give sth, provide** | **keep up, maintain, sustain** | **lose** ◇ *The team has lost ~ in recent weeks.* | **regain** | **slow**
MOMENTUM + VERB **build up, increase** | **carry sb/sth** ◇ *Her ~ carried her through the door.* | **go** ◇ *Their ~ has gone, and they feel they cannot fight any longer.*
PREP. **~ for** ◇ *We must keep up the ~ for reform.* | **~ towards/toward** ◇ *the irresistible ~ towards/toward reunification of the two countries*
PHRASES **keep the ~ going** ◇ *We have to keep the ~ of our sales operation going.*

monarch *noun*

ADJ. **reigning** | **absolute** | **constitutional**
MONARCH + VERB **reign, rule**
PHRASES **the power of the ~** ◇ *a new law which limited the power of the ~*

monarchy *noun*

ADJ. **strong, weak** | **absolute** | **constitutional, parliamentary** | **hereditary**
VERB + MONARCHY **establish, set up** | **have** ◇ *The country still has a strong ~.* | **abolish** ◇ *the arguments for abolishing the ~* | **overthrow** ◇ *rebels trying to overthrow the ~* | **restore**

monastery *noun*

ADJ. **great** ◇ *the great ~ of St-Quentin* | **ancient, medieval, old** | **ruined** | **Benedictine, Dominican, etc.** | **Buddhist, Tibetan, Zen**
VERB + MONASTERY **enter, go into, join** ◇ *He entered a ~ as a young man.* | **leave** | **found** ◇ *The ~ was founded in 1665.*
PREP. **at a/the ~** ◇ *You can stay at the ~.* | **in a/the ~** ◇ *He lived in a ~ for most of his life.*

Monday *noun* → Note at DAY

money *noun*

ADJ. **big** ◇ *There is big ~ in golf for the top players.* | **easy** ◇ *He started stealing as a way of making easy ~.* | **bonus, extra** ◇ *Whenever I have a little extra ~, I buy clothes.* | **hard-earned** | **federal** (*AmE*), **government, public, taxpayers'** ◇ *Is this a good way to spend taxpayers' ~?* | **private** | **corporate** | **pin, pocket** (*esp. BrE*), **spending** ◇ *Did your parents give you pocket ~ when you were little?* ◇ *I don't know how much spending ~ to take on honeymoon.* | **gas** (*AmE*), **lunch, petrol** (*BrE*), **rent** ◇ *She gave him $5 lunch ~.* ◇ *He spent their rent ~ on beer.* | **bail** | **prize** | **grant, scholarship** | **sponsorship** | **borrowed, stolen** | **dirty** | **bribe, ransom** ◇ *They demanded $1 million in ransom ~.* | **hush, protection** ◇ *The company paid hush ~ to the victims to keep them quiet.* | **soft** (*AmE*) ◇ *He contributed $180 000 in soft ~ (= unregulated political donations)to the party committee.* | **pension, retirement** | **seed** | **oil** ◇ *The new airport terminal was built with oil ~.* | **paper** ◇ *The collection box was full of coins and paper ~.* | **counterfeit, fake** (*esp. AmE*) | **Monopoly, play** (*esp. AmE*)

... OF MONEY **amount, sum** ◇ *the large sums of ~ we handle in this store*
VERB + MONEY **have** ◇ *I don't have any ~ left.* | **coin, print** | **count, count out** | **borrow, bring in, collect, earn, get, make, raise, receive** ◇ *He hoped the plan would bring in quite a bit of ~.* ◇ *Some people were in the street collecting ~ for charity.* ◇ *How much ~ did he earn last year?* ◇ *I'll have to get some more ~ from somewhere.* | **bank, deposit, pay in, pay into the bank, put in the bank, put into the bank** ◇ *The stallholders bank their ~ at the end of the day.* ◇ *I need to pay this ~ in today.* ◇ *I pay my ~ into the bank as soon as I get paid.* | **draw out, get out, take out, withdraw** | **divert, move, transfer** ◇ *The ~ was transferred into an offshore bank account.* | **pay out, shell out, spend** ◇ *I spent all the ~ on clothes.* | **fritter away, lose, squander, throw away, waste** ◇ *She lost a lot of ~ at the casino.* ◇ *He squandered his ~ on gambling.* | **run out of** ◇ *We ran out of ~ and had to come home early.* | **be careful with, hoard, save, set aside, stash away** ◇ *an old miser who hoarded his ~* ◇ *We're trying to set some ~ aside for a new car.* ◇ *She stashed the ~ away in the bank.* | **invest, tie up** ◇ *They sensibly invested their prize ~ rather than spending it.* ◇ *All their ~ was tied up in long-term investments.* | **pour, pump, put, sink** ◇ *Investors were pouring ~ into Internet start-ups.* ◇ *He sank most of his ~ into his struggling business.* | **contribute, donate, give sb, lend sb, loan sb** (*esp. AmE*), **pay (sb), provide (sb with), put up** ◇ *Half the ~ raised was donated to charity.* ◇ *He managed to persuade his friend to put up the ~ for the venture.* | **give (sb) back, pay (sb) back, refund (sb), repay (sb)** ◇ *I'll pay the ~ back next week, I promise.* ◇ *The manager was unwilling to refund my ~.* | **owe (sb)** ◇ *They owe lots of people ~.* | **pool, share** ◇ *The friends pooled their ~ to buy tickets.* | **accept, take** ◇ *I don't think they'll accept Mexican ~ on the plane.* ◇ *The stores were very happy to take his ~.* | **cost** ◇ *These cars cost a lot of ~.* ◇ *All these improvements will cost ~.* | **be worth** ◇ *That painting is worth a lot of ~.* | **change, exchange** ◇ *We changed our ~ into dollars at the airport.* | **allocate, earmark** ◇ *The quality of public health care depends on the amount of ~ allocated to it.* ◇ *This ~ has been earmarked for public projects.* | **channel, direct, funnel** (*AmE*) ◇ *Some of this ~ was funneled to secret CIA programs.* | **embezzle, extort, siphon off, steal** ◇ *Government officials were siphoning off ~ for personal gain.* | **launder** ◇ *He was charged with laundering ~.*
MONEY + VERB **come from sth** ◇ *Money for the extension to the gallery came from the sale of old exhibits.* | **go (on sth), go to** ◇ *I don't know where all the ~ goes!* ◇ *All his ~ went on women.* ◇ *Most of the ~ went to pay for food.* | **come in, flow in, pour in, pour into sth** ◇ *She had two children to support and no ~ coming in.* | **buy sth** ◇ *the best car that ~ can buy*
MONEY + NOUN **management** | **manager** ◇ *You could consider hiring a professional ~ manager.* | **problems** | **laundering** | **launderer** | **market** ◇ *He made a fortune dealing on the ~ markets.* | **supply** ◇ *The solution to inflation lies in the control of the ~ supply.* | **box** (*esp. BrE*) | **order** (*AmE*)
PREP. **for ~** ◇ *He'll do anything for ~!* | **~ for** ◇ *Where's the ~ for the milk?*
PHRASES **bet ~ on sth, put ~ on sth** ◇ *He's going to leave. I'd bet ~ on it.* | **get ~ off sth** ◇ *You might get some ~ off the price if it's an old model.* | **get your money's worth** ◇ *The boat trip lasts three hours, so you certainly get your money's worth.* | **on the ~** ◇ *His prediction was right on the ~.* | **put ~ in sb's pocket** ◇ *The Senate recognized the need to put more ~ in the pockets of dairy farmers.* | **the smart ~ is on sth, the smart ~ says sth** ◇ *The smart ~ is on Brazil to win.* | **take ~ off sth** ◇ *He felt sorry for her and took some ~ off her bill.* | **throw ~ at sth** ◇ *They tend to throw ~ at problems without trying to work out the best solution.* | **throw your ~ around** ◇ *He thinks he can make friends by throwing his ~ around.* | **value for ~** ◇ *The hotel gives value for ~.*
→ Special page at BUSINESS

monitor *noun*

1 television/computer screen

ADJ. **colour/color** | **digital** | **CCTV, computer, PC, television, TV, video** | **flat-panel, flat-screen, LCD, touch-screen**

PREP. **on a/the ~** ◇ *The security staff can see the outside of the building on their CCTV ~s.*

2 machine that records/checks sth

ADJ. **baby, foetal/fetal, heart, heart-rate, oxygen, pulse, radiation**
MONITOR + VERB **detect sth** | **display sth, show sth** ◇ *The heart ~ shows the strength of your pulse.* | **beep, flicker**
PHRASES **hooked up to a ~** ◇ *He was lying there hooked up to a heart ~.*

3 sb who checks sth is done fairly/correctly

ADJ. **UN** ◇ *UN ~s declared the referendum fair.* | **ceasefire, election** | **court-appointed** (*AmE*) | **hall** (*AmE*), **school**

monitor *verb*

ADV. **carefully, closely, rigorously** (*esp. BrE*), **strictly** ◇ *Television advertising is strictly ~ed.* | **periodically, regularly, routinely, systematically** | **constantly, continually, continuously** | **effectively, properly** | **automatically** | **remotely** | **electronically**
VERB + MONITOR **be able to** ◇ *We will now be able to ~ its progress more closely.* | **continue to** ◇ *The authorities will continue to ~ the situation.*
PREP. **for** ◇ *The workers are constantly ~ed for exposure to radiation.*

monitoring *noun*

ADJ. **careful, close, systematic** | **frequent, periodic, regular** | **long-term, ongoing** | **constant, continuous** | **routine** ◇ *The problem was discovered during routine ~.* | **independent** | **environmental** | **cardiac, foetal/fetal** | **electronic** ◇ *Many employers are resorting to electronic ~ of their workforce.* | **remote**
VERB + MONITORING **need, require** ◇ *It is a problem that requires constant ~.*
MONITORING + NOUN **agency, body, committee, group, network, organization, team, unit** ◇ *a UN ~ team* | **device, equipment** | **procedure, process, system** | **programme/ program** | **visit**

monk *noun*

ADJ. **Buddhist, Tibetan, Zen** | **Christian** | **Benedictine, Dominican, Trappist, etc.** | **medieval** | **novice**
VERB + MONK **become**
MONK + VERB **chant**

monkey *noun*

ADJ. **capuchin, howler, rhesus, etc.**
...OF MONKEYS **horde, troop**
MONKEY + VERB **chatter** | **hang, swing** ◇ *~s swinging from branch to branch*

monologue (*AmE also* monolog) *noun*

ADJ. **inner, interior, internal** | **extended, lengthy, long, rambling** | **short** | **comic, dramatic** | **opening**
VERB + MONOLOGUE **deliver, do, go into, launch into, recite** ◇ *She delivered her ~ in a deadpan voice.* ◇ *an entertainer who does comic ~s*
PREP. **~ about** ◇ *She launched into a long ~ about how wonderful the company was.* | **~ on** ◇ *He went straight into a rambling ~ on the state of the country.*

monopoly *noun*

1 control by one company

ADJ. **effective, near, virtual** | **absolute** (*esp. AmE*), **total** | **government, state** | **local, national** | **natural** ◇ *Water is a natural ~.*
VERB + MONOPOLY **enjoy, exercise, have, hold** ◇ *The company has a virtual ~ in world markets.* | **create, establish, gain, get, secure, set up** | **keep, maintain, preserve, retain** | **lose** | **give sb, grant sb** | **challenge** ◇ *companies who are challenging the state monopolies* | **break, break up, end** ◇ *attempts to break the company's ~ of the sugar industry*
MONOPOLY + NOUN **position** ◇ *The company was able to exploit*

its ~ position. | **control, power** ◇ *The company used its ~ control to charge exorbitant fees.*
PREP. **~ in** ◇ *They created a ~ in the export of wool.* | **~ of** ◇ *One company holds a ~ of the raw materials.* | **~ on** ◇ *The company lost its ~ on exporting beer to India.* | **~ over** ◇ *They will fight to maintain their ~ over local bus services.*

2 organization

ADJ. **public, state, state-controlled, state-owned** ◇ *the privatization of state-owned monopolies such as the gas and electricity industries* | **giant, powerful** | **private** | **statutory** | **gas, oil** ◇ *the giant gas ~ Gazprom* | **media** ◇ *It was one of the first new-media companies to take on Latin America's media monopolies.*

monster *noun*

ADJ. **big, giant, huge, large** | **hideous, horrible, ugly** | **bug-eyed, hairy** ◇ *cheap sci-fi movies with bug-eyed ~s* | **six-eyed, three-headed, etc.** | **evil, heartless, inhuman** ◇ *What sort of inhuman ~ could do such a thing?* | **alien, mythical, prehistoric** | **sea**
VERB + MONSTER **create** (*often figurative*) ◇ *The government has created a bureaucratic ~.* | **battle, defeat, destroy, fight, kill, slay, vanquish** (*often figurative*) ◇ *He wanted to fight the ~ of poverty.* | **be inhabited by** ◇ *a barren wilderness inhabited by ~s*
MONSTER + VERB **attack sb/sth, devour sb/sth, kill sb/sth** | **lurk** | **growl, roar**

month *noun*

ADJ. **last, past** ◇ *The past few ~s have been hectic.* | **preceding, previous, recent** | **current** | **coming, ensuing, following, future, next, upcoming** (*esp. AmE*) ◇ *Winning stories will be published in the magazine in future ~s.* | **consecutive, straight, successive** | **alternate** | **intervening** ◇ *To occupy the intervening ~s she took a temporary job.* | **entire, full, whole** ◇ *Performances were banned for the entire ~ of June.* ◇ *We've been here five whole ~s now.* | **short** ◇ *In just a few short ~s he was promoted to manager.* | **early, later** ◇ *the early ~s of 2003* | **closing, final** ◇ *Laura is in the final ~s of pregnancy with her first child.* | **cold, dry, hot, warm, wet** | **spring, summer, etc.** ◇ *hot summer ~s* | **holy** ◇ *the Muslim holy ~ of Ramadan* | **lunar** | **calendar** | **record** ◇ *This has been a record ~ for sales.* | **busy** ◇ *December is a busy ~ for most shops.*
VERB + MONTH **spend** ◇ *He spent about a ~ decorating the house.* | **take** ◇ *It took ~s to find another job.* | **wait** ◇ *I waited six ~s for them to reply to my letter.*
MONTH + VERB **elapse, go by, pass**
PREP. **by the ~** ◇ *paid by the ~* | **during a/the ~ of, in a/the ~ of** ◇ *The festival is always held in the ~ of May.* | **for a ~, for ~s** ◇ *It hasn't rained for ~s.* | **in a ~** ◇ *We're getting married in a ~/in a month's time.* | **over a ~, under a ~** ◇ *I've been working on the illustration for over a ~.* | **per ~** ◇ *What does the salary work out as per ~?* | **~ of** ◇ *The ~s of July and August are the hottest.*
PHRASES **the ~s leading up to sth** ◇ *The President was involved in discussions in the ~s leading up to the war.* | **time of the ~** ◇ *Our money's usually running low by this time of the ~.*
→ Note on following page

monument *noun*

ADJ. **ancient, historic, historical** | **national, public** | **great, important, major** | **famous** | **fitting** ◇ *The new boat is a fitting ~ to the crew members who lost their lives.* | **lasting** ◇ *The museum was built as a lasting ~ to the civil war.* | **funerary** | **architectural** | **religious** | **granite, stone, etc.**
VERB + MONUMENT **stand as** ◇ *The tower stands as a ~ to the invasion of the island.* | **commission** ◇ *A ~ has been commissioned in his memory.* | **build, construct, create, erect, put up** | **unveil** | **preserve, protect** ◇ *the best preserved Roman ~ in Britain* | **destroy, remove** ◇ *Monuments to the former ruler were all removed.*

mood

NOTE

Months

the month of . . . ◇ *The festival is held during the month of August.*

last . . . , next . . . , that . . . , this . . . , the coming . . . , this coming . . . ◇ *I'll be in Rio next January.* ◇ *She'll be 40 this coming September.*

. . . (of) last/next/that/this year, . . . (of) the/this coming year, . . . (of) the following/previous/same year ◇ *The construction work began in May of last year.*

early/late . . . ◇ *The strike began in late March.*

the beginning/end/middle of . . . ◇ *I'm going away on business at the end of April.*

the first/latter/second half of . . . ◇ *The first half of January was marked by intense diplomatic activity.*

the period . . . ◇ *Throughout the period November to February flocks of 500 or more are regularly present.*

the months/weeks/year to . . . ◇ *In the year to June, sales were up 12% on a year ago.*

spend . . . ◇ *He spent August abroad.*

. . . arrives, . . . comes ◇ *November came with especially nasty fog.*

. . . passes (into . . .) ◇ *January passed into February with the crime still a mystery.*

a . . . day, morning, night, etc. ◇ *a misty December morning*

the May edition, the May issue, May's edition, May's issue, etc. ◇ *His article will appear in the May issue of the magazine.*

about . . . , around . . . ◇ *We will get in touch with you again around August.*

after/before . . . ◇ *We expect to take delivery sometime after June.*

between . . . and . . . ◇ *The hotel is closed between October and April.*

through (*AmE*) ◇ *June through November is hurricane season.*

by . . . ◇ *The work should be completed by June.*

come . . . ◇ *It's back to school come September.*

during . . . ◇ *The museum attracted 2 000 visitors during March.*

for . . . ◇ *The congress is planned for February 2012.*

from . . . ◇ *The show is open from March to November.* (*BrE*) ◇ *The show is open from March through November.* (*AmE*)

in . . . ◇ *We're getting married in April.*

since . . . ◇ *She has played only four games since November.*

throughout . . . ◇ *The freezing weather continued throughout January.*

till . . . , to . . . , until . . . , up to . . . ◇ *The show runs until the end of October.*

MONUMENT + VERB **be, stand** ◇ *The ~ will stand just inside the cathedral.*
PREP. **as a ~** | **~ of** ◇ *~s of the army's past campaigns* | **~ to** ◇ *The statue was built as a ~ to victims of the war.*

mood *noun*

ADJ. **cheerful, cheery, good, happy, jovial, pleasant** ◇ *She was not in the best of ~s.* | **bullish** (*BrE*), **buoyant, confident** (*esp. BrE*), **jubilant** (*esp. BrE*), **optimistic, positive, upbeat** ◇ *She was in an upbeat ~ about the future of the company.* | **bad, black, foul, rotten, sour, terrible** | **negative, pessimistic** | **dark, depressed, gloomy, melancholy, sad, sombre/somber** | **bitchy** (*informal*), **grumpy, irritable** | **contemplative, introspective, pensive, reflective, serious, sober, thoughtful** | **expansive, talkative** | **mellow, relaxed** | **changing** ◇ *I can't keep up with his constantly changing ~s.* | **defiant** (*esp. BrE*) ◇ *The workers were in defiant ~ as they entered the tribunal.* | **generous** | **funny** (*esp. BrE*), **strange,**

weird ◇ *He's in a funny ~ today—who knows how he'll react?* | **playful** | **celebratory, festive** ◇ *It was Christmas and everyone was in a festive ~.* | **romantic** | **national, popular, public** ◇ *a president who can gauge the popular ~* | **general, overall** ◇ *The overall ~ was optimistic.* | **current, prevailing** ◇ *the prevailing ~ in the country at the time*
VERB + MOOD **be in** ◇ *Don't talk to Miranda today—she's in a terrible ~!* | **get sb in, put sb in** ◇ *The music helped to put them in a more relaxed ~.* | **create, evoke** | **affect** | **match, reflect, suit** ◇ *Choose clothes to match your ~.* ◇ *The weather seemed to reflect his dark ~.* | **convey** | **capture, catch** ◇ *a movie that has captured the ~ of the moment* | **gauge** | **read, sense** ◇ *Nicky seemed able to read her ~.* ◇ *He could sense her gloomy ~.* | **establish, set** ◇ *The right music sets the ~ for such a great moment.* | **break, kill, ruin, spoil** ◇ *His comments pretty much killed the ~ for the rest of the show.* | **dampen, darken** ◇ *Not wanting to dampen her good ~, I quickly changed the subject.* | **boost, brighten, elevate, enhance, improve, lift, lighten** ◇ *It immediately brightened her ~ and brought a smile to her face.* | **regulate** ◇ *Serotonin is a brain chemical which regulates ~.*
MOOD + VERB **change, shift** | **become . . . , grow . . . , turn . . .** ◇ *The crowd's ~ abruptly turned violent.* | **darken** | **brighten, improve, lift, lighten** ◇ *His ~ lifted as he concentrated on his driving.*
MOOD + NOUN **change, swing** ◇ *After the accident he suffered violent ~ swings.* | **state** ◇ *the challenge of coping with negative ~ states* | **disorder, disturbance** ◇ *Mood disorders can disrupt relationships.* | **symptoms**
PHRASES **be in no ~ for sth** ◇ *I tried to make him laugh, but he was in no ~ for jokes.* | **a change of ~** ◇ *Instantly he felt her change of ~.* | **when the ~ strikes you** ◇ *She could be a very funny girl when the ~ struck her.*

moon *noun*

ADJ. **bright** ◇ *A bright ~ shone high overhead.* | **pale** | **large, small** | **crescent, full, gibbous, half, harvest, new, quarter** | **waning, waxing** | **rising** | **icy** ◇ *Saturn's icy ~s*
VERB + MOON **cover, hide** ◇ *A large black cloud covered the ~.* | **fly to, go to, land on, reach** | **colonize** | **explore** | **orbit** | **discover** ◇ *Galileo discovered the ~s of Jupiter.*
MOON + VERB **appear, come out, rise** | **glow, shine** | **illuminate sth, light sth, light up sth** | **set** ◇ *The ~ had almost set and the night was now dark.* | **wane, wax** | **hang, hover** ◇ *The full ~ hung high in the night sky.* | **orbit sth** | **pass** ◇ *During the eclipse, the ~ passed between the sun and the Earth.* | **be reflected in sth, reflect off sth** ◇ *The ~ reflected perfectly off the surface of the water.* | **cast sth** ◇ *The ~ cast its soft glow on the earth below.*
MOON + NOUN **landing** | **base** ◇ *The agency wants to establish a permanent ~ base.* | **rocket** | **mission** ◇ *an astronaut who was killed during the first ~ mission* | **cycle, phase** ◇ *The calendar gives you sunset times as well as ~ phases.* | **god, goddess**
PREP. **on the ~** ◇ *the first man to walk on the ~* | **under a/the ~** ◇ *The road shone frostily under the full ~.*
PHRASES **the light of the ~** ◇ *They had to work by the light of the ~.* | **the surface of the ~**

moonlight *noun*

ADJ. **bright** | **dim, faint, pale, soft** | **silver**
... OF MOONLIGHT **shaft** ◇ *a single shaft of ~*
MOONLIGHT + VERB **filter, glint, shine, stream** ◇ *the faint ~ filtering through the stained glass windows* | **hit sth** ◇ *The ~ hit her face perfectly.* | **illuminate sth** | **reflect off sth** | **dance, fall** ◇ *The pale ~ danced across his skin.*
PREP. **by ~** ◇ *The castle looks fantastic by ~.* | **in the ~, under the ~** ◇ *The leaves were silver in the ~.*
PHRASES **be bathed in ~, gleam, glint, shine, etc. in the ~** ◇ *The fields were bathed in bright ~ that night.* ◇ *His helmet glinted in the ~.*

moor *noun* (*esp. BrE*)

ADJ. **bleak, desolate, open, wild, windswept**
PREP. **across the ~** ◇ *the wind blowing across the ~s* | **down from the ~** ◇ *the slopes leading down from the ~* | **on the ~**

◇ *We got lost on the ~s.* | **over the ~** ◇ *Don't walk over the ~s in bad weather.*
PHRASES **the edge of the ~**

mooring *noun*

VERB + MOORING **be torn from, break loose from, come loose from, slip** ◇ *During the storm several of our boats were torn from their ~s.* ◇ *The crowds cheered as the great ship slipped her ~s.*
MOORING + NOUN **line, post** (*esp. BrE*), **rope** (*esp. BrE*)

moral *noun*

1 practical lesson

VERB + MORAL **draw** ◇ *There are clear ~s to be drawn from the failure of these companies.*
PREP. **~ to** ◇ *There is a ~ to the story.*

2 morals principles

ADJ. **good, high, strong** | **loose, low** | **sexual** | **public** | **personal** | **Christian**
VERB + MORALS **have** ◇ *He has absolutely no ~s, that man!* | **instil/instill** ◇ *She was gradually instilling ~s into her children.* | **teach (sb)** | **corrupt**
PHRASES **a decline in ~s**

morale *noun*

ADJ. **good, high** ◇ *Morale is very high in the school.* | **low, poor** | **national** | **employee, faculty** (*esp. AmE*), **staff** | **civilian, troop** | **team**
VERB + MORALE **affect, be bad for, be damaging to, damage, hit** (*esp. BrE*), **hurt** (*esp. AmE*), **lower, sap, undermine** ◇ *These unfortunate incidents sapped both our ~ and our resources.* | **be good for, bolster, boost, build, do wonders for, help, improve, lift, raise, restore** ◇ *measures designed to boost the ~ of the police* | **keep up, maintain** ◇ *The bonus helped maintain ~ among the staff.* | **destroy**
MORALE + VERB **improve** | **decline, plummet, suffer** | **be at rock bottom, hit rock bottom** (*both esp. BrE*)
MORALE + NOUN **boost, booster** ◇ *Mail from home is a great ~ booster for our soldiers.* | **issue, problem** ◇ *The army has a major ~ problem.*
PREP. **~ among** ◇ *Morale among nurses is suffering.*
PHRASES **a crisis of ~, a loss of ~**

morality *noun*

ADJ. **conventional, traditional** | **strict** | **personal, private** | **common, public, social** | **political** | **sexual** | **human** | **Christian** | **biblical**
VERB + MORALITY **legislate** (*AmE*) ◇ *Should governments be legislating ~?* | **question** | **impose** ◇ *people who wish to impose their ~ on other people*
MORALITY + VERB **be based on sth** ◇ *He believes that ~ is based on instinct and feeling.*
PHRASES **standards of ~** ◇ *She criticized politicians' standards of personal ~.*

moratorium *noun*

ADJ. **six-month, etc.** | **national**
VERB + MORATORIUM **have, impose, place, put** ◇ *The city placed a ~ on industrial development in town.* | **lift** | **call for** | **announce, declare**
PREP. **~ on** ◇ *The government has called for a ~ on weapons testing.*

morning *noun*

ADJ. **this, tomorrow, yesterday** | **following, next** | **previous** | **Friday, Saturday, etc.** | **weekday, weekend** | **early, late** ◇ *The side of the mountain appeared pink in the early ~ light.* | **April, May, etc.** | **spring, summer, etc.** | **beautiful, bright, clear, fine, glorious, lovely, sunny, warm** | **chilly, cold, cool, crisp, dreary, foggy, frosty, grey/gray, misty, rainy, snowy** | **fateful** ◇ *After that fateful ~, my life changed.* | **lazy** ◇ *We had a lazy ~ at home.* | **peaceful, quiet** | **busy** | **typical** ◇ *On a typical ~, I'll have cereal for breakfast.*
VERB + MORNING **spend** ◇ *I spent the ~ doing some sightseeing.*
MORNING + VERB **arrive, come, dawn** ◇ *The ~ dawned bright*

and sunny. | **pass, progress, wear on** ◇ *As the ~ wore on she became more and more tired.* | **bring sth** ◇ *The ~ brought blue sky and golden clouds.*
MORNING + NOUN **coffee, tea** | **meal** (*esp. AmE*) | **prayer, service, worship** | **hours** | **rush, rush hour** | **flight, traffic, train** | **commute, drive, ride** | **jog, swim, walk, workout** | **chores** (*esp. AmE*) | **ritual, routine** | **shift** | **bath, shower** ◇ *I took my usual ~ shower and brushed my teeth.* | **news, newspaper, paper** | **briefing, meeting** | **programme/ program, show, television** (*all esp. AmE*) ◇ *He was a presenter on a ~ talk show.* | **call** | **class, session** | **air, breeze, dew, light, mist, sky, sun, sunlight, sunshine** | **sickness** | **person** ◇ *I'm not a ~ person* (= I don't like mornings).
PREP. **by ~** | **during the ~, in the ~** | **on Monday, etc. ~, on the ~ of sth** ◇ *We got the news on the ~ of the wedding.* | **towards/toward ~** ◇ *Towards/Toward ~ the snow turned to rain.*
PHRASES **first thing in the ~** ◇ *I'll see to it first thing in the ~.* | **from ~ till night, ~, noon and night** ◇ *It's all she talks about, ~, noon and night* (= all the time). | **good ~** ◇ *He didn't even say 'Good morning'.* | **the rest of the ~**

morsel *noun*

ADJ. **choice, delicious, juicy, tasty** (*all often figurative*) ◇ *a juicy ~ of gossip* | **little, tiny**
VERB + MORSEL **eat** ◇ *I couldn't eat another ~.*
PREP. **~ of** ◇ *a few tiny ~s of bread*

mortal *noun*

ADJ. **lesser, mere, ordinary** (*all usually humorous*) ◇ *I just assumed you were a mere ~ like the rest of us.* ◇ *a resort for celebrities as well as lesser ~s* | **foolish**

mortality *noun*

ADJ. **high, low** ◇ *Poor hygiene led to high ~ among children.* | **early, premature** ◇ *a condition that often results in premature ~* | **adult, child, infant, juvenile** | **childhood** | **hospital**
VERB + MORTALITY **cause** ◇ *The disease has caused widespread ~.* | **decrease, reduce** ◇ *measures that should reduce infant ~* | **increase**
MORTALITY + VERB **increase** | **decrease, fall**
MORTALITY + NOUN **level, rate** | **data, statistics** | **study** | **risk** | **increase, reduction**
PREP. **~ among** ◇ *Mortality among immigrant groups was higher than average.* | **~ from** ◇ *a lower annual ~ from cancer*
PHRASES **a decline in ~, an increase in ~**

mortgage *noun*

ADJ. **big, huge** | **small** | **cheap** ◇ *Banks often offer their employees cheap ~s.* | **endowment** (*BrE*), **repayment** (*BrE*), **reverse** (*AmE*) | **adjustable-rate** (*AmE*), **fixed-rate, variable-rate** (*BrE*) | **home, residential** | **first, second** ◇ *He raised the money by taking out a second ~ on his house.*
VERB + MORTGAGE **have, hold** ◇ *We have a big ~.* | **buy** (*AmE*), **get, take out** ◇ *They were having trouble getting a ~.* ◇ *We'll have to take out a second ~ to pay for this wedding!* | **pay, pay off, redeem** (*esp. BrE*), **repay** (*esp. BrE*) ◇ *He wasn't earning enough to pay the ~.* | **fall behind on** (*esp. AmE*), **fall behind with** (*BrE*), **get behind on** (*esp. AmE*) ◇ *They fell behind on/on their ~, so their home was repossessed.* | **sell** | **refinance**
MORTGAGE + NOUN **payment, repayment** (*BrE*) ◇ *They were struggling to keep up with their ~ payments.* | **application** | **loan** | **credit** | **debt** | **business, industry, market** | **banker, broker, company, lender** | **finance** | **product** | **insurance** | **interest, rate** ◇ *~ interest payments* (*esp. BrE*) ◇ *a rise in ~ rates* | **portfolio** | **refinancing**
PREP. **~ of** ◇ *a ~ of $800 000* | **~ on** ◇ *I couldn't get a ~ on the property.*

mosquito noun

ADJ. **infected** | **malaria**
... OF MOSQUITOES **swarm**
VERB + MOSQUITO **swat** ◊ *He swatted the ~ with a newspaper.* |
kill | **attract** | **repel** | **control**
MOSQUITO + VERB **fly** | **be out** (*esp. AmE*) ◊ *Stay indoors when
~es are out.* | **buzz** | **bite (sb)** | **carry sth, spread sth** ◊ *This
strain of ~ carries malaria and yellow fever.*
MOSQUITO + NOUN **bite** ◊ *I was awake all night scratching my ~
bites.* | **larva** ◊ *fish that feed on ~ larvae* | **species** |
population | **net** | **repellent** | **control**

motel noun

ADJ. **cheap** | **seedy** | **small** | **local**
VERB + MOTEL **check into, check out of** | **stay at, stay in** |
find
MOTEL + NOUN **room** | **owner**
PREP. **at a/the ~, in a/the ~** ◊ *We spent a night at a ~ on the
way.*

mother noun

ADJ. **lone, single, unmarried, unwed** ◊ *She felt proud that
she had raised four children as a lone ~.* | **married** |
widowed | **divorced** | **lesbian** | **biological, birth, natural,
real** | **surrogate** | **adoptive, custodial** (*AmE*), **foster** |
adolescent, teen (*esp. AmE*), **teenage, young** | **ageing/
aging, elderly, old** | **ailing, sick** ◊ *He has cared for his sick ~
for years.* | **dead, deceased, late** | **dying** | **caring, devoted,
excellent, good, loving, wonderful** | **proud** ◊ *the proud ~
of the bride* | **doting, overprotective** | **stern** | **domineer-
ing, overbearing** | **abusive** | **bad, unfit** ◊ *The court decided
she was an unfit ~.* | **anxious** (*esp. BrE*), **distraught, frantic,
worried** ◊ *Her distraught ~ had spent all night waiting by the
phone.* | **grieving** | **expectant, pregnant** | **first-time** | **new**
| **full-time, stay-at-home** | **working** | **welfare** (*AmE*) | **low-
income** | **breastfeeding, nursing** | **beloved, dear** ◊ *his
beloved ~*
VERB + MOTHER **resemble, take after** ◊ *The boys were like their
father, but Louise took after her ~.* | **inherit sth from** ◊ *She
inherited the urge to travel from her ~.*

motif noun

ADJ. **central, dominant** ◊ *Alienation is a central ~ in her
novels.* | **recurring** | **visual** | **simple** ◊ *The rug was
decorated with a simple flower ~.* | **decorative, ornamental**
| **fish, flower, etc.** ◊ *The jacket has a rose ~ on the collar.* |
floral
VERB + MOTIF **be decorated with, have**

motion noun

1 movement

ADJ. **smooth, steady** | **quick, rapid, swift** | **gentle** | **circular,
rocking, rolling, sliding, swaying, sweeping, twisting** |
bending, swinging, throwing, etc. ◊ *He made throwing ~s
with his hands.* | **rhythmic** | **graceful** | **jerky** | **exaggerated**
| **constant, continuous** | **repetitive** | **backward, down-
ward, forward, upward** | **side-to-side** | **anticlockwise**
(*BrE*), **clockwise, counterclockwise** (*AmE*) | **perpetual** ◊ *the
search for the secret of perpetual ~*
VERB + MOTION **feel** ◊ *She could feel the rolling ~ of the ship
under her feet.* | **detect** | **make, perform** ◊ *He made little
flapping ~s with his arms.* | **repeat** | **mimic, simulate** |
reverse | **restrict** ◊ *Too tight a grip will restrict the natural ~
in your hands.*
MOTION + NOUN **detector, sensor** | **exercise** ◊ *After surgery,
patients should begin a range of ~ exercises for the elbow.*
PREP. **into ~** ◊ *The insects are stirred into ~ by the heat of the
sun.* | **in ~** ◊ *Do not open the door when the train is in ~.*
PHRASES **in a circular, smooth, etc. ~** | **set sth in ~**

2 suggestion

VERB + MOTION **introduce** (*esp. AmE*), **propose, put** (*BrE*), **put
forward** (*BrE*), **table** (= *present*) (*BrE*) ◊ *Only delegates may*

introduce *~s and vote.* ◊ *The ~ was put before the conference.*
◊ *The board tabled a ~ calling for her resignation.* | **debate**
(*esp. BrE*), **discuss** ◊ *The ~ will be debated later today.* | **vote
on** | **be in favour/favor of, second, speak in favour/favor
of** (*esp. BrE*), **support, vote for** | **accept** (*esp. BrE*), **adopt,
approve, carry** (*BrE*), **pass** ◊ *The ~ was passed by 165 votes to
78.* | **be against, oppose, speak against, vote against** |
defeat, reject ◊ *The ~ was defeated by 51 votes to 43.* | **table**
(= *postpone*) (*AmE*)
MOTION + VERB **be carried** (*BrE*), **carry** (*AmE*) ◊ *The ~ (was)
carried.*
PHRASES **a ~ of no confidence** (*esp. BrE*) ◊ *He proposed a ~ of
no confidence in the government.*

motionless adj.

VERBS **be, hang, kneel, lie, remain, sit, stand, stay** ◊ *The flag
hung ~ on its pole.*
ADV. **absolutely, completely, perfectly** | **almost, virtually**

motivated adj.

VERBS **be, feel, seem** | **become** | **get sb** | **keep sb**
ADV. **extremely, fairly, very, etc.** | **highly, strongly, well** ◊ *a
highly ~ group of workers* ◊ *well-motivated students* | **poorly**
| **ideologically, politically, racially** ◊ *The attack was
thought to be racially ~.*

motivation noun

1 keenness and willingness to do sth

ADJ. **great, high, powerful, strong** ◊ *students with high ~* ◊
his strong ~ to succeed | **positive** | **low, poor** | **extra** |
student | **individual, personal, human** | **internal,
intrinsic**
VERB + MOTIVATION **have** ◊ *Many of the boys have very poor ~.*
| **lack** | **lose** ◊ *By this time the children had lost all their ~ for
writing poetry.* | **generate, provide** ◊ *high rewards that
generate the necessary ~ in the workers* | **enhance, improve,
increase, strengthen** | **reduce** | **maintain**
PHRASES **a lack of ~** | **level of ~** ◊ *students who have a low
level of ~*

2 a reason for doing sth

ADJ. **main, major, primary, prime** | **only, sole** | **real, true** |
original | **underlying** | **unconscious** | **great, powerful,
strong** | **economic, moral, political, psychological, re-
ligious, sexual**
VERB + MOTIVATION **have** ◊ *They had very different ~s for
creating the work.* | **understand** | **question** | **explain**
PREP. **~ for** ◊ *his main ~ for supporting the government* | **~ in**
◊ *my main ~ in making the suggestion* | **~ behind** ◊ *the
primary ~ behind the government's intervention*

motive noun

ADJ. **hidden, ulterior** | **good, strong** ◊ *I'd say he had a very
strong ~ for wanting her dead.* | **altruistic, high, noble,
pure** ◊ *He was acting from the noblest of ~s when he offered
her money.* | **base** (*formal*), **selfish** | **evil, sinister** |
questionable | **main, primary, prime** | **real, true** | **clear,
obvious** ◊ *There seemed to be no clear ~ for the attack.* |
underlying ◊ *She was not sure what his underlying ~s were.*
| **mixed** ◊ *We give aid to other countries with mixed ~s.* |
human | **personal** | **economic, financial, political, racial**
(*esp. BrE*), **religious** | **profit**
VERB + MOTIVE **be inspired by** (*esp. BrE*), **have** ◊ *She knew that
he was inspired by base ~s.* | **establish, find, find out,
suggest** ◊ *The police are still trying to establish a ~ for the
attack.* | **provide** ◊ *There must be something which provided
a ~ for these killings.* | **be suspicious of, examine, impugn**
(*formal*), **question, suspect** ◊ *He was suspicious of her ~s in
inviting him into the house.* ◊ *She should examine her ~s for
marrying him.* | **hide** ◊ *We've become adept at hiding our
true ~s.* | **explain** ◊ *However you explain the ~s behind his
actions, he was still wrong.* | **reveal** | **know, see, under-
stand** ◊ *Everyone can see your true ~s.*
MOTIVE + VERB **drive sb/sth** ◊ *speculation that less noble ~s
were driving the country's foreign policy*
PREP. **~ in** ◊ *What was their ~ in setting fire to the building?* |
~ behind ◊ *There is no doubt about the ~ behind it all.* | **~**

PHRASES **a variety of ~s** ◇ *I did it for a variety of ~s.*

motor *noun*

ADJ. **large, powerful** | **small, tiny** | **diesel, electric** | **outboard** ◇ *a boat with a powerful outboard ~* | **rocket** | **starter**
VERB + MOTOR **start, turn on** | **turn off** | **drive, power** | **build**
MOTOR + VERB **run, work** ◇ *He left the ~ running.* | **drive sth, power sth** ◇ *A powerful ~ drives the wheel.*

motorcycle *(BrE also motorbike) noun*

ADJ. **powerful** | **250 cc, 600 cc, etc.** | **vintage** *(esp. BrE)* ◇ *a collection of vintage ~s* | **police**
VERB + MOTORCYCLE **drive** *(esp. AmE)*, **ride** ◇ *He's learning to ride a ~.* | **race** | **climb on, get on** | **climb off, get off** | **come off** (= fall off) *(BrE)*, **fall off** ◇ *He died after falling off his ~.* | **park** | **rev, rev up** ◇ *a crowd of bikers all revving up their ~s*
MOTORCYCLE + NOUN **rider** | **cop** *(informal, esp. AmE)* | **maker, manufacturer** | **ride** | **race** | **accident, crash** | **safety** | **club, gang** | **helmet** | **apparel** *(esp. AmE)*, **boots, jacket** | **engine, parts**
PREP. **on a/the ~** ◇ *He was sitting on his ~.*
PHRASES **the back of a ~** ◇ *She climbed onto the back of my ~.*

motorway *noun (in the UK)* → See also FREEWAY

ADJ. **busy** | **four-lane, three-lane, etc.** | **orbital, urban** ◇ *the M25 London orbital ~*
VERB + MOTORWAY **join** | **leave, turn off** | **build**
MOTORWAY + NOUN **driving, traffic** | **network, system** | **bridge, junction** | **service area, service station** | **crash, pile-up** ◇ *Five people have been killed in a ~ pile-up.*
PREP. **along the ~, down the ~, up the ~** ◇ *She was driving along the ~.* ◇ *He sang as he rattled down the ~.* | **off the ~** | **on the ~, onto the ~** | **~ from, ~ to** ◇ *We were on the ~ to London.*

motto *noun*

ADJ. **company** *(esp. BrE)*, **family, school** *(esp. BrE)*, **state** *(AmE)* | **unofficial** | **new**
VERB + MOTTO **have** | **become** | **adopt, have sth as, use sth as** ◇ *He was the first to coin the ~ 'Make love, not war'.* ◇ *Let's use that as our ~*
PREP. **~ for** ◇ *a good ~ for gardeners*

mould *(BrE) (AmE mold) noun*

1 hollow container

ADJ. **jello** *(AmE)*, **jelly** *(BrE)* | **terrine** | **ring** | **prepared** ◇ *Fill the prepared ~s with ice cream.* | **plastic, rubber**
VERB + MOULD/MOLD **cast sth in, make sth in** ◇ *The statues were cast in clay ~s.* | **fill, pour sth into** | **use** | **create, make** | **remove**
PREP. **in a/the ~** ◇ *Leave the clay in the ~ overnight.* | **~ for** ◇ *a ~ for a bronze statue*

2 type of sth

ADJ. **old** *(esp. AmE)*, **traditional**
VERB + MOULD/MOLD **be cast in, be from, come from, fit, fit into** ◇ *She is clearly from a different ~ from her team mate.* ◇ *He doesn't fit into the usual ~ of bosses.* | **break** ◇ *Breaking the traditional ~ of local politics is not going to be easy.*
PREP. **in a/the ~** ◇ *a young politician in the ~ of the great statesmen of the past*

3 organic growth

ADJ. **bread, leaf, slime** | **toxic**
VERB + MOULD/MOLD **be covered in, be covered with** ◇ *The bread was covered in green ~.*
MOULD/MOLD + VERB **form, grow** | **kill**
MOULD/MOLD + NOUN **spore** | **growth** | **problem** ◇ *houses with ~ problems* | **contamination** | **exposure** | **allergy**

mound *noun*

1 small hill

ADJ. **high, large** ◇ *The church stands on a high ~ just outside the town.* | **low, small** | **grassy** | **burial** | **ant, termite**
PREP. **on a/the ~** ◇ *a small tree on a grassy ~*
PHRASES **the foot of a ~, the top of a ~**

2 pile

ADJ. **big, great, huge, large** | **little, small** ◇ *a small ~ of leaves*
PREP. **~ of** ◇ *a great ~ of paperwork*

mount *verb*

1 organize sth

ADV. **successfully** ◇ *The company successfully ~ed a takeover bid in 1996.*

2 increase

ADV. **quickly, rapidly** | **steadily** | **up** ◇ *The cost quickly ~s up.*
VERB + MOUNT **begin to, continue to**

3 picture, jewel, etc.

ADV. **beautifully** ◇ *The prints were beautifully ~ed.* | **carefully** | **directly** ◇ *The switch is ~ed directly on the wall.* | **horizontally, vertically** | **permanently**
PREP. **in** ◇ *The diamond is ~ed in gold.* | **on** ◇ *The specimens were ~ed on slides.*

mountain *noun*

1 very high hill

ADJ. **big, great, high, large, tall, towering** | **1 000 m, 3 000-foot, etc.** | **small** | **steep** | **low** | **beautiful, fine, majestic, mighty, spectacular** | **surrounding** ◇ *The surrounding ~s make the city difficult to evacuate.* | **distant** | **remote** | **volcanic** | **craggy, jagged, rocky, rugged** | **snow-capped, snow-covered, snowy** | **holy, sacred** ◇ *the holy ~ of the Lapp community*
... OF MOUNTAINS **chain, range** ◇ *a chain/range of ~s*
VERB + MOUNTAIN **ascend, climb, come up, go up, scale** | **come down, descend, go down, walk down** | **walk in** ◇ *We enjoy walking in the ~s.* | **cross** | **overlook** ◇ *a large window overlooking the ~s*
MOUNTAIN + VERB **rise, soar, tower** ◇ *The ~s here rise to well over 2 000 m.* | **loom** ◇ *Mountains loom in the distance.* | **surround sth** ◇ *Towering ~s surrounded the town.* | **overlook sth**
MOUNTAIN + NOUN **chain, range** | **area, country, environment, region, terrain** ◇ *Between the two towns was 50 miles of ~ country.* | **pass, path, road, route, track, trail** | **landscape, scenery** | **view, vista** | **face, peak, ridge, side, slope, top, valley, wall** | **cave** | **glacier** | **lake, stream** | **air** ◇ *Many people come simply to enjoy the fresh ~ air.* | **meadow, pasture** | **forest** | **town, village** | **fastness** *(literary)*, **fortress, stronghold** | **cabin, hut, lodge, resort, retreat** | **man** *(AmE)* | **folk, people** | **climbing, walking** *(BrE)* | **walk** *(BrE)* | **climber** | **guide** | **rescue** ◇ *a mountain-rescue team* | **bike** | **biker** | **biking** | **sickness** | **goat, gorilla, hare, lion** (= puma) *(AmE)*, **etc.**
PREP. **across the ~, over the ~, through the ~** ◇ *a pass through the ~s* | **down a/the ~, up a/the ~** ◇ *She arranged to meet the others halfway up the ~.* | **in the ~s** ◇ *This type of goat lives high up in the ~s.*
PHRASES **the flank of a ~, the side of a ~, the slope of a ~** | **the bottom of a ~, the foot of a ~, the top of a ~**

2 large amount/number of sth

ADJ. **great, massive** | **debt** *(esp. BrE)* | **paper** *(esp. BrE)* | **butter, sugar, etc.** *(BrE)* ◇ *They revealed a solution to reduce Europe's butter ~.*
VERB + MOUNTAIN **generate** | **reduce** *(esp. BrE)* | **face** ◇ *The school was facing a ~ of debt.*
PHRASES **a ~ of paper, a ~ of paperwork** ◇ *The investigation generated a ~ of paperwork.*

mourning noun

1 sadness about sb's death
ADJ. **deep** | **national, official** | **public**
VERB + MOURNING **be in, go into** ◇ *He was in deep ~ for his dead wife.*
MOURNING + NOUN **clothes**
PHRASES **a day of ~, a period of ~** ◇ *a day of ~ for the victims of the tragedy* | **a state of ~**

2 clothes
ADJ. **full**
VERB + MOURNING **wear**
PREP. **in ~** ◇ *She was still in full ~ six months after her son's death.*

mouse noun

1 animal
ADJ. **deer, field, house, etc.** | **laboratory** | **white**
VERB + MOUSE **chase** | **catch** | **kill** | **breed**
MOUSE + VERB **squeak** | **run, scurry** | **gnaw sth** ◇ *A ~ had gnawed its way through the cable.*
MOUSE + NOUN **droppings** | **hole** | **trap** (usually *mousetrap*)
PHRASES **as quiet as a ~** ◇ *She crept upstairs, as quiet as a ~.*

2 for a computer
ADJ. **optical, wireless**
VERB + MOUSE **click, double-click** | **use** | **drag, move**
MOUSE + NOUN **button** | **click** ◇ *Some of these mouse-click short cuts are worth learning.* | **cursor, pointer** | **mat** (*BrE*), **pad** (*esp. AmE*) | **port**
PREP. **with the ~** ◇ *You can move the cursor around the screen with the ~.*
→ Special page at COMPUTER

moustache (*BrE*) (*AmE* mustache) noun

ADJ. **thick, thin** | **long** | **small** | **bushy, curly, droopy, handlebar, neat** (*esp. BrE*), **pencil** (*BrE*), **toothbrush** (*BrE*), **walrus** (*esp. BrE*), **waxed** (*esp. BrE*) | **fake** (*esp. AmE*), **false** (*esp. BrE*)
VERB + MOUSTACHE/MUSTACHE **have, sport, wear** ◇ *Her fiancé sported a bushy ~.* | **grow** ◇ *He's trying to grow a ~.* | **trim** | **shave off** | **stroke, twirl** ◇ *He stroked his ~ thoughtfully.*

mouth noun

ADJ. **big, cavernous, enormous, huge, large, wide** | **small, tiny** | **beautiful, perfect, pretty, rosebud, sensual, sensuous** | **red** | **firm, hard, strong** ◇ *A smile played around his strong ~.* | **soft** | **hot, warm** | **slack** | **full** | **lipless, thin** | **toothless** | **wet** | **dry, tight** ◇ *A tight ~ was the only sign of her nerves.* | **gaping, half-open, open** | **closed** | **smiling** | **hungry** ◇ *She has four hungry ~s to feed.* | **sore, swollen**
VERB + MOUTH **open** | **clamp shut, close, shut, snap shut** | **cover** ◇ *He covered his ~ to hide his yawn.* | **cup, gag** ◇ *Suddenly a hand cupped her ~.* | **wipe** ◇ *He wiped his greasy ~ on his sleeve.* | **rinse, rinse out, wash out** | **fill, stuff** ◇ *He coughed as the blood filled his ~.* ◇ *He began to stuff his ~ with pasta.* | **foam at, froth at** ◇ *The dog was foaming at the ~ and near death.* | **burn** ◇ *The hot coffee burned her ~.* | **kiss** | **purse**
MOUTH + VERB **drop, drop open, fall open, gape, hang open, open, sag open** ◇ *Our ~s dropped open in surprise.* | **widen** ◇ *His ~ widened to a smile.* | **close, shut** | **clamp shut, snap shut** | **be contorted, be set, compress, contort, harden, purse, set, tighten, turn down, twist** ◇ *His ~ compressed into a thin, hard line.* ◇ *'Get out!' she shouted, her ~ contorted by emotion.* | *Her ~ suddenly set in a determined line.* | **curl, curve, lift, quirk** (*esp. AmE*), **stretch, tilt, turn up** ◇ *Her ~ curved into a smile.* ◇ *His ~ lifted in a wry smile.* | **droop, sag** | **pout** | **twitch** | **quiver, tremble** | **water** ◇ *My ~ started watering when I smelled the food.* | **be dry, go dry** | **taste like sth**
MOUTH + NOUN **sore, ulcer** (*BrE*) | **cancer** | **care** (*esp. AmE*) ◇ *Good ~ care is very important when you are having chemotherapy.* | **rinse**

PREP. **around your ~** ◇ *There were lines of tension around his ~.* | **across your ~** ◇ *A cool smile played across her ~.* | **in your ~** ◇ *I could taste blood in my ~.* | **over your ~** ◇ *She put her hand over her ~ to stifle the cough.*
PHRASES **the back of the ~, the roof of the ~** ◇ *I was so thirsty my tongue was sticking to the roof of my ~.* | **the corner of the ~, the side of the ~** ◇ *There was blood trickling from the corner of his ~.* ◇ *The corners of her ~ turned up in a slight smile.* | **keep your ~ shut** (= don't speak) | **(have) your ~ full** (= full of food) ◇ *Don't talk with your ~ full!* | **a ~ to feed** ◇ *Twins would mean two extra ~s to feed.*

mouthful noun

ADJ. **huge, large** | **first, last**
VERB + MOUTHFUL **drink, eat, gulp, gulp down, have, swallow, take** ◇ *She took a large ~ of bread and started to read the letter.* | **get** ◇ *She landed on her face, getting a ~ of sand.* | **chew** | **spit, spit out** | **choke on** ◇ *I choked on a ~ of tea.*
PREP. **between ~s** ◇ *He told the story between ~s.* | **through a ~** ◇ *She answered through a ~ of cake.* | **~ of** ◇ *a ~ of coffee*

mouthpiece noun

1 part of a telephone
VERB + MOUTHPIECE **cover, cover up, put your hand over** ◇ *He put his hand over the ~ and called his wife to the phone.*

2 sb/sth that informs the public about sb/sth's opinions
ADJ. **official, political**
VERB + MOUTHPIECE **act as, be**
PREP. **~ for, ~ of** ◇ *The media act as a ~ for the ruling party.*

move noun

1 action to achieve sth; change in ideas, etc.
ADJ. **big, important, major, radical, significant** | **decisive** | **astute, brilliant, clever, good, inspired, sensible, shrewd, smart, wise** | **bad** | **right** ◇ *She wondered whether she had made the right ~ in telling the truth.* | **false, wrong** ◇ *One false ~ could lead to war.* | **dumb** (*informal, esp. AmE*), **stupid, unwise** | **positive** | **aggressive, audacious, bold, brave, daring, strong** | **defensive** | **serious** | **desperate, drastic, dramatic, shock** (*BrE*) (used in journalism), **surprise, surprising, unexpected** ◇ *The company was put up for sale yesterday in an unexpected ~ by management.* | **unprecedented** | **obvious** | **interesting** | **unusual** | **controversial, conciliatory** (*esp. BrE*) | **popular** | **gradual** | **rapid** | **new** | **current** (*BrE*) ◇ *the current ~ towards/toward networked organizations* | **latest, recent** | **next** | **first, initial** ◇ *If he wants to see me, he should make the first ~.* | **strategic, tactical** | **logical** | **unilateral** | **diplomatic** (*esp. BrE*), **legal, military, political** | **pre-emptive** | **cost-cutting** | **career** ◇ *Getting a job in advertising was a good career ~.*
VERB + MOVE **be, represent** ◇ *The talks represented the first significant ~ towards/toward peace.* | **make** ◇ *The management has made no ~ to settle the strike.* | **pull** (*informal*) ◇ *Don't you dare pull a ~ like that again.* | **prompt** | **initiate** | **signal** ◇ *The new legislation signals a ~ away from government involvement in telecommunications.* | **spearhead** ◇ *The ~ is spearheaded by a prominent lawyer.* | **back, encourage, support** | **applaud, welcome** | **condemn, criticize** | **oppose, reject, resist** | **block** | **consider, contemplate, ponder** | **calculate, plan, plot** ◇ *Now we must plot our next ~.* | **decide, decide on** ◇ *They are waiting for the results of the opinion polls before deciding their next ~.* | **anticipate** | **announce** ◇ *The government announced its ~ to ban smoking in public spaces.*
MOVE + VERB **take place** | **be afoot, be underway** (*esp. BrE*) ◇ *Moves are afoot to increase car insurance premiums.* | **fail** | **pay off** | **prove sth** ◇ *The ~ proved a disaster.* | **be aimed at sth, be designed to do sth** ◇ *a ~ designed to control inflation* | **allow (sb/sth) sth** | **give (sb) sth** ◇ *The ~ gave her career a boost.* | **mean sth** ◇ *The ~ meant lower costs.* | **reflect sth** ◇ *The ~ reflects a change in approach to research.* | **surprise sb**
PREP. **in a/the ~** ◇ *In a ~ which surprised everyone, the bosses*

fired several managers. | **~ against** ◇ a ~ against drug dealers | **~ away from** ◇ a ~ away from the old Hollywood style of movie | **~ back to** ◇ a ~ back to old teaching styles | **~ to, ~ towards/toward** ◇ a ~ towards/toward greater trade liberalization

PHRASES **a ~ in the right direction** ◇ The new environmental regulations represent a ~ in the right direction.

2 change of place

ADJ. **false** ◇ One false ~ and I'll shoot! | **sudden** | **quick, swift** | **smooth** | **deft, nifty** | **graceful** | **finishing** | **acrobatic, dance, wrestling**

VERB + MOVE **make** ◇ We should make a ~ (= leave). | **execute, perform** | **bust** (informal) ◇ Flavio and I were busting some ~s on the dance floor. | **complete** | **practise/practice** | **master** | **block** ◇ The soldier blocked the ~ with his free hand.

PREP. **~ to, ~ towards/toward** ◇ She made a ~ towards/toward the door.

PHRASES **on the ~** ◇ His career as an engineer has kept him on the ~ (= moving from place to place). | **watch sb/sth's every ~, watch sb/sth's every ~** ◇ The cubs watched their mother's every ~. | **get a ~ on** ◇ We're leaving, so you'd better get a ~ on (= hurry)! | **make a ~ for sth** (informal) ◇ He made a ~ for (= in the direction of) the door.

3 change of house/job

ADJ. **permanent** | **lateral** (esp. AmE), **sideways** (BrE) ◇ His new job was a lateral/sideways ~ rather than a promotion. | **house** | **off-season** (AmE, sports) | **impending**

MOVE + VERB **take place**

PREP. **~ from, ~ to** ◇ a ~ from Ohio to Kansas

4 in a board game

ADJ. **brilliant, good** | **bad** | **opening** | **chess**

VERB + MOVE **learn** ◇ She learned all the chess ~s when she was four. | **play**

PREP. **on a/the ~** ◇ She captured the queen with her bishop on the 32nd ~.

movement noun

1 act of moving

ADJ. **big** | **little, slight, small, tiny** ◇ The eyes of predators are highly sensitive to the slightest ~. | **quick, rapid, swift** | **gentle, slow** | **fluid, graceful, smooth** ◇ She mounted the horse in one fluid ~. | **easy** ◇ The refrigerator unit has rubber wheels for easy ~. | **jerky** | **sudden** | **deft** | **controlled** | **free** ◇ the free ~ of goods across borders | **involuntary** | **random** | **constant, continuous** | **repetitive** | **rhythmic** | **backward, downward, forward, lateral, rearward** (esp. AmE), **rotational, sideways, upward** | **bodily, body** | **eye, hand, etc.** | **dance** | **currency, price** ◇ currency ~s in the foreign exchange markets | **troop** | **pincer** ◇ The army surrounded the town in a pincer ~.

VERB + MOVEMENT **execute** (formal), **make, perform, produce** ◇ He made a slight ~ with his right hand. ◇ Hydraulic jacks under the machine produce the ~. | **initiate** ◇ The brain is necessary to initiate ~ and control balance. | **allow** ◇ clothing that allows easy ~ | **control, coordinate, direct** ◇ As infants grow they become better able to direct their own ~s. | **govern, regulate** ◇ regulations governing the ~ of hazardous waste | **facilitate, promote** ◇ an attempt to facilitate the ~ of workers across national borders | **hinder, impede, inhibit, limit, restrict** | **slow** ◇ Blood loss and fatigue slowed their ~s. | **halt, stop** | **prevent** ◇ The striking farmers threatened to prevent the ~ of goods across the country. | **protest** (AmE) ◇ She winced as her muscles protested every ~. | **sense** ◇ She sensed a ~ in the dark beneath the stairs. | **notice, spot** | **detect** ◇ Sensors detect ~ or changes in temperature. | **monitor, track** ◇ They are monitoring the ~ of animals in and out of the country. | **measure** | **copy, imitate, mimic** | **reverse**

MOVEMENT + VERB **occur** ◇ Some ~ in the building will occur as it settles into the subsoil. | **catch your eye** ◇ A ~ caught his eye in the tangled undergrowth. | **startle sb** | **cause sth** ◇ Any slight ~ caused a sharp pain in his arm. | **slow** | **cease**

MOVEMENT + NOUN **pattern**

PREP. **in a ~** ◇ She kicked down the door in one swift ~. | **~**

away from, ~ from ◇ ~ from one level to the next | **~ to, ~ towards/toward** (figurative) ◇ Recently there's been a ~ (= a change in attitude) away from processed food towards/toward fresh food.

PHRASES **the direction of ~, the rate of ~, the speed of ~** | **freedom of ~** ◇ The decree allowed freedom of ~ for all citizens. | **the ~ of capital, the ~ of goods, the ~ of labour/labor** | **a sense of ~** (figurative) ◇ His music has a real sense of ~.

2 movements person's activities

ADJ. **troop**

VERB + MOVEMENTS **follow, observe, study, watch** ◇ The police are watching the suspect's ~s very closely. | **trace** ◇ The police have traced her ~s to the time of her death. | **synchronize**

3 group of people

ADJ. **radical** | **mass, popular, populist** | **burgeoning, growing, nascent** | **organized** ◇ The country has a well-organized consumer ~. | **international, national** | **artistic, literary** | **avant-garde** | **Modern, Romantic, etc.** ◇ Both architects were part of the Modern Movement. | **environmental, political, religious, social** | **feminist, women's** | **protest** | **anti-globalization, anti-nuclear, anti-war, etc.** | **peace** | **abolitionist** | **temperance** | **anti-abortion, pro-life** | **pro-choice** | **reform** | **civil rights, gay rights, human rights, suffrage** | **independence, liberation, opposition, resistance, revolutionary, secessionist, separatist** | **guerrilla** | **militant** | **conservative, democracy, democratic, fascist, nationalist, pro-democracy, socialist** | **labour/labor, trade-union** (BrE) | **consumer, student, working-class, youth, etc.** | **grass-roots** | **ecumenical, evangelical, fundamentalist, Islamic, Islamist, Zionist, etc.**

VERB + MOVEMENT **create, establish, found, launch, set up, start, start up** ◇ She started a ~ for agricultural reform. | **orchestrate, organize** | **join** | **embrace, support** | **promote** | **oppose** | **be involved in, be part of** | **lead, spearhead** | **direct** ◇ a protest ~ directed against exploitative trade practices | **spark** ◇ Ethical concerns can spark a mass ~. | **drive, energize, fuel** ◇ the optimism which fuels the environmental ~ | **galvanize, strengthen** | **influence** ◇ the philosophical writers who have influenced the ~ | **suppress**

MOVEMENT + VERB **arise, begin, emerge (out of sth), spring up** ◇ The ~ emerged out of concern for human rights abuses. | **develop, gain strength, gather momentum, grow** ◇ The ~ gained strength during the 1970s. | **peak, reach a peak** ◇ The student ~ reached its peak in 1968. | **succeed** | **be aimed at doing sth, focus on sth, seek sth** | **challenge sth**

PREP. **~ against** ◇ a mass ~ against the dictatorship | **~ for** ◇ He launched a ~ for children's rights.

PHRASES **the leader of a ~, a member of a ~** | **the rise of a ~** ◇ the rise of the peace ~ in the US

4 part of a long piece of music

ADJ. **first, opening** | **second, etc.** | **final, last** ◇ the last ~ of Brahms's fourth symphony | **slow**

VERB + MOVEMENT **perform, play**

PREP. **in a ~** ◇ There is a cello solo in the second ~. | **in … ~s** ◇ a symphony in five ~s

movie noun (esp. AmE) → See also FILM

ADJ. **fun, good, great, terrific, wonderful** | **bad, mediocre** | **romance, romantic** | **cheesy, sappy** (AmE, informal) | **entertaining, feel-good, funny, popcorn** | **scary** | **classic, cult** | **old** | **blockbuster, successful** | **big, big-budget, top** | **low-budget** | **made-for-TV, television, TV** | **DVD** | **pay-per-view** | **home** ◇ We watched a home ~ of my second birthday party. | **in-flight** | **drive-in** | **teen** | **mainstream** | **summer** | **silent** | **animated** | **black-and-white** | **comic-book** (esp. AmE) | **feature-length** | **live-action** | **gory, violent** | **action, disaster, gangster, heist, horror, monster, sci-fi, slasher, war, etc.** | **blue** (old-fashioned), **dirty, porn, porno, X-rated** | **Bollywood, Hollywood**

VERB + MOVIE **catch** (informal, esp. AmE), **see, view, watch** | **attend, go to (see), take sb to (see)** ◇ I'd never go to a ~ alone. | **rent** (esp. AmE) | **download** | **craft** (esp. AmE),

create, direct, edit, film, make, produce, shoot, write | remake | market, promote | release | distribute | air, screen, show | review | play ◇ *Her father played all the old home ~s.* | **pause** (*esp. AmE*) ◇ *Liz paused the ~ and walked over to the phone.* | **carry, steal** ◇ *an excellent actor who could easily carry the ~ all on his own* ◇ *Johnson really steals this ~ as Cassius.*
MOVIE + VERB **be based on sth** ◇ *a ~ based on the novel by Betty Munn* | **be called sth, be entitled sth, be titled sth** (*AmE*) ◇ *a ~ entitled 'Short Legs'* | **be set in sth** ◇ *The ~ is set in a New England school.* | **feature sb/sth, star sb** | **depict sb/sth, portray sb/sth, show sb/sth** | **follow sb/sth, revolve around sth/sb** ◇ *The ~ follows their lives on a small Arkansas farm.* | **contain sth** ◇ *The ~ contains a lengthy car chase through the streets of Paris.* | **open, start** ◇ *The ~ opens with a quote from the Buddha.* | **progress, unfold** | **end**
MOVIE + NOUN **actor, actress, director, maker, mogul, people, producer, star** ◇ *The former model is now mixing with ~ people in Hollywood.* | **audience** | **buff, fan, lover** | **critic** | **review** | **house, palace** (*old-fashioned*), **theater** (*all AmE*) | **premiere** | **clip, preview, trailer** | **company, studio** | **set** | **business, industry, world** | **career** | **channel** | **score, script** | **soundtrack** | **title** | **scene** | **plot** | **character** | **screen** | **rights** ◇ *the ~ rights to her autobiography* | **adaptation, version** ◇ *the ~ version of the well-known novel* | **musical** | **genre** | **camera** | **poster** | **tie-in** | **popcorn** | **night** ◇ *We're having a ~ night with pizza and beer.* | **piracy** | **magic**
PREP. **~ about** ◇ *a ~ about the life of Castro*

moving adj.

VERBS **be** | **find sth** ◇ *I found the story intensely ~.*
ADV. **deeply, extraordinarily, intensely, profoundly, very** ◇ *a deeply ~ account of life on the streets* | **quite**

mud noun

ADJ. **deep** | **thick** | **soft, sticky, wet** | **dried, dry** ◇ *footprints left in the hard dried ~* | **black, brown, red**
VERB + MUD **be caked in, be caked with, be covered with** ◇ *Her boots were caked in ~.* | **get/become bogged down in** (*esp. BrE*), **get stuck in** ◇ *Several cars got bogged down in the ~.* | **turn (sth) into, turn (sth) to** ◇ *The cars had turned the road into ~.* | **wallow in** ◇ *pigs wallowing in the ~* | **spatter (sb/sth with)**
MUD + VERB **ooze** ◇ *Wet ~ oozed up between their toes.* | **crack** ◇ *The ~ in the dried-up river bed had cracked.*
MUD + NOUN **brick, floor, house, hut, wall** | **flats** | **puddle** | **hole, pit** | **slide** ◇ *Flash floods and ~ slides struck three coastal towns.* | **fight, wrestling** | **bath** | **pie** ◇ *The kids were in the yard making ~ pies.*
PREP. **in the ~** ◇ *She fell in the ~.* | **through the ~** ◇ *We squelched through the ~.*
PHRASES **a layer of ~, a sea of ~**

muddle noun (esp. BrE)

ADJ. **awful** | **embarrassing** | **bureaucratic, financial**
VERB + MUDDLE **get (sb) in, get (sb) into** ◇ *I got into an awful ~ with my tax forms.* | **make** ◇ *The judge made a ~ of the case.*
PREP. **in a ~** ◇ *The house was in an awful ~ by the time the children left.* | **~ about, ~ over, ~ with** ◇ *There was a bureaucratic ~ over his appointment.*

muddled adj. (esp. BrE)

VERBS **be, feel** | **become, get**
ADV. **extremely, fairly, very, etc.** | **hopelessly** | **a little, slightly, etc.** ◇ *Her ideas are slightly ~.*
PHRASES **be ~ up, get ~ up**

muddy adj.

VERBS **be, look** | **become, get** | **get sth, make sth** ◇ *Don't get your shoes ~!* ◇ *The rain had made the field very ~.*
ADV. **extremely, fairly, very, etc.** | **all** ◇ *My boots were all ~.* | **a little, slightly, etc.** ◇ *We all got a little ~ and wet.*

mug noun

ADJ. **big, large** | **empty** | **chipped** | **hot, steaming, warm** ◇ *a hot ~ of tea* | **beer, coffee** | **pint** (*esp. BrE*) | **travel** (*esp. AmE*) | **commemorative, souvenir** (*both esp. BrE*) | **ceramic, china** (*esp. BrE*), **plastic, etc.**
VERB + MUG **fill, refill** ◇ *She filled her ~ with orange juice.* | **pour (sb), pour (sb) out** ◇ *Kyle got up and poured himself a ~ of soup.* ◇ *He poured out a ~ of tea.* | **pour sth into** ◇ *She poured hot water into the ~.* | **drink** ◇ *He drank a ~ of coffee and left.* | **sip** ◇ *She was sipping a ~ of coffee.* | **drain** ◇ *She drained her ~ and put it down.* | **drink sth from** ◇ *We had to drink the champagne from ~s.*
PHRASES **a ~ of beer, coffee, tea, etc.** | **the rim of a ~** ◇ *He ran his finger around the rim of the ~.*

multinational noun

ADJ. **big, giant, large** | **major** | **foreign**
MULTINATIONAL + VERB **operate** ◇ *foreign ~s operating in the UK*

multiply verb

ADV. **endlessly, indefinitely** | **greatly** | **exponentially, quickly, rapidly** ◇ *microorganisms that ~ rapidly* | **together** ◇ *Multiply these two figures together.*
PREP. **by** ◇ *2 multiplied by 4 is 8.* ◇ *2 multiplied by 4 makes 8.* (*BrE*)

mum (BrE) (AmE mom) noun (informal)

ADJ. **young** | **single, unmarried** | **lesbian** | **career, working** | **full-time, stay-at-home** | **welfare** (*AmE*) | **security, soccer** (*both AmE*) | **celebrity, TV** | **suburban** | **proud** | **busy** | **cool, good, great** | **expectant, pregnant** (also **mum-to-be** in *BrE*) | **new** ◇ *The group is aimed at new ~s with young babies.* | **surrogate** ◇ *The cat acted as a surrogate ~ to the chicks.* | **birth, real** ◇ *Ellie had always been there for him even though she wasn't his real ~.*
PHRASES **~ and dad**

mumble verb

ADV. **incoherently** | **quietly, softly** | **quickly** | **sleepily** | **angrily, bitterly** | **sarcastically**
PREP. **about** ◇ *I couldn't understand what he was mumbling about.* | **into** ◇ *She ~d something into her pillow.* | **to** ◇ *George ~d incoherently to himself.*

mumps noun → Special page at ILLNESS

mundane adj.

VERBS **be, seem, sound** | **become** | **find sth** ◇ *I found the job very ~.*
ADV. **extremely, fairly, very, etc.** | **utterly** (*esp. BrE*) | **relatively** ◇ *a relatively ~ task* | **apparently** (*esp. BrE*), **seemingly**

mural noun

ADJ. **giant, huge, large-scale** | **painted** | **colourful/colorful** | **wall**
VERB + MURAL **create, produce** | **paint** | **design**
MURAL + VERB **depict sth, show sth** ◇ *~s depicting Aesop's fables*

murder noun

ADJ. **barbaric, brutal, grisly, gruesome, horrific, savage, terrible, vicious, violent** | **cold-blooded, deliberate, premeditated, wilful/willful** (*law, esp. BrE*) ◇ *a verdict of wilful ~* | **senseless** | **shocking, tragic** | **perfect** ◇ *He committed the perfect ~ and left no forensic evidence.* | **indiscriminate, random** | **systematic** | **wholesale** ◇ *the wholesale ~ of innocent citizens* | **first-degree, second-degree** | **aggravated** | **attempted** | **alleged, suspected** | **double, mass, multiple, serial, triple** | **ritual** | **terrorist** | **gangland** (*BrE*) | **racial, racist, sectarian** | **politically motivated, racially motivated, sexually motivated** | **judicial, state-sanctioned, state-sponsored** | **high-profile,**

notorious | mysterious | unsolved | capital, felony, statutory (all AmE, law)
VERB + MURDER **carry out, commit, perpetrate** (formal) ◇ ~s committed by terrorists | **investigate, probe** (esp. BrE) | **solve** | **link** ◇ Detectives are linking the two ~s. | **imprison sb for, jail sb for** | **avenge** ◇ He vowed to avenge his brother's ~. | **witness** | **implicate sb in** ◇ new evidence that implicated her in the ~ | **mastermind, orchestrate, plan, plot** | **advocate** | **order** ◇ He ordered the ~ of his political opponents. | **admit, deny** | **get away with** (figurative) ◇ They let their children get away with ~! | **incite** | **condemn** | **condone, justify** ◇ Nothing justifies ~.
MURDER + VERB **happen, occur, take place** | **shock sb** ◇ It was a ~ which shocked the nation.
MURDER + NOUN **victim** | **suspect** | **detective, squad** | **case, hunt** (informal), **inquiry** (esp. BrE), **investigation, probe** | **charge** | **trial** | **conviction** | **attempt** | **plot** | **scene, site** | **weapon** | **campaign** (esp. BrE), **spree** | **count, rate, toll** ◇ a city that has the highest ~ rate in the US | **capital** ◇ The city used to be the ~ capital of the world. | **mystery, story** ◇ Her latest novel is a gripping ~ mystery.
→ Note at CRIME (for more verbs)

murder verb

ADV. **brutally, cruelly, in cold blood, savagely, violently** ◇ The boy was brutally ~ed. ◇ They were ~ed in cold blood. | **systematically** | **deliberately** | **allegedly**
VERB + MURDER **attempt to, try to** | **plan to, plot to**
PHRASES **admit ~ing sb, deny ~ing sb** | **be accused of ~ing sb, be charged with ~ing sb** ◇ She was arrested and charged with ~ing the two children. | **be convicted of ~ing sb, be found guilty of ~ing sb** | **be found ~ed** ◇ He was found ~ed in the cemetery.

murderer noun

ADJ. **accused** (esp. BrE), **alleged, suspected** | **convicted** | **potential, would-be** ◇ Does the death penalty deter would-be ~s? | **double, mass, multiple, serial** | **real** ◇ He protested his innocence and promised to help police track down the real ~. | **brutal, cold-blooded, ruthless, vicious** | **insane, psychopathic** | **infamous, notorious** | **child** | **axe/ax** | **suicide**
VERB + MURDERER **hunt, hunt down, hunt for, track down** | **catch, find, identify, reveal (sb as)** | **arrest** | **punish** | **sentence** | **execute, hang, kill**
MURDERER + VERB **strike** ◇ The ~ has struck again. | **kill sb**
PHRASES **bring a ~ to justice** | **the identity of the ~** ◇ The identity of her ~ has not yet been revealed.

murmur noun

1 sound of words that are spoken quietly
ADJ. **dull, faint, low, quiet, slight, soft** | **general** ◇ a general ~ of assent | **angry, excited**
VERB + MURMUR **give, let out** ◇ He gave a little ~ of relief. | **hear**
MURMUR + VERB **ripple through sth, run** ◇ A ~ of excitement rippled through the audience. ◇ A ~ of amusement ran around the room.
PREP. **in a ~** ◇ She answered in a low ~. | **with a ~** ◇ He took the mug of coffee with a ~ of thanks. | **without a ~** ◇ They did as they were told, without a ~. | **~ of**
PHRASES **the ~ of voices**
→ Note at SOUND

2 low, gentle, continuous sound
ADJ. **soft** | **low** | **distant**
VERB + MURMUR **hear**
PREP. **~ of** ◇ the distant ~ of traffic

murmur verb

ADV. **gently, quietly, silently, softly, under your breath** ◇ 'What a fool I've been,' he ~ed softly. | **aloud** | **huskily** | **sleepily** ◇ 'Night, night,' she ~ed sleepily. | **absently** | **weakly** | **sadly** | **apologetically, appreciatively, politely, soothingly, thoughtfully** ◇ 'Mmm,' she ~ed appreciatively. | **drily, sarcastically, wryly**
VERB + MURMUR **hear sb** ◇ She heard him ~ something under his breath.
PREP. **to** ◇ He held her tight and ~ed to her.

muscle noun

ADJ. **hard, powerful, strong** | **taut, tense, tight** | **relaxed** | **smooth** | **lean, ripped, toned** | **bulging, rippling** | **cramped** ◇ I walked up and down the aisle to stretch my cramped ~s. | **pulled, strained, torn** | **aching, sore, stiff, tired** | **abdominal, arm, calf, facial, heart, thigh, etc.** | **skeletal**
VERB + MUSCLE **clench, contract, flex, pump, squeeze, tense, tighten** ◇ He flexed his ~s, then set off to run. | **loosen, relax** ◇ Learn how to relax tense ~s. | **control** | **soothe** | **stretch** | **exercise, train, use, work** | **build, gain, strengthen, tone** ◇ diet supplements to build ~ | **sculpt** ◇ Lifting weights sculpts ~. | **damage, exhaust, fatigue, injure, overload, weaken** | **pull, strain, tear** ◇ I laughed so hard I almost pulled a ~. | **knead, massage** | **activate, stimulate** | **paralyse/paralyze**
MUSCLE + VERB **ache, burn, hurt** | **cramp** | **strain** | **clench, contract, flex, stiffen, tense, tighten** | **go limp, loosen, relax, slacken** | **stretch** | **quiver, ripple, tremble, twitch** ◇ His ~s rippled beneath his T-shirt as he worked. | **bulge** | **move, work** | **control sth** ◇ the ~s controlling speech production | **protest, scream** ◇ Suddenly my sore ~s protested and I let out a groan.
MUSCLE + NOUN **cell, fibre/fiber, tissue** | **mass** | **group** | **function** | **activity** | **ache, cramp, damage, disease, fatigue, pain, paralysis, soreness, stiffness, strain, weakness** | **loss, wasting** | **contraction, relaxation, spasm, tension, twitch** | **definition, tone** | **size** | **endurance, strength** | **repair** | **gain, growth** | **building** | **builder** | **man** (usually **muscleman**) | **shirt** (AmE)
PREP. **~ in** ◇ The ~s in my face tensed.

museum noun

ADJ. **excellent, fascinating** (esp. BrE), **great, interesting, major, prestigious** (esp. AmE), **world-class** ◇ one of the world's great ~s | **famous** | **historic** (esp. AmE), **historical** | **local, municipal, national, provincial** (esp. BrE), **regional, town** (esp. BrE) | **private, public** | **purpose-built** (BrE) | **open-air, outdoor** ◇ an open-air ~ of farming and the countryside | **living, working** (esp. BrE) ◇ Although the mill is no longer in commercial use, it is maintained as a working ~. | **heritage** | **virtual** ◇ The website's print gallery is a virtual ~. | **interactive** | **archaeological, art** (esp. AmE), **folk, industrial** (esp. BrE), **local history, maritime, military, railroad** (AmE), **railway** (BrE), **science, war** (esp. BrE), **etc.** ◇ Los Angeles County Art Museum
VERB + MUSEUM **go to, visit** | **tour** | **establish, found, open** ◇ He founded a ~ of modern art in his home town. | **fund** | **build, create, design** | **operate, run** | **house** ◇ The ~ is housed in a converted church.
MUSEUM + VERB **open** | **be dedicated to sb/sth, be devoted to sth, contain sth, feature sth, house sth** ◇ a ~ devoted to children's toys ◇ The ~ houses a fine collection of textiles. | **display sth, exhibit sth** | **acquire sth, buy sth** ◇ The first painting acquired by the ~ was by Hopper.
MUSEUM + NOUN **building, complex, gallery** | **space** | **collection, display, exhibit** (= exhibition) (AmE), **exhibition, show** | **artefact, exhibit, object, piece, specimen** ◇ All the planes are ~ pieces. | **archive, catalogue** | **boss** (BrE), **chief** (BrE), **curator, director, guard, guide, manager** (esp. BrE), **official, professional, staff, trustee** | **visitor** | **tour, visit** | **shop** (esp. BrE), **store** (AmE)
PREP. **at a/the ~** ◇ an exhibition of Chinese ceramics at the Ashmolean Museum | **in a/the ~** ◇ There's a gift shop in the ~. | **~ of** ◇ the Museum of Modern Art

mushroom noun

ADJ. **edible** | **poisonous** | **cultivated** | **wild** | **fresh** | **button, field, oyster, portobello, shiitake, etc.** | **hallucinogenic, magic, psychedelic** | **dried** | **stuffed**
VERB + MUSHROOM **cultivate, grow** | **pick** ◇ They went into the woods to pick wild ~s. | **chop, slice** ◇ Slice the ~s and add to the salad. | **cook, fry, grill, sauté**
MUSHROOM + NOUN **cap** | **omelette, risotto, sauce, soup** |

farm | grower, picker | compost | cloud (= of a nuclear explosion)
→ Special page at FOOD

music noun

1 arrangement of sounds for singing/playing

ADJ. **beautiful, fine, good, great, wonderful | loud | quiet, soft, sweet** ◊ *The soft background ~ made her feel sleepy.* | **ambient | heavy** ◊ *Heavy ~ thundered from the basement.* | **light | serious | cool, funky | dramatic, lively, upbeat | tonal | atonal, twelve-tone | contrapuntal, polyphonic | live | recorded | background | canned, elevator** (*esp. AmE*), **piped** (*BrE*) | **band, choral, instrumental, orchestral, symphonic | guitar, keyboard, organ, piano, vocal, etc.** | **chamber | church, liturgical, religious, sacred | secular | mood | film, movie** (*esp. AmE*) | **ballet, incidental, theme** ◊ *the incidental ~ for a radio play* | **acoustic, computer, digital, electronic, online** | **African, Indian, Irish, Western, etc.** | **mainstream, traditional | alternative, underground | urban | period** ◊ *The movie uses appropriate period ~.* | **experimental | avant-garde, Baroque, classical, contemporary, early, medieval, modern | popular | black, country, dance, disco, folk, gospel, heavy metal, hip-hop, house, indie, jazz, pop, rap, reggae, rock, soul, techno, world, etc.**
... OF MUSIC **piece | bar, line**
VERB + MUSIC **listen to** ◊ *Listening to ~ is a great way to relax.* | **hear** ◊ *She could hear loud ~ from the party upstairs.* | **make, perform, play, sing** ◊ *We love to make ~ as a family.* | **play, put on** ◊ *Put some ~ on, would you?* (= play a CD, etc.) | **blare, blare out, blast, blast out, pump out** ◊ *bars and nightclubs blaring ~ late into the night* | **download | turn down, turn up** ◊ *Could you turn that ~ down?* | **compose, write | arrange, score | put sth to, set sth to** ◊ *Schubert set several poems by Goethe to ~.* | **create, produce** ◊ *The city has produced a lot of good ~.* | **provide** ◊ *a beach party with ~ provided by a local band* | **release | distribute | broadcast | record | burn** ◊ *I use my laptop to burn ~ to a CD.* | **rip** ◊ *software that rips ~ from CDs* | **be into** (*informal*), **enjoy, like, love** ◊ *She's really into indie ~.* | **appreciate** ◊ *The ability to appreciate ~ is largely learnt.* | **pirate, steal**
MUSIC + VERB **sound** ◊ *The ~ sounded vibrant and loud.* | **play** ◊ *Calypso ~ played faintly in the distance.* | **blare, blast, boom, pound, pump** ◊ *disco ~ blaring out of the open windows of a car* | **come, drift, emanate, flow, waft** ◊ *The ~ was coming from next door.* | **fill sth** ◊ *Music filled the air.* | **drown sb/sth out | fade, fade away, fade out | accompany sth** ◊ *the ~ which accompanied the dance* | **emerge from sth** ◊ *the ~ emerging from the cities of America* | **evoke sth, inspire sth | reflect sth**
MUSIC + NOUN **biz** (*informal*), **business, industry | scene** ◊ *Rio's live ~ scene* | **world** ◊ *She is a rising star in the ~ world.* | **genre | press** ◊ *The album has been praised in the ~ press.* | **magazine | charts** ◊ *The band are number one in the ~ charts.* | **award | concert, event, festival | collection | appreciation | aficionado, buff, enthusiast, fan, lover | composer, critic, director, journalist, mogul, producer, promoter, teacher** ◊ *the choir's ~ director* | **group | legend, star** ◊ *~ legend, Elvis Presley* | **label | CD | video | download, file | album, track | channel, station | retailer, shop** (*esp. BrE*), **store** (*esp. AmE*) | **room, studio | venue | library | piracy | education | academy, college, school | class, lesson, workshop | therapy**
PREP. **to (the)** ~ ◊ *to dance to the ~*
PHRASES **in time to (the)** ~ ◊ *They did their exercises in time to the ~.* | **~ and song** ◊ *an evening of Scottish ~ and song* | **the sound of** ~ ◊ *The sound of pop ~ drifted through the open window.* | **a style of** ~ | **taste in** ~ ◊ *Her taste in ~ was eclectic.* | **words and** ~ ◊ *He made up the words and ~ for the song.*
→ Note at SUBJECT (for more verbs and nouns)

2 written signs that represent musical sounds

ADJ. **printed, sheet**
... OF MUSIC **bar, line, sheet**

VERB + MUSIC **read** ◊ *Can you read ~?*
MUSIC + NOUN **score | stand** ◊ *I pulled the lyrics out and laid them on the ~ stand.* | **publisher, publishing**
PREP. **~ for** ◊ *~ for piano, cello and voice* | **with ~, without ~** ◊ *He played the piece without ~.*

musical noun

ADJ. **hit, popular, successful | classic, modern | film** (*esp. BrE*), **movie** (*esp. AmE*), **stage | school | Bollywood, Broadway, Hollywood, West End | rock**
MUSICAL + VERB **be based on sth** ◊ *a ~ based on the life of Eva Perón*
→ Note at PERFORMANCE (for more verbs)

musician noun

ADJ. **accomplished, brilliant, excellent, fine, gifted, good, great, outstanding, talented, world-class | distinguished** (*esp. BrE*), **famous, legendary, renowned, well-known | aspiring, budding** (*esp. BrE*), **up-and-coming | struggling | local | traditional | contemporary | dedicated, serious, trained** ◊ *You have to be a very dedicated ~ to get to the top.* | **self-taught | amateur, performing, professional, working | orchestral | backing, backup** (*AmE*) ◊ *She had toured as a backing ~ for Madonna.* | **guest | blues, classical, folk, jazz, pop, rock, etc.**
MUSICIAN + VERB **perform (sth), play (sth), sing (sth) | practise/practice (sth), rehearse (sth) | compose sth, write sth | record sth**
→ Note at JOB

Muslim noun

ADJ. **devout, observant, pious, strict** (*esp. BrE*) | **Shia, Shiite, Sunni | practising/practicing | mainstream, moderate, orthodox | extremist, fundamentalist, militant, radical**

mustache noun (AmE) → See MOUSTACHE

mustard noun

ADJ. **hot, spicy** ◊ *Add some hot English ~.* | **mild | wholegrain | English, French** (*both esp. BrE*) | **brown, yellow** (*both esp. AmE*) | **honey | Dijon | dry**
VERB + MUSTARD **spread (sth with)** ◊ *Spread the bread thinly with ~.* | **add, mix (sth with)** ◊ *Mix together the ~ and olive oil.* | **eat sth with, serve sth with**
MUSTARD + NOUN **plant | seed | oil | powder | sauce, vinaigrette | colour/color, yellow**
→ Special page at FOOD

mutation noun

ADJ. **chance, random | common | rare | cell, gene, genetic | advantageous, beneficial | harmful, lethal**
VERB + MUTATION **carry, contain** ◊ *The protein contained a ~.* | **acquire, suffer** (*technical*), **undergo** ◊ *The genetic material has suffered a ~.* | **introduce** ◊ *Mutations were introduced in the region using various techniques.* | **cause, produce**
MUTATION + VERB **arise, occur | affect sth** ◊ *These cells carry a ~ affecting the prevention mechanism.* | **cause sth, lead to sth, result in sth**
MUTATION + NOUN **frequency, rate**

muted adj.

VERBS **be, seem, sound | remain**
ADV. **extremely, fairly, very, etc.** ◊ *Their reaction to the news was somewhat ~.* | **relatively | a little, slightly, etc. | curiously, strangely, surprisingly**

mutilate verb

ADV. **badly, horribly, severely** ◊ *A lot of the bodies had been badly ~d.*

mutiny noun

ADJ. **army, naval** (*esp. BrE*)
VERB + MUTINY **stage | lead | be faced with, face**
PREP. **~ against** ◊ *He led a military ~ against the senior generals.* | **~ by** ◊ *~ by the men*
→ Note at CRIME (for more verbs)

MUSIC

Playing

- a brass/keyboard/percussion/string/wind **instrument**
- a bass, clarinet, guitar, horn, keyboard, trumpet, etc. **player**
- an orchestral **player**
  an orchestra **player** (*esp.AmE*)

*She **plays** the piano very well.*
*I **play** lead guitar in rock band.*
*The clarinet **plays** the main theme.*
*The trumpets **sounded** to mark the queen's arrival.*
*She **plucked/strummed** the guitar.*
*He **banged/beat/pounded** the drums.*
*The hunters **blew** their **horns**.*
*Your **piano/violin** needs tuning.*

Learning

*My sister is **learning** the French horn.*
*I **practise/practice** the clarinet an hour a day.*
*He **studied** piano at the Royal College of Music.*
*My father **took up** the oboe in his retirement.*
*She **gave up** the violin when she was fifteen.*
(esp. BrE)
*She **quit** the violin when she was fifteen.*
(esp. AmE)
*He **teaches** flute.*
*He **teaches** the flute. (esp. BrE)*

- a music/piano/singing **lesson**
- a music/piano/singing **teacher**
- band, cello, choir **practice**
- an orchestra **rehearsal**
  an orchestral **rehearsal** (*esp. BrE*)

Prepositions

on (the) ~

She sang three songs and I accompanied her on the piano.
That was Miles Davis on trumpet.

for (the) ~

a work for cello, oboe and harpsichord

Artists and performers

- a brass/dance/military/rock **band**
- a classical/contemporary/modern **composer**
- an opera/orchestra **conductor**
- a chamber/pop (*esp.BrE*)/rock **group**
- a chamber/symphony **orchestra**
- a classical/concert/jazz/renowned/virtuoso **pianist**, **violinist**, etc.
- a jazz/string **quartet**
- a blues/folk/jazz/opera **singer**
- a solo **artist/performer**
- a concerto/instrumental/piano/violin/vocal **soloist**
- a clarinet/guitar/jazz/violin **virtuoso**

Performing

- to give a benefit/classical/pop (*esp.BrE*)/rock **concert**
- to do/play/perform/sing **a duet/a solo**
- to do a live **gig**
- a concert/debut/solo **performance**
- to give an organ/a piano/a solo/a vocal **recital**
- carol/choral/solo **singing**
- a guitar/drum/piano/violin **solo**
- a **solo** instrument/passage/piece/work

*The dancers will perform with live musical **accompaniment**.*
*She hummed the first few **bars** of the song.*
*The music rose to a deafening **crescendo**.*
*The orchestra played the opening **movement** of the symphony.*
*The song has a brisk/quick/upbeat **tempo**.*
*James Levine **conducts** the orchestra.*

Making and selling music

- a best-selling/debut/solo **album**
- a **chart** hit; to hit the **charts** (*both esp.BrE*)
- a best-selling/hit/number-one/smash/top-ten **single**

*The **lyrics** were written by Ira Gershwin.*
*The band is currently on **tour** in Japan.*
*The album was **produced** by Quincy Jones.*
*He wrote the **soundtrack** to the movie.*
*She played the title **track** from her new CD.*
*She sang backing **vocals** on most of the songs.*

mutter verb

ADV. **gruffly, harshly, hoarsely | through clenched teeth, through gritted teeth** ◊ *'I don't need a drink,' she ~ed through clenched teeth.* | **aloud | loudly | quietly, softly, under your breath | silently | sleepily | incoherently, vaguely, weakly | angrily, bitterly, crossly, darkly, fiercely, furiously, grimly, irritably, sourly, sullenly** ◊ *Helen began ~ing darkly about hospitals.* | **miserably, sadly | nervously | sheepishly | drily, sarcastically**
VERB + MUTTER **be heard to, hear sb** ◊ *A number of visitors were heard to ~ that it would not have happened at home.* ◊ *She heard him ~ an oath under his breath.*
PREP. **about** ◊ *She ~ed something about the incompetence of the office staff.* | **to** ◊ *He was ~ing incoherently to himself.*

mystery noun

ADJ. **big, great** ◊ *How the disease started is one of medicine's great mysteries.* | **little, minor, small** ◊ *one of life's little mysteries* | **complete, total** ◊ *She was a total ~ to him despite their long association.* | **whole** ◊ *He had found the clue to unlock the whole ~.* | **certain** ◊ *Her blue eyes had a certain ~.* | **genuine, real | central** ◊ *the central ~ of the story* | **deep, profound** ◊ *a place of deep ~ and enchantment* | **enduring, eternal, long-standing | ancient | dark | intriguing | impenetrable, unfathomable | insoluble** (*esp. BrE*)**, unsolvable** (*esp. AmE*) | **unexplained, unsolved | divine, religious, sacred | scientific | detective, murder** ◊ *He is the author of several murder mysteries.*
VERB + MYSTERY **be, present (sb with), remain** ◊ *How these insects actually communicate presents something of a ~.* | **have, hold** ◊ *It was easy to believe that the house held some great ~.* | **be cloaked in, be shrouded in** ◊ *The whole incident was shrouded in ~.* | **deepen** ◊ *The silence has deepened the ~ surrounding his work.* | **lose** ◊ *Air travel has lost much of its ~.* | **retain | clear up, crack, discover, explain, figure out, piece together, resolve, solve, uncover, unlock, unravel, unveil** ◊ *The police are close to solving the ~ of the missing murder weapon.* | **shed light on, throw light on** ◊ *The witness could shed no light on the ~ of the deceased's identity.* | **explore, fathom, grapple with, penetrate, probe, understand** ◊ *Her poetry attempts to penetrate the dark ~ of death.* | **contemplate, ponder, ponder on** ◊ *She pondered the ~ of the disappearing thief.*
MYSTERY + VERB **remain** ◊ *Mystery remains over who will star in the film.* | **deepen** ◊ *The ~ deepened when the police's only suspect was found murdered.* | **unfold, unravel | involve sb/ sth | surround sth** ◊ *the ~ surrounding her resignation*
MYSTERY + NOUN **man, woman** ◊ *Their suspect was a ~ man: a quiet, happily married man with no enemies.* | **caller** (*esp. BrE*)**, guest | shopper | benefactor** (*esp. BrE*) | **bidder, buyer** (*both esp. BrE*) | **prize** (*BrE*) | **tour** (*BrE*) | **bug, disease, illness, virus** (*all esp. BrE*) | **novel, story, thriller**
PREP. **~ about** ◊ *There's a bit of a ~ about this child.* | **~ as to** ◊ *It remains a ~ as to where he was buried.* | **~ to** ◊ *My sister is a complete ~ to me.*
PHRASES **an air of ~, an aura of ~** ◊ *Wearing dark glasses gives him an air of ~.* | **something of a ~ | take the ~ out of sth** ◊ *Modern weather forecasts try to take the ~ out of meteorology.*

mystified adj.

VERBS **be, look | remain**
ADV. **completely, totally | genuinely, truly** ◊ *She was genuinely ~ by her success.* | **rather, somewhat**

myth noun

1 story from ancient times
ADJ. **ancient, classical | religious | Biblical | Christian, Greek, Norse, Roman, etc. | creation** (= that explains how the world began) ◊ *the creation ~s of the Inuit*
PREP. **~ about** ◊ *the ~ about the golden apple*
2 idea/belief which is untrue/impossible
ADJ. **great** ◊ *There is a great ~ that people who wear glasses*

are more intelligent. | **common | powerful | enduring, persistent, prevailing | complete** (*esp. BrE*)**, total** ◊ *It's a total ~ that this causes blindness.* | **modern | folk, popular, urban, widespread | national** ◊ *The battle has become part of national ~.* | **historical, political** ◊ *The propaganda of both sides relies heavily on historical ~.* | **heroic, romantic | dangerous, pernicious | convenient**
VERB + MYTH **create, cultivate, establish, invent** ◊ *How did the ~ get so firmly established in the popular consciousness?* | **challenge, question | counter | bust** (*AmE, informal*)**, debunk, deconstruct, demolish, destroy, dispel, disprove, explode, expose, puncture, scotch** (*BrE*)**, shatter | bury, lay to rest, put to rest | feed, foster, keep alive, maintain, perpetuate, promote, propagate, reinforce | spread | peddle** (*BrE*) ◊ *Women have peddled the ~ that all decent men are either married or gay.* | **be based on** ◊ *People's faith in the Emperor was based on the ~ that he was infallible.* | **explore | believe**
MYTH + VERB **surround sth** ◊ *We are trying to lay to rest the ~s surrounding mental illness.* | **grow up** ◊ *A ~ has grown up that Fleming didn't realize the potential of penicillin.* | **persist, remain** ◊ *The ~ persists that men are more intelligent than women.*
PREP. **~ about** ◊ *a popular ~ about twins* | **~ of** ◊ *an attempt to perpetuate the ~ of racial superiority*

mythology noun

ADJ. **popular | personal | national | cultural, political | ancient, classical, old, traditional | modern, new | Greek, Hindu, Norse, Roman, etc.**
VERB + MYTHOLOGY **surround sb/sth** ◊ *the ~ that surrounds the princess* | **enter** ◊ *Stories about the ghost have entered the ~ of the town.* | **create** ◊ *She has created her own ~ in the books.*
PREP. **in (a/the) ~** ◊ *the characters in Greek ~* | **~ about** (*esp. BrE*)**, ~ of** ◊ *a whole ~ about how to get fit* ◊ *the national ~ of marriage and family*

N n

nail noun

1 on the fingers/toes → See also FINGERNAIL, TOENAIL
ADJ. **long, short | sharp | healthy, strong | brittle | broken | manicured | acrylic, artificial, fake, false** ◊ *I wore acrylic ~s for two months.* | **painted, polished**
VERB + NAIL **bite, chew | do, manicure** ◊ *Do your ~s after your bath as they will be softer.* | **clean | clip, cut, trim | file | paint, polish, varnish** (*BrE*) | **grow** ◊ *I was trying to grow my ~s.* | **examine, inspect, study** ◊ *She inspected her ~s casually.* | **break | dig, sink** ◊ *He screamed as she dug her ~s into his shoulders.* | **drag | tap** ◊ *I tapped my ~s against the glass.*
NAIL + VERB **grow | break, split | scrape sth, scratch sth | bite into sth, dig into sth**
NAIL + NOUN **care** (see also **nail polish**) | **brush | clippers, scissors | clippings | file | salon | technician | fungus, infection**
PREP. **under your ~** ◊ *There was dirt under his ~s.*
2 piece of metal
ADJ. **long | small | six-inch, etc. | loose | protruding | bent | rusty | brass, iron, etc. | galvanized | finishing | coffin, roofing**
VERB + NAIL **drive, hammer, knock** ◊ *He knocked the ~ into the wall.* | **drive in, hammer in, knock in | pull out, remove**
NAIL + VERB **stick out, stick up**
NAIL + NOUN **head | hole | bomb, gun**

nail polish (BrE also nail varnish) noun

ADJ. **chipped | clear | black, pink, etc.**
... OF NAIL POLISH **bottle**

VERB + NAIL POLISH **have on, wear** ◊ *She wore red ~.* | **apply, put on** | **remove, take off**
NAIL-POLISH + NOUN **remover** ◊ *a bottle of nail-polish remover*

naive (*also* naïve) *adj.*

VERBS **appear, be, prove, seem, sound** | **regard sth as** ◊ *He regarded the move as politically ~.*
ADV. **extremely, fairly, very, etc.** | **incredibly** | **hopelessly** | **a little, slightly, etc.** | **politically**
PHRASES **call sb ~** ◊ *Call me ~, but I believe him.*

naked *adj.*

VERBS **appear, be, feel, go, lie, look, stand** ◊ *Never had he felt so completely ~.* ◊ *He lay ~ on the bed.* | **get** (*informal*) | **strip** ◊ *She quickly stripped ~.* | **sleep** | **strip sb** | **leave sb** ◊ *She had been left ~ and alone.* | **find sb** | **see sb**
ADV. **completely, entirely, quite** (*esp. BrE*), **stark, totally** ◊ *She realized with a shock that she was stark ~.* | **almost, nearly, practically, virtually** | **half** ◊ *I suggest you don't make a habit of going around half ~.*

name *noun*

1 word/words sb/sth is known by

ADJ. **Christian** (*BrE*), **first, given** (*esp. AmE*) | **middle, second** (= middle name) (*BrE*) | **family, last** (see also *surname*), **second** (= last name) (*BrE*) | **full** ◊ *His full ~ was William Augustus Grove.* | **married** | **maiden** | **birth** (*esp. AmE*) ◊ *Muhammad Ali's birth ~ was Cassius Clay.* | **original** ◊ *St Petersburg has gone back to its original ~.* | **proper, real, true** | **pet** ◊ *His pet ~ for her was 'Fluff'.* | **assumed, fake** (*esp. AmE*), **false** | **official** | **joint** (*esp. BrE*) ◊ *The account is in joint ~s.* | **common** ◊ *'Smith' is a very common family ~.* | **double-barrelled** (*BrE*), **hyphenated** (*esp. AmE*) | **personal** | **pen** (usually *pen-name*), **professional, stage** ◊ *George Eliot was a pen-name; her real ~ was Mary Ann Evans.* | **brand, proprietary, trade** | **generic** | **company** | **scientific** ◊ *The scientific ~ for plants in this genus is Asclepias.* | **code** | **file** | **user** ◊ *Please enter your user ~.* | **domain** ◊ *You will need to register a domain ~ (= an individual Internet address).* | **place, street** | **band** ◊ *Their original band ~ was 'Cherry Five'*
VERB + NAME **have** ◊ *Do you have a middle ~?* | **bear, carry** ◊ *The Julian calendar was introduced by Julius Caesar and hence carries his ~.* | **be known by, go by** ◊ *The island is more commonly known by the ~ 'Krakatoa'.* ◊ *He goes by the ~ of Jonno.* | **use** ◊ *She uses a different ~ in her professional life.* | **share** ◊ *His wife and sister share the same ~, Sarah.* | **acquire, get, obtain** ◊ *The Brady bill acquired its ~ from its best-known sponsor, James Brady.* | **adopt, assume, take** ◊ *He was elected Pope in 1978 and took the ~ of John Paul II.* | **keep** ◊ *She decided to keep her maiden ~ for professional purposes.* | **abandon** | **change** | **carry on** ◊ *He wanted an heir to carry on the family ~.* | **immortalize** ◊ *His ~ was immortalized in 1992 when he scored three times in the space of five minutes.* | **choose, decide on, pick** | **give sb/sth** ◊ *She was given the ~ Maria, after her grandmother.* | **give sb, name, pass on** ◊ *Detectives believe that a hit man was sent to silence the witness before he could name ~s (= give evidence to the court/police).* | **reveal** | **call sb/sth by** ◊ *Please call me by my first ~.* | **call sb ~s** ◊ *Stop calling me ~s (= stop saying rude/insulting things about me)!* | **call, call out** ◊ *Somebody called out her ~ from below.* | **mention** ◊ *We cannot mention the suspect's ~ for legal reasons.* | **drop** ◊ *All he did was drop ~s (= mention the names of famous people to impress people).* | **invoke** ◊ *He invoked the ~ of Freud in support of his argument.* | **ask (sb)** ◊ *I asked him his ~.* | **hear** ◊ *I've heard that ~ mentioned before.* | **catch** ◊ *I'm sorry, I didn't catch your ~.* | **know** ◊ *How do you know my ~?* | **forget, remember** ◊ *I'm afraid I've forgotten your ~.* | **print, sign, write** | **spell** | **pronounce** | **enter, put down, register** ◊ *Have you put your ~ down for (= applied to take part in) the school play?* | **list** | **put forward** (*esp. BrE*) ◊ *They put his ~ forward (= chose him) as one of the five candidates for the post.*
NAME + VERB **appear** ◊ *The ~ of the artist appears on the vase.* | **sound ...** ◊ *His ~ sounds familiar.* | **imply sth, suggest sth** ◊ *As the ~ implies, Oxford was the place at which oxen could*

ford the river. | **be synonymous with sth** ◊ *His ~ is synonymous with the worst excesses of sixties architecture.* | **be associated with sth, be attached (to sth)** ◊ *I do not want my ~ associated with these products.* ◊ *He's been in four movies with Spielberg's ~ attached.* | **mean sth** | **come from** ◊ *Where does the band ~ come from?* | **ring a bell** (*figurative*) ◊ *'Does that ~ mean anything to you?' 'Yes, it does ring a bell (= it is familiar).'*
NAME + NOUN **badge, tag** | **plate** (usually *nameplate*) ◊ *She had her nameplate on the door.* | **recognition** ◊ *Coca Cola's global brand ~ recognition*
PREP. **by ~** ◊ *The teacher knows every student by ~.* | **by the ~ of** ◊ *an actor by the ~ of Tom Rees* | **in sb/sth's ~** ◊ *The tickets were booked in the ~ of McLean.* ◊ *I arrest you in the ~ (= on the authority) of the law.* | **under a/the ~** ◊ *The room was booked under (= using) a false ~.* | **~ for, ~ of** ◊ *The common ~ for the flower is 'pineapple lily'.*
PHRASES **a change of ~** | **give your ~ to sth** ◊ *The Huron people gave their ~ to one of the Great Lakes.* | **a list of ~s** | **~ and address** | **~s and faces** ◊ *I have a bad memory for ~s and faces.* | **put a ~ to sb/sth** ◊ *I couldn't put a ~ to the face (= didn't know or couldn't remember the person's name).* ◊ *He put his ~ to the business (= gave it his name).* | **take sb's ~ in vain** ◊ *to take the Lord's ~ in vain* ◊ *Have you been taking my ~ in vain (= showing lack of respect when using my name)?*

2 reputation

ADJ. **big** | **good** | **bad**
VERB + NAME **have** | **become** ◊ *She has become a big ~ in documentary photography.* | **make** ◊ *He made his ~ writing travel books.* ◊ *She's made quite a ~ for herself.* | **acquire, get** ◊ *The area got a bad ~ after a series of nasty murders.* | **protect** ◊ *They tried to protect the good ~ of the college.* | **clear** ◊ *Throughout his years in prison, he fought to clear his ~.* | **give sb** ◊ *This kind of conduct gives students a bad ~.* | **blacken** (*esp. BrE*), **damage** (*esp. BrE*), **sully** ◊ *These articles have damaged the good ~ of the newspaper.*
PREP. **~ for** ◊ *The company has a ~ for reliability.*
PHRASES **sb's ~ is mud** ◊ *If you tell our secret your ~ will be mud (= you will not be popular) around here.*

3 famous person/thing

ADJ. **big, familiar, famous, household, recognizable, well-known** ◊ *He is a big ~ in the world of rock music.*

name *verb* (often **be named**)

1 to give sb/sth a name

ADV. **originally** | **appropriately, aptly, suitably, well** | **correctly** ◊ *He correctly ~d the song from the clip played.* | **curiously, delightfully** (*esp. BrE*), **exotically, grandly, improbably, oddly, quaintly** (*esp. BrE*), **strangely, wonderfully** ◊ *the curiously ~d Egg Castle* | **unfortunately** | **confusingly** | **euphemistically** | **ironically** | **officially** ◊ *The ship will be officially ~d by the Queen before setting sail from her home port.*
PREP. **after** ◊ *I ~d my son after my father.* | **for** (*AmE*) ◊ *the dead sister for whom she had been ~d* | **in honour/honor of** ◊ *The hospital was ~d in honour/honor of its principal benefactor.*

2 to choose sb for a job/position

ADV. **formally, officially** ◊ *The President officially ~d Kirk as his choice to replace Timms.*
PREP. **to** (*AmE*) ◊ *She was recently ~d to the company's board of directors.*
PHRASES **newly ~d** ◊ *the newly ~d head coach*

nanny *noun*

ADJ. **live-in** ◊ *Board and lodging is part of the deal for live-in nannies.* | **full-time**
PREP. **~ for, ~ to** ◊ *She applied for the job of ~ to the Rickman family.*
→ Note at JOB

nap noun

ADJ. brief, little, quick, short | long | nice | afternoon, daytime, morning | power ◊ *A ten-minute power ~ can boost your productivity.*
VERB + NAP have, take ◊ *I had a short ~ after lunch.*

napkin noun

ADJ. folded | table ◊ *She dabbed her mouth with her table ~.* | cloth (*esp. AmE*), linen, paper | cocktail (*AmE*) | sanitary (*AmE*) (**sanitary towel** in *BrE*)
VERB + NAPKIN fold, unfold | tuck ◊ *He tucked his ~ under his chin.* | dab sth with, wipe sth on, wipe sth with
NAPKIN + NOUN holder, ring ◊ *~ rings made of silver*

nappy (*BrE*) noun → See also DIAPER

ADJ. clean | wet | dirty, soiled | smelly | disposable | reusable, washable | cloth, terry
VERB + NAPPY have on, wear | change ◊ *I'd just changed the baby's ~.* | put on | remove | wash | dispose of
NAPPY + NOUN change, changing | pin | rash
PREP. in ~ ◊ *Isn't he rather old to be still in nappies?*

narcotic noun

ADJ. mild, powerful | addictive | illegal, illicit (*esp. AmE*)
VERB + NARCOTIC use
NARCOTICS + NOUN agent, detective, officer, squad
→ Note at DRUG (for more verbs and nouns)

narrative noun

ADJ. popular | compelling | coherent | simple, straight-forward | complex, detailed | chronological, linear, sequential | first-person, third-person ◊ *The book is written in the style of first-person ~.* | autobiographical, personal ◊ *He provides a compelling personal ~ of his life.* | fictional, prose | film | traditional ◊ *The movie has a very traditional linear ~.* | biblical, historical | dominant ◊ *the dominant ~ of the Cold War* | grand, master (*esp. AmE*) ◊ *the grand ~s of history*
VERB + NARRATIVE construct, create, develop, produce, weave (*esp. AmE*), write ◊ *It's difficult to construct a ~ out of a series of fast-moving events.* | interrupt ◊ *The author interrupts her ~ to tell us that the idea for the book had not been well received.* | offer, present, provide ◊ *This book offers no coherent ~ of the American Civil War.* | weave sth into ◊ *The author weaves into this ~ many entertaining historical facts.*
NARRATIVE + VERB be based on sth
NARRATIVE + NOUN form, style, technique | framework, structure | flow, thread ◊ *interruptions to the ~ flow* | content | passage, sequence, text
PREP. in a/the ~ ◊ *events in the ~*

narrow verb

1 of a road/river/gap/range

ADV. considerably, significantly ◊ *The gap between the candidates has ~ed significantly.* | a little, slightly, etc. ◊ *The river ~s a little here.* ◊ *The trade deficit with China ~ed slightly.* | dramatically, sharply ◊ *The gap between the two parties ~ed sharply in the days before the election.* | gradually ◊ *Left untreated, the arteries will gradually ~, restricting the flow of blood.*
PREP. to ◊ *By the final round the gap had ~ed to three votes.*

2 of eyes

ADV. slightly ◊ *Her eyes ~ed slightly as she studied the woman.* | suddenly | dangerously, suspiciously ◊ *His blue eyes ~ed suspiciously.*
PREP. against ◊ *Lee's eyes ~ed against the harsh glare of the sun.* | at ◊ *His eyes suddenly ~ed at the sight of her.* | in ◊ *Her eyes ~ed in anger.* | to ◊ *His eyes ~ed to slits.* | with ◊ *His eyes ~ed with suspicion.*

narrow adj.

1 not wide

VERBS be, look, seem | become, get
ADV. extremely, fairly, very, etc. ◊ *The pass gets extremely ~ at its eastern edge.* | a little, slightly, etc. ◊ *The rear part of the casing is slightly narrower than the front.* | relatively

2 limited

VERBS be, seem | become
ADV. extremely, fairly, very, etc. | increasingly | a little, slightly, etc. | comparatively, relatively
PREP. in ◊ *people who are rather ~ in outlook*

nasty adj.

VERBS be, look, smell, sound, taste ◊ *He made it all sound very ~.* | become, get, turn ◊ *Things could turn ~* (= dangerous) *if we're not careful.*
ADV. extremely, fairly, very, etc. | particularly, thoroughly (*esp. BrE*) ◊ *He's a thoroughly ~ piece of work* (= a nasty person). (*BrE*)
PREP. about ◊ *She was ~ about everyone.* | to ◊ *Kevin seems to enjoy being ~ to his sisters.*
PHRASES cheap and ~ (*BrE*) ◊ *a room full of cheap and ~ ornaments* | ~ little ◊ *a ~ little man*

nation noun

ADJ. large | little, small | major | great, leading, powerful, strong | advanced, developed, industrial, industrialized | developing, emerging, Third-World | affluent, prosperous, rich, wealthy ◊ *the richest ~ on earth* | poor | modern | new, young | ancient, old | civilized | entire, whole ◊ *The entire ~ mourned her death.* | divided, united | free, independent, sovereign | democratic | capitalist, communist | Christian, Muslim, etc. | foreign | Western ◊ *the imperialist expansion of Western ~s in the 1880s* | Arab, European, French, etc. | island ◊ *The Soviet Union sent aid to the island ~ of Cuba.* | maritime, oil-producing, trading | nuclear | creditor, debtor ◊ *In 1950 the UK was the world's largest debtor ~ and the US the largest creditor.* | host ◊ *France was host ~ for the 1998 World Cup.* | member ◊ *the member ~s of the UN* | rogue ◊ *the threat of attack from terrorists or rogue ~s*
VERB + NATION build, create ◊ *They wanted to create a new ~.* | divide, unite ◊ *The fight against terrorism seemed to unite the ~.* | govern, lead | serve | defend, protect | shock ◊ *the savage murder that shocked the ~*
NATION + NOUN state
PREP. across a/the ~ ◊ *swings in public opinion across the ~* | among ~s ◊ *economic inequality among the ~s of the world* | in a/the ~, within a/the ~ ◊ *In the ~ as a whole there is no desire for war.* | ~ of ◊ *They are a ~ of food lovers.*
PHRASES the birth of a/the ~ | the interests of a/the ~ | the life of a/the ~ ◊ *They hoped that the exhibition would enhance the cultural life of the ~.* | the ~ as a whole, the ~ at large ◊ *The new economic policies were in the best interests of the ~ at large.* | the ~s of the world

nationalism noun

ADJ. extreme, radical | aggressive, militant, revolutionary | popular | religious, secular | black | American, Arab, etc. | cultural, economic, political
PHRASES the growth of ~, the rise of ~ | a resurgence of ~, a revival of ~ ◊ *a 19th-century resurgence of Finnish ~* | a tide of ~ ◊ *a tide of militant ~*

nationalist noun

ADJ. ardent, fervent | extreme, hard-line, radical | militant | moderate | liberal | conservative, right-wing | African, Basque, Irish, etc. | black

nationalistic adj.

VERBS be | become | remain
ADV. fiercely, intensely, strongly | increasingly

nationality noun

ADJ. various ◊ *cultural differences among various national-*

ities | **mixed** ◊ *The pupils are of mixed ~.* | **dual** ◊ *He has dual British and South African ~.* | **foreign** (*esp. BrE*) | **Argentinian, etc.**

VERB + NATIONALITY **have** | **acquire, adopt, assume, obtain, take** (*BrE*) ◊ *She is hoping to adopt Australian ~.* ◊ *a German-born composer who took British ~* | **change** | **renounce** | **lose** | **grant sb** (*BrE*) ◊ *He recently received the Spanish passport which grants him dual ~.*

NATIONALITY + VERB **be represented** ◊ *About 30 nationalities were represented at the tournament.*

PHRASES **on (the) grounds of ~** (*esp. BrE*) ◊ *He accused them of discrimination on the grounds of ~.*

natural *adj.*

1 not made by people

VERBS **be** ◊ *All the materials are ~.*
ADV. **completely, totally** ◊ *completely ~ materials* | **really** ◊ *Your highlights look really ~.*

2 usual/normal

VERBS **appear, be, feel, look, seem, sound** | **become**
ADV. **only, perfectly, quite** ◊ *It's only ~ that she should feel upset.* | **very** | **fairly**

nature *noun*

1 the physical world; plants, animals, etc.

ADJ. **Mother** ◊ *Mother Nature's way of dealing with overpopulation*
VERB + NATURE **commune with** ◊ *He believed in spending half an hour each day to relax and commune with ~.* | **be back to, get back to** ◊ *We built our house in the country because we wanted to get back (= be close) to ~.* | **be found in** ◊ *man-made substances not found in ~*
NATURE + VERB **endow (sb with) sth, give sb sth, provide (sb with) sth** ◊ *Nature had endowed her with exceptional vitality.* | **produce sth** ◊ *It's highly unlikely that this mound was produced by ~.*
NATURE + NOUN **conservation** | **preserve** (*AmE*), **reserve** | **trail** | **lover**
PREP. **close to ~** ◊ *people who live in the country and are close to ~* | **in ~** ◊ *We appreciate beauty in ~.*
PHRASES **the forces of ~, the laws of ~** | **a love of ~** ◊ *His love of ~ was expressed through his wildlife paintings.* | **let ~ take its course** ◊ *We can only treat the injury and then let ~ take its course.*

2 qualities/features of sb/sth

ADJ. **basic, essential, fundamental, intrinsic, real, true** | **artificial** | **exact, precise, specific** ◊ *I'm not clear about the exact ~ of their relationship.* | **general** | **selective** | **limited, restrictive** | **changing, seasonal, temporary, transitory** | **dynamic** | **uncertain, unpredictable** | **arbitrary, random** | **subjective** ◊ *the subjective ~ of perception* | **abstract** | **capricious, fickle** | **intractable** | **distinctive, unique, unusual** | **radical** | **complex** | **dual** ◊ *the dual ~ of man as a physical and spiritual being* | **special, specialist** (*BrE*) | **traditional** | **controversial** | **sensitive** ◊ *The victim has not been identified because of the sensitive ~ of the case.* | **contradictory** | **problematic** | **unsatisfactory** (*esp. BrE*) ◊ *the unsatisfactory ~ of the meeting* | **good** ◊ *People are always taking advantage of her good ~ (= her kindness).* | **human** ◊ *It's only human ~ to want more money.* | **divine** | **confidential, personal, private** | **public** | **international, local** ◊ *the international ~ of the business* | **repetitive** | **routine** (*esp. BrE*) ◊ *matters of a routine ~* | **detailed** ◊ *Because of the detailed ~ of the work, I have to use a very fine brush.* | **practical** | **physical, psychological, sexual** ◊ *They define sexual harassment as unwanted conduct of a sexual ~.* | **economic, legal, political, social** ◊ *Their problems are of an economic ~.* | **contemplative** | **inquisitive** | **competitive**
VERB + NATURE **have** ◊ *He has an inquisitive ~.* | **reveal** ◊ *The parties would not reveal the exact ~ of the dispute.* | **conceal** | **reflect, show** | **emphasize** | **belie** ◊ *The gentle lower slopes belie the true ~ of the mountain.* | **be against, be contrary to, go against** ◊ *It was against his ~ to tell lies.* | **alter, change** ◊ *This new information does not change the ~ of our findings.* | **acknowledge, be aware of, recognize** ◊

Are you aware of the ~ of the risks involved? | **define, specify** ◊ *It is important to define the ~ of the problem.* | **assess, consider, discuss, examine, explore, investigate** | **comprehend, realize, understand** ◊ *The Buddhist goal is to realize the true ~ of the world.* | **clarify, elucidate, explain** | **describe** | **determine** | **depend on** ◊ *The method employed will depend on the ~ of the task.* | **appeal to** ◊ *There was no point appealing to her better ~ (= kindness).*
PREP. **by ~** ◊ *He's not by ~ an inquisitive person.* | **concerning the ~ of** ◊ *a debate concerning the ~ of violence* | **considering the ~ of, given the ~ of** ◊ *Given the ~ of this matter, I am inclined to think it should be managed by you personally.* | **in ~** ◊ *Their strategy was essentially political in ~.* | **in sb/sth's ~** ◊ *It's not in his ~ to complain.* ◊ *A certain element of risk is in the ~ of the job.* | **of a ... ~** ◊ *The legal concept of insanity is of a different ~ from the medical.*
PHRASES **by its very ~** ◊ *By its very ~ a secret service is not open to public inspection.* | **the extent and ~ of sth** ◊ *We need to understand the true extent and ~ of the problem.* | **an insight into the ~ of sth** ◊ *His theory provides a remarkable insight into the ~ of the constitution.* | **a part of human ~** ◊ *Her view is that aggression is part of human ~.* | **a part of sb's ~** ◊ *the expressive part of his ~* | **a side of sb's ~, a side to sb's ~** ◊ *He had a vicious side to his ~.*

nausea *noun*

ADJ. **severe** | **mild, slight** | **sudden**
... OF NAUSEA **wave** ◊ *I was overcome by waves of ~.*
VERB + NAUSEA **experience, feel, have** ◊ *Some people have ~ and vomiting after surgery.* | **complain of** | **bring on, cause** | **reduce, relieve**
NAUSEA + VERB **come over sb, hit sb, sweep over sb** ◊ *A wave of ~ came over him.* | **pass** ◊ *The ~ had passed and I felt better.*
PHRASES **a feeling of ~**

navigate *verb*

ADV. **safely** ◊ *Only the best-trained captains could safely ~ these routes.* | **carefully** ◊ *Every day the ship carefully ~d through the channels of blue icebergs.* | **successfully** ◊ *She managed to successfully ~ the complex world of corporate finance.* (*figurative*) | **easily** ◊ *Customers will be able to ~ easily throughout the site.*
PREP. **by** ◊ *These birds ~ by the sun.* | **across, through** ◊ *She became expert in driving and navigating across the desert.* ◊ *Browsers are used to ~ through the Web.*
PHRASES **~ your way**

navigation *noun*

1 movement of ships, aircraft, etc.

ADJ. **accurate** | **safe** | **inland, ocean** (*esp. AmE*), **river, sea** (*esp. BrE*), **underwater** ◊ *Rail and inland ~ together account for 30–50% of the total delivered cost.* | **air, land, marine, maritime** | **GPS, radio, satellite** ◊ *Having used GPS ~, it's hard to go back to using maps.* | **in-car** ◊ *a maker of in-car ~ systems*
NAVIGATION + NOUN **system** ◊ *a global satellite ~ system for the Air Force* | **aids, chart, device, equipment, instruments, lights** ◊ *a GPS ~ device* | **beacon** ◊ *~ beacons for Allied aircraft* | **channel** ◊ *the main ~ channel on the far side of the island* | **satellite**
PREP. **~ in** ◊ *The stars were used for ~ in the desert.* | **~ of** ◊ *the ~ of our rivers*
PHRASES **an aid to ~** ◊ *small boats equipped with electronic aids to ~* | **freedom of ~, rights of ~** ◊ *freedom of ~ through international waters* | **an obstruction to ~** (*law, esp. BrE*) ◊ *the cost of removing obstructions to ~*

2 finding way your around a website

ADJ. **easy, good** ◊ *a well laid out design and easy ~* | **site, Web** ◊ *Make site ~ easy and intuitive.* ◊ *The software is designed to simplify Web ~.*
NAVIGATION + NOUN **bar, button, menu** ◊ *You can use the ~ bar at the bottom of the pictures to zoom in or out.*

PREP. **~ of** ◊ *Keep the ~ of your site really simple.* | **~ through** ◊ *~ through complex documents*
PHRASES **make ~ difficult, easy, etc.** ◊ *A mouse or joystick makes ~ simpler.*

navy *noun*

ADJ. **strong** | **merchant** (*BrE*) (**merchant marine** in *AmE*) | **Russian, US, etc.**
VERB + NAVY **have** | **build** ◊ *Germany had built a modern ~.* | **serve in** | **enter, join** ◊ *He joined the Navy in 1991.*
PREP. **in the ~** ◊ *He spent ten years in the US ~.*

neat *adj.* tidy and in order

VERBS **appear, be, look, seem** | **make sth** | **keep sth** ◊ *She kept her desk extremely ~.*
ADV. **extremely, fairly, very, etc.** | **surprisingly** ◊ *The handwriting was surprisingly ~.*
PHRASES **~ and tidy** ◊ *I've made the front lawn all ~ and tidy.*

necessary *adj.*

VERBS **appear, be, prove, seem** | **become** | **remain** | **make sth** ◊ *The cold weather has made it ~ to protect the crops.* | **believe sth, consider sth, deem sth, feel sth, find sth, regard sth as, see sth as, think sth** ◊ *Make any alterations you consider ~.* ◊ *You may find it ~ to readjust the wheels from time to time.*
ADV. **really, strictly** ◊ *I was determined not to stay in the hospital for any longer than was strictly ~.* | **absolutely** | **hardly** | **logically** | **medically**
PREP. **for** ◊ *qualifications which are ~ for work with the under-fives*
PHRASES **if ~** ◊ *These measures will be enforced, if ~, by the army.* | **as ~, when ~, where ~** ◊ *We are here to give help and support when ~.* ◊ *Editorial changes have been made where ~.*

necessity *noun*

1 fact that sth must happen; sth that cannot be avoided

ADJ. **absolute, fundamental** (*esp. BrE*), **sheer, vital** ◊ *Sleep is an absolute ~ for life.* | **dire, urgent** | **immediate** | **real** | **perceived** | **strategic** | **logical, physical, practical** ◊ *The people in the rural areas use mud bricks only as an immediate, practical ~.* | **business, economic, financial, historical, medical, military, political, social** ◊ *He argued that nuclear weapons were a political ~.*
VERB + NECESSITY **become** ◊ *A website has become a business ~.* | **recognize, see, understand** ◊ *She saw the ~ to make an immediate impression on him.* | **feel** ◊ *I've never felt the ~ to rely on such a strict rule.* | **accept (sth as), be convinced of** ◊ *They have accepted the ~ of greater state intervention.* | **avoid, obviate, remove** | **spare sb** ◊ *Mrs R has been spared the ~ of having to give evidence.* | **emphasize, highlight, stress** ◊ *Observers stressed the ~ for the ceasefire to be observed.* | **be born of, be born out of** ◊ *Culling of the animals was born out of the ~ for successful conservation.* | **be driven by** ◊ *Driven by financial ~, she decided to give up her writing career.*
NECESSITY + VERB **arise** ◊ *These animals don't like water but will swim if the ~ arises.* | **dictate (sth), require (sth)** ◊ *This rule is carried no farther than ~ requires.* | **force sth** ◊ *Necessity forced an urgent solution.*
PREP. **of ~** ◊ *The visit will, of ~, be brief.* | **out of ~** ◊ *He is changing jobs out of ~, not because he particularly wants to.* | **through ~** ◊ *Most of the women are forced, through economic ~, to work in part-time low-paid jobs.* | **without the ~ of** ◊ *Most disputes can be resolved without the ~ of going to court.* | **~ to** ◊ *There's no ~ for you to come.* | **~ to** ◊ *the ~ to earn a living*
PHRASES **any ~, no ~** ◊ *The company sees no ~ for a more cautious approach to investment.*

2 sth you must have

ADJ. **absolute** | **vital** | **real** | **urgent** ◊ *Policies which address*

---

these issues are an urgent ~. | **bare, basic** ◊ *They have nothing but the barest necessities.* | **daily**
VERB + NECESSITY **have** | **lack**
PHRASES **a ~ of life** ◊ *Food is a ~ of life.*

neck *noun*

1 part of the body

ADJ. **long, short** | **slender, slim, swan-like** (*literary*) | **scraggy** (*BrE*), **scrawny, thin** | **strong, thick** | **sore, stiff** | **broken**
VERB + NECK **crane, strain** ◊ *I craned my ~ to see what was happening at the front.* | **break, injure** | **rub** | **wring** ◊ *He killed the chicken quickly by wringing its ~.* ◊ *When he was late again I wanted to wring his ~.* | **risk** (*figurative*) ◊ *I'm not going to risk my ~ playing rugby with you!* | **save** (*figurative*) ◊ *He's out to save his own political ~* (= his political career).
NECK + VERB **ache, pain**
NECK + NOUN **muscle** | **brace, collar, support** ◊ *She's been wearing a ~ brace since her car crash.* | **injury**
PREP. **around your ~, round your ~** (*esp. BrE*) ◊ *I keep the key on a string around my ~.* | **in the ~** ◊ *The veins in his ~ stood out like knotted rope.*
PHRASES **the back of the ~, the nape of the ~** ◊ *The hairs on the back of my ~ prickled with fear.* | **a crick in your ~** ◊ *I had a crick in my ~ from staring up at the sky so long.* | **the scruff of the ~** ◊ *The cat picked up her kitten by the scruff of its ~.*

2 part of a piece of clothing

ADJ. **high, low** | **open** ◊ *He wore a casual shirt with an open ~.* | **boat** (*AmE*), **cowl, crew, halter, round, scoop, V** (usually **V-neck**) ◊ *He was wearing a black V-neck sweater.* | **polo** (*BrE*), **roll** (usually **roll-neck**) (*esp. BrE*), **turtle** (usually **turtleneck**) (*AmE*)

need *noun*

1 situation where sth is needed/necessary

ADJ. **big** (*esp. AmE*), **considerable** (*esp. BrE*), **great, strong** ◊ *There is a great ~ for English language classes.* | **special** ◊ *There is a special ~ for well-trained teachers.* | **overriding, overwhelming, paramount** | **burning, compelling, critical, crying, desperate, dire, driving, immediate, pressing, serious, urgent** ◊ *a crying ~ for skilled workers* ◊ *These children are in dire ~.* | **real** | **clear** | **basic, essential, fundamental** | **sudden** | **constant, continuing** ◊ *He's in constant ~ of treatment.* | **growing, increased, increasing** | **reduced** | **possible** | **perceived** | **common** ◊ *our common ~ for self-preservation* | **individual** | **human** ◊ *the human ~ to order existence* | **political, social**
VERB + NEED **feel, have** ◊ *I felt the ~ to do something.* | **express** ◊ *Several governments have expressed the ~ for a cautious approach to the conflict.* | **demonstrate, indicate, prove, show, suggest** ◊ *The incident proved the ~ for a continuing military presence in the area.* | **reflect** ◊ *a law reflecting a ~ for better social conditions* | **create** ◊ *The war created a ~ for national unity.* | **address, fill** (*esp. AmE*), **fulfil/fulfill, meet, satisfy** | **be driven by** ◊ *Research is currently driven by the ~ to reduce pollution.* | **avoid, eliminate, obviate, remove** ◊ *Early intervention frequently eliminates the ~ for surgery.* | **reduce** | **be aware of, be sensitive to** | **accept, acknowledge, perceive, recognize, see** ◊ *I see no ~ to do anything hasty.* | **emphasize, heighten, highlight, reaffirm, stress, underline, underscore** (*esp. AmE*) ◊ *She stressed the ~ for cooperation with the authorities.* | **support** ◊ *I understand and support their ~ to make a living.* | **ignore, overlook** | **deny** ◊ *The government has denied the ~ for economic reform.* | **understand** | **consider**
NEED + VERB **exist** ◊ *A ~ exists to bridge the gap between theory and practice in nursing.* | **arise** ◊ *The system can be switched to emergency power should the ~ arise.*
PREP. **in ~ (of)** ◊ *a campaign to help children in ~* ◊ *The room was sorely in ~ of a fresh coat of paint.* | **~ for** ◊ *the ~ for change*
PHRASES **any, little, no, etc. ~** ◊ *There's no ~ to worry.*

2 sth that sb requires

ADJ. **basic, essential, fundamental** | **particular, special,**

specific, unique ◇ *a school for children with special educational ~s* | **immediate, pressing** | **long-term** | **future** | **changing** | **conflicting** | **unmet** | **local** | **individual, personal** | **community, public** | **customer, patient, user,** etc. | **customers', patients', users',** etc. | **human** ◇ *Energy for cooking is a basic human ~.* | **humanitarian** | **material, physical** ◇ *material ~s of food and shelter* | **dietary** | **health, health-care, medical** | **biological, bodily, emotional, physical, psychological, sexual, spiritual** | **educational** | **political, social** | **business, economic, financial** | **operational** | **energy** | **information**

VERB + NEED **be responsive to, be sensitive to** | **address, cater for, cater to, cover, fill** (*esp. AmE*), **fit** (*esp. AmE*), **fulfil/ fulfill, meet, provide for, respond to, satisfy, serve, supply** ◇ *a new union set up to address the ~s of seasonal workers* ◇ *€25 a day was enough to cover all his ~s.* ◇ *We have now met most of the humanitarian ~s of the refugees.* | **suit, tailor sth to** ◇ *The coaching is informal and tailored to individual ~s.* | **identify** | **assess, consider** | **balance** ◇ *We try to balance the ~s of all our customers.*

PHRASES **~s and desires** | **sb's every ~** ◇ *Our staff will cater to your every ~.*

need verb

ADV. **badly, desperately, really, sorely, urgently** ◇ *She ~ed some money badly.* ◇ *Research is urgently ~ed into the causes of this illness.* | **certainly, definitely** | **probably** | **clearly, obviously** | **just, only, simply** ◇ *I just ~ some information.* | **hardly** ◇ *You hardly ~ me to tell you that your father is still very frail and must not be upset.* | **not necessarily** ◇ *These people require 24-hour attention, but they do not necessarily ~ to be in the hospital.* | **no longer** | **still**

VERB + NEED **be going to** | **be expected to, be likely to, may well** ◇ *You may well ~ to look outside your preferred area to find an affordable hotel.*

needle noun

1 for sewing, knitting, etc.

ADJ. **long** | **blunt** | **sharp** | **fine** | **darning, embroidery, knitting, sewing, tapestry**

VERB + NEEDLE **use** | **thread**

NEEDLE + VERB **prick sb/sth**

PHRASES **the eye of a ~** | **~ and thread** ◇ *She sewed it on with ~ and thread.* | **a ~ in a haystack** ◇ *Looking for one man in a city this size is like looking for a ~ in a haystack* (= difficult to find).

2 for drugs

ADJ. **hypodermic, syringe** | **injection** | **long** | **sharp** | **fine, thin** | **clean, sterile** | **contaminated, dirty, infected** (*esp. BrE*) | **used**

VERB + NEEDLE **inject, insert, jab (sb with), plunge, push, put, stick** ◇ *He saw her stick a ~ into her arm.* | **remove, withdraw** | **use** | **share** ◇ *the dangers of sharing ~s*

NEEDLE + VERB **go in** ◇ *The ~ went in easily.* | **pierce sth** ◇ *She winced when she felt the ~ pierce her skin.*

NEEDLE + NOUN **tip** | **exchange** ◇ *~ exchange schemes* (*BrE*) ◇ *~ exchange programs* (*AmE*) (= *where drug users can change used needles for clean ones*) | **biopsy**

PHRASES **the prick of a ~**

3 on a compass/instrument

ADJ. **magnetic** | **compass**

NEEDLE + VERB **move** ◇ *The ~ moved away from the wind.* | **point**

PHRASES **the ~ of a compass**

4 on a pine tree

ADJ. **conifer, pine**

VERB + NEEDLE **drop, lose**

needy adj.

VERBS **be, look** ◇ *a woman who looked ~*

ADV. **truly, very** | **emotionally, financially**

PHRASES **poor and ~** ◇ *the children of poor and ~ parents*

negative adj.

1 only thinking about/showing sb/sth's bad qualities

VERBS **be, feel, seem, sound** | **become** | **remain**

ADV. **extremely, fairly, very,** etc. | **decidedly, highly, profoundly, significantly** (*esp. AmE*), **strongly** ◇ *Their attitude was highly ~.* ◇ *the strongly ~ implications of these survey results* | **completely, entirely, purely, totally, wholly** ◇ *She spoke in entirely ~ terms.* | **largely, overwhelmingly, predominantly** | **increasingly** | **overly** ◇ *Some people have accused me of being overly ~.* | **uniformly** ◇ *Reaction to last night's attack was uniformly ~.* | **a little, slightly,** etc. | **apparently, seemingly** | **essentially** ◇ *Critical thinking is essentially ~ as it seeks to dissect and not to build.* | **potentially** | **generally**

PREP. **about** ◇ *He's been rather ~ about the idea.*

2 showing that sth has not happened/been found

ADV. **falsely**

VERBS **be, prove, test** ◇ *The antibody test proved ~.* ◇ *He tested ~ for HIV infection.*

PREP. **for** ◇ *The urine tests were ~ for protein.*

neglect noun

ADJ. **general, total** | **relative** | **benign** ◇ *The 18th-century interior of the building has survived through benign ~.* | **serious** (*esp. BrE*), **wilful/willful** | **emotional, physical** | **medical** ◇ *Medical ~ occurs when medical care is withheld.* | **child** ◇ *The maximum penalty for child ~ is ten years' imprisonment.* | **parental** ◇ *children who are victims of deliberate parental ~*

VERB + NEGLECT **suffer, suffer from** ◇ *The buildings suffered ~ for centuries.* | **be guilty of** ◇ *The doctor was guilty of serious ~ of duty.*

PREP. **by ~** ◇ *cruelty by ~* | **through ~** ◇ *the suffering of children through ~* | **~ of** ◇ *Abuse, domestic violence and ~ of children took place.* | **to the ~ of** ◇ *She had concentrated on her music to the ~ of her other studies.*

PHRASES **centuries of ~, years of ~** ◇ *After years of ~ the house is at last being restored.* | **~ of duty** ◇ *He was reprimanded for ~ of duty.*

neglect verb

ADV. **grossly** (*formal*), **seriously** | **completely, entirely, totally** | **largely** | **generally** ◇ *These are subjects generally ~ed by historians.* | **conveniently** (*ironic*), **deliberately, wilfully/willfully** (*esp. BrE*) ◇ *They conveniently ~ed their responsibilities.* | **hitherto, previously**

VERB + NEGLECT **tend to** | **cannot afford to** ◇ *This sector is one of the major growth areas and we cannot afford to ~ it.*

PREP. **in favour/favor of** ◇ *Local communities have been ~ed in favour/favor of private sector interests.*

neglected adj.

1 not given enough attention

VERBS **be, feel, lie, look, remain, seem, stand** ◇ *His tools lay ~ on the workbench.* | **become, get**

ADV. **badly, much, sadly, seriously, sorely, woefully** ◇ *It is a sadly ~ work.* ◇ *The building is sorely ~.* | **largely** | **comparatively, rather, relatively, somewhat** | **hitherto, previously** | **unjustly** ◇ *She is an excellent and unjustly ~ author.*

2 not given enough food, clothing, etc.

VERBS **be, look** ◇ *The group of street children looked ragged and ~.*

ADV. **badly, grossly, severely**

negligence noun (law)

ADJ. **gross** | **contributory** (*BrE*) ◇ *The plaintiff was guilty of contributory ~ for failing to wear a crash helmet.* | **medical, professional** | **criminal**

VERB + NEGLIGENCE **be guilty of** | **accuse sb of, allege, sue for**

◇ *The lawyer was accused of professional* ~. | **deny** | **prove** | **arise from** ◇ *death arising from* ~

NEGLIGENCE + NOUN **case** | **claim**

PREP. **by** ~ ◇ *His death was brought about by* ~ *on the doctor's part.* | **through** ~ ◇ *damage to company property through* ~ | ~ **in** ◇ ~ *in navigation*

PHRASES **a finding of** ~ ◇ *The court made a finding of criminal* ~. | **the result of (the)** ~ ◇ *The accident was the result of* ~ *on the part of the driver.*
→ Note at CRIME (for more verbs)

negligent *adj.* (law)

VERBS **be, seem**
ADV. **grossly** | **criminally**
PREP. **in** ◇ *The hospital was* ~ *in the way it cared for this young man.* | **over** ◇ *The court found him to be* ~ *over the loss of £18 million by the local authority.*

negligible *adj.*

VERBS **be, seem** | **become**
ADV. **by no means, far from** ◇ *Delays in the courts are far from* ~. | **almost**

negotiate *verb*

1 try to reach an agreement

ADV. **carefully** ◇ *a carefully* ~*d series of concessions* | **successfully** | **effectively** | **individually, separately** ◇ *Rents are individually* ~*d between landlord and tenant.* | **directly** ◇ *Theyt were forced to* ~ *directly with the rebels.* | **secretly** | **seriously** | **constantly, continually** ◇ *The parameters of the job are being continually* ~*d.* | **currently**
VERB + NEGOTIATE **be able to** | **be prepared to, be willing to** ◇ *Are the employers really willing to* ~? | **attempt to, seek to, try to** | **manage to** | **help (to)**
PREP. **between** ◇ *to* ~ *between the two sides* | **for** ◇ *We are negotiating for the release of the prisoners.* | **on** ◇ *They have refused to* ~ *on this issue.* | **on behalf of** ◇ *those negotiating on behalf of the government* | **with** ◇ *I managed to* ~ *successfully with the authorities.*

2 successfully get over/past sth

ADV. **easily, safely** (*esp. BrE*), **successfully** ◇ *He successfully* ~*d the slippery steps.*
VERB + NEGOTIATE **be difficult to** ◇ *The flight of steps was quite difficult to* ~ *with a heavy suitcase.*

negotiation *noun*

ADJ. **lengthy, protracted** | **ongoing** | **final** | **direct, face-to-face** | **successful** | **fruitless, unsuccessful** | **behind-the-scenes, secret** | **bilateral, multilateral** | **diplomatic, political** | **global, international** | **constant, continuous** | **difficult, tough** | **delicate** | **complex** | **intense, serious** ◇ *It's time for some serious* ~. | **formal** | **high-level** | **pay** (*esp. BrE*), **salary** (*esp. AmE*), **wage** (*esp. BrE*) | **peace, trade, etc.**
VERB + NEGOTIATION **enter into, open, start** | **break off** | **continue, reopen, resume** | **conduct** ◇ *Negotiations were conducted in secret.* | **handle** ◇ *Allen had handled the* ~*s himself.* | **lead** ◇ *Leading those* ~*s is Senator Susan Collins of Maine.* | **facilitate** | **complete, conclude** | **be open to, be subject to** ◇ *The final price is open to* ~.
NEGOTIATION + VERB **take place** ◇ *Union* ~*s take place behind closed doors.* | **begin, start** | **continue, go on** ◇ *Negotiations continued all day to try to avert a strike.* | **break down, collapse, fail**
NEGOTIATION + NOUN **process** | **skills** | **table** ◇ *They wanted to bring the conflicting parties back to the* ~ *table.*
PREP. **by** ~ ◇ *Rents are agreed by* ~. | **in** ~ **(with)** ◇ *She is in* ~ *with other heads of state on the question of oil prices.* | **through** ~ ◇ *The problem should be resolved through* ~. | **under** ~ ◇ *Contracts are under* ~. | ~ **between** ◇ *The alliance is the product of months of* ~ *between the two parties.* | ~ **for** ◇ *The problem is not the* ~*s for a contract.* | ~ **of** ◇ *the* ~ *of a new contract* | ~ **on** ◇ *international* ~*s on*

reducing carbon emissions | ~ **over** ◇ ~*s over the number of houses to be built* | ~ **with** ◇ ~*s with the other side*
PHRASES **a basis for** ~ | **a matter for** ~ | **months, years, etc. of** ~ ◇ *They signed the treaty after several years of* ~. | **a process of** ~ ◇ *Compromise is reached by a process of* ~. | **room for** ~ ◇ *There is considerable room for* ~ *on some of the details.*
→ Special page at MEETING

negotiator *noun*

ADJ. **good, skilled, tough** | **professional, trained** | **chief, lead, principal, senior, top** ◇ *the union's chief* ~ | **international** | **union** | **hostage** | **peace, trade**
→ Note at JOB

neighbour (*BrE*) (*AmE* neighbor) *noun*

1 person living nearby

ADJ. **friendly, good** ◇ *She's been a very good* ~ *to me.* | **nosy** | **noisy** | **elderly** | **close, immediate, near, next-door** ◇ *My nearest* ~ *lives a few miles away.* | **downstairs, upstairs** ◇ *She could hear her downstairs* ~ *moving around.* | **new**
VERB + NEIGHBOUR/NEIGHBOR **become** ◇ *The two men became* ~*s.* | **disturb, wake** ◇ *Shh! You'll wake the* ~*s.* | **help** | **meet** ◇ *I've just met our new* ~*s.* | **visit** | **invite** ◇ *He's having a barbecue and he's inviting all the* ~*s.*
NEIGHBOUR/NEIGHBOR + VERB **complain** ◇ *The* ~*s complained about his loud music.* | **move in** ◇ *Our new* ~*s moved in today.*
NEIGHBOUR/NEIGHBOR + NOUN **boy, girl, kid** (*informal*), **lady** (*all AmE*) ◇ *I borrowed the* ~ *kid's bike to get around.*
PHRASES **friends and** ~**s**

2 country that is next to another country

ADJ. **northern, southern, etc.** ◇ *England's northern* ~ *now has its own parliament.* | **hostile** ◇ *The country is vulnerable to attack from hostile* ~*s.* | **powerful, wealthy**
VERB + NEIGHBOUR/NEIGHBOR **attack, invade** | **threaten**

3 person sitting or standing next to another person

ADJ. **nearest** ◇ *She leaned over to her nearest* ~ *and whispered something.*

neighbourhood (*BrE*) (*AmE* neighborhood) *noun*

ADJ. **friendly, nice** | **safe** | **quiet** | **vibrant** | **bad, dangerous, rough, tough** ◇ *I lived in a tough* ~. | **crime-ridden** | **affluent, respectable, upscale** (*AmE*), **wealthy** | **depressed, disadvantaged, impoverished, low-income, poor, run-down** | **downtown** (*AmE*), **inner-city, suburban, urban** | **immediate, local, nearby, surrounding** ◇ *They often got together with other parents in the local* ~. | **residential** | **middle-class, working-class** | **good, great** | **ethnic, minority** | **diverse** | **gay** ◇ *a bar located in the middle of Chicago's gay* ~ | **Asian, black, Latino, white, etc.** | **real** (*esp. AmE*) ◇ *The place feels like a real* ~. | **entire, whole** ◇ *Before long the whole* ~ *knew about it.* | **segregated** | **historic**
VERB + NEIGHBOURHOOD/NEIGHBORHOOD **build, create, establish** ◇ *Our health depends on creating* ~*s that are conducive to walking.* | **move into** ◇ *A lot of new families have moved into the* ~. | **improve, revitalize, transform** | **destroy** ◇ *the criminals who are destroying our* ~ | **visit** ◇ *Tourists rarely visit that* ~. | **explore** | **canvass** (*esp. AmE*) | **patrol** ◇ *They hired a private police force to patrol the* ~. | **roam, wander** ◇ *stray dogs who roam the* ~ | **populate** ◇ *a* ~ *populated mainly by Mexican Americans*
NEIGHBOURHOOD/NEIGHBORHOOD + NOUN **resident** | **boy, children, kid** (*informal*) | **bully** | **leader** | **community** | **association, council, group, organization** | **watch** (= an arrangement by which people watch each other's houses to prevent crime) | **police, policing** | **cat, dog** | **bar, pub** (*BrE*), **restaurant, school, shop** (*esp. BrE*), **store** (*AmE*), **etc.** | **centre/center** | **park** | **street** | **party** (*esp. AmE*) ◇ *She volunteered to make a potato salad for the* ~ *party.*
PREP. **around the** ~, **round the** ~ (*esp. BrE*) ◇ *We used to ride bikes around the* ~. | **in a/the** ~ ◇ *There was a large school in the* ~. | **outside a/the** ~ ◇ *It was a car from outside the immediate* ~.

nerve *noun*

1 in the body

ADJ. **pinched** (*AmE*), **trapped** (*BrE*) | **sensitive** | **damaged** | **facial, optic, sciatic, spinal, etc.** | **peripheral** | **sensory**

VERB + NERVE **damage, pinch** (*AmE*), **strain, trap** (*BrE*) ◇ *He damaged a ~ in his spine.* | **sever** | **stimulate**

NERVE + VERB **go, lead, run** ◇ *The ~ runs from the eye to the brain.* | **transmit sth** ◇ *The ~s transmit pain.* | **supply sth** | **control sth** ◇ *The vagus ~ controls heart rate and breathing.*

NERVE + NOUN **bundle, cell, ending, fibre/fiber, sheath, tissue** | **pathway** | **activity, function** | **impulse, signal** | **stimulation** | **damage, injury** | **disease, dysfunction, paralysis** | **pain** | **gas**

PREP. **along a/the ~** ◇ *The message travels along the ~ to the brain.* | **~ in** ◇ *He's been off work with a trapped ~ in his back.* | **~ to** ◇ *Cutting the ~s to the stomach does not affect hunger.*

PHRASES **every ~ in sb's body** ◇ *Intense pain shot through every ~ in his body.* | **hit a ~, strike a (raw) ~, touch a (raw) ~** (*all figurative*) ◇ *My remarks about divorce had unwittingly touched a raw ~.*

2 nerves mental state

ADJ. **steady** | **bad, frayed, frazzled, jangled, shattered, taut** ◇ *At the end of a day's teaching, her ~s were absolutely shattered.*

VERB + NERVES **fray, stretch** ◇ *Her ~s were stretched to breaking point.*

NERVES + VERB **be on edge** ◇ *After the bomb, my ~s were on edge.* | **be shot** (*informal*) ◇ *Her ~s were shot from all the things happening around her.* | **jangle** ◇ *His ~s jangled every time the phone rang.* | **get the better of sb** ◇ *He uncharacteristically allowed ~s to get the better of him in yesterday's game.*

PHRASES **a battle of ~s, a war of ~s** ◇ *The union has been fighting a war of ~s with the management over pay.* | **get on sb's ~s** ◇ *His endless whining really gets on my ~s.* | **~s of steel** ◇ *You need ~s of steel to be a good poker player.* | **a strain on sb's ~s** ◇ *Caring for him while he was so ill has been a great strain on her ~s.*

3 nerves nervous state

ADJ. **exam** (*esp. BrE*), **first-night** (*BrE*) ◇ *I've never suffered from first-night ~s.* | **jittery** (*AmE*) ◇ *It gave me time to calm my jittery ~s before meeting her.*

VERB + NERVES **calm, control, ease, settle, soothe, steady** ◇ *She took a few deep breaths to calm her ~s.* | **suffer from**

PHRASES **an attack of ~s** ◇ *I had an attack of ~s just before I went on stage.* | **a bag of ~s, a bundle of ~s** ◇ *By the time of the interview, I was a bundle of ~s.*

4 courage

VERB + NERVE **have** ◇ *I didn't have the ~ to ask.* | **lack** | **lose** ◇ *At the last minute she almost lost her ~.* | **keep** ◇ *He kept his ~ to win a thrilling game.* | **find** ◇ *You must find the ~ to ask for more money.* | **gather, steel** ◇ *Steeling my ~, I jumped the first bar.* | **take** ◇ *It took a lot of ~ to stand up and speak.*

NERVE + VERB **break, fail (sb)** ◇ *At the last moment her ~ failed her.*

PHRASES **a failure of ~, a loss of ~** | **a test of ~** ◇ *Singing in front of so many people was a real test of ~.*

nervous *adj.*

VERBS **appear, be, feel, look, seem, sound** ◇ *Both men appeared ~.* | **become, get, grow** | **make sb** ◇ *Sit down—you're making me ~!*

ADV. **extremely, fairly, very, etc.** | **desperately, highly, incredibly** ◇ *He had worked himself up into a highly ~ state.* | **increasingly** | **almost** | **a little, slightly, etc.** | **suddenly** | **clearly, obviously, visibly** | **understandably**

PREP. **about** ◇ *~ about the wedding* | **at** ◇ *~ at what might happen* | **of** ◇ *I was slightly ~ of him.*

nervousness *noun*

ADJ. **extreme, great** ◇ *There has been great ~ about the future.* | **increasing** | **slight** | **initial**

VERB + NERVOUSNESS **feel** | **betray, show, show signs of** ◇ *She managed to speak without betraying her ~.* | **cover, cover**

up, hide ◇ *She laughed to hide her ~.* | **overcome** | **sense** ◇ *I could sense his ~.*

PREP. **from ~** ◇ *I was babbling from ~.* | **out of ~** ◇ *He found himself chattering away out of ~.* | **~ about** ◇ *her ~ about working with children* | **~ at** ◇ *He felt some ~ at the prospect of meeting her.*

PHRASES **a sign of ~** ◇ *Adjusting your tie is often a sign of ~.*

nest *noun*

ADJ. **ant's, bird's, wasp's, etc.**

VERB + NEST **build, construct, make** | **sit on** ◇ *The male and female take turns to sit on the ~.* | **occupy** ◇ *The litters of several different females often occupy the same ~.* | **abandon, desert, fly, leave** ◇ *Her children have flown the ~.* (*figurative*) | **defend, guard** | **disturb** ◇ *You should avoid disturbing the ~ until after the eggs are hatched.* | **destroy** | **find, locate**

NEST + NOUN **site** ◇ *The male uses song to attract a female to his ~ site.* | **hole** | **box** (usually *nesting box* in *BrE*) | **mate**

PREP. **away from a/the ~** ◇ *A rat took the egg while the mother was away from the ~.* | **in a/the ~, inside a/the ~** ◇ *The snake will attack if disturbed inside its ~.* | **on a/the ~** ◇ *The female spends all her time on the ~.*

nestle *verb*

ADV. **comfortably, safely** | **together** ◇ *My parents were ~d together on the couch.*

PREP. **against** ◇ *She sat back, nestling against his chest.* | **among** ◇ *The town ~s comfortably among the hills.* | **in** ◇ *a tiny village nestling in a valley* | **between**

net *noun*

ADJ. **fine, fine-mesh** | **safety** | **fishing** | **drift** | **mosquito** | **butterfly**

VERB + NET **mend** ◇ *The fishermen were mending their ~s.* | **cast, spread, spread out** | **haul in** | **slip through** (*often figurative*) ◇ *We tried to contact all former students but one or two slipped through the ~.*

PREP. **in a/the ~** ◇ *Unfortunately the animals are often caught in fishing ~s.* | **into a/the ~** ◇ *The ball went into the ~.* | **over the ~** ◇ *to hit the ball over the ~*

nettle *noun*

ADJ. **stinging**

...OF NETTLES **clump, patch**

NETTLE + VERB **grow** | **sting** ◇ *I was stung by ~s.*

PREP. **in ~s** ◇ *There was an old car half buried in the ~s.*

network *noun*

1 connections

ADJ. **extensive, large, vast, wide, widespread** ◇ *an extensive ~ of underground tunnels* | **complex, elaborate, intricate** | **dense** | **global, local, national, nationwide, regional, worldwide** | **neural** ◇ *the structure of the brain's neural ~s* | **bus** (*esp. BrE*), **motorway** (*in the UK*), **rail, railroad** (*AmE*), **railway** (*BrE*), **road, train** | **distribution** | **integrated**

VERB + NETWORK **build up, construct, create, develop, establish, set up** ◇ *They are establishing a ~ of pumps and pipelines to move the oil.* | **launch** | **form** ◇ *The new rail services will form a ~ connecting the capital and major cities.* | **join** ◇ *Once a supplier joins the ~, its shipping systems are integrated with the others.* | **use** | **operate, run** | **maintain, manage** | **expand** | **destroy, dismantle** ◇ *We are dismantling the financial ~s that have funded terrorism.*

NETWORK + NOUN **infrastructure**

PREP. **in a/the ~** ◇ *one of the depots in the company's ~* | **through a/the ~** ◇ *Drinking water is brought to the town through a ~ of underground pipes.* | **via a/the ~** ◇ *The newspapers are sent out via a national distribution ~.* | **~ of** ◇ *a ~ of threads*

2 group of people

ADJ. **strong** ◇ *a strong ~ of friends* | **supportive** | **informal** | **grass-roots** | **social** | **old boy** (*BrE, informal*) | **support** |

terror, terrorist ◇ *We must fight terrorist ~s and all those who support them.*
VERB + NETWORK **build up, create, form**
PREP. **in a/the ~** ◇ *Members are all linked together in a ~.* | **~ of** ◇ *a ~ of friends*

3 of computers, phones, etc.

ADJ. **computer** | **cellphone** (*esp. AmE*), **communications, mobile, phone, telephone** | **high-speed** | **corporate** | **peer-to-peer** | **Wi-Fi, wireless** ◇ *laptops connected to wireless ~s* | **wired** | **file-sharing, local area** (abbreviated to *LAN*), **wide area** (abbreviated to *WAN*) | **broadband, VoIP**
VERB + NETWORK **install, set up** | **maintain, manage, operate, run** ◇ *software to help you manage your ~* ◇ *They were unable to run the telephone ~ economically.* | **upgrade** | **access** | **secure** ◇ *Administrators can secure the ~ by segmenting it into zones.*
NETWORK + NOUN **administrator, controller, engineer, operator** | **access, address, connection, device, protocol, provider, security, server, traffic**
PREP. **across a/the ~** ◇ *Users can access data across a ~.* | **on a/the ~** ◇ *All computer users are connected on a ~.* | **over a/ the ~** ◇ *The files are accessible over a ~.*

4 radio/television stations

ADJ. **broadcast, news, radio, television** | **cable, digital, satellite**
NETWORK + NOUN **news, newscast** (*esp. AmE*), **show** (*esp. AmE*), **television** | **anchor** (*esp. AmE*)
PREP. **on a/the ~** ◇ *The show was first aired on the cable ~ Showtime.*
→ Note at ORGANIZATION

neurosis noun

ADJ. **anxiety**
VERB + NEUROSIS **have, suffer, suffer from**
PREP. **~ about** ◇ *the director's ~ about actors arriving late for filming*

neutral adj.

1 not supporting either side

VERBS **be** | **remain, stay**
ADV. **strictly** ◇ *The government maintained its strictly ~ policy.* | **completely** | **broadly** (*esp. BrE*) ◇ *The Russians took a broadly ~ position.* | **politically, religiously** ◇ *The meeting must be at a politically ~ location.*
PREP. **about** ◇ *~ about this issue*

2 not showing strong qualities, feelings, etc.

VERBS **be, seem** ◇ *Her expression seemed ~.* | **remain** | **keep sth** ◇ *Dolly kept her voice carefully ~.*
ADV. **perfectly** | **fairly, quite, relatively** ◇ *She chose fairly ~ make-up.* | **apparently** | **carefully**

3 not affected by sth

VERBS **be, seem**
ADV. **culturally, ethically, ideologically, morally, politically** ◇ *Our actions are never culturally ~.*

neutrality noun

ADJ. **political, religious** | **armed** ◇ *a policy of armed ~.* | **strict**
VERB + NEUTRALITY **declare** ◇ *Switzerland declared its ~.* | **maintain, preserve**
PREP. **~ between** ◇ *the commission's ~ between Sunnis and Shias*

neutralize (*BrE also* -ise) verb

ADV. **effectively** ◇ *This strategy effectively ~d what the party had hoped would be a vote-winner.*
PREP. **with** ◇ *Discarded acid should be ~d with alkali before disposal.*

new adj.

1 recently built/made

VERBS **be, look** ◇ *The car still looks ~.*
ADV. **brand, spanking** ◇ *a scratch on my brand ~ car* ◇ *very proud of their spanking ~ kitchen* | **fairly, relatively**

2 different/not familiar

VERBS **be** ◇ *These ideas are not entirely ~.*
ADV. **very** | **fairly** | **completely, entirely, quite, wholly** | **dramatically, radically** | **fundamentally** | **genuinely, truly** ◇ *genuinely ~ approaches to data recording* | **supposedly** | **hardly, not exactly** ◇ *City-based exhibitions are hardly ~.*
PREP. **to** ◇ *It was all very ~ and strange to me.* ◇ *She's still quite ~ to the job and needs a lot of help.*
PHRASES **nothing ~ about sth, nothing ~ in sth** ◇ *There is nothing ~ in teenagers wanting to change the world.*

news noun

1 new information

ADJ. **brilliant** (*BrE, informal*), **excellent, fantastic, good, great, happy, marvellous/marvelous** (*esp. BrE*), **terrific, tremendous** (*esp. BrE*), **welcome, wonderful** ◇ *The good ~ is that we've all been given an extra day's leave.* ◇ *Great ~! We've bought the house.* | **encouraging, positive** | **awful, bad, devastating, disappointing, grim, sad, terrible, tragic, unwelcome** | **disturbing, shock** (*BrE*), **shocking** | **big, dramatic, important, major** (*esp. AmE*), **momentous** (*esp. BrE*) | **breaking, hot, late, latest, recent** ◇ *Some late ~ has just come in.* | **old** | **exciting, interesting** | **hard** | **front-page, headline** ◇ *It was front-page ~ at the time.* | **online** | **domestic, local, national, regional** | **foreign, inter-national** | **business, City** (*BrE*), **economic, financial** | **celebrity** | **sports** | **football, etc.** | **shipping** (*AmE*) (*shipping forecast* in *BrE*)
... OF NEWS **bit, item, piece** ◇ *We've had a bit of good ~.*
VERB + NEWS **catch, get, have, hear, learn, receive** ◇ *You can catch all the latest ~ on our website.* ◇ *Have you heard the latest ~?* | **catch up on** ◇ *I want to catch up on all your ~.* | **follow** ◇ *I follow food industry ~ fairly closely.* | **announce, break, bring (sb), convey, deliver, give sb, relay, reveal, tell sb** ◇ *The police had to break the ~ to the boy's parents.* | **confirm** ◇ *The company refused to confirm the ~.* | **share, spread** ◇ *He shared his good ~ with everyone else in the office.* ◇ *She ran from office to office, spreading the ~.* | **print, publish** | **leak** ◇ *News of their engagement was leaked to the press.* | **release** ◇ *The actor's family released ~ of his death last night.* | **post** ◇ *The ~ was posted on the band's website.* | **bury, suppress** ◇ *Drug companies tend to bury ~ of drug failures.* | **report** ◇ *I don't really have any ~ to report.* | **carry, cover** ◇ *'The Daily Nation' carried ~ of the event.* | **gather, get** ◇ *It's the reporter's job to go out and gather ~.* | **await, expect, wait for** ◇ *They are waiting for ~ of their relatives.* | **digest** ◇ *He took a moment to digest the unbelievable ~.* | **greet, react to, welcome** ◇ *The ~ was greeted with astonishment.* | **celebrate** ◇ *Mrs Trowsdale will be celebrating the ~ with her family.* | **hit, make** ◇ *It was a very minor incident and barely made the ~.* | **dominate** ◇ *California's energy crisis dominated the ~.*
NEWS + VERB **come, come in, come through** ◇ *News is coming in of a large fire in central London.* | **break, emerge, leak out** ◇ *The ~ broke while we were away.* | **arrive, reach sb** | **filter through (sth)** | **spread, travel** ◇ *The ~ spread like wildfire.*
NEWS + NOUN **broadcast, bulletin, flash, programme/ program, show** ◇ *The schedules were interrupted for a ~ flash.* | **article, clip, exclusive** (*esp. BrE*), **footage, head-lines, item, release, report, round-up, story, update** | **digest** ◇ *a downloadable ~ digest* | **coverage** ◇ *News coverage of the fighting was extremely biased.* | **event** | **briefing** ◇ *He gave his first ~ briefing since being appointed.* (see also *news conference*) | **agency, organization, outlet, service** | **desk, room** | **channel, network, station** ◇ *Every ~ channel covered the story.* | **magazine** | **anchor** (*esp. AmE*), **broadcaster, crew** (*esp. AmE*), **editor, journalist, presenter, reporter** | **source** | **media** | **junkie** (*informal*) ◇ *If you're a ~ junkie, you can get updates mailed to you.* | **alert, ticker** ◇ *You can get ~ alerts through your cellphone.* | **website** | **blog**

PREP. **at the ~** ◇ *She went completely to pieces at the ~ of his death.* | **in the ~** ◇ *She's been in the ~ a lot lately.* | **with the ~** ◇ *Joan came in with the ~ that a pay rise had been agreed.* | **~ about** ◇ *I'm not interested in ~ about celebrities.* | **~ from** ◇ *And now with ~ from the Games, over to our Olympic correspondent.* | **~ of** ◇ *~ of fresh killings* | **~ on** ◇ *Is there any ~ on the car bomb attack?* | **~ to** ◇ *It was ~ to me that they were married.*

2 the news on TV or radio

ADJ. **radio, television, TV** | **evening, lunchtime** (*BrE*) | **ten o'clock, etc.** | **nightly** | **prime-time** (*esp. AmE*) | **local, national**

VERB + THE NEWS **hear, listen to, see, watch** | **turn on** | **broadcast** | **read** ◇ *The ~ is read by Katie Daly.*

PREP. **in the ~** ◇ *Our school was mentioned in the ~.* | **on the ~** ◇ *I heard it on the evening ~.*

news conference (*esp. AmE*) noun → See also PRESS CONFERENCE

ADJ. **formal** | **presidential** | **televised** | **prime-time** | **post-game, post-summit, etc.**

VERB + NEWS CONFERENCE **call** | **arrange, organize, plan** | **give, hold** | **tell** ◇ *The chairman told a ~ of the upcoming merger.*

PREP. **at a/the ~** ◇ *The proposed changes were outlined at a ~.* | **during a/the ~, in a/the ~** ◇ *The announcement was made in a ~ at the airport.*

newspaper noun

ADJ. **daily, evening** (*esp. BrE*), **morning, Sunday, weekly** | **today's, yesterday's** | **left-wing, right-wing** | **conservative, liberal** | **independent, state-run** | **local, national, provincial** (*esp. BrE*), **regional** | **prestigious, quality, reputable** (*esp. BrE*), **respectable** | **broadsheet** (*esp. BrE*), **tabloid** | **popular** | **leading, major, prominent** | **influential** | **mainstream** | **financial** | **folded, rolled-up** | **online** | **campus** (*esp. AmE*), **college, school, student**

...OF NEWSPAPER **copy** ◇ *Do you have a copy of yesterday's ~?* | **edition** ◇ *today's edition of the ~*

VERB + NEWSPAPER **buy, get, take** (*BrE, formal*) ◇ *Which ~ do you buy?* ◇ *Do you take a daily ~?* | **deliver** | **open** | **flick through** (*esp. BrE*), **flip through** (*AmE*), **peruse** (*formal*), **read, scan, scour** | **print, produce, publish** | **launch** ◇ *He launched a weekly ~ called 'The Challenge'.* | **edit, write for, write in** ◇ *Savage, writing in an Auckland ~, quotes an eminent academic.* | **own, run** ◇ *~s owned by the Tribune Company* | **appear in** ◇ *Her article appeared in the Saturday ~.* | **get into** | **sue** ◇ *She sued the ~ for publishing photos of her on the beach.*

NEWSPAPER + VERB **come out** ◇ *The ~ comes out every Saturday.* | **print sth, publish sth, report sth, reveal sth** | **carry sth, feature sth** ◇ *The ~ carried advertisements for several products.* | **cite sth, quote sb** | **announce sth, claim sth, declare sth** | **speculate sth** ◇ *The ~s speculated that the star was about to propose to his girlfriend.*

NEWSPAPER + NOUN **page** | **account, advertisement, article, cartoon, classifieds, column, coverage, editorial, interview, obituary, op-ed** (*AmE*), **poll, story** | **headline** | **clipping, cutting** (*BrE*) | **insert, supplement** | **baron** (*esp. BrE*), **executive, magnate, owner, proprietor** (*esp. BrE*), **tycoon** (*esp. BrE*) | **publisher** | **cartoonist, columnist, correspondent, critic, editor, journalist, photographer, reporter, writer** | **reader** | **circulation, readership** | **office** | **business, industry** | **group** ◇ *The company is a strong contender in the race for the Scottish ~ group.* | **kiosk, stand** | **seller** (*BrE*), **vendor**

PREP. **in a/the ~** ◇ *an article in a local ~* | **on a/the ~** ◇ *She got a job on a national ~.*

nice adj.

VERBS **be, feel, look, seem, smell, sound, taste** ◇ *I felt ~ and warm.* ◇ *That bread smells ~.* ◇ *His mother sounded very ~ on the phone.* | **make sth** ◇ *I cleaned the room to make it ~ for the others when they came home.*

ADV. **extremely, fairly, very, etc.** | **awfully, exceptionally, incredibly, terribly** (*esp. BrE*) ◇ *an awfully ~ man* | **perfectly, thoroughly** ◇ *I'm sure she's perfectly ~ really.* |

genuinely, truly | **not particularly** ◇ *It had not been a particularly ~ experience.* | **enough** ◇ *Some of the boys were ~ enough, but she didn't want to go out with them.*

PREP. **about** ◇ *He was incredibly ~ about it, though I am sure it caused him a lot of trouble.* | **for** ◇ *It's ~ for her to get out more.* | **to** ◇ *Can't you be ~ to each other for once?*

PHRASES **~ little** ◇ *It's a ~ little place you have here.*

niche noun

ADJ. **comfortable** | **distinctive, particular, special, specific, unique** | **little, small** ◇ *He had found his own little ~ in life.* | **growing** | **important** | **lucrative, profitable** | **market** | **ecological, environmental**

VERB + NICHE **have** ◇ *Each animal has its ecological ~.* | **find, identify, see, spot** ◇ *He saw a ~ in the market and exploited it.* | **carve out, create, develop, establish** ◇ *She's carved out quite a ~ for herself in fashion design.* | **fill, occupy** | **fit, serve** | **exploit**

NICHE + NOUN **market, marketing** | **business** | **audience** ◇ *a film intended for a ~ audience* | **film, magazine, product, vehicle, etc.**

PREP. **in a/the ~, into a/the ~** ◇ *Mammals moved into the ~ left vacant by the disappearance of the dinosaurs.* | **~ for** ◇ *There's a ~ for a small stylish car.* | **~ in** ◇ *women who dared question their ~ in society*

PHRASES **a ~ in the market**

nickname noun

ADJ. **childhood** | **affectionate** | **cute** (*esp. AmE*) | **little** (*esp. AmE*)

VERB + NICKNAME **have, use** ◇ *He used the ~ 'Brutus'.* | **give sb** | **acquire, gain, get** ◇ *He got his ~ 'Ash' from his heavy smoking.* | **earn (sb)** | **live up to** ◇ *Knockout Nat lived up to his ~.* | **hate**

NICKNAME + VERB **stick** ◇ *He got his ~ when he was at school and it stuck for the rest of his life.*

PREP. **~ for** ◇ *Their ~ for the club was 'Muscle Alley'.*

PHRASES **hence her/his ~** ◇ *He worked in a garage—hence his ~ 'Oily'.*

nicotine noun

VERB + NICOTINE **be addicted to, be dependent on** | **be stained with**

NICOTINE + NOUN **addiction, craving, dependence** | **use** | **exposure** | **addict** | **withdrawal** | **gum, inhaler, patch, replacement, spray** ◇ *~ replacement therapy* | **stain** ◇ *The ~ stains on his fingers told me he was under stress.*

night noun

1 when it is dark and most people sleep

ADJ. **last, tomorrow** | **the next, the previous** | **the entire, the whole** | **Friday, Saturday, etc.** | **early, late** ◇ *I think I'll have an early ~ (= go to bed early).* | **long** | **winter, etc.** | **bad, fitful, restless, rough, sleepless** | **restful** | **lonely** | **black, dark, moonless, pitch-black** | **clear, moonlit, starlit, starry** | **beautiful** | **cloudy** | **chilly, cold, foggy, freezing, rainy, snowy, stormy** | **humid, muggy, warm** | **wedding**

VERB + NIGHT **have** | **spend** ◇ *They spent the ~ in a hotel.* | **stay** ◇ *Ask your mother if you can stay the ~.*

NIGHT + VERB **come, fall** ◇ *The ~ fell quickly.* | **progress, wear on** ◇ *As the ~ wore on, it grew colder.*

NIGHT + NOUN **air, sky** | **breeze** | **duty, patrol, shift** | **sight, vision** | **sweats, terrors**

PREP. **at ~** ◇ *I lie awake at ~ worrying.* | **by ~** ◇ *Paris by ~* | **during the ~, in the ~** ◇ *I woke in the ~.* | **for a/the ~, on Friday, etc. ~, per ~** ◇ *The hotel costs €265 per person per ~.* | **through the ~, throughout the ~**

PHRASES **all ~ long** | **at this time of ~** | **day and ~, ~ and day** (= all the time) | **a good night's sleep** | **good ~** ◇ *She kissed him good ~.* | **in the dead of ~** (= in the middle of the night) | **morning, noon and ~** (= all the time)

2 time between late afternoon and when you go to bed

ADJ. **last, tomorrow** | **Friday, Saturday, etc.** | **weekday** | **the other** ◇ *I saw her the other ~ (= a few nights ago).* | **the next, the previous** | **lonely** ◇ *He spent another lonely ~ in front of the television.* | **busy, eventful** | **quiet** ◇ *He had plans to spend a quiet ~ at home.* | **fateful** ◇ *One fateful ~ he was involved in an accident that changed his life forever.*
NIGHT + NOUN **school**
PREP. **at ~** ◇ *She doesn't like to walk home late at ~.* | **by ~** | **on Friday, etc. ~**

3 evening when a special event happens

ADJ. **first, opening** | **last** ◇ *the last ~ of the play's run* | **big, eventful, fun, great, memorable** | **drunken** ◇ *a drunken ~ of partying* | **dance, election, karaoke, prom** (*AmE*), **quiz** (*esp. BrE*) | **Halloween**
PHRASES **make a ~ of it** ◇ *They decided to make a ~ of it and went on to a club.* | **a ~ out** ◇ *I was getting myself ready for a ~ out.* ◇ *a girls' ~ out*

nightclub noun → See also CLUB

ADJ. **hot** (*AmE*), **popular, top** (*BrE*) ◇ *the hottest ~ in town* ◇ *a top London ~* | **local** | **gay**
VERB + NIGHTCLUB **go to** | **own**
NIGHTCLUB + NOUN **bouncer** (*esp. BrE*), **owner, singer, staff** (*esp. BrE*) | **act** | **scene** ◇ *We all grew out of the ~ scene.*
PREP. **at a/the ~** ◇ *She's performing at a ~ in Paris.* | **in a/the ~** ◇ *He was murdered in a Bangkok ~.*

nightmare noun

1 bad dream

ADJ. **awful, horrible, terrible, terrifying** | **vivid** | **recurring**
VERB + NIGHTMARE **have, suffer, suffer from** | **wake from, wake up from** | **give sb** ◇ *The movie gave me ~s.* | **haunt** ◇ *The faces of all the people he had killed haunted his ~s.*
NIGHTMARE + VERB **haunt sb, plague sb**
PREP. **~ about** ◇ *I have ~s about drowning.*

2 bad/feared experience

ADJ. **awful, horrible, real, terrible** | **absolute, complete, total** | **ultimate, worst** ◇ *Losing a child is my worst ~.* | **personal** | **living** ◇ *The refugees had survived a living ~.* | **long** | **administrative, bureaucratic, financial** (*esp. BrE*), **logistical, etc.**
VERB + NIGHTMARE **endure, face, live, suffer, survive** | **become, prove** (*esp. BrE*), **turn into** ◇ *Their dream of living in the country turned into a ~.* | **create** | **escape, escape from** | **relive**
NIGHTMARE + VERB **be over** | **come true**
NIGHTMARE + NOUN **scenario, vision** ◇ *the ~ scenario of mass unemployment* ◇ *The writer evokes a ~ vision of a future on a polluted planet.* | **world** | **journey** (*esp. BrE*)

nipple noun

ADJ. **erect, hard, swollen** | **sensitive, sore** | **pierced**
VERB + NIPPLE **pinch** | **suck** | **squeeze**
NIPPLE + VERB **harden**

nod noun

ADJ. **brief, little, quick, slight, small** | **curt, perfunctory, terse** ◇ *He dismissed them with a curt ~.* | **approving, satisfied** ◇ *She inspected my work and gave a satisfied ~.* | **reassuring** | **knowing** | **passing** (*figurative*) ◇ *The house is white, in a passing ~ to Greek tradition.*
VERB + NOD **give (sb)** ◇ *My teacher gave me a ~ of reassurance and I began.* | **get, receive** ◇ *He's ready to play and just waiting to get the ~ from (= be approved by) the coach.* | **exchange** | **wait for**
PREP. **at a ~, with a ~** | **~ from** ◇ *At a ~ from Lawton, he gently turned the handle.* | **~ in the direction of, ~ of** ◇ *a ~ of approval* | **~ to, ~ towards/toward** ◇ *'I couldn't have done this alone,' he said with a ~ towards/toward his partner.*

PHRASES **a ~ of sb's/the head** ◇ *She answered with a slight ~ of the head.*

nod verb

ADV. **just, merely, only, simply** ◇ *Ashamed, I could only ~.* | **emphatically, furiously, vigorously** ◇ *'That's exactly it,' she said, nodding vigorously.* | **gently** ◇ *She nodded gently to herself.* | **almost imperceptibly, slightly** | **slowly** | **quickly** | **briefly, briskly, curtly, stiffly** ◇ *He nodded curtly and walked away.* | **dumbly, mutely, silently, wordlessly** ◇ *She could not speak but just nodded mutely.* | **absently, absent-mindedly, vaguely** ◇ *He nodded absently, his mind obviously on other things.* | **politely, respectfully** | **eagerly, happily** | **knowingly, sympathetically, understandingly** | **apprecia-tively, approvingly, encouragingly, enthusiastically, gratefully** | **hesitantly, reluctantly** | **meekly, weakly** | **grimly** | **glumly, miserably, sadly** | **gravely, sagely, seriously, solemnly, thoughtfully** ◇ *She nodded sagely as she listened.*
PREP. **at** ◇ *They nodded at us, so we nodded back.* | **in** ◇ *She nodded in agreement.* | **to** ◇ *She nodded to Duncan as she left.* | **towards/toward** ◇ *'Let's go!' he said, nodding towards/toward the door.* | **with** ◇ *He nodded with satisfaction.*

noise noun

ADJ. **deafening, loud** | **awful, horrible, terrible** | **faint, low, slight, small** ◇ *The slightest ~ will wake him.* | **sudden** | **funny, strange** | **background** ◇ *There was constant back-ground ~ from the road.* | **constant, incessant** | **banging, buzzing, clicking, hissing, etc.** | **muffled** | **aircraft, engine, traffic** | **ambient, white** | **rude** (*esp. BrE*) ◇ *One of the children made a rude ~.*
VERB + NOISE **create, emit, generate, let out, make, produce** ◇ *the ~ created by aircraft* ◇ *She was making a lot of ~.* | **hear, listen to** ◇ *We could hear funny little sucking ~s.* | **block out, drown out, reduce** ◇ *Wood is used to deaden the ~.* | **complain about**
NOISE + VERB **come from sth** ◇ *There were strange ~s coming from the kitchen.* | **become louder, get louder, grow louder, increase** | **die away, die down, fade, fade away** ◇ *The deafening ~ of the machine died away to a rumble.*
NOISE + NOUN **level** | **pollution** | **reduction**
PREP. **above the ~, over the ~** ◇ *We had to shout over the ~ of the traffic.* | **~ from** ◇ *the ~ from the engine room*

noisy adj.

VERBS **be** | **become, get, grow** ◇ *The party was starting to get a little ~.*
ADV. **extremely, fairly, very, etc.** | **particularly, terribly** | **a little, slightly, etc.**

nominate verb

ADV. **formally, officially**
VERB + NOMINATE **ask sb to, invite sb to** ◇ *Ten critics were asked to ~ their Book of the Year.*
PREP. **as** ◇ *He has now been formally ~d as presidential candidate.* | **for** ◇ *She was ~d for a special award.* | **to** ◇ *He has been ~d to the committee.*
PHRASES **the power to ~ sb, the right to ~ sb**

nomination noun

ADJ. **presidential** | **party** | **Democratic, Republican** | **gubernatorial** (*AmE*) | **judicial** (*AmE*) | **Grammy, Oscar, etc.**
VERB + NOMINATION **secure, win** | **stand for** ◇ *She is standing for the Democratic Party presidential ~.* | **accept** | **block, filibuster** (*AmE*), **oppose** | **withdraw** | **support** | **invite** ◇ *Nominations are invited for the post of party chairman.* | **seek** ◇ *She is seeking ~ as a candidate in the elections.*
NOMINATION + NOUN **form, paper** (*esp. BrE*) | **process** | **battle, fight** (*both esp. AmE*)
PREP. **~ as** ◇ *She has withdrawn her ~ as chairman.* | **~ for** ◇ *his ~ for the Best Actor award* | **~ to** ◇ *support for his ~ to the Supreme Court*

nominee noun

ADJ. presidential | Democratic, Republican | Grammy, Oscar, etc.
VERB + NOMINEE choose, select | appoint, confirm | support | block, filibuster (AmE), oppose
PREP. ~ for ◊ the ~s for Best Director

nonchalance noun

VERB + NONCHALANCE affect, feign ◊ She shrugged, feigning ~.
PREP. with ~ ◊ He declined the offer with cool ~.
PHRASES an air of ~ ◊ 'Oh, by the way…' she started, with a false air of ~.

non-existent adj.

VERBS be | become ◊ Typewriters have become almost ~ in offices.
ADV. completely ◊ The hotel turned out to be completely ~. | basically | almost, nearly, practically, virtually ◊ Crime is almost ~ in these communities.

nonsense noun

ADJ. absolute, arrant (old-fashioned), complete, pure, sheer, total, utter ◊ Most of his theories are arrant ~. | superstitious ◊ You don't believe that superstitious ~, do you?
VERB + NONSENSE spout, talk ◊ Don't talk ~! | put up with, stand for ◊ I'm not going to stand for any more of this ~. | stop ◊ Just stop this ~ of refusing to talk to anybody. | believe
PREP. ~ about ◊ What's all this ~ about you giving up your job?
PHRASES a load of ~, a lot of ~ ◊ People are talking a lot of ~ about him being the new Michael Jordan. | make a ~ of sth (BrE), make ~ of sth ◊ This decision makes ~ of all our hard work.

noon noun

ADJ. 12 ◊ The football action starts at 12 ~. | high ◊ the glaring light of high ~
PREP. around ~, at ~, by ~, till ~, until ~
PHRASES morning, ~ and night (= all the time)

noose noun

ADJ. hangman's
VERB + NOOSE fasten, tie ◊ They tied a ~ around her neck. | pull, tighten | make
NOOSE + VERB tighten
PREP. in a/the ~, into a/the ~ ◊ He put his head into the ~. | ~ around, ~ round (esp. BrE) ◊ The ~ tightened around her neck.

norm noun

ADJ. accepted, established | ethical, moral | cultural, social, societal | community, gender, group, peer
VERB + NORM be, become ◊ Small families are the ~ nowadays. | conform to ◊ Their appearance conforms to the group ~. | break from, challenge | be different from, deviate from, differ from, violate
PREP. above the ~, below the ~, over the ~ ◊ They want to discourage pay settlements over the ~. | ~ for ◊ On-screen editing has become the ~ for all student work. | ~ of ◊ accepted ~s of international law
PHRASES a departure from the ~, a deviation from the ~, an exception to the ~ ◊ The new design is a departure from the ~. | the ~ rather than the exception ◊ In these areas poverty is the ~ rather than the exception. | out of the ~ (esp. AmE) ◊ I saw nothing out of the ~.

normal noun

VERB + NORMAL be back to, go back to, return to ◊ After a week of festivities, life returned to ~.
PREP. above ~ ◊ The rainfall has been above ~ for this time of year. | below ~ ◊ Sales to December were well below ~. | near ~ ◊ His pulse rate had slowed to somewhere near ~.

normal adj.

VERBS be | become | feel | appear, look, seem | consider sth, regard sth as, view sth as ◊ It is now regarded as ~ for women to work outside the home.
ADV. very | completely, entirely (esp. BrE), perfectly, quite, totally ◊ It started out as a perfectly ~ day. | fairly, pretty ◊ I'd say it was pretty ~ to be upset if your house burned down. | relatively | apparently, seemingly
PREP. for ◊ The temperature is ~ for spring.
PHRASES as ~ ◊ First work out the answers as ~. | in the ~ way ◊ Go for your check-ups in the ~ way until you are six months pregnant. | in ~ circumstances, under ~ circumstances ◊ Under ~ circumstances Martin would probably have gone to college. | sb's ~ self ◊ Mandy doesn't seem her ~ self today.

normality (also **normalcy** esp. in AmE) noun

VERB + NORMALITY/NORMALCY restore, return to
PHRASES a return to ~ ◊ A complete return to ~ may take weeks. | a semblance of ~, some semblance of ~ ◊ By now any semblance of ~ had disappeared.

north noun

ADJ. magnetic, true | frozen ◊ the white expanses of the frozen ~
→ Note at DIRECTION (for more collocates)

nose noun

ADJ. big, bulbous, huge, large, long, prominent, strong | little, small, tiny | straight | aquiline, Grecian, Roman | crooked, hooked | pug (AmE), snub, turned-up, upturned | button, flat | pointed, sharp ◊ The sharp ~ and thin lips gave his face a very harsh look. | narrow, thin ◊ She had dark eyes and a long narrow ~. | aristocratic | cute, perfect | red, shiny ◊ She dressed up as a clown with a white face and red ~. | blocked, stuffy (esp. AmE) | runny, snotty (informal) ◊ a child with a runny ~ | bleeding, bloodied, bloody, broken, swollen | wet ◊ The dog pushed its wet ~ into my palm. | sensitive ◊ Cats have very sensitive ~s and rely heavily on scent markings. | pierced | fake (AmE), false ◊ She had to wear a false ~ for the role.
VERB + NOSE breathe through | blow, wipe | pick, rub, scratch | pinch | tap ◊ He tapped his ~ in a knowing gesture. | crinkle (esp. AmE), wrinkle ◊ She wrinkled her ~ as if she had just smelled a bad smell. | break
NOSE + VERB wrinkle ◊ His ~ wrinkled with distaste. | twitch | run ◊ She was weeping loudly and her ~ was running. | bleed
NOSE + NOUN job (informal) ◊ She wasn't happy with her appearance so she had a ~ job. | ring | bleed (usually nosebleed)
PREP. through the ~ ◊ Breathe in through your ~ and out through your mouth. | up your ~ ◊ The boy sat there with his finger up his ~.
PHRASES the bridge of the ~ ◊ He pushed his glasses up the bridge of his ~. | with your ~ in the air (often figurative) ◊ She walked in with her ~ in the air, ignoring everyone. | look down your ~ at sb (figurative) ◊ They tend to look down their ~s at people who drive small cars. | poke your ~ in/ into sth, stick your ~ in/into sth (both figurative) ◊ Stop poking your ~ into my business! | press your ~ against sth ◊ Charlie pressed his ~ against the window. | thumb your ~ at sb/sth (figurative) ◊ They thumb their ~s at all of our traditions. | turn up your ~ at sth (figurative) ◊ The children turn up their ~s at almost everything I cook.

nostalgia noun

ADJ. wistful ◊ She remembers her life as a singer with a certain wistful ~. | pure ◊ an evening of pure ~ | 80s, 90s, etc.
… OF NOSTALGIA wave ◊ A wave of ~ came over him.
VERB + NOSTALGIA feel ◊ He thought back to his time as a student and felt no ~ for any of it. | evoke | indulge in, wallow in

NOSTALGIA + NOUN **buff** ◇ *Nostalgia buffs gathered for the auction.* | **trip** ◇ *The college reunion was a great ~ trip.*
PREP. **with ~** ◇ *I remember it with great ~.* | **~ for** ◇ *She felt great ~ for the old way of life.*
PHRASES **a feeling of ~, a sense of ~**

nostril noun

VERB + NOSTRIL **fill** ◇ *The stench of the cellar filled my ~s.*
NOSTRIL + VERB **flare**
NOSTRIL + NOUN **hair**
PREP. **in your ~s** ◇ *The smell of decay lingered in her ~s.* | **through your ~s** ◇ *She drew on the cigarette and blew smoke through her ~s.*

notable adj.

VERBS **be**
ADV. **especially, particularly**
PREP. **for** ◇ *The birds are ~ for their rarity.*

note noun

1 short letter

ADJ. **brief, little, quick, short** ◇ *Just a quick ~ to wish you luck.* | **handwritten, scribbled** | **cover** (*AmE*), **covering** (*BrE*), **credit, delivery** (*BrE*), **love, promissory, ransom, sick** (*BrE*), **suicide, thank-you** | **Post-it**™, **sticky** (*esp. AmE*) ◇ *Never write your password on a sticky ~!* | **crumpled**
VERB + NOTE **scribble (sb), write (sb)** | **send (sb)** | **leave (sb)** ◇ *She left me a ~ to say my dinner was in the oven.* | **pass** ◇ *I saw you two passing ~s during class.* | **sign**
PHRASES **a ~ of thanks**

2 (often **notes**) words that you write down quickly

ADJ. **brief** | **copious, detailed, extensive** | **lecture** | **field** | **case, clinical** (*esp. BrE*), **medical** (*esp. BrE*)
VERB + NOTE **jot down, keep, make, take** ◇ *She kept detailed ~s of her travels.* | **go through, look through, read through, sift through** | **compare** (*usually figurative*) ◇ *Let's compare ~s on our experiences.*
PREP. **~ of** ◇ *I've made a ~ of the book's title.* | **~ on** ◇ *The booklet has full ~s on each artist.*
PHRASES **make a mental ~ (of sth/to do sth)** ◇ *She made a mental ~ to call them in the morning.*

3 (usually **notes**) extra piece of information

ADJ. **detailed, extensive** | **explanatory, helpful, informative** | **interesting** | **introductory** | **marginal, side** | **biographical** | **booklet, liner, sleeve** (*BrE*) | **briefing** (*esp. BrE*), **programme/program**

4 (*esp. BrE*) piece of paper money → See also BILL

ADJ. **five-pound, ten-euro, etc.** | **crumpled**
... OF NOTES **bundle, roll, wad** ◇ *a thick wad of ~s*

5 single musical sound

ADJ. **high, top** ◇ *She's a little wobbly on the top ~s.* | **low** | **right** | **wrong** | **musical** | **dissonant** | **whole, half, quarter, eighth, etc.** (*all AmE*)
VERB + NOTE **play, sing** | **hit, strike** | **hold**

6 quality/feeling

ADJ. **brighter, cheerful, happier, hopeful, lighter, optimistic, positive, upbeat** ◇ *On a brighter note…* | **related, unrelated** ◇ *On a completely unrelated note…* | **discordant, false, sad, sombre/somber, sour** | **faint** ◇ *a faint ~ of bitterness in his voice* | **serious** | **right** ◇ *His opening remarks struck the right ~.* | **odd** | **cautionary, warning** ◇ *He sounded a cautionary ~.* | **personal**
VERB + NOTE **hit, sound, strike** | **inject, introduce** ◇ *His remarks injected a ~ of levity into the proceedings.* | **detect** ◇ *I detected a faint ~ of weariness in his voice.* | **end on** ◇ *The conference ended on an optimistic ~.*
NOTE + VERB **creep into sb's voice, enter sb's voice**
PREP. **~ of** ◇ *A ~ of suspicion entered his voice.*
PHRASES **a ~ in sb's voice** ◇ *There was a sad ~ in her voice.*

7 notice/attention

ADJ. **careful**
VERB + NOTE **take** ◇ *He took careful ~ of the suspicious-looking man in the corner of the bar.*
PHRASES **worthy of ~** ◇ *The sculptures are worthy of ~.*

note verb

ADV. **carefully** | **briefly, in passing** ◇ *He ~d in passing that the government's record on unemployment was not very good.* | **duly** ◇ *Your objections have been duly ~d.* | **above, already, earlier, previously** ◇ *These policies, as ~d above, are not always successful.* | **approvingly** | **ruefully** | **drily, pointedly, wryly**
VERB + NOTE **should** ◇ *Visitors should ~ that the tower is not open to the public.* | **be important to** | **be interesting to** | **be pleased to** ◇ *I was pleased to ~ that my name had been spelled correctly for once.*
PHRASES **be worth noting** ◇ *There are a few points here that are worth noting.* | **it must be ~d that…, it should be ~d that…** | **a point to ~** ◇ *There are two other points to ~ from this graph.*

notebook noun

ADJ. **bound, leather-bound, spiral, spiral-bound** | **loose-leaf** | **pocket** | **reporter's** | **English, math, science, etc.** (*all AmE*) | **lab** (*informal*), **laboratory** | **blank** | **battered, tattered**
VERB + NOTEBOOK **jot sth (down) in, record sth in, scribble (sth) in, write sth (down) in** | **get out, pull out, take out** ◇ *She drew a ~ from her bag.* | **tear a page from, tear a sheet from** | **fill** | **carry** | **keep** ◇ *She kept a ~ during the trip.*
NOTEBOOK + NOUN **paper** (*esp. AmE*) | **computer**
PREP. **in a/your ~**
PHRASES **an entry in a ~**

noted adj.

VERBS **be** | **become**
ADV. **particularly**
PREP. **for** ◇ *The lake is also ~ for its bird population.*

noteworthy adj.

VERBS **be, seem** | **make sth** ◇ *the thing that makes this era so ~* | **consider sth, deem sth** ◇ *His reign has never been considered particularly ~.*
ADV. **especially, particularly**
PREP. **for** ◇ *The bridge is ~ for its sheer size.*

notice noun

1 attention

ADJ. **public** ◇ *The disease came to public ~ in the 80s.*
VERB + NOTICE **take** ◇ *Take no ~ of what you read in the papers.* | **catch** (*AmE*) ◇ *I caught ~ of a small scrap of paper on my desk.* | **come to** ◇ *Normally such matters would not come to my ~.* | **bring to** | **attract** ◇ *The change was too subtle to attract much ~.* | **escape** ◇ *It won't have escaped your ~ that I'm feeling rather pleased with myself.*

2 written statement

ADJ. **warning**
VERB + NOTICE **issue, place, post, put up** ◇ *The company has issued warning ~s saying that all water should be boiled.* | **take down** | **read, see**
NOTICE + VERB **appear, go up** ◇ *The ~ about his resignation went up this morning.* | **say sth, tell sb sth**
PREP. **~ about** ◇ *There are ~s about where to park.*

3 information given in advance

ADJ. **eviction** | **written** | **advance, prior** | **short** | **reasonable**
VERB + NOTICE **file** (*esp. AmE*), **give (sb), hand in your** ◇ *She's given ~ that she intends to leave.* | **serve (sb with)** ◇ *The tenants could soon be served with eviction ~s.* ◇ *This new law serves ~ that criminals will not go unpunished.* (*figurative*) | **send** | **have, receive** | **need, require** ◇ *The bank requires three days' ~.*
PREP. **without ~** ◇ *They cut off the electricity without ~.* | **~ of**

◇ *A landlord must give reasonable ~ of his intention to inspect the property.*
PHRASES **at a moment's ~ ◇** *The team is ready to go anywhere in the world at a moment's ~.* | **at short ~** (*esp. BrE*), **on short ~** (*AmE*) ◇ *It's the best we can do at/on such short ~.* | **~ to quit** ◇ *His landlord gave him two months' ~ to quit.*

notice *verb*

ADV. **not even** ◇ *My mother probably won't even ~ I'm gone.* | **not really** ◇ *Nobody really ~d the changes.* | **barely, hardly, scarcely** (*esp. BrE*) | **(only) just** ◇ *I must go! I've only just ~d how late it is.* | **suddenly** | **at once, immediately, instantly** ◇ *He ~d at once that something was wrong.* | **quickly, soon** | **eventually, finally**
VERB + NOTICE **fail to** | **not appear to, not seem to** ◇ *He didn't seem to ~ her.* | **pretend not to**
PHRASES **can't help but ~ sth, can't help noticing sth** ◇ *You couldn't help noticing how his eyes kept following her.* | **the first thing I, he, etc. ~d** ◇ *The first thing I ~d about him was his eyes.*

noticeable *adj.*

VERBS **be** | **become**
ADV. **extremely, fairly, very, etc.** | **especially, particularly** | **barely, hardly** | **immediately** ◇ *The smell was immediately ~ when you walked in the front door.* | **easily**
PREP. **in** ◇ *These changes are more ~ in women than in men.* | **to** ◇ *This may not be ~ to people from outside New York.*

notification *noun*

ADJ. **formal, official** | **email, written** | **immediate** | **advance, prior** | **parental** (*esp. AmE*) ◇ *The drugs were prescribed without parental ~.*
VERB + NOTIFICATION **have, receive** | **give (sb), send (sb)**
PREP. **without ~** ◇ *The police are entitled to inspect the premises without ~.* | **~ of** ◇ *They failed to give ~ of their intention to demolish the building.*

notify *verb*

ADV. **forthwith** (*BrE*), **immediately, promptly** | **in advance** | **by email, via email** | **by mail** (*esp. AmE*), **by post** (*BrE*), **in writing** | **formally, officially** | **automatically**
VERB + NOTIFY **be obliged to, be required to, must, should** ◇ *If you see anything suspicious you should ~ the police immediately.* | **fail to**
PREP. **of** ◇ *The family had been notified of the department's decision.* | **to** (*esp. BrE*) ◇ *Changes must be notified to the chairman.*

notion *noun*

ADJ. **absurd, foolish, misguided, ridiculous, silly** | **foggiest, vague** ◇ *I haven't the foggiest ~ of how to get there.* | **romantic** | **accepted, common, conventional, popular, traditional** | **preconceived** | **basic, general** ◇ *There seems to be a general ~ that nothing can be done about the problem.* | **simple, simplistic** | **false**
VERB + NOTION **have** ◇ *He has a very vague ~ of who his customers are.* | **challenge, debunk, dismiss, dispel** ◇ *We must dispel this ~ that you can rely on the state for everything.* | **accept, entertain** ◇ *They refused to entertain the ~.* | **reinforce, support**
PREP. **~ of** ◇ *They have come to reject the traditional ~ of womanhood.*

notoriety *noun*

ADJ. **a certain, considerable** | **international, public**
VERB + NOTORIETY **have** | **achieve, earn, gain** ◇ *He achieved sudden ~ when the details of his private life were revealed.* | **bring**
PREP. **~ for** ◇ *This make of car has a certain ~ for rust problems.*

noun *noun*

ADJ. **plural, singular** ◇ *'Sheep' is both a singular and a plural ~.* | **countable** | **mass, uncountable** | **feminine, masculine, neuter** ◇ *Most feminine ~s in Polish end in the letter 'a'.*

| **common, proper** ◇ *Proper ~s begin with a capital letter.* | **abstract, concrete** ◇ *'Happiness' is an abstract ~.* ◇ *'Car' is a concrete ~.* | **collective** ◇ *'Flock' is a collective ~.*
VERB + NOUN **decline, inflect** ◇ *English ~s are not usually inflected.* | **modify, qualify** ◇ *a prepositional phrase qualifying a ~* | **follow** ◇ *The ~ is followed by an intransitive verb.* | **precede** ◇ *an adjective preceding the ~*
NOUN + VERB **end in sth** ◇ *Most English plural ~s end in an 's'.* | **follow sth** | **precede sth**
NOUN + NOUN **class, phrase**

nourish *verb*

PHRASES **properly ~ed, well ~ed** ◇ *Patients recover quickly if they are well ~ed.*

nourishment *noun*

ADJ. **adequate, proper** ◇ *lack of adequate ~* | **emotional, intellectual, spiritual**
VERB + NOURISHMENT **need** | **draw, get, receive, take** ◇ *Every animal in the food chain draws ~ from other animals or plants.* | **deprive sb/sth of, provide (sb/sth with)**

novel *noun*

ADJ. **hardback, hardcover** (*esp. AmE*), **paperback** | **debut** | **first, second, etc.** ◇ *a prize for the best first ~ of the year* | **latest, new, recent** | **unfinished, unpublished** | **good, great** ◇ *One day I'm going to write the great American ~.* | **original** | **acclaimed** ◇ *his critically acclaimed ~* | **famous** | **classic** | **literary** | **best-selling, popular** | **dime** (*AmE, old-fashioned*), **pulp, trashy** | **contemporary, modern** | **19th-century, Victorian** | **adult, children's** | **autobiographical** | **adventure, comic, epic, epistolary, graphic, historical, romantic, satirical** | **fantasy, gothic, horror, sci-fi, science-fiction** | **crime, detective, mystery, spy**
...OF A NOVEL **copy** ◇ *I took a copy of a Graham Greene ~ on the train with me.*
VERB + NOVEL **produce, write** | **publish** | **read** | **complete, finish** ◇ *She completed her first ~ at the age of 53.* | **inspire** ◇ *the events that inspired the ~* | **translate** | **adapt** ◇ *the process of adapting the ~ for television* | **review**
NOVEL + VERB **be based on sth** ◇ *The ~ was based on a true life story.* | **be set, take place** ◇ *The ~ was set in a small town in France.*
PREP. **~ about** ◇ *a ~ about growing up*

novel *adj.*

VERBS **be, sound** ◇ *The plan sounded rather ~.*
ADV. **extremely, fairly, very, etc.** | **completely, totally, etc.** | **relatively** | **essentially**

novelist *noun*

ADJ. **great, leading** (*esp. BrE*) ◇ *one of the country's greatest contemporary ~s* | **acclaimed, famous** | **best-selling, popular** ◇ *his ambition to become a best-selling ~* | **aspiring** | **prolific** (*esp. BrE*) | **contemporary** | **19th-century, Victorian** | **crime, graphic, historical, mystery, romance, romantic**
NOVELIST + VERB **write sth** ◇ *A prolific ~, she wrote more than forty books.*

novelty *noun*

ADJ. **great** ◇ *This tropical fruit is still a great ~ in the north.* | **sheer** ◇ *The sheer ~ of the band's performance won them many fans.*
NOVELTY + VERB **wear off** ◇ *The ~ of her new job soon wore off.*
NOVELTY + NOUN **value** ◇ *A trip down a mine has great ~ value for most people.*
PHRASES **be something of a ~** ◇ *At that time, recorded sound was still something of a ~.*

November *noun* → Note at MONTH

novice *noun*

ADJ. **complete, total** | **young** | **political**
NOVICE + NOUN **user** ◇ *The on-screen manual shows the ~ user the basics of the program.* | **pilot, sailor, teacher, etc.**
PREP. **~ at** ◇ *I'm still a ~ at the sport.* | **~ in** ◇ *a ~ in politics*

nuance *noun*

ADJ. **fine, little, slight, subtle** ◇ *A baby is sensitive to the slightest ~s in its mother's voice.* ◇ *the painting's subtle ~s of light and dark* | **expressive** | **emotional** | **cultural, social** ◇ *It took a while to get used to the social ~s of the office.*
VERB + NUANCE **appreciate, understand** ◇ *Spectators may not understand all the ~s of the game.* | **capture**

nude *adj.*

VERBS **be, lie, sit, stand** ◇ *She was lying ~ on a towel.* | **appear, pose** ◇ *He refused to appear ~ in the movie.*
ADV. **completely, totally** | **nearly**

nudge *noun*

ADJ. **gentle, little, slight**
VERB + NUDGE **give sb** ◇ *She gave me a gentle ~ in the ribs to tell me to shut up.* | **feel**

nudge *verb*

ADV. **gently, playfully**
PHRASES **~ sb in the ribs** ◇ *She ~d him playfully in the ribs.*

nuisance *noun*

ADJ. **great, real** | **minor** | **public** ◇ *He was charged with committing a public ~.*
PREP. **~ to** ◇ *I don't want to be a ~ to you.*
PHRASES **make a ~ of yourself**

null *adj.* null and void

VERBS **be** | **become** | **render sth** ◇ *Their actions rendered the contract ~ and void.* | **declare sth, deem** ◇ *They declared the agreement ~ and void.*

numb *adj.*

1 unable to feel pain

VERBS **be, feel** ◇ *Robin's hand felt ~ with cold.* | **become, go, grow, turn** ◇ *His fingers were beginning to go ~.*
ADV. **almost** | **comfortably** ◇ *After two drinks I was feeling comfortably ~.*
PREP. **from** ◇ *My legs were ~ from kneeling.*
PHRASES **~ with (the) cold** ◇ *Their fingers were going ~ with cold.*

2 unable to feel/think/react

VERBS **be, feel** | **leave sb** ◇ *The news left us ~.*
PREP. **with** ◇ *He felt ~ with shock.*

number *noun*

1 symbol/word

ADJ. **three-digit, 16-digit** | **cardinal, ordinal** | **even, odd** ◇ *Houses on this side of the road have even ~s.* | **binary, decimal** | **complex, imaginary, irrational, prime, rational, real, whole** (*mathematics*) | **negative, positive** | **random** | **lucky, unlucky** ◇ *Many people think 13 is an unlucky ~.* | **winning** ◇ *the winning ~s in tonight's lottery* | **correct, right**
VERB + NUMBER **calculate** | **add, add together, divide, multiply, subtract, take away** ◇ *Add all the ~s together, divide by ten, and then take away twelve.* | **double, triple** | **crunch** | **enter, write, write down** | **pick, think of**
PHRASES **in round ~s** (*esp. BrE*) ◇ *There were about 150 there, in round ~s.* | **~ crunching** (= doing calculations) ◇ *There's more to an accountant's job than just ~ crunching.*

2 quantity/amount

ADJ. **big, high** ◇ *high ~s of unemployed teachers* | **low** | **considerable, good, great, high, large, substantial, unlimited** | **enormous, huge, impressive, incredible, inordinate, overwhelming, staggering, unprecedented, vast** | **alarming** | **sheer** | **record** ◇ *a record ~ of responses* | **disproportionate, surprising** | **fair, reasonable, significant** ◇ *We've had a fair ~ of complaints about the new phone system.* | **finite, infinite** ◇ *There are an infinite ~ of solutions to the problem.* | **equal** ◇ *The candidates received an equal ~ of votes.* | **maximum, minimum** | **average, mean, median** | **adequate, sufficient** | **insufficient** | **limited, low, modest, small, tiny** | **growing, increasing, rising** | **increased** | **reduced** | **declining** | **actual, exact, precise** ◇ *Many people have died in the epidemic—the precise ~ is not known.* | **certain** | **indefinite, unspecified** | **unknown** | **approximate** | **fixed, set** | **final, overall, total** | **expected** | **real, true** | **poll** (*AmE*)
VERB + NUMBER **grow in, increase in** ◇ *Factories had increased in ~ between the wars.* | **decrease in, reduce in** | **increase** ◇ *The Pentagon increased the ~ of troops in Iraq to about 145 000.* | **double** | **cut, decrease, reduce** | **control, limit, restrict** | **calculate, count, determine, estimate, measure, record** ◇ *Anna counted the ~ of men standing around outside.*
NUMBER + VERB **go up, grow, increase, jump, rise** | **double** | **decline, diminish, drop, dwindle, fall, fall off** ◇ *Shark ~s have dwindled as a result of hunting.* | **vary**
PREP. **in ~** ◇ *The paintings, twelve in ~, are over 200 years old.* | **~ of** ◇ *the ~ of children who wear glasses*
PHRASES **a decline in ~s, a drop in ~s** ◇ *The decline in ~s of young people means that fewer teachers will be needed.* | **a growth in ~s, an increase in ~s** | **few in ~, limited in ~, small in ~** ◇ *Wild dogs are now few in ~.* | **put the ~ (of sth) at sth** ◇ *Conference organizers put the ~ of attendees at around 500.*

3 for identifying sb/sth

ADJ. **model, serial** | **account, credit-card, membership, passport, PIN, reservation, social-security** | **ID, identification, identity** | **license** (*AmE*), **license plate** (*AmE*), **registration** (*BrE*) (= of a car) | **flight** | **page** | **apartment** (*esp. AmE*), **flat** (*BrE*), **house, room**
VERB + NUMBER **assign sth, give sth**
PREP. **at ~** ◇ *We live at ~ 21.*

4 telephone, etc.

ADJ. **fax, phone, telephone** | **home, office, work** | **wrong** ◇ *I keep getting the wrong ~.* | **Freephone** (*BrE*), **toll-free** (*AmE*) | **daytime, evening** | **emergency** | **contact**
VERB + NUMBER **call, dial, phone** (*esp. BrE*), **ring** (*BrE*) | **get** | **give sb**
NUMBER + VERB **be busy** (*AmE*), **be engaged** (*BrE*) | **be unobtainable** (*BrE*)
PHRASES **exchange ~s** ◇ *They exchanged ~s and agreed to go out for a drink one evening.* | **sb's name and ~**

number *verb*

ADV. **clearly** | **consecutively, sequentially** | **individually**
PREP. **according to, by** ◇ *Each key is clearly ~ed by room.* | **from, to** ◇ *Number the car's features from 1 to 10 according to importance.*

nurse *noun*

ADJ. **certified** (*AmE*), **experienced, licensed** (*AmE*), **qualified, registered, trained** | **staff** ◇ *the children's staff ~* | **ward** (*esp. BrE*) | **charge** | **head, senior** (*BrE*) | **auxiliary** (*BrE*), **practical** (*AmE*), **junior** (*BrE*), **novice** (*AmE*) | **student, trainee** (*BrE*) | **female, male** | **day, night** | **community, district** (*both BrE*) | **hospital, practice, school** ◇ *This is a job for the school ~.* | **emergency** | **emergency-room** (abbreviated to **ER**) (*AmE*) | **private** | **specialist** | **maternity, paediatric/pediatric, psychiatric, scrub** (= who helps a surgeon prepare for surgery), **triage, veterinary** (*BrE*) | **retired** | **practising/practicing** | **baby** (*AmE*), **nursery** (*BrE*) | **wet** (= who breastfeeds another woman's baby)

NURSE + NOUN **practitioner** | **educator** (*esp. AmE*), **manager**, **specialist** | **education**
→ Note at JOB

nursery school (*BrE also* **nursery**) *noun*

ADJ. **day** (*BrE*), **local**, **private**, **workplace**
NURSERY-SCHOOL + NOUN **class**, **education** | **assistant**, **manager**, **nurse**, **staff**, **teacher** | **care**, **facilities**, **provision** | **place** ◇ *nursery-school places for under-fives*
PREP. **at a/the ~** ◇ *The children are at ~ three days a week.* | **in a/the ~** ◇ *She works as an assistant in a ~.*

nursing *noun*

ADJ. **general** | **clinical** | **geriatric**, **psychiatric**, **surgical** | **community**, **district** (*both BrE*) | **home**, **hospital** | **private** (*BrE*)
NURSING + NOUN **profession** | **care**, **services**, **skills** | **home** | **staff** | **officer** (*BrE*) | **student** | **school** | **shortage** | **practice**
→ Note at SUBJECT (for verbs and more nouns)

nut *noun*

1 food

ADJ. **cashew**, **macadamia**, **pistachio**, **etc.** | **chopped**, **mixed**, **salted** | **tree** (*esp. AmE*)
VERB + NUT **crack**, **shell**
NUT + NOUN **allergy** ◇ *nut-allergy sufferers* | **oil** | **tree**

2 for screwing onto a bolt

VERB + NUT **put on**, **screw on**, **tighten** | **loosen**, **remove**, **unscrew**
PHRASES **~s and bolts** (*often figurative*) ◇ *a jar full of ~s and bolts* ◇ *The documentary focuses on the real ~s and bolts* (= the practical details) *of the film-making process.*

nutrition *noun*

ADJ. **adequate**, **balanced**, **good**, **proper** | **inadequate**, **poor** ◇ *Many children at the school were found to be suffering from inadequate ~.* | **human** | **sports**
VERB + NUTRITION **provide** | **receive** | **improve**
NUTRITION + NOUN **label** | **facts**, **information** | **consultant**, **expert**, **specialist** | **programme/program** | **bar** (*AmE*) | **education**, **research**
PHRASES **a source of ~**

O o

oar *noun*

VERB + OAR **take** ◇ *We each took an ~.* | **pull on** ◇ *We pulled hard on the ~s.*
OAR + NOUN **lock** (*usually* **oarlock**) (*AmE*) (**rowlock** *in BrE*)

oath *noun*

1 formal promise

ADJ. **sacred**, **solemn** | **blood** | **Hippocratic** ◇ *a doctor's Hippocratic ~* | **presidential** | **loyalty** (*esp. AmE*)
VERB + OATH **swear**, **take** ◇ *He took an ~ of allegiance to his adopted country.* | **sign** | **break**, **violate** | **keep**, **uphold**
PREP. **~ of** ◇ *an ~ of allegiance* ◇ *an ~ of loyalty*

2 in a court of law

VERB + OATH **administer** ◇ *Only a judge is allowed to administer the ~.*
PREP. **on ~** (*esp. BrE*), **under ~** ◇ *He swore on ~ that he had never seen me before.* ◇ *Witnesses must testify under ~.*

oats *noun*

ADJ. **whole** | **rolled** | **porridge** (*esp. BrE*)
... OF OATS **field**
VERB + OATS **grow** | **sow** | **harvest**
OATS + VERB **grow**

---

obedience *noun*

ADJ. **absolute**, **complete**, **perfect**, **strict** (*AmE*), **total** ◇ *He demands absolute ~ from his men.* | **blind**, **passive**, **unquestioning**
VERB + OBEDIENCE **command**, **demand**, **exact**, **expect**, **require** | **owe** ◇ *All clergy owed ~ to their superior.* | **pledge**
OBEDIENCE + NOUN **class**, **school** (*esp. AmE*), **training** (= for dogs)
PREP. **in ~ to** ◇ *She acted in passive ~ to her boss's directions.* | **~ to** ◇ *The slaves had to swear ~ to their masters.*

obey *verb*

ADV. **immediately**, **instantly**, **quickly** ◇ *She was used to having her orders instantly ~ed.* | **blindly**, **meekly** | **unquestioningly**, **without question** | **reluctantly**
VERB + OBEY **have to**, **must** | **refuse to** ◇ *He refuses to ~ the rules.* | **fail to** | **be willing to** | **promise to**
PHRASES **be only ~ing orders** ◇ *At the trial the soldiers made the excuse that they were only ~ing orders.* | **a duty to ~**, **an obligation to ~** ◇ *People have a moral duty to ~ the law.* | **a failure to ~** ◇ *She's being punished for failure to ~ a court order.* | **sth has to be ~ed**, **sth must be ~ed** ◇ *Rules are rules and they must be ~ed.*

obituary *noun*

VERB + OBITUARY **write** | **print**, **publish** | **read**
OBITUARY + NOUN **column**, **notice**, **page**

object *noun*

1 solid thing

ADJ. **inanimate** | **solid**, **three-dimensional** | **large**, **small** | **heavy**, **sharp**, **etc.** | **egg-shaped**, **V-shaped**, **etc.** | **man-made** | **common**, **everyday**, **familiar**, **household** ◇ *Her paintings are of ordinary everyday ~s.* | **decorative** | **flying**, **moving** | **stationary** | **distant** | **material**, **physical** | **sacred** | **foreign** ◇ *people who claim to have found foreign ~s in cans* | **sex**, **sexual** ◇ *He regards women as nothing more than sexual ~s.*

2 purpose

ADJ. **main**, **primary**, **principal** | **sole** ◇ *My sole ~ is to get to the bottom of this mystery.*
OBJECT + NOUN **lesson** ◇ *The plans are an ~ lesson in how to ruin a city.*
PHRASES **the ~ of the exercise** (*esp. BrE*), **the ~ of the game** ◇ *The ~ of the game is to score as many points as possible.* ◇ *It would defeat the ~ of the exercise if we paid someone to do it for us.*

object *verb*

ADV. **strenuously**, **strongly**, **vehemently**
VERB + OBJECT **can hardly** ◇ *It was your own idea in the first place, so you can hardly ~ now.* | **be entitled to** (*esp. BrE*), **have a/the right to**
PREP. **to** ◇ *a petition ~ing to the plan*
PHRASES **~ on the grounds that…** ◇ *I ~ed on the grounds that it was unkind to the animals.*

objection *noun*

ADJ. **serious**, **strenuous**, **strong** | **valid** | **main**, **major**, **primary**, **principal** | **fundamental** | **common** | **conscientious**, **ethical**, **moral**, **principled**, **religious** | **one**, **only** ◇ *My one ~ is that I don't think such an amendment is necessary.*
VERB + OBJECTION **file**, **lodge**, **make**, **raise**, **state**, **voice** | **have** ◇ *I'd like to open a window, unless anyone has any ~s.* | **address**, **answer**, **meet**, **overcome** | **drop**, **withdraw**
PREP. **over the ~s of** (*esp. AmE*) ◇ *She was appointed over the ~s of certain members of the board.* | **~ against** ◇ *a common ~ against nuclear power* | **~ to** ◇ *The committee has raised serious ~s to the plans.*
PHRASES **an ~ based on sth**

objective noun

ADJ. **first, key, main, major, primary, prime, principal** | **second, secondary** | **broad, overall, overriding, ultimate** | **limited, narrow** | **long-term, short-term** | **clear, specific** | **important** | **stated** ◊ *The legislation has failed to achieve its stated ~s.* | **desired** | **common** ◊ *The two groups are pursuing a common ~.* | **economic, educational, environmental, military, political, strategic** | **business, course, learning, mission, policy, research**

VERB + OBJECTIVE **have** | **accomplish, achieve, attain, complete, fulfil/fulfill, meet, reach, succeed in** ◊ *The department needs more money to achieve its ~s.* | **fail in** | **agree, define, establish, formulate, identify, set, specify** ◊ *a set of agreed ~s* ◊ *We need to establish a clear ~.* | **declare, state** | **promote, pursue, support**

PREP. **in an/the ~** ◊ *The party is radical in its ~s.* | **~ of** ◊ *We succeeded in our prime ~ of cutting costs.*

objective adj.

VERBS **be, seem** | **remain**

ADV. **truly, very** | **completely, entirely, purely, totally, wholly** ◊ *It is impossible to be completely ~.* | **fairly, reasonably** | **apparently** (*esp. BrE*), **seemingly** (*esp. AmE*) | **supposedly**

obligation noun

ADJ. **contractual, legal, statutory** | **ethical, moral, religious, social** | **debt, financial, pension** | **family** ◊ *I can't travel next month because of family ~s.* | **professional** | **treaty** | **mutual**

VERB + OBLIGATION **carry out, discharge, fulfil/fulfill, meet** ◊ *The builders failed to meet their contractual ~s.* | **comply with, honour/honor** | **have** ◊ *We have a moral ~ to help.* | **feel** | **owe** | **assume, carry, incur, take on** | **impose** | **ignore**

OBLIGATION + VERB **arise from sth** ◊ *~s arising from your contract of employment*

PREP. **under an ~** ◊ *I am under no ~ to tell you my name.* | **without ~** ◊ *Our mortgage advice is given free and without ~.* | **~ of** ◊ *the ~s of citizenship* | **~ to** ◊ *A lawyer owes an ~ of confidence to the client.* | **~ with respect to** ◊ *our moral ~s with respect to the law*

obligatory adj.

VERBS **be** | **become** | **remain** | **make sth** ◊ *The college authorities have now made these classes ~.*

ADV. **almost, practically** (*esp. BrE*) ◊ *It's almost ~ to have a blog nowadays.* | **morally**

PREP. **for** ◊ *It is ~ for vets to be registered.*

oblige verb

ADV. **duly** (*BrE*) ◊ *The fans were looking for another goal and Owen duly ~d* (= he scored). | **kindly** | **gladly, happily, willingly** | **grudgingly**

VERB + OBLIGE **be glad to, be happy to, be pleased to** (*esp. BrE*), **be willing to** ◊ *He asked me for advice, and I was only too happy to ~.* | *The staff are always willing to ~.*

PREP. **by** ◊ *Will you ~ by filling in this form?* | **with** ◊ *Would you be willing to ~ us with some information?*

obliged adj.

1 forced to do sth

VERBS **be, feel**

ADV. **by law** (*esp. BrE*), **contractually, legally** ◊ *Parents are ~ by law to send their children to school.* | **morally** ◊ *I felt morally ~ to do the best I could for her.*

2 grateful

VERBS **be, feel**

ADV. **much**

PREP. **for, to** ◊ *I'm much ~ to you for helping us.*

obliterate verb

ADV. **completely, entirely, totally** ◊ *The sect was totally ~d by the state.* | **almost, virtually**

oblivion noun

ADJ. **political** | **total**

VERB + OBLIVION **fade into, fall into, pass into, sink into, slide into** | **rescue sb/sth from, save sb/sth from** ◊ *a minor masterpiece, saved from ~* | **consign sb/sth to** ◊ *Most of his work has now been consigned to ~.*

PREP. **in ~** ◊ *He died in ~.*

oblivious adj.

VERBS **appear, be, seem** ◊ *Karen appeared ~ to the uproar.* | **become** | **remain** | **make sb** ◊ *His own arrogance made him ~ to the criticisms of others.*

ADV. **completely, quite, totally** | **almost** | **apparently, seemingly** | **clearly**

PREP. **of** ◊ *~ of the stares of the whole town* | **to** ◊ *She seemed almost ~ to the crowds of reporters.*

PHRASES **~ to the fact that…** ◊ *He seemed ~ to the fact that his wife was on the edge of a nervous breakdown.*

oboe noun → Special page at MUSIC

obscene adj.

VERBS **be, look** | **consider sth, deem sth** ◊ *The book was declared ~.*

ADV. **really** | **utterly** (*esp. BrE*) | **almost** | **allegedly** (*esp. AmE*)

PHRASES **something ~** ◊ *He muttered something ~ under his breath.*

obscenity noun

… OF OBSCENITY **stream, string**

VERB + OBSCENITY **mutter, scream, shout, yell** ◊ *He shouted a stream of obscenities.*

OBSCENITY + NOUN **charge, laws, trial**

obscure verb

ADV. **completely, totally** | **almost** | **largely** | **half, partially, partly, slightly, somewhat** | **deliberately** ◊ *All trace of his working-class background was deliberately ~d.* | **easily** ◊ *Solo passages in this register are very easily ~d by other instruments.*

VERB + OBSCURE **serve to, tend to** ◊ *The emphasis on social integration often served to ~ the real differences within the community.* | **allow sth to**

PREP. **behind** ◊ *The moon was ~d behind a wall of cloud.* | **in** ◊ *The right-hand side of the face is ~d in deep shadow.*

PHRASES **~ the fact that…** ◊ *These figures ~ the fact that a lot of older people live in poverty.* | **~ sth from view** ◊ *The house was ~d from view by a wall.*

obscure adj.

VERBS **be, seem** | **become** ◊ *The origins of the tradition have become ~.* | **remain** ◊ *The motives behind this decision remain somewhat ~.*

ADV. **extremely, fairly, very, etc.** | **completely, totally** | **largely** | **relatively** | **wilfully/willfully** (*esp. BrE*)

obscurity noun

ADJ. **complete, total** | **near, virtual** ◊ *He is now living in virtual ~.* | **comparative** (*esp. BrE*), **relative** | **professional**

VERB + OBSCURITY **fade into, sink into, slip into, vanish into** | **be plucked from, emerge from, rise from** ◊ *After many years, his scientific work emerged from ~.* ◊ *O'Neil rose from ~ to become an international sensation.* | **be relegated to** | **labor in** (*AmE*), **languish in**

PREP. **in ~** ◊ *He spent his early life in relative ~.*

PHRASES **go from ~ to celebrity, notoriety, fame, etc.**

observant adj.

VERBS **be, seem** | **become**

ADV. **extremely, fairly, very, etc.** | **acutely** (*esp. BrE*), **keenly** (*AmE*) ◊ *She was intelligent and highly ~.*

observation *noun*

1 examination

ADJ. **careful, close, detailed** | **direct, first-hand** | **systematic** | **casual** | **empirical, scientific** | **visual** | **clinical** | **astronomical** | **field** | **simple** ◇ *There's a lot to be learned from simple ~.*

PREP. **for ~** ◇ *She was admitted to the hospital for ~.* | **under ~** ◇ *The police have had him under ~ for several weeks.* | **~ of** ◇ *The survey was based on direct ~ of over 500 schools.*

PHRASES **powers of ~** ◇ *an artist with acute powers of ~*

2 remark

ADJ. **general** | **accurate, astute, insightful, keen, perceptive, shrewd** | **interesting** | **important** | **wry** | **sb's own, personal** | **common** | **early, initial, preliminary**

VERB + OBSERVATION **make, offer**

PREP. **~ about** ◇ *He smiled, and made some ~ about the weather.* | **~ from** ◇ *~s from one reader in Hawaii* | **~ on** ◇ *her witty ~s on life*

observe *verb*

1 notice/watch

ADV. **carefully, closely** | **precisely** | **directly** ◇ *It is not possible to ~ this phenomenon directly.* | **clearly** | **actually** ◇ *It is the parents who actually ~ these problems in their children.* | **just, simply** ◇ *You can learn a lot by simply observing.* | **generally, normally, typically, usually** | **repeatedly** | **quietly** ◇ *She stood there, quietly observing the domestic scene.* | **secretly** | **experimentally** ◇ *This phenomenon has been ~d experimentally.* | **recently**

VERB + OBSERVE **be able to** | **be possible to** | **be difficult to** | **be interesting to** ◇ *It is interesting to ~ the reaction of the children to these changes.* | **expect to** | **need to** | **get to** | **continue to**

PREP. **among** ◇ *A similar pattern was ~d among Hispanics.* | **for** ◇ *The patient should be ~d for signs of an allergic reaction.* | **from** ◇ *unaware that she was being ~d from the window*

PHRASES **be commonly ~d, be frequently ~d, be widely ~d** ◇ *This ritual is commonly ~d among several ethnic groups.* | **be easily ~d, be readily ~d** | **be occasionally ~d, be rarely ~d** | **an opportunity to ~ sb/sth, time to ~ sth**

2 make a remark

ADV. **astutely, correctly, keenly, rightly, shrewdly** ◇ *She correctly ~d that there was very little difference between the two parties on domestic policies.* | **drily, wryly** | **coolly** ◇ *'You took your time,' he ~d coolly.* | **mildly, quietly** | **sadly** | **famously** ◇ *The only certainties in this world, as Benjamin Franklin famously ~d, are death and taxes.*

PREP. **to** ◇ *'It's easy to say that,' she ~d to Michael, 'but can you prove it?'*

3 obey rules

ADV. **correctly, faithfully, scrupulously, strictly** ◇ *This procedure must be correctly ~d.*

VERB + OBSERVE **fail to**

PHRASES **failure to ~ sth** ◇ *Failure to ~ club rules may result in expulsion.*

observer *noun*

ADJ. **casual** ◇ *To the casual ~, it would have looked like any other domestic argument.* | **informed, knowledgeable** (*esp. AmE*) | **acute, astute, careful, close, keen, shrewd** | **experienced, long-time, seasoned** | **sceptical/skeptical** | **sympathetic** | **detached, impartial, neutral, objective, unbiased** | **reasonable** | **external, independent, outside** ◇ *Independent ~s will monitor the elections.* | **trained** | **foreign, international** | **American, Western, etc.** | **industry, legal, media, military, political** ◇ *some military ~s fear the US could get entangled in another war.* | **election** | **human** | **passive**

VERB + OBSERVER **send** ◇ *Observers were sent to check the conduct of the elections.* | **attend sth as** | **impress, puzzle, shock, strike, stun, surprise** ◇ *The suddenness of this move surprised ~s.*

OBSERVER + VERB **see sth** | **note sth, say sth** | **agree sth** |

---

believe sth, think sth | **expect sth, predict sth** | **attend sth** ◇ *The talks were attended by ~s from eight Arab countries and Israel.* | **monitor sth**

PHRASES **status** ◇ *The country was granted ~ status at the summit.* | **bias**

PREP. **as an ~** ◇ *I attended the conference as an ~.* | **~ of** ◇ *an ~ of the American cultural scene*

PHRASES **lead ~s to conclude, suggest, etc. sth** ◇ *Difficulties in the housing market have led some ~s to conclude that house prices will fall dramatically.*

obsession *noun*

ADJ. **dangerous, unhealthy** | **current** | **national** | **strange, weird** | **new**

VERB + OBSESSION **become** ◇ *Don't let this interest of yours become an ~.* | **have** ◇ *He thinks all women have an ~ with shoes.*

PREP. **~ with** ◇ *I don't understand television's current ~ with reality shows.*

obsolete *adj.*

VERBS **be** | **become** | **make sth, render sth** ◇ *Their work is now rendered ~ by machines.*

ADV. **completely, totally** | **increasingly** | **largely** | **almost, nearly** (*esp. AmE*), **virtually**

obstacle *noun*

ADJ. **big, major** | **chief, greatest, main** | **enormous, formidable, huge, serious, significant** ◇ *The attitude of the unions is a serious ~.* | **impossible** (*esp. AmE*), **insuperable** (*formal*), **insurmountable** (*formal*) ◇ *the joy of overcoming seemingly impossible ~s* ◇ *Lack of money has proved an almost insurmountable ~.* | **bureaucratic, legal, political**

VERB + OBSTACLE **be, become, constitute, prove, remain, represent** | **create, pose, present** | **come across** (*esp. BrE*), **encounter, face** | **avoid, overcome, remove, surmount** ◇ *He was determined to overcome all ~s in his way.*

OBSTACLE + NOUN **course**

PREP. **~ for** ◇ *Lack of childcare provision can be a major ~ for women wishing to work.* | **~ to** ◇ *The huge distances involved have proved an ~ to communication.*

PHRASES **an ~ in the path (of sb/sth), an ~ in the way (of sb/sth)** ◇ *The release of prisoners remains an ~ in the path of a peace agreement.*

obstruct *verb*

ADV. **partially** | **completely** | **deliberately** (*esp. BrE*), **wilfully** (*BrE, law*) ◇ *wilfully ~ing a police officer in the execution of his duty*

PREP. **in**

obstruction *noun*

ADJ. **physical** | **unlawful, wilful** (*both BrE, law*) | **bureaucratic** ◇ *The asylum seekers had to contend with continued bureaucratic ~.*

VERB + OBSTRUCTION **cause, create** ◇ *The car had been parked in front of the entrance, causing an ~.* | **clear, remove** ◇ *She had to have surgery to remove an ~ from her throat.*

PHRASES **~ of justice** (*law*) ◇ *She was charged with ~ of justice.*

obtain *verb*

ADV. **fraudulently, illegally, unlawfully** (*BrE, law*) | **legally** | **recently**

VERB + OBTAIN **be able to, be unable to** | **attempt to, endeavour/endeavor to** (*esp. BrE*) | **fail to** | **assist sb to, enable sb to** | **be easy to, be possible to** | **be difficult to, be impossible to** ◇ *goods which are difficult to ~* | **be necessary to, need to** ◇ *It is necessary to ~ the patients' consent.*

PREP. **by** ◇ *The company claims to have ~ed its database of names by legitimate means.* | **from** ◇ *Anglers are required to ~ prior authorization from the park keeper.*

PHRASES **be easily ~ed, be readily ~ed** ◇ *Such information is* *easily* ~*ed from the Internet.* | **sth can be ~ed, sth may be ~ed** ◇ *Details of this offer can be ~ed from any of our stores.* | **a means of ~ing sth, a method of ~ing sth, a way of ~ing sth**

obtainable *adj.*

VERBS **be** | **become**
ADV. **easily, readily**

obvious *adj.*

VERBS **appear, be, look, seem, sound** | **become** ◇ *It soon became ~ that the machine did not work.* | **make sth** ◇ *His manner made it ~ he didn't like her.*
ADV. **extremely, fairly, very, etc.** ◇ *I'm not going to tell Jim about this, for fairly ~ reasons.* | **blatantly, blindingly, glaringly, patently, transparently** (*esp. BrE*) | **completely, perfectly, quite** ◇ *The answer is perfectly ~!* | **increasingly** | **by no means, far from, less than, not at all, not entirely** ◇ *It was far from ~ how they were going to get off the island.* | **a little, slightly, etc.** | **apparently, seemingly** | **immediately** ◇ *It was immediately ~ that the bag was too heavy.* | **intuitively** ◇ *Avoid making intuitively ~ but unfounded assertions.* | **depressingly, painfully** ◇ *It was becoming painfully ~ that the two of them had nothing in common.* | **all too** ◇ *The ineptitude of the government was all too ~.*
PREP. **to** ◇ *It is ~ to me that you're unhappy in your job.*
PHRASES **be so ~ that ...** ◇ *The metaphor is so ~ that it's impossible to miss.*

occasion *noun*

1 time when sth happens

ADJ. **countless, many, multiple** (*esp. AmE*), **numerous** ◇ *It was the first of many such ~s.* | **a few, several, various** | **rare** | **previous** | **different, separate**
VERB + OCCASION **recall, remember**
PREP. **on an/the ~** ◇ *The police were called out on 24 separate ~s.* | **on ~, on ~s** ◇ *He has even been known to go shopping himself on ~.*
PHRASES **a number of ~s** ◇ *I have stayed there on a number of ~s.* | **on one ~** ◇ *On one ~ he even called me in the middle of the night.* | **on that ~, on this ~** ◇ *On this ~, as it happens, the engine started immediately.* | **on the odd ~** ◇ *They came to visit us on the odd ~, but only when they had nothing better to do.* | **a particular ~** ◇ *On this particular ~, Joe wasn't there.*

2 suitable time

ADJ. **right, suitable** (*esp. BrE*)
VERB + OCCASION **get, have** ◇ *I bought the camera last year, but never had the ~ to use it.*
OCCASION + VERB **arise** ◇ *I'll speak to him if the ~ arises.*
PREP. **~ for** ◇ *It should have been an ~ for rejoicing.*
PHRASES **be an ~ for sth, become an ~ for sth** ◇ *His death became an ~ for widespread discussion of his character.* | **have ~ to do sth** ◇ *Last year we had ~ to visit relatives in Florida.* | **provide an/the ~ for sth** ◇ *These workshops provide an ~ for talking about art.* | **take an ~ to do sth, use an ~ to do sth** ◇ *I want to use this ~ to thank you all for your hard work.*

3 special event

ADJ. **auspicious, big, great, historic, important, memorable, momentous, special** | **festive, happy, joyous** | **formal, sad, solemn** | **social** | **ceremonial, state** ◇ *Medals are usually worn only on ceremonial ~s.*
VERB + OCCASION **celebrate, mark** ◇ *a party to mark the ~ of their daughter's graduation* | **rise to** ◇ *The choir rose to the ~ and sang beautifully.*
OCCASION + VERB **call for sth** ◇ *I do sometimes dance if the ~ calls for it.*
PREP. **on ~** ◇ *I only wear my silk dress on special ~s.* | **~ of** ◇ *the ~ of his 50th birthday*
PHRASES **for all ~s, for every ~** ◇ *We sell cards and notepaper*

for all ~s. | **a sense of ~** ◇ *On the day of the wedding there was a real sense of ~.*

occupant *noun*

ADJ. **original** | **current, present** | **former, previous** | **future, next** | **only, sole** ◇ *The sole ~ of the car was an elderly man.* | **building** (*AmE*), **vehicle**

occupation *noun*

1 job

ADJ. **full-time** | **current** | **main** | **dangerous, hazardous** | **female, male** ◇ *Agricultural work is traditionally seen as a male ~.* | **managerial, professional, technical** | **skilled, unskilled** | **manual, non-manual** (*both esp. BrE*) | **blue-collar, white-collar** | **service** ◇ *service ~s such as cleaning and catering* | **civilian** ◇ *He left the army in 1999 and chose a civilian ~.*
VERB + OCCUPATION **choose, find** | **follow** (*BrE*) ◇ *The people interviewed followed a variety of ~s*
PHRASES **list sb's ~ as sth** ◇ *Her ~ is listed as 'homemaker'.* | **a range of ~s** ◇ *The college provides training in a wide range of ~s.*

2 control of another country

ADJ. **foreign** | **continued, continuing** | **military** | **post-war** | **colonial** | **brutal** | **illegal**
VERB + OCCUPATION **begin** | **end** ◇ *The invaders have ended their ~ of large parts of the territories.* | **maintain** | **fight, resist** | **oppose, protest** | **support**
OCCUPATION + VERB **begin, end** | **continue**
OCCUPATION + NOUN **force**
PREP. **during the ~** ◇ *During the ~, the church was used as a mosque.* | **under ~** ◇ *Part of Britain was under Roman ~.* | **~ of** ◇ *the ~ of territory*

3 living in a room, house, etc.

ADJ. **land** | **illegal, unlawful** (*BrE*) ◇ *illegal ~ of the building*
VERB + OCCUPATION **take up** (*BrE*) ◇ *You can only take up ~ once the tenancy has been signed.* | **exclusive** (*BrE, law*) | **multiple** (*BrE, law*) ◇ *the conversion of big old buildings to multiple ~*
PREP. **in ~ of** (*BrE, law*) ◇ *He intends to remain in ~ of the building for as long as possible.*
PHRASES **ready for ~** (*esp. BrE*) ◇ *The houses will be ready for ~ by March.*

occupied *adj.*

1 being used by sb

VERBS **be**
ADV. **densely** ◇ *the most densely ~ areas of the country* | **entirely** ◇ *The sofa was entirely ~ by two large cats.* | **permanently** | **illegally**

2 busy

VERBS **be** | **become** | **keep sb** ◇ *We need something to keep the children ~.*
ADV. **fully** (*esp. BrE*) | **happily**
PREP. **in** ◇ *You will be mainly ~ in checking sales records.* | **with** ◇ *She was happily ~ with reading.*

occur *verb*

ADV. **commonly, frequently, often, regularly, repeatedly** | **generally, normally, typically, usually** | **infrequently, rarely** | **occasionally, sometimes** | **randomly, sporadically** | **mainly, mostly, predominantly, primarily** | **exclusively, only** | **naturally** ◇ *These chemical changes ~ naturally.* | **spontaneously** ◇ *Opportunities for learning ~ spontaneously every day.* | **simultaneously, together** | **independently** | **quickly, rapidly** | **slowly**
VERB + OCCUR **be likely to, tend to** | **be unlikely to**
PREP. **among** ◇ *the problems that ~ among people living together* | **in** ◇ *A significant improvement occurred in patients given the drug.*

occurrence *noun*

ADJ. **common, everyday, widespread** | **daily, frequent, regular** | **rare, uncommon** | **isolated, random** | **freak,**

strange, unexpected, unusual | natural, normal | actual | new | high, low ◇ *the low ~ of heart disease in this particular group*
VERB + OCCURRENCE **prevent | reduce | increase | predict | document, record, report | explain**
PREP. **~ in** ◇ *These mild fits are quite a common ~ in babies.* | **~ of** ◇ *a past ~ of breast cancer*
PHRASES **a common ~, a regular ~** ◇ *His visits became a regular ~.* | **a daily ~** | **frequency of ~** ◇ *words with a high frequency of ~*

ocean *noun*

ADJ. **deep | vast | great** ◇ *a vessel which can explore the depths of the great ~s* | **blue | open** ◇ *A storm started up once we got out into the open ~.* | **calm, rough | endless** (*literary*) ◇ *Before him lay the vast, endless ~.* | **cold, frozen | tropical, warm | southern** ◇ *penguins of the southern ~s* | **coastal** (*AmE*)
VERB + OCEAN **cross, sail | explore | go in, swim in** (*both esp. AmE*) | **overlook** (*esp. AmE*) ◇ *a beach house overlooking the ~*
OCEAN + NOUN **depths** ◇ *the darkness of the ~ depths* | **surface | bed, bottom, floor | basin | water | ecosystem | wave** ◇ *a life on the ~ wave* (= at sea) | **current, tides | air, breeze** (*both esp. AmE*) | **voyage | liner | view | blue**
PREP. **across the ~** ◇ *trade across the Atlantic Ocean* | **in the ~** ◇ *Various toxic substances have been dumped in the ~.*
PHRASES **the bottom of the ~, the depths of the ~, the middle of the ~, the surface of the ~** | **the ~s of the world, the world's ~s** ◇ *great ships that sailed the ~s of the world*

October *noun* → Note at MONTH

odd *adj.*

VERBS **be, feel, look, seem, smell, sound, taste | consider sth, find sth, think sth** ◇ *I find it ~ that she takes so long to do that job.* ◇ *I didn't think it ~ at the time.*
ADV. **extremely, fairly, very, etc. | decidedly, distinctly** ◇ *There's something distinctly ~ about her.* | **especially, particularly | a little, slightly, etc.**
PHRASES **how ~** ◇ *How ~ that he should come from the same town as me.* | **it is ~ to think** ◇ *It's ~ to think I will never see her again.* | **something ~** ◇ *There's something ~ going on.*

odds *noun*

ADJ. **considerable, great, impossible, incredible, insurmountable, overwhelming, terrible** ◇ *She struggled against terrible ~ to overcome her illness.* | **good | high, low | long, short** (*esp. BrE*) ◇ *Sometimes an outsider will win at long ~, but not often.* ◇ *The bookmakers are offering only short ~ on the favourite.* (*BrE*)
VERB + ODDS **offer, quote | lay** ◇ *I'll lay ~ we never see him again.* | **reduce, shorten | improve, increase | beat, defy, overcome** ◇ *She defied the ~ to beat the clear favourite/favorite.* | **calculate**
ODDS + VERB **fall, go down, lengthen** (*esp. BrE*) | **go up, increase, shorten** (*esp. BrE*) | **favour/favor sb**
PREP. **against the ~** ◇ *The movie is a heart-warming tale of triumph against the ~.* | **~ against** ◇ *The ~ against making a profit in this business are huge.* | **~ of** ◇ *They were offering ~ of ten to one.* | **~ on** ◇ *The ~ on the outsider were 100–1.*
PHRASES **against all ~, against all the ~** ◇ *Against all the ~, we managed to get through to the final.* | **face impossible ~, face insurmountable ~** | **the ~ are stacked against sb, the ~ are stacked in favour/favor of sb** ◇ *He will try hard to win, although he knows the ~ are stacked against him.*

odour (*BrE*) (*AmE* odor) *noun*

ADJ. **foul, offensive, unpleasant | musty, stale | pungent, strong | faint | sweet | characteristic, distinct** (*esp. AmE*), **distinctive, familiar, unmistakable | strange | body**
VERB + ODOUR/ODOR **smell** ◇ *I smelled the distinct ~ of something burning.* | **emit, give off, produce | eliminate, remove**
ODOUR/ODOR + VERB **come from sth, emanate from sth**

PREP. **~ from** ◇ *~s from the local brewery*

offence (*BrE*) (*AmE* offense) *noun*

1 illegal act
ADJ. **grave, heinous, major, serious | lesser, minor, petty, trivial | alleged | first | federal** (*AmE*), **statutory** (*BrE*) | **arrestable** (*BrE*), **bookable** (in football/soccer) (*BrE*), **capital, firing** (*AmE*), **impeachable** (*AmE*), **imprisonable** (*BrE*), **indictable** (*BrE*), **punishable, sackable** (*BrE*) ◇ *The ~ is punishable by up to three months' imprisonment.* | **criminal, disciplinary** (*BrE*) | **driving** (*BrE*), **political, sex, sexual, terrorist** ◇ *Motorists may be fined on the spot for driving ~s such as speeding.* | **felony** (*AmE*) | **non-violent** (*esp. AmE*), **violent | drug, drug-related**
VERB + OFFENCE/OFFENSE **be, constitute | commit**
PREP. **~ against** ◇ *~s against public decency*
→ Note at CRIME (for verbs)

2 hurt feelings
VERB + OFFENCE/OFFENSE **cause, give | take**
PREP. **~ at** ◇ *He takes ~ at the slightest joke against him.* | **~ to** ◇ *I didn't mean to give ~ to anyone.*
PHRASES **no ~, no ~ intended, no ~ meant** ◇ *No ~ intended, but are you sure your calculations are right?*

3 (*AmE*) attacking players; attacking play
ADJ. **opposing** ◇ *the ability to disrupt opposing ~s* | **balanced**
VERB + OFFENSE **spark** ◇ *The move didn't spark the ~ as hoped.* | **initiate** ◇ *competent passers who can initiate the ~* | **disrupt** ◇ *their ability to disrupt the ~*

offend *verb*

ADV. **deeply, gravely, greatly** ◇ *He knew that he had ~ed her deeply.* | **mortally | slightly | easily** ◇ *He was very sensitive and easily ~ed.*
VERB + OFFEND **be likely to** ◇ *Omit anything that is likely to ~ people.* | **be anxious not to, be careful not to, not mean to, take care not to** ◇ *She stopped mid-sentence, anxious not to ~ him.*
PREP. **against** ◇ *Viewers complained that the broadcast ~ed against good taste.*
PHRASES **feel, look, sound, etc. ~ed** ◇ *She sounded ~ed when she replied.*

offender *noun*

1 person who commits a crime
ADJ. **alleged | convicted | first, first-time** ◇ *As a first ~, he received a lenient sentence.* | **persistent** (*esp. BrE*), **repeat | non-violent, violent | adult, juvenile, young | sex, sexual | drug**
VERB + OFFENDER **sentence**

2 sb/sth that causes trouble
ADJ. **main, worst** ◇ *As regards pollution, old diesel-engined vehicles are the worst ~s.*

offensive *noun*

ADJ. **all-out, full-scale, large-scale, major, massive** ◇ *In 1941, Hitler launched an all-out ~ against the Soviet Union.* | **military** ◇ *a military ~ against the insurgents* | **guerrilla, terrorist | air, bombing | ground | diplomatic, government, propaganda | charm** (*figurative*) ◇ *The politician has launched a charm ~ in an attempt to clean up his image.*
VERB + OFFENSIVE **launch, mount | plan | be on, go on, take** ◇ *She took the ~, challenging her critics to prove their allegations.*
PREP. **~ against** ◇ *The government is launching an all-out ~ against the drug cartels*

offensive *adj.*

VERBS **be, seem | become | consider sth, deem sth, find sth, think sth** ◇ *He's always making rude remarks about women. I find that deeply ~.*
ADV. **extremely, fairly, very, etc. | deeply, downright,**

grossly, highly | potentially | deliberately | patently (AmE, law) ◇ *The material is patently ~ as measured by the standards for the broadcast medium.* | morally | racially
PREP. to ◇ *This sort of attitude is very ~ to women.*

offer noun

1 of help or sth that is needed

ADJ. generous, kind | conditional, unconditional (both esp. BrE) ◇ *The company has made a conditional ~.* ◇ *She received a conditional ~ from the University of Warwick. (BrE)* | job | peace (usually *peace offering*)
VERB + OFFER make (sb) ◇ *He made me an ~ I simply couldn't refuse.* | withdraw | get, have, receive | accept, take, take up | decline, refuse, turn down | consider
PREP. on ~ ◇ *the range of goods on ~* | ~ from ◇ *I had to turn down a job ~ from a publisher because the pay was too low.* | ~ of ◇ *They refused our ~ of help.*

2 special price/deal

ADJ. special | cheap (BrE) ◇ *The council do cheap ~s on compost bins.* | free ◇ *I got the conditioner in a free ~ with my shampoo.* | introductory ◇ *Your first order is delivered free as an introductory ~.*
PREP. on ~ (BrE) ◇ *We have a number of bargains on ~.*

3 amount of money

ADJ. acceptable, attractive, fair, good, reasonable ◇ *The company says it has made a good ~ which cannot be improved upon.* ◇ *$500 is my best ~ (= the highest price I will offer).* | tempting | high, low ◇ *We realized we would not get a higher ~.* | first, initial ◇ *Don't just accept the first ~.* | final | firm, formal ◇ *No one has made a firm ~.* | lucrative | pay (BrE) ◇ *The union has voted for industrial action after rejecting a pay ~.* | takeover | cash (esp. BrE) | tender (both business) ◇ *a cash ~ of $21 a share* | contract (sports) ◇ *The Rams have made him a two-year contract ~.*
VERB + OFFER make (sb), put in | withdraw | get, receive | consider, listen to ◇ *I'll listen to any reasonable ~.* | accept, take | reject, turn down | increase, up ◇ *They just kept upping their ~ until I had to say yes.* | match ◇ *We should be able to match their ~ for the player.*
OFFER + NOUN
PREP. under ~ (BrE) ◇ *The property is currently under ~ to a client.* | ~ for ◇ *Several people put in an ~ for the house.* | ~ of ◇ *They accepted our ~ of £80 000.*
PHRASES be open to ~s (esp. BrE) ◇ *The asking price is £500 but I'm open to ~s.* | or best ~ (abbreviated to *o.b.o*) (AmE) ◇ *Excellent condition. $1000 or best ~.* | or near ~, or nearest ~ (abbreviated to *o.n.o*) (BrE) ◇ *They are selling their car for £2 500 or near ~.*

offer verb

1 give/provide sth; ask if sb would like sth

ADV. generously, graciously, kindly ◇ *She graciously ~ed to get pizza so I wouldn't have to cook.* | helpfully | freely ◇ *Hospitality was freely ~ed to refugees.*
VERB + OFFER be able to, be unable to, can ◇ *the protection that life insurance can ~* | appear to, seem to ◇ *The plan seemed to ~ real advantages.* | fail to | be pleased to (formal), would like to ◇ *I refer to your recent application and interview and am pleased to ~ you the post of editor.* | aim to, seek to | claim to ◇ *They claim to ~ a more comprehensive service than other companies.* | be expected to, be likely to ◇ *This investment is likely to ~ a higher return.* | be compelled to, be forced to, be obliged to | feel compelled to, feel obliged to ◇ *She felt obliged to ~ him a bed for the night.* | have little to, have a lot to, have nothing to, have something to, etc. ◇ *This player has proved that he still has a lot to ~ (= can still play well).* | have sth to ◇ *a chance to see what the college has to ~ students*
PREP. to ◇ *She ~ed drinks to her guests.*

2 say that you will pay a certain amount

VERB + OFFER be able to, be unable to, can | be prepared to,

be ready to, be willing to ◇ *Would they be prepared to ~ any more?*
PREP. for ◇ *They have ~ed over £500 000 for the house.*

offering noun

1 something produced for other people

ADJ. latest, new, recent | current | standard ◇ *the hot dog vendor's standard ~s of mustard, relish and ketchup* | innovative ◇ *Suzuki's latest innovative ~ could well be the road to take.* | literary, musical ◇ *Her latest literary ~ is full of tales of murder and deception.* | initial public (abbreviated to *IPO*), share (esp. BrE), stock (esp. AmE) (all business) ◇ *The insurance company raised $854 million in its initial public ~.*
VERB + OFFERING broaden, enhance, expand ◇ *We are expanding our ~ to include smaller, less expensive prints.* | launch ◇ *Microsoft launched its newest ~.*
OFFERING + VERB include sth, range from sth to sth ◇ *The company's ~s range from the very cheap to the hideously expensive.*
PREP. ~ from ◇ *The latest ~ from this young band is their best album yet.* | ~ to ◇ *our ~s to consumers*

2 something given to a god

ADJ. burned, sacrificial, votive | traditional | peace (figurative) ◇ *I think the present she sent you was intended as a peace ~.*
VERB + OFFERING make | bring ◇ *Look, I've brought a peace ~.* | accept
PREP. ~ of ◇ *~s of food* | ~ to ◇ *They made sacrificial ~s to the gods.*

office noun

1 room/building where work is done

ADJ. big, huge, large, spacious | cramped, small, tiny | plush | high-rise ◇ *London has relatively few high-rise ~ buildings compared to cities in the US.* | five-storey/five-story, ten-storey/ten-story, etc. | glass-fronted (esp. BrE), glass-walled (esp. AmE) | busy | open-plan | corner | back, front | air-conditioned | paperless | permanent, temporary ◇ *The company set up its first permanent ~s in Manhattan.* | private ◇ *The prime minister arranged a meeting in his private ~.* | central, head, main, national | corporate, executive | area, branch, county, district, field (esp. AmE), local, overseas, regional, satellite | congressional, federal | council (esp. BrE), government, state | administrative, editorial, press, sales, etc. | newspaper | medical (AmE) | dentist's, doctor's, nurse's, physician's, surgeon's, etc. (all AmE)
VERB + OFFICE manage, run | come to, go to | arrive at, get to | leave ◇ *What time do you usually leave the ~?* | come into, go into ◇ *I sometimes go into the ~ on Saturdays when we're busy.* | call, contact, reach ◇ *You can contact our sales ~ at this number.* | establish, open ◇ *We plan to open a New York ~ in the near future.* | close
VERB + OFFICE overlook sth ◇ *an ~ overlooking the Hudson River*
OFFICE + NOUN job, work | hours ◇ *Call this number outside normal ~ hours.* | colleague, staff, worker | life | gossip, politics | party ◇ *We have an ~ party every Christmas.* | administrator, assistant, cleaner (esp. BrE), clerk, manager | boy, girl, junior (BrE) (all old-fashioned) | chair, computer, desk, door, equipment, furniture, software, stationery (esp. BrE), supplies | system, technology | environment ◇ *Working in a busy ~ environment can be stressful.* | accommodation (BrE), area, block (BrE), building, complex, development, park, premises (BrE), space, suite, tower ◇ *The old warehouses have been redeveloped as ~ buildings.* | facilities, services ◇ *The hotel provides ~ facilities such as computers and faxes.* | expenses | administration, management | skills | procedures | visit (AmE) ◇ *the bill from an ~ visit to the doctor*
PREP. at the ~ ◇ *I sometimes have to stay late at the ~.* | in the ~ ◇ *I'm sorry, Mr Anders is not in the ~ today.*

2 official position

ADJ. high, important | minor | lucrative | elected, elective

| national, public | ecclesiastical, judicial, ministerial (*esp. BrE*), political

VERB + OFFICE **run for, stand for** (*BrE*) ◇ *He ran for ~ in the last presidential election.* | **seek** ◇ *She has never sought public ~.* | **hold, remain in, retain, stay in** ◇ *The president holds ~ for a period of four years.* | **be appointed to, be elected to** | **be re-elected to, be returned to** ◇ *The government was returned to ~ by a large majority.* | **win** | **assume, be sworn into, come into, come to, enter, take, take up** (*esp. BrE*) ◇ *Mr Martens was sworn into ~ as prime minister in March.* ◇ *The party took ~ in 1997.* | **give up, leave, lose, relinquish, resign from, retire from, vacate** | **be driven from, be forced from, be forced out of, be removed from, be suspended from** (*esp. BrE*), **be turned out of**
OFFICE + NOUN **holder**
PREP. **in ~** ◇ *The government seemed likely to remain in ~ for the next five years.* | **out of ~** ◇ *The party has broken all the promises it made when out of ~.*
PHRASES **a candidate for ~** | **duties of the ~** | **an ~ of state** ◇ *the three great ~s of state: the prime minister, the chancellor and the foreign secretary* (*BrE*) | **a term of ~** ◇ *to be re-elected for a second term of ~*

officer *noun*

1 in the army, navy, etc.

ADJ. **air-force, army, military, naval** | **commanding, high-ranking, ranking, senior, superior** ◇ *The decision rests with the ranking ~* (= the most senior officer present). | **junior, petty** ◇ *a former navy chief petty ~* | **commissioned, non-commissioned** | **warrant** | **staff** | **recruiting** | **duty** ◇ *He telephoned the duty ~ at regimental headquarters.* | **intelligence** ◇ *He's a retired Army intelligence ~.* | **uniformed** | **retired**
VERB + OFFICER **salute** ◇ *to salute a superior ~*
OFFICER + VERB **command sth** ◇ *the ~ commanding the infantry* | **serve** ◇ *a former army ~ who served in Bosnia*
OFFICER + NOUN **corps** | **cadet** (*esp. BrE*), **candidate** (*AmE*) | **training**
→ Note at RANK

2 in the government or other organization

ADJ. **chief, principal, senior** | **full-time, part-time** | **presiding, responsible, supervising** (*esp. BrE*) ◇ *Report the incident to the responsible ~.* ◇ *the ~ responsible for implementing the plan* | **regional** | **administrative, customs, environmental health** (*BrE*), **financial, liaison, medical, press, probation, security, trading standards** (*BrE*), **training, welfare** (*esp. BrE*) ◇ *an education welfare ~* (*BrE*) | **chief executive** (abbreviated to *CEO*), **chief financial** (abbreviated to *CFO*), **chief information, chief investment, chief marketing, chief operating, chief technology, etc.** (*all business*)
VERB + OFFICER **be, work as** | **become** | **appoint (sb)** ◇ *Khan has been appointed chief executive ~.* | **have** ◇ *The charity has a full-time press ~ working with the national newspapers.*

3 policeman/policewoman → See also POLICEMAN

ADJ. **chief, senior, superior** | **junior** | **law enforcement, police** | **arresting, investigating** | **duty** ◇ *We spoke to the duty ~ at the police station.* | **uniformed** | **plain-clothes** | **undercover**
OFFICER + VERB **investigate sth** ◇ *~s investigating the murder* | **patrol sth** | **raid sth, swoop on sth** (*BrE, informal*) ◇ *Officers raided an address in the Pittsburgh area.* ◇ *100 ~s swooped on various south Essex locations.* | **seize sth** | **arrest sb**

official *noun*

ADJ. **high-ranking, prominent, senior, top** | **junior, minor** | **local, provincial, regional** | **public** | **administration, departmental, federal, government, state** ◇ *a senior Bush administration ~* | **full-time** ◇ *full-time union ~s* | **retired** | **elected** | **responsible** ◇ *Report the incident to the responsible ~.* ◇ *the ~ responsible for handling the case* | **corrupt** | **bank, city, company, corporate, council, court, customs, health, intelligence, judicial, law enforcement** (*esp. AmE*), **military, ministry** (*esp. BrE*), **party, royal, union** ◇ *the FBI and other law enforcement ~s* ◇ *his background as a union ~*

VERB + OFFICIAL **appoint (sb)** | **consult, consult with** (*esp. AmE*), **meet, meet with** (*esp. AmE*) ◇ *She is due to meet with local ~s to discuss possible relief projects.* | **bribe** ◇ *He attempted to bribe local ~s.*

off-putting *adj.* (*informal, esp. BrE*)

VERBS **be** | **find sth** ◇ *I find it very ~ when people don't look me in the eye.*
ADV. **extremely, fairly, very, etc.** ◇ *The noise was extremely ~.* | **distinctly** | **a little, slightly, etc.**

offset *verb*

ADV. **largely, substantially** ◇ *The carbon emissions are largely ~ by planting trees.* | **completely, exactly, fully** | **more than** ◇ *The company's losses in the US were more than ~ by gains everywhere else.* | **partially, partly**
VERB + OFFSET **help (to)** ◇ *The money will help to ~ big medical bills.*
PREP. **against** (*BrE*) ◇ *Your donations to charity can be ~ against tax.* | **by** ◇ *The loss was partially ~ by increases in revenues elsewhere.*

offside (*AmE also* offsides) *adj.*

VERBS **be, look** | **jump** (in American football) | **catch sb, rule sb** (in football/soccer) ◇ *an attempt to catch an opponent ~* ◇ *He was ruled ~ by the referee.* | **rule sth out for** (in football/soccer) ◇ *He had a goal ruled out for ~.*

oil *noun*

1 used as fuel/to make machines work smoothly

ADJ. **heavy** | **light** | **crude** | **refined** | **offshore** | **mineral** | **engine, fuel, heating, lubricating, motor** | **linseed** | **paraffin** (usually just *paraffin*) (*BrE*) (*kerosene* in *AmE*) ◇ *Use a rag soaked in paraffin ~.*
...OF OIL **barrel** | **film** ◇ *a rod coated with a film of ~* | **drop**
VERB + OIL **extract, obtain, produce** | **drill for** ◇ *The company is drilling for ~ in the North Sea.* | **discover, find, strike** | **pump** | **export, import** | **burn, use** | **change, check** (in a car, etc.) | **soak sth in** | **smell of** ◇ *The place smelled of ~.*
OIL + NOUN **company, producer** | **man** (usually *oilman*) | **baron, magnate, sheikh** | **industry, production** | **drilling, exploration** | **field, rig, well** | **pipeline** | **drum** | **tanker** | **refinery** | **prices, revenue** | **reserves, supplies** | **slick, spill, spillage** ◇ *a seven-mile-long ~ slick off the Alaskan coast*

2 used in cooking

ADJ. **cooking** | **hydrogenated** (*esp. AmE*), **polyunsaturated** | **rancid** | **coconut, canola** (*AmE*), **corn, groundnut** (*BrE*), **olive, palm, peanut, rapeseed** (*esp. BrE*), **sesame, soya bean** (*BrE*), **soybean** (*AmE*), **sunflower, vegetable** ◇ *a bottle of extra virgin olive ~* | **salad**
VERB + OIL **heat** | **boil sb/sth in, cook sth in, fry sth in** | **drizzle, pour** ◇ *Toast the bread, rub with garlic and drizzle over a little olive ~.*
PREP. **in ~** ◇ *Fry the potato in a little sunflower ~.*
→ Special page at FOOD

3 used as a cosmetic/fragrance/medicine

ADJ. **aromatic, fragrant, scented** | **essential** ◇ *essential ~s extracted from flowers* | **natural** | **body, hair** | **baby, bath** | **aromatherapy, massage** | **cod liver, fish, omega-3** ◇ *A daily dose of omega-3 fish ~ will help children to concentrate better.* | **castor, evening primrose, flaxseed, lavender, tea tree, etc.**
VERB + OIL **massage, rub** ◇ *She rubbed a scented ~ into her hair.* | **massage sth with, rub sth with** | **anoint sb/sth with** ◇ *The sick were anointed with ~.* | **extract**
PREP. **~ of** ◇ *~ of rosemary*

ointment *noun*

...OF OINTMENT **tube**
VERB + OINTMENT **apply, put on, rub on** ◇ *He put some ~ on the cut.* | **use**

OK (also okay) adj., adv.

VERBS **be, feel, look, seem, smell, sound, taste** | **do** ◊ *I think I did ~ in the exam.* (*BrE*) ◊ *I think I did ~ on the exam.* (*AmE*) | **go, turn out** ◊ *I hope the meeting goes ~.*
ADV. **perfectly, quite** (*esp. BrE*), **really, totally** (*esp. AmE*) ◊ *I'm perfectly ~ now, thanks.*
PREP. **by sb** ◊ *John has suggested meeting at six, and that's ~ by me.* | **with sb/sth** ◊ *Is it ~ with you if I come around six?* ◊ *Are you sure you're ~ with the arrangement?*

old adj.

1 age

VERBS **be, feel, look, seem** ◊ *You are as ~ as you feel.*
ADV. **enough** ◊ *He's ~ enough by now to manage his own affairs.*
PHRASES **six months, ten years, etc. ~**

2 not young

VERBS **be, feel, look, seem, sound** ◊ *The way the young people rushed around made her feel ~.* ◊ *He was beginning to look ~.* | **become, get, grow** ◊ *We're all getting older.* ◊ *As they grow older, they develop new interests.*
ADV. **extremely, fairly, very, etc.** ◊ *She was fairly ~ when she got married.*

3 not new

VERBS **be**
ADV. **extremely, fairly, very, etc.** ◊ *It's a very ~ tradition.*
PHRASES **oldest known** ◊ *These are some of the oldest known fossil remains.* | **oldest remaining, oldest surviving** ◊ *It's one of the oldest remaining parts of the church.* ◊ *the world's oldest surviving ship*

4 shows affection/lack of respect

PHRASES **boring ~, silly ~** (*esp. BrE*) ◊ *boring ~ history books* ◊ *He's a silly ~ fool!* | **dear ~, good ~** ◊ *Good ~ Dad!* | **funny ~** ◊ *It's a funny ~ world.* | **plain ~** ◊ *Why drink plain ~ water when you can have something better?* | **poor ~** ◊ *You poor ~ thing!* | **same ~** ◊ *It's always the same ~ faces.*

old age noun

ADJ. **advanced, extreme** | **happy** ◊ *She can look forward to a happy ~.* | **lonely** (*esp. BrE*) ◊ *fears about a lonely ~*
VERB + OLD AGE **live to, reach, survive into, survive to** ◊ *My grandparents survived into advanced ~.* | **approach** | **die of**
OLD-AGE + NOUN **pension, pensioner** (*both BrE*) ◊ *I'll soon be drawing my old-age pension.*
PREP. **in (your) ~** ◊ *Loss of hearing often occurs in ~.* ◊ *He took up golf in his ~.* | **into ~** ◊ *She was now well into ~.*
PHRASES **the grand ~ of sth, the ripe ~ of sth** ◊ *She lived to the ripe ~ of 98.*

old-fashioned adj.

VERBS **be, look, seem** | **become** | **consider sth, regard sth as, see sth as** ◊ *Wearing a hat is now regarded as rather ~.*
ADV. **extremely, fairly, very, etc.** | **hopelessly, terribly** (*esp. BrE*) | **plain** | **a little, slightly, etc.** | **curiously** (*esp. BrE*) ◊ *His clothes were curiously ~.*
PREP. **in** ◊ *She's somewhat ~ in her attitudes.*
PHRASES **call me ~** ◊ *Call me ~, but I still believe in good manners.* | **a good old-fashioned…** ◊ *At heart, it's just a good ~ detective story.*

ombudsman noun

ADJ. **financial, health-service, insurance, local-government, parliamentary, pensions** (*all BrE*) ◊ *A pensions ~ has been appointed.*
VERB + OMBUDSMAN **appoint**

omen noun

ADJ. **good** | **bad, evil, ill** ◊ *They took the storm as a bad ~.*
VERB + OMEN **take sth as**
PREP. **~ for** ◊ *The smiling faces were a good ~ for the future of the restaurant.* | **~ of** ◊ *an ~ of death*

omission noun

ADJ. **important, major, serious, significant** | **complete** | **glaring, notable, obvious** ◊ *There were no glaring ~s in the report.* | **curious, surprising** | **deliberate**
VERB + OMISSION **correct, rectify, remedy** | **notice** ◊ *I notice one glaring ~ from your list.* | **point out** ◊ *I feel compelled to point out two ~s.*
PREP. **by ~** ◊ *A lie by ~* (= by not saying something) *is still a lie.* | **~ from** ◊ *her ~ from the guest list* | **~ of** ◊ *the ~ of the author's name*
PHRASES **an act or ~** (*law*) ◊ *The accident was not caused by any act or ~ of the gas company.* | **errors and ~s, errors or ~s** (*both formal*) | **a sin of ~** (*formal*)

omit verb

ADV. **altogether, completely, entirely** ◊ *This scene is usually cut down or omitted altogether.* | **accidentally, inadvertently** ◊ *The acknowledgements were inadvertently omitted from the article.* | **deliberately** | **conveniently** ◊ *This fact had been conveniently omitted from his account of events.* | **conspicuously**
PREP. **from** ◊ *Some important details were deliberately omitted from the report.*

one-sided adj.

VERBS **be, seem**
ADV. **pretty, rather, somewhat, very** ◊ *Their relationship seems rather ~.* | **completely, entirely, totally, wholly** (*BrE*) ◊ *Her article is entirely ~ and subjective.* | **a little, slightly, etc.**

onion noun

ADJ. **raw** | **caramelized, pickled** (*esp. BrE*) ◊ *a jar of pickled ~s* | **chopped, diced, sliced** ◊ *Put the chopped ~ and garlic in the pan…* | **green** (*AmE*), **spring** (*BrE*) | **cocktail, pearl** (*esp. AmE*), **red, sweet** (*esp. AmE*), **Vidalia™** (*AmE*), **etc.**
VERB + ONION **chop, peel, slice** | **brown, soften** | **cook, fry, grill** (*esp. AmE*), **sauté** | **garnish sth with** ◊ *Garnish with a little chopped ~.* | **grow**
ONION + NOUN **ring** | **soup** | **dip** (*esp. AmE*) | **skin** | **set** (*technical*) | **dome** ◊ *the ~ domes of St Basil's Cathedral*
PHRASES **cheese and ~** (*BrE*) ◊ *cheese and ~ flavoured crisps* | **sage and ~** (*BrE*) ◊ *sage and ~ stuffing*
→ Special page at FOOD

onset noun

ADJ. **rapid, sudden** ◊ *the sudden ~ of the disease* | **acute** (*medical*) ◊ *Symptoms include the acute ~ of pain.* | **slow** | **early** | **delayed, late**
VERB + ONSET **delay** | **prevent** | **mark, signal** ◊ *His first hit record marked the ~ of an astonishing career.* ◊ *The development of pubic hair signals the ~ of puberty.*
PREP. **after the ~** ◊ *after the ~ of sleep* | **at the ~** ◊ *at the ~ of the war* | **before the ~, prior to the ~** | **since the ~**

onslaught noun

ADJ. **sudden** ◊ *She could not withstand such a sudden ~.* | **initial** | **renewed** | **relentless** ◊ *the relentless ~ of modernism* | **fierce, vicious** ◊ *England faced a fierce ~ from South Africa for much of the game.* ◊ *His approach was met with a vicious ~.* | **verbal** ◊ *She unleashed a verbal ~ on her critics.* | **media**
VERB + ONSLAUGHT **face** ◊ *to face the verbal ~ of an angry teenager* | **resist, survive, withstand** | **launch, unleash** ◊ *The leadership launched an ~ against Trotsky and his supporters.* | **continue** | **stop**
PREP. **~ against, ~ on** ◊ *a renewed ~ against the proposed bill* | **~ from** ◊ *the latest ~ from the Russian team*

ooze verb

ADV. **slowly** | **out** ◊ *Cream ~d out at the sides.*
PREP. **from** ◊ *Blood ~d slowly from his wound.* | **out of** | **with** (*figurative*) ◊ *He was oozing with contempt for us.*

opaque adj.

1 not clear enough to see through

VERBS **be, look** | **become** ◊ *As the lens becomes more ~, the patient notices a falling off in vision.*
ADV. **completely** ◊ *These crystals are completely ~ and nearly black.* | **almost, nearly** | **slightly, somewhat** ◊ *The glasses looked slightly ~.*
PREP. **with** ◊ *The windows were nearly ~ with grime.*

2 difficult to understand

VERBS **be** | **become** | **remain**
ADV. **extremely, fairly, very, etc.** ◊ *Both question and answer are rather ~.* ◊ *The complex administrative arrangements mean that the decision-making process remains somewhat ~.* | **completely** ◊ *The system is completely ~ to non-specialists.* | **relatively** | **a little, slightly, etc.**

open verb

1 door, window, box, etc.

ADV. **fully, wide** ◊ *She ~ed all the windows wide to let some fresh air in.* | **gingerly** ◊ *Fred ~ed the box gingerly and peered inside.* | **quickly, suddenly** | **slowly** | **automatically** ◊ *The glass doors ~ed automatically for him.* | **out, up** ◊ *I ~ed out the map and laid it on the table.* ◊ *'Open up!' He shouted, hammering on the door.*
VERB + OPEN **try to** | **manage to** | **fail to** ◊ *Her parachute failed to ~.*

2 building, road, etc.

ADV. **formally, officially** | **up** ◊ *the opportunity to ~ up new markets*
VERB + OPEN **be due to, be expected to, be scheduled to** ◊ *The museum is due to ~ next year.* | **hope to, intend to, plan to, want to, wish to**
PHRASES **newly ~ed, recently ~ed** ◊ *the newly ~ed gallery of Western decorative art*

open adj.

1 not closed

VERBS **be, gape, hang, lie, stand** ◊ *She stared at him, her mouth hanging ~.* ◊ *The book lay ~ in front of him.* ◊ *The door stood ~.* | **burst, creak, fall, flutter, fly, shoot, slide, snap, swing** ◊ *The bag fell ~.* ◊ *Suddenly the door flew ~.* ◊ *The gate swung ~.* | **remain** | **break sth, cut sth, fling sth, flip sth, get sth, prise/prize sth** (*esp. BrE*), **pry sth** (*esp. AmE*), **pull sth, push sth, rip sth, tear sth, throw sth, wrench sth, yank sth** ◊ *She flung the door ~ and rushed in.* ◊ *She flipped ~ Chris's diary.* ◊ *I tried to pry ~ the locket.* ◊ *He tore the letter ~.* | **have sth, hold sth, keep sth, leave sth** ◊ *She held the door ~ for them.* | **find sth, see sth** ◊ *I found the door ~.*
ADV. **fully, wide** ◊ *The door was wide ~.* | **partially** | **slightly**

2 honest and willing to talk

VERBS **be, seem**
ADV. **extremely, fairly, very, etc.** | **completely**
PREP. **about** ◊ *She's very ~ about her mistakes.* | **with** ◊ *I don't think you've been completely ~ with me.*

3 available for people to use

VERBS **be** | **remain, stay** ◊ *In spite of the snow, the roads remained ~.* ◊ *Some of the supermarkets stay ~ till ten.* | **keep sth** ◊ *We want to keep the school ~.*
PREP. **to** ◊ *The pool is only ~ to residents.*

4 having begun

VERBS **be** | **declare sth** (*esp. BrE*) ◊ *The Australian premier declared the Olympic Games ~.*
ADV. **officially** ◊ *The bridge is officially ~ now.*

opening noun

1 beginning

ADJ. **successful** ◊ *It was the most successful ~ of any British movie ever.* | **chess**
PREP. **~ to** ◊ *the famous ~ to the novel*

2 hole; way in/out

ADJ. **large, wide** | **narrow, small** | **window**
VERB + OPENING **cut** | **create, make** | **block, cover, seal**

PREP. **~ in** ◊ *to cut an ~ in the fence* | **~ to** ◊ *the ~ to the kitchen*

3 opportunity; job which is available

ADJ. **new** | **possible** | **clear** (*sports*) ◊ *He missed one of the clearest ~s in the game.* | **job, political**
VERB + OPENING **create, provide** ◊ *Cooper created the ~ for Russell to shoot the first goal.* | **give sb** | **fill** ◊ *She is the strongest candidate to fill this ~.*
PREP. **~ for, ~ in** ◊ *career ~s for biologists in industry*

4 ceremony

ADJ. **grand** | **formal** | **official, royal, state** ◊ *the state ~ of Parliament* (*in the UK*)
VERB + OPENING **attend** | **celebrate** | **mark**
OPENING + NOUN **ceremony**

openness noun

ADJ. **greater, more** ◊ *There is a need for greater ~ in government.* | **complete** | **new** ◊ *He talked with a new ~ about his own life.*
VERB + OPENNESS **demonstrate, show** | **require**
PREP. **~ about** ◊ *her ~ about her marital problems* | **~ to, ~ towards/toward** ◊ *He demonstrated an ~ to change.*

opera noun

ADJ. **comic, grand, light**
VERB + OPERA **compose, write** | **sing**
OPERA + NOUN **singer, star** | **composer** | **company** | **house** | **season** | **buff, lover**
→ Note at PERFORMANCE (for more verbs)

operate verb

1 machine

ADV. **effectively, efficiently, reliably** | **normally, properly** ◊ *The equipment was not operating properly.* | **continuously** ◊ *The machine can ~ for 15 hours continuously at full power.* | **electrically, electronically, hydraulically, manually, remotely** (= by remote control) ◊ *The doors can be manually ~d in the event of fire.*
VERB + OPERATE **be designed to** ◊ *systems designed to ~ at the highest speeds* | **be easy to** ◊ *The machinery is easy to ~.*

2 business/system

ADV. **effectively, efficiently, smoothly** | **profitably, successfully** | **normally** ◊ *The hospital was operating normally.* | **currently** ◊ *The airline currently ~s 115 routes to 39 airports in 13 countries.* | **autonomously, independently** | **differently** | **commercially** ◊ *The laboratory is still owned by the government but is now commercially ~d.*
VERB + OPERATE **be able to** | **be allowed to** | **continue to**
PREP. **according to** ◊ *The government does not ~ according to fixed rules.* | **as** ◊ *We ~ as an advisory service for schools.* | **under** ◊ *The industry ~s under rigid guidelines.* | **within** ◊ *Local authorities ~ within a wider political system.*

operation noun

1 medical

ADJ. **major** | **minor, small** | **life-saving, vital** | **emergency** | **routine** (*esp. BrE*) | **delicate** ◊ *a delicate eye ~* | **exploratory** | **surgical, transplant** | **heart, knee, etc.**
VERB + OPERATION **have, undergo** ◊ *He had an ~ to remove a growth.* | **come through, survive** ◊ *She came through the ~ well.* | **carry out, perform** ◊ *the surgeon performing the ~*
PREP. **during a/the ~** ◊ *She woke during the ~.* | **~ for** ◊ *an ~ for a kidney problem* | **~ on** ◊ *a major ~ on his heart*

2 organized activity

ADJ. **big, large-scale, major, massive** | **covert, undercover** | **combined, joint** (*esp. BrE*) ◊ *a tricky rescue ~* | **successful** | **combat, intelligence, military, naval, police** | **air, flight, ground, land, sea** ◊ *US forces had to conduct ground and air ~s.* ◊ *The airline has appointed a new director of flight ~s.* | **guerrilla** | **clean-up, counter-terrorist, drilling, mining, mopping-up, offensive, peace-**

keeping, relief, rescue, salvage, security, tactical ◇ *UN troops supervised the relief ~s.* | banking, building, business, commercial ◇ *restrictions placed on business ~s* | psychological ~s, special ~s ◇ *Special ~s forces were on the ground in Afghanistan.*

VERB + OPERATION begin, launch, mount, undertake ◇ *The authorities launched a massive security ~ in the city.* | carry out, conduct, run | oversee, supervise

PREP. during a/the ~ ◇ *during joint military ~s*

PHRASES a theatre/theater of ~s (= where military operations take place)

3 fact of sth functioning

ADJ. effective, efficient, smooth | normal | daily, day-to-day ◇ *the smooth day-to-day ~ of the department*

VERB + OPERATION come into ◇ *A ceasefire came into ~ in May.* | bring sth into (*esp. BrE*), put sth into | cease ◇ *The factory will cease ~ at the end of the year.*

PREP. during ~ ◇ *The machine can get very hot during ~.* | in ~ ◇ *The current tax system has been in ~ for ten years.*

PHRASES in full ~, into full ~ ◇ *the only reactor in full ~*

operational *adj.*

VERBS be | become | remain | keep sth ◇ *They plan to keep the telescope ~ until the end of the decade.* | declare sth ◇ *The weapon system was declared ~ in June 2004.*

ADV. fully ◇ *The equipment is now fully ~.*

operative *adj.*

VERBS be | become | remain

ADV. fully ◇ *The new system will not become fully ~ until next year.*

operator *noun*

1 person who connects telephone calls

ADJ. switchboard, telephone

OPERATOR + VERB connect sb, put sb through ◇ *I asked the ~ to put me through to her office.*

2 person who works a machine, etc.

ADJ. experienced, skilled | machine, plant | camera, computer, lathe, radio, etc.

3 person/company that does particular business

ADJ. big, large | small | private | independent | holiday (*BrE*), tour, travel (*esp. BrE*) | cable, cable-television | cellular (*AmE*), mobile (*BrE*), mobile-phone (*BrE*), network | satellite, telecommunications | airline (*esp. BrE*), bus (*esp. BrE*), charter, coach (*BrE*), ferry (*esp. BrE*) ◇ *The budget airline ~ is to operate a new route to Northern Ireland.*

4 sb who is good at getting what they want

ADJ. shrewd, smooth

opinion *noun*

1 what you think about sb/sth

ADJ. good, high | low, poor | strong | conflicting, different, mixed ◇ *There are conflicting ~s regarding genetically modified food.* | same | honest ◇ *If you want my honest ~, I think the book is awful.* | expert, informed, professional | considered | personal, subjective | objective | contrary, dissenting | majority | minority | second ◇ *If in doubt about your diagnosis, get a second ~.*

VERB + OPINION have, hold | air, express, give (sb), offer (sb), state, venture, voice ◇ *The meeting will give people the chance to voice their ~s on the matter.* | share ◇ *I don't share your ~ of his ability.* | ask sb, seek ◇ *He asked me for my ~ of the course.* | want ◇ *I don't trust her, if you want my honest ~.* | get | form ◇ *I formed the ~ that he was not to be trusted.* | change

OPINION + VERB change | differ, vary ◇ *Opinions differ as to when this wine should be drunk.*

OPINION + NOUN piece ◇ *He writes an ~ piece in the 'New York Times'.*

PREP. in your ~ ◇ *In my ~, golf is a dull sport.* | ~ about, ~

on ◇ *She holds strong ~s on education.* | ~ as to ◇ *~s as to the merits of the plan* | ~ of ◇ *He has a very high ~ of your work.*

PHRASES be of the ~ that... (= to believe or think that) (*formal*) | a difference of ~ ◇ *a genuine difference of ~ between the experts* | in my humble ~ (*humorous*) | a matter of ~ ◇ *'Miami is wonderful.' 'That's a matter of ~.'*

2 what people in general think about sth

ADJ. prevailing | general, popular, public ◇ *Contrary to popular ~, not all of Hitchcock's movies were great.* | international, local, national, world ◇ *The country's government appears disdainful of world ~.* | expert, informed, professional | academic, legal, medical, political

... OF OPINION body ◇ *This view is supported by a growing body of professional ~.*

VERB + OPINION mould/mold, shape, sway ◇ *attempts to shape public ~*

OPINION + VERB be against sth, be in favour/favor of sth ◇ *Prevailing local ~ is against the new road proposals.* | be divided ◇ *Public ~ is divided on the subject of capital punishment.*

OPINION + NOUN poll | former (*esp. BrE*), leader

PREP. ~ among ◇ *Opinion among doctors is that the medication is safe.*

PHRASES climate of ~ ◇ *in the present climate of ~* | shades of ~ ◇ *all shades of political ~*

opium *noun*

VERB + OPIUM smoke

OPIUM + NOUN poppy | den

→ Note at DRUG (for more verbs and nouns)

opponent *noun*

1 person who plays against sb

ADJ. chief, main | dangerous, tough | worthy

VERB + OPPONENT attack, hit | fight | beat, defeat | hold to sth (*AmE, sports*) ◇ *This season the team is holding ~s to 88.9 points per game.* | get past, outmanoeuvre/outmaneuver, outwit | face ◇ *Today she faces her toughest ~.* | tackle | throw (*sports*) | knock down, knock out ◇ *He has knocked out 15 ~s in 20 fights.* | bring down, foul (*esp. BrE*)

→ Special page at SPORTS

2 sb who disagrees with sb's actions/plans/beliefs

ADJ. chief, leading, main | bitter, fierce, formidable, staunch, strong, vigorous | outspoken, vocal, vociferous ◇ *She's an outspoken opponent of the government.* | worthy | political

opportunity *noun*

ADJ. ample, considerable, plenty of ◇ *We'll have plenty of ~ to talk later.* | limited, little, not much | big, excellent, favourable/favorable, golden, good, great, marvellous/marvelous, real, tremendous, welcome, wonderful ◇ *a golden ~ to invest in new markets* | exciting | ideal, perfect | suitable | reasonable ◇ *We need to give them a reasonable ~ to look at the display.* | available | every ◇ *Students should take every ~ to widen their experience.* | new | historic, once-in-a-lifetime, rare, unique, unparalleled, unprecedented, unrivalled/unrivaled (*esp. BrE*) | lost, missed, wasted | career, educational, employment, job, training | business, commercial, economic, growth, investment, market, sales ◇ *a missed sales ~* | photo (= an opportunity to take photographs of famous people) | equal opportunities (*BrE*), equal ~ (*esp. AmE*) (= the principle of treating all people the same, regardless of sex, race, etc.) ◇ *We are dedicated to the principle of equal ~.* ◇ *an equal-opportunities employer* (*BrE*) ◇ *an equal-opportunity employer* (*AmE*)

VERB + OPPORTUNITY have | find, get ◇ *We didn't get much ~ to swim.* | afford, create, give sb, offer (sb), open up, present, provide (sb with) ◇ *to provide better educational opportunities* | see ◇ *He saw a great ~ to make some money.* | grasp, seize, take, take advantage of, take up, use ◇ *May I take this ~ to congratulate Ruth on her promotion.* | lose,

miss ◇ *He lost no ~ to vent his anger on those around him.* |
pass up
OPPORTUNITY + VERB **exist** | **arise, come, occur, present itself**
◇ *When the ~ came, I seized it with both hands.*
PREP. **~ for** ◇ *The job will offer you excellent opportunities for
promotion.*
PHRASES **at the earliest ~, at the first (possible) ~** | **at every
available ~, at every ~, at every possible ~** | **equality of
~** | **the ~ of a lifetime** | **a window of ~** ◇ *The ceasefire has
created a window of ~ to rescue the peace process.*

oppose *verb*

ADV. **adamantly, bitterly, fiercely, firmly, resolutely** (*esp.
BrE*), **strenuously, strongly, vehemently, vigorously, vio-
lently** ◇ *We would vigorously ~ such a policy.* | **totally** ◇ *We
totally ~ the use of gas to kill any animal.* | **actively** |
openly, publicly | **successfully, unsuccessfully** (*esp. BrE*) ◇
Environmental lobby groups successfully ~d the plan. |
initially ◇ *The ban was initially ~d by the US.* | **consistently**
◇ *The president has consistently ~d any relaxation in the law.*
VERB + OPPOSE **vote to** | **continue to**

opposed *adj.*

1 opposed to disagreeing strongly with sth
VERBS **be** | **remain**
ADV. **adamantly, bitterly, deeply, fiercely, firmly, fundamentally, implacably, resolutely, strongly, vehemently,
very, very much, vigorously, violently** | **absolutely,
completely, directly, totally, utterly** (*esp. BrE*), **wholly** (*esp.
BrE*) | **largely** | **actively, openly, publicly** ◇ *the party most
openly ~ to military rule* | **personally** (*esp. AmE*)
2 very different from sth
VERBS **be, seem, stand** | **remain**
ADV. **completely, diametrically, directly, entirely, fundamentally, utterly** (*esp. BrE*) ◇ *Our views are diametrically ~
on this issue.* | **mutually** ◇ *The two sets of values seemed
mutually ~.*
PREP. **to** ◇ *His actions seemed directly ~ to the values of the
company.*

opposite *noun*

ADJ. **complete, direct, exact, precise, total, very** | **polar**
OPPOSITE + VERB **be the case, be true** ◇ *Most people look
forward to the weekend, but with him the ~ is true.*
PREP. **the ~ of, the ~ to** ◇ *'Light' is the ~ of 'heavy'.* ◇ *In
temperament, she was the complete ~ to her sister.*
PHRASES **exactly the ~, just the ~, quite the ~** ◇ *The effect
was exactly the ~, what he intended.* | **~s attract**

opposition *noun*

1 disagreeing with sth/trying to change sth
ADJ. **bitter, considerable, determined, fierce, serious, stiff,
strong, vehement** | **violent** | **growing, mounting** |
effective, powerful | **vocal** | **direct** ◇ *a statement in direct ~
to party policy* | **active** | **organized** | **political** | **public** |
widespread
VERB + OPPOSITION **express, voice** ◇ *Many people have voiced
their ~ to these proposals.* | **mount, put up** (*esp. BrE*) ◇ *They
mounted an effective ~ to the bill.* | **lead** | **arouse, draw** |
crush, overcome, stifle, suppress, wear down (*esp. BrE*) |
be up against, come up against (*BrE*), **encounter, face,
meet, meet with, run into, run up against** (*esp. BrE*) ◇ *He is
up against stiff ~ from his colleagues.* | **brook** ◇ *We will
brook no ~ to the strategy.* | **strengthen** | **weaken** | **drop** ◇
The Democrats are unlikely to drop their ~ to his nomination.
OPPOSITION + VERB **come from sb** ◇ *Opposition came
primarily from students.*
OPPOSITION + NOUN **force, group, movement**
PREP. **against ~, in the face of ~** ◇ *She won against
determined ~ from last year's champion.* | **despite ~, in
spite of ~** ◇ *The authorities succeeded despite bitter ~ from
teachers.* | **in ~ to** ◇ *The warring factions had united in ~ to
the common enemy.* | **~ from** ◇ *The proposals met with
violent ~ from the environmental lobby.* | **~ to** ◇ *There was
fierce public ~ to the plan.*

2 parties not in government
ADJ. **loyal** ◇ *They see their role as a loyal ~.* ◇ *the leader of Her
Majesty's loyal Opposition* (*in the UK*) | **democratic**
OPPOSITION + NOUN **party** | **candidate, leader, member, MP**
(*in the UK*), **politician, spokesman** (*esp. BrE*) | **bench** (*in the
UK*)
PREP. **in ~** ◇ *The party is now in ~.*
PHRASES **the Leader of the Opposition** (*in the UK*)

oppression *noun*

ADJ. **class, economic, political, racial, religious, sexual,
social** | **black, colonial, women's** | **male, white**
VERB + OPPRESSION **face, suffer** ◇ *ethnic minorities suffering ~
at the hands of occupying forces* | **fight, fight against, resist**
◇ *years of resisting colonial ~* | **escape**

optician *noun* (*BrE*) → See also OPTOMETRIST

ADJ. **dispensing, ophthalmic**
PHRASES **at the optician's, to the optician's** ◇ *I've got to go to
the optician's tomorrow.*
→ Note at DOCTOR (for verbs)

optimism *noun*

ADJ. **considerable, great, tremendous** (*esp. BrE*) | **sunny** (*esp.
AmE*) | **some** | **cautious, guarded** | **false, misplaced** ◇ *Her
~ turned out to be misplaced.* | **naive** (*esp. AmE*) | **early,
initial** ◇ *By 1960, the initial ~ had evaporated.* | **renewed**
... OF OPTIMISM **wave** ◇ *The news caused a wave of ~.* | **note** ◇
There was a note of ~ in his voice.
VERB + OPTIMISM **express** | **share** ◇ *I find it hard to share
his ~.*
OPTIMISM + VERB **prevail** (*esp. AmE*), **reign** ◇ *Despite the crisis,
a cautious ~ reigned.* | **evaporate**
PREP. **with ~** ◇ *We can look to the future with considerable ~.* |
~ about, ~ over ◇ *The government expressed ~ about the
success of the negotiations.* | **~ among** ◇ *renewed ~ among
mortgage lenders* | **~ for** ◇ *great ~ for the future*
PHRASES **cause for ~, grounds for ~, reason for ~** ◇ *There
are now very real grounds for ~.* | **full of ~** ◇ *When the 1970s
began, we were still full of ~.* | **a mood of ~, a sense of ~, a
spirit of ~**

optimist *noun*

ADJ. **eternal, incurable** | **cockeyed** (*informal, esp. AmE*)
PHRASES **ever the ~** ◇ *Carlos, ever the ~, said things were
bound to improve.*

optimistic *adj.*

VERBS **appear, be, feel, look, seem, sound** | **become** |
remain, stay
ADV. **extremely, fairly, very, etc.** | **highly** ◇ *He remained
highly ~ that an agreement could be reached.* | **excessively,
hopelessly, incredibly, overly, unduly, wildly** ◇ *These
estimates were wildly ~.* | **a little, slightly, etc.** | **reasonably**
| **generally** ◇ *a generally ~ view of the future* | **cautiously,
guardedly, quietly** (*esp. AmE*) ◇ *I don't want to exaggerate
our chances, but I'm cautiously ~.*
PREP. **about** ◇ *He's very ~ about his chances.*

option *noun*

1 freedom to choose
VERB + OPTION **have** ◇ *You have the ~ of working full-time or
part-time.* | **give sb**
PREP. **with the ~ of, without the ~ of** ◇ *He was jailed without
the ~ of a fine.*
PHRASES **have little ~ but to, have no ~ but to** ◇ *We had no ~
but to leave without them.*
2 sth you choose/can choose
ADJ. **available, possible, viable** | **real, realistic** | **attractive,
good** ◇ *Deciding on your best ~ is not easy.* | **preferred** |
only ◇ *Resignation was her only ~.* | **limited** | **practical** |
easy, soft (*esp. BrE*) ◇ *A life of chastity is not an easy ~.* ◇ *He*

thought General Studies would be a soft ~. | **cheap,
expensive** | **policy** | **nuclear** | **menu** (= on a computer)
VERB + OPTION **choose, exercise, select, take** ◊ Look at the on-
screen menu and select the 'File' ~. | **give sb, offer (sb),
provide** | **limit** | **consider, look at, weigh** ◊ Let's look at all
the ~s available.
PHRASES **keep your ~s open, leave your ~s open** (= to
avoid making a decision now so that you still have a choice
later)

3 right to buy/sell sth at some time in the future
ADJ. **first** | **share** (BrE), **stock** (AmE)
VERB + OPTION **have** | **exercise, take, take up** ◊ She took up
an ~ in her contract to buy three million shares.
PREP. **~ on** ◊ He's promised me first ~ on his car.

optometrist noun (AmE) → See also OPTICIAN

VERB + OPTOMETRIST **go to, visit** ◊ I went to visit my ~.
→ Note at DOCTOR (for verbs)

orange noun

ADJ. **juicy** | **sour, sweet** | **navel** | **mandarin** (AmE) (just
mandarin in BrE)
...OF ORANGE **segment** (esp. BrE)
VERB + ORANGE **eat, have, squeeze** | **peel**
ORANGE + NOUN **segment, slice, wedge** (AmE) | **pip** (esp. BrE),
seed (esp. AmE) | **peel, rind, zest** ◊ Add a little grated ~ peel.
| **juice** | **squash** (BrE)
→ Special page at FRUIT

orange adj., noun → Special page at COLOUR

orbit noun

ADJ. **circular, elliptical** | **eccentric** ◊ Mercury's ~ is fairly
eccentric. | **high, low** | **stable** | **planetary** | **Earth**
VERB + ORBIT **enter, go into** | **reach** | **put sth into, send sth
into** | **complete, make** ◊ The spaceship made an ~ of the
moon. | **leave**
PREP. **in ~** ◊ The satellite will remain in ~ for several years. | **~
around, ~ round** (esp. BrE) ◊ the moon's ~ around the earth

orchestra noun

ADJ. **large, small** | **full** ◊ The full ~ includes two harps. |
great, major (esp. AmE), **top** (esp. BrE) | **live** | **amateur,
professional** | **symphony** | **chamber, jazz, string** | **school,
youth**
VERB + ORCHESTRA **conduct** | **lead** | **join**
ORCHESTRA + VERB **perform (sth), play (sth)** | **strike up (sth)** ◊
The ~ struck up a lively march. | **tune up**
ORCHESTRA + NOUN **pit**
PREP. **in a/the ~** ◊ She plays viola in a string ~. | **~ under** ◊
the Ulster Orchestra under Philip Ledger
PHRASES **the leader of the ~** (BrE) (**concertmaster** in AmE)

ordeal noun

ADJ. **long** | **entire** (esp. AmE), **whole** ◊ My family has
supported me through this whole ~. | **dreadful** (esp. BrE),
horrible (esp. AmE), **terrible, terrifying** (esp. BrE)
VERB + ORDEAL **endure, face, go through, suffer** (esp. BrE),
undergo | **subject sb to** (esp. BrE) ◊ She was subjected to a
terrible six-day ~. | **survive** | **recover from** | **be spared** (esp.
BrE)
PREP. **~ of** ◊ They were spared the ~ of giving evidence in
court.
PHRASES **an ~ at the hands of sb** (esp. BrE) ◊ their 20-hour ~
at the hands of a gunman

order noun

1 way in which people/things are arranged
ADJ. **correct, proper, right** | **wrong** | **logical** ◊ The
paragraphs are not in a logical ~. | **ascending** ◊ arranged in
ascending ~ of size | **descending** | **alphabetical, chrono-
logical, numerical, random, reverse** | **pecking** ◊ the

pecking ~ among the hospital staff | **rank** ◊ the top ten
groups, in rank ~ | **word** | **running** ◊ Where am I in the
running ~? | **batting** (sports)
VERB + ORDER **change** ◊ I think you should change the ~ of
these paragraphs.
PREP. **in ~** ◊ The winners were announced in reverse ~. | **in ~
of** ◊ I've listed the tasks in ~ of priority. | **out of ~** ◊ The
episodes were shown out of ~.

2 organized state
ADJ. **apple-pie** (= perfect) (old-fashioned, esp. AmE) ◊ The
accounts were in apple-pie ~.
VERB + ORDER **bring, create, impose** ◊ to bring ~ out of chaos
◊ She attempted to impose some ~ on the chaos of her files. |
put sth in, set sth in
PREP. **in ~** ◊ My notes are in ~.
PHRASES **in good ~** ◊ The house is in good ~.

3 when laws, rules, authority, etc. are obeyed
ADJ. **civil, public**
VERB + ORDER **keep, maintain, preserve** | **restore** | **keep sb/
sth in** ◊ Some teachers find it difficult to keep their classes in
~. | **call sth to** ◊ The argument continued until the chairman
called the meeting to ~ (= ordered them to obey the formal
rules).
PREP. **in ~** (= acceptable) ◊ Would it be in ~ for us to examine
the manuscript? | **out of ~** ◊ The objection was ruled out of
~ (= not allowed by the rules). ◊ He accepted that he'd been
out of ~ (= he had behaved unacceptably). (BrE, informal)
PHRASES **law and ~** | **a point of ~** ◊ One of the committee
members raised a point of ~.

4 way a society is arranged
ADJ. **established, existing, old** ◊ He was seen as a threat to
the established ~. | **new** | **natural** ◊ the natural ~ of things |
economic, moral, political, social | **international, world** ◊
a new world ~

5 instruction/demand
ADJ. **direct, specific, strict** | **executive** | **sealed** ◊ He opened
his sealed ~s. | **court** | **gag, gagging** (BrE) | **exclusion** (BrE),
maintenance (BrE), **preservation** (BrE), **restraining** (esp.
AmE) ◊ a wildlife preservation ~ ◊ The court issued a
restraining ~ against Pearson.
VERB + ORDER **give, issue, make** (law, esp. BrE) ◊ The captain
gave the ~ to fire. ◊ The judge made an ~ for the costs to be
paid. | **sign** | **slap** ◊ The building has had a preservation ~
slapped on it. (BrE) | **enforce** | **await** | **get, receive** | **obtain**
◊ His lawyer had to obtain a court ~ to get access to her
client. | **carry out, execute, follow, obey, take** ◊ The local
civilians don't take ~s from the military. | **disobey, ignore,
violate** | **cancel** | **countermand, rescind, revoke** (esp. BrE)
(all formal) | **bark, bark out, shout, shout out** ◊ He barked
out ~s as he left.
PREP. **by ~ of** (formal) ◊ by ~ of the police | **on sb's ~s** ◊ The
ship was to set sail at once, on the admiral's ~s. | **under ~s
from** ◊ A group of soldiers, under ~s from the president, took
control of the television station. | **~s for** ◊ The colonel had
given ~s for the spy's execution.
PHRASES **doctor's ~s** ◊ I'm not to drink any alcohol—doctor's
~s! | **get your marching ~s** (= be ordered to leave), **give
sb their marching ~s**

6 request for sth to be made/supplied/delivered
ADJ. **bulk, large, record** (esp. BrE) | **small** | **firm** | **advance** |
back, outstanding (esp. BrE) | **repeat** | **tall** (= difficult to
fulfill; unreasonable) ◊ That's a tall ~! | **mail, money,
postal** (BrE), **standing** | **purchase** | **export**
VERB + ORDER **place, put in, send** ◊ I've placed an ~ for the CD.
| **cancel** | **get, receive, win** ◊ The company won a $10
million ~ for oil-drilling equipment. | **have** | **complete, fill,
fulfil/fulfill, meet** ◊ We're trying to fill all the back ~s. |
make sth to ◊ kitchen cupboards made to ~
ORDER + NOUN **form** | **book** (usually figurative) ◊ We have a
full ~ book for the coming year.
PREP. **on ~** ◊ We have ten boxes on ~. | **to ~** ◊ The chairs can
be made to ~ (= when a customer orders one). | **~ for** ◊ We
have a firm ~ for ten cases of wine.

ADJ. **side** ◇ *a side ~ of mixed salad* | **short** (= that can be prepared quickly) ◇ *a short-order cook* | **last ~s** (*esp. BrE*) ◇ *Last ~s at the bar now, please!*
VERB + ORDER **take** ◇ *The waiter finally came to take their ~s.* | **give sb**
PREP. **~ for** ◇ *an ~ for steak and fries*

8 group of people living in a religious community

ADJ. **monastic, religious** | **contemplative** | **closed** (= with little or no contact with the outside world) | **Benedictine, Cistercian, etc.**

order verb

1 tell sb to do sth

ADV. **specifically** | **immediately** | **personally** ◇ *The general had personally ~ed the raid.* | **formally** | **about** (*esp. BrE*), **around** ◇ *Stop ~ing me around!* | **back, home, off, out** ◇ *He was ~ed off for bringing down the striker.* (*BrE, sports*)
PREP. **off, out of** ◇ *All foreign journalists have been ~ed out of the country.*

2 ask for sth

ADV. **direct, directly** | **online** ◇ *All our products can be ~ed online.*
PREP. **for** ◇ *We can ~ the book for you, if you like.* | **from** ◇ *You can ~ the book direct from the publisher.*

3 organize/arrange sth

ADV. **alphabetically, chronologically, hierarchically, logically** ◇ *The entries are ~ed alphabetically.*
PREP. **according to** ◇ *Different senses of a word are ~ed according to frequency.*
PHRASES **highly ~ed, well ~ed** ◇ *She led a highly ~ed existence, with everything having its own time and place.*

orderly adj.

VERBS **be**
ADV. **very** | **fairly, relatively**
PHRASES **in an ~ fashion, in an ~ manner, in an ~ way** ◇ *We want to bring about this change in an ~ fashion.*

ordinary adj.

VERBS **be, look, seem** | **become**
ADV. **very** ◇ *The wines produced were at best very ~.* | **perfectly, quite** ◇ *It was a perfectly ~ day.* | **fairly, pretty, rather** ◇ *The meal was pretty ~.*

ore noun

ADJ. **rich** | **high-grade, low-grade** | **metal, mineral** | **copper, gold, iron, uranium, etc.**
...OF ORE **vein** | **lump**
VERB + ORE **extract, mine** | **extract sth from, process, refine, smelt** ◇ *~ smelted with charcoal*
ORE + NOUN **deposits** | **mineral**

organ noun

1 part of the body

ADJ. **internal** | **bodily** | **important, major, vital** ◇ *The colon is an important ~ for the absorption of nutrients.* ◇ *to preserve blood flow to the vital ~s* | **abdominal, genital** | **digestive, olfactory, reproductive, sense, sensory, sex, sexual, etc.** | **human** | **donor, replacement** ◇ *He is waiting for a suitable donor ~.*
VERB + ORGAN **donate** | **transplant** | **harvest** | **affect, damage**
ORGAN + NOUN **donation, donor** | **transplant, transplantation** | **damage, failure**

2 musical instrument

ADJ. **pipe** | **electric, Hammond™** | **barrel, mouth** | **church, fairground** (*BrE*)
ORGAN + NOUN **pedal, pipe, stop** | **loft**
→ Special page at MUSIC

3 official organization

ADJ. **central, major** ◇ *the central ~s of state* | **administrative, constitutional** (*BrE*), **judicial** (*esp. BrE*), **political, security**

organic adj.

VERBS **be** | **become, go**
ADV. **completely, fully** (*esp. BrE*), **totally** ◇ *The farm went fully ~ in 1996.*
PHRASES **buy ~** ◇ *I try to buy ~ whenever possible.*

organism noun

ADJ. **developing, growing, living** | **simple** | **complex, higher** | **biological** | **human** | **aquatic, marine** | **microscopic**

organization (*BrE also* -isation) noun

1 organized group of people

ADJ. **large, major, mass** | **small** | **community, international, local, national** | **government, state** | **official** | **party, political** | **professional** | **non-governmental** (abbreviated to *NGO*) | **grass-roots** | **private** | **voluntary** | **charitable, philanthropic** | **non-profit, not-for-profit** | **commercial** | **faith-based** (*esp. AmE*), **religious** | **civil rights, environmental, human rights, labour/labor, relief, research** | **student, women's, youth** | **media, news** | **terrorist** | **umbrella** | **front** ◇ *a front ~ for drug trafficking*
VERB + ORGANIZATION **disband** (For more verbs see note.)
PREP. **in a/the ~** ◇ *There are several talented people in that ~.*
→ Special page at BUSINESS

2 way in which sth is organized

ADJ. **effective, efficient** ◇ *I admire her effective ~ of the campaign.* | **poor** ◇ *Most of these mistakes were the result of poor ~.* | **internal** | **social**
...OF ORGANIZATION **degree** ◇ *a high degree of ~*
VERB + ORGANIZATION **lack**
PHRASES **a lack of ~**

NOTE

Organizations

create..., **establish**..., **form**..., **found**..., **set up**..., **start**... ◇ *an association created to promote local industry* ◇ *The company was founded in 1981.*
dissolve... (*law*) ◇ *She sought a court order to have the partnership dissolved.*
run... ◇ *He runs his own publishing company.*
manage... ◇ *The executive committee manages the group on a day-to-day basis.*
be/become a member of..., **join**... ◇ *She became a member of the golf club.*
leave... ◇ *The country plans to leave the organization.*

---

organize (*BrE also* -ise) verb

ADV. **effectively, efficiently, properly, successfully, well** | **badly, poorly** | **carefully, neatly** | **locally** | **centrally** | **jointly** ◇ *They ~d the festival jointly with the tourism office.* | **separately** | **independently, privately** | **formally**
VERB + ORGANIZE **seek to, try to** | **help (to)** | **be able to** | **manage to** | **fail to** | **learn (how) to** | **be difficult to, be easy to** | **be possible to**
PREP. **according to** ◇ *We need to ~ the work according to the availability and skills of each volunteer.* | **around** ◇ *We're organizing the evening around a Japanese theme.* | **into** ◇ *It was difficult to ~ the men into teams.*

organized (*BrE also* -ised) adj.

1 arranged/planned

VERBS **be, seem**
ADV. **extremely, fairly, very, etc.** | **highly** ◇ *Although it doesn't look like it, the whole thing is highly ~.* | **carefully,**

efficiently, properly, superbly, well | badly, poorly | neatly | rigidly, tightly | loosely, weakly ◇ *a loosely ~ confederacy of allies* | **specially** ◇ *a specially ~ meeting* | **centrally, locally, nationally** | **separately** | **independently, privately** | **formally** ◇ *Often there is no formally ~ system of childcare.* | **traditionally** | **systematically** | **hierarchically, sequentially** ◇ *Each department is hierarchically ~.* | **chronologically** | **socially**

2 able to plan things well

VERBS **be, seem** | **get** ◇ *You need to get ~.*
ADV. **extremely, fairly, very, etc.** | **highly**

orgasm *noun*

ADJ. **female, male** | **multiple** | **simultaneous**
VERB + ORGASM **achieve, have, reach** | **fake, simulate**

orgy *noun*

ADJ. **drunken, sex, sexual** | **wild**
VERB + ORGY **have**
PREP. **~ of** ◇ *an ~ of looting and vandalism*

oriented (*BrE also* orientated) *adj.*

VERBS **be, seem** | **become** | **remain**
ADV. **strongly, very** | **correctly** ◇ *Make sure all the components remain correctly ~.* | **academically, politically, socially, technically** ◇ *The organization is not politically ~.*
PREP. **to, towards/toward** ◇ *The service is not sufficiently ~ to the needs of those who use it.*

origin *noun*

1 time/place/reason that sth starts

ADJ. **common** | **independent** | **doubtful** (*esp. BrE*), **obscure, unknown** ◇ *a letter of doubtful ~* | **true** | **ancient, early** | **recent** ◇ *The term 'carbon footprint' is of very recent ~.* | **immediate** ◇ *The development had its immediate ~s in discussions with management.* | **African, English, etc.** | **foreign** | **local** | **mixed** | **natural** | **supernatural** | **evolutionary, geographical, historical, intellectual** | **animal, human, plant** ◇ *foods of animal ~* ◇ *We shouldn't forget our animal ~s.*
VERB + ORIGIN **have, share** ◇ *The vases share common ~s.* | **investigate, trace** | **owe** ◇ *Population genetics owes its ~ to Francis Galton.* | **explain** | **reflect** | **suggest** ◇ *The name suggests a possible African ~.*
ORIGIN + VERB **go back to sth, lie in sth** ◇ *The ~s of the city go back to the 10th century.*
PREP. **in ~** ◇ *The rock is volcanic in ~.* | **of ... ~** ◇ *a painting of unknown ~*
PHRASES **country of ~, place of ~** ◇ *The label tells you the country of ~.* | **have its ~ in sth** ◇ *The custom has its ~ in an ancient festival.*

2 family, race, class, etc, that a person comes from

ADJ. **African, English, etc.** | **foreign** | **mixed** | **class, ethnic, national, racial, social** | **middle-class, noble, peasant, slave, working-class** | **humble, lowly** ◇ *He had risen from humble ~s through hard work.*
VERB + ORIGIN **trace** ◇ *Their family can trace its ~s back to the Norman Conquest.* | **betray** ◇ *Her accent betrayed her working-class ~s.*
PREP. **by ~** ◇ *He is a Londoner by ~.* | **in ~** ◇ *Her family is Portuguese in ~.* | **of ... ~** ◇ *He was of humble ~s.*
PHRASES **sb's country of ~**

original *noun*

VERB + ORIGINAL **pass sth off as** ◇ *He copied paintings of famous artists and passed them off as ~s.*
PREP. **in the ~** ◇ *to read Tolstoy in the ~*

original *adj.*

VERBS **be**
ADV. **extremely, fairly, very, etc.** | **highly, startlingly** (*esp. BrE*), **truly** ◇ *She has a highly ~ mind.* ◇ *a startlingly ~ idea* |

completely ◇ *They are tackling the problem in a completely ~ way.*

originality *noun*

ADJ. **great**
VERB + ORIGINALITY **have** | **display, show** | **be lacking in, lack**
ORIGINALITY + VERB **lie in sth** ◇ *His ~ as a painter lies in his representation of light.*
PREP. **~ in** ◇ *The government has shown great ~ in its foreign policy.*
PHRASES **a spark of ~** (*esp. BrE*) | **a lack of ~**

ornate *adj.*

VERBS **be**
ADV. **extremely, fairly, very, etc.** | **highly, richly**

orphan *noun*

ADJ. **little** | **poor** ◇ *a poor little ~* | **war** | **AIDS**
VERB + ORPHAN **be left** ◇ *She was left an ~ at the age of five.* | **adopt**
ORPHAN + NOUN **boy, child, girl**

orthodox *adj.*

VERBS **be** ◇ *His ideas are all fairly ~.*
ADV. **extremely, fairly, very, etc.** ◇ *I am not a very ~ kind of teacher.* | **highly, strictly** ◇ *This is the strictly ~ view.* | **religiously** (*esp. AmE*)

orthodoxy *noun*

ADJ. **rigid, strict** | **current, new, prevailing** | **Catholic, Christian, etc.** | **communist, liberal, etc.** | **party** | **economic, political, religious, scientific, etc.**
VERB + ORTHODOXY **challenge** ◇ *a speech that challenges prevailing economic ~*

ounce *noun* → Note at MEASURE

outage *noun* (*AmE*)

ADJ. **power** ◇ *intermittent power ~s up and down the East Coast*
VERB + OUTAGE **have** | **cause**
OUTAGE + VERB **occur**
PREP. **during an/the ~** ◇ *The baby was born during a power ~.*

outbreak *noun*

ADJ. **large, major, serious, severe** | **fresh** (*esp. BrE*), **further** (*esp. BrE*), **new, recent** | **occasional, periodic, sporadic** | **recurrent, repeated** | **sudden** | **disease** | **cholera, flu, salmonella, etc.**
VERB + OUTBREAK **cause, lead to** ◇ *the events that led to the ~ of war* | **prevent**
OUTBREAK + VERB **occur**
PREP. **~ of** ◇ *A new ~ of smallpox occurred in 1928.*
PHRASES **an ~ of disease** | **~s of rain** (*BrE*) | **an ~ of war, fighting, hostilities, violence, etc.**

outburst *noun*

ADJ. **sudden** | **spontaneous** | **occasional** ◇ *her occasional ~s of temper* | **little** ◇ *Sorry for that little ~ earlier.* | **angry, furious, violent** | **emotional, hysterical, passionate**
PREP. **~ against** ◇ *A player was cautioned for his angry ~ against the referee.* | **~ of** ◇ *an ~ of anger/laughter/temper/violence*

outcast *noun*

ADJ. **social** ◇ *He was treated as a social ~.*
VERB + OUTCAST **make sb** ◇ *Her criminal past made her an ~.* | **treat sb as, treat sb like**
PREP. **~ from** ◇ *an ~ from society*

outcome *noun*

ADJ. **desirable, desired, favourable/favorable, good, happy, positive, satisfactory, successful** | **adverse, bad, negative, poor, unfortunate, unsatisfactory** | **fatal, tragic** | **possible**

| likely, probable | different | anticipated, expected, inevitable, intended, logical, predicted | unexpected | immediate | actual, eventual, final, long-term, ultimate | **direct** ◇ *a direct ~ of the strike* | **practical** | **educational, electoral, political, etc.** (*all technical*)
VERB + OUTCOME **affect, change, influence** | **decide, determine** | **predict** ◇ *We use a computer model to predict the ~ of different scenarios.* | **know** ◇ *We may not know the ~ until tomorrow.* | **achieve, have, produce** ◇ *Their strategy produced the desired ~.* | **evaluate, measure** (*technical*) ◇ *The aim is to evaluate possible ~s.*
PREP. **~ of** ◇ *the ~ of the election*
PHRASES **whatever the ~** ◇ *Whatever the final ~ of the talks, the war should end soon.*

outcry noun

ADJ. **great, huge, massive** | **immediate** | **public** | **national** | **international**
VERB + OUTCRY **cause, prompt, provoke, spark** ◇ *The bombing caused an international ~.* | **raise** (*esp. AmE*) ◇ *His comments raised an ~ from religious leaders.*
PREP. **~ against, ~ over** ◇ *There was a massive public ~ against the harsh prison sentence.* | **~ from** ◇ *an immediate ~ from workers over pay reductions*

outfit noun

1 set of clothes worn together

ADJ. **complete** | **new** | **summer, winter** | **designer** | **interview, party, wedding, etc.** | **clown, cowboy, etc.** | **revealing, sexy, skimpy** | **matching** ◇ *The pair arrived in matching white ~s.*
VERB + OUTFIT **wear** | **choose, pick, pick out** | **buy** | **complete** ◇ *I'm looking for a necklace to complete my ~.*
PREP. **in a/the ~** ◇ *He looked very good in his new ~.*

2 organization, company, etc.

ADJ. **large** | **small** | **professional** | **cowboy, dodgy** (*both BrE*) | **computer, publishing, etc.**

outing noun

ADJ. **little** | **special** | **day's** (*esp. BrE*), **summer, weekend** | **annual** | **family, school, social**
VERB + OUTING **arrange, plan** | **enjoy**
PREP. **on ~** ◇ *We're going on an ~ tomorrow.* | **~ from** ◇ *The children were on an ~ from school.* | **~ to** ◇ *a family ~ to the mountains*

outlay noun

ADJ. **considerable, huge, large, massive** | **modest** (*esp. BrE*), **small** | **initial** ◇ *The revenue from the farm could repay the initial ~ within three years.* | **total** | **capital, cash, financial, investment**
VERB + OUTLAY **make** | **require** ◇ *The project would require little financial ~.* | **recoup, recover** (*both esp. BrE*)
PREP. **~ on** ◇ *The company had made a considerable capital ~ on property.*

outlet noun

1 place that sells goods of a particular company/type

ADJ. **specialist** (*BrE*) | **high-street** (*BrE*), **local** | **major** | **commercial, distribution, fast-food, media, news, retail, sales**
OUTLET + NOUN **mall** (*AmE*), **store**
PREP. **~ for** ◇ *a retail ~ for exotic plants*

2 means of releasing energy/strong feeling/talents

ADJ. **emotional** | **creative**
VERB + OUTLET **have** | **find** | **provide (sb with)** ◇ *Basketball provided an ~ for his energy.* | **need**
PREP. **~ for** ◇ *She needs an ~ for her talents.*

3 pipe/hole

ADJ. **sewage** (*BrE*), **water**
OUTLET + NOUN **pipe**

4 (*AmE*) for electricity

ADJ. **AC, electric, electrical, power** | **110-volt, 240-volt, etc.**

| **wall** | **standard** ◇ *The appliance can be connected to any standard ~.*

outline noun

1 line that shows the shape/outside edge of sb/sth

ADJ. **clear, sharp** ◇ *The sharp ~ of the island had become blurred.* | **dim, faint, vague** | **simple**
VERB + OUTLINE **draw, make, trace** ◇ *The children made an ~ of their hands.* | **make out, see** ◇ *I could just make out the dim ~s of the house in the mist.* | **soften**
OUTLINE + NOUN **drawing, map**
PREP. **around the ~, round the ~** (*esp. BrE*) ◇ *to cut around the ~* | **in ~** ◇ *He sketched the street in ~ only.* | **~ of**

2 most important facts/ideas about sth

ADJ. **bare, basic, brief, rough** ◇ *a brief ~ of Chinese history* | **broad, general** | **course**
VERB + OUTLINE **give (sb), provide (sb with), write** ◇ *Write an ~ for your essay.*
PREP. **in ~** ◇ *Here's the plan in ~.* | **~ for, ~ of**

outline verb

ADV. **briefly** | **clearly** | **roughly** ◇ *He roughly ~d the plot of the opera.* | **here** | **above, earlier, previously** ◇ *the plan ~d above* | **below**
VERB + OUTLINE **attempt to, seek to, try to**
PREP. **to** ◇ *She ~d to Mona the details of her mother's relationship.*

outlook noun

1 attitude to life

ADJ. **optimistic, positive, rosy, sunny** | **bleak, negative, pessimistic** | **general** | **broad** ◇ *Having children gave her a broader ~ on life.* | **different, differing** | **mental** | **moral, philosophical, religious**
VERB + OUTLOOK **have** | **give sb** | **change** | **broaden** ◇ *Travel broadens your ~.*
PREP. **in ~** ◇ *She is rather cautious in ~.* | **of (a)…~** ◇ *people of widely differing religious ~s* | **~ on** ◇ *Losing his job changed his whole ~ on life.*

2 what will probably happen

ADJ. **bright, good** | **bleak, gloomy, grim** ◇ *The ~ for people on low incomes is grim.* | **uncertain** | **business, economic, political** | **long-term, short-term** | **global, international**
VERB + OUTLOOK **improve** ◇ *The drug improves the long-term ~ of migraine sufferers.* | **worsen**
PREP. **~ for** ◇ *a brighter ~ for the economy*

outnumber verb

ADV. **easily, far, greatly, heavily, vastly** ◇ *Their failures vastly ~ their successes.* | **almost** | **slightly**
PREP. **by** ◇ *Females ~ males by a wide margin.*
PHRASES **be hopelessly ~ed** ◇ *The Spanish were hopelessly ~ed in the battle.*

output noun

ADJ. **high, large, massive** | **greater, increased** | **steady** | **low** | **aggregate, gross, overall, total** ◇ *10% of the country's total ~* | **net** | **average** | **annual, monthly, etc.** | **maximum** | **current** | **national, world** | **prodigious, prolific** ◇ *her prodigious literary ~* | **agricultural, industrial, manufacturing** | **data** | **artistic, creative, literary**
…OF OUTPUT **level** ◇ *changes in the level of ~*
VERB + OUTPUT **produce** | **double, expand, increase** ◇ *The plant plans to increase ~ to 10 000 cars a year.* | **reduce**
OUTPUT + VERB **increase, rise** | **decrease, fall**
PREP. **~ of** ◇ *a steady ~ of new ideas*
PHRASES **a drop in ~, a fall in ~** ◇ *the fall in ~ due to outdated equipment* | **a growth in ~, an increase in ~, a rise in ~**

outrage noun

1 great anger

ADJ. **genuine** | **widespread** | **international** | **public** | **moral** ◊ *Media reports generated moral ~.*
VERB + OUTRAGE **be greeted with, cause, generate, provoke, spark** ◊ *The news was greeted with ~.* | **feel** | **express, voice** ◊ *Shopkeepers voiced their ~ at the new tax.*
OUTRAGE + VERB **be directed at sb/sth** ◊ *Much of the ~ was directed at foreign nationals.*
PREP. **in ~** ◊ *The guests all shouted in ~.* | **with ~** ◊ *She was trembling with ~.* | **~ at** ◊ *Campaigners have expressed ~ at the decision.* | **~ over** ◊ *There is widespread public ~ over the massacre.*
PHRASES **cries of ~, howls of ~** ◊ *The announcement provoked howls of ~.* | **a feeling of ~, a sense of ~**

2 cruel/shocking act

VERB + OUTRAGE **commit, perpetrate** ◊ *the ~s committed by the invading army*
PREP. **~ against** ◊ *The new law on pensions is an ~ against the elderly.*

outrageous adj.

VERBS **be** | **consider sth, regard sth as, see sth as** ◊ *She considered it absolutely ~ that he should be promoted over her.*
ADV. **absolutely, completely, quite, totally** | **morally**

outsider noun

1 not a member of a group

ADJ. **complete** | **political, social**
VERB + OUTSIDER **feel** (*esp. BrE*), **feel like** ◊ *I started to feel like a complete ~.*
PREP. **~ to** ◊ *an ~ to the group*

2 competitor who will probably not win

ADJ. **complete, rank**
PREP. **~ in** ◊ *The company has gone from being an ~ in the market to being a market leader.*

outskirts noun

ADJ. **city** | **northern, etc.**
VERB + OUTSKIRTS **reach**
PREP. **in the ~** ◊ *a school in the ~ of Athens* | **on the ~** ◊ *They live on the ~ of Chennai.* | **through the ~** ◊ *We were driving through the ~ of Baghdad.*

outstanding adj.

1 excellent

VERBS **be** | **consider sth**
ADV. **particularly, really, truly** | **absolutely, quite** ◊ *That was a quite ~ performance!*

2 not yet paid or done

VERBS **be, remain** ◊ *Two or three tasks still remain ~.* | **leave sth** ◊ *We decided to leave the debt ~.*
ADV. **still** ◊ *75% of the amount originally borrowed is still ~.*

outweigh verb

ADV. **easily, far, greatly, heavily, more than, vastly** ◊ *The benefits would surely far ~ the risks.* ◊ *The advantages of this plan more than ~ the costs involved.*

oval adj.

VERBS **be**
ADV. **perfectly** ◊ *her delicate, perfectly ~ face* | **almost** ◊ *The leaves are long and almost ~.* | **roughly**
PHRASES **~ in shape** ◊ *The handle is ~ in shape.*

ovation noun

ADJ. **enthusiastic, huge, long, loud, thunderous** (*esp. AmE*) | **standing** ◊ *The audience gave her a standing ~ for her performance.* | **three-minute, five-minute, etc.**

VERB + OVATION **give sb** | **get, receive** ◊ *He received the longest ~ of the evening.* | **earn, win**
PREP. **to an ~** ◊ *He came off the field to a huge ~.* | **~ from** ◊ *The final piece won her an enthusiastic ~ from the audience.*

oven noun

ADJ. **electric, gas, microwave** | **hot, low, moderate, warm** ◊ *Bake them in a warm ~ until risen and golden brown.* | **preheated** | **convection, conventional, fan** (*BrE*), **toaster** (*esp. AmE*) | **domestic** (*esp. BrE*) | **self-cleaning** | **bread** | **clay** ◊ *Tandoori food is cooked in a clay ~.*
VERB + OVEN **turn on** | **heat, preheat** ◊ *Preheat the ~ to 250°.* | **bake sth in, cook sth in** | **put sth in** | **remove sth from, take sth out of** | **clean**
OVEN + VERB **heat, heat up** ◊ *Turn on the ~ and let it heat up.* | **cool, cool down**
OVEN + NOUN **dish** | **glove** (*esp. BrE*), **mitt** (*esp. AmE*) | **temperature** | **door, rack** | **timer** | **cleaner** | **chips** (*BrE*)
PREP. **in an/the ~** ◊ *bread baked in the ~*
→ Special page at FOOD

overcoat noun

ADJ. **long** | **heavy, thick** | **dark**
→ Special page at CLOTHES

overcome verb

1 defeat/conquer sb/sth

ADV. **completely** | **successfully** | **not entirely** ◊ *These problems were never entirely ~.* | **largely** | **partially** | **easily** | **quickly** | **gradually** | **eventually, finally** ◊ *He eventually overcame his disability.*
VERB + OVERCOME **be able to** | **help (to), help sb (to)** ◊ *Therapy helped her to ~ her fear.* | **be designed to** ◊ *methods designed to ~ these problems* | **attempt to, battle to, struggle to, try to** | **manage to**
PHRASES **an attempt to ~ sth**

2 be overcome become weak; lose control

ADV. **completely, quite** ◊ *She was quite ~ by their kindness.* | **almost, nearly** ◊ *She was almost ~ by a tide of relief.* | **suddenly**
PREP. **by** ◊ *Several firefighters had been ~ by smoke and fumes.* | **with** ◊ *He was suddenly ~ with remorse for the harm he had done.*

overcrowded adj.

VERBS **be** | **become, get**
ADV. **extremely, very** | **severely**

overdose noun

ADJ. **massive** | **drug, drugs** (*BrE*) | **heroin, etc.** | **fatal, lethal** | **accidental**
VERB + OVERDOSE **take** | **die from, die of**
PREP. **~ of** ◊ *She took an ~ of sleeping pills.*

overdraft noun (esp. BrE)

ADJ. **enormous, huge, large** | **agreed, authorized** | **unauthorized** | **free** (*BrE*) ◊ *We offer a free £400 ~.* | **bank** (*BrE*)
VERB + OVERDRAFT **have** | **get, take out** | **run up** ◊ *He ran up a huge ~ during his year in office.* | **arrange** | **extend** (*BrE*), **give sb, offer (sb)** | **pay off** | **increase** | **reduce** | **exceed** ◊ *They exceeded their ~ by £200 000.*
OVERDRAFT + NOUN **facility** | **limit**

overdue adj.

VERBS **be** | **become**
ADV. **long** ◊ *These reforms are long ~.*
PREP. **for** ◊ *This system is ~ for reform.*
PHRASES **months, weeks, years, etc. ~** ◊ *These changes are years ~.*

overestimate verb

ADV. **considerably, greatly, grossly, seriously, vastly** |

consistently ◇ *The department consistently ~d its budget deficits.*
VERB + OVERESTIMATE **tend to** | **be easy to** ◇ *It is easy to ~ the cost of this kind of research.* | **be difficult to, be hard to**
PREP. **by** ◇ *We ~d the cost by about 2%.*
PHRASES **sth cannot be ~d** ◇ *The importance of this group cannot be ~d.*

overgrown *adj.*
VERBS **be** | **become, get**
ADV. **extremely, fairly, very, etc.** | **thickly** | **completely** ◇ *The path was completely ~.*
PREP. **with** ◇ *The canal bank was thickly ~ with bushes.*

overhaul *noun*
ADJ. **complete, major, massive, thorough** | **radical**
VERB + OVERHAUL **have, undergo** ◇ *The tax system has undergone a complete ~.* | **give sth** | **need, require**

overhaul *verb*
ADV. **drastically, radically** ◇ *Within a year the party had drastically ~ed its structure.* | **completely, thoroughly** ◇ *The plan was completely ~ed.*

overhead *adj., adv.*
VERBS **be** | **appear, circle, fly, gather, hover, pass, soar, wheel** ◇ *The seagulls circled ~.* ◇ *Storm clouds were gathering ~.* | **buzz, roar, scream, whirr** ◇ *Helicopters buzzed ~.* | **shine** ◇ *The sun shone ~.*
ADV. **directly** ◇ *The storm must be directly ~.* | **nearly** | **high** ◇ *The moon was high ~.* | **low** ◇ *aircraft passing low ~*

overhear *verb*
ADV. **accidentally**
PHRASES **couldn't help ~ing sth** ◇ *Excuse me for interrupting, but I couldn't help ~ing what you were saying.*

overjoyed *adj.*
VERBS **be, look, seem, sound**
ADV. **not exactly** ◇ *She was not exactly ~ to see us again.*
PREP. **about** ◇ *They're all ~ about it.* | **at** ◇ *He was ~ at the thought of having a son.* | **by** ◇ *We are ~ by this decision.* | **with** ◇ *Patrick was ~ with his success.*

overlap *verb*
ADV. **almost** | **partially, partly, slightly, to some extent** ◇ *Put the two pieces of paper together so that they ~ slightly.* ◇ *The two categories ~ to some extent.* | **clearly**
PREP. **in** ◇ *terms which ~ slightly in meaning* | **with** ◇ *a world which ~s with the newspaper world*

overload *verb*
PREP. **with** ◇ *Their staff are heavily ~ed with work.*
PHRASES **be heavily ~ed, be seriously ~ed**

overlook *verb*
ADV. **completely, entirely** | **largely** | **frequently, often** | **easily** | **conveniently** ◇ *Conveniently ~ing the fact that she wouldn't be able to meet the commitment, she agreed.*
VERB + OVERLOOK **cannot, cannot afford to, should not** ◇ *We should not ~ this possibility.* | **be inclined to, tend to** ◇ *Hospitals have tended to ~ this need.* | **seem to** | **be prepared to, be willing to** ◇ *I was prepared to ~ her mistakes this time.* | **be easy to** ◇ *It is easy to ~ the significance of this change.* | **be impossible to**
PHRASES **be easily ~ed** ◇ *another fact which is all too easily ~ed* | **sth should not be ~ed** ◇ *The importance of this should not be ~ed.*

oversee *verb*
ADV. **directly** | **personally** ◇ *He personally oversaw the design of all the rooms.*
VERB + OVERSEE **be appointed to, be created to, be set up to** ◇ *A committee has been appointed to ~ the work.*
PHRASES **be responsible for ~ing sth** ◇ *the committee that is*

responsible for ~ing the day-to-day implementation of this policy

oversight *noun*
ADJ. **unfortunate** | **administrative**
PREP. **by (an) ~** ◇ *By an ~, we did not send out the agenda for the meeting.* | **due to (an) ~** ◇ *The mistake was due to an unfortunate ~ on my part.* | **through (an) ~** ◇ *Through ~, the bill was still unpaid.*

overthrow *noun*
ADJ. **attempted** | **violent**
VERB + OVERTHROW **bring about, lead to** | **plot**
PREP. **~ of** ◇ *to bring about the ~ of the military dictatorship*

overtime *noun*
1 work
ADJ. **excessive** ◇ *Doctors work excessive unpaid ~.* | **paid, unpaid** | **forced, mandatory** (*both AmE*)
VERB + OVERTIME **do, put in, work** ◇ *I do about five hours' ~ a week.* ◇ *She puts in a lot of ~.*
OVERTIME + NOUN **earnings** (*BrE*), **pay, payments** (*esp. BrE*), **rate** | **ban** (*esp. BrE*) ◇ *The union imposed an ~ ban in protest at the firing of two workers.*
2 (*AmE*) **sport**
ADJ. **first, second, etc.** ◇ *He scored with only seven seconds remaining in the second ~.* | **sudden-death**
VERBS **go into** ◇ *The game went into ~.* | **force** ◇ *Stanford scored two goals in the last minute to force ~.*
OVERTIME + NOUN **period** ◇ *The first ~ period ended with no scoring.* | **victory, win** ◇ *an impressive ~ win against Denver* | **loss**
PREP. **in ~** ◇ *We were unlucky to lose in ~.*

overtone *noun*
ADJ. **strong** ◇ *a play with strong religious ~s* | **serious** | **negative** ◇ *The word 'cheap' has negative ~s.* | **emotional, moral, political, racial, religious, sexual** | **racist**
VERB + OVERTONE **carry, have** | **take on** ◇ *The organization's cultural activities took on political ~s.*

overture *noun*
1 (usually **overtures**) **friendly approach**
ADJ. **friendly** | **diplomatic, peace** | **romantic, sexual**
VERB + OVERTURE **make** | **respond to** | **reject, resist, spurn** ◇ *She spurned his ~s of love.*
PREP. **~s of** ◇ *~s of friendship* | **~s to** ◇ *He made friendly ~s to the new people next door.*
2 piece of music
ADJ. **concert, operatic**
PREP. **~ to** ◇ *the ~ to Mozart's 'Don Giovanni'*

overturn *verb*
ADV. **completely** ◇ *She completely ~ed my preconceptions about movie stars.*
VERB + OVERTURN **seek to, try to** ◇ *He is seeking to ~ his conviction for armed robbery.* | **fail to**
PHRASES **be easily ~ed** ◇ *This argument seems convincing, but is easily ~ed.*

overview *noun*
ADJ. **brief, concise, quick, short** | **broad, general** | **complete, comprehensive** | **detailed, in-depth** | **critical** | **balanced** | **historical** ◇ *The opening chapter gives a brief historical ~ of the subject.* | **useful**
VERB + OVERVIEW **give (sb), offer (sb), present, provide (sb with)** | **have** ◇ *Only the head of sales has an ~ of the situation worldwide.*
PREP. **~ of, ~ on** ◇ *The seminar aims to provide an ~ on new media publishing.*

overweight adj.

VERBS **be, look** ◇ *You don't look ~.* | **become, get** ◇ *Don't let yourself get ~.*
ADV. **extremely, fairly, very, etc.** | **grossly, seriously** | **a little, slightly, etc.**
PHRASES **a few pounds, etc. ~**

overwhelm verb

ADV. **absolutely, completely, totally** | **quite, rather** | **almost, nearly** | **suddenly**
VERB + OVERWHELM **threaten to** ◇ *Deal with stress fast whenever it threatens to ~ you.*
PREP. **with** ◇ *The children pressed around him eagerly, ~ing him with questions.*
PHRASES **~ed by sth** ◇ *We were totally ~ed by the response to our appeal.* | **absolutely ~ed, completely ~ed, totally ~ed** ◇ *She felt completely ~ed.* | **a bit ~ed, a little ~ed** | **almost ~ed, nearly ~ed**

overwhelming adj.

VERBS **be, seem** | **become**
ADV. **completely, quite** | **almost** ◇ *The urge to look was almost ~.* | **a little, pretty** (*esp. AmE*) ◇ *All these new experiences were a little ~.* | **apparently, seemingly** ◇ *seemingly ~ obstacles*

owl noun

ADJ. **barn, spotted, etc.** | **stuffed** | **wise** (*often figurative*) ◇ *He's a wise old ~.* | **night** (*figurative*) ◇ *I was a night ~ when I was younger, but these days I'd rather go to bed early.*
OWL + VERB **fly** | **hoot, screech** | **catch sth, prey on sth** ◇ *Owls prey on small rodents.* | **nest, perch, roost**
OWL + NOUN **pellet**

own verb

ADV. **independently** | **formerly, once, originally, previously** ◇ *The car was once ~ed by Elvis Presley.* | **legally** ◇ *He committed the crime with a gun that he legally ~ed.* | **communally, jointly** ◇ *She ~s the house jointly with her husband.*
PHRASES **directly ~ed by sb, indirectly ~ed by sb** | **~ your own boat, home, etc.** ◇ *They dreamed of ~ing their own home.* | **partly ~ed by sb, wholly ~ed by sb** ◇ *The company is a wholly ~ed subsidiary of SNL Research.* | **privately ~ed, publicly ~ed** ◇ *The museum is privately ~ed.*

owner noun

ADJ. **sole** | **part** ◇ *I'm part ~ of the restaurant.* | **joint** | **former, original, previous** | **current, present** | **new** | **future, prospective** | **lawful, legal, rightful** ◇ *The stolen painting has now been returned to its rightful ~.* | **private** | **lucky, proud** ◇ *the proud ~ of a new camera* | **business, car, dog, factory, home, land, property**
VERB + OWNER **have** ◇ *The car had only one previous ~.* | **find, trace** ◇ *The police have been unable to trace the ~ of the vehicle.* | **become** ◇ *Their daughter became the ~ of the farm in 1892.*

ownership noun

ADJ. **full** | **sole** | **collective, common, fractional** (*AmE, law*), **joint, shared** | **new** | **legal** | **private** | **corporate** | **public, state** | **foreign** | **car, home, land**
VERB + OWNERSHIP **change, transfer** ◇ *The business has changed ~ several times.* ◇ *He transferred the legal ~ of his property to his children.* | **pass into** ◇ *The estate passed into public ~.* | **acquire, assume, seize, take, take over** | **retain** | **claim**
OWNERSHIP + VERB **pass** ◇ *Ownership of the land passed from father to son.*
PREP. **under (the)** ~ ◇ *The cafe is under new ~.*
PHRASES **a change in ~**

oxygen noun

ADJ. **pure** | **liquid** | **atmospheric**
VERB + OXYGEN **carry, contain** ◇ *the blood which carries ~ to the brain* | **absorb, breathe, consume, take in, use up** | **generate, produce, release** ◇ *After dark the plants stop producing ~.* | **administer, give sb** | **get, receive** ◇ *The patient didn't seem to be getting enough ~.* | **deprive sb/sth of, starve sb/sth of** ◇ *There was a risk the brain might be starved of ~.*
OXYGEN + NOUN **atom, molecule** | **level, supply** | **consumption** | **deprivation** | **mask** | **cylinder, tank**
PHRASES **a lack of ~** | **a supply of ~**

ozone noun

ADJ. **atmospheric, ground-level, stratospheric**
VERB + OZONE **deplete, destroy** | **form, produce**
OZONE + VERB **thin** | **disappear**
OZONE + NOUN **layer** ◇ *The ~ layer is disappearing over northern Europe.* | **depletion, destruction, loss** | **hole** | **pollution** | **concentration, levels**
PHRASES **damage to the ~ layer, depletion of the ~ layer, destruction of the ~ layer** | **a hole in the ~ layer**

P p

pace noun

1 one step

VERB + PACE **take, walk** ◇ *Take two ~s forward.* | **step back** ◇ *Step back three ~s.*
PREP. **~ behind** ◇ *Two bodyguards remained a couple of ~s behind the president.* | **~ from** ◇ *I stopped a few ~s from the edge of the cliff.*

2 speed

ADJ. **blistering, breakneck, breathtaking, brisk, cracking** (*esp. BrE*), **fast, frantic, frenetic, frenzied, furious, good, great, hectic, lightning, lively, rapid** | **gentle, glacial, leisurely, relaxed, slow, unhurried, walking** ◇ *the slow ~ of economic reform* | **even, measured, moderate, steady**
VERB + PACE **gather, increase, quicken** ◇ *The project had a slow start, but is now gathering ~.* ◇ *Thinking that she was being followed, she quickened her ~.* | **slacken, slow down** | **dictate, set** ◇ *Brown set the ~ in the first mile.* | **keep, keep up, maintain** ◇ *The younger children struggled to keep ~ with the older ones.* ◇ *She kept up a ~ of ten miles an hour.* | **stand** (*BrE*) ◇ *You shouldn't have such a job if you can't stand the ~.*
PACE + VERB **increase** | **slow**
PREP. **at a … ~** ◇ *They set off at a blistering ~.* | **~ of** ◇ *The ~ of change means that equipment has to be constantly replaced.* ◇ *The ~ of life is much slower on the islands.*
PHRASES **at sb's own ~** ◇ *The students work at their own ~.* | **at a snail's ~** ◇ *I set off at a snail's ~ to conserve my energy for later in the race.* | **a change of ~** ◇ *I try to get away at weekends for a change of ~.* | **a turn of ~** (*BrE*) ◇ *He's a skilful player with a good turn of ~.*

pace verb

ADV. **slowly** | **anxiously, nervously, restlessly** ◇ *She ~d restlessly up and down.* | **about** (*BrE*), **around, back and forth, round** (*esp. BrE*), **to and fro, up and down** ◇ *He ~d slowly back and forth.*
VERB + PACE **begin to**
PREP. **about** (*BrE*), **around, round** (*esp. BrE*)
PHRASES **begin pacing** ◇ *She began pacing around the room.*

pack noun

1 (*esp. AmE*) container holding goods

ADJ. **cigarette** (*esp. AmE*) (usually *cigarette packet* in BrE) | **blister** | **gift, sample** (*BrE*)
PACK + VERB **contain sth**

PREP. **in a/the ~** ◇ *How many needles are there in a ~?* | **~ of** ◇ *It comes in ~s of six.* ◇ *a ~ of cigarettes* ◇ *a ~ of gum*

2 things supplied together

ADJ. **action, information, resource** (*BrE*), **starter, training** (*BrE*)
PACK + VERB **contain sth, include sth** ◇ *Your information ~ includes addresses of leading manufacturers.*

3 things put together for carrying

ADJ. **heavy** | **fanny** (*AmE*) | **battery, power** ◇ *a rechargeable battery ~*
VERB + PACK **carry, sling**
PACK + NOUN **animal, horse, mule**
PREP. **in a/the ~** ◇ *The water in his ~ made it very heavy.*

4 group of animals, etc.

ADJ. **wolf** | **hunting** | **brat** (= a group of famous young people who sometimes behave badly)
VERB + PACK **lead**
PACK + NOUN **instinct**
PREP. **in a/the ~** ◇ *the dominant animal in the ~* | **in ~s** ◇ *The animals hunt in ~s.* | **~ of** ◇ *a ~ of dogs/wolves*
PHRASES **the leader of the ~**

5 (*BrE*) **playing cards** → See also DECK

VERB + PACK **shuffle** | **cut**
PREP. **in a/the ~** ◇ *There are 52 playing cards in a ~.*
PHRASES **the bottom of the ~, the top of the ~** ◇ *Take a card from the top of the ~.* | **a ~ of cards**

pack verb

1 put things into containers

ADV. **carefully, neatly** | **tightly** ◇ *Live animals are transported across the continent, ~ed tightly into trucks.* | **quickly** | **away, together, up** ◇ *The passengers were ~ed together like cattle.* ◇ *I think we might as well ~ up and go home.*
PREP. **in, into** ◇ *She ~ed her clothes into a suitcase.*

2 fill a place/sth

PREP. **into** ◇ *Crowds of people ~ed into the hall.*
PHRASES **be ~ed full of sth** ◇ *Our new brochure is ~ed full of inspirational ideas.* | **be ~ed out** (*esp. BrE*) ◇ *The stadium was ~ed out.* | **be ~ed to bursting** (*esp. BrE*), **be ~ed to capacity, be ~ed to overflowing** (*esp. BrE*) ◇ *The hall was ~ed to capacity.* | **be ~ed to the brim, be ~ed to the gills, be ~ed to the rafters** (*esp. BrE*) ◇ *The hostel was ~ed to the rafters.* | **be ~ed with sb** ◇ *The place was ~ed with conference attendees.* | **closely ~ed, densely ~ed, tightly ~ed**

package noun

1 (*esp. AmE*) **something wrapped in paper, etc.** → See also PARCEL

ADJ. **big, bulky, compact, neat, small** | **wrapped** | **plastic** (*AmE*) | **cigarette** (*AmE*) (usually *cigarette pack* in *AmE*, *cigarette packet* in *BrE*), **food** | **suspect** (*BrE*), **suspicious** ◇ *Police destroyed the suspicious ~ in a controlled explosion.*
VERB + PACKAGE **open, unwrap, wrap** | **mail** (*AmE*), **post** (*BrE*), **send** | **deliver** | **receive, sign for**
PACKAGE + VERB **contain** | **arrive**
PREP. **in a/the ~** ◇ *I sent the books in one big ~.* | **~ of** ◇ *a ~ of cookies/meat* (*AmE*)

2 set of proposals

ADJ. **basic** | **complete, comprehensive, entire, full, integrated, overall, total, whole** | **attractive, excellent, generous** | **reform** | **benefits, compensation, financial, incentive, pay, remuneration** ◇ *a comprehensive benefits ~* | **retirement, travel, vacation** | **redundancy** (*BrE*), **severance** | **aid, assistance, rescue** | **training**
VERB + PACKAGE **offer, produce, provide, put together** ◇ *The IMF has put together a rescue ~ for the country's faltering economy.* | **accept, approve** | **reject**
PACKAGE + VERB **consist of sth, contain sth, include sth** | **be aimed at sth** ◇ *a jobs ~ aimed at helping the unemployed*
PACKAGE + NOUN **holiday** (*BrE*), **tour** | **deal**
PREP. **in a/the ~** ◇ *the measures included in the ~* | **under a/**

the **~** ◇ *Under the reform ~, spending on health will increase.* | **~ of** ◇ *a ~ of measures to assist industry*
PHRASES **part of a ~** ◇ *The pay freeze forms part of a ~ of budget cuts.*

3 computer software

ADJ. **software** | **integrated** ◇ *an integrated business software ~* | **application, desktop-publishing, drawing, graphics, word-processing** | **accounting, business**
VERB + PACKAGE **download, install** | **use** | **develop**

packaging noun

ADJ. **fancy** ◇ *Many customers are influenced by designer names and fancy ~.* | **original** ◇ *Keep your sales receipt and the original ~.* | **recyclable** | **plastic** | **flexible, rigid** | **food, product, etc.**
VERB + PACKAGING **recycle**
PACKAGING + NOUN **materials** | **technology** | **waste** | **company, firm, group, manufacturer** | **industry**

packet noun

ADJ. **empty** | **cereal, cigarette** (*cigarette pack* in *AmE*), **cornflake, crisp** (*all BrE*) | **ketchup, mustard, sugar** (*all AmE*) | **seed** | **pay, wage** (*both BrE*) ◇ *a weekly pay ~* (= wage) *of £200* | **math** (= work to do in the holiday/vacation) (*AmE*) ◇ *My kids have summer math ~s from their schools.*
VERB + PACKET **open**
PACKET + VERB **contain sth** ◇ *a ~ containing seeds*
PACKET + NOUN **soup**
PREP. **on a/the ~** ◇ *Follow the instructions on the ~.* | **~ of** ◇ *a ~ of crisps* (*BrE*) ◇ *a ~ of sugar* (*AmE*)

packing noun

VERB + PACKING **do** ◇ *When shall we do the ~?* | **finish** ◇ *She finished her ~ and zipped up the bag.*
PACKING + NOUN **case** (*BrE*)
PHRASES **postage and ~** (*BrE*) (*postage and handling* in *AmE*) ◇ *All prices include postage and ~.*

pact noun

ADJ. **bilateral, mutual** | **defence/defense, security** | **non-aggression, peace** | **stability** | **electoral** (*esp. BrE*), **free-trade** (*esp. AmE*), **social, trade** | **suicide**
VERB + PACT **have** | **conclude, enter into, form, make** ◇ *The Liberals formed a secret ~ with the Independents.* | **sign** ◇ *The Soviet Union had signed a non-aggression ~ with Germany.* | **negotiate** | **break**
PREP. **in a/the ~** ◇ *She died with her lover in a suicide ~.* | **under a/the ~** ◇ *conditions under the recently signed non-aggression ~.* | **~ between** ◇ *a security ~ between Pakistan and France* | **~ with** ◇ *She made a ~ with her friend never to tell anyone what had happened.*
PHRASES **a ~ with the devil** (usually *a deal with the devil* in *AmE*) ◇ *He accused them of making a ~ with the devil by allowing soldiers to be stationed in the region.*

pad noun

1 pieces of paper fastened together at one edge

ADJ. **memo, note** (usually *notepad*), **scratch** (*AmE*) | **drawing, sketch** | **writing** | **prescription**
PREP. **on a/the ~** ◇ *She doodled on a ~ as she spoke.*

2 thick piece of soft material

ADJ. **thick** | **adhesive** | **cotton** (*AmE*), **cotton-wool** (*BrE*), **foam, gauze, gel, rubber** | **polishing, scouring, steel-wool** | **menstrual** (*esp. AmE*), **sanitary** | **incontinence** (*esp. BrE*) | **mattress, sleeping** (*both AmE*) | **mouse** (*esp. AmE*) (usually *mouse mat* in *BrE*) ◇ *Every computer user should have a good mouse ~.*

pad verb

1 be padded be filled/covered with soft material

ADV. **heavily** ◇ *She was wearing a warm coat and heavily padded gloves.* | **well**
PREP. **with** ◇ *The shoulder straps are padded with foam.*

2 move quietly

ADV. **quietly, silently, softly** | **barefoot** | **about** (*esp. BrE*), **around** ◇ *He padded around in his socks eating cereal.*
PREP. **about** (*esp. BrE*), **around** ◇ *She padded softly around the house.* | **across** ◇ *He padded barefoot across the carpet.* | **along** ◇ *The cat padded silently along the track.* | **to, towards/toward**

page noun

1 in a book, etc.

ADJ. **back, front** | **facing, opposite** ◇ *There's a photo of him on the opposite ~.* | **inside** | **left-hand, right-hand** | **following, next, preceding, previous** | **first, opening** | **final, last** | **new** ◇ *Write each answer on a new ~.* | **blank, empty** | **full** | **loose** | **dog-eared** | **torn** | **yellowed** | **glossy** ◇ *the glossy ~s of magazines* | **printed, typed, typewritten** ◇ *The speech did not transfer well to the printed ~.* | **handwritten, written** | **single-spaced** | **contents, title** | **introductory** | **advertising, business, editorial, financial, gossip, obituary, op-ed** (*AmE*), **opinion, problem** (*BrE*), **sports** (all in a newspaper, etc.) ◇ *the problem ~s of magazines* | **calendar, scrapbook**
VERB + PAGE **read** | **scan, skim** ◇ *She began to skim the ~s for something of interest.* | **peruse** (*formal or humorous*) | **write** ◇ *He wrote fifty ~s in five hours.* | **edit** | **turn, turn over, turn to** ◇ *I turned the dog-eared ~s of my old address book.* ◇ *Turn to ~ 30 in the coursebook.* | **flick through** (*esp. BrE*), **flip through** (*esp. AmE*), **leaf through** ◇ *She sat idly flipping through the ~s of a fashion magazine.* | **skip** ◇ *He skipped a few ~s and carried on reading.* | **rip, rip out, tear, tear out** | **splash sth across** ◇ *The headlines were splashed across the front ~ of every newspaper.* | **dedicate, devote** ◇ *Particularly sad are the ~s devoted to the death of his mother.* | **fill** ◇ *Beautiful pictures fill the ~s.* | **dominate** ◇ *The news dominated the ~s of the local newspaper.* | **grace** ◇ *Phyllis graced the ~s of 'Life' magazine in 1953.*
PAGE + VERB **contain sth, describe sth, detail sth, explain sth, feature sth, include sth, list sth, provide sth** ◇ *The front ~ features a warning about the dangers of drugs.* ◇ *The ~ provides information about the company.*
PAGE + NOUN **number** | **design, layout** | **size** | **count**
PREP. **at (a/the) ~, to (a/the) ~** ◇ *Open your books at ~ 14.* (*esp. BrE*) *Open your books to ~ 14.* (*AmE*) ◇ *The murder takes place in the opening ~s of the novel.* | **on a/the ~** ◇ *The crossword is on the back ~.* | **over the ~** ◇ *Her eyes skimmed over the ~.* ◇ *The article continues over the ~* (= on the other side of the page). (*BrE*)
PHRASES **at the bottom of the ~, at the foot of the ~** | **at the head of the ~, at the top of the ~** ◇ *Write your name at the top of each ~.* | **... pages long** ◇ *The story is thirty ~s long.* | **run your eye down a ~, run your finger down a ~** ◇ *I ran my finger down the ~ until I found the name I was looking for.*

2 on the Internet

ADJ. **HTML, Internet, web** | **home, main** | **landing, splash** | **linked** | **FAQ, index, login, search**
VERB + PAGE **read** | **scan, scroll down, skim** ◇ *She began to scroll down the ~ looking for the address.* | **dedicate, devote** ◇ *web ~s devoted to people's cats* | **create, design** | **customize** | **access, view, visit** | **display, download, load** | **refresh, update** ◇ *The ~ is automatically updated every five minutes.* | **bookmark, post** | **upload**
PAGE + VERB **load** ◇ *It takes a few seconds for the web ~ to load.*
PAGE + NOUN **link**
PREP. **on a/the ~** ◇ *The information you need is on the same ~.*

paid adj.

VERBS **be**
ADV. **highly, well** ◇ *a well-paid job* | **badly, poorly** ◇ *poorly ~ workers*

pail noun (*esp. AmE*) → See also BUCKET

ADJ. **empty, full** | **five-gallon, ten-gallon** | **metal, plastic** | **garbage** (*AmE*) ◇ *She threw all the scraps into a garbage ~.* | **diaper** (*AmE*) | **lunch** (= for carrying your lunch) (*AmE*)
VERB + PAIL **fill** ◇ *She filled the ~ with fresh water.* | **carry** | **fetch, lug** (*informal*) ◇ *Women in some villages had to trudge miles to fetch one ~ of water.*
PAIL + VERB **be full of sth, hold sth** | **overflow**
PREP. **in a/the ~** | **~ of** ◇ *~s of soapy water*
PHRASES **a shovel and ~** (*AmE*) ◇ *The children played on the beach with their shovels and ~s.* | **mop and ~** ◇ *a worker equipped with a mop and ~*

pain noun

1 physical pain

ADJ. **acute, agonizing, awful, blinding, excruciating, extreme, great, immense, intense, severe, terrible, unbearable, unimaginable** | **aching, burning, cramping, numbing, piercing, searing, sharp, shooting, stabbing, stinging, throbbing** ◇ *She had a burning ~ in one eye.* | **dull, little, mild, slight** | **debilitating** | **chronic, constant, nagging, persistent** | **sudden** | **intermittent** | **recurrent** | **bodily, physical** | **abdominal, back, chest, joint, leg, muscle, pelvic, shoulder, stomach** ◇ *She's been in bed with back ~.* ◇ *He went to the doctor with chest ~s.* | **menstrual, period** (*esp. BrE*) | **arthritis** | **labor pain** (*AmE*), **labour/labor pains** (*BrE, AmE*) | **growing ~s** | **phantom** ◇ *the phantom ~ of a lost limb*
...OF PAIN **spasm, stab**
VERB + PAIN **be in, be racked with, experience, feel, get, go through, have, suffer, suffer from** ◇ *He was obviously in a great deal of ~.* ◇ *Can you feel any ~?* ◇ *Marathon runners are used to going through ~.* ◇ *He was taken to the hospital suffering from severe abdominal ~.* | **cause, give sb, inflict** ◇ *His back gives him a lot of ~.* ◇ *It's wrong to inflict ~ on any animal.* | **aggravate, exacerbate, increase, make worse** | **alleviate, block out, deaden, dull, ease, help, kill, lessen, numb, reduce, relieve, soothe, stop** ◇ *These pills should ease the ~.* | **control, manage** ◇ *The treatments helped manage his ~.* | **minimize** | **treat** ◇ *Doctors used to treat back ~ with rest.* | **bear, endure, put up with, stand, take, withstand** | **ignore** | **cry out in, cry with, groan with, scream with** | **be contorted with, contort in** ◇ *His face was contorted with ~ as he crossed the finish line.*
PAIN + VERB **begin, come, occur, start** ◇ *The ~s began shortly after she started work as a gardener.* | **erupt, flare, flare up** | **hit sb/sth, strike sb/sth** ◇ *A sharp ~ hit the middle of my chest and I collapsed.* | **course through sb/sth, flash through sth, flood sth, lance through sb/sth** (*literary, esp. AmE*), **radiate from sth to sth, rip through sb/sth, rush through sb/sth, rush up sb/sth, sear through sb/sth, shoot through sth, shoot up sth, stab sb/sth, surge through sb/sth, sweep over sb/sth, sweep through sb/sth, tear through sb/sth, throb, wash over sb** ◇ *A sharp ~ shot up his leg.* | **overwhelm sb, wrack sb/sth** ◇ *Pain wracked her frail body once more.* | **grow stronger, increase, intensify, worsen** | **disappear, ease, fade, go, recede, stop, subside** ◇ *Has the ~ gone yet?* | **persist** ◇ *If the ~ persists, see your doctor.* | **come back, return**
PAIN + NOUN **control, management, relief** | **killer** (usually *painkiller*), **medication, medicine, pill** (*esp. AmE*), **reliever** | **sufferer** | **symptoms** | **specialist** | **clinic** | **threshold, tolerance** | **level** | **intensity, severity** | **sensation**
PREP. **~ in** ◇ *a ~ in her side*
PHRASES **aches and ~s** ◇ *Eucalyptus oil is good for easing muscular aches and ~s.* | **a cry of ~** | **a threshold for ~** (*esp. AmE*), **a threshold of ~** ◇ *I have a very low threshold for ~.*

2 unhappiness

ADJ. **great, immense, intense, terrible** | **numbing** | **indescribable, unspeakable** | **emotional**
VERB + PAIN **cause (sb), give sb, inflict** ◇ *Through her drug*

addiction she had inflicted a lot of ~ on the family. | **feel**, **go through** | **know** ◇ *She knew the ~ of separation.* | **get over** ◇ *It took him several years to get over the ~ of losing his job.* | **dull**, **ease**, **lessen**, **numb** | **heal** ◇ *Nothing could heal the ~ of her son's death.* | **spare sb** ◇ *We hoped to spare her the ~ of having to meet her attacker.* | **express** | **share** ◇ *It was lovely to have someone there to share both the ~ and the joy.* | **conceal**, **hide**, **mask** ◇ *He tried to conceal his ~ from her.* | **forget** ◇ *For a few moments she forgot the ~ he had caused her.* | **bear**, **endure**, **withstand** | **relive** ◇ *I don't want to relive the ~ of losing her.* | **sense** ◇ *I could sense her ~ and put my arm around her.* | **prolong**
PHRASES **the ~ etched on sb's face** ◇ *Ellen saw the ~ etched on his face when he mentioned his ex-wife's name.*

pained *adj.*

VERBS **be**, **look**, **seem**, **sound**
ADV. **slightly** ◇ *a slightly ~ expression on his face*

painful *adj.*

VERBS **be**, **look**, **seem** | **become**, **get** | **find sth** ◇ *She found it unbearably ~ to speak.*
ADV. **extremely**, **fairly**, **very**, etc. | **acutely**, **excruciatingly**, **horribly**, **incredibly**, **intensely**, **terribly**, **unbearably** | **particularly** | **increasingly** | **almost** | **a little**, **slightly**, etc. | **potentially** | **emotionally**, **physically**
PREP. **to** ◇ *The subject of his failed marriage was quite ~ to him.*

painless *adj.*

VERBS **be** ◇ *The operation was relatively ~.*
ADV. **completely**, **totally** | **fairly**, **pretty** | **almost** | **relatively**

paint *noun*

ADJ. **thick**, **thin** | **fresh** | **old** ◇ *Old ~ was chipping off the outside walls.* | **dry**, **wet** | **chipped**, **loose**, **peeling** | **non-toxic** | **emulsion** (*BrE*), **enamel**, **flat** (*esp. AmE*), **gloss**, **matt/matte**, **metallic**, **spray** | **lead**, **lead-based**, **oil-based**, **water-based** | **latex**, **acrylic**, **oil**, **poster**, **watercolour/watercolor** ◇ *an artist working with acrylic ~s* | **craft** (*AmE*) | **milk** (*AmE*), **tempera** | **exterior**, **interior** | **fabric**, **house**
... OF PAINT **blob**, **speck**, **splash**, **spot** ◇ *Specks of ~ found at the scene were found to match the accused's car.* | **coat** ◇ *I'll give the walls a fresh coat of ~.* | **layer** ◇ *The artist has used several layers of ~ to create the stormy sky.* | **lick** (*informal*) ◇ *A lick of ~ will do wonders for the room.* | **jar**, **pot**, **tube** | **bucket** (*AmE*), **can** (*AmE*), **tin** (*BrE*) | **box**, **set** ◇ *a set of oil ~s*
VERB + PAINT **apply**, **put on**, **spray** | **daub with** (*esp. BrE*), **splash with**, **splatter with** | **remove**, **scrape off**, **strip**, **strip off** | **mix** | **pour**
PAINT + VERB **dry** | **chip**, **flake**, **flake off**, **peel** ◇ *Paint was peeling from the walls.*
PAINT + NOUN **colour/color** | **finish** ◇ *The stove is available in two metallic ~ finishes.* | **brush** (usually **paintbrush**), **roller** | **gun** | **tray** | **bucket** (*esp. AmE*), **can** (*AmE*), **pot** | **thinner** | **remover**, **stripper** | **chip** (*AmE*) | **application**, **coat** (*AmE*) (usually **coat of paint** in *AmE* and always in *BrE*), **layer** | **sample** | **manufacturer**, **shop** (*BrE*), **store** (*AmE*) | **scheme** ◇ *The aircraft have been repainted in the original red and black ~ scheme.* | **job** ◇ *We did a quick ~ job on the car and hoped the damage wasn't noticeable.*

paint *verb*

ADV. **carefully**, **delicately**, **meticulously** | **well** | **badly**, **crudely** ◇ *The walls had been ~ed very badly.* ◇ *a crudely ~ed human figure* | **beautifully**, **exquisitely** | **brightly**, **gaily** (*old-fashioned*) ◇ *the cheerful, brightly ~ed doors*
PREP. **in** ◇ *an artist who usually ~s in oils* | **on** ◇ *I like to ~ on canvas.* | **with** ◇ *Paint the box all over with varnish.*
PHRASES **freshly ~ed**, **newly ~ed** | **~ sth blue**, **white**, etc. ◇ *We ~ed the walls light green.*

painter *noun*

1 person whose job is to paint buildings, walls, etc.
ADJ. **self-employed** | **house** | **sign**

PHRASES **~ and decorator** (*BrE*) ◇ *He now works as a ~ and decorator.*

2 artist who paints pictures
ADJ. **celebrated**, **distinguished**, **famous**, **great**, **leading**, **master**, **renowned**, **well-known** ◇ *some of the great ~s of the last century* ◇ *the Dutch master ~ Jan Vermeer* | **accomplished**, **good**, **talented** | **successful** | **amateur**, **professional** | **self-taught** | **contemporary**, **modern**, **modernist** ◇ *an exhibition of works by contemporary ~s* | **16th-century**, etc. | **court** ◇ *Rudolf II's court ~* | **oil**, **watercolour/watercolor** (*esp. BrE*) | **abstract**, **animal** (*esp. BrE*), **figurative**, **fresco** (*esp. BrE*), **genre**, **landscape**, **miniature**, **portrait**, **realist**, **still-life** | **Cubist**, **Impressionist**, **Romantic**, etc.
→ Note at JOB

painting *noun*

1 act of painting
ADJ. **acrylic**, **oil**, **watercolour/watercolor** | **miniature** | **abstract**, **decorative**, **figurative**, **genre**, **landscape**, **portrait**, **representational**, **still-life**, **surrealist** | **mural** | **contemporary**, **modern** | **traditional** ◇ *He studied traditional Japanese ~ at the Kano school.*
VERB + PAINTING **do** ◇ *I'll do some ~ this afternoon.* | **take up** (*esp. BrE*) ◇ *When she retired she took up ~.* | **study** ◇ *He went to Europe to study ~.*
PAINTING + NOUN **style**, **technique**
PHRASES **~ and decorating** (*BrE*) ◇ *The firm specializes in ~ and decorating.*

2 picture
ADJ. **beautiful**, **fine**, **good**, **great** | **famous**, **well-known** | **valuable** | **original** ◇ *The design is based on an original ~ by Matisse.* | **early**, **late** ◇ *His early ~s were light, expressive compositions.* | **recent** | **miniature** | **Cubist**, **Impressionist**, etc. | **avant-garde** | **contemporary** | **17th-century**, etc. | **abstract**, **decorative**, **figurative**, **figure**, **genre**, **landscape**, **religious**, **still-life**, **surrealist** | **cave**, **ceiling**, **fresco**, **mural**, **wall** | **acrylic**, **oil**, **watercolour/watercolor** | **monochrome** | **colourful/colorful** | **large**, **large-scale**, **small** | **easel** | **untitled** | **finished**, **unfinished** | **framed**
... OF PAINTINGS **series** | **collection**, **exhibition**
VERB + PAINTING **create**, **do**, **execute**, **make**, **paint**, **produce**, **work on** ◇ *Degas did several ~s of ballet dancers.* | **compose** | **complete**, **finish** | **frame** | **hang**, **put up** | **display**, **exhibit**, **present**, **show** | **view** | **collect** ◇ *She collects ~s by 19th-century Australian artists.* | **clean**, **restore** | **copy**, **reproduce** | **commission** | **buy**, **purchase**, **sell** | **donate** | **admire**
PAINTING + VERB **depict sb/sth**, **feature sb/sth**, **portray sb/sth**, **show sb/sth** | **evoke sth** ◇ *Rauch's ~s evoke memories of a bygone era.* | **reflect sth**, **represent sth**, **reveal sth**, **suggest sth** ◇ *His ~s reflect the joy and beauty in all he saw around him.* | **hang** ◇ *His most famous ~s hang in the Louvre.*
PREP. **in a/the ~** ◇ *The woman in the ~ is the artist's mistress.* | **by** ◇ *a ~ by Gauguin* | **~ in** ◇ *a fine ~ in oils* | **~ of** ◇ *~s of flowers*
→ Note at ART

pair *noun*

1 two things the same
ADJ. **matching** ◇ *a matching ~ of vases* | **identical** | **clean** ◇ *a clean ~ of socks*
PREP. **in a/the ~** ◇ *Answer one question in each ~.* | **in ~s** ◇ *These candles only come in ~s.* | **~ of** ◇ *a ~ of shoes*
PHRASES **one of a ~** ◇ *This sculpture was originally one of a ~ owned by the King of France.*

2 people who are connected
ADJ. **happy** (= a newly married couple) | **odd** ◇ *They make an odd ~.*
VERB + PAIR **match** ◇ *The ~ were matched for age.* | **make** ◇ *I*

thought they would make a good ~ so I arranged for them to meet.
PREP. **in a/the ~** ◇ *The students worked in ~s.*

3 male and female animal

ADJ. **breeding, mating | nesting | monogamous** (*biology*)
PAIR + VERB **breed, mate**
PREP. **~ of** ◇ *a ~ of swans nesting by the river*

pajamas *noun* (*AmE*) → See PYJAMAS

palace *noun*

ADJ. **ancient | 14th-century, etc. | imperial, papal, presidential, royal | beautiful, grand, great, huge, magnificent, sumptuous** (*esp. BrE*) **| pleasure | summer**
VERB + PALACE **build | live in**
PALACE + VERB **stand** ◇ *The ~ stands on the west bank of the river.*
PALACE + NOUN **complex, compound | courtyard, gardens, grounds | door, gates | walls | life** ◇ *She found it hard to adjust to ~ life.* **| aide, guard, official** (*esp. BrE*), **spokesman** (*esp. BrE*), **staff | servant | coup, revolution** (*esp. BrE*) ◇ *The king was deposed by his son in a ~ coup.*
PREP. **at a/the ~, in a/the ~**

palate *noun*

1 part of the mouth

ADJ. **hard | soft | cleft** ◇ *Their baby had an operation to repair a cleft ~.*

2 sense of taste

ADJ. **discerning, discriminating, sophisticated | jaded** (*esp. BrE*) ◇ *Here is a dish that will revive jaded ~s.*
VERB + PALATE **have** ◇ *She has a discerning ~.* **| appeal to, please, suit** ◇ *This kind of food appeals to more sophisticated ~s.* **| cleanse** ◇ *Have an apple to cleanse your ~.*

pale *adj.*

VERBS **appear, be, look, seem | become, go, grow, turn** ◇ *Ruth went ~ as the news sank in.*
ADV. **extremely, fairly, very, etc. | deathly, ghostly, sickly** (*esp. AmE*) ◇ *He turned deathly ~.* **| a little, slightly, etc. | strangely, unnaturally, unusually**
PHRASES **~ and drawn** ◇ *He looked ~ and drawn.*

pallor *noun*

ADJ. **deathly, sickly** ◇ *the deathly ~ of her face*
VERB + PALLOR **have** ◇ *He had a sickly ~.*

palm *noun*

1 flat part of the front of your hand

ADJ. **soft | sweaty | warm | flat, open | upturned | outstretched | left, right**
VERB + PALM **hold up, raise** ◇ *He held up a ~ for silence.* **| extend | open, spread** ◇ *He spread his ~s in a gesture of openness.* **| cup** ◇ *He cupped his empty ~s together.* **| lay, place, put, rest** ◇ *He went over to the wall and placed his ~ on it.* **| press** ◇ *I pressed my ~ to the wound to stop the bleeding.* **| slam, slap** ◇ *She slapped her ~ against the desk in anger.* **| rub, wipe** ◇ *He rubbed his ~s against his jeans.* **| run** ◇ *He ran his ~ up and down Holly's shoulder.* **| read** ◇ *She read people's ~s and told fortunes.*
PALM + NOUN **sweat | face** ◇ *Hold out your arms with your ~s facing down.* **| rest** ◇ *His right ~ was resting against my neck.*
PALM + NOUN **reader, reading | print**
PREP. **against your ~s** ◇ *The metal felt hot against my ~s.* **| between your ~s** ◇ *He took her hand between his ~s and squeezed it.* **| in your ~** ◇ *He showed me the coins in his ~.*

2 tree

ADJ. **coconut, date, oil | fan | potted**
PALM + NOUN **tree | branch, frond, kernel, leaf | grove | fruit, oil | wine**

pamphlet *noun*

ADJ. **political | informational** (*AmE*)
VERB + PAMPHLET **print, produce, publish, write | circulate, distribute, hand out | read**
PAMPHLET + VERB **be called sth, be entitled sth**
PREP. **in a/the ~** ◇ *accusations that were made in the ~*

pan *noun*

1 with a handle → See also POT, SAUCEPAN

ADJ. **chip** (*BrE*), **fry** (usually *frypan*) (*AmE*), **frying, sauté | non-stick | heavy-based** (*BrE*), **heavy-bottomed** (*esp. BrE*) **| aluminium/aluminum, cast-iron, copper | large, small | hot**
VERB + PAN **heat** ◇ *Heat a large ~ and fry the vegetables.* **| cover**
PHRASES **pots and ~s**

2 (*AmE*) for cooking food in the oven → See also TIN

ADJ. **cake, loaf, pie, pizza, tart | baking, roasting | sheet | springform | deep, shallow | prepared** ◇ *Turn the batter into the prepared ~ and bake for 40 minutes.* **| ovenproof | non-stick | metal**

pancake *noun*

ADJ. **blueberry, chocolate-chip | potato**
VERB + PANCAKE **cook, make | flip, toss** (*BrE*)
PANCAKE + NOUN **batter | mix | breakfast** (*AmE*) **| house** (= restaurant which serves pancakes)

pane *noun*

ADJ. **broken | glass | window**
VERB + PANE **break, shatter, smash** (*esp. BrE*)
PREP. **against a/the ~, to a/the ~** ◇ *Her face was pressed against the ~.* **| down a/the ~** ◇ *The rain ran down the window ~.* **| on a/the ~** ◇ *There was dirt on the ~.*
PHRASES **a ~ of glass** ◇ *The burglars got in by breaking a ~ of glass in a door.*

panel *noun*

1 group of people

ADJ. **all-star** (*AmE*), **blue-ribbon** (*AmE*), **distinguished, outstanding** ◇ *a distinguished ~ of academics* **| expert | independent | international | bipartisan** (*AmE*) **| advisory, arbitration, consensus, judging, review | interview, interviewing, selection** (*all esp. BrE*) **| jury** (*esp. AmE*)
VERB + PANEL **appoint, assemble, convene, create, establish, organize, select, set up | join** ◇ *He joins our ~ of journalists.* **| attend | chair, moderate | head, lead** ◇ *Raphael will head a ~ to discuss the topic.* **| meet | ask** ◇ *We asked a ~ of experts to review the products.*
PANEL + VERB **be drawn from sb/sth** ◇ *a ~ of scientists drawn from universities* **| consist of sb/sth, include sb/sth** ◇ *The ~ consists of ten attorneys.* **| investigate sth, review sth | recommend sth, suggest sth | approve sth | conclude sth** ◇ *The ~ concluded that there was no scientific basis for the claim.* **| note sth | rule sth** ◇ *The ~ ruled that the men must remain in prison.* **| vote** ◇ *The ~ voted unanimously for its approval.*
PANEL + NOUN **member | moderator | interview | discussion | presentation | session | report, review, study | game** (*BrE*) ◇ *The comedian will chair a new TV ~ game.*
PREP. **on a/the ~** ◇ *The head of department serves on the advisory ~.* **| ~ on** ◇ *an independent ~ on takeovers and mergers*
PHRASES **a member of a ~ | a ~ of experts, a ~ of judges** ◇ *The winners were chosen by a ~ of judges.*

2 part of a door, wall, etc.

ADJ. **ceiling, door, wall | sliding | removable | recessed | secret | glass, wood, etc. | decorative | solar**
VERB + PANEL **attach, fit, install | remove**
PANEL + VERB **depict sth** ◇ *The central ~ depicts St George.*

3 section of vehicle body

ADJ. **front, rear | body** ◇ *A rear body ~ needed replacing after the accident.*

4 surface containing controls

ADJ. **control, display, instrument**
PREP. **on a/the ~** ◊ *A red light flashed on the control ~.*

pang noun

ADJ. **sharp** | **little, slight, small** | **sudden** | **first** ◊ *He felt the first ~s of desire when he saw his new teacher.* | **familiar** | **hunger** | **birth ~s** (*figurative*) ◊ *the birth ~s of the new technology*
VERB + PANG **experience, feel, suffer** ◊ *He experienced a sudden ~ of conscience.*
PREP. **with a ~** ◊ *With a ~ she recalled the last time she had seen him.* | **~ of** ◊ *She felt a little ~ of jealousy.*

panic noun

ADJ. **blind, complete, mad** (*esp. BrE*), **pure, sheer, total, utter** | **mild, minor** (*esp. BrE*), **slight** | **momentary** | **growing, mounting** (*esp. BrE*), **rising** | **mass, widespread** | **public** | **general** | **sudden** | **last-minute** ◊ *There was a last-minute ~ when nobody could find the tickets.* | **financial, moral** ◊ *a moral ~ over rising crime rates*
... OF PANIC **surge, wave** ◊ *I felt a surge of ~ when I realized my mistake.*
VERB + PANIC **feel** ◊ *He felt ~ rising within him.* | **get into** (*esp. BrE*), **go into** ◊ *She went into a blind ~ when she couldn't find the exit.* | **cause, create, spread** | **fill sb with, throw sb into** ◊ *The thought of being in charge threw him into a mild ~.*
PANIC + VERB **break out, spread across, through, etc. sth, sweep over, through, etc. sth** ◊ *Panic swept through the crowd.* | **fill sb/sth, grip sb, seize sb, set in** | **grow, rise, well up** | **subside** | **ensue** ◊ *In the ensuing ~, they lost each other.*
PANIC + NOUN **attack** ◊ *She still has ~ attacks two years after the accident.* | **disorder** ◊ *people suffering from depression and ~ disorders* | **reaction, symptoms** | **button** ◊ *The shopkeeper pressed the ~ button and the police arrived in minutes.* | **room** ◊ *The house includes a ~ room which you can run to if intruders enter the house.* | **mode** ◊ *Eli was clearly in ~ mode.* | **buying** (*esp. BrE*) ◊ *Panic buying turned the shortage into a crisis.*
PREP. **in (a) ~** ◊ *He jumped out of the car in a ~.* ◊ *People fled in ~.* | **with ~** ◊ *Her mind went blank with ~.* | **~ about** ◊ *~ about food contamination* | **~ among** ◊ *~ among the population* | **~ over** ◊ *The keys were lost during the ~ over the fire alarm.*
PHRASES **a feeling of ~, a sense of ~** | **in a state of ~** | **a look of ~** ◊ *A look of ~ spread across the boy's face.* | **a moment of ~, a moment's ~** (*esp. BrE*)

pant verb

ADV. **heavily, loudly** | **slightly, softly**
PREP. **for** ◊ *He was ~ing for breath.* | **with** ◊ *She was ~ing with the effort of carrying the suitcase.*
PHRASES **puff and ~** ◊ *Mason puffed and ~ed up the stairs.*

panties noun (esp. AmE) → See also KNICKERS

ADJ. **cotton, lace**
... OF PANTIES **pair**
VERB + PANTIES **wear** | **pull down** | **pull on, pull up**
PHRASES **bra and ~**

pantomime noun (in the UK)

ADJ. **Christmas**
PANTOMIME + NOUN **cow, dame, horse, villain** | **season** → Note at PERFORMANCE (for verbs)

pants noun

1 (*BrE*) underwear → See also PANTIES, UNDERPANTS
... OF PANTS **pair**
VERB + PANTS **pull on, pull up** | **drop, pull down** | **wet** ◊ *He was so frightened that he wet his ~.* (*BrE, AmE*)
PHRASES **bra and ~**

2 (*esp. AmE*) outer clothing covering the legs → See also TROUSERS

ADJ. **long, short** | **corduroy, cotton, denim, flannel, leather, linen, polyester, silk, wool, etc.** | **stretch** | **pinstriped, plaid** (*AmE*), **striped** | **jogging** (*esp. BrE*), **sweat** (usually **sweatpants**) | **riding** | **cargo** (*BrE, AmE*), **flared, flat-front, low-rise, pleated** | **cropped** | **ripped** | **tailored** | **casual, dressy** | **dress** | **camo** (*informal*), **camouflage** | **parachute** (*AmE*) | **baggy, loose, loose-fitting** | **skintight, tight** | **drawstring** | **pajama** (*AmE*) | **matching** ◊ *a brown vest with matching ~*
... OF PANTS **pair**
VERB + PANTS **unbutton, undo, unzip** | **drop, pull down** | **pull on, pull up**
PANT + NOUN **leg, pocket** | **suit**
PREP. **in ~**
→ Special page at CLOTHES

pantyhose noun (AmE) → See also TIGHTS

ADJ. **sheer** | **fishnet** | **control-top**
... OF PANTYHOSE **pair** ◊ *a pair of black ~*
VERB + PANTYHOSE **wear**
PREP. **in ~**
→ Special page at CLOTHES

paper noun

1 material

ADJ. **thick, thin** | **plain** | **lined** | **graph** | **A3, A4, etc.** (*not in the US*) | **executive, legal, letter** (*all AmE*) | **blank** ◊ *I stared at the blank ~, not knowing how to start the letter.* | **printed** ◊ *There is a special rate for printed ~.* | **loose** ◊ *pieces of loose ~* | **brown, coloured/colored** ◊ *a brown ~ package of books* | **Manila** | **acid-free** | **kraft** (*AmE*) | **butcher** (*AmE*) | **parchment** | **greaseproof** (*BrE*), **wax, waxed** | **glossy, shiny** | **scrap, scratch** (*AmE*), **waste** ◊ *I made some notes on a piece of scrap ~.* | **recycled** | **handmade** | **decorative** | **computer** | **notebook** | **drawing, writing** | **blotting** | **tracing** | **wrapping** | **crêpe** | **tissue** | **photographic** | **filter** | **kitchen** (*BrE*) (**paper towel** in *AmE*) | **toilet** | **cigarette** (*esp. BrE*), **rolling** (*esp. AmE*) ◊ *a packet of cigarette ~s* (*BrE*) ◊ *a pack of rolling ~s* (*AmE*) | **litmus** | **crumpled, folded**
... OF PAPER **bit** (*esp. BrE*), **piece, scrap, sheet, slip, strip** ◊ *I scribbled down his number on a scrap of ~.* | **roll** ◊ *a roll of toilet ~* | **side** ◊ *The essay filled seven sides of ~.*
VERB + PAPER **fold** ◊ *Fold the ~ in half.* | **unfold** | **rip, shred, tear** | **crumple, crumple up, screw up** (*esp. BrE*) ◊ *He crumpled the ~ into a ball.* ◊ *I screwed up the ~ and threw it away.* | **recycle**
PAPER + VERB **be scattered** ◊ *Scraps of wrapping ~ were scattered around.* | **flutter** ◊ *A piece of ~ fluttered to the floor.*
PAPER + NOUN **bag, cup, plate, sack** | **napkin, towel** | **aeroplane** (*BrE*), **airplane** (*AmE*), **ball, doll, hat, lantern** | **currency, money** | **document, map, receipt, ticket** ◊ *the advantages of ~ maps over online maps* | **copy, version** ◊ *He kept a ~ copy of his account information.* | **edition** | **cut-out** | **mill** | **pulp** | **industry** | **shredder**
PREP. **on ~** ◊ *I've had nothing on ~* (= in writing) *to say that I've been accepted.*
PHRASES **put pen to ~** ◊ *I've thought about what I'm going to write, but I haven't yet put pen to ~.* | **a waste of ~** ◊ *This report is a waste of ~.*

2 newspaper

ADJ. **daily, evening** (*esp. BrE*), **morning, Sunday, weekly** | **today's, yesterday's** | **independent, left-wing** (*esp. BrE*), **right-wing** (*esp. BrE*) | **hometown** (*esp. AmE*), **local, national** | **school** (*esp. AmE*) | **broadsheet** (*esp. BrE*), **quality** (*BrE*) | **tabloid** (*esp. BrE*)
... OF PAPER **copy** ◊ *Do you have a copy of yesterday's ~?* | **edition** ◊ *today's edition of the ~*
VERB + PAPER **buy, get, take** (*esp. BrE*) ◊ *Do you take a daily ~?* | **flick through** (*esp. BrE*), **flip through** (*esp. AmE*), **read** ◊ *What ~ do you usually read?* | **print, produce, publish** |

paperback

edit, write for, write in | appear in | get into ◇ *The story got into the ~s.*
PAPER + VERB come out ◇ *The ~ comes out every Saturday.* | report sth ◇ *The ~ reported that several people had seen UFOs.*
PAPER + NOUN shop (*BrE*) | boy, girl | round (*BrE*), route (*AmE*) ◇ *Many kids do a ~ round.* ◇ *Many kids have ~ routes.*
PREP. in a/the ~ ◇ *I read about his arrest in the ~.* ◇ *I read about his arrest in the ~s.* (*esp. BrE*) | on a/the ~ ◇ *She got a job on the local ~.*

3 (usually **papers**) official document

ADJ. necessary | official | ID, identification, identity | personal, private | court, legal | adoption, divorce | ballot
... OF PAPERS pile, sheaf
VERB + PAPER sign ◇ *Teresa signed the adoption ~s.* | show ◇ *Be prepared to show your identity ~s at the border.* | shuffle ◇ *He shuffled the ~s on his desk.* | file ◇ *legal ~s filed in London*

4 (*BrE*) exam

ADJ. exam, examination, question, test (*BrE, AmE*) | written ◇ *I did well on the oral but not on the written ~.* | English, history, etc.
VERB + PAPER do, sit, take | set ◇ *The exam ~s are set by experienced teachers.* | mark | turn over ◇ *You may now turn over your ~s.*
PREP. in a/the ~ ◇ *the questions in the physics ~* | on a/the ~ ◇ *You must not write on the question ~.*

5 piece of writing

ADJ. draft (*esp. BrE*) | consultation (*esp. BrE*), discussion, position, working | research, scientific, technical | scholarly | term (*AmE*) ◇ *I wrote a term ~ on eating disorders.* | seminal | peer-reviewed | published, unpublished | influential
VERB + PAPER deliver, give, present, read, submit | author, draft, prepare, produce, write | co-author | issue, publish, release | cite
PAPER + VERB consider sth, deal with sth, examine sth, explore sth, focus on sth, look at sth ◇ *The ~ looks at the future of university education.* | outline sth | argue sth, propose sth | demonstrate sth | conclude sth | describe sth, outline sth, present sth | report sth ◇ *This ~ reports the results of a two-year field experiment.* | be called sth, be entitled sth, be titled sth (*esp. AmE*)
PREP. in a/the ~ ◇ *Freud first mentioned this concept in his ~ 'On Narcissism'.* | ~ on ◇ *a ~ on the development of the novel*

paperback *noun*

ADJ. mass-market (*esp. BrE*) ◇ *the demand for mass-market ~s* | trade
VERB + PAPERBACK read | come out in ◇ *The novel has just come out in ~.*
PAPERBACK + VERB come out ◇ *The ~ came out in June.*
PAPERBACK + NOUN book, copy, edition, novel, version | rights
PREP. in ~ ◇ *The book is now available in ~.*

paperwork *noun*

ADJ. proper | necessary | legal
VERB + PAPERWORK deal with, do, get through, go through, handle, prepare, process ◇ *I need to get this ~ done by tonight.* ◇ *I have a lot of ~ to get through.* | complete, finish | sign | involve ◇ *The project involved an enormous amount of ~.* | fill in (*BrE*), fill out (*esp. AmE*) | file, submit ◇ *He filed the necessary ~ to establish the club's business name.* | reduce
PREP. ~ for ◇ *Have you done all the necessary ~ for the sale?*
PHRASES a backlog, mountain, pile, etc. of ~

parachute *noun*

VERB + PARACHUTE deploy, use | open | pack

PARACHUTE + VERB deploy, open | fail to deploy (*esp. AmE*), fail to open (*esp. BrE*)
PARACHUTE + NOUN drop, jump ◇ *He made his first ~ jump at the age of seventy.* | instructor (*esp. BrE*)
PREP. by ~ ◇ *Supplies were dropped by ~.*

parade *noun*

ADJ. big, grand (*esp. BrE*) | colourful/colorful | fashion | military, victory | Thanksgiving Day (*in the US*) | gay pride | ticker-tape (*AmE*) | street | annual | inaugural | identification, identity (*both BrE*) (*line-up* in *AmE*)
VERB + PARADE have, hold, stage ◇ *They held a ~ to mark the soldiers' return.* ◇ *The ~ is held every year.* ◇ *The police held an identity ~.* (*BrE*) | go on (*esp. BrE*) ◇ *The battalion went on ~ to welcome the new commander-in-chief.* | lead | watch
PARADE + VERB take place (*esp. BrE*)
PARADE + NOUN ground | route | float | organizer
PREP. at a/the ~ ◇ *Thousands of people were at the ~.* | on ~ ◇ *The soldiers will be on ~ tomorrow.*

paradise *noun*

1 heaven

VERB + PARADISE enter, go to ◇ *They all expected to go to ~.*
PREP. in ~ ◇ *an angel in ~*

2 perfect place

ADJ. beautiful (*esp. AmE*) | lost ◇ *the lost ~ of childhood* | earthly, island, tropical
VERB + PARADISE create ◇ *She worked on the garden until she had created her own little ~.* | find ◇ *They moved to the country hoping to find ~.*
PARADISE + NOUN island
PREP. in (a) ~ ◇ *We found ourselves in a tropical ~.* | ~ for ◇ *The airport is a ~ for pickpockets.* | ~ of ◇ *a ~ of golden beaches*
PHRASES a ~ on earth

paradox *noun*

ADJ. apparent, seeming (*esp. AmE*) | great | central, fundamental | curious, interesting, strange
VERB + PARADOX create, pose, present ◇ *The facts pose something of a ~.* | address, explore | reveal | explain, resolve, solve
PREP. about ◇ *The ~ about time is that it seems to go faster as we become older and less active.* | ~ between ◇ *the ~ between the real and the ideal* | ~ in ◇ *the ~ in the relationship between creativity and psychosis* | ~ of ◇ *The author tackles one of the deepest ~es of life.*
PHRASES by a curious ~ ◇ *By a curious ~, the team became less motivated the more games it won.*

paradoxical *adj.*

VERBS appear, be, seem, sound
ADV. somewhat | apparently, seemingly ◇ *the scientists' seemingly ~ findings*

paragraph *noun*

ADJ. new | introductory, opening | closing, concluding, final | penultimate | preceding, previous | following, next | brief, short | single | key ◇ *This is the key ~ in the article.* | lead
VERB + PARAGRAPH begin, start ◇ *Start each ~ on a new line.* | read, reread | write | quote | add | skip
PARAGRAPH + VERB describe sth, explain sth, say sth | contain sth | begin with sth
PREP. in a/the ~ ◇ *The identity of the murderer is revealed in the very last ~.* | in accordance with ~ 3, etc., under ~ 9, etc. (*law*) ◇ *Cancellation charges will apply in accordance with ~ 4 above.* | ~ about ◇ *a ~ about the writer's reaction to his mother's death*

parallel *noun*

ADJ. direct, exact | clear, close, obvious, strong | interesting, striking | important, significant | historical
VERB + PARALLEL have ◇ *This weather pattern of the southern hemisphere has no ~ in the north.* | find, note, see | draw,

make ◇ *He drew an interesting ~ with religious practices in Japan.* | **offer, show, suggest** ◇ *The move west suggests a ~ with the earlier American pioneer experience.* | **provide**
PARALLEL + VERB **exist** ◇ *Parallels do exist between the author's family and that of Francie Coffin.*
PREP. **without ~** ◇ *a speed of development without ~ in post-war Europe* | **~ between** ◇ *a ~ between economic and cultural advancement* | **~ in** ◇ *We found a direct ~ in the attitudes of children in other countries.* | **~ to** ◇ *A close ~ to this mating pattern is found in dolphins.* | **~ with** ◇ *She saw an obvious ~ with her sister's predicament.*

parallel *adj.*

VERBS **be, run**
ADV. **exactly** | **almost, nearly** | **roughly**
PREP. **to** ◇ *The canal is roughly ~ to the main road.* | **with** ◇ *The road runs ~ with the coast.*

paralyse *(BrE)* *(AmE* **paralyze***) verb*

ADV. **completely, totally** | **partially** ◇ *He was partially ~d by the fall.* | **almost, nearly, virtually** | **temporarily** ◇ *Hannah was temporarily ~d on the right side.*
PHRASES **leave sb ~d** ◇ *The accident left her ~d.* | **be ~d from the neck, waist, etc. down** | **be ~d with fear**

paralysis *noun*

1 being unable to move your body or a part of it
ADJ. **complete** | **partial** ◇ *stroke patients who have suffered partial ~* | **permanent, temporary** | **facial, muscle**
VERB + PARALYSIS **suffer from** | **cause, induce** ◇ *Polio can cause ~ and sometimes death.*
2 being unable to work in the normal way
ADJ. **complete** ◇ *The country was on the verge of complete ~ due to the strike.* | **emotional, political** ◇ *The crisis over the constitution may lead to political ~.*

paranoia *noun*

ADJ. **rampant** | **extreme, severe** ◇ *The regime is in the grip of severe ~.* | **mild, slight** ◇ *I was guilty perhaps of mild ~.* | **increasing** | **irrational** | **anti-communist** ◇ *the anti-communist ~ of the 1950s*
VERB + PARANOIA **suffer from** | **border on, verge on** ◇ *Her passion for cleanliness borders on ~.* | **induce** ◇ *The drugs can induce ~.* | **fuel** ◇ *External threats will just fuel ~ among those in power.*
PARANOIA + VERB **kick in, set in** ◇ *The ~ is setting in.* | **grip sb** ◇ *He was gripped by ~.*

parasite *noun*

ADJ. **common** | **dangerous, deadly** ◇ *These flies carry a dangerous ~.* | **external, internal** | **human** | **intestinal** | **malaria**
VERB + PARASITE **carry, have** | **pick up** ◇ *Pets do sometimes pick up intestinal ~s.* | **transmit** ◇ *Your contaminated fingers can transmit the ~ to many surfaces.* | **be found in** ◇ *the most common intestinal ~ found in humans* | **kill**
PARASITE + VERB **infect sb/sth** | **cause sth** ◇ *the ~ that causes malaria*

parcel *noun (esp. BrE)*

1 something wrapped in paper, etc. → See also PACKAGE
ADJ. **large** | **little, small** ◇ *We left little ~s outside each person's door.* | **brown-paper** | **gift-wrapped, tissue-wrapped, etc.** | **clothing, food**
VERB + PARCEL **post** *(BrE)*, **send** | **deliver** ◇ *The courier tried to deliver a ~ yesterday but I'd already left.* | **get, receive** | **collect** ◇ *She went to collect her ~ from the depot.* | **wrap, wrap sth in** | **open, unwrap**
PARCEL + VERB **arrive** ◇ *This morning a ~ arrived containing a signed copy of his new book.* | **contain sth**
PARCEL + NOUN **delivery** ◇ *a parcel-delivery business* | **tape** *(BrE)* ◇ *I sealed up the box with brown ~ tape.* | **bomb** *(BrE)* ◇ *A young girl was injured by a ~ bomb.*
PREP. **in a/the ~** | **~ from, ~ to**

2 food wrapped in leaves, pastry, etc.
ADJ. **neat** ◇ *Place the fish on top, tucking any tail ends under to make neat ~s.* | **baked, crispy** | **filo, pasta, pastry, etc.** ◇ *a pastry ~ of brie and asparagus in a creamy sauce*
PARCEL + VERB **be stuffed with sth** ◇ *baked filo ~s stuffed with feta cheese*

pardon *noun*

ADJ. **full** | **conditional** | **general** ◇ *The king issued a general ~ to all those involved in the rebellion.* | **free** *(BrE)* | **posthumous** ◇ *posthumous ~s granted to soldiers shot for cowardice* | **presidential, royal**
VERB + PARDON **give sb, grant sb** | **offer sb** ◇ *The government offered a free ~ to the rebels.* | **get, obtain, receive** | **ask** *(esp. BrE)*, **ask for, seek** ◇ *I ask your ~ for my actions.* | **refuse**
PREP. **~ for** ◇ *She asked for a ~ for her crime.*

parent *noun*

ADJ. **married, unmarried** | **divorced** | **lone** *(BrE)*, **single** ◇ *single-parent families* | **absent** | **aged, aging, elderly** | **deceased, surviving** | **prospective, would-be** | **expectant** | **first-time, new** | **biological, birth, natural, real** | **adopted, adoptive, foster** ◇ *the identities of the adoptive ~s* | **surrogate** | **custodial, non-custodial** *(law)* | **female, male** | **gay, heterosexual, lesbian** | **low-income, poor** | **rich, wealthy, well-to-do** | **middle-class, working-class** | **immigrant** | **working** ◇ *The government has promised a better deal for working ~s.* | **stay-at-home** | **good** | **involved, supportive** ◇ *The study showed that children with involved ~s do better at school.* | **proud** ◇ *They have just become the proud ~s of a baby girl.* | **caring, devoted, loving** | **doting, fond, indulgent** | **overprotective** | **stern, strict** | **bad, unfit** | **abusive** | **neglectful** | **angry, anxious, concerned, distraught, distressed, grieving**
PARENT + NOUN **company** *(business)* ◇ *The subsidiary eventually outgrew its ~ company and took it over.*

parenthesis *noun*

1 parentheses *(esp. AmE)* marks around extra information in writing → See also BRACKET
VERB + PARENTHESES **enclose sth in parentheses, give sth in parentheses, put sth in parentheses** ◇ *The prices are given in parentheses.*
PREP. **in parentheses, inside parentheses, within parentheses** ◇ *The words in parentheses should be deleted.* | **outside parentheses** ◇ *The numbers outside the parentheses are the sales figures.*
2 extra information in a sentence, etc.
ADJ. **long** ◇ *After a long ~, she returned to the matter in hand.*
PREP. **in ~** ◇ *I add, in ~, that I doubt whether such a place exists.*

parenthood *noun*

ADJ. **lone** *(BrE)*, **single** ◇ *the stresses of lone ~* ◇ *the disintegrating nuclear family and the rise in single ~* | **responsible** ◇ *education about family planning and responsible ~*
PHRASES **preparation for ~**

park *noun*

ADJ. **local, neighbourhood/neighborhood** *(esp. AmE)* | **city, downtown** *(AmE)*, **municipal, urban** | **public** | **country** *(BrE)* | **county** *(AmE)*, **national, state** *(AmE)* ◇ *The mountain has been designated as a national ~.* ◇ *the national ~s system* | **beautiful** | **historic** | **25-acre, 45-acre, etc.** | **dog** *(AmE)* | **memorial, sculpture** | **waterfront** | **game, marine, safari** *(esp. BrE)*, **wildlife** | **amusement, leisure** *(BrE)*, **recreational** *(esp. AmE)*, **theme, water** | **indoor, outdoor** *(both AmE)* ◇ *an indoor ~ for skateboarders* | **ball** *(usually* **ballpark***)*, **baseball** *(both AmE)*, **skate, skateboard** | **mobile-home** *(esp. AmE)*, **RV** *(AmE)*, **trailer** *(esp. AmE)* | **business, industrial, office** *(esp. AmE)*, **retail** *(BrE)*

VERB + PARK **go to, visit** ◇ *They go to the* ~ *most Sundays.* | **design, landscape, lay out** ◇ *a beautifully landscaped* ~ | **build, create, develop** ◇ *He built* ~*s and highways in New York.* | **manage** ◇ *a* ~ *managed by the Department of Parks and Recreation* | **overlook** ◇ *a cafe overlooking the* ~
PARK + NOUN **bench** | **entrance** | **boundary** | **area** | **service, system** (*AmE*) ◇ *I work as a ranger in the city's* ~ *system.* | ~**s department** ◇ *She works for the* ~*s department.* | **employee, manager, official, ranger** ◇ *The lion was shot dead by a* ~ *ranger.* | **visitor**
PREP. **at a/the** ~ ◇ *We met at Hyde Park.* (*BrE*) | **in a/the** ~ ◇ *They went for a walk in the* ~. ◇ *We met in Central Park.*

park *verb*

ADV. **carefully** | **neatly** ◇ *All the cars were neatly* ~*ed on the street.* | **badly** | **quickly** | **illegally** (*esp. BrE*) ◇ *Motorists* ~*ed illegally are fined £50.*

parking *noun*

ADJ. **convenient, easy** | **ample** ◇ *The hotel has ample* ~. | **free** | **off-road** (*BrE*), **off-street** (*esp. BrE*), **on-street** (*esp. BrE*), **roadside** (*BrE*), **street** ◇ *The town has free on-street* ~. | **underground** | **long-stay** (*BrE*), **long-term** (*AmE*), **short-stay** (*BrE*), **short-term** (*AmE*) | **illegal** | **car** (*esp. BrE*) | **valet** | **daily, hourly, etc.**
PARKING + NOUN **area, facilities** (*esp. BrE*), **facility** (*esp. AmE*) | **deck, garage, lot, ramp, structure** (*all AmE*) | **bay** (*BrE*), **place, space, spot** ◇ *a restaurant with ample* ~ *space* ◇ *I spent half an hour looking for a* ~ *space.* | **brake, light** (*both AmE*) | **meter** | **fee** (*esp. AmE*) | **fine** (*esp. BrE*) | **ticket** | **permit, sticker** (*esp. AmE*) ◇ *The cost of a residents'* ~ *permit is due to rise.* | **restrictions** (*esp. BrE*) | **problem** ◇ *The influx of tourists could cause traffic congestion and* ~ *problems.* | **attendant** (*esp. BrE*)
PREP. ~ **for** ◇ ~ *for 300 cars*

parliament *noun*

ADJ. **current, present** | **new** | **outgoing** | **bicameral, unicameral** | **elected** | **hung** (*BrE*) ◇ *The election resulted in a hung* ~, *followed by the resignation of the prime minister.* | **federal, national, provincial, regional, state**
VERB + PARLIAMENT **stand for** (*esp. BrE*) ◇ *He first stood for Parliament in 2001.* | **enter, get into** | **be in, sit in** ◇ *He sat in Parliament for over forty years.* | **elect (sb to)** ◇ *a popularly elected* ~ | **return sb to** (*esp. BrE*) ◇ *He was returned to Parliament in 2001 as MP for Appleby.* | **represent sb/sth in** | **address** ◇ *The President will address the Canadian* ~ *during his trip.* | **bring sth before** (*esp. BrE*), **introduce sth into** (*esp. BrE*), **present sth to, put sth before** (*esp. BrE*) | **be before, come before, go before** (*all esp. BrE*) ◇ *The bill will come before Parliament next month.* | **get through, go through, pass through** | **force sth through, push sth through, put sth through** ◇ *The government was accused of forcing the bill through Parliament.* | **lobby, petition** (*esp. BrE*) | **mislead** (*esp. BrE*) | **convene** | **recall** | **dissolve, prorogue** (*BrE*) ◇ *The bill has to be passed before* ~ *is prorogued.* | **suspend** | **be accountable to, be responsible to** | **dominate** ◇ *The ruling National Democratic Party dominates* ~. | **storm** ◇ *Angry protestors stormed the* ~.
PARLIAMENT + VERB **adopt sth, approve sth, enact sth, lay sth down, pass sth, ratify sth** ◇ *The Commission is guided by rules laid down by Parliament.* | **reject sth** | **vote (on sth)** | **debate sth** | **legislate (on sth)** ◇ *Parliament may legislate on any matter of penal law.* | **be in session, convene, meet, sit** (*esp. BrE*) ◇ *Parliament will be in session until December.* | **rise** (*BrE*) ◇ *the day Parliament rises for the summer recess* | **reconvene, resume** ◇ *Parliament reconvenes next month.*
PARLIAMENT + NOUN **building** | **chamber** (*esp. BrE*) ◇ *The floor of the Scottish* ~ *chamber contains seating for 128 members.* | **minister, official** (*both esp. BrE*) ◇ *a senior* ~ *official*
PREP. **in** ~ ◇ *her first year in Parliament*
PHRASES **an Act of Parliament** (*BrE*) | **a house of** ~ ◇ *The National Assembly is the lower house of the French*

parody *noun*

1 writing/speech/music

ADJ. **brilliant, clever** | **funny, hilarious** | **cruel** | **song** (*esp. AmE*)
VERB + PARODY **write** | **do**
PREP. **through** ~ ◇ *He attacked her ideas through* ~. | ~ **of** ◇ *She has written a cruel* ~ *of his book.* | ~ **on** ◇ *The show included a* ~ *on Hollywood action movies.*

2 bad example

ADJ. **grotesque**
PREP. **in a** ~ **of** ◇ *He sighed in a* ~ *of deep emotion.* | ~ **of** ◇ *She has become a grotesque* ~ *of her former elegant self.*

parole *noun*

ADJ. **early**
VERB + PAROLE **be on** | **give sb, grant sb** | **get** ◇ *She got* ~. | **let sb out on, release sb on** ◇ *She was released on* ~ *after serving just half of her sentence.* | **break, violate** ◇ *He broke (his)* ~. | **be eligible for, be up for, come up for** ◇ *Her case comes up for* ~ *in September.*
PAROLE + NOUN **board, system** | **officer** | **hearing** | **violation**
PREP. **on** ~ ◇ *He committed a burglary while on* ~. | **with** ~ ◇ *With* ~, *he could be out in two years.* | **without** ~ ◇ *sentenced to life imprisonment without* ~

parsley *noun*

ADJ. **chopped** | **fresh** | **curly, flat-leaf**
... OF PARSLEY **sprig**
VERB + PARSLEY **chop** | **add** | **garnish sth with, sprinkle (sth with)** ◇ *The eggs are sprinkled with coarsely chopped* ~.
→ Special page at FOOD

part *noun*

1 piece, area, period, division, etc. of sth

ADJ. **big, good, greater, huge, large, major, significant, substantial** ◇ *We spent a good* ~ *of the day rehearsing.* ◇ *The greater* ~ *of the building has been refurbished.* | **minor, small** | **equal** ◇ *Cut it into four equal* ~*s.* | **important, main, principal** | **basic, central, critical, crucial, essential, fundamental, key, necessary, vital** | **integral, intrinsic** | **interchangeable** | **best, worst** ◇ *The worst* ~ *was having to wait three hours.* | **early** ◇ *In the early* ~ *of his career he worked in India.* | **latter** ◇ *the latter* ~ *of the century* | **first, last, middle, second** | **upper, uppermost** ◇ *the upper* ~ *of the spine* | **lower** | **inner, outer** | **anterior** (*technical*), **front** | **back, posterior** (*technical*) | **northern, southern, etc.** | **remote** | **different, distinct, various** | **separate** | **inseparable** | **component, constituent** ◇ *Break it down into its constituent* ~*s.* | **body** | **difficult, hard, tough, tricky** ◇ *I gave up once I got to the hard* ~. | **easy** | **fun** ◇ *Now comes the fun* ~. | **scary** | **funny** | **sad** ◇ *The sad* ~ *was that he didn't really care.* | **interesting**
VERB + PART **comprise, constitute, fall into, form** ◇ *The book falls into three distinct* ~*s.* | **break sth down into, divide sth into, split sth into**
PREP. **in** ~ ◇ *Your salary depends in* ~ *on your qualifications.* ◇ *The movie is good in* ~*s.* ◇ *a serial in four* ~*s* | ~ **of** ◇ *Part of me wants to stay and* ~ *of me doesn't.*
PHRASES **the** ~**s of the body** | **foreign** ~**s** (*esp. BrE*) ◇ *They're always off to foreign* ~*s.* | **private** ~**s** (= sexual organs)

2 a piece of a machine

ADJ. **replacement, spare** ◇ *Where can I get spare* ~*s for my bike?* | **auto** (*esp. AmE*), **automotive** (*esp. AmE*), **car, motorcycle** | **moving**
VERB + PART **manufacture** | **assemble**
PART + NOUN ~**s dealer,** ~**s maker,** ~**s supplier** ◇ *an auto* ~*s*

maker | **number** ◇ *The adaptors being recalled contain the ~ number 02K65 on their labels.*

3 role in a play, film/movie, etc.

ADJ. **big** | **bit, small, walk-on** | **speaking**
VERB + PART **act, have, play, take** | **sing** ◇ *Annette Markert sings the ~ of Medea.* | **learn** | **fit** ◇ *Walken stars as Shannon and he fits the ~ well.*
PREP. **in the ~** ◇ *He's very good in the ~.* | **~ of** ◇ *She played the ~ of Juliet.*
PHRASES **act the ~, dress the ~, look the ~** ◇ *He acts and dresses the ~ of a gentleman.* ◇ *He was a pirate in the school play and certainly looked the ~.*

4 share in an activity, event, etc.

ADJ. **big, huge, leading, major** ◇ *Luck played a big ~ in it.* | **minor** | **central, significant, vital** | **active**
VERB + PART **have** ◇ *He had no ~ in the scam.* | **do, play, take** ◇ *She did her ~ in bringing them back together.*
PREP. **~ in** ◇ *They took little ~ in the discussion.*

partial *adj.*

1 not complete

VERBS **be** | **remain**
ADV. **only** ◇ *His efforts met with only ~ success.* | **somewhat** ◇ *The information we have is somewhat ~.* | **necessarily** ◇ *The resulting assessment is necessarily ~ and subjective.*

2 liking sth

VERBS **be, become** ◇ *He's become ~ to vodka since coming to Russia.*
ADV. **very** | **especially** ◇ *I'm especially ~ to the Latin American music.* | **somewhat**
PREP. **to** ◇ *He's very ~ to ice cream.*

participant *noun*

ADJ. **full** | **active, passive** ◇ *We want people to become active ~s in the political process.* | **unwilling, willing** ◇ *She was an unwilling ~ in his downfall.* | **volunteer** (*AmE*) | **enthusiastic** | **interested, potential, prospective** | **eligible** | **regular** ◇ *She's a regular ~ in the show.* | **key, leading, main, major** | **individual** | **fellow** ◇ *He was talking with fellow ~s before the competition.* | **course, programme/program, workshop** | **focus-group, research, study, survey, trial** | **conference, forum, seminar, summit, symposium** | **chat** ◇ *online chat ~s*
VERB + PARTICIPANT **attract** ◇ *Protests on Monday attracted thousands of ~s.* | **select** | **ask, instruct** ◇ *The ~s were asked to indicate their attitudes to science.* | **interview** | **debrief**
PARTICIPANT + VERB **attend sth** | **experience sth** | **describe sth, indicate sth, report sth, state sth** | **rate sth** | **range from sth to sth** ◇ *Participants ranged in age from 35 to 55.*
PREP. **~ in** ◇ *an active ~ in the discussion*

participate *verb*

ADV. **fully** | **actively** ◇ *Local residents actively ~d in the decision-making process.* | **directly, personally** | **effectively, meaningfully** ◇ *We teach students how to ~ effectively in our society.* | **frequently, regularly** | **voluntarily, willingly** ◇ *Twenty-four subjects voluntarily ~d in the study.* | **eagerly, enthusiastically** ◇ *The women ~d enthusiastically in literacy classes.* | **equally**
VERB + PARTICIPATE **be able to, have the opportunity to** | **be allowed to, be encouraged to, be invited to** ◇ *Other countries were invited to ~ in the project.* | **agree to** | **refuse to**
PREP. **in** ◇ *They will have the opportunity to ~ actively in the process.*

participation *noun*

ADJ. **full** | **broader, greater, increased** | **mass, widespread** ◇ *We have to improve and increase mass ~ in sports.* | **limited** | **continued** | **active, direct** ◇ *active citizen ~ in governance* | **voluntary** | **effective, meaningful** | **individual, joint** | **equal** | **democratic, political** | **civic** (*esp. AmE*), **community, popular, public** ◇ *the decline in voting and civic ~* | **citizen, student, voter, worker** | **labor-force** (*AmE*), **labour-**market/labor-market ◇ *The labor-force ~ of mothers has risen steadily since 1976.* | **audience** ◇ *Some of the magic tricks called for audience ~.* | **athletics, sports** | **parental** | **foreign, international**
... OF PARTICIPATION **degree, extent, level** ◇ *We were very pleased with the high level of ~ in the charity events.*
VERB + PARTICIPATION **encourage, facilitate, foster, invite, promote, solicit** ◇ *The club encourages ~ in sporting activities.* ◇ *Teachers were asked to solicit student ~.* | **discourage** | **broaden, increase** | **limit, restrict** ◇ *He has a bad knee that will limit his ~ in training.* | **decline, refuse** (*both esp. AmE*) ◇ *Those who declined ~ were excused and sent back to the classroom.*
PARTICIPATION + VERB **increase**
PARTICIPATION + NOUN **level, rate**
PREP. **~ in** ◇ *direct ~ in the running of the country*

parting *noun*

ADJ. **final** | **amicable** ◇ *It was an amicable ~ and we greatly value the years we spent together.* | **bitter** ◇ *The divorce was a bitter ~ that cost him financially as well as emotionally.*
PHRASES **the moment of ~** ◇ *She was already dreading the moment of ~.* | **a/the ~ of the ways** ◇ *We've come to a ~ of the ways.*

partition *noun*

ADJ. **movable** (*esp. BrE*), **sliding** ◇ *Sliding glass ~s separate the main cafe and covered terraces.* | **folding** | **glass**
VERB + PARTITION **build, create, erect, put up** | **remove, take down**
PARTITION + VERB **divide sth, divide sth up, separate sth** ◇ *The restaurant was divided up by glass ~s.*
PARTITION + NOUN **wall**
PREP. **~ between** ◇ *There were no ~s between the showers.*

partner *noun*

1 in a marriage/relationship

ADJ. **former, one-time** | **dominant** ◇ *She was the dominant ~ in the relationship.* | **female, male** | **gay, homosexual, lesbian, same-gender** (*esp. AmE*), **same-sex** | **heterosexual** | **marital, marriage** ◇ *the choice of marriage ~* | **romantic** | **intimate, sex, sexual** | **committed, steady** ◇ *Most of those questioned said they wanted a steady ~ for emotional support.* | **domestic** ◇ *The organization offers health benefits to the domestic ~s of employees.* | **unmarried** ◇ *Local government workers have been refused pensions for their unmarried ~s.* | **life, long-time** | **casual, multiple ~s** ◇ *People who have had multiple ~s are more at risk from sexually transmitted diseases.* | **abusive** ◇ *reasons for divorce such as having an abusive ~* | **mating** (*biology*)
VERB + PARTNER **have** | **seek** | **find** | **marry**

2 in an activity

ADJ. **bridge, doubles, tennis, etc.** ◇ *I need a doubles ~ for the table tennis tournament.* | **climbing, dancing, playing, training, travelling/traveling, writing, etc.** | **conversational** | **sparring** (*figurative*) ◇ *The old political sparring ~s are now firm friends.* | **drinking** | **lab** (*informal, esp. AmE*) | **long-time** ◇ *He penned the script with his long-time writing ~.* | **former, one-time** | **equal** ◇ *They wanted to be seen as equal ~s in the creative relationship.*
VERB + PARTNER **choose, find** ◇ *The teacher asked the students to choose a ~ for the next activity.* | **change, switch** ◇ *All change ~s for the next dance!*

3 in business

ADJ. **full** ◇ *He was made a full ~ in his father's firm.* | **equal** | **active, managing** | **general** (*esp. AmE*), **limited** ◇ *He is a general ~ in a consulting firm.* ◇ *She and her husband became limited ~s in the team's ownership.* | **junior, senior** | **business, corporate** | **retail** ◇ *AOL remains the company's only online retail ~.* | **founding** | **silent** (*AmE*), **sleeping** (*BrE*) ◇ *The government is technically a silent ~ with almost no control over contractor spending.*

VERB + PARTNER **make sb** | **find, seek**

PARTNER + NOUN **company, institution, organization** ◇ *We are working with ~ companies on wireless technologies.*

PREP. **~ in** ◇ *He has recently been made a junior ~ in the family business.*

4 in international relations

ADJ. **biggest, main, principal** | **foreign** | **alliance, coalition** | **strategic, trading** ◇ *France's principal trading ~s*

PREP. **~ in** ◇ *Britain's ~ in the aeronautic project*

partnership noun

1 relationship between companies, organizations, etc.

ADJ. **close** | **limited** ◇ *They formed a limited ~.* | **effective, good, great, strong, successful** ◇ *We look forward to a long and successful ~ with them.* | **creative, innovative, productive** ◇ *Local historical societies are trying to establish creative ~s with schools.* | **unique** | **true** | **collaborative, cooperative, exclusive, joint** ◇ *a joint ~ between the Department of Energy and the State of Illinois* | **equal** ◇ *an equal ~ of men and women in government* | **working** ◇ *We are trying to develop a working ~ between local schools and industries.* | **long-term** ◇ *The two companies have formed a long-term ~ to develop and sell these products together.* | **global, international, multinational, transatlantic** | **community** | **business, corporate, professional** | **private, public-private** ◇ *The Channel Tunnel was an excellent public-private ~.* | **educational, marketing, promotional, research, strategic, etc.**

VERB + PARTNERSHIP **have** | **build, create, develop, establish, forge, form, set up** (*esp. BrE*) | **enter into, go into, strike** ◇ *The company has gone into ~ with Swiss Bank Corporation.* | **encourage, foster, promote, strengthen** | **expand** | **continue, maintain** | **seek** | **take sb into** (*esp. BrE*) ◇ *We took him into ~ in 2002.* | **break up, dissolve, end** ◇ *They dissolved their successful ~ in 1980.*

PARTNERSHIP + NOUN **agreement, arrangement, deal** ◇ *The two radio stations signed a five-year ~ agreement today.* | **programme/program** | **law**

PREP. **in ~ with** ◇ *They are in ~ with Apex software.* ◇ *The fund has been set up in ~ with banks.* ◇ *We are working in close ~ with our Japanese clients.* | **~ between** ◇ *a ~ between the university and schools* | **~ in** ◇ *She has a ~ in the business.* | **~ of** ◇ *a unique ~ of private companies and unions* | **~ with** ◇ *a ~ with an American company*

→ Note at ORGANIZATION

2 relationship between two people

ADJ. **civil** (*esp. BrE*), **domestic** (*AmE*) ◇ *Civil ~s or gay unions are now legal in Britain.* | **gay, homosexual, same-sex**

VERB + PARTNERSHIP **enter** ◇ *They registered their intention to enter a civil ~.* | **dissolve**

PARTNERSHIP + NOUN **benefits, rights** ◇ *civil unions that give legal recognition and ~ benefits to gay couples* ◇ *a bill extending domestic ~ benefits to same-sex couples* (*AmE*) | **status** ◇ *You can apply for ~ status after two years.*

party noun

1 political group

ADJ. **political** | **centre/center, centre-right/center-right, left-wing, right-wing** | **centrist, fascist, leftist, nationalist, populist, progressive, radical, reactionary, revolutionary, social democratic, socialist** | **Communist, Conservative, Democratic, Labour, Liberal, Republican, etc.** | **opposing, opposition** | **parliamentary** ◇ *members of the parliamentary ~* (= MPs, not ordinary party members) (*BrE*) | **main, major** ◇ *both main political parties* | **majority, minority** ◇ *the majority ~ in both Houses* | **governing, incumbent, ruling**

VERB + PARTY **build, establish, form, found** | **dissolve** ◇ *The ~ was officially dissolved in 1927.* | **weaken** | **split** ◇ *a bitter dispute which finally split the ~* | **unite** | **head, lead** | **belong to, join** | **be affiliated to, have links with** (*both esp. BrE*) ◇ *He was accused of having strong links with the*

Communist Party. | **leave, resign from** ◇ *She left the ~ in 2000.* | **expel sb from** | **vote for** | **elect, return to power** ◇ *The ~ was returned to power in 2001.*

PARTY + VERB **come to power, gain power, win (sth)** | **control sth** ◇ *The Liberal ~ controlled the Senate at this time.* | **dominate sth** | **lose (sth), lose power** ◇ *The ~ lost the vote on this important issue.* | **contest sth** ◇ *the parties contesting the elections* | **support sb/sth** | **nominate sb** | **emerge** ◇ *From 1991 new political parties emerged to challenge the governing ~.*

PARTY + NOUN **conference** (*esp. BrE*), **congress, convention** ◇ *Gordon Brown's speech at the Labour ~ conference* | **committee** | **activist, candidate, faithful** (= loyal members of the party), **member** ◇ *Mr Cameron was cheered by the ~ faithful.* | **chair, chairman, leader, leadership, official** | **affiliation** | **platform** ◇ *policies that would be out of place in the Republican ~ platform* | **line** ◇ *She refused to follow the ~ line* (= the official view of the party). | **politics**

PHRASES **the leader of a/the (…) ~, a member of a/the (…) ~** ◇ *She became the leader of the ~ in 2008.* | **the left wing of the ~, the right wing of the ~**

2 social occasion

ADJ. **surprise** ◇ *a surprise birthday ~* | **impromptu** | **lavish** ◇ *He loves throwing lavish parties.* | **all-night** | **cocktail, dinner, tea** | **birthday, Christmas, Halloween, holiday** (*AmE*) | **engagement, wedding** | **farewell, going-away, leaving** (*esp. BrE*) ◇ *We had a farewell ~ for Michelle when she left the company.* | **graduation** | **coming-out** (*esp. AmE*) | **launch** ◇ *They attended the launch ~ for the new film.* | **house-warming** | **garden, house, office, pool, street** | **costume** (*AmE*), **fancy-dress** (*BrE*), **toga** | **sleepover, slumber** (*AmE*) ◇ *The girls were having a slumber ~.* | **bachelor** (*AmE*), **bachelorette** (*AmE*), **hen** (*BrE*), **stag** (*BrE*) ◇ *She turned up at her fiancé's bachelor ~.* | **frat, fraternity, sorority** (*all AmE*) | **Tupperware™** | **private** | **tailgate** (*AmE*)

VERB + PARTY **give, have, hold, host, throw** ◇ *On moving in they threw a huge house-warming ~.* | **organize, plan** | **invite sb to** | **attend, go to** | **leave** | **crash, gatecrash** (*BrE*) | **ruin, spoil**

PARTY + VERB **go on** ◇ *There was a ~ going on next door.* | **be in full swing** (= be very busy and noisy) ◇ *By now the ~ was in full swing.* | **break up** ◇ *The ~ broke up around midnight.*

PARTY + NOUN **guest** | **girl** ◇ *She is a hard-drinking, non-stop ~ girl.*

PREP. **at a/the ~** ◇ *I was at a ~ in London that night.* | **~ for** ◇ *I'm organizing a surprise ~ for my sister.*

3 group of people working/doing sth together

ADJ. **boarding, hunting, landing, raiding, rescue, scouting, search, welcoming, working** ◇ *The captain told the crew to prepare to receive a boarding ~.* | **coach** (*BrE*) | **bridal, wedding** ◇ *The wedding ~ climbed into the carriages.* | **advance** ◇ *An advance ~ settled at Salem in 1628.*

PREP. **~ of** ◇ *She arrived with a ~ of helpers.*

4 person in a legal case

ADJ. **guilty, innocent** | **aggrieved, injured, wronged** | **offending** | **warring** | **concerned, interested, involved** ◇ *First we must notify all the interested parties.* | **disinterested, neutral, third** ◇ *You must sign the document in the presence of an independent third ~*

VERB + PARTY **notify** | **be binding on** (*esp. BrE*), **bind** ◇ *This agreement is binding on both parties.* ◇ *This agreement binds both parties.*

pass noun

1 in sports

ADJ. **deep, long** | **short** | **good, perfect** | **dropped, errant, incomplete** ◇ *Robson had pounced on a dropped ~.* | **careless** (*esp. BrE*), **sloppy** | **crisp, quick** | **back, cross-field, square** (all in football/soccer) | **forward** (in rugby) ◇ *The referee disallowed the try for a forward ~.* | **bounce, inbounds, lob, no-look, outlet** (in basketball) | **screen, swing, touchdown** (in American football)

VERB + PASS **play** ◇ *Lafferty played a ~ down the right to Gallagher.* | **deliver** | **get, pick up, receive** ◇ *He picked up a back ~ from one of his defenders.* | **complete, throw** (both

in American football) ◇ *McNabb has completed 57% of his
~es with five touchdowns.* | **catch, drop** (both in American
football) | **block, defend** ◇ *His long reach enables him to
block ~es.* ◇ *The Dolphins are among the NFL's best at
defending the ~.* | **intercept**
PREP. **~ from** ◇ *Owen picked up a long ~ from Beckham to
score.* | **~ to** ◇ *He played a back ~ to the goalkeeper.*

2 (*esp. BrE*) success in exam/course
ADJ. **good** (*BrE*) | **exam, examination** | **A level, GCSE, etc.**
VERB + PASS **get** (*BrE, AmE*), **obtain, scrape** ◇ *She barely
scraped a ~ in chemistry.*
PASS + NOUN **mark** (*BrE*), **rate** (*BrE, AmE*) ◇ *The ~ mark is 40%.*
PREP. **~ at** ◇ *It's difficult to obtain a ~ at A Level.* | **~ in** ◇ *He
should get a good ~ in mathematics.* (*BrE*)

3 official piece of paper
ADJ. **free** | **day, monthly, weekend, yearly** | **two-day, three-
day, etc.** | **bus, rail, railway** (*BrE*) ◇ *a monthly rail ~* |
security | **boarding** ◇ *The flight attendant asked to see my
boarding ~.* | **hall** (*AmE*) ◇ *The teacher wrote out a hall ~ and
handed it to her.* | **backstage** | **press, VIP**
VERB + PASS **have** | **use** | **give sb, issue (sb with)** ◇ *The visitors
were issued with day ~es.* | **produce, show**
PREP. **on a ~** ◇ *soldiers on a weekend ~* | **~ to** ◇ *We bought a
two-day ~ to Disneyland.*

4 way through mountains
ADJ. **high, low** | **narrow** | **mountain**
VERB + PASS **cross, take**
PREP. **over a/the ~** ◇ *They had to struggle over the ~ with their
donkeys.* | **through a/the ~** ◇ *A road was built through the
~.* | **~ over** ◇ *We took the high ~ over the ridge.*
PHRASES **the head of the ~, the summit of the ~, the top of
the ~**

pass *verb*

1 of time
ADV. **quickly, rapidly, soon, swiftly** ◇ *The time ~ed quickly.* |
slowly | **peacefully, uneventfully** ◇ *The days ~ed unevent-
fully.*
VERB + PASS **help (to)** ◇ *We played games to help ~ the time.*

2 law
ADV. **unanimously** | **overwhelmingly** | **narrowly** ◇ *The
Kansas State House narrowly ~ed the legislation last year.*
PREP. **by…to…** ◇ *The bill was ~ed by 360 votes to 280.*

3 happen
ADV. **peacefully**
VERB + PASS **come to** (*formal or old-fashioned*) ◇ *How did such
a disaster come to ~?* | **let sth** ◇ *I don't like it, but I'll let it ~*
(= will not object).
PREP. **between** ◇ *They'll never be friends again after all that
has ~ed between them.*
PHRASES **~ unnoticed** ◇ *In the confusion her departure ~ed
unnoticed.*

passage *noun*

1 narrow way through
ADJ. **long, short** | **narrow, small** | **winding** | **connecting,
side** | **subterranean, underground** | **dark** | **hidden, secret**
VERB + PASSAGE **clear** ◇ *to clear a ~ for ships through the ice* |
force ◇ *He forced a ~ for the singer through the crowd.*
PASSAGE + VERB **lead** ◇ *There was a bedroom with a small ~
leading off to a bathroom.*
PREP. **along a/the ~, down a/the ~, through a/the ~** ◇ *We
ran through the dark ~.* | **in a/the ~, into a/the ~** ◇
Someone was waiting outside in the ~. | **~ between** ◇ *the ~
between the two houses* | **~ from** ◇ *There is an underground
~ from the church to the house.* | **~ through** ◇ *a narrow ~
through the bushes* | **~ to**
PHRASES **the end of a ~** ◇ *There was a door at the end of the ~.*
| **a maze of ~s** ◇ *the maze of secret ~s which wound their
way under the building*

2 tube in the body
ADJ. **nasal** | **air** | **back** (= rectum)
VERB + PASSAGE **block, obstruct** | **clear**

3 extract from a book/speech
ADJ. **lengthy, long** | **brief, short** | **opening** | **famous, well-
known** | **key** | **relevant** ◇ *I'll dig out the relevant ~s in St
Augustine.* | **descriptive, expository, purple** | **biblical,
Gospel, scriptural**
VERB + PASSAGE **cite, quote, read, recite** ◇ *I have quoted this ~
at length.* | **reread** | **write** | **interpret** | **translate**
PASSAGE + VERB **describe sth, illustrate sth, indicate sth,
suggest sth** ◇ *His writings are filled with poignant ~s
describing winter winds.* | **contain sth**
PREP. **in a/the ~** ◇ *There's a lot of slang in this ~.* | **~ from** ◇ *a
~ from the Bible*

4 extract from a piece of music
ADJ. **lengthy, long** | **brief, short** | **opening** | **final** | **fast,
slow** | **loud** | **quiet, soft** | **solo** | **musical** | **instrumental,
lyrical**
VERB + PASSAGE **play**
PREP. **in a/the ~** | **~ from**

5 movement/progress
ADJ. **rapid, speedy** | **slow** | **safe** | **smooth** | **free** ◇ *The
Security Council has demanded free ~ for families fleeing
from the fighting.*
VERB + PASSAGE **deny sb, refuse (sb)** ◇ *The ship had been
denied ~.* | **block, prevent** | **allow, permit** | **facilitate** |
ensure ◇ *Escort ships were needed to ensure safe ~ on the
seas.* | **mark** ◇ *rituals which mark the ~ of the seasons*
PREP. **~ across** ◇ *the slow ~ of a snail across the veranda* | **~
down** ◇ *Steps cut in the hillside give walkers an easy ~ down
the mountain.* | **~ from…to…** ◇ *We are not aware of our ~
from consciousness to sleep.* | **~ into** ◇ *Portugal's ~ into the
next round of the tournament* | **~ out of** ◇ *a safe ~ out of the
war zone* | **~ over** ◇ *State-of-the-art suspension guarantees a
smooth ~ over the bumpiest road.* | **~ through** ◇ *They denied
him ~ through the territory.*
PHRASES **the ~ of time** ◇ *The problems only got worse with the
~ of time.* | **a rite of ~** ◇ *Marriage is seen as a rite of ~.*

6 voyage by ship
ADJ. **long, short** | **rough** | **homeward, outward** ◇ *If the men
resigned, they had to pay their outward ~s.* | **ocean** (*esp.
AmE*), **sea** (*esp. BrE*)
VERB + PASSAGE **have** | **book, secure** ◇ *She had secured ~ on a
ship heading for England.* | **work** (*BrE*) ◇ *He worked his ~*
(= worked on the ship to pay for his ticket) *to Australia.*
PREP. **during a/the ~** ◇ *During the ~, she taught herself basic
Arabic.* | **on sb's/the ~** ◇ *We met him on our outward ~.* | **~
across** ◇ *a rough ~ across the Atlantic* | **~ to** ◇ *We had a
stormy ~ to India.*

7 of a bill
ADJ. **smooth** | **stormy** ◇ *The bill is expected to face a stormy ~
in both houses.* | **speedy** | **final** ◇ *Starr voted for the final ~
of the bill.*
VERB + PASSAGE **begin, complete** ◇ *The bill will complete its ~
in November.* | **block** ◇ *They have launched a campaign to
block ~ of the bill.* | **ensure, facilitate, secure** (*all esp. AmE*)
◇ *He deserves credit for ensuring the ~ of the Civil Rights Act.*
| **gain, win** (*both AmE*) ◇ *The bills did not gain ~ in the
Senate.*
PREP. **during the ~** ◇ *There was much controversy during the
~ of the bill.* | **~ through** ◇ *a strategy to ensure the bill's
smooth ~ through Parliament*

passenger *noun*

ADJ. **business-class, coach** (= the cheapest seats in a plane
or train) (*AmE*), **economy-class, first-class** | **front-seat** |
back-seat (*esp. AmE*), **rear-seat** (*esp. BrE*) | **air, airline, bus,
coach** (= on a coach/bus) (*BrE*), **ferry, rail, subway** (*AmE*),
train, underground (*BrE*) | **cruise** | **pillion** (= riding on the
back of a motorcycle) (*BrE*) | **fellow** ◇ *I soon got talking to
my fellow ~s.*
VERB + PASSENGER **carry, fly, transport** ◇ *Last year the airline
carried 4.6 million ~s.* | **board** (*esp. AmE*), **let on, pick up,
take on** ◇ *Flight 717 began boarding ~s.* ◇ *A taxi was picking*

up a ~ *outside the hotel.* | **drop off, let off, let out** ◇ *The bus stopped to let its ~s off.* | **screen** ◇ *All airports in the country screen ~s for illicit drugs.* | **accommodate** ◇ *The ship can accommodate 450 ~s.* | **evacuate** ◇ *All the ~s had to be evacuated.*
PASSENGER + VERB **wait** ◇ *The ~s were waiting to board the plane.* | **be aboard (sth), fly, go in sth, go on sth, ride sth** (*AmE*), **ride in sth** (*AmE*), **travel in sth, travel on sth** ◇ *the first-class ~s aboard steamboats* | **board (sth), come aboard (sth), embark (on sth), get on (sth), go aboard (sth)** | **disembark, get off, get out** | **arrive** | **be stranded** ◇ *Thousands of ~s were stranded last night at Heathrow airport.*
PASSENGER + NOUN **cabin, compartment** | **door, window** | **seat, side** ◇ *There is no airbag on the ~ side.* | **comfort, safety** | **aircraft, ferry, jet, liner, plane, ship, train, vehicle** | **car, van** (*both AmE*) ◇ *Sales of ~ cars grew by 22% last year.* | **flight, services** | **numbers, traffic, volume** ◇ *Global air ~ traffic rose over 20%.* | **capacity, load** | **area, station, terminal** | **list, records**
PREP. **~ for** ◇ *Will all ~s for Mumbai please go to Gate 21.* | **~ in** ◇ *the ~s in her car* | **~ on** ◇ *all the ~s on the ferry*

passing *noun*

ADJ. **untimely**
VERB + PASSING **lament, mourn** ◇ *Few will mourn his ~.* | **mark** ◇ *Her death marks the ~ of an era.* | **note**
PHRASES **the ~ of the years, the ~ of time** ◇ *The wood darkens with the ~ of time.*

passion *noun*

ADJ. **grand, great** ◇ *She didn't believe in grand ~ or love at first sight.* ◇ *She was his first great ~.* ◇ *a woman of great ~* | **all-consuming, burning, consuming, deep, fierce, fiery, intense** | **animal** (*old-fashioned*), **physical, romantic, sexual** | **secret** ◇ *He had a secret ~ for poetry.* | **considerable, deep, real, strong** ◇ *There were moments of real ~ in the game.* | **unbridled, violent** | **renewed** ◇ *The team has been playing with renewed ~ this season.* ◇ *his renewed ~ for the game* | **abiding, genuine, lifelong** ◇ *his lifelong ~ for flying* | **personal** | **shared** ◇ *Elliot and Nina discovered a shared ~ for poetry.* | **human** | **youthful** | **intellectual, moral, political, religious**
...OF PASSION **surge, wave**
VERB + PASSION **arouse, awaken, ignite, inflame** ◇ *No one had ever aroused his ~ as much as Sandra.* | **rekindle** | **be filled with, feel** ◇ *the great ~ he felt for her* | **develop, have** ◇ *A writer should have ~.* | **fuel, rouse, stir** ◇ *This issue always rouses ~.* | **discover** | **share** ◇ *They shared a ~ for food.* | **express** | **feel** | **lack** | **indulge, pursue** ◇ *She had very little time to indulge her ~ for painting.*
PASSION + VERB **cool, wane** ◇ *As time went by the ~ cooled.* | **drive sb** ◇ *That ~ drove me to get to the top.*
PREP. **with ~** ◇ *They kissed with ~.* ◇ *He argued his case with great ~.* | **~ between** ◇ *The ~ between them had cooled.* | **~ for** ◇ *his all-consuming ~ for her* ◇ *He developed a real ~ for acting.*
PHRASES **a crime of ~** ◇ *She killed her husband's lover in a crime of ~.* | **full of ~** ◇ *a speech full of ~* | **a night of ~** ◇ *They spent a night of ~ in a hotel.* | **the object of sb's ~** ◇ *the young girl who was the object of his ~*

passive *adj.*

VERBS **be, seem** | **become** | **remain**
ADV. **extremely, fairly, very, etc.** | **completely, totally** ◇ *TV is a completely ~ activity.* | **merely, purely** ◇ *It is often assumed that the learner is merely ~.* | **relatively** | **essentially** ◇ *The heroine plays an essentially ~ role in the drama.*

passport *noun*

ADJ. **valid** | **full** (*BrE*) ◇ *a full British ~* (= one showing that sb has all the rights of British citizenship) | **fake, false, forged** | **Canadian, Mexican, Swiss, etc.** | **foreign** | **diplomatic** |

biometric, machine-readable ◇ *The European Parliament voted to adopt biometric ~s.*
VERB + PASSPORT **apply for** | **renew** | **get, obtain** | **be in possession of, carry, have, hold, travel on** ◇ *I usually travel on my Irish ~.* | **give sb, issue sb, issue sb with** | **ask for** | **hand sb, produce, show (sb)** ◇ *You have to show your ~ at the border.* | **check** | **stamp** | **hand back, hand over** ◇ *He examined my face carefully before handing back my ~.* | **surrender** ◇ *The Embassy made him surrender his ~.* | **confiscate, seize** | **steal**
PASSPORT + VERB **be valid** | **expire**
PASSPORT + NOUN **photo, photograph, picture** | **number** | **holder** | **agency, office** ◇ *the UK Passport Agency* | **control** ◇ *These sensors will cut the delays at ~ control.* | **application**
PREP. **~ into** (*figurative*) ◇ *The gold medal is his ~ into professional boxing.* | **~ to** (*figurative*) ◇ *A high score in the test is a ~ to success.*

password *noun*

ADJ. **correct, valid** | **user** ◇ *Please supply a valid user ~.* | **secret**
VERB + PASSWORD **know, remember** | **choose** | **give** ◇ *You must give the ~ before they'll let you in.* | **enter, provide, supply, type, type in** | **change, reset** | **crack, guess** ◇ *a software tool developed by hackers to crack ~s*

past *noun*

1 time before the present
ADJ. **immediate, recent** | **ancient, dim and distant** (*BrE*), **distant, remote** ◇ *Many modern festivals can be traced back to an ancient ~.* ◇ *It all happened in the distant ~.*
VERB + PAST **cling to, live in, relive** ◇ *We're going to have to stop living in the ~ and invest in new technology if the company is to survive.* | **reconstruct, recreate** ◇ *Archaeology provides us with tools for reconstructing the ~.* | **erase, forget** | **belong in, belong to** ◇ *Those memories belong to the ~ and I don't want to think about them.*
PREP. **from the ~** ◇ *Memories from the ~ came flooding back to him.* | **in the ~** ◇ *I admit that I have made mistakes in the ~.* | **into the ~** ◇ *events stretching back many years into the ~* | **of the ~** ◇ *great artists of the ~*
PHRASES **be all in the ~** ◇ *Don't worry about it—it's all in the ~ now.* | **a break with the ~** ◇ *In an effort to make a complete break with the ~, she went to live in Morocco.* | **a glimpse of the ~** ◇ *The uncovering of the buried town gives us a unique glimpse of the ~.* | **a link with the ~** ◇ *The old market is a living link with the ~, unchanged for hundreds of years.* | **nostalgia for the ~** | **a thing of the ~** ◇ *a new device that makes such problems a thing of the ~*

2 sb/sth's history
ADJ. **historic** (*esp. BrE*), **historical** | **forgotten** ◇ *He was forced to confront his forgotten ~.* | **colourful/colorful, rich** | **chequered/checkered, murky** (*esp. BrE*), **painful, sordid, troubled** | **mysterious** | **criminal** | **glorious, illustrious** (*esp. BrE*) ◇ *Few remnants remain of the city's glorious ~.* | **cultural, political** | **ancestral, evolutionary** | **colonial, imperial, industrial** ◇ *These customs are a relic of the country's colonial ~.*
VERB + PAST **reflect on** | **recapture** ◇ *He tried in vain to recapture his ~.* | **erase, escape from, forget, put behind you, wipe out** ◇ *Political parties cannot escape from their ~s any more than individuals can.* ◇ *Therapy helped Dan put the ~ behind him.*
PREP. **from your ~** ◇ *ghosts from his ~* | **in your ~** ◇ *at some time in her ~*

pasta *noun*

ADJ. **fresh** | **dried** | **egg, wholegrain** (*AmE*), **wholemeal** (*BrE*), **wholewheat** | **cooked** | **home-made**
VERB + PASTA **boil, cook** | **drain** | **stir, toss** ◇ *Toss the ~ with the hot sauce.* | **eat**
PASTA + NOUN **shapes, shells, etc.** | **sauce** | **dish, salad** | **bowl, pot** | **dough** | **machine, maker**
→ Special page at FOOD

paste noun

ADJ. **stiff** (*esp. BrE*), **thick** | **smooth** | **wallpaper** | **curry, fish, tomato, etc.**
VERB + PASTE **make, make up, mix, mix sth into, mix sth to, mix up** ◊ *Mix the sugar mixture to a smooth ~.* | **form** ◊ *Mix the flour with enough water to form a thick ~.* | **apply, put on** ◊ *Apply the wallpaper ~ with a roller.* | **add** ◊ *Add the tomato ~ and cook for a further 25 minutes.*

pastime noun

ADJ. **enjoyable, pleasurable** | **favourite/favorite, popular** | **dangerous** | **national** ◊ *Eating out is the national ~ in France.*
VERB + PASTIME **enjoy, indulge in, pursue**
PREP. **~ among** ◊ *Fighting is a popular ~ among some of the town's boys.* | **~ for** ◊ *Fishing is an enjoyable ~ for people of all ages.*

pastor noun

ADJ. **Lutheran, Methodist, Presbyterian, etc.** | **ordained** | **associate, senior** ◊ *He was the associate ~ at a church in Portland.* | **retired**
VERB + PASTOR **appoint (sb), ordain (sb)** ◊ *He was ordained a ~ in the Lutheran Church.*
PASTOR + VERB **pray, preach** | **serve** ◊ *a ~ serving a mainly Hispanic congregation*

pastry noun

1 (*esp. BrE*) mixture of flour and water
ADJ. **crisp, light** ◊ *Bake until the ~ is crisp and golden.* | **soggy** (*BrE*) | **golden, golden-brown** | **ready-made** (*BrE*) | **sweet** | **choux, filo, flaky, puff** (*BrE, AmE*), **shortcrust** (*BrE*)
VERB + PASTRY **make** | **cut, knead, roll out** ◊ *Cut the filo ~ into 10 cm strips.* | **line sth with** ◊ *Line the tin with the ~.* | **brush** ◊ *Brush the ~ with a little water.* | **wrap sth in** ◊ *mushrooms wrapped in filo ~*
PASTRY + NOUN **base** (*esp. BrE*), **case, parcel** (*BrE*), **shell** (*BrE, AmE*) | **dough** (*esp. AmE*) | **board, cutter** | **chef** (*BrE, AmE*)

2 small cake
ADJ. **Danish, French** (*esp. AmE*) | **filled, fried** | **breakfast** (*esp. AmE*)

pat noun

ADJ. **affectionate, friendly** | **reassuring** | **congratulatory** | **comforting** (*AmE*)
VERB + PAT **give sb/sth** ◊ *He gave the dog a ~.*
PREP. **~ on** ◊ *He gave her a reassuring ~ on the shoulder.*

pat verb

ADV. **gently, lightly** | **affectionately** | **awkwardly** (*esp. AmE*) ◊ *I threw my arms around him and he awkwardly patted my back.*
PREP. **on** ◊ *He patted her gently on the shoulder.*

patch noun

1 material over a hole
VERB + PATCH **have** ◊ *Her jeans have ~es all over them.* | **sew on/onto** ◊ *She wore a jacket with bright ~es sewn onto it.*
PREP. **~ on** ◊ *dancers with ~es on their costumes*

2 part of a surface that is different
ADJ. **irregular** | **clear, coloured/colored, dark** | **damp, wet** | **dry** | **sweat** | **icy** ◊ *icy ~es on the roads* | **bald** ◊ *He has a small bald ~ on the crown of his head.* | **rough**
PREP. **in ~es** ◊ *The velvet curtains were faded in ~es.* | **~ of** ◊ *There were some ~es of clear blue sky.* | **~ on** ◊ *A large damp ~ had appeared on the ceiling.*
PHRASES **a ~ of colour/color** ◊ *Flowers provide bright ~es of colour/color.*

3 piece of land
ADJ. **isolated** ◊ *an isolated ~ of forest* | **grassy** | **bare** | **berry** (*AmE*), **cabbage, potato, pumpkin** (*esp. AmE*), **strawberry, vegetable** | **briar** (*often figurative, esp. AmE*) ◊ *The track passes through dense weeds and briar ~es.* ◊ *This led Nixon into a political briar ~* (= painful situation difficult to escape).
PREP. **in a/the ~** ◊ *I spent Sunday working in my vegetable ~.* | **on a/the ~** ◊ *located on a small ~ of flat ground*
PREP. **~ of** ◊ *We found a nice ~ of grass to sit on.*

4 (*informal*) period of time
ADJ. **bad, difficult, rocky, rough, soft** (*BrE*), **sticky** (*BrE*) | **purple** (*BrE*) ◊ *The team has hit a purple ~, with nine wins from their last ten games.*
VERB + PATCH **go through, have, hit** ◊ *Their business hit a sticky ~ last year.*
PREP. **~ of** (*esp. BrE*) ◊ *I was going through a ~ of poor health.*

5 (*AmE*) piece of material sewn onto clothes or uniform
VERB + PATCH **sport, wear** ◊ *He wears a ~ from his employer, Verizon.* | **sew on, stitch on** ◊ *It has a UPS ~ sewn on the right shoulder.*
PREP. **~ on** ◊ *Students were wearing American flag ~es on their sleeves.*

6 solution to a computing problem
ADJ. **security**
VERB + PATCH **apply, deploy** | **download, install** | **issue, release**

patent noun

VERB + PATENT **apply for, file** ◊ *In 1843 Bain filed a ~ for his fax machine.* | **get, obtain, take out** | **protect sth by** ◊ *Genetically engineered plants can be protected by ~.* | **award (sb), grant (sb), issue, license** | **refuse** ◊ *A ~ will be refused if details of the item have already been released to the public.* | **have, hold** | **infringe, violate** | **enforce**
PATENT + VERB **expire** | **cover, protect**
PATENT + NOUN **application** | **protection** | **law** ◊ *a leading authority on ~ law* | **office** ◊ *the US Patent Office*
PREP. **~ for** ◊ *In 1995 he was granted a ~ for his invention.* | **~ on** ◊ *Edison took out a ~ on the light bulb.*
PHRASES **~ pending** (= waiting to be issued) ◊ *The item is Patent Pending No. 11092001.*

path noun

1 way across land
ADJ. **long** | **narrow** | **steep** | **winding** | **cobblestone** (*esp. AmE*), **dirt** (*esp. AmE*), **gravel, paved, rocky** | **wooded** | **cliff, coast, coastal** (*all esp. BrE*) | **forest, garden, woodland** (*esp. BrE*) | **pedestrian, public** (*esp. BrE*) | **bike** (*AmE*), **cycle** (*BrE*) | **bridle**
VERB + PATH **follow, take** ◊ *Follow this ~ for about 100 yards, and it's on your right.* | **go along, go down, go up** | **climb** | **keep on, keep to, stay on** | **leave, stray from, stray off** | **retrace** ◊ *They retraced the ~ they had taken earlier that day.* | **clear, make** ◊ *A ~ was cleared through the jungle.*
PATH + VERB **go, run** ◊ *That ~ goes down to the river.* | **descend** (*esp. BrE*) | **follow sth** ◊ *The ~ follows the stream for quite a way.* | **branch off, leave sth** ◊ *The ~ left the river bank and wound its way into the woods.* | **divide, fork** | **go to sth, lead (to) sth** ◊ *Where does this ~ lead?* | **wind, zigzag** ◊ *Then the ~ zigzags steeply uphill for a while.* | **be marked (sth)** ◊ *The ~ is clearly marked.* | **narrow, widen**
PREP. **along a/the ~, down a/the ~, up a/the ~** ◊ *The children ran along the ~.* | **on a/the ~** ◊ *I think we're on the ~ we used yesterday.* | **~ along, ~ beside, ~ by** ◊ *the ~ along the canal* | **~ for** ◊ *a ~ for cyclists* | **~ from** ◊ *the ~ from the hotel to the beach* | **~ through** ◊ *I took the ~ through the park.* | **~ to**
PHRASES **off the beaten ~** (= not in a place that most people go to) (*AmE*) ◊ *The museum is located well off the beaten ~.*

2 line of movement
ADJ. **correct, right** | **flight** ◊ *The pilot was instructed to change his flight ~.* | **direct** ◊ *The building was in the direct ~ of the missile.* | **circular, straight** ◊ *The object continued in its circular ~.*
VERB + PATH **steer** ◊ *He steered a ~ through the crowd.* | **trace** ◊ *Scientists can trace the ~ of the tornado.* | **block, obstruct,**

stand in ◇ *You're standing in my ~!* | **cross** ◇ *A peacock crossed our ~.*
PREP. **across sth's ~** ◇ *The car pulled right across the ~ of another vehicle.* | **in sth's ~, into sth's ~** ◇ *She stepped into the ~ of an oncoming car.* | **out of sth's ~** ◇ *I managed to jump out of the ~ of the bike just in time.* | **~ through** ◇ *Footsteps had scored a diagonal ~ through the snow.* | **~ to** ◇ *He moved quickly to block her ~ to the door.*
PHRASES **everything in sb's/sth's ~** ◇ *The tornado destroyed everything in its ~.*

3 way of achieving sth

ADJ. **well-trodden, well-worn** ◇ *Her education followed the usual well-worn ~ of rich youngsters in the 1930s.* | **clear, direct, straight** ◇ *She saw the plan as a direct ~ to her goals.* | **chosen** | **different, divergent** ◇ *The two friends followed divergent ~s in life.* | **career** | **spiritual** ◇ *the challenge of staying on his spiritual ~ while surrounded by temptation* | **evolutionary** ◇ *the evolutionary ~ that humans have followed*
VERB + PATH **choose, find** ◇ *Everyone has to find their own ~ in life.* | **follow, pursue, tread, walk** ◇ *Can a person who has walked a ~ of evil all his life really change?* | **blaze, carve, carve out, chart, forge** ◇ *He aimed to forge a new ~ between traditional left-wing and right-wing politics.* | **deviate from** | **clear, ease, smooth** ◇ *This cleared the ~ for them to marry.*
PREP. **on a/the ~** ◇ *His feet were now firmly on the ~ to success.* | **~ of** ◇ *The ~ of true love is never easy.* | **~ to** ◇ *the ~ to happiness*
PHRASES **cross ~s (with sb)** (= meet sb in the course of your life, work, etc.) ◇ *I hope to cross ~s with him again some day.* | **obstacles in sb/sth's ~**

pathologist noun

ADJ. **consultant** (*BrE*) | **forensic, surgical** (*AmE*) | **Home Office** (*in the UK*)
PATHOLOGIST + VERB **examine sth** | **confirm sth** (*esp. BrE*) ◇ *The ~ confirmed that death was due to poisoning.* | **review sth** (*esp. AmE*) ◇ *Four experienced ~s reviewed all the diagnoses.*
PHRASES **pathologist's report** (*esp. BrE*)

patience noun

ADJ. **endless, great, infinite** | **little** ◇ *I have little ~ with fundamentalists of any kind.*
VERB + PATIENCE **exercise, have, show** ◇ *They thanked him for showing so much ~.* | **lack** | **be out of, lose, run out of** ◇ *It is clear that they are out of ~ with me.* ◇ *We eventually ran out of ~ with him.* | **keep** ◇ *I find it hard to keep my ~ with them.* | **demand, need, require, take** ◇ *Above all, fishing requires great ~.* | **exhaust, strain, stretch, tax, test, try** ◇ *The children were beginning to try my ~.* | **counsel, preach** (*esp. AmE*) ◇ *His advisers are trying to counsel ~.*
PATIENCE + VERB **be exhausted, run out, snap, wear thin** ◇ *Meg could see Kirk's ~ was running out, so she shut up.* ◇ *Her ~ snapped and she walked out.* | **be rewarded** ◇ *Our ~ was finally rewarded and we got the band's autographs.*
PREP. **with ~** ◇ *She listened with infinite ~ to his excuses.* | **~ for** ◇ *He has little ~ for people who don't work.* | **~ with** ◇ *The fans were losing ~ with the team.*
PHRASES **the ~ of a saint** ◇ *These endless meetings are enough to tax the ~ of a saint.*

patient noun

ADJ. **AIDS, cancer, cardiac, diabetic, heart, etc.** | **surgical, transplant** ◇ *developments that will help surgical ~s recover more quickly* | **mental, psychiatric** | **depressed, mentally ill** | **seriously ill, severely ill, terminally ill** | **high-risk** (*esp. AmE*), **vulnerable** (*esp. BrE*) | **hospital** | **private** (*esp. BrE*) ◇ *He only takes private ~s.* | **elderly, older** | **adult, child** | **paediatric/pediatric**
VERB + PATIENT **assess, examine, see, treat** ◇ *She sees an average of 35 ~s every day.* | **admit** ◇ *The ~ was admitted to*

hospital yesterday. | **discharge** ◇ *~s waiting to be discharged from hospital* | **refer (to sb/sth), transfer (to sth)**
PATIENT + VERB **develop sth, have sth, suffer from sth** ◇ *The ~ has a severe heart condition.* | **suffer sth** ◇ *~s who have suffered a heart attack* | **be diagnosed with sth** ◇ *The ~ was first diagnosed with malaria.* | **present with sth** ◇ *Many ~s present with conditions that cannot be easily diagnosed.* | **respond (to sth)** ◇ *These ~s are responding well to the new drug.* | **improve** | **receive sth, undergo sth** ◇ *Patients undergoing chemotherapy may be at a higher risk of infection.*
PATIENT + NOUN **care**
PREP. **~ with** ◇ *~s with liver disease*

patient adj.

VERBS **be, sound** | **remain**
ADV. **extremely, fairly, very, etc.** | **incredibly** | **endlessly** (*esp. BrE*), **infinitely**
PREP. **about** ◇ *She's been extremely ~ about it all.* | **with** ◇ *He was endlessly ~ with the children.*

patriotic adj.

VERBS **be** | **become, feel**
ADV. **extremely, fairly, very, etc.** | **fiercely, intensely** | **unabashedly** (*AmE*), **unashamedly** (*BrE*) ◇ *The party framed its message in unashamedly ~ language.*

patrol noun

ADJ. **routine** | **special** (*BrE*) | **armed** | **foot** ◇ *Every police car and foot ~ in the area is on full alert.* | **mounted** | **reconnaissance** | **dawn, night** | **air, army, military, naval, police, security** | **enemy** | **border** | **coastal, harbour/harbor** (*esp. AmE*), **maritime, shore** | **highway** (*AmE*), **traffic** (*BrE*) ◇ *The highway ~ has sealed off the area.* ◇ *helicopters used for traffic ~s* | **safety** (*AmE*) (= to help children cross the street, etc.)
VERB + PATROL **carry out, conduct, fly, go on** ◇ *The Italians flew regular ~s over the desert.* | **maintain** ◇ *They maintain a continuous ~ of the oceans with three submarines.* | **send out** ◇ *They sent out four-man ~s to scout the area.* | **ambush, attack** ◇ *One soldier was killed when his ~ was ambushed.*
PATROL + NOUN **aircraft, boat, car, craft, vehicle, vessel** | **duty**
PREP. **on ~** ◇ *police officers on ~*

patron noun

ADJ. **influential, powerful** | **generous** | **aristocratic, wealthy**
PHRASES **a ~ of the arts** ◇ *The company is a major ~ of the arts.*

patter verb

ADV. **gently, lightly, softly** | **down** ◇ *The rain ~ed down softly.*
PREP. **across** ◇ *Footsteps ~ed across the floor.* | **against** | **along** ◇ *The child's feet ~ed along the landing.* | **on** ◇ *Rain ~ed lightly on the window.*

pattern noun

1 arrangement of lines, shapes, sounds, etc.

ADJ. **intricate** | **abstract, geometric** | **camouflage, floral, striped, etc.** | **regular, repeated, repeating** ◇ *wallpaper with a repeating ~ of interlocking shapes* | **random** | **drum, rhythmic, sound** ◇ *The music contains repeated rhythmic ~s.*
VERB + PATTERN **have** ◇ *The sweater has a geometric ~ on it.* | **form, produce** ◇ *The roof beams form a star-like ~.* | **create, design, make, print, weave**
PREP. **in a/the ~** ◇ *He had arranged the glasses in a ~ on the table.* | **~ on** ◇ *the ~ on the carpet* | **~ in** ◇ *She drew ~s in the sand.*

2 usual manner

ADJ. **basic, existing, familiar, normal, set, traditional, usual** ◇ *There is no set ~ for these meetings.* | **consistent, predictable, regular** | **same, similar** ◇ *Portuguese colonial rule followed a similar ~ to that of other powers.* | **changing, ever-changing** | **complex** | **clear** ◇ *The ~ is clear: obesity is associated with lower incomes.* | **main** | **overall** ◇ *The*

overall ~ of our life changes little. | **behaviour/behavior,**
behavioural/behavioral | **speech** ◇ *Her speech ~s are very*
distinctive. | **breathing, sleep** | **voting** | **consumption,**
spending, usage ◇ *They analyzed employees' email usage ~s.*
| **migration, settlement** | **employment** | **weather**
VERB + PATTERN **discern, identify, notice, recognize, trace** ◇
We can trace a familiar ~ to these events. | **establish, set** |
follow, repeat ◇ *Their actions follow a very predictable ~.* |
fall into, fit into ◇ *ideas that do not fit neatly into his ~s of*
thought | **exhibit, show** ◇ *67% of patients showed a similar*
~ of improvement. | **alter, change** ◇ *People have changed*
their spending ~s in response to changing conditions.
PATTERN + VERB **develop, emerge** ◇ *Similar ~s are emerging*
all over Eastern Europe. | **change**
PREP. **~ for** ◇ *the normal ~ for a boy/girl relationship* | **~ in** ◇
the main ~s in English spelling | **~ of** ◇ *~s of behaviour/*
behavior

patterned *adj.*

VERBS **be**
ADV. **heavily, highly, richly** ◇ *a highly ~ fabric* | **beautifully** |
boldly, brightly | **delicately, intricately**
PREP. **with** ◇ *~ with flowers*

pause *noun*

ADJ. **brief, momentary, short, slight, small** | **lengthy, long** |
frequent ◇ *He made frequent ~s to catch his breath.* |
awkward, uncomfortable | **pregnant** | **dramatic** |
thoughtful | **silent**
VERB + PAUSE **take** ◇ *Shall we take a ~ here?*
PAUSE + VERB **follow** ◇ *In the ~ that followed, I noticed that he*
was shaking.
PAUSE + NOUN **button** (on a video camera, etc.)
PREP. **after a/the ~** ◇ *'I don't know,' he said after a long ~.* |
in a/the ~ ◇ *Everyone nodded in agreement in the ~s*
between his sentences. | **with a/ the ~** ◇ *He read very slowly*
and with frequent ~s. | **without a/the ~** ◇ *She read the*
whole text without a ~. | **before** ◇ *There was a long ~*
before he spoke again. | **~ between** ◇ *in the ~s between his*
jokes | **~ for** ◇ *a ~ for breath* | **~ in** ◇ *during a ~ in the*
conversation

pause *verb*

ADV. **briefly, (for) a moment, momentarily, (for) a second** ◇
She ~d a moment and then walked away. | **mid-sentence,**
mid-stride ◇ *She ~d mid-stride when the doorbell rang.* |
occasionally ◇ *She ~d occasionally to smell the flowers.*
| **barely, hardly** ◇ *He spoke for two hours and barely*
~d for breath. | **deliberately** ◇ *She ~d deliberately, her eyes*
holding his. | **dramatically, meaningfully** | **expectantly** |
reflectively, thoughtfully | **uncertainly** | **awkwardly,**
uncomfortably
PHRASES **~ for breath, ~ for thought** | **~ only long enough**
to do sth, ~ only to do sth ◇ *Pausing only to put out her*
cigarette, she left the room. | **~ to consider, look, reflect,**
etc. ◇ *Just ~ to think before giving me your answer.* |
without pausing ◇ *Without pausing to knock, she opened the*
door.

pavement *noun* (BrE) → See also SIDEWALK

ADJ. **wide** | **narrow** | **hard** | **broken, uneven** | **crowded** |
empty
VERB + PAVEMENT **step off, step onto** | **keep to** | **mount** ◇ *The*
car mounted the ~ and crashed into a lamp post.
PAVEMENT + NOUN **cafe, table, terrace**
PREP. **along the ~, down the ~, on the ~** ◇ *There was a car*
parked on the ~ and we couldn't get by. | **up the ~**
PHRASES **the edge of the ~**

pay *noun*

ADJ. **hourly, monthly, weekly** | **full, half** (both esp. BrE) ◇ *He*
has taken leave on half ~. | **high** | **low, poor** ◇ *workers on*
low ~ | **average** | **equal** ◇ *equal ~ for men and women* |
base (AmE), **basic** | **gross** | **take-home** ◇ *the average take-*
home ~ of a manual worker | **holiday** (BrE), **vacation** (AmE) |
maternity (BrE) | **overtime** | **redundancy** (BrE), **severance**

(esp. AmE) | **retirement** (esp. AmE) | **sick** (esp. BrE), **sickness**
(BrE) | **back** ◇ *The workers are demanding their back ~.* |
merit (AmE), **performance** (esp. BrE), **performance-related**
(esp. BrE) | **bonus** (esp. AmE), **incentive** (AmE)
... OF PAY **level, rate** ◇ *The job offers good rates of ~ and*
excellent conditions.
VERB + PAY **earn, get, receive** | **give sb** | **cut, dock, slash** ◇ *He*
cut management ~ by 15%. | **boost, double, increase, raise**
◇ *He doubled his ~ by accepting bribes.*
PAY + NOUN **day** | **cheque** (BrE) (**paycheck** in AmE), **packet**
(BrE) ◇ *the money in my weekly ~ packet* | **package** ◇ *His ~*
package including bonuses was worth at least $12 million. |
slip (BrE), **stub** (AmE) | **hike** (esp. AmE), **increase, raise**
(AmE), **rise** (BrE) | **cut** | **freeze** ◇ *claim, demand*
(both esp. BrE) | **bargaining, negotiations** (both BrE) |
agreement, award, deal, offer, settlement (all esp. BrE) |
dispute (esp. BrE), **strike** (BrE) | **levels, rates** ◇ *industrial*
unrest over ~ levels in the public sector | **grade, scale,**
structure (esp. BrE) ◇ *He's at the top of his company's ~ scale.*
| **equity** (AmE), **parity** (BrE) ◇ *Women are still decades*
away from achieving ~ equity with men. | **differential,**
disparity
PREP. **on ... ~** ◇ *Women are eligible for 18 weeks maternity*
leave on full ~. | **with ~** ◇ *a day off with ~* | **without ~** ◇ *He*
has been suspended without ~.
PHRASES **a cut in ~, an increase in ~, a reduction in ~**

pay *verb*

ADV. **handsomely, well** ◇ *She ~s her workers very well.* |
dearly (figurative) ◇ *He will ~ dearly for what he did.* | **gladly**
◇ *I would gladly ~ for the benefits such a tax would bring.* |
typically ◇ *Clients typically ~ about $2 400 per month.* | **up**
◇ *I had a hard time getting him to ~ up.*
VERB + PAY **have to, must** | **be able to, can, can afford to** ◇
help for those who are genuinely not able to ~ | **be unable**
to, cannot, can't afford to | **expect (sb) to** ◇ *You can expect*
to ~ £200 a night at this hotel. | **be liable to** (esp. BrE) ◇ *It is*
for the courts to decide who is liable to ~ damages. | **be**
ordered to, be required to ◇ *The company was ordered to ~*
the workers £5 000 in compensation each. | **agree to, be**
prepared to, be willing to, offer to, promise to | **fail to,**
neglect to ◇ *He was made bankrupt for failing to ~ debts of*
over £2 million. | **refuse to** | **help (to)** ◇ *The revenue will be*
used to help ~ for environmental improvements. | **get sb to,**
make sb ◇ *If he had killed Caroline, then Mac was going to*
make him ~ the price. | **let sb** ◇ *She wouldn't let me ~ for my*
ticket.
PREP. **for** ◇ *How much did you ~ for your new car?* | **to** ◇ *We ~*
£200 a week to our landlord.
PHRASES **ability to ~** ◇ *Taxation should be based on the ability*
to ~.

payable *adj.* (esp. BrE)

VERBS **be** | **become** (BrE) ◇ *the date on which the rent becomes*
~ | **make sth** ◇ *Cheques should be made ~ to Brighton*
Borough Council. (BrE) ◇ *Include a check made ~ to the Texas*
Department of Transportation. (AmE)
ADV. **immediately** (BrE) ◇ *This amount is ~ immediately.*
PREP. **by** ◇ *the costs ~ by a client* | **on** ◇ *No tax is ~ on these*
earnings. | **to** ◇ *An initial fee is ~ to the franchiser.*
PHRASES **~ in instalments/installments**

payment *noun*

1 paying/being paid

ADJ. **immediate** (esp. BrE), **prompt** | **late** ◇ *penalties for late ~*
of tax | **early** (esp. BrE) | **full, part** (esp. BrE) | **partial** (esp.
AmE) ◇ *I enclose $65.50, in full ~ of the bill.*
VERB + PAYMENT **make** ◇ *How do you want to make ~?* (esp.
BrE) ◇ *I made the ~ in cash.* ◇ *The department makes ~s to*
farmers for providing improvement to water quality. |
authorize ◇ *The buyer is required to enter a code to*
authorize ~. | **arrange for** | **accept, take** ◇ *Do you accept ~*
by credit card? | **get, receive** | **stop, suspend, withhold** ◇ *I*
have authorized the bank to stop ~ of the cheque/check. |

refuse sb | **defer, delay** ◇ *We may have to defer ~ for a week.* | **demand** | **guarantee** ◇ *The only way to guarantee ~ is to sign a contract.*
PAYMENT + VERB **be due**
PAYMENT + NOUN **option, plan, schedule** ◇ *Some mortgage plans offer a bimonthly ~ schedule.*
PREP. **in ~** ◇ *He requested $8 000 in ~.* | **in ~ for, in ~ of** (*BrE*) ◇ *Credit cards are accepted in ~ for virtually anything.* ◇ *She wrote out a cheque in ~ of the fees.* | **on ~ of** ◇ *He was released on ~ of the ransom.* | **~ for** ◇ *~ for work done* | **~ from, ~ to** ◇ *~ to the company from its customers*
PHRASES **a method of ~** | **~ in advance** ◇ *The hostel requires full ~ in advance.* | **~ in full** ◇ *He demanded ~ in full of the $300 000 owed to him.*

2 amount of money paid

ADJ. **annual, monthly, etc.** | **regular** | **one-off, one-time** (*AmE*), **single** ◇ *All families of the victims will receive a one-off ~ of $100 000.* | **cash, lump-sum** | **token** | **generous** | **minimum** ◇ *She was finding it difficult to make even the minimum ~ on her credit card.* | **advance, upfront** | **down, initial** | **additional, further, subsequent** (*both esp. BrE*) | **interim** (*esp. BrE*) | **final** | **credit-card** | **debt, loan** | **insurance, interest, lease** (*esp. AmE*), **mortgage, rent, tax, tuition** (*AmE*) | **alimony** (*esp. AmE*), **benefit, child-support, compensation, disability** (*esp. AmE*), **maintenance** (*BrE*), **royalty, severance, welfare**
VERB + PAYMENT **afford, keep up, meet** ◇ *My client was unable to meet her rent ~s.* | **increase** | **lower, reduce** ◇ *You could lower your monthly mortgage ~s by $160.* | **collect** ◇ *It was my job to collect ~ for the trip.* | **deduct** ◇ *Companies deduct interest ~s from their taxable income.* | **guarantee** ◇ *The company guaranteed royalty ~s of at least $590 million.*
PREP. **in ~s** ◇ *an extra $9 million in interest ~s* | **~ for** ◇ *a generous ~ for his services* | **~ from** ◇ *~s to the landlord from his tenants* | **~ to**
PHRASES **the balance of ~s** (*economics*) ◇ *measures designed to reduce the balance of ~s deficit*

pea *noun*

ADJ. **canned** (*esp. AmE*), **dried, fresh, frozen, tinned** (*BrE*) | **green** | **snow** (*AmE*), **sugar snap** | **mushy** (*BrE*) | **black-eyed** (*AmE*) | **split**
VERB + PEA **eat, have** | **shell** | **cook** | **grow, plant, sow**
PEA + NOUN **soup** | **pod, shoot**
→ Special page at FOOD

peace *noun*

1 not war

ADJ. **durable, lasting, permanent** | **fragile, uneasy** | **negotiated** ◇ *A negotiated ~ would be preferable to a protracted war.* | **relative** ◇ *The country is in a state of relative ~ after ten years of fighting.* | **world** ◇ *obstacles in the way of world ~*
VERB + PEACE **bring (about), establish, make, secure** ◇ *England finally made ~ with France.* | **broker, negotiate** ◇ *The UN has resumed its efforts to broker ~.* | **keep, maintain, preserve** ◇ *UN troops are trying to keep the ~ in the region.* | **restore** | **promote** ◇ *We aim to promote world ~ by encouraging links between nations.* | **threaten** ◇ *His country's actions threaten ~ in the region.*
PEACE + VERB **come** | **prevail, reign** ◇ *An uneasy ~ prevailed in the first days of the ceasefire.*
PEACE + NOUN **conference, congress, negotiations, process, talks** ◇ *This must not be allowed to hold up the ~ process.* | **efforts, initiative** | **plan, proposal** | **accord, agreement, deal, pact, settlement, treaty** | **broker, envoy, negotiator** | **mission** ◇ *The president is visiting the country on a ~ mission.* | **activist, advocate** (*AmE*), **campaigner** (*esp. BrE*) | **marcher** (*esp. AmE*), **protester** | **group, movement** | **camp, march, protest, rally, vigil** | **offering** ◇ *The Greeks hid inside a wooden horse left as a ~ offering.*
PREP. **at ~ (with)** ◇ *Although the two countries were officially at ~, fighting continued.* | **~ between** ◇ *~ between the warring factions in the area*

2 state of being calm

ADJ. **inner** | **perfect** | **eternal**
VERB + PEACE **find, seek** ◇ *She finally found inner ~ and happiness.* | **enjoy** ◇ *He was enjoying the ~ of his study.* | **disturb, shatter** ◇ *The ~ of the afternoon was suddenly shattered by a police siren.* | **leave sb in** ◇ *Go away and leave me in ~!* | **make** ◇ *a scene in the movie where Harry tries to make ~ with his mother*
PEACE + VERB **reign** ◇ *She stopped shouting, and ~ reigned supreme once again.* | **descend on sth, settle over sth** ◇ *Peace descended once more on the little town.*
PREP. **at ~** ◇ *Her father is at ~ (= dead) now.* | **at ~ with** ◇ *For the first time in months, she felt calm and at ~ with the world.* | **in ~** ◇ *to live in ~ and harmony*
PHRASES **~ and quiet, ~ and tranquillity** ◇ *The island is a haven of ~ and tranquillity.* | **~ of mind** ◇ *The computer comes with a three-year guarantee for ~ of mind.*

peaceful *adj.*

1 without war/violence

VERBS **be** | **become** | **remain**
ADV. **extremely, fairly, very, etc.** | **largely, mostly** | **comparatively, reasonably, relatively**

2 quiet and calm

VERBS **be, feel, look** | **become** | **remain**
ADV. **extremely, fairly, very, etc.** | **utterly** | **comparatively, relatively** | **remarkably, strangely, surprisingly** | **blissfully** ◇ *The time without her in the house had been blissfully ~.*

peak *noun*

1 mountain top

ADJ. **high, lofty, towering** | **craggy, jagged, rocky, sharp** | **snow-capped, snow-covered, snowy** | **distant** | **mountain**
VERB + PEAK **climb, conquer, scale**
PEAK + VERB **loom, rise, tower** ◇ *We looked up at the rocky ~s towering above us.*
PREP. **on a/the ~** ◇ *climbers on the distant mountain ~s*

2 highest level, rate, etc.

ADJ. **all-time** ◇ *The share index rose to a new all-time ~ of 2112.* | **seasonal** | **summer, winter, etc.** ◇ *The influx of tourists has reached its summer ~.* | **sharp** ◇ *The graph shows two very sharp price ~s.*
VERB + PEAK **rise to, rise towards/toward** ◇ *Production is rising back towards/toward its 1999 ~.* | **hit, reach** | **fall below, fall from, pass** | **be past** ◇ *Her performance is just past its ~.*
PEAK + NOUN **hours, period, season, time, year** | **demand** ◇ *at times of ~ demand* | **rate** ◇ *peak-rate phone calls* | **level** | **efficiency, performance** ◇ *The engine is tuned to ~ efficiency.* | **fitness** (*esp. BrE*), **form**
PREP. **at a/the/your ~** ◇ *The crisis was now at its ~.* ◇ *At his ~ he was the best player in the world.* | **~ of** ◇ *She is at the ~ of her popularity.* ◇ *The party's numbers reached a ~ of 40 000 in 2001.*
PHRASES **in ~ condition** ◇ *You want your hair to look in ~ condition.* | **~s and troughs** ◇ *Economic life moves in cycles of ~s and troughs.*

peal *noun*

ADJ. **deafening, loud**
VERB + PEAL **burst into, give, let out** ◇ *He burst into ~s of laughter.* ◇ *She let out a ~ of laughter.* | **ring, ring out** ◇ *The bells of the cathedral rang out their loud ~.* | **hear**
PEAL + VERB **ring out**
PREP. **with a ~** ◇ *The bishop was welcomed to the church with a ~ of bells.* | **~ of**
PHRASES **a ~ of bells, laughter, thunder, etc.**
→ Note at SOUND

peculiar *adj.*

VERBS **be, feel, look, seem, smell, sound, taste** | **become** |

find sb/sth, regard sb/sth as, think sb/sth ◇ *I find her attitude a little ~, to say the least.*
ADV. **most** (*esp. BrE*), **very** ◇ *He is a most ~ man!* | **quite, rather, somewhat** ◇ *The meat tasted rather ~.* | **a little, slightly, etc.**

peculiarity *noun*

ADJ. **individual** | **local**
VERB + PECULIARITY **have** ◇ *The area has a few local peculiarities.*
PREP. **~ about** ◇ *I noticed a certain ~ about his appearance.*

pedal *noun*

ADJ. **accelerator, brake, clutch, gas** (*esp. AmE*) | **foot** ◇ *To stop the machine push the foot ~.* | **bicycle, bike** (*informal*) | **organ, piano** | **wah-wah** ◇ *Some guitarists tend to overuse the wah-wah ~.*
VERB + PEDAL **depress, press, push, put your foot on, step on, use, work** ◇ *Her foot was working the ~ of the sewing machine.* | **floor** (*AmE*), **slam on, stamp on** ◇ *He floored the ~ and drove off at high speed.* | **release, take your foot off**
PEDAL + VERB **control sth, operate sth**
PEDAL + NOUN **boat, car, cycle** (*BrE*) | **bin** (*BrE*)
PREP. **on a/the ~** ◇ *with one foot on the ~*

pedal *verb*

ADV. **fast, frantically, furiously, hard** ◇ *You have to ~ hard to get anywhere.* | **away**
PREP. **along, down, up** ◇ *He refused to ~ up the hill.*

pedigree *noun*

ADJ. **long** ◇ *Hereford cattle have a long ~.* | **distinguished, illustrious, impeccable, impressive** | **artistic, intellectual, literary** ◇ *These ideas have a long and distinguished intellectual ~.*
VERB + PEDIGREE **prove, show** ◇ *The champions really showed their ~ today.*
PEDIGREE + VERB **stretch back** ◇ *These trees have ~s stretching back thousands of years.*

peek *verb*

ADV. **cautiously** ◇ *Daniel ~ed cautiously over his shoulder.* | **out** ◇ *He ~ed out from behind the door.*
PREP. **around** ◇ *I was tempted to ~ around the corner.* | **at** ◇ *She ~ed at the clock to see the time.* | **into** ◇ *I wandered around the house, ~ing into various rooms.* | **through** ◇ *The child ~ed through a crack in the door.* ◇ *The sun was ~ing through the clouds.*

peek *noun*

ADJ. **little, quick, sneak** ◇ *a sneak peak at the new cartoon*
VERB + PEEK **have** (*esp. BrE*), **take** | **get** | **sneak** ◇ *Brooke couldn't help but sneak a ~ at him.* | **chance, dare**
PREP. **~ at** ◇ *Go ahead and take a ~ at your presents.* | **~ behind** ◇ *a fascinating ~ behind the scenes of the Oprah Winfrey Show* | **~ into** ◇ *We got a ~ into rooms that are normally closed to the public.* | **~ through** ◇ *I dared a little ~ through a crack in the door.*

peep *verb*

ADV. **cautiously** ◇ *He ~ed out cautiously from behind the door.* | **out**
PREP. **at** ◇ *She was tempted to ~ at the letter.* | **through** ◇ *The child ~ed through a crack in the door.*

peep *noun*

1 quick look

ADJ. **quick**
VERB + PEEP **have, take** | **get**
PREP. **~ at** ◇ *I noticed him take a little ~ at his watch.* | **~ behind** ◇ *The movie gives us a ~ behind the curtain at a Broadway musical.* | **~ into** ◇ *a ~ into the private life of a world leader* | **~ through** ◇ *I took a ~ through the keyhole.*

2 quiet sound

VERB + PEEP **utter** | **hear**
PHRASES **(not) a ~** ◇ *He didn't dare utter a ~.* ◇ *Not a ~ of protest was heard from the State Department.* (*figurative*)

peer *noun*

1 person of the same age/status

ADJ. **academic** (*esp. AmE*), **professional** ◇ *She is highly respected by her professional ~s.*
VERB + PEER **outperform** ◇ *We have seen several women who can outperform their male ~s physically.* | **impress** ◇ *teenagers trying to impress their ~s*
PEER + NOUN **group** ◇ *She was rejected by her ~ group.* | **influence, pressure** ◇ *Children often take up smoking because of ~ pressure.* | **interaction, relations, relationship** ◇ *Some children fail to develop normal ~ relations.* | **culture** ◇ *Children generally develop a strong ~ culture.* | **network** ◇ *an extended family and ~ network* | **rejection, victimization** | **acceptance** ◇ *Peer acceptance is particularly important for teenagers.* | **evaluation, review** ◇ *Research data will be subjected to ~ review.* | **mediation** | **counsellor/counselor, educator, mentor, tutor** (*all esp. AmE*)
PREP. **among sb's ~s** ◇ *They adopt attitudes that are more socially acceptable among their ~s.*

2 (*in the UK*) **person of noble rank**

ADJ. **Conservative, Labour, etc.** | **hereditary** | **life** ◇ *The Act made it possible for a woman to be created a life ~.*
PHRASES **a ~ of the realm**

> **NOTE**
>
> ### Aristocratic titles
>
> **first..., second...**, etc. ◇ *the 17th Earl of Lauderdale*
> **become..., be created..., be made...** ◇ *She was made a baroness in 1992.*
> **succeed (sb) as...** ◇ *He was succeeded as third Baron Northwick by his nephew.*

peer *verb*

ADV. **closely, intently** | **anxiously, carefully, cautiously, nervously, slowly** | **curiously** | **suspiciously** | **ahead, around, back, down, in, inside, out, round** (*esp. BrE*), **up** ◇ *A face was ~ing down at him.*
VERB + PEER **try to**
PREP. **around, round** (*esp. BrE*) ◇ *She ~ed around the corner.* | **at** ◇ *His pale blue eyes ~ed anxiously at Vic.* | **into** ◇ *He ~ed into the darkness.* | **out of** ◇ *She ~ed out of the window.* | **over** ◇ *She tried to ~ over her shoulder.* | **through** ◇ *I ~ed through the letter box.*

peg *noun*

ADJ. **wooden** | **clothes** (*BrE*) (*clothespin* in *AmE*) | **tent**

pelvis *noun*

ADJ. **broken, fractured** | **narrow, wide**
VERB + PELVIS **thrust, tilt** | **break, crush, fracture**

pen *noun*

ADJ. **ballpoint, feather** (*AmE*), **felt, felt-tip, felt-tipped, fountain, gel, highlighter** (*esp. BrE*), **ink, marker** (*esp. BrE*), **marking** (*AmE*), **quill** | **calligraphy** | **coloured/colored** | **digital**
VERB + PEN **use, write (sth) with** | **grab** (*esp. AmE*) ◇ *I grabbed a ~ and began taking notes.* ◇ *Let me grab a ~.* | **cap, uncap** | **tap, twirl** | **borrow** ◇ *Can I borrow your ~?* | **wield** (*figurative*) ◇ *The President has yet to wield his veto ~ to block a bill.* (*AmE*)
PEN + VERB **write** ◇ *This ~ won't write.* | **run out** ◇ *My pen's run out* (= has no more ink). | **be poised** ◇ *His ~ was poised, ready to sign his name.*

PEN + NOUN **nib** | **cap** | **ink** (*esp. AmE*) | **holder** | **mark** | **drawing** | **portrait** (= written description of sb) (*BrE*)
PHRASES **~ and ink** ◇ *pen-and-ink drawings*

penalize (*BrE* also **-ise**) *verb*

ADV. **heavily, severely** | **unfairly** ◇ *He claims that he was unfairly ~d.*
PREP. **for** ◇ *Students will be ~d for mistakes in spelling and grammar.*

penalty *noun*

1 punishment

ADJ. **harsh, heavy, hefty, severe, stiff, strict, substantial, tough** | **draconian** | **light** | **maximum, minimum** | **ultimate** ◇ *These crimes carried with them the ultimate ~ of execution.* | **automatic** (*esp. BrE*), **fixed** (*BrE*), **mandatory** ◇ *a new system of fixed penalties for most traffic offences* ◇ *The legislation sanctions harsh mandatory penalties for weapons possession.* | **financial, monetary, tax** ◇ *the heavy financial penalties of paying off the loan early* | **exit, redemption** (*both BrE*) ◇ *There are redemption penalties if you pay off the mortgage early.* | **death** ◇ *the movement for the abolition of the death ~* | **civil, criminal**
VERB + PENALTY **impose, introduce** (*esp. BrE*), **levy** | **reintroduce, restore** ◇ *calls to restore the death ~* | **apply, give, hand down, hand out** (*esp. BrE*) | **issue** (*esp. BrE*) ◇ *The ~ handed down was disproportionate to the crime committed.* | **exact** (*formal*), **implement** (*esp. BrE*) ◇ *From time to time, the death ~ was exacted for murder.* | **charge** (*esp. BrE*) ◇ *Some lenders charge heavy penalties for early settlement.* | **enforce, prescribe** | **threaten** | **receive** | **seek** ◇ *He was seeking financial penalties against the company.* | **deserve** | **risk** | **increase, stiffen, toughen** | **reduce** | **attract** (*BrE*), **carry** ◇ *crimes which carry severe penalties* | **face, incur** | **avoid, escape** | **waive** ◇ *Credit card companies will waive penalties for flood victims who are unable to pay on time.* | **eliminate**
PENALTY + NOUN **fee** | **notice, ticket** (*both BrE*) ◇ *You will be given a fixed ~ notice if you fail to renew insurance on time.* | **fine** (*BrE*) ◇ *There is a fixed ~ fine of £50 for allowing your dog to foul public places.* | **point** (*BrE*) ◇ *Penalty points are given to drivers who speed.* | **payment** (*esp. BrE*) | **clause** (*esp. BrE*) | **system**
PREP. **on ~ of, under ~ of** ◇ *The Romans prohibited the teaching of the Torah on ~ of death.* ◇ *The application should be signed under ~ of perjury.* | **~ for** ◇ *the ~ for murder* | **~ on** ◇ *He threatened stiffer penalties on young offenders.*

2 disadvantage

VERB + PENALTY **pay, suffer** ◇ *He's now paying the ~ for his misspent youth.* ◇ *People who lose their jobs are suffering the penalties for longer periods.* | **accept**
PREP. **~ for** ◇ *You must accept the ~ for your rash actions.* | **~ of** ◇ *It's just one of the penalties of fame.*

3 in football/soccer

ADJ. **controversial, disputed, dodgy** (*BrE, informal*), **dubious** | **winning** | **well-struck** | **missed** | **first-half, injury-time, second-half** | **early, late** | **last-minute** | **12th-minute, etc.**
VERB + PENALTY **award (sb), give (sb)** | **concede, give away** ◇ *They were leading until Cole gave away a ~.* | **appeal for** | **be awarded, be given, earn, get, have, land, win** ◇ *We were unlucky not to get a ~.* | **boot, dispatch, kick, strike, take** | **score from** ◇ *Owen scored from a first-half ~.* | **net, slot home** ◇ *Ricketts netted his third ~ of the season to put his team ahead.* | **miss** | **save**
PENALTY + NOUN **area, box, corner, spot** | **award** | **kick** | **shoot-out** | **goal** | **miss** | **save** | **taker** | **chance, opportunity** | **attempt**
PREP. **~ by, ~ from** ◇ *They won, thanks to a late ~ from Fry.*
→ Special page at SPORTS

penance *noun*

ADJ. **public**

VERB + PENANCE **do, pay** ◇ *Has anyone ever paid a higher ~ for telling a lie?*
PREP. **as a ~** ◇ *He devoted his life to helping the poor as a ~ for his past crimes.* | **in ~** ◇ *She kneeled at her mother's feet in ~.* | **~ for** ◇ *He decided to do public ~ for his sins.*
PHRASES **an act of ~**

pencil *noun*

ADJ. **blunt, sharp** | **soft** | **sharpened** | **stubby** | **broken** | **coloured/colored** ◇ *a box of coloured/colored ~s* | **charcoal** (*esp. AmE*), **graphite** (*esp. AmE*), **grease** (*AmE*), **lead** | **#2** (*in the US*), **HB** (*in the UK*), **etc.** | **mechanical** | **colouring/coloring** | **eye, eyebrow, eyeliner, lip**
VERB + PENCIL **draw (sth) with, use, write (sth) with** | **sharpen** | **tap, twirl** | **grab** ◇ *Grab a ~ and write down this number.* | **borrow**
PENCIL + NOUN **lead, sharpener** | **eraser** | **shavings** | **stub** | **box, case, holder** | **drawing, sketch** | **line, mark**
PREP. **in ~** ◇ *margin notes in ~*

penetrate *verb*

ADV. **deep, deeply, far** ◇ *caves penetrating deep into the hills* | **completely, fully** | **barely** ◇ *The sunlight barely ~d the inner room.* | **quickly** | **slowly** ◇ *The news slowly ~d his consciousness.* | **easily, readily** ◇ *These so-called secret societies were easily ~d by intelligence agents.* | **successfully**
VERB + PENETRATE **be able to, can** | **be difficult to** | **seem to** ◇ *The cold seemed to ~ his bones.* | **fail to** | **allow sth to ~** ◇ *Cut two slashes on each side of the fish to allow heat to ~.*
PREP. **into** ◇ *It is not yet known how deeply the radiation has ~d into the soil.* | **through** ◇ *The light could not ~ through the thick curtains.* | **to** ◇ *The dust had ~d to all corners of the room.*

penetration *noun*

1 making a way into sth

ADJ. **deep** | **greater, high** ◇ *The country has the highest cellphone ~ in Europe.* | **import** (*esp. AmE*), **market** ◇ *Our aim is to achieve greater market ~.* | **broadband, Internet, PC** ◇ *Broadband ~ in the country is likely to hit 31 million households.* | **cellphone** (*AmE*), **mobile-phone** (*BrE*) | **water** | **daylight, light**
VERB + PENETRATION **achieve** | **facilitate** | **allow** | **improve, increase** | **prevent** | **resist**

2 sexual act

ADJ. **sexual** | **anal, vaginal**

penis *noun*

ADJ. **erect, hard** | **flaccid** | **6-inch, etc.** | **circumcised, uncircumcised**
VERB + PENIS **insert** | **stroke, suck** | **expose** | **enlarge**
PENIS + VERB **get/go hard**
PENIS + NOUN **envy** | **length, size** | **enlargement**

penniless *adj.*

VERBS **be, die** ◇ *He died ~ in Paris.* | **find yourself** ◇ *Laura found herself virtually ~.* | **leave sb** ◇ *The legal dispute left them ~.*
ADV. **totally**

pension *noun*

ADJ. **adequate, big, decent, generous, good** (*all esp. BrE*) | **inadequate, meagre/meager, small** (*all esp. BrE*) | **basic** (*esp. BrE*) | **full** (*esp. BrE*) ◇ *Only half of all women qualify for a full state ~.* | **state** (*BrE*) | **company, occupational** (*both esp. BrE*) | **personal, private** (*both esp. BrE*) | **stakeholder** (*BrE*) | **contributory, non-contributory** (*both BrE*) | **index-linked** (*BrE*) | **final-salary** (*BrE*) | **guaranteed** (*esp. BrE*) | **annual** (*esp. BrE*), **monthly, weekly** (*BrE*) | **employee** | **old-age, retirement** (*both BrE*) | **disability** (*esp. BrE*) | **invalidity** (*BrE*)
VERB + PENSION **collect** (*BrE*), **draw** (*BrE*), **get, receive** ◇ *He draws his ~ at the post office.* | **enjoy** (*esp. BrE*) ◇ *Employees enjoy generous retirement ~s.* | **buy** (*BrE*) | **sell** (*BrE*) | **award sb** (*esp. BrE*), **give sb** (*esp. BrE*), **pay sb** (*esp. BrE*), **provide (sb**

with) | **claim** (*BrE*), **qualify for** (*esp. BrE*) ◇ *You will have to find out whether or not you qualify for a ~.* | **live on** (*BrE*) ◇ *She lives on her ~ and her savings.* | **fund** ◇ *State ~s are funded by taxpayers.* | **boost, increase, raise, supplement** (*all esp. BrE*) | **cut, reduce** (*both esp. BrE*) | **lose** (*esp. BrE*) ◇ *workers who have lost all their ~s as a result of company insolvencies* | **guarantee, secure** (*esp. BrE*)
PENSION + NOUN **age** (*BrE*) ◇ *The state ~ age for men and women will be 65.* | **contributions** (*esp. BrE*), **fund, pot** (*BrE*) ◇ *the company ~ fund* | **savings** (*esp. BrE*) | **costs** | **payment, payout** | **benefits** | **deficit, shortfall** | **plan, scheme** (*BrE*) | **arrangements** (*BrE*) | **provision** (*esp. BrE*) | **provider** (*esp. BrE*) | **holder** (*esp. BrE*) | **entitlement** (*esp. BrE*) | **obligations** (*esp. AmE*) | **rights** (*esp. BrE*) | **policy** (*esp. BrE*) | **reform** | **~s adviser** (*esp. BrE*), **~s consultant, ~s expert** (*esp. BrE*) | **~s industry** (*BrE*)
PREP. **on a ~** ◇ *He is now retired and on a ~.*

people noun

1 more than one person

ADJ. **young** | **elderly, old** | **common, normal, ordinary** | **real** ◇ *All the characters in the book are based on real ~.* | **important** ◇ *a line of limousines carrying very important ~* | **famous** | **middle-class, working-class** | **business, professional, working** | **unemployed** | **poor** | **rich, wealthy** | **blind, deaf, disabled** ◇ *access for disabled ~* | **gay** | **innocent** ◇ *Many innocent ~ were killed.* | **healthy, sick** | **vulnerable** (*esp. BrE*) | **homeless** | **happy** | **creative, intelligent, smart** (*esp. AmE*), **talented** | **stupid** | **decent, good, interesting, lovely** (*esp. BrE*), **nice, wonderful** | **bad** | **strange** | **single**
VERB + PEOPLE **meet** | **attract** ◇ *The local tourist board is trying to attract more ~ to the town.*

2 of a particular place/race

ADJ. **local** | **country** | **indigenous, native** | **primitive** ◇ *These artists derived much of their imagery from the art of so-called primitive ~s.* | **tribal** | **nomadic** | **Aboriginal, Arab, Japanese, Slavic, etc.** ◇ *the culture of the Basque ~* | **black, white** | **diverse** ◇ *Australia is a collectivity of diverse ~s.* | **civilized** | **oppressed** | **marginalized** | **colonial, colonized, conquered** | **displaced** | **prehistoric**
VERB + PEOPLE **represent** ◇ *I was elected to represent the ~ of Bristol.* | **bring together, unite** ◇ *The EU was intended to unite the ~s of Europe.*
PHRASES **the ~s of the world**

pepper noun

1 spice

ADJ. **crushed, ground** ◇ *freshly ground black ~* | **cracked** | **black, white** | **cayenne** | **lemon**
VERB + PEPPER **add, put in, put on, season sth with, sprinkle** ◇ *He put some ~ on his steak.* | **grind**
PEPPER + NOUN **grinder, mill, pot** (*esp. BrE*), **shaker** (*AmE*) | **powder** (*esp. AmE*) | **spray**
PHRASES **salt and ~** ◇ *Add salt and ~ to taste* (= in the quantity preferred). ◇ *salt-and-pepper hair* (= with some white hair)

2 vegetable

ADJ. **bell** (*AmE*), **sweet** | **chilli/chili, jalapeño** | **hot** | **green, red, yellow** | **stuffed** ◇ *He gave me a great recipe for stuffed ~s.* | **grilled, roasted** | **fresh**
VERB + PEPPER **chop, cut, slice** | **stuff with sth** ◇ *~s stuffed with meat and rice* | **roast**
PEPPER + NOUN **sauce** | **plant, tree**
→ Special page at FOOD

perceive verb

ADV. **clearly, distinctly** | **dimly** ◇ *The remedy for the problem was only dimly ~d by scientists until recently.* | **directly** ◇ *the world of directly ~d objects* | **differently** ◇ *Risks are ~d differently by different people.* | **easily, readily** ◇ *The industrial bias of canal building can be readily ~d by looking at Figure 7.3.* | **accurately, correctly** | **wrongly** | **immediately**

VERB + PERCEIVE **be able to, can** | **be unable to** | **fail to** | **be difficult to**
PREP. **as** ◇ *The General's words were ~d as a threat by countries in the region.*
PHRASES **commonly ~d, generally ~d, typically ~d, widely ~d** ◇ *It is widely ~d as a women's health problem, but it does also affect men.* | **a failure to ~ sth, an inability to ~ sth**

> ### NOTE
>
> #### Financial indicators
>
> **... is down, ... is up** ◇ *With prices down, it might be time to start buying.* ◇ *The index was up 18.84 points.*
> **... reaches sth, ... stands at sth** ◇ *Consumer confidence reached a 30-year high.* ◇ *Second-quarter sales stood at $18 billion.*
> **... is/remains unchanged** ◇ *The five-year Treasury yield was unchanged at 2.68%.*
> **... gains (sth)** ◇ *Gold stocks gained 6% this week.*
> **... suffers (sth)** ◇ *Profit margins suffered when the company lowered prices to remain competitive.*
> **... climbs, ... edges up, ... goes up, ... increases, ... jumps, ... rises, ... rockets, ... shoots up, ... skyrockets, ... soars** ◇ *Earnings per share climbed from 3.5p to 5.1p.* ◇ *The Brazilian real has increased in value relative to the euro.* ◇ *Profits have shot up by a staggering 25%.* ◇ *Oil prices have skyrocketed.*
> **... comes/goes down, ... crashes, ... declines, ... decreases, ... dives, ... drops, ... falls, ... plummets, ... plunges, ... shrinks, ... slips, ... slumps** ◇ *Banana exports crashed nearly 50%.* ◇ *The pound fell to a 14-year low against the dollar.* ◇ *Net income plummeted to $3.7 million.*
> **... increases in value, ... decreases in value** (for currencies)
> → See also the note at CURRENCY

per cent (*esp. BrE*) (*AmE usually* percent) noun

VERB + PER CENT **account for, amount to, be equal to, comprise, constitute, equal, represent** ◇ *Overseas earnings accounted for 9% of the total last year.* | **contain** ◇ *Roman coins containing about 25% zinc* | **hit, reach, stand at, total** ◇ *Their share of the vote reached 6.5% in 1998.* | **exceed, top** ◇ *Sales have already exceeded 25% of the predicted annual turnover.* | (All the verbs in the following collocate groups may be followed by *by, from* or *to* plus *per cent/percent*. Sometimes the word *by* is left out.), **be up, climb, expand, go up, grow, improve, increase, jump, leap, rise, shoot up, soar, surge** ◇ *Prices rose by 12% in 1998.* ◇ *Prices rose 12%.* | **be down, come down, decline, decrease, dip, drop, fall, go down, plummet, plunge, shrink, slide, slip, slump** (*esp. BrE*) ◇ *Profitability is down from 16% to 12.2%.* | **boost sth, increase sth, raise sth** ◇ *We're hoping to boost sales by 10%.* | **cut sth, reduce sth, slash sth** ◇ *Operating expenses were slashed 54.2%.*
PREP. **about five, ten, etc. ~, around five, ten, etc. ~** | **by five, ten, etc. ~** ◇ *They aim to cut carbon dioxide levels by 20% in 15 years.* | **over five, ten, etc. ~** | **up to five, ten, etc. ~** ◇ *a process that can reduce the cost by up to 15%* | **~ of sth** ◇ *In 40% of all cases, the parents had no idea of their child's problem.*
PHRASES **a boost of five, ten, etc. ~, an improvement of five, ten, etc. ~, an increase of five, ten, etc. ~, a jump of five, ten, etc. ~, a rise of five, ten, etc. ~** ◇ *a jump of 8% in cases of the disease* | **a cut of five, ten, etc. ~, a decline of five, ten, etc. ~, a decrease of five, ten, etc. ~, a drop of five, ten, etc. ~, a fall of five, ten, etc. ~, a reduction of five, ten, etc. ~** ◇ *a fall of 12% in cases of the disease* | **only five, ten, etc. ~** ◇ *Only 10% of the teenagers agreed with this statement.* | **fewer than five, ten, etc. ~, less than five, ten, etc. ~, more than five, ten, etc. ~** ◇ *Profits rose by*

more than 50% last year. | **growth of five, ten, etc. ~** ◊ *Growth of 11% is forecast.* | **in the bottom five, ten, etc. ~,** in the top five, ten, etc. ~ ◊ *His son was in the top 2% of his class.* | **five, ten, etc. ~ less, five, ten, etc. ~ more** ◊ *New cars use about 35% less fuel.* | **five, ten, etc. ~ of all, five, ten, etc. ~ of a total** ◊ *The tribe's land now amounts to around 50% of the total land area.*

percentage noun

ADJ. **considerable, high, huge, large, overwhelming, significant, sizeable, substantial** ◊ *The area has a high ~ of unemployed men.* | **greater** ◊ *The disease affects a greater ~ of men than women.* | **growing, increasing** | **low, small, tiny** | **fair, reasonable** ◊ *A fair ~ of their business comes from people using the airport.* | **disproportionate** ◊ *Disabled passengers make up a disproportionate ~ of the cruise company's customers.* | **relative** | **fixed** | **maximum, minimum** | **average, mean** | **overall, total**

VERB + PERCENTAGE **calculate, determine, estimate, measure** | **express sth as** ◊ *This figure can be expressed as a ~ of the total.* | **comprise, make up** ◊ *Young women comprise a large ~ of our clients.*

PERCENTAGE + VERB **decline, decrease, drop, fall** | *That ~ declined to 49.7 in 2006.* | **grow, increase, rise** | **range from sth to sth, vary** ◊ *Medical expenditure ~s ranged from 3.9% in Arizona to 9.8% in Delaware.* | **indicate sth, represent sth, show sth**

PERCENTAGE + NOUN **point** ◊ *Unemployment has fallen by two ~ points this month.* | **rate** ◊ *Insurance contributions are paid at a fixed ~ rate on all earnings.* | **figure** (*esp. BrE*) | **score, value** | **gain, increase, rise** ◊ *the ~ rise in the average salary* | **decline, decrease, drop, reduction** | **share**

PREP. **~ of** ◊ *What ~ of women own a car?*

PHRASES **in ~ terms** ◊ *The numbers are relatively low in ~ terms.* | **on a ~ basis** ◊ *The artist's agent receives commission on a ~ basis.*

perception noun

ADJ. **clear, distinct, keen** (*esp. AmE*) | **common, general, popular, widely held, widespread** | **growing** | **accurate** | **distorted, erroneous** (*esp. AmE*), **false, inaccurate, mistaken** | **negative, positive** | **altered, changing** ◊ *The book explores the changing ~s about gender.* | **heightened** ◊ *heightened ~ caused by drugs* | **conscious** | **selective** | **overall** ◊ *The company wanted to boost the overall ~ of the brand.* | **public** | **human** | **individual** | **consumer, parental** | **cultural** | **subjective** | **auditory, extrasensory** (abbreviated to *ESP*), **sense, sensory, visual** | **depth, spatial** | **hazard** (*BrE*) | **risk** (*esp. AmE*) | **threat** (*AmE*) ◊ *If we improve drivers' hazard ~, road deaths will fall.* ◊ *cultural differences in risk ~ between European students and their American counterparts*

VERB + PERCEPTION **have** ◊ *I was shocked to learn of the ~ people have of me.* | **create** ◊ *Your brand name should create a distinctive ~ in the customer's mind.* | **affect, influence, shape** ◊ *These developments hardly affected the public ~ of the crisis.* | **Movies have shaped our ~ of many historical events.** | **alter, change, shift, transform** ◊ *The computer changes our ~s of place and time.* | **colour/color, distort, skew** | **correct** | **counter, dispel** ◊ *This study dispels the ~ that men are better drivers.* | **confirm** | **overcome** ◊ *a marketing strategy to overcome negative public ~ of the company* | **enhance, improve** | **challenge** ◊ *This film challenges traditional ~s of older people.* | **assess, examine, explore** | **fuel, heighten** | **reflect** ◊ *The survey reflects the ~s of business people around the world.*

perceptive adj.

VERBS **be**

ADV. **extremely, fairly, very, etc.** | **highly** ◊ *a highly ~ analysis of the problem*

PREP. **about** ◊ *He's very ~ about people.*

perch verb

ADV. **precariously** ◊ *The hotel was ~ed precariously on a steep hillside.*

PREP. **on** ◊ *The birds ~ed on nearby buildings.*

PHRASES **be ~ed high above sth, be ~ed high on sth** ◊ *The castle is ~ed high above the valley.* | **be ~ed on the edge of sth, ~ on the edge of sth** ◊ *I ~ed on the edge of his desk to listen to him.* | **be ~ed on top of sth, ~ on top of sth**

percussion noun

ADJ. **tuned, untuned** | **live** | **electronic** | **tribal**

PERCUSSION + NOUN **instrument** | **player** | **section** | **band, ensemble**

→ Special page at MUSIC

perfect adj.

VERBS **be, look, seem** | **make sth** ◊ *The town's position in the region makes it ~ for touring.*

ADV. **absolutely, completely, just, quite** (*BrE*), **really, simply, totally, truly, utterly** | **far from, hardly, less than** ◊ *The treaty is far from ~, but it is clearly the way forward.* | **almost, near, nearly, practically, virtually** | **impossibly** ◊ *He flashed a smile revealing a set of impossibly ~ teeth.* | **too** ◊ *He seemed too ~ to be real.* | **seemingly** ◊ *a seemingly ~ alibi* | **otherwise** ◊ *He had high blood pressure but was in otherwise ~ health.* | **once** ◊ *He had brought chaos to her once ~ life.* | **already** ◊ *Her high heels emphasized her already ~ legs.* | **morally, physically** | **technically**

PREP. **for** ◊ *The day seemed ~ for a picnic.*

perfection noun

ADJ. **great** | **absolute, pure, sheer, ultimate, utter** | **near** | **moral, physical, spiritual, technical** | **divine, human**

... OF PERFECTION **degree**

VERB + PERFECTION **achieve, attain, bring sth to, find, reach** | **approach** ◊ *a dance troupe whose work approaches ~* | **demand, expect, pursue** (*esp. BrE*), **require, seek, strive for** ◊ *She strives for ~ in everything.* | **fall short of**

PREP. **close to ~** ◊ *The cooking was close to ~.* | **to ~** (= *perfectly*) ◊ *The dress fitted to ~.* | **towards/toward ~** ◊ *a sequence of developmental stages towards/toward the ~ of his violin technique*

PHRASES **a point of ~** ◊ *He brought the art of photography to the highest point of ~.* | **a model of ~** ◊ *The building became the model of ~ that architects sought to emulate.* | **the pursuit of ~** ◊ *She sometimes stayed up painting all night in her pursuit of ~.* | **a quest for ~, a search for ~**

perform verb

1 do a task/duty/piece of work

ADV. **effectively, efficiently, properly** (*esp. BrE*), **successfully, well** ◊ *Who ensures that tasks are properly ~ed?* | **poorly** | **adequately, competently, reliably, satisfactorily** | **correctly** | **safely** | **duly** (*BrE*), **faithfully** ◊ *He duly ~ed his own half of the bargain and expected the others to do likewise.* ◊ *those who faithfully ~ their duties* | **annually** | **regularly, routinely** | **automatically** | **manually**

VERB + PERFORM **be able to, be unable to** ◊ *The prince is no longer able to ~ his duties.* | **be expected to**

PHRASES **failure to ~ sth** ◊ *failure to ~ a duty*

2 work/function/play

ADV. **admirably, beautifully, brilliantly, efficiently, excellently, faultlessly, flawlessly, impressively, magnificently, solidly, strongly, superbly, well** ◊ *One or two of the players ~ed brilliantly.* ◊ *The company has been ~ing strongly over the past year.* | **badly, dismally** (*esp. BrE*), **poorly** ◊ *The car ~ed poorly at high speeds.* | **adequately, competently, reliably, satisfactorily** | **consistently**

VERB + PERFORM **be able to, be unable to** | **be expected to** ◊ *students who are expected to ~ well*

3 give a performance

ADV. **live** ◊ *The group will be ~ing live on tonight's show.* | **in public, publicly** | **professionally** | **together** ◊ *The two artists have never ~ed together before.* | **annually**

PHRASES **first ~ed** ◊ *The play was first publicly ~ed in 1872.* |

NOTE

Performing arts

write… ◇ *He's written a new Broadway musical.*

do…, perform…, present…, produce…, put on…, stage… ◇ *The drama club is doing a show.* ◇ *We are proud to present the play 'Rocket to the Moon'.*

direct… ◇ *She is directing 'La Traviata' at La Scala next year.*

act in…, appear in…, perform in…, sing in…, star in… ◇ *He starred in the musical 'Mamma Mia'.*

rehearse…, rehearse for… ◇ *We had no time to rehearse for the play.*

go to the… ◇ *How often do you go to the theatre/theater?*

see… ◇ *Have you seen that new production of 'Macbeth'?*

…opens ◇ *'The Nutcracker' opens in December.*

…plays, …runs ◇ *The show has been playing to packed houses.* ◇ *The show ran for years on Broadway.*

…closes ◇ *The musical closes this week after a record number of performances.*

a play/show folds ◇ *The play folded after poor reviews.*

at the… ◇ *We met at the opera.*

in a/the… ◇ *the characters in the play*

…by ◇ *a comedy by Molière*

rarely ~ed | see sth ~ed ◇ *I've never seen this play ~ed before.*

performance *noun*

1 sth performed

ADJ. **live | public | evening, matinee | amateur, professional | cameo** (*esp. BrE*) **| solo | debut | repeat** ◇ *The party is dreading a repeat ~ of its defeat in the last election.* **| ballet, concert, dance, dramatic, musical, opera, theatrical, vocal** ◇ *The singer is renowned for his live concert ~s.* **| benefit, charity** (*esp. BrE*) **| school**
VERB + PERFORMANCE **give, put on, stage** ◇ *The company is putting on a ~ of the popular musical 'Cats'.* **| attend, go to | see, watch**
PERFORMANCE + VERB **feature sb/sth**
PERFORMANCE + NOUN **art, poetry | artist, poet | troupe** (*esp. AmE*) **| piece | venue | anxiety** (*esp. AmE*)
PREP. **in ~** ◇ *The course aims to develop the children's appreciation of music in ~.*

2 way in which sth is done

ADJ. **brilliant, convincing, dazzling, electrifying** (*esp. BrE*), **excellent, exceptional, extraordinary, fine, good, great, impressive, inspired, magnificent, outstanding, remarkable, sparkling** (*esp. BrE*), **standout, stellar, sterling** (*esp. BrE, formal*), **stunning, superb, terrific, virtuoso, wonderful** ◇ *The recording gives the most convincing ~ of Stravinsky's 'Rite' to date.* ◇ *Finney gives a virtuoso ~ as a psychopath.* **| powerful, strong** ◇ *the country's strong economic ~ over the last two years* **| solid | creditable** (*esp. BrE*) **| flawless, polished | gutsy, spirited | energetic | bad, disappointing, dismal, lacklustre/lackluster, poor, weak | mediocre | satisfactory | improved | consistent | central** (*esp. BrE*) ◇ *Mel Gibson's central ~ in the movie as Hamlet* **| memorable | all-around** (*AmE*), **all-round** (*BrE*), **overall** ◇ *He got top marks for overall academic ~.* **| business, economic, financial, sales | academic, school | environmental | athletic | team** (*esp. BrE*)
VERB + PERFORMANCE **deliver, give, produce, put in** (*esp. BrE*) ◇ *The band gave a great ~ at the festival.* ◇ *The team put in an excellent ~.* **| affect, influence | hinder, impair | boost, improve | analyse/analyze, assess, evaluate, measure | monitor, track**
PERFORMANCE + NOUN **benchmark, indicator, level, parameter, standard** ◇ *The agency has developed a set of core ~ indicators to compare schools.* **| appraisal, assessment, evaluation, measure, measurement, review | goal, target | bonus, incentive | rating, score | enhancement, improvement | enhancer | style**

PREP. **~ as** ◇ *her fine ~ as Ophelia* **| ~ from** ◇ *The movie has a great ~ from Jack Lemmon.* **| ~ on** ◇ *his flawless ~ on the piano*
PHRASES **a level of ~, a measure of ~, a standard of ~** ◇ *to maintain a high level of ~* **| the quality of a ~** ◇ *The quality of his ~ was unmatched.* **| on past ~** ◇ *Sales forecasts were based on past ~.* **| the proper ~ of your duties** (*BrE*)

3 of a machine

ADJ. **high | maximum, optimal, peak | low, poor | engine**
VERB + PERFORMANCE **affect, influence | assess, measure | boost, enhance, improve, increase | maximize, optimize | hinder, impair**
PERFORMANCE + NOUN **boost**

performer *noun*

ADJ. **key, star, top** ◇ *The star ~ of the game was Holly, who scored 26 points.* **| accomplished, consummate** (*formal*), **fine, gifted, good, great, high-class** (*BrE*), **impressive** (*esp. BrE*), **outstanding, skilled, solid, standout, stellar, talented, top-notch** (*esp. BrE*), **virtuoso, world-class** (*esp. BrE*) **| poor | experienced, seasoned, veteran** ◇ *She's a seasoned concert ~.* **| legendary, well-known | proven | versatile | charismatic | live | solo | featured, guest | amateur, professional | circus, drag, jazz, musical, stage, street, television** (*esp. BrE*), **vaudeville** ◇ *The president was a polished television ~.*

perfume *noun*

1 liquid with a sweet smell that you put on your body

ADJ. **expensive | cheap | strong | subtle | sweet**
…OF PERFUME **bottle**
VERB + PERFUME **use, wear | spray** ◇ *She sprayed some ~ on her wrist.* ◇ *The letter had been sprayed with ~.* **| smell**
PERFUME + NOUN **bottle | oil | counter** ◇ *She works on the ~ counter.* **| company, industry**
PHRASES **a waft of ~, a whiff of ~** ◇ *He caught a faint whiff of her expensive ~.*

2 pleasant smell

ADJ. **sweet | heady, strong**
VERB + PERFUME **smell** ◇ *You could smell the ~ of the lilies.*
PERFUME + VERB **fill sth** ◇ *The ~ of the roses filled the room.*

peril *noun*

1 great danger

ADJ. **deadly, dire, grave, great, mortal, serious | imminent | financial**
VERB + PERIL **be in | put sth in**
PREP. **~ of** ◇ *All aboard were in grave ~ of drowning.*
PHRASES **at your ~** ◇ *Ignore these warnings at your ~.*

2 sth dangerous

ADJ. **great** ◇ *the great ~s facing the environment* **| immediate** (*AmE*) **| potential**
VERB + PERIL **face** ◇ *We face the immediate ~ of being bought out by another company.* **| pose** ◇ *the ~s posed by global warming* **| highlight** (*esp. BrE*), **illustrate** ◇ *a campaign illustrating the ~s of drug abuse* **| avoid**
PERIL + VERB **face sth**

perimeter *noun*

ADJ. **inner, outer | northern, southern, etc. | entire | defensive, security | airport, base**
VERB + PERIMETER **establish, form, mark** ◇ *The river marks the eastern ~ of our land.* **| defend, guard, secure | patrol, walk | breach** ◇ *The gunman did not breach the security ~ around the White House.*
PERIMETER + NOUN **fence, fencing, wall | security | road | defender, player, shooter** (all in basketball)
PREP. **along the ~** ◇ *I lugged my suitcase along the ~ of the square.* **| around the ~, round the ~** (*esp. BrE*) ◇ *We walked around the ~ of the prison.* **| inside the ~, outside the ~** ◇

They demonstrated just outside the ~ of the embassy. | **on the**
~ ◇ *Many of the offices are located on the ~ of the site.*

period noun

1 length of time

ADJ. **extended, lengthy, long, prolonged, sustained** | **brief,**
limited, short ◇ *The offer is only available for a limited ~.* |
six-month, two-year, etc. | **entire, full** ◇ *You have been paid*
for the full ~ of your employment with us. | **fixed, set,**
specified ◇ *The medication is prescribed for a fixed ~ of time.*
| **indefinite** | **early, late** ◇ *the late Victorian ~* | **initial** |
busy | **happy** ◇ *a happy ~ in her life* | **dark, difficult, lean**
(*esp. BrE*) ◇ *a dark ~ in the country's history* | **critical,**
crucial ◇ *a critical ~ in the development of the project* |
interim, intervening | **transition, transitional** | **off-peak,**
peak | **Christmas** (*esp. BrE*), **festive** (*esp. BrE*), **holiday** | **Cold**
War, medieval, Tudor, etc. | **inter-war, post-war** |
accounting | **cooling-off, grace** ◇ *The customer has the*
right to cancel the contract during the seven-day cooling-off
~. | **consultation** (*esp. BrE*) | **formative** ◇ *The most*
formative ~ of life is childhood. | **gestation, incubation** |
rest | **honeymoon** ◇ *The view is that the government's*
honeymoon ~ is over. | **training** | **waiting** | **trial** ◇ *You can*
use the software free for a 30-day trial ~. | **time**
VERB + PERIOD **cover, span** ◇ *the ~ covered by the book* ◇ *The*
film spans a ~ of 40 years of Castro's rule. | **begin, enter** ◇
Eastern Europe entered a ~ of transition in the 1990s. | **end** |
endure, experience, undergo | **extend, prolong** | **shorten**
| **dominate, mark** ◇ *The ~ was marked by a succession of*
financial crises.
PERIOD + VERB **begin, commence** | **elapse, end** | **last**
PERIOD + NOUN **costume, furniture**
PREP. **after a ~** ◇ *after a long ~ of waiting* | **during the ~,**
throughout the ~ ◇ *during the intervening ~* | **for a ~** ◇ *We*
lived in Caracas for a brief ~. | **in a/the ~, within a/the ~** ◇
Sales have gone up in the last-five-year ~. | **over a/the ~** ◇
There will be a reduced bus service over the Christmas ~. ◇
Changes were monitored over a ~ of two months. | **within a/**
the ~ ◇ *We visited five different cities within a two-day ~.* | **~**
between ◇ *the ~ between his resigning and finding a new job*
| **~ from…to…** ◇ *the ~ from July 1 to December 31*
PHRASES **the beginning of a ~, the start of a ~** | **the end of a**
~ | **a ~ in history, a ~ of history** | **sb's ~ of office** ◇ *Public*
spending was cut during his ~ of office. | **a ~ of silence, a ~**
of study ◇ *Try breaking your ~ of study into 20-minute*
blocks. | **a ~ of time** ◇ *The balance must be paid within an*
agreed ~ of time. | **a ~ of change, a ~ of transition** ◇ *a ~ of*
transition from a totalitarian regime to democratic govern-
ment

2 menstruation

ADJ. **heavy, light** | **menstrual** | **monthly**
VERB + PERIOD **have** ◇ *When did you last have a ~? ◇ I have my*
~ and don't feel too great. | **start** ◇ *I was thirteen when I*
started my ~s. (*BrE*) ◇ *I was thirteen when I started my ~.*
(*AmE*) | **miss, skip** ◇ *Missing a ~ is often one of the first signs*
that a woman is pregnant.
PERIOD + VERB **start** | **stop** | **last**
PERIOD + NOUN **cramps** (*esp. AmE*), **pains** (*esp. BrE*)

permanent adj.

VERBS **be, prove, seem** | **become** | **make sth** ◇ *We decided to*
make the arrangement ~.
ADV. **almost** ◇ *They are living in an almost ~ state of fear.* |
relatively | **seemingly** | **not necessarily**

permissible adj.

VERBS **be** | **consider sth**
ADV. **perfectly** ◇ *This is perfectly ~ under the new regulations.*
| **constitutionally** (*esp. AmE*), **legally, morally**

permission noun

ADJ. **full** | **special** | **explicit, express** ◇ *Staff may not leave*
early without the express ~ of the director. | **tacit** | **formal,**
government, legal, official | **parental** | **written** |
necessary ◇ *They chopped the trees down without having*
been granted the necessary ~. | **specific** | **prior** ◇ *He was not*
allowed to leave the city without the prior ~ of the
authorities. | **proper** | **outline** (*BrE*) ◇ *The council granted*
outline ~ for the construction of a house on the land. |
planning ◇ *You will need to obtain planning ~ if you want to*
extend your house.
VERB + PERMISSION **have** | **gain, get, obtain, receive, secure,**
win (*esp. BrE*) | **give (sb), grant (sb)** | **deny sb, refuse sb** |
revoke, withdraw (*both esp. BrE*) | **need, require** | **apply**
for (*esp. BrE*), **ask, ask for, request, seek** | **await**
PREP. **with sb's ~, without sb's ~** ◇ *The information was*
published with the full ~ of Amnesty International. | **~ for** ◇
She was given ~ for a three-month visit to Asia. ◇ *I did not*
give ~ for anyone to print it or copy it. ◇ *The council refused*
planning ~ for the erection of a block of flats. (*BrE*) | **~ to** ◇ *~*
to park
PHRASES **by ~ of sb** ◇ *The illustrations are reproduced by kind*
~ of the library.

permissive adj.

VERBS **be** | **become**
ADV. **extremely, fairly, very, etc.** | **sexually** ◇ *a society that is*
sexually ~

permit noun

ADJ. **federal, government** | **temporary** | **special** | **valid** |
necessary, proper (*esp. AmE*) | **export, import** | **emissions,**
pollution | **residence, resident's** (*both esp. BrE*) | **work** |
travel | **entry** | **visitor's** (*esp. BrE*) | **building, construction**
(*esp. AmE*), **driving, fishing** (*esp. BrE*), **operating** (*esp. AmE*),
parking
VERB + PERMIT **have, hold** | **buy** | **give (sb), grant (sb), issue** |
acquire (*esp. AmE*), **get, obtain, receive, secure** | **approve** |
deny sb | **revoke** | **renew** | **apply for, request, seek** |
need, require
PERMIT + VERB **expire** | **allow sth**
PERMIT + NOUN **holder** | **application** | **fee** | **scheme** (*BrE*),
system
PREP. **by ~** ◇ *Entry is by ~ only.* | **with a ~, without a ~** ◇ *You*
can't film here without a ~. | **~ for** ◇ *They applied for a ~ for*
a street demonstration.

permit verb

ADV. **legally** | **generally, normally, usually** ◇ *Development is*
not normally permitted in conservation areas. | **explicitly,**
expressly | **specifically** | **knowingly** (*esp. BrE*) | **thereby**
VERB + PERMIT **refuse to** | **be designed to** ◇ *The bill was*
designed to ~ new fathers to take time off work.

perpendicular adj.

1 pointing straight up

VERBS **be**
ADV. **almost, nearly** ◇ *an almost ~ staircase*

2 at an angle of 90° to sth

VERBS **be**
ADV. **approximately** | **almost** | **mutually** ◇ *two mutually ~*
directions
PREP. **to** ◇ *The axis of the moon will now be exactly ~ to that of*
the earth.

perpetuate verb

ADV. **just, merely, only, simply** ◇ *Giving these events a lot of*
media coverage merely ~s the problem. | **thereby**
VERB + PERPETUATE **help (to)** | **serve to, tend to** ◇ *Schools tend*
to ~ the myth that boys are better at science than girls. |
seek to

perplexed adj.

VERBS **be, feel, look, sound**
ADV. **extremely, fairly, very, etc.** | **completely, deeply,**
genuinely, utterly | **a little, slightly, etc.** ◇ *Gary looked a*
little ~.

persecution noun

ADJ. **systematic** | **brutal, severe** | **political, racial, religious**
VERB + PERSECUTION **be subject to, be subjected to, endure, experience, face, suffer, suffer from** ◊ *Some students returning to the country may face political ~.* | **avoid, escape from, flee from** | **fear** ◊ *He feared ~ by the military.* | **end**
PERSECUTION + NOUN **complex** ◊ *She started to have a ~ complex when she couldn't get a job.*
PHRASES **delusions of ~, feelings of ~** | **(a) fear of ~** | **a victim of ~**

perseverance noun

ADJ. **great, incredible, sheer** | **dogged, untiring**
VERB + PERSEVERANCE **have** ◊ *Does she have the ~ to finish the work?* | **demonstrate, display, show** ◊ *He showed great ~ by staying in the job.* | **require, take** ◊ *It may take some ~ to find the right people.* | **reward** ◊ *Her ~ was ultimately rewarded.*
PERSEVERANCE + VERB **pay off**
PREP. **with ~** ◊ *Anyone can learn Japanese with ~.* | **~ in the face of** ◊ *his courage and ~ in the face of serious illness* | **~ with** ◊ *His ~ with the new technique paid off.*

persist verb

1 continue doing sth

ADV. **doggedly, stubbornly**
PREP. **in** ◊ *If you ~ in upsetting her, I will have to punish you.* | **with** ◊ *The detective stubbornly ~ed with his questions.*

2 continue to exist

ADV. **still, to this day** ◊ *a belief that ~s to this day* | **indefinitely**
VERB + PERSIST **be likely to** | **tend to** | **be allowed to** ◊ *This situation cannot be allowed to ~.* | **continue to** ◊ *Drought conditions continue to ~ from Maine to Georgia.*
PREP. **beyond** ◊ *The condition almost always ~s beyond childhood.* | **despite, in spite of** ◊ *The trade network ~ed in spite of the political chaos.* | **during** ◊ *the problems that ~ed during the three-day conference* | **for** ◊ *If symptoms ~ for more than a few days, see a doctor.* | **into** ◊ *These practices ~ed into the Middle Ages.* | **through, throughout** ◊ *The depression ~ed through much of the 1930s.* | **until** ◊ *The snows ~ed until the second month of the new year.*

persistence noun

ADJ. **dogged, stubborn** | **great, remarkable, sheer**
VERB + PERSISTENCE **demonstrate, show** | **require, take** ◊ *a challenge that requires ~ and skill*
PERSISTENCE + VERB **be rewarded, pay off** ◊ *My ~ in demanding my rights finally paid off.*
PREP. **by ~** ◊ *By sheer ~, I eventually got her to change her mind.* | **through ~** ◊ *He achieved success through dogged ~.*

persistent adj.

VERBS **be**
ADV. **extremely, incredibly, really, remarkably, very** ◊ *The weeds were very ~.* | **stubbornly** ◊ *a stubbornly ~ unemployment problem* | **quite, rather** ◊ *Some infections can be quite ~.*

person noun → See also PEOPLE

ADJ. **young** | **elderly, old** | **married, single** | **gay** ◊ *an openly gay ~ working in business* | **black, white** | **poor, rich** | **decent, good, lovely** (*esp. BrE*), **nice** | **caring, gentle, kind, warm** | **bad, evil, wicked** | **happy, outgoing** | **rational, reasonable, sensible** ◊ *Any reasonable ~ can see that it is not fair.* | **intelligent, smart** (*esp. AmE*) | **talented** | **average, normal, ordinary** | **private** ◊ *She is a warm but very private ~.* | **blind, deaf, disabled** | **ill** (*esp. BrE*), **sick** ◊ *a terminally ill ~* (*BrE, AmE*) ◊ *a mentally ill ~* (*BrE, AmE*) | **sane** ◊ *Robbie did what any other sane ~ would do in this situation.* | **missing** ◊ *to file a missing ~s report* | **displaced** | **homeless** | **unemployed** | **dead** | **famous** | **important** | **innocent** ◊ *the imprisonment of an innocent ~* | **right, wrong** ◊ *She's the right ~ for the job.* ◊ *The police now realize*

that they had the wrong ~. | **religious** ◊ *I'm not a religious ~.* | **business**
PREP. **as a ~** ◊ *What's she like as a ~?* | **in ~** ◊ *She appeared in ~ to collect her prize.* | **~ from** ◊ *a ~ from the same family as Gina* ◊ *a ~ from Vietnam* | **in the ~ of** ◊ *Help arrived in the ~ of my brother.*
PHRASES **the ~ concerned** ◊ *The disciplinary panel will notify the ~ concerned of its findings.* | **the ~ in charge** ◊ *Can I speak to the ~ in charge, please?* | **the ~ responsible** ◊ *Police think they have found the ~ responsible for the muggings.* | **from ~ to ~** ◊ *The virus is spread from ~ to ~.*

personal adj.

VERBS **be, feel, seem, sound** ◊ *It felt too ~ to tell you.* | **become, get** ◊ *Am I getting too ~ with them?* | **make sth** ◊ *Then he made it rather ~ and pulled my family into it.*
ADV. **deeply, intensely** | **purely, strictly** ◊ *The views expressed here are purely ~.* ◊ *This is a strictly ~ decision.* | **uniquely** ◊ *The movie is a uniquely ~ exploration of the effects of war.* | **extremely, highly, very** ◊ *highly ~ information* | **rather**

personality noun

1 character

ADJ. **bright, bubbly, extrovert** (*esp. BrE*), **jovial, lively, outgoing, sparkling, vibrant, vivacious** | **attractive, charming, lovely** (*esp. BrE*), **nice, pleasant, warm** | **charismatic, colourful/colorful, larger-than-life** | **engaging, magnetic, winning** | **easy-going** ◊ *her amiable nature and easy-going ~* | **dominant, dynamic, forceful, formidable, powerful, strong** | **authoritarian** | **vulnerable** (*BrE*), **weak** ◊ *a troubled man who had a vulnerable ~* | **distinct, distinctive, individual, unique** ◊ *She manages to project a very distinct ~.* | **quirky** | **complex** | **volatile** | **creative** | **dual, multiple, split** ◊ *He developed a split ~ after the crash.* | **addictive** ◊ *Addictive personalities can run in families.* | **antisocial**
VERB + PERSONALITY **be, have** ◊ *Barbara is/has a very forceful ~.* | **develop** | **shape** ◊ *The events of her early life shaped her ~.* | **express, reflect** ◊ *His choice of clothes reflects his ~.* | **bring out** ◊ *She has brought out her husband's ~ since their relationship began.* | **add** (*esp. AmE*) ◊ *Interesting displays can add ~ to your store window.* | **lack** ◊ *He had no screen presence and lacked any real ~.* | **fit, match, suit** ◊ *The job didn't really suit my ~.*
PERSONALITY + NOUN **type** | **characteristic, quirk** (*esp. AmE*), **trait** | **disorder, flaw, problem** | **development** | **change** | **assessment** (*esp. AmE*), **profile, test** ◊ *From your ~ profile, it seems you're interested in politics.* ◊ *All candidates have to undergo a ~ test.* | **clash, conflict** ◊ *There was a ~ clash between two members of the committee.* ◊ *~ conflicts between a faculty member and a student*
PHRASES **an aspect of sb's ~, a side of sb's ~** ◊ *For the first time she was seeing the more unpleasant aspects of her husband's ~.* | **a clash of personalities** | **the force of sb's ~, the power of sb's ~, the strength of sb's ~** ◊ *He has achieved success by the sheer strength of his ~.* | **impose your ~ on sth, stamp your ~ on sth** ◊ *She stamped her ~ on the company.*

2 famous person

ADJ. **famous, great, important, leading, popular, prominent, top, well-known** | **political, sports** | **media, radio, television, TV** | **on-air** (*AmE*) ◊ *a broadcast network with well-known on-air personalities*
PERSONALITY + NOUN **cult** ◊ *the ~ cult surrounding Stalin*

personnel noun

1 staff

ADJ. **experienced, professional, qualified, skilled, trained** | **key** | **non-essential** ◊ *The area was evacuated of all non-essential ~.* | **senior** | **management** | **authorized** ◊ *Only authorized ~ have access to the computer system.* | **company** | **armed-forces, army, enlisted** (*AmE*), **intelligence, military, naval, navy, security, service** ◊ *an employment agency* for ex-service ~ | **uniformed** ◊ *the functions accomplished by uniformed* ~ | **law enforcement** (*esp. AmE*), **police** | **rescue** (*esp. AmE*), **support** ◊ *firefighters and other rescue* ~ ◊ *groups of support* ~, *engineers and medics* | **civilian** | **embassy, government** | **emergency, emergency-service, health, health-care, hospital** (*esp. AmE*), **medical** ◊ *police, fire and emergency medical* ~ ◊ *the training of key health* ~ | **airline, airport** | **school** (*AmE*) | **agency, office** | **administrative, maintenance, technical**

2 department of a company

VERB + PERSONNEL **be in, work in** ◊ *He's is in* ~, *isn't he?*
PERSONNEL + NOUN **department, office** | **director, manager, officer** | **management** | **files, records** | **decision** | **policy**

perspective noun

1 in art

ADJ. **distorted** | **horizontal, vertical**
PREP. **in** ~, **out of** ~ ◊ *That tree is out of* ~.
PHRASES **the laws of** ~

2 attitude to sth

ADJ. **alternative, different, fresh, new** | **broader, wider** | **narrow** ◊ *his desire to broaden his narrow* ~ | **proper, true** ◊ *We can now see things in their true* ~. | **balanced, objective** ◊ *The author brings a balanced* ~ *to these complex issues.* | **personal** ◊ *We'll be looking at fatherhood issues from a personal* ~. | **unique** ◊ *This latest study explores stress from a unique* ~. | **multiple** ◊ *stories told from multiple* ~*s* | **female, male** | **cultural, historical, political, social, theoretical, etc.** | **global** ◊ *multicultural education based on a global* ~
VERB + PERSPECTIVE **have** ◊ *He has a different* ~ *on what art can be.* | **get sth in/into, keep sth in, place sth in/into, put sth in/into, see sth in** ◊ *Let's get this into* ~. ◊ *I just need to keep things in* ~. ◊ *Her death put everything else into* ~. | **gain, get, put** ◊ *When you reach middle age you get a different* ~ *on life.* ◊ *This website puts a completely different* ~ *on world news.* | **add, bring, give, offer, present, provide** ◊ *women who bring a feminist* ~ *to their works* ◊ *This lively book presents a refreshing new* ~ *on a crucial period in our history.* | **keep, maintain** | **adopt, take** ◊ *The book adopts a historical* ~. | **lose** | **change, shift** | **broaden**
PREP. **from the** ~ **of** ◊ *We should view this from the* ~ *of the people involved.* | **in** ~ ◊ *This will require a shift in* ~. | **into** ~ | ~ **in** ◊ *a feminist* ~ *in philosophy* | ~ **on** ◊ *It's easy to lose* ~ *on things when you are under stress.*
PHRASES **a sense of** ~

perspiration noun

... OF PERSPIRATION **bead, drop** ◊ *Great beads of* ~ *trickled down his forehead.*
VERB + PERSPIRATION **wipe** ◊ *He wiped the* ~ *from his brow.* | **absorb** | **wick away** (*esp. AmE*) | **be bathed in, be drenched in, be soaked in** ◊ *My shirt was soaked in* ~. | **be damp with, be wet with, glisten with** ◊ *Her face was wet with* ~.
PERSPIRATION + VERB **drip down sth, run down sth, trickle down sth** ◊ *Perspiration ran down his face.* | **break out, form** ◊ *Perspiration broke out on my skin.* ◊ *Beads of* ~ *had formed on his forehead.* | **glisten**

perspire verb

ADV. **heavily, profusely** ◊ *He had been working hard and was perspiring profusely.* | **freely** | **excessively** | **a little, slightly, etc.**
PREP. **with** ◊ *She was perspiring a little with the heat.*

persuade verb

ADV. **successfully** | **almost** | **eventually, finally, ultimately** | **quickly** | **easily** ◊ *She was easily* ~*d to accompany us.* | **gently** ◊ *Dictators can sometimes be gently* ~*d to leave power with special deals that guarantee their safety.* | **somehow** ◊ *He somehow* ~*d the studio to let him make the movie.*
VERB + PERSUADE **attempt to, seek to, try to, work to** | **hope**

to | **be able to, be unable to, can** | **manage to** ◊ *He eventually managed to* ~ *the caretaker to let him in.* | **help (to)** | **be difficult to** | **fail to**
PREP. **into** ◊ *She was* ~*d into buying an expensive dress.* | **of** ◊ *We must* ~ *the government of the need for change.* | **out of** (*esp. BrE*) ◊ *There was no way to* ~ *him out of it.* ◊ *Why not invite Larry, if he can be* ~*d out of hibernation?*
PHRASES **an attempt to** ~ **sb, an effort to** ~ **sb** ◊ *an unsuccessful attempt to* ~ *her colleagues* | **be fully** ~**d** ◊ *I am not fully* ~*d by these arguments.* | **be reluctantly** ~**d** ◊ *I was reluctantly* ~*d to join the committee.* | **have difficulty (in) persuading sb** ◊ *They had difficulty in persuading the two sides to sit down together.*

persuasion noun

1 persuading

ADJ. **gentle** | **a little** ◊ *I think with a little* ~ *we can get her to come here.*
VERB + PERSUASION **use** ◊ *I had to use a little gentle* ~ *to get her to agree.* | **need, take** ◊ *She didn't need much* ~. | **be open to** ◊ *She is uncertain of what she wants and is open to* ~.
PHRASES **the art of** ~ ◊ *She is very charming, and skilled in the art of* ~. | **a means of** ~ ◊ *He will use every means of* ~ *to make her stay.* | **sb's powers of** ~ ◊ *I used all of my powers of* ~ *to get Jay to come back.*

2 set of beliefs

ADJ. **political, religious** | **sexual** ◊ *discrimination on the grounds of a person's sexual* ~
PHRASES **of all, different, varying, etc.** ~**s** ◊ *The meeting is open to people of all political* ~*s.* | **of ... persuasion** ◊ *He was basically of liberal* ~. | **of every** ~ ◊ *young people of every* ~

persuasive adj.

VERBS **be, prove, seem, sound** ◊ *Her arguments proved* ~ *to the court judges.* | **find sth** | **make sth** ◊ *What makes his case so* ~?
ADV. **extremely, fairly, very, etc.** | **highly** ◊ *His analysis is in many ways highly* ~. | **enough, sufficiently** ◊ *The evidence was not really* ~ *enough.* | **not entirely** ◊ *His arguments strike me as not entirely* ~.

pertinent adj.

VERBS **be, seem** | **become** | **remain**
ADV. **extremely, fairly, very, etc.** | **especially, highly, particularly** | **directly** ◊ *These examples are directly* ~ *to the question asked.*
PREP. **to** ◊ *The issues dealt with in the report are highly* ~ *to our own situation.*

pervasive adj.

VERBS **be, prove** | **become** | **remain**
ADV. **very** | **increasingly** ◊ *the increasingly* ~ *subculture in modern society*

perverse adj.

VERBS **be, seem, sound**
ADV. **extremely, fairly, very, etc.** | **deeply** ◊ *This kind of reasoning is deeply* ~. | **almost** | **a little, slightly, etc.** | **mildly, vaguely** | **deliberately, wilfully/willfully** ◊ *Had you truly forgotten or were you just being deliberately* ~?

perversity noun

ADJ. **sheer** ◊ *She's marrying him out of sheer* ~. | **wilful/willful** | **sexual** ◊ *a sordid tale of sexual* ~
PREP. **out of** ~

pessimism noun

ADJ. **deep, widespread** ◊ *the widespread* ~ *among young people today* | **undue** ◊ *He warned against the dangers of undue* ~.
VERB + PESSIMISM **express, reflect** ◊ *The article reflects the* ~ *of its author.* | **overcome**
PREP. ~ **about** ◊ *There were good grounds for* ~ *about future progress.*
PHRASES **a mood of** ~

pessimistic *adj.*

VERBS **be, feel, look, prove, seem, sound** ◇ *These figures look quite ~.* | **become, grow** | **remain**
ADV. **extremely, fairly, very, etc.** | **deeply, terribly** | **increasingly** | **overly, unduly, unnecessarily** ◇ *His predictions proved unduly ~.* | **generally**
PREP. **about** ◇ *I am deeply ~ about the future.*

pest *noun*

ADJ. **common** | **major, serious** | **destructive** | **agricultural, crop, garden, plant** | **insect** | **sex** (in newspapers) (*BrE*) ◇ *Police are looking for a sex ~ who is frightening early-morning joggers.*
VERB + PEST **control, repel** ◇ *These birds provide a useful function in controlling insect ~s.* | **eradicate, kill**
PEST + NOUN **control, controller** (*esp. BrE*), **management** ◇ *a ~ control officer* (*BrE*) ◇ *a ~ control operator* (*AmE*) | **population** | **infestation**

pesticide *noun*

ADJ. **chemical, synthetic** ◇ *the threat to human health from chemical ~s in our food* | **organic** | **agricultural** | **dangerous, harmful, hazardous, toxic** | **approved, banned**
... OF PESTICIDE **level** ◇ *It is claimed that current levels of ~ do not pose a threat to health.* | **trace** ◇ *Traces of ~ in the water were ten times above permissible levels.*
PESTICIDE + NOUN **use** | **levels** | **residues** | **exposure** ◇ *the risk of ~ exposure among farm workers* | **contamination, pollution** ◇ *tests for ~ contamination in food* | **poisoning** | **application, spray**
PHRASES **resistance to ~s** ◇ *Some weeds have developed resistance to agricultural ~s.* | **the use of ~s**

pet *noun*

ADJ. **domestic, family, house, household** | **beloved** ◇ *the loss of a beloved ~* | **abandoned, unwanted** | **lost** ◇ *if you need help locating your lost ~* | **exotic** ◇ *the booming trade in exotic ~s* | **virtual** ◇ *the latest wave of toy technology: virtual ~s*
VERB + PET **have, keep, own** | **allow** ◇ *The apartment we live in doesn't allow ~s of any kind.* | **feed** ◇ *Feed your ~ a healthy diet.*
PET + NOUN **shop** (*esp. BrE*), **store** (*esp. AmE*) | **cat, dog, rabbit, etc.** | **owner** | **sitter** ◇ *Some ~ sitters charge on a per-visit basis.* | **care** ◇ *the ~ care industry* | **trade** ◇ *the smuggling of endangered species for the ~ trade* | **food** | **dander** (*esp. AmE*), **hair** ◇ *a vacuum cleaner that can tackle ~ hair* | **allergy** ◇ *kids with ~ allergies* | **carrier** ◇ *She bundled Daisy into her ~ carrier.*

petition *noun*

1 document asking court for sth

ADJ. **court** (*esp. AmE*) | **bankruptcy, divorce, habeas corpus** (*AmE*) ◇ *She filed a habeas corpus ~ on Padilla's behalf.*
VERB + PETITION **file, submit** | **hear** ◇ *The ~ will be heard tomorrow.* | **accept, approve, grant** ◇ *Her ~ for divorce was granted.* | **deny, dismiss, oppose, reject** ◇ *The district court has opposed the ~ by the local electricity company.*
PREP. **~ for** ◇ *He can file a ~ for writ of habeas corpus.* | **~ on behalf of** ◇ *a divorce ~ on behalf of Terri Jones*

2 document signed by many people

ADJ. **protest** (*esp. BrE*) ◇ *10 000 people signed a protest ~.* | **online** | **nominating, recall** (*both AmE, politics*) ◇ *The deadline for filing nominating ~s for the primary election was Tuesday.* ◇ *Two million people signed the recall ~.*
VERB + PETITION **sign** | **draft, launch, organize, raise** (*esp. BrE*), **start, write** ◇ *We've started an online ~.* | **draw up, get up** (*esp. BrE*), **set up** (*esp. BrE*) ◇ *The players drew up a ~ and presented it to the coach.* ◇ *They've threatened to get up a ~ against the plan.* | **circulate** ◇ *The company had actively circulated ~s to get rid of the union.* | **support** | **deliver, present, send, submit** ◇ *They delivered ~s with nearly 20 000 signatures to the Senate.*
PETITION + VERB **ask sth, ask for sth, call for sth, demand sth,**

request sth, seek sth, urge sth ◇ *a ~ asking him to reconsider* | **oppose sth** ◇ *The ~ opposes the closures.* | **support sth** ◇ *The ~ supports the plan to rebuild the road.*
PREP. **~ against** ◇ *We're organizing a ~ against the proposed building plans.* | **~ by, ~ from** ◇ *a ~ by local residents* | **~ for** ◇ *Local government supports the ~ for a new hospital.* | **~ in favour/favor of** ◇ *a ~ in favour/favor of reform*

petrol *noun* (*BrE*) → See also GAS, GASOLINE

ADJ. **lead-free, ultra-low sulphur, unleaded** ◇ *The price of a litre of unleaded ~ has risen.* | **leaded, lead replacement** | **high-octane**
... OF PETROL **litre, tankful**
VERB + PETROL **fill (sth) up with, fill sth with** | **run on, take, use** ◇ *My car runs on unleaded ~.* | **run out of** ◇ *We ran out of ~ and had to walk to the nearest garage.* | **douse sb/sth in, douse sb/sth with, pour** ◇ *Thugs poured ~ over a homeless man and tried to set him alight.* | **smell** ◇ *Can you smell ~?* | **smell of** ◇ *The air smelled of ~.*
PETROL + VERB **burn, ignite**
PETROL + NOUN **engine, tank** | **car** | **gauge, pump** | **station** | **tanker** | **fumes** | **prices** | **tax** | **bomb**

pharmacy *noun*

ADJ. **community, hospital, local** | **Internet, mail-order, online** | **dispensing, retail**
PHARMACY + NOUN **business, chain** | **counter, shelf** ◇ *Research is bringing more effective new drugs to ~ shelves.*
PHRASES **available at pharmacies** (*AmE*), **available from pharmacies** (*BrE*), **available in pharmacies** (*AmE*) ◇ *The cream is available at/from/in pharmacies without a prescription.*

phase *noun*

ADJ. **early, first, initial, preliminary, primary** | **start-up** ◇ *The co-op is still in the start-up ~.* | **second, secondary, etc.** | **current, latest, new, present** | **final, last** | **intermediate, transition** | **temporary** | **critical, crucial, important** ◇ *the critical ~ of the operation* | **distinct** ◇ *The period can be divided into three distinct ~s.* | **acute, chronic** (*both medical*) ◇ *the acute ~ of the disease* | **recovery** (*medical*) | **experimental, testing** ◇ *The process is still in its testing ~.* | **planning** ◇ *during the planning ~ of an operation* | **design** ◇ *early in the project's design ~*
VERB + PHASE **begin, enter, initiate, launch, open, start** ◇ *Society has entered a technological ~ of evolution.* | **go through** ◇ *It's just a ~ he's going through.* | **reach** ◇ *as the team reaches the later ~s of product development* | **mark** ◇ *the main Catholic rituals that mark important ~s in a person's life* | **complete, pass**
PREP. **during a/the ~** ◇ *During the first ~ of expansion staff will move to the new offices.* | **in a/the ~** ◇ *In the earliest ~ of mental disorder, relatives feel confused.* | **~ in** ◇ *a new ~ in the European economy* | **~ of** ◇ *a calendar highlighting the ~s of the moon*

phenomenal *adj.*

VERBS **be, look, sound**
ADV. **absolutely, quite, simply, truly** ◇ *This plant has truly ~ healing powers.*

phenomenon *noun*

ADJ. **common, universal, widespread** | **global, worldwide** ◇ *The unfolding energy crisis is very much a global ~.* | **natural** | **well-known** | **isolated, rare, unique** | **growing** ◇ *the growing ~ of air rage* | **new, novel, recent** | **contemporary, modern** | **amazing** ◇ *amazing natural phenomena* | **fascinating, interesting** | **bizarre, curious, inexplicable, mysterious, peculiar, remarkable, strange, unusual** | **complex** | **observable** | **biological, cultural, economic, historical, linguistic, mental, physical, political, psychological, religious, social, urban** | **paranormal, psychic, supernatural** ◇ *He conducted a scientific investigation into*

paranormal phenomena. | **cult** ◊ *The movie has become a bona fide cult ~.*
VERB + PHENOMENON **investigate** ◊ *His job is to investigate supernatural phenomena.* | **examine, observe, study** ◊ *I observed a similar ~ in Bolivia.* | **explain** ◊ *How does one explain this incredible ~?* | **understand** | **become** ◊ *The movie has become a summer ~.*
PHENOMENON + VERB **arise, emerge, happen, occur** ◊ *The ~ occurs in the early stages of pregnancy.* | **exist** ◊ *She proved scientifically that such phenomena exist.*

philosopher *noun*

ADJ. **distinguished, eminent, famous, great, important, leading, prominent** ◊ *the great ~s of ancient Greece* | **ancient, classical, Enlightenment, medieval, etc.** | **contemporary, modern** | **17th-century, 18th-century, etc.** ◊ *the 17th-century Dutch ~ Spinoza* | **Eastern, Western** | **Christian, Greek, Jewish, Muslim, etc.** | **professional** | **analytic, feminist, legal, moral, political, social** ◊ *a talk by a distinguished moral ~*
PHRASES **a ~ of religion, science, etc.**

philosophical *adj.*

1 of philosophy
VERBS **be** | **become, get, wax** ◊ *The debate was getting too ~ for me.* ◊ *I could wax ~ on all the injustices of life.*
ADV. **purely** ◊ *a purely ~ argument* | **deeply** ◊ *Roth's story is deeply ~.* | **rather**

2 calm and accepting
VERBS **be** ◊ *Try to be ~ about it.* | **remain**
ADV. **very** | **quite**
PREP. **about** ◊ *Dad's being quite ~ about the whole thing.*

philosophy *noun*

1 study of ideas about the meaning of life
ADJ. **ancient, classical, Enlightenment, medieval** | **contemporary, modern** | **Buddhist, Chinese, Christian, Greek, Hindu, Islamic, etc.** | **Eastern, Western** | **judicial, moral, natural** (*historical*) | **political, religious, social, etc.** ◊ *the attraction of Marxism as a social ~* | **analytic, existential, feminist, postmodern, etc.**
PHRASES **the ~ of history, religion, science, etc.**
→ Note at SUBJECT (for verbs and nouns)

2 particular system of beliefs
ADJ. **competing, differing** | **governing, guiding, prevailing** ◊ *humanism—the prevailing ~ today in the Western world* | **basic, core, general, underlying** | **homespun** (*esp. BrE*) | **simple** ◊ *the homespun ~ that kept her going during this difficult period* | **personal** | **corporate, conservative, liberal** | **design, economic, educational, management, market, political, religious, social** ◊ *a furniture-maker's design ~*
VERB + PHILOSOPHY **develop, formulate** ◊ *Over the years he has developed his own personal ~.* | **articulate** | **adopt, embrace, espouse, follow** | **share** ◊ *We share the same guiding ~.* | **reflect** ◊ *Does this in any way reflect your own ~?* | **reject** | **base sth on** ◊ *These ideas are based on his political ~.*
PHILOSOPHY + VERB **guide sth, influence sth, inform sth, underlie sth, underpin sth** ◊ *the ~ underlying the education system*
PREP. **~ behind** ◊ *The new measures were introduced with no explanation of the ~ behind them.*
PHRASES **a ~ of life, a ~ of mind**

phobia *noun*

ADJ. **needle, social, water, etc.** ◊ *I have a severe needle ~.*
VERB + PHOBIA **have, suffer from** | **develop** | **treat** | **overcome** ◊ *Hypnotherapy is often used to overcome ~s.*
PREP. **~ about sth, ~ of sth** ◊ *He has a ~ of snakes.*

phone *noun* → See also TELEPHONE

ADJ. **cell** (usually ***cellphone***) (*esp. AmE*), **cellular** (*esp. AmE*), **mobile** (*BrE*) | **pay** (usually ***payphone***), **public** ◊ *There's a public payphone in reception.* | **office** | **home, private** ◊ *I called his cellphone and then his home ~.* | **landline** | **car** | **cordless** | **hands-free, speaker** (usually ***speakerphone***) ◊ *I switched over to speakerphone.* | **digital** | **satellite** | **camera** | **clamshell** (*BrE*), **flip** (*AmE*) | **3G** (*BrE*), **Bluetooth™, smart** (usually ***smartphone***), **VoIP** (= Voice over Internet Protocol), **WAP, Web-enabled, wireless** (*esp. AmE*), **etc.**
VERB + PHONE **be on** ◊ *She's on the ~ at the moment.* | **use** ◊ *Can I use your ~?* | **call (sb on)** ◊ *I called his cellphone but no one answered.* ◊ *He called me on my mobile ~.* | **answer, get** (*informal*), **grab** (*informal*), **lift, pick up** ◊ *If the ~ rings, don't answer it.* ◊ *Can you get the ~?* ◊ *I grabbed the ~ and called Josie's number.* | **hang up, put down, replace** ◊ *I hung up the ~ when he started shouting at me.* | **slam down** ◊ *She slammed the ~ down in a rage.* | **cradle, hold** ◊ *She cradled the ~ between her ear and shoulder.* ◊ *a £30 fine if caught holding a ~ while driving* | **be wanted on** ◊ *Dad, you're wanted on the ~.* | **call sb to** ◊ *He was called to the ~ just as he was leaving.* | **connect** | **disconnect, unplug** | **bug, tap** ◊ *I think our ~ is being tapped.* | **wait by** ◊ *She waits by the ~ all day but he doesn't call.* | **leave off the hook, take off the hook** ◊ *I couldn't get through because you'd left the ~ off the hook.* | **switch off, switch on, turn off, turn on** ◊ *Please switch off all mobile ~s.* ◊ *I turned on my ~.*
PHONE + VERB **go** (*esp. BrE*), **go off, ring, vibrate** ◊ *My mobile ~ went off during the movie.* ◊ *Vincent's cell ~ vibrated in his pocket.* | **ring off the hook** ◊ *The ~ was ringing off the hook* (= ringing continuously). | **be busy** (*esp. AmE*), **be engaged** (*BrE*) ◊ *The ~ was busy when I called.* ◊ *His ~ is almost permanently engaged.* | **be off the hook** | **go dead** ◊ *The ~ suddenly went dead in the middle of our conversation.*
PHONE + NOUN **number** | **book, directory** | **bill** | **call, conversation, interview, message** | **user** | **operator** | **card** (usually ***phonecard***) | **company, network, service** | **bank** (*esp. AmE*) ◊ *She was working a ~ bank for the Democrats.* | **booth, box** (*BrE*) | **line** ◊ *The modem links the computer to a ~ line.* | **keypad** | **handset, receiver** ◊ *the modern business of selling ~ handsets* ◊ *I picked up the ~ receiver and pressed it to my ear.* | **cord** | **charger** ◊ *I've lost my ~ charger.* | **records** ◊ *The search of the ~ records yielded nothing.*
PREP. **by ~** ◊ *We keep in contact by ~ but we rarely see each other.* | **on the ~** ◊ *We spoke on the ~ the other day.* | **over the ~** ◊ *I haven't seen her but we spoke over the ~.*

photo *noun* → See also PHOTOGRAPH

ADJ. **exclusive** ◊ *The magazine has exclusive ~s of the wedding.* | **autographed** (*esp. AmE*), **signed** ◊ *His most treasured possession is an autographed ~ of his basketball hero.* | **yearbook** (*AmE*) | **nude, pornographic, topless**
VERB + PHOTO **snap** (*esp. AmE*)
PHOTO + NOUN **call** (*esp. BrE*), **session, shoot** | **op** (*informal, esp. AmE*), **opportunity** ◊ *The press followed the President around the hospital, waiting for a ~ opportunity.* | **editor** | **booth** ◊ *We found a ~ booth on the station.* | **agency, shop** | **essay** (*esp. AmE*), **spread, story** ◊ *Her wedding got a big ~ spread in the magazine.* | **caption** | **gallery, studio** | **exhibit** (*AmE*), **exhibition** | **archive, collection** | **ID, identification** ◊ *the name on the ~ ID* | **finish** ◊ *The race ended in a ~ finish.*

photocopy *noun*

ADJ. **black-and-white, colour/color**
VERB + PHOTOCOPY **do** (*informal*), **make, take** (*BrE*) ◊ *Could you make a ~ of this letter for me, please?*

photograph (*also* photo) *noun*

ADJ. **old, recent** | **early, vintage** | **black-and-white, colour/color, sepia** ◊ *We looked through her old black-and-white ~s.* | **blurred, blurry, fuzzy, grainy, out-of-focus** ◊ *a fuzzy black-and-white ~* ◊ *The newspaper published a grainy ~ of her.* ◊ *This ~ is out of focus.* | **faded** | **clear, sharp** ◊ *The ~s were clear and sharp.* | **still** | **action** ◊ *The book is illustrated with 96 action ~s.* | **beautiful, excellent, good, great, lovely, stunning, superb, wonderful** | **good-quality, high-quality, high-resolution** | **glossy** | **framed** | **signed** |

studio | group, team (*esp. BrE*) | portrait | family | wedding | school (*esp. BrE*) (usually *school picture* in *AmE*) | cover, magazine, newspaper, press ◇ *The cover ~ of one magazine showed a dying soldier.* | publicity | documentary | archival (*AmE*), archive (*BrE*) | historic, historical, period | famous ◇ *the famous ~ of Che Guevara* | fashion | passport, passport-sized | enlarged | close-up | still ◇ *Frame the subject in the video viewfinder as you would for a still ~.* | aerial, satellite ◇ *satellite ~s of Beijing* | digital, Polaroid™ | infrared | indecent (*BrE, law*), pornographic ◇ *He admitted offences of possessing indecent ~s of children.*
VERB + PHOTOGRAPH get, shoot, take ◇ *I got some great ~s of the party.* | *Can I have my ~ taken with you?* ◇ *I spent the day taking ~s of the city.* | compose | pose for ◇ *We posed for a group ~.* | make ◇ *The sun rising over the horizon would have made a good ~.* | copy, develop, print ◇ *I can't wait till the ~s have been printed.* ◇ *I prefer to print my digital ~s.* | blow up, enlarge ◇ *A ~ of them is blown up to fill two full pages.* ◇ *editing software that enables you to enlarge and crop ~s* | touch up ◇ *The ~ has been touched up to conceal her scar.* | crop | mount ◇ *I cropped the ~ and mounted it on some card.* | scan, scan in ◇ *I scanned in some ~s of the family to send to friends by email.* ◇ *She scans each ~ into her computer.* | download, upload ◇ *Upload your ~s to one of these sites.* | post ◇ *I'm learning how to post ~s on my blog.* | store ◇ *the ~s stored on the memory card* | publish, release ◇ *The next day they published ~s of the kidnappers.* ◇ *a couple of ~s released by news agencies* | feature ◇ *The first issue featured a ~ of Martha Graham on the cover.*
PHOTOGRAPH + VERB appear ◇ *Her ~ appeared in all the papers.* | depict sth, document sth, illustrate sth, reveal sth, show sth | capture sth ◇ *The ~ manages to capture the excitement of the occasion.*
PHOTOGRAPH + NOUN album | frame
PREP. in a/the ~ ◇ *The wing is assembled as shown in the ~ below.* ◇ *Tell me who everyone is in the ~.* | ~ of ◇ *An aerial ~ of the field shows clearly where the buildings were.* ◇ *a ~ of my son Edmund*
→ Note at ART

photographer *noun*

ADJ. accomplished, award-winning, famed, famous, leading, renowned, top, well-known | brilliant, experienced, good, great, master, successful, talented, veteran | keen | amateur | commercial, freelance, professional, staff (*esp. AmE*) ◇ *a staff ~ at the 'New York Times'* | official | newspaper, press | police | celebrity, combat (*esp. AmE*), documentary, fashion, fine-art, landscape, nature, news, portrait, sports, war, wedding, wildlife, etc.
VERB + PHOTOGRAPHER pose for | hire ◇ *They had hired another ~ for the wedding.*
PHOTOGRAPHER + VERB shoot sth, take pictures, take shots ◇ *The ~ shot the usual roll of pictures.* | snap sb/sth, snap away at sb/sth ◇ *She didn't think much of the ~s snapping away at her.* | capture sb/sth ◇ *Photographer Darren Kidd captured the unique atmosphere of the event.*
PHRASES a photographer's gallery, a photographer's studio
→ Note at JOB

photography *noun*

ADJ. black-and-white, colour/color | digital | flash | infrared | aerial, satellite | underwater | close-up | still | trick | time-lapse ◇ *the shifting clouds caught in time-lapse ~* | amateur, professional | documentary, news | commercial | stock (*esp. AmE*) ◇ *a commercial stock ~ archive* | contemporary | fine-art ◇ *an exceptional online source for fine-art ~* | fashion, landscape, nature, portrait, sports, street, war, wedding, wildlife, etc.
PHOTOGRAPHY + NOUN collection, exhibit (*AmE*), exhibition | gallery, studio | book, magazine | competition | editor

phrase *noun*

ADJ. colloquial, idiomatic | key ◇ *'Start slowly' is the key ~ for the first-time marathon runner.* | common, familiar, famous, popular | catch-all, empty, hackneyed, meaningless, stock ◇ *He just comes out with the same old stock ~s.* | apt, catchy (*informal*), colourful/colorful, descriptive, memorable, telling, well-turned | catch (usually *catchphrase*), signature (*AmE*) ◇ *the show's best known catchphrase* | buzz ◇ *A current popular buzz ~ is 'Think outside the box'.* | code (*esp. AmE*) ◇ *'Law and order' was most often a code ~ for repressive measures.* | musical | adjectival, adverbial, noun, prepositional, verb
VERB + PHRASE employ, turn, use ◇ *She can certainly turn a ~.* | coin ◇ *Who coined the ~ 'desktop publishing'?* | borrow | utter | quote, repeat | trademark ◇ *In 1998, he trademarked the ~ 'Freedom of Expression'.*
PHRASE + NOUN book ◇ *I bought a Spanish ~ book.*
PREP. in a/the ~ ◇ *She was, in her own memorable ~, 'a woman without a past'.*
PHRASES a choice of ~ ◇ *Her unfortunate choice of ~ offended most of the audience.* | a turn of ~ ◇ *He is meticulous in his choice of words and turns of ~.*

phrase *verb*

ADV. carefully ◇ *The statement was very carefully ~d.* | differently ◇ *I should have ~d my question differently.* | beautifully ◇ *The concerto's slow movement was beautifully ~d.*

physical *noun* (*esp. AmE*) → See also MEDICAL

ADJ. complete | annual, routine ◇ *Pilots undergo routine ~s.*
VERB + PHYSICAL have, undergo | fail, pass ◇ *He was accepted onto the course after passing the ~.*

physical *adj.*

VERBS be ◇ *The problem is purely ~, not mental.* | become, get, turn ◇ *Mikey and Jacob's fight had started to get ~.*
ADV. purely ◇ *Our relationship was purely ~.* | almost ◇ *The shock of the darkness was almost ~.*

physical therapist, physical therapy

(*AmE*) → See PHYSIOTHERAPIST, PHYSIOTHERAPY

physician *noun* (*formal, esp. AmE*)

ADJ. family (*AmE*), general, hospital (*esp. BrE*), occupational (*BrE*), primary-care ◇ *Dr Dennett is a practicing family ~ in Atlanta.* | attending, practising/practicing, prescribing, referring, treating | experienced, licensed (*AmE*), qualified | senior | consultant (*BrE*) | emergency | personal, private, resident, royal (*esp. BrE*) ◇ *He became the President's personal ~.* | Ayurvedic, homeopathic, naturopathic, etc. | eminent (*BrE*)
PREP. ~ to ◇ *He was ~ to George Washington.*
→ Note at DOCTOR (for verbs)

physicist *noun*

ADJ. brilliant, distinguished, eminent, famous, great, leading, prominent | classical, modern | experimental, theoretical | atomic, mathematical, medical, nuclear, particle, quantum ◇ *Niels Bohr, the leading quantum ~ of his time*
→ Note at JOB

physics *noun*

ADJ. classical, Newtonian | modern ◇ *Einstein restructured modern ~.* | applied, experimental, theoretical | fundamental ◇ *the frontiers of fundamental ~* | atomic, mathematical, medical, nuclear, particle, quantum, statistical | college, undergraduate, university ◇ *the undergraduate ~ curriculum* ◇ *university ~ departments* | high-school (*in the US*), school
PHRASES the laws of ~
→ Note at SUBJECT (for verbs and nouns)

physiotherapist (*BrE*) (*AmE* physical therapist)
noun

ADJ. licensed (*AmE*), qualified (*BrE*), trained
→ Note at DOCTOR (for verbs)

physiotherapy (*BrE*) (*AmE* physical therapy) *noun*

ADJ. **intensive** | **regular**
VERB + PHYSIOTHERAPY/PHYSICAL THERAPY **provide** | **have, receive, undergo** ◇ *I'm undergoing regular ~ for a back problem.*
PHYSIOTHERAPY/PHYSICAL-THERAPY + NOUN **clinic, department** | **appointment, session** | **treatment** | **equipment** | **student**

physique *noun*

ADJ. **good, ideal, impressive, magnificent** | **athletic, muscular, powerful, strong** | **lean, slender**
PREP. **~ for** ◇ *She doesn't have the ~ for a dancer.*

piano *noun*

ADJ. **baby grand, concert grand, grand, upright** | **acoustic, digital, electric, electronic** | **toy**
VERB + PIANO **tune** | **make** ◇ *a ~ made by Steinway*
PIANO + NOUN **key, lid** | **strings, wire** ◇ *a length of ~ wire* | **stool** | **tuner** | **bar** ◇ *There is a ~ bar for evening entertainment.*
PREP. **at the ~** ◇ *He was sitting at the ~, ready to play.* | **on the ~** ◇ *The piece can also be played on the ~.*
→ Special page at MUSIC

pick *noun*

VERB + PICK **have** ◇ *She had her ~ of the single men.* | **take** ◇ *Which do you want? Take your ~.*
PHRASES **get first ~, take first ~** ◇ *I got the first ~ of the prizes because I was the oldest.*

pick *verb*

1 choose sb/sth

ADV. **at random, randomly** ◇ *Names were ~ed at random out of a hat.* | **out** ◇ *He was ~ed out as the best player.*
PREP. **as** ◇ *They ~ed Jane as the captain.* | **for** ◇ *Have you been ~ed for the team?*

2 take sth from the place where it is growing

PHRASES **freshly ~ed** ◇ *freshly ~ed strawberries*

PHR V pick sth up

ADV. **carefully, gingerly** ◇ *Rather gingerly, George ~ed up the tiny bundle.* | **absently, idly** ◇ *I idly ~ed up a magazine and leafed through it.* | **gently, slowly** ◇ *She gently ~ed up a plate and examined it.* | **hurriedly** ◇ *I hurriedly ~ed up the receiver.*
VERB + PICK UP **try to** | **bend to, bend down to, stoop to, stoop down to** ◇ *She stooped down to ~ up a stone.*
PREP. **by** ◇ *He ~ed the pan up carefully by the handle.* | **from, off** ◇ *She stooped to ~ the book up off the floor.*

picket *noun*

ADJ. **mass** | **flying** (*BrE*) ◇ *Flying ~s arrived from all over the country.*
VERB + PICKET **organize** ◇ *They organized a mass ~ of the governor's palace.*
PICKET + NOUN **duty** | **line** ◇ *Abuse was hurled at workers who crossed the ~ line.* | **sign** (*esp. AmE*) ◇ *angry people with ~ signs*

picnic *noun*

ADJ. **family** | **school** | **church, Sunday-school** (*both esp. AmE*) | **company** (*esp. AmE*)
VERB + PICNIC **go for** (*esp. BrE*), **go on** (*esp. AmE*), **have** ◇ *Let's have a ~ down by the river.* | **organize, plan** | **enjoy** | **make** ◇ *Will you help me make a ~?* | **bring, take** ◇ *We took a ~ and spent the day watching the races.* | **pack**
PICNIC + NOUN **basket, bench, blanket, hamper** (*BrE*), **rug** (*BrE*), **table** | **lunch, tea** (*BrE*) | **area, ground** (*AmE*), **site** (*esp. BrE*), **spot**

picture *noun*

1 painting/drawing/photograph

ADJ. **beautiful, lovely, pretty, striking, stunning, wonderful** | **blurred, blurry, fuzzy, grainy** | **black-and-white, colour/color** | **digital** | **baby, family** | **school** (*esp. AmE*) (usually **school photograph** in *BrE*) | **holiday** (*BrE*), **vacation** (*AmE*), **wedding** | **naked, nude**
VERB + PICTURE **draw, paint** | **compose** | **colour/color** ◇ *The book has simple stories and ~s to colour/color.* | **frame, hang** | **display, exhibit** (*esp. BrE*), **show** | **pose for, sit for** | **get, snap, take** ◇ *I got some good ~s of the procession.* | **print** | **email sb, send sb** | **download, upload**
PICTURE + VERB **depict sth, show sth** | **hang**
PICTURE + NOUN **frame** | **book, postcard** | **gallery** | **hook, rail** (*both esp. BrE*) | **editor**
PREP. **in a/the ~** ◇ *I can't see you in the ~.* ◇ *The story is told in ~s.* | **~ of** ◇ *It's a ~ of the Grand Canyon.*
→ Note at ART

2 pictures on TV, in films/movies, etc.

ADJ. **moving** | **live, satellite, television**

3 description; mental image

ADJ. **compelling, dramatic, vivid** ◇ *The book gives a vivid ~ of life in modern Japan.* | **clear** | **pretty** ◇ *He didn't paint a very pretty ~ of city life.* | **complete, comprehensive, full, general, overall, total, whole** ◇ *The documentary didn't give the full ~.* | **big** ◇ *Because she's not involved, she can see the bigger ~.* | **incomplete** | **broad** ◇ *My visits enabled me to build up a broad ~ of the culture.* | **composite** ◇ *a composite ~ of life a hundred years ago* | **accurate, balanced, realistic, true** | **false, misleading** | **idealized, optimistic** (*esp. BrE*), **rosy** | **bleak, dismal, gloomy, grim** ◇ *The report paints a dismal ~ of the government's economic record.* | **distorted** | **confusing** | **detailed** | **complex, complicated** | **disturbing** | **mental** ◇ *I tried to form a mental ~ of the building being described.*
VERB + PICTURE **build, build up, construct, create, develop, establish** (*esp. BrE*), **form, gain, get, obtain, put together** ◇ *They're trying to build up a detailed ~ of the incident.* | **give (sb), paint, present, project, reveal** ◇ *The figures reveal a disturbing ~ of the state of our schools.* | **complete** | **conjure, conjure up** ◇ *The smell of the sea conjures up ~s of my youth.*
PICTURE + VERB **emerge** ◇ *What emerges is a complex ~ of family rivalry.*

4 film/movie

ADJ. **motion** (*esp. AmE*) | **action** | **great, major** (*AmE*) | **best** ◇ *the award for best ~*
PICTURE + VERB **direct, make** | **release**
VERB + PICTURE **star sb** ◇ *a major motion ~ starring Brent Everett*
PREP. **in ~s** (*AmE, old-fashioned*) ◇ *I believe her husband's in ~s (= he acts in movies or works in the industry).*

pie *noun*

ADJ. **apple, chicken, meat** (*esp. BrE*), **pumpkin** (*esp. AmE*), **etc.** | **mud** (= mud in the shape of pies, made by children)
...OF PIE **piece, slice**
VERB + PIE **bake, cook, make**
PIE + NOUN **filling** | **dish** (*esp. BrE*), **pan** (*AmE*), **plate** (*AmE*)
PREP. **in a/the ~** ◇ *What's the filling in these ~s?*
→ Special page at FOOD

piece *noun*

1 separate amount; parts of sth

ADJ. **big, huge, large, long** | **little, short, small, tiny** ◇ *The plate smashed into little ~s on the stone floor.* | **bite-size, bite-sized** ◇ *The book breaks the information into bite-sized ~s.* (*figurative*) | **equal** | **missing** | **odd** ◇ *She makes her sculptures out of odd ~s of scrap metal.* | **jigsaw** (*BrE*), **puzzle**
VERB + PIECE **assemble, glue (back) together, put (back) together** | **scatter**
PREP. **in ~s** ◇ *The vase was now in ~s on the kitchen floor.* | **~ of** ◇ *a ~ of bread* ◇ *A few ~s of the puzzle were missing.*
PHRASES **bits and ~s** ◇ *The album is made up of bits and ~s*

from previous albums. | **break into** ~s, **smash into** ~s ◇ *The cake just broke into* ~s *when I cut it.* | **come to** ~s ◇ *This chair comes to* ~s. | **fall to** ~s ◇ *My old dictionary is falling to* ~s. | **~ by** ~ ◇ *We'll need to take the engine apart,* ~ *by* ~. | **blow sth to** ~s, **shoot sth to** ~s, **smash sth to** ~s | **take sth to** ~s (*esp. BrE*) ◇ *I had to take the car to* ~s *in order to repair it.* | **tear sth into** ~s, **tear sth to** ~s ◇ *She tore the letter into tiny* ~s.

2 of art, music, writing, etc.

ADJ. **amazing, beautiful, brilliant, excellent, fine, good, impressive, lovely, magnificent, marvellous/marvelous, remarkable, superb, wonderful** ◇ *The best* ~s *include three paintings by El Greco.* | **effective, powerful** ◇ *This is an effective* ~ *of writing.* | **atmospheric, dramatic** | **interesting** | **favourite/favorite** | **important** | **ambitious** | **original** ~ *an original* ~ *written specifically for the producer* | **short** ◇ *a short* ~ *by Will Simons on television satire* | **finished** | **modern, period, traditional** | **choral, orchestral** | **flute, piano, etc.** | **conversation** | **museum** | **occasional** ◇ *an occasional* ~ *on the lives of ordinary people* | **op-ed** (*AmE*), **opinion** | **companion** ◇ *a companion* ~ *to the portrait of Gauguin's empty chair* | **party** (*BrE*), **set** | **puff** (*AmE*)
VERB + PIECE **compose, produce, write** ◇ *He hasn't produced a single* ~ *of writing this year.* | **commission** | **perform, play, sing** | **hear, read** | **publish** | **display, exhibit, show**
PIECE + VERB **be called sth, be entitled sth, be titled sth** (*esp. AmE*)
PREP. **~ by** ◇ *They are exhibiting two important* ~s *by Calder.* | **~ for** ◇ *a* ~ *for symphony orchestra* | **~ from** ◇ *She read a* ~ *from 'Alice in Wonderland'.*
PHRASES **a ~ of music, a ~ of sculpture, a ~ of work, a ~ of writing**
→ Note at ART

pig *noun*

1 animal

ADJ. **domestic** | **feral, wild** | **suckling**
VERB + PIG **breed** | **keep, raise** | **feed** | **fatten** ◇ *The* ~s *were being fattened for slaughter.* | **kill, slaughter**
PIG + VERB **grunt, squeal**
PIG + NOUN **farm, farmer**

2 person

ADJ. **fat** | **disgusting** | **greedy** | **male chauvinist, sexist**
PHRASES **make a ~ of yourself** ◇ *We cooked up some pasta and all made* ~s *of ourselves.*

pigeon *noun*

ADJ. **carrier, homing, racing** (*esp. BrE*) | **clay** (*BrE*) ◇ *clay* ~ *shooting*
... OF PIGEONS **flock**
PIGEON + VERB **fly** | **nest, roost** | **coo**
PIGEON + NOUN **droppings, shit** (*slang*) | **coop** (*esp. AmE*), **loft** (*esp. BrE*) | **breeder** (*esp. AmE*), **fancier** (*BrE*)

pile *noun*

ADJ. **big, enormous, great, huge, large, massive** | **little, small** | **neat, tidy** (*esp. BrE*) | **untidy** (*esp. BrE*)
VERB + PILE **place sth in/into/on, put sth in/into/on** ◇ *I put the letter in the envelope and placed it on the* ~. ◇ *I've put the books into three separate* ~s. | **dump** ◇ *He dumped a* ~ *of dirty clothes onto the floor.* | **add sth to** ◇ *Just add that application to the* ~. | **flick through** (*esp. BrE*), **flip through** (*esp. AmE*), **look through, shuffle through, sort through** ◇ *I sorted through the* ~ *of documents until I found it.*
PREP. **amid a/the ~** ◇ *The money lay amid a* ~ *of unopened letters.* | **behind a/the ~** ◇ *He was busy behind a* ~ *of papers on his desk.* | **beneath a/the ~, under a/the ~** ◇ *I pulled my diary from beneath a* ~ *of files.* | **in a/the ~** ◇ *The clothes were in a* ~ *on the floor.* | **on a/the ~** ◇ *She closed the magazine and threw it back on the* ~. | **~ of** ◇ *a* ~ *of books* ◇ *I had* ~s *of work to do.*
PHRASES **be reduced to a ~ of sth** ◇ *The house was reduced to a* ~ *of rubble.* | **the bottom of the ~, the top of the ~** ◇ *I grabbed a shirt from the top of the* ~. ◇ *At the bottom of the* ~

were the prostitutes and drug dealers. (*figurative*) | **sort sth into** ~s ◇ *I sorted the clothes into two* ~s.

pile *verb*

ADV. **neatly** | **haphazardly** | **up** ◇ *We* ~d *the boxes up neatly.*
PREP. **against** ◇ *We* ~d *sandbags against the door.* | **on, onto** ◇ *She* ~d *food onto our plates.* | **on top of** ◇ *They* ~d *stones on top of the mound.* | **with** ◇ *a table* ~d *high with magazines*
PHRASES **~d high**

pile-up *noun*

ADJ. **multi-car** (*AmE*), **multiple** (*BrE*) ◇ *a multiple/multi-car* ~ *involving five cars* | **massive** | **eight-vehicle, five-car, etc.** | **highway** (*in the US*), **motorway** (*in the UK*)
PILE-UP + NOUN **cause**
PREP. **in a/the ~** ◇ *A young man died in a four-car* ~ *last night.*

pilgrimage *noun*

ADJ. **annual** | **religious, spiritual**
VERB + PILGRIMAGE **go on, make** ◇ *She made a* ~ *to visit the place where her hero was born.*
PILGRIMAGE + NOUN **route** | **destination** (*esp. AmE*), **site**
PREP. **during a/the ~** ◇ *There was a ban on political protests during the* ~. | **on a/the ~** ◇ *She was on a* ~ *to the Holy Land when she got sick.* | **~ to** ◇ *His parents made the* ~ *to Mecca.*
PHRASES **a centre/center of ~** (*esp. BrE*), **an object of ~**, **a place of ~** ◇ *The shrine was an object of* ~.

pill *noun*

1 medicine

ADJ. **diet, sleeping, vitamin** | **prescription** (*esp. AmE*)
... OF PILLS **bottle**
VERB + PILL **pop** (*informal*), **swallow, take** | **give sb, prescribe (sb)** ◇ *The doctor prescribed her some* ~s *to help her sleep.*

2 the pill to avoid becoming pregnant

ADJ. **birth-control** (*esp. AmE*), **contraceptive** | **abortion, morning-after**
VERB + THE PILL **be on, go on, use** | **prescribe (sb), put sb on** ◇ *Her doctor put her on the* ~ *at 16.* | **take sb off** | **come off** (*esp. BrE*), **stop taking**

pillar *noun*

ADJ. **giant, huge, massive** | **tall** | **supporting** | **concrete, marble, stone**
PILLAR + VERB **stand** | **hold sth up, support sth** ◇ *The roof is supported by eight massive stone* ~s.
PREP. **behind a/the ~** ◇ *I hid behind a* ~ *when I saw my former teacher.* | **~ of** ◇ *a* ~ *of rock/smoke*

pillow *noun*

ADJ. **down, feather** | **satin, silk, velvet, etc.** (*all esp. AmE*) | **fluffy, soft** | **lumpy** | **throw** (*AmE*) (*scatter cushion* in *BrE*)
VERB + PILLOW **fluff, fluff up, plump, plump up, punch** ◇ *She plumped up the* ~s *for her daughter.* | **fall back against/on, lie back against/on, sink back against/on** ◇ *He lay back on his* ~s *and closed his eyes.* | **be propped (up) on** | **bury your face in, bury your head in** ◇ *She buried her head in the* ~ *and wept.*
PILLOW + NOUN **case, slip** (usually *pillowcase, pillowslip*) | **fight**

pilot *noun*

ADJ. **experienced, licensed, professional, qualified, trained** | **inexperienced, trainee** | **instructor** | **airplane** (*AmE*), **bomber, fighter, glider, helicopter, jet** | **aerobatic** | **private** | **airline, civilian, commercial** | **combat, military** | **air-force, navy** | **downed** | **automatic** ◇ *The aircraft was set on automatic* ~. ◇ *She worked on automatic* ~, *her hands carrying out the necessary movements.* (*figurative*)
PILOT + VERB **fly (sth)** | **crash (sth)** | **bail out, eject** ◇ *The* ~ *bailed out as the aircraft crashed into the ocean.*

PILOT + NOUN **error** ◇ *The air crash is thought to have been caused by ~ error.*
→ Note at JOB

pimple *noun* → See also SPOT

ADJ. **red**
VERB + PIMPLE **have | break out in** (*AmE*), **get | pop** (*AmE*)

pin *noun*

1 sharp-pointed object for fastening things

ADJ. **safety | bobby** (*AmE*), **hair** (usually *hairpin*) | **bent, straight** (*both AmE*) | **drawing** (*BrE*), **push** (*AmE*) (usually *pushpin*) | **tie** (usually *tiepin*) (*esp. BrE*) | **diamond, jewelled/jeweled, metal, silver, steel | clothes** (usually *clothespin*) (*AmE*) (*clothes peg* in *BrE*)
VERB + PIN **drive in, insert, stick in** ◇ *The map had a lot of little ~s stuck into it.* | **pull out, remove**

2 (*AmE*) object worn to show support

ADJ. **lapel | flag** ◇ *an American flag lapel ~*
VERB + PIN **wear**

pin *verb*

1 fasten sth with a pin

ADV. **carefully, neatly** ◇ *She carefully pinned the two pieces of cloth together.* | **firmly, securely | back, on, together, up** ◇ *Her hair was pinned back.* | *pictures pinned up on the walls*
PREP. **onto** ◇ *The poster had been pinned onto a large board.* | **to** ◇ *Maps were pinned to the walls.*
PHRASES **~ sth in place**

2 hold sb in one position

ADV. **helplessly | down** ◇ *He was pinned down on the floor.*
PREP. **against** ◇ *He pinned her against the wall.* | **behind** ◇ *His arms were pinned behind his back.* | **to** ◇ *She was pinned helplessly to the desk.*

PHR V **pin sth down**
ADV. **exactly, precisely** ◇ *The difference between the two approaches is hard to ~ down precisely.*
VERB + PIN **be difficult to, be hard to**

pinch *verb*

ADV. **gently, lightly | playfully | together** ◇ *Apply pressure to the nose by ~ing the nostrils firmly together.*
PREP. **between** ◇ *He ~ed the leaf between his thumb and forefinger.* | **on** ◇ *He ~ed me sharply on the arm.*

pineapple *noun*

ADJ. **canned, tinned** (*BrE*) | **fresh**
PINEAPPLE + NOUN **chunks, rings | juice**
→ Special page at FRUIT

pink *adj., noun*

VERBS **glow** ◇ *The western sky was glowing ~.* | **go, grow, turn** ◇ *She could feel herself going ~.*
ADJ. **fluorescent, hot | baby, delicate, dusky** (*esp. BrE*), **dusty, pastel, rosy | bubblegum, candy, coral, rose, salmon, shocking**
PREP. **with** ◇ *He was ~ with anger.*
→ Special page at COLOUR

pinnacle *noun*

VERB + PINNACLE **reach** ◇ *He had reached the ~ of his military career.*
PREP. **at the ~ of** ◇ *She is at the ~ of her profession.*

pinpoint *verb*

ADV. **exactly, precisely**
VERB + PINPOINT **can** ◇ *With this you can ~ the precise location of the sound.* | **be difficult to, be hard to**
PREP. **as** ◇ *Stress at work was ~ed as the cause of his illness.*

pint *noun*

1 measure of liquid
→ Note at MEASURE

2 (*BrE*) pint of beer

VERB + PINT **consume, drink, have | sip | down, drain, finish, knock back** (*informal*), **sink** (*informal*) ◇ *He could sink a ~ faster than anyone else I knew.* | **draw (sb), draw off, pull (sb)** ◇ *I got the barman to pull me another ~.* | **buy (sb), order, stand sb** ◇ *He stood me a ~ in the pub after work.*
PINT + NOUN **glass**

pioneer *noun*

ADJ. **early | true**
PIONEER + NOUN **spirit**
PREP. **~ in, ~ of** ◇ *the early ~s in plastic surgery* ◇ *one of the ~s of modern art*

pipe *noun*

1 hollow tube that carries gas/liquid

ADJ. **underground | gas, sewage, waste, water** ◇ *the hot and cold water ~s* | **drain** (usually *drainpipe*), **drainage, exhaust, heating, outlet, overflow, plumbing** (*esp. AmE*), **service** (*BrE*), **supply | broken, burst, cracked, frozen, leaking, leaky | blocked** (*esp. BrE*), **clogged** (*AmE*) | **concrete, copper, iron, lead, metal, plastic, PVC, steel**
... OF PIPE **length** ◇ *to join two lengths of ~ together* ◇ *Copper ~ is sold in lengths.*
VERB + PIPE **install, lay, run** ◇ *He laid the ~s under the floorboards.* | **connect | insulate, lag** (*BrE*) ◇ *Insulating your ~s will save on your heating bills.*
PIPE + VERB **lead, pass through sth, run** ◇ *The ~s lead into the river.* ◇ *The ~s will have to pass through the wall.* | **burst, freeze, leak**
PREP. **through a/the ~** | **~ for** ◇ *the ~ for the hot water* | **~ from, ~ to** ◇ *The ~ from the boiler to the bathtub.*

2 used for smoking tobacco, etc.

ADJ. **clay | peace | crack, opium, etc.**
VERB + PIPE **smoke | light | fill | draw on, puff away at, puff away on, puff on**
PIPE + NOUN **smoker | smoke | tobacco | cleaner**
PHRASES **the bowl of a ~, the stem of a ~**

pipeline *noun*

ADJ. **gas, oil, water**
VERB + PIPELINE **build, construct, lay**
PIPELINE + VERB **supply sth** ◇ *The ~ supplies Jordan with 15% of its crude oil.* | **cross sth, pass through sth, run through sth** ◇ *The ~ runs through central Mozambique.* | **link sth** ◇ *The ~ links the refinery with the port.*
PIPELINE + NOUN **route | network**
PREP. **in the ~** (= being discussed or prepared) ◇ *Important changes are already in the ~.*

pistol *noun*

ADJ. **automatic, machine, semi-automatic | double-action, single-action | 9 mm, .45-calibre/.45-caliber | compact, pocket** (*both AmE*) | **service** (*AmE*) | **loaded | silenced | air, water | duelling/dueling, starting, target** ◇ *runners waiting for the starting ~*
VERB + PISTOL **load, reload | draw, produce, pull, pull out, whip out** ◇ *He drew his ~, aimed and fired.* | **cock | aim, brandish, level, point, raise | fire | carry** ◇ *There were two of them, both carrying ~s.*
PISTOL + NOUN **shot | cartridge | grip**

pit *noun*

1 hole

ADJ. **deep, shallow | bottomless | black, dark | chalk** (*esp. BrE*), **gravel, tar** ◇ *a disused gravel ~*
VERB + PIT **dig**

2 coal mine

ADJ. **open** ◇ *They extract the mineral from open ~s.*

VERB + PIT **go down** (*BrE*) ◇ *He went down the ~ at the age of fifteen.*
PIT + NOUN **village** (*BrE*) ◇ *There's no more work in these ~ villages.* | **closure**
PREP. **in a/the ~** ◇ *Most boys in the town worked in the ~s.*

3 (*esp. AmE*) of fruit

ADJ. **apricot, peach, etc.**
VERB + PIT **remove**

pitch noun

1 (*BrE*) sports field → See also FIELD

ADJ. **all-weather, grass, synthetic | waterlogged | cricket, football, hockey, rugby**
VERB + PITCH **invade, run onto** ◇ *The ~ was invaded by angry fans.*
PITCH + NOUN **invasion** ◇ *Police could do nothing to stop the ~ invasion.*
PREP. **off the ~** ◇ *The players have just come off the ~.* ◇ *Negotiations about his transfer are continuing off the ~.* | **on a/the ~** ◇ *He was the best player on the ~ today.*

2 strength of feeling

ADJ. **fever, high** (*esp. BrE*) ◇ *Excitement rose to fever ~ the day before the game.* ◇ *Excitement rose to a fever ~ the day before the game.* (*AmE*)
VERB + PITCH **reach, rise to**
PREP. **~ of** ◇ *to reach a high ~ of excitement*

3 of a musical note

ADJ. **high, low | correct** ◇ *The instrument is not tuned to the correct ~.*
VERB + PITCH **fall in, rise in** ◇ *Her voice fell in ~ as she grew older.* | **change**
PHRASES **have perfect ~** (= be able to recognize or produce any given note)

4 talk/proposal

ADJ. **sales | good, strong**
VERB + PITCH **deliver, do** (*informal*), **give, make** ◇ *a strong ~ delivered by advertising executives* ◇ *Marcelo will be making his ~ to a small number of potential clients.*
PITCH + NOUN **meeting**
PREP. **~ for** ◇ *The executives listened open-mouthed as she seamlessly delivered a ~ for their business.* | **~ to** ◇ *Farley was about to make a ~ to a big client.* ◇ *His ~ to the business community was based on common sense.*

5 in baseball

ADJ. **wild**
VERB + PITCH **deliver, hit, make, throw | miss | call**

pitch verb

1 throw sb/move suddenly

ADV. **violently** ◇ *The explosion ~ed her violently into the air.* ◇ *The boat ~ed violently in a heavy swell.* | **forward, headlong**
PREP. **from** ◇ *There was a loud bang and he was ~ed from his seat.* | **into** ◇ *If they hit any unseen obstacle they would be ~ed headlong into the snow.* | **out of**

2 set sth at a particular level

ADV. **deliberately** ◇ *Estimates have been deliberately ~ed on the conservative side.*
PREP. **at** ◇ *The test is ~ed at a high standard.*
PHRASES **~ sth high, ~ sth low** ◇ *The price has been ~ed very high.*

3 in baseball

ADV. **effectively, well** ◇ *Perez has ~ed effectively this spring.* | **poorly**
PREP. **for** ◇ *My dream was to ~ for the Yankees.*

pitcher noun

1 (*AmE*) container for liquid with a lip → See also JUG

ADJ. **water | ceramic, glass, plastic**
VERB + PITCHER **fill**

2 person who throws the ball in baseball

ADJ. **baseball | star** ◇ *the Houston Astros' star ~* | **left-handed, right-handed | starting | opposing | relief**
VERB + PITCHER **face** ◇ *Left-handed hitters usually prefer facing right-handed ~s.* | **acquire, sign**
PITCHER + VERB **throw (sth)** ◇ *The ~ threw a hard fastball.*

pitfall noun

ADJ. **obvious | common | hidden | possible, potential** ◇ *We need to be alert to potential ~s.*
VERB + PITFALL **be fraught with, be full of, have** ◇ *Trading in a foreign country can be fraught with ~s.* | **avoid**
PITFALL + VERB **await sb** ◇ *Numerous ~s await unsuspecting investors.*
PREP. **~ for** ◇ *Buying property holds many ~s for the unwary.* | **~ in** ◇ *~s in the interpretation of statistics* | **~ of** ◇ *She avoids the ~ of sensationalism.*

pity noun

1 feeling of sadness for sb/sth

VERB + PITY **be filled with, be full of, feel, have | show | arouse, evoke, inspire** ◇ *an unfortunate man who inspires ~* | **deserve**
PREP. **out of ~** ◇ *I threw the child some money out of ~.* | **without ~** ◇ *a cruel leader without ~* | **~ for** ◇ *She was full of ~ for him.*
PHRASES **a feeling of ~, a sense of ~, have ~ on sb** ◇ *We begged him to have ~ on us.* | **an object of ~** ◇ *Deaf people do not want to be seen as objects of ~.* | **take ~ on sb** ◇ *I took ~ on him and allowed him to stay.*

2 a pity sth that makes you feel disappointed

ADJ. **great, real**
PREP. **~ about** ◇ *The place was great, but it was a ~ about the weather.*
PHRASES **a bit of a ~** (*BrE*), **such a ~** ◇ *That would be such a ~, wouldn't it?* | **what a ~** ◇ *What a ~ you didn't tell me earlier!*

pizza noun

ADJ. **takeaway** (*BrE*), **takeout** (*AmE*) **| frozen | large, medium, small**
... OF PIZZA **piece, slice** ◇ *a slice of pepperoni ~*
PIZZA + NOUN **sauce** (*AmE*), **topping | joint** (*AmE*), **parlour/parlor, place, restaurant** ◇ *Let's go to that new ~ place tonight.* | **delivery | pie** (*AmE*)
PREP. **on a/the ~** ◇ *What do you want on your ~?*

place noun

1 particular position/area

ADJ. **convenient, good, great, ideal, perfect | horrible, terrible** ◇ *It was a terrible ~ to live.* | **dangerous, safe** ◇ *Keep your purse in a safe ~.* | **appropriate, right, suitable** ◇ *I happened to be in the right ~ at the right time.* | **wrong | beautiful, nice** ◇ *It's a nice ~ you've got here.* | **interesting | busy, crowded | peaceful, quiet | strange | faraway, godforsaken, out-of-the-way, remote** ◇ *trips to faraway ~s* | **public | gathering** (*esp. AmE*), **hiding, meeting, resting**
VERB + PLACE **mark** ◇ *I forgot to mark my ~* (= in a book). | **lose** ◇ *I've lost my ~ in the script.*
PLACE + NOUN **name**
PREP. **at a/the ~, in a/the ~** ◇ *We had dinner at a crowded ~ in Chelsea.* | **in ~** ◇ *It was held in ~ with tape.* ◇ *There will be rain in ~s.* | **into ~** ◇ *She tapped the lid into ~.* | **out of ~** ◇ *Some of these files seem to be out of ~.*
PHRASES **all over the ~** (= everywhere) **| no ~, not the ~** ◇ *This is not the ~ for an argument.* | **sb's ~ of birth** ◇ *Please state your date and ~ of birth.* | **sb's ~ of business, sb's ~ of work | a ~ of learning, a ~ of worship**

2 seat/position for sb/sth

VERB + PLACE **sit (down) in, take** ◇ *We took our ~s around the table.* | **go back to, return to** ◇ *The boy returned to his ~* | **keep (sb), save (sb) | lose** ◇ *I lost my ~ in the queue.* (*BrE*) ◇ *I* lost my ~ in line. (AmE) | **give up** | **change, swap** (esp. BrE), **switch** (esp. AmE) ◊ He changed ~s with me. | **show sb to** ◊ She showed them to their ~s. | **lay** (BrE), **set** ◊ I've set four ~s for dinner.

PLACE + NOUN **card, mat, setting**

PHRASES **the ~ of honour/honor** ◊ He took the ~ of honour/honor on his hostess's right.

3 role/position/function

ADJ. **central, important, prominent** | **special** ◊ He holds a special ~ in her affections. | **proper, rightful**

VERB + PLACE **have, hold, occupy** ◊ Housing occupied a prominent ~ in the discussions. | **secure** ◊ His victory secured him a ~ in history. | **know** ◊ She knows her ~. | **forget** ◊ I'm sorry—I was forgetting my ~. | **restore sth to** ◊ He has been restored to his rightful ~ in the community. | **put sb in** ◊ At first he tried to take charge of the meeting but I soon put her in her ~.

PREP. **~ in** ◊ Dance has a central ~ in their culture. | **~ to** ◊ It's not your ~ to correct her. | **a ~ in history** ◊ a statesman who is assured a ~ in history

PHRASES **it's not sb's ~ to** ◊ It's not your ~ to correct her. | **a ~ in history** ◊ a statesman who is assured a ~ in history

4 opportunity to play for a team, etc.

VERB + PLACE **get** | **offer sb** | **lose**

PREP. **~ on** ◊ He lost his ~ on the team. (esp. AmE) ◊ He lost his ~ in the team. (esp. BrE)

5 (BrE) opportunity to study at a college, etc.

ADJ. **college, nursery, school, university**

VERB + PLACE **get, win** | **award sb, offer sb**

PREP. **~ at, ~ in** ◊ He was awarded a ~ at Leeds University. | **~ on** ◊ She got a ~ on the French course.

6 sb's position at the end of a race, competition, etc.

VERB + PLACE **finish in, get, take** ◊ She took third ~.

PLACE + VERB **go to sb** ◊ Second ~ went to the Moroccan athlete.

place verb (often be placed)

ADV. **carefully, neatly** | **randomly** ◊ The books were ~d randomly on the shelf. | **firmly** ◊ She produced a long silver whistle and ~d it firmly between her lips. | **delicately, gently, gingerly, lightly** | **centrally, prominently** ◊ The table was ~d centrally. | **directly, squarely** ◊ The blame was ~d squarely on the doctor. | **conveniently, ideally** (esp. BrE), **perfectly, uniquely** (esp. BrE), **well** ◊ The hotel is well ~d for restaurants, bars and clubs. ◊ The company is perfectly ~d to win the contract. | **highly** ◊ highly ~d officials in the government | **strategically** ◊ There are candles strategically placed—in case we have another blackout. | **side by side** ◊ The boots were neatly ~d side by side.

VERB + PLACE **attempt to, try to**

PREP. **between, in, inside, on, over, under, etc.** ◊ He ~d the letter in a drawer. ◊ an attempt to ~ the question firmly back on the political agenda

plague noun

ADJ. **bubonic** | **great** ◊ Nearly a third of the population died in the Great Plague.

...OF PLAGUE **outbreak** ◊ a decline in population following outbreaks of ~

VERB + PLAGUE **suffer** ◊ The region has just suffered a ~ of locusts. | **spread** ◊ Fleas spread ~ from animals to humans. | **be decimated by, be destroyed by**

PLAGUE + VERB **break out, start, strike (sth)** ◊ Bubonic ~ struck London in 1665. | **spread**

PREP. **~ of** ◊ The city is suffering a ~ of rats.

→ Special page at ILLNESS

plain noun

ADJ. **open** ◊ The horses galloped across the open ~s. | **rolling** ◊ miles of rolling ~, made fertile by the river | **great, vast** | **flat, flood** | **fertile** ◊ fertile ~s suitable for farming | **arid, barren** | **grassy** | **coastal**

VERB + PLAIN **cross, roam** ◊ Herds of buffalo roamed these ~s.

PREP. **across a/the ~** ◊ Cattle move freely across the grassy ~. | **in a/the ~** | **on a/the ~** ◊ Nothing grew on the ~.

plain adj.

1 simple/not decorated

VERBS **be, look, seem**

ADV. **extremely, fairly, very, etc.** ◊ The food was fairly ~, but well cooked. | **completely** ◊ The dress was completely ~, but quite stunning.

PHRASES **~ blue, white, etc.** ◊ a ~ white shirt

2 clear

VERBS **be, seem** | **become** | **make sth** ◊ They made it ~ that they were against the idea.

ADV. **fairly, very, etc.** | **absolutely, perfectly, quite** ◊ Within weeks, it became perfectly ~ that we were in the grip of a tyrant. | **increasingly** | **reasonably** (esp. BrE)

PREP. **to** ◊ It is all very ~ to me.

plaintiff noun

VERB + PLAINTIFF **represent** | **compensate**

PLAINTIFF + VERB **bring an action (against sb), sue sb** | **allege sth, argue sth, claim sth, contend sth, seek sth** ◊ The ~ claimed that the correct procedures had not been followed. | **obtain sth** (BrE) ◊ The ~s obtained an injunction in the High Court.

PREP. **against the ~** ◊ Costs were awarded against the ~. | **on behalf of the ~** ◊ the lawyer appearing on behalf of the ~

plan noun

1 for future

ADJ. **ambitious, audacious, grand, grandiose** ◊ The government has ambitious ~s for prison reform. | **future** | **long-range** (esp. AmE), **long-term, three-year, etc.** | **immediate** ◊ What are your immediate ~s? | **new** | **original** | **five-point, three-point, etc.** ◊ a three-point action ~ to improve hygiene at work | **definite, firm** (BrE) ◊ A spokeswoman confirmed there was no definite ~ to stage a concert in the park. | **comprehensive, detailed** | **good** ◊ The best ~ is for me to meet you at the airport. | **best-laid** ◊ Even the best-laid ~s can go wrong. | **brilliant, clever, cunning, devious, elaborate, fiendish, ingenious** | **evil** | **realistic, sound** ◊ We need to develop a sound business ~. | **controversial** | **master** | **backup, contingency** ◊ Do you have any contingency ~s if there is a delay? | **secret** | **action, battle, game, ground, operational, strategic** ◊ What is their game ~ for winning the election? | **Plan A, Plan B** ◊ If Plan A fails, go to Plan B. | **business, career, corporate, development** | **budget, economic, financial, spending** | **flight, travel** | **marriage, wedding** | **treatment** | **training** | **expansion, recovery, restructuring** | **disaster, emergency, escape, evacuation** | **diet, eating, meal** ◊ a six-week low-fat eating ~ | **birth** | **peace** | **war**

VERB + PLAN **have** | **come up with, create, design, develop, devise, draft, draw up, figure out** (AmE), **form, formulate, hatch, make, prepare, put together, work out** ◊ I like to make ~s well in advance. | **consider, discuss, present, propose, put forward, set out** | **file** (AmE), **submit** ◊ The airline intends to file a reorganization ~ within three months. | **adopt, agree, approve** ◊ The moves contravene the peace ~ agreed by both sides. | **finalize, put in place** | **announce, detail, launch, outline, reveal, unveil** ◊ A new ~ for reducing traffic accidents was unveiled. | **carry out, execute, implement** | **put in motion, put into action, put into effect, put into operation, set in motion** | **forge ahead with, go ahead with, move ahead with, press ahead with** | **follow, keep to, stick to** ◊ Let's stick to our original ~. | **cancel, change, rethink, review, revise** | **abandon, cancel, drop, reject, scrap, shelve** | **disrupt, set back** | **derail, foil, ruin, scupper** (BrE), **spoil, thwart** (BrE) ◊ The strike ruined my travel ~s. | **support** | **fight** (esp. BrE), **oppose** ◊ Local residents have vowed to fight ~s to build a new road. ◊ Senators signed a letter opposing the ~.

PLAN + VERB **be afoot** ◊ Plans are afoot to stage a new opera. | **be aimed at sth** ◊ The government launched a five-year ~ aimed at diversifying the economy. | **call for sth, envisage sth** (esp. BrE), **envision sth** (esp. AmE), **involve sth** ◊ The ~

calls for massive investment in the region. | **contain sth, include sth** ◇ The ~ *contains four main elements.* | **come to fruition, succeed, work** | **fail, fall through, founder, go awry, go wrong**
PREP. **~ for** ◇ ~*s for the future* ◇ *The president will now press ahead with his* ~*s for reform.* | **~ to** ◇ *Plans to build a dam have been shelved following protests.*
PHRASES **go to ~** ◇ | **a ~ of action, a ~ of attack, a ~ of campaign** ◇ *To change anything in this organization, we'll need a ~ of action.*

2 way of investing money or paying for sth
ADJ. **pension, retirement** | **savings** | **insurance** | **health, health-care** | **instalment/installment, payment**
PLAN + VERB **set up**

3 map
ADJ. **street, town** | **seating** | **floor, ground, site**
VERB + PLAN **draw** | **file** (*AmE*) ◇ *Site* ~*s were filed with the city this week.*
PLAN + VERB **show sth** ◇ *The* ~ *shows the exact location of the house.*

plan *verb*
ADV. **ahead, in advance** | **initially, originally** ◇ *The government had originally planned to launch the review in June.* | **carefully, meticulously** | **well** | **rationally** | **centrally** ◇ *centrally planned economies*
VERB + PLAN **have to, need to** ◇ *You will need to* ~ *your shopping carefully in advance.*
PREP. **for** ◇ *We must* ~ *for the future.* ◇ *A meeting has been planned for early next year.* | **on** ◇ *I had planned on staying here for two or three years.*
PHRASES **be all planned out** ◇ *He thought his life was all planned out before him.* | **have sth all planned out** ◇ *I had it all planned out.* | **go as planned** ◇ *Everything went exactly as planned.* | **~ sth (down) to the last detail** ◇ *Everything has been planned down to the last detail.*

plane *noun*
1 → See also AEROPLANE, AIRPLANE
ADJ. **light, small** | **commercial, passenger** ◇ *the first generation of passenger* ~*s, like the Boeing 707* | **cargo, transport** ◇ *a military cargo* ~ | **fighter, spy** | **jet** | **private**
VERB + PLANE **catch, get, take** ◇ *She caught the first* ~ *out.* | **miss** | **board, get on** | **get off, step off** ◇ *I fell in love with the city the moment I stepped off the* ~. | **fly, pilot** | **land** | **charter** | **build** | **hijack** | **crash** | **shoot down** ◇ *The Soviets shot down our U-2 spy* ~.
PLANE + VERB **take off** | **come down, land** | **crash, go down** | **cruise, fly** ◇ *The* ~ *was cruising at 20 000 feet.* | **carry sb/sth** ◇ *The* ~ *was carrying 350 people.*
PLANE + NOUN **crash** | **ticket**
PREP. **by** ~ ◇ *We left by* ~ *for Beijing.* | **in a/the** ~ ◇ *I've never flown in a* ~. | **on a/the** ~ ◇ *The president was never on the* ~ *at all.*

2 flat surface
ADJ. **flat, horizontal, parallel, vertical**
3 standard/level of thought/activity
ADJ. **higher** ◇ *With practice, an athlete can reach a higher* ~ *of achievement.* | **mental, spiritual**
PHRASES **be on a different** ~, **operate on a different** ~ ◇ *Like all talented musicians, he operates on a different* ~ *from most people.*

planet *noun*
ADJ. **distant** | **alien, unknown** | **inner, outer** ◇ *the outer* ~*s of our solar system* | **extrasolar** (= outside our solar system) (*technical*) ◇ *Hubble has found around 100 new extrasolar* ~*s.* | **Earth-like** ◇ *the search for Earth-like* ~*s* | **rocky** ◇ *rocky* ~*s like Venus and Mars* | **another, different** (*figurative, humorous*) ◇ *He looked like something from another* ~*!*
VERB + PLANET **be in orbit around, orbit** ◇ *The spacecraft is currently in orbit around the red* ~. | **destroy, save** ◇ *We are destroying the* ~ *with our fossil-fuel lifestyle.* ◇ *Will recycling help save the* ~*?*

PLANET + VERB **orbit** ◇ *How many* ~*s orbit the sun?*
PREP. **from a/the** ~ ◇ *creatures from an alien* ~ | **on a/the** ~ ◇ *She believes there is life on other* ~*s.*

plank *noun*
1 flat piece of wood
ADJ. **wooden** | **loose** | **rotten**
PHRASES **a ~ of wood**
2 main point in a policy
ADJ. **central, key, main, major** ◇ *The proposed law was a central* ~ *in the manifesto.*
PREP. **~ in** ◇ *Health and security will be key* ~*s in the party's election campaign.* | **~ of** ◇ *the main* ~ *of the strategy*

planning *noun*
ADJ. **careful, detailed, meticulous, thoughtful** | **poor** | **initial** ◇ *the initial* ~ *stage* | **advance, forward** ◇ *The trip calls for careful advance* ~. | **contingency** ◇ *Costs can be reduced by effective contingency* ~. | **central** ◇ *the Soviet system of central* ~ | **long-range, long-term** | **short-term** | **corporate** | **family** ◇ *They give free advice on contraception at the family* ~ *clinic.* | **city, town, urban** | **business, economic, educational, environmental, financial, military, strategic** | **retirement** | **estate** (*esp. AmE*) ◇ *an attorney who specializes in estate* ~
VERB + PLANNING **call for, need, require, take** ◇ *This can be done, but it will take careful* ~. | **do** ◇ *The industry needs to do some long-term* ~.
PLANNING + NOUN **phase, stage** ◇ *The idea is still at the* ~ *stage.* | **process** | **decisions, issues** | **services** | **meeting** | **application** (*BrE*) | **approval, consent, permission** (*all esp. BrE*) ◇ *We've applied for* ~ *permission to build an extension to the house.* | **authority** (*BrE*), **committee** (*esp. BrE*), **department** (*esp. BrE*) ◇ *The plans were considered by the local* ~ *authority.*
PREP. **in the** ~ ◇ *The festival was four years in the* ~. | **~ for** ◇ *Planning for future development is vital for the community.*

plant *noun*
1 living thing
ADJ. **delicate** | **wild** | **native** | **rare** | **garden, house, indoor, potted** | **exotic, tropical** | **medicinal** | **food** ◇ *The butterfly's sole food* ~ *is wild lupine.* | **crop** | **poisonous** | **perennial** | **aquatic, desert, marsh, water** | **bedding, climbing, flowering, ornamental** | **woody** | **herbaceous, leguminous** (*both technical*) | **strawberry, tomato, etc.**
VERB + PLANT **cultivate, grow** | **water** | **protect**
PLANT + VERB **develop, grow** | **flourish** | **die** | **absorb sth** ◇ *Plants absorb carbon in the form of carbon dioxide.* | **produce sth**
PLANT + NOUN **roots** | **growth** | **life** ◇ *Much of the local* ~ *life has been destroyed by the chemicals.* | **species, variety** | **population** | **material, matter, tissue** | **cell** | **pot** | **food** | **science**

2 factory
ADJ. **industrial** | **assembly, manufacturing, production** | **auto** (*AmE*), **car** (*esp. BrE*) | **nuclear, power** | **coal-fired** | **processing, reprocessing, sewage, treatment, water, water-treatment** ◇ *a waste reprocessing* ~ | **chemical, petrochemical**
VERB + PLANT **build** | **manage, run**
PLANT + VERB **produce sth**
PLANT + NOUN **manager**

plant *verb*
1 put plants/seeds in the ground to grow
ADV. **carefully** | **deliberately** ◇ *weeds that had not been deliberately* ~*ed*
PREP. **in** ◇ *Carefully* ~ *your cutting in the soil.* | **with** ◇ *The garden was* ~*ed with roses and other shrubs.*
PHRASES **densely** ~**ed** ◇ *The Bordeaux area is densely* ~*ed with*

vine. | **newly ~ed, recently ~ed** ◇ *recently ~ed maples* | **widely ~ed** ◇ *Zinfandel is California's most widely ~ed red grape.*

2 put sth firmly in a place/position

ADV. **firmly, squarely** ◇ *She ~ed a kiss squarely on his cheek.*
PREP. **on** ◇ *He was determined to keep both feet firmly ~ed on dry land.*

plantation *noun* for growing a crop

ADJ. **coconut, coffee, cotton, rubber, sugar, tea, etc.**
VERB + PLANTATION **work, work on** ◇ *Hundreds of slaves worked on the ~s.* | **own**
PLANTATION + NOUN **owner, worker** | **economy, system** | **house**

plaque *noun*

1 on the wall

ADJ. **commemorative, memorial** | **brass, bronze, etc.**
VERB + PLAQUE **put up** ◇ *The local historical society put up a ~ at the site of the battle.* | **unveil** | **present (sb with)** | **receive**
PLAQUE + VERB **be dedicated to sb, commemorate sb/sth, honour/honor sb** | **mark sth, record sth** ◇ *A ~ marks the place where the first printing press was built.*
PREP. **on a/the** ◇ *Some Latin words were engraved on the ~.* | **~ on** ◇ *a ~ on the wall* | **~ to** ◇ *There is a commemorative ~ to those lost at sea.*

2 substance on teeth

ADJ. **dental**
VERB + PLAQUE **remove**
PLAQUE + VERB **build up** ◇ *Gum disease happens when ~ builds up.*
PHRASES **a/the build-up of ~** ◇ *Brushing prevents a build-up of ~ and tartar on the teeth.*

plaster *noun*

1 smooth covering for a wall

ADJ. **fresh** | **cracked, crumbling, peeling**
... OF PLASTER **chunk** ◇ *Each blow of the hammer removed a great chunk of ~.*
VERB + PLASTER **apply** ◇ *Apply the ~ evenly.*
PLASTER + VERB **come off (sth), fall off (sth), peel off (sth)** ◇ *Plaster was peeling off the ceiling.*
PLASTER + NOUN **cast** ◇ *A ~ cast of Madame Fournier stood in the artist's studio.* | **wall**

2 (*BrE*) for covering a cut → See also BAND-AID™

ADJ. **sticking**
VERB + PLASTER **put on** | **peel off, take off**

3 (*BrE*) for protecting broken bones

PLASTER + NOUN **cast** ◇ *Her broken leg was put in a ~ cast.*
PREP. **in ~** ◇ *Your arm will have to be in ~ for at least six weeks.*

plastic *noun*

ADJ. **heavy-duty, reinforced, strong** | **thin** | **flexible, rigid** | **moulded/molded** | **clear, see-through, transparent** | **shiny** | **biodegradable, recycled** ◇ *The handles are made from 100% recycled ~.*
VERB + PLASTIC **make, produce** | **recycle** | **make sth from/in/ of/out of, mould/mold sth from/in/of/out of** ◇ *chairs made from ~* | **cover sth with, wrap sth in**

plate *noun*

1 for food

ADJ. **dessert, dinner, serving, side, soup** | **paper** | **clean, dirty** ◇ *The sink was full of dirty ~s.* | **empty, full**
VERB + PLATE **clear, empty** ◇ *I could see how hungry she was from the way she cleared her ~.* | **clear, clear away, collect, take** | **clean**
PREP. **on a/the ~** ◇ *She ate everything on her ~.* | **~ of** ◇ *a ~ of rice*

2 piece of metal with writing on

ADJ. **licence/license** (*esp. AmE*), **number** (*BrE*) ◇ *The driver was arrested for having false licence/license ~s on his car.* | **name** ◇ *He read the brass name ~ by the door.*

plateau *noun*

ADJ. **high** | **broad, vast** | **central** | **rocky** | **windswept** ◇ *The summit is a windswept ~ of scattered rocks.*
VERB + PLATEAU **reach** ◇ *The children's standard of reading seems to have reached a ~.*
PLATEAU + VERB **overlook sth**
PREP. **across a/the** ◇ *A terrible storm swept across the ~.*

platform *noun*

1 raised floor

ADJ. **high, raised** | **wooden**
VERB + PLATFORM **mount, stand on** ◇ *The king mounted the ~ to loud cheers.* | **appear on, speak from, speak on** | **share** ◇ *Union leaders shared the ~ with business leaders in a debate on the future of the industry.*

2 at a station

ADJ. **railway** (*BrE*), **station, subway** (*AmE*), **tube** (*BrE*)
PREP. **along a/the** ◇ *He ran along the ~ to catch the train.* | **at ~** ◇ *The train at ~ 3 is the 13.15 service to Liverpool.* | **from ~** ◇ *The next train to depart from ~ 2 is the 10.30 for London Paddington.* | **on ~** ◇ *the waiting room on ~ 7*

3 in politics

ADJ. **political** | **party** | **election, electoral**
PREP. **in a/the ~** ◇ *the promises in their election ~* | **on a/the ~ of** ◇ *They fought the election on a ~ of economic reform.*

platonic *adj.*

VERBS **be** | **remain**
ADV. **purely, strictly** ◇ *Their friendship remained purely ~.*

plausible *adj.*

VERBS **be, seem, sound** | **make sth** | **find sth, think sth** ◇ *He did not think it ~ that all the differences could be explained in this way.*
ADV. **extremely, highly, very** | **entirely, perfectly, quite** ◇ *a perfectly ~ theory* | **equally** ◇ *an equally ~ explanation* | **not remotely** ◇ *There was no way the story could be made to sound even remotely ~.* | **hardly** | **reasonably** | **superficially** | **intuitively** ◇ *This view seems intuitively ~ and has a long history.*

play *noun*

1 activity done for fun

ADJ. **outdoor** | **creative, imaginative, pretend**
PLAY + NOUN **area** | **equipment** | **house** (usually ***playhouse***) | **room** (usually ***playroom***) | **group** (usually ***playgroup*** in *BrE*), **scheme** (*BrE*) ◇ *The local council runs some good ~ schemes.*
PREP. **at ~** ◇ *Children spend hours at ~.* | **in ~** ◇ *I only said it in ~* (= not seriously).

2 drama

ADJ. **one-act** | **stage** | **radio, television** | **musical** | **miracle, morality, mystery, nativity** (*esp. BrE*), **passion** ◇ *The children always perform a nativity ~ every Christmas.* | **school**
VERB + PLAY **review** ◇ *The ~ is reviewed in most of today's papers.*
PREP. **~ about** ◇ *a ~ about teenage runaways*
→ Note at PERFORMANCE (for more verbs)

3 in sports

ADJ. **excellent, good** | **bad, poor** | **fair** | **dangerous, dirty, foul, rough, violent** ◇ *He was sent off for foul ~.*
VERB + PLAY **stop** ◇ *Rain stopped ~ 40 minutes into the match.*
PREP. **in ~** ◇ *The ball is still in ~.* | **out of ~** ◇ *He kicked the ball out of ~.*
PHRASES **at close of ~, at start of ~** (in cricket) ◇ *At close of ~ he had scored 38 not out.*

4 (*AmE*) an action or move in a game

ADJ. **big** ◇ *A double ~ ended the inning and the Red Sox were up.* | **final** ◇ *the final ~ of the first half* | **defensive, offensive** (both in American football) | **running** (in American football) | **double, triple** (both in baseball) ◇ *There were ten double ~s completed.*
VERB + PLAY **execute, make, run** (in American football) ◇ *the team's ability to execute a ~* ◇ *He made several nice defensive ~s.* ◇ *They ran 10 ~s inside the 30 in the fourth quarter.* | **call** (in American football) ◇ *The offensive coordinator has called 60 running ~s and 44 passes.*

play *verb*

1 of children

VERB + PLAY **let sb** ◇ *The other children wouldn't let him ~.*
PREP. **at** (*BrE*) ◇ *Let's ~ at pirates!* | **with** ◇ *The little girl was ~ing with her toys.*

2 game/sport

ADV. **brilliantly, superbly, well** | **badly, poorly**
VERB + PLAY **learn to** | **teach sb to** | **be difficult to, be easy to** | **see sb, watch sb**
PREP. **against** ◇ *These guys make the team very difficult to ~ against.* | **at** ◇ *I've never ~ed John at tennis.* | **for** ◇ *He ~s for the Chicago Bears.* | **in** ◇ *She has ~ed in every game this season.* | **with** ◇ *She was ~ing cards with her mother.*

3 music

ADV. **beautifully, brilliantly, excellently, superbly, well** | **badly** | **together** | **live** ◇ *The band will be ~ing live in the studio.*
VERB + PLAY **learn to** ◇ *I'm learning to ~ sax.* | **teach sb to** | **be easy to, be difficult to** ◇ *a piece that is relatively easy to ~* | **hear sb** ◇ *Have you ever heard her ~?*

player *noun*

1 of a game

ADJ. **accomplished, brilliant, dangerous, excellent, exciting, fine, gifted, good, great, outstanding, strong, talented, top, world-class** ◇ *one of the country's top tennis ~s* | **star** ◇ *The club was forced to sell their star ~.* | **poor** ◇ *He's a poor ~, but he tries very hard.* | **average** ◇ *These golf clubs are for the professional rather than for the average ~.* | **experienced** | **former** | **college** (*esp. AmE*), **professional** | **aggressive** | **defensive, offensive** (*both esp. AmE*) | **attacking, midfield** (both in football/soccer) | **handicap, scratch** (both in golf) | **baseball, basketball, bridge, chess, football, rugby, tennis, etc.**
VERB + PLAYER **draft** (*AmE*), **sign** ◇ *The team has drafted some good ~s in recent years.*

2 of a musical instrument

ADJ. **accomplished, gifted, great, outstanding, talented** | **bass, horn, keyboard, piano, sax, etc.**

3 in business

ADJ. **big, key, leading, major**
PREP. **~ in** ◇ *Their company is a major ~ in the London property market.*

playground *noun*

ADJ. **children's** | **adventure** (*esp. BrE*) | **school** ◇ *an elementary school ~*
PLAYGROUND + NOUN **bully, bullying** (*both esp. BrE*) | **equipment** | **duty** (*esp. BrE*) ◇ *teachers on ~ duty*
PREP. **in a/the ~** ◇ *children in the school ~*

playgroup (*BrE*) *noun*

ADJ. **nursery, preschool** | **local** | **voluntary**
VERB + PLAYGROUP **attend, go to** | **run** | **start** ◇ *She started a ~ in her own house.* | **start, start at** ◇ *He'll grow in confidence once he starts at ~.*
PLAYGROUP + NOUN **leader**
PREP. **at ~** ◇ *She goes shopping while her little girl's at ~.*

plea *noun*

1 request

ADJ. **desperate, strong, urgent** | **emotional, heartfelt, impassioned, passionate** ◇ *She made an emotional ~ for her daughter's killer to be caught.* | **repeated** | **final** ◇ *a final ~ for his life* | **personal**
VERB + PLEA **make** | **issue** | **ignore**
PREP. **despite a/the ~** ◇ *Despite ~s from his mother, the gunman refused to give himself up.* | **~ by, ~ from** ◇ *Hospital visiting hours were extended in response to ~s from patients.* | **~ for** ◇ *The director of the charity made an impassioned ~ for help.*

2 statement in court

ADJ. **guilty** | **not guilty** | **insanity** (*AmE*)
VERB + PLEA **enter** | **hear** | **change** | **accept** ◇ *The prosecution accepted a ~ of manslaughter.* | **support** (*esp. BrE*) ◇ *These facts cannot support a ~ of diminished responsibility.* | **reject**
PLEA + NOUN **bargain, bargaining** (usually *plea-bargaining*) ◇ *They received suspended prison sentences after plea-bargaining by their lawyers.* | **agreement** (*AmE*) ◇ *The terms of the ~ agreements weren't disclosed.*
PREP. **~ for** ◇ *A senior judge heard a ~ for damages on behalf of the accident victims.* | **~ of** ◇ *Her lawyer entered a ~ of guilty on her behalf.*
PHRASES **cop a ~** (= admit in court to being guilty of a small crime in the hope of receiving less severe punishment for a more serious crime) (*AmE, informal*) ◇ *The feds said that if I didn't cop a ~, I'd get about 15 years.*

plead *verb*

1 ask sb for sth in a very serious way

ADV. **almost** ◇ *She was almost ~ing with him.* | **silently** | **successfully** (*esp. BrE*) ◇ *She successfully ~ed their cause with the mayor.* | **desperately** ◇ *The teacher was today desperately ~ing for news of her son who has disappeared.*
PREP. **for** ◇ *They ~ed for mercy.* | **with** ◇ *His eyes silently ~ed with her.*

2 say that you are guilty/not guilty

PHRASES **~ guilty, ~ not guilty** ◇ *He ~ed not guilty to the murder.*

pleasant *adj.*

VERBS **be, feel, look, seem, sound** | **find sth** | **make sth**
ADV. **extremely, fairly, very, etc.** | **perfectly, reasonably** ◇ *His colleagues were perfectly ~ and friendly but they had their own lives to lead.* | **less than, not altogether, not entirely, not exactly, not particularly** ◇ *It was not a particularly ~ experience.* | **almost** | **enough** ◇ *It was a ~ enough day.*
PREP. **to** ◇ *He has always been extremely ~ to me.*

please *verb*

ADV. **enormously** ◇ *The result ~d us enormously.*
VERB + PLEASE **be difficult to, be hard to, be impossible to** ◇ *Some children are very difficult to ~.* | **be easy to** | **be eager to** ◇ *He's always very eager to ~.* | **try to** | **fail to** ◇ *The planning policy failed to ~ anyone.*
PHRASES **there's no pleasing sb** ◇ *There's just no pleasing some people* (= some people are impossible to please).

pleased *adj.*

VERBS **appear, be, feel, look, seem, sound**
ADV. **extremely, fairly, very, etc.** | **especially, genuinely, immensely, inordinately, more than, only too, particularly, well** | **far from, not at all, not best** ◇ *She seemed surprised and not at all ~ to see him.* | **reasonably** (*esp. BrE*) | **enough** ◇ *They seemed ~ enough with the result.* | **apparently** | **clearly, obviously** | **quietly, secretly** | **oddly** | **always** ◇ *I am always ~ to hear from former students.*
PREP. **about** ◇ *~ about the move* | **at** ◇ *She seemed ~ at our success.* | **by** ◇ *You must be ~ by their confidence in you.* | **for**

◇ *I'm very ~ for you both.* | **with** ◇ *We are immensely ~ with this result.*

pleasing *adj.*

VERBS **be** | **find sth**
ADV. **extremely, fairly, very, etc.** | **aesthetically** ◇ *aesthetically ~ combinations*
PREP. **to** ◇ *a design which is ~ to the eye*

pleasurable *adj.*

VERBS **be** | **become** | **make sth** | **find sth** ◇ *activities which they find ~ and rewarding*
ADV. **extremely, fairly, very, etc.** ◇ *Summertime gardening can be very ~.* | **highly, intensely** ◇ *The whole experience was intensely ~.*

pleasure *noun*

1 enjoyment

ADJ. **considerable, deep, enormous, great, intense** ◇ *It gives me enormous ~ to welcome my next guest.* | **genuine, real** | **pure, sheer** | **quiet** ◇ *The audience nodded with quiet ~ at her remark.* | **obvious** | **endless** ◇ *Children find endless ~ in playing with water.* | **malicious, perverse, sadistic** | **personal** ◇ *She takes personal ~ in tormenting her students.* | **vicarious** ◇ *He gained vicarious ~ from watching people laughing and joking.* | **aesthetic, physical, sensual, sexual**
VERB + PLEASURE **give (sb), give (sb)** | **derive, find, gain, get, take** ◇ *My grandfather got immense ~ out of life until the end.* | **experience, feel**
PREP. **for ~** ◇ *Some people read for ~, and others read to study.* | **with ~** ◇ *His eyes lit up with ~.* | **~ at** ◇ *He beamed with ~ at seeing her.* | **~ from** ◇ *She was deriving a perverse ~ from his discomfort.* | **~ in** ◇ *They took great ~ in each other's company.*
PHRASES **business and ~, business or ~, etc.** ◇ *I often meet useful people at parties, so I combine business with ~.* ◇ *Are you in Chicago for business or ~?* | **for your listening, reading, viewing, etc. ~** ◇ *The photographs are now available for your viewing ~.* | **have the ~ of sth** ◇ *May I have the ~ of the next dance?* | **~ and pain** ◇ *These memories bring both ~ and pain.*

2 sth that makes you happy

ADJ. **great** | **dubious** ◇ *the dubious ~ of growing up in the public eye* | **little, simple, small** ◇ *one of life's little ~s* | **fleeting, momentary, temporary** | **guilty** ◇ *Daytime TV is one of his guilty ~s.*
VERB + PLEASURE **have** (*formal*) ◇ *I hope to have the ~ of meeting you again.* | **enjoy** | **forgo**
PLEASURE + NOUN **boat, craft** | **cruise**
PHRASES **the ~s of life** ◇ *She enjoys the simple ~s of life.* | **the ~s of the flesh** ◇ *Priests promise to forego the ~s of the flesh.* | **To what do I owe the ~?** (= why are you visiting me?) (*formal, old-fashioned*)

pledge *noun*

ADJ. **campaign** (*esp. AmE*), **election** (*esp. BrE*), **manifesto** (*BrE*) ◇ *The party's election ~ was to cut income taxes by a third over the next five years.* | **spending** (*BrE*) ◇ *spending ~s given by the government* | **abstinence, virginity** (*both esp. AmE*) ◇ *He took a virginity ~ as a teenager.*
VERB + PLEDGE **give (sb), make, sign, take** | **fulfil/fulfill, honour/honor** | **break, go back on, renege on** | **recite, say** ◇ *They recited the Pledge of Allegiance.* (*in the US*)
PREP. **~ on** ◇ *manifesto ~s on greater public spending*
PHRASES **a ~ of support**

plight *noun*

ADJ. **desperate, sad, sorry, tragic** ◇ *the desperate ~ of flood victims* | **current** | **economic, financial**
VERB + PLIGHT **recognize, see, understand** | **draw attention to, highlight, publicize** ◇ *He has been sleeping rough in the*

streets to highlight the ~ of the homeless. | **alleviate, ease** | **ignore**
PREP. **~ of** ◇ *the ~ of the 1.5 million refugees*

plot *noun*

1 plan

ADJ. **evil, fiendish** | **alleged** | **assassination, coup, murder, terrorist**
VERB + PLOT **hatch** | **uncover** | **foil**
PREP. **~ against** ◇ *They had taken part in a ~ against the king.* | **~ by** ◇ *The police claim to have uncovered a ~ by terrorists to assassinate the president.*

2 events in a story

ADJ. **simple** | **complex, complicated** | **basic** | **main**
VERB + PLOT **construct** ◇ *She has constructed a complicated ~, with a large cast of characters.* | **advance** ◇ *This car chase does nothing to advance the ~.* | **give away** ◇ *I don't want to give away the ~ to anyone who hasn't seen the movie.*
PLOT + VERB **develop, unfold** | **involve, revolve around** ◇ *The main ~ revolves around a suspicious death.*
PLOT + NOUN **development** | **twist** ◇ *There is a clever ~ twist near the end of the film.* | **device**
PHRASES **a twist in the ~, a twist of the ~** ◇ *There are several unexpected twists in the ~ before the murderer is revealed.*

3 piece of land

ADJ. **garden, vegetable** | **farm** | **building** (*esp. BrE*) | **burial** | **small** | **10-acre, 12-acre, etc.** ◇ *They own a five-acre ~ of land.* | **family, private**
VERB + PLOT **work**
PLOT + VERB **measure sth** ◇ *a ~ measuring 10 m by 20 m*
PHRASES **a ~ of land**

plot *verb*

1 make secret plans

ADV. **allegedly** | **secretly** | **carefully** ◇ *The killings were carefully plotted and not impulsive.*
PREP. **against** ◇ *He was arrested on suspicion of plotting against the king.* | **with** ◇ *Taylor plotted with his daughter to murder her husband.*
PHRASES **accuse sb of plotting sth**

2 mark sth on a chart

ADV. **accurately** ◇ *The positions of the finds are accurately plotted.*
PREP. **against** ◇ *Greenhouse temperature can be plotted against plant growth.* | **on** ◇ *The figures are plotted on a graph.*

plough (*BrE*) (*AmE* plow) *noun*

ADJ. **heavy** | **horse-drawn, ox-drawn** ◇ *the demise of the horse-drawn ~*
VERB + PLOUGH/PLOW **draw, pull** ◇ *They need two horses to pull these heavy ~s.*
PLOUGH/PLOW + NOUN **horse, team** | **furrow**

ploy *noun*

ADJ. **clever, effective, good** | **deliberate** (*esp. BrE*), **tactical** | **favourite/favorite, old** | **cynical** | **advertising, marketing, sales** | **political**
VERB + PLOY **resort to, try** | **devise** ◇ *She devised a clever ~ to hold off her opponents.*
PLOY + VERB **work**
PREP. **~ for** ◇ *a ~ for deflecting criticism*

plug *noun*

1 electric

ADJ. **electric, power** (*AmE*) | **mains** (*BrE*) | **three-pin, two-pin** ◇ *The iron is fitted with a three-pin ~.* | **jack** (*BrE*) ◇ *I pushed the jack ~ into the amp.*
VERB + PLUG **pull out, remove, take out** | **fit, wire** (*BrE*) | **be fitted with** | **change**
PLUG + NOUN **adapter** | **socket** (*esp. BrE*) ◇ *My room only has one ~ socket.*

ADJ. **bath** (*BrE*), **bathtub** (*AmE*), **sink**
VERB + PLUG **put in** | **pull, pull out** ◊ *I got out of the bath and pulled out the ~.* (*BrE*) ◊ *I got out of the bathtub and pulled the ~.* (*AmE*) ◊ *They decided to pull the ~ on the project* (= cancel it). (*figurative*)
PLUG + NOUN **hole** (usually *plughole*) (*BrE*)

plumbing *noun*

ADJ. **domestic** (*BrE*), **household** | **indoor**
VERB + PLUMBING **put in** ◊ *They're going to have to put in new ~.* | **fix**
PLUMBING + NOUN **system** | **fittings, fixtures** | **work** ◊ *He's worked for several companies doing ~ work.*

plunge *noun*

ADJ. **cold** ◊ *Bathers would go straight from the hot room to take a cold ~.* | **downward, headlong** (*both figurative*) ◊ *the economy's downward ~* ◊ *his headlong ~ into shame and hypocrisy*
VERB + PLUNGE **survive** ◊ *How did he survive his icy ~?* | **take** (*usually figurative*) ◊ *She prepared to take the ~ into the cold waters of Lake Ontario.* ◊ *He finally took the ~ and gave in his notice.*
PREP. **~ into** ◊ *a ~ into the icy water* | **~ to** ◊ *a ~ to the ground*

plunge *verb*

ADV. **ahead** (*AmE, often figurative*), **back, downwards/downward, forward, head first, headlong** ◊ *City officials are plunging ahead with plans for a new convention center.* ◊ *The car ~d headlong into the river.* | **in** ◊ *The pool was declared open and eager swimmers ~d in.*
PREP. **down** ◊ *The bus came off the road and ~d down an embankment.* | **from** ◊ *He ~d from a tenth floor window.* | **into** (*often figurative*) ◊ *She ~d straight into her story.* | **off** ◊ *The car had ~d off the road.*
PHRASES **~ to your death** ◊ *A climber ~d 300 feet to his death.*

plutonium *noun*

ADJ. **radioactive** | **weapons-grade**
VERB + PLUTONIUM **extract, produce, recover** ◊ *one ton of ~ extracted from spent nuclear fuel* | **reprocess** ◊ *the capability to enrich uranium or reprocess ~*
PLUTONIUM + NOUN **fuel** | **production** | **bomb** ◊ *the plane that dropped a ~ bomb on the city of Nagasaki*

pneumonia *noun*

ADJ. **severe** | **bronchial, double** ◊ *She died from bronchial ~.* | **bacterial**
... OF PNEUMONIA **bout**
VERB + PNEUMONIA **have, suffer from** | **catch, contract, develop, get** | **die from, die of** | **cause**
→ Special page at ILLNESS

pocket *noun*

1 for keeping things in
ADJ. **bulging** ◊ *tourists with bulging ~s* | **deep** | **zip** (*BrE*), **zipped, zippered** (*AmE*) | **jean** (*esp. AmE*), **jeans, pants** (*AmE*), **trouser** (*esp. BrE*) | **coat, jacket, shirt, vest** (*AmE*), **waistcoat** (*BrE*), **etc.** | **back, breast, chest** (*AmE*), **front, hip, inner, inside, outer, side, top** | **door** (*esp. BrE*), **seat** ◊ *Please read the safety leaflet in the seat ~ in front of you* (= on a plane). | **hidden, secret** ◊ *Forged passports were found in a secret ~ in the suitcase.*
VERB + POCKET **check, feel in, fish in, fumble in, go through, rummage in, search** ◊ *He went through all his ~s looking for his key.* | **pat** ◊ *My cellphone rang and I patted my ~s looking for it.* | **reach in** ◊ *She reached in her ~ and pulled out her phone.* | **dip into** (*figurative*) ◊ *Once again club members have had to dip into their ~s* (= spend their own money) *to buy new equipment.* | **fish sth from/out of, get sth from/out of, pull sth from/out of, take sth from/out of** ◊ *I fished the list out of my ~.* | **empty, turn out** ◊ *The security guard made them empty their ~s.* | **put sth in/into, stuff sth in/into, thrust sth in/into** ◊ *She stuffed the money into her ~ and walked out.* ◊ *He walked past with his collar turned up and his hands thrust into his ~s.* | **fill, stuff** ◊ *We filled our ~s with apples.* | **line** (*figurative*) ◊ *Dishonest officials have been lining their ~s with public funds.* | **pick** ◊ *He caught a boy trying to pick his ~ on the bus.*
POCKET + VERB **bulge** ◊ *My ~s were bulging with loose change.*
POCKET + NOUN **lining**
PREP. **in the/your ~** ◊ *My wallet was in the back ~ of my jeans.* | **out of the/your ~** ◊ *He took a few coins out of his ~.*
PHRASES **hands in ~s, with your hands in your ~s** ◊ *He stood there, hands in ~s.* | **the lining of a ~**

2 small area/group
ADJ. **large, small** ◊ *The country has large ~s of unemployment.* | **isolated**
PHRASES **a ~ of resistance** ◊ *Government forces are mopping up the last ~s of resistance.*

pocketbook (*AmE*) *noun*

VERB + POCKETBOOK **open** (*often figurative*) ◊ *The government opened its ~ to the US military.* ◊ *Increased maintenance costs are hitting building owners in the ~s.*
POCKETBOOK + NOUN **issue** ◊ *Unemployment is the leading ~ issue for most voters.*

poem *noun*

ADJ. **beautiful, fine, good, great** | **famous** | **collected, selected** ◊ *His collected ~s were published after the war.* | **anonymous** | **autobiographical** | **long, short** | **dramatic, epic, heroic, lyric, narrative** | **prose** | **love, war** | **humorous, nonsense, satirical**
... OF POEMS **anthology, collection**
VERB + POEM **compose, write** | **read** ◊ *She read the ~ aloud.* | **recite** | **know by heart, learn by heart** (*esp. BrE*) | **dedicate** ◊ *He dedicated the ~ to his mother.* | **publish**
POEM + VERB **be addressed to sb**
PREP. **in a/the ~** ◊ *Wordsworth describes his boyhood in his autobiographical ~ 'The Prelude'.* | **~ about** ◊ *a ~ about cultural differences*

poet *noun*

ADJ. **accomplished, good, great** | **distinguished, famous, well-known** | **foremost** ◊ *the foremost ~ of his generation* | **minor** | **unknown** | **aspiring** | **contemporary, modern** | **epic, lyric** | **metaphysical, Modernist, Romantic, etc.** | **17th-century, 18th-century, etc.**
VERB + POET **inspire** ◊ *These river banks have inspired ~s for many centuries.*
POET + VERB **write sth**

poetic *adj.*

VERBS **be, sound** | **wax** (*AmE*) ◊ *It's very easy to wax ~* (= speak in a poetic way) *about the sport of baseball.*
ADV. **very, wonderfully** | **truly** ◊ *The piece ends with a truly ~ slow movement.* | **almost** | **quite** | **self-consciously** ◊ *His writing is self-consciously ~.*

poetry *noun*

ADJ. **good, great** | **bad** | **classical** | **contemporary, modern** | **experimental** | **18th-century, etc.** | **dramatic, epic, lyric, narrative** | **Modernist, Romantic, symbolist, etc.** | **love, pastoral, war, etc.**
... OF POETRY **line** ◊ *He began his speech with a few lines of ~.* | **piece** | **anthology, book, collection, volume**
VERB + POETRY **compose, write** | **read** | **recite** | **know by heart, learn by heart** ◊ *At school we had to learn a lot of ~ by heart.* | **publish**
POETRY + NOUN **book, collection** | **reading** ◊ *She invited me to one of her ~ readings.* | **competition, contest, slam** | **workshop** | **group** | **scene** ◊ *the New York ~ scene*
PREP. **in ~** ◊ *an essay on imagery in ~*

poignant adj.

VERBS **be, seem, sound** | **become** | **make sth** ◇ *The presence of the rest of the family made John's absence even more ~.* | **find sth**

ADV. **extremely, very** | **deeply, especially, particularly, unbearably** ◇ *I found his speech deeply ~.* | **quite** | **oddly, strangely** ◇ *The performances are by turns uproarious and oddly ~.*

point noun

1 thing said as part of a discussion

ADJ. **excellent, good, interesting, valid** | **important** | **minor** | **subtle** | **moot** | **central, critical, crucial, key, major, salient** | **controversial** | **sore** ◇ *This was a sore ~ for Hemingway.* | **action** ◇ *The committee recommended a number of action ~s to avoid such problems in the future.* | **talking** ◇ *The possibility of an interest rate cut is a major talking ~ in the City. (BrE)* ◇ *Senate Democrats issued these talking ~s. (AmE)* | **final** ◇ *I do agree with her final ~.*

VERB + POINT **have** ◇ *She has a ~.* | **see, take** ◇ *I see your ~.* ◇ *Point taken.* | **concede** | **address, cover, make, raise** ◇ *He covers the key ~s in his introduction.* ◇ *She made some interesting ~s.* | **argue, discuss** ◇ *They argued the ~ for hours.* | **illustrate** | **get across, make, prove** ◇ *He had trouble getting his ~ across.* ◇ *That proves my ~.* | **clarify** | **belabour/belabor** (esp. AmE), **drive home, emphasize, hammer home, highlight, labour/labor** (esp. BrE), **press, reinforce, reiterate, stress, underline, underscore** (AmE) ◇ *She banged on the table to emphasize her ~.* ◇ *I understand what you're saying—there's no need to labour/labor the ~.*

PHRASES **a case in ~** (= an example relevant to the matter being discussed) | **the ~ at issue** | **a ~ of agreement, a ~ of disagreement** | **a ~ of law**
→ Special page at MEETING

2 the point essential aspect of sth

ADJ. **basic** ◇ *The basic ~ is that…*

VERB + THE POINT **come to, get to** ◇ *Hurry up and get to the ~!* | **get** ◇ *It took me a few minutes to get the ~.* | **miss** | **wander from, wander off** (both esp. BrE)

PREP. **beside the ~** (= not relevant) ◇ *That's beside the ~.* | **to the ~** ◇ *His remarks were brief and to the ~.*

PHRASES **more to the ~** (= what is more important) ◇ *More to the ~, did they get away?*

3 meaning/reason/purpose of sth

ADJ. **whole** ◇ *That's the whole ~.*

VERB + POINT **have** ◇ *It doesn't have any ~ to it.* | **see** ◇ *I don't see the ~ in arguing.* | **get, understand** ◇ *I didn't get the ~ of the story.*

PREP. **~ in, ~ of** ◇ *There's absolutely no ~ in complaining now.* ◇ *What's the ~ of worrying?*

4 item/detail/feature

ADJ. **finer, good, strong** ◇ *We discussed the finer ~s of growing roses.* | **bad, weak** | **salient** | **selling** ◇ *the major selling ~ of the line*

PHRASES **a ~ of difference** ◇ *There is only one ~ of difference between the two models.* | **a ~ of interest**

5 particular time/moment

ADJ. **high, low** ◇ *He had reached the high ~ of his career.* | **halfway** ◇ *by the time the movie has reached its halfway ~* | **breaking, bursting, saturation** ◇ *to fill a bag to bursting ~* | **jumping-off** ◇ *jumping-off ~s for further research* | **break-even** ◇ *well below its financial break-even ~* | **plot** ◇ *from one improbable plot ~ to another* | **boiling, freezing, melting** | **critical** ◇ *This is definitely a critical ~ in my life right now.* | **choke** (AmE), **sticking** ◇ *a sticking ~ in the potential deal* | **flash** ◇ *Their anger finally reached the flash ~.*

VERB + POINT **get to, reach** ◇ *I've reached the ~ (= in a book, etc.) where his father is dying.*

POINT + VERB **come** ◇ *There comes a ~ in most people's lives when they want to settle down.*

PREP. **at a/the ~** ◇ *At one ~ he looked like winning.* | **on the ~ of** ◇ *on the ~ of departure* | **to the ~ of** ◇ *We worked all night to the ~ of collapse.* | **up to a ~** ◇ *I agree with you up to a ~.*

PHRASES **a ~ in time** ◇ *At this ~ we can't give you a final answer.* | **the ~ of no return** (= after which it is impossible to go back/undo what you have done)

6 particular place/position

ADJ. **central, focal** ◇ *the focal ~ of his life* | **fixed** | **beginning** (esp. AmE), **starting** ◇ *This website is an excellent beginning ~ for any pianist.* | **ending, stopping** ◇ *the starting and ending ~ for most safaris* | **one stopping ~ on their tour of the shrines** | **halfway, midway** ◇ *a convenient midway ~ between Memphis and St. Louis* | **access, entry** ◇ *an excellent access ~ into Glacier National Park* | **assembly, rallying** | **meeting, rendezvous** | **crossing** ◇ *Baja California is the crossing ~ for most illegal immigrants to the US.* | **vantage** | **reference** | **pivotal, turning** ◇ *This proved to be the turning ~ of the game.* | **tipping** ◇ *The technology has reached a tipping ~.* | **cut-off** | **vanishing** | **price** (business) ◇ *The product sold at about a $100 price ~.* | **acupuncture, pressure** ◇ *Acupuncture ~s are believed to stimulate the central nervous system.* ◇ *pressures ~s on the foot*

VERB + POINT **arrive at, reach** | **provide** ◇ *The book provides a focal ~ for such discussions.*

PHRASES **a ~ of contact** | **a ~ of reference**

7 punctuation

ADJ. **decimal** | **exclamation** (AmE) | **bullet** ◇ *Break up your text with bullet ~s.*

8 in a game/sports competition

ADJ. **match, set** ◇ *It's set ~ to Nadal.* | **bonus** ◇ *Name the film and, for a bonus ~, name the actress.*

…OF POINT **tally** ◇ *a personal tally of 28 ~s*

VERB + POINT **accumulate, earn, gain, get, notch** (AmE), **notch up, rack up, score, tally** (AmE), **win** ◇ *After players accumulate enough ~s, they may exchange them for a wide variety of merchandise.* | **average** ◇ *She's averaged 19 ~s per game in her last seven games.* | **lose** | **award** ◇ *Points are awarded to the winner of each round.* | **deduct** ◇ *I'm deducting a ~ from the total score.*

PHRASES **beat sb on ~s, win on ~s**

9 measurement

ADJ. **basis, percentage** ◇ *The ten-year Treasury yield declined 9 basis ~s to 4.0%.* ◇ *Interest rates fell by one percentage ~.*

VERB + POINT (All these verbs may be followed by **by, from** or **to** plus *point*. Sometimes the word **by** is left out.), **be up, go up, improve, increase, jump, rise, shoot up, soar** ◇ *The Nikkei index rose 710 ~s to 14894.* ◇ *His popularity rose by 18 ~s in public opinion polls.* | **be down, come down, decline** (esp. AmE), **decrease, drop, fall, go down, plunge** ◇ *The CAC-40 index is down 67 ~s at 4413.*

PHRASES **about five, ten, etc. ~s, around five, ten, etc. ~s** | **only five, ten, etc. ~s** ◇ *The index was down only 4.6 ~s at the close.* | **over five, ten, etc. ~s** | **up to five, ten, etc. ~s** | **an improvement of five, ten, etc. ~s, an increase of five, ten, etc. ~s, a jump of five, ten, etc. ~s, a rise of five, ten, etc. ~s** ◇ *The target is for an average rise of two ~s a year from 2010 to 2020.* | **a drop of five, ten, etc. ~s, a fall of five, ten, etc. ~s, a reduction of five, ten, etc. ~s**

10 thin sharp end of sth

ADJ. **fine, sharp**

point verb

ADV. **accusingly** ◇ *Lee ~ed accusingly at Tyler.* | **downwards/downward, upwards/upward** | **ahead**

PREP. **at, in the direction of** ◇ *He ~ed in the direction of the beach.* | **to, towards/toward** ◇ *The toddler ~ed to the toy he wanted.* | **with** ◇ *She ~ed with her finger at the map.*

PHRASES **~ straight at sb/sth** ◇ *The gun was ~ing straight at me.* | **~ the way** ◇ *'You must cross that field,' she said, ~ing the way.*

PHR V **point sth out**

ADV. **correctly, rightly** ◇ *As you so rightly ~ed out, our funds are not unlimited.* | **helpfully** | **repeatedly** ◇ *as repeatedly ~ed out by President Bush*

VERB + POINT OUT **must, should** ◊ *I should ~ out that not one of these paintings is original.* | **try to** | **hasten to** ◊ *Let me to hasten to ~ out that this is not a marketing book.* | **fail to** | **hesitate to** ◊ *They would not hesitate to ~ out anything they found objectionable.* | **be at pains to, be keen to** (*esp. BrE*), **be quick to** ◊ *She was at pains to ~ out that she was no newcomer to the area.* | **be right to** ◊ *You were right to ~ out that this is only one of the difficulties we face.* | **be important to**
PREP. **to** ◊ *She tried in vain to ~ out to him the unfairness of the situation.*

point to sth
ADV. **clearly** ◊ *Fragments of woven cloth at the site clearly ~ to the production of textiles.* | **directly** ◊ *The symptoms ~ directly to appendicitis.*
VERB + POINT TO **seem to** ◊ *The evidence all seems to ~ to one conclusion.*

pointer *noun*

1 advice/indications
ADJ. **good, important** | **clear, obvious** | **practical, useful**
VERB + POINTER **give (sb), offer (sb), provide (sb with)** ◊ *He offered a few ~s on starting your own business.* | **get** ◊ *I was trying to get some ~s on what I should do.*
PREP. **~ for** ◊ *The examiner's comments include ~s for future study.* | **~ on** ◊ *Here are a few ~s on designing such facilities.* | **~ to** ◊ *His symptoms gave no obvious ~ to a possible diagnosis.* | **~ towards/toward** ◊ *~s towards/toward a new political agenda*
PHRASES **a ~ to the future**

2 sth used for pointing
ADJ. **mouse** ◊ *Move the mouse ~ to the menu bar.* | **laser** ◊ *She used a laser ~ during her presentation.*

pointless *adj.*

VERBS **be, seem** | **become** | **consider sth, find sth, think sth** ◊ *She considered it ~ to plan in too much detail.* | **make sth, render sth** ◊ *This renders the project ~.*
ADV. **absolutely, completely, entirely, quite, totally, utterly** ◊ *The whole discussion was utterly ~.* | **almost, fairly, pretty, rather, somewhat** | **a little, slightly, etc.** | **apparently, seemingly** | **ultimately** ◊ *The film is entertaining but ultimately ~.*

point of view *noun*

ADJ. **alternative, different** ◊ *He listened patiently to what we all had to say before putting across an alternative ~.* | **particular, unique** | **objective** ◊ *We can count on him for an objective ~.* | **personal, subjective** | **aesthetic, moral, practical, technical, theoretical** | **business, commercial, economic, historical, legal, medical, military, philosophical, political, psychological, religious, safety, scientific, security, strategic, etc.** ◊ *From a purely economic ~, the reforms make a great deal of sense.* | **conservative, liberal, socialist, etc.** | **Buddhist, Catholic, Islamic, etc.** | **American, European, Western, etc.**
VERB + POINT OF VIEW **have** | **adopt, take** ◊ *He always seems to take the opposite ~ to me.* | **accept, appreciate, support** | **respect** ◊ *I appreciate and respect your ~.* | **express, get across, present, put** (*esp. BrE*), **put forward** (*esp. BrE*) ◊ *We aren't shy about expressing our ~.* ◊ *A union representative was present to put the farmers' ~.* | **speak from, tell sth from** | **consider sth from, look at sth from, see (sth from), understand** ◊ *I can see your ~, but I think we have to consider the long-term implications.* ◊ *Try to see the situation from my ~.* | **agree with, share** | **come around to, come round to** (*esp. BrE*) ◊ *If we can talk to her for an hour I'm sure she'll come around to our ~.* | **disagree with** ◊ *I completely disagree with this ~.* | **reflect, represent** ◊ *I do not think the article reflects the ~ of the majority of the population.*
PREP. **from a/sb's ~** ◊ *From a purely personal ~, I'd like to see cars banned from the city.* | **from the ~ of** ◊ *The book tells the story of a murder investigation from the ~ of the chief suspect.* ◊ *From the ~ of safety, a lower speed limit would certainly be a good thing.* | **~ about** ◊ *We may always have a*

different ~ about what happened.* | **~ on** ◊ *I don't have a ~ on this issue.*

poise *noun*

ADJ. **natural** ◊ *the natural ~ and balance of the body* | **social** ◊ *She never lost her social ~, however awkward the situation.* | **extraordinary, great, remarkable, tremendous**
VERB + POISE **retain, show** ◊ *He showed ~ and maturity beyond his years.* | **lose** | **recover, regain** ◊ *She hesitated briefly but quickly regained her ~.*

poised *adj.*

VERBS **appear, be, look, seem, stand** ◊ *She stood ~ for a moment.* | **remain**
ADV. **delicately, finely** | **perfectly** ◊ *His manner was perfectly ~ between gravity and teasing.*
PREP. **above, over** ◊ *Peter hesitated, his hand ~ above the telephone.* | **between, for** ◊ *They hovered by the door, ~ for flight.*
PHRASES **~ on the brink of sth, ~ on the edge of sth, ~ on the threshold of sth** ◊ *The two countries were ~ on the brink of war.*

poison *noun*

ADJ. **potent, powerful, strong, virulent** | **deadly, lethal** | **pure** (*usually figurative*) ◊ *These words were pure ~ to me.* | **nerve, rat** | **chemical**
...OF POISON **trace**
VERB + POISON **administer, give sb, inject** | **lace sth with, put in, put on** ◊ *She had laced his drink with ~.* ◊ *She had put ~ in his wine.* | **spread** (*figurative*) ◊ *groups that are spreading the ~ of sectarianism* | **put down** (= put somewhere to kill animals) ◊ *The farmer had put down some rat ~.* | **drink, swallow, take** | **suck out** ◊ *He sucked most of the ~ from the wound.*
POISON + NOUN **gas, pill** | **arrow, dart**

poisoning *noun*

ADJ. **acute, chronic, severe** ◊ *I had severe food ~.* | **fatal** | **accidental** ◊ *to protect children from accidental ~* | **blood** | **food** ◊ *a bad case of food ~* | **alcohol, arsenic, carbon monoxide, chemical, lead, mercury, pesticide, radiation, etc.**
...OF POISONING **case**
VERB + POISONING **have** ◊ *My mother had blood ~.* | **get** ◊ *How did you get food ~ anyway?* | **cause** ◊ *Listeria can cause fatal blood ~.* | **die from, die of**

poisonous *adj.*

VERBS **be** | **become**
ADV. **deadly, extremely, highly, very**
PREP. **to** ◊ *The leaves of these trees are ~ to cattle.*

polarized (*BrE also* -ised) *adj.*

VERBS **be** | **become** | **remain**
ADV. **deeply, highly, sharply** ◊ *The country is deeply ~.* ◊ *Public opinion is sharply ~ on this issue.* | **increasingly** | **politically, racially**
PREP. **between** ◊ *In this period politics became ~ between extreme right and left.*

pole *noun*

ADJ. **North, South** | **geographic, geomagnetic, magnetic** ◊ *The north magnetic ~ lies to the west of the geographic North Pole.* | **opposite** (*figurative*) ◊ *The two authors represent the opposite ~s of fictional genius*
PREP. **between the (two) ~s of** (*figurative*) ◊ *an artistic compromise between the ~s of abstraction and representation* | **from ~ to ~** ◊ *The meridian is an imaginary line drawn from ~ to ~.*
PHRASES **be ~s apart** (*figurative*) ◊ *In temperament, she and her sister are ~s apart* (= completely different).

police noun

ADJ. **armed, mounted** | **plain-clothes, uniformed** | **undercover** | **riot, traffic** | **military, paramilitary, secret, security** | **airport, border, campus** (*esp. AmE*), **city** (*esp. AmE*), **county, federal, local, national, state** | **fashion, thought** (*both figurative*) ◇ *Following this rule will keep the fashion ~ off your tail.*
VERB + POLICE **call, contact** | **alert, inform, notify, tell** | **involve** ◇ *I'd really rather not involve the ~.* | **elude, evade**
POLICE + VERB **arrest sb, detain sb** | **catch sb** | **charge sb** ◇ *The ~ charged him with impaired driving.* | **patrol sth** | **raid sth** ◇ *The ~ raided his shop.* | **arrive, respond** ◇ *The ~ arrived to break up the battle.* | **interview sb, question sb** | **investigate sth** | **harass sb** | **appeal for sth** (*esp. BrE*) ◇ *Police have appealed for witnesses to come forward.*
POLICE + NOUN **captain, chief, commissioner** (*esp. AmE*), **constable** (*BrE*), **detective, inspector, lieutenant, officer** | **spokesman** | **investigator, official** | **department, headquarters, station** | **academy** (*esp. AmE*) | **cell** (*BrE*) ◇ *He spent the night in a ~ cell after his arrest.* | **report** ◇ *Police reports state that at around 6.30 p.m. Poole and a relative had an argument in his backyard.* ◇ *Contact your local ~ department to file a ~ report.* (*AmE*) | **blotter** (*AmE*) ◇ *His name has never shown up on the ~ blotter* (= written record of arrests). | **record** ◇ *I had a ~ record.* | **car, cruiser** (*esp. AmE*), **helicopter, van** (*BrE*), **vehicle** ◇ *an unmarked ~ car* | **siren** | **driver** (*BrE*), **marksman** | **dog, horse** | **uniform** | **authorities, force, service** | **unit** | **enquiries** (*BrE*), **investigation** | **interrogation, surveillance** | **escort** ◇ *The visiting fans returned to the station under ~ escort.* | **patrol** ◇ *A routine ~ patrol spotted signs of a break-in at the offices.* | **raid** ◇ *Nine arrests were made in a series of ~ raids across the city.* | **presence** ◇ *There was a huge ~ presence at the demonstration.* | **protection** ◇ *All prosecution witnesses were given ~ protection.* | **barricades, cordon, lines** ◇ *Some protesters managed to break through the ~ cordon.* | **checkpoint, roadblock** | **chase** | **shooting** | **informant, informer** | **abuse, brutality, corruption, harassment, misconduct, violence** | **state** ◇ *The country looks more and more like a ~ state.*
PHRASES **helping the ~ with their enquiries** (*BrE*) ◇ *No arrest has been made, but a man is helping the ~ with their enquiries.* | **in ~ custody** ◇ *He was held in ~ custody for a month*

policeman noun

ADJ. **senior** | **ordinary** ◇ *the duties of the ordinary ~* | **local** | **uniformed** | **plain-clothes, undercover** | **armed** | **military** | **traffic** | **border** | **off-duty**
VERB + POLICEMAN **call** ◇ *A ~ was called to the house just after midnight.*
POLICEMAN + VERB **patrol sth** | **raid sth** | **arrest sb, stop sb**
→ See also OFFICER

policy noun

1 plan of action

ADJ. **clear, coherent** | **explicit, specific** | **strict** | **conscious, deliberate** ◇ *a deliberate ~ to involve people of all ages* | **effective** | **sensible** | **controversial** | **flawed, misguided, short-sighted** ◇ *the need to reform our flawed agricultural ~* | **disastrous** | **official, public** | **federal, government, party** | **company** | **editorial** ◇ *The magazine has a misguided editorial ~.* | **domestic, internal, national, regional** | **foreign, international** | **expansionist, interventionary, protectionist,** etc. | **open-door** ◇ *an open-door ~ for migrant workers* | **affirmative-action** (*AmE*) ◇ *affirmative-action policies that aim to help members of historically disadvantaged groups* | **zero-tolerance** ◇ *We have a zero-tolerance ~ for drugs.* | **agricultural, defence/defense, drug, drugs** (*BrE*), **economic, education, educational, employment, energy, environmental, financial, fiscal, health, housing, immigration, macroeconomic, monetary, security, social, tax, trade, transport** (*esp. BrE*), etc. |

admissions ◇ *Some have criticized universities for their admissions policies.*
VERB + POLICY **design, develop, formulate, frame, influence, shape** | **determine, dictate** ◇ *a doctrine that would dictate American foreign ~ for some time to come* | **establish, implement, institute, introduce, set** | **adopt, carry out, enact, enforce, follow, pursue** ◇ *The government followed a ~ of restraint in public spending.* | **have, operate** ◇ *The company operates a strict no-smoking ~.* | **advocate, approve, endorse, favour/favor, promote, support** | **oppose** | **reverse** | **abandon**
POLICY + VERB **be aimed at sth, be designed to do sth** ◇ *a ~ aimed at halting economic recession* ◇ *policies designed to support and encourage marriage* | **govern sth** ◇ *policies governing the management of the environment* | **affect sb/sth** ◇ *Their economic policies affect us all.* | **prohibit sth** ◇ *a ~ prohibiting sexual harassment*
POLICY + NOUN **decision, making** | **proposal, recommendation** | **objective** | **issue** ◇ *the need to address public ~ issues at the national level* | **change, reform, review** | **agenda** | **document, statement** | **adviser, analyst, expert, maker, wonk** (*esp. AmE*) ◇ *a ~ adviser who made his name as a health reformer*
PREP. **~ of** ◇ *The company's ~ of expansion has created many new jobs.* | **~ on** ◇ *the party's ~ on housing*
PHRASES **a matter of ~** ◇ *It is a matter of company ~ that we do not disclose the names of clients.*

2 insurance contract

ADJ. **insurance** | **buildings and contents** (*BrE*), **home and contents** (*AmE*), **home contents** (*BrE*), **household contents** (*BrE*) | **auto** (*AmE*), **motor** (*BrE*) | **life, life-assurance** (*BrE*), **life-insurance** | **endowment, pension** (*both BrE*)
VERB + POLICY **take out** | **renew**
POLICY + VERB **cover sb/sth** ◇ *The ~ covers (you for) accidental loss or damage.* | **expire**
POLICY + NOUN **holder** | **schedule** (*BrE*)
PREP. **in a/the ~** ◇ *risks defined in the ~* | **under a/the ~** ◇ *the types of claims covered under the ~*

polio (*also formal* poliomyelitis) noun

VERB + POLIO **have** | **contract** | **immunize sb against, vaccinate sb against**
POLIO + NOUN **vaccination, vaccine** | **virus** | **victim**
→ Special page at ILLNESS

polish noun → See also NAIL POLISH

ADJ. **boot, furniture, metal, nail, shoe, silver** | **French** | **wax**
VERB + POLISH **apply** ◇ *Apply ~ with a soft brush.* | **give sth** (*esp. BrE*) ◇ *You'll need to give your shoes a good ~.* | **remove** ◇ *Use acetone to remove ~.*

polished adj.

VERBS **be**
ADV. **brightly, highly, well** ◇ *the brightly ~ brasses* ◇ *She slipped on the highly ~ floor.* | **beautifully, finely, nicely, perfectly** ◇ *the finely ~ wood table* | **freshly, newly**

polite adj.

VERBS **be, seem, sound** | **remain**
ADV. **extremely, fairly, very,** etc. | **perfectly, scrupulously, unfailingly** | **overly** (*esp. AmE*) ◇ *an overly ~ smile* | **coolly** ◇ *His manner was coolly ~ and impersonal.*
PREP. **to** ◇ *She was scrupulously ~ to him.*

politeness noun

ADJ. **common, conventional** ◇ *It's no more than common ~ to hear what she has to say.* | **formal** | **social** | **exaggerated, excessive**
PREP. **out of ~** ◇ *They accepted the food more out of ~ than because they were hungry.* | **with ~** ◇ *They greeted their visitor with formal ~.*
PHRASES **a veneer of ~** (*esp. BrE*) ◇ *His veneer of ~ concealed a ruthless determination.*

political adj.

VERBS **be** | **become, get** ◇ *We have no intention of getting ~.*
ADV. **highly, very** ◇ *This whole issue has become highly ~.* | **explicitly, overtly** | **purely** ◇ *the first purely ~ decision taken by the EU* | **inherently** ◇ *The royal family has an inherently ~ role.*

political asylum noun

VERB + POLITICAL ASYLUM **apply for, ask for, claim, seek** | **grant sb, offer sb** ◇ *He was granted ~ in Sweden.*
PHRASES **an application for ~, a claim for ~**

politician noun

ADJ. **leading, popular, prominent, senior** | **experienced, veteran** ◇ *a veteran ~ of the left* | **influential, powerful** | **successful** | **charismatic, astute, clever, shrewd** | **corrupt, crooked** | **career, professional** | **conviction** (*esp. BrE*) | **consummate** ◇ *Marcos was a consummate ~: energetic and ruthless.* | **elected** | **local** | **left-wing, right-wing** | **conservative, liberal, progressive** | **Conservative, Labour, etc.** | **Democratic, Republican** | **Opposition**
VERB + POLITICIAN **elect** | **bribe** | **lobby** ◇ *His job will be primarily to lobby ~s on airport and security issues.*

politics noun

ADJ. **domestic, internal** ◇ *the country's internal ~* ◇ *the internal ~ of the legal profession* | **county, local, national, regional** ◇ *She was active in local ~ for many years.* | **global, international, world** | **democratic, electoral, multiparty, parliamentary, party** | **presidential** | **contemporary, modern** | **mainstream** | **conservative, extreme, left-wing, liberal, progressive, radical, right-wing, etc.** ◇ *His manners were as mild as his ~ were extreme.* | **personal** ◇ *My personal ~ are pretty simple.* | **practical** ◇ *He argued that it was not practical ~ to abolish private schools.* | **power** ◇ *They took the view that Casper was playing power ~ with their jobs at stake.* | **consensus** ◇ *Consensus ~ places a high value on existing political institutions.* | **partisan** (*disapproving, esp. AmE*) ◇ *The Democrats are simply engaging in partisan ~.* | **dirty** ◇ *He used dirty ~ to trash his opponent's record.* | **conviction** (*esp. BrE*) | **identity** ◇ *multiculturalism and the rise of identity ~* | **nationalist, sectarian** | **cultural, environmental, feminist, gay, gender, racial, sexual, working-class** | **office** ◇ *I don't want to get involved in office ~.*
VERB + POLITICS **enter, go into** ◇ *They went into ~ in the hope of changing society.* | **abandon, retire from** ◇ *He abandoned ~ and went into business.* | **be interested in, follow** ◇ *I have always followed ~ closely.* | **understand** ◇ *I don't understand the ~ of it all.* | **be active in, be engaged in, be immersed in, be involved in, engage in, participate in** | **become active in, get immersed in, get involved in** | **dabble in, play** (*informal*) | **get embroiled in** | **discuss, talk** (*informal*), **talk about** ◇ *Let's not talk ~ now.* | **dabble in, interfere in, intervene in, meddle in** (*esp. BrE*) ◇ *As a churchman, he was accused of interfering in ~.* | **dominate** ◇ *the issues which have dominated Irish ~* | **influence, reshape, shape** ◇ *reforms that are intended to reshape Italian ~*
POLITICS + VERB **dominate sth, drive sth, motivate sth** ◇ *In their world ~ dominates everything.* ◇ *The legislation has been driven by populist ~.* | **affect sth** | **surround sth** ◇ *the ~ surrounding reproduction and fertility* | **play a role** ◇ *the role ~ played in daily life*
PHRASES **sb's involvement in ~, sb's participation in ~** | **the world of ~**

poll noun

1 survey of opinion

ADJ. **local, national, nationwide, statewide** (*AmE*) | **opinion** | **political, popularity** | **tracking** (*AmE*) ◇ *The latest tracking ~ shows the Democrats leading by four percentage points.* | **pre-election** | **exit** ◇ *Exit ~s suggest a big majority for the party.* | **informal, straw** ◇ *I took a straw ~ among my colleagues to find out how many can use chopsticks.* | **latest, recent** | **magazine, online, telephone**
VERB + POLL **carry out** (*esp. BrE*), **conduct, do, run, take** |

commission | **lead, lead in** ◇ *The party is leading in the ~s.* | **read, see** ◇ *I don't read opinion ~s.* ◇ *Have you seen the latest ~?* | **publish, release**
POLL + VERB **confirm sth, find sth, indicate sth, reveal sth, say sth, show sth, suggest sth** | **ask (sb) sth** ◇ *The ~ asked voters what was the most important moral issue that affected their vote.*
POLL + NOUN **numbers, rating, results** ◇ *The president's ~ numbers are sinking fast in the West.* | **data** ◇ *~ data on consumer attitudes* | **question** ◇ *the results generated by the ~ question* | **watcher** (*AmE*) ◇ *Missouri requires the parties to register ~ watchers before election day.* | **respondent** ◇ *Only 22% of ~ respondents say they have a positive opinion of him.*
PREP. **in the ~s** ◇ *success in the ~s*
PHRASES **be ahead in the ~s, be behind in the ~s** ◇ *With a week to go until polling day, the party is still behind in the ~s.* | **a lead in the ~s** ◇ *Clearer policies might have widened our lead in the ~s.*

2 (usually **the polls**) voting in an election

ADJ. **presidential**
VERB + POLL **go to** ◇ *In five days, the nation goes to the ~s to elect the next president.*
POLL + VERB **open** | **close** ◇ *Counting will begin as soon as the ~s close.*
PREP. **at the ~s** ◇ *She was defeated at the ~s.*

pollen noun

VERB + POLLEN **collect, gather** ◇ *bees gathering ~* | **produce** | **shed** ◇ *the few weeks a year that corn ~ is shed* | **spread**
POLLEN + NOUN **grain** | **count** ◇ *Hay fever sufferers have a worse time when the ~ count is high.* | **analysis** | **record** ◇ *The ~ record shows that this plant was never common on the island.*

pollutant noun

ADJ. **air, atmospheric, environmental, water** | **biological, chemical, hazardous, organic, toxic** | **major** | **common** ◇ *Both are common ~s and suspected carcinogens.* | **industrial** | **airborne**
VERB + POLLUTANT **discharge, emit, release** | **reduce** ◇ *a washable filter to reduce air ~s* | **remove**
PREP. **~ from** ◇ *~s from nearby industries* | **~ in** ◇ *~s in exhaust gases*
PHRASES **the emission of ~s, the release of ~s**

polluted adj.

VERBS **be** | **become, get** ◇ *The rivers became ~ as the result of industrial waste.*
ADV. **badly, heavily, highly, seriously, severely**
PREP. **with** ◇ *The air is heavily ~ with traffic fumes.*

pollution noun

ADJ. **air, atmospheric, environmental, marine, river, water** | **agricultural, chemical, industrial, toxic** | **lead, mercury, oil, ozone, smoke, traffic, etc.** | **light, noise** | **airborne**
VERB + POLLUTION **cause** | **create, emit, generate, produce** ◇ *They emit 90% less ~ than standard models.* | **avoid, eliminate, prevent** | **combat, control, fight, tackle** (*esp. BrE*) ◇ *a convention on combating atmospheric ~* ◇ *The government has announced plans to tackle light ~.* | **cut, limit, minimize, reduce** ◇ *The summit ended with a joint pledge to limit ~.* | **monitor**
POLLUTION + NOUN **level** | **abatement, control, prevention, reduction** | **limits** | **standards** ◇ *a tightening of water ~ standards* | **incident** (*esp. BrE*), **issue, problem** | **laws, legislation, regulations** | **offence** (*BrE*) | **sources** ◇ *The computer model assesses the likely impact of new ~ sources.* | **credits** (*AmE*) ◇ *a new market in ~ credits*
PHRASES **the cost of ~** ◇ *the cost of air ~ in health and other terms* | **the effects of ~** ◇ *Many athletes feel the effects of air ~ during outdoor exercise.* | **a risk of ~** ◇ *Environmentalists say there is a high risk of ~ from the landfill site.* | **a source**

of ~ ◊ *Heavy traffic flow is a major source of noise ~ in urban areas.*

polythene (*BrE*) (*AmE* **polyethylene**) *noun*

VERB + POLYTHENE/POLYETHYLENE **cover sth with, line sth with, wrap sth in**
POLYTHENE/POLYETHYLENE + NOUN **bag** | **film** (*AmE*)

pond *noun*

ADJ. **big, large** | **little, small** | **shallow** | **stagnant** | **muddy** | **frozen** | **village** (*BrE*) | **backyard** (*AmE*), **garden** | **ornamental** (*esp. BrE*) | **duck, fish, lily** | **retention** (*AmE*) ◊ *Five retention ~s were constructed to increase storage capacity.*
VERB + POND **build, construct, dig** | **fill** | **stock** ◊ *The ~s are fully stocked with rainbow trout.* | **drain, empty** ◊ *The ~ is drained every year.* | **have** ◊ *The Carters had a ~ in their back yard.*
POND + NOUN **life, water**
PREP. **across a/the ~** ◊ *She swam across the ~.* | **in a/the ~** ◊ *There are goldfish in the ~.* | **into a/the ~** ◊ *Her sunglasses had fallen into the ~.* | **on a/the ~** ◊ *There were some ducks swimming on the ~.*
PHRASES **the bottom, edge, middle, surface, etc. of a ~** ◊ *The dog raced around to the other side of the ~.*

ponder *verb*

ADV. **carefully, deeply, hard, seriously** | **(for) a moment** ◊ *She ~ed for a moment before replying.* | **quietly, silently** | **aloud** ◊ *She ~ed aloud the question of what should be done.*
VERB + PONDER **leave sb to** ◊ *He walked out of the room, leaving me to ~ what he had just said.* | **be forced to** | **pause to, stop to** ◊ *Spencer stopped to ~ the thought.*
PREP. **about** ◊ *This was something I had been ~ing about for some time.* | **on** ◊ *I walked up the stairs, ~ing on her reaction to my news.* | **over** ◊ *I ~ed hard over the reply to his letter.*

pony *noun*

ADJ. **wild** | **polo** | **pit** (*BrE, historical*) ◊ *Pit ponies were used in most mines at the turn of the last century.*
VERB + PONY **ride** | **lead** | **groom** | **saddle** | **shoe**
PONY + VERB **whinny** | **canter, gallop, trot**
PONY + NOUN **club** | **ride** | **riding, trekking** (*both esp. BrE*)
PHRASES **a ~ and trap** (*esp. BrE*)

pool *noun*

1 swimming pool, etc.

ADJ. **bathing, paddling** (*BrE*), **swimming, wading** (*AmE*) | **big** | **little, small** | **deep** | **empty** | **indoor** | **open-air** (*BrE*), **outdoor** | **heated** | **backyard** (*AmE*) | **in-ground** (*AmE*) | **Olympic, Olympic-size** | **baby** (*esp. AmE*), **children's, kiddie** (*esp. AmE*) | **inflatable** ◊ *We gave the children an inflatable ~ for Christmas.* | **lap** (*AmE*) ◊ *a 25 m lap ~* | **diving** (*esp. BrE*) ◊ *I left the diving ~ after my session on the springboards.* | **wave** ◊ *a unique new wave ~* | **plunge** ◊ *a sauna and plunge ~* | **birthing** (*BrE*) ◊ *babies born in birthing ~*
VERB + POOL **swim in** | **dive into, jump into, plunge into** | **fill** | **drain** ◊ *You won't have to drain the ~ so often.*
POOL + NOUN **deck** (*esp. AmE*) ◊ *I slipped on the wet ~ deck and fell down.* | **attendant** (*esp. BrE*), **boy** (*AmE*) ◊ *Jack works there as a ~ boy.* | **party** ◊ *A girl invited me over to her ~ party.*
PHRASES **the bottom, edge, middle, side, etc. of the ~** | **a length of the ~** ◊ *He swam three lengths of the ~.*

2 small shallow area of water

ADJ. **big, large** | **little, small** | **bottomless, deep** | **shallow** | **stagnant, still** | **muddy** ◊ *Rhinos are fond of wallowing in muddy ~s and sandy riverbeds.* | **freshwater, saltwater** | **rock** (*BrE*), **tide** (*AmE*) | **ornamental, reflecting** (*esp. AmE*)
PREP. **in a/the ~** ◊ *The children waded in the shallow rock ~s.* | **~ of** ◊ *~s of water*

3 small area of liquid/light

ADJ. **big** | **little, small** | **dark** | **mud** ◊ *The park is full of hot water springs and bubbling mud ~s.*
VERB + POOL **lie in** ◊ *The body lay in a dark ~ of blood.*
PREP. **in a/the ~** ◊ *The wick floated in a ~ of oil.* | **~ of** ◊ *~s of light*

4 supply of sth

ADJ. **big, huge, large, vast** ◊ *a vast ~ of knowledge on best practices* | **limited, small** ◊ *They will share a limited ~ of money with other defendants.* | **growing, shrinking** ◊ *a growing ~ of data* ◊ *a shrinking ~ of assets* | **available** ◊ *the available ~ of really good people* | **common** ◊ *They draw on funds from a common ~.* | **diverse** ◊ *this nation's diverse talent ~* | **car, labour/labor, motor** (*esp. AmE*), **typing** | **applicant** (*AmE*), **recruiting** (*esp. AmE*) ◊ *We need to increase our applicant ~.* | **talent** ◊ *There's a great talent ~ in the business community.* | **jury** (*AmE*) | **press** (*esp. AmE*) ◊ *A member of the press ~ shouted out a question to the president.* | **gene** ◊ *They share a common gene ~.*
VERB + POOL **build, create, form** | **broaden, expand, increase** ◊ *Supporting a diverse work force broadens our ~ of talent.* ◊ *a method of expanding the ~ of potential investors*
PREP. **~ of** ◊ *a strong ~ of talent in the company* ◊ *a large ~ of cheap labour/labor*

pop *noun*

1 short sharp sound

ADJ. **loud** | **sudden**
PREP. **with a ~** ◊ *The cork came out with a loud ~.*

2 popular music

ADJ. **classic, indie, mainstream** | **melodic, psychedelic, synth** | **teen** ◊ *The eight compilations range from teen ~ to classical.* | **60s, 80s, etc.**
VERB + POP **play** | **listen to**
POP + NOUN **classic, hit, music, song, tune** | **artist, singer, star** | **diva, icon, idol, princess** | **act, band, group** | **concert, festival** (*esp. BrE*) | **album, record, video** | **fan** | **charts** | **culture**
PREP. **in ~** ◊ *He was an important figure in ~ during the seventies.*

pope *noun*

VERB + POPE **elect** | **become** ◊ *He became ~ in 1958.* | **meet** ◊ *people who have met the Pope*
PHRASES **an audience with the ~** ◊ *He was granted an audience with the Pope.*

popular *adj.*

VERBS **be, prove, seem** | **become, get, grow** ◊ *They seem to be getting quite ~.* | **remain, stay** | **make sth** ◊ *What makes this subject so ~?*
ADV. **extremely, fairly, very, etc.** | **enormously, especially, exceedingly, extraordinarily, highly, hugely, immensely, incredibly, massively, overwhelmingly, particularly, phenomenally, tremendously, wildly** | **increasingly** | **less than, not exactly** ◊ *Jack was not exactly ~ after the incident with the fire extinguisher.* | **equally** ◊ *Alec and I are equally ~ with the show's viewers.* | **relatively** | **deservedly** ◊ *The restaurant is deservedly ~ with all who enjoy Mexican food.* | **instantly** ◊ *He was one of those people who are instantly ~.* | **newly** (*esp. AmE*) | **always, enduringly, ever, perennially** ◊ *Socks are always ~ as presents.* ◊ *a concert featuring the ever-popular entertainer* | **widely** | **universally** | **politically**
PREP. **among** ◊ *~ among young people* | **as** ◊ *These animals are quite ~ as pets.* | **for** ◊ *a restaurant that is ~ for light meals* | **with** ◊ *This area is immensely ~ with tourists.*

popularity *noun*

ADJ. **considerable, enormous, great, huge, immense, massive, overwhelming, tremendous, widespread** | **unprecedented** ◊ *The French president is enjoying unprecedented ~ due to his anti-war stance.* | **growing, increased, increasing, rising** | **continued, continuing, enduring** |

current, recent | new-found | personal | global, wide, worldwide
VERB + POPULARITY achieve, win | deserve ◇ *The movie deserves its ~.* | enjoy | gain, gain in, grow in ◇ *Organic produce appears to be gaining in ~.* | maintain, retain | regain | boost ◇ *He'll do anything he can to boost his ~.* | explain ◇ *This helps explain the ~ of underwater photography.* | lose ◇ *when the style loses ~*
POPULARITY + VERB grow, soar | decline, wane
POPULARITY + NOUN contest, poll ◇ *He still tops national ~ polls.* | rating
PREP. ~ among ◇ *The current system has never enjoyed ~ among teachers.* | ~ with ◇ *She enjoys huge ~ with the voters.*
PHRASES a decline in ~, a drop in ~ | an increase in ~, a rise in ~, a surge in ~, an upsurge in ~ ◇ *the recent upsurge in the ~ of folk music* | in the ~ stakes (*esp. BrE*) ◇ *We want to remain high in the ~ stakes.* | the peak of (sb/sth's) ~ ◇ *At the peak of its ~ in the late nineties, the band sold ten million albums a year.*

populated adj.

VERBS be
ADV. densely, heavily, highly, thickly ◇ *the most densely ~ part of the island* | sparsely, thinly ◇ *the most sparsely ~ areas in England*
PREP. with ◇ *The prison was ~ with people of every trade and profession.*

population noun

ADJ. dense, large | small, sparse | overall, total ◇ *The country has a total ~ of 65 million.* | growing ◇ *the growing Hispanic ~ in the United States* | global, local, national, world | indigenous, native | immigrant | resident | adult, ageing/aging, elderly, young, youthful | female, male | black, white | Hispanic, Latino, etc. | active, working ◇ *Most of the economically active ~ is employed in the primary industries.* | student | civil, civilian | prison, school | rural, urban | homeless | general ◇ *The general ~ was against the measures.* | natural ◇ *natural ~s of plants and animals* | diverse, heterogeneous ◇ *a diverse ~ of over 100 nationalities* | human ◇ *plagues that can destroy human ~s* | bird, fish, plant, etc. | breeding ◇ *The estuary is home to the largest breeding ~ of birds in Australia.*
POPULATION + VERB be sth, stand at sth ◇ *The ~ now stands at about 4 million.* | reach sth | exceed sth | double, grow, increase, rise | fluctuate ◇ *The ~ fluctuated between 16 000 and 31 000.* | decline, decrease, dwindle, fall, shrink | comprise sth, consist of sth | inhabit, live, reside ◇ *The majority of the ~ lives in these two towns.* ◇ *A quarter of the ~ was residing in rural areas.* | age ◇ *As ~s age, funding retirement becomes more expensive.*
POPULATION + NOUN levels, size | density | data, estimate, figures, projections, statistics, trends ◇ *No reliable ~ estimates exist.* | study | growth, increase ◇ *India's ~ growth rate has been more than twice that of China's.* | boom, explosion ◇ *the ~ boom which followed World War Two* | decline, decrease, loss, reduction | change, movement, shift ◇ *the major factors of ~ change* | huge ~ shifts within metropolitan regions | control ◇ *research in matters of sexual health and ~ control* | census, survey | centre/center ◇ *major ~ centres/centers along the coast*
PHRASES a decline in ~, an increase in ~ | the growth of ~ ◇ *The rapid growth of ~ led to an acute shortage of housing.* | per head of ~ (*esp. BrE*) ◇ *The income per head of ~ was under £1000 per annum.*

porcelain noun

ADJ. fine | white | Chinese, Meissen, etc.
...OF PORCELAIN piece ◇ *some fine pieces of Chinese ~*
PORCELAIN + NOUN factory | bowl, doll, vase

porch noun

1 entrance to a building
ADJ. entrance (*esp. BrE*) | church | back, front
PORCH + NOUN door, light

PREP. in the ~ ◇ *She stood in the ~ and rang the doorbell.*
2 (*AmE*) platform in front of a house
ADJ. back, front | side | wrap-around | covered | wooden
PORCH + NOUN step | light | swing
PREP. on the ~ ◇ *They were sitting out on the ~ in the cool evening air.*

pore noun

ADJ. blocked (*esp. BrE*), clogged (*esp. AmE*) | open
VERB + PORE block, clog (*esp. AmE*) | open ◇ *A hot bath opens the ~s.* | close

pork noun

ADJ. fresh | roast, salt, smoked | ground, pulled (*both AmE*)
...OF PORK bit (*esp. BrE*), piece, slice | belly, leg, loin, shoulder, tenderloin (*all esp. BrE*) ◇ *roast leg of ~*
PORK + NOUN chop, pie (*BrE*) | sausage | belly, loin, shoulder, tenderloin | butcher (*esp. BrE*) | producer (*esp. AmE*) | rinds (*esp. AmE*), scratchings (*BrE*) ◇ *a bag of ~ rinds* ◇ *a packet of ~ scratchings*
PHRASES sweet-and-sour ~

pornography (*also informal* porn) noun

ADJ. hard-core, soft, soft-core | child | Internet
PORNOGRAPHY + NOUN industry | site | porn star | porn ring

port noun

ADJ. bustling, busy | major | coastal, foreign, home, sea | Channel, Gulf, etc. | cargo, coal (*BrE*), commercial, ferry, fishing
VERB + PORT come into, enter, reach ◇ *The vessel reached ~ the next morning.* | leave
PORT + NOUN area, city, town | authority | facilities | security
PREP. in ~ ◇ *Bad weather kept the ship in ~ for three more days.* | into ~ ◇ *She tried to steer the boat into ~.*
PHRASES a ~ of call ◇ *Our next ~ of call was Bermuda.* | a ~ of entry (= where people or goods can enter a country officially) ◇ *Foreign visitors are fingerprinted at the ~ of entry.*

portable adj.

VERBS be
ADV. easily, highly, very ◇ *a machine that is designed to be easily ~*

porter noun

1 helps lift and carry things
ADJ. hospital, kitchen, railway (*all BrE*)
PORTER + VERB carry sth
2 (*BrE*) in charge of the entrance of a large building
ADJ. head | hall, hotel | night | uniformed
PHRASES porter's desk, porter's lodge
→ Note at JOB

portion noun

1 part/share
ADJ. considerable, good, huge, large, major, significant, sizeable, substantial | small | central, lower, southern, top, upper, etc. | first, second, etc. | remaining
VERB + PORTION make up, take up
PREP. ~ of ◇ *Salaries take up a considerable ~ of our total budget.*
2 of food
ADJ. double, generous, large ◇ *a generous ~ of vegetables* | small, tiny | individual
VERB + PORTION eat ◇ *Eat smaller ~s at regular intervals.*
PREP. ~ of ◇ *He asked for a large ~ of salad.*
PHRASES divide sth into ~s

portrait noun

1 a painting or photograph

ADJ. **full-length, half-length** | **oil, pastel, etc.** | **photographic** | **equestrian, family, group, royal**
VERB + PORTRAIT **do, draw, paint** | **sit for** | **commission** | **write** | **display, exhibit, show**
PORTRAIT + VERB **hang** ◊ *Ancient family ~s hung on the walls of the staircase.*
PORTRAIT + NOUN **gallery** | **artist, painter, photographer** ◊ *a fashionable ~ painter* | **bust**
PREP. **~ by, ~ of** ◊ *a ~ of the writer by Picasso*
→ Note at ART

2 detailed description

ADJ. **intimate** | **vivid** ◊ *The novel provides a vivid ~ of the Holberg family.* | **pen** (*esp. BrE*) ◊ *The letters contained many deft pen ~s of his colleagues.*
VERB + PORTRAIT **create, draw** ◊ *The book drew a stark ~ of Quebec's urban poor.* | **offer, present**

portray verb

ADV. **accurately** | **clearly** | **graphically, vividly** ◊ *an incident that graphically ~s the dangers associated with this sport* ◊ *The museum collection vividly ~s the heritage of 200 years of canals.* | **convincingly**
VERB + PORTRAY **attempt to, try to**
PREP. **as** ◊ *They try to ~ themselves as the victims.*

portrayal noun

ADJ. **accurate, realistic, vivid** | **moving** | **negative** ◊ *Much television news gives a negative ~ of politics.* | **media**
VERB + PORTRAYAL **give, offer, provide** ◊ *The movie gives an accurate ~ of the newspaper business.*
PREP. **in the, its, etc. ~** ◊ *She shows a full range of emotions in her ~ of an ambitious politician.* | **~ of** ◊ *His novel is a vivid ~ of life in a mining community.*

position noun

1 place

ADJ. **correct, exact** | **central** | **geographical** | **relative** | **military, strategic** | **defensive** | **scoring** (*sports, esp. AmE*) | **original, starting** | **new**
VERB + POSITION **take, take up** ◊ *The guards took up their ~s on either side of the door.* | **jostle for** ◊ *Hordes of journalists jostled for ~ outside the conference hall.* | **play** (*sports*) ◊ *What ~ does he play?* | **indicate** ◊ *Arrows indicate the ~s of the aircraft.* | **determine**
PREP. **in ~** ◊ *Fix the pieces in ~ before gluing them together.* | **into ~** ◊ *Please get into ~.* | **out of ~** ◊ *Nakata had to play out of ~ when the defender was injured.*

2 way of sitting, standing, etc.

ADJ. **comfortable, uncomfortable** | **crouched, kneeling, sitting, standing** | **sleeping** | **horizontal, upright, vertical** | **prone, supine** (*both formal*) | **foetal/fetal**
VERB + POSITION **assume** | **change, shift**

3 situation

ADJ. **business, economic, financial, legal** | **dominant, impregnable** (*esp. BrE*)**, strong** | **favourable/favorable, good, ideal, perfect** | **enviable** | **invidious** | **competitive** | **strategic** | **precarious, vulnerable, weak** ◊ *He left the club in a precarious financial ~ with debts of £36 million.* | **awkward, difficult, embarrassing, impossible** | **unique** | **same, similar** | **different** | **current, present** | **bargaining, negotiating** | **trading** ◊ *the trading ~ of the Chilean economy*
VERB + POSITION **achieve, attain, reach** ◊ *It has taken years to achieve the ~ we are now in.* | **put sb in** ◊ *It put me in an awkward ~ when he asked me to keep a secret.* | **strengthen** ◊ *Their obvious desperation strengthens our bargaining ~.*
PREP. **in a/the ~** ◊ *We may be in a ~ to help you.* ◊ *I was in the embarrassing ~ of having forgotten her name.* | **~ of**

4 opinion

ADJ. **extreme** | **ideological, philosophical, political, theoretical** | **official** ◊ *The country's official ~ is that there is no famine in the area.*
VERB + POSITION **adopt, take** | **defend, support**
PREP. **~ on** ◊ *He took an extreme ~ on religious matters.*

5 rank

ADJ. **first, second, etc.** | **dominant, high, important, influential, pre-eminent** | **inferior, lowly** | **privileged, secure** | **social**
VERB + POSITION **establish, gain, secure** | **maintain** | **hold, occupy** ◊ *They occupy a lowly ~ in society.* | **use**
PREP. **~ among** ◊ *This latest novel confirms her pre-eminent ~ among today's writers.* | **~ in** ◊ *The firm gained a dominant ~ in the market.*
PHRASES **a ~ of authority, a ~ of influence, a ~ of power**

6 job

ADJ. **full-time, part-time** | **current, present** | **new** | **key, responsible, senior, top** | **leadership** | **junior** | **official** | **skilled** | **administrative, management, managerial** | **staff** | **faculty** (*esp. AmE*)
VERB + POSITION **have, hold, occupy** | **apply for** | **find, obtain** | **assume, take, take up** ◊ *She has taken up a key ~ in our head office.* | **fill** | **offer sb** | **accept** | **resign**
PREP. **in a/the ~** ◊ *How long were you in your previous ~?* | **~ at** ◊ *a faculty ~ at Iowa State University* | **~ in, ~ within** ◊ *his new ~ in the firm* | **~ of** ◊ *She was offered the ~ of sales manager.*

position verb (often be positioned)

ADV. **centrally** ◊ *The markers were not ~ed centrally.* | **carefully** | **correctly, properly** | **wrongly** (*esp. BrE*) | **favourably/favorably** (*esp. BrE*)**, well** | **ideally, perfectly, uniquely** ◊ *The company is uniquely ~ed to compete in foreign markets.* | **strategically**
PREP. **at, behind, between, in, in front of, near, on, etc.** ◊ *Police marksmen were ~ed on the roof.*

positive adj.

1 certain

VERBS **be, seem, sound**
ADV. **absolutely, quite** (*esp. BrE*) ◊ *I'm absolutely ~ it was him.* | **fairly** | **almost** (*esp. AmE*)
PREP. **about** ◊ *She seemed fairly ~ about it.* | **of** ◊ *Are you ~ of your facts?*

2 hopeful and confident/encouraging

VERBS **appear, be, feel, seem, sound** | **remain**
ADV. **extremely, fairly, very, etc.** | **highly, overwhelmingly** ◊ *He took a highly ~ view of the matter.* | **entirely, wholly** | **moderately** (*AmE*) | **generally** | **apparently**
PREP. **about** ◊ *He sounded very ~ about his chances.*

3 showing that sth has happened/is present

VERBS **be, prove, test** ◊ *The test proved ~.*
ADV. **strongly, weakly** (*both technical*)
PREP. **for** ◊ *He tested ~ for HIV.*

possession noun

1 having/owning sth

ADJ. **exclusive, sole** ◊ *They had exclusive ~ of the property as tenants.* | **illegal, unlawful** (*esp. BrE*) (*both law*) ◊ *They were charged with unlawful ~ of firearms.* | **drug** | **cannabis** (*esp. BrE*)**, marijuana** (*esp. AmE*)**, etc.**
VERB + POSSESSION **gain, get, obtain** | **have** | **take** ◊ *When do you take ~ of your new house?* | **keep, retain** ◊ *The team was struggling to retain ~ of the ball.* | **lose**
POSSESSION + NOUN **order** (*BrE, law*) ◊ *The judge made a ~ order against the tenant.*
PREP. **in ~ of sth** ◊ *Passengers must be in ~ of a valid passport.* | **in your ~** ◊ *They have in their ~ some very valuable pictures.*
PHRASES **in full ~ of sth** ◊ *Anyone in full ~ of the facts would see that we are right.*

2 sth that sb has/owns

ADJ. **family, personal, private** | **precious, prized, treasured, valuable, valued** ◊ *The sports car was her proudest ~.* | **material, worldly** ◊ *He carried all his worldly ~s in an old suitcase.* | **colonial, overseas** ◊ *the country's overseas ~s* (= colonies).
VERB + POSSESSION **acquire** | **have** | **collect** (*esp. BrE*) | **sell** | **lose**

possessive *adj.*

VERBS **be, feel** | **become, get** ◊ *Loretta's starting to get ~ and jealous.*
ADV. **extremely, fairly, very, etc.**
PREP. **about** ◊ *Why should he feel so ~ about some old photos?* | **of** ◊ *She had always been ~ of her brother.*

possibility *noun*

ADJ. **exciting, interesting, intriguing** | **endless, many** ◊ *The resort offers endless possibilities for entertainment.* | **only** | **further, other** | **new** | **different, various** | **future** | **distinct, good, great, real, serious, strong** ◊ *There's a strong ~ that it will rain today.* | **likely** ◊ *A more likely ~ is that it will be a tie.* | **reasonable** | **faint** (*esp. BrE*) | **remote, vague** ◊ *There is a remote ~ that he got the wrong day.* | **practical** | **theoretical** | **obvious**
VERB + POSSIBILITY **allow sb, create, offer sb, open up, raise, suggest** | **see** | **consider, discuss, examine, explore, investigate, study, test** ◊ *Have you explored the possibilities of setting up your own business?* | **accept, acknowledge, admit, concede, countenance** (*esp. BrE*), **entertain, recognize** | **ignore, overlook** | **deny, discount, dismiss, eliminate, exclude, preclude, rule out** ◊ *We cannot rule out the ~ of mistaken identity.* | **face** ◊ *The team is facing the real ~ of losing.* | **risk** ◊ *We don't want to risk the ~ of losing all our money.* | **allow for, cover** ◊ *Our resources may be inadequate to cover all possibilities.* | **avert, lessen, reduce** | **remain** ◊ *Bankruptcy remains a distinct ~.*
POSSIBILITY + VERB **exist, remain** ◊ *The ~ exists that she may never make a full recovery.*
PREP. **~ for** ◊ *She was quick to see the possibilities for making money that her new skills gave her.* | **~ of** ◊ *Careful checks will reduce the ~ of unpleasant surprises.*
PHRASES **not beyond the bounds of ~** (*esp. BrE*), **within the realm of ~** ◊ *It's not beyond the bounds of ~ that a similar situation could arise again.* | **a number of possibilities, a range of possibilities** ◊ *The course offers a wide range of possibilities for personal development.*

possible *adj.*

VERBS **be, seem, sound** | **become** | **make sth** ◊ *New technology has made it ~ to communicate more easily.* | **think sth** (*esp. BrE*) ◊ *In those circumstances, I thought it ~ to work with him.*
ADV. **entirely, perfectly, quite, very** | **just** ◊ *It is just ~ that he's still here.* | **still** | **humanly** ◊ *I think that what he's suggesting is not humanly ~.* | **theoretically** ◊ *It's theoretically ~ but highly unlikely ever to happen.*
PHRASES **as far as ~, as long as ~, as much as ~** ◊ *She did as much as ~ to help him.* | **as quickly as ~, as soon as ~** ◊ *Please come as soon as ~.* | **if at all ~, if ~** ◊ *I'd like the money back by next week if ~.*

post *noun*

1 (*BrE*) postal system → See also MAIL

ADJ. **first-class, second-class** | **registered** | **inland**
PREP. **by ~** ◊ *I sent it by first-class ~.* | **in the ~** ◊ *My application for the job is in the ~.*
PHRASES **by return of ~** ◊ *Orders will be sent by return of ~.*

2 (*BrE*) letters, parcels, etc. → See also MAIL

ADJ. **first, last** ◊ *If you hurry you'll just catch the last ~.*
VERB + POST **check, open** ◊ *She arrived at the office early and checked her ~.*
POST + NOUN **box** (usually ***postbox***)

---

poster

619

3 job

ADJ. **senior** | **full-time, part-time** (*esp. BrE*) | **permanent, temporary** | **vacant** | **managerial** (*esp. BrE*), **teaching** ◊ *He took up a teaching ~ at Basle University.* | **government, university** | **diplomatic** (*AmE*) (***diplomatic posting*** in *BrE*) | **overseas** (*AmE*) (***overseas posting*** in *BrE*) | **hardship** (= a job abroad where conditions are difficult) (***hardship posting*** in *BrE*)
VERB + POST **apply for** | **get** | **take, take up** | **hold** | **leave, quit, resign** | **appoint sb to, fill** | **dismiss sb from, relieve sb of** (*esp. BrE*) ◊ *He was dismissed from his ~ when he was found to have accepted bribes.*
PREP. **~ as** ◊ *He quit his ~ as chief executive.* | **~ of** ◊ *She applied for the new ~ of training officer.*

4 place where sb is on duty

ADJ. **army, police** | **command, observation** | **border, frontier**
VERB + POST **take up** ◊ *The guard took up his ~ at the gate.* | **desert** ◊ *The sentries had deserted their ~s.*
PREP. **at your ~** ◊ *The gun crew were at their ~s.*

5 upright piece of wood, etc.

ADJ. **fence** | **finishing** (*BrE*), **winning** | **goal** (usually ***goalpost***) | **far, near** (both in football/soccer) ◊ *He steered a shot between the goalkeeper and the near ~.* | **high, low** (both in basketball)
PHRASES **be pipped at the ~, pip sb/sth to the ~** (*both BrE*) ◊ *She led for most of the way before being pipped at the ~.*

6 message sent to a discussion group on the Internet

ADJ. **blog** | **earlier, original, previous** | **last, new, recent** | **good, great, interesting** | **long**
VERB + POST **make, write** ◊ *I want to apologize for not making a ~ on Friday.* | **read, see** ◊ *To respond to your comments, please see my previous ~.*
POST + VERB **be entitled sth, be titled sth** (*esp. AmE*) ◊ *Seth made a blog ~ titled 'Rules of Engagement'.*
PREP. **~ about, ~ on** ◊ *More info can be found in my first ~ on the subject.*

postage *noun*

VERB + POSTAGE **pay** ◊ *I had to pay $4 ~.* | **cover** (*esp. BrE*) ◊ *Add £3 to each order to cover ~.* | **include**
POSTAGE + NOUN **meter** (*AmE*) | **stamp** | **costs, rates**
PREP. **for ~** ◊ *It costs €60, plus €5 for ~.* | **in ~** ◊ *Sending those books cost me a fortune in ~!* | **on ~** ◊ *What's the ~ on this package?*
PHRASES **~ and handling** (*AmE*), **~ and packing** (*BrE*) ◊ *All prices include ~ and packing/handling.* | **~ paid** (*esp. AmE*) ◊ *Send a check or money order for $7, ~ paid, to this address.* ◊ *a postage-paid envelope*

postcard *noun*

ADJ. **picture** | **holiday** (*BrE*)
VERB + POSTCARD **write** ◊ *I hate writing ~s.* | **mail** (*AmE*), **post** (*BrE*), **send (sb)** | **get, receive** | **buy, sell**
POSTCARD + VERB **arrive** (*esp. BrE*), **come** ◊ *A ~ came for you today.* | **depict sth** (*esp. BrE*), **show sth**
PREP. **on a/the ~** ◊ *Write your answers on a ~.* | **~ from, ~ of** ◊ *I sent him a ~ of the cathedral.* | **~ to**

poster *noun*

ADJ. **campaign, circus, election, film** (*esp. BrE*), **movie** (*esp. AmE*), **propaganda** | **vintage** (*esp. AmE*) ◊ *He collects vintage movie ~s.* | **wanted** ◊ *The police have put up wanted ~s describing the man.*
VERB + POSTER **display, hang, hang up, put up, stick up** | **be covered with, be plastered with** ◊ *His walls are plastered with ~s of rock stars.* | **take down** | **design, make** | **print**
POSTER + VERB **appear, go up** ◊ *Huge election ~s suddenly went up all over the town.* | **hang** ◊ *Assorted ~s hung on the walls.* | **depict sth, feature sth, show sth** | **say sth** ◊ *The wanted ~ said 'Dead or Alive'.* | **advertise sth**
POSTER + NOUN **campaign** ◊ *Detectives have launched a*

massive ~ *campaign to help in the search for two killers.* |
board (*esp. AmE*) | **presentation, session** | **boy, child, girl**
(*all esp. AmE*) (= a person who represents a particular
quality or activity) ◇ *He was the ~ boy for indie rock.*
PREP. **on a/the ~** ◇ *the picture on the ~* | **~ for** ◇ *~s for
tonight's concert* | **~ of** ◇ *a ~ of James Dean*

posting noun

1 message sent to a discussion group on the Internet

ADJ. **Internet, online** | **blog** | **job** ◇ *online job ~s on the
website* | **earlier, original, previous** | **last, new, recent**
VERB + POSTING **make, write** ◇ *I've made a couple of ~s about
identity theft.* | **read, see** ◇ *Have you read my ~?*
PREP. **~ about** ◇ *a ~ about cats* | **~ on** ◇ *~s on our message
board*

2 (*esp. BrE*) being sent to a place for work

ADJ. **diplomatic** | **foreign, overseas** | **hardship** (= a job
abroad where conditions are difficult) (**hardship post** in
AmE) | **three-month, two-year, etc.**
VERB + POSTING **get, take up** ◇ *She was unable to take up the
Bangkok ~.*
PREP. **~ as** ◇ *She has now accepted a ~ as ambassador to
Latvia.* | **~ to** ◇ *He received a ~ to Japan as soon as his
training was finished.*

postman, postwoman noun (*esp. BrE*)

ADJ. **local, village**
POSTMAN, POSTWOMAN + VERB **deliver sth**
→ Note at JOB

post-mortem noun

VERB + POST-MORTEM **carry out** (*esp. BrE*), **conduct, do** | **have,
hold** (*esp. BrE*) ◇ *The coroner says we will have to hold a ~.*
POST-MORTEM + VERB **reveal sth, show sth**
POST-MORTEM + NOUN **examination**
PREP. **~ on** ◇ *They're doing a ~ on her today.*

post office noun

ADJ. **head** (*BrE*), **main** | **local, village** (*esp. BrE*)
VERB + POST OFFICE **go to**
POST OFFICE + NOUN **clerk, worker** | **counter** (*BrE*)
PREP. **at a/the ~** ◇ *You can buy stamps at the ~.*

postpone verb

ADV. **indefinitely** ◇ *The event has been ~d indefinitely due to
lack of interest.* | **merely, only** ◇ *The inevitable conflict was
merely ~d till the next meeting.*
VERB + POSTPONE **agree to, decide to** | **be forced to** | **ask sb
to** ◇ *Ruth wrote at once, asking Maria to ~ her visit.*
PREP. **for** ◇ *Our visit had been ~d for several weeks.* | **from, to**
◇ *The game has been ~d from Wednesday night to Friday
night.* | **till, until** ◇ *The meeting has been ~d until next week.*

postponement noun

ADJ. **indefinite**
VERB + POSTPONEMENT **ask for, call for, request** ◇ *They are
calling for a further ~ of the election date.* | **announce** |
force
PREP. **~ until** ◇ *The death of one of the candidates forced ~ of
the voting until June 1.*

posture noun

1 position of the body

ADJ. **correct, good, perfect** (*esp. AmE*), **proper** | **bad, poor** |
erect, upright ◇ *the normal upright ~* | **stiff** | **body** | **yoga**
VERB + POSTURE **have** ◇ *She has very good ~.* | **adopt, take,
take up** | **maintain** | **change, improve** | **straighten** (*esp.
AmE*)
PREP. **in a/the ~** ◇ *He sat in a ~ of absolute respect.* | **~ for** ◇ *a
poor ~ for driving*

---

2 attitude

ADJ. **defensive** | **aggressive, threatening** | **military**
VERB + POSTURE **adopt, assume, take, take up** | **maintain** |
regain (*esp. AmE*) ◇ *Michael gulped as he struggled to regain
his ~.*
PREP. **~ towards/toward** ◇ *to adopt a threatening ~ towards/
toward an opponent*

pot noun

1 for cooking

ADJ. **cooking**
VERB + POT **cover** ◇ *Cook gently in a covered ~ for 3–4 hours.* |
stir
POT + VERB **boil, bubble** ◇ *He could hear the ~ bubbling on the
stove.*
POT + NOUN **pie** (*AmE*) | **roast**
PREP. **for the ~** (*esp. BrE*) ◇ *Local people kill these animals for
the ~ (= to eat).* | **in a/the ~, into a/the ~** ◇ *Put all the
ingredients in a large ~.* | **~ of** ◇ *a ~ of soup*
PHRASES **~s and pans** ◇ *I sat in the kitchen, among the dirty ~s
and pans.*

2 for tea/coffee

ADJ. **steaming** | **fresh** | **coffee, tea** (usually **teapot**)
VERB + POT **brew, make, put on** ◇ *I'll make a fresh ~ of tea.* |
fill ◇ *She filled the ~ with boiling water.*
PREP. **in a/the ~** ◇ *Is there any more tea in the ~?* | **~ of**

3 container for storing things, growing plants, etc.

ADJ. **ceramic, clay, earthenware, iron, plastic, terracotta** |
flower, plant | **paint, pepper** (*esp. BrE*) (usually **pepper
shaker** in *AmE*) | **chamber** | **chimney** | **lobster**
VERB + POT **grow sth in, plant sth in** | **fill**
POT + VERB **be filled with sth, be full of sth, contain sth** ◇ *a
clay ~ full of oil*
POT + NOUN **plant** (*BrE*)
PREP. **in a/the ~, into a/the ~** ◇ *Plants in ~s require more
water than you might think.* | **~ of** ◇ *a ~ of glue* (*BrE*) ◇ *a ~ of
geraniums*

potato noun

ADJ. **baking** (*esp. BrE*), **new** | **sweet** | **seed** | **baked, boiled,
fried, jacket** (*BrE*), **mashed, roast** (*esp. BrE*), **roasted** (*esp.
AmE*), **sauté** (*BrE*), **sautéed** (*esp. AmE*) ◇ *baked ~es with sour
cream and chives*
...OF POTATOES **sack**
VERB + POTATO **eat, have** | **peel** | **chop, mash, slice** | **bake,
boil, cook, fry, roast, sauté** ◇ *~es baked in their jackets* (*BrE*)
◇ *~es baked in their skins* (*AmE*) | **grow**
POTATO + NOUN **chip** (*AmE*), **crisp** (*BrE*), **pancake** (*AmE*), **purée,
salad** | **peelings** | **peeler** | **skins, wedges** ◇ *a plate of fried
~ skins* | **crop, harvest**
→ Special page at FOOD

potent adj.

VERBS **be** | **become** | **remain**
ADV. **extremely, fairly, very, etc.** ◇ *The vodka must have been
pretty ~ stuff.* | **especially, highly, particularly**

potential noun

ADJ. **considerable, enormous, great, high, huge, limitless,
tremendous, vast** | **full, maximum** ◇ *You aren't using your
computer to its full ~.* | **real, true** | **unfulfilled, untapped** |
future, long-term | **commercial, economic** | **growth** |
creative | **human** ◇ *He believes that religion allows us to
develop our human ~.*
VERB + POTENTIAL **demonstrate, have, show** ◇ *This young
man has enormous ~.* | **hold, offer** ◇ *The new business offers
great ~ for growth.* | **be aware of, recognize, see** ◇ *John
Cadbury could see the ~ for his product.* | **develop, exploit,
explore, unlock** ◇ *They were among the first companies to
exploit the ~ of the Internet.* | **achieve, fulfil/fulfill,
maximize, reach, realize** ◇ *his dream of fulfilling his true ~*
| **increase, reduce**
PREP. **with ~** ◇ *We're looking for a trainee with ~.* | **~ as** ◇ *She*

showed great ~ as an actor. | **~ for** ◇ *an industry that has the ~ for growth*

power

pottery noun

ADJ. **glazed** | **fine** (*esp. BrE*)
... OF POTTERY **fragment** (*esp. BrE*), **piece, shard** ◇ *shards of Iron Age ~*
VERB + POTTERY **make, manufacture** (*esp. BrE*), **produce** | **fire** ◇ *the kilns in which the ~ is fired*
POTTERY + NOUN **kiln** (*esp. BrE*)
→ Note at ART

poultry noun

ADJ. **free-range** (*esp. BrE*) | **domestic**
VERB + POULTRY **keep** (*esp. BrE*), **raise** (*AmE*) ◇ *He keeps/raises rabbits and ~.* ◇ *They keep/raise ~ on the farm.*
POULTRY + NOUN **farm, farming, industry** | **dish** ◇ *a wine that goes well with fish and ~ dishes*

pound noun

1 measure of weight → Note at MEASURE

2 money → Note at CURRENCY

pour verb

ADV. **carefully** | **quickly** | **gradually, slowly** | **out** ◇ *Helen ~ed out two stiff drinks.*
PREP. **from, into, on, onto, out of, over, etc.** ◇ *Pour the sauce over the pasta.*

pout verb

ADV. **slightly** | **cutely, playfully, prettily** (*all esp. AmE*)
PREP. **at** ◇ *She ~ed prettily at him.*

poverty noun

ADJ. **abject, absolute, extreme, grinding, severe** | **widespread** | **global, world** | **rural, urban** | **child**
VERB + POVERTY **alleviate, combat, fight, reduce** | **eliminate, end, eradicate** ◇ *a plan to eradicate urban ~* | **escape** ◇ *his struggle to escape the grinding ~ of his childhood*
POVERTY + NOUN **trap** ◇ *Caught in the ~ trap, they are unable to save money for business ventures.* | **rate** | **reduction**
PREP. **in ~** ◇ *Most of the population lives in grinding ~.* | **~ among** ◇ *the true extent of ~ among the unemployed* | **~ of** ◇ *His work displays a ~ of imagination.*
PHRASES **above/below/under the ~ level** (*AmE*), **above/below/under the ~ line** ◇ *families living below the ~ line/level* | **at the ~ level** (*AmE*), **at the ~ line** (*AmE*), **on the ~ line** (*BrE*)

powder noun

ADJ. **fine** | **chilli/chili, cocoa, curry, milk, protein** | **baking** | **soap, washing** (*both BrE*) | **baby, face, talcum** | **dusting, laundry** (*both AmE*)
VERB + POWDER **grind sth into** ◇ *The seeds are ground into a fine ~ before use.* | **dust sth with, sprinkle on** ◇ *Before the photo dries, the image is dusted with a special ~.* | **apply, put on** ◇ *She quickly put some ~ on her cheeks.* | **add, mix sth with, stir in** ◇ *Add a teaspoonful of curry ~.*
POWDER + NOUN **snow**
PHRASES **in ~ form** ◇ *The medication is also available in ~ form.*

power noun

1 authority/control

ADJ. **absolute, ultimate** | **considerable, enormous, tremendous** | **real** ◇ *The emperor held no real ~.* | **limited** | **arbitrary** | **economic, legal, legislative, political** | **corporate** | **executive** ◇ *He sits on the board but has no executive ~.* | **veto** | **popular** | **secular** | **federal** | **imperial** | **higher** ◇ *belief in a higher ~*
VERB + POWER **come to, rise to** ◇ *When did this government come to ~?* | **assume, gain, get, seize, take** ◇ *The prince assumed ~ in his father's place.* | **return to** | **restore sb to, return sb to** | **have, hold** ◇ *The court has no ~ to order a*

psychiatric examination of the child's parents. ◇ *They held ~ for 18 years.* | **share** | **exercise, use, wield** | **demonstrate, show** | **abuse** | **confer, give sb, grant sb** ◇ *certain ~s that were granted to the government* | **limit** | **lack** | **fall from, lose** ◇ *They fell from ~ in 1992.* | **give up, relinquish, renounce** | **delegate, devolve** (*esp. BrE*) ◇ *Some states delegate police ~ to municipalities.*
POWER + VERB **be concentrated in (the hands of sb/sth), flow from sb/sth, lie with sb/sth, rest with sb/sth** ◇ *The real legislative ~ still rests with the lower chamber.*
POWER + NOUN **struggle** ◇ *Who will get the upper hand in this ~ struggle?* | **relations, structure** | **base** ◇ *The party's ~ base is in the industrial north of the country.* | **broker**
PREP. **in ~** ◇ *the party in ~* | **in sb's ~** ◇ *They held us in their ~.* | **~ of** ◇ *the ~ of veto* | **~ over** ◇ *The government has limited legal ~s over television.*
PHRASES **abuse of ~** | **the balance of ~** ◇ *The war brought about a shift in the balance of ~.* | **a bid for ~** | **the exercise of ~** | **a position of ~** ◇ *the father's position of ~ and influence in the home* | **the ~ behind the throne** (= the person who is really in control) ◇ *People say that the First Lady is the ~ behind the throne.* | **a transfer of ~** ◇ *the transfer of ~ from a military to a civilian government*

2 ability to do sth

ADJ. **air, combat, military, naval, sea** (*esp. BrE*) ◇ *an increase in China's air ~* | **fire** ◇ *weapons with enormous fire ~* | **bargaining** | **computing, processing** | **healing** ◇ *the healing ~ of sleep* | **buying, earning, purchasing** | **staying** ◇ *Having served in four governments, he has the greatest staying ~ of any politician today.* | **special** | **magic, magical, mystical, psychic, supernatural** ◇ *They believe he has supernatural ~s.*
VERB + POWER **have, possess** | **use** | **develop** | **increase, limit, reduce** | **lack** | **lose** ◇ *Religion is rapidly losing its ~ to shape our lives.* | **underestimate** ◇ *Don't underestimate my ~s of persuasion.*
PREP. **beyond sb/sth's ~** ◇ *a task still beyond any computer's ~* | **in sb's ~, within sb's ~** ◇ *I'm afraid it's not within my ~ to help you.* | **through the ~ of** ◇ *He wants to change the world through the ~ of prayer.* | **~s as** ◇ *a tribute to his ~s as a teacher* | **~ of** ◇ *her ~s of observation* ◇ *I lost my ~ of speech for a while after the accident.*
PHRASES **at the height of your ~s, at the peak of your ~s, at the zenith of your ~s** ◇ *In 1946 Dalí was at the peak of his ~s.* | **do all in your ~, do everything in your ~** ◇ *He did everything in his ~ to find us somewhere to live.*

3 country with influence

ADJ. **great, major** | **world** | **foreign** | **allied, enemy** | **occupying** | **victorious** | **European, Western, etc.** ◇ *major European ~s such as France and Germany* | **colonial, imperial, industrial, naval**

4 force/strength

ADJ. **awesome, great, real, tremendous** ◇ *It was a performance of great ~* | **raw** ◇ *the raw ~ of their music* | **destructive, terrible** ◇ *the destructive ~ of a hurricane* | **star** (*esp. AmE*) ◇ *She exudes star ~ whenever she's on screen.*

5 energy

ADJ. **full** ◇ *The plane was still climbing at full ~.* | **reduced** ◇ *The transmitter is operating on reduced ~.* | **electric, electrical, hydroelectric, nuclear, solar, steam, tidal, water, wind**
VERB + POWER **generate, produce** ◇ *They use these streams to generate ~ for the mill.* | **provide (sb/sth with), supply (sb/sth with)** ◇ *This wheel provides the ~ to the cutting machine.* | **use** | **harness** | **turn on** | **cut off, turn off**
POWER + VERB **drive sth, run sth** ◇ *Wind ~ is used to drive the machinery.* | **go off, go out** (*esp. AmE*) ◇ *She was in the elevator when the ~ went off.*
POWER + NOUN **cable, grid, line, point** (*BrE*), **source, supply, system** | **tool** ◇ *Power tools make many jobs so much easier.* | **plant, station** (*BrE*) | **worker** | **cut** (*BrE*), **failure, outage** (*AmE*) | **consumption**

PREP. ~ for ◇ *The generator supplies ~ for lighting,*
PHRASES **a source of** ~

powerful *adj.*

VERBS **be, feel, look, seem** | **become, get, grow** | **make sb/ sth**
ADV. **extremely, fairly, very, etc.** | **enormously, especially, exceptionally, extraordinarily, immensely, incredibly, particularly, remarkably, surprisingly, tremendously, unusually** | **increasingly** | **relatively** | **enough, sufficiently** ◇ *She had a voice ~ enough not to need a microphone.* | **equally** | **potentially** | **economically, politically** ◇ *a politically ~ figure*

powerless *adj.*

VERBS **appear, be, feel, prove, seem** | **become** | **remain** | **leave sb, make sb, render sb** ◇ *If he took control, they would be rendered virtually ~.*
ADV. **completely, quite** (*esp. BrE*), **totally, utterly** | **essentially, largely, relatively, virtually**
PREP. **against** ◇ *They were completely ~ against such a large group.* | **in the face of** ◇ *They felt ~ in the face of disaster.* | **over** ◇ *People feel ~ over the problem.*

practicable *adj.* (*formal*)

VERBS **be, prove, seem** | **become**
ADV. **perfectly** | **reasonably** ◇ *We will do this as soon as is reasonably ~.* | **not very**
PHRASES **as far as (is) ~, so far as (is) ~** ◇ *to reduce smoking as far as is reasonably ~* | **as soon as (is) ~, at the earliest ~ date, time, etc.** ◇ *The decision will be made at the earliest ~ date.* | **to the extent ~** ◇ *We aim to reduce, to the maximum extent ~, the discharge of pollutants.* | **where ~, wherever ~**

practical *noun* (*BrE*)

ADJ. **chemistry, physics, etc.** | **laboratory**
VERB + PRACTICAL **sit** (*BrE*), **take** | **fail, pass** ◇ *I passed the written exam but failed the ~.*

practical *adj.*

VERBS **be, prove, seem, sound** | **become, get** ◇ *It's time to get ~!* | **make sth** ◇ *a feature that makes the system more ~* | **do sth** ◇ *I'll do something ~ now and answer some mail.*
ADV. **extremely, fairly, very, etc.** ◇ *She always adopted a very ~ tone.* | **eminently, highly, intensely** | **entirely, purely, strictly** ◇ *For entirely ~ reasons, children are not invited.* | **hardly**

practice *noun*

1 actual doing of sth

VERB + PRACTICE **put sth into** ◇ *I can't wait to put what I've learned into ~.*
PREP. **in** ◇ *The idea sounds fine in theory, but would it work in ~?*

2 doing sth many times

ADJ. **basketball, batting, football, piano, soccer** (*esp. AmE*), **swim** (*AmE*), **etc.** | **target** | **daily** ◇ *hard work and daily ~*
VERB + PRACTICE **do, get, get in, have** ◇ *I'll be able to get in a bit of ~ this weekend.* ◇ *I've had a lot of ~ in saying 'no' recently!* | **need, require, take** ◇ *Don't worry if you can't do it at first—it takes ~!* | **give sb** ◇ *This chapter gives students ~ in using adjectives.*
PRACTICE + NOUN **facilities, field** (*esp. AmE*), **ground** | **game, session** | **drill** ◇ *We watched the swimmers go through their ~ drills.*
PREP. **out of ~** ◇ *If you don't play regularly, you soon get out of ~.* | **with ~** ◇ *His accent should improve with ~.* | **~ at** ◇ *at swimming underwater* | **~ in** ◇ *The children need more ~ in tying their shoelaces.*
PHRASES **be good ~ for sth** ◇ *It will be good ~ for later, when you have to make speeches in public.* | **~ makes perfect** (*saying*)

3 way of doing sth

ADJ. **good, recommended, sound** ◇ *advice on adopting current best ~ in your business* ◇ *environmentally sound ~s* | **safe, unsafe** | **ethical** | **corrupt, deceptive, fraudulent, questionable, shady, sharp** (*esp. BrE*), **unethical, unfair** ◇ *shady business ~s* | **discriminatory, restrictive** | **actual** ◇ *the complications that arise in actual ~* | **everyday** | **contemporary, current** | **accepted, customary, established, long-standing, traditional** | **common, general, normal, routine, standard, usual** ◇ *the company's general ~ of selling through agents* ◇ *It is standard ~ not to pay bills until the end of the month.* | **universal, widespread** | **local** | **sustainable** ◇ *sustainable land-use ~s* | **clinical, cultural, legal, medical, nursing, religious, sexual, social, spiritual, etc.** ◇ *the medical ~s of ancient Egypt* | **accounting, administrative, business, employment, hiring** (*esp. AmE*), **management, working** ◇ *They carried out a study of Japanese working ~s.*
VERB + PRACTICE **introduce** ◇ *The ~ of community policing was introduced in the 1970s.* | **adopt, employ, follow, implement, use** | **advocate, encourage, endorse, promote, recommend** | **challenge, question** | **defend, support** ◇ *Some prisoners defend this ~ as the only way to survive.* | **condemn, discourage** ◇ *This ~ was roundly condemned by the World Medical Association.* | **abandon, abolish, ban, eliminate, end, forbid, halt, outlaw, prevent, prohibit, reject, stop** | **continue** ◇ *The bank has continued its ~ of charging late fees.* | **alter, change, improve, modify, transform** ◇ *Established ~s are difficult to modify.* | **affect, govern, guide, influence, inform, shape** ◇ *the decisions that govern our ~ and our conduct* ◇ *We use this information to inform clinical ~.*
PRACTICE + VERB **exist** ◇ *Certain ~s exist in both public and private schools.* | **begin** | **continue** ◇ *the ancient custom of log rolling, a ~ which continues to this day* | **change, develop, evolve** | **differ, vary** ◇ *Religious ~s differ from group to group.* | **reflect sth** ◇ *Such ~s do not reflect our values.*
PREP. **~ among** ◇ *This is now common ~ among ethnographers.* | **~ for** ◇ *safe medical ~s for children* | **~ in** ◇ *good ~ in undergraduate education* | **~ of** ◇ *the ~ of acupuncture* | **~ regarding** ◇ *questionable accounting ~s regarding the sale of hardware* | **~ within** ◇ *ethical ~ within the profession*
PHRASES **a change in ~** ◇ *changes in employment ~s* | **a code of ~** (*esp. BrE*) ◇ *voluntary codes of ~ between sellers and customers* | **make a ~ of sth** ◇ *I don't make a ~ of forgetting to pay my bills, I assure you!*

4 work/office of a professional person

ADJ. **successful** | **clinical, legal, medical, professional** | **family** (*esp. AmE*), **general** (*both medicine*) ◇ *a physician in family ~* (*AmE*) ◇ *a doctor in general ~* (*BrE*) | **private** ◇ *a psychologist in private ~* | **group** ◇ *It's a group ~, so you can easily change doctors.*
VERB + PRACTICE **be in, go into, set up in** ◇ *She wants to go into general ~.* | **retire from** | **suspend sb from** ◇ *He has been suspended from ~.* | **begin, establish, open, start** ◇ *Martin began his own ~ in 1993.* ◇ *She has opened a new ~ in the town.* | **run** ◇ *He runs a successful legal ~ in Ohio.* | **maintain** ◇ *She maintains a private ~ as a mental health consultant.* | **join** ◇ *A new partner has joined the ~.* | **leave**

practise (*BrE*) (*AmE* **practice**) *verb*

1 to train regularly to improve

ADV. **diligently, hard** ◇ *She diligently ~d her piano every day.* | **regularly**
PREP. **for** ◇ *She's practising hard for the piano competition.* | **on** ◇ *I learned hairdressing by practising on my sister.*
PHRASES **be well ~d (in sth)** ◇ *He was well ~d in meditation.*

2 to do sth as part of normal behaviour/behavior

ADV. **commonly, routinely, widely** ◇ *This model of education is widely ~d.* | **rarely** ◇ *Polygamy is legal, but it is very rarely ~d.* | **currently** ◇ *whaling as currently ~d* | **freely, openly** ◇ *Both Protestants and Catholics could freely ~ their religion.*
PHRASES **(be) ~d today** ◇ *These methods are still ~d today.*

pragmatic *adj.*

VERBS **be, seem** | **become** | **remain**
ADV. **extremely, fairly, very, etc.** | **highly** | **entirely, purely, strictly, utterly** | **ruthlessly** ◇ *We must be ruthlessly ~ and intensely focused.* | **essentially, largely** ◇ *Our approach is essentially ~.*
PREP. **about** ◇ *They're ~ about the spending cuts.*

prairie *noun*

ADJ. **high** | **open, rolling, vast, wide** | **northern, western, etc.** | **native** ◇ *Only about 5% of native ~ is left in Kansas.* | **tall-grass** (*esp. AmE*)
VERB + PRAIRIE **cross** ◇ *a train of covered wagons crossing the wide American ~s*
PRAIRIE + NOUN **grass** | **fire** (*AmE, figurative*) ◇ *His charges spread like a ~ fire.*
PREP. **across the ~** ◇ *their route across the ~* | **on the ~** ◇ *settlers' houses on the ~s of Canada*

praise *noun*

ADJ. **considerable, effusive, extravagant, fulsome, glowing, great, high, lavish, special, unstinting, warm** ◇ *The speech earned him lavish ~ from the press.* | **faint** ◇ *My comment sounds like damning with faint ~* (= *praise so little that you seem to be criticizing*). | **widespread** | **universal** | **critical** (= *praise from the critics of art, music, etc.*) ◇ *The novels have won widespread critical ~.* | **public** ◇ *His accomplishments won him wide public ~.*
VERB + PRAISE **be full of, be fulsome in** (*esp. BrE*), **be gushing in** (*esp. BrE*), **be unstinting in, gush with** (*esp. AmE*) ◇ *The critics were full of ~ for the movie.* ◇ *He was unstinting in his ~ of his teacher.* ◇ *He has great ~ for his co-stars.* | **single sb out for** ◇ *The team's coach singled his goalkeeper out for ~.* | **heap, lavish, shower (sb with)** ◇ *an article heaping ~ on the government* | **come in for, receive** | **attract, draw, earn, garner, get, win** ◇ *The play has attracted universal ~.* | **deserve** ◇ *These artists deserve ~ for the clarity of their visions.*
PREP. **beyond ~** ◇ *This book is beyond ~.* | **in ~ of** ◇ *He wrote many poems in ~ of his wife.* | **~ for** ◇ *They earned ~ for their efforts.* | **~ from** ◇ *The decision also won ~ from local people.* | **~ of** ◇ *her ~ of his skill* | **~ to** ◇ *much joyous singing and ~ to God*
PHRASES **a chorus of ~, a paean of ~** (*literary*) ◇ *The French manager led the chorus of ~ for the German team.* | **have nothing but ~ for sb/sth** ◇ *The patients interviewed had nothing but ~ for the hospital staff.* | **sing sb's ~s** ◇ *The newspapers were singing the president's ~s.* | **a word of ~** ◇ *There were words of ~ for the show's designer.*

praise *verb*

ADV. **effusively, highly, lavishly, warmly** ◇ *He ~d all his staff highly.* | **publicly** | **justly, rightly** ◇ *Her achievements in this field have been rightly ~d.* | **repeatedly** ◇ *She repeatedly ~d him and his works.*
VERB + PRAISE **be quick to** ◇ *The defeated captain was quick to ~ the winning team.*
PREP. **for** ◇ *They ~d him for his cooking.*
PHRASES **be unanimously ~d, be universally ~d, be widely ~d** ◇ *The album has been universally ~d for its creativity.* | **~ sb/sth to the skies** ◇ *Her manager ~d her to the skies.*

pram (*BrE*) *noun* → See also BABY CARRIAGE

VERB + PRAM **push, wheel**
PREP. **in a/the ~** ◇ *She was pushing her baby along in a ~.*

pray *verb*

ADV. **desperately, earnestly, fervently, hard** ◇ *He thought if he ~ed hard enough God might eventually listen.* | **humbly** | **quietly, silently** ◇ *I silently ~ed for my release.* | **aloud** | **together** | **secretly** ◇ *He was secretly ~ing that his offer would be rejected.* | **always, constantly, regularly** ◇ *My parents would always ~ for rain.*
PREP. **for** ◇ *He ~ed for good weather.* | **over** ◇ *Diane ~ed over the body for a moment.* | **to** ◇ *I ~ed to God for guidance.* | **with** ◇ *She asked the priest to ~ with her.*

PHRASES **hope and ~** ◇ *We can hope and ~ that no one gets hurt.* | **let us ~** ◇ *'Let us ~.' The congregation bowed their heads.* ◇ *Let's ~ Mick doesn't find out.*

prayer *noun*

ADJ. **little, quick, short** ◇ *She whispered a little ~.* | **private, quiet, silent** ◇ *She uttered a silent ~.* | **special** | **fervent, heartfelt** | **unanswered** | **afternoon, bedtime, evening, midday, morning, noon** | **daily** | **ritual** ◇ *the five daily ritual ~s of Islam* | **Friday** ◇ *Muslims attend Friday ~s at the mosque.* | **Christian, Jewish, etc.** | **family** | **school** (*esp. AmE*) ◇ *the contentious issue of school ~*
VERB + PRAYER **give, offer, offer up, pray, say, send up, utter** ◇ *He gave a ~ of thanks to the troops.* ◇ *I sent up a quick ~ and entered the interview room.* | **mutter, whisper** ◇ *Whenever I pass a temple, I mutter a quick ~.* | **chant, read, recite** ◇ *Priests chanted ~s and read from sacred texts.* | **remember sb in** ◇ *Let us remember them in our ~s today.* | **hear** | **answer** ◇ *Does God answer our ~s?* | **grant** ◇ *Thankfully, his ~s were granted.* | **kneel in** ◇ *The congregation kneeled in ~.* | **join in, meet for** ◇ *Local groups meet for ~.* | **have** ◇ *We had family ~s before breakfast.* | **attend** ◇ *Students are required to attend ~s twice a week.* | **lead** ◇ *An imam leads the ~ and usually gives a sermon.*
PRAYER + NOUN **book | beads** ◇ *He fiddled with his ~ beads.* | **mat, rug** | **shawl** ◇ *a Jewish ~ shawl* | **flag** ◇ *Buddhist ~ flags fluttering in the breeze* | **wheel** ◇ *Tibetan monks use a ~ wheel.* | **meeting, service, session, vigil** | **breakfast** (*AmE*) | **circle, group** | **leader** ◇ *a ~ leader at the mosque* | **hall, room** ◇ *a multi-faith ~ room in the college*
PREP. **at ~** ◇ *He spends an hour each day at ~.* | **in ~** ◇ *She moved her lips in silent ~.* | **~ for** ◇ *a ~ for peace* | **~ of** ◇ *I said a ~ of grateful thanks to God.* | **~ over** ◇ *He spoke a brief ~ over their meal.* | **~ to**
PHRASES **the answer to sb's ~s** (= *exactly what sb needs*) ◇ *The letter was the answer to all her ~s.* | **not have a ~** (= *be sure to fail*) ◇ *This never had a ~ of working.*

preacher *noun*

ADJ. **charismatic, dynamic, famous, good, great, popular, well-known** | **fundamentalist, radical** ◇ *He was a radical ~ who inspired peasants to rebel.* ◇ *right-wing Christian fundamentalist ~s* | **fiery, fire-and-brimstone, firebrand, hellfire** ◇ *a Southern hellfire ~* | **evangelical** | **Christian, Muslim, etc.** | **Baptist, Methodist, etc.** | **lay** | **woman** ◇ *clergymen who adamantly opposed women ~s* | **local** | **itinerant** ◇ *His father was an itinerant Methodist ~.* | **guest** ◇ *a series of guest ~s* | **radio, television, TV** ◇ *a charismatic TV ~*
VERB + PREACHER **hear, listen to**

precaution *noun*

ADJ. **sensible, wise** | **adequate, appropriate, proper, reasonable** | **necessary** ◇ *Condoms are a necessary ~.* | **elaborate, great** ◇ *the need to take great ~s to protect sources* | **basic, normal, simple, standard** ◇ *You'll be safe if you observe certain basic ~s.* | **every** ◇ *We take every ~ to ensure your safety.* | **added, additional, extra, special** | **fire, safety, security**
VERB + PRECAUTION **follow, observe, take, use** ◇ *Remember to use all necessary safety ~s.*
PREP. **as a ~** ◇ *She had to stay in hospital overnight, just as a ~.* | **~ against** ◇ *a ~ against customers who try to leave without paying* | **~ for** ◇ *Staff are expected to take reasonable ~s for their own safety.* | **~ of** ◇ *I took the ~ of turning the water supply off first.*

precede *verb*

ADV. **directly, immediately** ◇ *in the moments which immediately ~d the earthquake* | **generally, often, typically, usually** ◇ *Victories are often ~d by minor setbacks.*

precedence

precedence *noun*

ADJ. **historical**
VERB + PRECEDENCE **have, take** | **give sb/sth** ◇ *You should give your schoolwork ~.* | **claim** ◇ *The French kings claimed ~ over those of Spain.*
PREP. **~ over** ◇ *The needs of the patient take ~ over those of the student doctor.*
PHRASES **in order of ~** ◇ *The guests were seated strictly in order of ~.*

precedent *noun*

ADJ. **bad, dangerous, terrible, unfortunate** | **good, important, strong** ◇ *There is a strong ~ for such a strategy.* | **ample** ◇ *There is ample ~ for this tactic.* | **clear, obvious** ◇ *There is no obvious ~ for this law.* | **established, historical, past, prior** | **new** ◇ *This would have set a dangerous new ~.* | **court, judicial, legal** ◇ *There was a federal court ~ for this.* | **binding** ◇ *The ruling does not set a binding ~.* | **literary** ◇ *There are many literary ~s for this strategy.*
VERB + PRECEDENT **serve as** ◇ *This case could could serve as a ~ for others against the tobacco companies.* | **have** | **create, establish, provide, set** ◇ *This lowering of standards sets a dangerous ~ for future developments.* | **cite** | **find** | **base sth on, use sth as** ◇ *The judge based his decision on ~s set during the previous century.* | **follow** | **ignore** | **break, overturn** ◇ *Overturning a legal ~ is no easy matter.*
PREP. **without ~** ◇ *The achievements of this period were without ~ in history.* | **~ for** ◇ *Many ~s can be found for this decision.*

precinct *noun*

1 (*BrE*) commercial area where cars cannot go
ADJ. **shopping** ◇ *the £1.3-million redevelopment of the shopping ~.* | **pedestrian** | **town-centre**

2 (*AmE*) police district; a police station
ADJ. **police** ◇ *He was handcuffed and taken down to the police ~.* | **17th, 102nd, etc.** | **local** ◇ *I went down to my local ~ to make a report.*
PRECINCT + NOUN **house** ◇ *He wrote yesterday from a police ~ house in New Orleans.* | **commander** ◇ *The former Queens ~ commander has slashed crime.*

3 (*AmE*) part of a town or city for elections
ADJ. **key, targeted** ◇ *Campaigners walked door-to-door in targeted ~s.* | **Democratic, Republican** | **African-American, Hispanic, etc.**
VERB + PRECINCT **walk** ◇ *Did you walk your ~ on the day of the vote?* | **target** ◇ *Republicans have targeted ~s throughout the country.*
PRECINCT + NOUN **caucus** ◇ *A number of issues will be discussed at the ~ caucus.* | **captain, chairman, committeeman** ◇ *The ~ captains were able to round up 6 000 volunteers.* | **returns** ◇ *The ~ returns show that the support received by both men was remarkable.*
PREP. **in ~** ◇ *You can register to vote in your ~ by showing proof of residence.*
PHRASES **the ~ level** ◇ *We're literally organizing leadership down to the ~ level.*

4 area around a building
ADJ. **sacred** ◇ *the sacred ~ of Apollo* | **inner, outer** | **abbey, castle, palace, shrine, temple, etc.**
VERB + PRECINCT **enter** ◇ *It was forbidden to enter the temple ~s.*
PREP. **in ~** ◇ *The event was held in the ~s of the parish church.* | **within ~** ◇ *He took up residence in chambers within the ~ of a monastery.*

precious *adj.*

VERBS **be** | **become** | **seem** ◇ *The people in his life seemed so ~ to him now.*
ADV. **extremely, very** | **incredibly, infinitely**
PREP. **to** ◇ *You are infinitely ~ to me.*

precise *adj.*

VERBS **be** | **become** ◇ *These estimates will become more ~.* | **make sth** ◇ *We've tried to make the process as ~ as possible.*
ADV. **extremely, incredibly, infinitely** | **highly, incredibly, very** | **absolutely** | **increasingly** | **reasonably** | **enough, sufficiently** ◇ *Are the measurements ~ enough?* | **insufficiently** | **mathematically, surgically, technically** ◇ *You need to use legally ~ terms.*
PREP. **about** ◇ *You have to be ~ about the numbers.* | **in** ◇ *to be more ~ in my analysis*

precision *noun*

ADJ. **absolute, deadly, perfect, pinpoint** ◇ *The captain struck again with deadly ~.* ◇ *The rebels launched missiles with pinpoint ~.* | **extreme, great, high, utmost** ◇ *We can now choose our targets with greater ~.* ◇ *high ~ measurement tools* ◇ *The movements are executed with the utmost ~.* | **analytical, mathematical, military, scientific, surgical, technical** ◇ *He organized the team with military ~.*
... OF PRECISION **degree** ◇ *Chimps are able to manipulate objects with a high degree of ~.*
VERB + PRECISION **call for, demand, require** ◇ *surgery which requires great ~* | **improve, increase** | **lack** ◇ *His rambling writing style just lacks ~.*
PRECISION + NOUN **engineering** | **instrument, tool** ◇ *the finest timepieces and ~ instruments* | **measurement** ◇ *~ measurements of these atoms* | **bombing, strike** ◇ *They back their forces with ~ air strikes.* | **weapons** ◇ *high-tech ~ weapons*
PREP. **with ~** ◇ *These items cannot be dated with any ~.* | **~ in** ◇ *a new era of ~ in engineering*
PHRASES **a lack of ~** ◇ *Any lack of ~ in the contract could give rise to a dispute.*

preconception *noun*

VERB + PRECONCEPTION **have** | **fit, fit in with** ◇ *The facts refused to fit my ~s.* ◇ *They like this approach because it fits in with their own ~s.* | **challenge, defy, shatter** ◇ *It is important to challenge society's ~s about disabled people.*
PREP. **with ~s, without ~s** ◇ *It's important that you come to this task with no ~s.* | **~ about** ◇ *Most people have ~s about old age.* | **~ of** ◇ *her ~s of life in the country*

predicament *noun*

ADJ. **awful, difficult, dire, terrible, worse** ◇ *Other companies are in an even worse ~ than ourselves.* | **current, present** | **financial** ◇ *the team's dire financial ~* | **personal** | **similar** ◇ *When I was your age, I was in a similar ~.* | **human** ◇ *a portrayal of the human ~*
VERB + PREDICAMENT **be caught in, be in, face, find yourself in, get into** ◇ *Many young people find themselves in this ~.* | **place sb in, put sb in** | **escape, escape from, get out of** ◇ *How were we to escape this awful ~?* | **realize, understand** | **consider, ponder** | **explain** ◇ *She was searching for the right words to explain her ~.* | **solve**
PREP. **in a/the ~** ◇ *Now I really was in a dire ~.*

predict *verb*

ADV. **correctly, reliably, successfully** | **incorrectly, wrongly** | **accurately, exactly, precisely, with accuracy, with precision** ◇ *You cannot ~ the weather with absolute accuracy.* | **boldly, confidently, with certainty, with confidence** ◇ *The author boldly ~s the end of the Communist Party's rule.* ◇ *It is not possible to ~ with any certainty what effect this will have.* ◇ *We can ~ with absolute confidence how the newspapers will react.* | **reasonably, safely** ◇ *We can reasonably ~ what is going to happen.* ◇ *I think I can safely ~ that they will fight the verdict.* | **easily** ◇ *Every step in the movie is easily ~ed.* | **initially, originally** | **consistently**
VERB + PREDICT **be able to, be unable to, can** | **attempt to, try to** | **dare (to)** ◇ *Few would have dared to ~ such a landslide victory.* | **fail to** | **be early to** ◇ *It is still too early to ~ the degree to which prices will rise.* | **be difficult to, be hard to, be impossible to** | **be easy to, be possible to** | **be reasonable to, be safe to** ◇ *It is safe to ~ that this trend will persist.* | **use sth to** ◇ *a computer model used to ~ future weather patterns* | **allow sb to, enable sb to, help (sb) (to)** ◇

Newton's theories allow us to ~ the flight of a ball. ◇ *Computer programs are used to help ~ the weather.*
PREP. **from** ◇ *We can ~ from this information what is likely to happen next.*
PHRASES **be widely ~ed** ◇ *This result had been widely ~ed by the opinion polls.*

predictable *adj.*

VERBS **be, seem** | **become, get** ◇ *I'm getting too ~.* | **make sth** ◇ *Recent changes make the future even less ~.*
ADV. **extremely, fairly, very, etc.** | **easily, highly** | **completely, entirely, perfectly, quite** (*esp. BrE*), **totally, utterly, wholly** ◇ *The results were utterly ~.* | **almost** | **largely** | **reasonably, relatively** | **sadly** ◇ *The government's reaction was sadly ~.*
PREP. **from** ◇ *He asked whether this was ~ from previous performances.*

prediction *noun*

ADJ. **accurate, correct, good, precise, right, successful** ◇ *the best available ~ of future interest rates* ◇ *It turned out my ~ was right.* | **false, incorrect** | **dire, gloomy** (*esp. BrE*), **grim** ◇ *the dire ~s by economists of a worldwide recession* | **optimistic** ◇ *The sales results exceeded even the most optimistic ~s.* | **long-term** | **reliable, safe** | **bold, confident** | **definite, firm, specific** ◇ *In this study, we made no specific ~s about likely outcomes.* | **theoretical** ◇ *the discrepancy between the theoretical ~s and the results* | **computer** | **earthquake, weather**
VERB + PREDICTION **make** | **give, offer** ◇ *Could the panel give their ~ as to who he will appoint to the post?* | **test** ◇ *This study tests these ~s.* | **confirm, fulfil/fulfill, support** ◇ *The results of the experiment confirmed their ~s.* | **confound, contradict, defy** ◇ *Their success defies the ~s made by most experts.*
PREDICTION + VERB **prove sth, turn out to be sth** ◇ *Our ~ turns out to be correct.* | **be borne out, come true**
PREP. **amid ~s** (*esp. BrE*) ◇ *Six hundred workers there lost their jobs today, amid gloomy ~s that there could be worse to come.* | **contrary to a/the ~** ◇ *Contrary to almost all ~s, however, the government did not fall.* | **despite a/the ~** ◇ *Despite earlier dire ~s, shares remained steady.* | **~ about** ◇ *I've learned not to make ~s about the weather.* | **~ for** ◇ *the government's ~ for unemployment* | **~ of** ◇ *their ~s of future growth* | **~ on** ◇ *Let me get your ~s on the final score.*

prefer *verb*

ADV. **greatly, much, overwhelmingly, strongly, vastly** ◇ *I greatly ~ this version.* ◇ *I much ~ the orchestra's 1998 recording of the symphony.* | **just, simply** ◇ *You may simply ~ just to sit on the terrace with a cocktail.* | **really** ◇ *I would really ~ to teach girls.* | **rather, slightly** | **certainly, definitely** ◇ *Egg pasta is certainly preferred by many chefs.* | **clearly, obviously** | **apparently** ◇ *Huge majorities apparently ~ reducing unemployment to fighting inflation.* | **generally, normally, typically, usually** | **naturally** ◇ *Employers naturally ~ candidates with some previous experience of the job.* | **personally** | **still**
VERB + PREFER **would** ◇ *We can eat out if you like, but I would ~ to stay in.* | **tend to** ◇ *Industries still tend to ~ virgin raw materials to recycled ones.* | **appear to, seem to** | **happen to** ◇ *I happen to ~ action movies myself.*
PREP. **over** ◇ *A son is usually preferred over a female heir.* | **to** ◇ *I ~ his earlier paintings to his later ones.*

preferable *adj.*

VERBS **be, seem** | **become, remain** | **make sth** | **consider sth, deem sth** | **find sth**
ADV. **far, greatly, highly, infinitely, much, vastly** ◇ *This technique is far ~ to any alternative.* ◇ *The new policies are infinitely ~ to what went before.* | **clearly** | **environmentally** (*AmE*) ◇ *We are committed to purchasing environmentally ~ products whenever possible.*
PREP. **for** ◇ *The summer months are ~ for weddings.* | **to** ◇ *Death was considered vastly ~ to surrender.*

preference *noun*

ADJ. **clear, definite, marked, strong** | **slight** | **individual, personal** ◇ *It's a matter of personal ~.* | **consumer, customer, user, voter** | **policy, political** ◇ *His policy ~s are pretty centrist.* | **dietary, food** ◇ *modern children's food ~s* | **gender, racial** (*both AmE*) ◇ *his consistent opposition to racial ~s while a legislator* | **sexual** ◇ *discrimination based on race, religion, gender or sexual ~* | **aesthetic, cultural** | **first, second, etc.** ◇ *My first ~ is for the applicant from Hong Kong.* ◇ *Most local voters gave West second ~.* (*BrE*)
VERB + PREFERENCE **have** ◇ *Do you have any particular ~?* | **demonstrate, display, exhibit, indicate, reflect, reveal, show** ◇ *designs that reflect their individual ~s* ◇ *Learners show a ~ for one learning style over others.* | **express, state** ◇ *Older people tend to express a ~ for dark chocolate.* | **give sb** ◇ *Preference is given to students who have passed mathematics and chemistry.* | **receive** ◇ *Some countries receive ~ over others.* | **affect, determine, influence, shape** ◇ *A combination of factors determined ~.* | **fit, fit with, satisfy, suit** ◇ *She was happy to arrange her schedule to suit their ~s.*
PREP. **for ~** ◇ *I travel by plane, for ~.* | **in ~ to** ◇ *They bought French planes in ~ to British ones.* | **~ as to, ~ with regard to** ◇ *He has not expressed a ~ as to which school he wants to go to.* | **~ between** ◇ *people's ~s between brown and white bread* | **~ for sth (over sth)** ◇ *the government's ~ for tax cuts over greater public spending* | **~ in** ◇ *changing ~s in furniture styles* | **~ regarding** ◇ *their ~s regarding websites* | **~ towards/toward** ◇ *student ~s towards/toward the various activities*
PHRASES **in order of ~** ◇ *List the candidates in order of ~.*

pregnancy *noun*

ADJ. **early** | **late** | **full-term, post-term** | **healthy, normal** | **successful** | **difficult** ◇ *She had a difficult ~ with her first child.* | **high-risk** | **ectopic** ◇ *emergency surgery for an ectopic ~* | **multiple** ◇ *twins or other multiple pregnancies* | **first, second, etc.** | **teen** (*esp. AmE*), **teenage** | **out-of-wedlock, unwed** (*both esp. AmE*) | **unintended, unplanned, unwanted** ◇ *There are thousands of unwanted teenage pregnancies every year.*
VERB + PREGNANCY **have** | **avoid, prevent** ◇ *They took no precautions to avoid ~.* | **plan** ◇ *50% of all pregnancies are not planned.* | **confirm** ◇ *The doctor confirmed my ~ and told me to come back at 12 weeks.* | **continue, continue with** ◇ *the difficult decision about whether to continue with a ~* | **hide** ◇ *I tried hard to hide my ~.* | **abort, end, terminate** ◇ *the right of a woman to terminate her ~*
PREGNANCY + VERB **progress** ◇ *Here's what can happen as your ~ progresses.* | **go to full term, go to term** ◇ *women whose pregnancies have gone to term*
PREGNANCY + NOUN **test** ◇ *a home ~ test kit* | **rate** ◇ *Teen ~ rates have fallen.* | **complications**
PREP. **during (a/the) ~, in (a/the) ~** ◇ *Lower blood pressure is common in early ~.* | **throughout (a/the) ~** ◇ *You will be tested throughout your ~.*
PHRASES **carry a ~ to term** ◇ *a woman who intends to carry her ~ to term*

pregnant *adj.*

VERBS **be, look** ◇ *When I found out I was ~, I didn't know what to do.* | **become, fall, get** | **get sb, make sb** ◇ *He got her ~.*
ADV. **heavily, very** | **visibly** | **newly** ◇ *She was newly ~ at the time.*
PREP. **by** ◇ *She was ~ by a former client.* | **with** ◇ *She was ~ with twins.*
PHRASES **six weeks, three months, etc. ~**

prejudice *noun*

ADJ. **deep, deep-rooted, deep-seated, strong** | **blatant** | **serious** (*esp. BrE*), **unfair** (*esp. BrE*) | **personal** | **popular** ◇ *She has not been afraid to challenge popular ~s.* | **old** ◇ *It's hard to break down old ~s.* | **blind, irrational** | **anti-Catholic, anti-gay, etc.** | **class, colour/color** (*esp. AmE*),

cultural, ethnic, political, race (*esp. AmE*), racial, religious, sexist, social
VERB + PREJUDICE **have, hold** ◊ *We all have ~s of some kind.* | **air, express** ◊ *He sat there airing his personal ~s.* | **appeal to, pander to** ◊ *We must not pander to the irrational ~s of a small minority.* | **confirm, reinforce** | **encounter** ◊ *She had never encountered such deep ~ before.* | **confront, face** | **suffer** | **challenge, fight** | **overcome, put aside** ◊ *It's time to put aside our old ~s.* | **break down, eliminate, eradicate**
PREP. **without ~** ◊ *The tale is told without ~ or bias.* | **~ about** ◊ *a book written to challenge ~s about disabled people* | **~ against** ◊ *deep-rooted ~ against homosexuals* | **~ among** ◊ *~ among ignorant people* | **~ towards/toward** ◊ *~ towards/toward immigrants*
PHRASES **a victim of ~**

prejudice *verb*

1 cause sb to have a prejudice

ADV. **unfairly**
PREP. **against, in favour/favor of** ◊ *Newspaper reports had unfairly ~d the jury in her favour/favor.*

2 (*law*) **weaken sth/make it less fair**

ADV. **seriously, severely, substantially** ◊ *This could seriously ~ her safety.* | **unduly**
VERB + PREJUDICE **be likely to** ◊ *She did not disclose evidence that was likely to ~ her client's case.*

prejudiced *adj.*

VERBS **be, seem**
ADV. **extremely, fairly, very, etc.** | **deeply, highly** | **a little, slightly, etc.** ◊ *I was a little ~ against him because of his background.* | **racially**
PREP. **against** ◊ *He's deeply ~ against women.*

preliminary *noun*

ADJ. **essential** (*esp. BrE*), **necessary** | **usual** (*esp. BrE*) ◊ *After the usual preliminaries the meeting began.*
PREP. **as a ~** ◊ *The two presidents met today, as a ~ to resuming the peace talks.* | **~ to** ◊ *an essential ~ to serious research*
PHRASES **without preliminaries** ◊ *She began speaking intensely, without preliminaries.*

prelude *noun*

1 short piece of music

ADJ. **instrumental, orchestral** ◊ *the orchestral ~ to the cantata* | **organ, piano** | **brief** | **opening** ◊ *the opening orchestral ~* | **B major, D minor, etc.**
VERB + PRELUDE **open with** ◊ *'The Magnificat' opens with a long organ ~.*
PREP. **~ for** ◊ *seven ~s for piano* | **~ to** ◊ *The theme recalls the ~ to Wagner's 'Lohengrin'.*

2 sth that happens before a more important event

ADJ. **essential, inevitable, necessary** ◊ *a necessary ~ to privatization*
VERB + PRELUDE **serve as** ◊ *This analysis will serve as a ~ to a more extended examination.* | **consider sth, see sth as**
PREP. **as a ~** ◊ *events held as a ~ to the Christmas festivities* | **~ for** ◊ *the ~ for the battles ahead* | **~ to** ◊ *He considered the strikes a ~ to the great socialist revolution.*
PHRASES **a ~ to war** ◊ *the fear that any peace was merely a ~ to war* | **be but a ~ to sth, be just a ~ to sth, be merely a ~ to sth, be only a ~ to sth** ◊ *Every life is but a ~ to a death.* ◊ *This is just a ~ to a larger attack.*

premier *noun*

ADJ. **acting, deputy** | **former** | **British, Chinese, etc.** | **Conservative, Labour, etc.** | **state**
VERB + PREMIER **appoint (sb), appoint sb as, elect (sb), elect sb as, swear sb in as** ◊ *She was sworn in as ~ last week.* | **succeed sb as, take over as**
PREP. **as ~** ◊ *during his 25 years as Liberal ~*

premiere *noun*

ADJ. **world** | **American, British, etc.** | **film** (*esp. BrE*), **movie** (*esp. AmE*), **television, TV** | **stage, theatrical** (*esp. AmE*) ◊ *the stage ~ of John Adams's opera* ◊ *the movie's theatrical ~* (*AmE*) | **season** (*esp. AmE*) ◊ *Did you catch the season ~ of 'The Sopranos'?* | **gala** ◊ *the gala world ~ of the movie* | **glittering, glitzy, star-studded** (*all esp. BrE*) ◊ *London hosted the star-studded ~ of 'Harry Potter'.*
VERB + PREMIERE **attend** ◊ *They attended the ~ together.* | **host, present** | **conduct** ◊ *He conducted the world ~ of the symphony.* | **give (sth its)** ◊ *The opera was given its ~ by the New York City Opera.* | **receive** ◊ *The movie receives its American ~ on November 16.*
PREMIERE + NOUN **episode, issue** (*both esp. AmE*) ◊ *the ~ episode of 'Angel'* ◊ *the ~ issue of a new journal* | **party** ◊ *the movie's ~ party*

premises *noun*

ADJ. **new** ◊ *The company moved to new purpose-built ~ in Mumbai.* | **suitable** | **bigger, larger** ◊ *We are moving to larger ~ next month.* | **existing** | **alternative** ◊ *The congregation has been looking for alternative ~ for some time.* | **cramped, modest** | **city-centre** (*BrE*) | **purpose-built** | **adjoining, neighbouring/neighboring** | **temporary** | **rented** | **private, residential** | **licensed, unlicensed** (*both BrE*) ◊ *Persons under eighteen should not be served alcohol in licensed ~.* | **business, church, club, commercial, company, factory, hospital, hotel, industrial, office, retail, school, shop** (*esp. BrE*)
VERB + PREMISES **enter** ◊ *The police have the power to enter the ~ at any time.* | **find** | **own** | **acquire, lease** | **move to** | **occupy, use** | **leave, vacate**
PREP. **off the ~** ◊ *Police were called to escort her off the ~.* | **on the ~** ◊ *Smoking is strictly forbidden on school ~.*

premium *noun*

1 extra value/price

ADJ. **hefty, high** ◊ *The company is charging a pretty hefty ~ for access to their network.* | **small** | **additional, extra** | **price**
VERB + PREMIUM **pay** ◊ *Electricity companies pay a ~ for renewable energy.* | **charge** | **place, put** | **command** | **collect, earn, receive**
PREP. **at a ~** ◊ *Good hotels are at a ~* (= difficult to obtain and therefore expensive). | **~ of** ◊ *bought at a ~ of 40% above the current market price* | **~ on** ◊ *The company places a high ~ on customer loyalty.*

2 payment for insurance

ADJ. **annual, monthly, regular** (*esp. BrE*) | **high, low, small** ◊ *Intense competition has kept ~s low.* | **insurance** | **risk** ◊ *There's a risk ~ of probably $10 a barrel built into oil prices.* | **equity** ◊ *equity risk ~s* | **health-care** (*esp. AmE*), **health-insurance** | **malpractice** (*esp. AmE*) ◊ *the rising cost of medical malpractice insurance ~s*
VERB + PREMIUM **pay** | **afford** | **keep up** ◊ *We're struggling to keep up our ~s.* | **increase, raise** ◊ *The insurance company has increased our ~s.* | **cut, lower, reduce**
PREMIUM + VERB **go up, increase, rise** ◊ *My insurance ~s increase each year.* | **fall, go down** | **cost sth** ◊ *The additional ~ costs $1 800 a year.*
PREMIUM + NOUN **payment, rate** | **increase**
PREP. **~ for** ◊ *the ~s for your pension plan* | **~ on** ◊ *Premiums on many cars will go up this year.*

premonition *noun*

ADJ. **eerie, spooky**
VERB + PREMONITION **feel, get, have**
PREP. **~ about** ◊ *Perhaps he had a ~ about what might happen in London.* | **~ of** ◊ *I wonder if she had a ~ of her own fate.*

preoccupation *noun*

ADJ. **current, present, recent** | **central, chief, main, major** ◊ *Their chief ~ was how to feed their families.* | **intense** | **constant, continuing** | **lifelong** ◊ *his lifelong ~ with Chinese art forms* | **growing** | **excessive, obsessive, unhealthy** ◊ *our society's unhealthy ~ with women's bodies*

preoccupied adj.

VERBS **appear, be, look, seem** | **become** | **remain**
ADV. **extremely, fairly, very, etc.** | **deeply** | **completely, entirely, totally** | **increasingly** | **overly, too** ◇ *He was too ~ to notice.* | **a little, slightly, etc.**
PREP. **by** ◇ *We live in a world ~ by sport.* | **with** ◇ *He was too ~ with his own problems to worry about hers.*

preparation noun

1 getting sth ready

ADJ. **careful, thorough** | **elaborate** | **intense** ◇ *two years of intense ~* | **good** ◇ *He found it good ~ for the diplomatic skills needed in his new job.* | **proper** ◇ *As with any business, proper ~ is required.* | **adequate** | **inadequate, poor** ◇ *He had received inadequate ~ for a professional career.* | **initial** ◇ *It is the initial ~ that takes the time.* | **advance, prior** ◇ *An awful lot of advance ~ must have gone into this summit.* ◇ *Prior ~ is vital for achieving success.* | **mental, physical** ◇ *her mental ~ for the games* | **academic, educational** (both esp. AmE) ◇ *individuals who do not have the money or academic ~ to attend college* | **teacher** (AmE) ◇ *a college-based teacher ~ program* | **food, meal** ◇ *food ~ and food handling tips*
VERB + PREPARATION **need, require** ◇ *a dish that requires no elaborate ~ or cooking* | **do** ◇ *He's done a lot of ~ for this meeting.* | **receive** ◇ *They receive a fine ~ for college.* | **oversee** ◇ *the agency that oversees the ~ of the budget*
PREPARATION + NOUN **time** ◇ *This simple dish takes very little ~ time.* | **course** (esp. AmE), **programme/program** (esp. AmE) ◇ *Many Taiwanese children take ~ courses for the SATs.* ◇ *Teacher ~ programs train teachers to become effective instructors of children.* ◇ *The ~ program was well designed.*
PREP. **in ~ for** ◇ *Get a good night's sleep in ~ for the drive.*

2 preparations things done to get sth ready

ADJ. **elaborate, meticulous, special** | **extensive** ◇ *extensive ~s for war* | **necessary** | **final, last-minute** | **Christmas, wedding, etc.** | **military, war** ◇ *military ~s for full-scale action* ◇ *War ~s intensified.*
VERB + PREPARATIONS **make** ◇ *We're making the final ~s for the party.* | **begin, start** | **continue, go ahead with** | **be busy with** | **oversee** ◇ *She flew in from Paris to oversee final ~s.* | **complete, finalize, finish**
PREPARATIONS + VERB **begin** ◇ *A week before the ceremony, wedding ~s began.* | **be in hand** (BrE), **be underway** ◇ *Preparations are now in hand to close half the factories.* | **continue** | **be complete**
PREP. **~ for** ◇ *The family can now go ahead with ~s for the funeral.*

prepare verb

ADV. **adequately, properly** | **fully** | **carefully, meticulously, painstakingly** ◇ *The lectures were carefully ~d.* | **busily, hastily, quickly** ◇ *I was busily preparing a salad for the evening meal.* | **lovingly** ◇ *the chicken casserole I had so lovingly ~d for her* | **mentally** ◇ *How do you go about mentally preparing yourself for a project?*
VERB + PREPARE **help (sb), help (sb) to** | **need to** ◇ *Penn needs to ~ for a medical school interview.* | **fail to** ◇ *He had failed to ~ adequately for the task before him.* | **be easy to, be quick to, be simple to** ◇ *a meal that is very quick and easy to ~* | **be designed to** ◇ *The course is designed to ~ graduates for management careers.*
PREP. **according to** ◇ *Just ~ according to package directions.* | **for** ◇ *We all set about preparing for the party.*
PHRASES **~ for the worst** ◇ *The family are preparing for the worst.* | **time to ~ (sth)** ◇ *I haven't had time to ~ my arguments properly.*

prepared adj.

1 ready and able to deal with sth

VERBS **be, feel, seem** | **get** ◇ *I'd had three weeks to get ~.* | **come** ◇ *I came ~ (= with everything I might need).*
ADV. **perfectly, properly, thoroughly, well** ◇ *I was well ~ for*

the job. | **completely, fully, totally** | **badly, inadequately, poorly** ◇ *They were inadequately ~ for their role in society.* | **adequately, sufficiently** | **emotionally, mentally, physically, psychologically** ◇ *I feel mentally ~ to handle this situation.* | **academically** ◇ *They are poorly ~ academically.*
PHRASES **be ~ for the worst** ◇ *I want you to be ~ for the worst.* | **be ~ for any eventuality** ◇ *She was always one to be ~ for any eventuality.*

2 done, made, etc. in advance

ADV. **carefully, meticulously** ◇ *She's clearly reading from carefully ~ notes.* | **hastily, quickly** ◇ *hastily ~ newspaper reports* | **specially** ◇ *a table full of specially ~ food* | **freshly** ◇ *freshly ~ vegetables* | **commercially** ◇ *Commercially ~ food is often loaded with saturated fat.*

prerequisite noun

ADJ. **absolute, essential, fundamental, important, indispensable, necessary, vital** ◇ *Self-control is an absolute ~ for command.* ◇ *These qualities are necessary ~s for success.* | **basic, first**
PREP. **~ for** ◇ *Training is a ~ for competence.* | **~ to** ◇ *Recognition is a ~ to understanding.*

prerogative noun

ADJ. **exclusive, sole** ◇ *Making such decisions is not the sole ~ of managers.* | **constitutional, judicial, managerial, presidential, royal** | **personal** | **male** ◇ *women who challenge male ~s*
VERB + PREROGATIVE **enjoy, have** ◇ *one of the ~s enjoyed by the president* | **assert** (esp. AmE), **exercise, use** ◇ *The President has asserted the full ~s of his office.* ◇ *You can of course exercise your ~ to leave at any time.* | **defend, preserve, protect** ◇ *The tsar protected his personal ~s.* | **challenge** ◇ *those who challenge the ~s of the elite* | **retain** ◇ *Baker retained the ~ to craft solutions himself.* | **give up, surrender**

prescribe verb

1 drugs

ADV. **legally** ◇ *The drug can no longer be legally ~d.* | **commonly, frequently, routinely, widely** ◇ *These drugs are widely ~d to control high blood pressure.* | **medically**
PREP. **as** ◇ *It can be ~d as a form of preventive medicine.* | **for** ◇ *drugs ~d for high blood pressure* ◇ *This drug is often ~d for women with heart trouble.* | **to** ◇ *a drug ~d to patients with an obsessive compulsive disorder*

2 what should be done

ADV. **narrowly, rigidly, strictly** ◇ *The curriculum is rigidly ~d from an early age.* ◇ *Everything about her life was strictly ~d (= there were strict rules about what she could do).*
PHRASES **culturally ~d, socially ~d** ◇ *culturally ~d gender roles*

prescription noun

ADJ. **medical** | **free** ◇ *You are entitled to free ~s.* | **repeat** (BrE) ◇ *I just get a repeat ~ every month.* | **drug** ◇ *the rising rate of drug ~s for emotional and psychological complaints* | **antibiotic, antidepressant, etc.**
VERB + PRESCRIPTION **give sb, write, write out** | **fill, refill** (both esp. AmE) ◇ *The pharmacist refused to refill a ~ for birth control pills.* | **dispense, make up** (BrE) ◇ *The pharmacist dispenses ~s for antidepressants.* ◇ *Would you like to wait while the pharmacist makes up your ~?*
PRESCRIPTION + NOUN **charges** (esp. BrE) ◇ *people who are exempt from ~ charges* | **cost** ◇ *Physicians often underestimate retail ~ costs.* | **benefit, coverage** (both AmE) ◇ *The drug will be covered by Medicare's new ~ benefit.* | **drug, medication, medicine** ◇ *addicted to ~ drugs* | **contraceptive, painkiller, etc.** | **pad** ◇ *She scribbled on her ~ pad and handed me a sheet.*
PREP. **by ~** (AmE), **on ~** (BrE) ◇ *Some drugs are only available by/on ~.* | **without (a) ~** ◇ *The new medication is currently available without a ~.* ◇ *Nicotine patches are sold without ~.*

| ~ for ◇ *the usual ~ for asthma* ◇ *She gave him a ~ for antibiotics.*

presence *noun*

1 being present

ADJ. **mere** ◇ *The mere ~ of children in the room is enough to upset him.* | **constant, continued, continuing, permanent | growing, increased, increasing** ◇ *the increased ~ of Asian actors in Hollywood* | **significant, strong, substantial** ◇ *The company now has a strong ~ in Germany.* | **dominant** ◇ *He remained a dominant ~ in the art world.* | **overwhelming** ◇ *the overwhelming ~ of the church in daily lives* | **pervasive, ubiquitous** ◇ *the pervasive ~ of the Web* ◇ *He's become a ubiquitous ~ on talk shows.* | **comforting** ◇ *Her comforting ~ made him feel safe.* | **physical** ◇ *the physical ~ of actors among the audience* | **visible** ◇ *the visible ~ of campus security* | **online, Web** ◇ *Fox's efforts to create a Web ~ for the movie.* | **human** ◇ *I could see no signs of human ~.*
VERB + PRESENCE **indicate, reveal, show, suggest** ◇ *These chemicals could indicate the ~ of water on the planet.* | **confirm** ◇ *Tests confirmed the ~ of the disease.* | **acknowledge** ◇ *He acknowledged our ~ with a nod of his head.* | **request, require** ◇ *The King requested our ~ this morning.* | *Your ~ is required two days from now.* | **detect** | **have** ◇ *a small business that doesn't have a Web ~* | **establish** ◇ *Establishing a strong ~ on the Internet is a top priority.* | **expand, increase** ◇ *The company plans to expand its ~ in emerging markets.* | **grace sb with** (*ironic or humorous*) ◇ *How nice of you to grace us with your ~!*
PREP. **in sb's ~** ◇ *He should never have made those remarks in your ~.*
PHRASES **make your ~ felt, make your ~ known** ◇ *She certainly made her ~ felt in the boardroom.*

2 number of people

ADJ. **constant, continuing, permanent** ◇ *a permanent American ~ overseas* | **military, naval, police** ◇ *There was a strong police ~ throughout the demonstration.*
VERB + PRESENCE **have** ◇ *The United States has a substantial military ~ in the country.* | **maintain** ◇ *The army maintains a constant ~ in the area.*

3 force of personality

ADJ. **charismatic, commanding, dominating, formidable, great, imposing, intimidating, powerful, strong** ◇ *She was a formidable ~ on the set.* ◇ *He was still an intimidating ~.* | **screen, stage** ◇ *He has a commanding screen ~.*
VERB + PRESENCE **have**

4 (*literary*) a person or spirit that you cannot see

ADJ. **alien, ghostly** ◇ *I felt as though there was some ghostly ~.* | **divine** ◇ *Flame has always symbolized a divine ~.* | **evil** ◇ *She sensed an evil ~, and it was growing stronger.*
VERB + PRESENCE **feel, sense** ◇ *She felt a ~ in the room.*

present *noun*

ADJ. **Christmas, holiday** (*AmE*) | **anniversary, birthday, graduation** (*esp. AmE*), **house-warming, wedding | going-away** (*esp. AmE*), **leaving** (*esp. BrE*) | **unwanted** (*esp. BrE*) ◇ *Customers may return unwanted ~s in exchange for vouchers.*
VERB + PRESENT **buy | get, receive | bring sb, give sb, send sb | exchange** ◇ *At Christmas, family and friends exchange ~s.* | **hand out** ◇ *Santa Claus handed out ~s to the children.* | **wrap | open, unwrap**
PREP. **~ for** ◇ *a ~ for my daughter* | **~ from, ~ to** ◇ *It's a ~ to us all from Granny.*
PHRASES **make sb a ~ of sth** ◇ *My nephew loves this bike so I'm going to make him a ~ of it.*

present *verb*

ADV. **clearly, well** ◇ *The arguments were well researched and clearly ~ed.* | **attractively, neatly | briefly** ◇ *The papers are only briefly ~ed here.* | **graphically** ◇ *The results are ~ed graphically in Figure 2.* | **orally, visually** ◇ *The results can be ~ed visually in the form of a graph.* | **formally** ◇ *The launch is to be formally ~ed to trade partners in early summer.*
VERB + PRESENT **aim to, attempt to, seek to, strive to, try to** ◇ *We have tried to ~ both sides of the debate.* | **be designed to** ◇ *Hotel brochures are designed to ~ the most attractive aspects of the hotel.* | **fail to** ◇ *This book fails to ~ her story in a coherent manner.*
PREP. **as** ◇ *He likes to ~ himself as a radical politician.* | **for** ◇ *These two techniques are ~ed for illustration only.* | **to** ◇ *He ~ed the information to his colleagues.*

present *adj.*

VERBS **be | remain**
ADV. **ever** ◇ *the ever ~ risk of pollution* | **physically** ◇ *Simply to be physically ~ was all that was required.* | **naturally** ◇ *Bacteria are naturally ~ in the environment.*
PHRASES **past and ~** ◇ *a list of all club members, past and ~*

presentable *adj.*

VERBS **be, look | make sb** ◇ *Could you try and make yourself a little more ~?*
ADV. **very | perfectly** ◇ *She was not exactly good-looking, but perfectly ~.* | **halfway** (*esp. AmE*), **quite, reasonably, somewhat** (*esp. AmE*)

presentation *noun*

1 of a gift or prize

ADJ. **annual | official | special | farewell, retirement | award**
VERB + PRESENTATION **make**
PRESENTATION + NOUN **ceremony, dinner, evening** (*esp. BrE*), **night** ◇ *the school's annual ~ evening*
PREP. **~ to** ◇ *The president made a ~ to the businesswoman of the year.*

2 informative talk

ADJ. **formal | effective | slick | upbeat | business, sales | keynote** ◇ *The conference will begin with a keynote ~ by a leading industry figure.* | **audio-visual, multimedia, PowerPoint™, slide, video**
VERB + PRESENTATION **do, give, make**
PRESENTATION + NOUN **skills | software**
PREP. **~ on** ◇ *Candidates have to give a short ~ on a subject of their choice.*

3 way sth is presented

ADJ. **excellent, good | bad, poor | clear, simple | oral, visual | dramatic, effective**

presenter *noun* (*BrE*) → See also ANNOUNCER

ADJ. **radio, television, TV | programme, sports** ◇ *a BBC sports ~*
→ Note at JOB

preservation *noun*

ADJ. **building, railroad** (*AmE*), **railway** (*BrE*), **etc. | environmental, wildlife | farmland, wetland, wilderness** (*all esp. AmE*) | **historic**
PRESERVATION + NOUN **order** (*BrE*), **ordinance** (*AmE*) ◇ *The local authority has placed a ~ order/ordinance on the building.*
PHRASES **a state of ~** ◇ *Most of the buildings are in an excellent state of ~.*

preservative *noun*

ADJ. **food, wood | artificial, chemical, synthetic** ◇ *Our products contain no artificial ~s.*
VERB + PRESERVATIVE **apply, treat sth with** ◇ *Make sure the panels are treated with a wood ~.* | **contain** ◇ *The snacks contain no artificial ~s, sugar, or salt.*
PHRASES **additives and ~s, additives or ~s** ◇ *a range of traditional cakes made with no additives or ~s*

preserve *noun* (*AmE*) → See also RESERVE

ADJ. **forest, nature, wilderness, wildlife** ◇ *This land is protected as a wildlife ~.* | **game, hunting**
PREP. **in a/the ~** ◇ *She decided to go for a walk in the forest ~.*

preserve verb

ADV. **carefully, faithfully, lovingly** ◊ *She carefully ~d all his letters.* | **perfectly** ◊ *The style of the original film is ~d perfectly.*

VERB + PRESERVE **seek to, try to** | **be anxious to, want to, wish to** ◊ *We were anxious to ~ the original character of the house.* | **help (to)** ◊ *We need to take action to help ~ fish stocks.* | **fight to** ◊ *campaigners fighting to ~ a historic building* | **be designed to, be intended to** ◊ *The Act contained provisions designed to ~ the status quo.* | **be important to**

PREP. **as** ◊ *The prison is ~d as a tourist attraction.* | **for** ◊ *The collection has been sold to the British Museum where it will be ~d for the nation.* | **from** ◊ *an attempt to ~ the corpse from decomposition*

PHRASES **an attempt to ~ sth** | **beautifully, exquisitely, well, wonderfully, etc. ~d** ◊ *They were thrilled to discover a beautifully ~d specimen of Roman pottery.* | **be ~d intact** ◊ *The bones had all been ~d intact.* | **be worth preserving** ◊ *You need to say why the building is worth preserving.* | **poorly ~d** ◊ *The iron coins are poorly ~d and have rusted.*

presidency noun

ADJ. **executive** | **vice** (*AmE*) (*vice-presidency* in *BrE*) ◊ *He became a candidate for the vice ~.* | **rotating** ◊ *Greece then held the rotating ~ of the European Union.* | **one-term, eight-year, two-term, etc.**

VERB + PRESIDENCY **be nominated for, run for, stand for** | **be elected to, win** | **assume, take on, take over** | **hold** ◊ *She held the ~ of the association for three years.* | **resign** ◊ *That year he resigned his ~ of the Academy.*

PREP. **into sb's ~** ◊ *Three years into his ~, he is more popular than ever.* | **under sb's ~** ◊ *under the ~ of Gerald Ford*

president noun

1 leader of a republic

ADJ. **American, French, etc.** | **Democrat, Democratic, Republican** | **vice** (*AmE*) (*vice-president* in *BrE*) | **~ elect** (usually *president-elect*) | **incoming, outgoing** | **current, incumbent, sitting** | **former, previous** | **lame-duck** | **acting, interim, provisional** | **civilian, military**

VERB + PRESIDENT **elect, elect sb (as), re-elect, swear sb in as** ◊ *He was sworn in as President on August 31.* | **advise, brief** | **run for** | **serve as** | **impeach, oust, remove, topple, unseat** (*esp. AmE*) | **assassinate**

PRESIDENT + VERB **appoint sb, nominate sb** | **authorize sth, sign sth** | **announce sth, declare sth, propose sth** | **veto sth** | **intervene (in sth)**

PREP. **~ of** ◊ *the President of the United States*

2 person in charge of an organization

ADJ. **acting, honorary, interim** | **founding** | **deputy, vice** (*vice-president* in *BrE*) | **incoming, outgoing** | **former, past** | **company** (*AmE*) | **association, club, party** (*BrE*) | **team** (*AmE*) | **borough, council** (*both AmE*) | **college, university** (*both AmE*) | **national** ◊ *Bill Crane, national ~ of Omega Psi Phi Fraternity*

VERB + PRESIDENT **appoint, appoint sb (as), name sb (as)** ◊ *In 2007 Raymonds was appointed (as) ~ of PSWA.*

PRESIDENT + VERB **resign**

PREP. **~ of** ◊ *She is ~ of the Irish Olympic Council.*

press noun

1 media

ADJ. **foreign, international, local, national, provincial** (*BrE*) | **gutter** (*BrE*), **mainstream, popular, quality** (*esp. BrE*) | **tabloid** | **left-wing, liberal, right-wing** ◊ *The right-wing ~ tried to stir up prejudice against immigrants.* | **financial, gay, music, etc.** | **free** ◊ *A free ~ is fundamental to democracy.*

VERB + PRESS **alert, brief, tell** ◊ *Someone must have alerted the ~ that she was going to be there.* | **meet** ◊ *The president was briefed before meeting the ~.* | **censor, muzzle** ◊ *They introduced measures including muzzling the ~ and illegal detainment.* | **intimidate, manipulate, mislead** ◊ *Did the senator deliberately mislead the ~?*

PRESS + NOUN **briefing, release, statement** ◊ *He issued a ~ statement insisting on his innocence.* (see also **press conference**) | **corps** ◊ *The spokesman addressed an international ~ corps.* | **attention, coverage** ◊ *extensive ~ coverage of the event* | **account, report** | **clippings, cuttings** (*BrE*) ◊ *He kept a scrapbook containing ~ cuttings of his concerts.* | **office** ◊ *The company's ~ office did not return the call.* | **agent, officer, secretary, spokesman** | **photographer** | **agency** | **badge** (*esp. AmE*), **credentials, pass** ◊ *She showed the doorman her ~ pass.* | **box** ◊ *We got to sit in the ~ box since my dad would be writing about the game.* | **preview, screening** | **campaign** (*esp. BrE*) | **freedom**

PREP. **in the ~** ◊ *There was no mention of the incident in the national ~.*

PHRASES **get a good, bad, etc. ~** (*BrE*), **get good, bad, etc. ~,** **have a good, bad, etc. ~** (*BrE*), **have good, bad, etc. ~** ◊ *His latest novel didn't get (a) very good ~* (= was not praised in the media).

2 machine for printing

ADJ. **printing**

VERB + PRESS **go to** ◊ *The newspaper goes to ~ at 6 o'clock.*

PRESS + VERB **roll** ◊ *The ~es are already rolling.*

PREP. **in** ◊ *Their new book is in ~.*

PHRASES **hot off the ~, hot off the ~es** (*esp. AmE*) ◊ *We've just received a copy of her latest book, hot off the ~.* | **stop the ~, stop the ~es** (= a major event has happened) (*often ironic*) ◊ *Stop the ~es! Dan has had a haircut!*

press verb

1 push sth firmly

ADV. **firmly, forcefully, hard** ◊ *She ~ed down hard on the gas pedal.* | **gently, lightly, softly** ◊ *Her lips softly ~ed my cheek.* | **close, closely** ◊ *He ~ed up closer against the wall, terrified of being seen.* | **tightly** ◊ *She curled up, her knees ~ed tightly to her chest.* | **back, down, forward, together, up, etc.** ◊ *The crowd ~ed forward.* ◊ *She ~ed her lips together.*

PREP. **against** ◊ *She ~ed her face against the window.* | **into** ◊ *Bella ~ed her face into the pillow.* | **on** ◊ *She ~ed on the doorbell.* | **to** ◊ *He ~ed a finger gently to her lips.*

PHRASES **~ sth flat, ~ sth open, ~ sth shut** ◊ *He ~ed the lid firmly shut.*

2 try to persuade sb

ADV. **strongly** ◊ *In the interview he strongly ~ed his point of view.* | **consistently, continually, repeatedly** | **gently** ◊ *'Are you sure?' she ~ed gently.* | **further** | **successfully**

VERB + PRESS **continue to**

PREP. **for** ◊ *The party will continue to ~ the case for a new electoral system.* | **on** ◊ *I did not ~ him further on the issue.*

3 iron sth

PHRASES **immaculately ~ed, neatly ~ed** ◊ *his immaculately ~ed suit*

PHR V **press on**

PREP. **with** ◊ *They ~ed boldly on with their plan.*

PHRASES **~ on regardless** (*esp. BrE*) ◊ *The weather was dreadful but we ~ed on regardless.*

press conference (*esp. BrE*) noun → See also NEWS CONFERENCE

ADJ. **joint** | **impromptu** | **post-match, post-summit, etc.**

VERB + PRESS CONFERENCE **call** | **arrange, organize, plan** | **give, hold** | **tell** ◊ *The chairman told a ~ of the forthcoming merger.*

PREP. **at a/the ~** ◊ *The proposed changes were outlined at a ~.* | **during a/the ~, in a/the ~** ◊ *The announcement was made in an impromptu ~ at the airport.*

pressure noun

1 force produced by pressing

ADJ. **gentle, light** | **firm** | **downward**

VERB + PRESSURE **apply, exert, put** | **alleviate, reduce, relieve** ◊ *Reducing the swelling will relieve the ~ on her spine.*

PRESSURE + NOUN **sensor** ◇ *Pressure sensors in the seats tell the system which ones aren't occupied.*

2 force of a gas or liquid

ADJ. **elevated, high, low** | **air, blood, water** ◇ *an instrument for measuring blood ~* | **atmospheric, barometric** | **tyre/tire**
PRESSURE + VERB **build up, increase, rise** | **maintain** | **ease, fall**
PRESSURE + NOUN **gauge** | **valve** | **cooker**

3 stress

ADJ. **considerable, constant, intolerable** (*esp. BrE*) | **relentless, undue, unrelenting** | **added, increased, increasing** ◇ *Retailers face added ~ to have the products available by Christmas.* | **commercial, competitive, economic, financial, political, social** ◇ *The economic ~s on small businesses are intense.* | **external** ◇ *His own desires conflict with external ~s to conform.* | **downward, upward** ◇ *This puts upward ~ on prices.*
VERB + PRESSURE **place sb under, put sb under** | **create** ◇ *When more people move into an area, that creates ~s.* | **cope with, handle, withstand** | **escape, get away from** ◇ *It's an ideal place in which to relax and escape the ~s of modern life.* | **alleviate, ease, reduce, relieve** ◇ *They are looking for ways to ease the ~ of their stress-filled, competitive existence.* | **heighten, intensify** ◇ *There is a constant drive to exploit workers and intensify the ~ of work.*
PRESSURE + VERB **build up, increase**
PREP. **under ~** ◇ *He's felt under ~ since his wife had the operation.* | **~ on** ◇ *There's a lot of ~ on the soldiers preparing for battle.*
PHRASES **~ of work** ◇ *The cruise was a welcome relief from the ~ of work.*

4 attempt to persuade/influence sb

ADJ. **enormous, great, intense, strong, tremendous** ◇ *There is intense ~ on her to resign.* | **growing, increased, increasing, mounting** | **popular** ◇ *The government bowed to popular ~ and repealed the law.* | **international** ◇ *the use of the Internet to put international ~ on authoritarian regimes* | **peer, peer-group** (*esp. BrE*) ◇ *She started smoking because of peer ~.*
VERB + PRESSURE **bring to bear, exert, generate, place, put** ◇ *This concession would not have happened but for the ~ that was brought to bear on the authorities.* | *My parents never put any ~ on me to get a job.* | **place sb under, put sb under** | **be brought under, be under, come under, experience, face** ◇ *Hospital staff are coming under ~ to work longer hours.* | **heighten, intensify** ◇ *This has heightened ~ for economic sanctions against the regime.* | **resist, withstand** | **bow to, give in to, respond to** ◇ *The editor bowed to ~ from his staff, and the article was suppressed.*
PRESSURE + VERB **intensify, mount**
PRESSURE + NOUN **group** | **tactic** ◇ *Large companies were criticized for using ~ tactics against small suppliers.*
PREP. **under ~** ◇ *Management is under ~ to set an example on pay restraint.* | **~ for** ◇ *~ for change in the country's economy* | **~ from** ◇ *~ from religious groups* | **~ on** ◇ *on foreign diplomats*
PHRASES **keep the ~ on sb** (*AmE*), **keep up the ~ on sb, maintain the ~ on sb** ◇ *Farmers need to keep (up) the ~ on Congress.*

prestige *noun*

ADJ. **considerable, enormous, great, high, immense** ◇ *Winning the prize carries immense ~.* | **low** | **international, national** | **occupational** (*AmE*), **personal** | **academic, intellectual, political, social**
VERB + PRESTIGE **enjoy, have** ◇ *an international company that enjoys immense ~* | **lack** | **acquire, derive (from sth), gain, get** ◇ *Lavish hospitality allows the host to gain ~.* | **accord sb/sth, attach to sb/sth, give sb/sth** ◇ *Different jobs are accorded different levels of ~.* | **bring, carry, confer, lend** ◇ *Owning landed property confers ~.* | **lose** | **boost, enhance,**
increase, raise | **damage, lower** ◇ *The couple's ~ was damaged by the allegations.*
PREP. **~ among, ~ with** ◇ *the party's ~ among the public* | **~ within** ◇ *The post carried great ~ within the police force.*
PHRASES **a loss of ~** ◇ *Doctors have suffered a loss of ~ following a spate of scandals.*

prestigious *adj.*

VERBS **be**
ADV. **extremely, fairly, very, etc.** | **highly** ◇ *She won a highly ~ award.*

presume *verb*

ADV. **correctly** | **wrongly** ◇ *I had ~d wrongly that Jenny would be there.* | **reasonably** (*esp. BrE*) | **automatically**
PHRASES **be ~d dead** ◇ *Harrison disappeared and was ~d dead.* | **be ~d guilty, be ~d innocent** ◇ *They must be ~d innocent until proven guilty.*

presumption *noun*

ADJ. **strong** | **general** ◇ *There is a general ~ that fatty foods are bad for your heart.* | **correct** ◇ *It seems his ~s were correct.* | **false** (*esp. AmE*) ◇ *We must ensure the discussion is not based on false ~s.*
PREP. **~ about** ◇ *The argument is based on certain ~s about human nature.* | **~ against** (*law*) ◇ *There is a strong ~ against changes in the common law.* | **~ of** ◇ *a strong ~ of guilt*
PHRASES **the ~ of innocence** ◇ *The ~ of innocence is constitutionally protected.*

pretence (*BrE*) (*AmE* pretense) *noun*

ADJ. **elaborate** ◇ *It was all an elaborate ~.* | **flimsy, slight** ◇ *There is not even the slightest ~ of trying to make it realistic.*
VERB + PRETENCE/PRETENSE **keep up, maintain, sustain** (*BrE*) ◇ *I don't know how long I can keep up this ~ of happiness.* | **abandon, drop, give up**
PRETENCE/PRETENSE + VERB **be over** ◇ *Now that the ~ was over, he could tell them what he really thought.*
PREP. **under the ~ of** ◇ *He tried to get close to her under the ~ of examining the pictures on the wall.* | **~ at** ◇ *His ~ at friendliness fooled no one.* | **~ of** ◇ *He was hanged without even the ~ of a proper trial.*
PHRASES **abandon all ~, abandon any ~** ◇ *She abandoned all ~ of neutrality and began to cheer.* | **make a ~, make no ~** ◇ *I make no ~ to be an expert on the subject.* | **by false ~s, under false ~s** ◇ *He was accused of obtaining money under false ~s.*

pretend *verb*

ADV. **otherwise** ◇ *You know what this is all about. Why ~ otherwise?* | **at least** ◇ *Couldn't you at least ~ to enjoy it?* | **just, merely, simply** ◇ *They decided to just ~ it never happened.*
VERB + PRETEND **can no longer** | **try to** | **be dishonest to, be foolish to, be idle to** (*BrE*) ◇ *It would be foolish to ~ that there are no risks involved.*
PREP. **to** ◇ *He ~ed to his boss that he'd written the article.*
PHRASES **go on ~ing** ◇ *I can't go on ~ing any longer.* | **just ~ing, only ~ing** ◇ *Maria knew he was only ~ing.* | **let's ~** ◇ *Let's ~ it never happened.* | **stop ~ing** | **there's no point in ~ing, there's no point ~ing** (*esp. BrE*)

pretext *noun*

ADJ. **flimsy** ◇ *Several schools banned the game on flimsy ~s.* | **false** ◇ *This was a false ~ to attack another country.*
VERB + PRETEXT **give sb, provide (sb with)** | **find, invent** ◇ *He considered inventing some ~ for calling her.*
PREP. **on a/the ~** ◇ *He disappeared into his study on the ~ that he had work to do there.* | **under a/the ~** ◇ *Under the ~ of checking her identity, the man had copied down her credit card details.* | **~ for** ◇ *He used his research as a ~ for going to Hungary.*
PHRASES **at the slightest ~, on the slightest ~** ◇ *He keeps popping into my office on the slightest ~.*

pretty *adj.*

VERBS **be, feel, look** ◇ *She felt ~ wearing her mother's earrings.*

ADV. **extremely, fairly, very, etc.** | **awfully, exceptionally** | **conventionally** ◇ *She's very attractive, though not conventionally ~.* | **almost** | **undeniably**

prevail *verb*

ADV. **always, usually** ◇ *Her happy outlook always ~ed.* | **eventually, finally, in the end, ultimately**

VERB + PREVAIL **must, should, will, etc.** ◇ *Common sense must ~ in the end.*

PREP. **against** ◇ *The wishes of 20 million people ought to ~ against those of 200 thousand.* | **over** ◇ *His view eventually ~ed over theirs.*

prevent *verb*

ADV. **effectively** ◇ *This new legislation effectively ~s us from trading.* | **reliably, successfully** ◇ *a study to determine whether the brace can reliably ~ knee injuries* | **possibly, potentially** ◇ *Better intelligence could have possibly ~ed the attack.* | **completely** ◇ *These barriers completely ~ new companies from entering the market.* | **forcibly, physically** | **thereby** ◇ *The drug inhibits the replication of cancer cells, thereby ~ing their spread.*

VERB + PREVENT **be able to, be unable to, can** ◇ *No one can ~ you from attending this meeting.* | **attempt to, seek to, take action to, take steps to, try to** | **help (to)** ◇ *A good sunscreen will help ~ sunburn.* | **be designed to** | **be nothing to, do nothing to** ◇ *There's nothing to ~ these guys from copying our idea.* ◇ *The whole affair is an outrage and the authorities have done nothing to ~ it.*

PREP. **from** ◇ *They took action to ~ the disease from spreading.*

PHRASES **aimed at ~ing sth** ◇ *new measures aimed at ~ing accidents* | **action to ~ sth, measures to ~ sth** | **an attempt to ~ sth** | **in order to ~ sth** ◇ *Action must be swift in order to ~ further damage.*

preventable *adj.*

VERBS **be** | **become**

ADV. **entirely** ◇ *These injuries are entirely ~.* | **easily** | **largely** | **potentially** ◇ *Many potentially ~ cancers are currently missed.*

prevention *noun*

ADJ. **accident, crime, disease, drug, fire, flood, pollution, pregnancy** (*esp. AmE*) ◇ *drug ~ policies* | **AIDS, cancer, HIV, osteoporosis, etc.**

PREVENTION + NOUN **efforts, measures, programme/program, scheme** (*BrE*), **strategy** ◇ *crime ~ strategies*

preview *noun*

ADJ. **press** ◇ *a press ~ of a new movie* | **sneak** ◇ *Journalists have been given a sneak ~ of the singer's latest album.* | **exclusive** ◇ *On today's show, we'll have exclusive ~s of some of the best new music.*

VERB + PREVIEW **get, have** | **see** | **give sb**

PREVIEW + NOUN **audience** | **screening**

prey *noun*

ADJ. **easy** ◇ *Teenagers are easy ~ for unscrupulous drug dealers.* | **helpless** (*esp. AmE*), **unsuspecting** ◇ *They watched a hawk swoop down on its unsuspecting ~.*

VERB + PREY **chase, circle, hunt for, look for, pursue, stalk** | **spot** | **capture, pounce on** ◇ *a cat pouncing on its ~* | **devour, kill**

PREP. **~ for** ◇ *The young deer are ideal ~ for the leopard.* | **~ to** (*figurative*) ◇ *She was ~ to all kinds of conflicting emotions.*

PHRASES **a beast of ~, a bird of ~** | **be ~ to sth, fall ~ to sth** (*both figurative*) ◇ *The new government has fallen ~ to corruption and fraud.*

price *noun*

ADJ. **exorbitant, high, inflated, prohibitive, steep** ◇ *They charge exorbitant ~s for their goods.* ◇ *The ~ of fuel is prohibitive.* | **rising, soaring** | **falling** | **cheap, low** | **bargain, budget, discounted, knock-down** (*BrE*), **reduced, rock-bottom** ◇ *designer clothes at bargain ~s* | **affordable, attractive, competitive, decent, fair, reasonable, right** ◇ *We sell quality tools at the right ~.* | **good** ◇ *I managed to get a good ~ for my old car.* | **average** | **asking, purchase** ◇ *What's the asking ~ for this house?* ◇ *You need to pay a deposit of 10% of the purchase ~ of the property.* | **recommended** (*esp. BrE*), **suggested** (*esp. AmE*) ◇ *The suggested retail ~ of the DVD is $19.99.* | **retail, sale, sales, selling** | **wholesale** | **cost** (*esp. BrE*) ◇ *They are selling off summer shoes at cost ~.* | **base** (*esp. AmE*) ◇ *The car has a base ~ of $28 640.* | **full, half** ◇ *Children travel half ~ until age ten.* | **fixed** ◇ *They sell cars at fixed ~s, with no haggling.* | **market** ◇ *This website tells you the market ~ of all makes of second-hand car.* | **admission, ticket** ◇ *admission ~s at the museum* | **consumer** | **bond, commodity, gold, share** (*esp. BrE*), **stock** (*esp. AmE*) | **food** | **house, housing** (*esp. AmE*), **land, property** (*esp. BrE*), **real estate** (*esp. AmE*) | **electricity, energy, fuel, gas, gasoline** (*AmE*), **oil, petrol** (*BrE*)

VERB + PRICE **command, fetch, go for** ◇ *Property in the area is now fetching ridiculously high ~s.* | **give sb, quote sb** ◇ *I got a number of suppliers to quote me their best ~s.* | **agree, agree on, negotiate** ◇ *Banding together allows growers to negotiate a better ~ for their crop.* | **charge, fix, set** | **compare** ◇ *It's always worth comparing ~s before you buy.* | **boost, double, increase, push up, raise** ◇ *The deal would boost gas ~s.* | **bring down, cut, drop, lower, mark down, push down, reduce, slash** ◇ *The campaign urged retailers to drop their ~s.* | **adjust** ◇ *We need to adjust our ~s to reflect our actual costs.* | **go up in, increase in, rise in** ◇ *Oil is set in go up in ~.* | **come down in** | **range in, vary in** ◇ *These computers range in ~ from £1 300 to £2 000.* | **undercut**

PRICE + VERB **climb, double, go up, increase, jump, rise, shoot up, skyrocket, soar, spike** (*esp. AmE*) ◇ *House ~s went up by 5% last year.* ◇ *Prices soared during the war.* | **collapse, drop, fall, go down, plummet, plunge, slump, tumble** ◇ *If ~s slump further, the farmers will starve.* | **fluctuate, swing** | **go from… to…, range from… to…, start at, vary** ◇ *Prices go from $30 for the standard model to $150 for the de luxe version.*

PRICE + NOUN **level, range** | **hike** (*informal*), **increase, rise, spike** | **cut, drop** | **change, fluctuation, movement, volatility** | **stability** | **war** | **tag** ◇ *I got a shock when I looked at the ~ tag.* | **list** | **index** ◇ *the share ~ index*

PREP. **at/the ~** ◇ *Food is available, at a ~ (= at a high price).* ◇ *I can't afford it at that ~.* | **in ~** ◇ *Cigarettes have remained stable in ~ for some time.*

PHRASES **a drop in ~, a fall in ~, a reduction in ~** | **an increase in ~, a rise in ~** | **pay a heavy ~ (for sth), pay a high ~ (for sth), pay the ~ (for sth)** ◇ *The team paid a heavy ~ for its lack of preparation.* | **place a ~ on sth, put a ~ on sth** ◇ *You can't put a ~ on happiness.* | **the ~ of freedom, success, etc.** (= the unpleasant things you must suffer to have freedom, success, etc.) | **~ per gallon, pound, etc.** ◇ *The average ~ per gallon was $2.09.* | **a small ~ to pay (for sth)** ◇ *The cost of a policy premium is a small ~ to pay for peace of mind.*

→ Note at PER CENT (for more verbs)

price *verb* be priced

ADV. **exorbitantly, highly, outrageously** | **aggressively, cheaply** | **affordably, attractively, competitively, economically, fairly, moderately, modestly, realistically, reasonably, sensibly** ◇ *a wide range of competitively ~d office furniture* | **comparatively, similarly** ◇ *It has a much longer battery life than other comparatively ~d laptops.* | **accordingly** ◇ *This is considered a luxury item and is ~d accordingly.*

PREP. **at** ◇ *The car is ~d at $60 000.* | **between** ◇ *Tickets for the concert are ~d between £15 and £35.* | **from, to** ◇ *The kits are ~d from £8.50 to £20.*

PHRASES **be ~d high, be ~d low** ◇ *The house was ~d much too high.*

pride noun

1 feeling of being proud of sb/sth

ADJ. **fierce, great** | **justifiable** ◊ *She took justifiable ~ in her son's achievements.* | **fatherly** ◊ *He smiled with fatherly ~.*
VERB + PRIDE **feel, have, swell with** ◊ *They have a fierce ~ in their traditions.* ◊ *He swelled with ~ as he held the trophy.* | **express**
PREP. **with ~** ◊ *I wear my policeman's uniform with ~.* ◊ *'My daughter's a writer,' he added with ~.* | **~ in** ◊ *She expressed ~ in her child's achievement.*
PHRASES **a cause for ~, a matter for ~** ◊ *Their reputation for fairness is a matter for ~.* | **a source of ~** | **take (a) ~ in sth** ◊ *She takes great ~ in her work.*

2 self-respect

ADJ. **great** | **family, masculine, personal, professional** ◊ *His masculine ~ would not let him admit that a girl had defeated him.* | **civic, local, national, patriotic** ◊ *Businesses rushed to include images of patriotic ~ in their marketing.* | **ethnic** (*esp. AmE*), **gay, racial** ◊ *the politics of racial ~ and Black Power* | **dented** (*BrE*), **hurt, injured, wounded** ◊ *He was nursing his hurt ~.* | **foolish, stubborn** ◊ *It was foolish ~ that prevented me from believing her.*
VERB + PRIDE **have** ◊ *I don't want your money—I have my ~, you know!* | **hurt, wound** ◊ *I didn't mean to hurt your ~.* | **restore, salvage** ◊ *We want to restore ~ in our public services.* ◊ *They managed to salvage some ~ with a late goal.* | **sacrifice** (*esp. AmE*), **swallow** ◊ *She swallowed her ~ and called him.*
PREP. **out of ~** ◊ *She refused their help out of ~.* | **through ~** ◊ *It would be stupid to refuse through ~.*
PHRASES **a matter of ~** ◊ *It is a matter of ~ for him that he has never accepted money from his family.* | **a sense of ~** ◊ *They have a strong sense of ~ in their work.* | **with your ~ intact** ◊ *She refused his offer tactfully, allowing him to go away with his ~ intact.*

priest noun

1 in Christianity

ADJ. **local, parish, village** (*esp. BrE*) | **celibate** | **married** | **woman** | **ordained** | **Anglican, Catholic, Jesuit, etc.**
VERB + PRIEST **become, be ordained (as)**
PRIEST + VERB **celebrate sth, officiate (at sth)** ◊ *the ~ who was celebrating Mass*

2 in some other religions

ADJ. **chief, high** ◊ *a ceremony led by the High Priest* ◊ *He was considered the high ~ of finance at that time.* (*figurative*) | **temple** | **Brahman, Buddhist, etc.**

prime minister noun

ADJ. **deputy** | **acting, caretaker, interim, transitional** | **incumbent, present** | **former, previous** | **outgoing** | **strong** | **beleaguered** (*esp. BrE*) ◊ *The beleaguered ~ is coming under more pressure.* | **Conservative, Labour, etc.**
VERB + PRIME MINISTER **appoint, appoint sb (as), elect, elect sb (as)** | **serve as** ◊ *He served briefly as ~ from 1920 to 1921.* (For more verbs see the entry for *minister*.)
PREP. **under a/the ~** ◊ *She held office under two different ~s.*

principal noun

ADJ. **college** (*BrE*), **school** (*esp. AmE*) | **elementary-school, high-school, middle-school** (*all AmE*) | **independent-school, private-school, public-school** (*all AmE*) | **assistant, vice**
→ Note at JOB

principle noun

1 basic general rule

ADJ. **basic, broad, central, fundamental, general, underlying** ◊ *the basic ~s of car maintenance* | **bedrock** (*esp. AmE*), **cardinal, core, essential, key** | **universal** | **organizing** ◊ *His novels reject chronology as an organizing ~.* | **abstract,**

theoretical ◊ *She is interested in actual human relationships rather than abstract ~s.* | **constitutional, democratic, legal, market, political** | **mathematical, physical, scientific**
VERB + PRINCIPLE **violate** ◊ *This violates every ~ of good writing.* | **embody, embrace, illustrate, incorporate** ◊ *The house incorporates many ~s of modern environmentally aware design.* | **discover, establish, formulate, lay down** | **apply, invoke** | **articulate, explain, outline**
PRINCIPLE + VERB **apply** ◊ *This ~ applies to all kinds of selling.* | **underlie sth, underpin sth** ◊ *the ~s underlying Western philosophy*
PREP. **in ~** ◊ *I agree with you in ~, but we'll need to discuss the details.* | **~ behind** ◊ *She went on to explain the ~s behind what she was doing.*
PHRASES **the pleasure ~, the precautionary ~, the uncertainty ~** ◊ *Does everything we do come down to the pleasure ~?*

2 moral rule

ADJ. **high** | **founding, guiding** ◊ *Freedom is the founding ~ of our Republic.* | **Biblical, religious** | **Christian, Islamic, etc.** | **ethical, moral** ◊ *He was a man of high moral ~s.*
VERB + PRINCIPLE **abandon, betray, compromise** ◊ *I refuse to compromise my ~s by eating meat.* | **adhere to, stick to, uphold** ◊ *She sticks to the ~ that everyone should be treated equally.* | **be enshrined in sth** ◊ *The ~ of equality is enshrined in our Constitution.*
PREP. **against your ~s** ◊ *Eating meat was against her ~s.* | **on ~** ◊ *She's opposed to abortion on ~.*
PHRASES **a matter of ~** ◊ *They reject the proposal as a matter of ~.* | **a man/woman of ~** (= person with high moral standards)

print noun

ADJ. **large** | **fine, small** ◊ *Always read the small ~ in a contract before signing.* | **clear** | **bold**
VERB + PRINT **read** ◊ *I had to squint to read the tiny ~ on the screen.*
PRINT + NOUN **journalism, media** | **ad, advertisement, campaign** (*esp. AmE*) | **edition, version** ◊ *They make more money from online subscriptions than from selling the ~ version.* | **journalist, reporter** (*esp. AmE*), **worker** (*esp. BrE*) | **industry** (*esp. BrE*) (usually ***printing industry*** in *AmE*), **union** (*BrE*) | **run** ◊ *The initial ~ run for her book was 6 000 copies.*
PREP. **in ~** ◊ *All her books are still in ~.* | **out of ~** ◊ *I'm afraid that book is now out of ~.*

print verb

ADV. **beautifully** ◊ *The book is beautifully ~ed on good quality paper.* | **badly** | **cheaply** ◊ *He was handing out cheaply ~ed business cards.* | **correctly** ◊ *I couldn't get the graphics to ~ correctly.* | **boldly, clearly, legibly, neatly** | **indelibly** (*BrE, figurative*) ◊ *The incident was indelibly ~ed in her memory.* | **professionally** ◊ *We had the first issue of the newsletter professionally ~ed.* | **privately** ◊ *She had the memoir privately ~ed in a limited edition.* | **specially** ◊ *We had the T-shirts specially ~ed with the company's logo.* | **digitally** ◊ *The images are scanned onto computers and digitally ~ed.*
PREP. **from** ◊ *Photographs can be ~ed from a digital file or from a negative.* | **in** ◊ *The message was ~ed in blue ink.* | **on** ◊ *a leaflet ~ed on recycled paper* | **with** ◊ *a dress ~ed with blue flowers*

printer noun

1 person/company that prints books, etc.

ADJ. **book** | **commercial** | **master** | **jobbing** (*BrE*)
PRINTER + VERB **print sth, run sth off** ◊ *The ~ has run off 2 000 copies of the leaflet.*
→ Note at JOB

2 machine

ADJ. **black-and-white, colour/color, monochrome** | **computer** | **office** | **desktop** | **dot matrix, inkjet, laser** | **wide-format** (*AmE*) | **compatible**
VERB + PRINTER **configure, install** | **control, drive** | **attach,**

connect, plug in ◇ *Connect the ~ to your PC.* | **network** ◇ *You can print to any networked ~ in the building.*
PRINTER + VERB **print (sth), work** ◇ *The ~ won't print for some reason.*
PRINTER + NOUN **cartridge, ink, toner** | **paper** | **tray** | **cable** ◇ *Can you check to see if the ~ cable is still plugged into your computer?* | **port** | **driver** | **icon**
→ Special page at COMPUTER

priority noun

ADJ. **high, main, major, number-one, top** | **first, immediate, urgent** ◇ *Getting food, medicine and blankets to flood victims is the most urgent ~.* | **low** ◇ *Material possessions have always been a low ~ for Mike.* | **budget, budgetary, legislative** (*esp. AmE*), **spending, strategic** ◇ *Using the Internet is one of the company's top strategic priorities.*
VERB + PRIORITY **choose, decide on, determine, establish, identify, set, sort out** ◇ *You need to sort out your priorities before making a decision about the future.* | **get, have, take** ◇ *When hospital funds are being allocated children take ~.* | **assign, give** ◇ *We assign a high ~ to research and development.* ◇ *The bank seems to give ~ to new customers.* | **re-evaluate** (*AmE*), **reorder, rethink** ◇ *To reduce stress you may have to rethink your priorities in life.*
PREP. **~ over** ◇ *Her family takes ~ over her work.*
PHRASES **a list of priorities** | **order of ~** ◇ *List the tasks in order of ~.* | **place a high ~ on sth, place a low ~ on sth** ◇ *We need to place a higher ~ on family and social issues.*

prison noun

ADJ. **local** | **federal** | **overcrowded** | **high-security** (*esp. BrE*), **maximum-security** (*esp. AmE*), **supermax** (*AmE*) | **minimum-security** (*AmE*) | **closed** (*BrE*), **open** (*esp. BrE*) ◇ *Open ~s prepare prisoners for life back in the community.* | **private** | **women's** | **debtors'** (*historical*) | **military**
VERB + PRISON **go to** ◇ *He went to ~ for tax evasion.* | **put sb in, send sb to, throw sb into** ◇ *She was sent to ~ for leaking state secrets.* ◇ *He was immediately seized and thrown into ~.* | **be discharged from, be released from, come out of, get out of** ◇ *When did he get out of ~?* | **escape from** ◇ *A dangerous criminal has escaped from a maximum-security ~.* | **avoid, escape** ◇ *You only escaped ~ (= escaped being sent to prison) because of your previous good character.* | **face** ◇ *She was told by magistrates she could now face ~.* | **build, design** ◇ *Building new ~s is not going to help lower our incarceration rate.* | **operate, run** ◇ *It is one of several companies running private ~s across Britain.*
PRISON + NOUN **sentence, term** | **cell, hospital, yard** | **conditions** | **population** | **inmate** | **authorities, chaplain, governor** (*BrE*), **guard** (*esp. AmE*), **officer** (*esp. BrE*), **staff, warden** (*esp. AmE*), **warder** (*BrE*) | **service** (*BrE*), **system** | **reform**
PREP. **at a/the ~** ◇ *The police are investigating disturbances at the ~.* | **in (a/the) ~** ◇ *How long has her father been in ~?* ◇ *There have been riots in the ~.*

prisoner noun

ADJ. **virtual** ◇ *Without a wheelchair, she is a virtual ~ in her own home.* | **political** | **life** (*esp. BrE*), **long-term** (*BrE*) | **short-term** (*BrE*) | **remand** (*BrE*) | **condemned, convicted** (*esp. BrE*) | **death-row** | **escaped** | **captured** (*esp. AmE*) | **released** | **model** ◇ *He was a model ~, and was released after serving only half of his five-year sentence.* | **fellow** ◇ *They were allowed only limited contact with their fellow ~s.*
VERB + PRISONER **capture, take** ◇ *They had captured over 100 ~s.* | **detain, hold, incarcerate** (*esp. AmE*) ◇ *Over 2 million ~s are currently incarcerated in the US.* | **free, release** | **rehabilitate** | **execute**
PHRASES **hold sb ~, keep sb ~** ◇ *They were kept ~ in a basement room for eight months.* | **a ~ of conscience** ◇ *The former ~ of conscience was elected president of the new democracy.* | **a ~ of war** | **be taken ~** ◇ *Many soldiers were taken ~.*

privacy noun

ADJ. **absolute, complete, total** | **relative** ◇ *I was able to say goodbye to him in relative ~.* | **individual, personal** |

consumer, patient ◇ *We need to have access to health records while protecting patient ~.*
VERB + PRIVACY **ensure, guarantee, preserve, protect, respect, safeguard** | **guard, value** ◇ *He has always jealously guarded his ~.* | **disturb, intrude on, invade, violate** ◇ *I hope I'm not intruding on your ~.*
PREP. **in ~** ◇ *I want to be left in ~.* | **in the ~ of** ◇ *She longed to be in the ~ of her own room.* | **~ from** ◇ *~ from prying eyes*
PHRASES **an intrusion of ~** (*esp. BrE*), **an invasion of ~** ◇ *These phone calls are a gross invasion of ~.* | **an intrusion on (sb's) ~**

privatization noun

ADJ. **large-scale, mass** | **partial** | **electricity, rail, water, etc.**
VERB + PRIVATIZATION **oppose**
PRIVATIZATION + NOUN **plan, programme/program, proposal**

privilege noun

1 special right

ADJ. **exclusive, special** ◇ *Club members have special ~s, like free use of the pool.* | **class** | **diplomatic** ◇ *diplomatic ~s* | **attorney-client, doctor-patient** (*both AmE*)
VERB + PRIVILEGE **enjoy, exercise, have** | **accord sb, give sb, grant sb** | **abuse** ◇ *He was accused of abusing his diplomatic ~s.* | **revoke, withdraw**

2 opportunity to do sth pleasant

ADJ. **enormous** (*esp. BrE*), **great, rare, real** ◇ *It is a great ~ to be attending this conference.* | **dubious** (*esp. BrE*) ◇ *I was given the dubious ~ of organizing the summer fair.*
VERB + PRIVILEGE **have** ◇ *She had the rare ~ of a viewing of his private art collection.* | **give sb**

privileged adj.

VERBS **be, feel** | **consider sb/yourself** ◇ *I consider myself highly ~ to have this opportunity.*
ADV. **extremely, fairly, very, etc.** | **highly** | **uniquely** ◇ *a uniquely ~ position in the American workforce* | **quite, relatively** | **economically, socially** ◇ *She came from a socially ~ background.*

prize noun

ADJ. **big, great, prestigious** | **fabulous** | **special** | **ultimate** ◇ *The presidency is the ultimate ~.* | **coveted** ◇ *She was the first woman to win this coveted ~.* | **glittering** (*esp. BrE*) ◇ *He strove for the glittering ~s of politics.* | **first, first-place** (*AmE*), **grand, top** | **runner-up** (*esp. BrE*), **second** | **consolation** | **booby** ◇ *The booby ~ was awarded to the worst singer in the competition.* | **cash, monetary** (*esp. AmE*), **money** (*esp. BrE*) | **$1-million, etc.** | **raffle**
VERB + PRIZE **award (sb), give (sb)** | **offer** | **present** ◇ *The ~ was presented by the mayor.* | **capture, claim, collect, get, receive, take, win** | **accept** | **share** ◇ *De Klerk shared the peace ~ with Nelson Mandela in 1993.*
PRIZE + VERB **go to sb/sth** ◇ *The ~ went to the long-haired cat.* | **be worth sth, total sth** ◇ *a ~ worth over $3 000*
PRIZE + NOUN **winner** (*usually* ***prizewinner***) | **money** | **competition, draw** (*BrE*)
PREP. **~ for** ◇ *He won the Nobel Prize for Literature.* | **~ in** ◇ *~s in chemistry, physics and medicine*

prize verb

PREP. **above** ◇ *a precious thing to be ~d above all else* | **as** ◇ *The library is ~d as the finest of its kind in England.* | **for** ◇ *The berries are ~d for their healing properties.*
PHRASES **highly ~d, much ~d** ◇ *two fruits that are much ~d on the island*

probability noun

ADJ. **high, real, strong** ◇ *There is a high ~ that it will snow tonight.* | **greater, increased** | **low** | **equal** ◇ *All callers had an equal ~ of being chosen.* | **relative**

... OF PROBABILITY **degree** ◊ *We can say with a high degree of ~ that the poem was written by Shakespeare.*
VERB + PROBABILITY **have** | **increase** | **decrease, reduce** | **assess, calculate** | **predict** | **estimate** | **determine** | **affect, influence** ◊ *genetic factors that influence the ~ of becoming sick*
PREP. **~ for** ◊ *measures to increase the ~ for a sustained recovery* | **~ of** ◊ *This surgical procedure has a high ~ of success.*
PHRASES **in all ~** ◊ *In all ~ she wouldn't come even if we invited her.* | **on a/the balance of probabilities** (BrE) ◊ *On the balance of probabilities, the pilot suffered a stroke before the crash.*

probable adj.

VERBS **be, look, seem**
ADV. **highly, very** | **increasingly** | **quite** | **equally** ◊ *The two outcomes are equally ~.*

probation noun

VERB + PROBATION **give sb, place sb on, put sb on, sentence sb to** ◊ *He was placed on ~ for two years.* ◊ *She was sentenced to a year's ~.* | **get, receive** ◊ *She received ~ upon completing a drug rehab course.* | **release sb on** | **violate** ◊ *He was sentenced to eight months in jail for violating his ~.*
PROBATION + NOUN **order** (esp. BrE) ◊ *He was under a ~ order for attacking a photographer.* | **officer** | **department** (AmE), **office, service** (BrE) | **hostel** (BrE) | **period** ◊ *Once your ~ period is successfully completed, you will be offered a contract.* | **supervision** ◊ *the effectiveness of regular ~ supervision* | **violation**
PREP. **on ~** ◊ *The judge put her on ~ for a year.* ◊ *He joined the company on six months' ~.*

probe verb

ADV. **deep, deeply** ◊ *Scientists are probing deeper and deeper into the secrets of the universe.* | **further** | **carefully, gently**
PREP. **for** ◊ *The bird uses its long beak to ~ for worms.* | **into** ◊ *The police were probing into her personal life.* | **with** ◊ *He ~d the mud with his knife.*

problem noun

1 sth that causes difficulties

ADJ. **acute, big, enormous, grave, great, huge, important, major, serious, significant** ◊ *Our greatest ~ is the lack of funds.* | **global** ◊ *The traffic in illegal drugs is a global ~.* | **terrible** ◊ *The accident poses a terrible ~ for the family.* | **real** | **perceived** | **little, minor, petty, slight** | **complex, complicated, difficult, knotty, thorny, tough** | **growing** | **basic, central, fundamental, key, main, major, number-one** (esp. AmE) ◊ *Access to capital is often the number-one ~ for many entrepreneurs.* | **underlying** ◊ *the underlying ~ that's causing your high blood pressure* | **annoying, vexing** (esp. AmE) | **common** | **pressing, urgent** | **unforeseen** ◊ *Unforeseen ~s often arise.* | **immediate** | **possible, potential** ◊ *Fortunately, it's easy to avoid any potential ~s.* | **insoluble, insuperable** (formal), **insurmountable** (formal), **intractable** (formal) ◊ *Depression is a natural feeling if your ~s seem intractable.* | **unresolved, unsolved** ◊ *The role of the sun in climate change is still a big unsolved ~.* | **age-old, long-standing, long-term, perennial** | **chronic, ongoing, persistent, recurring** | **inherent** ◊ *the inherent ~s of merging two very different companies* | **logistical, practical** | **mechanical, technical** | **systemic** ◊ *Systemic security ~s have been identified.* | **attitude, behaviour/behavior, behavioural/behavioral, developmental, emotional, mental, mental-health, psychiatric, psychological** ◊ *His teachers say he has an attitude ~.* | **family, personal** ◊ *Her new job had taken her mind off her family ~s for a while.* | **communication** ◊ *We had communication ~s.* | **fertility, health, medical, physical, sexual, sleep** | **back, heart, knee** | **alcohol, drink** (BrE), **drinking** (AmE), **drug, gambling, substance-abuse** ◊ *She had serious substance*

abuse ~s with both cocaine and heroin.* | **social** | **housing** | **economic, financial, money** ◊ *They sold their car to ease their financial ~s.* | **environmental** | **political** | **legal** | **marital, marriage** | **ethical, moral** ◊ *Most people can see the ethical ~ with accepting such an offer.*

... OF PROBLEMS **host, set** ◊ *We're faced with a whole host of new ~s.* ◊ *an elegant solution to a very complex set of ~s*
VERB + PROBLEM **be, pose, present (sb with), remain** ◊ *Inadequate resources pose a ~ for all members of staff.* | **have** | **develop** ◊ *He developed a drinking ~.* | **bring, cause, create, pose** ◊ *Success brings its own ~s.* ◊ *Staff shortages cause ~s for the organization.* | **complicate, compound** | **be beset with, be confronted by, be confronted with, be dogged by** (esp. BrE), **be faced with, be fraught with, confront, encounter, experience, face, run into, suffer** ◊ *He has been faced with all sorts of ~s in his new job.* ◊ *The plan has been fraught with ~s from the start.* | **battle** ◊ *an important step in battling the terrorist ~* | **attribute, blame** ◊ *the ~s attributed to capitalism* ◊ *They blame the ~ on the new prescription drug law.* | **raise** ◊ *She raised the ~ of falling sales at the last meeting.* | **see** ◊ *He doesn't really see the ~.* | **define** | **acknowledge, admit, recognize** ◊ *I'm glad you finally admitted your ~.* | **understand** ◊ *He doesn't seem to understand my ~.* | **anticipate, foresee** ◊ *I don't anticipate any future ~s in that regard.* | **detect, discover, identify, isolate, pinpoint, spot** | **indicate, point out** ◊ *These symptoms may indicate a serious ~.* | **assess, examine, investigate, study** ◊ *They created a task force to study this ~.* | **diagnose, figure out** (esp. AmE), **work out** | **consider, debate, discuss, look at, look into** | **describe, frame** (esp. AmE) ◊ *Framing the ~ is an important step.* | **address, approach, attack, combat, come to grips with, counter, get to grips with, grapple with, handle, manage, tackle** ◊ *The next meeting will address the ~ of obesity.* | **illustrate** ◊ *This illustrates another potential ~.* | **highlight, underscore** (esp. AmE) ◊ *This underscores the biggest ~ with electronic voting.* | **mask** ◊ *All the anti-depressant does is mask the ~.* | **avoid, circumvent, find a way around, find a way round** (esp. BrE), **get around, get round** (esp. BrE), **prevent, sidestep** | **ignore** | **overlook** ◊ *For years I've tried to overlook this ~.* | **forget** ◊ *I forgot my ~s for a moment.* | **clear up, correct, cure, deal with, eliminate, fix** (esp. AmE), **iron out, overcome, rectify, remedy, repair, resolve, settle, solve, sort out, troubleshoot** ◊ *He had to undergo surgery to cure the ~ with his knee.* | **alleviate, ease, minimize, mitigate, reduce, relieve, simplify** | **aggravate, exacerbate, exaggerate, magnify, worsen** | **analyse/analyze, explore**
PROBLEM + VERB **arise, come up, crop up, emerge, occur, surface** ◊ *~s arising from poor ventilation* | **exist** | **begin, originate** ◊ *No one ever asked why or how the ~ originated.* | **persist, remain** ◊ *If the ~ persists you should see a doctor.* ◊ *The basic ~ remains the lack of available housing.* | **afflict sb, beset sb, confront sb, face sb, plague sb** | **lie in sth** ◊ *The ~ lies in the lack of communication between managers and staff.* ◊ *Therein lies the ~.* | **result from sth, stem from sth** ◊ *a ~ resulting from technical inadequacy*
PROBLEM + NOUN **area, spot** | **behaviour/behavior** | **child** | **drinker, gambler** ◊ *One out of every five people is a ~ drinker.* | **drinking, gambling** ◊ *a new approach to ~ drinking* | **page** (BrE) (= in a magazine, containing letters about readers' problems)
PREP. **~ about** ◊ *I didn't imagine there would be a ~ about getting tickets.* | **~ for** ◊ *The rail strike is a ~ for all commuters.* | **~ of** ◊ *the ~ of poverty* | **~ with** ◊ *Do you have a ~ with her?*
PHRASES **an approach to a ~** | **the crux of the ~, the heart of the ~, the root of the ~** ◊ *We need to get to the root of the ~ before we can solve it.* | **the answer to a ~, a remedy to a ~, a solution to a ~** ◊ *He believes he may have found the answer to his ~.* ◊ *He believes he may have found a solution to the ~.* | **the scale of a ~**

2 question to be solved

ADJ. **complicated, difficult** | **easy, simple** | **math** (AmE), **mathematical, maths** (BrE) ◊ *the ability to solve simple mathematical ~s*

VERB + PROBLEM **do, find the answer to, solve, work out** ◇ *I have five ~s to do for homework.*
PROBLEM + NOUN **set** (*AmE*)

procedure noun

ADJ. **complex, complicated** | **simple, straightforward** | **common, correct, normal, proper, recommended, standard, usual** ◇ *There are standard ~s for dismissing staff.* | **agreed** (*esp. BrE*), **established, routine** | **formal** ◇ *a formal ~ such as an audit* | **strict** ◇ *the strict legal ~s for adoption* | **alternative, experimental, new** | **sampling, testing** ◇ *the use of animals in experimental ~s* | **necessary** | **special** | **administrative, appeal** (*esp. BrE*), **appeals** (*esp. AmE*), **application, assessment, complaints** (*esp. BrE*), **court, criminal, disciplinary, emergency, evacuation, grievance** (*esp. BrE*), **operating, parliamentary, safety, scientific, security, selection, voting** | **legal, medical** | **cosmetic, diagnostic, non-invasive, non-surgical, screening, surgical** ◇ *the most popular cosmetic ~ in the nation* ◇ *a minor surgical ~* | **invasive** ◇ *invasive surgical ~s* | **abortion, biopsy, sterilization, transplant, etc.**
VERB + PROCEDURE **adopt, apply, carry out, conduct, employ, follow, implement, use** ◇ *All animal ~s were conducted in accordance with the recommendations.* ◇ *Did you follow the emergency ~ when you heard the alarm?* | **recommend** ◇ *This ~ is usually recommended only for children.* | **approve** | **perform** ◇ *He could no longer perform delicate ~s such as angioplasty.* | **complete** ◇ *The pilots completed the emergency ~s.* | **review** ◇ *Banks began to review their credit ~s.* | **repeat** | **undergo** ◇ *Women who undergo the ~ may be unable to breastfeed.* | **establish** ◇ *A straightforward complaints ~ must be established from the outset.* | **standardize** ◇ *An attempt was made to standardize the ~.* | **simplify** | **describe, outline**
PREP. **under a/the ~** ◇ *under a ~ established by legislation* | **~ for** ◇ *the correct ~ for hiring staff*

proceed verb

ADV. **apace, quickly, rapidly** ◇ *Work is now ~ing apace.* | **slowly** | **carefully, cautiously, with caution** ◇ *It will be necessary to ~ with caution.* | **smoothly** | **normally** ◇ *At first everything ~ed normally.* | **directly** ◇ *In some cases appeals may ~ directly from the High Court to the House of Lords.* | **accordingly** ◇ *I will remember your advice and ~ accordingly.* | **further** | **forward, onward** (*esp. AmE*) ◇ *With no more questions, he ~ed onward.* | **back** ◇ *She ~ed back to her office.*
VERB + PROCEED **be able to** | **decide to, intend to, want to, wish to** | **allow sb/sth to, enable sb/sth to** ◇ *This project cannot be allowed to ~.* | **instruct sb to, tell sb to** ◇ *I will instruct my lawyer to ~ with the preparation of draft contracts.* | **be unable to**
PREP. **along** ◇ *Proceed along the Botley Road.* | **down, into** ◇ *These students then ~ out into the world to positions of leadership.* | **through, to** ◇ *students who wish to ~ to college* | **towards/toward** ◇ *Jacob ~ed towards/toward the steps.* | **up** ◇ *I nodded and ~ed up the stairs.* | **with** ◇ *She decided not to ~ with the treatment.*
PHRASES **~ on the basis of sth** ◇ *The council must ~ on the basis of the vote.*

proceedings noun

ADJ. **court, criminal, judicial, legal** | **bankruptcy, divorce, extradition, impeachment, libel** | **appeal** (*BrE*), **civil, committal** (*BrE*), **summary** (*BrE*)
VERB + PROCEEDINGS **bring, initiate, instigate, institute, take** | **begin, commence, start** | **close, end, halt, stop**
PROCEEDINGS + VERB **begin, commence**
PREP. **in ~** ◇ *decisions made in court ~* | **~ against** ◇ *She is bringing divorce ~ against her husband.* | **~ before** ◇ *~ before a tribunal* | **~ between** ◇ *~ between the four parties involved*

proceeds noun

ADJ. **total** | **gross** | **net** | **sale**
VERB + PROCEEDS **use** ◇ *The ~ will be used to improve the school playground.* | **invest** | **split** | **donate**

PROCEEDS + VERB **benefit sth** (*AmE*), **go to sth** ◇ *All ~ benefit the Georgia Cancer Coalition.* ◇ *All the ~ will go to a local charity.*
PREP. **on the ~** ◇ *I sold my house and I'm planning to retire on the ~.* | **with the ~** ◇ *They bought a new minibus with the ~ from the auction.* | **~ from**
PHRASES **your share of the ~** ◇ *She bought a new car with her share of the ~.*

process noun

ADJ. **gradual, lengthy, long, slow, time-consuming** | **constant, continuous, ongoing** | **complex, complicated** | **arduous, difficult, gruelling/grueling, laborious, painstaking** ◇ *a painstaking ~ of trial and error* | **natural** | **normal** ◇ *The bylaws are amended through the normal ~es.* | **formal** ◇ *The company doesn't have a formal complaints ~.* | **due** ◇ *the due ~ of law* | **painful** ◇ *Removing the splinters from the wound was a long and painful ~.* | **tedious** ◇ *the tedious ~ of creating receipts and invoices* | **consultation, consultative, decision-making, management, planning** | **nomination, voting** | **registration** ◇ *As part of the registration ~, the applicant will report certain information.* | **collaborative** ◇ *Design is a collaborative ~.* | **cognitive, creative, design, learning, mental, thought** ◇ *Teachers are trained to stimulate the child's cognitive ~es.* ◇ *I was beginning to understand his thought ~es.* | **assessment, selection, testing** | **review** ◇ *the long review ~ for his application* | **democratic, electoral, political** ◇ *Churches are taking a key role in the democratic ~.* | **chemical, industrial, manufacturing, production** | **ageing/aging, biological, developmental, evolutionary, grieving, healing, physical, thinking** ◇ *Students use thinking ~es and skills to gain a knowledge of history.* | **judicial, legal, legislative** | **approval, screening, vetting** ◇ *They all have to go through a vetting ~.* | **bidding** ◇ *the bidding ~ for media rights* | **editorial** | **peace** ◇ *a stalemate in the peace ~* | **historical, social** | **three-step, two-step, etc.** ◇ *A two-step ~ was used to test this hypothesis.*
VERB + PROCESS **go through, undergo** ◇ *Each time we have to go through the whole decision-making ~ again.* | **accelerate, drive, expedite, hasten, speed up, stimulate** ◇ *Excessive exposure to sunlight speeds up the ageing/aging ~ of the skin.* | **slow, slow down** ◇ *Disputes and negotiations have slowed down the ~.* | **disrupt** ◇ *Protests disrupted the electoral ~ in the southern region.* | **begin, initiate, start** ◇ *She began the long ~ of clearing up all the reports.* | **complete** ◇ *The entire ~ was completed in less than 24 hours.* | **repeat** | **reverse** ◇ *places where the ~ of urbanization is being reversed* | **simplify, streamline** ◇ *e-commerce solutions to streamline the ~* | **facilitate** ◇ *The Web facilitates an interactive ~ of learning.* | **oversee** | **affect, influence** | **control, guide, regulate** ◇ *calls for the law to regulate the warrant ~ effectively* | **automate** ◇ *Most of the ~ is automated.*
PROCESS + VERB **occur, take place, unfold** ◇ *The selection ~ takes place over a period of two weeks.* | **begin, start** | **continue** | **evolve** ◇ *Any design ~ evolves over time as new information surfaces.* | **culminate, result in sth** ◇ *The ~ will culminate in December 2010.* | **call for sth, require sth** ◇ *These ~es require careful scheduling.* | **work** ◇ *Here's how the ~ works in Finland.*
PREP. **~ for** ◇ *a legal ~ for dealing with defrauders* | **~ of** ◇ *the ~ of change*
PHRASES **(a) part of the ~** ◇ *This is part of the ~ by which musical works are created.* | **a ~ of elimination** ◇ *I will prove this to you by a ~ of elimination.* | **a stage in the ~, a stage of the ~**

process verb

ADV. **efficiently** | **specially** ◇ *tobacco specially ~ed to reduce nicotine* | **correctly, properly** ◇ *properly ~ed black-and-white photographs* | **fully** ◇ *It was a second later when I fully ~ed what he had said.* | **quickly, slowly** ◇ *My brain slowly ~ed the fact that I was free to leave.* | **automatically** |

digitally ◇ *The image is ~ed digitally by computer software.* | routinely

PREP. **by** ◇ *This information is ~ed by the computer.* | **for** ◇ *The plant is then ~ed for dye.* | **into** ◇ *The berries are ~ed into juice or sauce.*

PHRASES **highly ~ed** ◇ *highly ~ed foods*

procession noun

ADJ. **grand, great, large, long** | **little, small** | **public, street** | **slow, solemn, stately** | **colourful/colorful** | **ceremonial, formal** | **triumphal** | **constant, endless, never-ending, steady** ◇ *We've had an endless ~ of new secretaries through the office since Amy left.* | **candlelit** (*BrE*), **torchlight** | **funeral, religious, wedding**

VERB + PROCESSION **head, lead** ◇ *The mayor of the town led the ~ to the central square.* | **form** | **join** ◇ *Heavily laden donkeys joined the ~ of jeeps and trucks.*

PROCESSION + VERB **make its way, march, move, pass, wind, wind its way** ◇ *The funeral ~ moved slowly down the avenue.* ◇ *The solemn ~ wound its way through the narrow streets.* | **begin, leave, move off, set off** (*BrE*) | **reach sth** ◇ *when the ~ reached the edge of the village*

PREP. **in (a/the) ~** ◇ *The children marched in ~ behind the band.* | **~ of** ◇ *a ~ of circus performers* | **~ through** ◇ *a ~ through the heart of Hong Kong*

proclaim verb

ADV. **loudly** | **formally, officially** | **openly, publicly** | **proudly, triumphantly** | **boldly** ◇ *She boldly ~ed that her goal was to win the championship.* | **hereby** (*often humorous*) ◇ *I hereby ~ June 12 as a computer-free day.* | **repeatedly** ◇ *She repeatedly ~ed her devotion to the cause.*

VERB + PROCLAIM **seem to** ◇ *His boyish looks seemed to ~ his inexperience.* | **continue to** ◇ *They continue to ~ their innocence.*

PREP. **as** ◇ *Everyone is ~ing him as the next president.* | **to** ◇ *She ~ed her innocence to the world.*

proclamation noun

ADJ. **official, presidential, public, royal** | **bold** (*esp. AmE*)

VERB + PROCLAMATION **issue, make** | **sign** ◇ *The President signed a ~ declaring martial law.*

PROCLAMATION + VERB **announce sth, declare sth**

PREP. **by ~** ◇ *The government restricted the use of water by ~.*

produce noun

ADJ. **fresh** | **home-grown** (*esp. BrE*), **local** | **supermarket** | **seasonal** | **agricultural, dairy** (*esp. BrE*), **farm, garden, organic** ◇ *fresh farm ~* | **conventional, non-organic** | **quality** ◇ *There was limited access to quality ~.*

VERB + PRODUCE **grow** | **export, market, sell** | **buy** ◇ *I buy my ~ directly from farmers.* | **eat** ◇ *I'm eating more fresh ~ than ever.*

produce verb

ADV. **domestically, locally** ◇ *fruit and vegetables that are ~d locally* | **commercially, industrially** | **artificially, synthetically** | **naturally** | **organically** ◇ *organically ~d food* | **sustainably** ◇ *the sale of sustainably ~d timber* | **annually** ◇ *the 700 million bottles of Bordeaux ~d annually* | **typically** ◇ *the sounds that are typically ~d by an American orchestra* | **consistently** ◇ *The changes have not consistently ~d the desired results.* | **efficiently, slickly** ◇ *These goods are more efficiently ~d in small associations.* ◇ *a slickly ~d thriller* | **beautifully, handsomely, lavishly** ◇ *this handsomely ~d reference work* | **professionally** ◇ *a professionally ~d CD* | **independently** | **cheaply** ◇ *The series was obviously cheaply ~d.*

VERB + PRODUCE **be able to, can, manage to** | **be unable to, cannot** | **may, might** | **be expected to, be likely to** ◇ *Which method is likely to ~ the best results?* | **help (to)** | **intend to** ◇ *He moved to California intending to ~ a third novel.* | **combine to, interact to** ◇ *All of these processes combine to ~*

a particular form of language.* | **be designed to** | **use sth to** ◇ *The technology can be used to ~ interactive educational programs.*

PREP. **from** ◇ *The wine is ~d from Chardonnay grapes.* | **with** ◇ *The letter has been ~d with digital technology.*

producer noun

1 sb/sth that makes/grows sth

ADJ. **big, large, large-scale, leading, major, primary** ◇ *one of the world's largest meat ~s* | **second-largest, third-largest, etc.** ◇ *the world's fifth-largest wine ~* | **small, small-scale** | **efficient** ◇ *a very efficient wine ~* | **prolific** | **domestic, local** | **foreign** | **private** | **specialist** (*esp. BrE*) ◇ *specialist ~s of high-quality British beef* | **commercial** ◇ *the commercial pork ~s in the region* | **organic** ◇ *organic ~s of meat, eggs and dairy products* | **low-cost** | **agricultural** | **beef, cattle, dairy, hog** (*AmE*), **livestock, milk, oil, pork, poultry, power** (*esp. AmE*), **software, steel, etc.**

2 sb that organizes a play, film/movie, etc.

ADJ. **film, movie** (*esp. AmE*), **radio, television, TV** | **documentary** | **music, record** | **BBC, Hollywood, etc.** | **news** | **independent** ◇ *We commission TV shows from independent ~s.* | **co-executive, executive, senior** | **assistant, associate** | **legendary** | **award-winning, top** ◇ *He's been a top ~ and mixer for the past decade.*

PHRASES **the role of ~** ◇ *She was willing to take on the role of ~.*

→ Note at JOB

product noun

1 sth that is made or formed

ADJ. **good, right** ◇ *We have a good ~, but it needs to be marketed better.* ◇ *the right ~ in the right place at the right time* | **innovative** | **high-end, quality** | **marketable** | **everyday** | **perishable** | **defective** | **natural** | **manufactured** | **finished** ◇ *the manufacture of chocolate from cocoa bean to the finished ~* | **commercial, consumer** | **branded, brand-name, proprietary** | **generic, own-brand, store-brand** (*esp. AmE*) | **premium** ◇ *We are introducing premium ~s to all our clients.* | **niche, specialty** (*AmE*) ◇ *They offer a range of niche ~s online.* ◇ *an expensive specialty ~* | **flagship** ◇ *the company's flagship ~* | **promotional** ◇ *agencies giving out promotional ~s* | **competing** ◇ *It's hard to find a competing ~ that is as compelling.* | **high-tech** | **domestic, household, industrial** ◇ *everyday household ~s* | **cleaning** ◇ *non-toxic cleaning ~s* | **styling** ◇ *Ken uses the very best styling ~s for Jessica's fine hair.* | **waste** | **agricultural, animal, beef, cereal, cheese, dairy, food, meat, milk, pork, poultry** | **organic** | **nutritional** | **medical, pharmaceutical** | **tobacco** ◇ *cigarettes and other tobacco ~s* | **software** | **beauty, cosmetic, hair-care, skincare**

VERB + PRODUCT **buy, purchase** | **sell** | **advertise, market, promote** | **showcase** ◇ *This new catalogue showcases our ~.* | **use** ◇ *Those who used the ~s were generally satisfied with the quality.* | **introduce** ◇ *The group says it will introduce nine new ~s before the end of the year.* | **endorse** ◇ *an athlete who endorses a ~* | **offer** ◇ *~s offered by our insurance companies* | **manufacture, produce** ◇ *They produce a ~ that meets the customer's quality requirements.* | **create, design, develop** | **customize, tailor** ◇ *Our research enables companies to customize and tailor ~s to suit individual tastes.* | **deliver, distribute** ◇ *the people who create and deliver the ~s and services* | **export, import** | **launch** | **package** ◇ *They put a lot of time and money into packaging ~s.* | **label** | **test** ◇ *Most companies haven't tested their ~s on humans yet.*

PRODUCT + NOUN **area, category, group, line, line-up, range, sector, type** ◇ *We are expanding the ~ line-up.* | **placement** ◇ *We are using a lot of outside agencies to help us do ~ placement.* | **offering** ◇ *the company's new ~ offerings* | **design, innovation** | **mix** ◇ *The company is diversifying its ~ mix to attract new customers.* | **development** | **manager** | **management** ◇ *She is president of ~ management.* | **package** | **portfolio** | **description, information** ◇ *Ensure you have adequate ~ descriptions.* | **launch** ◇ *the most successful new ~ launches of 2003* | **price** | **quality** |

liability | life cycle ◊ short ~ life cycles | safety ◊ for those still concerned about ~ safety
PHRASES **a range of ~s** ◊ a wide range of beauty ~s
→ Special page at BUSINESS

2 result

ADJ. **end, final** ◊ A complicated string of chemical reactions leads to the end ~. | **natural**
PREP. **~ of** ◊ Like many of his generation, he was a ~ of Japan's obsession with technology.

production noun

1 making/growing sth

ADJ. **full, full-scale** ◊ The machine will go into full ~ in November 2002. | **large-scale, mass, volume** | **increased** | **peak** ◊ the days of peak oil ~ | **small-scale** | **efficient** | **annual** | **domestic** | **global, worldwide** | **automobile** (esp. AmE), **car** (esp. BrE) | **coal, electricity, energy, gas, oil** | **cotton, textile** | **agricultural, beef, corn, crop, food, fruit, hog** (AmE), **livestock, meat, milk, pork, poultry, wheat** | **factory, industrial** | **steel** | **organic** ◊ These substances are not allowed in organic ~. | **sustainable** ◊ sustainable crop ~ | **artistic** | **antibody, egg, hormone, insulin, mucus, testosterone,** etc.
... OF PRODUCTION **level, volume** ◊ The increase in volume of ~ brought down the price of the goods. | **rate** ◊ The rate of ~ was greater in Saskatchewan than in Alberta.
VERB + PRODUCTION **be in** ◊ That particular model is no longer in ~. | **go into** | **go out of** | **begin, enter, start** ◊ The new model will enter ~ in 2009. ◊ They are going to start ~ of the car next year. | **resume** ◊ The country has resumed normal oil ~. | **boost, encourage, expand, improve, increase, maximize, promote, step up, stimulate** | **control, regulate** | **cut, cut back, cut back on** | **block, decrease, disrupt, hinder, inhibit, reduce, suppress** ◊ Green tea inhibits the ~ of this enzyme. | **cease, halt, stop** | **speed up** | **outsource** ◊ Buyers have increasingly outsourced ~ to lower-cost regions.
PRODUCTION + VERB **increase, rise** | **fall**
PRODUCTION + NOUN **facility, line, plant** ◊ a car ~ plant | **methods, process, system, technique** | **design** | **schedule** ◊ a tough ~ schedule | **run** ◊ special ~ runs of key components | **assistant, company, crew, designer, director, manager, staff, team, worker** | **costs** | **capacity, level, quota, volume** | **quality** ◊ the movie's direction and ~ quality
PHRASES **a cut in ~, a fall in ~** | **an increase in ~, a rise in ~** | **the means of ~** ◊ They believed that power largely derives from ownership of the means of ~.
→ Special page at BUSINESS

2 play, film/movie, etc.

ADJ. **successful** | **controversial** | **lavish** | **low-budget, low-cost** | **original** ◊ I had seen the original ~ in 1956. | **amateur, professional** | **stage** | **studio** ◊ This is not a big studio ~. | **Broadway, off-Broadway, West End,** etc. | **local** ◊ a local amateur ~ of 'The Sound of Music' | **touring** ◊ a touring ~ of 'Cats' | **school** | **television, TV, video** | **film** (esp. BrE), **movie** (esp. AmE) | **theatre/theater, theatrical**
→ Note at PERFORMANCE (for verbs)

productive adj.

VERBS **be, prove, seem** ◊ Internet sources have proved extremely ~. | **feel** ◊ It makes them feel ~ even if it is not a paying job. | **become** | **make sb/sth** ◊ Daylight makes people more ~. | **do sth** ◊ I just wish he would do something ~ with his life. | **remain, stay** ◊ The bush must be pruned to remain ~.
ADV. **extremely, fairly, very,** etc. | **enormously, exceptionally, highly, incredibly, remarkably** ◊ It was a highly ~ meeting. | **potentially** | **consistently** | **economically** ◊ economically ~ workers

productivity noun

ADJ. **high, low** | **enhanced, greater, improved, increased, maximum** | **improving, increasing, rising** | **decreased, lost, reduced** ◊ The strike took a heavy toll in lost ~. ◊ It cost the company $25 million in reduced ~. | **agricultural,**

economic, industrial, manufacturing | **employee, labour/labor, personal, worker** | **overall**
... OF PRODUCTIVITY **level** ◊ Farmers are struggling to maintain a level of ~ that generates an acceptable income.
VERB + PRODUCTIVITY **boost, enhance, improve, increase, raise** | **maximize** | **decrease, reduce** | **lose** ◊ Organizations today just can't afford to lose ~. | **maintain** ◊ the key strategies for maintaining the ~ of American workers | **affect** ◊ the mechanisms through which investment in information technology affects ~ and growth | **measure** ◊ Few employers measure employee ~.
PRODUCTIVITY + VERB **go up, grow, improve, increase, rise, soar** ◊ Productivity is growing at a very healthy rate. | **slow, slow down** | **decline, decrease, drop, fall, go down**
PRODUCTIVITY + NOUN **level** | **boom** (AmE), **enhancement** (AmE), **gains, growth, improvement, increase**
PHRASES **a decline in ~, a reduction in ~** | **a gain in ~, an improvement in ~, an increase in ~** | **growth in ~** ◊ Wage increases outpaced growth in ~.

profession noun

ADJ. **chosen** | **noble** (esp. AmE) ◊ We are members of an old and noble ~. | **caring** (BrE), **health-care** (esp. AmE), **helping** (AmE) ◊ She always wanted to work in the caring ~s. ◊ training programs for the helping ~s | **legal, medical, nursing, teaching,** etc.
VERB + PROFESSION **practise/practice** ◊ In the 1930s he was forbidden to practise/practice his ~. | **enter, go into, join** ◊ She entered the legal ~ after college. | **learn** ◊ a job where people can learn the ~ | **advance** (esp. AmE) ◊ Nurses advance the ~ through active involvement in their professional organizations. | **serve** (esp. AmE) ◊ He has served the medical ~ admirably. | **regulate** ◊ the licensing laws that regulate the ~ | **change** ◊ It's time to change your ~ for something more exciting. | **leave** ◊ the primary reason why nurses leave the ~
PREP. **by ~** ◊ He was a physician by ~. | **in a/sb's/the ~** ◊ She's making an impact in her chosen ~.
PHRASES **a choice of ~** ◊ She was shocked at her daughter's choice of ~. | **the top of sb's ~** ◊ He reached the top of his ~ in very little time. | **the oldest ~** (= prostitution)

professional noun

ADJ. **consummate, dedicated** ◊ She's a consummate ~. | **certified** (esp. AmE), **educated, experienced, licensed** (esp. AmE), **qualified, seasoned, trained, well-educated** | **competent, skilled** ◊ highly educated and skilled ~s | **real, true** ◊ This is the work of a real ~. | **leading, senior, top** ◊ a top golf ~ | **independent** ◊ The survey should be performed by an independent ~. | **fellow** ◊ an actor revered by his fellow ~s | **industry** ◊ workshops led by industry ~s from around the US | **business, computer, design, education** (esp. AmE), **financial, health, health-care, information-technology, legal, marketing, media, medical, nursing, security, tax, teaching** | **golf, tennis,** etc. | **busy** ◊ a manageable read for busy ~s
→ Note on following page

professional adj.

1 connected with a job

VERBS **be** | **keep sth** ◊ We keep everything ~ at work. | **remain** ◊ He tried very hard to remain ~.
ADV. **purely, strictly** ◊ He insisted that his relationship with the duchess was purely ~.

2 extremely skilled

VERBS **be, look, seem, sound** ◊ Their designs look very ~.
ADV. **extremely, fairly, very,** etc. | **highly, truly** ◊ He dealt with the problem in a highly ~ way. | **thoroughly, totally** | **increasingly** | **almost**

3 done as a paid job, not a hobby

VERBS **be** | **become, go, turn**
ADV. **fully** ◊ He wants to turn fully ~.

professor

NOTE

Professionals

be…, practise/practice as… ◇ *He is able to practise/ practice as a therapist.*

act as… ◇ *She is acting as architect on this project.*

have… ◇ *The group does not have an internal auditor.*

need… ◇ *We need an engineer to design something better.*

find… ◇ *It pays to find a good accountant.*

appoint…, appoint sb (as)…, employ… (*esp. AmE*), engage… (*esp. BrE*), get…, instruct… ◇ *Appoint a lawyer to act on your behalf.*

consult…, consult with… (*AmE*), get/take advice from…, go to…, see…, speak to…, talk to… ◇ *I demand to speak to my lawyer!*

…acts for sb, …defends sb, …represents sb (used of lawyers) ◇ *an in-house lawyer acting for a major company*

…advises ◇ *His accountant has advised him to close down his business.*

→ See also the note at JOB

professor *noun*

ADJ. **distinguished, eminent** | **respected** ◇ *a respected law ~ at a prestigious university* | **absent-minded, eccentric, mad** ◇ *He fitted perfectly the stereotype of the absent-minded ~.* | **college, university** | **adjunct, assistant, associate, full, junior, senior** (*all AmE*) | **tenured** (*esp. AmE*) | **research** (*esp. AmE*) ◇ *a research ~ at the University of Southern California* | **visiting** ◇ *I spent six months as a visiting ~ at Brown University.* | **retired** | **emerita** (*AmE*), **emeritus** ◇ *Jennifer Bradbery, emeritus professor/professor emeritus of surgery* (*BrE*) ◇ *Jennifer Bradbery, emerita professor/professor emerita of surgery* (*AmE*) | **history, law, etc.**
PREP. **~ of** ◇ *an eminent ~ of English*
→ Note at JOB

proficiency *noun*

ADJ. **great, high** ◇ *Not all students were developing high ~ in Spanish.* | **limited** ◇ *Many of them had only limited ~ in English.* | **academic, technical** | **language, oral, reading, written** | **English, Spanish, etc.** | **cycling** (*esp. BrE*), **skiing, etc.**
…OF PROFICIENCY **degree, level** ◇ *He taught himself to carve to a high degree of ~.*
VERB + PROFICIENCY **achieve, attain, develop, increase** ◇ *He acquired greater ~ after a three-month intensive course.* | **demonstrate, show** | **assess** ◇ *The test has been widely used for assessing English ~.*
PROFICIENCY + NOUN **assessment, examination, test** ◇ *a language ~ test* | **level, standard**
PREP. **~ in** ◇ *a certificate for ~ in English*

proficient *adj.*

VERBS **be, seem** | **become**
ADV. **extremely, fairly, very, etc.** | **highly** | **fully** | **reasonably** | **technically** ◇ *a technically ~ performance of the piece*
PREP. **at** ◇ *very ~ at sign language* | **in** ◇ *She's fairly ~ in Italian.*

profile *noun*

1 face seen from the side

ADJ. **handsome** | **strong** | **three-quarter**
VERB + PROFILE **present** | **examine, study**
PREP. **in** ◇ *The painting shows her in ~.*

2 description of sb/sth

ADJ. **detailed, in-depth** ◇ *an in-depth ~ of Boris Spassky and his career* | **age, career, personality, psychological** |

company, customer | demographic, financial, social | DNA, genetic
VERB + PROFILE **build, build up, construct, create, develop, generate** | **write** ◇ *Margo was told to write a ~ about him.* | **fit, match** ◇ *He fits the ~ of the managers we're looking for.* | **check, check out, study**
PREP. **~ of** ◇ *The data will enable us to construct a ~ of the company's customers.*

3 public image

ADJ. **high, low** ◇ *She decided to keep a low ~ until the scandal had died down.* | **public** | **political** | **corporate**
VERB + PROFILE **have** | **give sb/sth** ◇ *The story was given a low ~ in today's papers.* | **boost, improve, increase, raise** ◇ *a campaign to raise the ~ of the city as a cultural leader* | **lower** | **keep, maintain** | **adopt**

profit *noun*

ADJ. **big, considerable, decent, enormous, fat, good, greater, handsome, healthy, hefty, high, huge, large, massive, maximum, record, strong, substantial, tidy** | **increasing, rising** | **obscene** ◇ *At whose expense are those obscene ~s made?* | **low, modest, reasonable, small** ◇ *They closed down after years of low ~s.* | **declining, falling** | **overall, total** | **average, steady** ◇ *a commodity that produced steady ~s* | **additional, excess, extra** | **lost, unrealized** ◇ *Damaged goods mean lost ~.* | **quick** ◇ *He's only interested in making a quick ~.* | **pure** ◇ *$700 million of almost pure ~* | **expected** ◇ *The expected ~s have not materialized.* | **potential** ◇ *the potential ~s from insider trading* | **future** | **gross, pre-tax** (*esp. BrE*) | **after-tax, clear, net, post-tax** (*esp. BrE*) | **taxable** | **reported** | **interim** (*BrE*) | **short-term** | **annual, quarterly** ◇ *an annual ~ of £50 000* | **first-quarter, full-year, half-year** (*esp. BrE*), **second-quarter, etc.** | **corporate, group** | **operating, trading** | **personal** ◇ *Jakob had realized a personal ~ of $240 000.*
VERB + PROFIT **bring, bring in, deliver, earn, generate, make, produce, realize, reap, return, turn, yield** ◇ *The CD generated record ~s.* | **boost, increase** | **double** | **maximize** | **post, report** ◇ *The company posted second-quarter ~s of $570 million.* | **show** ◇ *The company started to show a ~ in its first year.* | **take** ◇ *Investors will take the ~s.* | **guarantee** | **share, split**
PROFIT + VERB **climb, grow, increase, jump, rise, soar, surge** ◇ *Profits surged 41% to £13 million.* | **decline, drop, fall, plummet, plunge** | **accrue, arise** ◇ *~s accruing to the taxpayer from the sale of property*
PROFIT + NOUN **margin, rate** | **sharing** | **motive** ◇ *the pharmaceutical companies' ~ motive* | **maximization** ◇ *We are continuing our strategy of ~ maximization.* | **centre/ center**
PREP. **against ~s** ◇ *The company made losses of $500 000 against ~s of $750 000.* | **at a ~** ◇ *We should be able to sell the piano at a ~.* | **for ~** ◇ *The goods were sold for ~.* | **~ from** ◇ *~s from property investments* | **~ on** ◇ *Did you make a ~ on your house when you sold it?*
PHRASES **a decline in ~s, a fall in ~s** | **an increase in ~s, a rise in ~s** | **~ after tax, ~ before tax** ◇ *Profit before tax increased by 40% on last year.*
→ Note at PER CENT (for more verbs)
→ Special page at BUSINESS

profitability *noun*

ADJ. **high, low** | **greater** | **declining** ◇ *concerns about the declining ~ of the industry* | **overall** | **long-term, short-term** | **future** | **potential** | **business, corporate**
…OF PROFITABILITY **level**
VERB + PROFITABILITY **achieve, reach** ◇ *measures to achieve greater ~* | **maintain, sustain** | **restore** | **boost, enhance, improve, increase** | **maximize** | **reduce**
PHRASES **a decline in ~** | **an increase in ~** | **a return to ~** ◇ *The company is now showing signs of a return to ~.*
→ Note at PER CENT (for more verbs)

profitable *adj.*

1 making a profit

VERBS **appear, be, prove, seem** ◇ *confident that the venture*

will prove ~ | **find sth** | **become** | **remain, stay** | **make sth** | **keep sth** ◇ *What can be done to keep the business ~?*
ADV. **extremely, fairly, very,** etc. | **enormously, highly, hugely, immensely, incredibly** ◇ *a highly ~ chain of stores* | **barely** | **enough, sufficiently** ◇ *The business is not really ~ enough.* | **potentially** | **consistently** | **financially**

2 helpful

VERBS **be** | **find sth** ◇ *Some churches have found it ~ to hold services during the week.*
ADV. **very** | **mutually** ◇ *Cooperation could be mutually ~.* | **potentially**

program *noun*

1 set of instructions for a computer

ADJ. **computer, software** | **analysis, database, design, desktop-publishing, drawing, graphics, simulation, spreadsheet, word-processing,** etc. | **shareware**
VERB + PROGRAM **run, use** | **create, design, develop, write** ◇ *a ~ designed to evaluate road safety measures* | **download, execute, install, load** | **uninstall** | **copy** | **support** ◇ *The developer is no longer supporting this DOS ~.* | **upgrade**
PROGRAM + VERB **crash** ◇ *I lost half a morning's work when the ~ crashed.* | **allow sth** ◇ *This ~ allows you to edit and catalogue digital photographs.* | **contain sth** ◇ *The ~ contains powerful new features.* | **provide sth** ◇ *This ~ provides everything you need to prepare your own publication.* | **require sth** ◇ *This ~ requires at least 24Mb of RAM.* | **create sth** ◇ *The ~ creates simulations of real-life driving conditions.* | **operate, run** | **close**
PROGRAM + NOUN **file**
PREP. **in a/the ~** ◇ *There may be a bug in the ~.* | **~ for** ◇ *a ~ for debugging*
→ Special page at COMPUTER

2 *(AmE)* → See PROGRAMME

programme *(BrE)* (*AmE* program) *noun*

1 plan of things to do

ADJ. **ambitious, innovative** | **broad, comprehensive, intensive, major, massive, radical** ◇ *a comprehensive ~ of economic reform* | **modest** | **long-term** | **regular** | **varied** ◇ *a varied ~ of entertainment* | **pilot** ◇ *The pilot ~ of vaccination proved successful.* | **party, political** | **government** | **collaborative, joint** ◇ *joint ~s between government and industry* | **national, nationwide** | **action, development, improvement, modernization, privatization, research** | **recycling** | **economic, expenditure, financial, investment, marketing, recovery, spending** ◇ *Mr Brown called for a national recovery ~.* | **austerity, closure** *(BrE)*, **cost-cutting** (*esp. BrE*) ◇ *The company began a major cost-cutting ~ which involved 1700 job losses.* | **aid, assistance, relief, welfare** | **mentoring** (*esp. AmE*), **outreach** ◇ *Support is provided through the community outreach ~.* | **instructional, tutoring** *(both AmE)* | **assessment, testing** | **care, health, health-care** ◇ *a community-care ~ for psychiatric patients* | **screening, treatment, vaccination** ◇ *a diabetes treatment ~* ◇ *large-scale screening ~s of newborns* | **rehab** *(informal)*, **rehabilitation** ◇ *She helped him get into a drug rehab ~.* | **inpatient, outpatient** | **residential** ◇ *a residential drug treatment ~* | **crime-prevention, drug-prevention,** etc. | **breeding, building, conservation, defence/defense, missile, nuclear, rebuilding, weapons** ◇ *Female seals are needed for the breeding ~.* | **exercise, weight-loss, workout** (*esp. AmE*) | **internship** *(AmE)*, **residency** (*esp. AmE*) ◇ *a residency ~ for artists* | **accredited, certificate, certification** *(all AmE)* ◇ *students in an accredited journalism ~* | **college, school** *(both esp. AmE)* | **graduate, undergraduate** *(both esp. AmE)* | **degree, doctoral, Master's** *(all esp. AmE)* ◇ *students enrolled on the two-year MA degree ~* | **academic** (*esp. AmE*), **education, educational, literacy, training, vocational** | **English, history, physics, science,** etc. *(all esp. AmE)* | **after-school** (*esp. AmE*) ◇ *an after-school science ~ that promotes science literacy* | **online** (*esp. AmE*) ◇ *The foundation's online learning ~ brings the classroom to you.* | **two-year, three-year,** etc. *(all esp. AmE)* ◇ *a two-year master's ~*

VERB + PROGRAMME/PROGRAM **agree, agree on, develop, draw up, establish, have, initiate, institute, organize, plan, set up** | **outline** ◇ *The course leader outlined the ~ we would be following.* | **administer, carry out, conduct, implement, launch, run** | **expand** | **offer** ◇ *The college offers a wide variety of ~s of study.* | **finance, fund** ◇ *How is the ~ to be financed?* | **begin, embark on, enter, start, undertake** | **enrol/enroll in, enrol/enroll on** *(both esp. AmE)* ◇ *She enrolled in a Master's ~ in American history* | **attend** ◇ *He must attend a sex offenders' ~.* | **follow, pursue** | **complete** | **cancel, scrap** ◇ *The government says it will scrap all of its nuclear ~s.* | **coordinate, oversee** ◇ *He is coordinating a Europe-wide research ~ into treatments for prostate cancer.*
PROGRAMME/PROGRAM + VERB **aim to, allow (sb) sth, be aimed at sb/sth, be designed to** ◇ *The ~ aims to increase employment.* | **include sth, involve sb/sth** | **offer sth, provide sth** | **target sb/sth** ◇ *an exercise ~ targeting those weak points* | **focus on** ◇ *a graduate ~ that focuses on a chosen profession*
PREP. **in a/the ~, on the/your ~** ◇ *What's on your ~ today* (= *What are your plans*)? | **~ for** ◇ *What's the ~ for* (= *What are we going to do*) *tomorrow?* | **~ of** ◇ *a ~ of lectures* ◇ *a program of study* *(AmE)*
PHRASES **the aim of a ~, the objective of a ~, the purpose of a ~**

2 radio/television show

ADJ. **radio, television, TV** | **current-affairs, documentary, factual** *(all esp. BrE)* | **news** | **comedy** | **children's** | **cookery** *(BrE)*, **cooking** *(AmE)*, **music, religious, wildlife,** etc. | **call-in** *(AmE)*, **phone-in** *(BrE)* | **digital** | **flagship** (*esp. BrE*) ◇ *BBC radio's flagship news ~*
VERB + PROGRAMME/PROGRAM **see, watch** | **listen to** | **record** | **do, make** | **host, present** ◇ *a news ~ hosted by Freddie Greenan* | **air, broadcast, screen, show** | **sponsor** | **cancel, scrap**
PREP. **in a/the ~** ◇ *In today's ~, we'll be giving you advice on how to manage your money.* | **on a/the ~** ◇ *He appeared on the ~ last night.* | **~ about, ~ on** ◇ *I saw a good ~ on owls last night.*

3 booklet for a play/concert/event

ADJ. **concert, theatre/theater** | **match, race**
PREP. **in the ~** ◇ *Her name doesn't appear in the concert ~.*

4 order of events

ADJ. **exciting, interesting** | **musical, sporting** *(BrE)*
VERB + PROGRAMME/PROGRAM **arrange, draw up, plan, organize** ◇ *We're planning an exciting ~ of activities.*
PROGRAMME/PROGRAM + VERB **consist of sth, include sth**
PREP. **~ of** ◇ *a ~ of 17th-century music*
PHRASES **a ~ of events** ◇ *The ~ of events also includes a parade and poetry recitations.*

programmer *noun*

ADJ. **lead** *(AmE)*, **senior** | **experienced, skilled, talented** | **freelance** | **computer, database, software, Web**
PROGRAMMER + VERB **create sth, develop sth, write sth**
→ Note at JOB

progress *noun*

ADJ. **considerable, dramatic, excellent, genuine, good, great, impressive, real, remarkable, significant, substantial, tremendous** ◇ *We have made significant ~ in the fight against HIV/AIDS.* | **limited, little** | **fast, rapid, swift** | **inexorable** (*esp. BrE*) | **slow, stately** (*esp. BrE*) ◇ *We watched the ship's stately ~ out of the docks.* | **adequate, satisfactory** | **incremental, steady** | **continued, further** | **forward** | **student** | **academic, educational** | **economic, evolutionary, industrial, medical, scientific, social, technical, technological** | **human** | **material** | **moral, spiritual**
VERB + PROGRESS **achieve, make** | **chart, follow, monitor, observe, trace, track, watch** ◇ *Regular tests enable the teacher to monitor the ~ of each child.* | **assess, check, check on, evaluate, gauge, measure, review** | **demonstrate, show** | **see** | **mark** | **block, hamper, hinder, impede,**

obstruct, slow, slow down | hold back | halt, stop | accelerate, facilitate
PROGRESS + VERB **continue** | **slow, stall**
PROGRESS + NOUN **report** | **note** (= written by a doctor about a patient) (*AmE*)
PREP. **in ~** ◇ *There was a tennis match in ~.* | **~ from … to …** ◇ *The book traced his steady ~ from petty theft to serious crime.* | **~ in** ◇ *He's making good ~ in reading.* | **~ on** ◇ *How much ~ have the builders made on the house?* | **~ towards/toward** ◇ *Who can halt his inexorable ~ towards/toward yet another championship?* | **~ with** ◇ *She's making steady ~ with her thesis.*
PHRASES **a lack of ~** ◇ *I was frustrated by my apparent lack of ~.* | **the march of ~** ◇ *the onward march of technological ~* | **a rate of ~** ◇ *At the present rate of ~ we won't be finished before July.* | **work in ~** ◇ *I have a file for work in ~.*

progress *verb*

ADV. **nicely, satisfactorily, smoothly, well** ◇ *The talks are ~ing very well.* | **further** ◇ *He felt he still needed to ~ further in his learning.* | **fast, quickly, rapidly** ◇ *to ~ rapidly in your career* | **slowly** ◇ *The work is ~ing slowly.* | **gradually, steadily** | **normally**
VERB + PROGRESS **fail to**
PREP. **beyond** ◇ *Samir failed to ~ beyond this first step on the ladder.* | **from, through** ◇ *Students ~ through the stages of the course.* | **to** ◇ *She soon ~ed from the basics to more difficult work.* | **towards/toward** ◇ *to ~ towards/toward a new kind of art* | **up** ◇ *his ambition to ~ up the career ladder* | **with** ◇ *They are anxious to ~ with the plan.*

progression *noun*

ADJ. **rapid** | **gradual, slow, steady** | **smooth** | **linear, logical, natural** ◇ *It seemed like a natural ~ from singing to acting as a career.* | **career** | **chord, harmonic**
VERB + PROGRESSION **inhibit, slow** | **halt, prevent** | **accelerate** | **monitor**
PREP. **~ from … to …** ◇ *his ~ from awkward teenager to handsome movie star* | **~ through** ◇ *Her ~ through the ranks of the company had been rapid.* | **~ within** ◇ *his steady upward ~ within the company*
PHRASES **the ~ of a disease** ◇ *one of the later stages in the ~ of the disease*

prohibit *verb*

ADV. **strictly** ◇ *Smoking in public areas is strictly ~ed.* | **clearly, explicitly, expressly, specifically** ◇ *The law specifically ~s any group from spending money for political purposes.* | **effectively** ◇ *The regulations effectively ~ the entry of seeds into the country.* | **constitutionally** (*esp. AmE*), **legally** ◇ *The president is constitutionally ~ed from serving more than two terms in office.*
PREP. **from** ◇ *The treaty ~s nations from making claims in outer space.*

prohibition *noun*

ADJ. **absolute, blanket, total** | **strict** | **general** | **constitutional** (*esp. AmE*), **federal** (*AmE*), **legal, statutory** | **criminal** | **alcohol, drug, etc.**
VERB + PROHIBITION **impose** | **enforce** | **lift, repeal** | **violate**
PROHIBITION + NOUN **notice, order** (*both BrE*) ◇ *The ~ order meant that the book could not be sold in this country.* | **law** | **movement** | **the Prohibition era** ◇ *a Prohibition-era speakeasy*
PREP. **~ against** ◇ *~ against sales to under-16s of cigarettes* | **~ of** ◇ *a treaty for the ~ of nuclear tests* | **~ on** ◇ *the ~ imposed on the sale of arms* | **under a/the ~** ◇ *Companies are under strict ~s about divulging confidential information.*

project *noun*

1 planned piece of work

ADJ. **ambitious, big, huge, large, large-scale, major, massive** ◇ *He embarked on an ambitious ~ to translate all the works*

of Plato.* | **small** | **exciting, important, interesting** | **new** | **worthwhile** | **successful** | **failed, unsuccessful** | **collaborative, cooperative, joint** | **solo** | **community, public** | **pilot** ◇ *a successful six-month pilot ~* | **long-term, ongoing** | **research** ◇ *They've set up a research ~ to investigate the harmful effects of air pollution.* | **building, construction, renovation, restoration** ◇ *At present there are five major new building ~s being undertaken nationwide.* | **housing** (*AmE*) | **capital, investment** | **development, educational, environmental** | **pet** ◇ *The wedding became her pet ~, and she spent hours organizing it.*
VERB + PROJECT **get off the ground, implement, initiate, set up, start** ◇ *He needed some financial assistance from the bank to get his ~ off the ground.* | **carry out, undertake** | **coordinate, lead, manage, oversee, run** | **complete, finish** | **conceive, design, develop, plan** | **launch** | **finance, fund, sponsor, support** | **abandon**
PROJECT + VERB **aim to, be aimed at sth** ◇ *The ~ aims to reduce homelessness.*
PROJECT + NOUN **management** | **coordinator, director, leader, manager, team** | **architect, engineer, etc.** | **budget, cost, schedule, specifications** | **work**
PHRASES **the aim of the ~** ◇ *The aims of the ~ are threefold …* | **sb's current ~, sb's latest ~, sb's next ~**
→ Special page at BUSINESS

2 piece of school work

ADJ. **class, school** | **French, history, etc.** | **thesis** (*AmE*)
VERB + PROJECT **do**
PROJECT + NOUN **work**
PREP. **~ on** ◇ *My class is doing a ~ on medieval towns.*

projection *noun*

ADJ. **current, latest** | **initial, original** | **future, long-term** | **demographic, population** | **budget, financial, growth, profit, revenue, sales** | **optimistic, realistic**
VERB + PROJECTION **make** | **revise** | **exceed, meet**
PHRASES **base a ~ on sth** ◇ *The divisions revenue ~ is based on net customer growth.*
PREP. **on … ~s** ◇ *On current ~s, there will be more than fifty million people over 65 in 2020.* | **~ about** ◇ *He declined to make ~s about the next quarter's earnings.* | **~ for** ◇ *They presented profit ~s for the rest of the year.* | **~ of** ◇ *We revised our ~s of funding requirements upwards/upward.*

projector *noun*

ADJ. **overhead** | **film, movie** (*AmE*), **slide, video** | **digital, LCD**
VERB + PROJECTOR **switch off, switch on** | **use**
PROJECTOR + NOUN **screen**

prolong *verb*

ADV. **significantly** | **indefinitely** ◇ *Might it be possible to ~ life indefinitely?* | **artificially** | **deliberately** ◇ *Doctors commented that some patients deliberately ~ their treatment.* | **unnecessarily** ◇ *We do not want to ~ the meeting unnecessarily.*

prominence *noun*

ADJ. **great** | **growing, increased, increasing** | **equal** | **special** ◇ *a performance which gives a special ~ to the part of Hamlet's mother* | **due, undue** (*both esp. BrE*) | **international, national** | **political, public**
VERB + PROMINENCE **achieve, come into, come to, gain, rise to, shoot to** (*esp. BrE*) ◇ *She came to national ~ as an artist in the 1960s.* | **bring sb/sth into, bring sb/sth to, give sb/sth** ◇ *His account gives due ~ to the role of the king.*
PHRASES **a place of ~, a position of ~** ◇ *The former rebels were given positions of ~ in the new government.* | **a rise to ~** ◇ *The city's rise to ~ as a port began in the early 19th century.*

prominent *adj.*

VERBS **be** | **become** | **remain**
ADV. **extremely, fairly, very, etc.** | **especially, particularly** | **increasingly** | **nationally** (*esp. AmE*) | **socially** (*esp. AmE*)
PREP. **as** ◇ *~ as a player and coach* | **in** ◇ *~ in the trade unions*

promise noun

1 statement that you will do sth

ADJ. **big** ◊ *He makes all kinds of big ~s he has little intention of keeping.* | **rash** | **broken, unfulfilled** | **empty, false, hollow** | **vague** | **binding, firm** | **solemn** | **pinky** (= made by linking your little finger with another person's) (*AmE, informal*) | **campaign, election, pre-election** (*esp. BrE*) | **brand** (= printed on a product) (*esp. AmE*)

VERB + PROMISE **give sb, make (sb)** ◊ *You gave me your ~ I could use the car tonight.* ◊ *I'll consider it, but I make no ~s.* | **hold out** ◊ *Organic food seems to hold out the ~ of healthy living.* | **fulfil/fulfill, honour/honor, keep** | **break, go back on** | **extract** ◊ *We extracted a ~ from them that they would repay the money by May.* | **hold sb to** ◊ *Politicians should be held to their ~s.*

PROMISE + NOUN **ring** (= showing sb's promise to be faithful)

PREP. **~ about** ◊ *They've made all sorts of ~s about reforming the health system.* | **~ of** ◊ *~s of support*

2 signs that sb/sth will be successful

ADJ. **considerable, enormous, great, real, tremendous** ◊ *This new venture holds great ~ for the future.* | **little** | **youthful** (*esp. BrE*) | **early, initial** | **future**

VERB + PROMISE **hold, show** | **fulfil/fulfill, live up to** ◊ *His career failed to live up to its early ~.*

PREP. **of ~** ◊ *a pianist of ~* | **~ as** ◊ *She showed great ~ as a runner.*

PHRASES **full of ~** ◊ *The year began so full of ~, and ended in disappointment.*

promise verb

ADV. **faithfully** ◊ *She ~d faithfully that she would come.* | **solemnly** | **initially, originally** | **repeatedly** ◊ *He repeatedly ~d to cut taxes in his campaign.*

VERB + PROMISE **can** ◊ *I can definitely ~ you that I'll do all I can to help.* | **cannot** ◊ *I can't ~ I'll be there.* | **seem to** ◊ *The plan seemed to ~ a new beginning.*

PREP. **to** ◊ *I've ~d my old computer to Jane.*

PHRASES **as ~d** ◊ *I am sending you information on hotels, as ~d.* | **I can't ~ anything** ◊ *I can't ~ anything, but I hope to have it finished next week.*

promising adj.

VERBS **be, look, seem, sound**

ADV. **extremely, fairly, very, etc.** | **highly, particularly** | **far from** (*esp. BrE*) ◊ *The outlook is far from ~.*

promote verb

1 encourage sth

ADV. **strongly** ◊ *Human rights are strongly ~d by all our members.* | **actively, directly** | **indirectly** | **effectively, successfully** | **deliberately, intentionally** ◊ *They claimed that the authorities had deliberately ~d the violence.*

VERB + PROMOTE **aim to, seek to, try to** | **help (to)** ◊ *Basketball stars have helped ~ the sport overseas.* | **be designed to** ◊ *measures designed to ~ economic growth* | **be likely to** | **serve to** ◊ *Bonus payments to staff serve to ~ commitment to the company.* | **tend to**

PREP. **through** ◊ *Young people's awareness of the issues is ~d through publicity material.*

PHRASES **a campaign to ~ sth, a scheme to ~ sth** (*BrE*) | **be aimed at promoting sth** | **be widely ~d** | **efforts to ~ sth, measures to ~ sth**

2 advertise sth

ADV. **aggressively, heavily, vigorously** ◊ *The new products have been very heavily ~d.* | **widely**

PREP. **as** ◊ *The country is now being ~d as a travel destination.* | **through** ◊ *The company's products have been ~d mainly through advertising in newspapers.*

promotion noun

1 to a higher position

ADJ. **rapid** | **internal** ◊ *The company encourages internal ~.*

VERB + PROMOTION **earn, gain, get, receive, win** ◊ *If I can't get ~ soon, I'll look for another job.* | **deserve** ◊ *We congratulate*

James on his well-deserved ~ to Chief Executive. | **recommend sb for** | **offer sb** | **deny sb** | **announce** | **seek, want**

PROMOTION + NOUN **opportunities, prospects** (*BrE*) | **race** (*BrE, sports*) ◊ *With three matches remaining, there are six teams in the ~ race.*

PREP. **~ from, ~ to** ◊ *her ~ from assistant to associate professor*

PHRASES **chance of ~, chances of ~** ◊ *She felt she had little chance of ~ in her job.* ◊ *The team's chances of ~ took a knock when they lost at home.* (*BrE*)

2 advertising

ADJ. **special** | **marketing, sales, trade** | **book** | **health** ◊ *The new health ~ clinic will provide free check-ups.* | **in-store, on-air, online** | **seasonal** | **consumer**

VERB + PROMOTION **do** ◊ *We're doing a special book ~ at key stores this week.*

prone adj.

VERBS **be, seem** | **become** | **leave sb/sth, make sb/sth** ◊ *Sun removes the oil and wax, leaving the leather ~ to cracking.*

ADV. **extremely, fairly, very, etc.** | **especially, highly, particularly** | **increasingly** | **notoriously** ◊ *The road is notoriously ~ to fog.* | **genetically** ◊ *people who are genetically ~ to putting on weight*

PREP. **to** ◊ *She seems very ~ to chest infections.*

pronoun noun

ADJ. **plural, singular** | **first-person, second-person, etc.** | **anaphoric, definite, demonstrative, indefinite, interrogative, personal, possessive, reflexive, relative** | **object, subject** | **feminine, masculine**

pronounce verb

1 make the sound of a word/letter

ADV. **clearly, distinctly** | **correctly, properly**

VERB + PRONOUNCE **can, know how to** ◊ *I don't know how to ~ the name of the town.* | **be difficult to**

PREP. **as** ◊ *'Gone back' is sometimes ~d as 'gom back'.* | **as in** ◊ *She ~d the 'o' as in 'no'.*

2 state sth

ADV. **officially** ◊ *Reality TV was officially ~d dead by the critics.*

PREP. **in favour/favor of** ◊ *The committee has ~d in favour/favor of the merger.* | **on, upon** ◊ *I do not feel competent to ~ on this matter.*

PHRASES **be ~d dead** ◊ *She was ~d dead upon arrival at the hospital.* | **~ yourself sth** ◊ *He ~d himself delighted with the judge's decision.*

pronounced adj.

VERBS **be** | **become**

ADV. **extremely, fairly, very, etc.** ◊ *He walks with a fairly ~ limp.* | **especially, particularly**

pronunciation noun

ADJ. **correct, good, proper** | **bad, incorrect** | **alternative, different, variant** | **standard** | **American, Australian, etc.**

VERB + PRONUNCIATION **correct** ◊ *She doesn't like having her ~ corrected.*

PRONUNCIATION + NOUN **drill, exercise, practice**

proof noun

ADJ. **clear, convincing, direct, good, positive, real** ◊ |*Do you have positive ~ that she took the money?* ◊ *I have no real ~ that he was in the country at the time.* | **concrete, empirical, solid, tangible** | **absolute, conclusive, definitive, incontrovertible, irrefutable** | **ample, sufficient** | **further** | **final, ultimate** ◊ *The photo was final ~ of her husband's infidelity.* | **documentary, written** | **photographic** | **legal** | **scientific** | **formal, mathematical** | **living** ◊ *I am living ~ that the treatment works.*

VERB + PROOF **be, constitute** | **have** | **give sb, offer (sb),**

present (sb with), produce, provide (sb with), show (sb) | find, get, obtain, see | need, require | demand, want
PREP. without ~ ◇ *He is unlikely to make wild accusations without ~.* | ~ of ◇ *Her account gives us no concrete ~ of his guilt.*
PHRASES the burden of ~, the onus of ~ ◇ *The burden of ~ lies on us to prove negligence.* | a lack of ~ ◇ *The men were acquitted for lack of ~.* | ~ of identity, ~ of purchase ◇ *Proof of purchase must be provided before a refund can be made.* | a standard of ~ (*law*) ◇ *Civil proceedings require a lower standard of ~ than criminal cases.*

propaganda *noun*

ADJ. government, official, party, state | corporate, political, religious | Communist, Conservative, socialist, etc. | left-wing, right-wing | anti-American, anti-Semitic, etc. | enemy, war, wartime | covert | pure
VERB + PROPAGANDA broadcast ◇ *The pirate radio station broadcasts anti-government ~.* | counter | spread | believe
PROPAGANDA + NOUN battle, campaign, effort, exercise (*esp. BrE*), ploy (*esp. AmE*), war | victory | department, machine ◇ *the lies that were spewed out by the regime's ~ machine* | film, leaflet, material, piece, poster | tool, weapon | purposes ◇ *The movie was made in 1938 for ~ purposes.* | value ◇ *The Olympics were of great ~ value to the regime.*
PHRASES sb's own ~ ◇ *He has been listening to his own ~ for so long that he is in danger of believing it.*
PREP. ~ about ◇ *The papers were full of political ~ about nationalization.* | ~ against ◇ *Soviet ~ against Fascism*

proper *adj.*

VERBS be, seem ◇ *It seemed ~ to pay tribute to her in this way.* | consider sth, deem sth, think sth ◇ *It was not considered ~ for young ladies to go out alone.*
ADV. very | entirely, perfectly, quite ◇ *The tribunal decided that his actions were perfectly ~.* | morally
PHRASES (only) right and ~ ◇ *It is only right and ~ that you should attend his funeral.* | prim and ~ ◇ *She has a reputation for being prim and ~.*

property *noun*

1 possessions

ADJ. personal, private | common, public | intellectual ◇ *Companies should protect their intellectual ~ with patents and trademarks.* | stolen | lost (*BrE*) ◇ *I called the lost-property office to see if someone had found my bag.*
VERB + PROPERTY protect | dispose of ◇ *The market was known as a place where people disposed of stolen ~.* | confiscate, seize | steal | damage, destroy
PROPERTY + NOUN rights ◇ *The company was found to have infringed intellectual ~ rights.*
PHRASES be the exclusive ~ of sb, be the sole ~ of sb ◇ *Charisma isn't the exclusive ~ of movie stars.*

2 land/building

ADJ. freehold, leasehold (*both BrE*) | adjacent, adjoining, neighbouring/neighboring | detached, semi-detached (*both BrE*) | separate | two-bedroom, three-bedroom, etc. (*all esp. BrE*) | business, commercial, hotel, residential | investment | rental | private | church, school, etc. ◇ *Students are not allowed on school ~ outside of school hours.* | council, council-owned (*both BrE*) | family | beachfront, waterfront | desirable
VERB + PROPERTY hold, own | acquire, buy, invest in, purchase | inherit | sell | lease, let (*esp. BrE*), rent out ◇ *They decided to rent out the ~ while they were in New Zealand.* | rent ◇ *They are living in rented ~.* (*BrE*) | view ◇ *We have a potential buyer who wants to view the ~.* | value ◇ *The ~ was valued at $750 000.* | put on the market ◇ *Once the tenants have left, the ~ will be put on the market.*
PROPERTY + NOUN market, prices, values | company, developer | owner | tax | law | boundary, line (*esp. AmE*) | crime, damage

3 characteristic

ADJ. biological, chemical, electrical, magnetic, mechanical, physical, structural | antiseptic, healing, health-giving (*BrE*), medicinal ◇ *The medicinal properties of the leaves of this tree have been known for centuries.* | individual | general | inherent, intrinsic | basic, essential, important
VERB + PROPERTY have, possess | display, exhibit | alter, modify | examine, study
PHRASES have properties similar to sth ◇ *The substance has properties similar to plastic.*

prophecy *noun*

ADJ. self-fulfilling ◇ *low expectations that become a self-fulfilling ~* | Biblical, Messianic, Old Testament | ancient | false
VERB + PROPHECY make | fulfil/fulfill | become | create
PREP. ~ about ◇ *Macbeth believed the witches' ~ about his future.* | ~ of ◇ *The poem contains a bleak ~ of war and ruin.*
PHRASES the gift of ~

prophet *noun*

ADJ. false, true ◇ *Some believe that he was not a true ~.* | great | biblical, Old Testament
PHRASES a ~ of doom (*informal*) ◇ *In spite of the ~s of doom, her business proved very successful.*

proportion *noun*

1 part/share of a whole

ADJ. appreciable (*esp. BrE*), considerable, good, great, high, huge, large, overwhelming, significant, sizeable, substantial ◇ *A significant ~ of the funding is likely to come from government.* | fair, reasonable (*esp. BrE*) | low, small, tiny | certain | equal ◇ *The company employs men and women in roughly equal ~s.* | equivalent, similar | different, differing, varying | fixed | exact | approximate | average | overall | growing, increasing, rising | declining, decreasing, diminishing
VERB + PROPORTION calculate, estimate | express sth as ◇ *The chart shows government spending expressed as a ~ of national income.* | grow as, increase as, rise as | decline as, decrease as, diminish as, fall as ◇ *The unskilled section of the working class was diminishing as a ~ of the workforce.*
PROPORTION + VERB grow, increase, rise | decline, decrease, fall

2 relationship between the size/amount of two things

ADJ. correct | direct | inverse ◇ *The human population in the region is expanding in inverse ~ to the wildlife.* | relative
VERB + PROPORTION keep sth in ◇ *Try to keep your view of the situation in ~ (= not think it is more serious than it is).*
PREP. in ~ (to) ◇ *The cost of insurance increases in ~ to the performance of the car.* | out of ~ (to) ◇ *The costs of the plan are out of ~ to the budget available.* | ~ of sth to sth ◇ *The ~ of sand to cement used was three to one.*
PHRASES be blown, exaggerated, etc. out of all ~ (*esp. BrE*), be blown, exaggerated, etc. out of ~ ◇ *This issue was about to be blown out of ~.* ◇ *The problem has been exaggerated out of all ~.* | a sense of ~ ◇ *Try to keep a sense of ~ (= of the relative importance of different things).*

3 proportions size and shape of sth

ADJ. biblical, enormous, epic, gargantuan, generous, gigantic, heroic, huge, immense, major, mammoth, massive, monumental, staggering | modest | manageable ◇ *The computer brings the huge task of stock control down to more manageable ~s.* | alarming | crisis, epidemic | classic, perfect ◇ *an entrance hall of perfect ~s*
VERB + PROPORTIONS reach ◇ *The food shortage had reached crisis ~s.*

proportional *adj.*

VERBS be
ADV. approximately, roughly ◇ *The amount of food a child needs is roughly ~ to her size.* | directly ◇ *The speed of the*

glider is directly ~ to the speed of the wind. | **inversely** ◇ *The amount of force needed is inversely ~ to the rigidity of the material.*
PREP. **to**

proposal *noun*

1 plan
ADJ. **concrete** | **detailed** | **draft** ◇ *Under the draft ~s, the Commission will be significantly strengthened.* | **controversial** | **ambitious, bold, radical** | **modest** | **compromise** | **peace, reform, research, etc.** | **legislative** | **initial, original** | **formal**
... OF PROPOSALS **package** (*esp. BrE*), **set** ◇ *The government outlined a new set of ~s on human rights.*
VERB + PROPOSAL **develop, draft, formulate, put together, write** | **outline** | **bring forward, make, offer, present, put forward, submit** | **back, support, welcome** ◇ *I welcome the ~ to reduce taxes for the poorly paid.* | **accept, approve, endorse** | **block, oppose, reject, vote against** | **push through** ◇ *The government tried to push through the controversial ~s.* | **drop, withdraw** | **consider, discuss, review**
PREP. **~ concerning, ~ relating to** ◇ *~s concerning the use of land* | **~ for** ◇ *The department submitted a ~ for lower speed limits.*
→ Special page at MEETING

2 offer of marriage
ADJ. **marriage**
VERB + PROPOSAL **make** | **get, receive** | **accept** ◇ *She accepted his ~ of marriage.* | **turn down** ◇ *She turned down his ~.*
PHRASES **a ~ of marriage**

propose *verb*

ADV. **seriously** ◇ *Are you seriously proposing that we allow this situation to continue?* | **formally** | **first, initially, originally** ◇ *The plan originally ~d was ruled unrealistic.*
PREP. **as** ◇ *The measures have been ~d as a way of improving standards.* | **for** ◇ *He was ~d for the job of treasurer.*
PHRASES **newly ~d** (*esp. AmE*), **recently ~d** ◇ *the newly ~d amendments* ◇ *the recently ~d standards*

proposition *noun*

1 arrangement/offer/suggestion
ADJ. **attractive, tempting, win-win** | **feasible, practical, viable** | **business, commercial, economic, paying** | **losing** (*esp. AmE*)
VERB + PROPOSITION **put to sb** ◇ *Ring up your agent in New York and put your ~ to him.* | **consider** | **accept** | **reject**

2 thing to be done
ADJ. **difficult, tough, tricky** | **simple** ◇ *Getting a job is not always a simple ~.* | **expensive** | **all-or-nothing** (*AmE*) | **dangerous, dicey** (*AmE*), **risky** | **different** ◇ *Running the business was one thing. Getting it to make a profit was a different ~ altogether.*

3 idea/opinion
ADJ. **basic, central, fundamental** | **true** | **abstract, empirical, existential, general, theoretical** | **dubious** | **simple**
... OF PROPOSITIONS **set**
VERB + PROPOSITION **advance, express, put forward** | **test** | **support**
PROPOSITION + VERB **concern sth, relate to sth**
PREP. **~ about** ◇ *The book puts forward a number of ~s about the nature of language.*

proprietor *noun*

ADJ. **hotel, newspaper, restaurant** | **landed** | **sole** ◇ *He is now sole ~ of the business.*

pros and cons *noun*

VERB + PROS AND CONS **consider, discuss, weigh up** ◇ *Before making a decision, you need to weigh up the ~ of the situation.*
PREP. **~ of**

prose *noun*

ADJ. **clear, lucid, plain, simple, straightforward** | **elegant, flowing, lyrical, poetic** | **flowery, purple** (= elaborate or exaggerated in style) | **descriptive** | **continuous** ◇ *I plan out an essay in note form before writing it up in continuous ~.* | **academic, literary**
... OF PROSE **piece**
VERB + PROSE **write, write in** | **craft**
PROSE + NOUN **works, writing** | **writer** | **style** | **narrative** | **passage, piece, text** | **fiction**
PREP. **in ~** ◇ *a passage in ~*

prosecution *noun*

1 trying to prove sb's guilt in court
ADJ. **criminal, federal** (*AmE*), **private** (*BrE*) | **successful** | **possible** ◇ *He faces possible ~.*
VERB + PROSECUTION **bring, initiate** | **be liable to, face, risk** | **avoid, escape** | **lead to, result in**
PREP. **~ against** ◇ *The police brought a ~ against the driver involved.* | **~ for** ◇ *Prosecutions for water pollution more than doubled.*
PHRASES **immunity from ~**

2 the prosecution lawyers trying to prove sb's guilt
PROSECUTION + VERB **prove sth** | **allege sth, claim sth, present sth** ◇ *The ~ alleged that he murdered his wife.* | **call sb**
PROSECUTION + NOUN **case, evidence** | **counsel** (*BrE*), **lawyer, team, witness** | **costs** (*BrE*)
PREP. **for the ~** ◇ *a witness for the ~*

prosecutor *noun*

ADJ. **public** | **county, federal, government, local, state** (all in the US) | **independent** (*esp. AmE*) | **special** (in the US) | **chief, lead** (*AmE*) | **criminal** (*esp. AmE*)
PROSECUTOR + VERB **charge sb with sth, indict sb** (*esp. AmE*) | **allege sth, argue sth, claim sth** | **investigate sth**

prospect *noun*

1 chance that sth will happen
ADJ. **realistic, reasonable** | **immediate**
VERB + PROSPECT **have** | **offer**
PREP. **in ~** ◇ *Major developments are in ~ for the company.* | **~ of sth** ◇ *There is little ~ of any improvement in the weather.*

2 idea of what may/will happen
ADJ. **attractive, exciting, intriguing** | **bleak, daunting** | **frightening, scary**
VERB + PROSPECT **be excited at, relish, welcome** ◇ *I don't relish the ~ of having to share an office.* | **dread** | **be faced with, face** | **consider** | **raise**

3 prospects chances of being successful
ADJ. **bright, excellent, exciting, good** | **limited, poor** | **future, long-term** | **development, economic, growth** | **career, employment, job, promotion** (*esp. BrE*) (usually **prospects for promotion** in *AmE*) | **election, electoral, re-election** | **survival**
VERB + PROSPECTS **have** | **offer (sb)** ◇ *This position offers excellent promotion ~s.* | **boost, enhance, improve** ◇ *Getting the right qualifications will enhance your employment ~s.* | **blight** (*BrE*), **damage, diminish, ruin, wreck** | **assess, examine, review**
PROSPECTS + VERB **improve**
PREP. **with ~s, without ~s** ◇ *At 25 he was an unemployed musician with no ~s.* | **~s for** ◇ *Long-term ~s for the economy have improved.* | **~s of** ◇ *Their ~s of employment look better than last year.*

4 sb/sth likely to be successful
ADJ. **bright, hot, top** | **new, young** ◇ *a list of the hot new prospects on the literary scene*

prosperity noun

ADJ. **economic, material** | **great, unprecedented** | **growing, increasing, rising** | **relative** | **future, lasting, long-term** | **general, global, national** | **personal**
... OF PROSPERITY **level** ◇ *an area with a level of ~ higher than the national average*
VERB + PROSPERITY **enjoy** | **bring, create** ◇ *The growth of tourism brought ~ to the island.* | **achieve** | **share**
PROSPERITY + VERB **depend on sth** ◇ *The island's ~ depends on its fishing industry.*
PHRASES **a period of ~**

prostitute noun

ADJ. **common** ◇ *She was arrested and charged with being a common ~.* | **child, teenage, underage** | **female, male** | **former** ◇ *a book written by a former ~* | **high-class, street**
VERB + PROSTITUTE **be, work as** | **go to, hire, solicit** (*esp. AmE*), **use, visit** ◇ *the men who use ~s*
PROSTITUTE + VERB **solicit** (*esp. BrE*) ◇ *The ~s solicit openly here.*

prostitution noun

ADJ. **child** | **male** | **legal, legalized** | **forced**
VERB + PROSTITUTION **be involved in** | **enter, turn to** ◇ *Some turned to ~ in order to survive.* | **decriminalize, legalize**
PROSTITUTION + NOUN **ring** ◇ *They sold the young girl into a ~ ring.*

protect verb

ADV. **completely, fully** | **adequately, properly, well** ◇ *A cardboard box would ~ the product better.* | **inadequately** | **carefully** | **effectively, successfully** | **jealously** (*esp. BrE*) ◇ *a star who jealously ~s her right to privacy*
VERB + PROTECT **need to** | **seek to, strive to, try to** | **act to, fight to** ◇ *Each company is fighting to ~ its own commercial interests.* | **take steps to** ◇ *We must take steps to ~ the region as a manufacturing base.* | **help (to)** | **serve to** | **be designed to**
PREP. **against** ◇ *a cream that helps to ~ your skin against the sun* | **from** ◇ *The new measures are designed to ~ the public from people like these.* | **with** ◇ *Protect the exposed areas of wood with varnish.*
PHRASES **be aimed at ~ing sth** | **constitutionally ~ed** (*esp. AmE*), **federally ~ed** (*AmE*), **legally ~ed, officially ~ed, specially ~ed** ◇ *a constitutionally ~ed right of freedom of speech* ◇ *a federally ~ed game preserve* ◇ *Many of these sites—of immense scientific interest—are not legally ~ed.* | **a desire to ~ sb/sth, a need to ~ sb/sth, a need to ~ sb/sth** ◇ *He felt it was his duty to ~ the child.* | **heavily ~ed, highly ~ed** ◇ *The Far Eastern markets are heavily ~ed (= with high taxes for imported goods).* | **poorly ~ed, well ~ed** ◇ *Keep the camera well ~ed at all times.* | **measures to ~ sb/sth** | **be ~ed by copyright** ◇ *Some pieces of music are ~ed by copyright.* | **be ~ed by law, be ~ed under law** ◇ *The equality of women is ~ed under law.*

protection noun

ADJ. **adequate, effective, good, great** | **added, additional, extra** | **special** | **complete, full, maximum** | **basic** | **constitutional, legal** | **police** ◇ *Witnesses at the trial were given police ~.* | **animal, child, consumer, data, environmental, personal, privacy, wilderness** (*AmE*), **wildlife, witness** ◇ *She carries a gun in her bag for personal ~.* ◇ *a witness-protection scheme* (*BrE*) ◇ *a witness-protection program* (*AmE*) | **fire, flood** ◇ *Fire-protection equipment must be available on all floors.* | **sun, UV** ◇ *sun-protection products* | **bankruptcy** | **copy, copyright, patent** | **anti-virus, password**
... OF PROTECTION **degree** ◇ *A helmet affords the rider some degree of ~ against injury.*
VERB + PROTECTION **afford (sb), ensure (sb), give (sb), offer (sb), provide (sb with)** | **need, require** | **seek, want** | **have**
PREP. **under the ~ of** ◇ *The site is under the ~ of UNESCO.* | **~ against** ◇ *Fill the cooling system with antifreeze as a ~*

~ for ◇ *Governments must provide ~ for their workers.* | **~ from** ◇ *The wall gives the plants ~ from the wind.*
PHRASES **a means of ~** ◇ *The skunk releases a pungent smell as a means of ~.* | **for sb's own ~** ◇ *She was put into a psychiatric hospital for her own ~.*

protective adj.

VERBS **be, feel** | **become**
ADV. **fiercely, highly, very** ◇ *Lionesses are fiercely ~ of their young.* | **overly** ◇ *an overly ~ father*
PREP. **of** ◇ *He's too jealous and ~ of her.* | **towards/toward** ◇ *She felt suddenly very ~ towards/toward her mother.*

protein noun

ADJ. **essential** | **natural** | **animal, vegetable**
VERB + PROTEIN **contain, supply** ◇ *Cereals supply essential ~ and vitamins.* | **be high in, be rich in** | **produce**
PROTEIN + VERB **be found in sth** ◇ *Gluten is a ~ found in wheat and other grains.*
PROTEIN + NOUN **content** | **level** | **intake** | **deficiency**
PHRASES **a source of ~**

protest noun

ADJ. **angry, strong, violent** | **non-violent, peaceful** | **sit-down** (*BrE*) | **mass** | **massive** | **formal, official** | **popular, public, student** | **anti-government, anti-war, etc.** | **political, social** | **continuing** | **rooftop** (*BrE*), **street** ◇ *a rooftop ~ by prison inmates* ◇ *street ~s by residents* | **widespread**
... OF PROTEST **storm, wave** ◇ *The new tax sparked a wave of public ~.*
VERB + PROTEST **organize, stage** | **lead** | **lodge, make, register** ◇ *The Samoan team lodged a formal ~ against the decision.* ◇ *The government has made an official ~.* | **lead to, spark** | **ignore**
PROTEST + NOUN **group, movement** | **demonstration, march, meeting, rally** | **strike** (*esp. BrE*) | **petition** (*esp. BrE*) | **vote** | **song**
PREP. **in ~** ◇ *Prisoners shouted and hurled slates in ~.* | **under ~** ◇ *The strikers returned to work, but under ~.* | **without ~** ◇ *The crowd dispersed without ~.* | **~ about** ◇ *a ~ about the new bypass* | **~ against** ◇ *There had been a number of public ~s against the new tax.* | **~ over** ◇ *a student ~ over tuition fees*
PHRASES **a chorus of ~, a cry of ~, a howl of ~** ◇ *The announcement brought cries of ~ from the crowd.* | **a letter of ~** | **in ~ at** (*esp. BrE*), **in ~ of** (*AmE*) ◇ *The party boycotted the election in ~ at alleged vote rigging.* ◇ *Winters quit the company board in ~ of Eisner's plans.*

protest verb

ADV. **strongly, vehemently, vigorously** | **formally** | **publicly** | **loudly** | **mildly** | **weakly** | **peacefully** ◇ *the right to ~ peacefully* | **angrily, bitterly, indignantly**
VERB + PROTEST **begin to, try to** ◇ *When he tried to ~, she insisted.* | **gather to** ◇ *Crowds gathered to ~ about the police violence.*
PREP. **about, over** ◇ *Many people ~ed over the tax increase.* | **against** ◇ *They were ~ing against the proposed agreement.* | **at** ◇ *Many people have ~ed at the cuts in state benefits.* | **to** ◇ *We have ~ed to the government.*
PHRASES **the freedom to ~, the right to ~** ◇ *They were exercising their lawful right to ~.*

protester noun

ADJ. **student** | **animal rights** (*esp. BrE*), **environmental, peace, political** | **anti-globalization, anti-government, anti-war, etc.** | **pro-hunt** (*BrE*), **pro-life, etc.** | **non-violent** (*esp. AmE*), **peaceful, unarmed** | **angry**
VERB + PROTESTER **arrest**
PROTESTER + VERB **call for sth, demand sth** | **march** | **demonstrate, gather** | **clash, fight** ◇ *Protesters clashed with police outside the embassy.*
PREP. **~ against** ◇ *The streets were crowded with ~s against the war.*

prototype noun

ADJ. **early** ◇ *They created an early ~ using this software.* | **working** | **pre-production**

VERB + PROTOTYPE **build, create, develop, make, produce** | **have** ◇ *We have a working ~ that is ready to demonstrate.* | **test**

PROTOTYPE + NOUN **stage** ◇ *The car is presently at the ~ stage.*

PREP. **~ for** ◇ *The team is developing a ~ for a digital compact camera.* | **~ of** ◇ *He is working on the ~ of a new type of ventilator.*

proud adj.

VERBS **be, feel, look, seem, sound** | **make sb**

ADV. **extremely, fairly, very, etc.** | **enormously, especially, fiercely, immensely, inordinately, intensely** (*esp. BrE*), **particularly, terribly, tremendously** ◇ *She was fiercely ~ of family traditions and continuity.* ◇ *He was tremendously ~ of himself.* | **almost** ◇ *He seemed almost ~ of his practical incompetence.* | **justifiably, justly, rightly** | **quietly** ◇ *He was not vain, but he was quietly ~ of his achievements.* | **secretly** | **once** ◇ *What has become of this once ~ nation?*

PREP. **of** ◇ *We are all really ~ of you!*

PHRASES **have every reason to be ~, have every right to be ~** ◇ *All those involved have every reason to be ~ of their achievement.*

prove verb

ADV. **conclusively, definitively** ◇ *All this ~s conclusively that she couldn't have known the truth.* | **scientifically** ◇ *This theory cannot be ~d scientifically.* | **just, only** ◇ *Their reaction just ~s my point.* | **otherwise** ◇ *The deaths are being treated as suspicious until we can ~ otherwise.*

VERB + PROVE **be difficult to, be impossible to** | **be easy to** | **be able to** | **try to** ◇ *What are you trying to ~?* | **be determined to** | **have sth to** ◇ *I certainly don't have anything to prove—my record speaks for itself.*

PREP. **to** ◇ *He tried to ~ his theory to his friends.*

PHRASES **a chance to ~ sth** | **~ sb right, ~ sb wrong** ◇ *I was determined to ~ my critics wrong.*

proven adj.

VERBS **be**

ADV. **well** | **conclusively, fully** ◇ *No funding will be available until the technology is completely ~.* | **not yet** | **clinically, scientifically, statistically** ◇ *The juice is clinically ~ to reduce cholesterol.* ◇ *a scientifically ~ method for increasing stamina*

provide verb

ADV. **kindly** ◇ *a buffet dinner, kindly ~d by club members* | **free, free of charge** ◇ *Careers advice is ~d free of charge.*

VERB + PROVIDE **be able to, can** | **aim to, seek to, try to** ◇ *We try to ~ the best possible medical care.* | **fail to** | **be designed to, be intended to** ◇ *The grants were intended to ~ financial help to unemployed workers.* | **be expected to** ◇ *The report was not expected to ~ any answers.* | **be likely to, be unlikely to**

PREP. **for** ◇ *The organization ~s food and shelter for refugees.* | **to** ◇ *The agency ~s legal services to farmers.* | **with** ◇ *He ~d us with a lot of useful information.*

province noun

1 region

ADJ. **northern, southern, etc.** | **central, coastal, frontier, remote** ◇ *the central ~ of Ghor* | **autonomous**

2 the provinces (*BrE*) not the capital city

VERB + THE PROVINCES **tour** ◇ *The show is currently touring the ~s with a new cast.*

PREP. **from the ~** ◇ *She's from the ~s and not familiar with Rome.* | **in the ~** ◇ *There are a number of press agencies based in London and in the ~s.*

3 (*formal*) person's area of knowledge/responsibility

ADJ. **exclusive, sole** ◇ *Love should no longer be the sole ~ of the poet.*

VERB + PROVINCE **become** | **remain** | **consider sth as, regard**

sth as ◇ *Creativity was once considered the ~ of a chosen few.* ◇ *Spirituality is no longer regarded as the exclusive ~ of organized religion.*

PHRASES **once the ~ of …** ◇ *Once the ~ of IT departments, these devices are emerging as consumer products.*

provision noun

1 supply

ADJ. **federal, private, state** | **childcare, educational, housing, nursery, pension, service, welfare, etc.** (*all esp. BrE*)

PREP. **~ of** ◇ *Several companies are responsible for the ~ of cleaning services.*

2 for a future situation; in a legal document

ADJ. **full** | **adequate** ◇ *It is important to make adequate ~ for your retirement.* | **detailed** | **express** (*esp. BrE*), **particular, special, specific** | **relevant** | **key** | **constitutional, legal, legislative, statutory** | **sunset** (*law, esp. AmE*) ◇ *The law contained a sunset ~, requiring Congress to re-authorize it in 2008.*

VERB + PROVISION **make** | **contain, include** ◇ *~s contained in the contract*

PROVISION + VERB **apply** ◇ *The same ~s apply to foreign-owned companies.* | **allow sth, require sth**

PREP. **~ against** ◇ *They had made all kinds of ~s against bad weather.* | **~ for** ◇ *The Act contains detailed ~s for appeal against the court's decision.*

3 provisions food and drinks

VERB + PROVISIONS **buy, stock up on, stock up with** ◇ *We went into town to stock up on ~s.*

provocation noun

ADJ. **extreme** | **deliberate**

… OF PROVOCATION **element** ◇ *The victim's conduct had involved an element of ~.*

VERB + PROVOCATION **respond to** | **constitute** (*law*) ◇ *Words alone can constitute ~.*

PREP. **under ~** ◇ *The crime was committed under ~.* ◇ *The defendant was not acting under ~.* | **without ~** ◇ *She attacked him without ~.*

PHRASES **at the slightest ~** ◇ *He would lose his temper at the slightest ~.*

provocative adj.

1 intending to cause an argument

VERBS **be, seem** | **consider sth**

ADV. **extremely, fairly, very, etc.** | **highly** | **deliberately, intentionally** ◇ *The book's epilogue is deliberately ~.* | **needlessly, unnecessarily**

2 intending to cause sexual excitement

VERBS **be, look**

ADV. **highly, very** | **sexually** ◇ *Models find themselves wearing sexually ~ clothing.*

provoke verb

ADV. **deliberately** | **inevitably** (*esp. BrE*) ◇ *The suggestion inevitably ~d outrage from student leaders.* | **immediately** | **eventually, finally**

VERB + PROVOKE **try to** | **be likely to** ◇ *The report is likely to ~ discussion of this issue.* | **be designed to, be intended to**

PREP. **into** ◇ *She had been trying to ~ her sister into an argument.* | **to** ◇ *Their laughter ~d him to anger.*

PHRASES **easily ~d** ◇ *He was sensitive and easily ~d.*

prowess noun

ADJ. **academic, athletic, intellectual, manufacturing, military, physical, sexual, sporting** (*esp. BrE*), **technical, technological, etc.**

VERB + PROWESS **demonstrate, display, show** ◇ *a parade aimed at demonstrating the country's military ~* | **boast about, boast of** | **prove** ◇ *He proved his athletic ~ with two*

convincing wins. | **match** ◇ *His academic performance does not match his athletic ~.*
PREP. **~ as** ◇ *He boasted of his ~ as a lover.* | **~ at** ◇ *her ~ at tennis* | **~ in** ◇ *The Gurkhas are famed for their ~ in battle.* | **~ with** ◇ *Singh demonstrated his ~ with the bat last season.*

proximity noun

ADJ. **close** | **geographic** (*esp. AmE*), **geographical, physical, spatial**
PREP. **in** | **~ to** ◇ *The site is in close ~ to an airport.* | **~ to** ◇ *House prices in the area are elevated by its ~ to London.*

proxy noun

VERB + PROXY **appoint** ◇ *You may appoint a ~ to vote for you.* | **act as, serve as** ◇ *She is acting as ~ for her husband.*
PROXY + NOUN **vote, voting** ◇ *Our practice is to delegate ~ voting to managers.* | **form** ◇ *It is important that members send their ~ forms in.* | **war** ◇ *The Cold War also saw ~ wars fought throughout the developing world.* | **battle, fight** (*both business*) ◇ *a ~ battle to get shareholders to overturn the board's decision*
PREP. **by ~** ◇ *If you will not be able to vote on election day, you may vote by ~.* | **~ for** ◇ *Husbands are discouraged from voting as ~ for their wives.*
PHRASES **as a ~** ◇ *I am here as a ~ for my father.*

prudent adj.

VERBS **be, seem** | **consider sth, think sth** (*esp. BrE*) ◇ *We thought it ~ to telephone first.*
ADV. **very** | **reasonably** | **financially, fiscally** ◇ *These investments are responsible as well as financially ~.* | **politically**

prune verb

ADV. **drastically, hard** (*esp. BrE*), **heavily, severely** ◇ *Prune the trees hard in the winter.* ◇ *Their budgets have been drastically ~d.* (*figurative*) | **back** ◇ *The roses had been ~d back more severely.*

pseudonym noun

VERB + PSEUDONYM **adopt, use** ◇ *He used various ~s.*
PREP. **under a/the ~** ◇ *Eric Blair wrote under the ~ of George Orwell.*

psychiatrist noun

ADJ. **leading, senior, top** ◇ *a leading child ~* | **practising/ practicing** | **consultant** (*esp. BrE*), **research** | **clinical** | **child** | **forensic**
PHRASES **the psychiatrist's couch** ◇ *the secrets revealed on the psychiatrist's couch*
→ Note at DOCTOR (for verbs)

psychiatry noun

ADJ. **clinical, community, forensic** | **adolescent, child, geriatric**
PHRASES **a department of ~, an institute of ~**
→ Note at SUBJECT (for verbs and nouns)

psychological adj.

VERBS **be**
ADV. **purely** ◇ *The symptoms are purely ~.*

psychologist noun

ADJ. **eminent, leading** | **clinical, consultant** (*BrE*), **professional** ◇ *He is now a clinical ~ with a major hospital.* | **chartered** (*BrE*), **licensed** (*AmE*) | **school** (*esp. AmE*) ◇ *I made an appointment with the school ~.* | **academic, experimental** | **behavioural/behavioral, child, cognitive, developmental, educational, evolutionary, forensic, occupational, social, sports**
→ Note at DOCTOR (for verbs)

psychology noun

1 study of the mind/the way people behave
ADJ. **clinical, professional** | **academic, experimental** | **applied** | **cognitive, developmental, educational, evolutionary, health, social, sports** | **child** | **Gestalt** | **Freudian, Jungian, etc.**
→ Note at SUBJECT (for verbs and nouns)

2 type of mind that a person/group has
ADJ. **individual, own** ◇ *The answers we give will reflect our own ~.* | **crowd, group** ◇ *Watching the shoppers at the sales gave her a first-hand insight into crowd ~.* | **human**

pub noun (BrE)

ADJ. **excellent, good** | **favourite** | **local, nearby, nearest** ◇ *The local ~ is quite good.* | **crowded** | **smoky** ◇ *I had to sing in crowded, smoky ~s.* | **cosy** ◇ *the atmosphere of a cosy country ~* | **friendly** | **country, village** | **city-centre, town-centre** | **riverside** | **historic, traditional** | **modern** | **theme** ◇ *It's one of those modern theme ~s.*
VERB + PUB **go down** (*informal*), **go down to, go round to, go to** ◇ *Let's go down the ~ for a drink.*
PUB + NOUN **food, lunch, meal** | **landlady, landlord**
PREP. **at a/the ~, in a/the ~** ◇ *He spent all afternoon in the ~.*

puberty noun

VERB + PUBERTY **enter, hit** (*informal*), **reach** ◇ *She hit ~ a year before any of her friends.* ◇ *He reached ~ at the age of fourteen.* | **approach** | **go through** ◇ *I was going through ~.*
PREP. **at ~** ◇ *Girls start menstruating at ~.* | **during ~** ◇ *The body undergoes many changes during ~.*
PHRASES **the age of ~** | **the onset of ~**

public noun

1 the public people in general
ADJ. **general**
VERB + THE PUBLIC **educate, inform** ◇ *The government was slow to inform the ~ about the health hazards of asbestos.* | **protect** | **serve** | **mislead** ◇ *He accused the administration of deliberately misleading the ~ on this issue.* | **be open to** ◇ *The house is open to the ~.*
PREP. **in ~** ◇ *He rarely appears in ~ these days.*
PHRASES **a member of the ~**

2 group of people with sth in common
ADJ. **book-buying, movie-going, paying, reading, sporting** (*esp. BrE*), **theatre-going/theater-going, travelling/travelling, viewing, voting, etc.** ◇ *Satellite television has provided the viewing ~ with a wide choice.* | **broader, larger, wider** ◇ *Her work is now available to a wider ~.*

publication noun

1 of a book, etc.
ADJ. **posthumous** ◇ *the posthumous ~ this year of his unedited journals* | **electronic, online, print** ◇ *the lower cost of electronic ~*
VERB + PUBLICATION **begin** | **cease, stop** | **delay** | **prepare sth for** | **be due for, be scheduled for** ◇ *The book is scheduled for ~ in the spring.* | **accept sth for**
PUBLICATION + NOUN **date**
PHRASES **the date of ~, the time of ~**

2 book, magazine, etc.
ADJ. **new, recent** | **forthcoming** | **leading, major** | **mainstream** | **national** | **online, print** ◇ *His writing has appeared in many other print and online ~s.* | **sister** ◇ *Our German sister ~, 'Diese Woche', went out of business.* | **government, official** | **specialist** (*esp. BrE*) | **glossy** (*esp. BrE*) ◇ *The glossy ~ is being mailed to 4 000 companies.* | **academic, business, industry, scholarly, scientific, trade, etc.**
PREP. **~ about** ◇ *specialist ~s about bees* | **~ on** ◇ *She has several ~s to her name on local history.*

publicity noun

1 media attention

ADJ. **considerable, enormous, extensive, greater, wide, widespread** ◊ *The papers have begun to give greater ~ to the campaign against GM food.* | **maximum** ◊ *The release of the report was timed to generate maximum ~.* | **favourable/favorable, good, positive** | **adverse, bad, negative, unfavourable/unfavorable, unwanted, unwelcome** (*esp. BrE*) | **free** | **international, local, national**
VERB + PUBLICITY **give sb/sth** | **gain, garner, get, receive** | **attract, generate** | **seek** | **avoid, shun**
PUBLICITY + VERB **surround sth** ◊ *There was a lot of negative ~ surrounding the movie.*
PREP. **~ about** ◊ *There has been a lot of negative ~ about the hospital.* | **~ for** ◊ *Taking part in the event will be good ~ for our school.* | **~ over** ◊ *The company had received bad ~ over a defective product.*
PHRASES **a blaze of ~** (*esp. BrE*), **a storm of ~** ◊ *The movie stars were married amid a blaze of ~.* ◊ *The chairman resigned in a storm of ~ over the bonus payments.* | **the glare of ~** ◊ *He carried on his life in the full glare of ~.*

2 advertising

ADJ. **advance**
PUBLICITY + NOUN **material, photograph, shot** ◊ *He's better-looking in his ~ shots than he is in real life.* | **campaign** | **stunt** ◊ *The actress denied that her marriage was just a ~ stunt.* | **agent, department, officer** (*BrE*) | **machine** ◊ *The record company's ~ machine was working flat out.*
PREP. **~ about** ◊ *I read some ~ about vaccinations while waiting my turn at the doctor's.* | **~ for** ◊ *There have been months of advance ~ for the show.*
PHRASES **a lack of ~**

publicize (BrE also -ise) verb

ADV. **well** | **widely**
VERB + PUBLICIZE **help (to)**
PHRASES **little ~d** | **highly ~d, much ~d** ◊ *her highly ~d affair with a leading politician*

publish verb

ADV. **recently** | **originally, previously** | **extensively** (*esp. AmE*), **widely** ◊ *He has ~ed extensively on medieval education.* ◊ *Her books have never been widely ~ed in the US.* | **posthumously** ◊ *Her last book was ~ed posthumously in 1948.* | **anonymously** | **online** ◊ *The study was ~ed online.*
VERB + PUBLISH **decide to** | **intend to, plan to** | **refuse to** | **be free to** ◊ *The press should be free to ~ and comment on all aspects of political and social life.* | **dare (to)** ◊ *Freud had not dared to ~ the third chapter of his book in Vienna.*
PHRASES **newly ~ed** ◊ *a newly ~ed series of essays*

publisher noun

ADJ. **big, large, leading, major** ◊ *one of the country's biggest book ~s* | **small** | **independent** | **mainstream** | **commercial** | **local** ◊ *He's writing a history of the town for a local ~.* | **specialist** (*BrE*) | **print** | **electronic, online, Web** | **art, book, magazine, music, newspaper, software** | **academic, educational, trade**
VERB + PUBLISHER **find, have** ◊ *Finding a ~ is hard for all writers.* ◊ *She now has a ~ for her book.*

publishing noun

ADJ. **book, newspaper, etc.** | **academic, scholarly** | **medical, music, scientific, etc.** ◊ *She works in music ~.* | **desktop** | **electronic, online**
VERB + PUBLISHING **work in**
PUBLISHING + NOUN **agreement, deal** | **arm, company, group, house** ◊ *The Cranfield Press is the ~ arm of the Cranfield Institute.* | **business, industry, world** ◊ *The ~ world is extremely competitive.*

puff noun

1 of air/smoke/wind

ADJ. **little, small, tiny**
PREP. **~ of** ◊ *a little ~ of smoke*

2 on a cigarette, pipe, etc.

ADJ. **long** | **short**
VERB + PUFF **have, take** ◊ *He took a long ~ at his cigar and began his story.*
PREP. **~ on** ◊ *a ~ on her cigarette*

puff verb

1 smoke

ADV. **furiously** | **contentedly, happily** | **thoughtfully** | **away** ◊ *He ~ed away at his cigar.*
PREP. **at** ◊ *She ~ed furiously at her cigarette.* | **on** ◊ *My father sat ~ing contentedly on his pipe.*

2 breathe loudly

ADV. **hard** ◊ *She was ~ing quite hard by the time she reached the office.* | **loudly**
PREP. **along, from** ◊ *She was still ~ing from the climb.* | **up** ◊ *He came ~ing up the hill.*
PHRASES **huff and ~, ~ and pant** ◊ *She ~ed and panted behind the others.* | **~ing and blowing** ◊ *Far behind us, ~ing and blowing, came Matt.*

pull noun

1 act of pulling

ADJ. **sharp** | **strong** | **gentle, slight** | **downward** | **gravitational** ◊ *the earth's gravitational ~* | **magnetic** (*figurative*) ◊ *The magnetic ~ of the city was hard to resist.* | **emotional** ◊ *It is hard to deny the emotional ~ of this music.*
VERB + PULL **give sth** ◊ *I gave the door a sharp ~.* | **exert** ◊ *The Moon exerts a gravitational ~ on the Earth, creating tides.* | **feel** (*figurative*) ◊ *She felt the ~ of her homeland.*
PREP. **~ at** ◊ *A gentle ~ at her sleeve got her attention.* | **~ on** ◊ *He felt a strong ~ on the rope.*

2 on a cigarette/drink

ADJ. **long**
VERB + PULL **take** ◊ *She took a long ~ on her cigarette and sighed.*
PREP. **~ at** ◊ *a ~ at his flask* | **~ on**

pull verb

ADV. **gently, hard** ◊ *He got hold of the rope and ~ed hard.* | **quickly, slowly** | **apart, off, on, out, over** ◊ *She ~ed off her boots.* ◊ *He ~ed his sweater on.* | **along, away, back** ◊ *She took his arm and ~ed him along.* ◊ *The dog snapped at her and she ~ed back her hand.*
VERB + PULL **try to** ◊ *He tried to ~ away.* | **manage to**
PREP. **at** ◊ *He ~ed at her coat sleeve.* | **on** ◊ *She ~ed on the lever.* | **towards/toward** ◊ *She ~ed him gently towards/toward her.*
PHRASES **~ (yourself) free** ◊ *John finally managed to ~ himself free.* | **~ yourself to your feet**

pullover noun (esp. BrE)

ADJ. **woollen/woolen, woolly** (*BrE*) | **sleeveless** (*BrE*) | **V-neck** | **fleece** (*esp. AmE*), **knitted** ◊ *She was wearing a knitted ~.*
VERB + PULLOVER **knit**
PULLOVER + NOUN **sweater** (*AmE*)
→ Special page at CLOTHES

pulse noun

ADJ. **fast, racing, rapid** | **slow** | **steady** | **strong** | **faint, weak**
VERB + PULSE **check, feel, take** ◊ *Last time I took my ~, it was a little fast.* | **check for, feel for** ◊ *She reached in through the driver's broken window and checked for a ~.* | **find** | **have** ◊ *The doctor felt to see if he had a ~.* | **quicken** ◊ *There was little to quicken the ~ in his dull routine.*
PULSE + VERB **beat** | **quicken, race** ◊ *She felt her ~ quicken as she recognized the voice.* | **slow**
PULSE + NOUN **rate** ◊ *My at-rest ~ rate is usually about 80 beats per minute.*

punch

648

punch noun

ADJ. **good, hard, powerful** | **killer** (*BrE, figurative*), **knockout** ◊ *Aluko landed a knockout ~.* ◊ *This policy will deliver a knockout ~ to the tourism industry* (*figurative*) | **sucker** (= an unexpected punch) ◊ *He was knocked flat by a sucker ~.* | **one-two** (*AmE, usually figurative*) ◊ *the devastating one-two ~ of Hurricanes Katrina and Rita* | **emotional** (*figurative*) ◊ *The film packs a heavy emotional ~.*
VERB + PUNCH **deliver, give sb, land, pack** (*usually figurative*), **swing, throw** ◊ *She gave him a ~ on the nose.* ◊ *The X37 engine packs a powerful ~.* ◊ *He can throw a powerful ~.* | **pull** ◊ *He pulled his ~es to avoid hurting his sparring partner.* ◊ *She pulls no ~es* (= she says exactly what she thinks). (*figurative*) | **get, take** ◊ *Be careful what you say or you'll get a ~ on the nose.* ◊ *a boxer who knows how to take a ~*
PREP. **~ in** ◊ *a ~ in the stomach* | **~ on** ◊ *She gave him a ~ on the nose.* | **~ to** ◊ *a ~ to the jaw*

punch verb

ADV. **hard** | **lightly** | **playfully** ◊ *She playfully ~ed him on the arm.* | **repeatedly**
PREP. **in** ◊ *His attacker had ~ed him hard in the face.* | **on** ◊ *She ~ed him on the nose.*
PHRASES **kick and ~, ~ and kick** ◊ *He was repeatedly kicked and ~ed as he lay on the ground.*

puncture noun (BrE) small hole in a tyre/tire → See also BLOWOUT

ADJ. **slow** ◊ *The tyre had a slow ~ and had to be pumped up every day.*
VERB + PUNCTURE **get, have, suffer** ◊ *She suffered a ~ in the fifth lap.* | **fix, mend, repair**
PUNCTURE + NOUN **repair kit**

punish verb

ADV. **harshly, severely** | **justly** | **unfairly** | **duly** ◊ *Those who had opposed the court were duly ~ed.* | **physically**
VERB + PUNISH **want to** | **try to** ◊ *He was trying to ~ her for deserting him all those years ago.* | **be designed to** ◊ *Damages are not designed to ~, but to compensate for the loss sustained.*
PREP. **by** ◊ *Never ~ children by making them go hungry.* | **for** ◊ *They will be severely ~ed for their crimes.* | **with** ◊ *Offenders will be ~ed with a £1000 fine.*
PHRASES **be ~ed accordingly** ◊ *Those found guilty will be ~ed accordingly.*

punishment noun

ADJ. **cruel, harsh, heavy, severe** | **unusual** ◊ *the constitutional prohibition on cruel and unusual ~* | **appropriate, fitting** | **capital** | **corporal, physical** | **collective**
VERB + PUNISHMENT **administer, dish out** (*informal*), **dole out** (*informal*), **hand out, impose, inflict, mete out** ◊ *It is unlawful for a teacher to inflict corporal ~ on students.* ◊ *Harsh ~ is expected to be meted out to the murderer.* | **face, receive, suffer** | **accept, take** ◊ *Take your ~ like a man.* | **avoid, escape** | **deserve**
PREP. **as ~ (for)** ◊ *He had his privileges withdrawn as ~ for fighting with another prisoner.* | **~ for** ◊ *Punishments for killing the king's deer were severe.*
PHRASES **crime and ~** ◊ *the sociology of crime and ~* | **the ~ fits the crime** ◊ *The victim's family do not believe that this ~ fits the crime.* | **reward and ~** ◊ *They use a system of reward and ~ to discipline their children.*

pupil noun

1 (*esp. BrE*) child in school

ADJ. **able, bright, good, star** ◊ *Daniel is the star ~ at school.* | **disruptive, unruly** | **first-year, second-year, etc.** | **older, senior** | **younger** | **former** (also **ex-pupil**) | **private** | **school** | **primary, secondary** ◊ *the parents of secondary school ~s*
VERB + PUPIL **teach** | **exclude, expel**

PUPIL + NOUN **attendance, numbers** | **assessment** | **performance** | **behaviour/behavior**

2 of the eye

ADJ. **dilated**
VERB + PUPIL **dilate, enlarge**
PUPIL + VERB **dilate, enlarge**

puppet noun

1 model of a person/animal

ADJ. **finger, glove** (*BrE*), **hand, shadow, sock** | **wooden**
VERB + PUPPET **manipulate, work** ◊ *a ~ controlled by strings* ◊ *How do you work these ~s?* | **make**
PUPPET + NOUN **play, show** | **theatre/theater** | **master**

2 sb whose actions are controlled by sb else

ADJ. **mere** (*esp. BrE*)
VERB + PUPPET **control, manipulate** ◊ *He's become a ~ manipulated by the government.*
PUPPET + NOUN **government, king, regime, state**

purchase noun

1 buying sth

ADJ. **cash** | **credit** | **online** ◊ *Make sure all online ~s are made through a secure server.* | **bulk** ◊ *the bulk ~ of paper* | **outright** ◊ *Companies are moving away from outright ~ of company cars to leasing.* | **compulsory** (*BrE*) ◊ *The council applied for a compulsory ~ order on the the tennis courts.* | **advance** | **hire** (= a method of buying an article by making regular payments for it over several months or years) (*BrE*) ◊ *He entered a hire ~ agreement with a car dealer.* | **arms, equipment, home, house, land, share**
PURCHASE + NOUN **price** | **tax** | **order**
PHRASES **the cost of ~** ◊ *You can resell books and cut the original cost of ~.* | **the date of ~, the time of ~** ◊ *I did not notice the defects at the time of ~.* | **the place of ~, the point of ~** ◊ *Ticket holders should return to the point of ~ for a refund.* | **proof of ~** ◊ *Keep your receipt as proof of ~.*

2 sth bought

ADJ. **big-ticket** (*AmE*), **expensive, large, major** ◊ *big-ticket ~s such as cars or refrigerators* | **impulse** ◊ *Consumers make a lot of impulse ~s.* | **consumer** ◊ *The company uses software to analyze consumer ~s.*
VERB + PURCHASE **make** ◊ *some ways to encourage customers to make a ~* | **pay for**

purchase verb

ADV. **newly, recently** | **compulsorily** (*BrE*) ◊ *The land was compulsorily ~d from the owner to make way for the new road.* | **online** ◊ *Tickets can be ~d online.*
VERB + PURCHASE **agree to, be willing to** | **wish to** | **can afford to, cannot afford to**
PREP. **for** ◊ *They ~d the land for $1 million.* | **from** ◊ *They ~d the house from an elderly couple.*

purity noun

ADJ. **absolute** ◊ *the absolute ~ of her love* | **great, high** ◊ *high-purity silver* | **ideological** | **racial** | **moral, sexual**
VERB + PURITY **maintain, preserve** ◊ *He struggled to preserve his ideological ~.*
PHRASES **~ of blood** ◊ *Hitler's belief in the ~ of blood of the German people* | **~ of form, ~ of style** ◊ *a classical ~ of form* | **~ of heart** ◊ *She has a ~ of heart that inspires others.*

purple adj., noun

ADV. **almost** | **slightly**
ADJ. **bright, vivid** | **dark, deep, rich** | **light, pale**
PHRASES **~ in the face, ~ with rage** ◊ *He turned ~ with rage.*
→ Special page at COLOUR

purpose noun

1 aim/function

ADJ. **limited** | **chief, main, primary, prime, principal** | **true** | **sole** | **whole** | **original** | **practical, useful** ◊ *These bars serve no useful ~.* | **legitimate** | **general** ◊ *a general-purpose* cleaning fluid | **common** ◊ *a group of individuals sharing a common* ~ | **particular, special, specific** | **dual** ◊ *a toy with the dual* ~ *of entertaining and developing memory skills* | **intended, stated** | **social** ◊ *the view that art should serve a social* ~

VERB + PURPOSE **have** | **lack** | **accomplish, achieve, fulfil/ fulfill, serve, suit** ◊ *The plan achieved its primary* ~, *if nothing else.* | **defeat** ◊ *Computer-animated cartoons that depict humans realistically seem to defeat the whole* ~ *of animation.*

PREP. **for a/the** ~ ◊ *I put the chair there for a* ~. ◊ *a measure introduced for the* ~ *of protecting the interests of investors* | **on** ~ (= intentionally) ◊ *He slammed the door on* ~.

PHRASES **at cross** ~s (= not understanding or having the same aims, etc. as each other) ◊ *I finally realized that we were talking at cross* ~s. | **for the express** ~ **of sth, with the express** ~ **of sth** ◊ *The school was founded with the express* ~ *of teaching deaf children to speak.* | **for (all) practical** ~s ◊ *Nominally she is the secretary, but for all practical* ~s *she runs the place.* | **your** ~ **in life** ◊ *She saw being a doctor as her* ~ *in life.* | **put sth to (a/some)** ~ ◊ *The same information can be put to many* ~s | **a sense of** ~ ◊ *Encouraged by her example, they all set to work with a fresh sense of* ~. | **strength of** ~ ◊ *They had great confidence and strength of* ~.

2 purposes requirements of a particular situation

ADJ. **administrative, business, commercial, domestic, educational, insurance, legal, medical, medicinal, political, research, tax, teaching, training** ◊ *You will need to have the vehicle valued for insurance* ~s. | **comparative** ◊ *For comparative* ~s, *the populations of three other cities are also shown.*

PREP. **for…** ~ ◊ *The drug can be sold for medicinal* ~s *only.* | **for the** ~s **of** (also **for the purpose of** in *AmE*) ◊ *Let's assume he knows, for the* ~s *of our argument.*

purse noun

1 (*esp. BrE*) for carrying money

ADJ. **leather** | **change** (*AmE*)

VERB + PURSE **open** | **snatch, steal** ◊ *She had her* ~ *snatched.*

PREP. **in sb's** ~ ◊ *What do you keep in your* ~?

2 money available to an organization/government

ADJ. **public**

VERB + PURSE **drain** ◊ *The reforms had drained the public* ~.

PURSE + NOUN **strings** ◊ *Who holds the* ~ *strings in your house?* ◊ *The government will have to tighten the* ~ *strings* (= spend less).

PREP. **in the** ~ (*esp. BrE*) ◊ *There is no money in the* ~ *for this.*

3 (*AmE*) bag for carrying things → See also HANDBAG

ADJ. **bulging** ◊ *She handed him a bulging velvet* ~. | **leather, silk, etc.** | **matching** ◊ *She wore pink heels with a matching clutch* ~. | **clutch**

VERB + PURSE **clutch, hold** ◊ *Both women clutched their* ~s *close to their bodies.* | **carry** | **grab, pick up, snatch** ◊ *She grabbed her* ~ *and headed out the door.* | **open** | **dig in, dig into, dig through, reach into, rummage through** ◊ *I dug in my* ~ *to find my respirator.* ◊ *I rummaged through my* ~ *for my lip gloss.* | **snatch, steal** ◊ *She had her* ~ *snatched.*

PURSE + NOUN **snatcher**

PREP. **in sb's** ~ ◊ *What do you keep in your* ~?

PHRASES **sling a** ~ **over your shoulder, throw a** ~ **over your shoulder** ◊ *She slung her black leather* ~ *over her shoulder.*

pursue verb

1 continue sth/try to achieve sth

ADV. **further, still** | **actively, aggressively, energetically, vigorously** | **doggedly, relentlessly** ◊ *He was still doggedly pursuing his studies.* | **successfully** ◊ *How can we successfully* ~ *these aims?* | **seriously**

VERB + PURSUE **decide to** ◊ *We have decided not to* ~ *the matter further.* | **intend to, want to, wish to** ◊ *How do you decide which career you wish to* ~? | **be inclined to, be interested in pursuing, feel inclined to** | **be reluctant to** | **be able to, be free to** | **continue to**

PHRASES **the ability to** ~ **sth, the freedom to** ~ **sth, the opportunity to** ~ **sth, the right to** ~ **sth** ◊ *the freedom to* ~

her own interests | **be not worth pursuing** ◊ *I decided the matter was not worth pursuing further.*

2 chase sb

ADV. **relentlessly** ◊ *He* ~d *her relentlessly, refusing to take 'no' for an answer.*

PHRASES **closely** ~d **by sb, hotly** ~d **by sb** ◊ *He ran past, hotly* ~d *by two policemen.*

pursuit noun

1 attempt to find sth

ADJ. **aggressive, dogged, relentless, single-minded, vigorous** | **endless** ◊ *the endless* ~ *of wealth*

VERB + PURSUIT **be engaged in**

PREP. **in** ~ **of** ◊ *people leaving their homes in* ~ *of work* | ~ **of** ◊ *He is engaged in the ruthless* ~ *of pleasure.* ◊ *He devoted his waking hours to the single-minded* ~ *of his goal.*

PHRASES **the** ~ **of excellence, happiness, knowledge, pleasure, truth, etc.**

2 attempt to catch sb/sth

ADJ. **close** | **police**

VERB + PURSUIT **give** (*formal*) ◊ *The police gave* ~. | **continue** | **abandon**

PREP. **in** ~ (**of**) ◊ *Two boys ran past with a security guard in* ~. ◊ *The guard set off in* ~ *of the thief.*

PHRASES **in close** ~, **in hot** ~ ◊ *Away ran the deer, with the hunters in hot* ~.

3 (usually **pursuits**) pastime

ADJ. **active, energetic** ◊ *active leisure* ~s | **leisure, recreational** | **favourite/favorite** (*esp. BrE*), **popular** | **individual** | **academic, artistic, cultural, educational, intellectual, scholarly, spiritual** | **country** (*BrE*), **outdoor, sporting** (*BrE*) | **sexual** (*esp. AmE*)

VERB + PURSUIT **follow** ◊ *She has time now to follow her various artistic* ~s.

pus noun

ADJ. **green, yellow**

VERB + PUS **ooze** ◊ *The wound had not healed properly and was oozing* ~.

PUS + VERB **ooze, ooze out**

push noun

1 act of pushing

ADJ. **big, hard** | **gentle, little, slight**

VERB + PUSH **give sb/sth** ◊ *She gave him a gentle* ~.

PHRASES **at the** ~ **of a button** ◊ *The machine washes and dries at the* ~ *of a button.*

2 effort to do/obtain sth

ADJ. **big, extra, major, strong** | **renewed** | **final**

VERB + PUSH **make** ◊ *The company is making a strong* ~ *to expand its distribution.*

PREP. ~ **against** ◊ *the final* ~ *against the enemy* | ~ **for** ◊ *There has been a big* ~ *for higher standards in schools.* | ~ **towards/toward** ◊ *a* ~ *towards/toward organic food*

push verb

1 use physical force

ADV. **firmly, hard** ◊ *You'll have to* ~ *harder if you want it to move.* | **angrily, roughly, violently** | **gently, lightly, playfully** | **carefully** | **deliberately** ◊ *He was deliberately* ~ed *into the path of the vehicle.* | **blindly, frantically** | **hastily, hurriedly, quickly** | **slowly** | **suddenly** | **just, merely, simply** ◊ *Jack flung himself at Steve, but he simply* ~ed *him away.* | **aside, away, back, down, over, together, etc.** ◊ *She leaned on the box and* ~ed *it aside.* ◊ *They* ~ed *the two desks together.*

VERB + PUSH **try to** | **manage to** | **begin to**

PREP. **against** ◊ *The fans* ~ed *against the barrier.* | **at** ◊ *She* ~ed *at the door but it wouldn't budge.* | **out of** ◊ *He* ~ed *her roughly out of the door.* | **through** ◊ *I tried to* ~ *through the* crowd. | **to** ◇ *The woman had been ~ed violently to the ground.* | **towards/toward**, **under** ◇ *She found a note ~ed under the door.*

PHRASES **~ sth open**, **~ sth shut** ◇ *He managed to ~ the window open a few inches.*

2 put pressure on sb/yourself

ADV. **aggressively**, **hard** ◇ *Lucy should ~ herself a little harder.* | **too far** ◇ *Her parents are very tolerant, but sometimes she ~es them too far.* | **around** ◇ *Don't allow yourself to be ~ed around by that bully.*

PREP. **into** ◇ *Her parents ~ed her into accepting the job.* | **for** ◇ *The two governments are ~ing for economic reform in the region.*

PHRASES **~ sb/yourself to the limit** ◇ *He felt he was being ~ed to the limit of his self-control.*

pushchair (*BrE*) *noun* → See also STROLLER

ADJ. **collapsible**, **folding**
VERB + PUSHCHAIR **push**, **wheel** | **push along**, **wheel along** | **collapse**, **fold**, **fold up**
PREP. **in a/the ~**

put *verb* express

ADV. **cleverly** (*BrE*), **eloquently**, **well** ◇ *I thought you ~ your points very well.* | **badly** | **gently**, **tactfully** | **bluntly**, **crudely** | **simply**, **succinctly** ◇ *Put simply, we accept their offer or go bankrupt.* | **mildly** (*ironic*) ◇ *I was annoyed, to ~ it mildly* (= I was extremely angry).

PHRASES **to ~ it another way** ◇ *He was too trusting—or, to ~ it another way, he had no head for business.*

puzzle *noun*

1 sth that is difficult to understand

ADJ. **great** | **perplexing** | **scientific**, **theoretical**
VERB + PUZZLE **crack** (*BrE*), **figure out** (*esp. AmE*), **piece together**, **solve** | **remain** ◇ *What happened to the ship remains a ~.*
PUZZLE + VERB **remain** ◇ *The ~ remains of what happened to the ship.*
PREP. **~ about** ◇ *There is a ~ about how the plant first came to Britain.* | **~ of** ◇ *They're trying to solve the ~ of how gravity works.*
PHRASES **a piece of the ~** ◇ *Another piece of the ~ fell into place.* | **the key to a ~** ◇ *Traces of explosives found among the wreckage were the key to the ~.* | **a piece in the ~** ◇ *The police didn't know what the message meant, but it was another piece in the ~.* | **a solution to a ~**, **something of a ~** ◇ *The origin of the word is something of a ~.*

2 game that tests your skill, intelligence, etc.

ADJ. **crossword**, **jigsaw** (*BrE*) | **logic**, **number**, **picture**, **word** | **complicated**
VERB + PUZZLE **complete**, **do**, **put together** (*esp. AmE*), **solve**
PUZZLE + NOUN **book** | **game** | **piece**

puzzled *adj.*

VERBS **be**, **feel**, **look**, **seem**, **sound** | **become**, **get** ◇ *We were becoming more and more ~ by the minute.* | **remain**
ADV. **extremely**, **fairly**, **very**, etc. | **a little**, **slightly**, etc. | **faintly** | **completely** (*AmE*) | **genuinely** | **clearly**, **obviously**
PREP. **about** ◇ *You look very ~ about something.* | **at** ◇ *I was somewhat ~ at his unwillingness to help.* | **by** ◇ *Mrs Sykes seemed slightly ~ by this.*

pyjamas (*BrE*) (*AmE* **pajamas**) *noun*

ADJ. **cotton**, **flannel** | **warm**
PYJAMAS/PAJAMA + NOUN **jacket**, **top** | **bottoms**, **pants** (*AmE*), **trousers** (*BrE*) ◇ *He was wearing only his pyjama bottoms.*
...OF PYJAMAS/PAJAMAS **pair**
→ Special page at CLOTHES

Q q

qualification *noun*

1 (often **qualifications**) allowing sb to work, study, etc.

ADJ. **formal**, **paper** (*BrE*) | **basic**, **minimum** | **entry** | **appropriate**, **necessary** | **special**, **specialist** | **management**, **professional**, **vocational** (*BrE*) ◇ *The aim of the reform is to give more status to vocational ~s.* | **further** | **academic**, **educational**, **postgraduate** (*BrE*) ◇ *Many of those selected lack the academic ~s to teach.* | **technical** (*esp. BrE*) | **legal**, **medical**, **secretarial**, **teaching** (*all esp. BrE*)
VERB + QUALIFICATION **acquire**, **gain**, **obtain** | **have**, **hold**, **possess** ◇ *Only two of the applicants had the necessary ~s.* | **meet** (*esp. AmE*) | **lack**
QUALIFICATION + NOUN **period** ◇ *The job usually has a three-year ~ period.*
PREP. **~ for** ◇ *the minimum entry ~ for admission* | **~ in** ◇ *He held no formal ~ in law.*

2 weakening of a statement

ADJ. **important**
VERB + QUALIFICATION **add** | **need**, **require** ◇ *The term 'population' as used here requires ~.*
PREP. **with ~s** ◇ *I agree with his view, with a few ~s.* | **without ~** ◇ *The committee supported her proposal, without ~.*

qualified *adj.*

1 having completed a course of study

VERBS **be** | **become**, **get**
ADV. **highly**, **well** ◇ *The teaching staff are all highly ~.* | **fully**, **properly** (*esp. BrE*) ◇ *a fully ~ electrician* | **newly**, **recently** (*both BrE*) ◇ *newly ~ doctors* | **appropriately**, **suitably** (*both esp. BrE*) ◇ *Applications are invited from suitably ~ individuals.* | **sufficiently** | **academically** (*esp. AmE*), **legally**, **medically**, **professionally** (*esp. BrE*) ◇ *He is a medically ~ doctor.* ◇ *She is a professionally ~ social worker.*
PREP. **as** ◇ *She is now ~ as a teacher.* (*BrE*)

2 having the skill needed to do sth

VERBS **be**, **feel** ◇ *Elaine did not feel ~ to comment.*
ADV. **eminently**, **ideally**, **uniquely**, **well** ◇ *My father was well ~ to act the part of a head teacher.* | **technically** ◇ *I'm not technically ~ to say anything.*

3 limited in some way

VERBS **be**
ADV. **heavily** (*esp. BrE*) ◇ *The proposals received heavily ~ approval.*

qualify *verb*

1 have/give sb the right to sth

ADV. **automatically**
PREP. **for** ◇ *You will automatically ~ for a pension.*

2 for a sports competition

ADV. **easily**
VERB + QUALIFY **fail to**
PREP. **for** ◇ *England failed to ~ for the final.*

3 fit a description

ADV. **barely**, **hardly**
PREP. **as** ◇ *A three-week course hardly qualifies as sufficient training.*

quality *noun*

1 how good/bad sth is

ADJ. **excellent**, **exceptional**, **good**, **high**, **outstanding**, **superior**, **top** ◇ *All our cakes are made with top-quality ingredients.* | **inferior**, **low**, **poor** | **variable**, **varying** | **product**, **service** | **audio**, **recording**, **sound** | **image**, **picture**, **video** | **air**, **water** | **food** | **artistic**, **technical**
VERB + QUALITY **maintain** | **enhance**, **improve**, **raise** | **affect**,

compromise, impact (*AmE*), impact on, impair (*esp. BrE*), reduce, sacrifice ◇ *How can we increase production without sacrificing ~?* | assess, determine, evaluate, judge, measure, monitor, rate, test | deliver ◇ *We aim to deliver ~ to our customers.*
QUALITY + VERB vary | improve | go down, suffer ◇ *When costs are cut, product ~ suffers.*
QUALITY + NOUN control | assurance | standards
PREP. of ... ~ ◇ *The photos are of variable ~.*
PHRASES ~ of life ◇ *Advances in technology would, it was hoped, improve the ~ of life.*

2 characteristic

ADJ. admirable, desirable, endearing, fine, good, great, positive | negative | redeeming ◇ *I found him thoroughly unpleasant, with no redeeming qualities whatsoever.* | individual, personal | inherent, innate, intrinsic | distinctive, particular, special, unique, wonderful | elusive, rare, star ◇ *a singer with that elusive ~ that sells records* ◇ *They have real star ~.* | essential, important | aesthetic, artistic, literary | dreamlike, magical, timeless | moral, spiritual | physical | feminine, masculine | leadership
VERB + QUALITY have, possess | display, show | lack | give ◇ *The music gives the movie a dreamlike ~.*

quantity *noun*

ADJ. considerable, enormous, great, huge, immense, large, massive, sheer, significant, substantial, vast | copious, generous, prodigious, vast ◇ *copious quantities of champagne* | limited, minute, modest, small, tiny | maximum, minimum | increasing | average | sufficient ◇ *Gas was detected in sufficient ~ to warrant careful monitoring.*
PREP. in ~ ◇ *There is a discount for goods bought in ~.* | ~ of ◇ *A ~ of fertilizer was stolen from the farm.*

quarantine *noun*

ADJ. strict
VERB + QUARANTINE enforce | keep sb/sth in, put sb/sth in
QUARANTINE + NOUN period | zone | facility, station | regulations, restrictions
PREP. in ~ ◇ *The animals are still in ~ at the port.*

quarrel *noun*

ADJ. bitter, serious, violent | family, internal, lovers' | personal, private | long-standing, old
VERB + QUARREL have | pick, provoke ◇ *I don't want to pick a ~ with her.* | be involved in, become involved in, get involved in (*all esp. BrE*) | make up (*BrE*), patch up (*BrE*), settle
QUARREL + VERB break out
PREP. ~ about ◇ *a ~ about money* | ~ between ◇ *a ~ between family members* | ~ over ◇ *a ~ over the ownership of a piece of land* | ~ with ◇ *Our ~ is not with the people, but with their leader.*
PHRASES have no ~ with sb/sth ◇ *We have no ~ with their plans, in fact we support them.*

quarrel *verb*

ADV. bitterly, fiercely, violently (*all esp. BrE*)
PREP. about, over ◇ *Companies always ~ about the exact terms of the agreement.* ◇ *What did you two ~ about?* ◇ *We tend to ~ over money.* (*esp. BrE*) | with ◇ *I didn't want to ~ with Tyler over weekend plans.* ◇ *Why must you always ~ with your sister?* (*esp. BrE*)

quarter *noun*

1 one of four equal parts into which sth is divided
→ See also FOURTH

VERB + QUARTER break sth into ~s, cut sth into ~s, divide sth into ~s, fold sth into ~s
PREP. ~ of ◇ *a ~ of a century/mile/million* ◇ *a ~ of an hour* ◇ *a ~ of all potential customers*

2 period of three months

ADJ. first, second, third, fourth ◇ *Profits fell during the third ~.* | last, opening | fiscal (*AmE*) ◇ *the current fiscal ~* |

current, past, previous | consecutive ◇ *six consecutive ~s of improved earnings*
PREP. during the ~

3 part of a town

ADJ. historic, old | Arab, Chinese, Latin, etc. | diplomatic, residential

4 quarters place to live in

ADJ. comfortable, spacious | confined, cramped | private ◇ *the president's private ~s* | living, sleeping | officers', servants' | married ◇ *The corporal and his family lived in married ~s.*
VERB + QUARTERS be confined to ◇ *He was confined to ~s as a punishment.*

queen *noun*

1 female ruler/wife of a king

ADJ. rightful | future | homecoming, prom (*both AmE*) ◇ *She was nominated for prom ~ in high school.*
VERB + QUEEN become | crown (sb), make sb, proclaim sb ◇ *She was crowned ~ at the age of fifteen.*
QUEEN + VERB reign, rule, rule sb/sth, rule over sb/sth | abdicate ◇ *the queen's decision to abdicate*
PREP. under a/the ~ ◇ *England under Queen Elizabeth I* | ~ of ◇ *the Queen of Thailand*
PHRASES ~ consort (= the wife of a king)

2 playing card
→ Note at CARD

query *noun*

ADJ. customer | email | search
VERB + QUERY have ◇ *If you have any queries regarding this offer, simply call our helpline.* | raise | email, pose (*esp. AmE*), post, send in, submit ◇ *I posted my ~ on the website and got an immediate reply.* | forward, refer | put (*esp. BrE*) ◇ *I've a ~ to put to the last speaker.* | answer, deal with, field, handle, reply to, resolve, respond to
PREP. ~ about, ~ as to, ~ concerning, ~ on, ~ regarding, ~ relating to ◇ *Have you any queries about what you're supposed to do?* ◇ *We regret that we cannot deal with queries on individual cases.* | ~ from ◇ *We had queries from people all over the country.*

quest *noun*

ADJ. endless, eternal, never-ending, relentless | continuing, lifelong, ongoing | personal | noble | religious, spiritual
VERB + QUEST begin, embark on, go on, set off on, set out on | continue, pursue ◇ *The team will continue its ~ for Olympic gold this afternoon.* | abandon
PREP. in a/the ~ ◇ *an important stage in their ~ for truth* | in ~ of ◇ *We set off in ~ of the perfect wedding dress.* | ~ for ◇ *her ~ for a better life*

question *noun*

1 sentence, etc. that asks sth

ADJ. awkward, difficult, embarrassing, hard, tough, tricky | pointed, probing, searching ◇ *He became embarrassed when a journalist asked him pointed ~s about his finances.* | open, open-ended, unanswered | personal | academic, hypothetical, rhetorical | leading, loaded, trick ◇ *The judge told him not to ask the witness leading ~s.* | good, interesting, pertinent, relevant | basic, big, fundamental, important, key, serious | silly, stupid | complex, simple | quick ◇ *Can I ask a quick ~?* | obvious | direct, straight (*esp. BrE*) ◇ *I wanted to find out how old he was without asking him a direct ~.* | specific | legal, philosophical, technical | exam, multiple-choice, quiz, test
VERB + QUESTION ask (sb) | have ◇ *Does anyone have any ~s for our speaker?* | address, put ◇ *I'd like to put a ~ to the first speaker.* | bombard sb with, fire ◇ *The children bombarded us with ~s.* ◇ *The interview panel fired ~s at me from all*

angles. | **frame, phrase** ◊ *I need to phrase my ~ rather carefully.* | **face** | **answer, reply to, respond to** | **do** (used only about written questions) ◊ *I couldn't do Question 6.* | **field** ◊ *The chairperson fielded technical ~s that she could not answer herself.* | **avoid, dodge, evade, ignore** ◊ *He easily evaded all the interviewer's most probing ~s.*

PREP. **~ about** ◊ *She refused to answer ~s about her private life.* | **~ as to** ◊ *Don't be afraid to ask ~s as to why things are done in the way they are.* | **~ concerning to, ~ regarding to, ~ relating to** ◊ *The official faced ~s concerning his role in the affair.* | **~ on** ◊ *In the exam there's sure to be a ~ on energy.*

2 issue

ADJ. **burning, challenging, controversial, difficult, vexed, vexing** ◊ *We come now to the vexed ~ of pension rights.* | **central, crucial, fundamental, important, key** | **related** | **delicate, sensitive** | **economic, ethical, moral, political**

VERB + QUESTION **bring up, pose, raise** ◊ *The new play poses some challenging ~s.* | **consider, discuss, examine, explore, ponder** | **address, deal with, face, tackle** | **answer, decide, find a solution to, resolve, settle** | **avoid, ignore** | **come to**

QUESTION + VERB **arise** | **go unanswered, remain unanswered** ◊ *Only one ~ remains unanswered.*

PREP. **~ about** ◊ *fundamental ~s about the nature of our society* | **~ for** ◊ *one of the crucial ~s for the jury* | **~ of** ◊ *~s of national security* ◊ *Now it's just a ~ of getting the wording right.*

3 doubt

VERB + QUESTION **come into** | **call into** ◊ *It does call into ~ the decision to send troops into the area.* | **be open to** ◊ *The government's handling of the whole affair remains open to ~.*

PREP. **beyond ~** ◊ *Her loyalty is beyond ~.* | **in ~** ◊ *His sincerity is not in ~.* | **without ~** ◊ *It was, without ~, the worst day of my life.* | **~ about** ◊ *There is no ~ about her enthusiasm for the job.* | **~ as to** ◊ *I did have some ~s as to his motive in coming.*

question verb

ADV. **openly, seriously** ◊ *People openly ~ whether he is right for the job.* | **closely**

PREP. **about** ◊ *She was closely ~ed about her whereabouts on the night of the murder.* | **in connection with** ◊ *A man is being ~ed in connection with the robbery.* | **on** ◊ *He was ~ed on his role in the affair.*

questionable adj.

VERBS **be** | **become** | **remain**

ADV. **extremely, fairly, very, etc.** | **highly** ◊ *Their motives for undertaking this study are highly ~.* | **ethically, morally**

questioning noun

ADJ. **careful, close** (*esp. BrE*) | **direct** ◊ *She decided to confront her boss about the situation with direct ~.* | **intensive** | **aggressive, hostile, tough** | **constant, repeated**

VERB + QUESTIONING **face** | **be wanted for** | **be detained for, be held for** ◊ *Four suspects have been detained for ~ in connection with the incident.*

PREP. **under ~** ◊ *The suspect remained silent under ~.* | **~ about, ~ on, ~ over** ◊ *The disaster prompted ~ about safety standards.* | **~ by** ◊ *The man was released after ~ by detectives.* | **~ from** ◊ *The group chairman faced hostile ~ from angry shareholders.*

question mark noun

ADJ. **big, huge, major**

VERB + QUESTION MARK **put** ◊ *His arrival clearly puts a huge ~ over the future of the present team captain.*

QUESTION MARK + VERB **hang over sth, remain** ◊ *A big ~ hangs over the wisdom of the move.*

PREP. **~ against** (*BrE*) ◊ *A slight ~ against her character remains.* | **~ over** ◊ *There is now a serious ~ over his leadership ability.*

questionnaire noun

ADJ. **brief, short, simple** | **detailed, lengthy** | **standardized** | **follow-up** | **online** | **mailed** (*AmE*), **postal** (*BrE*) | **self-administered, self-report**

VERB + QUESTIONNAIRE **design, develop, prepare** | **distribute, send, send out** | **administer, give sb** | **receive** | **complete, fill in** (*BrE*), **fill out** (*esp. AmE*) | **reply to, respond to, return, send, send in** ◊ *Most of the people who responded to the ~ were supportive.* | **analyse/analyze**

PREP. **~ about** ◊ *Local companies were asked to complete a ~ about their exports.* | **~ concerning** ◊ *~s concerning people's leisure preferences* | **~ on** ◊ *a ~ on the environment*

queue noun (BrE) → See also LINE

ADJ. **endless, long** | **growing, lengthening** | **orderly** ◊ *Please form an orderly ~.* | **bus, checkout, cinema, etc.** | **bread, dinner, food** ◊ *the country's soaring prices and growing food ~s* | **traffic** | **dole** ◊ *More unemployed people are joining the dole ~ each week.*

VERB + QUEUE **form, line up in** | **join, stand in, wait in** ◊ *He had to join the ~ for the toilets.* | **jump** ◊ *Don't jump the queue—take your turn like everyone else!*

QUEUE + VERB **form** | **build up, grow** ◊ *Long ~s are building up on the city's exit roads.* | **move** ◊ *The queue's not moving at all.* | **stretch** ◊ *The ~ stretched for more than a mile.*

PREP. **in a/the ~** ◊ *the people in the ~* | **~ for** ◊ *the ~ for tickets* | **~ of** ◊ *a long ~ of shoppers*

PHRASES **the back of the ~, the end of the ~** | **the front of the ~, the head of the ~**

queue verb (BrE)

ADV. **patiently** | **up** ◊ *People ~d up outside.*

VERB + QUEUE **have to**

PREP. **for** ◊ *We had to ~ for tickets.*

quick adj.

VERBS **be, seem** ◊ *We'd better be ~.* | **become, get**

ADV. **extremely, fairly, very, etc.** ◊ *an extremely ~ worker* | **particularly** | **reasonably, relatively** | **amazingly, remarkably, surprisingly** | **mercifully** ◊ *It was a mercifully ~ end for those condemned to die.*

PREP. **at** ◊ *I was getting quite ~ at designing websites.*

PHRASES **~ and easy** ◊ *meals that are ~ and easy to prepare*

quiet noun

ADJ. **relative** ◊ *a period of comparative ~* | **sudden** | **awful, eerie**

VERB + QUIET **break** (*esp. AmE*), **pierce** (*esp. AmE*), **shatter** ◊ *A machine gun shattered the ~.*

QUIET + VERB **follow** ◊ *in the sudden ~ that followed the gunshot*

PHRASES **peace and ~** ◊ *I'm going home now for a bit of peace and ~!*

quiet adj.

1 with little or no noise; not talking

VERBS **be** | **become, fall, go, grow** | **keep, lie, remain, sit, stay** ◊ *Just sit ~ for a moment, there's a good boy.* | **keep sb/sth** ◊ *Keep that dog ~, will you!*

ADV. **extremely, fairly, very, etc.** | **all** ◊ *Suddenly the room went all ~.* | **awfully, remarkably, unusually** ◊ *Everyone went awfully ~.* | **absolutely, completely, perfectly** | **deathly, eerily** ◊ *The house was eerily ~.* | **dangerously** ◊ *His voice was dangerously ~ as he asked the question.* | **oddly, strangely, unnaturally** ◊ *She went back to a strangely ~ house.* | **surprisingly, uncharacteristically**

PREP. **about** ◊ *I knew I had to keep ~ about it.*

PHRASES **nice (and) ~** ◊ *I was looking forward to a nice ~ afternoon.*

2 without much activity

VERBS **be, look, seem** | **become** | **lie, remain, sit** ◊ *Lie ~ for an hour and you'll feel better.* | **keep sb/sth** ◊ *Keep the patient as ~ as possible.*

ADV. **extremely, fairly, very, etc.** | **reasonably** (*esp. BrE*),

quilt *noun* → See also DUVET

ADJ. **antique | handmade | crazy** (*AmE*), **patchwork** ◇ *a crazy ~ of regulations* (*figurative*) | **thick**
VERB + QUILT **create, make, sew, stitch | pull up**
QUILT + NOUN **pattern | cover** (*BrE*)

quirk *noun*

ADJ. **personal, personality | odd, strange, weird | annoying | little**
VERB + QUIRK **have** ◇ *The system has some odd little ~s.*
PREP. **by a ~ of** ◇ *By a strange ~ of fate, she later married the first boyfriend she'd ever had.* | **~ in** ◇ *as a result of some ~ in the social order*
PHRASES **a ~ of fate**

quit *verb*

ADV. **altogether** ◇ *I thought about working part-time, or quitting altogether.* | **abruptly, suddenly**
VERB + QUIT **try to** ◇ *I'm still trying to ~ smoking.* | **decide to | be ready to, threaten to | be forced to, have to**
PREP. **as** ◇ *He was forced to ~ as the team's manager.* | **over** ◇ *Their longest-serving employee is threatening to ~ over pay.*
PHRASES **give notice to ~, issue notice to ~** (*both esp. BrE*) ◇ *Landlords are normally required to give 28 days' written notice to ~.* | **know when to ~** ◇ *In this job you have to know when to ~.*

quiz *noun*

1 competition or game

ADJ. **pub** (*BrE*), **radio, television, TV | interactive, online | general-knowledge** (*BrE*), **music, news, sports, etc. | pop** (= given to students without warning) (*AmE*) ◇ *We had a pop ~ in science class today.*
VERB + QUIZ **compile | hold** (*esp. BrE*) | **complete, do, take | enter, take part in** (*both BrE*) | **win** (*esp. BrE*)
QUIZ + NOUN **programme/program** (*esp. BrE*), **show | evening, night** (*both BrE*) ◇ *We have a ~ night every Wednesday.* | **question**
PREP. **~ about** ◇ *a ~ about the week's news*

2 (*AmE*) test given to students

ADJ. **geography, math, etc. | multiple-choice**
VERB + QUIZ **take | retake | flunk** (*informal*)
QUIZ + NOUN **question, score**

quota *noun*

ADJ. **full** ◇ *He never takes his full ~ of days off.* | **strict | annual, daily, monthly, weekly | national** (*esp. BrE*) | **fishing, milk, etc.** ◇ *the introduction of fishing ~s* | **export, import, production | gender, racial** (*both esp. AmE*)
VERB + QUOTA **allocate** (*esp. BrE*), **establish, impose, introduce** (*esp. BrE*), **set | increase | reduce | fill, fulfil/ fulfill, meet, reach** ◇ *We had to increase our output to fill the ~ by the end of the year.* | **exceed** ◇ *Many countries are still exceeding their ~s.*
QUOTA + NOUN **system**
PREP. **~ for** ◇ *~s for oil production* | **~ on** ◇ *national ~s on imports of cars*

quotation *noun*

1 words taken from a book, etc.

ADJ. **famous, memorable | direct, verbatim** ◇ *a direct ~ from a recent speech by the president* | **illustrative | selective | biblical, scriptural**
VERB + QUOTATION **take** ◇ *My ~ is taken from 'Hamlet'.* | **attribute | cite**
QUOTATION + VERB **come from sth** ◇ *Where does that ~ come from?*
QUOTATION + NOUN **marks** ◇ *If you take text from other sources, place it in ~ marks.*
PREP. **~ from** ◇ *It's a ~ from a poem by Keats.*

2 (*esp. AmE*) price that will be charged for a piece of work → See QUOTE

ADJ. **written | free | detailed**
VERB + QUOTATION **give (sb), provide (sb with), supply (sb with)** ◇ *Most builders will give you a free ~.* | **get, obtain | accept**
PREP. **~ for** ◇ *Always get several ~s for the job.*

quote *noun*

1 words taken from a book, etc.

ADJ. **famous, memorable, quotable | direct, exact, verbatim** ◇ *a direct ~ from this morning's paper* | **anonymous**
VERB + QUOTE **take** ◇ *~s taken from various lifestyle magazines* | **attribute**
QUOTE + VERB **come from sth** ◇ *The ~ of the week comes from Mae West.*
PREP. **~ from** ◇ *a ~ from Albert Einstein*

2 price that will be charged for a piece of work → See QUOTATION

ADJ. **written | free**
VERB + QUOTE **give (sb) | get, obtain** ◇ *Always get a written ~ before proceeding with work.* | **accept**
PREP. **~ for** ◇ *a ~ for the rental of the equipment*

3 quotes punctuation marks showing speech

ADJ. **double, single**
PREP. **in ~s** ◇ *If you take text from other sources, place it in ~s.*

quote *verb*

1 repeat exactly what sb has said/written

ADV. **at length, extensively** ◇ *She ~s extensively from the author's diaries.* | **in full** ◇ *The passage is ~d in full.* | **accurately, exactly | directly | selectively | approvingly, with approval | above, below, earlier, here, previously** ◇ *The new text of Article 92, ~d above, gives member states more discretion on this issue.*
PREP. **as** ◇ *She is wrongly ~d as saying 'Play it again, Sam.'* | **from** ◇ *He ~d from Shakespeare.* ◇ *They ~d from the Bible.*

2 give sth as an example

ADV. **frequently, often**
PREP. **as** ◇ *an example that is often ~d as evidence of mismanagement* | **on** ◇ *Don't ~ me on this but I think the figure is in excess of £2 billion.*
PHRASES **widely ~d** ◇ *the most widely ~d and influential study in this field*

R r

rabbit *noun*

VERB + RABBIT **catch, chase, hunt, shoot** (*esp. BrE*), **trap** (*esp. BrE*) | **skin**
RABBIT + VERB **hop, jump | breed** ◇ *Rabbits breed very fast.*
RABBIT + NOUN **fur, skin | hole, hutch, warren** (*often figurative*) ◇ *The building was a real ~ warren of corridors.*

race *noun*

1 contest to find the fastest person, car, etc.

ADJ. **big** ◇ *I get very nervous before a big ~.* | **close, tight | long-distance | 10-mile, 24-hour, 7-lap, etc. | gruelling/ grueling, hard, tough | relay, road | men's, women's | boat, yacht, etc. | bicycle, bike** (*informal*), **car, motor** (*esp. BrE*), **motorbike** (*BrE*), **motorcycle, etc. | dog, horse, etc. | drag, turf** (*esp. AmE*) | **play-off** (*esp. AmE*)
VERB + RACE **have, hold, organize** ◇ *Let's have a ~!* | **be in, compete in, do** (*informal*), **enter, go in for, run in, take part in** ◇ *Is she running in the big ~ on Saturday?* | **drop out**

of, pull out of, withdraw (sth) from ◇ *He dropped out of the ~ with a pulled muscle after two laps.* ◇ *She had to pull out of the ~ at the last minute.* | **lead, win** ◇ *I was leading the ~ until the half-way point.* ◇ *She has won the ~ for the last five years.* | **lose** | **come first in, come second in, etc.** | **beat sb/sth in** | **fix** ◇ *People are saying that the ~ was fixed.* | **throw** (= to lose deliberately) ◇ *He was paid $10 000 to throw the ~.*

RACE + VERB **be held, be run, take place**

RACE + NOUN **meet** (*esp. AmE*), **meeting** (*BrE*) ◇ *The horse was withdrawn from today's ~ meeting with an injured leg.* | **winner** | **official, organizer**

PREP. **in a/the ~** ◇ *I'm not in this ~.* | **out of a/the ~** | **~ against, ~ with** ◇ *the ~ against the Danish team* | **between** ◇ *A close ~ between the top two boats is expected.* | **~ over** ◇ *a ~ over two miles*

2 competitive situation

ADJ. **close, tight** | **two-horse** ◇ *Although there are five candidates, realistically it is a two-horse ~.* (*figurative*) | **congressional, gubernatorial** (*AmE*), **presidential, Senate** | **arms, space** ◇ *the halting of the nuclear arms ~*

VERB + RACE **be in, be involved in, join** ◇ *The rival TV companies are in a ~ to bring out the first film drama of his life.* | **be ahead in, lead, win** ◇ *Who will win the ~ for the White House?* | **be left behind in, lag behind in, lose**

PREP. **in a/the ~** ◇ *He is lagging behind in the ~ for the presidency.* | **~ between** ◇ *a ~ between the developing countries* | **~ for** ◇ *the ~ for nuclear supremacy* | **~ with** ◇ *the ~ with their rivals*

3 racial group

ADJ. **human** | **alien** | **mixed** ◇ *a child of mixed ~* | **Irish, Jewish, Latin, etc.** | **master** ◇ *the ideology of the master ~*

RACE + NOUN **relations** ◇ *Immigration and ~ relations were key political issues at the time.* | **equality** | **discrimination, preference, prejudice** | **riot**

PREP. **among ~s** ◇ *The disease is more common among European ~s.* | **between ~s** ◇ *greater understanding between nations and ~s* | **from a ~** ◇ *children from all ~s and religions* | **of a ~** ◇ *people of different ~s and cultures* | **regardless of ~** ◇ *We can all work together, regardless of ~.* | **~ of** ◇ *The Amazons were a ~ of female warriors.*

PHRASES **on the basis of ~, on (the) grounds of ~** ◇ *There is no excuse for discrimination on the grounds of ~.*

race verb

ADV. **frantically, madly, wildly** ◇ *She ~d frantically to catch the train.* | **ahead, away, back, by, downstairs, off, out, past, upstairs** ◇ *Farms and towns ~d by.*

PREP. **across, after, along, around, down, for, into, out of, round** (*esp. BrE*), **through, to, towards/toward, up** ◇ *He ~d madly up the stairs.*

PHRASES **come racing** ◇ *Two boys suddenly came racing around the corner.* | **~ against the clock, ~ against time** ◇ *Most of these movies have characters racing against the clock to save the day.*

racing noun

1 sport of racing horses

ADJ. **horse, thoroughbred** | **flat, jump**

RACING + NOUN **results** | **tip** (*esp. BrE*) | **expert, tipster** (*BrE*) ◇ *Her ~ tipster got the Derby winner right.* | **fan** ◇ *Racing fans adore statistics on horses, jockeys, and performance.* | **manager, trainer** (*esp. BrE*) | **career** | **stable** | **calendar, programme/program, season** ◇ *He organizes his life according to the ~ calendar.* | **business, game, industry** ◇ *He has ridden horses all his life, but he was a late starter in the ~ game.* | **circles, scene** ◇ *He's known in ~ circles as a fierce competitor.* ◇ *She's a familiar face on the ~ scene.* | **correspondent** ◇ *the ~ correspondent of 'The Times'*

2 sport of taking part in races

ADJ. **competitive** ◇ *Today's event marks his return to competitive ~.* | **auto** (*AmE*), **car, drag** (*esp. AmE*), **motor,**

NASCAR (*AmE*), **stock-car** (*BrE*) | **dog, greyhound** | **bicycle, bike** (*informal*), **yacht, etc.** | **Grand Prix** | **road, track**

RACING + NOUN **champion** | **legend, star** ◇ *~ legend Ayrton Senna* | **cyclist** (*esp. BrE*), **driver** | **team** | **event** | **programme/program, season** | **scene** | **career, days** | **debut** ◇ *He made his ~ debut for Ferrari three years ago.* | **car** (*BrE*) (**race car** in *AmE*) | **circuit, track** ◇ *The bikes sped by on the ~ circuit.* | **enthusiast, fan**

racism noun

ADJ. **blatant, overt** ◇ *I was shocked by the blatant ~ of his remarks.* | **covert, subtle** | **pervasive, rampant, virulent** (*esp. AmE*) ◇ *Racism is rampant in the armed forces.* | **inherent, institutional, institutionalized, systemic** | **anti-Arab, anti-Black, etc.**

VERB + RACISM **be a victim of, experience** ◇ *Many immigrants have experienced ~.* | **combat, fight, fight against, tackle** (*esp. BrE*) ◇ *measures to combat ~* | **end, eradicate, stamp out** (*esp. BrE*) | **challenge, confront**

PREP. **against ~** ◇ *the fight against ~* | **~ in** ◇ *There is a shocking amount of ~ in society.*

PHRASES **a form of ~**

rack noun

ADJ. **display, storage** | **cooling, drying** | **bicycle, bike** (*informal*), **coat, luggage, magazine, plate, spice, toast, towel, vegetable, wine, etc.** | **roof** ◇ *We mounted the canoe onto the car's roof ~.*

VERB + RACK **hang sth on, put sth on, put sth onto, put sth in, put sth into, stack sth in, stack sth on, store sth in, store sth on** ◇ *The wine is stored in special ~s.*

RACK + VERB **contain sth, hold sth** ◇ *The ~s along the wall held most of the costumes.*

PREP. **in a/the ~** ◇ *He replaced the CD in the ~.* | **on a/the ~** ◇ *Spread the flowers out to dry on a ~.* | **~ for** ◇ *a ~ for storing apples* | **~ of** ◇ *~s of magazines*

racket noun

1 noise

ADJ. **deafening, frightful, infernal** (*esp. BrE*), **terrible** ◇ *Stop that infernal ~!*

VERB + RACKET **make** ◇ *Do you kids have to make such a terrible ~?* | **hear** ◇ *I heard a ~ coming from upstairs.*

PREP. **above the ~, over the ~** ◇ *He had to shout over the ~.*

2 illegal way of making money

ADJ. **extortion, numbers** (*AmE*), **protection, smuggling, etc.** | **illegal** ◇ *The gang operated an illegal immigration ~.*

VERB + RACKET **operate, run** ◇ *He ran a protection ~ which demanded thousands from local businesses.* | **be involved in**

PREP. **in a/the ~** ◇ *the other people in this ~* | **~ in** ◇ *a ~ in stolen goods*

3 (*also* **racquet**) **piece of sports equipment**

ADJ. **badminton, squash, tennis** | **graphite, wooden**

VERB + RACKET **swing** | **smash** ◇ *He smashed his ~ into the clay*

RACKET + NOUN **sports** | **abuse** ◇ *McEnroe received a warning for ~ abuse in the second set.*

radar noun

ADJ. **enemy, police** | **airborne, ground, ground-based** | **long-range**

VERB + RADAR **be equipped with**

RADAR + NOUN **operator** | **station, system** | **antenna, detector, equipment, instrument, receiver, scanner, transmitter** | **screen** | **beam, signal** | **image**

PREP. **by ~** ◇ *navigation by ~* | **on ~** ◇ *The submarine is impossible to detect on ~.*

PHRASES **off the ~, on the ~** ◇ *The aircraft suddenly went off the ~.* ◇ *He's barely on the ~ of most movie-goers.* (*figurative*)

radiation noun

ADJ. **background** | **low-level** | **damaging, harmful** | **electromagnetic, gravitational, microwave, nuclear, thermal** | **gamma, infrared, ultraviolet** (abbreviated to *UV*) | **UVA, UVB** | **cosmic, solar** ◇ *fluctuations in the cosmic microwave background ~*

rage

...OF RADIATION **dose** ◇ *Patients receive high doses of ~ during cancer treatment.*
VERB + RADIATION **emit, give off** | **absorb** ◇ *The ozone layer absorbs solar ~.* | **block, protect from, reflect** ◇ *Ozone protects the Earth from harmful ultraviolet ~.* | **detect, measure, monitor** | **expose sb to** ◇ *Nuclear testing has exposed millions of people to ~.*
RADIATION + VERB **leak, leak out** ◇ *~ leaking from nuclear power stations*
RADIATION + NOUN **sickness** | **dose, level** | **leak, leakage** (*esp. AmE*) ◇ *the threat of ~ leaks* | **exposure** | **source** | **detector** | **therapy, treatment**
PREP. **~ from** ◇ *~ from computer screens*
PHRASES **levels of ~** ◇ *The counter showed high levels of ~.*

radiator noun

1 equipment used for heating a room
VERB + RADIATOR **turn off, turn on** | **bleed** ◇ *You'll need to bleed the ~s to remove the airlocks.*
RADIATOR + VERB **leak**
RADIATOR + NOUN **key** (*esp. BrE*), **valve**

2 equipment for keeping an engine cool
ADJ. **car**
VERB + RADIATOR **fill, fill up** ◇ *He filled his car ~ with water.*
RADIATOR + NOUN **cap, grille, hose**

radical adj.

VERBS **be, seem, sound** | **become**
ADV. **extremely, fairly, very, etc.** | **increasingly** | **equally** | **insufficiently** | **genuinely, truly** ◇ *a truly ~ concept* | **potentially** | **politically, socially** ◇ *When I was young, I was more politically ~.*

radio noun

ADJ. **car** ◇ *He was singing along with the car ~.* | **CB, hand-held, portable, transistor, two-way** | **clock** ◇ *According to my clock ~ it was 3.30 in the morning.* | **FM, long-wave, short-wave** | **digital, Internet, satellite, terrestrial** (*esp. AmE*) | **army, police** | **community, local, national, state** | **commercial, public** (*esp. AmE*) | **pirate** | **drive-time, talk**
VERB + RADIO **listen to, tune in to** | **tune** ◇ *His ~ is permanently tuned to Radio 1.* | **switch on, turn on** | **switch off, turn off** | **turn down, turn up**
RADIO + VERB **announce sth, report sth** ◇ *The ~ announced that the president had been assassinated.* | **play (sth)** | **blare, blare out, blast, blast out** ◇ *He drove along with his windows open and the ~ blaring.* | **crackle**
RADIO + NOUN **alarm** | **receiver, set** | **dial** | **signal, waves** | **communication, contact, message** | **operator** | **system** | **antenna, transmitter** | **silence** ◇ *The troops maintained a strict ~ silence while they moved into position.* | **static** ◇ *A crackle of ~ static came back through the earpiece.* | **broadcaster, network, station** ◇ *the largest ~ broadcaster in the US* | **broadcast, programme/program, show, spot** (*esp. AmE*), **transmission** | **ad, advertisement, interview, news, report, talk show** (*esp. AmE*) | **announcer, DJ, host** (*esp. AmE*), **personality, reporter** | **listener** | **airplay** ◇ *The song is currently getting heavy ~ airplay.* | **frequency** | **amateur, ham** ◇ *The distress call was picked up by a young ~ ham.* | **chatter** ◇ *It was fascinating to listen to the ~ chatter from the ships.* | **drama, play** | **astronomy, telescope**
PREP. **by ~** ◇ *The message was sent by ~.* | **on the ~** ◇ *We were listening to a show on the ~.*

radioactive adj.

VERBS **be** | **become** | **remain**
ADV. **dangerously, highly** | **slightly**

radioactivity noun

...OF RADIOACTIVITY **level** ◇ *The soil contains 30 times the acceptable level of ~.*
VERB + RADIOACTIVITY **produce, release** ◇ *the amount of ~ released by nuclear power plants* | **detect, determine, measure, monitor**
RADIOACTIVITY + NOUN **levels**

raffle noun

ADJ. **charity**
VERB + RAFFLE **have, hold, organize, run** (*esp. BrE*) ◇ *The office is holding a ~ to raise money for the local hospital.* | **enter, enter sb/sth in, enter sb/sth into** ◇ *You can enter the ~ and win some amazing prizes.* ◇ *Workers were entered into a ~ every time they bought a cup of coffee.* | **win** | **draw** (*esp. BrE*) ◇ *The club secretary will now draw the ~.*
RAFFLE + NOUN **ticket** ◇ *the winning ~ ticket* | **prize**
PREP. **in a/the ~** ◇ *I won a bottle of wine in the office Christmas ~.* | **~ for** ◇ *He's organizing a ~ for the school appeal fund.*

raft noun

ADJ. **life** | **inflatable, rubber** | **makeshift**
VERB + RAFT **build, make** ◇ *They built a ~ of logs.* | **inflate** ◇ *The two airmen inflated the life ~.* | **paddle** ◇ *We paddled the ~ to the shore.*
RAFT + VERB **float** ◇ *The ~ floated away down the river.* | **capsize, overturn**
RAFT + NOUN **race** (*esp. BrE*)
PREP. **on a/the ~, onto a/the ~** ◇ *He was found floating on a ~.*

rag noun

ADJ. **clean** | **dirty, filthy, oily, old, tattered** | **bloodstained, bloody** | **damp, wet** (*both esp. AmE*) ◇ *Wipe the board with a damp ~.* | **cleaning, dish** (usually **dishrag**), **wash** (usually **washrag**) (*all AmE*) ◇ *She grabbed a washrag and wiped the floor.*
...OF RAGS **bundle, heap, pile** ◇ *He noticed what looked like a bundle of ~s beside the road.*
VERB + RAG **be dressed in, wear** ◇ *I saw people dressed in ~s begging on the street.* | **be wrapped in** ◇ *The gun was wrapped in a dirty ~.*
PREP. **on a/the ~** ◇ *He wiped his hands on an oily ~.* | **with a ~** ◇ *I cleaned the board with an old ~.* ◇ *You can wipe the stains off with a ~.* (*esp. AmE*)

rage noun

1 great anger
ADJ. **blind, pure** | **blinding, boiling, burning, seething, uncontrollable** | **homicidal** (*esp. AmE*), **murderous** | **helpless, impotent** ◇ *She was burning with impotent ~.* | **pent-up, suppressed**
...OF RAGE **bout, burst, fit** ◇ *He punched the wall in a fit of ~.*
VERB + RAGE **be full of, feel, fill sb with** ◇ *He was filled with ~.* | **be beside yourself with, be boiling with, burn with, explode with, fume with, seethe with** ◇ *He glared at me, quite beside himself with ~.* ◇ *Her eyes were burning with ~.* ◇ *I was seething with ~.* | **be contorted with, contort with** ◇ *'How dare you!' she said, her face contorted with ~.* | **shake with, tremble with** ◇ *He was literally shaking with ~.* ◇ *Her voice was trembling with ~.* | **be red with, be white with** ◇ *express, unleash, vent* ◇ *The people vented their ~ on government buildings.* | **fuel** ◇ *His answer only seemed to fuel her ~.* | **channel, control, master** ◇ *He managed to master his ~.*
RAGE + VERB **boil, boil over, boil up, burn** ◇ *Ron felt ~ boil up inside him.* ◇ *Her ~ boiled over as she burst into tears.* | **build up, grow** ◇ *She felt the ~ building up inside her.* | **consume sb, fill sb** ◇ *Blind ~ consumed him.* | **erupt** ◇ *His ~ suddenly erupted.* | **subside** ◇ *His ~ was beginning to subside.*
PREP. **with ~** ◇ *She was speechless with ~.* | **at** ◇ *He was boiling with ~ at the unfairness of it all.*
PHRASES **a bellow of ~, a cry of ~, a roar of ~, a scream of ~** ◇ *He gave a roar of ~ and punched me in the face.* | **tears of ~**

2 sudden display of great anger
ADJ. **blind, terrible, towering** | **violent** ◇ *He was prone to violent ~s.* | **jealous** | **drunken** ◇ *She started hitting him in a*

drunken ~. | **air, road,** etc. ◇ *A motorist was assaulted in a road ~ attack.*

VERB + RAGE **be in, fly into, get in** ◇ *If something's too difficult she gets in a ~.*

PREP. **in a ~** ◇ *She killed him in a ~ of despair.* | **~ about** ◇ *He was in a towering ~ about his lost watch.* | **~ at** ◇ *He flew into a ~ at the insult.* | **~ of** ◇ *He left in a ~ of humiliation.*

rage verb

1 show great anger

ADV. **inwardly**

PREP. **about** ◇ *She was still raging about the treatment she had received.* | **against** ◇ *I ~d inwardly against his injustice.* | **at** ◇ *The team was left raging at the referee's decision.*

2 continue with great force

ADV. **on, still** ◇ *The argument still ~s on.*

PREP. **around** ◇ *Even the dogs were quiet while the heated quarrel ~d around them.* | **through** ◇ *Fire ~d through the forest.* | **within** ◇ *She tried to control the fury raging within her.*

PHRASES **~ unabated** ◇ *The storm ~d unabated.*

raid noun

1 surprise attack

ADJ. **daring** | **major** | **punitive, retaliatory** | **dawn, daylight, night, predawn** | **hit-and-run, surprise** ◇ *Guerrillas were carrying out hit-and-run ~s on the troops.* | **cross-border** | **air, bombing** | **commando, guerrilla**

VERB + RAID **carry out, conduct, make** ◇ *bombers carrying out daylight ~s over the city* | **launch, mount, stage** | **lead sb in**

PREP. **during a/the ~, in a/the ~** ◇ *Five civilians died in the ~.* | **on a/the ~** ◇ *He led his men on a cross-border ~.* | **~ against** ◇ *The ~s against military targets continued.* | **~ by** ◇ *The town suffered several ~s by Vikings.* | **~ on** ◇ *air ~s on Liverpool*

2 surprise visit by the police

ADJ. **dawn, early-morning, predawn** | **police** | **drug** (*esp. AmE*), **drugs** (*BrE*) | **armed**

VERB + RAID **carry out, launch, stage** ◇ *Police staged an early-morning ~ on the building.*

PREP. **during a/the ~** ◇ *He was injured during a police ~ on his nightclub.* | **in a/the ~** ◇ *the drugs seized in last night's ~* | **~ by** ◇ *a ~ by drugs squad detectives* | **~ on** ◇ *~s on houses in the south of the city*

3 robbery from a building

ADJ. **bank** (*esp. BrE*), **post office** (*BrE*), **shop** (*BrE*) | **armed** (*esp. BrE*), **smash-and-grab** (*BrE*)

VERB + RAID **plan** | **carry out, foil** (*BrE*) ◇ *Two customers foiled a ~ on a local post office.*

PREP. **during a/the ~, in a/the ~** ◇ *the jewels stolen in the ~* | **~ on** ◇ *She was shot during an armed ~ on a security van.*

rail noun

1 bar

ADJ. **guard, safety** | **curtain, picture, towel** (*all esp. BrE*) | *heated towel ~s* | **altar, balcony, banister, porch** (*esp. AmE*), **stair** | **bottom, top** ◇ *She climbed onto the top fence ~.* | **steel, wooden,** etc.

VERB + RAIL **grab, grasp, grip, hold on to, lean on** ◇ *She held tightly on to the ~.* | **hang from** ◇ *Lace curtains hung from the brass ~s over the bed.* | **fit, fix**

PREP. **on a/the ~** ◇ *She sat on the ~.* | **over a/the ~** ◇ *He folded the towel over the ~.*

2 (usually rails) tracks

VERB + RAIL **run along ~s, run on ~s** ◇ *Trams run along ~s.*

PREP. **along (the) ~s** ◇ *The train thundered along the ~s.* | **between the ~** ◇ *Weeds grew between the ~s.* | **on (the) ~s** ◇ *The gun is mounted on ~s.*

PHRASES **come off the ~s, go off the ~s** ◇ *The train came off the ~s.* ◇ *She was worried her son was going to go completely*

off the ~s. (*figurative*) | **ride the ~s** (= travel around by train) (*AmE*)

3 system of trains

ADJ. **high-speed, light** ◇ *Many business people now opt for high-speed ~ rather than flying.* | **commuter, freight, passenger** (*all esp. AmE*) ◇ *He uses a combination of commuter ~ and subway to get to work.*

RAIL + NOUN **fare, ticket** (*both esp. BrE*) | **network, system** ◇ *efforts to modernize the ~ network* | **route** | **timetable** (*esp. BrE*) | **service** | **connection, link** ◇ *the Channel Tunnel ~ link* | **line, track** | **journey** (*esp. BrE*), **trip** | **station, terminal** | **car** (*esp. AmE*) | **commuter, passenger, traveller/traveler, user** (*all esp. BrE*) | **transit** (*AmE*), **transport** (*esp. BrE*), **transportation** (*esp. AmE*), **travel** | **traffic** | **freight** | **bridge** | **accident, crash, disaster** (*all esp. BrE*) | **staff** (*BrE*), **worker** | **union** (*BrE*) | **enthusiast** (*BrE*)

PREP. **by ~** ◇ *We went from Paris to Budapest by ~.*

railway (BrE) (AmE railroad) noun

ADJ. **mainline** (*esp. BrE*) | **high-speed** | **disused** (*BrE*) | **narrow-gauge, standard-gauge** | **miniature** (*BrE*), **model** ◇ *He created a model ~ in his basement.* | **funicular** (*esp. BrE*) ◇ *Tourists can take the funicular ~ to the top of the mountain.* | **commuter, passenger, tourist** | **freight** (*esp. AmE*) | **private, regional, state** | **short-line** (*AmE*), **transcontinental** | **electric, steam**

VERB + RAILWAY/RAILROAD **manage, operate, run** | **nationalize, privatize** (*both BrE*) | **build, construct** | **close, open** | **regulate**

RAILWAY/RAILROAD + VERB **run** | **carry sth** ◇ *The ~s carry millions of tons of freight every year.*

RAILWAY/RAILROAD + NOUN **car** (*AmE*), **carriage** (*BrE*), **coach** (*esp. BrE*), **train, wagon** (*BrE*) | **depot, station, terminus** (*esp. BrE*), **yard** | **platform** (*esp. BrE*) | **ticket** (*esp. BrE*) | **timetable** (*esp. BrE*) | **service** (*esp. BrE*) | **connection** | **journey, travel** (*both esp. BrE*) ◇ *the pleasures of ~ travel* | **passenger, traveller** (*BrE*) | **employee, porter, staff** (*BrE*), **worker** | **architect, engineer** | **authorities** (*BrE*), **company** | **network, system** | **line** (*esp. BrE*), **track** | **junction, sidings** | **bridge, crossing, tunnel, viaduct** (*esp. BrE*) | **enthusiast** (*esp. BrE*) ◇ *He is a lifelong ~ enthusiast.* | **accident** | **age** (*esp. BrE*) ◇ *Such speed was unimaginable before the ~ age.*

PREP. **on a/the ~** ◇ *They are doing maintenance work on the ~.* ◇ *He works on the ~s.* | **between** ◇ *the ~ between Funchal and Monte* | **from, ~ to**

rain noun

ADJ. **driving, hard, lashing** (*esp. BrE*), **pelting, pounding** (*esp. AmE*) | **drenching, heavy, pouring, torrential** | **steady** | **drizzling, fine, gentle, light, soft** ◇ *The fine ~ turned to mist in the early evening.* ◇ *The forecast is for wind and light ~.* | **warm** | **cold, freezing, icy** | **constant, continuous, incessant, persistent** | **intermittent, patchy** (*BrE*) | **overnight** ◇ *Overnight ~ had freshened up the grass.* | **monsoon, tropical** ◇ *The monsoon ~s started early this year.* | **spring, summer,** etc. | **acid**

... OF RAIN **drop** | **inch, shower, spot** (*esp. BrE, informal*) ◇ *We had three inches of ~ last night.* ◇ *A few spots of ~ had fallen.* ◇ *We could do with a spot of ~.* (*BrE*)

VERB + RAIN **forecast** ◇ *Rain is forecast for tomorrow.* | **look like, threaten** ◇ *It looks like ~* (= it looks as though it is going to rain). ◇ *Black clouds threatened ~.* | **pour (down)** (*AmE*), **pour (down) with** (*BrE*) ◇ *It poured with ~ all afternoon.* | **get caught in** ◇ *We got caught in the ~ on the way home.*

RAIN + VERB **come down, fall, pour down, trickle** | **beat, drum, lash, pelt, pound** (*esp. AmE*) ◇ *Rain beat against the roof all night.* ◇ *The ~ pounded down on her.* | **drip, patter, splash** ◇ *She listened to the ~ pattering against the window.* | **drench sb/sth, soak sb/sth** ◇ *Heavy ~ drenched us.* | **come, set in, start** ◇ *The ~ came just as we set off.* ◇ *The ~ had set in steadily by the time we got home.* | **cease, let up, stop** ◇ *The ~ didn't let up all day.* | **continue** ◇ *The ~ continued for most of the day.* | **threaten** ◇ *With ~ threatening, we headed home as fast as we could.* | **drive sb** ◇ *The ~ drove the players off the court.*

RAIN + NOUN **cloud** | **drop** (usually **raindrop**), **water** (usually **rainwater**) | **shower, storm** (usually **rainstorm**) | **barrel,**

gutter (both AmE) | **gear** (esp. AmE) ◇ None of us had proper ~ gear. | **gauge**
PREP. **in the ~** ◇ We found her sitting in the pouring ~. | **out of the ~** ◇ Come in out of the ~. | **through the ~** ◇ We drove slowly through the driving ~.
PHRASES **come ~ or shine, ~ or shine** (figurative) ◇ We work outside every day, ~ or shine.

rain verb

ADV. **hard, heavily | a little, lightly, slightly | non-stop, solidly** (esp. BrE), **steadily** ◇ It had ~ed solidly for four days. ◇ It's been ~ing steadily all day.
VERB + RAIN **begin to, start to | be going to** ◇ I don't think it's going to ~.
PHRASES **start ~ing, stop ~ing**

rainfall noun

ADJ. **abundant, excessive, heavy, high** ◇ There have been heavy ~s this month. | **low | moderate | normal | annual | average | local | seasonal | summer, winter**
VERB + RAINFALL **have, receive** ◇ The area has a high annual ~. | **measure** ◇ Her work includes measuring the local ~.

rally noun

1 political meeting

ADJ. **big, huge, large, major, mass, massive | public | indoor, outdoor** ◇ a massive outdoor ~ in Buenos Aires | **pep** (AmE) ◇ a pep ~ before the homecoming game | **campaign** (esp. AmE), **election** (esp. BrE), **political | opposition, protest | peace | anti-government, anti-war,** etc. | **pro-government, pro-war,** etc.
VERB + RALLY **have, hold, stage** ◇ The demonstrators marched to Trafalgar Square where they held a ~. | **call for, organize, plan | attend, take part in** ◇ About 5 000 people attended a ~ calling for peace. | **address, speak at | ban** ◇ The government banned all rallies.
RALLY + VERB **take place | end | call for sth** ◇ a ~ calling for a boycott of the January elections
PREP. **at a/the ~** ◇ She spoke at a public ~ in Hyde Park. | **~ against** ◇ a mass ~ against the treaty | **~ for** ◇ a ~ for the winning candidate | **~ in support of** ◇ a ~ in support of the strike

2 recovery

ADJ. **bear-market, market, stock-market** (all business) ◇ The US dollar is now ending its bear-market ~. | **dollar, euro,** etc. | **recent | late** ◇ The visiting team staged a late ~.
VERB + RALLY **mount, stage**
PREP. **~ in** ◇ the recent ~ in the Treasury market

3 in tennis

ADJ. **long, short**
VERB + RALLY **play | win | lose**

4 (BrE) **motor race**

ADJ. **club, international | motor, motorcycle**
VERB + RALLY **hold, organize | compete in, enter | win**
RALLY + NOUN **circuit | driver, driving**
PREP. **on a/the ~** ◇ He will join the team on the ~ next week.

rally verb

ADV. **around, round** (esp. BrE) ◇ Everyone rallied around and offered to help.
VERB + RALLY **try to** ◇ The team captain vainly tried to ~ his troops.
PREP. **around, behind, round** (esp. BrE) ◇ She urged everyone to ~ behind the President. | **to** ◇ Friends rallied to her.
PHRASES **~ around the flag** ◇ We were at war and everyone was ~ing around the flag. | **~ to sb's defence/defense** ◇ BBC leaders rallied to his defence. | **~ to sb's/the cause** ◇ Friends and colleagues have rallied to her cause.

ram verb

ADV. **hard | deliberately**
PREP. **into** ◇ He deliberately rammed his truck into the back of the one in front.

PHRASES **~ sth down sb's throat** (figurative) ◇ People are sick of having advertising rammed down their throats.

random adj.

VERBS **be, seem**
ADV. **completely, entirely, purely, quite, totally | almost | fairly, pretty, somewhat | truly | essentially | apparently, seemingly** ◇ a seemingly ~ sequence of numbers

range noun

1 different things within the same category

ADJ. **broad, enormous, extensive, great, huge, large, vast, wide | complete, comprehensive, entire, full, whole | infinite | excellent, exciting, good, superb** (esp. BrE) ◇ You can enjoy an excellent ~ of leisure and sporting facilities. | **astonishing, extraordinary, impressive, remarkable | diverse** ◇ people from a diverse ~ of backgrounds | **acceptable | limited, restricted | new** ◇ Come and see our new ~ of furniture. | **product** ◇ For more information about our product ~, call your local office.
VERB + RANGE **have, stock** ◇ They stock a very wide ~ of gardening tools. | **make, produce | offer (sb), provide (sb with), supply (sb with)** ◇ We provide a full ~ of financial services. | **choose (sth) from, try out** ◇ Students can choose from a wide ~ of options. | **display, exhibit | reflect, represent** ◇ The artists have been chosen to represent a ~ of styles. | **create, develop, launch** ◇ The company is launching a new ~ of cosmetics. | **broaden, expand, extend**
RANGE + VERB **include sth** ◇ Our comprehensive ~ of benefits includes pension and health insurance.
PREP. **in a/the ~** ◇ the other models in their new ~
PHRASES **the bottom of the ~, the middle of the ~, the top of the ~** ◇ This is a top-of-the-range refrigerator.

2 amount between particular limits

ADJ. **broad, wide | narrow | normal | ability, age, price, size, temperature,** etc.
VERB + RANGE **cover, encompass, feature, include, span** ◇ The books cover the full ~ of reading abilities. | **show** ◇ The experiments show a surprisingly wide ~ of results. | **extend, increase** ◇ These books are designed to extend the ~ of children's language. | **limit, restrict** ◇ Many factors limit women's ~ of job choices.
PREP. **across a/the ~** ◇ There is considerable variation in ability across the ~. | **in a/the ~** ◇ Most of the students are in the 17–21 age ~. | **outside a/the ~** ◇ No, that's completely outside my price ~. | **within a/the ~** ◇ The level of mistakes is within the acceptable ~ of standards for a public organization. | **~ of** ◇ a broad ~ of abilities

3 distance that it is possible to travel, see, etc.

ADJ. **long** ◇ The missiles are effective over a long ~. | **close, point-blank, short** ◇ He shot her at point-blank ~. | **medium** ◇ a gun for precision shooting at medium ~ | **maximum** ◇ The receiver has a maximum ~ of about 30 feet. | **hearing, visual** (both esp. AmE) ◇ I listened, but the voices were just out of hearing ~.
PREP. **beyond ~** ◇ This car is beyond the ~ of most people's pockets. | **in ~, within ~** ◇ Are we within ~ of the local transmitter? | **out of ~** ◇ Don't shoot yet—he's still out of ~. | **outside a/the ~** ◇ It's outside my ~ of vision.

4 area of land for a particular purpose

ADJ. **archery, bombing, firing, shooting** ◇ shooting ~s where competitors shoot at targets | **driving, practice** (both in golf) ◇ an 18-bay floodlit driving ~
PREP. **on a/the ~** ◇ He hit balls on the practice ~ yesterday.

5 (AmE) **piece of equipment for cooking food** → See also COOKER, STOVE

ADJ. **electric, gas | cooking, kitchen**
PREP. **on a/the ~** ◇ Many chefs prefer to cook on a gas rather than an electric ~.

range verb

ADV. **enormously, widely**
PREP. **across** ◇ *The opinions they expressed ~d right across the political spectrum.* | **between** ◇ *The town's population ~d between 15 and 20 000.* | **from** ◇ *Her scores ~d from 23% up as high as 88%.* | **in** ◇ *The disease ~s widely in severity.* | **over** ◇ *Her lecture ~d over a number of topics.* | **through** ◇ *an array of lilies, ranging through yellow to purple* | **to** ◇ *prices ranging from about $10 to $500* | **up to** ◇ *Their ages ~ up to 84.*

> **NOTE**
>
> **Ranks in the armed forces**
>
> an air force…, an army…, a navy… ◇ *an air force/an army sergeant* ◇ *an army/a navy captain*
>
> air marshal, field marshal *(both in the UK)*
>
> a naval captain/commander/lieutenant/officer ◇ *a handsome young naval officer*
>
> have/hold the rank of…, serve as… ◇ *She joined the navy and held the rank of captain.* ◇ *He served as a lieutenant in the Marine Corps.*
>
> be appointed…, become…, be made… ◇ *He became a colonel at the age of 40.* ◇ *She ought to have been made sergeant by now.*
>
> under… ◇ *383 men under General Miles attacked the camp.*
>
> the rank of… ◇ *She was promoted to the rank of colonel.*

rank noun

1 level of importance

ADJ. **high, senior, superior, top, upper** | **middle** | **inferior, junior, low** ◇ *the lowest ~s of the army* | **first, second** ◇ *He is in the first ~ of designers.* | **social** | **Cabinet, ministerial** *(BrE)* ◇ *a politician of Cabinet ~*
VERB + RANK **achieve, attain, be promoted to, get to, reach, rise to** ◇ *She joined the navy, where she rose to the ~ of captain.* | **have, hold** ◇ *He held officer ~ in the air force for many years.* | **assign sb, award sb** ◇ *He was assigned the ~ of Commander.* | **be stripped of** ◇ *He was stripped of his ~ by a military court.*
PREP. **above a/the ~** ◇ *He never rose above the ~ of lieutenant.* | **below a/the ~** ◇ *police officers below the ~ of sergeant* | **in ~** ◇ *He is higher in ~ than I am.* | **~ in** ◇ *all ~s in society* | **~ of** ◇ *She reached the ~ of captain.*
PHRASES **of high, low, etc. ~** ◇ *officers of senior ~*

2 group of things/people

ADJ. **front, rear** ◇ *a poet who belongs in the front ~ of Latin American literature (figurative)* | **massed, serried** *(both esp. BrE)* ◇ *the serried ~s of hotel staff*
PREP. **along a/the ~** ◇ *The president moved slowly along the ~s of men.* | **in a/the ~** ◇ *He was standing in the second ~.* ◇ *The soldiers marched in three ~s of ten.*
PHRASES **break ~s** (= to leave a line of soldiers, police, etc.) ◇ *The police broke ~s and started hitting people with their batons.* ◇ *He broke ~s with his fellow Republicans and opposed the war. (figurative)* | **close ~s** *(figurative)* ◇ *When the establishment is attacked, it closes ~s.* (= unites to protect itself) | **~ upon ~ (of sth)** ◇ *Rank upon ~ of caravans filled the field.*

3 ranks members of a large group

ADJ. **growing, swelling** ◇ *These products appeal to the growing ~s of middle-class consumers.* | **amateur, pro** *(AmE)*, **professional** *(all sports)* ◇ *He spent two years on the college golf team before joining the professional ~s.*
VERB + RANKS **enter, fill, join, swell** ◇ *More women are now filling the ~s of the medical profession.* ◇ *Each month thousands more swell the ~s of the unemployed.* | **be admitted into, be admitted to** | **infiltrate** ◇ *A CIA operative had infiltrated their ~s.* | **deplete, thin** ◇ *Death and disease*

were thinning their ~s. | **serve in** ◇ *They had served in the ~s of the army.* | **climb, come up from, come up through, rise from, rise through** ◇ *He came up through the ~s to become a general.*
PREP. **among the ~s of, within the ~s of** ◇ *There is much disaffection among the ~s of the party.* | **beyond the ~s, outside the ~s** ◇ *The group has little influence over those outside its own ~s.* | **in the ~s** ◇ *There are few women in the highest ~s of the organization.*
PHRASES **the ~ and file** ◇ *Communication worked well at management level, but didn't always make it down to the ~ and file.*

rank verb

ADV. **high, highly, low** ◇ *These subjects ~ed low for most students.* ◇ *high-ranking officials*
PREP. **above** ◇ *She ~s above any other musician of her generation.* | **ahead of** ◇ *The dandelion ~s ahead of both broccoli and spinach in nutritional value.* | **alongside** ◇ *This city ~s alongside London as one of the great tourist attractions of the world.* | **among** ◇ *He ~s among the greatest boxers of all time.* | **as** ◇ *Their performance ~s as the best of the year.* | **below** | **with** ◇ *This ~s with the great paintings of the 19th century.* | **according to, by** ◇ *The children were ~ed according to academic ability.*
PHRASES **be nationally ~ed** *(AmE)* ◇ *We beat a nationally ~ed team.* | **be ~ed number two, three, etc., ~ number two, three, etc., ~ second, third, etc.** ◇ *the tennis player ~ed number two in the world* ◇ *The company ~s second among food manufacturers.* | **~ sth in order of sth** ◇ *~ed in order of size* | **~ in the top 10, 100, etc.** ◇ *She is now ~ed in the top five hockey players in Britain.*

ransom noun

VERB + RANSOM **hold sb for, hold sb to, kidnap sb for** ◇ *She was kidnapped and held for ~.* ◇ *The company refused to be held to ~ by the union. (figurative)* | **demand** | **pay**
RANSOM + NOUN **demand, note** | **money, payment**
PREP. **for ~** ◇ *They stole cattle for ~.*

rap verb

ADV. **loudly, sharply** ◇ *He rapped sharply on the door.* | **gently, lightly**
PREP. **on, with** ◇ *He rapped on the window with his stick.*

rape noun

ADJ. **alleged** | **attempted** | **marital, spousal** *(esp. AmE)* | **acquaintance** *(esp. AmE)*, **date, gang** | **brutal, forcible, violent** | **statutory** *(AmE)*
RAPE + NOUN **victim** | **suspect** | **accusation, allegation, charge** | **case, trial** | **scene** ◇ *a ~ scene from the movie*
→ Note at CRIME (for verbs)

rape verb

ADV. **brutally, viciously, violently** ◇ *She was attacked and brutally ~d.* | **repeatedly** | **allegedly** | **at gunpoint, at knifepoint** ◇ *She was viciously ~d at knifepoint.*
VERB + RAPE **attempt to, try to**
PHRASES **be ~d, get ~d** ◇ *She was worried about getting ~d on her way home.* | **be accused of raping sb, be charged with raping sb** | **be convicted of raping sb, be found guilty of raping sb** | **deny raping sb**

rapid adj.

VERBS **be, seem** | **become**
ADV. **extremely, fairly, very, etc.** | **extraordinarily, unusually** | **relatively** | **increasingly**

rapidity noun

ADJ. **alarming, amazing, astonishing, bewildering, great, remarkable** ◇ *The styles change with bewildering ~.* | **increasing**
PREP. **with ~**

rapist noun

ADJ. **potential, would-be** | **accused, alleged** | **convicted** | **serial** ◇ *The serial ~ has struck again.*
RAPIST + VERB **attack (sb), strike**

rapport noun

ADJ. **close, easy, friendly, good, great** | **personal** | **immediate, instant**
VERB + RAPPORT **build, create, develop, establish** | **enjoy, have** | **feel**
PREP. **~ between** ◇ *She felt an instant ~ between them* | **~ with** ◇ *He had enjoyed a personal ~ with the former president.*

rare adj.

VERBS **be, seem** | **become, get** | **remain** | **be considered** ◇ *19 species of the bird are considered ~.*
ADV. **extremely, fairly, very, etc.** | **especially, exceedingly, exceptionally, extraordinarily, incredibly, particularly, surprisingly** | **increasingly** | **comparatively, relatively** | **enough, sufficiently** ◇ *The stamps were not ~ enough to be interesting.*

rash noun

ADJ. **skin** | **itchy** | **red, scaly** | **allergic** | **diaper** (*AmE*), **nappy** (*BrE*) | **heat** | **poison ivy** (*esp. AmE*) | **nettle** (usually **nettlerash**) (*BrE*)
VERB + RASH **have** | **break out in, come out in, develop, get** ◇ *When I'm stressed I break out in a ~.* | **cause** ◇ *Some pesticides can cause ~es and burns.*
RASH + VERB **appear, come out, develop, spread** ◇ *The ~ most commonly appears on the back.*
PREP. **~ on** ◇ *He has a slight ~ on his chest.*

raspberry noun

... OF RASPBERRIES **pint** (*AmE*), **punnet** (*BrE*) ◇ *I bought a punnet/pint of fresh raspberries.*
RASPBERRY + NOUN **cane** ◇ *rows of ~ canes*
→ Special page at FRUIT

rat noun

ADJ. **black, brown** | **lab** (*informal*), **laboratory** | **sewer** | **water**
RAT + VERB **scurry, scuttle** ◇ *A brown ~ scurried across the road.* | **gnaw** ◇ *Rats had gnawed through the wires.* | **carry disease, spread disease**
RAT + NOUN **catcher** ◇ *The dog was a useful ~ catcher in the warehouse.* | **droppings** | **poison**

rate noun

1 speed/frequency

ADJ. **constant, expected, regular, steady, unchanged** | **slow** ◇ *the slow ~ of change* | **fast, rapid** | **alarming, phenomenal** ◇ *The costs of the project are rising at an alarming ~.* | **low** ◇ *There is a low survival ~ among babies born for 22 weeks.* | **elevated, high, increased** | **ever-increasing, rising** ◇ *anxiety over rising divorce ~s* | **success** | **divorce, marriage** | **death, fatality, mortality** | **recovery, survival** | **relapse** | **birth, fertility** | **accident** | **crime, murder, recidivism** (*technical, esp. AmE*), **suicide** | **jobless, unemployment** | **attrition** (*esp. AmE*), **dropout** (*esp. AmE*), **turnover** ◇ *Medical students had a high dropout ~.* | **graduation** (*AmE*) ◇ *Michigan's high-school graduation ~* | **growth, inflation** | **heart, metabolic, pulse, respiratory** ◇ *We need to eat less as we get older and our metabolic ~ slows down.*
VERB + RATE **accelerate, improve, increase, speed up** | **double** ◇ *The US has doubled its ~ of recycling in ten years.* | **cut, decrease, hold down, lower, reduce, slow down** ◇ *Educating girls has the effect of lowering birth ~s.* | **stabilize** | **maintain** | **calculate, determine, estimate, measure** ◇ *how to calculate your resting metabolic ~*
RATE + VERB **be up, go up, shoot up** | **grow, increase, jump, rise, rocket, skyrocket, soar** | **be down, come down, go**

rating noun

down | decline, decrease, drop, fall, plummet, plunge, slip, slow
PREP. **at a/the ~** ◇ *The water was escaping at a ~ of 200 gallons a minute.* | **~ of** ◇ *the ~ of salmonella infections* | **~ per** ◇ *the accident ~ per 10 000 flight hours*

2 amount of money paid

ADJ. **cheap, competitive, low, moderate, reasonable** ◇ *We have a wide range of vehicles available for hire at competitive ~s.* ◇ *Calls are cheap ~ after 6 p.m.* (*BrE*) | **extortionate** (*esp. BrE*), **high** ◇ *credit companies that charge extortionate ~s of interest* | **rising** ◇ *Borrowers want protection against rising interest ~s.* | **excellent, good** | **poor** ◇ *The account offers a poor ~ of interest.* | **fixed, flat** ◇ *You can opt to pay a flat ~ for unlimited Internet access.* | **usual** | **going** ◇ *I'll pay you at the going ~* (= the present usual rate of payment). | **variable** | **annual, hourly, weekly** | **base, basic, standard** | **top** ◇ *I pay the top ~ of tax.* | **average** | **market** ◇ *current market ~s for borrowing* | **group, preferential** (*esp. BrE*) ◇ *Ask about the special group ~s for entrance to the museum.* | **discounted, reduced** | **bank, exchange, interest, lending, mortgage, tax**
VERB + RATE **determine, fix, peg, set** ◇ *Global banks have pegged interest ~s at 1%.* | **hike, increase, lift, put up, raise** | **exceed** ◇ *The deficit has recently exceeded the peak ~s of the 1980s.* | **cut, halve, lower, reduce, slash** | **hold** ◇ *We will hold these ~s until April.* | **charge** ◇ *They charge the usual ~ of interest.* | **pay** | **give (sb), offer (sb)**
RATE + VERB **climb, go up, increase, jump, jump up, rise, shoot up** ◇ *Their hourly ~s have gone up.* ◇ *Mortgage ~s jumped to 15%.* | **come down, decline, dip, drop, fall, go down** | **differ, fluctuate, vary** ◇ *Exchange ~s are fluctuating wildly.* | **apply to sth** ◇ *Standard ~s of interest apply to these loans.*
PREP. **at a/the ~** ◇ *money borrowed at a high ~ of interest* | **~ for** ◇ *the average ~ for an unskilled worker* | **~ of** ◇ *an increase in the ~ of taxation*
PHRASES **a drop in ~s, a rise in ~s** ◇ *a one-point rise in base lending ~s* | **a ~ of return** ◇ *safe investments which give a good ~ of return*
→ Note at PER CENT (for more verbs)

rate verb

ADV. **highly** ◇ *Silver was ~d more highly than gold.* | **consistently** ◇ *This airport is consistently ~d as the worst in the world.*
PREP. **among** ◇ *a golf course that is ~d among the top ten in America* | **as** ◇ *It is ~d as one of the city's best hotels.* | **for** ◇ *a university that is highly ~d for its research work*
PHRASES **~ sth on a scale** ◇ *The difficulty of each exercise is ~d on a scale of 1 to 5.*

rating noun

1 measurement of how good sb/sth is

ADJ. **high, top** | **low, poor** | **overall** ◇ *The overall performance ~ puts the new model well ahead of its main rivals.* | **favourable/favorable, unfavourable/unfavorable** (both *esp. AmE*) ◇ *He's currently enjoying a favourable/favorable ~ with more than 50% of the electorate.* | **approval, favorability** (*AmE*), **opinion-poll, poll, popularity** ◇ *He has the highest opinion-poll ~ of any president this century.* | **performance** | **two-star, three-star, etc.** ◇ *The hotel achieved a four-star ~.* ◇ *The hospital has retained its top three-star ~.* (*BrE*) | **credit** ◇ *Most countries try to preserve their international credit ~ in order to secure necessary loans.* | **personal, subjective**
VERB + RATING **have** | **assign (sb/sth), give (sb/sth)** | **achieve, earn, get, obtain, receive, score** ◇ *The university scored a top ~ among students.* | **preserve** | **improve** | **downgrade, lower** (*business*) ◇ *Standard & Poor's lowered its credit ~ for the company from A to BBB.*
RATING + VERB **climb, improve, rise, rocket, soar** ◇ *The president's ~s have suddenly rocketed.* | **drop, fall, plummet**
RATING + NOUN **scale, system**

PREP. **in a/the ~** ◇ *a drop of 50 points in her personal ~* | **~ for** ◇ *The resort got a low ~ for children's facilities.* | **~ on** ◇ *The judges gave her the maximum ~ on style.*

2 ratings number of TV viewers, etc.

ADJ. **good, high** | **low, poor** | **audience, TV** | **prime-time** (*esp. AmE*) ◇ *The network's prime-time ~s are up 150%.*
VERB + RATINGS **garner** (*esp. AmE*), **get, have** ◇ *The show continues to garner high ~s.* ◇ *At this stage the series was getting good ~s.* | **boost** ◇ *Bringing her on the show was a cynical attempt to boost the ~s.*
RATINGS + VERB **go up, improve, pick up, shoot up, soar** ◇ *The ~s went shooting up overnight.* | **dip, drop, fall, go down** ◇ *The show's ~s have dipped sharply.*
RATINGS + NOUN **battle, war** | **success** ◇ *His new sitcom was a ~s success.*
PREP. **in the ~s** ◇ *It has been ousted from top spot in the TV ~s.*

ratio *noun*

ADJ. **high, low** | **gender, sex** ◇ *Some universities take steps to keep their gender ~ 50–50.* | **staffing** ◇ *Staffing ~s were generally better in smaller hospitals.* | **male-female, nurse-patient, student-teacher, etc.** | **benefit-to-risk, power-to-weight, etc.** | **price-earnings, price-to-earnings** (*both business*) ◇ *The stock's price-earnings ~ has dropped to 24.*
VERB + RATIO **achieve, have** ◇ *They have a high ~ of imports to exports.* | **improve, increase** ◇ *The hospital is trying to improve its staff/patient ~.* | **reduce** | **calculate, compute, determine, find, work out**
RATIO + VERB **improve** | **worsen** ◇ *the worsening student/teacher ~ in our schools* | **differ, range (from … to …), vary** ◇ *Waist-to-hip ~s vary according to body type.*
PREP. **in a/the ~** ◇ *We mixed the oil and water in a ~ of one to five.* | **~ between** ◇ *the ~ between the amount of time spent on the work and the profit produced* | **~ of sth to sth** ◇ *the ~ of house prices to incomes*

ration *noun*

ADJ. **daily, monthly** | **full** | **double, extra** ◇ *Pregnant women received a double ~ of milk.* | **meagre/meager** ◇ *The refugees waited for their meagre/meager ~s of soup.* | **emergency, humanitarian, short, starvation, wartime ~s** ◇ *We've been put on short ~s.* | **food, gasoline** (*AmE*), **petrol** (*BrE*), **water, etc.**
VERB + RATION **give sb, hand out, provide (sb with)** | **get, receive** | **consume, eat, have, use, use up** ◇ *You've had your ~ of chocolate for the day!* | **cut, reduce** ◇ *The guards are going to cut our ~s again.*
RATION + NOUN **book, card, coupon**
PREP. **on a/the ~** ◇ *They are living on starvation ~s.* | **~ of** ◇ *our daily ~ of bread*

ration *verb*

ADV. **strictly** ◇ *These foods had to be strictly ~ed.*
PREP. **to** ◇ *They were ~ed to one bottle of water each per day.*

rational *adj.*

VERBS **be, seem** ◇ *It all seemed quite ~ to me.*
ADV. **highly, very** | **completely, eminently** (*formal*), **entirely, fully, perfectly, quite** ◇ *At the time she was perfectly ~.* | **purely, strictly** | **essentially** ◇ *Humans are essentially ~ beings.* | **apparently** | **economically**
PREP. **about** ◇ *Try to be ~ about it.*

rationing *noun*

ADJ. **strict** | **bread, credit, food, fuel, gas** (*AmE*), **petrol** (*BrE*), **etc.** | **wartime**
VERB + RATIONING **have** | **bring in, introduce** ◇ *The government introduced meat ~ in May.* | **end**
RATIONING + VERB **be in force, exist**
RATIONING + NOUN **system**
PREP. **~ of** ◇ *Strict ~ of basic foodstuffs was still in force.*

ray *noun*

ADJ. **powerful** | **blinding, bright, brilliant** ◇ *a blinding ~ of light* | **golden** ◇ *They basked in sun's warm golden ~s.* | **soft, warm** | **burning, damaging, harmful** | **dying, last** ◇ *the dying ~s of a winter sun* | **cathode, cosmic, gamma, heat, infrared, light, ultraviolet** (abbreviated to *UV*), **etc.** ◇ *the invention of the cathode ~ tube* | **the moon's, the sun's**
VERB + RAY **emit, give off, send out** ◇ *gamma ~s given off by plutonium* | **cast, shine** ◇ *The moon cast pale ~s of light on the ground.* | **expose sb/sth to** | **block, filter out, protect sb/sth from, shield sb/sth from** ◇ *sunscreens which filter out harmful ultraviolet ~s* | **absorb** ◇ *A car window absorbs almost all UVB ~s.* | **bend, catch, deflect, reflect** ◇ *Her ring caught the ~s of the setting sun.*
RAY + VERB **filter through sth, pass through sth, penetrate sth, travel** ◇ *the moon's ~s filtering through the trees* | **shine, shine down, shine on sth** ◇ *The last of the sun's ~s shone on the grass.* | **hit sth, strike sth** ◇ *When the sun's ~s hit the earth, a lot of heat is reflected back into space.* | **damage sth** ◇ *Ultraviolet ~s damage the skin.*
PREP. **in the ~s of** ◇ *a stream sparkling in the ~s of the June sun*
PHRASES **a ~ of light** (*sometimes figurative*), **a ~ of sunlight, a ~ of sunshine** (*sometimes figurative*) ◇ *The one ~ of light in this whole affair is that justice has been done.* ◇ *A ~ of sunlight fell on the table.* ◇ *My nephew is a little ~ of sunshine.* | **the ~s of the sun**

razor *noun*

ADJ. **blunt** | **cut-throat** (*esp. BrE*), **disposable, electric, safety, straight-edge** (*AmE*) ◇ *a mugger who slashed a man with a cut-throat ~* | **open** ◇ *He appeared with an open ~ in his hand.*
VERB + RAZOR **cut sb/sth with, shave with, slash sb/sth with, use** ◇ *We used a ~ to cut the string.*
RAZOR + NOUN **blade** | **wire**
PREP. **with a/the ~** ◇ *He slashed his wrists with a ~.*

reach *noun*

1 distance over which you can stretch, travel, etc.

ADJ. **long** ◇ *Gorillas have a very long ~.*
VERB + REACH **have**
PREP. **beyond (sb/sth's) ~** ◇ *The latch was just beyond her ~.* | **in (sb/sth's) ~, within (sb/sth's) ~** ◇ *The riverbank was almost in ~.* ◇ *There was a knife within his ~.* ◇ *a beach resort within ~ of Bangkok* ◇ *The house is within easy ~ of the train station.* | **out of sb/sth's ~** ◇ *Keep all medicines out of ~ of children.*
PHRASES **within arm's ~** ◇ *I always keep my phone within arm's ~.*

2 power/influence

ADJ. **vast, wide** ◇ *The organization has a wide ~.* | **global** ◇ *The global ~ of the Internet has exceeded what anyone could have predicted.* | **geographic, geographical** ◇ *The business is looking at ways to extend its geographic ~.*
VERB + REACH **have** ◇ *The company has a worldwide ~.* | **broaden, expand, extend, increase** ◇ *Humans have extended their ~ into space.* | **limit** ◇ *As an artist, his ~ was not limited to Britain.*
PREP. **beyond (sb/sth's) ~** ◇ *He fled abroad, beyond the ~ of German prosecutors.* | **in sb/sth's ~, within sb/sth's ~** ◇ *Our $30 000 target is now well within our ~.* | **out of sb/sth's ~** ◇ *The price puts it out of the ~ of most people.*

3 reaches far place

ADJ. **far, farthest, furthest** | **nether, outer, outermost, upper, uppermost** ◇ *the upper ~es of the river* ◇ *the upper ~es of the music charts* (*figurative*) | **northern, southern, etc.** | **northernmost, southernmost, etc.**
VERB + REACHES **explore** ◇ *He dreamed of exploring the outermost ~es of space.*
PREP. **~ of** ◇ *the farthest ~es of our universe*

reach *verb*

1 arrive at a place/condition

ADV. **eventually, finally** | **easily, quickly** ◇ *The cost can easily*

~ six figures. | almost, nearly ◇ *The city's population had nearly ~ed a million by 1920.* | barely ◇ *He had barely ~ed the door when he collapsed.*
VERB + REACH attempt to, try to | be expected to, be likely to, expect to ◇ *Profits are expected to ~ £2 billion this year.* | be unlikely to | be able to | be unable to, fail to ◇ *The jury was unable to ~ a verdict.*

2 stretch out your arm to touch/get sth
ADV. gingerly, hesitantly, tentatively | slowly ◇ *Slowly he ~ed out and picked up the gun.* | automatically, instinctively ◇ *He instinctively ~ed for his camera.* | blindly ◇ *She ~ed blindly for the light switch.* | across, down, forward, out, over ◇ *He ~ed out gingerly to touch it.* | *A hand ~ed down to help her up the ladder.*
PREP. for ◇ *She ~ed for the telephone and picked it up.* | inside ◇ *I ~ed inside my pocket for a pen.* | into ◇ *He ~ed into his bag and took out a book.*

3 be able to touch sth
ADV. easily ◇ *She had arranged her desk so that she could ~ everything easily.* | almost, nearly ◇ *Her skirt almost ~ed the ground.* | halfway ◇ *His hair ~ed halfway to his waist.*
VERB + REACH can ◇ *I can't ~ the top shelf.*

react *verb*
ADV. strongly | favourably/favorably, positively, well ◇ *people who ~ positively to change* | adversely, badly, negatively, poorly, unfavourably/unfavorably | aggressively, angrily, defensively, sharply, violently | emotionally | cautiously, coolly | calmly, rationally | appropriately | strangely | immediately, instantly | quickly, rapidly, swiftly ◇ *The police must be able to ~ swiftly in an emergency.* | slowly | differently | accordingly ◇ *His insensitive remarks hurt and she ~ed accordingly.* | automatically, instinctively, spontaneously | physically | chemically ◇ *Silicon ~s chemically like carbon.*
VERB + REACT tend to | be slow to ◇ *The industry has been slow to ~ to these breakthroughs in technology.* | not know how to ◇ *He did not know how to ~ to her sudden mood swings.*
PREP. against ◇ *Many young people ~ against traditional values.* | by ◇ *The government ~ed by increasing taxation.* | to ◇ *The committee ~ed positively to the proposals.* | with ◇ *Her family ~ed with horror when she told them.*

reaction *noun*
1 response
ADJ. extreme, strong, violent | favourable/favorable, positive | adverse, hostile, negative | mixed ◇ *The speech got a mixed ~.* | angry | first, immediate, initial | delayed ◇ *Her outburst was a delayed ~ to an unpleasant letter she'd received that morning.* | chain ◇ *The change of plan set off a chain ~ of confusion.* | common, general, public | natural, normal, understandable ◇ *His ~ is completely understandable.* | automatic, gut, instinctive, knee-jerk, spontaneous ◇ *The incident calls for a measured response, avoiding knee-jerk ~s.* | nervous | emotional, visceral | critical ◇ *The critical ~ to his first novel has been positive.*
VERB + REACTION get, have, meet with ◇ *The play met with a mixed ~ from the critics.* | experience ◇ *I believe she is experiencing a post-traumatic stress ~.* | bring, cause, elicit, induce, produce, provoke, set off, spark, spark off, trigger, trigger off ◇ *She was surprised at the ~ brought by the mention of his name.* | gauge, judge ◇ *He eyed her cautiously, trying to gauge her ~.* | judge by, judge from ◇ *Judging by her ~, she liked the present.*
PREP. in ~ to ◇ *There's been a drop in ticket sales in ~ to the review.* | ~ against ◇ *Her rebellious attitude is just a ~ against her strict upbringing.* | ~ to ◇ *the public ~ to the news*

2 (usually reactions) ability to react quickly
ADJ. fast, good, lightning, quick ◇ *Keenan showed lightning ~s.* | slow
VERB + REACTION have ◇ *She has very quick ~s.* | speed up | slow down ◇ *Alcohol has the effect of slowing down your ~s.*

REACTION + NOUN time ◇ *Your ~ time increases when you are tired.*
3 chemical reaction
ADJ. chain | chemical, nuclear, thermonuclear, etc. | fission, fusion | reversible
VERB + REACTION cause, initiate, produce, start, trigger | catalyse/catalyze (*science*) | stop | slow down, speed up
REACTION + VERB occur, take place
PREP. during a/the ~, in a/the ~ ◇ *the energy given out during the ~* | ~ between ◇ *I am studying the ~s between certain gases.* | ~ with ◇ *the fuel's chemical ~ with the surrounding water*

4 physical reaction
ADJ. adverse, bad, severe | mild, slight | delayed ◇ *a delayed ~ to the drugs* | allergic | inflammatory
VERB + REACTION experience, have, suffer ◇ *She had a very bad allergic ~ to the peanuts.* | cause, induce, produce
PREP. ~ to ◇ *A small minority of patients suffer an adverse ~ to the treatment.*

reactor *noun*
ADJ. nuclear, nuclear-power | breeder, fast, fast-breeder, fission, fusion, gas-cooled, light-water, etc.
VERB + REACTOR build | operate, run | close, close down, decommission, shut down
REACTOR + VERB operate, run
REACTOR + NOUN building, site | design | coolant, fuel | core | accident, meltdown | safety | shutdown

read *noun*
1 activity of reading
ADJ. good | quiet | quick ◇ *The program is simple to use after a quick ~ of the manual.*
VERB + READ have ◇ *I had a good ~ of the paper before they arrived.*
2 writer/book
ADJ. enjoyable, entertaining, fun (*esp. AmE*), good, great, terrific | compelling, engaging, engrossing, fascinating, gripping, interesting | easy, quick | worthwhile
VERB + READ be, make ◇ *The story made an interesting ~.* | enjoy ◇ *I know you'll enjoy the ~.*

read *verb*
ADV. aloud ◇ *I listen to my children ~ing aloud.* | silently | carefully, with interest ◇ *He ~ her letter with interest.* | avidly, voraciously, widely ◇ *She ~ avidly from an early age.* | regularly ◇ *I regularly ~ 'Time'.* | critically ◇ *We teach students to ~ critically.* | correctly ◇ *Make sure you ~ the instructions correctly.* | fluently, well ◇ *He speaks and ~s Arabic fluently.* | just, lately, recently ◇ *I've just ~ your interesting article.* | out ◇ *Shall I ~ this out to you?*
VERB + READ be able to, can ◇ *Most children can ~ by the age of seven.* | learn to, learn how to | teach sb to, teach sb how to
PREP. about ◇ *Hogan had ~ about her death in the paper.* | from ◇ *She ~ from the letter.* | in ◇ *He remembers everything he ~s in books.* | of ◇ *I had ~ of the case in the local newspaper.* | over ◇ *She spent the morning ~ing over her script.* | through ◇ *I ~ through the first paragraph again.* | to ◇ *I ~ a story to my son every night.*
PHRASES ~ and write ◇ *She had great difficulty learning to ~ and write.* | ~ for fun, ~ for pleasure ◇ *He's not someone who ~s for pleasure.*

readable *adj.*
1 enjoyable to read
VERBS be | make sth
ADV. extremely, fairly, very, etc. | compulsively, eminently, highly, immensely ◇ *a stimulating and highly ~ account* | quite

2 able to be read

VERBS **be**
ADV. **clearly, easily** ◊ *The figures should be clearly ~.* ◊ *printed in large, easily ~ type*

reader *noun*

ADJ. **careful, competent, fast, fluent, good, proficient | poor, slow | alert, astute, attentive, eagle-eyed, observant** ◊ *Alert ~s may have noticed the misprint in last week's column.* | **interested** ◊ *The book is accessible to the interested ~ with basic knowledge of the subject.* | **reluctant | discerning, informed, knowledgeable, sophisticated | uninformed | avid, great, voracious | omnivorous | faithful, long-time** (*esp. AmE*), **loyal, regular** ◊ *regular ~s of this magazine* | **casual | adult, female, male, women, young | specialist | general, lay, non-specialist** ◊ *a book that will be too difficult for the general ~* | **newspaper, tabloid** (*esp. BrE*) | **Newsweek, Times, etc.**
PREP. **~ of** ◊ *a voracious ~ of science fiction*
PHRASES **dear ~** (*humorous*) ◊ *And so, dear ~, our tale comes to its end.*

readiness *noun*

ADJ. **greater | constant | combat, military, operational** ◊ *The troops were in a state of combat ~.* | **school** (*AmE*) ◊ *the importance of early learning for school ~*
VERB + READINESS **declare, demonstrate, express, indicate, show, signal** ◊ *Hungary has indicated its ~ to sign the treaty.*
PREP. **in ~ (for)** ◊ *Service the car in ~ for the trip.* | **~ for** ◊ *to express a ~ for change*
PHRASES **hold sb/sth in ~** ◊ *They were holding themselves in ~ to wage war.* | **a state of ~**

reading *noun*

1 sth you can read

ADJ. **compelling, compulsive, fascinating, good, interesting | worthwhile** ◊ *The book is worthwhile ~ for anyone interested in the Industrial Revolution.* | **depressing, disturbing | heavy, serious | light | assigned** (*AmE*), **compulsory** (*esp. BrE*), **essential, mandatory** (*esp. AmE*), **required** ◊ *Her assigned ~ for English class was 'Great Expectations'.* ◊ *His article should be compulsory ~ for law students.* | **recommended, suggested | background | further | beach** (*esp. AmE*), **bedtime, holiday** (*BrE*) ◊ *Horror is hardly my idea of bedtime ~.* ◊ *some light holiday ~*
VERB + READING **be, make, make for** ◊ *Their story makes compulsive ~.* | **assign** (*AmE*) ◊ *We assign ~s from different contexts and periods of history.*
READING + NOUN **list | comprehension**

2 activity of reading

ADJ. **extensive** ◊ *After extensive ~ on the subject she set to work on an article.* | **careful, close, critical** ◊ *A close ~ of the text reveals several contradictions.* | **cursory | serious | map** ◊ *My map-reading skills are not the best.*
VERB + READING **do, get down to** ◊ *I haven't had time to do much ~ lately.* ◊ *I need to get down to some serious ~.*
READING + NOUN **material, matter | habits** ◊ *He asked her about her ~ habits.* | **ability, age, knowledge, skills** ◊ *He has a ~ age of eight.* ◊ *She has a good ~ knowledge of Russian.* | **disability** (*AmE*) | **glasses, light, room**
PREP. **~ about, ~ on** ◊ *His ~ about Ruskin led him to the works of Turner.*

3 way of understanding

ADJ. **allegorical, literal** ◊ *He draws his morality from a literal ~ of the Old Testament.* | **insightful, sensitive** ◊ *her attentive and insightful ~ of the manuscript*
VERB + READING **give, offer, provide** ◊ *Longinus provides a sensitive ~ of Sappho's poem.* | **invite, suggest** ◊ *These paintings often invite an allegorical ~.*

4 reading in public

ADJ. **public | staged** (*esp. AmE*) ◊ *I saw a staged ~ of the new play 'Light'.* | **Bible, poetry**
VERB + READING **give** ◊ *Dickens gave many public ~s from his works.*
PREP. **at a/the ~** ◊ *We met at a ~ of his poetry.* | **~ from, ~ of** ◊ *~s from the Psalms*

5 figure/measurement shown on an instrument

ADJ. **high, low | normal | accurate, correct | false | meter, thermometer | blood-pressure, pressure, temperature**
VERB + READING **get, obtain, take | give** ◊ *The dials were giving higher ~s than we had expected.* | **record** ◊ *Temperature ~s were recorded throughout the day.*
PREP. **~of** ◊ *A ~ of 25 or more is abnormally high.*

ready *adj.*

1 prepared

VERBS **appear, be, feel, look, seem, stand** ◊ *The suitcases were standing ~ by the front door.* | **remain, stay** (*AmE*) ◊ *Our troops keep training all the time to remain ~.* | **get** ◊ *We were getting ~ to go out.* | **get sb/sth, make sth** ◊ *I'm trying to get the children ~ to leave.* ◊ *I'll get all the boxes ~.* ◊ *The warships were soon made ~.* | **have sth, hold sth, keep sth, leave sth** ◊ *Please have your tickets ~ for inspection.* ◊ *He held his gun ~.* ◊ *I've left everything ~ in the kitchen.* | **consider sb/sth, declare sb/sth, deem sb/sth, judge sb/sth** ◊ *The plane was repaired and declared ~ for service again.* ◊ *She was concerned to protect the children from the truth until she judged them ~ to hear it.*
ADV. **all, completely, totally** ◊ *I was all ~ to leave when the phone rang.* | **definitely, truly** ◊ *We're definitely ~ for the show tonight.* | **not quite** ◊ *He didn't feel quite ~ for marriage.* | **about, almost, just about, nearly, practically** ◊ *I think we're just about ~ to start.* | **always, ever | not yet | at last, finally** ◊ *At last, they were ~ to go.* | **emotionally, mentally, physically** ◊ *Though Paul had wanted a child, he wasn't emotionally ~ for it.*
PREP. **for** ◊ *I feel ~ for anything!* ◊ *The cases are ~ for delivery.* | **with** ◊ *He's always ~ with a quick answer.*

2 willing

VERBS **appear, be, seem | remain**
ADV. **more than, only too, very** ◊ *Connors was more than ~ to oblige.* ◊ *She was only too ~ to believe the worst of him.* | **always, ever | apparently | clearly, obviously**
PHRASES **~ and willing** ◊ *always ~ and willing to help*

real *adj.*

VERBS **be, look, seem | become**
ADV. **all too, very** ◊ *Her suffering was all too ~.* ◊ *the very ~ danger of war* | **frighteningly** ◊ *The possibility of being arrested was frighteningly ~.* | **enough** ◊ *The pearls looked ~ enough.*
PHRASES **~ and/or imaginary, ~ and/or imagined** ◊ *~ or imagined threats to national security*

realism *noun*

ADJ. **political | gritty, stark** ◊ *the stark ~ of Loach's films* | **literary | magic, magical, psychological, social, socialist** (*all literature*) ◊ *a complex novel of psychological ~* ◊ *the Soviet adoption of socialist ~ in art*
... OF REALISM **degree, level** ◊ *The computer animation offers an unprecedented level of ~.* | **dose, element** ◊ *They should temper their enthusiasm with a healthy dose of ~.*
VERB + REALISM **add, bring, lend** ◊ *Clever lighting and sound effects brought greater ~ to the play.* | **achieve** ◊ *Children can get frustrated when they are unable to achieve ~ in their drawings.*
PREP. **~ about** ◊ *the band's ~ about their chances of success* | **~ in** ◊ *~ in Dutch art*
PHRASES **a sense of ~**

realistic *adj.*

1 showing acceptance of the facts of a situation

VERBS **be, seem | keep sth** ◊ *Try to keep your ambitions ~.*

ADV. **extremely, very** | **fairly, quite** | **enough** ◇ *He was ~ enough to know this success could not last.*

PREP. **about** ◇ *My friends were quite ~ about my problems.* | **in** ◇ *You're not being very ~ in your expectations.*

PHRASES **it is not ~ to expect, think, etc. sth** ◇ *It's not ~ to expect people to pay more.*

2 showing things as they really are

VERBS **appear, be, look, seem, sound** ◇ *The special effects seem very ~.* | **become** | **make sth** ◇ *You could make the hands a little more ~.*

ADV. **extremely, fairly, very, etc.** | **highly, truly** ◇ *beautifully drawn, highly ~ flowers* | **amazingly, incredibly** | **grimly** ◇ *his grimly ~ first novel about drug addicts*

reality *noun*

ADJ. **sad, sobering, unfortunate, unpleasant** ◇ *We were faced with the unpleasant ~ of having nowhere to live.* | **bitter, brutal, cold, cruel, grim, gritty, hard, harsh, painful, stark, ugly** ◇ *The novel describes the harsh realities of racism and life on the road.* | **complex** | **underlying** ◇ *He has no illusions about the underlying ~ of army life.* | **objective, practical** ◇ *the practical realities of running a children's home* | **daily, day-to-day, everyday, mundane** | **external, material, physical** ◇ *Painters at the time were largely concerned with reproducing external ~.* | **ultimate** | **commercial, economic, historical, political, psychological, social** ◇ *the harsh economic realities of life as a student* | **virtual** ◇ *the use of virtual ~ in computer games* | **alternate** (*esp. AmE*) ◇ *The movie portrays a kind of alternate ~.*

VERB + REALITY **become** ◇ *One day her dream will become a ~.* | **make sth** ◇ *It's our task to make the proposals a ~.* | **accept, acknowledge, confront (sb with), grasp, perceive, recognize, understand, wake up to** ◇ *She will have to face ~ sooner or later.* ◇ *I don't think you have quite grasped the realities of our situation!* | **capture, depict, reflect, represent** ◇ *a book that captures the ~ of life during wartime* | **construct, create** ◇ *The director creates a believable, gritty ~.* | **bear little, no, etc. relation to, bear little, no, etc. resemblance to, have little to do with, not have much to do with** ◇ *Most people's ideas of the disease do not have much to do with the ~.* | **be cut off from, be divorced from, be out of touch with, be removed from** ◇ *They are out of touch with the realities of modern warfare.* | **escape from** | **deny, ignore** | **bring sb back to, come back to, get back to, return to** ◇ *He called for the committee to stop dreaming and return to ~.* | **alter, distort, obscure** ◇ *Most comedy relies on distorting ~.* | **protect sb from, shelter sb from, shield sb from** ◇ *Her parents always tried to shield her from the realities of the world.*

REALITY + NOUN **check** ◇ *It's time for a ~ check: are these goals really achievable?* | **television, TV**

PREP. **in ~** ◇ *The media portray her as happy and successful, but in ~ she has a difficult life.* | **~ of** ◇ *I don't think he understands the ~ of the situation.*

PHRASES **a grasp of ~, a grasp on ~** ◇ *He has a rather tenuous grasp of ~.* | **a perception of ~, a sense of ~**

realization (*BrE also* -isation) *noun*

ADJ. **full** | **dawning, growing** | **gradual, slow** | **belated** | **sudden** | **startling** | **awful, grim, horrible, painful, stark, terrible** | **sobering**

VERB + REALIZATION **come to** ◇ *He came to the ~ that he would never make a good teacher.*

REALIZATION + VERB **come (to sb), dawn (on sb), hit sb, sink in, strike sb** ◇ *The ~ that the murderer must have been a close friend came as a shock.* ◇ *We saw the terrible ~ of what she'd done dawn on her face.*

realize (*BrE also* -ise) *verb*

ADV. **fully** | **dimly** ◇ *She dimly ~d that she was trembling.* | **suddenly** | **quickly, soon** | **immediately, instantly, now** | **for the first time** ◇ *I ~d for the first time how difficult this would be.* | **at first** ◇ *The situation was more complicated than they had at first ~d.* | **gradually, slowly** | **at last,**

belatedly, eventually, finally | never ◇ *I never ~d how much it meant to you.*

VERB + REALIZE **begin to, come to** | **make sb** ◇ *The experience made me ~ that people did care.* | **seem to** ◇ *You don't seem to ~ the seriousness of the situation.* | **fail to** | **be important to**

PREP. **with** ◇ *He ~d with horror that he had forgotten his passport.*

PHRASES **without realizing (sth)** ◇ *They are constantly learning, without even realizing it.*

realm *noun*

1 area of activity/interest/knowledge

ADJ. **whole** ◇ *the whole ~ of human intellect* | **new** | **international** | **public** | **domestic, private** | **political, social** | **earthly, material, physical** | **divine, fantasy, heavenly, magical, spiritual, supernatural**

VERB + REALM **be in, belong in, belong to, lie in** | **open up** ◇ *The research has opened up new ~s for investigation.* | **enter, move into** | **descend into, descend to** (*both disapproving*) ◇ *Most readers are likely to lose interest when he descends into the ~s of* (= starts discussing) *rhetorical terminology.* | **move from, move out of** ◇ *The euro moved from the ~s of theory into reality.*

PREP. **beyond the ~ of, out of the ~ of, outside the ~ of** ◇ *His ambitions are way beyond the ~s of possibility.* | **in the ~ of, within the ~ of** ◇ *The idea belongs in the ~ of science fiction.*

PHRASES **the ~ of art, politics, science, etc.** ◇ *In the ~ of politics different rules sometimes apply.* | **the ~s of fantasy, the ~s of possibility, the ~s of reality**

2 (*formal*) country ruled by a king/queen

VERB + REALM **defend**

PREP. **beyond the ~, outside the ~** | **in the ~, within the ~** ◇ *peace within the ~* | **throughout the ~**

PHRASES **a part of the ~** | **the defence/defense of the ~**

realtor™ *noun* (*AmE*)

ADJ. **local** | **licensed** ◇ *As a licensed realtor, he also earns $15 000 a year in commissions.*

VERB + REALTOR **call** ◇ *I called the realtor to inquire about selling the house.* | **meet, meet with**

reappraisal *noun*

ADJ. **fundamental, major** (*esp. BrE*), **radical** | **complete** | **critical** ◇ *a critical ~ of existing ideas and social institutions*

VERB + REAPPRAISAL **force, prompt, trigger** ◇ *This research has prompted a ~ of his legacy.* | **lead to** ◇ *Her theory is that disillusionment with employment leads to ~ of career goals.*

rear *noun*

VERB + REAR **bring up** ◇ *Three drummers brought up the ~* (= were last in the parade). | **attack (sb/sth) from** | **cover, guard, protect** | **face** ◇ *Car seats for young babies should face the ~.*

PREP. **at the ~** ◇ *The socket for the printer cable is located at the ~ of the computer.* | **from the ~** | **in the ~** ◇ *The radio is loudest in the ~ of the car.* | **to the ~, towards/toward the ~** ◇ *A high gate blocks the only entrance to the ~.*

rear *verb*

ADV. **intensively** (*esp. BrE*) ◇ *intensively ~ed beef cattle* | **naturally** ◇ *naturally ~ed pork and beef* | **successfully**

reason *noun*

1 cause/motive/justification; explanation of sth

ADJ. **cogent, good, sound, strong** | **compelling, convincing** | **plausible** | **adequate, sufficient** | **bona fide, legitimate, valid** | **wrong** ◇ *He married her for all the wrong ~s.* | **opposite** ◇ *Tom's problem was that he lacked confidence; Ed failed for precisely the opposite ~.* | **important** | **special** | **big, chief, key, main, major, primary, principal** ◇ *There's* one big ~ why this won't work: cost. | **only, simple, sole** ◇ *The only ~ I didn't become a professional golfer was because of my family commitments.* ◇ *I was never good at school for the simple ~ that I never studied.* | **several, various** ◇ *I can think of several ~s why this might happen.* | **common** ◇ *Isolation and loneliness are common ~s for depression.* | **real, underlying** ◇ *She did not tell him the real ~ for her change of heart.* ◇ *The underlying ~s for these differences will be explored in depth in the next chapter.* | **possible** | **cited, ostensible, stated** ◇ *The company's stated ~ for firing him was misconduct.* | **exact, very** ◇ *You're asking me to help, and that's the exact ~ I came.* | **apparent, particular** ◇ *He was attacked for no apparent ~.* | **no earthly, no possible** ◇ *Surely there is no earthly ~ why you wouldn't want to come with us?* | **clear, obvious** ◇ *The ~s for her decision soon became clear.* | **unclear** | **logical, rational** | **understandable** | **justifiable** | **unspecified** | **unconnected** ◇ *dismissal for ~s unconnected with misconduct.* | **personal** | **sentimental** | **selfish** | **professional** | **commercial, economic, financial, legal, political, social, technical** | **practical, pragmatic, security** | **health** | **altruistic, humanitarian**

VERB + REASON   **be aware of, see** ◇ *He saw many ~s to be hopeful.* | **have** ◇ *I don't know why he did that, but I'm sure he had his ~s.* ◇ *I have no ~ to believe that she was lying to me.* | **cite, give (sb/sth), outline, provide, set out, state** ◇ *Give me one good ~ why I should help you.* ◇ *In the letter she carefully set out her ~s for leaving.* | **list** ◇ *This article lists the most common ~s why people pay too much tax.* | **offer, suggest** | **articulate, explain** | **cite sth as, give sth as, offer sth as** | **discuss, explore** | **understand** | **guess** | **discover, find, find out, uncover** | **pinpoint** ◇ *It's difficult to pinpoint the ~s for her success.*

PREP.   **by ~ of** (*formal*) ◇ *persons in need of care by ~ of* (= because of) *old age* ◇ *He was found not guilty by ~ of insanity.* (*law*) | **for a/the ~** ◇ *procedures carried out for ~s of national security* | **for ~ of** (*formal*) ◇ *For ~s of security, you are requested to keep your baggage with you at all times.* | **with ~, without ~** ◇ *They complained about the food, and with good ~* (= rightly)*.* | **~ against** ◇ *There are obvious ~s against such a move.* | **~ behind** ◇ *We are trying to uncover the ~s behind her decision.* | **~ for** ◇ *They didn't give any ~ for the delay.*

PHRASES   **all the more ~** ◇ *If he's unwell, that's all the more ~ to go and see him.* | **all sorts of ~s** ◇ *People buy things for all sorts of ~s.* | **every ~, little ~, some ~** ◇ *I know you're angry with me, and you have every ~* (= very good reasons) *to be.* ◇ *You have little ~ to be pleased with yourself.* | **no ~, not any ~** ◇ *He got angry for no ~.* ◇ *You don't have any ~ to complain.* | **for ~s best known to yourself** ◇ *For ~s best known to herself she has turned down the offer.* | **for some inexplicable ~, for some odd ~, for some strange ~, for some unfathomable ~** ◇ *For some odd ~, he found it really funny.* | **for unexplained ~s, for unknown ~s** ◇ *For unknown ~s, the ship sank in the middle of the ocean.* | **for whatever ~** ◇ *people who, for whatever ~, are unable to support themselves* | **a number of ~s, a variety of ~s** | **rhyme or ~** ◇ *There's no rhyme or ~* (= logic) *to the new opening hours.* | **not see any ~, see no ~** ◇ *We see no ~ why this band shouldn't be a huge success.* ◇ *I don't see any ~ why you can't come with us.* | **there is ample ~, there are ample ~s** ◇ *There is ample ~ to be optimistic about the economy.*

2 power to think logically; what is possible/right

ADJ.   **human**

VERB + REASON   **lose** ◇ *He seems to have lost all sense and ~.* | **be open to, listen to, see** ◇ *I tried to persuade her, but she just wouldn't listen to ~.* | **defy** ◇ *Sometimes he does things that defy ~.*

PREP.   **beyond ~** ◇ *He was beyond all ~.* | **within ~** ◇ *I'll lend you the money you need—within ~, of course!*

PHRASES   **an appeal to ~** ◇ *The residents hope that an appeal to ~* (= asking the rioters to be reasonable) *will end the rioting.* | **faculty of ~, sense of ~** ◇ *We possess the human faculty of ~.* | **it stands to ~** ◇ *It stands to ~* (= it is logical)

---

that she wouldn't want them to find out about her personal problems. | **the voice of ~** ◇ *She was always the voice of ~, persuading him not to buy things they couldn't afford.*

reasonable *adj.*

VERBS   **appear, be, look, seem, sound** | **consider sth, judge sth, regard sth as, think sth**

ADV.   **extremely, fairly, very, etc.** | **eminently** | **entirely, perfectly, totally** (*esp. AmE*) ◇ *The police apparently thought this explanation perfectly ~.* | **enough** ◇ *Her request sounded ~ enough to me.* | **only** ◇ *If companies expect work during personal time, it's only ~ to allow personal time at work.*

reasoning *noun*

ADJ.   **careful, sound** | **circular, faulty, flawed, specious** (*formal*) | **underlying** | **abstract** | **practical** | **logical** | **deductive, inductive** | **non-verbal, verbal** | **ethical, judicial, legal, mathematical, moral, scientific, theological** | **human**

...OF REASONING   **piece** ◇ *a rather confused piece of ~*

VERB + REASONING   **adopt, apply, employ, use** ◇ *the ~ adopted by the court* | **follow, understand** ◇ *I can't quite follow your ~.* | **accept** | **reject** | **explain**

REASONING + VERB   **apply** ◇ *The same ~ applies to the current situation.* | **be based on** ◇ *Their ~ is based on a false analogy.* | **suggest** ◇ *This ~ suggests the education process is simpler than it actually is.* | **lead sb/sth to sth** ◇ *I cannot accept the ~ that led the trial court to its decision.*

REASONING + NOUN   **process** | **ability**

PREP.   **in your ~** ◇ *the circularity in their ~* | **~ about** ◇ *~ about art* | **~ behind** ◇ *Many people challenged the ~ behind the proposal.*

PHRASES   **a flaw in your ~** | **a form of ~, a kind of ~, a line of ~** ◇ *The implication of this line of ~ is that globalization of capital is destructive.* | **power of ~** ◇ *She seemed to have lost her powers of ~.*

reassurance *noun*

ADJ.   **great** | **a little** ◇ *Consumers need a little ~ after all this bad publicity.* | **little** ◇ *She received little ~ or sympathy.* | **further** | **constant** | **calm** ◇ *Continual calm ~ should be given.* | **false** ◇ *A negative test result may give false ~.*

VERB + REASSURANCE   **have** ◇ *We have had some ~s from the council that the building will be saved.* | **need, want** | **look for, seek** ◇ *He glanced at her, seeking ~.* | **find, get, receive** ◇ *She found ~ in the high attendance at her lectures.* | **bring (sb), give (sb), offer (sb), provide (sb with)** ◇ *A system of beliefs can bring you ~ at times of stress.*

PREP.   **despite ~** ◇ *She kept looking in the mirror despite my constant ~s that her hair looked fine.* | **for ~** ◇ *He held onto her hand for ~.* | **in ~** ◇ *I patted her shoulder in ~.* | **~ about, ~ on** ◇ *The company tried to offer ~ on the safety of its products.* | **~ from** ◇ *~s from the researchers about their work*

reassure *verb*

ADV.   **constantly** ◇ *He was constantly reassuring himself that he had acted for the best.* | **quickly**

VERB + REASSURE   **be able to, can** | **help (to)** | **seek to, try to** | **hasten to** | **do little to, do nothing to** | **do a lot to, do much to** (*esp. BrE*) ◇ *The report will do much to ~ parents of children at the school.*

PREP.   **about** ◇ *They tried to ~ the public about the safety of public transport.* | **of** ◇ *She needed to be ~d of his love for her.* | **with** ◇ *He ~d her with a pat on the arm.*

PHRASES   **feel ~d** ◇ *Kate nodded, but she didn't feel ~d.* | **need reassuring** ◇ *Often parents simply need reassuring that their children are happy at school.*

reassuring *adj.*

VERBS   **be** | **find sth**

ADV.   **extremely, fairly, very, etc.** | **immensely** | **hardly, not exactly** ◇ *Her comment—'You can always try again if you fail'—was hardly ~.* | **vaguely** | **oddly, strangely** | **somehow**

PHRASES   **it is ~ to hear, know, see, etc.**

rebate *noun*

ADJ. **big, generous, substantial** | **full, maximum** | **cash** (*esp. AmE*) ◇ *The maximum cash ~ available is about $4 800.* | **rate** (*BrE*), **rent** (*esp. BrE*), **tax** ◇ *She's claiming a 100% tax ~.*
VERB + REBATE **be eligible for, be entitled to** (*esp. BrE*) ◇ *People on low incomes are entitled to a ~ of up to 80%.* | **apply for** (*esp. BrE*), **claim** | **get, receive** | **give sb, grant sb** | **offer** | **introduce**
REBATE + NOUN **scheme, system** (*both BrE*)
PREP. **~ on** ◇ *~s on the new tax*
PHRASES **a system of ~s** (*BrE*)

rebel *noun*

ADJ. **anti-government** | **leftist** (*esp. AmE*), **left-wing, right-wing** | **separatist** | **Communist, Maoist, etc.** | **former** | **armed** | **back-bench** (*BrE, politics*) ◇ *The Education Secretary has made further concessions to the back-bench ~s.*
... OF REBELS **band, group**
VERB + REBEL **back, help, support** ◇ *They sent in troops to back the ~s.* | **attack, fight** | **defeat** | **join** | **lead**
REBEL + VERB **be based ...** ◇ *The ~s were based in camps along the border.* | **advance** | **attack sth, fight** | **capture sth, gain control (of sth), regain control (of sth), seize sth, seize control (of sth), take control (of sth)** ◇ *The ~s seized control of the national radio headquarters.*
REBEL + NOUN **faction, group, movement** | **army, fighters, force, forces, militia, soldiers, troops** | **commander, leader** | **control** ◇ *The southern parts of the country had fallen into ~ control.* | **base, camp, position, stronghold** | **activity, advance, assault, attack, invasion** | **cause, movement** ◇ *new recruits to the ~ cause*
PREP. **against the ~** ◇ *military operations against the ~s* | **~ against** ◇ *a group of ~s against the emperor*
PHRASES **a bit of a ~, something of a ~** (*esp. BrE*) ◇ *He's a bit of a ~* (= he doesn't like to obey rules).

rebellion *noun*

1 attempt to change the government

ADJ. **full-scale, major** | **minor, small** | **open** | **armed** | **bloody, violent** | **military** | **grass-roots, popular** ◇ *A grass-roots ~ has flared nationwide against the proposed law.* | **peasant, slave** | **internal** ◇ *The country has been plagued by wars, civil wars, and internal ~s.*
VERB + REBELLION **rise in, rise up in** ◇ *The slaves rose up in ~.* | **launch, raise** (*literary, esp. BrE*), **stage** ◇ *They staged a ~ against Spanish rule in Mexico.* | **set off, spark off, start** ◇ *The re-introduction of conscription sparked off a major ~.* | **foment, incite, provoke** ◇ *attempts to foment ~ in the government* | **provoke sb/sth to** ◇ *The new taxes provoked the population to open ~.* | **threaten** ◇ *The party members threatened ~.* | **join** | **take part in** | **lead** | **support** | **crush, put down, quell, suppress**
REBELLION + VERB **occur** ◇ *Peasant ~s occurred throughout the 16th century.* | **begin, break out** ◇ *Rebellion broke out in India.* | **fail**
PREP. **in ~** ◇ *They are in ~ against the conservative hierarchy of the Church.* | **~ against** ◇ *a ~ against the new regime* | **~ over** ◇ *a ~ over an increase in taxes*

2 opposition to authority

ADJ. **adolescent, teenage, youth, youthful**
PREP. **~ against** ◇ *against their parents*
PHRASES **an act of ~** | **a form of ~**

rebuff *noun*

ADJ. **sharp** | **humiliating** | **electoral** (*BrE*) ◇ *The party suffered a humiliating electoral ~ in 1945.*
VERB + REBUFF **meet (sth) with, receive, suffer** ◇ *Her efforts were met with a sharp ~.*
PREP. **a ~ to** ◇ *In a ~ to the president, Congress voted against the bill.* | **~ from** ◇ *She suffered a ~ from her manager when she raised the matter.*

rebuild *verb*

ADV. **completely, entirely, totally** ◇ *The hall had to be completely rebuilt after the fire.* | **virtually** (*esp. BrE*) ◇ *The whole structure was virtually rebuilt.* | **extensively, largely, substantially** | **quickly, slowly** | **partially, partly** | **painstakingly**
VERB + REBUILD **begin to, start to** ◇ *She was just beginning to ~ her life.* | **try to** | **help (to)** ◇ *The international community must step in to help ~ the country.*
PHRASES **newly rebuilt, recently rebuilt** | **~ sth from scratch** ◇ *Much of the damaged vehicle had to be rebuilt from scratch.*

rebuke *noun*

ADJ. **harsh, scathing, sharp, stern, stinging, strong** | **gentle, mild** | **silent** | **implicit** (*esp. AmE*), **implied** | **public**
VERB + REBUKE **receive** | **draw, earn (sb)** ◇ *Even one minute's lateness would earn a stern ~.* | **accept** ◇ *He meekly accepted the ~.* | **deliver, offer** ◇ *Urban voters might deliver a sharp ~ to Congress.*
PREP. **~ for** | **~ from** ◇ *They received a public ~ from Secretary General for their handling of the matter.* | **~ to** ◇ *He hit back with a stinging ~ to his critics.*

rebuke *verb*

ADV. **sharply** | **gently** | **publicly**
PREP. **for** ◇ *She ~d herself sharply for her stupidity.*

recall *verb*

ADV. **clearly, distinctly, vividly, well** ◇ *I well ~ walking the five miles to school every morning.* | **dimly, faintly, vaguely** | **accurately, correctly** ◇ *If I ~ correctly, he lives in Luton.* | **easily** ◇ *She could easily ~ the smell of the orange groves.* | **suddenly** | **fondly, wistfully** ◇ *I am old enough now to wistfully ~ moments of my youth.* | **still** ◇ *Becky could still ~ that first meeting clearly.*
VERB + RECALL **seem to** ◇ *I seem to ~ that she said she was going away.* | **be able to, can** | **be unable to, cannot** ◇ *I couldn't quite ~ the date.* | **try to**
PHRASES **~ how ...** ◇ *She ~ed how she would go for walks along the beach late at night.* | **~ seeing, reading, hearing, etc. sth** ◇ *I ~ reading in an interview that he loved to cook.*

recede *verb*

ADV. **a bit, a little, slightly, somewhat** ◇ *His fine dark hair was receding a little.* | **further** | **gradually, slowly** ◇ *The pain was gradually receding.* | **fast, quickly, rapidly** ◇ *The January flood waters ~d as fast as they had risen.* | **back** ◇ *The water ~d back to its mysterious depths.*
PREP. **from** ◇ *These worries now ~d from his mind.*
PHRASES **~ into the background, ~ into the distance** ◇ *His footsteps ~d into the distance.*

receipt *noun*

1 piece of paper showing what was paid for

ADJ. **ATM** (*esp. AmE*), **credit-card** | **original** | **paper** ◇ *The machine issues a paper ~ on request.*
VERB + RECEIPT **ask (sb) for** | **need** ◇ *Do you need a ~?* | **get, obtain** | **receive** | **have** ◇ *Could I have a ~ for that please?* | **make out, write, write out** ◇ *a ~ made out for £5* | **sign** | **give sb, issue** | **print, print out, provide** | **keep, save** ◇ *You can claim a refund provided you keep the ~.* | **produce, submit** ◇ *The original ~ must be produced in order to reclaim your goods.*
RECEIPT + VERB **show** ◇ *His credit-card ~s show he was in New York at the time.*
RECEIPT + NOUN **book** | **printer** (*AmE*) ◇ *There was a little ~ printer on the counter.*
PREP. **~ for** ◇ *She issued a ~ for the goods.*

2 act of receiving sth

VERB + RECEIPT **acknowledge** ◇ *I would be grateful if you would acknowledge ~ of this letter.*
PREP. **in ~ of** ◇ *organizations in ~ of UN funding* | **on ~ of, upon ~ of** (*both esp. BrE*) ◇ *The goods will be sent on ~ of your payment.*
PHRASES **the date for ~** ◇ *The closing date for ~ of your*

application is July 14. | **~ of payment** *(esp. BrE)* ◇ *Upon ~ of payment by the bank, the goods will be dispatched.* | **within 7, etc. days of ~** ◇ *Items should be paid for within 14 days of ~.*

3 receipts money received

ADJ. **gross, total** ◇ *Cash income is calculated by subtracting total trading income from total ~s.* | **net** | **annual** | **capital** *(BrE)* | **corporate tax** *(esp. AmE)*, **federal tax** *(AmE)*, **income tax, tax** | **cash** | **dollar, euro, etc.** | **box-office, gate, match-day** *(BrE)*

VERB + RECEIPTS **receive**

RECEIPTS + VERB **rise** ◇ *Tax ~s rose 2.5%.* | **reach sth** ◇ *Cash ~s reached £70 million.* | **decline, fall, slump** ◇ *Gate ~s have fallen compared to last season.*

PREP. **~ from** ◇ *~s from land sales*

PHRASES **~s and expenditure, ~s and expenditures** *(both esp. AmE)* ◇ *an estimation of the ~s and expenditure for this financial year* | **~s and payments**

receive *verb*

1 get/accept sth

ADV. **regularly** | **automatically** ◇ *You will automatically ~ updates by text message.* | **currently** ◇ *They currently ~ subsidies from the government.* | **just, recently** ◇ *I just ~d a call from a concerned parent.* | **gratefully** ◇ *Any help or donations will be gratefully ~d.*

VERB + RECEIVE **be entitled to** ◇ *You might be entitled to ~ housing benefit.* | **expect to** ◇ *You can expect to ~ compensation for all direct expenses arising out of the accident.*

PREP. **from** ◇ *I ~d a package from my mother.*

PHRASES **send and ~, transmit and ~** ◇ *a device for sending and receiving electronic signals*

2 react to sth in a particular way

ADV. **enthusiastically, favourably/favorably, warmly, well** ◇ *The play was very well ~d.* | **badly** ◇ *The speech was badly ~d by Republican leaders.*

PREP. **with** ◇ *The news was ~d with dismay.*

receiver *noun*

1 part of a telephone

ADJ. **phone, telephone**

VERB + RECEIVER **lift, pick up** ◇ *She took a deep breath and lifted the ~ off its hook.* | **grab, snatch up** | **hold** | **cover** ◇ *He covered the ~ and mouthed, 'It's him.'* | **put back, put down, replace** | **bang down, slam down** ◇ *He slammed the ~ down and burst into tears.* | **drop**

RECEIVER + VERB **dangle** ◇ *The ~ was dangling from the payphone.*

PREP. **over the ~** ◇ *'It's your mother on the phone again!' said Juan with his hand over the ~.*

PHRASES **hold the ~ to your ear, put the ~ to your ear** ◇ *She picked up the ~ and put it to her ear.*

2 piece of radio/television equipment

ADJ. **hand-held, portable** | **GPS** | **HDTV, satellite, television** | **FM, radio, stereo**

RECEIVER + NOUN **module, unit** ◇ *To change channels, select the desired number on the ~ unit.* | **antenna**

3 person in charge of a bankrupt company

ADJ. **official** *(BrE)* | **court-appointed** *(AmE)* | **administrative** *(BrE)*

VERB + RECEIVER **appoint, appoint sb (as)** | **call in** *(esp. BrE)* ◇ *They had to lay off 200 staff and call in the ~s.*

PHRASES **in the hands of the ~** *(esp. BrE)* ◇ *The company remained in the hands (= under the control) of the ~.*

recent *adj.*

VERBS **be**

ADV. **very** | **comparatively, fairly, pretty, quite, rather, relatively** ◇ *a relatively ~ development*

reception *noun*

1 *(esp. BrE)* area in a building

VERB + RECEPTION **report to** ◇ *All delegates should report to the ~ on arrival.* | **call, call down to, phone, ring** *(BrE)*

RECEPTION + NOUN **area, lobby** *(AmE)* | **counter, desk** *(AmE, BrE)* | **hall** | **staff**

PREP. **at ~** *(BrE)*, **at the ~** ◇ *The man at the ~ says there's a call for you.* ◇ *I've left the keys at ~.* | **in ~** ◇ *Please wait for me downstairs in ~.* ◇ *The documents are in ~.* | **on ~** ◇ *I've been on ~ (= working at the reception desk) the whole morning.*

2 formal party

ADJ. **big, large** | **lavish** | **small** | **formal, informal** | **official** | **special** | **gala** | **evening** | **opening, welcome** *(esp. AmE)* ◇ *The opening ~ of the exhibition was attended by many well-known figures from the art world.* | **civic** *(BrE)*, **diplomatic, wedding** | **champagne** *(esp. BrE)*, **cocktail** *(esp. AmE)* ◇ *a White House cocktail ~*

VERB + RECEPTION **attend** | **give, have, hold, host** ◇ *Are you having a big ~ after the wedding?* | **organize** | **invite sb to** ◇ *Friends and family are invited to a ~ after the ceremony.*

RECEPTION + NOUN **room** ◇ *Tables were set out in the embassy's beautiful ~ room.*

PREP. **at a/the ~** ◇ *We met at a ~.* | **~ for** ◇ *a ~ for the Japanese trade delegation*

3 type of welcome given to sb/sth

ADJ. **enthusiastic, favourable/favorable, friendly, good, great, positive, rapturous, rousing, sympathetic, warm** | **lukewarm, mixed, tepid** | **bad, chilly, cold, cool, frosty, hostile** | **critical** ◇ *critical ~ to a movie* | **public**

VERB + RECEPTION **enjoy, get, have, meet, meet with, receive** ◇ *The plan has had a somewhat mixed ~ from local people.* ◇ *The returning soldiers received a rousing ~.* | **expect** ◇ *The managers did not expect a sympathetic ~ from the striking workers.* | **give sb/sth** ◇ *She was given a rapturous ~ by the crowd.*

RECEPTION + NOUN **party** ◇ *A ~ party of soldiers was there to greet the visiting head of state.* | **centre/center** ◇ *a ~ centre/center for visitors* ◇ *a ~ centre for children who have run away from home* *(BrE)*

PREP. **~ by** ◇ *the book's ~ by reviewers* | **~ from** ◇ *a cool ~ from the crowd* | **~ into** ◇ *~ into the monastic order* | **~ to** ◇ *the positive ~ to the speech*

4 quality of radio/television signals

ADJ. **good, strong** ◇ *Television ~ is very good in this area.* | **bad, poor, weak** | **radio, satellite, television, TV**

recess *noun*

1 period when a parliament, etc. does not meet

ADJ. **August** *(AmE)*, **Christmas** *(esp. BrE)*, **Easter** *(esp. AmE)*, **holiday** *(AmE)*, **summer, Whitsun** *(BrE)*, **winter** *(AmE)* ◇ *Congress returns from its August ~ Tuesday.* ◇ *Parliament is taking the Christmas ~ a little early this year.* ◇ *The bill has to be passed before the holiday ~.* | **congressional, parliamentary** | **brief, short** *(both esp. AmE)* ◇ *The Senate will go into ~ after Thanksgiving.* ◇ *Parliament is due to rise for the summer ~ on July 20.* ◇ *The Florida court stands in ~.* | **return from** | **call** ◇ *The judge called a short ~.*

VERB + RECESS **go into, rise for** *(BrE, formal)*, **stand in** *(AmE, formal)*, **take** ◇ *The Senate will go into ~ after Thanksgiving.* ◇ *Parliament is due to rise for the summer ~ on July 20.* ◇ *The Florida court stands in ~.* | **return from** | **call** ◇ *The judge called a short ~.*

PREP. **in ~** ◇ *Congress has been in ~ for over a month.*

2 *(AmE)* a period of time between classes at school

ADJ. **lunch**

VERB + RECESS **spend** | **have**

RECESS + NOUN **bell** | **time** ◇ *I believe kids need more ~ time.*

PREP. **at ~** ◇ *He wouldn't play with me at ~.*

3 part of sth that is farther back

ADJ. **deep** | **shallow, small** | **dark** | **window**

VERB + RECESS **create**

PREP. **in ~, inside ~** ◇ *blinds fitted inside a window ~* | **~ in** ◇ *There are small ~es in the wall beside the door.*

4 (usually **recesses**) part furthest from the light

ADJ. **dark, deep, dim** ◊ *He stared into the dark ~es of the room.* | **far, inner, innermost** (*figurative*) ◊ *He searched the innermost ~es of his soul.* | **hidden**
VERB + RECESS **hide in, lurk in** (*figurative*) ◊ *fears lurking deep in the ~es of our minds* | **push sth into, push sth to** (*both figurative*) ◊ *I had continually pushed my doubts to the darker ~es of my mind.*
PREP. **in the ~ of, within the ~ of** ◊ *The statue was in the inner ~es of the temple.*
PHRASES **the ~es of your brain, heart, soul, etc.** (*figurative*)

recession noun

ADJ. **bad, deep, major, serious, severe, sharp, steep** ◊ *It was the worst ~ since the war.* | **mild, shallow** | **double-dip** (= a second decrease after a period of improvement) (*esp. AmE*) ◊ *The US managed to avoid a double-dip ~.* | **long, prolonged** | **short, short-lived** | **impending, looming** | **deepening** | **global, international, national, world, worldwide** | **economic, industrial**
VERB + RECESSION **cause, induce, trigger** | **enter, go into, move into** | **fall into, plunge (sth) into, push sth into, sink into, slide into, slip into, throw sth into, tip (sth) into** ◊ *A rise in interest rates plunged Britain deeper into ~.* | **experience, suffer, suffer from** ◊ *Germany was suffering a steep ~.* | **deepen, prolong** ◊ *These reforms will only deepen the ~.* | **combat, fight** | **avoid, beat, prevent** | **climb out of, come out of, emerge from, get (sth) out of, lead sth out of, move out of, pull (sth) out of** ◊ *active policies to pull the country out of ~* | **end** | **escape, escape from** | **ride out, survive, weather** ◊ *As dozens of companies go out of business, others are riding out the ~.* | **worsen**
RECESSION + VERB **begin, start** | **end** | **loom** ◊ *With a ~ looming, consumers are spending less.* | **hit sth** ◊ *The country has been hit by ~.* | **bottom out**
PREP. **in (a/the)** ◊ *The economy is in deep ~.*
PHRASES **the depth of the ~** | **the effects of the ~, the impact of the ~** | **in the depths of a ~, in times of ~** | **recovery from (the) ~, a way out of the ~**
→ Special page at BUSINESS

recipe noun

ADJ. **good** | **delicious, mouth-watering, tasty** | **healthy, low-fat** ◊ *Each month we feature easy low-fat ~s.* | **favourite/favorite** | **basic** ◊ *The basic ~ can be adapted by adding grated lemon peel.* | **easy, simple** | **complicated** | **new** ◊ *I tried a new ~ and it was a great success.* | **authentic, classic, old, original, traditional** ◊ *The ales are brewed to an original Yorkshire ~.* | **secret, special** | **family** | **vegetarian** | **Italian, Mexican, etc.** | **cake, sauce, etc.** | **perfect** (*usually figurative*) ◊ *It's the perfect ~ for business success.* | **sure, sure-fire** (*both figurative*) ◊ *That sounds like a sure-fire ~ for disaster.*
VERB + RECIPE **get, have** ◊ *I have a good ~ for fudge.* | **give** ◊ *This is delicious—can you give me the ~?* | **cook, make, prepare** ◊ *This ~ can also be made with ricotta cheese.* | **try, try out** ◊ *I enjoy trying out new ~s.* | **read** | **follow, stick to, use** ◊ *If you want the dish to turn out right you should follow the ~.* | **adapt** | **create, devise** ◊ *All the ~s in the book have been devised by our team of experts.* | **discover, find** ◊ *He is credited with having discovered the first ~ for gin back in the 1600s.* | **share** ◊ *They talk and share their ~s.* | **feature, offer, print, publish** ◊ *The website offers cocktail ~s and tips.*
RECIPE + VERB **call for sth, require sth, use sth** ◊ *She always said that if a ~ calls for cream you shouldn't use yogurt instead.* | **contain sth, include sth** ◊ *The ~ contains lots of fat.* | **make sth, serve sb** ◊ *This ~ makes about thirty cookies.* ◊ *This ~ serves four people.*
RECIPE + NOUN **book, card** | **idea** ◊ *a magazine filled with ~ ideas*
PREP. **to a ~** ◊ *The dish is made to a traditional Italian ~.* | **for** ◊ *a ~ for leek soup* ◊ *To live every day to the full is a ~ for happiness.* (*figurative*)
PHRASES **a ~ for disaster, a ~ for success**

recipient noun

ADJ. **largest** | **main, major** | **intended** ◊ *She was not the intended ~ of the reward.* | **ultimate** ◊ *the ultimate ~ of the money* | **suitable** ◊ *the difficulties of matching a donor kidney with the most suitable ~* | **worthy** ◊ *He was a worthy ~ of the Nobel Prize.* | **passive** ◊ *We are passive ~s of information from the world around us.* | **unwilling** | **lucky** ◊ *Our 1000th member will be the lucky ~ of a mystery gift.* | **benefit** (*BrE*) | **welfare** (*esp. AmE*) | **organ, transplant** | **award, grant, scholarship** (*all esp. AmE*)
PREP. **~ of** ◊ *He was the ~ of a distinguished service award.*

recital noun

ADJ. **solo** | **lunchtime** (*esp. BrE*) | **organ, piano, etc.** | **poetry, song** | **ballet, dance** (*both esp. AmE*)
VERB + RECITAL **give, perform, play** | **attend, go to** | **listen to**
PREP. **~ by** ◊ *a ~ by the Grieg Trio* | **in ~** ◊ *Anna Netrebko in ~*

recognition noun

1 remembering/identifying sb/sth

ADJ. **immediate, instant** | **early, prompt** ◊ *the early ~ of a disease* | **dawning** | **brand, name** ◊ *One of the main goals of marketing is name ~.* | **word** ◊ *a tale of children's word ~* | **character, face, fingerprint, handwriting, speech, text, voice** | **automatic, computer** ◊ *the automatic ~ of handwriting by computer*
... OF RECOGNITION **flicker, sign** ◊ *She stared directly at the witness but he did not show a flicker of ~* (= he did not show that he recognized her).
VERB + RECOGNITION **show** | **avoid** ◊ *He pulled the hood of his cloak over his head to avoid ~.* | **allow, facilitate** ◊ *The monitoring system allows ~ of pollution hot spots.*
RECOGNITION + VERB **dawn** ◊ *Recognition slowly dawned, and I remembered her from my college days.*
RECOGNITION + NOUN **software, system, technology**
PREP. **beyond (all) ~** (*figurative*) ◊ *Many of those interviewed said their job had changed beyond ~* (= changed completely) *over the past five years.* | **out of (all) ~** (*figurative*) ◊ *The equipment and methods of production have improved out of all ~* (= greatly improved). | **without ~** ◊ *He looked up, glanced at them without ~, and went on his way.*
PHRASES **~ in sb's eyes** ◊ *There was no ~ in his eyes* (= he did not look as if he recognized her).

2 accepting that sth exists/is true; public praise/reward

ADJ. **full** | **special** ◊ *The judges selected three projects for special ~.* | **appropriate, due, proper, well-deserved** | **insufficient** | **greater, growing, increasing** ◊ *There needs to be a greater ~ of corporate crime as a social problem.* | **clear, explicit, overt** | **implicit** | **apparent** | **positive** | **equal** ◊ *equal ~ for the work women do* | **mutual** | **immediate, instant** | **belated, overdue** ◊ *The award is being made in belated ~ of her services to the industry.* ◊ *Recognition of his talent was long overdue.* | **individual, personal** ◊ *personal ~ for your achievements* | **general, universal, wide, widespread** ◊ *The young talent at the club deserves wider ~.* | **international, national, worldwide** | **public, social** | **professional** | **diplomatic** | **formal, legal, legislative, official** | **federal, government, state** | **de facto** ◊ *Twelve states have accorded de facto ~ to the new regime.*
VERB + RECOGNITION **achieve, attain, earn sb, gain, garner** (*esp. AmE*)**, get, obtain, receive, win** ◊ *His recitals have earned him ~ as a talented performer.* | **deserve, merit** | **require** ◊ *Both of these perspectives are valid and require ~.* | **imply** ◊ *They claim that signature of the peace accord did not imply ~ of the state's sovereignty.* | **ask for, call for, demand, request, seek** | **apply for** ◊ *to qualify for UN ~ as an International Biosphere Reserve* | **accord sb/sth, give sb/sth, grant sb/sth** | **deny sb/sth, refuse sb/sth**
RECOGNITION + VERB **come** ◊ *Official ~ of the change came fast.*
PREP. **in ~ of** ◊ *an award in ~ of his outstanding work* | **without ~** ◊ *She has worked actively but without ~.* | **as ~** ◊ *a country that has long sought ~ as a major power* | **~ by, ~**

from ◊ ~ *by his superiors of the service he had performed* | **for** ◊ *They received ~ for their 20-year commitment to safety at sea.*
PHRASES **a lack of ~** | **~ of the importance of sth, ~ of the need for sth** | **a struggle for ~**

recognizable (*BrE also* -**isable**) *adj.*
VERBS **be** | **become** | **remain** | **make sb/sth** ◊ *the mannerisms that make him instantly ~*
ADV. **clearly, completely, easily, highly, immediately, instantly, quite, readily** ◊ *John's car was easily ~.* ◊ *a building that was immediately ~ as a prison* | **universally** ◊ *The brand has a universally ~ logo.* | **barely, hardly, scarcely** (*esp. BrE*)
PREP. **as** ◊ *a language barely ~ as English* | **by** ◊ *~ by their distinctive uniforms* | **to** ◊ *The project's benefits were ~ to all interest groups.*

recognize (*BrE also* -**ise**) *verb*
1 know sb/sth again
ADV. **immediately, instantly** ◊ *I immediately ~d the building.* | **correctly, well** ◊ *She ~d the song correctly.* | **easily** ◊ *This is the only species of flamingo in the region, easily ~d by its pink plumage.* | **barely, hardly** ◊ *Stella hardly ~d her brother.* | **vaguely** ◊ *I vaguely ~d his voice, but couldn't think of his name.*
VERB + RECOGNIZE **learn to** ◊ *You learn to ~ the calls of different birds.* | **be easy to**
PREP. **as** ◊ *He ~d the man as one of the police officers.* | **by** ◊ *I ~d her by her red hair.* | **from** ◊ *I ~d them from a television show.*

2 understand or acknowledge sth
ADV. **clearly, fully** ◊ *They fully ~ the need to proceed carefully.* | **belatedly, finally** ◊ *The government has belatedly ~d the danger to health of passive smoking.* | **readily** ◊ *He readily ~s the influence of Freud on his thinking.* | **rightly** ◊ *The 1970s are rightly ~d as a golden era of Hollywood film-making.*
VERB + RECOGNIZE **must, need to** | **begin to** | **be slow to** ◊ *The company had been slow to ~ the opportunities available to it.* | **fail to**
PREP. **as** ◊ *This issue must be ~d as a priority for the next administration.*
PHRASES **be commonly ~d, be generally ~d, be universally ~d, be widely ~d** | **be increasingly ~d** ◊ *The strength of this argument is being increasingly ~d.* | **failure to ~ sth** | **it is important to ~ sth** ◊ *It's important to ~ that obesity isn't necessarily caused by overeating.*

3 accept sth officially
ADV. **clearly** ◊ *The law clearly ~s that a company is separate from those who invest in it.* | **federally** (*AmE*), **formally, legally, officially** | **internationally, nationally** ◊ *The estuary is ~d internationally as an important area for wildlife.* | **publicly** ◊ *The company should publicly ~ its mistake.* | **explicitly, implicitly** ◊ *The court explicitly ~d the group's right to exist.* ◊ *Criminal law implicitly ~s a difference between animals and property.* | **currently** ◊ *Do any US states currently ~ gay marriage?*
VERB + RECOGNIZE **agree to** | **refuse to**
PREP. **as** ◊ *All rivers should be officially ~d as public rights of way.*
PHRASES **be legally ~d** ◊ *A bill of exchange is a legally ~d document.* | **a refusal to ~ sth**

recoil *verb*
ADV. **a bit, a little, slightly** | **instinctively** ◊ *As he leaned forward she instinctively ~ed.* | **instantly** | **violently**
PREP. **at** ◊ *Carlos ~ed a little at the sharpness in my voice.* | **from** ◊ *She felt him ~ from her, frightened.* | **in** ◊ *He ~ed in apparent disgust.*

recollection *noun*
ADJ. **clear, distinct, vivid** | **dim, faint, hazy, vague** | **earliest**

| **childhood** | **sudden** | **painful** | **fond** ◊ *He has fond ~s of his first visit to Europe.* | **personal**
VERB + RECOLLECTION **have (no)** ◊ *I have only a vague ~ of sunshine and sand.* ◊ *I have absolutely no ~ of the incident.* | **share** ◊ *It was great to meet with old friends and share ~s.* | **smile at, smile in** ◊ *He smiled fondly at the ~.* ◊ *She smiled faintly in ~ of all the fun times they'd had together.*
PREP. **in ~** ◊ *She stared at him in sudden ~.* | **~ from** ◊ *~s from Eliot's own life* | **~ of** ◊ *The novel is based on ~s of his childhood in Shanghai.*
PHRASES **to the best of your ~** ◊ *To the best of my ~ (= if I remember correctly), he was not there that day.*

recommend *verb*
1 say that sb/sth is good
ADV. **highly, thoroughly** ◊ *This book is highly ~ed by teachers.* | **certainly, definitely** ◊ *I definitely ~ this movie.* | **enthusiastically, heartily, unreservedly, warmly, whole-heartedly** | **personally** ◊ *Consult a lawyer who is personally ~ed to you.*
PREP. **for** ◊ *Who would you ~ for the job?* | **to** ◊ *I can ~ this book to anyone interested in food.*
PHRASES **sth has a lot to ~ it, sth has much to ~ it** ◊ *Your idea has much to ~ it.*

2 advise sb to do sth
ADV. **strongly** ◊ *I would strongly ~ that you get professional advice.* | **particularly, specifically** | **commonly, generally, routinely, typically** ◊ *In the 1990s, doctors routinely ~ed hormone replacement therapy.* | **unanimously** ◊ *The commission unanimously ~ed the proposal.*
PREP. **for** ◊ *Food supplements are sometimes ~ed for diabetic patients.* | **to** ◊ *Here are a few safeguards I ~ to my clients.*

recommendation *noun*
1 official suggestion
ADJ. **firm, strong** | **clear** | **unanimous** | **detailed** | **specific** | **broad, general** ◊ *The committee put forward broad ~s for the improvement of safety at swimming pools.* | **far-reaching, wide-ranging** (*esp. BrE*) ◊ *The report made wide-ranging ~s for government.* | **important** | **central, key, main, major, principal** | **positive** | **practical** ◊ *What are your practical ~s for a healthy diet?* | **first, initial** | **final** | **further** | **draft** | **written** | **medical, official, practical** | **policy, safety, treatment** | **dietary**
... OF RECOMMENDATIONS **list, series, set**
VERB + RECOMMENDATION **come up with, develop, formulate, make, produce** ◊ *The committee has produced a set of ~s on ethics in health care.* | **give, issue, offer, present, provide, put forward, submit** | **publish, release** | **outline, summarize** | **consider, discuss, review** | **agree with** | **disagree with** | **accept, adopt, approve, endorse** ◊ *The UN Security Council endorsed the ~ submitted by the Secretary General.* | **reject** | **act on, carry out, follow, implement** ◊ *The government gave assurances that it would implement the ~s in full.* | **enforce** | **support** | **oppose** | **ignore** | **be in accordance with, be in line with** ◊ *to develop a plan in line with the ~s of national policy* | **base sth on** ◊ *The design of the breakwater was based on the ~s of an engineering study.*
RECOMMENDATION + VERB **arise from sth, be based on sth, follow sth, follow from sth, relate to sth** ◊ *a detailed set of ~s following a comprehensive examination of the subject* | **call for sth, propose sth, state sth, suggest sth** ◊ *The Senate ~ stated that the privatization of public hospitals should stop.* | **be aimed at sth** ◊ *~s aimed at achieving a more equitable admissions policy*
PREP. **at sb/sth's ~, on sb/sth's ~, upon sb/sth's ~** ◊ *At the ~ of a psychiatrist, the accused will remain under observation.* ◊ *I had the operation on the ~ of my doctor.* | **~ about, ~ as to, ~ concerning, ~ on** ◊ *~s on how health and safety standards might be improved* | **~ by, ~ from** ◊ *~s by the judges* | **~ for** ◊ *~s for improving the quality of service* | **~ to** ◊ *the board's ~s to the minister* | **~ with regard to, ~ with respect to** ◊ *~s with regard to management procedures*
→ Special page at MEETING

2 saying sb/sth is good/suitable

ADJ. **enthusiastic, glowing, high** ◇ *These two albums get my highest ~.* | **personal** ◇ *It's best to find a builder through personal ~.* | **word-of-mouth** ◇ *Many companies hire through word-of-mouth ~s from existing employees.*

VERB + RECOMMENDATION **give sb/sth** | **get, receive** | **come on, come with** ◇ *The new housekeeper came on the highest ~.* ◇ *The chef comes with her ~.*

RECOMMENDATION + NOUN **letter** (*AmE*) ◇ *Will you write me a ~ letter?*

PREP. **at sb's ~, on sb's ~, upon sb's ~** ◇ *We went to Malibu on your ~* (= because you recommended it).

PHRASES **a letter of ~** (*esp. AmE*) ◇ *I sent them a résumé and three letters of ~.*

reconciliation *noun*

ADJ. **genuine, true** | **full** | **national** | **political, racial** (*AmE*)

VERB + RECONCILIATION **seek** ◇ *He sought ~ with those he had stolen from.* | **attempt** ◇ *The pair are bravely attempting a ~.* | **achieve, bring** (*esp. AmE*), **bring about, effect, make** ◇ *the power of love to bring renewal and ~* ◇ *He is striving to bring about a ~ between the two conflicting sides.* | **promote, work for** | **call for** ◇ *The rebel leader called for ~ with the armed forces.*

RECONCILIATION + NOUN **agreement** | **process**

PREP. **~ between** ◇ *They aimed to secure a lasting ~ between the two countries.* | **~ with** ◇ *She attempted ~ with her estranged brother.*

PHRASES **an attempt at ~** | **a gesture of ~** ◇ *In a bold gesture of ~, the government released the rebel leader.* | **a policy of ~, a spirit of ~**

reconnaissance *noun*

ADJ. **initial, preliminary** | **maritime, military** | **aerial, air, satellite** ◇ *Spotter planes made a preliminary aerial ~ of the island.*

VERB + RECONNAISSANCE **carry out, conduct, do, make, perform** | **provide**

RECONNAISSANCE + VERB **reveal sth** ◇ *Reconnaissance revealed not a single large ship.*

RECONNAISSANCE + NOUN **flight, mission, operation** | **party, patrol, team, unit** | **aircraft, plane** | **satellite**

reconstruct *verb*

ADV. **completely** | **partially** | **carefully, painstakingly** ◇ *Every aspect of the original has been closely studied and painstakingly ~ed.* | **accurately**

VERB + RECONSTRUCT **attempt to, try to** | **be possible to** ◇ *It is not possible to ~ the complete symphony from these manuscript sketches.*

PREP. **from** ◇ *Local historians have ~ed from contemporary descriptions how the hall may have looked in 1300.*

PHRASES **an attempt to ~ sth**

reconstruction *noun*

ADJ. **major** | **complete, total** | **radical** | **large, large-scale, life-size** ◇ *a life-size ~ of a Viking longboat* | **accurate** | **three-dimensional** | **dramatic** (*esp. BrE*) ◇ *a dramatic ~ of school life in the 1940s* | **national** ◇ *The country faces a huge task of national ~ following the war.* | **post-conflict, post-war** | **economic, historical, political, social** | **surgical** ◇ *surgical ~ of his mouth* | **breast, facial, etc.**

VERB + RECONSTRUCTION **undergo** ◇ *The bombed city is now undergoing extensive ~.* | **undertake** ◇ *A group of enthusiasts have undertaken the ~ of a steam locomotive.* | **perform, stage** (*BrE*) ◇ *The police staged a ~ of the events leading up to the murder.* | **oversee** | **require**

RECONSTRUCTION + NOUN **period** | **effort, work** | **contract** ◇ *companies bidding for post-war ~ contracts* | **plan, programme/program, project, scheme** (*BrE*) ◇ *a large-scale urban ~ project* | **method, technique** | **cost** ◇ *~ costs following the cyclone* | **aid, assistance, money** | **fund** | **surgery** ◇ *breast ~ surgery*

PHRASES **a ~ based on sth** ◇ *a historical ~ based on contemporary documents*

---

record

record *noun*

1 account

ADJ. **formal** ◇ *No formal ~ of the marriage now survives.* | **official, public** | **permanent** | **accurate, careful, exact** ◇ *There is no exact ~ of the number of accidents.* | **up-to-date** | **adequate, proper, reliable** | **inadequate, incomplete** | **brief** | **complete, comprehensive, detailed, extensive** | **verbatim** (= exactly as written or spoken) ◇ *a verbatim ~ of the meeting* | **confidential** | **daily** | **personal** | **documentary, handwritten, paper, written** | **computerized, electronic** | **photographic, pictorial** | **early** | **archival, historical** | **archaeological, fossil, geological** ◇ *This period is poorly represented in the geological ~.* | **dental, health, hospital, medical, patient** | **accounting, administrative, departmental, financial, payroll, personnel** | **birth, census, tax, voting** | **court, library, school** | **cellphone** (*esp. AmE*), **mobile phone** (*BrE*), **phone** ◇ *There are cellphone ~s that prove we were not even in the apartment.*

VERB + RECORD **keep, maintain** ◇ *He has always kept an accurate ~ of his spending.* | **compile, create** | **provide** | **access** | **check, consult, examine, read, search, search through, study** ◇ *I checked the ~s but nobody by that name had worked here.* | **review** | **destroy, erase** ◇ *Medical ~s should not be destroyed.* | **file** | **update** | **correct** | **seize, subpoena** (*esp. AmE*) ◇ *Prosecutors had subpoenaed his phone ~s.* | **be on, go on** ◇ *She is on ~ as saying that she once took drugs.* ◇ *He is the latest public figure to go on (the) ~ about corruption in politics.*

RECORD + VERB **contain sth, include sth** ◇ *The ~s contain the bank details of all employees.* | **indicate sth, reveal sth, show sth** ◇ *The ~s showed that the building had not been inspected for ten years.* | **provide sth** | **suggest sth** ◇ *Fossil ~s suggest that the region was covered in water until relatively recently.* | **exist, survive** ◇ *No ~ exists of a battle on this site.* | **date back, go back** ◇ *The university ~s go back as far as the 13th century.* | **be available**

PREP. **in the ~, in the ~s** ◇ *evidence in the geological ~* ◇ *The historic agreement is preserved in the university ~s.* | **off the ~, on the ~** ◇ *Off the ~, he told the interviewer what he thought of his colleagues.* | **on ~** ◇ *It was the driest summer on ~.* | **~ of** ◇ *a ~ of achievement* | **~ on** ◇ *~s on children's progress*

PHRASES **access to the ~s** ◇ *Under the law, every citizen has access to their official ~s.* | **have a ~ of sth** ◇ *Do you have a ~ of how much you spent?* | **have no ~ of sth, not have any ~ of sth** ◇ *We have no ~ of your conversation with Mr Smith.* | **put the ~ straight, set the ~ straight** ◇ *She called a press conference to set the ~ straight about her disappearance.*

2 best result, highest level, etc.

ADJ. **club, course, national, Olympic, track, world** | **unbeaten, unbroken** | **current** | **new** | **old, previous** | **long-standing** ◇ *Bob Beamon's long-standing ~ for the long jump was eventually broken.* | **all-time** | **career, lifetime** (*AmE*) (*both sports*) ◇ *He compiled a lifetime ~ of 209–161.* | **scoring** | **all-comers** (= anyone who wants to take part in a sport or competition) (*BrE*) | **speed**

VERB + RECORD **hold** ◇ *Who holds the 100 m sprint ~?* | **establish, set** ◇ *She has just set a new world ~.* | **beat, better, break** ◇ *If she continues like this she could beat the ~.* | **eclipse, shatter, smash, top** | **equal, match, tie** ◇ *He hopes to equal the Olympic ~.*

RECORD + VERB **stand** ◇ *His mile ~ stood for twelve years.* | **fall**

RECORD + NOUN **book** ◇ *Bubka rewrote the pole-vault ~ books during his career.* | **attempt** | **breaker, holder** | **high, low** ◇ *Unemployment has reached a ~ high* (= the highest level ever). | **amount, level, number** ◇ *There was a ~ number of candidates for the post.* | **pace, speed, time** ◇ *The US saw its trade deficit shrink at a ~ pace in September.* | **attendance, crowd, turnout** | **earnings, sales**

PREP. **~ for** ◇ *These viewing figures are an all-time ~ for a single broadcast.* | **~ with** ◇ *Lewis established a new world ~ with a time of 9.86 seconds.*

PHRASES **in ~ time** ◇ *I got to work in ~ time.*

3 sb's performance in a particular area

ADJ. **past, track** | **distinguished, enviable, fine, good, impressive, proven, solid, strong** | **excellent, exceptional, exemplary, formidable** (*esp. BrE*), **outstanding, remarkable, stellar** (*esp. AmE*) | **unique, unparalleled, unrivalled/unrivaled** (*esp. BrE*) | **abysmal, appalling** (*esp. BrE*), **atrocious, bad, dismal, mediocre, poor, sorry** | **unenviable** ◇ *He has an unenviable ~ of poor health.* | **satisfactory** | **long** | **consistent** | **mixed, patchy, spotty** (*AmE*) ◇ *Given the patchy track ~ of previous international declarations, is it worthwhile to have such ambitious goals?* ◇ *He has a spotty military ~.* | **clean, unblemished** ◇ *Apart from a parking ticket ten years before, she had an unblemished driving ~.* | **academic, college, educational, school** | **military** | **attendance** ◇ *The teacher spoke to her about her poor attendance ~.* | **economic, environmental, human rights** ◇ *the government's economic ~* | **disciplinary** | **arrest** (*esp. AmE*), **criminal, police** ◇ *He has a long arrest ~.* ◇ *teenagers with a criminal ~* | **accident, safety** ◇ *The airline's accident ~ makes it among the safest.* | **driving**

VERB + RECORD **have, possess** | **establish** | **keep, maintain** ◇ *The company has maintained an accident-free ~ since it started business.* | **improve**

RECORD + VERB **demonstrate sth, show sth** ◇ *Her ~ shows that she is able to compete under great pressure.* | **compare with sth** ◇ *Our ~ compares well with that of any similar-sized company.* | **speak for itself** ◇ *When it comes to quality, our ~ speaks for itself.*

PREP. **~ among** ◇ *They have the worst human rights ~ among member countries.* | **~ for** ◇ *They have a good ~ for recognizing emerging talent.* | **~ in** ◇ *The ideal candidate will have a proven track ~ in project management.* | **~ on** ◇ *the government's abysmal ~ on crime*

4 (*old-fashioned*) **music**

ADJ. **long-playing, LP** (usually just *LP*) | **gramophone** | **vinyl** | **classical, hip-hop, jazz, pop, rock, etc.** | **best-selling, hit** ◇ *The band had a hit ~ in 1973.* | **favourite/favorite** | **good, great** | **bad** | **solo** | **debut, first** | **gold, platinum** ◇ *The album earned him his second gold ~.* ◇ *Her walls became lined with gold and platinum ~s.*

VERB + RECORD **write** | **cut, make, produce, record** | **release** ◇ *They released their first ~ in 1963.* | **sell** | **buy** | **listen to, play, put on** ◇ *I'll put on one of my old ~s.*

RECORD + NOUN **company, industry, label** | **producer** | **contract, deal** ◇ *The band signed their first ~ deal a year after forming.* | **collection** | **shop** (*esp. BrE*), **store** (*esp. AmE*) | **player** | **cover, sleeve** | **album**

record verb

1 information

ADV. **carefully, meticulously** | **accurately, correctly, properly** ◇ *The weights must be ~ed accurately.* | **faithfully** ◇ *It was all there, faithfully ~ed in his uncle's formal style.* | **duly** ◇ *The contract is witnessed by others and duly ~ed.* | **automatically, routinely** ◇ *The mother's occupation was not routinely ~ed on the birth certificate.* | **officially** | **electronically, manually** | **vividly** ◇ *The event is vividly ~ed in his journal.*

PREP. **as** ◇ *The time of the accident is ~ed as 6.23 p.m.*

PHRASES **be ~ed for posterity** ◇ *The names of those who died are ~ed for posterity on a tablet at the back of the church.* | **be ~ed in history** ◇ *the most famous and deadly influenza outbreak ~ed in history* | **historically ~ed** ◇ *historically ~ed events* | **poorly ~ed, well ~ed** ◇ *The geographical spread of the industry in the 16th century is hard to ascertain, for much of it is poorly ~ed.*

2 sound/pictures

ADV. **secretly** ◇ *She secretly ~ed the conversation.* | **originally** ◇ *The songs were originally ~ed on tape.*

PREP. **from** ◇ *a concert she had ~ed from the radio* | **on** ◇ *movies ~ed on videotape*

PHRASES **beautifully ~ed, well ~ed** ◇ *This CD has been beautifully ~ed.* | **digitally ~ed**

recorder noun → Special page at MUSIC

recording noun

ADJ. **excellent, fine, good** | **accurate, careful, detailed** ◇ *an accurate ~ of time* | **complete** ◇ *a complete ~ of Mozart's piano sonatas* | **last, later, latest, new, recent** ◇ *the band's latest ~* | **modern** | **early, old** | **first, original** ◇ *to enhance the quality of the original ~* | **commercial** ◇ *one of the first commercial ~s of the artist* | **professional** | **home** | **live, studio** | **audio, video** | **cassette, tape** | **analogue/analog, digital** | **mono, stereo** | **electrical, magnetic** ◇ *The principles of magnetic ~ have been around for a long time.* | **music, sound** ◇ *before the invention of sound ~* | **orchestral, piano, etc.** | **field** ◇ *field ~s of folk music from Asia*

VERB + RECORDING **do (sb), make (sb), produce** ◇ *Make a few test ~s before you start the session in earnest.* | **play (sb), play (sb) back** ◇ *I want to play you a ~ of the rehearsal.* | **hear, listen to** | **view, watch** | **release** | **obtain**

RECORDING + VERB **give sth, show sth** ◇ *The ~ gives an account of his kidnapping.* | **sound …** ◇ *The ~ sounds just like a live performance.*

RECORDING + NOUN **process** | **session** | **facility** (*esp. AmE*), **facilities** (*esp. BrE*), **studio** ◇ *a state-of-the-art digital ~ facility* ◇ *state-of-the-art digital ~ facilities* | **device, equipment, system** | **engineer** | **artist** | **career** ◇ *The clarinet player launched her ~ career in 2005.* | **contract, deal** | **company** | **industry**

PREP. **~ by** ◇ *a ~ by the Tokyo Quartet*

recount verb

ADV. **vividly** ◇ *The story of his life is vividly ~ed in this new book.* | **briefly** (*esp. AmE*) ◇ *Let me briefly ~ some personal experiences.* | **in detail** ◇ *The murders are ~ed in gruesome detail.*

recourse (*formal*) noun

ADJ. **constant, frequent** | **limited** (*esp. BrE*), **little** ◇ *Drivers have little ~ but to wait until the weather clears.* | **no other, only** ◇ *I have no other ~ than to inform the police.* | **direct** ◇ *The study of these creatures has been conducted without direct ~ to living specimens.* | **legal**

VERB + RECOURSE **have** ◇ *The mother of an illegitimate child had no legal ~ to the father.* ◇ *workers who have no ~ to trade unions* | **seek** ◇ *An order was made against which he sought ~ in the supreme court.* | **avoid** ◇ *Their system of dispute resolution avoids ~ to the courts.*

PREP. **by ~ to** ◇ *people who deal with emotional pain by ~ to drugs and alcohol* | **with (no) ~ to, without ~ to** ◇ *a charity for women with no ~ to public funds* ◇ *They tried to settle the dispute without ~ to the courts.* | **~ against** ◇ *Citizens have learned that they do have ~ against governments.* | **~ to** ◇ *She often had ~ to her dictionary.*

PHRASES **~ available to sb** ◇ *There is no ~ available to the victim.*

recover verb

ADV. **completely, fully** | **partially** | **mostly** (*esp. AmE*) | **only just** | **hardly, never quite, never really, not quite** ◇ *She had hardly ~ed from the birth of her last baby.* | **nicely, well** ◇ *Your baby is ~ing well.* | **enough, sufficiently** ◇ *After a minute she ~ed enough to speak.* | **easily** | **fast, quickly, rapidly, soon** | **gradually, slowly** | **eventually, finally** | **apparently** | **never** | **miraculously**

VERB + RECOVER **help sb (to)** | **struggle to** ◇ *Yates is struggling to ~ from a serious knee injury.*

PREP. **from** ◇ *Mrs Burton was still ~ing from her injuries in the hospital.*

recovery noun

ADJ. **amazing, astonishing** (*BrE*), **dramatic, excellent, miraculous, remarkable** ◇ *Laura made a miraculous ~.* | **good, robust, significant, strong, substantial** (*esp. BrE*) ◇ *There is a robust ~ in the markets.* ◇ *The world economy staged a strong ~.* ◇ *The company has made a substantial ~ over the past 12 months.* | **complete, full** | **limited, modest, partial** ◇ *The index staged a modest ~ to be 6.5 points down.*

| fragile | fast, quick, rapid, speedy, swift | gradual, slow | steady | eventual | successful | continuing | lasting (*esp. BrE*), long-term, sustained | spontaneous | global, national | economic, industrial ◇ *The global economic ~ has strengthened significantly.* | price, profits | jobless (*esp. AmE*) | physical ◇ *Mr Fisher made a full physical ~.* | post-operative | disaster ◇ *a disaster ~ plan* | post-war

VERB + RECOVERY **achieve, make, show, stage** ◇ *Many people make remarkable recoveries after strokes.* | **aid, enhance, facilitate, help, improve, maximize, promote, stimulate** ◇ *a reduction in interest rates to stimulate global economic ~* | **accelerate, hasten, speed, speed up** ◇ *A good rest would speed his ~.* | **allow, enable, ensure, permit** (*formal*) | **sustain** | **delay, hamper, hinder, impede, slow** | **affect** | **wish sb** ◇ *We wish them all a speedy ~.* | **expect, predict** | **see**

RECOVERY + VERB **depend on sth** | **be on the way, begin, come** ◇ *The economic circumstances are right and ~ is on the way* (= recovery will occur soon). ◇ *A ~ will come only when deflation is conquered.* | **be underway, occur, take place** | **continue**

RECOVERY + NOUN **time** ◇ *His injuries have returned as there was insufficient ~ time between games.* | **rate, speed** | **period, phase** | **process** | **effort, operation** | **plan, programme/program, strategy** | **area** (*esp. AmE*), **centre/center** (*esp. AmE*), **room** ◇ *After the operation she was taken to the ~ room.* | **position** (*esp. BrE*) ◇ *Continue resuscitation until the person starts breathing and then place them in the ~ position.*

PREP. **beyond ~** ◇ *The region has been damaged by acid rain and rivers are fouled almost beyond ~.* | **in ~** ◇ *He's in ~ from the disease.* | **~ from** ◇ *~ from his illness* | **~ in** ◇ *the recent ~ in consumer spending* | **~ to** ◇ *a slow ~ to full health*

PHRASES **be on the road to ~, be on the way to ~** ◇ *She is well on the road to ~* (= making good progress). | **hope of ~, a prospect of ~** ◇ *There is no hope of ~.* ◇ *the prospects of economic ~* | **a sign of ~** ◇ *The economy is showing the first signs of ~.*

recreation *noun*

ADJ. **popular** | **informal** (*BrE*) | **physical** (*esp. BrE*) | **outdoor, wilderness** (*AmE*) | **community** (*AmE*) ◇ *adult education and community ~ programs*

RECREATION + NOUN **area, centre/center** (usually *rec center* in *AmE*), **facilities, ground** (*BrE*), **room** ◇ *the construction of new parks and ~ areas*

PREP. **for ~** ◇ *She cycles for ~.*

PHRASES **a form of ~** ◇ *His only form of ~ is playing cards.*

recruit *noun*

ADJ. **latest, new, raw, recent** ◇ *raw ~s marching up and down with the drill instructor* | **potential, prospective** | **young** | **graduate** (*esp. BrE*) | **army, military, police**

VERB + RECRUIT **find** ◇ *A common way for companies to find new ~s is by taking a stand at a job exhibition.* | **attract** ◇ *It's difficult to attract ~s when working conditions are so poor.* | **enlist, gain, sign up** ◇ *Thousands of ~s had been enlisted and partly trained.* ◇ *She tried to gain ~s for the party.* | **train** ◇ *Army ~s are all trained in first aid.* | **provide** ◇ *Their business schools provide ~s for domestic industry.*

PREP. **~ to** ◇ *new ~s to the party*

recruit *verb*

ADV. **directly** ◇ *The specialist institutions directly ~ their own staff.* | **actively** | **aggressively** (*esp. AmE*) ◇ *Senior managers are being aggressively ~ed by companies.* | **heavily** (*esp. AmE*) ◇ *GM ~ed heavily in the South.* | **locally** ◇ *Most of the workers will be ~ed locally.* | **personally** ◇ *She personally ~ed the teachers.* | **specially** (*esp. BrE*) ◇ *Staff were ~ed specially for the event.* | **successfully**

VERB + RECRUIT **need to** | **seek to, try to**

PREP. **as** ◇ *Tony Ancona has been ~ed as Sales Manager.* | **for** ◇ *A hundred patients were ~ed for the study.* | **from** ◇ *Soldiers were ~ed from the local villages.* | **into** ◇ *Some of the men were ~ed into the army.* | **to** ◇ *Ten new members were ~ed to the committee.*

PHRASES **newly ~ed, recently ~ed** | **~ and retain sb** ◇ *a drive to ~ and retain federal employees*

recruitment *noun*

ADJ. **large-scale** | **labour/labor, staff** | **executive, faculty** (*AmE*), **teacher, volunteer** ◇ *She has set up her own executive ~ business in Paris.* ◇ *His responsibilities as associate provost will include faculty ~.* | **graduate** (*BrE*), **student** | **army, military, police** | **ethnic-minority, minority** (*esp. AmE*) ◇ *the need to increase ethnic-minority ~* | **active** (*esp. AmE*) ◇ *the active ~ of women* | **forced** ◇ *the forced ~ of children as soldiers* | **successful** ◇ *the successful ~ of a new chairman*

RECRUITMENT + NOUN **policy** | **strategy** | **procedure, process** | **method** | **campaign, drive, effort, programme/program** | **tool** ◇ *The website is an effective ~ tool for the organization.* | **market** (*BrE*) | **agency, consultancy, firm, service** (all *esp. BrE*) ◇ *You can get good IT staff by going to ~ agencies.* ◇ *She runs a ~ consultancy.* | **consultant** (*esp. BrE*), **manager** (*BrE*), **officer, specialist** (*BrE*) ◇ *the company's ~ officer* | **centre/center** | **site, website**

PREP. **~ by** ◇ *~ by large companies* | **~ into, ~ to** ◇ *large-scale ~ to the new industries*

PHRASES **a method of ~** | **~ and retention** ◇ *~ and retention of workers with essential skills*

recur *verb*

ADV. **constantly, frequently, repeatedly** ◇ *This is a constantly recurring problem which we must deal with.*

VERB + RECUR **be likely to** | **tend to**

PREP. **throughout** ◇ *a theme that ~s throughout the book*

PHRASES **keep recurring**

recurrence *noun*

ADJ. **frequent** | **cancer, disease, tumour/tumor, ulcer, etc.**

VERB + RECURRENCE **avoid, prevent** | **decrease, reduce** | **develop, experience, have, suffer** ◇ *He has suffered a ~ of his hamstring injury.*

RECURRENCE + VERB **be common, be frequent**

RECURRENCE + NOUN **rate** ◇ *a potentially fatal disease with a high ~ rate*

PHRASES **the likelihood of a ~, the risk of ~** ◇ *a high risk of ~*

recyclable *adj.*

VERBS **be**

ADV. **easily** ◇ *Paper is easily ~.* | **100%, completely, fully** ◇ *Glass products are completely ~.*

recycle *verb*

ADV. **endlessly** (usually figurative) ◇ *They endlessly ~ the same worn-out arguments.*

PREP. **from** ◇ *made of plastic ~d from old packaging material* | **into** ◇ *These materials are ~d into other packaging products.*

PHRASES **can be ~d** ◇ *The packaging can be ~d.* | **~d waste, paper, materials, etc.**

recycling *noun*

ADJ. **doorstep** (*BrE*), **kerbside/curbside** (*esp. BrE*) ◇ *kerbside/curbside ~ bins* | **paper, plastic, waste** ◇ *a paper-recycling bin* ◇ *opportunities for waste ~*

RECYCLING + NOUN **program** (*AmE*), **scheme** (*BrE*) ◇ *a curbside ~ program.* ◇ *a kerbside ~ scheme* | **bin** | **centre/center** ◇ *I take all my waste paper to the ~ centre/center.* ◇ *Garden waste can be taken to household ~ centres.* (*BrE*)

red *adj., noun*

1 colour/color

VERBS **glow** ◇ *The coals glowed ~ in the dying fire.* | **go, turn** ◇ *The traffic light turned ~.* | **paint sth**

ADV. **really, very** | **completely** | **slightly** ◇ *The leaves looked slightly ~.*

ADJ. **bright, brilliant, fiery, flaming, vibrant, vivid** ◇ *flaming*

~ **hair** | **dark, deep, rich** | **light, pale** | **dull** | **blood, brick, cherry, fire-engine, ruby** ◇ *her ruby ~ lips*
PHRASES **~ and blotchy** (= of skin or eyes), **~ and puffy** (= of eyes) ◇ *Her eyes were ~ and puffy, as if she'd been crying.* | **~ and swollen** (= of injured part of body)
→ Special page at COLOUR

2 of the face

VERBS **be, look** | **become, flush, get, go, grow, turn** ◇ *Mr Gruber was growing redder and redder in the face.*
ADV. **very** | **quite** | **rather, slightly**
ADJ. **bright, fiery** ◇ *He could feel himself going bright ~.*
PREP. **~ with** ◇ *Ross flushed ~ with embarrassment.*
PHRASES **as ~ as a beet** (*AmE*), **as ~ as a beetroot** (*BrE*) | **~ in the face** ◇ *Charles was rapidly turning ~ in the face.*

redemption noun being saved from the power of evil

VERB + REDEMPTION **be in need of, need** ◇ *She believes that humanity is in need of ~.* | **seek** | **find** | **offer (sb)**
PREP. **beyond ~** ◇ *Washington journalism is corrupt beyond ~.* | **~ from** ◇ *~ from evil*

redistribution noun

ADJ. **major** (*esp. BrE*), **massive, significant** ◇ *The new regime carried out a major ~ of land.* | **equitable** ◇ *an equitable ~ of wealth* | **income, land, wealth**
VERB + REDISTRIBUTION **bring about** ◇ *The tax brought about a significant ~ of wealth.*
PREP. **~ of** ◇ *a ~ of income* | **~ from, ~ to** ◇ *~ from the rich to the poor*

red tape noun

ADJ. **administrative, bureaucratic** | **government, governmental** (*AmE*)
VERB + RED TAPE **cut, reduce** | **be entangled in, be tied up in, be snarled in** (*esp. AmE*), **be snarled up in** (*esp. BrE*) | **cut through** | **deal with** ◇ *How do we deal with all this ~?*

reduce verb

ADV. **considerably, dramatically, drastically, greatly, markedly, severely, sharply, significantly, substantially** | **successfully** | **further** | **slightly** ◇ *We need to ~ the speed slightly.* | **gradually, progressively** ◇ *Legislation progressively ~d the number of situations in which industrial action could be taken.* | **quickly, rapidly**
VERB + REDUCE **aim to, attempt to, seek to, try to** | **help (to)** ◇ *Giving up smoking helps ~ the risk of heart disease.* | **manage to** | **be designed to, be intended to** | **be expected to, be likely to**
PREP. **by** ◇ *Pollution from the works has been ~d by 70%.* | **in** ◇ *I noticed that my belly had drastically ~d in size.* | **from, to** ◇ *The price is ~d from 99 cents to 85 cents.*
PHRASES **an attempt to ~ sth, an effort to ~ sth** | **measures to ~ sth** | **~ sth to a minimum** ◇ *The risks must be ~d to the absolute minimum.*

reduction noun

ADJ. **big, considerable, great, large, major, marked, significant, substantial** ◇ *The changes may result in a greater ~ in employee numbers than we had previously expected.* | **dramatic, drastic, huge, massive, remarkable, severe** ◇ *a sale with massive ~s on selected items* | **minor, modest, slight, small** | **tenfold, fiftyfold, etc.** | **further** | **possible** | **actual, net, overall, real** | **across-the-board, general** | **rapid, sharp, steep** | **slow** | **immediate, sudden** | **gradual, progressive, steady** | **initial, recent** | **long-term, permanent** | **proposed** | **percentage** ◇ *A small percentage ~ in the cost of materials would mean a significant increase in profit.* | **cost, debt, deficit, pay, price, tariff, tax, wage** | **emission, noise, pollution, waste** | **harm, pain, risk, stress** ◇ *a drug strategy which prioritizes harm ~* | **poverty** ◇ *The IMF claims to put poverty ~ at the heart of its policies.* | **size, weight** ◇ *The result is a 75 to 80%*

size ~. | **breast** ◇ *She had a breast ~ last year.* | **staff** | **arms, troop**
VERB + REDUCTION **achieve, make, secure** ◇ *The government has found it difficult to make real ~s in spending.* ◇ *Every effort is made to secure the highest possible ~ in casualties.* | **cause, lead to, make, produce, result in** ◇ *These simple changes will make a substantial ~ in the fat content of your diet.* | **avoid** | **ask for, demand, seek** ◇ *I asked for a ~ as the dress was damaged.* | **require** | **get, receive** ◇ *Guests staying 14 nights will receive a 10% ~.* | **experience, have** ◇ *The company has had a ~ in sales.* | **suffer** ◇ *They suffered a severe ~ in income.* | **accept, welcome** (*esp. BrE*) ◇ *I welcome the ~ in road traffic fatalities.* | **give (sb), offer (sb)** | **propose** ◇ *She proposed a ~ in the state president's powers.* | **notice, observe, see** ◇ *Police said they had noticed a significant ~ in crime last year.* | **announce** ◇ *The gas company has announced price ~s for all customers.* | **mean, represent** ◇ *Our average margins dropped to 35%, which represents a ~ in gross margins of £109 million.* | **demonstrate, show** ◇ *Figures just released show a steady ~ in levels of emissions over the last four years.*
REDUCTION + VERB **occur, take place**
REDUCTION + NOUN **target** ◇ *the government's waste ~ targets*
PREP. **through a/the ~** ◇ *economic growth through a ~ in interest rates* | **~ by** ◇ *~ by 30%* | **~ from, ~ in** ◇ *There has been a sharp ~ in the number of accidents on our roads.* | **~ of** ◇ *a ~ of carbon dioxide emissions* | **~ on** ◇ *a 25% ~ on normal subscription rates* | **~ to** ◇ *a ~ in the speed limit from 50 to 40 miles per hour*
PHRASES **a ~ in numbers** ◇ *Asian elephants have experienced a 50% ~ in numbers over the last three generations.* | **a ~ in the amount of sth, a ~ in the number of sth, a ~ in the size of sth** ◇ *the ~ in the number of hospital beds*

redundancy noun (BrE)

ADJ. **large-scale, major, mass, massive** ◇ *The closure of the mine led to large-scale redundancies.* | **possible, threatened** | **compulsory, voluntary** | **staff** | **further**
... OF REDUNDANCIES **round, wave** ◇ *a fresh wave of redundancies*
VERB + REDUNDANCY **make** ◇ *The bank will be making 3 500 redundancies over the next five years.* | **lead to, result in** | **avoid** | **announce** | **rule out** | **be threatened by, be threatened with, face** ◇ *Sixty workers at the factory face ~.* | **be offered** | **accept, take, volunteer for** ◇ *34 members of staff have taken voluntary ~.*
REDUNDANCY + NOUN **programme** | **notice** ◇ *Redundancy notices have been sent to 200 workers.* | **package, terms** | **money, pay, payment** | **costs** ◇ *Most of the companies' losses stemmed from ~ costs.*
PHRASES **the threat of ~**

redundant adj.

1 (*BrE*) no longer needed for a job

VERBS **be** | **become** | **make sb** ◇ *the decision to make 800 employees compulsorily ~*
ADV. **compulsorily**

2 not necessary or wanted

VERBS **be, feel, seem** | **become** | **declare sth** (*BrE*), **make sth, render sth** ◇ *The chapel was declared ~ in 1995.*
ADV. **completely** | **partially** | **virtually** (*BrE*) ◇ *The boom in mobile phones has made phone boxes virtually ~.* | **largely** | **a bit, somewhat**

refer verb

PHRV **refer to sb/sth**
ADV. **briefly, in passing** ◇ *He referred to the report in passing.* | **specifically, commonly** ◇ *The disease was commonly referred to as 'the green sickness'.* | **constantly, frequently, often, repeatedly** | **generally, usually** | **sometimes** | **always** | **never** | **henceforth, hereafter, hereinafter** (*all formal*) ◇ *Kaminsky and Reinhart—hereafter referred to as KR* | **jokingly** | **affectionately, lovingly** | **collectively** | **directly, explicitly**
VERB + REFER TO **be used to** ◇ *The term 'alexia' is used to ~ to any acquired disorder of reading.*

referee *noun*

1 official who controls a game

ADJ. **basketball, boxing, football, soccer** (*esp. AmE*), **etc.** | **match** (*esp. BrE*), **meet** (*AmE*), **tournament** ◊ *decisions taken by the tournament ~* | **international** | **top** | **professional** (*esp. BrE*) ◊ *my 20 years as a professional ~* | **assistant** (in football/soccer) ◊ *an assistant ~ flagged for a penalty* | **guest** (*esp. AmE*) ◊ *He was acting as a guest ~ in the main wrestling event.*

REFEREE + VERB **award sb sth** ◊ *The ~ awarded a free kick to the home team.* | **blow his/her/the whistle** | **stop sth** | **book sb, send sb off** (both in football/soccer) (*both BrE*) ◊ *The ~ booked three players for offensive behaviour.*

PHRASES **the referee's decision**

2 (*BrE*) recommends sb for a job → See also REFERENCE

ADJ. **academic**

VERB + REFEREE **act as, be**

PREP. **~ for** ◊ *His former employer agreed to act as a ~ for him.*

reference *noun*

1 mentioning sb/sth

ADJ. **extensive** | **brief, casual, passing** | **occasional** | **frequent, repeated** | **constant** | **further** ◊ *They could find no further ~ to Mr LaMotte in the records.* | **general** | **particular, special, specific** ◊ *She won a grant to study political science with special ~ to China.* | **direct, explicit, express** (*law, esp. BrE*) | **overt** | **cryptic, indirect, oblique, obscure, subtle, vague, veiled** | **clear, obvious** | **ambiguous** | **early** ◊ *one of the earliest ~s to the game of chess* | **biblical, cultural, historical, literary, religious** | **written**

VERB + REFERENCE **contain, have, include** ◊ *Her diary contains no ~ to the alleged appointment.* | **drop, make** ◊ *He dropped casual ~s to the legacy of his great work.* ◊ *The article makes no ~ to his first marriage.* | **delete, drop, omit, remove** ◊ *The new constitution dropped all ~ to previous wars.* | **avoid** | **find** | **get, understand** ◊ *The audience didn't get the ~s to colonialism.*

PREP. **in a/the ~** ◊ *In an obvious ~ to the president, he talked of corruption in high places.* | **in ~ to, with ~ to** (in letters) ◊ *I am writing with ~ to your job application.* | **~ to** ◊ *The summary should be comprehensible without ~ back to the source work.* ◊ *The book is filled with ~s to God.*

2 consulting sb/sth for advice/help/information

ADJ. **easy, quick** ◊ *The book is organized alphabetically for easy ~.* | **further, future**

PREP. **by ~ to** ◊ *Our charges are calculated by ~ to an hourly rate.* | **for ~** ◊ *Retain a copy of the form for future ~.* | **without ~ to** ◊ *The decision was made without ~ to local managers.*

PHRASES **for sb's own ~, for sb's personal ~** ◊ *I made a copy of your work, just for my own ~.* | **for ~ purposes** ◊ *She needs the book for ~ purposes.* | **a source of ~** ◊ *The book is an invaluable source of ~ for the art historian.*

3 book containing facts/information

ADJ. **general** ◊ *The book is by far the best general ~ on natural history.* | **comprehensive** | **essential** | **handy, useful** | **excellent, good** | **standard** | **online** ◊ *an online ~ tool*

REFERENCE + NOUN **book, guide, manual, material, source, text, work** | **tool** | **library** | **section** ◊ *You'll find the information in the ~ section of your local library.* | **desk** (= in a library) (*esp. AmE*) | **librarian** (*esp. AmE*)

4 number/note/symbol

ADJ. **copious** | **full** ◊ *For full ~s of all books cited, see Appendix B.* | **appropriate** ◊ *Please quote the appropriate ~ in your letter.* | **bibliographic, bibliographical** | **page** | **grid, map**

VERB + REFERENCE **quote** | **cite, give** ◊ *References to original sources are given at the end of each chapter.* | **check**

REFERENCE + NOUN **number**

PREP. **in a/the ~** ◊ *The date of publication should be included in the ~.* | **~ to** ◊ *a ~ to page 17*

PHRASES **a list of ~s**

5 letter about your character/abilities

ADJ. **glowing, good** | **bad** | **character**

VERB + REFERENCE **ask for** | **need** | **give (sb), provide (sb with), write (sb)** | **follow up, take up** (*BrE*) ◊ *They've taken up my ~s* (= contacted the people who provided them)*, so they must be interested in me.*

PREP. **~ from** ◊ *a ~ from your current employer*

PHRASES **a letter of ~**

6 (*esp. AmE*) recommends sb for a job → See also REFEREE

VERB + REFERENCE **act as, be** | **contact**

PREP. **~ for** ◊ *His former employer agreed to act as a ~ for him.*

7 standards by which sth is judged

REFERENCE + NOUN **point** | **group** ◊ *Gene frequencies were calculated then compared with the Finnish population as a ~ group.* | **sample** (*science*)

PHRASES **a frame of ~** ◊ *People interpret events within their own frame of ~.* | **a point of ~** ◊ *Unemployment serves as a useful point of ~ in examining social problems.* | **terms of ~** (*esp. BrE*) ◊ *The matter was outside the committee's terms of ~.*

referendum *noun*

ADJ. **planned, proposed** | **popular, public** | **national, nationwide, statewide** (*esp. AmE*) | **constitutional, independence**

VERB + REFERENDUM **conduct, hold** ◊ *The ~ will be held on July 14th.* | **put sth to** ◊ *The proposals were put to a ~.* | **call** ◊ *The president called a ~ that he hoped would confirm him in power.* | **call for, demand, propose** ◊ *The group called for a ~ on the death penalty.* | **force** | **oppose** | **boycott** ◊ *The unions urged people to boycott the ~.* | **organize** | **approve, pass** (*both esp. AmE*) ◊ *California voters passed a ~ allocating $22 billion for school facilities.* | **vote against, vote for, vote on** (*all esp. AmE*) ◊ *The president won a ~ on his rule.* | **win** ◊ *The president won a ~ on his rule.* | **be adopted by/in, be approved by/in, be confirmed by/in** ◊ *a new constitution adopted by ~* ◊ *The agreement was approved in a ~.*

REFERENDUM + VERB **show sth** ◊ *A popular ~ showed that the majority of people want reform.* | **approve sth** | **fail**

REFERENDUM + NOUN **proposal** ◊ *The Democrats rejected the ~ proposal.* | **campaign, process** | **result**

PREP. **in a/the ~** ◊ *The issue will be decided in a national ~.* | **~ on** ◊ *a ~ on a new constitution*

PHRASES **the result of a ~**

refine *verb*

ADV. **slightly** | **greatly** | **further** | **increasingly** | **constantly, continually, continuously** ◊ *The information system is constantly ~d and updated.* | **gradually**

VERB + REFINE **attempt to, try to** | **continue to** | **help (to)**

PREP. **into** ◊ *Sugar cane is ~d into sugar.*

PHRASES **highly ~d** ◊ *supplies of the highly ~d white sugar*

refinement *noun*

1 improvement to/on sth; process of improving sth

ADJ. **considerable, great** ◊ *A greater ~ of the categorization is possible.* | **extra, further** | **constant, continuous, progressive** ◊ *the progressive ~ of their accounting technique* | **useful** ◊ *It is possible to add a few useful ~s to the basic system.* | **technical** | **modern**

... OF REFINEMENT **degree, level**

VERB + REFINEMENT **need, require** ◊ *The technology requires a great deal of ~.* | **add, introduce**

PREP. **~ in** ◊ *a ~ in the masonry* | **~ on** ◊ *a ~ on previous methods* | **~ to** ◊ *to add a further ~ to the computer system*

2 being polite/well educated; clever in design

ADJ. **great** ◊ *a woman of great ~ and beauty*

VERB + REFINEMENT **lack** ◊ *The kite was star-shaped and lacked the ~ of current designs.*

PREP. **~ in** ◊ *a lack of ~ in engine design*

PHRASES **a lack of ~**

reflect verb

1 send back light/heat/sound

ADV. **dimly, dully** ◊ *The sun ~ed dully off the stone walls.* | **directly** ◊ *Light ~s directly off a face of a crystal.* | **back**
PREP. **from** ◊ *The screen ~s light from the sun.* | **off**

2 show/express sth

ADV. **clearly** | **directly** | **accurately, closely, correctly, faithfully, well** ◊ *Does this opinion poll accurately ~ the public mood?* | **adequately** ◊ *The punishment should adequately ~ the revulsion felt by most people for this appalling crime.* | **merely, simply** ◊ *This year's budget simply ~s the fact that we have fewer people out of work.* | **not necessarily** ◊ *The views expressed in this article do not necessarily ~ those of the editor.* | **badly, poorly** ◊ *This kind of conduct ~s very poorly on you.* | **negatively** ◊ *information that may ~ negatively on research participants* | **strongly** ◊ *Senegalese culture strongly ~s influences from Islamic rulers.*
VERB + REFLECT **be designed to** ◊ *The exhibition is designed to ~ the diversity of the nation and its regions.*
PREP. **in** ◊ *The condition of the house is ~ed in its low price.*

3 think deeply

ADV. **bitterly, ruefully** (*esp. BrE*), **wryly** ◊ *He ~ed ruefully that the his money didn't buy as much as it used to* ◊ *One good thing, he ~ed wryly, was that none of his colleagues would find out.* | **critically** ◊ *an opportune time to ~ critically on the city's past*
VERB + REFLECT **pause to** | **leave sb to** ◊ *He was left to ~ on the implications of his decision.*
PREP. **on, upon** ◊ *She paused to ~ on what she had achieved.*
PHRASES **time to ~** ◊ *I need time to ~.*

reflection noun

1 image in a mirror, etc.

ADJ. **clear** | **dim, faint** | **blurred, distorted**
VERB + REFLECTION **catch, catch a glimpse of, catch sight of, glimpse, see** ◊ *I caught his ~ in the window.* ◊ *He caught sight of her ~ in the window.* | **glance at, look at** | **gaze at, stare at, watch** | **admire, examine, inspect, study** ◊ *She caught him admiring his ~ in the mirror.* | **show** ◊ *The mirror showed her ~.*
REFLECTION + VERB **look ...** ◊ *Her ~ in the mirror looked distorted.* | **appear** ◊ *Kyle's ~ appears in the glass.* | **stare (back)** ◊ *My ~ stared back at me.*
PREP. **in a/the ~** ◊ *In the ~ on the glass door he could see the class behind him.* | **~ in** ◊ *I saw my ~ in the polished marble.* | **~ on** ◊ *the ~ of the mountains on the calm waters of the lake*

2 sending light/heat/sound back from a surface

ADJ. **heat, light, sound**
PREP. **~ from** ◊ *There is ~ of heat from the metal surface.*
PHRASES **the angle of ~**

3 indication/description of sth

ADJ. **accurate, fair, good, perfect, true** | **inadequate** | **mere, pale** ◊ *This account is only a pale ~ of the true state of affairs.* | **poor, sad** ◊ *The movie is a poor ~ of Kerouac's work.* | **direct, simple** ◊ *Young people's conduct is a direct ~ of adults'.* | **clear** ◊ *This was a clear ~ of Marc's personality.*
VERB + REFLECTION **give (sb), provide** ◊ *Such studies do not give a true ~ of population needs.*
PREP. **~ of, ~ on, ~ upon** ◊ *His low level of performance is no ~ on his general ability.*

4 careful thought about sth

ADJ. **careful, deep, mature, profound, serious, sober** | **further** | **quiet** | **personal** | **thoughtful** ◊ *Such decisions may be made after thoughtful ~.* | **critical, ethical, moral, philosophical, spiritual, theological, theoretical**
VERB + REFLECTION **encourage, invite, prompt, stimulate** ◊ *Teachers should encourage ~ on the part of their students.*
REFLECTION + VERB **show sb/sth** ◊ *A moment's ~ will show you that that can't be true.*
PREP. **after ~, on ~, upon ~** ◊ *On further ~, I'm not so sure it's a good idea.* | **~ about, ~ on, ~ upon** ◊ *The party needs a period of sober ~ about what went wrong.*
PHRASES **a moment of ~, a moment's ~** | **a period of ~** | **a period for ~, time for ~**

5 written or spoken thoughts about sth

ADJ. **interesting** | **poignant** | **brief**
VERB + REFLECTION **have** | **offer** ◊ *They took a few minutes to offer their personal ~s.*
PREP. **~ about, ~ on, ~ upon** ◊ *She has some interesting ~s about the spiritual state of the country.*

reflective adj.

VERBS **be** | **become**
ADV. **highly, truly, very** | **merely** ◊ *I fear my comments are merely ~ of a larger problem.*

reflex noun

ADJ. **fast, good, lightning, quick** ◊ *He reacts with lightning fast ~es.* | **poor** | **automatic** | **natural** | **conditioned**
VERB + REFLEX **trigger** ◊ *The rapid movement of an object close to the eye triggers an automatic ~.* | **control** | **hone, sharpen** ◊ *The training is designed to sharpen the fighter's ~es.* | **slow** ◊ *Alcohol can slow your ~es.* | **suppress** | **test** ◊ *The doctor tested her ~es.*
REFLEX + NOUN **action, response** ◊ *Almost as a ~ action, I grab my pen as the phone rings.*
PREP. **by ~** ◊ *Almost by ~, he helped himself to a drink.*

reform noun

ADJ. **dramatic, drastic, fundamental, great, important, major, radical, significant, substantial** | **broad, comprehensive, far-reaching, sweeping, wholesale, wide-ranging** ◊ *The Prime Minister promised sweeping ~s of the banking system.* | **genuine, meaningful, real** | **minor, modest** | **piecemeal** | **new** | **proposed** | **further** | **immediate** | **rapid** | **lasting** | **necessary, needed, overdue** ◊ *much-needed ~s* ◊ *Health-care ~ is long overdue.* | **effective** | **practical** | **moral, political, social** | **democratic, liberal** | **domestic, institutional, internal** | **procedural, structural** ◊ *There remains reluctance to undertake the structural ~s advocated by Mr Smith.* | **administrative, governmental, regulatory** | **policy** | **constitutional, election, electoral, judicial, law, legal, legislative, tort** (*esp. AmE*) ◊ *The country desperately needs broad political and constitutional ~.* | **intelligence** ◊ *our debate on intelligence ~* | **penal, prison** | **curriculum, education, educational, school** | **health-care, pension, social-security, welfare** ◊ *advocates of health-care ~* | **banking, economic, finance, financial, fiscal, market, monetary, tax** ◊ *The government instituted a tax ~ to stimulate demand.* | **corporate, media** ◊ *the battle for corporate ~* | **agrarian, agricultural, environmental, land** | **immigration** ◊ *Top on his list was immigration ~.*
... OF REFORMS **package**
VERB + REFORM **adopt, bring about, initiate, introduce, pass** | **push through** ◊ *They wanted to push through radical ~s.* | **carry out, enact, implement, institute, make, put in place, put into practice, undertake** ◊ *His administration carried out economic ~s.* | **accelerate** ◊ *efforts to accelerate the structural ~ of the economy* | **delay** | **block** ◊ *The conservative coalition could delay further ~s or block them altogether.* | **oppose, resist** | **accept, embrace, welcome** | **advocate, call for, press for, promote, propose, pursue, push for, seek** ◊ *They have issued a statement advocating ~ of the legal system.* ◊ *Publishers continue to push for sweeping ~s.* | **demand** | **back, encourage, support** ◊ *We are committed to supporting democracy and ~ in the region.* | **require** ◊ *The practice of global politics requires ~.* | **plan** | **discuss**
REFORM + VERB **go through** ◊ *The ~s went through in spite of opposition from teachers.* | **be aimed at sth** ◊ *tax ~s aimed at encouraging land development* | **fail** ◊ *His economic ~s failed to improve their lives.*
REFORM + NOUN **process** | **movement** | **agenda, initiative, package, plan, programme/program, proposal** | **measure, policy** | **act, bill, law, legislation** ◊ *The House narrowly passed the education ~ bill.* | **school** (*esp. AmE*)

PREP. **~ in** ◊ *~s in housing and education*
PHRASES **the need for ~ | the pace of ~ | a programme/
program of ~**

reform *verb*

ADV. **drastically, fundamentally, radically, truly** ◊ *The
education system must be radically ~ed.* ◊ *the near
impossibility of truly ~ing the system*
VERB + REFORM **attempt to, push to, seek to, try to**
PHRASES **attempts to ~ sth, efforts to ~ sth, proposals to ~
sth | a need to ~ sth**

refrain *noun*

ADJ. **constant | common, familiar** ◊ *Complaints about school
food have become a familiar ~.*
VERB + REFRAIN **sing, take up** ◊ *The choir's sopranos took up
the ~.* | **echo, repeat | hear** ◊ *I kept hearing the same ~.*
REFRAIN + VERB **go** ◊ *Can you remember how the ~ goes?*

refrain *verb*

ADV. **carefully, deliberately** ◊ *He deliberately ~ed from
expressing his opinion on the matter.* | **wisely | barely** ◊
Priscilla could barely ~ from clapping her hands together.
PREP. **from** ◊ *I ~ed from laughing.*

refreshing *adj.*

VERBS **be, feel | find sth**
ADV. **extremely, really, very, wonderfully** ◊ *The water was
cold and wonderfully ~.* | **quite** (*esp. BrE*)

refreshment *noun*

ADJ. **light | liquid** (*humorous*)
VERB + REFRESHMENT **need | enjoy, get, take | pause for, stop
for** ◊ *We stopped for ~ after an hour.* | **bring, offer, provide
(sb with), serve** ◊ *Light ~s will be served in the interval.*
REFRESHMENT + VERB **be available**
REFRESHMENT + NOUN **area, centre/center, kiosk** (*esp. BrE*),
room, stand, table | facilities
PREP. **for ~** (*esp. BrE*) ◊ *We're allowed twenty minutes for ~.* |
for ~s ◊ *What are we going to have for ~s?*

refrigerator *noun* (*formal or AmE*) → See also FRIDGE

ADJ. **home, household | empty, full | mini, small | walk-in
| stainless-steel | wine** (*esp. AmE*)
VERB + REFRIGERATOR **raid** (*informal*) ◊ *I'll raid your ~ while we
talk.* | **fill, stock** ◊ *I stocked the ~ with fruit.* ◊ *a ~ stocked
with food* | **open** ◊ *I opened the ~ to take out some orange
juice.* | **defrost**
REFRIGERATOR + VERB **hum** ◊ *The ~ was humming in the corner.*
REFRIGERATOR + NOUN **door | magnet | box** (*AmE*)
PREP. **in the ~** ◊ *Place the dough in the ~ overnight.*

refuge *noun*

ADJ. **safe | temporary | wildlife | mountain** ◊ *a monk living
in a mountain ~* | **last** (*figurative*) ◊ *They looked to the
country as the last ~ of liberty.* | **welcome** ◊ *Many children
consider the facility a welcome ~.*
VERB + REFUGE **take** ◊ *They took ~ in the embassy.* | **look for,
seek** ◊ *They sought ~ in the mountains.* | **find** ◊ *They were
hoping to find a safe ~ for the night.* ◊ *They found ~ from the
bright sun.* | **become** ◊ *a town that became a ~ for a number
of dissident artists* | **create, establish | open | give (sb),
offer | provide (sb with)**
PREP. **~ against** (*figurative*) ◊ *Home is a ~ against the pressures
of work.* | **~ from** ◊ *The cave provided ~ from the storm.*
PHRASES **a place of ~**

refugee *noun*

ADJ. **genuine | would-be** (*esp. BrE*) ◊ *the government's
strategy in dealing with would-be ~s* | **former, returning |
displaced, homeless** (*both esp. AmE*) ◊ *A flood of displaced
~s fled west.* | **economic, environmental, political, war** ◊
*Many claimed to be environmental ~s, leaving for the sake of
their health.* | **civilian | child**
VERB + REFUGEE **qualify as** (*esp. BrE*) ◊ *Those who did not*
qualify as ~s were returned to their home countries.* | **be
considered (as)** ◊ *They should be considered economic ~s.* |
accept, repatriate, resettle, take, take in ◊ *The government
has agreed to take only 150 ~s.* | **expel, return | take back |
house | assist, help**
REFUGEE + VERB **flee sth** ◊ *~s fleeing political persecution* | **be
displaced** ◊ *~s displaced by the civil war* | **arrive | flood,
flow, pour** ◊ *Hundreds of ~s are pouring over the border.* |
live ◊ *~s living in camps along the border* | **return**
REFUGEE + NOUN **crisis, issue, problem, question, situation |
flows** (*AmE*), **movement** ◊ *The ~ flows alone would be a huge
upheaval.* | **resettlement | programme/program | status** ◊
She has been refused ~ status. ◊ *He does not qualify for ~
status.* | **claim | agency, group, organization, worker |
camp, centre/center** ◊ *He was born in a ~ camp.* | **children,
community, family, population**
PREP. **among ~** ◊ *Unemployment among the ~s has risen
sharply.* | **~ from** ◊ *~s from civil wars*
PHRASES **a flood of ~s, a influx of ~s** ◊ *a new influx of ~s
from the combat zone* | **the flow of ~s | the plight of ~s |
the return of ~s**

refund *noun*

ADJ. **full | partial | 10%, 50%, etc. | cash | tax | prompt**
VERB + REFUND **give (sb), issue, make** (*BrE*), **pay, provide** ◊
They'll only give you a ~ if you have the receipt. | **offer (sb) |
refuse (sb)** ◊ *He has been refused a ~ on his air ticket.* | **be
entitled to** ◊ *You're entitled to a full ~ if you change your
mind.* | **ask (sb) for, claim, demand, request, seek | get,
obtain, receive**
PREP. **~ for** ◊ *There will be no ~ for cancellations.* | **~ of** ◊ *a
full ~ of the registration fee* | **~ on** ◊ *She received a ~ on the
unused tickets.* | **~ to** ◊ *~s to 10 000 customers across the
country*

refund *verb*

ADV. **in full** ◊ *Your money will be ~ed in full.* | **gladly |
promptly**
PREP. **to** ◊ *If you are not satisfied with the goods, the price will
be ~ed to you.*

refusal *noun*

ADJ. **absolute, adamant, blank** (*BrE*), **blunt, complete, flat,
outright, point-blank, utter** ◊ *the panel's point-blank ~ to
release the information* ◊ *her utter ~ to do anything to help* |
**continued, continuing, deliberate, obstinate, persistent,
repeated, resolute, staunch, steadfast, stubborn, wilful/
willful** ◊ *the enemy's steadfast ~ to accept defeat* | **polite |
apparent | initial | first** (*BrE*) ◊ *If you decide to sell your car,
I hope you'll give me first ~* (= the opportunity to buy it
before it is offered to others).
VERB + REFUSAL **be met by, be met with** ◊ *Her appeals for
funds to support the cause were met with outright ~s.* |
accept ◊ *He accepted my ~ with a shrug.*
PREP. **~ by, ~ of** ◊ *a ~ by a patient to accept the recommended
treatment*
PHRASES **a ~ of consent** (*law, BrE*) ◊ *a ~ of consent to blood
transfusions* | **~ on … grounds** (*esp. BrE*) ◊ *their ~ on
religious grounds to perform military service*

refuse *noun*

ADJ. **domestic, household** (*both esp. BrE*) | **human**
... OF REFUSE **heap, pile**
VERB + REFUSE **dump** ◊ *People just dump their ~ in the street.* |
collect (*esp. BrE*) ◊ *Refuse is collected on Fridays.*
REFUSE + NOUN **collection, disposal | collector** (*BrE*) ◊ *I had a
part-time job as a ~ collector.* | **dump, heap** (*esp. AmE*)

refuse *verb*

ADV. **absolutely, utterly | adamantly, obstinately, reso-
lutely, staunchly** (*esp. AmE*), **steadfastly, stubbornly,
vehemently | categorically, flatly, point-blank, simply** ◊
Gerard ~d point-blank to cooperate. | **explicitly** (*esp. AmE*),

pointedly ◊ *The demand for an apology was pointedly ~d.* | **politely** | **consistently** | **repeatedly** ◊ *The Court has repeatedly ~d to bend on this point.*
VERB + REFUSE **cannot** ◊ *They made me an offer I couldn't ~.* | **can hardly** | **be entitled to, have the right to** ◊ *Workers should be entitled to ~ to work under these conditions.* | **be churlish to, seem churlish to** (*both BrE*) ◊ *She offered them tea and it seemed churlish to ~.* | **dare to** ◊ *He didn't dare to ~.* | **continue to**

regain *verb*

ADV. **completely, fully** ◊ *He hadn't completely ~ed his strength.* | **quickly, rapidly** | **soon** ◊ *She soon ~ed her composure.* | **gradually, slowly** | **eventually, finally** | **never** ◊ *He was severely injured and never ~ed consciousness.*
VERB + REGAIN **attempt to, battle to, fight to, struggle to, try to** ◊ *She struggled to ~ her composure.* | **be desperate to, be determined to, hope to** ◊ *He was determined to ~ what his father had lost.* | **help sb (to)** | **manage to** | **be unable to, fail to**
PHRASES **an attempt to ~ sth, a bid to ~ sth, an effort to ~ sth** ◊ *He is making a bid to ~ his number-one ranking.* | **a chance to ~ sth, an opportunity to ~ sth** ◊ *a chance to ~ the lead in the contest*

regard *noun*

1 attention to/thought for sb/sth

ADJ. **particular, special, specific** | **scant** ◊ *They paid scant ~ to my views.* | **due, full** (*BrE*), **proper** (*esp. BrE*) (*all law*) ◊ *The decision reached has due ~ for the safety of the public.*
VERB + REGARD **have** ◊ *When exercising its discretion, the court will have ~ to all the circumstances.* ◊ *They have no ~ for the values of our community.* ◊ *These people had little ~ for the environment.* | **pay, show** ◊ *The manifesto pays scant ~ to green issues.*
PREP. **in ~ to, with ~ to** ◊ *I am writing with ~ to your recent order.* | **without ~ for, without ~ to** ◊ *an attempt to plan the future of an industry without due ~ to market forces* | **~ for** ◊ *a proper ~ for human dignity*
PHRASES **in that ~, in this ~** ◊ *I have nothing further to say in this ~* (= in regard to what has just been said). | **a lack of ~** ◊ *a lack of ~ for public safety* | **little, no, etc. ~ for sb/sth, little, no, etc. ~ to sb/sth**

2 respect/admiration for sb

ADJ. **deep** (*esp. AmE*), **great, high** ◊ *He has a high ~ for truth.* ◊ *The composer was held in high ~ in England.* | **insufficient, low** | **mutual** | **critical**
VERB + REGARD **have, hold sb/sth in** ◊ *I have the greatest ~ for his abilities.* ◊ *He is held in the highest ~ by his colleagues.*

3 regards used in letters to send greetings to sb

ADJ. **best, kind, warm** ◊ *The letter ended, 'Kindest ~s, Felicity.'*
VERB + REGARDS **give (sb), send (sb)** ◊ *David sends his warmest ~s to your parents.*
PREP. **~ to** ◊ *My ~s to your aunt* (= please give my regards to your aunt).

regard *verb*

1 (often **be regarded**) **think of sb/sth in a particular way**

ADV. **highly, well** ◊ *She was highly ~ed as a sculptor.* | **generally, universally, widely** ◊ *The project was widely ~ed as a success.* | **commonly, popularly, usually** | **conventionally, traditionally** ◊ *Rabbits were traditionally ~ed as vermin.* | **legitimately, properly, reasonably, rightly** ◊ *The crash could be reasonably ~ed as an opportunity to invest.* | **long** ◊ *an agency long ~ed as ineffectual* | **hitherto** | **still** | **no longer**
VERB + REGARD **appear to, seem to** ◊ *He seemed to ~ the whole thing as a joke.* | **tend to** ◊ *They tend to ~ the open expression of emotion as being soft and feminine.* | **come to** ◊ *I had come to ~ him as a close friend.* | **continue to** | **be tempted to** ◊ *The successful are often tempted to ~ their*

success as a kind of reward. | **be tempting to** | **be a mistake to, be wrong to** ◊ *It would be a mistake to ~ the incident as unimportant.*
PREP. **as** ◊ *Many of her works are ~ed as classics.* | **with** ◊ *They ~ed people outside their own town with suspicion.*

2 look steadily at sb/sth

ADV. **steadily** | **intently** | **curiously, suspiciously, thoughtfully, warily**
VERB + REGARD **continue to** ◊ *His eyes continued to ~ her steadily.*
PREP. **with** ◊ *She ~ed the mess with distaste.*

regime *noun*

1 system of government

ADJ. **new** | **old** ◊ *Crowds celebrated the downfall of the old ~.* | **current, established, existing, present** | **ruling** | **former, previous** | **ousted** ◊ *An interim government was elected to replace the ousted ~.* | **interim** | **political** | **conservative, liberal, radical** | **authoritarian, autocratic, despotic, dictatorial, fundamentalist, totalitarian, tyrannical, undemocratic** ◊ *dictatorships and autocratic ~s* ◊ *The tyrannical ~ violently repressed any opposition.* | **brutal, hard-line, harsh, murderous, oppressive, repressive** | **corrupt** | **hostile** | **outlaw, rogue** ◊ *the threat posed by rogue ~s* | **communist, democratic, fascist, nationalist, socialist** | **constitutional, parliamentary** | **revolutionary** | **military** | **colonial** | **secular, theocratic** ◊ *a harsh and unrelenting theocratic ~* | **puppet** ◊ *In 1940 a puppet ~ was established by the invaders.*
VERB + REGIME **establish, install, set up** | **defeat, destroy, overthrow, topple** | **change, remove, replace** ◊ *the day he and his ~ are removed from power* | **bolster, strengthen** ◊ *Education was seen as a way of bolstering the existing ~.* | **destabilize, undermine** | **back, support** | **challenge, criticize, oppose** | **head, lead** ◊ *a military ~ headed by the general*
REGIME + VERB **exist** | **come to power** ◊ *The communist ~ came to power in 1975.* | **emerge** | **collapse, fall** | **govern, rule** | **pose a danger, pose a threat** ◊ *These ~s pose a grave and growing danger.*
REGIME + NOUN **change** ◊ *the real war aim of ~ change*
PREP. **against a/the ~** ◊ *She called for sanctions against the ~.* | **under a/the ~** ◊ *He spoke of the abhorrent crimes that had been committed under the ~.* | **~ under** ◊ *a military ~ under Franco*
PHRASES **a change of ~** | **the collapse of a ~, the fall of a ~, the overthrow of a ~** | **a member of a ~**

2 set of rules/procedures

ADJ. **harsh, rigorous, strict** | **new** | **special** | **exercise, fitness, health, training** | **dietary** | **drug, treatment** | **economic, financial, fiscal, legal, monetary, regulatory** ◊ *a financial ~ imposed by the government* | **tax, trade, trading** | **safety** (*esp. BrE*) ◊ *the company's outstanding safety ~* | **non-proliferation** ◊ *a challenge to the global nuclear non-proliferation ~* | **sanctions** ◊ *the UN-enforced sanctions ~*
VERB + REGIME **create, set up, start** ◊ *It will be necessary to create a ~ to monitor compliance with the agreements.* | **impose** ◊ *A strict ~ of exercise was imposed on the children.* | **follow** ◊ *He suggested to me that I follow his fitness ~.*
REGIME + VERB **be based on sth** ◊ *a ~ based on discipline and training*
PREP. **under a/the ~** ◊ *Under the new ~ you will be liable for automatic penalties for late submission of tax returns.* | **~ for** ◊ *the new ~ for accounting for charities*

regimen *noun* (*medical or formal*)

ADJ. **strict** | **combined** | **daily** ◊ *a sensible daily ~ of vitamin supplements* | **dietary** | **exercise, fitness, training, workout** ◊ *a strenuous training ~* | **drug** | **treatment** | **antibiotic, chemotherapy, etc.** | **dosage, dose**
VERB + REGIMEN **use** ◊ *We used a combined ~ of chemotherapy and radiation therapy.* | **follow** ◊ *She follows a strict fitness ~.* | **begin, start** ◊ *He began a new fitness ~.* | **continue, maintain** ◊ *It is important to maintain a training ~.*

region *noun*

1 area of land/part of a country

ADJ. **large** | **small** | **entire**, **whole** | **distinct**, **particular**, **specific** | **northern**, **southern**, etc. | **central** | **border**, **far-flung**, **outlying**, **peripheral**, **remote** ◇ *oil exploration in remote ~s of the Russian Far East* | **neighbouring/neighboring**, **surrounding** | **unexplored** | **geographic** (*esp. AmE*), **geographical** | **arid**, **coastal**, **desert**, **equatorial**, **mountain**, **mountainous**, **polar**, **subtropical**, **tropical** | **Arctic**, **Gulf**, **Himalayan**, **Mediterranean**, **Pacific**, etc. | **autonomous** ◇ *the autonomous ~s of the People's Republic of China* | **metropolitan**, **urban** | **rural** | **populated** ◇ *a sparsely populated ~* | **economic** | **developed**, **industrial** | **developing** | **depressed**, **poor**, **underdeveloped** ◇ *the poorer ~s of the continent* | **prosperous**, **rich** ◇ *Italy's richest ~* | **oil-producing**, etc. | **troubled** ◇ *an attempt to bring peace and stability to a troubled ~*
VERB + REGION **inhabit**, **live in**, **occupy**, **populate** ◇ *Nomads have inhabited this ~ for thousands of years.* | **characterize** ◇ *This tropical forest ~ is characterized by frequent heavy rainfall.* | **work in** | **study**, **survey** | **leave** | **explore**, **visit** | **divide into** ◇ *The country is divided into 17 autonomous ~s.* | **confine sb/sth to** ◇ *This bird is largely confined to the southern ~s of the country.*
REGION + VERB **cover sb/sth** ◇ *The champagne-producing ~ covers 34 500 hectares.*
PREP. **across a/the ~** ◇ *Sports events across the ~ have been affected by the weather.* | **from a/the ~** ◇ *Twenty participants from the Asia-Pacific ~ will be invited to the seminar.* | **in a/the ~**, **within a/the ~** ◇ *The animal is found in the northern ~s of Sweden.* | **in the ~ of** (*figurative*) ◇ *She earns in the ~ of* (= approximately) *£200 000.* | **throughout a/the ~** ◇ *The plant is found throughout the western ~s of the country.*
PHRASES **sth varies from ~ to ~** ◇ *Sanitary facilities varied widely from ~ to ~.*

2 part of the body

ADJ. **distinct**, **particular**, **specific** | **abdominal**, **brain**, **lumbar**, etc.
PREP. **from a/the ~** ◇ *tissue from the mouth ~* | **in a/the ~**, **within a/the ~** ◇ *cells in a particular ~ of the brain*

register *noun*

1 list of names

ADJ. **full** (*esp. BrE*) | **annual** (*esp. BrE*) | **central**, **federal**, **national**, **public** (*esp. BrE*) | **statutory** (*BrE*) | **professional** (*esp. BrE*), **social** ◇ *CEOs who were listed in a social ~* | **attendance** (*BrE*) ◇ *the keeping of an attendance ~* | **electoral** (*esp. BrE*) ◇ *residents listed on the electoral ~* | **medical** (*BrE*) ◇ *Dr Shaw was struck off the medical ~ for misconduct.* | **birth**, **marriage** | **class**, **school** (*both BrE*) | **church**, **parish** (*both esp. BrE*) | **guest** (*esp. AmE*), **hotel** (*esp. BrE*) | **check** (*AmE*) ◇ *ways of reconciling bank statements with check ~s* | **land** (*esp. BrE*), **share** (*BrE*) | **sex offenders'** (*BrE*) ◇ *He has been placed on the sex offenders' ~.*
VERB + REGISTER **appear on**, **be on** (*both esp. BrE*) ◇ *All those appearing on the ~ must notify the authorities of any change of address.* | **join** (*esp. BrE*) | **remain on** (*BrE*) | **keep** (*esp. BrE*), **maintain** ◇ *They keep a ~ of all those who have contributed to the fund.* | **call**, **take** (*both BrE*) (*take attendance* in *AmE*) ◇ *The teacher takes the ~ at the beginning of each class.* | **compile** (*esp. BrE*), **create**, **draw up** (*esp. BrE*), **establish** (*esp. BrE*) ◇ *She was asked to draw up a ~ of suitable sites.* | **add sb/sth to** | **enter sb/sth in**, **enter sb/sth on**, **~ sth in**, **~ sth on** (*all esp. BrE*) ◇ *Their names had been entered in the ~ as owners of the company.* | **remove sb from**, **strike sb from**, **strike sb off** (*all BrE*) ◇ *He was struck off the medical ~ for professional misconduct.* | **sign** (*esp. BrE*) ◇ *The bride and bridegroom signed the ~.*
REGISTER + VERB **contain sth**, **include sth** ◇ *a ~ containing details of four million cars*
REGISTER + NOUN **office** (*in the UK*) ◇ *The Leas married in a ~ office.*

PREP. **in a/the ~** ◇ *It was the last entry in the ~.* | **on a/the ~** ◇ *There are 36 children on the ~.*
PHRASES **an entry in a ~**, **an entry on a ~** (*esp. BrE*)

2 range of notes of a voice/an instrument

ADJ. **high**, **low**, **middle**, **upper** ◇ *the lower ~ of the piano* | **vocal** | **chest**, **head**
PREP. **in a/the ~** ◇ *boy trebles singing in high ~s*

3 level/style of a piece of writing/speech

ADJ. **formal**, **informal**
VERB + REGISTER **adopt** (*BrE*) ◇ *He has adopted an informal ~ so as not to alienate his audience.*

4 (*AmE*) **machine used for money in a shop/store** → See CASH REGISTER

register *verb*

1 put sb/sth on an official list

ADV. **formally**, **officially** | **properly** ◇ *They had not properly ~ed as required by state law.* | **legally** | **fully** (*esp. BrE*) | **duly** ◇ *As I reached my eighteenth birthday I duly ~ed for military service.* | **automatically** | **online** ◇ *Players must ~ online before playing the game.*
VERB + REGISTER **be required to**, **have to**, **must**, **need to**, **should** ◇ *You must ~ the death within three days.* | **be eligible to** | **fail to** | **refuse to**
PREP. **as** ◇ *the number of people officially ~ing as unemployed* | **at** ◇ *He ~ed at his local university.* | **for** ◇ *There is still time to ~ for English classes.* | **with** ◇ *Students living away from home are required to ~ with a local doctor.*
PHRASES **newly ~ed** ◇ *the preferences of newly ~ed voters*

2 notice sth

ADV. **barely**, **hardly** ◇ *She had barely ~ed his presence.* | **dimly**, **vaguely** ◇ *He vaguely ~ed that the women had gone.* | **slowly** ◇ *The words ~ed slowly in her mind.*
VERB + REGISTER **fail to**, **not seem to** ◇ *His eyes failed to ~ Susan's surprise.* ◇ *The pain that stung her hand did not seem to ~.* | **begin to** ◇ *Slowly, my mind began to ~ where I was: in the hospital.*

registration *noun*

ADJ. **full** | **limited** | **formal** | **compulsory**, **mandatory** | **complimentary**, **free** ◇ *a complimentary ~ for the 2002 meeting of the society* | **advance** | **same-day** (*AmE*) ◇ *states that allow same-day voter ~* | **on-site** (*AmE*) ◇ *on-site ~ for this week's events* | **online** | **civil** ◇ *civil ~ of births* | **birth**, **death** (*both esp. BrE*) | **class**, **course**, **student** | **voter** | **car**, **company** (*BrE*), **domain-name**, **gun**, **land**, **product**, **trademark**, **vehicle** | **VAT** (*BrE*) | **conference**, **convention**, **meeting** | **party** (*AmE*) ◇ *my Democratic party ~*
VERB + REGISTRATION **require** | **apply for**, **file**, **seek**, **submit** | **conduct** (*AmE*) ◇ *The organization will conduct voter ~ for overseas nationals.* | **obtain**, **receive** | **accept**, **grant sb** ◇ *Under the new regulation we can grant full ~ to foreign lawyers.* | **renew** | **cancel**
REGISTRATION + VERB **be required**
REGISTRATION + NOUN **requirement** ◇ *a failure to comply with the ~ requirements* | **period** | **deadline** ◇ *The ~ deadline is November 4.* | **procedure**, **process** | **scheme** (*BrE*), **system** | **database**, **records** ◇ *I traced my family history using the civil ~ records.* | **list**, **roll** (*both AmE*) ◇ *the information on the ~ roll* | **application**, **form** | **card**, **document**, **papers** | **statement** | **number** ◇ *I gave the ~ number of the car to the police.* (*BrE*) ◇ *You must have the voter ~ number on the form.* (*AmE*) | **plate** (*BrE*) (*license plate* in *AmE*) ◇ *The police are looking for a black car with German ~ plates.* | **sticker** (*AmE*) | **officer** (*BrE*) | **fee** | **counter** (*AmE*), **desk**, **office** ◇ *I headed to the ~ desk to find out where the talk was.* | **campaign**, **drive** ◇ *a voter ~ campaign*
PREP. **on ~** ◇ *You will receive a free CD on ~ with the club.* | **~ as** ◇ *~ as a political party* | **~ by** ◇ *the ~ of the vehicle by the appropriate authority* | **~ for** ◇ *Registration for this event ends on December 10.* | **~ with** ◇ *Registration with the council is compulsory.*

PHRASES **an application for ~** (*esp. BrE*) | **a certificate of ~**

registry *noun*

ADJ. **central** ◇ *a central ~ for all applicants* | **district** (*BrE*), **national, regional** | **land** (*BrE*) ◇ *The deed of transfer must be entered at the land ~.* | **bridal, gift, wedding** (*all AmE*) ◇ *the growth of online gift registries* | **patient** (*AmE*) ◇ *the available data in the patient ~* | **sex offender** (*AmE*) ◇ *He was forced to register in the sex offender ~.*
VERB + REGISTRY **register sth at, register sth in, register sth with** ◇ *The certificate will have to be lodged at the ~.* | **create, establish**
REGISTRY + NOUN **office** (*in the UK*) ◇ *They got married in a ~ office.* | **entry** | **database**

regret *noun*

ADJ. **big, bitter, deep, genuine, great, profound, real, sincere** ◇ *Her biggest ~ was that she had never had children.* ◇ *She expressed deep ~ at the incident.*
... OF REGRET **pang, stab, tinge** (*esp. BrE*), **twinge** (*esp. AmE*)
VERB + REGRET **feel, have** ◇ *I have absolutely no ~s about resigning.* | **express, show** | **send** ◇ *He sends his ~s about missing our 45th reunion.*
PREP. **to your ~** ◇ *To my ~, I lost touch with her years ago.* | **with ~** ◇ *It is with deep ~ that we announce the death of Mr Fred Fisher.* | **without ~** ◇ *She thought of them without ~.* | **~ about, ~ over** ◇ *She showed no ~ about leaving her country.* | **~ at** ◇ *my sincere ~ at what has happened* | **~ for** ◇ *She enjoyed living alone, but felt a tiny pang of ~ for her mother's cooking.*
PHRASES **expression of ~** ◇ *The police offered no expression of ~ at his wrongful arrest.* | **a matter for ~** (*BrE*), **a matter of ~** (*esp. BrE*) ◇ *I never learned to play an instrument and that's a matter of some ~.* (*BrE*)

regret *verb*

ADV. **bitterly, deeply, greatly, really, seriously, sincerely, truly, very much** ◇ *The president said that his country deeply regretted the incident.* | **rather** | **immediately, instantly** ◇ *I immediately regretted not asking for his name and address.* | **quickly, soon** ◇ *It was a decision she would soon ~.* | **later** ◇ *Pierre told them some things he later regretted telling.* | **never**
VERB + REGRET **begin to** | **come to, grow to, live to** ◇ *She knew that she would live to ~ this decision.* | **seem to**

regrettable *adj.*

VERBS **be, seem**
ADV. **deeply, extremely, highly, truly, very** ◇ *a deeply ~ incident* ◇ *It is highly ~ that the delegate cannot be here in person.* | **rather** | **especially, particularly** ◇ *His death is particularly ~ because this condition could have easily been treated.*

regular *adj.*

1 frequent

VERBS **be, seem** | **become**
ADV. **very** | **fairly, pretty** (*esp. AmE*), **quite, reasonably** ◇ *a pretty ~ customer* | **increasingly** ◇ *She enjoyed his increasingly ~ visits.*
PHRASES **at ~ intervals** ◇ *His blood pressures was taken at ~ intervals.* | **on a ~ basis** ◇ *The paintings are changed on a ~ basis.*

2 following a pattern

VERBS **be**
ADV. **highly, very** ◇ *highly ~ patterns* | **perfectly** ◇ *Her face was perfectly ~.* | **fairly**

3 (*AmE*) ordinary

VERBS **be, seem** ◇ *Everything seemed ~.*
ADV. **fairly, pretty** ◇ *He's a pretty ~ guy.* | **perfectly** ◇ *She comes from a perfectly ~ middle-class family.*

regularity *noun*

ADJ. **depressing, monotonous, predictable** ◇ *Rows over funding that broke out with depressing ~.* | **alarming** ◇ *The same mistakes reoccur with alarming ~.* | **amazing, remarkable** | **great, increasing** ◇ *Financial crises erupt with increasing ~.*
... OF REGULARITY **degree** ◇ *Sons followed their fathers' trade with a high degree of ~.*
VERB + REGULARITY **maintain** ◇ *The idea is to maintain the ~ of the heartbeat.*
PREP. **with (a) ~** ◇ *He exercised with a ~ that amazed us.* | **~ in** ◇ *Is there any ~ in English word stress?*
PHRASES **with ... regularity** ◇ *She seems to change jobs with amazing ~.*

regulate *verb*

ADV. **closely, heavily, strictly, tightly** ◇ *The use of these chemicals is strictly ~d.* | **carefully, properly** | **lightly, loosely** | **poorly** | **federally** ◇ *Tobacco is a federally ~d product.*
VERB + REGULATE **attempt to, seek to** | **be designed to, be intended to** ◇ *a code of conduct intended to ~ press reporting on the royal family*
PHRASES **an attempt to ~ sth** | **~d by law, ~d by statute**

regulation *noun*

1 control of sth

ADJ. **strict, tight, tough** ◇ *those opposed to tighter ~ of banks* | **increased** | **excessive** ◇ *Businesses should be free from excessive government ~.* | **federal, government, governmental, international, official, professional, public, state** | **legal, statutory** | **voluntary** | **economic, environmental, financial** | **price, temperature**
VERB + REGULATION **call for, demand** ◇ *They are calling for tighter ~ of the industry.* | **introduce** | **be subject to** ◇ *Food additives are subject to government ~.*
PREP. **~ by** ◇ *~ by local authorities* | **~ of** ◇ *the ~ of the medical profession*

2 (usually **regulations**) law/rule

ADJ. **strict, stringent, tight, tough** ◇ *The act imposes more stringent ~s on atmospheric pollution.* | **Tighter ~s come into force next year.** | **burdensome** (*esp. AmE*), **restrictive** | **lax** ◇ *The company took advantage of the country's lax environmental ~s.* | **draft, proposed** | **new** | **current, existing** | **emergency** | **statutory** | **building** (*esp. BrE*), **fire, highway** (*AmE*), **hygiene** (*esp. BrE*), **planning** (*esp. BrE*), **safety, traffic, etc.** ◇ *The restaurant owner admitted 13 breaches of food hygiene ~s.* | **EU, federal, government, international, official** | **prison, school**
VERB + REGULATION **comply with, conform to, meet, observe, satisfy** ◇ *To comply with government hygiene ~s, there must be a separate sink for hand washing.* | **breach, break, contravene, flout, violate** | **adopt, bring in, enact** (*both esp. AmE*), **impose, introduce, issue, make** ◇ *States are enacting new laws and ~s.* ◇ *These restrictions are set out in ~s made by the minister.* | **liberalize, relax** ◇ *The government is under pressure to relax censorship ~s.* | **tighten** | **enforce** ◇ *In practice, the ~s are rarely enforced.*
REGULATION + VERB **be designed to** ◇ *The ~s are designed to encourage lower consumption of water.* | **control sth, govern sth, protect sth** ◇ *~s governing trade and industry* | **dictate sth, impose sth, mandate sth** (*esp. AmE*), **prescribe sth, require sth, specify sth, stipulate sth** ◇ *There will be stricter ~s dictating which foods are allowed in schools.* ◇ *Regulations require water authorities to test sea water for bacteria.* | **limit sth, restrict sth** | **ban sth, forbid sth, prohibit sth** ◇ *The ~s ban the use of genetically modified organisms.* | **permit sth** | **apply (to sth)** ◇ *These ~s apply to all cows sold after June 1998.* | **come into force**
REGULATION + NOUN **uniform** ◇ *She was wearing the ~ school uniform.*
PREP. **against (the) ~s** ◇ *It's against safety ~s to leave these doors open.* | **in (the) ~** ◇ *The limits are specified in the ~s.* | **under (the) ~** ◇ *Under the new ~s, each worker must have a rest every two hours.* | **~s concerning, ~s regarding** ◇ *There*

are strict ~s concerning the adoption of children. | ~ **on** ◇ ~s
on hygiene
PHRASES **a breach of the** ~s | **compliance with a** ~ | **in
accordance with (the)** ~s ◇ The notice is in accordance with
Regulation 7. | **rules and** ~s

rehabilitation noun

ADJ. **medical, physical, social** | **alcohol, drug** ◇ a specialist
drug and alcohol ~ unit | **cardiac, pulmonary, stroke, etc.**
(all medical)
REHABILITATION + NOUN **centre/center, clinic, unit** ◇ a drug ~
centre/center | **services** | **process, programme/program,
scheme** (BrE) ◇ He entered an alcohol ~ programme/
program.

rehearsal noun

ADJ. **dress** ◇ a dress ~ for a Broadway play | **wedding** ◇ I
attended my friend's wedding ~. | **band, choir, choral,
orchestra, orchestral, play** ◇ I'll see you at band ~ on
Monday!
VERB + REHEARSAL **conduct, do, have, hold** ◇ We only had one
full ~. | **attend, go to**
REHEARSAL + VERB **take place** | **go** ◇ How did the ~ go?
REHEARSAL + NOUN **hall** (esp. AmE), **room, space, studio** |
schedule, time | **dinner** (AmE) ◇ The wedding ~ dinner is
tonight.
PREP. **at (a/the)** ~ ◇ He apologized for his outburst at ~. |
during (a/the) ~ ◇ During the dress ~ she suddenly forgot her
lines. | **in** ~ ◇ They're performing every night and they have
another production in ~. | ~ **for** ◇ ~s for 'Romeo and Juliet' |
~ **of** ◇ a ~ of the final scene

rehearse verb

ADV. **carefully** | **mentally** ◇ She mentally ~d what she would
say to Jeff.
PREP. **for** ◇ We're rehearsing for the show.
PHRASES **well** ~d ◇ He had his speech well ~d.

reimburse verb

ADV. **fully, in full** (esp. BrE) ◇ His costs in recovering the lost
suitcase were fully ~d. ◇ All monies received will be ~d in full.
PREP. **for** ◇ You will be ~d for your expenses.

rein noun

1 (often **reins**) for controlling a horse

VERB + REIN **hold** ◇ Can you hold the ~s for a minute? |
gather, gather up, pick up ◇ Sean gathered up the horse's
~s. | **grab, grab at, grip** | **pull on, tug, tug at, tug on** ◇ She
pulled sharply on the ~s. | **give sb, hand sb, let go of** |
loosen, tighten
PREP. **on a** ~ ◇ She had the horse on a long ~.
PHRASES **give free** ~ **to sth, give full** ~ **to sth** (= give sb
freedom of action) ◇ The designer was given free ~.

2 the reins being in control/the leader of sth

VERB + THE REINS **hold** ◇ It's the accountants who effectively
hold the ~s. | **grasp, seize, take up** ◇ The vice-president was
forced to take up the ~s of office. | **hand over** | **loosen,
tighten** ◇ Parents need to loosen the ~s as the child grows.
PHRASES **the** ~s **of government, the** ~s **of office, the** ~s **of
power** ◇ He seized the ~s of power.

reinforce verb

1 support sth that already exists

ADV. **greatly, powerfully, strongly** ◇ This report strongly ~s
the view that the system must be changed. | **further** |
merely, only, simply ◇ All this simply ~s my earlier point. |
constantly, continually | **subtly** ◇ Our prejudices are subtly
~d in many different ways. | **mutually** ◇ Violence and
rejection by society are mutually reinforcing. | **unwittingly** |
positively
VERB + REINFORCE **help (to), serve to, tend to**

2 make sth stronger

ADV. **heavily**
PREP. **with** ◇ The door was built of oak, heavily ~d with iron.

reinforcement noun

1 supporting/strengthening sth

ADJ. **powerful** | **negative, positive** ◇ The children respond
well to praise and positive ~. | **steel**
VERB + REINFORCEMENT **provide** ◇ The instructor provides ~ to
elicit the desired response. | **receive** | **have** ◇ The windows
have steel ~. | **need**

2 reinforcements extra soldiers, etc.

ADJ. **police, troop**
VERB + REINFORCEMENTS **call for, call in, request, send for** ◇
The crowd was very large and police ~s were called in. | **need**
◇ We need urgent ~s. | **bring in, send**
REINFORCEMENTS + VERB **arrive** ◇ Reinforcements arrived too
late.

reject verb

ADV. **decisively, emphatically, firmly, resoundingly,
roundly, soundly, strongly, vehemently, vigorously** ◇
Voters emphatically ~ed the proposals. ◇ She firmly ~ed the
suggestion that she had lied. | **categorically, completely,
flatly, unequivocally, utterly** | **out of hand, outright,
summarily** ◇ Don't just ~ their suggestions out of hand. |
overwhelmingly | **unanimously** | **narrowly** ◇ Voters
narrowly ~ed the plan. | **initially** | **immediately, instantly** |
quickly | **consistently, constantly, repeatedly** | **eventually,
finally, ultimately** ◇ We considered offering him the job, but
finally ~ed him. | **deliberately** | **explicitly, expressly,
specifically** ◇ The paper expressly ~ed charges that it had
invented the story. | **formally** | **publicly** | **automatically** ◇
The organs are automatically ~ed by the immune system. |
rightly ◇ It was a badly researched product that consumers
rightly ~ed.
VERB + REJECT **vote to** | **be free to, have the right to** ◇
Consumers have the right to ~ faulty goods and demand a
refund. | **urge sb to** ◇ He urged the committee to ~ the plans.
PREP. **as** ◇ The proposal was ~ed as too costly. | **in favour/
favor of** ◇ Their design was ~ed in favour/favor of one by a
rival company.
PHRASES ~ **sth on … grounds** ◇ The plan was ~ed on economic
grounds.

rejection noun

ADJ. **outright, total, wholesale** | **explicit** | **deliberate** |
knee-jerk ◇ There is often a knee-jerk ~ of new ideas.
VERB + REJECTION **fear** ◇ Children who have had bad
experiences fear ~. | **risk** | **cope with, deal with, handle,
take** ◇ It takes a strong personality to cope with ~.
REJECTION + NOUN **letter, slip** ◇ a publisher's ~ slip
PREP. ~ **by** ◇ the ~ of the child by its mother
PHRASES **fear of** ~ | **feelings of** ~ | **the** ~ **of an idea, a
proposal, a theory, etc.**

rejoicing noun

ADJ. **great, much** | **general**
PREP. **amid** ~ ◇ The bridge was completed in 1811 amid much
~. | ~ **at** ◇ general ~ at the team's victory
PHRASES **a cause for** ~ ◇ She had a personal cause for ~. | **an
occasion for** ~ ◇ Finding a job should have been an occasion
for ~. | **scenes of** ~ ◇ There were scenes of ~ at the news.

relapse noun

ADJ. **acute**
VERB + RELAPSE **experience, suffer** | **cause, precipitate,
trigger** ◇ A wide range of emotionally stressful events may
trigger a ~. | **prevent**
RELAPSE + VERB **occur**
RELAPSE + NOUN **prevention** ◇ A drug counsellor/counselor
advises patients on ~ prevention. | **rate** (medical) ◇ The
therapy can reduce the ~ rate for multiple sclerosis.
PREP. **in** ~ (medical) ◇ Even in ~ there will be times when the
patient's general condition improves.
PHRASES **a risk of** ~

relate

relate *verb*

ADV. **closely** | **directly, specifically** ◊ *The issues raised in the report ~ directly to Age Concern's ongoing work in this area.* | **somehow** ◊ *All these works ~ somehow to the artist's emotional life.* | **primarily** ◊ *Our work primarily ~s to product design.*

VERB + RELATE **be able to, can** | **attempt to, try to** | **be difficult to, find sth difficult to** ◊ *I found it difficult to ~ the two ideas in my mind.*

PREP. **to** ◊ *Our product needs an image that people can ~ to.*

PHRASES **the ability to ~ to sb/sth** | **an attempt to ~ sth** ◊ *Attempts to ~ studies on animals to those on humans are not really comparing like with like.*

related *adj.*

1 connected

VERBS **be, seem**

ADV. **closely, integrally, intimately, strongly** ◊ *The two ideas are very closely ~.* | **significantly** ◊ *Scores in the test were not significantly ~ to gender.* | **inextricably** | **loosely** | **not necessarily** | **not remotely** ◊ *What she was reading was not remotely ~ to her work.* | **largely** | **partly** | **directly, linearly** | **indirectly, tangentially** ◊ *Tax rates were indirectly ~ to income.* | **specifically** | **positively** | **inversely, negatively** ◊ *The traditional approach has tended to regard unemployment and inflation as being inversely ~.* | **apparently** | **clearly, obviously** | **causally, contextually, functionally, logically, structurally, thematically** ◊ *Is unemployment causally ~ to crime?*

PREP. **to** ◊ *The occurrence of the disease is apparently ~ to standards of hygiene.*

2 of the same family

VERBS **be**

ADV. **closely** | **distantly** | **biologically, evolutionarily, genetically** ◊ *All the bees in the colony are genetically ~.*

PREP. **to** ◊ *He claims to be distantly ~ to the British royal family.*

relation *noun*

1 connection between two or more things

ADJ. **causal** | **direct** ◊ *The energy an animal uses is in direct ~ to speed and body mass.* | **complex** ◊ *the complex ~ between business and society* | **close, intimate** ◊ *The study shows the close ~ between poverty and ill health.* | **significant** | **spatial** ◊ *The right side of the brain deals with spatial ~s between objects.*

VERB + RELATION **bear, have** ◊ *The movie bore no ~ to (= was very different from) the book.* ◊ *The fee bears little ~ to the service provided.* | **establish, show** ◊ *He established a ~ between asthma and certain types of work.* | **analyse/analyze, explore** ◊ *Her work explores the ~ between technology and culture.*

PREP. **in ~ to** ◊ *Similar policies were pursued in the 1970s, particularly in ~ to health services.* | **~ between, ~ to** ◊ *the ~ of the subject to the object*

2 member of sb's family

ADJ. **close, near** | **distant** | **blood** | **poor** (*often figurative*) ◊ *Other sparkling wines are often considered the poor ~s of champagne.*

VERB + RELATION **visit**

PREP. **~ to** ◊ *What ~ is Rita to you?*

PHRASES **friends and ~s**

3 **relations** between people/groups/countries

ADJ. **close, intimate** | **cordial, friendly, good, harmonious** | **improved** ◊ *a period of improved trade ~s* | **difficult, poor, strained** ◊ *Relations between the two countries are strained.* | **bilateral, diplomatic, foreign, international, political, trade** ◊ *The US broke off diplomatic ~s with Cuba's communist government.* | **industrial, labour/labor** ◊ *The change of government led to improved industrial ~s.* | **class, gender, race** | **economic, power, social** | **public** ◊ *a public ~s exercise* | **customer, investor** | **human, interpersonal,**

personal | **family, marital** ◊ *a breakdown of marital ~s leading to divorce* | **sexual** | **parent-child, student-teacher, etc.** | **Anglo-American, East-West, etc.**

VERB + RELATIONS **cultivate, develop, establish, foster, maintain** ◊ *the need to establish good ~s with our European partners* | **break off, sever, suspend** ◊ *Diplomatic ~s have been broken off between the two countries.* | **damage, poison, sour** ◊ *The move soured ~s between Washington and Moscow.* | **improve, strengthen** ◊ *Renewed efforts are being made to improve the strained ~s between the two countries.* | **normalize** (*esp. AmE*), **repair** | **re-establish, restore, resume** ◊ *Venezuela re-established diplomatic ~s with Cuba.* | **govern, regulate** ◊ *the system governing social ~s in India*

RELATION + VERB **improve** ◊ *Relations between the two states have improved.* | **deteriorate, sour, worsen**

PREP. **~ among, ~ between, ~ with**

PHRASES **an improvement in ~s**

relationship *noun*

1 between people/groups/countries

ADJ. **friendly, good, happy, harmonious, healthy, strong** ◊ *They have a very healthy father-son ~.* | **broken, difficult, failed, fragile, poor, rocky, stormy, strained, troubled, uneasy, volatile** ◊ *Their ~ has always been a stormy one.* | **close, intense, intimate, special** ◊ *Britain's special ~ with the US* | **committed, enduring, lasting, long-standing, long-term, monogamous, permanent, serious, stable, steady** ◊ *He was not married, but he was in a stable ~.* | **brief, casual** | **caring, love-hate, loving** | **abusive** | **family, human, interpersonal, one-to-one, personal** | **doctor-patient, parent-child, etc.** | **business, contractual, financial, formal, professional, social, working** | **marital, physical, romantic, sexual** | **platonic** | **gay, heterosexual, homosexual, lesbian, same-sex** | **power** ◊ *The play is about power ~s at work.*

VERB + RELATIONSHIP **enjoy, have** ◊ *They enjoyed a close working ~.* ◊ *The school has a very good ~ with the community.* ◊ *He had brief ~s with several women.* | **begin, build, build up, cultivate, develop, establish, forge, form, foster** ◊ *Building strong ~s is essential.* ◊ *They established a ~ of trust.* | **cement, improve, strengthen** | **continue, maintain** | **deal with, handle, manage** ◊ *He's not very good at handling personal ~s.* | **break off, end** ◊ *She broke off the ~ when she found out about his gambling.* | **destroy, ruin** ◊ *Lack of trust destroys many ~s.*

RELATIONSHIP + VERB **exist** ◊ *We want to improve the ~ that exists between the university and industry.* | **deepen, develop, evolve, progress** | **blossom, flourish, work** ◊ *I tried everything to make our ~ work.* | **continue, last** | **deteriorate, go wrong, worsen** | **break down, break up, end, fail**

RELATIONSHIP + NOUN **difficulties, problems** | **breakdown** (*esp. BrE*) | **goals** | **counsellor/counselor** (*esp. BrE*)

PREP. **in a/the ~** ◊ *In normal human ~s there has to be some give and take.* ◊ *At the moment he isn't in a ~.* | **~ among** ◊ *The focus is on ~s among European countries.* | **~ between, ~ to** ◊ *their ~ to each other* | **~ with**

PHRASES **the breakdown of a ~** | **a network of ~s, a web of ~s**

2 family connection

ADJ. **blood, family, kin, kinship** | **distant** ◊ *He claimed to have a distant ~ with royalty.*

PREP. **~ between** ◊ *'What's the ~ between you and Tony?' 'He's my cousin.'* | **~ to** ◊ *What ~ are you to Pat?*

3 connection between two or more things

ADJ. **close** ◊ *There's a close ~ between increased money supply and inflation.* | **direct** | **clear** | **complex, complicated** | **significant** | **true** | **particular** | **inverse, negative** ◊ *the inverse ~ between gas consumption and air temperature* | **positive** | **causal, dynamic, reciprocal, symbiotic** ◊ *the symbiotic ~ between corals and algae* | **linear, spatial** | **economic, functional, legal** | **natural, organic** | **symbolic**

VERB + RELATIONSHIP **bear, have** ◊ *The fee bears little ~ to the service provided.* | **analyze, assess, evaluate, examine, explore, investigate, look at, study** ◊ *His latest book examines the ~ between spatial awareness and mathematical*

ability. | **determine, discover, establish, find** ◇ *They discovered a ~ between depression and lack of sunlight.* | **demonstrate, show** | **see, understand** | **describe**
RELATIONSHIP + VERB **exist** ◇ *No statistically significant ~ existed between the occurrences.* | **emerge** ◇ *A clear ~ emerged in the study between happiness and level of education.*
PREP. **in a/the ~** ◇ *The different varieties of the language are in a dynamic ~ with each other.* | **~ among** ◇ *Our research will explore the ~s among these variables.* | **~ between** ◇ *I can't see the ~ between the figures and the diagram.* | **~ to** ◇ *the ~ of a parasite to its host* | **~ with**
PHRASES **the nature of the ~** | **stand in a … relationship to sth** ◇ *Women and men stand in a different ~ to language.*

relative noun
ADJ. **close, near** ◇ *The succession passed to the nearest surviving ~.* | **distant** | **blood, family** ◇ *If you die without a will, only a husband, wife, children and blood ~s are entitled to inherit your property.* | **immediate** ◇ *The deceased's immediate ~s will inherit her estate.* | **living, surviving** | **deceased** | **elderly, old** | **young** | **female, male** | **long-lost** ◇ *He greeted me like a long-lost ~.* | **poor** *(often figurative)* ◇ *He believes that interior design is the poor ~ of* (= inferior to) *architecture.* | **dependent** *(esp. BrE)* ◇ *the increase in dependent elderly ~s* | **disabled, ill, sick** ◇ *people who care for a sick or disabled ~* | **bereaved, grieving** *(both esp. BrE)*
VERB + RELATIVE **have** ◇ *I have no parents or close ~s.* | **lose** ◇ *an organization that helps people who have lost ~s* (= whose relatives have died) | **care for, give support to, help, look after** *(esp. BrE)*, **support, take care of** *(esp. AmE)* ◇ *She's caring for an elderly ~.* | **live with** | **stay with, visit** | **find, trace** *(esp. BrE)* ◇ *The police are trying to find the ~s of the deceased.* | **contact, inform** ◇ *The names of the victims are being withheld until the ~s have been informed.*
PHRASES **friends and ~s, friends or ~s** ◇ *an intimate reception for close friends and ~s* | **a ~ by marriage**

relax verb
ADV. **completely, fully, totally** | **a little, slightly** | **just, simply** ◇ *Just ~ and take it easy.* | **gradually, slowly** ◇ *He gradually ~ed and began to enjoy himself.* | **immediately, instantly** ◇ *She instantly ~ed at the sight of him.* | **consciously** ◇ *She realized how tense she was and consciously ~ed.* | **visibly**
VERB + RELAX **begin to** | **try to** ◇ *Just try to ~ completely.* | **learn to** | **help sb (to)** ◇ *Use music to help you ~.* | **make sb** | **appear to, seem to** ◇ *Julie seems to be ~ing a little now.*
PREP. **against** ◇ *Jenna ~ed against the pillows.* | **into** ◇ *His severe expression ~ed into a half-smile.* | **on** ◇ *He was ~ing on the couch with a book.*
PHRASES **lie back and ~, sit back and ~** | **~ and enjoy sth/yourself, ~ and unwind**

relaxation noun
1 time spent resting/sth you do to rest
ADJ. **deep, great** | **complete, total** | **muscle, muscular** ◇ *an ointment that helps muscle ~* | **mental** ◇ *an environment that promotes physical and mental ~*
VERB + RELAXATION **aid, cause** *(medical)*, **induce, promote** ◇ *Some people take up yoga to aid ~.* ◇ *drugs that cause the ~ of the muscle* ◇ *a popular herb known to induce ~*
RELAXATION + NOUN **exercise, technique** | **tape** ◇ *Try listening to a ~ tape before you go to sleep.* | **therapy** | **class** ◇ *He goes to ~ classes.*
PREP. **for ~** ◇ *She listens to classical music for ~.* | **~ from** ◇ *a chance for ~ from work*
PHRASES **a form of ~, a kind of ~** | **rest and ~** | **a state of ~**
2 making rules/controls less strict
ADJ. **further** | **general** | **slight** | **temporary** *(esp. BrE)* | **gradual**
VERB + RELAXATION **call for** *(esp. BrE)* ◇ *Financiers are calling for a ~ of these stringent measures.*
PREP. **~ in, ~ of** ◇ *a ~ in the rules*

release

relaxed adj.
VERBS **appear, be, feel, look, seem** | **keep sb**
ADV. **extremely, fairly, very, etc.** | **deeply** | **completely, perfectly, totally** | **apparently, seemingly** | **visibly** | **enough** ◇ *You need to ensure that a patient feels ~ enough to discuss things fully.*
PREP. **about** ◇ *I was very ~ about the decision.*

relay noun
ADJ. **4 by 400, etc.** | **freestyle, medley, sprint**
VERB + RELAY **run, run in, swim** ◇ *She ran in the 4 by 400 ~.* | **win**
RELAY + NOUN **race** | **squad, team** | **medallist/medalist**

release noun
1 freeing sb from prison, etc.
ADJ. **immediate** ◇ *There have been calls for his immediate and unconditional ~.* | **imminent** | **early** | **unconditional** | **supervised** *(AmE)* ◇ *On completing his prison sentence Smith will serve three years of supervised ~.*
VERB + RELEASE **demand** ◇ *The outraged public demanded her ~.* | **grant sb** ◇ *He was granted early ~.* | **secure** ◇ *A public outcry secured her ~ from detention.* | **negotiate** ◇ *He negotiated the ~ of American prisoners of war.*
RELEASE + NOUN **date**
PREP. **~ from** ◇ *his ~ from hospital*
PHRASES **~ sb on bail, ~ sb on parole**
2 freeing sb from an emotion, a pain, etc.
ADJ. **welcome** ◇ *She saw death as a welcome ~ from pain.* | **emotional, sexual**
VERB + RELEASE **give (sb)** ◇ *Crying gave some emotional ~.* | **need** ◇ *Sometimes we just need some ~ from the pressure.*
RELEASE + NOUN **valve** *(figurative)* ◇ *Laughter is an important ~ valve for feelings of frustration.*
PREP. **~ from**
PHRASES **a feeling of ~, a sense of ~** | **a ~ of tension** ◇ *All societies have social mechanisms for the ~ of tension.*
3 book, film/movie, music, piece of news, etc.
ADJ. **latest, new, recent** | **forthcoming, future, upcoming** *(esp. AmE)* ◇ *a publicity tour for the upcoming ~ of her autobiography* | **previous, subsequent** | **commercial** | **official** | **cinema** *(BrE)*, **theatrical** *(AmE)* ◇ *The film never got a theatrical ~ but went straight to video.* | **news, press** | **album, book, film** *(esp. BrE)*, **movie** *(esp. AmE)*, **record** | **CD, DVD, video**
VERB + RELEASE **authorize** ◇ *The judge authorized the ~ of the information.* | **demand** ◇ *The senator demanded the immediate ~ of the full report.* | **announce** ◇ *He has announced the ~ of his new album.* | **anticipate, await** ◇ *I am anxiously awaiting the ~ of the next volume.* | **block, delay, prevent** ◇ *The controversy threatens to delay the movie's ~.*
RELEASE + VERB **be out, come out** ◇ *The new CD ~s will be out on Friday.*
RELEASE + NOUN **date, schedule** ◇ *Under the current ~ schedule, the series will be available on DVD early next year.*
PREP. **~ on** ◇ *I've been eagerly awaiting this film's ~ on DVD.*
PHRASES **in general ~** *(AmE)*, **on general ~** *(BrE)* ◇ *The movie is already in/on general ~.* ◇ *The film will go on general ~ in November.*

release verb
1 allow sb to be free
ADV. **quickly** | **immediately** | **eventually, finally** | **conditionally, unconditionally**
PREP. **from** ◇ *She was ~d from prison last week.*
PHRASES **newly ~d, recently ~d** | **~ sb on bail, ~ sb on parole, ~ sb on licence** *(BrE, law)*, **~ sb on probation, ~ sb on their own recognizance** *(AmE, law)* ◇ *He was ~d on his own recognizance and could face up to four years in jail.* | **~ sb unharmed** ◇ *The hostages were ~d unharmed.*

2 let sth go or escape

ADV. **accidentally** ◊ *The factory had accidentally ~d a quantity of toxic waste into the sea.* | **slowly** ◊ *The compound slowly ~s iron into the bloodstream.* | **quickly, suddenly** ◊ *The dam suddenly ~d millions of gallons of water.* ◊ *She laughed, the tension inside her suddenly ~d.*

PREP. **from** ◊ *the gases that are ~d from spray cans* | **into** ◊ *How much radiation was ~d into the air?*

3 make sth available

ADV. **officially** ◊ *Figures to be officially ~d this week reveal that long-term unemployment is still rising.* | **commercially, publicly** | **theatrically** (*esp. AmE*) ◊ *The film was never ~d theatrically in the US.* | **recently** | **shortly, soon** ◊ *The new version is expected to be ~d shortly.*

VERB + RELEASE **refuse to** ◊ *Police have refused to ~ the name of the dead man.* | **be expected to** ◊ *The committee is expected to ~ its findings this summer.* | **plan to** ◊ *He's planning to ~ a solo album.*

PREP. **in, on** ◊ *The book has not yet been ~d in paperback.* ◊ *The album has not been ~d on CD.* | **to** ◊ *Details of the attack have not yet been ~d to the public.*

PHRASES **newly ~d, recently ~d** ◊ *newly ~d recordings* | **originally ~d, previously ~d** ◊ *The album was originally ~d in 1974.*

relevance noun

ADJ. **considerable, great, wider** | **limited, marginal** ◊ *This debate has limited ~ to our current concerns.* | **dubious, questionable** | **direct, immediate** | **continued, continuing** ◊ *the continuing ~ of art to our daily lives* | **obvious** | **real** | **possible, potential** | **general** | **particular, special** | **contemporary** ◊ *He claims that the laws are antiquated and have no contemporary ~.* | **practical** | **political**

VERB + RELEVANCE **be of, remain of** ◊ *The book is of particular ~ to student nurses.* | **bear, have** ◊ *The theory bears little ~ to practice.* | **lack, lose** ◊ *Her ideas have lost all ~ to the modern world.* | **ensure** ◊ *Constant revision of the curriculum must be undertaken to ensure its continuing ~.* | **increase** | **see** | **demonstrate, establish** ◊ *Skim the book in order to establish its ~ to your needs.* | **emphasize, underline** (*esp. BrE*), **underscore** (*AmE*) ◊ *A Marxist approach emphasizes the ~ of class power.* | **assess, consider, examine, explore, judge** | **question**

PREP. **~ for, ~ to** ◊ *I can't see the ~ of his comment to the debate.*

relevant adj.

VERBS **be, seem** | **become** | **consider sth, deem sth, regard sth as, see sth as**

ADV. **especially, extremely, highly, particularly, very** | **hardly, not really** ◊ *Past imperial glories are hardly ~ to the present day.* | **marginally** ◊ *The article was only marginally ~.* | **not necessarily, not strictly** ◊ *Resist the temptation to discuss topics that are not strictly ~ to the essay question.* | **directly** | **immediately** | **no longer** | **potentially** | **clearly, obviously** | **personally** ◊ *If a story is personally ~, people are more likely to remember it.* | **culturally, morally, politically, socially** ◊ *Is there a morally ~ difference between human life and animal life?*

PREP. **to** ◊ *information ~ to this case*

reliability noun

ADJ. **high** | **greater, greatest** | **poor** | **absolute** | **improved, increased** | **statistical**

... OF RELIABILITY **degree, level**

VERB + RELIABILITY **assure** (*esp. AmE*), **ensure** ◊ *Changes in design will ensure the quality and ~ of the printer.* | **enhance, improve, increase, maximize** | **reduce** | **assess, evaluate, judge** ◊ *It is important to assess the ~ of the data.* | **demonstrate** | **measure** ◊ *The ~ of the statistical estimates can be measured.* | **doubt, question** ◊ *Many experts question the ~ of these figures.*

RELIABILITY + VERB **improve, increase**

reliable adj.

VERBS **be, prove, seem** | **become** | **consider sth**

ADV. **extremely, fairly, very, etc.** | **highly** ◊ *It has a highly ~ control system.* | **absolutely, completely, perfectly, totally, utterly** ◊ *He's a good musician and totally ~.* | **not entirely, not wholly** | **reasonably** | **enough, sufficiently** ◊ *These measurements are ~ enough for most purposes.* | **statistically**

PREP. **as** ◊ *This statement is not ~ as evidence.*

reliance noun

ADJ. **complete, exclusive, sole, total** | **great, heavy, strong** ◊ *Too heavy a ~ on a particular market may be dangerous for the company.* | **excessive, undue** | **continued, continuing** | **growing, increasing** | **increased** | **reduced**

... OF RELIANCE **degree** ◊ *a high degree of ~ on newspaper reports*

VERB + RELIANCE **place** ◊ *I don't think you should place too much ~ on these figures.* | **increase** | **decrease, lessen, reduce** | **eliminate** ◊ *the means by which individuals might reduce or eliminate ~ on the state* | **encourage** ◊ *They believe that modern farming techniques encourage an excessive ~ on harmful chemicals.* | **lead to**

PREP. **~ on, ~ upon** ◊ *the increased ~ of the university on private funds*

reliant adj.

VERBS **be** | **become** | **remain**

ADV. **heavily** ◊ *The service has become heavily ~ on government support.* | **completely, entirely, totally, wholly** (*esp. BrE*) | **overly** | **increasingly** | **quite** (*esp. BrE*)

PREP. **on, upon** ◊ *The charity is completely ~ on public donations.*

relic noun

ADJ. **ancient** | **last** ◊ *It was the last ~ of the old system.* | **quaint** ◊ *He seemed to view her as a quaint ~ of the past.* | **historic, historical** | **precious, priceless** | **holy, religious, sacred**

VERB + RELIC **discover, unearth** ◊ *The ~s were discovered in a lead box in the ruins of an abbey.* | **preserve**

RELIC + VERB **survive** ◊ *This silver belt buckle is the only ~ of the battle that survives.*

PREP. **~ from** ◊ *Most of these guns are ~s from the Boer War.*

PHRASES **a ~ of an age, a ~ of a time** ◊ *~s of a bygone age* ◊ *a ~ of the time when people hunted their own food* | **a ~ of the past** ◊ *They believe that hunting is a ~ of the past and are calling for it to be banned.*

relief noun

1 removal of anxiety/pain

ADJ. **considerable, deep, enormous, great, huge, immense, intense, overwhelming, tremendous** | **certain** ◊ *The news of his appointment was received with a certain ~ by most people.* | **sheer** | **complete** | **short-lived, short-term, temporary** ◊ *The drugs only provided temporary ~ from the pain.* | **fast, immediate, instant** | **evident, obvious, palpable** ◊ *She smiled with evident ~.* ◊ *Their ~ at the news was palpable.* | **blessed, much-needed, sweet, welcome** | **pain** ◊ *The injection gives complete pain ~.* | **symptom, symptomatic** (*both medical*) ◊ *Your doctor can give you symptomatic ~, but there is no cure.* | **stress** ◊ *Exercise is good for stress ~.*

VERB + RELIEF **bring (sb), give (sb), offer (sb), provide (sb with)** ◊ *Morning brought no ~ from the heat.* | **come as** ◊ *The news came as a welcome ~ to Bobby.* | **seek** ◊ *She sought ~ in vodka.* | **find, get** ◊ *He found ~ from his fears in a world of fantasy.* | **experience, feel** ◊ *I felt enormous ~ when he walked through the door.* | **sense** ◊ *She could sense his ~ when she said she wouldn't be leaving.* | **express**

RELIEF + VERB **come** ◊ *He believes that ~ only comes from helping others with their suffering.* | **flood through sb, sweep over sb, wash over sb** ◊ *Relief flooded through me as the plane landed safely.*

RELIEF + NOUN **valve** (*esp. AmE*) ◊ *a pressure ~ valve*

PREP. **in** ◊ *She smiled in ~.* | **out of ~** ◊ *He hugged her out of sheer ~.* | **to your ~** ◊ *To my great ~, she didn't notice that*

anything was wrong. | **with ~** ◊ *He sighed with ~.* | **~ at** ◊ *~ at not having been made a fool of* | **~ from** ◊ *~ from hunger* | **~ to** ◊ *The news was a huge ~ to her.*
PHRASES **a cry of ~, a sigh of ~, tears of ~** ◊ *He breathed a sigh of ~.* | **a sense of ~, a wave of ~**

2 food/money/medicine given to people in need

ADJ. **humanitarian** | **disaster, emergency** | **famine, flood, hurricane, tsunami** | **short-term** ◊ *We need long-term solutions as well as short-term emergency ~.*
VERB + RELIEF **give sb, provide (sb with), send (sb)** ◊ *The organization provides emergency famine ~.*
RELIEF + NOUN **work** ◊ *She said that the fighting has halted almost all ~ work in the area.* | **effort, operation** ◊ *There was a huge international ~ effort to bring help to the stricken area.* | **package, programme/program** ◊ *Congress has agreed an $11 million ~ package for victims of the hurricane.* | **aid, supplies** | **agency, fund, organization** | **worker** | **convoy, flight**

3 reduction in the amount of tax, etc. you have to pay

ADJ. **debt, interest** (*BrE*), **tax** ◊ *the abolition of mortgage interest ~*
VERB + RELIEF **get, obtain, receive** ◊ *You can get income tax ~ for gifts to charity.* (*BrE*) | **grant** | **be entitled to, qualify for** | **apply for, claim, seek** (*all esp. BrE*)
RELIEF + VERB **be available** ◊ *No tax ~ is available in respect of this loss.*

4 sth interesting that replaces sth boring

ADJ. **light** | **comic**
VERB + RELIEF **give (sb), provide (sb with)** ◊ *The scene provided some comic ~ for the audience.*
PREP. **for ~** ◊ *The comical characters are brought into the story for a little light ~.*
PHRASES **a moment of ~**

5 way of decorating wood, stone, etc.

ADJ. **high** ◊ *The scene has been carved in high ~.* | **bas, low** | **carved** | **bronze, marble, plaster, etc.** | **classical, Greek, Roman, etc.**
VERB + RELIEF **carve (sth) in**
RELIEF + NOUN **carving, sculpture** | **panel**
PREP. **in ~** ◊ *a sculpture in high ~*

6 making sth noticeable

ADJ. **bold, sharp, stark**
VERB + RELIEF **bring sth into, throw sth into** (*often figurative*) ◊ *The proximity of the wealthy suburb to the squatter camp throws the plight of the squatters into even sharper ~.* | **stand out in** ◊ *The snow-capped mountains stood out in sharp ~ against the blue sky.*

relieve verb

ADV. **temporarily** | **completely, partially**
VERB + RELIEVE **attempt to, try to** ◊ *They try to ~ the symptoms of depression by drinking.* | **help (to)** ◊ *Her jokes helped to ~ the tension.* | **be designed to, be intended to** ◊ *Respite care is intended to ~ parents of the burden of caring for disabled children.*

relieved adj.

VERBS **be, feel, look, seem**
ADV. **extremely, fairly, very, etc.** | **greatly, hugely, immensely, incredibly, mightily** (*esp. BrE*) | **completely, totally** (*both esp. AmE*) | **almost** | **a little, slightly, etc.** | **clearly, obviously, visibly** | **secretly** ◊ *I was secretly ~ when Tony said it was time to turn back.*
PREP. **at** ◊ *We were greatly ~ at the news of their safe return.*

religion noun

ADJ. **great, major** | **universal, world** ◊ *Judaism is one of the great world ~s.* | **ancient, established, old, old-time** (*esp. AmE*), **traditional** ◊ *These faiths draw on the traditional ~s of indigenous peoples.* | **new** | **contemporary** | **dominant, mainstream, popular** ◊ *the leaders of all the mainstream ~s* ◊ *This popular ~ is a blend of Confucianism, Buddhism and Taoism with spirit beliefs.* | **minority** | **official, state** | **institutional, organized** ◊ *I believe in God, but I don't belong*

to any organized ~. | **orthodox** ◊ *Darwinism contradicted orthodox ~.* | **fundamentalist** | **false, true** | **alternative** ◊ *Football has become an alternative ~ for many people.* | **folk, native, primitive** | **pagan** | **monotheistic, polytheistic** | **Eastern** ◊ *Eastern ~s such as Shintoism* | **Hindu, Jewish, etc.** | **Catholic, evangelical, Orthodox, Protestant**
VERB + RELIGION **belong to, have** ◊ *She has no ~.* | **follow, practise/practice** ◊ *Do you still practise/practice your ~?* | **adopt** ◊ *The majority of children adopt the ~ of their parents.* | **embrace, find** (= become interested in), **get** (*informal, esp. AmE*) ◊ *He reportedly embraced ~ and became a vegetarian.* ◊ *As a result of her brother's death, Maria found ~.* ◊ *We're waiting for the company to get ~ on recycling.* (*figurative*) | **change** | **abandon, reject** | **defend** ◊ *She believed that her ~ needed to be defended by philosophy and logic.* | **endorse** (*esp. AmE*), **promote** ◊ *The law prohibits the government form endorsing a particular ~.* | **impose** ◊ *I don't think the government should try to impose ~ on our society.* | **found** ◊ *He founded a new ~.* | **preach** ◊ *The teachers started preaching the Christian ~ to us at every opportunity.* | **spread** | **study, teach** | **discuss** ◊ *They never discussed ~ or politics.* | **respect** ◊ *I believe we should respect all ~s of the world equally.*
RELIGION + VERB **be based on sth** ◊ *a ~ based on reason* | **originate from sth** ◊ *He believes that all ~s originated from a single source.* | **develop** | **spread** | **teach sth** | **forbid sth** | **give sth, offer sth** ◊ *Almost all ~s offer the idea of sacred space.*
PREP. **by** ◊ *These people are predominantly Russian Orthodox by ~.* | **in a/the ~** ◊ *In their ~, mountains are sacred.*
PHRASES **an adherent of a ~, an follower of a ~** | **a form of ~, a kind of ~**

> **NOTE**
>
> ### Religions
>
> **accept…, adopt…, convert to…, embrace…, follow…, turn to…** ◊ *He converted to Judaism when he got married.* ◊ *people who follow Hinduism*
> **abandon…, reject…** ◊ *He rejected Christianity and became a Buddhist.*
> **…spreads** ◊ *Islam spread rapidly through North Africa.*
> **…preaches sth, …proclaims sth, …teaches sth** ◊ *Christianity preaches that sinners can be forgiven.*
> **a follower of…** ◊ *followers of Sikhism*
> **the rise of…, the spread of…** ◊ *the rise of Christianity in the 1st century*
> **the teachings of…, the tenets of…** ◊ *the basic tenets of Buddhism*

religious adj.

VERBS **be** | **become**
ADV. **extremely, fairly, very, etc.** | **deeply, devoutly, highly, intensely, profoundly** ◊ *a deeply ~ person* | **strictly** ◊ *He distanced himself from the strictly ~ aspects of the music.* | **essentially, fundamentally, inherently** ◊ *Yoga is essentially ~ and not just physical.* | **specifically** ◊ *the specifically ~ goals of the college* | **explicitly, overtly**

relinquish verb

ADV. **voluntarily** ◊ *They will never voluntarily ~ their independence.* | **finally** ◊ *Adrian finally ~ed Eva's hand from his grip.*
VERB + RELINQUISH **be forced to** ◊ *He was forced to ~ control of the company.* | **refuse to** | **be willing to** | **be reluctant to** | **persuade sb to**
PREP. **to** ◊ *She has ~ed the post to her cousin.*

relish verb

ADV. **positively** (*esp. BrE*), **really** | **not particularly** ◊ *He did not particularly ~ the prospect of a meeting with his boss.* |

clearly, obviously | secretly ◊ *She secretly ~ed the thought of being alone with him.*
VERB + RELISH **appear to, seem to**

reluctance noun

ADJ. **considerable, deep, extreme, great, marked** | **a certain** ◊ *I noticed a certain ~ among the teachers.* | **clear, evident, obvious** | **apparent** | **initial** | **growing, increasing** | **continued, continuing** | **general** | **natural, understandable**
VERB + RELUCTANCE **have** | **display, express, indicate, reflect, show** ◊ *His designs indicate a ~ to conform to fashion.* ◊ *She showed considerable ~ to leave.* | **pretend** | **overcome** | **notice, sense** | **understand** ◊ *I can quite understand your ~ to talk about what happened to you.* | **explain** ◊ *These political tensions explain the ~ of financiers to invest in the region.*
PREP. **with ~** ◊ *With great ~, we have come to the decision to close the hospital.* | **~ by, ~ on the part of** ◊ *~ by insurers to keep paying out heavy claims*

reluctant adj.

VERBS **appear, be, feel, look, seem** ◊ *Students may feel ~ to ask questions.* | **become** | **remain**
ADV. **extremely, fairly, very, etc.** | **decidedly, deeply, remarkably** | **increasingly** | **a little, slightly, etc.** | **almost** ◊ *For a moment, he felt almost ~ to leave.* | **apparently, seemingly** | **clearly** | **initially** | **curiously, strangely** ◊ *She was curiously ~ to talk about the experience.* | **understandably** ◊ *Children are sometimes understandably ~ to wear glasses.*

rely verb

PHR V **rely on/upon sb/sth**
1 need sb/sth
ADV. **heavily, a lot, strongly** ◊ *countries that ~ heavily on food aid* | **completely, entirely, exclusively, solely** ◊ *I advise you to think rationally and not to ~ solely on your intuition* | **increasingly** | **largely, mainly, mostly, primarily** | **traditionally** | **typically**
VERB + RELY ON/UPON **be forced to, have to, must** ◊ *people who are forced to ~ on public transport/transportation* | **tend to**
PREP. **for** ◊ *They relied entirely on these few weapons for their defence.*
2 trust sb/sth
ADV. **safely** ◊ *You can safely ~ on the report's conclusions.* | **simply** ◊ *Most historians simply ~ on archives.* | **generally** ◊ *I generally ~ on instinct when pairing wine and food.*
VERB + RELY ON/UPON **can** ◊ *Who can you ~ on these days?* ◊ *You can always ~ on Holly to say the wrong thing.* ◊ *The party could no longer ~ on its traditional supporters.*
PREP. **for** ◊ *I couldn't ~ on John for information.*

remains noun

ADJ. **abundant, considerable, extensive, substantial** ◊ *abundant ~ of marine algae* ◊ *the extensive ~ of an Aztec pyramid* | **impressive** | **fragmentary** | **visible** | **existing, surviving** | **ancient, prehistoric** | **Greek, Roman, etc.** | **battered, mangled, shattered, tattered** ◊ *the mangled ~ of the bomber's van* | **burned, burned-out, charred, cremated, smouldering/smoldering** | **physical** | **earthly, human, mortal** ◊ *This tomb holds the mortal ~ of a great pharaoh.* | **animal, archaeological, fossil, fossilized, organic, plant, skeletal**
VERB + REMAINS **discover, find, locate, reveal, uncover, unearth** ◊ *While excavating the site, workers unearthed the ~ of several dinosaurs.* | **identify** ◊ *The ~ have been identified as those of Carl Rider.* | **excavate, exhume, recover, remove** ◊ *They are excavating the ~ of an Iron Age settlement.* ◊ *Marie Curie's ~ were exhumed and interred in the Pantheon.* | **examine, study** | **bury, inter** (*formal*) | **preserve** | **dump,**

scatter, throw | burn | feed on ◊ *Gulls often feed on the ~ of seal kills.*
REMAINS + VERB **survive** ◊ *Considerable ~ survive of the great city walls.* | **lie** ◊ *Her ~ lie in an unmarked grave.* | **date from…** ◊ *The burned-out ~ date from the 19th century.*
PREP. **among the ~, in the ~** ◊ *The body was found among the ~ of a burned-out house.*

remand noun

VERB + REMAND **be held on** ◊ *He was held on ~, charged with causing malicious damage to property.*
REMAND + NOUN **centre, home** (*both BrE*) | **prisoner**
PREP. **on ~** ◊ *I was in prison on ~ for three weeks.*

remark noun

ADJ. **brief, passing** | **occasional** | **casual, chance, off-the-cuff, throwaway** | **prepared** (*esp. AmE*) ◊ *He had a set of prepared ~s.* | **careless, inappropriate** ◊ *the sad consequences of one careless ~* | **catty, caustic** (*esp. AmE*), **cutting, derogatory, disparaging, insulting, nasty, offensive, pointed, scathing, snide** ◊ *He made some snide ~s about his opponent's skill.* | **complimentary, encouraging, kind** | **innocent** | **critical** | **sarcastic** | **smart** (*esp. AmE*) ◊ *There is no room for jokes and smart ~s.* | **flippant, offhand** ◊ *a conflict that comes about through someone's offhand ~ or careless mistake* | **controversial** | **inflammatory, provocative** | **famous** | **cryptic** | **odd, strange** | **silly, stupid** | **funny, witty** ◊ *He's always making witty ~s.* | **anti-Semitic, homophobic, racist, sexist** ◊ *Racist or sexist ~s are never acceptable in the workplace.* | **crude, obscene, rude** | **defamatory** | **personal** ◊ *How dare you make personal ~s!* | **general** | **introductory, opening, preliminary** | **closing, concluding, final** ◊ *I agreed with most of what he said at the beginning of the speech but not with his closing ~s.*
VERB + REMARK **deliver** (*esp. AmE*), **give** (*esp. AmE*), **make, offer** (*esp. AmE*), **pass, utter** ◊ *The Pope delivered his ~s before boarding his plane.* ◊ *I gave my ~s at the benefit.* ◊ *She made a disparaging ~ about men.* ◊ *Candice would have liked to offer a smart ~ at that moment.* | **withdraw** (*esp. BrE*) ◊ *He was expelled from the party for failing to withdraw his controversial ~s.* | **address, direct** ◊ *Who were those rude ~s addressed to?* | **add** ◊ *She was just about to add some sarcastic ~ when her phone rang.* | **preface** ◊ *I must preface my ~s with a confession.* | **begin** ◊ *He began his ~s with a prayer.* | **conclude** ◊ *The President concluded his ~s by thanking everyone who had helped.* | **clarify** | **hear, read** | **interpret, take** ◊ *Please don't interpret my ~s as support for the current system.* ◊ *The White House said it took such ~s very seriously.* | **ignore, take no notice of** ◊ *I just ignored her last ~.*
REMARK + VERB **apply to sb/sth** ◊ *These ~s apply equally to doctors.* | **be directed at/to sb** ◊ *The ~ was directed at him.* | **suggest sth** ◊ *Her ~s suggest that the negotiations may be successful.* | **reflect sth** ◊ *The General's ~s do not reflect the view of the government.* | **provoke sth** ◊ *The ~ provoked an angry response from the crowd.*
PREP. **in a/the ~** ◊ *He made a few factual errors in his ~s on Rembrandt.* | **~ about, ~ concerning, ~ on** ◊ *I shall keep my ~s on the subject brief.* | **~ by, ~ from** ◊ *~s by officials* | **~ to** ◊ *a casual ~ to his father*

remark verb

ADV. **casually** ◊ *She ~ed casually that she was leaving her job.* | **pointedly** | **lightly, mildly** | **drily, sarcastically, wryly** | **ruefully** | **jokingly** | **cheerfully** | **coolly** | **snidely** | **famously**
VERB + REMARK **be heard to**
PREP. **on, upon** ◊ *Several people ~ed on her outfit.* | **to** ◊ *He ~ed to Jane that he had not heard from Sally for a long time.*

remarkable adj.

VERBS **be, seem**
ADV. **absolutely, just** (*esp. AmE*), **most, quite, really, truly, very** ◊ *What they have achieved is just ~.* ◊ *a most ~ musician* ◊ *a truly ~ discovery* | **fairly, pretty, rather** | **equally** ◊ *Equally ~ is the transformation he has undergone personally.* | **especially, particularly**

PREP. **for** ◇ *These cars are ~ for the quietness of their engines.*

remedy noun

1 treatment/medicine

ADJ. **effective, good** | **common, popular** ◇ *Ginger is a popular ~ for morning sickness.* | **traditional** | **ancient, old** | **folk** | **home** | **alternative, herbal, homeopathic, natural** | **over-the-counter** | **cold, cough, hangover** ◇ *The player insists that he merely took a cold ~ and not a banned substance.*
... OF REMEDY **dose** ◇ *One dose of the ~ is sufficient.*
VERB + REMEDY **take, use** | **need** | **try** | **give sb** ◇ *The ~ was given in different strengths to a group of volunteers.* | **prescribe (sb)** | **prepare** ◇ *The remedies are all prepared from wild flowers.* | **find** ◇ *They're hoping to find a ~ for the condition.*
REMEDY + VERB **be available** | **work** ◇ *She tried various remedies, but none of them worked.*
PREP. **~ for** ◇ *He took a herbal ~ for his hay fever.*

2 way of dealing with a problem

ADJ. **adequate, effective, good** ◇ *Your best ~ is to go to the small claims court.* | **appropriate, proper, suitable** | **easy, simple** ◇ *There's no easy ~ for unemployment.* | **common, usual** | **desperate, drastic** | **proposed** | **judicial**
VERB + REMEDY **have** | **pursue, seek** ◇ *They will have to seek a judicial ~ for breach of contract.* | **find** | **resort to** ◇ *Desperate remedies were resorted to in the search for food.* | **exhaust** ◇ *They advised him to exhaust all other remedies before applying to court.* | **offer** | **propose, suggest** | **afford (sb), grant sb, provide (sb with)** *(all law, esp. BrE)* ◇ *remedies afforded to creditors by a bankruptcy order*
REMEDY + VERB **be available** | **lie in sth** ◇ *When the reservoir becomes blocked, the only ~ lies in cleaning the entire system.*
PREP. **~ against** ◇ *The agreement states that he has a ~ against the subcontractor.* | **~ for** ◇ *remedies for breach of contract* | **~ in** ◇ *You have a ~ in civil law.*
PHRASES **rights and remedies** *(BrE, law)* ◇ *The Act created rights and remedies for consumers.*

remedy verb

ADV. **easily** ◇ *This could easily be remedied if the authorities were willing.*
VERB + REMEDY **attempt to, seek to, take steps to, try to** ◇ *The government should have taken steps to ~ the situation.*

remember verb

ADV. **clearly, distinctly, vividly, well** ◇ *I distinctly ~ Jane saying that the show started at eight.* ◇ *I ~ Miss Scott very well.* | **dimly, faintly, vaguely** | **barely, hardly, scarcely** | **easily** ◇ *To this day, people can easily ~ the show.* | **correctly, rightly** ◇ *If I ~ correctly, you were supposed to collect the keys on your way here.* | **exactly, precisely** ◇ *I don't exactly ~ what she said.* ◇ *I can't ~ exactly what happened.* | **specifically** ◇ *I specifically ~ her saying she would be visiting today.* | **especially, particularly** | **mostly, primarily** ◇ *I mostly ~ the art nouveau decor of her living room.* | **certainly, definitely** | **fondly** ◇ *She fondly ~ed her early years in India.* | **still** | **always, forever** ◇ *I'll always ~ you.* ◇ *This is an experience that the kids will enjoy and ~ forever.* | **suddenly** | **finally** ◇ *She finally ~ed what she was going to say.* | **back** ◇ *I ~ed back to the time I saw her last.*
VERB + REMEMBER **can** ◇ *I can't ~ her name.* | **try to** | **be important to**
PREP. **as** ◇ *He still ~ed her as the lively teenager he'd known years before.* | **for** ◇ *She is best ~ed for her first book, 'In the Ditch'.*

remind verb

ADV. **always, constantly, continually, frequently, often, repeatedly** ◇ *I am often ~ed of my former boss.* | **just, simply** ◇ *I simply ~ them that the choice is theirs.* | **suddenly** ◇ *Reading the note suddenly ~ed me of my appointment with Angela.* | **immediately, instantly** | **quickly** ◇ *I quickly ~ed him that I had said 'maybe'.* | **gently** ◇ *She gently ~ed him that the baby was getting cold and should be taken indoors.* |

painfully ◇ *The terrorist attack painfully ~ed the Americans that they are vulnerable even at home.*
VERB + REMIND **not have to, not need to** ◇ *I'm sure I don't need to ~ you that we have lost our last ten games.* | **serve to** ◇ *An event like this serves to ~ us that we do not have control over nature.*
PREP. **about** ◇ *I called to ~ him about the party.* | **of** ◇ *She looked at her watch to ~ him of the time.*
PHRASES **keep ~ing sb**
PHR V **remind sb of sb/sth**
ADV. **forcefully, forcibly, strongly, vividly** ◇ *The building ~ed me strongly of my old school.* | **vaguely** ◇ *Gabriel vaguely ~s me of my father.* | **suddenly** ◇ *I was suddenly ~ed of a tiger defending its cubs.* | **immediately, instantly** ◇ *He was instantly ~ed of the time he and Edna had visited Paris.* | **always** ◇ *Mrs Nolan always ~ed Marie of her own mother.*

reminder noun

ADJ. **good, potent, powerful, strong** | **lasting, permanent** | **constant, continual, daily** | **further** | **graphic, sharp, stark, vivid** | **visible, visual** | **physical, tangible** | **chilling, grim, harsh, painful** | **poignant, sad, sobering** | **salutary** *(esp. BrE)* | **timely** ◇ *This is a timely ~ of the importance of the retail sector to our economy.* | **important** | **gentle, little, quick, subtle** | **final** ◇ *It always took a final ~ to get her to pay her share of the rent.* | **helpful, useful** ◇ *The list serves as a useful ~ of the issues to consider.* | **welcome** | **email** ◇ *We will send email ~s to committee members.*
VERB + REMINDER **act as, be, offer, provide, serve as** ◇ *The ruined church acts as a constant ~ of the war.* | **become** | **give sb, issue, send (sb), send out** ◇ *She gave him a gentle ~ that payment was due.* | **get, have, receive** ◇ *You can get email ~s every week.* | **need**
REMINDER + NOUN **letter, note, postcard** *(AmE)* | **system**
PREP. **~ about** ◇ *We were sent a ~ about the next meeting.* | **~ of** ◇ *It was a cruel and tragic ~ of how dangerous mountaineering can be.* | **~ to** ◇ *a timely ~ to people that leaving their doors open is an invitation to thieves*

reminiscent adj.

VERBS **be**
ADV. **highly, strongly, very** ◇ *This painting is strongly ~ of da Vinci's 'Annunciation'.* | **faintly, slightly, somewhat, vaguely** | **eerily, oddly, strangely** | **strikingly**
PREP. **of**

remnant noun

ADJ. **small** | **last, surviving** ◇ *The museum is one of the last ~s of the 17th-century palace.* | **shattered, tattered** ◇ *the tattered ~s of the flag* ◇ *She still has a chance to scrape together the shattered ~s of her life and move on.* *(figurative)*
PREP. **~ from** *(figurative)* ◇ *Their outdated attitudes are a ~ from colonial days.*
PHRASES **a ~ from the past, a ~ of the past**

remorse noun

ADJ. **deep, genuine, great, real**
... OF REMORSE **pang, stab**
VERB + REMORSE **be filled with, be full of, be overcome with, be stricken with, feel, have, suffer** ◇ *She knew that the next day she would be full of ~.* ◇ *I suffered no ~.* | **display, express, show**
PREP. **without** ◇ *He died without ~.* | **~ at** ◇ *He felt some ~ at his actions.* | **~ for** ◇ *She was filled with ~ for the crime.* | **~ over** ◇ *She felt a sharp pang of ~ over the incident.*
PHRASES **buyer's ~** *(= after buying sth that you do not really need, like, etc.)* *(esp. AmE)* ◇ *After spending $720 on the shoes, she suffered buyer's ~.* | **a feeling of ~**

remote adj.

VERBS **appear, be, feel, look, seem**
ADV. **extremely, fairly, very, etc.** ◇ *a fairly ~ possibility* | **impossibly, infinitely** ◇ *Adulthood and responsibility seemed*

impossibly ~. | **totally** (*esp. AmE*) | **increasingly** | **relatively** ◇ *rural areas that are relatively* ~ | **geographically, physically** ◇ *geographically* ~ *areas*
PREP. **from** ◇ *Jane felt* ~ *from what was going on around her.*

removal *noun*

ADJ. **complete, total, wholesale** | **partial** | **permanent, temporary** | **effective, successful** | **immediate, speedy** ◇ *his immediate* ~ *from power* | **easy** ◇ *a liquid for the easy* ~ *of coffee stains* | **forced, forcible** ◇ *the forcible* ~ *of the protesters' barricades.* | **physical** | **surgical** | **hair, stain, tattoo** ◇ *the process of laser hair* ~ | **debris, snow, tree, etc.**
VERB + REMOVAL **call for, demand, seek** ◇ *They demanded her* ~ *from office.* | **order** ◇ *In a symbolic move, the new government ordered the* ~ *of the dictator's statue.* | **force** | **necessitate, require** ◇ *His condition required the* ~ *of a kidney.* | **allow** | **arrange for** ◇ *to arrange for the* ~ *and disposal of waste.* | **facilitate** | **prevent**
PREP. ~ **from** ◇ *The law does not allow the* ~ *of sand from the beach.* | ~ **to** ◇ *the collection's temporary* ~ *to storage*
PHRASES ~ **from office**

remove *verb*

ADV. **altogether, completely, entirely** | **partially** | **effectively** ◇ *Translation software should effectively* ~ *all barriers to communication between people.* | **successfully** | **permanently, temporarily** | **hastily, quickly, rapidly** | **gradually, slowly** | **easily** ◇ *The old cladding can be easily* ~*d using a hammer.* | **painlessly** | **safely** | **carefully** | **forcibly** ◇ *people who have been forcibly* ~*d from their homes* | **surgically** ◇ *Unsightly moles can be* ~*d surgically.* | **manually, physically**
VERB + REMOVE **try to** | **be possible to** | **be difficult to** ◇ *These stains can be difficult to* ~.
PREP. **for** ◇ *Fittings should be completely* ~*d for cleaning.* | **from** ◇ *She* ~*d the dirty dishes from the table.* | **with** ◇ *Bee stings should be* ~*d with tweezers.*

rendezvous *noun* arrangement to meet sb

ADJ. **secret** | **romantic** | **midnight** | **little**
VERB + RENDEZVOUS **have** | **arrange** | **keep** ◇ *Although it was late, there was still enough time to keep the* ~. | **make** ◇ *She made the* ~ *with only minutes to spare.*
RENDEZVOUS + NOUN **point** ◇ *The platoon made its way to the prearranged* ~ *point in the desert.*
PREP. ~ **with** ◇ *I have a* ~ *with Peter at a restaurant.*

renew *verb*

ADV. **completely** | **annually** ◇ *Membership must be* ~*ed annually.* | **periodically, regularly** | **constantly, continually, repeatedly** | **automatically**
VERB + RENEW **decide to** | **agree to** | **refuse to**
PHRASES **a chance to** ~ **sth, an opportunity to** ~ **sth** ◇ *a chance to* ~ *acquaintance with old friends* | **need** ~**ing** ◇ *The paintwork will need* ~*ing every five years.*

renewal *noun*

1 making valid for a further period of time

ADJ. **annual** | **automatic** | **contract, licence/license, membership**
VERB + RENEWAL **seek** ◇ *He sought* ~ *of the grant.* | **apply for** | **be due for, come up for** ◇ *Her contract is coming up for* ~ *in the spring.*
RENEWAL + NOUN **date** | **notice** ◇ *You can contact us at the number shown on your last* ~ *notice.* | **fee** | **process** | **option**

2 improving/repairing

ADJ. **cultural, economic, national, physical, religious, spiritual, urban** ◇ *urban* ~ *projects in the city* | **community** (*esp. AmE*)
VERB + RENEWAL **seek** ◇ *to seek spiritual* ~ | **bring, bring about** ◇ *They felt the need to bring about a* ~ *of society.*
RENEWAL + NOUN **programme/program, project**

renovate *verb*

ADV. **extensively** | **completely** ◇ *The hotel has been completely* ~*d.*
PHRASES **newly** ~**d, recently** ~**d** ◇ *the newly* ~*d synagogue*

renovation *noun*

ADJ. **extensive, major** ◇ *The building has undergone major* ~. | **complete, total** | **£40-million, $90-million, etc.** | **recent** | **building, home, house**
VERB + RENOVATION **carry out, do** (*esp. AmE*), **make** ◇ *They are to carry out extensive* ~*s to the building.* | **complete** | **oversee** | **be in need of, need, require** ◇ *The old house is in need of* ~. | **be closed for** ◇ *The gallery is closed for* ~. | **undergo** | **approve** (*esp. AmE*) ◇ *The city approved* ~*s for the mall.*
RENOVATION + NOUN **work** | **programme/program, project** | **process** | **plans** | **costs**
PREP. ~ **to** ◇ ~ *to the town hall*

rent *noun*

ADJ. **exorbitant, high** ◇ *The tenants were not prepared to pay the higher* ~*s demanded.* | **affordable, cheap, low** | **nominal, peppercorn** (*BrE*) | **free** (*esp. AmE*) ◇ *They get free* ~ *in return for taking care of the house.* | **fair** | **reduced** | **increased** | **rising** ◇ *Discontent resulted from sharply rising* ~*s.* | **fixed** | **market** ◇ *They weren't paying market* ~ *on the properties.* | **annual, monthly, weekly** (*esp. BrE*) | **initial** ◇ *The initial* ~ *will be reviewed annually.* | **back, unpaid** | **apartment** (*esp. AmE*), **ground** (*in the UK*), **house, housing, land, office**
VERB + RENT **pay** | **afford** ◇ *He couldn't afford the* ~ *by himself.* | **be behind with, fall behind with, owe** ◇ *You put your tenancy at risk if you fall behind with the* ~. | **charge** ◇ *The* ~ *charged depends largely on the size and locality of the property.* | **collect** ◇ *The landlord came around to collect the month's* ~. | **receive** ◇ *The company receives* ~ *on local property that it owns.* | **fix** ◇ *The* ~ *will be fixed at 18% of the market value of the property.* | **increase, push up, put up** (*esp. BrE*), **raise** ◇ *The large stores have pushed up the* ~*s in the area.* ◇ *The new lease will put her* ~ *up to £200 a week.* | **calculate, determine**
RENT + VERB **be due, be payable** (*esp. BrE*) ◇ *The* ~ *is due on the last day of the quarter.* | **go up, increase, rise** ◇ *Their* ~ *has increased from $25 200 to $28 600 a year.* | **fall**
RENT + NOUN **money, payment** | **book** (*BrE*) ◇ *We gave tenants* ~ *books.* | **arrears** (*BrE*) | **levels** (*esp. BrE*) ◇ *They took the landlord to court over increasing* ~ *levels.* | **increase, rise** (*esp. BrE*) | **review** (*BrE*) | **allowance** (*esp. BrE*), **rebate** (*BrE*), **subsidy** (*esp. AmE*) | **control** (*esp. in AmE*) | **collection** | **collector, man** (*BrE*) | **strike**
PREP. **in** ~ ◇ *The company has paid out a lot of money in* ~. | ~ **for** ◇ *The* ~ *for the house is affordable.* | ~ **from** ◇ *They earned* ~ *from their property in London.* | ~ **on** ◇ *the* ~ *on a factory*
PHRASES **arrears of** ~ (*BrE, law*) ◇ *to be liable for arrears of* ~ | **for** ~ (*esp. AmE*) ◇ *There was a sign saying 'Room for rent'* | **a month's, a year's, etc.** ~ | **the non-payment of** ~, **the payment of** ~ ◇ *The movement advocated the non-payment of* ~ *and taxes.*

rental *noun*

ADJ. **annual, monthly, weekly** | **short-term** (*AmE*) ◇ *Some landlords have resorted to short-term* ~*s.* | **free** ◇ *the broadband package includes 6 months free line* ~ (*BrE*) | **DVD, movie** (*AmE*), **video** ◇ *a coupon for a free movie* ~ | **line** (*BrE*) ◇ *The phone bill gives a breakdown of the cost of the line* ~ *and of calls.* | **equipment, ski** (*both esp. AmE*) | **bicycle, bike** (*informal*), **boat, car, truck** (*all esp. AmE*)
RENTAL + NOUN **company** | **terms** | **charge, fee, payment** | **income** | **market** ◇ *The local* ~ *market is booming.* | **accommodation** (*BrE*), **property** | **car** (*esp. AmE*)

reorganization *noun*

ADJ. **fundamental, major, massive, radical** | **financial, structural** | **corporate, internal** | **bankruptcy** (*AmE*) | **government**

VERB + REORGANIZATION **undergo** ◇ *The company has undergone a major ~.* | **carry out** | **announce**
REORGANIZATION + VERB **take place**
REORGANIZATION + NOUN **plan**

reorganize (*BrE* also **-ise**) *verb*

ADV. **completely, totally** | **systematically**
PREP. **as** ◇ *The laboratory was ~d as a separate establishment.* | **into** ◇ *Their headquarters was ~d into five regional offices.*

repair *noun*

ADJ. **extensive, major** | **minor** | **essential, necessary, vital** | **emergency, immediate, urgent** | **quick, rapid** | **costly, expensive** | **constant** | **temporary** | **running** (*BrE*) ◇ *The drivers carried small toolkits for making running ~s.* | **warranty** | **building, home** (*esp. AmE*), **house, housing** (*BrE*), **roof, structural** | **car, engine, vehicle** | **highway** (*in the US*), **motorway** (*in the UK*), **road** | **electrical, TV** | **shoe** | **muscle, tissue** ◇ *nutrients needed for energy and tissue ~*
VERB + REPAIR **carry out, do, make, perform** | **complete** ◇ *It is unlikely that the ~s will be completed on time.* | **be in need of, need, require** | **be closed for** ◇ *The museum is currently closed for structural ~s.* | **undergo** ◇ *The highway is undergoing major ~s.*
REPAIR + VERB **cost sth**
REPAIR + NOUN **work** | **job** ◇ *The damage meant a nine-month ~ job.* | **project** | **service** ◇ *They provide a 24-hour ~ service.* | **business** | **bill, cost** | **centre/center, facility, garage, shop, yard** ◇ *a ~ yard for fishing boats* | **guy** (*informal, esp. AmE*), **man** (usually **repairman**), **technician** (*esp. AmE*) ◇ *Why don't you get a TV repairman to have a look at it before you buy a new one?* | **crew, team** | **part** (*AmE*) | **kit** | **manual** (*esp. AmE*)
PREP. **beyond ~** ◇ *The vase was damaged beyond ~.* | **for ~** ◇ *I took my bike in for ~.* | **under ~** ◇ *We were given a courtesy car to use while our car was under ~.* | **~ to** ◇ *to carry out ~s to the track*
PHRASES **a backlog of ~s** ◇ *Investment is needed to reduce the backlog of ~s.* | **in good ~, in poor ~** ◇ *The tools are old but in good ~.* | **keep sth in good ~, keep sth in ~** (*formal, esp. BrE*) ◇ *As a tenant you are required to keep the house in good ~.* | **~ and maintenance** ◇ *They are responsible for the ~ and maintenance of the buildings.* | **a … state of ~** ◇ *The barn was in a poor state of ~.*

repair *verb*

ADV. **properly, successfully** ◇ *Most of the damage has now been successfully ~ed.* | **poorly** | **completely, fully** | **quickly** | **easily**
VERB + REPAIR **try to** | **help (to)** ◇ *Natural vitamins in the shampoo will help ~ damaged hair.*
PHRASES **the cost of ~ing sth** ◇ *They estimate the cost of ~ing the damaged roads at £1 million.* | **have sth ~ed** ◇ *I'm having my car ~ed next week.* | **surgically ~ed** (*esp. AmE*) ◇ *His surgically ~ed knee is bothering him.*

repatriate *verb*

ADV. **forcibly**
PREP. **from, to** ◇ *The refugees were forcibly ~d from Hong Kong to Vietnam.*

repatriation *noun*

ADJ. **compulsory** (*esp. BrE*), **forced, forcible** ◇ *The party advocates compulsory ~ of immigrants who commit a crime.* | **voluntary**
VERB + REPATRIATION **await, face** ◇ *refugees awaiting ~* ◇ *Mexican American workers faced forced ~.*
REPATRIATION + NOUN **programme/program** | **process** (*esp. AmE*)
PREP. **~ from** ◇ *voluntary ~ of people from the disputed territory to their homes* | **~ to**
PHRASES **the ~ of profits**

repay *verb*

1 pay back money

ADV. **fully, in full** ◇ *The loan must be repaid in full by December 31.*
VERB + REPAY **be able to, can, can afford to** | **be unable to** | **use sth to** ◇ *The proceeds from the sale will be used to ~ the loan.*
PREP. **to** ◇ *This money must be repaid to the bank.*

2 (*BrE*) bring you sth in return for your efforts

ADV. **amply, more than, well** ◇ *The charter can be seen in the town museum, which more than ~s a visit.*
PREP. **for** ◇ *I felt that I had been amply repaid for my exertions.*

repayment *noun*

ADJ. **full** | **partial** | **early** ◇ *Interest will be refunded in the event of early ~ of the loan.* | **regular** | **monthly, weekly, etc.** | **capital, principal** | **interest** | **debt, loan, mortgage** (*BrE*)
VERB + REPAYMENT **make** ◇ *The ~s can be made directly from your current account.* | **keep up** (*BrE*), **meet** (*esp. BrE*) ◇ *They are struggling to keep up their loan ~s.* | **demand** ◇ *The bank has demanded ~ of the loan.* | **be due for** (*BrE*) ◇ *The loans are due for ~ in July 2015.* | **spread** ◇ *Repayments can be spread over 25 years.* | **calculate**
REPAYMENT + NOUN **period** | **plan, schedule, terms** | **option** ◇ *a ten-year ~ option* | **rate** | **loan, mortgage** (*both BrE*)
PREP. **~ on** ◇ *~s on the mortgage* | **~ to** ◇ *~ to the fund*

repeat *verb*

ADV. **just, merely, simply** ◇ *There is no point in merely ~ing what we've done before.* | **again** | **ad nauseam, constantly, continually, endlessly, indefinitely, over and over, over and over again** ◇ *That message was still being ~ed ad nauseam on the radio.* ◇ *They constantly ~ the same mistakes.* ◇ *A single note ~ed over and over again, throbbing in my head.* | **consistently, frequently, often, persistently, regularly** | **exactly, faithfully, word for word** ◇ *She faithfully ~ed everything he had told her.* ◇ *He ~ed what she had said word for word.* | **mechanically** | **slowly** | **quietly, softly** | **loudly** | **patiently** | **stubbornly** | **firmly**
VERB + REPEAT **can only** ◇ *I can only ~ what I have already said to other journalists.* | **be necessary to, need to** ◇ *It may be necessary to ~ the dose several times to effect a cure.*
PREP. **after** ◇ *The students ~ed each sentence after their teacher.* | **to** ◇ *You must not ~ this to anyone.*
PHRASES **keep ~ing sb/sth** ◇ *She kept ~ing it over and over again like a robot.*

repellent *adj.*

VERBS **be** | **find sb/sth**
ADV. **extremely, fairly, very, etc.** | **utterly** (*esp. BrE*) | **a little, slightly, etc.**
PREP. **to** ◇ *His arrogance was utterly ~ to her.*

repent *verb* (*formal*)

ADV. **genuinely, sincerely, truly** ◇ *In order to be saved one must truly ~.*
VERB + REPENT **come to** ◇ *He came to ~ his hasty decision.*
PREP. **for** (*esp. AmE*), **of** ◇ *I will spend the rest of my life trying to ~ for my actions.* ◇ *She has ~ed of her sins.*

repentance *noun*

ADJ. **genuine, sincere, true** | **deathbed**
VERB + REPENTANCE **show** ◇ *They refused to showed ~ for their crimes.* | **preach**

repercussion *noun*

ADJ. **considerable, important, major, serious, severe, significant** ◇ *A fall in oil production would have severe ~s for the global economy.* | **wide, widespread** | **international** ◇ *The international ~s are still being felt today.* | **economic,**

financial, legal, political, social | negative | possible, potential ◇ *These actions have potential ~s.*
VERB + REPERCUSSION **have** | **feel, suffer** ◇ *Anne felt the ~s of the earlier incident.* | **fear**
REPERCUSSION + VERB **be felt** ◇ *The ~s of the change in policy will be felt throughout the world.*
PREP. **~ for** ◇ *Changes in the industry had major ~s for the local community.* | **~ on** ◇ *The pay cuts are likely to have serious ~s on productivity.*
PHRASES **for fear of ~s, without fear of ~s** ◇ *a resident who did not want to be named for fear of ~s*

repertoire noun

ADJ. **broad, extensive, large, vast, wide** | **diverse, varied** | **full, rich** | **limited, small** | **standard** | **classical** ◇ *ballets from the classical ~* | **contemporary** | **emotional** ◇ *An actor has to build a character and extend his own emotional ~.* | **music, musical** | **concert, opera, operatic** | **guitar, piano, vocal, etc.**
VERB + REPERTOIRE **have** ◇ *She has a rather limited ~.* | **add (sth) to, broaden, build, build up, develop, expand, extend, increase** ◇ *He has added considerably to his piano ~.* ◇ *She needs to build up a ~ of pieces.* | **perform, play** | **enter** ◇ *The piece has deservedly entered the violin ~.*
REPERTOIRE + VERB **include sth** ◇ *His ~ includes a large number of Scottish folk songs.*
PREP. **in the/your ~** ◇ *a key piece in the standard concert ~*

repetition noun

ADJ. **exact** | **frequent** | **constant, endless** | **mindless, rote** (*esp. AmE*) ◇ *the mindless ~ of the official line* ◇ *the rote ~ of mythological formulas*
VERB + REPETITION **use** ◇ *Blues is a musical form that uses a lot of ~.* | **avoid, prevent** ◇ *She said I should avoid ~ of words in my essay.* | **complete, perform** (*in exercising*) ◇ *If you can, perform multiple ~s of this exercise on each hand.*

repetitive adj.

VERBS **be, seem** | **become, get**
ADV. **extremely, fairly, very, etc.** | **highly** | **endlessly** ◇ *a boring and endlessly ~ task* | **a little, slightly, etc.**

replace verb

1 take the place of sb/sth; exchange sb/sth

ADV. **completely, entirely, fully, totally** | **largely** | **partially** | **merely, simply** ◇ *Putting in a new kitchen can cost very little if you are simply replacing an old one.* | **easily** ◇ *These losses are not easily ~d.* | **effectively** ◇ *These guidelines effectively ~d the official procedure.* | **immediately, quickly, rapidly** | **gradually, slowly** | **eventually, finally, ultimately** | **temporarily** ◇ *Williams has temporarily ~d Reed on the first team.*
VERB + REPLACE **can** ◇ *Machines can't ~ people in this work.* | **can afford to** | **be built to, be designed to, be intended to, be meant to, be used to** ◇ *It was built to ~ the old jail.* | **decide to** | **appoint sb to, elect sb to, nominate sb to** (*esp. AmE*) ◇ *She has been nominated to ~ Justice O'Connor on the Supreme Court.* | **attempt to, try to** | **be costly to, be expensive to** ◇ *Halogen lamps give excellent service, but the bulbs are expensive to ~.* | **be difficult to, be hard to, be impossible to**
PREP. **as** ◇ *She ~d Jane Stott as Managing Director.* | **by** ◇ *Many of the workers have been ~d by machines.* | **with** ◇ *We ~d the old television set with a newer one.*

2 put sth back in the right place

ADV. **carefully, gently**
PREP. **in** ◇ *She ~d the dress in the wardrobe.* | **on** ◇ *He carefully ~d the vase on the shelf.*

replacement noun

1 replacing one thing with another

ADJ. **complete, full** ◇ *Complete ~ of the roof tiles would be*

very costly. | **partial** | **direct** ◇ *The series III gearbox is a direct ~ for a series II.* | **gradual** | **eventual**
VERB + REPLACEMENT **be in need of, need, require** ◇ *The original furnishings are now in need of ~.*
REPLACEMENT + NOUN **programme/program** | **cost, value** ◇ *Rare instruments are usually insured for their full ~ value.* | **equipment**
PHRASES **hormone ~ therapy** (*abbreviated to **HRT***)

2 sb/sth that replaces sb/sth else

ADJ. **permanent** | **temporary** | **immediate** | **last-minute, late** ◇ *She served as a last-minute ~ for the woman originally selected.* | **likely** ◇ *He is the most likely ~ for the captain.* | **possible, potential** | **ideal** | **adequate** | **appropriate, suitable** | **hip, joint, knee** | **valve** | **meal** (*esp. AmE*) ◇ *low-calorie meal ~s*
VERB + REPLACEMENT **appoint, bring in (sb/sth as), hire** ◇ *We'll have to see how bad the injury is before deciding whether to bring in a ~.* | **name (sb as)** ◇ *She was named as a possible ~ for the head of sales.* | **choose, select** | **need** | **look for, seek** | **find** ◇ *We need to find a ~ for Jan when she goes on maternity leave.* | **get** | **come in as, come on as** (*both BrE*) ◇ *He came on as a ~ for the injured player.* | **have, undergo** ◇ *She had a hip ~ six years ago.*
REPLACEMENT + NOUN **worker** (*esp. AmE*) | **part, product, unit** ◇ *Do you know where I can get the ~ part?* | **car, vehicle**
PREP. **as ~** ◇ *Trams are now often preferred as ~s for buses.* | **~ by** ◇ *the president's temporary ~ by the Chief of Staff* | **~ for**

replay noun

1 playing again of a short section of video, etc.

ADJ. **action** (*BrE*), **instant** (*AmE*) ◇ *Instant ~s can occasionally prove the referee wrong.* | **slow-motion** | **endless** ◇ *the endless television ~s of the attack* | **television, TV, video**
VERB + REPLAY **see, view, watch** ◇ *He has watched a video ~ of his fall on numerous occasions.* | **show** ◇ *On the big screen they showed the ~.* | **use** ◇ *The ~ is used on disputed decisions.*
REPLAY + VERB **show sth** ◇ *The ~ shows that it was a handball.*

2 football (soccer) game that is played again

ADJ. **final, first-round, quarter-final, etc.** | **cup**
VERB + REPLAY **earn, force** ◇ *They earned a ~ with their 1–1 draw.*
PREP. **~ against, ~ with** ◇ *a ~ against Real Madrid* | **~ between** ◇ *the ~ between Liverpool and Portsmouth*

replica noun

ADJ. **exact** | **accurate, perfect** | **full-scale, full-size, life-size** | **half-scale, etc.** | **miniature, small**
VERB + REPLICA **build, construct, create, make, produce** ◇ *She made a half-scale scale ~ of Captain Cook's ship.*
PREP. **in ~** ◇ *The original library has been rebuilt in ~.*

reply noun

ADJ. **brief, monosyllabic** (*esp. BrE*) | **blunt, curt, short, terse** ◇ *His ~ was short and to the point.* | **sarcastic, scathing** | **only** ◇ *A non-committal grunt was his only ~.* | **simple** ◇ *Her ~ was simple: 'No.'* | **standard, usual** ◇ *'No comment' is his standard ~ to most questions.* | **straight** ◇ *She refused to give a straight ~, deciding rather to defer the question.* | **evasive, non-committal** | **proper, satisfactory** (*esp. BrE*) | **suitable** | **correct** | **affirmative, positive** | **negative** | **early, immediate, prompt, quick** | **formal** | **individual, personal** | **written** | **polite** | **thoughtful** ◇ *Many thanks for your thoughtful ~, we greatly appreciate it.* | **witty** | **muffled** ◇ *'I'm in here!' came the muffled ~.*
VERB + REPLY **get, have, receive** ◇ *Have you had a ~ to your letter yet?* | **give sb, make, offer** ◇ *He made no ~, but simply walked away.* ◇ *Grace could offer no ~.* | **post, send, send back, type, write** ◇ *I'll post the replies later on my web page.* ◇ *I must write my letter in time for them to send back a ~.* | **elicit, produce** ◇ *The report elicited a formal ~ from the department.* ◇ *The questionnaire produced 9 000 replies.* | **grunt (sth in), mumble (sth in), mutter (sth in)** ◇ *'Mmm!' she grunted in ~.* | **wait for** | **await, expect** (*both formal*) (*in*

letters) ◇ *I await your ~ with interest.* | **hear, read** ◇ *She heard no ~.*

REPLY + VERB **come, come back** ◇ *'No!' came the ~.* ◇ *A ~ came back the next day.* | **be forthcoming** ◇ *No ~ seemed to be forthcoming.*

REPLY + NOUN **card, envelope, form, slip** (*BrE*) ◇ *Please complete the ~ card and return it to us as soon as possible.* | **button** (= in email) ◇ *It's easy to just hit the ~ button.*

PREP. **in ~ (to sth)** ◇ *What did they say in ~?* ◇ *I am writing in ~ to your request for information on hotels in Italy.* | **~ from** ◇ *a ~ from the minister* | **~ to** ◇ *my ~ to your query*

PHRASES **a/the right of ~** (*esp. BrE*) ◇ *I am grateful to you for having given me a right of ~* (= the opportunity to respond) *to the article in your magazine about my company.*

reply *verb*

ADV. **merely, simply** ◇ *He simply replied that he hadn't the faintest idea.* | **directly** ◇ *She did not ~ directly to the allegations.* | **personally** ◇ *Well, you weren't expecting him to ~ personally, were you?* | **at once, immediately** | **hastily, hurriedly, promptly, quickly** | **slowly** | **at length** ◇ *She replied at length, but not to the point.* | **briefly, briskly, curtly, gruffly, shortly** | **abruptly, sharply** | **bluntly, flatly** ◇ *'No, you're not!' Graham replied bluntly.* | **firmly** | **gently, politely, soothingly** | **lightly** | **seriously** | **quietly, softly** | **angrily, bitterly, crossly, indignantly, sourly** ◇ *'It was your fault!' she replied angrily.* | **coldly, coolly, icily** | **cautiously, defensively, guardedly, hesitantly, nervously** | **calmly, evenly, mildly** | **meekly** | **haughtily, smugly** | **sternly, stiffly** | **brightly, cheerfully, happily** | **innocently** | **grimly, sadly** | **drily, sarcastically, sardonically, sweetly** (*ironic*), **tartly** | **absently, distractedly, vaguely** | **casually, non-chalantly** ◇ *'I really don't care!' he replied nonchalantly.* | **matter-of-factly** ◇ *'I know!' she replied matter-of-factly.* | **honestly, truthfully** | **confidently** | **evasively** | **sheepishly** | **shyly** | **tiredly, wearily** | **in kind** ◇ *Calvin was insulted and replied in kind* (= by insulting them back).

VERB + REPLY **not bother to** ◇ *She didn't even bother to ~.*

PREP. **to** ◇ *He did not ~ to my letter.* | **with** ◇ *She replied with a smile.*

PHRASES **a chance to ~** ◇ *She quickly left the room before he had a chance to ~.*

report *noun*

1 written/spoken account of sth

ADJ. **groundbreaking, important, influential, landmark, major** | **lengthy** | **brief, short** | **12-page, 140-page, etc.** | **complete, comprehensive, extensive, full, wide-ranging** (*esp. BrE*) ◇ *I will have to make a full ~ of the situation to my superiors.* | **detailed, in-depth** | **general** | **summary** (*esp. AmE*) ◇ *the company's summary ~ for the second quarter of this year* | **encouraging, excellent, favourable/favorable, glowing, positive** | **adverse, bad, critical, damning, disturbing, hard-hitting** (*esp. BrE*), **negative, scathing** | **sensational** | **latest, new, recent, updated, up-to-date** | **previous** | **first, original** ◇ *There have been many new findings since the original ~.* | **early, initial, interim, preliminary** | **follow-up, further, later, subsequent** | **periodic, regular** | **annual, daily, monthly, quarterly, weekly** | **final** | **draft** | **status** ◇ *daily status ~s as to how and what we were doing* | **formal** | **written** | **oral, verbal** | **published, unpublished** | **special** | **standard** | **verbatim** | **credible, reliable** | **erroneous, false, misleading** | **conflicting** ◇ *There have been conflicting ~s on the number of people killed.* | **factual** | **anecdotal** | **live** ◇ *We'll have a live ~ from Manila in about 30 minutes.* | **exclusive** | **eyewitness, first-hand** | **second-hand** | **anonymous** | **unconfirmed** ◇ *unconfirmed ~s of a shooting in the capital* | **independent** | **joint** | **official** | **classified, confidential, secret** | **internal** ◇ *a damaging internal ~ on the department's organization* | **public** | **congressional, federal, government, parliamentary, Senate** | **intelligence, police** ◇ *Reliable intelligence ~s suggest that the terrorists have bases in five cities.* | **investigative** ◇ *investigative news ~s about glitches in the system* | **media, press** | **magazine, newspaper, radio, television** | **news, traffic, weather** | **commission, committee** | **company** | **credit, economic,**

financial, market | **expense** (*AmE*) ◇ *fired for falsifying an expense ~* | **consumer** ◇ *the consumer ~ for this 1993 model* | **employment** (*AmE*) ◇ *the government's latest employment ~* | **environmental** | **clinical, medical, psychiatric, scientific, technical** | **lab** (*informal*), **laboratory** | **inspection** ◇ *the inspection ~ sent to the committee* | **case, research, survey** | **enquiry** (*esp. BrE*) | **accident, incident, autopsy** | **progress, status** | **probation** (*esp. BrE*) | **audit** | **law** (*esp. BrE*) ◇ *The case has not yet been reported in the law ~s.*

VERB + REPORT **deliver, give sb, make, present** ◇ *The committee presented its ~ to the Attorney General.* | **compile, complete, do, draw up** (*esp. BrE*), **prepare, produce, type, type up, write** ◇ *I typed up a ~ about the morning's events for our clients.* | **generate** ◇ *The sites generate detailed travel ~s.* | **file, give (sb/sth), let sb have, provide, send sb/sth, submit** ◇ *Our correspondent in Kabul files a ~ most days.* ◇ *I'll let you have a ~ as soon as I can.* | **issue, release** ◇ *Auditors normally issue a ~ as to whether the company accounts have been prepared correctly.* | **leak** ◇ *a confidential ~ leaked to the press* | **have, hear, obtain, receive** ◇ *We've had ~s of a gang shooting in the city.* | **commission, request** ◇ *The government commissioned a ~ on the state of agriculture in the country.* | **launch** (*esp. BrE*) | **accept, approve, endorse** ◇ *Following discussion, the annual ~ was accepted unanimously.* | **dismiss, reject** | **confirm, corroborate** | **deny** ◇ *They could neither confirm nor deny ~s that the chairperson was to be replaced.* | **cite, quote** ◇ *They replied citing a ~ from the finance department.* | **read, see** | **consider, discuss, examine, review** ◇ *We have reviewed all ~s from today's battle.* | **investigate** ◇ *We're investigating ~s of an explosion in this area.* | **publish** | **appear in** ◇ *A large number of tables and figures appear in the ~.*

REPORT + VERB **be based on sth** ◇ *This ~ is based on the analysis of 600 completed questionnaires.* | **address sth, concern sth, cover sth, deal with sth, detail sth, examine sth, focus on sth, look at sth, relate to sth** ◇ *The ~ looks at the health risks linked to obesity.* | **comprise sth, contain sth, include sth** | **present sth, provide sth** ◇ *The chairman's ~ provides a summary of operations.* | **comment on sth, declare sth, describe sth, document sth, explain sth, express sth, indicate sth, mention sth, outline sth, say sth, state sth, summarize sth** ◇ *Reports have indicated that a growing number of medium-sized companies are under financial pressure.* | **cite sth, list sth, note sth, quote sth** ◇ *The ~ notes evidence that secondary smoke harms unborn children.* | **add sth, continue…, go on…** ◇ *The ~ continued in similar vein.* ◇ *The ~ went on to list her injuries.* | **acknowledge sth, admit sth, admit to sth** ◇ *The ~ admits to several outstanding questions about the safety of the waste dumps.* | **allege sth, assert sth, claim sth, contend sth** | **argue sth** | **demonstrate sth, identify sth, illustrate sth, show sth** | **reveal sth** ◇ *The riots could have been avoided, a ~ revealed yesterday.* | **predict sth** | **fail to do sth** ◇ *The ~ fails to explain his decision.* | **draw attention to sth, emphasize sth, highlight sth, point sth out, stress sth** ◇ *The ~ draws attention to the appalling conditions in the country's prisons.* | **warn sth** ◇ *The ~ warns that more job losses are likely.* | **confirm sth** | **conclude sth, find sth, link sth with sth** ◇ *a ~ linking ill health with industrial pollution* | **advise sth, advocate sth, call for sth, propose sth, recommend sth, suggest sth, support sth, urge sth** ◇ *The ~ called for sweeping changes in the education system.* | **question sth** ◇ *Her ~ questions the scientific validity of the experiment.* | **accuse sb/sth, attack sb/sth, blame sb/sth, criticize sb/sth** | **be called sth, be entitled sth, be titled sth** (*esp. AmE*) ◇ *a ~ entitled 'Kick-start'* | **be issued, be out, be released, come out** ◇ *Criticism has been directed at local businesses in a ~ out* (= published) *today.* | **come in** ◇ *First ~s of the accident are coming in.* | **be circulating** ◇ *I based my statement on ~s circulating at the time.* | **appear, emerge, surface** ◇ *These ~s surfaced throughout the summer.*

REPORT + NOUN **author, writer, writing** | **results**

PREP. **according to a/the ~** ◇ *According to this evening's* weather ~, there will be snow tomorrow. | amid ~s ◊ The rally came amid ~s of dissatisfaction among army officers. | in a/the ~ ◊ The findings are summarized in the ~. | ~ about, ~ into, ~ on ◊ The department has launched a ~ into the bombing. ◊ an official ~ on the accident | ~ by ◊ a ~ by scientists | ~ from ◊ a ~ from the select committee | ~ to ◊ a ~ to the academic community

2 (BrE) (AmE **report card**) written statement about a student's work

ADJ. **good** | **bad** | **school**
VERB + REPORT/REPORT CARD **get** ◊ She got a better ~ this time. (BrE) ◊ She got a better ~ card this time. (AmE)

report verb

ADV. **back** ◊ The reconnaissance party ~ed back that the town was heavily fortified. | **erroneously, falsely, incorrectly** | **accurately, correctly** | **initially, originally** | **publicly** ◊ if the facts that have been ~ed publicly are true | **dutifully** ◊ She had dutifully ~ed this to her superiors.
VERB + REPORT **be expected to, be likely to, expect to** ◊ The company is expected to ~ record profits this year. | **be delighted to, be glad to, be happy to, be pleased to, be proud to** ◊ I am pleased to ~ that the plan is going well. | **be sad to, regret to** ◊ I am sad to ~ that she is not very well. | **have to** ◊ It is with regret that I have to ~ the death of one of our members. | **be reluctant to** ◊ Companies are sometimes reluctant to ~ economic espionage. | **fail to** ◊ He was charged with careless driving and failing to ~ an accident.
PREP. **from** ◊ This is John Hutchins, ~ing from Zimbabwe. | **on** ◊ Tonight we ~ on the situation in central Africa. | **to** ◊ Report the theft to the police as soon as possible.
PHRASES **be widely ~ed** ◊ The incident was widely ~ed in the press. | **~ing for duty** ◊ This is Dan Baker, ~ing for duty.

reporter noun

ADJ. **chief, senior** | **cub, junior, trainee** (BrE) | **foreign** | **local, national** (esp. AmE) | **beat** (AmE) ◊ the beat ~ of a leading financial daily | **embedded** ◊ an embedded ~ with the combat team | **roving** | **ace, enterprising, intrepid** | **magazine, newspaper, radio, television, TV** | **online, Web** | **print** (AmE) ◊ a print ~ from the 'Washington Post' | **tabloid** | **court, crime, entertainment, financial, media, news, police** (AmE)**, political, sports, etc.** | **investigative** | **undercover** | **freelance** | **pool** (AmE)**, staff** (esp. AmE) ◊ The pool ~ assigned to cover the event. ◊ a staff ~ for a major paper
VERB + REPORTER **brief, speak to, speak with** (AmE)**, talk to, talk with** (AmE)**, tell** ◊ We were warned not to talk to ~s. | **assign, send**
PREP. **~ at** ◊ a business ~ at the largest daily paper in Finland | **~ for, ~ with** ◊ She then became a crime ~ with a national newspaper. | **~ from** ◊ The secret was leaked to a ~ from the 'New York Times'. | **~ on** ◊ the chief ~ on the 'Herald'
→ Note at JOB

represent verb

1 be a member of a group

ADV. **strongly, well** ◊ Local businesses are well ~ed on the committee. | **equally** ◊ Women and men were ~ed equally on the teams. | **poorly** | **adequately** | **disproportionately** ◊ Women are disproportionately ~ed among welfare recipients.

2 act/speak officially for sb

ADV. **legally** (BrE) ◊ The suspect must appear and may be legally ~ed. | **ably, adequately, truly** ◊ We have been ably ~ed in our efforts by our attorney. ◊ How can we all be adequately ~ed by one political party? ◊ leaders who truly ~ the interests of working families
VERB + REPRESENT **choose sb to, elect sb to, select sb to** ◊ He was chosen to ~ Scotland in three consecutive World Cup Finals. | **claim to, pretend to** ◊ organizations claiming to ~ farmers

3 show sth

ADV. **accurately, faithfully** ◊ Representing an image accurately requires a great many bytes of digital information. | **fairly** | **falsely** | **diagrammatically** (esp. BrE)**, graphically, schematically, visually** ◊ The data can be ~ed graphically in a line diagram. | **symbolically**
VERB + REPRESENT **be intended to** ◊ It is not clear what these symbols were intended to ~. | **purport to, seek to** ◊ The book purported to ~ the lives of ordinary people.
PREP. **as** ◊ The movie ~s women as victims.

representation noun

1 sth that shows/describes sth

ADJ. **accurate, faithful, good, true** | **inaccurate** | **simplified** | **stereotypical** | **diagrammatic, graphic, graphical, photographic, pictorial, schematic, visual** | **two-dimensional, etc.** | **written** ◊ the written ~ of a spoken text | **artistic, cinematic, fictional, literary** ◊ artistic ~s of the parent/child relationship | **media** ◊ contemporary media ~s of youth | **abstract, symbolic** | **literal, realistic** ◊ a realistic cinematic ~ of the Depression
VERB + REPRESENTATION **create, generate, produce** ◊ There are many ways of generating a two-dimensional ~ of an object. | **offer, present** ◊ The film offers a realistic ~ of life in rural Spain. | **show** ◊ a book showing graphic ~s of the periodic table
PHRASES **a form of ~, a means of ~**

2 having representatives to speak/vote for you

ADJ. **broad, large** ◊ The task force had broad ~ with members drawn from different departments. | **increased** | **strong** | **effective** | **adequate** | **balanced, equal, fair** | **disproportionate** | **direct** ◊ direct ~ in Parliament | **democratic, proportional** | **collective** ◊ Textile workers wanted collective ~. | **parliamentary, political** | **black, female, minority** | **legal** | **diplomatic** | **union** | **employee**
VERB + REPRESENTATION **have** ◊ They had a strong ~ in government. | **be entitled to** ◊ Whether guilty or innocent, we are still entitled to legal ~. | **achieve, secure, win** ◊ All parties won ~ in the national assembly. | **ensure, guarantee** ◊ He claims that their electoral system ensures fair ~ of all parties. | **increase** ◊ The party has increased its ~ in Parliament. | **reduce** | **allow sb, provide (sb with)** ◊ The accused was not allowed legal ~. | **seek** ◊ workers that seek union ~ | **get, obtain**
PREP. **~ by** ◊ ~ by a lawyer | **~ for** ◊ ~ for employees | **~ from** ◊ ~ from all parties | **~ on** ◊ shareholder ~ on the boards of directors
PHRASES **a system of ~**

3 representations (formal, esp. BrE) formal statements

ADJ. **false** | **oral, written**
VERB + REPRESENTATIONS **make** | **receive**
PREP. **~ to** ◊ They may make ~s to government on matters affecting their organization.

representative noun

ADJ. **chief, leading, main** | **senior** | **sole** ◊ I was the sole ~ of the committee. | **appointed, designated, elected** | **authorized, official** | **field** (AmE)**, international, local, national, regional, state** | **British, US, etc.** | **personal** | **legal** | **congressional, parliamentary, political** | **council, government** | **diplomatic** | **UN** | **special** ◊ the UN special ~ for Cyprus | **permanent** ◊ the Algerian permanent ~ at the UN | **military** | **business, company, corporate, industry, management, marketing, trade** | **customer-service, sales** (also informal **rep**) ◊ She's a sales rep for sports equipment. | **financial, insurance, media, pharmaceutical** ◊ his success as a full-time financial ~ ◊ a panel of media ~s | **employee, labour/labor, union, worker** | **class, student** | **community, public** | **NGO** | **club, committee** | **church**
VERB + REPRESENTATIVE **appoint, appoint sb (as), choose (sb as), elect, elect sb (as), nominate** (esp. BrE)**, nominate sb (as)** (esp. BrE)**, select, select sb (as)** | **send** ◊ The association is sending ~s to the conference. | **consult, consult with, meet, meet with** (esp. AmE) ◊ Management are obliged to

consult with union ~s about changes to conditions. | **discuss (sth) with**
REPRESENTATIVE + VERB **attend sth** ◇ *The negotiations were attended by ~s of several states.* | **vote**
REPRESENTATIVE + NOUN **body** ◇ *The country has a new supreme ~ body.*
PREP. **~ for** ◇ *a ~ for international shipping companies* | **~ from, ~ of** ◇ *~s from citizens' groups* | **~ on** ◇ *a nursing ~ on the infection control committee* | **~ to** ◇ *~s to a conference*
→ Note at JOB

representative *adj.*

VERBS **be, seem** | **consider sb/sth**
ADV. **highly, very** | **fully, truly** | **not necessarily** | **broadly, fairly, reasonably** ◇ *a broadly ~ sample* | **widely** ◇ *Exhibits include a widely ~ collection of Greek vases.* | **statistically** | **nationally** ◇ *a nationally ~ picture of the employment situation*
PREP. **of** ◇ *Is this group of people fully ~ of the population in general?*

repress *verb*

ADV. **barely** ◇ *She could barely ~ a sigh of relief.* | **brutally, harshly, violently** ◇ *The organized opposition has been brutally ~ed.* | **systematically** ◇ *a country that systematically ~es human rights*
VERB + REPRESS **try to** | **be unable to**

repressed *adj.*

VERBS **be** | **become**
ADV. **extremely, fairly, very, etc.** | **severely** | **a little, slightly, etc.** | **barely** ◇ *His eyes flashed with barely ~ anger.* | **sexually** ◇ *people who are sexually ~*

repression *noun*

1 using force to control people
ADJ. **extreme, harsh, massive, severe** | **bloody, brutal, ruthless, violent** | **political, religious, social** ◇ *her attempts to combat censorship and political ~* ◇ *the religious ~ during his rule* | **government, military, police, state**
VERB + REPRESSION **suffer, suffer from** ◇ *The trade unions suffered brutal ~ after the coup.* | **subject sb/sth to** ◇ *Reports claimed that civilians were being subjected to ruthless ~.* | **escape, flee** ◇ *Streams of migrants are fleeing war, ~ and poverty.*
PREP. **~ against** ◇ *~ against ethnic minorities* | **~ by** ◇ *~ by the state*
PHRASES **a target for ~, a target of ~**
2 controlling strong emotions/desires
ADJ. **emotional, sexual**

reprieve *noun*

ADJ. **brief, temporary** | **welcome** | **last-minute** ◇ *He was saved from the electric chair by a last-minute ~.*
VERB + REPRIEVE **earn, gain, get, receive, win** | **offer, provide** (*esp. AmE*) ◇ *This house offers no ~ from the heat.* | **give sb/sth, grant (sb/sth)** ◇ *The school was granted a six-month ~.*
PREP. **~ from** ◇ *The family has won a temporary ~ from eviction.*

reprimand *noun*

ADJ. **severe** | **gentle** ◇ *His gentle ~ shamed her sufficiently.* | **public** | **verbal, written** | **formal, official**
VERB + REPRIMAND **earn (yourself), get, receive** ◇ *The manager earned himself a severe ~ for criticizing the referee.* | **give sb, issue (sb with)** ◇ *She was given a ~ for leaking the news.*
PREP. **~ for** ◇ *a ~ for a breach of the rules* | **~ from** ◇ *Jen's reply earned her a ~ from her mother.*

reprimand *verb*

ADV. **severely, sternly** | **gently** | **formally, officially** | **publicly**
PREP. **by** ◇ *~ed by the judge* | **for** ◇ *She was severely ~ed for accepting the money.*

reprisal *noun*

ADJ. **bloody, brutal, savage, violent** | **military** ◇ *The government responded with harsh military ~s.* | **economic, legal, political** ◇ *boycotts and economic ~s* ◇ *The people live in fear of political ~s.*
VERB + REPRISAL **take** ◇ *The gang threatened to take ~s against them.* | **threaten (sb with)** | **suffer** ◇ *She tried to persuade the soldiers that they would not suffer ~s if they surrendered.* | **expect, fear** | **face**
REPRISAL + NOUN **attack, raid**
PREP. **in ~ for** ◇ *A dozen hostages were shot in ~ for the killing of an army officer.* | **~ against** ◇ *~s against witnesses for the evidence they have given* | **~ for** ◇ *Workers won't face ~s for their decisions.* | **~ from** ◇ *~s from angry fans*
PHRASES **fear of ~s**

reproach *noun*

ADJ. **bitter** | **mild** ◇ *There was mild ~ in his tone.*
PREP. **above ~, beyond ~** ◇ *Her conduct had always been beyond ~.* | **with ~** ◇ *He glanced at her with ~.* | **~ to** ◇ *Paul saw this as a ~ to himself.*
PHRASES **full of ~** ◇ *Her voice was full of ~.* | **a look of ~** ◇ *He gave Helen a look of bitter ~.* | **a word of ~** ◇ *She had never uttered a word of ~.*

reproduce *verb*

1 produce a copy of sth; produce sth again
ADV. **accurately, exactly, faithfully** ◇ *The painting is ~d very accurately.* ◇ *The book's characters are faithfully ~d in the movie.* | **well** ◇ *They do not ~ well in print.* | **easily** ◇ *Photographs can be easily ~d with a negative.* | **merely, simply** ◇ *In her own work she simply ~s the very conventions that she claims to despise.*
VERB + REPRODUCE **be able to, can** | **be unable to** | **be easy to, be possible to** | **be difficult to, be hard to, be impossible to** ◇ *It is difficult to ~ a signature exactly.*
PREP. **from** ◇ *The map is ~d here from a 19th-century original.*
PHRASES **an attempt to ~ sth** ◇ *Writing grew out of an attempt to ~ speech in a permanent form.* | **beautifully ~d** ◇ *The photos are beautifully ~d.* | **~d (by) courtesy of sb/sth** ◇ *The painting is ~d here courtesy of the National Gallery.* ◇ *The interview is ~d by courtesy of 'Attitude'.* | **~d with sb's permission, ~d without sb's permission** ◇ *The article may not be ~d without written permission of the author.* | **widely ~d** ◇ *These works were popular and widely ~d.*
2 produce young
ADV. **asexually, sexually** | **naturally** ◇ *The salmon would begin reproducing naturally.* | **successfully** ◇ *a frog species successfully reproducing*
VERB + REPRODUCE **be able to, be likely to, can** ◇ *The offspring have to be able to ~ in their turn.* | **be unable to, fail to**
PREP. **by** ◇ *Many single cell organisms ~ by splitting in two.*

reproduction *noun*

1 producing babies/animals/plants
ADJ. **animal, human, plant** | **biological** | **asexual, sexual** | **artificial, assisted** ◇ *advanced techniques for assisted ~* | **natural** | **successful** ◇ *successful ~ in birds*
REPRODUCTION + VERB **occur, take place**
PHRASES **a method of ~**
2 act/process of producing a copy/recording
ADJ. **accurate, faithful, good-quality, high-quality, quality** | **colour/color, digital, mechanical, photographic, sound** ◇ *the age of mechanical ~* ◇ *Using a wide tape gives better quality sound ~.* | **mass** ◇ *the mass ~ of images*
VERB + REPRODUCTION **give, provide** | **ensure** ◇ *The craftsmen have ensured faithful ~ of the original painting.*
3 sth that has been reproduced
ADJ. **exact, excellent, faithful, good, perfect** ◇ *an exact ~ of an ancient building* | **large** | **black-and-white, colour/color** | **digital, mechanical, photographic** ◇ *digital ~s of*

masterworks ◇ *The quality of a photographic ~ decreases with time.* | **art, fine-art** ◇ *a publisher of fine-art ~s*
REPRODUCTION + NOUN **antique, furniture** (= made as a copy of an earlier style)
PREP. **~ from** ◇ *a ~ from an old book* | **~ of** ◇ *~s of well-known old-master paintings*

republic noun

ADJ. **new, young** | **former** ◇ *the former Yugoslav ~s* | **autonomous, free, independent, sovereign** | **breakaway** ◇ *the breakaway ~s of the former Soviet empire* | **constitutional, democratic, federal, Islamic, people's, secular, socialist** ◇ *a constitutional ~ based on the principles of democracy* ◇ *the People's Republic of China* | **banana** *(disapproving, offensive)*
VERB + REPUBLIC **become** ◇ *the year that Guyana became a socialist ~* | **build, create, establish, form, found** | **defend, preserve, save** | **declare (sth), proclaim (sth)** ◇ *They have declared themselves an independent democratic ~.* | **recognize (sth as)** | **overthrow**

repulsive adj.

VERBS **be, look, seem, smell** ◇ *The very thought seems ~.* | **find sb/sth**
ADV. **extremely, fairly, very, etc.** | **deeply** ◇ *She found the idea deeply ~.* | **completely, totally** *(esp. AmE)*, **utterly** | **a little, slightly, etc.** | **morally, physically, sexually**
PREP. **to** ◇ *He was utterly ~ to her.*

reputable adj.

VERBS **be**
ADV. **extremely, fairly, very, etc.** | **highly** ◇ *a highly ~ company* | **less** ◇ *Customers who are tired of waiting turn to less ~ suppliers.* ◇ *He spent a lot of time hanging around the less ~ bars in Chicago.* | **less than** ◇ *Some of the men looked less than ~.*

reputation noun

ADJ. **considerable, enviable, excellent, fine, good, great, high, impeccable** ◇ *She has built up an enviable ~ as a writer.* | **legendary, outstanding, stellar** *(esp. AmE)*, **sterling** *(esp. AmE)*, **unrivalled/unrivaled** ◇ *the player's legendary ~ for accuracy* | **awesome** *(esp. BrE)*, **fearsome, formidable, strong** | **deserved, well-deserved, well-earned** | **undeserved** ◇ *his undeserved ~ for stinginess* | **bad, poor, terrible, unenviable** *(esp. BrE)*, **unsavoury/unsavory** ◇ *The club has an unenviable ~ for attracting trouble.* ◇ *The town's unsavoury/unsavory ~ was bad for business.* | **dubious, questionable** | **tarnished** ◇ *America is struggling to restore its tarnished ~.* | **infamous, notorious** ◇ *He has a notorious ~ of womanizing.* | **negative, positive** *(both esp. AmE)* ◇ *The company has built up a positive ~.* | **established, long-standing, solid** | **intact** *(only after reputation)* ◇ *He emerged from the trial with his ~ intact.* | **growing** | **international, national, worldwide** | **personal, public** ◇ *the need to save his political life and personal ~* | **corporate, professional** ◇ *They may be damaging their corporate ~.* | **academic, literary, scholarly, scientific** ◇ *the school's academic ~* | **historical, posthumous** ◇ *Franklin's historical ~ has fluctuated.* ◇ *Her posthumous ~ has begun to grow.*
VERB + REPUTATION **enjoy, have** ◇ *He has the ~ of being a hard worker.* | **acquire, build, build up, develop, earn, establish, forge, gain, garner, get, make, win** ◇ *Her international ~ is built on an impressive list of publications.* ◇ *She garnered a ~ as an incisive commentator.* | **bolster, enhance, improve** ◇ *Her extensive research enhanced her ~.* | **damage, destroy, hurt, lose, ruin, sully, tarnish** ◇ *It seems that nothing can tarnish his ~.* | **defend, maintain, preserve, protect, secure, uphold** | **salvage, save** ◇ *He can still salvage his ~ if he acts quickly.* | **restore** ◇ *If the profession wishes to restore its ~, it must get its act together.* | **cement, solidify** ◇ *This cemented his ~ as a civil rights militant.* | **deserve, live up to** ◇ *November is certainly living*

up to its reputation—we've had nothing but rain all week.* | **live down** ◇ *She found it hard to live down her ~ as a second-rate actress.* | **risk, stake** ◇ *He has staked his ~ on the success of the play.* | **shed** ◇ *The country has definitively shed its ~ for economic mismanagement.*
REPUTATION + VERB **grow** | **suffer** ◇ *The company's ~ suffered when it had to recall thousands of products.* | **depend on sth, rest on sth** ◇ *My ~ rests on the success of this party!* | **be based on sth** ◇ *That ~ is based on hard work.*
PREP. **by** ◇ *He was by ~ difficult to please.* | **~ among, ~ with** ◇ *the publisher's ~ among critics* ◇ *It has given them a good ~ with their customers.* | **~ as** ◇ *You've made quite a ~ for yourself as a rebel!* | **~ for** ◇ *The company has a well-deserved ~ for being reliable.* | **~ of** ◇ *our ~ of excellence in journalism*
PHRASES **a loss of ~** | **sb's ~ precedes them** ◇ *His ~ preceded him* (= we had heard about him before we met him).

request noun

ADJ. **special** | **legitimate, reasonable** | **unreasonable** | **formal, official** | **polite** | **direct** ◇ *I could not deny a direct ~ like that.* | **simple** | **odd, strange, unusual** | **initial, original** ◇ *I made my initial ~ for material in February.* | **final, last** ◇ *Her last ~ before she died was that she be buried at sea.* | **numerous, repeated** | **urgent** | **explicit, particular, specific** | **email, written** ◇ *I got a couple of email ~s for it.* | **interview** ◇ *He has refused all interview ~s.* | **budget, funding** *(both esp. AmE)* ◇ *the State Department budget ~* | **extradition** ◇ *an extradition ~ by the US*
VERB + REQUEST **make, put in, send, submit** ◇ *I've put in a ~ for a room with a view of the sea.* | **get, have, receive** ◇ *We have had repeated ~s for a pedestrian crossing near the school.* | **consider, review** ◇ *The judge will now consider this ~ from the plaintiffs.* | **accept, agree to, grant** | **accommodate, comply with, fulfil/fulfill** *(esp. AmE)*, **honour/honor, meet** ◇ *His ~ was always met with the same answer.* | **approve** ◇ *The Commission approved a ~ for $700 000 in tax refunds.* | **answer, respond to** | **deal with, handle** | **ignore** | **decline, deny, refuse, reject, turn down** | **repeat**
PREP. **at sb's ~** ◇ *The book was withdrawn at the author's ~.* | **by ~** ◇ *The writer's name was withheld by ~* (= because the writer had asked for this to be done). | **on ~, upon ~** ◇ *Additional copies will be made available on ~.* | **~ for** ◇ *The helpline was inundated with ~s for information on the crash.*
PHRASES **available on ~, available upon ~** ◇ *A detailed list of our publications is available on ~.* | **by popular ~** *(esp. BrE)* (usually **by popular demand**) ◇ *The movie is being shown again by popular ~.* | **a number of ~s**

request verb

ADV. **explicitly, specifically** | **formally, officially** | **politely** | **simply** ◇ *She had left him a message, simply ~ing that he call her back.* | **reasonably** *(law, esp. BrE)* ◇ *Auditors will be required to provide any information reasonably ~ed by the bank.* | **urgently** | **repeatedly**
PREP. **from** ◇ *We have ~ed some information from the company.*

require verb

ADV. **urgently** ◇ *Many of the refugees urgently ~ medical treatment.* | **reasonably** *(law, esp. BrE)* | **generally, normally, typically, usually** | **frequently, often** | **rarely** | **eventually** | **specifically** | **legally** | **absolutely** *(esp. AmE)* ◇ *These plants absolutely ~ shade.*

requirement noun

ADJ. **absolute** ◇ *There's no absolute ~ to disclose your age.* | **necessary** | **core, important, key, main** | **essential, fundamental** ◇ *An open system of criminal justice is a fundamental ~ of any democratic society.* | **demanding, strict, stringent** | **detailed** | **exact, precise** | **reasonable** | **basic** | **minimum** | **additional, further** | **general** | **special** | **certain, particular, specific** | **individual, personal** | **unique** | **annual, daily** ◇ *your daily ~ of vitamin C* | **current, future** | **changing** | **constitutional, contractual, federal, formal, legal, legislative, mandatory, procedural,** regulatory, statutory | business | borrowing (*esp. BrE*) ◊ *The public sector borrowing ~ is expected to rise.* | **customer, market, user** | academic, course, curriculum, education (*AmE*), educational, graduation (*AmE*) ◊ *core curriculum ~s* | entrance, entry | eligibility | technical | environmental | safety, security | visa | residency (*AmE*) | dietary, food, nutritional ◊ *patients with special dietary ~s* | data, information | labour/labor, manpower | capital, energy, housing (*BrE*), maintenance, performance, space, storage | operational

VERB + REQUIREMENT **have** ◊ *I have some very simple ~s.* | **comply with, fit, fulfil/fulfill, match, meet, satisfy, suit** ◊ *We can arrange a honeymoon to meet your ~s exactly.* | **exceed** | **impose, lay down** (*esp. BrE*), **set out** ◊ *The government has imposed strict safety ~s on fairground rides.* | **define, determine, establish, identify, specify** | **enforce** | **violate** | **relax, waive** ◊ *to relax university entrance ~s* (*BrE*) ◊ *The initial investment ~ is often waived for existing customers.* | **eliminate**

PREP. **for your ~** ◊ *We grow enough vegetables for our own ~s.* | **to your ~** ◊ *Our porches can be designed to your exact ~s.* | **~ for** ◊ *Large buildings have specific ~s for fire-service access.* | **~ of** ◊ *the ~s of the law*

PHRASES **subject to the ~s (of sth)** ◊ *The school can decide which students will be given priority, subject to the ~s of the law.* | **surplus to ~s** (= more than is needed) (*esp. BrE*) ◊ *Workers at the factory have been told they are surplus to ~s.*

rescue *noun*

ADJ. **dramatic** | **daring** | **emergency** | **attempted** | **successful** | **air-sea** (*esp. BrE*), **mountain, ocean** (*AmE*), **sea** (*esp. BrE*), **water** | **hostage** | **helicopter** | **financial**

VERB + RESCUE **attempt** ◊ *Her own boat capsized after she attempted a ~.* | **come to, go to, rush to** ◊ *No one came to their ~ until the following day.* | **perform** | **await**

RESCUE + NOUN **attempt, effort, mission, operation** | **crew, party, squad** (*AmE*), **team, unit** ◊ *a mountain ~ team* | **service** | **personnel** (*esp. AmE*), **worker** | **work** | **boat, helicopter, ship, vehicle, vessel** | **dog** | **swimmer** (*AmE*) | **equipment** | **centre/center** ◊ *an animal ~ centre/center* | **bid** (*BrE*), **package, plan, scheme** (*BrE*) ◊ *a financial ~ package for the company*

PREP. **to sb's/the ~** ◊ *Her wails of distress brought him running from the house, like a knight to the ~.* | **~ from** ◊ *his ~ from a burning building* | **~ of** ◊ *the ~ of a man from a burning building*

PHRASES **fire and ~** ◊ *New Zealand fire and ~ services carried out several extensive searches for survivors.* | **search and ~** ◊ *The navy are on a search and ~ mission.*

research *noun*

ADJ. **careful, detailed, in-depth, meticulous, painstaking, rigorous, thorough** | **considerable, exhaustive, extensive** ◊ *He has carried out extensive ~ into renewable energy sources.* | **basic** | **applied** | **original** | **latest, new, recent** | **current, present** | **existing** | **further** | **ongoing** | **future** | **earlier, past, previous, prior** | **cutting-edge, ground-breaking, innovative, pioneering** ◊ *pioneering ~ into skin disease* | **collaborative** | **empirical, experimental** | **laboratory** | **Internet, online** | **academic, scholarly** (*esp. AmE*) | **graduate, undergraduate, university** | **clinical, educational, historical, medical, military, scientific, social, space** | **AIDS, cancer, etc.** | **animal** ◊ *Extremists called for a ban on animal ~.* | **market** | **field** ◊ *For his PhD he conducted field ~ in Indonesia.*

... OF RESEARCH **piece** ◊ *a startling piece of historical ~*

VERB + RESEARCH **carry out, conduct, do, perform, pursue, undertake** ◊ *She's doing ~ on Czech music.* | **produce, provide, present, publish** | **be based on** ◊ *One paper based on ~ conducted at Oxford suggested that the drug may cause brain damage.* | **fund, sponsor, support** | **direct, lead, oversee** | **continue** | **need, require** ◊ *Further ~ is needed.* | **encourage, promote, stimulate** | **cite** | **discuss** | **review**

RESEARCH + VERB **demonstrate sth, find sth, identify sth, indicate sth, reveal sth, show sth, suggest sth, support sth** ◊ *~ which identifies the causes of depression* ◊ *What has their*

~ *shown?* ◊ *The ~ does not support these conclusions.* | **demonstrate that…, find that…, indicate that…, reveal that…, show that…, suggest that…** ◊ *Research demonstrates that women are more likely than men to provide social support to others.* | **link sth to sth, link sth with sth** ◊ *the ~ done in the 1950s that linked smoking with cancer* | **confirm sth, prove sth** | **produce sth, yield sth** ◊ *Recent ~ on deaf children has produced some interesting findings.* | **examine sth, explore sth, focus on sth, investigate sth** | **involve sth** | **be part of sth**

RESEARCH + NOUN **degree** | **effort, programme/program, project, study, work** ◊ *Who is directing the group's ~ effort?* | **agenda** | **methodology, methods** | **tool** | **findings, results** | **purposes** ◊ *Copies of the tape can be made for ~ purposes.* | **centre/center, facility, lab** (*informal*), **laboratory, station, unit** | **company, firm, institute, institution, organization, university** | **analyst, assistant, associate, director, fellow, scientist, student, worker** | **group, team** | **funding, grant** | **paper, report** | **data** | **interests** | **question** | **subject, topic** | **library** | **budget**

PREP. **~ in** ◊ *Most ~ in the field has concentrated on the effects on children.* | **~ into, ~ on** ◊ *They are carrying out ~ into the natural flow patterns of water.*

PHRASES **an area of ~** | **focus your ~ on sth** ◊ *He focused his ~ on the economics of the interwar era.* | **sb's own ~** ◊ *They lack the resources to do their own ~.* | **~ and development** (abbreviated to *R & D*) ◊ *spending on military ~ and development*

research *verb*

ADV. **carefully, exhaustively, extensively, fully, meticulously, properly, thoroughly, well** | **poorly** ◊ *The book has been poorly ~ed.*

PREP. **for** ◊ *She is currently ~ing for her next novel.* | **into** ◊ *I spent two years carefully ~ing into his background.*

researcher *noun*

ADJ. **experienced, leading, prominent, renowned** | **chief, lead, senior** | **young** | **early** ◊ *She based her work on that of earlier ~s.* | **independent** | **academic** | **postdoctoral, postgraduate** | **university** | **AIDS, cancer, clinical, health, medical** | **educational, scientific, social** | **market**

... OF RESEARCHERS **group, team**

RESEARCHER + VERB **analyse/analyze sth, compare sth and sth, examine sth, explore sth, focus on sth, investigate sth, look for sth, study sth, work in sth, work on sth** ◊ *~s working in different disciplines* ◊ *~s working on the biochemistry of the brain* | **conduct sth, measure sth, test sb/sth** | **believe sth, claim sth, note sth, say sth, suggest sth, think sth** | **determine sth, discover sth, find sth, identify sth** ◊ *Researchers found 17% of their random sample to be severely depressed.* | **observe sth, report sth, show sth** | **conclude sth** ◊ *The ~s have concluded that further studies are needed.*

PHRASES **~s in the field** ◊ *The book is written by experts who are well known as ~s in the field.*

→ Note at JOB

resemblance *noun*

ADJ. **close, great, marked, remarkable, striking, strong** | **eerie** (*esp. AmE*), **uncanny** ◊ *She has an uncanny ~ to her sister.* | **obvious** | **faint, passing, slight, superficial** | **little** ◊ *two actors bearing little ~ to each other* | **physical** | **family**

VERB + RESEMBLANCE **bear, have, show** ◊ *The story of the movie bears more than a passing ~ to 'Tom Sawyer'.* | **note, notice, see** ◊ *I can see the family ~.*

RESEMBLANCE + VERB **end** ◊ *They are both called Brad, but there the ~ ends* (= they are not similar to each other in any other way).

PREP. **~ between** ◊ *There is a close ~ between her and her daughter.* | **~ to** ◊ *Crocodiles still have a strong ~ to their ancestors.*

resemble

694

resemble verb

ADV. **closely, greatly, strongly, very much** ◊ *He very much ~s a friend of mine.* | **in no way, not remotely** ◊ *He does not ~ his brother in any way.* ◊ *I have never seen anything remotely resembling the horrors of that day.* | **barely** | **faintly, rather, somewhat, superficially, vaguely** | **in some respects, in some ways** | **oddly, uncannily** | **physically** | **increasingly**
VERB + RESEMBLE **be designed to** ◊ *The house was designed to ~ a church.* | **tend to**
PREP. **in** ◊ *The meat ~s chicken in texture.*
PHRASES **anything resembling sth** ◊ *Neither achieved anything resembling their former success.* | **something resembling sth** ◊ *a fight for something resembling justice*

resent verb

ADV. **bitterly, deeply, greatly, really** ◊ *She bitterly ~ed the fact that her husband had been so successful.*

resentful adj.

VERBS **be, feel, look, seem, sound** | **become, grow, remain** ◊ *They grew bitter and ~.*
ADV. **extremely, fairly, very, etc.** | **bitterly, deeply** ◊ *They were bitterly ~ of the fact that they had to work such long hours.* | **increasingly** | **a little, slightly, etc.**
PREP. **about, at** ◊ *She felt ~ at the way she had been treated.* | **of** ◊ *He was very ~ of their success.* | **towards/toward** ◊ *He felt deeply ~ towards/toward his ex-wife.*

resentment noun

ADJ. **bitter, considerable, deep, deep-seated, great, lingering, seething, smouldering/smoldering** | **growing** | **old** ◊ *She felt all her old ~ flaring up.* | **class, racial** (*both esp. AmE*)
VERB + RESENTMENT **feel, harbour/harbor, hold** ◊ *I felt no ~ towards/toward him.* | *You seem to be harbouring/harboring some ~ against your boss.* | **express, show** | **hide** ◊ *He struggled to hide his ~.* | **arouse, breed, cause, create, fuel, generate, lead to, provoke, stir** ◊ *Inequality breeds ~.*
RESENTMENT + VERB **grow**
PREP. **~ about, ~ over** ◊ *Maggie was filled with ~ about her treatment.* | **~ against** ◊ *the growing ~ against foreigners* | **~ among** ◊ *The measures will fuel ~ among students.* | **~ at** ◊ *I felt great ~ at having to work such long hours.* | **~ between** ◊ *the bitter ~ between the two brothers* | **~ towards/toward** ◊ *their ~ towards/toward each other*
PHRASES **a cause of ~, a source of ~** | **a feeling of ~, a sense of ~** | **~ and anger**

reservation noun

1 arrangement for a seat/room

ADJ. **airline, flight, travel** | **hotel, room** (*AmE*) | **dinner, restaurant** (*both esp. AmE*) | **online**
VERB + RESERVATION **have** ◊ *Do you have a ~?* | **book** (*AmE*), **make** | **get** | **confirm** | **cancel** | **recommend** ◊ *Reservations are recommended, especially during the busy holiday weekends.* | **need, require** (*formal*) | **accept** (*AmE*)
RESERVATION + NOUN **service, system** | **centre/center** | **form**
PREP. **~ at** ◊ *We have ~s at a restaurant at six tonight.* | **~ for** ◊ *I'd like to make a ~ for four people for Friday night, please.*

2 feeling of doubt about sth

ADJ. **considerable** (*esp. BrE*), **deep, grave, major, serious, strong** | **minor, slight** | **certain** ◊ *I have certain ~s regarding several of the clauses in the contract.* | **initial** | **mental** (*esp. AmE*)
VERB + RESERVATION **have** | **express, voice** ◊ *NATO generals voiced ~s about making air strikes.*
PREP. **despite ~s** ◊ *Despite his initial ~s, he came to love London.* | **with ~s** ◊ *The employees are backing the reorganization plans, with ~s.* | **without ~** ◊ *I can recommend her without ~.* | **~ about, ~ concerning, ~ over, ~ regarding** ◊ *They have expressed ~s concerning the provisions of the treaty.*

PHRASES **one ~, only ~** ◊ *My one ~ concerns the performance of the vehicle in wet conditions.*

reserve noun

1 supply of sth available to be used in the future

ADJ. **great, huge, large, substantial, vast** | **adequate, sufficient** | **low, small** | **existing** | **additional** | **last** ◊ *It took my last ~s of strength and will to swim to the lifeboat.* | **untapped** ◊ *The region is thought to have some of the world's largest untapped oil ~s.* | **hidden** ◊ *She had hidden ~s of courage.* | **known, proven** ◊ *proven oil ~s* | **capital, cash, currency, financial, foreign-currency, foreign-exchange, gold, international** ◊ *In the face of a severe crisis relating to international ~s, the government devalued the currency twice.* | **dollar, sterling, etc.** | **coal, energy, fuel, gas, oil, petroleum** (*esp. AmE*) | **food** | **fat** ◊ *The birds build up fat ~s to help them survive the winter.*
VERB + RESERVE **have** ◊ *We have only a small ~ of coal.* | **hold sth in, keep sth in, maintain** ◊ *The crack troops were held in ~ behind the front line.* | **dig into** (*BrE*), **dip into, draw on, draw upon, tap, use** ◊ *He had to draw on ~s of strength just to finish the race.* | **accumulate, build, build up, increase** | **deplete, exhaust** ◊ *The company has depleted its ~s to make the purchase.* | **take**
RESERVE + VERB **be available** | **dwindle, fall** | **rise**
RESERVE + NOUN **assets, currency, funds** | **requirement** | **tank** ◊ *The plane was fitted with fuel ~ tanks for long-distance flights.* | **account** | **power**
PREP. **in ~** ◊ *The rail company has two trains in service and one in ~.* | **~ of** ◊ *the world's ~s of oil*

2 protected area → See also PRESERVE

ADJ. **national** | **bird** (*BrE*), **forest, game, marine, natural, nature, wildlife**
VERB + RESERVE **create, establish**

3 quality/feeling

ADJ. **deep** | **natural** (*esp. BrE*) ◊ *They made him feel at ease, despite his natural ~.*
PREP. **with ~** ◊ *Any contract should be treated with ~ until it has been checked.* | **without ~** ◊ *She trusted him without ~* (= completely).

4 extra player; second team

VERB + RESERVE **play in** (*BrE*) ◊ *He will continue to train and may play in the ~s next season.*
RESERVE + NOUN **side** (*BrE*), **team** | **goalkeeper** (*BrE*), **outfielder** (*AmE*), **striker** (*BrE*), **etc.** | **game, match** (*BrE*) | **role** (*AmE*) ◊ *Bautista could be traded or moved into a ~ role.*

5 extra military force

ADJ. **air-force, army, marine, naval** | **strategic** | **volunteer**
RESERVE + NOUN **army, force, police** | **component, unit** | **officer, personnel, soldier, troops** | **duty**

reserve verb

ADV. **exclusively, only, specially, specifically, strictly** ◊ *The star has a ski slope ~d exclusively for her.* | **generally, normally, traditionally, typically, usually** ◊ *a ceremony normally ~d for heads of state* | **previously**
PREP. **for** ◊ *The parking spaces are ~d for customers.*

reserved adj.

VERBS **be, seem** ◊ *She seems very ~.*
ADV. **extremely, fairly, very, etc.** ◊ *his fairly ~ manner*
PHRASES **quiet and ~, ~ and quiet**

reservoir noun

1 where water is stored

ADJ. **natural** | **artificial, man-made** | **underground** | **water** | **large**
PREP. **in a/the ~**

2 amount of sth that can be used

ADJ. **deep, huge, vast**
VERB + RESERVOIR **tap, tap into**
PREP. **~ of** ◊ *We can tap into the vast ~ of information available on the Internet*

residence *noun*

1 house

ADJ. **desirable** (*BrE*) | **palatial** | **official** | **royal** | **personal** (*AmE*), **private** | **main, primary** (*esp. AmE*), **principal** ◇ *Tax breaks are often available to those buying a primary ~.* | **current, former** | **summer** | **country, town** (*esp. BrE*) | **family, student** | **new**
VERB + RESIDENCE **build** | **maintain** | **change**

2 living in a particular place

ADJ. **long** | **permanent** | **temporary** | **normal** (*BrE, law*) | **legal**
VERB + RESIDENCE **establish, take up** ◇ *The family took up temporary ~ in the manor house.*
RESIDENCE + NOUN **permit** ◇ *He has applied for a ~ permit.* | **hall** (*AmE*)
PREP. **in ~** ◇ *The flag flying above the palace indicates that the Queen is in ~.*
PHRASES **a change of ~** | **sb's city of ~, sb's country of ~, sb's place of ~** ◇ *The notice was addressed to her last known place of ~.* | **a hall of ~** (*BrE*) (*dormitory* in *AmE*) ◇ *The university has two halls of ~ for its postgraduate students.*

resign *verb*

ADV. **formally** | **abruptly** | **immediately**
VERB + RESIGN **be forced to, be obliged to** (*BrE*), **have to** ◇ *He was forced to ~ due to ill health.* | **intend to** | **offer to, threaten to** ◇ *Daniels offered to ~ as team chief.* | *Some judges have threatened to ~ over this issue.* | **decide to** | **refuse to** | **call on sb to** ◇ *They called on her to ~ as chief executive.*
PREP. **as** ◇ *He ~ed as chairman.* | **from** ◇ *She formally ~ed from the government.* | **over** ◇ *Three members of the committee ~ed over the issue.*

resignation *noun*

1 giving up your job; letter of resignation

ADJ. **immediate** | **shock** (*BrE*), **sudden, surprise, unexpected** (*esp. BrE*) | **forced** | **mass**
VERB + RESIGNATION **hand in, submit, tender** ◇ *She handed in her ~ following the dispute over company policy.* | **announce** | **withdraw** | **offer (sb), proffer** (*formal*) | **threaten** | **lead to, prompt, provoke** (*BrE*) ◇ *The accusation prompted the ~ of the party leader.* | **force** ◇ *Illness forced his ~ from the team.* | **call for, demand** ◇ *The protesters called for his immediate ~.* | **accept** ◇ *She has refused to accept the ~ of her deputy.* | **reject**
RESIGNATION + VERB **be effective, become effective** ◇ *My ~ is effective from May 1.*
RESIGNATION + NOUN **letter** | **announcement** ◇ *His ~ announcement was widely expected.* | **speech, statement**
PREP. **~ as** ◇ *her ~ as party leader* | **~ from** ◇ *A scandal led to his ~ from office.*
PHRASES **a call for sb's ~** | **a letter of ~** | **~ on (the) grounds of sth** (*BrE*) ◇ *~ on grounds of ill health*

2 willingness to accept a difficult situation

ADJ. **weary** | **quiet**
PREP. **in ~** ◇ *Hearing that the train was running late, he sighed in weary ~.* | **with ~** ◇ *She spoke with ~.* | **~ to** ◇ *~ to fate*
PHRASES **a look of ~, a sigh of ~**

resilience (*also less frequent* **resiliency**) *noun*

ADJ. **amazing, extraordinary, great, remarkable, tremendous** | **natural** | **emotional, mental, psychological**
VERB + RESILIENCE **have** | **demonstrate, show** | **build, increase, promote**
PREP. **~ to** ◇ *She has shown great ~ to stress.*
PHRASES **~ in the face of sth** ◇ *Abandoned children display ~ in the face of their plight.* | **strength and ~**

resilient *adj.*

VERBS **be, prove, seem** | **become** | **make sth** | **remain**
ADV. **extremely, fairly, very, etc.** ◇ *a pretty ~ plant* | **amazingly, highly, incredibly, remarkably** ◇ *a remarkably ~ woman*

PREP. **to** ◇ *The body of the camera makes it highly ~ to outdoor use.*

resist *verb*

ADV. **fiercely, firmly, resolutely, strenuously, strongly, vigorously** | **successfully** ◇ *They successfully ~ed pressure from their competitors to increase prices.* | **naturally** ◇ *People naturally ~ change.* | **stubbornly** | **actively** | **at first, initially, so far** ◇ *He has so far ~ed pressure to resign.*
VERB + RESIST **be able to, can, manage to** | **be unable to, cannot** ◇ *Trends in the national economy confront companies with pressures they are unable to ~.* | **can hardly, cannot easily** ◇ *She could hardly ~ the urge to turn and run.* | **can never, can no longer** | **be difficult to, be hard to** | **be impossible to** | **try to** | **be determined to** | **be helpless to, be powerless to** ◇ *She was powerless to ~ the attraction that she felt to him.* | **tend to**
PHRASES **the strength to ~ sth**

resistance *noun*

1 trying to stop sth

ADJ. **considerable, great, massive, stiff, strong, substantial** | **determined, fierce, heroic, serious, spirited** (*esp. BrE*), **stubborn** | **effective** | **token** | **active** | **passive** | **collective, organized** | **widespread** | **armed, military** | **non-violent, violent** | **political** | **popular, public** | **guerrilla, peasant** | **initial**
VERB + RESISTANCE **mount, offer, put up** ◇ *They mounted stiff ~ to the proposal.* | **encounter, face, find, meet, meet with, run into** ◇ *The advancing army met with little ~.* | **break, break down, crush, overcome**
RESISTANCE + VERB **stiffen** | **collapse, crumble** | **be futile**
RESISTANCE + NOUN **movement** | **fighter, forces, group, leader, member, worker** (*esp. BrE*)
PREP. **without ~** ◇ *The attacks did not take place without ~.* | **~ against** ◇ *armed ~ against the invaders* | **~ to** ◇ *There was fierce ~ to the new laws.*
PHRASES **the line of least ~, the path of least ~** (= the easiest way of doing sth) | **a pocket of ~** (= an area of resistance)

2 to a disease/drugs

ADJ. **high** | **increased** | **low** | **disease** | **antibiotic, drug, pesticide** | **bacterial**
VERB + RESISTANCE **have** | **build up, develop** ◇ *You need to build up your ~ to colds.* | **lower**
PREP. **~ to** ◇ *AIDS lowers the body's ~ to infection.*

resistant *adj.*

VERBS **be, prove** | **become** | **make sth, render sth**
ADV. **extremely, fairly, very, etc.** | **highly, particularly, remarkably** | **completely** | **increasingly** | **moderately, relatively** | **naturally**
PREP. **to** ◇ *a metal that is highly ~ to corrosion*

resolution *noun*

1 formal decision taken after a vote

ADJ. **draft** | **formal** | **proposed** | **joint** ◇ *a joint US-British ~* | **unanimous** | **ordinary** (*BrE*) | **emergency, special** | **compromise** | **affirmative, negative** (*both BrE, law*) ◇ *An affirmative ~ of both Houses of Parliament is needed.* | **non-binding** | **second** | **congressional, Security Council, Senate, shareholder, UN** | **war** | **budget** (*AmE*)
VERB + RESOLUTION **draft** | **introduce, issue, present, propose, put forward, sponsor, submit, table** | **vote on** | **back, support** | **agree** (*esp. BrE*), **agree on, agree to, approve, carry** (*BrE*), **pass** ◇ *The legislature has approved a ~ calling for the removal of such advertising.* ◇ *The ~ was carried unanimously.* | **adopt, implement** | **block, oppose, reject, veto** | **enforce**
RESOLUTION + VERB **ask for sth, be aimed at sth, call for sth, demand sth** ◇ *The ~ called for the resumption of negotiations.* | **declare sth, say sth, state sth** ◇ *a ~ declaring*

independence | **approve sth, authorize sth, endorse sth, give (sb) sth** ◊ *The assembly adopted a ~ approving the plan.* | **condemn sth, oppose sth** ◊ *a ~ condemning the invasion* | **support sth** | **urge sth**
PREP. **under (a/the) ~** ◊ *weapons banned under Resolution 687* | **~ on** ◊ *The General Assembly rejected the ~ on the subject of arms control.*
→ Special page at MEETING

2 settling a dispute

ADJ. **early, quick, rapid** | **eventual, final, ultimate** | **peaceful** ◊ *Hopes of a peaceful ~ to the conflict were fading.* | **effective, satisfactory, successful** | **easy** | **complete** | **conflict, dispute** ◊ *methods of conflict ~* | **problem**
VERB + RESOLUTION **need, require** | **press for, seek, want** ◊ *The government is pressing for an early ~ of the hostage crisis.* | **achieve, find, reach** | **offer, provide** | **facilitate** | **await**
PREP. **~ of** ◊ *the non-violent ~ of conflict* | **~ to** ◊ *the likelihood of achieving a satisfactory ~ to the problem*

3 being firm and determined

ADJ. **great, strong**
VERB + RESOLUTION **have** | **show** ◊ *She showed great ~ in her dealings with management.* | **lack**

4 firm decision to do/not to do sth

ADJ. **firm, good** | **New Year** (*esp. BrE*)**, New Year's**
VERB + RESOLUTION **make** ◊ *I made a New Year's ~ to give up smoking.* | **keep**

5 power to give a clear image

ADJ. **good, high** ◊ *high-resolution graphics* | **low, poor** | **maximum** | **image, screen** | **pixel** ◊ *a monitor capable of a 1024 by 768 pixel ~* | **24-bit, 32-bit,** etc.

resolve verb

ADV. **completely, fully** ◊ *The matter is not yet fully ~d.* | **partially** | **successfully** | **adequately, satisfactorily** | **amicably, peacefully** ◊ *We hope that the dispute can be ~d peacefully.* | **easily, readily** | **quickly, rapidly, speedily** (*BrE*) | **immediately** | **soon** | **eventually, finally, ultimately**
VERB + RESOLVE **attempt to, take steps to, try to** | **be unable to, fail to** ◊ *The two countries have failed to ~ their differences on this.* | **help (to)** | **be difficult to**
PREP. **by, through** ◊ *The crisis was finally ~d through high-level negotiations.*
PHRASES **an attempt to ~ sth, an effort to ~ sth** ◊ *They met in a last-ditch attempt to ~ their differences.* | **a means of resolving sth, a method of resolving sth, a way of resolving sth** | **~ itself** ◊ *The family feuding could ~ itself.*

resort noun

ADJ. **fashionable, favourite/favorite, popular** | **attractive** | **bustling, lively** (*both esp. BrE*) | **modern** | **health, holiday** (*BrE*)**, ski, spa, tourist, vacation** (*AmE*) | **beach, coastal, island, lakeside, mountain, seaside** | **casino, golf** | **destination** (*AmE*) ◊ *destination ~s such as Atlantis in the Bahamas* | **all-inclusive** | **summer, winter** | **exclusive, fancy** (*esp. AmE*)**, luxurious, luxury, posh** | **big, large, major**
RESORT + NOUN **area, destination, island, town** | **hotel** | **community**
PREP. **at a/the ~, in a/the ~** ◊ *They spent a month at a fashionable ski ~ in Vermont.*

resource noun

ADJ. **abundant, considerable, enormous, great, large, major, rich, significant, substantial, vast** ◊ *The library is an enormous ~ for historians of the period.* | **important, necessary, vital** | **adequate, sufficient** | **limited, meagre** (*BrE*)**, scarce** | **renewable, sustainable, unlimited** | **finite, limited, non-renewable** | **available** | **additional, extra** | **invaluable, precious, useful, valuable** ◊ *Time is your most*

valuable ~, especially in examinations. | **excellent** | **untapped** | **natural** | **material, physical** | **energy, food, mineral, oil, water** | **capital, economic, financial** ◊ *The school has limited financial ~s.* | **human, manpower, staff** | **educational, information, learning, library, teaching** ◊ *The database could be used as a teaching ~ in colleges.* | **computer, electronic, technical** | **Internet, online, Web** | **cultural** | **national, public** | **inner, personal** ◊ *She is someone of considerable personal ~s.* | **shared** | **local**
VERB + RESOURCE **be rich in, have** ◊ *Australia is a country rich in natural ~s.* ◊ *We do not have the ~s (= the money) to update our computer software.* | **lack** | **combine, pool, share** ◊ *We'll get by if we pool our ~s.* | **allocate, distribute, provide** | **commit, dedicate, devote** ◊ *More ~s need to be committed to the development.* | **concentrate, focus** ◊ *They are focusing their ~s on improving the infrastructure.* | **pour, put** ◊ *Resources are being poured into the Olympic site.* | **divert, reallocate, redistribute** ◊ *the government's role in diverting ~s into social policies* | **consume, draw on, expend, exploit, tap, use, utilize** | **mobilize** ◊ *to mobilize ~s in the community to provide shelter for the homeless* | **manage** ◊ *We need to manage our ~s better.* | **access** | **deplete, drain, exhaust, use up** | **strain, stretch** ◊ *The Olympics may stretch the country's ~s to breaking point. (BrE)* ◊ *The Olympics may stretch the country's ~s to the breaking point. (AmE)* | **squander, waste** | **conserve** | **acquire** | **protect**
RESOURCE + NOUN **centre/center** | **base** | **guide** | **exploitation, use, utilization** | **allocation, management, planning** | **depletion** | **availability** | **constraints, implications, limitations**
PHRASES **access to ~s** | **the allocation of ~s, the distribution of ~s, the provision of ~s** | **the exploitation of ~s, the use of ~s** ◊ *We must make the most efficient use of the available ~s.* | **a lack of ~s** ◊ *Lack of ~s has prevented the company from investing in new technology.* | **the ~s at sb's disposal** | **time and ~s**

respect noun

1 admiration

ADJ. **considerable, deep, enormous, great, high, profound, tremendous** | **grudging** | **mutual** ◊ *a relationship based on mutual ~* | **new, new-found** | **healthy** | **genuine**
VERB + RESPECT **feel, have, hold sb in** ◊ *She held him in considerable ~.* | **command, earn (sb), gain (sb), garner** (*esp. AmE*)**, get, inspire, win (sb)** ◊ *a society in which age commands great ~* | **demand, deserve** | **lose**
PREP. **~ for** ◊ *He felt a grudging ~ for her talents as an organizer.*

2 respectful behaviour/behavior

ADJ. **great, utmost** | **little** | **due, proper** ◊ *the ~ due to his great age* | **decent** (*AmE*) | **equal**
VERB + RESPECT **accord sb/sth, pay (sb/sth), show (sb/sth), treat sb/sth with** ◊ *the ~ accorded to her memory* ◊ *He treats his grandparents with great ~.* ◊ *The chainsaw is a dangerous tool—it should be treated with ~. (esp. BrE)* | **want**
PREP. **out of ~** ◊ *We observed a minute's silence out of ~ for the disaster victims.* | **with ~** ◊ *With all due ~, I think you've misunderstood what he said.*
PHRASES **a lack of ~** ◊ *to show a lack of ~ for authority* | **a mark of ~, a sign of ~, a token of ~**

3 detail/point

ADJ. **certain** | **different** | **crucial, important, key, significant** | **material**
VERB + RESPECT **differ in** ◊ *There was one ~, however, in which they differed.* | **be alike in, be identical in, be similar in, resemble sth in**
PREP. **in … ~** ◊ *The report is accurate in all material ~s.* | **in ~ of** (= concerning) ◊ *A writ was served on the company in ~ of their unpaid bill.* | **with ~ to** (= concerning) ◊ *The two groups were similar with ~ to income and status.*
PHRASES **in all, many, some, several,** etc. **~s, in every ~** ◊ *In many ~s she is like her mother.* ◊ *The marriage was a disaster in every ~.* | **in this ~** ◊ *In this ~ he cannot be criticized.*

respect *verb*

1 admire sb/sth

ADV. **deeply, greatly, really, very much | truly**
PREP. **as** ◇ *She is widely ~ed as a politician.* | **for** ◇ *She was much ~ed for her knowledge of herbs.*
PHRASES **be highly ~ed, be much ~ed, be very ~ed, be well ~ed** ◇ *a highly ~ed doctor* | **be internationally ~ed, be universally, be widely ~ed** ◇ *WWF is internationally ~ed for its conservation work.*

2 pay attention to sth

ADV. **fully**
VERB + RESPECT **promise to, undertake to** (*esp. BrE*) ◇ *The government has promised to ~ human rights.* | **fail to** ◇ *Her daughters failed to ~ her last wishes.*
PHRASES **a duty to ~ sth | failure to ~ sth**

respectability *noun*

ADJ. **bourgeois, middle-class | academic, intellectual, political, scientific, social | international** ◇ *The country has again achieved international ~ after years of isolation.*
VERB + RESPECTABILITY **achieve, gain** ◇ *The theory has now gained scientific ~.* | **give sth | seek**
PHRASES **an air of ~, a veneer of ~**

respectable *adj.*

VERBS **be, look, seem | become**
ADV. **extremely, fairly, very, etc. | eminently, highly** ◇ *It was an eminently ~ boarding school.* | **entirely** (*esp. BrE*), **perfectly | almost | enough** ◇ *She seems ~ enough.* | **apparently** (*esp. BrE*), **seemingly | academically, intellectually**

respite *noun*

ADJ. **brief, little, momentary, short, temporary** ◇ *a brief ~ from the ringing of the phone* | **much-needed, welcome**
VERB + RESPITE **enjoy, have | bring (sb), give (sb), offer (sb), provide (sb with)** ◇ *The morphine brought temporary ~ from the excruciating pain.* | **need, seek**
RESPITE + NOUN **care**
PREP. **without ~** ◇ *The storm continued for two hours without ~.* | **~ from** ◇ *They had no ~ from the demands of their children.*
PHRASES **a period of ~**

respond *verb*

1 react

ADV. **immediately, instantly | promptly, quickly, rapidly, swiftly | slowly | favourably/favorably, positively, readily, successfully, well** ◇ *Both sides have ~ed positively to the plan.* | *Their son is ~ing well to the treatment.* | **eagerly, enthusiastically | forcefully, strongly, vigorously | adequately, appropriately, constructively, effectively, intelligently, properly | normally | adversely, negatively, poorly | aggressively, angrily | cautiously, coolly | sensitively, sympathetically | generously | magnificently** (*esp. BrE*) ◇ *The teams ~ed magnificently to the challenge.* | **accordingly** ◇ *The government needs to listen to the public and ~ accordingly.* | **readily** ◇ *The plants readily ~ to these stimuli.* | **directly | automatically, instinctively | flexibly | differently | similarly | merely, simply** ◇ *We do not have a strategy. We merely ~ to ideas from local people.* | **emotionally, imaginatively** ◇ *The music seems to ~ emotionally to the landscape.* | **in kind** ◇ *The terrorists declared all-out war on the government and the government ~ed in kind.*
VERB + RESPOND **be able to, be unable to | be likely to** ◇ *She wasn't sure how he was likely to ~.* | **fail to** ◇ *His condition failed to ~ to the treatment.* | **be slow to | enable sb to** ◇ *The system enables teachers to ~ flexibly to the needs of their students.*
PREP. **by** ◇ *The government ~ed by tightening the law on gun ownership.* | **to** ◇ *Companies have to ~ to the changing economic climate.* | **with** ◇ *The demonstrators threw stones and the police ~ed with tear gas.*
PHRASES **an ability to ~, a capacity to ~, a willingness to ~ |**

a failure to ~ | **~ in a… manner, ~ in a… way** ◇ *We ~ to business problems in creative ways.*

2 say sth in reply

ADV. **politely | angrily | calmly, casually, coolly, easily | coldly, sharply | drily, sarcastically | quietly, softly | flatly | cheerfully, warmly | thoughtfully | honestly | affirmatively | correctly | personally**
PREP. **to** ◇ *He ~ed politely to her questions.* | **via** ◇ *You can ~ via email or phone.* | **with** ◇ *He ~ed with a smile when she spoke.*

response *noun*

ADJ. **affirmative** (*esp. AmE*), **encouraging, enthusiastic, favourable/favorable, good, positive | lukewarm** (*esp. BrE*), **muted, tepid** (*esp. AmE*) | **poor | aggressive, angry, negative | adequate, appropriate, correct, proper, satisfactory | normal** ◇ *This is a normal ~ to feeling abandoned.* | **desired** ◇ *He was not getting the desired ~ from the audience.* | **logical** ◇ *That's the only logical ~.* | **imaginative | sympathetic | individual, subjective | inadequate, inappropriate, incorrect** ◇ *incorrect ~s in a multiple-choice test* | **strong** ◇ *These images are likely to evoke a strong ~ in the viewer.* | **direct | effective | prompt, quick, rapid | slow | automatic, immediate, instinctive, knee-jerk** ◇ *my knee-jerk ~ to the story* | **measured, thoughtful | initial** ◇ *My initial ~ was one of anger.* | **emergency | delayed** ◇ *his delayed ~ to the event* | **public | official** ◇ *The World Bank has postponed an official ~ to the report.* | **natural | rational | possible** ◇ *These are just a few of the possible ~s to this question.* | **behavioural/behavioral, conditioned, emotional, fight-or-flight, physiological | political | verbal, written | allergic, antibody, immune** ◇ *the immune ~ to viral infections*
VERB + RESPONSE **give, make | formulate | get, have, receive** ◇ *Have you had any ~s to the advertisement yet?* | **bring forth, call forth, draw, elicit, evoke, generate, induce, produce, prompt, provoke, stimulate, trigger, yield** ◇ *His comments drew an angry ~ from the crowd.* | **await, wait for | predict | mount** ◇ *The immune system springs into action to mount a ~ against the virus.* | **exhibit, show** ◇ *Dawn showed no ~ at all.* | **coordinate** ◇ *We'll coordinate emergency ~s from now on.* | **affect, influence | assess, examine, gauge, observe | post** ◇ *He has posted his ~ on the organization's website.*
RESPONSE + NOUN **rate, time** ◇ *We sent out over 100 letters but the ~ rate was low* (= few people replied).
PREP. **in ~ (to)** ◇ *In ~, she stormed out of the room.* | **~ from** ◇ *The ~ from local businesses has been muted.* | **~ to** ◇ *What was their ~ to the question?*
PHRASES **(a) lack of ~** ◇ *Due to lack of ~ we have had to cancel the event.*

responsibility *noun*

1 being responsible

ADJ. **complete, full, total | awesome, big, enormous, grave, great, heavy, huge, important, serious, tremendous, weighty** ◇ *It is a great ~ caring for other people's children.* | **direct | primary | overall, ultimate** ◇ *Ultimate ~ rests with the president.* | **special | diminished** (*law, esp. BrE*) ◇ *He was found not guilty of murder on the grounds of diminished ~.* | **exclusive, sole | collective, communal, joint, mutual, shared | individual, personal | corporate | criminal | security | constitutional, political | environmental, ethical, financial, fiscal, legal, moral, social**
VERB + RESPONSIBILITY **have** ◇ *She has ~ for public spending.* | **accept, acknowledge, assume, bear, carry, recognize, shoulder, take, take on, take over** ◇ *The bank refuses to accept ~ for the mistake.* ◇ *Will you take ~ for arranging the food?* | **feel** ◇ *He feels a ~ to his community.* | **share | lay, place** ◇ *The government of the time placed ~ for the poor on the Church.* | **assign, delegate, devolve, give sb, hand over** ◇ *Responsibility is devolved down to the people who are affected.* | **retain** ◇ *We retain all ~ for any shortcomings.* |

abdicate, escape, evade, shift ◇ *They wanted to shift ~ for the failure onto their employees.* | admit, claim ◇ *No organization has yet claimed ~ for the bomb attack.* | deny, disclaim, duck ◇ *Ducking ~ is fatal in a democracy.* | allocate, assign (sb), give sb | attribute ◇ *He attributed ~ for the killing to the secret service.* | burden sb with | absolve sb from, absolve sb of
RESPONSIBILITY + VERB fall on sb, fall to sb, lie with sb, rest with sb | come with sth ◇ *With great power comes great ~.*
PREP. ~ for ◇ *Full ~ for the fiasco lies with the PR department.* | ~ towards/toward ◇ *He feels a strong sense of ~ towards/ toward his parents.*
PHRASES the age of criminal ~ (*BrE, law*) | the burden of ~ ◇ *Governors carry a special burden of ~.* | do sth on your own ~ (= without being told to and being willing to take the blame if it goes wrong) | a position of ~ | a feeling of ~, a sense of ~

2 job/duty
ADJ. heavy, major, onerous | basic, fundamental | added, additional, increased | main ◇ *What are the main responsibilities in your job?* | departmental, ministerial (*BrE*), professional, public, teaching | caring (*esp. BrE*), childcare, domestic, family, household, parental, public, social | fiduciary (*esp. AmE*), financial | administrative, command, management, managerial, oversight (*AmE*), supervisory ◇ *The sergeant assumed his command responsibilities.* | adult ◇ *people on the verge of assuming adult responsibilities* | contractual, statutory | particular, special | daily, day-to-day
VERB + RESPONSIBILITY have | carry out, discharge, fulfil/ fulfill, meet ◇ *an obligation to meet family responsibilities* | accept, face up to, take on, undertake ◇ *He seems unwilling to face up to his responsibilities as a father.* ◇ *I don't feel ready to take on new responsibilities.* | juggle ◇ *She juggled the competing responsibilities of family and work.* | handle ◇ *The assistants were handling their responsibilities in the only way they could.* | exercise | delegate, relinquish, transfer | abandon, avoid, escape, evade, neglect, shirk | relieve sb of
PREP. ~ for ◇ *The heads of school departments have particular responsibilities for the curriculum.* | ~ to, ~ towards/ toward ◇ *The club has a ~ to its members.*
PHRASES duties and responsibilities, rights and responsibilities ◇ *parental rights and responsibilities*

responsible adj.
1 having the job/duty of doing sth
VERBS be | become | remain | make sb ◇ *I am making you ~ for the cooking.* | leave sb ◇ *I'm leaving you ~ for Juliet's protection.*
ADV. completely, entirely, fully, totally, wholly | chiefly, largely, mainly, primarily | directly ◇ *Thompson is directly ~ for all aspects of the business unit.* | personally | solely ◇ *if you're solely ~ for your family's welfare* | collectively, equally, jointly ◇ *Members of the committee are collectively ~ for all decisions taken.* ◇ *Both parents are equally ~ for raising the children.* | formally, legally | nominally ◇ *the person nominally ~ for staff training* | ultimately ◇ *The board is ultimately ~ for policy decisions.* | financially
PREP. for ◇ *They're ~ for cleaning the engine.*
2 being the cause of sth/to blame for sth
VERBS be, feel, seem ◇ *No single pathogen seems wholly ~ for the disease.* | become | believe sb (to be), consider sb, deem sb, find sb, hold sb, regard sb as, see sb as, think sb ◇ *A man arrested in Madrid is believed to be ~ for the bombings.* ◇ *They held him ~ for the failure of the policy.*
ADV. completely, entirely, fully, wholly | chiefly, largely, mainly, primarily, principally ◇ *It's been one of the factors chiefly ~ for improved public health.* | in part, partially, partly, somewhat | equally ◇ *We are all equally ~ for its success.* | directly | indirectly | personally | single-handedly, solely ◇ *He was almost single-handedly ~ for the*

flourishing drug trade in the town.* | ultimately | somehow ◇ *Did he think her somehow ~ for Mario's death?* | morally | criminally
PREP. for ◇ *Who was ~ for the mistake?*
3 having to report to sb/sth
VERBS be
ADV. directly | ultimately ◇ *a complex web of party bodies ultimately ~ to the Central Committee*
PREP. to ◇ *The prime minister is directly ~ to Parliament.*
4 showing/needing good sense and reliability
VERBS be, seem | become | consider sb ◇ *In California you have to be 21 to be considered ~ enough to drink.* | make sb ◇ *their efforts to make the industry more ~ and responsive to concerns*
ADV. extremely, fairly, very, etc. | highly | ecologically, environmentally ◇ *The organization needs to become more environmentally ~.* | ethically, morally, politically, socially ◇ *Resources must be allocated in a morally ~ way.* | financially, fiscally (*esp. AmE*)
PREP. with ◇ *They are not very ~ with money.*

responsive adj.
VERBS be, seem | become | remain | make sb/sth ◇ *What conditions can make governments more ~ to the public?*
ADV. extremely, fairly, very, etc. | highly ◇ *The company is highly ~ to changes in demand.* | fully | immediately | culturally (*AmE*) ◇ *culturally ~ classroom management* | emotionally (*esp. AmE*) | sexually | socially
PREP. to ◇ *She's fairly ~ to new ideas.*

rest noun
ADJ. complete | good, long | brief, little, short | well-deserved, well-earned | much-needed | adequate, proper, sufficient ◇ *The body requires a healthy diet and adequate ~.* | nice | beauty (*AmE*) ◇ *I need my beauty ~.* | bed ◇ *She's on complete bed ~, antibiotics and plenty of fluids.* ◇ *I was hospitalized many times and put on bed ~ for six months.*
VERB + REST find (*formal*), get, have, take ◇ *Her heart would find no ~ until she knew the truth.* ◇ *Get some ~ while you can.* ◇ *I had a good long ~ before the party.* | need | deserve ◇ *You deserve some ~.* | disturb ◇ *I apologize for disturbing your ~.* | come to ◇ *The ball rolled down the hill and came to ~ against a tree.*
REST + NOUN break, day, interval (*AmE*), period, time | area, stop (*both AmE*) | room (usually *restroom*) (= room with a toilet) (*AmE*) | home (= for old or sick people)
PREP. at ~ ◇ *At ~ (= when not moving) the insect looks like a dead leaf.* | ~ from ◇ *The doctor advised him to take a complete ~ from the gym.*
PHRASES a day of ~

rest verb
ADV. casually, gently, lightly, loosely, softly | heavily | comfortably ◇ *Her head was ~ing comfortably against his chest.* | peacefully, quietly | safely ◇ *He could ~ safely in this place.* | lazily ◇ *His hand was ~ing lazily against the steering wheel.* | briefly, momentarily | awhile
VERB + REST let sth ◇ *She let his hand ~ heavily on hers.* | have to, need to | want to, would like to | stop to ◇ *I stopped to ~ on one of the benches.*
PREP. against ◇ *She ~ed the ladder against the wall.* | atop (*esp. AmE*) ◇ *Her thin hands were ~ing atop the quilted bed cover.* | in ◇ *I settled back, my hands ~ing in my lap.* | on, upon ◇ *His hands ~ed lightly on her shoulders.*
PHRASES ~ easy ◇ *I can ~ easy (= stop worrying) knowing that she's safely home.*
PHR V rest on/upon sth
ADV. solely, squarely ◇ *It is rare for the responsibility for causing conflict to ~ solely on one side.* | entirely ◇ *The decision ~s entirely upon how good a fighter you think she is.* | largely, primarily ◇ *The success or failure of the film ~s largely on the talents of the cast.* | firmly ◇ *Our trade policy ~s firmly on the foundation of free and open markets.*

ADV. **squarely** ◇ *Surely the blame ~s squarely with Sir Ralph?* | **ultimately** ◇ *The decision ultimately ~s with the council.*

restaurant noun

ADJ. **large** | **little, small** ◇ *a little ~ I know in Paris* | **five-star, four-star, etc.** | **decent, excellent, good, great, wonderful** | **classy, elegant, exclusive, fancy, fine, fine-dining** (*esp. AmE*), **gourmet, high-end** (*AmE*), **posh** (*informal*), **smart** (*esp. BrE*), **stylish** (*esp. BrE*), **top, upscale** (*AmE*) | **cool** (*esp. AmE*), **hip, hot** (*esp. AmE*), **trendy** (*all informal*) ◇ *some of the hottest ~s in New York* | **casual** | **cheap, expensive** | **popular** | **chain** (*esp. AmE*) ◇ *the country's most successful chain ~s* | **theme** (*esp. AmE*) | **hotel** ◇ *She eats at the hotel ~ when she travels on business.* | **area** (*AmE*), **local, nearby, neighbourhood/neighborhood** (*esp. AmE*) | **downtown** (*AmE*) | **busy, crowded** | **family** | **candlelit** (*AmE*), **intimate, romantic** | **à la carte** (*esp. BrE*) | **full-service** (*AmE*) | **self-service** | **sit-down** (*AmE*) | **takeaway** (*BrE*), **takeout** (*AmE*) | **outdoor** | **licensed** (*BrE*) | **ethnic** | **Chinese, French, etc.** | **fish, pizza, seafood, sushi** | **fast-food, organic, vegetarian, etc.**
VERB + RESTAURANT **go out to, go to, visit** ◇ *If you're too tired to cook, let's go to a ~.* | **frequent** ◇ *She frequented the ~ on almost a weekly basis.* | **try** ◇ *We're going to try this Italian ~ that just opened.* | **recommend** ◇ *We would recommend this ~ to anyone.* | **leave, walk out of** ◇ *They walked out of the ~ without paying.* | **open, start** ◇ *She decided to open her own ~.* | **manage, run** ◇ *She runs a family fish ~.* | **operate** (*esp. AmE*), **own** ◇ *It operates 79 ~s in 26 states.* | **close**
RESTAURANT + VERB **offer sth, serve sth, specialize in sth** ◇ *a ~ offering a wide variety of local specialities* ◇ *The hotel ~ serves a buffet breakfast.* ◇ *an Asian ~ specializing in Thai cuisine* | **cater for, cater to** ◇ *the few local shops and ~s catering to summer visitors* | **open** | **close**
RESTAURANT + NOUN **employee, manager, operator, owner, patron** (*esp. AmE*), **staff, worker** ◇ *Restaurant workers are often badly paid.* | **chain, group** | **business, industry** ◇ *hygiene standards in the ~ industry* | **food, menu** | **meal** ◇ *the increasing cost of ~ meals* | **dining** (*AmE*) ◇ *We don't do a lot of ~ dining.* | **table** | **guide, review** | **critic** | **reservation** | **kitchen**
PREP. **at a/the ~** ◇ *They argued the whole time we were at the ~.* | **in a/the ~** ◇ *We had a quick meal in a small local ~.*

restoration noun

1 returning sth to its original condition

ADJ. **complete, full** | **extensive, major** ◇ *Many of the older paintings have undergone extensive ~.* | **partial** | **ecological, ecosystem, forest, habitat, prairie, wetland** (*all esp. AmE*)
VERB + RESTORATION **carry out** (*esp. BrE*), **undertake** | **undergo** | **facilitate** (*esp. AmE*) ◇ *The government did much to facilitate these ~s.* | **await, be in need of, need, require** ◇ *This historic building is currently awaiting ~.* | **begin** | **complete**
RESTORATION + NOUN **activities** (*esp. AmE*), **effort, plan, process, programme/program, project, work** | **ecology** (*AmE*)
PREP. **for ~** ◇ *The palace is closed for ~.* | **under ~** ◇ *a steam engine under ~*

2 bringing sth back into use/existence

ADJ. **full** ◇ *the full ~ of Sino-US relations* ◇ *Protesters called for the full ~ of civil liberties.*
PHRASES **the ~ of the monarchy**

restore verb

1 bring back a situation/feeling

ADV. **quickly, soon** ◇ *Order was quickly ~d.*
VERB + RESTORE **need to** ◇ *We need to ~ public confidence in the industry.* | **attempt to, seek to, try to, work to** | **help (to)** | **manage to** | **fail to** | **be designed to, be intended to**
PREP. **to** ◇ *Peace has now been ~d to the area.*
PHRASES **an attempt to ~ sth, an effort to ~ sth** ◇ *an attempt to ~ the company's finances* | **be aimed at restoring sth** | **measures to ~ sth** | **a way of restoring sth, a way to ~ sth**

2 repair/rebuild sth

ADV. **completely, fully** | **partially, partly** | **beautifully** | **carefully, faithfully, lovingly, meticulously, painstakingly** | **successfully, sympathetically** | **extensively** ◇ *The interior has recently been extensively ~d.* | **digitally** ◇ *The film has been digitally ~d and remastered.*
PREP. **to** ◇ *The train has been ~d to full working order.*
PHRASES **newly ~d, recently ~d** | **~ sth to its former glory** ◇ *The buildings have now been ~d to their former glory.*

restrain verb

ADV. **barely** ◇ *I barely ~ed myself from hitting him.* | **properly** ◇ *The horse must be properly ~ed in a location where it would not hurt itself.* | **forcibly, physically** ◇ *She had to be physically ~ed.*
VERB + RESTRAIN **be unable to, can no longer, cannot** ◇ *She could not ~ a flash of pride.* | **attempt to, seek to, try to** | **manage to** | **help (to)**
PREP. **from** ◇ *He ~ed himself from shouting at her.*
PHRASES **an attempt to ~ sb, an effort to ~ sb**

restrained adj.

VERBS **be**
ADV. **extremely, fairly, very, etc.** | **remarkably** ◇ *I thought she was remarkably ~ in the circumstances.*

restraint noun

1 limit/control on sth

ADJ. **voluntary** ◇ *agreements on voluntary export ~s* | **conventional** ◇ *What happens when the conventional ~s on human cruelty are removed?* | **physical** ◇ *Sometimes the care workers need to use physical ~ on the hospital patients.* | **budget, budgetary, economic, financial, fiscal, monetary, pay** (*esp. BrE*), **spending, wage** (*esp. BrE*) ◇ *the government's need to exercise fiscal ~* ◇ *talks on voluntary wage ~* | **constitutional, government, judicial, legal, political, regulatory** | **cultural, moral, social** | **unconstitutional, unlawful** ◇ *guilty of the charge of unlawful ~* | **time** ◇ *We did the best we could within the limited time ~s.* | **prior** ◇ *They balked at the notion of prior ~s on research.*
VERB + RESTRAINT **impose, use** | **remove**
PREP. **without ~** ◇ *Prices continued to rise without ~.* | **~ on, ~ upon** ◇ *The government imposed ~s on spending.*

2 behaving in a calm/moderate way

ADJ. **considerable, great, remarkable** | **admirable** | **emotional, sexual**
VERB + RESTRAINT **have** ◇ *Somehow I had the ~ not to tell Peter that.* | **exercise, practise/practice, use** ◇ *Journalists have exercised remarkable ~ in not reporting all the sordid details of the case.* ◇ *The media should have used more ~ in disclosing his private life.* | **demonstrate, exhibit, show** | **call for, urge** ◇ *The role requires a certain ~.* | **abandon** ◇ *He abandoned all ~ and yelled at the top of his lungs.*
PREP. **with ~** ◇ *They reacted with ~.* | **without ~** ◇ *Finally he was able to cry properly, without ~.* | **~ by** ◇ *The government called for ~ by both sides.*

restrict verb

ADV. **greatly, seriously** (*esp. BrE*), **severely, sharply** (*esp. BrE*), **significantly** | **further** ◇ *The government is considering new laws which will further ~ people's access to firearms.* | **effectively, largely** ◇ *The authors largely ~ their attention to three issues.* | **unduly** (*esp. BrE*), **unnecessarily**
VERB + RESTRICT **attempt to, seek to, try to** | **need to** ◇ *He needs to ~ his intake of red meat.* | **tend to** ◇ *Having small children tends to ~ your freedom.*
PREP. **to** ◇ *I'm ~ing myself to one glass of wine a day.*
PHRASES **an attempt to ~ sth** ◇ *attempts to ~ the sale of alcohol* | **measures to ~ sth**

restricted adj.

VERBS **be** | **become** ◇ *The US may become more ~ in its use of economic sanctions.* | **feel** ◇ *She felt ~ in her uniform.* | **remain**
ADV. **extremely, fairly, very, etc.** | **greatly, heavily** (*esp. BrE*), **highly, seriously** (*esp. BrE*), **severely, tightly** ◇ *New heavy industries were concentrated in tightly ~ areas.* ◇ *He has a severely ~ diet.* | **increasingly** | **largely** | **relatively** | **apparently** | **normally, typically, usually** | **unduly** (*esp. BrE*) ◇ *Access to higher education has been unduly ~ for people with disabilities.*
PREP. **to** ◇ *Access to the documents remains ~ to civil servants.*

restriction noun

ADJ. **draconian, harsh, severe, strict, stringent, strong, tight, tough** | **major, significant** | **petty** (*esp. BrE*) ◇ *The removal of petty ~s has made life easier.* | **arbitrary** ◇ *arbitrary ~s on medicines* | **reasonable** | **absolute** | **additional, further** | **new** | **artificial** ◇ *free movement of goods between member countries without any artificial ~s* | **self-imposed** | **proposed** | **international** | **local, state** | **contractual** (*esp. BrE*) | **constitutional** (*esp. AmE*), **federal, government, governmental** (*esp. AmE*), **legal, legislative, regulatory** (*esp. AmE*), **statutory** (*esp. BrE*) | **access, security** | **budgetary, financial** | **copyright, deed** (*AmE*), **land-use** (*AmE*), **ownership** (*esp. AmE*) | **age, height, speed, time, weight** | **abortion** (*esp. AmE*), **advertising, environmental, gun, parking, reporting** (*BrE*) | **export, import, trade** | **flight, immigration, travel, visa** | **religious, social** (*esp. AmE*), **speech** (*AmE*) | **food, water** | **dietary** ◇ *the dietary ~s of Judaism* ◇ *By following certain dietary ~s, these children can lead normal lives.* | **calorie** ◇ *the health benefits of calorie ~*
VERB + RESTRICTION **create, impose, introduce, place, put, set** ◇ *plans to create further vehicle ~s in the city* ◇ *The government has introduced tough new import ~s.* ◇ *He doesn't put any ~s on me.* | **enforce** ◇ *They have the potential to enforce ~s such as no smoking policies.* | **tighten** ◇ *a Senate bill that seeks to tighten ~s on coal plant emissions* | **ease, loosen** (*esp. AmE*), **relax** ◇ *The ~ was relaxed in 2002.* | **eliminate** (*esp. AmE*), **lift, remove** ◇ *The press asked for ~s on reporting the war to be lifted.* | **accept** | **be subject to** ◇ *The right of sale is subject to certain ~s.*
RESTRICTION + VERB **affect sth, apply** ◇ *The 30 mph speed ~ applies in all built-up areas.* | **limit sth** ◇ *~s that limit access to land and raw materials* | **prevent sth** ◇ *Confidentiality ~s prevent me from giving any names.*
RESTRICTION + NOUN **order** (*BrE, law*)
PREP. **with ~** ◇ *They had to live for a month with certain ~s on their freedom of movement.* | **with no ~, without ~** ◇ *Citizens of the EU can travel without ~ within the EU.* | **~ of** ◇ *another instance of the ~ of basic civil liberties* | **~ on, ~ upon** ◇ *The regulations were seen as a ~ on personal freedom.*

restrictive adj.

VERBS **be, seem** | **become** ◇ *In time, the changes become ~.* | **make sth** ◇ *their attempts to make drug legislation more ~ and repressive*
ADV. **extremely, fairly, very, etc.** | **highly** | **overly, too** | **increasingly** | **unduly, unnecessarily** ◇ *He argued that the law was unduly ~.*

restroom noun (AmE)

ADJ. **public** | **ladies', men's, women's**
VERB + RESTROOM **find** ◇ *He went off to find the ~.* | **enter** | **exit, leave** | **go to, use** ◇ *Do you need to use the ~?*
PREP. **in a/the ~, into a/the ~, out of a/the ~**

result noun

1 outcome/effect

ADJ. **beneficial, encouraging, favourable/favorable, good, positive** ◇ *the beneficial ~s of the reforms to the economy* ◇ *For best ~s buy one of the more expensive brands.* | **acceptable, satisfactory** ◇ *If you can't get satisfactory ~s on your own, remember that professional help is available.* | **catastrophic, disastrous, unfortunate** | **disappointing, poor** ◇ *a series of disappointing financial ~s* ◇ *The company blamed the poor ~s on bad weather.* | **mixed** ◇ *He wrote and directed the movie, to very mixed ~s.* | **direct, indirect** | **net** | **end** ◇ *The end ~ is a great album.* | **long-term, short-term** ◇ *Here's how to get the best long-term ~s from your mutual funds.* | **final** ◇ *When I showed my customer the final ~ he was thrilled.* | **overall** ◇ *The overall ~ is impressive and persuasive.* | **inevitable, logical** | **predictable** ◇ *It was the predictable ~ of their negligence.* | **expected** ◇ *Sales were some 40% above this year's expected ~s.* | **amazing, dramatic, excellent, impressive, incredible, outstanding, spectacular, superior, surprising** | **lasting** | **desired** ◇ *And did your intervention produce the desired ~?* | **financial** ◇ *He reviewed quarterly financial ~s.* | **interim** ◇ *On March 4 the company announces its interim ~s.* | **second-quarter, third-quarter, etc.** | **search** ◇ *the first page of search ~s*
VERB + RESULT **deliver, have, produce, provide, yield** ◇ *My interference had a rather unfortunate ~.* | **achieve, get, obtain** ◇ *This was not the ~ we had hoped to achieve.* | **announce, publish, release, report** ◇ *Companies are required by law to report their financial ~s on a quarterly basis.*
PREP. **as a/the ~** ◇ *These actions were taken as a direct ~ of the strike.* | **with a/the ~** ◇ *Parking restrictions were lifted, with the ~ that the road is permanently blocked by cars.*

2 desired effect

ADJ. **concrete, tangible** ◇ *We have yet to see any concrete ~s from the research.*
VERB + RESULT **come up with, deliver, get, produce, provide, yield** ◇ *Her commitment to excellence yields ~s.* | **give, show** ◇ *When is all your effort going to show some ~s?*

3 (often **results**) final position in a competition

ADJ. **election, electoral, poll, referendum** (*esp. BrE*) | **sports** (*BrE*) | **football, racing, etc.** (*BrE*) | **inconclusive** ◇ *the inconclusive election ~* | **final** ◇ *The final ~s saw Canada holding on to first over Italy.* | **official** ◇ *We'll bring you the official ~s as soon as we get them.*
VERB + RESULT **announce, read out** ◇ *The announcer read out the ~s.* | **influence** ◇ *He aimed at influencing the ~ of the presidential elections.*

4 (*BrE*) (usually **results**) mark given for an examination

ADJ. **encouraging, excellent, good** | **disappointing, poor** | **exam, examination, test** | **degree** | **A level, IELTS, etc.**
VERB + RESULT **get, have** ◇ *When do you get your exam ~s?*

5 of an experiment, a medical test, an investigation, etc.

ADJ. **early, initial, preliminary** | **interim** | **final** ◇ *He expects to have final ~s later this year.* | **experimental, research, study** | **conclusive** | **clinical, lab** (*informal*), **laboratory, test, X-ray** ◇ *Clinical ~s have been very encouraging.* | **survey** | **empirical, statistical** | **conflicting, contradictory, inconsistent, varying** ◇ *Researchers have found conflicting ~s on the effects of the drug.* | **misleading** ◇ *Such approaches may give misleading ~s.* | **inconclusive** | **encouraging, promising** ◇ *The team has achieved promising ~s during testing.* | **significant** ◇ *statistically significant ~s* | **negative, positive** ◇ *Scientists tested 20 drugs, all with negative ~s.* | **abnormal** ◇ *if a woman receives an abnormal ~ on a blood test* | **measurable** ◇ *Measurable ~s are the key to motivation on any diet.* | **accurate, reliable** | **inaccurate** ◇ *There are 3 ways to obtain more accurate ~s in cases such as this.*
VERB + RESULT **await, wait for** ◇ *The doctor is still waiting for my ~s.* | **get, have, receive** ◇ *I haven't had the X-ray ~s yet.* | **find** ◇ *We found some puzzling ~s.* | **observe** | **analyse/analyze, evaluate, interpret** | **review** | **achieve, deliver, generate, give, produce, provide, yield** ◇ *Different labs will come up with different ~s.* ◇ *The study produced inconclusive ~s.* | **announce, present, publish, release, report** ◇ *They hope to publish their ~s next month.* | **confirm, verify** ◇ *We ran the test again to verify the ~.* | **affect, influence** | **bias, skew** ◇ *That could bias study ~s.*

retirement

RESULT + VERB **demonstrate sth, illustrate sth, reflect sth, reveal sth, show sth** | **imply sth, indicate sth, suggest sth** ◊ *Preliminary ~s suggest that there is no cause for concern.* | **agree with sth, confirm sth, support sth** | **differ from sth** ◊ *These ~s differ somewhat from those reported by previous studies.* | **provide sth** ◊ *The ~s provide many insights into the mating rituals of these animals.* | **highlight sth** ◊ *These ~s highlight the growing threat posed by this infection.*
PREP. **pending the ~ of** ◊ *Work on the plan has been halted, pending the ~s of a judicial investigation.* | **~ from** ◊ *The ~s from various recent surveys were evaluated.*

result verb

PHR V **result in sth**
ADV. **inevitably** ◊ *This move will inevitably ~ in the loss of a lot of jobs.* | **typically** | **conceivably, possibly, potentially** ◊ *The charges could have potentially ~ed in a death sentence.* | **not automatically** (*esp. BrE*), **not necessarily** | **easily** ◊ *Complacency could easily ~ in tragedy.* | **quickly** | **eventually, finally, ultimately**
VERB + RESULT IN **be certain to** ◊ *the approach that is most certain to ~ in failure* | **be expected to, be liable to** (*esp. BrE*), **be likely to** ◊ *Such measures are likely to ~ in decreased motivation of the workforce.* | **be unlikely to**

résumé noun (*AmE*) record of education, jobs, etc.
→ See also CURRICULUM VITAE

ADJ. **impressive** | **brief, short** | **extensive, long** | **online** ◊ *An online ~ allows you to use the Internet to assist you in your job hunt.*
…OF RÉSUMÉS **pile, stack**
VERB + RÉSUMÉ **update** | **create, prepare, write** | **submit** | **email, mail, send** | **post** ◊ *You can post your ~ on the website free of charge.* | **receive** ◊ *I received an unsolicited ~ from someone asking me to hire him.* | **sift through** | **read, review, scan** ◊ *Yes, I've read your ~. Very impressive.* | **build** ◊ *I have been building my ~ by interning at various law firms.* | **pad** ◊ *He padded his ~ in order to appear more experienced.*
PREP. **in a ~** ◊ *There's still a glaring hole in his ~.*

resuscitation noun

ADJ. **cardiopulmonary** (abbreviated to *CPR*), **emergency** (*esp. BrE*), **mouth-to-mouth**
VERB + RESUSCITATION **give sb, perform** ◊ *We gave him mouth-to-mouth ~ and heart massage.* | **require** ◊ *Mouth-to-mouth ~ was required to revive him.*
RESUSCITATION + NOUN **equipment** | **technique**

retailer noun

ADJ. **big, giant, large** | **leading, major, top** ◊ *the country's biggest food ~* | **small** | **local** | **high-street** (*BrE*) ◊ *High-street ~s reported a marked increase in sales before Christmas.* | **big-box** (= that sells large items) (*AmE*) | **mass** (*AmE*), **mass-market** | **multiple** | **independent** | **niche** (*esp. BrE*), **specialist** (*BrE*), **specialty** (*AmE*) | **high-end** (*AmE*), **luxury** (*esp. AmE*), **upscale** (*AmE*) | **discount** | **brick-and-mortar** (*AmE*), **bricks-and-mortar** (*AmE*), **traditional** | **Internet, online, Web** | **apparel** (*AmE*), **clothing, DIY** (*BrE*), **electrical** (*BrE*), **electronics, fashion, food, furniture, grocery, music, toy,** etc.

retain verb

ADV. **nonetheless, still, yet** | **no longer** | **somehow** ◊ *Despite the decay the mosque somehow ~ed a profound grandeur.* | **successfully** ◊ *He has successfully ~ed his position as national president of the society.* | **largely** ◊ *Her new music largely ~s the distinctiveness of the old.*
VERB + RETAIN **be eager to, be keen to** (*esp. BrE*), **hope to, want to, wish to** | **attempt to, fight to, seek to, struggle to, try to** ◊ *He struggled to ~ control of the situation.* | **be unlikely to** | **be likely to** | **manage to** | **help (to)** | **be allowed to, be entitled to** (*BrE*), **have the right to** ◊ *He was allowed to ~ his parliamentary seat.* (*BrE*) ◊ *The immigrants have a right to ~ their language.* | **be important to** | **fail to**
PREP. **as** ◊ *The president ~ed her as his chief adviser.*

retaliation noun

ADJ. **massive** | **brutal, violent** | **physical** | **swift** | **immediate, instant** | **possible** ◊ *contingency plans to deter possible nuclear ~* | **economic, trade** | **military** | **nuclear**
VERB + RETALIATION **invite, prompt, provoke, trigger** ◊ *a casual remark that brought swift ~ from her boyfriend* | **face** ◊ *She may face ~ for speaking out.* | **suffer** ◊ *He knows he will suffer ~.* | **threaten** | **fear**
PREP. **in ~** ◊ *He never said a single word in ~.* | **in ~ for** ◊ *They killed two men in ~ for a bomb attack the previous day.* | **~ against** ◊ *Retaliation against government troops is feared.* | **~ by, ~ from** ◊ *the possibility of ~ by other governments* | **~ for** ◊ *~ for the bombing of civilians*
PHRASES **an act of ~** | **~ in kind** ◊ *They decided not to use chemical weapons as ~ in kind.*

retarded adj. (*old-fashioned, offensive*)

VERBS **be, look**
ADV. **severely** ◊ *Many of the children are severely ~.* | **mildly, slightly** | **emotionally, mentally, socially** ◊ *a mentally ~ child*

rethink noun

ADJ. **complete** | **fundamental, major, radical, serious**
VERB + RETHINK **have**
PREP. **~ of** ◊ *to have a fundamental ~ of policy*

rethink verb

ADV. **fundamentally, radically, seriously** | **completely** | **constantly**
VERB + RETHINK **force sb to, make sb** | **have to, need to** ◊ *I think we may have to ~ our policies fairly radically.* | **begin to, start to**

retire verb

ADV. **early** ◊ *He is hoping to ~ early on medical grounds.* | **recently** ◊ *She recently ~d from teaching.* | **officially** ◊ *he officially ~d from the day-to-day operations of his company.* | **comfortably** ◊ *She's on course to ~ quite comfortably by the time she's 55.*
VERB + RETIRE **be forced to, be obliged to** (*BrE*), **have to** ◊ *Anderson was forced to ~ because of injury at the age of 26.* | **be due to, plan to** ◊ *Mr McNeil is due to ~ later this month.* | **hope to** ◊ *I'm hoping to ~ in about five years.* | **be ready to** ◊ *As for me, I am quite ready to ~.* | **choose to, decide to** | **be eligible to** ◊ *In a few years, I'll be eligible to ~.* | **afford to** ◊ *She simply couldn't afford to ~ at sixty.*
PREP. **as** ◊ *He recently ~d as CEO of the company.* | **at** ◊ *Most employees ~ at 60.* (*BrE*) ◊ *Most employees ~ at age 60.* (*esp. AmE*) | **from** ◊ *She ~d from the bank last year.*
PHRASES **newly ~d, recently ~d** ◊ *a newly ~d couple* | **be medically ~d** ◊ *He was medically ~d at the age of 55.*

retirement noun

ADJ. **early, premature** ◊ *A knee injury forced him into premature ~.* | **active** | **comfortable, happy, secure** ◊ *He provided for a comfortable ~ by selling the business.* | **compulsory, enforced** (*esp. BrE*), **forced** (*AmE*), **mandatory** (*esp. AmE*) ◊ *compulsory ~ at 60* ◊ *her enforced ~ from the sport* | **voluntary** ◊ *She took voluntary ~ in 2001.* | **imminent, impending, pending** (*AmE*), **upcoming** ◊ *She announced her impending ~.* | **official** ◊ *his official ~ in 2012*
VERB + RETIREMENT **consider, contemplate, think about, think of** | **look forward to** | **approach, be close to, near** | **delay, postpone** | **plan, plan for, prepare for** ◊ *The website helps you plan your ~.* | **finance, fund, provide for** ◊ *investments to fund their ~* | **reach** | **announce** | **enter, go into** ◊ *It was their final concert before entering ~.* | **come out of** ◊ *He is going to come out of ~ for this one last concert.* | **force, force sb into** ◊ *In 1996 health problems forced her ~.* | **mark** ◊ *They presented him with a watch to mark his ~.* | **enjoy, spend** ◊ *I intend to spend my ~ playing golf.*
RETIREMENT + NOUN **age** | **date** ◊ *Her official ~ date is March*

changing business conditions. | **women's, writers'** | **family** (*esp. AmE*)
VERB + RETREAT **attend, do, go on** ◇ *She goes on a spiritual ~ for two weeks every summer.* | **go into** ◇ *He went into ~ at his country home to escape the attention of the media.* | **hold** ◇ *The family held its first ~ last October.* | **offer** ◇ *Zen Mountain offers numerous wilderness ~s.*

retreat verb

ADV. **hastily, quickly, rapidly, swiftly** | **slowly** ◇ *Sandy ~ed slowly, wary of what the man might do.* | **further** | **back** ◇ *He ~ed hastily back to his car.*
VERB + RETREAT **try to** | **order sb to** ◇ *The army has been ordered to ~.*
PREP. **before** ◇ *They ~ed before the Americans.* | **behind** ◇ *He ~ed behind the table.* | **down** ◇ *I heard her footsteps ~ down the hall.* | **from** | **in the face of** ◇ *He ~ed in the face of strong opposition.* | **into** ◇ *He ~ed into his own world.* | **to** ◇ *She ~ed from the busy office to her own room.*

retribution noun

ADJ. **just** | **terrible** | **violent** | **legal, political** ◇ *Political ~ will fall swiftly on any president who fails in that task.* | **swift** ◇ *Retribution will be swift if you cross me.* | **divine**
VERB + RETRIBUTION **demand, seek** | **exact** | **bring** | **fear**
RETRIBUTION + VERB **come, follow** ◇ *Violent ~ soon followed.*
PREP. **in** ◇ *His armies invaded their lands in ~.* | **~ against** ◇ *~ against wrongdoers* | **~ for** ◇ *He saw his suffering as ~ for the sins of his past life.* | **~ from** ◇ *The celebrity couple clearly feared ~ from their fans.* | **~ on** ◇ *She saw the sentence as just ~ on the man who had assaulted her.*
PHRASES **an act of ~** | **fear of ~** ◇ *The victim did not report the incident for fear of ~.*

return noun

1 coming/going back; giving sth back

ADJ. **complete, full** ◇ *a full ~ to health* | **gradual** | **eventual** ◇ *his eventual ~ to Budapest* | **long-awaited** ◇ *The championships made their long-awaited ~ to the West Coast.* | **imminent** | **unexpected** ◇ *the unexpected ~ of her long-lost niece* | **timely** ◇ *Will he be saved by the timely ~ of Simone?* | **early** | **welcome** ◇ *This is a welcome ~ to form for one of the best athletes in the sport.* | **possible, potential** ◇ *He does not rule out a possible ~ to the concert world.* | **fast, prompt, quick, rapid, speedy, swift** ◇ *The new treatment means patients can expect a shorter hospital stay and a faster ~ to work.* | **brief** | **safe** ◇ *They offered up a prayer of thanks for her safe ~.* | **triumphant** ◇ *She made a triumphant ~ to Broadway earlier this year.* | **successful** ◇ *He made a successful ~ to the game after several years of retirement.* | **emotional, happy, nostalgic** ◇ *The photos were taken during his nostalgic ~ to Redwood Creek.* | **dramatic** | **miraculous** ◇ *Today, the whole village celebrates Elizabeth's miraculous ~.*
VERB + RETURN **make** ◇ *Shevchenko made an emotional ~ to his former team.* | **mark** ◇ *The victory marked Williams's ~ to top form.* | **herald, signal** ◇ *The takeover heralded a ~ to a strong central administration.* | **await, wait for** | **anticipate, expect** ◇ *The cooperative anticipates a ~ to profitability later in the year.* | **announce** | **greet** (*esp. BrE*) ◇ *The smell of cooking greeted his ~ home.* | **welcome** ◇ *Thousands will welcome the ~ of this national treasure.* | **celebrate** | **facilitate** ◇ *The organization facilitates the ~ of refugees and displaced persons.* | **delay** | **request** | **demand** ◇ *He demanded the ~ of his money.* | **advocate, support** ◇ *a cult whose members advocated a ~ to traditional living* | **seek, want** ◇ *He continued to seek the ~ of his property.* | **call for** ◇ *The UN continued to call for a ~ to civilian rule.*
RETURN + NOUN **date** | **flight, journey, trip** ◇ *When is your ~ flight?* | **ticket** (= for the return trip) ◇ *I lost my ~ ticket and was stranded in Thailand.* | **address** | **envelope** | **call, phone call** ◇ *She hoped she'd get a ~ call soon.* | **email, message**
PREP. **in ~ (for)** ◇ *She gave them all the help she could, and asked for nothing in ~.* | **on sb's ~** ◇ *He promised to visit us on his ~.* | **~ from** ◇ *The date of their ~ from India is a*

---

12. | **benefits, package, pension** (*esp. BrE*) | **plan, programme/program** (*esp. AmE*) | **savings** ◇ *They have about $14 800 in ~ savings.* | **account** (*AmE*) ◇ *the benefits of private ~ accounts* | **fund** | **income, money** (*esp. AmE*), **pay** (*esp. AmE*) ◇ *He has a good ~ income.* | **portfolio** (*esp. AmE*) ◇ *Thanks to his diligence, his ~ portfolio is flourishing.* | **security** ◇ *important matters like health care and ~ security* | **gift, party** | **facility** (*AmE*), **home** | **community** (*AmE*), **village** ◇ *older adults who relocate to ~ communities* | **years** ◇ *I've been thinking about where I might like to spend my ~ years.*
PREP. **after (your) ~, before (your) ~** ◇ *After her ~ from the stage she began to drink.* | **at (your) ~** ◇ *Your pension plan provides a cash lump sum at ~.* | **for (your) ~** ◇ *She's saving for her ~.* | **in (your) ~** ◇ *His father was now living in ~ in France.* ◇ *She has found a new hobby in her ~.* | **on (your) ~** ◇ *a gift from the company on his ~* | **until (your) ~** ◇ *He remained in the post until his ~ last year.* | **~ as** ◇ *her ~ as sales director* | **~ at** ◇ *~ at fifty* (*BrE*) ◇ *~ at age fifty* (*esp. AmE*) | **~ from** ◇ *his ~ from football*
PHRASES **the age of ~** ◇ *The age of ~ for all employees is 60.* | **take early ~** ◇ *The company suggested that he should take early ~.* | **a long and happy ~**

retort noun

ADJ. **quick, sharp** | **clever, witty** | **sarcastic, scathing** | **angry**
VERB + RETORT **come up with, make** ◇ *He opened his mouth to make a sarcastic ~.* | **bite back** ◇ *He bit back a sharp ~.* | **bring, draw, meet with** ◇ *Her remark drew angry ~s from the unemployed workers.*

retort verb

ADV. **quickly** | **angrily, furiously, heatedly, hotly** ◇ *'How dare you!' he ~ed angrily.* | **bitterly, harshly, sarcastically, scathingly, sharply** | **defensively, indignantly** | **calmly, coldly, coolly** | **drily, playfully** | **childishly**

retreat noun

1 retreating/leaving

ADJ. **hasty, headlong, quick, rapid** ◇ *I decided to beat a hasty ~.* | **humiliating, ignominious** (*formal*) | **orderly, strategic, tactful, tactical** ◇ *I made a tactful ~ before they started arguing.*
VERB + RETREAT **beat, make** | **lead** | **call** (*AmE*), **order, sound** | **force, force sb into** ◇ *Eventually the police forced the crowd into ~.* | **block, cut off** | **cover** ◇ *We covered his ~ with bursts of gunfire.*
PREP. **in** ◇ *The enemy was now in ~.* | **on the ~** ◇ *fresh evidence that trade unionism is on the ~* | **~ from** ◇ *He took part in the ~ from Paris.* | **~ into** ◇ *her ~ into a fantasy world of her own* | **~ to** ◇ *an ignominious ~ to the River Vistula*
PHRASES **be in full ~** ◇ *On the eastern front the army was in full ~.* | **a line of ~** ◇ *We succeeded in cutting off the enemy's line of ~.*

2 quiet and private place

ADJ. **favourite/favorite, idyllic, perfect** ◇ *the perfect ~ for a romantic honeymoon* | **private, secret** | **peaceful, quiet** | **country, mountain, rural, wilderness** (*esp. AmE*) ◇ *designed as a gentleman's country ~* | **summer, winter** | **holiday** (*BrE*), **vacation** (*AmE*), **weekend** | **presidential** ◇ *Camp David, the presidential ~ in Maryland*
VERB + RETREAT **turn sth into, use sth as** ◇ *She plans to use it as a winter ~.*
PREP. **~ for** ◇ *a summer ~ for the rich* | **~ from** ◇ *They are staying here at their secret ~ from life in the city.*

3 quiet place; time spent there

ADJ. **Buddhist, meditation, religious, spiritual, yoga, Zen** | **silent** ◇ *I went on a ten-day silent ~.* | **annual** ◇ *I went off on one of my annual ~s.* | **two-day, week-long, etc.** | **business, corporate, executive, management** (*all esp. AmE*) ◇ *A successful executive ~ can be a powerful tool for addressing*

month from now. | **~ to** ◇ *Jones is hoping for an early ~ to racing after her injury.*
PHRASES **by ~** (*BrE*), **by ~ mail** (*AmE*), **by ~ of post** (*BrE*) ◇ *All orders will be sent by ~ of post/by ~ mail.*

2 (also **returns**) profit

ADJ. **attractive, big, excellent, good, great, high, maximum, substantial** | **increasing** ◇ *increasing ~s from educational investment* | **acceptable** (*esp. BrE*), **adequate, decent, fair, healthy, modest, positive, reasonable, solid** | **disappointing** | **low, marginal, meagre/meager, negative, poor, small** | **decreasing, diminishing** ◇ *the law of diminishing ~s* | **10%, 30%, etc.** | **total** | **average** ◇ *an average ~ of 16%* | **economic, financial** ◇ *They are counting on a big financial ~.* | **overall** | **investment** ◇ *They're looking for new sources of investment ~.* | **immediate** | **fast, quick** ◇ *The software had to demonstrate a fast ~.* | **early** ◇ *Venture capitalists currently see few prospects of early ~s.* | **future** | **long-term, short-term** | **annual, monthly, etc.** | **expected, likely, projected, possible, potential** | **guaranteed** ◇ *The plan provides a guaranteed ~.* | **gross** (*esp. BrE*) | **after-tax, net** | **actual, real** ◇ *future real ~s from global equities* | **tax-free** (*esp. BrE*) | **risk-adjusted** (*AmE*) | **amended** (*AmE*) | **annualized** (*esp. AmE*) | **shareholder** | **stock** (*AmE*) | **excess** (*AmE*)
VERB + RETURN **achieve, bring, earn, get, make, receive** ◇ *You should get a good ~ on this investment.* | **average** ◇ *The group has averaged ~s of 3.8% a year over the past five years.* | **boost, enhance, improve, increase, maximize** ◇ *to maximize ~s to shareholders* | **calculate** | **expect, forecast, predict** ◇ *She expects a 100% ~ within 18 months.* | **look for, seek** ◇ *investors seeking better ~s in an era of low inflation* | **deliver, generate, give (sb), offer (sb), produce, provide, realize, show, yield** ◇ *Gold shares could realize ~s of 15% per annum.* ◇ *The venture yielded a net ~ of £15 million.* | **ensure, guarantee** ◇ *The employer guaranteed a certain ~ on retirement investment.* | **represent** ◇ *These figures represent a ~ of 8.5% per annum.*
RETURN + VERB **increase** | **decline**
RETURN + NOUN **rate** (*esp. AmE*) ◇ *We're getting a high ~ rate.*
PREP. **~ from** ◇ *Their goal is to improve economic ~s from irrigation.* | **~ on** ◇ *the ~ on capital/investment/savings*
PHRASES **a rate of ~** ◇ *We're getting a high rate of ~.*

3 (*BrE*) ticket to travel to a place and back again → See also ROUND TRIP

ADJ. **day, period** | **business-class, economy, first-class, standard, tourist-class**
RETURN + NOUN **ticket** | **flight, journey**

return *verb*

ADV. **recently** | **shortly** | **promptly** ◇ *See that the documents are ~ed promptly, please.* | **immediately, instantly** ◇ *His headache ~ed instantly.* | **quickly** ◇ *She quickly ~ed to the car and sped off.* | **slowly** ◇ *My strength was slowly ~ing to me.* | **suddenly** | **gradually** | **eventually, finally** | **subsequently** ◇ *The patient subsequently ~ed for surgery.* | **periodically** ◇ *Her symptoms ~ed periodically.* | **frequently** | **repeatedly** ◇ *His conversation ~s repeatedly to the same subjects.* | **briefly** ◇ *Let me ~ briefly to this question.* | **safely** ◇ *Our aircraft all ~ed safely to their bases.* | **gladly, happily** ◇ *Kevin gladly ~ed her hug.* | **reluctantly** ◇ *Charlie reluctantly ~ed to his seat.* | **triumphantly** ◇ *Ali ~ed triumphantly to boxing in 1970.* | **unexpectedly** ◇ *We locked the door in case Mary ~ed unexpectedly.* | **voluntarily** | **forcibly** ◇ *The asylum seekers are to be forcibly ~ed to their home countries.* | **directly** ◇ *I will have to ask that you ~ directly to your houses.* | **home**
VERB + RETURN **be due to** ◇ *She is due to ~ to school in a week.* | **be expected to, be likely to, be set to, look set to** (*BrE*) | **be allowed to** | **choose to, decide to, expect to, hope to, intend to, opt to, plan to, vote to, want to, wish to, yearn to** | **can't wait to** ◇ *I couldn't wait to ~ from my travels.* | **agree to, promise to** | **prepare to** ◇ *She was preparing to ~ to El Salvador.* | **offer to** ◇ *I offered to ~ his Christmas gift to me.* | **fail to** ◇ *Suspicions were aroused when he failed to ~ to work on Monday morning.* | **not bother to** ◇ *He hadn't bothered to ~ her messages.* | **refuse to** ◇ *He refused to ~ our*

money. | **forget to** ◇ *Don't forget to ~ his handkerchief.* | **force sb to** ◇ *Lack of cash forced her to ~ to work.* | **threaten to** ◇ *the tears that threatened to ~*
PREP. **from** ◇ *She had recently ~ed from Paris.* | **to** ◇ *She never ~ed the book to me.*

reunion *noun*

ADJ. **emotional, tearful, touching** ◇ *It was an emotional ~ after 25 years apart.* | **happy, joyful, joyous** | **alumni** (*esp. AmE*), **class, college, high-school** (*esp. AmE*), **school** (*esp. BrE*) | **five-year, twenty-year, etc.** | **family** | **annual** | **big, grand** (*esp. BrE*) | **little** ◇ *I think it's time to arrange a little ~.*
VERB + REUNION **have, hold, plan, stage** ◇ *The ~ is held every two years.* | **arrange, organize** | **attend, go to** | **celebrate** ◇ *Let's have a party to celebrate our ~.*
REUNION + VERB **take place**
REUNION + NOUN **dinner, event, lunch** (*BrE*) | **party** | **weekend** | **album, concert, show, tour** ◇ *He left the group during the 1997 ~ tour.* | **movie** (*AmE*)
PREP. **at a/the ~** ◇ *At the ~ I met a friend I hadn't seen for twenty years.* | **~ between** ◇ *an emotional ~ between mother and son* | **~ for** ◇ *We organized a ~ for former company employees.* | **~ of** ◇ *the ~ of two old friends* | **~ with** ◇ *a tearful ~ with his family*

revealing *adj.*

VERBS **be**
ADV. **extremely, fairly, very, etc.** | **highly, particularly** ◇ *some deeply ~ insights into his life*
PREP. **about** ◇ *The book is very ~ about young people's views of themselves.*

revelation *noun*

ADJ. **amazing, astonishing** (*esp. BrE*), **embarrassing, sensational, shock** (*BrE*), **shocking, startling, sudden** | **big, great** ◇ *There are no great ~s in the final chapter.* | **fresh** (*esp. BrE*), **latest, new, recent** | **divine** ◇ *He claimed to know these things by divine ~.* | **personal**
VERB + REVELATION **come as, prove** ◇ *To many members of her audience, these performances must have come as a ~.*
REVELATION + VERB **come** ◇ *The embarrassing ~s came just hours before he was to make his speech.*
PREP. **~ about, ~ concerning** ◇ *new ~s concerning their private lives* | **~ for** ◇ *The demonstration proved something of a ~ for our teachers.* | **~ from** ◇ *He claimed to have had a ~ from God.* | **~ to** ◇ *His acting ability was a ~ to us all.*

revenge *noun*

ADJ. **sweet** ◇ *This was sweet ~ for our defeat earlier in the season.* ◇ *Revenge is sweet, so they say.*
VERB + REVENGE **seek, want** | **plot** ◇ *For ten years he has been plotting his ~.* | **vow** | **exact, get, have, take, wreak** ◇ *He vowed to take his ~ on the man who had killed his brother.*
REVENGE + NOUN **attack, killing** | **fantasy**
PREP. **in ~** ◇ *The attack was in ~ for the deaths of two prisoners.* | **~ for** ◇ *for the insult* | **~ on** ◇ *She desperately wanted to take ~ on her attacker.*
PHRASES **an act of ~** ◇ *The bombing was an act of ~ for the shooting of two young boys.* | **a desire for ~** ◇ *The accusations were driven by a desire for ~.*

revenue *noun*

ADJ. **annual, yearly** | **expected, potential, projected** ◇ *the company's expected annual ~* | **general** (*esp. AmE*), **overall, total, worldwide** | **local** (*esp. AmE*) | **gross, net** | **additional, extra** | **increased** | **substantial** | **lost** ◇ *Tax fraud costs the country millions in lost ~.* | **federal, government, public, state, tax** ◇ *the main sources of public ~* | **advertising, export, oil, sales, tourism, tourist**
VERB + REVENUE **depend on, need, rely on** ◇ *These companies rely on advertising ~ for their funds.* | **earn, get, raise** | **collect** ◇ *The central government collects the tax ~.* | **spend, use** | **bring in, generate, produce, yield** ◇ *The project will*

not generate any ~ until 2018. | **boost, increase** | **maximize** | **reduce** | **lose**
REVENUE + VERB **be derived from sth, come from sth** ◊ *Their government's ~s come mainly from direct taxes.* | **go up, grow, increase, rise** | **drop, fall, go down**
REVENUE + NOUN **stream** ◊ *Licensing the technology has created a new ~ stream for the company.* | **share**
PREP. **~ from** ◊ *~s from the sale of oil*
PHRASES **loss of ~** | **a source of ~** ◊ *Tourism is the island's main source of ~.*
→ Special page at BUSINESS

reverence *noun*

ADJ. **deep, great** | **due** (*esp. BrE*)
VERB + REVERENCE **have** | **show** | **hold sb in** ◊ *He is still held in great ~ throughout the country.* | **inspire** ◊ *a painting that inspires deep ~ for nature*
PREP. **in ~** ◊ *I closed my eyes in ~.* | **with ~** ◊ *She spoke of them with profound ~.* | **~ for** ◊ *~ for human life* | **~ to, ~ towards/toward** ◊ *Children are taught to show ~ towards/toward their elders.*

reversal *noun*

ADJ. **complete, total** | **dramatic, sharp, sudden** | **apparent** | **policy** | **role** ◊ *Role ~ is a common feature of modern relationships.*
VERB + REVERSAL **mark, represent** ◊ *This represents an apparent ~ of previous policy.* | **bring about, lead to, result in** | **suffer**
PREP. **~ in** ◊ *the dramatic ~ in population decline* | **~ of** ◊ *a ~ of current trends*
PHRASES **a ~ of fortunes** ◊ *Cheaper imports played a part in the company's ~ of fortunes.*

reverse *noun*

1 opposite

ADJ. **exact**
VERB + REVERSE **do** ◊ *If you tell children to do something, they will often do the exact ~.*
PREP. **on the ~** (= on the opposite side) ◊ *The coin has a date on one side and the emperor's head on the ~.*

2 gear

VERB + REVERSE **put sth in, put sth into, throw sth into** ◊ *I put the car in ~.*
REVERSE + NOUN **gear**

3 failure/defeat

ADJ. **major, serious**
VERB + REVERSE **have, suffer** ◊ *Their forces have suffered serious ~s in recent months.*

reverse *verb*

1 change sth to the opposite

ADV. **dramatically** | **completely, exactly, totally** ◊ *The decline in this industry has now been completely ~d.* | **almost** | **partially** | **simply** ◊ *To solve the puzzle, simply ~ the order of the numbers.* | **quickly, rapidly** | **suddenly**
VERB + REVERSE **seek to, try to** | **fail to**

2 move back

ADV. **slowly** ◊ *She slowly ~d up the narrow driveway.* ◊ *She slowly ~d the van up the narrow driveway.* (*BrE*) | **in, out**
PREP. **into** ◊ *The car ~d into a hedge.* | **out of** ◊ *He ~d slowly out of the garage.* ◊ *He ~d the car slowly out of the garage.* (*BrE*)

reversible *adj.*

VERBS **be** ◊ *The operation is easily ~.*
ADV. **easily, readily** | **completely**

review *noun*

1 considering sth again

ADJ. **careful, complete, comprehensive, detailed, extensive, full, full-scale** (*esp. BrE*)**, fundamental** (*esp. BrE*)**, in-depth, major, overall, systematic, thorough, wide-ranging** | **brief, quick, rapid, short** | **urgent** (*esp. BrE*) | **annual, periodic, regular** ◊ *the government's annual policy ~* | **constant, continuous** | **critical** ◊ *The first chapter presents a critical ~ of the existing nursery education system.* | **government, independent, internal, judicial** | **peer** ◊ *All papers submitted to the journal undergo a process of peer ~.* | **literature** | **financial, performance, policy, rent** (*BrE*) | **pay** (*esp. BrE*)**, salary**
VERB + REVIEW **ask for, call for, seek** ◊ *Greenpeace will seek a judicial ~ if a full public investigation is not held.* | **announce** (*esp. BrE*)**, order** | **carry out** (*esp. BrE*)**, complete, conduct, do, hold, perform, undertake** | **present, provide**
REVIEW + VERB **take place** | **cover sth, deal with sth** | **conclude sth, indicate sth, propose sth, recommend sth, suggest sth**
REVIEW + NOUN **board, body** (*esp. BrE*)**, committee, group** | **process**
PREP. **under ~** ◊ *The matter is still under ~.* | **up for ~** ◊ *These rules will soon be up for ~.* ◊ *The rent is up for ~.* | **~ by** ◊ *a ~ by the court*

2 report on a film/movie, restaurant, etc.

ADJ. **enthusiastic, excellent, favourable/favorable, glowing, good, positive, rave, wonderful** | **bad, hostile, negative, poor, scathing** ◊ *The show has good audience figures despite poor ~s in the press.* | **critical** | **mixed** ◊ *The book received mixed ~s.* | **book, film** (*esp. BrE*)**, movie** (*esp. AmE*)
VERB + REVIEW **do, write** ◊ *I'm doing a ~ for the local paper.* | **give sth** | **get, have, receive, win** | **post, publish** | **open to** ◊ *Their new musical opened to glowing ~s.* | **read, see** ◊ *Did you see the ~ in 'Phase'?*
REVIEW + VERB **appear** ◊ *His ~ appeared in yesterday's paper.*
REVIEW + NOUN **copy** | **article**

3 (*AmE*) studying

VERB + REVIEW **do**
REVIEW + NOUN **class, session** | **materials** | **question**
PREP. **~ for** ◊ *we need to do the ~ for the test tomorrow.*

review *verb*

1 examine sth again

ADV. **comprehensively, fully, thoroughly** | **extensively, widely** | **carefully** | **briefly** | **urgently** (*esp. BrE*) ◊ *Safety procedures are being urgently ~ed after a chemical leak at the factory.* | **currently** ◊ *We are currently ~ing the situation.* | **constantly, regularly** | **annually, periodically** ◊ *This figure will be ~ed periodically in the light of inflation.* | **critically** ◊ *Pull out your budget and critically ~ each line on it.*
VERB + REVIEW **agree to, promise to** | **ask sb to** | **decline to, refuse to**
PREP. **for** (*AmE*) ◊ *Jonas helped me ~ for the test.*
PHRASES **~ sth in the light of sth** ◊ *This case should be ~ed in the light of the new evidence.*

2 write a report of a book, film/movie, etc.

ADV. **favourably/favorably** ◊ *The movie has been favourably/favorably ~ed on various websites.* | **critically**

revise *verb*

ADV. **drastically, extensively, heavily, radically, substantially** ◊ *The text has been radically ~d.* | **completely, fully, thoroughly** | **slightly** | **constantly, continually** ◊ *The procedures are continually revised—it is very difficult to keep up with the latest version.* | **periodically** | **newly, recently** | **downwards/downward, upwards/upward** ◊ *Sales forecasts will have to be ~d downwards/downward.*
VERB + REVISE **be forced to, have to** ◊ *The estimate for the building work had to be ~d.* | **be necessary to**
PREP. **from, to** ◊ *The figure has now been ~d from $1 million to $2 million.* | **for** (*BrE*) ◊ *Have you ~d for the test tomorrow?*

revision *noun*

1 making changes

ADJ. **complete, drastic, extensive, fundamental, major, radical, substantial, thorough** | **minor** | **constant** | **final** | **latest, recent** | **downward, upward** ◊ *an upward ~ of government expenditure plans* | **policy, treaty** (*esp. BrE*)

VERB + REVISION **propose, recommend, suggest** | **call for, demand** ◊ *They called for ~s to the treaty.* | **be open to, be subject to** ◊ *Our conclusions are always open to ~ in the light of fresh evidence.* | **need, require** ◊ *These guidebooks require constant ~.* | **undergo** ◊ *The plan has recently undergone drastic ~.* | **announce, approve** ◊ *A ~ of the budget was approved in October.* | **lead to, result in** | **complete, make, undertake**

PREP. **~ in** ◊ *This has brought about a radical ~ in the style of school management.* | **~ to** ◊ *~s to the plan*

PHRASES **the process of ~** ◊ *The process of ~ continued at rehearsals.*

2 (*BrE*) **studying** → See also REVIEW

VERB + REVISION **do** ◊ *I've got to do some history ~ tonight.*

REVISION + NOUN **class, course, lesson** | **question**

PREP. **~ for** ◊ *~ for tomorrow's history exam*

revival *noun*

ADJ. **great, major** | **modern, recent** | **current** | **cultural, economic, literary** (*esp. BrE*), **religious, etc.** ◊ *The late 19th century was a time of religious ~.*

VERB + REVIVAL **enjoy, experience, undergo** ◊ *His work is enjoying a ~ in popularity.* | **stage** (*esp. BrE*) ◊ *The economy has staged something of a ~ in the last year.* | **bring about, lead to, spark, stimulate** ◊ *The exhibition has sparked a ~ of interest in the Impressionists.* | **lead** | **see, witness** ◊ *The period saw a great ~ in the wine trade.*

PREP. **~ in** ◊ *a ~ in the fortunes of the Democratic Party* | **~ of** ◊ *a ~ of ancient skills*

PHRASES **a ~ of interest** ◊ *the ~ of interest in radio* | **signs of (a) ~** ◊ *He claimed the market was showing signs of a ~.*

revive *verb*

1 bring sth back

ADV. **quickly** ◊ *Banks and businesses are quickly reviving business activities in China.* | **recently**

VERB + REVIVE **try to** ◊ *They are trying to ~ some of the old customs.* | **help (to), help sb (to)** ◊ *The good harvest helped ~ the economic fortunes of the country.*

PHRASES **an attempt to ~ sth, an effort to ~ sth** ◊ *attempts to ~ falling sales* | **be aimed at reviving sth** (*esp. BrE*) ◊ *an initiative aimed at reviving talks on the country's political future*

2 make sb conscious again

VERB + REVIVE **try to**

PREP. **with** ◊ *They ~d him with cold water.*

PHRASES **an attempt to ~ sb, an effort to ~ sb** ◊ *Attempts to ~ her failed and she was dead on arrival at the hospital.*

revolt *noun*

ADJ. **mass, popular, serious** (*esp. BrE*), **widespread** (*esp. BrE*) ◊ *There was a widespread ~ against the party leadership.* | **open** ◊ *Parliament came out in open ~ against the president.* | **armed** | **peasant, peasant's, shareholder's, slave, student, etc.** | **tax**

VERB + REVOLT **cause, provoke** (*esp. BrE*), **spark** | **lead** ◊ *a student-led ~* | **organize, stage** | **crush, deal with** (*esp. BrE*), **put down, suppress** ◊ *The ~ was suppressed with total ruthlessness.* | **face** ◊ *The party leadership is facing open ~.*

REVOLT + VERB **break out** ◊ *Revolt broke out when the government decided to raise the price of bread.* | **spread** | **overthrow sb/sth** ◊ *The regime was finally overthrown by a popular ~.*

PREP. **in ~** ◊ *The farmers rose in ~.* | **~ against** ◊ *the ~ against the new tax* | **~ by** ◊ *a ~ by backbenchers* (*BrE*) | **~ over** ◊ *the farmers' ~ over imported meat* | **~ within** ◊ *~ within the party*

revolution *noun*

1 changing the political system

ADJ. **successful** | **bloody, violent** ◊ *Thousands of people were killed in the bloody ~ that toppled the government.* | **bloodless, peaceful** | **popular** | **political** | **communist, democratic, socialist, etc.** | **bourgeois, proletarian** | **world** ◊ *Some Marxists still believe that socialism will one day triumph through world ~.*

VERB + REVOLUTION **carry out, fight, foment, stage** ◊ *The activists were charged with fomenting ~.* | **lead** | **crush, put down** | **call for**

REVOLUTION + VERB **break out** | **spread** | **overthrow sth, topple sth** ◊ *the ~ which overthrew the old regime* | **fail** ◊ *the failed 1911 ~*

PREP. **~ against** ◊ *a ~ against communist rule*

PHRASES **the outbreak of the ~** | **~ from above, ~ from below** (= *by people already in power/by people without political power*) | **the threat of ~** (*esp. BrE*)

2 complete change in methods, opinions, etc.

ADJ. **quiet** ◊ *There has been a quiet ~ in the way writing is taught.* | **complete** | **virtual** | **minor** | **agrarian, agricultural, computer, cultural, digital, economic, electronic, industrial, information, Internet, political, scientific, sexual, social, technological**

VERB + REVOLUTION **achieve, begin, bring, bring about, create, launch, spark, start** ◊ *The coming of the Internet brought about a ~ in people's leisure activities.* | **lead** | **go through, undergo** ◊ *Marketing has undergone a ~ in recent years.* | **see** ◊ *The last decade has seen a ~ in telecommunications.* | **embrace, welcome** (*esp. BrE*) ◊ *Doctors have welcomed the fitness ~.*

REVOLUTION + VERB **occur, take place** ◊ *As the 18th century wore on, an agricultural ~ took place.* | **go on** ◊ *There has been a ~ going on in farming during the last five years.* | **transform sth** ◊ *The computer ~ has transformed the workplace.*

PREP. **~ in** ◊ *He achieved a virtual ~ in the way music is recorded.*

3 movement around sth; one complete turn

ADJ. **complete, full** ◊ *One full ~ of the knob will open the hatch.*

VERB + REVOLUTION **complete, make**

PREP. **through a ~** ◊ *The earth turns through one complete ~ every 24 hours.* | **~ about** (*BrE*), **~ around** ◊ *Jupiter makes a complete ~ around the sun every 12 years.*

PHRASES **~s a minute, ~s per minute**

revolver *noun*

ADJ. **service** | **double-action, single-action**

VERB + REVOLVER **load** | **draw, pull out** | **aim** | **fire** | **shoot sb with** | **be armed with, carry**

revulsion *noun*

ADJ. **deep, utter** | **widespread** ◊ *The killing caused widespread ~.* | **moral** (*esp. AmE*)

VERB + REVULSION **be filled with, feel** | **cause** | **express**

PREP. **in ~, with ~** ◊ *The children shrank back from him in ~.* | **~ against** ◊ *public ~ against violence in our society* | **~ at** ◊ *He tried to conceal his instinctive ~ at the idea.* | **~ for** ◊ *He was filled with hatred and ~ for everything about her.* | **~ towards/toward** ◊ *She seems to feel ~ towards/toward her own children.*

PHRASES **a feeling of ~, a sense of ~**

reward *noun*

1 for effort, etc.

ADJ. **great, high, huge, rich** ◊ *Top athletes enjoy rich ~s.* | **fitting, just** | **poor, scant** (*both esp. BrE*) ◊ *It was a poor ~ for years of devoted service.* | **tangible** ◊ *Victory brought glory as well as more tangible ~s.* | **immediate** | **potential** | **economic, financial, material, monetary**

VERB + REWARD **earn, enjoy, gain, get, obtain, reap, receive** ◊

We are just starting to reap the ~s of careful planning. | **bring, have, provide, yield** ◊ *Hard work usually brings its own ~s.* | **promise** | **deserve** ◊ *You deserve a ~ for all your efforts.*
REWARD + NOUN **system**
PREP. **as a ~** ◊ *Give yourself some time off as a ~.* | **~ for** ◊ *a ~ for hard work* ◊ *~s for employees who do their jobs well*
PHRASES **~ enough** ◊ *The look on her face when I told her was ~ enough.* | **~ and punishment** | **be its own ~, have its own ~** ◊ *Virtue is its own ~.*

2 for helping the police
ADJ. **big, huge, large, substantial** | **$20 000, £10 000, etc.** | **cash**
VERB + REWARD **offer, put up** (*esp. BrE*) | **give sb, pay sb** | **claim** | **collect, get, receive**
REWARD + NOUN **money**
PREP. **~ for** ◊ *There is a ~ for information leading to an arrest.*

reward *verb* (often **be rewarded**)

ADV. **amply, generously, greatly** (*esp. AmE*), **handsomely, highly, richly, well** ◊ *You will be handsomely ~ed for your loyalty.* ◊ *highly ~ed occupations* (= those that pay well) | **poorly** | **duly, properly** ◊ *We must make sure that effort is properly ~ed.* | **justly** | **immediately** | **eventually, finally**
PREP. **for** ◊ *He was duly ~ed for his outstanding contribution to the arts.* | **with** ◊ *The rats are ~ed with food when they press the lever.* ◊ *Her efforts were ~ed with a medal.*

rewarding *adj.*

VERBS **be, prove** | **find sth** ◊ *I found it immensely ~ working with the less able children.*
ADV. **extremely, fairly, very, etc.** | **highly, immensely, particularly, richly** | **intrinsically** ◊ *I did not expect the job to be intrinsically ~.* | **potentially** | **mutually** ◊ *a mutually ~ partnership* | **financially** ◊ *a satisfying as well as a financially ~ career*

rewrite *verb*

ADV. **extensively, substantially** (*esp. BrE*) | **completely**
PHRASES **an attempt to ~ sth** ◊ *attempts to ~ history*

rhetoric *noun*

ADJ. **empty, mere** ◊ *Her speech was just empty ~.* | **fiery, inflammatory, powerful, radical** | **government, official, public** | **campaign** | **nationalist, patriotic, political, revolutionary** | **religious**
VERB + RHETORIC **adopt, employ, engage in, resort to, use** ◊ *He was prepared to use militant ~ in attacking his opponents.*
PREP. **behind the ~, beneath the ~** ◊ *Behind all the ~, his relations with the army are tense.* | **despite the ~** ◊ *Little has changed, despite the ~ about reform.* | **~ about, ~ on** ◊ *official ~ on the virtues of large families*

rhyme *noun*

1 using words that have the same sound as each other
ADJ. **internal**
RHYME + NOUN **scheme**
PREP. **in ~** ◊ *a story in ~*
2 word that has the same sound as another
ADJ. **half**
PREP. **~ for** ◊ *Can you think of a ~ for 'tragic'?*
3 short piece of writing with rhyming words
ADJ. **little** | **nonsense** | **nursery, old**
VERB + RHYME **recite, sing** ◊ *The children sang a nursery ~.* | **make up**
PREP. **~ about** ◊ *The kids made up a ~ about a frog.*

rhythm *noun*

ADJ. **fast, slow** | **constant, good, perfect, regular, steady** ◊ *the steady ~ of his heartbeat* | **abnormal, irregular, staccato**,

complex, intricate | **syncopated** | **strong** | **easy** ◊ *Cleaning up the house in the morning fell into an easy ~.* | **natural, normal** ◊ *part of the natural ~ of life* | **driving, insistent, pounding, pulsating** | **African, dance, Latin, reggae, samba, etc.** | **biological, body, circadian** ◊ *My body ~s had not yet adapted to the ten-hour time difference.* | **cardiac, heart** | **daily** ◊ *changes to our daily ~s* | **hypnotic**
VERB + RHYTHM **develop, fall into, get into, settle into** ◊ *She soon settled into a regular ~.* | **have** | **lack** | **create, make** ◊ *Her feet made a steady ~ as she walked.* | **find, get** ◊ *Williams is having trouble finding her ~ on the serve.* | **follow** ◊ *The movie follows the ~s of a year on the farm.* | **keep, maintain** | **break, disrupt** ◊ *Try to disrupt your opponent's ~.* | **lose** | **beat, beat out, clap, tap out** ◊ *Her pencil tapped out a staccato ~ on the desk top.* | **clap to** ◊ *Clap to the ~ of th music.*
RHYTHM + NOUN **section** ◊ *the band's ~ section*
PREP. **in (a) ~** ◊ *He was snapping his fingers in ~.* | **to a/the ~** ◊ *I found myself swaying to the ~ of the music.* | **with a/the ~** ◊ *I like music with a good ~.* | **~ in** ◊ *There's ~ in her movements.*
PHRASES **a lack of ~** | **a sense of ~**

rib *noun*

ADJ. **broken, bruised, cracked, fractured** ◊ *He sustained a broken ~.*
VERB + RIB **break, bruise, crack, crush** | **dig sb in, nudge sb in, poke sb in, prod sb in**
RIB + NOUN **cage** | **injury**
PREP. **against the/your ~s, in the/your ~s** ◊ *I woke him up with a poke in the ~s.*

ribbon *noun*

ADJ. **long** | **wide** | **narrow, thin** | **satin, silk, velvet** | **hair**
... OF RIBBON **length, piece** ◊ *He cut off a length of ~.*
VERB + RIBBON **tie, tie sth with** ◊ *He tied some gold ~ around the present.* ◊ *Her hair was tied back with a black silk ~.* | **tie sth back with, tie sth up with, tie sth with** | **undo, untie** | **cut** ◊ *The Mayor cut a ~ to launch the celebrations.* | **have, wear** ◊ *She had a pink ~ in her hair.* ◊ *She was wearing a pink hair ~.*

rice *noun*

ADJ. **brown, red** (*esp. AmE*), **white** | **long-grain, short-grain** | **basmati** | **wild** | **boiled, fried, steamed** | **pilau** (*esp. BrE*) | **dirty** (*AmE*) (= cooked with chicken liver, etc.) | **sticky**
... OF RICE **grain** | **bag, sack** | **bowl**
VERB + RICE **cultivate, grow, produce** | **harvest** | **boil, cook, steam** | **drain**
RICE + NOUN **crop, production** | **farmer, grower, producer** | **field, paddy** | **cake, pudding, salad, wine** | **pilaf** (*esp. AmE*) | **dish** ◊ *a spicy ~ dish* | **cooker**

rich *adj.*

1 with a lot of money
VERBS **be, feel, look** | **become, get, grow** ◊ *people who want to get ~ quickly* | **make sb** ◊ *This discovery never made her ~.*
ADV. **extremely, fairly, very, etc.** | **enormously, fabulously, filthy** (*informal*), **immensely, incredibly, seriously, stinking** (*informal*) ◊ *He's fabulously ~, one of the richest men in the world.* ◊ *She's filthy ~, you know.* | **relatively** | **newly** ◊ *a newly ~ businessman*
2 containing/providing sth
VERBS **be**
ADV. **extremely, fairly, very, etc.** | **especially, exceptionally, extraordinarily, particularly, unusually** ◊ *the exceptionally ~ fishing grounds of the North Pacific* | **fairly, quite, relatively** | **potentially** | **culturally** ◊ *a culturally ~ nation*
PREP. **in** ◊ *Oranges are ~ in vitamin C.*
3 of food
VERBS **be**
ADV. **very, wonderfully** ◊ *The wine gives the dish a wonderfully ~ aroma.*

ride noun

1 in a vehicle, on a horse, etc.

ADJ. **long, short** ◇ *We have a long ~ ahead of us tomorrow.* | **leisurely** ◇ *We went for a leisurely ~ along the canal.* | **comfortable, easy, smooth** *(all often figurative)* ◇ *The new legislation did not have a smooth ~ through Parliament.* | **bumpy, rough, uncomfortable** ◇ *It was a bumpy ~ along the farm track.* ◇ *The new teacher was given a rough ~ by the class.* *(figurative)* | **wild** ◇ *He took her for a wild ~ on the back of his motorcycle.* | **fun** | **free** ◇ *The rats hitch a free ~ on ships.* | **bike, bus, cab, car, cycle** *(BrE)*, **subway** *(AmE)*, **taxi, train, etc.** | **boat, ferry, plane** | **camel, donkey, pony, etc.**

VERB + RIDE **have, take** ◇ *Visitors can take a ~ on a miniature train.* | **go for** ◇ *She's gone for a ~ on her bike.* | **enjoy**

PREP. **~ from** ◇ *The ~ from our house to my parents' takes about an hour.* | **~ to**

2 at a fair

ADJ. **amusement** *(esp. AmE)*, **amusement-park, carnival** *(esp. AmE)*, **fairground** *(esp. BrE)*, **funfair** *(BrE)*, **helter-skelter** *(BrE)*, **roller-coaster, white-knuckle** ◇ *The day had been a roller-coaster ~ of emotions.* *(figurative)*

VERB + RIDE **go on** ◇ *I went on every ~ in the amusement park.*

3 *(AmE)* **free ride in a car, etc.** → See also LIFT

ADJ. **free**

VERB + RIDE **get** ◇ *She hitched a ~ to the station.* | **ask for, bum** *(informal)*, **catch, get, hitch, thumb** ◇ *I managed to hitch a ~ with someone going in my direction.* | **need, want** | **give sb, offer sb** | **accept**

PHRASES **a ~ back, a ~ home** ◇ *He gave me a ~ home after the party.*

ride verb

ADV. **fast, hard** ◇ *They rode hard all night.* | **slowly** | **well** | **steadily** | **bareback, side-saddle** | **around, away, back, home, off, on, out, over, past** ◇ *At the end of the movie they ~ off into the sunset.* | **together**

VERB + RIDE **learn to** | **teach sb to, teach sb how to**

PREP. **along, down, from, on, through, to, up, etc.** ◇ *We were riding along a dusty trail.*

PHRASES **go horseback riding** *(AmE)*, **go riding**

ridicule noun

ADJ. **public**

VERB + RIDICULE **attract** *(esp. BrE)*, **receive** | **expose sb/sth to, hold sb/sth up to, treat sb/sth with** | **be open to, face, invite, risk** | **endure**

PHRASES **an object of ~, a target for ~, a target of ~** ◇ *The president was becoming an object of ~.*

ridiculous adj.

VERBS **be, feel, look, seem, sound** | **become, get** ◇ *This is getting ~!*

ADV. **really** | **absolutely, completely, downright, quite, simply, totally, utterly** ◇ *It's downright ~ that the library isn't open on Mondays!* | **pretty, rather, somewhat** | **almost** | **a little, slightly, etc.** | **faintly** | **patently** ◇ *The whole idea was patently ~.*

PHRASES **a sense of the ~** *(esp. BrE)* ◇ *The whole situation appealed to her sense of the ~.*

riding noun

ADJ. **horse** *(BrE)*, **horseback** *(AmE)*

VERB + RIDING **go** ◇ *We went horse ~.* *(BrE)* ◇ *We went horseback ~.* *(AmE)*

RIDING + NOUN **boots, breeches, crop, hat** *(esp. BrE)* | **centre** *(BrE)*, **school, stables**

rifle noun

ADJ. **automatic, bolt-action, semi-automatic, single-shot** | **high-powered** | **.22, etc.** | **army, assault, hunting, sniper, sporting** | **air** | **Kalashnikov, M-16, etc.**

VERB + RIFLE **grab** | **load, reload** | **raise** | **aim** | **fire** | **shoot sb/sth with** | **be armed with, carry**

RIFLE + NOUN **barrel, butt** | **bullet, cartridge** | **fire, shot** | **club, range** | **company, platoon** *(both AmE)*

rift noun

ADJ. **deep, growing, serious** | **public** | **family**

VERB + RIFT **cause, create, lead to** | **deepen, widen** ◇ *His actions only deepened the ~ between himself and Congress.* | **heal, mend, repair**

RIFT + VERB **develop, occur, open up** ◇ *A ~ had opened up within the party.* | **deepen** *(esp. BrE)*, **grow, widen**

PREP. **~ among, ~ between** ◇ *new evidence of a ~ between the two countries* | **~ in, ~ within** ◇ *The debate has succeeded only in widening ~s within the Church.* | **~ over** ◇ *a ~ over public spending* | **~ with** ◇ *He tried to heal the ~ with his brother.*

right noun

1 what is morally good

PREP. **in the ~** (= having justice and truth on your side) ◇ *There's no doubt that he's in the ~ on this.*

PHRASES **have ~ on your side** *(esp. BrE)* ◇ *I appealed against the decision because I knew I had ~ on my side.* | **know ~ from wrong** ◇ *Children of that age don't know ~ from wrong.* | **~ and wrong** ◇ *She doesn't understand the difference between ~ and wrong.* | **the ~s and wrongs of sth** ◇ *We sat discussing the ~s and wrongs of the prison system.*

2 entitlement

ADJ. **basic, fundamental, inalienable, unalienable** *(esp. AmE)* ◇ *the basic ~s of all citizens* | **absolute, perfect** ◇ *I have a perfect ~ to park here if I want to.* | **equal** | **exclusive, sole** | **full** | **automatic** ◇ *Any employee who is fired has an automatic ~ to appeal.* | **animal, human** ◇ *animal ~s campaigners* ◇ *human ~s violations* | **constitutional, legal, statutory** | **contractual** | **moral** ◇ *You have a moral ~ to that money.* | **natural** ◇ *A man had a natural ~ to subsist off the crops he grew on his own land.* | **citizenship, civil** ◇ *the civil ~s movement* ◇ *the individual ~s of its constituents* | **individual** ◇ *the individual ~s of its constituents* | **gay, lesbian, women's** | **parental** ◇ *The local authority exercises parental ~s over the children until foster homes are found.* | **abortion** | **visitation, visiting** *(esp. BrE)* ◇ *Many prisoners lost visitation ~s and had their mail confiscated.* | **privacy** ◇ *laws covering privacy ~s* | **squatters'** *(BrE)* ◇ *The teenagers claimed squatters' ~s and were allowed to remain in the building.* | **pension** *(BrE)* | **voting** | **divine, God-given** ◇ *the old idea of the divine ~ of kings* ◇ *I suppose you think you have some God-given ~ to tell me what to do?* | **sovereign** ◇ *We have a sovereign ~ to conduct scientific research on our soil.*

VERB + RIGHT **enjoy, have, retain** ◇ *They have no ~ to come onto my land.* | **assert, claim, demand** | **know** ◇ *You can't do that to me—I know my ~s.* | **establish** ◇ *The new president undertook to establish full ~s for all minorities.* | **fight for, stand up for** ◇ *You should stand up for your ~s and insist that they pay you.* | **reserve** ◇ *I reserve the ~ to leave at any time I choose.* | **gain, get** | **confer on sb, give sb, grant sb** ◇ *We were granted the exclusive ~s to produce the software in Malaysia.* | **extend** ◇ *The government extended voting ~s to everyone over the age of 18.* | **curtail, limit, restrict** ◇ *Abortion ~s have been restricted in some places.* | **exercise** | **enforce** ◇ *The landlord enforced his ~ to enter the property.* | **abdicate** *(esp. AmE)*, **give up, relinquish, renounce** ◇ *He renounced his ~ to the throne.* | **waive** ◇ *They gave me my uncle's money, on condition that I waived all ~s to his property.* | **forfeit, lose** | **affirm, champion, defend, guarantee, preserve, promote, protect, safeguard, support, uphold** ◇ *The constitution guarantees basic human ~s.* ◇ *We promote the ~s of communities.* | **acknowledge, recognize, respect** | **affect, infringe** ◇ *These additional guarantees do not affect your statutory ~s.* *(BrE)* | **deny sb, trample** *(esp. AmE)*, **trample on, violate** | **abolish** | **restore**

PREP. **as of ~** *(BrE)*, **by ~** ◇ *The property belongs to her as of ~.* ◇ *The property belongs to her by ~.* | **by ~ of** ◇ *The Normans ruled England by ~ of conquest.* | **within your ~s** ◇ *You're*

right

acting entirely within your ~s. | **~ of** ◊ the ~ of assembly/ asylum/citizenship/free speech/ownership | **~ over** ◊ He claimed full ~s over the discovery. | **~s for** ◊ equal ~s for all | **~ to** ◊ Do I have any ~ to compensation?
PHRASES **have every ~** ◊ She has every ~ to feel bitter. | **~ of way** ◊ roads where bikes have the ~ of way (= cars must allow them to pass first) ◊ There is no public ~ of way across the fields. (BrE)

3 rights legal authority/claim to sth

ADJ. **film** (esp. BrE), **movie** (esp. AmE), **television** | **translation** | **foreign** | **land, property** | **intellectual property** | **patent** ◊ They acquired her patent ~s. | **inheritance** | **mineral** | **fishing** | **grazing** | **bragging** (AmE) ◊ The team earned the bragging ~s by taking first place in all three events.
VERB + RIGHTS **acquire, buy, get, obtain, purchase, secure** ◊ Altman secured the movie ~s. | **sell** ◊ He sold the movie ~s for $2 million. | **sign away** | **have, hold, own** ◊ Lucas owned the marketing ~s. | **reserve** ◊ He has reserved the movie ~s. | **grant** ◊ The company was granted offshore oil-drilling ~s.
PHRASES **all ~s reserved** (= protected or kept for the owner of the rights) (law)

4 right side/direction

VERB + RIGHT **hang** (AmE, informal), **take** ◊ Take a ~ at the traffic lights.
PREP. **from the ~** ◊ Look out for traffic coming from the ~. | **on the ~** ◊ Ours is the first house on the ~. | **to the ~** ◊ Keep over to the ~. | **to the ~ of** ◊ a hallway immediately to the ~ of the front door
PHRASES **the first, second, etc. ~** ◊ Take the first ~, and then it's the second on your left. | **from left to ~, from ~ to left** ◊ The books are numbered from ~ to left.

5 the right in politics

ADJ. **extreme, far, radical** | **Christian, religious**
PREP. **on the ~** ◊ He's on the extreme ~ of the party.

right adj.

1 acting entirely...

VERBS **be, feel, look, seem, sound, taste** ◊ The meat doesn't taste ~ to me. | **come, go, turn out** ◊ I'm sure it'll all turn out ~ in the end. | **get sth** ◊ He never gets anything ~. | **make sth** ◊ It may be a very easy way to make money, but that doesn't make it ~.
ADV. **absolutely, dead** (esp. BrE), **exactly, just, perfectly, quite** ◊ You're dead ~. There's nothing we can do. ◊ She needs to get everything exactly ~ for her guests. ◊ There's something not quite ~ about these figures. | **almost, more or less, mostly, nearly, partially** ◊ Don't worry about it—that's more or less ~. | **probably** | **morally**
PREP. **about** ◊ You were quite ~ about the weather.
PHRASES **what you think is ~** ◊ James did what he thought was ~.

rigid adj.

1 not able/willing to change

VERBS **appear, be, seem** | **become, grow** ◊ He grew even more ~ and uncompromising as he got older.
ADV. **extremely, fairly, very, etc.** ◊ We operate within fairly ~ parameters. | **entirely** ◊ An entirely ~ system is impractical. | **increasingly** | **excessively, overly, relatively**

2 stiff

VERBS **be, feel, lie, look, sit, stand** ◊ She feigned sleep, lying ~ in bed. | **become, go, turn** | **remain**
ADV. **very** | **absolutely, completely, quite** | **almost**
PREP. **with** ◊ He went absolutely ~ with shock.

rigour (BrE) (AmE rigor) noun

1 strictness

ADJ. **academic, analytical, formal, intellectual, logical, mathematical, methodological, scholarly, scientific** | **full** (BrE) ◊ The crime will be treated with the full ~ of the law.
VERB + RIGOUR/RIGOR **lack** ◊ Their analysis lacks ~. | **apply** ◊ I can only hope that they are applying ~ to these ideas and

discoveries. | **maintain** (esp. AmE) ◊ methodology guidelines to maintain scientific ~
PREP. **with ~** | **~ in** ◊ There is a need for academic ~ in approaching this problem.

2 rigours/rigors severe conditions

VERB + RIGOURS/RIGORS **be subjected to, face** ◊ computers that are subjected to the ~s of the office environment | **avoid, escape** ◊ The town managed to escape the ~s of war. | **handle, stand up to, survive, withstand** ◊ He quickly proved he could handle the ~s of the job. | **prepare sb/sth for, protect (sb/sth) against** ◊ The thick coat of the mountain goat protects it against the ~s of winter.

ring noun

1 piece of jewellery/jewelry

ADJ. **engagement, eternity** (esp. BrE), **promise** (esp. AmE), **purity** (esp. AmE), **signet, wedding** | **diamond, gold, silver, etc.** ◊ She wore a diamond engagement ~. | **belly-button, eyebrow, lip, navel, nipple, nose, tongue, etc.** ◊ She had a small nose ~. | **pinky** (AmE) | **championship, Super Bowl™** (both AmE) ◊ He has earned three Super Bowl ~s in the last four years.
VERB + RING **have on, sport, wear** ◊ He had a signet ~ on his little finger. ◊ His right ear sported a gold ~. | **put on, slide on, slip on** ◊ He slipped the ~ on her finger. | **pull off, slide off, slip off, take off** | **exchange** ◊ They exchange ~s and wedding vows. | **kiss** ◊ She kissed the great ~ of the archbishop of Chicago.
RING + NOUN **finger** (= the finger next to the little finger, esp. on the left hand) | **box** (esp. AmE) ◊ I pulled the small ~ box out of my pocket.

2 circle

ADJ. **inner, innermost** | **outer, outermost** | **concentric** ◊ The street plan of the city has evolved as a series of concentric ~s. | **black, dark** ◊ He had dark ~s around his eyes. | **smoke** ◊ He can blow smoke ~s. | **tree** | **onion** ◊ a plate of onion ~s | **teething** | **napkin**
VERB + RING **form, stand in** ◊ The children formed a ~ around their teacher.
PREP. **~ of** ◊ a ~ of fire/smoke/stones | **in a/the ~** ◊ The children sat on the floor in a ~.

3 where a performance, match, etc. takes place

ADJ. **boxing, bull, circus, show, wrestling**
VERB + RING **enter** ◊ He entered the ~ wearing his usual outfit. | **leave** ◊ Ashton left the ~ with a nasty cut to the right eye.
PREP. **in the ~, into the ~** ◊ He was back in the ~ (= the boxing ring) only a month after the injury.
PHRASES **retire from the ~** (= stop boxing)

4 people involved in sth secret/illegal

ADJ. **drug** (esp. AmE), **drugs** (BrE), **money-laundering, prostitution, smuggling, spy**
VERB + RING **be involved in** | **break up, bust** (esp. AmE) ◊ Customs officials have broken up a major drug ~.

5 (BrE) telephone call

VERB + RING **give sb** ◊ I'll give you a ~ once I get home.

rinse noun

1 act of rinsing

ADJ. **good** | **final** | **cream** | **mouth, oral** (both AmE)
VERB + RINSE **give sth** ◊ Give your hair a good ~ after shampooing it.
PREP. **~ in, ~ with** ◊ a ~ with cold water

2 liquid for hair, teeth, etc.

ADJ. **cream** | **hair** (esp. AmE) | **blue** (esp. BrE) | **mouth, oral** (both esp. AmE)
VERB + RINSE **use** ◊ Use a cream ~ after each shampoo.

rinse verb

ADV. **well** | **thoroughly** ◊ Always ~ your hair thoroughly. | **quickly** | **away, off, out** ◊ She ~d out her coffee cup. ◊ Make sure you ~ all the soap out.
PREP. **from** ◊ He ~d the flour from his hands. | **in** ◊ She ~d her

riot *noun*

ADJ. **major, serious** | **full-scale** | **bloody, violent** | **deadly** (*esp. AmE*) | **inner-city** (*esp. BrE*), **street, urban** | **prison** | **race** | **political, religious** | **anti-American, anti-war, etc.** | **student** | **bread, food** ◊ *Shortages eventually led to food ~s.* | **draft** (*esp. AmE*) ◊ *the violent draft ~s during the Civil War* | **laugh** (*AmE*) ◊ *The movie is a laugh ~.*
VERB + RIOT **cause, incite, instigate, provoke, spark** (*esp. BrE*), **start, trigger** ◊ *The city's housing and unemployment problems provoked serious ~s.* | **put down, quell, stop** | **have** ◊ *The city had the worst race ~ in history.*
RIOT + VERB **begin, break out, erupt, happen, occur, start** ◊ *Prison ~s broke out over worsening conditions.* | **ensue, follow**
RIOT + NOUN **cop** (*esp. AmE*), **police, squad** | **gear, gun** (*esp. AmE*), **helmet** (*esp. AmE*), **shield** | **control**
PREP. **during a/the ~, in a/the ~** ◊ *He was killed in the ~s.* | **~ against, ~ over** ◊ *a ~ against bread prices*
PHRASES **run ~** ◊ *Local youths ran ~ after the attack.*

ripe *adj.*

VERBS **be, feel, look, smell, taste**
ADV. **really, very** ◊ *a really ~ strawberry* | **fully, perfectly, quite** ◊ *Make sure the plums are fully ~ before you eat them.* ◊ *Some of the apples were not quite ~.* | **almost, just, nearly** ◊ *The crops were just about ~.*
PHRASES **~ for the picking, ~ for the plucking, ~ for the taking** (*all usually figurative*) ◊ *The army has withdrawn, leaving the country ~ for the picking.*

ripple *noun*

ADJ. **little, slight, small, tiny**
VERB + RIPPLE **cause, set off** ◊ *The decision caused ~s of concern among the parents.* | **create, make** ◊ *The problems in one place create ~s elsewhere.* ◊ *The Internet is making ~s in people's lives.* | **send** ◊ *I dropped the pebble in the water, sending ~s across the pond.* ◊ *His remarks sent a ~ of laughter through the audience.* | **feel** ◊ *He felt a small ~ of fear pass through him.*
RIPPLE + VERB **pass through sb/sth, run through sb/sth** | **spread across sth** ◊ *He watched the ~s spread across the pool.*
RIPPLE + NOUN **effect**
PREP. **~ of** ◊ *A ~ of unease passed through her.*

ripple *verb*

ADV. **gently** | **out** ◊ *The effects ~ out through the community.*
PREP. **across** ◊ *Small waves ~d gently across the pond.* | **through** ◊ *Shock ~d through her.*

rise *noun*

1 increase

ADJ. **big, dramatic, huge, large, massive, sharp, strong, substantial** | **modest, slight, small** | **threefold, 80%, etc.** | **significant** | **alarming** ◊ *the alarming ~ in obesity in the US* | **abrupt, exponential, rapid, steep, sudden** | **gradual, slow** | **steady, continued, continuing** | **inexorable** (*esp. BrE*) ◊ *the inexorable ~ of oil prices* | **general, overall** | **global, worldwide** | **concomitant** (*formal*), **corresponding** ◊ *the deterioration of our trade balance and the corresponding ~ in protectionism* | **annual, monthly** | **temperature** | **sea-level** | **interest-rate, pay, price, tax, wage** (*all esp. BrE*) ◊ *The union is demanding a pay ~ of 5%.*
PREP. **on the ~** (= rising) ◊ *Crime is on the ~.* | **~ in** ◊ *a twofold ~ in prices* | **~ on** (*BrE*) ◊ *a ~ on last year's levels*

2 becoming more powerful/important

ADJ. **meteoric, quick, spectacular, swift** ◊ *That is the quickest ~ to power I have ever seen.* | **initial** ◊ *the initial ~ of a women's emancipation movement*
PREP. **~ from** ◊ *his ~ from the music halls into a beloved star* | **~ of** ◊ *the ~ of capitalism* | **~ to** ◊ *His swift ~ to the national team surprised everyone.*

PHRASES **the ~ and fall of sth** ◊ *the ~ and fall of the Roman Empire* | **sb's ~ to fame, sb's ~ to power, sb's ~ to prominence** ◊ *her meteoric ~ to fame*

rise *verb*

1 move upwards

ADV. **majestically** ◊ *the cliffs which ~ majestically from the ocean* | **up** ◊ *Lush green mountains ~ up behind the airport.*
PREP. **from** ◊ *Smoke rose from the chimney.* | **into** ◊ *Tall chimneys ~ into the air.*

2 stand up

ADV. **slowly** | **abruptly** ◊ *Adam rose abruptly from the table.* | **stiffly** | **shakily, unsteadily** ◊ *She rose unsteadily to her feet.*
VERB + RISE **make to, try to** ◊ *He made to ~ but found his legs were not strong enough to support him.* | **manage to** ◊ *Somehow he managed to ~ to a sitting position.* | **be unable to**
PREP. **from** ◊ *She rose slowly from her chair to greet us.*
PHRASES **~ to your feet** ◊ *She rose shakily to her feet and looked around.* | **~ to your full height** ◊ *He rose to his full height and leaned across the table.*

3 get out of bed

ADV. **early, late** ◊ *He rose early and went for a walk.*

4 increase

ADV. **considerably, dramatically, markedly, sharply, significantly, steeply, substantially** ◊ *House prices have risen sharply in recent months.* | **a little, slightly, etc.** | **further, higher** | **steadily** | **gradually** | **exponentially, fast, quickly, rapidly** ◊ *The cost of health care is rising faster than ever.*
VERB + RISE **be expected to, be likely to, be predicted to, be projected to, be set to** ◊ *Entry standards into the profession are set to ~ further.* | **be unlikely to** | **begin to, start to** | **continue to**
PREP. **above** ◊ *Air pollution has risen above an acceptable level.* | **by** ◊ *Unemployment has risen by 25 000 this month.* | **from, in** ◊ *Gas rose in price.* | **in line with** ◊ *Pensions will ~ in line with inflation.* | **to** ◊ *Inflation rose from 2% to 5% last year.*

risk *noun*

ADJ. **big, considerable, enormous, grave, great, high, huge, major, serious, significant, substantial, terrible, tremendous** ◊ *high-risk patients* ◊ *a major ~ to livestock* | **good** | **bad, poor** | **low, minimal, slight, small** | **added, additional, elevated, extra, heightened, increased, increasing** | **decreased, reduced** | **genuine, real** | **attendant, inherent, possible, potential** ◊ *Standards of hygiene have fallen, with all the attendant ~s of disease.* ◊ *There are considerable ~s inherent in the policy.* | **long-term, short-term** | **lifetime** | **overall** | **personal** ◊ *They do their patriotic duty at great personal ~.* | **political** ◊ *They run great political ~s by opposing him.* | **relative** | **perceived** ◊ *The perceived ~ is far greater than reality.* | **unacceptable, unnecessary, unreasonable** | **acceptable, moderate** ◊ *its judgment of what constitutes an acceptable ~* | **calculated** ◊ *I take calculated ~s but never gamble.* | **commercial, credit, environmental, financial, fire, health, insurance, safety, security** ◊ *Those old boxes in the corridor are a fire ~.* ◊ *He's a good insurance ~.* | **cancer, cardiovascular, disease, heart-disease, HIV, mortality, stroke** | **suicide** ◊ *He is not a current suicide ~.* | **flight** (*esp. AmE*) ◊ *His lawyer argued that he was not a flight ~* (= that he would not try to run away, leave the country, etc.).
... OF RISK **degree, level** | **element** ◊ *The operation carries an element of ~.*
VERB + RISK **face, run, take** ◊ *If you don't study, you run the ~ of failing.* ◊ *I'm not prepared to take risks—I want the equipment thoroughly checked.* | **carry, create, entail, incur, involve, pose, present** ◊ *Pollutants in the river pose a real ~ to the fish.* | **heighten, increase, raise** | **double** ◊ *Smoking doubles the ~ of having a stroke.* | **cut, decrease, diminish, lessen, limit, lower, minimize, mitigate, reduce** ◊ *Com-*

panies can mitigate the ~s of losing valuable data. | **avoid, eliminate** | **assess, calculate, determine, evaluate, measure, weigh, weigh up** (BrE) ◇ The directors will have to assess our credit ~. ◇ You have to weigh ~s and benefits. | **know, understand** ◇ I think you know the ~s of your choices. | **identify** ◇ They try to identify every possible ~. | **indicate** | **estimate, predict** | **manage** ◇ Farmers invest in irrigation to manage ~ in drought years. | **address** ◇ solutions to address security ~s more effectively | **accept, assume, bear** ◇ The lawyers are assuming all the financial ~. | **spread** ◇ These funds spread the ~ among different countries. | **outweigh** ◇ The benefits outweigh the ~s. | **justify** ◇ The rewards may well justify the ~s. | **be considered** ◇ He is no longer considered a security ~ in the State of California.

RISK + VERB **outweigh sth**

RISK + NOUN **group** ◇ Miners are a high ~ group for certain types of gastric cancer. | **factor** ◇ Cigarette smoking is a ~ factor for this disease. | **assessment** | **analysis** | **level** ◇ investors' assessments of overall ~ levels | **category** ◇ Young male drivers are a higher ~ category compared to mature ladies and even women of the same age. | **mitigation** (esp. AmE), **reduction** | **management** | **manager** | **aversion, avoidance** ◇ the strategies of ~ avoidance that people practice in their everyday lives | **tolerance** ◇ Consider your own ~ tolerance. How many chances are you willing to take? | **behaviour/behavior** (esp. AmE) ◇ efforts to persuade the public to reduce ~s behavior | **premium** ◇ a big jump in the ~ premium on corporate bonds

PREP. **at ~** ◇ ~ to put someone's life at ~ | **at ~ from, at ~ of** ◇ Journalists in the zone are at serious ~ of being kidnapped. | **at ~ for** (esp. AmE) ◇ Children are at greater ~ for these diseases. | **at the ~ of** ◇ At the ~ of sounding rude, don't you think you'd better change for the party? | **at ~ to** ◇ He saved the child at considerable ~ to himself. | **by** ◇ He knew he was taking a big ~ by going skiing. | **for** (esp. AmE) ◇ a reduced ~ for heart disease | **from** ◇ a ~ from contaminated water | **in** ◇ I was taking a big ~ in lending her the money. | **~ of** ◇ a higher ~ of stomach cancer | **~ to** ◇ a ~ to health

PHRASES **at your own ~** ◇ The building is unsafe—enter at your own ~. | **an increase in ~, a reduction in ~** | **~s and benefits, ~s and rewards** ◇ the ~s and benefits of a drug

risk verb

VERB + RISK **cannot, dare not, not want to, would not** ◇ I simply can't ~ being seen there. ◇ I didn't want to ~ being late. | **be prepared to, be willing to** ◇ He was prepared to ~ everything in order to achieve his ambition. | **choose to, decide to** | **refuse to** ◇ I refuse to ~ being hurt.

PREP. **for** ◇ I am not ~ing my neck for anyone! | **on** ◇ I wouldn't ~ my money on this investment.

PHRASES **~ it** ◇ I knew I would be in trouble if I was found out, but I decided to ~ it anyway. | **~ life and limb** ◇ the brave tourist who ~s life and limb for adventure | **~ losing sth** ◇ families who ~ losing their homes

risky adj.

VERBS **be, look, prove, seem, sound** | **become, get** | **consider sth, deem sth**

ADV. **extremely, fairly, very, etc.** | **especially, highly, particularly** ◇ It all sounds highly ~ to me. | **increasingly** | **a little, slightly, etc.** | **inherently** ◇ All business activities are inherently ~. | **potentially** | **financially, politically**

ritual noun

ADJ. **ancient, primitive** | **traditional** | **daily, nightly** | **Sunday, etc.** | **family** ◇ Eating around the table was a family ~ that could not be broken. | **tribal** | **little** ◇ A cognac before bed is one of our little nightly ~s. | **elaborate, solemn** | **bizarre, strange** | **empty** ◇ Bargaining at the markets is now just an empty ~. | **secret** ◇ secret ~s in the sacred forest | **magical, religious** | **public, social** | **sacred** | **Catholic, Hindu, Jewish, etc.** | **pagan, satanic, shamanic, voodoo** | **burial, cleansing, courtship, fertility, funerary, healing, initiation, mating, mourning, purification** | **hazing** (AmE)

VERB + RITUAL **conduct, do, enact, go through, hold, perform** ◇ She had to go through the ~ of kissing the toys before her son would go to sleep. ◇ ~s performed by druids on Midsummer's Day | **undergo** ◇ Boys undergo a circumcision ~ to usher them into adulthood. | **follow, observe, practise/ practice** ◇ Their funerals follow the ~s of the Catholic church. ◇ They practise/practice certain ~s in connection with rites of passage. | **complete** ◇ It takes several days to complete the ~. | **begin** ◇ Jake began the evening ~ of asking about everyone's day. | **make** ◇ He makes an elaborate ~ of washing the car. | **become** ◇ Her visits to her aged father have become a ~.

RITUAL + VERB **take place**

PREP. **in a/the ~** ◇ Women's roles in the ~s of many religions have been limited.

rival noun

ADJ. **bitter, close, deadly** (BrE), **fierce, formidable, great, hated, powerful, serious, tough** | **biggest, chief, largest, leading, main, major, nearest, primary, principal, top** (also **arch-rival**) | **long-time, old, traditional** ◇ They're old political ~s. | **former, one-time** | **new** ◇ The business needed to revive profits and compete with new ~s. | **potential** ◇ She is now regarded as the greatest potential ~ to Hu. | **jealous** | **friendly** ◇ Those two have been friendly ~s since they first met. | **romantic** ◇ They wind up as romantic ~s for the same woman. | **foreign, international** ◇ The company is well equipped to compete with its international ~s. | **business, political** | **presidential** | **Conservative, Democratic, etc.**

VERB + RIVAL **have** ◇ She has no ~s for the job. | **face** ◇ The company faces big ~s in Europe and Asia. | **beat, defeat** | **eliminate** ◇ He eliminated his ~s with brutal efficiency.

RIVAL + NOUN **candidate** | **clan, faction, gang, group, tribe** | **company, firm, organization** | **bid, offer** | **claim** | **theory**

PREP. **~ for** ◇ They were ~s for her love. | **~ in** ◇ They were ~s in love. | **~ to** ◇ Grand it may be, but this cathedral is no ~ to the great cathedral of Amiens.

rivalry noun

ADJ. **big, bitter, fierce, great, heated, intense** ◇ the bitter ~ that existed between them | **ancient, long-standing, old** | **traditional** | **friendly** | **petty** | **international, local, regional** | **internal, inter-service** (esp. AmE) | **sibling** | **ethnic, personal, political, professional, religious** ◇ Bitter ethnic rivalries within the region have grown in recent years. | **football**

RIVALRY + VERB **grow**

PREP. **~ among, ~ between** ◇ the increasing ~ among competitors in the industry ◇ ~ between the army and the police | **~ for** ◇ ~ for the party leadership | **~ in** ◇ the fiercest ~ in professional sports | **~ over** ◇ ~ over who is to head the delegation | **~ with** ◇ ~ with foreign companies

river noun

ADJ. **broad, great, large, long, mighty, wide** ◇ the mighty River Nile ◇ The ~ was too wide to swim across comfortably. | **major** ◇ major ~s such as the Congo | **little, narrow, small** | **deep** | **shallow** | **high** ◇ The ~ is still high after the recent rain. | **low** | **fast-flowing** | **raging, rushing, white-water, wild** | **flowing, free-flowing** | **lazy, slow-moving, sluggish** | **frozen, icy** | **meandering, winding** | **swollen** ◇ The ~ was swollen after the floods. | **navigable** ◇ The ~ is navigable by vessels of up to 90 tons. | **underground** | **coastal, mountain** | **freshwater** | **tidal** | **polluted** | **sacred** ◇ the Ganges and other sacred ~s | **salmon**

VERB + RIVER **cross, ford, get across** ◇ We crossed the ~ by boat. ◇ How are we going to get across the ~? | **swim** ◇ We had to swim the ~. which is deep and very rapid. | **follow** ◇ I had decided to follow the ~ to my destination. | **bridge** ◇ They've bridged the ~ at four points. | **span** ◇ The bridge once spanned the ~ Serein. | **dam** ◇ Wildlife groups are protesting against the proposal to dam the ~. | **divert** ◇ plans to divert the ~ further north | **dredge** ◇ They're dredging the ~ to make it safer for larger boats. | **navigate** ◇ The rocks make the ~ hard to navigate.

RIVER + VERB **flow, run, wind** ◇ *This ~ flows into the Gulf of Mexico.* ◇ *A ~ runs through the field.* ◇ *The ~ winds its way through the hills.* | **rise** ◇ *The ~ has risen with the rains.* ◇ *The ~ rises in central Africa.* | **be in flood** (*BrE*), **burst its banks, flood (sth), overflow sth** ◇ *The ~ had overflowed its banks.* | **dry up** ◇ *This ~ dried up long ago.*

RIVER + NOUN **bank** | **bed, bottom** | **water** | **level** ◇ *when the ~ level is low* | **basin, channel, delta, mouth, plain, valley** | **system** | **crossing** | **barge, boat, steamer** | **traffic** | **cruise, trip** | **rock** (*esp. AmE*) ◇ *as smooth as ~ rocks* | **city, port, town** ◇ *a ~ town in Borneo*

PREP. **across a/the ~** ◇ *There's a bridge across the ~.* | **along a/the ~, down a/the ~** ◇ *We walked along the ~.* ◇ *They sailed down the ~.* | **down by a/the ~, down to a/the ~** ◇ *Let's go down to the ~ at sunset.* | **into a/the ~** ◇ *He dived into the ~.* | **in a/the ~** ◇ *Trout live in this ~.* | **on a/the ~** ◇ *There was a boat on the ~.* | **up a/the ~** ◇ *We were sailing up the ~.* | **~ of** (*figurative*) ◇ *a ~ of lava*

PHRASES **the banks, bottom, middle, side, surface, etc. of a ~, the river's edge** ◇ *They were waiting for us on the other side of the ~.* | **a bend in the ~** | **the course of a ~, the direction of a ~**

road noun

ADJ. **broad, wide** | **narrow** | **busy, congested** | **clear, deserted, empty, lonely, quiet** ◇ *Let's leave when the ~s are clear.* | **direct** ◇ *The airport's near here but there's no direct ~.* | **straight** | **curvy** (*AmE*), **twisting, twisty, winding, windy** | **steep** | **scenic** | **asphalt, blacktop** (*AmE*), **cobbled, cobblestone** (*esp. AmE*), **flat, gravel, metalled** (*esp. BrE*), **paved, Tarmac™** (*esp. BrE*) | **good, smooth** | **passable** ◇ *All main ~s were passable with care.* | **bad, bumpy** (*often figurative*), **dirt** (*esp. AmE*), **poor, rough, rutted, unmade** (*BrE*), **unpaved** ◇ *a bumpy ~ through the forest* | **dangerous, difficult, hard, rocky, tough** (*all usually figurative*) ◇ *Bringing up a handicapped child can be a long and hard ~.* | **easy** (*often figurative*) ◇ *It isn't going to be an easy ~ for him.* | **safe** | **slick** (*AmE*), **slippery** | **dusty, icy, muddy, snowy, wet** | **fast** | **dark** (*often figurative*) | **long** (*often figurative*), **main, major, national, trunk** (*BrE*) | **back, local, minor** (*esp. BrE*), **secondary, small, unclassified** (*BrE*) | **old** ◇ *the old dirt ~ to the village* | **new** ◇ *the building of new ~s* | **one-lane, two-lane, etc.** | **single-track** (*BrE*) | **country, rural** | **urban** (*esp. BrE*) | **county** (*esp. AmE*) | **residential** (*esp. BrE*) | **tree-lined** | **private, public** | **dead-end** (*often figurative*) ◇ *The government's policy on education is a dead-end ~.* | **open** ◇ *We'll be able to go faster once we're out on the open ~.* | **right, wrong** ◇ *We took the wrong ~ and had to turn back.* ◇ *It does appear we are on the right ~ to success.* (*figurative*) | **east-west, etc.** | **canyon** (*AmE*), **coast** (*esp. BrE*), **coastal, country, desert, forest, mountain** | **logging** | **airport** | **access, arterial** (*esp. BrE*), **bypass, feeder, frontage** (*AmE*), **perimeter, ring** (*BrE*), **side, slip** (*BrE*) | **high, low** | **toll**

VERB + ROAD **follow, go down** ◇ *Follow the ~ around to the left.* ◇ *We have discussed privatization, but we would prefer not to go down that ~.* (*figurative*) | **take, turn into** (*BrE*), **turn onto** ◇ *Take the next ~ on the right.* ◇ *Turn right into Harpes Road.* ◇ *Turn left onto the coastal ~.* | **turn off** | **pull (out) into** (*BrE*), **pull (out) onto** ◇ *He was hit by another car as he pulled out onto the ~.* | **leave, pull off** ◇ *They stopped in a forest, leaving the main ~.* ◇ *The car left the ~ and slid to a halt.* ◇ *I pulled off the ~ for a rest.* | **drive** (*esp. AmE*), **travel** (*also figurative*), **walk** (*esp. AmE, often figurative*) ◇ *I must have driven the back ~s for half an hour.* ◇ *They have travelled/traveled the long, lonely ~ of exclusion.* ◇ *He walks a ~ filled with shadow and doubt.* | **choose** ◇ *We have chosen the ~ of peace.* | **cross, get across** | **join, meet** (*esp. AmE*) ◇ *The track joins the main ~ just south of the town.* | **block, block off** (*esp. AmE*), **blockade, close, cordon off** (*BrE*) ◇ *Angry farmers blocked the ~ with their tractors.* ◇ *Police cordoned off the ~ and diverted commuter traffic.* | **clog, clog up** (*BrE*) ◇ *Traffic clogs the ~s.* | **clear** ◇ *The crowd eventually cleared the ~.* ◇ *They cleared the ~s of snow.* | **build, construct, rebuild** | **maintain, mend** (*BrE*), **repair** | **pave, resurface** (*BrE*), **surface** (*BrE*) | **widen** | **line** ◇ *Huge eucalyptuses lined the ~.* ◇ *The crowds lined the ~s for his triumphal entry.*

ROAD + VERB **go, lead, run** ◇ *Where does this ~ go?* ◇ *The ~*

runs parallel to the river. | **stretch** ◇ *the ~ stretched out before them.* ◇ *The ~ stretches off into the distance.* | **bend** (*BrE*), **curve, turn, twist, wind** ◇ *The ~ twists and turns up the hillside.* | **climb** ◇ *The ~ climbs steeply from the beach.* | **cross sth** ◇ *The ~ crosses the river further up the valley.* | **connect sth, link sth** ◇ *the ~ connecting Irado and Calla Ayda* | **branch** (*esp. BrE*), **branch off, fork** ◇ *Our ~ branches off to the left just past the woods.* | **narrow, widen** ◇ *The ~ narrowed and turned into this dirt trail.*

ROAD + NOUN **atlas, map** | **markings, sign** | **intersection, junction** | **bridge, crossing, tunnel** | **closure** | **block** (*usually roadblock*), **blockade** | **bump, hump** (*BrE*) (*usually speed humps* in *BrE*, *speed bumps* in *AmE*) ◇ *Road bumps have been laid down to limit the speed of cars.* | **infrastructure, network, system** ◇ *the surrounding ~ system* | **layout** (*BrE*), **access, link** ◇ *There is still no ~ access to the island.* | **development, plan** (*esp. BrE*), **programme/program** (*esp. BrE*), **project, proposal** (*BrE*), **scheme** (*BrE*) | **building, construction** ◇ *loans for ~ construction and infrastructure development* | **maintenance, repair** ◇ *the cost of ~ maintenance* | **improvements** | **surface** | **journey** (*esp. BrE*), **trip** (*informal, esp. AmE*) | **accident, crash** (*esp. BrE*), **smash** (*BrE*), **traffic accident** | **safety** | **deaths, fatalities** (*both esp. BrE*) | **conditions** | **salt** | **traffic, vehicles** | **race** | **racer** | **course** | **bike** | **test** | **engineer** (*esp. BrE*) | **haulier** (*BrE*) (**hauler** in *AmE*) | **haulage** (*BrE*) | **sweeper** (*esp. BrE*) | **pricing, tax** (*in the UK*), **toll** (*esp. BrE*) ◇ *Road tax is set to rise in next month's budget.* ◇ *Road tolls can make driving expensive.* | **user** | **hog** (*informal*) | **warrior** (*esp. AmE*) | **crew** | **rage** ◇ *A man has been stabbed to death in a road-rage attack.* | **manners, sense** (*both esp. BrE*) ◇ *poor driving standards and lack of ~ manners* | **kill** (*usually roadkill*) ◇ *scavengers that feed off roadkill* | **rash** (= scratches on the skin from falling from a bicycle) (*AmE*) ◇ *She was treated for ~ rash.* | **movie**

PREP. **across the ~** ◇ *The house across the ~ is for sale.* | **along the ~** ◇ *He was walking along the ~ when he was attacked.* | **by ~** ◇ *It takes three hours by ~* (= driving). | **down the ~, up the ~** ◇ *They live down the ~ from us.* | **in the ~** ◇ *There was a dog in the ~ so we stopped.* ◇ *We live in Pinsley Road.* (*BrE*) ◇ *We live on Pinsley Road.* (*BrE, AmE*) | **into the ~** ◇ *She stepped out into the ~ without looking.* | **off the ~** ◇ *My car's off the ~ at the moment while I recondition the engine.* | **on a/the ~** ◇ *There's something lying on the ~.* ◇ *There was a lot of traffic on the ~ this morning.* ◇ *on the ~ to Damascus* ◇ *My car is back on the ~* (= is working) *again.* ◇ *We'd been on the ~ since dawn and needed a rest.* | **~ along, ~ over, ~ through** ◇ *the main ~ through the town* | **~ from, ~ to** ◇ *the ~ to Acapulco* ◇ *to be on the ~ to recovery/success* (*figurative*)

PHRASES **at the side of the ~** (*esp. BrE*), **by the side of the ~, on the side of the ~** | **the bottom of the ~** (*BrE*), **the top of the ~** | **the end of the ~** (*often figurative*) ◇ *This latest disagreement could mean the end of the ~ for the band.* | **a bend in the ~, a fork in the ~, a turn in the ~** ◇ *We came to a fork in the ~.* | **the middle of the ~** ◇ *A dog was sitting in the middle of the ~, so we stopped.* | **the middle ~** (*figurative*) ◇ *Kaufman has opted to travel the middle ~.* | **a stretch of ~** ◇ *a notoriously dangerous stretch of ~* | **hit the ~** ◇ *The following spring I hit the ~.*

roadblock noun

1 barrier across a road

ADJ. **army, military, police**

VERB + ROADBLOCK **set up** ◇ *Police set up a ~ on the road to the capital.* | **remove**

PREP. **at a/the ~** ◇ *They were stopped at a ~ leaving the city.* | **through a/the ~** ◇ *The truck drove through the ~ at 100 mph.*

2 (AmE) problem

ADJ. **big, major** ◇ *Funding has been a major ~.* | **potential** ◇ *The proposed merger is already facing potential ~s.* | **political**

VERB + ROADBLOCK **remove** | **encounter, hit** ◇ *The company*

hit its first ~ last year. | **face** | **create, put up, throw up** ◊ *This bill would create a ~ for women.* | **overcome**
PREP. **up against a ~** ◊ *No sooner had they celebrated their victory than they came up against a new ~.* | **~ in** ◊ *I was hitting a ~ in my personal work.* | **~ to** ◊ *self-defeating beliefs and other ~s to happiness*

roam *verb*

ADV. **free, freely** ◊ *The animals were allowed to ~ free.* | **widely** ◊ *the wild dog's instinct to ~ widely* | **aimlessly** ◊ *He'd ~ed aimlessly for a few hours.* | **about** (*esp. BrE*), **around**
VERB + ROAM **allow sb/sth to, let sb/sth**
PREP. **about** (*esp. BrE*), **around** ◊ *They're ~ing around the countryside.* | **across** ◊ *Wild camels ~ across the country.* | **over** ◊ *Her eyes ~ed over him, assessing him.* | **through** ◊ *Bears ~ through the town at night.*
PHRASES **the freedom to ~, the right to ~** (*esp. BrE*) ◊ *Ramblers are calling for the right to ~ to be made law.* | **~ the earth** ◊ *when dinosaurs ~ed the earth*

roar *noun*

ADJ. **almighty, deafening, ear-splitting, great, huge, loud, mighty, thunderous, tremendous** ◊ *The lion let out a great ~.* | **angry, fierce, terrible** ◊ *The shouting grew into an angry ~.* | **deep, low** | **dull, faint, muffled** | **throaty** ◊ *the throaty ~ of the engine* | **distant** ◊ *the distant ~ of the sea* | **sudden**
VERB + ROAR **give, let out** | **hear** | **become** ◊ *The low rumble had become a ~.*
ROAR + VERB **erupt, go up** ◊ *A mighty ~ went up from the crowd as the home team scored.* | **echo** ◊ *The sound of a distant ~ echoed over the plains.* | **fill sth** ◊ *A loud ~ filled the air around them.*
PREP. **above the ~, over the ~** ◊ *She couldn't make herself heard over the ~ of the engines.* | **with a ~** ◊ *The car sped off with an almighty ~.* | **~ from** ◊ *There was a crash and a ~ from the kitchen.* | **~ of** ◊ *a ~ of applause* ◊ *a ~ of laughter*
→ Note at SOUND

robber *noun*

ADJ. **armed, masked** (*esp. BrE*) | **bank, train** | **grave, tomb** | **highway** | **would-be** (*esp. BrE*) ◊ *The would-be ~ fled empty-handed.*
... OF ROBBERS **band, gang**
VERB + ROBBER **chase, hunt** (*BrE*), **search for** ◊ *Police are searching for the ~s.* | **catch**
ROBBER + VERB **hold sb/sth up** ◊ *Robbers held up a bank at gunpoint.* | **snatch sth** (*esp. BrE*), **steal sth, take sth** | **escape with sth, get away with sth, make off with sth** ◊ *Robbers escaped with $30 000.*

robbery *noun*

ADJ. **attempted, botched, bungled** (*esp. BrE*), **failed** | **armed** | **bank, highway, street** (*esp. BrE*), **train**
VERB + ROBBERY **commit, take part in** | **foil** ◊ *He was shot as he tried to foil a bank ~.*
ROBBERY + NOUN **attempt** | **charge** | **suspect**
PHRASES **~ with violence** (*BrE, law*) ◊ *He was sentenced to four years in prison for ~ with violence.*
→ Note at CRIME (for more verbs)

robe *noun*

ADJ. **long** | **loose, voluminous** | **billowing, flowing** ◊ *a ghostly figure in flowing ~s of white* | **rich** ◊ *The emperor was clad in a rich ~ encrusted with jewels.* | **embroidered** | **traditional** | **ceremonial, choir** (*esp. AmE*), **clerical, coronation** (often with *robes*), **graduation** (*AmE*), **judicial, priestly, royal**
VERB + ROBE **don, slip on** | **wear**
PREP. **in a/the ~** ◊ *an old man swathed in ~s*
→ Special page at CLOTHES

rock *noun*

1 hard, stony part of the earth

ADJ. **hard, solid** ◊ *Solid ~ is broken down by weathering.* | **soft** | **jagged, rough, sharp** | **smooth** | **flat** | **slippery** ◊ *The ~s were slippery as I tried to climb them.* | **weathered** | **bare, barren, exposed** ◊ *Ahead the vegetation broke into bare ~.* | **sheer, steep** ◊ *The river runs between walls of sheer ~.* | **overhanging** | **liquid, molten** | **crushed** | **loose** ◊ *an avalanche of loose ~* | **falling** ◊ *Signs warn of the perils of falling ~.* | **igneous, metamorphic, sedimentary, volcanic** | **permeable** (*esp. BrE*), **porous**
... OF ROCK **chunk, lump, piece, slab**
VERB + ROCK **form** | **climb, skip** (*AmE*), **skip over** ◊ *Lars taught me to skip ~s.*
ROCK + VERB **form** ◊ *~s that formed beneath the sea* | **jut out** ◊ *A great ~ jutted out into the water.*
ROCK + NOUN **type** | **formation, structure** | **layer, strata** | **cliff, ledge, outcrop, outcropping** (*AmE*) | **face, surface, wall** | **crevice** | **debris, dust, fragment, sample, specimen** | **fall, slide** ◊ *The path had been blocked by a ~ fall.* | **crystal, salt** | **climber, climbing** | **pool** (*esp. BrE*) (usually **tide pool** in *AmE*) ◊ *Children were looking for crabs in the ~ pools.* | **quarry** | **pile** | **art, carvings, painting** | **garden**
PHRASES **as hard as a ~** (*esp. AmE*), **as hard as ~** (*esp. BrE*) | **a layer of ~, an outcrop of ~** ◊ *The castle is perched on a massive outcrop of ~.* | **sleep like a ~** (*AmE*) ◊ *You slept like a ~ last night.*

2 (*AmE*) **small stone; stone that can be thrown**

ADJ. **large, small** | **heavy**
... OF ROCKS **mound, pile**
VERB + ROCK **pick up** | **pelt sb with, throw** ◊ *Protesters pelted the soldiers with ~s.* ◊ *They used to throw ~s at neighborhood dogs.*

3 music

ADJ. **live** | **acid, alternative, arena** (*esp. AmE*), **blues, classic, country, folk, garage, glam, hard, heavy, indie, mainstream, modern, pop, progressive, psychedelic, punk, soft** | **60s, 80s, etc.**
ROCK + NOUN **anthem, ballad, number, riff, song, tune** | **lyrics, music** | **album, CD, record, video** | **act, band, group, outfit** | **concert, festival, gig** (*esp. BrE*) | **musical, opera, show, soundtrack** | **club, venue** | **scene** ◊ *one of the biggest bands on the ~ scene* | **artist, drummer, guitarist, musician, singer** | **guitar** | **hero, icon, idol, legend, star** | **stardom** | **critic** ◊ *influential ~ critics* | **fan** | **chick** ◊ *She was a ~ chick through and through.* | **culture, history** | **radio, station** ◊ *Ryan changed the radio to a ~ station.*
PHRASES **~ and roll** ◊ *the king of ~ and roll*

rock *verb*

ADV. **violently** ◊ *The boat ~ed violently in the huge waves.* | **gently, slightly** ◊ *She gently ~ed the baby in her arms.* ◊ *The boat ~ed slightly.* | **slowly** | **back and forth, backwards and forwards, from side to side, to and fro** ◊ *He ~ed back and forth in his chair.*

rocket *noun*

1 spacecraft

ADJ. **space**
VERB + ROCKET **launch**
ROCKET + VERB **blast off, lift off, take off** | **land**
ROCKET + NOUN **booster, engine, motor** | **fuel** | **launch** | **flight** | **ship** | **scientist** (*often humorous*) ◊ *You don't have to be a ~ scientist* (= very clever) *to do this job.* | **science** (*often humorous*) ◊ *Come on, it's not ~ science.*

2 weapon

ADJ. **long-range** | **anti-aircraft, anti-tank** | **artillery** | **guided, unguided** | **conventional, nuclear**
VERB + ROCKET **fire, shoot**
ROCKET + VERB **explode** | **hit sth, strike sth** | **fire, launch**
ROCKET + NOUN **attack** | **launcher, pod** | **artillery**

role noun

1 in a play, film/movie, etc.

ADJ. **lead, leading, starring, title** ◇ *He has the starring ~ in the movie.* ◇ *She sings the title ~ in Tosca.* | **big** ◇ *Lee began to get big ~s in movies.* | **principal** | **dramatic** | **meaty, substantial** ◇ *the chance to sink her teeth into the meaty ~ of femme fatale Margaret* | **plum** ◇ *This is the plum ~ in the play.* | **small** | **supporting** | **lesser** | **comic, tragic** | **female, male** ◇ *a starring female ~* | **cameo** | **stereotypical** ◇ *one of his stereotypical action hero ~s* | **thankless** ◇ *Ethan Hawke does a solid job in a thankless ~.* | **film** (*esp. BrE*), **movie** (*esp. AmE*), **television, TV**
VERB + ROLE **assume, perform, play, take** ◇ *In the series, Smith assumes the ~ of the go-between.* ◇ *John's playing the leading ~ in this year's play.* | **underplay** ◇ *Walken carefully underplays the ~.* | **fill** ◇ *The supporting ~s are filled by British actors.* | **reprise** ◇ *Most of the original cast are reprising their ~s.* | **handle** ◇ *Sbaraglia handles this difficult ~ well.* | **get, land, win** ◇ *It took her three years to land her first film ~.* | **cast sb in** | **interpret** ◇ *She interprets the ~ as more tragic than I expected.* | **dance, sing** ◇ *Dean Ely sings the title ~.*
PREP. **in the ~** (of) ◇ *He was very good in the ~.*

2 position and importance

ADJ. **big, huge, large, substantial** ◇ *Small businesses have a substantial ~ to play in keeping the economy buoyant.* | **important, influential, instrumental, integral, powerful, prominent, significant, special** ◇ *an area where national rivalries play a powerful ~* | **central, dominant, key, lead, leading, main, major, pivotal, primary** ◇ *Migrant workers played a central ~ in the state's prosperity.* | **critical, crucial, decisive, essential, fundamental, vital** ◇ *Economic factors played a decisive ~ in the outcome of the war.* | **useful** | **expanded, greater, increased** ◇ *the expanded ~ of the federal government* | **diminished, limited, small** ◇ *the limited ~ of women in the church* | **minor, secondary, subordinate, subservient** | **backup, supporting** ◇ *He may have to settle for a backup ~.* | **constructive, full** (*esp. BrE*), **meaningful, positive, useful, valuable** | **active, proactive** | **passive** | **direct** | **clear, defined, distinct, exact, particular, specific, unique** ◇ *Every member of staff must have a clear ~.* ◇ *the specific ~ of calcium in preventing disease* | **different, dual, multiple, various** ◇ *She has a dual ~ as principal and French teacher.* ◇ *Many staff perform multiple ~s.* | **traditional** | **changing** | **conflicting** ◇ *her conflicting ~s as mother and manager of a large company* | **advisory, consultative, managerial, regulatory, supervisory** | **leadership** | **maternal, parental, parenting, paternal** | **protective** ◇ *Their brother plays a protective ~.* | **caregiving** (*AmE*) ◇ *The caregiving ~ is still overwhelmingly a female one.* | **economic, educational, military, peacekeeping, political, social, strategic** ◇ *the economic ~ of small towns* ◇ *Adult education often serves an important social ~.* | **symbolic** | **possible, potential** ◇ *Supervising elections is a possible ~ for the UN.* | **gender** ◇ *essays that question gender ~s in a patriarchal culture* | **female, male** ◇ *the views prevalent in society about female ~s*
VERB + ROLE **have, occupy, perform, play, serve** ◇ *Regional managers occupy a crucial ~ in developing a strategic framework.* | **provide** | **provide sb/sth with** | **adopt, assume, take, take on** ◇ *I've had to take on the ~ of mother in her absence.* | **accept** ◇ *I accepted the executive editor ~ at the magazine.* ◇ *They have to be willing to accept their ~s as caregivers and not managers.* | **resume** | **embrace, relish** ◇ *She embraced her ~ as ruler of the country.* | **fulfil/fulfill** ◇ *The fighting has prevented the UN troops from fulfilling their ~ as peacekeepers.* | **fill** ◇ *He filled several governmental ~s.* | **handle** ◇ *We are waiting to see if he can handle an expanded ~.* | **carve out, establish** ◇ *He is trying to carve out a new ~ for himself.* | **assign sb, cast sb in, give sb** ◇ *He has been cast in the ~ of chief apologist for the government.* | **reverse** ◇ *Traditional gender ~s are reversed in their household.* | **find** ◇ *We need to find a useful ~ for the volunteers in the campaign.* | **clarify, define, elucidate, redefine** ◇ *a clearly defined ~ within the group* | **analyse/analyze, assess, evaluate, examine, explore, investigate** ◇ *The paper examines the ~ of various institutions.* | **emphasize,**

highlight, stress ◇ *The authors emphasized the ~ of the slave trade in the economic development of the New World.* | **understand** ◇ *We need to better understand the ~ of cold regions in the global climate system.* | **acknowledge, appreciate, recognize** ◇ *Politicians acknowledge the key ~s that young people play in the country.* | **determine, identify** ◇ *We will meet with them to determine individual ~s.* | **address** ◇ *He addressed the ~ of tradition in design.* | **downplay** ◇ *Thomas downplays the ~ of these letters as historical evidence.* | **expand** ◇ *They decided to expand the ~ that new technologies play at the hospital.* | **increase, strengthen** ◇ *He is looking for ways to strengthen his ~ in the business.* | **fit** ◇ *I feel I can fit any ~ this team needs me to.* | **swap** (*esp. BrE*), **switch**
ROLE + NOUN **model** | **reversal** | **expectation** (*esp. AmE*) ◇ *methods for exploring gender ~ expectations* | **conflict** (*esp. AmE*) ◇ *This ~ conflict can quickly escalate.*
PREP. **in a/the ~** ◇ *She has joined the team in a consultative ~.* | **~ as** ◇ *the teacher's ~ as instructor* | **~ at** ◇ *He assumed a conspicuous ~ at the new arts agency.* | **~ for** ◇ *The new prime minister promised a greater ~ for women in government.* | **~ in, ~ within** ◇ *Pressure groups played a major ~ in bringing about the reforms.* ◇ *the opportunity to assume a leadership ~ within your organization*

roll noun

1 bread

ADJ. **bread** | **crusty, soft** | **dinner, finger** (*BrE*), **kaiser** (*AmE*), **morning** (*BrE*), **sub** (*AmE*), **submarine** | **brown** (*esp. BrE*), **white** (*esp. BrE*), **wholegrain, wholemeal** (*BrE*), **wholewheat** | **sweet** | **cinnamon** | **buttered, filled** (*BrE*) | **cheese, ham, lobster** (*AmE*), **etc.**

2 list of names

ADJ. **blog, honour/honor** (*esp. AmE*), **jobless** (*AmE*), **membership, registration, school, tax** (*esp. AmE*), **welfare** (*AmE*) ◇ *My daughter's grades improved and she made the honor ~.* (*AmE*) | **electoral** (*BrE*), **voter** (*AmE*), **voting** (*AmE*) | **falling** (*BrE*) ◇ *Falling ~s could lead to smaller class sizes.*
VERB + ROLL **remove sb from** ◇ *Eligible voters had been removed from the voting ~s.* | **call, take** ◇ *The chairman called the ~* (= to see if everyone was present)*.*
ROLL + NOUN **call** ◇ *Staff evacuated the building and a ~ call was taken outside.*
PREP. **on (the) ~** ◇ *There are 340 children on the school ~.*
PHRASES **a ~ of honour** (*BrE*) ◇ *Her name was engraved on sport's ~ of honour.*

roll verb

1 move by turning over

ADV. **slowly** | **quickly** ◇ *He quickly ~ed over and got to his feet.* | **gently** | **smoothly** ◇ *The black car ~ed smoothly down the street.* | **lazily** ◇ *She lazily ~ed her head on the pillow.* | **easily** ◇ *The boulder easily ~ed aside.* | **along, around, away, back, backwards/backward, down, forward, over** ◇ *The tigers ~ed over and over in the mud.*
PREP. **down** ◇ *A tear ~ed slowly down her cheek.* | **off**

2 make sth into the shape of a ball/tube

ADV. **tightly** ◇ *She carried the magazine tightly ~ed up in her hand.* | **up**
PREP. **into** ◇ *He ~ed the paper into a tight ball.*

3 of a ship/plane

ADV. **heavily** (*BrE*) | **slightly**

romance noun

1 love affair

ADJ. **brief** | **broken** | **whirlwind** ◇ *They married after a whirlwind ~.* | **budding** ◇ *the budding ~ between Richard and Elise* | **holiday** (*BrE*), **summer** | **office** ◇ *Have you ever had an office ~?* | **online** ◇ *Everyone knows that online ~s never work out.* | **teenage** | **interracial** (*esp. AmE*) ◇ *We're seeing more interracial ~s in the movies.* | **fairy-tale** ◇ *It*

ruined their perfect fairy-tale ~. | **real-life** ◇ *the true story of a real-life ~* | **doomed** | **failed** ◇ *He was still recovering from a failed ~.*
VERB + ROMANCE **have** ◇ *They had a brief ~ in the eighties.* | **begin, start**
ROMANCE + VERB **blossom** | **begin** | **end**

2 romantic feeling

ADJ. **true** | **interracial** (*esp. AmE*)
VERB + ROMANCE **find** ◇ *People find ~ in strange places.*
ROMANCE + VERB **be in the air** ◇ *Could ~ be in the air for the young prince?* | **bloom**
PHRASES **love and ~** ◇ *Most of her songs are about love and ~.*

romantic noun

ADJ. **great** (*esp. BrE*), **real, true** | **old** (*esp. BrE*) | **hopeless, incurable**
PHRASES **be a ~ at heart**

romantic adj.

VERBS **be, feel, look, seem, sound** | **become, get** ◇ *You're getting very ~ in your old age!*
ADV. **extremely, fairly, very, etc.** | **highly** ◇ *highly ~ notions of marriage* | **incredibly, terribly, wildly, wonderfully**

roof noun

ADJ. **conical, flat, gabled, mansard, pitched, pointed, sloped** (*esp. AmE*), **sloping, steep** | **corrugated-iron** (*esp. BrE*), **corrugated-metal** (*AmE*), **glass, metal, slate, steel, thatched, tiled, tin** | **leaky** | **retractable, sun** | **car, church, etc.**
VERB + ROOF **support** ◇ *The ~ is supported by stone columns.* | **cover** ◇ *The ~ was covered with red clay tiles.*
ROOF + VERB **slope** ◇ *The ~ slopes down to the top of the windows.* | **cave in, collapse, fall in** ◇ *Five people were killed when the ~ fell in.* | **leak**
ROOF + NOUN **space** (*esp. BrE*) ◇ *The burglars removed tiles to climb into the ~ space.* | **covering, slate** (*esp. BrE*), **tile** | **beams, rafters, structure, timbers** (*esp. BrE*) | **top** (usually **rooftop**) ◇ *A figure appeared on a nearby rooftop.* | **insulation** | **deck** (*esp. AmE*), **garden, terrace** ◇ *The hotel has a charming ~ garden.* | **rack**
PREP. **in a/the ~** ◇ *There are small windows in the ~.* | **on a/the ~** ◇ *There's a cat on the ~.* | **under your ~** (= in your house) ◇ *I won't have that man under my ~ again!*
PHRASES **under one ~, under the same ~** (= in the same building) ◇ *We're good friends but we could never live under the same ~.*

room noun

1 in a house/building

ADJ. **big, cavernous, enormous, high, high-ceilinged, large, spacious, vast** | **cramped, little, low** (*BrE*), **low-ceilinged, narrow, small, tiny** ◇ *The ~s are cramped and narrow.* | **L-shaped** | **north-facing, south-facing, etc.** | **airy** | **airless, claustrophobic, stuffy, windowless** | **bright** | **dark, darkened, dim, dimly lit, dingy, pitch-black, shadowed, shadowy** | **dreary** | **chilly, cold, draughty/drafty** (*esp. BrE*) | **hot, warm** | **clean, tidy** (*esp. BrE*) | **dirty, dusty, messy, shabby, smelly** | **comfortable, cosy/cozy** | **attractive, beautiful, elegant, handsome, impressive, luxurious, magnificent, pretty** | **bare, bleak, empty** | **book-lined** | **tiled, wood-panelled/wood-paneled** | **crowded** | **smoke-filled, smoky** | **quiet, silent** | **private** | **locked** | **adjacent, adjoining, next** | **attic, back, basement, downstairs, front, upstairs** ◇ *I was renting a tiny basement ~ at that time.* | **first-floor, second-floor, etc.** | **guest, spare** ◇ *Our guests are sleeping in the spare ~.* | **hotel, motel** | **double, family, single** | **dorm** | **bedsitting** (*BrE*) | **rented** | **breakfast, dining, drawing, living, main, reception, sitting** (*BrE*), **utility** | **laundry** | **dressing, make-up, rehearsal** | **control** | **fitness, weight, weights** (*BrE*) | **news, press** ◇ *He emailed his report back to the news ~.* | **committee, conference, meeting** | **break** (*AmE*) | **storage,**

store (usually **storeroom**) | **incident** (*BrE*), **interview** ◇ *Police have set up an incident ~ at the scene of the murder.* | **changing** (*esp. BrE*), **locker, shower** | **emergency** (*AmE*), **first-aid, hospital, medical, operating** (*AmE*), **recovery, treatment** | **waiting** | **common, lecture, reading, seminar, staff** (usually **staffroom**) | **boiler, engine** | **computer** | **throne**
VERB + ROOM **burst into, come into, creep into, enter, go into, hurry into, march into, reach, run into, rush into, slip into, sneak into, step into, storm into, stride into, walk into, wander into** ◇ *Suddenly Katie burst into the ~.* | **back out of, come out of, creep out of, exit, flounce out of, go out of, hurry out of, leave, march out of, run out of, rush out of, slip out of, step out of, storm out of, stride out of, walk out of** ◇ *As soon as the teacher left the ~ there was uproar.* | **show sb to, usher sb into** | **cross** | **go around, go round** (*esp. BrE*) | **wander around, wander round** (*esp. BrE*), **wander through** ◇ *I wandered restlessly around my ~.* | **walk, walk around, walk round** (*esp. BrE*) | **pace, pace around, pace round** (*esp. BrE*) ◇ *He was pacing the ~ nervously.* | **prowl, prowl around, prowl round** (*esp. BrE*) ◇ *She prowled around the ~ like a caged tiger.* | **echo around, echo round** (*esp. BrE*), **echo through, run around, run round** (*esp. BrE*) ◇ *A ripple of laughter ran around the ~.* | **glance around, glance round** (*esp. BrE*) | **look around, look round** (*esp. BrE*), **scan** | **search** | **fill** | **clean, tidy** (*esp. BrE*) | **decorate, paint** ◇ *a ~ decorated with flowers* ◇ *a ~ decorated in pastel shades* (*BrE*) | **air, air out** (*AmE*), **ventilate** | **light** ◇ *a ~ lit by one dusty light bulb* | **share** ◇ *I used to share a ~ with my sister.* | **occupy** | **vacate** ◇ *Guests are requested to vacate their ~s by 11 a.m.* | **set aside** ◇ *a ~ set aside for quiet study* | **book, hire** (*esp. BrE*), **rent** ◇ *We hired a ~ for the party.* ◇ *I rented a ~ while looking for a house to buy.*
ROOM + VERB **adjoin sth, face sth, overlook sth** ◇ *The ~ adjoins the hotel kitchens.* | **contain sth** ◇ *The ~ contained little more than a table and chair.* | **be crammed with sth, be filled with sth, be full of sth** | **be equipped with sth, be furnished with sth, have sth** ◇ *The patient was in a private ~ equipped with bathroom and TV.* | **measure sth** ◇ *a ~ measuring 28 feet by 34* | **darken** | **fall silent, go quiet, go silent, grow quiet** ◇ *The ~ fell silent as she rose to speak.* | **smell** ◇ *The ~ smelled of stale sweat and coffee.* | **spin, sway** ◇ *She felt sick and the ~ was spinning.*
ROOM + NOUN **key** | **number** | **lights** | **mate** (usually **room-mate**) | **service** | **temperature** ◇ *This wine should be served at ~ temperature.* | **rates** ◇ *Soaring ~ rates have put tourists off visiting the city.*
PREP. **around a/the ~, round a/the ~** (*esp. BrE*) | **from ~ to ~** ◇ *She flew from ~ to ~ looking for the fire extinguisher.* | **in a/the ~, inside a/the ~, into a/the ~**

2 space; enough space

ADJ. **ample, considerable, enough, sufficient** | **insufficient** (*esp. BrE*) | **extra** | **head, leg** (usually **headroom, legroom**) | **wiggle** (= opportunity to make adjustments) ◇ *There is some wiggle ~ for varying interpretations.*
VERB + ROOM **find, leave, make** ◇ *We had to move the furniture to make ~ for the piano.* | **have** ◇ *Do you have enough ~?* | **give sb**
PREP. **~ for** ◇ *Will there be enough ~ for that dishwasher in your kitchen?* ◇ *The sales figures are good, but there is still ~ for improvement.* (*figurative*)
PHRASES **~ for manoeuvre/maneuver**

root noun

1 of a plant

ADJ. **deep, shallow** | **gnarled** | **plant, tree**
VERB + ROOT **develop, grow** | **put down, take** ◇ *I hope those cuttings will take ~.* | **plant**
ROOT + VERB **grow**
ROOT + NOUN **system** | **ball** | **crops, vegetables** | **growth**
PREP. **by its/the ~s** ◇ *She pulled the shrub out by its ~s.*

2 roots place where you feel you belong

ADJ. **humble** ◇ *Despite his wealth, he never forgot his humble ~s.* | **strong** | **cultural** ◇ *severed from our cultural ~s by* industrialization | working-class | African, French, Scottish, etc.

VERB + ROOTS **get back to, go back to, return to** ◇ *My husband wants to go back to his Irish ~s.* | **trace** ◇ *They can trace their ~s back to the 16th century.* | **put down** ◇ *We haven't been here long enough to put down ~s.* | **be cut off from, forget**

3 cause/source

ADJ. **deep, strong** | **very** | **common, same** ◇ *The two languages share a common ~.* | **historical**

VERB + ROOT **have** | **explore, find, get at, get to, go to** ◇ *I've spent months trying to get to the ~ of the problem.* | **lie at**

ROOT + VERB **be planted in sth** ◇ *Jazz's ~s are firmly planted in African tradition.* | **go back** ◇ *The company's ~s go back to the 18th century.*

ROOT + NOUN **cause**

PREP. **at (the ~ of)** ◇ *It is a moral question at ~.* ◇ *His fears of loneliness lay at the very ~ of his inability to leave.* | **~ in** ◇ *The unrest has ~s in religious differences.*

PHRASES **the ~ of all evil** ◇ *They consider globalization to be the ~ of all evil.* | **the ~ of the matter, the ~ of the problem** ◇ *I expect money is at the ~ of the matter.*

rooted *adj.*

VERBS **be** | **become** | **remain**
ADV. **deeply** | **firmly**
PREP. **in** ◇ *His problems are deeply ~ in his childhood experiences.*

rope *noun*

ADJ. **strong** | **guy** (*esp. BrE*), **mooring** (*esp. BrE*), **tow** ◇ *I tripped over the guy ~ of the tent in the dark.* | **jump** (*AmE*), **skipping** (*BrE*) | **velvet** (*AmE*) ◇ *One of the bouncers lifted the velvet ~ to let us enter the club.*
... OF ROPE **length, piece** | **coil**
VERB + ROPE **knot, tie (sth together with)** ◇ *He tied the planks together with a strong ~.* | **untie** | **tighten** | **loosen** | **coil, coil up** | **pull, pull at, pull on** | **cut** | **grab, grab hold of, hold, take, take hold of**

rose *noun*

ADJ. **pink, red, yellow, etc.** | **climbing, rambling, shrub** | **long-stemmed** | **fresh** ◇ *She put fresh ~s in the vases.* | **wild**
ROSE + NOUN **garden** | **bed** | **bush** | **petals** | **bowl**
PHRASES **a bed of ~s** | **a dozen ~s** | **the scent of a ~, the smell of a ~**
→ Note at FLOWER (for verbs)

roster *noun*

ADJ. **impressive** ◇ *The firm has built up an impressive ~ of clients over the past ten years.* | **duty** ◇ *All names should be listed on the duty ~.* | **active** (*AmE*) ◇ *The team has ten rookies on the active ~.*
VERB + ROSTER **fill, fill out** (*AmE*) | **make** (*AmE*) ◇ *Kelly has an excellent chance of making the opening-day ~.*

rota *noun* (*BrE*)

ADJ. **daily, weekly, etc.** | **duty** | **cleaning**
VERB + ROTA **have** | **draw up, work out** ◇ *I've been asked to draw up the cleaning ~.*
ROTA + NOUN **scheme, system**
PREP. **on the ~** | **~ for** ◇ *Are you on the ~ for cooking?*
PHRASES **on a ~ basis** ◇ *We share the babysitting duties on a ~ basis.*

rotate *verb*

ADV. **quickly, rapidly** | **gently, slowly** | **freely** | **back and forth**
VERB + ROTATE **allow sth to** ◇ *It is best to allow the rotor to ~ freely.*
PREP. **around** ◇ *The blades ~ around a central point.* | **on** ◇ *The earth ~s on its axis.* | **through** ◇ *The handle ~s through 360 degrees.*

round *noun*

1 series of events

ADJ. **endless, long** ◇ *Life to him was one long ~ of parties.* | **fresh, further, latest, new** | **earlier, previous**
VERB + ROUND **begin, start** | **hold** | **complete**
PREP. **~ of** ◇ *a fresh ~ of peace talks*

2 regular series of visits, etc.

ADJ. **daily, weekly** (*esp. BrE*) | **milk, paper** (*both BrE*)
VERB + ROUND **do, make** ◇ *The milkman does his ~ very early.* (*BrE*) | **complete**
PREP. **on sb's ~** (*esp. BrE*) ◇ *a doctor on his ~*

3 number of drinks

VERB + ROUND **buy, order** ◇ *I bought the last ~.*
PHRASES **it's my ~** (= it's my turn to buy the drinks) | **a ~ of drinks** ◇ *We just had time for one more ~ of drinks.*

4 part of a competition

ADJ. **first, second, etc.** ◇ *Italy qualified for the second ~ of the tournament by beating Germany.* | **early, last, next, previous** | **opening, preliminary** | **final** | **qualifying**
VERB + ROUND **make, reach** ◇ *He has never made the fourth ~ of the tournament.* | **win** ◇ *Ali won the next ~ convincingly.* | **lose**
PREP. **in a/the ~** ◇ *China was knocked out in the second ~.*

5 (in golf) one game

ADJ. **practice** ◇ *I finished the practice ~ and went in to have lunch.*
VERB + ROUND **have, play, shoot**
PHRASES **a ~ of golf** ◇ *We had a good ~ of golf today.*

6 bullets

ADJ. **live** | **blank** | **artillery, mortar**
VERB + ROUND **fire** ◇ *The soldiers fired several blank ~s into the crowd.*
PHRASES **a ~ of ammunition**

round *verb*

PHR V **round sth off**
ADV. **nicely** (*esp. BrE*) ◇ *A coffee would ~ the meal off nicely.*
PREP. **with** ◇ *We ~ed off the day with a picnic.*

rounded *adj.*

1 having a round shape

VERBS **be**
ADV. **gently, slightly, softly** | **beautifully, nicely, perfectly** ◇ *beautifully ~ arches*

2 complete and balanced

VERBS **be**
ADV. **well** | **fully** ◇ *a fully ~ education*

round trip *noun*

ADJ. **25-mile, etc.** | **two-hour, etc.** | **daily** (*esp. AmE*), **etc.** ◇ *I have a daily ~ of three hours.*
VERB + ROUND TRIP **make** ◇ *It took two days to make the ~.*
PREP. **~ from** ◇ *a 300-mile ~ from Los Angeles to Palm Springs* | **~ to**

rout *noun*

VERB + ROUT **become, turn into** ◇ *The game ended in a total ~.* | **put sb to** ◇ *They put the rebel army to ~.* | **start** (*esp. BrE*) | **complete** (*esp. BrE*)

route *noun*

ADJ. **fast, quick, short** ◇ *The shortest ~ home is along the shore.* | **convenient, easy** | **best** | **long** | **direct** | **circuitous, circular, indirect, roundabout, tortuous** (*esp. BrE*) ◇ *a circuitous ~ through the narrow side streets* | **dangerous, safe** | **attractive, beautiful** (*esp. BrE*), **scenic** ◇ *We had plenty of time so we took the scenic ~.* | **accessible** | **alternate** (*AmE*), **alternative, different** ◇ *The snow forced us to take an alternative ~.* | **main, major, trunk** (*esp. BrE*) |

air, overland, sea | bus, cycle (*BrE*) | shipping, supply, trade | coastal | east-west, southerly, southern, etc. | transatlantic (*esp. BrE*), transcontinental (*esp. AmE*), etc. | tourist | migration | well-travelled/well-traveled | traditional | access | escape | parade

VERB + ROUTE follow, go, take, use | choose, find, map out, plan, work out ◇ *You'll have to plan your ~ carefully.* | try | know ◇ *The bus driver did not seem to know the ~.* | trace | retrace ◇ *We retraced our ~ in an attempt to get back on the right path.* | fly, travel ◇ *The airline currently flies this ~ twice a day.*

ROUTE + VERB cross sth, follow sth, go, pass through sth, run, take sb ◇ *The alternative ~ takes you along the river.* | turn (*esp. BrE*) | lead | lie ◇ *Our ~ lay straight ahead and downhill.* | connect sth, link sth ◇ *the trade ~s linking Persia and China*

ROUTE + NOUN map

PREP. along the ~ ◇ *There are plenty of hotels along the ~.* | on the ~ ◇ *We live on the school bus ~.* | ~ between ◇ *the most direct ~ between Bangkok and Chiang Mai* | ~ from ◇ *the air ~ from Berlin to Beijing* | ~ through ◇ *a scenic ~ through the south of France* | ~ to ◇ *the shortest ~ to Manila* ◇ *the best ~ to success*

PHRASES en ~ (= on the way) ◇ *We'll stop for lunch en ~.*

routine noun

1 normal order/way of doing things

ADJ. set | strict | dull, humdrum (*esp. BrE*), monotonous | familiar, normal, old, regular, same, usual ◇ *a break in my usual ~* | daily, day-to-day, morning | domestic, school, work

VERB + ROUTINE establish, fall into, get into, settle into ◇ *It took me a week to settle into a ~.* | follow, go through ◇ *We go through the same old ~ every morning.* | begin, start | break, change, vary | have ◇ *Everyone has their own morning ~.* | know ◇ *I'm sure you know the ~ by now.*

PHRASES a change from the ~, a change in ~, a change of ~ ◇ *The children were confused by the change of ~.* | a matter of ~ ◇ *Bags of all visitors to the museum are searched as a matter of ~.*

2 series of movements, jokes, etc.

ADJ. comedy, stand-up | dance | exercise, fitness, training, workout

VERB + ROUTINE learn | perform

row¹ noun

ADJ. bottom, middle, top | back, front | first, second, etc. | horizontal, vertical | double, single | neat ◇ *She arranged the chairs in two neat ~s.* | long | endless ◇ *endless ~s of identical houses*

PREP. in a/the ~ ◇ *The children stood in a ~.* ◇ *It rained for five days in a ~* (= without a break). ◇ *We have seats in the front ~.* | ~ of ◇ *a long ~ of houses*

PHRASES the end of the ~, the middle of the ~ | ~s and ~s, ~ upon ~ ◇ *He looked down at ~ upon ~ of eager faces.*

row² noun (*informal, esp. BrE*)

ADJ. almighty, awful, big, bitter, blazing, fearful, ferocious, fierce, flaming, furious, great, huge, major, serious, terrible, tremendous, unholy (*BrE*), violent ◇ *We had a blazing ~ over who should do the cooking.* | domestic, family | stand-up ◇ *A couple was having a stand-up ~ in the street.* | public | drunken | long-running | diplomatic, political

VERB + ROW have | kick up (*BrE*) ◇ *I'm going to kick up a ~ if I don't get my money back.* | cause | get into

ROW + VERB blow up, break out, develop, erupt ◇ *A ~ blew up over salary increases.* | go on, rage, rage on

PREP. in a/the ~ ◇ *He came to prominence in the ~ over defence policy.* | ~ about, ~ over ◇ *Carol and I had a terrible ~ about how much money she spends.* | ~ between ◇ *a ~ between the left and right wings of the party* | ~ with ◇ *a ~ with my mother*

royalty noun

1 members of a royal family

ADJ. minor (*esp. BrE*)

PHRASES in the presence of ~ ◇ *She behaved as if she were in the presence of ~.*

2 (usually royalties) money paid to an author, etc.

ADJ. performance | unpaid (*esp. BrE*)

VERB + ROYALTY pay | collect, earn, get, receive | charge

ROYALTY + NOUN cheque/check, fee, payment | rate

PREP. in ~s ◇ *She earns a lot in royalties.* | ~ from, ~ on ◇ *He has received royalties on previous inventions.*

PHRASES an advance against royalties, an advance on royalties

rub verb

ADV. hard, vigorously ◇ *He rubbed his face vigorously with the towel.* | well ◇ *Put a little cream onto each hand and ~ it in well.* | gently, lightly ◇ *He gently rubbed his swollen nose.* | slowly ◇ *She rubbed her chin thoughtfully.* | absently (*esp. AmE*) | in, together ◇ *He began to ~ his hands together in glee.*

VERB + RUB begin to

PREP. against ◇ *The cat rubbed against my legs.* | at ◇ *She stood up, rubbing at her back.* | into ◇ *Rub the cream well into your skin.* | on ◇ *She rubbed her hands on her apron.* | with ◇ *I rubbed my glasses with my handkerchief.*

rubbish noun → See also GARBAGE, TRASH

1 (*esp. BrE*) waste material

ADJ. domestic, household | garden

...OF RUBBISH bag, pile | tons

VERB + RUBBISH put out ◇ *I forgot to put the ~ out last night.* | collect, remove, take away ◇ *The ~ is collected on Tuesdays.* | clear, clear out, dispose of, dump, throw, throw away, throw out ◇ *He's clearing ~ out of the attic.* ◇ *Someone had dumped their ~ by the road.* ◇ *Throw the ~ in the bin.* | leave ◇ *Don't leave your ~ on the bus.* | strew, strew around (both usually passive) ◇ *There was ~ strewn around everywhere.* | pick up

RUBBISH + VERB decay, rot

RUBBISH + NOUN bag, bin, skip | dump, heap, tip | collection, disposal | chute

2 (*BrE*) sth that you think is bad/silly/wrong

ADJ. absolute, complete, total, utter ◇ *The film was absolute ~.* | worthless ◇ *Many critics see the paintings as worthless ~.* | old ◇ *The antique shop was just full of old ~.*

VERB + RUBBISH talk ◇ *Don't talk such ~!*

PREP. ~ about ◇ *the usual ~ about his undiscovered talents*

PHRASES a load of ~ ◇ *What he said was just a load of old ~.* | what ~!

rubble noun

ADJ. building (*esp. BrE*)

...OF RUBBLE heap, pile ◇ *What was once a house was now a crumbling heap of ~.*

VERB + RUBBLE be reduced to ◇ *The school was reduced to ~.* | clear, clear away | search, search through, sift through ◇ *Rescue workers are searching the ~ for survivors.* | Police sifted through the ~ looking for clues.

PREP. amid the ~, among the ~ ◇ *She stood among the ~ left by the earthquake.* | beneath the ~, under the ~ ◇ *Our car was buried somewhere under the ~.* | in the ~ ◇ *Several people were trapped in the ~.*

rucksack (*BrE*) noun → See also BACKPACK

VERB + RUCKSACK pack | open | put on, shoulder | sling ◇ *She slung her ~ over her shoulder.* | pull off, take off | carry, have on, wear ◇ *He had a large ~ on.*

PREP. in a/the ~ ◇ *He had very little in his ~.*

rude adj.

VERBS appear, be, feel, seem, sound | become | consider sth, find sb, think sb/sth ◇ *I hope you won't think me ~ if I leave early.*

ADV. **extremely, fairly, very, etc.** | **downright, incredibly, plain, terribly** ◇ *He wasn't just impolite–he was downright ~.* | **a little, slightly, etc.**
PREP. **about** ◇ *He's very ~ about her cooking.* | **to** ◇ *Don't be so ~ to your mother!*

rug *noun*

ADJ. **hearth** (usually *hearthrug*) | **oriental, Persian**
VERB + RUG **make, weave**
RUG + VERB **cover sth** ◇ *A Persian ~ covered the polished floor.*

rugby *noun*

ADJ. **amateur, professional** | **competitive, representative** | **junior** (*esp. BrE*), **school, student, youth** | **senior** | **club** (*esp. BrE*), **league** | **first-class** (*esp. BrE*), **international, test, world** | **touch** | **wheelchair** | **running** (*BrE*) ◇ *The crowd enjoyed the Fijians' running ~.*
... OF RUGBY **game**
VERB + RUGBY **play** | **watch**
RUGBY + NOUN **scrum, tackle** | **club, side** (*esp. BrE*), **team** | **championship, game, international, match** | **tour** | **ball, posts** | **boots** (*esp. BrE*), **jersey, shirt** | **field, pitch** (*BrE*) | **forward, international, player** ◇ *the former ~ international, Serge Blanco* | **coach** | **official** | **career** | **season** | **buff, enthusiast, fan, follower, supporter** | **circles, community, fraternity, people** | **country, nation**
PHRASES **Rugby League, Rugby Union**
→ Special page at SPORTS

ruin *noun*

1 spoiled state

ADJ. **complete, utter**
VERB + RUIN **fall into, go to** ◇ *The house gradually fell into ~.*
PHRASES **be the ~ of sb/sth** ◇ *Drinking has been the ~ of her.* | **go to rack and ~** (*esp. BrE*) ◇ *They've let the house go to rack and ~.*

2 end of success, hopes, etc.

ADJ. **economic, financial**
VERB + RUIN **face** ◇ *The company faces ~ over the new road plans.* | **bring, lead to, mean, spell** ◇ *The cost would have meant financial ~ for us.* | **save from**
PHRASES **on the brink of ~, on the verge of ~** | **the road to ~** ◇ *He's on the road to political ~.*

3 damaged building, town, etc.

ADJ. **ancient, old** | **charred, smoking, smouldering/ smoldering** ◇ *the charred ~s of their home* | **crumbling** | **castle, temple, etc.**
VERB + RUIN **be in ~s, lie in ~s** ◇ *The church now lies in ~s.* | **leave sth in ~s** ◇ *The earthquake left the town in ~s.*
PREP. **~s of** ◇ *the ancient ~s of Jericho*

ruin *verb*

ADV. **completely, totally** ◇ *The experience has completely ~ed her life.* | **nearly** | **effectively** | **financially** ◇ *The long legal battle ~ed him financially.*
VERB + RUIN **threaten to** ◇ *A knee injury threatened to ~ her Olympic hopes.* | **be going to** ◇ *All this mud is going to ~ my shoes.*

rule *noun*

1 what you can or cannot do, say, etc.

ADJ. **basic, cardinal, first, fundamental, golden** | **ground ~s** ◇ *You and your room-mates should establish some ground ~s.* | **general** | **special** | **formal, official, written** | **informal, unspoken, unwritten** | **old, traditional** ◇ *the traditional ~s of grammar* | **current, existing** | **proposed** | **new** | **rigid, strict, stringent** | **absolute, hard and fast** ◇ *There are no hard and fast ~s when it comes to choosing a typeface.* | **clear** | **simple** ◇ *Follow these few simple ~s, and you won't go far wrong.* | **arbitrary** | **petty** (*esp. BrE*) ◇ *He made his children's lives a misery with all his petty ~s.* | **club, company, competition, house, school, union, etc.** | **federal, global, international** ◇ *federal ~s on campaign fund-raising* | **cultural, ethical, legal, moral, social** | **accounting,**
disciplinary, immigration, privacy (*esp. AmE*), **safety, tax** | **grammar, grammatical**
... OF RULES **set** ◇ *The aim is to get each member country to adhere to a single set of ~s.*
VERB + RULE **create, develop, draw up, establish, formulate, impose, issue, lay down, make, set out, write** ◇ *The ~s were drawn up to make it fair for everyone.* ◇ *You don't make the ~s, you know.* | **abide by, accept, adhere to, follow, go by, obey, observe, play by, stick to** ◇ *If he wanted a loan he would have to play by the bank's ~s.* | **be in line with, conform to** ◇ *The packaging does not conform to EU ~s.* | **have** ◇ *The sport has strict ~s for player safety.* | **be in breach of, break, disregard, fall foul of** (*BrE*), **flout, ignore, violate** ◇ *Their action was in breach of Stock Exchange ~s.* | **apply, enforce** ◇ *The referee applied the ~s to the letter* (= very strictly). | **adopt, use** | **bend, relax** ◇ *Couldn't they just bend the ~s and let us in without a ticket?* | **waive** | **tighten up** ◇ *The ~s on claiming have been tightened up.* | **change, rewrite** ◇ *The Internet has changed the ~s of business.* ◇ *The ~s of dating have had to be rewritten, thanks to the movies.* | **be bound by, be governed by** ◇ *Employees are bound by ~s of confidentiality.* | **know, learn, remember** ◇ *You should know the ~s by now.* | **read** | **explain** | **interpret, understand** ◇ *The punishment depends on how the umpire interprets the ~s.*
RULE + VERB **apply, be applicable, operate** | **come into effect, come into force** ◇ *New accounting ~s come into force next year.* | **dictate sth, provide sth** (*formal*), **require sth, say sth, state sth, stipulate sth** ◇ *The competition ~s provide that a cash alternative may be given.* | **govern sth** ◇ *the ~s governing the importing of livestock* | **allow sth, allow for sth, permit sth** ◇ *The existing ~s allow for some flexibility.* | **forbid sth, prevent sth, prohibit sth** | **limit sth, restrict sth** ◇ *~s limiting imports* | **change** ◇ *The ~s keep changing.*
RULE + NOUN **book** ◇ *The officials went strictly by the ~ book.* | **change** ◇ *Several proposed ~ changes have been announced.*
PREP. **according to the ~s** ◇ *According to the ~s, no alcohol can be consumed on the premises.* | **against the ~s, contrary to the ~s** ◇ *Tackling a player without the ball is against the ~s.* | **in accordance with the ~s** ◇ *The music was turned off at midnight, in accordance with the ~s.* | **outside the ~s** ◇ *conduct which is outside the ~s* | **under a/the ~** ◇ *Under this ~, only full members of the club are entitled to vote.* | **within the ~s** ◇ *I believed I was acting within the ~s.* | **~ about, ~ concerning, ~ on, ~ regarding, ~ relating to** ◇ *What are the school ~s about dress?* | **~ for** ◇ *There seems to be one ~ for the rich and another for the poor.* ◇ *What is the ~ for forming plurals?* | **~ of** ◇ *the ~s of the game*
PHRASES **a breach of the ~s, a violation of the ~s** | **a body of ~s, a code of ~s, a system of ~s** | **respect for the ~s** | **~s and regulations** | **~ of thumb** (= a practical method of doing or measuring sth)

2 what is usual

ADJ. **general** ◇ *There are few exceptions to the general ~ that bars close at midnight.*
PREP. **as a ~** ◇ *As a ~, hardly anybody uses this road.*
PHRASES **be the ~** ◇ *Among her friends, casual dress and a relaxed manner are the ~.*

3 government

ADJ. **authoritarian, harsh** | **direct, indirect** | **emergency** ◇ *The president imposed emergency ~ following the riots.* | **majority** | **one-party** | **Communist, Labour, Republican, etc.** | **colonial, imperial** | **home** | **civilian, military** | **presidential** | **constitutional, democratic** | **mob** ◇ *the lawless days of mob ~*
VERB + RULE **impose**
PREP. **under...~** ◇ *The country remained under direct ~ by the occupying powers.*
PHRASES **the ~ of law** ◇ *a society based on the ~ of law*

rule *verb*

ADV. **justly**

PREP. **by** ◇ *the president's powers to ~ by decree* | **over** ◇ *He left his son to ~ over Saragossa.*
PHRASES **~ supreme** | **~ with an iron fist**, **~ with an iron hand**, **~ with a rod of iron** (*esp. BrE*) (= control a person or group of people very severely)

PHR V **rule sth out**
ADV. **altogether**, **categorically**, **completely**, **definitely** (*esp. BrE*), **entirely**, **totally** ◇ *This theory cannot be ~d out altogether.* | **virtually** (*esp. BrE*) | **effectively** ◇ *His age effectively ~d him out as a possible candidate.* | **apparently** | **automatically** ◇ *Infringement of this regulation would automatically ~ you out of the championship.* | **immediately** | **previously** (*esp. BrE*)
VERB + RULE OUT **cannot**, **refuse to** ◇ *We cannot ~ out the possibility of a recession.*
PREP. **as** ◇ *Police have now ~d her out as the killer.*

ruler *noun*

ADJ. **great** | **effective**, **good**, **powerful**, **strong** | **weak** | **enlightened** | **absolute** ◇ *an absolute ~ who will tolerate no opposition* | **authoritarian**, **autocratic**, **despotic** | **sovereign** | **supreme** | **hereditary** (*esp. BrE*) | **legitimate**, **rightful** | **independent** (*esp. BrE*) | **former** | **current** | **new** | **future** | **colonial**, **military** | **local** | **secular**
PREP. **under a/the ~** ◇ *The country was finally united under one ~.* | **~ over** ◇ *He eventually became ~ over all Egypt.*

ruling *noun*

ADJ. **authoritative** (*esp. BrE*), **definitive** | **unanimous** | **adverse** | **favourable/favorable** (*esp. AmE*) | **controversial** | **important** | **preliminary** | **original** | **final** | **previous**, **recent** | **court**, **judicial**, **legal** | **federal**
VERB + RULING **give**, **hand down**, **issue**, **make** | **overturn**, **reverse** ◇ *The court overturned the original ~.* | **uphold** | **base on sth** ◇ *The judge's ~ is based on legal precedent.* | **follow** | **appeal**
PREP. **~ against** ◇ *the European Court's ~ against detention without trial* | **~ by** ◇ *the ~ by the High Court* | **in favour/favor of** ◇ *The newspaper said that this was a ~ in favour/favor of freedom of speech.* | **~ on** ◇ *The House will make a final ~ on the case next week.*

rumble *noun*

ADJ. **deep**, **low** | **dull** | **loud** | **faint**, **soft** | **distant** | **ominous**
VERB + RUMBLE **give**, **let out** | **hear** | **feel**
PREP. **with a ~** ◇ *The door slid shut with a ~.* | **~ of**
PHRASES **the ~ of thunder** ◇ *We could hear the distant ~ of thunder.*
→ Note at SOUND

rumour (*BrE*) (*AmE* rumor) *noun*

ADJ. **malicious**, **nasty**, **scurrilous**, **ugly**, **vicious** | **baseless**, **false**, **unconfirmed**, **unfounded**, **unsubstantiated**, **wild** | **persistent**, **strong**, **widespread** | **trade** | **Internet**
VERB + RUMOUR/RUMOR **start** | **fuel** ◇ *His lengthy absence will fuel ~s that he has been fired.* | **spread** | **hear** | **believe** | **deny** | **confirm** ◇ *The actor confirmed ~s that he will be leaving the series.* | **quash**, **scotch** (*esp. BrE*), **silence** ◇ *The Chief Executive issued a statement to quash ~s of financial problems.*
RUMOUR/RUMOR + VERB **circulate**, **get around**, **go around**, **go round** (*esp. BrE*), **spread** | **abound**, **be flying**, **be flying about** (*esp. BrE*), **be flying around**, **be rife** ◇ *Rumours about an impending divorce were rife.* | **sweep sth** (*esp. BrE*), **sweep through sth** (*esp. AmE*) ◇ *The ~ quickly swept the town.* | **persist**
RUMOUR/RUMOR + NOUN **factory** (*BrE*), **mill** ◇ *The Washington ~ mill suggests the money changed hands illegally.*
PREP. **amid ~s** ◇ *The manager resigned suddenly amidst ~s of misconduct.* | **~ about**, **~ concerning**, **~ surrounding** ◇ *~s surrounding the closure of the hospital* | **~ of** ◇ *There were persistent ~s of drug-taking among staff.*
PHRASES **~ has it that…** ◇ *Among the other employees, ~ has*

it that he was fired from his last job. | **there is no truth in the ~** ◇ *There is no truth in the ~ that she is about to resign.*

run *noun*

1 on foot
ADJ. **five-mile**, **etc.** | **fun**, **sponsored** (*esp. BrE*) ◇ *The school has organized a two-mile fun ~ for charity.* | **training** | **record**, **record-breaking** ◇ *The Ethiopian is aiming to produce his second record-breaking ~ of the week.*
VERB + RUN **go for**, **have** ◇ *Let's go for a ~ before dinner.* | **go on** ◇ *I'm going on a fun ~ tomorrow.* | **break into** ◇ *When he saw me he broke into a ~.* | **take** ◇ *He took a ~ at the wall and just managed to clear it.*
PREP. **at a ~** ◇ *She took the stairs at a ~.* | **on the ~** ◇ *The prisoners have now been on the ~ (= escaping by running) for three days.* ◇ *I usually eat breakfast on the ~ (= while going somewhere).*
PHRASES **make a ~ for it** (= escape by running)

2 of success/failure
ADJ. **bad**, **disappointing**, **disastrous**, **dismal**, **poor** | **excellent**, **fine**, **good**, **remarkable**, **successful** | **unbeaten**, **winning** | **record-breaking**
VERB + RUN **enjoy**, **have** ◇ *Spurs have had a winning ~ of ten games.* | **begin** | **end** ◇ *Manchester United have finally ended their ~ of victories.*
RUN + VERB **begin** | **end**
PREP. **~ of** ◇ *a ~ of good/bad luck*

3 of a play, film/movie, etc.
ADJ. **theatrical** (*AmE*) | **long** | **short** | **eight-week**, **six-month**, **etc.** | **successful** | **sell-out**
VERB + RUN **have** ◇ *The play had a long ~ in the West End.* | **begin**, **end** ◇ *They play began its ~ last June.* | **extend** ◇ *The show has had its ~ extended till March.*
RUN + VERB **begin** | **end**

4 way things are/happen
ADJ. **common**, **general**, **ordinary**, **usual** ◇ *She was very different from the general ~ of American movie stars.* ◇ *In the normal ~ of things the only exercise he gets is climbing in and out of taxis.*
PHRASES **against the ~ of play** (*BrE*) ◇ *Villa scored in the 15th minute against the ~ of play (= although the other team had seemed more likely to score).*

5 of product
ADJ. **print**, **production** ◇ *a print ~ of 20 000*

6 in sports
ADJ. **home** | **play-off**, **stretch** (*both AmE*)
VERB + RUN **get**, **hit**, **make**, **play** (*AmE*), **score** ◇ *They've scored another ~!* ◇ *He's only made four home ~s all season.* | **be on**, **have** ◇ *Our team is on 90 ~s.* | **allow**
RUN + NOUN **defense**, **game**, **support** (*all AmE*)

7 attempt/practice
ADJ. **dry**, **dummy**, **practice**, **trial**

8 attempt to win political office
ADJ. **presidential**
PREP. **~ for** ◇ *Senator Blake's ~ for the presidency*

run *verb*

1 move quickly on foot
ADV. **fast**, **quickly** ◇ *John can ~ very fast.* ◇ *She ran quickly downstairs.* | **blindly**, **headlong** | **frantically** | **away**, **off**, **out** | **home** | **downstairs**, **upstairs**
VERB + RUN **begin to**, **start to** | **get up and**, **jump up and**, **turn and**, **turn to** | **want to** ◇ *He just wanted to ~ away and hide.*
PREP. **down** ◇ *She turned and ran blindly down the street.* | **into** ◇ *He ran headlong into an enemy patrol.* | **out of** ◇ *He ran out of the house.* | **to**, **towards/toward**, **up**, **etc.**

2 manage sth
ADV. **efficiently**, **properly**, **well** | **badly** ◇ *a badly ~ company* | **professionally** | **privately** | **jointly** ◇ *The school is jointly ~ with the local parish.* | **independently** ◇ *The group is ~ independently of college authorities.*

VERB + RUN **try to** ◊ *Stop trying to ~ my life for me.* | **manage to** | **help (to), help sb (to)**

3 work

ADV. **efficiently, smoothly** ◊ *The engine was running very smoothly.* | **continuously**
PREP. **on** ◊ *Our car only ~s on unleaded.*
PHRASES **be up and running** ◊ *We soon had the sound system up and running.*

4 happen

ADV. **smoothly** ◊ *Things ran very smoothly for a while.* | **concurrently, consecutively, simultaneously** ◊ *He was given two twelve-month sentences to ~ concurrently.* | **in parallel, in tandem** ◊ *The two experiments ~ in parallel.*

5 buses/trains

ADV. **regularly** ◊ *Local buses ~ regularly to and from the school.* | **late** ◊ *The train was running late, as usual.*
PREP. **between, from, to**

6 (esp. AmE) be a candidate in an election

ADV. **successfully, unsuccessfully** ◊ *He ran unsuccessfully for the Senate in New York.*
PREP. **for** ◊ *He hopes to ~ for president in 2016.*

runner noun

ADJ. **fast, good, great, powerful, top** | **distance, long-distance, marathon, middle-distance** | **cross-country, fell** (BrE) | **Olympic** | **base, pinch, route** (all AmE) | **fancied** (BrE) ◊ *one of the fancied ~s in today's race* | **front** (often figurative) ◊ *He is currently the front ~ for the Democratic Party presidential nomination.*

running noun

1 activity/sport

ADJ. **cross-country, fell** (BrE) | **distance, long-distance, marathon, middle-distance**
RUNNING + NOUN **event, race** | **gear** | **clothes** (AmE), **pants** (AmE), **shoe, shorts, tights** (AmE), **vest** (BrE) | **track**

2 management of business, etc.

ADJ. **efficient, smooth** ◊ *Careful planning is needed to ensure the smooth ~ of the event.* | **day-to-day**
VERB + RUNNING **be involved in, be responsible for**
RUNNING + NOUN **costs, expenses**

rural adj.

VERBS **be**
ADV. **extremely, fairly, very, etc.** | **largely, mainly, mostly, predominantly** ◊ *Sri Lanka's predominantly ~ population*

ruse noun

ADJ. **clever, elaborate**
PREP. **~ by sb** ◊ *The attack may merely be a ~ by the enemy to distract our forces.*

rush noun

1 sudden movement or emotion

ADJ. **headlong, sudden** | **adrenalin, sugar** ◊ *Nothing can beat that adrenalin ~.*
VERB + RUSH **experience, feel** ◊ *She felt a ~ of blood to her face.*
PREP. **~ for** ◊ *The movie ended, and there was a ~ for the exits.* | **~ of** ◊ *A ~ of water came from the burst pipe.* ◊ *She experienced a sudden ~ of emotion.*

2 busy period

ADJ. **awful, big, frantic, great, mad** | **sudden** | **last-minute** | **Christmas, holiday** (esp. AmE) | **gold** (= rush to find gold in a particular place)
VERB + RUSH **avoid** ◊ *Do your Christmas shopping early and avoid the ~.*
RUSH + NOUN **decision** | **job** ◊ *You can see that the painting was a ~ job.* | **hour** ◊ *During ~ hour the drive may take up to twice as long.*
PREP. **in a ~** ◊ *I've been in a mad ~ all day.* | **~ for** ◊ *a last-minute ~ for tickets* | **~ of** ◊ *a sudden ~ of tourist traffic*

PHRASES **have a ~ on** ◊ *We've had a ~ on at the office, dealing with the backlog of orders.*

rush verb

ADV. **headlong, madly** ◊ *a train ~ing headlong down the track* | **quickly** | **immediately** | **suddenly** | **downstairs, upstairs** | **about** (esp. BrE), **around, back, forward, home, in, off, out, over, past** ◊ *She was ~ing around madly looking for her bag.*
PREP. **along, from, into, out of, through, to, etc.** ◊ *A surge of joy ~ed through her body.* ◊ *He was ~ed to hospital.*
PHRASES **come ~ing, go ~ing** ◊ *Two men came ~ing into the room.* | **~ to sb's rescue, ~ to the rescue** ◊ *Whenever her little brother was upset, Jane ~ed to the rescue.*

rust noun

VERB + RUST **get off, remove, scrape off**
RUST + NOUN **spot, stain** | **remover** | **belt** (= a region where many factories have closed) (esp. AmE)
PHRASES **covered with ~** ◊ *The lock was covered with ~.*

rust verb

ADV. **badly** | **away, through** ◊ *The car had been ~ing away in his garage for years.*

rustle noun

ADJ. **faint, gentle, slight, soft**
VERB + RUSTLE **hear**
PREP. **with a ~** ◊ *With a ~ of wings the bird landed on the window ledge.* | **~ of** ◊ *I heard a soft ~ of leaves.*

rustle verb

ADV. **gently, slightly, softly** ◊ *the sound of the leaves rustling softly*
PREP. **in** ◊ *The wind ~d in the bushes.* | **through** ◊ *the sound of their feet rustling through the grass*

rut noun

ADJ. **deep** | **wheel** | **wagon** (esp. AmE)
PREP. **in a ~, into a ~** (both figurative) ◊ *My job bores me—I feel I'm in a ~.* ◊ *I got into a ~, cooking the same things week after week.* | **out of a ~** (figurative) ◊ *Moving to San Francisco gave her the chance to get out of a ~.*

S s

sabbath noun

ADJ. **Jewish, Muslim, etc.**
VERB + SABBATH **keep, observe** | **break, violate**
SABBATH + NOUN **day, holiday** | **rest** | **dinner** | **candles** | **prayer** | **observance**
PREP. **on the ~** ◊ *It was considered a sin to work or play on the Sabbath.*
PHRASES **observance of the Sabbath** ◊ *The speaker advocated a less austere observance of the Sabbath.*

sabotage noun

ADJ. **deliberate** | **economic, industrial** ◊ *They conducted a campaign of economic ~.* | **computer, pipeline**
SABOTAGE + NOUN **attempt** | **attack, campaign**
PREP. **~ of** ◊ *The low levels of production were caused by ~ of the northern pipeline.*
PHRASES **an act of ~**

sabotage verb

ADV. **deliberately** ◊ *They accused him of deliberately sabotaging the peace talks.*

VERB + SABOTAGE **attempt to, try to** ◇ *They had tried to ~ our plans.*

sack noun

1 large bag

ADJ. **bulging, heavy** ◇ *bulging ~s of toys* | **burlap** (*AmE*), **gunny** (*AmE*), **hessian** (*esp. BrE*), **leather, paper, plastic** | **flour, mail, potato** | **refuse** (*BrE*) (*garbage bag* in *AmE*) | **bivvy** (*AmE*)
VERB + SACK **empty, fill** ◇ *They filled the ~s with potatoes.* | **carry, drag, haul, heave, pull** | **carry sth in, put sth in**
SACK + VERB **be filled with sth, be full of sth**
SACK + NOUN **lunch** (*AmE*) | **race** (= a race in which the competitors jump forward inside a sack)
PREP. **in a/the ~** | **~ of** ◇ *a ~ of coal* ◇ *two ~s of groceries* (*AmE*)

2 the sack (BrE) dismissal from your job

VERB + THE SACK **get** (*BrE, AmE*) ◇ *She got the ~ after 20 years of service.* | **give sb** | **be threatened with, face** ◇ *Hundreds of postal workers are facing the ~.*

3 the sack (informal, esp. AmE) bed

VERB + THE SACK **hit** ◇ *I decided to hit the ~ (= go to bed) and have an early night.*
PREP. **in the ~** ◇ *He caught them in the ~ together.*

sacred adj.

VERBS **be** | **become** | **remain** | **consider sth, deem sth, hold sth, regard sth as** ◇ *Certain animals were regarded as ~.* ◇ *the feeling that all life should be held ~*
ADV. **absolutely** | **almost**
PREP. **to** ◇ *The place was ~ to the Apaches.*
PHRASES **~ and profane**

sacrifice noun

1 giving sth up

ADJ. **big, considerable, enormous, great, heavy, huge, real, tremendous** | **financial, personal** | **heroic, noble** | **final, supreme, ultimate** ◇ *Soldiers who die for their country have made the supreme ~.*
VERB + SACRIFICE **be** ◇ *I know it's a ~ for you, but please try to understand.* | **make** | **involve, mean, require** ◇ *Completing the course will require ~.*

2 part of a ceremony

ADJ. **animal, human** | **pagan, religious, ritual** | **blood**
VERB + SACRIFICE **perform** | **offer (sth as)**
PREP. **~ to** ◇ *Food and wine were offered as ~s to the gods.*

sacrifice verb

ADV. **gladly, willingly**
VERB + SACRIFICE **be forced to, be obliged to, have to** | **be prepared to, be ready to, be willing to** ◇ *She was prepared to ~ having a family in order to pursue her career.*
PREP. **for** ◇ *soldiers who ~d their lives for their country* | **to** ◇ *In her writing, clarity is sometimes ~d to (= for the sake of) brevity.*
PHRASES **~ sth for the sake of sth** ◇ *Comfort has been ~d for the sake of improved performance.*

sad adj.

1 unhappy

VERBS **appear, be, feel, look, seem, sound** | **become, get, grow, turn** | **make sb** ◇ *This music always makes me ~.*
ADV. **extremely, fairly, very, etc.** | **all, desperately, immensely, particularly, profoundly, unbearably** ◇ *I called Dad, sounding all ~ and pathetic.* | **a little, slightly, etc.** | **strangely**
PREP. **about** ◇ *She was still feeling very ~ about her father's death.*

2 causing unhappiness

VERBS **be, seem** | **find sth**

ADV. **extremely, fairly, very, etc.** ◇ *an extremely ~ story* | **deeply, incredibly, intensely, particularly, profoundly, terribly, unutterably** ◇ *a deeply ~ occasion* | **a little, slightly, etc.**

sadden verb

ADV. **deeply, greatly, profoundly, terribly** ◇ *I was deeply ~ed by his death.* | **slightly, somewhat**

sadness noun

ADJ. **deep, great, overwhelming, profound, real**
... OF SADNESS **hint, tinge, touch** ◇ *There was a hint of ~ in her voice.*
VERB + SADNESS **be filled with, be full of, feel** ◇ *Claudia felt a deep ~.* | **hear, notice, see, sense** ◇ *He saw the ~ on her face.* | **express, show** | **hide** | **bring (sb)** ◇ *I had brought nothing but ~ to my family.* | **be tinged with** ◇ *Our joy was tinged with ~.*
SADNESS + VERB **fill sth** ◇ *A deep ~ filled his heart.* | **creep over sb, overcome sb, overwhelm sb, wash over sb, well up inside sb**
PREP. **with ~** ◇ *It was with great ~ that we learned of his death.* | **~ about, ~ at, ~ over** ◇ *He expressed his ~ about what had happened.* | **~ for** ◇ *Kate felt a great ~ for those who had lost their houses.*
PHRASES **an air of ~, an aura of ~** ◇ *a lonely place with an air of ~* | **a note of ~** | **a feeling of ~, a sense of ~**

safe noun

ADJ. **bank, hotel, office** | **wall**
VERB + SAFE **open** | **close, lock** | **break into, crack**

safe adj.

VERBS **be, feel, seem** | **become** | **keep, remain, stay** | **make sth, render sth** ◇ *The army experts made the bomb ~.* | **keep sth** ◇ *Keep your money ~ by carrying it in an inside pocket.* | **consider sth, declare sth, deem sth** ◇ *The water was not considered ~ to drink.*
ADV. **extremely, fairly, very, etc.** | **absolutely, completely, entirely, perfectly, quite, totally** ◇ *a completely ~ and secure environment for young children* ◇ *The woods are never entirely ~ for women on their own.* | **comparatively, reasonably, relatively** | **enough** ◇ *You should be ~ enough, but don't go too far.* | **inherently, intrinsically** | **environmentally** ◇ *an environmentally ~ form of energy*
PREP. **from** ◇ *They were ~ from attack.* | **with** ◇ *Your money will be ~ with me.*
PHRASES **better ~ than sorry** | **play it ~, play ~** (*BrE*) ◇ *I decided to play it ~ and wore a formal suit.* | **~ and sound** ◇ *They returned from their adventure ~ and sound.*

safeguard noun

ADJ. **adequate, effective, proper, sufficient** ◇ *Does the procedure provide adequate ~s against corruption?* | **appropriate, necessary** | **added, additional, extra, further** | **inadequate** | **environmental, nuclear** | **constitutional, democratic, legal, procedural**
VERB + SAFEGUARD **implement, introduce** (*BrE*), **put in place** | **provide** | **provide sb with** | **build in, build into sth, include** ◇ *Appropriate ~s would have to be built into the procedures to avoid abuses.*
SAFEGUARD + VERB **be in place** ◇ *The elections will go ahead, provided that adequate ~s are in place.*
PREP. **~ against** ◇ *The credit agreement includes a ~ against overcharging.* | **~ for** ◇ *Any agreement must provide ~s for minority rights.*

safeguard verb

ADV. **adequately, properly** ◇ *This legislation does not adequately ~ the rights of consumers.*
VERB + SAFEGUARD **be necessary to** | **help (to)** | **be designed to, be intended to, be meant to, be supposed to** | **take steps to**
PREP. **against** ◇ *We must take steps to ~ our environment against these threats.* | **from** ◇ *Try to ~ the young plants from frost.*

safety noun

ADJ. **added, extra, greater, increased** ◊ *The seat is bolted in place for added ~.* | **comparative, reasonable, relative** ◊ *A blizzard forced the climbers back to the relative ~ of their tents.* | **complete, perfect** ◊ *Walkways allow visitors to enter the caves in perfect ~.* | **long-term, temporary** | **child, passenger, patient, worker** ◊ *The house will have to be rearranged with a view to child ~.* | **personal, physical, public** | **fire, food, nuclear, etc.** | **air, aviation, road, traffic, etc.** | **environmental, home, industrial, occupational, workplace** | **firearm, gun**
VERB + SAFETY **assure, ensure, guarantee** | **enhance, improve, increase** | **compromise, endanger, jeopardize, risk, threaten** | **fear for** ◊ *Police fear for the ~ of the missing children.* ◊ *We fear for their ~.* | **find, get to, make it to, reach** ◊ *They thought they would never reach ~.* | **leave** ◊ *What made her leave the ~ of her apartment?*
SAFETY + NOUN **tips** | **controls, improvements, limits, measures, precautions, procedures, provisions** | **codes** (*esp. AmE*), **guidelines, laws, legislation, levels, policy, recommendations, regulations, requirements, rules, standards** ◊ *a violation of ~ codes* ◊ *New ~ legislation will be introduced next year.* | **violation** (*AmE*) | **hazard, risk** | **check, inspection** | **inspector, officer, official** ◊ *The plan was rejected by the ~ inspectors.* | **record** | **concerns, considerations, implications, issues, matters** | **aspect, factor** | **awareness** ◊ *a safety-awareness campaign* | **campaign, initiative, training** | **belt, equipment, features, glasses** (*esp. AmE*), **goggles, harness, helmet, rope** ◊ *The car has many ~ features, including anti-skid braking.* | **catch** (*esp. BrE*), **device, valve** | **barrier, curtain, net** (*often figurative*) ◊ *A national insurance system provides a ~ net for the very poor.* | **glass, pin, razor, seat**
PREP. **for ~** ◊ *The stairs are fitted with a handrail for ~.* | **for your own ~** ◊ *The police gave him protection for his own ~.* | **in ~** ◊ *The people want to be able to walk the streets in ~.* | **to ~** ◊ *We managed to run to ~ before the building collapsed.* | **~ of** ◊ *She finally made it to the ~ of her room.*
PHRASES **for ~ reasons** ◊ *The building was evacuated for ~ reasons.* | **health and ~** ◊ *The company was fined by the health and ~ inspectors.* | **on ~ grounds** ◊ *The playground was closed down on ~ grounds.* | **a place of ~** ◊ *The refugees finally reached a place of ~.* | **~ first** ◊ *When operating machinery, remember: ~ first.*

sag verb

ADV. **a bit** (*esp. BrE*), **slightly** | **visibly** ◊ *She seemed to visibly ~ at the thought of what lay ahead.* | **limply** ◊ *All she could do was ~ limply in his arms.* | **back, down, forward** ◊ *Martin sighed and sagged back in his chair.* ◊ *Helga's body sagged forward.*
PREP. **against** ◊ *She sagged against the door.* | **under** ◊ *The shelf sagged under the weight of hundreds of volumes.*
PHRASES **~ in the middle** ◊ *a mattress that was beginning to ~ in the middle*

saga noun

ADJ. **continuing, ongoing** | **long, long-running** | **epic, extraordinary** | **sad, sorry, terrible** | **complicated** | **entire, whole** ◊ *This whole ~ has been a pretty significant victory for truth.* | **family**
SAGA + VERB **continue**
PREP. **in a/the ~** ◊ *His suicide is the latest chapter in this terrible ~.*

sail noun

ADJ. **main** (usually *mainsail*) | **canvas**
VERB + SAIL **hoist, raise, rig** | **drop, lower** | **adjust, trim** | **fill** ◊ *The dinghy gathered speed as the wind filled her ~s.* | **reef, shorten** | **furl, unfurl**
SAIL + VERB **billow, flap, flutter** ◊ *The bay was full of boats with billowing ~s.* | **fill** | **hang** ◊ *The white canvas ~ hung limply against the mast.* | **catch the air, catch the wind** ◊ *The ~s caught the wind once more and they were on their way.*
SAIL + NOUN **boat** (usually *sailboat*) (*AmE*)
PHRASES **the days of ~** ◊ *The boat is preserved as a monument*

to the days of ~. | **in full ~, under full ~** ◊ *a pirate ship under full ~* | **set ~ (for…)** ◊ *We set ~ for France at first light.* | **under ~** ◊ *The ship came in under ~ and anchored near us.*

sail verb

ADV. **gracefully, serenely, smoothly** | **single-handed** ◊ *to ~ single-handed around the world* | **away, back, off, on, out, past** ◊ *The boat ~ed gracefully on into the distance.*
VERB + SAIL **know how to** | **learn to** | **teach sb to**
PREP. **across** ◊ *He ~ed across the Atlantic.* | **around, round** (*esp. BrE*) ◊ *to ~ around the world* | **for** ◊ *The ferry ~ed for Staten Island.* | **from, to** ◊ *We were ~ing from Dover to Calais.*

sailing noun

ADJ. **dinghy** (*BrE*)
VERB + SAILING **go**
SAILING + NOUN **club, school** | **regatta** | **holiday** (*BrE*), **trip** | **boat** (*BrE*) (*sailboat* in *AmE*), **craft, dinghy** (*BrE*), **ship, vessel**

sailor noun

ADJ. **avid** (*AmE*), **keen** (*BrE*) | **experienced, good** | **inexperienced** | **merchant** | **drunken** | **drowned, shipwrecked**
SAILOR + NOUN **outfit** (*esp. AmE*), **suit** | **hat** (*sailor's hat* in *BrE*)

saint noun

ADJ. **patron** ◊ *St Nicholas is the patron ~ of children.* | **Buddhist, Catholic, Christian, etc.**
VERB + SAINT **canonize** | **venerate** | **become**

salad noun

ADJ. **fresh** | **crisp, crunchy** | **delicious, tasty** | **pasta, potato, rice, tomato, etc.** | **chicken, egg, ham** (*esp. BrE*), **taco** (*esp. AmE*), **tuna, etc.** | **Caesar, chef** (*AmE*), **chef's** (*AmE*), **garden** (*AmE*), **green, mixed** | **Greek, Russian** | **fruit** | **side** ◊ *Is the steak served with a side ~?* | **cold, warm** | **tossed** (*esp. AmE*)
VERB + SALAD **eat** | **make, prepare** | **dress, toss** ◊ *She tossed and dressed the ~.* | **serve sth with** | **come with**
SALAD + NOUN **greens, leaves** | **cream** (*BrE*), **dressing** | **garnish** (*BrE*) ◊ *The sandwiches came with a ~ garnish.* | **spinner** | **bowl, plate** (*AmE*) | **fork, servers** | **bar**
→ Special page at FOOD

salary noun

ADJ. **big, generous, good, handsome, high, huge, large, top** ◊ *Top salaries are liable for a higher rate of tax.* | **six-figure, seven-figure, etc.** | **low, meagre/meager, modest, small** | **competitive, decent, reasonable** | **average, median** (*AmE*) | **annual, monthly, yearly** | **base** (*esp. AmE*), **basic** (*BrE*) | **minimum** | **gross, net** | **starting** | **final** ◊ *Your pension will be based on a proportion of your final ~.* | **current** | **severance** (*AmE*) (usually *severance pay* in *BrE* and *AmE*) ◊ *He was entitled to one year of severance ~.* | **pensionable** (*BrE*) | **tax-free**
VERB + SALARY **pay (sb)** | **command, earn, receive** ◊ *US tech workers command six-figure salaries.* | **draw** ◊ *Mr Kerry continued to draw his ~ during the time of his absence.* | **boost, increase, raise** ◊ *She raised his ~ to $36 000.* | **cut, slash** | **double, triple**
SALARY + VERB **increase, rise** (*BrE*)
SALARY + NOUN **package** ◊ *The position is rewarded with a generous ~ package.* | **hike** (*esp. AmE*), **increase, raise** (*AmE*), **rise** (*BrE*) ◊ *The school district gave teachers a 12% ~ increase.* | **cut** | **level** | **review** | **band** (*BrE*), **grade, range** | **cap** ◊ *The ~ cap will be set at $49.5 million.* | **scale, structure** | **bill** (*esp. BrE*), **costs**
PREP. **on a ~** ◊ *It's impossible to bring up a family on such a low ~.*
PHRASES **an increase in ~, a raise in ~** (*AmE*), **a rise in ~** (*BrE*)

| a cut in ~, a drop in ~ (*BrE*) ◇ *Workers are being asked to take a cut in ~.*

sale noun

1 act of selling sth; occasion when things are sold

ADJ. **quick** ◇ *The price is low to ensure a quick ~.* | **illegal** ◇ *the illegal ~ of alcohol* | **art** | **bond, share, stock** | **auction, bake** (*AmE*), **bring-and-buy** (*BrE*), **car boot** (*BrE*), **estate** (*AmE*), **garage, jumble** (*BrE*), **rummage** (*esp. AmE*), **tabletop** (*BrE*), **tag** (*AmE*), **yard** (*AmE*)
VERB + SALE **hold** | **ban, block, halt, prevent, prohibit, restrict, stop** | **approve** | **close, complete, make** ◇ *If we don't close this ~, we're out of business.* | **lose** | **announce**
SALE + VERB **make sth, realize sth** ◇ *The bake ~ made $358 for cancer research.* | **go ahead, go through, proceed** | **fall through** ◇ *The ~ of the house fell through when the buyer pulled out.*
SALE + NOUN **price**
PREP. **for** ~ ◇ *I see their house is for ~.* | **on** ~ ◇ *The new stamps are now on ~ at post offices.*
PHRASES **conditions of** ~ ◇ *The conditions of ~ were posted up around the auction room.* | **a contract of** ~ | **point of** ~ ◇ *promotional posters shown at the point of ~* | **the proceeds from a** ~, **the profits from a** ~ ◇ *All proceeds from the ~ of the book will go to charity.* | **(on)** ~ **or return** (*BrE*) ◇ *The novels are delivered to outlets on a ~ or return basis.* | **up for** ~ ◇ *The land has come up for ~ again.*

2 sales activity of selling things; amount sold

ADJ. **good, healthy, high, huge, massive, record, strong** | **increased** | **disappointing, poor** | **annual, quarterly** | **first-quarter, second-quarter, etc.** | **high-street** (*BrE*), **over-the-counter, retail** ◇ *High-street ~s have fallen for the fifth consecutive month.* | **direct, telephone** ◇ *Direct ~s, by mail order, were up by 15%.* | **Internet, online** | **domestic** | **local** | **export, foreign, international, overseas** | **global, overall, total, world, worldwide** | **gross, net** | **unit, volume** | **CD, DVD, PC, ticket, etc.** | **home, house, land, property, real estate** (*AmE*) | **auto** (*AmE*), **car, vehicle** | **arms**
... OF SALES **level, value, volume** ◇ *The high volume of ~s makes the low pricing policy profitable.*
VERB + SALES **achieve, have** | **generate, rack up** (*esp. AmE*) ◇ *The advertising campaign generated massive ~s.* | **boost, drive, drive up, expand, increase, push, push up, spur** ◇ *Low interest rates pushed ~s to a record in 2006.* | **hurt** ◇ *Lower consumer confidence could hurt PC ~s.* | **double, triple, etc.** | **expect, project** | **report** ◇ *The company reported strong ~s for May.*
SALES + VERB **account for sth** ◇ *North American ~s account for 40% of the worldwide market.* | **amount to sth, reach sth, total sth** ◇ *~s amounting to over £4 million* ◇ *Sales failed to reach 10 000 units.* | **exceed sth** | **be up, climb, go up, grow, improve, increase, jump, rise, rocket, skyrocket, soar, surge** ◇ *Sales of ice cream are up because of the hot weather.* | **be down, decline, drop, fall, fall off, go down, slump**
SALES + NOUN **force, people, personnel, staff, team** | **agent, department, office** | **director, manager, rep** (*informal*), **representative** | **assistant, clerk** (*AmE*) | **campaign, drive, effort, promotion** | **strategy, tactics, technique** | **patter** (*BrE*), **pitch, talk** ◇ *an aggressive ~s pitch from the company rep* | **estimates, projections** | **data, figures, levels, performance, revenue, targets, volume** | **growth** | **slump** ◇ *The factory was forced to shed jobs following a dramatic ~s slump.* | **conference** | **presentation** | **report** | **tax** (*esp. AmE*) ◇ *It sells for $50 plus ~s tax and shipping.* | **receipt, slip** (*both AmE*)
PREP. **~s of** ◇ *Sales of VCRs have plummeted.* | **in ~s** ◇ *I work in ~s* (= in the sales department).
PHRASES **a decline in ~s, a drop in ~s, a fall in ~s, a slowdown in ~s, a slump in ~s** | **an increase in ~s, a jump in ~s, a rise in ~s, a surge in ~s, an upturn in ~s** | **growth in ~s** | **~s and marketing**
→ Note at PER CENT (for more verbs)
→ Special page at BUSINESS

3 period of reduced prices

ADJ. **after-Christmas** (*AmE*), **annual, January** (*BrE*), **summer, winter** | **clothing, furniture, etc.** | **clearance, closing-down** (*BrE*), **fire, going-out-of-business** (*AmE*)
VERB + SALE **hold**
SALE + VERB **begin, end**
SALE + NOUN **rack** (*AmE*) | **prices**
PREP. **in a/the** ~ ◇ *I got these shoes in the Bloomingdales ~.* | **at the ~s, in the ~s** (*both BrE*) ◇ *I bought it at the winter ~s.* | **on** ~ (*AmE*) ◇ *All video equipment is on ~ today and tomorrow.*

salesman noun

ADJ. **good, successful** | **door-to-door, travelling/traveling** | **car, computer, double-glazing** (*BrE*), **insurance, used-car** | **snake-oil** (= a person who sells sth that is not effective or useful) (*informal, esp. AmE*)
→ Note at JOB

saliva noun

VERB + SALIVA **produce, secrete** | **swallow** | **wipe** ◇ *I wiped the ~ off my mouth.*
SALIVA + VERB **dribble, drip** | **flow**

salmon noun

ADJ. **fresh** | **wild** | **farm** (*AmE*), **farm-raised** (*AmE*), **farmed** | **smoked** | **canned, tinned** (*BrE*) | **pink, red** | **Alaskan, Atlantic, Scottish, etc.**
VERB + SALMON **eat, have** | **bake, cook, grill, poach, roast** | **fish for** | **catch, land** | **farm**
SALMON + VERB **migrate** | **return** ◇ *Salmon return to these waters to spawn.* | **spawn** | **swim**
SALMON + NOUN **fillet/filet, steak** | **mousse, paste** (*BrE*) | **farm, farming, fishery, fishing** | **river, run, stream** | **pink** ◇ *a salmon-pink shirt*
PHRASES **a fillet/filet of** ~

salon noun

ADJ. **beauty, hair, hairdressing, nail, tanning** | **local** | **professional, top**
VERB + SALON **go to, visit**

salt noun

ADJ. **mineral, rock, sea** | **common, table** | **kosher** (*esp. AmE*) | **celery, garlic** | **acid, potassium, sodium** | **soluble ~s** | **bath ~s, Epsom ~s, liver ~s, smelling ~s** | **bile ~s**
... OF SALT **grain** | **pinch**
VERB + SALT **taste** ◇ *He could taste the ~ from the water in his mouth.* | **add, put in, put on, season sth with, sprinkle (sth with)** ◇ *Don't put so much ~ on your food!* | **dissolve** ◇ *When ~ is dissolved in water, it alters the properties of the water.* | **contain** ◇ *Most foodstuffs contain some ~.* | **pass** ◇ *Could you pass the ~, please?*
SALT + NOUN **crystals** | **solution** | **content** ◇ *foods with a high ~ content* | **intake** ◇ *He wants to reduce his ~ intake.* | **cellar** (*esp. BrE*), **shaker** (*AmE*) | **air, spray, water** ◇ *I could smell the ~ air as it whipped through my hair.* | **flats, marsh, pan** | **mine** | **truck** (*AmE*)
PHRASES **high in** ~, **low in** ~ ◇ *a diet low in ~* | **~ and pepper** ◇ *Add ~ and pepper to taste* (= in the quantity preferred).
→ Special page at FOOD

salute noun

1 military gesture

ADJ. **military, naval** | **fascist, Nazi** | **crisp** (*esp. AmE*), **sharp** (*esp. AmE*), **smart** | **casual, half-hearted, sloppy** | **mock**
VERB + SALUTE **give (sb), snap** (*AmE*), **throw** (*AmE*) ◇ *The sentry gave a smart ~ and waved us on.* ◇ *The Admiral snapped a sharp ~.* | **acknowledge, return** | **take** (*BrE*) ◇ *The Queen took the ~ as the guardsmen marched past.*

2 action of respect or welcome

ADJ. **final, last** | **21-gun, etc.** | **triumphant, victory**
PREP. **in** ~ ◇ *The guests raised their glasses in ~.* | **from** ◇ *The retiring editor received a special ~ from the local*

salute *verb*

ADV. **crisply** (*esp. AmE*), **sharply** (*esp. AmE*), **smartly** ◊ *The captain stood to attention and ~d smartly.*
PREP. **with** ◊ *He ~d her with a graceful bend of his head.*

salvation *noun*

ADJ. **individual, personal** | **universal** | **eternal**
VERB + SALVATION **bring, offer** | **seek** | **achieve, attain, find**
PREP. **~ from** ◊ *~ from sin*

same *adj., pron.* the same

VERBS **be, feel, look, seem, smell, sound, taste** ◊ *They both taste just the ~ to me.* | **remain, stay**
ADV. **exactly, just, precisely** ◊ *I had exactly the ~ experience.* | **not altogether, not quite** ◊ *That's not quite the ~ thing, is it?* | **almost, basically, broadly, essentially, more or less, nearly, practically, pretty much, roughly, substantially, virtually** ◊ *Your new job will be essentially the ~ as your old one.*
PREP. **as** ◊ *Your dress is nearly the ~ as mine.*
PHRASES **one and the ~** ◊ *In his work, form and meaning are one and the ~.*

sample *noun*

1 people in a survey

ADJ. **large, small** | **total** | **population** | **national** | **random, representative** | **clinical, non-clinical**
VERB + SAMPLE **draw, select** ◊ *a random ~ drawn from men aged 35–40*
SAMPLE + VERB **comprise sth, consist of sth** ◊ *Our ~ comprised 250 office workers.*
SAMPLE + NOUN **size** ◊ *A larger ~ size yields more reliable data.* | **survey** | **group**
PREP. **~ from** ◊ *The research was based on ~s from 29 populations.* | **~ of** ◊ *a wide ~ of people*

2 small quantity of sth tested to provide information

ADJ. **blood, faecal/fecal, serum, stool, tissue, urine** | **DNA, RNA** | **rock, soil, water** | **control** | **biopsy**
VERB + SAMPLE **collect, obtain, take** | **provide** ◊ *All the athletes had to provide a urine ~.* | **analyse/analyze, study, test**
SAMPLE + VERB **contain** | **show**
PREP. **~ of** ◊ *~s of tissue*

3 small quantity of sth tried to see what it is like

ADJ. **free** ◊ *They're giving out free ~s of the new toothpaste.*
SAMPLE + NOUN **book** ◊ *We looked at ~ books to choose the fabric.*
PREP. **~ of** ◊ *I'd like to see a ~ of your work.*

sanction *noun*

1 (usually **sanctions**) punishment

ADJ. **economic, financial, military, trade** | **civil, criminal, disciplinary** | **legal, penal, social** | **international, UN** | **severe, strict** | **punitive** | **effective**
VERB + SANCTION **apply, enforce, impose, use** | **end, lift** | **call for** | **threaten**
PREP. **~ against** ◊ *The UN called for ~s against the invading country.* ◊ *There were strict ~s against absenteeism.* | **~ for** ◊ *Employers imposed heavy ~s for union activity.*
PHRASES **the imposition of ~s** | **the lifting of ~s** | **a threat of ~s**

2 official permission

ADJ. **government, official** ◊ *The movement was first given official ~ in the 1960s.* | **divine, religious**
VERB + SANCTION **give sth** ◊ *The conference gave its official ~ to the change of policy.*
PREP. **with sb/sth's ~, without sb/sth's ~** ◊ *No decision can be taken without the ~ of the committee.*

sanction *verb*

ADV. **officially** | **legally, socially** ◊ *Slavery was once socially ~ed.* | **divinely**
VERB + SANCTION **refuse to**

sanctuary *noun*

1 safety and protection

VERB + SANCTUARY **seek** ◊ *Thousands of refugees have sought ~ over the border.* | **find, take** ◊ *In former times, criminals could take ~ inside a church.* | **leave** ◊ *He was reluctant to leave the ~ of his bedroom.* | **provide** | **give sb, offer (sb)**
PREP. **~ from** ◊ *It had been built as a ~ from World War II bombs.* | **~ of** ◊ *She retreated swiftly to the ~ of her room.*

2 area for wild birds, animals, etc.

ADJ. **animal, bird, marine, wildlife**

sand *noun*

ADJ. **coarse, fine** ◊ *a beach of fine golden ~* | **hard, soft** | **damp, moist, wet** | **dry** | **burning, hot, warm** | **cool** | **black, golden, silver, white, yellow** | **beach, desert** ◊ *the burning desert ~s* | **drifting, loose, shifting**
... OF SAND **grain** | **layer** | **handful** | **patch, stretch, strip** | **cloud**
VERB + SAND **brush off, dust off** | **kick** | **sink into**
SAND + VERB **blow, fly** ◊ *The ~ was flying everywhere.* | **cover sth** | **cling to sth, stick to sth**
SAND + NOUN **beach, dune** | **bank** (usually *sandbank*), **bar** (usually *sandbar*), **box** (usually *sandbox*) (*AmE*), **pit** (usually *sandpit*) (*BrE*) | **castle** (usually *sandcastle*) | **storm** (usually *sandstorm*)
PREP. **in the ~** ◊ *The children played happily in the ~.* | **on the ~** ◊ *We found her asleep on the ~.*
PHRASES **covered in ~, covered with ~** ◊ *All my clothes were covered with ~.*

sandal *noun*

ADJ. **high-heeled, platform** | **flat, low-heeled** | **open, open-toed** | **strappy** | **thong** (*AmE*) | **plastic, rubber**
... OF SANDALS **pair**
VERB + SANDAL **kick off** | **slip on**
→ Special page at CLOTHES

sandwich *noun*

ADJ. **cheese, ham, peanut butter, etc.** | **jam** (*BrE*), **jelly** (*AmE*) ◊ *a peanut butter and jelly ~* | **toasted** | **open** (*BrE*), **open-faced** (*AmE*) | **submarine** (*AmE*) | **club** | **deli** (*esp. AmE*)
... OF SANDWICHES **plate** | **round** (*BrE*)
VERB + SANDWICH **make** ◊ *He made two plates of peanut butter and jelly ~es.* | **order** | **eat, grab, have** | **bite into, munch, take a bite of**
SANDWICH + NOUN **filling** | **bag, box** (*BrE*) | **bar, shop**
PREP. **in a/the ~** ◊ *What would you like in your ~?*

sane *adj.*

VERBS **be, seem** | **remain, stay** | **keep sb** ◊ *Having that little bit of time to myself is what keeps me ~.*
ADV. **completely, perfectly, quite** ◊ *She seems perfectly ~ to me.* | **reasonably, relatively** | **not entirely**

sanitation *noun*

ADJ. **inadequate, poor** | **adequate, basic, good, improved, proper** | **public**
SANITATION + NOUN **facility, services, system** | **department** (*esp. AmE*) | **engineer, worker** (*both esp. AmE*)
PHRASES **lack of ~** ◊ *the direct link between disease and lack of adequate ~*

sanity *noun*

VERB + SANITY **doubt, question** ◊ *There were moments when he doubted his own ~.* | **fear for** ◊ *I fear for her ~ if this continues much longer.* | **keep, maintain, preserve, retain,**

save ◇ *Getting away at weekends is the only way I can retain my ~.* | **lose** | **recover, regain** | **threaten** ◇ *The pace of city life threatens our ~.* | **bring** ◇ *We need to bring some ~ to this issue.*
SANITY + VERB **return** ◇ *Stock-market trading slowly settled down as ~ returned.* | **prevail** ◇ *We still hope that ~ will prevail.*
PREP. **for sb's ~** ◇ *Such a move is essential for the ~ of all concerned.*
PHRASES **voice of ~** ◇ *He was a voice of ~ in the Republican Party.*

sarcasm *noun*

ADJ. **biting, bitter, heavy** | **obvious** | **dry** (*esp. AmE*) ◇ *I love him for his cutting wit and dry ~.* | **slight**
... OF SARCASM **hint, note, tinge, touch, trace** ◇ *He made the remark without a hint of ~.*
VERB + SARCASM **be full of, be heavy with, drip, drip with** (used about sb's voice) ◇ *His voice dripped (with) ~.* | **catch, note, notice** ◇ *James caught the ~ in her voice.*
SARCASM + VERB **drip** ◇ *'Great!' she said, ~ dripping from her voice.*
PREP. **with ~** ◇ *'Your skills amaze me,' she said, with heavy ~.* | **~ in** ◇ *I detected a touch of ~ in his remarks.*

satellite *noun*

ADJ. **commercial, research** | **military, reconnaissance, spy** | **meteorological, weather** | **communications, GPS** | **artificial** | **geostationary**
VERB + SATELLITE **launch** | **put into orbit, send into orbit** | **put into space, send into space**
SATELLITE + VERB **be in orbit, orbit sth** ◇ *About 100 Russian ~s are orbiting the earth.* | **detect sth, monitor sth, track sth** ◇ *a new ~ that monitors changes in the environment* | **provide** ◇ *American reconnaissance ~s provide images of the earth.*
SATELLITE + NOUN **image, imagery, photo, photograph, picture** ◇ *high-resolution ~ imagery* | **broadcast** | **data** | **feed, link** ◇ *The pictures are broadcast through a live ~ link with Tokyo.* | **communications, system, technology** | **dish, receiver** | **phone, radio, television, TV** | **navigation** | **broadcaster, channel, company, provider** (*esp. AmE*), **station**
PREP. **from a/the ~** ◇ *images from ~s* | **via ~** ◇ *The game will be broadcast via ~.*

satire *noun*

ADJ. **biting, dark, savage** | **brilliant, funny, hilarious** | **political, social** ◇ *the recent boom in political ~*
PREP. **~ on** ◇ *The movie is a brilliant ~ on Hollywood.*

satisfaction *noun*

ADJ. **complete, deep, great, immense** | **overall** ◇ *Clients are asked to rate their overall ~.* | **evident, obvious** | **grim, perverse, smug** | **quiet** | **mutual, personal** | **job, life** (*esp. AmE*) | **emotional, marital** (*AmE*), **sexual** | **client, customer, employee, patient**
... OF SATISFACTION **level** ◇ *My current level of job ~ is pretty low.*
VERB + SATISFACTION **derive, feel, find, gain, get, have, take** ◇ *He derived great ~ from knowing that his son was happy.* ◇ *Although we didn't win, we were able to take some ~ from our performance.* | **bring (sb), give sb, provide (sb with)** | **express**
SATISFACTION + NOUN **rating, score** | **level, rate**
PREP. **in ~** ◇ *She watched in ~ as he opened the present.* | **to sb's ~** ◇ *The matter was resolved to our general ~.* | **with ~** ◇ *He nodded with evident ~.* | **~ at** ◇ *her deep ~ at seeing justice done* | **~ in** ◇ *I find ~ in helping people.* | **~ of** ◇ *I had the ~ of proving him wrong.* | **~ with** ◇ *Both parties expressed their complete ~ with the decision.*
PHRASES **a certain ~** ◇ *She felt a certain ~ in keeping him waiting.* | **a grin of ~, a look of ~, a smile of ~, a smirk of ~** | **a feeling of ~, a sense of ~** | **a source of ~** ◇ *The children were a major source of ~.*

satisfactory *adj.*

VERBS **appear, be, look, prove, seem, sound** | **consider sth, find sth, regard sth as**
ADV. **highly, most, very** ◇ *It was all most ~.* | **completely, fully, perfectly, quite** | **far from, less than, not altogether, not entirely, not totally, not wholly** ◇ *The results were not entirely ~.* | **generally** | **mutually** ◇ *The arrangement has proved mutually ~.*
PREP. **to** ◇ *We hope this proposal is ~ to you.*

satisfied *adj.*

VERBS **appear, be, feel, look, seem** | **declare yourself, pronounce yourself** ◇ *He declared himself ~ with the results.*
ADV. **extremely, fairly, very, etc.** | **more than, well** ◇ *I felt well ~ with my day's work.* | **completely, fully, perfectly, quite, thoroughly, totally** | **far from, not entirely, not wholly** | **generally, reasonably** | **enough, sufficiently** ◇ *Her parents seemed ~ enough with her progress.* | **apparently**
PREP. **with** ◇ *She seemed ~ with the arrangements.*

satisfy *verb*

VERB + SATISFY **have to, must, should** ◇ *The education system must ~ the needs of all children.* | **be able to, can** ◇ *Nothing could ~ his desire for power.* ◇ *We could never ~ all their requests* | **be unable to** ◇ *The owners were unable to ~ all the demands of the workers.* | **seem to** ◇ *His answer seemed to ~ her.* | **be enough to, be sufficient to** ◇ *Her description of events was not enough to ~ the court.* | **fail to** ◇ *The meal failed to ~ his hunger.*

satisfying *adj.*

VERBS **be** | **find sth**
ADV. **deeply, eminently** (*esp. AmE*), **extremely, highly, immensely, profoundly, really, richly** (*esp. BrE*), **very** ◇ *There's something deeply ~ about eating vegetables that you have grown yourself.* | **particularly** | **completely, quite, thoroughly, wholly** | **personally** ◇ *the need for a personally ~ set of beliefs* | **mutually** ◇ *a mutually ~ relationship* | **emotionally, intellectually, musically, sexually**

saturation *noun*

ADJ. **market, media** | **colour/color, light**
VERB + SATURATION **approach, be close to, near** ◇ *The company's sales are now close to ~ in many western countries.* | **reach**
SATURATION + NOUN **level, point** ◇ *Demand for the product has reached ~ point.* | **coverage** ◇ *television's ~ coverage of the Olympics* | **bombing**

Saturday *noun* → Note at DAY

sauce *noun*

ADJ. **thick, thin** | **buttery, creamy** | **hot, rich, spicy, tangy** | **savoury/savory, sweet** | **smooth** | **home-made** | **lumpy** | **chilli/chili, mustard, peanut, pepper, etc.** | **barbecue, Béarnaise, brown, curry, hollandaise, sweet-and-sour, white, etc.** ◇ *fish in white ~* | **Tabasco™, Worcester, etc.** | **fish, oyster, soy** | **cheese, chocolate, tomato, etc.** | **dipping, pasta**
VERB + SAUCE **make, prepare** | **reduce, thicken** | **add** | **pour on sth, pour over sth, put on sth, spoon on sth, spoon over sth** ◇ *Pour the ~ over the pasta.* | **mix, stir** | **taste**
SAUCE + NOUN **boat** (*esp. BrE*) | **bottle**
PREP. **in ~** ◇ *chicken in peanut ~* | **with ~** ◇ *We had lamb with mint ~.*
→ Special page at FOOD

saucepan *noun* (*esp. BrE*) → See also PAN, POT

ADJ. **non-stick** | **heavy, heavy-based, heavy-bottomed, thick-bottomed** | **large, medium-sized, small**
VERB + SAUCEPAN **cover** ◇ *Cover the ~ and remove from the heat.* | **put sth in, put sth into**
SAUCEPAN + NOUN **lid**

PREP. **in a/the ~, into a/the ~** ◊ *Heat one tablespoon of oil in a ~.* ◊ *Strain the sauce into a ~.*

saunter *verb*

ADV. **casually, slowly | away, back, by, down, in, off, out, over, past, up** ◊ *She ~ed over and said hello.*
PREP. **into, out of | through** ◊ *He ~ed casually through the door.* | **over to, up to**

sausage *noun*

ADJ. **blood, garlic, pork, etc. | smoked | vegetarian | spicy**
VERB + SAUSAGE **eat, have | cook, fry, grill | slice | make**
SAUSAGE + VERB **sizzle**
SAUSAGE + NOUN **meat, skin | link** (*AmE*), **patty** (*AmE*), **roll** (*BrE*), **sandwich**
→ Special page at FOOD

save *noun* in football/soccer, hockey, etc.

ADJ. **brilliant, excellent, fine, good, great, magnificent, outstanding, smart, spectacular, stunning, superb | crucial, important, vital | diving, one-handed, reflex | double**
VERB + SAVE **make, produce, pull off** ◊ *Casillas made some spectacular ~s.*
PREP. **~ by, ~ from** ◊ *some great ~s from both goalkeepers*

save *verb*

1 keep sb/sth safe

ADV. **single-handedly | possibly, potentially, probably | literally**
VERB + SAVE **be able to, can** ◊ *Nothing could ~ us from disaster.* | **be unable to | may, might** ◊ *It's a trick that might just ~ us from total disaster.* | **help (to), try to** ◊ *She helped ~ my career.* | **battle to, be determined to, be on a mission to, fight to** ◊ *Doctors battled to ~ the little boy's life.* | **find a way to, manage to** ◊ *We managed to ~ the animals from being put down.*
PREP. **from** ◊ *They ~d the paintings from destruction.*
PHRASES **an attempt to ~ sth, an effort to ~ sth** ◊ *a last desperate attempt to ~ his marriage* | **a battle to ~ sth, a bid to ~ sth, a campaign to ~ sth, a fight to ~ sth | be responsible for saving sb/sth** ◊ *He is responsible for saving the lives of the aircrew.* | **beyond saving** ◊ *The furniture was beyond saving.*

2 not spend money

ADV. **up** ◊ *I'm saving up to buy a new car.*
VERB + SAVE **look to, try to | manage to**
PREP. **for** ◊ *We're trying to ~ up for our honeymoon.* | **on** ◊ *They're hoping to ~ on printing costs.*
PHRASES **scrimp and ~** ◊ *We scrimp and ~ to send our children to a private school.* | **thereby saving** ◊ *We use video conferencing for our meetings, thereby saving thousands in travel expenses.*

3 in football/soccer, hockey, etc.

ADV. **brilliantly, superbly | bravely, comfortably**

saving *noun*

1 amount not used or wasted

ADJ. **big, considerable, great, huge, major, significant, substantial | estimated, potential, projected** ◊ *The potential ~s are enormous.* | **total | net | cost, financial | efficiency** (*BrE*) | **energy, fuel, power** ◊ *the advantages of energy ~*
VERB + SAVING **find, identify** (*esp. BrE*) ◊ *We need to find ~s of around €30 million.* | **mean, represent, result in** ◊ *For a family of four this can mean a ~ of around $500.* | **deliver, generate, give (sb), offer (sb), produce, yield** ◊ *This smart new design offers considerable ~s in fuel efficiency.* | **achieve, make, realize** ◊ *We need to see where financial ~s can be made.* | **increase | pass on** ◊ *We will pass on this ~ to our customers.* | **offset** ◊ *Crushing fuel costs are offsetting other ~s.*
SAVING + VERB **come from sth, result from sth** ◊ *The major ~s come from reduced costs.*

PREP. **~ for** ◊ *a ~ for club members* | **~ from** ◊ *~s from the use of the new technology* | **~ in** ◊ *a significant ~ in energy costs* | **~ of** ◊ *average ~s of 30%* | **~ on** ◊ *You can have all the benefits of membership while making a big ~ on price.* | **~ to** ◊ *This represents a ~ to businesses of about £175 million a year.* | **with a ~** ◊ *This was done, with a ~ of 40% in staff costs.*

2 savings money saved in a bank, etc.

ADJ. **life, pension, retirement | household** (*esp. AmE*), **personal, private | long-term**
VERB + SAVINGS **have** ◊ *I don't have any ~s.* | **invest | put** ◊ *My grandfather refused to put his ~s in the bank.* | **take out, withdraw | dip into | boost, build up, increase** ◊ *I was determined to build up some ~s.* | **spend, use, use up | live off, live on** ◊ *She lost her job and had to live on her ~s.* | **lose** ◊ *The couple lost their entire life ~s on the venture.* | **wipe out** ◊ *The war had wiped out the family ~s.*
SAVINGS + VERB **grow**
SAVINGS + NOUN **account, bank | bond, certificate** (*BrE*) | **plan, product** (*BrE*), **scheme** (*BrE*), **vehicle | rate | ratio** (*esp. BrE*)
PHRASES **access to your ~s** ◊ *The card gives you instant access to your ~s.*

saviour (*BrE*) (*AmE* savior) *noun*

ADJ. **potential, would-be | personal | unlikely**
VERB + SAVIOUR/SAVIOR **acclaim sb as, hail sb as, see sb/sth as** ◊ *The people clearly saw her as their ~.*
PREP. **~ of** ◊ *He was hailed as the ~ of the nation.*

say *verb*

ADV. **aloud, out loud | loudly | gently, quietly, softly | gruffly, huskily | at once | at last, at length, finally | simply** ◊ *'I am home,' he said simply.* | **hastily, hurriedly, quickly | slowly | abruptly, suddenly | briskly, curtly, shortly, tersely | angrily, bitterly, crossly** (*esp. BrE*) | **fiercely, sharply** ◊ *'I don't know,' she said crossly.* | **bluntly, flatly, matter-of-factly, plainly | firmly, weakly | harshly, sternly | kindly, sweetly | brightly, cheerfully, cheerily, happily | enthusiastically | with a grin, with a smile** ◊ *'You'll see!' Lianne said with a smile.* | **with a smirk, with a wink | with a chuckle, with a laugh | with a frown, with a shrug, with a sigh** ◊ *'Well, at least we tried!' he said with a shrug.* | **miserably, sadly | gravely, grimly, seriously, solemnly | airily, casually, lightly, nonchalantly, smoothly** ◊ *'There's nothing wrong with him,' she said airily.* | **stiffly | proudly | smugly | thoughtfully | conversationally | calmly, evenly, mildly | impatiently, patiently | defensively, indignantly | politely | soothingly | apologetically, sheepishly | awkwardly, hesitantly, lamely, nervously | jokingly, teasingly | drily, mockingly, sarcastically | coldly, coolly, icily | breathlessly | absently | honestly, sincerely, truthfully** ◊ *Can you honestly ~ you're sorry?*
VERB + SAY **be about to, be going to** ◊ *I've forgotten what I was going to ~.* | **hasten to | long to, want to** ◊ *I want to ~ how much we have all enjoyed this evening.* | **hate to** ◊ *I hate to ~ it, but I think Stephen may be right.* | **dare (to)** ◊ *I dared not ~ a word about it to anyone.* ◊ *I dare ~ they she'll come to the wedding.* | **suffice it to, suffice to** ◊ *Suffice it to ~, I refused to get involved.* | **be fair to** ◊ *It is fair to ~ a considerable amount of effort went into the project.* | **have nothing to, have something to** ◊ *Be quiet, I have something to ~.* | **hear sb** ◊ *I heard him ~ they were leaving tomorrow.*
PREP. **about** ◊ *Do you have anything to ~ about this?* | **to** ◊ *That's not what he said to me.*
PHRASES **be quoted as ~ing sth** ◊ *A government spokesman was quoted as ~ing that they would take steps to restore order.* | **a thing to ~** ◊ *That was a very cruel thing to ~.* | **I have to ~, I must ~** ◊ *I have to ~ I didn't expect it to be so good.* | **it has to be said** ◊ *She wasn't at her best, it has to be said.* | **needless to ~** ◊ *Needless to ~, it all went smoothly in the end.*

saying noun

ADJ. **common, famous, popular, well-known** | **old, traditional** | **wise** | **favourite/favorite** ◇ *one of my mother's favourite/favorite ~s* ◇ *My boss's favourite/favorite ~ is 'Don't work harder, work smarter'.*
PREP. **~ about** ◇ *traditional ~s about the weather*
PHRASES **as the ~ goes** ◇ *'Practice makes perfect', as the old ~ goes.*

scaffolding noun

VERB + SCAFFOLDING **erect, put up** | **remove, take down** | **climb, climb up**
SCAFFOLDING + NOUN **pole**
PREP. **on the ~** ◇ *There are several builders working on the ~.*

scale noun

1 size/extent

ADJ. **full** ◇ *It was several days before the full ~ of the accident became clear.* | **big, considerable, epic, grand, greater, huge, large, mass, massive, monumental, vast, wide** | **modest, small** | **sheer** ◇ *It is difficult to comprehend the sheer ~ of the suffering caused by the war.* | **unprecedented** ◇ *a misuse of presidential power on an unprecedented ~* | **ambitious, lavish** ◇ *Do they always entertain on such a lavish ~?* | **global, international, local, national, regional, world** | **commercial** ◇ *The dolls are now produced on a commercial ~.* | **human** ◇ *The final building is realized on a human ~.*
VERB + SCALE **expand, increase** ◇ *They plan to expand the ~ and scope of their operations.* | **reduce** | **match** | **assess, determine** ◇ *We need to determine the ~ of the problem.* | **reveal, show** | **appreciate, comprehend, realize** | **underestimate**
PREP. **~ of** ◇ *the ~ of the disaster/destruction/problem* ◇ *the ~ of the project/task* | **in ~** ◇ *The paintings are small in ~.* | **on a ~** ◇ *pollution on a massive ~*
PHRASES **an economy of ~** ◇ *Economies of ~ enable the larger companies to lower their prices.* | **given the ~ of** ◇ *Given the ~ of the changes, it is essential that all managers familiarize themselves with the details.*

2 range of values

ADJ. **fixed** | **sliding** ◇ *Benefits are paid on a sliding ~ according to family income.* | **five-point, six-point, etc.** | **rating** ◇ *Patients were asked to state their level of anxiety on a 10-point rating ~.* | **time** ◇ *Can you give me any sort of time ~ for the completion of the building work?* | **evolutionary, social** | **pay, salary, wage** (*esp. BrE*) ◇ *The company has a five-point pay ~.* | **Beaufort, Richter, etc.** ◇ *The earthquake measured 6.4 on the Richter ~.*
VERB + SCALE **use** | **construct, develop** | **go up, move up, rise up** ◇ *He has risen up the social ~ from rather humble beginnings.* | **go down, move down**
SCALE + VERB **go from… to…, range from… to…** ◇ *a ~ ranging from 'utterly miserable' to 'deliriously happy'* | **be based on** ◇ *a sliding ~ based on income*
PREP. **on a/the ~** ◇ *Where do birds come on the evolutionary ~?* | **~ of… to…** ◇ *On a ~ of 1 to 10, he scores 7.*
PHRASES **the bottom of the ~, the end of the ~, the top of the ~** ◇ *After ten years, she had worked her way to the top of the pay ~.*

3 relation between actual size and size of a map, etc.

VERB + SCALE **draw sth to** | **have**
SCALE + NOUN **drawing, model** ◇ *He's made a ~ model of the Eiffel Tower.*
PREP. **to ~** ◇ *The plan of the building is not drawn to ~.* | **~ of… to…** ◇ *The map has a ~ of one inch to the mile.* ◇ *a ~ of 1 : 25 000*

4 in music

ADJ. **major, minor**
VERB + SCALE **play, sing** | **practise/practice** ◇ *We could hear her practising/practicing her ~s.*
PREP. **~ of** ◇ *the ~ of C major*

5 on a fish, etc.

ADJ. **overlapping** | **fine, thin** | **armoured/armored** | **fish**
VERB + SCALE **be covered in, be covered with**

6 (*AmE*) machine for weighing → See SCALES

scales (*AmE usually* scale) noun

ADJ. **weighing** (*esp. BrE*) | **bathroom, kitchen**
…OF SCALES **pair** (*esp. BrE*), **set** (*BrE*) ◇ *a pair of kitchen ~*
VERB + SCALES **put sth on, put sth onto, weigh sth on** | **get on, get onto, stand on, step on, step onto** | **tilt, tip** ◇ *At birth, she tipped the ~ at a healthy 7 lb 9 oz.* | **balance**
SCALES + VERB **tip (in favour/favor of sb/sth), tip (towards/ toward sb/sth)** (*figurative*) ◇ *At the moment the scales tip in favour of the Russians.* (*BrE*) ◇ *At the moment the scale tips in favor of the Russians.* (*AmE*)
PREP. **on the ~** ◇ *I had a shock when I stood on the ~.*
PHRASES **tip the ~ (in favour/favor of sb/sth), tip the ~ (towards/toward sb/sth)** (*figurative*) ◇ *That last goal has tipped the ~ towards/toward the Brazilians.*

scalp noun

ADJ. **bald** | **dry** | **itchy** | **flaky**
VERB + SCALP **massage** | **scratch**
SCALP + VERB **itch** | **prickle, tingle**

scan noun

1 examination by a machine

ADJ. **body, whole-body** | **bone, brain, iris, retina, retinal** | **CAT, CT, MRI, PET, ultrasound** | **antivirus, virus** | **routine**
VERB + SCAN **get, have, obtain, undergo** | **carry out, do, perform, run, take** | **order** | **interpret**
SCAN + VERB **confirm sth, indicate sth, reveal sth, show sth** ◇ *A ~ revealed a small fracture in the hip area.*
SCAN + NOUN **data, results**
PREP. **~ of** ◇ *The doctors took a ~ of his thigh bone.*

2 quick look

ADJ. **cursory, quick** ◇ *A quick ~ of the local paper revealed nothing.*
PREP. **~ of**

scan verb

1 look

ADV. **carefully** | **anxiously, frantically, nervously** ◇ *She scanned the street nervously, looking for the two men.* | **slowly** | **briefly, quickly, rapidly** | **constantly** | **mentally, visually**
PREP. **for** ◇ *I scanned the paper for news.* | **across, around, down, through** ◇ *My eyes scanned across the horizon.* ◇ *He scanned through the web pages.*

2 copy using a scanner

ADV. **automatically** | **digitally, electronically, optically**

scandal noun

ADJ. **big, great, major** | **current, recent** | **national, public** | **abuse, accounting, bribery, corporate, corruption, doping, drug** (*esp. AmE*), **drugs** (*esp. BrE*), **financial, political, sex, sexual** ◇ *a sex-abuse ~* ◇ *the prisoner-abuse ~* | **real** ◇ *The real ~ is that nothing has been done to make sure it doesn't happen again.*
…OF SCANDALS **series, spate, wave** ◇ *The government was rocked by a series of ~s.*
VERB + SCANDAL **cause, create** | **avoid, prevent** | **investigate** | **expose, reveal, uncover** | **cover up, hush up** | **be embroiled in, be implicated in, be involved in** ◇ *There have been calls for the resignation of the official involved in the sex ~.*
SCANDAL + VERB **be brewing** (*esp. AmE*), **break, develop, erupt, unfold** ◇ *The ~ broke on the front pages of all the papers the next day.* | **rock sth** | **involve sb/sth** | **engulf sb/ sth** (*esp. BrE*), **surround sb/sth** ◇ *financial ~s surrounding the government*
SCANDAL + NOUN **sheet** (= a newspaper that publishes stories intended to shock the public)

PREP. **in a/the ~** ◊ *He was imprisoned for his part in the bribery ~.* | **~ over** ◊ *the ~s over corruption in public life*
PHRASES **the centre/center of a ~** ◊ *The apartment was paid for by the bank at the centre/center of the ~.* | **a hint of ~, a suggestion of ~** ◊ *Until the story was published there had been no hint of ~.* | **in the wake of a ~** ◊ *In the wake of recent accounting ~s, new cases have come to light.*

scapegoat noun
ADJ. **convenient, easy**
VERB + SCAPEGOAT **become** | **find** | **make sb, use sb as** ◊ *He has been made a ~ for the company's failures.*
PREP. **~ for** ◊ *They are being made the ~s for all the ills of society.*

scar noun
ADJ. **deep, large, long** | **small, thin** | **faint, visible** | **jagged** | **nasty, ugly** | **permanent** | **emotional, mental, psychological** ◊ *Her mental ~s will take time to heal.* | **acne, bullet** | **battle**
VERB + SCAR **leave** | **bear** (*often figurative*) ◊ *The countryside still bears the ~s of the recent hurricane.* | **expose, reveal** | **hide**
SCAR + VERB **remain** | **form** | **fade, heal** | **run** ◊ *She had a long ~ running down her face.*
SCAR + NOUN **tissue**
PREP. **~ on** ◊ *The cut left a permanent ~ on his arm.*

scar verb (often be scarred)
ADV. **badly, deeply, heavily, hideously** ◊ *His face was badly scarred by the fire.* | **emotionally, mentally, physically, psychologically** ◊ *She was both physically and mentally scarred by the accident.* | **forever, permanently**
PREP. **with** (*figurative*) ◊ *Their minds were scarred with bitterness.*
PHRASES **be scarred for life, leave sb scarred** ◊ *The accident left him permanently scarred.*

scarce adj.
VERBS **be, seem** | **become, get, grow** ◊ *Medical supplies were growing ~.* | **remain**
ADV. **extremely, fairly, very, etc.** ◊ *Money was extremely ~ after the war.* | **increasingly, particularly** ◊ *Skilled workers were becoming increasingly ~.*

scarcity noun
ADJ. **great** | **growing, increasing** | **relative** | **artificial** | **food, land, resource, water**
SCARCITY + NOUN **value** ◊ *Old properties in the town have acquired a ~ value.*
PREP. **~ of** ◊ *There is a great ~ of food in the drought-stricken areas.*
PHRASES **in times of ~** ◊ *In times of ~, lions will travel great distances in search of food.*

scare noun
ADJ. **major, nasty, terrible** ◊ *a major health ~* | **food, health** | **AIDS, cancer, etc.** | **pregnancy** | **bomb** | **terror, terrorism, terrorist**
VERB + SCARE **cause** | **give sb** ◊ *It wasn't a serious heart attack, but it gave him a terrible ~.* | **get, have**
SCARE + NOUN **campaign, story, tactics** ◊ *The ad uses ~ tactics to get people to stop smoking.*
PREP. **~ about, ~ over** ◊ *the ~ over bird flu*
PHRASES **a bit of a ~, quite a ~** ◊ *I got quite a ~ when the police called me.*

scare verb
ADV. **really** | **easily** ◊ *He doesn't ~ easily.* | **away, off** ◊ *His name ~s off a lot of people.*
VERB + SCARE **try to, want to** | **start to**
PREP. **into** ◊ *They're just trying to ~ us into letting out the secret.* | **with** ◊ *You don't ~ me with your threats!*
PHRASES **~ sb silly, ~ sb stiff, ~ sb to death** (*all informal*) ◊ *The very thought of flying ~s me stiff.* | **~ the life out of sb, ~ the living daylights out of sb** (*both informal*) ◊ *You ~d the*

life out of me, hiding like that!* | **~ the pants off sb** (*informal, esp. AmE*)

scared adj.
VERBS **be, be running** (*figurative*), **feel, look, seem, sound** ◊ *They had their opponent running ~.* | **get**
ADV. **extremely, fairly, very, etc.** | **a little, slightly, etc.** | **dead** | **just, plain** ◊ *He wasn't sick, Sophie decided. He was just plain ~.* | **genuinely**
PREP. **about** ◊ *It's only a little injection. It's nothing to be ~ about.* | **at** ◊ *I'm feeling a little ~ at the thought of the operation.* | **of** ◊ *I'm really ~ of heights.*
PHRASES **~ out of your wits, ~ stiff** (*informal*), **~ to death** (*informal*)

scarf noun
ADJ. **long, thick** | **cashmere, chiffon, silk, wool** (*esp. AmE*), **woollen/woolen** | **knitted** | **striped, stripy** (*BrE*) | **matching** | **head** (usually *headscarf*), **neck** | **college, football** (*both esp. BrE*)
VERB + SCARF **wind around sth, wrap around sth** ◊ *He wrapped his ~ around his neck.* | **knot, tie** ◊ *She had a ~ tied over her head.* | **unwind, unwrap** (*esp. AmE*) | **pull** ◊ *She pulled her ~ over her mouth.* | **knit**
SCARF + VERB **cover sth** ◊ *Her hair was covered by a silk ~.*
→ Special page at CLOTHES

scarlet adj., noun
1 bright red
ADJ. **bright, brilliant, vivid**
→ Special page at COLOUR
2 red in the face
VERBS **be** | **blush, flush, go, turn**
ADJ. **bright** ◊ *She flushed bright ~.*
PREP. **with** ◊ *He had gone ~ with embarrassment.*

scattered adj.
VERBS **be, lie** | **find sth**
ADV. **liberally** ◊ *Large vases of flowers were liberally ~ around the room.* | **randomly** | **thinly** (*esp. BrE*) | **widely** ◊ *The people live in widely ~ communities.* | **everywhere**
PREP. **about** (*esp. BrE*), **across, along, among, around, on, over** ◊ *Broken glass lay ~ over the floor.* | **throughout, with** ◊ *The whole area was ~ with debris.*

scenario noun
ADJ. **likely, plausible, possible, realistic** ◊ *The more likely ~ is that interest rates will rise.* | **unlikely** | **common, familiar, typical** | **future, hypothetical** | **optimistic, rosy** | **best-case, ideal, perfect, win-win** (*esp. AmE*) | **frightening, grim, pessimistic** | **apocalyptic, doomsday, nightmare, worst, worst-case** | **dramatic, interesting** | **alternative, different** | **similar**
VERB + SCENARIO **consider, imagine** | **construct, create, develop** | **describe, outline, paint, present** ◊ *the ~ painted by some sections of the Western press* | **offer, propose, suggest** | **enact, play out** ◊ *He enjoyed playing out the various ~s in his own mind.*
SCENARIO + VERB **play out** (*esp. AmE*), **unfold** ◊ *Similar ~s are playing out across the country.*
PREP. **in a/the ~** ◊ *In a worst-case ~, the disease will reach epidemic proportions.* | **under a/the ~** ◊ *Under any of these ~s, the company will run into debt.*

scene noun
1 place where sth happened
ADJ. **accident, crash, crime, murder** ◊ *footprints found near the murder ~*
VERB + SCENE **attend, be on** ◊ *A police officer attended the ~.* | **arrive at, arrive on, reach** ◊ *An ambulance soon arrived at the ~ of the accident.* | **return to, rush to** | **flee, leave** | **be**

called to ◇ *The police were called to the ~.* | **cordon off** (*esp. BrE*)

PREP. **at the ~** ◇ *Police say the man died at the ~.* ◇ *a gun found at the ~ of the crime* | **on the ~** ◇ *Photographers were on the ~ in seconds.* | **~ of** ◇ *The criminal often revisits the ~ of the crime.*

2 what you see around you

ADJ. **beautiful, charming, idyllic, peaceful, picturesque** | **bucolic, pastoral** | **grisly, gruesome, horrific** | **appalling, distressing** | **touching** | **bizarre, extraordinary, strange** ◇ *She opened the door on an extraordinary ~ of disorder.* | **familiar** | **domestic** ◇ *a touching domestic ~* | **city, country, rural, street** | **nativity**

VERB + SCENE **stare at, survey, watch, witness** ◇ *He surveyed the ~ with horror.* | **imagine, picture** | **recall, remember, replay** ◇ *I replayed the ~ in my mind.* | **describe**

SCENE + VERB **occur, unfold** ◇ *We sat in horror watching the ~s of violence unfold before us.* | **be reminiscent of sth** ◇ *Paramedics tended the wounded in ~s reminiscent of wartime.*

PREP. **amid ~s of** ◇ *The star arrived amidst ~s of excitement.* | **in a/the ~** | **~ from** ◇ *~s from Greek mythology* | **~ of** ◇ *He painted ~s of country life.* ◇ *The battlefield was a ~ of utter carnage.*

PHRASES **a change of ~** (*esp. BrE*) (usually **a change of scenery** in *AmE*) ◇ *You're exhausted. What you need is a complete change of ~.*

3 one part of book, play, etc.

ADJ. **opening** | **climactic, final, last** | **dramatic, funny, romantic, steamy, touching, tragic** ◇ *The movie has several steamy bedroom ~s.* | **courtroom, crowd** | **action, battle, chase, fight** | **bedroom, kissing, love, sex** | **death** | **cut, deleted**

VERB + SCENE **act, play** ◇ *She plays the love ~s brilliantly.* | **rehearse, run through** ◇ *We ran through the final ~ again.* | **recreate** | **write** | **film, shoot** | **stage** | **set** ◇ *The ~ is set in the first paragraph with an account of Sally's childhood.* | **steal** ◇ *The little girl stole the ~ from all the big stars.*

SCENE + VERB **feature sb** | **depict sth, show sth** | **begin** | **take place** | **shift** ◇ *Then the ~ shifts to the kitchen.*

SCENE + NOUN **change**

PREP. **in a/the ~** ◇ *He appears in the opening ~.* | **~ between** ◇ *There is a dramatic fight ~ between the two brothers.*

PHRASES **behind the ~s** (= behind the stage) | **a change of ~**

4 public display of anger, etc.

ADJ. **big, little** | **angry** (*esp. BrE*), **terrible, ugly, unpleasant** | **emotional, violent**

VERB + SCENE **cause, create, make** ◇ *Quiet! Don't make a ~!*

PREP. **~ between** ◇ *There have been a couple of ugly ~s between him and the manager.*

5 area of activity

ADJ. **burgeoning, flourishing, lively** | **contemporary** | **international, local, world** | **art, arts, cultural, literary, music, musical, theatre/theater** ◇ *He is heavily involved in the local art ~.* | **club, dance** | **fashion, political, social** | **dating, singles** | **gay** | **drug** (*esp. AmE*), **drugs** (*esp. BrE*), **underground** | **folk, jazz, pop, rap, rock, etc.**

VERB + SCENE **be involved in, be part of** | **appear on, arrive on, come on, come onto** ◇ *A new face has arrived on the South African literary ~.* | **burst onto, explode onto** | **vanish from** ◇ *Many of the stars of the nineties have completely vanished from the music ~.* | **dominate**

PREP. **on the ~, onto the ~** ◇ *the eruption of Cuban music onto the world ~*

PHRASES **a newcomer to the ~** ◇ *The movie's director is a newcomer to the Hollywood ~.* | **not your ~** (*informal*) ◇ *Hillwalking is not my ~, so I stayed at home.*

scenery noun

1 features of the countryside

ADJ. **lovely, nice, picturesque, pretty** | **beautiful, breath-**

taking, dramatic, fantastic, gorgeous, magnificent, spectacular, stunning, wonderful** | **changing, varied** | **surrounding** ◇ *The town is charming and the surrounding ~ superb.* | **passing** | **local** | **coastal, mountain, natural**

VERB + SCENERY **admire, enjoy, look at, take in** ◇ *An observation deck lets you take in the passing ~.* | **see** | **watch** ◇ *She watched the passing ~.*

SCENERY + VERB **change**

PREP. **amid (the) ~, in (the) ~** ◇ *The hotel lies amid spectacular mountain ~.* | **through (the) ~** ◇ *The train passes through some magnificent ~.*

PHRASES **the beauty of the ~** ◇ *We stopped to admire the beauty of the ~ around us.* | **a change of ~** ◇ *For a complete change of ~, take a ferry out to one of the islands.*

2 on stage

VERB + SCENERY **set up** | **change**

PREP. **~ for** ◇ *That table is part of the ~ for Act 2.*

scent noun

1 pleasant smell

ADJ. **heady, heavy, intoxicating, pungent, rich, sharp, strong** ◇ *the heavy ~ of Indian cooking* | **delicate, faint, soft** | **lingering** | **sweet** | **beautiful, delicious, lovely, pleasant** | **fresh** ◇ *the fresh ~ of flowers* | **warm** | **floral, flowery** | **jasmine, lavender, pine, etc.** | **musky, spicy** | **exotic** ◇ *Frank inhaled the exotic floral ~ of her perfume.* | **familiar**

VERB + SCENT **have** ◇ *This flower has no ~.* | **be filled with** ◇ *The air was filled with the ~ of lilac.* | **give off, release** ◇ *The flowers give off a heady ~ at night.* | **breathe in, inhale, smell**

SCENT + VERB **come, drift, waft** ◇ *From the vine outside came the ~ of honey.* | **fill sth** ◇ *The ~ of pine filled the room.* | **linger** ◇ *The ~ of incense lingered in the air.*

2 smell that an animal/a person leaves behind

ADJ. **body, human, masculine, personal, sexual**

VERB + SCENT **be on, have** ◇ *The dog was on the ~ of a rabbit.* ◇ *The hounds have the ~.* | **leave** ◇ *The cat had left its ~ on the sofa.* | **catch, pick up** ◇ *One of the hounds had picked up the ~ of a fox.* | **lose** | **follow**

SCENT + NOUN **gland** | **mark, marking** | **trail**

scented adj.

VERBS **be**

ADV. **heavily, highly, powerfully, richly, strongly** ◇ *richly ~ flowers* | **delicately, faintly, lightly** ◇ *the delicately ~ writing paper* | **sweetly**

PREP. **with** ◇ *The air was ~ with the smell of pines.*

sceptic (*BrE*) (*AmE* skeptic) noun

ADJ. **hardened**

VERB + SCEPTIC/SKEPTIC **convince, win over** ◇ *He has managed to convince even the ~s.* | **confound, defy, refute, silence**

SCEPTIC/SKEPTIC + VERB **argue sth, claim sth, point out sth, say sth** ◇ *Sceptics will argue that no such plan has ever proved successful.* | **think sth** | **doubt sth, question sth, wonder sth**

PREP. **~ about** ◇ *She is a ~ about the dangers of global warming.*

PHRASES **prove the ~s right, prove the ~s wrong** ◇ *Events since the elections have proved the ~s right.*

sceptical (*BrE*) (*AmE* skeptical) adj.

VERBS **be, look, sound** | **remain** | **become**

ADV. **extremely, fairly, very, etc.** | **deeply, highly** | **increasingly** | **a little, slightly, etc.** ◇ *I'm a little ~ of these claims.* | **naturally, understandably** ◇ *They remain understandably ~ about her promises of improvement.* | **initially**

PREP. **about** ◇ *He is deeply ~ about the value of teaching poetry.* | **as to** ◇ *Many were ~ as to whether the plan would succeed.* | **of** ◇ *They are highly ~ of political leaders.*

scepticism (*BrE*) (*AmE* skepticism) noun

ADJ. **considerable, deep, extreme, great** | **healthy** | **growing** | **general, widespread** | **public** | **initial** ◇ *My initial ~ was replaced with respectful admiration.*

... OF SCEPTICISM/SKEPTICISM **degree, great deal** ◇ *I regard their press releases with a degree of ~.* | **healthy dose** ◇ *The President's claim must be regarded with a healthy dose of ~.*
VERB + SCEPTICISM/SKEPTICISM **have** ◇ *She has a healthy ~ towards/toward the claims in the company's report.* | **express, voice** | **share** ◇ *Some attorneys share her ~ about the new plan.* | **be greeted with, be met with, be treated with, be viewed with** ◇ *This claim has often been met with ~.*
PREP. **with ~** ◇ *This theory was initially received with great ~ by her fellow scientists.* | **~ about, ~ over, ~ towards/toward** ◇ *He expressed a great deal of ~ about the value of psychoanalysis.*

schedule noun

1 plan of work to be done

ADJ. **daily, weekly, etc.** | **current** | **normal, regular** | **ambitious, busy, demanding, full, gruelling/grueling, heavy, hectic, punishing** (*esp. BrE*), **rigorous, tight** | **rigid, strict** | **flexible** | **delivery, development, payment, production, training, work, etc.** | **filming, recording, shooting**
VERB + SCHEDULE **have, maintain** ◇ *She has a very demanding ~.* | **arrange, design, draw up, establish, make, plan, prepare, work out** | **adjust, alter, juggle** (*AmE*), **rearrange** | **check** | **keep to, meet, stay on, stick to** ◇ *We had to work a lot of overtime to meet the strict production ~.* | **be ahead of, run ahead of** | **interrupt, take time out of** ◇ *The president took time out of his busy ~ to visit our school.* | **fit sth into** ◇ *I'm trying to fit everything into my busy ~.*
SCHEDULE + VERB **have a ~ to keep** (*AmE*) ◇ *We have a tight ~ to keep.*
PREP. **according to ~** ◇ *At this stage everything is going according to ~.* | **behind ~** ◇ *We're starting to slip behind ~.* | **in the ~** ◇ *Allow time in the ~ for sickness.* | **off ~** (*esp. AmE*) ◇ *We're five days off ~.* | **on ~** ◇ *The project is right on ~.*

2 (*AmE*) **list showing times of events** → See also TIMETABLE

ADJ. **class, course, exam, lecture, school** | **bus, train** ◇ *Connor checked the bus ~s for the day.* | **flight** ◇ *disruptions to flight ~s caused by the strike* | **racing**
VERB + SCHEDULE **check, compare, look at, scan**

3 list of television programmes/programs

ADJ. **television, TV** | **programme** (*BrE*), **programming** (*esp. AmE*) | **network** | **daytime, evening, prime-time** (*esp. AmE*), **weekday** | **spring, summer, etc.** | **Saturday, Sunday, etc.**

schedule verb

ADV. **currently** | **initially, originally** ◇ *The meeting was originally ~d for March 12.* | **provisionally, tentatively** | **regularly**
PREP. **for** ◇ *The movie is ~d for release next month.*
PHRASES **be ~d to begin, open, take place, etc.** ◇ *The Grand Prix is ~d to take place on July 4.* | **be ~d to appear, compete, speak, etc.**

scheme noun

1 plan for getting an advantage, etc. for yourself

ADJ. **crazy, hare-brained** ◇ *She's come up with a hare-brained ~ for getting her novel published.* | **elaborate** | **get-rich-quick, moneymaking** ◇ *This is not one of those get-rich-quick ~s that you see on the Internet.* | **money-laundering, Ponzi** (*AmE*), **pyramid** | **devious, diabolical, evil, fraudulent, nefarious**
VERB + SCHEME **concoct, devise, dream up, hatch** ◇ *He concocted a ~ to steal 1.9 million shares.* | **propose** | **crack, foil, thwart, uncover**
SCHEME + VERB **involve sth**

2 way sth is designed or organized

ADJ. **colour/color, decorating** (*AmE*), **lighting, paint** | **rhyme** ◇ *The poem's rhyme ~, which Dante invented, is known as 'terza rima'.* | **classification, labelling/labeling, naming, numbering** | **conceptual, organizational, regulatory**
VERB + SCHEME **design** | **choose**

PHRASES **in the grand ~ of things, in the great ~ of things, in the overall ~ of things** ◇ *In the grand ~ of things, one missing page doesn't matter.*

3 (*BrE*) **plan for doing sth**

ADJ. **major, multi-million-pound** | **ambitious, grandiose** | **controversial** | **imaginative, ingenious, innovative** | **successful** | **compulsory, voluntary** | **proposed** | **pilot** ◇ *The project is based on a successful pilot ~ in Glasgow.* | **incentive, insurance, pension, recycling, share, statutory, training**
VERB + SCHEME **have** ◇ *He has an ingenious ~ to attract funding.* | **come up with, design, devise, draw up, plan, prepare, propose** | **oppose, support** | **approve, reject** | **announce** | **establish, initiate, introduce, launch, organize, pilot, set up, start** ◇ *The government set up a ~ of limited public health assistance in 1992.* | **administer, adopt, carry out, implement, operate, run** | **back, finance, fund** ◇ *a government-backed ~* | **be in, join, participate in, take part in** | **use** | **abolish, wind up**
SCHEME + VERB **offer sth, provide sth** | **allow sth, enable sth** ◇ *The ~ allows customers to trade in their own computer against the cost of a new one.* | **aim to, be aimed at sth, be designed for sth, be designed to do sth, involve sth** ◇ *a ~ involving local libraries* | **be based on** | **apply to sth, cover sth** ◇ *The ~ applies to families with three or more children.* | **go ahead, proceed** ◇ *The ~ has been given approval to go ahead.* | **come into effect, come into force** | **succeed, work** | **collapse, fail**
PREP. **in a/the ~** ◇ *Schools in the ~ will receive an annual grant.* | **under a/the ~** ◇ *Under the ~, land would be sold to building companies.* | **~ for** ◇ *a training ~ for unemployed teenagers* | **~ whereby** ◇ *a ~ whereby the elderly will be provided with help in the home*

scholar noun

ADJ. **brilliant, great, leading, outstanding** | **distinguished, eminent, famous, noted, prominent, renowned** | **senior** | **visiting** | **contemporary, modern** | **conservative, feminist, Jewish, liberal, Muslim, Western, etc.** | **biblical, classical, French, history, literary, religious, etc.**

scholarship noun

ADJ. **college** (*esp. AmE*) | **student** (*AmE*) | **academic** (*AmE*), **athletic** (*AmE*), **sports** | **basketball, football, golf, etc.** (*esp. AmE*) | **full** (*AmE*) | **travelling** (*BrE*)
VERB + SCHOLARSHIP **earn** (*AmE*), **gain** (*BrE*), **get, obtain** (*BrE*), **receive, win** | **award (sb), give (sb), offer** ◇ *The Fund awards four ~s every year.*
SCHOLARSHIP + NOUN **programme/program, scheme** (*BrE*) | **student** | **exam, examination** (*both BrE*)
PREP. **on a ~** ◇ *Two of the boys are on football ~s.* | **~ to** ◇ *She was awarded a ~ to Columbia University.*

school noun → See also HIGH SCHOOL

ADJ. **nursery** | **comprehensive, first, grammar, junior, middle, prep, preparatory, senior** (*all in the UK*) | **elementary, grade** (*informal*), **high, junior high, middle** (*all in the US*) | **primary, secondary** (*both esp. BrE*) | **charter** (*AmE*), **fee-paying, independent, private, public, state** (*BrE*) (In Britain 'public schools' are private. In the US a public school is a free local school paid for by the government. In the UK, this type of free school is called a 'state school'.) | **special** ◇ *She attends a special ~ for children with learning difficulties.* | **coed** (*informal*), **co-educational, mixed** (*BrE*) | **single-sex** | **all-boys, all-girls, boys', girls'** | **boarding, residential** (*BrE*) | **day** | **faith** (*BrE*), **mainstream, religious** | **Catholic, Christian, Islamic, Muslim, etc.** | **Bible, Hebrew, Sunday** | **summer** | **inner-city, local, neighbourhood/neighborhood, parochial** (*AmE*), **rural, village** (*BrE*) | **night** (*old-fashioned*) | **finishing** | **prep, preparatory** (= a school that prepares students for college) (*in the US*) | **grad, graduate** (*both AmE*) | **trade, vocational** (*both AmE*) | **training** | **art, business, divinity** (*AmE*), **drama, film, law,** medical ~. | **understand** ◇ *our ability to understand the ~ of environmental degradation*

SCIENCE + NOUN **curriculum** | **education, research, teaching** | **experiment, project** | **lab** (*informal*), **laboratory** | **major** (*AmE*) | **researcher** | **adviser** ◇ *President Bill Clinton's ~ adviser* | **correspondent, editor, journalist, reporter** (*esp. AmE*), **writer** | **book, journal, textbook** | **policy** (*esp. AmE*) ◇ *The society provides advice on ~ policy.* | **community** (*esp. AmE*) (usually *scientific community* in *BrE* and *AmE*) | **museum, park** | **fair** (*esp. AmE*)

PREP. **~ of** ◇ *Meteorology is the ~ of the weather.*

PHRASES **the advancement of ~, the development of ~** | **the history of ~** | **the laws of ~** | **~ and technology** | **the world of ~** ◇ *His experiments have achieved notoriety in the world of ~.*

→ Note at SUBJECT (for verbs and more nouns)

scientific *adj.*

VERBS **be, seem, sound**

ADV. **highly** ◇ *It all looks highly ~!* | **truly** | **purely** ◇ *Her curiosity was purely ~.* | **not very** ◇ *His approach was not very ~.*

scientist *noun*

ADJ. **brilliant, good, great** | **distinguished, eminent, famous, leading, respected** | **serious** | **professional, trained** | **chief, senior, top** | **mad** (*often humorous*) ◇ *She had an image of a mad ~ working in his laboratory.* | **independent** | **government** | **fellow** ◇ *She gave a lecture to 2 000 fellow ~s in Kyoto.* | **research** | **natural, physical** | **agricultural, earth, environmental, food, marine, nuclear, soil** | **forensic, medical** | **behavioural/behavioral, political, social** | **computer** | **young** ◇ *a contest for young ~s*

...OF SCIENTISTS **group, team**

VERB + SCIENTIST **baffle, intrigue, puzzle** ◇ *a mystery that has baffled ~s for many years*

SCIENTIST + VERB **be interested in sth, be involved in sth, examine sth, specialize in sth, study sth, work (on sth)** ◇ *~s interested in Antarctic research* | **know sth** | **estimate sth** ◇ *The ~s estimate that nearly two thirds of the continent has become drier over the past 60 years.* | **argue sth, believe sth, claim sth, propose sth, say sth, suggest sth, warn sth, warn that…** ◇ *Scientists warned of even greater eruptions to come.* | **discover sth, find sth, identify sth, reveal sth** | **agree sth, agree on sth, conclude sth** | **disagree on sth** | **report sth** | **develop sth** ◇ *Scientists have developed an injection that doesn't use a needle.*

→ Note at JOB

scissors *noun*

ADJ. **blunt, sharp** | **kitchen** | **nail** | **small**

...OF SCISSORS **pair** ◇ *a pair of nail ~*

VERB + SCISSORS **cut sth with, use** ◇ *Don't use these ~ to cut paper or cardboard.*

SCISSORS + VERB **cut** ◇ *These ~ don't cut very well.*

scold *verb*

ADV. **gently, lightly** | **silently** | **severely**

PREP. **for** ◇ *Rose ~ed the child gently for being naughty.*

scope *noun*

1 opportunity

ADJ. **full** ◇ *In her new house she had full ~ for her passion for gardening.* | **ample, considerable, enormous, great, huge, tremendous** | **limited**

VERB + SCOPE **have** | **allow (sb), give sb, leave (sb), offer (sb), provide (sb with)** ◇ *These courses give students more ~ for developing their own ideas.* | **increase, reduce**

PREP. **~ for** ◇ *There is limited ~ for creativity in my job.*

2 range/extent

ADJ. **broad, wide** | **epic, vast** ◇ *This is a novel of epic ~ and grand passions.* | **global, international, national** | **sheer** ◇ *The sheer ~ of the project was impressive.* | **limited, narrow** ◇ *The ~ of the exhibition is disappointingly narrow.* | **proper** ◇ *the proper ~ of the criminal law* | **geographic** (*esp. AmE*),

---

med (*informal, esp. AmE*), **medical, military** | **dance, driving, language, riding** | **prestigious** | **beacon** (*BrE*), **magnet** (*AmE*) | **failing** ◇ *It is a failing ~ with some of the worst results in the city.*

VERB + SCHOOL **attend, go to** | **enter** (*esp. AmE*), **start** | **finish, leave** (*BrE*), **quit** (*AmE*) | **stay in** | **be expelled from, be kicked out of** (*esp. AmE*) ◇ *He was expelled from ~ for verbally abusing his teacher.* | **drop out of** | **bunk off** (*BrE, informal*), **ditch** (*AmE*), **play hooky from** (*AmE*), **play truant from** (*BrE*), **skip** | **be off** (*BrE*), **stay home from** (*AmE*), **stay off** (*BrE*) ◇ *Eric is off ~ again.* ◇ *My parents let me stay home from ~ yesterday.* ◇ *My parents let me stay off ~ yesterday.* | **keep sb home from** (*AmE*), **keep sb off** (*BrE*) ◇ *You don't need to keep your child home from ~ because of a cough.* ◇ *You don't need to keep your child off ~ because of a cough.* | **teach** (*AmE*) ◇ *She teaches elementary ~ in Atlanta.* | **run** ◇ *He runs a karate ~ in San Jose, California.*

SCHOOL + NOUN **child** (usually *schoolchildren*), **kid** (*informal*) (usually *schoolkids*) | **boy, girl** (usually *schoolboy, schoolgirl*) | **pupil** (*esp. BrE, becoming less frequent*) | **student** | **friend, mate** (usually *schoolmate*) (*both esp. BrE*) | **teacher** (usually *schoolteacher*) ◇ *She's a middle-school teacher.* | **master, mistress** (usually *schoolmaster, schoolmistress*) (*old-fashioned, esp. BrE*) | **head teacher** (*BrE*), **principal** (*AmE*) | **administrator, counselor** (*both AmE*) | **governor** (*esp. BrE*) | **auditorium** (*esp. AmE*), **building, classroom, hall, library** | **playground, yard** (usually *schoolyard*) (*AmE*) | **day** ◇ *The next day was Monday, a ~ day.* ◇ *It was just a typical ~ day.* | **semester** (*esp. AmE*), **term, year** | **holidays** (*BrE*), **vacation** (*AmE*) | **bus** | **run** (= the journey that parents make to take their children to school) (*BrE*) | **dinners** (*BrE*), **lunch** (*esp. AmE*), **meals** (*BrE*) | **rules** | **uniform** | **assembly** | **age** ◇ *children of ~ age* ◇ *school-age children* | **days** (usually *schooldays*) ◇ *She hadn't seen Laura since her schooldays.* | **district** (*AmE*) | **curriculum** | **voucher** (*AmE*)

PREP. **after ~** ◇ *We're going to play football after ~.* ◇ *a range of after-school activities* | **at (a/the) ~** (*BrE*) ◇ *She didn't do very well at ~.* ◇ *Their son's at the ~ near the station.* | **in (a/the) ~** ◇ *Are your children still in ~?* (*AmE*) ◇ *the cleverest child in the ~*

PHRASES **be on the way home from ~** | **get ready for ~** | **get out of ~** | **come home from, get home from** | **do well at ~** (*BrE*), **do well in ~** (*esp. AmE*) ◇ *Amy is doing extremely well in ~ and gets top marks in every class.* | **leave for ~**

schooling *noun*

ADJ. **good, proper** ◇ *She received the best ~ the town could offer.* | **poor** ◇ *Many children are disadvantaged by poor ~.* | **compulsory** ◇ *Compulsory ~ ends at sixteen.* | **formal** | **primary, secondary** (*both esp. BrE*) | **home, private** | **mainstream**

VERB + SCHOOLING **get, have, receive** ◇ *He has had no formal ~.* | **begin** | **continue, continue with** ◇ *She continued with her ~ after a long period of illness.* | **complete, finish**

SCHOOLING + VERB **suffer** ◇ *We will stay in this country, as we don't want her ~ to suffer.*

PHRASES **years of ~** ◇ *children's development in the early years of ~*

science *noun*

ADJ. **modern** | **bad, junk** (*informal*) ◇ *This rule is based on bad ~.* | **good, hard, real, sound** ◇ *His essay is not based on good ~.* | **exact, inexact** ◇ *Politics is as much an art form as an exact ~.* | **popular** ◇ *a writer of popular ~ books* | **advanced, basic** | **applied, empirical, experimental** | **pure, theoretical** | **biological, chemical, evolutionary, human, life, materials, mathematical, natural, physical** ◇ *The life ~s include biology and botany.* | **agricultural, earth, environmental, food, marine, soil** | **biomedical, forensic, medical, veterinary** | **behavioural/behavioral, cognitive, political, social** | **computer, information** | **space** | **management, sports** | **creation**

VERB + SCIENCE **advance** ◇ *Research is critical to advancing*

geographical ◇ *The geographical ~ of product markets has widened since the war.*
VERB + SCOPE **broaden, enlarge, expand, extend, increase, widen | limit, narrow, reduce, restrict | define, determine** ◇ *These criteria were used to determine the ~ of the curriculum.*
SCOPE + VERB **broaden, expand, extend, increase**
PREP. **beyond the ~ of, outside the ~ of** ◇ *The subject lies outside the ~ of this book.* | **in (sth's) ~** ◇ *The survey is too limited in (its) ~.* | **within the ~ of** ◇ *These disputes fall within the ~ of the local courts.*

score noun

1 in a game, competition, etc.

ADJ. **big, excellent, good, high, record, top | winning | bad, low, poor | average | close, level** ◇ *The ~ was close in the final game.* | **aggregate** (*BrE*), **overall, total | final, half-time | individual, team | basketball, football, etc. | box** (in baseball)
VERB + SCORE **achieve, earn, finish with, get, have | give (sb)** ◇ *He got around the course in 72, giving him an average ~ of 70.* | **make, take** ◇ *A late goal made the ~ 4–2.* ◇ *A late goal took the ~ to 4–2.* | **keep, record** ◇ *I'll keep (the) ~.* | **level, tie** ◇ *Gerrard struggled valiantly to level the ~.*
SCORE + VERB **be, stand at** ◇ *At half-time the ~ stood at 3–0.*
SCORE + NOUN **board** (usually **scoreboard**), **card** (usually **scorecard**), **sheet** (*BrE*) ◇ *The scoreboard showed we were in the lead.* ◇ *Inamoto failed to get his name on the ~ sheet (= failed to score).* | **draw** (*BrE*)
PREP. **~ against** ◇ *the best ~ for years against Italy*
PHRASES **bring the ~s level, keep the ~s level** (*both BrE*) ◇ *Ronaldo brought the ~s level at 2–2.*

2 (*esp. AmE*) in a test

ADJ. **excellent, good, high, perfect, record, top | bad, low, poor | average, mean, median, standard | combined, overall, total | IQ, SAT** (*AmE*), **test**
VERB + SCORE **achieve, get, have, obtain, receive | calculate | compare | give sb | boost, improve, increase** ◇ *The article claims that vitamins will boost your child's IQ ~.*
SCORE + VERB **indicate, reflect, show | range** ◇ *Most ten-year-olds had ~s ranging between 50 and 70.*
PREP. **~ for** ◇ *She got an unusually low ~ for creativity.*

3 written music

ADJ. **full | music, musical | orchestral, piano, vocal** ◇ *the vocal ~ of 'The Magic Flute'* | **ballet | film, movie** (*esp. AmE*) | **original** ◇ *The original ~ for the movie was composed by John Williams.*
VERB + SCORE **compose, play, read, write**
PREP. **in a/the ~** ◇ *a mistake in the piano ~*

score verb

1 win points, goals, etc.

ADV. **once, twice, etc. | nearly | easily** ◇ *Cunningham broke away and ~d easily.* | **heavily** (*BrE*) | **finally**
VERB + SCORE **try to | be able to, manage to | fail to, have yet to** ◇ *Walker has yet to ~ this season.* | **be ready to** (*esp. AmE*), **look likely to** (*esp. BrE*) ◇ *Schumacher is ready to ~ at his home track again.* ◇ *Villa always looked likely to ~.*
PREP. **against** ◇ *The crowd erupted when the Green Bay Packers ~d against the Denver Broncos.* | **for** ◇ *She has not yet ~d for her new team.*
PHRASES **come close to scoring** (*esp. BrE*) ◇ *It was Robertson who came closest to scoring.* | **have a/the chance to ~, have an/the opportunity to ~** ◇ *We had several chances to ~ in the second half.* | **open the scoring** ◇ *Ronaldinho opened the scoring in the seventh minute of the game.*

2 gain marks in a test, survey, etc.

ADV. **highly, well** ◇ *The company ~s highly on customer service.* | **consistently** ◇ *Women consistently ~d higher than men in this test.*

scorn noun

ADJ. **withering** ◇ *She reserved her most withering ~ for*

---

journalists. | **public** ◇ *He has suffered public ~ and humiliation.*
VERB + SCORN **heap, pour** ◇ *Abuse and ~ were heaped upon the new tax.* | **reserve** ◇ *He reserved particular ~ for the director.* | **deserve** ◇ *What have I done to deserve such ~?*
PREP. **with ~** ◇ *He stared with ~ at his interviewers.* | **~ for** ◇ *He didn't try to hide his ~ for our way of doing things.*
PHRASES **an object of ~** ◇ *His poetry was the object of ~.*

scowl noun

ADJ. **dark | angry | permanent | slight**
VERB + SCOWL **wear | give (sb) | be set in** ◇ *His face was set in a permanent ~.*
SCOWL + VERB **darken, deepen**
PREP. **in a ~** ◇ *Her brows drew together in a ~.* | **with a ~** ◇ *He looked up at me with a ~.*
PHRASES **have a ~ on your face**

scowl verb

ADV. **angrily, darkly, deeply, fiercely** ◇ *She ~ed darkly and muttered something under her breath.* | **slightly**
PREP. **at** ◇ *He ~ed at her before stalking out of the room.*

scramble noun

ADJ. **desperate, frantic, mad, undignified** (*esp. BrE*) ◇ *There was a mad ~ for the exits.*
PREP. **in a/the ~** ◇ *I lost my sister in the ~ for a seat.* | **~ down, ~ over, ~ up, etc.** ◇ *an undignified ~ down the slope* | **~ for** ◇ *a ~ for tickets for the game*

scramble verb

ADV. **desperately, frantically, quickly** ◇ *They ~d frantically over the piles of debris.* | **around, away, back, off**
VERB + SCRAMBLE **manage to**
PREP. **down, into, out of, over, through, up, etc.** ◇ *She managed to ~ over the wall.* ◇ *He ~d up the stairs.*
PHRASES **~ for cover** ◇ *We ~d for cover and hid underneath the truck.* | **~ to your feet** ◇ *He ~d awkwardly to his feet.* | **~ to safety**

scrap noun

1 small piece or amount

ADJ. **little, small, tiny** ◇ *She scribbled the address on a little ~ of paper.* | **last** ◇ *He removed the last ~s of food from his plate.* | **leftover | food, kitchen, table** (*AmE*) ◇ *The pigs are fed on food ~s.*
PREP. **~ of** ◇ *Every ~ of land in the town has been built on.*
PHRASES **every last ~** ◇ *He ate every last ~ of the food.*

2 recyclable items or material

...OF SCRAP **piece**
VERB + SCRAP **sell sth as, sell sth for** ◇ *The engine has been sold for ~.*
SCRAP + NOUN **iron, material, metal, paper, wood | heap, yard** (usually **scrapyard**) ◇ *My first computer has been consigned to the ~ heap.* | **dealer, merchant** (*BrE*) | **value** ◇ *The ~ value of the car is around $200.*

3 (*informal*) fight

VERB + SCRAP **get into, have**
PREP. **in a/the ~** ◇ *He looks like he's been in a ~.* | **~ with** ◇ *He had a bit of a ~ with the boy next door.*

scrape verb

ADV. **carefully, gently** ◇ *She carefully ~d away the top layer of paint.* | **away, back, off** ◇ *I ~d the dirt off.*
PREP. **against** ◇ *He ~d the car against the garage wall.* | **along** ◇ *Patrick lifted the gate to prevent it from scraping along the ground.* | **on** ◇ *I ~d my elbow on the wall as I went past.* | **with** ◇ *I ~d the carrots with a knife.*
PHRASES **~ sth clean** ◇ *The wood had been ~d clean.*

scratch noun

ADJ. **deep, long, nasty** | **light, little, minor, slight, small** ◇ *His only injuries were some minor ~es above his eye.* | **a few, numerous** | **cat**
VERB + SCRATCH **have** | **get** | **leave, make** ◇ *Powdered cleansers will leave ~es on the glass.*
SCRATCH + NOUN **mark**
PREP. **without a** ~ ◇ *She emerged from the wrecked vehicle without a ~.*

scratch verb

ADV. **badly** ◇ *The table had been badly ~ed.* | **absently** (*esp. AmE*) ◇ *He absently ~ed his head.* | **lightly**
PREP. **at** ◇ *He ~ed at his beard for a few seconds.* ◇ *I could hear the dog ~ing at the door.* | **on** ◇ *I ~ed my arm on a rose bush.* | **with** ◇ *She ~ed his face with her nails.*

scream noun

ADJ. **deafening, ear-piercing, ear-splitting, high-pitched, loud, piercing, shrill** | **muffled, stifled, strangled** | **agonizing, hysterical, terrible** | **agonized, terrified**
VERB + SCREAM **hear** | **emit, give, let out** | **muffle, stifle, suppress**
SCREAM + VERB **echo, ring out** ◇ *His ~s echoed through the empty house.* | **come from** ◇ *The ~ came from upstairs.*
PREP. **with a** ~ ◇ *She reacted to the news with hysterical ~s.* | ~ **for** ◇ *a ~ for help* | ~ **of** ◇ *~s of laughter* ◇ *~s of terror*

scream verb

ADV. **aloud** | **loudly** | **silently** ◇ *Despair shook him and he ~ed silently in the darkness.* | **hysterically, shrilly, wildly** | **almost, practically** | **back**
VERB + SCREAM **want to** ◇ *I was so bored I wanted to ~.* | **try to** | **begin to** | **hear sb**
PREP. **after** ◇ *Marion ~ed after them, 'Stop! Stop!'* | **at** ◇ *She ~ed at me to get out of the way.* | **for** ◇ *The trapped passengers ~ed for help.* | **in** ◇ *People ran for the exits, ~ing out in terror.* | **with** ◇ *People were staggering around, ~ing with pain.*
PHRASES **begin ~ing, start ~ing** | ~ **your head off** ◇ *The baby was ~ing its head off.* | **stop ~ing**

screen noun

1 on a TV, computer, etc.

ADJ. **big, giant, huge, large** | **small, tiny** | **blank** ◇ *I sat gazing at the blank ~, trying to think of something to write.* | **full, split** | **computer, laptop, radar, television, TV, video** | **display** | **projection, projector** | **colour/color** | **flat, wide** (usually *widescreen*) ◇ *a flat-screen TV* | **LCD, plasma** | **touch** | **17-inch, 48-inch, etc.**
VERB + SCREEN **fill** ◇ *The star's face filled the ~.* | **be glued to, gaze at, look at, stare at, watch**
SCREEN + VERB **show** | **flash, flicker** ◇ *The ~ flickered, and then everything went dark.* | **fade**
SCREEN + NOUN **saver** | **image** | **resolution, size** | **name**
PREP. **on (the)** ~ ◇ *Information can be viewed on ~ or printed out.* ◇ *The image came up on the ~ for a few seconds.*
PHRASES **go blank, go black** ◇ *The ~ suddenly went black.*

2 films/movies or television in general

ADJ. **cinema** (*esp. BrE*), **movie** (*esp. AmE*) | **big, small** ◇ *big-screen entertainment* (= at the cinema) ◇ *She appears regularly on the small ~* (= on television). | **silver** (= the film/movie industry) (*old-fashioned*)
VERB + SCREEN **appear on, grace** ◇ *the greatest comic actor ever to grace a movie ~* | **bring sth to** ◇ *Henry James's novel was brought to the ~ by director James Ivory.* | **share** ◇ *She shares the ~ with Nicole Kidman.*
SCREEN + NOUN **adaptation, version** ◇ *Neil Simon's ~ adaptation of his hit stage play* | **actor, beauty** (*esp. BrE*), **legend, star** ◇ *The film features ~ legends James Stewart and Grace Kelly.* | **persona** ◇ *Bogart's ~ persona as a cynical anti-hero* | **presence** | **appearance** ◇ *Marilyn Monroe's first ~ appearance* | **time** ◇ *De Niro is only given a few minutes of ~ time.* | **test** | **debut** | **career**
PREP. **off** ~ ◇ *They play deadly rivals in the show but they are good friends off ~.* | **on (the)** ~ ◇ *She is remembered mainly for her performances on ~.*
PHRASES **stage and** ~ ◇ *stars of stage and ~*

3 partition

ADJ. **folding** ◇ *The room was divided by a folding ~.* | **privacy** (*esp. AmE*), **security**
VERB + SCREEN **put up**
SCREEN + NOUN **door, window** (*both AmE*)
PREP. **behind a/the** ~ ◇ *His desk was discreetly placed behind a ~.* | ~ **between** ◇ *There is a ~ between the two beds.*

screen verb

1 check sb/sth for faults/illnesses

ADV. **carefully** ◇ *All foster parents are carefully ~ed.* | **routinely**
PREP. **for** ◇ *All pregnant women are to be ~ed for the infection.*

2 show sth on television or in a cinema/movie theater

ADV. **live** ◇ *The race will be ~ed live on TV.*

screw noun

ADJ. **wood** | **loose**
VERB + SCREW **turn** | **loosen, tighten** | **remove**

screw verb

ADV. **firmly, tightly** | **down, together** ◇ *Screw the drain cover down tightly.*
PREP. **into** ◇ *She ~ed the lock into the door.* | **on, onto** ◇ *I ~ed the lid back on the jar.* | **to** ◇ *The bed was ~ed to the floor.*
PHRASES ~ **sth in place,** ~ **sth into position** ◇ *I ~ed the curtain rail in place.*

scribble verb

ADV. **furiously, hastily, hurriedly, quickly** ◇ *The students were all scribbling away furiously.* | **away, down, out** ◇ *She hastily ~d out a note.*

script noun

1 text of a play, film/movie, etc.

ADJ. **draft** (*esp. BrE*) | **original** | **final** | **comedy, film** (*esp. BrE*), **movie** (*esp. AmE*), **radio, television, TV** | **good, great, well-written** | **shooting**
VERB + SCRIPT **prepare, write** | **co-write, rewrite** | **read**
SCRIPT + NOUN **editor** | **writer** (usually *scriptwriter*)
PREP. ~ **about** ◇ *a ~ about a farmer's life* | ~ **for** ◇ *a ~ for children's TV*

2 system/style of writing

ADJ. **neat** | **cursive, flowing** | **phonetic** | **Arabic, Cyrillic, Hebrew, etc.**
PREP. **in a/the** ~ ◇ *She writes in a neat, flowing ~.*

scripture noun (often scriptures)

ADJ. **holy, sacred** ◇ *the sacred ~ of the Buddhists* | **ancient** | **Buddhist, Christian, Hindu, Jewish, etc.**
... OF SCRIPTURE **passage, verse, words**
VERB + SCRIPTURE **read, read from** ◇ *She read from the ~s.* | **interpret** | **study** | **cite, quote, quote from**
PREP. **in the** ~s ◇ *You won't find this moral precept in the ~s.*

scrub noun

1 small trees growing in a dry area

ADJ. **desert** ◇ *miles of desert ~* | **low** ◇ *The vegetation consisted of low ~.* | **dense, thick**
... OF SCRUB **patch** ◇ *The horses stood near a patch of ~.*
VERB + SCRUB **be covered in, be overgrown with** ◇ *The mountain was covered in ~.*

2 cleaning

ADJ. **good** ◇ *I gave the table a good ~.*
VERB + SCRUB **give sb/sth**
SCRUB + NOUN **brush** (*AmE*) (*scrubbing brush* in *BrE*)

scrub verb

ADV. **furiously, vigorously** | **thoroughly** | **away, down, out**
PREP. **at** ◇ *She scrubbed at the child's face with a tissue.* |
from, off ◇ *He scrubbed the blood from his shoes.*
PHRASES **freshly scrubbed** ◇ *his freshly scrubbed face* | **~ sth clean** ◇ *The table had been scrubbed clean.*

scruples noun

ADJ. **moral, religious** ◇ *a man of few moral ~*
VERB + SCRUPLES **have** | **overcome** ◇ *Some persuasion would be required to overcome her ~.*
PREP. **without ~** ◇ *A man who can behave like that must be completely without ~.* | **~ about** ◇ *I don't have any ~ about telling her what I think.*

scrutinize (BrE also **-ise**) verb

ADV. **carefully, closely, intensely**
PREP. **for** ◇ *All parts of the aircraft are closely ~d for signs of wear or damage.*

scrutiny noun

ADJ. **careful, close, critical, detailed, intense, rigorous, serious, strict** ◇ *The company has come under intense ~ because of its environmental record.* | **increased** | **international, judicial, media, public, scientific** ◇ *The activities of the committee are subject to public ~.* | **congressional** (*in the US*), **parliamentary** (*in the UK*)
VERB + SCRUTINY **be subjected to, come under, submit to, undergo** | **be open to, be subject to, face** | **deserve, require, warrant** | **bear, stand up to, withstand** ◇ *The testimony of the chief witness doesn't stand up to ~.* | **avoid, escape**
PREP. **under ~** ◇ *The company is under ~ by the authorities.* | **~ by** ◇ *I realized I was being subjected to intense ~ by a group of children.*

scuffle noun

ADJ. **brief** | **little, minor**
VERB + SCUFFLE **be involved in**
SCUFFLE + VERB **break out** ◇ *A ~ broke out among people in the crowd.* | **ensue**
PREP. **in a/the ~** ◇ *He was injured in a ~ at the demonstration.* | **~ between** ◇ *a ~ between rival gangs* | **~ with** ◇ *He was involved in a ~ with photographers.*

sculptor noun

ADJ. **celebrated, famous, great, influential, leading, renowned** | **talented** | **abstract** | **contemporary, modern**
SCULPTOR + VERB **create sth, work (on sth)** ◇ *a classical Greek figure created by the ~ Polyclitus*
→ Note at JOB

sculpture noun

ADJ. **abstract, figurative** | **ancient, classical, modern** | **relief** ◇ *The frieze shows ancient Greek relief ~ at its most inventive.* | **monumental** ◇ *He worked on the symbolic monumental ~ for Oscar Wilde's tomb.* | **life-size** | **public** | **bronze, glass, ice, marble, metal, stone, wooden** | **kinetic, sound**
... OF SCULPTURE **piece** | **series** | **collection**
VERB + SCULPTURE **create, make** ◇ *She creates ~s out of scrap materials.* | **commission** | **display, exhibit**
PREP. **~ by** ◇ *a ~ by Henry Moore* | **~ of** ◇ *a ~ of a horse*
→ Note at ART

sea noun

1 area of salt water

ADJ. **calm** ◇ *a calm ~ after the storm* | **choppy, heavy, mountainous** (*esp. BrE*), **raging, rough, stormy** ◇ *A week of heavy ~s has created problems for fishermen.* ◇ *The ~ was too rough for sailing in small boats.* | **deep, shallow** | **blue, grey/gray** | **cold, frozen** | **warm** | **salty** | **inland** | **open** ◇ *The fishing boats headed for the open ~.*
VERB + SEA **cross** ◇ *Thousands of Haitians tried to cross the ~ to Florida.* | **roam, sail** ◇ *He has sailed the seven ~s.* | **go to** (= become a sailor) | **put out to, put to** ◇ *The ship put to ~ (=*

left port) in deteriorating weather conditions. | **be lost at** ◇ *They were lost at ~ when their ship sank en route for Madeira.* | **stare out to** ◇ *She stood on the cliff, staring out to ~.* | **overlook** ◇ *a house overlooking the ~*
SEA + VERB **rise** ◇ *In recent years the ~ has risen by a couple of inches.* | **recede** ◇ *The ~ has receded since the river was diverted.*
SEA + NOUN **water** | **bed, bottom, floor** | **level** ◇ *The island is sinking into the ocean due to rising ~ levels.* | **conditions** ◇ *treacherous ~ conditions around Greenland* | **air, breeze** | **ice** | **creature** | **otter, trout, turtle, urchin, etc.** | **port** (*usually **seaport***) | **voyage** | **cliff, front, view** | **chantey** (*AmE*), **shanty** (*BrE*) | **salt** | **power** ◇ *the rise of British ~ power in the 17th and 18th centuries*
PREP. **at ~** ◇ *We spent three weeks at ~.* | **across the ~** ◇ *We sailed across the Black Sea in a yacht.* | **by ~** ◇ *We sent our furniture by ~.* | **by the ~** ◇ *They live by the ~.* | **down to the ~** ◇ *We'll go down to the ~ for a swim before dinner.* | **in the ~, into the ~** ◇ *I love swimming in the ~!* | **on the ~** ◇ *three ships sailing on the ~* | **out to ~** ◇ *She fell overboard and was swept out to ~.*
PHRASES **the bottom of the ~, the depths of the ~, the edge of the ~, the middle of the ~, the surface of the ~** | **above ~ level, at ~ level, below ~ level** ◇ *The camp is situated 6 755 feet above ~ level.* | **on the high ~s** | **the seven ~s**

2 large amount of sth

ADJ. **endless, vast**
VERB + SEA **be surrounded by** ◇ *They were surrounded by a ~ of boxes.*
PREP. **~ of** ◇ *She scanned the vast ~ of faces below her.*

seafood noun

ADJ. **fresh** | **local**
VERB + SEAFOOD **eat** | **cook** | **serve**
SEAFOOD + NOUN **dish** ◇ *a good wine to drink with fish or ~ dishes* | **cocktail, platter, salad** | **chowder, soup, stew** (*all esp. AmE*) | **restaurant**
→ Special page at FOOD

seagull noun

... OF SEAGULLS **flock**
SEAGULL + VERB **circle, fly, wheel** | **swoop** | **cry, scream, screech, shriek**

seal noun

1 animal

ADJ. **baby**
VERB + SEAL **hunt** | **club** ◇ *The ad criticized hunters for clubbing baby ~s.* | **cull** (*esp. BrE*) ◇ *Environmentalists claim there is no reason to cull ~s.*
SEAL + VERB **bask**
SEAL + NOUN **pup** | **colony** | **cull** (*esp. BrE*) | **hunt**

2 for a document

ADJ. **wax** ◇ *an official-looking letter with a wax ~* | **presidential** (*esp. AmE*), **privy** (*BrE*), **royal**
VERB + SEAL **break** ◇ *He broke the ~ and opened the envelope.*
PHRASES **a/the sb's ~ of approval** ◇ *Her report was given the ~ of approval by senior management.*

seal verb

ADV. **carefully, properly, tightly, well** ◇ *The containers must be carefully ~ed so that no air can get in.* | **completely** ◇ *The unit is completely ~ed.* | **virtually** | **effectively** | **hermetically** ◇ *a hermetically ~ed container* | **away, in, off, up** ◇ *Police ~ed off the area.*
PREP. **from** ◇ *The nuclear plant would be effectively ~ed off from the world.* | **with** ◇ *He ~ed the bag tightly with tape.*

seam noun

1 in fabric

VERB + SEAM **sew, stitch** ◇ *She sewed the ~ with small neat stitches.* | **press** | **rip**
PHRASES **be bursting at the ~s** (*often figurative*) ◇ *This city is bursting at the ~s with would-be actors.* | **come apart at the ~s, fall apart at the ~s** (*both often figurative*) ◇ *Their marriage was coming apart at the ~s.*

2 of coal, etc.

ADJ. **coal** | **rich** ◇ *They're still mining a rich ~ of high-grade coal.* | **narrow**
VERB + SEAM **exploit** (*esp. AmE*), **mine** (*esp. BrE*) ◇ *The festival exploits a rich ~ of talent in the local area.* (*figurative*)

search noun

1 an attempt to find sb/sth

ADJ. **exhaustive, extensive, painstaking, systematic, thorough** | **major, massive, nationwide** | **desperate, frantic** | **constant** | **random** ◇ *random security ~es* | **fruitless, futile** | **ongoing** | **routine** ◇ *Police conducted a routine ~ of all the houses in the area.* | **illegal, warrantless** (*both AmE*) ◇ *The President could order warrantless ~es for national security purposes.* | **police** | **house-to-house** | **fingertip** (*BrE*) ◇ *A team of police officers did a fingertip ~ of the area.* | **body, strip** ◇ *I was subjected to a body ~ by customs officials.*
VERB + SEARCH **begin, initiate, launch, mount, start** ◇ *The police immediately launched a nationwide ~ for the killer.* | **prompt, spark, trigger** (*all esp. BrE*) ◇ *His disappearance prompted a week-long ~.* | **carry out, conduct, do, make** ◇ *The ~ for the missing men was conducted in poor weather conditions.* | **lead** ◇ *Inspector Binns is leading the ~ for the stolen paintings.* | **continue** | **abandon, call off** ◇ *The ~ was called off when it began to get dark.* | **resume** | **narrow, widen**
SEARCH + NOUN **operation** ◇ *The police mounted an extensive ~ operation.* | **area** (*AmE*) ◇ *to narrow the ~ area* | **party, team** ◇ *They sent out a ~ party to look for her.* | **warrant** | **committee** (*AmE*) ◇ *A ~ committee was established to help the President find his Supreme Court nominee.* | **firm** (*esp. AmE*) ◇ *an executive ~ firm*
PREP. **in ~ of** ◇ *We're constantly in ~ of new talent.* ◇ *Michael went off in ~ of another bottle of wine.* | **~ for** ◇ *the ~ for oil off the coast*
PHRASES **~ and seizure** (*AmE*) ◇ *The Constitution forbids unreasonable ~es and seizures.*

2 on a computer

ADJ. **quick, simple** ◇ *a quick ~ on the Internet* | **computer, database, Internet, online, Web** ◇ *I did an Internet ~ for free music sites.* | **advanced, keyword**
VERB + SEARCH **conduct, do, perform, run** | **narrow, refine** ◇ *You can refine a ~ using Boolean parameters.*
SEARCH + NOUN **engine** ◇ *This is one of the fastest Internet ~ engines.* | **box** ◇ *Type your domain name in the ~ box.* | **features** ◇ *A number of advanced ~ features are available.* | **technology, tool** | **query, term** ◇ *Companies try to identify the most popular ~ terms.* | **results** | **company**
PREP. **~ for**

search verb

ADV. **carefully, systematically, thoroughly** ◇ *The area has been thoroughly ~ed.* | **actively** ◇ *actively ~ing for something to keep the conversation going* | **desperately, frantically** | **fruitlessly, in vain, unsuccessfully, vainly** | **aimlessly, blindly** ◇ *For the rest of the morning he ~ed aimlessly through the town.* | **constantly** | **around** ◇ *I ~ed around for a thick stick.* | **online** ◇ *You can also ~ online for a job.*
PREP. **among** ◇ *We ~ed among the rocks for crabs.* | **for** ◇ *They are still ~ing for the missing child.* | **in** ◇ *He ~ed in his pocket and found a few coins.* | **through** ◇ *I ~ed through a drawer for my passport.*
PHRASES **~ far and wide, ~ sth from top to bottom** ◇ *We ~ed*

the house from top to bottom. | **~ high and low** ◇ *I have ~ed high and low and cannot find them.*

seaside noun (*esp. BrE*)

VERB + SEASIDE **go to, visit** ◇ *Every summer we went to the ~ for two months.*
SEASIDE + NOUN **resort, town, village** | **holiday** (*BrE*) | **postcard**
PREP. **at the ~** ◇ *Summers were spent at the ~.* ◇ *a day out at the ~* (*BrE*) | **by the ~** ◇ *They have a cottage by the ~.*
PHRASES **a trip to the ~**

NOTE

Seasons

have… ◇ *Perhaps we will have a good summer this year.*
spend… ◇ *I spent the winter indoors.*
… approaches ◇ *The days become longer and temperatures rise as spring approaches.*
… arrives, … begins, … comes ◇ *Winter arrived early that year.*
winter sets in ◇ *The aid must reach the refugees before winter sets in.*
… passes, … wears on (usually used of summer or winter) ◇ *As the summer wore on, food became scarce.*
… comes to an end, … ends (usually used of summer or winter) ◇ *Winter was coming to an end at last.*
… months, summer/winter period, spring/summer/ winter time (usually ***springtime***, etc.) ◇ *The museum is open daily during the summer months.* ◇ *It was springtime and the slopes were ablaze with almond blossoms.*
… day, … morning, … night, etc. ◇ *It's hard to sleep on hot summer nights.*
during (the)…, in (the)… ◇ *The woods are carpeted with flowers in spring.*
over the summer/winter ◇ *The repairs will be carried out over the summer.*
through (the)…, throughout (the)… ◇ *The meat is salted so it keeps through the winter.*
for (the)… ◇ *She's gone to Ireland for the summer.*
the… of 2008, etc. ◇ *The winter of 2001 was especially cold.*
a summer's day, a summer's night, etc., a winter's day, a winter's morning, etc. ◇ *a lazy summer's day*
all summer long, all winter long ◇ *It rained all summer long.*
the height of summer, the depths of winter ◇ *He always wore a short-sleeved shirt, even in the depths of winter.*

---

season noun

1 of the year

ADJ. **dry, hurricane, monsoon, rainy, wet** ◇ *In this climate there are no real changes of temperature, just a wet and a dry ~.* | **summer, winter, etc.**
VERB + SEASON **be in, come into** (*esp. AmE*) ◇ *Melons are in ~ right now.* | **be out of** ◇ *Lobster's out of ~ right now.*

2 period when an activity takes place

ADJ. **holiday** (= when people are on holiday/vacation) (*BrE*), **tourist** | **high** (*esp. BrE*), **peak** ◇ *The resort gets overcrowded in peak ~.* | **low, off** ◇ *The hotel is almost empty in the off ~.* | **coming, forthcoming** (*BrE*), **upcoming** (*esp. AmE*) | **breeding, mating, nesting** | **growing, harvest, planting** | **close** (*BrE*), **closed** ◇ *It is illegal to fish for salmon during the closed ~.* | **open** (*often figurative*) ◇ *The media have declared open ~ on the congressman and his private life.* | **political** (*esp. AmE*) | **campaign, election, primary** (*all AmE*) ◇ *The Senator has led in the polls for most of the primary ~.* | **conference** (*BrE*) ◇ *The party conference ~ gets under way this week.* | **silly** (*BrE*) ◇ *Fleet Street's silly ~ is upon us.* | **flu** (*esp. AmE*) ◇ *This year's flu ~ has been relatively mild.* | **movie, TV** (*both esp. AmE*) | **Christmas, festive** (*BrE*), **holiday** (= the time including Christmas, Hanukkah and

New Year) (AmE) ◇ Best wishes for the festive ~! ◇ I wished everyone a very happy holiday ~. | **panto** (informal), **pantomime** (both BrE)

PHRASES **the height of the ~**

3 period when a sport is played

ADJ. **baseball, cricket, football, hunting, racing, etc.** | **championship, league** ◇ Decker played nine major league ~s. (AmE) | **junior, senior, sophomore** (all AmE) | **debut** (esp. BrE), **rookie** (AmE) | **inaugural** ◇ The Denver Broncos' inaugural ~ was 1960. | **regular** (AmE) ◇ The Patriots won their last 12 games in the regular ~. | **full** ◇ He played a full ~ for West Ham. | **difficult, hard, tough** (all esp. BrE) ◇ It was the final race of a hard ~. | **outstanding, successful, undefeated** (esp. AmE), **winning** (esp. AmE) | **disappointing, disastrous, poor** (esp. BrE) | **coming, forthcoming** (BrE), **upcoming** (esp. AmE) ◇ He is busily preparing for the coming ~. | **close** (BrE), **off** (AmE) ◇ The team trained hard during the close/off ~. | **consecutive, successive** ◇ Our team won the trophy for the second successive ~.

VERB + SEASON **begin, open, start** ◇ We opened the ~ with five straight losses. | **end, finish** | **enter** ◇ He entered the ~ with 173 wins.

SEASON + VERB **begin, kick off** (esp. BrE), **start** | **end**

SEASON + NOUN **ticket** ◇ ~ ticket holders | **opener** (AmE) ◇ They played against the Celtics in the ~ opener.

season verb

ADV. **lightly, well**

PREP. **with** ◇ Season the meat well with salt and pepper.

PHRASES **highly ~ed** ◇ highly ~ed food

seat noun

1 for sitting on

ADJ. **available, empty, spare, vacant** ◇ There were no empty ~s left in the hall. ◇ Do you have a spare ~ in your car? | **comfortable, comfy** (informal) | **plush** | **cushioned, leather** | **bicycle, car** | **back, front, middle, rear** ◇ I always feel sick if I sit in the back ~ of the car. | **driver's** (AmE), **driving** (BrE), **passenger** | **bucket** ◇ I slid into the leather bucket ~ and fastened my ~ belt. | **booster, car, child** (esp. BrE), **safety** | **airline, theatre/theater** | **aisle, window** ◇ I always ask for an aisle ~ when I fly. | **front-row, good, ringside** ◇ I got to the concert early to get a good ~. ◇ We had ringside ~s for the boxing match. | **bleacher** (AmE) (usually just **bleachers**) | **bench** | **love** (= a comfortable seat for two people to sit on) (AmE) | **ejection** (AmE), **ejector** (esp. BrE) | **lavatory, loo** (BrE, informal), **toilet** | **usual** ◇ I took my usual ~ at the front of the classroom.

VERB + SEAT **find, get, grab** (informal), **have, take** ◇ Please take a ~. ◇ Is this ~ taken? | **occupy, sit on** ◇ The best ~s were occupied by the friends and families of the performers. ◇ It is very uncomfortable to sit on these ~s. | **get (up) out of, leave, rise from** | **give up, offer, vacate** ◇ He gave up his ~ on the bus to a pregnant woman. | **resume, return to** ◇ The audience resumed their ~s for the second half of the play. | **fill** ◇ Not all theatres/theaters can fill their ~s so easily. | **book** (esp. BrE), **reserve** ◇ Is it possible to reserve ~s for the play? | **save** ◇ Can you save me a ~ if you get there first? | **lean back in, recline in, settle back in** | **lean forward in** | **settle into** ◇ We had hardly settled into our ~s when the first goal was scored. | **slide into** ◇ She slid into the driver's ~. | **shift in** | **put back, recline**

SEAT + NOUN **cover** | **cushion** | **reservation** (BrE) ◇ Seat reservations are free. ◇ an electronic seat-reservation system

PREP. **in a/the ~** ◇ The man in the passenger ~ seemed to be asleep. | **on a/the ~** ◇ I found my gloves lying on the back ~. | **out of a/the ~** ◇ He leaped out of his ~ when he saw the rat. | **~ for** ◇ I managed to get some ~s for the ballet.

PHRASES **the best ~ in the house** ◇ We had the best ~s in the house for the concert. | **lean back in your ~, settle back in your ~** ◇ We settled back into our ~s and waited for the show to begin. | **on the edge of your ~** ◇ With two minutes to go before the end, I was on the edge of my ~.

2 in Parliament, Congress, etc.

ADJ. **congressional, House, Senate** (all in the US) ◇ Republicans won 52.7% of the House ~s. | **Commons,**

second

parliamentary (both in the UK) | **council** (BrE) | **board** ◇ the search for finance chiefs to fill board ~s | **marginal** (esp. BrE) | **open** (AmE) ◇ The Democrats captured 18 of the 30 open ~s. | **safe** | **Democratic, Labour, Republican, Tory, etc.**

VERB + SEAT **gain, pick up, secure, take** (BrE), **win** ◇ Republicans gained five ~s in the Senate. ◇ The Liberals took seven ~s from Labour. | **lose** ◇ He lost his ~ in the last election. | **hold, keep, retain** ◇ The party held the ~ with a 10 000 majority. | **regain, win back** | **contest** (esp. BrE), **fight** (BrE), **run for** (AmE) ◇ He has been selected to fight the ~ at the next election. ◇ She is running for a ~ in the New York State Assembly. | **defend** | **take** (= begin your duties in Parliament) (BrE) ◇ She took her ~ in Parliament as Britain's youngest MP. | **hold, occupy** ◇ Republicans currently hold 51 ~s in the Senate. | **resign, vacate**

PREP. **~ in** ◇ a ~ in Congress | **~ on** ◇ a ~ on the board

seat verb

ADV. **comfortably** ◇ He ~ed himself comfortably at the foot of the bed. ◇ The car ~s six comfortably.

PREP. **at** ◇ Ramirez was ~ed at a table near the window. | **in** ◇ The old woman was ~ed in a chair. | **on** ◇ She ~ed herself on the sofa.

PHRASES **be ~ed** ◇ Please be ~ed. | **be ~ed cross-legged** | **remain ~ed, stay ~ed** ◇ Please remain ~ed until your name is called.

seat belt (also safety belt) noun

VERB + SEAT BELT **have on, wear** ◇ By law you are obliged to wear ~s. | **buckle** (AmE), **fasten, put on** | **take off, unbuckle** (AmE), **undo, unfasten**

seating noun

ADJ. **comfortable** ◇ The auditorium has comfortable ~ and modern acoustics. | **outdoor** | **allocated** (BrE), **assigned** (AmE), **reserved**

VERB + SEATING **have** ◇ The stadium has ~ for less than 10 000. | **arrange** | **offer, provide**

SEATING + NOUN **area** | **arrangements, plan** ◇ We need to work out the ~ plan for the wedding. | **capacity**

PREP. **~ for** ◇ There is ~ for 250 people.

seclusion noun

ADJ. **complete, total** | **relative** ◇ I prefer the relative ~ of the countryside. | **quiet** ◇ She fled to a life of quiet ~, living on a farm in rural Virginia.

PREP. **in (the ~ of)** ◇ I live very much in ~ these days. ◇ He felt comfortable in the ~ of the forest. | **~ from** ◇ ~ from the outside world

second noun very short moment of time

ADJ. **brief, fleeting, mere** (esp. AmE), **split** ◇ I only saw the man for a split ~ as he ran past. ◇ I swam to the other shore in mere ~s. | **single** | **precious** ◇ She had wasted a few precious ~s. | **closing, dying** (BrE) ◇ His goal in the dying ~s of the game secured Rangers a 3–2 victory.

VERB + SECOND **take** ◇ This will only take a ~. | **have** ◇ Do you have a ~, Miss White? | **hang on, hold on, wait** ◇ Wait a second—this letter's been sent to me by mistake. | **spend** ◇ She wanted to spend every ~ with him.

SECOND + VERB **go by, pass, tick by** ◇ The ~s ticked by.

SECOND + NOUN **hand**

PREP. **for a ~** ◇ For a ~ I thought you were my mother. ◇ I hesitated for a ~ before speaking. | **in a ~** ◇ I'll be with you in a ~. | **in ~s, within ~s** ◇ Within ~s he had disappeared from view.

PHRASES **a couple of ~s** ◇ It took a couple of ~s to realize what was going on. | **a fraction of a ~** ◇ If he'd reacted a fraction of a ~ later, he would surely have died. | **a matter of ~s** ◇ The end of the game is only a matter of ~s away. | **count the ~s** ◇ I was counting the ~s until the bell. | **in the final ~s** ◇ The game was lost in the final ~s. | **(only) ~s left** ◇ We only have a few ~s left. ◇ We were three points behind with only ~s *left in the game.* | **with each passing ~, with every passing ~** ◊ *The room seemed to grow hotter with each passing ~.* → Note at MEASURE

secrecy *noun*

ADJ. **absolute, complete, total** | **great, strict, utmost** | **excessive** | **government, official**
VERB + SECRECY **maintain** | **be cloaked in, be shrouded in** | **be sworn to** ◊ *All the researchers on the project are sworn to absolute ~.*
SECRECY + VERB **surround sth**
PREP. **in ~** ◊ *The drugs squad operates in the greatest ~.* | **~ about** ◊ *The organization has managed to maintain ~ about its activities.*
PHRASES **a blanket of ~, a cloak of ~, a veil of ~** ◊ *A blanket of ~ surrounded the tribunals.* | **a culture of ~** *(esp. BrE)* ◊ *The Ministry of Defence must answer for its culture of ~.*

secret *noun*

1 sth that must not be known by others

ADJ. **big, great** | **little** | **closely guarded, well-kept** ◊ *a charming museum that is one of the city's best-kept ~s* (= that not many people know about) | **deep** *(esp. AmE)*, **hidden, inner, innermost, intimate** ◊ *That evening she had revealed many of her innermost ~s.* | **open** ◊ *Their affair is an open ~.* | **dark, dirty, guilty, shameful, terrible** | **family, military, nuclear, official, state, trade**
VERB + SECRET **have** | **guard, keep** ◊ *Can you keep a ~?* | **hide** ◊ *Uncle Charlie hides a dark ~.* | **betray, divulge, give away** | **let sb in on, let sb into** *(BrE)*, **reveal, share, tell sb** ◊ *She let us into her secret—she was engaged.* | **discover, find out, learn, uncover, unlock** | **know** | **remain** ◊ *Their relationship remained a ~.*
SECRET + VERB **be out, come out, get out** ◊ *How did the ~ get out?*
PREP. **in ~** ◊ *The stars were married in ~ to avoid publicity.* | **~ about** ◊ *There was some ~ about the source of his wealth.* | **~ from** ◊ *I have no ~s from you.*
PHRASES **make no ~ of the fact that…, not make a ~ of sth** ◊ *He refuses to make any ~ of his political allegiances.*

2 only/best way of doing/achieving sth

VERB + SECRET **reveal, tell sb** | **know** | **hold** ◊ *These animals may hold the ~ to combating the virus.*
PREP. **~ behind** ◊ *She revealed the ~ behind her extraordinary success.* | **~ of** ◊ *the ~s of staying healthy*
PHRASES **the ~ of (sb's) success**

secret *adj.*

VERBS **be** | **remain, stay** | **keep sth**
ADV. **highly, top, very** ◊ *a top-secret meeting* | **formerly, previously** ◊ *The text of the previously ~ treaty can now be revealed.* | **supposedly**
PREP. **from** ◊ *They managed to keep the party more or less ~ from Christine.*

secretary *noun*

1 person who works in an office

ADJ. **executive, legal** | **medical** | **press, publicity** | **personal, private** | **social** | **school**
→ Note at JOB

2 head of a government department in the US

ADJ. **deputy** ◊ *deputy ~ of agriculture in the Bush administration* | **assistant** ◊ *assistant ~ of commerce under President Clinton* | **acting** | **former** ◊ *former Treasury Secretary Lloyd Bentsen* | **cabinet** | **state** | **Agriculture, Commerce, Defence, Education, Health, Homeland Security, Interior, Labor, Transportation, Treasury, etc.**
VERB + SECRETARY **resign as** | **replace (sb as)**
PREP. **~ for** ◊ *the Treasury Department's Assistant Secretary for Economic Policy* | **~ of** ◊ *a former assistant ~ of defense*
PHRASES **Secretary of State** ◊ *the US Secretary of State*

3 government minister or assistant in the UK

ADJ. **permanent** | **former** ◊ *the former Secretary of State for Energy, Cecil Parkinson* | **cabinet, shadow** (= a senior British politician of the opposition party) *(BrE)* | **parliamentary** | **Agriculture, Defence, Economic, Education, Employment, Energy, Environment, Financial, Foreign, Health, Home, Transport, Treasury, etc.**
PREP. **~ to** ◊ *the Financial Secretary to the Treasury*
PHRASES **Secretary of State** ◊ *the Secretary of State for Education*

4 official of an organization

ADJ. **chief, first** ◊ *the First Secretary of the Communist Party* | **assistant, deputy** | **honorary** | **executive, general** | **branch, district, group, national, party, regional** | **club, company**
VERB + SECRETARY **resign as** | **elect** | **elect sb, elect sb as** | **replace** | **replace sb as**
SECRETARY + NOUN **General** ◊ *UN Secretary General, Ban Ki-moon*
PREP. **~ to** ◊ *~ to the Jockey Club*
PHRASES **the post of ~**

secretive *adj.*

VERBS **be** | **become**
ADV. **extremely, fairly, very, etc.** | **highly** ◊ *his highly ~ nature* | **notoriously**
PREP. **about** ◊ *They were very ~ about their plans.*

sect *noun*

ADJ. **religious** | **evangelical, fundamentalist, radical** | **dissenting** | **splinter** *(AmE)* | **Buddhist, Christian, Jewish, Muslim, etc.**
VERB + SECT **belong to** | **join** | **found**
SECT + NOUN **member** | **leader**
PHRASES **a leader of a ~, a member of a ~**

section *noun*

ADJ. **opening** | **concluding, final, middle** | **following, next, subsequent** | **preceding, previous** | **large, small** ◊ *Large ~s of the forest have been destroyed by acid rain.* | **long, short** ◊ *a long ~ of roadway* | **main** | **separate, special** | **business, entertainment, finance, news, travel, etc.** (of a newspaper, website, etc.) | **biology, fiction, history, reference, etc.** (in a library, bookshop/bookstore, etc.) | **brass, percussion, rhythm, string, wind, woodwind** (in an orchestra) | **cello, horn, etc.** (in an orchestra) | **tail** (of a plane)
VERB + SECTION **dedicate, devote** ◊ *A whole ~ is devoted to mental illness.* | **add, remove** ◊ *The new edition of the dictionary adds a ~ on phrasal verbs.* | **skip** ◊ *I skipped the ~ on garden design.* | **divide sth into** ◊ *The book is divided into chapters, ~s and subsections.*
SECTION + NOUN **leader, manager** *(esp. BrE)* (in a company, an organization, etc.)
PREP. **in a/the ~** ◊ *You'll find the book in the music ~.* | **in ~s** ◊ *The table comes in ~s.* | **under ~** (relating to a section of a law, etc.) ◊ *The case was the first prosecution under Section 3A of the Road Traffic Act 1988.*
PHRASES **a ~ of society** ◊ *an area populated largely by the poorer ~s of society*

sector *noun*

1 part of the business activity of a country

ADJ. **important, key** | **growing, growth** | **independent** *(BrE)* | **private** | **public, state** | **non-profit** *(esp. AmE)*, **voluntary** *(BrE)* | **economic, industry, market** ◊ *The survey covers a wide range of industry ~s.* | **agricultural, business, commercial, corporate, export, industrial, manufacturing, media, retail, service** | **banking, financial, financial services** *(esp. BrE)* | **energy, oil** | **electronics, high-tech, tech, technology, telecom** *(esp. AmE)*, **telecommunications, telecoms** *(BrE)* | **education, schools** *(BrE)*, **university** *(esp. BrE)* ◊ *the chronic underfunding of the education ~* | **health, health-care** | **tourism, tourist** *(esp. BrE)* | **consumer, household** *(esp. AmE)*

PREP. **in a/the ~** ◇ *He went on to a successful career in the private ~.* ◇ *employment opportunities in the higher education ~*

PHRASES **a ~ of the economy, a ~ of the industry, a ~ of the market**

2 part of an area or of a large group of people

ADJ. **rural, urban** | **northern, north-eastern, etc.**

VERB + SECTOR **divide sth into** ◇ *Berlin was divided into four ~s after the war.*

PHRASES **a ~ of the city** | **a ~ of society, a ~ of the population**

secular adj.

VERBS **be**

ADV. **completely, entirely, purely, strictly** ◇ *It began as a religious organization, but these days it is purely ~.* | **largely, mostly** ◇ *We live in a largely ~ society.* | **increasingly**

secure verb

1 fix/lock sth firmly

ADV. **firmly, properly, tightly**

PREP. **to** ◇ *The crates had not been firmly ~d to the truck.* | **with** ◇ *She ~d the boat with a rope.*

2 get/achieve sth

ADV. **easily** ◇ *Victory was not going to be easily ~d.* | **safely** ◇ *The police safely ~d the release of the youngster.* | **eventually, finally** | **thereby** ◇ *The party won 399 seats, thereby securing a majority in the Assembly.*

VERB + SECURE **be able to, manage to** | **fail to** ◇ *They failed to ~ the release of the prisoners.* | **help (to)**

PHRASES **an attempt to ~ sth, an effort to ~ sth** | **be aimed at securing sth** | **a chance of securing sth** ◇ *This could improve your chances of securing employment.* | **failure to ~ sth** ◇ *the failure to ~ public support for the project* | **in the hope of securing sth** (*esp. BrE*), **in hopes of securing sth** (*AmE*) | **be successful in securing sth**

secure adj.

VERBS **be, feel** | **become** | **make sth** | **keep sth** ◇ *It's important to keep your documents ~.*

ADV. **extremely, fairly, very, etc.** | **highly** | **absolutely, completely, perfectly, totally** | **enough, sufficiently** ◇ *I finally felt ~ enough in myself to have a child of my own.* | **economically, financially**

PREP. **against** ◇ *The house has been made ~ against intruders.* | **in** ◇ *We left, ~ in the knowledge that Mason was safe at home with his grandmother.*

PHRASES **safe and ~** ◇ *She felt safe and ~ in his arms.*

security noun

1 feeling safe/being free from worry

ADJ. **greater** | **emotional, psychological** | **economic, financial** | **job** | **energy, food**

VERB + SECURITY **have** ◇ *They have the ~ of a good home.* | **give (sb), provide (sb with)** ◇ *He gave her the emotional ~ she needed.*

SECURITY + NOUN **blanket** (= an object that a child holds in order to feel safe) (*often figurative*) ◇ *He clings to her like a ~ blanket.*

PHRASES **a false sense of ~** ◇ *The user will be lulled into a false sense of ~.* | **a feeling of ~, a sense of ~** | **~ of tenure** (*law, esp. BrE*)

2 to protect sb/sth from thieves, attack, war, etc.

ADJ. **heightened** | **strict, tight** | **lax** | **collective** | **domestic** (*esp. AmE*), **homeland** (*AmE*), **internal, national, state** | **airline, airport, aviation** | **border, port** | **personal** | **home** | **computer, data, information, Internet, network** | **long-term**

VERB + SECURITY **provide (sb with)** | **ensure, guarantee** | **protect** ◇ *a law to protect national ~* | **beef up** (*informal*), **improve, increase, strengthen, tighten, tighten up** ◇ *We need to tighten ~ around the hotel during the president's visit.* | **compromise, endanger, jeopardize, threaten, under-**

mine ◇ *The leaking of state secrets has compromised national ~.*

SECURITY + NOUN **apparatus, forces, services** | **adviser** (*esp. AmE*), **expert, guard, man, officer, official, personnel, staff** ◇ *a former national ~ adviser to President Clinton* | **arrangements, matters, measures, policy, system** | **issue, situation** | **concerns, interests** ◇ *our national ~ interests* | **risk, threat** | **breach** | **check** | **checkpoint** ◇ *Soldiers stand at ~ checkpoints.* | **clearance** ◇ *He lost his ~ clearance because he failed a lie-detector test.* | **camera, device, van** (*BrE*), **video**

PREP. **~ against** ◇ *The bars are to provide ~ against break-ins.*

PHRASES **for ~ reasons** ◇ *For ~ reasons, passengers are requested not to leave any baggage unattended.* | **a high level of ~** | **peace and ~** | **a threat to ~**

3 (*esp. BrE*) **when you borrow money**

VERB + SECURITY **put up (sth as)** | **use sth as** | **hold (sth as), take (sth as)**

PREP. **against the ~ of** ◇ *The bank will make a loan against the ~ of the lender's house.* | **as ~** ◇ *She pledged her necklace as ~ for a loan.* | **~ for**

4 securities financial documents

ADJ. **agency** (*esp. AmE*), **company, corporate** (*esp. AmE*), **government, Treasury** (*esp. AmE*) ◇ *foreign ownership of US government securities* | **foreign** (*esp. AmE*) | **gilt-edged** (*BrE*), **high-yield, top-rated** | **long-term, short-term**

VERB + SECURITIES **issue** | **buy, purchase** | **sell** | **trade**

SECURITIES + NOUN **company, firm** ◇ *Wall Street securities firms* | **market** ◇ *the faltering securities market* | **broker, lawyer** ◇ *a securities lawyer with Tinson and Zelkins*

sedation noun

ADJ. **deep, heavy** | **mild**

PREP. **under ~** ◇ *The attack victim is currently in hospital, under heavy ~.*

sedative noun

ADJ. **powerful, strong** | **mild** ◇ *The doctor gave her a mild ~ to help her sleep.*

VERB + SEDATIVE **administer, give sb, prescribe (sb)** | **take, use**

seductive adj.

VERBS **be, become, look, seem, sound**

ADV. **extremely, fairly, very, etc.** | **highly** | **dangerously, strangely** | **almost** ◇ *His words had a soothing, almost ~ quality.*

see verb

1 become aware of sth using your eyes

ADV. **clearly, easily, plainly** | **dimly, faintly** | **barely, hardly** ◇ *I could hardly ~ because of the smoke.* | **just** ◇ *We could just ~ the hotel in the distance.* | **suddenly** | **first-hand, personally** ◇ *He saw first-hand the impact of colonialism.* | **commonly** ◇ *This problem is commonly seen in young adults.*

VERB + SEE **be able to, can** ◇ *I could ~ the boat clearly now.* | **go to** ◇ *I went to ~ a movie.* | **get to** ◇ *I finally got to ~ them in concert.* | **turn around to, turn to** ◇ *She turned to ~ who it was.* | **be amazed to, be shocked to, be surprised to** ◇ *He was surprised to ~ Martha standing there.* | **be relieved to** | **be keen to** (*esp. BrE*) | **be delighted, be glad to, be happy to, be overjoyed to, be pleased to** ◇ *I'm glad to ~ that you're keeping well.* | **be sad to** | **would love to** ◇ *I'd love to ~ her win the gold medal.* | **wait to** ◇ *I can't wait to ~ his face!* ◇ *We'll have to wait to ~ if sales hold up.* | **expect to** ◇ *We expect to ~ an increase of 50–60%.* | **be likely to** | **be great to, be nice to** ◇ *It's nice to ~ the children playing together.* | **be interesting to** | **let sb** ◇ *A dolphin? Oh, let me ~! ◇ Let me ~ the evidence!*

PREP. **into** ◇ *She claims that she can ~ into the future.*

PHRASES **get a/the chance to ~, get an/the opportunity to ~**

| have a/the chance to ~, have an/the opportunity to ~ | only to ~ ◇ *I looked up, only to ~ Tommy chatting to someone.* | ~ at a glance ◇ *You can ~ at a glance if all is well.* | ~ with the naked eye ◇ *The star is bright enough to ~ with the naked eye.* | ~ (sth) with your own eyes ◇ *I know it's hard to believe but I saw it with my own eyes.*

2 visit sb

VERB + SEE **come to** ◇ *Veronica came to ~ him in prison.* | **come around to, come over to** ◇ *Logan came around to ~ me about a job.* ◇ *He came over to ~ me after my surgery.* | **go to** ◇ *She went to ~ the doctor about it.* | **want to, wish to** ◇ *What is it you want to ~ me about?* | **be here to** ◇ *I'm here to ~ Lisa Daniels.*
PREP. **about** ◇ *She's gone to ~ the mechanic about getting her car repaired.*

3 understand/realize sth

VERB + SEE **can** ◇ *I can ~ why you were so angry about it.* | **cannot, do not** ◇ *I don't ~ why she should get more money than the others.* | **be easy to** | **be difficult to, be hard to** ◇ *It is difficult to ~ how to get around this problem.* | **fail to** ◇ *I fail to ~ how this idea will help anyone.*

4 find out

VERB + SEE **want to** ◇ *I want to ~ how they'll react.* | **come over, go over, look over** ◇ *He came over to ~ what was going on.* | **let sb** ◇ *Let's ~ what happens.*
PHRASES **go and ~** *'Is the taxi here?' 'I'll just go and ~.'* | **wait and ~** *'Is he going to get better?' 'I don't know, we'll just have to wait and ~.'*

seed *noun*

1 from which a plant grows

ADJ. **grass, mustard, poppy, sesame, etc.** | **bird** (usually *birdseed*) | **bad** (*AmE, figurative*) ◇ *the transformation of Tracy from good girl to bad ~*
... OF SEEDS **packet**
VERB + SEED **plant, sow** | **produce, set** ◇ *This tree produces very hard ~s.* ◇ *The plant will set ~ in June.* | **grow sth from, raise sth from** ◇ *She grew all the plants from ~.* | **disperse, spread** ◇ *Most ~s are spread by the wind.* | **go to, run to** ◇ *Cutting weeds before they go to ~ will greatly reduce future weed problems.* | **contain** ◇ *Each fruit usually contains a single ~.* ◇ *He argued that capitalism contained the ~s of its own destruction.* (*figurative*) | **remove** ◇ *Peel the peppers and remove the ~s.*
SEED + VERB **germinate, grow, sprout**
SEED + NOUN **head, pod** | **packet, tray** | **bank, catalogue, merchant** (*esp. BrE*) | **corn, potato** | **money**
PHRASES **a variety of ~s** ◇ *The catalogue has hundreds of different varieties of ~s.*

2 player in a sports competition

ADJ. **first, second, etc.** | **number-one, number-two, etc.** | **top** ◇ *She was the top ~ at the US Open this year.*

seek *verb*

ADV. **aggressively** (*esp. AmE*), **avidly, eagerly, keenly** (*esp. BrE*) | **actively** ◇ *people who are unemployed and actively ~ing work* (*BrE*) | **desperately, urgently** ◇ *He was desperately ~ing a way to see her again.* | **deliberately** ◇ *He deliberately sought to expand his country's influence on the region.* | **always, consistently, constantly, continually** | **initially** ◇ *They initially sought to blame others for the disaster.* | **currently** ◇ *The developer is currently ~ing funding for the project.* | **successfully** | **in vain, unsuccessfully, vainly** ◇ *We sought in vain for a solution.*
VERB + SEEK **continue to**
PREP. **for** ◇ *We're ~ing for alternative materials which might bring the cost down.* | **in** ◇ *the answers she sought in those books*
PHRASES **highly sought after** ◇ *Jobs in Paris are highly sought after.*

seep *verb*

ADV. **gradually, slowly** | **away, back, out, through, up** ◇ *The power had gradually ~ed away.*
VERB + SEEP **begin to, start to**
PREP. **from** ◇ *Blood was ~ing slowly from the wound.* | **into, out of** ◇ *Water was ~ing out of the tank.* | **through** ◇ *The damp ~ed through her thin shoes.*

seethe *verb*

ADV. **inwardly, privately** ◇ *Inwardly she was seething, and vowed to get back at him.* | **quietly, silently** | **absolutely**
PREP. **at** ◇ *She was seething at the insult.* | **with** ◇ *He clenched his fists, seething with anger.*

segregate *verb*

ADV. **strictly**
PREP. **according to, by** ◇ *Jobs were strictly ~d by gender.* | **from** ◇ *The women were ~d from the male workers in the factory.* | **into** ◇ *The club was ~d into smoking and non-smoking areas.*
PHRASES **highly ~d** ◇ *Women's work has always been highly ~d.* | **racially ~d** ◇ *racially ~d schools*

segregation *noun*

ADJ. **racial, religious, residential, sex, social** ◇ *to bring an end to sex ~ within the school* | **complete** | **legal**
VERB + SEGREGATION **end, outlaw** | **enforce** | **practise/practice**
PREP. **~ between** ◇ *~ between students of different ethnic groups* | **~ by** ◇ *~ by race* | **~ within**

seize *verb*

1 take hold of sb/sth suddenly and firmly

ADV. **immediately, suddenly** ◇ *He was immediately ~d and thrown into prison.*
PREP. **by** ◇ *She ~d him by the arm.* | **from** ◇ *He ~d the book from her hand.*
PHRASES **~ hold of sb/sth** ◇ *The wrestlers try to ~ hold of each other.*

2 take sth

ADV. **immediately, instantly, quickly, suddenly** ◇ *She promptly ~d the opportunity his absence gave her.* | **eagerly**
VERB + SEIZE **be quick to, be ready to** ◇ *He was quick to ~ on this idea.* | **be determined to** | **attempt to, try to** | **fail to** ◇ *He had failed to ~ his chance.*
PREP. **on, upon** ◇ *The rumours/rumors were eagerly ~d on by the local press.*
PHRASES **an attempt to ~ sth** | **the power to ~ sth, the right to ~ sth** ◇ *We have the legal right to ~ his property.*

seizure *noun*

ADJ. **biggest, largest** | **drug** (*AmE*), **drugs** (*BrE*) | **cocaine, heroin, etc.** | **land**
VERB + SEIZURE **make** ◇ *Customs have made their biggest ever ~ of heroin.*
PHRASES **search and ~** (*law*) ◇ *The Act confers powers of search and ~ on the police.*

select *verb*

ADV. **carefully** | **specially, specifically** | **deliberately** | **arbitrarily, at random, randomly** ◇ *The winning entry will be ~ed at random by computer.* | **automatically** ◇ *The program automatically ~s and stores the most frequently used data.* | **manually** | **personally**
VERB + SELECT **allow sb to, enable sb to**
PREP. **according to** ◇ *Students ~ modules according to their interests.* | **as** ◇ *They were ~ed as finalists for this year's awards.* | **for** ◇ *She has been ~ed for the team.* | **from** ◇ *You can ~ goods from our catalogue.*
PHRASES **be ~ed on the basis of** ◇ *They were ~ed on the basis of size.* | **well ~ed** ◇ *This anthology is well ~ed and presented.*

selection noun

1 process of choosing/being chosen

ADJ. **careful** ◇ *the careful ~ of building materials* | **random** | **initial** | **final** | **judicial** (*esp. AmE*), **jury** | **team** | **Darwinian**, **natural**, **sexual** ◇ *Natural ~ is a key element of Darwin's theory of evolution.*
VERB + SELECTION **make** ◇ *She took a long time to make her ~.* | **base on** ◇ *Selection is based on standards of quality.* | **win** (*esp. BrE*) ◇ *She hopes to win ~ for the Olympic team.*
SELECTION + NOUN **criteria**, **policy** (*esp. BrE*) | **procedure**, **process** | **bias** ◇ *These results may have been caused by ~ bias.* | **board**, **committee**, **panel** (*esp. BrE*) | **pressure** ◇ *evolutionary ~ pressures*
PREP. **~ as** ◇ *his ~ as candidate for the party* | **~ for**

2 number of people/things that have been chosen

ADJ. **varied**, **wide** | **random** ◇ *We interviewed a random ~ of teenagers.* | **representative** | **judicious**, **well-chosen** | **final** ◇ *The final ~ of winners will be announced at the end of the event.*
VERB + SELECTION **contain**, **include** ◇ *The catalogue includes a ~ of his poetry.* | **play** ◇ *She played a ~ of waltzes.*
PREP. **from**, **~ of** ◇ *a ~ of hits from well-known musicals*

3 collection of things from which sth can be chosen

ADJ. **broad**, **comprehensive**, **extensive**, **huge**, **large**, **vast**, **wide** ◇ *We offer a broad ~ of products.* | **limited**, **poor**, **small** | **excellent**, **fine**, **good**, **great**, **interesting**, **nice**, **superb** | **menu**, **wine** ◇ *The wine ~ isn't bad.* | **musical**
VERB + SELECTION **offer** ◇ *The restaurant offers a wide ~ of cocktails.* | **find** ◇ *You'll find a good ~ of paints at this store.* | **feature** ◇ *Their website features a large ~ of photographs.* | **choose from**
PREP. **~ of**

selective adj.

VERBS **be**
ADV. **extremely**, **fairly**, **very**, etc. | **highly** | **increasingly** | **necessarily** ◇ *The list provided here is necessarily ~.* | **notoriously** ◇ *The human memory is notoriously ~.*
PREP. **about** ◇ *He is quite ~ about what he studies.* | **in** ◇ *Most of the girls are extremely ~ in their choice of boyfriends.*

self noun

ADJ. **whole** ◇ *He put his whole ~ into the performance.* | **real**, **true** | **inner**, **innermost** | **own** | **private**, **public** ◇ *Her private and public selves were vastly different.* | **normal**, **usual** | **other** | **former**, **old**, **past** ◇ *She knew that with a rest he would be back to his former ~.* | **new** | **younger** | **future** | **bubbly**, **cheerful**, **happy** ◇ *He's his usual cheerful ~ again.* | **better** ◇ *a book about reaching for one's better ~* | **conscious** | **physical** | **higher**, **spiritual** | **human**, **individual** | **good** (*humorous, esp. BrE*) ◇ *We look forward to seeing Mrs Brown and your good ~ this evening.*
VERB + SELF **reveal** ◇ *He was afraid to reveal his innermost ~.* | **discover**, **find** ◇ *a movie about a boy who falls in love and finds his true ~ in the process* | **express**
PHRASES **a loss of ~** | **a sense of ~** | **a shadow of your former ~** | **note to ~** ◇ *I was very thirsty (note to ~: bring water on walks!).*

self-assurance noun

ADJ. **new-found** | **blustery** | **masculine**
VERB + SELF-ASSURANCE **be lacking in**, **lack** | **exude** ◇ *In conversation she exudes wit and ~.*

self-confidence noun

ADJ. **enormous**, **great**, **supreme** | **growing**, **increased** | **new**, **renewed** | **national**
VERB + SELF-CONFIDENCE **have** | **exude**, **ooze**, **show** | **be lacking in**, **lack** | **gain** | **lose** | **give sb** ◇ *Living away from home has given him renewed ~.* | **boost**, **build**, **build up**, **develop**, **increase** ◇ *A few kind words might boost her ~.* | **undermine**
PHRASES **an air of ~** ◇ *She had an air of ~ that he admired.* | **a lack of ~** | **a sense of ~**

self-conscious adj.

VERBS **be**, **feel**, **look** | **become**, **get**, **grow** | **make sb** ◇ *He studied her in a way that made her very ~.*
ADV. **extremely**, **fairly**, **very**, etc. | **acutely** (*esp. BrE*), **overly**, **painfully** | **a little**, **slightly**, etc.
PREP. **about** ◇ *He started to get ~ about his weight.*

self-contained adj.

VERBS **be**, **seem**
ADV. **extremely**, **fairly**, **very**, etc. | **completely**, **entirely**, **fully**, **totally** ◇ *The flat is completely ~.* (*BrE*) | **largely** ◇ *a largely ~ community* | **relatively**

self-control noun

VERB + SELF-CONTROL **have** | **lack** | **lose** | **regain** | **keep** ◇ *She struggled to keep her ~.* | **exercise**, **practise/practice** ◇ *You should try exercising a little ~!* | **require**, **take** ◇ *It took all the ~ he had not to lose his temper.* | **develop**, **learn**
SELF-CONTROL + VERB **snap**
PHRASES **a lack of ~** | **a loss of ~** | **powers of ~** (*BrE*) ◇ *a person exercising ordinary powers of ~*

self-defence (BrE) (AmE self-defense) noun

ADJ. **collective** | **legitimate**
VERB + SELF-DEFENCE **learn** ◇ *The women learn ~ to protect themselves.* | **plead** ◇ *At his trial he will plead ~.*
SELF-DEFENCE/SELF-DEFENSE + NOUN **class**, **group** | **technique** | **instructor**, **teacher**
PREP. **for ~** ◇ *I own a gun for ~.* | **in ~** ◇ *He told police that he had acted in ~.* | **~ against** ◇ *~ against armed assailants*
PHRASES **an act of ~** | **the art of ~** | **the right of ~**

self-evident adj.

VERBS **appear**, **be**, **seem** | **become**
ADV. **by no means** ◇ *These ideas were by no means ~ when they were first suggested.* | **almost** | **fairly**
PREP. **to** ◇ *It was ~ to her that anything so wonderful could not have evolved accidentally.*

self-interest noun

ADJ. **enlightened**, **rational** | **economic**, **material** | **individual**, **national** | **naked**, **pure** | **narrow**
VERB + SELF-INTEREST **be motivated by** | **pursue your own**
PHRASES **act in ~**, **act out of ~** (*esp. BrE*) | **in your own ~** ◇ *Directors may be tempted to act in their own ~.* | **the pursuit of ~**

selfish adj.

VERBS **be**, **feel**, **seem**, **sound** ◇ *I know I'm being ~, but I can't help it.* | **become**
ADV. **extremely**, **fairly**, **very**, etc. ◇ *a very ~ attitude* | **incredibly** | **completely**, **entirely**, **purely**, **totally**, **utterly** ◇ *These people are completely ~.* | **a little**, **slightly**, etc.

selfishness noun

ADJ. **pure**, **utter** | **human**
PHRASES **an act of ~** ◇ *an act of pure ~* | **greed and ~**

self-pity noun

... OF SELF-PITY **wave** ◇ *He felt a sudden wave of ~.*
VERB + SELF-PITY **wallow in**
PHRASES **full of ~** | **tears of ~**

self-respect noun

VERB + SELF-RESPECT **have** ◇ *She has little ~.* | **lose** ◇ *You can't help but feel sorry for a man who has clearly lost all ~.* | **regain** | **keep** ◇ *He chose to resign to keep his ~.*

self-sufficient adj.

VERBS **be** | **become**

ADV. **completely, entirely, totally, wholly** | **almost** | **largely** | **economically, financially**
PREP. **in** ◇ *These people have now become almost ~ in grain crops.*

sell *verb*

ADV. **cheaply**
VERB + SELL **be able to, can** | **want to** | **plan to** | **try to** ◇ *They are still trying to ~ their house.* | **be expected to, expect to** ◇ *The novel was expected to ~ between 1 000 and 1 500 copies.* | **be willing to** | **be forced to** ◇ *The company has been forced to ~ land to recoup some of the losses.* | **be difficult to, be hard to** ◇ *It will be hard to ~ 3 000 tickets.* ◇ *The property was hard to ~.* | **have the right to ~** ◇ *Your broker has the right to ~ your shares.*
PREP. **at** ◇ *We ~ these little notebooks at €1 each.* | **for** ◇ *They sold their house for $847 000.* | **to** ◇ *She sold her car to a friend.*
PHRASES **~ sth at a discount, ~ sth at a loss, ~ sth at a premium, ~ sth at a profit** ◇ *Some of these cars are actually being sold at a loss.* | **be sold at auction** ◇ *The painting was sold at auction for $11.3 million.* | **be sold over the counter** ◇ *This medicine is sold over the counter.* | **buy and ~ (sth)** ◇ *Many banks are willing to buy and ~ shares on behalf of customers.* | **~ sb into slavery**

PHR V **sell sth off**
ADV. **cheaply** ◇ *Derelict inner-city sites could be sold off cheaply for housing.*

semblance *noun*

ADJ. **vague** ◇ *Brad had his emotions under a vague ~ of control.*
VERB + SEMBLANCE **have** | **lack** ◇ *The movie lacks any ~ of realism.* | **gain** | **lose** ◇ *He lost all ~ of dignity and rushed down the street after her.* | **keep, maintain, preserve, retain** | **bring, give sth** ◇ *She struggled to bring a ~ of order to the meeting.* | **regain, restore (sth to), return (sth) to**
PREP. **in a/the ~ of, into a/the ~ of** ◇ *She bared her teeth in a ~ of a smile.* | **~ of** ◇ *He tried to restore some ~ of normality to their home life.*
PHRASES **a/some ~ of control** | **a/some ~ of order**

semester *noun* (*esp. in the US*)

ADJ. **first, second** ◇ *the end of the first-semester course* | **fall, spring, summer** ◇ *His fall-semester grades were abysmal.* | **last, next** ◇ *a class I took last ~* | **following, previous** | **entire, whole** ◇ *I spent an entire ~ studying Chomsky.*
VERB + SEMESTER **spend** ◇ *I spent a ~ at the University of Madrid.* | **begin** | **complete, finish** ◇ *students completing all eight ~s of the program* ◇ *I was finishing my last ~ in college and trying to look for a job.*
SEMESTER + VERB **begin, start** ◇ *The new ~ started on February 3.* | **end**
SEMESTER + NOUN **break** ◇ *The ~ break had begun.* | **hour** ◇ *The total curriculum is 54 ~ hours.* | **credit hours, credits** ◇ *The course is worth 40 ~ credit hours.*

seminar *noun*

1 class at a university, etc.

ADJ. **weekly, etc.** | **freshman** (*AmE*), **graduate, senior** (*AmE*), **undergraduate** | **online**
... OF SEMINARS **series**
VERB + SEMINAR **conduct, give, teach** (*AmE*) ◇ *In spring 2006 I taught a ~ on Sappho.* | **attend, go to** | **be entitled** (*esp. BrE*), **be titled** (*esp. AmE*) ◇ *Architect Ken Bonner presented a ~ titled 'Elements of Design'.*
SEMINAR + NOUN **discussion, paper** | **room** | **programme/ program, series**
PREP. **at a/the ~, in a/the ~** ◇ *There was some lively debate at this week's ~.* | **~ on** ◇ *Professor Mackay will give a ~ on Pound's poetry.*

2 conference for discussion/training

ADJ. **all-day, half-day, weekend** | **one-day, two-day, etc.** | **annual** | **business, educational, management, training** | **free** | **special** | **international**
VERB + SEMINAR **hold, host, offer, organize, run** | **sponsor** | **do, present** | **lead** | **attend, go to**
SEMINAR + VERB **take place** | **focus on sth** ◇ *a ~ focusing on Africa*
SEMINAR + NOUN **participant** | **leader**
PREP. **~ for** ◇ *I recently spoke at an educational ~ for judges.*

senator *noun*

ADJ. **American, US** | **Democratic, Republican** | **conservative, liberal** | **junior, senior** | **state** ◇ *a Republican state ~* | **former** ◇ *the former US Senator, James Hurley* | **fellow** ◇ *He was pilloried by his fellow Senators.* | **key, leading** ◇ *We'll talk to two key ~s on the Intelligence Committee.*
VERB + SENATOR **elect, elect sb (as)** | **become** ◇ *In 1988 he became a US Senator.*
PHRASES **~s and congressmen, ~s and representatives** (*both AmE*) ◇ *Write your ~s and congressmen urging them to protect the US constitution.* | **~s on both sides of the aisle** (= Democrats and Republicans) (*AmE*)

senior *adj.*

VERBS **be**
ADV. **very** ◇ *a meeting of all the very ~ officers* | **fairly, quite, relatively** | **enough** ◇ *She wasn't ~ enough to take such a decision.*
PREP. **to** ◇ *Is Mark ~ to you?*

seniority *noun*

VERB + SENIORITY **have** | **lose**
SENIORITY + NOUN **system**
PREP. **by** ◇ *Promotion in the job was by ~.* | **~ over** ◇ *She had ~ over three members of the department.*
PHRASES **in order of ~** ◇ *On the death of the captain, the officer next in order of ~ assumed command.*

sensation *noun*

1 feeling

ADJ. **bodily, physical, tactile** | **delicious, pleasant, pleasurable, wonderful** | **painful, unpleasant** | **intense, overwhelming, strong** | **curious** (*esp. BrE*), **eerie, odd, peculiar, strange, weird** ◇ *I had a strange ~ in my leg.* | **familiar** | **burning, choking, prickling, stinging, tingling** | **cold** | **hot, warm** | **sinking** ◇ *She felt a sinking ~ in the pit of her stomach.* | **pain, taste** ◇ *For a special taste ~, try our gourmet coffee.*
VERB + SENSATION **experience, feel, have** ◇ *He felt a tingling ~ down his side.* ◇ *I had the eerie ~ that I was not alone.* ◇ *She had no ~ in her hands.* | **lose** | **produce** | **enjoy** ◇ *Most people enjoy the ~ of eating.* | **describe** ◇ *Rossi described the ~ of plunging downhill at 130 mph.*
SENSATION + VERB **come back** | **come over sb, fill sth, spread** ◇ *A strange ~ came over her.* ◇ *A warm tingling ~ spread to her fingers.* | **overwhelm** ◇ *A wonderful ~ filled his body.* ◇ *He was overwhelmed by a ~ of fear.*
PREP. **~ in** ◇ *Lisa felt a burning ~ in her eyes.* | **~ of** ◇ *the ~ of sand between your toes* ◇ *the ~ of being watched*

2 great excitement, etc.; person that causes this

ADJ. **great** | **overnight** | **international** | **literary, media, pop** (*esp. BrE*), **singing, tennis, etc.** ◇ *The series became a media ~ in the early 1950s.* | **rookie** (*AmE*), **teen, teenage** (*esp. BrE*) ◇ *Golf's latest teen ~ is 14-year-old Michael Woo.*
VERB + SENSATION **cause, create** ◇ *The movie caused a ~ among critics.* | **become**

sense *noun*

1 sight, hearing, etc.

ADJ. **acute, developed, good, keen** ◇ *Raccoons have a highly developed ~ of touch.* | **poor** | **sixth** ◇ *He has a sixth ~ when it comes to fashion.*
VERB + SENSE **have** ◇ *He has an acute ~ of smell.* | **lose** ◇ *She*

lost her ~ of hearing early in life. | **heighten, sharpen** | **dull** | **appeal to** ◇ Art should appeal to the ~s rather than the intellect.
SENSE + VERB **tell sb** ◇ When she came to, her ~s told her she was lying on a beach. | **reel, swim** ◇ Her ~s reeled as she fought for consciousness.
SENSE + NOUN **organ**
PREP. **through the ~s** ◇ Although he can't see, he learns a lot through his other ~s.
PHRASES **the five ~s** | **the ~ of hearing, the ~ of sight, the ~ of smell, the ~ of taste, the ~ of touch** | **an assault on the ~s** | **the evidence of your ~s**

2 feeling/awareness of sth

ADJ. **deep, great, keen, overwhelming, palpable, pervasive, powerful, profound, strong, tremendous** ◇ He felt a deep ~ of relief after the phone call. ◇ a palpable ~ of danger ◇ They feel a pervasive ~ of loss and longing. ◇ We felt a profound ~ of alienation from Western culture. | **genuine, real, true** | **basic, underlying** | **clear** ◇ He lacked a clear ~ of direction. | **growing, heightened** | **new-found** (esp. AmE), **renewed** ◇ Many felt a renewed ~ of purpose in the nation's war effort. | **general, overall** | **shared** ◇ We have a shared ~ of community. | **inner** | **slight, vague** ◇ a vague ~ of unease | **nagging** ◇ Patti had a nagging ~ of foreboding.
VERB + SENSE **experience, feel, have, possess** ◇ I experienced a new ~ of freedom. | **gain, get** ◇ I got the ~ that she wasn't very pleased to see us. ◇ Readers gain a real ~ of what life was like in the camp. | **display, show** | **convey** ◇ The music conveyed a ~ of loss. | **bring, give sb, provide** ◇ The conviction may bring a ~ of closure. | **create, develop, foster** ◇ Clubs try to create a ~ of community. | **keep, maintain, retain** | **lose** | **lack** | **heighten, sharpen**
PREP. **~ of** ◇ He seems to have lost his ~ of reality.
PHRASES **a false ~ of security** ◇ The public has been lulled into a false ~ of security.

3 understanding/ability to judge

ADJ. **good, great, wonderful** ◇ She had a great ~ of style. | **bad, poor** | **innate, intuitive, natural** ◇ a natural ~ of justice | **moral** | **business, dress, fashion** ◇ He has no dress ~. ◇ I have absolutely no fashion ~.
VERB + SENSE **have**
PREP. **~ of** ◇ a good ~ of direction ◇ a poor ~ of rhythm ◇ a great ~ of timing

4 sensible or practical reason/judgement

ADJ. **complete, perfect** ◇ It all makes perfect ~ (= is easy to understand). | **good** | **common, horse** (esp. AmE) ◇ Common ~ tells me I should get more sleep. | **business, economic, financial** ◇ Family-friendly policies make good business ~. | **intuitive, logical** ◇ These results seem to make intuitive ~.
VERB + SENSE **have** ◇ He at least had the ~ to call the police. | **display, show** | **lack** ◇ Meg is incredibly intelligent but she lacks common ~. | **make** ◇ This paragraph doesn't make ~. | **see** ◇ I tried to make him see ~, but he just wouldn't listen. | **talk** ◇ If you can't talk ~, I'm leaving!
PREP. **~ in** ◇ There's a lot of ~ in what he's saying.
PHRASES **have more money than ~** (esp. BrE) | **make little ~** ◇ It makes little ~ to discuss this now. | **(not) an ounce of ~** ◇ If you had an ounce of ~, you'd never have agreed to help him. | **knock some ~ into sb, talk ~ into sb** (esp. AmE) ◇ I'm trying to knock some ~ into her. ◇ We'll try and talk a little ~ into her. | **there's no ~ in sth** ◇ There's no ~ in going home before the concert.

5 your senses normal state of mind

VERB + SENSES **come to, regain** | **take leave of** ◇ Have you taken leave of your ~s? | **bring sb to**

6 meaning

ADJ. **broad, loose, wide** ◇ The novel is about education in its widest ~. | **certain** ◇ In a certain ~, justice was done. | **limited, narrow, strict** | **full** ◇ This is a tragedy in the fullest ~ of the word. | **accepted, classic, conventional, traditional** ◇ I am not writing poetry in the traditional ~. ◇ These teachings do not constitute a religion in the conventional ~. | **general, ordinary, usual** ◇ I don't have any friends in the usual ~ of the word. | **meaningful** ◇ He and I were no longer

friends in any meaningful ~. | **negative, positive** | **practical** | **figurative, metaphorical** | **literal** | **legal, technical** | **spiritual** | **pejorative**
VERB + SENSE **have** ◇ That word has three ~s.
PREP. **in a ~** ◇ In a ~, she's right.
PHRASES **in every ~ of the word, in a very real ~** ◇ In a very real ~, post-war repression was the continuation of the war. | **in the true ~ of the word**

sense verb

ADV. **immediately** ◇ I immediately ~d something was wrong. | **clearly, strongly** ◇ He clearly ~d that some points could be scored. ◇ I ~d very strongly that she was angry with me. | **dimly, vaguely** | **almost** ◇ Sandra could almost ~ the tension in the air. | **just** ◇ Maybe she could just ~ what I needed. | **apparently** ◇ She apparently ~d defeat was inevitable. | **intuitively**

senseless adj.

1 having no meaning

VERBS **be, seem**
ADV. **seemingly** | **absolutely, completely** ◇ It was a completely ~ act of violence.

2 unconscious

VERBS **beat sb, knock sb** ◇ The thugs beat him ~ with a baseball bat.

sense of humour (BrE) (AmE **sense of humor**) noun

VERBS **have, possess** | **keep, maintain, retain** (esp. BrE) ◇ I'm trying to keep a ~ about all of this. | **lose** | **lack** ◇ He seems to lack a ~.
ADJ. **good, great, wonderful** ◇ He had a keen ~. | **mischievous, wicked** ◇ the playwright's wicked ~ | **dark, dry, wry** | **goofy** (AmE), **offbeat** (esp. AmE), **quirky** ◇ Michael and I share a quirky ~. | **odd, strange, weird** | **sick, twisted, warped**
PREP. **with a ~** ◇ He seemed to take most things with a ~.

sensible adj.

VERBS **appear, be, seem, sound** ◇ This approach seems very ~ to me. | **become**
ADV. **extremely, fairly, very, etc.** ◇ Ben's usually very ~. | **eminently** (esp. BrE) | **entirely, perfectly** (both esp. BrE) ◇ In the state I was in, this seemed a perfectly ~ remark. | **hardly** ◇ Are you going out to search for it at this time of night? It seems hardly ~. | **enough** ◇ That advice sounds ~ enough.

sensitive adj.

1 aware of other people's feelings

VERBS **be** | **become** | **make sb** ◇ Her experiences had made her ~ to other people's troubles. | **remain**
ADV. **extremely, fairly, very, etc.** | **deeply, unusually** ◇ a deeply ~, caring man
PREP. **to** ◇ Horses are very ~ to their riders' moods.

2 reacting more than usual to sth; easily upset

VERBS **be, seem** | **become** | **remain** | **make sb/sth ~ (to sth)** ◇ These drugs can make skin extremely ~ to sunlight.
ADV. **extremely, fairly, very, etc.** | **acutely, deeply, highly, painfully, particularly** | **overly** | **increasingly** | **a little, slightly, etc.**
PREP. **about** ◇ Teenagers are often very ~ about their appearance. | **to** ◇ He was acutely ~ to criticism.

3 needing to be dealt with carefully

VERBS **be** | **become** | **remain** | **consider, deem** ◇ The information was deemed too ~ to be broadcast.
ADV. **extremely, fairly, very, etc.** ◇ an extremely ~ question | **highly** ◇ this highly ~ issue | **potentially** ◇ It is not known how the Russians obtained such potentially ~ information. | **commercially** (esp. BrE), **culturally** (esp. AmE), **ecologically**

(*esp. AmE*), **environmentally**, **politically** ◊ *commercially ~ information* ◊ *culturally ~ policies*

4 able to measure very small changes

VERBS **be** ◊ *The bat's hearing is remarkably ~.*
ADV. **extremely**, **fairly**, **very**, **etc.** | **especially**, **exquisitely**, **highly**, **incredibly**, **remarkably** ◊ *The equipment is highly ~.* | **enough**, **sufficiently** ◊ *The probe is ~ enough to detect the presence of a single microbe.*
PREP. **to** ◊ *~ to the slightest movement*

sensitivity *noun*

ADJ. **extreme**, **great**, **high** ◊ *This is a matter of great ~.* ◊ *a poet of great ~* | **low** ◊ *a tool that has been criticized for its low ~* | **heightened**, **increased** | **reduced** | **cultural**, **political**
... OF SENSITIVITY **degree** ◊ *Collective living depends on a degree of ~ to what is happening around us.*
VERB + SENSITIVITY **have** | **develop** | **display**, **show** ◊ *Migrating birds show extreme ~ to air currents.* | **be aware of** ◊ *The producers were aware of the ~ of the subject.* | **reduce** | **lack** ◊ *Many doctors lack ~ when dealing with their patients.*
SENSITIVITY + NOUN **training** (*esp. AmE*) ◊ *Sensitivity training for teachers is always useful.*
PREP. **with ~** ◊ *She broke the news to us with great ~.* | **~ about** ◊ *~ about racial issues* | **~ in** ◊ *She is not known for her ~ in dealing with complaints.* | **~ over** ◊ *There is deep ~ over the treatment of minority groups.* | **~ to** ◊ *The course teaches ~ to body language.* | **~ towards/toward** ◊ *the need for ~ towards/toward the views of the children*
PHRASES **a lack of ~**

sentence *noun*

1 group of words

ADJ. **long**, **short** ◊ *Try to keep your ~s short.* | **complete**, **whole** | **broken**, **incomplete** | **full** | **single** ◊ *The argument can be distilled into a single ~.* | **grammatical**, **ungrammatical** | **coherent** | **affirmative**, **declarative**, **negative** | **complex**, **simple** | **run-on** (*AmE*) | **opening** ◊ *the opening ~ of the novel* | **following** ◊ *I came across the following ~ in a paper recently…*
VERB + SENTENCE **begin** | **finish** ◊ *Peter finished Jane's ~ for her.* | **complete** ◊ *Complete the following ~: 'I love dictionaries because…'.* | **end** ◊ *He tells her not to end her ~s with prepositions.* | **speak**, **utter** ◊ *Troy uttered one last ~.* | **construct**, **form**, **formulate**, **string together**, **write** ◊ *He can barely form a grammatical ~.* ◊ *Cooke was so nervous he could barely string a ~ together.* | **parse** | **punctuate** (*usually figurative*) ◊ *She punctuated her ~ with a well-aimed kick at his right shin.* | **read** ◊ *I kept reading the same ~ over and over again.*
SENTENCE + VERB **contain sth**, **have sth** ◊ *Does the ~ contain an adverb?*
SENTENCE + NOUN **structure**

2 punishment given by a judge

ADJ. **maximum**, **minimum** ◊ *the mandatory minimum ~* (*AmE*) | **average** | **long**, **short** | **harsh**, **heavy**, **severe**, **stiff** | **lenient**, **light** | **reduced** ◊ *He turned state's evidence in return for a reduced ~.* | **indeterminate** (*esp. BrE*) | **appropriate** | **mandatory** ◊ *The judge imposed the mandatory ~ for murder.* | **suspended** | **jail**, **prison** | **criminal** | **custodial**, **non-custodial** (*both BrE*) | **death** | **life**
VERB + SENTENCE **hand down**, **impose**, **pass**, **pronounce** ◊ *The judge will pass ~ on the accused this afternoon.* | **be given**, **get**, **receive** | **begin** (*esp. BrE*) ◊ *He has begun a life ~ for Carol's murder.* | **serve** ◊ *He will have to serve a life ~.* | **carry out**, **complete** ◊ *ex-felons who have completed their ~s* | **await** (*esp. BrE*) ◊ *He spent a week in custody awaiting ~.* | **face** ◊ *She could face a long prison ~.* | **suspend** | **appeal** (*esp. AmE*), **appeal against** (*BrE*) | **review** | **commute**, **reduce** ◊ *The death ~ may be commuted to life imprisonment.* | **overturn**, **quash** (*BrE*) | **uphold** ◊ *The US Supreme Court recently upheld both of these ~s.* | **carry** ◊ *This type of assault carries a maximum ~ of six months in prison.*
PREP. **~ for** ◊ *an eight-year ~ for burglary*
PHRASES **under ~ of death** ◊ *He was imprisoned under ~ of death.*

sentiment *noun*

ADJ. **deep**, **strong** | **growing** | **common**, **general**, **prevailing** | **fine**, **lofty**, **noble** ◊ *All these noble ~s have little chance of being put into practice.* | **national**, **popular**, **public** | **consumer**, **investor** (*both esp. AmE*) | **bearish**, **bullish** (= concerning stock markets, etc.) (*both esp. AmE*) ◊ *There was a steep rise in bullish ~ as foreign investors rushed in.* | **nationalist**, **patriotic** | **anti-American**, **anti-Western**, **etc.** | **anti-government**, **anti-war**, **etc.** | **pro-American**, **etc.** | **racist** | **political** | **moral**, **religious** ◊ *The people are renowned for their deep religious ~.* | **mawkish** (*esp. BrE*) ◊ *The new movie is to be applauded for refusing to drift into mawkish ~.*
VERB + SENTIMENT **express**, **voice** | **agree with**, **endorse**, **share** ◊ *He agrees with the ~s expressed in the editorial.* | **echo**, **reflect** ◊ *I think his view reflects the ~ of a lot of fans.* | **disagree with** | **arouse**, **inflame** ◊ *These actions are likely to inflame anti-Western ~.* | **understand**
SENTIMENT + VERB **run** ◊ *In the 19th century, anti-Catholic ~ ran high.*
PREP. **~s about**, **~s on** ◊ *It would be a mistake to ignore their strong ~s on the issue.* | **~ against** ◊ *The killings helped arouse popular ~ against the organization.* | **~ among** ◊ *anti-war ~ among the civilian population* | **~ in favour/ favor of** ◊ *public ~ in favour/favor of state ownership* | **~ towards/toward** ◊ *critical ~ towards/toward government policy*
PHRASES **I, we, etc. appreciate the ~** ◊ *Even though I disagree with you, I appreciate the ~s that prompt you to speak out.* | **my ~s exactly** (= I agree) ◊ *'I don't see why we should change our plans just because of him.' 'My ~s exactly.'*

separate *verb*

1 move/keep people/things apart

ADV. **completely** | **carefully** | **clearly** ◊ *These two branches of the science have now become clearly ~d.* | **effectively** | **easily** ◊ *One cannot easily ~ moral, social and political issues.* | **formally** | **legally** | **mechanically** ◊ *Mechanically ~d meat made from cattle and sheep has now been banned.* | **geographically**, **physically**, **spatially**
VERB + SEPARATE **attempt to**, **try to** | **be difficult to**, **be hard to**, **be impossible to** ◊ *It was impossible to ~ the rival fans.*
PREP. **from** ◊ *The boys are ~d from the girls.* | **into** ◊ *I ~d the documents into two piles.*
PHRASES **sharply ~d**, **totally ~d**, **widely ~d** ◊ *The disciplines of science and engineering are not always sharply ~d.* ◊ *an island resort totally ~d from the mainland* ◊ *The two groups became widely ~d.*

2 stop living together

ADV. **legally** | **recently** ◊ *He had recently ~d from his wife.* | **forcibly** ◊ *Slave parents were forcibly ~d from their children.*
VERB + SEPARATE **decide to**
PREP. **from** ◊ *She is ~d from her husband.*

separate *adj.*

VERBS **be** | **become** | **remain** | **keep sb/sth** ◊ *The women are kept ~ from the men.* | **consider sth**
ADV. **somewhat**, **very** ◊ *I kept my two lives very ~.* | **essentially**, **largely** ◊ *The two groups are essentially ~ and independent.* | **completely**, **entirely**, **quite**, **totally**, **wholly** ◊ *The waste water is kept entirely ~ from the rainwater.* | **apparently** | **previously** ◊ *to merge the two previously ~ businesses* | **geographically**, **physically**
PREP. **from** ◊ *a lifestyle which is quite ~ from that of her parents*
PHRASES **go your ~ ways** ◊ *They decided to go their ~ ways after being together for five years.*

separation noun

1 being apart

ADJ. **complete, total** | **clear, rigid, strict** | **long** ◇ *She is visiting her family after a long ~.* | **physical, spatial** | **constitutional** ◇ *the constitutional ~ of church and state*
PREP. **~ between** ◇ *the clear ~ of powers between the executive and the legislature* | **~ from** ◇ *the ~ of children from their parents during the war*
PHRASES **~ anxiety** (= fear that a child feels when separated from its parents) | **~ of powers** ◇ *the constitutional principle of ~ of powers*

2 when a married couple lives apart

ADJ. **formal, judicial** (*BrE*), **legal** | **trial** | **parental** (*esp. AmE*)
SEPARATION + NOUN **agreement** (*esp. AmE*)
PREP. **~ between** ◇ *the ~ between Mary and her husband* | **~ from** ◇ *the ~ from his wife*

September noun → Note at MONTH

sequel noun

ADJ. **long-awaited** | **forthcoming** (*esp. BrE*), **upcoming** (*esp. AmE*) | **inevitable** | **direct** ◇ *The new movie is a direct ~ to the first, picking up the story where the original left off.* | **worthy** ◇ *The result is a worthy ~ to the original book.*
VERB + SEQUEL **do, make, work on, write** ◇ *She was asked to make a ~ to 'Peter Pan'.* | **spawn** ◇ *The film has spawned five ~s to date.*
SEQUEL + VERB **come out** ◇ *The ~ came out this spring.*
PREP. **in a/the ~** ◇ *Some important new characters appear in the ~.* | **~ to**

sequence noun

1 set of actions, etc.; order of appearance

ADJ. **complete, entire, whole** | **continuous, unbroken** | **complex** | **long, short** | **correct** | **specific** | **chronological, temporal** ◇ *The article describes the chronological ~ of events.* | **logical, random** | **chord** ◇ *a basic blues chord ~* | **amino acid, protein** | **DNA, gene, genetic, genome** ◇ *a representative cross section of the entire human genome ~* | **unbeaten, winning** (*both BrE*) ◇ *a remarkable winning ~ of games* | **losing** (*BrE*)
VERB + SEQUENCE **complete** ◇ *Complete the following ~: 1, 4, 8, 13…* | **repeat** ◇ *Repeat the entire ~ at least three times.* | **follow** ◇ *We had to follow a complex ~ of movements.*
PREP. **~ of**
PHRASES **in ~, out of ~** ◇ *The book is more satisfying if you read each chapter in ~.* ◇ *This article is out of ~ and belongs on page 57.* | **a ~ of events**

2 part of a film/movie

ADJ. **opening** | **climactic, closing, final** | **dramatic, exciting** ◇ *The movie includes a few exciting action ~s.* | **brilliant, great** | **impressive, memorable** ◇ *There were some very impressive underwater ~s.* | **dance, musical** | **action, battle, chase, fight** ◇ *The movie begins with an extended car-chase ~.* | **animated** | **dream, fantasy, flashback** | **credit, title** ◇ *the opening credit ~* | **extended, long** | **short**
VERB + SEQUENCE **film, shoot** | **choreograph** ◇ *The fight ~s were choreographed by Xin-Xin Xiong.*
SEQUENCE + VERB **feature, involve, show** ◇ *This ~ features some impressive skydiving action.*
PREP. **in a/the ~** ◇ *The heroine dies in the closing ~ of the movie.*

serene adj.

VERBS **be, become, feel, look, seem, sound** | **remain**
ADV. **very** | **perfectly, quite, utterly** | **almost** | **outwardly** ◇ *beneath the outwardly ~ surface*

serenity noun

ADJ. **peaceful, quiet**
VERB + SERENITY **achieve, find**
PREP. **with ~** ◇ *She was able to face death with ~.*
PHRASES **a feeling of ~** | **peace and ~** ◇ *My Japanese garden is a haven of peace and ~.*

sergeant noun

1 in the army/air force

ADJ. **army** | **drill** ◇ *He had a voice like a drill ~.* | **supply** (*in the US*) | **staff** | **platoon** | **chief master, first, master** (*all in the US*) | **gunnery** (*in the US*) | **flight** (*in the UK*) | **colour** (*in the UK*) | **recruiting** (*usually figurative*) ◇ *a powerful recruiting ~ for terrorist organizations*
→ Note at RANK

2 in the police

ADJ. **police** | **detective** (*in the UK*) ◇ *Detective Sergeant Peter Wiles* | **desk, duty** ◇ *Visitors to the police station should report to the duty ~.* | **custody** (*in the UK*)
PHRASES **the rank of ~**

series noun

1 number of things that come one after another

ADJ. **entire, whole** ◇ *He had a whole ~ of tests.* | **ongoing** | **recent** | **endless, long** | **complex** ◇ *a complex ~ of events* | **continuous** | **infinite** | **concert, lecture** | **time** ◇ *a time ~ showing the pattern of global warming*
PREP. **in a/the ~** ◇ *The quartet will be performing in a ~ of lunchtime concerts.* | **~ of** ◇ *a ~ of events/interviews/meetings/lectures* ◇ *a ~ of experiments/studies/tests*
PHRASES **the first of a/the ~, the last of a/the ~** | **the first in a ~, the latest in a ~**

2 on radio, TV, etc.

ADJ. **radio, television, TV** | **book, DVD, film, movie, video** ◇ *the Harry Potter book ~* | **comedy, crime, documentary, drama, reality** | **animated, anime, cartoon** | **hit, popular** ◇ *the hit comedy ~ 'Friends'* | **long-running** | **classic** | **original** | **new** | **forthcoming** (*BrE*), **upcoming** (*esp. AmE*) | **two-part, three-part, etc.** | **weekly** | **special** ◇ *In the first of a special two-part ~ on the economy…*
VERB + SERIES **film** | **commission** (*esp. BrE*) ◇ *The BBC has already commissioned a second ~.* | **broadcast, screen** | **release** ◇ *HBO has begun releasing the ~ on DVD.* | **be based on** ◇ *an anime ~ based on novels by Hiroyuki Morioka*
PREP. **in a/the ~** ◇ *She has a small part in a drama ~ for radio.* ◇ *the final book in the ~* | **~ about, ~ on** ◇ *We watched the final part of a ~ on Australian wildlife.*
PHRASES **an episode of a ~, a part of a ~**

3 a set of sports games

ADJ. **racing** | **World Series** (in baseball) | **championship, Test** (in cricket) ◇ *Australia won the Test ~ against England.* | **home** (esp. in cricket) | **play-off** (*AmE*) | **two-game, three-game, etc.** (*AmE*) | **season, weekend** (*both AmE*)
VERB + SERIES **lose, win** | **level** (*BrE*) ◇ *India must win to level the ~.*
PREP. **in the ~** ◇ *They took the first two games in the ~.* | **~ with** ◇ *The Bronx Bombers won two of three in a weekend ~ with the Red Sox.*

serious adj.

1 bad/dangerous

VERBS **be, look, seem, sound** | **become, get** ◇ *By this time the riots were getting ~.* | **remain**
ADV. **extremely, fairly, very, etc.** | **particularly, really, terribly** ◇ *These are terribly ~ allegations.* | **potentially**
PREP. **for** ◇ *This situation could be very ~ for her.*
PHRASES **nothing ~** ◇ *'Bob's sick.' 'Oh, I hope it's nothing ~.'* | **~ enough to warrant sth** ◇ *The crime is considered ~ enough to warrant a jail term.*

2 not joking

VERBS **be, look, sound** ◇ *Come on, be ~!* | **become, grow, turn** ◇ *He became ~ all of a sudden.* | **remain, stay** ◇ *Please try to stay ~!*
ADV. **extremely, fairly, very, etc.** | **absolutely, completely, entirely, perfectly, quite, totally** | **deadly, terribly** ◇ *Joe is deadly ~ in his beliefs.*
PREP. **about** ◇ *Are you ~ about resigning?*

seriousness noun

ADJ. **complete** (*esp. AmE*), **deadly** (*esp. BrE*), **deep**, **great**, **high** ◊ *He maintained an attitude of high ~.* | **mock** ◊ *'You didn't know?' he asked in mock ~.* | **underlying** ◊ *The joke did not obscure the underlying ~ of his point.* | **moral**
VERB + SERIOUSNESS **appreciate**, **grasp**, **realize**, **recognize**, **understand** ◊ *Only later did he realize the full ~ of his actions.* | **demonstrate**, **show** ◊ *The sentence imposed in this case demonstrates the ~ of environmental crimes.* | **downplay** | **treat sth with** ◊ *The problem was not treated with the ~ it deserved.*
PREP. **with ~** ◊ *She spoke with great ~ of the hardships she had endured.*
PHRASES **in all ~** ◊ *You can't in all ~ think they'll give you the job!* | **take, treat, etc. sth with the utmost ~**

sermon noun

ADJ. **fiery** | **weekly** | **long**
VERB + SERMON **deliver**, **give**, **preach**, **read** | **hear**
PREP. **during a/the ~, in a/the ~** ◊ *He fell asleep during the ~.* | **~ on** ◊ *She preached a ~ on forgiveness.*

servant noun

ADJ. **devoted**, **faithful**, **loyal**, **trusted** | **humble**, **obedient** | **good** | **female**, **male** | **hired** | **indentured** | **personal** | **domestic**, **farm** (*esp. BrE*), **house** (*esp. AmE*), **household** | **palace**, **royal** | **civil** (*esp. BrE*), **Crown** (*BrE, law*), **public** ◊ *a powerful committee of politicians and civil ~s*
VERB + SERVANT **employ**, **have** | **call** | **order**
SERVANT + VERB **serve sb**, **wait on sb** ◊ *An army of ~s waited on the general's household.* | **work** | **bustle**, **run**, **rush**, **scurry** ◊ *Servants scurried around him.* | **bow**
SERVANT + NOUN **boy**, **girl**
PREP. **~ to** ◊ *He banishes Kent, a loyal ~ to King Lear.*
PHRASES **an army of ~s** ◊ *The duchess arrived, surrounded by her army of ~s.* | **a ~ of the Crown** (*BrE*) | **a ~ of the people** | **a ~ of God** | **servants' quarters**

serve verb

1 give sb food or drink
ADV. **immediately** ◊ *Pour the sauce over the pasta and ~ immediately.*
VERB + SERVE **be ready to** ◊ *Cover and chill the salad until ready to ~.*
PREP. **to** ◊ *They ~d a wonderful meal to more than 50 delegates.* | **with** ◊ *The delegates were ~d with a wonderful meal.* ◊ *Serve the lamb with new potatoes and green beans.*
PHRASES **dinner is ~d** ◊ *'Dinner is ~d!' Katie announced.* | **~ sth chilled, ~ sth cold, ~ sth hot** ◊ *The quiche can be ~d hot or cold.*

2 work
ADV. **faithfully**, **loyally**, **well** ◊ *She ~d the family faithfully for many years* (= *as a servant*). | **better** ◊ *Let us know how we can better ~ your needs.* | **currently** ◊ *She is currently serving as special adviser to the American Ambassador.* | **previously**
VERB + SERVE **continue to**
PREP. **as** ◊ *I shall continue to ~ as a trustee.* | **in** ◊ *She ~d in the medical corps.* ◊ *to ~ in the army/military/navy* | **on** ◊ *I currently ~ on the Board of Directors.* ◊ *to ~ on the committee/jury/panel* | **under** ◊ *He ~d under President Reagan in the 1980s.*
PHRASES **if memory ~s you, if memory ~s (you) correctly, if memory ~s you right** ◊ *If memory ~s me right, we arrived on June 22, which was a Tuesday.* | **~ in a … capacity, ~ in this/that capacity** ◊ *She has ~d in an advisory capacity for a number of groups.* | **~ on active duty** (*esp. AmE*) ◊ *He ~d on active duty in the US Marine Corps.* | **~ with distinction** ◊ *He ~d with distinction in the First World War.*

3 be useful
ADV. **merely**, **only**, **simply** ◊ *This only ~d to complicate the situation further.* | **mainly**, **mostly**, **primarily** ◊ *The*

Declaration ~d primarily as a propaganda piece.* | **well** ◊ *This strategy has always ~d him well.*
PREP. **as** ◊ *The texts ultimately ~ as springboards for the artists' imagination.*

service noun

1 system that provides sth the public needs
ADJ. **efficient**, **excellent**, **good**, **valuable** | **adequate** | **bad**, **inadequate**, **poor**, **terrible** | **complete**, **comprehensive**, **full** | **standard** | **basic** | **free** | **premium** | **personalized** (*esp. AmE*), **specialized** ◊ *specialized ~s for the deaf and hard of hearing* | **backup**, **support** | **ambulance** (*esp. BrE*), **emergency**, **fire** (*BrE*) **police** (*BrE*), **rescue** (*esp. BrE*) ◊ *A passer-by called the emergency ~s* (= *the ambulance/fire/police service*). (*BrE*) | **essential** ◊ *Essential ~s* (= *the supply of water, gas, electricity*) *will be maintained.* | **vital** (*esp. BrE*) ◊ *paramedics who provide a vital ~ to the public* | **public** | **available** ◊ *Find out what ~s are available in your area.* | **Internet**, **online**, **Web**, **Web-based** ◊ *an online dating ~* | **broadband**, **dial-up**, **high-speed**, **wireless** ◊ *wireless Internet ~s* | **download** ◊ *The studio launches its own digital music download ~ next month.* | **messaging** ◊ *I typed my password into my instant messaging ~.* | **phone**, **telephone** | **satellite** | **subscription** | **advisory** (*esp. BrE*), **consulting** (*esp. AmE*), **counselling/counseling** | **health**, **health-care**, **medical**, **etc.** | **customs**, **diplomatic**, **foreign**, **library** (*esp. BrE*), **postal**, **prison** (*BrE*), **probation** (*BrE*), **prosecution** (*BrE*), **social** ◊ *She works for the social ~s* | **information**, **news**, **wire** (*esp. AmE*) | **banking**, **financial** | **intelligence**, **secret**, **security** | **dating**, **escort**
VERB + SERVICE **offer (sb)**, **provide (sb with)** ◊ *We offer a comprehensive ~ to home buyers.* | **operate**, **run** | **maintain** | **guarantee** | **improve** | **launch** | **expand**, **extend** ◊ *We need to expand this valuable ~ to other cities.* | **axe** (*BrE*), **cut**, **cut back**, **cut back on**, **suspend** ◊ *This government has systematically cut back public ~s since it took office.* | **restore** | **access**, **make use of**, **use** ◊ *The new system will enable people to access the ~ more easily.* ◊ *people who use the health-care ~* | **complain about**
SERVICE + VERB **improve** | **deteriorate**
SERVICE + NOUN **provider** ◊ *Internet ~ providers* | **business**, **company** ◊ *a financial ~s company* | **organization** (*esp. AmE*) | **economy**, **industry**, **sector** | **pack** (*computing*)
PREP. **~ for** ◊ *mental health ~s for young people* | **~ to** ◊ *The company provides products and ~s to customers in 145 countries.*
PHRASES **goods and ~s, products and ~s**

2 work of serving a customer
ADJ. **efficient**, **excellent**, **first-class**, **good**, **professional**, **quality** | **bad**, **poor**, **terrible** | **prompt**, **quick** | **slow** | **friendly**, **personal** | **customer** | **after-sales** (*esp. BrE*) ◊ *We offer excellent after-sales ~ on all our goods.* | **room** ◊ *If you would like a meal in your room, please call room ~.* ◊ *We ordered room ~.*
VERB + SERVICE **deliver sth (to sb)**, **give (sb)**, **offer (sb)**, **provide (sb with)** ◊ *Our main concern is to provide quality customer ~.* | **get**, **receive** | **improve** | **guarantee** ◊ *We guarantee first-class ~.* | **complain about** ◊ *I complained about the poor ~.*
SERVICE + NOUN **job** (*AmE*) | **worker** (*AmE*) ◊ *retail and food ~ workers*

3 working for a country, company, etc.
ADJ. **meritorious**, **outstanding** | **faithful** | **long** | **active** ◊ *He died on active ~.* | **military**, **national** (*esp. BrE*) | **selective** (*AmE*) | **domestic** ◊ *a job in domestic ~* | **civil** (*esp. BrE*), **community**, **public** ◊ *a public-service announcement* ◊ *public-service broadcasting* | **voluntary** (*esp. BrE*) | **jury** (*esp. BrE*) ◊ *available for jury ~*
VERB + SERVICE **do** ◊ *All 18-year-old males are required to do a year's military ~.* | **see** (*esp. BrE*) ◊ *He saw ~ during the First World War.* | **begin**, **enter** ◊ *The aircraft entered ~ with the Swedish Air Force in 1997.* | **leave** | **take sth out of** ◊ *The ship has been taken out of ~ for extensive cleaning.*
SERVICE + NOUN **member** (*AmE*), **personnel** ◊ *retired military ~ members* | **record** ◊ *his military ~ record during the Vietnam War*

PHRASES **conditions of** ~ | **in the ~ of your country, in the ~ of God**

4 work done for sb; help given to sb

ADJ. **great, invaluable, valuable | professional**
VERB + SERVICE **be of, do sb, perform, render** ◇ *May I be of ~ to you?* ◇ *You have done us a great ~.* ◇ *payment for ~s rendered* | **offer (sb), provide (sb with)** ◇ *She offered her ~s as a babysitter.* | **sell** ◇ *They sold their ~s to a major airline.* | **advertise** ◇ *a plastic surgeon advertising his ~s on the Internet* | **need, seek** ◇ *to seek the ~s of an attorney*
SERVICE + NOUN **charge, fee**
PREP. **at your ~** ◇ *The cabin staff are at your ~ throughout the flight.* | **~s of** ◇ *We need the ~s of a good lawyer.* | **~ to** ◇ *He was given an award for his ~s to the disabled.*

5 the services the armed forces

ADJ. **armed**
VERB + THE SERVICES **go into, join** ◇ *Most of the boys went straight into the ~s.*

6 (esp. BrE) bus, train, etc.

ADJ. **efficient, good, reliable | fast | frequent, regular | direct, non-stop** (*esp. AmE*) | **full | limited, reduced** ◇ *We will be operating a reduced ~ while engineering work takes place.* | **scheduled** ◇ *changes to scheduled ~s* | **bus, car, coach** (*BrE*), **ferry, rail, subway** (*AmE*), **taxi, train, tram** (*BrE*), **tube** (*BrE*), **underground** (*BrE*)
VERB + SERVICE **lay on, offer (sb), provide (sb with)** ◇ *Bus companies are planning to lay on extra ~s.* | **operate, run | add** (*AmE*), **extend, improve** ◇ *US Airways also added ~ recently to the Dominican Republic.* | **suspend | axe** (*BrE*), **cut | restore | use**
PREP. **in ~** ◇ *This bus is not in ~.* | **out of ~ | ~ between** ◇ *The company offers direct, fast and frequent ~s between large towns and cities.* | **~ from, ~ to** ◇ *~s from Bangkok to Chiang Mai*

7 religious ceremony

ADJ. **church, religious | funeral, marriage, memorial | afternoon, evening, morning**
VERB + SERVICE **attend, go to | hold**
PREP. **~ for** ◇ *memorial ~ for people killed in the attack*

service verb

ADV. **fully, properly** (*BrE*) ◇ *The car was fully ~d last month.* | **regularly** ◇ *A regularly ~d car will keep its value longer.*
VERB + SERVICE **continue to**
PHRASES **get sth ~d, have sth ~d** ◇ *You should get all gas appliances regularly ~d.*

session noun

1 meeting of a court, parliament, etc.

ADJ. **inaugural, opening | closing, final, last | current | joint | open, public** (*esp. BrE*) | **closed, closed-door** (*esp. AmE*), **private** ◇ *The board met in closed ~.* | **emergency, extraordinary** (*esp. AmE*), **special | full, plenary** ◇ *a full ~ of the peace talks* ◇ *a plenary ~ of the committee* | **follow-up** ◇ *A follow-up ~ was held a month after the initial meeting.* | **congressional, parliamentary | legislative** (*esp. AmE*) | **executive** (*AmE*) ◇ *The Council met in executive ~ for the purpose of selecting a new general secretary.*
VERB + SESSION **hold | attend | boycott | address** ◇ *The president addressed a closed ~ of Congress.* | **call** (*esp. AmE*) ◇ *The Governor called a special ~ of the Legislature.*
SESSION + VERB **convene, take place | begin, open | close, end | agree sth | call for sth**
PREP. **at a/the ~** ◇ *The statute was approved at the 1985 ~ of the Texas Legislature.* | **in a/the ~** ◇ *in the opening ~* | **in ~** ◇ *The court is now in ~.*

2 time spent doing an activity

ADJ. **lengthy, long | short | 30-minute, two-hour, etc. | all-day, all-night, late-night | early, late | daily, regular, weekly, etc.** | **bargaining, negotiating | briefing** (*esp. BrE*) | **question-and-answer | brainstorming | breakout** (*esp. AmE*) | **coaching** (*esp. BrE*), **practice, training, tutoring** (*esp. AmE*) | **one-to-one** ◇ *I had a one-to-one ~ with one of the*

instructors at the gym.* | **counselling/counseling, therapy | drop-in** (*BrE*) ◇ *The case worker will talk to refugees at drop-in ~s and by appointment.* | **photo, photographic** (*esp. BrE*) | **autograph | jam, jazz, recording | workout, yoga | drinking** (*esp. BrE*) ◇ *The man fell in the canal after a heavy drinking ~.*
VERB + SESSION **do, have, offer (sb), organize, provide (sb with), run** ◇ *The college runs training ~s every afternoon.* | **schedule** ◇ *Both ~s are scheduled for 10 o'clock.* | **attend | miss | begin, start | end, finish**
SESSION + VERB **take place | last** ◇ *Each ~ lasted approximately 15 minutes.*
SESSION + NOUN **guitarist, musician, singer** (*esp. BrE*), **etc.**
PREP. **~ on** ◇ *a ~ on remedial reading*

set noun

1 group of similar things

ADJ. **complete, entire, full, whole | broad, comprehensive, huge, large | common** ◇ *These two species share a common ~ of characteristics.* | **standard | matched, matching** ◇ *a necklace with a matching ~ of earrings* | **unique | closed, finite** ◇ *We have a finite ~ of options.* | **open | complex, diverse | data, instruction** ◇ *a computer's instruction ~* | **chemistry, chess, drum** (*esp. AmE*), **train | dinner, tea | box, boxed, DVD | two-disc/two-disk, three-CD, etc.** ◇ *The series is available in a three-DVD box ~.* | **skill** ◇ *This job requires a completely different skill ~.*
VERB + SET **complete** ◇ *She won a silver medal in the long jump to complete her ~ (= of all three types of medal).*
SET + VERB **comprise sth, consist of sth | contain | include**
PREP. **in a/the ~** ◇ *There are ten pictures in the ~.* | **~ of** ◇ *a ~ of clothes/doors/keys/stairs/tools* ◇ *a ~ of conditions/guidelines/instructions/principles/rules* ◇ *a ~ of beliefs/ideas/standards/values* ◇ *a ~ of circumstances/challenges/issues/problems/questions* ◇ *a ~ of data/facts/figures/numbers/results*
PHRASES **one of a ~, part of a ~** ◇ *The plate is part of a ~.*

2 scenery for play or film/movie

ADJ. **film** (*esp. BrE*), **movie** (*esp. AmE*), **stage, studio**
VERB + SET **design | build, construct**
SET + NOUN **design, designer** ◇ *The locations and ~ designs were fabulous.*
PREP. **off ~** ◇ *Off ~, the two actors became close friends.* | **on (the) ~** ◇ *The crew had a lot of fun on ~.*

3 in tennis

VERB + SET **play | clinch** (*BrE*), **win | level** (*BrE*) ◇ *She had two break points to level the ~.* | **lose**
SET + NOUN **point**
PHRASES **in straight ~s** ◇ *Nadal won in straight ~s (= his opponent won none).*

set adj.

1 ready

VERBS **be, look, seem | get** (used when starting a race) ◇ *Get set... Go!*
ADV. **all** ◇ *Are you all ~? Let's go!*
PREP. **for** ◇ *The Italian team looks ~ for victory.*

2 determined

VERBS **be**
ADV. **dead**
PREP. **against** ◇ *Her father is dead ~ against the marriage.* | **on** ◇ *The government is now ~ on increasing taxes.*

setback noun

ADJ. **temporary | early, initial | big, huge, major, serious, severe, significant | minor | unexpected | recent | financial, military, political**
... OF SETBACKS **series**
VERB + SETBACK **experience, face, have, receive** (*esp. BrE*), **suffer** ◇ *His research has suffered a temporary ~.* | **deal** (*esp. AmE*) | **overcome | represent** ◇ *That would represent a huge ~ in the fight to change our criminal justice system.*

PREP. **~ for** ◇ *a further ~ for the coal industry* | **~ to** ◇ *a serious ~ to his chances of re-election*

settee *(BrE)* noun

ADJ. **comfortable, comfy** *(informal)* | **leather, etc.** | **three-seater, two-seater**
VERB + SETTEE **sit (down) on** ◇ *He slumped down exhausted on the ~.* | **lie on** | **fall asleep on**
PREP. **on the ~** ◇ *She found her glasses lying on the ~.*
PHRASES **the arm of a ~, the back of a ~**

setting noun

1 place where sth happens

ADJ. **natural** ◇ *wild animals in their natural ~* | **attractive** *(esp. BrE),* **beautiful, ideal, idyllic, lovely** *(esp. BrE),* **magnificent** *(esp. BrE),* **perfect, picturesque** | **dramatic** | **peaceful, tranquil** | **intimate, romantic** | **formal, informal** | **appropriate** | **rural, urban** | **outdoor** | **contemporary** ◇ *biblical stories in a contemporary ~* | **public, social, work** ◇ *The French Club offers the chance to improve your language skills in a social ~.* ◇ *In a work ~, more formal language would be used.* | **clinical, experimental, hospital, institutional, laboratory, etc.** | **academic, classroom, educational, school** | **cultural, historical** | **domestic, family** ◇ *elderly people living in a domestic ~* | **unfamiliar, unlikely** ◇ *The hospital is an unlikely ~ for an art auction.*
VERB + SETTING **create, make, provide** ◇ *The park provides the perfect ~ for the play.*
PREP. **in a/the … ~** ◇ *a hotel in a beautiful mountain ~* | **~ for** ◇ *the perfect ~ for a picnic* | **~ in** ◇ *The site creates a dramatic ~ for the new building.* | **~ of** ◇ *the urban ~ of Manhattan*

2 of controls

ADJ. **high, low, medium** | **default, standard** | **adjustable** | **network, security** *(both computing)* | **difficulty** (= in computer games)
VERB + SETTING **adjust, alter, change, modify, tweak** | **increase, reduce** | **choose** | **save** *(computing)*
PREP. **at a/the ~** ◇ *The oven should be at a high ~.*

settle verb

1 end an argument

ADV. **amicably, peacefully** ◇ *Hopes of settling the conflict peacefully are fading.* | **eventually, finally** ◇ *The matter has not yet been finally ~d.* | **out of court** ◇ *The company has agreed to ~ out of court* (= come to an agreement without going to court).
VERB + SETTLE **attempt to, try to** | **agree to**
PREP. **for** ◇ *I ran well but still had to ~ for second.* | **on** ◇ *After much deliberation, he finally ~d on a fur rug.* | **with** ◇ *After six months the company finally ~d with the unions.*
PHRASES **an attempt to ~ sth**

2 choose a permanent home

ADV. **permanently** ◇ *He has now ~d permanently in London.* | **eventually, finally** | **happily**
VERB + SETTLE **decide to, intend to**
PHRASES **be densely ~d, be sparsely ~d** ◇ *a fertile area that was densely ~d in early times* | **be ready to ~ down** ◇ *She felt she wasn't yet ready to ~ down.*

3 make sb/yourself comfortable

ADV. **comfortably, happily, peacefully** ◇ *He ~d himself more comfortably in his chair.* | **quickly, soon** | **slowly**
VERB + SETTLE **be unable to, cannot** ◇ *Unable to ~, she trailed around the house all day.* | **allow sb to, let sb** ◇ *She kept fussing around, refusing to let him ~.* | **help (to), help sb (to)** ◇ *I took a pill to help ~ my nerves.*
PHRASES **~ down to do sth** ◇ *Finally they ~d down to watch an old movie.*

PHR V **settle in, settle into sth**
ADV. **happily, nicely** ◇ *The kids ~d happily into their new school.* | **quickly, soon**
PREP. **for** ◇ *They prepared to ~ in for the night.*

settlement noun

1 official/legal agreement

ADJ. **final** | **lasting, long-term, permanent** | **comprehensive** ◇ *a lasting and comprehensive peace* | **early** | **temporary** | **amicable, friendly** *(BrE),* **peaceful** | **just, reasonable, satisfactory** *(esp. BrE)* | **compromise** | **negotiated** | **global** *(law)* ◇ *a proposed $100-million global ~ of a class action suit* | **constitutional** *(esp. BrE),* **diplomatic, financial, legal, political** | **compensation** *(esp. BrE),* **divorce, marriage** *(esp. BrE)* | **out-of-court** | **generous** | **huge, large** ◇ *They signed away their legal rights for a large cash ~.* | **cash** | **peace** | **post-war** | **pay** *(esp. BrE),* **wage** *(BrE)* ◇ *Nurses refused to accept a pay ~ less than the rate of inflation.* | **dispute**
VERB + SETTLEMENT **achieve, agree, reach, secure** ◇ *Both parties hope to reach an amicable ~.* | **make** ◇ *They made a financial ~ with the family in order to prevent a civil lawsuit.* | **negotiate, produce** ◇ *The union has negotiated a temporary ~.* | **seek** ◇ *Lawyers are seeking an out-of-court ~.* | **offer, propose** | **accept** | **receive, win** ◇ *They won a ~ of $10.6 million.* | **pay** ◇ *The company had to pay multi-million-dollar ~s to victims.*
SETTLEMENT + NOUN **agreement** ◇ *negotiations for a final ~ agreement* | **offer** ◇ *a $50 000 pretrial ~ offer*
PREP. **~ of** ◇ *the peaceful ~ of a long-standing dispute* | **under a/the ~** ◇ *a beneficiary under the ~* | **~ with** ◇ *They have reached a ~ with the government.*
PHRASES **~ in ~ of** ◇ *They agreed to pay $8 million in ~ of the claim by Duqual.* ◇ *a cheque in ~ of the amount owing* *(BrE)* | **the terms of the ~**

2 place where people have come to live

ADJ. **ancient, early** | **land** | **agricultural, rural** | **urban** | **coastal** | **isolated, outlying** | **large, small** | **human** ◇ *the earliest urban human ~ in the world* | **European, Jewish, etc.** | **permanent** | **illegal** | **penal** *(esp. BrE)*
VERB + SETTLEMENT **establish, found** ◇ *The Romans established a ~ on the south shore.*
SETTLEMENT + VERB **grow up** ◇ *A ~ grew up around the castle.*
SETTLEMENT + NOUN **patterns** ◇ *early ~ patterns in South America* | **site** *(esp. BrE)*

settler noun

ADJ. **early, first, original** | **English, European, Jewish, etc.**
VERB + SETTLER **attract** ◇ *The islands attracted more ~s than mainland colonies.*
SETTLER + VERB **arrive, come** | **move in, move into sth** ◇ *When the first ~s moved into the area they faced immense hardships.* | **live, occupy sth** | **introduce sth** ◇ *British ~s introduced pigs to Virginia.* | **establish sth, found sth** ◇ *French ~s founded New Orleans.*
PREP. **~ from** ◇ *~s from France* | **~ in** ◇ *Dutch ~s in Cape Town*

severe adj.

VERBS **be, seem, sound** | **become, grow** | **remain**
ADV. **extremely, fairly, very, etc.** | **especially, exceptionally, particularly, unusually** ◇ *an exceptionally ~ frost* | **increasingly, moderately, relatively** ◇ *women affected by mild to moderately ~ symptoms*

severity noun

ADJ. **great** | **utmost** *(esp. BrE)* | **moderate** | **increasing** | **varying** | **mock** ◇ *She wagged her finger with mock ~.*
VERB + SEVERITY **assess, determine** | **reduce** ◇ *The medicine can reduce the ~ of symptoms.* | **increase** | **reflect** *(esp. BrE)* ◇ *The sentence passed today reflects the ~ of the crime.*

sew verb

ADV. **neatly** ◇ *The squares of fabric were all sewn neatly together.* | **together, up** ◇ *He ~ed up the tear with a needle*

and thread. | **back** ◇ *He had his partially severed ear sewn back on.*
PREP. **into** ◇ *The jewel was sewn into the lining of his coat.* | **onto** ◇ *He ~ed the patch onto the back of his jeans.*

sewage *noun*
ADJ. **raw, untreated** | **treated**
VERB + SEWAGE **discharge, dump, pump** ◇ *In some parts of the country raw ~ is pumped straight in the ocean.* | **treat** ◇ *Sewage should be treated in a proper disposal system.*
SEWAGE + NOUN **disposal, treatment** | **farm** (*BrE*), **plant** (*esp. AmE*), **works** (*BrE*) ◇ *a ~ treatment plant* | **system** | **pipe** | **discharge, effluent, sludge** | **pollution**

sewing *noun*
VERB + SEWING **do** ◇ *I haven't done any ~ for a long time.* | **take in** ◇ *She took in ~ to supplement her income.*
SEWING + NOUN **basket, kit** | **needle, thread** | **machine** | **room** (*esp. AmE*)

sex *noun*
1 male or female
ADJ. **female, male** | **opposite** ◇ *At that age they can start becoming shy with the opposite ~.* | **same** ◇ *people of the same ~* ◇ *same-sex couples/partners* ◇ *same-sex relationships/marriages/weddings* | **fair, fairer, gentle, weaker** (= women; some women may find these terms offensive) (*humorous*) ◇ *They tend to consider women as the weaker ~ in need of care and protection.*
VERB + SEX **determine** ◇ *ultrasound tests to determine the ~ of a baby* ◇ *Sex is determined by chromosomal content.* | **change** ◇ *For a long time I wanted to change my ~.* | **be attracted to** ◇ *to be attracted to the opposite ~*
SEX + NOUN **change** ◇ *to have a ~ change* ◇ *a sex-change operation* | **equality** ◇ *issues of ~ equality in the office* | **discrimination, inequality** | **ratio** | **difference** ◇ *The theory predicts ~ differences in the brain.* | **chromosome** ◇ *the X and Y ~ chromosomes* | **hormone**
PREP. **between the ~es** ◇ *differences/inequalities/relations between the ~es*
PHRASES **the battle of the ~es** ◇ *The quiz is a battle of the ~es between teams of male and female students.* | **equality between the ~es, equality of the ~es** | **on (the) grounds of ~** (*BrE*) ◇ *discrimination on grounds of ~* | **irrespective of ~, regardless of ~** ◇ *The word 'man' can refer to all humans, irrespective of ~.* | **a member of the opposite ~** ◇ *This will help us meet attractive members of the opposite ~.*

2 sexual intercourse
ADJ. **anal, oral, penetrative** (*esp. BrE*), **vaginal** (*esp. AmE*) | **gay, homosexual, lesbian** | **heterosexual, straight** | **good, great, hot, passionate, wild** | **rough** | **kinky** | **safe** ◇ *Always practise/practice safe ~!* | **unprotected, unsafe** | **consensual, non-consensual** | **extramarital, illicit, premarital** | **anonymous, casual, promiscuous** | **group** | **public** (= sex in public places) | **explicit, graphic, gratuitous, hard-core, steamy** ◇ *Movies containing scenes of explicit ~ are banned.* | **Internet, phone** | **underage, unlawful** (*BrE*) ◇ *He was convicted of having unlawful ~ with an underage girl.* | **teen** (*esp. AmE*), **teenage**
VERB + SEX **engage in, have** ◇ *She had never had ~ before.* | **consent to** | **refuse** | **get, obtain**
SEX + NOUN **life** ◇ *a healthy ~ life* | **drive, urge** ◇ *a low ~ drive* | **appeal** ◇ *Despite his age, he still has a lot of ~ appeal.* | **act** ◇ *photos showing ~ acts* | **therapist, therapy** | **partner** (*esp. AmE*) ◇ *I have had several ~ partners over the years.* | **organ** | **education** ◇ *She is an advocate of abstinence-only ~ education.* (*AmE*) ◇ *comprehensive ~ education* (*esp. AmE*) | **scandal** | **abuse, assault** (*esp. BrE*), **attack** (*BrE*), **crime, offence/offense** ◇ *He was arrested for ~ crimes.* | **fiend** (*informal*), **offender, pest** (*BrE, informal*) ◇ *convicted ~ offenders* ◇ *registered ~ offenders* | **addict, maniac** ◇ *He had a reputation of being a ~ maniac.* | **film, scene, show** | **comedy** | **kitten, symbol** ◇ *She wants to be known as a singer rather than as a ~ symbol.* | **object** ◇ *Women are viewed as ~ objects and exploited to sell products.* | **club, shop** | **aid, toy** | **industry** | **worker** ◇ *In this zone,*

---

prostitution is legal, but ~ workers must be at least 18. | **tourism** | **trafficking** ◇ *to crack down on international ~ trafficking* | **slave**
PREP. **~ between** ◇ *~ between consenting adults* | **~ with** ◇ *~ with her husband*
PHRASES **~, drugs and rock 'n' roll** (*humorous*) | **~ and violence** ◇ *~ and violence in today's liberal media* | **~ outside of marriage** ◇ *They teach that ~ outside of marriage is wrong.* | **~ sells** ◇ *Sex sells, the advertisers believe.*

sexism *noun*
ADJ. **blatant, rampant** ◇ *She was shocked by his blatant ~.* ◇ *Sexism is rampant in many institutions.*
VERB + SEXISM **fight, fight against** ◇ *efforts to fight ~ in the workplace*

sexuality *noun*
ADJ. **female, male** | **human** | **gay, lesbian** | **overt** ◇ *Her overt ~ shocked movie audiences.*
VERB + SEXUALITY **express** ◇ *Victorian women were rarely allowed to express their ~.* | **explore, question** | **discuss** | **come to terms with** ◇ *He couldn't come to terms with his ~.*

sexy *adj.*
VERBS **be, feel, look** | **find sb/sth**
ADV. **extremely, fairly, very, etc.** | **dead** (*informal, esp. BrE*), **incredibly**

shack *noun*
ADJ. **old** | **little, small, tiny** | **one-room, two-room** | **dilapidated, run-down, tumbledown** | **tin, wooden** | **guard** (*AmE*)
PREP. **in a /the ~** ◇ *He lives in a ~ in the middle of the woods.*

shade *noun*
1 area out of the sunlight
ADJ. **cool** | **deep** | **welcome** | **dappled** | **afternoon** | **partial** | **leafy** ◇ *in the leafy ~ of a fig tree*
...OF SHADE **patch** ◇ *I searched for a patch of ~ to rest in.*
VERB + SHADE **give (sb), offer (sb), provide (sb with)**
PREP. **in (the)** ◇ *a plant that grows well in ~* ◇ *I was sitting in the ~.* | **into the ~** ◇ *Let's move into the ~.* | **under the ~ of** ◇ *They were sitting under the ~ of an umbrella.* | **~ for** ◇ *the need to ensure adequate ~ for coffee plants* | **~ from** ◇ *The huge trees offered ~ from the sun.*
PHRASES **light and ~**

2 type of colour
ADJ. **delicate, light, muted, pale, pastel, soft, subtle** ◇ *The rooms were decorated in delicate pastel ~s.* | **dark, deep, rich, strong** ◇ *His face turned an even deeper ~ of red.* | **bright, brilliant, vivid** | **attractive, beautiful, lovely, nice** | **startling, stunning** ◇ *a room painted in startling ~s of pink and orange* | **natural, neutral, warm** ◇ *Towels in warm ~s can soften the room.* | **various** ◇ *various ~s of green*
VERB + SHADE **be available in, come in** ◇ *This wool is available in ten stunning ~s.*
PREP. **in a ~** ◇ *The ocean glistened in ~s of blue and emerald.* | **~ for** ◇ *our new range of ~s for lips and eyes* | **~ of** ◇ *He threw out his old suits, all in various ~s of brown.* ◇ *a word with various ~s of meaning* (*figurative*)
PHRASES **~s of opinion** (*figurative, esp. BrE*)

3 (*AmE*) on a window → See also BLIND
ADJ. **window** | **roller**
VERB + SHADE **close, draw, lower** | **pull** ◇ *His room was dark, the ~s pulled to block out the sun.* | **open**

shade *verb*
ADV. **completely** | **deeply** | **lightly, partially** ◇ *This plant prefers a lightly ~d position.*
PREP. **against** ◇ *She ~d her eyes against the fierce sun.* | **from** ◇ *We were completely ~d from the sun by the trees.* | **with** ◇ *a square ~d with trees*

shading noun

ADJ. **delicate, fine, light, subtle** ◇ *an effect that is achieved with subtle ~* | **dark, heavy**

shadow noun

ADJ. **dark, deep, dense, strong** ◇ *The house lay in dark ~.* | **black** | **faint, pale** (*figurative*) ◇ *The industry is a pale ~ of its former self.* | **giant, long** | **eerie, sinister, strange, terrible** | **dancing, flickering** ◇ *the flickering ~s of the flames*
VERB + SHADOW **cast, create, make, produce, throw** ◇ *The boat's sail cast a ~ on the water.* ◇ *Use a desk light to produce a strong ~.* ◇ *The candles on the table threw huge flickering ~s against the wall.* | **fill sth with ~s** ◇ *The streets were now filled with terrible ~s.* | **emerge from, move out of, step out from, step out of** ◇ *Suddenly a large figure emerged from the ~s.* | **move into, shrink into, slip into** ◇ *She shrank back into the ~s as the footsteps approached.* | **lurk in, wait in, watch from** ◇ *criminals lurking in the ~s*
SHADOW + VERB **fall, lie** ◇ *The evening ~s were beginning to fall.* ◇ *Deep ~s lay across the small clearing where they sat.* | **get longer, grow longer, lengthen** ◇ *As the ~s lengthened, the men drifted home.* | **creep, move, pass** ◇ *The ~s of the clouds passed over us.* | **loom** ◇ *A dark ~ loomed over her.* | **dance, flicker, leap** ◇ *A dark ~ leaped out of nowhere.*
PREP. **among the ~s** ◇ *an odd shape among the ~s* | **in the ~s** ◇ *I could just make out a figure in the ~s.* | **into the ~s** ◇ *I backed into the ~s until the car had passed.* | **in ~** ◇ *His face was in ~.* | **into ~** ◇ *The storm clouds threw the mountains into deep ~.* | **from the ~s, out of the ~s** ◇ *A huge figure stepped out of the ~s.* | **through the ~s**
PHRASES **live in the ~ of sb/sth** (*figurative*) ◇ *She had always lived in the ~ of her older sister.*

shaft noun

ADJ. **deep** | **vertical** | **narrow** | **elevator** (*AmE*), **lift** (*BrE*) ◇ *She almost fell down an elevator ~.* | **mine** (usually **mineshaft**) | **air, ventilation**
VERB + SHAFT **dig, drill, sink**
PREP. **down a/the ~** ◇ *The body had been thrown down a disused ~.* | **in a/the ~, into a/the ~** | **through a/the ~**
PHRASES **the bottom of a ~, the top of a ~**

shake noun

ADJ. **good, vigorous** ◇ *Give the tablecloth a good ~ before putting it away.* | **firm** | **violent** | **gentle, little, slight, small** | **quick** | **mental** ◇ *He gave himself a mental ~ and got down to work.*
VERB + SHAKE **give sb/sth**
PREP. **with a ~** | **~ of**
PHRASES **a ~ of your/the head**

shake verb

1 tremble

ADV. **badly, furiously, terribly, uncontrollably, violently** ◇ *Her hands were shaking so badly that she couldn't hold her glass.* | **a little, slightly, etc.** | **almost, practically** ◇ *He was almost shaking with the intensity of what he was saying.* ◇ *Roxy was practically shaking with anger.* | **literally, physically** ◇ *I was numb with dread. I was literally shaking.* | **visibly** | **nervously** ◇ *My hands started shaking nervously.*
PREP. **from** ◇ *My body was shaking from the cold.* | **with** ◇ *She was shaking with anger/fury/rage.* ◇ *to ~ with fear/laughter/sobs*
PHRASES **be shaking all over, be shaking from head to toe** ◇ *He was crying and shaking all over.* | **be shaking in your boots** (= be frightened), **be shaking like a leaf** | **find yourself shaking** ◇ *I found myself shaking uncontrollably with cold.* | **start shaking** ◇ *I started shaking with fear.* | **stop shaking** ◇ *I just couldn't stop shaking.*

2 move sb/sth from side to side, etc.

ADV. **hard, roughly, vigorously, violently** ◇ *He shook the blankets vigorously to get rid of the dust.* ◇ *She must have*

shaken the baby very violently to inflict such severe injuries. | **gently, lightly, slightly** | **well** ◇ *Shake well before use.* (instructions on a bottle of medicine, etc.) | **suddenly**
PREP. **by** ◇ *He shook her gently by the shoulders.*

3 your head

ADV. **decisively, emphatically, firmly** | **fiercely, furiously, vehemently, vigorously, violently, wildly** | **a little, gently, lightly, slightly** | **quickly** | **slowly** | **dismissively, impatiently** | **despairingly, desperately, helplessly, miserably, mournfully, regretfully, ruefully, sadly, sorrowfully** | **wearily** | **disbelievingly, doubtfully** | **just, merely, only, simply** ◇ *He merely shook his head.* | **silently** | **from side to side**
PREP. **at** ◇ *He shook his head at her disbelievingly.* | **in** ◇ *She shook her head in disbelief.*

4 sb's hand

ADV. **firmly, vigorously** | **warmly**
PHRASES **~ sb by the hand** ◇ *Our host shook each of us warmly by the hand.*

shaken adj.

VERBS **be, look, seem** | **be left** ◇ *the woman was left ~ by the attack.* ◇ *The experience left him deeply ~.*
ADV. **extremely, fairly, very, etc.** | **badly, deeply, profoundly, seriously, severely, thoroughly** ◇ *She was left badly ~ by her ordeal.* | **a little, slightly, etc.** ◇ *Are you all right? You look a little ~.* | **clearly, obviously, visibly** ◇ *He was visibly ~ by what had happened.*
PREP. **by** ◇ *She was visibly ~ by the news.*

shake-up noun

ADJ. **big, huge, major, massive** | **complete, wholesale** (*BrE*), **wide-ranging** | **controversial, radical** | **proposed** | **long-awaited** | **urgent** | **boardroom, government** (*BrE*), **management**
VERB + SHAKE-UP **need** | **call for** ◇ *The paper calls for an urgent ~ in the health-care system.* | **plan, promise** | **face, have, undergo** ◇ *Police forces face the biggest ~ in their 150-year history.* | **lead to** ◇ *This case could lead to a ~ of the prison system.*
PREP. **in a/the ~** ◇ *the posts that were scrapped in the recent ~* | **~ at** ◇ *a major ~ at the company* | **~ in** ◇ *a radical ~ in the chemical industry*

shallow adj.

1 not deep

VERBS **be, look** | **become, get** ◇ *The water gets ~ closer to the shore.* | **remain**
ADV. **extremely, fairly, very, etc.** ◇ *Don't worry, the water's very ~.* | **comparatively, relatively** | **enough, sufficiently** ◇ *Follow the south shore, crossing the river where it is ~ enough.*

2 not showing serious thought

VERBS **be, seem** ◇ *Tony seemed very ~ and immature.*
ADV. **extremely, fairly, very, etc.** | **exceedingly**

shame noun

1 feeling that you have lost the respect of others

ADJ. **deep** | **secret** ◇ *This is the secret ~ I have carried around for decades.* | **public** ◇ *He risked public ~ and possible imprisonment.* ◇ *All she wanted was to escape so that she would not have to face this public ~.* | **national** (*esp. BrE*) ◇ *It is a national ~ that our prisons serve as mental institutions.*
VERB + SHAME **be filled with, feel** | **bring, cause** ◇ *His arrest for stealing brought ~ on his family.* | **die of** (*figurative*) ◇ *I nearly died of ~!*
PREP. **from ~** ◇ *She wept from the ~ of having let everyone down.* | **in ~** ◇ *She shut her eyes in ~.* | **to your ~** ◇ *To my ~, I didn't tell Robert about the party.* | **without ~** ◇ *He had cried noisily and without ~ at the news of Esther's death.* | **with ~** ◇ *She blushed with ~.* | **~ about, ~ at** ◇ *She felt a flush of ~ at what she'd said.* | **~ for** ◇ *Do you feel no ~ for what you've done?* | **~ in** ◇ *There's no ~ in making an honest*

living. | **~ on** ◇ *Shame on you for doubting me!* | **~ over** ◇ *You feel absolutely no ~ over what you did, do you?*
PHRASES **bow your head in ~, hang your head in ~** | **a feeling of ~, a sense of ~** ◇ *He was being held by two security guards, his head bowed in ~.*

2 a shame sth that makes you feel disappointed

ADJ. **awful** (*esp. BrE*), **great, real, terrible** | **crying, damn, damned** (*all informal*)
PREP. **~ about** ◇ *It's a terrible ~ about Steve losing his job.*
PHRASES **a bit of a ~** (*esp. BrE*), **rather a ~** (*esp. BrE*), **such a ~, what a ~** ◇ *What a ~ you can't come!*

shame *verb*

ADV. **publicly** ◇ *The people who did this all deserve to be publicly ~d.*
PREP. **into** ◇ *An outcry from customers has ~d the company into lowering its prices.*

shampoo *noun*

1 liquid soap for washing hair

ADJ. **baby, gentle, medicated, mild, moisturizing** | **anti-dandruff, dandruff**
... OF SHAMPOO **bottle**
VERB + SHAMPOO **use, wash your hair with** | **rinse** ◇ *She rinsed the ~ out of her hair.*
SHAMPOO + NOUN **bottle**
PREP. **~ for** ◇ *a ~ for greasy hair*

2 act of washing hair

VERB + SHAMPOO **give sb/sth** | **have**

shape *noun*

1 physical outline

ADJ. **basic, simple** ◇ *The children cut the paper into various simple ~s.* | **overall** | **characteristic, distinctive, familiar, unique** ◇ *I recognized the distinctive ~ of a 747.* | **natural, normal** | **interesting, strange, unusual, weird** | **awkward** ◇ *The desk was an awkward ~ and wouldn't fit through the door.* | **original** | **geometric, geometrical** | **regular, symmetrical** | **complex** | **asymmetrical, irregular** | **abstract** | **odd, random** ◇ *tiles of random ~* | **solid, three-dimensional** | **aerodynamic** | **organic** ◇ *She drew inspiration from organic ~s in the surrounding landscape.* | **desired** ◇ *Draw the desired ~ onto white paper.* | **angular, circular, cone, conical, crescent, curved, cylindrical, diamond, dome, elliptical, elongated, hexagonal, oblong, oval, pyramid, rectangular, round, spherical, square, triangular, wedge** | **rounded, smooth** | **egg, heart, hourglass, pear, star, etc.** ◇ *The bruise was a sort of mushroom ~.* | **L, V, etc.** ◇ *The road forms an L ~.* | **blurred, ghostly, indistinct, shadowy, vague** | **huge, large, massive** | **black, dark, grey/gray** | **human** | **body** ◇ *You can't change your natural body ~.* | **face, facial** ◇ *Opt for a hairstyle to suit your face ~.*
VERB + SHAPE **cut out, draw, make, trace** ◇ *Fold the paper to make the ~ of a cone.* | **carve sth in, carve sth into, cut sth into, make sth in, produce sth in** ◇ *a log carved into the ~ of a fish* | **come in, have** ◇ *Tables come in various ~s.* | **assume, form, make, take on** ◇ *Ordinary things assumed different ~s in the mist.* | **hold, keep, maintain, retain** ◇ *These garments will retain their ~ even with repeated washing.* | **regain** | **change** | **lose** | **distort** ◇ *The lens distorts ~s.* | **distinguish, make out, see** ◇ *I could just make out the ~s of animals in the field.*
SHAPE + VERB **appear, emerge, loom** ◇ *Ghostly ~s loomed out of the fog.*
PREP. **~ for** ◇ *the optimum ~ for a plane* | **in the ~ of** ◇ *a doormat in the ~ of a cat*
PHRASES **all ~s and sizes** ◇ *T-shirts come in all ~s and sizes.* | **circular, hexagonal, oblong, rectangular, etc. in ~** ◇ *The island is roughly circular in ~.*

2 structure/nature of sth

ADJ. **general, overall** | **changing** | **final** | **future**
VERB + SHAPE **alter, change, determine, influence** ◇ *He did much to determine the ~ of Asia's political map.* | **take** ◇ *A*

wonderful idea began to take ~ in her brain. | **give** ◇ *the words we use to give a ~ to our feelings*
PHRASES **the ~ of things to come** ◇ *This new system could be the ~ of things to come.* | **in any ~ or form** (*esp. BrE*) ◇ *I can't stand insects in any ~ or form.*

3 good or bad condition

ADJ. **decent, excellent, fine, good, great** | **perfect, tip-top, top** (*esp. AmE*) | **bad, poor, rough** (*esp. AmE*), **terrible** ◇ *After the night before, he was in rough ~.* | **physical** ◇ *He's 64, but he's in better physical ~ than I am.* | **financial** ◇ *The company is in good financial ~.*
PREP. **~ for** ◇ *to be in good ~ for combat*
PHRASES **get sb/sth into ~, knock sb/sth into ~** (*esp. BrE*), **lick sb/sth into ~** (*BrE*), **whip sb/sth into ~** (*esp. AmE*) ◇ *Get your body into ~ for the summer!* | **be in good, excellent, etc. ~** ◇ *You are in pretty good ~ for your age.* | **get in ~, get into ~** ◇ *I need to get back into ~ after the Christmas holiday.* | **keep in ~, stay in ~** ◇ *She likes to stay in ~.* | **be out of ~**

shape *verb*

ADV. **decisively, fundamentally, powerfully, profoundly** ◇ *Memory can be profoundly ~d by subsequent experience.* | **largely** | **partly** | **actively, deliberately** ◇ *actively shaping the history of their country*
VERB + SHAPE **help (to)** | **continue to** ◇ *The fictional Capone has continued to ~ America's vision of the 1920s.*
PREP. **in** ◇ *a crudely carved python ~d in a spiral* | **into** ◇ *The dough is ~d into balls and fried.*
PHRASES **be a factor in shaping sth, be a force in shaping sth** ◇ *Work was an important factor in shaping their children's attitudes.* | **be important in shaping sth, be influential in shaping sth, have influence in shaping sth** ◇ *The media had great influence in shaping public opinion.* | **have a hand in shaping sth, have a part in shaping sth, have a role in shaping sth, play a role in shaping sth** ◇ *Economists had a direct hand in shaping government policy.* ◇ *Money played a major role in shaping his decision.* | **be responsible for shaping sth** ◇ *He was responsible for shaping my career.*

shaped *adj.*

VERBS **be**
ADV. **beautifully, perfectly** ◇ *her beautifully ~ mouth* | **differently, similarly** ◇ *Donkeys' hoofs are ~ differently from horses'.* | **irregularly** | **awkwardly** ◇ *All the rooms in the house were awkwardly ~.* | **abnormally, curiously, oddly, strangely** ◇ *an oddly ~ parcel* | **uniquely** | **specially** ◇ *You can buy specially ~ bricks for an arch.*
PHRASES **be ~ like sth** ◇ *curious vases ~ like birds and animals*

share *noun*

1 part of sth that has been divided

ADJ. **bigger, greater, higher, large, the lion's, major, significant, substantial** ◇ *The region receives a higher ~ of tax revenue than it raises.* | **full** | **small** | **modest** ◇ *a modest ~ of total exports* | **growing, increasing** | **5%, 10%, etc.** ◇ *The wife owns an 80% ~ of their second home.* | **equal** | **disproportionate** ◇ *The government devotes a disproportionate ~ of the budget to military expenditure.* | **proportionate** | **audience, market** ◇ *to lose market ~* ◇ *to win market ~* ◇ *The supermarket giant has continued to gain market ~.*
VERB + SHARE **get, have, receive, take** ◇ *You should receive a large ~ of the profits.* ◇ *Hospitals take the lion's ~ of the budget.* | **increase, reduce** | **lose** ◇ *Broadcast networks are losing ~ to cable networks.* | **be entitled to** ◇ *She may be entitled to a ~ of his future earnings.* | **claim** ◇ *Everyone wants to claim their ~ of fame and fortune.* | **contribute, do** ◇ *We must all do our ~ of the work.*
PREP. **~ of** ◇ *a reduced ~ of the vote* ◇ *I accept my ~ of the blame.*
PHRASES **do your ~ of sth, have your ~ of sth, see your ~ of sth** ◇ *He had done his ~ of partying in college.* ◇ *She has seen her ~ of suffering.* ◇ *The industry has had its fair ~ of*

problems. | **a ~ of the spoils** (*BrE*) ◇ *She won a ~ of the spoils at the last competition.*

2 in a company → See also STOCK

ADJ. **ordinary** (*BrE*) | **preference** (*BrE*), **preferred** (*AmE*) | **penny** (*BrE*) | **outstanding** | **additional** | **company's** ◇ *The company's ~s slumped 11%.*
VERB + SHARE **acquire, buy, get, invest in, purchase** | **have, hold** (*formal*), **own** | **dump** (*informal*), **sell** | **deal in, trade in** ◇ *a new company dealing in US ~s* | **float, issue** ◇ *The company has issued four classes of ~s.*
SHARE + VERB **trade** ◇ *The ~s were trading at $1.10.* | **go up, rise** ◇ *American ~s rose 2.7% the next day.* | **fall**
SHARE + NOUN **price, value** ◇ *Hong Kong ~ prices plunged.* | **valuation** | **certificate** | **portfolio** | **index** ◇ *the FTSE 100 ~ index* | **capital** | **option, scheme** (*both BrE*) ◇ *The Chief Executive's ~ option has earned him over £2 million.* | **ownership** | **transaction, transfer** | **purchase** | **buy-back** ◇ *The group recently announced a £300 m ~ buy-back.* | **issue, offer, offering, sale** ◇ *A ~ issue has been launched to finance the restoration of the building.* | **dealing** ◇ *allegations of illegal ~ dealings*
PREP. **~ in** ◇ *I have a few ~s in the gas compny.*
PHRASES **a class of ~s** | **stocks and ~s** (*BrE*) ◇ *I have some money in stocks and ~s.* | **the value of your ~s** ◇ *Will this affect the value of my ~s?*
→ Note at PER CENT (for more verbs)
→ Special page at BUSINESS

share *verb*

ADV. **fully** ◇ *knowledge that others cannot fully ~* | **equally** ◇ *We ~d the money equally between the three of us.* | **broadly, freely** ◇ *an environment where information is freely ~d*
VERB + SHARE **want to, would like to** | **be prepared to, be willing to** ◇ *experienced teachers willing to ~ their expertise with others* | **be reluctant to** | **be forced to, have to** | **agree to** | **refuse to** | **let sb** ◇ *She wished he would let her ~ his pain.*
PREP. **among** ◇ *The patterns are ~d among the potters.* | **between** ◇ *Responsibility is ~d between parents and teachers.* | **in** ◇ *He ~d in our enthusiasm for rowing.* | **with** ◇ *She had to ~ a bedroom with her sister.*
PHRASES **widely ~d** ◇ *These ideas are widely ~d in the community.*

shareholder *noun*

ADJ. **big, large, major, substantial** | **small** | **main, principal** | **controlling, majority** ◇ *The government is still a majority ~ in the industry.* | **minority** | **corporate, institutional** | **individual, ordinary, private** ◇ *He was voicing the concerns of ordinary ~s.* | **existing** ◇ *He has attracted new and existing ~s to invest in his company.*
VERB + SHAREHOLDER **defraud** | **reward**
SHAREHOLDER + VERB **vote** | **approve** ◇ *Company ~s approved the merger.*
PREP. **~ in** ◇ *the major ~s in the company*

shark *noun*

ADJ. **killer, man-eating**
SHARK + VERB **attack sb** | **bite sb** | **feed** | **circle** ◇ *The dark shapes of half a dozen ~s circled beneath the boat.* | **cruise**
SHARK + NOUN **attack** | **fin, tooth**

sharp *adj.*

1 having a fine edge or point

VERBS **be, feel, look, seem** | **stay** | **keep sth**
ADV. **extremely, fairly, very, etc.** | **exceptionally, wickedly** (*esp. AmE*) ◇ *a display of wickedly ~ teeth* | **surprisingly** ◇ *The picture is surprisingly ~ and clear.*
PHRASES **as ~ as a razor**

2 very great or sudden

VERBS **be**

ADV. **extremely, fairly, very, etc.** ◇ *a fairly ~ rise in the cost of living* | **particularly**

3 able to think quickly

VERBS **be, seem** | **stay**
ADV. **extremely, fairly, very, etc.**

4 angry; severe

VERBS **be, sound** ◇ *Her voice sounded rather ~.*
ADV. **extremely, fairly, very, etc.** | **suddenly** ◇ *'Stick to the facts,' said Romanov, his voice suddenly ~.*
PREP. **with** ◇ *She was very ~ with me when I talked during her lecture.*

shatter *verb*

1 break into very small pieces

ADV. **completely**
PREP. **into** ◇ *The bottle ~ed into little shards of glass.*
PHRASES **~ (sth) into pieces** ◇ *The mirror ~ed into a thousand pieces.*

2 destroy sth completely

ADV. **completely** ◇ *an event that completely ~ed her life* | **abruptly, instantly, suddenly** ◇ *The moment was abruptly ~ed by the sound of Mia's loud voice.* | **brutally, rudely**

shattered *adj.*

VERBS **be, feel** (*esp. BrE*), **look**
ADV. **absolutely** (*esp. BrE*), **completely, totally** ◇ *His run had left him feeling totally ~ (= very tired).* (*BrE*) | **emotionally, physically** (*esp. BrE*) ◇ *I felt drained and emotionally ~ after my ordeal.*

shave *noun*

ADJ. **clean, close, smooth** ◇ *You can get a really close, smooth ~ with this new razor.* | **quick** | **wet** (*BrE*) ◇ *an old-fashioned barber who does wet ~s*
VERB + SHAVE **need** ◇ *He badly needed a ~.* | **get, have** ◇ *He had a bath and a quick ~ first.* | **give sb**

shawl *noun*

ADJ. **heavy** | **light, thin** | **crocheted, knitted** | **embroidered, fringed** | **lace, silk, woollen/woolen, etc.** | **pashmina** | **prayer**
VERB + SHAWL **be draped in, be wrapped in** | **drape, throw, wrap** ◇ *Ellianne wrapped the ~ around her shoulders.* | **throw off** | **draw, pull** ◇ *She pulled her ~ about her protectively.* | **tie** ◇ *She was wearing a ~ tied around her waist.*
SHAWL + VERB **cover sth**
→ Special page at CLOTHES

shed *noun*

1 small simple building for keeping things in

ADJ. **wooden** | **lean-to** (*BrE*) | **storage** | **equipment, tool** | **bicycle, bike** (*informal, both esp. BrE*) | **garden, potting** (*both BrE*)
PREP. **in a/the ~**

2 (*esp. BrE*) large industrial or agricultural building

ADJ. **engine, railway** (*BrE*), **train** | **milking** | **packing** (*esp. AmE*) | **machine** (*AmE*)

sheep *noun*

ADJ. **hill** (*BrE*), **mountain** | **lost** (*often figurative*), **stray** ◇ *He sees it as his duty to take care of the lost ~ of the world.* | **dead** | **domestic, wild**
...OF SHEEP **flock, herd**
VERB + SHEEP **farm, keep, raise, rear** (*BrE*) ◇ *My grandfather used to raise ~ in Australia.* | **tend, watch** | **slaughter** | **shear** | **drive, herd, round up** (*esp. BrE*) ◇ *The dogs herded the ~ into the pen.*
SHEEP + VERB **graze** ◇ *There were a lot of ~ grazing high up on the mountain.* | **bleat**
SHEEP + NOUN **farm, ranch** (*AmE*), **station** ◇ *a 4 000-acre ~ station in New South Wales* | **farmer, rancher** (*AmE*)

PHRASES **a breed of ~**

sheet *noun*

1 large piece of fabric used on a bed

ADJ. **clean, crisp, fresh** ◊ *a pile of clean ~s* | **crumpled, rumpled** (*esp. AmE*) ◊ *She had slept in her bed–the ~s were crumpled.* | **white** | **cool** | **soft** | **cotton, linen, rubber, satin, silk** | **bed** | **double, single** | **fitted** | **bottom, top**
VERB + SHEET **change, fold, put on, tuck in** ◊ *She changed the ~s on all the beds.* ◊ *Could you put some fresh ~s on the bed?* | **climb between, climb under** | **slide between, slide under, slip between, slip under** ◊ *I slipped under the ~s and was asleep in an instant.* | **cover sb/sth with, wrap sb/sth in** ◊ *The police had covered the body with a ~.* | **wrap** ◊ *I simply wrapped the ~ around her.* | **pull back, pull over, pull up** ◊ *I pulled the ~ up over my nose.* | **throw, throw back** ◊ *I threw a ~ over the sofa.* ◊ *He threw back the ~s and rolled out of bed.*
SHEET + VERB **cover** | **hang** ◊ *~s hung on a line*
PREP. **beneath a/the ~, under a/the ~** | **between the ~s** ◊ *She lay between the cool ~s.*
PHRASES **~s and blankets** | **be white as a ~** (= look very pale)

2 piece of paper

ADJ. **blank, clean** ◊ *He grabbed a blank ~ of paper and began to write.* | **A3, A4, etc.** (*not in the US*) | **large** | **printed** ◊ *The advertisement was a single printed ~.* | **loose, separate, single** | **folded** | **cover** ◊ *a fax cover ~* | **answer, data, fact, information, instruction** (*esp. AmE*), **record, score** (*BrE*), **sign-up** (*AmE*), **spec, stat** (= statistics) (*AmE*), **time** ◊ *I sent for the free fact ~ on the disease.* | **balance** (= record of company's finances) | **charge** (*BrE*), **rap** (*informal, esp. AmE*) | **news** (usually ***news-sheet***), **scandal** | **cheat** (*esp. AmE*), **crib** ◊ *I need cheat ~s to help me cram for my exam.*
VERB + SHEET **take, use** ◊ *Take a clean ~ of paper and start again.* | **rip, tear** ◊ *She tore a ~ out of her notebook.*
SHEET + NOUN **music**
PREP. **~ of** ◊ *a ~ of blotting paper*
PHRASES **a ~ of paper**

3 flat thin piece of any material

ADJ. **flat, large** | **thick, thin** | **baking** (*BrE*), **cookie** (*AmE*) | **dust** (*BrE*) ◊ *The furniture was covered in dust ~s.* | **canvas, plastic, polythene** | **ice** ◊ *the Antarctic ice ~*
SHEET + NOUN **metal, steel, vinyl** ◊ *sheet-metal workers* | **rock** (*AmE*) ◊ *A wall of ~ rock was placed down the middle.* | **lightning** ◊ *The sky was lit up by great flashes of ~ lightning.*
PREP. **~ of** ◊ *a ~ of glass/plastic/metal* ◊ *Sheets of flame shot into the air.* (*figurative*)

shelf *noun*

ADJ. **high, low** | **deep** | **bottom, middle, top** ◊ *He took a book down from the top ~.* | **bare, empty** | **open** | **dusty** | **glass, metal, wooden** | **book** (usually ***bookshelf***), **CD, DVD, video** | **bathroom, kitchen, library, shop** (*BrE*), **store** (*esp. AmE*), **supermarket** ◊ *The supermarket shelves were bare.* | **closet** (*esp. AmE*)
VERB + SHELF **have** ◊ *The cabinet has three shelves.* | **build, put up** ◊ *She soon learned how to put up her own shelves.* | **arrange sth on, display sth on, put sth (back) on, replace sth on, return sth to, stack sth on** ◊ *I put the box back on the ~.* | **restock, stack** (*esp. BrE*), **stock** (*AmE*) ◊ *He has a job stacking/stocking shelves.* | **fill, line, pack** ◊ *The shelves were packed with dolls of every shape and size.* ◊ *Hundreds of books lined the shelves.* | **clear** ◊ *I've cleared a ~ in the bedroom for you.* | **get sth (down) from, get sth (down) off, pick sth from, pick sth off, remove sth from, take sth (down) from, take sth (down) off** ◊ *They immediately removed the product from their shelves.* | **fit on, fit onto, go on, remain on, sit on** ◊ *Souvenirs filled the shelves.* ◊ *Her diaries just sat on the ~ for years* (= nobody looked at them). | **browse, scan, scour, search** ◊ *She scanned the shelves of the library for new books.* | **reach** ◊ *I can't reach the top ~.* | **reach for** ◊ *She reached for the ~ next to the bed.*

SHELF + VERB **be full of sth, contain sth, hold sth** | **line** ◊ *Shelves lined the walls behind the long counter.*
SHELF + NOUN **space** | **life** ◊ *The medicine has a ~ life of six months.*
PREP. **off a/the ~** ◊ *I knocked it off the ~ by accident.* | **on a/the ~** ◊ *the books on the shelves* | **~ of** ◊ *a ~ of books on economics*
PHRASES **be filled with shelves, be lined with shelves** ◊ *The walls of her study were lined with shelves.* | **a place on your shelves** ◊ *The book deserves a place on everyone's shelves.* | **hit the shelves** (*figurative*) ◊ *Their new CD hits the shelves in May.* | **fly off the shelves** (*both figurative*) ◊ *The DVD is flying off the shelves.*

shell *noun*

1 on eggs/nuts/some animals

ADJ. **empty, hard, outer, protective, thick** ◊ *She had built up a protective ~ around herself.* (*figurative*) | **broken** | **egg** (usually ***eggshell***) | **sea** (usually ***seashell***) | **conch, cowrie, mussel, oyster, snail, tortoise** (usually ***tortoiseshell***) | **coconut, peanut, walnut**
VERB + SHELL **have** ◊ *creatures that have ~s* | **come out of, emerge from** (*both often figurative*) ◊ *He's really come out of his ~ since he met Marie.* | **go (back) into, retreat into, withdraw into** (*all often figurative*) ◊ *The snail went back into its ~.* | **remove sth from** ◊ *Remove the mussels from their ~s.* | **break (open), crack (open)** | **shed** ◊ *Male crabs shed their ~s twice a year.*

2 explosive weapon

ADJ. **unexploded** | **spent** ◊ *a heap of spent brass ~s from a machine gun* | **anti-aircraft, artillery, cannon, mortar, shotgun, tank** | **depleted uranium, high-explosive** ◊ *tank-busting guns that fired depleted uranium ~s* | **incoming** ◊ *The telltale sound of an incoming ~ was heard.*
VERB + SHELL **load** | **fire**
SHELL + VERB **fly** ◊ *A ~ flew over his head and exploded in front of him.* | **fall, land** | **burst, crash, explode** | **hit sth, strike sth** ◊ *Two ~s hit the roof.*
SHELL + NOUN **fire** ◊ *They braved heavy ~ fire to rescue the wounded.* | **shock** ◊ *soldiers suffering from ~ shock* | **case, casing, fragments, splinter** | **crater**

3 outer walls of a building

ADJ. **concrete** | **burned-out, empty, hollow** (*all often figurative*) ◊ *The fire reduced the school to a hollow ~.* ◊ *I had become a hollow ~.*

shelter *noun*

1 protection from danger/bad weather

VERB + SHELTER **afford (sb), give (sb), offer (sb), provide (sb with)** ◊ *The great trees gave ~ from the wind.* | **need** | **find, run for, seek, take** | **refuse sb** ◊ *The nuns won't refuse you ~.* | **leave** ◊ *We had to leave the ~ of the trees.*
PREP. **in the ~ of, under the ~ of** ◊ *She was standing in the ~ of the doorway.* | **~ from** ◊ *They tried to seek ~ from the rain.*
PHRASES **~ for the night**

2 small building that gives protection

ADJ. **makeshift, temporary** | **stone, underground, wooden** | **air-raid** (*BrE*), **bomb, bus, emergency, fallout** | **animal** | **homeless** ◊ *She works as a volunteer at a homeless ~.* | **tax** (*figurative*) ◊ *These tax ~s allow people to invest in shares without paying tax.*
VERB + SHELTER **build, construct, erect, make, put up** ◊ *The earthquake victims were forced to build temporary ~s.*
PREP. **in a/the ~** ◊ *You'll be safer in the ~.* | **~ for** ◊ *a ~ for cattle*

shield *noun*

1 used to protect the body when fighting

ADJ. **riot**
VERB + SHIELD **lower, raise** | **be armed with, be equipped**

with, carry, have, hold | **act as** ◊ *The car had acted as a ~, protecting him from the blast.*
PREP. **behind a/the ~** ◊ *a row of police officers behind their riot ~s* | **on a/the ~** ◊ *She did not recognize the coat of arms on his ~.*

2 used for protecting yourself

ADJ. **defensive, protective** | **human** | **missile-defence/ missile-defense, nuclear** | **heat, radiation, wind** (usually **windshield**) (*esp. AmE*) ◊ *The nose of the space capsule is protected by a heat ~.* | **face, gum** (usually **gumshield**) (*BrE*)
VERB + SHIELD **use sb/sth as** ◊ *They used 400 hostages as human ~s.* | **form** | **provide** ◊ *The software provides a ~ against hackers, worms and viruses.* | **penetrate**
SHIELD + VERB **protect** ◊ *A face ~ protects your eyes from harmful chemicals.*
PREP. **~ against** ◊ *The ozone layer forms a ~ against harmful solar rays.*

shield verb

ADV. **partially, partly** | **carefully** ◊ *He carefully ~ed the flame with his cupped hand.*
VERB + SHIELD **try to** ◊ *She tried to ~ the children from the full horrors of the war.*
PREP. **against** ◊ *She raised her hand to ~ her eyes against the sun.* | **from** ◊ *new laws to ~ companies from foreign competition* | **with** ◊ *He ~ed her with his body.*

shift noun

1 change

ADJ. **distinct, dramatic, fundamental, huge, important, major, marked, massive, profound, pronounced, radical, seismic, significant, substantial** ◊ *There has been a major ~ in the public's taste.* ◊ *a significant ~ in policy* | **discernible, perceptible** | **slight, subtle** | **gradual** | **abrupt, rapid, sudden** | **decisive, irreversible, long-term** | **climate, cultural, demographic, ideological, policy, population, power** | **paradigm** (= an important change in the way sth is thought about) ◊ *Einstein's theories caused a paradigm ~ in scientific thought.*
VERB + SHIFT **be, mark, represent** ◊ *These proposals represent a dramatic ~ in policy.* | **indicate, reflect, signal** ◊ *The moment signals a significant ~ in attitudes to the war.* | **show** | **detect, notice, observe, see, witness** ◊ *I detected a subtle ~ towards/toward our point of view.* | **bring about, cause, drive, lead to, produce, result in** | **experience, undergo** ◊ *The industry has undergone a fundamental ~ in recent years.* | **explain** ◊ *one factor which may explain the president's policy ~*
SHIFT + VERB **occur, take place** ◊ *These climate ~s occurred over less than a decade.*
PREP. **~ between** ◊ *the many ~s between verse and prose that occur in Shakespeare* | **~ (away) from** ◊ *the ~ away from direct taxation* | **~ in** ◊ *a ~ in public opinion* ◊ *a ~ in attitude/opinion/perspective* ◊ *a ~ in emphasis/mood/tone* ◊ *a ~ in direction/focus/policy/strategy* | **~ to** ◊ *a sudden ~ to the right in politics* | **~ towards/toward** ◊ *a ~ towards/ toward part-time farming*

2 division of the working day

ADJ. **double, long, split** (*esp. BrE*) ◊ *I agreed to work double ~s for a few weeks.* | **day, early** | **late, swing** (*AmE*) | **graveyard** (*esp. AmE*), **night, overnight** | **eight-hour, ten-hour, etc.** | **afternoon, evening, morning, weekend**
VERB + SHIFT **do, work** ◊ *I'm doing the early ~ this week.* ◊ *He works the night ~.* ◊ *I didn't realize that I'd have to work ~s.* | **be on, come on, go on** | **be off, come off, finish, go off** | **change** ◊ *It was 8 a.m. and the nurses were changing ~s. My husband changed his ~s from afternoons to nights.*
SHIFT + VERB **begin** (*esp. BrE*), **start** (*esp. AmE*) | **end** | **change** ◊ *The ~ change took place at 10 p.m.*
SHIFT + NOUN **work** | **manager, supervisor, worker** | **pattern, system** (*both BrE*) ◊ *They'd altered his ~ pattern twice in the past month.* | **change** ◊ *The ~ change took place at 10 p.m.*
PREP. **in ~s** ◊ *The clinic is staffed by ten doctors who work in ~s.* | **on a/the ~** ◊ *a decision for the chief nurse on each ~*

shift verb

1 move

ADV. **slightly** ◊ *Julie ~ed her position slightly and smiled.* | **impatiently, nervously, restlessly, uncomfortably, uneasily** ◊ *She ~ed uncomfortably in her chair.* | **away**
PREP. **from** ◊ *She ~ed her gaze away from the group of tourists.* | **onto** ◊ *He ~ed his weight onto his left foot.* | **to** ◊ *Her eyes ~ed to his face.*
PHRASES **~ from foot to foot** | **~ in your chair, ~ in your seat**

2 change

ADV. **dramatically, markedly, radically** ◊ *The emphasis has ~ed markedly in recent years.* | **slightly** | **effectively** | **simply** ◊ *We cannot simply ~ the responsibility onto someone else.* | **gradually, slowly** | **quickly, rapidly** | **suddenly** | **constantly, continually** ◊ *constantly ~ing alliances* | **away** ◊ *Government grants are being ~ed away from the capital to the regions.*
VERB + SHIFT **attempt to, try to** ◊ *They tried to ~ the blame onto the government.* | **tend to** | **begin to**
PREP. **(away) from** ◊ *I felt the advantage had suddenly ~ed away from us.* | **back, back and forth** ◊ *Like many plays, this one ~s back and forth in time and place.* | **into** ◊ *~ to ~ into second gear* | **out of** ◊ *In recent years, manufacturing has ~ed out of the US.* | **onto, to** ◊ *His sympathies rapidly ~ed to the side of the workers.* | **towards/toward** ◊ *These changes will ~ the balance more towards/toward science subjects.*

shin noun

VERB + SHIN **kick (sb in/on)** ◊ *I kicked him hard in the ~s to shut him up.* | **bang, bruise, hit, knock** ◊ *I banged my ~ on a tree stump.* | **rub**
SHIN + NOUN **bone** | **guard** (*esp. AmE*), **pad** (*BrE*) | **splints** (= sharp pains in the lower legs) ◊ *I have been suffering from ~ splints.*
PREP. **on the/your ~** ◊ *She had a nasty cut on her ~.*

shine verb

ADV. **brightly, brilliantly** ◊ *The sun was shining brightly.* | **faintly** | **briefly** | **directly** ◊ *A spotlight was shining directly into her eyes.* | **warmly** | **down, in, out** ◊ *Sunlight shone in through the window.*
VERB + SHINE **seem to** (*figurative*) ◊ *She seemed to ~ with an inner radiance.* | **make sth** ◊ *You've really made that floor ~!*
PREP. **at** ◊ *The watchman shone his torch at us.* | **from** (*figurative*) ◊ *Love and pride shone from her eyes.* | **in** ◊ *The water was shining faintly in the moonlight.* | **like** ◊ *The dark wood shone like glass.* | **on, upon** ◊ *The light shone on his face.* | **through, with** (*figurative*) ◊ *His dark eyes shone with excitement.*

ship noun

ADJ. **cruise, sailing** | **cargo, container, factory, hospital, supply, transport, whaling** ◊ *a factory ~ that is equipped for freezing and canning* | **civilian, commercial** (*esp. AmE*), **merchant, passenger** | **military, naval, navy, troop** | **enemy** | **amphibious, landing, surface** ◊ *missiles from surface ~s* | **ocean-going** | **wooden** | **passing** ◊ *The crew was rescued by a passing ~.* | **pirate, slave**
...OF SHIPS **fleet**
VERB + SHIP **board, come aboard, come on board, go aboard, go on board** | **be aboard, be on board** | **sail** | **manoeuvre/maneuver, pilot, steer** | **moor** ◊ *The ~ is now permanently moored in Buenos Aires.* | **command** | **build, launch** | **load, unload** ◊ *The ~ had already been unloaded.* | **load sth onto, unload sth from** ◊ *The dockers were loading the cargo onto the ~.* | **christen, name** | **abandon** ◊ *The captain gave the order to abandon ~.* | **go down with** ◊ *The captain went down with his ~.* | **scuttle, sink, torpedo** | **attack, damage, destroy** | **jump** ◊ *Some of the crew jumped ~* (= *left it illegally*) *and disappeared.*
SHIP + VERB **carry sb/sth** ◊ *a ~ carrying more than a thousand people* | **arrive, dock** | **anchor** ◊ *The ~ anchored in the bay.* | **be at anchor, lie at anchor** ◊ *Their ~ lay at anchor in the bay.* | **depart, go, leave, put out to sea, put to sea, sail, set**

shocking

sail | be wrecked, run aground | capsize | go down, sink | collide with sth, hit sth | be equipped for/with sth
PREP. aboard a/the ~, on a/the ~, on board a/the ~ ◇ *They are now on a ~ bound for New York.* | by ~ ◇ *There was no time to send the goods by ~.* | ~ bound for, ~ for, ~ to
PHRASES the bow of a ~, the deck of a ~, the stern of a ~ | the captain of a ~, the crew of a ~

shipment *noun*

1 quantity of goods sent from one place to another
ADJ. aid, arms, drug, food, fuel, oil, weapons, etc. | cargo (*esp. AmE*) | large, massive | illegal
VERB + SHIPMENT get, receive | deliver, send ◇ *a contract to deliver large ~s of bananas* | track ◇ *Customers can track a ~ over the Web.* | escort ◇ *An armed patrol boat will escort the ~.* | intercept, seize ◇ *Customs officers have seized a large ~ of cocaine.*
PREP. ~ of ◇ *a ~ of arms* | ~ from ◇ *to arrange a ~ from India*

2 act of transporting goods
ADJ. bulk | direct (*esp. AmE*)
VERB + SHIPMENT await ◇ *large quantities of food awaiting ~ to the worst-affected areas* | arrange, begin, make | ban, halt, stop, suspend | resume
PREP. ~ to ◇ *illegal ~ of arms to the Third World*

shirt *noun*

ADJ. clean | crisp, fresh ◇ *He wears a crisp white ~ to the office every day.* | long-sleeved, short-sleeved | sleeveless | button-down, collared, collarless | open-necked (*esp. BrE*), unbuttoned (*esp. AmE*) | cotton, denim, flannel, oxford (*AmE*), silk, etc. | dress, tuxedo (*AmE*) | check (*BrE*), checked, checkered (*AmE*), plaid (*AmE*), plain, striped | baggy, oversized | loose, tight | dress | football (*BrE*), golf (*esp. AmE*), polo, rugby, sport (*AmE*), sports, team | replica (*BrE*) ◇ *replica football ~s with Beckham's famous number 7* | Hawaiian ◇ *He sported a floral Hawaiian ~.* | muscle (= a T-shirt with very short or no sleeves, worn by men) (*AmE*) | night (usually *nightshirt*) (*esp. AmE*) | hair (= worn in the past by people who wished to punish themselves for religious reasons) (*often figurative*)
VERB + SHIRT button, button up, unbutton | pull off | tuck in ◇ *He tucked his ~ into his pants.* | wash | iron
SHIRT + NOUN button, collar, cuff, front, pocket, sleeve, tail | number (*esp. BrE*) ◇ *a footballer's ~ number*
PHRASES ~ and tie
→ Special page at CLOTHES

shiver *noun*

ADJ. little, slight, small | involuntary | sudden | cold, icy | delicious ◇ *a delicious ~ of pleasure*
VERB + SHIVER give ◇ *She gave a little ~ and laughed.* | feel ◇ *He felt a ~ of excitement.* | send ◇ *His appearance sent a cold ~ down her spine.* | suppress ◇ *She tried to suppress a ~ of anticipation.*
SHIVER + VERB go, pass, run ◇ *A ~ of unease ran through the audience.*
PREP. with a ~ ◇ *'I'm scared!' she admitted, with a ~.* | ~ of ◇ *a ~ of fear*
PHRASES get the ~s ◇ *I get the ~s when I think about it.* | give sb the ~s, send ~s down sb's spine ◇ *Just thinking about flying gives me the ~s.* ◇ *Her beautiful voice sends ~s down your spine.*

shiver *verb*

ADV. uncontrollably, violently | a little, slightly | involuntarily ◇ *She ~ed involuntarily as he approached her.* | visibly
VERB + SHIVER begin to, start to | make sb ◇ *His cruel and callous comments made me ~.*
PREP. at ◇ *He ~ed at the thought of it.* | from, in ◇ *to ~ in fear* | with ◇ *I was ~ing with cold.*
PHRASES ~ at the thought (of sth) (*figurative*) ◇ *He ~ed at the thought of having to run for election.*

shock *noun*

1 extreme surprise
ADJ. awful (*esp. BrE*), big, considerable (*esp. BrE*), dreadful (*esp. BrE*), great, huge, major, massive, nasty, real, rude, terrible, tremendous ◇ *Drivers could be in for a nasty ~ when they see the cost of renewing their insurance policies.* | absolute, complete, pure, total, utter (*esp. AmE*) | mild, slight | first, initial ◇ *Once the initial ~ had worn off, I got to like my new hairstyle.* | sudden | economic, emotional | culture ◇ *It was a bit of a culture ~ when I first came to this country.* | sticker (*AmE*) ◇ *Customers may experience sticker ~ when they see the prices of the new SUVs (= they may be shocked by the prices).*
VERB + SHOCK come as | feel, get, have, receive ◇ *She felt ~ that he would be capable of such an act.* ◇ *I got a terrible ~ when I saw him.* | give sb | be in for ◇ *If you think it's going to be easy, you're in for a ~!* | die of (*informal*) ◇ *I nearly died of ~ when your mother appeared.* | get over, recover from | express | feign | imagine ◇ *Imagine my ~ when I saw them kissing!*
SHOCK + NOUN tactics | value ◇ *The scene was clearly added for ~ value.* | jock (*informal, esp. AmE*) | troops | wave ◇ *The news sent ~ waves through the financial markets.* (*figurative*) | defeat, departure, exit (*all BrE, sports*) ◇ *United suffered a ~ defeat to Norwich.* | result, victory, win (*all BrE, sports*) | announcement, decision, resignation (*all BrE*)
PREP. in ~ ◇ *She looked around in ~.* | with a ~ ◇ *She realized with a sudden ~ that she was being followed.* | ~ at, ~ on ◇ *her ~ on seeing him with another woman* | ~ to ◇ *This news came as a great ~ to me.*
PHRASES a bit of a ~, quite a ~, something of a ~ | in a state of ~ ◇ *I think I'm still in a state of ~.* | a feeling of ~, a sense of ~ | ~ horror (*BrE, humorous*) ◇ *The article reports on a celebrity who—shock horror—has gained weight!* | the ~ of your life (*informal*) ◇ *I got the ~ of my life when she told me she was pregnant.* | a ~ to the system (*informal*) ◇ *The low salaries came as something of a ~ to her system.*

2 electric shock
ADJ. massive (*esp. BrE*), severe | mild ◇ *He gave himself a mild electric ~ while changing a light bulb.* | painful | electric (less often *electrical*)
VERB + SHOCK get, receive | give sb | administer ◇ *The guards would administer electric ~s to the inmates.*
SHOCK + NOUN therapy

3 extreme weakness caused by injury or shock
ADJ. deep, severe | mild | delayed (*esp. BrE*) | anaphylactic | shell ◇ *soldiers suffering from shell ~*
VERB + SHOCK be in, be suffering from, suffer ◇ *He was in deep ~ after the accident.* | go into ◇ *He had gone into ~ and was shaking violently.* | be treated for

shock *verb*

ADV. deeply, really ◇ *The news had ~ed her deeply.* | easily ◇ *He had old-fashioned ideas and was easily ~ed.*
PREP. into ◇ *The news ~ed her into action.*

shocked *adj.*

VERBS appear, be, feel, look, sound
ADV. extremely, fairly, very, etc. | badly (*esp. BrE*), deeply (*esp. BrE*), genuinely, greatly, profoundly, terribly, truly ◇ *The passengers were badly ~ but unharmed.* | absolutely, completely, thoroughly (*esp. AmE*), totally, utterly (*esp. AmE*) | almost | a little, slightly, etc. | mildly | clearly, visibly
PREP. at ◇ *They were ~ at how the children had been treated.* | by ◇ *She was visibly ~ by the conditions she witnessed in the camp.*

shocking *adj.*

VERBS be, seem, sound | find sth
ADV. extremely, fairly, very, etc. | deeply, especially,

genuinely, particularly, truly ◇ *a deeply ~ and painful discovery* | **absolutely, just** | **a little, slightly,** etc.
PREP. **to** ◇ *His attitude was ~ to her.*

shoe *noun*

ADJ. **heavy, stout** (*BrE*), **strong, sturdy** | **clumpy** (*BrE*), **clunky** (*AmE*) | **light** | **comfortable, sensible, soft** | **old, worn, worn-out** | **dirty, muddy** | **patent-leather, polished, shiny** | **matching** ◇ *She wore a dark blue dress with matching ~s.* | **designer, fashionable, stylish, trendy** | **casual** | **dress, dressy** (*informal, esp. AmE*), **fancy** (*esp. AmE*), **smart** (*esp. BrE*) | **open-toed, pointed, pointy** (*informal*) | **flat, high-heeled, low-heeled, platform** | **buckled, lace-up, slip-on, strappy** | **canvas, leather, rubber, suede,** etc. | **boat** (*esp. AmE*), **deck** | **court** (*BrE*) | **oxford** (*AmE*) | **athletic** (*AmE*), **gym, sports, training** (*BrE*) | **climbing, running, track** (*esp. AmE*), **walking** | **bowling, golf, skate** (= for skateboarding), **tennis** | **basketball, soccer** (*both AmE*) | **dancing** | **ballet, pointe, toe** (*esp. AmE*) | **tap** | **baby**
... OF SHOES **pair** ◇ *a sturdy pair of walking ~s*
VERB + SHOE **put on, slip on** | **kick off, pull off, slip off** | **tie, untie** (*both esp. AmE*) | **lace, lace up, unlace** | **break in** ◇ *to break in a new pair of ~s* | **reheel, repair, resole** ◇ *I've had my ~s resoled.* | **buff, clean, polish, shine** | **scuff**
SHOE + VERB **fit (sb)** | **pinch sth** ◇ *The ~s, though elegant, pinched her feet terribly.* | **squeak**
SHOE + NOUN **polish** | **size** ◇ *What's your ~ size?* | **shop** (*BrE*), **store** (*AmE*) | **repair** | **leather** | **company, designer, factory, maker** (usually **shoemaker**), **manufacturer** | **box, rack** | **insert** (*AmE*), **insole** ◇ *For her feet the doctor recommended ~ inserts.*
PHRASES **the heel of a ~, the sole of a ~, the toe of a ~**
→ Special page at CLOTHES

shoelace (*also* lace) *noun*

ADJ. **undone, untied** | **loose** | **knotted** ◇ *a tightly knotted ~*
... OF SHOELACES **pair**
VERB + SHOELACE **do up** (*BrE*), **knot, tie** ◇ *He's still a little young to tie his own ~s.* | **undo, untie** | **retie** (*AmE*) | **break**
SHOELACE + VERB **be undone, be untied** (*AmE*) | **come undone, come untied** (*AmE*)
→ Special page at CLOTHES

shoot *noun*

1 new part of a plant

ADJ. **fresh, green, new, tender, young** | **growing** | **flowering, leafy** | **lateral, side** | **bamboo**
VERB + SHOOT **have** ◇ *This plant has no ~s yet.* | **develop, produce, put out** (*esp. BrE*), **put up** (*esp. AmE*), **send out, send up** (*esp. AmE*) ◇ *These shrubs will need more light to produce flowering ~s.*
SHOOT + VERB **appear, come up, develop, emerge, grow** ◇ *Keep the bulbs in a cool dark place until ~s appear.*

2 occasion when you photograph sb/sth

ADJ. **commercial, cover, fashion, film** (*esp. BrE*), **magazine, movie** (*esp. AmE*), **photo, photographic** (*BrE*), **video** ◇ *a cover ~ for the September issue of Cosmopolitan* ◇ *a five-day photo ~ in Cyprus* | **location** | **night** | **one-day, two-day,** etc.
PREP. **on a/the ~** ◇ *He goes out on photo ~s with very little equipment.*

shoot *verb*

ADV. **accurately, straight** ◇ *She trained for days until she could ~ straight.* | **accidentally** ◇ *He accidentally shot himself in the foot.* | **fatally** ◇ *Four policemen were fatally shot in the incident.* | **summarily** ◇ *If caught, the men could be summarily shot as spies.* | **back** ◇ *The soldiers shot back at invading planes with rifles.* | **down** ◇ *The airliner was shot down near Korea.*
VERB + SHOOT **want to** | **threaten to** | **be about to, be going to** ◇ *I thought for a moment that he was going to ~.* | **try to** ◇ *The soldiers were ~ing at a target.* | **in** ◇ *He was*

shot in the back. | **into** ◇ *Troops shot into the air to stop the rioting.* | **with** ◇ *She was shot with a small automatic pistol.*
PHRASES **~ (sb) on sight** ◇ *Any intruders will be shot on sight.* | **~ sb dead** ◇ *The police shot him dead.* | **~ to kill** ◇ *The soldiers were told to ~ to kill.* ◇ *a shoot-to-kill policy* | **shot and killed** ◇ *Four protestors were shot and killed by police.* | **shot to death** ◇ *She was shot to death for a crime she did not commit.*

shop *noun* (*esp. BrE*) → See also STORE

ADJ. **corner** (*BrE*), **local, village** | **high-street** (*BrE*) | **busy** | **exclusive, expensive, fine, posh** (*BrE*), **smart** (*BrE*), **stylish, upmarket** (*BrE*) | **excellent, good, wonderful** | **well-stocked** | **trendy** | **old-fashioned, traditional** | **colourful/colorful** | **boarded-up, empty, vacant** | **butcher** (*AmE*), **butcher's, greengrocer's** (*BrE*), etc. | **book** (usually **bookshop**), **gift** (*BrE, AmE*), **gun** (*esp. AmE*), **pet** (*BrE, AmE*), **shoe, souvenir** (*BrE, AmE*), etc. | **electrical, photographic,** etc. | **specialist, specialty** (*AmE*) | **pro** (= at a golf club, etc.) (*AmE*) | **duty-free** (*BrE, AmE*) ◇ *She bought 400 cigarettes at the airport duty-free ~.* | **charity** (*BrE*), **thrift** (*AmE*) ◇ *I gave all my old books to a charity ~/thrift ~.* | **antique** (*BrE, AmE*), **junk** (*BrE, AmE*) | **betting** (*BrE*) | **mobile** (*BrE*) ◇ *Mobile ~s are invaluable to people in rural areas.* | **retail** | **repair** (*BrE, AmE*) | **barber** (usually **barbershop**) (*AmE*) | **pawn** (usually **pawnshop**) (*BrE, AmE*) | **one-stop** (*BrE, AmE*) ◇ *This is your one-stop ~ for all your skiing needs.* | **coffee** (*BrE, AmE*)
... OF SHOPS **parade** (*BrE*), **row** ◇ *The post office is at the end of the row of ~s.* | **chain** ◇ *The brothers opened a chain of electrical ~s in the eighties.*
VERB + SHOP **have, keep, own, run** | **open, set up** ◇ *She opened a flower ~ in the High Street.* ◇ *an area where many artists have set up ~* (*figurative*) | **close, close up, shut, shut up** (*BrE*) ◇ *At 5.30 she shuts up ~ and goes home.*
SHOP + VERB **sell sth** | **offer sth** ◇ *The ~ offers a large selection of leather goods at reasonable prices.* | **specialize in sth** | **advertise sth** | **display sth** | **open** | **close, shut**
SHOP + NOUN **assistant, manager, manageress** (*BrE*), **owner, staff, worker** | **counter, display, doorway, front, premises, shelves, sign, window**
PREP. **around a/the ~, round a/the ~** (*esp. BrE*) ◇ *I went around all the ~s but I couldn't find a present for him.* | **at a/the ~** ◇ *There was was a break-in at that new ~ last night.* | **in a/the ~** ◇ *She works part-time in a ~.*

shopkeeper *noun*

ADJ. **small** ◇ *an organization set up to help small ~s* | **independent** | **local, small-town** (*AmE*), **village** (*BrE*)
SHOPKEEPER + VERB **sell sth**
→ Note at JOB

shoplifting *noun*

... OF SHOPLIFTING **spate** (*esp. BrE*) ◇ *They installed cameras to halt a spate of ~.*
SHOPLIFTING + NOUN **spree** (*esp. BrE*) ◇ *They stole thousands of pounds' worth of goods in a two-day ~ spree.*
PHRASES **be arrested for ~**
→ Note at CRIME

shopper *noun*

ADJ. **average** ◇ *what the average ~ spends her money on* | **frequent** (*AmE*), **regular** (*esp. BrE*) | **local** | **disabled, elderly** (*both esp. BrE*) | **late-night, morning, Saturday, weekend** | **Christmas, festive** (*BrE*), **holiday** (*AmE*) | **last-minute** ◇ *last-minute ~s on Christmas Eve* | **city-centre** (*BrE*), **downtown** (*AmE*), **town-centre** (*BrE*) | **personal** (= sb you pay to do your shopping) | **mystery, secret** (= person who pretends to be a customer) (*AmE*) ◇ *A mystery ~ visits each branch every two weeks.* | **Internet, online, Web** | **grocery** (*AmE*), **mall** (*AmE*), **supermarket** (*esp. BrE*) ◇ *We are a nation of supermarket ~s.* | **savvy, smart** (*both esp. AmE*) ◇ *A savvy ~ can purchase the gem for about €2 000 per carat.* | **compulsive, frantic, frenzied** | **serious** ◇ *If you're a serious ~, this is the credit card for you.* | **happy** | **fellow** ◇ *I observed my fellow ~s rushing from store to store.*
... OF SHOPPERS **crowds, throngs** ◇ *The cheap deals brought out big crowds of ~s.*

VERB + SHOPPER **be crowded with, be filled with, be packed with, be thronged with** ◇ *The street was thronged with ~s.* | **attract, draw, encourage, lure, persuade, tempt** ◇ *special offers designed to tempt ~s* | **deter** (*esp. BrE*), **discourage, drive away, put off** (*esp. BrE*)

SHOPPER + VERB **rush** ◇ *Shoppers rushed to catch the sales.*

PHRASES **attractive to ~s** ◇ *Window displays are intended to be attractive to ~s.*

shopping *noun*

1 activity of shopping

ADJ. **late-night, morning, weekend** | **back-to-school** (*AmE*), **Christmas, holiday** (*esp. AmE*), **last-minute, sales** (*BrE*) ◇ *the back-to-school ~ season* | **a bit of** (*esp. BrE*), **a little** ◇ *I thought we'd do a little ~ before the show.* | **family** (*BrE*), **food, grocery** (*esp. AmE*), **supermarket, weekly** (*esp. BrE*) ◇ *I do the weekly ~ on a Saturday.* | **car, clothes, dress, etc.** | **catalogue, home, Internet, online** ◇ *the move to home ~ using your computer* | **duty-free, tax-free** | **comparison** ◇ *This website is a valuable resource for comparison ~.* | **convenience** (*esp. BrE*) | **one-stop** ◇ *the consumers' demand for one-stop ~* (= *buying all they need in one place*) | **quality** (*esp. BrE*) | **serious** (*humorous*) ◇ *Jenny went directly to town for some serious ~.* | **heavy, light** (*both esp. BrE*) | **compulsive** ◇ *to suffer from compulsive ~ disorder*

... OF SHOPPING **afternoon, day**

VERB + SHOPPING **be out, do, go, go out** ◇ *She's doing some last-minute Christmas ~.* ◇ *When shall I do the ~?* (*BrE*) ◇ *We do our ~ on Saturdays.* ◇ *I have to go ~ in town this afternoon.* | **come** | **take sb** ◇ *Jade wants me to take her ~ for a new outfit.*

SHOPPING + NOUN **bag, basket, cart** (*esp. AmE*), **trolley** (*BrE*) | **list** | **area, district** | **arcade** (*esp. BrE*), **complex, development** (*esp. BrE*), **mall** (*esp. AmE*), **parade** (*BrE*), **park** (*BrE*), **plaza** (*AmE*), **precinct** (*BrE*), **street** (*esp. BrE*), **strip** (*AmE*) ◇ *the town's main ~ street* (see also ***shopping centre***) | **facilities** (*esp. BrE*), **outlet** (*esp. BrE*) | **channel, network** (*esp. AmE*) ◇ *a home ~ network* | **site, website** ◇ *an Internet ~ site* | **service** ◇ *a personal ~ service* | **space** (*esp. BrE*) ◇ *Developers plan to build 4 000 square feet of ~ space here.* | **destination** ◇ *New York, the ultimate ~ destination* | **excursion, expedition, spree, trip** ◇ *She won £10 000 and immediately went on a ~ spree.* | **day, hours, season** ◇ *Only 22 ~ days left until Christmas!* ◇ *the Christmas ~ season* | **environment** (*esp. BrE*), **experience** ◇ *We ensure that our customers have an exceptional ~ experience.* | **habits** ◇ *detailed portraits of consumers' ~ habits* | **voucher** (*BrE*)

PHRASES **be on sb's ~ list** (*often figurative*) ◇ *A new car is on my ~ list.* ◇ *Improved electricity generation is one of the first things on the country's ~ list.*

2 (*esp. BrE*) food, etc. bought in shops/stores → See also GROCERIES

ADJ. **heavy**

VERB + SHOPPING **be laden with** | **carry** | **put away, unpack** ◇ *They unpacked the ~ and put it away.*

shopping centre (*AmE* shopping center) *noun*
→ See also MALL

ADJ. **big, huge, large, major** | **small** | **main, principal** | **new** | **modern, state-of-the-art** ◇ *Kendal boasts a modern ~ and a museum.* | **high-end, upscale** (*both AmE*) | **run-down** | **$10 million, £200 million, etc.** | **busy, crowded, thriving** | **district, downtown** (*AmE*), **high-street** (*BrE*), **local, neighbourhood** (*AmE*), **out-of-town** (*BrE*), **regional, suburban** ◇ *Local shops are facing fierce competition from out-of-town ~s.* | **strip** (*AmE*)

VERB + SHOPPING-CENTRE/SHOPPING-CENTER **build, develop** ◇ *A developer in this suburb of Phoenix plans to build a ~.* | **go to, visit**

SHOPPING-CENTRE/SHOPPING-CENTER + NOUN **car park** (*BrE*), **parking lot** (*AmE*) | **developer** | **manager**

shore *noun*

1 land along the edge of a sea/lake

ADJ. **golden, sandy** ◇ *on the golden ~s of beautiful Bali* | **lake, ocean, sea** (usually ***seashore***) | **rocky** | **barren, exposed,**

wilder (*figurative*) ◇ *a Belgian artist from the wilder ~s of Flemish nationalism* | **distant, far, farther, opposite, other** ◇ *Meg was pointing to the far ~.* | **near** | **east, north, etc.** ◇ *Lake Michigan's north ~* | **eastern, northern, etc.** ◇ *The path ran along the southern ~ of the lake.* | **lake**

VERB + SHORE **approach, reach** | **leave** | **follow, hug** ◇ *We sailed until midnight, hugging the ~.* | **line** ◇ *Four thousand spectators lined the ~s.* | **hit, lap, lap against** ◇ *the sound of waves lapping the ~* | **be found on, be washed up on** ◇ *A dolphin was found washed up on the ~.*

SHORE + NOUN **bird, crab** | **leave** ◇ *sailors on ~ leave* | **excursion**

PREP. **along the ~** ◇ *We walked along the ~s of the lake together.* | **around the ~ of** ◇ *The route goes around the ~ of Derwent Water.* | **at the ~** ◇ *We spent our vacation at the ~* (= *the beach*). (*AmE*) | **by the ~** ◇ *We strolled by the ~ after dinner.* | **close to the ~, near the ~** ◇ *The sea appears calm near the ~.* | **from (a/the) ~** ◇ *just a few miles from ~* ◇ *He waited, watching from the ~.* | **on (a/the) ~** ◇ *The others were now safely on ~.* ◇ *There are a lot of rocks on that ~.* | **on the ~s of** ◇ *The hotel is situated on the sheltered ~s of the Moray Firth.* | **to the ~, towards/toward the ~** ◇ *The hotel's gardens stretch down to the lake ~.* | **~ of** ◇ *the ~s of the Mediterranean*

2 shores particular country

ADJ. **British, US, etc.** | **foreign, native** | **our, these** ◇ *the ship in which Columbus first sailed to these ~s*

VERB + SHORES **arrive on, come to, grace** (*BrE*), **hit, reach, return to** ◇ *the most thought-provoking movie to hit these ~s in recent years* ◇ *He was glad to return to his native ~s.* | **leave** | **defend** ◇ *We will fight to the death to defend our ~s.*

PREP. **beyond the ~** ◇ *The decisions concerning the future of the company will be taken beyond these ~s.*

short *adj.*

1 not measuring much from one end to the other

VERBS **be, look, seem**

ADV. **extremely, fairly, very, etc.** | **comparatively, relatively** ◇ *a relatively ~ distance of 50 to 100 miles*

2 not lasting a long time

VERBS **be, feel, seem** | **become, get** ◇ *The days are getting shorter and shorter.* | **make sth** | **keep sth** ◇ *Do you mind if we keep the meeting ~?*

ADV. **extremely, fairly, very, etc.** | **remarkably, surprisingly** | **reasonably** | **comparatively, relatively** ◇ *It was all over in a relatively ~ space of time.* | **mercifully** ◇ *The interview was mercifully ~.* | **tragically** ◇ *a young woman whose life was cut tragically ~*

3 not having enough of what is needed

VERBS **be, look** ◇ *Our team was one player ~.* | **become, get** ◇ *We're getting ~ of funds.*

ADV. **extremely, fairly, very, etc.** ◇ *If space is very ~, that door can be moved.* | **terribly, woefully** ◇ *His performance was woefully ~ of conviction.* | **a little, slightly, etc.**

PREP. **of** ◇ *Mike was a little ~ of cash just then.*

PHRASES **in ~ supply** ◇ *Safe drinking water is in desperately ~ supply.*

shortage *noun*

ADJ. **acute, chronic, critical, desperate, dire, serious, severe** ◇ *the current acute ~ of teachers* | **growing, increasing** | **future, impending, looming** ◇ *a looming housing ~ in the city* | **general** | **national, nationwide, world** ◇ *the world ~ of coffee* | **current** | **wartime** | **supply** | **cash, electricity, energy, food, fuel, gas, gasoline** (*AmE*), **housing, oil, petrol** (*BrE*), **power, water** | **labour/labor, manpower, nursing, personnel** (*esp. AmE*), **skill, skills, staff, staffing, teacher**

VERB + SHORTAGE **cause, create, lead to, result in** | **be affected by, be hampered by, experience, face, have, suffer, suffer from** ◇ *Industry is facing a serious skills ~.* | **alleviate, ease** ◇ *The recent heavy rains have helped to ease the water ~.* | **address, deal with, fill, meet, overcome,**

solve, tackle | **exacerbate** ◊ *The energy ~s were exacerbated by the severe winter.*
SHORTAGE + VERB **occur** | **cause sth, lead to sth** ◊ *A ~ of resources has led to a cutback.*
PREP. **because of a/the ~, due to a/the ~** ◊ *Lives are being put at risk because of staff ~s.* | **~ in** ◊ *Their economy continued to suffer ~s in raw materials.* | **~ of** ◊ *a ~ of organ donors*

shortcoming *noun*

ADJ. **alleged, perceived** | **obvious** ◊ *There were obvious ~s in the report.* | **fundamental, main, major, serious, significant** | **minor** | **potential** | **sb's own, personal** | **methodological, technical** | **moral**
VERB + SHORTCOMING **have, suffer from** | **call attention to** (*esp. AmE*), **draw attention to** (*esp. BrE*), **expose, highlight, identify, point out, reveal** | **deflect attention from, divert attention from** | **acknowledge, recognize** | **be aware of** ◊ *They are well aware of their own ~s.* | **ignore, overlook** ◊ *The committee was willing to overlook her ~s.* | **address, compensate for, correct, make good** | **make up for, overcome, remedy** ◊ *Their proposal seeks to remedy the ~s of the current system.*
SHORTCOMING + VERB **stem from sth** ◊ *Not all these ~s stem from inadequate resources.*
PREP. **despite sb/sth's ~s, in spite of sb/sth's ~s** ◊ *Despite its obvious ~s, the plan was accepted.* | **~ in** ◊ *the ~ in the law*
PHRASES **~s on sb's part** (*esp. BrE*) ◊ *They said the accident was due to ~s on the part of the pilots.*

short cut *noun*

VERB + SHORT CUT **be** | **take** | **use sth as** | **provide** (*often figurative*) | **find, know**
PREP. **~ across, ~ through** ◊ *Take the ~ across the fields.* | **~ to** ◊ *There are no ~s to economic recovery.*
PHRASES **there are no ~s** (*figurative*) ◊ *There are no ~s when it comes to fitness.*

shorten *verb*

ADV. **considerably, dramatically, drastically, greatly, significantly** ◊ *The course has now been ~ed considerably.* | **slightly**
PREP. **by** ◊ *His driving ban has been ~ed by a year.* | **from, to** ◊ *The waiting time has been ~ed dramatically from eight weeks to just one week.*

shorthand *noun*

1 system of writing

VERB + SHORTHAND **learn** | **do** (*BrE*), **take** ◊ *Her secretary was taking ~.* | **take sth down in, write sth down in** ◊ *He took the speech down in ~.*
SHORTHAND + NOUN **typist, writer** (*both BrE*) ◊ *A ~ writer will make a transcript.* | **notes** | **notation**

2 quick way of talking about sth

ADJ. **convenient, useful** | **visual**
VERB + SHORTHAND **use sth as** | **become** ◊ *Smoking became visual ~ for 'cool and rebellious'.*
SHORTHAND + NOUN **description, term** | **way** ◊ *a ~ way of talking about this situation*
PREP. **~ for**

shortlist *noun*

ADJ. **final** | **all-women** (*BrE, politics*)
VERB + SHORTLIST **compile, draw up, make** ◊ *The interviewers have to draw up a ~ of five or six people.* | **put sb on** ◊ *I think we should put her on our ~.* | **choose from** ◊ *They will choose from a ~ of seven candidates.* | **announce**
PREP. **on a/the ~** | **~ for** ◊ *The movie is on the ~ for Best Picture.* | **~ of** ◊ *a ~ of three* ◊ *a ~ of candidates*

shorts *noun*

1 outer clothing

ADJ. **cut-off** (*esp. AmE*), **knee-length** | **baggy, loose** | **tight** | **long, short** | **athletic, basketball, bike** (*esp. AmE*), **board** (= for surfing) (*AmE*), **cycling** (*BrE*), **football** (*BrE*), **gym** (*esp. AmE*), **running, soccer** (*AmE*), **swim** (*AmE*), **swimming** | **Bermuda, cargo** (*esp. AmE*), **khaki, pajama** (*AmE*) ◊ *a pair of khaki cargo ~* | **denim, jean** (*AmE*) | **lycra, spandex** | **cheer** (= cheerleader) (*AmE*)
... OF SHORTS **pair**

2 (*AmE*) underwear

ADJ. **loose** | **tight** | **boxer** (*BrE, AmE*), **boy** (= for women) (*esp. AmE*), **jockey** (*AmE*)
... OF SHORTS **pair**
→ Special page at CLOTHES

shot *noun*

1 act of firing a gun

ADJ. **excellent, fine, good, well-placed** | **clean** ◊ *He killed them with a clean ~ to their heads.* | **lucky** | **random** | **fatal** | **warning** | **clear** | **first, opening** (*often figurative*) ◊ *the opening ~ in the election campaign* | **cheap, parting** (*both figurative*) | **cannon, gun, pistol, rifle** ◊ *I heard a pistol ~.* | **head** ◊ *That man fired the fatal head ~.*
... OF SHOTS **volley** ◊ *A volley of ~s rang out.*
VERB + SHOT **aim** | **fire, take** ◊ *I took a few more ~s at the target, but missed.*
SHOT + VERB **ring out** | **hit sb/sth, strike sb/sth** ◊ *The ~ hit him in the chest.* | **kill sb/sth** | **miss (sb/sth)**
PREP. **~ from** ◊ *a ~ from his rifle* | **~ to** ◊ *She was killed by a single ~ to the head.*

2 person who shoots a gun, etc.

ADJ. **crack, excellent, good** ◊ *She is a crack ~ with a rifle.* | **bad, poor**

3 act of kicking/hitting/throwing a ball

ADJ. **excellent, fine, good, great, superb** (*esp. BrE*), **well-placed** | **awesome** (*esp. BrE*), **brilliant** (*esp. AmE*) (*both informal*) | **errant** (*esp. AmE*), **poor, wayward** (*esp. BrE*) | **long, long-range** | **close-range** | **20-yard, 25-yard, etc.** | **low** | **game-winning** (*AmE*) | **trick**
VERB + SHOT **crack** (*esp. BrE*), **get in, have, take, try** ◊ *He cracked a terrific ~ into the bottom corner of the net.* ◊ *Go on—take another ~.* | **miss** | **scuff** (*BrE*) ◊ *He scuffed a ~ from the edge of the box.* | **block, parry** (*esp. BrE*), **save** ◊ *The goalkeeper parried his first ~ but he scored from the rebound.*
SHOT + VERB **be on target** (*esp. BrE*) | **go wide, miss** ◊ *My first ~ went wide, but my second was right on target.*
PREP. **~ at, ~ on** ◊ *Their captain tried a long ~ on goal.* | **~ from** ◊ *his right-footed ~ from outside the penalty area* ◊ *a superb ~ from Rivaldo*
→ Special page at SPORTS

4 photograph; picture in a film/movie

ADJ. **camera** | **close-up, long, medium** | **aerial, overhead, still** | **tracking, wide-angle, zoom** | **exterior, location** | **establishing, opening** | **action, crowd** | **money** (*figurative, esp. AmE*) | **fashion, publicity** | **cover** | **screen** (usually **screenshot**) (= from a computer) | **mug** (usually **mugshot**) (= photograph of sb's face kept by the police)
... OF SHOTS **series**
VERB + SHOT **get, take** ◊ *I got some great ~s of the runners as they crossed the line.* | **snap** ◊ *Kate snapped a few ~s with her camera through the window.*
SHOT + VERB **show sth** ◊ *a wide-angle ~ showing the Grand Canyon*
PREP. **~ from** ◊ *a ~ from a low angle* | **~ of** ◊ *a publicity ~ of the band performing*

5 (*esp. AmE*) injection of a drug

ADJ. **booster** | **allergy, flu, tetanus**
VERB + SHOT **give sb** | **get, have** ◊ *Have you had all your ~s for your expedition yet?*
PREP. **~ of** ◊ *a ~ of penicillin* ◊ *The applause acted on her like a ~ of adrenalin.*

shotgun noun

ADJ. **12-bore** (BrE), **12-gauge** (AmE), **double-barrelled/
double-barreled**, **pump** (AmE), **pump-action**, **sawed-off**
(AmE), **sawn-off** (BrE) ◇ The men were armed with sawn-off/
sawed-off ~s. | **loaded**
VERB + SHOTGUN **cock** | **fire** | **be armed with**, **carry**, **have**,
hold | **point**, **raise**, **threaten sb with** ◇ The ~ was pointed at
me. | **load**, **reload** | **aim** | **be blasted with**
SHOTGUN + NOUN **licence** (BrE) | **cartridge**, **pellet**, **shell** | **blast**
◇ The cause of death was a ~ blast at close range. | **wound**
PREP. **of a/the ~** ◇ the barrel of a ~ | **with a ~** ◇ He tried to
blow his brains out with a ~.

shoulder noun

1 part of the body

ADJ. **dislocated**, **fractured**, **frozen**, **injured**, **sore**, **wounded**
◇ His frozen ~ has stopped him from playing tennis.
SHOULDER + NOUN **injury** | **blade**, **bones**, **joint**, **muscle**,
socket ◇ The bullet hit him squarely between the ~ blades. |
height, **level** | **harness**, **sling**, **strap** | **pad** | **bag**
PREP. **over your ~** ◇ He slung the sack over his ~ and set off.
PHRASES **a pat on the ~** ◇ He gave me a reassuring pat on the
~. | **~ to ~** ◇ The route of the procession was lined with
police officers standing ~ to ~. | **tap sb on the ~** ◇ I tapped
the man on the ~ and asked him to move.

2 shoulders the part between the two shoulders

ADJ. **broad**, **huge**, **muscled**, **muscular**, **powerful**, **strong**,
wide | **delicate**, **slim** | **narrow**, **thin** | **square** | **round** |
bony | **bowed** | **bare** | **tense**, **tight**
VERB + SHOULDERS **shrug** ◇ When I asked him why he'd done it
he just shrugged his ~s. | **hunch** ◇ He hunched his ~s against
the cold wind. | **drop**, **relax** ◇ Inhale, drop your ~s and raise
your chest. | **roll**, **rotate** ◇ Roll your ~s forward and take a
deep breath. | **square**, **straighten** ◇ In an aggressive
situation, we stand tall and square our ~s.
SHOULDERS + VERB **be bent**, **be bowed**, **be stooped** ◇ She was
crouched with her head forward and her ~s bent. | **droop**,
drop, **sag**, **slump** ◇ My ~s dropped with relief. | **lift**, **shrug** ◇
Her ~s lifted in a vague shrug. | **heave**, **shake**, **twitch** ◇ His
broad ~s heaved with sobs. | **stiffen**, **tense**, **tighten** | **relax**
PREP. **on sb's ~s** ◇ The child sat on her father's ~s to watch the
parade go by.

shout noun

ADJ. **great**, **loud** | **faint**, **muffled** | **distant** | **sudden** | **angry**
| **joyous**, **triumphant** | **warning**
... OF SHOUTS **chorus**
VERB + SHOUT **give**, **let out** | **hear** ◇ I heard her warning ~ too
late. | **be greeted with** | **give sb** (figurative) ◇ Give me a ~ if
you'd like to come with us.
SHOUT + VERB **echo**, **go up**, **ring out** ◇ A great ~ of excitement
went up as she crossed the line.
PREP. **with a ~** ◇ With a ~ of pain, he pulled his hand away. |
~ from ◇ There were ~s of laughter from the crowd. | **~ of** ◇
a ~ of anger/laughter/victory
→ Note at SOUND

shout verb

ADV. **aloud** ◇ 'I'm done for!' he ~ed aloud. | **loudly** | **hoarsely**
| **frantically**, **hysterically**, **wildly** | **angrily**, **furiously** |
happily, **triumphantly** | **almost**, **nearly**, **practically** ◇ He
found he was almost ~ing. | **suddenly** | **back** ◇ 'Go on then!'
he ~ed back at them. | **out** | **down**, **up** ◇ Jorge ~ed up to her.
VERB + SHOUT **want to** | **try to** | **open your mouth to** ◇ He
opened his mouth to ~, but no sound came out. | **begin to**,
start to | **hear sb** ◇ I could hear him ~ing into the telephone.
PREP. **about** ◇ What were they ~ing about? | **above** ◇ We had
to ~ above the noise of the engines. | **after** ◇ We ~ed after
him, but he couldn't hear us. | **at** ◇ There's no need to ~ at
me! | **for** ◇ We ~ed for help. | **in** ◇ to ~ in anger/frustration/
pain | **over** ◇ Emily ~ed over the din of the alarms. | **to** ◇ He
~ed to the driver to stop. | **with** ◇ to ~ with delight/glee/joy
PHRASES **keep on ~ing**, **keep ~ing** | **~ and scream** ◇ They
were surrounded by people ~ing and screaming. | **~ at the
top of your lungs** (AmE), **~ at the top of your voice** (BrE) |
~ in unison ◇ The crowd ~ed back in unison. | **~ yourself**

hoarse ◇ She ~ed herself hoarse, cheering on the team. |
start ~ing, **stop ~ing**

shove noun

ADJ. **friendly**, **gentle**, **light**, **little**, **playful** | **good**, **hard**, **hefty**
(BrE), **mighty**, **powerful**, **violent**
VERB + SHOVE **give sb/sth** ◇ Harry gave him a hefty ~ and he
fell down.
PREP. **with a ~** ◇ She sent him off with a little ~.

shove verb

ADV. **forcefully**, **hard**, **roughly** ◇ I ~d hard until the door
opened. | **gently**, **playfully** | **practically** | **aside**, **away**, **back**
◇ He ~d me roughly aside. | **open** ◇ She ~d open the door.
PREP. **down**, **in** ◇ She ~d the letter in a drawer. | **into**, **out of**,
through ◇ A leaflet was ~d through my letter box. (BrE) ◇ A
leaflet was ~d through my mail slot. (AmE) | **to** ◇ He was ~d
to the ground.
PHRASES **push and ~** ◇ The crowd was pushing and shoving to
get a better view. | **~ your hands in your pockets**, **~ your
hands into your pockets** | **~ sb out of the way** | **~ your
way past sb/sth**, **~ your way through sth** ◇ We ~d our way
through the crowd.

show noun

1 on TV, radio, etc.

ADJ. **live**, **recorded** | **family** | **cable** (AmE), **network** (esp.
AmE), **radio**, **television**, **TV** | **award**, **breakfast**, **cookery**
(BrE), **cooking** (esp. AmE), **cop**, **dating**, **game**, **makeover**
(esp. BrE), **news** (esp. AmE), **quiz**, **reality**, **reunion** (AmE) |
comedy, **sketch** | **satirical**, **topical** | **chat** (esp. BrE), **talk**
(esp. AmE), **call-in** (AmE), **phone-in** (BrE) ◇ a radio phone-
in/call-in ~ | **animated** (BrE), **cartoon** | **pre-game** (AmE) |
one-off (esp. BrE), **special** | **daytime**, **late-night**, **lunchtime**,
morning, **prime-time** (esp. AmE) ◇ late-night talk ~s | **daily**,
nightly (esp. AmE), **weekly** | **forthcoming** (BrE), **upcoming**
(esp. AmE) | **long-running** | **original** ◇ I watched the original
~ as a kid. | **classic**, **entertaining**, **funny**, **great**, **hot** (esp.
AmE), **terrific** ◇ a hot new dating ~ | **cheesy** | **hit**, **popular**,
successful, **top-rated** (esp. AmE) ◇ a hit TV ~ | **award-
winning** ◇ the Emmy award-winning television talk ~ |
flagship (esp. BrE) | **sb's own** ◇ She finally got her own TV ~.
| **syndicated** (esp. AmE) ◇ a nationally syndicated radio ~ |
local, **national** (both esp. AmE) | **interactive**
VERB + SHOW **see**, **watch** ◇ Did you see the Late Show? | **host**
SHOW + VERB **feature sb/sth**, **star sb** ◇ a live ~ featuring the
best of Irish talent
SHOW + NOUN **business**
PREP. **from a/the ~** ◇ a character from the ~ | **on a/the ~** ◇ I
saw her on a news ~ yesterday.
PHRASES **the star of the ~** ◇ The dog was the real star of the ~.
→ Note at PERFORMANCE (for more verbs)

2 performance on stage

ADJ. **cabaret**, **comedy**, **magic**, **musical**, **stand-up** (esp. BrE),
talent, **variety** | **floor** | **stage** | **benefit** (esp. AmE), **charity**
(BrE) | **film** (BrE), **light**, **slide** | **Punch and Judy** (BrE),
puppet | **freak**, **peep** | **one-man**, **one-woman**, **solo** |
road, **touring**, **travelling/traveling** | **fringe** (BrE) | **en-
tertaining**, **great**, **spectacular** ◇ a spectacular light ~ | **sold-
out** | **half-time** (AmE) ◇ the Super Bowl half-time ~
PREP. **from a/the ~** ◇ songs from the ~ | **in a/the ~** ◇ one of
the acts in the ~

3 public display/exhibition

ADJ. **big**, **major** | **annual**, **spring**, **summer** | **local** | **private** |
agricultural (BrE), **flower** (esp. BrE), **horse**, **horticultural**
(BrE) | **boat**, **gun** (esp. AmE), **motor** (esp. BrE), **trade** | **air**,
bodybuilding, **dog** | **art**, **gallery** | **catwalk** (esp. BrE),
fashion, **runway** (AmE) | **pro** (esp. AmE) ◇ a pro bodybuilding
~ in California | **dog-and-pony** (= a complicated business
presentation) (AmE)
VERB + SHOW **have**, **hold**, **organize**, **put on** ◇ They are holding
a big fashion ~ at the Hilton tonight. | **attend**, **go to**

SHOW + VERB **feature sb/sth** ◊ *The ~ features the work of local artists.*
SHOW + NOUN **ring**
PREP. **at a/the ~** ◊ *There were more than 500 exhibitors at the trade ~.* | **on ~** ◊ *The paintings are on ~ until April.*

4 outward expression of an emotion/attitude

ADJ. **big, great** | **brave** | **public**
VERB + SHOW **make, put on** ◊ *Although she hated him, she put on a ~ of politeness.*
PREP. **for ~** ◊ *She pretends to be interested in opera, but it's only for ~.* | **~ of** ◊ *He made a great ~ of welcoming us.*
PHRASES **a ~ of force, a ~ of strength**

show verb

1 make sth clear; let sb see sth

ADV. **clearly, conclusively, convincingly, plainly** ◊ *The figures clearly ~ that her claims are false.* | **consistently, repeatedly** | **diagrammatically, graphically, schematically** ◊ *The results are shown graphically in Figure 2.*
VERB + SHOW **appear to, seem to** | **go to** ◊ *It just goes to ~ what you can do when you really try.* | **aim to, attempt to, seek to, try to** | **be expected to, be likely to** ◊ *Third-quarter figures are likely to ~ a further fall.* | **refuse to** ◊ *Lewis refused to ~ any emotion.* | **be anxious to, be eager to, be happy to, be keen to** (*esp. BrE*) ◊ *Lee was happy to ~ her how it should be done.* | **be designed to** | **let sb** ◊ *Let me ~ you on the map.*
PREP. **to** ◊ *She ~ed her new toy to her friends.*
PHRASES **a chance to ~ sth** ◊ *I'm giving him a chance to ~ what he can do.*

2 be visible

ADV. **hardly** ◊ *It's such a tiny mark, it hardly ~s.*
VERB + SHOW **begin to** | **let sth** ◊ *She tried not to let her disappointment ~.*

showdown noun

ADJ. **climactic, final** ◊ *The scene was set for the final ~.* | **dramatic, ultimate** | **long-awaited, looming** | **military, nuclear** | **Commons, political, Senate** | **courtroom, High Court, Supreme Court** | **championship, quarter-final, semi-final, title, etc.** (*sports*) | **relegation, winner-takes-all** (*both BrE, sports*)
VERB + SHOWDOWN **have** | **avert, avoid** | **face, head for** | **force, seek** ◊ *He was now strong enough to force a ~ with them.*
PREP. **~ against** ◊ *the ~ against Holland in April* | **~ between** ◊ *the title ~ between Brazil and France* | **~ over** ◊ *The government is heading for a ~ over the new proposals.* | **~ with** ◊ *the semi-final ~ with Australia last month*
PHRASES **it comes to a ~** (= a showdown happens) ◊ *Of course I'll support you if it comes to a ~.*

shower noun

1 for washing your body

ADJ. **cold, cool** | **hot, steaming, warm** | **brief, quick** ◊ *I'll just take a quick ~.* | **refreshing, relaxing** | **electric** (*esp. BrE*) | **power** | **en suite, private** | **stall** (*AmE*), **walk-in** | **communal, locker-room** (*AmE*) | **outdoor**
VERB + SHOWER **grab** (*AmE*), **have** (*esp. BrE*), **take** (*AmE*) | **hit** (*esp. AmE*) ◊ *After the game, the boys hit the ~s.*
SHOWER + VERB **run** ◊ *He could hear the ~ running in the bathroom.*
SHOWER + NOUN **cubicle** (*BrE*), **curtain, room, stall** (*AmE*), **unit** (*esp. BrE*) | **block** (*esp. BrE*) ◊ *The plans include changing facilities and ~ blocks.* | **door, head, tray** | **gel** | **cap**

2 of rain or snow

ADJ. **rain, sleet, snow** | **heavy, light** | **intermittent, occasional, odd** (*BrE*) | **scattered** | **frequent** | **blustery, squally** (*BrE*), **thundery** (*BrE*), **wintry** | **April, spring, summer**
VERB + SHOWER **brave** ◊ *They decided to brave the ~s and headed for the coast.*

SHOWER + VERB **die out** ◊ *Scattered ~s will die out by late evening.*

3 of small objects

ADJ. **dust, meteor**
VERB + SHOWER **send** ◊ *A light exploded, sending a ~ of sparks raining down.*
PREP. **~ of** ◊ *The grinding wheel sent out a ~ of sparks.*

4 (*AmE*) party to give presents

ADJ. **baby** | **bridal, wedding**
VERB + SHOWER **have, throw** | **give sb** | **plan, plan for** | **attend**
SHOWER + NOUN **invitation** ◊ *I got a ~ invitation from Katie.* | **gift**
PREP. **~ for** ◊ *a baby ~ for my sister*

showing noun

1 how sb/sth behaves or performs

ADJ. **good, impressive, respectable, strong** | **disappointing, disastrous** (*esp. BrE*), **dismal, lacklustre/lackluster, poor, weak** (*esp. AmE*) ◊ *the party's poor ~ in the election*
VERB + SHOWING **make, put up** ◊ *The opposing team put up a very strong ~.* | **improve on** ◊ *The team will have to improve on today's ~ if it is to survive in the competition.*
PREP. **on sb's ~** ◊ *On its present ~, the party should win the election.* | **~ against** ◊ *the euro's strong ~ against the dollar* | **~ by, ~ from** ◊ *It was a great ~ by the Brazilian team.*

2 of a film/movie, etc.

ADJ. **private, public** | **late-night, midnight** ◊ *a midnight ~ of a B-movie at the Phoenix* | **repeat** ◊ *a repeat ~ of the series on Channel 9*
VERB + SHOWING **attend, go to** ◊ *They attended a private ~ of the new Disney movie.* | **catch, see** | **get, have, receive** | **give sth**

showroom noun

ADJ. **car, carpet, furniture** | **retail** | **dealer**
VERB + SHOWROOM **go to, visit** | **open** | **hit, reach** ◊ *The new model hits ~s in November.*
SHOWROOM + NOUN **floor** ◊ *By the end of the decade these cars could be on the ~ floor.* | **price** | **condition** (*esp. BrE*) ◊ *He managed to find a second-hand Ferrari in ~ condition.* | **model** (*BrE*) ◊ *They took 10% off the price of the computer as it was a ~ model.*

shrapnel noun

ADJ. **flying** ◊ *He was hit in the arm by flying ~.* | **deadly**
... OF SHRAPNEL **piece**
VERB + SHRAPNEL **be hit by, be killed by, be wounded by, take** (*esp. AmE*) ◊ *He took ~ to his leg.* | **have** ◊ *She still has ~ in her left arm.* | **send** ◊ *The rocket sent ~ in every direction.* | **remove** ◊ *surgery to remove ~*
SHRAPNEL + VERB **fly** ◊ *The bomb exploded, sending ~ flying through the trees.* | **be lodged** ◊ *An air strike left him with ~ lodged in his chest.*
SHRAPNEL + NOUN **wound**
PREP. **~ from** ◊ *the ~ from the grenade* | **~ in** ◊ *a piece of ~ in her back*

shred noun

1 small thin piece of sth

ADJ. **fine, thin** | **tattered** ◊ *the tattered ~s of their flag*
PREP. **in ~s, into ~s** ◊ *Cut the orange peel into thin ~s.* ◊ *Their economy is in ~s.* (*figurative*) | **~ of** ◊ *Just a few ~s of cloth were left.*
PHRASES **cut, rip, tear, etc. sth to ~s** (*figurative*) ◊ *Their case was torn to ~s by the lawyer.*

2 very small amount of sth

ADJ. **every** ◊ *With her had gone every ~ of hope he had for the future.* | **last, remaining** ◊ *She was hanging on to the last remaining ~s of her reputation.* | **one, single, slightest** (all used in negative phrases) ◊ *There is not one ~ of evidence in this case.*
PREP. **~ of** ◊ *There is not a ~ of doubt in my mind that we will win.*

shriek noun

ADJ. **loud** | **little** ◇ *She gave a little ~ of delight.* | **blood-curdling, ear-piercing, high-pitched, piercing, shrill**
VERB + SHRIEK **emit, give, let out** | **stifle** | **hear**
PREP. **with a ~** ◇ *She fell to the floor with a ~ of pain.* | **~ of** ◇ *Shrieks of laughter came from the bedroom.*
PHRASES **a ~ of delight, a ~ of laughter, a ~ of pain, a ~ of rage**
→ Note at SOUND

shriek verb

ADV. **aloud, loudly** | **out** | **happily, hysterically** | **almost, nearly, practically** ◇ *He almost ~ed when he saw her.*
VERB + SHRIEK **hear sb**
PREP. **at** ◇ *Stop ~ing at me!* | **in** ◇ *She ~ed in terror.* | **with** ◇ *The audience ~ed with laughter.*
PHRASES **~ at the top of your lungs** (*AmE*)

shrine noun

ADJ. **hallowed, holy, religious, sacred** ◇ *This ~ is sacred to the Hindu god Vishnu.* | **Buddhist, Catholic, Muslim, Shinto, etc.** | **makeshift** ◇ *a makeshift ~ near the spot where he died* | **ancient** | **ancestral, family, household, national** | **roadside**
VERB + SHRINE **build, create, erect** | **turn sth into** | **become** | **dedicate** ◇ *a ~ dedicated to the sea goddess* | **go on a pilgrimage to, make a pilgrimage to, visit** ◇ *On his recovery he made a pilgrimage to the ~ of St John.*
SHRINE + NOUN **city** | **room**
PREP. **at a/the ~** ◇ *The people worshipped at wayside ~s.* | **~ of** ◇ *the ~ of St Cuthbert at Durham* | **~ to** ◇ *She had turned the room into a ~ to her dead son.*

shrink verb

1 become smaller
ADV. **considerably, dramatically, significantly** | **a little, slightly, etc.** | **further** | **fast, rapidly** ◇ *We are competing in a market that is ~ing fast.* | **gradually, slowly** | **steadily**
PREP. **by** ◇ *Their profits shrank by 4% last year.* | **from, to** ◇ *Their share of the market has shrunk from 14% to 5%.*
PHRASES **~ in size** ◇ *Households have been ~ing in size but increasing in number.*

2 move away
ADV. **a little** ◇ *He shrank a little at the sight of the blood.* | **visibly** | **instinctively** | **away, back, down**
VERB + SHRINK **try to**
PREP. **against** ◇ *He shrank back against the wall.* | **in** ◇ *She shrank back in terror.* | **into** ◇ *I shrank back into the shadows.* | **from** ◇ *She shrank from his touch.*

shroud noun

ADJ. **burial, funeral, mourning**
VERB + SHROUD **wrap sb in** ◇ *A human form lay there, wrapped in a ~.*
PREP. **in a/the ~** | **~ of** (*figurative*) ◇ *The nuclear project was cloaked in a ~ of secrecy.* ◇ *a ~ of darkness/mist*

shrub noun

ADJ. **deciduous, evergreen** | **dwarf, large, low, medium-sized, small, tall** | **spring, spring-flowering, etc.** | **flowering** | **thorny, woody** | **dense, thick** | **fast-growing, vigorous** | **native** | **ornamental, wall** | **overgrown**
VERB + SHRUB **grow** | **plant, put in** | **dig out** (*AmE*), **dig up, take out** | **replant** | **cut back, prune, trim** (*esp. AmE*) ◇ *Overgrown deciduous ~s can be cut back at this time of year.*
SHRUB + VERB **grow** | *These ~s don't grow well here.* | **flower**
SHRUB + NOUN **species** | **rose**
PHRASES **be planted with ~s** ◇ *The bed is planted with flowering ~s.* | **a variety of ~**

shrug noun

ADJ. **little, slight, small** | **simple** ◇ *The answer was a simple*

~. | **careless, indifferent** | **casual, nonchalant** | **dismissive** | **half-hearted, helpless, resigned** | **weary** | **apologetic** | **self-deprecating** | **mental** ◇ *With a mental ~, he decided to tell the truth.* | **Gallic** (*BrE*)
VERB + SHRUG **give** ◇ *The boy gave a slight ~ and walked away.*
PREP. **in a ~** ◇ *She lifted her shoulders in a little ~* | **with a ~** ◇ *'I don't know!' she said with a ~.* | **~ of** ◇ *a ~ of resignation*
PHRASES **a ~ of the/your shoulders** ◇ *He replied with a ~ of his shoulders.*

shrug verb

ADV. **lightly, slightly** | **carelessly, dismissively, indifferently, nonchalantly, offhandedly** ◇ *She shrugged nonchalantly and turned away.* | **casually** | **wearily** | **uncomfortably** | **apologetically, awkwardly, sheepishly** | **helplessly** ◇ *He shrugged helplessly and said nothing.* | **innocently, modestly** | **good-naturedly** | **just, merely, only, simply** ◇ *He merely shrugged his shoulders in reply.*

shudder noun

ADJ. **little, slight, small, tiny** | **deep, great, violent** | **involuntary**
VERB + SHUDDER **give** ◇ *She gave a little ~ when she touched his clammy hand.* | **feel** | **repress, suppress** ◇ *He suppressed a ~ of disgust.* | **send** ◇ *The sight of the body sent a ~ through him.*
SHUDDER + VERB **go through sb/sth, pass through sb/sth, rack sb/sth, run through sb/sth** ◇ *A ~ of pain racked his body.*
PREP. **with a ~** ◇ *He remembered that awful moment with a ~.* | **~ of** ◇ *a ~ of relief*

shudder verb

ADV. **convulsively, uncontrollably, violently** | **slightly** | **involuntarily** ◇ *She ~ed involuntarily as he approached her.* | **inwardly** | **visibly**
VERB + SHUDDER **make sb** ◇ *The sight of the dead body made them ~.*
PREP. **at** ◇ *She ~ed at the memory of school exams.* | **in** ◇ *Joe ~ed in disgust.* | **through** ◇ *A deep sigh ~ed through her body.* | **with** ◇ *His whole body ~ed with fury.*
PHRASES **~ at the thought (of sth)** ◇ *I ~ed at the thought of going back to school.*

shuffle verb

1 walk by sliding your feet along
ADV. **quickly, slowly** | **awkwardly** ◇ *Simon ~d awkwardly up to them.* | **quietly** | **along, away, back, forward, off, out, over, sideways** ◇ *The crowd ~d slowly forward.*
PREP. **across, down, into, out of, towards/toward, etc.**

2 move your body/feet around
ADV. **nervously, uncomfortably, uneasily** ◇ *She ~d nervously on the bench.* | **about** (*esp. BrE*), **around** ◇ *The boys ~d around uncomfortably.*
PHRASES **~ from foot to foot, ~ from one foot to the other** | **~ in your chair, ~ in your seat**

shut adj.

1 in a closed position
VERBS **be, look** | **bang, blow, clang, click, close, slam, slide, swing** ◇ *The window blew ~.* ◇ *The doors closed ~ behind me.* ◇ *The elevator door slid ~.* | **remain, stay** | **be clenched, be jammed** ◇ *His jaw was clenched ~.* | **clamp sth** ◇ *I clamped my mouth ~.* | **be bolted, be glued, be nailed, be screwed, be sealed, be sewn, be welded** ◇ *The windows were sealed ~.* | **bang sth, close sth, kick sth, pull sth, slam sth, slide sth, snap sth** ◇ *He slammed the case ~.* ◇ *She snapped ~ a file on her desk.* | **be drawn** ◇ *The curtains were drawn ~.* | **leave sth** ◇ *I'll leave the window ~ for now.* | **keep sth** ◇ *The gates are always kept ~.* ◇ *Afraid to ask seemingly stupid questions, I kept my mouth ~.* (*figurative*)
ADV. **firmly, properly, tightly** ◇ *The door was firmly ~.*

PHRASES **squeeze your eyes ~** ◇ *She squeezed her eyes ~ to keep the tears from coming.*

2 (*BrE*) not open to the public → See also CLOSED

VERBS **be, look** ◇ *The bars all look ~ to me.* | **remain**
PREP. **for** ◇ *The park is now ~ for the winter.*

shutter *noun*

1 cover for a window

ADJ. **closed, open** ◇ *He left the ~ open.* | **metal, steel, wooden** | **security** (*BrE*), **window** | **louvred/louvered**
VERB + SHUTTER **have** | **fling open, fold back, open, throw back, throw open** ◇ *He threw open the ~s to cool the room.* | **close, pull down, put up** (*esp. BrE*) ◇ *The store had put up the ~s for the night.* | **install**
SHUTTER + VERB **be down, come down** ◇ *All the ~s in the street were down.* ◇ *I could feel the ~s coming down in her mind.* (*figurative*)
PREP. **behind ~ a/the** ◇ *She could be seen waiting for him behind half-closed ~s.* | **through ~ a/the** ◇ *Daylight was filtering through the ~s when he woke up.*

2 part of a camera

ADJ. **camera**
VERB + SHUTTER **click, press**
SHUTTER + VERB **click** ◇ *You could hear hundreds of camera ~s clicking.*
SHUTTER + NOUN **speed** ◇ *You will need a fast ~ speed to photograph racing.* | **button, release** ◇ *to press the ~ release*

shuttle *noun*

1 plane/bus/train

ADJ. **airport, hotel**
VERB + SHUTTLE **catch, fly on, get, take**
SHUTTLE + NOUN **bus, flight, service, train** ◇ *The supermarket operates a complimentary ~ service.* | **diplomacy** (= international talks carried out by sb who travels between two or more countries)
PREP. **on a/the ~** ◇ *We'll fly up on the ~.* | **~ between** ◇ *the ~ between Adrar and Oran* | **~ from, ~ to** ◇ *I took the ~ from Washington to New York.*

2 spacecraft

ADJ. **space**
VERB + SHUTTLE **fly, launch**
SHUTTLE + NOUN **craft** | **crew** | **flight, mission** | **landing** | **fleet** | **commander, pilot**
PREP. **aboard the ~, on board the ~**

shy *adj.*

VERBS **be, feel, look, seem, sound** ◇ *Please don't be shy—I won't eat you!* | **become, get, grow**
ADV. **extremely, fairly, very, etc.** | **desperately, excessively, painfully, terribly** ◇ *As a teenager I was painfully ~.* | **all** ◇ *She went all ~ and hid behind her mother.* | **almost** | **a little, slightly, etc.** | **naturally** ◇ *He is a naturally ~, retiring man.* | **chronically** (*esp. BrE*)
PREP. **around** ◇ *She was terribly ~ around strangers.* | **of** ◇ *I was a little ~ of them at first.* | **with** ◇ *You don't have to be ~ with me, you know.*

shyness *noun*

ADJ. **natural** | **extreme, paralysing/paralyzing** | **initial**
VERB + SHYNESS **be overcome with, have** ◇ *He was suddenly overcome with ~.* | **conceal** (*esp. BrE*) | **forget, get over, lose, overcome** ◇ *She had to work very hard to overcome her ~.* | **cure**
SHYNESS + VERB **disappear**

sick *noun* the sick

ADJ. **chronic, long-term** (*both esp. BrE*)
VERB + THE SICK **visit** | **aid, care for, comfort, help, look after** (*esp. BrE*), **minister to, nurse, take care of, tend** ◇ *workers who are caring for the ~ and elderly* | **treat** | **cure, heal** ◇

the Church's mission to preach the gospel and heal the ~ | **pray for**
PHRASES **the ~ and wounded** ◇ *The ~ and wounded were evacuated from the war zone.*

sick *adj.*

1 not well → See also ILL

VERBS **be, look** | **become, fall** (*formal*), **get** (*esp. AmE*) ◇ *He fell ~ with yellow fever.* ◇ *She was afraid she would get ~ if she stayed in that place any longer.*
ADV. **chronically** (*esp. BrE*), **desperately, extremely, seriously, terribly, very** ◇ *The home has 20 chronically ~ and disabled residents.* ◇ *a very ~ woman in the next bed* | **mentally**
PREP. **from** ◇ *The workers got ~ from radiation exposure.* | **with** ◇ *She was ~ with cancer.*
PHRASES **be off ~** ◇ *John's not in the office today. He's off ~.*

2 (*esp. BrE*) wanting to vomit

VERBS **be** (*BrE*), **feel, look** ◇ *I was ~ three times in the night.* ◇ *Dad, I feel ~!* | **get** ◇ *I get ~ if I sit in the back seat.* | **make sb** ◇ *If you eat all that chocolate it'll make you ~.*
ADV. **horribly, very, violently** ◇ *He leaned sideways and was violently ~.* | **almost** | **continually** | **physically** ◇ *Every time I think about it I feel physically ~.*
PREP. **with** ◇ *Laura felt almost ~ with embarrassment.*
PHRASES **be as ~ as a dog** | **~ to your stomach** (*AmE*) ◇ *I feel ~ to my stomach just thinking about it.*

3 bored/disgusted/annoyed

VERBS **be** | **become, get** ◇ *I'm getting ~ of all these delays.* | **make sb** ◇ *Her attitude makes me ~.*
ADV. **heartily** (*esp. BrE*), **really** ◇ *He was getting heartily ~ of all the false sympathy.* | **absolutely, thoroughly** | **a bit, a little, pretty, rather** ◇ *She was getting a little ~ of his moaning.*
PREP. **of** ◇ *I'm getting ~ of you leaving things in a mess.*
PHRASES **~ and tired of sth, ~ to the back teeth of sth** (*BrE*), **~ to death of sth** | **(as) ~ as a parrot** (*BrE*)

4 cruel/in bad taste

VERBS **be, seem, sound** ◇ *You're really ~, you know that?*
ADV. **extremely, fairly, very, etc.**
PHRASES **~ in the head** ◇ *Whoever started the fire must be ~ in the head.*

sickness *noun*

1 state of being ill

ADJ. **chronic** | **long, long-term** (*esp. BrE*) ◇ *The policy includes long-term ~ cover.*
VERB + SICKNESS **feign** ◇ *I tricked my father by feigning ~.*
SICKNESS + NOUN **absence** (*BrE*) | **benefit** (*BrE*) | **cover, insurance** (*esp. BrE*) | **levels, rates** ◇ *Staff ~ rates are at record levels.*
PREP. **due to ~, owing to ~, through ~** ◇ *The Personnel Department keeps a record of employees absent through ~.*

2 (*esp. BrE*) nausea

VERB + SICKNESS **suffer, suffer from**
SICKNESS + VERB **rise** ◇ *The ~ rose inside him.*
PHRASES **a feeling of ~** ◇ *Several workers complained of feelings of ~ and headaches.*

3 particular type of illness

ADJ. **acute, chronic, severe** | **air, car, motion, sea** (usually **seasickness**), **travel** (usually **travel-sickness**) (*BrE*) | **altitude, mountain** | **decompression, radiation, sleeping** | **morning**
VERB + SICKNESS **cause, induce** ◇ *This activity may induce motion ~.* | **experience, get** | **prevent** | **cure, treat**
→ Special page at ILLNESS

side *noun*

1 flat surface of sth thin

ADJ. **flip, reverse** ◇ *The reverse ~ of the coin has a picture of a flower.*

2 either of the two parts of a place/object

ADJ. **far, opposite, other** ◇ *At the other ~ of the room, a group of people were clustered around the fire.* | **near** | **right, wrong** ◇ *A car was coming in their direction on the wrong ~ of the road.* | **left-hand, right-hand** ◇ *the left-hand ~ of the page* | **east, west, etc.** | **leeward, seaward, windward** ◇ *the sunny, leeward ~ of the island* | **port** (= left side of a boat), **starboard** ◇ *The ship was damaged on her starboard ~.* | **driver's, passenger** ◇ *She got in the passenger ~ of the car.*

PREP. **~ of** ◇ *the ~ of the road* | **at one ~, at the ~** ◇ *Some people were standing at one ~ of the room.* | **down one ~, down the ~** ◇ *A long bench runs down one ~ of the room.* | **from ~ to ~** ◇ *She shook her head from ~ to ~.* | **on the ~** ◇ *a factory on the west ~ of town* | **on one ~, to one ~** (= not in the middle) ◇ *He stood with his head cocked to one ~.*

PHRASES **sunny ~ up** (AmE) ◇ *I'd like my eggs sunny ~ up.*

3 right/left part of your body

ADJ. **left, left-hand, right, right-hand** ◇ *the right-hand ~ of the brain*

SIDE + VERB **ache** (often figurative), **hurt** ◇ *I laughed until my ~s ached.*

PREP. **down your ~** ◇ *He felt a pain down his left ~.* | **in the/your ~** ◇ *I've a pain in my ~.* | **on your ~** ◇ *I always sleep on my ~ because I'm not comfortable on my back.* | **onto your ~** ◇ *Emily turned onto her ~ and yawned.*

PHRASES **at sb's ~** ◇ *He rushed to be at her ~.* | **by ~** ◇ *The two sat ~ by ~ on the bench.* | **a pain in your ~** ◇ *I felt a sharp pain in my ~.* | **a thorn in the ~** (figurative) ◇ *The trade deficit is a thorn in the ~ of the US economy.*

4 aspect/quality of sb/sth

ADJ. **bright, plus, positive, sunny** (esp. AmE) ◇ *When things go badly, try to look on the bright ~.* (BrE) ◇ *Look at the bright side—you can spend more time at home.* (AmE) | **dark, negative, seamy, seedy, ugly** ◇ *This murder highlights the seamy ~ of Hollywood.* | **flip** (esp. AmE) ◇ *The flip ~ of nationalism is racism.* | **caring, creative, feminine** ◇ *She likes men who do not hide their feminine ~.* | **lighter** ◇ *Bob is hoping to show off his lighter ~.* | **business, commercial, financial, management, marketing** ◇ *I had nothing to do with the financial ~ of the company.* | **demand, supply** (both business) ◇ *What can we do on the supply ~ to make this market more competitive?*

VERB + SIDE **have** ◇ *He's usually very kind, but he has his less positive ~ too.* | **show** | **hide** | **see** ◇ *He had never seen this ~ of her before.*

PREP. **~ to** ◇ *There are two ~s to every story.*

PHRASES **sb's ~ of the story** ◇ *The book gave him the opportunity to give his ~ of the story.* ◇ *The book gave him the opportunity to put his ~ of the story.* (BrE) | **see the funny ~ (of sth)** (esp. BrE) ◇ *Fortunately, Julie saw the funny ~ when I spilled coffee on her.*

5 in a war, argument, etc.

ADJ. **opposing** | **losing, winning** | **Democratic, Republican**

VERB + SIDE **choose** ◇ *War forces people to choose ~s.* | **switch** ◇ *He switched ~s and joined the opposition.*

SIDE + VERB **accuse sb** ◇ *Each ~ accused the other of firing first.* | **argue sth** ◇ *Let both ~s argue their case.* | **want sth** | **agree, disagree**

PREP. **on ~** ◇ *He was on the losing ~.*

PHRASES **on both ~s** ◇ *There were casualties on both ~s of the conflict.*

6 (BrE) **team**

ADJ. **good, strong** | **full-strength** ◇ *France fielded a full-strength ~.* | **losing, winning** | **away, home** ◇ *The home ~ scored in the opening ten minutes.* | **League, Test** (in cricket)

VERB + SIDE **captain, skipper** (informal) | **lead, steer** ◇ *He steered his ~ to victory.* | **beat, bowl, bowl out, dismiss** (all often passive) ◇ *The away ~ were dismissed for 192.* | **field** ◇ *Sussex are likely to field a strong ~.*

SIDE + VERB **win (sth)** | **play** | **battle, clash** | **dominate (sth)** | **struggle** ◇ *Both ~s struggled to find any sort of form.* | **score** | **equalize, level** | **concede** ◇ *His ~ conceded two goals in their last match.*

PHRASES **let the ~ down** (figurative) ◇ *I felt I was letting the ~*

---

down by not going to the wedding. | **put your ~ ahead, put your ~ in front** ◇ *Lampard scored a goal to put his ~ ahead.*

side effect *noun*

ADJ. **common** | **possible, potential** | **adverse, bad, dangerous, debilitating, deleterious** (esp. AmE), **harmful, nasty, negative, toxic, undesirable, unexpected, unfortunate, unpleasant, unwanted** | **deadly, fatal** | **major, serious, severe, significant** | **mild, minimal, minor** | **beneficial, positive** | **long-term** | **physical** | **drug** | **known, reported** ◇ *This drug has no known ~s.*

VERB + SIDE EFFECT **cause, have, produce** ◇ *The treatment has some unfortunate ~s.* | **develop** | **experience, suffer** | **minimize, reduce**

PREP. **~ from** ◇ *The patient suffered severe ~s from the drug.* | **~ of** ◇ *The drug has the beneficial ~ of lowering the patient's blood pressure.* | **~ on** ◇ *The medication can have adverse ~s on the patient.*

sideline *noun*

ADJ. **little, lucrative, nice, profitable, useful** (all esp. BrE) ◇ *He decided to turn his hobby into a lucrative ~.* ◇ *He had found himself a nice little ~ painting windows.*

VERB + SIDELINE **have** | **develop**

PREP. **~ for** ◇ *Cider-making was a ~ for many farmers.* | **~ in** ◇ *She is developing a nice little ~ in babysitting for friends.* | **~ to** ◇ *The restaurant started out as a ~ to his main business.*

sidewalk *noun* (AmE) → See also PAVEMENT

ADJ. **city, public** | **busy, crowded** | **deserted, empty** ◇ *A handful of pedestrians walked down empty ~s.* | **narrow, wide** | **cracked, uneven** | **brick, cement, concrete, wooden** | **icy, snow-covered, wet**

VERB + SIDEWALK **line** ◇ *Elm trees lined the ~.* | **litter** ◇ *Newspapers and broken glass litter the ~.* | **sweep** ◇ *the hard-working neighbors who sweep the ~s in front of their houses* | **block** | **cover** ◇ *Snow covered the ~.* | **shovel** ◇ *In the winter he worked shoveling ~s.* | **sit on, stand on, step onto** | **walk, walk along, walk down, walk up** ◇ *As she walked the ~s of the campus, Jillie thought about Leo.*

SIDEWALK + VERB **lead (to sth)** ◇ *the ~ leading to her house*

SIDEWALK + NOUN **cafe** | **table** ◇ *They relaxed over wine at a ~ table.* | **vendor** | **chalk**

siege *noun*

ADJ. **lengthy, long, prolonged** (esp. BrE) | **four-day, ten-hour, etc.** | **armed, gun, police** (esp. BrE) | **economic, military** ◇ *Under military and economic ~, entire economic sectors have collapsed.*

VERB + SIEGE **lay** ◇ *An angry mob laid ~ to City Hall.* | **break** | **end, lift, raise, relieve** (= arrive to help the people in a siege) ◇ *The opposition pledged to lift a ~ of government buildings.* | **withstand** ◇ *This fortress could withstand a ~ for years if necessary.* | **survive**

SIEGE + VERB **last** ◇ *The ~ lasted two years.* | **begin, end** ◇ *The seven-hour armed ~ at the school ended peacefully.*

SIEGE + NOUN **warfare** | **engine, tower, weapon** | **mentality** (figurative) ◇ *His views are typical of the ~ mentality of this administration.*

PREP. **~ at/the ~** ◇ *soldiers wounded at the ~ of Charleston* | **during a/the ~** | **under ~** ◇ *At the very end of the war, the city again came under ~.* | **~ of**

PHRASES **a state of ~** ◇ *The police placed the city under a virtual state of ~.*

sieve *noun*

ADJ. **fine, large**

VERB + SIEVE **strain sth through** | **pass sth through, press sth through, push sth through** | **place sth in**

PREP. **in a/the ~** ◇ *Wash the rice in a ~ under cold running water.* | **through a/the ~** ◇ *Strain the cream through a fine ~ into the egg mixture.*

sift *verb* examine sth very carefully

ADV. **carefully** | **out** ◇ *They will try to ~ out the winners and the losers.*
PREP. **for** ◇ *He's mentally ~ing for truths.* | **through** ◇ *They spent days carefully ~ing through the evidence.*
PHRASES **spend hours ~ing through sth, spend time ~ing through sth** ◇ *I spent hours ~ing through those heavy art books.*

sigh *noun*

ADJ. **big, deep, great, heavy, huge** | **little, slight, small, soft** | **loud, quiet** | **audible, silent** ◇ *There was an audible ~ of relief when the news came through that nobody was hurt.* | **inward** ◇ *Nancy heaved an inward ~ but did as her son suggested.* | **exaggerated** | **long** | **exhausted, long-suffering, weary** | **defeated, resigned** | **wistful** ◇ *His departure prompted a few wistful ~s and the odd tear from admirers.* | **annoyed, exasperated, frustrated, irritated** (*esp. AmE*) | **relieved** | **contented, satisfied** | **collective** ◇ *The crowd breathed a collective ~ of relief.*
VERB + SIGH **breathe, give, heave, let out, release** ◇ *I breathed a ~ of relief.* | **hold back, repress, stifle, suppress** | **hear**
SIGH + VERB **escape sb** ◇ *A weary ~ escaped him.* | **come** ◇ *A heavy ~ came from her mother.*
PREP. **on a ~** ◇ *She let out her breath on a ~.* | **with a ~** ◇ *'I suppose we'd better get back to work!' he said with a heavy ~.* | **~ of** ◇ *She gave a deep ~ of contentment.*
PHRASES **a ~ of relief**
→ Note at SOUND

sigh *verb*

ADV. **deeply, heavily** ◇ *She ~ed heavily and sat down.* | **softly** | **audibly, loudly** | **inwardly** | **a little** | **contentedly, happily** ◇ *She looked at her son and ~ed happily.* | **dreamily** ◇ *The girl watching him ~ed dreamily.* | **dejectedly, sadly, wistfully** | **resignedly** | **wearily** ◇ *He ~ed wearily as he looked at the pile of work.* | **angrily, exasperatedly, impatiently**
PREP. **in** ◇ *He ~ed in exasperation.* | **with** ◇ *We ~ed with relief when the noise stopped.*

sight *noun*

1 ability to see → See also EYESIGHT

VERB + SIGHT **have** ◇ *She has very little ~ in her left eye.* | **lose** ◇ *He's lost the ~ of one eye.* | **regain** | **save** ◇ *The surgeons battled to save her ~.* | **restore**
SIGHT + VERB **deteriorate, fail, go** (*all esp. BrE*) ◇ *I think my ~ is beginning to go.* | **return** ◇ *His ~ returned by degrees.*
SIGHT + NOUN **test** (*BrE*) | **defects** (*BrE*), **problems** | **loss** (*BrE*) ◇ *This disease is the main cause of ~ loss among those aged 50 and over.*
PHRASES **the/your sense of ~**

2 act/moment of seeing sth

VERB + SIGHT **catch, get, have** ◇ *She suddenly caught ~ of the look on her mother's face.* ◇ *We will soon get our first ~ of the Statue of Liberty.* | **keep** ◇ *She kept ~ of him in her mirror.* | **lose**
SIGHT + NOUN **gag** ◇ *The movie is filled with dozens of funny ~ gags.*
PREP. **at the ~ (of)** ◇ *Her knees went weak at the ~ of him.* | **on ~** ◇ *Soldiers have been ordered to shoot looters on ~ (= as soon as they see them).*
PHRASES **at first ~** ◇ *He looked at first ~ like a tourist.* ◇ *It was love at first ~.* | **cannot bear the ~ of sth, cannot stand the ~ of sth** (= hate seeing sb/sth) ◇ *I can't stand the ~ of blood.* | **a clear ~ of sth** (*esp. BrE*) ◇ *He didn't shoot until he had a clear ~ of the goal.* | **know sb by ~** (= to recognize sb without knowing them well) | **the mere ~ of sb/sth, the very ~ of sb/sth** ◇ *The mere ~ of her sitting there made his heart beat faster.* | **sick of the ~ of sb/sth** (*esp. BrE*) ◇ *We've shared an office for too long and we're sick of the ~ of each*

other. | **~ unseen** ◇ *I bought it, ~ unseen (= without seeing it).*

3 position where sth can be seen

VERB + SIGHT **come into** ◇ *Then the towers of the castle came into ~.* | **disappear from, vanish from** ◇ *She watched until the car disappeared from ~.* | **block, block out** | **hide (sth) from, remove sth from** ◇ *I hid the papers from ~.*
PREP. **in ~** ◇ *Keep their car in ~ for as long as you can.* ◇ *The end is in ~ (= will happen soon).* (*figurative*) | **out of ~** ◇ *He kept out of ~ behind a pillar.* ◇ *You'd better stay out of ~ until they go.* | **within ~ of** ◇ *Her staff of 30 work in an industrial loft within ~ of Logan Airport.*
PHRASES **in full ~ of sb** ◇ *He tried to break into a car in full ~ of a policeman.* | **in plain ~** ◇ *They waited until the enemy was in plain ~.* | **be nowhere in ~** ◇ *Her father was nowhere in ~.* | **come in ~ of sb/sth** ◇ *At last we came in ~ of a few houses.* | **no end in ~** ◇ *The violence continues with no end in ~.* | **not leave sb's ~** ◇ *He won't let the children leave his ~.* | **sb's line of ~** ◇ *She was now standing just out of his line of ~.* | **not let sb/sth out of your ~** ◇ *Whatever you do, don't let them out of your ~!*

4 sth that you see

ADJ. **common, familiar, regular** (*esp. BrE*) ◇ *Tom was a pretty familiar ~ around the casino.* | **bizarre, odd, rare, strange, unexpected, unfamiliar, unlikely** (*esp. BrE*), **unusual** | **amazing, awe-inspiring, awesome, beautiful, breathtaking, extraordinary, fine, impressive, inspiring, magnificent, spectacular, splendid** (*esp. BrE*), **unforgettable, wonderful** | **depressing, pathetic, pitiful, sad, sorry, unedifying** (*BrE*) ◇ *He really did look a sorry ~, with his clothes covered in mud.* | **disturbing, ghastly, gruesome, horrible, horrific, horrifying, terrible, terrifying** | **welcome** ◇ *Dan's face was a welcome ~.*
VERB + SIGHT **behold, see, witness** ◇ *This is a ~ not often seen on concert stages in this country.* ◇ *I witnessed the awful ~ of children drinking dirty water from puddles.* | **look** (*BrE, informal*) ◇ *You look a ~ in that hat!* | **enjoy** ◇ *Who does not enjoy the ~ and sounds of birds in the country?*
SIGHT + VERB **greet** ◇ *An appalling ~ greeted her.*
PHRASES **be quite a ~** ◇ *The military parade was quite a ~.* | **be spared the ~ of sth** ◇ *Thankfully, we were spared the ~ of his naked body.* | **not a pretty ~** ◇ *I'm not a pretty ~ when I get out of bed in the morning.* | **~s and sounds** ◇ *The ~s and sounds of the city distracted her from her work.*

5 sights places of interest

ADJ. **famous, historic**
VERB + SIGHTS **see, take in, visit** ◇ *Let's get out of the hotel and see the ~s.*

6 on gun/telescope

ADJ. **gun** (usually *gunsight*) | **adjustable, fixed** | **optical, telescopic** | **night, thermal, thermal-imaging** | **laser** | **front, rear**
VERB + SIGHT **adjust, align** ◇ *to align the ~s on the target*
PREP. **in your ~** ◇ *He fixed the deer in his ~s and pulled the trigger.*

7 sights your aim, attention, etc.

VERB + SIGHTS **have sb/sth in, have sb/sth within** ◇ *Rossi has the defending champion in her ~s in tomorrow's race.* | **fix, train, turn** ◇ *She turned her ~s on Florida's adoption laws.* | **lower, raise** ◇ *After failing to get into college, he lowered his ~s and got a job in a bar.*
PHRASES **have your ~s set on sth, set your ~s on sth** ◇ *She has her ~s set on becoming a writer.* | **set your ~s high, set your ~s low** ◇ *He says he wants to win the trophy, but I think he's setting his ~s too high.*

sighting *noun*

ADJ. **confirmed, unconfirmed** | **possible** | **reported** | **rare** | **celebrity** (*AmE*), **UFO**
VERB + SIGHTING **have** ◇ *We now have three confirmed ~s of an enemy plane.* | **report** | **follow up** (*esp. BrE*), **investigate** ◇ *The police are now following up a reported ~ of the man's car.*
PREP. **~ of**

sightseeing *noun*

ADJ. **a little**
... OF SIGHTSEEING **day** ◊ *three days of ~ in Beijing*
VERB + SIGHTSEEING **do, go** ◊ *We did some ~ in the morning.* ◊ *It's too hot to go ~.*
SIGHTSEEING + NOUN **tour, trip**

sign *noun*

1 sth that shows that sth exists/may happen

ADJ. **classic, clear, definite, distinct, obvious, real, sure, telltale, unmistakable** ◊ *He displayed the classic ~s of post-traumatic stress disorder.* ◊ *the telltale ~s of drug abuse* | **telling** ◊ *The lack of interest in the media is a telling ~ of the industry's health.* | **subtle** ◊ *I detected the subtle ~s of disapproval.* | **external, outward, visible** ◊ *All the outward ~s of growth in the market are there.* | **tangible** | **early, first** ◊ *Strong dislikes of foods are early ~s of pregnancy.* | **increasing** | **encouraging, good, healthy, hopeful, positive, promising, welcome** ◊ *He was silent. It was a good ~.* | **bad, disturbing, troubling** (*esp. AmE*) | **danger, ominous, warning** ◊ *The warning ~s were present from the start.* ◊ *Are appliances you buy safe? We point out the danger ~s.* | **vital** ◊ *She checked his vital ~s and found that his pulse was slow.*
VERB + SIGN **bear, have** ◊ *The murder had all the ~s of a crime of passion.* | **betray, display, exhibit, give, show** ◊ *His face betrayed no ~ of emotion.* ◊ *By now the fish was showing ~s of distress.* | **point to sth** ◊ *Early ~s point to business improving.* | **detect, find, notice, see, spot** ◊ *We detected ~s that they were less than enthusiastic about their honeymoon.* | **miss** | **ignore** ◊ *He ignored the warning ~s of mounting health problems.* | **interpret (sth as), read, recognize, see sth as** | **look for, watch for** ◊ *Look carefully for ~s of damp.*
SIGN + VERB **appear, come** ◊ *The first ~s of spring appeared.* | **indicate sth, point to sth** ◊ *All the ~s pointed to it being more than just a coincidence.*
PREP. **at a/the ~** ◊ *He disappeared at the first ~ of trouble.* | **~ from** ◊ *The people regarded the earthquake as a ~ from God.* | **~ of** ◊ *This move will be seen as a ~ of weakness.* ◊ *There's no ~ of the snow stopping.*
PHRASES **~ of life** ◊ *There was no ~ of life in the house* (= there seemed to be nobody there). | **a ~ of the times** ◊ *It's a real ~ of the times: thirty small businesses face financial ruin this month.* | **a ~ of things to come** ◊ *I hope this incident isn't a ~ of things to come.* | **not the least ~ (of sb/sth), not the slightest ~ (of sb/sth)** ◊ *He spoke up without the slightest ~ of nervousness.* | **the ~s and symptoms** ◊ *Get this test if you have ~s and symptoms of diabetes.*

2 board, etc. giving information/a warning

ADJ. **flashing, illuminated** (*esp. BrE*), **neon** | **painted** | **faded** | **hand-lettered** (*AmE*), **handwritten** | **home-made** (*esp. AmE*) | **cardboard, wooden** | **exit** | **pub** (*BrE*), **shop** (*esp. BrE*), **store** (*esp. AmE*), **street** | **lawn, yard** (*both AmE*) ◊ *I put out a lawn ~ in my yard* (= to show political support). | **direction** (*esp. BrE*), **highway** (*esp. AmE*), **motorway** (*in the UK*), **road, traffic** | **warning** | **picket** (*AmE*) ◊ *He gets $300 a week from the union for carrying a picket ~.*
VERB + SIGN **erect, hang, hang out, hang up, place, post** (*esp. AmE*), **put up** ◊ *Someone had put up a 'For Sale' ~.* | **carry, hold up, wave** (*all esp. AmE*) ◊ *The demonstrators shouted and waved ~s.* | **wear** (*usually figurative*) ◊ *He might as well have been wearing a ~ saying 'I am a tourist'.* | **see, spot** | **read** | **ignore** ◊ *He yelled at us for ignoring the stop ~.* | **follow** ◊ *Just follow the ~s for Bridgend.*
SIGN + VERB **read sth** ◊ *The ~ read 'No Fishing'.* | **announce sth, proclaim sth, say sth, state sth, tell sb sth** | **bear sth** ◊ *hundreds of ~s bearing the single word 'Peace'* | **indicate sth, mark sth** ◊ *This ~ indicates that photography is allowed.* | **point** ◊ *The ~ pointed down a narrow road.* | **advertise sth** | **warn** ◊ *~s warning against trespass* | **hang** | **flash** ◊ *A neon ~ flashed above the door.*
PREP. **~ for, ~ to** ◊ *Follow the road and you'll see ~s for the turn-off.*

3 movement with a particular meaning

ADJ. **rude** | **peace, thumbs-up, V** (usually V-sign) ◊ *She made a peace ~ while having her picture taken.*
VERB + SIGN **give (sb), make** ◊ *She gave me a thumbs-up ~.* |

communicate through ◊ *They had to communicate through ~s and grunts.*
SIGN + NOUN **language, system** ◊ *We used ~ language to talk.*
PREP. **~ for** ◊ *the ~ for 'woman' in sign language*
PHRASES **make the ~ of the cross** ◊ *The priest made the ~ of the cross over the dead body.*

4 mark/symbol with a particular meaning

ADJ. **dollar, euro, pound, etc.** (In the US, the **pound sign** refers to '#'. In the UK, it refers to the currency sign '£'.) | **equals, minus, plus, etc.** | **peace** ◊ *a T-shirt with a peace ~ on it* | **call** ◊ *Bravo Two Zero was the call ~ of an eight-man SAS team.*
VERB + SIGN **draw** ◊ *He drew a huge dollar ~ on the paper.* | **use** ◊ *I used the Chinese ~ for 'father' instead of 'uncle'.*
SIGN + VERB **mean sth** ◊ *What does this ~ mean?*
PREP. **~ for** ◊ *I can't remember the ~ for 'square root'.*

5 star sign

ADJ. **birth, star** | **astrological, zodiac** ◊ *the twelve astrological ~s* ◊ *Mars rules the zodiac ~ of Aries.*
VERB + SIGN **be born under**
PREP. **~ of** ◊ *people born under the ~ of Gemini*
PHRASES **the ~s of the Zodiac**

sign *verb*

ADV. **duly** ◊ *One copy of this letter should be duly ~ed and returned to us.* | **formally, officially** | **personally** ◊ *a first edition of the book, personally ~ed by the author* | **online** | **up** ◊ *You can ~ up online for language classes.*
VERB + SIGN **be required to, have to, need to** ◊ *This is the contract you will be required to ~.* | **ask sb to, persuade sb to** | **agree to** | **refuse to** | **want to** | **be willing to**
PREP. **for** ◊ *The courier asked me to ~ for the parcel.*

signal *noun*

1 sign/action/sound that sends a message

ADJ. **clear, unmistakable** | **agreed, prearranged** | **conflicting, confusing, contradictory, mixed** | **wrong** ◊ *Laughing when you should be crying sends out the wrong ~s to people.* | **alarm, danger, distress, warning** | **hand, non-verbal, smoke, visual** | **turn** (*AmE*) | **busy** (*AmE*) (**engaged tone** in *BrE*) ◊ *All I get is a busy ~ when I dial his number.* | **buy, sell** (*both business*) ◊ *A strong buy ~ was issued to traders.*
VERB + SIGNAL **give (sb), make, send, send out** ◊ *When I give the ~, run!* | **interpret, read** ◊ *The brain interprets the ~s from the retina as light.* | **interpret sth as** ◊ *The remark was interpreted as a ~ that their government was ready to return to the peace talks.* | **pick up, respond to** ◊ *Interviewers quickly learn to pick up non-verbal ~s.* | **act as** ◊ *The insect's yellow spots act as a warning ~ to its predators.*
SIGNAL + VERB **come from sth** ◊ *Try to read the ~s coming from the patient.* | **indicate sth** ◊ *the ~s that can indicate danger*
PREP. **at a ~, on a ~** ◊ *At a prearranged ~, everyone started cheering.* | **~ for** ◊ *She made a ~ for the car to stop.* | **~ from, ~ to** ◊ *Wait for the ~ from the leader of your group.*

2 set of lights for drivers

ADJ. **railroad** (*AmE*), **railway** (*BrE*), **traffic**
VERB + SIGNAL **operate**
SIGNAL + VERB **be on red/green, be red/green** ◊ *The traffic ~s were on red.* | **fail**
SIGNAL + NOUN **box** (*BrE*) | **failure** (*BrE*)

3 series of radio waves, chemical messages, etc.

ADJ. **faint, weak** | **strong** | **high-frequency, low-frequency** | **input, output** | **acoustic, analogue/analog, audio, chemical, digital, electrical, electronic, GPS, light, radar, radio, satellite, sonar, sound, television, TV, video, wireless**
VERB + SIGNAL **carry, pass, relay** ◊ *The nerves carry these ~s to the brain.* | **amplify, boost** | **convert (sth into), scramble** ◊ *The ~ is scrambled into code before it is sent.* | **decode, encode** | **emit, generate, produce, send, transmit** | **detect, pick up, receive, respond to** ◊ *This equipment can*

detect very low-frequency ~s. | **block, jam** ◊ *It is possible to jam GPS ~s in battle.*
SIGNAL + VERB **travel** ◊ *The digital ~ travels down wires to the server.* | **fade**
SIGNAL + NOUN **intensity, strength**
PREP. **~ from** ◊ *a faint ~ from the satellite* | **~ to**

signal *verb*

1 move your arms to give a signal

ADV. **frantically** ◊ *I saw her ~ frantically to us.*
PREP. **for** ◊ *He raised his hand to ~ for the waiter.* | **to** ◊ *She tried to ~ to the bus driver to stop.*

2 show/mark sth

ADV. **clearly** ◊ *These changes clearly ~ the end of the welfare state as we know it.* | **effectively** (*esp. BrE*) | **not necessarily** ◊ *A fall in demand does not necessarily ~ the death of the industry.*
VERB + SIGNAL **appear to, seem to** ◊ *These events appeared to ~ the end of an era.* | **try to** | **be intended to, be meant to** ◊ *This address was meant to ~ a change in policy.*

signatory *noun*

ADJ. **first, original** | **authorized** (*BrE*) ◊ *The document must be signed by an authorized ~ of the company.*
... OF SIGNATORIES **list** ◊ *The public letter and list of signatories can be read here.*
VERB + SIGNATORY **require** ◊ *The Convention requires signatories to punish genocide when it occurs.*
SIGNATORY + VERB **agree sth** ◊ *Signatories agreed to support the nuclear test ban.* | **include** ◊ *The signatories included Spain, Italy and Portugal.*
SIGNATORY + NOUN **country, nation, state**
PREP. **~ of, ~ to** ◊ *the signatories to the treaty*

signature *noun*

1 written name

ADJ. **illegible** | **handwritten** | **valid** | **forged** | **digital, electronic** ◊ *The law recognizes a digital ~ for online transactions.*
VERB + SIGNATURE **put, scrawl, scribble, write** ◊ *We both refused to put our ~s to the agreement.* | **add, affix, append** | **witness** ◊ *Your ~ must be witnessed by two people.* | **recognize** | **check, verify** (*esp. AmE*) ◊ *The salesperson verifies the ~ by comparing it with the one on the card.* | **collect, garner, gather, get, obtain** ◊ *They collected over 1 000 ~s for the petition.* | **bear, carry** ◊ *The will bears her ~.* | **forge** | **require** ◊ *The form requires the ~s of two witnesses.*

2 quality that makes sth different

ADJ. **characteristic, distinctive, telltale, unique** ◊ *Each material has its own unique chemical ~.* | **chemical, genetic, etc.**
VERB + SIGNATURE **detect** | **bear** ◊ *Each song bears the ~ of its performer.* | **leave**
PREP. **~ of** ◊ *the genetic ~s of natural selection*

significance *noun*

ADJ. **considerable, cosmic, deep, enormous, great, historic, immense, major, profound, real** | **broader, full, general, universal, wider** ◊ *The scientists are cautious about the wider ~ of their findings.* | **limited, minor** (*esp. BrE*) | **particular, special** | **potential** | **real, true** ◊ *They failed to appreciate the true ~ of these discoveries.* | **functional, practical, statistical, strategic, symbolic, theoretical** | **cultural, economic, historical, moral, political, religious, social, spiritual**
VERB + SIGNIFICANCE **have** ◊ *The ceremony has great symbolic ~.* | **acquire, assume, gain, take on** ◊ *Suddenly the relationship took on a new ~.* | **attach** ◊ *Let us not attach too much ~ to these meetings.* | **assess, determine** | **appreciate, be aware of, grasp, recognize, understand** | **exaggerate** | **downplay** (*esp. AmE*), **minimize, play down** (*esp. BrE*), **underestimate**

SIGNIFICANCE + VERB **lie in sth** ◊ *The ~ of this lies in the fact that he had previously denied all knowledge of the fund.* | **attach to sth** ◊ *Does any ~ attach to the use of the technical terms?*
PREP. **~ for, ~ to** ◊ *a meal that has particular ~ for a Jewish family* | **of** ◊ *a policy of special ~ to women*
PHRASES **be of little, no, etc. ~**

significant *adj.*

VERBS **be, prove** | **become** | **remain** | **consider sth (as), deem sth, find sth, regard sth as, see sth as, think sth, view sth as** ◊ *The move was regarded as ~ in Japan.* | **make sth** ◊ *What makes this discovery ~ is that it goes against our theory.*
ADV. **extremely, fairly, very, etc.** | **deeply, highly** | **especially, particularly** | **potentially** | **equally** | **statistically** ◊ *These differences are not statistically ~.* | **biologically, culturally, historically, militarily, politically, etc.**
PREP. **for** ◊ *This development proved highly ~ for the whole town.* | **to** ◊ *rituals which are deeply ~ to Christians*

silence *noun*

1 quietness

ADJ. **lengthy, long, prolonged** | **brief, momentary, a moment's, short** ◊ *There was a moment's ~ before she replied.* | **deep, hushed** | **awed** ◊ *We sat and watched in awed ~ as she performed.* | **absolute, complete, dead, deadly, deathly, total, utter** ◊ *We sat in complete ~, save for the ticking of the clock.* ◊ *A deathly ~ hung over the town.* | **relative** ◊ *The rest of the trip passed in relative ~.* | **shocked, stunned** ◊ *Her comments were met with a stunned ~.* | **awkward, embarrassed, embarrassing, strained, uncomfortable, uneasy** ◊ *An awkward ~ followed.* | **heavy, ominous, oppressive, tense** | **brooding, thoughtful** ◊ *She fell into long, brooding ~s.* | **stony, sullen** | **eerie, unnerving** | **companionable** ◊ *They walked in companionable ~.* | **expectant, pregnant** | **sudden** | **radio** ◊ *The soldier had broken radio ~ to contact his aircraft.*
... OF SILENCE **moment**
VERB + SILENCE **maintain** ◊ *She maintained a stony ~.* | **break, interrupt, penetrate, pierce, punctuate, shatter** ◊ *Lewis finally broke the long ~ between them.* ◊ *Celeste's voice penetrated the ~.* ◊ *a ~ punctuated only by the occasional sniff from the children* | **lapse into, relapse into, retreat into, subside into, trail off into** (all used only about people) ◊ *He lapsed into a sullen ~.* | **stun sb into** ◊ *The boys were stunned into ~ by this news.* | **be met with** ◊ *Her question was met with an uneasy ~.* | **observe** (= as a sign of respect for the dead, etc.) ◊ *A minute's ~ for the victims will be observed.* | **fill** ◊ *She filled the ~ with music.*
SILENCE + VERB **come over sth, descend, fall, fall over sth, settle, settle over sth** ◊ *A sudden ~ fell over the room.* | **hang, prevail, reign** ◊ *Silence reigned.* | **linger** ◊ *A heavy ~ lingered in the air.* | **envelop sth, fill sth** ◊ *Silence filled the room.* | **ensue, follow** | **deepen, grow, lengthen, spread, stretch** ◊ *He thought for a moment, the ~ lengthening.* | **greet sth** ◊ *A stunned ~ greeted her announcement.*
PREP. **in (the) ~** ◊ *They ate their breakfast in ~.*
PHRASES **two minutes' ~, three minutes' ~** (*esp. BrE*) ◊ *They observed two minutes' ~ to remember the war dead.* ◊ *Countries throughout Europe held a three minutes' ~.*

2 not saying anything about sth

ADJ. **deafening** ◊ *The government's only response has been a deafening ~.* | **dignified** (*esp. BrE*) | **deliberate**
VERB + SILENCE **keep, maintain** ◊ *He has so far kept a dignified ~ on the subject.* | **take as** ◊ *I took her ~ as a no.*
SILENCE + VERB **surround** ◊ *a debate to break the ~ surrounding domestic violence*
PREP. **~ from** ◊ *There seems to have been a deliberate ~ from the newspapers.*
PHRASES **a conspiracy of ~, a wall of ~** ◊ *There is a conspiracy of ~ about what is happening* (= nobody is willing to talk about it). | **a vow of ~** ◊ *She has broken her vow of ~ on the issue.*

silence verb

ADV. **completely** | **effectively** ◇ *Criticism has now been effectively ~d.* | **immediately, quickly** | **abruptly, instantly** ◇ *Her scream was abruptly ~d.* | **momentarily, temporarily** | **forever** ◇ *A shot to the head ~d him forever.*
VERB + SILENCE **try to** | **manage to** | **fail to** ◇ *Even these improvements to the service failed to ~ a grumbling chorus of complaints.*
PREP. **with** ◇ *She ~d him with a glare.*

silent adj.

VERBS **be, seem** | **become, fall, go, grow** ◇ *The crowd fell ~ as she began to speak.* ◇ *The room grew ~ as the men entered.* | **keep, lie, remain, sit, stand, stay** ◇ *I could not keep ~ any longer.* ◇ *The street lay ~ and deserted.* ◇ *She sat ~ throughout the meal.*
ADV. **absolutely, completely, dead** (*informal, esp. AmE*), **entirely, perfectly, totally, utterly** | **almost, nearly** (*esp. AmE*), **virtually** ◇ *The new bus is virtually ~.* | **largely, mostly** ◇ *an issue about which the researchers are largely ~* | **notably, remarkably** | **curiously, uncharacteristically, unusually** | **deadly, eerily, oddly, strangely, unnaturally** ◇ *The street was strangely ~.* | **ominously** ◇ *This is a subject about which the official documents are ominously ~.* | **resolutely, stubbornly** ◇ *Len remained obstinately ~.*
PREP. **about** ◇ *They had kept remarkably ~ about their intentions.* | **on** ◇ *The report was ~ on that subject.*

silk noun

ADJ. **heavy** | **delicate, fine, thin** | **soft** | **pure** | **artificial** | **rich** ◇ *a drawing room decorated in rich blue and purple ~s* | **faded** | **watered** | **raw** | **Chinese, Thai, etc.**
VERB + SILK **wear** | **produce** ◇ *fine ~s produced in Italy* | **spin, weave** | **be lined with, be trimmed with**
SILK + NOUN **industry, mill** | **merchant** | **moth**
PREP. **in ~** (= wearing clothes made of silk) ◇ *ladies in ~s and satins* | **of ~** ◇ *an evening dress of pure white ~*

silt noun

ADJ. **fine** ◇ *The water contains fine ~.*
... OF SILT **deposit, layer** ◇ *The wreck was covered in a fine layer of ~.*
VERB + SILT **deposit** ◇ *During the annual floods the river deposits its ~ on the fields.* | **remove** | **be covered in, be covered with**
SILT + NOUN **deposit**
PREP. **with ~** ◇ *The tunnel had been blocked with ~.*

silver noun

1 metal

ADJ. **pure, solid** | **sterling** | **polished** ◇ *a knife with a polished ~ casing*
VERB + SILVER **extract, mine** ◇ *Silver is extracted from ore.* | **set sth in** ◇ *a gemstone set in ~*
SILVER + NOUN **ore** | **mine** | **plate** (= metal covered with a thin layer of silver) ◇ *The chain was available in ~ plate for $12.50.* ◇ *gold and ~ plate*

2 (*also* **the silver**) objects made of silver

ADJ. **family** (*esp. BrE, often figurative*) ◇ *He was forced to sell the family ~ to pay for the repairs to the house.* ◇ *They accused the government of selling off the family ~ to pay for their policies.*
VERB + SILVER **polish**

3 (*also* **silver medal**) in sports

ADJ. **Commonwealth, Olympic**
VERB + SILVER **be awarded, earn, get, land** (*BrE, informal*), **secure, take, win** ◇ *She got a ~ in the long jump.* ◇ *Her run was enough to secure ~ for the team.* ◇ *He took the ~ this year.* | **snatch** ◇ *She managed to snatch the ~ from the defending champion.*

similar adj.

VERBS **be, feel, look, sound, taste** | **appear, seem** | **become** | **remain**

ADV. **extremely, fairly, very, etc.** | **remarkably, strikingly** ◇ *The three portraits are remarkably ~.* | **basically, broadly, essentially, fundamentally, roughly, vaguely** ◇ *countries with broadly ~ characteristics* | **superficially** ◇ *Their experiences are superficially ~.* | **qualitatively, substantially** | **surprisingly** | **eerily, uncannily** ◇ *The scene in the picture was eerily ~ to what I had seen in my dream.*
PREP. **in** ◇ *The two houses are ~ in size.* | **to** ◇ *Snake meat tastes ~ to chicken.*

similarity noun

ADJ. **close, considerable, great, remarkable, strong** ◇ *the close ~ in our ages* | **clear, marked, obvious** | **eerie, striking, uncanny** | **significant** | **certain** | **basic, fundamental** | **apparent, perceived, superficial** | **broad, general** | **cultural, physical, structural**
... OF SIMILARITY **degree**
VERB + SIMILARITY **bear, have** ◇ *The area bears a superficial ~ to Tokyo.* | **reveal, show** | **find, note, notice, see, spot** | **highlight, point out** | **recognize** | **share** ◇ *These theories share certain similarities.* | **explain** ◇ *a route across the Pacific which may explain the ~ between the two cultures*
SIMILARITY + VERB **exist** | **end** ◇ *Here the ~ with Western politics ends.*
PREP. **between** | **~ in** ◇ *the striking ~ in their appearance* | **~ to** ◇ *the chimpanzee's ~ to humans* | **~ with** ◇ *The panel shows marked similarities with mosaics found elsewhere.*
PHRASES **a point of ~** ◇ *There are several points of ~ between the two cases.*

simmer verb

ADV. **gently, slowly** ◇ *Allow the soup to ~ gently for ten minutes.* | **quietly** (*figurative*) ◇ *She was still quietly ~ing from her argument with Nathan.*
VERB + SIMMER **allow sth to, leave sth to, let sth** ◇ *Turn the heat down and let it ~ for thirty minutes.*
PREP. **in** ◇ *a mixture of vegetables ~ed in yogurt*

simple adj.

VERBS **appear, be, look, prove, seem, sound** | **remain** | **keep sth, make sth** ◇ *When creating your design, keep it ~.* ◇ *Is all this technology making our lives simpler?* | **find sth** ◇ *I found the work fairly ~.*
ADV. **extremely, fairly, very, etc.** | **amazingly, breathtakingly** (*esp. BrE*), **incredibly, remarkably** | **devastatingly** (*esp. BrE*) ◇ *The logic of the plan was devastatingly ~.* | **comparatively, relatively** | **apparently, seemingly** ◇ *This seemingly ~ task ended up taking hours.* | **deceptively, disarmingly, surprisingly** ◇ *a deceptively ~ technique* | **beautifully, elegantly** ◇ *The engine design is elegantly ~.* | **brilliantly, wonderfully** (*both esp. BrE*) ◇ *It is a brilliantly ~ idea.* | **refreshingly** ◇ *Their approach is refreshingly ~ and direct.*

simplicity noun

ADJ. **elegant** | **extreme, great** | **stark** ◇ *The stage design is striking in its stark ~.* | **relative** | **apparent** ◇ *Don't be fooled by the music's apparent ~.* | **deceptive** | **childlike** ◇ *Her views of the world have a childlike ~.*
VERB + SIMPLICITY **have**
PREP. **~ of** ◇ *I find elegance in the ~ of approach.* | **for ~** ◇ *For ~, I shall continue to use the accepted term.*
PHRASES **be ~ itself** (= to be very simple) ◇ *His solution to the problem was ~ itself.* | **for simplicity's sake, for the sake of ~** ◇ *For the sake of ~, we will focus on the two most common cases.*

simplification noun

ADJ. **considerable, gross, radical** | **further**
VERB + SIMPLIFICATION **make**
PREP. **~ in** ◇ *He made a number of ~s in the taxation system.*

simplify verb

ADV. **considerably, greatly, radically, vastly** ◊ *The whole process has now been greatly simplified.* | **drastically, grossly** ◊ *He presents the theory in a grossly simplified form.* | **slightly** | **overly** ◊ *This analysis is overly simplified.*
VERB + SIMPLIFY **attempt to, try to** | **be designed to** ◊ *The changes are designed to ~ grant applications.*
PHRASES **highly simplified** ◊ *This is a highly simplified view of the economy.*

simulate verb

ADV. **accurately, closely** ◊ *The device ~s conditions in space very closely.*
VERB + SIMULATE **be designed to, be used to** ◊ *Models are used to ~ the workings of a real-life system.* | **try to**

simulation noun

ADJ. **computer, computerized, digital, real-time, virtual, virtual-reality** | **laboratory** | **historical** | **flight, training** | **realistic** | **sophisticated**
VERB + SIMULATION **carry out, conduct, perform, run** ◊ *To test the model under different conditions, it is necessary to run ~s on a computer.* | **create, develop** ◊ *His team created a computer ~ of the earthquake.* | **use**
SIMULATION + VERB **indicate sth, show sth**
SIMULATION + NOUN **model** ◊ *Simulation models are used to predict earthquake patterns.* | **program, software** | **techniques** | **exercise** (*esp. BrE*) | **experiment** | **game**
PREP. **in a/the ~** ◊ *the basic steps in the ~* | **through ~** ◊ *The pilot's skills are tested through ~.* | **~ of** ◊ *a virtual-reality ~ of a moon landing*

sin noun

ADJ. **cardinal, deadly, mortal** | **egregious** (*esp. AmE*), **grave, great, grievous, heinous** | **unforgivable, unpardonable** | **venial** | **original** ◊ *the Christian doctrine of original ~* | **past** ◊ *We have repented for past ~s. Now it's time to move on.*
VERB + SIN **commit** | **confess** ◊ *They had confessed their ~s and done their penance.* | **repent** | **expiate** ◊ *They would have to expiate their ~s through suffering.* | **wash away** | **forgive** | **punish** | **consider sth** ◊ *It's considered a ~ to be disrespectful to your parents.*
SIN + NOUN **tax** (*esp. AmE*) ◊ *~ taxes on cigarettes and alcohol* | **bin** (*BrE, sports*) ◊ *Both sides lost a player to the ~ bin just before the interval.*
PREP. **~ against** ◊ *a ~ against God* | **~ of** ◊ *the ~ of pride*
PHRASES **the forgiveness of ~, the forgiveness of ~s** ◊ *We believe in the forgiveness of ~s.* | **the seven deadly ~s** | **a ~ of commission** (= doing sth you should not do), **a ~ of omission** (= not doing sth you should do) | **the ~s of the fathers** ◊ *Our sons will pay for the ~s of their fathers.* | **the ~s of the flesh** (= sexual acts that you should not do) ◊ *Even politicians are not immune from the ~s of the flesh.*

sincere adj.

VERBS **appear, be, look, seem, sound**
ADV. **extremely, fairly, very, etc.** | **deeply** ◊ *the warm, deeply ~ note in her voice* | **absolutely, completely, entirely, perfectly, quite, totally, utterly** | **apparently, seemingly** (*esp. AmE*) | **enough** ◊ *Her protests seemed ~ enough.* | **most** ◊ *We offer our most ~ apologies.* | **painfully** ◊ *painfully ~ declarations of love*
PREP. **about** ◊ *his refusal to be ~ about his feelings* | **in** ◊ *Have they been ~ in their efforts to resolve the crisis?*

sincerity noun

ADJ. **complete, deep, great, total, utmost** | **genuine, heartfelt** | **fake, false, mock** | **apparent** ◊ *He spoke these words with apparent ~.* | **obvious** | **emotional** ◊ *a sense of emotional ~ in each song*
VERB + SINCERITY **doubt, question** ◊ *There seems no reason to doubt the ~ of his beliefs.* | **be convinced of** ◊ *She wasn't yet convinced of his ~.* | **demonstrate, prove, show**

PREP. **with ~** | **~ in** ◊ *He could hear the ~ in her voice.*
PHRASES **in all ~, with all ~** (*AmE*) ◊ *'Really?' he asked in all ~.* | **lack of ~** ◊ *His eyes betrayed his utter lack of ~.*

sing verb

ADV. **loud, loudly, lustily** ◊ *The birds sang louder than ever.* | **gently, quietly, softly** ◊ *He was ~ing quietly to himself.* | **beautifully, sweetly, well** | **badly** | **cheerfully, happily, joyfully, merrily** ◊ *Birds sang cheerfully in the trees.* | **a bit** (*esp. BrE*), **a little** ◊ *She could ~ a little and agreed to take part in the show.* | **live** ◊ *Have you ever heard the band ~ live?* | **professionally** | **together** ◊ *We played and sang together.*
VERB + SING **be able to, can** ◊ *I can't ~ very well.*
PREP. **about** ◊ *boy bands ~ing about love* | **to** ◊ *Shall I ~ to you?*
PHRASES **be sung to the tune of sth** ◊ *The lyrics were sung to the tune of the Beatles' 'Eleanor Rigby'.* | **~ at the top of your lungs** (*AmE*), **~ at the top of your voice** (*BrE*) | **~ like an angel** | **~ out of tune** ◊ *Unfortunately, he was ~ing out of tune.* | **~ sb to sleep** ◊ *Her mother sang her to sleep.*

singer noun

ADJ. **accomplished** (*esp. BrE*), **fine, good, great, talented, wonderful** | **chart-topping** (*BrE*), **famous, popular, well-known** | **legendary** | **aspiring, budding** ◊ *an aspiring concert ~* | **soulful** ◊ *a soulful jazz ~* | **amateur, professional** | **backing** (*esp. BrE*), **backup** (*AmE*), **lead** ◊ *an interview with the band's lead ~* | **guest** ◊ *She will perform with two guest ~s.* | **choral, solo** | **blues, country, folk, jazz, opera, pop, etc.** | **carol** | **cabaret, lounge** (*esp. AmE*), **nightclub, pub** (*BrE*) ◊ *I was just a lounge ~ in a Key West bar.* | **wedding** (*AmE*) ◊ *Our wedding ~s are the best in Las Vegas.* | **torch** (*esp. AmE*)
SINGER + VERB **belt sth out, sing (sth)** ◊ *A local ~ belted out the national anthem.* | **perform sth** ◊ *Singers took turns to perform songs they had written.* | **sound, sound like** ◊ *a ~ who sounds like Rufus Wainwright*

singing noun

ADJ. **beautiful, fine, good, great** | **carol, choral** | **communal** (*esp. BrE*), **community** (*BrE*), **congregational, devotional** (*esp. AmE*) | **solo, unaccompanied** (*esp. BrE*) | **backup** (*AmE*)
VERB + SINGING **lead** ◊ *The minister led the ~.* | **accompany** ◊ *Her brother accompanied her ~ on the piano.* | **be good at** ◊ *I'm not that good at ~.*
SINGING + NOUN **career** | **lesson** | **teacher** | **voice** ◊ *He has a lovely ~ voice.*

single noun

1 CD, tape, etc.

ADJ. **best-selling, hit, smash** | **number-one, top-ten** | **debut, first** | **lead, lead-off** (*AmE*) | **breakthrough** ◊ *Following the success of their breakthrough ~, a follow-up is planned.* | **comeback** (*esp. BrE*) ◊ *the classic comeback ~ from Take That* | **current, latest, new** | **dance, pop** | **catchy** (*informal*) ◊ *Her catchy first ~ was a hit.*
VERB + SINGLE **play** ◊ *The radio stations play her new ~ several times a day.* | **record** ◊ *The band has yet to record a hit ~.* | **produce** | **put out, release (sth as)** ◊ *They put out a ~ in time for Christmas.* | **The band later released this album track as a ~.** | **feature, include** ◊ *Her new album features her ~ 'Georgia Rain'.*
SINGLE + VERB **come out**
SINGLES + NOUN **~s chart** ◊ *number one in the ~s chart* | **~s collection, ~s compilation**
PHRASES **~ by** ◊ *It was voted the best ~ by a solo artist.* | **~ from** ◊ *the new ~ from the band*

2 singles in tennis

ADJ. **junior, men's, women's**
VERB + SINGLES **play** ◊ *I prefer playing ~s to doubles.* | **win** ◊ *She won the junior ~s.*
SINGLES + NOUN **championship, final, match, tournament** | **champion, player** | **title**
PHRASES **in the ~** ◊ *She decided not to play in the ~s.*

3 (*BrE*) ticket

VERB + SINGLE **buy, get** ◊ *I got a ~ to Birmingham.*
PREP. **~ to** ◊ *A ~ to Stratford, please.*

sinister *adj.*

VERBS **be, look, seem, sound** | **find sth**
ADV. **extremely, fairly, very, etc.** | **deeply, truly** | **almost** | **a little, slightly, etc.** | **faintly, vaguely** ◊ *I found his silence faintly ~.* | **somehow**

sink *noun*

ADJ. **bathroom** (*esp. AmE*), **kitchen** | **blocked** (*esp. BrE*), **clogged** (*AmE*) | **marble** (*esp. AmE*), **porcelain, stainless-steel** | **double** ◊ *The kitchen had a double ~.*
VERB + SINK **fill** ◊ *She filled the ~ with hot water.* | **block** (*esp. BrE*), **clog** (*AmE*) | **clear** (*esp. BrE*), **unblock** (*esp. BrE*), **unclog** (*AmE*) | **install** ◊ *You can install a new ~ in the kitchen.*
SINK + NOUN **unit** (*BrE*) | **plunger** (*BrE*) ◊ *I bought a ~ plunger to clear the blocked kitchen sink.* | **faucet** (*AmE*), **tap** (*BrE*) | **counter** (*AmE*) ◊ *the ~ counter in the bathroom*
PREP. **at the ~** ◊ *She was at the ~, washing the dishes.* | **down the ~** ◊ *Don't pour coffee grounds down the kitchen ~.* | **in the ~** ◊ *Put the dishes in the ~.*

sink *verb*

1 in water, mud, etc.

ADV. **slowly** | **fast** ◊ *Duane was in waist-deep and ~ing fast.* | **down** ◊ *She sank down into the soft soil.* | **deep** ◊ *His boots sank deep into the mud.* | **nearly** ◊ *The boat nearly sank under the increased weight.*
VERB + SINK **begin to, start to**
PREP. **below, beneath** ◊ *We watched the boat ~ beneath the waves.* | **into** ◊ *Our feet sank deep into the soft sand as we walked.* | **to, up to** ◊ *He sank up to his knees in the mud.*
PHRASES **~ like a stone** ◊ *The box sank like a stone.* | **~ or swim** (*figurative*) ◊ *In a situation like this, you either ~ or swim.* | **~ to the bottom (of sth)** ◊ *The ship had sunk to the bottom of the sea.* | **~ under the weight (of sth)** (*often figurative*) ◊ *The airline industry is ~ing under the weight of its losses.* | **~ without trace** ◊ *It seemed as though the ship had sunk without trace.*

2 fall/sit down

ADV. **wearily** | **gratefully** ◊ *I sank gratefully into the warm, dry bed.* | **gracefully** | **low** ◊ *The sun was ~ing lower.* | **back, down** ◊ *Dexter sank back into his seat.*
PREP. **into** ◊ *He sank lower into his chair.* | **onto** ◊ *She sank gracefully down onto a cushion at his feet.*
PHRASES **~ below the horizon** ◊ *The sun had sunk below the horizon.* | **~ to the floor, ~ to the ground** ◊ *She sank to the ground and started to cry.* | **~ to your knees** ◊ *He sank to his knees, grasping at his stomach.*

3 become weaker/worse

ADV. **quickly, rapidly** ◊ *Virgil rapidly sank into depression.* | **gradually** ◊ *The project gradually sank into oblivion.*
PREP. **into**
PHRASES **~ to a new low, ~ to new lows** (*both figurative*) ◊ *With this article the newspaper has sunk to a new low.*

sip *noun*

ADJ. **little, small, tiny** | **careful, cautious, tentative** | **quick, slow** | **large, long** | **noisy** | **first** | **final, last** ◊ *He took a final ~ of his coffee before leaving.*
VERB + SIP **drink, have, take** ◊ *I took a little ~ of my drink.*
PREP. **~ from** ◊ *He took a ~ from his glass.* | **~ of** ◊ *a ~ of coffee* | **in ~s** ◊ *He drank the brandy in ~s.*

sip *verb*

ADV. **slowly** | **quietly, silently** | **calmly, casually** ◊ *'Oh yes?' she asked, calmly sipping her drink.* | **daintily, delicately, gingerly** | **thoughtfully**
VERB + SIP **pause to** ◊ *She paused to ~ her tea.*
PREP. **at** ◊ *He sipped at his beer thoughtfully.* | **from** ◊ *She sipped from her glass of water.* | **on** ◊ *Luther continued sipping on his coffee.*

siren *noun*

ADJ. **approaching** ◊ *The cars had stopped at the sound of the approaching ~.* | **distant** | **blaring, wailing** ◊ *the blaring ~s of ambulances and police cars* | **air-raid, ambulance, emergency, fire, police, tornado** (*esp. AmE*), **warning**
VERB + SIREN **put on, sound, switch on** ◊ *The ships all sounded their ~s.* | **hear**
SIREN + VERB **go** (*BrE*), **go off, sound, start, start up** | **blare, scream, wail** ◊ *The ambulance sped off with its ~ wailing.*

sister *noun*

ADJ. **big, elder, older** | **baby, kid** (*informal*), **little, younger** | **twin** | **full** (= sharing both parents) | **adopted, adoptive** | **beloved, darling, dear** | **annoying, bratty** (*informal, esp. AmE*) ◊ *my bratty little ~* | **dead, deceased, late** | **long-lost** ◊ *a refugee who traced his long-lost ~* | **unmarried** | **sorority** (*AmE*) ◊ *Carolyn's sorority ~s at Indiana University*
PHRASES **brothers and ~s, brothers or ~s** ◊ *Brothers and ~s do not always get on.* ◊ *I have no brothers or ~s.* | **like ~s** ◊ *The two girls are so close, they're like ~s.*

sit *verb*

1 on a chair, etc.

ADV. **motionless, still** ◊ *Just ~ still!* | **quietly** ◊ *He would ~ quietly and watch what was happening.* | **in silence, silently** ◊ *We sat in silence for a few moments.* | **calmly, patiently** | **just, merely, simply** ◊ *She just sat there staring into space.* ◊ *He simply sat there not speaking.* | **comfortably, uncomfortably** | **cross-legged, Indian-style** (*AmE*), **with your legs crossed** ◊ *The children sat cross-legged on the floor.* ◊ *She was sitting in her chair with her legs crossed.* | **sideways** | **bolt upright, erect, straight, upright** ◊ *He sat bolt upright, hands folded in front of him.* | **awkwardly, demurely, primly, stiffly** ◊ *She sat primly on the edge of her chair.* | **proudly** | **happily** ◊ *Elmer was happily sitting in his high chair.* | **down** ◊ *Please ~ down and let me talk to you.* | **back** ◊ *Joan sat back in her chair.* ◊ *Just ~ back and enjoy the show.* | **around** ◊ *I hate to be sitting around doing nothing.* | **side by side, together** | **alone**
VERB + SIT **let sb** ◊ *Surely someone would stand up and let her ~ down?* | **gesture for sb to, gesture to sb to, motion sb to, motion for sb to, motion to sb to** ◊ *He motioned the young officer to ~ down.*
PREP. **against** ◊ *He was sitting against the wall.* | **around** ◊ *The kids sat around a campfire.* | **astride** ◊ *She was sitting astride a horse.* | **at** ◊ *We sat at a table in the corner.* | **behind** ◊ *The manager sat behind his desk.* | **beside** ◊ *She went and sat beside him.* | **in** ◊ *He sat back in his chair and started to read.* | **on** ◊ *Can I ~ on this chair?* | **opposite** ◊ *They sat opposite each other.* | **under** ◊ *She sat under an apple tree.*
PHRASES **a place to ~** ◊ *Ann found a place to ~.* | **~ down (with sb)** ◊ *I recently had a chance to ~ down with Britain's Foreign Secretary.* | **~ and..., ~ back and..., ~ idly by and...** (*figurative*) ◊ *How can you ~ back and watch him suffer?* ◊ *We can't ~ idly by and let this happen.*

2 seem right/not seem right

ADV. **comfortably** (*esp. BrE*), **easily** (*esp. BrE*), **happily, nicely, well** | **uneasily** (*esp. BrE*)
PREP. **with** ◊ *His views did not ~ well with the management line.*

PHR V **sit up**

ADV. **abruptly, quickly, suddenly** | **immediately** | **slowly** ◊ *She slowly sat up and looked around.* | **straight**
PHRASES **~ up and take notice** (*figurative*) ◊ *Their actions have forced us to ~ up and take notice.*

site *noun*

1 piece of land where a building was/is/will be

ADJ. **good, prime** (*esp. BrE*) ◊ *houses built on prime ~s with stunning views* | **designated, possible, potential, proposed, suitable** ◊ *some potential ~s for the new business* |

building (*esp. BrE*), construction (*esp. AmE*), development (*esp. BrE*) | demolition | derelict (*BrE*) | industrial, manufacturing | commercial | factory, hospital, school, etc. (*esp. BrE*) | protected | brownfield, greenfield (*both BrE*) | 5-acre, 20-hectare, etc.

VERB + SITE **allocate** (*BrE*), **choose**, **designate**, **earmark** (*BrE*), **select** ◇ *The ~ is designated for housing.* ◇ *The council has earmarked the ~ for possible redevelopment.* | **find, identify, locate, look for** | **acquire** (*esp. BrE*), **buy, purchase** ◇ *A local company has recently acquired the ~.* | **lease** (*esp. BrE*) ◇ *The ~ was leased from another company.* | **inspect** | **clear, prepare** ◇ *The ~ is being cleared for development.* | **build on, develop** ◇ *Nothing can be built on this ~.* | **occupy** ◇ *The ~ is presently occupied by offices.* | **stand on** ◇ *The school stands on the ~ of an ancient settlement.*

SITE + VERB **belong to sb**

SITE + NOUN **manager** (*esp. BrE*), **supervisor** | **owner** | **inspection**

PREP. **at a/the ~** ◇ *The factory will be built at a ~ to the north of the city.* | **in a/the ~** ◇ *The hotel is in a prime ~ overlooking the sea.* | **on (a/the) ~** ◇ *Hard hats must be worn on ~.* ◇ *He was injured on a construction ~.*

2 place where sth happened or that is used for sth

ADJ. **ancient, archaeological, historic, historical, prehistoric** | **important** | **holy, sacred** | **sensitive** ◇ *an extremely sensitive ~ of national importance* | **remote** | **accident, bomb, crash, disaster** | **civic-amenity** (*BrE*), **dump, landfill** (*BrE*), **waste-disposal** ◇ *a waste-disposal ~ on the edge of town* | **training** | **burial, grave** ◇ *Many of these ancient burial ~s were destroyed in the last century.* | **excavation** | **landing, launch** | **test** ◇ *the test ~ for the atom bomb* | **camp** (usually *campsite*), **camping, caravan** (*all BrE*) | **picnic** (*esp. BrE*) | **allotment** (*BrE*) | **dive, wreck** ◇ *Gozo has some of the best dive ~s in the Mediterranean.* | **breeding, nest, nesting** | **park-and-ride** (*BrE*)

VERB + SITE **visit** ◇ *The president is to visit the crash ~ later today.* | **disturb, remove sth from, steal sth from** ◇ *penalties for disturbing ancient ~s* | **excavate**

3 on the Internet → See also WEBSITE

ADJ. **Internet, online, Web** (usually *website*), **WWW** ◇ *online dating ~s* | **official** ◇ *the official website of the New York Yankees* | **personal** ◇ *I am redesigning my personal ~ this month.* | **free** ◇ *a free ~ devoted to tropical fish* | **home** | **major** ◇ *major news ~s* | **favourite/favorite** | **informative, useful** ◇ *Harvard Law has a very useful and informative ~.* | **interactive** | **portal, search** ◇ *one of the major search ~s* | **content** ◇ *entertainment content ~s* | **download** ◇ *a music download ~* | **business, commercial, corporate, e-commerce** | **government** | **auction, gambling, gaming, media, music, news, newspaper, review, shopping, travel** ◇ *online music review ~s* | **blog, chat, community, dating, social-networking** | **adult, porn** (*informal*), **pornographic** | **fan** ◇ *a Harry Potter fan ~* | **hate** ◇ *He saw the photo on a right-wing hate ~.* | **destination** | **linked** | **mirror** | **sister** ◇ *You can go to ePay Music, a music-specific sister ~ to ePay.* | **password-protected** ◇ *Users log onto a password-protected Internet ~.*

VERB + SITE **access, check, check out** (*informal*), **view, visit** | **browse, navigate, search, surf** ◇ *Their ~ is easy to navigate.* | **search for** | **crawl** ◇ *The search engine crawls the ~ for relevant keywords.* | **find, identify** | **build, create, design, develop, set up** | **maintain, operate, run** | **update** ◇ *The official ~ is updated on a regular basis.* | **redesign** | **host, own** | **bookmark** ◇ *I have bookmarked your ~ for future reading.* | **rank** ◇ *Search engines rank ~s through a variety of methods.* | **block** ◇ *The government tries to block foreign ~s deemed subversive.* | **promote**

SITE + VERB **be dedicated to sth, be devoted to sth** ◇ *a ~ devoted to health issues* | **contain sth, feature sth, include sth** ◇ *The ~ contains information on local services.* | **offer sth** ◇ *The ~ offers used equipment for sale.* | **link to sth** ◇ *the number of ~s that link to your website*

SITE + NOUN **map** ◇ *A ~ map lists and links to all pages on your*

website. | **design** | **content** | **link** | **search** | **administrator, owner** | **visitor** | **designer**

PREP. **at a/the ~** ◇ *At this ~ you'll find all the latest news and gossip.* | **in a/the ~** ◇ *Check out the links in our home ~.* | **on a/the ~** ◇ *The software sells on the ~ for $29.95.* | **~ about** ◇ *~s about Japan* | **~ for** ◇ *the most popular ~s for children* | **~ on** ◇ *I'm searching for ~s on aromatherapy.*

→ Special page at COMPUTER

sited *adj.*

ADV. **carefully, strategically** ◇ *The fence is strategically ~ to prevent anyone getting onto the beach.* | **appropriately, conveniently** | **insensitively** | **attractively** ◇ *The hotel is attractively ~ by a lake in a steep valley.* | **badly**

situated *adj.*

VERBS **be**

ADV. **beautifully, delightfully, ideally, picturesquely, pleasantly, superbly, well** ◇ *The hotel is delightfully ~ close to the waterfront.* | **conveniently, inconveniently** | **centrally** | **remotely** | **quietly**

PREP. **for** ◇ *ideally ~ for touring the country*

situation *noun*

ADJ. **general, overall, whole** | **current, immediate, present** | **international, local, national, world** | **actual, concrete, real, real-life, real-world** (*esp. AmE*) | **hypothetical, unlikely** | **favourable/favorable, happy** (*esp. BrE*), **healthy, ideal** | **satisfactory, stable** (*esp. BrE*), **chaotic, explosive, fluid, precarious, unstable, volatile** | **awkward, delicate, difficult, embarrassing, problematic, sticky** (*informal*), **stressful, tense, tough** (*esp. AmE*), **tricky, uncomfortable, unfortunate, unpleasant** ◇ *I always seem to get into sticky ~s.* | **dangerous, hazardous, life-threatening, perilous, risky, vulnerable** | **deteriorating, worsening** | **crisis, emergency, life-and-death, life-or-death** | **high-pressure, pressure** | **alarming, critical, desperate, dire, grave, serious, terrible, tragic, unhappy** (*esp. BrE*) | **disgraceful** (*esp. BrE*), **intolerable, untenable** | **catch-22** (*esp. BrE*), **hopeless, no-win** ◇ *We were placed in a hopeless ~.* | **lose-lose, win-win** | **absurd, bizarre, compromising, extraordinary, ludicrous** (*esp. BrE*), **novel, odd, paradoxical, ridiculous, strange, unique, unusual** | **complex, complicated, simple** | **social** ◇ *Do you feel awkward in social ~s?* | **work** | **domestic** | **employment, housing** | **economic, financial, legal, military, political, security** ◇ *the international political ~* | **strategic, tactical** | **combat, conflict, war** | **hostage**

VERB + SITUATION **bring about, create, lead to, result in** | **be faced with, be placed in, encounter, face, find yourself in, get into** ◇ *I found myself in rather an awkward ~.* | **avoid** | **comprehend, grasp, take in, understand** ◇ *She found it difficult to take in the ~.* | **analyse/analyze, appraise, assess, consider, discuss, evaluate, examine, judge, look at, monitor, ponder, review, size up, survey, take stock of, think about, weigh** (*esp. AmE*), **weigh up** (*esp. BrE*) | **clarify, describe, explain, outline, sum up** | **accept** | **address, be in control of, control, cope with, deal with, handle, respond to, take control of** ◇ *learning strategies to cope with difficult ~s* | **fit** ◇ *You can adapt your knowledge to fit your particular ~.* | **ameliorate** (*formal*), **calm, defuse, ease, help, improve** | **correct, rectify, remedy, resolve, stabilize** ◇ *The peacekeepers are trained to defuse potentially explosive ~s.* | **salvage** ◇ *She tried her best to salvage the ~.* | **exploit, manipulate, take advantage of** ◇ *He saw she was confused and he took full advantage of the ~.* | **lose control of** | **affect, change, influence, transform** | **aggravate, complicate, compound, exacerbate, inflame** (*esp. BrE*), **worsen** ◇ *Interfering now would only exacerbate the ~.* | **reverse** ◇ *What would the Republicans be doing if the ~ were reversed?*

SITUATION + VERB **arise, develop, occur, unfold** ◇ *We will deal with that if the ~ arises.* | **exist** | **continue, remain** | **change** | **deteriorate, escalate, worsen** ◇ *The ~ is deteriorating rapidly.* | **improve** | **stabilize** | **demand, require** ◇ *The ~ requires immediate action.*

SITUATION + NOUN **comedy** (usually *sitcom*)

PHRASES the gravity of the ~, the seriousness of the ~ ◇ Given the gravity of the ~, I'm not surprised she's panicking. | the reality of the ~ ◇ She was forced to confront the reality of the ~. | a way out of the ~ ◇ I was in trouble and I could see no way out of the ~.

size noun

1 how big or small sth is

ADJ. considerable, enormous, fair, good, great, impressive, large, massive, substantial, vast ◇ The kitchen is a fair ~. ◇ The vast ~ of the country made it difficult to govern. | compact, diminutive, limited, modest, small ◇ The unit's compact ~ makes it an ideal travel companion. ◇ The dog's diminutive ~ is attractive to many people. ◇ the reduced ~ of the show | increased | increasing | average, mean, medium | moderate, reasonable, sufficient | overall, total | sheer ◇ The sheer ~ of these dinosaurs was their main weapon. | appropriate, convenient, handy, manageable ◇ The ladder is a handy ~ for using in the house. ◇ classes of manageable ~ | optimal, optimum (esp. BrE), perfect | correct, right | wrong | comparable, equal, equivalent, similar | relative ◇ The relative ~ of the middle class has been steadily shrinking. | normal, standard, uniform ◇ Her knee swelled to twice its normal ~. ◇ The standard ~ for the tiles is 12 inches. | varying ◇ windows of varying ~s | maximum, minimum ◇ The fish grow to a maximum ~ of 50 cm. | actual, full, life ◇ The ring is shown actual ~ in the illustration. ◇ a life-size model of a Roman soldier | adult ◇ Only a limited number of the fish will grow to reach adult ~. | class, family, group, household, market, population, sample | portion, serving (AmE) ◇ The larger the serving ~, the more you're likely to eat. | physical | body, brain, etc. ◇ He eats a lot in proportion to his body ~. | screen, window

VERB + SIZE adjust, change, control | expand, increase | limit | decrease, reduce, shrink ◇ The company is reducing the ~ of its workforce. | double, treble (BrE), triple ◇ She has almost doubled the ~ of her investments. | determine ◇ A city's ~ is determined by the extent of its market area. | match | attain, grow to, reach | estimate, guess, guess at ◇ I had to guess at the ~ of the batteries. | overestimate, underestimate | calculate, determine, measure | compare

SIZE + VERB grow, increase | decline, decrease, fall | range from … to … | vary ◇ The ~ of her audience varied. | allow sth, allow for sth ◇ Their smaller ~ allowed for greater acceleration.

PREP. from the ~ of ◇ From the ~ of the crowds outside, it was a very good movie. | in ~ ◇ How do the samples compare in ~? ◇ The city has doubled in ~ in the last twenty years. ◇ These insects range in ~ from one to two inches. ◇ Houses increase in ~ as you travel further from the city. | in the ~ of ◇ the increase in the ~ of the population

PHRASES given the ~ of sth ◇ Given the ~ of the task, he won't have time to do anything else. | half the ~ of sth, two, three, etc. times the ~ of sth ◇ Their house is twice the ~ of ours. | relative to sb's/sth's ~ ◇ Their weight is small relative to their ~. | shapes and ~s, ~s and shapes (often figurative) ◇ Our customers come in all shapes and ~s. | ~ and scope ◇ Their website has grown in ~ and scope.

2 one of a number of fixed measurements

ADJ. large, medium, small ◇ The company is now going to make these products in larger ~s. | various ◇ Brushes come in various ~s. | two-gallon, four-pound, etc. ◇ The half-gallon ~ comes in a metal can. | imperial, metric ◇ New radiators come in metric ~s. | adult, children's, men's, women's | bust, chest, etc. ◇ XL fits chest ~s 44 to 50. | bra, collar, shoe | font ◇ I changed the font ~ on the document.

… OF SIZES range, variety

VERB + SIZE be, take, wear ◇ What ~ are you (= for shoes or clothes)? ◇ What ~ do you take? ◇ Michael wears ~ 10 shoes. | be available in, come in ◇ The bricks come in four ~s.

SIZE + VERB fit sb ◇ Children's ~s don't fit her any more.

PREP. in a/your ~ ◇ Does this dress come in a bigger ~? ◇ I couldn't find the blouse in my ~.

PHRASES be a ~ too big, small, etc. ◇ The jacket is several ~s

too large for him. | ~ matters ◇ In surfing, ~ matters: big waves are beautiful.

skating noun

ADJ. ice, roller | in-line (esp. AmE) | figure (usually figure-skating), speed | pair

VERB + SKATING go ◇ We used to go ~ on the lake in cold winters.

SKATING + NOUN championships, competition, event | rink | lesson | coach | world ◇ some of the ~ world's leading choreographers

→ Special page at SPORTS

skeleton noun

ADJ. dinosaur, fish, human, etc. | external, internal | complete, partial ◇ a partial ~ of an undiscovered species

VERB + SKELETON form | discover, find, uncover, unearth | preserve

SKELETON + VERB belong ◇ The other ~ belonged to a young man.

skeptic, skeptical, skepticism (AmE) → See SCEPTIC, SCEPTICAL, SCEPTICISM

sketch noun

1 quick drawing

ADJ. lightning, quick | rough, simple | detailed | preliminary, preparatory | initial, original ◇ the artist's original ~ | charcoal, ink, oil, pen-and-ink, pencil, watercolour/watercolor | composite (AmE) ◇ Police released a composite ~ of the suspect.

VERB + SKETCH do, draw, make

SKETCH + NOUN book (usually sketchbook), pad | map | plan (BrE) | artist (esp. AmE) ◇ The judge will ban ~ artists from the courtroom.

PREP. in a/the ~ ◇ The family house appears in several of her ~es. | ~ by ◇ a series of ~es by John Constable | ~ for ◇ to make a ~ for an oil painting | ~ of ◇ He did some rough ~es of the costumes.

→ Note at ART

2 short description

ADJ. brief, thumbnail ◇ The talk began with a thumbnail ~ of the political situation at that time. | biographical, character | historical ◇ He begins the tour with a brief historical ~ of the town.

VERB + SKETCH give sb

PREP. ~ of ◇ He gave us character ~es of all his relations.

3 short comic scene

ADJ. short | comedy, comic, satirical | revue (esp. BrE) ◇ The show sometimes feels like a university revue ~.

VERB + SKETCH do, perform | write

SKETCH + NOUN comedy | comedy show (AmE), show (BrE) ◇ a one-hour TV ~ (comedy) show | writer (esp. BrE) | group (AmE) ◇ I was in a ~ group for a couple of years.

PREP. ~ about ◇ a comedy ~ about a dead parrot

ski noun

ADJ. alpine, backcountry (AmE), cross-country ◇ Backcountry ~s are carefully designed to save weight. | powder, slalom | shaped

… OF SKIS pair

VERB + SKI put on | remove, take off | hire (BrE), rent | wax

SKI + NOUN pole, stick (BrE) | boot, jacket, mask, pants, suit | equipment | instructor | lesson | area, run, slope, trail | lift | jump | resort | season | chalet, lodge | holiday (BrE), trip, vacation (AmE) ◇ She was on a ~ trip in Colorado.

PREP. on ~s ◇ The children go to school on ~s.

skiing noun

ADJ. alpine, downhill | backcountry (AmE), cross-country, Nordic | dry-slope | off-piste (BrE)

VERB + SKIING go | **have** ◇ *The mountain regions have plenty of good* ~.

SKIING + NOUN accident | holiday (*BrE*), trip (*esp. BrE*) (usually *ski trip* in *AmE*), vacation (usually *ski vacation*) (*AmE*) | resort, season (*both BrE*) (usually *ski resort*, *ski season* in *AmE*) | conditions | technique ◇ *He taught us how to improve our* ~ *technique.* | champion | championship | event ◇ *their first ever medal in an alpine* ~ *event* → Special page at SPORTS

skilful (*BrE*) (*AmE* skillful) *adj.*

VERBS be | become

ADV. extremely, fairly, very, etc. | highly, incredibly, particularly | technically

PREP. at ◇ *I became* ~ *at drawing.* | in ◇ *highly* ~ *in his tactics*

skill *noun*

ADJ. considerable, consummate (*esp. BrE*), extraordinary, great, remarkable ◇ *He is a negotiator of considerable* ~. | superior ◇ *Holmes defeated Cooney with his superior boxing* ~*s.* | good, poor ◇ *She has good organizational* ~*s.* | basic ◇ *the basic* ~*s of reading, writing and arithmetic* | essential, important, necessary, requisite ◇ *He lacked the requisite* ~*s for the job.* | marketable, practical, transferable (*esp. BrE*), useful ◇ *training in problem-solving and other marketable* ~*s* | new, old ◇ *to learn some new* ~*s* | analytical, critical-thinking (*esp. AmE*), problem-solving | cognitive, motor ◇ *Alcohol can impact cognitive and motor* ~*s severely.* | coping ◇ *Her therapist hopes to improve her coping* ~*s.* | parenting | special, specialist (*esp. BrE*) ◇ *No special* ~*s or knowledge are required for the job.* | diplomatic, entrepreneurial, leadership, management, managerial, negotiating, organizational, professional ◇ *She displays excellent management* ~*s.* | communication, conversational, inter-personal, social, verbal ◇ *He had poor social* ~*s and often offended people.* | comprehension, linguistic, listening, literacy, reading, speaking, writing ◇ *The project will help to develop children's literacy* ~*s.* | business, computer, design, language, math (*AmE*), mathematical, maths (*BrE*), research, study, survival, teaching ◇ *It is important to develop good study* ~*s.* | athletic (*esp. AmE*), boxing, dribbling, footballing (*BrE*), martial-arts | combat, fight-ing, manual | acting, artistic, cooking, culinary, driving, medical, military, musical, political, tactical, technical ... OF SKILLS range, set ◇ *She had to develop a whole new set of* ~*s when she changed jobs.*

VERB + SKILL have, possess | combine ◇ *Veterinarians combine the* ~*s of a surgeon, radiologist, dietitian and much more.* | lack | need, require, take ◇ *a feat requiring* ~ *and patience* | match ◇ *I decided to find a career to match my* ~*s and abilities.* | acquire, develop, gain, learn, pick up | demonstrate, display, exhibit, show, show off, showcase | exercise, practise/practice | apply, harness, use, utilize ◇ *The manager must harness the* ~*s of the workers to firm objectives.* | broaden, enhance, hone, improve, increase, polish, refine, sharpen, upgrade ◇ *She attends regular training weekends to sharpen her* ~*s.* | master, perfect ◇ *School helps children to master the* ~*s necessary to live in our society.* | refresh, update | pool, share | assess, test ◇ *a course that will test the* ~*s of any golfer* | teach

SKILL + NOUN level | set ◇ *This work requires a different* ~ *set.* | acquisition, development, training | ~s shortage ◇ *The country is facing a* ~*s shortage.*

PREP. with ~ ◇ *She performed the task with great* ~. | ~ as ◇ *her* ~*s as a doctor* | ~ at ◇ *his* ~ *at painting* | ~ in ◇ *their* ~ *in selecting the best designs* | ~ of ◇ *the basic* ~*s of managing an office* | ~ with ◇ *his* ~ *with a sword*

PHRASES a degree of ~, a level of ~ ◇ *an operation that calls for a high degree of* ~ | a lack of ~ ◇ *I enjoy playing squash, despite my lack of* ~. | literacy and numeracy ~s (*BrE*) ◇ *School-leavers lacked basic literacy and numeracy* ~*s.* | a mastery of ~s ◇ *a mastery of basic language* ~*s*

skilled *adj.*

VERBS be | become

ADV. extremely, fairly, very, etc. ◇ *Interviewing is a very* ~ *job.* | especially, exceptionally, highly, particularly, remarkably ◇ *a highly* ~ *workforce* | enough, sufficiently | socially, technically ◇ *We have a shortage of technically* ~ *workers.*

PREP. at ◇ ~ *at needlework* | in ◇ ~ *in the basic techniques* | with ◇ *She wasn't very* ~ *with the camera yet.*

PHRASES ~ in the art (of sth) ◇ *They were* ~ *in the art of war.*

skillet *noun* (*AmE*)

ADJ. non-stick | cast-iron | 8-inch, 10-inch, etc. | large, medium, small | deep

VERB + SKILLET place ◇ *Place the* ~ *over medium heat.* | heat ◇ *Heat a* ~ *over medium-high heat.*

skin *noun*

1 covering of a human/animal body

ADJ. beautiful, clear, fine, flawless, good, healthy, perfect ◇ *You want clear, healthy* ~. | glowing, radiant ◇ *Keep your* ~ *radiant using creams and lotions.* | creamy, smooth, soft | thick, thin | translucent | supple, young, youthful | sagging, wrinkled | hard, leathery, rough, tough | delicate, sensitive | greasy, oily | moist | dry, flaky, scaly | flaking, peeling | black, brown, dark, ebony, golden, olive, tan | alabaster (*literary*), fair, ivory, light, milky, pale, porcelain (*literary*), white ◇ *Jenny is small and slender with porcelain* ~. | pallid, pasty, sallow | bronzed, tanned | sunburned | weathered | freckled | raw, tender ◇ *There was a patch of raw* ~ *on my back where the sun had burned it.* | itchy | blotchy | broken, damaged | hairless | facial | bare, exposed, naked ◇ *The sheets felt nice next to his bare* ~. ◇ *Wear clothing that protects all exposed* ~. | loose ◇ *I picked up the kitten by the loose* ~ *on its neck.* | outer | dead ◇ *A lot of dust is made up of particles of dead* ~.

VERB + SKIN break, burn, damage, irritate | protect | moisturize, nourish, soothe ◇ *This cream moisturizes dry* ~. | dry, dry out | exfoliate ◇ *Clean and exfoliate your* ~ *before applying make-up.* | remove ◇ *Exfoliate to remove dead* ~. | penetrate, pierce, puncture ◇ *The needle pierced my* ~. | shed ◇ *This snake sheds its* ~ *eight times a year.* | age ◇ *Smoking undoubtedly ages the* ~.

SKIN + VERB glisten, glow ◇ *Her* ~ *was glistening with sweat after her run.* | age ◇ *They claim that this cream makes the* ~ *age more slowly.* | hang, sag | blister, burn, peel | crawl, tingle ◇ *Just thinking about spiders makes my* ~ *crawl.*

SKIN + NOUN allergy, burns, cancer, complaint (*esp. BrE*), condition, damage, disease, disorder (*esp. AmE*), infection, irritation, lesion, problems, rash | graft | specialist (*esp. BrE*) | care ◇ *make-up and skin-care products* | cleanser, cream, lotion, products (*esp. AmE*) | colour/color, tone | texture | type | cells, tissue | contact ◇ *Avoid* ~ *contact with the glue.*

PREP. against the/your ~ ◇ *The sheets felt rough against her* ~. | beneath the/your ~ ◇ *Beneath his* ~, *the muscles were tight with tension.* | on the/your ~ ◇ *blisters on the* ~ | through the/your ~ ◇ *A network of veins showed through his* ~. | under the/your ~ ◇ *He discovered a lump under his* ~ *so he went to the doctor.*

PHRASES ~ and bone (*esp. BrE*), ~ and bones (*esp. AmE*) ◇ *The dog was little more than* ~ *and bone/bones.*

2 skin of an animal that has been removed

ADJ. animal | crocodile, goat, leopard, etc.

VERB + SKIN cure, tan

3 covering of some fruits/ vegetables

ADJ. banana, onion, potato, etc.

VERB + SKIN peel off, remove

skip *verb*

ADV. lightly, nimbly | happily, merrily | practically ◇ *Scott practically skipped home, he was so happy.* | along | away, off ◇ *She skipped off to play with her friends.* | back

PREP. down, up ◇ *He skipped lightly up the stairs.* | to ◇ *She skipped to the door.*

PHRASES **sb's heart ~s a beat** (*figurative*) ◊ *What I saw made my heart ~ a beat.*

skirmish *noun*

ADJ. **brief, little, minor, small** | **border** | **early, first, opening** ◊ *an opening ~ in the protracted media battle ahead*
SKIRMISH + VERB **break out** ◊ *Minor ~es broke out all along the border.* | **go on, happen, occur** | **continue**
PREP. **in a/the ~** ◊ *He was killed in a border ~.* | **~ between** ◊ *~es between the police and guerrillas* | **~ over** ◊ *a ~ over boundaries* | **~ with** ◊ *They were involved in a ~ with rival fans.*

skirt *noun*

ADJ. **long, short** ◊ *She was wearing a short denim ~.* | **ankle-length, calf-length, knee-length** | **tight** | **circular, flared, full, gathered, voluminous** ◊ *She tucked up her voluminous ~s to make room for Jane.* | **A-line, mini** (usually *miniskirt*), **pencil, straight** | **pleated, wrap-around** | **cotton, denim, linen, etc.** | **plaid** (*esp. AmE*), **tartan** ◊ *She wore the plaid ~ that was the uniform of her private school.* | **grass, hula** | **matching** ◊ *a green jacket with a matching ~*
VERB + SKIRT **hike up** (*esp. AmE*), **hitch up, lift, pick up, pull up** | **pull down** | **smooth, smooth down** ◊ *She sat down, smoothing her ~.* | **straighten**
SKIRT + VERB **billow, swirl** ◊ *Her full ~ billowed around her as she danced.* | **ride up** ◊ *Her ~ rode up her thighs when she sat down.* | **fall** ◊ *The ~ falls just above the knee.*
SKIRT + NOUN **length** | **suit** (*AmE*) ◊ *I've worn both ~ suits and pant suits to interviews.*
PHRASES **the hem of sb's ~** ◊ *I lifted the hem of my ~.*
→ Special page at CLOTHES

skull *noun*

ADJ. **human** | **thick, thin** | **fractured** ◊ *He suffered a fractured ~ in an accident in April.* | **grinning** ◊ *the angel of death with his grinning ~*
VERB + SKULL **crack, fracture** | **crush, shatter, smash**
SKULL + NOUN **fracture**
PHRASES **a fracture of the ~, a fracture to the ~** (*BrE*) | **suffer a fractured ~** (*esp. BrE*) ◊ *He suffered a fractured ~ in an accident in April.* | **~ and crossbones** ◊ *The ship was flying a pirate flag with the ~ and crossbones on it.*

sky *noun*

ADJ. **big, vast, wide** | **open** ◊ *We slept under the open ~.* | **empty** | **bright, clear, cloudless, sunny** ◊ *a week of cloudless skies* | **hazy, smoggy** | **cloudy, dull, overcast** | **stormy** | **star-filled, starlit, starry, star-studded** | **moonlit** | **dark, darkening, pale** | **azure, blue, cerulean** (*esp. AmE*) ◊ *I opened my shutters and saw a brilliant blue ~.* | **grey/gray, leaden** | **black, inky, moonless** ◊ *the pale moon in the inky night ~* | **morning, night, etc.** | **January, spring, winter, wintry, etc.** | **northern, southern, etc.** | **desert** ◊ *the vast desert skies*
... OF SKY **patch** ◊ *a patch of blue ~*
VERB + SKY **illuminate, light up** ◊ *The fireworks lit up the ~.* | **fill** ◊ *Flocks of flamingoes fill the ~.* | **scan, watch** ◊ *Astronomers scan the night skies for asteroids.* | **patrol**
SKY + VERB **clear, clear up, lighten** ◊ *The rain stopped and the skies cleared.* | **cloud over** (*esp. BrE*), **darken, turn grey/gray** ◊ *The afternoon ~ turned orange.* | **be streaked with sth** ◊ *The ~ was streaked with gold.* | **glow (with sth), light up (with sth)** ◊ *The ~ glows red with fire.* | **open** (= start raining) ◊ *The skies opened and rain poured down.*
PREP. **across the ~** ◊ *Black clouds spread across the ~.* | **against the ~** ◊ *The eagle was black against the morning ~.* | **beneath a…~, under a…~** ◊ *a ship tossing under a dark ~* | **from the ~, out of the ~** ◊ *A strange object dropped out of the ~.* | **in the ~** ◊ *There was a kite high up in the ~.* | **~ above** ◊ *A helicopter appeared in the ~ above them.* | **~ over** ◊ *to patrol the skies over the Atlantic*
PHRASES **high in the ~, low in the ~** ◊ *when the sun is low in the ~* | **the ~ above, the ~ overhead** ◊ *Swallows darted about in the ~ overhead.* | **the ~ is falling** (*figurative, esp. AmE*) ◊ *alarmists who claim that the ~ is falling* | **reach for the ~** (*often figurative*) ◊ *My philosophy has always been to*

reach for the ~. | **take to the skies** (= to go into the sky) ◊ *Some vintage aircraft will be taking to the skies at this weekend's fair.*

skyline *noun*

ADJ. **dramatic** | **city, downtown** (*AmE*) | **Manhattan, Tokyo, etc.** | **northern, western, etc.**
VERB + SKYLINE **dominate, fill** ◊ *The ~ is dominated by a power station.* | **change** ◊ *These buildings have already changed ~s from Los Angeles to Hong Kong.* | **break** ◊ *The ~ is broken by a water tower.*
PREP. **across the ~** ◊ *small white clouds sweeping gently across the ~* | **against the ~** ◊ *the moving figures he could see against the ~* | **below the ~** ◊ *The sun slipped below the ~.* | **on the ~** ◊ *There are many construction cranes on the ~.* | **over ~** ◊ *Clouds of smoke floated over the ~.*
PHRASES **a view of the ~** ◊ *The roof commands a spectacular view of the ~.*

skyscraper *noun*

ADJ. **giant, huge, tall, towering** ◊ *the world's tallest ~ in the shadow of the towering ~s of Manhattan* | **modern, new** | **downtown** (*AmE*) | **20-storey/20-story, 30-storey/30-story, etc.** | **glass** | **gleaming** ◊ *Chicago's skyline of gleaming ~s*
... OF SKYSCRAPERS **forest** ◊ *He found himself approaching a forest of ~s.*
VERB + SKYSCRAPER **build** | **surround** ◊ *a square surrounded by towering ~s*
SKYSCRAPER + VERB **loom, rise** ◊ *Tall ~s loomed above us.* | **tower above sb/sth, tower over sb/sth** ◊ *The ~ towered over the surrounding buildings.*

slab *noun*

ADJ. **great, huge, large** ◊ *They were unloading great ~s of rock.* | **thick** ◊ *thick ~s of meat* | **flat** | **paving** (*BrE*) | **mortuary** | **concrete, marble, stone, etc.**
PREP. **on a/the ~** ◊ *corpses laid out on cold mortuary ~s* | **~ of** ◊ *a ~ of butter/chocolate/concrete/meat*

slack *adj.*

1 loose
VERBS **be, feel, look, seem** | **become, fall, go** ◊ *Let the reins go ~.* | **leave sth** ◊ *Leave the thread slightly ~ to allow for movement.*
ADV. **very, fairly** | **completely** ◊ *Some of the ropes were completely ~.* | **a little, slightly, etc.**

2 not busy
VERBS **be, seem** | **become** | **remain** ◊ *The antiques business remained ~.*
ADV. **extremely, fairly, very, etc.** ◊ *This season has been pretty ~ for local hotels so far.*

3 lazy
VERBS **be** | **become, get**
ADV. **very** | **a bit, rather**
PREP. **in** ◊ *She knew she had been very ~ in her church attendance recently.*

slam *verb*

ADV. **hard** ◊ *She ran out of the room and slammed the door as hard as she could.* | **loudly** | **angrily, violently** | **repeatedly** ◊ *He repeatedly slammed the man's head against the wall.* | **back, down** ◊ *He said goodbye and slammed the phone down.*
VERB + SLAM **hear sth**
PREP. **against** ◊ *Kath's heart slammed against her ribs.* | **behind** ◊ *I heard the door ~ behind him.* | **into** ◊ *The car skidded and slammed into a tree.*
PHRASES **~ sth home** (*BrE, sports*) ◊ *He slammed home the penalty for goal number two.* | **~ on the brakes** ◊ *He slammed on the brakes to avoid hitting another car.* | **~ (sth) shut** ◊ *He slammed the lid shut.* ◊ *The door slammed shut.*

slander noun

ADJ. **gross** (*BrE*), **malicious, vicious, vile**
VERB + SLANDER **be guilty of** | **sue sb for**
SLANDER + NOUN **suit** (*esp. AmE*) ◇ *I might have grounds for a ~ suit.*
PREP. **~ against** ◇ *He was found guilty of ~ against his employers.* | **~ on** ◇ *Many teachers saw the statement as a vicious ~ on their profession.*

slang noun

ADJ. **current, modern** | **common** | **street** ◇ *The gang members use street ~.* | **hip-hop** | **army** (*esp. BrE*), **military** | **sexual** | **rhyming** ◇ *cockney rhyming ~*
VERB + SLANG **use**
SLANG + NOUN **expression, name, term, word**
PREP. **in ~** ◇ *in military ~* | **~ for** ◇ *'Woofy' is ~ for 'good-looking'.*

slant noun

1 leaning position

PREP. **at a ~** ◇ *They held their spears at a ~.*

2 way of thinking about sth

ADJ. **different, modern, new** | **negative, positive** | **definite, obvious** ◇ *The story has a definite liberal ~ to it.* | **overall** (*esp. AmE*) ◇ *the overall ~ of newspaper coverage of the campaign* | **your own, personal, unique** | **editorial** | **ideological, political** | **conservative, feminist, left-wing, liberal, rightward** (*esp. AmE*), etc.
VERB + SLANT **give sth, have, put, take** ◇ *He puts his own particular ~ on everything.*
PREP. **with a ...~** ◇ *an article with a right-wing ~* | **~ on** ◇ *That's a different ~ on the causes of the war.* | **~ to** ◇ *The story gives a new ~ to his character.*
PHRASES **a/sb's ~ on things** ◇ *I've tried to put my own ~ on things, even in the early songs.*

slap noun

ADJ. **gentle, light, little, playful** ◇ *She gave him a playful ~ on the arm as everyone laughed.* | **hard, painful, sharp, stinging** | **resounding** | **friendly, hearty** ◇ *He gave his brother a hearty ~ on the back to congratulate him.*
VERB + SLAP **deliver, give sb** ◇ *Her mother delivered a hard ~ and sent her to bed.* | **get, receive** | **deserve, need** ◇ *That boy needs a ~!*
PREP. **~ across** ◇ *He received a ~ across the face.* | **~ on** ◇ *They congratulated me with hearty ~s on the back.* | **with a ~** ◇ *He hit the water with a resounding ~.*
PHRASES **a ~ in the face** (*figurative*) ◇ *The closure of the school is a ~ in the face to the local community.* | **a ~ on the wrist** (*figurative*) ◇ *We're hoping that she gets off with a ~ on the wrist from the judge.*

slap verb

ADV. **hard** | **gently, lightly, playfully** | **away** ◇ *She slapped his hand away.*
PREP. **across** ◇ *The officer slapped him hard across the face.* | **on** ◇ *She slapped the boy on the leg.*
PHRASES **~ sb in the face** (*usually figurative*) ◇ *I felt like I had been slapped in the face.*

slash verb

1 cut

ADV. **wildly**
PREP. **at, through** ◇ *He ~ed through the rope.* | **with** ◇ *He ~ed wildly at me with a knife.*

2 reduce

ADJ. **dramatically, drastically** ◇ *The company dramatically ~ed its forecasts for annual profits.* | **aggressively** | **in half** ◇ *Inflation was ~ed in half.*
PREP. **by** ◇ *His salary was ~ed by 20%.* | **from, to** ◇ *The discount could be ~ed from 15% to 10%.*

slaughter noun

ADJ. **indiscriminate, mass, wholesale** ◇ *the indiscriminate ~ of civilians* | **brutal, senseless, terrible** | **ritual** | **animal** ◇ *humane forms of animal ~* | **halal, kosher**
VERB + SLAUGHTER **end, prevent, stop** ◇ *We were helpless to stop the ~.* | **ban** ◇ *federal legislation to ban horse ~* | **order** ◇ *Officials ordered the ~ of hundreds of animals.*
PREP. **for ~** ◇ *the transporting of live horses for ~*
PHRASES **the ~ of innocents** ◇ *the horrors of civil war and the ~ of innocents*

slaughter verb

1 kill an animal

ADV. **humanely** ◇ *The animals are all humanely ~ed.* | **ritually** | **illegally** ◇ *elephants illegally ~ed by poachers*
PREP. **for** ◇ *Thousands of birds were ~ed for their feathers.*

2 kill a large number of people

ADV. **brutally, cruelly** ◇ *Hundreds of innocent civilians were cruelly ~ed.* | **indiscriminately** | **systematically** ◇ *Thousands of people were systematically ~ed by their oppressors.*

slave noun

ADJ. **escaped, fugitive, runaway** | **emancipated, freed** | **former** ◇ *the son of former ~s* | **domestic, personal** | **plantation** | **galley** ◇ *galley ~s at the oars of Mediterranean ships* | **wage** ◇ *They work as wage ~s for 13 cents an hour.* | **sex** | **virtual** ◇ *She was forced to work as a virtual ~ for a rich family.*
VERB + SLAVE **become** | **have, keep, own** | **export, import** | **buy, take sb as** | **sell (sb as)** | **use (sb as)** | **treat** ◇ *He treated the ~s like animals.* | **emancipate, free, liberate** ◇ *landowners who freed their ~s voluntarily*
SLAVE + NOUN **labour/labor** ◇ *Without ~ labour/labor, the tobacco industry would have collapsed.* | **labourer/laborer** | **master, owner, trader** | **market, trade, traffic** ◇ *the abolition of the ~ trade* | **ship** | **population** | **society** ◇ *studies comparing ~ societies throughout history* | **state** ◇ *Virginia was the largest ~ state in the Union.* | **plantation** | **rebellion, revolt, uprising** | **quarters** ◇ *the ~ quarters at the rear of the house* | **girl, woman** | **wages** (*figurative*) ◇ *I'll be working long hours for ~ wages!*
PREP. **~ of** ◇ *a ~ of habit* | **~ to** ◇ *a ~ to fashion*

slavery noun

ADJ. **chattel** ◇ *the system of chattel ~* | **plantation** | **domestic** | **child, human** | **racial** | **antebellum** (= before the American Civil War) (*esp. AmE*) | **modern, modern-day** | **economic, wage** | **sex, sexual** ◇ *The women were sold into sexual ~.* | **virtual** ◇ *Poverty forces children into virtual ~.*
VERB + SLAVERY **establish, introduce** | **abolish, ban, end, outlaw, prohibit** ◇ *The Thirteenth Amendment abolished ~ in 1865.* | **condone, defend, justify, support** | **condemn, denounce, oppose** | **sell sb into** | **free sb from** | **be born into** | **escape**
SLAVERY + NOUN **reparations** ◇ *The Senate candidate now supports ~ reparations.* | **issue, question** | **ring** ◇ *The organization has helped to expose human ~ rings.*
PREP. **in ~** ◇ *They were living in ~ and poverty.* | **under ~** ◇ *conditions for children under ~*
PHRASES **the abolition of ~, the end of ~** | **the institution of ~** | **the legacy of ~**

sled noun (*esp. AmE*)

ADJ. **plastic, wooden** | **dog** ◇ *He explored Greenland on a dog ~.* | **snow**
VERB + SLED **drag, pull** | **drive, ride**
SLED + NOUN **dog** | **team** | **ride**
PREP. **on a ~** ◇ *I went down a hill on a ~.*

sledge (*BrE*) noun

ADJ. **dog**
VERB + SLEDGE **drag, pull** ◇ *She had to pull a 60-pound ~ across 200 miles.* | **drive**
PREP. **on a ~**

sleep noun

1 condition of rest

ADJ. **deep** | **light** | **much-needed** ◇ *I'm off to bed for some much-needed ~.* | **adequate** | **REM**
VERB + SLEEP **drift into, drift off to, drop off to, fall back to** (*AmE*), **get to, go to** ◇ *She turned over and went back to ~.* | **cry yourself to** | **catch, get, snatch** ◇ *Close your eyes and get some ~ now.* ◇ *I snatched a few hours' ~ in the afternoon.* | **need** | **survive on** ◇ *They seem to survive on only a few hours' ~ a night.* | **induce, promote** ◇ *the use of drugs to induce ~* | **lull sb to, send sb to** ◇ *The quiet music soon sent her to ~.* | **drift in and out of** ◇ *He drifted in and out of ~ all night.* | **lose** (*often figurative*) ◇ *Don't lose ~ over it—we'll sort everything out in the morning.* | **disrupt, disturb, interrupt** | **catch up on** ◇ *I used Saturday to catch up on my ~.* | **feign** ◇ *I feigned ~ when the nurse came around.*
SLEEP + VERB **come** ◇ *Sleep came to her in snatches.* | **overcome sb, overtake sb** ◇ *Sleep finally overtook me.*
SLEEP + NOUN **cycle, pattern, schedule** (*esp. AmE*) | **deprivation, loss** | **disorder** | **apnoea/apnea** | **aid** (*esp. AmE*) ◇ *the nation's most commonly prescribed ~ aid*
PREP. **during ~** ◇ *a decreased heart rate during ~* | **in your ~** ◇ *He often walks and talks in his ~.*
PHRASES **a lack of ~** ◇ *I was suffering from a lack of ~.* | **a wink of ~** ◇ *I won't get a wink of ~ with that noise downstairs.*

2 period of sleep

ADJ. **long** | **little, short** | **dead, deep, heavy, sound** | **uninterrupted** | **good, restful** | **light** | **disturbed, exhausted, fitful, restless, troubled, uneasy** ◇ *I woke up early after a disturbed ~.* | **dreamless, peaceful** | **drunken** | **beauty** ◇ *Sorry, but I need my beauty ~.*
VERB + SLEEP **need** | **have** ◇ *Did you have a good ~?* | **be in** ◇ *I was in a deep ~ when the phone rang.* | **drift into, fall into, sink into** ◇ *I immediately fell into a dead ~.* | **awake (sb) from, awaken (sb) from, wake (sb) from** ◇ *He woke from a fitful ~ with a headache.*
PHRASES **a good, poor, etc. night's ~** ◇ *You'll feel better after a good night's ~.*

sleep verb

ADV. **properly** (*esp. BrE*), **soundly, well** ◇ *The children were all ~ing soundly.* ◇ *Did you ~ well last night?* | **comfortably, peacefully, quietly, safely** | **easily, quiet** | **easy** ◇ *We can at least ~ easy at night, knowing that we are safe.* | **late, long** ◇ *Let them ~ late on Saturday morning if they want to.* ◇ *She scolded him for ~ing so long.* | **badly, fitfully, poorly, uneasily** | **deeply, heavily** ◇ *He was exhausted and slept deeply.* | **lightly** ◇ *She always slept very lightly so I had to be careful not to wake her.* | **barely, hardly** ◇ *She felt as if she had hardly slept.* | **a little** | **alone** | **together**
VERB + SLEEP **be unable to, cannot** ◇ *I couldn't ~ so I got up and went downstairs.* | **try to** ◇ *You must be very tired. Try to ~ a little.* | **let sb** | **put sb/sth to** ◇ *You should always put babies to ~ on their backs.* ◇ *We had to have our dog put to ~* (= humanely killed).
PREP. **for** ◇ *I only slept for four hours that night.* | **through** ◇ *She slept right through the storm.* ◇ *Very few babies ~ through the night* (= without waking up). | **with** ◇ *Everyone knows she ~s with the boss.*
PHRASES **have trouble ~ing** ◇ *I've been having trouble ~ing lately.* | **not ~ a wink** (= not sleep at all) ◇ *I didn't ~ a wink last night.* | **~ like a baby, ~ like a log** (= sleep very well) | **~ on your back, ~ on your front, ~ on your side, ~ on your stomach** ◇ *I had to ~ on my back for the first few days after the accident.* | **~ overnight** ◇ *We slept overnight at the beach.* | **~ outside, ~ rough** (*BrE*) ◇ *the problem of young people who ~ rough in the streets*

sleepy adj.

1 ready to go to sleep

VERBS **be, feel, look, sound** | **become, get, grow** | **make sb** ◇ *The alcohol was making him ~.*
ADV. **extremely, fairly, very, etc.** | **a little, slightly, etc.** ◇ *She was beginning to get a little ~.*

2 very quiet

VERBS **be, seem** | **remain** ◇ *The town remains ~ despite the activity all around it.*
PHRASES **~ little** ◇ *a ~ little fishing town*

sleeve noun

1 piece of clothing that covers arm

ADJ. **long, short** | **left, right** | **full, wide** | **three-quarter** (*esp. AmE*), **three-quarter length** | **rolled-up** | **coat, jacket, shirt, etc.** | **removable**
VERB + SLEEVE **push back, push up, roll up** ◇ *She rolled up her ~s and got down to work.* | **roll down** | **tug at, tug on** ◇ *I looked around to see who was tugging at my ~.*
PREP. **in…~s** ◇ *It was sunny, and everyone was in short ~s.* | **on a/the ~** ◇ *There's tomato on your ~.*

2 envelope for a CD, etc.

ADJ. **album, CD, DVD, record** | **cardboard, plastic** | **protective** | **inner, outer** | **gatefold**
VERB + SLEEVE **design** ◇ *He designed record ~s for the Rolling Stones.*
SLEEVE + NOUN **notes** ◇ *The music is explained in the extensive ~ notes.* | **design**

slender adj.

1 thin in an attractive way

VERBS **be, look**
ADV. **extremely, fairly, very, etc.** ◇ *Those jeans make you look very ~.*
PHRASES **long slender…** ◇ *She had long ~ fingers.*

2 small in amount/size

VERBS **be, seem** | **remain**
ADV. **fairly, pretty, rather**

slice noun

1 flat piece of food

ADJ. **big, generous, great, huge, large, thick** | **little, small, thin** | **cheese, lemon, pizza, etc.**
VERB + SLICE **cut** ◇ *She cut a thin ~ of lemon.* | **eat**
PREP. **in ~s** ◇ *The sausage is also sold pre-packed in ~s.* | **~ of** ◇ *a ~ of bread/cake/pizza/toast*
PHRASES **cut sth into ~s** ◇ *He cut the meat into thick ~s.*

2 part or share of sth

ADJ. **big, huge, large** | **fair, significant, sizeable, substantial** (*all esp. BrE*) ◇ *They spend a fair ~ of the budget on research and development.* | **narrow, small, tiny**
VERB + SLICE **carve, carve out** ◇ *The company has managed to carve out a ~ of the market for itself.* | **get, grab** ◇ *Many investors are hoping to grab a ~ of the action.*
PREP. **~ of** ◇ *The agency takes a large ~ of the profits.*
PHRASES **a ~ of life** ◇ *This drama provides a ~ of life in 1950s Connecticut.* | **a ~ of the action** | **a ~ of the pie** ◇ *Different groups of people will demand a bigger ~ of the pie.* | **a ~ of luck** (*BrE*) ◇ *He needed a large ~ of luck to win the game.*

slice verb

ADV. **finely** (*esp. BrE*), **thinly** ◇ *Slice the bread thinly.* | **thickly** | **neatly** (*esp. AmE*) | **cleanly** ◇ *The knife ~d cleanly through the flesh.* | **off, up** ◇ *Slice up the mushrooms and fry them.*
PREP. **into** ◇ *The blade ~d into her shoulder.* | **off** ◇ *He ~d pieces off the large steak.* | **through** ◇ *The knife ~d through his ear.*
PHRASES **~ sth in half, ~ sth in two** ◇ *Slice the onion in two.*

slide noun

1 in photography

ADJ. **colour/color** | **photographic**
VERB + SLIDE **show** | **develop**
SLIDE + NOUN **film** | **presentation, show** ◇ *He gave a fascinating ~ show on climbing in the Himalayas.* | **projector**

2 for use with a microscope

ADJ. **glass** | **microscope**
VERB + SLIDE **mount sth on**

3 change to a lower/worse condition

ADJ. **downhill, downward** | **inevitable, inexorable** | **long, slow, steady** | **steep** | **slippery** (esp. BrE) ◇ the start of a slippery ~ down to family breakdown | **economic, stock-market**
VERB + SLIDE **begin** | **continue** ◇ The country is continuing the ~ into chaos and violence. | **halt, prevent, stop** | **reverse**
PREP. **~ down** ◇ He began his ~ down the slippery slope of alcohol abuse. | **~ in** ◇ to stop the ~ in the dollar | **~ into** ◇ No one could prevent the inexorable ~ into war. | **~ towards/ toward** ◇ the market's recent ~ towards/toward panic

slide verb

ADV. **slowly** ◇ Tears slid slowly down his pale cheek. | **quickly** | **easily** | **smoothly** ◇ a vehicle that will ~ smoothly across snow | **gently** | **gracefully** | **noiselessly, quietly, silently** ◇ The moon slid silently behind a cloud. | **around, away, back, backwards/backward, down, forward, in, off, out, sideways** ◇ The drawers ~ in and out easily. | **downhill** (often figurative) ◇ The economy is sliding rapidly downhill.
PREP. **across, along, down, from, into, off, onto, out of, over, to, up, etc.** ◇ The Hong Kong economy was sliding into recession. | ◇ He slid off the couch and walked over to me.
PHRASES **~ open** ◇ The doors slid open.

slight adj.

1 very small in degree

VERBS **appear, be, seem**
ADV. **extremely, fairly, very, etc.** | **comparatively, relatively**
PHRASES **the slightest of ...** ◇ She gave the slightest of smiles.

2 thin and delicate

VERBS **be, look** ◇ She looked very ~, almost fragile.
ADV. **very** | **physically**

slim adj.

VERBS **be, look** | **become, get** (informal) ◇ dieters who get ~ using these methods | **keep, remain, stay** ◇ She works very hard to stay ~. | **make sb** ◇ Step exercises can help make you ~. | **keep sb**
ADV. **extremely, fairly, very, etc.**
PHRASES **tall and ~**

slime noun

ADJ. **thick** | **primeval, primordial** ◇ the primeval ~ from which all life developed | **pond** | **black, green, etc.**
VERB + SLIME **be covered in, be covered with** | **produce** ◇ Frogs produce ~ to keep their skin moist.
SLIME + VERB **ooze**
SLIME + NOUN **mould/mold** ◇ The organisms are a ~ mould/ mold.
PHRASES **a trail of ~** ◇ The snail left a trail of ~ along the floor.

slimy adj.

VERBS **be, feel, look** ◇ The seaweed felt cold and ~.
ADV. **a little, slightly, etc.** | **very** | **all** ◇ The walls were all ~ and green.
PREP. **with** ◇ The steps were ~ with moss.
PHRASES **cold and ~, wet and ~** ◇ The wall of the cave was wet and ~ to the touch.

sling verb

ADV. **loosely** | **carelessly, casually** ◇ His jacket was carelessly slung over one shoulder.
PREP. **across, around, in, on, over, round** (esp. BrE), **etc.**
PHRASES **~ mud at sb** (= criticize or accuse sb to damage their reputation) | **~ sth around sb's shoulders** ◇ He slung his arm around my shoulders. | **~ sth over your shoulder** ◇ She slung her bag over her shoulder.

slip noun

1 mistake

ADJ. **little, slight** | **unfortunate** | **accidental** | **occasional** | **Freudian, verbal**
VERB + SLIP **make** ◇ She made a couple of unfortunate ~s during the talk. | **afford** ◇ His team cannot afford any ~s.
PHRASES **a ~ of the tongue** ◇ I didn't mean to say that—it was just a ~ of the tongue.

2 piece of paper

ADJ. **rejection** (esp. BrE) ◇ He got fifty rejection ~s before his novel was published. | **betting, voting** (both BrE) | **permission** (esp. AmE) | **credit, credit-card, deposit** ◇ a bank deposit ~ | **pay, wage** (both BrE) | **blue** (AmE, politics) ◇ The Senator returns the blue ~ with an indication whether he or she supports or opposes the nominee. | **pink** (= to say that sb must leave their job) (AmE) | **compliments** (BrE) ◇ He sent his cheque with a compliments ~.
VERB + SLIP **sign** ◇ His father signed a permission ~ for a school field trip. | **give sb, hand sb** ◇ Thousands of workers were handed pink ~s. | **get, receive** | **return** ◇ Please detach and return the ~ below.
PREP. **on a/the ~** ◇ He wrote the address on a ~ of paper.
PHRASES **a ~ of paper**

slipper noun

ADJ. **bedroom, carpet** (BrE), **house** (esp. AmE) | **comfortable, comfy** (informal) | **old** | **fluffy** (BrE), **fuzzy** (AmE) | **leather, satin, sheepskin, silk, etc.** | **glass** ◇ Cinderella's glass ~ | **ballet**
... OF SLIPPERS **pair**
VERB + SLIPPER **slip on** | **kick off**
PHRASES **pipe and ~s** (BrE) ◇ a pipe and ~s, the traditional image of retirement
→ Special page at CLOTHES

slippery adj.

VERBS **be, feel, look** | **become, get** ◇ The concrete gets ~ when it's wet. | **make sth** ◇ The oil made the ground ~ and treacherous to walk on.
ADV. **extremely, fairly, very, etc.** | **a little, slightly, etc.** ◇ Watch out—the floor's a little ~. | **notoriously** ◇ International law is notoriously ~.
PREP. **with** ◇ rocks that were ~ with seaweed
PHRASES **~ when wet** ◇ Bathroom floors can become ~ when wet. | **wet and ~** ◇ The track was wet and ~ for the race.

slither verb

ADV. **silently** ◇ A snake was ~ing silently along the floor. | **slowly** | **away, off** ◇ The snake ~ed away. | **along** ◇ Zack ~ed along on his belly. | **back** ◇ It ~ed back down the drain.
PREP. **across, along, around, down, into, onto, out of, over, through, to, towards/toward, up, etc.**
PHRASES **~ its, his, etc. way along, over, etc. sth**

slogan noun

ADJ. **catchy** (informal), **snappy** | **popular** | **famous** | **new, old** | **simple** | **empty, hollow** ◇ The 'freedom to learn' has become just another one of the government's empty ~s. | **anti-government, anti-war, etc.** | **ad** (esp. AmE), **advertising, marketing** | **campaign, election** (esp. BrE), **political** | **patriotic, revolutionary** | **bumper-sticker** (esp. AmE), **T-shirt**
VERB + SLOGAN **coin, come up with, invent** | **adopt (sth as), have (sth as), use (sth as)** | **chant, shout** | **spout** ◇ The Left was still spouting old Marxist ~s. | **bear, be emblazoned with, carry** (esp. BrE) ◇ T-shirts bearing anti-war ~s | **daub, paint, write** ◇ Slogans had been daubed on the walls. | **be summed up by, be summed up in** ◇ The principle is summed up by the ~ 'Trade, not aid'.
SLOGAN + VERB **go, say** ◇ We switched the car stereo to WKTU, 'the beat of New York', as its ~ goes.
PREP. **on the ~** ◇ They fought the election on the ~ 'The time has come'. | **under a/the ~** ◇ They protested under the ~ 'When women stop, everything stops!' | **~ for** ◇ the ~ for the 2012 London Olympics | **~ of**

slope noun

ADJ. **precipitous** (*formal*), **steep** | **gentle, gradual, slight** | **long, short** | **downhill, downward** | **uphill, upward** | **higher, upper** ◇ *There was snow on the higher ~s of the mountain.* | **lower** | **northern, north-facing, etc.** ◇ *The vineyards on the south-facing ~s get more sunshine.* | **open** | **forested, grassy, icy, smooth, snow-covered, snowy, wooded** | **craggy, rocky, scree** (*esp. BrE*), **talus** (*esp. AmE*) | **mountain** | **dry** (*BrE*), **ski** ◇ *dry-slope skiing* | **bunny** (*AmE*), **nursery** (*BrE*) ◇ *ski lessons on the bunny ~* (*AmE*) ◇ *skiing lessons on the nursery ~* (*BrE*) | **negative, positive** ◇ *The unemployment-income curve on the graph has a negative ~.* | **40-degree, 45-degree, etc.** | **continental** ◇ *the continental ~ off the American coast*
VERB + SLOPE **ascend, clamber up, climb, climb up** ◇ *We clambered up the steep, rocky ~.* | **clamber down, descend** | **roll down, tumble down** ◇ *Rocks and boulders rolled down the ~s of the crater.* | **have** ◇ *The field has a ~ of about three feet.* | **hit** ◇ *She plans to hit the ski ~s this winter.* | **cover** ◇ *The vineyard covers the ~.*
SLOPE + VERB **lead to sth** ◇ *a ~ leading down to the river* | **rise** ◇ *The lower ~s rise quite gently.* | **level off, level out** | **overlook** ◇ *a west-facing ~ overlooking the river*
PREP. **down a/the ~** ◇ *I scrambled down the icy ~.* | **of a/the ~** ◇ *the steepness of the ~* | **on a/the ~** ◇ *We camped on an open mountain ~.* | **up a/the ~** ◇ *There were more skiers further up the ~.* | **~ of** ◇ *the ~ of a hill/mountain/roof* ◇ *the ~ of a curve/line*
PHRASES **the bottom of a ~, the foot of a ~, the top of a ~**

slope verb

ADV. **steeply** ◇ *The ground ~s away steeply at the back of the house.* | **gently, slightly** | **away, down, downwards/ downward, up, upwards/upward**
PREP. **to** ◇ *The field ~s down to a small river.* | **towards/ toward**

slot verb

ADV. **easily, neatly, simply** | **together** ◇ *The panels ~ together to make a box.* | **back** ◇ *He has slotted back into the role of being a second-in-command.*
PREP. **in, into** ◇ *He slotted the magazines neatly into the rack.*
PHRASES **~ (sth) into place** ◇ *All the pieces of the puzzle now slotted into place.*

slow verb

ADV. **considerably, dramatically, markedly, noticeably, sharply, significantly** ◇ *Sales have ~ed down quite markedly.* | **barely, hardly** ◇ *The roadblocks hardly ~ed them at all.* | **a little, slightly, etc.** | **gradually** | **eventually, finally** | **deliberately** ◇ *She very deliberately ~ed her steps.* | **down, up** ◇ *Slow down a little!*
VERB + SLOW **begin to** | **try to** ◇ *Rachel tried to ~ her breathing.* | **be expected to** ◇ *Economic growth is expected to ~.* | **seem to** ◇ *Time seemed to ~ down as she fell.*
PHRASES **~ to a crawl, ~ to a snail's pace, ~ to a walk** ◇ *I was nearing West Road when the traffic ~ed to a crawl.* | **~ to a halt, ~ to a standstill, ~ to a stop** | **~ to a trickle** | **~ your pace** ◇ *Bill ~ed his pace to allow her to catch up with him.*

slow adj.

VERBS **be, prove, seem** | **remain**
ADV. **extremely, fairly, very, etc.** | **incredibly, remarkably** | **considerably, noticeably, significantly** ◇ *My computer is noticeably slower than before.* | **a little, slightly, etc.** | **comparatively, relatively** | **agonizingly, desperately, excruciatingly, frustratingly, painfully, painstakingly** ◇ *Filming was painfully ~.* | **notoriously** ◇ *Civil court proceedings are notoriously ~.*
PREP. **at** ◇ *They are extremely ~ at reaching decisions.*
PHRASES **~ and steady** ◇ *She is showing a ~ and steady improvement in her reading ability.*

slum noun

ADJ. **crowded, overcrowded, teeming** | **sprawling, vast** | **poor** | **filthy** | **notorious** | **city, inner-city** (*esp. BrE*), **urban** | **tenement** | **rural** | **immigrant** (*esp. AmE*)
VERB + SLUM **clear** (*esp. BrE*), **demolish** | **live in** ◇ *25% of the city lives in ~s.*
SLUM + NOUN **conditions** | **area, district, neighbourhood/ neighborhood, street** | **dwelling, housing** (*esp. BrE*), **property, tenement** | **clearance** | **children, dwellers, kids** (*informal*) | **life** | **landlord** (*esp. BrE*) (**slumlord** in *AmE*)
PREP. **from the ~s** ◇ *a kid from the ~s* | **in a/the ~s** ◇ *born in the ~s of East London*

slump noun

ADJ. **global, world, worldwide** | **economic, price, property, stock-market** ◇ *The share-price ~ has wiped about $10 billion off the company's value.* | **current, recent** | **prolonged** ◇ *The economy is in a prolonged ~.* | **deep, disastrous, severe** ◇ *a severe ~ in much-needed foreign investment*
PREP. **in a ~** ◇ *The economy is in a ~.* | **into ~** ◇ *The industry is sinking into a ~.* | **~ in** ◇ *Investors were badly hit by the ~ in property prices.*

slump verb

1 decrease suddenly

ADV. **alarmingly, badly, dramatically, heavily** ◇ *Oil prices have ~ed quite badly in recent months.*
PREP. **by** ◇ *Profits ~ed by 70%.* | **from, to** ◇ *Shares in the company ~ed from £2.75 to £1.54.*

2 fall/sit down suddenly and heavily

ADV. **a little** | **forward, over** ◇ *She was sitting with her head ~ed forward.* ◇ *I walked in and saw him ~ed over.* | **back, down**
PREP. **against** ◇ *He ~ed against the wall.* | **in** ◇ *She ~ed back in her seat.* | **in front of** ◇ *Bart was ~ed in front of the TV.* | **into** ◇ *He ~ed down into a chair.* | **onto** ◇ *She ~ed onto the bed.* | **over** ◇ *She ~ed dejectedly over the wheel.* | **to** ◇ *She ~ed to the floor.*
PHRASES **be found slumped…** ◇ *He was found ~ed in a pool of blood by security guards.* | **lie slumped…, sit slumped…** ◇ *He lay ~ed over the steering wheel.*

slur noun

ADJ. **racial, racist, sexual** | **anti-gay, anti-Semitic, etc.**
VERB + SLUR **cast, make** ◇ *The comments cast a ~ on her character.* ◇ *He had made a series of racial ~s.*
PREP. **~ against, ~ on** ◇ *The joke was seen as a ~ against the mentally ill.* ◇ *a ~ on his good name*

smack noun

ADJ. **firm** (*BrE*), **good, hard** | **light** | **loud, resounding** ◇ *He landed with a loud ~.*
VERB + SMACK **give sb, land (sb)** ◇ *He longed to land her a good ~ in the face.* | **get**
PREP. **with a ~** ◇ *She brought her hand down on the water with a ~.*

smack verb

1 (*esp. BrE*) hit sb as a punishment

ADV. **hard** ◇ *I'll ~ you very hard if you do that again!*
PREP. **on** ◇ *She ~ed the boy on the leg.*

2 hit sb/sth

ADV. **accidentally** ◇ *I accidentally ~ed him in the face with a ruler.* | **hard** ◇ *I ~ed him hard across the face.*
PREP. **against, into** ◇ *He turned around and ~ed into a wall.*
PHRASES **~ sb across the face, ~ sb in the face, ~ sb on the shoulder, ~ sb upside the head** (*AmE*) ◇ *He ~ed me in the face.* ◇ *The teacher ~ed me upside the head.*

PHR V **smack of sth**
ADV. **a little, slightly, etc.** ◇ *This move ~s a little of desperation.* | **just** ◇ *It just ~s of paranoia.* | **strongly, too**

much ◊ *Today's announcement ~s strongly of a government cover-up.*

small *adj.*

VERBS **be, feel, look, seem** | **become, get, grow** ◊ *The gap seemed to be getting smaller.* ◊ *The kite grew smaller and smaller and finally disappeared altogether.* | **remain, stay** ◊ *Choose plants that will stay ~.* | **keep sth, make sth** ◊ *Technology has made the world smaller.*
ADV. **extremely, fairly, very, etc.** | **a little, slightly, etc.** | **relatively**
PREP. **for** ◊ *My coat was rather ~ for Bob.*
PHRASES **big and ~, large and ~** ◊ *Employers, large and ~, face massive fines.* | **smaller and smaller** ◊ *The phones are getting smaller and smaller.*

smart *adj.* (*esp. AmE*) intelligent

VERBS **be** | **look, seem, sound** | **become, get** ◊ *Companies are getting ~ about how they use corporate planes.* | **make sb** ◊ *A little information makes you smarter.*
ADV. **extremely, fairly, very, etc.** | **enough** ◊ *She's ~ enough to know what works and what doesn't.*

smash *noun*

1 breaking noisily into pieces
ADJ. **loud**
VERB + SMASH **hear**
PREP. **with a ~** ◊ *The plate hit the floor with a ~.* | **~ of** ◊ *He heard the ~ of breaking glass.*

2 (*BrE*) in a car, etc.
ADJ. **head-on** | **fatal** ◊ *Their car was involved in a fatal ~ with a stolen van.* | **horrific** | **hit-and-run** ◊ *a 20-year-old victim of a hit-and-run ~* | **high-speed** | **car, motorbike** | **rail, train** | **motorway, road** | **two-car, three-vehicle, etc.**
VERB + SMASH **have** | **cause**
SMASH + VERB **happen** ◊ *The ~ happened just before junction 13 of the M6.*
PREP. **in a/the ~** ◊ *Four people were seriously injured in a head-on ~ on the A45.*

3 in tennis
ADJ. **powerful** | **overhead** | **forearm**
VERB + SMASH **hit** ◊ *He can hit a powerful overhead ~.* | **miss** ◊ *He misses a ~ to hand Federer a 5–0 lead.*

4 song, film/movie, etc.
ADJ. **box-office** | **club, dance-floor** (*both BrE*) ◊ *the recent club ~, 'Rocking Music'* | **surprise** | **instant** ◊ *The comedy was an instant ~ with critics.* | **summer**
VERB + SMASH **be, become**
SMASH + NOUN **album, single** | **series, show, sitcom** ◊ *Bridges starred on the ~ sitcom 'Diff'rent Strokes'.* | **hit** | **film** (*esp. BrE*), **movie** (*esp. AmE*)

smear *noun*

1 mark
ADJ. **greasy**
VERB + SMEAR **leave**
PREP. **~ of** ◊ *His fingers left a ~ of sweat on the wall.*

2 lies about an important person
ADJ. **political** | **Democratic, Republican, etc.**
SMEAR + NOUN **campaign, tactic** ◊ *They have conducted a vicious ~ campaign against him.* | **job** (*AmE, informal*) ◊ *a ~ job on President Clinton* | **machine** (*AmE*) ◊ *the far-right ~ machine*
PREP. **~ against, ~ on** ◊ *campaign ~s against the socialist candidate*

3 medical test
ADJ. **cervical** (*BrE*), **Pap** (*AmE*) | **negative, positive** | **abnormal** ◊ *an abnormal ~ test* (*BrE*) ◊ *an abnormal Pap ~ test* (*AmE*)
VERBS **get, have**

smear *verb*

ADV. **liberally** ◊ *She ~ed the cream liberally on her face.*
PREP. **across, on, over, with** ◊ *The child had ~ed peanut butter all over her face.* ◊ *His hands were ~ed with blood.*

smell *noun*

ADJ. **overpowering, pervasive, pungent, rich, sharp, strong** ◊ *There was an overpowering ~ of burning rubber.* | **faint** | **distinct** | **distinctive, particular, unmistakable** | **funny, peculiar, strange, unusual** ◊ *What's that funny ~?* | **familiar** | **lingering** | **aromatic, delectable, delicious, fragrant, fresh, lovely, nice, pleasant, sweet, wonderful** ◊ *the sweet ~ of roses* | **warm** | **awful, bad, disgusting, evil, foul, horrible, nasty, offensive, terrible, unpleasant, vile** | **acrid, nauseating, noxious, putrid, rank, sickly** ◊ *An acrid ~ filled the air.* | **damp, musty, rancid, sour, stale** ◊ *the sour ~ of unwashed linen* | **chemical, earthy, fishy, masculine, metallic, musky, smoky, spicy** | **burning, cooking** ◊ *Cooking ~s drifted up from the kitchen.*
VERB + SMELL **be filled with, have** ◊ *The air was filled with a pervasive ~ of chemicals.* ◊ *The house had a musty ~ after being shut up over the winter.* | **give off** ◊ *The skunk gives off an unpleasant ~ when attacked.* | **catch, detect, notice** ◊ *As she walked into the house she detected the ~ of gas.* | **mask** ◊ *Fragrance dispensers are designed to mask unpleasant ~s.*
SMELL + VERB **come, drift, emanate, float, waft** ◊ *The ~ was coming from the kitchen.* ◊ *A delicious ~ of freshly baked bread wafted across the lawn.* | **fill sth, hang in the air** ◊ *The ~ of death hangs in the air.* | **hit sb** ◊ *Then the pungent ~ hit us—rotting fish and seaweed.*
PREP. **~ from** ◊ *the putrid ~ from the slaughterhouse* | **~ of** ◊ *the ~ of smoke*
PHRASES **sense of ~** ◊ *Deer have a keen sense of ~.* | **the sights, sounds and ~s of …** ◊ *The sights, sounds and ~s of Delhi stunned me.*

smell *verb*

1 notice/identify sth by using your nose
ADV. **almost, practically** ◊ *Snow fell so that you could almost ~ the cold.* ◊ *You could practically ~ the danger around us.*
VERB + SMELL **can** ◊ *Can you ~ gas?*

2 have a particular smell
ADV. **strongly** ◊ *His clothes ~ed strongly of fish.* | **faintly, slightly, vaguely** ◊ *He ~ed faintly of mason.*
PREP. **like** ◊ *It ~s like rotten meat!* | **of** ◊ *The kitchen ~ed sweetly of herbs and fruit.*

smile *noun*

ADJ. **big, bright, broad, huge, wide** ◊ *She had a big ~ on her face.* | **faint, slight, thin, wan, weak** | **beaming, beatific, cheerful, dazzling, happy, radiant, sunny, warm** ◊ *the warm ~ in his eyes* | **beautiful, charming, cute** (*esp. AmE*), **engaging, friendly, gentle, sweet, winning** ◊ *She has a beautiful ~.* | **infectious** ◊ *He had an infectious ~ that touched the lives of many people.* | **disarming, enigmatic, mischievous, mocking, rueful, sardonic, sly, wry** ◊ *She gave a wry ~.* | **sad** | **shy** | **apologetic, sheepish** | **encouraging, indulgent, reassuring** | **polite** | **beguiling, easy, ready** ◊ *She had a keen wit and a ready ~.* | **fake, fixed, forced** | **conspiratorial, knowing** | **grim** ◊ *a grim ~ of satisfaction* | **humourless/humorless, mirthless** ◊ *She suppressed a mirthless ~.* | **goofy** (*informal, esp. AmE*) ◊ *He had a goofy ~ plastered across his face.* | **crooked, lopsided** | **toothy** | **toothless**
… OF A SMILE **glimmer, hint, trace** ◊ *A trace of a ~ played across her lips.*
VERB + SMILE **have, wear** ◊ *She had a happy ~ on her face.* | **crack, flash (sb), give sb, smile** ◊ *He flashed her a disarming ~.* ◊ *She smiled a ~ of dry amusement.* | **manage** ◊ *She managed a weak ~.* | **return** ◊ *She returned his ~.* | **hide, suppress** ◊ *They had to hide their ~s.* | **force** ◊ *Her father forced a ~.* | **raise** (*esp. BrE*) ◊ *Mention of this subject is guaranteed to raise a ~.*
SMILE + VERB **fade, freeze, vanish** ◊ *Her sunny ~ vanished as she read the letter.* | **falter** ◊ *His ~ faltered slightly.* | **come across sth, come over sth, come to sth** ◊ *A ~ came to her*

lips. | **creep across sth, creep onto sth, creep over sth** ◊ *A wry ~ crept over his face.* | **cross sth** | **flicker across sth, flicker on sth, flicker over sth** ◊ *A faint ~ flickered across her face.* | **light sth up** ◊ *She got up immediately, a ~ lighting up her face.* | **play about sth** (*esp. BrE*), **play across sth, play on sth** ◊ *A small ~ played on his lips.* | **form** | **grow, spread, spread across sth, spread over sth, widen** ◊ *Her ~ grew radiant.* ◊ *A gentle ~ spread over her face.*
PREP. **with a ~** ◊ *'Oh, hello!' he said, with a ~.* | **~ of** ◊ *a ~ of approval*
PHRASES **have a ~ on your face** ◊ *She always has a ~ on her face.* | **bring a ~ to sb's face, put a ~ on sb's face** ◊ *It is a beautiful song that puts a ~ on your face.* | **keep the ~ off your face** ◊ *He could hardly keep the ~ off his face.* | **wipe the ~ off sb's face** ◊ *I'm going to wipe that ~ off your face* (= make you stop thinking this is funny). | **be all ~s** ◊ *Twelve hours later she was all ~s again.* | **be wreathed in ~s** ◊ *His face was wreathed in ~s.* | **(have) a ~ plastered across/on your face** ◊ *The little boy had a ~ plastered across his face.*

smile verb

ADV. **broadly, widely** ◊ *She put down her tools and ~d broadly.* | **faintly, slightly, thinly, wanly, weakly** ◊ *He looked at the mess and ~d weakly.* | **brightly, dazzlingly, happily, radiantly, warmly** ◊ *Lawrence nodded, smiling happily.* | **charmingly, gently, softly, sweetly, winningly** | **innocently** | **benignly, kindly, politely** | **merely, simply** ◊ *I simply ~d at him and said 'hi!'* | **shyly** | **encouragingly, indulgently, reassuringly** ◊ *The doctor ~d reassuringly.* | **apologetically, sheepishly** | **ruefully, wryly** ◊ *Molly ~d rather wryly and said nothing.* | **archly, enigmatically** | **conspiratorially** | **mischievously, slyly** | **sadly** | **grimly** | **humourlessly/humorlessly, mirthlessly** | **smugly, tri-umphantly** | **crookedly, lopsidedly** | **back** ◊ *He winked at her, and she ~d back.* | **always** ◊ *Gary is always smiling—he's so positive.*
VERB + SMILE **try to** | **manage to** | **make sb** ◊ *The memory still made her ~.*
PREP. **at** ◊ *He turned and ~d at me.* | **with** ◊ *She ~d with pleasure.*
PHRASES **~ down at sb, ~ up at sb** ◊ *She ~d up at him.* | **~ from ear to ear** | **~ to yourself** ◊ *She ~d to herself, picturing how surprised her mother would be to see her.*

smirk noun

ADJ. **arrogant, satisfied, self-satisfied, smug, triumphant** | **amused, knowing** | **playful** | **evil** | **little, slight, small** ◊ *He gave a slight ~.*
VERB + SMIRK **have, wear** ◊ *She had a self-satisfied ~ on her face.* | **give** ◊ *She gave a knowing ~.* | **conceal, hide** ◊ *He made no attempt to conceal his ~.*
SMIRK + VERB **appear on sth, come across sth, come to sth, cross sth, play across sth, play on sth** ◊ *A small ~ crossed his face.* ◊ *'What kept you?' He asked, a ~ playing on his lips.* | **grow, widen** ◊ *Her ~ grew wider.*
PREP. **with a ~** ◊ *'Comfortable?' he asked with a ~.* | **~ of** ◊ *a ~ of triumph*
PHRASES **wipe the ~ off sb's face** ◊ *I longed to wipe the smug ~ off his face.*

smog noun

ADJ. **heavy** | **urban** | **photochemical**
... OF SMOG **layer** ◊ *a layer of ~ over the city*
VERB + SMOG **reduce** ◊ *measures to reduce ~*
SMOG + NOUN **alert** | **level** ◊ *Smog levels are high today.*

smoke noun

ADJ. **dense, heavy, thick** | **black, blue, grey/gray, white, etc.** | **billowing** | **acrid, choking** | **stale** ◊ *the smell of stale cigarette ~ on your clothes* | **wood** | **cigar, cigarette, pipe, tobacco** | **second-hand** ◊ *Hundreds of people die each year as a result of exposure to second-hand ~* (= smoke from other people's cigarettes, cigars, etc.).
... OF SMOKE **cloud, column, haze, pall, plume, puff, spiral, wisp** ◊ *We sat drinking in a haze of cigarette ~.* ◊ *The witch disappeared in a puff of ~.*
VERB + SMOKE **belch, belch out, blow, emit** ◊ *The car ahead*

was belching out black ~. ◊ *Don't blow ~ in my face!* | **exhale, inhale** | **be wreathed in** ◊ *She sat there wreathed in cigarette ~.*
SMOKE + VERB **belch, billow, come, curl, drift, pour, rise** ◊ *Blue ~ curled up from her cigarette.* ◊ *Smoke rose into the sky.* | **fill sth** | **hang** ◊ *A pall of yellow ~ hung over the quarry.* | **clear** ◊ *When the ~ cleared we saw the extent of the damage.*
SMOKE + NOUN **plume, ring** ◊ *I taught myself to blow ~ rings.* | **signal** | **bomb, grenade** | **alarm, detector** | **inhalation** | **machine** ◊ *The club had a ~ machine and laser show.* | **break** (*informal, esp. AmE*) ◊ *I was taking a ~ break outside.*
PHRASES **go up in ~** ◊ *The barn went up in ~.* | **full of ~** | **thick with ~** ◊ *The bar was thick with stale tobacco ~.*

smoke verb

1 cigarette, pipe, etc.

ADV. **heavily** ◊ *He has always ~d heavily.* | **openly** ◊ *You see kids openly smoking in the streets.*
PHRASES **~ like a chimney** (= smoke a lot) ◊ *He ~s like a chimney.*

2 meat/fish/cheese

ADV. **heavily** | **lightly** ◊ *The ham is cured, then lightly ~d.*

smoker noun

ADJ. **chain, heavy** | **light** | **regular** | **pack-a-day, two-pack-a-day, etc.** (*AmE*) | **20-a-day, 40-a-day, etc.** (*BrE*) | **passive** (*BrE*) ◊ *the risk of lung cancer in passive ~s* | **former** ◊ *a former ~ who quit 20 years ago* | **cigar, cigarette, pipe** | **cannabis** (*esp. BrE*), **marijuana** (*esp. AmE*), **pot** (*informal*)
PHRASES **~s and non-smokers** ◊ *separate rooms for ~s and non-smokers* | **a smoker's cough**

smoking noun

ADJ. **chain, heavy** | **passive** (*BrE*) ◊ *the dangers of passive ~* | **teen** (*esp. AmE*), **teenage, underage** ◊ *The campaign aims to reduce teen ~.* | **cigar, cigarette, pipe, tobacco** | **cannabis** (*esp. BrE*), **marijuana** (*esp. AmE*)
VERB + SMOKING **start, take up** | **give up** (*esp. BrE*), **quit** (*esp. AmE*), **stop** ◊ *I'm trying to stop ~.* | **cut down on** (*esp. BrE*), **reduce** ◊ *The doctor advised me to cut down on ~ and alcohol.* | **ban** | **allow**
SMOKING + NOUN **habit** | **ban** ◊ *A total ~ ban has been imposed throughout the building.* | **room**
PHRASES **a ban on ~** | **the dangers of ~, the effects of ~** ◊ *a study of the harmful effects of ~* | **no ~** ◊ *The company has a strict no-smoking policy.* | **smoking-related death** | **smoking-related disease, smoking-related illness** (*esp. BrE*)

smooth verb

ADV. **carefully, gently** ◊ *She ~ed his hair gently.* | **away, out** ◊ *Use an iron to ~ out any creases.* | **back, down** ◊ *Her mother ~ed back Alice's hair.*

smooth adj.

1 without bumps

VERBS **be, feel, look** | **become** | **make sth, wear sth** ◊ *The steps had been worn ~ by the thousands of passing feet.* | **sand sth** ◊ *The surface should be sanded ~.*
ADV. **extremely, fairly, very, etc.** | **beautifully, exceptionally** ◊ *her beautifully ~ complexion* | **completely, perfectly** | **silky, velvety** ◊ *This cream makes even the roughest hands silky ~.* | **almost** | **deceptively** ◊ *the deceptively ~ surface of the glacier*

2 without problems

VERBS **be, look, seem** | **become**
ADV. **extremely, fairly, very, etc.** ◊ *a fairly ~ transition to democracy* | **incredibly, particularly, remarkably** ◊ *The project got off to a remarkably ~ start.* | **surprisingly** | **completely** | **not always, not entirely** ◊ *The process of negotiation was not entirely ~.*

smug *adj.*

VERBS **appear, be, feel, look, seem, sound** | **get** ◊ *Now don't get ~ just because you've won a couple of games.*
ADV. **extremely, fairly, very, etc.** | **incredibly** ◊ *the incredibly ~ expression on his face* | **almost** | **a little, slightly, etc.** | **annoyingly, insufferably, unbearably** ◊ *He is insufferably ~ and arrogant.*
PREP. **about** ◊ *What are you looking so ~ about?*

smuggle *verb*

ADV. **secretly** | **illegally** | **aboard, in, out** ◊ *He managed to ~ out a note from prison.*
VERB + SMUGGLE **try to** | **manage to**
PREP. **across** ◊ *Weapons are being ~d across the border.* | **into** ◊ *goods which have been ~d into Spain* | **out of** ◊ *Friends secretly ~d him out of the country.*

smuggling *noun*

ADJ. **illegal** | **cigarette, cocaine, diamond, drug, heroin, etc.** | **alien** (*AmE*), **human** (*esp. AmE*), **people** (*esp. BrE*) ◊ *They have been charged with people/alien ~.* | **nuclear** ◊ *policies to reduce the threat of nuclear ~*
SMUGGLING + NOUN **attempt** | **gang** (*esp. BrE*), **operation, racket** (*esp. BrE*), **ring** ◊ *The two sailors are caught up in a diamond-smuggling racket.* | **route**
PREP. **~ of** ◊ *the ~ of narcotics into the country*
→ Note at CRIME (for verbs)

snack *noun*

ADJ. **light, little, small** | **quick** ◊ *We stopped for a quick ~.* | **healthy, nutritious** | **delicious, tasty** | **salty, savoury/ savory** (*esp. BrE*) | **sugary, sweet** | **cold, hot** | **bedtime** (*esp. AmE*), **late-night, lunchtime, mid-afternoon, mid-morning, midnight** | **bar** ◊ *Order bar ~s with your drinks.*
VERB + SNACK **eat, get, grab, have** | **stop for** | **fix (sb)** (*esp. AmE*), **make (sb), prepare** ◊ *I fixed myself a light ~.* | **provide (sb with), serve** ◊ *A bar service provides drinks and ~s throughout the day.*
SNACK + NOUN **food** | **lunch, meal** (*both BrE*) ◊ *Most office staff prefer a ~ lunch to a sit-down meal.* | **time** | **bar, counter** | **machine** ◊ *I got a drink from the hotel ~ machine.*
→ Special page at FOOD

snag *noun*

ADJ. **big, major** | **little, minor, slight, small** ◊ *A minor ~ is that it's expensive.* | **one, only** ◊ *There is just one snag—his boss might not let him go.* ◊ *The only ~ is the price.* | **possible, potential** | **last-minute** | **technical**
VERB + SNAG **hit, run into** ◊ *We've hit a technical snag—the printer isn't compatible with my PC.*
PREP. **~ in** ◊ *one of the ~s in the plan* | **~ on** (*esp. AmE*) ◊ *I ran into a few ~s on my thesis.* | **~ to** ◊ *There is a ~ to the job: you have to work at weekends.* | **~ with** ◊ *I suddenly saw a major ~ with the whole idea.*

snail *noun*

ADJ. **edible** | **aquatic, land, marine, pond, sea, water**
SNAIL + NOUN **shell**
PHRASES **slugs and ~s** (*esp. BrE*) ◊ *the war with the slugs and ~s in my garden* | **(at) a snail's pace** ◊ *Traffic had slowed to a snail's pace.*

snake *noun*

ADJ. **deadly** ◊ *one of the world's deadliest ~s* | **poisonous, venomous** | **giant, huge, large** | **dead, live** ◊ *He had a live ~ draped over his shoulders.* | **pet** ◊ *He keeps a pet ~ that he lavishes with affection.* | **sea, tree, water** | **coiled** (*often figurative*) ◊ *The men sit like coiled ~s that are ready to strike.*
SNAKE + VERB **bite sb/sth, strike sth** ◊ *She was bitten by a ~ while walking through long grass.* ◊ *The ~ lifted up its head before striking its prey.* | **slide, slither, wind, wind its way** ◊ *A small green ~ slithered across the wet road.* ◊ *The ~ wound*

its way through the undergrowth. | **hiss, spit** | **shed its skin** | **coil around sth, coil itself around sth, curl up**
SNAKE + NOUN **bite** (usually ***snakebite***) | **charmer, handler** | **venom**
PHRASES **a ~ in the grass** (*figurative*) ◊ *I came to realize that he's just a ~ in the grass.*

snap *verb*

1 break suddenly with a sharp noise

ADV. **suddenly** ◊ *The branch suddenly snapped.* | **easily** | **off** ◊ *One of the table's legs had been snapped off.*
PHRASES **~ (sth) in half, ~ (sth) in two** ◊ *She picked up the pencil and snapped it in two.*

2 move quickly with a sharp noise

PHRASES **~ (sth) open, ~ (sth) shut** ◊ *She snapped the lid shut.* | **~ (sth) together** ◊ *The plastic pieces ~ together to make a replica of a dinosaur.*

3 speak in a quick angry way

ADV. **angrily, harshly, impatiently, irritably, sarcastically, sharply** | **back** ◊ *'How should I know?' Jen snapped back.*
PREP. **at** ◊ *He lost his temper and snapped irritably at the children.*

4 lose control

ADV. **finally** ◊ *My patience finally snapped.* | **suddenly** | **just, simply** ◊ *I guess he just snapped.*

snarl *verb*

ADV. **angrily, savagely, viciously** ◊ *He ~ed savagely at her.* | **almost**
PREP. **at** ◊ *A guard dog ~ed at us as we walked by.*

snatch *noun*

ADJ. **brief**
VERB + SNATCH **catch, hear, overhear** ◊ *We caught ~es of conversation from the room next door.* | **hum, sing** ◊ *He was humming a ~ of a song from 'Cabaret'.*
PREP. **in ~es** ◊ *She learned to sleep in brief ~es.*
PHRASES **a ~ of conversation, a ~ of dialogue, a ~ of music, a ~ of song**

snatch *verb*

ADV. **almost** | **quickly** | **away, back, up** ◊ *She ~ed her hand back.* ◊ *She leaped to her feet, ~ing up her bag.*
VERB + SNATCH **try to** ◊ *Someone tried to ~ her purse.*
PREP. **at** ◊ *He ~ed at her arm as she walked past.* | **from** ◊ *She almost ~ed the letter from my hand.* | **out of** ◊ *I ~ed it out of his hands.*

sneaker *noun* (*AmE*)

ADJ. **new** | **beaten-up, old, worn, worn-out** ◊ *a pair of worn canvas ~s* | **designer, stylish** | **basketball, high-top** ◊ *He wears white high-top ~s.* | **canvas, leather**
...OF SNEAKERS **pair**
VERB + SNEAKER **pull on, slip on** ◊ *I pulled on my ~s and headed out for a run.* | **kick off, pull off** | **lace up**
→ Special page at CLOTHES

sneer *noun*

ADJ. **arrogant** | **faint, slight**
VERB + SNEER **give** ◊ *He gave an arrogant ~.* | **curl into, turn into, twist into** ◊ *The smile slowly turned into a ~.* ◊ *Her lips twisted into a ~.* | **hide**
PREP. **with a ~**
PHRASES **a ~ in your voice** | **a ~ on sb's face**

sneeze *verb*

ADV. **loudly** ◊ *Someone ~d loudly at the back of the hall.* | **violently** | **uncontrollably**
VERB + SNEEZE **cause sb to, make sb** ◊ *The smoke reached her and made her ~.*
PREP. **on** ◊ *I ~d on him.*
PHRASES **coughing and sneezing** ◊ *Viruses can be spread through coughing and sneezing.* | **the urge to ~** ◊ *She suddenly felt the urge to ~.*

sniff noun

ADJ. **deep, good, long | little, slight, small | loud**
VERB + SNIFF **give** ◇ *She gave a loud ~ of disapproval.* | **hear | get, have, take** ◇ *to get a ~ of fresh air*
PREP. **between ~s** ◇ *'I'm sorry,' he said between ~s.* | **with a ~** ◇ *'I'm fine,' she said with a ~.* | **~ at** *The dog had a good ~ at the bushes.*
→ Note at SOUND

sniff verb

ADV. **loudly** ◇ *She wiped her eyes and ~ed loudly.* | **deeply | a little | carefully, delicately | appreciatively** ◇ *He ~ed appreciatively. 'Smells delicious. What is it?'* | **disdainfully, haughtily | suspiciously | back** ◇ *The woman ~ed back her tears.*
PREP. **at** ◇ *The dog ~ed at his shoes.*

snippet noun

ADJ. **brief, little, small** ◇ *brief ~s of interviews* | **interesting** ◇ *The guidebook is full of interesting ~s of information.* | **vocal** ◇ *vocal ~s in the background of the song*
VERB + SNIPPET **catch, get, hear** ◇ *I heard ~s of conversation.* | **read, see**
PREP. **~ from** ◇ *The article gave a few ~s from her forthcoming memoirs.* | **~ of** ◇ *~s of dialogue from the TV show*

snobbery noun

ADJ. **cultural, intellectual, musical | class, social** ◇ *She faced the twin barriers of class ~ and racial discrimination.* ◇ *the elitism and social ~ of the art world* | **petty** ◇ *her obsession with petty social snobberies* | **inverted** (*BrE*) ◇ *His dismissive attitude to the rich is just inverted ~.*
PREP. **~ about** ◇ *his ~ about mixing with people from other classes* | **~ towards/toward** ◇ *~ towards/toward electronic music*

snooker noun

ADJ. **professional**
... OF SNOOKER **frame, game** ◇ *We played a couple of frames of ~ in the evening.*
VERB + SNOOKER **play**
SNOOKER + NOUN **ball, cue, table** ◇ *He bought a a full-size ~ table.* | **ace, champion, player, star | club, hall, room | championship, match, tournament | world** ◇ *The ex-miner stunned the ~ world by winning his first tournament.*
→ Special page at SPORTS

snore verb

ADV. **loudly, noisily | gently, lightly, quietly, softly** ◇ *She was asleep in a chair and snoring gently.* | **peacefully** ◇ *He began to ~ peacefully.* | **away** ◇ *Grandma was snoring away in her bed.*
VERB + SNORE **begin to, start to** ◇ *Lily began to ~ loudly.*

snort noun

ADJ. **little, small | loud | derisive**
VERB + SNORT **give, let out** ◇ *He gave a ~ of contempt.* | **hear | stifle**
PREP. **with a ~** ◇ *'What a mess they made of it!' said Sam with a ~ of derision.* | **~ of**
PHRASES **a ~ of derision, a ~ of disgust | a ~ of laughter**
→ Note at SOUND

snort verb

ADV. **loudly | softly | angrily, contemptuously, derisively, impatiently, indignantly** ◇ *He ~ed indignantly and walked away.*
PREP. **at** ◇ *She ~ed at his suggestion.* | **in** ◇ *Calvin ~ed in disbelief.* | **with** ◇ *He ~ed with derision.* ◇ *Her friends ~ed with laughter.*

snow noun

ADJ. **heavy, thick | fine, light** ◇ *The plants were covered in fine ~.* | **deep | wet | compacted, crisp, frozen, hard, icy, packed** ◇ *The crisp ~ crunched as we walked through it.* ◇

The frozen ~ was treacherous to walk on. | **powder, powdery, slushy, soft | drifting, driving, falling, swirling** ◇ *They struggled on through the driving ~.* | **melted, melting | fresh, freshly fallen, new, newly fallen | first** ◇ *the first ~ of winter* | **spring, winter | artificial, fake** ◇ *They had to use artificial ~ at the Winter Olympics.* | **dirty**
... OF SNOW **flake | fall** (*esp. BrE*), **flurry | patch | dusting** ◇ *There was a light dusting of ~ on the ground.* | **blanket, carpet, layer | pile** ◇ *There were great big piles of ~ on the road outside.* | **foot, inch** ◇ *The porch is currently covered in three feet of ~.* | **handful** ◇ *He grabbed a handful of ~ and threw it at Kate.*
VERB + SNOW **be covered in** ◇ *The car was completely covered in ~.* | **blow** (*AmE*), **clear** (*esp. BrE*), **plough/plow** (*esp. AmE*), **shovel** (*esp. AmE*), **sweep** ◇ *She cleared the ~ from the path.* | **melt** ◇ *The sun came out and melted all the ~.* | **expect** ◇ *We're expecting ~ over the next few days.* | **get, have** ◇ *Southern Europe rarely gets ~.* | **struggle through, trudge through, walk through** ◇ *I trudged through the ~ and ice to the edge of town.*
SNOW + VERB **cover sth, lie, pile, pile up, settle** ◇ *Snow covered everything from horizon to horizon.* ◇ *Snow had piled up against the walls of the house.* ◇ *It was too warm for the ~ to settle.* | **come down, drift, drive, fall, swirl** ◇ *The heaviest ~ is coming down in Maine.* | **melt, thaw**
SNOW + NOUN **flurry, shower, storm** (usually ***snowstorm***) | **conditions** ◇ *The ~ conditions were excellent.* | **fall** (usually ***snowfall***) ◇ *a heavy snowfall* ◇ *a light snowfall* ◇ *an area of low snowfall* | **cover** ◇ *The glacier provides skiers with year-round ~ cover.* | **line** (usually ***snowline***) ◇ *animals that live above the snowline* | **bank, drift** (usually ***snowdrift***) ◇ *He got his car stuck in a snowdrift.* | **field** (usually ***snowfield***) | **slide** (usually ***snowslide***) (*AmE*) (***avalanche*** in *BrE*) | **day** (*AmE*) ◇ *Growing up in New York, I had my share of ~ days.* | **blower** (usually ***snowblower***), **plough/plow** (usually ***snowplough/snowplow***), **shovel | cannon** (*BrE*), **gun | blindness | chains, tyre/tire | shoe** (usually ***snowshoe***) | **globe** ◇ *She bought a plastic ~ globe with the Eiffel Tower inside.*
PREP. **across the ~** ◇ *We walked across the ~ to the road.* | **in ~, into ~** ◇ *The children are playing in the ~.* | **through ~** ◇ *We struggled through the deep ~ back to the chalet.* | **under ~** ◇ *The steps were buried under the ~.*

snow verb

ADV. **hard, heavily** ◇ *It had been ~ing heavily all night.* | **lightly | outside** ◇ *It looked to be ~ing outside.* | **overnight** ◇ *We woke up to find that it had ~ed overnight.*
VERB + SNOW **begin to, start to**
PHRASES **start ~ing, stop ~ing** ◇ *It started ~ing just as we were setting out.*

snowfall noun

ADJ. **heavy | light | annual | average, mean** ◇ *What's the average ~ for this region?* | **first** ◇ *the first ~s of November* | **fresh, new** ◇ *A fresh ~ had covered the ground.*
VERB + SNOWFALL **get, have** ◇ *We had a light ~ last night.*

snowflake noun

ADJ. **white | fluffy** ◇ *Fluffy white ~s began to fall from the sky.*
SNOWFLAKE + VERB **drift, fall, flutter** ◇ *Snowflakes slowly drifted down from the sky.* | **melt**

snub noun

ADJ. **deliberate** ◇ *a deliberate ~ to the ambassador* | **apparent | embarrassing, humiliating**
VERB + SNUB **deliver sb** (*BrE*) ◇ *He took the opportunity to deliver us another ~.* | **receive | interpret sth as, regard sth as, see sth as, take sth as** ◇ *These references were widely seen as a ~ to the President.* | **intend sth as, mean sth as** ◇ *It was never intended as a ~.* | **amount to, represent** ◇ *The deal amounts to something of a ~ for the rival online music company.*
PREP. **as a ~ | ~ by** ◇ *Some are suggesting that it was a ~ by*

the French. | **~ for, ~ to** ◇ *His withdrawal from the event was seen as a deliberate ~ to the organizers.* | **~ of** (*esp. AmE*) ◇ *an unintentional ~ of President Johnson*

snuggle *verb*

ADV. **close** ◇ *She slipped her arm through his and ~d close.* | **together** ◇ *We ~d up together on the couch.* | **down, up** ◇ *I ~d down in my bed.* | **back**
PREP. **against** ◇ *Claudia ~d against him.* | **into** ◇ *She ~d into her sleeping bag and closed her eyes.* | **under** ◇ *He ~d back under the covers.*

soak *verb*

ADV. **completely, thoroughly** | **overnight** ◇ *Leave the beans to ~ overnight.* | **off** ◇ *Place the jar in warm water to ~ the label off.* | **up** ◇ *Let the soil ~ up the water.*
VERB + SOAK **leave sth to, let sth** ◇ *I've left the clothes to ~ overnight.*
PREP. **in** ◇ *Soak the clothes in cold water.* | **into** ◇ *Water dripped off the table and ~ed into the carpet.* | **through** ◇ *The rain had ~ed through every layer of his clothing.* | **with** ◇ *He ~ed the cloth with kerosene.*

soaked *adj.*

VERBS **be, look** | **get**
ADV. **absolutely, completely, thoroughly** | **through** ◇ *The collar of my shirt was completely ~ through.*
PHRASES **~ to the bone** (*AmE*), **~ to the skin** ◇ *There was a sudden shower and we got ~ to the skin.*

soap *noun*

1 substance used for washing

ADJ. **gentle, mild** | **perfumed, scented** | **liquid** | **carbolic** (*esp. BrE*) | **antibacterial** ◇ *Clean the wound with mild antibacterial ~.* | **bar** (*AmE*) ◇ *I switched to liquid shower gel from bar ~.* | **bath, hand** (*esp. AmE*), **toilet** (*BrE*) | **dish, dishwashing, laundry** (*all AmE*) ◇ *I cleaned it with warm water and liquid dish ~.* | **saddle**
... OF SOAP **bar, cake** (*less frequent*)
VERB + SOAP **use, wash (sth) with**
SOAP + NOUN **powder** (*BrE*) | **bubble, suds** | **dish, dispenser**
PHRASES **~ and water**

2 → See SOAP OPERA

soap opera (*also* soap *informal*) *noun*

ADJ. **radio, TV** | **daytime, night-time** (*esp. AmE*), **prime-time** (*esp. AmE*) | **long-running** (*esp. BrE*) ◇ *a long-running TV ~.* | **hit, popular, top** | **teen** ◇ *He worked on the popular teen soap 'Dawson's Creek'.*
VERB + SOAP OPERA **watch** ◇ *I don't watch many soaps.*
SOAP + NOUN **star** ◇ *an Aussie soap star*

soar *verb*

1 increase very fast

ADV. **dramatically** ◇ *Profits have ~ed dramatically in recent months.*
VERB + SOAR **be expected to, be set to** ◇ *Borrowing is set to ~ to an astonishing £60 billion.*
PREP. **by** ◇ *Retail sales ~ed by 10% in the twelve months to November.* | **from, to** ◇ *Inflation has ~ed from 5% to 15%.* | **past** ◇ *The death toll ~ed past 100 000.* | **up** ◇ *This model will ~ up the sales charts.*
PHRASES **send sth ~ing** ◇ *The fuel shortage sent prices ~ing.* | **~ to new heights** ◇ *Property stock has ~ed to new heights.*

2 fly high in the air

ADV. **high** | **overhead** ◇ *A bird ~ed high overhead.* | **up, upwards/upward** ◇ *The cliffs ~ed upward.*
PREP. **above, across, into** ◇ *Rockets ~ed into the sky.* | **over** ◇ *an eagle ~ing high above them* | **past** ◇ *The ball went ~ing past my head.* | **through** ◇ *She stopped suddenly and her bag went ~ing through the air.* | **towards/toward**

sob *noun*

ADJ. **big, deep, great** | **little, small** | **loud** | **quiet, silent, soft** | **choked, hoarse, muffled, stifled, strangled** | **choking, gasping, heaving, racking, shuddering** ◇ *I couldn't hold back the heaving ~s.* | **dry**
VERB + SOB **give, let out** | **break (down) into, burst into** ◇ *My father broke down into ~s.* | **be racked by, be racked with, heave with, shake with** ◇ *Her body was racked with ~s.* | **choke back, hold back, muffle, stifle** ◇ *Choking back a ~, she ran to her father's chair.* | **hear**
SOB + VERB **break from sb/sth, come from, escape sb/sth** ◇ *A ~ escaped her lips.* | **rise** ◇ *A choked ~ rose in his throat.* | **catch** ◇ *A dry ~ caught in her throat.* | **rack sth, shake sth** ◇ *Deep racking ~s shook his whole body.* | **subside**
SOB + NOUN **story** ◇ *You can't expect me to believe this ~ story!*
PREP. **between ~s** ◇ *'I don't want to go!' she said between ~s.* | **on a ~** ◇ *Ellen choked on a ~ before admitting the truth.* | **through ~s** ◇ *He continued his story through stifled ~s.* | **with a ~** ◇ *'Why didn't you tell me?' she asked with a ~.* | **~ from** ◇ *a ~ from George*
PHRASES **a ~ of despair, a ~ of pain, a ~ of relief** ◇ *a great ~ of despair*
→ Note at SOUND

sob *verb*

ADV. **aloud** | **loudly** | **quietly, silently, softly** | **hysterically, uncontrollably, wildly** | **almost** ◇ *He was pleading, almost sobbing, first silently and then aloud.*
VERB + SOB **begin to, start to** ◇ *He began to ~ uncontrollably.* | **hear sb** ◇ *I heard a child ~ loudly.*
PREP. **into** ◇ *She began sobbing into her pillow.* | **with** ◇ *She was sobbing with pain and fear.*
PHRASES **~ your heart out** | **begin ~ing, start ~ing** ◇ *She started sobbing hysterically.*

sober *adj.*

VERBS **be, feel, look, seem** | **become, get** | **remain, stay** ◇ *She wanted a drink, but she had to stay ~.* | **keep sb** ◇ *Only the thought of her kept him ~.*
ADV. **completely, entirely, perfectly, quite, stone-cold, totally** | **not entirely** | **almost, fairly, pretty, reasonably, relatively** ◇ *By this time he felt reasonably ~ again.* | **enough** ◇ *At that point she was still ~ enough to ask sensible questions.*
PHRASES **clean and ~** (*esp. AmE*) ◇ *I've been clean and ~ for four years.*

soccer *noun* → See also FOOTBALL

ADJ. **amateur, pro** (*AmE*), **professional** | **top-class** | **junior, kids'** (*esp. AmE*), **senior, youth** (*esp. AmE*) ◇ *He played on the Irish junior ~ team.* | **women's** | **college, high-school, varsity** (*all AmE*) | **league, non-league** (*BrE*) | **international, national, world** | **competitive** | **five-a-side** (*esp. BrE*) | **indoor**
... OF SOCCER **game**
VERB + SOCCER **play** | **watch**
SOCCER + NOUN **ball** | **field, ground** (*BrE*), **pitch** (*BrE*), **stadium** | **game, match, tournament** | **goal** (*AmE*) | **league** | **club, team** | **season** (*esp. AmE*) | **ace** (*BrE*), **hero** (*esp. BrE*), **legend, player, star** | **boss** (*esp. BrE*), **coach, manager** | **management** | **official, referee** | **fan, supporter** (*esp. BrE*), **mom** (*AmE*) | **season** | **career** | **skills** | **practice** ◇ *The kids are at ~ practice.* | **jersey** (*AmE*), **shirt, shorts, strip** (*BrE*), **uniform** (*AmE*) ◇ *He was wearing a yellow Brazil ~ jersey.* | **cleats, shoes** (*both AmE*) ◇ *a pair of ~ cleats* | **hooligan, thug** (*both esp. BrE*) | **violence** | **magazine**
PHRASES **be on the ~ team** (*esp. AmE*) ◇ *He's on the ~ team.*

socialism *noun*

ADJ. **democratic, revolutionary, scientific** ◇ *Marx claimed that his was the first scientific ~.* | **market, state** | **international** | **Marxist**
VERB + SOCIALISM **build, establish** ◇ *They are trying to build ~ in their own country.*
PREP. **under ~** ◇ *They believed that these problems would disappear under ~.*

socialist noun

ADJ. **committed, dedicated** (*esp. BrE*), **lifelong, staunch** (*esp. BrE*), **strong** (*esp. BrE*) | **leading** ◇ *His father was a leading ~ in Germany.* | **radical, revolutionary** | **liberal** | **moderate** | **democratic**
SOCIALIST + VERB **come to power** ◇ *The ~s came to power in 1981.*

social security noun

1 (*BrE*) money paid by the government to people who are poor, unemployed, etc. → See also WELFARE
... OF SOCIAL SECURITY **system**
VERB + SOCIAL SECURITY **be entitled to, claim, receive** ◇ *If you are unemployed you can claim ~.*
SOCIAL-SECURITY + NOUN **provision, scheme, system** ◇ *plans to improve social-security provision for single parents* | **benefit, payments** | **contributions** ◇ *All people in work pay social-security contributions.* | **claimant** | **minister, office** | **budget, funds, spending**
PREP. **on ~** ◇ *He's out of work and on ~.*

2 Social Security (*AmE*) system of assistance for people who cannot work
VERB + SOCIAL SECURITY **apply for, be eligible for** | **get** ◇ *Teachers can get Social Security if they work in private industry.* | **depend on** ◇ *My wife and I are retired and depend on Social Security.* | **pay into** ◇ *He has paid into Social Security throughout his 35-year career.* | **privatize, reform** ◇ *the plan to privatize Social Security*
SOCIAL SECURITY + NOUN **number** ◇ *a list of workers' Social Security numbers* | **card** ◇ *You need ID such as a birth certificate or Social Security card.* | **benefits** | **contributions, payments, tax** ◇ *The current Social Security tax of 6.2% on workers.* | **program, system** | **privatization, reform**

society noun

1 people who have shared customs and laws

ADJ. **larger, wider** ◇ *the position of women within the family and the wider ~* | **entire, whole** | **contemporary, modern** | **traditional** | **mainstream** ◇ *a place for people excluded from mainstream ~* | **new** ◇ *He wanted to create a new ~.* | **advanced** ◇ *the role of women in an advanced industrial ~* | **primitive** | **complex** | **egalitarian, free, just, liberal, open** | **closed** | **civilized, good, humane** | **affluent** ◇ *the consumerist values of the affluent ~* | **consumer, consumerist** | **disposable** (*esp. AmE*), **throwaway** (*esp. BrE*) ◇ *Our disposable ~ must be encouraged to recycle.* | **permissive** | **diverse, multicultural, multiracial, pluralistic** ◇ *the celebration of a culturally diverse ~* | **divided, stratified** ◇ *Years of high unemployment have left ~ deeply divided.* | **civil** ◇ *the relationship between the state and civil ~* | **secular** | **human** ◇ *a theory on the basis of human ~* | **class** | **classless** | **tribal** | **matriarchal, patriarchal** | **male-dominated** | **bourgeois** | **high** ◇ *She was marrying into Rio's high ~.* | **capitalist, democratic, feudal, political, socialist, etc.** | **industrial, post-industrial, pre-industrial** ◇ *governments in the advanced industrial societies* | **agricultural, information, scientific, technological** ◇ *the global information ~* | **Islamic, Muslim, Western, etc.** | **rural, urban, village** (*BrE*) | **global** | **decent, polite** ◇ *Such language would not be used in polite ~.*
VERB + SOCIETY **build, create** ◇ *the struggle to build a just ~* | **change, shape, transform** | **become** ◇ *the path to becoming a secular ~* | **permeate, pervade** ◇ *the greed that pervades modern ~* | **dominate** ◇ *Prisoners often have problems fitting into ~ on their release.* | **live in** ◇ *We live in a ~ dominated by men.* | **polarize**
SOCIETY + VERB **be based on sth** ◇ *a ~ based on social justice* | **become** ◇ *US ~ is becoming more unequal.*
PREP. **in (a) ~, within (a) ~** ◇ *the role of television in modern Western ~*
PHRASES **a cross-section of ~** ◇ *The clinic deals with a wide cross-section of ~.* | **the fabric of ~** ◇ *The civil war tore apart the fabric of ~.* | **the higher echelons of ~, the top echelons of ~** ◇ *Officers were drawn largely from the top echelons of ~.* | **a level of ~, a rank of ~, a stratum of ~** ◇

Child cruelty exists at all levels of ~. | **a member of ~** ◇ *welfare reforms to protect the most vulnerable members of ~* | **an outcast from ~, an outcast of ~** ◇ *She devoted herself to helping the outcasts of ~.* | **a pillar of ~** ◇ *He considered himself to be a pillar of ~.* | **your place in ~, your rank in ~** ◇ *A person's job is one of the factors that determines their place in ~.* | **a contributing member of ~** (*esp. AmE*), **a productive member of ~** ◇ *We help offenders to become productive members of ~.* | **the rest of ~** ◇ *He felt isolated from the rest of ~.* | **a section of ~, a sector of ~, a segment of ~** ◇ *Every section of ~ must have access to education.* | **~ as a whole** ◇ *The research examines minorities and their relation to ~ as a whole.* | **~ at large** ◇ *Health standards have risen in ~ at large.* | **~ in general** ◇ *the benefits for ~ in general* | **the structure of ~** ◇ *the class structure of our ~*

2 organization formed for a particular purpose

ADJ. **debating, drama** (*esp. BrE*), **dramatic** (*esp. BrE*), **historical, horticultural** (*BrE*), **music, musical** (*esp. BrE*), **religious, etc.** ◇ *a member of an amateur dramatic ~* | **medical, professional, scientific, etc.** ◇ *He is a member of numerous professional societies.* | **local** ◇ *a local historical ~* | **secret**
VERB + SOCIETY **belong to** ◇ *She belongs to the historical ~.* | **become a member of, join** | **create, establish, form, found, set up, start**
PREP. **in a/the ~** ◇ *She was active in the Society for Women's Suffrage.* | **~ for** ◇ *a ~ for the prevention of cruelty to animals* | **~ of** ◇ *the Society of Motor Manufacturers and Traders*
→ Note at ORGANIZATION

sociology noun

ADJ. **classical, mainstream** | **economic, historical, industrial, medical, political, rural, urban, etc.**
→ Note at SUBJECT (for verbs and nouns)

sock noun

ADJ. **knee, knee-high, long** | **ankle** (*esp. BrE*), **short** | **thick, thin** | **white** | **athletic, gym, sweat, tube** (*all AmE*) ◇ *a pair of white tube ~s* | **sports** (*BrE*) | **argyle, bobby** | **dress** | **cotton** | **wool** (*esp. AmE*), **woollen/woolen, woolly/wooly** (*esp. BrE*) | **clean, dirty** | **old, smelly** | **mismatched** (*AmE*), **odd** (*BrE*) ◇ *He wore odd ~s, one red and one yellow.*
... OF SOCKS **pair**
VERB + SOCK **pull on, pull up** | **pull off** | **knit** | **darn, mend** (*esp. BrE*)
SOCK + NOUN **drawer** | **puppet** (*esp. AmE, often figurative*) ◇ *He is a man of integrity, not a ~ puppet taking orders from above.*
→ Special page at CLOTHES

socket noun

1 (*BrE*) for electricity → See also OUTLET
ADJ. **electric, electrical, light, mains, plug, power** | **aerial, earphone, headphone, phone** | **Scart, USB** | **standard, wall**
VERB + SOCKET **plug (sth) into** ◇ *The battery charger plugs into any mains ~.*
SOCKET + NOUN **outlet**

2 in the body
ADJ. **empty, hollow, sunken** | **arm, eye, hip, shoulder, tooth**
PREP. **in its ~** ◇ *His eyes bulged madly in their ~s.*

soda noun

1 (*AmE*) drink
ADJ. **club, cream** (*BrE, AmE*), **orange** | **diet, regular** | **ice-cream**
... OF SODA **bottle, can** | **glass** | **sip, swig**
VERB + SODA **drink, sip** | **get, grab** ◇ *I grabbed a ~ from the refrigerator.* | **order** | **open** | **pour** | **spill**
SODA + NOUN **water** (*BrE, AmE*) | **pop** (*AmE, old-fashioned*) | **bottle, can** | **machine** | **fountain** (*AmE*), **siphon** (*BrE*)

PHRASES **a Scotch and ~** (*BrE, AmE*)

2 chemical

ADJ. **caustic** | **baking** | **washing**
SODA + NOUN **lime** | **lake** (*technical*)

sofa noun

ADJ. **battered** | **comfortable, comfy** (*informal*), **plush, soft** |
overstuffed ◇ *Amy collapsed on her overstuffed leather ~.* |
deep, low-slung (*AmE*) ◇ *She sank into the deep ~.* | **chintz,**
leather, etc. | **three-seater, two-seater, etc.** | **convertible,**
sleeper (*AmE*) ◇ *The convertible ~ means that the apartment*
can sleep four. | **living-room** ◇ *I was lying on my living-*
room ~.
VERB + SOFA **collapse on/onto, flop (down) on/onto, settle**
(down) on, sink (down) into/on/onto, sit (down) on, slump
(down) on/onto ◇ *He slumped back on the ~ in tears.* | **be**
sprawled (out) on, lie on, lounge on, recline on, stretch
out on ◇ *I spent the evening sprawled on the ~, watching TV.*
| **get up from, jump up from, rise from** ◇ *He got up from*
the ~ to fetch some drinks. | **hide behind** ◇ *I might have to*
hide behind the ~ if the movie gets too scary!
SOFA + NOUN **bed** | **cushion**
PREP. **on the ~** ◇ *She was curled up on the ~.* ◇ *I fell asleep on*
the ~.
PHRASES **the arm of a/the ~, the back of a/the ~, the edge**
of a/the ~, the side of a/the ~

soft adj.

VERBS **be, feel, look** | **become, get, go, grow, turn** | **stay** ◇
Her skin had stayed ~ and supple.
ADV. **extremely, fairly, very, etc.** | **beautifully, incredibly,**
wonderfully ◇ *The fabric has a beautifully ~ texture.* | **all** ◇
These tomatoes have gone all ~. | **relatively** | **a little,**
slightly, etc.

soften verb

1 become/make sth softer/gentler

ADV. **considerably, a lot** | **a bit, a little, slightly, somewhat** ◇
His smile ~ed slightly. ◇ *I've ~ed somewhat in my advancing*
age.
PREP. **towards/toward** ◇ *Her anger ~ed towards/toward him.*

2 make sth seem less severe

ADV. **slightly, somewhat**
VERB + SOFTEN **try to** | **help (to)**
PHRASES **~ the blow (of sth)** ◇ *I should try to ~ the blow of this*
news. | **~ into a smile** ◇ *Her face ~ed into a smile.*

software noun

ADJ. **computer, PC** | **application** | **accounting, blogging,**
design, editing, educational, enterprise, management,
social, etc. | **character-recognition, handwriting-recogni-**
tion | **face-recognition, facial-recognition** | **speech-**
recognition, voice-recognition ◇ *Voice-recognition ~ takes*
your speech and turns it into text. | **antivirus, filtering,**
security | **proprietary** ◇ *Sony's proprietary PC ~* | **free,**
open-source | **latest** | **pirated** ◇ *He was arrested for selling*
pirated ~.
... OF SOFTWARE **piece** ◇ *an exciting piece of design ~*
VERB + SOFTWARE **run, use** ◇ *My PC isn't powerful enough to*
run that ~. | **create, design, develop, make, write** |
download, install | **buy, sell** | **update** ◇ *I updated my*
antivirus ~ last night.
SOFTWARE + VERB **run** ◇ *The ~ will run on most PCs.*
SOFTWARE + NOUN **application, applications, package,**
product, program, system, tool | **development, engin-**
eering | **developer, engineer** | **company, firm, house,**
maker | **giant** ◇ *Microsoft, the ~ giant* | **business, industry**
→ Special page at COMPUTER

soil noun

1 earth

ADJ. **deep** | **shallow, thin** | **fertile, good, rich** | **infertile,**
poor | **light** | **heavy** | **loose** | **compacted** | **dry** | **damp,**
moist, waterlogged, wet ◇ *Keep the ~ moist and fertilize*
weekly. | **well-drained** | **acid, acidic** | **alkaline** |
contaminated | **top** (usually ***topsoil***) | **potting** (*AmE*) ◇ *She*
bought a bag of potting ~. | **chalky, clay, clayey, loam,**
loamy, peaty ◇ *Rich loamy ~s produce the largest leeks.* |
rocky, sandy, stony | **alluvial, desert, forest, garden,**
volcanic
VERB + SOIL **cultivate, enrich, improve** | **dig, dig in, dig up,**
till, turn, work ◇ *fields of newly turned ~* ◇ *The clay ~s of the*
region are difficult to work. | **fertilize** | **drain** | **loosen**
SOIL + NOUN **conservation** | **degradation, erosion** |
conditions, fertility, quality ◇ *declining ~ fertility* |
moisture | **temperature** | **type** | **surface** | **sample** ◇ *Soil*
samples taken from the site revealed massive amounts of
radiation. | **science, scientist**
PREP. **in (the) ~** ◇ *The flowers do well in sandy ~.*

2 part of a country

ADJ. **native** | **foreign** | **American, British, etc.**
VERB + SOIL **set foot on** ◇ *the place where she first set foot on*
Canadian ~
PREP. **on ... ~** ◇ *protests over the siting of nuclear weapons on*
British ~
PHRASES **on home ~** (*sports, esp. BrE*) ◇ *England's first defeat*
on home ~ against Australia

solace noun

ADJ. **great** | **spiritual**
VERB + SOLACE **bring (sb), give sb, offer (sb), provide** ◇ *The*
news brought no ~ to the grieving relatives. | **find, take** ◇
Unable to leave his bed, he found some ~ in reading about
other people's travels. | **seek** ◇ *They sought ~ in religion from*
the harshness of their everyday lives.
PREP. **~ in** ◇ *I take ~ in the fact that he died in peace.*
PHRASES **turn to sb/sth for ~** ◇ *His career took a nosedive and*
he turned to drugs for ~.

soldier noun

ADJ. **brave, fine, good, great** ◇ *The president paid tribute to*
the brave ~s who had lost their lives. | **trained** |
experienced, veteran | **former, old, retired** | **decorated** ◇
a highly decorated ~ | **active-duty** ◇ *The number of active-*
duty ~s has continued to rise. | **child** ◇ *Boys are forced to*
become child ~s. | **career, professional, regular** | **citizen**
(*esp. AmE*), **volunteer** | **conscript** | **common, ordinary,**
private, rank-and-file ◇ *What was life like for the common*
~? | **fellow** ◇ *He was deeply affected by the death of one of*
his fellow ~s. | **loyal** ◇ *~s loyal to the president* | **dead,**
fallen, injured, wounded | **armed** | **combat** | **foot,**
mounted | **army** | **mercenary** | **enemy** | **American,**
British, etc. | **Allied, coalition, Confederate, etc.** |
government, rebel | **uniformed** | **toy**
... OF SOLDIERS **company** | **group**
VERB + SOLDIER **be, become, serve as** ◇ *Sharon has served as a*
~. | **enlist as** ◇ *He decided to enlist as a ~.* | **train** | **play** ◇
little boys playing ~s | **lead into battle, send into battle** ◇
He has led American ~s into battle.
SOLDIER + VERB **enlist** ◇ *The number of ~s enlisting has fallen*
dramatically. | **be stationed, serve** ◇ *~s serving in Germany*
| **march** | **fight (sb)** | **defend sth, guard sth** | **open fire (on**
sb) ◇ *At least 19 people were killed when ~s opened fire on a*
peaceful demonstration. | **be killed in action, die** | **be shot,**
be wounded | **be missing in action** | **be captured, be**
taken prisoner | **return** ◇ *~s returning from the war* |
desert
PREP. **as a ~** ◇ *his time as a ~*
PHRASES **a ~ of fortune** | **~s in uniform** ◇ *We saw very few*
enemy ~s in uniform. | **~s at war** ◇ *a realistic portrait of ~s*
at war | **~s in the field, ~s on the ground** ◇ *We don't have*
enough ~s in the field.

sole noun

ADJ. **thick, thin** | **leather, rubber** | **inner**
PHRASES **the ~ of your boot, the ~ of your shoe** ◇ *There's a*
hole in the ~ of my shoe. | **the ~s of your feet** ◇ *The sand*
was so hot I got blisters on the ~s of my feet.

solemn *adj.*

VERBS **be, look, seem, sound** ◊ *She usually had a smile on her face, but now she looked ~.* | **become, grow** ◊ *His face grew ~.* | **remain**
ADV. **extremely, fairly, very,** etc. ◊ *He addressed them all in very ~ tones.* ◊ *Her mood was rather ~.* | **most** ◊ *Our most ~ duty is to protect the public.*

solemnity *noun*

ADJ. **great** ◊ *The monument was unveiled with great ~.* | **mock** | **due**
... OF SOLEMNITY **air, sense** ◊ *An air of ~ hung over the event.*
PREP. **with ~** ◊ *I responded with due ~.*

solicitor *noun* (BrE) lawyer

ADJ. **competent, good** | **qualified** | **trainee** | **duty, practising** ◊ *There will be no court duty ~ today.* ◊ *She is still a practising ~ at the age of sixty-two.* | **instructing** ◊ *I discussed the matter with my instructing ~.* | **defence**
PHRASES **a firm of ~s**
→ Note at PROFESSIONAL (for verbs)

solid *adj.*

1 hard and firm/not hollow
VERBS **be, feel, look, seem** | **become, go** ◊ *If you put it in the freezer, it will go ~.* | **freeze** ◊ *The water was frozen ~.* | **make sb/sth**
ADV. **extremely, fairly, very,** etc. | **absolutely, completely** | **almost, nearly** | **enough** ◊ *The ice felt ~ enough.* | **apparently, seemingly** (esp. AmE)
2 reliable and strong
VERBS **appear, be, look, seem** | **become** | **remain**
ADV. **extremely, fairly, very,** etc. | **surprisingly** | **consistently** ◊ *The songwriting quality is consistently ~.* | **absolutely, rock** ◊ *Support for the plan remained rock ~.* | **reasonably, relatively** ◊ *There is pretty ~ evidence to show that the disease is caused by poor hygiene.*

solidarity *noun*

ADJ. **international, national** | **communal, community, social** | **class, family, group, human, political, racial, union, working-class**
... OF SOLIDARITY **expression, gesture, show** ◊ *Hospital staff staged a protest as a gesture of ~ with the striking nurses.* | **feeling, sense** ◊ *The strike fostered a sense of ~ among the workers.*
VERB + SOLIDARITY **feel** | **demonstrate, express, show** | **build, foster, promote**
PREP. **in ~ with** ◊ *Various other groups of workers went on strike in ~ with the train drivers.* | **~ against** ◊ *union ~ against management* | **~ among, ~ between** ◊ *The conflict fostered ~ among Arab oil states.* | **~ with** ◊ *He expressed his ~ with the miners.*

solitude *noun*

ADJ. **absolute, total** | **quiet**
VERB + SOLITUDE **seek** | **find** | **enjoy, prefer** ◊ *He enjoys the ~ of writing.*
PREP. **in ~** ◊ *to pray in ~* | **in the ~ of** ◊ *She enjoyed a few days of peace in the ~ of the mountains.*

solo *noun*

ADJ. **extended, lengthy, long** | **brief, short** | **brilliant, great** | **opening** ◊ *the opening piano ~* | **guitar, piano, violin,** etc. | **soprano, tenor,** etc.
VERB + SOLO **do, perform** | **dance, play, sing** | **feature, include** ◊ *The song features an extended guitar ~.*

soluble *adj.*

VERBS **be** | **become**
ADV. **highly, very** ◊ *It is a highly ~ gas.* | **easily, freely, readily** | **completely, totally** | **partially, partly, slightly**
PREP. **in** ◊ *The salt was easily ~ in water.*

solution *noun*

1 to a problem, difficult situation, etc.
ADJ. **complete, comprehensive** | **partial** | **effective, good, ideal, neat, optimal, perfect, real** ◊ *His plan does not offer a real ~ to the problem.* | **acceptable** | **satisfactory, workable** | **correct, right** | **easy, obvious, simple** | **possible** | **alternative** | **feasible, practical, realistic, viable** | **cost-effective** | **creative, imaginative, ingenious, innovative** | **drastic, radical** | **immediate, instant, quick, speedy** ◊ *The UN representative stressed the urgency of a speedy ~.* | **final, lasting, long-term, permanent, ultimate** | **interim, short-term, temporary** | **proposed** | **pragmatic** | **compromise, negotiated** | **diplomatic, peaceful, political** | **military, security** | **technical, technological, technology** (esp. AmE) ◊ *The industry needs to look for technological ~s to their problems.* | **software**
VERB + SOLUTION **look for, seek, work towards/toward** | **achieve, agree, agree on, agree upon, arrive at, come up with, find, produce, reach, work out** ◊ *attempts to find a comprehensive political ~ to the crisis* | **develop** | **propose, put forward, suggest** | **adopt** | **offer, provide**
PREP. **~ for** ◊ *a quick ~ for dealing with the paper shortage* | **~ to** ◊ *They were seeking an ultimate ~ to the city's traffic problem.*
PHRASES **part of the ~** ◊ *Either you're part of the ~ or part of the problem.*
2 liquid in which a solid has been dissolved
ADJ. **concentrated, strong** | **dilute, weak** | **saturated** | **acid** | **alkaline** | **aqueous** | **saline, salt** | **buffer** | **bicarbonate, sodium chloride,** etc.
SOLUTION + VERB **contain**
PREP. **in ~** ◊ *carbon dioxide in ~*

solve *verb*

ADV. **completely** ◊ *The mystery has not yet been completely ~d.* | **largely** | **half, partially, partly** | **hardly** | **actually, really** ◊ *It doesn't really ~ the problem.* | **not necessarily** ◊ *Being with friends does not necessarily ~ my problem.* | **adequately, satisfactorily** ◊ *This question has never been satisfactorily ~d.* | **effectively** | **easily, readily** | **quickly, neatly** | **magically, somehow** | **eventually, finally** | **never**
VERB + SOLVE **attempt to, try to** | **help (to), help sb (to)** ◊ *We were given clues to help us ~ the puzzle.* | **be designed to** ◊ *a plan designed to ~ the housing problem* | **fail to** | **be difficult to**
PREP. **by** ◊ *We hope the difficulty can be ~d by getting the two sides together to discuss the issues.* | **with** ◊ *The problem cannot be ~d with spending cuts alone.*
PHRASES **an attempt to ~ sth** | **be aimed at solving sth** ◊ *research aimed at solving the growing problem of child obesity* | **be good at solving sth** ◊ *She's really good at solving problems.* | **focus on solving sth** ◊ *We need to focus on solving the country's problem.* | **help in solving sth** ◊ *their appeal for help in solving the case*

sombre (BrE) (AmE somber) *adj.*

VERBS **be, look, seem** ◊ *Everyone looked very ~.* | **become, grow, turn** ◊ *His eyes grew ~.* ◊ *The mood turned ~.* | **remain** ◊ *The mood in the city remained ~.*
ADV. **extremely, fairly, very,** etc. ◊ *She was in a somewhat ~ mood.* | **suitably** ◊ *The funeral cortège passed, to suitably ~ music.*

son *noun*

ADJ. **baby, newborn** | **infant, little, small, young** | **teenage** | **adult** (esp. AmE), **grown-up** | **only** | **eldest, first-born, middle, oldest, youngest** | **elder, younger** | **six-month-old, two-year-old,** etc. | **legitimate** | **bastard** (old-fashioned), **illegitimate** ◊ *an illegitimate ~ of Louis XV* | **adopted** | **dutiful, good** | **beloved** | **fine, strong** | **long-lost, prodigal** ◊ *They welcomed me like a long-lost ~.* | **dead** | **unborn** ◊ *his wife and unborn ~* | **surviving** | **native** (esp. AmE) ◊ *a native ~ of Philadelphia*

VERB + SON **have** ◇ *They have three young ~s.* | **bear** (*formal*), **give birth to** ◇ *His wife bore him three ~s.* | **bring up, raise** (*esp. AmE*) ◇ *Trying to bring up a young ~ is no easy task.* ◇ *a single parent raising her ~ alone*
SON + VERB **grow up**

song *noun*

1 piece of music with words

ADJ. **beautiful, good, great** | **catchy** (*informal*), **memorable** | **classic, famous, popular** | **hit** ◇ *He had a string of hit ~s in the 1970s.* | **mournful, sad** | **traditional** | **blues, country, dance, folk, pop, rap, etc.** ◇ *an Irish folk ~* | **patriotic, protest, religious** ◇ *a protest ~ written in the sixties* | **love, slow, torch** ◇ *The band were still playing slow ~s.* ◇ *emotional ballads and heartfelt torch ~s* | **bawdy** (*BrE*), **drinking, football** (*BrE*), **rugby** (*BrE*) ◇ *After a few drinks, they were all singing bawdy ~s at the top of their voices.* | **children's** | **Christmas, novelty** ◇ *A Christmas novelty ~ was playing on the radio.* | **theme, title** ◇ *the theme ~ from 'The Godfather'* ◇ *the title ~ from the Beatles' album 'Help!'* | **signature** ◇ *She closed the concert by singing her signature ~.* | **cover, original** ◇ *He released an album of cover ~s.* | **siren** (*figurative*) ◇ *People can become vulnerable to the siren ~ of extremism.* | **swan** (usually ***swansong***) (= last piece of work or last performance by an actor, musician, etc.)
VERB + SONG **compose, write** | **do, make, perform, play, sing** ◇ *They performed another two ~s as encores.* ◇ *Sing us a ~, Susanna!* | **record** | **download** ◇ *I downloaded a ~ from the Internet.* | **listen to**
SONG + VERB **come on, play** ◇ *A rap ~ came on the radio.* | **go** ◇ *How does the ~ go?* | **sound** ◇ *The old ~s sound like Gregorian chants.* | **be called** ◇ *a ~ called 'Mona Lisa'*
SONG + NOUN **lyric, lyrics** | **title** | **writer** (usually ***songwriter***) ◇ *a singer-songwriter*
PREP. **in (a/the) ~** ◇ *Important historical events were commemorated in ~.* | **~ about** ◇ *a ~ about love*
PHRASES **the same old ~** (*esp. AmE, often figurative*) ◇ *They continue to sing the same old ~ they have been singing for years.*

2 act of singing

VERB + SONG **break into, burst into** ◇ *He strummed a couple of chords on the guitar and they all burst into ~.*
PREP. **in ~** ◇ *He heard voices raised in ~.*

soothing *adj.*

VERBS **be, feel, sound** ◇ *Her touch felt wonderfully ~.*
ADV. **very, wonderfully** | **quite** ◇ *There was something quite ~ about her being there.* | **oddly, strangely**

sophisticated *adj.*

VERBS **be, feel, look, seem** | **become, get, grow** ◇ *The software grows more ~ over time.*
ADV. **extremely, fairly, very, etc.** | **highly** ◇ *She was a highly ~ and elegant woman.* | **incredibly, remarkably** ◇ *incredibly ~ computers* | **increasingly** | **enough, sufficiently** | **technically, technologically** | **intellectually, philosophically, politically**

sophistication *noun*

ADJ. **considerable, great** | **growing, increased, increasing** | **cool** | **cultural, intellectual, musical, political, technical, technological, theoretical**
... OF SOPHISTICATION **degree, level** ◇ *Computers raised the level of ~ of these maps.*
VERB + SOPHISTICATION **have** ◇ *The decor has a cool ~.* | **demonstrate, show** | **lack** | **grow in** ◇ *Financial markets have grown in ~ as well as size.*
PREP. **with ~** ◇ *He writes with increasing ~ on the subject.*
PHRASES **an air of ~** ◇ *Despite her scruffy clothes, there was an air of ~ about her.* | **a lack of ~** ◇ *He felt people were contemptuous of his lack of ~.* | **a veneer of ~** (*esp. BrE*) ◇ *She adopted an upper-class accent to give herself a veneer of ~.*

sore *noun*

ADJ. **festering** (*often figurative*), **oozing, open, running** (*esp. BrE, often figurative*) ◇ *This issue is a festering ~ between the two countries.* ◇ *The border dispute was a running ~ in relations between the countries.* | **cold** ◇ *I have a recurrent cold ~ on my lip.* | **canker** (*AmE*) ◇ *canker ~s caused by biting the inside of your mouth* | **bed** (usually ***bedsore***), **pressure, saddle** ◇ *Many people in the care home have bedsores.*
VERB + SORE **cause** | **develop, get** ◇ *The patient developed pressure ~s on the toes of both feet.* | **have**

sorrow *noun*

ADJ. **deep, genuine, great, immense, profound, terrible, tremendous, unbearable** ◇ *He wrote to the dead man's mother expressing his deep ~.*
VERB + SORROW **feel** ◇ *I felt no ~ for her.* | **express** | **share** ◇ *She wanted to share his ~.* | **hide** ◇ *I couldn't hide my ~ and anger.* | **drown** (*figurative*) ◇ *Alex decided to drown his ~s in beer.* | **bring, cause** ◇ *The war brought ~ to millions.*
PREP. **to sb's ~** ◇ *To his great ~ he could not remember his mother.* | **with ~** ◇ *They accepted the decision with ~.* | **~ at** ◇ *his ~ at having to quit his job*
PHRASES **an expression of ~, a look of ~** ◇ *His eyes took on an expression of ~.* | **a feeling of ~, a pang of ~** ◇ *Claudia felt a deep pang of ~ for her sister.* | **full of ~** ◇ *He looked at Katherine, his eyes full of ~.* | **tears of ~** ◇ *Tears of relief were mixed with tears of ~.* | **a time of ~** ◇ *This is a time of great ~ for all the family.*

sorry *adj.*

VERBS **be, feel, seem, sound** | **make sb** ◇ *I'll make you ~ you were ever born!*
ADV. **extremely, fairly, very, etc.** | **awfully, deeply, desperately, dreadfully, genuinely, sincerely, terribly, truly** ◇ *I'm awfully ~ Jane can't come with us.* ◇ *I'm terribly ~. I didn't catch your name.* ◇ *He was sincerely ~ for the distress he had caused.* | **almost** ◇ *She was almost ~ to stop work.* | **a little, slightly, etc.** ◇ *Mitch felt slightly ~ for himself.*
PREP. **about** ◇ *I'm ~ about the noise.* ◇ *I'm ~ about your mother. I hope she'll soon be better.* | **for** ◇ *She is obviously deeply ~ for what she has done.* ◇ *I feel really ~ for John.*
PHRASES **be ~ to disappoint sb** ◇ *I am ~ to disappoint you.* | **be ~ to hear about sth/that…** ◇ *We were incredibly ~ to hear about his death.* | **be ~ to interrupt (sb/sth)** | **better safe than ~**

sort *noun*

ADJ. **best, worst** | **right, wrong** | **same, similar** | **different** | **funny, odd, strange** ◇ *He was friendly in a funny ~ of way.*
PREP. **~ of** ◇ *We sell all ~s of books.*

sort *verb*

1 put things into different groups/places

ADV. **busily**
PREP. **according to** ◇ *Sort the books according to their subject matter.* | **by** ◇ *The most common way of grouping was to ~ the children by ability.* | **into** ◇ *We ~ed the clothes into piles.* | **through** ◇ *She was busily ~ing through her clothes.*
PHRASES **begin ~ing sth, start ~ing sth** | **begin ~ing through sth, start ~ing through sth** ◇ *She started ~ing through the papers.*

2 (*esp. BrE*) **find an answer to a problem**

ADV. **out** ◇ *Someone will have to ~ this problem out.*
VERB + SORT **have to** | **try to** | **help to, help sb to** | **leave sb to** ◇ *Leave them to ~ it out among themselves.*
PHRASES **get sth ~ed** (*BrE*), **get sth ~ed out** ◇ *If he can't get his talk ~ed out, we'll have to ask someone else.*

soul *noun*

1 part of sb believed to exist after body is dead

ADJ. **eternal, immortal** | **dead** ◇ *The messenger god, Hermes, leads dead ~s into the underworld.* | **damned** | **human, individual** | **rational** | **pure** | **great**

VERB + SOUL **save** ◊ *Missionaries saw it as their task to save ~s.* | **sell** ◊ *to sell your ~ to the Devil*

PHRASES **a/the battle for sb's ~, a/the struggle for sb's ~** (*often figurative*) ◊ *a battle for the ~ of the country* | **have mercy on sb's ~** ◊ *May God have mercy on my ~.* | **God rest sb's ~** ◊ *God rest his ~.* | **the immortality of the ~** ◊ *an argument for the immortality of the ~* | **the ~s of the dead**

2 part of sb/sth that shows its true nature

ADJ. **very** ◊ *The plea touched him to his very ~.* | **whole** | **inner**

VERB + SOUL **lose** ◊ *In the process of being made into a movie, the story seemed to have lost its ~.* | **bare** ◊ *He bared his ~ to her.* | **search** ◊ *I searched my ~ for any malice that could have provoked his words, but found none.* | **be good for** ◊ *Laughter is good for the ~.*

PREP. **in your ~** ◊ *Deep in her ~ she knew she had to return to her country.*

PHRASES **body and ~** ◊ *She gave herself to him body and ~.* | **from the depths of sb's ~, in the depths of sb's ~** ◊ *He let out an anguished cry from the depths of his ~.* | **heart and ~** ◊ *He gave himself heart and ~ to the cause.* | **a part of sb's ~** ◊ *She was a part of his ~.*

3 deep feeling and thought

VERB + SOUL **have** | **lack**

PREP. **with ~** ◊ *She sang the song with passion and ~.*

4 person

ADJ. **little** ◊ *poor little ~* | **old** | **good** | **bad** | **lonely, lost, poor, unfortunate** | **innocent, simple** | **kindred** ◊ *They recognized each other as kindred ~s.* | **dear, generous, gentle, kind, kindly** ◊ *a kind old ~* | **sensitive** | **brave** | **hardy** (*esp. BrE*) ◊ *A few hardy ~s braved the icy conditions.* | **romantic** | **restless, tormented, tortured, troubled** | **living** ◊ *There was no other living ~ to be seen.* | **single** ◊ *I don't know a single ~ in this town.*

VERB + SOUL **not tell** ◊ *I will not tell a ~ about this.*

PHRASES **not a ~ in sight** ◊ *By midnight, there wasn't a ~ in sight.*

sound noun

1 sth you hear

ADJ. **big, deafening, loud, powerful** ◊ *We need a big powerful ~ from the trumpets in the final passage.* | **audible** | **faint, little, soft** | **high, high-pitched** | **deep, low** | **clean, clear, sharp** ◊ *He produces a good clean ~ on his flute.* | **piercing** | **muffled** | **amazing, beautiful, good, lovely, pleasing, sweet** ◊ *His film opens with the sweet ~ of birdsong.* | **awful, horrible, sickening** ◊ *There was a sickening ~ as his head made contact with the concrete.* | **familiar** | **different, strange** ◊ *We experimented with different ~s.* | **distinctive** | **haunting** | **beeping, booming, buzzing, clanking, clicking, etc.** | **metallic** | **electronic** | **hollow** | **distorted** | **distant** ◊ *the distant ~ of church bells* | **musical** | **guitar, piano, etc.** ◊ *She tried to describe what made a good guitar ~.* | **speech, vowel** | **natural** ◊ *the mixing of recorded and natural ~* | **ambient** ◊ *There's a lot of ambient ~ in this film.*

VERB + SOUND **hear, listen for, listen to** ◊ *He listened for ~s of movement.* | **emit, make, produce, pronounce, transmit, utter** ◊ *What's making that awful creaking ~?* ◊ *He didn't utter a single ~ throughout the meeting.* | **use** ◊ *She uses all the ~s available to a 21st-century composer.* | **be filled with** ◊ *The room was filled with the ~ of laughter.* | **awake to, be woken by, wake to, wake up to** ◊ *I awoke to the ~ of rain.* | **be interrupted by** | **jump at** ◊ *He jumped at the ~ of my voice.*

SOUND + VERB **carry, travel** ◊ *Sound carries well over calm water.* | **come** ◊ *A strange ~ came from the box.* ◊ *My mouth moved but no ~ came out.* | **echo, fill, ring out** ◊ *A hollow ~ echoed through the room.* | **die away, fade, fade away** | **grow louder**

SOUND + NOUN **wave** | **effect** | **bite** ◊ *As a politician he is a master of the 30-second ~ bite.*

PREP. **at the ~ of** ◊ *He turned around at the ~ of footsteps behind him.* | **without a ~** ◊ *The door opened without a ~.* | **~ of** ◊ *the ~ of breaking glass* | **~ from** ◊ *There was a strange ~ from downstairs.*

PHRASES **break the ~ barrier** | **the speed of ~**

2 the sound from TV, radio, etc.

ADJ. **mono, stereo, surround** | **recorded** | **great** ◊ *a game with good graphics and great ~*

VERB + SOUND **turn down, turn off, turn up** ◊ *Can you turn the ~ up?* | **get**

SOUND + NOUN **level, quality** | **system** ◊ *a stereo ~ system* | **recording** | **engineer** | **card**

3 of musicians

ADJ. **live** ◊ *The band developed a formidable live ~.* | **different, new, unique** | **beautiful, great** ◊ *Franz Ferdinand have a great ~ that's their own.* | **signature** ◊ *the band's signature ~*

VERB + SOUND **create, develop** ◊ *The Moog synthesizer created a whole new ~.*

> **NOTE**
>
> **Sounds**
>
> **give a…** ◊ *The dog gave a low growl.*
> **let out a…** ◊ *He let out a blood-curdling scream.*
> **hear…** ◊ *We heard the peal of church bells.*
> **with a…** ◊ *The vase fell to the ground with a great crash.*
> **…of** ◊ *a roar of laughter* ◊ *a snort of derision* ◊ *the whine of an engine*

---

sound adj.

1 in good condition

VERBS **be, look, seem**

ADV. **extremely, fairly, very, etc.** | **reasonably** ◊ *The roof is in reasonably ~ condition.* | **structurally** ◊ *Is the building structurally ~?*

PHRASES **safe and ~** (= not hurt) ◊ *We finally arrived home safe and ~.*

2 sensible

VERBS **be, seem**

ADV. **extremely, fairly, very, etc.** ◊ *That seems like fairly ~ advice.* | **perfectly** ◊ *She had a perfectly ~ reason for acting as she did.* | **basically, fundamentally** | **ecologically, environmentally, financially, ideologically, scientifically, technically, theoretically** ◊ *It was a financially ~ investment.*

soundtrack noun

ADJ. **film** (*esp. BrE*), **movie** (*esp. AmE*) | **original** ◊ *The original Japanese ~ is included with English subtitles.* | **musical** ◊ *a musical ~ conceived by Quincy Jones*

VERB + SOUNDTRACK **compose, create, make** | **listen to** | **provide** (*often figurative*) ◊ *Abba provided the ~ to my teenage years.*

SOUNDTRACK + VERB **feature** ◊ *The movie has a ~ featuring music by Strauss.*

PREP. **~ for, ~ of, ~ to** ◊ *She composed the ~s to several hit movies.*

soup noun

ADJ. **creamy, hearty, thick** ◊ *hearty vegetable ~* | **clear, thin** | **cold, hot** | **home-made** | **canned** (*esp. AmE*), **tinned** (*BrE*) | **dried, packaged** (*AmE*), **packet** (*BrE*) | **chicken, chicken noodle, miso, pea, tomato, vegetable, etc.** | **alphabet** (*often figurative*) ◊ *an alphabet ~ of other government agencies* (= used to say that their names consist of complicated abbreviations) | **bird's nest, shark fin, shark's fin** (*esp. BrE*) ◊ *the Chinese delicacy of shark fin ~* | **primordial** (*figurative*) ◊ *the emergence of life from the primordial ~ on the Earth*

…OF SOUP **bowl, cup, mug** (*BrE*) | **can, tin** (*BrE*) | **pot**

VERB + SOUP **cook, make, prepare** | **heat, heat up** | **drink, eat** (*Eat* is the normal verb when the soup is served in a

bowl.) | **slurp** ◇ *Don't slurp your ~!* | **ladle, ladle out, pour, serve** ◇ *He ladled out three bowls of ~.*
SOUP + NOUN **bowl, plate, pot** (*AmE*), **tureen** | **spoon** | **can** ◇ *Warhol's paintings of Campbell's ~ cans* | **kitchen** (= a place where soup and other food is supplied free to people with no money)
→ Special page at FOOD

sour *adj.*

VERBS **be, smell, taste** ◇ *The sauce tasted very ~.* ◇ *The milk smelled ~.* | **go, turn** (*both also figurative*) ◇ *By the next day the wine had turned ~.* ◇ *Their relationship quickly turned ~.*
ADV. **extremely, fairly, very, etc.** | **a little, slightly, etc.** ◇ *Their friendship has turned a little ~.*
PHRASES **leave a ~ taste in sb's mouth** (*figurative*) ◇ *The whole experience has really left a ~ taste in my mouth.*

source *noun*

1 where you get sth from

ADJ. **excellent, fertile, good, great, lucrative, reliable, rich, valuable** ◇ *a fertile ~ of ideas* ◇ *a lucrative ~ of income* ◇ *a rich ~ of vitamins* | **important, large, main, major, principal** | **cheap** ◇ *a cheap ~ of protein* | **external, foreign, outside** ◇ *Do you have any foreign ~s of income?* | **independent** ◇ *an independent ~ of funding* | **only, single** ◇ *The only ~ of light was the fire.* | **additional, alternative, different, new, other** ◇ *We need to look for alternative ~s of energy.* ◇ *to develop new ~s of revenue* | **same** | **likely, potential** ◇ *a potential ~ of conflict* | **unexpected** | **constant** ◇ *a constant ~ of irritation* | **natural** | **renewable, sustainable** ◇ *The town obtains all its energy from renewable ~s.* | **energy, food, fuel, heat, light, power, protein, water** | **funding, revenue**
VERB + SOURCE **be, constitute, prove, provide** ◇ *The census constitutes the principal ~ of official statistics.* ◇ *These crustaceans provide a valuable food ~ for some fish.* | **exploit, tap, tap into, use (as)** ◇ *The government hopes to tap new ~s of employment in the area of health.* | **find, identify, locate** ◇ *We tried to locate the ~ of the sound.*
PREP. **at ~** (*BrE*) ◇ *Is your salary taxed at ~ (= by your employer)?* | **~ of** ◇ *a ~ of income/revenue* ◇ *a ~ of inspiration/strength* ◇ *a ~ of energy/food/light*
PHRASES **a variety of ~s** ◇ *The research was funded from a wide variety of ~s.*

2 person, book, etc. that gives information

ADJ. **invaluable, useful, valuable** | **authoritative, informed, reliable, reputable** | **unreliable** | **original** | **independent** | **anonymous, confidential, unnamed** ◇ *his refusal to reveal the identity of a confidential ~* | **primary, secondary** | **multiple, several, various** ◇ *The evidence is corroborated by multiple ~s.* | **published** | **biographical, documentary, historical, literary, written** | **media, news** | **diplomatic, government, intelligence, military, official, police** ◇ *Intelligence ~s report a build-up of troops just inside the border.* | **data, information**
VERB + SOURCE **use (as)** | **cite, quote** ◇ *Researchers try to quote primary ~s wherever possible.* | **disclose, identify, name, reveal** ◇ *The police refused to reveal the ~ of their information.* | **protect**
SOURCE + VERB **claim sth, describe sth, disclose sth, indicate sth, report sth, reveal sth, say sth, suggest sth, tell sb sth** ◇ *Government ~s indicated that a compromise might be reached.* ◇ *One ~ said: 'We are angry at the way we have been treated.'* | **deny sth**
SOURCE + NOUN **material**
PREP. **according to ~s** ◇ *According to informed ~s, a takeover bid is planned for next month.* | **~ of** ◇ *Do you know the ~ of this rumour/rumor?*
PHRASES **~s close to sb** ◇ *Sources close to the player claim he won't be entering this year's championship.*

sovereignty *noun*

ADJ. **absolute, full, unlimited** ◇ *Demonstrators demanded full ~ for the self-proclaimed republic.* | **limited** | **joint, shared** (*both esp. BrE*) | **national, popular** | **British, Japanese, etc.** | **consumer, economic, legal, parliamentary** (*esp. BrE*), **political, state, territorial, tribal**
VERB + SOVEREIGNTY **exercise, have** ◇ *China exercises ~ over Hong Kong.* | **share** | **claim, establish** | **give sb/sth, grant sb/sth** | **cede, give up, relinquish, surrender, transfer, turn over** (*esp. AmE*) ◇ *In 1949 the Dutch ceded ~ of the Dutch East Indies to the Indonesian Republic.* | **recognize, respect** ◇ *We must respect the ~ of member states.* | **threaten** | **violate** | **defend**
SOVEREIGNTY + VERB **reside in sb/sth, reside with sb/sth** ◇ *Sovereignty resides with the people.*
PREP. **~ over** ◇ *The treaty gave Edward III ~ over Calais and the whole of Aquitaine.*
PHRASES **the handover of ~, the return of ~, the transfer of ~** ◇ *the handover of ~ to the new government* | **the loss of ~** ◇ *Politicians were alarmed over the potential loss of national ~.* | **a claim to ~** ◇ *Two countries have a claim to ~ over the islands.* | **the ~ of Parliament** (*esp. BrE*), **the ~ of the people** ◇ *This constitutes an attack on the ~ of Parliament.*

space *noun*

1 empty area

ADJ. **large, vast, wide-open** ◇ *She left a large ~ empty at the bottom of the page.* ◇ *He loved the wide-open ~s of Australia.* | **adequate, ample, enough, sufficient** ◇ *The new house has ample living ~.* | **limited, little, small, tiny** | **narrow** ◇ *the narrow ~ between the sofa and the wall* | **open** | **confined, enclosed** ◇ *Avoid using the cleaner in a confined ~.* | **available, free, vacant** ◇ *The exhibition takes up most of the available ~ in the gallery.* ◇ *I was looking for a free parking ~.* | **blank, empty, white** ◇ *Fill in the blank ~s in the table.* ◇ *The page layout included plenty of white ~.* | **storage** | **floor, roof, shelf, wall, etc.** | **crawl** (*AmE*) ◇ *the crawl ~ under my house* | **living** | **office, work** (usually ***workspace***) ◇ *an open-plan workspace* | **interior** | **parking** | **personal, private** ◇ *She moved out of the house because she wanted her own personal ~.* | **physical** | **sacred** | **public, social** | **green** ◇ *The inner residential areas don't have many green ~s.* | **urban** | **air** (usually ***airspace***) ◇ *The plane strayed into French airspace.* | **disk** | **ad** (*informal*), **advertising** ◇ *The magazine is struggling to fill all its advertising ~.* | **commercial, retail** | **exhibition, gallery**
... OF SPACE **amount** ◇ *a large amount of ~*
VERB + SPACE **fill, occupy** | **make use of, take up, use** ◇ *The potted plants take up too much ~.* | **share** ◇ *He was sharing office ~ with a lawyer.* | **create, make, provide** ◇ *They moved the sofa to make ~ for the piano.* | **waste** | **save** | **clear** ◇ *We'd better clear a ~ for the new computer.* | **fill, fill in** | **compete for, fight for, jostle for** ◇ *A motley collection of ornaments jostled for ~ on the crowded shelf.* | **stare into, stare off into** ◇ *She sat there motionless, staring into ~.*
PREP. **~ between** ◇ *the ~ between the bookshelves*
PHRASES **be short of ~, run short of ~** ◇ *I'm running short of disk ~.* | **time and ~** ◇ *The writer lacked the time and ~ to develop his idea fully.* | **a waste of ~** (*often figurative*) ◇ *You are a pathetic waste of ~!*

2 vast area containing planets, stars, etc.

ADJ. **deep** | **outer**
VERB + SPACE **go into**
SPACE + NOUN **exploration, programme/program, research, science** | **flight, tourism, travel** | **agency** | **mission** ◇ *They intend to begin manned ~ missions next year.* | **capsule, probe, rocket, ship** (usually ***spaceship***), **shuttle, station**
PREP. **in ~** ◇ *the first man in ~*
PHRASES **the depths of ~, the edge of ~** ◇ *these wonderful pictures from the edge of ~* | **~ and time** ◇ *the fabric of ~ and time* | **the vacuum of ~** | **the vastness of ~**

3 period of time

ADJ. **long** | **brief, short** | **two-second, ten-minute, etc.** ◇ *The*

recording includes a five-second ~ between tracks. | **breathing** (*figurative*) ◇ *The extension of the deadline gives us a breathing ~.*
PREP. **for the ~ of** ◇ *The job holder will be on probation for the ~ of six months.* | **in the ~ of, within the ~ of** ◇ *He fell asleep in the ~ of a few minutes.* | **~ of** ◇ *She returned to top-class tennis after a ~ of two years.*
PHRASES **a ~ of time** ◇ *They have achieved a great deal in a short ~ of time.*

space verb

ADV. **at intervals, equally, evenly, regularly** ◇ *The nails should be ~d at regular intervals.* ◇ *Make sure the posts are ~d evenly apart.* | **irregularly** | **closely** | **well, widely** | **apart, out** ◇ *The fruits should be well ~d out so that they are not touching each other.*
PREP. **along**

spacecraft noun

ADJ. **manned, unmanned** ◇ *An unmanned Chinese ~ has returned safely to Earth.* | **orbiting**
VERB + SPACECRAFT **launch, send** ◇ *They plan to send a ~ to the moon.* | **build**
SPACECRAFT + VERB **land** | **orbit sth** ◇ *a ~ orbiting the earth*
PREP. **in a/the ~, on a/the ~**

spade noun

1 tool for digging
ADJ. **garden** ◇ *There was a garden ~ in the shed.*
VERB + SPADE **use** ◇ *He dug a deep hole in the lawn with his ~.*
PHRASES **bucket and ~** (*BrE*) ◇ *children playing in the sand with their buckets and ~s* | **call a ~ a ~** (= to speak honestly and openly) ◇ *I believe in calling a ~ a ~.*

2 playing card
→ Note at CARD

span noun

1 length
ADJ. **full** | **broad, wide** ◇ *a broad ~ of interests* | **clear** ◇ *The bridge has a clear ~ of 120 feet.* | **15-foot, 500-metre/500-meter, etc.** | **wing** (usually **wingspan**) ◇ *The bird has a three-foot wingspan.*

2 length of time
ADJ. **long** | **brief, short** | **ten-day, two-week, etc.** | **entire** | **allotted** ◇ *The speech continued well beyond its allotted ~.* | **natural** (*esp. BrE*) ◇ *to prolong life beyond its natural ~* | **time** | **life** (usually **lifespan**) ◇ *The average lifespan of an American is 75 years.* | **attention, concentration** (*esp. BrE*) | **memory** ◇ *He has a short attention ~.*
VERB + SPAN **cover** ◇ *The book covers the entire ~ of Arab history.*
PREP. **over a/the ~** ◇ *Developments were monitored over a ~ of two years.*
PHRASES **a ~ of time, a ~ of years**

spare verb

1 make sth available
ADV. **barely, hardly** ◇ *She hardly ~d him a second glance.*
VERB + SPARE **can, could** ◇ *Can you ~ a second to give me a hand?*
PREP. **for** ◇ *Can you ~ some money for the homeless?*
PHRASES **to ~** ◇ *Have you any money to ~?* | *We should get there with half an hour to ~.*

2 allow sb/sth not to be harmed
ADV. **largely** ◇ *The storm largely ~d Houston and surrounding districts.* | **mercifully**
PREP. **from** ◇ *The children were ~d from the virus.*

spark noun

1 small bright piece of burning material/electric flash
ADJ. **tiny** | **flying** | **electric**
VERB + SPARK **emit, produce, send, send out, shower (sb with), strike** ◇ *The firework showered ~s all over the lawn.*
SPARK + VERB **flare, fly** | **ignite sth** ◇ *Flying ~s ignited the dry grass.* | **die**
PHRASES **a shower of ~s** ◇ *The grinding wheel sent a shower of ~s across the workbench.* | **a ~ of light**

2 small amount of a quality/feeling
ADJ. **little, tiny** ◇ *A tiny ~ of rebellion flared within her.* | **creative, divine, vital** (*esp. BrE*)
VERB + SPARK **have** ◇ *She didn't have a ~ of talent in her.* | **lack** ◇ *His performances lack that creative ~.* | **lose** | **add, create, provide** ◇ *Her performance added a little ~ to the movie.* | **feel** ◇ *She felt a little ~ of anger.* | **shoot** (*figurative*) ◇ *Her eyes shot ~s of contempt.*
SPARK + VERB **fly** ◇ *Sparks flew* (= people got angry) *at the meeting.*
PREP. **~ of** ◇ *He had kindled a ~ of interest within her.* ◇ *a ~ of hope/life*

sparkle noun

ADJ. **extra** | **a little** | **old** ◇ *She has lost none of her old ~ as a jazz singer.*
VERB + SPARKLE **have** | **lack** | **lose** | **add, put, put back** ◇ *A live band added extra ~ to the occasion.*
PHRASES **a ~ in sb's eyes**

spasm noun

ADJ. **sudden** | **involuntary, uncontrollable** ◇ *involuntary ~s of the nervous system* | **intense, violent** | **painful, severe** | **muscle, muscular** | **back** ◇ *He suffered a back ~ while playing football.*
VERB + SPASM **experience, feel, suffer** ◇ *He felt a ~ of panic sweeping over him.* | **cause** | **go into** (*esp. BrE*) ◇ *The muscle goes into ~, producing the symptom of cramp.*
SPASM + VERB **pass, stop**
PREP. **in ~** (*esp. BrE*) ◇ *She could not speak; her throat was in ~.* | **~ of** ◇ *He kicked the chair in a ~ of impatience.*
PHRASES **a ~ of pain**

speak verb

1 have a conversation
ADV. **briefly** ◇ *We spoke briefly on the phone.* | **at length** | **hardly** ◇ *Ben hardly spoke to me all evening.*
VERB + SPEAK **want to** | **refuse to** ◇ *The president refused to ~ to the waiting journalists.* | **dare (to)** ◇ *No one had ever dared to ~ to him like that before.*
PREP. **about, to** ◇ *I need to ~ to Joseph about this matter.* | **with** (*esp. AmE*) ◇ *Can I ~ with you for a minute?*
PHRASES **be on ~ing terms (with sb)** ◇ *We are still on ~ing terms after the argument.* | **a/the chance to ~, a/the opportunity to ~** ◇ *I didn't get a chance to ~ to him.* | **not be ~ing (to sb)** ◇ *Ed and Dave aren't ~ing at the moment.* | **~ing of ...** ◇ *Speaking of Brett, why isn't he here?*

2 use your voice to say sth
ADV. **loudly** | **quietly, softly** | **clearly** ◇ *You must ~ loudly and clearly on the stage.* | **slowly** | **calmly** | **briefly** | **at length** | **suddenly** | **hardly** | **eloquently, movingly** ◇ *She spoke eloquently about the need for action.* | **lovingly, soothingly, warmly** | **disparagingly, harshly, sharply, sternly** | **authoritatively, forcefully** | **earnestly** | **coherently, intelligibly** | **freely, openly, publicly** | **directly** ◇ *The main character ~s directly into the camera.* | **boldly** | **hesitantly**
VERB + SPEAK **be able to, be unable to, can (hardly)** ◇ *She was so moved she could hardly ~.* | **be allowed to** | **begin to, open your mouth to** ◇ *She opened her mouth to ~ and found she couldn't.* | **try to** | **not trust yourself to** ◇ *He nodded, not trusting himself to ~.* | **hear sb** ◇ *I heard him ~ at the debating society.* | **invite sb to** ◇ *She was invited to ~ at a Harvard conference.*
PREP. **about, on** ◇ *She ~s on women's issues.* | **against** ◇ *He spoke out against mismanagement.* | **for, on behalf of** ◇ *I ~ for all my colleagues.* ◇ *I ~ on behalf of many thousands of women.* | **in favour/favor of** ◇ *She spoke in favour/favor of*

the new tax. | **of** ◇ *He ~s very warmly of you.* | **to** ◇ *He will be ~ing to history students about the causes of war.*
PHRASES **the ability to ~** ◇ *He lost his ability to ~.* | **have the courage to ~** ◇ *They had the courage to ~ the truth.* | **the right to ~** ◇ *Everyone should have the right to ~ their mind.* | **~ from experience** ◇ *I'm ~ing from experience, having been there often.*

3 know a language
ADV. **fluently, well** ◇ *He ~s German fluently.*
VERB + SPEAK **be able to, can | be unable to, cannot | learn to** ◇ *the benefits of learning to ~ a foreign language* | **teach sb to**
PREP. **in** ◇ *Would you prefer it if we spoke in French?*
PHRASES **the ability to ~ sth** ◇ *The ability to ~ another language is a valued skill.*

speaker *noun*

1 person who makes a speech
ADJ. **brilliant** (*esp. BrE*), **good, great | featured** (*esp. AmE*), **keynote, main, principal | guest, invited, visiting | public** ◇ *She's a good public ~.* | **commencement** (*AmE*) ◇ *the commencement ~ at my graduation* | **after-dinner** (*BrE*) | **conference | motivational** (*esp. AmE*) ◇ *He makes his living as a motivational ~.*
VERB + SPEAKER **feature** ◇ *Each month's service features a different ~.* | **invite**
PREP. **~ at** ◇ *a keynote ~ at the Republican convention*

2 person who speaks a particular language
ADJ. **fluent** ◇ *He's a fluent Arabic ~.* | **native, non-native** ◇ *a native ~ of English* | **Japanese, Russian, etc. | non-English**
PREP. **~ of** ◇ *~s of English*

3 part of a radio, etc. that sounds comes out of
ADJ. **left, right | front, rear** ◇ *sound effects coming from the rear ~s* | **stereo** ◇ *The computer has built-in stereo ~s.*
... OF SPEAKER **set** ◇ *a new set of ~s*
SPEAKER + NOUN **system | phone** (usually **speakerphone**) ◇ *He put me on the speakerphone.*

spear *noun*

ADJ. **hunting**
VERB + SPEAR **be armed with, carry, hold, wield** ◇ *The tribesmen were armed with ~s and shields.* | **use | raise | brandish | hurl, throw | drive, thrust** ◇ *He drove his ~ through the creature's leg.*
SPEAR + NOUN **point** ◇ *a 5 000-year-old stone ~ point*
PHRASES **the point of a ~** ◇ *She had a fish impaled on the point of her ~.*

special *noun*

ADJ. **daily** ◇ *The restaurant has an extensive menu and daily ~s.* | **television, TV** ◇ *There are lots of TV Christmas ~s for children this year.* | **prime-time** (*esp. AmE*) | **Christmas, holiday** (*esp. AmE*) | **one-off** (*BrE*) ◇ *Eric Sykes returned with this one-off ~ for ITV.* | **reunion** (*AmE*) ◇ *the Dick Van Dyke Show reunion ~* | **after-school** (*AmE*) | **comedy | election | one-hour, two-hour, etc.**

specialist *noun*

ADJ. **leading, top** ◇ *a leading cancer ~* | **experienced, qualified, trained | independent | academic, industry, professional, research, technical | clinical, hospital, medical, public-health | cancer, ear, ear, nose and throat, eye, fertility, heart, mental-health, skin | finance, financial, marketing, property** (*BrE*) | **tax | recruitment** (*esp. BrE*) | **development, education, foreign-policy, technology** ◇ *a rural-development ~* | **communications, computer, information-technology** (abbreviated to *IT*), **software, systems | intelligence, security** ◇ *a new generation of computer security ~s*
VERB + SPECIALIST **bring in, hire** ◇ *They brought in an outside ~ to install the computer system.* | **consult, see** ◇ *He went to see a cancer ~.*

PREP. **~ in** ◇ *She is a ~ in children's literature.* | **~ on** ◇ *a ~ on the history of this city*
PHRASES **a group of ~s, a team of ~s | a ~ in the field** ◇ *The book is written by a noted ~ in the field.*
→ Note at DOCTOR, JOB

speciality (*BrE*) (also **specialty** *AmE, BrE*) *noun*

ADJ. **local, regional | house** ◇ *The drink is a house ~ prepared at the table.*
SPECIALITY/SPECIALTY + NOUN **food, product | retailer, shop, store** ◇ *You can find their product in ~ retailers.*

specialization *noun*

ADJ. **increased, increasing | academic, professional | economic** ◇ *There has been increased economic ~ throughout the country.* | **functional** (*technical*)
... OF SPECIALIZATION **degree** ◇ *The production line involves a high degree of ~.*
PREP. **~ in** ◇ *Her degree is in French, with ~ in 17th-century literature.*
PHRASES **an area of ~** ◇ *The company has gradually focused on its current areas of ~.*

specialized (*BrE* also **-ised**) *adj.*

VERBS **be** ◇ *These tools are very ~.* | **become**
ADV. **highly, very** ◇ *a job calling for highly ~ skills* | **increasingly**
PREP. **for** ◇ *This bird is highly ~ for eating fish.*

species *noun*

ADJ. **living | extinct | common | exotic, rare | different, distinct | new** ◇ *She identified and described 998 new ~ of crab.* | **related** ◇ *closely related ~ of beetle* | **native, non-native | alien | invasive** ◇ *the threat posed by non-native invasive ~* | **wild | dominant | endangered, imperilled/imperiled** (*esp. AmE*), **threatened | protected | animal, bird, fish, insect, mammal, mammalian, plant, tree, etc.** ◇ *The area is rich in different plant ~.* | **human** ◇ *the development of the human ~*
SPECIES + VERB **be found, grow, live, occur** ◇ *Similar ~ of fish occur in Mongolia.* | **become extinct, be threatened with extinction, die out, go extinct | survive**
PREP. **~ of** ◇ *a native ~ of fish*
PHRASES **a member of a ~**

specific *adj.*

VERBS **be** ◇ *Can you be a little more ~ in your instructions?*
ADV. **fairly, rather, very | highly** ◇ *Highly ~ instructions were issued.* | **culturally, historically** ◇ *These values are culturally ~, not naturally given.*
PREP. **about** ◇ *She was very ~ about the type she wanted.* | **to** ◇ *These heart issues are ~ to women.*

specification *noun*

ADJ. **complete, detailed, full | exact, precise | standard | high** (*esp. BrE*) ◇ *The yachts are built to the highest ~s.* | **original | design, performance, product, technical | customer | contract, job** (*both esp. BrE*) ◇ *The manager has drafted job ~s for each of the positions.*
VERB + SPECIFICATION **develop, draw up** (*esp. BrE*), **write | provide | have** ◇ *The prototype has the same basic ~s.* | **meet** ◇ *The aircraft have to meet the strict ~s laid down by the FAA.*
PREP. **according to the/your ~s, to the/your ~s** ◇ *Each vehicle can be equipped according to your ~s.*

specify *verb*

ADV. **clearly | fully | carefully | exactly, precisely** ◇ *She did not ~ precisely how many people were involved in the incident.* | **explicitly | correctly** ◇ *Are all the details correctly specified?* | **uniquely** ◇ *Each computer is uniquely specified by its serial number.* | **otherwise** ◇ *Unless otherwise specified, all fields have a maximum length of 20 characters.*
VERB + SPECIFY **allow sb to | require sb to | be difficult to**

specimen noun

1 example

ADJ. **large, small** | **beautiful, fine, good, healthy, magnificent, perfect, prize** (esp. BrE) ◇ This is a fine ~ of a walnut tree. | **living, preserved** ◇ well-preserved ~s of Homo erectus | **complete, incomplete** | **adult, juvenile** | **female, male** | **rare** | **physical**
VERB + SPECIMEN **find** ◇ He found two ~s of early humans.
SPECIMEN + NOUN **plant, tree**

2 small amount of sth used for testing

ADJ. **blood, urine, etc.**
VERB + SPECIMEN **collect, take** | **give, provide** ◇ The motorist may be required to give a urine ~. | **obtain**

spectacle noun

ADJ. **dramatic, grand** (esp. BrE), **great, magnificent** | **sad, sorry, unedifying** (esp. BrE) ◇ the sad ~ of him struggling to keep up with the younger players | **sheer** ◇ I attended solely to witness the sheer ~ of a political rally. | **public** ◇ Hangings took place outside the prison as a public ~. | **visual** ◇ The Olympics are a wonderful visual ~. | **media** | **sporting** (esp. BrE)
VERB + SPECTACLE **watch, witness** | **enjoy** | **create**
PHRASES **make a ~ of yourself** (= make yourself look ridiculous in public)

spectacles noun (formal, esp. BrE)

ADJ. **heavy** | **gold-rimmed, horn-rimmed, rimless, steel-rimmed, wire-framed, wire-rimmed** | **thick** | **tinted** (BrE) | **half-moon, round** | **reading**
... OF SPECTACLES **pair**
VERB + SPECTACLES **have on, wear** | **put on** | **take off** | **push** ◇ She pushed her ~ further up her nose and sighed. | **adjust** | **look through, peer through** | **look over, peer over** ◇ He peered at the waiter over his ~.
SPECTACLES + VERB **be perched on sth, perch on sth** ◇ Her wire-framed ~ were perched on the end of her nose.
PREP. **behind your ~, through your ~**

spectacular adj.

VERBS **be, look**
ADV. **fairly, rather, very** | **really, truly** | **absolutely, quite** ◇ The waterfall is truly ~. | **particularly** | **equally**

spectator noun

ADJ. **mere, passive, silent** | **interested** | **impartial** | **paying** | **virtual** (esp. BrE) ◇ He was rendered a virtual ~ for large parts of the game. | **football, sports, etc.**
... OF SPECTATORS **crowd**
VERB + SPECTATOR **attract, draw** ◇ This year's festival attracted 87 000 ~s. | **seat** ◇ The stadium will seat 60 000 ~s.
SPECTATOR + VERB **gather, turn up** (BrE) | **line sth** ◇ Spectators lined the route of the president's walkabout. | **cheer (sb/sth)**
SPECTATOR + NOUN **event, sport**

spectre (BrE) (AmE specter) noun

ADJ. **grim** (esp. BrE), **ominous** ◇ The grim ~ of terrorism cast its shadow. | **old** | **constant** | **looming** ◇ the looming ~ of a financial crisis | **twin** ◇ the twin ~s of addiction and violence
VERB + SPECTRE/SPECTER **evoke, invoke, raise** ◇ Wall Street's collapse raised ~s of the 1987 stock-market crash. | **face, see** | **banish, exorcize** ◇ an attempt to exorcize the ~ of poverty
SPECTRE/SPECTER + VERB **hang over sb/sth, haunt sb/sth, hover over sb/sth, loom, loom over sb/sth**
PREP. **~ of** ◇ The terrible ~ of civil war hung over the country once again.

spectrum noun

1 range of light waves, etc.

ADJ. **visible** ◇ These wavelengths correspond to red in the visible ~. | **colour/color, electromagnetic** | **broadcast, radio**
PHRASES **the colours/colors of the ~** ◇ Other species can perceive colours/colors of the ~ that are invisible to us. | **the ... end of the ~, the ... part of the ~, the ... portion of the ~, the ... region of the ~** ◇ the ultraviolet part of the ~

2 full or wide range

ADJ. **complete, full** ◇ The courses cover the full ~ of levels. | **broad, wide** | **narrow** | **entire, whole** | **ideological, political, social** | **age, income**
VERB + SPECTRUM **cover, span** | **represent** ◇ These thinkers represent a wide ~ of political perspectives.
PREP. **across the ~** ◇ There was consensus across the political ~. | **of** ◇ a wide ~ of interests
PHRASES **at one end of the ~, at the other end of the ~** | **both ends of the ~, opposite ends of the ~** ◇ The two speakers were chosen to represent opposite ends of the ~. | **a ~ of opinion** ◇ The newspaper covers a broad ~ of opinion.

speculate verb

ADV. **openly, publicly** ◇ Commentators are openly speculating on whether the accusation is false. | **widely** | **wildly** ◇ The British press ~d wildly about his disappearance.
VERB + SPECULATE **can only** | **be free to, feel free to** ◇ Both sides are free to ~ on the other's motives. | **decline to, refuse to** | **be interesting to, be tempting to** | **be possible to, be reasonable to** ◇ It would seem entirely reasonable to ~ that tribal loyalties influenced the outcome of the election. | **be premature to** ◇ It would be premature to ~ as to the outcome at this stage. | **be difficult to**
PREP. **about** ◇ There was no point in speculating about the possibility of them getting back together. | **as to** ◇ We can only ~ as to this man's identity. | **on, upon** ◇ He refused to ~ on her reasons for leaving.

speculation noun

1 making guesses about sth

ADJ. **considerable, intense, much, widespread** | **further, increasing, renewed** | **continuing** (esp. BrE), **endless** | **recent** | **pure** | **mere, sheer** ◇ Whether or not he will get the job is mere ~. | **wild** | **media, press** | **metaphysical, philosophical**
VERB + SPECULATION **cause, encourage, fuel, give rise to, increase, intensify, invite, lead to, prompt, raise** | **dampen** (esp. BrE), **dismiss, quash** (esp. BrE) | **end, put an end to** | **confirm** | **indulge in**
SPECULATION + VERB **be rife, run rampant** (esp. AmE) ◇ Speculation was rife as to who would be chosen as a successor. ◇ With a lack of credible answers, ~ is running rampant. | **grow, mount** ◇ Speculation is mounting that a new tax will be introduced. | **centre/center on, surround** ◇ Much ~ surrounds his role in the crisis. | **be based on** ◇ amateur ~ based on questionable assumptions | **link** (esp. BrE) ◇ There has been a lot of ~ linking the defender with a move to Chelsea.
PREP. **amid ~** ◇ He was dropped from the team amid ~ that he was sick. | **among** ◇ This issue has attracted a great deal of ~ among economists. | **~ about, ~ as to, ~ on, ~ over** ◇ There has been increasing ~ over the company's future.
PHRASES **a matter for ~** (esp. BrE), **a matter of ~, a subject of ~** | **on sb's part** ◇ This is just ~ on my part.

2 buying and selling for profit

ADJ. **financial** | **market, stock-market** (esp. AmE) | **currency, land, property** (esp. BrE), **real estate** (AmE), **etc.**
PREP. **~ in** ◇ ~ in oil | **~ on** ◇ ~ on the stock market

speech noun

1 speaking

ADJ. **slurred** ◇ She could tell by his slurred ~ that he had been drinking. | **clipped** | **casual** | **connected, continuous, fluent** | **natural, normal, ordinary** | **spontaneous** | **direct** | **indirect, reported** | **free** ◇ The demonstrators were demanding free ~. | **hate, hateful** (esp. AmE) ◇ racist hate ~ | **conversational, everyday** | **children's, human, etc.**
SPEECH + NOUN **pattern, style** ◇ He learned to successfully mimic American ~ patterns. | **defect** (esp. BrE), **impairment,**

impediment | therapist, therapy | community (technical) ◇ The members of a ~ community share many cultural attitudes. | recognition ◇ These computers are capable of ~ recognition. | code (esp. AmE) ◇ Speech codes have been instituted by some universities (= to stop language that is sexist, racist, etc.). | act (technical) | marks (esp. BrE) ◇ The author's punctuation goes outside ~ marks.

PREP. in ~ ◇ the use of language in everyday ~

PHRASES a figure of ~ ◇ When we say we're 'dead tired', it's just a figure of ~. | freedom of ~ ◇ the right of/to freedom of ~ | the power of ~ ◇ He temporarily lost the power of ~ after the accident.

2 formal talk

ADJ. brief, little, short | interminable, long, long-winded, rambling | keynote, major | eloquent, excellent, good | emotional, impassioned, rousing, stirring | boring | impromptu | public | televised | political | presidential | campaign, conference (esp. BrE), convention (esp. AmE), floor (AmE), stump (AmE) ◇ a Senate floor ~ ◇ The candidates gave their standard stump ~es. | Budget (BrE), inaugural, policy, State of the Union (AmE) ◇ George Washington's inaugural ~ ◇ the Chancellor's Budget ~ ◇ President Bush delivered his 2004 State of the Union ~. | acceptance, concession (AmE), farewell, resignation (esp. BrE), victory ◇ The prizewinner gave an emotional acceptance ~. | maiden (esp. BrE) ◇ her maiden ~ in the House of Commons | commencement (AmE), opening ◇ He delivered the com- mencement ~ at Notre Dame University. | closing (esp. BrE) | after-dinner (esp. BrE)

VERB + SPEECH deliver, give, make, read ◇ The President will deliver a major foreign-policy ~ to the United Nations. | broadcast ◇ His ~ was broadcast on national radio. | write

SPEECH + NOUN writer (usually speech-writer) ◇ the Prime Minister's speech-writers

PREP. in a/the ~ | ~ about, ~ on ◇ She gave a ~ on the economy. | ~ to ◇ He delivered his final ~ to Congress.

speechless adj.

VERBS be, remain, sit, stand ◇ Rachel stood ~. | leave sb, render sb ◇ The news left us all ~.

ADV. completely, totally | almost, practically | for a moment, momentarily, temporarily

PREP. with ◇ He was almost ~ with anger.

speed noun

ADJ. amazing, astonishing, breakneck, fast, good, great, high, incredible, lightning, phenomenal, remarkable, startling, surprising, terrific (esp. BrE) ◇ The new houses have been built with astonishing ~. ◇ He drove us to the hospital at breakneck ~. | low, slow | full, maximum, top, warp (informal, humorous, esp. AmE) ◇ Business is moving at warp ~. | excess ◇ 90% of car accidents involve excess ~. | constant, steady | average, normal | increased | operat- ing, processing, processor, running ◇ the increase in processor ~s for home computers | broadband, connection, download ◇ We offer subscribers a download ~ of 8 MB. | cruising, flying | supersonic ◇ jets flying at supersonic ~ | traffic (esp. BrE), etc. | air, wind | engine | shutter ◇ The camera will choose a fast shutter ~.

... OF SPEED burst ◇ The Kenyan runner put on a sudden burst of ~ over the last 50 yards. | rate (AmE) ◇ He was traveling at a high rate of ~.

VERB + SPEED attain, reach ◇ The car reaches a ~ of 60 miles per hour within five seconds. | build up, gain, gather, increase, pick up ◇ The train pulled out of the station, slowly gathering ~. | lose | kill, reduce ◇ Motorists are asked to reduce their ~ in wet conditions. | maintain ◇ The boat maintained a steady ~ while the sea was calm. | move at, run at, travel at ◇ The glacier moves at an average ~ of about six feet per day. ◇ Radio waves travel at the ~ of light. | measure

SPEED + VERB increase | decrease

SPEED + NOUN control, reduction, restriction (esp. BrE) |

record ◇ He set a new land ~ record in this car. | bump (esp. AmE), hump (BrE) | camera (BrE), trap

PREP. at ~ (= fast) ◇ The car was moving at ~ when the accident happened. ◇ at lightning ~ | in ~ ◇ a significant increase in ~ | with ~ ◇ Hedgehogs, though small, can move with surprising ~. | ~ of ◇ The ships have a maximum ~ of 18 knots.

PHRASES at full ~, full ~ ◇ He was running at full ~ when a tendon snapped in his leg. | full ~ ahead ◇ The boat can be brought to a stop from full ~ ahead within her own length. | the ~ of light, the ~ of sound ◇ Concorde crossed the Atlantic at twice the ~ of sound. | a turn of ~ (BrE) ◇ For a small car it has a good turn of ~.

speeding noun

VERB + SPEEDING fine sb for (esp. BrE), pull sb over for (esp. AmE), stop sb for ◇ He was pulled over for ~. ◇ The driver had been stopped twice for ~ on the same day.

SPEEDING + NOUN conviction, offence/offense (both esp. BrE) | fine (esp. BrE), ticket ◇ He was obliged to pay a £40 ~ fine. (see also speed limit)

PHRASES be/get caught ~, be done for ~ (BrE, informal)

speed limit noun

ADJ. high, low | legal | 50-mph, 60-mph, etc.

VERB + SPEED LIMIT drive (AmE), keep to, keep within, obey, observe | break, exceed ◇ Motorists can be fined on the spot for exceeding ~s. | set | raise | lower, reduce (esp. BrE)

PREP. above the ~, over the ~ ◇ He was driving over the 60 mph ~. | below the ~, under the ~, within the ~ (esp. BrE) ◇ You have to come down that hill in a low gear to keep within the ~.

spell noun

1 period of time

ADJ. lengthy (esp. BrE), long, prolonged | brief, short, five- minute, ten-day, etc. (esp. BrE) | good | bad ◇ He's going through a bit of a bad ~ at the moment. | quiet | barren, lean (both esp. BrE) ◇ Viera ended his barren ~ with a goal against Parma. | cold, dry, hot, mild, sunny (esp. BrE), warm, wet | dizzy, fainting ◇ The children began having dizzy ~s from hunger.

VERB + SPELL go through, have

PREP. during a ... ~ ◇ She managed to write a letter during a quiet ~ at work. | ~ as (esp. BrE) ◇ He had a brief ~ as ambassador to Turkey.

PHRASES a ~ of ... weather (esp. BrE) ◇ a ~ of sunny weather

2 magical effect

ADJ. magic, magical | powerful | hypnotic ◇ the hypnotic ~ of the cicadas singing in the trees

VERB + SPELL be under, come under, fall under | cast, perform, put, weave ◇ The witch cast a ~ on them. ◇ This place had woven its ~ over them. | break, remove ◇ She uttered the magic word, and the ~ was broken.

SPELL + NOUN book

PREP. under a/the ~ ◇ Sleeping Beauty was under a ~ when the prince found her. | under sb's ~ ◇ The audience was completely under his ~.

spell verb

ADV. correctly, right | wrongly | backwards/backward ◇ 'Nevaeh' is 'heaven' ~ed backwards/backward.

PREP. as ◇ The article ~ed 'survey' as 'servay'. | with ◇ Is 'necessary' ~ed with one 's', or two?

PHR V spell sth out

ADV. clearly | explicitly, fully, in detail | exactly, precisely ◇ She ~ed out precisely what she wanted.

VERB + SPELL OUT have to, need to

PREP. for ◇ Do I really have to ~ it out for you? | to ◇ His speech ~ed out a clear message to the car industry.

spelling noun

ADJ. correct, incorrect | conventional, proper, usual | alternate (esp. AmE), alternative, different, variant | original | American, English, etc. | phonetic

VERB + SPELLING **use** | **check** | **correct** | **improve**
SPELLING + NOUN **error, mistake** | **bee** (*esp. AmE*), **test** | **dictionary, rule** | **variant** | **reform**
PREP. **in…~** ◊ *In American ~ 'travelled' only has one 'l'.* | **~ for, ~ of** ◊ *The document uses the British ~ for caesium.*
PHRASES **be good, bad, etc. at ~**

spend *verb*

ADV. **wisely** ◊ *Try to ~ your money wisely.* | **freely, heavily, lavishly** | **annually**
PREP. **on** ◊ *The company spent a lot on advertising.* | **per** ◊ *the amount of money spent per student*
PHRASES **be money well spent** ◊ *It may seem expensive but it's money well spent.*

spending *noun*

ADJ. **total** ◊ *There has been an increase in total government ~.* | **high, low** | **additional, increased** | **annual, monthly, etc.** | **consumer, corporate, private** | **federal, government, local, public, state** | **defence/defense, domestic** (*esp. AmE*), **education, military, R & D, social** (*AmE*), **welfare, etc.** | **deficit, discretionary** (*esp. AmE*) ◊ *The President wants to increase discretionary ~ by 4%.* | **capital**
VERB + SPENDING **boost, increase** | **cut, cut back, cut back on, reduce** | **finance** ◊ *The government will finance its ~ through taxes.*
SPENDING + VERB **rise** | **fall** | **go to** ◊ *Three quarters of all federal ~ goes to Social Security.*
SPENDING + NOUN **level** | **plan, programme/program, target** | **bill** (*AmE*) ◊ *A military ~ bill is currently being considered in Congress.* | **cap** (*esp. AmE*), **cut, limit** | **increase** | **money** ◊ *How much ~ money are you taking with you?* | **power** | **spree** (*esp. BrE*) ◊ *The boys went on a two-day ~ spree with the stolen credit cards.* | **habits** ◊ *her husband's extravagant ~ habits*
PREP. **~ on** ◊ *More ~ on education was promised.*
PHRASES **a cut in ~, a reduction in ~** | **an increase in ~, a rise in ~**
→ Special page at BUSINESS

sperm *noun*

ADJ. **donated** | **frozen**
VERB + SPERM **produce** | **donate**
SPERM + VERB **fertilize sth** ◊ *The ~ fertilizes the egg.*
SPERM + NOUN **cell** | **count** ◊ *a high/low/normal ~ count* | **bank, donor** | **donation** | **production**

sphere *noun*

ADJ. **wider** ◊ *He wanted to spread his ideas to a wider ~ than the school.* | **separate** ◊ *In the novel, men and women enjoy separate ~s of action.* | **academic, cultural, domestic, economic, financial, military, political, social** ◊ *His work is little known outside the academic ~.* | **private, public**
PREP. **in sb's/the ~, within sb's/the ~** ◊ *The region is within the Russian ~ of influence.* | **outside sb's/the ~** ◊ *The matter is outside my ~ of responsibility.* | **~ of**
PHRASES **a ~ of activity** | **a ~ of influence** | **a ~ of life**

spice *noun*

1 flavour for food

ADJ. **ground** | **mixed** (*esp. BrE*) | **exotic** | **pumpkin, pumpkin pie** (*both AmE*)
SPICE + NOUN **mix, mixture, rub** (*AmE*) | **cake** | **cupboard, jar, rack**
PHRASES **herbs and ~s**

2 excitement and interest

ADJ. **extra** ◊ *That result added extra ~ to the game.*
VERB + SPICE **add, give** ◊ *The danger added ~ to their romance.*
PHRASES **the ~ of life**

spicy *adj.*

VERBS **be, smell, taste** ◊ *The soup tasted mildly ~.*
ADV. **extremely, fairly, very, etc.** | **a little, slightly, etc.** | **lightly, mildly** | **deliciously** ◊ *a deliciously ~ aroma*

spider *noun*

ADJ. **big, huge, large** | **giant** | **hairy** | **poisonous**
SPIDER + VERB **make a web, spin a web, weave a web** | **crawl, run, scuttle** | **hunt sth** | **catch sth** | **bite sb/sth** ◊ *I was bitten by a ~.* | **lurk**
SPIDER + NOUN **silk** | **web** (*esp. AmE*)
PHRASES **a spider's web** (*esp. BrE*)

spill *verb*

ADV. **almost** | **accidentally** | **out, over** ◊ *After the clubs closed, the drinkers ~ed out into the streets.* ◊ *He nodded, his tears ~ing over.*
VERB + SPILL **try not to** | **let sth** ◊ *He opened the curtains, letting the morning light ~ into the room.*
PREP. **across, down, from, into, on, onto, out of, over** ◊ *I accidentally ~ed my drink all over him.*

spin *noun*

1 fast turning movement

ADJ. **quick, rapid** | **slow** | **back, side, top** (usually ***topspin***, etc.) (*sports*) *She puts heavy topspin on her serve.*
VERB + SPIN **go into** ◊ *He had to stop the helicopter from going into a ~.* | **come out of** | **put sb/sth in, put sb/sth into, send sb/sth into** (*all figurative*) ◊ *The president's death sent the stock market into a ~.* | **give sth** ◊ *Give the clothes another ~.* | **impart, put** ◊ *How do you put more ~ on the ball?*
SPIN + NOUN **dryer** (*BrE*) | **cycle** ◊ *We stopped the washing machine before the ~ cycle.* ◊ *After a bitter divorce, the two actors were thrown into a media ~ cycle.* (*AmE, figurative*) | **bowler, bowling** (in cricket)

2 on information

ADJ. **negative, positive** | **different, fresh, interesting, (whole) new, unique** ◊ *She's put a whole new ~ on the theme of corporate greed.* | **contemporary, modern** | **media, political** | **Labour, Republican, etc.**
VERB + SPIN **add, give sth, put** ◊ *The chairman tried to put a positive ~ on the closure of the factory.*
SPIN + NOUN **doctor** ◊ *government ~ doctors* | **machine** ◊ *the government's ~ machine*
PREP. **with a ~** ◊ *The film retells the famous legend with a Marxist ~.*

spin *verb*

ADV. **fast, quickly, rapidly** ◊ *The blade ~s very fast.* | **freely** ◊ *The wheel can now ~ freely.* | **around, round** (*esp. BrE*) ◊ *He spun around to face her.* | **away, back**
VERB + SPIN **begin to, start to**
PHRASES **make sb's head ~** (*figurative*) ◊ *The wine made my head ~.* | **~ like a top** ◊ *The dinghy spun like a top and a huge wave came at me.* | **~ on its axis** ◊ *The Earth ~s on its axis once every 24 hours.* | **~ on your heel** (*esp. AmE*) ◊ *She spun on her heel and walked out of the room.* | **~ out of control** ◊ *The car spun out of control.*

spine *noun*

1 backbone

ADJ. **fractured** | **cervical, lumbar**
VERB + SPINE **bend, curve** | **straighten** | **break, damage** | **slide down, slide up** (*both figurative*) ◊ *An icy chill slid up my ~.* | **form** (*figurative*) ◊ *These speeches form the ~ of his election campaign.* | **stiffen** (*figurative*) ◊ *Their protests stiffened the ~s of party activists.* | **grow** (*AmE, figurative*) ◊ *The legislature must grow a ~ and demand this.*
PREP. **in the/your ~** ◊ *the nerves in the ~*
PHRASES **the base of the ~** | **the length of sb's ~** | **curvature of the ~** | **send shivers down sb's ~**

2 sharp point on some plants/animals

ADJ. **sharp** ◊ *Hedgehogs are covered with sharp ~s.* | **fine** | **poisonous, venomous**
VERB + SPINE **bear, have**

spin-off noun

ADJ. **movie, TV** | **positive** (*esp. BrE*) ◇ *The games will certainly have positive financial ~s for local companies.* | **lucrative** (*esp. BrE*) | **unexpected** (*esp. BrE*) | **commercial, economic** (*both esp. BrE*)
SPIN-OFF + NOUN **benefit** (*esp. BrE*) ◇ *The contract is likely to have ~ benefits for the aerospace business.* | **business, company** | **movie, series, show** ◇ *The show was so successful that it launched two ~ series.*
PREP. **~ from**

spiral noun

ADJ. **vicious** | **downward, upward** | **deflationary, inflationary** | **wage-price** | **death** (*AmE, figurative*) ◇ *The company has entered a death ~.*
VERB + SPIRAL **create, trigger** ◇ *There is a risk that the policy may trigger an inflationary ~.* | **continue** ◇ *The economy continued its downward ~.* | **halt, stop**
PREP. **~ of** ◇ *to halt the vicious downward ~ of drug abuse*

spirit noun

1 mind or feelings

ADJ. **human** ◇ *It is a testimony to the triumph of the human ~.*
PREP. **in ~** ◇ *I will be with you in ~.*

2 spirits morale

ADJ. **flagging** (*esp. BrE*)
VERB + SPIRITS **keep up, lift, raise** ◇ *We sang songs to keep our ~s up.* | **revive** | **break, dampen** ◇ *A string of defeats has failed to dampen the team's ~s.*
SPIRITS + VERB **lift, rise**
PHRASES **in good, high, low, poor, etc. ~s** ◇ *She isn't in the best of ~s today.* ◇ *My mother was in excellent ~s.*

3 person

ADJ. **guiding, leading** (*esp. BrE*), **moving** ◇ *She was a guiding ~ in primary education.* | **generous** | **mean** | **brave, proud** | **free, independent** | **kindred** ◇ *He found kindred ~s in the peace movement.*

4 courage/liveliness

ADJ. **great, tremendous** (*esp. BrE*) | **adventurous, competitive, fighting, indomitable, pioneer, pioneering** ◇ *the indomitable American ~*
VERB + SPIRIT **be full of, have** ◇ *She has plenty of fighting ~.* | **display, show** | **break**
PREP. **with ~** ◇ *He sang with great ~.*
PHRASES **broken in ~** ◇ *They tortured him until he was broken in ~.*

5 feelings of loyalty

ADJ. **community, party, public, team**
VERB + SPIRIT **have** | **develop, foster, promote**

6 attitude/mood

ADJ. **right** ◇ *They have the right ~!* | **essential, genuine, true** | **carefree** | **democratic, revolutionary** | **creative** | **entrepreneurial** | **can-do** (*informal, esp. AmE*) | **Christmas, festive** (*esp. BrE*), **holiday** (*esp. AmE*)
VERB + SPIRIT **have** | **enter into, get into** ◇ *I was just getting to the ~ of things when the party suddenly ended.* | **bring** ◇ *They brought the ~ of carnival to their concerts.* | **capture, embody, reflect, represent** ◇ *That song really captures the ~ of the times.* ◇ *She embodies the ~ of revolution.*
PREP. **in a ~ of** ◇ *Both sides have come together in a ~ of goodwill.* ◇ *They are all working together in a ~ of cooperation.* | **~ of** ◇ *a ~ of adventure*
PHRASES **be closer in ~ to sth, be similar in ~ to sth** | **be faithful to the ~ of sth, be true to the ~ of sth** ◇ *The movie is true to the ~ of the book.* | **a generosity of ~** ◇ *She exudes a warmth and generosity of ~.* | **in the right ~** | **the ~ of the age, the ~ of the times** | **the ~ of Christmas, the ~ of the season** ◇ *I'm trying to get in the ~ of the holiday season.*

7 real/intended meaning of a rule, an agreement, etc.

VERB + SPIRIT **obey** | **be against, be contrary to, go against,**

violate ◇ *an edict that violates the ~ of the Geneva Convention*
PHRASES **the ~ of the law** ◇ *The referee should try to obey the ~ as well as the letter of the law.*

8 soul/ghost

ADJ. **ancestral** | **evil, malevolent** | **restless** ◇ *Owls were believed to be restless ~s who had returned to earth.*
VERB + SPIRIT **conjure up, contact, invoke, summon, summon up** | **exorcize, ward off** ◇ *She slept with a cross under the pillow to ward off evil ~s.* | **be possessed by**
SPIRIT + VERB **live on** ◇ *Many people believe the ~ lives on after death.* | **move sb** (*often figurative*) ◇ *Make a donation to the charity if the ~ moves you.*
SPIRIT + NOUN **guide** ◇ *My ~ guide cares for me and protects me.* | **world**
PHRASES **body, mind and ~** ◇ *healing for body, mind and ~* | **the Holy Spirit** | **the ~s of the dead**

9 (esp. BrE) (usually spirits) strong alcoholic drink

... OF SPIRITS **bottle, measure** (*BrE*) ◇ *a single measure of ~s*
VERB + SPIRITS **drink**

spiritual adj.

VERBS **be**
ADV. **deeply, truly, very** ◇ *This is a deeply ~ piece of music.* ◇ *a truly ~ experience* | **purely** | **almost** ◇ *The music had an almost ~ quality.*

spite noun

ADJ. **pure, sheer** | **personal** (*esp. BrE*)
VERB + SPITE **be full of, feel** ◇ *She was angry and full of ~.* | **vent** (*esp. BrE*) ◇ *He vented his ~ on his grandfather.*
PREP. **out of ~** ◇ *She killed her boss's dog out of pure ~.* | **with ~** ◇ *'Your cooking is hard to forget,' he said with ~.* | **~ towards/toward** ◇ *I felt no ~ towards/toward her.*

splash noun

1 sound; amount of liquid

ADJ. **big, huge, large** | **little, small** | **loud** | **soft**
VERB + SPLASH **make** (*often figurative*) ◇ *She intended to make a big ~ with her wedding.* | **hear**
PREP. **~ of** ◇ *a ~ of cold water in the face* | **with a ~** ◇ *She jumped into the pool with a ~.*

2 area of colour/color, light, etc.

ADJ. **bold, bright** ◇ *a bold ~ of red*
PHRASES **a ~ of colour/color** ◇ *Window boxes of tulips added a ~ of colour/color to the street.* | **a ~ of light**

splash verb

ADV. **happily** ◇ *The baby was ~ing happily in the bathtub.* | **about** (*esp. BrE*), **around** ◇ *The children were ~ing around in the river.*
PREP. **against** ◇ *Rain ~ed against the window.* | **on, onto** ◇ *She ~ed some water onto the stain.* | **over** ◇ *She ~ed some water over her boots to clean them.* | **through** ◇ *They ~ed through the puddles.* | **with** ◇ *Her clean clothes were all ~ed with mud.*
PHRASES **be ~ed across the front page, be ~ed on the cover** ◇ *The next day his exploits were ~ed across the front page.*

splendid adj. (esp. BrE)

VERBS **be, look**
ADV. **really** ◇ *a really ~ evening* | **absolutely, most, perfectly, quite, rather, simply, truly** ◇ *The meal was quite ~!*

splendour (BrE) (AmE splendor) noun

ADJ. **full** ◇ *A butterfly emerged in its full ~ a week later.* | **glorious, great, regal** | **former, original** | **faded** | **architectural, scenic, visual** | **baroque, gothic, medieval, etc.** | **Edwardian, Victorian, etc.** ◇ *They have restored the building to its former Victorian ~.*
VERB + SPLENDOUR/SPLENDOR **have** ◇ *The hotel has the ~ of a 19th-century mansion.* | **lose** | **match** ◇ *No other palace could match the ~ of the Taj Mahal.* | **recapture, regain** ◇ *It will take a lot of repair work before the building regains its*

former ~. | **restore sth to** ◇ *The house has been restored to its original ~.*
PREP. **in ~** ◇ *They dined in a special suite in glorious ~.* | **in sb's/sth's ~** ◇ *There below lay Paris in all its ~.* | **of ~** ◇ *a castle of great ~* | **~s of** ◇ *I've only just discovered the ~s of the countryside.*
PHRASES **in solitary ~** ◇ *The castle rises in solitary ~ on the fringe of the desert.*

splinter noun

ADJ. **tiny** | **glass, metal, wood, wooden**
VERB + SPLINTER **get, have** | **pull out, remove, take out**
SPLINTER + VERB **lodge**
SPLINTER + NOUN **faction, group, party** (*all figurative*) ◇ *a radical ~ group of the organization*
PREP. **~ of** ◇ *A small ~ of metal had lodged in his thumb.*

split noun

1 disagreement

ADJ. **clear, deep, major, serious** ◇ *A serious ~ in the ruling coalition appeared soon after the election.* | **acrimonious, damaging** ◇ *Ten years after their acrimonious ~, the band has reformed.* | **growing** | **ideological** ◇ *an ideological ~ within the party*
VERB + SPLIT **cause, create, lead to**
SPLIT + VERB **appear, occur**
PREP. **~ between** ◇ *a ~ between the right and left wings of the party* | **~ in, ~ within** | **~ over** ◇ *a growing ~ in the Church over the issue of gay priests* | **~ with** ◇ *Mike's ~ with his wife*

2 division between things

ADJ. **even** ◇ *It's an even ~; some love it, some hate it.* | **two-way, three-way, etc.** (*esp. BrE*)

split verb

1 break into two or more parts

ADV. **easily** ◇ *Plastic ~s very easily.* | **apart** | **open** ◇ *The ripe seed pod ~s open and scatters the seeds.* | **down the middle, in half, in two** ◇ *The lid had ~ down the middle.* ◇ *Split the coconut in half.*
PREP. **into** ◇ *He ~ the log into several pieces.*

2 separate into different groups

ADV. **eventually, finally** | **apart, away, off, up** ◇ *The rock group ~ up last year.*
PREP. **from** ◇ *Several factions ~ from the party.* | **into** ◇ *In 1993 Czechoslovakia ~ into two independent states.* | **on, over** ◇ *The party finally ~ over the issue of gun control.*
PHRASES **be deeply ~** ◇ *The party is deeply ~ on this issue.*

3 divide/share sth

ADV. **equally, evenly**
PREP. **among, between** ◇ *The cost has been ~ equally between three countries.*
PHRASES **~ sth two, three, etc. ways** ◇ *The profit will be ~ three ways.* | **~ the difference** ◇ *I offered €200 but he wanted €300. In the end, we ~ the difference and I paid him €250.* | **~ your time between sth and sth** ◇ *She ~s her time between Madrid and Washington.*

spoil verb

1 make sth useless/unsuccessful/not very good

ADV. **completely, quite** ◇ *Her selfish reaction completely ~ed the party.* | **rather, slightly, somewhat**
VERB + SPOIL **hate to, not be going to, not want to** ◇ *I don't want to ~ things for everyone else.* | **be a pity to** ◇ *It would be a pity to ~ the surprise.* | **try to** | **not let sth** ◇ *Don't let the bad weather ~ your trip.*

2 a child

PREP. **with** ◇ *He ~s the children with expensive toys.*
PHRASES **be completely ~ed, be thoroughly ~ed, be utterly ~ed** ◇ *Those children are thoroughly ~ed!* | **~ sb rotten** ◇ *My grandparents used to ~ me rotten.* | **a ~ed brat, a ~ed child**

spoils noun

VERB + SPOILS **divide, share** ◇ *The soldiers began to divide the ~.* | **claim, take** | **enjoy** ◇ *He never sits back and enjoys the ~ of victory.*
PHRASES **a division of the ~, a share of the ~** ◇ *They fought for a share of the ~.* | **the ~ of victory, the ~ of war**

sponge noun

ADJ. **damp, wet** | **dry** | **bath** | **make-up**
VERB + SPONGE **squeeze, squeeze out**
SPONGE + VERB **absorb sth, fill with sth, soak sth up** ◇ *This ~ doesn't soak up water very well.*
PREP. **with a/the ~** ◇ *Wipe the surface with a damp ~.*

sponsor noun

ADJ. **big, major** | **chief, main, primary, principal** | **potential** | **private** | **official** | **state** ◇ *the list of state ~s of terrorism* | **commercial, corporate, industrial** | **title** ◇ *the title ~ of the rowing World Cup*
VERB + SPONSOR **look for, seek** | **attract, find, get** | **act as**
SPONSOR + VERB **back sb/sth, support sb/sth**
SPONSOR + NOUN **money** (*esp. BrE*)
PREP. **~ for, ~ of** ◇ *I need to find some more ~s for my charity bike ride.*
PHRASES **a/the bill's ~** (*politics, esp. AmE*)

sponsorship noun

ADJ. **generous, major** | **lucrative** (*esp. BrE*) | **arts** (*BrE*), **sports** | **business** (*esp. BrE*), **commercial, corporate, government, private, state** ◇ *state ~ of religious societies* | **tobacco** (*BrE*) ◇ *tobacco ~ of Formula One*
VERB + SPONSORSHIP **attract** (*esp. AmE*), **find, get, obtain, raise** (*esp. AmE*), **receive, secure, win** (*BrE*) | **collect** (*BrE*) ◇ *Many participants collect ~ from family, friends and colleagues.* | **look for, seek** | **withdraw, withdraw from** ◇ *The company has decided to withdraw from some of its sports ~.*
SPONSORSHIP + NOUN **agreement, deal, package, pro-gramme/program, scheme** (*BrE*) ◇ *The company has entered into a ~ agreement with the team.* | **opportunities** | **dollars** (*esp. AmE*), **money** (*esp. BrE*), **revenue** ◇ *Sponsorship dollars are rolling in as never before.* ◇ *He hopes to raise around £4 000 in ~ money for the hospital.* (*BrE*) | **form** (*BrE*) ◇ *Entry and ~ forms for the marathon are available at local post offices.* | **contract** (*esp. BrE*) ◇ *the four-year ~ contract*
PREP. **in ~** (*esp. BrE*) ◇ *She has raised about £500 in ~.* (*BrE*) | **through ~** (*esp. BrE*) ◇ *Two million pounds were raised through ~.* | **under (the) ~** ◇ *under commercial ~* | **with ~, without ~** ◇ *Without generous corporate ~, the ballet company would not have survived.* | **~ for, ~ of** ◇ *~ for next year's World Cup* | **~ from** ◇ *We have won ~ from one of the big banks.*

spontaneous adj.

VERBS **appear, be, seem**
ADV. **genuinely** | **quite, totally** | **apparently, seemingly**

spooky adj. (*informal*)

VERBS **be, feel, look, sound** | **become, get** ◇ *It got a little ~ when James started telling ghost stories.* | **find sth** ◇ *I find the whole place really rather ~.*
ADV. **dead** (*informal, esp. BrE*), **decidedly** (*esp. BrE*), **down-right** (*informal, esp. AmE*), **really, very** | **a little, slightly, etc.**

spoon noun

ADJ. **slotted** ◇ *Remove the onions with a slotted ~.* | **serving, soup, sugar** | **dessert, table, tea** (usually *dessertspoon*, etc.) | **measuring** ◇ *a 5 ml measuring ~* | **metal, plastic, silver, wooden**
VERB + SPOON **pick up** | **put down** | **hold** | **eat sth with, stir sth with, use** ◇ *I stirred my coffee with the sugar ~.* | **lick** ◇ *The children argued over who should lick the ~.*
PREP. **~ of** ◇ *two ~s of sugar*

sport noun

1 (*BrE*) (*AmE* **sports**) physical activity done for pleasure

ADJ. **amateur, pro** (*informal, esp. AmE*), **professional** | **organized** | **youth** | **high-school** (*AmE*), **school** (*esp. BrE*), **college** (*esp. AmE*), **collegiate** (*AmE*), **intercollegiate** (*AmE*) | **after-school** | **motor** (usually **motorsport** in *BrE*, **motor-sports** in *AmE*)

VERB + SPORT/SPORTS **do, play** ◊ *He does a lot of sport.* (*BrE*) | *We played sports together when we were kids.* (*esp. AmE*) | **be involved in, get involved in, participate in** ◊ *We encourage the children to get involved in sport/sports.* | **promote** ◊ *a campaign to promote sport/sports among women*

SPORTS + NOUN (The following nouns all follow **sports** in *BrE* and *AmE*.), **event** | **arena, bar, centre** (*BrE*), **club, facilities, field** (*esp. BrE*), **ground, hall** (*esp. BrE*), **pavilion** (*BrE*), **stadium, venue** ◊ *the construction of a new $250-million ~s arena* ◊ *The council has allocated an extra £11 million to a new community ~s club.* (*BrE*) | **league** (*esp. AmE*) | **day** (*BrE*) ◊ *the school ~s day* | **programme/program** (*esp. AmE*) ◊ *government funding for ~s programmes/programs for girls and women* | **figure, hero, person** (usually **sportsperson**), **personality, star** | **team** | **enthusiast, fan** | **commentator** | **channel, coverage, news, page, section** ◊ *Sports coverage in the local newspaper is good.* | **programme/program, show** (*esp. AmE*) | **columnist, correspondent, editor, journalist, photographer, reporter, writer** | **injury** | **medicine, nutrition** | **nutritionist, psychologist** | **bag** | **equipment** | **goods** (*BrE*) (**sporting goods** in *AmE*) | **bra, clothing** | **drink** | **book, movie** | **shop, store** | **betting** ◊ *~s betting on the Internet* | **marketing**

PREP. **in ~** ◊ *the use of drugs in sport* (*BrE*) ◊ *the use of drugs in sports* (*AmE*)

PHRASES **love for ~** (*BrE*), **love for ~s** (*AmE*), **love of ~** (*BrE*), **love of ~s** (*AmE*), **passion for ~** (*BrE*), **passion for ~s** (*AmE*) ◊ *She has a real passion for ~/~.* | **the world of ~** (*BrE*), **the world of ~s** (*AmE*)

2 particular type of sporting activity

ADJ. **mainstream, major, popular** ◊ *popular ~s such as football* | **minor, minority** (*BrE*) | **competitive, recreational** (*esp. AmE*) | **Olympic** | **contact, non-contact** ◊ *In theory, basketball is a non-contact ~.* | **active** | **dangerous, risky** | **spectator** | **indoor, outdoor** | **winter** (usually **winter sports**) | **individual, team** | **adventure, extreme** (usually **adventure sports, extreme sports**) ◊ *the inherent dangers of adventure ~s such as mountaineering* | **field** (*BrE*) | **country** (*BrE*) | **water** (usually **water sports**) | **combat** ◊ *Combat ~s such as karate and judo carry with them the risk of injury.* | **racket** | **equestrian** | **blood, cruel** (*esp. BrE*)

VERB + SPORT **take up** ◊ *I need to take up a ~ to get fit.* | **dominate** ◊ *In the 1960s, the Soviet Union dominated the ~ of gymnastics.* | **promote** ◊ *a campaign to promote the ~ among young people*

PREP. **~ of** ◊ *the ~ of boxing*

PHRASES **love for a ~, love of a ~, passion for a ~** ◊ *She has a real passion for the ~.*

sportsman, sportswoman noun (*esp. BrE*)

ADJ. **famous** | **great, outstanding** (*BrE*) ◊ *one of the greatest sportswomen this country has produced* | **all-round** (*BrE*) | **avid** (*AmE*), **keen** ◊ *They are all keen sportsmen.* | **amateur, professional**

spot noun

1 small mark on the skin → See also PIMPLE

ADJ. **beauty** ◊ *She had a small beauty ~ on the left side of her face.* | **liver**

VERB + SPOT **break out in** ◊ *The children all had measles, and had broken out in ~s.* | **scratch, squeeze** (*BrE*)

2 place/area

ADJ. **exact, particular, precise** | **convenient, good, ideal, perfect, right, suitable** ◊ *Take the time to find the right ~ to pitch your tent.* | **beautiful, beauty** (*BrE*), **idyllic** (*esp. BrE*),

lovely (*esp. BrE*), **pleasant** ◊ *It's a beautiful ~ to relax and enjoy the peaceful surroundings.* ◊ *The lake is one of the local beauty ~s.* | **favourite/favorite, popular** ◊ *a popular ~ for picnickers* | **deserted, desolate, isolated, lonely, remote** | **quiet, secluded** | **shady, sheltered** | **sunny** | **holiday** (*BrE*), **tourist, vacation** (*AmE*) | **picnic** | **skate, surf** (*both esp. AmE*) | **parking** | **sore, tender** | **sensitive** (*often figurative*) ◊ *From his angry reply it was obvious that I had touched a sensitive ~.* | **sweet** (*informal*) ◊ *It's easier to hit the sweet ~ on larger-faced golf clubs.* | **vulnerable, weak** ◊ *Check your house for weak ~s where a thief could get in.* | **blind** (*often figurative*) ◊ *I have a blind ~ where jazz is concerned* (= I don't understand it). | **danger, hot, trouble** ◊ *one of the world's major trouble ~s* | **bald** ◊ *He usually wears a hat to hide his bald ~.*

VERB + SPOT **mark** ◊ *On your map, X marks the ~ where the race begins.* | **point to** ◊ *point to a ~ on the map.* ◊ *The referee pointed to the ~* (= the penalty spot). (*BrE*) | **reach** | **be frozen to, be rooted to** ◊ *He stood rooted to the ~, unable to move.* | **find, pick** ◊ *They picked a good ~ for a picnic.*

PREP. **on the ~** ◊ *The police were on the ~ within minutes.*

PHRASES **an accident black ~** (*BrE*) | **a bright ~** (*figurative*) ◊ *The birth of my son was the one bright ~ in a terrible year.* | **a tight ~, a tough ~** (*figurative*) ◊ *The captain's knee injury leaves the team in a tight ~.*

3 position (in a sport, etc.)

ADJ. **high, top** | **number-one, number-two, etc.** ◊ *The album quickly reached the number-one ~ in the charts.* | **second, third, etc.** | **lead-off** (*AmE*), **starting** | **final** | **play-off** (*AmE*), **qualifying, runner-up** ◊ *The Korean team secured two qualifying ~s for the Olympic Games.* | **promotion, relegation** (*both BrE*) | **roster** (*AmE*) ◊ *That leaves one roster ~, and the team will need a versatile player to fill it.*

VERB + SPOT **claim, secure** ◊ *Glamorgan claimed the top ~ in the League.* | **earn** ◊ *She has earned a ~ on the national team.*

4 part of a show on TV, etc.

ADJ. **radio, TV** | **guest** | **promo** (*informal*), **promotional**

spot verb

ADV. **immediately, quickly, soon** | **easily** ◊ *Most of these fossils are too small to be easily spotted.* | **suddenly** | **eventually, finally**

VERB + SPOT **be difficult to, be hard to** | **be easy to** ◊ *The birds should be easy enough to ~.* | **fail to**

PHRASES **well spotted** (*esp. BrE*) ◊ *'There's a parking space over there.' 'Well spotted!'*

spotlight noun

1 lamp

VERB + SPOTLIGHT **shine** ◊ *They shone the ~ on a woman at the back of the audience.* | **step into** ◊ *He stepped into the ~ to the wild applause of the crowd.*

SPOTLIGHT + VERB **be on sb/sth, fall on sb/sth, shine on sb/sth**

PREP. **in the ~, under the ~** ◊ *It was hot under the ~s.*

2 public attention/interest

ADJ. **harsh** ◊ *After the defeat, he tried to avoid the harsh ~ of the media.* | **international, national, public** | **media, political**

VERB + SPOTLIGHT **come into, come under** (*both esp. BrE*) ◊ *This issue will come under the ~ at tomorrow's meeting.* | **be thrust into, step into, take** ◊ *She was suddenly thrust into the political ~.* | **bring sth into** | **focus, put, shine, throw, turn** ◊ *These revelations threw a ~ on the shakiness of the economy.* | **keep** ◊ *He will want to keep the ~ on the divisions within the party.* | **share** ◊ *The captain had to share the ~ with the new young star.* | **grab, hog, steal** ◊ *He accused her of hogging the ~.* | **shun, shy away from** ◊ *The President has never been one to shun the ~.*

SPOTLIGHT + VERB **be on sb/sth, fall on sb/sth, shine on sb/sth, turn on sb/sth**

PREP. **away from the ~** | **in the ~, under the ~** ◊ *The quality of our food is back in the ~.* | **out of the ~** ◊ *The affair is now out of the ~.*

SPORT

In British English you can **do sport** or **play sports**. In American English you **do** or **play sports**.
Do you do a lot of sport(s)?   We played sports together when we were kids.

You can also:

do	go	play
aerobics	bowling	baseball
athletics (*BrE*)/track (*AmE*)	cycling (*esp.BrE*)/biking (*esp.AmE*)	basketball
gymnastics	fishing	cricket
the high jump	mountaineering	football
judo	riding (*BrE*)/horseback riding (*AmE*)	golf
karate		hockey
the long jump	skateboarding	pool
the pole vault	skating	soccer
weightlifting	skiing	tennis
wrestling	swimming	**against** sb
yoga	**to** aerobics, judo, etc. (= to go to your aerobics, etc. class)	**for** a team

- beat, defeat, face an **opponent**
- be dropped from, be left out of, be selected for, get into (*esp.BrE*), get on/onto (*esp.AmE*), join, try out for (*esp.AmE*) a **team**
- capture, clinch, defend, lose, retain, take, win **the title**
- break, hold, set, shatter, smash **the world record**

American football

- carry, catch, fumble, snap, run, throw **the ball**
- catch, complete, drop, intercept, throw a **pass**
- call, make, run a **play**
- find, get in/into, reach, run into **the end zone**
- score **points/a touchdown**

Baseball

- cross, step (up) to **the plate**
- hit, make, take, throw a **pitch**
- throw a breaking/curve/ground/fly/foul **ball**
- swing the **bat**; be at **the bat**
- hit a **home run**
- reach, steal **bases**; play second **base**
- score **runs** in the bottom of the ninth inning

Golf

- chip, drive, hit, putt **the ball**
- hit an approach/a bunker/a chip/a tee **shot**
- hit, miss **the fairway/the green**
- hole, miss, sink a **putt**
- hook your drive into **the rough**

Basketball

- dribble, dunk, get, handle, have, move, pass, protect, receive, shoot, steal **the ball**
- block, get off, hit, make, miss, take a **shot**
- a blocked/foul/jump **shot**
- get, score an **easy basket**
- call, commit, draw a **foul**

Football/soccer

- chip, clear, cross, drive, give away, head, kick, lob, lose, pass, strike, win **the ball**
- score a **goal**
- book, foul; mark, send off, tackle **a player**
- award, concede, miss, take, win a **penalty**
- blast, block, fire, get in, have, save a **shot**

Tennis

- hit, return, run down, slice **the ball**
- have, miss, save a **match point**
- lose, play, win a **point/rally**
- drop, hold, return (a) **serve**
- hit a drop/passing **shot**

sprawl verb

ADV. **lazily** | **out** ◊ *He was ~ed out on the sofa.*
PREP. **across, in, on, over** ◊ *She ~ed lazily in an armchair.*
PHRASES **find sb ~ed across, on, etc. sth** ◊ *She found him ~ed across the doorstep.* | **go ~ing** ◊ *She went ~ing across the boat.* | **lie ~ed, sit ~ed** ◊ *She lay ~ed across the bed.* | **send sb ~ing** ◊ *The blow sent him ~ing.*

spray noun

1 drops of liquid

ADJ. **fine, light** | **salt, sea**
... OF SPRAY **cloud, plume** ◊ *The boat sent a cloud of ~ up behind it.*
VERB + SPRAY **send, send up, throw, throw up**
SPRAY + VERB **fly, fly up** ◊ *Spray flew up onto the rocks.*
PREP. **~ of** ◊ *a ~ of salt water*

2 substance in a container, released as drops of liquid

ADJ. **bug** (*AmE*), **fly** | **body, hair** (usually *hairspray*), **nasal** | **cooking** (*esp. AmE*) ◊ *a casserole dish sprayed with non-stick cooking ~* | **CS** (*BrE*), **pepper** ◊ *The police used pepper ~ on demonstrators.* | **aerosol, chemical** ◊ *A boy died aged just 13 after inhaling aerosol ~.*
VERB + SPRAY **apply, use**
SPRAY + NOUN **bottle, can** | **paint**

spread noun

1 increase in amount or number of sth

ADJ. **good, great, wide** | **rapid** | **gradual, slow** | **geographical, global** ◊ *The current survey will have a wider geographical ~.*
VERB + SPREAD **encourage, promote** ◊ *Such unhygienic conditions encourage the ~ of disease.* | **halt, prevent, stem, stop, tackle** | **combat, contain, control, curb, limit, reduce, slow** (*esp. AmE*)
PREP. **~ of** ◊ *the ~ of fire*

2 newspaper, magazine, etc.

ADJ. **centre/center** ◊ *A photograph of the star adorned the centre/center ~.* | **double, double-page** (*esp. BrE*), **two-page** | **five-page, 20-page, etc.** | **full-page** | **fashion, photo**
PHRASES **be featured in a ~, feature in a ~** ◊ *Her work featured in a two-page ~ in 'New Woman' magazine.*

spread verb

1 open sth so that you can see all of it

ADV. **carefully** | **out** ◊ *We ~ the rug out on the floor.*
PREP. **across, on, over**
PHRASES **~ sth open** ◊ *He had a newspaper ~ open on his knee.* | **~ your arms, legs, etc. out wide, ~ your arms, legs, etc. wide** ◊ *a bird with its wings ~ wide*

2 reach more people/wider area

ADV. **fast, like wildfire, quickly, rapidly, soon** ◊ *The news ~ like wildfire.* | **gradually, slowly** | **easily** ◊ *The disease ~s easily.* | **widely** ◊ *Allow plenty of space for this plant as its roots ~ widely.* | **far and wide** ◊ *His fame had ~ far and wide.* | **outwards/outward**
PREP. **(all) across, among, around, beyond, by, from, into, (all) over, through, throughout, to** ◊ *The effects of this policy ~ far beyond children now at school.* ◊ *The disease can be ~ by contact.* ◊ *The fire rapidly ~ to adjoining buildings.*
PHRASES **be thinly ~** ◊ *Expertise in this field is very thinly ~ across the country.* | **~ yourself too thin** ◊ *With four markets to manage, there's a danger that's she's ~ing herself too thin.*

3 cover a surface with a soft substance

ADV. **thickly** | **lightly, thinly** | **evenly** ◊ *Don't make the paste too thick, or it will not ~ evenly.*
PREP. **on** ◊ *He ~ marmalade on the toast.* | **with** ◊ *Spread each slice generously with butter.*

4 divide/share sth

ADV. **equally, evenly, uniformly** | **unevenly**

VERB + SPREAD **try to**
PREP. **among, between** ◊ *We tried to ~ the workload evenly between the departments.* | **over** ◊ *The course takes forty hours, ~ over twenty weeks.*

spreadsheet noun

ADJ. **computer, electronic** | **simple**
VERB + SPREADSHEET **create, do** (*informal*), **make** ◊ *I created a ~ to calculate my expenses.* | **use**
SPREADSHEET + VERB **show sth** ◊ *a ~ showing current spending*
SPREADSHEET + NOUN **application, program, software** | **file** | **data** | **format** ◊ *The information is saved in a ~ format for further analysis.*
PREP. **in a/the ~** ◊ *Sales are reported in a ~.* | **into a/the ~** ◊ *I entered the data into a ~ on my laptop.* ◊ *The figures are automatically imported into a ~.* | **on a/the ~** ◊ *I do a weekly update for managers on a ~.* | **~ with** ◊ *a ~ with the names and addresses of all my clients*

spree noun

ADJ. **massive** ◊ *a massive buying ~* | **buying, shopping, spending** | **acquisition, hiring** (*both business*) | **drinking** | **crime, killing, looting** (*esp. AmE*), **murder, shooting, wrecking** (*BrE*) ◊ *Hungry mobs went on a looting ~ in the city.* ◊ *Vandals went on a £10 000 wrecking ~.*
VERB + SPREE **go on** ◊ *He's gone on a drinking ~.*
PREP. **on a ~** ◊ *She's out on a shopping ~.*

spring noun

1 season

ADJ. **last, this past** (*esp. AmE*) | **the following, next, this, this coming** | **early, late** | **wet**
SPRING + NOUN **weather** | **sun, sunlight, sunshine** | **frost, rain, shower, wind** | **tide** | **equinox** | **day, morning** ◊ *a perfect ~ day* | **semester** (*esp. AmE*), **term** (*esp. BrE*) ◊ *The students spend the whole ~ term on teaching practice.* | **season** | **break** (*esp. AmE*) ◊ *high-school kids on ~ break* | **bloom, bulb, flower** ◊ *to plant ~ bulbs* | **clean** (*BrE*), **cleaning** (usually *spring-cleaning*) ◊ *They decided to give the attic a ~ clean.* ◊ *I want to do some spring-cleaning.* | **training** (*sports, esp. AmE*) | **conference** (*esp. BrE*) ◊ *the party's ~ conference* | **collection, exhibition, issue**
→ Note at SEASON (for more collocates)

2 coiled metal or wire

ADJ. **coiled** | **box** (*AmE*) ◊ *a box-spring mattress*
VERB + SPRING **break** ◊ *The children broke some ~s jumping on the bed.*
SPRING + VERB **break, go** ◊ *Most of the ~s have gone in the sofa.*

3 where water comes up

ADJ. **hot, thermal** | **bubbling** | **mineral, natural** | **mountain, underground**
SPRING + VERB **bubble** ◊ *A thermal ~ bubbled up out of the rocks.*
SPRING + NOUN **water** ◊ *deliciously cool ~ water*

spring verb

ADV. **suddenly** | **apart, away, back, forth** (*esp. AmE*), **forward, out, up** ◊ *He sprang back in alarm.*
VERB + SPRING **be ready to, be waiting to** ◊ *The lion crouched, ready to ~.*
PREP. **at** ◊ *Lisa sprang at him and kissed him on both cheeks.* | **into, off, onto, out of, upon** ◊ *He sprang out of the car.*
PHRASES **~ open** ◊ *The drawer sprang open.* | **~ to attention** ◊ *The sentry sprang to attention.* | **~ to your feet** ◊ *She sprang to her feet and ran to answer the doorbell.*

sprinkle verb

ADV. **lightly** | **evenly** | **liberally** (*often figurative*) ◊ *The screenplay is liberally ~d with jokes.*
PREP. **on, over** ◊ *Sprinkle sugar evenly over the top of the cake.* | **with** ◊ *Sprinkle the meat lightly with salt.*

sprint *noun*

ADJ. **quick, short** | **final** | **100-metre/100-meter, 40-yard, etc.**
VERB + SPRINT **break into, make** ◊ *The runners broke into a ~ a hundred yards from the finish.* ◊ *It started raining, so we made a ~ for a cafe.*
SPRINT + NOUN **race** | **relay** ◊ *Jamaica won the gold in the ~ relay.* | **finish** ◊ *Sato just pipped the Kenyan runner in a ~ finish.* | **champion** ◊ *Olympic ~ champion Marion Jones* | **hurdles** (*BrE*)
PREP. **in a ~** ◊ *This car could comfortably outpace its rivals in a ~.* | **~ for** ◊ *The Moroccan came out best in a frantic ~ for the line.*

spur *noun*

1 on horse rider's boots

... OF SPURS **pair**
VERB + SPUR **dig in, dig into sth** ◊ *He dug his ~s into the horse's flank.*

2 encouragement

ADJ. **great, powerful**
VERB + SPUR **act as, be** | **give (sb), provide (sb with)**
PREP. **~ for** ◊ *The research provided a ~ for reform.* | **~ to** ◊ *a ~ to action*

spurt *noun*

ADJ. **sudden** | **brief, little** | **initial** ◊ *an initial ~ of energy* | **final** | **growth** ◊ *Boys experience a growth ~ during puberty.*
VERB + SPURT **put on** (*BrE*) ◊ *She put on a ~ to get to the station in time.* | **feel** ◊ *He felt a ~ of resentment against his brother.*
PREP. **with a ~** ◊ *With one final ~, he reached the top of the hill.* | **~ in** ◊ *a ~ in capital spending* | **~ of**
PHRASES **in short ~s** ◊ *His breath came in short ~s.*

spy *noun*

ADJ. **enemy, foreign, government, industrial** | **suspected** | **top** ◊ *Britain's top ~* | **British, Soviet, etc.**
... OF SPIES **network**
VERB + SPY **act as, be, work as** ◊ *He denied acting as an enemy ~.* | **recruit (sb as)**
SPY + VERB **infiltrate** ◊ *Soviet spies who had infiltrated the American government*
SPY + NOUN **film** (*esp. BrE*), **movie** (*esp. AmE*), **novel, story, thriller** | **camera, plane, satellite** | **network, ring** ◊ *Counter-intelligence officers uncovered a ~ involving twenty agents.* | **agency** (*esp. AmE*) ◊ *the director of a top American ~ agency* | **chief**
PREP. **~ for** ◊ *He was a ~ for the government.*

squabble *noun*

ADJ. **minor, petty** | **bitter, unseemly** (*BrE*) | **domestic, family, marital** | **political** | **internal, public**
VERB + SQUABBLE **have** | **resolve, settle**
PREP. **~ about, ~ over** ◊ *~s about money* | **~ among, ~ between** ◊ *I always have to settle ~s between the children.* | **~ with** ◊ *a ~ with her publisher over royalties*

squad *noun*

1 police, soldiers, etc.

ADJ. **elite** ◊ *an elite combat ~* | **anti-terrorist** (*esp. BrE*), **bomb, bomb-disposal** (*BrE*), **crime** (*esp. BrE*), **drug** (*BrE*), **drugs** (*BrE*), **flying** (*BrE*), **fraud** (*BrE*), **infantry** (*AmE*), **murder** (*BrE*), **police, rescue** (*AmE*), **rifle** (*AmE*), **riot, vice** ◊ *The serious crime ~ have taken over the investigation.* (*BrE*) ◊ *an early-morning raid by a police ~*
VERB + SQUAD **lead**
SQUAD + NOUN **detective, officer** (*both BrE*) ◊ *a murder ~ detective* | **leader** | **car**
PREP. **in a/the ~** ◊ *He's working in the vice ~.*

2 sports team

ADJ. **good, strong** (*esp. BrE*) ◊ *They've got together a good ~ for the World Cup.* | **first-team** (*BrE*), **practice** (*AmE*), **training** (*esp. BrE*) | **football, rowing, etc.** | **cheer, cheerleading** (*both AmE*) ◊ *She was captain of the cheerleading ~.* |

national, Olympic | **16-strong, 22-strong, etc.** (*esp. BrE*) ◊ *They were part of a 36-strong ~.* | **12-man, 20-man, etc.** (*esp. BrE*)
VERB + SQUAD **lead** | **join, make** ◊ *Maria failed to make the Olympic ~.* | **assemble, build** (*both esp. BrE*) | **announce, name** (*both BrE*) ◊ *England named their ~ for the second Test against Australia.* | **bolster, boost, improve, strengthen** (*all BrE*)
SQUAD + NOUN **member, player**
PREP. **in a/the ~, on the ~** ◊ *He spent last season on the practice ~.*

3 group with particular task

ADJ. **firing** ◊ *He was led out at dawn to face a firing ~.* | **assassination, death, hit, suicide** ◊ *He sent a hit ~ after the chief.* | **demolition** | **truth** (*AmE, informal*) ◊ *He is a one-man truth ~ on the subject of intelligence.*
VERB + SQUAD **lead** | **form** ◊ *They started forming death ~s.*
SQUAD + NOUN **leader, member**

squalor *noun*

ADJ. **public, urban**
VERB + SQUALOR **live in**
PREP. **amid the ~ of, in the ~ of** ◊ *a beautiful park amid the ~ of the slums* | **in ~** ◊ *He was born in ~ next to the docks.*

square *noun*

1 shape

ADJ. **perfect** | **neat**
VERB + SQUARE **cut sth into, divide sth into** ◊ *Cut the sandwiches into neat ~s.*
PREP. **~ of** ◊ *A ~ of light shone from the skylight.*

2 open space in a town, etc.

ADJ. **central, main** | **public** | **city, town, village** | **market** ◊ *crowds in the market ~*
VERB + SQUARE **fill, throng** (*esp. BrE*) ◊ *The crowd filled the ~.*
PREP. **in a/the ~**
PHRASES **the centre/center of the ~, the middle of the ~, the side of the ~** ◊ *the east side of the ~*

squeak *noun*

ADJ. **little, small** | **high, high-pitched** | **frightened, terrified**
VERB + SQUEAK **give, let out** | **hear**
PREP. **with a ~** ◊ *The door opened with a ~.* | **~ of** ◊ *She gave a little ~ of surprise.*
PHRASES **not a ~** (*BrE, figurative*) ◊ *'Have you heard from them?' 'Not a ~ since yesterday.'* | **a ~ of protest** (*figurative, esp. BrE*) ◊ *The situation was allowed to continue without a ~ of protest from the government.* | **a ~ of surprise**
→ Note at SOUND

squeal *noun*

ADJ. **little** | **high-pitched**
VERB + SQUEAL **give, let out** ◊ *She gave a little ~ of delight.* | **hear**
PREP. **with a ~** ◊ *The car stopped with a ~ of brakes.* | **~ of**
PHRASES **a ~ of delight** | **the ~ of brakes**
→ Note at SOUND

squeeze *noun*

1 pressing with fingers

ADJ. **affectionate** | **comforting, reassuring** | **gentle, little, quick** ◊ *He gave her hand a gentle ~.*
VERB + SQUEEZE **give sb** ◊ *He gave his mother a comforting ~ as he left.*
PHRASES **~ of** ◊ *A ~ of her hand reassured him.*

2 in a small space

ADJ. **tight** ◊ *There were six of us in the car and it was a tight ~.*
PREP. **at a ~** (*BrE*) ◊ *We can get six in the car at a ~.* | **in a ~** (*AmE*) ◊ *Hospitals have been in a ~ for some time.*
PHRASES **a bit of a ~**

3 reduction in money

ADJ. **cash, credit, economic, financial, profit** (*esp. AmE*)
VERB + SQUEEZE **feel** ◊ *All manufacturers are feeling the ~.* |
put ◊ *The government is trying to put the ~ on high earners.*
PREP. **~ on** ◊ *a ~ on spending*

squeeze *verb*

1 press sth hard

ADV. **hard, tightly** | **gently, lightly** ◊ *'I know,' she said,
squeezing his hand gently.* | **together** ◊ *His legs were ~d
together.*
PREP. **from** ◊ *to ~ the juice from a lemon* | **out of** ◊ *I ~d the
last bit of toothpaste out of the tube.*
PHRASES **freshly ~d** ◊ *freshly ~d orange juice*

2 limit the money available

ADV. **hard** ◊ *High interest rates have ~d the industry hard.*

squirm *verb*

ADV. **uncomfortably** | **silently** | **visibly**
VERB + SQUIRM **make sb** ◊ *The very mention of her singing
made her ~ uncomfortably.*
PREP. **at** ◊ *He ~ed visibly at the thought of his secret being
revealed.* | **away from** ◊ *She ~ed away from his hands.* | **in,
with** ◊ *He ~ed with embarrassment.* | **out of** ◊ *I started to ~
out of his grasp.*
PHRASES **~ in your seat** ◊ *I ~ed in my seat, not knowing what
to do.*

stab *noun*

1 with a knife

ADJ. **quick**
VERB + STAB **make** ◊ *The boy made a ~ at the pig.*
STAB + NOUN **wound**
PREP. **~ at, ~ to** ◊ *a ~ to the chest*
PHRASES **a ~ to the heart** (*figurative*) ◊ *Each word felt like a ~
to the heart.*

2 sudden pain

ADJ. **sharp, sudden**
VERB + STAB **feel**
PHRASES **~ of** ◊ *He felt a sharp ~ of disappointment.* ◊ *a ~ of
pain*

3 attempt

ADJ. **brave, good** | **half-hearted** ◊ *She made a half-hearted ~
at medical school, and quickly withdrew.* | **wild** | **first** ◊ *He
took his first ~ at directing.*
VERB + STAB **have, make, take**
PREP. **~ at** ◊ *I had a ~ at answering the question.*
PHRASES **a ~ in the dark** (*figurative*) ◊ *It was only a ~ in the
dark, but I hoped I could learn something.*

stab *verb*

ADV. **repeatedly** ◊ *He is accused of repeatedly stabbing a 16-
year-old boy.* | **fatally** ◊ *He was fatally stabbed.* |
accidentally ◊ *Tina accidentally stabbed herself with her
pencil.*
VERB + STAB **threaten to** | **try to**
PREP. **at, in** ◊ *He was stabbed in the chest.* | **with** ◊ *I stabbed at
my meat with my fork.*
PHRASES **be found stabbed** ◊ *He was found stabbed in his car.*
| **~ sb to death**

stability *noun*

ADJ. **greater, increased** | **relative** | **overall** ◊ *These actions
may threaten the overall ~ of the system.* | **long-term** |
internal | **global, international, regional** | **economic,
financial, monetary, price** | **political, social** | **family** (*esp.
AmE*) ◊ *They believe that religion enhances family ~.* |
emotional, mental
... OF STABILITY **degree, level** ◊ *communities that have a high
degree of ~*

VERB + STABILITY **achieve, bring, ensure, give sb, provide (sb
with)** ◊ *The policy should bring greater monetary ~ to the
country.* | **enhance, improve, increase, promote** | **restore**
| **lack** | **threaten, undermine** | **maintain, preserve**
PHRASES **a lack of ~** | **peace and ~** ◊ *the need for peace and ~
in the Middle East* | **a period of ~** ◊ *The country was
enjoying a period of political ~.* | **a sense of ~** | **a threat to
~** ◊ *The conflict is becoming a threat to ~ in the region.*

stable *adj.*

1 not likely to move

VERBS **be, feel, look, seem** | **make sth** | **keep sth** ◊ *Put a
book under the table leg to keep it ~.*
ADV. **extremely, fairly, very, etc.** | **perfectly, quite** ◊ *Don't
worry—it's perfectly ~!* | **enough, sufficiently** ◊ *The unit is ~
enough on level ground.*

2 not likely to change suddenly

VERBS **be, look, seem** | **become** | **remain** | **keep sth** ◊
attempts to keep prices ~
ADV. **extremely, fairly, very, etc.** | **highly, remarkably** |
completely, perfectly ◊ *Animals rarely live in completely ~
environments.* | **comparatively, more or less, reasonably,
relatively, roughly** | **enough, sufficiently** ◊ *He was not
emotionally ~ enough to think through his decision.* |
apparently | **emotionally, financially, politically**

stack *verb*

ADV. **carefully, neatly** | **away, up** ◊ *The wood was collected up
and carefully ~ed away.* ◊ *Stack the chairs up over there.*
PREP. **against** ◊ *The cases were ~ed against the wall.* | **in** ◊ *The
paintings were ~ed in a corner of the room.* | **on** ◊ *The plates
were neatly ~ed on the draining board.* | **with** ◊ *shelves ~ed
with boxes*
PHRASES **be ~ed in piles** ◊ *Boxes were ~ed in piles all around
the room.*

stadium *noun*

ADJ. **packed** | **all-seater** (*BrE*) | **indoor** | **sports** | **Olympic** |
home ◊ *the home ~ of the New York Giants* | **baseball,
football, greyhound** (*BrE*), **soccer** (*AmE*) | **20 000-seat,
30 000-seat, etc.**
VERB + STADIUM **fill, pack, pack into** ◊ *Thousands packed into
the ~ to watch the final.* | **build** ◊ *The Reds are building a
new ~.*
PREP. **at a/the ~**

staff *noun*

ADJ. **full-time, part-time** | **permanent, temporary** (*esp. BrE*)
| **skeleton** ◊ *We'll be down to a skeleton ~ over Christmas.* |
experienced, professional, qualified, skilled, trained |
junior, senior | **ancillary, support** | **general** (= officers
assisting a military leader in administration and planning)
| **ground** ◊ *the ground ~ at the airport* ◊ *The Wimbledon
ground ~ pulled the covers over the courts.* (*BrE*) | **academic,
administrative, campaign** (*esp. AmE*), **editorial, news** (*esp.
AmE*), **etc.** ◊ *the campaign ~ of President Bush* | **nursing,
teaching** (*BrE*), **etc.** | **hospital, hotel, library, office, etc.** |
bar, catering (*esp. BrE*), **door, kitchen, wait** (*AmE*), **waiting**
(*BrE*), **etc.**
VERB + STAFF **employ, have** ◊ *The company has a ~ of fifty.* |
appoint, engage (*esp. BrE*), **hire, recruit, take on** (*esp. BrE*)
◊ *~ appointed to the project* ◊ *I've heard they're recruiting ~ at
the moment.* | **dismiss, fire, lay off, make redundant** (*BrE*),
sack (*BrE*) ◊ *The bank expects to make 15 000 ~ redundant
over the next three years.* | **retain** ◊ *Some companies are
struggling to retain skilled ~.* | **train** | **pay** ◊ *They pay their ~
weekly.* | **join** ◊ *He joined the editorial ~ in 1999.* | **leave**
STAFF + VERB **work** ◊ *The ~ are working under pressure.* (*BrE*) ◊
The ~ is working under pressure. (*AmE*) | **deal with sb/sth,
serve sb/sth, treat sb/sth** ◊ *The bar ~ can serve around a
hundred drinks an hour.* ◊ *the medical ~ who treated him
during his confinement* | **carry sth out** ◊ *Specialist training
is necessary for ~ carrying out this work.*
STAFF + NOUN **member** (*esp. AmE*), **person** (*AmE*) ◊ *There are
four full-time ~ members.* ◊ *a ~ person for a government
agency* | **position** (*esp. AmE*) ◊ *a ~ position at 'Life' magazine*

| levels, numbers (*esp. BrE*), resources | shortage | retention, turnover | cuts | appointment ◇ *The hospital is freezing ~ appointments as part of its cutbacks.* | development, training | wages (*BrE*) | accommodation (*BrE*) ◇ *There is separate ~ accommodation for the housekeeper.* | morale (*esp. BrE*) | meeting | association | canteen (*esp. BrE*), restaurant (*esp. BrE*), room (usually *staffroom*) | attorney, physician, scientist, etc. (*all AmE*) ◇ *She's a ~ scientist at the Research Institute.* | photographer, reporter, writer, etc. (*all esp. AmE*) ◇ *He's a ~ writer for The New Yorker.* | report (*AmE*) ◇ *a ~ report by the House Foreign Affairs Committee*
PREP. on the ~ (of) (*esp. BrE*) ◇ *She has been on the ~ of the hospital for most of her working life.*
PHRASES chief of ~ (= in the army, navy, etc.) | member of ~ (*esp. BrE*) ◇ *There are four full-time members of ~.*

staff verb be staffed

ADV. well | fully, properly ◇ *The ward is now fully ~ed.* | adequately, inadequately
PHRASES be ~ed by sb, be ~ed with sb ◇ *The office will be ~ed mainly with volunteers.* ◇ *The reception desk is ~ed entirely by experienced employees.*

stage noun

1 period/state in progress/development

ADJ. distinct ◇ *The process has three distinct ~s.* | beginning, early, initial, opening, preliminary | advanced, closing, final, last, late, latter, terminal ◇ *Her husband was in the advanced ~s of cancer.* | halfway (*esp. BrE*), intermediate, secondary | first, second, etc. | transitional | successive | critical, crucial, formative, important, key, main ◇ *a young entertainer at the formative ~s of his career* | difficult | delicate, vulnerable | life ◇ *the different life ~s of insects and fish* | growth, reproductive | adult, embryonic, juvenile, larval, mature, pupal | experimental, exploratory, testing | committee (*BrE, politics*), design, development, developmental, formative, planning ◇ *The project is still at the planning ~.* | knockout (*esp. BrE*) ◇ *Colombia's win sent them through to the knockout ~ of the tournament.* | quarter-final, semi-final, etc. (*esp. BrE*)
VERB + STAGE go through, move through, pass through ◇ *The water goes through three ~s of purification.* | enter, reach ◇ *We've entered a crucial ~ in the project.* | mark, represent ◇ *This adaptation represented an important ~ in human evolution.*
PREP. at a/the ~ ◇ *You should read this article at some ~.* | by ~s ◇ *a process that by ~s led to the Cold War* | during a/the ~, in a/the ~ ◇ *in the early ~s of the job* | in ~s ◇ *We renovated the house in two ~s.* | ~ in ◇ *an important ~ in her life* | ~ of ◇ *the latter ~s of the race*
PHRASES the beginning of a ~, the end of a ~ ◇ *Students are tested at the end of each ~ of the course.* | a ~ further, one ~ further ◇ *take the investigation one ~ further* | a ~ of development, a ~ of life

2 in a theatre/theater, etc.

ADJ. centre/center (*often figurative*) ◇ *He was always unwilling to take centre/center ~.* | main ◇ *They played the main ~ at Glastonbury.* | empty | revolving | makeshift ◇ *A group of tables were converted into a makeshift ~.* | concert ◇ *David Bowie returned to the concert ~ last week.* | political (*figurative*) ◇ *Gore has stepped back onto the political ~.* | global, international, national, world (*all figurative*) ◇ *China is now a major player on the world ~.*
VERB + STAGE go on, hit (*informal*), step on, step onto, take, take to ◇ *She was too nervous to go on ~.* ◇ *I was shaking as I took the ~.* | stand on | jump off, leave, step off ◇ *She left the ~ to tumultuous applause.* | jump on, jump onto ◇ *A fan jumped up onto the ~.* | return to | share ◇ *He once shared the ~ with Frank Sinatra.* | grace ◇ *She is one of the finest actors ever to grace the ~.* | set (*often figurative*) ◇ *The thrilling semi-finals set the ~ for what should be a great game.* | boo sb off ◇ *She was booed off the ~.*
STAGE + NOUN musical, play, production, show, work ◇ *Stravinsky's last ~ work* | adaptation, version ◇ *the ~ version of 'The Lion King'* | appearance, performance, role

| presence ◇ *It was hard to forget her powerful ~ presence.* | persona ◇ *His ~ persona was that of a foolish drunk.* | name ◇ *He adopted the ~ name Dixon Hare when he became a full-time actor.* | career, debut ◇ *She made her ~ debut at the age of four.* | lighting, lights | set ◇ *The ~ set is the most expensive ever built.* | floor | door ◇ *Fans hung around the ~ door hoping to meet the band.* | actor, crew, director, manager, etc. | management | direction ◇ *As the ~ directions indicate, it is early morning in Moscow.* | left, right | fright ◇ *Even experienced actors can suffer from ~ fright.* | whisper ◇ *'She's pregnant!' he said in a ~ whisper.*
PHRASES the back of the ~, the edge of the ~, the front of the ~, the side of the ~

stage verb

ADV. carefully ◇ *The event was very carefully ~d.* | elaborately ◇ *an elaborately ~d drama*
PHRASES well ~d ◇ *The action scenes are all well ~d.*

stagger verb

ADV. almost | a little, slightly, etc. | blindly ◇ *She ~ed blindly off into the darkness.* | about (*esp. BrE*), around, away, back, backwards/backward, forward, off, out
PREP. from, into, out of, through, towards/toward, under, etc. ◇ *He was ~ing under the weight of the sack.*
PHRASES ~ to your feet ◇ *She ~ed to her feet and tottered unsteadily across the room.*

staggering adj.

VERBS be, seem ◇ *The number of dead is truly ~.*
ADV. absolutely, quite, simply, truly ◇ *The public response was absolutely ~.* | pretty

stagnation noun

ADJ. economic, political
VERB + STAGNATION cause, lead to | avoid, prevent
PHRASES a period of ~, years of ~ ◇ *Poor economic policies led to a long period of ~.*

staid adj.

VERBS be, feel, look, seem | become, get ◇ *He had become ~ and dull.*
ADV. extremely, fairly, very, etc. ◇ *The locals were a very ~ lot.* | relatively ◇ *a relatively ~ and old-fashioned hotel* | normally ◇ *the normally ~ image of chess*
PHRASES the ~ world of... ◇ *the ~ world of business*

stain noun

ADJ. stubborn | dark | blood (usually *bloodstain*), coffee, grass, grease, ink, etc. | port wine (= a permanent red mark on sb's skin) (*BrE*) ◇ *a port wine ~, present at birth*
VERB + STAIN leave | get out, remove
STAIN + VERB spread ◇ *The glass fell and a dark ~ spread over the carpet.*
STAIN + NOUN remover
PREP. ~ on ◇ *The coffee left a ~ on his shirt.* ◇ *The scandal left a dark ~ on his reputation.* (*figurative*)

stain verb

PREP. with ◇ *The shirt was heavily ~ed with blood.*
PHRASES be badly ~ed, be heavily ~ed, be slightly ~ed | ~ sth green, red, etc. ◇ *The children's fingers were ~ed purple with juice.*

stair noun

1 stairs steps inside a building

ADJ. steep | wide | narrow | rickety | spiral | main | back | basement ◇ *My kids sat on the basement ~s.* | marble, metal, stone, wooden
...OF STAIRS flight ◇ *We went up three flights of ~s.*
VERB + STAIRS ascend, climb, mount | go up, run up, etc. |

descend | go down, run down, etc. | take, use ◇ *Take the back ~s.*
STAIRS + VERB **go down to sth, go up to sth, lead to sth** | **creak** ◇ *The ~s creaked as I went down.*
STAIR + NOUN **rod** (*esp. BrE*) ◇ *The carpet was held in place by brass ~ rods.* | **rail** (*AmE*) | **gate** (*esp. BrE*)
PREP. **under the ~s** ◇ *a cupboard under the ~s* (*BrE*) ◇ *a closet under the ~s* (*AmE*) | **~s down to, ~s to, ~s up to** ◇ *the ~s to the third floor*
PHRASES **the bottom of the ~s, the foot of the ~s, the head of the ~s, the top of the ~s** | **take the ~s two, etc. at a time** ◇ *He rushed up to the bedroom, taking the ~s two at a time.*

2 one step

ADJ. **top** | **bottom**
PREP. **on a/the ~** ◇ *He sat waiting on the bottom ~.*

staircase *noun*

ADJ. **steep** | **broad, wide** | **narrow** | **elegant, grand, great** | **rickety** | **curving, spiral, sweeping, twisting, winding** | **moving** | **central, main** | **outside** | **back** | **marble, metal, stone, wooden**
VERB + STAIRCASE **ascend, climb, mount** | **go up, run up, etc.** | **descend** | **go down, run down, etc.** | **take, use**
STAIRCASE + VERB **lead to sth** ◇ *The spiral ~ led to an upper gallery.*
PREP. **on the ~** ◇ *They passed each other on the ~.* | **~ to** ◇ *the ~ to the main floor*
PHRASES **the bottom of the ~, the foot of the ~, the top of the ~**

stake *noun*

1 (*also* **stakes**) amount that could be won/lost

ADJ. **big, high** | **low, small** | **personal** ◇ *He has a personal ~ in the outcome of the war.* | **emotional, political** ◇ *The political ~s are high.*
VERB + STAKE **play for** ◇ *They always play for high ~s.* | **raise** | **lower**
PREP. **at ~** ◇ *He will face the investigation with his reputation at ~.*
PHRASES **with so much at ~** ◇ *With so much at ~, we can't afford to make mistakes.*

2 share of a company, etc.

ADJ. **controlling, large, majority, significant, substantial** | **minority, small** | **direct** | **equity, financial, ownership** (*esp. AmE*) ◇ *IBM will take an 18% ownership ~ in the new company.* | **20%, 30%, etc.**
VERB + STAKE **have, own** | **acquire, buy, take** | **sell** | **build up, increase, raise** | **cut, reduce**
PREP. **~ in** ◇ *She acquired a 4% direct ~ in the company.*

3 (*esp. BrE*) situation involving competition

PHRASES **in the … stakes** ◇ *She was determined to win in the fashion ~s.* ◇ *Beckham was high in the popularity ~s.*

stale *adj.*

VERBS **be, look, seem, smell, taste** ◇ *The room smelled musty and ~.* | **become, get** (*usually figurative*), **go, grow** (*figurative*), **turn** ◇ *This bread's going ~.* ◇ *His subject matter has grown ~.*
ADV. **extremely, fairly, very, etc.** | **a little, slightly, etc.**
PREP. **with** ◇ *The atmosphere was ~ with cigarette smoke.*

stalemate *noun*

ADJ. **political** | **current**
VERB + STALEMATE **end in, reach, result in** ◇ *The talks reached a ~.* (*BrE, AmE*) ◇ *The talks reached ~.* (*BrE*) | **break, end** ◇ *Efforts to break the ~ in the peace talks continue.* | **be locked in** ◇ *Discussions are locked in ~.*
STALEMATE + VERB **continue**
PREP. **~ between** ◇ *a ~ between management and unions* | **~ in** ◇ *The ~ in the trade talks continues.* | **~ on, ~ over** ◇ *a ~ over economic issues*

stall *noun*

1 where things are sold → See also STAND

ADJ. **market, roadside** (*esp. BrE*) | **bric-a-brac, cake, charity, fish, flower** (*all esp. BrE*) | **book** (usually **bookstall**) (*BrE*)
VERB + STALL **have** ◇ *He has a flower ~ in the market.* | **put up** (*BrE*), **set out, set up** | **pack up** (*esp. BrE*) | **man, run** ◇ *Who's going to man the ~ at lunchtime?*
STALL + VERB **sell sth** ◇ *a ~ selling second-hand books*
STALL + NOUN **holder** (usually **stallholder**) (*BrE*), **keeper** (*AmE*)
PREP. **at a/the ~** ◇ *I bought this trout at the market fish ~.* | **behind the ~** ◇ *the man behind the ~*

2 small room/space

ADJ. **empty** | **bathroom, shower, toilet** (*all esp. AmE*) | **choir, horse** | **starting** (*esp. BrE*) ◇ *The horse refused to enter the starting ~s.*
VERB + STALL **clean, muck, muck out** ◇ *We had to muck out ~s and groom the horses.*
STALL + NOUN **door**

stall *verb*

ADV. **effectively** ◇ *Discussions were effectively ~ed by the union's refusal to participate.*
PHRASES **be currently ~ed, be temporarily ~ed** ◇ *The peace process is currently ~ed.* | **~ for time** ◇ *He asked them all kinds of pointless questions, ~ing for time.*

stamina *noun*

ADJ. **great** | **mental, physical**
VERB + STAMINA **have** ◇ *She didn't the ~ to complete the course.* | **lack** | **need, require** | **build, build up, improve, increase** ◇ *Aerobic exercise helps to build up ~.*
PHRASES **reserves of ~** (*esp. BrE*) ◇ *Waley had to call on all her reserves of ~ to win the marathon.* | **strength and ~** ◇ *He is working to improve his strength and ~.* | **a test of ~** (*esp. BrE*) ◇ *Final exams at college can be as much a test of ~ as of knowledge.*

stamp *noun*

1 on a letter/package

ADJ. **postage** (*formal*) | **first-class, second-class** (*both in the UK*) | **47p, 83-cent, etc.** | **Christmas, commemorative, special** | **food** (*AmE*) ◇ *These families receive food ~s to purchase food.*
… OF STAMPS **book, set, sheet** ◇ *a book of ten ~s*
VERB + STAMP **put, put on, stick, stick on** ◇ *Don't forget to put a ~ on.* ◇ *She stuck a ~ on the letter.* | **lick** | **issue** ◇ *The ~s were issued in 1863.* | **collect** ◇ *Do you collect ~s?*
STAMP + NOUN **album, collecting, collection, collector**

2 instrument for stamping a design, etc. on a surface

ADJ. **official** | **date, time** ◇ *The software uses digital time ~s.* | **rubber**
PHRASES **~ of approval** (*figurative*) ◇ *Congress has given its ~ of approval to the budget.*

3 character/quality

ADJ. **personal, unmistakable** | **indelible** (*esp. AmE*) ◇ *President Reagan left an indelible ~ on the nation.*
VERB + STAMP **bear, carry** ◇ *His work bears the unmistakable ~ of genius.* | **leave on, put on** ◇ *She left her ~ on the school.*
PREP. **~ of** ◇ *the ~ of authority*

stamp *verb*

1 put your foot down

ADV. **hard** | **impatiently** ◇ *She ~ed her foot impatiently.* | **about, around, down, off** ◇ *He ~ed off in disgust.*
PREP. **on** ◇ *She ~ed on my toe!*

2 print letters, etc. on sth

ADV. **indelibly** (*usually figurative*) ◇ *His personality was indelibly ~ed on the final product.*
PREP. **with** ◇ *Approved goods were ~ed with a hallmark.*
PHRASES **~ed all over sth** (*figurative*) ◇ *This is an album with 'epic' ~ed all over it.*

stance noun

1 position in which sb stands

ADJ. **correct, good** | **natural** | **rigid** | **relaxed** | **upright** | **defensive, fighting** | **narrow, wide** (*both esp. AmE*) | **batting, three-point** (*both AmE, sports*) ◇ *He lines up in a three-point ~ and rushes quarterbacks.*
VERB + STANCE **adopt, assume** (*esp. AmE*), **get into** (*AmE*), **go into** (*AmE*), **take up** ◇ *The boxer took up a fighting ~.* | **adjust, change** ◇ *Williams has adjusted his ~ and swing.* | **keep, maintain**
PREP. **in a ~** ◇ *She stood in a defensive ~.* | **~ of** ◇ *a ~ of deliberate contempt*

2 attitude

ADJ. **positive** | **critical, negative, oppositional** (*esp. AmE*) | **neutral** | **aggressive, firm, hard-line, hawkish, rigid, strong, tough, uncompromising** | **proactive** (*esp. AmE*) ◇ *Lawmakers should take a proactive ~ to protect these animals.* | **cautious** | **conservative** | **radical** | **ethical, ideological, moral, political** | **official, public** ◇ *Her public ~ was much tougher than her private feelings on the subject.* | **anti-war**
VERB + STANCE **adopt, assume** (*esp. AmE*), **make, take** | **alter, change, shift, soften** | **maintain** ◇ *the country maintained a neutral ~ during the war.*
PREP. **~ against** ◇ *The state has adopted a hard-line ~ against abortion.* | **~ on, ~ towards/toward** ◇ *He has changed his ~ on immigration.*

stand verb

1 be on your feet/be upright

ADV. **erect, tall, upright** | **motionless, still** ◇ *Stand still while I take your photo.* | **barefoot, naked** | **on tiptoe** ◇ *She stood on tiptoe to reach the shelf.* | **awkwardly, meekly, uncertainly** ◇ *He stood awkwardly in the doorway, not sure what to say.* | **rigidly, stiffly** | **quietly, silently** | **proudly** ◇ *Her parents stood proudly at her side.* | **around, there** ◇ *Don't just ~ there—do something.*
VERB + STAND **be able to, can** | **be unable to, cannot** ◇ *The roof was so low I couldn't ~ upright.* | **can barely, can hardly** ◇ *He felt so weak he could hardly ~.*
PHRASES **be left ~ing** ◇ *After the earthquake only a few houses were left ~ing.* | **~ rooted to the spot** ◇ *She stood rooted to the spot, too afraid to move or speak.*

2 tolerate sth

VERB + STAND **can** ◇ *I don't know how you can ~ the heat.* | **cannot** ◇ *I can't ~ that man!* | **can hardly**

3 (*esp. BrE*) be a candidate in an election → See also RUN

ADV. **successfully, unsuccessfully**
VERB + STAND **decide to** | **be allowed to**
PREP. **against** ◇ *Two candidates will be ~ing against her.* | **as** ◇ *She stood unsuccessfully as a candidate in the local elections.* | **for** ◇ *He is ~ing for Oxford East in the election.*
PHRASES **sb's decision to ~** | **~ for election**

PHR V **stand by**
ADV. **idly, passively** ◇ *Surely the world cannot ~ idly by and let this country go through the agony of war yet again?*
VERB + STAND BY **can**

stand up
ADV. **straight** ◇ *You'll look taller if you ~ up straight.* | **abruptly, quickly, suddenly** | **slowly** | **immediately**
VERB + STAND UP **try to** ◇ *I tried to ~ up and found myself in agony.*

stand noun

1 effort to resist opposition

ADJ. **brave, defiant, determined, firm, strong, tough** | **moral, principled** | **last, last-ditch** | **public**
VERB + STAND **make, take**
PREP. **~ against** ◇ *to make a ~ against industries that contribute to river pollution* | **~ on** ◇ *He has taken a public ~ on the issue of misuse of hospital funds.*

2 (*esp. AmE*) small shop → See also STALL

ADJ. **concession, farm, market** (*all AmE*) | **roadside** (*AmE*) | **news** (usually ***news-stand***), **newspaper** | **fruit** (*AmE*), **hamburger, hot-dog, lemonade** (*AmE*), etc.
VERB + STAND **set up**
PREP. **at a/the ~** ◇ *We can get a magazine at the newspaper ~.*
PHRASES **hit the ~s** ◇ *The magazine will hit the ~s in April.*

3 (*esp. BrE*) table at an exhibition

ADJ. **display, exhibition, trade** (*BrE*) | **information**
VERB + STAND **have** ◇ *Our company has a display ~ at this year's fair.* | **set up** | **man** ◇ *We took it in turns to man the exhibition ~.*
PREP. **at a/the ~, on the ~** ◇ *I'll be on the ~ for two hours.* ◇ *You'll find brochures of our new products on the ~.*

4 furniture/equipment for putting sth on

ADJ. **coat, hat** (usually ***hatstand***), **umbrella** | **mic** (*informal*), **microphone, mike** (*informal*) | **music** | **night** (usually ***nightstand***) (*AmE*) | **wooden**
PREP. **in a/the ~, on a/the ~** ◇ *There was some music open on the music ~.*

standard noun

1 level of quality

ADJ. **high** | **low, poor** | **certain, minimum** ◇ *Players have to be of a certain ~ to compete in the tournament.* | **acceptable, adequate, decent, proper, reasonable** ◇ *We must ensure proper ~s of care for the elderly.* ◇ *a decent ~ of living* | **improved, rising** | **new** ◇ *He set a new ~ of excellence in detective fiction.* | **current, modern** ◇ *The houses need to be brought up to modern ~s.* | **historical** | **clear** | **objective** ◇ *Judged by any objective ~s, the campaign was a disaster.* | **accepted** (*esp. BrE*), **official, required** (*esp. BrE*) | **conventional** (*esp. AmE*), **usual** | **common, consistent, uniform, universal** ◇ *They will adopt common ~s for dealing with asylum applications.* | **exacting, rigorous, strict, stringent** | **gold** (*figurative*) ◇ *Charles Schulz's 'Peanuts' is the gold ~ for comic strips.* ◇ *The newspaper has to offer a gold ~ for journalistic integrity.* | **professional** ◇ *The work has been done to a professional ~.* | **federal, international, national, state** (*AmE*) | **quality** ◇ *We have to try and achieve the quality ~s set by the project.* | **qualifying** ◇ *The Olympic qualifying ~ has been set at 64.50 m.* | **living** ◇ *The region enjoys the highest living ~s in Asia.* | **accounting, journalistic, labour/labor** (*esp. AmE*), **legal, safety, security, trading** (*BrE*), etc. | **academic, educational, environmental, health, performance, technical**, etc. | **industry** ◇ *The product has become an industry ~.* | **emission, emissions** ◇ *The bill established new emissions ~s for cars sold in the state.*
VERB + STANDARD **have** ◇ *The agency has very high ~s.* | **boast, enjoy** | **define, develop, establish, set** | **achieve, be up to, live up to, meet, reach** ◇ *The factory is struggling to meet national environmental ~s.* ◇ *She has reached an acceptable ~ of English.* | **bring sth up to** | **fall short of** ◇ *The hotel service fell short of the usual ~.* | **apply, enforce, provide** ◇ *It's impossible to apply the same academic ~s across the country.* | **judge sb/sth by** | **improve** (*esp. BrE*), **raise** | **lower** | **maintain, sustain**
PREP. **above (the) ~, below (the) ~** ◇ *Your work is below ~.* | **according to a/the ~, by…~s** ◇ *By today's ~s, he isn't a particularly fast runner.* | **to a…~** ◇ *The building work had not been completed to a satisfactory ~.* | **up to ~** ◇ *We need to bring our computer system up to ~.* | **~ in** ◇ *~s in safety*
PHRASES **by any** ◇ *She's a great violinist by any ~.* | **by the ~s of the day** ◇ *The army was massive by the ~s of the day.* | **a drop in the ~, a fall in the ~** ◇ *There has been a drop in the ~ of health care.* | **an increase in the ~, a rise in the ~** ◇ *There has been an increase in the ~ of service provided.* | **a ~ of living** ◇ *the fall in their ~ of living*

2 (usually **standards**) acceptable level of conduct

ADJ. **declining, falling** ◇ *My grandparents are always complaining about falling moral ~s.* | **double** ◇ *the double ~ frequently encountered in 19th-century attitudes to sex* | **ethical, moral**
VERB + STANDARD **prescribe** | **keep up, maintain** | **improve, raise**

STANDARD + VERB **drop, fall**
PHRASES **~s of behaviour/behavior, ~s of conduct | ~ of care**

standard *adj.*

VERBS **be, be fitted as** (*esp. BrE*), **come as** ◊ *Anti-lock brakes come as ~.* | **become**
ADV. **almost** ◊ *The stations were built to a simple, almost ~ design.* | **fairly, pretty, relatively** ◊ *a fairly ~ method of assessing employees*

standing *noun*

1 reputation

ADJ. **good, high | low | equal | current | public | international, national | academic, economic, financial, legal, moral, political, professional, social**
VERB + STANDING **have** ◊ *Professor Greenan has a high ~ in the academic world.* | **enhance, improve | damage, diminish**
STANDING + VERB **decline, fall | rise**
PREP. **of…~** ◊ *She married into a family of higher social ~.* | **~ among** ◊ *her low ~ among her fellow scientists* | **~ as** ◊ *His ~ as a movie director has risen in recent years.* | **~ in, ~ within** ◊ *his international ~ in cancer research* | **~ with** ◊ *She was appointed for her high ~ with the general public.*
PHRASES **in good ~ with sb** ◊ *a student in good ~ with the college* | **a member in good ~** (*AmE*) ◊ *a member in good ~ of the movement*

2 length of time that sth has existed

ADJ. **long | 25 years', many years', etc.** ◊ *Their relationship is of many years' ~.*
PREP. **of…~**

standpoint *noun*

ADJ. **different** ◊ *We must approach the problem from a different ~.* | **objective, personal | practical | ideological, theoretical | ethical, moral | economic, financial, historical, legal, military, political, religious, technical, etc.**
VERB + STANDPOINT **adopt** (*esp. BrE*) ◊ *We should try to adopt a more positive ~.* | **approach sth from, view sth from**
PREP. **from the ~ of, from this, that, etc. ~** ◊ *From the ~ of women, this looks like a policy of discrimination.*

standstill *noun*

ADJ. **complete, dead, total | near, virtual**
VERB + STANDSTILL **come to, grind to** ◊ *The train came to a complete ~.* | **bring sth to** ◊ *The roadworks brought the traffic to a ~.*
PREP. **at a ~** ◊ *The factory has been at a ~ for days.*

star *noun*

1 small point of light in the night sky

ADJ. **bright, brilliant | faint | distant | nearby, nearer, nearest | falling, shooting | evening, morning | massive**
…OF STARS **cluster** ◊ *a dense cluster of ~s at the galaxy's nucleus* | **canopy** ◊ *They lay down under a canopy of ~s.*
VERB + STAR **look up at**
STAR + VERB **be out | shine, twinkle** ◊ *A bright ~ shone in the east.* | **appear, come out**
STAR + NOUN **cluster**
PREP. **under the ~s** ◊ *We camped out under the ~s.*
PHRASES **the brightness of a ~, the density of a ~, the luminosity of a ~**

2 famous person

ADJ. **big, big-name, major** ◊ *There were several big Hollywood ~s at the function.* | **A-list, B-list, Z-list, etc. | real, true, undisputed | budding, emerging, rising, young | veteran** ◊ *veteran ~s of stage and screen* | **pop, rap, rock, etc. | basketball, football, soccer, track** (*AmE*), **etc.** ◊ *Through high school he was a track ~.* | **film** (*esp. BrE*), **Hollywood, media, movie** (*esp. AmE*), **screen, soap, TV | guest** ◊ *The show has plenty of guest ~s appearing each week.*

…OF STARS **array, galaxy, host** ◊ *Channel 8 has lined up a galaxy of ~s for the coming season.*
VERB + STAR **make sb** ◊ *That was the movie that made him a ~.*
STAR + NOUN **quality, status | power** (*esp. AmE*) | **role | actor, athlete** (*esp. AmE*), **performer, player | witness | attraction, turn** ◊ *He was the ~ turn at the celebrations.* | **system** ◊ *the Hollywood ~ system* | **vehicle** ◊ *The movie was nothing more than a ~ vehicle for Tom Hanks.*
PREP. **~ of** ◊ *the ~ of the show*

stardom *noun*

ADJ. **film** (*esp. BrE*), **movie** (*esp. AmE*), **TV | pop, rock | major-league, NBA, NFL** (*all AmE*) | **global, Hollywood, international**
VERB + STARDOM **achieve, rise to, rocket to, shoot to | rocket sb to, shoot sb to** ◊ *Her number one single shot her to ~.* | **be destined for, be tipped for** (*BrE*) ◊ *This young tennis player is being tipped for ~.* | **be groomed for** ◊ *He was groomed for ~ by his father.*
PHRASES **be on the brink of ~, be on the verge of ~** ◊ *The band was on the brink of rock ~.* | **sb's rise to ~** ◊ *her meteoric rise to ~* | **the road to ~** ◊ *He set out on the lonely road to ~ early in life.*

stare *verb*

ADV. **fixedly, hard, intently, unblinkingly** ◊ *I could see a man staring at me intently.* | **steadily | impassively | absently, blankly, uncomprehendingly, vacantly** ◊ *She ~d blankly at the brick wall in front of her.* | **disbelievingly, incredulously, open-mouthed, wide-eyed, wildly** ◊ *I ~d at him open-mouthed, unable to speak.* | **bleakly, gloomily, glumly, helplessly, morosely** ◊ *He ~d at me bleakly and said nothing.* | **coldly, coolly, defiantly, fiercely, stonily** ◊ *She ~d at him stonily as he came in.* | **curiously, quizzically, suspiciously, thoughtfully | silently | just, merely, simply | (for) a moment** ◊ *For a long moment they just ~d at each other.* | **still** ◊ *He was still staring at himself in the mirror.* | **across, ahead, around, back, down, out, straight ahead, up** ◊ *She ~d back at him.* ◊ *He ~d straight ahead and did not move.*
VERB + STARE **seem to | continue to | turn to** ◊ *Everyone in the room turned to ~ at her.* | **pause to, stop to**
PREP. **at | across, around, through | after** ◊ *She stalked off, leaving them all staring after her.* | **into, out of | in, with** ◊ *I ~d in horror at his bloody mouth.* ◊ *He just ~d at her with disbelief.*
PHRASES **sit staring, stand staring** ◊ *I sat staring at the ruins of the building.* | **sit and ~, stand and ~, stop and ~** ◊ *It was too cold to stand and ~.* | **~ into the abyss** (*figurative*) ◊ *His party was staring into the abyss.* | **~ into space** ◊ *She was just sitting there, staring into space.*

start *noun*

ADJ. **auspicious, bright** (*esp. BrE*), **decent, encouraging, excellent, fine, flying, good, great, impressive, promising, sound, strong, wonderful** ◊ *Despite a promising ~, we lost the game.* | **bad, disappointing, disastrous, poor, rocky, shaky, slow, sluggish, uncertain | running** (*esp. AmE*), **standing** (*both often figurative*) ◊ *The space project went from a standing ~ to the moon in ten years.* | **false** ◊ *After a couple of false ~s, she found the job that suited her.* | **head** (*usually figurative*) ◊ *All parents want to give their kids a head ~ in life.* | **fresh, new | early, late | very** ◊ *right from the very ~*
VERB + START **make** ◊ *I think it's time we made a ~.* | **get off to** ◊ *The company got off to an impressive ~ this year.* | **herald** (*esp. BrE*), **mark, signal**
START + NOUN **date, time | button, menu** (*computing*), **signal** ◊ *I clicked the icon in the ~ menu.* | **line, point, position** ◊ *The runners walked up to the ~ line.*
PREP. **at the ~ (of)** ◊ *Everyone was in a conciliatory mood at the ~ of the meeting.* | **from the ~** ◊ *She felt at home in her new job right from the ~.* | **prior to the ~** ◊ *He joined the team prior to the ~ of the season.* | **~ to** ◊ *The fine winter weather heralded a good ~ to the year.* | **~ in** ◊ *Moving to a good school gave Sally a fresh ~ in life.*
PHRASES **be doomed from the ~** ◊ *The project was doomed*

from the ~. | **from ~ to finish** ◇ *This is a thoroughly good book from ~ to finish.*

start verb

ADV. **suddenly** ◇ *Her heart suddenly ~ed to race.* | **immediately** | **just** ◇ *He has just ~ed at school.* ◇ *At that point I just ~ed to hate the man.* | **already** | **off, out** ◇ *We'll ~ off by doing some warm-up exercises.* | **up** ◇ *She ~ed up a conversation with the woman sitting next to her.* | **again, all over again, over** (*AmE*) ◇ *We'll just have to ~ all over again.*
VERB + START **decide to, expect to, hope to, intend to, plan to, want to** | **be due to, be expected to, be scheduled to, be supposed to** ◇ *Work is due to ~ this weekend.* | **be ready to** ◇ *By early evening he was ready to ~ work.* | **be about to, be going to** ◇ *A new term was about to ~.* | **had better, have to, need to** ◇ *You'd better ~ packing if you're to leave early tomorrow morning.*
PREP. **as** ◇ *It ~ed as a hobby and grew from there.* | **by** ◇ *Let's ~ by reviewing what we did last week.* | **from** ◇ *Start from the beginning and tell me exactly what happened.* | **on** ◇ *I've finished decorating the bathroom, so now I can ~ on the bedroom.* | **with** ◇ *Let's ~ with this first piece of music.*
PHRASES **get (sb/sth) ~ed** ◇ *It's already late, so I think we should get ~ed.* | **a good, great, etc. place to ~** ◇ *If you want to learn about frogs, this book is an excellent place to ~.* | **let's ~** | **~ from scratch** ◇ *I'll have to ~ again from scratch.* | **time to ~ sth** ◇ *It's time to ~ thinking about next year.*

starting point noun

ADJ. **excellent, good, ideal, perfect** | **convenient, useful** | **appropriate, logical, obvious, reasonable, suitable**
VERB + STARTING POINT **be, provide, serve as** | **take sth as, use sth as**
PREP. **from a/the ~** ◇ *They reached the same conclusion from different ~s.* | **~ for** ◇ *Your paper provides a useful ~ for the discussion.*

startled adj.

VERBS **appear, be, look, seem, sound**
ADV. **extremely, fairly, very, etc.** | **a little, slightly, etc.** | **for a moment, momentarily** ◇ *She was momentarily ~ by the sight before her.* | **suddenly** | **clearly, obviously**
PREP. **at** ◇ *She was obviously a little ~ at this idea.* | **by** ◇ *I was ~ by his sudden appearance in the doorway.*

starvation noun

ADJ. **prolonged, slow** | **mass, widespread** | **oxygen** ◇ *The pilot had lost consciousness because of oxygen ~.*
VERB + STARVATION **be threatened with, face, suffer from** | **save sb from** | **avoid, prevent** | **die from, die of**
STARVATION + NOUN **diet, rations** | **wages** ◇ *The workers lived in poor conditions and were paid ~ wages.* | **level** ◇ *Millions of people around the world live at or below ~ level.*
PHRASES **death by ~, death from ~**

starve verb

ADV. **slowly** | **literally** ◇ *She refused food and literally ~d herself to death.*
VERB + STARVE **leave sb to** ◇ *He locked them in a room and left them to ~.*
PREP. **for** (*usually figurative*) ◇ *He is starving for attention.* | **of** ◇ *The baby's brain had been ~d of oxygen.*
PHRASES **be half ~d** ◇ *The poor cat was half ~d.* | **keep sb from starving** ◇ *320 tons of food are needed each month to keep millions from starving.* | **~ in the streets, ~ on the streets** ◇ *Their policies will leave innocent children starving in the streets.* | **~ to death**

state noun

1 condition

ADJ. **acceptable, fit, good, healthy** ◇ *She managed to get the company's finances into a healthy ~.* | **appalling** (*esp. BrE*), **awful, bad, desperate, dire, dreadful, pitiful, poor, sorry, terrible** | **run-down** (*esp. BrE*) ◇ *We were shocked at the run-down ~ of the hospital.* | **emotional, mental, psychological** ◇ *He's not in a fit enough mental ~ to drive.* | **physical** ◇ *The*

803 **state**

inspectors assess the physical ~ of schools and equipment. | **financial** | **current, present** | **former, previous** | **natural** ◇ *You can either varnish the wood or leave it in its natural ~.* | **constant, continual, continuous, permanent, perpetual** ◇ *The country is in a perpetual ~ of anarchy.* | **advanced** ◇ *an advanced ~ of dehydration* | **altered** ◇ *a drug that produces altered ~s of consciousness* | **nervous, trance-like** ◇ *He goes into a trance-like ~ when he plays the guitar.* | **persistent vegetative** (*medical*)
VERB + STATE **get into, go into, reach** ◇ *The soul continues to be reborn until it has reached a ~ of perfection.* | **live in** ◇ *She continues to live in a ~ of denial.* | **get sb/sth into** | **create** ◇ *She uses music to create a particular emotional ~.* | **describe**
PREP. **in a ~** ◇ *Jane was in a terrible ~ after losing her job.* | **into a ~** ◇ *She slipped into a ~ of unconsciousness.* | **~ of** ◇ *His life seems to be in a constant ~ of chaos.*
PHRASES **be in a good, bad, etc. ~ of repair** (*BrE*) ◇ *The house was in a poor ~ of repair when we bought it.* | **given the ~ of sth** ◇ *Given the current ~ of knowledge, it will take years to find a solution.* | **a ~ of affairs** ◇ *The brothers' refusal to work together had brought about this sad ~ of affairs.* | **a ~ of emergency** ◇ *The government has declared a ~ of emergency in the flooded regions.* | **a ~ of flux** ◇ *The education system is still in a ~ of flux following the recent reform.* | **sb's ~ of health** ◇ *He's concerned about his mother's ~ of health.* | **a ~ of mind** ◇ *Public speaking can produce a ~ of mind similar to panic.* | **a ~ of shock** ◇ *The driver was just sitting there in a ~ of shock.* | **a ~ of siege, a ~ of war**

2 country/government

ADJ. **city, nation** | **independent, sovereign** | **foreign** | **client** | **failed, rogue** ◇ *rogue ~s that shelter terrorists* | **democratic, one-party, police, socialist, totalitarian** | **member** ◇ *member ~s of the European Union* | **powerful, strong** | **weak** | **neighbouring/neighboring** | **welfare** | **nanny** (*esp. BrE*) ◇ *This latest policy is an example of the nanny ~ gone mad.*
VERB + STATE **create, establish** ◇ *They created a modern nation ~.* | **become** ◇ *In 1949 China became a communist ~.*
STATE + NOUN **enterprise, monopoly** | **control, ownership** ◇ *The telephone network is still under ~ control.* | **property** ◇ *Every citizen could buy shares in privatized ~ property.* | **sector** (*esp. BrE*), **system** ◇ *Teachers in the ~ sector are asking for a 7% pay rise.* ◇ *schools outside the ~ system* | **education** (= paid for by the government) (*BrE*) | **school** (= paid for by the government) (*in the UK*) ◇ *Did you go to a ~ school or a private school?* | **school, university** (= managed by a state) (*in the US*) | **aid, funding, funds, subsidy, support** | **benefit, pension** (*both esp. BrE*) ◇ *unemployed people living on ~ benefits* ◇ *The ~ pension is barely enough to live on.* | **intervention** (*esp. BrE*) ◇ *large-scale ~ intervention in industry* | **power** ◇ *the legitimate exercise of ~ power* | **spending** ◇ *Some prefer tax cuts to greater ~ spending on health and social services.* | **employee** | **secret** ◇ *He was shot for passing ~ secrets to foreign powers.*
PHRASES **affairs of ~, matters of ~** ◇ *The president's wife is said to have a powerful hand in affairs of ~.* | **church and ~** ◇ *the separation of church and ~* | **an enemy of the ~** | **head of ~** ◇ *Visiting heads of ~ usually stay at the palace.* | **the power of the ~** | **the role of the ~**

3 part of a country

ADJ. **battleground, swing** ◇ *Both candidates have been campaigning in key battleground ~s.* | **blue, red** (*both AmE*) ◇ *New Jersey is a blue ~* (= votes for the Democrats). ◇ *red ~s for Republicans* | **border, slave** (*both AmE*) ◇ *opposition to the Civil War in Kansas and the other border ~s*
... OF STATES **handful** ◇ *A handful of ~s have introduced similar legislation.*
VERB + STATE **represent** ◇ *She was selected to represent the ~ of Texas at the conference.* | **win** ◇ *George W. Bush won the ~ of Florida.*
STATE + VERB **allow sth, require sth** ◇ *Most ~s require all drivers to carry a minimum level of insurance.* | **pass sth** ◇ *Thirty ~s have passed similar legislation.*

STATE + NOUN **capital, line** (*AmE*) ◇ *It can be a felony to transport wine across ~ lines.* | **court, prison** ◇ *I was a correctional officer out of Utah ~ prison.* | **law** | **constitution** | **budget, tax** | **agency, court, government, legislature** ◇ *Charities are required to register with a ~ agency.* | **attorney general** (*AmE*), **lawmaker, legislator, official, senator** | **police, trooper** (*AmE*)

PREP. **across the ~, throughout the ~** ◇ *He roamed throughout the ~.*

PHRASES **at the ~ level, on the ~ level** ◇ *The legislation must work at both the federal and ~ levels.* | **a corner of the ~** ◇ *a farm tucked into the far north-west corner of the ~*

state *verb*

ADV. **clearly, plainly** ◇ *Please ~ clearly how many tickets you require.* | **exactly, explicitly, expressly, precisely, specifically** ◇ *These facts were nowhere explicitly ~d.* | **categorically, unequivocally, with certainty** ◇ *She ~d categorically that she had no intention of leaving.* | **boldly, proudly** | **emphatically, firmly** | **bluntly, flatly, matter-of-factly** ◇ *'Alcohol doesn't solve problems,' she ~d flatly.* | **confidently, with confidence** | **accurately** | **correctly, rightly** | **falsely, incorrectly, wrongly** (*esp. BrE*) | **openly, publicly** ◇ *He ~d his own views quite openly.* | **formally, officially** | **briefly, succinctly** | **quietly** | **just, merely, simply** ◇ *I am merely stating the facts.* | **repeatedly**

VERB + STATE **go on to** ◇ *The report goes on to ~ that…* | **fail to** ◇ *The committee failed to ~ their reasons for this decision.* | **let sb**

PHRASES **as previously ~d, as ~d earlier, as ~d previously** ◇ *As previously ~d, the phrase has an ambiguous meaning.* | **~d above, ~d below** ◇ *We cannot accept this proposal for the reasons ~d above.* | **~ at the outset** ◇ *Let me ~ at the outset that this report contains little that is new.* | **~ for the record** ◇ *Let me ~ for the record that my knowledge of wine is almost non-existent.* | **~ the obvious** ◇ *At the risk of stating the obvious, people who have not paid cannot be admitted.* | **unless otherwise ~d, unless ~d otherwise** ◇ *All the photographs in this book, unless otherwise ~d, date from the 1950s.*

statement *noun*

1 something that you say or write

ADJ. **brief, short** ◇ *Saunder's lawyer made a brief ~ to the press outside the court.* | **bald, blunt, flat** ◇ *His bald ~ that he'd resigned concealed his anxiety about the situation.* | **comprehensive, definitive, detailed, full** | **explicit** ◇ *An explicit ~ of objectives is vital before the project begins.* | **clear, simple** | **bold, firm, positive, strong** | **explanatory** | **false, inaccurate, misleading** | **sweeping** ◇ *She made one of her sweeping ~s about foreigners.* | **joint** ◇ *The two heads of state issued a joint ~.* | **formal, government, official, press, public** | **political** ◇ *They decided to make a political ~ by refusing to vote.* | **oral, signed, sworn, written** | **witness** (*esp. BrE*) ◇ *He made a witness ~ to the police.* | **policy** | **mission, vision** ◇ *The company needed a mission ~ describing its core values.* | **fashion** (*figurative*) ◇ *He was making a fashion ~ by wearing a pink suit.*

VERB + STATEMENT **issue, put out, release** | **give, make** ◇ *He admitted giving a false ~ to the police.* | **read** ◇ *She read a ~ to reporters yesterday.* | **take** ◇ *The police will take a ~ from each of you.* | **retract, withdraw** | **contradict** | **deny**

STATEMENT + VERB **condemn** ◇ *a ~ condemning the death penalty*

PREP. **in a/the ~** ◇ *In a ~ released today, the Department of Health said…* | **~ about** ◇ *The clothes you wear are a ~ about yourself.* | **~ on** ◇ *a ~ on human rights* | **~ on behalf of** ◇ *She put out a ~ on behalf of the Government.* | **~ to** ◇ *a recent ~ to the press*

2 financial record

ADJ. **bank, credit-card, tax** (*AmE*) | **financial, income** (*AmE*), **trading** (*BrE*)

VERB + STATEMENT **prepare** | **publish** ◇ *The issuing banks published financial ~s.* | **file** ◇ *He filed false ~s with the SEC.*

statesman *noun*

ADJ. **great, leading** | **elder, senior** ◇ *Political power resided with the nation's elder ~ and party leader.* | **international, world** ◇ *his reputation as a world ~*

static *adj.*

VERBS **appear, be, seem** | **become** | **remain, stay**

ADV. **very** | **completely, totally** | **far from** | **almost, largely, more or less, virtually** (*esp. BrE*) ◇ *The population remained more or less ~.* | **essentially** | **fairly, rather, relatively, somewhat** ◇ *The economy is fairly ~ at the moment.*

station *noun*

1 place where trains/buses stop

ADJ. **rail, railroad** (*AmE*), **railway** (*BrE*), **train** | **bus, coach** (*BrE*) | **metro, subway** (*AmE*), **tube** (*BrE*), **underground** (*BrE*) | **next** ◇ *We get off at the next ~.*

VERB + STATION **get to, go to** ◇ *We got to the ~ just as the train was pulling out.* | **leave** ◇ *The bus leaves the ~ at 09.00 hours.* | **arrive at** ◇ *The train arrived at Pisa ~ twenty minutes late.*

STATION + NOUN **building** | **platform** | **car park** (*BrE*), **parking lot** (*AmE*) | **agent** (*AmE*), **manager** (*BrE*), **master** (usually *stationmaster*) (*BrE, old-fashioned*), **staff**

PREP. **at a/the ~** ◇ *He got off at the same ~.* ◇ *We waited for him at the bus ~.* | **in a/the ~** ◇ *There's a newspaper kiosk in the ~.*

2 radio/television company

ADJ. **radio, television, TV** | **foreign, local** | **digital, FM, pirate** ◇ *a digital radio ~* | **cable, satellite** | **commercial** | **news**

VERB + STATION **get, pick up, tune in to, tune to** ◇ *I can pick up a lot of foreign ~s on this radio.* | **listen to** | **operate, run**

STATION + VERB **air sth, broadcast sth, play sth** ◇ *The ~ airs 14 hours of local news per week.*

STATION + NOUN **manager** (*esp. AmE*)

3 place/building where service is organized

ADJ. **ambulance** (*esp. BrE*), **fire, lifeboat** (*BrE*), **police** | **polling** ◇ *I went into a polling ~ and cast my vote.* | **power** | **filling, gas** (*AmE*), **petrol** (*BrE*), **service** | **service** (*BrE*), **way** (*often figurative, esp. AmE*) ◇ *We stopped for a break at a motorway service ~.* ◇ *The UK post was a way ~ to retirement.* | **earth, space** | **radar, tracking, weather**

VERB + STATION **operate, run** | **close, open**

STATION + NOUN **house** (*AmE*) ◇ *The police led me into the ~ house.* | **forecourt** (*BrE*) ◇ *a petrol ~ forecourt* | **attendant, manager, owner** ◇ *a petrol ~ attendant* (*BrE*) ◇ *a gas ~ attendant* (*AmE*) | **chief** (*AmE*) ◇ *the CIA ~ chief in Vietnam* | **commander, officer** (*both esp. BrE*) ◇ *The meeting had to be abandoned after local fire ~ officer, Dave Temple, was called away to a fire.*

stationery *noun*

ADJ. **business, company, hotel, office, wedding** (*esp. BrE*) | **handmade** (*BrE*), **quality** ◇ *handmade wedding ~* | **letterhead** (*esp. BrE*) ◇ *The logo featured on the letterhead ~ for the Association.*

STATIONERY + NOUN **shop** (*esp. BrE*), **store** (*esp. AmE*), **supplier** | **cupboard** (*BrE*)

statistics *noun*

ADJ. **annual** | **latest** | **reliable** | **vital** | **raw** ◇ *The raw ~ tell us nothing about the underlying trends.* | **government, national, official, police** | **accident, crime, economic, employment, health, police, population, trade, unemployment, etc.** | **baseball** (*esp. AmE*), **career** ◇ *Her final international career ~ are impressive.* | **descriptive, summary** (*both technical*) ◇ *Table 1 presents descriptive ~ for cancer deaths in England.*

VERB + STATISTICS **have** ◇ *I don't have official ~ on the subject.* | **prepare, produce** | **keep** ◇ *We no longer keep ~ on former*

employees. | **release** | **provide** | **collect, compile** ◊ *They began compiling those ~ in 1985.* | **cite**
STATISTICS + VERB **indicate sth, prove sth, reveal sth, show sth, tell sb sth** | **suggest sth**
STATISTICS + NOUN **office**
PREP. **according to ~** ◊ *According to official ~, the island had 37 inhabitants.* | **~ on** ◊ *The government has released new ~ on the cost of living.*
→ Note at SUBJECT (for more verbs and nouns)

statue noun
ADJ. **colossal** (*esp. BrE*), **enormous, giant, huge, large** | **small** | **life-size, life-sized** | **equestrian** | **ancient** | **Buddhist, Greek, etc.** | **golden** | **bronze, marble, stone, etc.**
VERB + STATUE **erect, put up** | **unveil** | **topple** ◊ *The protestors toppled a ~ of King George III.*
STATUE + VERB **be, stand** ◊ *The ~ stands in one of the main squares.*
STATUE + NOUN **base** ◊ *the dedicatory inscription on the ~ base*
PREP. **~ of** ◊ *a ~ of David* | **~ to** ◊ *the unveiling of a ~ to Lord Brown*

stature noun
1 height
ADJ. **imposing, tall** | **diminutive, short, slight, small** | **physical**
VERB + STATURE **have**
PREP. **of…~** ◊ *He was a man of imposing ~ who carried himself well.*
PHRASES **a lack of ~** ◊ *Despite his lack of ~, he became a successful athlete.* | **small in ~** ◊ *Both her parents are fairly small in ~.*

2 importance
ADJ. **considerable, great, growing** | **heroic** | **full** | **public** | **international, world** | **political, social** | **moral** ◊ *a woman of great moral ~*
VERB + STATURE **have, lack** | **gain, gain in, grow in** ◊ *She has grown in ~ since winning the award.* | **achieve** ◊ *Geomorphology has now achieved full ~ as a branch of geology.* | **enhance** ◊ *The election result enhanced the party's ~.* | **diminish**
STATURE + VERB **grow, increase, rise** ◊ *His political ~ increased during the crisis.*
PREP. **of ~** ◊ *a writer of international ~*

status noun
ADJ. **elite** (*esp. AmE*), **great, high, superior** | **inferior, low, lowly** ◊ *low-status jobs* | **relative** ◊ *The relative ~ of the speakers affects what language is used.* | **equal** | **current** | **full** ◊ *The Institute has now achieved full ~ as part of the University.* | **privileged, special** | **insider, outsider** ◊ *My outsider ~ granted me special insights.* | **amateur** | **economic, educational, employment, financial, occupational, professional, social, socio-economic** ◊ *a payment made to every individual irrespective of employment ~* | **minority** ◊ *the minority ~ of Catholics in Virginia* | **marital** | **health, HIV** ◊ *He has told family and friends of his HIV ~.* | **legal** ◊ *They argued that the email had no signature and therefore no legal ~.* | **diplomatic** | **citizenship** (*esp. AmE*), **immigrant, immigration, refugee, resident** | **independent** ◊ *A majority voted for fully independent ~ for the region.* | **charitable, charity** (*both esp. BrE*) ◊ *The organization has charitable ~.* | **non-profit, not-for-profit** (*both esp. AmE*) | **college, foundation** (*both BrE*) ◊ *hospitals that have been given foundation ~* | **tax-exempt** (*esp. AmE*) | **international** | **superpower** ◊ *the United States' rise to superpower ~* | **celebrity, star, superstar** ◊ *He achieved celebrity ~ through his role in a popular sitcom.* | **canonical, classic, cult, legendary** ◊ *a car from the 50s that has acquired cult ~*
VERB + STATUS **enjoy, have** ◊ *The teaching profession has a low ~ in this country.* ◊ *This sort of bike has ~ among teenagers.* | **achieve, acquire, attain, gain, get** ◊ *Marrying a rich woman helped him achieve ~.* ◊ *They have acquired refugee ~.* | **bring sb, give sb** ◊ *Owning the yacht has given them ~.* | **accord, attach, confer, give** ◊ *High social ~ is attached to the legal profession.* | **recognize** | **befit** ◊ *At last James had*

an office that befitted his ~. | **enhance, improve, raise** ◊ *They are campaigning to raise the ~ of nurses.* | **elevate to** ◊ *The show has been elevated to cult ~.* | **lower** | **change** | **cement, confirm** ◊ *This performance confirmed her ~ as a world-class athlete.* | **maintain, retain** | **lose** ◊ *Churches seem to have lost some of their ~.* | **regain** | **apply for** ◊ *She applied for resident ~ but was turned down.* | **check, clarify, determine** ◊ *Officers could determine their legal ~.* | **deny sb, refuse sb** ◊ *Women are still denied equal ~ in the company.*
STATUS + NOUN **symbol** ◊ *Scars are ~ symbols among mountain-bike riders.*
PREP. **~ as** ◊ *China's ~ as an economic superpower* | **~ among** ◊ *The company has managed to maintain its ~ among retailers.* | **~ of** ◊ *the ~ of women*
PHRASES **change in ~** ◊ *the change in ~ of teachers*

status quo noun
VERB + STATUS QUO **defend, keep, maintain, preserve** ◊ *There are many people who wish to maintain the ~.* | **threaten, upset** | **change** | **restore**
PHRASES **a return to the ~** ◊ *They wanted a return to the ~ before the war.*

statute noun
ADJ. **legal** | **federal, parliamentary, state** | **criminal**
VERB + STATUTE **enact, pass** | **comply with, violate** | **uphold** ◊ *The Court upheld a federal ~.* | **interpret** ◊ *The Supreme Court interpreted the ~ in light of its recent rulings.* | **amend**
STATUTE + VERB **bar sth, prohibit sth** | **authorize sth, provide for sth** ◊ *The ~ provided for a maximum sentence of 53 months.* | **impose, require**
STATUTE + NOUN **law** ◊ *the obligations of the employer in common and ~ law* | **book** ◊ *This archaic law remained on the ~ books until last year.*
PREP. **by ~** ◊ *Local authorities are required by ~ to provide care homes for the elderly.* | **under (a/the) ~** ◊ *a trading company formed under ~*
PHRASES **~ of limitations** (*law*) ◊ *The judge threw out the case because the ~ of limitations had expired.*

stay noun
ADJ. **lengthy, long, prolonged** | **brief, short, temporary** | **indefinite** | **three-week, week-long, etc.** | **overnight** | **comfortable, enjoyable, pleasant** | **hospital, hotel** ◊ *In recent years the average hospital ~ for elderly patients has decreased.*
VERB + STAY **enjoy** ◊ *Did you enjoy your ~ in Prague?* | **shorten** | **extend, prolong** ◊ *She has extended her ~ by three days.*
PREP. **during a/the ~** ◊ *We did a lot of walking during our ~.* | **throughout a/the ~** ◊ *It poured throughout their ~.*
PHRASES **the duration of sb's ~, the length of sb's ~**

stay verb
ADV. **behind, on** ◊ *Alex ~ed behind when the others had gone.* ◊ *She failed her exam, and had to ~ on at school for another year.* (*BrE*) | **on** ◊ *My hat won't ~ on!* | **at home, home** (*AmE*), **indoors** ◊ *financial incentives for women to ~ at home with their children* | **away, out** | **here, there** | **late** ◊ *I'm ~ing late at the office tonight.* | **overnight** | **indefinitely** ◊ *We can't ~ here indefinitely.* | **together**
VERB + STAY **allow sb to** | **can, manage to** | **cannot** ◊ *I just couldn't ~ away.* | **want to** | **choose to, decide to** | **be going to, intend to** | **let sb** ◊ *Won't you let me ~?* | **ask sb to, beg sb to, plead with sb to** | **persuade sb to**
PREP. **at, in, on** | **for** ◊ *We ended up ~ing for lunch.* | **till, until** ◊ *I'm going to ~ until tomorrow.* | **with** ◊ *'Stay with me!' he pleaded.*
PHRASES **a place to ~** ◊ *He needs a place to ~.* | **a reason to ~** ◊ *I had no more reason to ~ in California.* | **~ and chat, help, etc.** ◊ *I'd love to ~ and chat but I must be going.* | **~ in one place** ◊ *He never ~s in one place for too long.* | **~ in place** ◊ *The tax cuts will ~ in place for two more years.* | **~ in touch** ◊ *Email is a great way to ~ in touch with friends.* | **~**

on top ◊ *the battle to ~ on top* ◊ *I try to ~ on top of musical trends.* | **~ the course** ◊ *He insists that he will not quit but will ~ the course.* | **~ the night (at sb's/with sb)** *(esp. BrE)* ◊ *She ~ed the night at Kathryn's.* | **~ this/that way** ◊ *At the moment, it's all fine. Let's hope it ~s that way!*

steady *adj.*

1 not moving or shaking
VERBS **be, feel, look, seem, sound** | **become** | **hold, remain, stay** ◊ *Inflation seems to be holding ~.* | **hold sb/sth, keep sb/sth** ◊ *Hold the ladder ~!*
ADV. **extremely, fairly, very, etc.** | **absolutely, perfectly, quite, rock** ◊ *His gaze was rock ~.* | **not quite** ◊ *She opened the letter with hands that were not quite ~.*

2 developing/happening at a regular rate
VERBS **be, seem** | **become** | **hold, remain** ◊ *Share prices have held ~ over the last few days.*
ADV. **remarkably, very** | **fairly, relatively**

steak *noun*
ADJ. **juicy, succulent** *(esp. BrE)*, **tender** | **tough** | **prime** *(esp. BrE)* ◊ *a good helping of tasty prime ~* | **lean** ◊ *A hamburger is far more fatty than lean ~.* | **12 oz, 18 oz, etc.** | **medium, medium-rare, rare, well done** ◊ *I like my ~ rare.* | **grilled** | **fillet/filet, flank** *(AmE)*, **loin** *(esp. BrE)*, **New York** *(AmE)*, **porterhouse** *(esp. AmE)*, **rib-eye, rump** *(esp. BrE)*, **Salisbury** *(AmE)*, **sirloin, strip** *(AmE)*, **T-bone, tenderloin** *(esp. AmE)* ◊ *a 12 oz New York strip ~* | **braising, stewing** *(both BrE)* | **beef** | **gammon** *(BrE)*, **salmon, tuna, etc.** | **chicken-fried** *(AmE)*
VERB + STEAK **eat, have** | **cook, fry, grill** ◊ *a lightly grilled ~*
STEAK + NOUN **knife** | **dinner** | **pie** *(BrE)*, **sandwich** | **house** (usually **steakhouse**)
→ Special page at FOOD

steam *noun*
ADJ. **hot**
... OF STEAM **cloud, jet** ◊ *The saucepan puffed little jets of ~.*
VERB + STEAM **generate, produce**
STEAM + VERB **come, escape** | **rise** ◊ *Steam rose from her mug of cocoa.* | **condense** | **drive sth** ◊ *The engine is driven by ~.* | **hiss**
STEAM + NOUN **power** | **engine, locomotive, ship** (usually **steamship**), **shovel** *(esp. AmE)*, **train, turbine** | **pipe** | **iron** | **bath, room** ◊ *The hotel has a ~ room.* | **age** *(esp. BrE)*
PHRASES **the age of ~** *(esp. BrE)*

steamer *noun*
ADJ. **coastal, lake, river** | **passenger, pleasure** *(both BrE)* | **tramp** | **paddle** *(BrE)*
VERB + STEAMER **board** ◊ *In 1926 they boarded the ~ for home.*
STEAMER + NOUN **trunk** *(esp. AmE)*
PREP. **by ~, on a/the ~, on board a/the ~**

steel *noun*
ADJ. **solid** | **forged, galvanized, mild, reinforced, rolled, stainless** ◊ *knives made of stainless ~* ◊ *a stainless-steel refrigerator*
VERB + STEEL **make, manufacture, produce** | **harden, temper, weld**
STEEL + NOUN **sheet** | **industry, manufacture** *(esp. BrE)* | **mill, plant, works** *(esp. BrE)*
PREP. **in ~** ◊ *the advantages of building in ~ and glass*

steep *adj.*
VERBS **be, look, seem** | **become, get, grow**
ADV. **extremely, fairly, very, etc.** | **impossibly, incredibly, terribly** ◊ *an incredibly ~ hill* | **increasingly** | **deceptively** ◊ *The terrain is often deceptively ~ (= steeper than you expect).*

steering *noun*
ADJ. **heavy, light** *(both BrE)* | **power, power-assisted** *(esp. BrE)* | **precise**
VERB + STEERING **have** ◊ *Does the car have power ~?*
STEERING + NOUN **column**

steering wheel *noun* → See also WHEEL
ADJ. **leather**

stem *noun*
ADJ. **long, tall** | **short** | **thick** | **slender, thin** | **main** | **flexible, strong** | **brittle, weak** | **flowering, woody** | **flower, plant** | **iris, rose, etc.**
VERB + STEM **break, cut, cut back, prune, prune back, remove, shorten, trim** ◊ *When the bush has finished flowering, cut back all the ~s.*
STEM + VERB **break**
PREP. **on a/the ~** ◊ *There are several leaves on each ~.*
PHRASES **the base of the ~** ◊ *Cut half an inch off the base of each ~.*

stench *noun*
ADJ. **overpowering, overwhelming, powerful, strong** | **unmistakable** | **appalling** *(esp. BrE)*, **awful, foul, horrible, nauseating, sickening, terrible, unpleasant** | **acrid, fetid, putrid**
VERB + STENCH **be filled with** ◊ *The air was filled with the overpowering ~ of decomposing vegetation.*
PREP. **~ of** ◊ *The ~ of death hung heavily over the land.*

step *noun*

1 in walking, running, etc.
ADJ. **large, small** | **heavy, light** | **quick, slow** | **hesitant** | **involuntary** ◊ *I gasped and took an involuntary ~ back.* | **careful** | **shaky, unsteady**
VERB + STEP **go, take** ◊ *He'd only gone a few ~s when he realized he'd left his keys behind.* | **retrace** ◊ *You might find your ticket if you retrace your ~s back to the car.*
PREP. **~ (away) from** ◊ *She was only a ~ away from the cliff edge.* | **~ towards/toward** ◊ *He took a hesitant ~ towards/ toward her.*
PHRASES **a spring in your ~** ◊ *I had a spring in my ~ when I walked into that office for the last time.* | **a ~ ahead, a ~ behind** *(both often figurative)* ◊ *He lagged a few ~s behind.* ◊ *She's always one ~ ahead of the competition.* | **a ~ back, a ~ backwards/backward** | **a ~ forward** | **a ~ sideways** | **a ~ closer** ◊ *We've moved a ~ closer to independence.* | **with each ~, with every ~** ◊ *He grew fainter with every ~.*

2 in dancing
ADJ. **dance** | **jive, tango, etc.**
VERB + STEP **execute, perform** ◊ *He executed some dance ~s for the judges.* | **learn** | **keep in** ◊ *She had trouble keeping in ~ with the others.*
PREP. **in ~, out of ~ (with)** ◊ *He was out of ~ with the music.*

3 action taken in order to achieve sth
ADJ. **big, considerable, giant, huge, massive** *(esp. BrE)* | **small** | **critical, crucial, decisive, essential, great, historic, important, key, major, significant, vital** | **first, initial, preliminary** | **final, last** | **additional, extra, further, next** ◊ *What's the next ~?* | **logical, necessary, reasonable** ◊ *We shall take all necessary ~s to prevent public disorder.* | **active** | **forward, positive** | **backward, retrograde** *(esp. BrE)* ◊ *The new law is seen by many as a backward ~.* | **bold, brave** | **dramatic, drastic, extraordinary, rare, unprecedented, unusual** | **irreversible, irrevocable** ◊ *It suddenly struck her that having a baby was an irrevocable ~.* | **careful, precautionary** | **faltering, tentative** ◊ *They have taken their first tentative ~s towards/toward democracy.* | **practical** | **welcome** | **immediate, urgent** ◊ *I shall take immediate ~s to have this matter put right.* | **false** ◊ *One false ~ could mean disaster.*
... OF STEPS **number, series**
VERB + STEP **go, make, take** | **follow** ◊ *If you follow all the ~s, nothing will go wrong.*
PREP. **~ in** ◊ *The move was a first ~ in establishing a union.* |

~ towards/toward ◊ *The talks mark a ~ towards/toward peace.*

PHRASES **a ~ closer (to sth)** ◊ *Greece moved a ~ closer to the final with last night's win.* | **a short ~ from sth to sth** ◊ *It's only a short ~ from disorder to complete chaos.* | **a ~ back, a ~ backwards/backward** ◊ *This can only be seen as a ~ backward.* | *The offer constitutes a considerable ~ forward.* | **step by step** ◊ *a step-by-step guide to setting up an aquarium* | **a ~ further** ◊ *If he goes one ~ further with this crazy idea, I'll resign.* | **a ~ in the right direction** ◊ *The new speed limit does not solve the problem, but it is a ~ in the right direction.* | **a ~ on the road to sth, a ~ on the way to sth**

4 on stairs, a ladder, etc.

ADJ. **bottom, top** | **door** (usually *doorstep*)
VERB + STEP **mind** (*esp. BrE*) ◊ *Mind the ~!*
PREP. **on a/the ~** ◊ *She paused on the top ~.*
PHRASES **a ~ down, a ~ up** ◊ *There are three ~s down to the kitchen.*

5 steps set of steps

ADJ. **front** | **back** | **porch** (*esp. AmE*) | **concrete, marble, wooden, etc.**
... OF STEPS **flight** ◊ *You have to go up four flights of ~s to get up to the roof.*
VERB + STEPS **go up, run up, walk up** ◊ *She went up the ~s to the side entrance.* | **ascend, climb, mount** | **descend** | **go down, run down, walk down** | **sit on**
STEPS + VERB **lead to sth** ◊ *The front ~s lead to an enormous terrace.*
PREP. **~ to** ◊ *the ~s to the roof* | **~ down to, ~ up to** ◊ *the ~s down to the pool*
PHRASES **the bottom of the ~s, the foot of the ~s, the top of the ~s**

step *verb*

ADV. **briskly, quickly** | **hastily, smartly** (*esp. BrE*) ◊ *He stepped back hastily from the edge.* | **slowly** | **quietly, silently** | **delicately, lightly** | **carefully, cautiously, gingerly** ◊ *He stepped gingerly over the cat.* | **boldly** | **aside, away, back, backwards/backward, close, down, forth** (*esp. AmE*), **forward, inside, out, outside, up** ◊ *Would you like to ~ inside for a few minutes?*
PREP. **across, from, in, in front of, into, on, onto, out of, over, towards/toward** ◊ *Don't ~ in the puddle.*

stereotype *noun*

ADJ. **common, popular, traditional, usual** | **negative** | **cultural, national, racial** | **gender, sexual** | **social** | **media** ◊ *the media ~ of Asian culture*
VERB + STEREOTYPE **hold** (*esp. AmE*) | **create, produce** | **use** | **confirm, perpetuate, reinforce** ◊ *Jokes perpetuate various national ~s.* | **conform to, fit** ◊ *Not all areas of the country fit the ~s.* | **break, challenge, defy** (*esp. AmE*), **dispel** (*esp. AmE*), **reject, shatter** ◊ *a writer who challenges sexual ~s*
PREP. **~ about** ◊ *common ~s about the French* | **~ of** ◊ *the ~ of women as passive victims*

sterile *adj.*

1 completely clean

VERBS **be** | **remain** | **make sth** | **keep sth** ◊ *This top fits over the bottle and keeps the teat ~.*
ADV. **completely**
PHRASES **under ~ conditions** ◊ *The experiment was performed under ~ conditions.*

2 not able to produce young animals/babies

VERBS **be** | **become** | **remain** | **leave sb, make sb, render sb**

3 with no interest or life

VERBS **be** | **become** ◊ *Their relationship had become ~ over the years.*
ADV. **very** | **increasingly** ◊ *the increasingly ~ debate on constitutional reform* | **largely** | **rather**

steward *noun*

ADJ. **chief, senior** | **air** (*BrE, old-fashioned*), **cabin, ship's** |

wine | **shop, union** (*both esp. BrE*) ◊ *She was elected a shop ~.* | **club** (*esp. BrE*) | **race** (*esp. BrE*), **state** (*AmE*), **track** (*AmE*) (*all sports*) ◊ *The race ~s will investigate the incident.* | **faithful, good, responsible** (*all esp. figurative*) ◊ *a faithful ~ of God's word*
VERB + STEWARD **act as** | **elect (sb)** (*esp. BrE*)
STEWARD + NOUN **steward's enquiry** (*BrE, sport*) ◊ *a steward's enquiry into Goodman's victory*
PREP. **~ to** ◊ *Moore was acting as ~ to Fleming.*
→ Note at JOB

stick *noun*

ADJ. **big, long** | **little, short** | **thick, thin**
... OF STICKS **bundle** | **pile**
VERB + STICK **carry, hold, wield** | **brandish, wave** ◊ *A mob came over the hill yelling and brandishing ~s.* | **throw**

stick *verb*

ADV. **just, simply** ◊ *He simply stuck a pin in at random among the names of candidates.*
PREP. **in, into, on, onto, through** ◊ *He stuck the note through her letter box.* (*BrE*) ◊ *He stuck the note through her mail slot.* (*AmE*)

PHR V **stick to sth**

ADV. **close, closely** | **rigidly, slavishly, strictly** ◊ *What is the point of ~ing slavishly to the rules?* | **doggedly, firmly, resolutely, stubbornly** ◊ *She simply made a decision and resolutely stuck to it.*
VERB + STICK TO **tend to** ◊ *I tended to ~ to tried and tested techniques.* | **decide to** | **be determined to**

sticky *adj.*

VERBS **be, feel** | **become, get** | **get sth, make sth**
ADV. **extremely, fairly, very, etc.** ◊ *It was covered in a really ~ mess.* | **all** ◊ *The rubber's gone all ~.* | **a little, slightly, etc.** ◊ *The paint was still slightly ~.*
PREP. **with** ◊ *His hair was ~ with blood.*
PHRASES **hot and ~** (*figurative*) ◊ *The air was hot and ~.*

stiff *adj.*

1 difficult to bend/move

VERBS **be, feel, lie, look, sit, stand** ◊ *She lay ~ and still beside him.* | **become, get, go** ◊ *My fingers had gone ~ with cold.*
ADV. **extremely, fairly, very, etc.** | **a little, slightly, etc.** | **all**
PREP. **with** ◊ *The clothes were ~ with dust and grease.*
PHRASES **(as) ~ as a board** ◊ *The captain stood as ~ as a board.*

2 having sore muscles

VERBS **be, feel** ◊ *He felt ~ all over.* | **get** ◊ *You'll get ~ if you don't have a hot bath.* | **leave sb, make sb** ◊ *All that digging made me really ~.*
ADV. **extremely, fairly, very, etc.** | **a little, slightly, etc.** | **all** ◊ *My arm's gone all ~.*
PREP. **from** ◊ *I was ~ from kneeling.*

3 strong/severe

VERBS **be, seem** ◊ *Their punishment seemed rather ~.*
ADV. **extremely, fairly, very, etc.** ◊ *in the face of some very ~ competition* | **a little, slightly, etc.**

4 not friendly or relaxed

VERBS **be, look, seem, sound** ◊ *She was aware that her words sounded ~.*
ADV. **extremely, fairly, very, etc.** ◊ *His manner seemed rather ~ and impersonal.* | **a little, slightly, etc.**

stigma *noun*

ADJ. **social**
VERB + STIGMA **bear, carry** ◊ *Being an unmarried mother used to carry a social ~.* | **suffer, suffer from** ◊ *He still suffered the ~ of having been rejected for the army.* | **avoid** | **overcome** ◊ *She had to overcome the ~ attached to mental illness.* | **reduce, remove** ◊ *Wider knowledge of the disease removed some of the ~ from it.*

STIGMA + VERB **be associated with sth, be attached to sth, surround** ◇ *There is still a lot of ~ attached to suicide.*
PREP. **~ to** ◇ *There is no ~ to losing your job.*

still *adj.*

1 not moving

VERBS **be, hold, keep, lie, sit, stand, stay** ◇ *Hold ~ a minute!* ◇ *Please sit ~!* | **hold sb/sth, keep sb/sth** ◇ *I held the cat ~ while the vet gave the injection.*
ADV. **very** | **absolutely, completely, perfectly, quite, stock-** ◇ *He stood stock-still, hardly daring to breathe.*

2 calm and quiet

VERBS **be** | **become, go** ◇ *Suddenly everything went ~.* | **remain**
ADV. **very** | **completely** ◇ *It was a completely ~, warm evening.* | **strangely** ◇ *The air was strangely ~ and silent.*

stillness *noun*

ADJ. **absolute, great, perfect, utter** | **sudden** ◇ *There was a sudden ~ in the air.* | **eerie** | **inner**
VERB + STILLNESS **break** ◇ *A voice behind the hedge broke the ~.*
PREP. **in (the) ~** ◇ *He lay in absolute ~.* ◇ *in the ~ of the night*

stimulate *verb*

ADV. **greatly, significantly, strongly** | **further** | **effectively** | **directly** ◇ *An interest rate increase directly ~s saving and reduces real expenditure.* | **in part** ◇ *The economy is recovering, ~d in part by government spending.* | **artificially** ◇ *This tax policy is artificially stimulating demand.* | **intellectually, sexually, visually** ◇ *These materials are designed to ~ students intellectually.* | **electrically**
VERB + STIMULATE **help (to)** | **be designed to, be intended to**

stimulating *adj.*

VERBS **be** | **find sb/sth**
ADV. **extremely, fairly, very, etc.** | **highly** | **intellectually, mentally, sexually, visually** ◇ *The documentary contains some visually ~ material.*

stimulation *noun*

ADJ. **direct** | **constant** | **electrical** ◇ *electrical ~ of nervous tissue* | **auditory, sensory, visual** | **sexual** | **intellectual, mental**
VERB + STIMULATION **need, require** | **get** ◇ *You don't get any intellectual ~ in this job.* | **give sb, provide (sb with)** ◇ *The camp provides plenty of ~ for the children.* | **respond to**
PHRASES **a lack of ~**

stimulus *noun*

ADJ. **great, major, powerful, strong** | **negative, positive** | **conditioned, unconditioned** | **environmental, external** ◇ *plant growth responses to environmental stimuli* | **initial** | **auditory, sensory, verbal, visual** | **emotional, intellectual, sexual** | **economic, fiscal, monetary**
VERB + STIMULUS **act as, give, provide** | **react to, respond to**
STIMULUS + VERB **come from sth** ◇ *The initial ~ came from a letter in the newspaper.*
STIMULUS + NOUN **bill, package, plan** (*all AmE*) ◇ *Congress passed the President's economic ~ package.*
PREP. **~ for** ◇ *The very act of lying down in bed should provide a strong ~ for sleep.* | **~ to** ◇ *A reduction in corporate tax should act as a ~ to economic activity.* ◇ *a response to a ~*
PHRASES **a response to a ~** ◇ *The pupils dilate in response to chemical stimuli.*

sting *noun*

1 of an insect, etc.

ADJ. **nasty, painful, sharp** | **bee, scorpion, wasp, etc.** | **nettle** | **deadly, fatal**
VERB + STING **have** ◇ *The scorpion has a ~ that can be deadly.* |

get ◇ *You can get a nasty ~ from a jellyfish.* | **give sb** | **feel** | **remove** | **be allergic to** ◇ *She's allergic to bee ~s.*

2 sharp pain

ADJ. **hot, sharp** ◇ *the hot ~ of tears*
VERB + STING **feel** ◇ *He felt the sharp ~ of the soap in his eyes.*

3 (*esp. AmE*) plan by police to catch criminals

ADJ. **undercover** | **FBI, police** | **drug**
VERB + STING **mount, set up** | **be arrested in, be caught by, be caught in** ◇ *She was arrested in an undercover ~ operation.*
STING + NOUN **operation**

stink *noun*

1 very unpleasant smell

ADJ. **acrid, overpowering**
STINK + NOUN **bomb**
PREP. **~ of** ◇ *the acrid ~ of cordite*

2 (*informal*) very strong complaint about sth

ADJ. **big, tremendous**
VERB + STINK **cause, kick up, make, raise** ◇ *Residents are kicking up a ~ about the amount of litter in the town.*

stint *noun*

ADJ. **long** | **brief, short** | **one-year, two-year, etc.**
VERB + STINT **do, serve** ◇ *She's doing a brief ~ at the World Bank.* ◇ *He later served a ~ in the Navy.* | **enjoy, have** ◇ *The singer enjoyed a short ~ at number one.* ◇ *He had three ~s as coach.* | **start** | **complete, finish** | **include** ◇ *His résumé includes a ~ as a professor of physics.*
PREP. **after a/the ~** | **during a/the ~** ◇ *She met her husband during her ~ at the London office.*

stipulation *noun*

VERB + STIPULATION **have, make** ◇ *The only ~ the bank makes is that you must be in employment.* | **include** ◇ *My contract includes the ~ that I have a seat on the board.* | **drop**
PREP. **with the ~** ◇ *He left all his money to the town, with the ~ that it be used to build a museum.* | **~ about, ~ as to** ◇ *There's no ~ as to the amount you can invest.*

stir *noun*

1 action of stirring

ADJ. **good** (*esp. BrE*)
VERB + STIR **give sth** ◇ *Give the mixture a good ~.*

2 general excitement or shock

ADJ. **big, considerable, great, real** | **media, political** (*both esp. AmE*)
VERB + STIR **cause, create**
PREP. **~ about, ~ over** ◇ *There was quite a ~ about the book.* | **~ among** ◇ *The discovery caused something of a ~ among physicists.*
PHRASES **quite a ~, something of a ~** (*esp. BrE*)

stir *verb*

1 mix a liquid

ADV. **thoroughly, well** | **carefully, gently** | **vigorously** | **gradually** | **all the time** (*BrE*), **constantly, continuously, frequently** ◇ *Boil the mixture, stirring frequently.* | **occasionally** | **together** | **in** ◇ *Gradually ~ in the beaten egg.*
PREP. **into** ◇ *Chop an onion and ~ it into the sauce.*
PHRASES **~ over a high, low, etc. heat** ◇ *Stir over a medium heat for three minutes.*

2 move

ADV. **barely, hardly** ◇ *The wind hardly stirred the surface of the water.* | **slightly** | **slowly** | **suddenly** | **restlessly** ◇ *The students stirred restlessly in their seats.* | **sleepily** | **uneasily**
PHRASES **~ in your sleep**

3 make sb feel an emotion

ADV. **deeply** ◇ *It was not music to set hearts on fire or deeply ~ the emotions.* | **up** ◇ *Going back there stirred up a lot of memories for her.*

stitch *noun*

1 in sewing

ADJ. **decorative, embroidery** | **hand, machine** | **blanket, chain, cross, running, satin, seam, straight, zigzag, etc.**
VERB + STITCH **do, put, sew** ◇ *Can you do chain ~?* | **sew with, use** ◇ *The edge was sewn with blanket ~.* | **remove, take out**

2 in knitting

ADJ. **garter, stocking, etc.**
VERB + STITCH **cast off, cast on** | **drop, pick up**

3 in a wound

ADJ. **dissolvable** | **butterfly**
VERB + STITCH **need, require** ◇ *He needed four ~es.* | **get, have, receive** ◇ *I had to have five ~es when I cut my finger.* | **insert** (*BrE*), **put in** ◇ *She had five ~es put in her cheek.* | **remove, take out** ◇ *He has now had the ~es taken out.* | **get out, have out** ◇ *When are you having your ~es out?*
STITCH + VERB **dissolve**
PREP. **~ in** ◇ *He had twenty ~es in a head wound.*

stock *noun*

1 available supply of sth

ADJ. **good, high, huge, large** | **low** | **adequate** | **declining, dwindling, falling** ◇ *declining fish ~s in the oceans* | **surplus** | **buffer, reserve** ◇ *A buffer ~ of grain was held in case of emergency shortages.* | **fresh, new** | **old** | **existing** | **breeding, fish, food, oil, etc.** | **film** | **housing** (*esp. BrE*) ◇ *The housing ~ is no longer large enough for the population.* | **capital, money** | **rolling** (*BrE*) ◇ *The rail company is investing in new rolling ~.*
VERB + STOCK **carry, have, hold, keep** ◇ *The big supermarkets carry huge ~s of most goods.* | **add to, increase** | **get rid of, reduce** ◇ *They're getting rid of their old ~.* | **maintain, protect** ◇ *laws to protect fish ~s* | **replace, replenish**
STOCK + VERB **be up, increase** | **be down, decline, dwindle, run low** ◇ *Stocks of coal are running dangerously low.* | **last** ◇ *The offer is only available while ~s last.*
STOCK + NOUN **room** (usually **stockroom**) | **levels** | **control** (*esp. BrE*)
PREP. **from ~** ◇ *We can supply the table from ~.* | **in ~** ◇ *Do you have futon beds in ~ or will I have to order one?* | **out of ~** ◇ *Red tights are out of ~.*

2 (*esp. AmE*) share in a company → See also SHARE

ADJ. **company** | **growth** | **domestic, foreign** | **common, dividend-paying, preferred, restricted** | **traded** ◇ *publicly traded ~* | **energy, financial, gold, high-tech, Internet, technology, etc.** | **tracking**
VERB + STOCK **acquire, buy, invest in, purchase** | **cash in, dispose of, sell** | **deal in, trade** | **have, hold, own** | **issue** | **value** ◇ *The ~s were valued at $100 000.*
STOCK + VERB **be down, be up** | **drop, fall, go down, plummet, plunge, sink** | **go up, rally, rise, soar** | **hit sth, reach sth** ◇ *The company's ~ hit an all-time high of $94.66.*
STOCK + NOUN **exchange, market** | **price** | **fund** | **index** | **option**
PREP. **in ~s** ◇ *She has about $30 000 in ~s.*
PHRASES **investment in ~s** | **~s and bonds** (*AmE*), **~s and shares** (*BrE*) | **the price of the ~s, the value of the ~s** ◇ *The total value of the ~s was over $3 million.*

3 liquid used for making soups, sauces, etc.

ADJ. **beef, chicken, fish, vegetable, etc.**
VERB + STOCK **make** | **dilute, reduce** | **flavour/flavor** ◇ *You can flavour/flavor the ~ with bay leaves.*
STOCK + NOUN **cube**
PREP. **in a/the ~** ◇ *Poach the fish in the ~.*

stock *verb* be stocked

ADV. **plentifully, well** | **fully, properly**
PREP. **with** ◇ *gift shops ~ed with cheap souvenirs*

stockbroker *noun* → See also BROKER

ADJ. **large** | **leading** | **private-client** (*BrE*) | **City** (*BrE*) | **online**
VERB + STOCKBROKER **consult**
STOCKBROKER + NOUN **belt** (*BrE*)

stomach

stock exchange *noun*

VERB + STOCK EXCHANGE **trade (sth) on** ◇ *The company's shares will be traded on the Stock Exchange.* | **float sth on** (*esp. BrE*) ◇ *The club may be floated on the ~.* | **be listed on, be quoted on** ◇ *Both companies are listed on the Stock Exchange.* | **be delisted from**
STOCK EXCHANGE + VERB **close, open** ◇ *Bahrain's ~ closed up 10.09 points today at 2160.09.*
PREP. **on the ~** ◇ *to lose money on the ~*

stockholder (*esp. AmE*) *noun*

ADJ. **sole** | **major, majority, principal** | **minority** | **preferred** ◇ *The company told its preferred ~s that it couldn't make its dividend payments.* | **existing** ◇ *the distribution of remaining stock to existing ~s*
VERB + STOCKHOLDER **cheat, defraud, mislead** ◇ *She was charged with having misled her ~s.* | **benefit, enrich, reward** ◇ *The corporations' goal is to enrich their ~s.*
STOCKHOLDER + VERB **vote**
STOCKHOLDER + NOUN **meeting** ◇ *the annual ~ meeting*
PREP. **~ in** ◇ *the major ~ in the company*

stocking *noun*

ADJ. **fishnet, sheer** | **laddered** (*BrE*) | **nylon, silk, etc.** | **Christmas** ◇ *trinkets you can use to fill a Christmas ~*
... OF STOCKINGS **pair**
VERB + STOCKING **pull on** | **ladder** (*BrE*), **rip** ◇ *She laddered her ~ on a bush.* ◇ *I've ripped my ~s again.* | **fill, stuff** (*esp. AmE*) ◇ *Santa will be filling the ~s at Christmas time.* | **hang** ◇ *The ~s were hung by the chimney.*
STOCKING + NOUN **filler** (*BrE*), **stuffer** (*AmE*) ◇ *This book is a light-hearted Christmas ~ filler/stuffer.*
→ Special page at CLOTHES

stomach *noun*

1 part of the body where food is digested

ADJ. **empty, full** ◇ *You shouldn't drink wine on an empty ~ (= without eating food).* | **dodgy** (*BrE, informal*), **queasy, upset** ◇ *She's been off work with an upset ~.* | **strong** ◇ *You need a strong ~ to go on the giant roller coaster.* | **sensitive, weak** | **rumbling** ◇ *the sound of my rumbling ~*
VERB + STOMACH **turn** ◇ *The smell of the dog turned his ~.* | **settle** ◇ *He ordered a sandwich to settle his ~.* | **settle in** ◇ *A feeling of nausea settled in her ~.* | **pump** ◇ *He had his ~ pumped after taking an overdose.*
STOMACH + VERB **churn, heave, lurch** ◇ *My ~ lurched as another big wave hit the boat.* | **growl, rumble** | **clench, knot** (*esp. AmE*), **knot up** (*esp. AmE*) | **tighten, turn, turn over, twist**
STOMACH + NOUN **ache, ailment** (*esp. AmE*), **bug, cancer, complaint** (*esp. BrE*), **cramps, disorder, illness** (*esp. BrE*), **pain, problems, ulcer, upset** ◇ *The drug can cause mild ~ upset.* ◇ *He had a ~ upset.* (*BrE*) | **lining, wall** | **acid, juices** | **contents** ◇ *Human remains were found among the ~ contents of the shark.* | **pump, tube**
PREP. **in the/your ~** ◇ *The pains in his ~ were becoming worse.* ◇ *enzymes in the ~*
PHRASES **the contents of your ~** ◇ *He violently emptied the contents of his ~.* | **feel sick to your ~, sth makes you sick to your ~** ◇ *It makes me sick to my ~ to hear such stupid attitudes.* | **the pit of your ~** ◇ *I felt a sickening feeling in the pit of my ~ when I saw the ambulance.* | **get a knot in your ~, have a knot in your ~** | **your ~ is in knots** (*esp. AmE*) ◇ *I would get knots in my ~ because I was so scared.*

2 front part of the body below the chest

ADJ. **firm, flat, toned, washboard** | **bulging, fat, flabby, large** | **bloated, swollen** | **bare**
VERB + STOMACH **hold in, pull in, suck in** ◇ *He sucked in his ~ as he walked along the beach.* | **lie on, roll (over) onto** | **clutch, hold** ◇ *'Call a doctor!' he said, clutching his ~.* | **pat,**

rub ◇ *'I'm eating for two now!' she said, patting her ~.* | **kick (sb in), punch (sb in), stab (sb in)**, etc. ◇ *He was stabbed in the ~ during a street brawl.*

STOMACH + VERB **protrude, stick out**

STOMACH + NOUN **muscles** | **injury** (*esp. BrE*), **strain** (*BrE*), **wound**

PREP. **on the/your ~** ◇ *I lay on my ~ on the beach.*

stone *noun*

1 hard solid substance

ADJ. **heavy** | **hard** | **rough, smooth** | **weathered** | **carved** ◇ *a carved ~ fireplace* | **dressed, polished** | **crushed** | **building**

...OF STONE **block, slab**

VERB + STONE **break, cut, hew (sth from/out of)** ◇ *Convicts were made to break ~ for the roads.* ◇ *The ~ is cut into blocks ready for building.* | **be built from/in/of/out of, be carved from/in/of/out of, be made from/in/of/out of** ◇ *names carved in ~* | **carve sth in**

STONE + NOUN **block, flag** (*BrE*), **slab** ◇ *The path's ~ slabs were worn and broken.* | **arch, archway, bridge, building, floor, house, pillar, stairs, structure, wall**, etc. | **monument, sculpture, tablet** | **axe/ax, tool** | **mason** (usually **stonemason**) ◇ *He went to work as a stonemason.*

PREP. **in ~** ◇ *He is a sculptor who works mainly in ~.*

PHRASES **be set in, be written in** (*both figurative*) ◇ *These rules are not set in ~.*

2 (*esp. BrE*) small piece of rock → See also ROCK

ADJ. **sharp** | **smooth** | **round** | **loose** ◇ *Some loose ~s tumbled down the slope behind her.*

...OF STONES **heap, pile**

VERB + STONE **cast** (*figurative*), **hurl, throw** ◇ *The boys were caught throwing ~s at passing trains.*

3 piece of stone shaped for a particular purpose

ADJ. **foundation** | **memorial** | **paving, stepping** | **cobble, kerb/curb** (usually **cobblestone**, etc.) | **grinding, sharpening** | **pumice** | **standing**

STONE + NOUN **circle** ◇ *The ~ circle at Avebury is larger than Stonehenge.*

4 precious stone

ADJ. **gem** (usually **gemstone**), **precious, semi-precious**

VERB + STONE **mine** | **cut** | **set** ◇ *She had the ~ set in a ring.*

STONE + VERB **glitter, shine**

5 (*BrE*) measure of weight

→ Note at MEASURE

stool *noun*

ADJ. **high, tall** | **small** | **three-legged** | **swivel** | **step** (*esp. AmE*) | **bar, drum, kitchen, milking, piano** | **wooden**

VERB + STOOL **be perched on, perch on, sit (down) on** ◇ *He was perched on a bar ~, ordering a beer.* | **get off** | **pull up** ◇ *She pulled up a ~ next to me.*

stop *noun*

1 stopping or staying

ADJ. **long** | **brief, short** | **overnight** | **abrupt, sharp, sudden** | **emergency** | **scheduled, unscheduled** | **bathroom** (*esp. AmE*), **toilet** (*BrE*) | **fuel, lunch, refuelling/refueling, rest**, etc. | **pit** ◇ *The cars made two pit ~s during the race.* ◇ *We made a pit ~ to buy a bottle of water.* (*AmE, figurative*) | **campaign** (*AmE*) ◇ *Cheney is making a campaign ~ in Lubbock, Texas.* | **traffic** (*AmE*) ◇ *The police found the drugs during a routine traffic ~.*

VERB + STOP **have, make** ◇ *We had a lunch ~ at Timperley.*

STOP + NOUN **light, sign**

PREP. **~ at** ◇ *There will be a ~ at Aboyne.* | **~ for** ◇ *a ~ for refreshments*

PHRASES **bring sth to a ~** ◇ *She brought the car to an abrupt ~.* | **come, draw, pull, slow**, etc. **to a ~** ◇ *The truck came to a sudden ~.* ◇ *At lunchtime everything comes to a complete ~.* | **put a ~ to sth** ◇ *to put a ~ to all the arguments*

2 for a bus, etc.

ADJ. **bus, subway** (*AmE*), **tram, tube** (*BrE*) | **request** (*BrE*)

VERB + STOP **get off at** | **miss** ◇ *We were chatting and missed our ~.* | **reach**

PREP. **at a/the ~** ◇ *We dropped the kids off at the bus ~.* | **between ~s** ◇ *You're not allowed to get off between ~s.*

stop *verb*

ADV. **abruptly, dead, immediately, in sb's tracks, short, suddenly** ◇ *Suddenly he stopped dead: what was he doing? The question stopped Alice dead in her tracks.* | **altogether, completely** ◇ *The sobs came less frequently, then stopped altogether.* | **for a moment, momentarily, temporarily** | **never** ◇ *That phone never ~s ringing!*

VERB + STOP **can** ◇ *He couldn't ~ thinking about her.* | **try to** | **be going to** ◇ *When is the violence going to ~?* | **want (sb/sth) to** ◇ *I was enjoying myself so much I didn't want to ~.* | **have to, must, need to** ◇ *We need to ~ making excuses.* ◇ *He's dangerous and needs to be stopped.*

PREP. **from** ◇ *They tried to ~ me from leaving.*

PHRASES **know how to ~, know when to ~** ◇ *He never knows when to ~.*

stopover *noun*

ADJ. **brief** | **extended, prolonged** | **one-night, two-hour**, etc.

VERB + STOPOVER **have, make**

STOPOVER + NOUN **point** ◇ *a ~ point on the way from Mexico to the Philippines*

PREP. **at a/the ~** ◇ *We had our tickets checked at each ~.* | **during a/the ~** ◇ *During our two-day ~ in Bangkok we saw most of the sights.*

storage *noun*

ADJ. **safe, secure** ◇ *the safe ~ of nuclear weapons* | **cold, dry** | **long-term, temporary** | **additional, extra** | **disk** ◇ *the available disk ~ capacity* | **food, fuel, water**, etc. | **data, information**, etc.

VERB + STORAGE **put sth in, put sth into** ◇ *The strawberries are put into cold ~ for several months.* | **take sth out of** | **provide** | **be used for** ◇ *The side rooms are used for ~.*

STORAGE + NOUN **facilities** | **device, medium, system** ◇ *digital ~ devices* | **area, capacity, space** | **building, depot, room, shed, site** | **cabinet, compartment, cupboard, locker, unit** ◇ *a handy ~ compartment below the oven* | **bin, container, jar, tank, vessel** | **heater** (*BrE*) | **battery** (*AmE*) | **costs** | **life** ◇ *The cheese has a ~ life of two months.*

PREP. **in ~** ◇ *All their furniture is in ~ until they come back from Africa.*

store *noun*

1 place where you can buy things → See also SHOP

ADJ. **big, large, major** (*esp. BrE*) | **small** | **retail** | **department** | **high-street** (*BrE*), **local, village** (*esp. AmE*) | **chain** | **online** ◇ *You can buy music from an online ~.* | **discount** | **convenience, corner** (*esp. BrE*), **general** | **specialty** (*AmE*) | **outlet** | **DIY** (*esp. BrE*), **electrical** (*esp. BrE*), **grocery** (*esp. AmE*), **hardware** (*esp. AmE*), **health-food** (*esp. AmE*), **liquor** (*AmE*), **record, toy, video**, etc. | **dime** (*AmE*) | **thrift** (*AmE*) | **flagship** ◇ *Ralph Lauren's flagship ~ on Madison Avenue*

...OF STORES **chain**

VERB + STORE **go to, visit** | **close, open** ◇ *The company plans to open two new ~s in Dublin.* | **operate, run** ◇ *The company operates four ~s in Maryland.* | **hit** ◇ *The CD will hit ~s in January.*

STORE + VERB **carry sth, offer sth, sell sth** ◇ *The ~ offers a comprehensive line of auto parts.* | **close, open**

STORE + NOUN **chain** | **account** (*AmE*), **card** (*BrE*) | **shelf, window** (*both esp. AmE*) ◇ *The new book has been flying off ~ shelves.* | **brand** (*esp. AmE*) ◇ *Buying ~ brands certainly works out cheaper.* | **sales** (*esp. AmE*) | **clerk, employee** (*both AmE*) | **manager, owner** | **detective** (*esp. BrE*)

PREP. **at a/the ~, in a/the ~**

PHRASES **the back of a/the ~, the front of a/the ~**

2 supply for future use

ADJ. **good, great, large, vast** | **small** | **food** | **energy, fat** ◇ *your body's fat* ~*s*
VERB + STORE **have, keep** | **build up**
STORE + NOUN **cupboard** (*BrE*), **room** (usually *storeroom*)
PREP. **~ of** ◇ *a vast ~ of knowledge*

3 place for keeping sth

ADJ. **cold, dry** ◇ *Beef and lamb are hung in a cold ~ for at least a week.* | **temporary** | **ammunition, equipment, grain,** etc.
STORE + VERB **hold sth** ◇ *The grain ~ holds several thousand tons.*
PREP. **in a/the ~** ◇ *You'll find a ladder in the equipment ~.* | **~ for** ◇ *We're using the shed as a temporary ~ for all our stuff.*

store verb

ADV. **carefully, properly** (*esp. BrE*), **safely, securely** ◇ *The paintings were carefully* ~*d in crates.* | **conveniently, easily** ◇ *Butane can be conveniently* ~*d as a liquid in a can.* | **permanently, temporarily** | **digitally, electronically** ◇ *electronically* ~*d information* | **separately** | **together** | **away, up**

storey (*esp. BrE*) (*AmE usually* **story**) noun

ADJ. **lower** | **top, upper** | **first, second,** etc. ◇ *He jumped out of the second-storey/second-story window.*
VERB + STOREY/STORY **have** ◇ *The house has three* ~*s.* | **occupy** ◇ *The kitchen occupies the lower* ~. | **add** ◇ *They plan to add an extra* ~.
PREP. **on a/the ~** ◇ *I live on the top* ~.
PHRASES **five, ten,** etc. **storeys/stories high, five, ten,** etc. **storeys/stories tall** (*esp. AmE*) ◇ *The building is four storeys/stories high.*

storm noun

1 period of bad weather

ADJ. **bad, big, devastating, ferocious, fierce, great, heavy, killer** (*informal, esp. AmE*), **major, monster** (*AmE, informal*), **raging, severe, terrible, tremendous, violent** | **perfect** (*figurative, esp. AmE*) ◇ *The company was hit by a perfect ~ of negative conditions that converged on it.* | **approaching, gathering** ◇ *the dark clouds of an approaching* ~ | **freak** | **summer, winter,** etc. | **tropical** | **monsoon** | **electric, electrical, lightning, thunder** (usually *thunderstorm*) | **hail, rain, snow, wind** (usually *hailstorm,* etc.) | **ice** (*esp. AmE*) | **dust, sand** (usually *sandstorm*) | **magnetic, solar**
VERB + STORM **be in for** ◇ *I think we're in for a ~* (= going to have one). | **brave** ◇ *She had to brave an ice ~ to get to the interview.* | **shelter from, wait out** (*esp. AmE*) ◇ *We tried to find a safe place to wait out the ~.* | **track** (*esp. AmE*) ◇ *We'll be tracking the ~ as it makes its way across the Gulf.*
STORM + VERB **hit (sth), strike (sth)** ◇ *It was the worst ~ to hit Sri Lanka this century.* ◇ *Where were you when the ~ struck?* | **rage** ◇ *The ~ raged all night.* | **be approaching, be brewing, be coming** ◇ *A ~ had been brewing all day.* | **blow up** (*esp. BrE*), **break** ◇ *The ~ broke while we were on the mountain.* | **blow in, move in** ◇ *A ~ blew in off the ocean.* | **move across, over,** etc. **sth, sweep across, over,** etc. **sth** ◇ *A major winter ~ is moving across the country today.* | **batter sth, lash sth, ravage sth, sweep sth** ◇ *a boat battered by the ~* ◇ *Winter* ~*s swept the coasts.* | **abate, blow itself out, blow over, clear, clear up, pass, subside** ◇ *The ~ blew over after a couple of hours.* | **last** ◇ *The ~ lasted for three days.*
STORM + NOUN **cloud** (*often figurative*) ◇ *In 1939 the ~ clouds gathered over Europe.* | **surge** (*esp. AmE*), **water** ◇ *We're forecasting 14 to 16 feet of ~ surge.* | **damage** ◇ *Insurance companies face hefty payouts for ~ damage.* | **warning** ◇ *a tropical ~ warning* | **door** (*AmE*), **drain, window** (*AmE*)
PREP. **during a/the ~, in a/the ~**
PHRASES **at the height of the ~** | **bear the brunt of the ~, take the brunt of the ~** ◇ *The east coast of Florida bore the brunt of the ~.* | **seek shelter from the ~** (*often figurative*), **take shelter from the ~** ◇ *I took shelter from the ~ in the*

clubhouse. | **the calm before the ~** (*figurative*) | **the eye of the ~** (*often figurative*)

2 violent display of strong feeling

ADJ. **approaching, coming, gathering** ◇ *a gathering ~ of discontent* | **media, political** | **fire** (usually *firestorm*) (*figurative, esp. AmE*) ◇ *His comments brought down a firestorm of criticism.*
VERB + STORM **arouse, cause, create, provoke** (*esp. BrE*), **raise, spark** (*esp. BrE*), **unleash** | **face** | **ride out, survive, weather** ◇ *The government is determined to ride out the political ~ caused by its new immigration policy.*
STORM + VERB **blow up, break, erupt** (*all esp. BrE*) ◇ *A ~ blew up between Britain and the US over Venezuela.* | **blow over, pass** ◇ *The [political ~ had blown over at last.*
PREP. **amid a/the ~** (*esp. BrE*) ◇ *The band toured Ireland amid a ~ of controversy.* | **~ between** | **~ of** ◇ *His comments created a ~ of protest in the media.*

story noun

1 account of events/people, true or invented

ADJ. **true** | **plausible** | **false, made-up** ◇ *She told the police a false ~ about being attacked.* | **fictional, real-life** | **untold** | **published** ◇ *his first published short ~* | **apocryphal** | **cock and bull, tall** (*esp. BrE*) ◇ *No one would believe such a tall ~.* | **official** ◇ *The official ~ was that the singer had broken his arm falling in the shower.* | **personal** | **wild** | **convincing** | **compelling, dramatic, exciting, fantastic, fascinating, good, great, interesting, intriguing, nice, touching, wonderful** | **amazing, bizarre, colourful/colorful, crazy** (*esp. AmE*), **extraordinary, incredible, outrageous, remarkable, strange** | **inspirational, inspiring** | **amusing, entertaining, feel-good, funny** | **epic** ◇ *the epic ~ of a family's escape from war* | **complex, elaborate** | **straightforward** | **awful, horrific, horrifying, nasty, shocking, terrible, tragic** | **sorry** (*esp. BrE*) ◇ *His life was a sorry ~ of betrayal and rejection.* | **depressing, heart-rending, moving, poignant, sad** | **well-known, familiar** ◇ *the familiar ~ of a star who turns to drink and drugs* | **popular** ◇ *There is one popular ~ in the town of a man-eating cat that lives in the forest.* | **life, success** ◇ *She told them her life ~.* | **coming-of-age, coming-out, rags-to-riches** ◇ *The movie is the rags-to-riches ~ of a country girl who becomes a famous singer.* | **hard-luck, sob** (*both disapproving*) ◇ *He was boring people with more of his hard-luck stories.* ◇ *She gave me some sob ~ about losing her credit cards.* | **coherent** ◇ *The movie lacks a coherent ~.* | **entire, full, whole** ◇ *I suspected he hadn't told us the whole ~.* | **short** ◇ *a collection of short stories* | **original** ◇ *The screenplay sticks to the original ~.* | **back** (usually *backstory*) ◇ *The writers have to create backstories for their characters.* | **children's** | **classic** | **bedtime** | **adventure, Bible, biblical, crime, detective, fairy** (*esp. BrE*), **ghost, horror, love, spy,** etc.
...OF STORIES **collection** ◇ *a collection of stories by modern writers*
VERB + STORY **hear** | **read (sb)** ◇ *My dad sometimes read me a ~ at bedtime.* | **write** | **narrate, recount, relate, retell, tell (sb)** | **embellish, embroider** | **believe** ◇ *The police didn't believe her ~.* | **stick to** ◇ *We must stick to our ~ about the accident.* | **change** ◇ *At first he denied everything, but then he changed his ~ and said it was an accident.* | **share (with sb), swap** ◇ *We swapped stories about our worst teachers.* | **spread** | **publish**
STORY + VERB **circulate, go around, go round** (*esp. BrE*), **spread** ◇ *A ~ was going around that the factory was in line for closure.* | **abound** ◇ *Stories abound of vandalism and looting.* | **emerge** | **begin, open, start** ◇ *The ~ opens with a man hiding from the police.* | **progress, unfold** ◇ *The motives of the hero become clearer as the ~ unfolds.* | **end** | **be called sth, be entitled sth, be titled sth** (*esp. AmE*) | **be set in...** ◇ *The ~ is set in India in the 1930s.* | **be based on sth** | **concern sth, involve sth, revolve around sth** | **contain sth** | **illustrate sth** ◇ *This ~ illustrates the dangers of living on credit.*
STORY + NOUN **teller** (usually *storyteller*) | **telling** (usually

storytelling) | **line** (usually *storyline*) ◇ *His novels always have the same basic storyline.*

PREP. **according to a/the ~** | **~ about** ◇ *a ~ about time travel* | **~ of** ◇ *the ~ of the Beatles* ◇ *a ~ of moral redemption*

PHRASES **a fragment of a/the ~**, **a part of a/the ~** ◇ *We had difficulty in piecing together the fragments of her ~.* | **the rest of the ~** | **but that's another ~** ◇ *Many years later I returned to Africa—but that's another ~* (= I am not going to talk about it now). | **(that's) a likely ~** (*ironic*) ◇ *He said he'd met Madonna. A likely ~.* | **it's a long ~** ◇ *'How come you only have one shoe on?' 'It's a long ~.'* | **sb's half of the ~**, **sb's side of the ~** ◇ *The teacher punished me without listening to my side of the ~.* | **tell a different ~** ◇ *Antidepressants are widely believed to be effective medications. The data, however, tell a different ~.* | **the moral of the ~** ◇ *The moral of this ~ is that you should never take things for granted.* | **the ~ goes (that…)** (= used to describe what people are saying although it may not be correct) ◇ *She never saw him again—or so the ~ goes.* | **the ~ of my life** ◇ *Out of work with no money—that's the ~ of my life.* | **to cut a long ~ short**, **to make a long ~ short** ◇ *Anyway, to cut a long ~ short* (= not to give all the details), *we had this argument and I haven't seen him since.* | **a version of a ~** ◇ *According to Rachel's version of the ~, they threw the key in the river.*

2 report in a newspaper, etc.

ADJ. **big, huge** (*esp. AmE*), **top** ◇ *The biggest ~ of the day was the signing of the peace agreement.* ◇ *And now back to our top ~ tonight…* | **exclusive** | **breaking** (*esp. AmE*) ◇ *We'll have more on this breaking ~ as developments come in to us.* | **feature** (*AmE*) ◇ *National Geographic ran a feature ~ on dinosaurs.* | **main** | **full** ◇ *Full ~ on page 3.* | **scare** ◇ *scare stories about the harmful effects of the vaccination* | **inside** ◇ *The magazine gives the inside ~ of life in a rock band.* | **sensational** | **lurid, sordid** ◇ *lurid stories of politicians' sexual adventures* | **cover, front-page, lead** ◇ *The magazine chose the peace process as its cover ~.* | **news** | **political** | **media, newspaper, wire** (*esp. AmE*)

VERB + STORY **file, write** ◇ *More than one correspondent filed a ~ about the incident.* | **carry, cover, print, publish, report, run** ◇ *Every newspaper carried the ~.* ◇ *He's covering the ~ in Gaza for CNN.* | **follow** ◇ *We will continue to follow this ~ and bring you the latest developments.* | **break** (*esp. AmE*) ◇ *The New York Times broke the ~ and others picked it up.*

STORY + VERB **break** (*esp. AmE*) ◇ *The ~ broke in January.*

PREP. **~ about,** | **~ of** ◇ *the ~ of his arrest*

3 (*AmE*) → See STOREY

stove *noun* → See also COOKER, RANGE

ADJ. **hot** | **kitchen** (*esp. AmE*) | **electric** (*esp. AmE*), **gas, wood, wood-burning** | **pot-bellied** (*AmE*) | **cast-iron, iron** (*both esp. AmE*) | **camp** (*AmE*), **camping** (*BrE*), **portable, Primus™** (*esp. BrE*)

VERB + STOVE **light** | **turn off, turn on** (*both esp. AmE*) | **touch** ◇ *Don't touch the ~! It's hot.*

PREP. **on the ~** ◇ *A pot of soup was cooking on the ~.*

PHRASES **slave over a hot ~** (*humorous*) ◇ *I've been slaving over a hot ~ all day for you!*

stow *verb*

ADV. **carefully, neatly, safely** | **quickly** | **away**

PREP. **in** ◇ *The suitcases were now safely ~ed away in the back of the truck.* | **on** ◇ *The containers were ~ed on deck.*

straight *adj.*

1 not bent or curved

VERBS **be, look** | **become** | **stay** | **keep sth** ◇ *Keep the car ~ when you're backing out.* | **hold sth** ◇ *She held herself very ~.*

ADV. **absolutely, completely, dead** (*esp. BrE*), **perfectly** ◇ *Keep going in a dead-straight line.* ◇ *His teeth were white and perfectly ~.* | **almost, more or less, nearly** | **fairly, relatively** | **naturally** ◇ *She had curled her naturally ~ hair.*

2 level/upright

VERBS **be, look** | **hang sth, put sth** ◇ *Can you hang that sign ~ for me?*

ADV. **absolutely, completely, perfectly, quite** | **almost, more or less, nearly**

3 (*esp. BrE*) tidy/in order

VERBS **be** | **get sth, put sth** ◇ *I'm trying to get the house ~ before the weekend.* ◇ *She tidied up and put the ornaments ~.* | **keep sth**

4 honest and truthful

VERBS **be** ◇ *I think he was pretty ~ with me.*

ADV. **absolutely, completely, totally** | **fairly, pretty**

PREP. **with** ◇ *Are you being completely ~ with her?*

5 clear/understood

VERBS **be** | **get sth** | **put sb** (*esp. BrE*), **set sb** (*esp. AmE*) ◇ *She soon set me ~ about what had happened.*

ADV. **absolutely** ◇ *Let's get this absolutely ~.*

straightforward *adj.*

1 clear and simple

VERBS **appear, be, look, prove, seem, sound** | **find sth** ◇ *I think you'll find it all quite ~.*

ADV. **extremely, fairly, very, etc.** | **perfectly, quite** ◇ *Look, it's perfectly straightforward—just multiply everything by five.* | **by no means** (*esp. BrE*), **far from, less than, not entirely** ◇ *Getting funding for the project was far from ~.* | **comparatively, reasonably, relatively** | **apparently, seemingly** | **deceptively, surprisingly** ◇ *The answer to this question is deceptively ~* (= more straightforward than it looks).

2 honest

VERBS **be, seem**

ADV. **very** | **quite** | **refreshingly** ◇ *a refreshingly ~ attitude*

PREP. **about, with** ◇ *He was very ~ with us about the difficulties involved.*

strain *noun*

1 severe demand on strength, resources, etc.

ADJ. **considerable, enormous, great, heavy, real, severe, terrible, tremendous** ◇ *It's a real ~ having to get up so early!* | **slight** | **increasing** | **constant** | **excessive, intolerable** (*esp. BrE*), **unbearable, undue** | **emotional, financial, mental, nervous, physical, psychological** ◇ *The mental ~ of sharing an office with Alison was starting to show.*

VERB + STRAIN **be under, come under, feel, suffer, suffer from** ◇ *Television newsreaders come under enormous ~.* ◇ *After weeks of overtime, she was starting to feel the ~.* | **cause, create, impose, place, put** ◇ *Increasing demand is placing undue ~ on services.* | **ease, reduce** | **cope with, stand, take** | **increase**

STRAIN + VERB **show, take its toll (on sb), tell (on sb)** (*BrE*) ◇ *After weeks of uncertainty, the ~ was beginning to take its toll.*

PREP. **under the ~** ◇ *The ice gave way under the ~.* ◇ *He broke down under the ~ of having to work twelve hours a day.* | **~ on** ◇ *Losing the business put a ~ on their relationship.*

PHRASES **a bit of a ~** ◇ *making conversation with her.* | **signs of ~** ◇ *After three years, their marriage was beginning to show signs of ~.* | **stresses and ~s** ◇ *the stresses and ~s of a long day* | **take the ~ off sb, take the ~ out of sth** ◇ *The Internet takes the ~ out of shopping.*

2 injury

ADJ. **bad** | **slight** | **back, eye** (*esp. BrE*), **muscle, thigh, etc.**

VERB + STRAIN **be suffering from, have** | **get** ◇ *You'll get eye ~ if you don't put the light on.* | **recover from, shake off** (*BrE*) ◇ *Gerrard will play if he can shake off a slight thigh ~.*

3 type of virus or bacteria

ADJ. **new** | **mutant** | **virulent** | **antibiotic-resistant, drug-resistant, resistant** | **bacterial, viral** | **flu, influenza**

VERB + STRAIN **discover, identify** | **analyse/analyze, examine, test**

PREP. **~ of** ◇ *H5N1 is a ~ of avian influenza.*

strain verb

1 make a great effort to do sth

ADV. **hard** ◇ *You could see he was ~ing hard to understand.* | **forward** ◇ *I ~ed forward to get a better view.*
VERB + STRAIN **have to**
PREP. **against** ◇ *The dogs were ~ing against the sled.* | **at** ◇ *Several men were ~ing at a rope, trying to move the stalled vehicle.* | **for** ◇ *Their ears ~ed for any slight sound.* | **under** *(often figurative)* ◇ *The company is already ~ing under the weight of a $12 billion debt.*
PHRASES **~ to hear sth, ~ to see sth** ◇ *We had to ~ to hear what was being said.*

2 put a lot of pressure on sth

ADV. **seriously, severely** ◇ *The dispute severely ~ed relations between the two countries.*
PHRASES **~ sth to breaking point** *(BrE)*, **~ sth to the breaking point** *(AmE)* ◇ *Our public health laboratories are ~ed to (the) breaking point.* | **~ sth to its limits, ~ sth to the limit**

strained adj.

1 worried and tense

VERBS **be, feel, look, seem, sound**
ADV. **extremely, fairly, very, etc.** ◇ *She looked rather ~ and miserable.* | **a little, slightly, etc.**

2 not natural or friendly

VERBS **be** | **become, grow** | **remain** ◇ *The atmosphere remained somewhat ~ all evening.*
ADV. **extremely, fairly, very, etc.** ◇ *Relations between us were rather ~.* | **severely** ◇ *Relations between the two countries had become severely ~.* | **increasingly** | **a little, slightly, etc.** | **already** ◇ *Their already ~ relationship was made worse by this incident.*

strait noun

1 narrow piece of water connecting seas, etc.

ADJ. **narrow**
VERB + STRAIT **go through, pass through** | **enter**
STRAIT + VERB **separate sth** ◇ *The oil terminal is in the narrow ~ that separates the island from the mainland.*
PREP. **across the ~** ◇ *a ship anchored in the Straits of Gibraltar.* | **in the ~** ◇ *a ship anchored in the Straits of Hormuz* | **on the ~** ◇ *The town is on the ~s between the Black Sea and the Mediterranean.* | **through the ~** ◇ *Many hundreds of vessels pass through the ~s each year.* | **~ between**

2 straits trouble

ADJ. **desperate, dire, serious** | **economic, financial**
PREP. **in ~** ◇ *The business is in dire financial ~s.*

strand noun

1 single thread, hair, etc.

ADJ. **long** | **thick, thin** | **loose, stray** ◇ *She pushed a stray ~ of hair out of her eyes.* | **single**
VERB + STRAND **twirl, twist), weave** ◇ *She wove the four ~s together into a ribbon.* | **twist together, weave together** ◇ *She wove the four ~s together into a ribbon.* | **tuck** ◇ *She tucked a ~ of long dark hair behind her ear.* | **brush, brush away, push, push away** ◇ *He brushed a ~ of hair from my face.*
PREP. **~ of** ◇ *a loose ~ of hair*

2 one part of a story, idea, etc.

ADJ. **important, main** | **different, disparate, various** ◇ *At the end, all the different ~s of the story are brought together.* | **distinct, individual, separate**
VERB + STRAND **bring together, draw together, pull together, weave together** | **disentangle, separate, unravel**
STRAND + VERB **come together**
PREP. **~ to** ◇ *There are three main ~s to the policy.* | **~ in, ~ within** ◇ *There are various ~s in feminist thinking.*
PHRASES **~s of opinion, ~s of thought**

stranded adj.

VERBS **be** | **become, end up, find yourself, get** ◇ *We ended*

up ~ *in Paris with no money.* ◇ *Some people found themselves ~ in the elevator as the power failed yet again.* ◇ *We got ~ on the island after we missed the last boat.* | **leave sb** ◇ *Thousands of air passengers were left ~ by the strike.*

strange adj.

VERBS **appear, be, feel, look, seem, smell, sound, taste** | **consider sth, find sth, regard sth as** *(esp. BrE)*, **think sth** ◇ *His actions were regarded as very ~.*
ADV. **extremely, fairly, very, etc.** | **incredibly** | **a little, slightly, etc.** ◇ *He's nice, but a little ~.*
PREP. **to** ◇ *Their accent was ~ to her ears.*
PHRASES **~ and wonderful** *(esp. AmE)* ◇ *He told all sorts of ~ and wonderful stories.*

stranger noun

ADJ. **complete, perfect, total** | **mysterious** | **beautiful, dark, handsome** ◇ *She said that I would meet a tall dark ~.* | **relative, virtual** | **passing**
PREP. **~ to** ◇ *He was a complete ~ to me.* ◇ *She was a ~ to the place.* ◇ *He was no ~ to controversy.* *(figurative)*
PHRASES **a ~ here** ◇ *You're a ~ here, aren't you?* | **a ~ in these parts, a ~ to these parts** ◇ *A ~ to these parts would be confused by some of the local customs.*

strangle verb

ADV. **almost, half, nearly, practically** | **slowly**
VERB + STRANGLE **try to**
PREP. **with** ◇ *He was ~d with a scarf.*
PHRASES **be found ~d** | **be ~d to death** | **~ sb/sth at birth** *(BrE, often figurative)* ◇ *This project should have been ~d at birth.*

strap noun

ADJ. **broad, thick, wide** | **narrow, spaghetti** *(esp. AmE)*, **thin** | **tight** | **loose** | **adjustable, detachable, removable, Velcro™** ◇ *The bag comes with a removable shoulder ~.* | **leather, nylon, etc.** | **elastic, padded** | **carrying** *(esp. AmE)*, **safety** ◇ *a portable radio with a carrying ~* | **ankle, chest, shoulder, wrist, etc.** | **bra, guitar, watch, etc.**
VERB + STRAP **buckle, buckle up, do up, fasten** | **unbuckle, undo, unfasten** | **tighten** | **loosen** | **adjust** | **attach, clip on, fit** ◇ *He clipped on his safety ~.* | **be fitted with** ◇ *The camera was fitted with a ~.*
PREP. **on a/the ~** ◇ *His binoculars were on a ~ around his neck.* | **~ across, ~ around, ~ round** *(esp. BrE)*, **etc.** ◇ *She had a wide leather ~ around her wrist.*

strap verb

ADV. **safely, securely** | **firmly, tightly** | **down, in, on** ◇ *He strapped his gun belt on.*
PREP. **around, round** *(esp. BrE)* ◇ *His money belt was securely strapped around his waist.* | **in, into** ◇ *Make sure that the child is strapped tightly into the seat.* | **to**

strategy noun

ADJ. **effective, good, sound** *(esp. AmE)*, **successful, winning** | **bad, poor** | **alternative, different** | **clear, coherent, simple** | **viable** | **future** | **long-term, medium-term, short-term** | **basic, broad, general, overall** ◇ *Their overall ~ is good, but one or two of the details could be improved.* | **key** ◇ *a key ~ to increase sales* | **comprehensive** | **global, international, national** ◇ *a global marketing ~* | **grand** | **draft** *(esp. BrE)* ◇ *The committee drew up a draft ~ for dealing with future floods.* | **dual, two-pronged** ◇ *The government has employed a dual ~ to achieve these two objectives.* | **innovative, radical** | **high-risk** *(esp. BrE)*, **risky** | **aggressive** ◇ *The company adopted aggressive marketing strategies to sell its products.* | **defensive, offensive** *(esp. AmE)*, **proactive** | **prevention, preventive** | **deliberate** ◇ *Her rudeness was a deliberate ~ to provoke him.* | **economics-based, market-oriented, etc.** ◇ *a customer-oriented business ~* | **anti-inflationary, anti-racist, etc.** | **coping** ◇ *We all have*

different coping strategies for times of stress. | **survival** | **exit** ◊ No one has yet come up with an exit ~ for the troops. | **defence/defense, military** | **campaign, election, electoral, government, political** | **instructional** (AmE), **pedagogic, teaching** | **learning** | **business, commercial, company, corporate, financial, investment, management, marketing, pricing, product, promotional, recruitment, research, sales** ◊ resource management strategies | **economic, energy, environmental, industrial, legislative,** etc.
VERB + STRATEGY **have** | **design, develop, devise, draw up, formulate, map out, plan, plot** (esp. AmE), **work out** ◊ A coherent ~ for getting more people back to work needs to be developed. ◊ The charity is drawing up a ~ to meet the needs of the homeless. ◊ The committee is meeting today in Washington to plot ~. (AmE) | **explore** ◊ It is certainly a ~ worth exploring. | **choose, decide, decide on** | **adopt, employ, execute** (esp. AmE), **follow, implement, pursue, use, utilize** (esp. AmE) ◊ They're pursuing a ~ of massive retaliation. | **describe, outline, set out, unveil** ◊ The document sets out the government's new ~. | **propose, suggest** | **discuss** | **change, rethink, revise** | **focus** ◊ The company will now focus its ~ on its core business areas. | **abandon**
STRATEGY + VERB **be based on sth** | **be aimed at sth, be designed to do sth** ◊ a ~ aimed at reducing the risk of accidents | **consist of sth, involve sth** | **depend on sth, hinge on sth** (esp. AmE), **rely on sth** ◊ This ~ relies on property prices continuing to rise. | **succeed, work** ◊ The company's financial ~ is not working. | **backfire, fail**
STRATEGY + NOUN **development, formulation** | **meeting, session** (esp. AmE) | **review** | **document, paper** | **game** ◊ a ~ game set during the Civil War
PREP. **in a/the** ~ ◊ the key idea in their ~ | ~ **for** ◊ to develop an effective ~ for change | ~ **on** ◊ the party's ~ on poverty | ~ **towards/toward** ◊ a comprehensive ~ towards/toward regional development
PHRASES **a change in** ~ ◊ The coming year may herald a change in ~ for major publishers. | **the adoption of a** ~, **the development of a** ~, **the formulation of a** ~ ◊ The money is earmarked for the development of new product and sales strategies. | **the implementation of a** ~, **the pursuit of a** ~ ◊ Their single-minded pursuit of this controversial ~ led to their fall from power. | **part of a** ~ ◊ He pretended that resigning was part of his long-term career ~.

straw noun

1 dried plant stems used for food, packaging, etc.

ADJ. **clean, fresh**
... OF STRAW **bale** ◊ I sat on a bale of ~ near the fire.
PREP. **in (the)** ~ ◊ The rat hid in the ~. | **on (the)** ~ ◊ The animals sleep on ~.

2 thin tube for drinking

ADJ. **drinking** | **bendy** | **plastic**
PREP. **through a** ~ ◊ She drank her milkshake through a ~.

strawberry noun

ADJ. **fresh** | **juicy** | **wild**
... OF STRAWBERRIES **carton** (AmE), **punnet** (BrE) ◊ I bought a carton/punnet of strawberries.
STRAWBERRY + NOUN **bed, plant**
→ Special page at FRUIT

stray verb

ADV. **far** ◊ The animals hadn't ~ed too far. | **never, rarely** ◊ He never ~ed far from his home. | **accidentally, involuntarily** ◊ Her eyes ~ed involuntarily. | **away** (often figurative) ◊ The teachers rarely ~ away from the approved textbook.
VERB + STRAY **allow sth to** ◊ new penalties for owners who allow their dogs to ~
PREP. **from** ◊ Be careful not to ~ from the path. | **into, off, to** ◊ His eyes ~ed to the telephone. | Her thoughts ~ed to the week ahead of her. (figurative)

streak noun

1 thin mark

ADJ. **dark** ◊ There were dark ~s down her cheeks where she had been crying. | **faint, pale** | **bright** | **blond, golden, grey/gray**
PREP. ~ **of** ◊ The last ~s of light faded from the sky.
PHRASES **a** ~ **of lightning** ◊ A ~ of lightning forked across the sky. | **a** ~ **of red, white,** etc. ◊ She had a few ~s of white in her black hair.

2 aspect of sb's character

ADJ. **strong** | **hidden** | **cruel, mean, nasty, ruthless, selfish, vicious, violent** | **independent, rebellious, stubborn** | **adventurous, competitive** | **puritanical**
VERB + STREAK **have** ◊ Most of the players have a strong competitive ~. | **reveal, show** ◊ She suddenly revealed a mean ~ in her character.
PREP. **with a** ~ ◊ trips for those with an adventurous ~ | ~ **of** ◊ There was a ~ of eccentricity in the family.

3 period of good/bad luck

ADJ. **hot** (esp. AmE), **lucky** | **unbeaten** (esp. AmE), **undefeated** (esp. AmE), **winning** ◊ The Yankees continued their six-game winning ~. | **losing, winless** | **scoreless** (AmE)
VERB + STREAK **be on, go on** (esp. AmE) ◊ The team has been on a winning ~ since it won against Lazio. | **continue, extend** | **break** (esp. AmE), **end, snap** (AmE)

stream noun

1 small river

ADJ. **little, small** | **shallow** | **clear** | **fast-flowing, rushing** | **bubbling** ◊ We picnicked beside a bubbling ~. | **trickling** | **meandering** | **mountain, underground** | **salmon, trout**
VERB + STREAM **cross, ford** | **pollute**
STREAM + VERB **flow, run, trickle** ◊ The ~ flows through a narrow valley.
STREAM + NOUN **bed**
PREP. **across a/the** ~ | **down a/the** ~, **up a/the** ~ | **in a/the** ~ ◊ There are small fish in the ~. | **on a/the** ~ ◊ a leaf floating on the ~
PHRASES **the edge of the** ~, **the side of the** ~

2 continuous flow of a liquid/gas/light

ADJ. **thin** | **air, gas** | **jet** ◊ The jet ~ in the northern hemisphere moves northward. | **blood** (usually **bloodstream**) ◊ The drug is not absorbed into the bloodstream.
VERB + STREAM **emit** | **let in**
STREAM + VERB **flow** ◊ A ~ of blood flowed from the wound.
PREP. ~ **of**

3 flow of people/vehicles/money/events

ADJ. **constant, continuous, endless, never-ending, steady, unending** ◊ a constant ~ of letters ◊ Cars filed past in an endless ~. | **funding, income, revenue** ◊ By licensing their works, artists can create an ongoing revenue ~. | **audio, data, video** ◊ You can listen to the live audio ~.
VERB + STREAM **generate** ◊ The computer generates a steady ~ of emails. | **send** | **let loose, let out** ◊ He let loose a ~ of abuse.
PREP. ~ **of** ◊ a ~ of racist abuse ◊ We have established several different ~s of funding. (esp. BrE)
PHRASES ~ **of consciousness** ◊ the stream-of-consciousness technique in modern literature

street noun

ADJ. **broad, wide** | **narrow** | **bustling, busy, congested, crowded** | **pedestrian, pedestrianized** (BrE) ◊ It really irritates me when people ride bicycles in pedestrian ~s. | **deserted, desolate, empty, lonely, quiet** | **noisy** | **dark, darkened** | **bright, well-lit** | **dim, dimly lit, gloomy** | **winding** | **steep** | **cobbled** (esp. BrE), **cobblestone** (esp. AmE), **paved** | **unpaved** | **clean** | **dirty, dusty, filthy, muddy** | **rainy** | **flooded** | **dangerous, mean, unsafe** ◊ He grew up on the mean ~s of one of the city's toughest areas. | **leafy** (esp. BrE), **tree-lined** | **one-way, two-way** | **dead-end** (esp. AmE) | **main, principal** | **back** (usually **backstreet**), **side** ◊ a rundown house in the backstreets of Cairo ◊ a bar in a side ~ off the Champs-èlysées | **city, village** (esp. BrE) | **right**

| **wrong** ◊ *You've taken the wrong ~.* | **shopping** (*esp. BrE*) ◊ *the town's main shopping ~* | **high** (*BrE*), **main** (*AmE*) ◊ *Sales on the UK high ~ are in decline.* ◊ *high-street retailers* ◊ *He works at a small store on Main Street.* | **downtown** (*AmE*), **residential, suburban, urban**

VERB + STREET **go along** (*esp. BrE*), **go down, go up, take, turn down, turn into, turn up** ◊ *Take the second ~ on the right after the bridge.* ◊ *We turned down a dead-end ~ by mistake.* | **cross** | **block, block off, clog** (*esp. BrE*), **clog up** (*BrE*) | **cordon off** (*esp. BrE*) | **patrol** ◊ *The police have been patrolling the ~s in this area since the murder.* | **stroll, stroll down, stroll through** | **walk, walk down** | **cruise, prowl, roam, wander** ◊ *Gangs roamed the ~s at night.* | **crowd, fill, flood, line, pack, throng** ◊ *Spectators lined the ~s.* | **clear** ◊ *Police were told to clear the ~s of drug dealers before the Olympics.* | **litter** ◊ *Dead bodies littered the ~s.* | **widen**

STREET + VERB **go, lead, run** | **bend, curve, turn** | **be lined with sth** ◊ *~s lined with cafes* | **be packed with sb, teem with sth** ◊ *The ~s were packed with people shopping.* ◊ *The ~s are teeming with traffic.* | **be named sth, be named after sb/sth** ◊ *Mozart is remembered by a ~ named after him.*

STREET + NOUN **corner** | **map, plan** | **layout, pattern** ◊ *the dense ~ pattern of the old town* | **name, number, sign** ◊ *Most ~ names were changed under the new regime.* | **lamp, light, lighting** | **crime, gang** | **punk, thug** (*both esp. AmE*) | **people** (*esp. AmE*) | **attack, battle, brawl, fight, fighting, robbery, violence** ◊ *He suffered extensive injuries in a ~ attack.* ◊ *~ fighting between police and stone-throwing youths* | **demonstration, protest** | **fair, festival, party** (*esp. BrE*), **procession** | **cleaner** (*esp. BrE*), **sweeper** | **door** (*esp. BrE*) ◊ *There were photographers outside the ~ door so she used a back entrance.* | **market** | **entertainer, entertainment, musician, performer, theatre/theater** | **dealer, pedlar/peddler, seller, trader** (*esp. BrE*), **vendor** (*esp. AmE*) | **hustler** (*esp. AmE*) ◊ *Tourists need to be wary of ~ hustlers near the station.* | **selling** (*AmE*), **trading** (*BrE*) ◊ *people engaged in informal ~ selling* ◊ *He pleaded guilty to illegal ~ trading.* | **cred, credibility** (*both informal*) ◊ *His spell in prison gained him a lot of ~ cred.* | **smarts** (*AmE, informal*), **wisdom** | **clothes** (*esp. AmE*), **culture, fashion, slang** ◊ *the ~ culture of working-class youth* | **life** | **scene** ◊ *a painting of a typical Parisian ~ scene* | **collection** (*BrE*) ◊ *The charity is having a ~ collection in aid of the local hospital.* | **child, kid** (*informal*), **urchin** ◊ *a charity set up to house ~ children* | **boy, girl** | **hustler** (*informal, esp. AmE*), **prostitute** | **price, value** ◊ *drugs with a ~ value of £5 million*

PREP. **across a/the ~** ◊ *He could see her across the ~.* | **along a/the ~** ◊ *They walked along the ~.* | **down a/the ~, up a/the ~** ◊ *A band was playing a little way down the ~.* ◊ *She lives just up the ~ here.* | **in a/the ~** ◊ *She parks her car in the ~.* ◊ *A couple were arguing out in the ~.* ◊ *We live in Barker Street.* (*BrE*) | **into a/the ~** ◊ *She stepped out into the ~.* ◊ *He turned into a side ~.* (*BrE*) | **off a/the ~** ◊ *a club just off William Street* ◊ *a plan to keep teenagers off the ~s* | **on a/the ~** ◊ *people dealing drugs on the ~* ◊ *I was living on 10th Street off Hudson.* (*AmE*) | **on the ~s, out on the ~s** ◊ *Thousands of people were out on the ~s for the protest.* | **onto a/the ~** ◊ *She was thrown onto the ~.* ◊ *He turned onto a side ~.* (*AmE*) | **through the ~s** ◊ *He wandered through the ~s of Calcutta.*

PHRASES **above ~ level, at ~ level, below ~ level** | **the end of the ~, the top of the ~** | **the other side of the ~** | **the ~ on the left, the ~ on the right** | **hit the ~s** (= start to be available or seen in public) ◊ *Her shocking autobiography is about to hit the ~s.* | **take to the ~s** ◊ *Argentinians took to the ~s in protest.*

strength noun

1 how strong sb/sth is

ADJ. **considerable, enormous, great, immense, incredible, tremendous** | **high** ◊ *The material has exceptionally high ~ for its weight.* | **greater, superior** ◊ *His superior physical ~ won him the title.* | **relative** ◊ *Profits have been helped by the relative ~ of the euro against the dollar.* | **maximum** | **growing, increased** | **new-found** | **continuing** ◊ *the continuing ~ of the pound* | **surprising, unexpected** | **superhuman, supernatural** | **brute, sheer** ◊ *He got the*

door open with brute ~. | **extra** ◊ *They are reinforced with steel for extra ~.* | **collective, combined, overall** ◊ *They believe their combined ~ will overwhelm the competition.* | **numerical** ◊ *the numerical ~ of the Chinese army* | **emotional, inner, mental, spiritual** | **muscle, muscular, physical** | **tensile** ◊ *The steel adds tensile ~ to the concrete.* | **arm, leg** ◊ *It's well known that cycling builds leg ~.* | **lower-body, upper-body** | **economic, electoral, financial, industrial, military** | **police, troop, union, etc.** ◊ *US troop ~ in Afghanistan dropped to 18 000.* | **bargaining** (*esp. BrE*) | **wind** | **signal** ◊ *The phone company aims to improve signal ~ within buildings.* | **alcoholic**

VERB + STRENGTH **have, possess** ◊ *He had just enough ~ to reach for the phone.* | **lack** | **find, muster** (*esp. AmE*), **summon, summon up** ◊ *I'm trying to summon up the ~ to do some more work.* | **draw, draw on, use** ◊ *She was able to draw on her immense inner ~.* | **put** ◊ *He put all his ~ into reorganizing the department.* | **take** ◊ *It took all his ~ to open the box.* | **boost, build, build up, improve, increase** ◊ *You need to try and build up your ~ before the winter.* | **gain, gather** ◊ *The opinion that the president should stand down has gained considerable ~.* | **gain in, grow in, increase in** | **add** | **conserve, maintain, save** | **lose** | **sap** ◊ *The series of steep hills sapped the cyclists' ~.* | **get back, recover, regain** | **give sb/sth, lend sb/sth** ◊ *Her love and support gave me ~.* ◊ *The metal reinforcement gives it the ~ to resist the high winds.* | **reduce, undermine** ◊ *Her unwillingness to answer questions undermined the ~ of her position.* | **assess, measure, test** ◊ *The Moroccan athlete ran a fast lap to test the ~ of the other runners.* | **underestimate** | **vary in** ◊ *These wines vary in ~ between 11% and 15%.*

STRENGTH + VERB **grow, increase** | **decline, drain, drain away, ebb, ebb away, fade, fail, falter, wane** ◊ *The country's economic ~ is declining.* ◊ *Her ~ was ebbing fast, so her children were called to her bedside.* | **return**

PREP. **up to ~** ◊ *The Korean team was not up to ~ for the final.* | **below ~, under ~** (*both BrE*) ◊ *The Chilean team was below ~ for the final.* | **with ~** ◊ *She pushed him away with unexpected ~.* | **~ in** ◊ *She gradually regained ~ in her legs.*

PHRASES **at full ~** ◊ *The orchestra was at full ~ for the Mahler symphony.* | **back to full ~** ◊ *I'm still not quite back to full ~ after my illness.* | **every ounce of ~** ◊ *She summoned up every ounce of ~ she possessed.* | **draw ~ from sth** ◊ *I draw great ~ from the support of my family.* | **a feat of ~** ◊ *He used to entertain people with his feats of ~.* | **a pillar of ~, a tower of ~** ◊ *He was a tower of ~ to his sisters when their father died.* | **a position of ~** ◊ *They are negotiating from a position of ~.* | **reserves of ~** ◊ *When she had twins, she discovered reserves of ~ that she didn't know she had.* | **a show of ~** ◊ *50 000 troops massed on the border in the biggest show of ~ to date.* | **a source of ~** ◊ *Her childhood memories were a great source of ~ when her mother was killed.* | **~ of character, ~ of purpose, ~ of will** | **~ of feeling** | **the ~ of sb's position** | **a test of ~, a trial of ~** ◊ *Today's vote is being seen as a test of ~ for the government.* ◊ *The dispute developed into a trial of ~ between management and the union.* | **with all your ~** ◊ *She threw the rope with all her ~.*

2 useful quality

ADJ. **great** ◊ *What's your greatest ~?* | **real** | **individual, personal, unique** | **combined** | **relative** ◊ *We want to learn more about the relative ~s of our students.* | **core, key** ◊ *The company's key ~ is its people.*

VERB + STRENGTH **capitalize on** (*esp. AmE*), **exploit, play to** ◊ *The team may not have the best players, but it plays to its ~s.* | **discover, identify**

STRENGTH + VERB **come from sth, lie in sth** ◊ *Her great ~ lies in her flexibility.*

PHRASES **~s and weaknesses**

strengthen verb

ADV. **considerably, enormously, greatly, significantly, substantially** ◊ *The success in the election ~ed the party's position considerably.* | **further** ◊ *This merger will further ~*

the company and ensure its continued success. | **merely** ◇ This temporary setback merely ~ed her resolve.

VERB + STRENGTHEN **help (to), serve to** | **be designed to, be used to** ◇ These exercises are designed to ~ your back muscles.

PREP. **against** ◇ The euro has ~ed against the dollar.

PHRASES **an attempt to ~ sth, an effort to ~ sth** | **be aimed at ~ing sth** ◇ The new law is aimed at ~ing protective measures for workers. | **measures to ~ sth**

stress noun

1 state of tension

ADJ. **considerable, extreme, great, high, incredible, intense, severe** ◇ Separation is a time of high emotional ~. | **acute, chronic** | **excessive, undue** ◇ compensation claims for undue ~ in the workplace | **added, greater, heightened, increased** | **low** | **daily** ◇ the daily ~ of teaching | **emotional, mental, psychological, social** | **post-traumatic** ◇ He has suffered post-traumatic ~ since the crash. ◇ treatment for post-traumatic ~ disorder | **occupational, work-related** | **family** (esp. AmE) ◇ The program helps workers with work-related and family ~. | **environmental** ◇ Different organisms react differently to environmental ~. | **economic, financial** ◇ The high mortgage payments put them under severe financial ~.

... OF STRESS **level** ◇ Many workers experience a high level of ~ in their daily life.

VERB + STRESS **cause, create** ◇ A divorce causes children great emotional ~. | **avoid, remove** | **add to, increase** | **alleviate, decrease, ease, lessen, minimize, reduce, relieve** ◇ There are many things an employer can do to ease employees' ~. | **be under, endure, experience, have, suffer, suffer from, undergo** ◇ He's been under a lot of ~ lately. | **cope with, handle, manage, stand, take** ◇ He's had to give up his job as leader of the project—he just couldn't take the ~.

STRESS + VERB **bring sth about, bring sth on, cause sth, trigger sth** ◇ an illness brought on by ~

STRESS + NOUN **level** ◇ high ~ levels | **control, management** ◇ Staff are encouraged to go on stress-management courses. | **response** ◇ The release of the stress hormone cortisol is part of the human ~ response. | **hormone** | **reduction, relief** | **buster** (informal), **reliever** (both esp. AmE) ◇ Physical exercise is a great ~ reliever.

PREP. **under ~** ◇ He broke under ~ and had to leave.

PHRASES **a source of ~** ◇ An overcrowded workplace can be a major source of ~. | **a symptom of ~** ◇ Tiredness is one of the most common symptoms of ~.

2 emphasis that shows importance

ADJ. **enormous, great** | **particular, special** | **equal** | **undue**

VERB + STRESS **lay, place, put** ◇ I must lay great ~ on the need for secrecy.

PREP. **with the ~ on** ◇ a study of child development, with the ~ on acquisition of social skills | **~ on** ◇ There's been a lot of ~ on getting drug sellers off the streets.

3 emphasis on a word, syllable, etc.

ADJ. **main, major, primary, strong** | **secondary, weak** | **sentence, word**

VERB + STRESS **carry, have, take** ◇ Italian words usually have the main ~ on the penultimate syllable in the word. ◇ The first syllable takes the ~. | **place, put** | **mark** ◇ Mark the primary ~ in each word.

STRESS + VERB **fall, go** ◇ Where does the ~ fall in 'psychological'?

STRESS + NOUN **pattern**

PREP. **~ on** ◇ There's a ~ on the second syllable.

4 physical force

ADJ. **enormous, high** | **low** | **constant** | **equal** ◇ There is equal ~ on all parts of the structure. | **undue** ◇ Avoid exercise that puts undue ~ on the knees. | **mechanical** ◇ The majority of sports injuries are due to excessive mechanical ~ on joints, ligaments and muscles.

VERB + STRESS **exert, set up** ◇ The tower exerts an enormous ~ on the walls. ◇ The movements set up ~es in the earth's crust.

| **apply, put, subject sth to** ◇ Stress is applied to the wood to make it bend. ◇ Standing all day puts ~ on your feet. ◇ The buttresses are subjected to constant ~. | **bear, take, withstand** | **increase, reduce** | **transfer, transmit** | **calculate** ◇ Engineers calculated the ~es borne by each of the bridge supports.

STRESS + NOUN **fracture** ◇ He was diagnosed with a ~ fracture in his right foot.

PREP. **~ on** ◇ Cycling puts very little ~ on the joints. | **under ~** ◇ Some woods warp under ~.

stress verb

ADV. **heavily, strongly** ◇ He ~ed the point very strongly that all these services cost money. | **constantly, continually, repeatedly** ◇ She has constantly ~ed the government's poor record in this area. | **rightly** ◇ Doctors have rightly ~ed the importance of exercise.

VERB + STRESS **must** ◇ I must ~ that we still know very little about this disease. | **tend to** ◇ Private schools tend to ~ the more academic subjects. | **be anxious to, be at pains to** (esp. BrE), **be careful to, be keen to** (BrE), **take pains to** ◇ She is at pains to ~ the cultural differences between the two countries.

PHRASES **I can't ~ enough, it can't be ~ed enough** ◇ I can't ~ enough that security is of the highest importance. | **be important to ~ sth, be worth ~ing sth** ◇ It is worth ~ing that this was only a relatively small survey.

stressed (also informal stressed out) adj.

VERBS **be, feel** | **look, seem, sound** | **become, get** | **make sb** ◇ She's just making herself more ~.

ADV. **extremely, fairly, very, etc.** | **completely, totally** ◇ I was just totally ~ out and afraid I couldn't continue. | **overly** (esp. AmE) ◇ She felt overly ~ and needed to calm down. | **a little, slightly, etc.** | **clearly, obviously**

PREP. **about** ◇ He's ~ out about money. | **over** (esp. AmE)

stressful adj.

VERBS **be, prove, sound** | **become, get** ◇ My job's getting more and more ~. | **find sth** ◇ I find these meetings rather ~.

ADV. **extremely, fairly, very, etc.** | **highly** | **a little, slightly, etc.** | **emotionally** ◇ It was an emotionally ~ time for him.

stretch noun

1 area of land or water

ADJ. **great, huge, large, long, open, vast, wide** ◇ A great ~ of ocean lay beneath them. | **15-mile, half-mile, etc.** | **narrow, short, small** | **straight** ◇ a straight ~ of road | **continuous, unbroken** | **beautiful, lovely** | **deserted, empty, lonely** ◇ an empty ~ of beach | **fast** | **dangerous, hazardous** | **coastal** ◇ a wild uninhabited coastal ~ | **final** ◇ She felt a renewed burst of energy for the final ~.

PREP. **along a/the ~** ◇ There are tailbacks along a ten-mile ~ of the road. | **on a/the ~** ◇ The festival is being held on a ~ of parkland near the river. | **~ of**

PHRASES **the home ~** (esp. AmE) ◇ The presidential race has now entered the home ~. (figurative)

2 period of time

ADJ. **long** | **short** | **final** ◇ The students have now entered the final ~ of their course. | **three-year, two-week, etc.** | **rough, tough** (both AmE) ◇ He went through a tough ~ last year but things are better now.

PREP. **~ of** ◇ She had been unhappy for long ~es of her life.

PHRASES **at a ~** ◇ He worked for three days and nights at a ~.

3 stretching

ADJ. **good** | **gentle**

VERB + STRETCH **do** ◇ First let's warm up by doing some ~es. | **have** ◇ Have a good ~ from time to time to prevent yourself getting stiff. | **hold** ◇ Hold the ~ for a count of ten.

PHRASES **at full ~** ◇ Her arms were at full ~.

stretch *verb*

1 pull sth tight

ADV. **taut, tautly** (*AmE*), **tight, tightly** ◊ *Make sure that the rope is ~ed tight.* ◊ *Stretch the fabric tightly over the frame.*
PREP. **across, between, over** ◊ *Striped awnings had been ~ed across the courtyard.*

2 your body/part of the body

ADV. **gently** | **lazily, luxuriously** ◊ *He stirred and ~ed lazily.* | **full-length** ◊ *Andrea turned out the light and ~ed full-length on the bed.* | **down, forward, out, up, upwards/upward** ◊ *She ~ed up to reach the top shelf.*
PREP. **on** ◊ *He ~ed out on the couch and watched TV.*
PHRASES **~ and yawn, yawn and ~** ◊ *She sat up, yawning and ~ing.*

3 cover a large area

ADV. **far** ◊ *The wood does not ~ very far.* | **endlessly, forever** ◊ *The fields ~ed forever into the distance.* | **ahead, away** ◊ *The road ~ed ahead.*
VERB + STRETCH **seem to** ◊ *The beach seemed to ~ endlessly.*
PREP. **along** | **beyond** | **from, to** ◊ *an area which ~es from London to the north* | **for** ◊ *The beach ~es for five miles.* | **into** ◊ *A line of cars ~ed into the distance.*

4 continue over a period of time

ADV. **endlessly** ◊ *The future ~ed out endlessly in front of me.* | **back, out** ◊ *The town's history ~es back to before 1700.*
PREP. **before** ◊ *Endless summer days ~ed out before us.* | **into** ◊ *The talks look set to ~ into a second week.*

5 your ability/intelligence

ADV. **really** | **severely** ◊ *The increase in demand has severely ~ed our resources.* | **fully** ◊ *We can't take on any more work—we're fully ~ed as it is.* | **thin, thinly** ◊ *Don't ~ yourself too thin financially.* ◊ *Our forces are too thinly ~ed to control the chaos.* | **financially** (*esp. BrE*)
PREP. **to** ◊ *This department is ~ed to its limit.*

stride *noun*

1 step

ADJ. **long, short** ◊ *In one short ~ he reached the window.* | **quick, slow** | **easy**
VERB + STRIDE **take**
PREP. **in a ~**

2 way of walking

ADJ. **loping** | **confident, determined, purposeful**
VERB + STRIDE **lengthen** ◊ *He lengthened his ~ to keep up with her.* | **shorten** | **break** ◊ *Without breaking her ~ she ducked the ball.* | **match** ◊ *He matched his ~ to her slower pace.*
PHRASES **find your ~** (*figurative*), **get into your ~** (*BrE, figurative*), **hit your ~** (*figurative, esp. AmE*) ◊ *The team took time to get into their ~.* ◊ *The show finally hit its ~ in the second season.*

3 progress

ADJ. **big, considerable, enormous, giant, great, huge, impressive, rapid, significant, tremendous**
VERB + STRIDE **make** ◊ *She's made enormous ~s in English this term.*
PREP. **~s in** ◊ *We have made great ~s in areas like employment and housing.*

stride *verb*

ADV. **briskly, quickly** | **confidently** | **purposefully** | **angrily** | **ahead, away, off, up, etc.** ◊ *He strode off in search of a taxi.*
PREP. **across, down, out of, past, through, towards/toward, etc.** ◊ *She strode purposefully across the stage.*
PHRASES **come striding** ◊ *He came striding up the path.*

strife *noun*

ADJ. **internal** | **ethnic, factional, internecine, sectarian** | **civil, industrial, labour/labor** (*esp. AmE*), **political, racial, religious, social** | **domestic, family, marital**
VERB + STRIFE **cause, create, foment** | **be torn apart by, be torn by, experience** ◊ *The country has been torn apart by years of civil ~.* | **end**

PREP. **during the ~, in the ~** ◊ *He lost his job during last year's industrial ~.* | **~ among, ~ between** ◊ *internecine ~ among the nationalities of the region*
PHRASES **a time of ~** | **years of ~**

strike *noun*

1 industrial protest

ADJ. **long** | **short** | **one-day, two-day, etc.** | **24-hour, 48-hour, etc.** | **indefinite** (*esp. BrE*) | **crippling, damaging, major** | **bitter** | **official** (*esp. BrE*) | **illegal, unofficial** (*esp. BrE*) | **token** (*BrE*) | **lightning** (*BrE*), **wildcat** ◊ *a series of wildcat ~s in parts of the coal industry* | **all-out** (*esp. BrE*), **general, mass** (*esp. BrE*), **national, nationwide** ◊ *A general ~ brought the country to a standstill.* | **hunger** | **sit-down** | **political** | **sympathy** ◊ *The shipyard voted to launch a sympathy ~ in support of the machinists.* | **pay** (*BrE*) | **rent** | **dock, miners', postal** (*BrE*) | **train** (*BrE*), **transit** (*AmE*), **tube** (*BrE*), **etc.** ◊ *The New York transit ~ is in its second day.*
... OF STRIKES **series, wave**
VERB + STRIKE **be on** | **come out on** (*esp. BrE*), **go on, go out on, join, take part in** (*esp. BrE*) | **call, organize, stage** ◊ *The union leaders called a ~.* | **call sb out on** ◊ *He called all the workers out on ~.* | **ballot for, vote for** (*both esp. BrE*) ◊ *Both unions have pledged to ballot for ~ action unless hours are cut.* | **avert, prevent** | **threaten** ◊ *More train ~s are threatened.* | **begin, start** | **call off, end** | **break, crush** ◊ *The army was used to help break the ~.* | **settle** | **ban** ◊ *The new government banned ~s.*
STRIKE + VERB **occur, take place** | **start** | **end** | **last** | **spread** ◊ *The ~ soon spread to other cities.* | **paralyse/paralyze sth** ◊ *The ~ paralysed/paralyzed the port.*
STRIKE + NOUN **action** ◊ *Prison officers are threatening to take ~ action.* | **threat** | **ballot** (*esp. BrE*) | **leader** | **breaker** (usually **strike-breaker**) | **committee, movement**
PREP. **during a/the ~** ◊ *There was a continual police presence during the ~.* | **~ against** ◊ *a ~ against poor conditions* | **~ by** ◊ *a ~ by air traffic controllers* | **~ for** ◊ *a ~ for a ten-hour day* | **~ in protest at** (*BrE*) ◊ *a ~ in protest at the government's economic policies* | **~ in support of** ◊ *Miners staged a one-day ~ in support of the steel workers.* | **~ over** ◊ *a ~ over pay*
PHRASES **a ballot for a ~** (*esp. BrE*), **a ballot for ~ action** | **the threat of ~s**

2 sudden military attack

ADJ. **air, missile, nuclear** | **military, terrorist** | **lightning, quick** | **pre-emptive** | **retaliatory** | **precision, surgical** | **massive**
VERB + STRIKE **carry out, launch, make**
STRIKE + NOUN **force** | **aircraft**
PREP. **in a/the ~** ◊ *The house was damaged in an air ~.* | **~ against, ~ on** ◊ *The aircraft carried out a pre-emptive ~ against bases in the north.*

strike *verb*

1 hit/attack sb/sth

ADV. **firmly, hard** ◊ *He struck her hard across the face.* | **deep** ◊ *The army struck deep into northern territory.* | **directly** | **without warning** ◊ *Earthquakes can ~ without warning.* | **repeatedly** | **home** (*often figurative*) ◊ *The remark struck home.*
VERB + STRIKE **be about to, be going to, be ready to, prepare to** ◊ *A hurricane is about to ~ Jamaica.*
PREP. **against** ◊ *The oar struck against something hard.* | **at** ◊ *He struck at me repeatedly with a stick.* | **on** ◊ *The ball struck her on the head.*
PHRASES **be struck by lightning, get struck by lightning** | **be struck down by sth, be struck down with sth** ◊ *He was struck down with food poisoning.*

2 come into your mind suddenly/give an impression

ADV. **immediately** | **suddenly** ◊ *It suddenly struck me how we could improve the situation.* | **just** ◊ *An awful thought has just struck me.* | **particularly, really** ◊ *I was particularly*

struck by the sound of the birds. ◇ *One thing that really struck me was how calm he appeared.* | **forcibly** ◇ *Joan was struck quite forcibly by the silence.*
PREP. **as** ◇ *He always struck me as being rather stupid.* ◇ *It struck me as strange that there was no one there.*

3 go on strike

VERB + STRIKE **threaten to** | **vote to** (*esp. BrE*) | **be set to** (*esp. BrE*) ◇ *Over 100 000 civil servants are set to ~ on Tuesday.*
PREP. **against, for** ◇ *The union has voted to ~ for a pay increase of 6%.* | **in protest at** (*esp. BrE*), **over** ◇ *Drivers are threatening to ~ over pay.*
PHRASES **the right to ~**

striking *adj.*

VERBS **be, look** ◇ *That hat looks very ~.*
ADV. **extremely, fairly, very, etc.** ◇ *She was tall and very ~.* | **especially, particularly** | **immediately** ◇ *What is immediately ~ is how resourceful the children are.*
PREP. **in** ◇ *The picture was ~ in its simplicity.*

string *noun*

1 thin cord

ADJ. **taut, tight** ◇ *He pulled the ~ tight.* | **loose** | **tangled** ◇ *He had hair like tangled yellow ~.*
... OF STRING **bit** (*esp. BrE*), **length, piece** ◇ *I cut a length of ~ to tie up the package.* | **ball**
VERB + STRING **tie, tie sth up with** ◇ *Tie the ~ around the package.* | **undo, untie** | **wind** ◇ *He wound the ~ into a ball.* | **dangle (sth) on** ◇ *Next to the phone, there was a pencil dangling on a ~.*
STRING + NOUN **vest** (*BrE*)
PREP. **in the ~** ◇ *There's a knot in the ~.* | **~ of** ◇ *a ~ of pearls*

2 on a musical instrument

ADJ. **open** | **guitar, violin, etc.** | **A, G, etc.**
VERB + STRING **tune** | **loosen, tighten** | **pluck** | **change, replace** | **break**
STRING + VERB **break** | **vibrate**
STRING + NOUN **instrument**
PREP. **on a/the ~** ◇ *Play it on the G ~.*

strip *noun*

1 long, narrow piece

ADJ. **long** | **narrow, thin, tiny** | **thick, wide** ◇ *Cut the meat into thick ~s.* | **plastic** | **magnetic** ◇ *a card with a magnetic ~ on the back* | **chicken** (*esp. AmE*) ◇ *grilled chicken ~s* | **test** ◇ *The kit contains five test ~s.* | **rumble** (*BrE*) | **coastal** | **landing** ◇ *This aircraft requires a good-sized landing ~.*
STRIP + NOUN **steak** (*AmE*)
PREP. **in ~s** ◇ *The wallpaper can then be torn off in ~s.* | **~ of** ◇ *a narrow ~ of leather*
PHRASES **cut sth into ~s, tear sth into ~s**

2 taking clothes off

STRIP + NOUN **bar, club, joint** (*esp. AmE*) | **show** | **poker** | **search**

strip *verb*

1 take off your/sb's clothes

PREP. **off** ◇ *We stripped off and went for a swim.* | **(down) to** ◇ *Office workers stripped down to their shirtsleeves in the heatwave.*
PHRASES **~ (sb) naked** ◇ *He was stripped naked and left alone in a cell.* | **~ to the waist** ◇ *He stripped to the waist and began to dig.*

2 take sth away

ADV. **completely** | **away, off, out** ◇ *Strip out any damaged wiring.*
PREP. **from** ◇ *The bark is stripped from the trees by hand.* | **of** ◇ *The president had been completely stripped of power.* | **off** ◇ *We stripped all the paint off the walls.*

PHRASES **~ sth bare** ◇ *The room had been stripped bare by the thieves.*

stripe *noun*

1 long narrow line

ADJ. **broad, wide** | **narrow, thin** | **bold, dark** | **subtle** | **distinctive** | **diagonal, horizontal, vertical**
STRIPE + VERB **run** ◇ *The butterfly is black and white with a blue ~ running down each wing.*
PREP. **with ~s** ◇ *a white tablecloth with red ~s* | **~ across, ~ down** ◇ *The toad has a distinctive yellow ~ down its back.*

2 (*esp. AmE*) **kind/type**

ADJ. **ideological, political** | **all, any, every, various**
PREP. **of ... ~** ◇ *Politicians of every ~ have demonstrated a thirst for power.*

strive *verb*

ADV. **hard, mightily** ◇ *He strove very hard to remain calm.* | **desperately** ◇ *They are desperately striving for some sort of dignity.* | **earnestly** | **always, constantly, continually, continuously**
PREP. **after** ◇ *I am constantly striving after artistic beauty.* | **against** ◇ *man striving against the elements* | **for** ◇ *The school constantly ~s for excellence in its teaching.* | **towards/toward** ◇ *companies that ~ towards/toward bigger profits*

NOTE

Swimming strokes

do (the) ... , swim (the) ... ◇ *a swimmer doing the crawl* ◇ *I can't swim butterfly.*
strike out in/with ... ◇ *She struck out for the shore with a strong crawl.*
a lap of ... (*AmE*), **a length of ...** ◇ *He did 15 lengths of backstroke every morning.*
100 metres/meters ... , 200 metres/meters ... , etc. ◇ *the 100 metres/meters butterfly*
men's ... , women's ... ◇ *the women's freestyle*
compete in ... , take part in ... (*esp. BrE*) ◇ *They're competing in the breaststroke.*
in the ... ◇ *He came first in the 200 metres/meters backstroke.*

---

stroke *noun*

1 of a brush, pen, etc.

ADJ. **long, short** | **broad** (*often figurative*), **thick** ◇ *I will outline in broad ~s our main ideas.* | **narrow, thin** | **bold, vigorous** ◇ *She caught his likeness with a few bold pen ~s.* | **even** | **deft** | **quick, slow** | **downward, upward** | **horizontal, vertical** | **brush** (usually **brushstroke**), **pen, pencil**
PHRASES **with a ~ of the pen** ◇ *With a ~ of the pen our names were removed from the register.*

2 in sports

ADJ. **fast, quick** | **slow, smooth** | **powerful** ◇ *The Romanian rowers pulled ahead with powerful ~s.* | **backhand, forehand** (in tennis, etc.) | **downward, upward**
VERB + STROKE **play** ◇ *He played some powerful backhand ~s throughout the game.*
PREP. **by a ~, two ~s, etc.** (in golf) ◇ *Woods leads by two ~s.*
PHRASES **a ~, two ~s, etc. ahead, a ~, two ~s, etc. behind** (in golf)

3 in swimming

ADJ. **swim** (*AmE*), **swimming** | **long, short** ◇ *He swam back with long, slow ~s.* | **fast, slow** | **powerful, strong**
VERB + STROKE **do, swim** ◇ *You can't swim more than four ~s before you reach the other side.*

4 sudden illness of the brain

ADJ. **acute, crippling, debilitating, disabling** (*esp. BrE*), **massive, serious** | **mild, minor, slight** | **fatal, non-fatal** |

recurrent ◇ *This regimen substantially reduces the risks of recurrent ~.*
VERB + STROKE **have, suffer** ◇ *She had a massive ~ and lost her speech.*
STROKE + VERB **leave sb…** ◇ *The ~ left him in a wheelchair.*
STROKE + NOUN **patient, survivor, victim | prevention**
→ Special page at ILLNESS

5 sth that happens unexpectedly
ADJ. **sudden** ◇ *I had a sudden ~ of inspiration.*
VERB + STROKE **have**
PREP. **at a ~, at one ~** ◇ *They lost half their fortune at a ~.* | **~ of** ◇ *a ~ of genius*
PHRASES **a ~ of bad luck, a ~ of fortune, a ~ of good fortune, a ~ of good luck, a ~ of luck**

stroke *verb*
ADV. **gently, lightly, slowly, softly, tenderly | thoughtfully** ◇ *He ~d his beard thoughtfully.* | **absently, absent-mindedly, idly** ◇ *She ~d his hair absently.* | **away, back** *(both esp. BrE)* ◇ *She gently ~d away his tears.* ◇ *He ~d back his hair.*

stroll *noun*
ADJ. **little, quick, short | five-minute, etc.** ◇ *The bars are only a ten-minute ~ away.* | **casual, easy** *(esp. BrE)*, **gentle** *(esp. BrE)*, **leisurely, long | pleasant | moonlit, romantic | midnight, night-time | afternoon, evening, lunchtime** *(esp. BrE)*, **morning, etc.** | **daily | Sunday**
VERB + STROLL **be out for, enjoy, go for, go out for, take** ◇ *They took a leisurely ~ along the river bank.*
PHRASES **a ~ away** *(esp. BrE)* ◇ *The beach is only a short ~ away.*

stroll *verb*
ADV. **casually, leisurely, slowly | about** *(esp. BrE)*, **around, away, back, down, over, etc.** ◇ *They ~ed down to the canal.*
PREP. **across, along, around, through, etc.** ◇ *He hummed to himself as he ~ed leisurely through the streets.*

stroller *noun (AmE)* → See also PUSHCHAIR
ADJ. **baby | double**
VERB + STROLLER **push** ◇ *parents pushing ~s*

strong *adj.*
VERBS **be, feel, look | become, get, grow | remain, stay | prove | stand** ◇ *We must stand ~ in the face of adversity.* | **finish** ◇ *The men's golf team finished ~ on Saturday.* | **make sb** ◇ *All that outdoor work has made him very ~.* | **keep sth** ◇ *This news helped keep the dollar relatively ~ today.* | **smell, taste**
ADV. **extremely, fairly, very, etc.** ◇ *He exerts an extremely ~ influence on his classmates.* | **exceptionally, immensely, incredibly | surprisingly** ◇ *Sales were surprisingly ~ in the second half of the year.* | **enough** ◇ *Don't try to go back to work before you are physically ~ enough.* | **physically**
PHRASES **be still going ~** ◇ *The business is still going ~.*

structure *noun*
ADJ. **basic, simple | complex, elaborate | coherent, logical | rigid, stable | flimsy** ◇ *The flimsy ~ of the vehicle could not withstand even mild impacts.* | **formal | internal, underlying | overall** ◇ *The overall ~ of the book is divided into three components.* | **solid, three-dimensional | concrete, steel, wooden, etc. | anatomical, body, bone, skeletal, skeleton | atomic, cell, cellular, chemical, genetic, molecular | grammatical, language, linguistic, sentence, syntactic | narrative | administrative, bureaucratic, command, committee, control, corporate, governance, hierarchical, institutional, management, organizational, power, etc.** ◇ *the US military command ~* | **economic, financial, political, social, etc.** ◇ *the social ~ of the town* | **democratic, federal, etc. | class | family, household | traditional** ◇ *policies that undermine the traditional family ~* | **pay, price, salary, tax, wage | career**
VERB + STRUCTURE **have | lack** ◇ *The job lacked a basic career ~.* | **need | be based on | build, create, develop, devise,**

establish ◇ *to devise a new management ~* | **form** ◇ *The cells are stacked up to form a honeycomb ~.* | **impose | alter, change**
STRUCTURE + VERB **be based on sth**
PREP. **of a…~** ◇ *The cell walls of plants are of a rigid ~.* | **in a/ the ~** ◇ *There are weaknesses in the ~ of the organization.*
PHRASES **a change in the ~, a change to the ~** ◇ *significant changes in the power ~* | **a lack of ~** ◇ *The novel suffers from a lack of ~.*

structure *verb*
ADV. **beautifully, carefully, clearly, properly** *(esp. BrE)*, **well** ◇ *She had ~d her arguments very carefully.* | **badly | loosely** ◇ *a loosely ~d organization* | **rigidly, tightly** ◇ *a tightly ~d drama* | **differently, similarly | formally, hierarchically, logically**
PREP. **according to** ◇ *The organization is ~d according to business principles.* | **around** ◇ *The teaching is ~d around three topics.* | **as** ◇ *The nation was ~d as a federation of states.* | **by** ◇ *Relations between women and men are ~d by gender.* | **into** ◇ *The company is ~d into two divisions.*
PHRASES **highly ~d** ◇ *a complex but highly ~d procedure*

struggle *noun*
1 fight
ADJ. **epic, great, life-and-death, titanic | bitter, desperate, fierce, heroic, violent** ◇ *There were the sounds of a desperate ~.* | **continuing, ongoing | protracted | unequal** *(esp. BrE)* | **armed** ◇ *The group supported the armed ~ against the dictator.* | **class, internecine** ◇ *Marx wrote about the class ~.* | **inner, internal** ◇ *The author illustrates the inner ~s of this complicated woman.* ◇ *The party is locked in an internal ~.* | **economic, ideological, leadership, liberation, political, power, revolutionary**
VERB + STRUGGLE **begin, end | join, take up** ◇ *They took up the ~ against racism.* | **carry on, wage | be engaged in, be locked in** ◇ *species engaged in a life-or-death ~ with the environment* | **lead | lose, win | put up** ◇ *If someone snatched your bag, would you put up a ~?*
STRUGGLE + VERB **ensue, take place | continue, go on | intensify**
PREP. **in a/the ~** ◇ *One of the guards was hurt in the ~.* | **without a ~** ◇ *She won't give up without a ~.* | **~ against** ◇ *the ~ against oppression* | **~ between** ◇ *the ~ between good and evil* | **~ for** ◇ *the long ~ for democracy* | **~ over** ◇ *a ~ over the property* | **~ with** ◇ *He was involved in a ~ with the police.*
PHRASES **a sign of a ~** ◇ *The police said that there was no sign of a ~ by the murder victim.* | **years of ~** ◇ *After 150 years of ~ against colonial rule, the country won its independence.*

2 great effort
ADJ. **great, hard, real, uphill** ◇ *It will be an uphill ~ to maintain exports at the current level.* | **long | ceaseless, constant, daily, endless** ◇ *the daily ~ for survival*
VERB + STRUGGLE **face, have** ◇ *We had a real ~ to get everything into the suitcase.* | **give up** ◇ *I've given up the ~ to keep my house clean.*
PHRASES **a bit of a ~** ◇ *It was a bit of a ~ for me to get there so early.*

struggle *verb*
1 try very hard to do sth
ADV. **desperately, hard, manfully, mightily** *(esp. AmE)*, **painfully, valiantly** ◇ *He ~d desperately to get to the shore.* ◇ *He ~d hard to keep the boat upright.* | **a little | constantly | on** ◇ *She ~d on despite the pain.*
VERB + STRUGGLE **have to**
PREP. **against** ◇ *The small boat ~d against the waves.* | **along, down, up** ◇ *They ~d up the hill.* | **for** ◇ *Shona ~d for breath.* | **through** ◇ *The family ~d through the next few years.*
PHRASES **~ to your feet** ◇ *She ~d to her feet and set off after him.*

2 have great difficulties

ADV. **badly** ◊ *The team ~d badly last season.* | **really** ◊ *He was really struggling in geometry.* | **clearly**, **obviously** | **financially** ◊ *I was unemployed and struggling financially.* | **defensively** (*esp. AmE*), **offensively** (*AmE*) (*both sports*)
PREP. **through**, **with** ◊ *I'm really struggling with this essay.*
PHRASES **~ to make ends meet** ◊ *For years, she ~d to make ends meet.*

3 fight sb/try to get away from sb

ADV. **fiercely**, **furiously**, **violently** ◊ *She ~d furiously but could not get away.* | **together** ◊ *Ben and Jack ~d together on the grass.*
PREP. **against** ◊ *She ~d against her attacker.* | **with** ◊ *He was hit in the mouth as he ~d with the raiders.*
PHRASES **~ free** ◊ *The attacker's victim managed to ~ free.*

stuck adj.

VERBS **be** | **become**, **get** | **remain** | **get sth** ◊ *She got the key ~ in the lock.*
ADV. **firmly** | **completely**, **fast** ◊ *I couldn't budge the drawer—it was ~ fast.* | **halfway** ◊ *He got ~ halfway up the rock face.*
PREP. **in**, **onto**, **to** ◊ *The tiles were ~ firmly to the wall.*

student noun

ADJ. **brilliant**, **good**, **straight-A**, **talented** ◊ *one of the best ~s the college has ever had* | **college**, **school**, **university** | **A level**, **sixth-form** (*both BrE*) | **full-time**, **part-time** | **prospective** | **first-year**, **second-year**, etc. | **graduate**, **postgraduate**, **research**, **undergraduate** | **doctoral**, **master's**, **PhD**, etc. | **mature** (*BrE*) ◊ *She studied metallurgy as a mature ~.* | **former**, **old** ◊ *She's a former ~ of mine who graduated in the 80s.* | **fellow** ◊ *He developed the website in collaboration with his fellow ~s.* | **foreign**, **international** (*esp. AmE*), **overseas** (*BrE*) | **exchange** ◊ *I first came to America as an exchange ~.* | **art**, **engineering**, **law**, **medical**, **music**, etc.
VERB + STUDENT **enroll** ◊ *Ninety-four ~s were enrolled in the class.* | **educate**, **instruct**, **prepare**, **teach** | **engage**, **motivate** ◊ *teachers who engage ~s in meaningful discussions* | **assist**, **encourage**, **help** ◊ *The ~s are encouraged to think creatively.*
STUDENT + NOUN **nurse**, **teacher** | **numbers**, **population** ◊ *Student numbers at the college have increased by 25%.* | **body** (*esp. AmE*), **council**, **government** (*AmE*), **group**, **organization** | **days** ◊ *She worked hard in her ~ days.* | **life** ◊ *I'm thoroughly enjoying ~ life.* | **participation** | **enrolment/enrollment** | **grant** (*esp. BrE*), **loan** ◊ *She had to take out a ~ loan to help her through college.* | **accommodation** (*BrE*), **dorm** (*informal*), **dormitory** | **newspaper** | **visa** | **activism**, **demonstration**, **protest**, **unrest** ◊ *He often takes part in ~ demonstrations.* | **activist**
PREP. **as a ~** ◊ *She first went to Paris as a ~.*

studio noun

ADJ. **art**, **artist's**, **design**, **photographer's**, **photographic**, **photography**, **portrait** | **animation**, **broadcast**, **film**, **movie** (*esp. AmE*), **production**, **radio**, **recording**, **sound**, **television**, **TV** | **dance**, **music** ◊ *She taught at a private dance ~.* | **rehearsal** | **home** ◊ *The CD was recorded in his home ~.* | **big**, **large**, **major** ◊ *a major movie ~* | **independent**, **private** (*both esp. AmE*)
STUDIO + NOUN **audience** ◊ *a ~ audience for a new television sitcom* | **executive**, **head** ◊ *He was a ~ executive at Paramount.* | **system** ◊ *the constraints of the Hollywood ~ system* | **album**, **recording** | **film** (*esp. BrE*), **movie** (*esp. AmE*) | **release**, **version** | **work** ◊ *I was doing a lot of ~ work and remixing.* | **space**, **time**
PREP. **in a/the ~** ◊ *The photograph was taken in a ~.*

study noun

1 learning

ADJ. **full-time**, **part-time** | **graduate**, **postgraduate** | **independent**, **private** ◊ *This grammar book is suitable both for classroom use and for independent ~.* | **academic** ◊ *The course integrates academic ~ and practical training.* | **language**
...OF STUDY **course**, **programme/program**
VERB + STUDY **take up** ◊ *Now that her children are all at school, she's going to take up full-time ~ again.*
STUDY + NOUN **group** ◊ *A ~ group meets every Sunday at the church.* | **programme/program** | **leave** (*BrE*) ◊ *The company allows its staff to take paid ~ leave.* | **skills** ◊ *The first part of the course is designed to develop students' ~ skills.* | **hall** (*AmE*), **period**
PREP. **~ for** ◊ *full-time ~ for an MA*
PHRASES **an area of ~**, **a field of ~** ◊ *Students do a foundation year before specializing in their chosen field of ~.*

2 studies sb's learning activities

ADJ. **further** ◊ *Many undertake further studies after college.*
VERB + STUDIES **begin**, **undertake** (*formal*) | **continue**, **pursue** | **complete**, **finish** ◊ *When he has completed his studies, he'll travel around the world.* | **resume**, **return to** ◊ *She returned to her studies when her children reached school age.*

3 studies subjects

ADJ. **area**, **business**, **cultural**, **management**, **media**, **religious**, **women's**, etc. ◊ *She's doing women's studies at Liverpool University.*
VERB + STUDIES **do** | **lecture in**, **teach** ◊ *He lectures in management studies.*
STUDIES + NOUN **department** ◊ *Princeton's African American studies department* | **course**, **programme/program** ◊ *the university's cultural studies course*

4 piece of research

ADJ. **current**, **new**, **present**, **recent** ◊ *The present ~ reveals an unacceptable level of air pollution in the city.* | **earlier**, **original**, **previous** | **future** | **careful**, **close**, **comprehensive**, **detailed**, **in-depth**, **intensive**, **serious** ◊ *a close ~ of energy prices* ◊ *She devoted herself to a serious ~ of the literature.* | **longitudinal** ◊ *a longitudinal ~ of children in low-income families* | **definitive**, **major** | **initial**, **pilot**, **preliminary** ◊ *A preliminary ~ suggested that the product would be popular.* | **research** ◊ *Research studies carried out in Italy confirmed the theory.* | **clinical**, **empirical**, **experimental**, **systematic**, **theoretical** | **anthropological**, **historical**, **literary**, **scientific**, **sociological**, etc. | **field** ◊ *This phenomenon has been observed in field studies.* | **feasibility** ◊ *The company undertook an extensive feasibility ~ before adopting the new system.* | **time-and-motion** | **case** ◊ *a detailed case ~ of nine companies* | **comparative** ◊ *a comparative ~ of the environmental costs of different energy sources* | **independent** ◊ *An independent ~ was commissioned by the department.*
VERB + STUDY **commission**, **fund**, **support** ◊ *a ~ commissioned by the World Bank* | **carry out**, **conduct**, **do**, **make**, **participate in**, **undertake**, **work on** ◊ *He has made a special ~ of the way that birds communicate.* | **publish**
STUDY + VERB **take place** | **aim at sth**, **aim to do sth**, **attempt to**, **be aimed at sth**, **be designed to**, **set out to** ◊ *The ~ aims to examine bias in television news coverage.* | **be based on sth** ◊ *a ~ based on a sample of male white-collar workers* | **concern sth**, **cover sth**, **deal with sth**, **examine sth**, **explore sth**, **focus on sth**, **investigate sth**, **look at sth** ◊ *The ten-year ~ covered 13 000 people aged 15-25.* | **compare sth** ◊ *The ~ compares the incidence of bone cancer in men and women.* | **conclude sth**, **confirm sth**, **demonstrate sth**, **document sth**, **find sth**, **indicate sth**, **prove sth**, **report sth**, **reveal sth**, **say sth**, **show sth**, **suggest sth**, **support sth**, **warn sth** ◊ *A new ~ shows that fewer students are ~ing science.* | **provide sth** ◊ *The ~ provided valuable insight into the development of the disease.* | **highlight sth**, **identify sth** ◊ *The ~ highlighted three problem areas.*
STUDY + NOUN **group** ◊ *The ~ group was selected from a broad cross section of the population.* | **session**
PREP. **according to a/the ~**, **in a/the ~** ◊ *In a recent ~, 40% of*

schools were found to be understaffed. | **under ~** ◇ *the biochemical process under ~* | **~ into** ◇ *a ~ into the viability of the mine* | **~ on** ◇ *a definitive ~ on medieval weapons*
PHRASES **an area of ~, a field of ~** | **the author of a/the ~** | **the objective of a/the ~, the purpose of a/the ~** | **the findings of a/the ~, the results of a/the ~** | **the subject of a/the ~** ◇ *Shakespeare is the subject of a new ~ by Kraft.*

study *verb*

1 spend time learning about sth
ADV. **hard** | **abroad**
PREP. **at** ◇ *to ~ at college* | **for** ◇ *She is ~ing hard for her exams.* | **under, with** ◇ *He studied under Professor Sager.*

2 examine sth carefully
ADV. **carefully, closely, in depth, in detail, intensively, intently** ◇ *She picked up the letter and studied it carefully.* ◇ *In the third year a number of areas are studied in detail.* | **extensively, widely** | **fully, thoroughly** | **systematically** | **thoughtfully** ◇ *He studied her thoughtfully, then smiled.*
PHRASES **be well studied** ◇ *This area has not been well studied.*

stuff *verb*

ADV. **frantically, hastily, quickly**
PREP. **down** ◇ *The police found the money that she'd ~ed down her dress.* | **in, into** ◇ *He hastily ~ed a few clothes into a bag.* | **inside, up, with, etc.** ◇ *She ~ed her case with presents for the kids.*
PHRASES **be ~ed full of sth** ◇ *Her briefcase was ~ed full of papers.* | **be ~ed to the brim (with sth), be ~ed to the gills (with sth)** ◇ *The room was ~ed to the gills with trophies.* | **~ your face (with sth), ~ yourself silly (with sth)** (*esp. BrE*) ◇ *He was ~ing his face full of chocolate.*

stumble *verb*

ADV. **almost, nearly** | **a little, slightly** ◇ *She ~d a little on the uneven path.* | **badly** (*often figurative*) ◇ *The economy ~d badly at the end of 2000.* | **blindly** ◇ *He ~d blindly on through the dark building.* | **along, away, back, on, etc.**
PREP. **down, from, into, out of, over, etc.** ◇ *They ~d over the field.*
PHRASES **~ over the/your words** ◇ *Josh was nervous and ~d over his words.* | **~ to your feet** ◇ *The train stopped, and several passengers ~d to their feet.*

PHR V **stumble across, into, on/upon sth**
ADV. **accidentally, by chance, unwittingly** ◇ *I ~d across the place quite by chance.* | **finally**

stumbling block *noun*

ADJ. **big, key, main, major, real** | **potential**
VERB + STUMBLING BLOCK **be, prove, prove to be** ◇ *Money could prove a ~ to the project.* | **become** | **hit** ◇ *The negotiations have hit a ~ over the price.* | **remove**
PREP. **~ to** ◇ *The question of disarmament proved a major ~ to agreement.*

stun *verb*

ADV. **briefly, momentarily**
PREP. **into** ◇ *The assault was so unexpected that he was briefly stunned into submission.*
PHRASES **~ sb into silence** ◇ *The guests were stunned into silence.*

stunned *adj.*

VERBS **appear, be, feel, look, seem, sit, sound, stand** ◇ *Morton stood ~, unable to believe his ears.* | **leave sb** ◇ *Leaving them all ~, she walked out of the bar.*
ADV. **absolutely, completely, quite, simply, totally, utterly** | **rather, somewhat** | **almost** | **a little, slightly, etc.** | **for a moment, momentarily, temporarily**
PREP. **at** ◇ *They seemed ~ at his outburst.* | **by** ◇ *She was a little ~ by the news.* | **with** ◇ *~ with grief*

stunning *adj.*

VERBS **be, look** | **find sth**

ADV. **really** ◇ *You look really ~ in that dress!* | **absolutely, quite, simply, truly** ◇ *The finished effect was absolutely ~.* | **visually** ◇ *a visually ~ movie*

stunt *noun*

1 sth done for attention
ADJ. **PR, promotional, publicity** | **media, political** | **little** (*disapproving*) ◇ *What was the point of tonight's little ~?* | **crazy, stupid**
VERB + STUNT **arrange, organize, stage** ◇ *She arranged a publicity ~ to make the public aware of the product.* | **pull** ◇ *What do you hope to gain by pulling a ~ like that?*
STUNT + VERB **backfire**
PREP. **as a ~** ◇ *They jumped off the bridge as a publicity ~.*

2 dangerous act
ADJ. **dangerous, daredevil, daring, death-defying** | **dramatic** (*esp. BrE*) | **spectacular** | **aerial**
VERB + STUNT **do, perform** ◇ *The actor performed all the ~s himself.* | **attempt**
STUNT + VERB **go wrong**
STUNT + NOUN **coordinator, man** (usually *stuntman*)**, woman** (usually *stuntwoman*) ◇ *a Hollywood stuntwoman* | **double** ◇ *He was Tom Cruise's ~ double.* | **driver, pilot, rider** | **work**

stupid *adj.*

VERBS **appear, be, feel, look, seem, sound** ◇ *I felt so ~ when I realized what had happened.* ◇ *My sister made me look ~ in front of all my friends.* | **get** ◇ *The situation is getting ~.* | **act, play** (*AmE*) ◇ *I decided it was best to act ~.* ◇ *Don't play ~, Carlos—what happened?* | **call sb** | **make sb** ◇ *Success has made him ~.*
ADV. **extremely, fairly, very, etc.** | **amazingly, exceptionally, incredibly, monumentally, particularly, ridiculously, truly, unbelievably** ◇ *a truly ~ thing to do* | **absolutely, completely, plain, simply, totally, utterly** ◇ *That was just plain ~!* | **not entirely** ◇ *I'm not entirely ~.* *I checked the train times before we came out.* | **a little, slightly, etc.** | **enough, sufficiently** ◇ *He's ~ enough to believe anything.*
PHRASES **be too ~ to do sth** ◇ *She's too ~ to realize that she'd be happier without him.*

stupidity *noun*

ADJ. **complete, crass** (*BrE*)**, incredible, plain, sheer, utter** ◇ *It's hard to know if it's corruption or just plain ~ by the authorities.* | **human**
VERB + STUPIDITY **can't believe** ◇ *I can't believe the ~ of some people.* | **realize** ◇ *I now realize the ~ of that statement.* | **curse** ◇ *He cursed his own ~.* | **demonstrate, show** ◇ *Her answer showed the most incredible ~.*
PREP. **through (your) ~** ◇ *Through his own ~, he missed an excellent opportunity.*
PHRASES **~ on sb's part** ◇ *It was sheer ~ on the part of the crew.*

stupor *noun*

ADJ. **alcoholic, dazed, drug-induced, drunken** ◇ *He fell into an alcoholic ~.*
VERB + STUPOR **drink yourself into, fall into, go into, sink into** ◇ *As the vodka took effect, he gradually fell into a drunken ~.* | **come out of, emerge from** | **rouse sb from, shake sb out of, snap sb out of** ◇ *The noise of someone banging at the door roused her from her ~.*
PREP. **in a ~** ◇ *He fell to the ground in a ~.*

style *noun*

1 way that sth is done/made
ADJ. **latest, modern, new** | **classic, classical, old, old-fashioned, period, traditional** ◇ *an old ~ of management* | **contemporary** ◇ *The house has been renovated and furnished in contemporary ~.* | **characteristic, distinctive, individual, inimitable, original, signature, typical, unique** ◇ *her inimitable personal ~* | **personal** | **musical, visual** |

acting, fighting, painting, playing, etc. | **architectural** | learning, teaching | **leadership**, **management**, **managerial** | **house** ◇ *a chain of bars which has developed its own house* ~ | **political** | **literary**, **narrative**, **prose**, **writing** | **elegant**, **lively** | **flamboyant** ◇ *a flamboyant* ~ *of dress* | **formal** | **casual** ◇ *She was dressed in casual* ~. | **conversational** ◇ *The article is written in a conversational* ~. | **aggressive** ◇ *His aggressive* ~ *of play sometimes gets him in trouble.* | **autocratic** ◇ *an autocratic* ~ *of leadership* | **18th-century**, etc. | **Gothic**, **Renaissance**, etc.

... OF STYLES **range**, **variety** ◇ *a wide range of musical* ~s

VERB + STYLE **have** ◇ *The two artists have radically different* ~s. | **develop**, **establish**, **evolve**, **find**, **form** ◇ *He evolved his* ~ *of painting while working as a magazine illustrator.* | **adapt**, **adjust**, **alter**, **change**, **modify** ◇ *He adapted his acting* ~ *to suit the material.* | **adopt**, **use** | **copy**, **emulate**, **follow**

STYLE + NOUN **sheet** (*computing*)

PREP. **in** ~ ◇ *very utilitarian in* ~ | **in a/the** ~ ◇ *The new houses have been built in a traditional* ~.

2 good quality

ADJ. **fine**, **great**, **real**, **terrific** (*esp. BrE*) | **certain**

VERB + STYLE **have** ◇ *He has a certain* ~. | **ooze** ◇ *The whole house just oozed* ~. | **add**, **give sb/sth**

PREP. **in** ~ ◇ *They celebrated in* ~ *by popping open a bottle of champagne.* ◇ *to arrive/go out/travel in* ~ | **with** ~ ◇ *Whatever she did, she did it with* ~.

PHRASES **like sb's** ~ ◇ *I like your* ~! *It shows real courage.* | **a sense of** ~ ◇ *his innate sense of* ~ | **a touch of** ~ (*esp. BrE*) ◇ *Curtains add a touch of* ~ *to the room.*

subject *noun*

1 topic or person under consideration

ADJ. **big**, **complex**, **complicated**, **vast** | **simple** | **excellent**, **fascinating**, **good**, **interesting** | **serious** ◇ *This chapter deals with a very serious* ~. | **controversial**, **delicate**, **difficult**, **embarrassing**, **sensitive**, **touchy** | **taboo** ◇ *Work is a taboo* ~ *when we go out for dinner.* | **closed** ◇ *I don't wish to discuss it any further—the* ~ *is closed.* | **different**, **diverse**, **various** ◇ *books on such diverse* ~s *as trains and ancient sculpture* | **chosen** ◇ *Each candidate has to speak for three minutes on her chosen* ~. | **favourite/favorite**, **pet** (*esp. BrE*) ◇ *Once he gets onto his pet* ~ *there's no stopping him.* | **control**, **healthy**, **human**, **normal**, **research**, **study**, **test** (*all science*) ◇ *research on human* ~s

VERB + SUBJECT **cover**, **debate**, **discuss**, **talk about**, **touch** (*esp. AmE*), **touch on** ◇ *We touched briefly on the* ~. | **address**, **deal with**, **tackle**, **treat** ◇ *I wasn't sure how to deal with the delicate* ~ *of money.* | **examine**, **explore**, **have a look at**, **investigate**, **look at**, **look into**, **pursue** ◇ *We want to have a fresh look at the difficult* ~ *of corporate fraud.* | **approach**, **bring up**, **broach**, **get onto**, **raise** | **drop** ◇ *Let's drop the* ~ *since we don't seem to be able to agree.* | **stick to** ◇ *I wish he'd stick to the* ~. | **get off**, **wander off** ◇ *She was supposed to be speaking about sales figures, but she kept wandering off the* ~. | **bring sb back to**, **get back to**, **return to** ◇ *Getting back to the* ~ *of lighting, does anyone have any suggestions for improvements?* | **avoid** | **change**, **switch** (*AmE*) ◇ *Don't change the* ~.

SUBJECT + VERB **arise**, **come up** ◇ *The* ~ *of gambling has come up several times recently.* | **range from sth to sth** ◇ *Internet courses on diverse* ~s *ranging from nursing to computers*

SUBJECT + NOUN **matter** ◇ *I like the way she writes, although I'm not interested in her* ~ *matter.*

PREP. **on a/the** ~ ◇ *While we're on the* ~ *of books, has anyone read 'The Corrections'?* | ~ **of** ◇ *the* ~ *of the new painting*

PHRASES **a range of** ~s ◇ *We discussed a wide range of* ~s. | **a variety of** ~s ◇ *She touches on a wide variety of* ~s.

2 area of study

ADJ. **difficult**, **easy** | **compulsory**, **core**, **main** | **additional**, **optional**, **special** | **specialist** | **technical** ◇ *students of technical* ~s | **research** | **art** (*AmE*), **arts** (*BrE*), **science** | **academic**

VERB + SUBJECT **take** ◇ *What* ~s *are you taking* (= studying)

this year? | **offer** ◇ *The department offers seven different* ~s *in all.* | **choose** | **study** ◇ *I have spent a lifetime studying this* ~. | **teach** ◇ *those who teach core* ~s *like English* | **fail**, **fail in**, **pass** ◇ *She was disappointed to fail in two of her four* ~s. | **drop** ◇ *Students are free to drop the* ~ *at age 14.*

SUBJECT + NOUN **area** ◇ *The syllabus is divided into five* ~ *areas.*

PREP. **in a/the** ~ ◇ *He did well in every* ~.

PHRASES **a choice of** ~, **a choice of** ~s ◇ *His unusual choice of* ~s *made it harder to find a job.* | **a range of** ~s

---

Subjects of study

do... (*BrE*), **read**... (*BrE, formal*), **study**... ◇ *She did physics and chemistry at school.* ◇ *She read classics at Cambridge.* ◇ *He studied German at school.* ◇ *She went on to study mathematics at college.*

choose..., **take**... ◇ *I'm taking philosophy and politics this year.*

fail..., **flunk**... (*AmE, informal*), **pass**... ◇ *I failed English.* ◇ *I flunked math.* ◇ *Did you pass history?*

drop... ◇ *I want to drop linguistics.*

lecture in... (*esp. BrE*), **teach**... ◇ *He taught music at a school in Cuba.*

a... **degree**, **a degree in**..., **a diploma in**... ◇ *a law degree* ◇ *a higher diploma in fine art*

... **class**, ... **course**, ... **lecture**, ... **lesson** (*esp. BrE*) ◇ *The genetics lectures are on a different campus.*

a/the... **department**, **a/the department of**... ◇ *All queries should be addressed to the Department of Architecture.*

... **graduate**, ... **student**, ... **undergraduate** ◇ *Some architecture graduates gain further qualifications in specialist fields.*

... **lecturer**, ... **teacher**, ... **tutor** (*esp. BrE*) ◇ *He's an English teacher at Orange Road School.*

a... **professor**, **(a) professor of**... ◇ *She's professor of linguistics at MIT.*

the study of... ◇ *The study of philosophy helps you to think critically.*

in... ◇ *He got As in history and art.*

subject *adj.* **subject to sth**

1 likely to be affected by sth

VERBS **be**, **seem** | **become** | **leave sb/sth**, **make sb/sth** ◇ *His illness left him* ~ *to asthma attacks.*

ADV. **particularly** | **frequently**, **increasingly** | **potentially** | **still** ◇ *At this stage these proposals are still* ~ *to change.*

2 under the authority of sb/sth

VERBS **be** ◇ *Everyone was* ~ *to the whim of the sheikh.* | **become** | **remain** | **make sb/sth**

ADV. **entirely** | **directly**

subjective *adj.*

VERBS **appear**, **be**, **seem**

ADV. **extremely**, **fairly**, **very**, etc. | **highly** ◇ *painted from a highly* ~ *point of view* | **completely**, **entirely**, **purely**, **totally**, **wholly** ◇ *The criticisms are purely* ~. | **essentially**, **largely** ◇ *Taste in art is essentially* ~. | **inherently**, **necessarily** ◇ *The process of selection is inherently* ~ *and deeply unfair.*

submarine *noun*

ADJ. **conventional** | **atomic**, **ballistic-missile**, **nuclear**, **nuclear-powered** | **midget**, **miniature** | **enemy** | **attack**

SUBMARINE + VERB **dive**, **sink** | **surface** | **sink sth** | **operate**, **patrol (sth)** ◇ *the problem of* ~s *operating too close to fishing vessels* | **be equipped with sth**, **carry sth** ◇ ~s *carrying nuclear warheads*

SUBMARINE + NOUN **captain**, **commander**, **crew** | **base**, **fleet** | **attack**, **warfare**

submerged *adj.*

VERBS **be**, **lie**, **remain** | **become**

ADV. **deeply | completely, fully, totally | almost, nearly | barely** ◇ *barely ~ antagonism* | **half, partially, partly**
PREP. **in** ◇ *The machine is totally ~ in water.* | **below, beneath, under** ◇ *The car was ~ under 20 feet of water.*

submission noun

1 accepting sb else's control

ADJ. **complete, total**
VERB + SUBMISSION **demand, expect** ◇ *The emperor demanded total ~ from his subjects.* | **get** | **beat sb into, bludgeon sb into, bomb sb into, force sb into, frighten sb into, intimidate sb into, pound sb into, scare sb into, starve sb into** ◇ *They bombed the town into ~.*
PREP. **~ to** ◇ *the patient's ~ to the demands of the hospital*

2 plan/statement

ADJ. **detailed, lengthy** ◇ *He prepared a detailed ~ for the directors to study.* | **joint** (*esp. BrE*) | **electronic, email, online** ◇ *The university is setting up a website to allow electronic ~ of manuscripts.* | **unsolicited** | **article, manuscript** | **new** ◇ *We're looking for new ~s.*
VERB + SUBMISSION **make | accept | reject | review | get, receive, take** ◇ *The agency got 15 ~s from 11 countries.* | **require | encourage, welcome** ◇ *We welcome ~s from writers and reviewers.* | **send** ◇ *Send ~s via email to the editor.*
PREP. **in a/the ~ | ~ for** ◇ *The Society invites ~s for a special issue.* | **~ to** ◇ *The companies have made a joint ~ to the president.*

3 (*BrE*) statement made to a judge

ADJ. **oral, written | closing**
VERB + SUBMISSION **consider, hear | support, uphold** ◇ *The judge upheld the defendant's ~.*

submit verb

1 give/propose sth so that it can be discussed

ADV. **formally** ◇ *He formally submitted his resignation.* | **respectfully** (*law, esp. BrE*) ◇ *May I respectfully ~ that this is not the right thing to do?* | **humbly | electronically, online** ◇ *21% of the votes were submitted online.* | **originally, previously** ◇ *the manuscript I originally submitted to them*
VERB + SUBMIT **ask sb to, invite sb to, require sb to** ◇ *Six groups were invited to ~ proposals for the research.* ◇ *Candidates for the degree are required to ~ a 30000-word thesis.* | **intend to, plan to**
PREP. **for** ◇ *They have submitted plans for our approval.* | **to** ◇ *She submitted her report to the committee.*

2 accept sb's power/control

ADV. **voluntarily, willingly** ◇ *He voluntarily submitted to their control.* | **meekly**
VERB + SUBMIT **refuse to | agree to, be prepared to, be willing to | be compelled to, be forced to, be obliged to** ◇ *They were forced to ~ to foreign rule.*
PREP. **to** ◇ *She refused to ~ to threats.*

subordinate adj.

VERBS **be | become | remain**
ADV. **completely, wholly | essentially** ◇ *He had an essentially ~ role.* | **directly** ◇ *She was directly ~ to the president.*
PREP. **to**

subscribe verb

PHR V **subscribe to sth**
ADV. **fully, wholeheartedly** ◇ *I ~ wholeheartedly to this theory.* | **personally** ◇ *I do not personally ~ to this idea.*

subscriber noun

ADJ. **newspaper | broadband, cable** (*esp. AmE*)**, digital, Internet, magazine, satellite, wireless | cellular** (*AmE*)**, mobile** (*esp. BrE*)**, mobile-phone** (*esp. BrE*)**, phone, telephone | regular | annual | long-time** (*esp. AmE*) | **new**
PREP. **~ to** ◇ *Subscribers to the magazine can take advantage of this special offer.*

subscription noun

ADJ. **annual, monthly, yearly, etc. | one-month, one-year, etc.** ◇ *a one-year ~ to this service* | **lifetime | full | paid** (*esp. AmE*) | **complimentary, free, gift** (*AmE*) | **trial** ◇ *a 30-day free trial ~* | **new** ◇ *The company has already sold 500 000 new ~s for the magazine.* | **individual, institutional, personal | Internet, online | journal, magazine, newspaper**
VERB + SUBSCRIPTION **buy, pay, purchase | take out | get, receive** ◇ *Customers receive a free ~ to our newsletter.* | **renew | cancel | require** ◇ *Most of the articles require a ~.*
SUBSCRIPTION + NOUN **fee, price, rate | service** ◇ *It is available through an annual ~ service.* | **list**
PREP. **for, ~ to** ◇ *a yearly ~ for a print version of the journal* ◇ *Do you wish to take out a full twelve-month ~ to the journal?*
PHRASES **a month's, year's, etc. ~** ◇ *The prize was a year's ~ to 'Newsweek'.*

subside verb

ADV. **quickly, rapidly, soon** ◇ *My laughter soon ~d.* | **gradually, slowly** ◇ *The storm gradually ~d.* | **a little, slightly, etc. | somewhat | eventually, finally**
VERB + SUBSIDE **begin to, start to**
PREP. **into** ◇ *Her tears ~d into sniffs.*

subsidence noun

ADJ. **rapid, slow**
VERB + SUBSIDENCE **suffer from** (*esp. BrE*) ◇ *A number of houses had suffered from ~.*
SUBSIDENCE + VERB **occur** (*esp. BrE*)

subsidiary noun

ADJ. **foreign, offshore** (*esp. AmE*)**, overseas** (*esp. BrE*) | **German, Madrid-based, etc. | wholly-owned** ◇ *a wholly-owned ~ of Millennium Graphics* | **banking, manufacturing, software, etc. | for-profit** (*AmE*) ◇ *The Association established two for-profit subsidiaries.*
VERB + SUBSIDIARY **operate as** ◇ *The company operates as a wholly-owned ~ of a large French company.* | **operate** ◇ *The company operates two subsidiaries.* | **have, own | create, establish, form, open** ◇ *their decision to open a ~ in India* | **acquire | close**
SUBSIDIARY + NOUN **company**
→ Note at ORGANIZATION

subsidize (*BrE also* -ise) verb

PHRASES **heavily ~d, highly ~d** ◇ *The airline is heavily ~d by the government.* | **federally ~d** (*AmE*)

subsidy noun

ADJ. **big, generous, heavy, huge, large, massive | small | direct | hidden, indirect** ◇ *The help that the government gives the industry amounts to an indirect ~.* | **annual | domestic, EU, federal, government, public, state | corporate** (*esp. AmE*)**, financial, tax** (*esp. AmE*)**, taxpayer** (*AmE*) | **agricultural, childcare, export, farm, food, housing | illegal**
... OF SUBSIDY **amount, level** ◇ *The level of ~ given to farmers is to be reduced.*
VERB + SUBSIDY **get, receive | lose | give sth, grant sth, offer, pay, provide (sth with)** ◇ *The Arts Council granted them a small ~.* | **increase | cut, phase out, reduce** ◇ *Export subsidies have been reduced by 20%.* | **abolish, eliminate** (*esp. AmE*)**, end, remove**
SUBSIDY + NOUN **payments | scheme** (*BrE*)**, system | cuts**
PREP. **~ for** ◇ *state subsidies for rice producers* | **~ on** ◇ *subsidies on basic goods and services* | **~ to** ◇ *subsidies to agriculture*
PHRASES **a cut in subsidies, a reduction in subsidies** ◇ *The government cut spending through reductions in state subsidies to industry.* | **the abolition of subsidies, the removal of subsidies, the withdrawal of subsidies** ◇

protests against the removal of subsidies on basic commodities

subsistence noun

ADJ. **bare**, **basic**
SUBSISTENCE + NOUN **agriculture**, **farming** | **farmer** | **economy** | **level** ◇ Most of the population lives at ~ level. | **needs** ◇ their family's basic ~ needs | **wage** (esp. BrE) ◇ She earns less than a ~ wage at the mail-order company.
PHRASES **a level of ~** ◇ They were living barely above the level of ~. | **means of ~** ◇ She had no means of ~ and was dependent on charity.

substance noun

1 material

ADJ. **addictive**, **cancer-causing** (esp. AmE), **carcinogenic**, **dangerous**, **harmful**, **hazardous**, **noxious**, **poisonous**, **radioactive**, **toxic** | **harmless**, **innocuous** ◇ Even innocuous ~s can sometimes register a positive result in a drug test. | **banned**, **controlled**, **illegal**, **illicit**, **prohibited** | **hallucinogenic**, **mind-altering**, **psychedelic**, **psychoactive**, **psychotropic** | **performance-enhancing** | **natural** ◇ a natural ~ found in the body of animals | **synthetic** | **chemical** | **inorganic**, **organic** | **pure** | **soluble**, **volatile** | **active**, **inactive**, **inert** | **crystalline**, **fatty**, **gooey** (informal), **oily**, **powdery**, **slimy**, **sticky**, **viscous**, **waxy** | **medicinal** | **foreign**, **unknown** ◇ foreign ~s that contaminated the experiments | **material**
VERB + SUBSTANCE **use** | **abuse** | **contain** | **produce** ◇ Some frogs produce toxic ~s in their skin. | **take** ◇ The athletes had taken banned ~s.
SUBSTANCE + NOUN **use** | **abuse**

2 important content

ADJ. **real** ◇ The real ~ of the report was in the third part. | **added** ◇ His disappearance has given added ~ to the argument that he stole the money.
VERB + SUBSTANCE **have** ◇ The image of him that the media have presented has no ~. | **add**, **give sth**, **lend sth** ◇ The letters lent ~ to the claims. | **lack**
PREP. **in ~** ◇ There's no difference in ~ between the two points of view. | **of ~** ◇ Nothing of ~ was achieved at the meeting. | **with ~** ◇ lyrics with ~ | **without ~** ◇ Their allegations were without ~. | **~ in** ◇ There's no ~ in the story. | **~ of** ◇ the ~ of the evidence against him | **~ to** ◇ There was little ~ to his claims.

substitute noun

ADJ. **good** | **acceptable**, **adequate**, **perfect**, **satisfactory**, **suitable** | **healthy** ◇ Carob is a healthy ~ for chocolate. | **close** | **imperfect** (esp. AmE), **poor** ◇ The television is a poor ~ for human companionship. | **cheap** | **meat**, **milk**, **sugar**, etc.
VERB + SUBSTITUTE **act as**, **serve as** ◇ His teacher acted as a father ~. | **use sth as** | **produce**, **provide** ◇ The company produces ~s for engine oil.
SUBSTITUTE + NOUN **teacher** (AmE)
PREP. **~ for** ◇ There's no ~ for hard work.

subtitle noun

ADJ. **English**, **French**, etc. | **optional** ◇ The film is presented in French with optional English ~s.
VERB + SUBTITLE **have** | **read**
PREP. **with ~s** ◇ a Japanese movie with English ~s

subtle adj.

VERBS **be**, **seem** | **become**
ADV. **extremely**, **fairly**, **very**, etc. | **extraordinarily**, **incredibly** | **infinitely** ◇ infinitely ~ tonal gradations | **not exactly**, **not too** ◇ He was not exactly ~ about it!

subtlety noun

ADJ. **extreme**, **great**, **real**

VERB + SUBTLETY **have** ◇ Her dancing has great ~. | **display**, **show** | **bring** ◇ His understanding of light brings great ~ to his painting. | **lack** | **appreciate**, **grasp**, **understand** ◇ She was too young to grasp the subtleties of the movie.
PREP. **with ~** ◇ He uses language with great ~.
PHRASES **a lack of ~** | **of great ~**, **of some ~** ◇ a pianist of great ~

suburb noun

ADJ. **outer**, **outlying** | **inner**, **inner-ring** (AmE) | **northern**, **southern**, etc. | **surrounding** ◇ people in the surrounding ~s and small towns | **Berlin**, **Tokyo**, etc. | **affluent**, **comfortable**, **exclusive**, **prosperous**, **rich**, **smart** (esp. BrE), **upmarket** (BrE), **upscale** (AmE), **wealthy** | **poor** | **middle-class**, **working-class** | **respectable** | **pleasant** | **leafy**, **quiet** | **garden** (esp. BrE) | **grey/gray** | **black**, **white** ◇ the mostly white ~ of Woodland Beach | **industrial**, **residential** | **sprawling** ◇ out beyond the sprawling ~s
VERB + SUBURB **move to** ◇ As soon as we can afford it, we'll move to the ~s.
SUBURB + VERB **grow** ◇ The middle-class ~s are growing fast.
PREP. **from the ~s** ◇ For a child from the ~s, a trip to the city was a great adventure. | **in a/the ~** ◇ She's renting in a ~ of Boston. | **in the ~s** ◇ People often prefer to live in the ~s and commute to work. | **~s of** ◇ the coastal ~s of the capital

subversive noun

ADJ. **dangerous** | **alleged**, **suspected**

subversive adj.

VERBS **be** | **consider sth**, **deem sth**, **regard sth as**, **see sth as**
ADV. **very** | **inherently** | **potentially** | **morally** | **politically**

subway noun

1 (AmE) underground train system → See also UNDERGROUND

ADJ. **crowded**
VERB + SUBWAY **ride**, **take**, **use** | **get on**, **hop on** | **get off**
SUBWAY + NOUN **car**, **train** | **platform**, **tunnel** | **station**, **stop** | **line**, **system** | **token** | **map** | **ride** ◇ Yankee Stadium is a 40-minute ~ ride from our house. | **rider** ◇ During the blackout, ~ riders were stranded and unable to get home.
PREP. **in the ~** ◇ rush hour in the ~ | **on the ~** ◇ I've never been on the ~.

2 (BrE) path under a road

ADJ. **pedestrian**
PREP. **along a/the ~**, **in a/the ~**, **through a/the ~** ◇ He ran through the pedestrian ~.

succeed verb

1 manage to achieve what you want; do well

ADV. **admirably**, **beautifully** (esp. AmE), **brilliantly**, **marvellously/marvelously** (esp. AmE), **well**, **wildly** (esp. AmE), **wonderfully** ◇ The book ~s beautifully in presenting the problem before us. ◇ The plan ~ed pretty well. | **not quite** | **nearly** ◇ They very nearly ~ed in blowing up the building. | **completely**, **fully**, **truly** | **largely**, **mostly** ◇ We feel that we have largely ~ed in our aims. | **partially**, **partly** | **rarely** ◇ This option has rarely ~ed in recent years. | **eventually**, **finally**, **ultimately** | **apparently** | **academically** ◇ the pressure on children to ~ academically
VERB + SUCCEED **be likely to**, **be unlikely to** ◇ The appeal is unlikely to ~. | **be determined to**, **hope to**, **want to** ◇ No company can hope to ~ at everything. | **attempt to**, **try to** | **manage to**
PREP. **against** ◇ to ~ against serious opposition | **at** ◇ She can teach you how to ~ at tennis. | **in** ◇ We ~ed in repairing the engine. | **with** ◇ hints on how to ~ with interior design

2 have a job/position after sb else

VERB + SUCCEED **appoint sb to**, **elect sb to** (esp. BrE) ◇ He was appointed to ~ Solti as head of the orchestra. | **be tipped to** (esp. BrE) | **be expected to** ◇ He was expected to ~ Jack Smith as CEO when he retired.

success noun

1 good results

ADJ. **enormous, great, immense, massive** | **considerable, real, tremendous** | **conspicuous, notable, remarkable, spectacular** | **extraordinary, incredible, phenomenal** | **amazing, astonishing, overwhelming, stunning, surprising** | **unparalleled, unprecedented** | **limited, moderate, modest, partial, relative** ◊ *The campaign had only limited ~.* | **mixed** ◊ *the mixed ~ of the project* | **popular, public** | **early, initial** | **subsequent** | **eventual, ultimate** ◊ *Their ultimate ~ has yet to be determined.* | **future** | **recent** ◊ *the recent ~ of films from Mexico* | **immediate** | **continued, continuing** | **long-term, short-term** | **overall** ◊ *the overall ~ of the project* | **apparent** ◊ *He was pleased with his apparent ~.* | **unexpected** | **artistic, business, commercial, economic, entrepreneurial, financial** | **academic, educational, electoral, literary, military, professional, etc.** | **material, worldly** ◊ *the immediate satisfaction of worldly ~* | **international, worldwide** ◊ *The company's excellent marketing has resulted in enormous international ~.*
...OF SUCCESS **amount, degree, level, rate** ◊ *Initially the venture enjoyed a fair amount of ~.*
VERB + SUCCESS **achieve, attain, enjoy, have, notch up** ◊ *She had little ~ in getting new customers.* ◊ *He is eager to notch up another ~.* | **celebrate** ◊ *We were celebrating our ~.* | **experience, find** ◊ *artists who have experienced some initial ~* | **bring** ◊ *A change of management failed to bring ~.* | **end in, lead to, result in** ◊ *The year-long fight for permission to build the house ended in ~.* | **assure, ensure, guarantee** ◊ *We can't guarantee immediate ~.* | **increase** | **assess, determine, evaluate, gauge, judge, measure** ◊ *These issues determine ~ in the global marketplace.* | **predict** ◊ *the test's ability to predict ~ in college* | **explain** | **be vital to** ◊ *Your contribution was vital to the ~ of the concert.* | **affect, influence** | **claim** ◊ *Researchers have claimed great ~ with this approach.* | **attribute** ◊ *He attributes his ~ to having a stable family life.* | **owe** ◊ *I owe my ~ to him.* | **repeat, replicate** | **maximize** | **report** ◊ *Several people have reported ~ with this approach.*
SUCCESS + VERB **come** ◊ *Success didn't come overnight–she struggled for years before making any money.* | **lie (in sth)** ◊ *Much of his ~ lies in his skill in handling staff.* | **depend on sth, hinge on sth, rely on sth, rest on sth** ◊ *The ~ or failure of the project depends on how committed the managers are.* ◊ *The bank's ~ rests on several factors.* | **breed sth** ◊ *That kind of financial ~ breeds confidence.*
SUCCESS + NOUN **rate** ◊ *The operation has a ~ rate of over 80%.* | **story** ◊ *The company has been one of the ~ stories of the past decade.* | **factor** ◊ *one of the key ~ factors*
PREP. **with ~** ◊ *It has already been used with great ~.* | **without ~** ◊ *She tried to persuade them, without ~.* | **~ in** ◊ *I've had some ~ in getting rid of the weeds.* | **~ with** ◊ *the secret of his ~ with women*
PHRASES **a chance of ~, a hope of ~** ◊ *What are our chances of ~?* ◊ *We're trying to get him to sponsor us, but there's not much hope of ~.* | **confident of ~** ◊ *She had worked hard and was confident of ~.* | **the key to ~, the secret of (sb's) ~** | **a lack of ~** | **a symbol of (sb's) ~**

2 sth that achieves its aim

ADJ. **resounding, roaring, rousing** (*AmE*)**, runaway, smashing** (*AmE*)**, tremendous** ◊ *The band's new album has been a runaway ~.* | **amazing, considerable, conspicuous, extraordinary, incredible, notable, outstanding, phenomenal, real, remarkable, spectacular, stunning** | **big, enormous, great, huge, immense, major, massive** | **complete, total** | **unparalleled, unprecedented, unqualified** | **moderate, modest, qualified** | **box-office, business, commercial, critical, economic, popular** ◊ *The book proved a major commercial ~.* | **international** | **immediate, instant, overnight** | **unexpected**
VERB + SUCCESS **be, prove** | **have** ◊ *We had one or two outstanding ~es.* | **judge sth** ◊ *The event was judged a ~ by its organizers.* | **make** ◊ *She's made a real ~ of that job.* | **score** ◊ *The movement has scored some notable ~es.*

successful adj.

VERBS **be, prove** | **appear, seem** | **become** | **feel** ◊ *Winning is the only way they can feel ~.* | **be considered, be deemed, be judged**
ADV. **extremely, fairly, very, etc.** | **enormously, extraordinarily, fabulously** (*esp. AmE*)**, highly, hugely, immensely, outstandingly** (*esp. BrE*)**, phenomenally, spectacularly, tremendously, truly, unusually, wildly** ◊ *his phenomenally ~ period as manager* | **amazingly, astonishingly, incredibly, remarkably, surprisingly** | **largely** | **not completely, not entirely, not wholly** ◊ *Their attempts had not been entirely ~.* | **marginally** (*esp. AmE*)**, moderately, modestly, partially, partly, reasonably, relatively** ◊ *The operation was only partially ~.* | **consistently** | **increasingly** | **initially** | **eventually, ultimately** ◊ *The alliance was ultimately ~ in getting its message across.* | **academically, commercially, economically, financially, politically** ◊ *a politically ~ move*
PREP. **at** ◊ *He has been remarkably ~ at keeping his private life private.* | **in** ◊ *We hope the party will be ~ in the elections.*

succession noun

1 series of people, things, etc.

ADJ. **endless, long, never-ending** | **constant, continuous, unbroken, uninterrupted** | **quick, rapid, rapid-fire** ◊ *We lost three secretaries in quick ~.* | **whole** ◊ *A whole ~ of presidents had tried to resolve the issue without success.*
PREP. **in ~** ◊ *There has been a rise in crime for the second year in ~.* | **~ of** ◊ *This set in motion a ~ of events.*

2 right to have an important position after sb else

ADJ. **orderly** ◊ *The party has always attempted to secure an orderly ~ of leaders.* | **disputed** | **dynastic, hereditary** | **presidential**
VERB + SUCCESSION **ensure, secure** ◊ *He wanted to have a son to ensure the ~.*
PREP. **in ~ to** ◊ *the manager in ~ to Edna Greenan*
PHRASES **the line of ~, the order of ~** ◊ *He is next in (the) line of ~ to the throne.* | **the right of ~** | **~ to the throne**

successor noun

ADJ. **logical, natural, obvious** | **rightful, worthy** ◊ *Their latest offering is a worthy ~ to their popular debut album.* | **chosen, designated, eventual** | **hand-picked** (*esp. AmE*)**| immediate** | **permanent** | **likely, possible, potential** | **would-be** ◊ *his would-be ~* | **spiritual**
VERB + SUCCESSOR **have** ◊ *He doesn't have an obvious ~ as party leader.* | **appoint, choose, elect, find, hand-pick** (*esp. AmE*)**, name, pick, select** | **groom** | **hand over to** (*esp. BrE*) ◊ *She will hand over to her ~ in one year's time.*
SUCCESSOR + VERB **take over**
PREP. **as sb's ~** ◊ *She has been appointed as his ~.* | **~ as** ◊ *Andrew Kirkham will be her ~ as Chief Executive.* | **~ to** ◊ *the challenge to create a worthy ~ to the old library building*
PHRASES **the appointment of a ~, the choice of a ~, the election of a ~** | **be tipped as a possible ~** (*esp. BrE*) ◊ *The former newsreader is being tipped as a possible ~ to the outgoing Head of Broadcasting.*

succumb verb

ADV. **almost** | **quickly, rapidly** | **gradually, slowly** | **eventually, finally, ultimately** | **easily, readily** ◊ *people who ~ easily to exploitation*
VERB + SUCCUMB **be likely to**
PREP. **to** ◊ *Malnourished children are more likely to ~ to infections.*

suck verb

ADV. **noisily** ◊ *She was noisily ~ing up milk through a straw.* | **away, in, out, up** ◊ *She ~ed away on her thumb.* ◊ *He cut the orange in half and ~ed out the juice.*

PREP. **at** ◇ *He ~ed at the wound on his hand.* | **from** ◇ *The machine ~s up mud and stones from the bottom of the pond.* | **on** ◇ *The baby ~ed on her bottle.* | **through** | **into**, **out of**

sue *verb*

ADV. **successfully** | **unsuccessfully** | **promptly** ◇ *Hammond promptly ~d Gray for libel.*
VERB + SUE **be able to**, **be entitled to**, **have the right to** | **be ready to**, **intend to**, **plan to** | **be likely to** | **threaten to**
PREP. **for** ◇ *He threatened to ~ the company for negligence.* | **over** ◇ *The water authority was successfully ~d over his illness.*

suffer *verb*

ADV. **a lot**, **badly**, **enormously**, **greatly**, **grievously**, **horribly**, **immensely**, **mightily**, **severely**, **terribly**, **tremendously** ◇ *This area ~ed very badly in the storms.* | **needlessly** ◇ *Thousands of children in the world today ~ needlessly.* | **disproportionately** ◇ *Poor families ~ disproportionately from asthma.* | **accordingly** | **unnecessarily** | **economically**, **financially** | **emotionally**, **mentally**, **physically** | **alone** ◇ *I'm sorry that you have to ~ alone like this.*
VERB + SUFFER **be likely to**, **tend to** ◇ *Premature babies are more likely to ~ from breathing difficulties in childhood.* | **continue to** | **deserve to** ◇ *No child deserves to ~ for a parent's mistakes.*
PREP. **for** ◇ *I played tennis yesterday and I know I shall ~ for it today.* | **from** ◇ *She ~s from asthma.* | **under** ◇ *people ~ing under repressive regimes* | **with** ◇ *He ~s terribly with migraines.*
PHRASES **~ in silence** ◇ *They were just expected to ~ in silence.*

sufferer *noun*

ADJ. **worst** ◇ *The worst ~s of the condition tend to live in highly polluted areas.* | **lifelong**, **long-term** | **fellow** ◇ *The sessions will enable you to discuss problems with fellow asthma ~s.* | **AIDS**, **allergy**, **arthritis**, **asthma**, **cancer**, **migraine**, etc. | **back**, **back-pain**
VERB + SUFFERER **help** ◇ *a support group to help cancer ~s*
PREP. **~ from** ◇ *He's been a lifelong ~ from hay fever.* | **~ of** ◇ *~s of major depression*

suffering *noun*

ADJ. **enormous**, **great**, **immense**, **intense**, **massive**, **real**, **terrible**, **unbearable**, **unimaginable**, **untold** | **needless**, **unnecessary** | **widespread** | **endless**, **prolonged** | **eternal** | **individual**, **personal** | **animal**, **human** | **emotional**, **mental**, **physical** ◇ *The taunts of her schoolmates caused her intense mental ~.*
... OF SUFFERING **amount**, **degree**, **level** ◇ *The West has contributed to the immense amount of ~ in underdeveloped countries.*
VERB + SUFFERING **cause (sb)**, **inflict** | **increase** | **prolong** | **alleviate**, **ease**, **minimize**, **reduce**, **relieve** ◇ *These pills should relieve his ~ for a couple of hours.* | **eliminate**, **end**, **stop** | **endure**, **experience** | **see**, **witness** | **share**, **share in**
PHRASES **pain and ~** ◇ *His life was one of pain and ~.*

sufficient *adj.*

VERBS **be**, **prove**, **seem** | **consider sth**, **deem sth**, **regard sth as**, **see sth as** ◇ *Do you really regard that explanation as ~?*
ADV. **quite** | **barely**, **hardly** ◇ *Our budget is hardly ~ to pay people, let alone buy any new equipment.* | **just**
PREP. **for** ◇ *The salary proved ~ for his needs.*

sugar *noun*

ADJ. **raw**, **unrefined** | **processed**, **refined** | **brown**, **white** ◇ *Add one cup of soft brown ~.* | **caster** (*BrE*), **confectioner's** (*AmE*), **cube** (*esp. AmE*), **demerara** (*BrE*), **granulated**, **icing** (*BrE*), **lump** (*BrE*), **powdered** (*AmE*), **table** (*AmE*) | **beet**, **cane**, **maple**, **palm** | **cinnamon** (*AmE*) | **spun** | **natural** ◇ *Fruit juices contain natural ~s.* | **complex**, **simple** (*both*

science) ◇ *simple ~s, such as glucose* | **blood** ◇ *to raise blood ~ levels*
... OF SUGAR **kilo**, **pound**, etc. | **lump**, **spoonful** | **cup**, **tablespoon**, **teaspoon** ◇ *Add 1 cup of white ~ and boil until dissolved.* (*esp. AmE*) | **bag** | **packet** (*AmE*), **sachet** (*BrE*)
VERB + SUGAR **add**, **put in**, **put on**, **sprinkle**, **stir in**, **stir into sth**, **take** (= in tea or coffee) ◇ *He stirred another spoonful of ~ into his tea.* ◇ *Do you take ~ in your tea?* | **contain** | **produce** | **dissolve** ◇ *Bring to a boil to dissolve the ~.*
SUGAR + VERB **dissolve**
SUGAR + NOUN **cube** (*esp. AmE*), **lump** (*BrE*) | **bowl** | **substitute** | **syrup** | **cookie** (*AmE*) | **content**, **intake**, **level** ◇ *a high ~ intake* | **craving** | **fix** | **high**, **rush** | **beet**, **cane** | **grower**, **planter**, **producer** | **industry**, **mill**, **plantation**, **production**, **refinery**
PHRASES **high ~ content**, **low ~ content**, **reduced ~ content** | **high in ~**, **low in ~** ◇ *Most junk food is high in ~.* | **no added ~** ◇ *apple juice with no added ~*

suggest *verb*

1 propose sth/state sth indirectly

ADV. **highly** (*esp. AmE*), **strongly** ◇ *I strongly ~ keeping personal and business accounts separate.* | **tentatively** ◇ *I tentatively ~ed that she might be happier working somewhere else.* | **gently**, **humbly**, **politely**, **respectfully**, **tactfully** ◇ *I would respectfully ~ a different explanation for the company's decline.* | **seriously** ◇ *You're not seriously ~ing that is a plausible explanation?* | **jokingly** | **hopefully** | **helpfully** ◇ *'Shall I tell them you're unwell?' Alice ~ed helpfully.* | **falsely**, **rightly** | **initially**, **originally**, **previously** | **merely** ◇ *I am merely ~ing that there is more than one way to view this matter.*
VERB + SUGGEST **seem reasonable to** ◇ *It seems reasonable to ~ that all life forms on earth share a common origin.* | **be far-fetched to**, **seem far-fetched to** ◇ *It is not far-fetched to ~ a connection between them.* | **be wrong to** | **be tempting to** | **dare (to)** ◇ *How dare you ~ such a thing?* | **hesitate to** | **not mean to** ◇ *I do not mean to ~ that the poem is purely biographical.*
PREP. **as** ◇ *She ~ed John as chairman.* | **for** ◇ *Who would you ~ for the job?* | **to** ◇ *He ~ed to the committee that they delay making a decision.*
PHRASES **can I suggest...**, **I suggest...**, **I would suggest...**, **may I suggest...** ◇ *I would ~ that you see your doctor about this.*

2 show sth in an indirect way

ADV. **certainly**, **clearly**, **strongly** ◇ *The evidence ~s quite strongly that the fire was caused by an explosion.* | **subtly** | **implicitly**, **indirectly** ◇ *The novel implicitly ~s that racism can explain the murder.* | **otherwise** ◇ *The evidence ~s otherwise.*
VERB + SUGGEST **seem to** ◇ *The evidence seems to ~ that he did steal the money.* | **be meant to** ◇ *The ending is meant to ~ a form of redemption.*

suggestion *noun*

1 proposal

ADJ. **constructive**, **excellent**, **good**, **helpful**, **interesting**, **intriguing**, **positive**, **practical**, **reasonable**, **sensible**, **useful**, **valuable** | **absurd**, **bizarre**, **preposterous**, **ridiculous**, **stupid** | **subtle**, **tentative**, **vague** | **provocative** ◇ *This is a book full of provocative ~s.* | **concrete**, **simple**, **specific** ◇ *They made three specific ~s.* | **alternative**
VERB + SUGGESTION **have** ◇ *Does anyone have any ~s for a title?* ◇ *I've had several helpful ~s from colleagues.* | **come up with**, **give sb**, **make**, **offer**, **provide**, **put forward** ◇ *Can you give us any ~s for a slogan?* ◇ *May I make a ~?* | **send**, **submit** ◇ *Please send your ~s via email to...* | **accept**, **act on**, **adopt**, **follow**, **implement**, **take up** (*esp. BrE*) ◇ *I think we might take up the ~ of printing the books in Hong Kong.* | **take sb up on** ◇ *May we take you up on your ~ of sharing the costs for the party?* | **deny**, **dismiss**, **ignore**, **reject**, **resist** ◇ *They dismissed the ~ that they hadn't worked hard.* ◇ *He rejected my ~ as impractical.* | **appreciate**, **welcome** ◇ *I'd appreciate any ~s you may have.* | **support** | **consider**, **look at**, **note** ◇ *We have noted your ~ and will give it due consideration.*

SUGGESTION + NOUN **box** ◊ *Employee ~ boxes invite raw ideas.*
PREP. **at the ~ of** ◊ *At the ~ of his boss, he resigned.* | **~ about, ~ as to, ~ concerning, ~ on, ~ regarding** ◊ *Management welcomes practical ~s on how to improve the facilities.* | **~ for** ◊ *~s for further reading*
PHRASES **amid ~s that …** (*esp. BrE*) ◊ *She left the country amid ~s that she had stolen from the company.* | **be open to ~, be open to ~s** ◊ *I'm open to ~s on how we should proceed.*
→ Special page at MEETING

2 communicating without stating directly
ADJ. **implicit** | **hypnotic**
PREP. **by ~, through ~** ◊ *There's no scientific basis to the method—it works by ~.*
PHRASES **the power of ~** ◊ *These healers claim to remove the pain by the power of ~.*

3 trace of sth
ADJ. **faint, mere, slightest, vague** | **strong** ◊ *Her eyes contained a strong ~ of mischief.*
VERB + SUGGESTION **carry, have**
PREP. **at the ~ of** ◊ *At the slightest ~ of criticism, he loses his temper.* | **~ of**

suggestive *adj.*

1 making you think of sth
VERBS **be, seem**
ADV. **highly** (*medical*), **richly, strongly, very** ◊ *The results were highly ~ of malignancy.* | **vaguely**
PREP. **of** ◊ *music that is ~ of warm summer days*

2 making people think about sex
VERBS **be, look, sound** | **become**
ADV. **extremely, fairly, very, etc.** | **mildly** | **sexually**

suicidal *adj.*

1 wanting to kill yourself
VERBS **be, feel, look, seem, sound** | **become, get** ◊ *He became very depressed and even got ~ at one point.*
ADV. **almost, nearly** (*esp. AmE*), **potentially**

2 likely to cause your failure
VERBS **be, prove** | **seem**
ADV. **financially, politically** ◊ *a move which would be politically ~* | **potentially, seemingly** ◊ *a seemingly ~ plan* | **downright** | **ultimately**
PREP. **for** ◊ *These policies would prove ~ for our economy.*

suicide *noun*

ADJ. **attempted** | **collective, double, mass** ◊ *Members of the sect committed mass ~.* | **adolescent, teen, teenage, youth** | **assisted, doctor-assisted** (*esp. AmE*), **physician-assisted** (*esp. AmE*) ◊ *the questions surrounding euthanasia and assisted ~* | **apparent** ◊ *Her death was ruled an apparent ~.* | **ritual** ◊ *the ritual ~ of a widow on her husband's funeral pyre* | **electoral, political** ◊ *Raising taxes before an election would be political ~.* | **economic, social** (*humorous*) ◊ *Wearing shoes like that would be social ~.* | **career** ◊ *That's asking them to commit career ~.*
VERB + SUICIDE **commit** | **attempt** | **consider, contemplate** | **threaten** | **prevent**
SUICIDE + NOUN **risk, threat** ◊ *There is no evidence that he is a ~ risk.* | **attempt, bid** (*BrE*) ◊ *He slashed his wrists in a failed ~ attempt.* | **pact** ◊ *The couple died together in a ~ pact.* | **terrorism** | **letter, note** ◊ *He died without leaving a ~ note.* | **watch** ◊ *He was put on ~ watch* (= checked to make sure he did not commit suicide) *earlier in his prison term.* | **prevention** | **rate** | **attacker, bomber, terrorist** | **bomb** | **attack, bombing, mission, operation** ◊ *a ~ bomb attack on a military convoy*

suit *noun*

1 set of clothes
ADJ. **designer, elegant, immaculate, smart** (*esp. BrE*), **well-cut** (*esp. BrE*), **well-tailored** (*esp. AmE*) | **ill-fitting** | **best, good** ◊ *He wore his one good ~ to the interview.* | **expensive** | **tailored** | **double-breasted, single-breasted** | **one-piece,**

two-piece, three-piece | **pinstripe, pinstriped** | **linen, seersucker** (*esp. AmE*), **tweed, wool, etc.** | **summer** | **business, dinner** (*BrE*), **dress, formal, lounge** (*BrE*), **morning, safari, zoot** | **pant** (usually *pantsuit*) (*AmE*), **trouser** (*BrE*) | **bathing, diving, swim** (usually *swimsuit*), **swimming** (*esp. AmE*) | **jogging** (*BrE*), **ski** | **leisure** (*AmE*), **shell** (*BrE*), **sweat** (usually *sweatsuit*) (*AmE*) | **warm-up** (*AmE*) | **biohazard, boiler** (*esp. BrE*), **hazmat** (*AmE*), **protective** | **flying, pressure** | **clown, gorilla**
SUIT + NOUN **coat** (*AmE*), **jacket, pants** (*AmE*), **trousers** (*esp. BrE*)
PREP. **in a ~** ◊ *Two men in ~s came out of the hotel.*
PHRASES **a ~ and tie** ◊ *They won't let you into the restaurant without a ~ and tie.* | **a ~ of armour/armor** ◊ *The cavalry wore a ~ of light armour/armor and carried a shield.* | **a ~ of clothes** (*old-fashioned*) ◊ *His parents had bought him a new ~ of clothes for the occasion.*

2 (*also* **lawsuit**) legal case
ADJ. **civil** (*esp. AmE*) | **class-action** (*AmE*) | **paternity** | **antitrust, discrimination, libel, malpractice** (*all esp. AmE*)
VERB + SUIT **bring, file** ◊ *A ~ has been filed against the company.* | **be involved in, pursue** | **drop** ◊ *They have agreed to drop their ~ against the Dutch company.* | **be faced with, face** ◊ *The company now faces several ~s over its failure to protect its employees.* | **defend** ◊ *She plans to defend the ~ vigorously.* | **win** | **lose** | **settle** ◊ *The two companies have settled the ~.* | **dismiss**
PREP. **in a/the ~** ◊ *They are seeking damages in a lawsuit.* | **~ against** ◊ *a ~ against her former husband* | **~ over** ◊ *a ~ over a disputed estate*

suit *verb*

ADV. **admirably** (*esp. BrE*), **fine, well** ◊ *Try out the various rackets to find out which one ~s you best.* ◊ *It would ~ me fine if I never have to see them again.* | **down to the ground** (*BrE, informal*), **perfectly** ◊ *This arrangement ~ed me perfectly.*
VERB + SUIT **seem to** | **adapt sth to, adjust sth to, be designed to, be tailored to** ◊ *a shampoo designed to ~ all hair types*
PHRASES **especially ~ed, ideally ~ed, particularly ~ed, uniquely ~ed** ◊ *a car that's ideally ~ed for urban living*

suitability *noun*

VERB + SUITABILITY **assess, demonstrate, determine** ◊ *to assess the ~ of the buildings for disabled people* | **ensure** | **doubt, have doubts about, question** | **test (sth for)** ◊ *Potential donors can be tested for ~.*
PREP. **~ for** ◊ *the greater ~ of women for the work*

suitable *adj.*

VERBS **be, look, prove, seem** | **make sth** ◊ *The book's format makes it ~ for self-study.* | **consider sb/sth, deem sb/sth, find sb/sth** ◊ *These properties are considered especially ~ for older people.*
ADV. **eminently, especially, highly, particularly, very** | **entirely, perfectly** | **quite** | **not entirely, not really** ◊ *This building is not really ~ for wheelchair users.* | **not necessarily** | **hardly** | **potentially** | **equally** ◊ *There are many other training courses that would be equally ~.*
PREP. **as** ◊ *It is not ~ as a word-processing program.* | **for** ◊ *The walk is ~ for all the family.* ◊ *The shampoo is ~ for everyday use.* | **to** ◊ *conditions ~ to their development*

suitcase (*also* case) *noun*

ADJ. **heavy, light** | **open** | **empty, full** | **packed** | **bulging** | **battered** ◊ *His only possession was a battered old ~ of clothes.* | **leather** | **rolling** (*AmE*), **wheelie** (*BrE*) | **carry-on**
VERB + SUITCASE **cram sth in/into, pack, stuff sth in/into, throw sth in/into** ◊ *Have you packed your ~ yet?* ◊ *He stuffed a few clothes in a ~ and left.* | **take sth out of, unpack** | **fasten, shut, snap shut** ◊ *She snapped her ~ shut and stuck on a label.* | **open** | **lift, pick up** ◊ *The ~ was too heavy to*

lift. | **grab** | **clutch, hold** | **carry, drag, heave, lug, pull** ◊ *She heaved her ~ down from the luggage rack.* ◊ *We had to lug our ~s around for a week.* | **drop, dump, put down** | **live out of** ◊ *He got tired of living out of a ~ and left his job as a sales rep.*

SUITCASE + VERB **be crammed with sth, be full of sth, be stuffed with sth, contain sth** ◊ *The ~ was full of drugs.*

PREP. **in a/the ~, inside a/the ~**

suite noun

1 of furniture

ADJ. **bathroom** (*BrE*), **bedroom** (*esp. BrE*) | **three-piece** (*BrE*) ◊ *We bought a three-piece ~ for the living room.*

PHRASES **a ~ of furniture**

2 set of rooms in a hotel, office block, etc.

ADJ. **private** | **luxury** | **bridal, family, honeymoon, master, penthouse, presidential** ◊ *a family ~ of two interconnecting rooms* | **executive** | **conference** (*esp. BrE*), **hospitality** | **hotel, office** | **delivery** (= in the maternity ward of a hospital) (*BrE*) | **computer, ICT** (*both BrE*) | **edit, editing** ◊ *a video editing ~* | **fitness** (*BrE*)

PHRASES **a ~ of offices, a ~ of rooms**

suited adj.

VERBS **appear, be, seem** | **make sth**

ADV. **admirably, eminently, especially, particularly, very, well** ◊ *land that is well ~ to dairy farming* | **ideally, perfectly, uniquely** ◊ *She was ideally ~ to the job.* | **ill, little, poorly** ◊ *a song ill ~ to male voices* | **naturally** | **temperamentally**

PREP. **for** ◊ *He was not really ~ for army life.* | **to** ◊ *an approach especially ~ to the adult learner*

sum noun

1 amount of money

ADJ. **considerable, generous, good, great, handsome, hefty, high, large, not inconsiderable** (*esp. BrE*), **princely** (*ironic*), **significant, sizeable, substantial, tidy** (*informal*) ◊ *It seemed an absurdly high ~ to pay for a coat.* ◊ *For his first book he received the princely ~ of $400.* ◊ *The team has raised substantial ~s for local charities.* | **astronomical, colossal** (*esp. BrE*), **enormous, exorbitant, huge, magnificent** (*esp. BrE*), **massive, record, staggering, vast** ◊ *£200 was an astronomical ~ of money in 1547.* ◊ *He joined the team two years ago for a record ~.* | **five-figure, six-figure, etc.** (*esp. BrE*), **modest, nominal, reasonable, small, token, trifling** ◊ *The charity pays a nominal ~ to lease the premises.* | **derisory, paltry** | **average** | **net** | **round** (*esp. BrE*) ◊ *€10 000 is a good round ~.* | **full** (*esp. BrE*), **overall, total** | **agreed** (*esp. BrE*), **fixed** | **undisclosed, unspecified** | **annual, monthly, etc.** | **regular** | **guaranteed** (*esp. BrE*) | **capital, cash** (*esp. BrE*), **lump** ◊ *My wife would receive a guaranteed lump ~ in the event of my death.* | **tax-free** (*esp. BrE*)

VERB + SUM **borrow, earn, fetch** (*esp. BrE*), **raise, recover** (*esp. BrE*) ◊ *Some of the paintings should fetch a tidy ~ at today's auction.* ◊ *You will have to go to court to recover these ~s.* | **get, receive** | **award sb** (*esp. BrE*), **contribute, give sb, offer sb, pay (sb), repay** (*esp. BrE*) ◊ *The judge awarded them an undisclosed six-figure ~ in damages.* ◊ *How can we repay such a large ~?* | **invest, spend** | **cost** ◊ *a project that cost vast ~s of public money* | **charge (sb)** | **agree, agree on** ◊ *We eventually agreed a ~ and I paid him.*

SUM + VERB **be due, be payable** (*both esp. BrE*) | **be equal to sth, be equivalent to sth** ◊ *The gangsters offered him a ~ equivalent to a whole year's earnings.* | **exceed sth**

PHRASES **a ~ of money**

2 calculation

ADJ. **difficult, easy**

VERB + SUM **do** ◊ *I did a quick ~ to work out how much it would cost.*

PHRASES **get your ~s right/wrong** (*BrE*) ◊ *The company got its*

~s wrong when estimating how many customers it would attract.

3 total

VERB + SUM **calculate, find, work out** ◊ *Calculate the ~ of the following figures.*

PREP. **~ of** ◊ *The ~ of two and five is seven.*

PHRASES **greater, less, more, etc. than the ~ of its/the parts** ◊ *The team is greater than the ~ of its parts.*

sum verb

PHR V **sum sth up**

ADV. **aptly, neatly, nicely, succinctly, well** | **perfectly** | **just about, pretty much** ◊ *'So we're stuck in this place with no food?' 'That just about ~s it up.'*

VERB + SUM UP **seem to** | **attempt to, try to** ◊ *The report attempts to ~ up recent economic trends.* | **be difficult to, be hard to** ◊ *The appeal of this city is hard to ~ up.*

PREP. **as** ◊ *She summed it up as 'the most brilliant lecture I've ever attended'.*

PHRASES **can be summed up as** ◊ *Her whole philosophy can be summed up as 'so what?'.*

summarize (*BrE also* -ise) verb

ADV. **briefly, succinctly** | **accurately** | **aptly, best, conveniently, neatly, nicely, usefully, well** ◊ *The research has been usefully ~d in an article by Greenwood.* | **easily**

VERB + SUMMARIZE **attempt to, try to** | **be possible to** | **be difficult to, be hard to**

PREP. **as** ◊ *The results of the survey can be ~d as follows…* | **in** ◊ *The costs are ~d in Table 5.*

summary noun

ADJ. **accurate, apt, clear, cogent** (*esp. AmE*), **excellent, fair, good, useful** ◊ *Is that a fair ~ of the situation?* | **comprehensive, detailed, full** | **general, overall** | **brief, concise, quick, short, succinct** | **executive** ◊ *He only reads the executive ~ of reports.* | **crude** | **financial, statistical** | **news, plot** ◊ *Details of new titles, with plot summaries, are included in the catalogue.*

VERB + SUMMARY **make, prepare, publish, write** ◊ *Could you make a short ~ of this article for me?* | **give (sb), offer, present (sb with), provide (sb with), supply (sb with)** ◊ *He has provided a useful ~ of the main categories.*

SUMMARY + NOUN **sheet, table** | **report, statement**

PREP. **in ~** ◊ *In ~, his views are out of date.* | **in a/the ~** ◊ *She decided not to include this incident in her ~ of the day's events.* | **~ of** ◊ *What follows is a brief ~ of the findings.*

PHRASES **in ~ form** ◊ *The information is shown in ~ form in the following tables.*

summer noun

ADJ. **last, this past** (*esp. AmE*) | **the following, next, this, this coming** | **early, late** | **high** ◊ *Seville is scorching in high ~.* | **good, hot, scorching** | **cool** | **dry, wet** | **humid** | **Indian** ◊ *We had an Indian ~ that year.* ◊ *She seems to be enjoying an Indian ~ of popularity.* (*figurative*) | **long**

SUMMER + NOUN **heat, temperature, weather** | **sun, sunlight, sunshine** | **rain, rains** | **breeze, wind** | **sky** | **solstice** | **camp** (*esp. AmE*), **course, school** | **term** (*esp. BrE*) ◊ *There are two new courses being run in the ~ term.* | **break, holiday** (*BrE*), **recess, vacation** (*AmE*) ◊ *I went home for the ~ holidays.* ◊ *I returned home for ~ vacation.* | **season** (*esp. AmE*) | **job** | **time** (*BrE*) ◊ *the extra light brought by British Summer Time* | **home** (*esp. AmE*), **house** | **garden** | **flower, clothes, clothing, dress** | **collection, exhibition, festival, programme/program, stock** (*AmE*), **tour** ◊ *He began his acting career in ~ stock.* | **blockbuster, film** (*esp. BrE*), **movie** (*esp. AmE*) | **Olympics, sports**

→ Note at SEASON (for more collocates)

summit noun

1 top of a mountain

ADJ. **high** ◊ *Maroon Peak is the highest ~ in its group.* | **very** (*esp. BrE*) | **rocky, snow-capped** | **mountain** | **2 000-foot, etc.** ◊ *a 2 030-foot ~*

VERB + SUMMIT **arrive at, climb, climb to, gain, get to, reach** ◇ *We finally arrived at the ~.* | **lead to**

SUMMIT + NOUN **attempt, bid** ◇ *The blizzard forced them to delay their ~ bid.*

PREP. **at the ~** ◇ *We were standing at the ~ of the highest mountain in India.* | **below the ~** ◇ *They reached base camp, 30 000 feet below the ~.* | **on the ~** ◇ *The climbers planted a flag on the ~.*

2 important meeting between leaders

ADJ. **annual** | **regular** | **crisis** (*BrE*), **emergency, special** | **two-day, etc.** | **global, international, regional** | **bilateral** | **Asian, Franco-German, etc.** | **EU, G8, NATO, etc.** | **presidential** | **earth, economic, peace**

VERB + SUMMIT **call, convene** ◇ *The President called a ~ at Camp David.* | **have, hold, host** ◇ *The 2016 ~ will be hosted by Japan.* | **attend, go to**

SUMMIT + NOUN **conference, meeting, talks** | **agenda** | **agreement, declaration** | **participant**

PREP. **at a/the ~** ◇ *These measures were decided at a ~ in July.* | **~ between** ◇ *annual ~s between the major nations* | **~ on** ◇ *a two-day international ~ on drugs*

summon verb

1 order a person to come to a place

ADV. **hastily, urgently** | **duly** (*esp. BrE*) | **back**

PREP. **for** ◇ *I was recently ~ed for jury duty.* | **from** ◇ *He has been ~ed from New York to give evidence at the trial.* | **to** ◇ *She was ~ed back to his office.*

2 find sth that you need

ADV. **barely** ◇ *He could barely ~ the strength to stand up.* | **forth** (*esp. AmE*), **up**

VERB + SUMMON **be able to, can** | **try to** | **manage to** ◇ *She managed to ~ up a smile.*

summons noun

1 order to go somewhere

ADJ. **urgent** | **royal**

VERB + SUMMONS **send, send out** | **await, expect** ◇ *I stayed at home that night awaiting her ~.* | **get, hear, receive** | **answer, obey, respond to** | **ignore**

SUMMONS + VERB **come** ◇ *She was ready when the ~ came.*

PREP. **~ from** ◇ *She responded immediately to the ~ from her boss.* | **~ to** ◇ *I received an urgent ~ to her office.*

PHRASES **a ~ to appear before sb** ◇ *He received a ~ to appear before the committee.*

2 order to go to a court of law

ADJ. **court** (*esp. BrE*) | **jury** (*AmE*), **witness** (*BrE*)

VERB + SUMMONS **issue, take out** (*BrE*) | **deliver, serve (sb with)** (*esp. BrE*) ◇ *The ~ can be served on either of the partners in the business.* | **get, receive**

PREP. **~ against** (*BrE*) ◇ *The landlord issued a ~ against her for non-payment of rent.* | **~ for**

PHRASES **a ~ to appear in court** ◇ *She received a ~ to appear in court.*

sun noun (usually the sun)

ADJ. **bright, brilliant, golden, red, yellow** | **hazy, pale, weak, wintry** | **high, low** ◇ *The wintry ~ was already low in the sky.* | **rising** | **dying, setting, sinking, western** ◇ *The distant mountains glowed in the light of the setting ~.* | **baking, blazing, burning, harsh, hot, scorching, strong, warm** | **direct, full** ◇ *This plant likes a dryish soil in full ~.* | **afternoon, early, early-morning, evening, late, midday, morning, noon, noonday** | **midnight** ◇ *They call Norway the land of the midnight ~.* | **spring, summer, etc.** | **August, February, etc.** | **desert, tropical** | **Californian, Caribbean, Italian, etc.**

VERB + SUN **block, block out, blot out, obliterate** ◇ *The clouds darkened, obliterating the ~.* | **soak up** ◇ *We were lying by the pool, soaking up the afternoon ~.* | **get** ◇ *The north side of the garden never gets any ~.* | **catch** (*esp. BrE*) ◇ *You've caught the ~ (= become slightly burned).* | **reflect, orbit** ◇ *Venus orbits the Sun in just under one Earth year.*

SUN + VERB **climb, come up, rise** ◇ *The ~ climbed higher in the sky.* ◇ *The ~ rises in the east.* | **dip, drop, go down, set, sink** ◇ *The ~ sets in the west.* ◇ *It was getting cooler as the ~ sank below the horizon.* | **be out, be up** ◇ *The ~ was up now, and strong.* | **move** ◇ *The ~ moved slowly westward.* | **appear, break through (sth), come out, emerge, peek out, peek through (sth)** ◇ *Just then, the ~ broke through the clouds.* | **beam, beat down, blaze down, burn, shine** ◇ *A brilliant ~ shone through the trees.* | **disappear, go in** ◇ *The ~ went in and it started to rain.* | **catch sth, glint off sth, glint on sth, hit sth, play on sth, sparkle (on sth)** ◇ *The ~ caught her dazzling copper hair.* ◇ *The ~ glinted on the blades.* | **stream in, stream through sth** ◇ *The evening ~ streamed in through the window.* | **strike sth, touch sth** ◇ *The ~ struck the steep blue slates of the roof.* | **reflect off sth, reflect on sth** ◇ *The ~ reflected off the water.* | **cast shadows over sth** ◇ *The setting ~ cast long shadows over the landscape.* | **warm sth** ◇ *The ~ warmed his face.*

SUN + NOUN **god** | **worshipper** (*usually figurative*) | **lounge** (*BrE*), **room** (*usually sunroom*), **terrace** (*esp. BrE*), **trap** (*usually suntrap*) (*esp. BrE*) | **bed** (*esp. BrE*), **lounger** (*usually sunbed, etc.*) (*BrE*) | **hat, visor** | **shade** (*usually sunshade*) | **tan** (*usually suntan*) | **block** (*usually sunblock*), **cream** (*BrE*), **protection, screen** (*usually sunscreen*) ◇ *On children, use a cream with a high ~ protection factor.* | **damage, exposure** ◇ *wrinkles caused by ~ damage*

PREP. **in the ~** ◇ *Don't sit in the ~ too long.* ◇ *The helmets were glinting in the ~.* ◇ *We've booked a holiday in the ~ (= in a place that is warm and sunny).* (*BrE*) | **into the ~** ◇ *We went out into the ~.* | **out of the ~** ◇ *We did our best to keep out of the ~.* | **under the ~** ◇ *an afternoon of lazing under the warm ~* ◇ *There is nothing new under the ~. (figurative)* | **~ in** ◇ *with the ~ in her eyes* | **~ on** ◇ *He was enjoying the feel of the ~ on his back.*

PHRASES **everything under the ~** (*figurative*) ◇ *We had discussions about everything under the ~.* | **exposure to the ~** ◇ *Try to avoid prolonged exposure to the ~.* | **the heat of the ~, the warmth of the ~** | **the light from the ~, the light of the ~** | **the rays of the ~, the sun's rays**

Sunday noun → Note at DAY

sunglasses noun

ADJ. **dark** | **aviator, wrap-around** | **mirrored** | **designer** | **cool, stylish**

... OF SUNGLASSES **pair**

VERB + SUNGLASSES **have on, wear** | **put on** | **remove, take off** | **adjust, push back, push up**

SUNGLASSES + VERB **be perched on sth, perch on sth** ◇ *Her ~ were perched on her head.*

PREP. **behind your ~** ◇ *She observed the goings-on from behind her mirrored ~.*

sunlight noun

ADJ. **blinding, bright, brilliant, harsh, hot, intense, scorching, strong, warm** ◇ *He emerged from the tunnel into blinding ~.* | **direct, full** ◇ *plants that do not like direct ~* | **pale, weak** | **dappled, golden** ◇ *the dappled ~ of the forest* | **reflected** | **afternoon, evening, morning** | **spring, summer, etc.**

... OF SUNLIGHT **beam, ray, shaft** | **patch, pool**

VERB + SUNLIGHT **block out** ◇ *a dank backyard with a wall that blocked out the ~* | **be exposed to** ◇ *Do not leave your skin exposed to ~ for too long.*

SUNLIGHT + VERB **come in, fall, filter, flood, penetrate sth, pierce sth, pour, shine, stream** ◇ *Sunlight filtered dustily through the slats of the door.* ◇ *in dark thickets where ~ could not penetrate* ◇ *She threw back the shutters and the ~ streamed in.* | **fill sth** ◇ *Bright ~ filled the room.* | **gleam, glimmer, glint, glitter, shimmer, sparkle** ◇ *the ~ sparkling on the water* | **be reflected from sth, reflect off sth, reflect on sth**

PREP. **in the ~** ◇ *waves sparkling in the ~* | **into the ~** ◇ *We came out into bright ~ again.*

PHRASES **gleam in the ~, glint in the ~, shimmer in the ~,** sparkle in the ~ ◊ *The sea shimmered in the ~.* | **blink in the ~, squint in the ~** ◊ *They emerged from their cells, blinking in the ~.*

sunny *adj.*

VERBS **be, look** | **become, get** | **remain, stay**
ADV. **brilliantly, very** ◊ *a brilliantly ~ day* | **pretty, quite** (*BrE*) | **mostly** | **beautifully, gloriously** (*esp. BrE*), **gorgeously** ◊ *a gloriously ~ morning*
PHRASES **bright ~ …** ◊ *It was a bright ~ day.*

sunset *noun*

ADJ. **beautiful, brilliant, glorious, gorgeous, lovely, spectacular, stunning** | **fiery, golden, orange, red**
VERB + SUNSET **admire, watch**
PREP. **against the ~** ◊ *The trees were black against the ~.* | **at ~** ◊ *We walked along the beach at ~.* | **~ over** ◊ *a beautiful ~ over the bay*
PHRASES **the glow of the ~** ◊ *They sat in the last glow of the ~.* | **ride off into the ~, sail off into the ~** (*both usually figurative*) ◊ *At the end of the movie, the hero rides off into the ~.*

sunshine *noun*

ADJ. **blazing** (*esp. BrE*), **bright, brilliant, dazzling** | **beautiful, glorious** ◊ *two weeks of glorious ~* | **hot, warm** | **hazy, pale, watery** (*BrE*) ◊ *It was a cool day with hazy ~.* | **afternoon, evening, morning** | **spring, summer, etc.** ◊ *She sat on the wall, enjoying the spring ~.*
… OF SUNSHINE **ray** ◊ *the last rays of ~ of the day*
VERB + SUNSHINE **bask in, enjoy, soak up** | **be bathed in** ◊ *The town was bathed in spring ~.*
SUNSHINE + VERB **beat down, flood, pour, stream** ◊ *The ~ came streaming in at the window.*
PREP. **in (the) ~** ◊ *The race was run in bright ~.* | **into the ~** ◊ *She followed us out into the ~.*

suntan *noun* → See also TAN

ADJ. **golden, good**
VERB + SUNTAN **have** | **show off, sport** (*esp. BrE*) ◊ *Everyone in the bar was sporting a ~.* | **get, work on** ◊ *He spent the mornings on the beach getting a ~.* ◊ *I'm going down to the pool to work on my ~!*
SUNTAN + NOUN **lotion, oil**

superb *adj.*

VERBS **be, look, sound** ◊ *She looked ~.*
ADV. **really** | **absolutely, quite** (*esp. BrE*), **simply** (*esp. BrE*), **truly** ◊ *The cuisine is absolutely ~.* | **technically** ◊ *His work for the company is technically ~.*

superficial *adj.*

VERBS **be, seem** | **remain**
ADV. **extremely, fairly, very, etc.** ◊ *The movie bears a fairly ~ resemblance to the original novel.* | **entirely, purely** ◊ *He began to feel he could cope, on a purely ~ level, at least.* | **largely**

superfluous *adj.*

VERBS **be, feel, seem** | **become** | **make sth, render sth** | **consider sth**
ADV. **completely, quite** (*esp. BrE*), **totally, wholly** ◊ *She gave him a look that made words quite ~.* | **almost** | **rather**

superior *noun*

ADJ. **direct, immediate** ◊ *The form has to be signed by your immediate ~.* | **intellectual, moral, social** | **military, religious**
VERB + SUPERIOR **inform, tell** | **report sb/sth to** ◊ *She threatened to report the assistant to his ~s.*

superior *adj.*

VERBS **be, look, prove (yourself), seem** | **feel (yourself)** ◊ *She felt (herself) ~ to the other children.* | **become** | **make sth** ◊ *What is it that makes this technique ~?* | **consider sth, see sth as** ◊ *I don't see either product as ~ to the other.*
ADV. **clearly, distinctly, far, greatly, markedly, vastly** ◊ *The new products are far ~ to the old ones.* ◊ *They defeated a greatly ~ Roman army.* | **altogether, infinitely** ◊ *Plainly, you possess an altogether ~ intellect.* | **rather, slightly, somewhat** | **inherently, intrinsically, naturally** | **supposedly** | **undoubtedly** | **numerically** ◊ *the numerically ~ (= larger in numbers) British forces* | **genetically, intellectually, morally, socially, technically, technologically** (*esp. AmE*)
PREP. **in** ◊ *a microwave that is vastly ~ in design to all other models* | **to** ◊ *She felt socially ~ to the rest of the group.*

superiority *noun*

ADJ. **absolute, overwhelming** | **effortless** ◊ *Driving the Jaguar gave him a feeling of effortless ~.* | **inherent, innate, natural** | **biological, cultural, intellectual, moral, numerical, physical, racial, social, technical, technological** ◊ *a discredited ideology of racial ~* | **male, white** ◊ *his air of male ~* | **air, military, naval**
VERB + SUPERIORITY **achieve, establish** ◊ *the enemy's attempts to establish air ~* | **enjoy, have** ◊ *For a long time France enjoyed overwhelming ~ in this field.* | **confirm, convince sb of, demonstrate, prove, show, underline** (*esp. BrE*) | **maintain** | **assert, assume, claim, imply** ◊ *The use of the words 'modern' and 'old' is not meant to imply the ~ of one over the other.* | **acknowledge** ◊ *Their team has had to acknowledge Australia's ~ in recent years.*
SUPERIORITY + NOUN **complex** ◊ *the perception that they have a ~ complex*
PREP. **~ in** ◊ *We should make use of our ~ in numbers.* | **~ over** ◊ *the company's clear technological ~ over its rivals* | **~ to** ◊ *The settlers remained convinced of their ~ to the native population.*
PHRASES **an air of ~** ◊ *He spoke with an air of ~.* | **a feeling of ~, a sense of ~**

supermarket *noun* → See also GROCERY STORE

ADJ. **leading, major, top** (*all esp. BrE*) | **high-street** (*BrE*), **local, neighborhood** (*AmE*) | **out-of-town** (*BrE*)
SUPERMARKET + NOUN **chain, giant, group** (*BrE*) | **development** (*BrE*) | **aisle, checkout, queue** (*BrE*), **shelf, trolley** (*BrE*) ◊ *An increasing amount of organic produce is to be found on ~ shelves.* | **car park** (*BrE*), **parking lot** (*AmE*) | **brand** | **assistant** (*BrE*), **clerk** (*AmE*), **manager** | **tabloid** (*AmE*)

superstition *noun*

ADJ. **popular** | **age-old, ancient, medieval, old** | **local** | **pagan, religious** | **primitive**
VERB + SUPERSTITION **have** ◊ *We have a lot of ~s about animals.* | **be riddled with** ◊ *The topic of birth is riddled with ~.* | **be based on** ◊ *These ideas are based on myths and ~s.* | **believe in** ◊ *I'm unwilling to believe in local ~s.* | **dismiss sth as, reject sth as**
PREP. **~ about** ◊ *primitive ~s about death*

supervise *verb*

ADV. **carefully, closely, directly, strictly, well** ◊ *The children will be closely ~d at all times.* | **fully, properly** ◊ *The pool is fully ~d by trained staff.* | **adequately** | **personally** ◊ *I will ~ the work personally.* | **internationally** ◊ *a proposal for an internationally ~d ceasefire*
VERB + SUPERVISE **appoint sb to** ◊ *An executive officer was appointed to ~ the arrangements.*
PHRASES **be responsible for supervising sth** ◊ *He was directly responsible for supervising the loading of the containers.*

supervision *noun*

ADJ. **careful, close, intensive, strict** | **adequate, effective, proper** | **inadequate** | **constant, day-to-day, regular** | **minimal** | **direct** ◊ *New employees are trained to work without direct ~.* | **general, overall** | **international** ◊ *The* elections will be held under international ~. | **adult, clinical, expert, medical, parental, personal** | **court, federal, judicial** ◊ He's now under court ~. ◊ the federal ~ of state elections

VERB + SUPERVISION **need, require** | **get, have, receive** | **exercise, give sb, offer (sb), provide (sb with)** ◊ The facilities offer only minimal ~ for young offenders. | **be responsible for** ◊ The head porter is responsible for the ~ and allocation of duties. | **keep sb/sth under** ◊ He needs to be kept under strict ~. | **improve, tighten, tighten up**

SUPERVISION + NOUN **order** (BrE) ◊ The local authority can apply for a ~ order for the child.

PREP. **under (sb's)** ~ ◊ under the close ~ of her teachers | **with** ~, **without** ~ ◊ Children are not allowed to swim without adequate ~. | **~ by** ◊ They still require ~ by colleagues. | **~ from** ◊ Trainees will receive personal ~ from experienced staff.

PHRASES **a lack of** ~

supervisor noun

ADJ. **senior** | **direct, immediate** (both esp. AmE) | **area** | **office** | **shift** | **account** (esp. AmE), **election(s), project** | **maintenance, production** | **music, technical** | **effects** ◊ a special effects ~ ◊ a visual effects ~ | **door** (BrE) ◊ a nightclub door ~ | **lunchtime** (BrE) ◊ She is a lunchtime ~ at the local school. | **city, county** (both AmE)

VERB + SUPERVISOR **act as**

PREP. **under a/the** ~ ◊ the people working under that ~
→ Note at JOB

supper noun

ADJ. **light** | **cold, hot** | **buffet** (esp. BrE) | **early, late** | **family** | **church, potluck** (both AmE) ◊ There'll be a potluck ~ Sunday night at the church. | **harvest** (BrE) ◊ There was always a harvest ~ for the farm workers. | **fish, fish-and-chip, pie, etc.** (BrE)

SUPPER + NOUN **dish** ◊ It can also be eaten as a ~ dish with a salad. | **table** ◊ Nell cleared the ~ table.

PHRASES **a bit of** ~ (BrE) ◊ They invited me over for a bit of ~.
→ Note at MEAL (for verbs)

supple adj.

VERBS **be, feel, look** ◊ The cream leaves your skin feeling soft and ~. | **become, get** ◊ He was gradually getting more ~. | **keep, remain, stay** ◊ exercises that will help you to keep ~ | **make sth** ◊ a cream that is used on dry skins to make them soft and ~ | **keep sth** ◊ You must exercise your joints to keep them ~.

ADV. **extremely, fairly, very, etc.**

PHRASES **soft and** ~

supplement noun

1 sth that is added

ADJ. **useful, valuable** | **colour/color** (= a magazine that comes with a newspaper) (esp. BrE), **magazine, newspaper, online, special, Sunday** (esp. BrE), **weekend** ◊ Our special ~ is packed with ideas for healthy hair. | **16-page, 20-page, etc.** | **diet, dietary, food, herbal, natural, nutritional** | **daily** ◊ women who take a daily ~ of folic acid | **mineral, protein, vitamin, etc.**

VERB + SUPPLEMENT **provide (sb/sth with)** | **add** ◊ The farmer adds a ~ to the horse's feed. | **take, use (sth as)** ◊ I take a vitamin ~ every day.

PREP. **~ to** ◊ This document is a ~ to the main report.

2 (esp. BrE) extra amount of money

ADJ. **additional, extra** | **$100, £50, etc.** ◊ A single cabin is available for a £20 ~. | **flight, single-room** (both esp. BrE) ◊ If you want to travel on a different day, a flight ~ is payable. | **means-tested** (BrE) ◊ means-tested ~s to the basic pension

VERB + SUPPLEMENT **add, charge** ◊ We charge a small ~ for this service. | **carry** (esp. BrE), **have** ◊ Weekend flights carry a ~. | **pay**

SUPPLEMENT + VERB **be payable**

PREP. **at a** ~ ◊ Single rooms are available at a ~. | **~ for** ◊ a €20 ~ for each extra night | **~ on** ◊ There is a ~ on rooms with a sea view.

supplier noun

ADJ. **big, key, largest, leading, main, major** | **small** | **official, preferred** | **sole** | **reliable** | **external, foreign, outside, overseas** | **local** | **independent** | **automotive** (AmE), **component, energy** (esp. BrE), **equipment, food, material, materials, software, etc.** ◊ People are encouraged to switch energy ~ to save money. ◊ building material ~s | **electricity, gas, oil** | **arms**

PREP. **~ of** ◊ the major ~s of foreign goods | **~ to** ◊ the leading arms ~ to the rebel forces

supply noun

1 sth that is supplied

ADJ. **total** ◊ It is impossible to measure the total ~ of money in circulation. | **available** | **endless, inexhaustible, infinite, limitless, never-ending, unending, unlimited** ◊ He has an endless ~ of corny jokes. | **abundant, bountiful, good, large, plentiful** | **adequate, ample, sufficient** | **excess** | **inadequate, limited, small** ◊ Hurry, as we only have a limited ~ of these TVs in stock! | **dwindling** | **constant, continuous, regular, steady** | **fresh** ◊ The body needs a fresh ~ of vitamin C every day. | **ready, reliable** ◊ a reliable ~ of clean water to communities | **domestic** | **air, blood, oxygen** ◊ A clot in the brain cut off her blood ~. | **food, milk, water, etc.** | **coal, electricity, energy, fuel, gas, oil, power, etc.** ◊ Domestic coal supplies were more plentiful in the 1950s. ◊ Turn off the mains electricity ~. (BrE) | **mains** (BrE) | **labour/labor** ◊ The farmers depend on a casual labour/labor ~ at harvest time. | **money** ◊ the country's problems with inflation and money ~

VERB + SUPPLY **have** ◊ Make sure you have an adequate ~ of brochures. | **get, lay in, obtain, receive** ◊ We should lay in a good ~ of beer for the party. | **produce, provide** ◊ The studio produced a steady ~ of good movies. | **ensure, maintain** | **cut off, disconnect, disrupt, stop** ◊ The electricity company disconnected our ~. ◊ The storm disrupted the town's power ~. | **deplete, exhaust, use, use up** ◊ By the end of the winter the ~ of grain was severely depleted. | **replenish, restock** (esp. AmE), **restore** | **increase** | **control, limit, reduce, restrict** | **exceed, outstrip** ◊ Demand for top-quality programmers exceeds ~, leading to extortionate salaries.

SUPPLY + VERB **increase** | **fall** | **exceed demand, meet demand** ◊ Supply did not increase to meet demand.

SUPPLY + NOUN **chain, line, network** | **system** ◊ the water ~ system | **contract** | **closet, room** (both AmE) | **depot, store** (esp. AmE) ◊ I went to the office ~ store. | **convoy, ship, train** | **route**

PREP. **~ of** ◊ a ~ of spare batteries | **~ to** ◊ to maintain an adequate water ~ to the city

PHRASES **be in short** ~ ◊ Food is in short ~ following the flooding. | **demand and** ~, ~ **and demand** ◊ laws of ~ and demand | **a fall in** ~, **a shortfall in** ~ ◊ There will soon be a shortfall in the ~ of qualified people. | **an increase in** ~

2 supplies amount of sth needed

ADJ. **abundant, plentiful** | **limited, meagre/meager** | **vital** | **basic** | **emergency, humanitarian, relief** | **arms, food** ◊ The Red Cross flew emergency food supplies into the war zone. | **medical, military** | **farm** (esp. AmE), **office, school** (esp. AmE) | **cleaning** (esp. AmE)

VERB + SUPPLIES **bring, bring in, lay in, provide (sb/sth with)** ◊ The money raised will provide vital medical supplies to refugee camps. | **deliver** | **be out of, be short of** | **run out of, run short of** | **threaten** ◊ Rebel action threatened relief supplies. | **buy** | **gather**

SUPPLIES + VERB **hold out, last** | **be depleted, be exhausted, run out** | **dwindle, run low, run short**

PREP. **~ of** ◊ The injured climbers had only meagre/meager supplies of water and peanuts to live off.

supply verb

ADV. **amply, well** ◊ The room was well supplied with reading material. | **adequately** ◊ Any room where gas is used must be adequately supplied with air. | **poorly** | **generously,**

helpfully, kindly ◇ *a buffet supper, generously supplied by club members* | **readily** ◇ *Calvin readily supplied the information.* | **free, free of charge**
VERB + SUPPLY **agree to** | **refuse to** | **fail to** | **ask sb to** ◇ *Each applicant is asked to ~ a portfolio of work at interview.*
PREP. **for** ◇ *goods supplied for private use* | **from** ◇ *The water was supplied from a tanker.* | **to** ◇ *They were accused of ~ing arms to the rebels.* | **with** ◇ *He refused to ~ the police with information.*
PHRASES **a contract to ~ sth** | **keep sb/sth supplied with sth** ◇ *She kept the guests well supplied with champagne.* | **with intent to ~ (sb/sth)** *(BrE, law)* ◇ *He was jailed for possession of heroin with intent to ~.*

support noun

1 help and encouragement

ADJ. **complete, full, total** | **firm, solid, strong** ◇ *The candidate enjoys the firm ~ of local industry.* ◇ *The plan received strong ~ from farmers.* | **considerable, generous, substantial** ◇ *the company's generous financial ~ of the arts* | **good, great, tremendous** | **active, enthusiastic** | **loyal** | **unconditional, unqualified, wholehearted** | **massive, overwhelming, unanimous** ◇ *The poll revealed massive ~ for the proposal.* | **unflagging, unstinting** *(esp. BrE)*, **unswerving** *(esp. BrE)*, **unwavering** ◇ *We would like to thank Ana for her unwavering ~ over the years.* | **growing, increased, increasing** | **continued, continuing, ongoing** | **broad, general** | **grass-roots, popular, public** | **majority, mass, wide, widespread** ◇ *The government has lost majority ~ in the Assembly.* | **community** | **main** | **limited, lukewarm, qualified, weak** ◇ *My idea only received lukewarm ~ from my colleagues.* | **adequate, sufficient** | **direct, indirect** | **long-term** ◇ *people who need long-term ~ at home* | **personal** ◇ *The proposal has the personal ~ of the president.* | **mutual** ◇ *The parents of the sufferers get together for mutual ~.* | **international** | **Democratic, Labour, Liberal, Republican, etc.** | **all-party** *(BrE)*, **bipartisan** *(esp. AmE)*, **cross-party** *(BrE)* | **parental** | **emotional, moral** ◇ *She took her sister with her to the interview for moral ~.* | **administrative, economic, electoral, financial, political, practical, technical, etc.** | **federal, government, official, state** | **air, intelligence, logistical, logistics, military, naval** | **customer, tech** (= company departments) | **life** ◇ *He's on life ~ at the moment.* ◇ *They turned off her life-support machine.*
VERB + SUPPORT **enjoy, have** ◇ *The policy has the ~ of the community.* | **derive, draw, get, receive** ◇ *Which groups does the party draw most of its ~ from?* | **enlist, find, gain, mobilize, secure, win** ◇ *Campaigners have enlisted the ~ of the local people.* | **attract, generate** | **drum up, garner, muster, rally, recruit, seek, solicit, whip up** | **give sb/sth, lend (sb/sth), offer (sb/sth), provide (sb/sth with)** ◇ *organizations that provide ~ and advice to small businesses* | **lose** | **cut, cut off, withdraw** | **need, require** ◇ *She will need a lot of emotional ~ at this difficult time.* | **count on, rely on** ◇ *Can I count on your ~?* | **deserve** | **announce, confirm, express, pledge, reaffirm, voice** ◇ *Many TV celebrities have already pledged their ~ to the appeal.* | **come out in, demonstrate, show** ◇ *one of the first scientists to come out in ~ of 'The Origin of Species'* | **acknowledge** ◇ *I wish to acknowledge the ~ of my family during the writing of this book.* | **appreciate** | **bolster, broaden, build, build up, increase, strengthen** ◇ *The government is trying to build popular ~ for an unwinnable war.* | **erode, weaken**
SUPPORT + VERB **come from sth** ◇ *Support came from all sections of the community.* | **grow, rise** ◇ *Support for the party has risen to 33%.* | **fall**
SUPPORT + NOUN **base, network** ◇ *He had no ~ base within the party.* | **group** ◇ *a local ~ group for single parents* | **services, system** | **personnel, staff, team** | **function, role**
PREP. **in ~ of** ◇ *an intense campaign in ~ of the proposal* | **with … ~, without … ~** ◇ *The pipeline is to be built with international ~.* | **~ against** ◇ *Farmers mobilized considerable ~ against plans to remove import restrictions.* | **~**

among ◇ *The party wishes to broaden its ~ among professionals.* | **~ between** ◇ *mutual ~ between local cooperatives* | **~ for** ◇ *The president has expressed his ~ for the project.* | **~ from** ◇ *The policy has broad ~ from industry.*
PHRASES **a base of ~** ◇ *Fears that instability would return gave the government a broad base of ~.* | **a cut in ~, a decline in ~** | **an expression of ~** ◇ *The rebel leader received expressions of ~ from all quarters.* | **a lack of ~** | **a source of ~** | **~ and encouragement** | **throw your ~ behind sb, throw your ~ to sb** *(AmE)* ◇ *She threw her full ~ behind him.* ◇ *They are now throwing their ~ to the other candidate.*

2 money to buy food, clothes, etc.

ADJ. **child, family, social, spousal** *(esp. AmE)* | **income** *(BrE)*
VERB + SUPPORT **claim** ◇ *Families earning below a certain amount can claim child ~.* | **pay**
PHRASES **a means of ~**

3 sth that carries the weight of sb/sth

ADJ. **firm** | **added, additional, extra** | **back, knee, etc.** | **roof** | **structural**
VERB + SUPPORT **give sth** ◇ *The piece of wood under the mattress is to give my back extra ~.*
SUPPORT + NOUN **beam, structure**
PHRASES **hold onto sb/sth for ~** ◇ *He held onto his wife for ~ as he left the hospital.*

support verb

1 help/encourage/agree with sb/sth

ADV. **overwhelmingly** ◇ *The people of this country overwhelmingly ~ their president.* ◇ *I strongly ~ the view that education should be available to everyone.* | **fervently, fully, strongly, wholeheartedly** | **unanimously** | **actively, enthusiastically, vigorously** ◇ *The group is actively ~ed by the administration.* | **consistently** ◇ *He has consistently ~ed the tax cuts.* | **directly** | **tacitly, openly, publicly** | **loyally** ◇ *He has ~ed the party loyally for over twenty years.* | **ably** ◇ *The soloists were ably ~ed by the University Singers.*
VERB + SUPPORT **agree to, pledge to, promise to** ◇ *He promised to ~ me at the meeting.* | **be prepared to, be willing to** | **fail to, refuse to**
PREP. **in** ◇ *Very few countries ~ed France in its action.*
PHRASES **be well ~ed, be widely ~ed** ◇ *These policies were widely ~ed in the country.* | **~ and encourage sb/sth** ◇ *Teachers should always ~ and encourage their students.*

2 show that sth is true/correct

ADV. **strongly, weakly** ◇ *The evidence strongly ~s his claims.* | **adequately** ◇ *The sample adequately ~s this conclusion.* | **directly, indirectly** ◇ *These results indirectly ~ the hypothesis.* | **partially** | **generally** ◇ *Research has generally ~ed these predictions.* | **clearly** ◇ *Our results clearly ~ this view.*
VERB + SUPPORT **appear to, seem to, tend to**
PHRASES **be ~ed by data, be ~ed by evidence** ◇ *His claim is not ~ed by any evidence.* | **be well ~ed** ◇ *He said the figures were questionable and not well ~ed.*

3 give sb money

ADV. **financially** | **generously** | **partially** ◇ *This work was partially ~ed by the government.*
VERB + SUPPORT **help (to)**
PREP. **through** ◇ *Her parents ~ed her all through college.*

supporter noun

ADJ. **active, ardent, avid, big, close, committed, diehard, enthusiastic, fanatical, fervent, great, keen** *(esp. BrE)*, **loyal, passionate, stalwart** *(esp. BrE)*, **staunch, strong** ◇ *an active ~ of democratic change* ◇ *diehard ~s of the old system* ◇ *Only stalwart ~s of the team stayed to the end.* *(BrE)* | **outspoken, vocal** | **core, leading, principal, prominent** | **lifelong, long-time** | **traditional** ◇ *an area of traditional Republican ~s* | **government, opposition, party, political** | **Conservative, Democratic, Labour, Republican, etc.** | **grass-roots** ◇ *The party has not been listening to the concerns of its grass-roots ~s.* | **football, rugby** *(both BrE)* | **gay rights, human rights, war, etc.**
… OF SUPPORTERS **army, band, crowd, group, legion, set** *(BrE)* ◇ *Both sets of ~s applauded the fantastic goal.*
VERB + SUPPORTER **have** | **attract, mobilize, rally** ◇ *to attract*

~s to the cause | **alienate** | **urge** ◊ *The party is urging ~s to keep up the pressure on the government.*
SUPPORTER + VERB **cheer** ◊ *a crowd of cheering ~s*

supportive *adj.*

VERBS **be, seem** | **become** | **remain** | **find sb**
ADV. **extremely, fairly, very, etc.** | **highly, incredibly, strongly, wonderfully** ◊ *strongly ~ of the government's approach* ◊ *All the hospital staff were wonderfully ~.* | **entirely, fully, totally, wholly** ◊ *We are totally ~ of this idea.* | **broadly** (*esp. BrE*), **generally, largely** | **mutually** ◊ *They have established a mutually ~ and caring relationship.*
PREP. **of** ◊ *fully ~ of the changes* | **to** ◊ *They were all extremely ~ to me.*

suppose *verb*

ADV. **mistakenly, wrongly** | **commonly, generally** ◊ *This combination of qualities is generally ~d to be extremely rare.*
VERB + SUPPOSE **be plausible to, be reasonable to** ◊ *It's reasonable to ~ that people go into this business in search of fame.* | **be absurd to, be a mistake to, be naive to, be unreasonable to**
PHRASES **reason to ~ sth** ◊ *There is no reason to ~ she's lying.*

supposition *noun*

ADJ. **reasonable** ◊ *It is a reasonable ~ that many mothers would welcome the offer of part-time work.* | **mere, pure** (*both esp. BrE*) ◊ *That is mere ~!*
VERB + SUPPOSITION **make** ◊ *We can make a ~ about how the accident happened.* | **be based on** | **confirm, support**
SUPPOSITION + VERB **be correct, be wrong** | **be based on sth**
PREP. **on (a/the) ~** ◊ *She was charged on the ~ that she had colluded with her husband in the murders.* | **~ about** ◊ *They are making all sorts of ~s about our possible reaction.* | **~ of** ◊ *a ~ of innocence*

suppress *verb*

1 stop sth by using force

ADV. **brutally, ruthlessly, violently** ◊ *A pro-democracy uprising was brutally ~ed.*
VERB + SUPPRESS **attempt to, seek to, try to** | **use sth to** ◊ *They often use violence to ~ opposition.*
PHRASES **an attempt to ~ sth**

2 stop sth from being seen/known

ADV. **completely** | **effectively** ◊ *The medication effectively ~ed the pain.* | **deliberately** ◊ *This information had been deliberately ~ed.* | **systematically**
VERB + SUPPRESS **attempt to, seek to, try to**
PHRASES **an attempt to ~ sth**

3 stop yourself doing/expressing sth

ADV. **barely, hardly** ◊ *He could hardly ~ his surprise.* ◊ *Her face was charged with barely ~ed anger.* | **instantly** ◊ *The disloyal thought was instantly ~ed.* | **quickly**
VERB + SUPPRESS **be unable to, cannot** ◊ *She was unable to ~ a giggle.* ◊ *He could no longer ~ his anger.* | **try to** | **manage to** | **be hard to**

suppression *noun*

ADJ. **total** | **bloody, brutal, ruthless, violent**
PREP. **during the ~ of, in the ~ of** ◊ *He was injured in the bloody ~ of the uprising.*

supremacy *noun*

ADJ. **absolute, total** | **unchallenged** | **global, world** | **air, military, naval** | **male, white** | **economic, political** | **racial** | **judicial** (*AmE, law*)
VERB + SUPREMACY **enjoy** (*esp. BrE*), **have** ◊ *a period when the British enjoyed ~ in international trade* | **lose** | **battle for, fight for, struggle for, vie for** | **assert, establish, gain** | **acknowledge, uphold** ◊ *to uphold the ~ of the country's own laws* | **give sb/sth** ◊ *Coal gave the region industrial ~.* | **maintain** | **challenge**
PREP. **~ in** ◊ *the battle for ~ in the world economic markets* | **~ of** ◊ *the ~ of international law* | **~ over** ◊ *By the end of the war, the warlord had established total ~ over all his rivals.* | **~ within** ◊ *factions fighting for ~ within the Church*
PHRASES **a battle for ~, a fight for ~, a struggle for ~** | **a challenge to sb/sth's ~, a threat to sb/sth's ~** | **a symbol of ~**

surcharge *noun*

ADJ. **small** | **hefty** | **fuel, tax** ◊ *a corporate tax ~* | **delivery** (*AmE*) ◊ *The price includes the delivery ~ of $15.*
VERB + SURCHARGE **have** | **add, impose, levy, put** ◊ *A ~ of €40 was added to our bill.* | **pay**
PREP. **~ for** ◊ *There is a ~ for excess baggage.* | **~ on** ◊ *There is a 2% ~ on credit-card users.*

sure *adj.*

VERBS **be, feel, seem, sound** ◊ *You don't seem very ~ to me.* | **make** ◊ *Make ~ no one finds out about this.* | **make sb** ◊ *What makes you so ~ she'll come back to you?*
ADV. **absolutely, completely, quite, totally, very** | **doubly** ◊ *To make doubly ~ they would not be disturbed she turned the key in the lock.* | **not altogether, not entirely, not exactly, not quite, not really, not so** ◊ *I'm not altogether ~ he would appreciate your efforts.* | **almost, fairly, pretty, reasonably**
PREP. **about** ◊ *Potts was confident of taking the American title, but less ~ about the world championship.* | **of** ◊ *You'd better be completely ~ of your facts.*

surf *noun*

ADJ. **crashing, pounding** | **big, heavy**
VERB + SURF **ride** ◊ *dolphins riding the ~*
SURF + VERB **break, crash** ◊ *the sound of ~ breaking on the beach*
PREP. **in the ~** ◊ *The children splashed around in the ~.*
PHRASES **the roar of (the) ~**

surface *noun*

ADJ. **even, flat, level, smooth** | **rough, uneven** | **curved** | **firm, hard, solid** | **soft** | **slippery** | **calm, glassy, polished, reflective, shiny** ◊ *the glassy ~ of the lake* | **frozen** ◊ *The ball rolled onto the frozen ~ of the pond.* | **inner, interior, internal** ◊ *the inner ~ of a bone* | **exterior, external, outer** | **lower, upper** | **water** | **floor, ground, land, ocean, road, rock, sea, wall** | **kitchen, work, working** ◊ *a cleaning product for all kitchen ~s*
VERB + SURFACE **come to, come up to, reach, rise to** | **hit** | **bring sth to** ◊ *The captain brought the submarine to the ~.* | **coat, cover** | **break, penetrate** | **smooth** ◊ *Smooth the ~ with a spatula.* | **scratch, skim, touch** (*all figurative*) ◊ *The investigation barely scratched the ~ of the city's drug problem.*
SURFACE + NOUN **area** | **level** | **layer** ◊ *the ~ layer of the skin* | **temperature, tension** | **water** ◊ *Surface water made driving conditions hazardous.*
PREP. **above the ~, on a/the ~, over the ~** ◊ *A trail of flowers floated on the ~ of the water.* ◊ *On the ~ his words were funny, but I detected a lot of anger behind them.* (*figurative*) | **below the ~, beneath the ~, under the ~** ◊ *The ring slowly sank beneath the ~ of the mud pool.* ◊ *She gives the impression of being rather conventional, but under the ~ she is wildly eccentric.* (*figurative*) | **across the ~, along the ~** | **in the ~** ◊ *Cracks began to appear in the ~ of the earth.*
PHRASES **the Earth's ~, the ~ of the Earth** ◊ *Visible light from the sun passes through the atmosphere to the Earth's ~.*

surge *noun*

1 of feeling

ADJ. **great, huge** | **sudden** | **initial** ◊ *His initial ~ of euphoria was quickly followed by dismay.* | **fresh, new, renewed** ◊ *She felt a fresh ~ of anger when he denied lying.* | **adrenalin**
VERB + SURGE **experience, feel, get, have** ◊ *He experienced a sudden ~ of excitement.* | **send** ◊ *The mention of her name sent a ~ of anger through me.*

SURGE + VERB **sweep sth, sweep over sb, sweep through sb** ◇ *A great ~ of emotion swept through him.*
PREP. **with a ~** ◇ *He thought of his old teacher with a ~ of affection.* | **~ of** ◇ *a sudden ~ of adrenalin*

2 movement/increase

ADJ. **big, dramatic, great, huge, massive** | **sudden, unexpected** | **temporary** | **last-minute, late, overnight, recent** ◇ *A last-minute ~ in ticket sales saved the show from closure.* | **power, storm, tidal** ◇ *The storm ~ caused widespread flooding.*
PREP. **~ in** ◇ *a dramatic ~ in the demand* | **~ of** ◇ *a ~ of electricity*
PHRASES **a ~ forward** ◇ *Police struggled to control the sudden ~ forward by the demonstrators.*

surgeon noun

ADJ. **distinguished, eminent, leading, renowned, top** | **brilliant, good, skilled** | **pioneering** (*esp. BrE*) | **chief, consultant** (*BrE*), **senior** | **qualified** | **general** | **specialist** (*BrE*) | **brain, cardiac, eye, heart, orthopaedic/orthopedic, transplant, trauma** | **cosmetic, plastic** ◇ *A plastic ~ successfully rebuilt his nose.* ◇ *a board-certified plastic ~* (*AmE*) | **dental, veterinary** | **army, flight** (*AmE*), **police** (*BrE*)
VERB + SURGEON **be, work as** | **become, qualify as** (*BrE*) ◇ *He is determined to qualify as a ~.* | **see**
SURGEON + VERB **operate, perform sth** ◇ *the ~ who will operate on you* ◇ *Surgeons performed two operations on him yesterday.* | **insert sth, place sth, remove sth** ◇ *Surgeons removed her right leg above the knee.* | **make an incision**
PHRASES **the surgeon's knife** (*often figurative*) ◇ *Many people are terrified at the thought of the surgeon's knife.*

surgery noun

1 medical treatment

ADJ. **major, radical** | **minor** | **extensive** | **further** | **successful, unsuccessful** | **keyhole, laser** | **invasive** ◇ *One of his specialities is minimally invasive ~.* | **elective, emergency, experimental, exploratory** ◇ *They discussed whether patients should have to pay for all elective ~.* | **day, outpatient** (*AmE*) | **cosmetic, plastic, reconstructive** | **cataract, eye** | **bypass, cardiac, heart, open-heart** ◇ *to undergo coronary bypass ~* | **abdominal, brain, gastric, orthopaedic/orthopedic, paediatric/pediatric, etc.** | **elbow, hip, knee, etc.** | **…replacement** ◇ *patients recovering from hip replacement ~* | **general**
VERB + SURGERY **get, have, undergo** ◇ *She had minor ~ on her knee.* ◇ *She had three surgeries over ten days.* (*AmE*) | **do, perform** ◇ *He has been performing heart ~ for ten years.* | **need, require** | **recommend** | **consider** | **come off** (used about sportspeople) (*AmE*) ◇ *a left-handed hitter coming off elbow ~*
PREP. **after ~, before ~, during ~** ◇ *She felt weak for six months after undergoing major abdominal ~.* | **~ for emergency ~ for appendicitis** | **~ on** ◇ *She had ~ on her knee.* | **~ to** ◇ *After the accident, she needed extensive plastic ~ to her face.*

2 (*BrE*) place/time a doctor/dentist sees patients

ADJ. **open** | **afternoon, evening, morning** | **dental, doctor's, GP's, veterinary**
VERB + SURGERY **do, have, hold** ◇ *She has a morning ~.* | **attend, go to** ◇ *those attending the doctor's ~ with physical symptoms*
SURGERY + NOUN **hours**
PREP. **in a/the ~** ◇ *Dr Smith isn't in the ~ today.*

surname noun (*esp. BrE*)

ADJ. **double-barrelled** (*BrE*) | **common** ◇ *Rossi is a common ~ in Italy.*
VERB + SURNAME **bear, have** | **address sb by, call sb by** ◇ *The teacher addresses the students by their ~s.* | **change** | **adopt, take, use** ◇ *On marriage most women still take their husband's ~.*

surpass verb

ADV. **far** | **easily** | **eventually, soon** ◇ *The death toll may eventually ~ two thousand.*
PREP. **in** ◇ *The second half easily ~ed the first in entertainment value.*

surplus noun

ADJ. **big, huge, large** ◇ *a large grain ~* | **small** | **projected** ◇ *a projected ~ of $5.6 trillion over ten years* | **agricultural, budget, current-account, federal, social-security** (*AmE*), **trade** | **consumer, producer** (*both economics*)
VERB + SURPLUS **have, run** (*esp. AmE*) ◇ *Japan runs a large current-account ~.* | **generate, produce** | **project** (*esp. AmE*)
SURPLUS + NOUN **cash, stock**
PREP. **in ~** ◇ *The pension fund is in ~.*

surprise noun

1 feeling of surprise

ADJ. **great, total, utter** | **mild, slight, some** | **initial** ◇ *After the initial ~ I got to like the place.* | **mock** ◇ *His eyebrows rose in mock ~.* | **genuine, real**
VERB + SURPRISE **express, register, show** | **feign** ◇ *He feigned ~ when I went up and said hello.* | **hide** ◇ *She was quick to hide her ~.* | **cause** ◇ *The president's remarks caused ~ and embarrassment.*
PREP. **in ~** ◇ *'Walk twenty miles!' repeated the old man in ~.* | **to sb's ~** ◇ *Much to her ~, she enjoyed the party.* | **with ~, without ~** ◇ *It was with some ~ that I read of his resignation.* | **~ at** ◇ *She showed no ~ at the news.*
PHRASES **an expression of ~, a look of ~** ◇ *I could not believe the look of ~ on his face.* | **a gasp of ~, a scream of ~, a shriek of ~** | **the element of ~** ◇ *The Egyptian team relied on the element of ~ to defeat their stronger opponents.* | **catch sb by ~, take sb by ~** ◇ *The storm took us completely by ~.* | **imagine my ~ when…** ◇ *Imagine my ~ when I found out he wasn't really a doctor.* | **surprise surprise** (*humorous*) ◇ *Bob turned up half an hour late, surprise surprise.*

2 sth that you did not expect

ADJ. **big, complete, genuine, great, huge, major, real, total** | **unexpected** | **lovely** (*esp. BrE*), **nice, pleasant, wonderful** | **nasty, unpleasant, unwelcome** | **little** ◇ *I have a little ~ for you!*
VERB + SURPRISE **be, come as** | **get, have** ◇ *I had a wonderful ~ when I saw Mark there.* | **give sb, spring** ◇ *Johnson sprung a ~ by winning the first round.* | **be in for** ◇ *Your mother's in for a bit of a ~ when she gets home.* | **ruin, spoil**
SURPRISE + NOUN **announcement, appearance, party, visit** | **hit, victory, win** | **defeat** | **attack** ◇ *They launched a ~ attack on the Russian fleet.* | **winner** ◇ *Roach was the ~ winner of the £10 000 first prize.* | **guest**
PREP. **~ for** ◇ *It was a complete ~ for me.* | **~ to** ◇ *His refusal came as no ~ to his boss.*
PHRASES **a bit of a ~, quite a ~** | **hold few, many, no, etc. ~s** ◇ *She feels that the future holds few ~s.*

surprise verb

ADV. **greatly, really** | **not at all** ◇ *The outcome did not ~ me at all.* | **hardly** | **a little, slightly**
VERB + SURPRISE **wouldn't** ◇ *It wouldn't ~ me if they got married.* | **seem to** | **want to** ◇ *They wanted to ~ their mother and get the breakfast ready.*

surprised adj.

VERBS **appear, be, feel, look, seem, sound**
ADV. **extremely, fairly, very, etc.** | **completely, greatly, most, terribly** | **hardly, not altogether, not at all, not entirely, not in the least, not particularly, not totally** ◇ *Her father didn't seem at all ~.* | **a little, slightly, etc.** | **mildly, vaguely** ◇ *She looked vaguely ~ at my remark.* | **genuinely, truly** | **clearly, evidently, obviously** | **secretly** | **constantly, continually** ◇ *I am constantly ~ by what my fourteen-month-old son understands.* | **pleasantly** ◇ *He was pleasantly ~ to discover that he was no longer afraid.*
PREP. **at** ◇ *He sounded ~ at this request.* | **by** ◇ *She appeared genuinely ~ by this gesture of affection.*

surprising *adj.*

VERBS **be, seem** | **make sth** | **find sth**
ADV. **extremely, fairly, very, etc.** | **a little, slightly, etc.** | **hardly, not altogether, not at all, not entirely, not really, not totally, scarcely** ◊ *It is hardly ~ that these stories continue to circulate.*

surrender *noun*

ADJ. **complete, total** | **unconditional** | **immediate**
VERB + SURRENDER **demand** ◊ *The allied commander demanded their immediate and unconditional ~.* | **force into, starve into** ◊ *The villagers were starved into ~.* | **accept** ◊ *The division accepted the ~ of a group of some 500 rebels.* | **negotiate**
PREP. **~ to** ◊ *the government's ~ to the nationalists' demands*
PHRASES **a flag of ~** ◊ *The rebels hoisted the white flag of ~.* | **in ~** ◊ *He raised his hands in mock ~.* | **terms of ~** ◊ *The rebels were offered easy terms of ~.*

surrender *verb*

ADV. **unconditionally** | **completely** ◊ *After three weeks under siege they ~ed completely.* | **immediately** | **eventually, finally** | **formally** ◊ *The British formally ~ed on May 31.* | **voluntarily**
VERB + SURRENDER **order sb to** ◊ *They were ordered to ~ their weapons to the police.* | **agree to** ◊ *They agreed to ~ their claim to the territory.* | **refuse to** | **be forced to**
PREP. **to** ◊ *He ~ed voluntarily to his enemies.* ◊ *The dictator ~ed power to Parliament.*

surrogate *noun*

VERB + SURROGATE **act as, be, become** | **use**
SURROGATE + NOUN **father, mother, parent** | **child**
PREP. **~ for** ◊ *He used the Internet as a ~ for contact with real people.*

surround *verb*

ADV. **completely, entirely, totally** | **almost, virtually** | **partially** | **quickly**
PREP. **with** ◊ *They ~ed the building with tanks.*

surroundings *noun*

ADJ. **beautiful, elegant, idyllic, lovely** (*esp. BrE*), **magnificent, pleasant** | **comfortable, luxurious** | **peaceful, quiet, tranquil** | **familiar** | **new, strange, unfamiliar** | **natural** ◊ *animals living in their natural ~* | **physical** | **immediate** | **rural, urban**
VERB + SURROUNDINGS **adapt to, be in harmony with, blend into, blend in with, blend with, fit into, fit in with** ◊ *The new hotel blends perfectly with the immediate ~.* | **examine, observe, scan, survey**
PREP. **amid …** ◊ *classic French cuisine served amid elegant ~* | **in …~** ◊ *We spent the afternoon relaxing in the beautiful ~ of my parents' home.*
PHRASES **the beauty of the ~**

surveillance *noun*

ADJ. **close, constant, regular, round-the-clock, routine** | **covert, secret** | **aerial, electronic, Internet, satellite, video** | **CCTV, closed-circuit television** (*both esp. BrE*) | **military, police** | **health, medical**
VERB + SURVEILLANCE **be under** ◊ *The suspects are under police ~.* | **keep sb/sth under, place sb/sth under, put sb/sth under** ◊ *The country's borders are kept under constant ~.* | **carry out, conduct, do** ◊ *The army carried out covert ~ of the building for several months.* | **increase, reduce**
SURVEILLANCE + NOUN **camera, device, equipment** | **footage, tape** (*AmE*), **video** ◊ *The images were covertly captured on ~ tape.* | **method, operation, programme/program, system** | **aircraft** | **flight** | **team**

survey *noun*

1 study of sth

ADJ. **comprehensive, detailed, extensive, full, in-depth, large-scale, major, systematic** | **brief, quick, informal** |

broad, general | **representative, sample** ◊ *a nationally representative ~ of the US population conducted each year* | **regular** | **annual, monthly, etc.** | **follow-up** ◊ *The fifth follow-up ~ provides the data for this study.* | **local** (*esp. BrE*), **national, nationwide, regional** | **independent** | **historical** ◊ *a historical ~ of children's clothing* | **mail** (*AmE*), **online, postal** (*BrE*), **questionnaire, telephone, Web-based** | **comparative** | **field** | **pilot** | **attitude, consumer, customer, customer-satisfaction, opinion** ◊ *A recent customer ~ showed widespread ignorance about organic food.* | **market, market-research, marketing** | **household** (*esp. AmE*)
VERB + SURVEY **administer** (*esp. AmE*), **carry out** (*esp. BrE*), **conduct, do, make, perform** (*esp. AmE*), **undertake** (*esp. BrE*) ◊ *The charity did a ~ of people's attitudes to the disabled.* | **commission** | **participate in, respond to, take** (*esp. AmE*), **take part in** ◊ *94% of people who took part in the ~ said they agreed.* | **complete, fill in** (*BrE*), **fill out** (*AmE*) | **return, send back** | **send out**
SURVEY + VERB **cover sth, deal with sth, examine sth** ◊ *The ~ covered 74 species.* | **ask sth** | **claim sth, conclude sth, confirm sth, disclose sth, find sth, highlight sth, identify sth, indicate sth, report sth, reveal sth, say sth, show sth, suggest sth** ◊ *A customer-satisfaction ~ highlighted the need for clearer pricing.*
SURVEY + NOUN **data, results** | **method, technique** | **participant** (*AmE*), **respondent** | **group** | **questionnaire** | **question** | **response**
PREP. **according to a/the ~** ◊ *According to the ~, many young adults have experimented with drugs of some kind.* | **in a/the ~** ◊ *the questions used in the ~* | **~ into** ◊ *a ~ into the state of English in universities* | **~ of** ◊ *a ~ of adults* | **~ on** ◊ *a ~ on drivers' attitudes to the police*
PHRASES **the findings of a/the ~, the results of a/the ~**

2 of land or a building

ADJ. **full** | **aerial** | **archaeological, geological, geophysical, land, seismic** | **structural** (*esp. BrE*) ◊ *A structural ~ of the property revealed serious defects.*
VERB + SURVEY **carry out** (*esp. BrE*), **do, make**

survey *verb*

ADV. **carefully** | **calmly, critically** ◊ *She ~ed his appearance critically.* | **briefly, quickly**
PREP. **from** ◊ *I ~ed the scene from my window.*

survival *noun*

ADJ. **long-term, short-term** | **continued, future** ◊ *They are working to ensure the continued ~ of this species.* | **day-to-day** | **improved** ◊ *The study showed improved ~ of patients using the drug.* | **miraculous** | **business, economic, human, national, physical, political**
VERB + SURVIVAL **fight for** | **assure** (*esp. AmE*), **ensure** ◊ *The campaign will hopefully ensure the ~ of the tiger.* | **improve, prolong** ◊ *Chemotherapy can prolong ~ in cancer patients.* | **threaten** ◊ *The arrival of this South American predator threatened the ~ of native species.* | **affect, influence** | **be critical for/to, be crucial for/to, be essential to, be necessary for, be vital for/to** ◊ *Adaptability is essential to ~ in a changing environment.*
SURVIVAL + NOUN **chances, rate** | **skills, strategy** | **guide** (= book), **kit** ◊ *The expedition members carried flares in their ~ kit.* | **instinct** | **advantage, benefit** ◊ *In rare cases, a mutation confers a ~ advantage to the organism.*
PREP. **~ against** ◊ *the struggle for ~ against such well-armed enemies* | **~ as** ◊ *his ~ as leader*
PHRASES **a battle for ~, a fight for ~, a struggle for ~** ◊ *Here, life is a battle for ~.* | **be a matter of ~, be a question of ~** ◊ *For the poorest people, life was merely a matter of ~.* | **a chance of ~, chances of ~** ◊ *Doctors gave him only a 50% chance of ~.* ◊ *Her chances of ~ are poor.* | **the instinct for ~** ◊ *He lacked the common instinct for ~.* | **~ of the fittest** ◊ *Darwin's theory of the ~ of the fittest* | **a threat to the ~ of sth** ◊ *The main threat to the ~ of these creatures comes from their loss of habitat.*

survive verb

ADV. **well** ◊ *The frescoes have ~d remarkably well.* ◊ *Seedlings ~ better in stony soil.* | **barely, hardly** ◊ *The islanders could barely ~ without an export crop.* | **just, just about, narrowly** ◊ *I can just about ~ on what I earn.* ◊ *He narrowly ~d several assassination attempts.* | **(for) long** ◊ *Nobody can ~ long without water.* | **still** ◊ *Only one copy of the book still ~s.* | **miraculously** ◊ *A young boy miraculously ~d a 25 000-volt electric shock.* | **somehow** | **economically, financially, politically** ◊ *Many of these teachers are struggling to ~ financially.*

VERB + SURVIVE **struggle to** ◊ *poor people struggling to ~* | **be able to, can, manage to** | **expect (sb/sth) to** ◊ *Doctors did not expect him to ~ the night.* | **hope to** ◊ *She cannot hope to ~ long in power.* | **be likely to, be unlikely to** | **be lucky to** ◊ *Lung cancer patients are lucky to ~ for five years.* | **enable sb to, help sb (to)**

PREP. **as** ◊ *Will she ~ as party leader?* | **from** ◊ *Very little has ~d from this period of history.* | **into** ◊ *Very few of the children ~d into adult life.* | **on** ◊ *They ~d on roots and berries.* | **through** ◊ *She ~d through two world wars.* | **to** ◊ *Four of their five chickens ~d to adulthood.* | **until** ◊ *The original apple tree ~d until 1911.*

PHRASES **the only surviving…, the sole surviving…** ◊ *the only surviving member of her family* | **~ and prosper, ~ and thrive** ◊ *Companies need to keep to deadlines if they are to ~ and thrive.* | **~ intact, ~ unscathed** ◊ *Few buildings ~d the war intact.*

survivor noun

ADJ. **the last, the only, a rare, the remaining, the sole** ◊ *This grand park is a rare ~ from the 18th century.* | **crash, Holocaust, rape, shipwreck, tsunami** | **cancer, stroke** ◊ *the recovery process for breast cancer ~s*

VERB + SURVIVOR **be** | **find, pick up, rescue** ◊ *The navy helped pick up the ~s.* | **look for, search for** ◊ *The emergency services searched all night for crash ~s.* | **leave** ◊ *The bomb blast left no ~s.* | **interview** | **help, treat**

SURVIVOR + NOUN **guilt** (*psychology*) ◊ *She is wrestling with ~ guilt.*

PREP. **~ from** ◊ *a ~ from the Titanic*

susceptible adj.

VERBS **be, prove, seem** | **become** | **remain** | **leave sb/sth, make sb/sth, render sb/sth** ◊ *The operation had left her ~ to infection.*

ADV. **extremely, fairly, very, etc.** | **easily, especially, highly, particularly, readily, unusually** ◊ *certain highly ~ individuals* | **increasingly** | **genetically**

PREP. **to** ◊ *Some dogs are genetically ~ to the disease.*

suspect noun

ADJ. **chief, key, main, number-one, primary** (*AmE*), **prime** ◊ *She has been identified as the chief ~.* | **likely, logical** (*AmE*), **obvious, possible, potential** | **usual** | **criminal, murder, terror, terrorism** (*esp. AmE*), **terrorist**

VERB + SUSPECT **have, identify (sb as), name (sb as)** ◊ *The police have several ~s.* | **apprehend, arrest, capture, catch, detain, hold, round up** ◊ *The army rounded up all the usual ~s.* | **interrogate, interview, question** | **charge** | **release** | **extradite, hand over**

PREP. **~ for** ◊ *The letter makes him a possible ~ for her murder.* | **~ in** ◊ *Two men were arrested as ~s in the bombing.*

suspect verb

1 believe that sth may happen/be true

ADV. **strongly** | **rather** (*esp. BrE*) ◊ *I rather ~ they were trying to get rid of me.* | **rightly, wrongly** | **all along, always** ◊ *These revelations only prove what I ~ed all along.* | **immediately** ◊ *He immediately ~ed the worst.*

VERB + SUSPECT **begin to** | **have reason to, have reasons to** ◊ *She had no reason to ~ that he had not been telling the truth.*

PHRASES **be widely ~ed** ◊ *It was widely ~ed that the cadets had been acting on orders.*

2 believe sb is guilty of sth

ADV. **rightly, wrongly**

PREP. **of** ◊ *He was wrongly ~ed of the crime.*

PHRASES **have grounds for ~ing sb/sth** (*esp. BrE*), **have grounds to ~ sb/sth** (*esp. BrE*), **have reason to ~ sb/sth, have reasons for ~ing sb/sth, have reasons to ~ sb/sth**

suspect adj.

VERBS **be, look, seem** | **render sth** ◊ *The theory is rendered ~ by its reliance on now discredited sources.*

ADV. **extremely, fairly, very, etc.** | **deeply, highly** ◊ *Some of the evidence was deeply ~.* | **increasingly** | **a little, slightly, etc.** | **inherently** | **constitutionally** (*esp. AmE*), **morally, politically**

suspend verb

1 delay sth

ADV. **immediately** | **indefinitely** | **temporarily** ◊ *Funding for the new building has been temporarily ~ed.* | **effectively**

VERB + SUSPEND **agree to, decide to, vote to** ◊ *They have decided to ~ production at the country's biggest plant.* | **threaten to** | **be forced to**

PHRASES **the power to ~ sth** ◊ *They have the power to ~ subsidy payments.*

2 stop sb from working, going to school, etc.

ADV. **automatically, formally** (*esp. BrE*) ◊ *The players will be automatically ~ed.* | **indefinitely, permanently** | **temporarily**

VERB + SUSPEND **threaten to**

PREP. **for** ◊ *We both got ~ed for fighting.* | **from** ◊ *The girls had been ~ed from school for five days.* | **pending** ◊ *She was ~ed pending the outcome of the police investigation.*

PHRASES **be ~ed on full pay** (*BrE*) ◊ *She has been ~ed on full pay following a disciplinary hearing.* | **be ~ed with pay, be ~ed without pay**

suspender noun

1 (*BrE*) for holding stockings up

SUSPENDER + NOUN **belt**

PHRASES **stockings and ~s**

2 suspenders (*AmE*) for holding trousers/pants up → See also BRACES

SUSPENDERS + VERB **hold sth up** ◊ *The ~s held up his trousers.* → Special page at CLOTHES

suspense noun

ADJ. **nail-biting, unbearable** | **genuine, real**

VERB + SUSPENSE **break, spoil** ◊ *Don't look at the end of the book yet—you'll spoil the ~.* | **build, build up, create, generate** | **stand** ◊ *She couldn't stand the ~ a moment longer.*

SUSPENSE + VERB **be killing sb** (*informal*) ◊ *I don't get the results till next week, and the ~ is killing me.*

SUSPENSE + NOUN **film** (*esp. BrE*), **movie** (*esp. AmE*), **story, thriller**

PREP. **~ about** ◊ *They were kept in ~ about joining the expedition for several weeks.*

PHRASES **a state of ~** | **keep sb in ~, leave sb in ~** ◊ *Don't keep us in suspense—did you get the job or not?*

suspension noun

1 stopping of activity

ADJ. **temporary** | **lengthy, long** | **immediate** | **automatic** ◊ *Another caution will result in his automatic ~ from the final.* | **one-match, two-match, etc.** (*esp. BrE*) | **one-game, two-game, etc.** (*esp. AmE*) | **five-day, seven-month, etc.**

VERB + SUSPENSION **give sb, impose** (*esp. BrE*), **order** (*esp. BrE*) ◊ *A four-day ~ was imposed on her.* | **face** | **get, receive** ◊ *He receive a five-day ~.* | **appeal** (*AmE*), **appeal against** (*BrE*) | **serve, serve out** (*BrE*) ◊ *He is serving a one-match ~.*

PREP. **under ~** ◊ *a detective under ~ from his job* | **~ for** ◊ *a*

sweat

five-game ~ *for violating the league's drug policy* | ~ **from** ◇ *his* ~ *from the club*

PHRASES **a period of** ~ ◇ *The athlete could face a lengthy period of* ~ *if found guilty.* | ~ **of disbelief** ◇ *Many movies require the viewer to engage in a willing* ~ *of disbelief.*

2 on a vehicle

ADJ. **front, rear** | **active, independent** | **air**
VERB + SUSPENSION **be fitted with** (*esp. BrE*), **have** ◇ *The new model has independent* ~.
SUSPENSION + NOUN **system**

suspicion *noun*

ADJ. **strong** ◇ *There is strong* ~ *on both sides that information is being withheld.* | **considerable, deep, grave, great** | **the slightest, vague** ◇ *I don't think he had the slightest* ~ *anything was wrong.* | **dark, nagging, nasty, sneaking, terrible, worst** ◇ *I have a nasty* ~ *he's organized a surprise party for me.* ◇ *My worst* ~*s were realized when I was fired.* | **lingering** | **growing** | **mutual** ◇ *an atmosphere of mutual* ~ | **false, unfounded** (*esp. BrE*) ◇ *Our* ~*s turned out to be unfounded.* | **widespread** | **initial**
... OF SUSPICION **degree, level**
VERB + SUSPICION **entertain, harbour/harbor, have** ◇ *We had our* ~*s as to who did it.* | **express, report, voice** | **be under, come under, fall under** ◇ *He fell under* ~ *of tax evasion.* | **arouse, cast, cause, create, draw, fuel, give rise to** (*esp. BrE*), **invite, raise, sow** ◇ *Parked vehicles that arouse* ~ *should be reported to the police.* ◇ *information that casts* ~ *on one of the most powerful figures in the party* ◇ *The parked car outside only served to fuel his* ~*s.* | **avoid** | **share** ◇ *She shared her* ~*s with no one but her diary.* | **confirm, heighten, justify, reinforce** ◇ *A telephone call confirmed my worst* ~*s.* | **allay, dispel** ◇ *She was anxious to allay any* ~ *that she had married for money.*
SUSPICION + VERB **arise** | **exist** ◇ *The* ~ *exists that Harris is stealing money from the company safe.* | **linger, remain** | **grow** | **fall on sb** ◇ *Strong* ~ *fell on the victim's boyfriend.*
PREP. **above** ~, **beyond** ~ ◇ *They thought the teacher was beyond* ~. | **on** ~ **of** ◇ *arrested on* ~ *of bribery* ◇ *to be arrested/detained/held/questioned on* ~ *of sth* | **with** ~ ◇ *They viewed the new plan with great* ~. | ~ **about,** ~ **as to** ◇ *his* ~*s about the candidate's background* | ~ **against** ◇ *Suspicions against the former leader remain.*
PHRASES **the finger of** ~ (*esp. BrE*) ◇ *The finger of* ~ *pointed to a close friend of the victim.* | **grounds for** ~ (*BrE*) ◇ *The police must have reasonable grounds for* ~ *before they can get a search warrant.* | **an object of** ~ ◇ *Boys were an immediate object of* ~ *to her.* | **under a cloud of** ~ ◇ *He ended his athletics career under a cloud of* ~.

suspicious *adj.*

1 not trusting sb

VERBS **be, feel, look, seem, sound** | **become, get, grow** ◇ *I think they're starting to get* ~. | **remain** | **make sb** ◇ *Something about her smile made him* ~.
ADV. **extremely, fairly, very, etc.** | **deeply, highly, particularly** ◇ *She remained deeply* ~ *of computers.* | **increasingly** | **a little, slightly, etc.** ◇ *His voice grew slightly* ~. | **immediately, instantly** | **naturally** ◇ *I have a naturally* ~ *mind.* | **rightly** ◇ *Voters are rightly* ~ *of attempts to save money in the area of education.* | **overly**
PREP. **about** ◇ *They were somewhat* ~ *about her past.* | **of** ◇ *She was highly* ~ *of his motives.*
PHRASES **be right to be** ~ (**of sb/sth**), **have reason to be** ~ (**of sb/sth**) | **have a right to be** ~ (**of sb/sth**) ◇ *Parents have every right to be* ~ *of what the experts tell them.*

2 making you feel that sth is wrong

VERBS **be, look, seem, sound** ◇ *We have to carry on as usual or it would look* ~. | **consider sth, find sth, regard sth as, treat sth as** ◇ *I find it very* ~ *that he left halfway through the morning.* | *Police are treating both fires as* ~.
ADV. **extremely, fairly, very, etc.** | **highly** ◇ *He was seen acting in a highly* ~ *manner.* | **a little, slightly, etc.**
PHRASES **hear anything** ~, **see anything** ~ ◇ *Inform the police immediately if you see anything* ~.

sustain *verb*

ADV. **no longer** ◇ *The soil was so badly eroded it could no longer* ~ *crop production.* | **barely** | **indefinitely** | **still**
VERB + SUSTAIN **be able to, can** | **be unable to, cannot** | **help (to)** | **be difficult to, be hard to** ◇ *This relationship would be very difficult to* ~. | **be impossible to** | **be enough to, be sufficient to** | **be necessary to**

swallow *verb*

1 food, drink, etc.

ADV. **hastily, quickly** | **accidentally** ◇ *She accidentally* ~*ed a glass bead.* | **easily** ◇ *Liquid food may be more easily* ~*ed.* | **down** ◇ *She* ~*ed down her breakfast in a hurry.* | **hard**
PHRASES ~ **sth whole** ◇ *Most snakes* ~ *their prey whole.*

2 move your throat muscles

ADV. **deeply, hard** | **convulsively, nervously, painfully, with difficulty** ◇ *She* ~*ed convulsively, determined not to cry.* | **back** ◇ *He* ~*ed back the lump in his throat.*
PHRASES **have difficulty** ~**ing, have trouble** ~**ing**

swap *noun*

ADJ. **house, job** (*esp. BrE*), **land** | **straight** (*BrE*) ◇ *Let's do a straight swap—your guitar for my bike.*
VERB + SWAP **do, make**
SWAP + NOUN **deal** (*BrE*) ◇ *The football managers agreed on* ~ *deals involving their star players.*
PREP. ~ **between** ◇ *a spy* ~ *made between East and West Germany* | ~ **with** ◇ *I did a* ~ *with my brother.*

sway *verb*

1 from side to side/backwards and forwards

ADV. **gently, lightly, a little, slightly** | **alarmingly** (*esp. BrE*), **dangerously, precariously** ◇ *The stage* ~*ed alarmingly under their weight.* | **dizzily, drunkenly, unsteadily** | **back and forth, from side to side** ◇ *He* ~*ed back and forth like a drunken man.*
VERB + SWAY **begin to**
PREP. **in** ◇ *The curtains* ~*ed gently in the breeze.* | **to** ◇ *Couples were* ~*ing to the rhythm of the music.*

2 influence sb/sth

ADV. **easily** ◇ *He will not easily be* ~*ed by argument.*

swear *verb*

1 use bad language

ADV. **loudly** | **quietly, silently, softly, under your breath** | **viciously, violently**
VERB + SWEAR **hear sb** ◇ *He heard her* ~ *under her breath.*
PREP. **at** ◇ *He swore loudly at her and left.*

2 make a serious promise; promise to tell the truth

ADV. **solemnly** ◇ *He swore solemnly that he would never hit her again.* | **on oath, under oath** | **up and down** (*AmE*) ◇ *He* ~*s up and down that he trusts me.*
VERB + SWEAR **be prepared to** ◇ *I would be prepared to* ~ *on oath that they didn't see me.* | **make sb** ◇ *He made her* ~ *on the Bible that she wouldn't leave him.*
PREP. **by** ◇ *I* ~ *by Almighty God to tell the truth.* | **on** ◇ *Do you* ~ *on your mother's life?* | **to** ◇ *I* ~ *to you, I don't know.*
PHRASES **be sworn into office** ◇ *Lincoln was sworn into office on March 4, 1861.* | ~ **sb to secrecy,** ~ **sb to silence** ◇ *We were all sworn to secrecy about the plan.*

sweat *noun*

ADJ. **heavy** | **light** | **clammy** ◇ *My shirt stuck to the clammy* ~ *on my back.* | **cold** | **stale** ◇ *The room smelled of stale* ~. | **good** ◇ *We worked up a good* ~ *carrying the boxes outside.* | **night** ◇ *Exercise can help reduce night* ~*s.*
... OF SWEAT **bead, drop, trickle**
VERB + SWEAT **break into, break out in, break out into** ◇ *She broke out in a cold* ~ *when she saw the spider.* | **work up** | **bring sb out in** (*BrE*) | **be bathed in, be covered in, be**

drenched in, be soaked in ◇ *The workmen were bathed in ~.* | **be beaded with** | **be damp with, be wet with** | **be dripping, be dripping with** ◇ *His forehead was dripping ~.* ◇ *He was dripping with ~.* | **glisten with** | **mop, wipe** ◇ *He mopped the ~ from his brow.*
SWEAT + VERB **appear, break out** ◇ *His hands trembled and ~ broke out all over his body.* | **glisten, stand out** ◇ *Sweat glistened on her forehead.* ◇ *Sweat stood out on his shoulders.* | **drip from/off sth, pour from/off sth, run from/off sth** ◇ *Water was dripping from the branches.* | **pour down sth, run down sth, trickle down sth** ◇ *Sweat was running down his back.* | **soak sth**
SWEAT + NOUN **gland**
PREP. **in a ~** ◇ *She woke up in a cold ~.*
PHRASES **break ~** (*BrE*), **break a ~** (*AmE*) ◇ *She beat me without even breaking (a) ~.*

sweat *verb*
ADV. **freely, heavily, a lot, profusely** | **slightly** | **away, off, out** ◇ *He's trying to ~ off a few pounds in the gym.* ◇ *You can ~ out toxins in the sauna.*
VERB + SWEAT **begin to, start to** | **make sb** ◇ *The heat was making us ~.*
PREP. **from** ◇ *We were ~ing profusely from the exertion.* | **with** ◇ *He awoke with a pounding heart, ~ing with fear.*
PHRASES **~ buckets, ~ bullets** (*AmE*), **~ like a pig** (*all informal*) ◇ *After two hours of digging he was ~ing like a pig.*

sweater *noun*
ADJ. **bulky** (*AmE*), **chunky** (*esp. BrE*), **heavy, thick** | **light, thin** | **baggy, oversized** (*esp. AmE*) | **warm** | **crew-neck, high-necked, polo-neck** (*BrE*), **roll-neck, turtleneck** (*AmE*), **V-neck** | **hooded** (*esp. AmE*) | **hand-knit** (*AmE*), **hand-knitted** (*esp. BrE*), **knit** (*AmE*), **knitted** | **angora, cashmere, cotton, wool, woollen/woolen** | **argyle, cable-knit** (*AmE*) | **cardigan, pullover, zip-up** (*all AmE*)
VERB + SWEATER **pull on** | **knit**
SWEATER + NOUN **vest** (*AmE*)
→ Special page at CLOTHES

sweaty *adj.*
VERBS **be, feel, look, smell** | **become, get**
ADV. **extremely, fairly, very, etc.** | **all** ◇ *Ugh! You're all ~ and horrible!* | **a little, slightly, etc.**
PREP. **from** ◇ *Her forehead was ~ from the pain.* | **with** ◇ *He felt ~ with embarrassment.*

sweep *noun*
ADJ. **great, long, wide** ◇ *The house overlooks the great ~ of the St Lawrence River.* | **single** | **comprehensive** ◇ *Her eyes made a comprehensive ~ of the room.* | **elegant, graceful** | **broad, dramatic, epic, grand** ◇ *the broad cultural ~ of Flaubert's novel* ◇ *He dismissed his assistant with a grand ~ of his hand.*
VERB + SWEEP **make, take** ◇ *We made a wide ~ south to the River Dee.*
PREP. **in one ~** (*figurative*) ◇ *Thousands of jobs were lost in one broad ~.* | **with a ~** ◇ *with a ~ of his arm*

sweet (*BrE*) *noun* → See also CANDY
ADJ. **chewy, jelly, sugary** | **boiled** | **cough, throat**
... OF SWEETS **bag, box, packet**
VERB + SWEET **eat, suck** ◇ *I was sucking a boiled ~.*
SWEET + NOUN **shop**

sweet *adj.*
1 tasting like sugar/smelling pleasant
VERBS **be, smell, taste** ◇ *The air smelled ~ and clean.* | **make sth** | **find sth** ◇ *I found the dessert a little ~ for my taste.*
ADV. **extremely, fairly, very, etc.** | **a little, slightly, etc.** | **enough** ◇ *Is the tea ~ enough for you?* | **sickly** ◇ *an overpowering, sickly ~ smell*

2 nice
VERBS **be, look, seem, sound** | **keep sb** (*informal*) ◇ *He'd promised her a new car, just to keep her ~* (= keep her in a good mood).
ADV. **awfully, really, terribly, very** | **sickeningly, sugary** ◇ *a sickeningly ~ smile*
PREP. **to** ◇ *She was really ~ to me.*
PHRASES **dear sweet ...** ◇ *My dear ~ sister Jillie.* | **short and ~** ◇ *I'll keep it short and ~* (= speak briefly). | **~ and innocent** ◇ *She looked so ~ and innocent.* | **~ little** ◇ *a ~ little smile*

sweetness *noun*
1 sweet smell/taste
ADJ. **natural** | **cloying** (*esp. BrE*), **sickly** ◇ *the sickly ~ of incense*
... OF SWEETNESS **hint** ◇ *This is a full-bodied wine with just a hint of ~.*
VERB + SWEETNESS **taste** | **add** ◇ *Vanilla adds ~ and creaminess to ice cream.*

2 pleasantness
ADJ. **great** | **cloying** (*esp. BrE*), **saccharine** (*esp. BrE*), **sugary** (*esp. AmE*) ◇ *She smiled with saccharine ~.*
VERB + SWEETNESS **taste** ◇ *to taste the ~ of military success*
PHRASES **all ~ and light** ◇ *People think she's all ~ and light, but she actually has a temper.* | **dripping with ~** (*esp. AmE*) ◇ *Her voice was dripping with ~.*

swell *noun*
1 movement of the surface of the sea
ADJ. **heavy** | **gentle, slight** | **10-foot, 20-foot, etc.** | **Atlantic, ocean** ◇ *The ship was bobbing up and down like a small boat in a heavy ocean ~.*
SWELL + VERB **break, come in, roll in, surge up** ◇ *The Atlantic ~ surged up under them.*
PREP. **in a/the ~** ◇ *The trawler rolled wildly in the heavy ~.* | **on the ~** | **with the ~** ◇ *The boat rose and fell with the ~.*

2 curve in sth
ADJ. **gentle, soft**
PREP. **~ of** ◇ *the gentle ~ of her breasts*

swell *verb*
ADV. **badly** ◇ *His sprained ankle had swollen badly.* | **slightly** | **up** ◇ *Her feet ~ed up after the long walk to the top of the hill.*
PREP. **to** ◇ *My fingers and thumbs ~ed to grotesque proportions.* | **with** ◇ *Her legs had swollen with the heat.*
PHRASES **~ shut** ◇ *His right eye had almost swollen shut.*

swelling *noun*
ADJ. **painful, severe** ◇ *There is severe ~ of the glands.* | **slight**
VERB + SWELLING **cause** | **prevent** | **reduce**
SWELLING + VERB **occur** | **go down, subside**

swerve *noun*
ADJ. **sudden** ◇ *The car made a sudden ~ to the left.*
VERB + SWERVE **make**

swerve *verb*
ADV. **sharply, violently** | **dangerously, wildly** | **suddenly** | **away**
PREP. **across** ◇ *The car veered out of control and ~d across the road.* | **around, into** ◇ *A van suddenly ~d into her path.* | **off** ◇ *The vehicle ~d off the road.*
PHRASES **~ to avoid sb/sth** ◇ *The car ~d sharply to avoid the bus.*

swim *noun*
ADJ. **evening, morning, regular** | **long, quick** ◇ *How about a quick ~ before breakfast?* | **nice**
VERB + SWIM **go for, have, take** (*esp. AmE*) ◇ *She got up early and went for a ~.*
SWIM + NOUN **suit** (usually *swimsuit*), **trunks** (*AmE*) | **coach, team** (*both AmE*) | **meet, practice** (*both AmE*)
PREP. **for a ~** ◇ *Are you joining us for a ~?*

swim verb

ADV. **strongly, vigorously** ◇ *A beaver swam vigorously upstream.* | **well** ◇ *He can't ~ well.* | **quickly, rapidly** | **slowly** | **underwater** | **out** | **ashore, back** ◇ *Exhausted, they swam ashore.* | **away, off** | **downstream, upstream** | **around**
VERB + SWIM **can, know how to** | **learn (how) to** | **teach sb (how) to**
PREP. **across** ◇ *to ~ across the river* | **in** ◇ *to ~ in the sea* | **to** ◇ *We swam out to the boat.* | **towards/toward** ◇ *She swam back towards/toward the shore.*
PHRASES **go swimming**

swimmer noun

ADJ. **good, keen** (*BrE*), **strong** ◇ *She's a strong ~.* | **poor** | **champion, great, top** | **competitive, Olympic** | **rescue** (*AmE*)

swing noun

1 change in public opinion, sb's mood, etc.

ADJ. **big, dramatic, huge, sharp, violent, wide** (*esp. AmE*) ◇ *violent ~s in policy* | **small** | **10%, etc.** | **sudden, wild** ◇ *his sudden ~s of mood* | **electoral, national** (*esp. BrE*) | **mood** ◇ *She suffers from severe mood ~s.*
VERB + SWING **need** ◇ *The party needs a ~ of only 2.5% to win.* | **represent** ◇ *This represents a ~ of 14% against the party.* | **suffer, suffer from**
SWING + NOUN **state, vote, voter** (*all esp. AmE*) ◇ *Ohio is a ~ state in the presidential election.*
PREP. **~ in favour of** (*BrE*), **~ to, ~ towards/toward** ◇ *signs of a late ~ to the Democrats* | **~ against** ◇ *a dramatic ~ against the socialists* | **~ away from** ◇ *the ~ away from science in schools* | **~ from** | **~ in** ◇ *a sharp ~ in the attitudes of economists*

2 swinging movement

ADJ. **wild** | **mighty** (*esp. AmE*), **powerful** | **backward, forward** | **golf** | **practice**
VERB + SWING **do, make, take** ◇ *the technique for making the perfect golf ~* | **change** | **practise/practice** ◇ *The golfers were practising/practicing their ~s.*
SWING + NOUN **bridge, door** (*both BrE*)
PREP. **~ at** ◇ *He took a wild ~ at the ball.* | **~ of** ◇ *There was a political ~ of the pendulum back to the right.* (*figurative*)

3 swinging seat

ADJ. **porch, tyre/tire** (*both esp. AmE*)
VERB + SWING **go on, play on, sit on** ◇ *Some kids were playing on the ~s.*
PREP. **on a/the ~** ◇ *Her dad pushed her on the ~.*

swing verb

1 move backwards and forwards/from side to side

ADV. **gently, slowly** | **violently, wildly** ◇ *She lashed out, her arm ~ing wildly.* | **freely** ◇ *Let your arms ~ freely at your sides.* | **back and forth, from side to side, to and fro** ◇ *The pendulum swung slowly from side to side.*
PREP. **from** ◇ *I could see him ~ing from the branch of a large tree.*

2 move smoothly

ADV. **slowly** | **suddenly** | **sharply** ◇ *The road swung sharply around.* | **across, around, away, back, down, forward, off, round** (*esp. BrE*), **up** ◇ *Hearing a sarcastic note in his voice, she swung around to face him.*
VERB + SWING **let sth** ◇ *She let the door ~ shut behind her.*
PREP. **from** ◇ *She swung down from the tree in one easy movement.* | **into** ◇ *He swung up into the saddle and rode off.* | **towards/toward** ◇ *Nick swung towards/toward her.*
PHRASES **~ open, ~ shut**

3 change quickly

ADV. **rapidly** | **suddenly** | **wildly** ◇ *The balance of power swung wildly from one party to the other.* | **heavily** ◇ *Opinion swung heavily to the left.*
PREP. **from, to** ◇ *Her mood could ~ rapidly from gloom to exhilaration.*

swipe noun

ADJ. **playful, satirical** | **side, sideways**
VERB + SWIPE **take** ◇ *She took a playful ~ at her brother.*
SWIPE + NOUN **card** (*esp. BrE*) ◇ *Students use ~ cards rather than cash for meals.*
PREP. **~ at** ◇ *The article takes a side ~ at the teachers.*

switch noun

1 small button/lever

ADJ. **master, power** ◇ *The master ~ is under the stairs.* | **electric, electrical** | **off, on, on-off** ◇ *I couldn't find the off ~ on the remote control.* | **dimmer, timer** (*esp. BrE*), **toggle** (*esp. AmE*) ◇ *We fitted dimmer ~es in all the bedrooms.* | **ignition, light, wall** (*AmE*)
VERB + SWITCH **flick, flip, hit, press, pull, throw, turn off, turn on** ◇ *Someone threw a ~ and the electricity went off.*
SWITCH + VERB **activate sth, control sth, operate sth** ◇ *This ~ controls the heating system.*
PREP. **by a ~** ◇ *The light operates by a timer ~.* | **on a ~** ◇ *The heater is on a timer ~.* | **~ for** ◇ *the ~ for the air conditioning*
PHRASES **at the flick of a ~** ◇ *in the days before electricity was available at the flick of a ~*

2 change that sb makes

ADJ. **abrupt, sudden** | **big** | **complete** | **tactical** (*esp. BrE*) ◇ *The team's manager made a shrewd tactical ~.*
VERB + SWITCH **make**
PREP. **~ away from, ~ from** ◇ *There will be no overnight ~ away from old voting habits.* | **~ her ~ from full-time to part-time work** | **~ back to, ~ over to, ~ to** ◇ *He's a classical singer who has made the ~ over to pop.* | **~ between** ◇ *the recent ~es between direct and indirect taxation* | **~ in** ◇ *their abrupt ~ in allegiance*

switch verb

ADV. **easily, readily, simply** | **suddenly** ◇ *My mind suddenly ~ed back to my conversation with Jeremy.* | **quickly** | **automatically** | **around, back, back and forth** (*esp. AmE*), **over, round** (*esp. BrE*)
VERB + SWITCH **decide to** ◇ *He decided to ~ tactics.*
PREP. **between** ◇ *The remote control allows you to ~ easily between TV channels.* | **away from, from** ◇ *He ~ed his allegiance from the British to the French.* | **to** | **with** ◇ *We asked them if they would ~ places with us.*

switchboard noun

ADJ. **telephone**
VERB + SWITCHBOARD **call, ring** (*BrE*) | **flood, jam** ◇ *The ~ was jammed with furious calls.* | **be on, man, work on**
SWITCHBOARD + VERB **light up**
SWITCHBOARD + NOUN **operator**
PREP. **on a/the ~** ◇ *the man on the ~* | **through a/the ~** ◇ *All calls must pass through the ~.*

swollen adj.

VERBS **be, feel, look, seem** | **become, get** ◇ *Her legs got ~ from standing up all day.* | **remain**
ADV. **extremely, fairly, very, etc.** ◇ *Her face was still very ~.* | **badly** ◇ *His ankle is bruised and quite badly ~.* | **all** ◇ *Her eyes were all red and ~ from crying.* | **a little, slightly, etc.**
PREP. **from**
PHRASES **be red and ~** ◇ *Her eyes were all red and ~ from crying.* | **~ shut** ◇ *One of her eyes was ~ shut.*

swoop verb

ADV. **low** ◇ *An eagle ~ed low over the trees.* | **suddenly** | **down, in**
PREP. **into, on, over, through, towards/toward** ◇ *Customs officers ~ed on several houses last night looking for drugs.* (*figurative*)

sword noun

ADJ. **long, short** | **sharp** | **double-edged, two-edged** (*both*

figurative) ◊ *The potential financial boost is a double-edged* ~ (= *has advantages and disadvantages*). | **ceremonial, dress** | **Samurai**
VERB + SWORD **be armed with, carry, hold, wear** | **draw, unsheathe** | **brandish, wield** | **cross** (*usually figurative*) ◊ *The Governor crossed* ~s *with Democrats over US policy.* | **thrust** ◊ *I thrust my* ~ *into his chest.* | **sheathe**
SWORD + NOUN **arm** | **belt** | **blade** | **stroke** | **fight**
PREP. ~ **of** (*often figurative*) ◊ *the* ~ *of justice*
PHRASES **be put to the** ~ ◊ *All the men were put to the* ~ (= *killed*). | **the blade, edge, hilt, tip, etc. of a** ~

syllable noun

ADJ. **first, second, third, etc.** | **final, last** | **middle** | **accented, stressed, strong** | **unstressed, weak** | **long, short** | **single** | **nonsense** ◊ *nonsense* ~s *such as 'fa-la'.*
VERB + SYLLABLE **consist of, contain, have** ◊ *words that have three or more* ~s | **pronounce** | **utter** ◊ *Before I could utter a single* ~, *she held up one warning finger.* | **accent, draw out, stress** ◊ *We stress the second* ~ *of the word.*
PHRASES ~ **in,** ~ **of** ◊ *the final* ~ *of 'Oregon'*
PHRASES **stress falls on a** ~, **stress is on a** ~ ◊ *Normally the stress falls on the first* ~ *of a word.* | **a word of one, two, etc.** ~s ◊ *You'll have to spell it out to him, using words of one* ~ (= *explain it in simple language*).

syllabus noun

ADJ. **class** (*esp. AmE*), **course** ◊ *Professors will want to develop their own course* ~es. | **exam, examination** (*both esp. BrE*) | **A level, FCE, GCSE, etc.** | **college, school** (*esp. BrE*), **university** (*esp. BrE*) | **geography, history, mathematics, etc.** | **online, sample** ◊ *sample* ~es *for undergraduate courses*
VERB + SYLLABUS **design, develop, write** | **follow, offer, teach, use** ◊ *The courses do not follow the* ~ *of any particular examination board.* | **follow, study** ◊ *Students follow different* ~es *according to their ability.* | **change, revise** (*esp. BrE*) ◊ *the need to revise the history* ~ | **cover, get through** ◊ *It was impossible to cover the* ~ *in a year.*
SYLLABUS + VERB **contain sth, cover sth, include sth** ◊ *Does the* ~ *cover modern literature?*
SYLLABUS + NOUN **design** | **content** (*BrE*)
PREP. **from** ~ ◊ *questions from last year's* ~ | **in a/the** ~ ◊ *Let's include that in this year's* ~. | **on a/the** ~ ◊ *Is calculus on the* ~? | ~ **for** ◊ *some* ~es *for basic courses in geography* | ~ **in** ◊ *the course* ~es *in arts subjects*

symbol noun

1 image/object/event that is a sign of sth

ADJ. **dramatic, important, perfect, potent, powerful, ultimate** ◊ *The Berlin wall was the ultimate* ~ *of the Cold War.* | **universal** ◊ *The dove is a universal* ~ *of peace.* | **outward, physical, visual** ◊ *The company car is an outward* ~ *of the employee's status.* | **ancient, traditional** | **national** | **cultural, political** | **religious, sacred** | **Christian, Hindu, etc.** | **fertility, phallic, sexual** ◊ *The people use fertility* ~s *to ensure a good harvest.* | **sex** (= *a person famous for being attractive*) ◊ *He is not most people's idea of a sex* ~. | **status** ◊ *A stressful job can actually be a status* ~.
VERB + SYMBOL **become** | **create** | **represent** ◊ *Guevara has come to represent a powerful* ~ *of defiance.* | **adopt sth as, consider sth, interpret sth as, regard sth as, see sth as, use sth as** ◊ *Eggs are seen as the* ~ *of new life.*
PREP. ~ **of** ◊ *a* ~ *of royal power*

2 letter/sign that has a particular meaning

ADJ. **abstract, geometric** | **graphic, written** | **chemical, Chinese, linguistic, mathematical, musical, phonetic** ◊ *A list of phonetic* ~s *is given in the front of the dictionary.*
VERB + SYMBOL **bear, be marked with, have** ◊ *The coin bears a Jewish* ~. ◊ *The bottle had a skull and crossbones* ~ *on it.* | **display, show, use** ◊ *Hotels that show this* ~ *offer activities for children.* | **decipher, interpret, understand**

SYMBOL + VERB **denote sth, indicate sth, mean sth, represent sth** ◊ *What does this little* ~ *mean?*
PREP. **in** ~s ◊ *a message written in* ~s | ~ **for** ◊ *O is the chemical* ~ *for oxygen.*

symbolic adj.

VERBS **be, seem** | **become** ◊ *The case became* ~ *of racial tension in society.* | **regard sth as, see sth as** ◊ *His refusal to accept the honour was seen as highly* ~.
ADV. **deeply, heavily, highly, very** ◊ *This is a gruesome and heavily* ~ *tale.* | **merely, purely** ◊ *The role of monarch is a purely* ~ *one.* | **largely, mainly** | **somehow**
PREP. **of** ◊ *These two objects are* ~ *of life and death.*

symbolism noun

ADJ. **Christian, pagan, religious** | **political** | **phallic, sexual**
VERB + SYMBOLISM **be full of, be rich in** ◊ *Her paintings are full of* ~. | **use** | **understand**

symmetrical (*also* symmetric) adj.

VERBS **appear, be, look** | **become**
ADV. **highly** ◊ *highly* ~ *crystals* | **perfectly** | **almost, nearly, roughly**

symmetry noun

ADJ. **perfect, pleasing** (*esp. BrE*) | **bilateral, rotational**
VERB + SYMMETRY **have, possess** | **lack** | **break, destroy** ◊ *The trees break the* ~ *of the painting.*
PREP. ~ **between** ◊ *the* ~ *between different forces*
PHRASES **an axis of** ~, **a line of** ~

sympathetic adj.

VERBS **appear, be, feel, look, seem, sound** | **become** | **find sb** ◊ *I found the doctors very* ~. | **make sb** ◊ *Her aggressive attitude makes me less* ~ *to her plight.* ◊ *The character's faults actually make him more* ~.
ADV. **extremely, fairly, very, etc.** | **deeply, genuinely, truly** ◊ *a patient and deeply* ~ *man* ◊ *He sounded genuinely* ~. | **entirely, highly** ◊ *He was speaking to a highly* ~ *audience.* | **not entirely** ◊ *He'd written a not entirely* ~ *article in the 'Globe'.* | **less than** ◊ *Her attitude to my situation was less than* ~. | **broadly, largely**
PREP. **about** ◊ *My boss is being very* ~ *about my problems.* | **to** ◊ *They were extremely* ~ *to my plight.* ◊ *The government is broadly* ~ *to our ideas.* | **towards/toward** ◊ *I did not feel* ~ *towards/toward them.*

sympathize (*BrE also* -ise) verb

ADV. **completely, deeply, fully** (*esp. BrE*), **really** ◊ *I completely* ~ *with the workers' situation.* ◊ *I* ~ *deeply with his family.*
VERB + SYMPATHIZE **can** ◊ *I can really* ~ *with John.* | **be easy to, be hard to** | **be hard not to** ◊ *It is hard not to* ~ *with her dilemma.*
PREP. **with** ◊ *We* ~d *with the bereaved family.* ◊ *I entirely* ~ *with this view.*

sympathy noun

ADJ. **considerable, deep, genuine, great, heartfelt, real, strong** | **little, scant** (*esp. BrE*) | **general, popular** (*esp. BrE*), **public, widespread** | **human** ◊ *a total lack of human* ~
VERB + SYMPATHY **feel, find, have** ◊ *She seemed to feel some* ~ *for the patients.* | **It's hard to find any** ~ *for such an evil man.* | **express, extend, give sb, offer (sb), show (sb)** ◊ *She expressed her deepest* ~ *for him.* ◊ *We extend our* ~ *to the families of the victims.* ◊ *She says I haven't given her enough* ~. | **waste** | **demand, want** ◊ *I don't want your* ~! | **look for** ◊ *I'm not looking for* ~. | **deserve, need** | **arouse, attract, create, earn, elicit, engage, evoke, gain, generate, get, win** ◊ *Their plight aroused considerable public* ~. ◊ *He didn't get much* ~ *from anyone.* | **lose**
SYMPATHY + VERB **go out to sb, lie with sb** ◊ *Our deepest* ~ *goes out to his wife and family.* ◊ *My* ~ *lies with his wife.*
PREP. **in** ~ **with** ◊ *Nurses came out on strike in* ~ *with the doctors.* | **out of** ~ ◊ *She married him more out of* ~ *than love.* | **with** ~ ◊ *Desmond eyed her anguished face with* ~. | ~ **for** ◊ *He has a total lack of* ~ *for young people.* | ~ **to** ◊

The government showed ~ to their cause. | **~ towards/ toward** ◊ He acted with some ~ towards/toward his victim. | **~ with** ◊ She had every ~ with him.

PHRASES **a feeling of ~, a pang of ~** ◊ I felt a pang of ~ for her. | **full of ~** | **a lack of ~** | **have every ~ for sb** (esp. BrE) | **you, they, etc. have my ~**

symphony noun

ADJ. **first, second, etc.** | **C major, D minor, etc.**
VERB + SYMPHONY **compose, write** | **conduct, perform, play** ◊ Bruckner's fourth ~, conducted by Hugh Wolff
SYMPHONY + NOUN **orchestra** ◊ the Chicago Symphony Orchestra | **concert** | **hall** (esp. AmE)

symptom noun (usually symptoms)

ADJ. **characteristic, classic, common, typical** | **clinical** | **minor, secondary** | **acute, chronic** | **intermittent, recurrent** | **distressing, negative, serious, severe, unpleasant** | **mild** | **visible, visual** ◊ These virus infections display obvious visual ~s. | **physical, physiological** ◊ the physical ~s that are the result of stress | **withdrawal** | **abdominal, respiratory, urinary** | **allergic, allergy, asthma, asthmatic, flu, flu-like, menopausal** | **behavioural/behavioral, mental, psychiatric, psychological, psychosomatic** | **depressive, neurotic, schizophrenic, stress**
VERB + SYMPTOM **display, exhibit, experience, have, present with** (medical), **show, suffer, suffer from** ◊ She had all the classic ~s of the disorder. ◊ The patient was admitted presenting with flu-like ~s. | **describe, report** ◊ Can you describe your ~s? | **develop, get** ◊ Not all carriers of the disease develop ~s. | **bring about, bring on, cause, produce** | **aggravate, exacerbate** ◊ Cigarettes can aggravate the ~s of a cold. | **ignore** ◊ He had been ignoring the ~s for years. | **detect, diagnose, identify, interpret, recognize** ◊ Nurses are taught how to identify and treat the ~s of poisoning. | **alleviate, control, ease, improve, reduce, relieve, suppress, treat** | **be free from**
SYMPTOM + VERB **appear, arise, develop, occur** | **persist, recur** ◊ If ~s persist, consult your doctor. | **worsen** | **improve** ◊ If ~s do not improve after a week, see your doctor. | **disappear**
PHRASES **the onset of ~s** ◊ 40% of patients were treated within three hours of the onset of ~s.

synchronize (BrE also -ise) verb

ADV. **perfectly** | **carefully** | **automatically**
PREP. **with** ◊ The timing of the attack was ~d with the ambassador's arrival.

syndicate noun

ADJ. **crime, criminal, drug** | **lottery** (BrE) | **organized** ◊ an organized crime ~
VERB + SYNDICATE **form** | **run** | **join** | **lead**
PREP. **in a/the ~** ◊ I'm in a lottery ~ at work.
PHRASES **a member of a ~**

syndrome noun

ADJ. **acute** | **clinical** | **Asperger's, chronic fatigue, etc.**
VERB + SYNDROME **have, suffer from** | **develop** | **cause, produce** | **diagnose, recognize** | **treat** | **be known as** ◊ This phenomenon has become known as the 'Californian syndrome'.
SYNDROME + VERB **affect sb, be present in sb, occur** ◊ This ~ mostly affects women in their forties. | **be characterized by**

synonymous adj.

VERBS **be, seem** | **become** | **remain** | **make sth** ◊ His deeds had made his name ~ with victory. | **consider sth, regard sth as, see sth as, treat sth as**
ADV. **exactly** | **almost, largely, more or less, roughly, virtually**
PREP. **with** ◊ The Delson name is ~ with excellence in audio.

syringe noun

ADJ. **clean, sterile** | **contaminated, dirty, used** ◊ a beach

scattered with used ~s | **disposable** | **hypodermic** | **glass, plastic**
VERB + SYRINGE **fill, prepare** | **draw sth into** ◊ The doctor drew a dose of morphia into the ~. | **share** | **use**
SYRINGE + NOUN **exchange** (AmE) ◊ a syringe-exchange program

system noun

1 set of ideas/rules for organizing sth

ADJ. **current, existing** ◊ We're looking to replace the existing ~. | **modern, new** | **old-fashioned, outdated** | **traditional** | **standard** | **complex, complicated, elaborate, intricate, sophisticated** ◊ The new ~ is overly complex. | **simple** | **comprehensive** | **coherent** | **integrated** ◊ an integrated transport ~ (BrE) ◊ an integrated transportation ~ (AmE) | **effective, efficient** | **viable, workable** | **inefficient, wasteful** | **flexible** | **rigid** | **stable** | **foolproof** | **imperfect, perfect** | **unique** | **centralized, decentralized** | **closed, open** ◊ a closed ~ with a rigidly defined set of choices | **bureaucratic** | **hierarchical** | **authoritarian, oppressive, repressive** | **equitable, fair** | **corrupt, unjust** | **bankrupt** ◊ The governor referred to a prison ~ that was bankrupt of compassion. | **public, state** ◊ schools within the state ~ (BrE) ◊ schools within the public ~ (AmE) | **local-government** (esp. BrE), **parliamentary, political** | **electoral, voting** | **banking, economic, financial, monetary** | **tax, taxation** | **educational, examination, school, university** | **court, criminal justice, judicial, justice, legal, penal, prison** | **benefit, benefits, health-insurance, pension, social-insurance, social-security, welfare** | **care, health, healthcare** | **rail, railway** (BrE), **subway, transport** (esp. BrE), **transportation** (esp. AmE) | **communication** | **cable** | **detection, monitoring, warning** | **security, surveillance** | **backup, support** | **accounting, administrative** | **delivery** | **control** | **disciplinary** | **agricultural** | **commercial, market** | **cultural, social** | **scoring** ◊ The game has a complex scoring ~. | **grammatical, language** | **classification, filing** | **storage** | **belief, value** | **capitalist, caste, communist** | **multiparty, two-party** | **two-tier**
VERB + SYSTEM **build, create, design, develop, devise, establish, set up** | **have** | **adopt, apply, deploy, implement, introduce** ◊ We are implementing a new ~ of stock control. | **advocate** | **join** | **be part of** ◊ They are all part of the corrupt ~ we need to change. | **manage, operate, run** | **maintain** | **manipulate, play, use** ◊ He played the legal ~ to his own advantage. | **organize** ◊ How is the ~ organized? | **adapt, change, transform** | **tinker with** | **test** | **improve, modernize, overhaul, refine, reform, reorganize, simplify, streamline, strengthen** ◊ the need to modernize the judicial ~ | **perfect** | **perpetuate** ◊ The so-called reforms merely perpetuate an unjust ~. | **clog, clog up** ◊ a backlog of cases clogging up the ~ | **destabilize, disrupt, undermine, weaken** ◊ attempts to disrupt the rail ~ | **dismantle, abandon, do away with, scrap** | **destroy, overthrow** | **replace** | **restore** | **criticize, fight, rebel against** ◊ She spent her years at school fighting the ~. | **defend, support** | **understand** | **beat, buck** ◊ You can never beat the ~! | **bypass** ◊ an attempt to bypass the bureaucratic ~ | **blame** ◊ It's not your fault—blame the ~.
SYSTEM + VERB **exist** | **be based on sth, rest on sth** ◊ Every political ~ rests on certain fundamentals. | **be aimed at sth, be geared to sth** | **allow sth, enable sth** ◊ This ~ allows you to study at your own speed. | **offer sth, provide sth** | **be in operation, be operational, function, operate, work** ◊ This case proves that the ~ works effectively. | **break down, collapse, fail**
PREP. **in a/the ~** ◊ at another point in the education ~ | **under a/the ~** ◊ Under the new ~, all children will be monitored by a social worker. | **~ for** ◊ They devised an appropriate ~ for presenting the required information.

2 group of things/parts that work together

ADJ. **sophisticated** | **automated, automatic, computer, computer-based, computerized, electronic, manual, mechanical** | **audio, sound, stereo** | **air-conditioning,**

table

842

alarm, electrical, exhaust, heating, life-support, plumbing, public address (abbreviated to *PA*), sprinkler, ventilation | electronic mail, email, mail, phone, telephone, voicemail | satellite | global positioning, guidance, navigation | propulsion | missile, weapons | drainage, irrigation | river, road

VERB + SYSTEM **build, create, develop** | **improve, streamline** | **install** ◇ *For this month only, installing the ~ is free.*

SYSTEM + VERB **function, operate, work** | **break down, fail** ◇ *The air-conditioning ~ failed.*

PREP. **in a/the ~, with a/the ~** ◇ *a fault in the sound ~*

3 the body, or parts of it that work together

ADJ. **auditory, biological, cardiovascular, circulatory, digestive, immune, nervous, reproductive, respiratory, sensory, visual** ◇ *the central nervous ~*

PREP. **in a/the ~** ◇ *a valve in the circulatory ~*

PHRASES **a shock to the ~** ◇ *Returning to work after a long break can be a terrible shock to the ~.*

4 workings of a computer

ADJ. **advanced, powerful** | **interactive** | **online** | **digital, optical, wireless** | **compatible, incompatible** | **computer, PC** | **operating, operational** | **database, file, information, management** | **processing, recognition, retrieval, storage** ◇ *an information retrieval ~* | **server, software** | **parallel**

VERB + SYSTEM **install** | **boot, boot up, reboot** ◇ *Just reboot the ~ and try again.* | **build, design, develop** ◇ *We're designing a voice-recognition ~.* | **launch** | **upgrade**

SYSTEM + VERB **run** ◇ *The ~ runs on this workstation.* | **crash, fail, go down** ◇ *The entire computer ~ went down.*

SYSTEM + NOUN **software** | **design** | **performance** | **administrator** | **failure** | **backup** | **reboot**

PREP. **in a/the ~** ◇ *faults in the data-processing ~*

T t

table noun

1 piece of furniture

ADJ. **big, high, huge, large, long** | **little, low, small** | **circular, oval, rectangular, round, square** | **coffee, folding, side, trestle** (*esp. BrE*) ◇ *We arranged the party food on a trestle ~ on the patio.* | **candlelit, glass-topped, whiteclothed** | **glass, mahogany, marble, metal, oak, oaken, plastic, steel, wooden** | **polished, scrubbed** | **rickety, rough** | **empty** ◇ *We found an empty ~ at the back of the restaurant.* | **bare** | **dining, dining-room, kitchen** ◇ *She often does her homework at the kitchen ~.* | **breakfast, dinner, lunch** ◇ *We never discuss politics at the breakfast ~.* | **banquet, buffet, picnic, refreshment** | **cafe, cafeteria, restaurant** | **corner, end, window** ◇ *We'll take the corner ~ near the bar, please.* | **bedside** (*esp. BrE*), **dressing, night** (*AmE*) | **writing** | **bargaining** (*esp. AmE*), **conference, drafting** (*AmE*), **negotiating** ◇ *They spent hours around the negotiating ~.* | **examination** (*BrE, AmE*), **examining** (*AmE*) | **massage, operating** | **air-hockey, billiard, foosball**™ (*AmE*), **ping-pong/Ping-Pong**™ (*esp. AmE*), **pool, snooker, table-tennis** (*BrE*) | **blackjack, card, gaming, roulette** | **makeshift** ◇ *We turned the box upside down and used it as a makeshift ~.*

VERB + TABLE **be seated around, be seated at, be seated round** (*esp. BrE*), **occupy, sit around, sit (down) at, sit round** (*esp. BrE*) ◇ *They were all five of them sitting around the kitchen ~.* | **lean across, lean over, reach across** | **get up from, leave** ◇ *He left the ~ in a hurry.* | **lay** (*BrE*), **set** ◇ *Please set the ~ for six.* | **clear, wipe** ◇ *You clear the ~ and I'll wash the dishes.* | **book, reserve** ◇ *We booked a ~ at the restaurant for 8 p.m.* | **overturn** | **wait ~s** (*AmE*)

TABLE + VERB **be piled with sth, be strewn with sth**

TABLE + NOUN **decorations** | **edge, leg** | **mat** (*BrE*) | **cloth** (usually *tablecloth*), **linen, napkin** | **lamp** | **manners**

PREP. **across the ~** ◇ *She leaned across the ~ and kissed him.* | **around the ~, round the ~** (*esp. BrE*) ◇ *We gathered around the ~ to hear his news.* | **at the ~** ◇ *to sit down at the ~* | **on the ~** ◇ *She put the vase on the ~.* | **out from under the ~** ◇ *James crawled out from under the ~.* | **over the ~** ◇ *They flirted over the dinner ~.* | **under the ~** ◇ *The potato rolled under the ~.*

PHRASES **the centre/center of the ~, the middle of the ~** ◇ *My father always sits at the head of the ~.* | **the edge of the ~, the end of the ~, the head of the ~**

2 list of facts/figures

ADJ. **statistical** | **league** (*BrE*) ◇ *The league ~ shows the Danish team in first place with eight points.* ◇ *school league ~s* (*BrE*) | **multiplication, periodic**

VERB + TABLE **compile** | **consult, see** ◇ *See Table XII for population figures.*

TABLE + VERB **show sth**

PREP. **in a/the ~** ◇ *He showed the price fluctuations in a statistical ~.*

PHRASES **the bottom of the ~, the top of the ~**

tablet noun

1 (*esp. BrE*) pill → See also PILL

ADJ. **Ecstasy, paracetamol, sleeping, vitamin, etc.** ◇ *Take two paracetamol ~s with water.*

VERB + TABLET **swallow, take**

PHRASES **in ~ form** (*BrE, AmE*) ◇ *The drug is now available in ~ and capsule form.*

2 slab

ADJ. **clay, stone, wax, etc.** | **ancient** | **memorial** ◇ *We had a memorial ~ put up on the church wall.*

tabloid noun

ADJ. **daily, weekly** (*esp. AmE*) | **local** (*esp. AmE*), **national** (*esp. BrE*) | **popular** | **supermarket** (*AmE*)

VERB + TABLOID **read**

TABLOID + NOUN **format** | **journalism, magazine** (*AmE*), **newspaper, press** ◇ *He believes that the ~ press has behaved disgracefully.* | **headlines, report, story** | **editor, journalist, reporter** | **television, TV** (*esp. AmE*)

PREP. **in a/the ~** ◇ *You shouldn't believe everything you read in the ~s.*

taboo noun

ADJ. **powerful** | **cultural, religious, sexual, social** | **incest**

VERB + TABOO **break, shatter, violate**

TABOO + NOUN **subject**

PREP. **~ about** ◇ *~s about divorce in society* | **~ against** ◇ *the ~ against marrying a foreigner* | **~ on** ◇ *The play violates several ~s on sexuality.* | **~ surrounding** ◇ *~s surrounding menstruation*

taboo adj.

VERBS **be** | **become** | **remain** | **consider sth** ◇ *Sex is considered ~ as a topic for discussion.*

ADV. **strictly, virtually** ◇ *The subject of death was strictly ~ in their society.*

PREP. **to** ◇ *Such work was ~ to women.*

tack noun way of achieving sth

ADJ. **right, wrong** | **different, opposite** | **same** | **new**

VERB + TACK **adopt, go off on, take, try** ◇ *New research is taking a different ~.* ◇ *The interviewer decided to try another ~.* | **change, switch** ◇ *She suddenly changed ~, taking him by surprise.*

PREP. **on a/the ~** ◇ *I think you're on the wrong ~ with that approach.*

PHRASES **a change of ~**

tackle noun

1 movement in sports

ADJ. **hard, strong** | **high** ◇ *Their captain was sent off for a*

high ~ on Cooper. | **bad, crunching, late** (all BrE) | **cover, scything, sliding** (all BrE) | **brave, skilful** (both BrE) | **flying** ◊ A security guard brought him down with a flying ~. | **football** (AmE), **rugby**
VERB + TACKLE **execute** (BrE), **make** | **break** (AmE) | **miss**
PREP. **~ from** ◊ a crunching ~ from her opponent | **~ against, ~ on** (BrE) ◊ He bruised his arm making a ~ against the Browns. ◊ He was booked for a ~ from behind on Morris. | **in a/the ~** ◊ She lost the ball in a ~.

2 position in American football
ADJ. **defensive, offensive** | **left, right** | **nose**
VERB + TACKLE **play** | **draft**

tackle verb
1 deal with sth difficult
ADV. **properly** (BrE), **seriously** | **directly** (esp. BrE), **head-on** ◊ The drugs problem has to be ~d head-on. | **effectively, successfully**
VERB + TACKLE **attempt to, try to** | **help (to)** | **fail to** ◊ We are failing to ~ the key issues.
PREP. **with** ◊ The problem is being ~d with a range of measures.
PHRASES **~ sb to the floor, ~ sb to the ground** (both AmE)

2 in sports
ADV. **hard** ◊ He can run fast and ~ hard.

tact noun
ADJ. **great**
VERB + TACT **have** | **call for, need, require** ◊ The situation called for considerable ~. | **display, exercise, show, use** ◊ Employees are trained to show ~ and patience with difficult customers. | **lack**
PREP. **with ~** ◊ The incident should have been handled with more ~ by the police.
PHRASES **a lack of ~, ~ and diplomacy**

tactic noun
ADJ. **subtle** | **legitimate** ◊ Some players see injuring their opponent as a legitimate ~. | **devious, dubious, stealth, underhand** | **extreme, scare, shock, terror** | **guerrilla, militant, revolutionary, violent** | **aggressive, bully-boy** (BrE), **bullying, hardball** (AmE), **heavy-handed, strong-arm** | **non-violent, softly-softly** | **intimidation, psychological** | **interrogation** | **smear** | **avoidance, delaying, diversionary, spoiling, stalling** ◊ Children are adept at delaying ~s. | **negative, time-wasting** ◊ The coach was criticized for his negative ~s. | **short-term** | **campaigning, marketing, negotiating, promotional, sales** | **military, naval, parliamentary, police, political**
VERB + TACTIC **decide on, discuss, plan, talk (about), work out** ◊ She decided on a stalling ~. | **adopt, apply, deploy, employ, try, use** ◊ the temptation to use underhand ~s ◊ They were desperate enough to try shock ~s. | **resort to, stoop to** ◊ I refuse to stoop to such bullying ~s. | **change, rethink, shift, switch** ◊ They would do well to switch ~s. | **demand, require** ◊ Longer races demand different ~s.
TACTIC + VERB **pay off, succeed, work** ◊ His strong-arm ~s paid off. | **backfire, fail**
PREP. **~ for** ◊ Teachers learn ~s for dealing with aggressive children.
PHRASES **a variety of ~s** ◊ We use a variety of ~s to make learning fun.

tag noun label
ADJ. **identification, identity, name, price** ◊ The baby had a plastic name ~ on its ankle. ◊ Despite a price ~ of £100 000, the car was sold in two days. | **metal, plastic** | **security** | **baggage** (esp. AmE), **luggage** (esp. BrE) | **gift** | **electronic** | **dog** (= metal name tag worn by soldiers) (AmE, slang) | **ear**
VERB + TAG **attach, put** ◊ I still have to put gift ~s on all the presents. | **remove**
PHRASES **sth carries a price ~ of …, sth has a price ~ of …** ◊ This suit carries a price ~ of £2 000.

tail noun
1 of an animal, a bird, etc.
ADJ. **long, short** | **bushy, curly, forked, pointed** | **muscular, prehensile**
VERB + TAIL **flick, swish, thrash, wag** ◊ The dog wagged its ~ furiously. | **chase** ◊ My dog loves to chase his ~. | **dock**
TAIL + VERB **swish, twitch, wag, wave** ◊ The dog ran out with its ~ wagging madly.
TAIL + NOUN **bone** (usually **tailbone**) | **feathers, fin**
PHRASES **the tip of its/his/her ~** ◊ It was black from its nose to the tip of its ~.

2 of a thing
TAIL + NOUN **section** ◊ The plane's ~ section had broken off. | **fin, light**
PREP. **at the ~** ◊ the truck at the ~ of our convoy
PHRASES **nose to ~** ◊ Traffic which used to be nose to ~ now flows freely.

tailor verb
ADV. **carefully** | **exactly** | **individually, narrowly** (AmE), **specially, specifically** ◊ We identify your needs, and ~ your training accordingly.
PREP. **for** ◊ a system that is specially ~ed for small companies | **to** ◊ The account offered by the bank will be ~ed exactly to your needs.

takeover noun
ADJ. **attempted, proposed** | **hostile** | **company, corporate** | **communist, military**
VERB + TAKEOVER **attempt, engineer, launch** | **plot** | **prevent**
TAKEOVER + NOUN **attempt, bid** ◊ a hostile ~ bid | **offer** | **battle** ◊ The consortium won a fierce ~ battle for the engineering group. | **bait** (AmE), **target**
PREP. **~ of** ◊ the attempted ~ of an oil company

takings noun (esp. BrE)
ADJ. **the day's, the week's** | **weekly** | **gross, net** | **cash** | **record** ◊ Store managers are predicting record ~ this Christmas. | **bar, box-office**
VERB + TAKINGS **add up, check, count, count up** | **boost** ◊ The shop's new look has boosted its ~ considerably. | **cut**
TAKINGS + VERB **be up, rise** ◊ Box-office ~ are up by 40% on last year. | **be down, drop** ◊ Takings dropped a little this week.
PREP. **in ~** ◊ She was losing about £100 a week in ~. | **~ from** ◊ the ~ from wines and beers
→ Special page at BUSINESS

tale noun
ADJ. **long, rambling** | **familiar** | **amazing, bizarre, curious** (esp. BrE), **extraordinary, fantastic, magical, marvellous/ marvelous, strange** | **awful** (esp. BrE), **sad, sorry, terrible, tragic** ◊ the sorry ~ of his marriage breakdown | **chilling, gruesome, hair-raising, harrowing, horror, macabre** | **lurid, sordid, tawdry** | **dark** ◊ a dark ~ of sexual obsession | **mysterious, spooky** | **funny, humorous, witty** (esp. BrE) | **fascinating, interesting** | **heart-warming** | **simple** | **fanciful, incredible, tall, unlikely** (esp. BrE) ◊ a tall ~ that would fool no one | **true** | **old wives'** | **coming-of-age, rags-to-riches** ◊ the rags-to-riches ~ of an orphan who becomes a star | **epic, heroic** ◊ an epic ~ of courage and heroism | **cautionary, moral, morality** | **classic, folk, old, traditional** | **childhood** | **fairy** (often figurative) ◊ Winning the French Open was a fairy-tale end to her career. | **gothic, romantic** | **original**
VERB + TALE **narrate, recount, regale sb with, relate, tell (sb)** ◊ She regaled us with ~s of her wild youth. | **hear** | **make up, spin, weave** | **read, write** | **begin**
TALE + VERB **begin** | **unfold** | **concern sb/sth, involve sb/sth** | **be set in …** ◊ a ~ set in 19th-century Moscow | **be based on sth**

PREP. **~ about** ◇ *a ~ about a hungry snake* | **~ of** ◇ *~s of adventure* ◇ *the strange ~ of the man who sold his hair*
PHRASES **a ~ of woe** (= about failure, bad luck, etc.) | **(have) a ~ to tell** ◇ *Each of the survivors had a terrible ~ to tell.* | **tell ~s** (= to say things about sb that are untrue or that they would prefer to be secret) *(BrE)*

talent *noun*

ADJ. **amazing, considerable, enormous, extraordinary, formidable, genuine, great, immense, incredible, major, obvious, outstanding, prodigious, real, remarkable, tremendous, true, undoubted** (*esp. BrE*) | **exceptional, rare, special, unique** | **God-given, inborn, innate, natural, raw** ◇ *Hard work is important, but it is no substitute for raw ~.* | **individual** | **hidden, undiscovered** | **mediocre** | **fresh, new** ◇ *The company is always looking out for new ~.* | **young** | **precocious** | **home-grown, local** ◇ *one of the few teams that relies on home-grown ~* | **best, top** ◇ *We are losing our top ~ to other countries who pay more.* | **acting, artistic, athletic** (*esp. AmE*), **creative, literary, managerial, musical, scientific, sporting** (*BrE*), **vocal, writing**
VERB + TALENT **have, possess** ◇ *The boy has undoubted ~.* | **lack** | **demonstrate, display, reveal, show, showcase** | **put to use** ◇ *He has been putting his artistic ~s to good use.* | **show off** ◇ *The banquet gave the chef a chance to show off his ~s.* | **direct, turn** ◇ *After making her name as a singer, she turned her ~s to acting.* | **discover, find, recognize, see, spot, unearth** (*esp. BrE*) ◇ *She has a keen eye for spotting ~.* | **attract, bring in** ◇ *The festival attracts ~ from all over the world.* | **build on, cultivate, develop, harness, make the most of, nurture, realize, tap, use, utilize** ◇ *an effort to develop his creative ~s to the full* | **squander, waste** ◇ *His parents accused him of wasting his ~s and abilities.* | **take** ◇ *It takes real ~ to write a great pop song.*
TALENT + VERB **lie** ◇ *Her ~s lay in organization.* | **come from** ◇ *Where does her musical ~ come from?* | **come through** ◇ *There is a shortage of new comedy ~ coming through.*
TALENT + NOUN **agent, scout, spotter** | **agency** | **competition, contest, show** | **pool** | **level** (*esp. AmE*)
PREP. **of** ◇ *He is a violinist of exceptional ~.* | **with ~, without ~** ◇ *kids with musical ~* | **~ for** ◇ *You have a natural ~ for storytelling.*
PHRASES **a man, woman, etc. of many ~s, a pool of ~** ◇ *Hollywood directors have an amazing pool of acting ~ to draw from.* | **a wealth of ~** ◇ *There is a wealth of ~ out there in our schools.*

talented *adj.*

VERBS **be, seem**
ADV. **extremely, fairly, very, etc.** | **amazingly, enormously, exceptionally, extraordinarily, highly, hugely, immensely, incredibly, prodigiously, supremely, truly, wonderfully** ◇ *an extraordinarily ~ designer* ◇ *Some of these young musicians are hugely ~.* | **not particularly** | **precociously** (*esp. BrE*) ◇ *a precociously ~ youngster* | **artistically, musically**

talk *noun*

1 a conversation

ADJ. **brief, little** (*often ironic*), **short** ◇ *I will have to have a little ~ with that young lady* (= tell her that I disapprove of sth). | **good, long, serious** | **heart-to-heart**
VERB + TALK **have**
TALK + NOUN **show** (*esp. AmE*) | **radio** (*esp. AmE*)
PREP. **~ about** ◇ *I enjoyed our ~ about the old days.* | **~ with** ◇ *I need to have a heart-to-heart ~ with her.*

2 talking

ADJ. **excited** ◇ *There was excited ~ of emigrating to America.* | **crazy** (*esp. AmE*), **wild** ◇ *There is wild ~ of her breaking the world record soon.* | **careless** (*esp. BrE*), **idle, loose** | **fighting** (*BrE*), **tough** | **war** ◇ *The US authorities have increased the war ~.* | **straight** ◇ *She likes straight ~ and hates hypocrites.* | **double** ◇ *The president's true agenda was hidden in*

political double ~. | **open** ◇ *There is open ~ of a leadership challenge.* | **public** ◇ *There has been much public ~ about bilingual education.* | **dirty** ◇ *the crusade against dirty ~ on TV* | **trash** (= a way of talking intended to insult sb and make them feel less confident) (*AmE, informal*) | **sweet** (= trying to persuade sb to do sth by praising them and telling them things they like to hear) | **cheap, empty, mere** ◇ *The chairman's boasts about future profits were just cheap ~.* | **big, fancy** (*esp. AmE*), **fine** (*ironic*) ◇ *What all the fine ~ came down to was hard cash.* | **baby** ◇ *I never used baby ~ to my little girl.* | **girl** ◇ *We can have some girl ~ until Joe gets here.* | **pillow** ◇ *the pillow ~ of lovers* | **shop** ◇ *Don't you get enough shop ~ at work?*
VERB + TALK **hear** ◇ *You often hear ~ of the north-south divide.*
TALK + VERB **turn to sth** ◇ *Talk turned to money and tempers began to fray.*
PREP. **~ about/of** ◇ *All this ~ of the boss resigning is nonsense!*
PHRASES **be all ~** ◇ *He's all ~. He's too scared to do anything.* | **be just ~** ◇ *'You think it's just ~?' 'No, I think it's true.'* | **for all the ~ of sth** ◇ *For all their ~ of equality, the boys ended up not doing any cooking.* | **(to exchange/make) small ~** (= to talk politely about unimportant things) ◇ *He was never very good at making small ~ with her parents.*

3 (*also* talks) discussions between official groups

ADJ. **lengthy** (*esp. BrE*) | **high-level, top-level** | **informal** | **formal, official** | **private, secret** | **direct, face-to-face** | **wide-ranging** | **all-party** (*BrE*), **etc.** | **bilateral, multilateral, round-table** (*esp. BrE*) | **global** (*esp. AmE*) | **fresh** (*esp. BrE*), **further** | **crisis, emergency, urgent** (*all esp. BrE*) | **exploratory** (*esp. BrE*), **preliminary** | **political** | **arms** (*esp. BrE*), **peace** | **merger, pay** (*BrE*), **trade**
... OF TALKS **round** ◇ *A further round of ~s is expected in March.*
VERB + TALK **conduct, have, hold** ◇ *The two governments held secret ~s on the nuclear threat.* | **broker, host** | **attend, enter** | **begin, initiate, open, start** | **continue** | **break off, pull out of, walk out of** ◇ *The union has broken off ~s with the management.* | **cancel, end, suspend** | **reopen, restart, resume**
TALK + VERB **be scheduled** ◇ *Talks were scheduled for Rome the following month.* | **take place** ◇ *The peace ~s will take place in Cairo.* | **begin, open** (*esp. BrE*), **start** | **end** | **continue, go on** | **resume** | **be aimed at sth, be designed to** (*esp. BrE*) ◇ *the latest round of ~s aimed at ending the civil war* | **centre/center on sth, concentrate on sth, cover sth, deal with sth, focus on sth** ◇ *The ~s centred on bilateral trade.* | **produce sth** ◇ *Talks produced agreement on an end to the occupation.* | **be deadlocked** (*esp. BrE*), **break down, collapse, fail, founder** (*esp. BrE*), **stall** (*esp. BrE*) ◇ *The ~s remain deadlocked over spending plans.* ◇ *The ~s foundered on the issue of compensation.*
PREP. **during ~** ◇ *The agreement was concluded during ~s in Beijing.* | **in ~** ◇ *He is currently in ~s with two football clubs.* | **~ about, ~ on, ~ over** ◇ *Talks are being held over the political future of the province.* | **~ between** ◇ *the failure of ~s between the two communities* | **~ with** ◇ *The delegation arrived for ~s with their government.*

4 lecture

ADJ. **entertaining** (*esp. BrE*), **informative** (*esp. BrE*), **interesting** | **introductory** (*esp. BrE*) | **brief, short** | **chalk** (*AmE*), **motivational, pep, team** (*esp. BrE*) | **radio, television, TV** | **illustrated** (*BrE*) ◇ *She gave an illustrated ~ on Roman architecture.*
VERB + TALK **deliver, give, present** | **begin** | **end** ◇ *Let me end my ~ with a prediction.* | **attend, go to**
TALK + VERB **be entitled sth, be titled sth** (*esp. AmE*) ◇ *She gave a very entertaining ~ entitled 'My life and hard times'.*
PREP. **~ about, ~ on** ◇ *Did you go to the ~ on Peru?*

talk *verb*

ADV. **loudly** | **quietly, softly** | **at length** | **constantly, continuously, endlessly, incessantly, non-stop** | **briefly** | **candidly, freely, openly** ◇ *She ~ed quite freely about her work.* | **privately, publicly** | **exclusively** ◇ *Bruce Springsteen has agreed to ~ exclusively to our reporter about his life.* | **directly** ◇ *I think you'd better ~ directly to my manager.* | **animatedly, enthusiastically, excitedly** | **specifically** |

vaguely ◇ *He had ~ed vaguely of going to work in Japan.* | **casually** | **politely** | **earnestly, seriously** ◇ *a group of students ~ing earnestly* | **sensibly** ◇ *Let's ~ sensibly about this.* | **wildly**
VERB + TALK **be able to, can** ◇ *I can't ~ about it just now.* | **need to, want to** ◇ *I need to ~ to you.* | **begin to** | **be easy to** ◇ *He was so easy to ~ to.* | **be difficult to, be hard to** | **hear sb, listen to sb, overhear sb** ◇ *I loved to hear him ~ about the old days.* | **make sb** ◇ *The police questioned him for four hours, trying to make him ~.* | **let sb** ◇ *Just shut up and let me ~ for a minute.*
PREP. **about** ◇ *All they ~ about is clothes.* | **of** (*formal*) ◇ *We often ~ed of the war.* ◇ *Talking of Joe, I met his new boyfriend last week.* (*BrE*) | **to** ◇ *I'll ~ to Mario this afternoon.* | **with** ◇ *I've ~ed with him on the telephone.*
PHRASES **start ~ing, stop ~ing** | **~ a good game** (*AmE*) ◇ *The senior managers ~ a good game about customer relations (= they say the right things), but really they don't care about the customer.* | **~ the ~** (*esp. AmE*) ◇ *You can ~ the talk, but can you walk the walk (= can you do what you say)?*

tall *adj.*
VERBS **be, look, seem** | **become, get, grow** | **stand** ◇ *Suddenly he seemed to stand taller.*
ADV. **extremely, fairly, very, etc.** ◇ *She is quite ~ for her age.* | **exceptionally, freakishly, unusually**

tame *adj.*
1 not afraid of people
VERBS **be, look, seem** | **become**
ADV. **extremely, fairly, very, etc.** | **almost**
2 boring
VERBS **appear, be, look, seem, sound** ◇ *The recent violence makes previous uprisings look ~ by comparison.* | **become** | **find sth** ◇ *I found office work very ~ after army life.*
ADV. **extremely, fairly, very, etc.** ◇ *To us it was all pretty ~ stuff.* | **relatively** ◇ *Most of the jokes are relatively ~.* | **surprisingly** ◇ *I found the violence in the film surprisingly ~.* | **a little, slightly, etc.**

tan *noun* → See also SUNTAN
ADJ. **dark, deep, golden** | **light** | **healthy** | **all-over** (*esp. BrE*), **perfect** (*esp. AmE*) | **fake, spray-on** | **natural**
VERB + TAN **have** | **show off, sport** ◇ *Show off your ~ in this little white top.* | **get, top up** (*BrE*), **work on** ◇ *I want to top up my ~ on the sunbed.*
PREP. **against your ~** ◇ *His teeth were a gleaming flash of white against his ~.*

tangle *noun*
ADJ. **confused** | **dense, thick** ◇ *a dense ~ of undergrowth* | **complex, vast** ◇ *a complex ~ of loyalties* | **legal**
... OF TANGLES **mass** (*esp. AmE*) ◇ *her hair was a mass of ~s*
VERB + TANGLE **get in/into** ◇ *He got into a ~ with his budget figures.* | **sort out** (*esp. BrE*), **unravel** ◇ *The legal ~ was never really unravelled/unraveled.* | **brush out, remove** ◇ *She brushed the ~s out of her hair.* | **run your fingers through** ◇ *She ran her fingers through the ~s in her hair.* | **fight (your way) through, pick (your way) through, work (your way) through** ◇ *I had to pick my way through the ~ of bodies.*
PREP. **in a ~** ◇ *This string's in a ~.* | **~ of** ◇ *a ~ of wires*

tank *noun*
1 container
ADJ. **empty, full** | **glass, steel** | **4-foot, 50-gallon, 80-litre/ 80-liter, etc.** | **fuel, oil, oxygen, water** ◇ *the hot and cold water ~s* | **gas, gasoline** (*AmE*), **petrol** (*BrE*), **propane** (*esp. AmE*) (In the US, *gas tank* usually refers to the part of a car or motorbike that contains petrol/gasoline. In the UK, it refers to a container for a gas.) | **holding, storage** ◇ *a water storage ~* | **main** | **septic** | **fish**
VERB + TANK **fill, refill** | **drain, empty** | **puncture, rupture** ◇ *The truck crashed into a wall and ruptured a fuel ~.* | **clean, clean out** ◇ *I cleaned out the fish ~ today.*
TANK + VERB **contain sth**

PREP. **in a/the ~, into a/the ~** ◇ *Put a little fish food into the ~.* | **~ of** ◇ *a full ~ of petrol* (*BrE*) ◇ *a full ~ of gasoline/gas* (*AmE*)
2 military vehicle
ADJ. **armoured/armored, army, battle**
VERB + TANK **climb into, get into** | **drive** | **employ, use** | **destroy**
TANK + VERB **roll** ◇ *Tanks rolled in to end the siege.* | **advance, attack** | **fire**
TANK + NOUN **battalion, company** (*esp. AmE*), **corps, platoon** (*AmE*), **regiment** (*esp. BrE*) | **commander, crew**

tanker *noun*
1 ship carrying oil or petrol/gasoline
ADJ. **giant, huge, large** | **gas, oil**
TANKER + VERB **carry sth, transport sth** ◇ *a ~ carrying thousands of tons of crude oil* | **run aground** ◇ *The ~ ran aground in heavy seas.* | **spill sth** ◇ *A damaged ~ has spilled millions of gallons of oil into the sea.*
TANKER + NOUN **disaster, spill** ◇ *the worst year for ~ spills for ten years* | **fleet**
2 heavy vehicle for carrying liquids
ADJ. **fuel, gasoline** (*AmE*), **milk, petrol** (*BrE*), **water** | **road** (*BrE*)
VERB + TANKER **drive**
TANKER + VERB **carry sth**
TANKER + NOUN **driver** (*BrE*) | **aircraft, truck** (*esp. AmE*)

tanned (*also* **suntanned**) *adj.*
VERBS **be, look** | **become, get**
ADV. **deeply, very, well** ◇ *His blue eyes glittered in his deeply ~ face.* | **lightly, slightly** | **evenly, perfectly** ◇ *her perfectly ~ skin* | **nicely** | **naturally** ◇ *She was naturally ~ with black hair.*

tantrum *noun*
ADJ. **temper** | **major** (*esp. AmE*) | **little** ◇ *He had a little temper ~ yesterday.* | **occasional** ◇ *All kids have the occasional ~.*
VERB + TANTRUM **have, throw** ◇ *He threw a ~ on the school bus.* | **deal with** | **ignore**

tap *noun*
1 (*esp. BrE*) **for water, etc.** → See also FAUCET
ADJ. **hot, hot-water** | **cold, cold-water** | **mixer** (*BrE*) | **dripping, running** ◇ *the sound of a dripping ~* | **leaky** | **bath, bathroom, kitchen**
VERB + TAP **turn** ◇ *Turn the ~ clockwise.* | **turn off, turn on** | **run** ◇ *You have to run the ~ a long time before the hot water comes.*
TAP + VERB **drip, run** ◇ *Someone has left the ~ running.* | **leak**
TAP + NOUN **water** (*BrE, AmE*) | **washer**
2 quick gentle blow; the sound it makes
ADJ. **gentle, light, little, slight, soft** | **sharp** | **quick**
VERB + TAP **give sb/sth** | **feel** | **hear** ◇ *She heard a ~ at the door.*
PREP. **~ at** ◇ *There was a little ~ at the door.* | **~ on** ◇ *He gave her a ~ on the shoulder.*

tap *verb*
ADV. **gently, lightly** ◇ *She tapped her fingers gently on the table.* | **impatiently** | **away** ◇ *She tapped away at her keyboard.* | **home** (*BrE*) (in football/soccer) ◇ *He tapped home his second goal from close range.*
PREP. **against, at, on** ◇ *He was tapped on the shoulder by a soldier.* | **with** ◇ *She tapped the ice with a stick.*

tape *noun*
1 magnetic material used for recording
ADJ. **magnetic** ◇ *The data is stored on the magnetic ~.* |

audio, computer, video (usually *videotape*) | **recording** | **backup** ◇ *Email messages are stored on backup ~s for years.*
VERB + TAPE **store sth on** | **capture sth on, get sth on, record sth on** ◇ *Police are examining the incident, which was captured on ~.* | **splice**
TAPE + NOUN **recording** | **loop** ◇ *~ loops of the same spoken phrase* | **machine, player** ◇ *a reel-to-reel ~ player* | **backup** ◇ *Most companies already create ~ backups and archives.*
PREP. **on ~** ◇ *I got the whole concert on ~.*

2 cassette with magnetic tape on it

ADJ. **cassette** | **audio, music, sound** | **VHS™** (*esp. AmE*), **video** (usually *videotape*) | **demo, master, original** | **compilation, mix** ◇ *a compilation ~ featuring new bands* | **blank** | **pre-recorded** | **bootleg, pirate** (*esp. BrE*), **pirated** (*esp. BrE*) ◇ *bootleg ~s of Hollywood blockbusters* | **surveillance**
VERB + TAPE **make** ◇ *I made another ~ to play in the car.* | **play, play back, put on** ◇ *The police will be able to play back the videotape for clues.* | **listen to, review, see, watch** | **release** ◇ *The panel released audio ~s of the attack.* | **fast-forward, pause, replay, rewind, start, stop, wind back** | **erase, wipe** ◇ *Someone had deliberately erased the ~s.*
TAPE + VERB **contain sth, have sth, show sth** ◇ *The ~ contained damning evidence.* ◇ *What does this ~ have on it?*
TAPE + NOUN **deck, player, recorder** | **cassette** | **recording**

3 long narrow strip of fabric/paper

ADJ. **adhesive, Scotch™** (*AmE*), **sticky** (*esp. BrE*) | **duct** (*AmE*), **gaffer** (*BrE*), **masking, packing** | **electrical** (*esp. AmE*), **insulating** (*esp. BrE*) | **measuring** | **paper, plastic** | **ticker** (*esp. AmE*) | **double-sided**
... OF TAPE **piece, strip** | **roll**
VERB + TAPE **seal sth (up) with** ◇ *I sealed up the package with strong adhesive ~.* | **use** | **apply, put on** | **remove**
TAPE + NOUN **measure** ◇ *Use a steel ~ measure to measure the dimensions of the room.* | **dispenser** (*AmE*) ◇ *an adhesive ~ dispenser*

tape *verb*

ADV. **firmly** ◇ *The wires are ~d firmly together.* | **down, together, up** ◇ *The lid was ~d down to hold it in place.* ◇ *The box was all ~d up.* | **off** ◇ *The area had been ~d off by police.*
PREP. **onto, to** ◇ *Someone had ~d a note onto my door.*

target *noun*

1 sb/sth that you try to destroy, hurt, steal, etc.

ADJ. **favourite/favorite, frequent, important, likely, natural, obvious, perfect, possible, potential, prime, suitable** ◇ *The President is a favourite/favorite ~ of comedians.* | **attractive, tempting** ◇ *Trains are attractive ~s for terrorists.* | **specific** | **real** ◇ *The real ~ of his satire is religion.* | **easy, sitting, soft, tempting, vulnerable** ◇ *The stationary trucks were sitting ~s for the enemy planes.* | **legitimate** | **intended** | **fixed, stationary** | **moving** | **ground** | **enemy, military, strategic** | **civilian, non-military** | **high-value** | **terrorist** | **takeover** ◇ *The company could become a takeover ~.*
VERB + TARGET **choose, identify, pick** | **aim at, attack, engage, go for, shoot at** | **find, locate** | **hit, reach, strike** ◇ *The bomb reached its intended ~ ten seconds later.* | **miss, overshoot** ◇ *The flare overshot its ~ and set fire to a hotel.* | **destroy** ◇ *The missile is intended to destroy military ~s.* | **track** ◇ *The radar beam can track a number of ~s simultaneously.* | **present** ◇ *The damaged ship presented a tempting ~.* | **make** ◇ *The casino made an easy ~ for thieves.*
TARGET + NOUN **site** ◇ *It should be possible to deliver the drug direct to the ~ site.*
PREP. **off ~** ◇ *The missile veered way off ~ and landed in the sea.* | **on ~** ◇ *Politically speaking, his jibes were right on ~.* | **~ for** ◇ *an easy ~ for thieves*

2 object that you shoot at

VERB + TARGET **put up, set up** ◇ *The archers were setting up their ~s.* | **aim at, shoot at** | **hit** | **miss** | **use sth as** ◇ *The boys used an old tree stump as a ~.*

TARGET + NOUN **area, range** | **practice**
PREP. **off ~** ◇ *Patton was just off ~ with his shot.* | **on ~** ◇ *His first shot was bang on ~.* | **wide of the ~** ◇ *The shot went wide of the ~.*

3 result, person, etc. that you aim to reach

ADJ. **achievable, attainable** (*esp. BrE*), **low, modest, realistic** | **ambitious, challenging** (*esp. BrE*), **demanding** (*esp. BrE*), **difficult, high, tough, unrealistic** ◇ *She has always set herself very high ~s.* | **impossible** | **new** | **clear, specific** | **chief, key, main, major, primary, prime, principal** | **annual** | **immediate, initial** | **future, long-term, ultimate** | **economic, financial, growth, inflation, performance, price, production, profit, recruitment, sales, spending** ◇ *Hospital performance ~s will not be met.*
VERB + TARGET **set** ◇ *Managers must set ~s that are realistic.* | **aim for** ◇ *Students should be given a ~ to aim for.* | **achieve, meet, reach** | **stay on/within** ◇ *in a desperate attempt to stay within budget ~s* | **exceed** ◇ *The company pays bonuses to workers who exceed production ~s.* | **fall short of**
TARGET + NOUN **audience, demographic** (*esp. AmE*), **group, market, population** ◇ *The film's ~ demographic is women aged 18–49 years.* | **date** ◇ *to meet a ~ date of May 2002* | **figure** (*esp. BrE*), **level, price, range, weight**
PREP. **above (a/the) ~** ◇ *Sales so far this year are 20% above ~.* | **off ~** ◇ *These figures are way off ~.* | **on ~** ◇ *We are still right on ~.* | **within ~** ◇ *We are well within our ~ for trains arriving on time.* | **over (a/the) ~** ◇ *Many pay agreements reached were over the original ~ of 4%.* | **towards/toward (a/the) ~** ◇ *We are working towards/toward a ~ of twenty cars a week.* | **~ for** ◇ *The CEO has set new ~s for growth.*

target *verb*

ADV. **deliberately, intentionally, particularly, specifically** ◇ *Children are deliberately ~ed.* | **actively** (*esp. BrE*), **directly** ◇ *Police are actively ~ing known offenders.* ◇ *an exercise that directly ~s the back muscles* | **carefully, precisely** ◇ *a carefully ~ed marketing campaign* | **unfairly** ◇ *The authority was accused of unfairly ~ing minority groups.* | **primarily**
PREP. **at** ◇ *The products are ~ed at young people.* | **for** ◇ *This hospital is ~ed for additional funding.* | **on** ◇ *Tax cuts should be ~ed on the poor.* | **towards/toward** ◇ *We ~ our services towards/toward specific groups of people.*

tariff *noun*

ADJ. **high, low** | **preferential, protectionist, protective** ◇ *British industry was sheltered from foreign competition by protective ~s.* | **punitive, retaliatory** ◇ *The European Union has threatened retaliatory ~s.* | **external** | **internal** | **import** | **agricultural, industrial** | **steel, textile, etc.** | **across-the-board** ◇ *a 27% across-the-board ~ on all goods from China*
... OF TARIFFS **level** ◇ *a 40% level of ~s on imports*
VERB + TARIFF **fix, set** (*both esp. BrE*) ◇ *The agreement fixed ~s for foreign goods coming into Japan at 5%.* | **impose, introduce, levy** (*esp. AmE*), **slap** (*informal*) ◇ *The US could impose punitive ~s of up to 100% on some countries' exports.* | **pay** | **increase, raise** | **cut, lower, reduce** | **abolish, eliminate, lift, remove**
TARIFF + NOUN **reduction, reform** | **structure, system** | **policy** | **level, rate** | **barrier, protection** ◇ *the aim of removing all ~ barriers by next year*
PREP. **~ on** ◇ *They set a ~ of 36% on British wool cloth.*
PHRASES **a reduction in ~/~s**

tarnish *verb*

1 become/make sth less bright

ADV. **badly** ◇ *The mirror had ~ed quite badly.* | **slightly**

2 spoil sth

ADV. **severely** ◇ *their severely ~ed reputation* | **slightly, somewhat** | **unfairly** | **forever**

tart *noun* open pie

ADJ. **chocolate, fruit, jam** (*BrE*), **treacle** (*BrE*) | **almond, apple, lemon, etc.**
VERB + TART **make**

task noun

ADJ. **awesome, challenging, daunting, enormous, formidable, great, Herculean, huge, mammoth** (*esp. BrE*), **massive, monumental** | **arduous, demanding, difficult, hard, laborious, onerous, stiff** (*BrE*), **time-consuming, tough, uphill** (*esp. BrE*) | **dangerous, hazardous** (*esp. BrE*) | **basic, easy, simple, small, trivial** ◇ *the simple ~ of making a sandwich* | **menial, mundane, repetitive, routine, tedious** | **complex, complicated** | **delicate, tricky** | **hopeless, impossible** | **daily, day-to-day, everyday, routine** | **central, fundamental, important, main, major, primary, principal** ◇ *The primary ~ of the chair is to ensure the meeting runs smoothly.* | **critical, crucial, essential, key, vital** | **immediate, urgent** | **pleasant** | **thankless, unenviable, unpleasant** | **grim** ◇ *the grim ~ of identifying the dead* | **administrative, domestic, household, manual** | **self-appointed**

VERB + TASK **handle, take on, take upon yourself** (*esp. BrE*), **undertake** ◇ *Nobody was willing to take on such a thankless ~.* | **approach, face, get to grips with** (*esp. BrE*), **tackle** ◇ *How do you tackle a ~ like that?* | **begin, start** | **carry out, do, fulfil/fulfill, get on with, perform** ◇ *I left her to get on with the ~ of correcting the errors.* | **accomplish, complete, finish, succeed in** | **cope with** | **fail, fail at, fail in** | **allocate, assign (sb), delegate, entrust sb with, give sb, set sb** ◇ *She failed to complete the ~ that she had been set.* | **be charged with, be faced with, have** ◇ *She was charged with the important ~ of telling the children.* | **be engaged in** ◇ *I was engaged in the delicate ~ of clipping the dog's claws.* | **help in, help sb with** | **be suited to** ◇ *His thick fingers were not well suited to the ~.*

TASK + VERB **involve sth, require sth** ◇ *The ~ requires a variety of skills and experience.* | **fall to sb** ◇ *The unenviable ~ of telling my parents fell to my teacher.* | **confront sb, face sb** ◇ *The team have no illusions about the size of the ~ confronting them.*

PREP. **~ for** ◇ *a hard ~ for the committee* | **~ in** ◇ *one of the first ~s in language learning*

PHRASES **be no easy ~** ◇ *Translating the letter was no easy ~.* | **the ~ ahead, the ~ at hand** (*esp. AmE*), **the ~ before us, the ~ in hand** (*BrE*) ◇ *We need to think realistically about the ~ ahead.* ◇ *We should stop chatting and get back to the ~ in/at hand.*

task force noun

ADJ. **special** | **government** (*esp. BrE*), **presidential** (*esp. AmE*), **etc.** | **naval, police, etc.** | **joint** ◇ *a joint ~ of local, state, and FBI officers* | **energy, health, etc.** | **drug, terrorism, etc.** | **anti-drug, anti-terrorism, etc.**

VERB + TASK FORCE **appoint** (*esp. AmE*), **create, establish, form, set up** | **head, lead**

TASK-FORCE + NOUN **member** (*esp. AmE*), **team**

PREP. **~ on** ◇ *The government has set up a special ~ on health-care reform.*

PHRASES **the head of a/the ~**

taste noun

1 flavour/flavor

ADJ. **delicious, fresh, nice, pleasant, refreshing** | **distinctive** | **pungent, rich, strong** | **bland, mild** | **foul, nasty, unpleasant** | **bitter, creamy, metallic, salty, sharp, smooth, sour, spicy, sweet** | **authentic** ◇ *You need to use fresh herbs to get the authentic Italian ~.*

VERB + TASTE **have** ◇ *The soup had a very salty ~.* | **leave** ◇ *The drink left a bitter ~ in his mouth.* ◇ *The whole business left a bad ~ in my mouth.* (*figurative*) | **affect** | **spoil** ◇ *Don't have a cigarette now—you'll spoil the ~ of your food!* | **enhance, improve** | **enjoy, savour/savor** ◇ *She was enjoying the ~ of the champagne.* | **disguise, take away** ◇ *I had a strong coffee to take away the nasty ~ of the food.* | **feel** ◇ *He could feel the ~ of blood in his mouth.*

TASTE + NOUN **buds**

2 a taste small amount

ADJ. **brief, little, small** | **real** ◇ *That job gave me my first real ~ of teaching.* | **first**

VERB + TASTE **get, have, taste** (*esp. AmE*) ◇ *Have a ~ of this cake.* | **give sb, offer (sb), provide (sb with)**

PREP. **~ of** ◇ *This was her first ~ of success.*

PHRASES **a ~ of things to come** ◇ *The new appraisal plan is only a ~ of things to come.*

3 liking

ADJ. **catholic** (*esp. BrE*), **eclectic, varied** | **simple** | **refined, sophisticated** | **expensive, extravagant** | **eccentric, esoteric** (*esp. BrE*), **strange** | **acquired** ◇ *Modern art is an acquired ~.* | **changing** ◇ *the changing ~s of consumers* | **natural** | **local, national** | **modern** | **individual, personal** | **aesthetic, artistic, cultural, literary, musical, reading, sexual** | **audience, consumer, contemporary, popular, public, Western** ◇ *Her music appeals to popular ~.*

VERB + TASTE **have** ◇ *They have a ~ for adventure.* | **like, share** ◇ *You obviously share her ~ in reading.* | **acquire, cultivate, develop, get** | **lose** ◇ *I've lost my ~ for exotic trips.* | **indulge** ◇ *Now he is retired he has time to indulge his ~s for writing and politics.* | **demonstrate, display** ◇ *Her choice of outfit demonstrated her ~ for the outrageous.* | **appeal to, cater for** (*esp. BrE*), **cater to** (*esp. AmE*), **match, meet, satisfy, suit** ◇ *a range of hotels to suit all ~s and budgets*

TASTE + VERB **lie** ◇ *It all depends on where your ~s lie.* | **run** ◇ *His ~s run to the exotic.* | **change, differ, vary** ◇ *Lifestyles differ and ~s vary.*

PREP. **for sb's ~** ◇ *The music was too modern for my ~.* | **to ~** (= according to how much of sth as you want) ◇ *Add salt and pepper to ~.* | **to your ~** ◇ *If fishing is not to your ~, there are many other leisure activities on offer.* | **~ for** ◇ *People with a ~ for complex plots will enjoy this book.* | **~ in** ◇ *young people's ~s in music*

PHRASES **a man/woman of ... tastes** ◇ *a man of advanced ~s* | **a matter of (personal) ~** ◇ *What type of bicycle you should buy is very much a matter of personal ~.* | **a wide range/variety of ~s**

4 ability to make good choices

ADJ. **excellent, exquisite, fine, good, great, impeccable** ◇ *Her work is executed with impeccable ~.* | **appalling** (*esp. BrE*), **bad, dubious, poor, questionable, terrible**

VERB + TASTE **reflect, show** ◇ *The house reflected his ~.* | **exercise** ◇ *The designer has exercised good ~ in her choice of fabrics.*

PREP. **in ... ~** ◇ *That joke was in very poor ~.* | **with ~** ◇ *The room had been decorated with great ~.* | **~ in** ◇ *She has terrible ~ in clothing.*

PHRASES **an arbiter of ~** (*esp. BrE*) ◇ *Contemporary arbiters of ~ dismissed his paintings as rubbish.* | **in the best possible ~, in the worst possible ~** ◇ *The love scenes are all done in the best possible ~.* | **a lack of ~** ◇ *The remark showed a real lack of ~.* | **a man/woman of ~** | **~ and decency** (*BrE*) ◇ *The play was judged to offend against standards of public ~ and decency.*

taste verb

ADV. **strongly** ◇ *The water ~d strongly of chemicals.* | **faintly, slightly** ◇ *The fish ~d faintly of garlic.*

PREP. **like** ◇ *The fruit ~d rather like mango.* | **of** ◇ *a cake which ~d of almonds*

PHRASES **~ awful, ~ bad, ~ bitter, ~ disgusting, ~ foul, ~ horrible, ~ terrible, ~ vile** | **~ delicious, ~ fine, ~ good, ~ great, ~ sweet, ~ wonderful** | **~ funny**

tatters noun

VERB + TATTERS **lie in** (*figurative*) ◇ *Her marriage now lay in ~.* | **hang in** ◇ *Everywhere wallpaper hung in ~.* | **leave sth in** (*figurative*) ◇ *an injury that left his dreams in ~*

PREP. **in ~** ◇ *Her clothes were in ~.* ◇ *With their plans now in ~, they gave up.* (*figurative*)

PHRASES **rags and ~**

tattoo noun

ADJ. **distinctive** (*esp. BrE*) ◇ *He had a distinctive snake ~ on his*

neck. | **temporary** ◊ *I took to wearing a temporary ~ on my ankle.* | **henna** | **dragon, heart,** etc.
VERB + TATTOO **do** ◊ *She's having a ~ done on her leg.* | **get** | **have** | **sport** ◊ *He sported a barbed-wire ~ on his left arm.* | **be covered in** ◊ *His arms were covered in ~s.* | **remove** ◊ *I've decided to get my ~ removed.*
TATTOO + NOUN **parlour/parlor** | **artist**
PREP. **~ of** ◊ *She had a ~ of a swallow on her shoulder.*

taunt noun

ADJ. **racist** | **playground** (*esp. BrE*), **schoolyard** (*AmE*) | **cruel**
VERB + TAUNT **shout** | **be subjected to, endure, suffer** ◊ *He had to endure the racist ~s of the crowd.* | **hear** | **ignore**

taut adj.

VERBS **be, feel** | **become, go, grow** ◊ *Her body went as ~ as a bowstring.* | **remain, stay** ◊ *Exercise helps your muscles to stay ~.* | **make sth** | **draw sth, pull sth, stretch sth** ◊ *His skin was stretched ~ over his cheekbones.* | **hold sth, keep sth** ◊ *Try to keep the leash ~, as it will help your puppy to learn.*
PREP. **with** (*figurative*) ◊ *a voice ~ with anger*

tax noun

ADJ. **high, low** | **direct, indirect** | **flat** | **basic-rate, higher-rate** (*both BrE*) | **progressive, redistributive, regressive** | **stealth** (*BrE*) | **windfall** ◊ *a windfall ~ on the profits of the last few years* | **back** (*informal*) ◊ *The ~ office demanded £80 000 in back ~es.* | **council** (*BrE*), **poll** (*esp. BrE*) | **federal, local, national, state** | **capital, capital gains, death** (*AmE*), **dividend** (*AmE*), **estate** (*AmE*), **income, inheritance, land, payroll, profits, property, social-security, wealth** | **consumption, luxury, purchase** (*BrE*), **sales, value added** (= VAT) (*BrE*) | **personal** | **company** (*BrE*), **corporate, corporation** | **car, road** (*BrE*), **vehicle** ◊ *It's time to renew your car ~.* | **carbon, energy, fuel, gas** (*AmE*), **gasoline** (*AmE*), **petrol** (*BrE*) | **excise, import** | **environmental, green**
VERB + TAX **pay** | **owe** | **charge, impose, introduce, levy, put** ◊ *The government may put an indirect ~ on books.* | **collect** ◊ *the government department responsible for collecting ~es* | **deduct** ◊ *Your employer will deduct the ~ for you.* | **calculate** | **increase, put up, raise** | **cut, keep down, lower, reduce** | **abolish, repeal** | **eliminate** | **overpay** | **claim back, reclaim** (*BrE*) | **offset sth against, set sth off against, write sth off against** (*all BrE*) ◊ *Claims for expenses can be set off against ~.* | **avoid, escape** | **evade** ◊ *She was charged with conspiracy to evade ~es.*
TAX + VERB **go up, increase, rise** ◊ *Taxes look set to rise again.* | **come/go down, fall** | **be chargeable** (*BrE*), **be payable** ◊ *the amount on which capital gains ~ is payable*
TAX + NOUN **payer** (usually **taxpayer**) ◊ *a higher-rate ~ payer* | **preparer** (*AmE*) | **authority/authorities, man** (usually **taxman**) (*informal*), **office** ◊ *She owes the taxman £10 000.* | **law, legislation, measures, package, policy, reform, structure, system** | **season** ◊ *April is ~ season.* | **year** (*BrE*) ◊ *The ~ year begins in April.* | **cut, reduction** | **hike, increase** | **band** (*BrE*), **bracket, code, rate, threshold** ◊ *Her salary puts her in the highest ~ bracket.* | **dollars, money, receipts, revenue, yield** | **collection** | **assessment, form, return** ◊ *You have to fill in your ~ return by tomorrow.* | **advantage, allowance, benefit, break, concession, credit, exemption, incentive, perks** (*BrE*), **rebate, refund, relief, saving** ◊ *There are ~ advantages to working freelance.* ◊ *You will only receive ~ relief on the first $30 000.* | **deduction** | **affairs, arrangements** (*both BrE*) ◊ *His ~ affairs are under investigation by the police.* | **records** | **preparation** (*esp. BrE*) | **avoidance** | **loophole** ◊ *Her accountant was good at exploiting ~ loopholes.* | **shelter** | **dodge, evasion, fraud** ◊ *He gave the Porsche to his mother as a ~ dodge.* | **dodger** | **exile** (*esp. BrE*) ◊ *She is living as a ~ exile in Monaco.* | **haven** ◊ *The island is a popular ~ haven for the very rich.* | **assessor** (*AmE*), **collector, consultant, inspector** (*BrE*) | **bill, charge, payment** | **arrears** (*BrE*) ◊ *He was ordered to pay £2 million in ~ arrears.* | **liability** ◊ *an increase in ~ liability on*

company cars | **burden** ◊ *He was criticized for putting a new ~ burden on the poor.* | **base** ◊ *By broadening the ~ base (= making more people pay tax) the chancellor could raise more revenues.*
PREP. **after ~, before ~** ◊ *Profits after ~ were $562 000.* | **in ~** ◊ *Collectively, smokers pay over £15 000 a day in ~.* | **~ on** ◊ *to introduce a 60% ~ on alcohol*
PHRASES **for ~ purposes** ◊ *He is non-resident for ~ purposes.* | **the rate of ~** ◊ *an increase in the basic rate of ~* | **inspector of ~es** (*BrE*)

tax verb

ADV. **heavily, highly** ◊ *Many self-employed people are heavily ~ed.* ◊ *goods which are most highly ~ed* | **lightly**
PREP. **according to** ◊ *Drinks would be ~ed according to their alcoholic strength.* | **at** ◊ *Many goods were ~ed at 17.5%.* | **on** ◊ *You will be ~ed on all your income.*

taxation noun

ADJ. **excessive, heavy, high** ◊ *the heavy ~ on smokers and drinkers* | **low** | **direct, indirect** | **progressive, redistributive** | **double** ◊ *the proposal to eliminate the double ~ of dividends* | **corporate, income** (*esp. AmE*), **property** ◊ *changes in corporate ~* | **general, personal** (*both esp. BrE*) | **federal, local, state**
... OF TAXATION **level, rate** ◊ *a promise to reduce the overall level of ~*
VERB + TAXATION **levy** ◊ *the inability to levy sufficient ~ to meet the costs of government* | **increase, raise** ◊ *If the government raises direct ~, it will lose votes.* | **cut** (*BrE*), **reduce** | **eliminate** (*esp. BrE*) | **avoid** | **be exempt from** ◊ *Any profits made are totally exempt from ~.*
TAXATION + NOUN **policy, system**
PREP. **after ~, before ~** (*BrE*) ◊ *The loss before ~ was £2.7 million.* | **from ~** ◊ *The hospital was funded from ~.* | **out of ~** (*esp. BrE*), **through ~** ◊ *the power to raise funds through ~* | **~ on** ◊ *increased ~ on oil companies*
PHRASES **the burden of ~** ◊ *The party's policy is to reduce the burden of ~ on the poor.* | **a form of ~** ◊ *The charge was seen as just another form of ~.* | **for ~ purposes** (*esp. BrE*) ◊ *They were treated as a married couple for ~ purposes.*

taxi noun

ADJ. **air, water** ◊ *a water ~ heading for Venice*
VERB + TAXI **take** ◊ *I took a ~ back home.* | **book (sb)** (*esp. BrE*) | **call (sb), get (sb), order (sb), phone for** (*esp. BrE*) ◊ *I'll get my secretary to call you a ~.* | **find** ◊ *We had some difficulty finding a ~.* | **catch, flag, flag down, grab** (*informal, esp. AmE*), **hail** ◊ *We caught a ~ to the airport.* | **get into, get out of** | **drive** | **pay for** | **share** | **hire** (*esp. BrE*) ◊ *We hired a ~ for the day and went all over the island.*
TAXI + NOUN **cab** | **company, firm** (*BrE*) | **ride** | **service** | **fare** | **driver** | **rank** (*BrE*), **stand** (*AmE*)
PHRASES **by ~** ◊ *a five-minute trip by ~* ◊ *I prefer to travel by ~.*

tea noun

1 drink

ADJ. **fresh** ◊ *There's some fresh (= just made) ~ in the pot.* (*BrE*) | **stewed** (= very strong) (*BrE*), **strong** | **weak** | **cold, hot, lukewarm, scalding** | **milky** (*esp. BrE*) | **white** (usually after **tea**) ◊ *I'll have tea—white, no sugar, please.* | **black** (*esp. BrE*) | **sugary** (*esp. BrE*), **sweet** | **morning** | **decaffeinated** | **China** (*BrE*), **Chinese, Indian,** etc. | **Earl Grey, green,** etc. | **fruit, herbal** | **camomile, jasmine, lemon, mint,** etc. | **ice** (*AmE*), **iced**
... OF TEA **cup, flask** (*BrE*), **mug, pot, Thermos™**
VERB + TEA **drink** ◊ *I don't drink ~.* | **have** | **take** ◊ *How do you take your ~?* | **sip** ◊ *She sipped her hot ~ slowly.* | **take a mouthful of, take a sip of** | **brew, get (sb), make (sb), mash** (*BrE*) ◊ *I'll make you some ~.* ◊ *All rooms have tea-making facilities.* (*BrE*) | **bring sb, ply sb with** (*humorous, esp. BrE*), **serve (sb), take sb** ◊ *I'll bring you a cup of ~ in a few minutes.* | **pour (sb), pour (sb) out** (*esp. BrE*) ◊ *Pour me a cup of ~ please.* | **stir** | **sweeten**
TEA + VERB **brew** ◊ *You haven't let the ~ brew long enough.* | **cool** ◊ *Allow the ~ to cool before you drink it.*

TEA + NOUN **kettle** (usually *teakettle*) (*esp. AmE*), **pot** (usually *teapot*), **urn** (*esp. BrE*) | **cosy/cozy** | **service, set** ◊ *a bone china ~ service* | **cup** (usually *teacup*) | **cart** (usually *teacart*) (*AmE*), **tray, trolley** (*BrE*), **wagon** (*AmE*) | **bar** (*esp. BrE*), **garden, house, room** (*esp. BrE*), **shop** (*esp. BrE*) ◊ *The hospital ~ bar is run by volunteers.* ◊ *an authentic Japanese ~ house* | **boy** (*offensive when used of an older man*), **lady** (*both BrE*) | **drinker, drinking** | **break** (*esp. BrE*) | **party** | **ceremony**

PREP. **in your ~** ◊ *Do you take sugar in your ~?*
PHRASES **~ and coffee, ~ or coffee** ◊ *Would you like ~ or coffee?* | **~ and biscuits** (*BrE*) | **~ and sympathy** (*esp. BrE*) ◊ *He tried to alleviate their disappointment by inviting them in for ~ and sympathy.* | **~ for two** (*esp. BrE*) ◊ *'Tea for two,' said Mary, 'and a slice of your delicious chocolate cake.'*

2 leaves for making tea

ADJ. **loose** (= tea that is not in bags)
... OF TEA **box** (*AmE*), **packet** (*BrE*)
VERB + TEA **grow**
TEA + VERB **grow**
TEA + NOUN **leaf** | **bag** | **caddy** (*esp. BrE*) | **strainer** | **estate** (*BrE*), **plantation** | **chest** (*BrE*) ◊ *He stores his books in a ~ chest.*

3 (*esp. BrE*) **light meal**

ADJ. **afternoon, cream, high** ◊ *I decided to treat myself to a cream ~ in the ~ room next door.* | **birthday, funeral**
TEA + NOUN **time** (usually *teatime*) | **things** ◊ *I cleared away the ~ things.*
→ Note at MEAL (for verbs)

teach verb

ADV. **effectively, well** ◊ *information which helps the teacher ~ more effectively* | **commonly, widely** ◊ *the languages that are commonly taught in schools today*
VERB + TEACH **try to** ◊ *I'm trying to ~ my daughter to behave.* | **be qualified to** ◊ *I am not qualified to ~ this subject.* | **be designed to** ◊ *training courses designed to ~ managerial techniques* | **help (to), help sb (to)**
PREP. **about** ◊ *Children are taught about the world around them.* | **to** ◊ *She ~es English to Polish students.*

teacher noun

ADJ. **excellent, great, outstanding** | **competent, good, inspired, popular, skilled** | **bad, incompetent** | **sympathetic** | **fellow** | **former, retired** | **female, woman** | **male** | **school** (usually *schoolteacher* when used on its own) ◊ *She was a public school ~* (= paid for by the government). (*AmE*) | **kindergarten** (*esp. AmE*), **nursery** (*BrE*), **nursery-school, preschool** | **elementary, elementary-school, grade-school, high-school, junior-high, junior-high-school, middle-school** (*all in the US*) | **primary, primary-school, secondary, secondary-school** (*all esp. BrE*) | **college, university** (*esp. BrE*) | **first-grade, second-grade, etc.** (*all AmE*) | **head** (*BrE*), **senior** ◊ *She held the post of deputy head ~ at a school in Leeds.* | **certified** (*AmE*), **qualified, experienced, inexperienced** | **in-service, pre-service** (*both AmE*) | **student, trainee** (*BrE*) | **master** (*esp. AmE*) | **full-time, part-time** | **substitute** (*AmE*), **supply** (*BrE*), **support** (*esp. BrE*) | **class, classroom, homeroom** (*AmE*) | **special-education** (*AmE*), **special-needs** (*BrE*) | **non-specialist, specialist** (*both esp. BrE*) | **subject** (*esp. BrE*) | **language** | **art, English, gym, history, math** (*AmE*), **maths** (*BrE*), **music, PE, science, etc.** | **EFL** (*BrE*), **ESL** | **dance, piano** | **Sunday-school** | **spiritual**
VERB + TEACHER **have** ◊ *I'm good at cooking. I had a good ~.* | **train**
TEACHER + VERB **teach sth** | **work with sb** ◊ *~s working with less able students*
TEACHER + NOUN **education, preparation** (*AmE*), **training** ◊ *~ preparation programs* ◊ *She's been accepted at ~ training college.* (*BrE*) | **trainer** | **union** | **shortage** | **ratings** (*AmE*) ◊ *~ ratings of reading ability*
→ Note at JOB

849

team

teaching noun

1 work/profession of a teacher

ADJ. **effective, good** | **poor** | **classroom** ◊ *a system that rewards good classroom ~* | **whole-class** (*BrE*) | **individual, one-on-one** (*AmE*), **one-to-one** (*esp. BrE*) | **collaborative, team** | **formal, traditional** ◊ *the formal ~ of grammar* | **creative** | **school** (usually *schoolteaching* when used on its own) ◊ *secondary school ~* | **primary, secondary** (*both esp. BrE*) | **college, undergraduate, university** | **English, language, music, etc.** | **student** (= practical experience for people training to be teachers) (*AmE*)
VERB + TEACHING **get into, go into** ◊ *He's going to go into ~.* | **promote** ◊ *The aim of the campaign is to promote the ~ of science.*
TEACHING + NOUN **method, strategy, style, technique** | **aid, material, resource** ◊ *She used puppets as ~ aids.* | **objective, point** ◊ *Write each ~ point on the whiteboard.* | **ability, skills** | **experience, qualification** (*BrE*) ◊ *Applicants must hold a recognized ~ qualification.* | **job, post** | **career** ◊ *Mr Murphy retired at the end of a 30-year ~ career.* | **practice** (= practical experience for people training to be teachers) (*BrE*) | **profession, staff** ◊ *They have left the ~ profession, demoralized and undervalued.* | **assistant, fellow** ◊ *He served as a ~ assistant at South Dakota State University.* | **duties, load, responsibilities, role** ◊ *Lecturers who have heavy ~ loads.* | **centre/center, institution** | **environment, situation** ◊ *a ~ environment where English is not the first language* | **programme/program, session, year** ◊ *The ~ year runs from October to May.* | **time** ◊ *Critics say that these tests waste ~ time.* | **hospital**
PREP. **in ~** ◊ *I've been in ~ for ten years.*
PHRASES **an approach to ~** ◊ *the modern approach to language ~* | **a method of ~, a style of ~**

2 ideas and beliefs that are taught by sb

ADJ. **ancient, traditional** | **official** ◊ *the official ~ of the Church* | **fundamental** ◊ *the fundamental ~s of the Buddha* | **biblical, church, moral, religious, social** | **Buddhist, Christian, etc.**
VERB + TEACHING **follow** ◊ *He followed the ~s of the Bible on this subject.* | **contradict** | **accept, reject** | **explain, interpret** | **pass on, spread** ◊ *the disciples who passed on Jesus's ~* | **base sth on** ◊ *the great moral ~s on which our culture is based*
PREP. **in the ~** ◊ *the source of goodness in the ~s of Confucius* | **~ about, ~ on** ◊ *the Church's ~ on forgiveness*

team noun

1 group of people who play a sport together

ADJ. **home, hometown** | **away** (*esp. BrE*), **opposing, rival, visiting** | **decent, strong, successful, winning** | **weak, losing** | **dream** ◊ *The manager has chosen his dream ~ for the World Cup.* | **junior, senior, youth** | **under-16, etc.** | **A, B, first, second, etc.** | **international, local, national, Olympic** | **England, Ireland, Scotland, US** | **French, Japanese, etc.** | **baseball, basketball, football, relay, etc.** | **college, school, varsity** (*esp. AmE*) | **display** (*BrE*) ◊ *a parachute display ~* | **special** (in American football) | **five-man, five-person, five-strong, five-woman, etc.** ◊ *Spain are fielding a three-man ~ in this race.* | **men's, mixed, women's**
VERB + TEAM **field, have** | **choose, get together, organize, pick, put together** ◊ *Can you get a ~ together by Saturday?* | **coach, manage** | **be in, be on, play for, play in** (*esp. BrE*), **play on** (*esp. AmE*) ◊ *I'm playing for the first ~ this week.* | **be called up to** (*BrE*), **be selected for, get into** (*esp. BrE*), **get on** (*esp. AmE*), **get onto** (*AmE*), **make** ◊ *Cole has been selected for the ~ to meet Italy next week.* ◊ *You didn't make the ~, I'm afraid.* | **be dropped from, be left out of** | **join, sign for** (*BrE*), **sign up for** (*esp. AmE*), **sign with** (*esp. AmE*) ◊ *He is looking to sign for a Conference League ~.* ◊ *I signed up for the school basketball ~.* ◊ *He hopes to sign with an NFL ~.* | **play, play against** | **beat** | **lead** | **support**
TEAM + VERB **enter** (*esp. AmE*), **get into, make it into** |

compete (in sth), take part (in sth) (*esp. BrE*) ◇ *The ~ competes in a local league.* | *There are six ~s taking part.* | **play** | **play sb, play against sb** | **win (sth)** | **lose (sth)** ◇ *Our ~ lost the final.*

TEAM + NOUN **game, sport** | **captain, coach, manager, owner, president** (*esp. AmE*) | **official** (*esp. AmE*) | **mate** (usually **teammate**) ◇ *He apologized to his teammates for his mistake.* | **championship, competition, event, prize** | **effort, performance** | **selection** | **talk** (*BrE*) ◇ *The lads were given a rousing half-time ~ talk by the coach.* | **roster** (*AmE*), **sheet** (*BrE*) (= the list of players chosen for the team)

PREP. **in a/the ~, on a/the ~** ◇ *I'll have you on the first ~.* | *Whose ~ are you in?* (*BrE*) ◇ *Whose ~ are you on?* (*AmE*) | **~ for** ◇ *She's in the ~ for the World Championships.*

→ Special page at SPORTS

2 group of people who work together

ADJ. **joint** ◇ *a joint ~ of European and North American economists* | **five-strong** | **husband-and-wife** | **campaign, creative, design, development, editorial, investigation, management, marketing, production, project, research, sales** ◇ *a member of the senior management ~* | **legal, medical, surgical** | **multidisciplinary** | **special** ◇ *A special ~ of police officers will patrol the town.* | **crack** ◇ *a crack ~ of lawyers* | **rescue, SWAT** (*esp. AmE*)

VERB + TEAM **assemble, build, form, put together, train** ◇ *Willing volunteers formed ~s of helpers to carry everything in.* ◇ *a specially trained ~ of advisers* | **make** ◇ *You and I make a good ~.* | **head, lead, manage, run** | **send** ◇ *The charity sent a ~ to the area hit by the earthquake.* | **join** ◇ *She has recently joined our sales ~.* | **leave** | **work as** ◇ *We're learning to work together as a ~.*

TEAM + VERB **comprise sb, consist of sb** ◇ *The ~ consisted of six investigators and two secretaries.* | **develop sth, operate, work on sth** ◇ *the ~ that developed this microchip* | **work with sb/sth** ◇ *The ~ will work closely with other government departments.*

TEAM + NOUN **leader, member** | **player** (= sb who works well as part of a team) (*informal*) | **meeting** | **approach** | **building, development** ◇ *The survival course was intended as a team-building exercise.* | **chemistry** (*esp. AmE*), **dynamics** ◇ *We have a great ~ chemistry.* | **spirit** | **effort** ◇ *It took a tremendous ~ effort to finish the project on time.*

PREP. **in a/the ~** (*esp. BrE*), **on a/the ~** (*esp. AmE*) ◇ *There are 20 people in/on the ~.* | **~ of** ◇ *a ~ of scientists*

PHRASES **a member of a ~, part of a ~**

teamwork noun

ADJ. **effective, good, great**

VERB + TEAMWORK **emphasize, encourage, foster, promote** ◇ *The company says the aim is to encourage ~.* | **require**

PREP. **through ~** ◇ *achieving our success through effective ~*

tear¹ noun from the eyes

ADJ. **angry, bitter, emotional** ◇ *There were angry ~s in Lily's eyes.* | **happy** | **burning, fresh, hot, salty, warm** ◇ *Her eyes were blinded by scalding ~s.* | **genuine, real, wet** (*esp. AmE*) | **crocodile** (= not sincere) ◇ *They weep crocodile ~s for the poor, but do nothing to help.* | **great, huge, large** | **single, solitary, stray** ◇ *I wiped a stray ~ from my eye.* | **silent** | **helpless, sudden, uncontrollable** | **unshed** ◇ *His eyes were bright with unshed ~s.*

VERB + TEAR **cry, shed** (*also figurative*), **weep** ◇ *I won't shed any ~s when Moira retires.* ◇ *She wept silent ~s when she heard his name.* | **brush, brush away, dry, wipe, wipe away** ◇ *I picked the little girl up and helped dry her ~s.* ◇ *She wiped a ~ from her eye.* | **blink back, choke back, fight back, hold back** ◇ *He had to fight back ~s of frustration.* | **stop** ◇ *I couldn't stop the ~s.* | **hide** ◇ *He turned away to hide his ~s.* | **break down in ~s, burst into ~s** ◇ *She broke down in ~s in court.* | **move sb to ~s, reduce sb to ~s** ◇ *His father's angry shouting reduced the little boy to ~s.* | **brim with ~s, fill with ~s** ◇ *His eyes filled with ~s.* | **end in ~s** (= to have an unhappy result)

TEAR + VERB **appear, brim in sb's eyes, come, escape, fill sb's eyes, form, gather, spill from sb's eyes, spill over, spring into/to sb's eyes, start, well, well up** ◇ *He could never read the letter without ~s coming to his eyes.* ◇ *Her ~s spilled over her cheeks.* | **drip, drop, fall, flow, overflow, stream (from sth)** ◇ *She ran out of the room, ~s streaming from her eyes.* | **course down sth, flood down sth, pour down sth, roll down sth, run down sth, slide down sth, slip down sth, spill down sth, stream down sth, trickle down sth** ◇ *A single ~ rolled slowly down her cheek.* | **stain sth, streak sth** ◇ *Tears streaked her face.* | **glisten** | **stand** ◇ *Tears stood in Oliver's eyes.* | **blur sth, cloud sth** ◇ *Tears blurred his vision.* | **burn (sth), prick sth, prick at sth, prick in sth, sting sb's eyes** ◇ *She felt ~s pricking her eyelids.* | **dry, dry up**

TEAR + NOUN **duct, gland** | **gas** ◇ *The police fired ~ gas at the protesters.*

PREP. **in ~s** ◇ *He came to me in ~s.* | **through your ~s** ◇ *She tried to smile through her ~s.* | **~ for** ◇ *He shed no ~s for his lost youth.* | **~ of** ◇ *~s of happiness* | **~ over** ◇ *It turned out to be a lot of ~s over nothing.*

PHRASES **bring ~s to sb's eyes** ◇ *It brings ~s to your eyes to see them having such fun.* | **close to ~s, near to ~s** ◇ *More than once I came near to ~s.* | **a flood of ~s, floods of ~s** ◇ *We were in floods of ~s at the end of the movie.* | **a mist of ~s** ◇ *I watched it all through a mist of ~s.* | **on the verge of ~s** | **with ~s in your eyes** | **wet with ~s** ◇ *Her cheeks were wet with ~s.*

tear² noun in fabric, paper, etc.

VERB + TEAR **have** | **make** | **fix, mend** (*esp. BrE*)

PREP. **~ in** ◇ *This sheet has a ~ in it.*

PHRASES **wear and ~** (= the damage to objects, furniture, etc. that is the result of normal use)

tear³ verb

ADV. **badly** ◇ *His clothes were badly torn.* | **easily** ◇ *Careful—the fabric ~s very easily.* | **almost, nearly, practically** ◇ *The storm nearly tore the roof off.* | **apart** (*also figurative*), **asunder** (*literary, figurative*), **off, out, up** ◇ *The dogs tore the fox apart.* ◇ *We tore the other team apart in the second half.*

VERB + TEAR **threaten to**

PREP. **at** ◇ *The fabric snagged and tore at the seams.* | **from** ◇ *I tore another sheet from the pad.* | **off** ◇ *She tore the label off the suitcase.* | **on** ◇ *She tore her skirt on a nail.* | **out of** ◇ *Several pages had been torn out of the book.*

PHRASES **~ free, ~ loose** ◇ *She tore herself free.* | **~ sth in half, ~ sth in two** ◇ *She tore the piece of paper in half.* | **~ sb limb from limb** ◇ *He threatened to ~ me limb from limb.* | **~ sth open** ◇ *She tore the letter open.* | **~ sth to pieces, ~ sth to shreds** (*often figurative*) ◇ *The critics tore his last movie to shreds.*

tease verb

ADV. **mercilessly** | **playfully** | **a little, gently, lightly** | **constantly**

VERB + TEASE **used to**

PREP. **about** ◇ *His friends used to ~ him about his clothes.* | **with** ◇ *They ~d her mercilessly with remarks about her weight.*

PHRASES **be just teasing, be only teasing** ◇ *Don't get upset—I was only teasing.*

technical adj.

VERBS **be, sound** | **become, get** ◇ *The conversation was getting a little ~ for me.*

ADV. **extremely, fairly, very, etc.** | **highly** ◇ *A lot of the discussions were highly ~.* | **a little, slightly, etc.** | **overly, too** ◇ *Without getting too ~, this is basically how it works.* | **purely** ◇ *This is a purely ~ problem.*

technicality noun

ADJ. **mere, minor** | **legal, procedural** ◇ *His conviction was reversed by the US Supreme Court on a procedural ~.*

VERB + TECHNICALITY **understand** | **discuss, get into, go into** (*esp. BrE*) ◇ *I don't want to go into all the technicalities just now.*

technician *noun*

ADJ. **chief, senior** | **experienced, skilled** | **qualified, trained** | **trainee** (*BrE*) | **lab** (*informal*), **laboratory** | **dental, medical** | **computer** | **lighting, sound** ◊ *He works as a sound ~ in a recording studio.* | **ultrasound, X-ray, etc.** (*esp. AmE*) | **maintenance, service, support** ◊ *a computer support ~* | **ambulance** (*BrE*)
VERB + TECHNICIAN **train** ◊ *a need to train ~s in construction methods*
→ Note at JOB

technique *noun*

ADJ. **effective, powerful, useful** | **popular** | **basic, simple** | **conventional, established, proper, standard, traditional** | **alternative, experimental, innovative, new** | **advanced, modern, sophisticated** | **ingenious** | **building, construction, farming, manufacturing** | **assessment, communication, dating, evaluation, exam, interrogation, interview, management, marketing, problem-solving, relaxation, research, sales, teaching, training** ◊ *She needs to work on her interview ~ if she's going to get a job.* | **analytical, diagnostic, mathematical, medical, photographic, scientific, statistical, surgical** | **narrative**
VERB + TECHNIQUE **have** ◊ *He has an ingenious ~ for dealing with problems of that sort.* | **adopt, apply, deploy, employ, implement, try, use, utilize** ◊ *On the walls I applied the same ~ as I had used for the ceiling.* | **develop, devise, introduce, pioneer** ◊ *The ~ was pioneered in California.* | **acquire, learn, master, practise/practice** ◊ *The students were struggling to master the new ~.* | **teach** | **adapt, improve, perfect, refine, work on** | **demonstrate, describe**
TECHNIQUE + VERB **allow sth, enable sth** ◊ *Modern freezing ~s enable the chickens to be stored for weeks.* | **work** ◊ *The new ~ works better than the one it has replaced.* | **be based on sth, be derived from sth** ◊ *singing ~s derived from Tibetan music*
PREP. **~ for** ◊ *~s for the storage of data* | **~ in** ◊ *They employ the latest ~s in farm management.*

technology *noun*

ADJ. **current, existing** | **emerging, the latest, modern, new** ◊ *small businesses that are involved with emerging technologies* | **basic, low** | **core** | **advanced, complex, cutting-edge, high, leading-edge, sophisticated, state-of-the-art, up-to-date** | **alternative, innovative** ◊ *a car based on alternative ~* | **efficient** | **computer, digital, electronic, energy, information, management, manufacturing, nuclear, production, satellite, software** | **communication, communications, telecommunications** | **Bluetooth™, broadband, DSL, interactive, Internet, wireless** | **educational, environmental, medical, military**
VERB + TECHNOLOGY **have** ◊ *We now have the technologies to transplant limbs.* | **adopt, apply, embrace, employ, exploit, implement, introduce, take advantage of, use, utilize** ◊ *We need to exploit existing technologies more fully.* | **create, develop, improve** | **be based on, incorporate** ◊ *a car engine based on ~ developed for planes* | **invest in** ◊ *The company is investing heavily in new technologies.*
TECHNOLOGY + VERB **advance, develop, evolve** ◊ *Telecommunications ~ is developing fast.* | **exist** ◊ *The ~ already exists to do this.* | **allow sth, enable sth** ◊ *This ~ enables computers to read handwriting.*
PREP. **~ for** ◊ *the ~ for the extraction of iron ore*
PHRASES **advances in ~** ◊ *recent advances in medical ~* | **the impact of (a) ~** | **science and ~**

tedious *adj.*

VERBS **be, seem, sound** | **become, get** ◊ *Her visits were starting to get a little ~.* | **make sth** | **find sth** ◊ *He found committee meetings extremely ~.*
ADV. **extremely, fairly, very, etc.** | **incredibly, mind-numbingly** | **a bit, slightly, etc.** | **increasingly** ◊ *The joke became increasingly ~.*

teenager *noun*

ADJ. **older, young** ◊ *a young ~ of fourteen* | **normal, typical** ◊ *She's just acting like a normal ~.* | **awkward, gawky, shy** | **fresh-faced** | **impressionable** | **moody, rebellious, stroppy** (*BrE, informal*), **sulky, surly, troublesome** | **angst-ridden, depressed, troubled** | **bored** | **drunken, rowdy, unruly** ◊ *Residents have been disturbed by large groups of rowdy ~s.* | **horny** (*informal*) | **pimply, spotty** (*BrE*) | **gangly** ◊ *He had grown from a tall, gangly ~ to a handsome young man.* | **lovesick** (*often figurative*) ◊ *He's acting like a lovesick ~.*

teens *noun*

ADJ. **early** ◊ *a girl in her early ~* | **late**
VERB + TEENS **reach** ◊ *He didn't want to share a room with his brother once he reached his ~.*
PREP. **during your ~** ◊ *His parents divorced during his ~.* | **in your ~** ◊ *All my children are in their ~.* | **since your ~** ◊ *She's had skin problems since her ~.*

telecommunications (*also informal* telecoms) *noun*

ADJ. **global, national, world** | **public** ◊ *a public ~ system* | **broadband, mobile, wireless**
TELECOMMUNICATIONS + NOUN **infrastructure, network, services, system** ◊ *modernizing their postal and ~ networks* | **device, equipment, products, satellite, technology** | **carrier, company, firm, giant, group, operator, provider** ◊ *Japan's ~ giant, NTT* | **business, industry, market, sector**

telephone *noun* → See also PHONE

ADJ. **public** | **office** ◊ *The office ~s were all out of order.* | **cellular, cordless, digital, mobile, portable, wireless** | **radio, satellite**
VERB + TELEPHONE **use** ◊ *Can I use your ~?* | **be on** ◊ *Don't pester me now—I'm on the ~.* | **have** ◊ *Excuse me, do you have a ~?* | **answer, get** (*informal*), **pick up** ◊ *Hang on—I'll just get the ~.* | **hang up, put down** ◊ *She put down the ~ and burst into tears.* | **call sb to** ◊ *He was called to the ~ just as he was leaving.* | **bug** (*BrE*), **tap** | **connect, install** | **disconnect**
TELEPHONE + VERB **ring** ◊ *The ~ was ringing furiously.*
TELEPHONE + NOUN **number** ◊ *All letters should include an address and a daytime ~ number.* | **book, directory** | **bill, call, message** | **conference, conversation, enquiry** (*BrE*), **interview, poll, survey** | **contact** ◊ *She is in ~ contact with headquarters.* | **helpline** (*BrE*), **hotline, support** ◊ *The charity has set up a 24-hour ~ hotline.* | **company** | **banking** (*esp. BrE*), **service** | **charges** | **cord, handset, headset, receiver** | **cable, line, pole** (*AmE*), **wire** | **exchange, network, switchboard, system** | **operator** | **booth, box** (*BrE*), **kiosk** (*BrE*) | **tapping**
PREP. **by ~** ◊ *Can I get in touch by ~?* | **on the ~** ◊ *She sounded very distant on the ~.* | **over the ~** ◊ *I don't want to talk about this over the ~.*

telescope *noun*

ADJ. **powerful** | **60 mm, etc.** | **ground-based, optical, radio, space** ◊ *images from the Hubble space ~*
VERB + TELESCOPE **use** | **point** ◊ *We can't simply point a ~ at a star and see its orbiting planets directly.* | **set up** ◊ *She set up her ~ on the balcony.* | **build** ◊ *They've built the largest ~ in the world.*
PREP. **through a/the ~** ◊ *I looked at the moon through a ~.* | **with a ~, without a ~** ◊ *These stars are too faint to been seen without a ~.*
PHRASES **the wrong end of a ~** ◊ *He felt as if he were seeing things through the wrong end of a ~.*

television *noun*

ADJ. **broadcast** (*esp. AmE*), **cable, closed-circuit, digital, high-definition, satellite, terrestrial** (*esp. BrE*) | **commercial, network** (*esp. AmE*), **public** (*AmE*), **state** | **local, national** | **live** ◊ *Millions watched the events on live ~.* | **daytime,**

tell

prime-time | interactive, reality | black-and-white, colour/color | flat-screen, plasma, plasma-screen, wide-screen | portable
VERB + TELEVISION **watch** ◇ *The children watched ~ for most of the evening.* | **switch on, turn on** | **switch off, turn off**
TELEVISION + VERB **broadcast sth, screen sth** ◇ *The trial was broadcast by local ~.*
TELEVISION + NOUN **broadcast, production, programme/program, series, show** | **debate, interview, report** | **chat show** (*BrE*), **comedy, documentary, drama, film** (*esp. BrE*), **movie** (*esp. AmE*), **news, sitcom, special, talk show** (*esp. AmE*) | **ad, advert** (*BrE*), **advertisement, commercial, spot** (*esp. AmE*) | **adaptation** ◇ *a ~ adaptation of the popular novel* | **audience, viewer** | **commentator, critic, journalist, reporter** | **personality, presenter, star** | **character** | **actor, director, producer** | **cameraman, crew** | **appearance, spot** ◇ *She recalled her first ~ appearance forty years ago.* | **career** | **coverage, exposure** ◇ *The Olympics receive extensive ~ coverage.* | **ratings** | **camera** | **channel, network, station, studio** | **licence** (*BrE*) | **business, company, industry, service** | **monitor, receiver, set** | **screen** | **aerial** (*BrE*), **antenna** (*AmE*)
PREP. **in ~** ◇ *She works in ~.* | **in front of the ~** ◇ *He spends hours in front of the ~ every night.* | **on ~** ◇ *We were watching the news on ~.*

tell *verb*

1 give sb information

ADV. **bluntly, curtly, flatly** ◇ *She told me bluntly it was my own fault.* | **gravely, seriously** | **smugly** | **honestly, truthfully** | **gently, quietly, softly** | **falsely**
VERB + TELL **want to** | **be going to** ◇ *I was going to ~ you—I just didn't get around to it.* | **try to** | **hate to** ◇ *I hate to ~ you this but I've broken your phone.* | **let sb** ◇ *I tried to ~ them but they wouldn't let me.*
PREP. **about** ◇ *I told him about the money.* | **of** ◇ *No one had told her of the dangers.* | **to** ◇ *He told the story to all his friends.*

2 order sb

ADV. **firmly, sternly** ◇ *'Calm down,' he told her firmly.*

temper *noun*

1 tendency to become angry easily

ADJ. **bad, explosive, fierce, fiery, hot, nasty, terrible, violent, volatile** | **quick, short** | **uncontrollable**
... OF TEMPER **display, fit, flash, outburst** ◇ *He broke the chair in a fit of violent ~.*
VERB + TEMPER **have** ◇ *He has a nasty ~.* | **control, keep** ◇ *I only just managed to keep my ~ with him.* | **lose** ◇ *She loses her ~ easily.*
TEMPER + VERB **flare, rise** ◇ *Tempers flared as the traffic jam became worse.* | **cool, cool down**
TEMPER + NOUN **tantrum**
PREP. **in a ~** ◇ *She stormed out of the room in a ~.*
PHRASES **keep your ~ in check, keep your ~ under control** ◇ *He had to learn to keep his ~ under control before he could become a teacher.*

2 way you are feeling

ADJ. **bad, filthy** (*esp. BrE*), **foul, ill, terrible** ◇ *Peter's comments were responsible for her ill ~.* | **good** | **frayed** ◇ *Frayed ~s at the end led to three players being sent off.*
VERB + TEMPER **improve**
TEMPER + VERB **improve** | **fray**
PREP. **in a ~** ◇ *He stormed out of the room in a ~.*

temperament *noun*

ADJ. **fiery, violent, volatile** | **fragile** (*esp. BrE*), **high-strung** (*AmE*), **highly strung** (*BrE*), **nervous** (*esp. BrE*) | **cool, even, good, sanguine** (*BrE*), **unflappable** | **docile** (*esp. BrE*) | **sunny** | **difficult** | **right** ◇ *He doesn't have the right ~ for the job.* | **romantic** | **artistic, judicial** (*AmE*), **scientific, etc.**

VERB + TEMPERAMENT **have**
PREP. **by ~, in ~** ◇ *She was fiery by ~.*

temperature *noun*

1 how hot or cold sth is

ADJ. **high, hot, warm** ◇ *Yesterday the town reached its highest ever February ~.* | **cold, cool, low, sub-zero** | **moderate** | **normal** | **extreme** ◇ *Avoid exposing the instrument to extreme ~s.* | **boiling, freezing, melting** ◇ *the boiling ~ of the solvent* | **maximum, minimum** | **average, mean** | **constant, stable, steady** | **daytime** | **annual, daily** | **summer, winter, etc.** | **April, July, etc.** | **global** ◇ *The increase in the mean global ~ will be about 0.3°C per decade.* | **air, ocean** (*esp. AmE*), **sea** (*esp. BrE*), **water, etc.** | **ambient, room** ◇ *The product can be stored at room ~.* | **oven** | **body** | **surface** ◇ *the surface ~ of our planet* | **external, internal**
VERB + TEMPERATURE **have** ◇ *Some places had ~s in the forties during the heatwave.* | **heat sth to, increase, raise** ◇ *Heat the oven to a ~ of 200°C.* | **decrease, lower, reduce** | **reach** | **control, maintain, regulate** | **measure, monitor, record** | **expose sth to** | **withstand** ◇ *These instruments can withstand ~s of 180°C.*
TEMPERATURE + VERB **go up, increase, rise, soar** | **dip, drop, fall, go down, plummet** ◇ *Overnight the ~ fell to minus 30°C.* | **range** ◇ *Water ~s ranged from 12 to 15°C.* | **exceed sth, reach sth** | **change, vary**
TEMPERATURE + NOUN **conditions** | **change, difference, drop, increase, rise** | **fluctuation, gradient, range, variation** ◇ *a ~ range of 60–74°F* | **extremes** ◇ *The desert is a place of ~ extremes.* | **control, regulation** | **data, measurement, reading** | **gauge, sensor**
PREP. **at ... ~** ◇ *Serve the wine at room ~.* | **in a ~** ◇ *This plant grows well in ~s above 55°F.* | **~ above, ~ below** ◇ *Temperatures below freezing are common here.* | **~ between** ◇ *a ~ between 35 and 37°* | **~ of** ◇ *The fish prefer a ~ of 24–27°C.*
PHRASES **a change in ~, a variation in ~** | **a range of ~** | **a drop in ~** | **an increase in ~, a rise in ~**

2 fever

ADJ. **high** | **slight**
VERB + TEMPERATURE **have, run** ◇ *She's running a ~.* | **take** ◇ *The nurse produced a thermometer and took my ~.* | **bring down** ◇ *They used ice packs to bring down her ~.*
TEMPERATURE + VERB **go up, rise** | **come down**
PREP. **~ of** ◇ *He's in bed with a ~ of 102°.*

temple *noun*

1 building used for worship

ADJ. **great** ◇ *the great ~s of Egypt* | **ancient, classical** | **Greek, Roman, etc.** | **holy, sacred** | **pagan** | **ruined** | **Buddhist, Hindu, etc.**
VERB + TEMPLE **dedicate** ◇ *a ~ dedicated to Venus*
TEMPLE + NOUN **priest, priestess** | **complex, precincts** ◇ *These deities prevent evil spirits from entering the ~ precincts.* | **worship**
PREP. **in a/the ~** ◇ *They went to pray in the ~.* | **to ~** (= to the synagogue) (*AmE*) ◇ *to go to ~*

2 part of the head

ADJ. **left, right** | **throbbing**
VERB + TEMPLE **massage, rub**
TEMPLE + VERB **throb**
PREP. **at sb's/the ~s** ◇ *He's going white at the ~s.* | **in sb's ~s** ◇ *There was a throbbing in her ~s.*

tempo *noun*

1 speed of an activity/event

VERB + TEMPO **increase, raise** (*esp. BrE*), **step up, up** (*esp. BrE*) ◇ *We need to step up the ~ of our information campaigns.* | **slow, slow down** | **vary** | **control, dictate, set** ◇ *The Kenyan runner set the ~ from the start.*
TEMPO + VERB **quicken** | **slow** | **change**
PREP. **~ of** ◇ *the ~ of the game*

2 speed of a piece of music

ADJ. **brisk, fast, quick, upbeat** | **slow** | **moderate** | **waltz,** etc.
VERB + TEMPO **change**
TEMPO + NOUN **indication, markings** | **change, shift**
PREP. **at a … ~** ◇ *They took the last movement at an unusually slow ~.*

tempt *verb*

VERB + TEMPT **could, may, might** | **try to**
PREP. **into** ◇ *Charlotte was ~ed into parting with $50 for the painting.* | **with** ◇ *restaurants ~ing us with delicious cakes*
PHRASES **be almost ~ed, be half ~ed** ◇ *I was almost ~ed to strip off and plunge straight into the pool.* | **be ~ed, feel ~ed** ◇ *Did you ever feel ~ed to cheat?* | **be seriously ~ed, be severely ~ed** (*esp. BrE*), **be sorely ~ed, be strongly ~ed, be very ~ed** ◇ *She was sorely ~ed to throw the wine in his face.*

temptation *noun*

ADJ. **great, huge, overwhelming, strong** | **irresistible** | **constant** | **sexual**
VERB + TEMPTATION **feel, have** ◇ *I had the constant ~ to look out of the window.* | **avoid, fight, overcome, resist** | **give in to, succumb to, yield to**
PHRASES **in temptation's way, out of temptation's way** (*both esp. BrE*) | **put ~ in sb's way** ◇ *Keep your valuables locked away so as not to put ~ in the way of thieves.*

tenancy *noun*

ADJ. **joint** | **shorthold** (*BrE*) ◇ *The flat could be let on an assured shorthold ~ for about £800 a month.* | **assured, protected, secure** (*all BrE*) | **business, council** (*both BrE*)
VERB + TENANCY **hold** (*esp. BrE*) | **hold sth in, hold sth on** (*esp. BrE*) ◇ *The ~ is held in joint names.* | **take over** (*BrE*) | **grant (sb)** (*BrE*) | **terminate** (*BrE*) | **renew** (*BrE*)
TENANCY + VERB **end, expire** (*both BrE*)
TENANCY + NOUN **agreement**
PREP. **under a/the ~** (*BrE*) ◇ *The club occupies the land under a protected ~.*

tenant *noun*

ADJ. **current, existing, sitting** (*esp. BrE*) ◇ *She is taking legal action to evict a sitting ~.* | **incoming, outgoing** (*both esp. BrE*) | **potential, prospective** | **secure** (*BrE*) | **joint** | **business** (*esp. BrE*), **commercial** | **private** (*BrE*) | **council, council-house, housing-association** (*all BrE*) | **public-housing** (*AmE*)
VERB + TENANT **find** | **have** | **evict**
TENANT + VERB **occupy sth** ◇ *The property is currently occupied by a ~.*
TENANT + NOUN **farmer**
PHRASES **landlord and ~** ◇ *conflicts that might arise between landlord and ~*

tend *verb*

ADV. **carefully, lovingly** ◇ *She lovingly ~ed her garden.*
PREP. **to** ◇ *He ~ed to her every need.*
PHRASES **well-tended** ◇ *well-tended lawns*

tendency *noun*

ADJ. **clear, great, marked, pronounced, strong** | **slight** | **greater, growing, increased, increasing** ◇ *There's a growing ~ for women to marry later.* | **broad, common, general** | **inbuilt** (*esp. BrE*), **inherent, innate, natural, underlying** | **human** ◇ *our natural human ~ to group all the things we don't like together* | **alarming, dangerous, unfortunate, worrying** ◇ *The later model has an unfortunate ~ to collapse after a few weeks' use.* | **contradictory** | **centrifugal** ◇ *The civil war reinforced the centrifugal tendencies at work within the economy.* | **aggressive, destructive, homicidal, psychopathic, suicidal, violent** | **artistic, criminal, etc.** ◇ *He displayed artistic tendencies at an early age.* | **homosexual, lesbian**
VERB + TENDENCY **have** | **display, exhibit, reflect, reveal,**

show | **increase, reinforce** | **curb, reduce** | **overcome, resist**
PREP. **~ among** ◇ *a worrying ~ among the abused to become abusers* | **~ for** ◇ *There is a ~ for farm sizes to increase.* | **~ on the part of** ◇ *The ~ on the part of the children is to blame their parents for everything.* | **~ towards/toward** ◇ *Industry showed a ~ towards/toward increasingly centralized administration.*

tender *adj.*

1 kind and loving

VERBS **be, feel, seem** | **become**
ADV. **achingly, very** ◇ *The letters to Penelope are achingly ~.* | **almost** ◇ *Her expression became soft, almost ~.*
PREP. **towards/toward** ◇ *He felt ~ and loving towards/toward her.*

2 soft and easy to cut/bite

VERBS **be, seem** | **become**
ADV. **beautifully** (*esp. BrE*), **deliciously** (*esp. BrE*), **exceptionally, meltingly, very** ◇ *This meat is beautifully ~.* | **just** ◇ *Boil the potatoes in salted water until just ~.* | **almost**

3 painful when touched

VERBS **be, feel, look** ◇ *The back of my neck feels very ~.* | **become**
ADV. **extremely, fairly, very, etc.** | **a little, slightly, etc.**

tenderness *noun*

ADJ. **deep, great** | **genuine, real, true** | **surprising**
… OF TENDERNESS **wave** ◇ *She felt a wave of ~ sweep over her.*
VERB + TENDERNESS **feel, have** | **reveal, show**
PREP. **with (a) ~** ◇ *He spoke with real ~.* | **~ for** ◇ *She felt great ~ for him.* | **~ towards/toward**
PHRASES **~ in sb's eyes, voice, etc.** ◇ *There was ~ in his face as he looked at her.*

tendon *noun*

ADJ. **damaged, torn** | **Achilles, hamstring**
VERB + TENDON **pull, rupture, sever, tear** | **repair**
TENDON + NOUN **injury**
PREP. **~ in** ◇ *He had surgery for a torn ~ in his elbow.*

tenement *noun*

ADJ. **cramped, overcrowded, squalid** | **crumbling, dilapidated, old, ramshackle, run-down** | **abandoned**
TENEMENT + NOUN **apartment** (*esp. AmE*), **block** (*esp. BrE*), **building, flat** (*BrE*), **house, housing**
PREP. **in a/the ~** ◇ *families living in overcrowded ~s*

tennis *noun*

ADJ. **men's, women's** | **junior** | **professional** | **international, world** (*esp. BrE*) | **competitive** ◇ *Williams' return to competitive ~ after injury* | **doubles, singles** | **lawn** | **court** (*AmE*), **real** (*BrE*)
… OF TENNIS **game**
VERB + TENNIS **play** | **watch**
TENNIS + NOUN **ball, racket** | **dress, shoe, shorts** | **court, facilities** | **camp, centre/center, club** | **circuit, scene, tour, world** ◇ *She is a popular figure on the international ~ circuit.* | **championship, competition, event, match, tournament** | **ace** (*esp. BrE*), **champion, coach, legend, player, pro, star** | **team** | **fan** | **commentator** (*esp. BrE*) | **career** | **practice** | **lesson**
→ Special page at SPORTS

tense *noun*

ADJ. **future, past, present** | **verb**
VERB + TENSE **use** | **form** ◇ *The '-ed' ending is used to form the past ~ of regular verbs.*
TENSE + NOUN **marker** ◇ *the present ~ marker 's'*
PREP. **in the … ~** ◇ *In the sentence 'I fed the cat', 'fed' is in the past ~.*

tense *adj.*

VERBS **be, feel, look, seem, sound** | **become, get, grow** ◇ *The situation grew increasingly* ~. | **remain**
ADV. **extremely, fairly, very, etc.** | **incredibly, particularly** | **increasingly** | **a little, slightly, etc.** ◇ *I was feeling a little* ~ *and restless.* | **visibly** ◇ *Relations between the two leaders are visibly* ~.
PREP. **about** ◇ *There's no point in getting* ~ *about the situation.*

tension *noun*

1 inability to relax

ADJ. **inner** | **emotional, nervous, sexual** ◇ *He suffers from nervous* ~. | **muscle, muscular** | **premenstrual**
VERB + TENSION **feel, suffer from** ◇ *I feel some* ~ *in my shoulders.* | **sense** ◇ *As soon as he entered, he sensed a* ~ *in the air.* | **cause, create** | **relieve** | **release**
TENSION + NOUN **headache**
PREP. ~ **in** ◇ *The hot bath eased the* ~ *in his body.*
PHRASES **a release of** ~ ◇ *Laughter can be a great release of* ~. | **a sign of** ~ ◇ *Horses are very sensitive to signs of* ~ *in humans.*

2 bad feeling between people, countries, etc.

ADJ. **considerable, great, high** ◇ *More police have been sent to areas of high political* ~. | **palpable, real** | **slight** | **escalating, growing, heightened, increased, increasing, mounting, rising** | **constant, continuous** | **continuing, ongoing** | **unresolved** | **renewed** | **fundamental, inherent, underlying** | **ethnic, political, racial, religious, social** | **communal, family, internal, international, national, regional** | **creative, dynamic** ◇ *the creative* ~ *between democracy and business interests*
VERB + TENSION **cause, create, generate** | **defuse, ease, reduce, release, resolve** ◇ *She often used humour/humor to defuse* ~ *in meetings.* | **exacerbate, heighten**
TENSION + VERB **build up, grow, increase, mount, rise** | **ease** | **arise** ◇ *In the early 1960's, new* ~s *arose between the United States and the USSR.* | **exist** | **run high** ◇ *Racial* ~s *in the town were running high.*
PREP. ~ **among** ◇ *The* ~ *among the audience was palpable.* | ~ **between** ◇ ~ *between local youths and the police* | ~ **in,** ~ **within** ◇ *The job losses caused greater* ~s *within the company.* | ~ **over** ◇ *There has been increased* ~ *over the border incident.* | ~ **with** ◇ *renewed* ~ *with France*
PHRASES **a source of** ~ ◇ *Money was always a source of* ~ *between her parents.*

3 of rope, wire, etc.

ADJ. **string**
VERB + TENSION **adjust** ◇ *This old racket needs its string* ~ *adjusted.* | **release**
PREP. **in** ~ ◇ *The metal is weak in* ~. | **under** ~ ◇ *Stay clear of cables which are under* ~. | ~ **on** ◇ *The sudden* ~ *on the line told me I had hooked a fish.*

4 feeling of excitement in a film/movie, etc.

ADJ. **dramatic** ◇ *The movie lacks dramatic* ~.
VERB + TENSION **build, heighten, increase** ◇ *the use of editing to heighten the* ~ | **keep, keep up, maintain** | **break**
TENSION + VERB **build, grow, mount** ◇ *Tension builds around the mystery of what will happen to Freddie.*

tent *noun*

ADJ. **camping** (*AmE*) | **A-frame, dome, frame** (*BrE*), **pup** (*AmE*), **ridge** (*BrE*), **wall** (*AmE*) | **three-person, two-person, etc.** | **makeshift** ◇ *The refugees had been living in makeshift* ~s *for a year.* | **leaky** | **flimsy** | **canvas** | **circus** | **beer, dining, food, hospitality, mess, refreshment** (*esp. BrE*), **tea** (*BrE*) | **cook, cooking** (*both esp. AmE*) | **press, VIP** ◇ *The reporters were waiting for Tiger Woods to come to the press* ~. | **hospital** | **oxygen**
... OF TENTS **row**
VERB + TENT **erect, pitch, put up, set up** ◇ *They pitched their* ~ *in a little clearing in the woods.* | **unzip, zip up** | **take down** | **pack, pack up** | **fold, fold up** | **share**

TENT + VERB **blow down, collapse** | **blow away**
TENT + NOUN **camp, city** ◇ *a* ~ *city housing refugees from the war* | **door, flap, peg, pole, rope, wall**
PREP. **in a/the** ~

term *noun*

1 word or group of words

ADJ. **specific** | **blanket, broad, general, generic, umbrella** | **descriptive** | **common** | **basic, key** | **correct, preferred** | **precise** | **ambiguous, vague** | **mild, strong** ◇ *His objection was couched in the strongest* ~s. | **colloquial, slang** | **derogatory, pejorative** ◇ *'Nerd' is a pejorative* ~ *for someone who likes computers.* | **technical** | **search** ◇ *Try entering the search* ~ *'classical music'.* | **clinical, legal, medical, musical, etc.**
VERB + TERM **use** | **be couched in** | **define, explain** | **coin, introduce, invent** ◇ *The* ~ *'acid rain' was coined in the 19th century.* | **borrow** | **prefer** ◇ *I prefer the* ~ *'network' to 'community'.* | **apply** ◇ *I think we can apply the* ~ *'genius' to the painter.*
TERM + VERB **connote sth, denote sth, describe sth, mean sth** | **apply to sth, be applied to sth, cover sth, refer to sth** ◇ *The* ~ *'renewable energy' is applied, for example, to energy deriving from solar radiation.*
PREP. ~ **for** ◇ *'Old man' is a slang* ~ *for 'father'.* | ~ **of** ◇ *a* ~ *of abuse/endearment*
PHRASES **in glowing** ~s ◇ *The chairman spoke of the achievements of the company in glowing* ~s. | **in no uncertain** ~s ◇ *I let them know in no uncertain* ~s *how disappointed I was.* | **in simple** ~s | **in the following** ~s

2 in…**terms** showing what aspect of something you are considering

ADJ. **absolute, material, practical, real** ◇ *Income has increased in real* ~s *by 5%.* | **relative** ◇ *Iceland has had a mild winter, in relative* ~s. | **broad, general** | **clear, concrete** ◇ *The law should be set out in clear* ~s. | **abstract** | **international** | **negative** ◇ *She tends to perceive herself in purely negative* ~s. | **cultural, economic, financial, historical, money, political, scientific, social, etc.** ◇ *In money* ~s, *the event was a disaster.*

3 (usually **terms**) of an agreement/a relationship

ADJ. **favourable/favorable, unfavourable/unfavorable** | **express, implied** (*both BrE, law*) ◇ *the breach of an express* ~ *in the contract* | **contract, credit, peace**
VERB + TERM **dictate, negotiate, set** ◇ *Our opponents set the* ~s *of the debate.* | **accept, agree on, agree to** | **violate** | **extend**
PREP. **under the** ~s **of** ◇ *Under the* ~s *of the alliance, Japan was not obliged to enter the war.*
PHRASES **on amicable** ~s, **on friendly** ~s, **on good** ~s ◇ *The dispute was resolved on amicable* ~s. | **on equal** ~s ◇ *It is a sport in which the top men and women can compete on equal* ~s. | **on familiar** ~s, **on first-name** ~s ◇ *I'm on first-name* ~s *with my boss.* | **on speaking** ~s ◇ *They haven't been on speaking* ~s *since they had that big row.* | ~s **and conditions** ◇ *A wide range of accounts are available, with varying* ~s *and conditions.*

4 (*esp. BrE*) period of a school/university year → See also SEMESTER

ADJ. **college, school, university** (*BrE*) | **spring, summer, etc.**
TERM + NOUN **paper** (*AmE*) ◇ *I was working on a* ~ *paper for a geography class.*
PREP. **during (the)** ~ ◇ *It's hard to get away during* ~. | **in the** ~ ◇ *We have exams in the summer* ~.
PHRASES **the beginning of (the)** ~, **the end of (the)** ~ ◇ *It's the end of* ~. (*BrE*) ◇ *It's the end of the* ~. (*AmE*)

5 period of time

ADJ. **long, short** ◇ *a long* ~ *of imprisonment* | **full** (*medical*) ◇ *The pregnancy went to full* ~ (= *lasted the normal length of time*). | **fixed** ◇ *The contract was for a fixed* ~ *of five years.* | **jail, prison** | **presidential** | **first, second** ◇ *The president wants to make tax reform a top priority during his second* ~.
VERB + TERM **serve** ◇ *He served a five-year prison* ~. | **seek** ◇ *She is now seeking her second* ~ *in the Senate.* | **win** ◇ *Blair won a third* ~ *of office.* | **begin, complete**

TERM + VERB **run** ◊ *Her current ~ runs until January 2014.* | **expire, run out** ◊ *His ~ expires at the end of May.*
PREP. **at ~** *(medical)* ◊ *Her baby was born at ~.*
PHRASES **in the long ~, in the medium ~, in the near ~, in the short ~** ◊ *In the long ~, our efforts will pay off.* | **a ~ of imprisonment, a ~ of office** ◊ *The president was sworn in for his second ~ of office.* | **a ~ of years** ◊ *The lease is granted for a set ~ of years.*

term *verb* be termed

ADV. **aptly** | **accurately** | **broadly, loosely** | **commonly, generally, often** | **variously** ◊ *This material is variously ~ed ash, clinker, cinders or slag.* | **collectively** | **euphemistically** *(esp. BrE)* | **hereafter** *(formal)* ◊ *The sampling units (hereafter ~ed 'local areas') are towns.*
PREP. **as** ◊ *His condition would be more accurately ~ed as 'chronic fatigue'.*

terminal *noun*

1 place/building that handles goods/passengers

ADJ. **international** | **air, airport** | **rail, subway** *(AmE)*, **train** | **bus** | **cruise, cruise-ship, ferry** | **passenger** | **container, freight** *(esp. BrE)* | **gas, oil**, etc.
TERMINAL + NOUN **building**
PREP. **at a/the ~, in a/the ~** ◊ *We met up at the bus ~.*

2 computer equipment

ADJ. **computer, Internet** | **network** | **display** | **data** ◊ *The larger financial institutions have over 200 news and data ~s in their offices.* | **mobile, portable, wireless**
VERB + TERMINAL **connect** ◊ *The computer ~s are connected to a central network.* | **install** ◊ *Internet ~s have been installed at most libraries.* | **use**
TERMINAL + NOUN **screen, server**
PREP. **at a/the ~** ◊ *There were two students at each ~.* | **on a/the ~** ◊ *All she did was press a few keys on the ~.*

terminate *verb*

ADV. **abruptly, prematurely** ◊ *His contract was abruptly ~d.* | **immediately** | **automatically** | **lawfully** *(esp. BrE)* ◊ *The agreement was lawfully ~d under clause 34.* | **effectively** ◊ *This federal intervention effectively ~d the strike.*
VERB + TERMINATE **be entitled to** *(esp. BrE)* | **decide to** ◊ *She decided to ~ the pregnancy.*
PHRASES **the decision to ~ sth, the right to ~ sth** ◊ *Either party has the right to ~ the agreement.*

termination *noun*

1 ending of sth

ADJ. **early, premature** | **abrupt** | **wrongful** ◊ *She sued the company for wrongful ~.*
VERB + TERMINATION **face** | **justify, permit** ◊ *His negligence justified immediate ~ of the contract.*
TERMINATION + NOUN **date**
PHRASES **notice of ~** ◊ *The landlord gave notice of the ~ of tenancy.* | **~ of a contract, ~ of employment** ◊ *You are required to give the company six weeks' notice of ~ of employment.*

2 abortion

ADJ. **early** | **pregnancy**
VERB + TERMINATION **have, undergo** *(esp. BrE)* ◊ *She chose to have an early ~.*
PHRASES **a ~ of (a) pregnancy**

terminology *noun*

ADJ. **modern, new** | **basic, common, standard** | **correct, proper** | **precise** | **specialized, technical** | **computer, legal, medical, scientific**, etc.
VERB + TERMINOLOGY **use** ◊ *The article uses rather specialized musical ~.* | **adopt, borrow** | **standardize** | **understand**
PREP. **in … ~** ◊ *The outer walls, in building ~, are 'double skin'.*

terrace *noun*

1 flat area of stone next to a restaurant, etc.

ADJ. **covered, outdoor** | **shaded, sunny** | **rear, upper** | **raised** | **viewing** | **garden, pool** *(esp. BrE)* | **roof, rooftop** | **sun**
VERB + TERRACE **open onto** ◊ *The dining room opens onto a garden ~.*
TERRACE + VERB **overlook sth** ◊ *The hotel has a roof ~ overlooking the sea.*
TERRACE + NOUN **garden** | **bar, cafe, restaurant** *(all esp. BrE)*
PREP. **on a/the ~** ◊ *There's a table free on the ~.*

2 *(BrE)* line of joined houses

ADJ. **long** | **two-storey/two-story, three-storey/three-story**, etc. | **Georgian, Victorian**
TERRACE + NOUN **home, house, property** (usually **terraced home**, etc.)
PREP. **in a/the ~** ◊ *Our house is in a long Victorian ~ in north London.*
PHRASES **a ~ of houses**

terrain *noun*

ADJ. **flat** | **steep** | **hilly, mountainous, rocky, rough, rugged, uneven** | **arid, barren, desert** | **boggy, marshy, swampy** *(esp. AmE)* | **difficult, harsh, inhospitable, treacherous** | **difficult ~ for walking** | **familiar, unknown** | **open** ◊ *Tank warfare dominated campaigns in open ~.* | **urban**
VERB + TERRAIN **cross, navigate, negotiate, traverse** | **explore** | **know** ◊ *local fighters who know the ~*
PREP. **across … ~, over … ~** ◊ *It took us the whole day to trek across the rocky ~.*

terrible *adj.*

VERBS **be, feel, look, seem, sound**
ADV. **really, truly** ◊ *I thought something really ~ had happened.* | **absolutely, just, quite, simply** ◊ *He suddenly collapsed—it was simply ~.* | **pretty, rather** | **very** ◊ *Nothing very ~ happened.*
PREP. **for** ◊ *It must have been ~ for the survivors.*

terrified *adj.*

VERBS **be, feel, look, seem**
ADV. **really, truly** | **absolutely, completely, positively, quite, utterly** | **clearly, obviously**
PREP. **at** ◊ *She was absolutely ~ at the thought of jumping off the bridge.* | **of** ◊ *He's ~ of spiders.*

territory *noun*

1 area of land that belongs to one country, etc.

ADJ. **vast** | **new** ◊ *The explorers set off to conquer new territories.* | **former** ◊ *former French territories* | **neighbouring/neighboring, surrounding** | **home, national** | **alien, foreign, overseas** | **enemy, hostile** | **friendly** | **neutral** | **colonial, dependent** *(esp. BrE)*, **trust** *(esp. BrE)* ◊ *a UN trust ~ administered by New Zealand* | **sovereign** ◊ *Troops were stationed on sovereign German ~.* | **annexed, conquered, lost, occupied** ◊ *a town in British-occupied ~* | **contested, disputed** | **familiar, home** *(both figurative)* ◊ *The writer is back on home ~ with his latest novel.* | **uncharted, unexplored, unfamiliar, unknown, virgin** *(all often figurative)* | **dangerous** *(often figurative)*
VERB + TERRITORY **hold** | **annex, capture, conquer, invade, occupy, recapture, take** | **control, govern, rule** ◊ *The ~ had been controlled by Azerbaijan for many years.* | **cede, surrender** | **lose** | **enter, stray into** ◊ *The soldiers strayed into hostile ~.* | **leave** | **settle** ◊ *The ~ was never densely settled.* | **stake out** *(often figurative)* ◊ *The parties have been staking out their ~ on education.* | **chart, explore, map out** *(all often figurative)* ◊ *Tired of writing detective novels, she began to explore new ~.* | **cover** *(often figurative)* ◊ *Many books have covered this ~ before.*

2 of an animal

ADJ. **breeding**, **nesting**
VERB + TERRITORY **defend**, **patrol**, **protect** | **establish**, **mark**, **mark out** ◇ *The male establishes a ~ and attracts a female.*

terror noun

1 great fear

ADJ. **abject**, **absolute**, **pure**, **real**, **sheer**, **utter** | **constant**
VERB + TERROR **be filled with**, **feel**, **have** ◇ *He was filled with absolute ~ at the sight.* ◇ *He had a real ~ of darkness.* | **shake with**, **tremble with** | **inspire** ◇ *He inspired ~ in everyone he met.* | **bring**, **inflict**, **sow**, **spread**, **unleash**, **wreak** ◇ *The explosion brought ~ to hundreds of local residents.* | **live in** ◇ *She lived in ~ of her father.*
PREP. **from ~** ◇ *She was trembling from ~ and excitement.* | **in ~** ◇ *He was found hiding in ~.* ◇ *The shots sent the crowd fleeing in ~.* ◇ *He cried out, out of pure ~.* | **with ~** ◇ *His face was white with ~.*
PHRASES **a state of ~** ◇ *The three kids lived in a state of ~.* | **strike ~ into (the heart of) sb** ◇ *Its fearsome appearance struck ~ into their hearts.*

2 violent action for political purposes

ADJ. **political** | **state** | **global**
VERB + TERROR **resort to**, **use** ◇ *The group has resorted to ~ to try to get what it wants.* | **combat**, **fight** ◇ *He said that the whole world must unite to fight ~ in all its forms.* | **give in to** | **defeat**, **stop** | **sponsor**, **support**
TERROR + NOUN **campaign**, **war** | **plot** | **alert**, **warning** | **threat** | **tactics** | **cell**, **gang**, **group**, **network**, **organization** | **suspect**
PHRASES **an act of ~** ◇ *people who carry out acts of ~* | **a campaign of ~** ◇ *The bombing formed part of a nationwide campaign of ~.* | **a reign of ~** ◇ *The dictator's ten-year reign of ~ left over 100 000 dead.* | **the war on ~**

terrorism noun

ADJ. **urban** | **global**, **international**, **transnational** (*esp. AmE*) | **cross-border** | **state**, **state-sponsored** | **domestic** | **anti-American**, **anti-Western** | **fundamentalist**, **radical** | **nuclear**
VERB + TERRORISM **combat**, **fight** | **defeat**, **prevent**, **stop** | **give in to** ◇ *This government will not give in to ~.* | **sponsor**, **support** ◇ *states that actively sponsor ~*
TERRORISM + NOUN **analyst**, **expert** | **investigation** | **suspect** | **charges**, **offences/offenses** ◇ *He is to stand trial on ~ charges.* | **threat**
PREP. **against ~** ◇ *Public cooperation is vital in the fight against ~.*
PHRASES **an act of ~**
→ Note at CRIME (for more verbs)

terrorist noun

ADJ. **alleged**, **potential**, **suspected** | **convicted**, **known** | **would-be** ◇ *the recruitment of young would-be ~s* | **so-called** ◇ *the so-called wine ~s of the Languedoc* | **domestic**, **foreign**, **international** ◇ *The bomb attacks have been attributed to a group of international ~s.* | **armed** | **suicide** | **fundamentalist**, **radical**, **right-wing**, etc.
TERRORIST + NOUN **band**, **cell**, **faction**, **gang**, **group**, **network**, **organization**, **unit** | **camp** | **state** | **act**, **action**, **activity**, **atrocity**, **attack**, **bomb**, **bombing**, **campaign**, **explosion**, **incident**, **murder**, **operation**, **strike**, **violence** ◇ *an increase in ~ activity* ◇ *the victim of a ~ atrocity* | **threat** | **plot** | **target** ◇ *Aircraft remain likely ~ targets.* | **victim** | **charge** (*esp. BrE*), **crime**, **offence/offense** (*esp. BrE*) | **suspect** | **leader**

test noun

1 examination of sb's knowledge/ability

ADJ. **demanding**, **difficult**, **gruelling/grueling** | **easy**, **simple** | **fair**, **good**, **objective** ◇ *This type of exam does not provide a fair ~ of the student's knowledge.* | **standardized** | **class**

(*BrE*), **take-home** (*AmE*) | **listening**, **oral**, **practical**, **written** | **essay** (*AmE*) | **cloze**, **multiple-choice** | **aptitude**, **SAT**™ (*in the US*) | **intelligence**, **IQ**, **mental** | **achievement**, **endurance**, **proficiency** ◇ *The recruits were put through a week of demanding endurance ~s.* | **language**, **memory**, **spelling** | **placement** ◇ *He scored well in the placement ~ and was put in the most advanced class.* | **driver's** (*AmE*), **driving**, **road** (*AmE*) | **screen** ◇ *Three actors out of a hundred were chosen from the screen ~.*
VERB + TEST **do** (*BrE*), **sit** (*BrE*), **take** ◇ *I took my driving ~ last week.* | **review for** (*AmE*), **revise for** (*BrE*), **study for** | **complete** | **pass** | **fail** | **give**, **set** | **administer** | **monitor** | **grade** (*esp. AmE*), **mark** (*esp. BrE*)
TEST + NOUN **result**, **score** | **conditions** ◇ *As a final practice for the exam, they had to write two essays under ~ conditions.* | **paper**, **questions**
PREP. **in a/the ~** (*BrE*), **on a/the ~** (*AmE*) ◇ *a good mark in the ~* (*BrE*) ◇ *a good grade on the ~* (*AmE*) | **~ in** ◇ *a ~ in mathematics* | **~ on** ◇ *a ~ on the French Revolution*

2 experiment; medical examination

ADJ. **exhaustive** (*esp. BrE*), **extensive**, **rigorous**, **stringent**, **thorough** | **initial**, **preliminary** | **routine**, **standard** | **statistical** | **empirical**, **experimental** | **field**, **lab** (*informal*), **laboratory** | **successful** | **negative**, **positive** | **medical** | **screening** ◇ *screening ~s for cancer* | **diagnostic** | **forensic** ◇ *Forensic ~s showed that the man had been poisoned.* | **eye**, **sight** (*BrE*) | **hearing** | **blood**, **DNA**, **genetic**, **skin**, **urine** | **dope** (*esp. BrE*), **drug**, **drugs** (*BrE*) | **fitness** | **breath**, **breathalyser/Breathalyzer**™ | **Pap** (*AmE*), **Pap smear** (*AmE*), **smear** (*BrE*) ◇ *a campaign advising women of the need for regular Pap/smear ~s* | **AIDS**, **HIV** | **pregnancy** | **paternity** | **personality**, **psychological**, **psychometric** | **ink-blot**, **Rorschach** | **lie-detector**, **polygraph** | **means** | **flight**, **road**, **safety** | **crash** | **atomic**, **nuclear** | **alpha**, **beta** ◇ *The new system goes into beta ~ this month.*
... OF TESTS **number**, **series** ◇ *She had a series of blood ~s.*
VERB + TEST **have**, **undergo** | **carry out**, **conduct**, **do**, **perform**, **run** ◇ *Rigorous safety ~s are being carried out on the new jet.* | **apply**, **use** ◇ *The judge applied the wrong ~ in coming to his decision.* ◇ *The ~ used in detecting the disease carries its own risks.* | **fail** ◇ *Three athletes were sent home after failing drugs ~s.*
TEST + VERB **take place** | **confirm sth**, **demonstrate sth**, **indicate sth**, **measure sth**, **reveal sth**, **show sth** ◇ *The urine ~ showed some sort of infection.* | **prove negative**, **prove positive** | **come into force** ◇ *The new safety ~ came into force last month.* | **be designed to** ◇ *a ~ designed to detect bowel cancer*
TEST + NOUN **result** ◇ *a negative/positive ~ result* | **data**, **statistics** | **conditions** ◇ *The machine refused to perform correctly under ~ conditions.* | **bed**, **platform** ◇ *The company is using the library as a ~ bed for its new software.* | **range**, **site** ◇ *protesters at nuclear ~ sites* | **facility** | **drive**, **flight**, **run** ◇ *He's taken the car out on a ~ run.* | **driver**, **pilot** | **aircraft**, **car** | **trial** ◇ *The new drink went down well in the ~ trials.* | **methods**, **procedures** | **system** | **performance** | **subject** | **equipment**, **instruments**, **kit**, **machine** | **samples**, **substances** | **strip** ◇ *Dip the ~ strip in the urine sample.* | **programme/program** | **period**, **phase**, **stage** ◇ *The software is still at the ~ stage.* | **ban** ◇ *negotiations on a nuclear ~ ban* | **session** ◇ *Subjects had to attend ten ~ sessions on different days.* | **certificate** (*BrE*) ◇ *The vehicle did not have a current ~ certificate at the time of the accident.* | **case** ◇ *This was the first action taken by a cancer sufferer against a tobacco company, and was seen as a ~ case.*
PREP. **~ for** ◇ *a ~ for diabetes* | **~ on** ◇ *a ~ on the engine*

3 shows how good, strong, effective, etc. sb/sth is

ADJ. **good** | **critical**, **crucial**, **key**, **real**, **supreme**, **true**, **ultimate**, **vital** (*esp. BrE*) ◇ *a real ~ of character* | **serious**, **severe**, **stiff**, **tough** | **simple** | **objective** | **subjective** | **political**
VERB + TEST **pose**, **provide** ◇ *The calls for tax reform pose a severe ~ to the government.* | **put sb/sth to the ~** ◇ *The latest pay dispute has really put her management skills to the ~.* | **face** ◇ *The new president is facing his toughest political ~ so far.*
TEST + NOUN **case**

PHRASES **the acid ~, the litmus ~** (= a way of deciding whether sth is successful or true) ◊ *Whether he would accept a pay cut would be the acid ~ of his loyalty to the company.* | **stand the ~ of time** ◊ *Whether this new technology will stand the ~ of time remains to be seen.*

test verb

1 examine sth to find out if it is working/what it is like

ADV. **adequately, properly** ◊ *The product had not been adequately ~ed before being put on the market.* | **extensively, fully, rigorously, thoroughly** | **systematically** | **periodically, regularly, routinely** ◊ *You should ~ your brakes regularly.* | **independently, individually, separately** | **simultaneously** | **formally** | **successfully** ◊ *The exercise successfully ~ed the procedures for dealing with a serious oil spillage.* | **clinically, empirically, experimentally, scientifically** ◊ *the importance of empirically ~ed research* | **statistically** | **out** ◊ *a good way to ~ out his hypothesis*
VERB + TEST **decide to** ◊ *We decided to ~ the theory experimentally.* | **attempt to, seek to, try to** | **be designed to, be intended to** | **be used to** | **be difficult to** ◊ *It is difficult to ~ a potential cure when a disease is ill-defined.*
PREP. **for** ◊ *Squeeze the fruit to ~ for ripeness.* | **on** ◊ *We only sell products that have not been ~ed on animals.*
PHRASES **get sth ~ed, have sth ~ed** ◊ *I'm having my eyes ~ed this week.* | **~ negative/positive** ◊ *Two of the athletes ~ed positive for illegal drugs.* | **~ sth to the limit** ◊ *The training ~ed his body to the very limit.* | **tried and ~ed** ◊ *tried and ~ed techniques*

2 require all sb's strength, ability, resources, etc.

ADV. **seriously, severely, sorely** ◊ *Neither player was seriously ~ed in the contest.* ◊ *There were times when my temper was sorely ~ed.*

testament noun

ADJ. **fitting** (*esp. BrE*), **good, great, true** | **powerful, remarkable** | **living** ◊ *Adams is a living ~ to the power of following one's dreams.* | **sad** ◊ *The decline of the port is sad ~ to the state of the shipping industry.* | **mute, visible** ◊ *The crumbling ruins bear mute ~ to the ravages of war.*
VERB + TESTAMENT **be, bear** (*esp. BrE*) ◊ *That so many people came is (a) ~ to her powers of persuasion.*
PREP. **~ to** ◊ *The monument is a worthy ~ to the courage of the men who fought in the war.*

testify verb

ADV. **falsely, truthfully** ◊ *The basis for the perjury conviction was he had testified falsely under oath.* | **publicly** | **personally**
VERB + TESTIFY **ask sb to, call sb to, call upon sb to, subpoena sb to** (*esp. AmE*) ◊ *The president's former aides were called to ~ at his trial.* | **compel sb to, force sb to** | **agree to, be prepared to, be willing to** | **refuse to** | **come forward to** ◊ *Several witnesses have come forward to ~ against her.* | **be allowed to** | **be expected to, be scheduled to** | **take the stand to** ◊ *He took the stand to ~ at the trial of his colleague.*
PREP. **against** ◊ *She refused to ~ against her brother.* | **before** ◊ *She was willing to ~ before Congress.* | **for** ◊ *a Mafia member who was prepared to ~ for the authorities* | **to** ◊ *A senior officer testified to the existence of police hit squads.* ◊ *A large number of witnesses testified to the tribunal.*
PHRASES **~ in court, ~ under oath** (*esp. AmE*)

testimony noun

1 formal statement that sth is true

ADJ. **credible, reliable** | **uncorroborated** | **false, perjured** | **sworn** | **oral, written** | **video, videotaped** | **eyewitness, personal, witness** | **expert** | **court, trial** ◊ *a transcript of the trial ~* | **public** (*AmE*) | **congressional, grand jury** (*both AmE*)
VERB + TESTIMONY **hear** | **give, offer, present, provide** | **corroborate** ◊ *Her ~ was corroborated by the other witnesses.* | **undermine** | **coerce, compel** (*both AmE*) ◊ *The government was able to compel his ~.*

PREP. **by your ~** ◊ *He had by his own ~ taken part in the burglary.* | **in ~** ◊ *In ~ before the Crown Court, she described her movements on the day of the murder.* | **~ about** ◊ *Witnesses were called to give ~ about the effects of smoking.* | **~ against** ◊ *The court heard her ~ against the accused.* | **~ before** ◊ *his ~ before a Senate committee*

2 proof

ADJ. **ample, clear, eloquent, powerful, remarkable**
VERB + TESTIMONY **bear, stand as** | **offer, provide**
PREP. **~ to** ◊ *His thick, swollen fingers bore ~ to a lifetime of toil.*

text noun

1 written words

ADJ. **complete, full** ◊ *The newspaper printed the full ~ of the interview.* | **draft** | **final** | **original** | **main** ◊ *The illustrations are printed separately from the main ~.* | **accompanying** ◊ *The catalogue consists of reproductions of the paintings with accompanying ~.* | **electronic, handwritten, printed, written** | **plain** (*computing*) ◊ *Save the file in plain ~ format.*
...OF TEXT **block, body, chunk, line, page, piece, portion** ◊ *Hand symbols in the main body of the ~ cross-refer the reader to the appendices.* ◊ *Use the mouse to move chunks of ~ from place to place.*
VERB + TEXT **create, produce, provide, write** | **edit** | **highlight** | **cut, delete** | **insert, move, paste** | **scan, scan in** | **handle, manipulate, process** ◊ *computer programs that process ~* | **set** | **print** | **publish** | **post** ◊ *I posted the full ~ for free on my site.* | **read** | **transcribe** | **translate**
TEXT + VERB **accompany** ◊ *The photographs are accompanied by ~.*
TEXT + NOUN **file** ◊ *The program allows you to import ~ files.* | **editor** ◊ *one of the best HTML ~ editors available* | **message, messaging** ◊ *The ~ message just said 'Hope 2CU@the party'.* | **box** ◊ *When you point at the icon, a small ~ box appears.* → Special page at COMPUTER

2 book or piece of writing to be studied

ADJ. **basic, introductory** | **key, main, primary, standard** | **canonical, classic** | **authoritative, influential** | **ancient, classical** | **explanatory** | **primary, secondary** ◊ *The book exhibits a close reading of primary ~s as well as scholarly commentaries.* | **recommended, set** (*esp. BrE*) ◊ *Her books appear on lists of recommended ~s in universities.* | **prepared** ◊ *He stood up and began reading from a prepared ~.* | **academic, biblical, dramatic, historical, legal, literary, poetic, religious, sacred, scientific, etc.** ◊ *We're studying dramatic ~s by Mexican playwrights.* | **biology, mathematics, etc.**
VERB + TEXT **read, read from** | **analyse/analyze, deconstruct, interpret, study** | **understand** | **annotate**
TEXT + VERB **contain sth, describe sth, emphasize sth, indicate sth, provide sth, reveal sth, suggest sth**
TEXT + NOUN **analysis**
PREP. **in a/the ~** ◊ *We discussed the use of metaphor in the ~.* | **~ about, ~ on** ◊ *a poetic ~ about growing up in the South.*

textbook noun

ADJ. **basic, elementary, introductory** | **general, standard** ◊ *Do you have the standard ~ on the subject?* | **leading, popular** | **biology, economics, medical, physics, psychology, etc.** | **college** (*esp. AmE*), **school, university** (*esp. BrE*)

textile noun

ADJ. **embroidered, printed, woven** | **cheap, fine** ◊ *a producer of fine cotton ~s* | **cotton, silk, etc.**
TEXTILE + NOUN **business, company, factory, firm, industry, manufacture, manufacturer, manufacturing, mill, trade, worker** | **exports, imports** | **design, designer**
PREP. **in ~s** ◊ *She has a job in ~s.*
PHRASES **the manufacture/production of ~s**

texture *noun*

ADJ. **dense, firm, thick** | **delicate, fine, light, soft** ◇ *Sponge cakes have a light ~.* | **coarse, crumbly, crunchy, gritty, rough** ◇ *the gritty ~ of sand* | **chewy, meaty** ◇ *the chewy ~ of Portobello mushrooms* | **creamy, silky, smooth, velvety** ◇ *It's a pungent little wine with a velvety ~.* | **different, varied** | **interesting, rich** ◇ *She enjoyed the rich ~ of the beer.* | **hair, skin** | **soil** | **surface** ◇ *She pays great attention to the surface ~ of her paintings.* | **visual** ◇ *the movie's stunning visual ~* | **instrumental, musical, orchestral**
VERB + TEXTURE **have** | **feel** | **add, create, give sth** ◇ *I use a styling gel to give ~ to my hair.*
PREP. **in ~** ◇ *The cloth was rough in ~.* | **with a …~** ◇ *a piece of music with a dense choral ~*

thank *verb*

ADV. **gratefully, heartily, profusely, warmly** ◇ *He ~ed her warmly for the meal.* | **sincerely** ◇ *I would like to ~ you all most sincerely.* | **properly** | **graciously, politely** | **personally** | **publicly**
VERB + THANK **must, want to, would like to** ◇ *I wanted to ~ him personally.*
PREP. **for** ◇ *I haven't ~ed Bill for his present yet.*

thankful *adj.*

VERBS **be, feel, seem**
ADV. **extremely, incredibly, really, truly, very** | **eternally, forever** ◇ *I'll be forever ~ to John. He saved my life.* | **just** ◇ *I'm just ~ that my mother never lived to see this.*
PREP. **for** ◇ *We were ~ for the chance to rest.*

thanks *noun*

ADJ. **heartfelt, sincere, warm** | **grateful** (*esp. BrE*) | **personal** ◇ *Please accept my personal ~.* | **special** ◇ *Special ~ to all of you who supported our fund-raising campaign.* | **additional, extra**
VERB + THANKS **express, extend, give, offer** ◇ *We would like to express our warmest ~ for all you've done.* | **owe (sb)** ◇ *I owe you my ~.* | **nod, smile** ◇ *She smiled her ~ as the car drove off.* | **get, receive** ◇ *You'll get little ~ from him for all your trouble.* | **accept** | **deserve** ◇ *Their generosity deserves our grateful ~.*
THANKS + VERB **go to sb** ◇ *Thanks go to Claire Potter for making the hall available to us.*
PREP. **as ~ for, in ~ for** ◇ *He got a bottle of wine in ~ for his cooperation.* | **~ to** ◇ *He gave ~ to God for the safe return of his son.*
PHRASES **a letter of ~, a vote of ~** (*esp. BrE*), **a word of ~ ◇** *The chairperson proposed a vote of ~ to the volunteers.* | *I'd like to say a word of ~ to our hosts.* | **many ~** ◇ *Many ~ for the flowers.* | **~ be to God** ◇ *We were all pulled out alive, ~ be to God.*

thank you *noun*

ADJ. **big, huge, special** | **heartfelt** | **personal** ◇ *I would just like to say a personal ~ to all the people who contributed to this appeal.* | **simple**
VERB + THANK YOU **give, say** ◇ *He didn't even say ~.* ◇ *We said our ~s and goodbyes to the hosts.* | **get**
THANK-YOU + NOUN **card, letter, note** ◇ *He didn't even send a thank-you letter.*
PREP. **~ for** ◇ *She got a special ~ for all her hard work.* | **~ to** ◇ *a big ~ to the hospital staff*

thaw *noun*

ADJ. **slow** | **sudden** | **spring, summer** ◇ *The arctic shore remains frozen until the summer ~.*
THAW + VERB **arrive, begin, come** ◇ *The plants will be ready for use when the spring ~ arrives.*
PREP. **during a/the ~** ◇ *The river often floods during the ~.*

thaw *verb*

ADV. **completely** ◇ *Make sure the meat has ~ed completely*

before cooking. | **partially** | **rapidly, slowly** | **a little** (*figurative*) ◇ *Relations between the two countries ~ed a little after the talks.* | **out** ◇ *Has the meat ~ed out yet?*

theatre (*BrE*) (*AmE* theater) *noun*

1 where you go to see plays, etc. → See also CINEMA

ADJ. **large** | **little, small** | **500-seat, etc.** | **crowded, packed** ◇ *The ~ was packed for the opening night.* | **community, local, provincial** (*esp. BrE*), **regional** | **off-Broadway, West End** (= central London) | **open-air** | **purpose-built** (*BrE*) ◇ *The city's first purpose-built ~ is nearing completion.* | **puppet** ◇ *The pier has a unique little puppet ~.* | **movie** (*AmE*) ◇ *The documentary opens tomorrow in movie ~s nationwide.* | **drive-in** (*AmE*) | **darkened** (*AmE*) | **art-house** (*AmE*) | **home** (*AmE*)
VERB + THEATRE/THEATER **go to, visit** ◇ *I haven't been to the ~ for a long time.* | **enter, leave**
THEATRE/THEATER + NOUN **seat, ticket** | **design, production** | **audience** | **manager, owner** | **scene** ◇ *the Toronto ~ scene*
PREP. **at a/the ~** ◇ *We were at the ~ last night.* | **in a/the ~** ◇ *There's a bar in the ~.*

2 drama

ADJ. **good, great** ◇ *He writes the sort of dialogue that makes good ~.* | **live** | **commercial, professional** | **amateur** (*esp. BrE*) | **fringe** (*BrE*), **repertory** ◇ *There was some good fringe ~ at the festival.* | **classical, contemporary, experimental, modern, popular** | **dance** | **music, musical** | **street** ◇ *We saw some good street ~ while we were in Paris.* | **children's, community, youth** (*esp. BrE*) | **Elizabethan, Jacobean, etc.** | **political** (*figurative*) ◇ *His speech was a great piece of political ~.*
… OF THEATRE/THEATER **piece**
VERB + THEATRE/THEATER **study** ◇ *He is studying Greek ~.*
THEATRE/THEATER + NOUN **studies** | **critic** | **piece** (*esp. BrE*) ◇ *an hour-long ~ piece*

3 work of acting in/producing plays

VERB + THEATRE/THEATER **be in, work in** | **go into** ◇ *He wants to go into the ~ when he finishes university.*
THEATRE/THEATER + NOUN **director, impresario** (*esp. BrE*), **producer** | **company, group, troupe**

4 (*BrE*) in a hospital

ADJ. **operating**
VERB + THEATRE **take to** ◇ *He's already been taken to ~ for the operation.*
THEATRE + NOUN **nurse, sister** | **staff**
PREP. **in (the) ~** ◇ *She was in the operating ~ for two hours.*

theft *noun*

ADJ. **petty** | **grand** (*AmE*) | **attempted** (*esp. BrE*) ◇ *the crime of attempted ~.* | **large-scale, outright, wholesale** ◇ *the wholesale ~ of copyrighted music* | **retail** | **auto** (*AmE*), **car, cattle, laptop, etc.** | **data** | **ID, identity** ◇ *the potential victims of identity ~*
… OF THEFTS **series, spate** (*esp. BrE*), **string** ◇ *a spate of ~s over the Christmas period*
PREP. **~ from** ◇ *He is accused of ~ from his employer.* | **~ of** ◇ *She admitted the ~ of three pairs of shoes.*
→ Note at CRIME (for verbs)

theme *noun*

ADJ. **basic, central, dominant, important, key, main, major, overriding, underlying** | **broad, general, overall** | **common, popular, universal** ◇ *universal ~s of love and loneliness* | **consistent, constant, familiar, favourite/favorite, recurrent, recurring** | **related** | **overarching, unifying** | **contemporary** | **historical, religious, etc.** | **campaign, conference, research** | **musical** ◇ *The movie's haunting musical ~ stayed in my head for days.*
VERB + THEME **address, continue, develop, discuss, examine, explore, have, introduce, reflect** ◇ *His later novels develop the ~ of alienation.* | **warm to** (*esp. BrE*) ◇ *'Our work', he continued, warming to his ~, 'will be a milestone in scientific history.'* | **identify**
THEME + VERB **emerge** ◇ *Several familiar ~s emerged from the*

discussion. | **run through sth** ◊ *The same ~s run through all her novels.*
THEME + NOUN **music, song** (*esp. AmE*), **tune** (*esp. BrE*) | **park, pub** (*BrE*), **restaurant** | **party**
PREP. **on the ~ of** ◊ *He gave a talk on the ~ of teenage unemployment.*
PHRASES **variations on a ~** ◊ *Most of the essays appear to be variations on a few central ~s.*

theology noun

ADJ. **dogmatic, liberal, traditional** | **moral, natural, practical, systematic** | **biblical** | **liberation** ◊ *Latin American liberation ~* | **academic** ◊ *the rarified world of academic ~* | **medieval** | **eastern, western** | **Christian, Islamic, Jewish, etc.** | **Catholic, Orthodox, Protestant, etc.** | **ecumenical**
→ Note at SUBJECT (for verbs and nouns)

theoretical adj.

VERBS **be** | **remain**
ADV. **highly** | **merely** | **purely** ◊ *This research is purely ~.* | **largely**

theory noun

ADJ. **complete, unified** ◊ *a grand unified ~ of the physical forces governing matter* | **general** | **coherent** | **current, modern, new** | **classical** ◊ *Keynes misinterpreted the classical ~ of interest.* | **pet** ◊ *One of her pet theories is that people who restrict their calorie intake live longer.* | **alternative, conflicting** | **abstract** ◊ *His comments are just abstract ~ and show little understanding of the realities of the situation.* | **economic, legal, linguistic, literary, political, scientific, social, etc.** | **critical** | **feminist, Marxist, postmodern, structuralist, etc.** ◊ *Current feminist ~ consists of several different trends.* ◊ *the dominant strand of postmodern ~* | **chaos, evolutionary, game, number, probability, quantum, string, etc.** | **conspiracy** ◊ *a conspiracy ~ about the princess's death*
...OF THEORIES **set** ◊ *Each school has its own set of theories.*
VERB + THEORY **have, hold** | **advance, develop, formulate, present, produce, propose, put forward** | **work on** ◊ *Police are working on the ~ that the murderer was known to the family.* | **refute, reject** | **accept** | **confirm, prove, support** | **disprove** | **challenge, test** | **apply, use**
THEORY + VERB **hold sth, suggest sth** | **explain sth, predict sth** | **be based on sth**
PREP. **in ~** ◊ *In ~, these machines should last for ten years.* | **~ about** ◊ *He has a ~ about why dogs walk in circles before going to sleep.*
PHRASES **put (the) ~ into practice, ~ and practice** ◊ *the distinction/relationship between ~ and practice*

therapist noun

ADJ. **experienced** | **certified** (*AmE*), **licensed** (*AmE*), **qualified, trained** | **family** | **beauty** (*esp. BrE*), **comple-mentary** (*BrE*), **massage** (*esp. AmE*), **occupational, physical** (*AmE*) (**physiotherapist** in *BrE*), **sex, speech** | **behavioural/behavioral, cognitive**
→ Note at DOCTOR, JOB

therapy noun

ADJ. **alternative, complementary** | **occupational, physical** (*AmE*) (**physiotherapy** in *BrE*) | **drug, gene, hormone, radiation** | **hormone replacement** | **art, aversion, relaxation, shock, etc.** | **retail** (*humorous*) ◊ *She indulged in a bit of retail ~.* | **speech** | **behaviour/behavior, behav-ioural/behavioral, cognitive** ◊ *the efficacy of cognitive behavioural/behavioral ~* | **family, group, individual** ◊ *They discuss their problems in group ~ sessions.*
...OF THERAPY **course**
VERB + THERAPY **need, require, seek** | **be given, have, receive, undergo** ◊ *He will have to have speech ~.* | **be in, go into** ◊ *I went into ~ because my doctor suggested it.*
THERAPY + NOUN **group, session**
PHRASES **a form of ~** ◊ *the use of hypnosis as a form of ~*

thermometer noun

ADJ. **accurate** | **clinical** | **digital, mercury** | **ear, oral, rectal** | **candy** (*AmE*), **sugar** (*BrE*) | **meat** ◊ *Check that the roast is cooked right through, using a meat ~.* | **oven**
VERB + THERMOMETER **insert, place in, stick in** (*informal*) ◊ *He stuck a ~ in her mouth.* | **read**
THERMOMETER + VERB **measure sth, read sth** ◊ *If the ~ reads 98.6°F, then you don't have a fever.*
THERMOMETER + NOUN **reading**
PREP. **on a/the ~** ◊ *the reading on the ~*

thesis noun

1 part of a university/college degree

ADJ. **doctoral, honors** (*AmE*), **MA, Master's, MSc, PhD, senior** (*AmE*), **etc.** | **research** | **unpublished**
VERB + THESIS **do, work on, write, write up** | **complete, finish** | **submit** | **present** ◊ *He presented this ~ for his PhD.* | **publish**
THESIS + NOUN **project** (*AmE*), **research, topic** | **work** ◊ *her ~ work on skin cancers* | **statement** (*AmE*) | **defense** (*AmE*) ◊ *Many departments require their students to do a ~ defense.* | **committee** (*AmE*) ◊ *Three Caltech professors served on my ~ committee.* | **adviser** (*AmE*) ◊ *her ~ adviser at MIT*
PREP. **in a/the ~** ◊ *research presented in a ~* | **~ about, ~ on** ◊ *He wrote a doctoral ~ on set theory.*

2 statement of an idea/a theory

ADJ. **basic, central, fundamental, general, main, principal** | **controversial, provocative**
VERB + THESIS **prove, support** ◊ *The results of the experiment support his central ~.* | **disprove, undermine** | **advance, present** ◊ *He advanced the ~ that too much choice was burdensome to people.* | **develop, illustrate** | **challenge, reject** | **accept** | **defend**
PREP. **~ about** ◊ *a ~ about the effects of new technology on skills*

thick adj.

1 of solid things/growing things

VERBS **be, feel, look, seem**
ADV. **extremely, fairly, very, etc.** ◊ *Use fairly ~ wads of newspaper.*

2 of liquid

VERBS **be, look, seem** | **become, get** ◊ *The paint is getting too ~. I'll have to thin it down.*
ADV. **extremely, fairly, very, etc.**

3 of fog/smoke/air

VERBS **be, feel, look, seem** | **become, grow** ◊ *The air had grown ~ and smoky.*
ADV. **extremely, fairly, very, etc.**
PREP. **with** ◊ *The air was ~ with dust.* ◊ *The atmosphere was ~ with tension.* (*figurative*)

thief noun

ADJ. **would-be** ◊ *The alarm is usually sufficient to deter a would-be ~.* | **common, petty** | **professional** | **master** | **opportunist, sneak** (*both BrE*) | **convicted, suspected** | **car, identity, jewel, etc.**
...OF THIEVES **gang**
VERB + THIEF **catch**
THIEF + VERB **snatch sth** (*esp. BrE*), **steal sth, take sth** ◊ *A ~ snatched her handbag containing her wages.* | **escape with sth** (*esp. BrE*), **get away with sth, make off with sth** | **break in, break into sth** | **strike** (*esp. BrE*) ◊ *The ~ struck while the family were out.*

thigh noun

ADJ. **fat, flabby, huge, thick** (*AmE*) | **muscular, powerful, strong, sturdy** | **firm, hard, toned** | **slender, slim** | **bare, naked** | **inner** | **lower, upper**
THIGH + NOUN **bone, muscle** | **injury, strain** (*BrE*)

thin *adj.*

1 of solid things: not thick

VERBS **be, feel, look, seem** | **become, wear** ◊ *The fabric was wearing ~.* ◊ *That joke is wearing a little ~.* (*figurative*)
ADV. **extremely, fairly, very, etc.** | **incredibly** | **a little, slightly, etc.**

2 not fat

VERBS **be, look** | **become, get, grow** | **stay** ◊ *How do you manage to stay so ~?*
ADV. **extremely, fairly, very, etc.** ◊ *She's tall and rather ~.* | **dangerously, painfully** ◊ *The old horse was painfully ~.*

3 of liquids

VERBS **be, look, seem** ◊ *The paint looks a little ~.* | **become, get** ◊ *Be careful that the mixture doesn't get too ~.*
ADV. **extremely, fairly, very, etc.** | **a little, slightly, etc.**

4 of poor quality

VERBS **be, seem** ◊ *The evidence seems awfully ~.* | **become, grow, run** ◊ *My patience is running ~.* | **remain**
ADV. **extremely, fairly, very, etc.** | **dangerously, perilously** ◊ *The team is dangerously ~ at wide receiver.*
PHRASES **spread sth (too) ~, stretch sth (too) ~** ◊ *You can spread yourself too ~, often leading to poor choices.* ◊ *His management team was stretched ~.* | **~ on the ground** (*BrE*) ◊ *Jobs were still a bit ~ on the ground* (= not many were available). | **~ on top** ◊ *He's getting a little ~ on top* (= losing his hair).

thing *noun*

1 used instead of the name of an object

ADJ. **basic, essential** ◊ *I need to buy a few basic ~s like bread and milk.*
VERB + THING **make** ◊ *He makes ~s out of wood.*

2 things objects/clothing/tools

ADJ. **breakfast, lunch, etc.** (*all esp. BrE*) ◊ *He hadn't washed up the dinner ~s yet.* | **swimming, tennis, etc.** (*all esp. BrE*)
VERB + THINGS **get together, pack** ◊ *Come on kids, get your ~s together—we're going.* | **put on, take off** ◊ *Hang on a second—I'll just take off my painting ~s* (= clothes). | **put away** | **clear away, clear up, stow** (*esp. AmE*), **tidy away** (*esp. BrE*), **tidy up** (*esp. BrE*) ◊ *Clear your painting ~s* (= materials) *away.*

3 a thing (used with negatives) anything

VERB + A THING **hear, know, notice, see** ◊ *I can't see a ~ without my glasses.* | **miss** ◊ *I'm going to arrive early because I don't want to miss a ~.* | **do** ◊ *She's tricked you, and you can't do a ~ about it.* | **eat** ◊ *I haven't eaten a ~ all day.* | **say** ◊ *Nobody said a ~ when he appeared with a wig on.* | **mean** ◊ *Fame and fortune don't mean a ~ if you don't have happiness.*

4 fact/event/situation/action

ADJ. **good, great, positive** ◊ *It's a good ~ you remembered to turn off the gas!* ◊ *The best ~ would be to apologize straight away.* ◊ *If she works hard she's capable of great ~s.* ◊ *Try to look on your rejection as a positive ~.* | **beautiful, cool** (*informal*), **lovely** (*esp. BrE*), **nice, wonderful** | **bad, negative** ◊ *Too much studying can be a bad ~.* ◊ *It's no bad ~ to express your anger.* | **appalling** (*esp. BrE*), **awful, dreadful, horrible, terrible** ◊ *That was a horrible ~ to say to her.* | **sad** | **amazing, curious, exciting, extraordinary, funny, interesting, odd, remarkable, startling, strange, striking, surprising, weird** ◊ *The amazing ~ is, he wouldn't accept any money!* | **frightening** | **annoying** | **foolish, ridiculous, silly, stupid** ◊ *I admit it was a foolish ~ to do.* | **clever** (*esp. BrE*), **smart** (*esp. AmE*) ◊ *That wasn't a very smart ~ to do!* | **big, crucial, important, key, main, vital** ◊ *The key ~ is to remain calm.* | **little, the slightest, small, trivial** ◊ *I give thanks for every little ~.* ◊ *He loses his temper at the slightest ~.* ◊ *It's such a small ~ to ask.* | **easy, simple** ◊ *Apologizing is never the easiest ~ to do.* | **difficult, hard** | **brave, dangerous, risky** | **sure** (*esp. AmE*) ◊ *His new film seems like a sure ~* (= a certain success). | **natural** ◊ *Entertaining people is the most natural ~ in the world for her.* | **close** (*esp. BrE*), **close-run** (*BrE*) ◊ *I managed to get on the train, but it was a close ~* (= I almost missed it). | **rare** | **everyday** ◊ *She helped with the everyday ~s like shopping and cooking.* | **usual** ◊ *I did my usual ~ of losing my keys.* | **nearest, next-best** ◊ *He's the nearest ~ to a movie star I've ever met.* ◊ *I wanted to be a musician, but teaching music is the next-best ~.* | **first** ◊ *She said the first ~ that came into her head.* | **next** ◊ *What's the next ~ you want me to do?* | **last** ◊ *The last ~ she wanted was to upset her parents.* | **real** ◊ *It's just a practice, not the real ~.* | **the whole** ◊ *Let's forget the whole ~.*
... OF THINGS **loads** (*esp. BrE*), **lots, plenty, tons** ◊ *I have loads of ~s to do today.* ◊ *There are plenty of ~s to say about it.*
VERB + THING **do** ◊ *He has a funny way of doing ~s.* ◊ *It's impossible to get ~s done when you're taking care of a baby.* | **make up, say** ◊ *Who's been saying ~s about me?* | **be hearing/imagining/seeing** ◊ *There's nobody at the door—you must have been imagining ~s!*
THING + VERB **go on, happen, occur** ◊ *There are some weird ~s going on in that house.* ◊ *A funny ~ happened to me this morning…*
PREP. **~ about** ◊ *The best ~ about Alan is he's always honest.*
PHRASES **among other ~s** ◊ *Among other ~s, I have to deal with mail and keep the accounts.* | **have better ~s to do** ◊ *I've better ~s to do than stand here chatting all day!* | **kind/ sort of ~** ◊ *They go canoeing, climbing, that sort of ~.* | **know/learn/teach sb a ~ or two** ◊ *Jack knows a ~ or two about kids—he has five.* | **the next big ~** ◊ *Advertising on blogs is going to be the next big ~.* | **no such ~** ◊ *There's no such ~ as ghosts* (= they don't exist). | **one ~ leads to another** ◊ *One ~ led to another and we ended up dating.* | **such a ~/a ~ like that** ◊ *People defraud their companies every day, but Mike would never do such a ~!* | **a ~ of the past** ◊ *Books may one day become a ~ of the past.*

5 things general situation, as it affects sb

VERB + THINGS **think over/through** ◊ *She's taken a few days off to think ~s over.* | **look at, see** ◊ *Try to look at ~s from my point of view.* | **discuss, talk over, talk through** ◊ *We arranged to meet and talk ~s over.* | **explain** | **accept** ◊ *You should suggest changes, rather than accept ~s as they are.* | **change** | **arrange, deal with, fix, handle, look after** (*esp. BrE*), **run, sort out, take care of** ◊ *I want to get ~s sorted out before I go away.* ◊ *Who's going to take care of ~s while you're away?* | **straighten out** | **work out** ◊ *I have to work ~s out my own way.* | **mess up, spoil** | **complicate** ◊ *Sorry, I didn't mean to complicate ~s.* | **patch up** ◊ *They patched ~s up a week after their quarrel.* | **speed along/up** ◊ *It might speed ~s up if you call them.* | **hold up, slow down**
THINGS + VERB **stand** ◊ *As ~s stand at present, he seems certain to win.* | **be going** ◊ *He asked me how ~s were going.* | **change** | **go according to plan, go to plan, go well, work, work out** ◊ *I just don't know if ~s are going to work out.* | **get better, improve, look up** ◊ *We were in trouble but now ~s are looking up.* | **look bright, look good, look promising, look rosy** ◊ *There was a week to go to the deadline and ~s were looking good.* | **look bleak, look grim** ◊ *Things looked bleak for the future of the factory.* | **be in a mess, get into a mess, get out of control, get out of hand, go wrong** | **get worse, go downhill** | **turn out** ◊ *I'm sure ~s will turn out OK.* | **come to a head** ◊ *Things came to a head when money was found to be missing from the account.* | **get to sb** ◊ *Try not to let ~s get to you.*
PHRASES **all ~s being equal, other ~s being equal** ◊ *All other ~s being equal, the bigger fighter should win.* | **all ~s considered** ◊ *All ~s considered, I think we've done a good job.* | **get/keep ~s going, get/keep ~s moving** ◊ *They hired temporary staff to keep ~s going over the summer.* | **get ~s straight, put ~s straight, set ~s straight** ◊ *I marched into his office to get a few ~s straight.* | **get ~s under control, have ~s under control, keep ~s under control** ◊ *He offered to help, but she assured him she had ~s under control.* | **have ~s on your mind** ◊ *We chatted about school, but I could tell she had other ~s on her mind.* | **let ~s slide, let ~s slip** ◊ *She'd started the term studying hard, but now was beginning to let ~s slip.* | **let ~s run their course, let ~s happen, let ~s take their course** ◊ *Don't worry about it—just let ~s take*

their course. | **make ~s better, easier, difficult, worse, etc.**
◇ *Her apology only served to make ~s worse.* | **put ~s right** ◇
He apologized, and asked for a chance to put ~s right. | **~s to
come** ◇ *The pay cut was just a taste of ~s to come.*

6 what is needed/socially acceptable

ADJ. **proper, right** ◇ *He did the right ~ and went back to his
wife.* ◇ *I did all the right ~s but I couldn't get the engine to
start.* | **wrong** ◇ *She always manages to say the wrong ~.* |
logical, obvious, prudent, sensible ◇ *Calling a doctor
seemed the logical ~ to do.* | **decent, done** (*esp. BrE*) |
honourable/honorable ◇ *He did the decent ~ and resigned.*
◇ *It's not the done ~ to ask someone how much they earn.* |
very ◇ *Iced tea—the very ~!*
VERB + THING **do** | **say**
PHRASES **just the ~, not quite the ~** ◇ *It wouldn't be quite the
~ to turn up in running gear.*

7 a person/an animal

ADJ. **little** ◇ *The baby's a pretty little ~.* | **pretty, sweet** ◇ *Abby
is just the sweetest little ~!* | **old, young** | **silly** | **poor** ◇ *You
must be starving, you poor ~!*

think *noun*

ADJ. **hard** (*esp. BrE*), **long** ◇ *I've had a long, hard ~ about it.*
VERB + THINK **have**
PREP. **~ about**

think *verb*

1 have an opinion

ADV. **really** | **personally** ◇ *I personally ~ it's all been a lot of
fuss over nothing.* | **honestly, seriously** ◇ *Did you honestly ~
I would agree to that?* | **never, sometimes** ◇ *I never thought
you would carry out your threat.* | **differently, otherwise** ◇
That's my opinion, but you might ~ otherwise.
VERB + THINK **be inclined to** ◇ *I'm inclined to ~ we've been a
little harsh on her.*
PREP. **about** ◇ *I still don't know what he really ~s about it.* | **of**
◇ *What did you ~ of the movie?*

2 have an idea

ADV. **suddenly**
PREP. **of** ◇ *I suddenly thought of a way I could help.*

3 consider/reflect

ADV. **carefully, deeply, hard, long and hard, seriously** ◇ *She
thought long and hard before accepting his offer.* | **fast** |
clearly, rationally ◇ *He seemed to have lost the ability to ~
rationally.* | **frantically** ◇ *What can I do now? he thought
frantically.* | **bitterly, dully, glumly, grimly, irritably,
miserably** | **ruefully, wistfully, wryly** | **again** ◇ *You really
should ~ again about that.* | **twice** ◇ *You should ~ twice
about employing someone you've never met.*
VERB + THINK **dread to, hate to, shudder to** ◇ *I hate to ~ what
would have happened if we hadn't arrived.*
PREP. **about** ◇ *Think about what you are going to do next.* | **of**
◇ *I often ~ of Jane.*
PHRASES **not ~ straight** ◇ *The drugs were affecting her and she
couldn't ~ straight.* | **~ big** ◇ *You need to ~ big if you want to
run this business.*

thinker *noun*

ADJ. **brilliant, great** ◇ *Einstein was one of the world's greatest
~s.* | **influential, leading** | **deep, profound, serious** | **big**
(*esp. AmE*) | **clear, logical** | **quick** | **creative, original** |
critical, free, independent | **contemporary, modern** |
19th-century, classical, medieval, etc. | **strategic** |
political, religious, scientific, etc. | **conservative, liberal,
radical, etc.** | **Christian, feminist, western, etc.**
PREP. **~ on** ◇ *a leading ~ on constitutional law*

thinking *noun*

1 using your mind to think

ADJ. **deep, hard, serious** ◇ *This topic requires a lot of deep ~.* |
good ◇ *Yes, I'll email her instead—that's good ~ (= a good
idea).* | **clear, logical, rational** | **muddled** (*esp. BrE*) | **quick**
| **forward** ◇ *The school would have made better use of the
money with a little forward ~.* | **positive** | **abstract,**

analytical, critical | **creative, independent, innovative,
original** | **lateral** | **wishful** ◇ *His claims to be a millionaire
are just wishful ~.*
... OF THINKING **piece** (*esp. BrE*) ◇ *a brilliant piece of lateral ~*
VERB + THINKING **do** ◇ *We have some hard ~ to do before we
agree to the plan.* | **apply, use** ◇ *The book shows you how to
apply critical ~ to your studies.* | **encourage, promote,
stimulate** ◇ *She believes in encouraging creative ~ in the
classroom.* ◇ *We hope that her book will stimulate ~ about
this subject.*
PREP. **~ behind** ◇ *It was difficult to see what the ~ was behind
their eventual decision.*

2 opinion

ADJ. **contemporary, current, modern** | **fresh, new** |
conventional, old, traditional | **divergent** | **government**
(*esp. BrE*) ◇ *The latest announcement marks a major shift in
government ~.* | **Labour, Republican, etc.** | **economic,
historical, political, scientific, etc.** ◇ *Traditional educa-
tional ~ placed importance on learning by rote.* | **feminist,
socialist, etc.** | **military, strategic**
VERB + THINKING **develop, influence, shape** | **clarify, explain**
| **change** ◇ *They are unlikely to have changed their ~ so soon.*
| **dominate** ◇ *His writings on motorized warfare dominated
strategic ~ in the 1930s.*
PREP. **in... ~** ◇ *contemporary trends in feminist ~* | **~ about,
~ on** ◇ *What is the current party ~ on welfare benefits?*
PHRASES **a shift in sb's ~** ◇ *There's been a shift in government
~ on genetically modified food.* | **to sb's way of ~** (= in sb's
opinion) ◇ *To my way of ~, it would just be a massive waste
of money.*

third *noun*

ADJ. **first** | **middle** | **final, last** ◇ *the last ~ of the novel* |
remaining | **bottom, lower** | **top, upper** ◇ *Most of the
students' scores were in the upper ~ of the range.*
VERB + THIRD **divide sth into** ◇ *He divided the money into ~s.*
PREP. **~ of** ◇ *Over a ~ of sales were made over the Internet.*
PHRASES **about a ~, almost a ~, at least a ~, over a ~** ◇ *Over
a ~ of people questioned said they would consider cosmetic
surgery.* | **between a ~ and a half, a ~ to (a) half** ◇ *The
discount is a ~ to a half of the full price.*

thirst *noun*

1 desire to drink

ADJ. **great, intense, raging, terrible, unquenchable**
VERB + THIRST **quench, slake** (*literary*) | **die of** | **work up** ◇
After walking five miles, they had worked up a great ~.

2 strong desire

ADJ. **great, insatiable, unquenchable** ◇ *He has an
unquenchable ~ for knowledge.*
VERB + THIRST **have** | **satisfy**
PREP. **~ for**

thought *noun*

1 sth that you think

ADJ. **comforting, good, happy, pleasant, positive** ◇ *It was a
comforting ~ that at least her father hadn't suffered.* | *Before
going on stage, I breathe deeply and think positive ~s.* |
**anxious, awful, bad, black, dark, depressing, disturbing,
evil, gloomy, horrible, negative, sad, scary, sobering,
terrible** ◇ *A disturbing ~ suddenly struck me.* | **confused,
crazy, strange** | **interesting, intriguing** | **original** ◇ *This is
hardly an original ~.* | **first, immediate, initial** ◇ *My
immediate ~ was that he must be joking.* | **final** ◇ *Do you
have any final ~s?* | **sudden** | **random** ◇ *Let me share a few
random ~s with you.* | **fleeting, passing** | **intrusive** |
suicidal ◇ *patients that are suffering from depression and
suicidal ~s* | **conscious** | **unspoken** | **waking** ◇ *She occupied
all his waking ~s.* | **inner, innermost, private**
VERB + THOUGHT **have, think** ◇ *I've just had a ~ (= an idea).* ◇
He remained aloof, thinking his own ~s. | **have, hear, know**
◇ *Let me have your ~s on the report.* | **express, share, write**

down | collect, gather ◇ *She paused to collect her ~s before speaking.* | clear ◇ *He shook his head to clear his ~s.* | read ◇ *She often seems to know what I'm thinking, as though she can read my ~s.* | interrupt | brush aside, brush away, push aside, push away, push from your mind, push out of your mind ◇ *An image of his boss came into his mind, but he brushed the ~ aside.* | dread, not be able to bear, not like, not relish ◇ *She said she couldn't bear the ~ of living alone in the house.* ◇ *I don't like the ~ of you walking home alone.*
THOUGHT + VERB **come into sb's head, come into sb's mind, come to sb, cross sb's mind, enter sb's head, enter sb's mind, hit sb, occur to sb, pop into sb's head, pop into sb's mind, strike sb** ◇ *The ~ crossed my mind that Jim might know the answer.* ◇ *Such a ~ never entered my head.* | **flash through sb's mind, go through sb's mind, pass through sb's mind, race through sb's mind, run through sb's mind** ◇ *All kinds of ~s raced through my mind.* | **sb's ~s turn to sth** ◇ *My ~s turned to home.* | **sb's ~s drift back to** ◇ *Her ~s drifted back to that night.*
PREP. **~ about** ◇ *He lay there thinking gloomy ~s about life and death.* | **~ of** ◇ *He shuddered at the ~ of going to the dentist.* | **~ on** ◇ *They asked him what his ~s were on the government's announcement.*
PHRASES **just a ~** ◇ *Would Mark be able to help? It's just a ~.* | **keep your ~s to yourself** ◇ *He's not the kind of man to keep his ~s to himself.* | **the mere ~ of sth, the very ~ of sth** ◇ *The mere ~ of lice makes my head itch.*

2 process/act of thinking

ADJ. **careful, proper** (*esp. BrE*), **serious** ◇ *You should give the offer serious ~.* | **deep, profound** | **little** ◇ *He gave little ~ to the impact of his actions on his family.* | **coherent** ◇ *He was so upset, he was incapable of coherent ~.* | **logical, rational** | **analytical, critical** | **abstract** | **creative** | **free, independent, original** | **conscious** ◇ *My job is so repetitive, it does not require much conscious ~.* | **fresh** ◇ *We have to give the matter fresh ~.* | **second** ◇ *I accepted the offer without a second ~.*
VERB + THOUGHT **give sb/sth, spare (sb)** ◇ *I've given the matter careful ~.* ◇ *Don't give it another ~* (= to tell sb not to worry after they have said they are sorry). ◇ *Spare a ~ for us—we'll be working through the night to finish the report.* | **direct, turn** ◇ *I tried to turn my ~s to pleasanter things.* | **provoke** ◇ *The article was intended to provoke ~.* | **be deep in, be lost in** ◇ *She was deep in ~ and didn't hear me call her.*
THOUGHT + VERB **go into sth** ◇ *Not enough ~ has gone into this essay.*
THOUGHT + NOUN **pattern, process** ◇ *I couldn't see what ~ processes led him to that conclusion.* | **experiment** ◇ *A simple ~ experiment may serve to illustrate my point.* | **bubble** ◇ *I can see the comic ~ bubble forming over your head.*
PREP. **without ~** ◇ *They had acted rashly, without ~.*
PHRASES **after a moment's ~** ◇ *After a moment's ~, I accepted his offer.* | **freedom of ~** ◇ *The constitution guarantees freedom of ~ and belief.* | **a line of ~, a mode of ~, a train of ~** ◇ *That line of ~ can only lead to one conclusion.* ◇ *He hesitated, as though he had lost his train of ~.* | **with no ~ for sth** ◇ *He ran into the burning house with no ~ for his own life.*

3 ideas

ADJ. **modern** | **19th-century, etc.** | **Eastern, Western** | **intellectual, philosophical, religious, scientific** | **economic, political** | **Christian, feminist, liberal, socialist, etc.**
THOUGHT + NOUN **crime** (*figurative*) | **police** (*figurative*) ◇ *They accused their opponents of being 'politically correct ~ police'.*
PHRASES **a school of ~** ◇ *They belong to different schools of ~.* | **a strand of ~** ◇ *three different strands of scientific ~*

4 kindness

ADJ. **kind** (*esp. BrE*), **nice** ◇ *Thank you for the flowers—it was a very kind ~.*

thrash *verb*

1 hit sb many times

ADV. **soundly** ◇ *That boy deserves to be soundly ~ed!*
PREP. **with** ◇ *He ~ed the poor servant with his stick.*

2 move your arms and legs in an uncontrolled way

ADV. **violently, wildly** | **about** (*esp. BrE*), **around** ◇ *The cow fell on its side and ~ed about wildly.*

3 (*esp. BrE*) defeat sb easily in a game

ADV. **comprehensively, soundly, thoroughly** ◇ *The visiting side were soundly ~ed.*

thread *noun*

1 piece of cotton, etc.

ADJ. **strong** | **delicate** (*usually figurative*), **fine, fragile** (*usually figurative*), **thin** ◇ *Our lives hang by a fragile ~.* | **loose** | **matching** | **cotton, gold, silk, etc.** | **embroidery, sewing** | **warp, weft**
...OF THREAD **length, piece**
VERB + THREAD **spin** | **pull** ◇ *You've pulled a ~ in your sweater.* | **cut**
PHRASES **hanging by a ~** (*often figurative*) ◇ *The player's career is hanging by a ~ after this latest injury to his knee.* | **needle and ~**

2 connection between ideas, parts of a story, etc.

ADJ. **central, main** | **common, connecting** | **consistent, continuous** | **narrative, plot** | **loose** ◇ *Apart from one or two loose ~s, the police now had the complete picture of what happened.*
VERB + THREAD **have** ◇ *These stories have no real common ~.* | **follow, trace** ◇ *I found it hard to follow the main ~ of his argument.* | **find** ◇ *Police have not been able to find a common ~ linking the victims.* | **lose** ◇ *The speaker lost his ~ halfway through the talk.* | **keep** ◇ *She struggled against all the interruptions to keep the ~ of her argument.* | **draw together, pick up, pull together, weave** ◇ *The author eventually picks up the various ~s of the plot and weaves them into a masterly conclusion.*
THREAD + VERB **run through sth** ◇ *A continuous ~ runs through all the versions of the legend.* | **connect, link** | **emerge** ◇ *On studying the different historians' accounts, common ~s emerge.* | **unravel** ◇ *As the movie progresses, the ~s of the plot slowly begin to unravel.*

3 series of connected messages

ADJ. **comment, discussion**
VERB + THREAD **open, start**

threat *noun*

1 expression of intention to do harm/punish

ADJ. **dire, terrible** ◇ *Despite dire ~s of violence from extremist groups, the protest passed off peacefully.* | **empty, idle** ◇ *The kids took no notice of the teacher's idle ~s.* | **credible** | **implied, veiled** ◇ *The company's pay offer was accompanied by thinly veiled ~s if it was rejected.* | **explicit** | **physical, violent** | **verbal** | **bomb, death, suicide**
VERB + THREAT **issue, make, utter** | **receive** | **carry out** ◇ *It's unwise to make ~s that you cannot carry out.* | **lift, withdraw** ◇ *Teachers have lifted their ~ of strike action.* | **give in to** ◇ *The government refused to give in to the hijackers' ~s.*
PREP. **~ against** ◇ *The accused made death ~s against a notable politician.*

2 possible danger

ADJ. **big, considerable, dangerous, deadly, grave, great, major, real, serious, significant** | **main** | **growing, increasing** | **constant, continual, ever-present, permanent** | **new** | **renewed** ◇ *The national park is under renewed ~ from road-building schemes.* | **direct, immediate, imminent** ◇ *The opposition presents no immediate ~ to the government.* | **insidious** | **long-term, short-term** | **possible, potential** | **apparent, perceived** | **external** ◇ *The government was faced with internal rebellion as well as external ~s.* | **physical** | **political** | **environmental, health** | **military, nuclear, security, terror, terrorist**

VERB + THREAT **be, constitute, pose, present, represent** ◇ *the environmental ~ posed by oil spillages* | **consider sth (as), perceive sth as, regard sth as, see sth as, view sth as** ◇ *Translators do not yet perceive computers as a ~ to their livelihood.* | **address, face, meet** | **reduce** | **counter, eliminate**
THREAT + NOUN **assessment, level**
PREP. **under ~** ◇ *Many wild plants are under ~ of extinction.* | **~ from** ◇ *the ~ from overfishing* | **~ of** ◇ *a ~ of violence* | **~ to** ◇ *The junta reacted violently to the perceived ~ to its authority.*

threaten *verb*

1 warn sb that you may hurt, kill or punish them
ADV. **publicly** | **personally, physically** ◇ *He says he was physically ~ed in an attempt to get him to sign over his rights.* | **repeatedly** ◇ *She had repeatedly ~ed to commit suicide.* | **allegedly, reportedly**
PREP. **with** ◇ *She ~ed him with a gun.*
PHRASES **feel ~ed** ◇ *I never felt ~ed by him.*

2 be likely to harm/destroy sth
ADV. **gravely** (*esp. AmE*), **seriously, severely** ◇ *Our way of life is gravely ~ed.* ◇ *social unrest which seriously ~s the stability of the whole area* | **increasingly** | **directly** | **constantly, continually** ◇ *Our marriage was constantly ~ed by his other women.* | **potentially**
VERB + THREATEN **could** | **appear to, seem to**
PHRASES **be ~ed with sth** ◇ *Many species are now ~ed with extinction.*

threatening *adj.*

VERBS **appear, be, seem, sound** | **become** | **find sth** | **regard sth as, see sth as**
ADV. **extremely, fairly, very, etc.** ◇ *I found an extremely ~ message on my answering machine.* | **increasingly** | **almost** | **potentially**

threshold *noun*

1 doorway
VERB + THRESHOLD **cross**
PREP. **across the ~, over the ~** ◇ *He hesitated before stepping across the ~.* | **on the ~** ◇ *She stood on the ~, unsure whether to enter.*

2 level
ADJ. **high, low** | **maximum, minimum** | **critical** | **poverty** | **tax** (*esp. BrE*) | **boredom** (*esp. BrE*), **pain** ◇ *He has an extremely low pain ~.*
VERB + THRESHOLD **have** | **reach** ◇ *The number of people with the disease is reaching a critical ~.* | **meet** | **cross, exceed** | **determine, set** ◇ *They earn wages below the ~ set by the government.* | **raise** | **lower**
THRESHOLD + NOUN **level, value** ◇ *Below a certain ~ level a person will not be able to detect sound.*
PREP. **above a/the ~, below a/the ~** ◇ *Her wages are below the income tax ~.*

thrill *noun*

ADJ. **big, great, real** ◇ *Meeting him was a real ~ for me.* | **little** | **cheap** | **vicarious** ◇ *He gets vicarious ~s from watching people bungee jumping.* | **visceral** ◇ *The movie certainly provides the audience with some visceral ~s.*
VERB + THRILL **enjoy, experience, feel, get, have** | **give sb**
THRILL + NOUN **seeker** | **ride**
PREP. **for a/the ~** ◇ *He used to steal just for the ~ of it.* | **~ from, ~ out of** ◇ *He used to get cheap ~s out of frightening the girl next door.* | **~ of** ◇ *She felt a ~ of excitement as the mountains came into view.*

thrilled *adj.*

VERBS **be, feel, look, seem**
ADV. **really** | **absolutely, quite, totally, utterly** | **not exactly, not too** ◇ *He's not exactly ~ at the prospect of working for his old rival.* | **secretly**

PREP. **at** ◇ *I was secretly ~ at the prospect of going there again.* | **with** ◇ *I'm really ~ with the results.*
PHRASES **~ to bits** (*BrE*), **~ to pieces** (*AmE*) ◇ *I was ~ to bits/pieces when my son won.*

thriller *noun*

ADJ. **gripping** (*esp. BrE*), **taut** | **best-selling** | **classic** | **action, comedy, crime, erotic, legal, mystery, noir, political, psychological, science-fiction, spy, supernatural, suspense** ◇ *a gripping political ~*
VERB + THRILLER **craft** ◇ *his renown for crafting ~s* | **direct, write** ◇ *She had always wanted to write a spy ~.* | **read, watch**
THRILLER + NOUN **writer** | **genre**
PREP. **in a/the ~** ◇ *one of the characters in the ~* | **~ by** ◇ *a new ~ by this American writer*

thrive *verb*

ADV. **positively** (*esp. BrE*) ◇ *a culture which positively ~s on new ideas* | **still** ◇ *The glass industry still ~s there.*
VERB + THRIVE **seem to** | **continue to** ◇ *These traditions continued to ~.* | **fail to** (*medical*)
PREP. **on** ◇ *Some people seem to ~ on stress.*
PHRASES **failure to ~** (*medical*) ◇ *concerned about their baby daughter's failure to ~*

throat *noun*

1 front part of the neck
VERB + THROAT **cut, slash, slit** | **rip out** ◇ *I wanted to rip his ~ out.*
PREP. **by the ~** ◇ *She seized her attacker by the ~.*

2 passage down which air and food pass
ADJ. **bad** (*BrE*), **scratchy** (*esp. AmE*), **sore, strep** (*AmE, informal*) ◇ *symptoms of a cold such as a runny nose and a scratchy sore ~* ◇ *I have a sore ~.* | **dry, parched**
VERB + THROAT **clear** ◇ *She cleared her ~, then began to speak.* | **escape** ◇ *A small cry escaped his ~.* | **burn** ◇ *She felt the smoke burn her ~.*
THROAT + VERB **ache, hurt** | **close, close up, constrict, tighten** ◇ *His ~ constricted with fear when he saw the knife.* | **dry, go dry** | **burn**
THROAT + NOUN **infection, irritation** ◇ *The chemical causes eye, nose and ~ irritations.* | **cancer** | **lozenge, pastille** (*esp. BrE*)
PREP. **down the/sb's ~** ◇ *She felt the cold water trickle down her ~.*
PHRASES **the back of your ~** ◇ *The medicine left a sour taste in the back of my ~.* | **a lump in your ~** ◇ *He felt a lump in his ~, and tears forming in his eyes.*

throb *noun*

ADJ. **dull** | **steady** ◇ *the steady ~ of the engine* | **bass** ◇ *the opening bass ~s of the song*
VERB + THROB **feel, hear**
PREP. **~ of** ◇ *a ~ of pain*

throb *verb*

ADV. **painfully** ◇ *The vein at his temple throbbed angrily.*
VERB + THROB **begin to, start to** | **make sth** ◇ *The noise made my head ~.*
PREP. **with** ◇ *Her head throbbed with pain.*

throne *noun*

ADJ. **empty, vacant** | **imperial, papal, royal**
VERB + THRONE **ascend, assume, come to, gain, inherit, succeed to, take** ◇ *Elizabeth I came to the ~ in 1558.* | **claim** | **seize, usurp** | **occupy** | **abdicate, give up, renounce** | **lose** | **reclaim, regain** | **put sb on** | **topple sb from** ◇ *Left-wing revolutionaries toppled the king from his ~.* | **restore sb to** | **be in line to** ◇ *The prince is second in line to the ~ behind his brother.*

Steps thudded on the stairs. | **with** ◇ *His heart thudded with excitement.*

PREP. **on the ~** ◇ *Queen Victoria remained on the ~ for over sixty years.*
PHRASES **sb's accession to the ~** | **a claimant to the ~, a pretender to the ~** ◇ *a claimant to the vacant Spanish ~* | **sb's claim to the ~, sb's right to the ~** | **an heir to the ~** ◇ *The marriage failed to produce an heir to the ~.* | **the power behind the ~** (*figurative*) ◇ *The managing director's secretary is the real power behind the ~.* | **the succession to the ~**

throng noun

ADJ. **assembled, gathered**
VERB + THRONG **join** ◇ *people coming from all directions to join the ~*
PREP. **among/through the ~** ◇ *He made his way slowly through the ~.* | **in the ~** ◇ *She was lost in the ~.* | **into the ~** ◇ *He disappeared into the ~.*

throw verb

ADV. **angrily** | **carelessly, casually** ◇ *He threw the keys casually down on the table.* | **quickly, suddenly** | **literally, practically** ◇ *We were literally thrown out of our bunks.* | **overboard** ◇ *The ship's cargo was thrown overboard.* | **around, aside, away, back, backwards/backward, down, forward, out** ◇ *She threw her head back and laughed.*
VERB + THROW **be ready to, be tempted to, want to** | **threaten to** ◇ *He threatened to ~ her in the river if she screamed.* | **be going to**
PREP. **at** ◇ *He threw a stone at the window.* | **in, into** ◇ *I just wanted to ~ myself into his arms and cry.* | **to** ◇ *She threw the ball to him.* | **towards/toward**
PHRASES **~ sth open** ◇ *He threw the double doors open in a dramatic gesture.*

thrust noun

1 strong push

ADJ. **backward, downward, forward, upward** | **powerful** | **quick** | **knife, sword** ◇ *The realization that she was gone was like a knife ~.* | **pelvic**
VERB + THRUST **deliver, make** ◇ *The army made an aggressive ~ towards/toward the front line.* | **parry**
PREP. **~ into** ◇ *a ~ into the unknown*

2 the thrust main part/ideas

ADJ. **basic, broad** (*esp. BrE*), **central, general, main, major, overall, primary** (*esp. AmE*), **whole** ◇ *She explained the broad ~ of the party's policies.* | **dramatic, narrative, political** ◇ *The dramatic ~ of the movie centres around the conflict between the brothers.*
PREP. **~ of** ◇ *the main ~ of his argument*

thrust verb

ADV. **deep, deeply** | **hard** | **quickly, suddenly** ◇ *She suddenly ~ out her arm.* | **aside, away, back, forward, out, up, upwards/upward**
PREP. **at** ◇ *He ~ a piece of paper at me.* | **into** ◇ *She ~ her hands deep into her pockets.*
PHRASES **~ your way** ◇ *She ~ her way through the dense undergrowth.*

thud noun

ADJ. **heavy, loud, resounding** | **dull, muffled, soft** | **sickening**
VERB + THUD **give** ◇ *She felt her heart give an extra ~.* | **make** ◇ *The boot made a dull ~ as it hit the ground.* | **hear** | **feel**
PREP. **with a ~** ◇ *He hit the floor with a sickening ~.*
PHRASES **the ~ of a heart, the ~ of hooves**

thud verb

ADV. **hard, painfully, wildly** (all only used with *heart*) ◇ *Her heart thudded wildly inside her chest.* | **heavily, loudly**
PREP. **against** ◇ *The waves thudded against the side of the ship.* | **into** ◇ *The sniper's bullets thudded into the wall.* | **on** ◇

thug noun

ADJ. **teenage, young** | **street** (*esp. AmE*) | **murderous, vicious, violent** | **drunken, mindless** (*esp. BrE*) | **hired** | **armed, knife-wielding** (*esp. BrE*) | **jackbooted** | **fascist, Nazi, racist, right-wing** | **football, soccer** (*both esp. BrE*)
... OF THUGS **bunch, gang** ◇ *He was beaten up by a gang of ~s.*

thumb noun

VERB + THUMB **suck** | **flick, jab, jerk** ◇ *'What'll we do with them?' he asked, jerking his ~ at the suitcases.* | **raise, stick out** ◇ *He smiled and raised a ~ in greeting.* ◇ *I stuck out a ~ and a car stopped immediately.* | **twiddle** (*often figurative*) ◇ *I sat there twiddling my ~s until the manager finally appeared.*
THUMB + NOUN **nail** (usually *thumbnail*)
PHRASES **between finger and ~, between ~ and forefinger** ◇ *I picked up the beetle carefully between finger and ~.* | **~s up** ◇ *He made a thumbs-up sign through the window to tell us everything was fine.*

thump noun

ADJ. **heavy, loud** | **dull, muffled, soft**
VERB + THUMP **give sb/sth** (*BrE*) ◇ *She gave the television a good ~, and the picture came back.* | **feel, hear**
PREP. **with a ~** ◇ *The sack hit the ground with a loud ~.*

thump verb

1 hit sb/sth with your fist

ADV. **hard** ◇ *He ~ed Jack hard in the face.* | **down** ◇ *He ~ed his fist down onto the table.*
PREP. **with** ◇ *She ~ed the desk with her fist.*

2 of the heart

ADV. **hard, heavily, loudly, painfully, wildly**
VERB + THUMP **begin to** ◇ *Her heart began to ~ wildly in her chest.*
PREP. **against** ◇ *He spun around, his heart ~ing against his ribs.*

thunder noun

ADJ. **loud** ◇ *The ~ was getting louder and louder.* | **rolling, rumbling** | **distant** ◇ *the rumble of distant ~*
... OF THUNDER **clap, crack, crash, peal, roll, rumble**
THUNDER + VERB **boom, crack, crash, roar** ◇ *Thunder boomed in the sky overhead.* | **growl, roll, rumble, sound** ◇ *A crash of ~ sounded in the distance.* | **echo** | **rattle sth, shake sth** ◇ *The windows were shaken by a tremendous crash of ~.*
THUNDER + NOUN **clap** (usually *thunderclap*) | **cloud** (usually *thundercloud*)
PREP. **~ of** (*figurative*) ◇ *She could hear the ~ of hoofs approaching.*
PHRASES **the sound of ~, ~ and lightning**

thunderstorm noun → See STORM

Thursday noun → Note at DAY

thwart verb

ADV. **easily** | **successfully** | **constantly, repeatedly** ◇ *Plans to expand the company have been constantly ~ed.*
VERB + THWART **attempt to, try to**
PREP. **in** ◇ *They were ~ed in their attempt to gain overall control of the company.*

tick verb

1 of a clock, etc.

ADV. **loudly** | **relentlessly** | **away** ◇ *The clock ~ed relentlessly away on the mantelpiece.*

2 (*BrE*) **put a mark (✓) next to sth** → See also CHECK

ADV. **simply** ◇ *To take advantage of this extra bonus offer, simply ~ the box on your order form.* | **mentally** | **off** ◇ *She* mentally ~ed off the names of the people she had already spoken to.

PHR V **tick over** (*BrE*)
ADV. **nicely** ◇ *The business is ~ing over nicely at the moment.* | **still**
PHRASES **keep things ~ing over** ◇ *Morrison had kept things ~ing over in my absence.*

ticket *noun*

1 for travel, an event, etc.

ADJ. **one-way** (*esp. AmE*), **single** (*BrE*) | **return** (*BrE*), **round-trip** (*AmE*) | **day, season, weekly** (*BrE*) ◇ *an annual season ~* | **business-class, coach-class** (*AmE*), **economy-class, first-class, second-class** (*esp. BrE*), etc. ◇ *a first-class rail ~* | **valid** | **complimentary, free** ◇ *I had complimentary ~s for the show.* | **adult, family** (*both esp. BrE*) ◇ *A family ~ for two adults and two children costs £27.* | **advance** ◇ *Use the coupon below to reserve advance ~s for the exhibition.* | **admission, entrance, entry** | **air, airline, bus, plane, rail** (*BrE*), **train**, etc. | **cinema** (*BrE*), **movie** (*AmE*) | **concert**
VERB + TICKET **buy, get, obtain, purchase** | **sell** | **have, hold** ◇ *You must hold a valid ~ before boarding the train.* | **book, reserve** | **collect** | **hand (sb), show (sb)** ◇ *He showed the guard his ~.* | **punch, take**
TICKET + VERB **be priced, cost** | **go on sale**
TICKET + NOUN **agency, agent, booth, counter, machine, office, window** | **line** ◇ *Phone the ~ line on this number.* | **price** | **sales** | **holder** | **collector, inspector** (*both BrE*) | **scalper** (*AmE*), **tout** (*BrE*) | **barrier** (*BrE*) | **stub**
PREP. **by ~** ◇ *admission by ~ only* | **~ for** ◇ *I bought a ~ for the concert.* ◇ *a ~ for Saturday* | **~ to** ◇ *I have a free ~ to the game.* ◇ *a plane ~ to New York*

2 for a lottery, etc.

ADJ. **winning** | **lottery, raffle**
... OF TICKETS **book** (*esp. BrE*) ◇ *I bought a whole book of raffle ~s and I still didn't win anything.*

3 giving a penalty

ADJ. **parking, speeding, traffic** (*AmE*) | **fixed-penalty** (*BrE*)
VERB + TICKET **give sb, issue** | **get, receive**
PREP. **~ for** ◇ *The police officer gave us a ~ for going through a red light.*

4 (*esp. AmE*) list of candidates in an election

ADJ. **national, party, presidential** | **Democratic, Republican** | **split, straight** ◇ *I generally vote a split ~.*
VERB + TICKET **run on** ◇ *He ran on the Republican ~.* | **join, support** | **drop sb from, put sb on** ◇ *There had been talk of Kennedy dropping LBJ from the ~ in '64.* | **vote, vote for** ◇ *I'm voting the straight Democratic ~.*
PREP. **on ~** ◇ *There are three candidates on the national ~.*

tide *noun*

1 change in the level of the sea

ADJ. **strong** | **flood, incoming, rising** | **ebb, outgoing** | **high, low** | **neap, spring** | **ocean** (*esp. AmE*) | **rip** ◇ *If caught in a rip ~, strong swimmers should swim for shore.*
VERB + TIDE **catch** ◇ *We have to get up early to catch the ~ (= leave at the same time as the tide goes out).*
TIDE + VERB **be in** | **be out** | **come in, rise** | **ebb, fall, go out, recede, retreat** (*esp. BrE*) | **be on the turn** (*BrE*), **turn** | **occur** ◇ *the time of day when the highest ~s occur* | **wash sb/sth up** ◇ *The body was washed up by the ~ the next day.*
TIDE + NOUN **line, mark** ◇ *the high ~ mark* | **pool** ◇ *When the sea recedes, ~ pools reveal a bewildering diversity of marine life.*
PREP. **at ... ~** ◇ *Seals lie on the rocks at low ~.* | **on a/the ~** ◇ *We went out to sea on the ebb ~.*

2 movement of opinion; sudden increase

ADJ. **growing, rising** ◇ *the rising ~ of crime* | **shifting** | **political** ◇ *He didn't have the courage to swim against the political ~.*
VERB + TIDE **go with, ride** | **go against, swim against** | **reverse, stem, turn, turn back** ◇ *attempts to stem the ~ of revolution*
TIDE + VERB **run** ◇ *Seeing the ~ was now running in his*

direction, he renewed his campaign for reform. | **carry sb/sth along** | **turn** ◇ *The ~ of public opinion seems to be turning at last.*
PREP. **against a/the ~** ◇ *It takes courage to speak out against the ~ of public opinion.* | **on a ~** ◇ *They were carried along on a ~ of euphoria.* | **~ against, ~ in favour/favor of** ◇ *Civil liberties groups helped to turn the ~ against industrial violence.*
PHRASES **the ~ of history** ◇ *the shifting ~s of history* | **the turn of the ~** ◇ *In the early 1990s there was a marked turn of the ~.*

tidy *adj.* (*esp. BrE*)

VERBS **be, look, seem** | **stay** ◇ *Why does nothing ever stay ~ around here?* | **get sth, make sth** | **keep sth** ◇ *I hope you're going to keep your room ~.*
ADV. **extremely, fairly, very,** etc. ◇ *The living room is fairly ~.* | **immaculately** ◇ *It was a neatly furnished and immaculately ~ room.* | **obsessively**
PHRASES **clean and ~, neat and ~** (*BrE, AmE*)

tie *noun*

1 worn around the neck with a shirt

ADJ. **undone** ◇ *His ~ was undone.* | **loose** | **askew** ◇ *His ~ was askew and his hair uncombed.* | **loud** | **bow, kipper** (*BrE*), **neck** (usually **necktie**) (*AmE*) | **bolo** (*AmE*), **bootlace** (*BrE*) | **black, white** (= a black/white bow tie as part of formal dress) ◇ *a black-tie dinner* | **silk** | **club, regimental, school** (*all esp. BrE*)
VERB + TIE **wear** | **knot, tie** | **loosen** | **adjust, straighten**
TIE + NOUN **pin** (usually **tiepin**), **tack** (*AmE*)
PHRASES **collar and ~, jacket and ~, shirt and ~, suit and ~** → Special page at CLOTHES

2 (usually **ties**) sth that connects you with sb/sth

ADJ. **close, strong** | **loose, weak** | **direct, indirect** | **blood, family** | **emotional** | **personal** | **business, commercial, economic, financial** | **cultural, diplomatic, historical, political, social, traditional**
VERB + TIE **have** ◇ *We have close economic ~s with other countries in the region.* | **develop, establish, forge** | **maintain** | **cement, strengthen** | **break, cut, sever** ◇ *He cut all ~s with the Church.* | **loosen, weaken**
PREP. **~ between** ◇ *There is a strong ~ between her and her daughters.* | **~ of** ◇ *~s of kinship* | **~ to, ~ with** ◇ *to establish diplomatic ~s with China*

3 in a game/competition

VERB + TIE **end in, result in** ◇ *The match ended in a ~.*
TIE + NOUN **break** (usually **tiebreak**) (*BrE*), **breaker** (usually **tiebreaker**) (*AmE*) | **game** (*AmE*)
PREP. **~ between** ◇ *a ~ between Egypt and France* | **~ for** ◇ *There was a ~ for first place.*

tie *verb*

1 attach/fasten sb/sth with string/rope

ADV. **firmly, securely, tightly** ◇ *Did you ~ the balloons on tightly?* | **loosely** ◇ *He wore plimsolls, loosely ~d with bits of string.* | **carefully** | **neatly** ◇ *Tie the cords neatly.* | **back, on, together, up**
PREP. **around, round** (*esp. BrE*) ◇ *He ~d his bathrobe firmly around him.* | **in(to)** ◇ *Her hair was ~d into a loose ponytail.* | **onto** ◇ *I ~d the bundle onto the end of the string.* | **to** ◇ *She ~d the rope securely to a tree.* | **with** ◇ *Katie ~d her hair back with a ribbon.*

2 connect sb/sth with sb/sth else

ADV. **closely, intimately** ◇ *Their company's future is closely ~d to our own.* | **directly** | **firmly** | **inextricably** | **in, together, up** ◇ *Production and consumption are inextricably ~d together.*
PREP. **to** ◇ *You can't stay ~d to her forever.*

tiger noun

ADJ. **man-eating** | **sabretooth/sabertooth, sabre-toothed/saber-toothed** | **paper** *(figurative)* ◇ *They view America as a paper ~ (= something that seems powerful or dangerous but is not really).*
TIGER + VERB **growl, roar** | **spring** | **maul sb** ◇ *The zookeeper was mauled to death by a ~.* | **prowl** ◇ *A ~ was often seen prowling around the village.*
TIGER + NOUN **cub** | **skin, stripes** | **print** ◇ *a tiger-print skirt* | **hunt** | **population**

tight adj., adv.

1 not loose

VERBS **be, feel, look, seem** | **become, get, go** ◇ *Those jeans are getting too ~ for me.* ◇ *The rope suddenly went ~.* | **hold, hold on** ◇ *'Hold ~!' She increased her grip.* | **clamp sth, clench sth, close sth, draw sth, pull sth, shut sth, squeeze sth, stretch sth, tie sth, wrap sth** ◇ *His jaw was clenched ~.* ◇ *Every muscle in her face was drawn ~.* ◇ *Shut your eyes ~.* ◇ *The cloth was stretched ~ over the frame.* | **keep sth, make sth** ◇ *Keep the rope ~.* | **clutch sb/sth, grip sb/sth, hold sb/sth, hug sb/sth** ◇ *He held his children ~.*
ADV. **extremely, fairly, very, etc.** | **a little, slightly, etc.**

2 with not much time/money to spare

VERBS **be, look, seem** | **get** ◇ *I think we'd better leave—time's getting very ~.*
ADV. **extremely, fairly, very, etc.** | **a little, slightly, etc.**

3 controlled very strictly

VERBS **be, seem** | **become** | **remain** ◇ *Security at the airport remains ~.*
ADV. **extremely, fairly, very, etc.** | **incredibly** | **increasingly**

tighten verb

ADV. **a little, slightly, etc.** | **considerably** | **gradually, slowly** | **suddenly** | **instinctively, involuntarily, unconsciously** ◇ *Her fingers ~ed unconsciously with every jolt she received.* | **painfully** | **up** ◇ *Can you ~ up the bolts for me?*
VERB + TIGHTEN **seem to** | **feel sth** ◇ *He felt his stomach ~.* | **make sth** ◇ *His words made her throat ~.*
PREP. **about** *(BrE)*, **around, round** *(esp. BrE)* ◇ *His hand ~ed painfully around her wrist.* | **on** ◇ *Her grip seemed to ~ on the door handle.* | **in** ◇ *He saw his father's jaw ~ in irritation.* | **into** ◇ *His mouth ~ed into a thin hard line.* | **with** ◇ *Her face ~ed with pain.*

tights noun → See also PANTYHOSE

ADJ. **opaque, thick** | **ribbed** | **sheer** *(BrE)* | **black, flesh-coloured** *(BrE)*, **etc.** | **stripy** | **fishnet** | **nylon** | **wool** *(AmE)*, **woollen** *(BrE)*, **woolly** *(BrE)* | **15-denier, etc.** *(BrE)* | **support** | **ballet** | **laddered** *(BrE)*
...OF TIGHTS **pair** *(BrE)*
VERB + TIGHTS **pull on** | **ladder** *(BrE)*
TIGHTS + VERB **ladder** *(BrE)*
PHRASES **a hole in your ~, a ladder in your ~** *(BrE)* → Special page at CLOTHES

tile noun

ADJ. **broken, cracked, damaged, loose, missing** | **decorative, glazed, hand-painted, plain** | **ceramic, clay, linoleum, marble, mosaic, quarry, slate, stone, terracotta, vinyl, etc.** | **floor, pool, wall** | **carpet, ceiling, roof** | **bathroom, kitchen**
VERB + TILE **cover sth with, fit, lay** ◇ *I'm laying ceramic floor ~s in the kitchen.*

till noun *(BrE)* → See also CASH REGISTER

ADJ. **computerized, electronic**
TILL + VERB **ring** ◇ *a sales idea that has set ~s ringing all over the country*
TILL + NOUN **receipt, roll**
PREP. **at the ~, behind the ~, on the ~** ◇ *The supermarket didn't have enough people working on the ~s.* | **in a/the ~,**

---

into a/the ~ ◇ *Put the money straight into the ~.* | from a/the ~, out of a/the ~ ◇ *He gave her £10 from the ~.*

tilt verb

ADV. **a little, gently, slightly** | **back, down, forward, sideways, up, etc.** | **sharply** ◇ *The ground ~ed sharply downwards/downward.* | **slowly**
PREP. **away from** ◇ *Tilt the mirror away from you.* | **towards/toward** ◇ *Her face was ~ed towards/toward the sky.*
PHRASES **~ed to one side** ◇ *She thought for a minute, her head ~ed to one side.*

timber noun

1 trees grown for building

VERB + TIMBER **cut, fell, harvest** | **sell**
TIMBER + NOUN **company, industry, production, trade** | **harvest** | **sale, supply**

2 *(BrE)* wood for use in building/carpentry

ADJ. **heavy** | **solid** ◇ *a solid ~ door* | **rough** | **decayed, rotten, rotting** | **seasoned, treated** | **unseasoned, untreated**
...OF TIMBER **length, piece**
VERB + TIMBER **dress, season, treat**
TIMBER + VERB **decay, rot**
TIMBER + NOUN **product** | **merchant, yard** | **construction, frame, structure, support** | **beam, building, floor, etc.**

3 (usually **timbers**) piece of wood used in a building

ADJ. **heavy** | **exposed** ◇ *The house has exposed oak ~s.* | **roof** | **oak** | **ship's**

time noun

1 what is measured in minutes, hours, days, etc.

TIME + VERB **elapse, go by, pass** ◇ *As ~ went by we saw less and less of each other.* ◇ *The changing seasons mark the passing of ~.* | **fly** ◇ *How ~ flies!* | **go** ◇ *Where does the ~ go?* | **drag** ◇ *Time drags in this job.* | **heal sth** ◇ *Time heals all wounds.*
PREP. **in ~** ◇ *The play takes us back in ~ to the 1940s.* | **over ~** ◇ *Perceptions change over ~.* | **through ~** ◇ *travel through ~*
PHRASES **a matter of ~** ◇ *It was only a matter of ~ before someone tried to kill him.* | **the mists of ~** ◇ *The origins of this custom are lost in the mists of ~.*

2 time shown on a clock

ADJ. **good, perfect** ◇ *My watch keeps good ~.* | **local** ◇ *The attacks were launched at 9 p.m. local ~.* | **daylight saving** | **British Summer, Eastern Standard, Greenwich Mean, etc.**
VERB + TIME **tell** ◇ *Can he tell the ~ yet?* *(BrE)* ◇ *Can he tell ~ yet?* *(AmE)* | **have** ◇ *Do you have the ~?* ◇ *What ~ do you have?* *(AmE)* | **make** ◇ *What ~ do you make it?* *(BrE)* | **look at** ◇ *Look at the ~! We'll be late.* | **check** ◇ *Let me just check the ~.* | **keep**
TIME + NOUN **zone**
PREP. **ahead of... ~, behind... ~** ◇ *10 hours behind Pacific Standard Time*
PHRASES **at... time in the morning/afternoon/evening, at... time of the morning/afternoon/evening/night** ◇ *There's less traffic at this ~ of day.* ◇ *What are you doing out of bed at this ~ of night?* | **~ of year, ~ of the year** ◇ *The leaves start to turn red at this ~ of (the) year.* | **this ~ tomorrow, etc.** ◇ *This ~ tomorrow I'll be in Canada.*

3 time when sth happens/should happen

ADJ. **peak** ◇ *There are extra buses at peak ~s.* | **prime** | **closing, opening** | **arrival, departure**
VERB + TIME **fix** *(BrE)*, **set** ◇ *We need to set a ~ for the next meeting.* | **change**
TIME + VERB **come** ◇ *You'll feel differently about it when the ~ comes.*
PREP. **ahead of ~** ◇ *We had everything worked out ahead of ~.* | **behind ~** *(BrE)* ◇ *The plane took off an hour behind ~.* | **by the ~** ◇ *By the ~ you get there the meeting will be over.* | **in ~** ◇ *We got home in ~ to see the end of the game.* | **on ~** ◇ *The trains are rarely on ~.* | **~ for** ◇ *It's ~ for dinner.*

4 amount of time

ADJ. **considerable, long** | **little, short** | **limited** | **total** | **reasonable** | **precious** ◇ *We're wasting precious ~.* | **idle** |

free, leisure, spare | quality | journey, travel, travelling/
traveling | running ◇ *the movie's two-hour running ~* |
playing (esp. AmE), screen ◇ *The coach plans to give younger
players more playing ~.* ◇ *De Niro makes the most of limited
screen ~.* | lead, waiting ◇ *There is a long lead ~ between
order and delivery of the product.*
...OF TIME amount, length, period ◇ *Have you lived overseas
for any length of ~?* | great deal ◇ *A great deal of ~ has been
spent on developing this software.*
VERB + TIME have ◇ *Do you have ~ for a chat?* ◇ *I had no ~ to
think.* | need ◇ *Do you need more ~?* | give sb/sth ◇ *I can
certainly do the job if you give me ~.* | take (sb) ◇ *It takes ~ to
make changes in the law.* ◇ *It took her a long ~ to read the
report.* ◇ *Take your ~* (= take as much time as you like). |
spend ◇ *She spends much of her ~ reading.* ◇ *I hope to spend
more ~ with my family.* | kill, pass, while away ◇ *It helps to
pass the ~.* | fritter away, idle away | devote, put, use ◇
She devotes all her spare ~ to gardening. ◇ *He put all his ~
into the show.* | allow, leave ◇ *They didn't allow much ~ for
discussion.* ◇ *This doesn't leave much ~ for us to get ready.* |
find, make ◇ *I can never find ~ to write letters.* ◇ *I can
probably make the ~ to see them.* | wait ◇ *We had to wait
some ~ before the bus arrived.* | gain, save ◇ *You would save
~ with a dishwasher.* | reduce ◇ *measures to reduce waiting
~s* | waste | lose, run out of ◇ *We have no ~ to lose* (= we
must hurry). ◇ *I didn't finish the test—I ran out of ~.* | be
pressed for, be short of | be out of | play for ◇ *Not
knowing what to do, she played for ~ by going to the
bathroom.*
TIME + VERB be up, run out ◇ *Sorry, your ~ is up.*
TIME + NOUN frame, interval, period, scale, span | limit | lag
PREP. at a ~ ◇ *He surfs the Internet for hours at a ~.* | for a ~
◇ *I lived there for a ~.* | in ~ ◇ *You'll get used to the work in
~.* | over ~, with ~ ◇ *Her skills improved with ~.*
PHRASES all in good ~ (= sth will happen when the time is
right) ◇ *Be patient, Emily! All in good ~.* | all the ~ ◇ *The
letter was in my pocket all the ~* (= while I was looking for
it). ◇ *She leaves the lights on all the ~* (= always/repeatedly).
| the entire ~, the whole ~ | for quite some ~ ◇ *He'd been
thinking about quitting his job for quite some ~.* | if ~
permits ◇ *We will discuss this matter later, if ~ permits.* | in
the fullness of ~ (= when the time is right, usually after a
long period) | in good ~, in plenty of ~ ◇ *Get to the
airport in good ~* (= plenty of time before the plane leaves).
| in next to no ~, in no ~ at all | in ten minutes', three
hours', etc. ~ (esp. BrE) ◇ *I'll be back in ten minutes' ~.* | in
your own good ~, in your own ~* (= taking as long as you
want/need) | most of the ~ | a race against ~ ◇ *Finishing
the book was a race against ~.* | a long ~ ago, some ~ ago ◇
Her parents died a long ~ ago. | a waste of ~ ◇ *What a waste
of ~!*

5 (often **times**) period in the past/present
ADJ. good, great, happy | bad, difficult, hard, rough, sad,
tough, troubled, unhappy ◇ *Times are hard for the
unemployed.* | ancient, early, former, old ◇ *in ancient ~s* |
modern, recent | medieval, prehistoric, etc.
TIME + VERB change ◇ *Times have changed since Grandma was
young.*
PREP. at a/the ~ ◇ *He lived at the ~ of the Civil War.* ◇ *At one ~
Mary was my best friend.* | before sb's ~ ◇ *The Beatles were
before my ~.* | in sb's ~ ◇ *Mr Curtis was the manager in my ~*
(= when I was working there). | in ~s ◇ *in ~s of trouble*
PHRASES from ~ immemorial, since ~ immemorial (= for a
very long time) | of all ~ ◇ *the greatest hockey player of all
~* | a sign of the ~s ◇ *It's a sign of the ~s when sports stars
earn more than movie stars.* | ~ was when ◇ *Time was when*
(= there was a time when) *we never needed to lock our
house at night.*

6 occasion
ADJ. that, this ◇ *I'm determined to pass this ~.* | final, last ◇
When was the last ~ you saw her? | another, next ◇ *Next ~
you're here let's have lunch together.* | one | each, every ◇
Every ~ I hear that song I feel happy. | only | same ◇
appropriate, good, suitable ◇ *Is this an appropriate ~ to
discuss my salary?* | appointed, right | bad, wrong ◇ *This
would be a bad ~ to tell her.* | first, second, etc. ◇ *For the
first ~ in history, more than half of us now live in cities.* |

umpteenth | countless, many ◇ *I've told you countless ~s.* |
several
...OF TIME couple | number
VERB + TIME remember ◇ *I can remember the first ~ I met her.*
| bide ◇ *We'll have to bide our ~ until the rain stops.*
TIME + VERB come ◇ *Your ~ will come.* | be ripe ◇ *The ~ is ripe
for revolution.*
PREP. at a/the ~ ◇ *The chairlift can take four people at a ~.* ◇
At the ~ of writing, a ceasefire is under discussion. ◇ *Hot
water is available at all ~s.* ◇ *He can be rather moody at ~s.* |
by the ~ ◇ *She'll have gone by the ~ we get there.* | for
the...~ ◇ *I told her not to do it for the umpteenth ~.*
PHRASES at the present ~ | for the ~ being (= temporarily)
| a number of ~s | x ~s out of x ◇ *three ~s out of ten*

7 when you experience sth in a particular way
ADJ. enjoyable, fun, good, grand (esp. BrE), great,
marvellous/marvelous, pleasant, splendid (esp. BrE),
wonderful ◇ *It was a fun ~ for us girls.* | awful, dreadful
(esp. BrE), horrible, miserable, sad, terrible | difficult,
hard
VERB + TIME have ◇ *Did you have a good ~ in Spain?* ◇ *We had
a great ~ at the party.* | enjoy

8 time taken in a race, etc.
ADJ. fast | record ◇ *He completed the course in record ~.*
VERB + TIME clock up, record ◇ *She clocked up one of the
fastest ~s of the year.*
TIME + NOUN trial

9 musical rhythm
ADJ. waltz | double, quick
VERB + TIME beat, keep ◇ *The conductor beat ~ with a baton.*
TIME + NOUN signature
PREP. in ~, in ~ to, in ~ with, out of ~ with ◇ *Kelly played
guitar and everyone clapped their hands in ~.* ◇ *They were
clapping in ~ to the music.*

time verb
ADV. conveniently, well ◇ *This campaign is well ~d.* |
beautifully (esp. BrE), perfectly, to perfection ◇ *a beauti-
fully ~d entrance* ◇ *We had ~d our arrival to perfection.* |
badly, poorly | carefully ◇ *The schedule must be carefully
~d.* | precisely
PREP. for ◇ *The meeting is ~d for 3 o'clock.*
PHRASES be ~d to coincide with sth ◇ *The show is ~d to
coincide with the launch of her new book.*

timetable noun
1 (esp. BrE) list showing the time of events → See also
SCHEDULE
ADJ. busy, full ◇ *a full ~ of teaching* | college, school, etc. |
exam, examination | bus, train, etc.
VERB + TIMETABLE consult, look at
PREP. according to the ~ ◇ *According to the ~, the bus should
have come in at 9.00.* | in a/the ~ ◇ *It said in the ~ that a
train was due at 5.30.*

2 plan of events
ADJ. detailed (BrE), precise, specific | strict | realistic (esp.
BrE) | overall (BrE)
VERB + TIMETABLE have | agree on, draw up, establish,
outline, set, set out | adhere to, follow, keep to ◇
Implementation of the reforms was kept to a very strict ~.
PREP. ~ for ◇ *The administration refused to set out a specific ~
for troop withdrawal.*

timing noun
ADJ. exact, precise ◇ *There is disagreement within the
government over the exact ~ of the referendum.* | con-
venient, fortuitous ◇ *The ~ of the meeting is not convenient.*
| inconvenient, unfortunate ◇ *the unfortunate ~ of the
announcement* | accurate, careful, good, great, impec-
cable, perfect | right ◇ *He knew the ~ was right for a*

comeback. | **bad, poor** | **split-second** | **comedic** (*esp. AmE*), **comic**

VERB + TIMING **have** ◇ *He has the split-second ~ all good players need.*

PREP. **with…~** ◇ *The punchline was delivered with perfect comic ~.*

PHRASES **get the ~ right, get the ~ wrong** | **a matter of ~** ◇ *Using press releases to good effect is a matter of ~.* | **a sense of ~** ◇ *She has a wonderful sense of ~.*

tin *noun* (*BrE*) metal container → See also CAN, PAN

ADJ. **baking, roasting** | **cake, flan, loaf** (= for baking cakes, etc.) | **biscuit** (*BrE*), **cookie** (= for storing biscuits/cookies) (*AmE*)

TIN + NOUN **opener** (usually **tin-opener**)

PREP. **in a/the ~** ◇ *Store the seeds in an airtight ~.* | **~ of** ◇ *a ~ of beans*

tinge *noun*

ADJ. **faint, slight** ◇ *blue with a slight ~ of purple* | **blue, bluish, etc.** ◇ *a slight reddish ~*

VERB + TINGE **have** | **feel** ◇ *She felt a ~ of guilt.*

PREP. **~ of** ◇ *a ~ of regret* | **~ to** ◇ *The sky had a slight pink ~ to it.*

tint *noun*

ADJ. **dark** | **light, pale** | **blue, bluish, etc.** | **faint, slight** (*esp. AmE*)

VERB + TINT **have**

PREP. **~ of** ◇ *The branches of the trees were barely showing their first ~ of green.*

tiny *adj.*

VERBS **be, feel, look, seem** | **become**

ADV. **extremely, fairly, very, etc.** | **comparatively, relatively** ◇ *her comparatively ~ budget*

PHRASES **little ~, ~ little** ◇ *Look at his little ~ fingers. Aren't they cute?*

tip *noun*

1 pointed end

ADJ. **northern, etc.** ◇ *We took a bus to the northern ~ of the island.* | **pointed, sharp** | **very** ◇ *The cat was black except for a patch of white on the very ~ of its tail.* | **finger** (usually **fingertip**), **wing**

PREP. **~ of** ◇ *the ~s of your fingers/toes*

2 money

ADJ. **big, generous, good, large** | **small**

VERB + TIP **give sb, leave sb** ◇ *He left the waitress a large ~.* | **get** ◇ *We get fewer ~s on weeknights.*

3 advice

ADJ. **good, handy, helpful, practical, useful** | **quick, simple** | **hot** ◇ *He said he'd been given a hot ~ for that afternoon's race.* | **beauty, fashion, gardening, money-saving, safety, etc.** | **racing** (*esp. BrE*) | **anonymous** (*AmE*) ◇ *Police received an anonymous ~ from a caller.*

VERB + TIP **have** | **give sb, offer (sb), pass on, provide** | **take, use** ◇ *Take a safety ~ from me—get that light fixed!* | **follow** ◇ *Follow these ~s to improve your communication skills.* | **pick up** ◇ *I picked up some useful ~s from my ski instructor.*

PREP. **~ for** ◇ *some handy ~s for gardeners* | **~ on** ◇ *Do you have any ~s on buying a second-hand car?*

tip *verb* (often **be tipped**) (*BrE*)

ADV. **hotly, strongly** | **widely**

PREP. **as** ◇ *He has been widely tipped as a future CEO.* | **for** ◇ *The band is being hotly tipped for the top.*

tip-off *noun* (*esp. BrE*) secret information given to the police

ADJ. **anonymous** | **intelligence** | **telephone**

VERB + TIP-OFF **give sb** | **get, receive** | **act on** ◇ *Acting on a ~, police raided the house.*

PREP. **after ~** ◇ *He was arrested after a ~ to police.* | **~ about** ◇ *Customs officers had received a ~ about a shipment of cocaine.*

tire *noun* (*AmE*) → See TYRE

tire *verb*

ADV. **easily, quickly** ◇ *She found herself tiring more quickly these days.* | **eventually** | **out** ◇ *The long walk had really ~d me out.*

VERB + TIRE **begin to** ◇ *After an hour Rick began to ~.*

tired *adj.*

1 needing rest

VERBS **be, feel, look, seem, sound** | **become, get** | **leave sb, make sb** ◇ *The walk left me ~ out.*

ADV. **extremely, fairly, very, etc.** | **awfully, bone** (*informal, esp. AmE*), **dead, desperately, terribly** ◇ *Polly suddenly felt awfully ~.* | **overly** | **a little, slightly, etc.** | **just** ◇ *Of course I'm not ill. I'm just ~.* | **mentally, physically** | **visibly** | **out**

PREP. **from** ◇ *I'm still a little ~ from the flight.*

PHRASES **~ and drawn** ◇ *He looked ~ and drawn.*

2 tired of sb/sth feeling you have had enough

VERBS **be** | **become, get, grow** ◇ *She had grown heartily ~ of his company.*

ADV. **extremely, fairly, very, etc.** | **a little, slightly, etc.**

PHRASES **sick and ~** (*informal*) ◇ *I'm sick and ~ of listening to you complain.*

tiredness *noun*

ADJ. **desperate, extreme, overwhelming** | **chronic, severe** | **constant** (*esp. BrE*) | **physical**

VERB + TIREDNESS **feel, suffer from** (*esp. BrE*)

TIREDNESS + VERB **set in** (*esp. BrE*) ◇ *A desperate ~ set in after hours of waiting.*

PHRASES **a sign of ~** ◇ *The team showed no signs of ~.*

tissue *noun*

1 organic material

ADJ. **living** | **healthy, normal** ◇ *Vitamin C helps maintain healthy ~.* | **damaged, diseased** | **animal, human, plant** ◇ *Dyes were extracted by boiling the plant ~.* | **body, brain, intestinal, lung, muscle, etc.** | **connective, scar** | **surrounding** | **fat, fatty, fibrous, soft** ◇ *She treats skin and soft ~ injuries in casualty.*

VERB + TISSUE **damage** | **remove**

2 paper handkerchief

ADJ. **paper** | **toilet**

... OF TISSUES **box, pack, package** (*AmE*), **packet, wad** ◇ *She grabbed a wad of ~s from the box.*

VERB + TISSUE **use** | **take**

PREP. **on a/the ~** ◇ *He wiped his nose on a ~.* | **with a/the ~** ◇ *She gently dabbed her eyes with a ~.*

title *noun*

1 name of a book, film/movie, etc.

ADJ. **album, book, chapter, film** (*esp. BrE*), **movie** (*esp. AmE*), **song** | **original** | **working**

VERB + TITLE **give sth**

TITLE + NOUN **page** | **sequence** ◇ *the opening ~ sequence of the movie* | **character, role** ◇ *She sang the ~ role in 'Carmen'.* | **song, track** ◇ *'Take me', the ~ track of his latest album*

PREP. **under a/the ~** ◇ *She published her poetry under the ~ 'Homecoming'.*

2 book, magazine, etc.

ADJ. **new** ◇ *40% of new ~s were actually new editions of existing books.* | **best-selling** | **book, game, etc.** ◇ *Sony has released six new game ~s.*

VERB + TITLE **publish, release** ◇ *The company is publishing fewer ~s than last year.*

3 name of a rank/profession

ADJ. **grand, long** ◊ *She bears the grand ~ 'Divisional President'.* | **courtesy** (*esp. BrE*), **honorary, honorific, official** ◊ *The justices are accorded the courtesy ~ 'Lord'.* | **job** ◊ *His job ~ is Special Projects Officer.* | **full** ◊ *Count Victor Oldenburg and Hess, to give him his full ~*
VERB + TITLE **bear, have, inherit** ◊ *She has a ~ (= is of noble birth).* | **take** | **deserve, earn** ◊ *Bessie Smith earned the ~ 'Empress of the Blues'.* | **award, bestow, confer, give sb** ◊ *He was given the ~ of 'wise man'.*

4 championship win

ADJ. **European, national, world, etc.** | **championship, division, league, etc.** | **heavyweight, middleweight, etc.** | **batting** (in baseball) | **back-to-back, consecutive, successive** (*esp. BrE*) ◊ *Suzuki won seven consecutive batting ~s in Japan's Pacific League.* | **overall**
VERB + TITLE **capture, claim, clinch, take, win** ◊ *Deportivo clinched the ~ with a goal in the final seconds of the last game of the season.* | **hold, keep** ◊ *He held the world heavyweight ~ until last year.* | **defend** | **retain** | **lose**
TITLE + NOUN **challenge** (*esp. BrE*), **shot** ◊ *He has been building up fitness for his world ~ challenge.* | **defence/defense** | **bout, fight, game** (*AmE*), **match** | **holder** | **challenger** (*esp. BrE*), **contender** | **sponsor** ◊ *Dodge was the ~ sponsor of the Darlington race.*
→ Special page at SPORTS

toast noun

1 bread

ADJ. **brown** (*esp. BrE*), **white, wholemeal** (*BrE*), **wholewheat** (*AmE*), **dry** | **burned** | **buttered** | **cinnamon, French, Melba, etc.**
... OF TOAST **piece, round** (*BrE*), **slice**
VERB + TOAST **make** ◊ *I'm making ~ for breakfast.* | **butter, spread** ◊ *buttered ~* ◊ *She ate two slices of ~ spread with honey.* | **burn** ◊ *I can smell burned ~.*
PREP. **on ~** ◊ *For lunch we had cheese on ~.* (*BrE*)

2 drink

ADJ. **champagne**
VERB + TOAST **make, propose, raise** (*AmE*) ◊ *He raised his glass as if to make a ~.* | **drink**
PREP. **~ to** ◊ *The bridegroom ended his speech by proposing a ~ to the hosts.*

tobacco noun

ADJ. **strong** | **stale** | **pipe** | **chewing, rolling** (*esp. BrE*)
VERB + TOBACCO **chew, smoke** | **use** ◊ *Native Americans had used ~ since time immemorial.* | **be addicted to** | **grow**
TOBACCO + NOUN **addiction, consumption, use** | **smoke** ◊ *The air was thick with ~ smoke.* | **business, company, firm, industry, manufacturer, producer** | **lobby** ◊ *The ban on cigarette advertising will upset the ~ lobby.* | **products** | **market** | **sales** | **advertising** (*esp. BrE*), **sponsorship** (*BrE*) ◊ *the ban on ~ advertising* | **control** | **settlement** (*esp. AmE*) ◊ *a multi-billion-dollar ~ settlement* | **pouch, tin** | **grower, plantation** | **leaf, plant**

toe noun

ADJ. **big** ◊ *The shoe pressed painfully against her big ~.* | **little, pinky** (*AmE*) | **bare** ◊ *Under his bare ~s the floor felt gritty.* | **broken, stubbed** ◊ *the pain of a stubbed ~*
VERB + TOE **stand on, step on, tread on** (*esp. BrE*) ◊ *She stood on her ~s to kiss him.* ◊ *Ouch! That was my ~ you just trod on.* ◊ *She trod on a lot of ~s when she joined the company.* (*figurative*) | **stub** | **break** | **dip** ◊ *I dipped my ~ in the river to test the temperature.* ◊ *So far they have only dipped their ~ in the potentially vast computer market.* (*figurative*) | **point** | **curl** | **wiggle** | **tap** ◊ *She tapped her ~s to the music.* | **touch** ◊ *Can you touch your ~s (= while keeping your legs straight)?*
TOE + VERB **curl** (*often figurative*) ◊ *The man's broad smile made her ~s curl (= made her feel uncomfortable).*
TOE + NOUN **injury**
PREP. **between the/your ~s** ◊ *He had some kind of fungus between his ~s.* | **on your ~s** ◊ *He moved lightly on his ~s like*

a boxer. ◊ *The threat of inspections kept us all on our ~s (= made sure we kept everything up to standard and were ready).* (*figurative*)
PHRASES **from head to ~, from top to ~** ◊ *He gave himself a good scrub from head to ~.* | **the tips of your ~s** ◊ *I stood on the tips of my ~s to look through the window.* | **the ~ of your boot, the ~ of your shoe**

toenail noun

ADJ. **ingrowing** (*BrE*), **ingrown** | **painted**
VERB + TOENAIL **clip, cut, trim** | **paint**
TOENAIL + NOUN **clippings** | **clippers**

toil noun

ADJ. **back-breaking, grinding, hard** (*esp. BrE*) | **ceaseless, endless, unceasing** | **daily** | **physical** | **honest**
PHRASES **hours, years, etc. of ~** ◊ *a lifetime of physical ~* | **sweat and ~** ◊ *a day of sweat and ~*

toilet noun

1 bowl with a seat, used for passing solid waste

ADJ. **flush, flushing** ◊ *The caravan is equipped with a sink and a flush ~.* | **portable** | **chemical, compost** (*BrE*), **composting** (*AmE*)
VERB + TOILET **go to** (*BrE*), **use, visit** (*esp. BrE*) ◊ *I need to go to the ~.* | **be desperate for** (*esp. BrE*), **need** ◊ *Do you need the ~?* | **flush (sth down)** ◊ *Someone's forgotten to flush the ~.* ◊ *He flushed the letter down the ~.* | **block, clog** | **unblock**
TOILET + NOUN **bowl, seat** | **paper, roll** (*BrE*), **tissue** | **brush, cleaner** | **facilities** | **training**
PREP. **in the ~, on the ~**

2 (*BrE*) room, etc. with a toilet or toilets

ADJ. **public** | **communal, shared** ◊ *There was a communal ~ on the landing for the four flats.* | **indoor, inside** | **outside** | **gents', ladies', men's, women's** | **disabled**

token noun

ADJ. **small** | **love** | **book** (*BrE*)
PREP. **as a ~ of, in ~ of** (*formal*) ◊ *She presented them with a small gift in ~ of her thanks.* ◊ *We hope you will accept this book as a small ~ of our appreciation.*

tolerable adj.

VERBS **be** | **become** | **make sth, render sth** | **find sth** ◊ *She inspected the rooms and found them perfectly ~.*
ADV. **barely** ◊ *In August the heat is barely ~.* | **almost** ◊ *A nice breeze made the desert almost ~.* | **quite** ◊ *This wine is really quite ~ considering it cost only $4 a bottle.*

tolerance noun

1 able to tolerate other opinions, actions, etc.

ADJ. **great** ◊ *The policy required greater ~ of foreigners.* | **political, racial, religious** | **zero** (of crime) ◊ *Howard County has a zero-tolerance policy on alcohol use by teenagers.*
... OF TOLERANCE **degree, level**
VERB + TOLERANCE **have** | **show** | **learn** | **foster, preach, promote, teach (sb)**
PREP. **~ for** ◊ *He has no ~ for people who are not like him.* | **~ of** ◊ *a plea for greater ~ of religious diversity* | **~ towards/ toward** ◊ *She was showing greater ~ towards/toward her younger sister than before.*
PHRASES **a lack of ~** ◊ *Your lack of ~ is disappointing.*

2 ability to suffer pain, cold, etc.

ADJ. **high, low** | **decreased, increased** | **pain** | **drought, heat, stress, etc.** ◊ *We group plants according to their light and heat ~s.*
... OF TOLERANCE **level**
VERB + TOLERANCE **have** | **develop, improve, increase**
TOLERANCE + NOUN **level**

PREP. **~ for** ◊ *He proved his high ~ for pain.* | **~ to** ◊ *Tolerance to alcohol decreases with age.*

tolerant *adj.*

VERBS **be, seem** | **become, grow**
ADV. **extremely, fairly, very, etc.** | **highly, remarkably, surprisingly** ◊ *Mary was surprisingly ~ of his annoying habits.* | **relatively** ◊ *He's relatively ~ of my faults.* | **religiously** ◊ *an area known to be religiously ~*
PREP. **of** ◊ *They learn to be ~ of other people.* | **towards/ toward** ◊ *They are more ~ towards/toward minorities now.*

tolerate *verb*

1 allow sth you do not like

ADV. **barely** | **just, merely** ◊ *She actually seemed pleased to see him: most of her visitors she merely ~d.* | **grudgingly** | **officially** ◊ *Union activity was officially ~d but strongly discouraged.* | **widely** ◊ *It is technically illegal but widely ~d.* | **no longer** ◊ *The government is not prepared to ~ this situation any longer.*
VERB + TOLERATE **be unable to, cannot** | **not be prepared to** (*esp. BrE*), **not be willing to, will not** ◊ *I will not ~ this conduct!* | **find sth difficult to**

2 not be affected by difficult conditions

ADV. **readily, well** ◊ *This plant will readily ~ some acidity.* ◊ *She ~d the chemotherapy well.* | **poorly**
VERB + TOLERATE **be unable to, cannot** | **will not** | **find sth difficult to, make sth difficult to** ◊ *The condition makes it difficult to ~ bright light.*

toleration *noun*

ADJ. **religious** | **mutual**
...OF TOLERATION **degree, measure** ◊ *Religious minorities were allowed a wide measure of ~.*
PREP. **~ for** ◊ *He preached ~ for all religions.*

toll *noun*

1 money that you pay to use a road, bridge, etc.

ADJ. **highway** (*in the US*), **motorway** (*in the UK*), **road**
VERB + TOLL **charge, collect, exact, impose, levy** ◊ *the possibility of imposing ~s on some roads* | **pay**
TOLL + NOUN **bridge, highway** (*in the US*), **motorway** (*in the UK*), **road** | **booth** (usually **tollbooth**), **plaza, station** (*both AmE*) | **charge**

2 amount of damage done/number of people killed

ADJ. **devastating, enormous, great, heavy, high, huge, terrible, tragic** | **mounting, rising** ◊ *the mounting death ~* | **final** | **casualty, death, injury** (*esp. BrE*) | **civilian, human** | **emotional, physical, psychological**
VERB + TOLL **exact, take** ◊ *The pressure of fame can take a terrible ~.* ◊ *The recession is taking its ~.* | **estimate**
TOLL + VERB **mount, rise** ◊ *The death ~ from yesterday's crash is still rising.* | **reach sth** ◊ *The casualty ~ could reach 200.* | **stand at sth** ◊ *The death ~ stands at 37.*
PREP. **~ on** ◊ *Illness has taken a heavy ~ on her.*
PHRASES **bring the ~ to** ◊ *This brings the death ~ to 86.* | **put the ~ at** ◊ *The latest estimates put the death ~ at 15 000.*

tomato *noun*

ADJ. **fresh, ripe** | **rotten** | **chopped, sliced** | **green, red** | **beef** (*BrE*), **beefsteak** (*AmE*), **cherry, heirloom** (*AmE*), **plum** | **organic, sun-dried, vine-ripened** | **canned** (*esp. AmE*), **tinned** (*BrE*)
VERB + TOMATO **eat, have** | **chop, dice, slice** | **grow** | **pick** | **throw** ◊ *Demonstrators threw rotten ~es at the car.*
TOMATO + NOUN **juice, ketchup** (*esp. BrE*), **paste, purée, salad, sauce, soup** | **slice** | **plant**

ton *noun* → Note at MEASURE

tone *noun*

1 quality of a sound, esp. of the human voice

ADJ. **deep, low** | **hushed, quiet, subdued** ◊ *Why is everyone speaking in hushed ~s?* | **breathy, gravelly, husky** | **clear, ringing** | **sharp, shrill, stentorian, strident** | **dry, even, flat, level, measured, neutral** ◊ *The question was posed in a flat ~.* | **normal, reasonable** | **brisk, businesslike, matter-of-fact** ◊ *She answered him in a brisk, matter-of-fact ~.* | **commanding, defiant, firm** | **formal** | **serious, solemn** | **dramatic, urgent** | **casual** | **bright, conversational** | **calm, friendly, gentle, mild, pleasant, soft, soothing, sympathetic, warm** ◊ *Her ~ was mild, almost conversational.* | **sweet** ◊ *the sweet ~ of the flute* | **dulcet, honeyed, mellifluous** (*formal*) (*all often ironic*) ◊ *the dulcet ~s of the sergeant* | **clipped, cold, cool, curt, hard, harsh, icy** ◊ *In cool, clipped ~s, he told her what had happened.* | **aggressive, biting, bitter, condescending, contemptuous, disapproving, dismissive, ironic, mocking, patronizing, playful, sarcastic, sardonic, scathing, teasing** ◊ *His ~ was faintly mocking.* | **threatening** | **angry, annoyed, exasperated** | **aggrieved, shocked, worried** | **bantering, conciliatory, conspiratorial, reverential**
VERB + TONE **adopt, speak in, strike, take, use** ◊ *When she heard my accent, she adopted a warmer ~.* ◊ *The President struck a defiant ~.* ◊ *Don't you take that ~ with me.* | **soften** | **change** | **hear, notice** | **interpret** ◊ *Her ~ was hard to interpret.* | **not like** ◊ *Excuse me, I don't like your ~.*
TONE + VERB **change** ◊ *His ~ changed dramatically when he saw the money.* | **soften** | **convey sth, imply sth, indicate sth, suggest sth** | **sound sth** ◊ *Her ~ sounded sincere but I knew she was lying.* | **betray sb/sth, give away sb/sth** ◊ *Her ~ betrayed her impatience.*
PREP. **in a/the ~** ◊ *'You ought to have thought of them,' she said in a reproachful ~.* | **in ~s of** ◊ *'I don't believe it!' cried Henry in ~s of utter amazement.*
PHRASES **a ~ of voice** ◊ *I didn't like his ~ of voice; I felt he was being condescending.*

2 general quality/style of sb/sth

ADJ. **dominant, general, overall, prevailing** ◊ *The general ~ of the report was positive.* | **moral, political** ◊ *The newspaper sets a high moral ~ in its editorial about politicians' private lives.* | **negative** | **comic, humorous** | **serious**
VERB + TONE **establish, set** ◊ *Her enthusiastic speech set the ~ for the day's conference.* | **have** ◊ *The movie has a jokey ~ throughout.* | **maintain** | **lighten** ◊ *He uses humour/humor to lighten the ~ of the novel.* | **match** ◊ *The music perfectly matches the ~ of the movie.*
PREP. **in ~** ◊ *His letter was very negative in ~.*
PHRASES **a change in ~, a change of ~** ◊ *There is a marked change of ~ in the second half of the book.*

3 shade of a colour

ADJ. **light, muted, neutral, pale, pastel, soft** ◊ *muted ~s of brown and green* | **dark, deep** | **rich, warm** | **earthy, flesh, grey/gray, natural** | **colour/color** | **skin** ◊ *What is your natural skin ~?*
VERB + TONE **match** ◊ *You should use a foundation that matches your skin ~.*

4 on the telephone

ADJ. **dial** (*AmE*), **dialling** (*BrE*) | **engaged** (*BrE*) (**busy signal** in *AmE*) | **ring** (usually **ringtone**)
VERB + TONE **get** ◊ *I keep getting the engaged ~.*
TONE + VERB **sound** ◊ *The dial ~ sounded.*

tongue *noun*

1 soft part inside the mouth

ADJ. **long** | **forked** | **loose, sharp** (*both figurative*) ◊ *Everyone knows now, thanks to Ken's loose ~* (= he could not keep the secret). ◊ *He has a reputation for having a sharp ~.*
VERB + TONGUE **poke out, put out, stick out** ◊ *It's very rude to stick your ~ out at people.* | **run** ◊ *He ran his ~ nervously over his lips.* | **click** | **bite, hold** (*both figurative*) ◊ *She was dying*

to say something sarcastic to him, but bit her ~ and stayed silent. | **free, loosen** (both figurative) ◇ The wine had loosened his ~. | **roll off, slip off, trip off** ◇ It's not a name that exactly trips off the ~ (= is easy to say).

TONGUE + VERB **hang out** ◇ The dog lay in a patch of shade with its ~ hanging out. | **flick, flicker** ◇ The snake's ~ flicked out of its mouth. | **wag** (figurative) ◇ This is a small island and ~s are beginning to wag (= people are beginning to gossip). | **find** (figurative) ◇ Before she could find her ~ (= speak) the door had closed behind him. | **watch** (figurative) ◇ You just watch your ~ (= be careful what you say)!

TONGUE + NOUN **piercing**

PHRASES **a slip of the ~** (figurative) ◇ He said it was a slip of the ~ (= a mistake in speaking) and apologized. | **be on the tip of your ~** (figurative) ◇ It was on the tip of her ~ to refuse. | **get your ~ around sth, get your ~ round sth** (BrE, figurative) ◇ He was having trouble getting his ~ around my name. | **a ~ of fire, a ~ of flame** ◇ Tongues of flame licked up the walls.

2 a language

ADJ. **mother, native** ◇ She speaks English, though her native ~ is German. | **common** | **foreign** | **strange**

VERB + TONGUE **speak** ◇ They were speaking a foreign ~.

PREP. **in a/the ~** ◇ She could hear the men whispering in a foreign ~.

PHRASES **speak in ~s** (= to speak in unknown languages, esp. at a religious ceremony)

tonne noun → Note at MEASURE

tool noun

1 instrument for making/repairing things

ADJ. **general-purpose, multi-purpose** | **basic, primitive, simple, standard, traditional** ◇ craftsmen using traditional ~s | **sophisticated, special** | **right** ◇ Do you have the right ~s for the job? | **sharp** | **rusty** | **cutting, drawing, measuring** | **cordless, hand, machine, power** | **agricultural, engineering, farm, farming, garden, gardening, industrial, woodworking**

... OF TOOLS **set**

VERB + TOOL **use** | **sharpen** | **down ~s** (BrE) ◇ Workers downed ~s (= stopped work) in protest at poor safety standards in the works.

2 sth that helps you do/achieve sth

ADJ. **new** | **effective, essential, handy, important, indispensable, invaluable, key, major, necessary, powerful, primary, useful, valuable, vital** | **blunt** | **educational, learning, pedagogical, teaching** | **reference, research** ◇ This dictionary is an invaluable reference ~ for advanced learners. | **analysis, analytical, conceptual, diagnostic, investigative, practical** ◇ a valuable diagnostic ~ for physicians | **legal, negotiating, political, propaganda** ◇ We must ensure that education is not used as a political ~. | **communication, management, marketing** | **design, development, drawing, multimedia, presentation** | **blogging, desktop, digital, online, programming, software**

VERB + TOOL **become** ◇ The Internet has become a vital ~ for many artists. | **develop, provide**

PHRASES **the ~s of the/sb's trade** ◇ Sympathy and compassion are the ~s of his trade.

tooth noun

1 individual tooth

ADJ. **broken, chipped, missing** | **bad, decayed, rotten** | **loose** | **capped, gold** | **canine, eye** (AmE) | **wisdom**

VERB + TOOTH **extract, pull out, remove** | **have out** ◇ I've just had a ~ out at the dentist's. | **knock out** | **lose** ◇ I lost three teeth in the fight. | **break** | **fill** | **cut** ◇ The baby's crying because he's cutting a new ~ (= a new one is coming through). ◇ a reporter who cut her teeth working in Soweto (figurative)

TOOTH + VERB **be through, come through** ◇ Billy's first ~ is now through. | **fall out** | **ache**

TOOTH + NOUN **decay, loss** | **abscess** | **enamel** | **fairy** ◇ Does the ~ fairy really exist?

2 teeth set of teeth

ADJ. **big, huge** | **gappy** (BrE) ◇ She wore a brace to correct her gappy teeth. | **buck, prominent** ◇ I used to be self-conscious of my prominent teeth. | **even, straight** | **crooked, jagged** (often figurative), **misshapen, pointy** (informal) ◇ Her smile showed crooked teeth. ◇ Skyscrapers rose like jagged teeth. | **good, healthy, pearl-white, pearly, perfect, strong, white** | **yellow** | **false** | **needle-sharp, razor-sharp, sharp** ◇ Mink have razor-sharp teeth. | **clenched, gritted** ◇ Alan hissed from behind his clenched teeth. | **back, front** | **bottom, top** | **baby, milk** (BrE) ◇ I still have one of my baby teeth. | **adult** | **real** | **permanent**

VERB + TEETH **have** | **brush, clean** | **rot** ◇ Sugar rots your teeth. | **bare, reveal, show** ◇ The dog bared its teeth at us and growled. ◇ The man smiled, revealing perfect white teeth. | **clamp, clench, grit** ◇ He broke off what he was saying, clamping his teeth together. ◇ She answered through clenched teeth (= opening her mouth only a little because of anger). | **clamp sth between, clamp sth in** ◇ His pipe was firmly clamped between his teeth. | **gnash, grind** | **sink** ◇ The cat sank its teeth into his finger.

TEETH + VERB **bite sb/sth, sink into sb/sth, snap together** | **chatter** ◇ Their teeth were chattering with cold. | **flash, gleam, glint, shine** ◇ Her teeth flashed as she smiled.

PREP. **against the/your ~** ◇ He clattered the spoon against his teeth as he ate. | **between the/your ~** ◇ She answered the phone with a cigarette between her teeth. | **in the/your ~** ◇ The cat came in with a mouse in its teeth. | **through the/your ~** ◇ 'Come here now!' she growled through her teeth.

top noun

1 highest part/surface of sth

ADJ. **extreme, very** ◇ We didn't climb to the very ~ of the mountain, but close enough. | **cliff, hill, mountain, roof, tree** (usually **clifftop, hilltop**, etc.) | **counter** (esp. AmE), **stove** (AmE), **table** (usually **countertop**, etc.)

PREP. **at the ~, on ~** ◇ Each cake had a cherry on ~. ◇ There was a vase on ~ of the bookcase. | **to the ~**

PHRASES **from ~ to bottom** ◇ I'm going to clean the house from ~ to bottom this weekend.

2 highest/most important rank/position

VERB + TOP **get to, make it to, reach, rise to** ◇ Few of the trainees make it to the ~. ◇ She rose to the ~ of her profession within ten years.

PREP. **at the ~** ◇ The company has an unusually high proportion of young people at the ~. | **on ~, to the ~**

PHRASES **~ of the agenda** ◇ Pay was now (at the) ~ of the employees' agenda. | **~ of the class** ◇ She was ~ of the class in geography.

3 cover that you put on sth in order to close it

ADJ. **bottle**

VERB + TOP **lift, lift off, pop** (AmE, informal), **pop off** (informal, esp. AmE), **pull off, unscrew** ◇ He popped the ~ of a soda can. | **put back on, screw on**

4 piece of clothing

ADJ. **halter, hooded** (esp. BrE), **long-sleeved, low-cut, sleeveless, strapless** | **baggy, loose** | **tight** | **skimpy** | **matching** ◇ She wore a pink skirt with a matching ~. | **crop, tank, tube** (AmE), **vest** (BrE) | **bikini, pyjama/pajama** | **football, tracksuit** (both BrE)
→ Special page at CLOTHES

top adj.

VERBS **be** | **come** ◇ She came ~ in the exams.

PREP. **in** ◇ All the doctors here are ~ in their field. ◇ She was ~ in English. (BrE) | **of** ◇ He was ~ of his class.

topic noun

ADJ. **chosen, selected** | **particular, specific** | **related** ◇

articles on religious art and related ~s | **broad, general, large, wide** ◇ *She spoke on the broad ~ of 'discipline'.* | **diverse, wide-ranging** ◇ *The book covers such diverse ~s as diving and first aid.* | **narrow** | **central, important, key, main, major** | **favourite/favorite, hot** (*informal*), **popular** ◇ *Pensions are a hot ~ at the moment.* | **interesting** | **complex, difficult** | **controversial, sensitive, taboo** ◇ *It might be better to avoid such a controversial ~.* | **conversational, discussion, essay, research** | **historical, philosophical, scientific, social,** etc.
VERB + TOPIC **address, approach, broach, consider, cover, deal with, explore, focus on, look at, tackle** ◇ *In the next chapter the writer focuses on the ~ of adoption.* | **debate, discuss** | **research** | **speak on, write on** | **choose, pick** | **raise** | **change** ◇ *I did my best to change the ~ (= of conversation).*
TOPIC + VERB **range from sth to sth** ◇ *We discussed ~s ranging from foreign policy to economics.* | **come up** ◇ *This ~ comes up every year.*
TOPIC + NOUN **area, heading** ◇ *There will be workshops on four main ~ areas.*
PREP. **on a/the ~** ◇ *Mr Graham will speak on the ~ of dogs.* | **~ for** ◇ *the ~ for discussion*
PHRASES **a choice of ~** ◇ *She was an excellent speaker, but I found her choice of ~ strange.* | **a range of ~s, a variety of ~s** | **a ~ of conversation, a ~ of discussion** ◇ *His main ~ of conversation is football.*

topless *adj.*

VERBS **be, go** ◇ *Do you dare to go ~ on the beach?* | **sunbathe** | **appear, dance, perform, pose** ◇ *There was talk that she had posed ~ for a magazine.* | **show sb**

torch *noun*

1 (*BrE*) electric light → See also FLASHLIGHT
ADJ. **powerful** | **electric**
VERB + TORCH **carry, have** | **switch off, turn off** | **switch on, turn on** | **flash, point, shine** ◇ *The policeman flashed his ~ over the men's faces.* ◇ *I shone my ~ through the crack.*
TORCH + VERB **flash, shine** ◇ *A powerful ~ shone in their direction.*
TORCH + NOUN **beam**
PHRASES **the beam of a ~** | **the light from a ~, the light of a ~** ◇ *We struggled to read the map by the light of the ~.*
2 piece of burning wood carried to give light
ADJ. **blazing, burning, flaming, flickering** | **Olympic**
VERB + TORCH **light** ◇ *They lit their ~es from the fire.* | **carry, hold** ◇ *Servants were carrying lighted ~es.* | **pass, pass on** (*both figurative*) ◇ *I'm ready to pass the ~ on to the next generation.*
TORCH + VERB **light** ◇ *The path was lit by blazing ~es.* | **burn** ◇ *The ~es were burning fiercely.* | **flare, flicker** | **go out** ◇ *The ~ flickered and went out.*

torment *noun*

ADJ. **great** | **emotional, inner, mental, personal, physical, psychological** | **eternal** ◇ *Hell as a place of eternal ~*
VERB + TORMENT **endure, suffer** ◇ *She has suffered great mental ~.* | **escape** | **inflict on sb** ◇ *the ~ inflicted on a young girl by her mother*
PREP. **in ~** ◇ *He was a man in ~.*
PHRASES **be released from ~**

tornado *noun*

ADJ. **deadly, powerful** | **possible** ◇ *McMullen County is expecting a possible ~.*
TORNADO + VERB **hit sth, strike sth** ◇ *The town was hit by a ~ last night.* | **come down, touch down** (*both esp. AmE*) ◇ *A powerful ~ touched down in Evansville, Indiana.* | **damage sth, destroy sth, devastate sth** | **come through (sth), rip through sth** (*esp. AmE*), **sweep across sth, sweep through sth** ◇ *A huge ~ ripped through two states.*
VERB + TORNADO **cause, produce, spawn** (*esp. AmE*) ◇ *Tropical storm Bonnie spawned ~es in North Carolina.* | **chase** ◇ *The group meets every spring to chase ~es.*
TORNADO + NOUN **warning** ◇ *We had a ~ warning earlier in the evening.* | **watch** (*esp. AmE*) ◇ *There are ~ watches in effect all across eastern Alabama.* | **siren**
PREP. **in a/the ~** ◇ *The building was badly damaged in a ~.*

torpedo *noun*

VERB + TORPEDO **carry** ◇ *enemy planes carrying ~es* | **fire, launch** | **drop**
TORPEDO + VERB **hit sth, strike sth**
TORPEDO + NOUN **tube** | **boat, bomber**

torrent *noun*

1 large amount of water moving very quickly
ADJ. **raging, rushing** ◇ *After heavy rain, the little stream becomes a raging ~.*
PREP. **in ~s** ◇ *The rain poured down in ~s.*
PHRASES **a ~ of rain, a ~ of water**
2 large amount of sth that comes suddenly
VERB + TORRENT **let loose, release, unleash** ◇ *The sight of her father unleashed a ~ of emotions.* | **generate, produce**
PREP. **in a ~** ◇ *Her pent-up anger was released in a ~ of words.* | **~ of** ◇ *a ~ of abuse/criticism/tears*

torso *noun*

ADJ. **bare, naked** | **tanned** | **lower, upper** | **human** | **headless** ◇ *The headless ~ of a man was found in some bushes.*
VERB + TORSO **reveal** ◇ *He took off his T-shirt to reveal his tanned ~.*

torture *noun*

ADJ. **brutal** | **systematic** | **mental, physical, psychological**
VERB + TORTURE **inflict** | **endure, suffer**
TORTURE + NOUN **camp, chamber, room** | **device** | **method, technique** | **victim**

torture *verb*

ADV. **badly, brutally, severely** | **routinely** ◇ *The prisoners were routinely ~d.*
PHRASES **~ sb to death**

toss *noun*

1 of the head
PREP. **with a ~**
PHRASES **a ~ of your/the head** ◇ *'Of course not!' she said with a ~ of her head.*
2 the toss (*esp. BrE*) of a coin
VERB + THE TOSS **lose, win** ◇ *England won the ~ and chose to kick off.* | **call** ◇ *The team captains called the ~.*
PREP. **with a ~**
PHRASES **the ~ of a coin** ◇ *The order of play was decided by the ~ of a coin.* ◇ *The venue will be decided on the ~ of a coin.* (*BrE*)

toss *verb*

1 throw sth carelessly
ADV. **carelessly, casually** ◇ *She picked up the package and casually ~ed it into her bag.* | **unceremoniously** ◇ *The bodies were unceremoniously ~ed into mass graves.* | **around** (*often figurative*), **aside, away, back, out, over** ◇ *It's an idea that gets ~ed around from time to time.* ◇ *She ~ed back her blonde hair.* | **overboard** (*often figurative*) ◇ *The improvements had to be ~ed overboard because of lack of money.*
PREP. **into, out of, to** ◇ *He ~ed the letter over to me.*
2 keep moving up and down/from side to side
ADV. **restlessly** ◇ *She ~ed around restlessly all night with a high fever.* | **about** (*BrE*), **around** ◇ *He was ~ed around in his boat.*
PHRASES **~ and turn** ◇ *He ~ed and turned all night, unable to sleep.*

3 cover food in a sauce

ADV. **gently, lightly | well | together**
PREP. **in** ◊ *Toss the vegetables lightly in olive oil.*

total noun

ADJ. **annual, daily, monthly | current | combined, cumulative, grand, overall, sum** ◊ *His two goals give him a grand ~ of 32 for the season.* ◊ *The sum ~ of my knowledge is not impressive.* | **estimated | running** ◊ *Players keep a running ~ of the score.* | **final | high, huge** (*esp. BrE*), **record** ◊ *a record ~ of victories* | **low | national, world | jobless** (*esp. BrE*) ◊ *Britain's jobless ~ rose by 20 000 last month.* | **vote** (*AmE*) ◊ *We had an early vote ~ of about 1.7 million people.* | **career** (*sports*) ◊ *He won a career ~ of 19 gold medals.* | **point, run, win, etc.** (*sports*)
VERB + TOTAL **add up to, give, make, make up** ◊ *Their earnings were €250, €300 and €420, giving a ~ of €970.* | **earn, receive | pay, spend | bring, take** ◊ *A donation of $250 has been received, bringing the ~ to $3 750.* | **achieve, reach, win** ◊ *The Greens achieved a ~ of 18 seats.*
TOTAL + VERB **rise | fall**
PREP. **in ~** ◊ *In ~, they spent 420 hours on the project.* | **out of a ~ of** ◊ *180 vehicles out of a ~ of 900 examined were not roadworthy.* | **~ of**

touch noun

1 act of touching sb/sth

ADJ. **delicate, gentle, light, slight** ◊ *The slightest ~ will set off the alarm.*
PREP. **at sb/sth's ~** ◊ *The door swung open at his ~.* ◊ *You can now shop at the ~ of a button.*
PHRASES **be cold, hot, soft, etc. to the ~** ◊ *The solid rock was warm to the ~.*

2 small detail

ADJ. **final, finishing | decorative, festive, homely** (*BrE*), **romantic** ◊ *The family photos add a homely ~.* ◊ *The candles gave the table a romantic ~.* | **humorous | classy, lovely** (*esp. BrE*), **nice, professional** ◊ *Giving her flowers was a nice ~.* | **feminine, human, individual, personal | little, small, subtle** ◊ *The decor includes many individual little ~es.*
VERB + TOUCH **add, give sth, put** ◊ *She's just putting the finishing ~es to her painting.*

3 particular ability

ADJ. **golden, magic | deft, sure** (*esp. BrE*) ◊ *She seemed to have a deft ~ with comedy.* ◊ *With students she had a sure ~ and showed great personal sensitivity.* | **light** ◊ *He handles this controversial subject with a light ~.* | **political** ◊ *He found his old political ~ when the crisis emerged.* | **shooting** (*AmE*) (in basketball) ◊ *He must regain his shooting ~.*
VERB + TOUCH **have | find | lack | lose** ◊ *Maybe the champion is losing her magic ~.*
PHRASES **the common ~** ◊ *a politician who lacked the common ~*

4 small amount of sth

ADJ. **little, subtle | welcome | right** ◊ *He has just the right ~ of arrogance for the role.*
VERB + TOUCH **add, bring** ◊ *Her speech brought a welcome ~ of frivolity to the evening.*
PREP. **with a ~ of** ◊ *'Thanks,' she said, with a ~ of sarcasm.* | **~ of**

5 contact

ADJ. **close** ◊ *The security staff were in close ~ with the local police.*
VERB + TOUCH **get in** ◊ *I'm trying to get in ~ with Jane. Do you have her number?* | **keep in, stay in** ◊ *It is important to keep in ~ with the latest research.* ◊ *Let's keep in ~.* | **put sb in** ◊ *I'll put you in ~ with someone in your area.* | **lose** ◊ *I've lost ~ with all my old friends.*
PREP. **in ~** ◊ *Are you still in ~ with your friends from college?* | **out of ~** ◊ *This government is increasingly out of ~ with ordinary voters.* | **~ with**

touch verb

1 put your hand on sb/sth; be in contact with sb/sth

ADV. **(not) actually, not even, not quite** ◊ *He did not actually ~ the substance, but may have inhaled it.* | **barely, hardly, scarcely** ◊ *You've hardly ~ed your food* (= not eaten it). | **almost, nearly, practically** ◊ *Their faces were almost ~ing.* | **just | briefly** ◊ *His fingers briefly ~ed hers.* | **gently, lightly | gingerly | accidentally, inadvertently** ◊ *He accidentally ~ed a live wire.* | **never** ◊ *He said I kicked him, but I never ~ed him!*
VERB + TOUCH **want to | (not) dare (to)** ◊ *Don't you dare ~ me!* | **reach out, over, up, etc. to** ◊ *Her hand reached out to ~ his cheek.* | **let sb** ◊ *He wouldn't let me ~ the wound.*
PREP. **on** ◊ *He ~ed her gently on the arm.* | **with** ◊ *She ~ed him with her hand.*
PHRASES **(be) careful not to ~ sth** ◊ *She hugged him, being careful not to ~ his broken wrist.* | **close enough to ~ sb/sth** ◊ *He was close enough to ~ her.*

2 make sb feel a strong emotion

ADV. **deeply** ◊ *The story ~ed me very deeply.*
PHR V **touch on/upon sth**
ADV. **briefly | just, merely** ◊ *Photography is merely ~ed on in the book.*
VERB + TOUCH ON/UPON **want to** ◊ *I want to ~ briefly on another aspect of the problem.*

touchdown noun in American football

ADJ. **defensive, offensive | rushing | game-winning, winning**
VERB + TOUCHDOWN **score** ◊ *He failed to score a ~ for the third consecutive game.*
TOUCHDOWN + NOUN **run** ◊ *a 25-yard ~ run* | **pass** ◊ *Manning and Brett threw nine ~ passes between them.*

touched adj.

VERBS **be, feel, look, seem**
ADV. **extremely, fairly, very, etc. | deeply, genuinely, incredibly, really, truly | especially** ◊ *She was especially ~ by the chairman's appeal.*
PREP. **by** ◊ *We were deeply ~ by your concern.*

tough adj.

1 difficult/unpleasant

VERBS **be, seem | get | remain | find sth** ◊ *He may find it ~ to pursue his plans.* | **make sth** ◊ *The strong dollar has made it ~ for small businesses.*
ADV. **extremely, fairly, very, etc. | particularly, really** ◊ *Things were really ~ at first.* | **a little, slightly, etc.**
PREP. **on** ◊ *It's very ~ on the wives when the husbands leave.*

2 strict/firm

VERBS **be | become, get**
ADV. **extremely, fairly, very, etc. | particularly | enough** ◊ *Has the government been ~ enough on polluters?*
PREP. **on** ◊ *The government has promised to get ~ on crime.* | **with** ◊ *You have to be ~ with these young thugs.*

3 strong

VERBS **appear, be, feel, look, seem, stand** (*informal*) | **become, get, grow | act, play, talk** (*all informal*) ◊ *Then this guy started acting ~.*
ADV. **extremely, fairly, very, etc. | incredibly, really, remarkably | enough** ◊ *Are you sure you're physically ~ enough for this job?* | **mentally, physically**

tour noun

1 trip

ADJ. **foreign** (*esp. BrE*), **international, national, nationwide, overseas, world | American, European, UK, etc. | two-city, three-country, etc.** ◊ *The group will shortly go on a ten-city European ~.* | **whirlwind, whistle-stop** ◊ *The band completed a whirlwind ~ of North America in two months.* |

tour

874

gruelling/grueling, lengthy, long | official ◇ *the couple's
first official overseas ~* | grand ◇ *He took his degree in 1665
before embarking on the grand ~ (= a tour of Europe lasting
several months).* | package ◇ *an all-inclusive package ~ of
Austria* | mystery *(= where the destination is not known)*
(BrE, often humorous) | bike *(esp. AmE),* bus *(AmE),* coach
(BrE), cycle *(esp. BrE),* walking | camping | cricket, rugby
(both BrE) | pro, senior *(both in golf)* | book, concert,
lecture, speaking, study, theatre/theater | sell-out *(esp.
BrE),* sold-out *(esp. AmE),* successful ◇ *The band is just back
from a sell-out Asian ~.* | comeback, farewell, reunion ◇
Simon and Garfunkel's 2003 reunion ~ | promotional,
publicity ◇ *a promotional ~ for her new book*
... OF TOUR leg, part, stage ◇ *He was now on the last leg of his
book ~.*
VERB + TOUR do, go on, make, undertake *(esp. BrE)* | embark
on, set off on *(esp. BrE)*
TOUR + NOUN company, operator | date, schedule ◇ *details
of the band's ~ dates* | stop | leader, manager ◇ *Our ~
leaders are all fluent in English.* ◇ *The team's ~ manager
called a press conference.* | party, squad *(both BrE)* ◇ *He
wasn't selected for England's ~ party to Australia.* | player,
pro *(both in golf)* | bus, van ◇ *Dolly Parton's ~ bus*
PREP. on (a) ~ ◇ *We met a group of Italians on a ~ in Peru.* ◇
The band is currently on ~ in the States. | ~ of ◇ *I'd like to do
a ~ of Belgium on foot.*
PHRASES ~ of duty ◇ *The soldiers were returning from a six-
month ~ of duty in Northern Ireland.*

2 short visit

ADJ. brief, quick ◇ *Our host gave us a quick ~ of the house.* |
extensive | grand *(humorous)* ◇ *Come on, I'll give you the
grand ~ of the backyard.* | conducted, guided, self-guided |
bus, helicopter, etc. ◇ *an open-top bus ~ of the city* | city,
factory | sightseeing | ghost ◇ *She takes tourists on ghost
~s of Edinburgh.* | virtual ◇ *A virtual ~ is available on the
Web.*
VERB + TOUR do, make ◇ *I made a quick ~ of the office to say
goodbye.* | conduct, lead | give sb, take sb on | arrange,
organize | offer ◇ *Garden ~s are offered throughout the
summer.*
TOUR + NOUN guide | group | boat, bus, etc.
PHRASES ~ of inspection ◇ *The boss started his ~ of inspection
with my office.*

tour *verb*

ADV. extensively, widely | internationally | currently
VERB + TOUR plan to
PREP. all over ◇ *We plan to ~ all over the country.* | in ◇ *She
has ~ed extensively in the US.* | with ◇ *She is currently ~ing
with her new band.*

tourism *noun*

ADJ. global, international, overseas | mass, package *(esp.
BrE)* | increased | environmental, green, responsible,
sustainable | cultural, farm *(BrE),* heritage *(esp. AmE),* sex,
space
VERB + TOURISM boost, encourage, increase, promote | hurt
| be dependent on, depend on, rely on ◇ *The island's
economy is largely dependent on ~.*
TOURISM + VERB boom, increase ◇ *With the expansion of air
travel, ~ boomed.* | decline, fall
TOURISM + NOUN business, operator ◇ *the world's first
commercial space ~ operator* | industry, market, sector |
dollars, revenue *(BrE),* revenues *(AmE)* | development,
promotion | agency, bureau, office | officer *(BrE),* official
| boss, chief *(both BrE, informal)* ◇ *Tourism chiefs in York are
drawing up plans to attract more people.* | potential ◇ *The
city is finally realizing its ~ potential.*
PREP. through ~ *(esp. BrE)* ◇ *The town survives mainly
through ~.*
PHRASES a decline in ~, a downturn in ~, a drop in ~ | an
increase in ~, a rise in ~ | the growth in ~, the growth of
~ | the development of ~, the promotion of ~ | income
from ~, revenue from ~ | the impact of ~

tourist *noun*

ADJ. foreign, Western | American, Japanese, etc. | modern
| sex, space ◇ *the exploitation of women by sex ~s*
... OF TOURISTS busload, coachload *(BrE),* group, party
VERB + TOURIST attract, bring, draw ◇ *The story of the Loch
Ness Monster has attracted many ~s to the area.*
TOURIST + VERB come to sth, flock to sth, frequent sth, visit
sth ◇ *the part of town most frequented by ~s*
TOURIST + NOUN area, centre/center, destination, resort,
site, spot, town, trap ◇ *Recently Shanghai has become a
popular ~ destination.* | attraction, facility, sight ◇ *Pompeii
is one of Italy's prime ~ attractions.* ◇ *The theme park is the
region's most popular ~ facility.* | route, trail *(esp. BrE)* ◇ *The
town is off the usual ~ route.* | hotel, shop | business,
industry, trade | board, office | information ◇ *the local ~
information office* | guide ◇ *I bought a ~ guide to Paris.* ◇
She works as a ~ guide. | map | traffic ◇ *the reduction in ~
traffic due to the violence* | dollars ◇ *Their economy is
dependent on ~ dollars.* | season | visa | bus, coach *(BrE)*
PHRASES influx of ~s ◇ *The festival is accompanied by a huge
influx of ~s.*

tournament *noun*

ADJ. basketball, chess, golf, poker, tennis, etc. | qualifying,
ranking, World Cup | European, international, local,
national, regional, world | major | one-day *(in cricket)* |
knockout, round-robin *(both esp. BrE)* | doubles, five-a-
side, seven-a-side, etc. *(in football/soccer),* sevens *(in
rugby),* singles | indoor | club, open | amateur,
professional | pre-season *(esp. BrE)*
VERB + TOURNAMENT enter, play, play in, take part in *(esp.
BrE)* ◇ *The ~ was played under floodlights.* ◇ *Several top
teams have agreed to play (in) the ~.* | win | hold, host,
organize
TOURNAMENT + VERB take place
TOURNAMENT + NOUN victory, win ◇ *her first ~ win of the
season* | leader, winner | final, game | director, organizer,
sponsor | referee *(esp. BrE)* | player, professional *(esp. BrE)*
◇ *the ~ professional at the local golf club* | golf ◇ *She retired
from ~ golf last year.*
PREP. in a/the ~ ◇ *the strongest player in the ~* | out of a/the
~ ◇ *The loser will be out of the ~.*

tow *noun*

VERB + TOW give sb ◇ *A truck driver gave me a ~ to the nearest
garage.*
TOW + NOUN bar, line *(usually* **towline***),* rope | truck *(esp.
AmE),* vehicle
PREP. in ~ *(usually figurative)* ◇ *a harassed mother with three
small children in ~* | under ~ ◇ *The ship, whose engine had
failed, is now safely under ~.*

towel *noun*

ADJ. clean, fresh | damp, wet | dry | hot, warm | rolled
(AmE), rolled-up | fluffy, soft, thick | cotton, paper, terry
(esp. AmE), terry-cloth *(AmE)* | bath, bathroom, beach, dish
(usually **dishtowel***) (AmE),* hand, kitchen *(esp. BrE),* tea
(BrE) | sanitary *(BrE) (***sanitary napkin** *in AmE)*
VERB + TOWEL drape, wrap ◇ *He had a ~ draped across his
shoulders.*
TOWEL + VERB hang ◇ *Several ~s hung over the side of the bath.*
TOWEL + NOUN rack *(AmE),* rail *(BrE)* ◇ *a heated ~ rail/rack* |
dispenser ◇ *a paper ~ dispenser*

tower *noun*

ADJ. high, high-rise *(BrE),* lofty *(literary),* massive, tall | two-
storey/two-story, 20-storey/20-story, etc. | 30-foot, 100-
foot, etc. | round, square | ancient, Gothic, medieval |
fortified | ruined | control, guard, lookout, observation,
watch *(usually* **watchtower***)* ◇ *Armed guards manned the
lookout ~s.* | bell, clock | cooling, water | cell, cellphone
(both AmE) | radio, television | apartment, office,
residential *(all esp. AmE)* | conning *(esp. BrE)* | castle,
cathedral, church | glass | ivory *(figurative)* ◇ *academics
sitting in their ivory ~s*

TOWER + VERB **collapse, fall** | **stand** ◇ *the spot where the ~s once stood*
TOWER + NOUN **block** (*BrE*)

town *noun*

1 place with many streets and buildings

ADJ. **big, large, major** | **little, small, tiny** (*esp. AmE*) | **nearby, neighbouring/neighboring, surrounding** | **ancient, historic, medieval, old** | **new** ◇ *It was built as a new ~ in the 1960s.* (*BrE*) | **company** (*esp. AmE*), **factory** (*esp. AmE*), **farm** (*esp. AmE*), **industrial, mill, mining** ◇ *a 19th-century mill ~ that used to produce cotton* | **busy** ◇ *a busy market ~* | **boom, thriving** ◇ *Rio was a boom ~ and trade was thriving.* ◇ *a thriving mining ~* | **dusty, sleepy** ◇ *the dusty border ~ of Eagle Pass, Texas* ◇ *a sleepy provincial ~ in southern France* | **remote** | **country, provincial, rural** | **county** (*BrE*) ◇ *Exeter, the county ~ of Devon* | **home, native** ◇ *She has gone back to live in her home ~.* | **border, frontier** | **mountain, prairie** (*esp. AmE*) | **beach** (*esp. AmE*), **coastal, seaside** (*esp. BrE*) ◇ *the sun-drenched beach ~s of Southern California* | **holiday** (*BrE*), **resort** | **cathedral, college** (*AmE*), **market, university** (*esp. BrE*) | **dormitory** (*BrE*), **satellite** | **fortified** ◇ *Kitzbühel is an ancient fortified ~.* | **shanty** | **ghost** ◇ *It's been a ghost ~ since the gold rush ended.* | **twin** (*BrE*) ◇ *Darlington's twin ~ of Amiens*
VERB + TOWN **build, found** | **live in** ◇ *How many people live in the ~?* | **get out of, leave, move out of, skip** (*informal, esp. AmE*) ◇ *He left ~ yesterday for a conference in Cape Town.* ◇ *They wanted to move out of ~ and start a new life in the country.* | **surround** ◇ *the rolling hills that surround the ~*
TOWN + VERB **flourish, grow**
TOWN + NOUN **centre** (*BrE*) | **hall, square, walls** | **council** | **meeting** | **life** | **planning**
PREP. **in ~** ◇ *They'll be back in ~ tomorrow.* | **out of ~** ◇ *I was out of ~ last week.* | *an out-of-town superstore* | **outside (the) ~** ◇ *a lake just outside the ~*
PHRASES **the centre/center of (the) ~, the middle of (the) ~** | **the edge of (the) ~, the outskirts of (the) ~** | **from town to town** ◇ *I spent years moving from town to town.*

2 main part of a town, with the shops/stores, etc.

VERB + TOWN **go into, hit** (*informal*) ◇ *I'm going into town—can I get you anything?* ◇ *Millie hit the ~, looking for excitement.*
PREP. **in ~** ◇ *Dad's in ~ shopping.*

toxic *adj.*

VERBS **be, prove, stay** ◇ *Black walnuts can prove ~ to other plants.* | **become** | **remain**
ADV. **extremely, fairly, very, etc.** | **highly, particularly** | **potentially** ◇ *potentially ~ chemicals*
PREP. **to** ◇ *This chemical is ~ to many forms of life.*

toy *noun*

ADJ. **cuddly** (*BrE*), **fluffy** (*esp. BrE*), **plush** (*AmE*), **soft** (*BrE*), **stuffed** | **clockwork** (*esp. BrE*), **electronic, mechanical, wind-up** | **plastic, wooden** | **construction, educational, learning** | **squeaky** | **favourite/favorite** ◇ *My son has lost his favourite/favorite ~.* | **expensive, new, shiny** (*all often humorous*) ◇ *He loved buying cars and expensive ~s.* ◇ *My husband's abandoned me for his shiny new ~.* | **child's, children's** | **executive** (*esp. BrE*) ◇ *Desktop publishing is probably the best executive ~ ever invented.* | **boy** (*informal*) ◇ *She introduced me to her handsome boy ~ (= younger lover).* (*AmE*) ◇ *Forty-two-year-old James showed us his favourite boy ~: a train set.* (*BrE*) | **sex**
VERB + TOY **play with** | **grab** (*esp. AmE*), **snatch** (*esp. BrE*) ◇ *Stop grabbing Debbie's ~s!* ◇ *Freddie kept snatching ~s from the other children.* | **pick up** (*esp. AmE*), **put away, tidy away** (*esp. BrE*), **tidy up** (*esp. BrE*)
TOY + NOUN **department, library** (*BrE*), **shop** (*esp. BrE*), **store** (*esp. AmE*) ◇ *All kinds of games can be borrowed from the ~ library.* | **company, industry, maker, manufacturer, retailer** | **box, chest, cupboard** (*BrE*) | **car, gun, piano, soldier, etc.** | **boy** (*BrE, informal*) ◇ *She has a 17-year-old ~ boy.*

trace *noun*

1 mark/sign that shows sb/sth happened/existed

ADJ. **archaeological, historical** | **indelible, permanent** | **memory** (*technical*)
VERB + TRACE **leave** ◇ *The burglar had left several ~s of his presence.* ◇ *Little ~ is left of how Stone Age people lived.* | **bear, reveal, show** | **discover, find** ◇ *The search party had found no ~ of the missing climbers.* | **erase, obliterate, remove** ◇ *Remove all ~s of rust with a small wire brush.*
TRACE + VERB **remain** ◇ *Traces still remain of the old brewery.*
PREP. **with a ~ of sth, without a ~ of sth** ◇ *'No thanks,' she said, with a ~ of irritation in her voice.* | **without ~** (*BrE*), **without a ~** ◇ *The plane was lost without a ~ over the Atlantic.* ◇ *The ship seems to have sunk without ~.*

2 very small amount of sth

ADJ. **discernible** (*esp. BrE*), **faint, minute, slight, small, tiny** ◇ *There was not the faintest ~ of irony in her voice.* | **unmistakable**
VERB + TRACE **contain** ◇ *The water was found to contain ~s of cocaine.* | **detect, find**
TRACE + NOUN **amount** | **element, gas, metal, mineral** ◇ *Seaweed is rich in vitamins and ~ elements.*
PREP. **~ of** ◇ *a ~ of amusement/anxiety/a smile*

trace *verb*

1 find out where sth is/where it comes from

ADV. **successfully**
VERB + TRACE **be able to, be unable to, can** ◇ *Police have been unable to ~ her movements during her final days.* | **attempt to, try to** | **help (to)** | **fail to** | **be difficult to** | **be possible to**
PREP. **to** ◇ *The stolen paintings have been successfully ~d to a London warehouse.*

2 find/describe the cause/origin of sth

ADV. **carefully** | **easily** ◇ *Words have over the centuries acquired meanings not easily ~d in dictionaries.* | **directly** | **back**
VERB + TRACE **can** | **attempt to, try to** | **be difficult to** ◇ *The origins of the custom are difficult to ~.* | **be possible to**
PREP. **to** ◇ *The book ~s the history of the game back to an incident in 1863.*

3 mark where the line of sth is with a thin object

ADV. **gently, lightly** | **slowly**
PREP. **with** ◇ *She lightly ~d the outline of his face with her finger.*

track *noun*

1 marks left behind by a car/a person/an animal

ADJ. **deep** | **fresh** | **animal, car, tyre/tire** ◇ *The beach is criss-crossed with animal ~s.*
VERB + TRACK **leave, make** ◇ *Rabbits had left ~s in the snow.* | **cover, hide** (*both often figurative*) ◇ *He had been careless, and had done little to cover his ~s.* | **follow**
TRACK + NOUN **marks**
PREP. **on the ~ of** (*often figurative*) ◇ *She felt the excitement of a journalist on the ~ of a good story.*
PHRASES **freeze in your ~s, halt in your ~s, stop in your ~s** (*all figurative*) | **halt sb/sth in their/its ~s, stop sb/sth in their/its ~s** (*all figurative*) ◇ *The disease was stopped in its ~s by improved hygiene.* | **make ~s** (*figurative*) ◇ *It's getting late—I'd better make ~s (= leave).*

2 path/rough road

ADJ. **narrow** | **wide** | **steep** | **bumpy** (*esp. BrE*), **dusty, muddy, rough, rutted, sandy, stony** (*esp. BrE*) | **ancient** | **cinder** (*esp. BrE*), **dirt, mud** | **cart** (*esp. BrE*), **cycle, sheep** (*esp. BrE*), **ski** | **single** ◇ *a single-track road with passing places* (*BrE*) | **farm, forest, forestry** (*BrE*) | **mountain** | **perimeter** ◇ *A few planes were parked on the perimeter ~ of the airfield.* | **main**
VERB + TRACK **follow**

TRACK + VERB **lead** ◇ *The ~ leads across a field.* | **fork** ◇ *When the ~ forks, take the left fork.*

PREP. **along a/the ~, down a/the ~, up a/the ~** ◇ *Continue along the farm ~ for another hundred yards.*

PHRASES **off the beaten ~** (= not in a place that most people go to) | **on the right ~, onto the right ~** (both figurative) ◇ *The new manager successfully got the team back onto the right ~.* | **on the wrong ~** (figurative) ◇ *The police were on the wrong ~ when they treated the case as a revenge killing.*

3 special path, often in a circle, for racing

ADJ. **race** (usually **racetrack**), **running** | **indoor, outdoor** | **all-weather** | **training, warm-up** | **flagship** (AmE) | **oval** | **fast** | **eighth-mile, one-mile, etc.** | **dog, greyhound** | **harness** (AmE)

VERB + TRACK **build** | **operate, own** ◇ *The company already operates a greyhound ~.*

TRACK + NOUN **race** | **announcer** (AmE) | **official, super-intendent** (AmE), **worker** | **operator, owner** | **surface** | **condition**

4 (AmE) **athletics**

TRACK + NOUN **championship, event, meet** (see also **track and field**) | **practice** ◇ *Yesterday I had ~ practice.* | **athlete, runner** | **champion, star** | **team** | **coach**

5 metal rails on which a train runs

ADJ. **rail, railroad** (AmE), **railway** (BrE), **train, tram** | **double, single** | **elevated** | **eastbound, westbound, etc.** | **narrow-gauge, standard-gauge**

VERB + TRACK **lay** | **cross** | **come off** (BrE), **jump** (AmE), **leave** ◇ *The train had left the ~s.*

TRACK + NOUN **layout**

6 direction/course that sb/sth takes

ADJ. **fast, inside** ◇ *an inside ~ to the ear of government* | **parallel, twin** ◇ *a twin-track approach to crime* | **career** ◇ *She decided to change her career ~.* | **forecast** (= the track that a storm, hurricane, etc. is predicted to take)

VERB + TRACK **switch** ◇ *He switched ~s and went back to college.*

PREP. **along a/the ~** ◇ *Sculpture developed along a similar ~ to painting.* | **on (a/the) ~** ◇ *A UN spokesman insisted that the implementation of the peace plan is back on ~.* ◇ *The ship was on a southerly ~.* | **~ for** ◇ *She seems to be on the fast ~ for promotion.* | **~ to** ◇ *The country is on the fast ~ to democracy.*

PHRASES **keep ~ of sth** (= to know what is happening, where sth is, etc.) ◇ *Keep ~ of all your payments by writing them down in a book.* | **lose ~ of sth** (= to not know what is happening, where sth is, etc.) ◇ *I was so absorbed in my work that I lost ~ of time.*

7 single song/piece of music

ADJ. **album** | **live** | **pre-recorded** | **title** | **lead, lead-off** (AmE), **opening** | **closing, final** | **main** | **unreleased** | **original** | **bonus** | **dance, disco** | **backing** | **drum, guitar, instrumental, rhythm, solo, vocal** (see also **soundtrack**) | **standout** (AmE) ◇ *This song is easily the disc's standout ~* (= the best track).

VERB + TRACK **create, cut, lay down, mix, produce, record** ◇ *She had already cut a couple of ~s as lead singer with her own group.* | **write** | **remix** | **release** | **download** | **play** | **listen to**

TRACK + VERB **feature sb/sth, include sth**

TRACK + NOUN **title** | **list, listing**

track and field noun (AmE) → See also ATHLETICS

ADJ. **indoor, outdoor** | **international**

VERB + TRACK AND FIELD **compete in, do** ◇ *My daughter wants to compete in ~.*

TRACK-AND-FIELD + NOUN **competition, event, athlete** ◇ *college track-and-field athletes* | **coach** | **star** | **team**

track record noun

ADJ. **good, impressive, proven** | **poor**

VERB + TRACK RECORD **have, possess**

PREP. **~ for** ◇ *If possible, select pairs of fish that already have a ~ for breeding.* | **~ in** ◇ *Applicants should have a proven ~ in telesales.*

tractor noun

ADJ. **agricultural, farm** | **lawn** (AmE) | **diesel** (esp. AmE)

VERB + TRACTOR **drive** | **use**

TRACTOR + VERB **plough/plow, work** ◇ *the sound of a ~ working in the field nearby*

TRACTOR + NOUN **driver** | **shed** | **tyre/tire** | **trailer**

PREP. **on a/the ~** ◇ *a farmer on his ~*

PHRASES **a ~ and trailer**

trade noun

1 buying/selling of goods/services

ADJ. **booming, brisk, burgeoning, expanding, flourishing, lively, roaring, thriving** ◇ *All around the pyramids, sales-people were doing a roaring ~ in souvenirs.* | **increased** | **lucrative, profitable** | **cross-border, external, foreign, global, international, overseas, transatlantic, world** | **domestic, internal, interstate, regional** | **export, import, import-export** | **direct, indirect** | **free, liberalized** | **fair** ◇ *The organization promotes fair ~ with developing countries.* | **legal, legitimate** | **illegal, illicit** ◇ *attempts to curb the illicit ~ in exotic species* | **private** | **coastal, maritime** | **agricultural, commercial** | **merchandise, retail, wholesale** ◇ *It has been a bad year for the retail ~.* | **book, fur, ivory, timber, wildlife, wine, etc.** | **sex, slave** | **drug, heroin, opium** | **tourist** ◇ *the area's dependence on the tourist ~* | **evil** (esp. BrE) ◇ *the evil ~ in drugs*

VERB + TRADE **conduct, do, engage in, ply** ◇ *All manner of street sellers were plying their ~.* | **boost, build up, develop, expand, increase, promote** ◇ *a bid to boost foreign ~* ◇ *He built up a ~ in seeds, corn and manure.* | **facilitate** | **damage, harm** ◇ *A bitterly cold winter damaged industrial output and ~.* | **lose** ◇ *The store has lost a day's ~.* | **ban, restrict** | **liberalize** | **control, govern, regulate** | **dominate** ◇ *They already dominated the domestic ~ in raw jute.*

TRADE + VERB **boom, expand, flourish, grow, increase, pick up** | **decline, fall**

TRADE + NOUN **balance, figures, performance, statistics** | **surplus** | **deficit, gap, imbalance** | **adjustment** | **barrier, blockade, boycott, embargo, restrictions, sanctions** | **tariff** | **dispute, war** ◇ *The countries were locked in a ~ war, refusing to allow imports of each other's goods.* | **liberal-ization** | **benefits, concessions** | **accord, agreement, deal, pact, protocol, treaty** | **negotiations, talks** | **cooperation, links, network, relations** | **partner** | **agenda, policy, practice** ◇ *The US was accused of employing unfair ~ practices.* | **law, legislation, regime, rules** | **bloc** ◇ *The five countries formed a regional ~ bloc.* | **delegation, mission** ◇ *Several local companies took part in a ~ mission to Spain.* | **commissioner, minister, negotiator, official, representa-tive** ◇ *talks between ~ officials from the two countries* | **mark** (usually **trademark**), **name** | **promotion** | **exhibition, fair, show** | **centre/center** | **route** ◇ *The road has been an important ~ route since prehistoric times.* | **cycle** ◇ *the boom and slump periods of a ~ cycle* | **association, body, group, organization** ◇ *the ~ body representing water companies* | **directory** | **journal, magazine, paper, press, publication** | **information, secret** ◇ *The employees were fired for divulging ~ secrets to a competitor.*

PREP. **in a/the ~** ◇ *She's in the wholesale fruit ~.* ◇ *These flour sacks are known in the ~ as 'pockets'.* | **~ between** ◇ *Trade between the Adriatic ports and their hinterland had grown.* | **~ in** ◇ *Steps were taken to ban the ~ in ivory.* | **~ with** ◇ *The US has restricted ~ with India.*

→ Special page at BUSINESS

2 job

ADJ. **skilled** | **building** ◇ *Work in the building ~s became scarce.*

VERB + TRADE **learn** | **carry on, exercise, follow, practise/practice** ◇ *the tools needed to carry on a ~*

PREP. **by ~** ◇ *She is a carpenter by ~.*

PHRASES **a jack of all ~s** (= a person who can do many

different types of work), **the tricks of the ~** ◇ *The experienced artisan would pass on the tricks of the ~ to the apprentice.*

trade *verb*

ADV. **profitably, successfully** | **actively** | **openly** ◇ *The company openly ~d in arms.* | **publicly** ◇ *publicly ~d securities* | **widely** | **freely** ◇ *He claimed that all businesses should be able to ~ freely on Sundays.* | **directly** | **illegally** | **fairly** | **internationally** | **online**
VERB + TRADE **continue to** | **cease to**
PREP. **as** ◇ *They now ~ as a partnership.* | **in** ◇ *countries trading illegally in rhinoceros horn* | **with** ◇ *Early explorers ~d directly with the Indians.*
PHRASES **cease trading, continue trading** ◇ *The company has now ceased trading.* | **~ under the name (of) sth** ◇ *The company ~s under the name 'Language Solutions'.*

trader *noun*

ADJ. **large** ◇ *China is now one of the largest ~s in the world.* | **free** | **small, small-scale** ◇ *small market ~s* | **local** | **foreign, international** | **wealthy** | **market, street** | **itinerant** | **sole** (*BrE*) ◇ *You can set up in business as a sole ~, in partnership or as a limited company.* | **independent, private** (*both esp. BrE*) | **professional** | **retail** | **cattle, fur, motor** (*BrE*), **slave, etc.** | **commodity, currency, futures, options** | **floor** (in a stock exchange)

tradesman *noun*

ADJ. **skilled** ◇ *This is a job for a skilled ~.* | **local** | **self-employed** | **respectable** | **wealthy**
PHRASES **tradesmen's entrance** ◇ *All deliveries should be made to the tradesmen's entrance.*

trade union (*also* trades union) *noun* (*BrE*) → See
UNION

trading *noun*

ADJ. **busy, heavy, hectic, intensive** ◇ *In heavy ~, the index closed down 38 points.* | **quiet** | **day, late** | **electronic, online** | **free** | **fraudulent, illegal, improper, insider** ◇ *a Wall Street dealer jailed for insider ~* | **global, international, world** | **stock-market** | **commodity, currency, equity, foreign-exchange, share, stock**
TRADING + VERB **begin, open** | **close**
TRADING + NOUN **partner**

tradition *noun*

ADJ. **age-old, ancient, centuries-old, deep-rooted, old, time-honoured/time-honored** | **long, long-established, long-standing** | **enduring, living, unbroken, well-established** | **distinguished, fine, great, honourable/honorable, venerable** | **proud** | **cherished, hallowed** | **dominant, powerful, strong** | **rich** ◇ *Japan's rich cultural ~ and history* | **ancestral, family** | **inherited** | **indigenous, local, national, native, vernacular** | **folk, popular** | **oral, storytelling** | **Catholic, Christian, Islamic, pagan, etc.** | **faith** ◇ *people of all faith ~s* | **Eastern, English, European, etc.** | **19th-century, etc.** | **classical, medieval, modernist, etc.** | **academic, artistic, culinary, cultural, historical, ideological, intellectual, literary, military, musical, philosophical, political, religious, spiritual, sporting** (*esp. BrE*), **theatrical** ◇ *This region has a great musical ~.* | **biblical** | **mystical** | **democratic, liberal, radical, revolutionary**
VERB + TRADITION **have** | **become** ◇ *It became an annual ~ for me to ice the cake.* | **cherish, continue, defend, follow, follow in, honour/honor, keep alive, maintain, perpetuate, preserve, respect, uphold** ◇ *Following in the Hitchcock ~, he always appears in the movies he directs.* ◇ *The locals get together every year to keep this age-old ~ alive.* | **hand down** ◇ *an oral ~ handed down from generation to generation* | **inherit** ◇ *They have inherited a rich ~ of music and dance.* | **abandon, break, break with, buck, defy, go against, ignore, reject** ◇ *He broke with the family ~ and did not go down the mines.* | **challenge** ◇ *The girl had challenged the ~s*

of her patriarchal tribe.* | **establish, start** | **embody** | **extend, reinterpret, revive** | **celebrate** | **share**
TRADITION + VERB **continue, die hard, exist, remain, survive** ◇ *Old habits and ~s die hard.* | **date back to, go back to** ◇ *The ~ dates back to the 16th century.* | **dictate sth, emphasize sth, hold sth, say sth, teach sth**
PREP. **according to (a/the)** ~ ◇ *According to ~, a tree grew on this spot.* | **by** ~ ◇ *By ~, ships are often referred to as 'she' in English.* | **in (a/the)** ~ ◇ *In time-honoured/time-honored ~, a bottle of champagne was smashed on the ship.* ◇ *He's a politician in the ~ of* (= similar in style to) *Kennedy.*
PHRASES **bound by** ~ ◇ *He made it clear he was not going to be bound by ~.* | **a departure from** ~ ◇ *In a departure from ~, the bride wore red.* | **in the best ~s of sth** ◇ *The building was constructed in the best ~s of church architecture.* | **respect for** ~ ◇ *His education gave him a lasting respect for ~.*

traffic *noun*

1 vehicles going somewhere

ADJ. **bad, bumper-to-bumper, busy, congested, heavy, terrible** ◇ *The ~ was terrible on the way here.* | **light** | **fast, fast-flowing** | **slow-moving** | **stop-and-go** (*AmE*) | **passing** ◇ *She waved her arms at the passing ~, pleading for someone to stop.* | **automobile** (*AmE*), **lorry** (*BrE*), **motor, road, truck** (*esp. AmE*), **vehicle, vehicular** | **foot, pedestrian** | **air, airline** ◇ *an air ~ controller* | **boat, maritime, river, sea** | **rail, railroad** (*AmE*), **railway** (*BrE*) | **freeway** (*in the US*), **highway** (*in the US*), **interstate** (*in the US*), **motorway** (*in the UK*) | **commercial, freight, goods, industrial, passenger** | **city, city-centre** (*BrE*), **downtown** (*AmE*), **local, town-centre** (*BrE*), **urban** | **international** | **commuter, tourist** | **morning, rush-hour** | **holiday** | **oncoming** ◇ *I stood waiting for a gap in the oncoming ~.* | **through** ◇ *Through ~ is directed around the bypass.* | **northbound, southbound, etc.** | **inbound, outbound** | **one-way, two-way**
... OF TRAFFIC **stream**
VERB + TRAFFIC **generate, increase** ◇ *Building larger roads could generate more ~.* | **cut, reduce** | **slow down** | **block, disrupt, hold up, obstruct, snarl, stop, tie up** ◇ *Traffic was held up for six hours by the accident.* | **control, direct** | **divert** | **avoid, beat** ◇ *We set off early to beat the ~.* | **navigate** ◇ *The driver calmly navigated the heavy ~.* | **watch**
TRAFFIC + VERB **build up, thicken** (*esp. AmE*) ◇ *Traffic was already building up as early as 3 p.m.* | **grow, increase** ◇ *Traffic has increased by 50% in ten years.* | **clog sth** ◇ *Traffic clogs the streets of the city.* | **thin** (*esp. AmE*) ◇ *Traffic thins noticeably after 9 a.m.* | **flow, move, speed, travel** ◇ *The road is being widened to keep ~ moving.* | **go by, pass** | **stop** | **head** ◇ *We joined the ~ heading north.* | **roar, rumble**
TRAFFIC + NOUN **accident** | **fatality** | **hazard** ◇ *Sheep are a ~ hazard in the hills.* | **chaos, congestion, delays, disruption, hold-ups, jam, problems, queues** (*BrE*), **snarl** (*esp. AmE*) | **fumes, pollution** | **noise** | **flow, speed** ◇ *Widening the road would improve ~ flow.* | **levels, volume** | **calming** (*BrE*), **management, restraint, safety** | **sign, signal** | **laws, legislation, regulations** | **court** (*AmE*) | **system** | **offence/offense** (*esp. BrE*), **violation** (*esp. AmE*) | **ticket** (= an official notice to pay a fine) (*AmE*) | **camera** | **stop** (*AmE*) ◇ *The cop was shot during a routine ~ stop.* | **bollard** (*BrE*), **circle** (*AmE*), **cone, island** ◇ *A ~ island at the junction separates left- and right-turning vehicles.* | **artery** (*formal*), **route** | **lane** | **information, report, survey, update** | **cop, officer, police, policeman, warden** (*BrE*) | **engineer, planner** (*BrE*) | **duty** ◇ *a policeman on ~ duty*
PHRASES **the volume of** ~

2 messages, signals, etc.

ADJ. **radio, telephone** | **data, voice** | **network** | **email, Internet, Net, search-engine, site, Web, website** ◇ *Our company will help you generate site ~.* | **targeted** ◇ *These tips should help you generate more targeted ~ to your website.* | **real-time** | **inbound, incoming** | **outbound, outgoing**
VERB + TRAFFIC **boost, build, generate** | **receive, send** |

attract, draw | carry | handle, manage | monitor | encrypt | redirect, re-route, route
TRAFFIC + VERB **flow** | **grow, increase**
TRAFFIC + NOUN **pattern** | **load** | **capacity**

3 illegal buying and selling of sth

ADJ. **illegal** | **arms, drug** | **international**
PREP. **~ in sth** ◊ *the ~ in arms*

traffic jam *noun*

ADJ. **huge, massive**
VERB + TRAFFIC JAM **be/get caught in, be/get stuck in, sit in** ◊ *Our bus was caught in a ~ and arrived late.* | **cause**

traffic light *(also light) noun*

ADJ. **amber** (*BrE*), **green, red, yellow** (*AmE*) | **temporary** ◊ *There are temporary ~s because of the roadworks.*
... OF TRAFFIC LIGHTS **set** ◊ *Turn left at the third set of ~s.*
VERB + TRAFFIC LIGHT **go through, jump** ◊ *He was stopped by the police for going through a red light.*
TRAFFIC LIGHT + VERB **change (to sth), go green, etc., turn green, etc., turn to green, etc.** ◊ *A line of vehicles waited for the ~s to change.* ◊ *Stop when the lights change to red.* | **be green, etc., be on green, etc.** (*both esp. BrE*) ◊ *The lights were on red but she didn't stop.* | **work** ◊ *The ~s weren't working.*
PREP. **at the ~s** ◊ *There was a hold-up at the lights.*

tragedy *noun*

1 event/situation that causes great sadness

ADJ. **absolute, appalling** (*esp. BrE*), **awful, big, enormous, great, horrible, horrific, major, real, terrible, unspeakable** | **family, human, personal, private** | **national** | **recent**
VERB + TRAGEDY **end in** ◊ *A family's outing ended in ~ when their boat capsized.* | **be dogged by** (*esp. BrE*), **experience, face, suffer** | **cause** ◊ *We don't know what caused the ~.* | **avert, avoid, prevent** | **overcome** | **survive** | **see, witness** | **exploit**
TRAGEDY + VERB **befall sb, happen, occur, strike (sb)** ◊ *Tragedy struck when their eight-year-old daughter was knocked down by a car.* | **unfold** ◊ *She had seen the ~ unfold.* | **affect sb/sth, touch sb**
PREP. **~ for sb** ◊ *The closure of the factory is a ~ for the whole community.*

2 serious play with a sad ending

ADJ. **classical, Greek, Jacobean, Shakespearean** | **revenge**
VERB + TRAGEDY **write**

tragic *adj.*

VERBS **be, seem**
ADV. **particularly, really, terribly, truly, very** ◊ *a genuinely ~ figure in the play* | **quite, rather** ◊ *a rather ~ story*

trail *noun*

1 line/smell that sb/sth leaves behind

ADJ. **scent** ◊ *Ants follow a scent ~ laid down previously.* | **blood, smoke, vapour/vapor** | **faint, thin** | **long** | **muddy** | **wet** | **false**
VERB + TRAIL **lay, leave, make, produce** ◊ *The couple laid a false ~ to escape the press photographers.* ◊ *The tourists left a ~ of empty cans behind them.* | **find, pick up** ◊ *The dog had picked up the ~ of a rabbit.* | **notice, see** | **follow** | **lose** ◊ *The fox had crossed a stream, and the hounds lost the ~.* | **cover**
TRAIL + VERB **go cold** ◊ *They had to find the kidnappers before the ~ went cold.*
PREP. **on sb's ~** ◊ *Detectives had found several new clues and were back on the murderer's ~.*
PHRASES **a ~ of blood, a ~ of devastation** ◊ *The hurricane passed, leaving a ~ of devastation in its wake.* | **a ~ of smoke**

2 path/route

ADJ. **forest, mountain, nature, wooded, woodland** | **cross-country** | **10-km, 5-mile, etc.** | **bike, biking, cycle** (*BrE*), **hiking, jogging, mountain-bike, ski, snowmobile, walking** | **cross-country** | **tourist** ◊ *This restaurant is off the tourist ~.* | **narrow, rough, steep, winding** | **dusty, rocky** | **dirt** | **lighted, marked, paved** | **groomed** (*AmE*) | **scenic** | **main** | **campaign, comeback, presidential, winning** (*BrE*) (*all figurative*) ◊ *After a disastrous few seasons, the team are on the comeback ~.*
VERB + TRAIL **follow, hit, take** ◊ *I like to hit the ~ early and be finished by eight.* | **hike, ride, walk** (*all AmE*) | **do** (*informal*) ◊ *We did the Inca ~.*
TRAIL + VERB **go, lead, run, wend its way, wind** ◊ *The ~ wends its way through dark forests.* | **begin, start** | **cross sth, follow sth, pass sth**
PREP. **along a/the ~**

trail *verb*

1 move/walk slowly

ADV. **slowly** | **wearily** | **closely (behind)**
PREP. **after** ◊ *I ~ed wearily after the others.* | **around, round** (*esp. BrE*) ◊ *They spent their lives ~ing around the country.* | **(along) behind**

2 have a lower score than the other player/team

ADV. **badly** ◊ *The team is now ~ing badly in the league.* ◊ *Tyler is ~ing badly in the polls.* | **slightly**
PREP. **by** ◊ *They were ~ing by 12 points until the last few minutes of the game.*

trailer *noun*

1 container with wheels

ADJ. **lorry** (*BrE*), **truck** (*esp. AmE*) | **car** (*AmE*) | **boat** | **horse** | **flatbed** (*esp. AmE*) | **camping** (*AmE*) | **semi** (*AmE*)
VERB + TRAILER **load** | **pull, tow**
TRAILER + TRAILER **carry sth** ◊ *a ~ carrying a motor boat*
TRAILER + NOUN **hitch** | **truck**
PREP. **on a/the ~, onto a/the ~** ◊ *a broken-down car on a ~*
PHRASES **a tractor and ~**

2 (*AmE*) vehicle with no engine, where people live or work

ADJ. **travel** | **house** | **construction** | **30-foot, 53-foot, etc.**
VERB + TRAILER **live in** | **buy**
TRAILER + NOUN **home, house** | **park** | **trash** (*informal*) | **hitch**

3 an advertisement for a film/movie, etc.

ADJ. **preview** | **promotional** | **theatrical** (*AmE*)
VERB + TRAILER **see, watch**
PREP. **~ for** ◊ *He featured in the ~ for the movie.* | **in a/the ~**

train *noun*

1 engine pulling coaches/cars

ADJ. **railroad** (*AmE*), **railway** (*BrE*) | **metro, subway** (*AmE*), **tube** (*BrE*), **underground** (*esp. BrE*) | **intercity, long-distance** | **local, suburban** | **express, fast, direct, through** ◊ *I got the through ~ to Manchester.* | **slow, stopping** (*BrE*) | **special** | **early, evening, midnight, morning, night, over-night** | **two o'clock, 10.45, etc.** | **rush-hour** | **outbound** (*AmE*), **return** ◊ *What are the times of the return ~s?* | **first, last, next** ◊ *The last ~ leaves at 00.30.* | **Moscow to Beijing, etc.** ◊ *the Paris to Brussels ~* | **Denver-bound, etc.** | **northbound, southbound, etc.** | **inbound** (*AmE*) | **crowded, full** | **empty** | **moving, stationary** | **speeding** | **runaway** | **approaching, oncoming** ◊ *the sound of an approaching ~* ◊ *He was pushed into the path of an oncoming ~.* | **passing** ◊ *the roar of a passing ~* | **departing** ◊ *She ran alongside the departing ~, waving goodbye.* | **delayed, late-running** | **luxury, Pullman** | **four-car** (*AmE*), **four-coach** (*BrE*), **etc.** | **bullet, high-speed** | **diesel, electric, steam** | **elevated** | **coal, commuter, freight, goods, mail, passenger** | **transit** | **wagon** | **troop** | **model, toy** | **ghost** (= at a funfair) (*BrE*)
VERB + TRAIN **take, travel by** ◊ *From Germany we'll travel by ~ to Poland.* | **ride** (*AmE*), **travel on** ◊ *She travels on the same ~ as you.* | **use** | **catch, get, make** ◊ *We had to get up early to*

make the 6 o'clock ~ for Richmond. | **miss** | **wait for** | **run for** ◇ I was late and had to run for my ~. | **board, get on, hop on, jump aboard, jump on** ◇ We jumped on the ~ just as it was about to leave. | **jump from, jump off, jump out of** ◇ She tried to kill herself by jumping off a moving ~. | **alight from** (esp. BrE), **exit** (esp. AmE), **get off, leave** | **meet, meet sb off** ◇ I'm going to the station to meet her off the ~. | **change** ◇ You'll have to change ~s at Cambridge. | **operate, run** ◇ The company plans to run ~s on key intercity routes. | **cancel** ◇ The 10.19 ~ has been cancelled/canceled. | **drive** | **haul** ◇ a ~ hauled by a steam locomotive | **stop** | **derail** | **fall under, throw sb under** ◇ Driven to despair, he threw himself under a ~.

TRAIN + VERB **run** ◇ In summer the ~s run as often as every ten minutes. | **start** | **terminate** ◇ The ~ terminated in Baltimore. | **be bound for...** ◇ an express ~ bound for Edinburgh | **be due** ◇ The next ~ is due at 9.45. | **be delayed, be held up, be late, run late** ◇ Most ~s are running late because of the accident. | **arrive, come in, come into sth, draw in, draw into sth, pull in, pull into sth** ◇ The next ~ to arrive at Platform 2 is the 12.30 from Leeds. (BrE) ◇ The 15.18 Amtrak ~ to Chicago will be arriving on track 3. (AmE) ◇ The ~ came in and I got on. ◇ The ~ drew into the station. | **come, go** ◇ We didn't want to leave the platform in case the ~ came. | **reach** ◇ The ~ reached Tokyo at half past six. | **return** | **depart, draw out (of sth), leave, pull away, pull out (of sth), start, start off** ◇ The ~ pulled out of the station. | **head...** ◇ The ~ headed out of Mumbai. | **stand** (BrE), **wait** ◇ The ~ now standing at Platform 3 is the 16.50 to Brighton. ◇ a ~ waiting at a signal | **move** ◇ Slowly the ~ began to move. | **travel** ◇ The high-speed ~ travels at 120 mph. | **chug, roll, trundle** (esp. BrE) ◇ The ~ chugged slowly forward. | **gather speed, hurtle, rush, speed, steam** (esp. BrE) ◇ a picture of the bullet ~ speeding past Mount Fuji | **slow, slow down** | **brake** | **be brought to a halt, come to a halt, halt, stop** | **rattle, rumble, thunder, whistle** ◇ The ~ rattled into the station. | **jerk, jolt, lurch, shudder** ◇ The ~ jolted into motion. | **approach** | **pass** | **enter sth** ◇ The ~ entered the tunnel. | **collide (with sth), crash, hit sb/sth** | **derail** | **be loaded with sth, carry sth**

TRAIN + NOUN **journey** (esp. BrE), **ride, trip** | **service** | **system** | **traffic** | **station** | **stop** | **platform** | **route** | **schedule** (AmE), **times, timetable** (BrE) | **fare** | **ticket** | **conductor, crew, driver, engineer, guard** (BrE) | **staff** | **travel, travellers/travelers, travelling/traveling** | **accident, collision, crash, disaster, wreck** (esp. AmE) | **derailment** | **bombing** | **window** | **car** (AmE), **carriage** | **compartment** | **whistle** | **depot, shed, yard** | **line, track** | **robber, robbery** | **set** ◇ I saved up to buy an electric ~ set.

PREP. **aboard a/the ~, on a/the ~, on board a/the ~** ◇ the people on the ~ | **by ~** ◇ It's quicker by ~. | **~ between** ◇ ~s between Cape Town and Pretoria | **~ for, ~ to** ◇ He was leaving on the early ~ for Zaragoza. | **~ from** ◇ the ~ from Toronto to Calgary

PHRASES **a ~ to catch** ◇ I can't stop now, I have a ~ to catch.

2 number of people/animals moving in a line

ADJ. **camel, mule, wagon** | **supply**

3 series of events/actions/thoughts

VERB + TRAIN **set sth in** ◇ That telephone call set in ~ a whole series of events. | **bring sth in** (figurative) ◇ Unemployment brings greater difficulties in its ~ (= causes great difficulties). | **break, interrupt** ◇ A knock on the door interrupted his ~ of thought. | **lose** ◇ I lose my ~ of thought when there are distractions.

PHRASES **a ~ of events** (esp. BrE) ◇ an initial omission which set in motion a ~ of events leading to the crime | **a ~ of thought** ◇ The telephone rang and she lost her ~ of thought.

PREP. **in sb's ~** (figurative) ◇ In the ~ of (= following behind) the rich and famous came the journalists.

train verb

ADV. **hard, intensely** | **seriously** ◇ He's been ~ing seriously for over a year now. | **extensively** | **effectively, successfully** | **regularly** | **consistently**

PREP. **for** ◇ The team is ~ing hard for the big match.

trained adj.

VERBS **be**

ADV. **highly, superbly** ◇ a highly ~ army | **well** ◇ The animals have all been well ~. | **fully, properly, rigorously, thoroughly** ◇ It is important that staff should be properly ~. | **adequately, sufficiently** | **badly, inadequately, poorly** | **appropriately, suitably** | **specially, specifically** | **formally** | **academically, medically, professionally** | **classically** ◇ classically ~ dancers | **militarily** | **newly** ◇ newly ~ officers

trainee noun

ADJ. **management** | **graduate** (esp. BrE) ◇ Many companies recruit graduate ~s to train as managers. | **new**

VERB + TRAINEE **employ** (esp. BrE), **hire** (esp. AmE), **recruit** (esp. BrE), **take on** (esp. BrE)

TRAINEE + VERB **work**

TRAINEE + NOUN **accountant, manager, nurse, solicitor, teacher** (all BrE)

PREP. **as a ~** ◇ She joined as a management ~.

trainer noun

1 person who trains sb/sth

ADJ. **teacher** | **athletic** (AmE), **boxing, football, etc.** | **fitness** | **animal, dog, horse, racehorse** | **champion, winning** | **experienced, veteran** | **assistant** | **personal, private** ◇ He works out every morning with his personal ~. | **corporate** | **certified** | **professional**

→ Note at JOB

2 (BrE) (usually **trainers**) sports shoe

...OF TRAINERS **pair**

VERB + TRAINER **lace up, unlace**

→ Special page at CLOTHES

training noun

1 learning skills

ADJ. **basic, initial, preliminary** ◇ New recruits undergo six weeks' basic ~ at the base. | **advanced, high-level** | **comprehensive, in-depth, rigorous, systematic, thorough** | **extensive, lengthy** | **intense, intensive** | **focused** | **essential, necessary** | **minimum** | **appropriate** | **adequate, proper** ◇ No one must operate the machinery without proper ~. | **inadequate** | **minimal** ◇ Using spreadsheets requires minimal ~. | **excellent, first-class, high-quality** | **special, specialist, specialized** | **supervised** | **hands-on, practical** | **theoretical** | **continuous, long-term, ongoing** | **individual, one-on-one** (esp. AmE), **one-to-one** (BrE) | **formal, informal** ◇ He is good at selling, although he has had no formal ~. | **job, job-related, occupational, professional, vocational, work-related** | **in-service, on-the-job** | **external** | **in-house, internal, on-site** | **field** | **computer-based, Web-based** | **mental, moral, physical, social** | **tactical** | **academic, clinical, educational, industrial, intellectual, journalistic, legal, management, medical, military, musical, scientific, technical** | **classical** | **first-aid** | **combat** | **assertiveness** | **potty** (= when a child learns to use a potty) | **staff, teacher** | **doctoral, postdoctoral, postgraduate** | **collective, joint**

VERB + TRAINING **attend, do, get, have, receive, undergo** ◇ You have to do a year's intensive ~ to become a paramedic. | **complete, finish** | **give sb, provide (sb with)** | **oversee, supervise** | **require** | **lack**

TRAINING + VERB **prepare sb for sth** | **focus on sth** | **consist of sth, include sth, involve sth**

TRAINING + NOUN **base, camp, centre/center, college, establishment, facility, school** ◇ an army ~ base ◇ a teacher ~ college | **activity, course, exercise, initiative, package, plan, programme/program, project, scheme** (BrE), **strategy, system** ◇ The soldiers were building a bridge as a ~ exercise. | **methods, policy, procedures, process, skills, techniques** | **needs, objectives, requirements** | **opportunities, provision** | **aid, device, equipment, material** | **manual** | **instructor, manager, officer** | **body** (BrE),

company, department, organization, provider, service | place, placement (BrE) | event, session, workshop | day, period, etc. | budget, costs, fees (esp. BrE)
PREP. **by ~** ◆ She's an accountant by ~. | **in ~** ◆ I am delighted with the work he has done in ~. | **~ for** ◆ Training for nurses was on strictly formal lines. | **~ in** ◆ Employees should be given ~ in safety procedures.
PHRASES **counselor in ~** (AmE)
2 physical exercises

ADJ. **hard, intense, intensive, rigorous, serious, strict, tough** ◆ She did six months' hard ~ before the marathon. | **athletic** (esp. AmE), **physical, resistance, strength** | **aerobic, cardiovascular** | **cross** (usually **cross-training**), **interval** | **pre-season** | **spring, summer, etc.**
VERB + TRAINING **do**
TRAINING + NOUN **run, session, stint** (esp. BrE) | **regime, regimen, routine, schedule** | **partner** | **ground** (also figurative), **pitch** (BrE), **track** ◆ This local newspaper has been a ~ ground for several top journalists.
PREP. **in ~** ◆ Nevis is in serious ~ for the Olympics. | **~ for**

trait noun

ADJ. **admirable, attractive, desirable** | **negative, undesirable** | **human** ◆ Her boss did not display any human ~s. | **characteristic, defining, distinctive, dominant, individual** | **common** | **family, genetic, hereditary, inherited** | **behavioural/behavioral, character, personal, personality** | **mental, psychological** | **physical** | **stylistic** ◆ the composer's stylistic ~s | **female, feminine, male, masculine** | **cultural, national**
VERB + TRAIT **have, possess** | **lack** | **share** ◆ She shares several character ~s with her father. | **display, exhibit, reveal, show** | **acquire, develop, inherit** ◆ We do not know which ~s are inherited and which acquired. | **identify, recognize**
TRAIT + VERB **(be) associated with** ◆ a collection of ~s associated with schizophrenia

traitor noun

VERB + TRAITOR **turn** ◆ He turned ~ and joined the opposition. | **brand sb as, call sb, denounce sb as, label sb as**
PREP. **~ to** ◆ He is seen as a ~ to the cause.

tram noun (BrE) → See also TROLLEY

ADJ. **electric**
VERB + TRAM **catch, take** | **miss** | **board, get on** | **get off**
TRAM + VERB **run** ◆ The last ~ ran through Glasgow in September 1962. | **rattle** | **stop**
TRAM + NOUN **network, service, system** | **route** | **stop** | **ride** | **driver** | **car** (usually **tramcar**) | **shed** | **line, rail, track** | **ticket**
PREP. **by ~** ◆ There is easy access to the city by ~. | **on a/the ~** ◆ They sat together on the rattling ~. | **~ from, ~ to**

trample verb

ADV. **nearly** ◆ I was nearly ~d to death by the crowd. | **down** ◆ crops that have been ~d down by walkers' feet | **underfoot** ◆ He saved a little girl from being ~d underfoot in the rush for the fire exit.
PREP. **on** (often figurative) ◆ The government is trampling on the views of ordinary people. | **over** ◆ Police officers had been trampling all over the ground.
PHRASES **be ~d to death**

trance noun

ADJ. **deep** | **light** | **hypnotic, mesmeric** | **ecstatic, meditative**
VERB + TRANCE **enter, enter into, fall into, go into** | **put sb into** | **induce** | **break** | **awake from, come out of, wake from**
TRANCE + NOUN **state**
PREP. **in a ~** ◆ In a deep ~, the subject is taken back to an earlier stage of their life.

tranquil adj.

VERBS **be, look, seem** ◆ The town looked ~ in the evening sunlight. | **become** | **remain**
ADV. **extremely, fairly, very, etc.** | **wonderfully** | **perfectly, quite** | **relatively** | **normally, usually** ◆ The normally ~ town awoke to the sound of gunfire.

transaction noun

ADJ. **cross-border, international** | **private** | **fraudulent** (esp. BrE), **illegal, suspicious** ◆ The president had entered into fraudulent property ~s. | **secure** ◆ secure Internet ~s | **cash, credit** | **credit-card, debit-card** | **electronic, Internet, online** | **business-to-business, e-commerce, over-the-counter** ◆ Electronic banking may make over-the-counter ~s obsolete. | **banking, business, commercial, consumer, economic, financial, market, monetary** | **currency, foreign-exchange** ◆ foreign currency ~s | **property** (esp. BrE), **real estate** (AmE) | **share** (esp. BrE), **stock** (esp. AmE)
VERB + TRANSACTION **carry out** (esp. BrE), **conduct, do** (esp. AmE), **enter into** (esp. BrE), **make** | **handle, process** ◆ to handle a ~ for a client | **complete** | **record**
TRANSACTION + VERB **proceed, take place** ◆ to ensure the ~ proceeds smoothly
TRANSACTION + NOUN **charges** (esp. BrE), **cost** ◆ Using the Internet can significantly reduce ~ costs.
PREP. **~ between** ◆ The system records all ~s between the company and its suppliers. | **~ over** ◆ ~s over the Internet
→ Special page at BUSINESS

transcript noun

ADJ. **complete, entire, full, verbatim** | **edited, partial** | **official** | **radio** | **interview** | **court, trial** | **college, school** (AmE)
VERB + TRANSCRIPT **read** | **make** | **post** (esp. AmE), **print, publish** ◆ The White House posted a ~ of the speech on its website. | **release** (esp. AmE)

transfer noun

1 change of place/situation

ADJ. **massive** ◆ The war caused a massive ~ of population. | **efficient, smooth, successful** ◆ the smooth ~ of power to the new government | **net** ◆ There has been a net ~ of lower-paid people away from the inner cities. | **permanent** ◆ Her boss recommended a permanent ~ overseas. | **direct** ◆ Employees are paid by direct ~ to a bank account. | **data, information, knowledge** | **land, property** | **wealth** (esp. AmE) | **population** | **resource** | **technology** | **file** | **digital, electronic, telegraphic** (BrE) | **balance** (esp. BrE), **bank, capital, cash, credit, financial, money, share** (esp. BrE), **stock** | **embryo, gene** | **charge, electron, energy, heat, nuclear, thermal**
VERB + TRANSFER **do, effect** (formal), **make** ◆ I did a file ~ from one PC to another. ◆ Only the owner can make a ~ of goods. | **allow, facilitate**
TRANSFER + VERB **occur, take place**
TRANSFER + NOUN **rate, speed** ◆ data ~ rates of 6.4 GB per second | **process** | **student** ◆ The law schools accept a large number of second-year ~ students.
PREP. **~ between** ◆ the ~ of property between private buyers | **~ from, ~ of** ◆ the ~ of power/sovereignty | **~ to**

2 (BrE) **in sports**

ADJ. **free** | **permanent**
VERB + TRANSFER **give sb** ◆ His club have given him a free ~.
TRANSFER + NOUN **list, market, system** | **fee, payment, price** | **budget, kitty** | **deadline, window** | **deal**

transfer verb

ADV. **carefully** | **directly** ◆ Skills cannot be transferred directly from a trainer to a trainee. | **easily** ◆ Data is easily transferred electronically. | **successfully** | **simply** | **immediately** | **quickly, rapidly** | **gradually** | **eventually** | **temporarily** | **formally** ◆ Sovereignty was formally transferred on December 27. | **automatically** | **electronically** | **abroad** (esp. BrE), **overseas** ◆ Assets can be transferred overseas. | **back, out**

PREP. **across, between** ◇ *Can the disease be transferred across species?* | **from, into** ◇ *She transferred the gravy into a gravy boat.* | **onto, out of, to** | **through, via**

transferable *adj.*

VERBS **be** | **become**
ADV. **easily, freely, highly, readily** ◇ *The shares are freely ~.* | **fully** | **not necessarily**
PREP. **between** ◇ *Tickets are ~ between members of the same family.* | **from, to** ◇ *skills which are ~ from one environment to another*

transform *verb*

ADV. **considerably, dramatically, fundamentally, profoundly, radically** ◇ *The riots radically ~ed the situation.* | **completely, entirely, totally, utterly** | **quickly, rapidly** | **gradually, slowly** | **suddenly** | **magically, miraculously** ◇ *He seems to have been miraculously ~ed into a first-class player.* | **overnight** ◇ *Things cannot be ~ed overnight.*
VERB + TRANSFORM **help (to)** | **be used to**
PREP. **from, into** ◇ *The place was ~ed from a quiet town into a busy port.*
PHRASES **the ability to ~ sb/sth, the power to ~ sb/sth** ◇ *the power of religion to ~ our hearts and minds*

transformation *noun*

ADJ. **amazing, complete, dramatic, fundamental, magical, major, miraculous, profound, radical, remarkable, revolutionary, startling, total** | **subtle** | **gradual** | **immediate, instant, rapid, sudden** | **cultural, economic, historical, institutional** (*esp. AmE*), **intellectual, personal, physical, political, social, spiritual, structural, technological**
... OF TRANSFORMATIONS **series**
VERB + TRANSFORMATION **go through, undergo** ◇ *The way we work has undergone a radical ~ in the past decade.* | **make** ◇ *He was struggling to make the ~ from single man to responsible husband.* | **achieve, bring about, carry out, cause, effect, lead to** ◇ *Going to college brought about a dramatic ~ in her outlook.* | **accelerate** | **complete** | **witness**
TRANSFORMATION + VERB **begin** | **happen, occur, take place** ◇ *A startling cultural ~ occurred in post-war Britain.*
TRANSFORMATION + NOUN **process**
PREP. **~ from** ◇ *The ~ from disused docks into cultural venue took three years.* | **~ in** ◇ *This decision marked a fundamental ~ in policy.* | **~ into** ◇ *Japan's ~ into an economic superpower* | **~ to** ◇ *Russia's ~ to a market economy*
PHRASES **a/the process of ~**

transfusion *noun*

ADJ. **blood** | **emergency**
VERB + TRANSFUSION **get, have, receive** | **give sb, perform** | **need, require**
TRANSFUSION + NOUN **unit**

transit *noun*

1 process of transporting sth
TRANSIT + NOUN **point** ◇ *The port has become a ~ point in the drug trade.* | **camp** ◇ *a ~ camp for refugees* | **lounge** ◇ *The passengers had been transferred into the ~ lounge.* | **visa** (*esp. AmE*)
PREP. **in ~** ◇ *The goods were damaged in ~.* | **~ between** ◇ *goods in ~ between factory and store* | **~ from, ~ to** ◇ *in ~ from factory to store*
2 (*AmE*) system for moving people
ADJ. **mass, public** ◇ *An improved mass ~ system would cut traffic on the roads.* | **rapid** | **rail** | **city, local, regional, urban**
TRANSIT + NOUN **system** ◇ *The city has acquired a light rail ~ system.* | **hub, station** | **agency, authority** | **officer, official, police, worker** | **union** | **strike** ◇ *The New York ~ strike is in its second day.* | **bus, train**

transition *noun*

ADJ. **abrupt, rapid, sudden** | **direct** | **gradual, slow** | **awkward, difficult, painful** | **easy, seamless, smooth** | **successful** | **orderly, peaceful** | **democratic**
VERB + TRANSITION **bring about** ◇ *The negotiators hoped to bring about a smooth ~ to an interim administration.* | **complete, make** ◇ *The company was slow to make the ~ from paper to computer.* | **undergo** | **mark** ◇ *The ceremony marks the ~ of the student to graduate status.* | **ease, smooth**
TRANSITION + VERB **occur, take place** | **be complete** ◇ *Her ~ from girl to woman was complete.*
TRANSITION + NOUN **period, process** | **phase** | **committee, team**
PREP. **during (the) ~** ◇ *He will remain head of state during the ~ to democracy.* | **in ~** ◇ *The country is in ~ from an agricultural to an industrial society.* | **~ between** ◇ *This training course aims to smooth the ~ between education and employment.* | **~ from, ~ to**
PHRASES **a period of ~, a time of ~** | **a process of ~** | **a state of ~**

translate *verb*

1 change sth from one language to another
ADV. **literally** ◇ *'Tiramisù' literally ~s as 'pull-me-up'.* | **accurately, correctly** | **freely, loosely, roughly** | **generally, usually** | **variously** ◇ *a Greek word variously ~d as 'summit', 'top' and 'finishing stroke'*
VERB + TRANSLATE **attempt to, try to** | **be difficult to** ◇ *This word is difficult to ~.*
PREP. **as** ◇ *The word 'sensus' can be ~d as 'feeling'.* | **for** ◇ *I don't speak Italian—can you ~ for me?* | **from** ◇ *The book has been ~d from the Japanese by Livia Yamaguchi.* | **into** ◇ *an expression that is difficult to ~ into English*
PHRASES **widely ~d** ◇ *The novel has been widely ~d.*
2 change into a different form
ADV. **well** ◇ *The story ~s well to the screen.* | **easily, readily** | **automatically** ◇ *Teacher expectations do not automatically ~ themselves into student results.* | **not necessarily** ◇ *Higher sales won't necessarily ~ into profits.* | **effectively, directly** | **ultimately** (*esp. AmE*) ◇ *The lost trade revenue ultimately ~d into job losses at home.*
VERB + TRANSLATE **attempt to, try to** ◇ *They tried to ~ the theory into simple concepts.* | **be difficult to**
PREP. **into** ◇ *A small increase in local spending will ~ into a big rise in council tax.*
PHRASES **~ sth into action, ~ sth into practice** ◇ *The group attempts to ~ these ideas into action.*

translation *noun*

ADJ. **accurate, correct, exact, faithful, good** | **approximate, free, loose, rough** | **bad, poor** | **direct, literal, word-for-word** | **prose, verse** | **literary, poetic, vernacular** | **English, Japanese, etc.** | **simultaneous** ◇ *There will be simultaneous ~ in English and Chinese.* | **automatic, machine** ◇ *advances in machine ~*
VERB + TRANSLATION **do, make, produce** ◇ *I have a ~ to do for Friday.* ◇ *She tried making her own ~ of the contract.* | **provide** | **work on** | **read** | **survive** ◇ *The poems do not survive the ~ into English.*
TRANSLATION + VERB **read** ◇ *The ~ of the Latin motto reads 'Not for oneself, but for others'.*
TRANSLATION + NOUN **process** | **service, work** | **facilities** (*esp. BrE*) | **equivalent**
PREP. **in ~** ◇ *I read the book in ~.* | **~ from, ~ into** ◇ *Simultaneous ~ into English is available to delegates.*
PHRASES **lose sth in ~** ◇ *The irony is lost in ~.*

translator *noun*

ADJ. **Dutch, Japanese, etc.** | **professional** | **online**
TRANSLATOR + VERB **~ from sth (to sth)** ◇ *~s from Portuguese to English* | **render sth as sth** ◇ *The ~ renders the French 'C'est-à-dire' as 'That is to say'.*

PREP. **through** ~ ◊ *He spoke through a* ~.
→ Note at JOB

transmission *noun*

1 sending out/passing on

ADJ. **direct, indirect | onward** (*BrE*) ◊ *An extra copy of each document was supplied for onward* ~ *to head office.* | **data, information, voice | facsimile, fax | light, power | money** (*esp. BrE*) | **cable, radio, satellite, television | analogue/ analog, digital, electronic, wireless | live, simultaneous** ◊ *There will be simultaneous* ~ *of the concert on TV and radio.* | **genetic, oral, sexual | human-to-human, mother-to-child, person-to-person | disease, HIV, malaria, STD | cultural**
VERB + TRANSMISSION **prevent | reduce | facilitate | block**
TRANSMISSION + NOUN **equipment, technology | belt** (*figurative*), **mechanism, network, system** ◊ *The associations serve as* ~ *belts for party policy.* | **route** ◊ *The virus's usual* ~ *route is by sneezing.*
PREP. ~ **among** ◊ *HIV* ~ *among homosexual men* | ~ **between** ◊ ~ *between patients* | ~ **by** ◊ ~ *by satellite* | ~ **from,** ~ **of** ◊ *the* ~ *of knowledge* | ~ **to** ◊ ~ *from one aircraft to another* | ~ **through** ◊ *HIV* ~ *through blood transfusion*
PHRASES **a mode of** ~, **a risk of** ~ ◊ *There is a risk of* ~ *of the virus between hypodermic users.*

2 TV/radio show

ADJ. **radio, television, TV | live, satellite | test**
VERB + TRANSMISSION **receive**
PREP. ~ **from** ◊ *a live* ~ *from Sydney*

3 in a car, etc.

ADJ. **automatic, manual | 4-speed, 5-speed, etc.**
TRANSMISSION + NOUN **system**

transmit *verb*

1 pass sth from one person to another

ADV. **easily, readily | genetically, orally, sexually** ◊ *the study of genetically transmitted diseases*
PREP. **from, through** ◊ *The disease cannot be transmitted through sneezing.* | **to** ◊ *The infection can be transmitted from a mother to her baby.* | **via** ◊ *The virus is easily transmitted via needles.*

2 send out radio signals, etc.

ADV. **automatically | electronically**
PREP. **from, over** ◊ *Movies can be transmitted over the Internet.* | **to** ◊ *The data will be automatically transmitted from one part of the system to another.*

transmitter *noun*

ADJ. **radar, radio, television, TV | FM, short-wave, VHF | powerful | ground, satellite, wireless**
VERB + TRANSMITTER **be equipped with, be fitted with**
TRANSMITTER + VERB **emit sth, send sth, send out sth** ◊ *The receiver picks up pulses emitted by the* ~.

transparent *adj.*

VERBS **appear, be, look, seem | become | make sth**
ADV. **very | completely, entirely, fully, perfectly, quite, totally** ◊ *They are so thin that they are quite* ~. | **almost, nearly, partially** ◊ *Her eyelids were blue and almost* ~. | **fairly, rather | slightly**

transplant *noun*

ADJ. **organ | bone-marrow, heart, kidney, liver, lung, stem-cell, etc.**
VERB + TRANSPLANT **need, require | wait for** ◊ *patients waiting for heart* ~s | **get** (*informal*), **have, receive, undergo** ◊ *She will have to have a kidney* ~ *within 48 hours.* | **carry out** (*esp. BrE*), **do, perform | reject** ◊ *It is likely that such a* ~ *will be rejected in older people.*
TRANSPLANT + NOUN **operation, surgery | surgeon | team | centre/center, unit** (*esp. BrE*) | **donor** ◊ *A suitable* ~ *donor has been found.* | **candidate, patient, recipient**
PREP. **for** ~ ◊ *a shortage of kidneys for* ~

transplant *verb*

ADV. **successfully**
PREP. **from, into** ◊ *Organs are* ~*ed from donors into patients who need them.* | **to** ◊ *The Dutch successfully* ~*ed trees to the East Indies.*

transport *noun*

1 (*esp. BrE*) **system for moving people or goods** → See also TRANSIT, TRANSPORTATION

ADJ. **public** ◊ *to travel by/on public* ~ | **cheap, efficient | private | city, local, rural, urban | motor | air, ground, land, rail, road, sea, water | passenger | cargo** (*AmE*), **freight**
VERB + TRANSPORT **use | arrange | provide**
TRANSPORT + NOUN **facilities, provision** (*BrE*), **services | infrastructure, network, system | hub, interchange** (*BrE*) | **business, company, group, industry, operator | boss** (*BrE*), **chief, manager, officer, official | planner | project, scheme** (*BrE*), **strategy | bill, policy | budget | minister, secretary, spokesman, spokeswoman | authority, committee, department** ◊ *He sits on the passenger* ~ *authority.* | **needs | sector | costs, fares | user | worker | links, routes | police | union**
PREP. **without** ~ ◊ *The car broke down, leaving us without* ~.
PHRASES **access to** ~ ◊ *people who have no access to private* ~ | **a form of** ~, **a means of** ~, **a method of** ~, **a mode of** ~ | ~ **to and from…** ◊ *We provide* ~ *to and from school.* | **your own** ~ ◊ *Applicants for the job must have their own* ~.

2 vehicle used for carrying soldiers

ADJ. **army, military | cargo, troop**
TRANSPORT + NOUN **aircraft, helicopter, plane, vehicle, etc.**

transportation *noun* (*esp. AmE*) → See also TRANSIT, TRANSPORT

ADJ. **mass, public** ◊ *Many destinations can be reached by public* ~. | **private | local, state | cheap, efficient | reliable | air, ground, highway** (*AmE*), **land, rail, railroad** (*AmE*), **road, sea, space, surface | cargo, freight | interstate** (*AmE*)
VERB + TRANSPORTATION **take** (*AmE*), **use** ◊ *You can take public* ~ *to the office.* | **arrange | provide**
TRANSPORTATION + NOUN **facilities, services | infrastructure, network, system | hub | industry, sector | company | official | project | bill, policy** ◊ *a federal* ~ *bill* | **committee, department | needs, requirements | costs | worker | links, route**
PREP. **without** ~
PHRASES **access to** ~ ◊ *Do you have access to* ~? ◊ *The neighborhood offers easy access to public* ~. | **a form of** ~, **a means of** ~, **a method of** ~, **a mode of** ~ | ~ **to and from…** ◊ *We provide* ~ *to and from school.* | **your own** ~ (*AmE*) ◊ *Volunteers must provide their own* ~.

trap *noun*

1 hidden equipment used for catching sb/sth

ADJ. **animal, bear, mouse** (usually ***mousetrap***), **etc. | radar** (*BrE*), **speed** ◊ *Slow down—there are speed* ~s *along this stretch of road.*
VERB + TRAP **be caught in, get caught in | free sth from** ◊ *The fox had managed to free itself from the* ~. | **lay, set, set up | bait** ◊ *The* ~s *are traditionally baited with cheese.*

2 sth that tricks you; unpleasant situation

ADJ. **hidden, obvious | potential | booby | deadly, death** ◊ *The overhead cable is a potential death* ~ *for birds.* | **fire** ◊ *This building is a fire* ~. | **debt, poverty | liquidity** (*business, esp. AmE*) | **sand** (in golf) (*AmE*)
VERB + TRAP **lay, set, set up | spring | lure sb into | be caught in, fall into, get caught in, walk into** ◊ *It is easy to fall into the* ~ *of taking out a loan you cannot afford.* | **avoid, escape**

trappings *noun*

ADJ. **external, outer** (*AmE*), **outward, visible** ◊ *She scorns the visible* ~ *of success, preferring to live unnoticed.* | **traditional, usual** ◊ *the usual* ~ *of wealth*

trash *noun (AmE)* → See also GARBAGE, RUBBISH

1 waste material

VERB + TRASH **dump, empty, throw away** | **take out** ◇ *Can you take out the ~?* | **talk** *(figurative)* ◇ *He was talking ~ about my family.*

TRASH + NOUN **bin, can** | **bag** | **heap** *(often figurative)*, **pile** ◇ *His theories were relegated to the ~ heap of history.* | **talk** *(figurative)*

2 offensive term for poor people

ADJ. **gutter, street, trailer, white** *(all esp. AmE)* ◇ *poor white ~*

trauma *noun*

ADJ. **major, severe** | **emotional, mental, physical, psychological, sexual** | **childhood** ◇ *The phobia may have its root in a childhood ~.* | **historical**

VERB + TRAUMA **experience, face, go through, suffer** | **get over, recover from**

TRAUMA + NOUN **patient, survivor, victim** | **centre/center**

PHRASES **a history of ~** ◇ *patients who have histories of childhood ~*

traumatic *adj.*

VERBS **be** | **become, get**

ADV. **extremely, fairly, very, etc.** | **deeply, particularly, really** ◇ *this deeply ~ incident in his past* | **potentially** | **emotionally**

travel *noun*

ADJ. **air, airline** *(esp. AmE)*, **airplane** *(esp. AmE)*, **automobile** *(AmE)*, **bus, car, coach** *(BrE)*, **jet, rail, sea, train** | **domestic** *(esp. AmE)*, **foreign, international, overseas, transatlantic, world** | **long-distance** | **business, corporate** *(esp. AmE)* | **adventure** *(esp. AmE)*, **leisure** | **holiday, vacation** *(AmE)* | **cheap, concessionary** *(BrE)*, **discount** *(esp. AmE)*, **free** | **first-class** | **return** *(esp. BrE)*, **round-trip** *(AmE)* | **frequent** ◇ *The job involves frequent ~.* | **extensive** | **interplanetary, interstellar, space** | **time**

TRAVEL + NOUN **agency, agent, business, company, firm** *(esp. BrE)*, **industry, market, service** ◇ *an online ~ agent* | **arrangements, plans** | **allowance** *(esp. BrE)*, **budget, costs, expenses** | **insurance** | **document** | **itinerary, schedule** *(esp. AmE)* | **destination** ◇ *Mexico's top ~ destinations* | **ban, restrictions** | **time** ◇ *The new road will reduce ~ time to the airport.* | **season** *(AmE)* ◇ *the holiday ~ season* | **sickness** *(esp. BrE)* | **book, brochure, guide** | **literature, writing** | **writer** | **bag** | **companion** *(esp. AmE)*

PREP. **~ from, ~ to** ◇ *The price includes ~ from Bangkok to Phuket.*

PHRASES **a/the direction of ~** *(often figurative in BrE)* ◇ *The party needs to set out a clear direction of ~ for health care.* | **a/the means of ~, a/the mode of ~** ◇ *The bus is their preferred mode of ~.*

travel *verb*

ADV. **fast, quickly** ◇ *News ~s fast these days.* | **slowly** | **regularly** ◇ *business people who ~ regularly to the US* | **widely** ◇ *She ~s widely in her job.* | **freely** ◇ *The dissidents were unable to hold meetings or ~ freely.* | **independently** ◇ *I prefer to ~ independently.* | **alone, together** | **separately** ◇ *We had to ~ separately as we couldn't get seats on the same flight.* | **first class, tourist class, etc.** ◇ *I always ~ first class.* | **extensively, far, far and wide** ◇ *information for the backpacker who wants to ~ farther afield* ◇ *a writer who ~s far and wide* | **abroad, overseas** ◇ *The job gives her the opportunity to ~ overseas.* | **home** | **back, back and forth, down** ◇ *He ~s back and forth across the Atlantic.* | **north, northwards, etc.**

PREP. **across, along, around, at** ◇ *to ~ at the speed of light* | **between, by** ◇ *We decided to ~ by car.* | **around, from, into, round** *(esp. BrE)*, **through** ◇ *We plan to ~ through Thailand*

and into Cambodia. | **to, with** ◇ *He ~s with a huge entourage.*

PHRASES **freedom to ~** | **go travelling/traveling** ◇ *When I finished college I went travelling/~ing for six months* (= *spent time visiting different places*). | **~ all over the world, ~ around the world** | **~ back in time** ◇ *In the film, he ~s back in time to the '50s.* | **~ light** ◇ *She ~s light, choosing to use as little equipment as possible.*

traveller *(esp. BrE)* *(AmE usually* **traveler***) noun*

ADJ. **business, corporate** *(AmE)* | **commercial** *(BrE, old-fashioned)*, **leisure** | **holiday** *(esp. AmE)* | **budget** | **frequent** ◇ *Attractive discounts are available to frequent ~s.* | **foreign, international, world** | **long-distance** | **avid** *(esp. AmE)*, **great** *(esp. BrE)*, **inveterate, keen** *(BrE)*, **seasoned** ◇ *I'm not a great ~. I'm happiest staying at home.* | **adventurous, intrepid** | **independent** *(esp. BrE)* ◇ *Independent ~s often steer clear of the most touristy spots.* | **lone** | **discerning** | **fellow** ◇ *I got to know my fellow ~s quite well in the course of the three-day journey.* | **weary** | **unwary** ◇ *Stations can be dangerous places for the unwary ~.* | **air, rail** *(esp. BrE)*, **train** | **space, time** | **armchair** (= *sb who does not travel but likes to read about distant places*) ◇ *His travel books have given pleasure to generations of armchair ~s.*

VERB + TRAVELLER **attract, deter** | **cater to** ◇ *hotels that cater to business ~s* | **guide** ◇ *Local tribesmen earn their living guiding ~s across the mountains.*

tray *noun*

ADJ. **breakfast, dinner, lunch** | **cafeteria, deli** *(both esp. AmE)* | **drinks, tea** | **bed** *(AmE)* | **hospitality, serving** | **plastic, silver, etc.**

VERB + TRAY **bear, carry** | **pick up** | **balance** ◇ *He balanced the ~ on his knees.* | **place, put down, set down** | **drop**

PREP. **on a/the ~** ◇ *A waitress came in, carrying tea on a ~.* | **~ of** ◇ *waiters bearing ~s of champagne*

treacherous *adj.*

VERBS **be, prove** | **become** | **remain**

ADV. **extremely, fairly, very, etc.** | **potentially** | **notoriously** ◇ *the mountain's notoriously ~ face*

tread *noun*

1 sound you make when you are walking

ADJ. **heavy** ◇ *I heard his heavy ~ moving about upstairs.* | **light, soft** | **measured, slow, steady**

VERB + TREAD **hear**

PREP. **with a … ~** ◇ *A policeman walked by with a slow, measured ~.*

2 on a tyre/tire

ADJ. **tyre/tire, wheel** | **worn** ◇ *The tyre/tire ~ is worn below the legal limit.* | **tank** *(esp. AmE)*

TREAD + NOUN **depth, pattern**

tread *verb*

ADV. **heavily** ◇ *He came down the stairs, ~ing as heavily as he could.* | **gently, lightly, softly** | **carefully, cautiously, gingerly, warily** ◇ *The government will have to ~ carefully in handling this issue.* *(figurative)* ◇ *She trod gingerly. It would be risky to hurry.* | **with care, with caution** | **down** ◇ *She planted the seeds and trod the earth down.*

PREP. **in** *(BrE)* ◇ *Billy trod in a big puddle.* | **into** *(BrE)* ◇ *Some cake crumbs had been trodden into the carpet.* | **on** *(BrE)* ◇ *Be careful not to ~ on the flowers.*

treason *noun*

ADJ. **high**

PREP. **~ against** ◇ *an act of high ~ against the English crown*

PHRASES **an act of ~**

→ Note at CRIME

treasure noun

1 collection of very valuable objects

ADJ. **buried, hidden, lost, sunken** | **pirate, royal** | **vast** ◇ *a vast ~ of medieval manuscripts*
VERB + TREASURE **hunt for, look for, search for** | **dig up, discover, find, uncover, unearth** | **steal** | **bury, hide**
TREASURE + NOUN **chest, house, trove** (*figurative*) ◇ *This book is a ~ house of information on Arctic birds.* | **map** | **hunt, hunter, hunting**
PHRASES **a hoard of ~**

2 sth that is very valuable

ADJ. **great, precious, priceless, valuable** | **rare** | **ancient** | **forgotten, hidden, secret, unexpected** ◇ *Many forgotten ~s have been discovered in old houses.* | **archaeological, architectural, historic, historical** | **art, artistic, cultural** | **family** | **national**
VERB + TREASURE **discover, find, uncover, unearth**

treasurer noun

ADJ. **assistant** | **honorary** (*BrE*) ◇ *the honorary ~ of the rugby club* | **corporate** | **church, class** (*AmE*), **club** (*BrE*), **party** (*esp. BrE*) | **campaign** (*esp. AmE*) | **county, state** (*both AmE*)
VERB + TREASURER **act as, be, serve as** ◇ *He agreed to act as ~.* | **appoint, appoint sb (as), elect, elect sb (as)**
PHRASES **treasurer's report** ◇ *The treasurer's report gives a breakdown of the club's income and expenditure.*

treat noun

ADJ. **big, great, real, special** | **little** ◇ *I like to give the girls a little ~ every now and then.* | **occasional, rare** | **birthday** (*esp. BrE*), **Christmas** (*esp. BrE*), **festive** (*esp. BrE*), **holiday** (*esp. AmE*) | **family** | **delicious, sweet, tasty** ◇ *Snails are a tasty ~ for hedgehogs.* | **frozen** (*AmE*) | **musical, visual** | **dog** (*esp. AmE*)
VERB + TREAT **give sb** | **deserve** | **get**
PREP. **as a ~, for a ~** ◇ *I took the kids to the zoo for a special ~.*
PHRASES **be in for a ~, have a ~ in store** (*esp. BrE*) ◇ *If their latest album is half as good as their last one, we've a real ~ in store.*

treat verb

1 handle sb/sth in a particular way

ADV. **equally, equitably, fairly, humanely, kindly, leniently, sympathetically, well** | **abominably, badly, harshly, roughly, shabbily, unfairly, unjustly** ◇ *They ~ their animals quite badly.* | **seriously** ◇ *These allegations are being ~ed very seriously indeed.* | **accordingly** ◇ *He is guilty and should be ~ed accordingly.* | **in the same way** | **differently** | **separately**
VERB + TREAT **tend to** ◇ *Parents still tend to ~ boys differently from girls.*
PREP. **as** ◇ *the tendency to ~ older people as helpless* | **like** ◇ *Don't ~ me like a child!* | **with** ◇ *He ~ed the idea with suspicion.*
PHRASES **deserve to be ~ed** ◇ *They deserve to be ~ed with patience and respect.*

2 give sb medical treatment

ADV. **easily** | **appropriately, properly** | **effectively, successfully** | **medically, surgically**
VERB + TREAT **be difficult to** | **use sth to**
PREP. **for** ◇ *She was ~ed for cuts and bruises.* | **with** ◇ *We can ~ this condition successfully with antibiotics.*
PHRASES **be effective in ~ing sth** ◇ *The drug is effective at ~ing depression.*

3 use a substance to protect sth

ADV. **chemically** ◇ *Chemically ~ed hair can become dry and brittle.*
PREP. **for** ◇ *You need to ~ this wood for woodworm.* | **with** ◇ *The timber has been ~ed with chemicals to preserve it.*

treatment noun

1 way you treat sb/sth

ADJ. **favourable/favorable, preferential, special, VIP** ◇ *She was given the VIP ~ after winning a gold medal.* | **generous, lenient** | **equal, fair** | **good, humane** | **sensitive, sympathetic** | **discriminatory, poor, unequal, unfair, unjust** | **brutal, cruel, degrading, harsh, inhuman, inhumane, rough** ◇ *He claims he suffered inhuman ~ at the hands of prison officers.* | **shabby** ◇ *You shouldn't put up with such shabby ~.*
VERB + TREATMENT **get, have, receive, suffer** | **deserve** ◇ *He had done nothing to deserve such cruel ~.* | **give sb, mete out (to sb)** (*esp. BrE*) ◇ *The ~ meted out to captured soldiers was harsh.* | **accept, put up with**

2 medical care

ADJ. **emergency, immediate, prompt, urgent** (*esp. BrE*) | **first-line** (*AmE*), **primary** | **follow-up, further** | **long-term** | **effective, successful** | **conventional, orthodox, recommended, standard** | **experimental** | **alternative, holistic, homeopathic** | **hospital** (*esp. BrE*) | **inpatient, outpatient** | **free, NHS** (*in the UK*) | **private** (*esp. BrE*) | **specialist** (*BrE*) | **clinical, dental, medical, psychiatric, veterinary** (*esp. BrE*) | **surgical** | **non-surgical** | **acupuncture, antibiotic, drug, hormone, laser, radiation, shock** (*often figurative*) | **addiction, cancer, fertility** | **dietary** | **beauty** (*esp. BrE*), **hair, spa**
...OF TREATMENT **course**
VERB + TREATMENT **get, have, receive, undergo** ◇ *She is still undergoing medical ~.* | **administer, give sb, provide (sb with)** ◇ *paramedics trained in administering emergency ~* | **be effective in, be used in** ◇ *a herbal drug that is used in the ~ of dizziness* | **be approved for** ◇ *drugs approved for AIDS ~* | **need, require** | **seek** ◇ *When his depression worsened, he decided to seek ~.* | **prescribe, recommend, suggest** | **refuse** | **begin, enter** (*esp. AmE*) | **complete** | **discontinue** | **benefit from, respond to** ◇ *He responded well to ~ and is now walking again.*
TREATMENT + NOUN **decision, option** | **centre/center, room** | **method, procedure, process, technique** | **course, plan, programme/program, regime, regimen, schedule** | **provider** (*esp. AmE*), **services**
PREP. **in ~** ◇ *He's in ~ for cocaine addiction.* | **~ for** ◇ *She is receiving ~ for a heart condition.*

3 process for cleaning/protecting sth

ADJ. **sewage, water**
TREATMENT + NOUN **facility, plant, works** (*BrE*)

4 discussion of a subject, work of art, etc.

ADJ. **exhaustive, systematic** | **lengthy** | **cursory, superficial** | **philosophical, theoretical**

treaty noun

ADJ. **global, international, regional, union** | **bilateral, multilateral** | **formal** | **draft** | **commercial, trade** | **climate, environmental** ◇ *the 1997 Kyoto climate ~* | **unequal** | **cooperation, friendship** | **non-aggression, peace** | **arms, arms-control, disarmament, non-proliferation** ◇ *A multilateral nuclear non-proliferation ~ was to be signed.* | **defence/defense** | **human rights** | **extradition**
VERB + TREATY **draft, draw up** | **negotiate** | **become a party to, conclude, enter into, make, sign** ◇ *In September 1871 Japan entered into a commercial ~ with China.* | **be a party to** ◇ *Indonesia was not a party to this ~.* | **vote on** | **accept, approve, ratify, vote for** ◇ *All the members have voted to ratify the ~.* | **reject, vote against** | **oppose** | **amend** | **adhere to, support** | **be in breach of** (*esp. BrE*), **breach** (*esp. BrE*), **break, violate** ◇ *These methods violate international treaties.* | **abrogate** (*technical*), **repudiate** (*esp. BrE*) | **enforce** | **impose** ◇ *The people felt the ~ had been imposed on them by their government.* | **be bound by** | **be laid down by, be laid down in** (*both esp. BrE*) ◇ *the criteria laid down in the ~*
TREATY + VERB **come into force** ◇ *The ~ comes into force at midnight on December 31.* | **provide for** ◇ *The ~ provides for UN inspection of all countries' weapons systems.* | **guarantee sth** | **govern sth, regulate sth** | **create sth, establish sth** |

recognize sth | require sth | ban sth, prohibit sth | end sth ◇ *In 1713 the Treaty of Utrecht ended the War of the Spanish Succession.*
TREATY + NOUN **party** (*law*) | **amendment, changes, revision** (*esp. BrE*) | **negotiations** | **provision** | **agreement** (*esp. AmE*) | **terms** | **law** | **commitment, obligation** | **rights** | **relationship**
PREP. **by ~** ◇ *Certain areas had been ceded by ~.* | **under a/the ~** ◇ *These arrangements under the ~ apply to the whole of Europe.* | **~ between** ◇ *a bilateral ~ between the US and Mexico* | **~ on** ◇ *an international ~ on climate change* | **~ with** ◇ *The government concluded a peace ~ with the rebels.*
PHRASES **an article of a ~, an clause of a ~** | **the provisions of a ~, the terms of a ~** | **the ratification of a ~**

treble verb (*esp. BrE*) → See also TRIPLE
ADV. **more than** | **almost, nearly**
PREP. **in** ◇ *Some goods have almost ~d in price.* | **to** ◇ *The figure has more than ~d to 67%.*

tree noun
ADJ. **deciduous, evergreen** | **coniferous** | **native** | **exotic, tropical** | **ornamental** | **forest, woodland** (*esp. BrE*) | **big, giant, great, high, huge, large, massive, mighty, tall** | **low, small, stunted** | **mature** | **old, young** | **bare, leafless** | **shady** ◇ *We sat beneath a shady ~.* | **shade** ◇ *It was a small town of dust lanes and wide shade ~s.* | **hollow** | **gnarled** ◇ *a gnarled old apple ~* | **fallen** ◇ *A fallen ~ was blocking the road.* | **dead** | **fruit** | **apple, cherry, maple, peach, pear, etc.** | **beech, oak, palm, pine, willow, etc.** | **Christmas**
... OF TREES **clump, copse, grove** | **avenue** (*esp. BrE*), **belt** (*esp. BrE*), **line**
VERB + TREE **grow, plant** | **climb** | **chop down, cut down, fell** ◇ *Protesters formed a human blockade to stop loggers felling ~s.* | **uproot** ◇ *The floods left a tide of mud and uprooted ~s.* | **prune** | **be shaded by**
TREE + VERB **grow** | **stand** ◇ *An enormous oak ~ stands at the entrance to the school.* | **line sth, surround sth** ◇ *Palm ~s line the broad avenue.* | **sway** ◇ *Trees swayed gently in the breeze.* | **be blown down, blow down, fall** | **bear sth, produce sth** ◇ *The ~ produces tiny white blossoms.* | **provide sth**
TREE + NOUN **bark, branch, leaves, limb, root, stump, trunk** | **tops** (usually **treetops**) | **canopy** ◇ *dappled shafts of light which struggled through the ~ canopy* | **cover** ◇ *Tree cover would prevent further soil erosion.* | **felling, planting** | **trimmer** | **species** | **line** (usually **treeline**) ◇ *Above the treeline, take a grassy path leading steeply to the summit.* | **belt** ◇ *The ~ belt around the fields acts as a windbreak.* | **growth** | **rings** ◇ *The forest can be dated by studying ~ rings.* | **damage** ◇ *~ damage caused by acid rain* | **nursery** ◇ *He bought tools and seeds with the aim of setting up a ~ nursery.* | **surgeon** | **hugger** (usually **tree-hugger**) (= sb who is anxious to protect the environment) (*disapproving, humorous*)
PREP. **in a/the ~** ◇ *a bird in a ~* | **on a/the ~** ◇ *fruit on a ~* | **under a ~** ◇ *We sat under a ~, in the shade.* | **up a/the ~** ◇ *The cat got stuck up a ~.*

trek noun
ADJ. **long, marathon** (*esp. BrE*) | **20-mile, etc.** | **3-day, 10-hour, etc.** | **arduous, gruelling/grueling, strenuous** | **short** | **cross-country**
VERB + TREK **go on, make, take** ◇ *The family made the long ~ west in 1890.* | **begin** | **continue**
PREP. **on a/the ~**

tremble verb
ADV. **badly, violently** | **uncontrollably** | **a little, slightly** | **inside** | **still** ◇ *His voice was still trembling.*
VERB + TREMBLE **begin to, start to** ◇ *I began to ~ uncontrollably.* | **make sb** ◇ *The thought made him ~ inside.*
PREP. **at** ◇ *She ~d at the thought of going back through those prison doors.* | **in** ◇ *He was still trembling in fear.* | **with** ◇ *She was trembling with anger.*
PHRASES **~ all over, ~ from head to foot, ~ from head to toe** | **~ like a leaf**

tremor noun
1 small earthquake
ADJ. **minor, slight** | **severe** | **earth**
2 shaking movement
ADJ. **faint, slight, small** ◇ *He felt a tiny ~ of excitement as he glimpsed the city lights.* | **violent** | **nervous** | **hand, muscle**
VERB + TREMOR **send** ◇ *Her expression sent a ~ of anxiety through him.* | **cause** | **feel** ◇ *She felt a ~ run down her back when she saw him.* | **control** ◇ *He couldn't control the ~ in his voice.*
TREMOR + VERB **run** ◇ *A ~ ran through the audience.* | **shake sb/sth** ◇ *An uncontrollable ~ shook his mouth.*
PREP. **with a ~, without a ~** ◇ *He managed to make his short speech without a ~.* | **~ of** ◇ *a ~ of fear*

trench noun
ADJ. **deep, narrow, shallow** | **muddy** | **defensive** | **enemy** | **communication, front-line, slit**
VERB + TRENCH **dig**
TRENCH + NOUN **warfare** | **foot** ◇ *The soldiers had to be treated for ~ foot.*
PREP. **in the ~** ◇ *life in the ~es in the First World War*

trend noun
ADJ. **strong** | **consistent, steady** | **accelerating, growing, increasing** | **underlying** ◇ *Despite this month's disappointing figures, the underlying ~ is healthy.* | **big, dominant, main, major, prevailing** | **current, latest, new, recent** | **long-term** | **gradual** | **clear, marked, significant important** | **general, overall** | **apparent, discernible** | **global, international, national, worldwide** | **larger, wider** ◇ *The increase in crime in the capital was just part of a wider ~.* | **positive, upward** | **downward, negative** | **opposite** | **healthy, welcome** | **adverse, dangerous, disturbing, unfortunate, worrying** | **fashion** | **demographic, population** | **cultural, social** | **evolutionary, historical** | **economic, market** | **growth, inflationary** ◇ *The latest figures show a clear growth ~ in the service sector.*
VERB + TREND **begin, create, set, start** ◇ *In the 1960s, Britain set the fashion ~s.* | **continue** | **follow** ◇ *We are following the ~ for more flexible working conditions.* | **reinforce** | **buck, counteract, go against** ◇ *efforts to buck the current downward ~ in sales* | **reverse** | **halt** | **detect, identify, notice, observe, see** ◇ *I can see a worrying ~ in these results.* | **indicate, reflect, show, suggest** ◇ *The data indicates a ~ towards/toward earlier retirement.*
TREND + VERB **develop, emerge** | **continue** | **indicate sth, reflect sth, show sth, suggest sth** ◇ *Current ~s suggest that cities will continue to grow.* | **grow**
PREP. **on ~** ◇ *Linen is on ~ again this summer.* | **~ away from** ◇ *a ~ away from narrow specialization* | **~ for** ◇ *A ~ for nostalgia has emerged.* | **~ in** ◇ *future ~s in the volume of employment* | **~ towards/toward** ◇ *the ~ towards/toward privatization*

trial noun
1 in a court of law
ADJ. **fair, unfair** ◇ *The men claim they did not receive a fair ~.* | **full** | **criminal** | **fraud, impeachment** (*esp. AmE*) | **libel, murder, rape, etc.** | **court, jury** | **Crown Court, High Court** (*in the UK*) | **federal, state** (*both esp. AmE*) | **civil** | **public** | **show** ◇ *A series of show ~s of former senior officials* | **summary** (*esp. BrE*) ◇ *The rebels were brutally executed after summary ~s.* | **controversial, notorious, sensational**
VERB + TRIAL **come to, face, go on, go to, stand** ◇ *He never came to ~ for the robbery.* ◇ *She died before the case came to ~.* ◇ *A man has gone on ~ accused of murdering his girlfriend.* | **bring sb to, commit sb for** (*BrE*), **put sb on** ◇ *Four people had been arrested and committed for ~.* | **await** ◇ *He is in prison awaiting ~ on drugs charges.* | **get** ◇ *She does not believe she got a fair ~.* | **attend** ◇ *As a journalist he attended every murder ~ of note.* | **order** ◇ *The judge ordered a new ~*

on the grounds that evidence had been withheld. | **hold** | **adjourn** (*esp. BrE*) | **halt**, **stop** ◊ *The judge halted the ~ when it emerged witnesses had been threatened.* | **tell** (*BrE*) ◊ *The ~ was told that death threats had been made against him.*

TRIAL + VERB **proceed**, **take place** | **begin**, **open** | **continue**, **go on**, **resume** | **collapse** (*esp. BrE*) ◊ *The ~ collapsed after a key witness admitted lying.*

TRIAL + NOUN **attorney** (*AmE*), **court**, **judge**, **jury**, **lawyer** | **verdict** | **procedure**, **proceedings**, **process** | **date** ◊ *A ~ date has been set for May 10.*

PREP. **at the ~** ◊ *More than a hundred witnesses gave evidence at the ~.* | **during the ~** ◊ *The letters that were shown during his ~ turned out to be forgeries.* | **on ~** ◊ *She is presently on ~ at the Old Bailey.* | **without ~** ◊ *Opposition leaders had been jailed without ~.* | **~ by** ◊ *The president faces ~ by television tonight when he takes part in a live debate.* | **~ for** ◊ *She faces ~ for murder.* | **~ over** ◊ *Three people are to stand ~ over the deaths of a young couple.*

2 act of testing sb/sth

ADJ. **clinical**, **experimental**, **field** ◊ *If clinical ~s are successful the drug could be on the market early next year.* | **human** ◊ *Human ~s of the vaccine could begin within two years.* | **full-scale**, **large**, **large-scale** | **ongoing** | **controlled**, **double-blind**, **randomized** | **free** ◊ *There's a 30-day free ~ of the software available.* ◊ *We've got this vacuum cleaner on ten days' free ~.* | **speed** (*BrE*), **time** (*both sports*) | **Olympic**

VERB + TRIAL **carry out**, **conduct**, **do**, **hold** | **complete** | **take part in** | **have** (*BrE*) ◊ *He had a ~ with Chelsea when he was young.*

TRIAL + VERB **demonstrate sth**, **show sth** ◊ *The ~ showed a dramatic reduction in side effects.* | **find sth** | **involve sb/ sth**, **use sth** ◊ *a ~ involving hundreds of patients*

TRIAL + NOUN **period** ◊ *She agreed to employ me for a ~ period.* | **run** ◊ *They are treating this as a ~ run for their marathon later this month.* | **data**, **results** | **version** ◊ *You can download a free 30-day ~ version of the software.* | **project** (*esp. BrE*), **scheme** (*BrE*) | **balloon** (= sth that you say to find out what people think about it before you do it) (*AmE*) ◊ *The President may simply be floating a ~ balloon.* | **game** (*esp. BrE*) ◊ *Gates played his second ~ game in midfield.* | **separation** ◊ *The couple agreed on a ~ separation.*

PREP. **on ~** ◊ *We had the machine on ~ for a week.* | **under ~** (*esp. BrE*) ◊ *A new stocktaking system is currently under ~ in the store.*

PHRASES **on a ~ basis** ◊ *The new system will be introduced on a ~ basis.* | **~ by fire** (*figurative, esp. AmE*) ◊ *My first day at work was a ~ by fire.* | **~ and error** ◊ *We discovered the ideal mix of paint by ~ and error.* | **a ~ of strength** ◊ *The dispute was regarded as a ~ of strength by the unions.*

3 experience/person that causes difficulties

ADJ. **real** ◊ *She was a real ~ to her family at times.*

PREP. **~ to**

PHRASES **~s and tribulations** ◊ *the ~s and tribulations of married life*

triangle noun

1 shape

ADJ. **equilateral**, **isosceles**, **right** (*AmE*), **right-angled** (*BrE*), **scalene** | **inverted** ◊ *a large region resembling an inverted ~*

VERB + TRIANGLE **construct** (*technical*), **draw** ◊ *Use your protractor to construct an equilateral ~.* | **form** | **cut sth into** ◊ *I cut the sandwiches into ~s.*

PHRASES **the apex of a ~**

2 musical instrument

→ Special page at MUSIC

tribe noun

ADJ. **aboriginal**, **indigenous**, **native** | **local**, **neighbouring/ neighboring** | **desert**, **hill** | **nomadic** | **barbarian** | **primitive** | **hostile**, **warring**

VERB + TRIBE **belong to**

PHRASES **a member of a ~**

tribunal noun

1 court of justice

ADJ. **international**, **local** (*esp. BrE*) | **special** | **higher**, **highest** | **inferior** (*BrE*) | **judicial** (*esp. BrE*), **military** | **ad hoc**, **revolutionary** | **criminal**, **war crimes**

VERB + TRIBUNAL **create**, **establish**, **set up** ◊ *A war crimes ~ was set up to prosecute those charged with atrocities.* | **convene** | **appear before**, **face** ◊ *He could face a military ~.* | **be tried by** ◊ *The conspirators were tried by a military ~ and found guilty.*

TRIBUNAL + VERB **indict sb**, **sentence sb** ◊ *The ~ sentenced him to twenty years in prison.* | **rule sth**

PREP. **at a/the ~** ◊ *The police gave evidence at the ~.* | **before a/the ~** ◊ *He stood trial before an international ~.* | **by ~** ◊ *He was put on trial by military ~.*

2 (*BrE*) **official body to settle dispute**

ADJ. **impartial**, **independent** | **expert** | **employment**, **industrial**, **transport** | **appeal**, **arbitration**, **disciplinary** | **medical** | **fact-finding**

VERB + TRIBUNAL **establish** | **go to** ◊ *The case went to a ~.* | **apply to** | **bring sb/sth before**, **refer sth to**, **take sth to** ◊ *The case was referred to an industrial ~.* ◊ *She took her case to a ~.* | **appear before**, **face** | **tell** ◊ *She told the ~ that she was a victim of sex discrimination.* | **satisfy** ◊ *The employer must satisfy the ~ on several matters.*

TRIBUNAL + VERB **consider sth**, **hear sth** | **accept sth** | **dismiss sth**, **reject sth** | **conclude sth**, **decide sth**, **find sth** ◊ *The ~ found for her employers* (= judged that they were right). | **order sth**, **rule sth**, **uphold sth** ◊ *The disciplinary ~ upheld an earlier ruling.* | **be entitled** ◊ *The ~ was entitled to reach this conclusion.*

TRIBUNAL + NOUN **case**, **claim** ◊ *an employment ~ claim* | **hearing**, **proceedings** | **decision** | **chairman**, **member**, **panel**

PREP. **at a/the ~**, **before a/the ~**, **by ~** ◊ *The fee for the player will be decided by ~.*

tributary noun

ADJ. **main**, **major**

TRIBUTARY + VERB **drain sth**, **drain into sth**, **feed sth**, **flow into sth** ◊ *The river is fed by several small tributaries.*

TRIBUTARY + NOUN **river**, **stream**

tribute noun

1 sth you say/do to show you respect/admire sb/sth

ADJ. **anniversary**, **birthday**, **memorial** | **final** | **fine**, **fitting** | **lasting** | **affectionate**, **emotional**, **heartfelt**, **moving**, **touching**, **warm** | **generous** (*esp. BrE*), **glowing** (*esp. BrE*), **loving** (*esp. AmE*), **special** | **silent** (*esp. BrE*) ◊ *Thousands of people stood in silent ~ to the dead.* | **musical** | **floral** (*BrE*) ◊ *Floral ~s were piled up outside the church.*

VERB + TRIBUTE **pay** ◊ *The couple paid ~ to the helicopter crew who rescued them.* | **give**, **write** | **lead** (*esp. BrE*) ◊ *The President led the ~s to 'a great statesman and a decent man'.*

TRIBUTE + VERB **flood in**, **pour in** (*both esp. BrE*) ◊ *Tributes flooded in when her death was announced.*

TRIBUTE + NOUN **album**, **concert**, **show** | **act** (*esp. BrE*), **band** ◊ *He'll be on the road with a Beatles ~ band.*

2 sign of how good sb/sth is

ADJ. **great**, **remarkable**

PREP. **~ to** ◊ *The bridge is a remarkable ~ to the skill of the early engineers.*

trick noun

1 deception

ADJ. **cheap**, **cruel**, **dirty**, **mean**, **nasty** ◊ *The press accused the president of dirty ~s in his election campaign.* | **stupid** | **funny** | **little** | **con** (*informal*), **confidence** (*both BrE*)

VERB + TRICK **play**, **pull**, **try**, **use** ◊ *We decided to play a little ~ on the teacher.* | **fall for** ◊ *She won't fall for such a stupid ~.* | **know**, **learn** ◊ *He's learned a ~ or two in his time working in the tax office.*

TRICK + VERB **work**

TRICK + NOUN **question**

a ~ of the light ◊ *A ~ of the light made it look like she was pregnant.* | **a ~ or two** ◊ *I could teach him a ~ or two* (= show him a better way to do things). | **every ~ in the book** (= all methods, honest or not)

2 clever way of doing sth that works well

ADJ. **special** | **clever, good, neat** ◊ *Another neat ~ is to add lemon peel to the water.* | **handy, nifty** (*informal*), **useful** | **old** ◊ *He used the old ~ of attacking in order to defend himself.* | **real** ◊ *The real ~ is predicting the market two years down the line.*

PREP. **~ for** ◊ *a ~ for getting out red wine stains* | **~ to** ◊ *There's no ~ to it—you just need lots of practice.*

PHRASES **have a ~ up your sleeve** (= a plan to use if necessary) ◊ *I have a few ~s up my sleeve.* | **the ~ is to…** ◊ *The ~ is to keep your body still and your arms relaxed.* | **the ~s of the trade**

3 skilled act

ADJ. **clever, difficult** | **simple** | **card, conjuring, disappearing, magic** | **parlour/parlor** (*old-fashioned, esp. AmE*), **party** | **camera** | **rhetorical** ◊ *These rhetorical ~s are common in political speeches.* | **accounting** ◊ *the kinds of accounting ~s that get CEOs into trouble*

VERB + TRICK **do, employ, perform** ◊ *Very few camera ~s are employed.* | **learn** | **teach sb**

TRICK + VERB **work**

TRICK + NOUN **photography**

PHRASES **(you can't) teach an old dog new ~s** (= it is difficult to make people change their ideas, etc.)

trickle noun

ADJ. **small, thin** | **constant, steady** ◊ *a constant ~ of water* | **slow** | **mere** ◊ *The flood of offers of help had dwindled to a mere ~.*

VERB + TRICKLE **dwindle to, slow to**

PREP. **~ of** ◊ *He felt a warm ~ of blood run down his arm.*

trigger noun

VERB + TRIGGER **press, pull, squeeze** | **tighten on** ◊ *Her finger tightened on the ~ as she heard footsteps approaching.*

TRIGGER + NOUN **finger** | **guard** | **mechanism**

PHRASES **have your finger on the ~** (= to be ready to shoot)

trim verb

ADV. **carefully, neatly, perfectly** ◊ *his neatly trimmed beard* | **away, off** ◊ *Trim away the lower leaves.* | **back, down** (*figurative*) ◊ *We need to ~ the hedge back.* ◊ *The board will be trimmed down to eight members.* | **into** ◊ *We trimmed the bush into a heart shape.*

PHRASES **get your hair trimmed, have your hair trimmed**

trip noun → See also JOURNEY

ADJ. **extended, long** | **brief, little, quick, short** | **day, overnight, weekend, week-long** ◊ *We went on a day ~ to the beach.* | **four-day, two-week, etc.** | **frequent, occasional, rare, regular** ◊ *He makes frequent ~s to Poland.* | **annual, weekly, etc.** | **forthcoming** (*esp. BrE*), **upcoming** (*esp. AmE*) | **fantastic, good, great, nice, pleasant** | **safe** ◊ *Well, have a safe ~ back!* | **successful, worthwhile** ◊ *The food alone made the ~ worthwhile.* | **memorable** | **dream** ◊ *her dream ~ to New Zealand* | **uneventful** ◊ *The rest of our ~ was uneventful.* | **special** ◊ *Don't make a special ~ just to get my newspaper.* | **free** ◊ *The first prize is a free ~ to New York.* | **return, round** ◊ *From São Paulo to Rio and back is a round ~ of five hundred miles.* | **foreign, overseas** | **round-the-world, world** (*both esp. BrE*) | **European, Korean, etc.** | **away** (*BrE, sports*) ◊ *In their last two away ~s, Everton were defeated by Spurs.* | **boat, bus, coach** (*BrE*), **train, etc.** | **bicycle, bike** (*informal*), **cycle** (*BrE*) | **road** ◊ *He set off on a road ~ from Rhode Island to California.* | **business, camping, fishing, golf, hunting, pleasure, shopping, sightseeing, etc.** | **school** ◊ *a school ~ to Washington, DC* | **field** ◊ *a geography field ~ to study a limestone landscape* ◊ *a field ~ to the Science Museum* (*AmE*) | **family** | **study**

VERB + TRIP **be (away) on, do, go on, make, take** ◊ *She's away on a business ~.* ◊ *From here visitors can take a boat ~*

along the coast. | **have** ◊ *Did you have a good ~?* | **come back from, return from** | **be back from** ◊ *He's just back from a ~ to Alaska.* | **complete** ◊ *They are hoping to complete the ~ in four days.* | **arrange, organize, plan** | **book** | **cancel** | **extend** | **cut short** ◊ *I had to cut short my ~ when my wallet was stolen.* | **enjoy** ◊ *Enjoy your ~!* | **survive**

PREP. **on ~** ◊ *My wife is away on a business ~.* | **~ by** ◊ *a five-minute ~ by taxi* | **~ to** ◊ *a ~ to Tokyo*

PHRASES **a ~ abroad** (*esp. BrE*) ◊ *My last ~ abroad was two years ago.* | **the ~ home** ◊ *The ~ home took us five hours!* | **the ~ of a lifetime** ◊ *They saved for years for their ~ of a lifetime to Hawaii.*

trip verb

1 knock your foot on sth and fall

ADV. **accidentally** | **almost, nearly** | **over, up** (*BrE*) ◊ *One of the boys tripped over and crashed into a tree.* ◊ *Be careful or you'll ~ up.*

PREP. **on** ◊ *She tripped on the loose stones.* | **over** ◊ *I nearly tripped over the cat.*

PHRASES **~ and fall** ◊ *Don't leave toys on stairs where someone could ~ and fall.*

2 walk lightly

ADV. **lightly** | **out**

PREP. **along** ◊ *She went tripping along the path.* | **down** ◊ *She came tripping lightly down the stairs.* | **up**

PHRASES **come tripping**

triple verb → See also TREBLE

ADV. **more than** | **almost, nearly** | **roughly**

PREP. **in** ◊ *Some homes have almost ~d in value.* | **to** ◊ *The figure has more than ~d to 67%.*

triumph noun

ADJ. **great, major, real, remarkable** (*esp. BrE*), **resounding** | **memorable** ◊ *The team enjoyed a memorable ~ last night.* | **little, minor, small** | **eventual, final, ultimate** | **artistic, diplomatic, electoral, military, political** | **personal**

VERB + TRIUMPH **score** ◊ *The union scored a ~ in negotiating a minimum wage within the industry.* | **hail sth as, see sth as** ◊ *They hailed the signing of the agreement as a major diplomatic ~.* | **celebrate** | **represent** ◊ *This result represents a personal ~ for the party leader.*

PREP. **in ~** ◊ *The leading runner raised his arms in ~.* | **~ against** ◊ *their recent ~ against Brazil* ◊ *~ against seemingly insuperable odds* | **~ for** ◊ *The match was a personal ~ for Rivaldo.* | **~ in** ◊ *their ~ in the general election* | **~ of** ◊ *the ~ of the human spirit* | **~ over**

PHRASES **a/sb's moment of ~** ◊ *This was her moment of ~.* | **a sense of ~** | **a/sb's ~ over adversity** ◊ *Her victory was hailed as a ~ over adversity.*

triumph verb

ADV. **eventually, finally, ultimately** | **always** ◊ *He believes that good will always ~ in the end.*

PREP. **over**

PHRASES **~ over adversity** ◊ *She was confident that she would ultimately ~ over adversity.*

triumphant adj.

VERBS **appear, be, feel, look, seem, sound** | **emerge, return** ◊ *The Democrats have emerged ~ from the political crisis.* | **reign** ◊ *At that time, this brand of liberalism reigned ~.* | **stand** ◊ *In the painting, St George stands ~ over the dragon.*

ADV. **almost** | **ultimately** ◊ *Hers is a moving and ultimately ~ story.*

trivial adj.

VERBS **appear, be, look, seem, sound** | **render sth** | **consider sth, deem sth, regard sth as**

ADV. **extremely, fairly, very, etc.** | **completely, utterly** | **almost** | **comparatively** (*esp. BrE*), **relatively** | **essentially** (*esp. BrE*) ◇ *He made a few essentially ~ changes.* | **apparently, seemingly** ◇ *Apparently ~ clues may turn out to be important.*

trolley noun

1 (*BrE*) small vehicle → See also CART

ADJ. **laden, loaded** ◇ *The waiter was pushing a laden sweet ~ towards our table.* | **drinks, tea** | **dessert, sweet** | **hostess** | **baggage, luggage, shopping** | **hospital, supermarket** | **abandoned** ◇ *the problem of abandoned ~s littering the countryside*
VERB + TROLLEY **load, pile** ◇ *Passengers with ~s piled high with luggage waited at the check-in desk.* | **push, wheel**
TROLLEY + NOUN **service** ◇ *On many trains, refreshments are provided by a ~ service.* | **dash** ◇ *The club sold tickets for a ~ dash at the supermarket to raise money for charity.*
PREP. **on a/the ~** ◇ *They brought breakfast to the room on a ~.*

2 (*AmE*) vehicle driven by electricity → See also TRAM

VERB + TROLLEY **catch, ride, take** ◇ *We took the ~ over to the hotel.*
TROLLEY + NOUN **bus** (usually ***trolleybus***) (*BrE*), **car** (*old-fashioned*) | **line, system, track**

trombone noun

ADJ. **muted** | **bass, tenor** | **slide**
→ Special page at MUSIC

troops noun

ADJ. **crack** (*BrE*), **elite** | **additional, extra** | **armed** ◇ *a division of up to 6 000 heavily armed ~* | **enemy, foreign, rebel** | **friendly, loyal** ◇ *~ loyal to the government* | **army, auxiliary, paramilitary, regular, reserve** | **allied, coalition, federal** (*esp. AmE*), **government** | **international** | **combat, fighting** | **shock** (= trained to make sudden attacks on the enemy) | **reconnaissance** | **peacekeeping, security** | **airborne, ground** | **border, front-line, garrison**
VERB + TROOPS **deploy, mass, put in, send, send in** ◇ *They are massing ~ on the border.* | *The UN is sending peacekeeping ~ into the trouble spot.* | **commit, provide (sb with), supply (sb with)** ◇ *The army has provided ~ for the UN all over the world.* | **pull out, withdraw** ◇ *Washington is talking about pulling out its ~ next year.* | **bring home** ◇ *It's time to bring our ~ home.* | **command, lead, order** ◇ *He ordered ~ to shoot to kill if attacked.* | **call in** | **station** ◇ *The US had stationed over 300 000 ~ in Japan.* | **transport** | **rally** | **support** ◇ *We must always support our ~.* | **train**
TROOPS + VERB **fight (sb), kill sb** | **die** | **be based, be positioned, be posted, be quartered, be stationed** ◇ *~ based in East Timor* ◇ *Five hundred ~ were quartered in a town just behind the front line.* | **serve** ◇ *British ~ serving in the Gulf* | **advance, march, move in, move into sth** ◇ *Allied ~ were advancing on the capital.* | **arrive, cross into sth, enter sth, land, reach sth** ◇ *Iraqi ~ crossed into Kuwaiti territory.* | **cross sth** ◇ *Troops crossed the border with Georgia.* | **mass** ◇ *Government ~ have massed on the northern border.* | **guard sth, patrol sth** ◇ *~ patrolling the border* | **occupy sth** | **attack (sb), invade (sth), overrun sth, storm sth, surround sth** ◇ *Rebel ~ stormed the presidential palace.* | **fire on sb/sth, open fire, shoot sb** | **leave sth, pull out, withdraw** | **come home**
TROOP + NOUN **deployment, levels, numbers, presence, strength** ◇ *Various figures for US troop presence in Iraq were quoted.* | **build-up** | **reductions** | **withdrawal** | **movements** | **carrier, ship, train, transport** | **commander** | **morale**
PHRASES **the deployment of ~, the withdrawal of ~**

trophy noun

ADJ. **coveted, prestigious** | **major** (*esp. BrE*) | **winning** (*esp. BrE*) | **sporting** (*esp. BrE*), **sports** (*esp. AmE*) | **basketball, bowling, football, etc.** | **domestic** (*BrE*)
VERB + TROPHY **lift** (*esp. BrE*), **pick up, receive, take, win** ◇ *Britain has not lifted the ~ since it last hosted the event.* |

hold ◇ *Europe currently holds the ~.* | **award, present** | **defend** ◇ *Portugal will be defending the ~ they won last year.*
TROPHY + NOUN **cabinet** (*esp. BrE*), **case** (*esp. AmE*) | **room** | **winner** | **wife** (*informal, disapproving*)
PREP. **~ for** ◇ *He picked up a ~ for best news editor.*

trot noun a trot

ADJ. **brisk, fast** | **gentle, slow**
VERB + A TROT **break into** ◇ *When the horses reached the field they broke into a brisk ~.* | **slow to**
PREP. **at a ~** ◇ *We set off at a fast ~.* | **into a ~** ◇ *He kicked his horse into a ~.*

trot verb

ADV. **briskly, quickly** | **happily** | **obediently** ◇ *Anne trotted obediently beside her mother.* | **across, along, back, off, over** ◇ *He trotted off to greet the other guests.*
PREP. **down, up** ◇ *She trotted quickly down the stairs.*

trouble noun

1 problems

ADJ. **bad, big, deep, desperate** (*esp. BrE*), **dire, huge** (*esp. AmE*), **major, real, serious, terrible** ◇ *We're in deep ~ now!* | **endless** | **potential** | **current, recent** | **ongoing** | **domestic, family, marital** | **financial, money** ◇ *She got into serious financial ~ after running up large debts.* | **legal, political** | **back, hamstring** (*sports*), **heart, etc.** | **boyfriend, girl, man, etc.** ◇ *He was obviously upset, and muttered something about girlfriend ~.* | **car, engine** | **foul** (*AmE*) (in basketball) ◇ *Most of the game we were in foul ~.*
VERB + TROUBLE **mean, spell** ◇ *She knew that a hygiene inspection could spell ~ for her restaurant.* | **have, suffer from** ◇ *He has had back ~ since changing jobs.* | **get (yourself) into, run into** ◇ *The company soon ran into financial ~.* | **keep out of, stay out of** | **cause, lead to** ◇ *The printer's causing ~ again.* | **avoid** | **forget, leave behind, put behind you** ◇ *They are hoping to leave their recent ~s behind.* ◇ *He put his past ~s behind him and built up a successful new career.*
TROUBLE + VERB **come** ◇ *Trouble often comes when you're least expecting it.* | **begin, start** ◇ *Her ~s began last year when she lost her job.*
PREP. **in ~** ◇ *When she saw the teacher coming she knew she was in big ~.* | **~ for** ◇ *He got into ~ for not doing his homework.* | **~ with** ◇ *I've had endless ~ with my car.* ◇ *He is in ~ with the law again.*
PHRASES **a cause of ~, a source of ~** | **a history of … trouble** ◇ *She has a history of back ~.* | **have ~ doing sth** ◇ *I've had ~ sleeping recently.* | **in times of ~** ◇ *In times of ~ she always turns to her mother.* | **teething ~s** (*figurative, esp. BrE*) ◇ *After some teething ~s, the system is now up and running.* | **~ ahead** ◇ *I can see ~ ahead.*

2 arguing/violence

ADJ. **crowd** (*esp. BrE*)
VERB + TROUBLE **cause, make** ◇ *He had a reputation for making ~ in the classroom.* | **start** ◇ *Just don't start any ~.* | **be asking for, be looking for, court, stir up** ◇ *He was asking for ~ when he insulted their country.* ◇ *Fans wandered the town after the match looking for ~.* | **want** ◇ *Look, we don't want any ~, so we'll leave.*
TROUBLE + VERB **be brewing** ◇ *There was ~ brewing among the workforce.* | **begin, blow up** (*BrE*), **flare** (*BrE*), **start** ◇ *Trouble blew up when the gang was refused entry to a nightclub.* ◇ *We left before the ~ started.*
TROUBLE + NOUN **spot** ◇ *Extra journalists have been sent to the main ~ spots.*
PREP. **~ between** ◇ *~ between the races*

3 extra work

ADJ. **considerable, enormous** (*esp. BrE*), **great** ◇ *They went to enormous ~ to make her stay a pleasant one.*
VERB + TROUBLE **bring (sb), cause (sb), give sb, make, put sb to** ◇ *I don't want to make ~ for her.* ◇ *I don't want to put you to any ~.* | **go to, take** ◇ *We took the ~ to plan our route in advance.* | **be worth** ◇ *Do you think it's worth the ~ of booking seats in advance?* | **save sb** ◇ *Why don't we bring a*

pizza to save you the ~ of cooking? | **thank sb for** ◊ *Thank you very much for all your ~.*
PHRASES **be more ~ than it's worth** ◊ *Growing your own vegetables is more ~ than it's worth.*

trouble *verb*

ADV. **deeply, greatly** ◊ *This latest news ~d him deeply.*
VERB + TROUBLE **be sorry to, hate to** ◊ *I hate to ~ you, but could you move your car?*
PHRASES **be ~d with sth** ◊ *He has been ~d with a knee injury.*

troubled *adj.*

VERBS **be, feel, look**
ADV. **extremely, fairly, very, etc.** ◊ *a singer with an extremely ~ past* | **deeply, greatly, particularly** | **a little, slightly, etc.** | **vaguely** ◊ *She still felt vaguely ~ by it all.* | **increasingly** | **emotionally, financially** ◊ *financially ~ companies*
PREP. **at, by** ◊ *He was deeply ~ by the news.*

trough *noun*

1 container for animal feed/water
ADJ. **drinking, feeding, watering** (*esp. AmE*) | **feed** (*esp. AmE*), **water** | **cattle, horse, pig** | **metal, stone, wooden, etc.**
2 low point
ADJ. **deep, shallow**
VERB + TROUGH **reach** ◊ *The economy is unlikely to reach its ~ until the turn of the year.*
PHRASES **the peaks and ~s** ◊ *the peaks and ~s of economic cycles*

trousers *noun* (*esp. BrE*) → See also PANTS

ADJ. **long, short** (*BrE*) ◊ *I was still in short ~ (= still only a boy) at the time.* | **baggy, loose** | **tight** | **drainpipe** (*BrE*), **flared** | **camouflage, combat** | **pyjama/pajama, tracksuit** (*BrE*) | **corduroy, cotton, leather, linen**
... OF TROUSERS **pair**
VERB + TROUSERS **pull on, pull up** ◊ *He quickly pulled on his ~ and a T-shirt.* | **drop, pull down, unzip**
TROUSER + NOUN **bottoms, leg, pocket** ◊ *He tucked his trouser bottoms into his socks.*
PREP. **in ~** ◊ *He disapproves of women in ~.*
→ Special page at CLOTHES

trout *noun*

ADJ. **fresh** | **smoked** | **wild** | **farmed** | **lake, river** (*esp. BrE*), **sea**
VERB + TROUT **fish for** | **tickle** (*BrE*) | **catch, hook, land** (*esp. BrE*) ◊ *He hooked several ~ from the stream.*
TROUT + VERB **spawn** ◊ *The ~ spawn in late summer or autumn.*
TROUT + NOUN **fishing** | **farm, fishery** | **stream** | **population, stocks** ◊ *the collapse of sea ~ stocks*
→ Special page at FOOD

truancy *noun* (*esp. BrE*)

ADJ. **persistent**
VERB + TRUANCY **combat, tackle** ◊ *measures to combat persistent ~ in our schools* | **cut, reduce** ◊ *a government campaign to cut ~* | **condone** ◊ *parents who condone their children's ~*
TRUANCY + NOUN **level, rate** | **crackdown** | **patrol, sweep** (*both BrE*) ◊ *A ~ sweep found 168 children skipping school.*

truant *noun* (*esp. BrE*)

ADJ. **persistent** | **school**
VERB + TRUANT **play** (*BrE*) ◊ *She often played ~ and wrote her own sick notes.*
TRUANT + NOUN **officer** (*BrE, AmE*)

truce *noun*

ADJ. **brief, temporary** ◊ *A temporary ~ had been reached earlier that year.* | **permanent** | **three-day, week-long, etc.** | **fragile, uneasy**
VERB + TRUCE **call, declare, offer, propose** ◊ *The guerrillas*

have called a one-month ~. | **agree, agree on, agree to, arrange, broker, conclude, make, negotiate, reach** ◊ *The priest helped to negotiate a ~ between the warring sides.* | **sign** | **maintain** | **break, violate**
TRUCE + VERB **hold, last, prevail** | **collapse** ◊ *The two-day ~ collapsed in intense shellfire.* | **expire** ◊ *They renewed the war as soon as the ~ expired.*
PREP. **during a/the ~** | **~ among, ~ between** ◊ *An uneasy ~ prevailed between them at dinner.* | **~ with** ◊ *the fragile ~ with France*
PHRASES **a flag of ~**

truck *noun*

1 (*esp. AmE*) large heavy vehicle → See also LORRY
ADJ. **big, heavy, heavy-duty, huge, large** | **light** ◊ *sales of cars and light ~s* | **17-ton, etc.** | **diesel** | **refrigerated** | **articulated, trailer** (*AmE*) | **flatbed, open, pickup** | **full-size, semi** (*both AmE*) | **cargo** (*AmE*), **commercial, delivery, transport** | **mail** (*AmE*) | **breakdown** (*BrE*) | **cement, dump** (*AmE*), **dumper** (*BrE*) | **farm, forklift, logging, tow** (*AmE*) | **fire** (*AmE*) | **garbage** (*AmE*), **refuse** (*BrE*) | **fuel, tanker** ◊ *Behind them, the fuel ~ exploded.* | **armoured/armored, army, gun** (*AmE*), **military** | **moving** (*AmE*) ◊ *A band of moving ~s hauls all of the furniture out of the house* | **ice-cream** (*AmE*) | **monster** ◊ *a monster ~ rally* | **toy** ◊ *Zach was playing with a toy ~ on the floor.*
... OF TRUCKS **convoy, fleet**
VERB + TRUCK **drive** | **park** | **load, unload**
TRUCK + VERB **drive, roll, rumble** ◊ *A convoy of heavy ~s rumbled past.* | **carry sth, haul sth** ◊ *a ~ carrying sacks of vegetables* | **park** ◊ *She heard the ~ parking in front of the building.*
TRUCK + NOUN **driver** | **stop** (*AmE*) | **bed** (*AmE*), **cab, chassis, tyre/tire** | **convoy, fleet** | **load** (usually **truckload**) | **bomb**
2 (*BrE*) open wagon pulled by train
ADJ. **railway** | **cattle, coal, goods**
VERB + TRUCK **pull**

trudge *verb*

ADV. **slowly** ◊ *She ~d slowly back to the office.* | **wearily** ◊ *He ~d wearily on down the road.* | **dejectedly, disconsolately** (*esp. BrE*) ◊ *Following a heavy defeat, the players ~d disconsolately back to the showers.* | **along, away, back, home, off, on, onwards/onward, out** ◊ *We ~d along in silence.* ◊ *A hot sun beat down on them as they ~d onward.*
PREP. **across, along, around, down, into, through, towards/ toward, up** ◊ *We ~d slowly through the fields.*

true *adj.*

1 right or correct
VERBS **be, ring, seem, sound** ◊ *Her explanation doesn't ring quite ~.* | **come** ◊ *All her wishes came ~.* ◊ *It was like a dream come ~.* | **remain** | **hold** ◊ *This principle holds ~ for all states.* | **prove** ◊ *We hope that this will prove ~.*
ADV. **especially, particularly, very** ◊ *This is particularly ~ of older women.* | **absolutely, completely, perfectly, quite, totally** ◊ *It's perfectly ~ that I didn't help much, but I was busy.* | **certainly, clearly, demonstrably, indisputably, obviously, undeniably, unquestionably** ◊ *While this is certainly ~ for some, it is not the case for others.* | **definitely, surely, undoubtedly** ◊ *That is undoubtedly ~.* | **actually, indeed, in fact, really** ◊ *This is in fact ~ in most situations.* | **by no means, far from, not at all** ◊ *This degree of inequality was by no means ~ of all 19th-century marriages.* ◊ *'That's not ~ at all,' he said firmly.* | **hardly, not completely, not entirely, not exactly, not necessarily, not quite, not really, not strictly** ◊ *It's hardly ~ to call your job a 'profession'.* ◊ *That's not strictly ~, I'm afraid.* | **almost, basically, essentially, generally, largely, more or less, partially, partly, pretty much** ◊ *The story is more or less ~.* | **factually, objectively** | **literally** ◊ *It is literally ~ that I never heard of him until I was in my late twenties.* | **technically** ◊ *While technically ~, this is unfair.* | **doubly, equally** ◊ *What applies*

at a local level holds doubly ~ at a national level. ◇ *What is true for buyers is equally ~ for sellers.*

2 faithful

VERBS **be** | **feel** ◇ *I have never felt more ~ to myself.* | **remain, stay** ◇ *He has stayed ~ to his word.*
ADV. **absolutely**
PREP. **to** ◇ *She stayed ~ to her principles.*
PHRASES **~ to your word** ◇ *He was ~ to his word, and turned up on time.*

trumpet noun

ADJ. **muted**
VERB + TRUMPET **blow, sound**
TRUMPET + VERB **blare, sound**
TRUMPET + NOUN **blast, call, fanfare**
PHRASES **a blast of the ~** ◇ *the shrill blast of a ~* | **a fanfare of ~s, a flourish of ~s** ◇ *A wreath was laid on the monument to a fanfare of ~s.*
→ Special page at MUSIC

trunk noun

1 part of a tree

ADJ. **massive, thick** | **gnarled** | **fallen** | **hollow, hollowed-out** ◇ *an instrument made from a hollowed-out tree ~* | **tree**

2 (*AmE*) **of a car, etc.** → See also BOOT

ADJ. **car**
VERB + TRUNK **open, pop** ◇ *She popped the ~ and we tossed the stuff inside.* | **close, slam** ◇ *He slammed the ~ shut.* | **load, unload**
PREP. **in the ~** ◇ *What's in the ~?*

3 trunks for swimming

ADJ. **bathing, swim** (*AmE*), **swimming**
... OF TRUNKS **pair** ◇ *I need a new pair of ~s.*
→ Special page at CLOTHES

4 strong box with a lid

ADJ. **old** | **tin, wooden** | **steamer**
VERB + TRUNK **pack, unpack**
PREP. **in a/the ~**

trust noun

1 relying on sb/sth

ADJ. **great** ◇ *They have placed great ~ in him as a negotiator.* | **absolute, complete, perfect, total** | **blind, implicit** ◇ *They followed the instructions in blind ~ that all would turn out well.* | **little** ◇ *They had little ~ for outsiders.* | **basic** | **mutual** | **personal** (*esp. AmE*) ◇ *The President needs to rebuild his personal ~ with the electorate.* | **consumer, public, social** (*esp. AmE*) ◇ *a campaign to build consumer ~ in the quality of dairy products* ◇ *the need to restore public ~* | **sacred** ◇ *They accepted the responsibility as a sacred ~* (= sth that had been trusted to them). | **fragile** ◇ *the fragile ~ that existed between them* | **misplaced**
VERB + TRUST **have** ◇ *We have absolute ~ in the teachers.* ◇ *Does the plan have the ~ and cooperation of the workers?* | **place, put** | **establish** | **build, build up, develop** | **earn, foster, gain, win** | **engender, inspire** ◇ *This girl does not exactly inspire ~.* | **deserve** ◇ *I will do all I can do to deserve your ~.* | **abuse, betray, break, destroy, violate** (*esp. AmE*) ◇ *He claimed the government had betrayed the ~ of the people.* | **erode, undermine** ◇ *He undermined public ~ in his office.* | **lose** | **keep, maintain** ◇ *It's good that you kept her ~.* | **rebuild, regain, restore** | **be based on** ◇ *a relationship based on ~*
TRUST + VERB **exist**
PREP. **~ among, ~ between** ◇ *This requires a certain level of ~ among the community's members.* ◇ *efforts to promote mutual ~ between nations* | **~ for** ◇ *their love and ~ for one another* | **~ in** ◇ *His ~ in them was misplaced.*
PHRASES **a breach of ~, a lack of ~, a position of ~** ◇ *As a teacher, you are in a position of ~.*

2 financial arrangement/company

ADJ. **offshore** (*esp. BrE*) | **investment, unit** (*BrE*) ◇ *a publicly traded real estate investment ~* ◇ *Investing in a unit ~ reduces risks for small investors.* (*AmE*) | **family**
VERB + TRUST **hold sth in, hold sth on, keep sth in** ◇ *The proceeds will be held in ~ for the children until they are eighteen.* | **create, establish, form, set up** ◇ *They set up a ~ for their grandchildren's education.* | **invest in**
TRUST + NOUN **account, assets, fund** | **deed** | **property** | **status** | **manager** | **company** | **beneficiary**
PREP. **in ~** ◇ *His father put the money in ~ for him until he was 21.* | **~ for**

3 (*esp. BrE*) **a charity organization**

ADJ. **independent** | **charitable, non-profit, not-for-profit** | **hospital** (*BrE*) | **land** (*AmE*)
VERB + TRUST **manage, run** ◇ *They ran the ~ as a non-profit making concern.*
TRUST + VERB **own** ◇ *The ~ owns the land and the buildings.* | **manage, run** ◇ *a heritage site that is run by a charitable ~*
PREP. **~ for** ◇ *the Cecil Houses Trust for old people*

trust verb

ADV. **implicitly** ◇ *I ~ you implicitly.* | **blindly** ◇ *In my position I cannot risk blindly ~ing anyone.* | **completely, fully, really, totally, truly** ◇ *the only person I truly ~ed* | **not entirely, not fully, not necessarily, not quite, not really** ◇ *You can never entirely ~ even a 'tame' leopard.*
VERB + TRUST **be able to, can** ◇ *I knew I could ~ John.* | **be unable to** | **be prepared to, be ready to, be willing to** | **be reluctant to, be unwilling to** ◇ *I was reluctant to ~ the evidence of my senses.* | **be afraid to** ◇ *I was afraid to ~ anyone after that.*
PREP. **in** ◇ *You have to ~ in the competence of others.* | **to** ◇ *I stumbled along in the dark, ~ing to luck to find the right door.* | **with** ◇ *I'd ~ her with my life.*
PHRASES **not to be ~ed** ◇ *He is not to be ~ed with other people's money.* | **tried and ~ed** (*esp. BrE*) ◇ *tried and ~ed techniques*

trustee noun

ADJ. **joint** (*BrE*), **sole** ◇ *He acts as sole ~ of the fund.* | **independent** | **public** | **professional** | **bankruptcy** | **pension, pension-fund** | **museum** | **college, university** (*both AmE*)
VERB + TRUSTEE **act as, be, become, serve as** | **appoint, appoint sb (as)** | **remove (sb as)** | **resign as**
PREP. **~ for** ◇ *They hold the land as ~s for the infant.* | **~ of** ◇ *a ~ of the museum* | **~ to** ◇ *executor and ~ to the estate of his sister*
PHRASES **a board of ~s**

truth noun

1 what is true

ADJ. **absolute, gospel** (*informal*), **honest** (*informal*), **real** ◇ *She takes everything she reads in the paper as gospel ~.* | **complete, entire, full, whole** ◇ *It still doesn't make sense to me—I don't think he's told us the whole ~.* | **exact, literal** | **naked, plain, simple** ◇ *The simple ~ is he's lost his job.* | **pure, unvarnished** ◇ *the plain unvarnished ~* | **hidden, secret** ◇ *the hidden ~ behind the events of the last four years* | **underlying** | **awful, bitter, brutal, cruel, dreadful, grim, hard, harsh, horrible, painful, sad, shocking, terrible, ugly, uncomfortable, unfortunate, unpalatable** (*esp. BrE*), **unpleasant, unwelcome** ◇ *the shocking ~ about heroin addiction among the young* ◇ *The sad ~ is he never loved her.* | **factual, objective** | **empirical, historical, moral, poetic, psychological, religious, scientific, spiritual** ◇ *It's a good movie but contains little historical ~.* | **divine, revealed** ◇ *the revealed ~ of God*
... OF TRUTH **element, germ, glimmer, grain, kernel, nugget, ounce, shred** ◇ *There may have been a grain of ~ in what he said.*
VERB + TRUTH **know** ◇ *So now you know the ~.* ◇ *If the ~ be known, I was afraid to tell anyone.* | **admit, convey, expose, speak, tell (sb)** ◇ *He was reminded of his duty to speak the ~*

when questioned in court. ◇ I'm sure she's telling the ~. ◇ To tell you the ~, I'm rather dreading his return. | **establish, discern, discover, find out, get, get at, get to, learn, reveal, uncover** ◇ She was determined to discover the ~ about her boss. ◇ We're going to try to get the ~ out of this boy. ◇ The journalist protested that he was only trying to get at the ~. | **seek** ◇ a man on a journey seeking the ~ about God and humanity | **guess** | **accept, acknowledge, face (up to), grasp, realize** ◇ He realized the ~ in Adam's words. | **doubt** ◇ The police doubt the ~ of his statement. | **conceal, cover up, hide, suppress** ◇ You've been hiding the ~ from me! | **deny** ◇ Dare anyone deny the ~ of what we have said? | **bend, distort, stretch, twist** ◇ Lawyers distorted the ~ about the deal. | **handle** ◇ He was too fragile to handle the ~.
TRUTH + VERB　**be, lie** ◇ We are examining the matter to see where the ~ lies. | **come out, emerge** ◇ Almost at the end of the letter the cruel ~ emerged. | **dawn on sb** ◇ The awful ~ suddenly dawned on her.
PREP.　**in ~** ◇ She laughed and chatted but was, in ~, not having much fun. | **~ about** ◇ She would later find out the ~ about her husband. | **~ behind** ◇ What's the ~ behind all the gossip? | **~ in** ◇ There is no ~ in these allegations.
PHRASES　**an/the arbiter of ~** ◇ They claim to be the arbiters of sacred ~. | **be economical with the ~** (= not to tell the whole truth) (esp. BrE) | **moment of ~** ◇ Finally the moment of ~ will be upon you. | **nothing could be further from the ~** ◇ I know you think she's mean, but nothing could be further from the ~. | **the pursuit of (the) ~** ◇ They were motivated by the pursuit of the ~. | **the quest for (the) ~, the search for (the) ~** | **a ring of ~** ◇ His explanation has a ring of ~ to it. | **a seeker after ~** (literary) ◇ seekers after divine ~ | **a semblance of ~** | **the ~ of the matter** ◇ The ~ of the matter is we can't afford to keep all the staff on. | **the ~ will come out, the ~ will out** (saying)

2 fact that is true

ADJ.　**basic, central, common, essential, eternal, fundamental, general, great, immutable, important, profound, simple, timeless, ultimate, universal** ◇ in search of the eternal ~s of life | **ancient** | **obvious, self-evident, undeniable** ◇ We hold these ~s to be self-evident… | **deep** ◇ the deeper ~s that often go unspoken | **underlying** | **half, partial** ◇ His evidence was a blend of smears, half ~s and downright lies. | **harsh, home, painful, uncomfortable, unpalatable** (esp. BrE), **unpleasant, unwelcome** ◇ It's time we told him a few home ~s about sharing a house. | **necessary** | **moral, philosophical, scientific** | **biblical, divine, spiritual, theological, transcendent** ◇ Science, like theology, reveals transcendent ~s about a changing world.
VERB + TRUTH　**establish, reveal, uncover** | **tell sb** | **accept, acknowledge, face up to**
PREP.　**~ about** ◇ She was forced to face up to a few unwelcome ~s about her family.

truthful adj.

VERBS　**be** | **sound**
ADV.　**very** | **absolutely, completely** | **not entirely, not quite** ◇ I don't think you are being entirely ~.
PREP.　**about** ◇ She was completely ~ about her involvement in the affair. | **in** ◇ Gwen was ~ in her answer.

try noun

1 attempt

ADJ.　**good, nice** ◇ Never mind—it was a good ~. Better luck next time. | **another** | **first, second, etc.** ◇ She passed the test on the first ~. | **her second ~** at a Broadway musical
VERB + TRY　**have** ◇ Can I have a ~? | **give sth** ◇ It looks difficult, but let's give it a ~. | **be worth** ◇ It may not work, but it's certainly worth a ~.
PREP.　**~ at** ◇ She's having another ~ at the marathon.

2 scoring move in rugby

ADJ.　**dazzling, excellent, good, great, splendid, superb, well-taken** | **opening** | **last-minute, late** | **decisive, winning** | **penalty** | **pushover**
VERB + TRY　**get, go over for, score** | **convert**

PREP.　**~ against** ◇ He scored three tries against New Zealand. | **~ by, ~ from** ◇ an excellent ~ by winger Neil Lang
→ Special page at SPORTS

try verb

ADV.　**desperately, frantically, furiously, hard, mightily** (esp. AmE) ◇ She was ~ing desperately to stay afloat. ◇ Sam was ~ing hard not to laugh. | **gamely, valiantly** ◇ She tried valiantly to smile through her tears. | **actively** ◇ Do you actively ~ to get involved in other people's projects? | **consciously, deliberately, intentionally, purposely** ◇ I wondered if he was purposely ~ing to avoid me. | **constantly, continually, repeatedly** ◇ I'm constantly ~ing to make things better. | **clumsily** ◇ I clumsily tried to make amends. | **hurriedly** ◇ I hurriedly tried to unlock the door. | **feebly** | **at least** ◇ Can you guys at least ~ and be nice to her? | **fruitlessly, futilely** (esp. AmE), **in vain, unsuccessfully, vainly** | **allegedly** ◇ a treason charge for allegedly ~ing to overthrow the government by force
VERB + TRY　**decide to** ◇ I decided to ~ again. | **dare (sb) to** ◇ I dare you to ~ and stop her. | **bother to** ◇ She didn't even bother to ~ to check on her son. | **continue to** ◇ We have to continue to ~ to learn more about this. | **hesitate to** ◇ He wouldn't hesitate to ~ and kill them. | **be going to** ◇ I hope you're not going to ~ and deny it. | **be tempted to** ◇ be tempting to** | **let sb** ◇ Can't you do it? Let me ~.
PHRASES　**be just ~ing to do sth, be only ~ing to do sth** ◇ I was just ~ing to help! | **give up ~ing** ◇ I've given up ~ing to persuade her. | **~ your best, ~ your hardest, ~ your utmost** ◇ I tried my best not to laugh.

T-shirt (also tee shirt) noun

ADJ.　**baggy, loose, oversized** | **fitted, tight** | **long-sleeved, short-sleeved, sleeveless** | **crew-neck, V-neck** | **faded, old, ratty** (AmE, informal) ◇ He was wearing a faded pair of blue jeans and a ratty old ~. | **plain** | **tie-dye, tie-dyed** | **cotton**
→ Special page at CLOTHES

tub noun (esp. AmE) large container for washing your body

ADJ.　**bath** (usually **bathtub**) | **wash** (usually **washtub**) | **hot** | **claw-foot** | **Jacuzzi™, whirlpool**
VERB + TUB　**lie in, soak in** ◇ I love soaking in a hot ~. | **climb in, climb into, get into** | **climb out of, get out of** | **fill** | **drain, empty**

tube noun

1 long hollow pipe

ADJ.　**fine, narrow, thin** | **hollow** | **flexible** | **closed, sealed** | **inner** (= on a bicycle wheel) | **fluorescent** (= a kind of light) | **cardboard, copper, glass, metal, plastic, rubber, steel, etc.** | **cathode ray, vacuum** | **test** | **breathing, feeding, ventilation** | **bronchial, capillary, Eustachian, Fallopian, neural, etc.** | **pollen** | **torpedo**
PREP.　**down a/the ~** ◇ She poured the liquid down the ~. | **in a/the ~, into a/the ~** ◇ I put the poster back into its ~. | **through a/the ~** ◇ He gave the lamb its food through a ~. | **up a ~**

2 (usually the tube) (BrE) the London Underground

ADJ.　**London**
VERB + TUBE　**catch, go on, take, travel by, travel on** ◇ I often travel by ~ ◇ I often travel on the ~
TUBE + NOUN　**line, network, station** | **carriage, train** ◇ I had to cram myself into a packed ~ carriage. | **map, ticket** | **driver, worker** | **journey** ◇ my ~ journey to work
PREP.　**by ~** ◇ I go to work by ~. | **on the ~** ◇ I bumped into him on the ~.

tuck verb

ADV.　**carefully, discreetly, neatly** | **gently** | **firmly** | **tightly** ◇ knees ~ed tightly against her chest | **cosily/cozily, safely, snugly** ◇ The children were safely ~ed up in bed. | **securely** ◇

He had securely ~ed his phone away in his pocket. | **away, in, up** ◇ *The boys ~ed their shirts in.*
PREP. **behind** ◇ *The pool was ~ed away behind a screen of trees.* | **beneath** ◇ *the pillow that was gently ~ed beneath her head* | **between** ◇ *a puppy with its tail ~ed between its legs* | **inside** ◇ *He ~ed the map inside his shirt.* | **into** ◇ *He ~ed his jeans neatly into his boots.* | **under, underneath** ◇ *She ~ed the newspaper under her arm.*

Tuesday *noun* → Note at DAY

tug *noun*
ADJ. **good, hard, sharp** ◇ *All it needed was a good ~.* | **firm** | **gentle, little, slight, small** | **quick, sudden**
VERB + TUG **give (sth)** | **feel**
PREP. **with a ~** ◇ *She started the engine with one ~ of the starter rope.* | **~ at** ◇ *She felt a sharp ~ at her sleeve.* | **~ on** ◇ *She gave a little ~ on the rope.*

tug *verb*
ADV. **gently, lightly** ◇ *He tugged lightly at my wrist.* | **hard** ◇ *He tugged harder, but it was caught fast.* | **nervously** ◇ *She nervously tugged at her long brown hair.* | **playfully** ◇ *She playfully tugged at his shirt.*
PREP. **at** ◇ *She tugged at his arm to get his attention.* | **by** ◇ *He tugged me by the sleeve.* | **on** ◇ *Alexis was up in a flash, tugging on his arm.*

tuition *noun*
1 (*esp. BrE*) teaching
ADJ. **private** | **individual, one-to-one, personal** | **daily** | **extra** | **free** ◇ *The foreign students receive free ~ and accommodation.* | **advanced** | **expert** ◇ *The students get expert ~ in small groups.* | **language, music, etc.**
VERB + TUITION **give (sb), offer (sb), provide (sb with)** | **get, have, receive**
TUITION + NOUN **fees** ◇ *the controversy over university ~ fees*
PREP. **under sb's ~** ◇ *She had become expert in Chinese cooking under the ~ of her aunt.* | **~ for** ◇ *~ for beginners* ◇ *extra ~ for the exams* | **~ from** ◇ *He is receiving ~ from a well-known artist.* | **~ in** ◇ *~ in Italian*
2 (*AmE*) money paid for teaching at college, etc.
ADJ. **college, university** ◇ *How can we make college ~ affordable for everyone?* | **in-state, out-of-state** | **full** ◇ *They pay full ~.*
VERB + TUITION **afford, cover, pay, raise** ◇ *He won't be able to finish his education unless someone pays his ~.* | **charge** | **increase**
TUITION + NOUN **rate** (*AmE*) | **hike, increase** (*both AmE*) | **assistance** (*AmE*) ◇ *The program includes about $5 000 in ~ assistance.*

tummy *noun* (*informal*)
1 part of the body where food is digested
ADJ. **empty, full** | **upset**
TUMMY + VERB **rumble** | **ache**
TUMMY + NOUN **ache, bug, trouble, upset** (*all BrE*) ◇ *I had a slight ~ upset.* | **button** (*BrE*)
PREP. **in the/your ~** ◇ *I get a fluttery feeling in my ~ before meeting new people.*
2 front part of the body below the chest
ADJ. **bulging, fat, flat**
VERB + TUMMY **pull in** | **pat, rub, tickle**
TUMMY + NOUN **muscles** | **tuck** ◇ *cosmetic surgery like facelifts and ~ tucks*
PREP. **on the/your ~**

tumour (*BrE*) (*AmE* tumor) *noun*
ADJ. **cancerous, malignant** | **benign** | **primary** | **inoperable** | **brain, breast, kidney, etc.**

VERB + TUMOUR/TUMOR **diagnose** | **remove** | **shrink** | **treat** | **develop** ◇ *He developed a brain ~.*
TUMOUR/TUMOR + NOUN **cell, tissue** | **formation, growth**
PREP. **~ in** ◇ *a primary ~ in the breast* | **~ of** ◇ *tumors of the central nervous system* | **~ on** ◇ *a malignant ~ on the eyelid*

tune *noun*
ADJ. **little** ◇ *He hummed a little ~ as he washed the dishes.* | **good, great, nice** | **happy, jaunty, lively, merry, upbeat, uplifting** | **haunting, melancholy, sad** | **classic, familiar, favourite/favorite, old, popular, traditional, well-known** ◇ *a collection of classic ~s* | **catchy** (*informal*), **memorable** | **dance, show** | **folk, jazz, pop, etc.** ◇ *an old jazz ~* | **hymn** | **signature** (*BrE*), **theme** (*esp. BrE*)
VERB + TUNE **hum, play (sb), sing, whistle** ◇ *He softly hummed the ~ to himself.* ◇ *She played us a ~ on the piano.* | **spin** (*informal*) ◇ *DJs spinning the coolest ~s* | **hum along with, sing along with** | **compose, write** | **pick out** ◇ *The kids were picking out a ~ on the old piano.* | **carry, hold** ◇ *He wasn't allowed in the choir because he couldn't hold a ~.*
PHRASES **to the ~ of sth** ◇ *The crowd were singing 'Give us jobs!' to the ~ of 'Happy Birthday'.*

tune *verb*
1 adjust an engine, a machine, etc.
ADV. **perfectly, precisely** | **carefully, properly**
PREP. **to**
PHRASES **finely ~d, highly ~d** ◇ *a finely ~d engine*
2 adjust a TV, radio, etc.
ADV. **permanently** ◇ *His radio was permanently ~d to Radio KVB.* | **automatically** ◇ *Most phones will automatically ~ to the strongest network signal.* | **regularly** ◇ *Ten million people regularly ~ in to see his show.* | **in** ◇ *Don't forget to ~ in to our special news coverage this evening.*
PREP. **for, into** ◇ *200 000 people ~ into the station each week.* | **to** ◇ *I ~d to the BBC for the late news.*
PHRASES **badly ~d** ◇ *He heard everything through a screen of interference, like on a badly ~d radio.* | **stay ~d** ◇ *Stay ~d for the news.*

tunnel *noun*
ADJ. **long, short** | **narrow, wide** | **dark** | **winding** ◇ *the end of the long, winding ~* | **subterranean, underground** | **connecting, entrance, escape, service** | **hidden, secret** ◇ *a vast network of secret underground ~s* | **rail, railroad** (*AmE*), **railway** (*BrE*), **road, subway** (*AmE*), **tube** (*BrE*) | **sewer** | **wind** ◇ *a wind ~ for aerodynamic experiments*
VERB + TUNNEL **go through, use** | **disappear into, enter, go into** ◇ *The train disappeared into a ~.* | **come out of, leave** | **bore, build, construct, dig, drill, excavate, make** ◇ *They've built a new ~ through the mountain.* ◇ *The initial section of ~ had to be dug by hand.*
TUNNEL + VERB **run** ◇ *A service ~ runs between the two buildings.* | **lead** ◇ *a ~ leading into the hill* | **connect** ◇ *Adriana hid in the ~ connecting the house with the stables.* | **open out, open up** ◇ *The ~ opened out into a large cavern.*
TUNNEL + NOUN **entrance, floor, mouth, roof, wall** | **system** ◇ *the ~ system below the building*
PREP. **through a/the ~**
PHRASES **a labyrinth of ~s, a maze of ~s, a network of ~s, a series of ~s, a system of ~s** ◇ *We got lost in the maze of ~s.*

turf *noun*
1 grass/lawn
ADJ. **green** | **soft, springy** (*esp. BrE*) | **artificial** | **home** ◇ *the team's first success of the season on home ~* (= in their own stadium) | **hallowed** (*BrE*) ◇ *the hallowed ~ of Wembley*
...OF TURF **piece, sod** ◇ *primitive dwellings made of sods of ~ and sticks*
VERB + TURF **cut** ◇ *They still cut ~ here for fuel.* | **lay** ◇ *We laid ~ to create a lawn.*
TURF + NOUN **field** (*AmE*) ◇ *The training area includes a synthetic ~ field,*

2 (*esp. AmE*) place where sb lives, works, etc.; area of expertise

ADJ. **home** ◊ *We finally met on his home ~.* ◊ *The orchestra is on home ~ in this repertoire.* (*figurative*) | **familiar** ◊ *Supercomputers are familiar ~ for IBM.*
VERB + TURF **defend**, **protect** ◊ *We all protect our own ~.* | **invade** (*AmE*) ◊ *I don't want to invade his ~.*
TURF + NOUN **battle**, **war** ◊ *~ wars between different factions*
PHRASES **(on) sb's own ~**

turkey noun

ADJ. **lean** | **Christmas**, **Thanksgiving** | **traditional** ◊ *the traditional ~ with all the trimmings* | **frozen** | **roast**, **smoked** | **stuffed** | **ground** (*AmE*), **minced** (*BrE*) | **leftover** | **free-range**, **wild** (*esp. AmE*)
VERB + TURKEY **breed** | **raise** ◊ *We raise ~s mainly for the Christmas market.* | **serve** | **stuff** | **cook**, **roast** | **baste** | **carve**, **slice**
TURKEY + VERB **gobble**
TURKEY + NOUN **farm** | **breast**, **leg** | **bacon** (*AmE*), **burger**, **meat**, **sausage** (*esp. AmE*) | **sandwich** | **dinner** | **baster**, **fryer** (*AmE*)
→ Special page at FOOD

turmoil noun

ADJ. **constant** ◊ *Her mind was in a state of constant ~.* | **great** | **emotional**, **inner**, **internal**, **mental**, **personal** | **economic**, **financial**, **political**, **social** | **domestic**, **global**, **international** | **current**, **recent**
VERB + TURMOIL **cause**, **create** | **plunge sb/sth into**, **send sb/sth into**, **throw sb/sth into** ◊ *Her emotional life was thrown into ~.* | **experience**
PREP. **in ~** ◊ *He came to a stop, his thoughts in ~.* | **~ of** ◊ *a ~ of emotions* | **~ over** ◊ *The university had been in ~ over anti-war protests.*
PHRASES **a state of ~**

turn noun

1 act of turning sb/sth around

ADJ. **complete**, **full**, **half**, **quarter** ◊ *It slowly spun for three complete ~s.* ◊ *a full ~ of the handle to the right* | **90-degree**, **180-degree**, etc. | **quick** ◊ *a quick ~ of his head* | **slight** ◊ *He quickly gives the handle a slight ~.*
VERB + TURN **give sth** ◊ *Give the knob a ~.*

2 change of direction

ADJ. **left**, **left-hand**, **right**, **right-hand** | **abrupt**, **sharp**, **tight** ◊ *Tinker makes the tight ~s look easy.* | **wide** | **sudden** | **three-point** (see also *U-turn*) | **handbrake** (*BrE*) | **flip** (*AmE*) (in swimming) ◊ *Every time she did a flip ~, she made a large splash.*
VERB + TURN **do**, **make**, **negotiate** ◊ *She stopped talking as she negotiated a particularly sharp ~.* | **execute** ◊ *Syd executed each ~ perfectly.*
PHRASES **at every ~** (*figurative*) ◊ *At every ~ I met with disappointment.* | **a ~ to the left**, **a ~ to the right** ◊ *He made a sudden ~ to the right.* | **twists and ~s** (*figurative*) ◊ *It's impossible to follow all the twists and ~s of the plot.*

3 (*esp. AmE*) bend/corner in a road → See also TURNING

ADJ. **next** | **wrong** | **hairpin** (*AmE*), **tight** ◊ *The car skidded around a hairpin ~.* ◊ *There was a screech as the car rounded a tight ~.*
VERB + TURN **make**, **take** ◊ *He took a wrong ~ and ended up on the coast road.* | **miss** | **approach**, **enter**, **round** ◊ *Slow down as you enter the ~.*
PHRASES **a ~ on the left**, **a ~ on the right** ◊ *Take the next ~ on the right.* | **twists and ~s** ◊ *a road full of twists and ~s*

4 time when you must or may do sth

VERB + TURN **have**, **take** ◊ *Can I have a ~?* ◊ *I'll take a ~ making the dinner—you have a rest.* ◊ *The children took ~s on the swing.* | **miss** ◊ *If you can't put any cards down you have to miss a ~.* | **give sb** ◊ *Give Sarah a ~ on the swing.* | **await**, **wait** ◊ *Be patient and wait your ~!* | **come to** ◊ *By the time it came to my ~ to sing, I was very nervous.*

TURN + VERB **come** ◊ *When my ~ finally came, I was shaking with nerves.*
PREP. **in ~** (= one after the other) ◊ *They gave their names in ~.* | **in sb's ~** (*esp. BrE*) ◊ *She had not been friendly to Pete and he, in his ~, was cold to her when she came to stay.* | **out of ~** (= before or after your turn) ◊ *Batista had batted out of ~.*

5 change

ADJ. **abrupt**, **sudden** ◊ *He seems to have taken an abrupt career ~ with his new movie.* | **dramatic**, **remarkable** | **decisive**, **drastic**, **radical** ◊ *Schuler's life took a radical ~ when he became obsessed with horses.* | **different**, **new** | **interesting** ◊ *The video market took an interesting ~ in the mid 1980s.* | **bizarre**, **ironic**, **odd**, **shocking**, **strange**, **surprising**, **unexpected** ◊ *The trial has taken an even more bizarre ~ today.* ◊ *Events took a surprising ~.* | **ugly**, **unfortunate** ◊ *The battle took an unfortunate ~.* | **downward**
VERB + TURN **take** ◊ *Her career took an unexpected ~ when she moved to Vancouver.* | **mark**, **signal** ◊ *It marks a major ~ in this presidency.*
PREP. **by ~**, **by ~s** ◊ *This movie is by ~ (= alternately) terrifying and very funny.* | **on the ~** (= changing) ◊ *Our luck is on the ~.*
PHRASES **take a ~ for the better**, **take a ~ for the worse** ◊ *I'm afraid Grandma has taken a ~ for the worse.* | **a ~ of events** ◊ *In a dramatic ~ of events she took the company into her own hands.*

turning noun (*BrE*) → See also TURN

ADJ. **next** | **wrong**
VERB + TURNING **take** ◊ *She took a wrong ~ and ended up lost.* | **miss**

turning point noun

ADJ. **big**, **dramatic**, **great**, **major** ◊ *It marks a great ~ in your lives.* | **critical**, **crucial**, **decisive**, **historic**, **important**, **key**, **real**, **significant**, **true** ◊ *This win could prove to be a historic ~ (= one that will be remembered) in the fortunes of the team.* | **possible**, **potential** | **historical**, **political** ◊ *The industrial revolution was a major historical ~.*
VERB + TURNING POINT **be**, **become**, **constitute**, **prove (to be)** | **provide**, **serve as** | **indicate**, **mark**, **represent**, **signal** ◊ *The election represented a major ~ in American history.* | **consider sth (to be)**, **see sth as** | **reach** ◊ *In 2001 the world reached a ~ in its history.*
TURNING POINT + VERB **come** ◊ *The ~ came when reinforcements arrived from the south.*
PREP. **at a ~** ◊ *The process of disarmament is at a crucial ~.* | **~ in**

turn-off noun

1 road that leads away from another

ADJ. **next**
VERB + TURN-OFF **take** ◊ *Take the next ~.* | **miss**, **overshoot** ◊ *We were chatting and overshot our ~.*
PREP. **~ for** ◊ *the ~ for Freiburg*

2 (*informal*) sb/sth that is not attractive or exciting

ADJ. **big**, **major** ◊ *These public arguments are a big ~ for voters.*
VERB + TURN-OFF **be**, **prove** | **become**
PREP. **~ for** ◊ *The wet conditions proved a ~ for some spectators.* | **~ to** ◊ *The advertisement was a real ~ to customers.*

turnout noun

1 number of people who vote in an election

ADJ. **good**, **heavy** (*esp. AmE*), **high**, **huge**, **massive**, **strong** | **record** ◊ *a record ~ for an election* | **low**, **poor** | **40%**, **70%**, etc. | **electoral**, **voter** ◊ *Voter ~ was high at the last election.*
VERB + TURNOUT **depress**, **suppress** (*both AmE*) ◊ *That could depress ~ in a few states.* | **boost**, **increase**

PHRASES **a decline in ~, a fall in ~, an increase in ~**

2 number of people who go to a meeting, event, etc.

ADJ. **big, fantastic, good, great, impressive, large | disappointing, poor**
VERB + TURNOUT **attract** (esp. BrE) ◇ The concert attracted a large ~. | **get, have** ◇ I think we will have the biggest ~ we've had for quite some time.

turnover noun

1 (esp. BrE) amount of business a company does

ADJ. **high, low | company, group** (both BrE) | **combined, total** ◇ The combined ~ of both businesses has doubled in the last two years. | **gross, net | annual, daily, etc. | global, worldwide**
VERB + TURNOVER **boast, have** ◇ The company boasts an annual ~ of £240 m. | **record** ◇ The company recorded a ~ of €70 million last year. | **boost, increase**
TURNOVER + VERB **be up | be down** ◇ Turnover was down compared with last year's figures. | **double, grow, increase, rise** ◇ The company's ~ increased 30% to $10 million. | **drop, fall** ◇ Turnover fell from £12 million to £11 million. | **reach sth** ◇ Turnover reached $2 billion in the 12 months to September. | **exceed sth, top sth** ◇ The company's worldwide ~ exceeds $5 billion.
TURNOVER + NOUN **figure, growth, rate**
PHRASES **a decline in ~, an fall in ~ | an increase in ~, a rise in ~**
→ Special page at BUSINESS

2 rate at which people come and go from a job/place

ADJ. **fast, rapid | high, large | low | employee** (esp. AmE), **job** (esp. AmE), **labour/labor, management, personnel, staff** ◇ The new offices have reduced the very high rates of staff ~. | **population** ◇ The city has a rapid population ~.
VERB + TURNOVER **have | reduce**
TURNOVER + NOUN **rate**
PREP. **~ in** ◇ We've had very little ~ in our sales personnel.

tussle noun

ADJ. **brief, little | legal**
VERB + TUSSLE **have** ◇ Anna and her conscience had a little ~. | **be engaged in, be involved in**
PREP. **in a/the ~** ◇ They found themselves in a legal ~ with a big corporation. ◇ He broke his leg in a ~ for the ball. (in football/soccer) | **~ between** ◇ a ~ between the two countries | **~ for** ◇ There is a ~ for power before the Congress convenes. | **~ over** ◇ a ~ over the closure of the local hospital | **~ with** ◇ We are engaged in a legal ~ with a large pharmaceutical company.

tutor noun

ADJ. **good | full-time, part-time | personal, private | peer** (AmE) ◇ advanced students who act as peer ~s | **online | assistant, senior** (both BrE) | **college, university** (both BrE) | **course** (BrE) | **art, English, etc.**
VERB + TUTOR **act as | become** ◇ He became ~ to the prince. | **employ, engage** (BrE), **hire** (esp. AmE) ◇ His father hired a private ~ for him.
PREP. **~ for** ◇ She works part time as a ~ for Spanish. | **~ in** ◇ a ~ in mathematics | **~ to** ◇ He became a ~ to some of the sport's top players.
→ Note at JOB

tutorial noun

1 (esp. BrE) lesson at a university, college, etc.

ADJ. **group, individual**
VERB + TUTORIAL **have** ◇ I have two ~s today. | **prepare for | go to | miss | give (sb)** ◇ He gives one lecture and two ~s a week.
TUTORIAL + NOUN **class, group**
PREP. **at a/the ~, during a/the ~, in a/the ~ | ~ on** ◇ a ~ on the rise of the novel

2 book or computer program

ADJ. **excellent, good | detailed, step-by-step | interactive, online, video, Web-based** ◇ The website provides a nice online ~.
VERB + TUTORIAL **include, offer, provide** ◇ Some sites offer step-by-step ~s. | **go through** ◇ I spent an hour or two going through the ~.
TUTORIAL + VERB **walk sb through sth** (esp. AmE) ◇ A short ~ walks you through the software.
PREP. **~ on**

tuxedo noun (esp. AmE)

ADJ. **formal, traditional | double-breasted | rented**
VERB + TUXEDO **rent**
TUXEDO + NOUN **jacket, pants** (AmE), **shirt**
→ Special page at CLOTHES

twang noun

ADJ. **slight | nasal | American, Cockney, Southern, etc.** ◇ She had a slight Southern ~ to her voice.
VERB + TWANG **have, speak with** ◇ She had a slight Australian ~. | **hear**
PREP. **with a ~** ◇ The words came out with an Irish ~ to them.

twig noun

ADJ. **dry | bare | dead | broken** ◇ She ran, treading on broken ~s and stumbling over roots. | **birch, willow, etc.**
VERB + TWIG **break, break off, snap, snap off** ◇ She broke a ~ from a nearby tree and began poking it into the soft ground.
TWIG + VERB **break, snap** ◇ A ~ snapped under her feet.

twilight noun

ADJ. **gathering**
TWILIGHT + NOUN **sky** ◇ They gazed up at the ~ sky. | **hour** (often figurative) ◇ in the ~ hour before dawn ◇ He had the courage to spend his ~ hours acknowledging his misdeeds. | **world** (figurative) ◇ the ~ world of the occult | **zone** (figurative) ◇ the ~ zone between living and merely existing | **years** (figurative) ◇ a forgotten man who spent his ~ years alone
PREP. **at ~, in the ~, into the ~** ◇ She stared into the gathering ~.
PHRASES **in the ~ of your career, life, etc.**

twin noun

ADJ. **identical, monozygotic** (technical) | **dizygotic** (technical), **fraternal, non-identical | conjoined, Siamese | long-lost** ◇ His long-lost ~ was searching for him. | **older, younger** ◇ I was the older ~. | **female, male | evil** ◇ the plot device of giving a character an evil ~
...OF TWINS **pair, set** ◇ a pair of identical ~s
VERB + TWIN **be carrying, be pregnant with, expect | give birth to, have** ◇ My sister had ~s. ◇ He had a ~ (= a twin brother or sister). | **raise** ◇ adult ~s who were raised apart | **separate** ◇ The ~s were separated at birth. ◇ an operation to separate conjoined ~s
TWIN + NOUN **boys, girls** ◇ She had ~ girls. | **daughters, sons | brother, sister**

twinge noun

ADJ. **sharp | little, slight** ◇ I felt a slight ~ of disappointment. | **sudden | occasional** ◇ I still get the occasional ~ of pain.
VERB + TWINGE **experience, feel, get, have, suffer** ◇ She still has ~s of resentment about it. | **give sb** ◇ The letter still gives him a ~ when he thinks of it.
PREP. **~ of** ◇ a ~ of guilt

twinkle noun

ADJ. **amused, mischievous, wicked | slight**
VERB + TWINKLE **notice, see, spot** ◇ I could see the ~ in his eyes.
PREP. **~ of** ◇ There was a slight ~ of mischief in her eyes.
PHRASES **a ~ in sb's eye**

twist noun

1 act of twisting sth

ADJ. **little, slight** | **quick, sharp** | **wry** ◇ *'You're brave' she said, with a wry ~ of the mouth.*
VERB + TWIST **give sth** ◇ *Give the lid another ~.*
PREP. **~ of** ◇ *He finished him off with a quick ~ of the knife.* | **~ to** ◇ *a wry ~ to her lips*

2 change/development

ADJ. **final, latest** ◇ *the latest ~ in the saga of high-level corruption* | **added, extra, further** | **fresh, modern, new** ◇ *The movie gives this old legend a real modern ~.* | **clever, interesting, intriguing, neat, nice** | **bizarre, curious, dramatic, ironic, odd, strange, surprise, surprising, unexpected, unique, unusual, weird** | **cruel, shocking, vicious** ◇ *a cruel ~ of fate* | **little, slight** ◇ *That adds a slight ~ to this battle* | **plot**
VERB + TWIST **give sth** ◇ *The writer takes well-known fairy tales and gives them an ironic ~.* | **have, offer** ◇ *The movie has some unexpected ~s.* | **add** ◇ *I added my own ~ to the whole thing.* | **take** ◇ *The scandal has taken a new ~ this week.*
TWIST + NOUN **ending** (esp. AmE) ◇ *horror movies with ~ endings*
PREP. **in a ~, with a ~** ◇ *classic French dishes with a ~* (= with a difference) | **~ in** ◇ *a ~ in the plot* | **~ on** ◇ *I thought it would be an interesting ~ on the zombie movie.* | **~ to** ◇ *In a bizarre ~ to the evening the police came at eleven and arrested our host.*
PHRASES **a ~ in the tale** ◇ *I find this latest ~ in the tale most intriguing.* | **a ~ of fate** | **~s and turns** ◇ *the ~s and turns in the economy*

3 in a road, river, etc.

ADJ. **sharp**
PREP. **~ in** ◇ *a sharp ~ in the road*
PHRASES **~s and turns** ◇ *the ~s and turns of the river*

twist verb

ADV. **slightly** ◇ *She ~ed slightly in her chair to look up at him.* | **gently** ◇ *Gently ~ off the green stalks.* | **quickly, slowly** ◇ *She placed her hand on the doorknob and ~ed slowly.* | **violently** ◇ *She fired again and saw the creature ~ violently.* | **badly** (esp. BrE), **painfully** ◇ *She badly ~ed her ankle on the high jump.* | **bitterly** ◇ *His mouth ~ed bitterly.* | **nervously** ◇ *Amanda nervously ~ed her hair.* | **away, off, together, up** ◇ *Her black hair was ~ed up into a knot on top of her head.* | **sideways** ◇ *He ~ed sideways to face her.*
PREP. **around, round** (esp. BrE) ◇ *I ~ed the bandage around his leg.* | **into** ◇ *My stomach ~ed into knots.* ◇ *Nicola's face ~ed into a grimace of disgust.* | **with** ◇ *His face was ~ed with rage.*
PHRASES **~ and turn** ◇ *The road ~s and turns along the coast.* | **~ (yourself) free** ◇ *He managed to ~ himself free.* | **~ sth out of shape** ◇ *Her mouth was ~ed out of shape by grief.*

twitch noun

ADJ. **nervous** | **little, slight** ◇ *His mouth gave a slight ~.* | **involuntary** | **muscle**
VERB + TWITCH **have** ◇ *He has a ~ in his right eye.* | **develop** | **give**

twitch verb

ADV. **convulsively, violently** ◇ *The body ~ed violently and then lay still.* | **involuntarily, uncontrollably** | **a little, slightly** | **nervously** ◇ *Her fingers ~ed nervously.*
PREP. **in, with** ◇ *The corner of his mouth ~ed in amusement.* ◇ *His shoulders ~ed with suppressed laughter.*

tycoon noun

ADJ. **business, media, newspaper, oil, property** (BrE), **publishing, real estate** (AmE), **shipping**

type noun

1 kind/sort

ADJ. **distinct, distinctive, specific, well-defined** | **certain, particular** ◇ *certain ~s of cancer* | **diverse** | **broad** ◇ *Two*

broad ~s of approach can be identified. | **main, major, predominant, principal** | **basic, common, conventional, standard, traditional** | **extreme** | **alternative** | **novel** ◇ *a novel ~ of sculpture* | **favourite/favorite, popular** | **ideal** ◇ *the ideal ~ of helmet for caving* | **body, personality, physical** | **blood, cell, hair, skin, tissue, etc.** | **product** | **habitat, rock, soil, vegetation**
VERB + TYPE **distinguish, identify, recognize** | **represent** | **classify, define, determine** | **choose, select, specify** | **revert to** ◇ *The boss came back to work all relaxed, but now he's reverting to ~.*
PREP. **in ~** ◇ *The recession is similar in ~ to that of ten years ago.* | **of a ~** ◇ *a motel of a ~ that has all but vanished* | **~ of** ◇ *There are various ~s of daffodil(s).*
PHRASES **of its ~** ◇ *This exercise is the hardest of its ~.* | **a range of ~s, a variety of ~s**

2 person

ADJ. **adventurous, athletic, sporty** | **quiet, shy, silent** ◇ *He must be the strong silent ~.* | **jealous, marrying, old-fashioned** ◇ *I am definitely not the marrying ~.* ◇ *He was the old-fashioned ~, well-mannered and always in a suit and tie.* | **artistic, creative, literary, media** ◇ *West Coast media ~s* | **City** (= a person who works in finance in the City of London) (BrE), **corporate, Wall Street** (esp. AmE) ◇ *The bar was crowded with corporate ~s in suits.*
PHRASES **true to ~** (esp. BrE) ◇ *True to ~, Adam turned up an hour late.* | **(not) your ~** ◇ *She's not really my type–she's a little too serious.*

3 printed letters

ADJ. **bold, boldface** | **italic** | **roman**
VERB + TYPE **print sth in, set sth in** ◇ *Key paragraphs of the report are set in italic ~.* | **use**
PREP. **in…~** ◇ *The important words are in bold ~.*

type verb

ADV. **correctly** | **neatly** | **quickly, rapidly** | **furiously** ◇ *He was sitting at his desk typing furiously.* | **out, up** ◇ *I've written the report and will ~ it up next week.* | **in** ◇ *She ~d her password in.* | **away** ◇ *Sam ~d away for a few minutes.* | **back** (esp. AmE) ◇ *She quickly ~d back a response.*
PREP. **into** ◇ *She ~d the details into the computer.* | **on** ◇ *This letter was ~d on an electronic typewriter.*

typhoon noun

TYPHOON + VERB **hit sth, strike sth** ◇ *The town was hit by a ~.* | **damage sth, destroy sth, devastate sth** ◇ *The plantation was devastated by a ~.*
PREP. **in a/the ~** ◇ *His home was destroyed in a ~.*

typical adj.

VERBS **be, look, seem, sound** | **become** | **consider sth, regard sth as, take sth as** ◇ *You must not take this attitude as ~ of English people.*
ADV. **extremely, fairly, very, etc.** | **highly** | **absolutely, altogether, entirely, just** ◇ *That's altogether ~ of Tom!* ◇ *They're going to be late? Now, isn't that just ~?* | **by no means, not necessarily** ◇ *Cape Town is by no means ~ of South Africa.*
PREP. **of** ◇ *Julia is fairly ~ of her age group.*

typing noun

ADJ. **touch** (usually **touch-typing**)
VERB + TYPING **do** ◇ *Could you do some ~ for me?*
TYPING + NOUN **error** | **skills** | **speed** | **pool**

typist noun

ADJ. **fast, good** | **copy, shorthand** (both BrE) | **touch** (usually **touch-typist**)
→ Note at JOB

tyranny noun

ADJ. **petty** | **brutal** | **judicial** (esp. AmE), **political, religious**

VERB + TYRANNY be free of, be freed from, escape, escape from, overthrow | impose (*often figurative*) ◊ *An artist's need for money imposes the ~ of popular taste.* | fight, oppose, resist | defeat, end
PREP. ~ over ◊ *her ~ over her staff*

tyrant noun

ADJ. brutal, cruel, evil, murderous, ruthless, vicious | great | petty ◊ *Some of the prison officers were petty ~s.*
VERB + TYRANT become | overthrow
TYRANT + VERB rule sth ◊ *The country was ruled by ~s.*
PREP. under a/the ~

tyre (*BrE*) (*AmE* tire) noun

ADJ. flat, punctured (*esp. BrE*) ◊ *I got a flat ~ soon after setting off.* | blown (*AmE*), burst (*BrE*) | bald, worn | defective | old, scrap (*esp. AmE*), used | recycled | spare | front | back, rear | nearside, offside (*both BrE*) ◊ *The front nearside ~ was unroadworthy.* | fat ◊ *trucks with fat ~s and reinforced springs* | balloon, pneumatic, radial, snow, whitewall ◊ *an off-road vehicle fitted with balloon ~s* ◊ *Her truck had snow ~s.* | off-road, road | bicycle, car, etc.
... OF TYRES/TIRES set
VERB + TYRE/TIRE change, replace | inflate, pump (*AmE*), pump up | deflate, let down (*BrE*) ◊ *Someone let the ~s down overnight as a joke.* | fit, fit sth with ◊ *This car is fitted with radial ~s.* | blow (*esp. AmE*), burst (*esp. BrE*) ◊ *He was going so fast he blew a ~.* | fix ◊ *He fixed a flat ~ on his bike.* | check ◊ *She checked the ~s and oil before setting off.* | slash ◊ *Vandals had slashed the ~s and broken the side mirror.*
TYRE/TIRE + VERB be deflated, be punctured, deflate, go flat | get a puncture, have a puncture, suffer a puncture (*all esp. BrE*) ◊ *My front ~ had a slow puncture.* | blow, blow out, burst (*esp. BrE*) ◊ *A back ~ blew after half an hour tearing along a rocky road.* | crunch, screech, squeal ◊ *The ~s crunched to a standstill on the gravel.* ◊ *She braked suddenly, her ~s squealing in protest.*
TYRE/TIRE + NOUN mark, tracks | pressure, size | tread | iron (*AmE*) ◊ *The victim had been beaten with a ~ iron.* | chain (*esp. AmE*) ◊ *For working in snow, ~ chains are essential.* | swing ◊ *She had been sitting on the ~ swing rocking back and forth.*
PHRASES a crunch of ~s, a screech of ~s, a squeal of ~s ◊ *He roared up the drive with a screech of ~s.*

U u

ugly adj.

1 unattractive
VERBS be, feel, look
ADV. extremely, fairly, very, etc. | hideously, horribly, incredibly ◊ *The witch was hideously ~.* | downright, plain (*both informal*) ◊ *It's just plain ~.*
2 dangerous/threatening
VERBS be, look, sound | become, get, turn
ADV. extremely, fairly, very, etc. ◊ *A fight started and things got pretty ~.* | a little | potentially

ultimatum noun

VERB + ULTIMATUM deliver, give sb, issue, present (sb with), send sb ◊ *The government denied that it had presented the union with an ~.* | get, receive | accept, comply with | ignore
ULTIMATUM + VERB demand sth

umbrella noun

ADJ. rolled | beach, sun | golf | nuclear, protective (*both figurative*) ◊ *the American nuclear ~ over Europe* | corporate (*figurative, esp. AmE*) | broad (*figurative*) ◊ *the broad ~ of alternative medicine*
VERB + UMBRELLA open, put up, unfurl | fold | carry, hold
UMBRELLA + NOUN stand | stroller (*AmE*) | body (*esp. BrE*), company, group, organization (*all figurative*) ◊ *an ~ group including members of opposition parties* | name, term, title (*all figurative*) ◊ *'Herb' is an ~ term covering many types of plant.*
PREP. under an/the ~ ◊ *She was fast asleep under a big beach ~.* ◊ *the two areas brought together under the ~ of the committee (figurative)*

unable adj.

VERBS appear, be, feel, prove, seem | become | remain | find yourself, leave sb, make sb, render sb ◊ *She found herself ~ to meet his gaze.* ◊ *The accident left him ~ to walk.* | consider sb/sth ◊ *He was considered ~ to cope with the pressure of the job.*
ADV. completely, quite, totally, utterly, wholly | increasingly | almost, nearly, virtually | generally, largely | apparently, seemingly ◊ *He went on, apparently ~ to stop.* | clearly | simply ◊ *The staff were simply ~ to cope.* | somehow ◊ *They are somehow ~ to make the choices necessary.* | genuinely (*esp. BrE*) | temporarily ◊ *Clare nodded, temporarily ~ to speak.* | still | currently | constitutionally, physically ◊ *He seemed constitutionally ~ to keep quiet.*
PHRASES unwilling or ~ ◊ *He remained silent, unwilling or ~ to say what was in his mind.*

unacceptable adj.

VERBS be, prove, seem | become | remain | make sth ◊ *The cost of these proposed changes makes them ~.* | consider sth, deem sth, find sth, regard sth as, see sth as ◊ *Most people would consider such risks wholly ~.*
ADV. absolutely, completely, entirely, just, quite, simply, totally, utterly, wholly | clearly | morally, politically, socially ◊ *socially ~ conduct*
PREP. to ◊ *Such a solution would be quite ~ to the majority of people.*

unaffected adj.

VERBS appear, be, seem | remain
ADV. completely, entirely, totally, wholly | almost, virtually | essentially, largely | relatively | apparently, seemingly ◊ *She was seemingly ~ by his presence.*
PREP. by ◊ *He appeared totally ~ by this experience.*

unanimous adj.

VERBS be
ADV. almost, nearly, virtually
PREP. about ◊ *Doctors are ~ about the dangers of this drug.* | in ◊ *They were ~ in this decision.* | on ◊ *The experts are not ~ on this point.*

unavoidable adj.

VERBS be, prove, seem | become | make sth ◊ *This latest incident makes his dismissal ~.*
ADV. absolutely, simply | probably | almost, largely, virtually | seemingly

unaware adj.

VERBS appear, be, seem | remain
ADV. completely, entirely, quite, totally, utterly, wholly | almost, virtually | generally, largely | apparently, seemingly | evidently, obviously | blissfully, blithely ◊ *They remained blissfully ~ of his true intentions.*
PREP. of

unbalanced adj.

1 slightly crazy
VERBS be, seem | become
ADV. a little, slightly, etc. | emotionally, mentally ◊ *She became mentally ~ after the accident.*

2 not fair to all ideas or sides of sth

VERBS **be, seem** | **become**

ADV. **extremely, fairly, very, etc.** ◇ *a somewhat ~ account of the events* | **dangerously, seriously** ◇ *The stock-market boom is dangerously ~.* | **completely, wholly** ◇ *The report is completely ~.* | **a little, slightly, etc.**

unbearable adj.

VERBS **be, feel, seem** | **become, get** | **make sb/sth** ◇ *His arrogance made him absolutely ~.* | **find sb/sth** ◇ *They found the heat ~.*

ADV. **absolutely, just, quite** (*esp. BrE*) | **completely, totally** (*both esp. AmE*) | **almost, nearly**

unbeatable adj.

VERBS **be, look, seem** ◇ *The French team looks ~.* | **become** | **remain** ◇ *United remain ~ at the top of the League.*

ADV. **almost, nearly, practically, virtually** ◇ *He now has an almost ~ lead over his rivals.* | **seemingly**

unbelievable adj.

VERBS **be, seem, sound** | **become** | **find sth** ◇ *I find his story quite ~.*

ADV. **really** | **absolutely, completely, quite, totally, truly** | **just, simply** | **almost** | **pretty**

PREP. **to** ◇ *It's simply ~ to me.*

unbroken adj.

VERBS **be** | **remain** | **continue** ◇ *an intimacy that continued ~ until the following spring*

ADV. **almost, largely, virtually** ◇ *a tradition of government involvement which remained virtually ~ until the 1990s*

uncertain adj.

1 not confident

VERBS **be, feel, look, seem, sound** | **become** | **leave sb** ◇ *His research into the incident has left him ~ as to exactly where responsibility lay.* | **make sb**

ADV. **deeply** (*esp. BrE*)**, very** ◇ *I feel deeply ~ about the future.* | **rather, somewhat** | **a little, slightly, etc.**

PREP. **about, as to** ◇ *He seemed strangely ~ as to how to continue.* | **of** ◇ *We were rather ~ of the direction it came from.*

2 not known exactly

VERBS **be, look** | **become** | **remain, seem** | **make sth** ◇ *immigration policies that made employment status ~*

ADV. **extremely, fairly, very, etc.** | **highly** ◇ *Cost estimates are highly ~ in this business.* | **increasingly** | **still** ◇ *Whether diet is an important factor in this illness is still ~.* | **inherently** ◇ *The world is inherently ~.*

uncertainty noun

ADJ. **considerable, great, high** (*esp. AmE*)**, significant, substantial** ◇ *The 1990s were a period of high ~ for businesses.* | **fundamental** ◇ *It still leaves us with fundamental uncertainties about why the famine happened.* | **inherent** ◇ *the inherent ~ in economic and budgetary forecasts* | **current** | **growing, continuing, lingering** | **economic, financial, legal, political, scientific**

...OF UNCERTAINTY **amount, degree, element**

VERB + UNCERTAINTY **cause, create, generate, give rise to** (*esp. BrE*)**, introduce, lead to** | **add, add to, increase** ◇ *Her comments will add to the ~ of the situation.* ◇ *Her comments will add ~ to an already complicated situation.* | **reduce** | **eliminate, end, remove, resolve** | **bring an end to** (*BrE*)**, put an end to** (*esp. BrE*) | **express, show** ◇ *I expressed some ~ on the point.* ◇ *Her expression showed her ~.* | **face** ◇ *They are facing some ~ about their jobs.*

UNCERTAINTY + VERB **surround sth** ◇ *the ~ surrounding the proposed changes in the law* | **exist** ◇ *Some ~ still exists about the safety of the new drug.* | **remain** ◇ *Considerable ~ remains about this approach.*

PREP. **~ about** ◇ *a feeling of ~ about his future* | **~ as to** ◇ *There's considerable ~ as to whether the government's job*

creation strategies will work. | **~ in** ◇ *There is considerable ~ in our understanding of global warming.* | **~ over** ◇ *~ over the safety of the drug* | **~ regarding** ◇ *This will remove any uncertainties regarding possible contamination.*

PHRASES **an area of ~** ◇ *One area of ~ remains: who will lead the team?* | **an atmosphere of ~, a climate of ~** ◇ *a climate of global economic ~* | **a feeling of ~, a moment of ~** ◇ *Chris experienced a moment of ~.* | **a period of ~, a source of ~** ◇ *The economy became a source of ~ and discontent.*

unchanged adj.

VERBS **appear, be, look** | **continue, remain, stay** | **leave sth**

ADV. **completely, totally** | **almost, nearly** (*esp. AmE*)**, practically, virtually** | **largely, mostly, pretty much, substantially** | **basically, essentially, fundamentally** ◇ *The school appeared essentially ~ since my day.* | **relatively**

PREP. **by** ◇ *She was the only one of us ~ by events.*

uncharacteristic adj.

VERBS **be, seem**

ADV. **very** | **completely, quite, totally** | **rather**

PREP. **of** ◇ *The houses were totally ~ of the area.*

uncle noun

ADJ. **beloved, favourite/favorite** | **rich** | **crazy** (*esp. AmE*)**, drunken, eccentric** | **bachelor** | **elderly, old** | **dead, late** ◇ *the fortune left to her by her dead ~* ◇ *He looks so much like his late ~.* | **maternal, paternal** | **great** (usually **great-uncle**)

uncomfortable adj.

1 not comfortable

VERBS **be, feel, look, seem** | **become, get** | **make sth** ◇ *Sharp stones on the path made walking barefoot rather ~.* | **find sth** ◇ *I find these chairs incredibly ~.*

ADV. **extremely, fairly, very, etc.** | **downright, incredibly, most, terribly** | **physically**

2 feeling/causing worry/embarrassment

VERBS **appear, be, feel, look, seem, sound** | **become, get, grow** ◇ *He started to get a little ~ as the conversation continued.* | **remain** ◇ *A few remain highly ~ with the idea of same-sex marriage.* | **make sb** ◇ *The way he looked at her made her distinctly ~.* | **leave sb** ◇ *This discussion leaves them ~.* | **find sth**

ADV. **extremely, fairly, very, etc.** | **acutely, decidedly, deeply, distinctly, downright, highly, horribly, incredibly, most, profoundly, terribly** | **increasingly** | **a little, slightly, etc.** | **mildly, vaguely** | **clearly, obviously, visibly** | **suddenly** ◇ *I noticed that Elisa was suddenly ~ and blushing.*

PREP. **about** ◇ *She was a little ~ about this situation.* | **at** ◇ *He looked ~ at the news.* | **with** ◇ *Planners seem a little ~ with the current guidelines.*

uncommon adj.

VERBS **be** | **become**

ADV. **extremely, fairly, very, etc.** | **by no means, far from, not at all** ◇ *Such attitudes were not at all ~ thirty years ago.* | **relatively** | **still** ◇ *Such technologies were still ~ in the US.*

unconcerned adj.

VERBS **act, appear, be, look, seem, sound** ◇ *I tried to act ~.* | **remain**

ADV. **completely, quite, totally, utterly** | **blissfully, blithely** | **remarkably** | **largely, relatively** | **apparently, seemingly**

PREP. **about** ◇ *They appeared completely ~ about what they had done.* | **by** ◇ *He was apparently ~ by his failure to get the job.* | **with** ◇ *Bennett is ~ with such matters.*

unconscious adj.

1 in a state that is like sleep

VERBS **appear, be, lie, look** ◇ *They found her lying ~ on the*

floor. | **become, fall, go** (*esp. AmE*) ◊ *She fell ~ after breathing in the gas.* | **remain** | **batter sb** (*esp. BrE*), **beat sb, kick sb, knock sb, render sb** ◊ *He was knocked ~ by the impact.* | **find sb** ◊ *The paramedics found me ~ on the floor.* | **leave sb** ◊ *The attack left her ~.*
ADV. **deeply** | **completely** | **almost** | **still**

2 unconscious of sb/sth not aware of sb/sth
VERBS **appear, be, seem**
ADV. **quite** (*BrE*), **totally** ◊ *Parents are often quite ~ of the ways in which they influence their children.*

3 done without you being aware of it
VERBS **be, seem**
ADV. **deeply** | **quite, totally, wholly** ◊ *These impulses are often totally ~.* | **almost** | **largely**

unconsciousness *noun*
ADJ. **deep** | **blissful**
VERB + UNCONSCIOUSNESS **drift into, fall into, lapse into, sink into, slip into**

uncontrollable *adj.*
VERBS **be, seem** | **become**
ADV. **completely, totally** | **almost, virtually** ◊ *an almost ~ urge to laugh* | **apparently, seemingly**

undecided *adj.*
VERBS **be, seem** | **remain** | **leave sth** ◊ *The question cannot be left ~.*
ADV. **truly** ◊ *Only about 5% of the voters are truly ~.* | **still** | **as yet** (*esp. BrE*) ◊ *She is as yet ~ about her career.*
PREP. **about** ◊ *He is still ~ about what to do.* | **as to** ◊ *They are ~ as to whether to buy a new car.* | **on** ◊ *The government remains ~ on this issue.*

underbrush *noun* (*AmE*) → See also UNDERGROWTH
ADJ. **dense, thick** ◊ *In some places, the dense ~ becomes so thick that it's nearly impassable.* | **tangled, thorny**
VERB + UNDERBRUSH **clear, clear away, clear out** ◊ *The government wants to clear ~ near populated areas.*
PREP. **~ of** ◊ *the ~ of the forest*

underestimate (*also* underestimation) *noun*
ADJ. **gross, serious, significant** ◊ *The official figures are a gross ~ of the true number.* | **slight**
PREP. **~ of**

underestimate *verb*
ADV. **badly, considerably, greatly, grossly, massively, seriously, severely, significantly, substantially, vastly, woefully** ◊ *I realized that he had seriously ~d their strength.* | **consistently, systematically** ◊ *We consistently ~ the resources and motivation of our adversaries.* | **completely, totally** | **clearly** | **slightly**
VERB + UNDERESTIMATE **tend to**
PHRASES **sth should not be ~d** ◊ *The importance of these feelings should not be ~d.*

undergraduate *noun*
ADJ. **college, university** | **Harvard, Oxford, etc.** | **first-year, second-year, etc.** (*esp. BrE*) | **chemistry, history, etc.** | **full-time, part-time**
UNDERGRADUATE + NOUN **course, curriculum, degree, education, programme/program** (*esp. AmE*), **studies** | **major, minor** (*both AmE*) | **research, thesis, work** (*all esp. AmE*) ◊ *He completed his ~ work at Rutgers University.* | **chemistry, mathematics, etc.** | **college, institution, school** (*all AmE*) | **admissions, enrolment /enrollment** (*esp. AmE*) | **population, student** | **class** (*esp. AmE*) | **teaching** | **career** ◊ *memoirs of his ~ career at the University of Toronto* | **days, years** ◊ *during her ~ years at the University of California* | **level** | **grant**

underground *noun* (*BrE*) → See also SUBWAY
VERB + UNDERGROUND **go by, go on, take, travel by, travel on** ◊ *We went by ~.* | ◊ *I often travel on the ~.*
UNDERGROUND + NOUN **station, train, tunnel** | **system** ◊ *It brought the whole ~ system to a halt.*
PREP. **in the ~** ◊ *I always seem to get lost in the ~.* | **on the ~** ◊ *passengers on the ~*

undergrowth (*BrE*) *noun* → See also UNDERBRUSH
ADJ. **deep, dense, lush, tangled, thick**
... OF UNDERGROWTH **patch, tangle**
VERB + UNDERGROWTH **clear**
PREP. **into the ~** ◊ *The snake slithered off into the ~.* | **in the ~** ◊ *I noticed someone hiding in the ~.* | **through the ~** ◊ *I could hear him crashing through the ~.*

underline (*also* underscore *esp. in AmE*) *verb*
1 draw a line under a word
ADV. **heavily** ◊ *The word 'not' was heavily ~d.*
2 emphasize sth
ADV. **clearly** | **just, merely, only, simply** ◊ *This disaster merely ~s the need for caution.* | **further** (*BrE*)
VERB + UNDERLINE **serve to** | **seem to**
PHRASES **~ the fact that…**

undermine *verb*
ADV. **greatly, radically, seriously, severely, significantly** ◊ *His position within the government has been seriously ~d.* | **completely, totally** | **ultimately** ◊ *It ultimately ~d his ability to play.* | **rather, somewhat** | **further** | **effectively** | **actively** | **fatally** | **subtly** | **systematically** | **gradually, increasingly, progressively** | **eventually** | **potentially** | **constantly**
VERB + UNDERMINE **threaten to** | **attempt to, seek to, try to** | **conspire to, help (to), serve to, tend to** | **be likely to** | **be designed to, be intended to** ◊ *a terror attack intended to ~ the morale of citizens*

underpants *noun*
ADJ. **men's, women's** (*AmE*)
... OF UNDERPANTS **pair**
PREP. **in your ~** ◊ *He came to the door dressed only in his ~.*
→ Special page at CLOTHES

underscore *verb* (*esp. AmE*) → See UNDERLINE

undershirt *noun* (*AmE*) → See also VEST
ADJ. **sleeveless** | **thermal** | **cotton**
PREP. **in (your) ~** ◊ *He was standing there in his ~ and shorts.*
→ Special page at CLOTHES

understand *verb*
ADV. **clearly, well** | **completely, fully, perfectly, quite, thoroughly, totally, truly** ◊ *I fully ~ the reason for your decision.* | **better** ◊ *These categories help us to better ~ our readers.* | **not really, not truly** ◊ *Her actions wounded him in a way he did not really ~.* | **not necessarily** ◊ *They won't necessarily ~ the pros and cons of the matter.* | **not entirely, partially** ◊ *a complex topic which I only partially ~* | **barely, hardly** ◊ *I could barely ~ a word of his story.* | **adequately** | **accurately, correctly, precisely, properly, rightly** ◊ *If I've understood you correctly…* | **easily, readily** ◊ *The reasons for this decision are not easily understood.* | **immediately, instantly, quickly, suddenly** ◊ *The girl ~s immediately and promises to be more careful.* | **finally** ◊ *I finally understood what she meant.* | **instinctively, intuitively** ◊ *She intuitively understood his need to be alone.*
VERB + UNDERSTAND **be able to, can** ◊ *I can't ~ what all the fuss is about.* | **be unable to, fail to** | **attempt to, hope to, seek to, strive to, try to** ◊ *Only specialists can hope to ~ them.* | **struggle to** ◊ *a woman struggling to ~ an incomprehensible situation* | **help (to), help sb (to)** | **begin to, start to** | **come to, learn to** ◊ *We came to ~ why certain things happened in certain ways.* | **appear to, seem to** |

claim to ◊ *I don't claim to ~ it.* | **be easy to, be simple to** | **be difficult to, be hard to** ◊ *It is difficult to ~ why he reacted in that way.*
PREP. **about** ◊ *We ~ little about this disease.* | **as** ◊ *These beliefs are best understood as a form of escapism.*
PHRASES **be commonly understood, be generally understood, be popularly understood** ◊ *What is generally understood by 'democracy'?* | **be imperfectly understood, be incompletely understood, be poorly understood** ◊ *The effects of these chemicals on the body are still poorly understood.* | **be universally understood, be widely understood**

understandable *adj.*

1 seeming normal and reasonable
VERBS **be, seem** | **become**
ADV. **very** | **completely, entirely, perfectly, quite, totally, wholly** | **fairly, somewhat** ◊ *His frustration is somewhat ~.* | **certainly** ◊ *It is certainly ~ that he would be so devoted to his home and family.* | **perhaps**

2 easy to understand
VERBS **be, seem** | **make sth** ◊ *The author makes complex topics ~ by using simple words and examples.*
ADV. **easily, readily** ◊ *Warning notices must be readily ~.*
PREP. **to** ◊ *The instructions must be ~ to the average user.*

understanding *noun*

1 knowledge of a subject, of how sth works, etc.
ADJ. **complete, comprehensive, full** ◊ *He showed a full ~ of the sequence of events.* | **growing** | **accurate, clear, deep, detailed, fundamental, in-depth, intimate, keen, profound, proper, real, solid, sophisticated, thorough, true** ◊ *You need to read more widely to gain a proper ~ of the issue.* | **adequate, basic, broad, general, sufficient** | **limited, rudimentary, superficial** ◊ *She has only a limited ~ of what the job involves.* | **incomplete, poor** ◊ *He had a poor ~ of international law.* | **better, deeper, greater, improved, increased, richer** ◊ *an improved ~ of the mechanisms involved* | **conceptual, critical, rational, theoretical** | **historical, musical, scientific, etc.** | **contemporary, modern** | **conventional, traditional** | **instinctive, intuitive** | **collective, common** ◊ *Some religions have a common ~ of the nature of a divine being.* | **popular, public** ◊ *with a view to increasing public ~ of the functions and institutions of government*
... OF UNDERSTANDING **degree, level** ◊ *It allowed him to deepen his degree of ~ even further.* ◊ *The students seem to have a reasonable level of ~ of how genes work.*
VERB + UNDERSTANDING **have, possess** | **demonstrate, show** | **reflect** ◊ *This change of policy reflects a growing ~ of the extent of the problem.* | **lack** | **achieve, acquire, arrive at, gain, obtain** | **create, provide** ◊ *This creates a better ~ of organic farming.* | **give sb** | **facilitate** | **inform, shape** ◊ *All of this research informs our ~ of how disease processes work.* | **alter, change** | **advance, broaden, deepen, develop, enhance, enrich, expand, extend, further, improve, increase, refine** ◊ *a book that will deepen your ~ of global warming* | **seek** ◊ *Scientists are seeking a better ~ of the process.*
PREP. **~ about** | **~ of** ◊ *The book aims to give children a balanced ~ of food and the environment.*
PHRASES **a lack of ~**

2 intelligence
ADJ. **human**
VERB + UNDERSTANDING **pass** ◊ *a level of cruelty that passes human ~*
PREP. **beyond (your) ~** ◊ *How children change so quickly is beyond my ~.*

3 ability to feel sympathy and trust
ADJ. **deeper, great** | **common, mutual, shared** | **sympathetic** ◊ *She gave me a look filled with sympathetic ~.* | **international** | **cross-cultural** (*esp. AmE*), **cultural**
VERB + UNDERSTANDING **show** ◊ *He didn't show much ~ towards/toward her when she lost her job.* | **bring, bring about** (*esp. BrE*), **develop, lead to** ◊ *Greater contact between*

the two groups should lead to a better mutual ~. | **have** | **gain, grow in** ◊ *After spending a month living together, they have gained a better ~ of each other.* | **build** ◊ *Our goal was to build shared ~ between the two communities.* | **foster, promote**
PREP. **~ among** ◊ *a force for ~ among the races* | **~ between** ◊ *The association fosters a deeper ~ between prisons and the public.* | **~ for** ◊ *She suddenly had a new ~ for her mother.*

4 informal agreement
ADJ. **written** | **verbal** | **implicit, tacit, unspoken** ◊ *There is an unspoken ~ that Hugh will be in charge while Jane is away.*
VERB + UNDERSTANDING **have** | **come to, reach** ◊ *They came to an ~ on when final payment was to be made.*
PREP. **~ between** ◊ *an ~ between the companies to fight against the proposed tax reform* | **~ on** ◊ *a tacit ~ on the need for a pay rise* | **~ with** ◊ *I have a clear ~ with any lawyer I hire.* | **on the ~** ◊ *I thought you gave me the book on the ~ that I could keep it.*

understatement *noun*

ADJ. **gross, massive, vast** ◊ *'A little strange' is a gross ~.* | **typical** ◊ *with typical British ~*
PHRASES **a bit of an ~, something of an ~** | **the ~ of the century, the ~ of the year** (*both informal*) ◊ *To say he wasn't amused must be the ~ of the year.*

undertaking *noun*

1 piece of work/business
ADJ. **big, considerable** (*esp. BrE*), **large, major** | **enormous, great, huge, massive, monumental, tremendous** (*esp. AmE*) | **ambitious, important, serious** | **worthwhile** | **hazardous, risky** | **complex, difficult** | **costly, expensive** | **joint** ◊ *the first joint ~ of the two societies* | **commercial** ◊ *We have to decide if this is a worthwhile commercial ~.*

2 (*esp. BrE, law*) formal promise
ADJ. **solemn** | **express** | **irrevocable** | **voluntary** | **written** | **contractual** | **public**
VERB + UNDERTAKING **give (sb), make** ◊ *He gave an ~ not to leave the country before the trial.* | **seek** | **obtain** | **honour/honor** ◊ *The factory failed to honour/honor its ~ to stop dumping waste into the local river.* | **sign**

undertone *noun*

ADJ. **dark, sinister** | **subtle** | **bitter, sarcastic** | **racist, sexual** ◊ *The article was full of racist ~s.* | **political, religious** ◊ *There are hints of political ~s throughout the movie.*
VERB + UNDERTONE **carry, have** ◊ *His voice carried bitter ~s.*
PREP. **in an ~** ◊ *'I don't think she's been told yet,' he said in an ~.* ◊ *The couple at the next table were speaking in ~s.*

underwear *noun*

ADJ. **long** | **skimpy** | **thong** (*esp. AmE*) | **bikini** (*AmE*) | **thermal, warm** | **cotton, lace, lacy, silk** | **sexy** | **ladies', women's** | **men's** | **clean, fresh** | **dirty**
... OF UNDERWEAR **change, set** ◊ *She packed a fresh set of ~ and her toothbrush.* | **pair** (*esp. AmE*)
PREP. **in your ~** ◊ *I'm getting cold standing around in my ~.*
→ Special page at CLOTHES

underworld *noun*

ADJ. **dark, murky** (*esp. BrE*), **seedy, shadowy, sinister** ◊ *the dark ~ of smuggling* | **criminal**
UNDERWORLD + NOUN **boss, figure** | **contact** ◊ *He ran an import-export business and had ~ contacts in Japan.*
PREP. **in the ...~** ◊ *She was a shady figure in the Dublin ~.*

undesirable *adj.*

VERBS **be, seem** | **make sth** | **consider sth, deem sth, regard sth as, see sth as**
ADV. **extremely, fairly, very, etc.** | **highly** ◊ *a situation which is highly ~* | **totally** | **clearly, obviously** ◊ *It is clearly ~ for*

the issue to be ignored.· | **economically, politically, socially** ◇ *Why is he mixing with socially ~ types?* ◇ *It was felt that big cars were socially and economically ~.*

undignified *adj.*

VERBS **be, feel, look, seem** | **become**
ADV. **extremely, fairly, very, etc.** | **most** | **thoroughly** | **a little, slightly, etc.**

undone *adj.*

1 not fastened or tied

ADV. **slightly**
VERBS **be** | **come** ◇ *My button's come ~ again.* | **leave sth** ◇ *He was wearing a white shirt with the first few buttons left ~.* | **get sth** ◇ *I can't get this knot ~.*

2 not done

VERBS **be** | **remain** | **leave sth** ◇ *We left the cleaning ~ and went out for the day.*

undressed *adj.*

VERBS **be, feel** ◇ *She felt ~ without her hat.* | **get** ◇ *He got ~ and ready for bed.*
ADV. **half, partly** ◇ *He was half ~ when the doorbell rang.* | **completely, fully**

unease *noun*

ADJ. **considerable, deep, great, growing, profound** | **certain, some, vague** ◇ *She felt a vague ~.* | **slight** | **general, public**
VERB + UNEASE **feel** | **express, show** ◇ *They expressed their deep ~ about the lack of security arrangements.* | **hide** ◇ *I smiled to hide my ~.* | **sense** ◇ *He sensed a certain ~ in her.* | **cause, create, generate**
UNEASE + VERB **grow**
PREP. **~ about, ~ at, ~ over** ◇ *Many felt ~ about the methods used.* | **~ with** ◇ *his ~ with the situation*
PHRASES **a feeling of ~, a sense of ~, a source of ~** ◇ *He looked in vain for the source of his ~.*

uneasy *adj.*

VERBS **appear, be, feel, look, seem, sound** | **become, get, grow** ◇ *We were starting to grow slightly ~.* | **remain** | **leave sb, make sb (feel)**
ADV. **extremely, fairly, very, etc.** | **decidedly, deeply, distinctly, profoundly** | **a little, slightly, etc.** | **increasingly** | **vaguely**
PREP. **about** ◇ *I felt distinctly ~ about lending her so much money.* | **with** ◇ *She always felt ~ with her body shape.*

unemployed *noun* the unemployed

ADJ. **long-term**
PREP. **among the ~** ◇ *The party's policies were popular among the ~.*
PHRASES **the ranks of the ~** ◇ *He graduated with a good degree, only to join the ranks of the ~.*

unemployed *adj.*

VERBS **be, be counted as** (*esp. AmE*), **be registered (as)** (*BrE*) | **become** | **remain, stay** | **leave sb, make sb** (*esp. BrE*) ◇ *The closure of the factory left hundreds of men ~.*
ADV. **currently** | **newly** | **still** | **temporarily** | **chronically** (*AmE*), **permanently** | **officially**

unemployment *noun*

ADJ. **double-digit** (*esp. AmE*), **high, huge, mass, massive, severe, widespread** | **low** | **growing, rising** | **falling** | **chronic** | **involuntary** | **long-term** | **seasonal** (*esp. BrE*) | **structural** | **graduate, youth** | **rural** (*esp. BrE*), **urban**
...OF UNEMPLOYMENT **level, rate**
VERB + UNEMPLOYMENT **be faced with, face** | **cause, create** |

alleviate, bring down, cut, reduce | **increase** | **combat, tackle**
UNEMPLOYMENT + VERB **climb, double, increase, rise, soar** ◇ *Unemployment climbed above two million.* | **decline, fall** | **average sth, remain sth, remain at sth, stand at sth** ◇ *Unemployment averaged 15% across the country.* | **hit sth, reach sth** ◇ *Unemployment hit 10% in 1982.* ◇ *Unemployment reached 30%.*
UNEMPLOYMENT + NOUN **benefit** (*BrE*), **benefits** (*esp. AmE*), **compensation** (*AmE*), **cover** (*BrE*), **insurance** (*esp. AmE*) ◇ *New claims for ~ benefits remain low.* | **claims** (*esp. AmE*), **data, figures, levels, numbers, percentage, rate, statistics, total** ◇ *The county's ~ rate has dropped to 9%.* | **black spot** (*BrE*) ◇ *This former mining town is now an ~ black spot.*
PREP. **~ among** ◇ *Unemployment among graduates is falling steadily.*
PHRASES **a period of ~** | **a rise in ~, an increase in ~** | **a fall in ~**

unexpected *adj.*

VERBS **be**
ADV. **most, very** ◇ *Help came from a most ~ quarter.* | **completely, quite, totally, wholly** | **not entirely** ◇ *His death was not entirely ~.* | **a little, rather, somewhat** ◇ *It happened in rather ~ circumstances.*

unfair *adj.*

VERBS **be, seem** | **consider sth, regard sth as, think sth** ◇ *She thought it most ~ that girls were not allowed to take part.*
ADV. **extremely, fairly, very, etc.** | **blatantly, grossly, patently, terribly** ◇ *I thought the decision was grossly ~.* | **totally, utterly, wholly** (*esp. BrE*) | **a little, slightly, etc.**
PREP. **to** ◇ *He was terribly ~ to the younger children.*

unfamiliar *adj.*

VERBS **be, feel, look, sound**
ADV. **very** | **completely, quite** (*esp. AmE*), **totally** | **not entirely** | **largely, relatively**
PREP. **to** ◇ *The language was completely ~ to me.* | **with** ◇ *We were quite ~ with the town.*

unfashionable *adj.*

VERBS **be** | **become** | **remain**
ADV. **deeply, distinctly, terribly, very** | **completely** | **rather** (*esp. BrE*) ◇ *She lived in a rather ~ part of London.*

unfit *adj.*

1 unsuitable for sth/not capable of sth

VERBS **be, look** | **become** | **make sb/sth, render sb/sth** ◇ *His conduct made him ~ to act as director of a company.* | **consider sb/sth, declare sb/sth, deem sb/sth, find sb/sth** ◇ *The house was declared quite ~ for human habitation.*
ADV. **completely, quite, totally** | **medically, mentally, morally, physically**
PREP. **for** ◇ *completely ~ for our purposes* ◇ *She was found ~ for work.* ◇ *The prison service was declared 'unfit for purpose'.* (*BrE*)

2 (*esp. BrE*) not in good physical health

VERBS **be, feel, look** | **become**
ADV. **very** | **completely, quite** | **slightly**

unforgettable *adj.*

VERBS **be**
ADV. **absolutely, simply, totally, truly** ◇ *It was a truly ~ experience.*

unfortunate *adj.*

VERBS **be, seem** | **consider sb/sth**
ADV. **extremely, fairly, very, etc.** | **most, particularly** ◇ *It was a most ~ choice of expression.* | **doubly** ◇ *This comment was doubly ~ for Bob as he lost friends and further antagonized enemies.*

unfounded adj.

VERBS **be, prove** | **seem**
ADV. **completely, entirely, quite, simply** (esp. AmE), **totally, wholly** (esp. BrE) ◇ These claims were completely ~. | **largely** | **manifestly** (BrE, law) ◇ The claim is manifestly ~.

unfriendly adj.

VERBS **appear, be, look, seem** | **become**
ADV. **extremely, fairly, very, etc.** | **decidedly, really** ◇ a distinctly ~ tone of voice | **environmentally** ◇ the use of environmentally ~ products (= that harm the environment)
PREP. **to** ◇ She was really ~ to me.

unhappiness noun

ADJ. **deep, great** | **general, widespread** (esp. BrE) | **personal** | **marital**
VERB + UNHAPPINESS **express** | **cause, lead to** ◇ Bottling up your anger can only lead to ~.
PREP. **~ about** ◇ He expressed his ~ about the arrangements. | **~ at** ◇ the great ~ she felt at having to leave the town | **~ with** ◇ his deep ~ with the situation
PHRASES **a cause of ~**

unhappy adj.

VERBS **be, feel, look, seem, sound** | **become, grow** ◇ She grew more ~ as the years went by. | **remain** | **make sb** ◇ It makes me very ~ to see you so miserable.
ADV. **extremely, fairly, very, etc.** | **decidedly, deeply, desperately, distinctly, most** (esp. BrE), **really, terribly** ◇ She is deeply ~. ◇ He described it as 'a most ~ and distressing case'. | **increasingly** | **a little, slightly, etc.** | **clearly, obviously** | **equally** ◇ He was equally ~ with the alternative.
PREP. **about** ◇ He sounded a little ~ about the extra work he had to do. | **at** ◇ She was very ~ at the idea of staying in Sydney. | **with** ◇ They were terribly ~ with the arrangements.

unheard-of adj.

VERBS **be**
ADV. **absolutely, completely, quite, totally** ◇ At that time, it was completely ~ for girls to go to college. | **almost, practically, virtually** | **hitherto, previously** ◇ He was sentenced to a hitherto ~ seven life terms in prison.

unification noun

ADJ. **European, German, etc.** | **national** | **economic, monetary, political**
VERB + UNIFICATION **achieve**
UNIFICATION + NOUN **process**

uniform noun

ADJ. **full** | **smart** (BrE) | **regulation** ◇ the regulation ~ of tunic, hat and tie | **standard** (figurative) ◇ They wore the standard ~ of the American office worker. | **traditional** | **dress** ◇ a man in the full dress ~ of the Marines | **camouflage, combat** | **army, military, naval, prison** | **maid's** (esp. AmE), **nurse's, waitress** (esp. AmE) | **school** | **baseball, basketball, cheerleading, football, soccer, etc.** (all AmE)
VERB + UNIFORM **don** ◇ men and women who don military ~ to defend their country | **be dressed in**
PREP. **in (a/the) ~** ◇ The limousine was driven by a chauffeur in ~. ◇ A man in a ~ stopped us entering. | **out of ~** ◇ a soldier out of ~
→ Special page at CLOTHES

uniformity noun

ADJ. **relative** | **great** | **bland** | **cultural, religious**
... OF UNIFORMITY **degree**
VERB + UNIFORMITY **achieve, ensure, impose**
PREP. **~ in** ◇ Inspections ensure a high degree of ~ in standards.
PHRASES **a/the lack of ~**

uninhabitable adj.

VERBS **be** | **become** | **make sth, render sth** ◇ houses made ~

by radioactive contamination | **declare sth** ◇ Fifty homes were declared ~.
ADV. **completely** | **virtually**

uninhibited adj.

VERBS **be, feel, seem** ◇ The loud music made him feel totally ~. | **become**
ADV. **extremely, fairly, very, etc.** ◇ I'm a fairly ~ sort of person. | **completely, totally, utterly**

unintelligible adj.

VERBS **be, sound** | **become** | **render sth** ◇ These amendments will render the law ~.
ADV. **completely, quite, totally** | **almost, practically, virtually** | **largely** | **mutually** ◇ mutually ~ languages
PREP. **to** ◇ Dolphin sounds are ~ to humans.

uninterested adj.

VERBS **appear, be, look, seem, sound** | **remain**
ADV. **completely, totally, utterly** | **largely** (esp. AmE)
PREP. **in** ◇ She was completely ~ in her career.

union noun

1 act of joining; state of being joined

ADJ. **close** ◇ Some of the member states wanted a closer ~ rather than the loose confederation that developed. | **loose** | **full** ◇ a move in the direction of full political ~ | **economic, monetary, political** | **currency, customs**
VERB + UNION **create, form** | **dissolve**
PREP. **~ between** ◇ currency ~ between the two countries | **~ with** ◇ the ~ with East Germany

2 workers' organization

ADJ. **labor** (AmE), **trade** (esp. BrE), **trades** (BrE) | **public-sector, public-service, public-services** (all BrE) | **government-employee, public-employee** (both AmE) | **free, independent** | **official** | **big, large, major** ◇ France's biggest ~ | **militant, strong** | **local, national** | **industrial** (esp. AmE) | **electricians', faculty** (AmE), **teachers', etc.** ◇ She became active in the teachers' ~. | **engineering, health, rail, teaching, transport, etc.** (all BrE) | **student, students'**
VERB + UNION **form, organize** (esp. AmE), **set up** | **join** | **belong to** | **recognize**
UNION + VERB **be affiliated to sth** | **represent sb/sth** ◇ The ~ represents 40% of all hospital workers. | **negotiate (sth)** ◇ The nurses' ~ negotiated a new contract. | **accept sth, agree (to sth)** | **refuse sth, reject sth, threaten sth** ◇ The ~ threatened strike action if its demands were not met. | **claim sth, express sth** ◇ Several ~s expressed support for the strike. | **support sb/sth**
UNION + NOUN **confederation, federation, movement, organization** | **branch** (esp. BrE), **local** (AmE) | **action, activism, activity, militancy** (esp. BrE), **power** | **rights** | **activist, member, official, rep, representative** | **spokesman, spokesperson, spokeswoman** | **boss, chief, leader, organizer, president, secretary** (esp. BrE), **shop steward** (BrE), **steward** (BrE) | **leadership, membership, representation** | **conference** (esp. BrE), **election** | **shop** (AmE) | **card, dues** (esp. AmE) ◇ He paid his ~ dues to Local Union 98. | **law** | **contract** (AmE)
→ Note at ORGANIZATION

3 between two people

ADJ. **civil, legal** | **holy, spiritual** | **sexual** | **gay, same-sex**
VERB + UNION **allow, recognize** ◇ states where same-sex ~s are recognized

unique adj.

VERBS **be** | **make sb/sth** ◇ The magnificent light make this place ~.
ADV. **completely, quite, totally, truly** ◇ The city has an atmosphere which is quite ~. | **fairly, pretty, rather, somewhat** | **by no means, far from, hardly** ◇ Although

such a case is rare, it is by no means ~. | **almost, virtually** | **apparently**
PREP. **to** ◇ *This monkey is ~ to the island.*

unit *noun*

1 single thing

ADJ. **large, small** | **basic, fundamental** ◇ *The family is the basic ~ of society.* | **discrete, individual, single** | **cohesive** ◇ *to change a collection of individuals into a cohesive ~* | **family, social** ◇ *the role of the family ~ in the community*
VERB + UNIT **break sth down into, divide sth into** ◇ *Large departments were broken down into smaller ~s.*
PHRASES **~ of analysis** ◇ *This study's ~ of analysis is the individual hospital.*

2 fixed amount

ADJ. **basic, standard** | **monetary** | **linguistic**
VERB + UNIT **produce** ◇ *China produced 65 million ~s last year.* | **sell** ◇ *The manufacturer sold 73 000 ~s in the first quarter.*
UNIT + NOUN **cost, length, weight** ◇ *the average ~ cost of all products* | **sales**
PREP. **~ of** ◇ *a ~ of currency* ◇ *a ~ of length* ◇ *fifty ~s of electricity*
PHRASES **per ~** ◇ *Electricity is ten pence per ~.*

3 group of people

ADJ. **policy** (*esp. BrE*) | **research** | **business, production**
VERB + UNIT **be attached to** ◇ *The research ~ is attached to the local university.* | **create, form**

4 in a hospital

ADJ. **intensive care** | **accident and emergency, casualty** (*both BrE*) | **psychiatric, surgical** | **baby, maternity** (*both BrE*) ◇ *She works in the maternity ~ at the local hospital.* | **burn** (*AmE*), **burns** (*BrE*), **stroke** (*BrE*)

5 in the army, police, etc.

ADJ. **army, combat** (*esp. AmE*), **infantry, military** | **intelligence** | **enemy** | **police, road policing** (*BrE*)
UNIT + NOUN **commander** (*esp. AmE*)

6 piece of furniture/equipment

ADJ. **kitchen** (*esp. BrE*), **storage** (*esp. AmE*), **vanity** (*BrE*), **wall** | **air-conditioning, control, power, processing, shower** (*BrE*) ◇ *the central processing ~ in a computer*
VERB + UNIT **install** ◇ *We're having new kitchen ~s installed.*

7 house/building

ADJ. **dwelling** (*formal, esp. AmE*), **housing, residential** ◇ *a single dwelling ~* ◇ *A city council member pledged to build 500 affordable housing ~s.* | **business, industrial, retail** (*all esp. BrE*)
VERB + UNIT **build**

united *adj.*

VERBS **be, seem, stand** ◇ *Our nation needs to stand ~.* | **become** | **remain**
ADV. **closely, firmly** | **absolutely, entirely, fully, totally** ◇ *The members of the team were absolutely ~ in their common goal.* ◇ *obstacles to a fully ~ Europe* | **largely** | **legally, politically** ◇ *a politically ~ federation*
PREP. **against** ◇ *Everyone was ~ against a common enemy.* | **in** ◇ *~ in their aims* | **with** ◇ *We ask others to stand ~ with us.*

unity *noun*

ADJ. **complete** ◇ *Complete political ~ is impossible to achieve.* | **greater** | **essential, fundamental, underlying** | **organic** ◇ *the organic ~ of Raphael's picture* | **Arab, Christian, European, etc.** | **cultural, economic, national, party, political, racial** (*esp. AmE*), **religious, social** ◇ *a government of national ~*
VERB + UNITY **achieve, bring, bring about, create, foster, promote** ◇ *She brought ~ to her people.* | **maintain, preserve** | **destroy, shatter** | **restore** ◇ *He restored peace and ~ in the country after years of civil war.* | **call for, seek** ◇ *The party is calling for greater economic ~.*

PREP. **in ~** ◇ *live together in ~* | **~ among** ◇ *The dispute has destroyed ~ among the workers.* | **~ between** ◇ *a degree of ~ between faculty and students*
PHRASES **a sense of ~** ◇ *a leader who gave her people a strong sense of ~* | **a show of ~** | **~ in diversity** ◇ *The organization promotes ~ in diversity.*

universal *adj.*

VERBS **be, seem** | **become** | **remain**
ADV. **truly** | **by no means, far from** ◇ *Some of the teachers are technical specialists, but this is far from ~.* | **almost, near, nearly, virtually** | **apparently** | **supposedly** ◇ *supposedly ~ standards*
PREP. **among** ◇ *These practices remain ~ among the islanders.* | **in** ◇ *a plan that is ~ in scope*

universe *noun*

ADJ. **entire, whole** | **vast** | **expanding** | **material, physical** | **moral** (*figurative*) | **observable, visible** | **known** ◇ *the outer regions of the known ~* | **alternate** (*esp. AmE*), **alternative, parallel** (*all usually figurative*) ◇ *The characters exist in a parallel ~.* | **fictional**
VERB + UNIVERSE **create**
UNIVERSE + VERB **expand** ◇ *The ~ is still expanding.*
PREP. **in the ~** ◇ *Is there be intelligent life elsewhere in the ~?*
PHRASES **the beginning of the ~, the origin of the ~, the origins of the ~** | **the expansion of the ~**

university *noun*

ADJ. **elite, leading, major, prestigious, top** | **ancient** (*esp. BrE*) | **modern, new, red-brick** (*BrE*) | **Catholic, private, public** (*all esp. AmE*) | **land-grant** (*AmE*) | **local, provincial** (*BrE*), **state** (*AmE*) | **research**
VERB + UNIVERSITY **attend, go to, study at** ◇ *He goes to Princeton University.* | **apply to** ◇ *I applied to three universities.* ◇ *I'm applying to ~ this year.* (*BrE*) | **enter** ◇ *King entered Montana State University in 2002.* ◇ *Young people may be deterred from entering ~.* (*BrE*) | **finish** (*BrE*), **graduate from, leave** ◇ *She graduated from the University of Michigan in 1999.* ◇ *I graduated from ~ last year.* (*BrE*)
UNIVERSITY + NOUN **lecturer** (*esp. BrE*), **professor, researcher, staff, teacher** | **graduate, student** | **course, degree, education** | **research** | **fees** (*BrE*), **tuition** (*AmE*) ◇ *the government's decision to introduce ~ top-up fees* ◇ *those who can afford ~ tuition* | **funding** (*esp. BrE*) | **term** (*BrE*), **year** | **vacation** | **admission, admissions, entrance, entry** (*esp. BrE*), **place** (*esp. BrE*) ◇ *a ~ entrance exam* ◇ *There is stiff competition for ~ places.* | **chair** ◇ *His aim was to obtain a ~ chair.* | **department** | **accommodation** (*BrE*), **buildings, campus, library** | **chancellor, vice chancellor** | **dean, president, provost** (*all in the US*) | **administration, authorities** (*BrE*) | **administrator, official** (*both esp. AmE*) | **faculty** (= those who teach) (*esp. AmE*), **staff** (= those who teach and those who provide services) (*BrE*) | **staff** (= those who provide services) (*AmE*) | **hospital, laboratory, medical centre/center, press** | **level** ◇ *All the staff are educated to ~ level.* | **system** | **life** (*esp. BrE*) ◇ *the pressures of ~ life* | **days, years** (*both esp. BrE*) ◇ *I often think of my ~ days.* | **town**
PREP. **at (the) ~** ◇ *She teaches botany at Syracuse University.* ◇ *She's at ~, studying engineering.* (*BrE*)

unknown *noun*

1 place/thing that you know nothing about

ADJ. **big, great** ◇ *What the weather will be like on the day is, as always, the great ~.*
VERB + UNKNOWN **explore, face, step into, venture into**
PHRASES **a journey into the ~, a leap into the ~, a voyage into the ~** ◇ *This action represents a leap into the ~.* | **fear of the ~**

2 sb who is not well known

ADJ. **complete** ◇ *The championship was won by a complete ~.* | **relative, virtual** ◇ *a cast of virtual ~s*

unknown adj.

VERBS **be** | **remain** ◇ These sites remain largely ~ to the British public.
ADV. **completely, entirely, quite** (BrE), **totally, utterly** (esp. AmE) ◇ His whereabouts were quite ~ during this period. | **almost, practically, virtually** ◇ This drug was practically ~ in Britain. | **largely, mostly** | **comparatively, relatively** ◇ a comparatively ~ actor ◇ She was then still relatively ~. | **as yet, currently, still** | **heretofore** (formal, esp. AmE), **hitherto, previously** ◇ a period of democratic development previously ~ in their country | **apparently** | **otherwise** ◇ He cites the works of two otherwise ~ authors.
PREP. **to** ◇ Gold was totally ~ to their civilization.
PHRASES **for parts ~, to parts ~** ◇ She departed for parts ~. | **for reasons ~, for ~ reasons**

unlikely adj.

VERBS **appear, be, look, sound** ◇ The takeover bid now looks ~ to succeed. | **become** | **remain, seem** | **make sth, render sth** | **consider sth, deem sth, find sth, think sth** ◇ He thought it ~ that she would refuse.
ADV. **extremely, fairly, very, etc.** | **exceedingly, highly, most** | **increasingly** | **a little, slightly, etc.** | **inherently** (BrE) ◇ An economic collapse is inherently ~.

unlimited adj.

VERBS **appear, be, seem**
ADV. **almost, nearly** (esp. AmE), **virtually** ◇ This new technology opens up almost ~ possibilities. | **apparently, seemingly** | **essentially** (esp. AmE) | **potentially**

unlucky adj.

VERBS **be, seem, sound** | **consider sb/sth** ◇ The number thirteen is traditionally considered ~.
ADV. **extremely, fairly, very, etc.** | **desperately** (esp. BrE) ◇ She was desperately ~ to fall as badly as she did. | **a little, slightly, etc.** | **enough** ◇ soldiers who were ~ enough to be captured
PREP. **for** ◇ a date that is ~ for that family | **in** ◇ He was ~ in love. | **with** (esp. BrE) ◇ She has been very ~ with injuries this year.

unmoved adj.

VERBS **appear, be, seem** | **remain** | **leave sb** ◇ Her daughter's accident had left her curiously ~.
ADV. **completely, totally** | **largely, relatively** | **apparently**
PREP. **by** ◇ He was quite ~ by my anger.

unnecessary adj.

VERBS **appear, be, prove, seem** | **become** | **make sth, render sth** | **consider sth, deem sth, regard sth as**
ADV. **completely, entirely, quite, totally, utterly, wholly** ◇ No, no, that's quite ~. | **largely** | **rather, somewhat** | **a little**
PREP. **to** ◇ the possession of items strictly ~ to survival

unnoticed adj.

VERBS **be, go, lie, pass** ◇ The ticket lay ~ in my desk drawer for a week. ◇ His remark passed ~. | **remain** | **enter, escape, slip, slip away** ◇ She slipped away ~ from the party.
ADV. **completely, entirely, totally** ◇ There's a good chance my absence will go completely ~. | **almost, practically, virtually** | **largely, mostly, relatively** | **hitherto, previously** ◇ a hitherto ~ detail

unpleasant adj.

VERBS **be, feel, look, seem, smell, sound, taste** | **become, get, turn** ◇ Things started to get ~ when the police were called. | **make sth** ◇ He may make life ~ for the rest of us. | **find sb/sth** ◇ I found the atmosphere in there extremely ~.
ADV. **extremely, fairly, very, etc.** | **decidedly, deeply, distinctly, downright, highly, most, particularly** ◇ His clothes smelled most ~. | **thoroughly** ◇ a thoroughly ~ man | **not altogether, not entirely** ◇ The overall feeling was a strange mixture of sensations, not altogether ~. | **a little, slightly, etc.**

PREP. **for** ◇ tests which are ~ for patients | **to** ◇ He was very ~ to my friends.

unpopular adj.

VERBS **be, prove** | **become** | **remain** | **make sb/sth** ◇ His views made him ~ with many.
ADV. **extremely, fairly, very, etc.** | **deeply, highly, hugely, particularly, wildly** (esp. AmE) | **increasingly** | **generally, widely** | **politically** ◇ Cuts in government expenditure are politically ~.
PREP. **among** ◇ Highly priced shares are ~ among investors. | **with** ◇ He's ~ with the students.

unpopularity noun

ADJ. **growing, increasing**
VERB + UNPOPULARITY **increase**
PREP. **~ among** ◇ Her close relationship with the teacher increased her ~ among her schoolmates. | **~ with** ◇ the great ~ of the policy with teachers

unprecedented adj.

VERBS **be**
ADV. **entirely, quite, totally, truly** | **by no means, hardly** | **almost, virtually** | **historically** ◇ a historically ~ growth in retirement at a fixed age

unprovoked adj.

VERBS **be**
ADV. **completely, totally** ◇ a totally ~ attack | **apparently** (BrE), **seemingly**

unreal adj.

VERBS **be, feel, look, seem, sound** | **become**
ADV. **very** | **completely, quite, totally** | **almost** | **a little, slightly, etc.** | **somehow** | **strangely** ◇ She felt strangely ~, as if she were in a dream.

unreasonable adj.

VERBS **appear, be, seem, sound** ◇ She did not want to appear ~. | **become, get** ◇ His demands were becoming more and more ~. | **consider sth, deem sth, find sb/sth, hold sth (to be)** (law), **judge sth** (law), **regard sth as** (esp. BrE), **think sth** ◇ I find her a little ~ at times. ◇ This clause in the contract was held ~.
ADV. **extremely, very** | **completely, entirely, quite, totally, utterly, wholly** | **a little, slightly, etc.** | **apparently**
PREP. **about** ◇ He was totally ~ about it.

unrest noun

ADJ. **great, serious** | **violent** | **widespread** ◇ There was widespread industrial ~ in the north. | **domestic, internal** ◇ The incident led to domestic ~ in the cities. | **popular, public** | **growing, mounting** | **further** ◇ The murder of a boy by police sparked further ~ in the occupied zone. | **civil, economic, ethnic, industrial, labour/labor, political, racial, social** | **peasant, student**
... OF UNREST **period, wave** ◇ The increase in fees sparked a new wave of student ~. | **state**
VERB + UNREST **cause, create, foment, provoke, spark, spark off, stir up** (esp. BrE), **trigger** | **deal with, quell** ◇ The government's attempts to quell serious popular ~ led to civil war.
PREP. **during (the) ~** ◇ Many businesses were looted during the ~. | **~ among** ◇ a wave of democratic ~ among the masses | **~ over** ◇ growing ~ over pay levels

unscathed adj.

VERBS **be, be left, come out (of sth), emerge, escape, get away, remain, return, survive, walk away** ◇ The children escaped ~.
ADV. **remarkably** | **completely, entirely, totally** ◇ Amazingly, the driver walked away from the accident completely ~. |

almost, virtually | largely | relatively | apparently, seemingly ◇ *The company came through the crisis apparently ~.* | miraculously
PREP. by ◇ *The old town was left ~ by the riots.*

unscrupulous *adj.*

VERBS be, seem | become
ADV. completely, quite, thoroughly (*esp. BrE*) ◇ *In his desire for power, he has become completely ~.* | pretty (*esp. BrE*)

unstable *adj.*

1 likely to change suddenly; likely to move or fall

VERBS appear, be, seem | become | remain | make sth, render sth ◇ *Prison order is rendered ~ by young inmates serving short sentences.*
ADV. extremely, fairly, very, etc. | highly | increasingly | relatively | inherently | potentially | notoriously ◇ *The building trade is notoriously ~.* | dangerously | economically, financially, politically ◇ *a politically ~ region*

2 not mentally normal

VERBS be, seem | become
ADV. extremely, fairly, very, etc. | highly | emotionally, mentally, psychologically ◇ *vulnerable, emotionally ~ individuals*

unsuitable *adj.*

VERBS be, prove | make sth, render sth ◇ *The size of the rooms made the house ~ for conversion into apartments.* | consider sth, deem sth, find sth ◇ *Many tasks were considered ~ for women.*
ADV. extremely, fairly, very, etc. | highly, most (*BrE*) | completely, entirely, quite, totally, wholly | manifestly
PREP. for

unsure *adj.*

VERBS be, feel, look, seem, sound ◇ *I felt a little ~ about him.* | remain | leave sb, make sb ◇ *His sudden change of heart left Brenda ~ once more.*
ADV. extremely, fairly, very, etc. | completely, totally | a little, slightly, etc. | clearly, obviously | genuinely | still
PREP. about ◇ *If you're still ~ about what you are supposed to do, speak up!* | as to ◇ *We were ~ as to what to do next.* | of ◇ *She was rather ~ of her reception.*

unthinkable *adj.*

VERBS be, seem | make sth | consider sth ◇ *This would have been considered ~ only a decade ago.*
ADV. absolutely, completely, literally, quite, simply | almost, nearly (*esp. AmE*), practically, virtually | hitherto, previously ◇ *A hitherto ~ question was asked.* | politically
PREP. for ◇ *It's ~ for something like this to happen.* | to ◇ *This course of action would have been ~ to the generals.*

untidy *adj.*

VERBS be, look, seem | become, get ◇ *I've become more ~ since I stopped going out to work.* | leave sth (*esp. BrE*), make sth ◇ *Books and magazines lying around make the place very ~.*
ADV. extremely, fairly, very, etc. | a little, slightly, etc.

unused *adj.*

VERBS appear, be, go, lie, look, remain, sit, stand ◇ *The church has lain empty and ~ since 1994.* | leave sth ◇ *The meeting rooms are left ~ for long periods.*
ADV. largely | virtually | heretofore (*AmE, formal*), hitherto, previously ◇ *a mass of hitherto ~ material*

unused to *adj.*

VERBS appear, be, seem | become, grow ◇ *He had grown ~ this sort of attention.*

ADV. completely, quite ◇ *She was quite ~ this way of life.* | still ◇ *She is still ~ her new powers.*

unusual *adj.*

VERBS appear, be, look, seem, strike sb as | become | consider sth, find sth ◇ *It was considered ~ for a woman to study medicine.*
ADV. extremely, fairly, very, etc. | decidedly, distinctly, highly, most, particularly, truly (*esp. AmE*) ◇ *This is a highly ~ case.* | relatively | a little, slightly, etc. | by no means, hardly, not at all ◇ *It's not at all ~ to feel very tired in the early months of pregnancy.* | enough, sufficiently
PREP. for ◇ *It's ~ for a woman to do this job.* | in ◇ *The organization is ~ in several respects.*

unwarranted *adj.*

VERBS be, seem ◇ *The delay did seem ~.*
ADV. completely, quite (*esp. BrE*), totally, wholly ◇ *a wholly ~ smear campaign*

unwell *adj.* (*esp. BrE*)

VERBS appear, be, feel, look, seem, sound ◇ *He complained of feeling ~.* | become | make sb
ADV. extremely, really, seriously, very | a little, vaguely (*BrE*) ◇ *patients who just feel a little ~* | mentally
PREP. with ◇ *You should delay vaccination if you are ~ with a fever.*

upbringing *noun*

ADJ. conventional ◇ *Mine was a conventional family ~.* | good, proper | sheltered, strict | religious | Catholic, Jewish, etc. | cultural | middle-class, etc. | privileged
VERB + UPBRINGING have ◇ *He had a normal middle-class ~.* | give sb ◇ *They gave their children a strict Catholic ~.*
UPBRINGING + VERB give sb sth ◇ *Her ~ had given her the social skills to cope with such situations.*
PHRASES part of your ~ ◇ *Part of his ~ had been not to question his elders.*

update *noun*

1 the most recent information

ADJ. daily, monthly, weekly, etc. | frequent, periodic, regular | constant, continuous | the latest, recent ◇ *The 6 o'clock news provides the latest ~s.* | final | quick, short ◇ *Here's a quick ~ on the travel situation.* | live ◇ *We'll have a live ~ on the storm's progress from the experts.* | email, online | news, weather | business, stock (*AmE*), trading (*BrE*)
VERB + UPDATE give (sb), offer, provide (sb with) ◇ *The report gives an ~ on the currency crisis.* | issue | do | post, send ◇ *Employees post ~s on their progress to a website.* | get, have, receive ◇ *I get regular ~s by email.* | read, write
UPDATE + NOUN list ◇ *I added your name to my ~ list.*
PREP. ~ on ◇ *an ~ on the political crisis* | ~ to ◇ *We need an ~ to the mailing list.*

2 new improvements to a computer program

ADJ. the latest | regular | automatic ◇ *In Windows you can set up automatic ~s.* | antivirus, security | critical
VERB + UPDATE download, install ◇ *You have to download the ~ and save it to your hard drive.* | issue, release ◇ *Google had to release an ~ for the toolbar.*

update *verb*

ADV. constantly, continually, continuously | frequently, often | on a regular basis, periodically, regularly ◇ *The official site is ~d on a regular basis.* | annually, monthly, etc. | recently ◇ *They have just recently ~d their server software.* | fast, quickly | fully ◇ *The road map has been fully ~d.* | automatically ◇ *The program automatically ~s your antivirus settings.*
VERB + UPDATE try to | need to
PREP. on ◇ *Could you ~ me on how the work is progressing?* | to ◇ *Ensure that your site is ~d to the latest version of the software.* | with ◇ *The files are continuously ~d with new information.*

upgrade verb

ADV. **significantly, substantially** (AmE) | **constantly, continually** ◇ We are constantly upgrading our software to meet customers' needs. | **recently** | **easily** ◇ Users can easily ~ to the new version.

PREP. **from, to** ◇ customers who want to ~ from version 4.2 to version 4.5 | **with** ◇ All the machines can be ~d with the new processors.

upheaval noun

ADJ. **big, enormous, great, major, massive** | **cultural, economic, emotional, political, social** | **violent** | **revolutionary**

VERB + UPHEAVAL **cause** | **experience, go through, undergo** ◇ The company underwent a massive ~ after the takeover.

PREP. **during the ~, in the ~** ◇ He rose to power during the political ~s of the 1990s.

PHRASES **a period of ~**

uphold verb

ADV. **consistently, firmly, rigorously, vigorously** | **unanimously** ◇ Three judges unanimously upheld the sentence.

VERB + UPHOLD **have a duty to** | **be determined to** ◇ We are determined to ~ the law. | **seek to** | **promise to** | **vote to** ◇ The IWC voted to ~ the ban on commercial whaling. | **fail to**

upkeep noun

VERB + UPKEEP **require** ◇ The pond requires minimal ~. | **contribute (sth) towards/toward** (esp. BrE), **go towards/toward, pay for, pay (sth) towards** (BrE) ◇ The money will go towards/toward the ~ of the centre. ◇ Our taxes help pay for the ~ of the roads. ◇ My ex-husband pays a mere £163 a month towards the ~ of our son. | **afford** (esp. BrE) ◇ He says he can no longer afford the ~ of his 2 000-acre estate.

PHRASES **the maintenance and ~ of sth** ◇ the maintenance and ~ of the monuments | **responsibility for the ~ of sth** ◇ The university has responsibility for the ~ of the buildings.

uplifting adj.

VERBS **be, feel** | **find sth**

ADV. **incredibly, really, very, wonderfully** ◇ a wonderfully ~ ending for the movie | **genuinely, truly** | **oddly, strangely, surprisingly** | **ultimately** ◇ It is a warm-hearted and ultimately ~ movie. | **morally, spiritually**

upright adj.

VERBS **be, sit, stand** ◇ rows of children sitting ~ at their desks | **come, jerk, shoot, spring** ◇ Slowly the boat came ~. ◇ Polly jerked ~, wild-eyed and blinking. | **remain, stay** ◇ The flag pole wouldn't stay ~. | **haul sb/sth, heave sb/sth, jerk sb/sth, place sth, prop sth, pull sb/sth, push sb/sth** ◇ Pulling himself ~, he squared his shoulders. | **hold sb/sth, keep sth**

ADV. **completely, fully, perfectly** ◇ a fully ~ posture | **almost** | **relatively** | **rigidly, stiffly** ◇ She held herself rigidly ~.

PHRASES **sit bolt ~, stand bolt ~** (= to sit/stand with your back straight) ◇ He was sitting bolt ~ on his chair, looking very tense.

uprising noun

ADJ. **failed** ◇ the failed ~ of 1830 | **mass, national, popular** | **massive** | **bloody, violent** | **armed** | **revolutionary** | **military** | **peasant, slave, student** | **prison** | **spontaneous**

VERB + UPRISING **provoke, spark, spark off** | **stage** | **lead** ◇ an ~ led by a rebel cleric | **crush, put down, quell, suppress**

PREP. **during the ~, in the ~** ◇ He was killed in the Soweto ~. | **~ against** ◇ the 1951 ~ against colonial rule

uproar noun

ADJ. **big, great, huge** | **public** ◇ a huge public ~ over taxation plans | **international** | **ensuing** ◇ A shot was fired and in the ensuing ~ the prisoner escaped.

VERB + UPROAR **cause, create, provoke** | **imagine** ◇ Can you imagine the ~ if alcohol was banned?

PREP. **amid (an/the) ~** ◇ The trial proceeded amid ~. | **in (an/the) ~** ◇ Financial markets were in ~ after the crash of the

rouble. ◇ The classroom was in an ~. | **~ over** ◇ There was a great ~ over plans to pull down the old library.

upset noun

ADJ. **big, huge, major** | **minor** | **emotional**

VERB + UPSET **have** ◇ We had our first major ~ when Rogers was taken off with a leg injury. | **cause**

upset verb

ADV. **badly, deeply, really, terribly** | **easily** ◇ She was sensitive and easily ~.

VERB + UPSET **not mean to, not want to, not wish to** (formal) ◇ I'm sorry—I didn't mean to ~ you. ◇ Keep the volume down—we don't want to ~ the people next door! | **be likely to** ◇ This decision is likely to ~ a lot of people.

upset adj.

VERBS **appear, be, feel, look, seem, sound** | **become, get** ◇ Don't get so ~ about it! | **remain** | **leave sb, make sb** ◇ The incident had left him visibly angry and ~.

ADV. **extremely, fairly, very, etc.** | **deeply, desperately** (esp. BrE), **greatly, particularly, seriously, terribly** ◇ She's obviously deeply ~ by his comments. | **genuinely, truly** | **thoroughly** | **a little, slightly, etc.** | **clearly, obviously, visibly** | **understandably** | **emotionally**

PREP. **about** ◇ She was still ~ about her divorce. | **at** ◇ He was ~ at missing all the excitement. | **with** ◇ I think she may be a little ~ with you.

upsurge noun

ADJ. **dramatic, great, huge, massive** (esp. BrE) | **sudden** | **recent**

PREP. **~ in** ◇ an ~ in violent crime

uptight adj.

VERBS **be, feel, look, seem, sound** | **get** ◇ Try to laugh at it instead of getting ~. | **make sb**

ADV. **extremely, fairly, very, etc.** | **all** (informal) ◇ He gets all ~ if anyone criticizes him! | **a little, slightly, etc.**

PREP. **about** ◇ He's feeling a little ~ about his exam tomorrow.

up to date adj.

1 modern/most recent

VERBS **be** | **bring sth** ◇ We'll have to bring our equipment ~. | **keep sth**

ADV. **extremely, fairly, very, etc.** ◇ a fairly up-to-date image | **bang** (informal, esp. BrE)

2 having the most recent information about sth

VERBS **be, seem** | **keep** ◇ It is difficult to keep ~ with all the developments. | **bring sb** | **keep sb**

ADV. **completely, fully** ◇ Make sure the information is completely ~.

PREP. **on** ◇ Bring me ~ on their progress. | **with** ◇ We can keep you fully ~ with your financial position.

upturn noun

ADJ. **dramatic, sharp** | **slight** | **economic**

VERB + UPTURN **be on** (esp. BrE), **take** ◇ Sales are on the ~. ◇ Their fortunes have taken an ~ in recent months. | **expect, predict** | **see** ◇ Many companies are seeing an ~ in business.

UPTURN + VERB **come** (esp. BrE) ◇ We expect to be in a good position for the ~ when it comes.

PREP. **~ in** ◇ a sharp ~ in oil prices

urge noun

ADJ. **desperate, great, incredible, intense, irresistible, overpowering, overwhelming, powerful, strong, uncontrollable** | **strange** | **violent** | **sudden** ◇ I felt a sudden ~ to smash the teapot against the wall. | **instinctive, natural** ◇ an instinctive ~ to tap your feet to the beat of the music | **primal, primeval, primitive** ◇ the primal ~ to reproduce |

human ◊ *the human* ~ *to control the environment* | **biological, creative, sexual**
VERB + URGE **experience, feel, get, have** | **avoid, bite back** (*esp. AmE*), **control, fight, fight back, hold back, repress, resist, restrain, stifle, suppress** ◊ *She resisted the* ~ *to kiss him.* ◊ *I suppressed a strong* ~ *to yawn.* | **overcome** ◊ *He overcame his* ~ *to run from the room.* | **ignore** | **satisfy**
PREP. ~ **for** ◊ *Leaving him off the guest list satisfied her* ~ *for revenge.*

urge *verb*

ADV. **strongly** | **gently** | **constantly, repeatedly** ◊ *He has repeatedly* ~*d the government to do something about this.* | **publicly** | **quietly, silently**

urgency *noun*

ADJ. **desperate, extreme, great, utmost** ◊ *a matter of the utmost* ~ | **added, new** ◊ *The murders have given added* ~ *to the debate about violent crime.* | **particular, special** ◊ *The policy was pursued with special* ~ *in the 1990s.* | **sudden** | **moral**
... OF URGENCY **note** ◊ *There was a note of* ~ *in her voice.*
VERB + URGENCY **add to sth, give sth, inject into sth** (*esp. BrE*), **lend sth** ◊ *The bomb attack lent a new* ~ *to the peace talks.* | **increase** | **stress**
PREP. **with** ~ ◊ *We need to act with* ~ *to ensure his safety.* | ~ **about** ◊ *Is there any* ~ *about this?* | ~ **in** ◊ *There was an* ~ *in her movements.*
PHRASES **a lack of** ~ ◊ *We waited in the car while he checked the oil with an irritating lack of* ~. | **a matter of** ~ ◊ *The refugee situation must now be addressed as a matter of* ~. | **a sense of** ~

urgent *adj.*

VERBS **be, seem, sound** ◊ *Can you come to the phone—it sounds* ~. | **become**
ADV. **extremely, fairly, very, etc.** ◊ *Don't forget that one, it's rather* ~. | **increasingly** ◊ *the increasingly* ~ *political situation at home*

urine *noun*

ADJ. **stale** ◊ *I gagged at the stench of stale* ~.
... OF URINE **drop, stream**
VERB + URINE **pass**
URINE + NOUN **sample, specimen** | **analysis, screen** (*esp. AmE*), **test, testing** ◊ *a* ~ *drug screen for cocaine* | **output, production, volume** | **retention** | **flow** | **infection** (*BrE*) (**urinary infection** in *AmE*)
PREP. **in (the/your)** ~ ◊ *sugars in* ~
PHRASES **a smell of** ~, **a stench of** ~

usage *noun*

1 way/amount that sth is used
ADJ. **heavy, high** ◊ *high energy* ~ | **low** | **normal** ◊ *With normal* ~, *the equipment should last at least five years.* | **increased** | **widespread** | **drug** ◊ *Drug* ~ *by teenagers has increased in recent years.* | **electricity, energy, fuel, power, water** | **computer, email, Internet, Web** | **cellphone** (*AmE*), **mobile-phone** (*BrE*) | **condom**
VERB + USAGE **increase** | **reduce** | **restrict** | **monitor, track** | **measure**
USAGE + VERB **go up, grow, increase** | **drop, go down**
USAGE + NOUN **pattern** | **level, rate** | **data, information**
PREP. ~ **of** ◊ *Usage of computers in schools is increasing.*
2 way that words are used
ADJ. **common, everyday, general, normal, ordinary, popular** ◊ *That word is no longer in common* ~. | **contemporary, current, modern** ◊ *a book on current English* ~ | **actual** ◊ *Actual* ~ *of the word is different from the meaning given in the dictionary.* | **correct, proper** | **American, English, etc.** | **language, linguistic, word** | **colloquial** | **figurative**

VERB + USAGE **come into, enter** ◊ *The term 'ecotourism' entered common* ~ *in the 1990s.*
PREP. **in** ~ ◊ *The word has a slightly different meaning in popular* ~.
PHRASES **pattern of** ~ ◊ *Dictionaries show typical patterns of* ~.

use *noun*

1 using; being used
ADJ. **considerable, extensive, great, heavy, liberal** | **full, maximum** ◊ *He made full* ~ *of the opportunity to travel.* | **excessive** ◊ *a style of writing with an excessive* ~ *of metaphor* | **increased, increasing** | **constant, continued, daily, everyday, frequent, regular, repeated, routine** ◊ *the daily* ~ *of a deodorant* | **long-term, prolonged** ◊ *There is a high risk of developing side effects from prolonged* ~ *of the drug.* | **lifetime** ◊ *lifetime* ~ *of cigarettes* | **future** ◊ *The prints remain on file for future* ~. | **wide, widespread** ◊ *a campaign to encourage wider* ~ *of public transport* | **common, current, general, normal, ordinary** ◊ *This software is no longer in common* ~. | **limited** | **occasional** | **effective, efficient, good, judicious, optimum** ◊ *an efficient* ~ *of resources* ◊ *Holding a party was not the best* ~ *of scarce funds.* ◊ *The layout of the furniture makes optimum* ~ *of the space available.* | **appropriate, correct, fair, legitimate, proper** ◊ *the fair* ~ *of copyrighted material* | **clever, innovative, skilful/skillful** | **selective** | **careful, safe** | **inappropriate, indiscriminate, poor** | **illegal, illicit, improper, unauthorized** | **sustainable** ◊ *the sustainable* ~ *of natural resources* | **personal, private** | **external, internal** ◊ *This antiseptic is for external* ~ *only.* | **home** ◊ *fire extinguishers for home* ~ | **recreational** | **clinical, commercial, industrial, non-commercial** | **official** | **exclusive** ◊ *for the exclusive* ~ *of club members* | **free** ◊ *Guests have free* ~ *of the hotel pool.* | **immediate** ◊ *Only half the land was fit for immediate* ~. | **alcohol, drug, heroin, substance, etc.** ◊ *Drug* ~ *in this age group is on the increase.* | **condom, contraceptive** | **pesticide** | **land** | **language** | **energy** | **Internet**
VERB + USE **make** ◊ *We made* ~ *of the car while you were away.* | **bring sth (back) into, come into** ◊ *a technology which came into* ~ *at the end of the last century* | **go out of** ◊ *The expression went out of* ~ *some time ago.* | **enable** ◊ *Advances in battery technology would enable more widespread* ~ *of solar energy.* | **facilitate** | **allow, permit** | **legalize** | **ban, forbid, outlaw, prohibit** ◊ *the first country to ban the* ~ *of antidepressants in children* | **regulate** | **preclude** | **curb, curtail, limit, restrict** | **maximize, minimize** | **increase** | **decrease, reduce** | **discontinue** ◊ *If side effects occur, discontinue* ~. | **advocate, encourage, promote, recommend** ◊ *I don't recommend the* ~ *of chemicals in home gardens.* | **condone, sanction** | **approve, endorse, favour/favor, support** ◊ *The study showed that 75% of people favoured/favored the* ~ *of ID cards.* | **discourage, oppose** | **pioneer** | **justify** ◊ *You can't justify the* ~ *of violence.*
PREP. **for** ~ ◊ *This phone number is only for* ~ *in an emergency.* | **in** ~ ◊ *The phone is in constant* ~.
PHRASES **ease of** ~ ◊ *This model has been designed for greater ease of* ~. | **for** ~ **as** ◊ *The CD is intended for* ~ *as background music.* | **ready for** ~ ◊ *This room is now ready for* ~.
2 purpose for which sth is used
ADJ. **different** | **new** | **intended** | **potential** ◊ *The product has several potential* ~*s.* | **medicinal** ◊ *Water was reserved for drinking or medicinal* ~*s.*
VERB + USE **have** ◊ *This herb has a variety of* ~*s.* | **find, put sth to** ◊ *Can you find a* ~ *for this old table?* ◊ *Don't throw that box away—I'm sure I could put it to some* ~.
PHRASES **a variety of** ~*s* | **what** ~ **is...?, what's the** ~ **of...?** ◊ *What* ~ *is a mouse without a computer?* ◊ *What's the* ~ *of denying it?*
3 ability/permission to use sth
ADJ. **full** ◊ *the full* ~ *of your mental faculties*
VERB + USE **have** ◊ *Since his stroke he hasn't had the* ~ *of his left hand.* | **give sb, offer (sb)** ◊ *We gave them the* ~ *of our house while we were away.* | **deny sb** ◊ *They denied us* ~ *of*

the college library. | **lose** | **recover, regain** ◇ *After a while she regained the ~ of her fingers.*
PREP. **~ of** ◇ *She lost the ~ of her legs in a car accident.*

4 how useful sth is
ADJ. **practical**
VERB + USE **be of** ◇ *Could this old coat be of ~ to you?* | **have** ◇ *I have no ~ for my golf clubs any more.*
PREP. **of … ~** ◇ *It's of no practical ~ to me.* | **~ to** ◇ *Is it any ~ to you?*
PHRASES **be no ~** ◇ *It's no ~ running—the train has already gone.*

use verb
ADV. **appropriately, correctly, properly** ◇ *Credit cards, ~d appropriately, are a great financial tool.* | **effectively, efficiently, successfully** | **improperly** (*esp. BrE*), **inappropriately, indiscriminately** | **carefully, cautiously, judiciously, responsibly, selectively, sparingly** ◇ *This paint is very expensive, so please ~ it sparingly.* | **safely** | **interchangeably, synonymously** ◇ *'Ethics' and 'morality' are often ~d interchangeably.* | **concurrently, simultaneously** | **consistently, frequently, generally, habitually, normally, regularly, routinely, typically, usually** ◇ *Do you habitually ~ display screen equipment in your job?* | **mainly, primarily** ◇ *a technique that is pimarily ~d in eye surgery* | **exclusively** ◇ *an etching technique ~d exclusively by Picasso* | **liberally** | **infrequently, occasionally, rarely** | **originally** | **conventionally, traditionally** | **commercially** | **up** ◇ *The oil had all been ~d up.*
VERB + USE **be easy to, be simple to** ◇ *These garden shears are lightweight and easy to ~.* | **be difficult to, be hard to** | **be ready to** | **be likely to, tend to** ◇ *the factors that make people likely to ~ heroin* ◇ *Manufacturers tend to ~ disks made in the US.* | **allow sb to, be entitled to, let sb, permit sb to** ◇ *Candidates are not allowed to ~ dictionaries in the exam.* | **forbid sb to** | **teach sb to**
PREP. **as** ◇ *The church is sometimes ~d as a concert venue.* | **for** ◇ *chemicals that are ~d for cleaning*
PHRASES **permission to ~ sth**

used adj.
VERBS **be, look** ◇ *The board game looked ~.*
ADV. **commonly, extensively, frequently, regularly, well, widely** ◇ *a widely ~ technique for assessing the strength of metals* | **little, rarely** ◇ *a little-used path through the woods*

used to adj.
VERBS **be, seem, sound** | **become, get, grow** ◇ *Don't worry, you'll soon get ~ your new school.* ◇ *She had gradually grown ~ him.*
ADV. **very, well** | **quite** | **pretty**

useful adj.
VERBS **be, look, prove, seem** | **become** | **make yourself** ◇ *She told Fred to make himself ~.* | **consider sth, find sth** ◇ *some leaflets which you might find ~*
ADV. **extremely, fairly, very, etc.** | **enormously, especially, exceptionally, highly, immensely, incredibly, more than** (*informal*), **particularly, terribly, tremendously** ◇ *She has made an exceptionally ~ contribution to the debate.* | **genuinely, truly** ◇ *It needs to give more information to be truly ~.* | **increasingly** | **equally** ◇ *The same information is equally ~ when negotiating.* | **generally, universally** ◇ *This method has proved the most generally ~.* | **potentially** | **practically** ◇ *The subject is practically ~ and will stand you in good stead when looking for a job.* | **certainly, undoubtedly** ◇ *an undoubtedly ~ skill* | **economically, politically, socially** ◇ *to provide rewarding and socially ~ employment*
PREP. **as** ◇ *It was ~ as a short-term measure.* | **for** ◇ *This tool is ~ for a variety of purposes.* ◇ *Internet booking is ~ for people who want a short break.* | **in** ◇ *She was very ~ in dealing with foreign visitors.* | **to** ◇ *information which will be ~ to new mothers*

usefulness noun
ADJ. **limited, some** | **general** | **practical** | **potential**

uterus

VERB + USEFULNESS **have** | **increase** | **diminish, limit, reduce** ◇ *Badly written questions limit the ~ of questionnaires.* | **lose** ◇ *Many people claim that the word has lost its ~.* | **assess, determine, evaluate, examine** | **question** | **demonstrate, prove** | **outlive** ◇ *The advisory group has outlived its ~.*
PREP. **of … ~** ◇ *The theory is of limited ~.* | **~ for** ◇ *the exam's ~ for ranking students* | **~ in** ◇ *the drug's ~ in the treatment of cancer* | **~ to** ◇ *The report is of potential ~ to the government.*

useless adj.
1 of no use
VERBS **be, feel, prove** ◇ *Her efforts to avoid him proved ~.* | **become** | **leave sth, make sth, render sth** ◇ *The condition rendered her legs virtually ~.*
ADV. **absolutely, completely, entirely, quite, totally, utterly, wholly** (*esp. BrE*) | **worse than** ◇ *A computer program with too many icons is worse than ~.* | **all but, almost, nearly, practically, virtually** | **largely, mostly** | **basically, essentially** | **fairly, pretty, rather** | **seemingly** | **equally** ◇ *There are two manuals, both of them equally ~.*
PREP. **as** ◇ *A candle is practically ~ as a light source.* | **for** ◇ *The land is ~ for cattle.* | **in** ◇ *This drug is ~ in the treatment of patients with AIDS.* | **to** ◇ *The information was ~ to him.*
2 (*informal*) **weak/not successful**
VERBS **be**
ADV. **absolutely, completely** | **pretty**
PREP. **at** ◇ *I'm pretty ~ at this job.*

user noun
ADJ. **avid** (*esp. AmE*), **heavy, large** ◇ *heavy ~s of credit* ◇ *The larger ~s of the service have to pay more.* | **small** | **daily, frequent, regular** | **occasional** | **casual** ◇ *a casual ~ of cocaine* | **active** | **potential** | **current, existing** ◇ *Existing ~s will be able to upgrade their software at a reduced price.* | **first-time, novice** ◇ *They offer a short course to first-time ~s of the software.* | **experienced** | **end** (usually **end-user**) ◇ *The company supplies its computers direct to the end-user.* | **authorized, unauthorized** | **registered** | **malicious** (*computing*) ◇ *These security holes allow malicious ~s to hijack your account.* | **computer, desktop, PC** | **Internet, Web** | **remote** | **broadband, dial-up, wireless** ◇ *We'll have about 500 million wireless ~s accessing the Internet.* | **cellphone** (*AmE*), **mobile-phone** (*BrE*) | **business, corporate, home** ◇ *a computer intended for business and home ~s* | **car, public-transport** (*BrE*), **rail, road** | **wheelchair** ◇ *A special entrance is being built for wheelchair ~s.* | **library** | **service** ◇ *a survey of health service ~s* | **electricity, energy** | **drug, heroin, substance, tobacco, etc.**

usual adj.
VERBS **be** | **become**
ADV. **quite** (*esp. BrE*), **very** (*esp. AmE*) ◇ *Don't worry—it's quite ~ to have a few problems at first.* ◇ *It's very ~ for people to leave books and papers behind.* | **far from** ◇ *This kind of reaction is far from ~ in children of this age.*
PREP. **for** ◇ *It's ~ for the man to propose marriage.*
PHRASES **as per** (*informal*) ◇ *Everyone blamed me as per ~.* | **as ~, like ~** (= in the same way as what happens most of the time or in most cases) ◇ *Steve, as ~, was the last to arrive.* | **business as ~** (= things will continue as normal in spite of a difficult situation) ◇ *It's business as ~ at the factory, even while investigators sift through the bomb wreckage.* | **in the ~ way** ◇ *The metal can then be painted in the ~ way.*

uterus noun → See also WOMB
ADJ. **female**
PREP. **in the/sb's ~, within the/sb's ~** ◇ *the baby growing in her ~* ◇ *A scan determines the position of the baby in the ~.* | **out of the/sb's ~**
PHRASES **the lining of the ~, the neck of the ~, the wall of the ~**

utility *noun*

1 usefulness

ADJ. **great, high** | **limited, low** | **potential** | **overall** | **practical** | **clinical, military, social** ◇ *He argued that the arts have great social ~.*
VERB + UTILITY **have** | **maximize** | **enhance, improve, increase** | **limit** | **assess, evaluate, examine, investigate** | **question** | **demonstrate, illustrate, show** ◇ *A number of researchers have demonstrated the ~ of this approach.*
PREP. **of … ~** ◇ *This computer is of low ~ for the home user.*

2 (*esp. AmE*) service provided for the public

ADJ. **municipal, public, state-owned** | **investor-owned** (*AmE*), **privatized** | **regulated** | **large, major** | **local** | **electric** (*AmE*), **electrical, power, water** ◇ *a privatized power ~*
UTILITY + NOUN **company** (*BrE, AmE*) | **bill** (*BrE, AmE*) | **commission** (*AmE*) ◇ *regulatory agencies such as public ~ commissions*

utilize (*BrE also* **-ise**) *verb*

ADV. **commonly, extensively, widely** ◇ *an oil commonly ~d in aromatherapy* | **frequently, often** | **increasingly** | **fully, to the full** ◇ *The new computer system is not being fully ~d yet.* | **effectively, efficiently, successfully** ◇ *Are our resources being effectively ~d?* | **properly** | **primarily**
PREP. **as** ◇ *Concrete had long been ~d as a bonding material.*

U-turn *noun*

1 movement in a car

VERB + U-TURN **do, execute** (*esp. BrE*), **make, pull** (*AmE*)

2 (*informal*) sudden change of plan

ADJ. **complete** | **dramatic, spectacular** (*BrE*) | **embarrassing, humiliating** | **government, policy**
VERB + U-TURN **do, make, perform** (*BrE*) ◇ *The government has made a spectacular ~ on taxes.*
PREP. **~ on** ◇ *a ~ on education policy* | **~ over** ◇ *a government ~ over plans to cut social security payments*

V v

vacancy *noun*

ADJ. **unfilled** | **suitable** ◇ *The agency will let you know if they have any suitable vacancies.* | **casual, temporary** | **job, staff** (*esp. BrE*) | **office** (*esp. AmE*) ◇ *high office ~ rates and stagnant housing prices*
VERB + VACANCY **have** | **create, leave** ◇ *Her going on maternity leave will create a temporary ~.* | **fill**
VACANCY + VERB **arise** (*esp. BrE*), **exist** (*esp. BrE*), **occur** ◇ *A ~ has arisen in our sales department.*
VACANCY + NOUN **rate**
PREP. **~ for** ◇ *a ~ for head chef* | **~ in** ◇ *a ~ in the IT department*

vacant *adj.*

VERBS **be** | **become, fall** (only used of jobs) ◇ *A seat became ~ and he took it.* ◇ *A job fell ~ in the accounting department.* | **remain** | **leave sth** ◇ *The office of treasurer had been left ~ since her retirement.* | **keep sth** ◇ *The job will be kept ~ for a few more weeks.*

vacation *noun* → See also HOLIDAY

1 (*AmE*) period of time away from home for pleasure

ADJ. **summer, winter** ◇ *The sisters are on summer ~ with their family.* | **annual** | **three-day, two-week, etc.** | **month-long, week-long, etc.** | **extended, long** ◇ *I may go on an extended ~ to Bermuda.* | **little, short** ◇ *She needed a little ~ to clear*

her head. | **all-inclusive** | **family** | **beach, cruise, golf, ski** | **exotic, tropical** | **Caribbean, European, etc.** | **great, nice** | **relaxing** | **dream, perfect** ◇ *A Nile cruise is high on my list of dream ~s.* | **well-deserved** | **working** ◇ *The President cut short his working ~ by two days.* | **real** ◇ *He hadn't taken a real ~ in years.*
VERB + VACATION **get, go on, have, take** ◇ *She took a well-deserved ~ to Mexico.* | **spend** ◇ *She was going to spend her ~ in Hawaii all by herself.* | **come back from, get back from, return from** | **plan** | **book** | **cancel** | **could use, need** | **enjoy** | **ruin** ◇ *I hope the bad weather didn't ruin your ~.*
VACATION + NOUN **trip** | **destination, resort, spot** ◇ *Orlando is a popular ~ resort for British tourists.* | **cottage, home, house, property, villa** | **plans** | **photos, pictures** | **season**
PREP. **on ~**

2 (*esp. AmE*) period of rest from work/school

ADJ. **school** | **paid** ◇ *Military personnel receive a month of paid ~.* | **spring, summer, winter** | **annual** | **month-long, week-long, etc.** | **one-month, two-week, etc.** ◇ *Students had a two-week ~ at the end of December.* | **long** ◇ *The long summer ~ breaks the rhythm of instruction.*
VERB + VACATION **use**
VACATION + NOUN **day, leave, time** ◇ *Employees no longer have a fixed number of ~ days.* ◇ *I wasn't able to use all of my ~ time last year.* ◇ *I have put in for ~ time.* | **pay**
PREP. **on ~**

vaccination *noun*

ADJ. **flu, measles, MMR, rubella, smallpox, etc.** | **routine** | **emergency** | **compulsory, mandatory** (*esp. AmE*) | **voluntary** | **mass, widespread** | **childhood** | **booster** ◇ *I had a routine tetanus booster ~ last year.*
VERB + VACCINATION **have** | **give sb**
VACCINATION + NOUN **campaign, programme/program, schedule** (*esp. AmE*) | **rate** ◇ *Vaccination rates remain below 75% of the at-risk adult population.*
PREP. **~ against** ◇ *a ~ against tetanus*

vaccine *noun*

ADJ. **effective, safe** | **flu, measles, rubella, etc.** ◇ *The polio ~ has saved millions of lives.* | **live** ◇ *a live ~ containing the polio virus*
… OF VACCINE **dose** ◇ *one dose of BCG ~*
VERB + VACCINE **give sb** | **have, receive** | **develop**
VACCINE + VERB **protect sb** ◇ *The ~ protects babies and children against tuberculosis.* | **prevent sth** ◇ *a ~ to prevent rubella*
VACCINE + NOUN **development, research, trial** ◇ *$28 million raised for AIDS ~ research* | **production** | **maker, manufacturer** | **programme/program** | **supply** | **shortage**
PREP. **~ against** ◇ *Researchers are trying to develop a ~ against the disease.* | **~ for** ◇ *a ~ for meningitis*

vacuum *noun*

ADJ. **perfect** | **cultural, moral, political, spiritual** ◇ *The writer criticized the moral ~ in society.* | **power** ◇ *Her resignation left a power ~ in the government.* | **leadership** | **security**
VERB + VACUUM **create, leave, produce** ◇ *The machine then creates a ~.* | **fill** ◇ *Other gases rush in to fill the ~.*

vagina *noun*

VERB + VAGINA **enter, penetrate**
PREP. **in the/your ~, inside the/your ~, into the/your ~**

vague *adj.*

VERBS **be, look, sound** ◇ *'Where did you leave it?' Isobel looked ~.* | **become, get** ◇ *She seems to be getting rather ~ as she grows older.* | **remain** | **leave sth** ◇ *The identity of the city in the novel is deliberately left ~.*
ADV. **extremely, fairly, very, etc.** | **hopelessly** ◇ *Her directions were hopelessly ~.* | **a little, slightly, etc.** | **enough, sufficiently** ◇ *It was a ~ enough suggestion for everyone to be happy with it.* | **suitably** | **deliberately, intentionally** ◇ *You're being deliberately ~.* | **necessarily** ◇ *Since the officers knew little themselves their reassurances*

were necessarily ~. | **notoriously** ◇ *The law is notoriously ~ on this point.* | **frustratingly**

PREP. **about** ◇ *I am ~ about what happened during the rest of the night.* | **as to** ◇ *I was suitably ~ as to exactly how I had acquired the money.* | **in** ◇ *The statement was ~ in its wording.*

valid *adj.*

1 legally acceptable

VERBS **be** | **become** | **remain, stay** | **deem sth, hold sth** ◇ *The original written contract was held ~.*

ADV. **still** ◇ *Is your passport still ~?* | **no longer** | **legally** ◇ *Is the contract legally ~?*

PREP. **for** ◇ *These discounts are ~ for travel within the continental United States.*

2 strong and convincing

VERBS **be, seem** | **become** | **remain** | **accept sth as, consider sth, deem sth, regard sth as** ◇ *We accepted several different approaches as ~.*

ADV. **extremely, fairly, very, etc.** | **absolutely, completely, perfectly, quite** ◇ *This is a perfectly ~ question to raise.* | **not entirely** | **reasonably** | **equally** ◇ *We use a different, but equally ~, technique.* | **universally** ◇ *a universally ~ set of moral principles* | **not necessarily** (*esp. BrE*), **not strictly** (*esp. AmE*) ◇ *The agreement is not necessarily ~ in other countries.* ◇ *That argument is not strictly ~ in this case.* | **still** | **no longer** ◇ *The old assumptions are no longer ~.* | **logically, scientifically, statistically** ◇ *a logically ~ deduction*

validity *noun*

ADJ. **great** | **equal** ◇ *Don't you think that both views have equal ~?* | **doubtful, dubious, questionable** | **face** ◇ *The theory has the face ~ of being consistent with recent findings.* | **legal, scientific, statistical** ◇ *The legal ~ of the claims has been challenged.*

VERB + VALIDITY **have** | **give sth, lend sth** ◇ *His reputation lends a certain ~ to the approach that it might not deserve.* | **assess, check, determine, establish, evaluate, investigate, test** ◇ *to assess the scientific ~ of new treatments* | **confirm, uphold** ◇ *The judges upheld the ~ of the previous judgement.* | **accept, acknowledge, recognize** | **demonstrate, prove, show** | **cast doubt on, challenge, deny, doubt, question, undermine**

PREP. **of ... ~** ◇ *The results are of doubtful ~.* | **~ for** ◇ *the theory's ~ for parent-child relationships*

valley *noun*

ADJ. **broad, deep, high, large, long, steep, wide** | **little, narrow, shallow, small** | **steep** | **lower, upper** | **fertile, forested, green, lush, wooded** | **remote** | **mountain, river** | **Missouri, Thames, etc.**

VERB + VALLEY **enter, leave, reach** | **form** ◇ *The rivers Rhône and Rhine rise here and form broad ~s.* | **overlook** ◇ *The castle is situated on a hill overlooking a ~.* | **dominate** ◇ *a high hill that dominates the mineral-rich ~s of this region.* | **surround** ◇ *a ~ surrounded by mountains* | **fill** ◇ *A large cloud filled the ~ and obscured vision.*

VALLEY + NOUN **bottom, floor, side, wall**

PREP. **in a/the ~** ◇ *The house was in a wooded ~.*

valour (*BrE*) (*AmE* valor) *noun*

ADJ. **great, uncommon** (*AmE*) ◇ *a soldier famed for his great ~*

VERB + VALOUR/VALOR **demonstrate** (*esp. AmE*), **exhibit, show** ◇ *He showed ~ and skill on the battlefield.*

PHRASES **an act of ~, a display of ~** ◇ *a display of uncommon valor and gallantry* (*AmE*)

valuable *adj.*

1 worth a lot of money

VERBS **be, look** | **become** | **remain**

ADV. **extremely, fairly, very, etc.** | **commercially, economically** ◇ *commercially ~ expertise*

2 very useful

VERBS **be, prove, seem** | **become** | **remain** | **make sb/sth** ◇

They have skills and qualities which make them highly ~. | **consider sth**

ADV. **extremely, fairly, very, etc.** | **enormously, especially, exceptionally, highly, immensely, incredibly, most, particularly, tremendously, truly** | **uniquely** | **increasingly** | **equally** ◇ *The subject could be equally ~ for scientists.* | **intrinsically** ◇ *The Romantics believed that the life of the imagination was intrinsically ~.* | **potentially** | **scientifically, socially** ◇ *ecologically ~ species*

PREP. **as** ◇ *The survey was ~ as an indicator of local opinion.* | **for** ◇ *Good eyesight is a quality which is extremely ~ for a hunting animal.* | **to** ◇ *documents that are enormously ~ to historians*

valuation *noun*

ADJ. **high, low** | **detailed** | **independent** | **current** | **actuarial** (*finance*) | **market** | **land, mortgage, property** | **asset, equity, share, stock**

VERB + VALUATION **carry out** (*esp. BrE*), **do, make, prepare** (*esp. BrE*) | **get** | **base** ◇ *The ~ was based on earnings forecasts for the company in 2008.*

VALUATION + NOUN **fee, report** (*both BrE*) | **method, technique**

value *noun*

1 amount of money that sth is worth

ADJ. **high, low** ◇ *the high ~ of the pound* | **full, total** | **real, true** | **average** | **estimated** | **monetary** | **nominal** ◇ *a share with a nominal ~ of $50* | **face** ◇ *At yesterday's auction an old coin sold for many times more than its face ~.* | **residual** ◇ *a residual ~ of 10% of its original cost* | **resale** ◇ *Regular servicing will add to the resale ~ of your car.* | **rental** | **market** ◇ *Use current market ~s to determine the worth of your assets.* | **land, property** | **shareholder**

VERB + VALUE **place, put, set** ◇ *It's hard to put a ~ on a company with large assets and turnover but low profits.* | **add** | **boost, increase, inflate, raise** ◇ *They were accused of artificially inflating the ~ of the company's securities.* | **maximize** | **double, triple, etc.** ◇ *Dramatic developments on the stock market tripled the ~ of his shares.* | **diminish, lower, reduce** | **hold, keep, retain** ◇ *The piano has held its ~.* | **calculate, determine, estimate, measure, work out** | **overestimate, underestimate**

VALUE + VERB **double, triple, etc.** | **appreciate, go up, increase, rise** | **exceed sth** | **decline, decrease, depreciate, fall, go down**

PREP. **in ~** ◇ *The land has dropped in ~.* | **to the ~ of** ◇ *Paintings to the ~ of two million euros were stolen last night.*

PHRASES **an increase in ~, a rise in ~** | **a drop in ~, a fall in ~, a reduction in ~**

2 how much sth is worth compared with its price

ADJ. **excellent, good, great, outstanding** | **poor**

VERB + VALUE **deliver, offer, provide** ◇ *Our products deliver ~.*

PHRASES **~ for money** ◇ *Though a little more expensive, the larger model gives better ~ for money.*

3 importance

ADJ. **enormous, great, high, immense, incalculable, inestimable, tremendous** | **added** ◇ *It has an added ~ for native speakers of English.* | **doubtful, dubious, limited, low** ◇ *His published account of his travels is of dubious ~ to other explorers.* | **lasting** | **main, real, true** | **intrinsic** | **practical, sentimental, symbolic** | **aesthetic, entertainment** | **nutritional, nutritive** ◇ *the nutritional ~ of eggs*

VERB + VALUE **have** ◇ *The stolen necklace only had sentimental ~ for her.* | **attach, place, put, set** ◇ *He places a high ~ on marriage.* | **appreciate, realize, recognize, understand** ◇ *We began to recognize the ~ of advice from others.* | **demonstrate, prove, show** ◇ *a program which demonstrates the ~ of education* | **measure** | **question** ◇ *Many people question the social ~ of talk shows.* | **overestimate, underestimate** ◇ *You can't underestimate the ~ of networking.* | **diminish** | **enhance** ◇ *This would greatly enhance the*

~ of the book as a resource for scholars. | **emphasize**, **underline** (esp. BrE), **underscore** (esp. AmE)
VALUE + VERB **be, lie** ◇ The real ~ of the book lies in its wonderful characterization.
VALUE + NOUN **judgement** ◇ Evolutionary psychology does not make a ~ judgement about the way we behave.
PREP. **of ~** ◇ He didn't say anything of ~. | **~ to** ◇ Pottery fragments are of great ~ to historians.

4 values set of beliefs

ADJ. **dominant** ◇ the dominant ~s of a society | **conservative**, **conventional**, **traditional** | **common**, **shared**, **universal** ◇ What shared ~s do you have with your friends? | **human** | **aesthetic**, **cultural**, **educational**, **political**, **social** | **Christian**, **ethical**, **moral**, **religious**, **spiritual** ◇ We need to be guided by our moral ~s. | **family** ◇ The party's election campaign emphasized its belief in family ~s. | **middle-class**, **Victorian**, **Western** | **parental** ◇ the rejection of parental ~s by a child | **democratic**, **liberal**
... OF VALUES **set** ◇ a prevailing set of cultural ~s
VERB + VALUES **have, hold** ◇ They hold very middle-class ~s. | **cherish, encourage, foster, promote** ◇ Is it the role of schools to foster spiritual ~s? | **instil/instill** ◇ Families adhered to the ~s instilled by the church. | **embody** ◇ the principles and ~s embodied in the Constitution | **hold onto, preserve, uphold** ◇ a society that has failed to preserve its traditional ~s | **compromise** ◇ I won't compromise my artistic ~s. | **share** ◇ the cultural ~s shared by all the ethnic groups
VALUE + NOUN **system** ◇ a common ~ system
PHRASES **production ~s** ◇ a movie with high production ~s

value verb think sb/sth is very important

ADV. **greatly, highly, particularly** | **increasingly** | **positively** | **equally** | **rightly** ◇ the fear of losing the independence that they rightly ~
VERB + VALUE **come to, learn to** ◇ During my illness I learned to ~ the ordinary things in life.
PREP. **as** ◇ I ~ her very highly as a friend. | **for** ◇ Tulips are ~d for their beauty.

valueless adj.

VERBS **be, seem** | **become** | **render sth**
ADV. **completely, intrinsically** ◇ Our shares became completely ~ overnight.
PREP. **as** ◇ Some of the royal forests had become ~ as hunting grounds.

van noun

ADJ. **delivery** (esp. BrE) | **camper, transit** (both BrE) | **panel** | **burger, ice-cream, kebab** (all BrE) | **furniture, removal** (both BrE) | **cargo, moving** (both AmE) | **armoured/armored, police** (esp. BrE) | **detector, prison, riot, security** (all BrE) ◇ a TV detector ~ going round the area | **tour** (esp. AmE) ◇ Each band had a tour ~. | **news** (esp. AmE) ◇ A TV news ~ was parked at the entrance. | **15-passenger, family** (both AmE)
VERB + VAN **drive** | **park** | **load, unload**
VAN + NOUN **driver** (esp. BrE)

vandal noun

ADJ. **teenage, young** | **mindless** | **graffiti** (esp. BrE) ◇ young graffiti ~s who blight the city with their scrawls
VERB + VANDAL **deter, discourage, stop** ◇ The windows are covered with grilles to deter ~s. | **be plagued by** ◇ The station is plagued by ~s.
VANDAL + VERB **strike** ◇ The ~s struck at about 7.30 p.m. yesterday. | **attack sth, damage sth, deface sth, destroy sth, smash sth, wreck sth** | **target sth** ◇ Her statue has been targeted by ~s. | **break into sth** ◇ Vandals broke into the factory and set fire to a cabin. | **cause damage (to sth)** ◇ Vandals caused more than £4000 worth of damage. | **go on a rampage, go on a smashing spree, go on a wrecking spree** (all BrE) ◇ The pool had to close after ~s went on a

£10 000 wrecking spree. | **throw bricks, stones, etc. (at sth)** ◇ The ~s throw stones at the building.
VANDAL + NOUN **attack** ◇ This is the latest in a spate of ~ attacks on fire crews.

vandalism noun

ADJ. **mindless, wanton** | **minor, petty** | **cultural, environmental**
VERB + VANDALISM **combat, deter, discourage, prevent, stop, tackle** | **commit** | **cause** | **be blighted by, be plagued by**
VANDALISM + NOUN **attack, spree** (both BrE) ◇ The trouble-makers embarked on a £30 000 ~ spree.
PHRASES **an act of ~**

vanish verb

1 disappear suddenly and completely

ADV. **just, simply** ◇ I turned around and she had simply ~ed. | **abruptly, instantly, promptly, suddenly** | **quickly, rapidly** ◇ Her feelings of shyness rapidly ~ed. | **mysteriously** ◇ a man who mysteriously ~ed from his home last month
VERB + VANISH **seem to** | **make sb/sth**
PREP. **from** ◇ All thoughts of romance ~ed from his mind. | **into** ◇ She ~ed into the mist.
PHRASES **~ from the face of the earth, ~ from sight, ~ into thin air** ◇ At a stroke she could make things ~ into thin air. | **~ without trace**

2 disappear over a period of time

ADV. **altogether, completely, entirely, totally** ◇ Many of these old cinemas have now ~ed altogether. | **all but, almost, nearly, virtually** ◇ a way of life that has now all but ~ed | **long since** ◇ The people who built this temple have long since ~ed. | **forever** ◇ Much of the land we loved has ~ed forever. | **away**
PREP. **from** ◇ This plant is ~ing from our countryside.

vanity noun

ADJ. **human, personal** | **female, feminine, male**
VERB + VANITY **appeal to, flatter** ◇ My suggestion appealed to her ~.

vapour (BrE) (AmE **vapor**) noun

ADJ. **water**
... OF VAPOUR/VAPOR **cloud** ◇ There was a hissing sound, and clouds of ~ were emitted.
VERB + VAPOUR/VAPOR **form, turn to** ◇ The particles then form a ~. | **emit, give off**
VAPOUR/VAPOR + VERB **condense**

variability noun

ADJ. **considerable, extreme, great, high, wide** ◇ There is considerable ~ in all the test scores. | **low** | **genetic, natural**
... OF VARIABILITY **degree**
VERB + VARIABILITY **demonstrate, exhibit, show**
PREP. **~ among, ~ between** ◇ ~ among different health authorities | **~ in** ◇ ~ in crop yields

variable adj.

VERBS **be, seem** | **become**
ADV. **extremely, fairly, very, etc.** | **highly, widely** ◇ Polar habitats are harsh and highly ~. | **infinitely** ◇ These systems are infinitely ~.
PREP. **in** ◇ ~ in shape

variation noun

ADJ. **considerable, dramatic, enormous, extreme, great, major, marked, significant, substantial, tremendous, wide** | **minor, slight, small, subtle** ◇ subtle ~s of light and texture | **numerous** | **endless, infinite** | **natural** | **complex** | **random** | **systematic** | **local, regional** | **climatic, cultural, environmental, genetic, geographic, geographical, linguistic** | **annual, daily, day-to-day, seasonal, year-to-year**
... OF VARIATION **amount, degree, level**
VERB + VARIATION **reflect, show** ◇ The businesses showed a dramatic ~ in how they treated their staff. | **find, observe,**

see ◇ *Considerable ~ was found in the terms offered by different banks.* | **analyse/analyze** | **account for, explain**
VARIATION + VERB **occur**
PREP. **~ according to** ◇ *~ according to the time of year* | **~ across** ◇ *She is studying linguistic ~ across the social range.* | **~ among** ◇ *~ among the students in terms of ability* | **~ between** ◇ *~ between different accents* | **~ by** ◇ *There is little ~ by sex or social class in these attitudes.* | **~ in** ◇ *slight ~s in pressure* | **~ on** ◇ *the story is a ~ on 'Treasure Island'* | **~ with** ◇ *temperature ~ with altitude* | **~ within** ◇ *There may be striking ~s within a species.*
PHRASES **a range of ~** | **a ~ on a theme** ◇ *His numerous complaints are all ~s on a theme.*

varied *adj.*

VERBS **be** | **become**
ADV. **extremely, fairly, very, etc.** | **enormously, highly, immensely, richly, tremendously, widely, wonderfully** ◇ *a richly ~ cultural life* | **endlessly, infinitely** ◇ *an endlessly ~ repertoire of songs* | **wildly** | **increasingly** | **enough, sufficiently**
PHRASES **many and ~** ◇ *The opportunities the job offers are many and ~.* | **rich and ~** ◇ *The country has a rich and ~ culture.*

variety *noun*

1 not being the same; different kinds of sth

ADJ. **amazing, astonishing, bewildering, broad, considerable, endless, enormous, extraordinary, fascinating** (*esp. BrE*)**, good, great, huge, impressive, incredible, infinite, large, remarkable, rich, surprising, tremendous, vast, wide, wonderful** ◇ *The market sold a bewildering ~ of cheeses.* ◇ *the rich ~ of the local bird life* | **sheer**
VERB + VARIETY **add, give, offer** ◇ *Dealing with customers adds ~ to the job.*
PREP. **of … ~** ◇ *a country of great ~* | **~ in** ◇ *There is wide ~ in taste.* | **~ of** ◇ *The restaurants offer a good ~ of seafood.*

2 particular type of sth

ADJ. **distinctive** | **common or garden** (*BrE*)**, garden** (*AmE*)**, standard** | **rare, unusual** | **different** ◇ *There are hundreds of different varieties of apple.* | **new, old** ◇ *Old varieties of rose can be less resistant to diseases.* | **cultivated, indigenous** ◇ *cultivated varieties such as the damask rose* | **disease-resistant, resistant** | **high-yielding** ◇ *high-yielding varieties of rice* | **hybrid** | **grape, rice, wheat, etc.**
VERB + VARIETY **develop** ◇ *breeders who develop new varieties* | **grow, plant**

varnish *noun*

ADJ. **clear, transparent** | **gloss, glossy** | **discoloured/discolored** ◇ *The painting was obscured by discoloured/discolored ~ and a heavy layer of grime.* | **protective**
… OF VARNISH **coat** ◇ *The table needed two coats of ~.*
VERB + VARNISH **apply** ◇ *Apply the ~ evenly over the whole surface.* | **remove, scrape away, scrape off, strip, strip off**
VARNISH + VERB **dry** | **protect sth** ◇ *You need a good quality ~ to protect the timber.*

vary *verb*

ADV. **considerably, dramatically, enormously, extensively, a great deal, greatly, a lot, markedly, significantly, substantially, tremendously, widely, wildly** | **hardly** ◇ *The speed of the car hardly varied.* | **(a) little, slightly, somewhat** | **constantly, continuously** ◇ *the continuously ~ing intensities of natural light* | **never** | **inevitably, necessarily** ◇ *What can be found will inevitably ~ according to the area under study.* | **naturally, obviously** ◇ *Personal preference naturally varies.* | **systematically** | **accordingly** ◇ *The drug is available in several forms, and dosages ~ accordingly.* | **inversely** ◇ *The availability of good medical care tends to ~ inversely with the need for it.* | **geographically, historically, regionally** ◇ *Voting patterns ~ geographically.*
VERB + VARY **can, may** ◇ *Prices can ~ enormously.* | **be likely to, tend to**
PREP. **according to** ◇ *The leaf's size varies widely according to the area where it grows.* | **by** ◇ *Access to this information*

varies by social class. | **depending on** ◇ *Costs are likely to ~ depending on where you live.* | **with** ◇ *The danger of a heart attack varies with body weight.* | **across** ◇ *Gender roles ~ across cultures.* | **among** ◇ *Services offered ~ among the main banks.* | **between** ◇ *The rate of growth varies considerably between different industries.* ◇ *The doses used ~ between 2 and 10mg/kg.* | **from … to …** ◇ *The situation varies slightly from country to country.* ◇ *Its speed varies from 20 mph to 35 mph.* | **in** ◇ *The rooms ~ in size.*
PHRASES **~ over time, ~ with time** ◇ *a study of how moral values ~ over time*

vase *noun*

ADJ. **flower** | **china, crystal, cut-glass, glass, porcelain, silver, stone** | **Attic, Chinese, Greek, Ming, etc.**
VERB + VASE **break, shatter, smash**
VASE + VERB **be filled with sth, contain sth, hold sth** | **stand** ◇ *A silver ~ stood on the mantelpiece.*
VASE + NOUN **painter, painting** ◇ *Greek ~ paintings*
PREP. **in a/the ~** ◇ *flowers arranged in a ~* | **~ of** ◇ *a ~ of fresh flowers*

vault *noun*

1 strong, underground room

ADJ. **secure** | **subterranean, underground** | **hidden, secret** | **bank, museum** | **storage**
VERB + VAULT **keep sth in, store sth in** | **lock** | **open, unlock**
PREP. **in a/the ~** ◇ *The jewels were kept in a bank ~.*

2 room under a church where dead people are buried

ADJ. **burial, family** (*esp. BrE*)**, royal** (*esp. BrE*)
VERB + VAULT **bury sb in** ◇ *She is to be buried in the family ~.*

veer *verb*

ADV. **sharply, wildly** ◇ *The missile ~ed wildly off course.* | **(to the) left, (to the) right** | **off course** | **around, away, off, round** (*esp. BrE*) ◇ *The plane ~ed away to the left.*
PREP. **between** (*figurative*) ◇ *He ~ed between the extremes of optimism and pessimism.* | **from** (*figurative*) ◇ *The play ~s from loopy comedy to serious moralizing.* | **off** ◇ *The car ~ed off the road.* | **to** ◇ *The path ~s sharply to the right.* | **towards/toward** ◇ *He ~ed left towards/toward home.*
PHRASES **~ close to sth** (*figurative*) ◇ *His poetry ~ed dangerously close to sentimentalism.*

vegetables *noun*

ADJ. **green, leafy, root, salad** (*esp. BrE*) ◇ *The children don't eat enough green ~.* | **crisp** ◇ *a salad of crisp, raw ~* | **raw** | **cooked, grilled, steamed, stir-fried, etc.** | **overcooked** | **canned** (*esp. AmE*)**, fresh, frozen, pickled, tinned** (*BrE*) | **mixed** ◇ *roast pork with mixed ~* | **organic** | **seasonal** | **spring, summer, winter** | **rotten**
VERB + VEGETABLES **grow** ◇ *They grow all their own ~.* | **plant** | **pick** | **eat, have** | **add** | **wash** | **boil, cook, grill, roast, sauté, steam, stir-fry** | **chop, cut, peel, purée**
VEGETABLES + VERB **grow** ◇ *~ which grow in cooler climates* | **contain sth** ◇ *Green ~ contain calcium.*
VEGETABLE + NOUN **bed, garden, patch** (*esp. BrE*)**, plot** (*esp. BrE*) | **market, stall** | **grower** | **peeler** | **crop** | **produce** | **broth, dish, juice, soup, stew, stock** | **curry, lasagne, samosa, etc.** | **fat, oil** | **protein** | **dye** | **fibre/fiber, matter**
→ Special page at FOOD

vegetarian *noun*

ADJ. **strict** ◇ *They are strict ~s.*
VERB + VEGETARIAN **become**
VEGETARIAN + NOUN **dish, food, meal** | **cookery** (*BrE*)**, cooking** | **diet** | **restaurant**
PHRASES **suitable for ~s** (*esp. BrE*) ◇ *All our cheeses are suitable for ~s.*

vegetation *noun*

ADJ. **green** | **dense, lush, thick** | **scrub, sparse** ◇ *As we came*

closer to the desert, the ~ became sparser. | **decaying, rotting** ◊ piles of rotting ~ | **natural** ◊ Removal of the natural ~ has resulted in a loss of nutrients in the soil. | **native** | **forest, woodland** | **aquatic** | **tropical**
VERB + VEGETATION **be covered in, be covered with** ◊ The hills are covered in lush green ~. | **destroy** | **clear, clear away, remove**
VEGETATION + VERB **grow**
VEGETATION + NOUN **cover**

vehicle noun

1 used for transporting people or things
ADJ. **moving, oncoming, passing** ◊ She was blinded by the lights from an oncoming ~. | **parked, stationary** (esp. BrE) ◊ The bus crashed into a stationary ~. | **unattended** | **abandoned** | **stolen** ◊ The thieves escaped in a stolen ~. | **horse-drawn, motor** ◊ deaths from motor ~ accidents (AmE) | **electric, fuel-cell, hybrid** | **diesel, gas** (AmE), **gasoline** (AmE), **petrol** (BrE) | **fuel-efficient, gas-guzzling** | **tracked, wheeled** | **road** | **four-by-four** (esp. BrE), **four-wheel-drive** | **all-terrain, off-road, sport utility** (abbreviated to **SUV**) (esp. AmE) | **vintage** (esp. BrE) | **luxury** | **private** | **passenger** | **recreational** (esp. AmE) | **private-hire** (BrE) ◊ taxis and private-hire ~s | **commercial, delivery** (esp. BrE), **goods** (BrE), **heavy goods** (abbreviated to **HGV**) (BrE) | **emergency, rescue** | **police** | **amphibious, armoured/armored, fighting, light armoured/armored, military**
... OF VEHICLES **convoy** ◊ The president's car was being followed by a convoy of ~s.
VERB + VEHICLE **own** | **hire** (esp. BrE), **rent** (esp. AmE) ◊ Hire a four-wheel-drive vehicle—there are lots of spots to discover off the beaten track. ◊ We rented an SUV. | **drive, operate** | **park** | **impound, tow** (AmE), **tow away** (BrE) ◊ The ~ was impounded as part of the police investigation. ◊ car owners whose ~s have been towed (away) | **abandon** ◊ Sniffer dogs were brought in to follow the men after they abandoned the ~ in a ditch. | **enter, exit** (esp. AmE)
VEHICLE + VERB **break down** | **collide, crash (into sth)** ◊ Two drivers escaped injury when their ~s collided. | **run on sth** ◊ ~s running on biodiesel | **be equipped with sth** ◊ a ~ equipped with a GPS receiver
VEHICLE + NOUN **emissions** ◊ tighter controls on ~ emissions | **development, manufacture, production** | **sales** (esp. AmE) ◊ Total ~ sales increased 5% from last year. | **crime** (BrE) ◊ Vehicle crime has dropped by 16%. | **registration number** (esp. BrE) ◊ He was seen driving away and his ~ registration number was given to the police.
PHRASES **the front of a ~, the rear of a ~, the side of a ~** | **the inside of a ~, the interior of a ~**

2 sth used for communicating ideas/achieving sth
ADJ. **excellent, ideal, perfect** | **important, main, major** | **investment**
PREP. **~ for** ◊ The play is a perfect ~ for her talents. | **~ of** ◊ the main ~ of communication for students

veil noun

1 piece of material for covering a woman's head
ADJ. **thin** | **black, white** | **bridal, wedding** ◊ The bridal ~ was fringed with lace. | **Islamic**
VERB + VEIL **wear** | **take** ◊ to take the ~ (= become a nun) | **lift, pull back, remove, take off**
VEIL + VERB **cover sth, hide sth** ◊ A ~ covered her face.
PREP. **behind a/the ~** ◊ I couldn't see her face behind the ~.

2 sth that stops you knowing the full truth about sth
ADJ. **discreet** (BrE) ◊ I'll draw a discreet ~ over the rest of the proceedings.
VERB + VEIL **lift** ◊ The government has decided to lift the ~ on its plans. | **penetrate, pierce** | **draw, throw** ◊ It would be better to draw a ~ over what happened next (= not talk about it).
PREP. **behind a ~ of, under a ~ of** ◊ The work is carried out behind a ~ of secrecy.

vein noun

1 tube carrying blood in the body
ADJ. **blue** ◊ A blue ~ throbbed in his forehead. | **broken** (esp. BrE), **spider** (esp. AmE), **thread** (esp. BrE), **varicose** ◊ She uses make-up to hide the thread ~s in her cheeks. | **jugular** | **hepatic, pulmonary, renal, etc.** (all medical)
VERB + VEIN **course through, flow through, pump through, race through, run through, rush through, surge through** ◊ He felt the adrenalin coursing through his ~s. | **cut, open, sever** ◊ The philosopher Seneca opened his ~s in his bath. | **inject sth into**
VEIN + VERB **pulse, throb** | **bulge, pop out, stand out** ◊ The ~s stood out on her throat and temples.
PHRASES **... blood in sb's ~s** ◊ There's a drop of Irish blood in her ~s.

2 particular style/quality
ADJ. **rich**
VERB + VEIN **hit, strike** ◊ The team have hit a rich ~ of form recently. | **mine, tap, tap into**
PREP. **~ of** ◊ The writer tapped into a rich ~ of sentiment in the play.
PHRASES **in a different ~, in a lighter ~, in a more serious ~** ◊ Fortunately, the rest of the evening continued in a lighter ~. | **in a related ~, in the same ~, in a similar ~**

velocity noun

ADJ. **high** | **low** | **constant, uniform** | **average, mean** | **initial** | **maximum, terminal**
VERB + VELOCITY **achieve, attain, reach** ◊ Eventually, the star attained the ~ of light. | **move with** ◊ to move with a uniform ~ | **increase, raise** | **reduce** | **maintain**
VELOCITY + VERB **decrease, increase**
PREP. **at a/the ~** ◊ Light travels at a constant ~.

velvet noun

ADJ. **heavy, thick** | **soft** | **luxurious, rich** | **faded, worn** | **crushed**
PREP. **of ~** ◊ curtains of heavy crimson ~

vendetta noun

ADJ. **personal, political**
VERB + VENDETTA **conduct, pursue, wage** | **settle**
PREP. **~ against** ◊ For years he pursued a ~ against the Morris family.

veneer noun

ADJ. **thin**
VERB + VENEER **acquire, add** | **maintain** | **peel away, peel back, strip, strip away, strip off** ◊ The lyrics strip the ~ of respectability from the music | **strip sb/sth of**
VENEER + VERB **hide sth, mask sth** ◊ He managed to acquire a thin ~ of knowledge to mask his real ignorance. | **crack** ◊ For the first time her ~ of politeness began to crack.
PREP. **behind a/the ~, beneath a/the ~, under a/the ~** ◊ They're brutal people behind their civilized ~. | **~ of** ◊ He concealed his darker side behind a ~ of respectability.

vengeance noun

ADJ. **terrible**
VERB + VENGEANCE **exact, take, wreak** ◊ She is determined to wreak ~ on those who killed her cousin. | **be bent on, demand, seek, want** ◊ He stormed out, eyes blazing, bent on ~. | **swear, vow**
PREP. **~ against** ◊ He sought ~ against those who had humiliated his country. | **~ for** ◊ ~ for the murder of the princess | **~ on, ~ upon** ◊ He silently vowed ~ on them all.

venom noun

1 poisonous fluid from a snake, etc.
ADJ. **deadly, potent** | **scorpion, snake, spider, etc.**
VENOM + VERB **inject** ◊ The snake injects the ~ immediately after biting its prey.
VENOM + NOUN **gland**

2 extreme anger or hatred

ADJ. **pure, real** ◇ *a look of pure ~*
VERB + VENOM **spew** (*AmE*), **spit** ◇ *She surveyed him coldly with eyes that spat ~.* | **be filled with, be full of, drip with** ◇ *His voice dripped with ~.* | **direct** ◇ *Most of her ~ was directed at the President.* | **reserve** ◇ *He reserved his ~ for the company's bosses.*
PREP. **with ~** ◇ *She said it quickly and with ~.*

vent *noun*

ADJ. **air, air-conditioning, heating** | **exhaust** | **roof, side** | **steam, volcanic**
VERB + VENT **close, open** | **block, cover** | **install**
PREP. **through a/the ~** ◇ *Air passes through a ~.*

ventilate *verb*

ADV. **adequately, properly, well** ◇ *Make sure that the room is well ~d.* | **poorly** | **naturally** ◇ *The building is naturally ~d.*

ventilation *noun*

ADJ. **adequate, good, proper** ◇ *Inspectors checked that there was adequate ~.* | **inadequate, poor** | **artificial, mechanical** | **natural**
VERB + VENTILATION **allow, give, provide** ◇ *Holes up the sides of the jacket give good ~.* | **improve**
VENTILATION + NOUN **system** | **duct, hole, pipe, shaft, tube**

venture *noun*

ADJ. **exciting** | **latest, new** | **profitable, successful** | **costly, expensive, unprofitable** | **failed, ill-fated, unsuccessful** | **ambitious, bold, high-risk, risky, speculative** | **collaborative, cooperative, joint** ◇ *a joint-venture company* | **private, solo** | **entrepreneurial, start-up** | **business, commercial, corporate, financial, moneymaking** | **Internet, publishing**
VERB + VENTURE **embark on, undertake** ◇ *The directors of the company refused to undertake such a risky ~.* | **establish, launch, set up, start** ◇ *The company has set up a joint ~ with a company in Austria.* | **finance, fund** | **join, join in, join sb in** ◇ *His son Mark will be joining him in the new ~.*
VENTURE + NOUN **capital, funding, funds, money** | **capitalist**
PREP. **~ by** ◇ *a cooperative ~ by companies at the science park*
→ Special page at BUSINESS

venture *verb*

ADV. **cautiously** ◇ *She ~d cautiously into the room.* | **never, occasionally, rarely, seldom** ◇ *They never ~d from their buildings after sunset.* | **far, further/farther, further/farther afield** ◇ *Some of the men ~d farther out to sea.* | **close, deep** ◇ *He ~d deeper into the forest.* | **abroad** (*esp. BrE*), **back, down, forth, inside, off, out, outside** ◇ *We ~d down to the south coast over the weekend.* ◇ *A few people ~d out into the street.*
VERB + VENTURE **dare (to)** ◇ *She would not have dared ~ here alone.* | **decide to**
PREP. **away from, beyond, down, into, out of, to** ◇ *They rarely ~d beyond their local town.*

venue *noun*

ADJ. **major, popular, premier, prestigious, top** ◇ *Europe's top ~ for indoor athletics* | **appropriate, great, ideal, perfect, suitable** (*esp. BrE*) | **alternative** (*esp. BrE*) ◇ *The club must find an alternative ~ for the games.* | **unlikely** | **public** | **intimate** ◇ *With room for only 200 people, this is an intimate ~.* | **500-seater, all-seater, etc.** (*all BrE*) | **outdoor** | **home, neutral** (*both esp. BrE*) ◇ *The match will be played at a neutral ~.* | **local** | **tourist** | **concert, conference, entertainment, exhibition, music, performance, rock, sporting** (*esp. BrE*), **sports, wedding** | **Olympic**
VERB + VENUE **be, offer, provide** ◇ *The Holiday Inn provided the ~ for this year's conference.* | **find** | **change** | **hire** (*BrE*) | **play** ◇ *This is the most intimate ~ the band has played for years.* | **pack** (*esp. BrE*), **pack out** (*esp. BrE*) ◇ *The musical has been packing out ~s around the world.*
PREP. **at a/the ~** ◇ *The meeting will be held at a ~ in the south*

of the city. | **in a/the ~** ◇ *She has performed in ~s around Europe.* | **~ for** ◇ *The hall is a popular ~ for weddings.*
PHRASES **a change of ~**

verb *noun*

ADJ. **plural, singular** | **intransitive, transitive** | **active, passive** | **irregular, regular** | **main** ◇ *What's the main ~ of the sentence?* | **finite** | **auxiliary, linking, modal** | **phrasal**
VERB + VERB **use** ◇ *In this essay he has used the same ~s over and over again.* | **take** ◇ *'Government' can take a singular or plural ~.* | **agree with** ◇ *The subject doesn't agree with the ~.* | **conjugate, inflect** ◇ *Do you know how to conjugate the ~ 'seek'?* | **modify, qualify** ◇ *Adverbs modify ~s.*
VERB + VERB **take sth** ◇ *Transitive ~s take a direct object.* | **agree with sth, inflect** ◇ *Add an ending to make the ~ agree with the subject.* | **end in sth**
VERB + NOUN **ending** | **form, tense** | **phrase**

verdict *noun*

1 decision in a court of law about whether sb is guilty

ADJ. **adverse, favourable/favorable** ◇ *In the case of an adverse ~, the company could lose millions.* | **guilty, not guilty, not proven** (*BrE*) | **majority** (*esp. BrE*), **unanimous** ◇ *a unanimous ~ of not guilty* | **split** (*esp. AmE*) | **formal** ◇ *The jury returned a formal ~ after direction by the judge.* | **narrative** (*BrE*) | **jury, trial** | **appeal, inquest** (*BrE*) | **manslaughter** (*esp. BrE*), **murder** | **accident, accidental death, misadventure, suicide** (*all BrE*) | **open** (*BrE*) ◇ *An open ~ was the only appropriate one.*
VERB + VERDICT **consider** ◇ *The judge sent the jury away to consider its ~.* | **agree, agree on, arrive at, reach** ◇ *They reached a ~ after hours of deliberation.* | **announce, bring in, deliver, give, hand down, issue, pass, pronounce, read, read out, record** (*esp. BrE*), **render** (*esp. AmE*), **return** ◇ *The ~ was delivered in front of a packed courtroom.* ◇ *The coroner recorded a ~ of accidental death.* ◇ *The jury returned a ~ of guilty at the end of the trial.* | **accept** | **appeal** (*AmE*), **appeal against** (*esp. BrE*) | **overturn, quash** (*esp. BrE*), **reverse, set aside, throw out** (*esp. AmE*) ◇ *His family always insisted that the original 'guilty' ~ should be overturned.* | **uphold** ◇ *The ~ was upheld at appeal.*
VERDICT + VERB **be in sb's favour/favor** | **be in, come down, come in** (*all esp. AmE*) ◇ *The ~ came in this afternoon.*
PREP. **~ of** ◇ *a ~ of accidental death* | **~ against, ~ in favour/favor of** ◇ *We believe that the ~ against him was unfair.*
PHRASES **the court's ~, the judge's ~, the jury's ~** ◇ *The jury's ~ was unanimous.*

2 decision/opinion

ADJ. **final** ◇ *The panel will give its final ~ tomorrow.* | **general, overall** (*esp. BrE*), **unanimous** ◇ *The unanimous ~ was that the picnic had been a great success.* | **damning** (*esp. BrE*)
VERB + VERDICT **give**
PREP. **~ on** ◇ *What's your ~ on her new book?*

verge *noun*

1 very close to an extreme state

PHRASES **be on the ~ of sth** ◇ *She was on the ~ of a nervous breakdown when she finally sought help.* ◇ *He looked as if he was on the ~ of tears.* | **be poised on the ~ of sth, stand on the ~ of sth, teeter on the ~ of sth** ◇ *The company is teetering on the ~ of bankruptcy.* | **bring sb/sth to** ◇ *This action brought the country to the ~ of economic collapse.*

2 (*BrE*) piece of grass at side of a road, etc.

ADJ. **grass** | **motorway, roadside**
VERB + VERGE **mount** ◇ *The vehicle crossed white lines and mounted a ~ before being stopped by police.* | **hit**

verification *noun*

ADJ. **empirical, experimental, scientific** | **independent** | **additional, further** | **credit-card, ID, identity**
VERB + VERIFICATION **need, require** | **await** | **obtain** | **provide**

VERIFICATION + NOUN **procedures, process | purposes** ◊ *Please give your phone number for ~ purposes.*
PREP. **for ~** ◊ *The documents must be submitted for ~.*
PHRASES **subject to ~** ◊ *The credit card is then accepted, subject to ~ of the signature.*

vermin *noun*

VERB + VERMIN **consider sth, regard sth as** ◊ *Farmers regard foxes as ~.* | **attract | control, deal with, shoot**
VERMIN + VERB **infest**

versatile *adj.*

VERBS **be, prove**
ADV. **extremely, fairly, very, etc. | amazingly, highly, incredibly, remarkably, wonderfully** ◊ *This machine is amazingly ~.*

verse *noun*

ADJ. **humorous, light, nonsense, satirical | alliterative, blank, free, metred/metered, metrical, rhyming**
VERB + VERSE **compose, write | recite**
VERSE + NOUN **form | drama**
PREP. **in ~** ◊ *a play in ~*

version *noun*

1 sth based on sth else

ADJ. **current, latest, modern, new, recent, updated, up-to-date | beta** (*computing*), **early, initial, original, preliminary, prototype** ◊ *an earlier ~ of this computer software* | **demo, trial | future, later, subsequent | definitive, final** ◊ *the final ~ of the architectural plans* | **future** ◊ *A future ~ of the camera is currently being developed.* | **basic, standard | generic** ◊ *the less expensive generic ~ of the drug* | **primitive, simplified | amended, enhanced, improved, modified, refined, revamped | advanced, complex, elaborate, sophisticated** ◊ *a more advanced ~ of the initial concept* | **customized | de luxe, expensive, luxury | cheap | miniature | enlarged, larger | abbreviated** (*esp. AmE*), **shortened | compact, cut-down** (*esp. BrE*), **portable, scaled-down, shorter, stripped-down | full-blown, full-length, full-size**
VERB + VERSION **develop | bring out, come out with, come up with, create, introduce, launch, offer, present, produce, release, roll out, unveil** ◊ *The company will roll out an enhanced ~ of its operating system in the new year.* | **download, install** ◊ *You can download a free trial ~ from the website.*
VERSION + VERB **be out, come out** ◊ *The new ~ comes out next year.* | **be due out | be based on sth**

2 play, film/movie, book, piece of writing, etc.

ADJ. **draft, rough** ◊ *Keep a copy of the rough ~ of your essay.* | **abridged, condensed, edited, short, simplified | complete, full, unabridged** ◊ *Only one newspaper printed the full ~ of the speech.* | **expanded, extended | revised | official** ◊ *This is the official ~ of the painter's biography.* | **unauthorized, unofficial | hardback, paperback | print, printed, published | audio | CD-ROM, DVD, electronic, interactive, online | big-screen, film, movie** (*esp. AmE*), **musical, screen, stage, television** ◊ *The screen ~ does not live up to the original novel.* | **cover** (= of a song) ◊ *The band does a lively cover ~ of 'Johnny B. Goode'.*
VERB + VERSION **choreograph, stage | do**
PREP. **in a/the ~** ◊ *They read the novel in its abridged ~.*

3 way sth is seen/done by sb

ADJ. **accurate, faithful | popular | extreme, radical | watered-down, weak** ◊ *Theirs is a watered-down ~ of socialism.*
VERB + VERSION **sb's ~ of events, sb's ~ of the story** ◊ *She agreed to give her ~ of events to journalists.*

vessel *noun*

1 ship/boat

ADJ. **stranded, stricken | seaworthy | sailing, steam | ocean-going, seagoing | fishing | cargo, commercial, container, freight** (*esp. BrE*), **merchant | naval | escort, patrol, supply, support, survey, transport | passenger | research | foreign | enemy | high-speed**
VERB + VESSEL **operate** ◊ *He was accused of operating the ~ while drunk.* | **register** ◊ *The ~ was registered in Bermuda.* | **charter | steer | anchor, berth** (*BrE*), **moor | sink | refloat** ◊ *A salvage team failed to refloat the ~.* | **intercept, seize** ◊ *The Navy seized any ~ caught trading with the enemy.* | **board** ◊ *Police boarded and searched the ~.* | **ram** ◊ *The captain of the boat was accused of ramming a patrol ~.* | **attack**
VESSEL + VERB **be afloat** ◊ *It was one of the largest ~s afloat.* | **sail** ◊ *The damaged ~ sailed on for another 50 miles.* | **be bound for sth** ◊ *a French ~ bound for Nigeria* | **enter sth** ◊ *The ~ finally entered port after thirty days at sea.* | **leave sth | carry sb/sth** ◊ *The ~ carried a crew of 130.* | **go aground, run aground, sink** ◊ *The ~ flooded and began to sink.*
PREP. **aboard a/the ~** ◊ *They managed to haul the survivors aboard the ~.* | **alongside a/the ~** ◊ *A rescue boat managed to come alongside the crippled ~.* | **on a/the ~, on board a/the ~** ◊ *A fire broke out on board the ~.*

2 container for liquids

ADJ. **drinking | empty** ◊ *It is a scientific fact that empty ~s make the most noise.* | **ritual, sacred** ◊ *ancient bronze ritual ~s* | **bronze, ceramic, glass, pottery, wooden, etc.**
VERB + VESSEL **fill**
VESSEL + VERB **contain sth** → See also BLOOD VESSEL

vest *noun*

1 (*BrE*) → See also UNDERSHIRT

ADJ. **sleeveless | string | thermal | running**
PREP. **in your ~** ◊ *What are you doing, standing there in your ~?*

2 special clothing covering the upper body

ADJ. **bulletproof, stab-proof** (*BrE*), **Kevlar™ | armoured/armored** (*esp. AmE*), **protective, safety, tactical** (*AmE*) | **fluorescent** (*BrE*), **reflective**

3 (*AmE*) sleeveless piece of clothing worn over a shirt → See also WAISTCOAT

ADJ. **sleeveless | matching** ◊ *She wore a navy blue skirt with a matching ~.* | **denim, down, fleece, leather, etc. | embroidered | sweater**
→ Special page at CLOTHES

vestige *noun*

ADJ. **final, last, remaining** ◊ *The government has to remove any last ~s of corruption.* | **all** ◊ *The Supreme Court ruled that states had to remove all ~s of past discrimination.*
VERB + VESTIGE **lose, shed | destroy, eliminate, remove | retain** ◊ *I'm struggling to retain any ~ of belief in his innocence.*
PREP. **without a ~** ◊ *He looked at her without a ~ of sympathy.* | **~ of**

vet (*esp. BrE*) *noun* → See also VETERINARIAN

ADJ. **qualified | chief | practising/practicing | country** (*BrE*), **local | emergency**
VERB + VET **call, call out** (*BrE*), **contact** ◊ *I think we'll have to call the ~.* | **consult, go to, see, take sth to** ◊ *We had to take the dog to the ~.* | **speak to, talk to**
VET + VERB **recommend sth | examine sth, treat sth**
→ Note at JOB

vet *verb*

ADV. **carefully | fully, thoroughly**
PREP. **for** ◊ *All goods are carefully vetted for quality before they leave the factory.*
PHRASES **vetting procedure** (*esp. BrE*) ◊ *We are introducing new security vetting procedures.*

veteran *noun*

1 sb who has served in the army, navy, etc.

ADJ. **combat** (*esp. AmE*), **war** | **army, military, navy** | **decorated** (*esp. AmE*) | **battle-hardened** | **ageing/aging, old** | **retired** | **disabled, wounded** | **returning** (*esp. AmE*) | **Vietnam, World War Two**, etc.
VERB + VETERAN **honour/honor** ◊ *Were ~s honoured and adequately rewarded for their sacrifice?*
VETERAN + VERB **fight, serve** ◊ *~s who served in Vietnam* | **return** ◊ *Veterans returned to heroes' welcomes.*
PREP. **~ of** ◊ *a ~ of World War Two*

2 sb with long experience of an activity, etc.

ADJ. **battle-scarred, grizzled, long-time** (*esp. AmE*), **seasoned** ◊ *He's a seasoned ~ of the political establishment.* | **wily** | **eight-year, seven-year**, etc. ◊ *an eight-year ~ of the New York Yankees* | **industry**
VETERAN + NOUN **campaigner, leader, politician** | **broadcaster, reporter** | **actor, director** | **defender, pitcher, player, quarterback**, etc. (*sports*)
PREP. **~ of** ◊ *a ~ of numerous political campaigns*

veterinarian *noun* (*AmE*) → See also VET

ADJ. **licensed, qualified** | **chief** ◊ *the chief ~ for the Kruger National Park* | **practicing** | **local, state** | **holistic**
VERB + VETERINARIAN **call, contact** ◊ *Contact your ~ to discuss medications.* | **consult, consult with, go to, take sth to, talk to, talk with, visit** ◊ *Consult your ~ if your cat is still not eating.*
VETERINARIAN + VERB **recommend sth** | **examine sth, treat sth** ◊ *The ~ examined my pony before giving her diagnosis.*
→ Note at JOB

veto *noun*

ADJ. **effective** | **government, gubernatorial** (*AmE*), **presidential** | **line-item** (*AmE*)
VERB + VETO **have, wield** | **exercise, use** ◊ *The board can exercise its ~ to prevent the decision.* | **threaten** | **override, overturn**
VETO + NOUN **power, rights** | **threat** | **pen** (*AmE*) ◊ *The President hasn't yet used his ~ pen.*
PREP. **~ against** ◊ *The nobles had a virtual ~ against peasant candidates.* | **~ on** ◊ *The opposition parties effectively have a ~ on constitutional reform.* | **~ over** ◊ *a ~ over all political appointments*
PHRASES **a/the power of ~, a/the right of ~**

veto *verb*

ADV. **effectively** ◊ *The president effectively ~ed this measure.*
VERB + VETO **threaten to**
PHRASES **the power to ~ sth, the right to ~ sth**

viability *noun*

ADJ. **continued, future, long-term** ◊ *She is very negative about the long-term ~ of the project.* | **commercial, economic, financial, political**
VERB + VIABILITY **assess, determine, test** | **ensure** | **maintain, preserve, safeguard** (*esp. BrE*) ◊ *measures to preserve the ~ of small businesses* | **improve** | **question** ◊ *The company has questioned the commercial ~ of the mine.* | **threaten, undermine**

viable *adj.*

VERBS **be, prove, seem** ◊ *None of the projects proved financially ~.* | **become** | **remain** | **make sth** ◊ *It is only their investment that makes the project economically ~.* | **consider sth, regard sth as**
ADV. **extremely** (*esp. AmE*), **truly** | **perfectly** ◊ *a perfectly ~ form of political organization* | **potentially** | **still** | **no longer** | **commercially, economically, financially, politically**

vibrate *verb*

ADV. **gently, slightly, softly** | **violently**
VERB + VIBRATE **seem to**

PREP. **through** ◊ *The thuds ~d through the car.* | **with** ◊ *The atmosphere seemed to ~ with tension.*

vibration *noun*

ADJ. **slight** | **sound** | **low** | **high-frequency, low-frequency** | **engine, mechanical** | **seismic**
VERB + VIBRATION **cause, create, produce** | **send, transmit** | **absorb, dampen, minimize, reduce** | **detect, feel, hear, sense** ◊ *Their instruments can detect the slightest ~.* ◊ *Certain animals can feel ~s in the sand.*
VIBRATION + NOUN **frequency** | **level**
PREP. **~ from** ◊ *~s from heavy traffic*

vice *noun*

ADJ. **secret**
VERB + VICE **have** ◊ *He had only two ~s: smoking and women.* | **indulge, indulge in** ◊ *He used his inheritance to indulge his ~s of drinking and gambling.*

vicinity *noun*

ADJ. **close, immediate, near** | **general** ◊ *The murder occurred in the general ~ of where the bodies were found.*
VERB + VICINITY **leave** ◊ *The police suggested that he leave the ~ of the property.*
PREP. **in the ~ (of)** ◊ *There is no hospital in the immediate ~.*

vicious *adj.*

VERBS **be, look, sound** | **become, get, turn** ◊ *The computer wars are going to get ~ over the next few years.*
ADV. **extremely, fairly, very**, etc. | **especially, particularly** ◊ *a particularly ~ and brutal crime* | **increasingly**

victim *noun*

ADJ. **hapless, helpless, innocent, poor, unfortunate, unwilling** ◊ *He defrauded his innocent ~s of millions.* | **unsuspecting, unwitting** | **easy** ◊ *Tourists are easy ~s for pickpockets.* | **passive** | **willing** ◊ *In his fantasies, women became passive and sometimes even willing ~s.* | **intended, potential** ◊ *The intended ~s were selected because they seemed vulnerable.* | **alleged** | **primary** ◊ *Boys are the primary ~s of corporal punishment.* | **child, elderly, young** ◊ *the child ~s of the war* | **female, male** | **civilian** | **injured** | **AIDS, cancer, heart-attack, plague, stroke** | **burn** (*esp. AmE*), **burns** (*BrE*) | **genocide, Holocaust** | **bomb, bombing** | **accident, crash** | **disaster, earthquake, famine, flood, hurricane, tsunami** ◊ *The government is sending aid to flood ~s.* | **abuse, assault, crime, domestic-violence, homicide** (*esp. AmE*), **identity-theft, incest, kidnap, lynching** (*esp. AmE*), **murder, rape, terror, torture**, etc. ◊ *The helpline takes calls from child-abuse ~s.* | **the failure to protect domestic-violence ~s** | **gunshot** | **suicide** | **sacrificial** | **fashion** ◊ *She's a fashion ~ (= wears the newest fashions even if they do not suit her).*
VERB + VICTIM **be, become, fall** ◊ *ways to avoid becoming a ~ of fraud* ◊ *Her son fell ~ to tuberculosis.* | **portray sb as** ◊ *In his trial, he tried to portray himself as the ~ of an uncaring society.* | **claim** ◊ *The train crash claimed its tenth ~ yesterday when the driver died in hospital.* | **compensate** ◊ *a bill aimed at compensating ~s of air pollution* | **blame** ◊ *The cut in benefits for the unemployed is a classic case of blaming the ~.* | **aid, assist, help** | **rescue, save** | **treat** | **stalk** | **lure** ◊ *He managed to lure ~s into his car.* | **choose, select, target** ◊ *He targeted younger ~s, often single women.* | **identify** ◊ *Not all ~s have been identified yet.* | **commemorate, honour/honor, remember** ◊ *a service to remember the ~s of the terrorist attacks* | **bury**
VICTIM + VERB **die** | **survive (sth)** | **suffer (sth)** ◊ *The ~ suffered severe cuts to the upper lip.*
VICTIM + NOUN **culture, mentality** ◊ *This ~ mentality is sadly all too prevalent in our country.* | **status** ◊ *groups claiming ~ status* | **impact statement** | **advocate** (*AmE*)
PREP. **~ of** ◊ *They were the ~s of a cruel hoax.*
PHRASES **play the ~** ◊ *Stop playing the victim—you knew*

exactly what was happening. | **a ~ of your/its own success** ◇ *The small company became a ~ of its own success when it could not supply all its orders on time.*

victor noun

ADJ. **clear** | **worthy** (*esp. BrE*) | **likely** ◇ *China is looking a likely ~ at these championships.* | **surprise** (*esp. BrE*) | **eventual, ultimate**
VERB + VICTOR **be, emerge (as)** ◇ *The team emerged as clear ~s in the competition.*
PREP. **~ in** ◇ *the ~ in the contest* | **~ over**

victorious adj.

VERBS **be, come out, emerge, prove** ◇ *Osborne emerged ~ after the second round of voting.*
ADV. **eventually, ultimately** ◇ *Against all the odds, Frederick was ultimately ~.*
PREP. **in** ◇ *The socialists were ~ in the election.* | **over** ◇ *The Reds were ~ over the Whites.*

victory noun

ADJ. **big, famous, glorious, great, historic, huge, impressive, major, notable, outstanding** (*esp. BrE*), **remarkable, sensational, significant, superb** (*esp. BrE*), **tremendous** | **clear, clear-cut, comfortable, convincing, crushing, easy, emphatic** (*esp. BrE*), **handsome** (*BrE*), **landslide, overwhelming, resounding, sweeping** ◇ *His party won a landslide ~ in the elections.* | **complete, comprehensive** (*esp. BrE*), **outright, total** | **conclusive, decisive** ◇ *The army won the decisive ~ that changed the course of the war.* | **bloodless** ◇ *This series of bloodless victories won him widespread domestic support.* | **partial** | **small** ◇ *He saw it as a small ~ over the increasingly repressive policies.* | **narrow** | **dramatic, thrilling** | **shock** (*BrE*), **stunning, surprise, unexpected, upset** (*AmE*) ◇ *He surprised the nation with an upset ~ over the incumbent leader.* | **crucial, important, vital** (*BrE*) | **hard-fought** | **deserved, well-deserved** | **first-round, second-round, etc.** (*sports*) | **final-round, play-off, semi-final, etc.** (*sports*) | **back-to-back, consecutive, straight** ◇ *Of their nine consecutive victories, five have been at home.* | **hollow, Pyrrhic** | **symbolic** | **electoral, legislative** (*AmE*), **military, moral, political, tactical** | **election, re-election**
VERB + VICTORY **achieve, capture, clinch, notch up** (*esp. BrE*), **post, pull off, record, score, secure, snatch, win** ◇ *The Hungarians pulled off a surprise ~ against the Italian champions.* | **eke out** (*esp. AmE*) ◇ *Bush barely eked out a ~ in 2000.* | **assure, ensure** ◇ *They would do anything to ensure ~ for themselves.* | **seal** ◇ *A goal in the final seconds of the game sealed their ~.* | **taste** ◇ *The team has tasted ~ for the first time this season.* | **end in** | **romp to** (*BrE*), **storm to, sweep to** ◇ *The party swept to ~ in the 2008 election.* | **hail sth as** | **hail** ◇ *Union leaders hailed the socialists' ~ as a huge step forward.* | **celebrate** | **enjoy, savour/savor** | **claim** ◇ *The outcome left both sides claiming ~.* | **announce, declare, proclaim** | **gain sb, give sb, hand sb** | **deny sb** ◇ *The Dutch champions were denied ~ in a tough 2–2 draw at Porto.* | **bring, deliver, produce** ◇ *Any mistake by the Democrats could deliver a Republican ~.* | **seek**
VICTORY + NOUN **celebration, parade, party** | **speech** | **dance, salute, sign** ◇ *She made a ~ sign with her two fingers.* | **lap** ◇ *The winners took a ~ lap after the race.* | **margin** ◇ *a 98 000-vote ~ margin*
PREP. **~ against** ◇ *a ~ against racism* | **~ for** ◇ *The case was hailed as a ~ for the common man.* | **~ over** ◇ *their resounding ~ over India*
PHRASES **snatch ~ from the jaws of defeat**

video noun

1 system of recording moving pictures and sound

ADJ. **live, real-time** | **interactive** | **analogue/analog, digital** | **high-definition** | **full-motion**

VERB + VIDEO **stream** ◇ *You need a broadband Internet connection to stream ~ online.*
VIDEO + NOUN **camera, card** (*computing*), **equipment, player, projector, recorder** | **monitor, screen** | **clip, film** (*BrE*), **footage, image, montage, picture, recording, sequence** ◇ *The jury watched ~ footage of the riots.* | **nasty** (*BrE*) ◇ *The infamous ~ nasty is now a cult film.* | **playback** | **diary, documentary, interview, series** ◇ *She started making a ~ diary of her life.* | **shoot** ◇ *The band are in Iceland doing a ~ shoot.* | **channel** ◇ *I can't find the ~ channel on this television.* | **file** ◇ *Video files can be readily transmitted over digital broadband.* | **format** | **game** | **gamer** | **arcade** | **conferencing, teleconferencing** | **conference, presentation, teleconference** | **link** ◇ *The speech was broadcast via a ~ link to thousands standing outside.* | **signal** | **surveillance** | **archive** | **installation** (= type of art) | **artist**
PREP. **on ~** ◇ *The movie is already out on ~.*

2 film recorded on disk, tape, etc.

ADJ. **hour-long, ten-minute, etc.** | **amateur, home** ◇ *An amateur ~ of the crash failed to reveal the cause.* | **educational, instructional** ◇ *They produce educational ~s for learning languages.* | **music, pop** | **hip-hop, rap, rock, etc.** | **corporate** (*esp. BrE*) | **promotional** | **training** | **exercise, fitness, yoga** | **documentary** | **adult, porn, pornographic, sex** | **police** (*esp. BrE*), **security** | **online** | **accompanying** ◇ *This article and the accompanying ~ takes you through each stage step by step.*
VERB + VIDEO **create, do, film, make, record, shoot** | **manufacture, produce** | **direct** | **release** ◇ *The group's new ~ will be released next month.* | **air, broadcast** | **download, post, upload** ◇ *He posted a ~ on his website* | **capture sb/sth on, catch sb/sth on** ◇ *The thief was caught on ~ as he pocketed watches and rings.* | **rent** ◇ *We rent ~s nearly every weekend.* | **see, view, watch** ◇ *The children can sit for hours watching ~s.* | **show (sb)** ◇ *Their teacher showed them a ~ about the Inuit.* | **play** | **fast-forward, forward, rewind** | **edit**
VIDEO + NOUN **cassette, tape** (usually *videotape*) | **library, shop** (*esp. BrE*), **store** (*esp. AmE*) | **rental** | **release** ◇ *a review of the latest ~ releases* | **production** | **maker, producer**
PREP. **~ of** ◇ *a security ~ of the attack*

3 (*BrE*) video recorder

VERB + VIDEO **programme, set** ◇ *Did you remember to set the ~ for 'EastEnders'?*

view noun

1 opinion/idea about sth

ADJ. **current, prevailing** | **general, popular, widely held** ◇ *The prevailing ~ is that he has done a good job in difficult circumstances.* | **personal** ◇ *The author's personal ~s are pretty clear.* | **conflicting, contrary, contrasting, differing, divergent, opposing** ◇ *The debate brings together experts with conflicting ~s.* | **alternative** ◇ *It's well worth considering alternative ~s.* | **dissenting** | **clear, forthright** (*esp. BrE*), **strong** ◇ *He's a doctor with clear ~s on how to prevent illness.* | **favourable/favorable** ◇ *Many Americans have a favourable/favorable ~ of the Democratic nominee.* | **idealized, optimistic, positive, romantic, rosy** ◇ *Her rosy ~ of life in the country seems rather naive.* | **cynical, jaundiced, negative, pessimistic** ◇ *After his experience in jail, he has a pretty jaundiced ~ of the penal system.* | **myopic, naive, simplistic** | **realistic** | **balanced** ◇ *a balanced ~ of the subject* | **distorted** ◇ *He has a very distorted ~ of life in general.* | **correct, wrong** ◇ *So which ~ is correct?* | **broad, comprehensive, holistic** | **narrow** | **conventional** ◇ *The conventional ~ is that work is pleasant and rewarding.* | **unorthodox** | **minority** | **philosophical, political** | **Christian, religious** | **liberal, modern, progressive, radical** | **moderate** | **conservative, reactionary, traditional** | **extreme, extremist, hard-line** | **stereotypical** | **informed, uninformed** | **world** ◇ *His world ~ revolves around a battle between rich and poor.*
VERB + VIEW **have, hold** | **adopt, take** ◇ *I took the ~ that an exception should be made in this case.* | **air, articulate, communicate, convey, expound, express, make known, outline, present, put forward** (*esp. BrE*), **state, voice** ◇ *The*

meeting gave everyone the chance to air their ~s. ◇ She picked up the phone and made her ~s known to her boss. | **clarify, explain** | **discuss, exchange, share** ◇ At the meeting, we hope people will exchange ~s freely. | **advance, advocate, endorse, espouse** (formal), **favour/favor, promote** | **challenge, question** ◇ His music challenges the ~ that modern jazz is inaccessible. | **dismiss, refute, reject** | **defend** | **accept, adhere to, agree with, embrace** | **contradict, counter** | **be consistent with** ◇ Their research is consistent with the ~s expressed in this paper. | **confirm, corroborate, echo, reinforce, reiterate, support** ◇ His ~ was echoed by industry experts. | **alter, change, modify** ◇ The experience changed my ~ of myself. | **reconsider, rethink, revise** ◇ Maybe he'll revise his ~s on that a little. | **affect, colour/color, shape** ◇ the experiences which shape our ~ of the world | **canvass** (esp. BrE) | **base** ◇ They based this ~ on studies done in the 1990s. | **reflect, represent** ◇ His letter to the management did not reflect the ~s of his colleagues. | **impose** ◇ He never imposes his own ~ on others. | **respect** ◇ It's important to respect other people's ~s. | **broaden**

VIEW + VERB **prevail** ◇ This ~ prevailed in medical writing for many years. | **reflect sth** ◇ His ~s reflected those of the political leaders. | **differ (from sth)** ◇ The Reagan ~ differed radically. | **change** ◇ Nothing indicates that his ~s have changed.

PREP. **according to ~** ◇ According to this ~, economic growth occurs in protracted spurts. | **in your ~** ◇ In my ~ it was a waste of time. | **~ about** ◇ Teachers generally keep their ~s about politics hidden. | **~ on** ◇ Experts hold widely differing ~s on this subject.

PHRASES **an exchange of ~s** ◇ It's good to have a full and frank exchange of ~s. | **a point of ~** ◇ From a teacher's point of ~, activities that can be done with minimal preparation are invaluable. | **take a dim ~ of sth** (= have a poor opinion of sth) ◇ My mother takes a pretty dim ~ of my cooking skills.

2 ability to see/be seen from a particular place

ADJ. **good, grandstand** (esp. BrE), **wonderful** | **clear, unimpeded, uninterrupted, unobstructed** | **aerial** | **bird's-eye** | **back, front, rear, side** ◇ The picture shows a front ~ of the car. | **close, close-up** | **public** ◇ Tensions within the band remained hidden from public ~. | **overall** (figurative) ◇ The staff handbook gives an overall ~ of the company. | **long, long-term** (both figurative) ◇ We take a long-term ~ of the business.

VERB + VIEW **get, have** ◇ The pillar prevented me getting a clear ~ of the action. | **give sb** ◇ The patio gave an unimpeded ~ across to the ocean. | **block, obscure, obstruct** ◇ A woman in a very large hat was blocking my ~ of the parade. | **come into** ◇ A large truck suddenly came into ~. | **disappear from** ◇ They stood waving on the platform, until the train disappeared from ~. | **be hidden from**

PREP. **in ~** ◇ There was nobody in ~. | **on ~** ◇ The carriage was put on ~ for the public to see.

PHRASES **in full ~ (of sth), in plain ~ (of sth)** (esp. AmE) ◇ He was shot in full ~ of a large crowd.

3 scenery

ADJ. **breathtaking, fine, lovely** (esp. BrE), **magnificent, picturesque, scenic, spectacular, splendid, stunning, superb** (esp. BrE), **wonderful** ◇ a room with a breathtaking ~ across the bay | **commanding, dramatic, expansive, panoramic, sweeping** | **mountain, ocean** (esp. AmE), **sea** (esp. BrE), **etc.**

VERB + VIEW **afford, boast, command, enjoy, give, have, offer, provide** ◇ Most rooms enjoy panoramic ~s of the ocean. | **The large windows give fine ~s of the surrounding countryside. | admire, enjoy** ◇ a place to unwind and enjoy the ~ | **paint** ◇ On his visits he painted ~s of the town and the surrounding countryside.

PREP. **~ across, ~ over** ◇ a ~ over the valley | **~ from** ◇ the ~ from his apartment | **~ of**

PHRASES **a room with a ~**

view verb

ADV. **favourably/favorably, positively** | **negatively, un-favourably/unfavorably** | **cautiously, suspiciously, with**

suspicion ◇ These results should be ~ed cautiously. | **differently** | **objectively** ◇ Try to ~ the situation objectively. | **personally**

VERB + VIEW **tend to** | **try to**

PREP. **as** ◇ This conduct is not ~ed as acceptable. | **from** ◇ Try to ~ the situation from an American perspective. | **with** ◇ They tend to ~ foreigners with suspicion.

PHRASES **generally ~ed as sth, largely ~ed as sth, primarily ~ed as sth, typically ~ed as sth, widely ~ed as sth** ◇ He is widely ~ed as a possible leader. | **historically ~ed as sth, traditionally ~ed as sth** ◇ Slaves were traditionally ~ed as their masters' property. | **a way of ~ing sth**

viewer noun

ADJ. **television, TV** | **cable, satellite** ◇ Most cable ~s have a few channels that they watch regularly. | **casual** ◇ The first series is probably the one best remembered by fans and casual ~s alike. | **avid, loyal, regular** | **adult, young** | **average, typical** ◇ Many producers have a low opinion of the average viewer's intelligence. | **contemporary, modern** | **armchair** (esp. BrE), **home** (AmE) ◇ While fewer people are attending live sports events, armchair ~s are growing in number. | **online** | **attentive**

VERB + VIEWER **attract, draw, draw in, pull, pull in** ◇ The evening news is to change its serious image in a bid to attract more ~s. | **entice, lure** ◇ attempts to lure younger ~s to the channel | **reach** ◇ Advertisers want to reach younger ~s. | **be a hit with** ◇ The new sitcom has been a big hit with ~s. | **inform, tell** ◇ The announcer informed ~s that the game had been postponed. | **offer sth, present with sth, provide with sth** ◇ We want to present ~s with something they haven't seen before. | **entertain** | **shock** ◇ a major new drama series that looks set to shock television ~s | **alienate** ◇ The presenter's style may alienate some ~s.

VIEWER + VERB **see sth, watch sth** ◇ TV ~s saw the giant funnel of a tornado speeding across the fields. ◇ It is estimated that four million ~s watched the show. | **tune in** ◇ More than six million ~s tuned in to see the game. | **switch off, switch to sth** | **call, call in, phone, phone in, ring** (BrE) ◇ Hundreds of ~s called in to complain after the show. | **email, write, write in** | **vote** ◇ Viewers can vote for their favourite/favorite performer.

viewpoint noun

ADJ. **alternative, different, differing, diverse, opposite** ◇ The magazine likes to publish articles with alternative ~s. | **personal** | **objective, subjective** | **interesting** | **political, religious, scientific** | **conservative, liberal, minority**

VERB + VIEWPOINT **have, hold** ◇ Fischer holds a similar ~. | **express, offer, present, provide** | **reflect, represent** ◇ Individuals interviewed represented different ~s. | **adopt, take** ◇ He always takes the opposite ~ to the rest of the group. | **get** ◇ It's good to get all the ~s. | **share** ◇ I understand her ~, but do not share it. | **support** ◇ He quoted recent test results to support his ~. | **change** | **understand**

PREP. **from a/the ~** ◇ Seen from the student's ~, the exam can be frightening. ◇ From the ~ of teachers, there has been a great increase in work.

PHRASES **from a purely… viewpoint** ◇ From a purely commercial ~, the movie was a failure.

vigil noun

1 when you stay awake to care for sb, etc.

ADJ. **24-hour, all-night, constant, round-the-clock** (BrE) ◇ Since the accident, the boy's parents have kept a constant ~ at his bedside. | **bedside** (esp. BrE) ◇ His fiancée kept a bedside ~ during his weeks in intensive care. | **lonely** ◇ For three nights he maintained his lonely ~.

VERB + VIGIL **keep, maintain, stand**

PREP. **~ over** ◇ the husband's ~ over his dying wife

2 silent political protest; time of prayer

ADJ. **candlelight** (esp. AmE), **candlelit** (esp. BrE) ◇ Protesters

held a candlelight/candlelit ~ against the war. | **silent** ◇ *a silent ~ outside the presidential palace* | **prayer** | **peace**
VERB + VIGIL **hold** | **organize** | **attend**
PREP. **~ for** ◇ *a ~ for the murdered politician*

vigilance noun

ADJ. **constant, continued, eternal** | **extra, heightened, increased** ◇ *You should exercise extra ~ about locking your car.*
VERB + VIGILANCE **exercise, increase, maintain** | **relax** ◇ *The birds cannot afford to relax their ~ against predators.* | **require**
PREP. **~ against** ◇ *~ against shoplifters* | **~ on the part of sb** ◇ *Guaranteeing the safety of students requires continued ~ on the part of teachers.*
PHRASES **a need for ~**

vigilant adj.

VERBS **be, keep, remain, stay** | **become**
ADV. **extremely, very** | **especially, particularly** | **constantly, ever** ◇ *The organization is ever ~ for threats to the habitats of birds.*
PREP. **about** ◇ *Be extra ~ about what you eat or drink.* | **against** ◇ *You need to be ~ against garden pests.*

vigorous adj.

VERBS **be** | **become**
ADV. **extremely, fairly, very, etc.** ◇ *They are leading a very ~ campaign to get the chairman removed.* | **particularly**
PREP. **in** ◇ *The group is not ~ enough in its opposition to the proposals.*

vigour (BrE) (AmE vigor) noun

ADJ. **increased, increasing** | **fresh, new, renewed** ◇ *He returned to work with a sense of renewed ~.* | **great** | **youthful** | **intellectual, physical**
VERB + VIGOUR/VIGOR **regain, restore** | **lack**
PREP. **with ~** ◇ *The government gave assurances that the investigation would be pursued with ~.*
PHRASES **full of ~** ◇ *She was a wonderful, bubbly girl, full of ~.* | **vim and ~** ◇ *He set to his task with renewed vim and ~.* | **with equal ~** ◇ *She attacked both parties with equal ~.*

villa noun

ADJ. **grand, luxurious, luxury, magnificent, sumptuous** (*esp. BrE*) | **country, seaside** (*esp. BrE*), **suburban** | **private, rental** (*AmE*), **rented** | **holiday** (*BrE*), **self-catering** (*BrE*), **vacation** (*AmE*) | **four-bedroom, two-storey/two-story, etc.** | **detached** (*BrE*) | **Roman** | **Italian, Mediterranean, Tuscan, etc.**
VERB + VILLA **have, own** | **build** | **rent** | **live in, stay in**
VILLA + NOUN **holiday** (*BrE*)
PREP. **in a/the ~** ◇ *He invited Brad to stay in his Italian ~.*

village noun

ADJ. **big, large** | **little, small, tiny** | **ancient, historic, medieval, old** | **poor** | **attractive, beautiful, picturesque, pretty, quaint** | **peaceful, quiet, sleepy** | **local, nearby, neighbouring/neighboring, surrounding** ◇ *The flood affected the town and surrounding ~s.* | **isolated, outlying, remote** | **country, rural** | **urban** | **coastal, seaside** (*esp. BrE*) | **mountain** | **abandoned, deserted** | **home** (*esp. BrE*), **native** ◇ *She married a man from her home ~.* | **agricultural, farming, fishing, mining** | **holiday** (*BrE*) | **retirement** | **Olympic** | **global** (*figurative*) ◇ *Technology has turned the world into a global ~.*
VILLAGE + NOUN **community, life** | **church, green** (*esp. BrE*), **hall** (*esp. BrE*), **market, post office** (*esp. BrE*), **pub** (*BrE*), **school, shop** (*esp. BrE*), **square, street** | **centre/center** | **resident** | **baker, blacksmith, priest, etc.** | **chief, elder, leader** | **council** | **idiot**
PREP. **in a/the ~** ◇ *They live in a farming ~.* | **outside a/the ~** ◇ *Our cottage is just outside the ~.*

villain noun

ADJ. **movie, pantomime** (*BrE*), **screen** ◇ *He doesn't fit the standard stereotype of a movie ~.* | **evil** | **great** ◇ *The Queen in 'Snow White' is one of film's greatest ~s.* | **real, true** ◇ *He felt that the insurance companies were the real ~s in all this.*
VERB + VILLAIN **cast sb as** ◇ *She seems to have cast me as the ~ in her latest emotional upheaval.* | **play** ◇ *He has played ~s in most of his movies.* | **catch** (*esp. BrE*) ◇ *The police still haven't caught the ~.*
PHRASES **the ~ of the piece** ◇ *He changed his story to make his wife appear the ~ of the piece.*

vintage noun

ADJ. **fine, great, superb** (*esp. BrE*) | **rare** | **recent** ◇ *a film of such recent ~*
PREP. **~ of** ◇ *the youngest ~s of wines*

violate verb

ADV. **blatantly, flagrantly** ◇ *They have flagrantly ~d the treaty.* | **clearly** ◇ *Some companies have clearly ~d the rules.* | **allegedly** | **repeatedly, routinely, systematically** ◇ *The peace of this island community has been repeatedly ~d.*

violation noun

ADJ. **blatant, clear, flagrant, obvious** ◇ *The attack on civilians is a flagrant ~ of the peace agreement.* | **egregious** (*formal, esp. AmE*), **grave, gross, major, massive, serious** | **minor** | **direct** ◇ *practices that are in direct ~ of the Geneva Conventions* | **technical** (*esp. AmE*) ◇ *a technical ~ of law* | **systematic, wholesale** (*esp. AmE*), **widespread** | **continued, repeated** | **alleged** | **civil liberties** (*esp. AmE*), **civil rights** (*esp. AmE*), **human rights** | **privacy** | **ethical** (*esp. AmE*) | **code, law, rule** (*all esp. AmE*) ◇ *He had been fined for building code ~s.* ◇ *arrests for drug law ~s* | **criminal** (*esp. AmE*) | **drug** (*AmE*) ◇ *Nearly 60% of all arrests are for drug ~s.* | **traffic** | **copyright, trademark** | **parole, probation** (*both esp. AmE*) | **immigration, visa** (*both esp. AmE*) | **safety, security** (*both esp. AmE*) ◇ *fines for safety ~s* | **antitrust** (*AmE*)
VERB + VIOLATION **commit** ◇ *The army was accused of committing ~s against the accord.* | **be, constitute** ◇ *This action constitutes a ~ of international law.* | **report** | **detect, find** | **investigate** | **ignore** | **avoid, prevent**
PREP. **in ~ of** ◇ *There is plenty of evidence that her actions were in ~ of an earlier contract.* | **~ against** ◇ *~s against minimum wage agreements*

violence noun

1 hurting other people physically

ADJ. **considerable, excessive, extreme, great, large-scale, serious** | **fresh** ◇ *There are fears of fresh ~ if the strike continues.* | **escalating, growing** | **continuing, ongoing** | **gratuitous, unnecessary** ◇ *Letters poured in complaining about the gratuitous ~ on the show.* | **indiscriminate, random, mindless, senseless, wanton** | **brutal, deadly, horrific, lethal** ◇ *We need to bring an end to the deadly ~ in the region.* | **graphic** ◇ *There was surprisingly little graphic ~ in the film.* | **criminal, unlawful** (*BrE*) | **endemic, widespread** ◇ *attempts to rescue the country from endemic ~* | **sporadic** ◇ *In spite of sporadic ~, polling was largely orderly.* | **physical, sexual** | **domestic, family, marital** (*AmE*), **partner** (*AmE*) | **hate** ◇ *a wave of hate ~ and discrimination against migrant workers* | **interpersonal** | **communal, ethnic, racial, sectarian** | **anti-gay, anti-Semitic, etc.** | **drug-related, gang-related, etc.** | **insurgent, political, revolutionary, terrorist** | **school, workplace** | **urban** | **gun** | **gang, mob** | **male, teen** (*AmE*), **teenage, youth**
... OF VIOLENCE **level**
VERB + VIOLENCE **commit, employ, engage in, inflict, perpetrate, resort to, turn to, use** ◇ *people who inflict ~ on animals* ◇ *~ perpetrated by the army* ◇ *The peasants believed their only choice was to resort to ~.* ◇ *Under no circumstances should police use ~ against protesters.* | **suffer** ◇ *She had*

suffered years of ~ and abuse. | **witness** ◊ *Children who witness ~ between parents often develop problems.* | **encourage, fuel, incite, promote, provoke** | **advocate** | **condemn, denounce, hate, reject, renounce** | **threaten** ◊ *Charlie was threatening ~ against them both.* | **condone, justify** ◊ *They use their religion to justify ~* | **glorify** ◊ *Don't buy toys that glorify ~.* | **breed** ◊ *Hatred breeds ~.* | **spill over into** ◊ *The enthusiasm of the protest spilled over into ~.* | **contain, control** ◊ *UN peacekeepers are struggling to contain the escalating ~.* | **curb, end, quell, stop** ◊ *Troops were called in to quell the ~.* | **be capable of** ◊ *We are all capable of ~ in certain circumstances.*

VIOLENCE + VERB **break out, erupt, flare, occur, take place** ◊ *Violence erupted outside the prison last night.* | **affect sb/sth** | **kill sb** ◊ *Political ~ killed 29 people last week.* | **mar sth** ◊ *The demonstration was marred by ~.* | **threaten sth** ◊ *TV ~ threatens the health and welfare of young people.* | **escalate, increase, intensify** ◊ *Observers have warned that the ~ could escalate into armed conflict.* | **spread** | **continue**

PREP. **~ against** ◊ *~ against police officers* | **~ among** ◊ *~ among young men* | **~ between** ◊ *~ between rival ethnic groups* | **~ towards/toward** ◊ *~ towards/toward ethnic minorities* | **~ within** ◊ *~ within the family*

PHRASES **an act of ~** ◊ *Any act of ~ against another player must be punished.* | **an end to ~** ◊ *The former leader of the terrorist group has called for an end to the ~.* | **an eruption of ~, an outbreak of ~, an upsurge in ~, a wave of ~** ◊ *The police are bracing themselves for an outbreak of ~.* | **fear of ~** | **a life of ~** ◊ *It was a predictable death for a man who had lived a life of ~.* | **men of ~** ◊ *the men of ~ who start wars* | **an outburst of ~** ◊ *He had a short temper and was prone to outbursts of ~.* | **the threat of ~** | **a victim of ~** ◊ *a refuge for victims of domestic ~* | **violence begets violence, violence breeds violence** ◊ *We have to make people realize that violence only begets more violence.*

2 physical/emotional force

ADJ. **suppressed**
PREP. **with (a) ~** ◊ *He kissed her with suppressed ~.*

violent *adj.*

1 using physical strength intended to hurt/kill

VERBS **be** | **become, get, grow, turn** ◊ *She started to get ~.*
ADV. **extremely, fairly, very, etc.** | **exceptionally, incredibly, particularly** | **increasingly** | **gratuitously** ◊ *The movie is contrived, sentimental and gratuitously ~.* | **potentially** ◊ *Employees are trained to deal with potentially ~ incidents.* | **inherently** ◊ *the question of whether humans are inherently ~* | **physically, sexually** | **graphically** ◊ *a range of graphically ~ video games*
PREP. **to, towards/toward** ◊ *He was ~ towards/toward his wife on several occasions.*

2 very strong

VERBS **be** | **become**
ADV. **extremely, fairly, very, etc.** | **exceptionally** ◊ *an exceptionally ~ storm* | **almost** ◊ *He felt a strong, almost ~, dislike for the stranger.*

violin *noun*

ADJ. **first, second** (in an orchestra) | **solo** ◊ *Bach's sonatas and partitas for solo ~* | **Stradivarius** | **electric**
VERB + VIOLIN **tune**
VIOLIN + NOUN **bow, string** | **case** | **family** ◊ *The cello is a member of the ~ family.*
→ Special page at MUSIC

virginity *noun*

VERB + VIRGINITY **lose** | **take, take away** (*both literary*) ◊ *the man who had taken her ~*

virtue *noun*

ADJ. **cardinal, great, important, real** | **chief, primary** | **heroic** | **inherent** ◊ *There is, of course. no inherent ~ in moderation.* | **old-fashioned, traditional** ◊ *He understands the traditional ~ of hard work.* | **Christian, ethical, moral, theological** ◊ *the theological ~s of faith, hope and charity* |

intellectual, political, social | **civic, public** | **domestic** ◊ *She was seen as a paragon of domestic ~.* | **personal** (*esp. AmE*), **private** | **human** | **female, feminine, manly, masculine** | **easy** ◊ *women of easy ~* (= with low standards of sexual morality)

VERB + VIRTUE **have, possess** ◊ *Her book has the cardinal ~ of simplicity.* | **embody** ◊ *Philippe embodies the French ~s of charm and grace.* | **cultivate, practise/practice** ◊ *He taught his children to practise/practice the ~s of temperance and chastity.* | **espouse, extol, preach, promote, tout** (*esp. AmE*) ◊ *He never stops extolling the ~s of the free market.* | **inculcate, teach** | **celebrate** ◊ *a story celebrating the ~s of democracy*

PHRASES **make a ~ of necessity** (= to manage to gain an advantage from sth you have to do and cannot avoid) | **a paragon of ~** ◊ *It would have taken a paragon of ~ not to feel jealous.*

virus *noun*

1 sth that causes disease; a disease

ADJ. **deadly, killer, lethal** | **nasty** | **virulent** | **infectious** | **AIDS, flu, hepatitis, herpes, HIV, measles, etc.** | **airborne** | **live** | **computer, email**
VERB + VIRUS **be infected with, catch, contract, get** | **carry** | **pass, pass on, spread, transmit** ◊ *An infected person can pass the ~ to others.* | **isolate** | **inactivate** | **fight** | **detect, discover, identify**
VIRUS + VERB **infect sb/sth** | **attack sb/sth, kill sb/sth** ◊ *The ~ attacks cells in the body.* | **cause sth** | **mutate** | **spread** | **replicate (itself)**
VIRUS + NOUN **infection** | **vaccine** | **transmission**

2 computer virus

ADJ. **computer, email**
VERB + VIRUS **be infected with** | **create, develop, write** ◊ *to write computer ~es*
VIRUS + VERB **attack sth, destroy sth** | **spread**
VIRUS + NOUN **threat, warning** | **protection, scanner** | **writer**

visa *noun*

ADJ. **entry, exit, transit** | **student, tourist, travel, work** | **permanent, temporary** | **valid**
VERB + VISA **get, obtain** ◊ *I obtained a ~ after hours of waiting at the embassy.* | **extend, renew** | **give sb, grant (sb), issue, issue sb, issue sb with** | **deny sb, refuse sb** ◊ *She was refused a ~ because of her criminal record.* | **revoke** | **need, require** ◊ *Do Brazilians need a ~ to go to France?* | **stamp** | **check** | **overstay** ◊ *He was arrested for overstaying his ~.*
VISA + VERB **expire** ◊ *Her ~ expired six months ago.*
VISA + NOUN **regulations, requirements, restrictions** | **application** | **applicant, holder** | **violation** | **waiver** ◊ *a ~ waiver program*
PREP. **on a ~** ◊ *She entered the country on a student ~.* | **~ for** ◊ *Do you need a ~ for Egypt?*

visibility *noun*

1 how far you can see

ADJ. **clear** (*esp. BrE*), **excellent, good** | **limited, low, poor, zero**
VERB + VISIBILITY **reduce** ◊ *The sand reduced ~ to a hundred yards.*
VISIBILITY + VERB **be down to sth** ◊ *Visibility was down to 25 yards.*
PREP. **in … ~** ◊ *We set a course in good ~ and calm seas.*

2 fact of being well known by the public

ADJ. **good, high** | **greater, increased, increasing** | **public** | **international, national**
VERB + VISIBILITY **enhance, improve, increase, raise** ◊ *We aim to raise the ~ of ethnic minorities in our organization.* | **gain** | **give, provide**

visible *adj.*

VERBS **be** | **become** | **remain, stay** ◊ *The scars remained ~ all*

her life. | **leave sth, make sth** ◇ *We cut the trees down to make the lake ~ from the house.*
ADV. **all too, clearly, easily, highly, particularly, plainly, readily, very** ◇ *His relief was all too ~.* ◇ *The election poster was clearly ~ from the street.* ◇ *Italy has a highly ~ environmental movement.* | **completely, fully, quite** ◇ *The tide was now out, leaving the wreck fully ~.* ◇ *Ellie's quite ~ embarrassment* | **just** ◇ *The mountains were just ~, dusky and black.* | **barely, hardly, scarcely** ◇ *The flat boats were barely ~.* | **almost** | **partially** | **dimly, faintly** ◇ *A figure was dimly ~ in the evening gloom.* | **immediately** ◇ *Women are advised to wait where they are not immediately ~ to approaching traffic.* | **still** | **no longer**
PREP. **from** ◇ *Their house is not ~ from the street.* | **through** ◇ *Visible through the window is a row of small houses.* | **to** ◇ *Its contents were ~ to all of them.*
PHRASES **~ to the naked eye** ◇ *tiny spiders that are hardly ~ to the naked eye*

vision noun

1 ability to see

ADJ. **20/20, excellent, perfect** ◇ *The eye test shows she has perfect ~.* | **normal** | **clear, sharp** (*esp. AmE*) ◇ *The rain prevented her having clear ~ of the road ahead.* | **blurred, blurry** (*esp. AmE*), **distorted, impaired, poor** | **double, tunnel** (*often figurative*) | **binocular, stereoscopic** | **heat, X-ray** | **distance** ◇ *I can read without glasses, but my distance ~ is poor.* | **night** | **colour/color** | **peripheral** ◇ *Use your peripheral ~ widely when moving from place to place.* | **machine**
VERB + VISION **have** | **give (sb)** | **block, obscure, restrict** | **distort, impair** | **blind, blur, cloud** ◇ *The tears blurred her ~.* | **fill, flood** | **clear, improve, sharpen** | **correct** | **lose** | **restore** | **regain**
VISION + VERB **blur, fade, swim** | **go black, go blank, go blurry** | **clear** ◇ *Her ~ cleared and she realized Niall was standing beside her.* | **disappear** | **return**
PREP. **across your ~** ◇ *A bird shot across her ~.*
PHRASES **your field of ~** ◇ *She was aware of shapes moving across her field of ~.* | **your line of ~** ◇ *Someone was standing in my line of ~ so I couldn't see the screen.*

2 picture in your imagination

ADJ. **disturbing, horrible, nightmarish, strange** | **bleak** | **inner, mental, spiritual** | **mystic, mystical, prophetic, religious** ◇ *A young girl in the town experienced a prophetic ~.* | **poetic** | **apocalyptic** ◇ *an apocalyptic ~ of the end of civilization* | **sudden**
VERB + VISION **experience, have, receive** ◇ *I had ~s of us getting hopelessly lost.* | **conjure, conjure up** ◇ *The name 'Las Vegas' conjures up a ~ of casinos.*
VISION + VERB **disappear, fade** ◇ *As he approached, the ~ faded and there was no one there.*
PREP. **in a/the ~** ◇ *The idea came to her in a ~.* | **~ of**

3 ability to see/plan for the future

ADJ. **grand, great** | **artistic, creative, imaginative** | **alternative** | **singular, unique** | **broad, comprehensive, global, wide** ◇ *The company needs to develop a global ~.* | **narrow** | **overall** | **personal** | **clear** ◇ *The engineers had a clear ~ of what they wanted to achieve.* | **compelling** | **bold, radical** | **common, shared** ◇ *They share a common ~ for the development of health services.* | **strategic** | **political** | **revolutionary** | **moral** | **romantic, Utopian** | **long-term**
VERB + VISION **have, possess** | **lack** | **create, develop** | **achieve, fulfil/fulfill, implement, realize** | **articulate, communicate, convey, describe, lay out, outline, present** ◇ *He outlined his ~ for the new economic order.* | **promote** | **pursue** | **impose** ◇ *The new leader set about imposing his ~ on the party.* | **offer** | **share** | **embrace** | **cloud** ◇ *He was determined not to let emotions cloud his ~.*
PREP. **of ~** ◇ *a statesman of great ~* | **~ for** ◇ *a ~ for the future* | **~ of** ◇ *an alternative ~ of society*
PHRASES **breadth of ~** ◇ *His plans for the country's future show a remarkable breadth of ~.*

ADJ. **brief, fleeting** (*esp. BrE*), **flying** (*BrE*), **quick, short** | **little** ◇ *I think it's time we paid him a little ~.* | **extended, lengthy, long** | **eight-day, hour-long, weekend, etc.** | **regular** | **routine** | **frequent, repeated** ◇ *She enjoyed the frequent ~s of her grandchildren.* | **infrequent, occasional, periodic, rare** | **annual, daily, twice-weekly, etc.** | **repeat** | **recent** | **last, previous** | **forthcoming** (*esp. BrE*), **impending, upcoming** (*AmE*) ◇ *The President has been briefed in preparation for his forthcoming ~ to Russia.* | **exchange** (*esp. BrE*), **reciprocal, return** ◇ *Exchange ~s between company and school have kept the project going.* ◇ *They came here last week, and we'll pay them a return ~ in the summer.* | **surprise, unannounced, unexpected** | **planned, scheduled** | **unwelcome** | **casual** | **formal, ministerial** (*esp. BrE*), **official, presidential, royal, state** | **high-profile** | **family, private, social, unofficial** | **foreign, overseas** (*both esp. BrE*) | **personal** ◇ *Following her letter of complaint, she received a personal ~ from the store manager.* | **home** (*BrE*) ◇ *You should receive a home ~ from your midwife within a month.* | **hospital, prison** | **dental, doctor's, emergency-room, medical, office** (*all AmE*) | **first, initial** | **follow-up** | **educational** (*esp. BrE*), **study** | **fact-finding** (*esp. BrE*), **research** | **inspection** | **on-site, site** | **campus** (*AmE*), **school** | **memorable**
VERB + VISIT **conduct** (*formal*), **go on, make, pay sb, take, undertake** (*formal, esp. BrE*) ◇ *We used to go on school ~s to museums and historical buildings.* ◇ *How many doctors are still able to make home ~s?* ◇ *Pay us a ~ next time you're in town.* | **get, have, receive** | **look forward to** ◇ *I'd been looking forward to my friend's ~ for some time.* | **arrange, organize, plan, schedule** | **postpone** | **cancel** | **cut short** ◇ *He was forced to cut short a ~ to North America.* | **announce** ◇ *We received a letter announcing a ~ from government inspectors.* | **be (well) worth** ◇ *If you're staying in Rome, Ostia is well worth a ~.*
PREP. **during a/the ~, on a/the ~** ◇ *On one of her regular ~s home, she told her parents she was engaged.* | **~ from** ◇ *We had a ~ from somebody collecting for charity.* | **~ to** ◇ *a ~ to the dentist* | **~ with** (*AmE*) ◇ *He thought back to his ~ with the doctor.*

visit verb

ADV. **frequently, often, regularly** | **occasionally, sometimes** | **rarely** | **personally** | **online**
VERB + VISIT **come to, go to** ◇ *My parents are coming to ~ me next week.* ◇ *We've just been to ~ my grandparents.* | **decide to, hope to, intend to, plan to, promise to, want to, wish to** | **be expected to, be likely to** ◇ *A million people are expected to ~ the museum over the next 12 months.* | **invite sb to, urge sb to**
PREP. **with** ◇ *Come and ~ with me sometime.*

visitor noun

ADJ. **frequent, regular** | **occasional** | **seasonal** | **rare** | **casual** | **first-time** ◇ *First-time ~s to Spain are often surprised by how late people eat.* | **welcome** | **surprise, unexpected** | **uninvited, unwanted, unwelcome** | **potential, prospective** ◇ *The latest crime figures are likely to put off prospective ~s to the city.* | **foreign, international, overseas** | **important** | **annual** | **business** (*esp. BrE*), **holiday** (*BrE*) | **museum, park** | **home, hospital, prison** (*all esp. BrE*) | **health** (*BrE*) ◇ *The baby's weight is monitored by the health ~.* | **site, website**
VERB + VISITOR **get, have, receive** ◇ *Do you get many ~s?* | **expect** ◇ *I could see he was expecting ~s.* | **greet, welcome** | **entertain** ◇ *The front room was used mainly for entertaining ~s.* | **attract, bring, bring in, draw, lure** ◇ *The festival brings 5 000 ~s to the town every year.* | **want** | **deter** (*esp. BrE*) ◇ *The lack of facilities in the town may deter the casual ~.* | **admit** ◇ *The college only admits ~s in organized groups.*
VISITOR + VERB **come, flock, turn up** (*BrE*) ◇ *Visitors flocked to see the show.* | **be interested in sth**
VISITOR + NOUN **bureau** (*AmE*), **centre/center** ◇ *Pick up a free map of the town from the ~ centre/center.* | **attraction** | **information** | **experience** | **numbers**
PHRASES **encourage ~s to do sth, invite ~s to do sth** ◇

Visitors are invited to browse around the farm site. | **give ~s sth, offer ~s sth** ◇ *The museum gives ~s a glimpse of the composer's life.*
PREP. **~ from** ◇ *Visitors from Ireland will find much that reminds them of home.* | **~ to** ◇ *~s to the museum*

visualize (BrE also **-ise**) verb

ADV. **easily**
VERB + VISUALIZE **be able to, be unable to, can** ◇ *I could ~ the scene in the office.* | **try to** | **be easy to** | **be difficult to, be hard to** ◇ *It is difficult to ~ how the town must have looked years ago.*
PREP. **as** ◇ *I ~d him as a typical businessman.*

vital adj.

VERBS **be, prove, seem** | **become** | **remain** | **consider sth, regard sth as** (*esp. BrE*), **see sth as**
ADV. **particularly, really, very** | **absolutely** | **strategically** ◇ *the strategically ~ industrial zone*
PREP. **for** ◇ *Team spirit is ~ for success.* | **to** ◇ *These nutrients are absolutely ~ to good health.*

vitality noun

ADJ. **enormous, great, sheer, tremendous** ◇ *You have to admire the sheer ~ of his performance.* | **renewed** | **continued, continuing** | **cultural, economic, rhythmic** (of music)
VERB + VITALITY **burst with** ◇ *They came back from their honeymoon bursting with ~.* | **restore** | **maintain** | **increase** | **lack** | **lose**
PHRASES **full of ~** | **a lack of ~**

vitamin noun

ADJ. **essential, important** | **antioxidant, fat-soluble** | **prenatal** (*AmE*) | **multiple** (*AmE*) | **~ A, ~ B, etc.** ◇ *~ D pills*
VERB + VITAMIN **take** ◇ *The doctor told me to take ~s regularly.* | **contain** ◇ *Most foods contain ~ E.* | **provide** ◇ *Potatoes provide ~s A and C, as well as calcium.* | **be rich in** ◇ *Fish is rich in ~s and minerals.* | **enrich sth with, fortify sth with** ◇ *breakfast cereals fortified with ~s* | **get** ◇ *Some people are getting too much ~ A.* | **add**
VITAMIN + VERB **be found in sth**
VITAMIN + NOUN **pills, supplements, tablets** (*esp. BrE*) | **deficiency** ◇ *Vitamin C deficiency can ultimately lead to scurvy.* | **supplementation** | **content** ◇ *strawberries' high ~ C content* | **requirement** ◇ *your daily ~ C requirement* | **intake** | **therapy, treatment** | **level**
PHRASES **~s and minerals**

vivid adj.

1 very bright
VERBS **be**
ADV. **extremely, fairly, very, etc.**

2 very clear
VERBS **be** | **remain**
ADV. **extremely, fairly, very, etc.** | **extraordinarily, wonderfully** ◇ *a wonderfully ~ imagination* | **still**
PHRASES **~ in sb's mind**

vocabulary noun

ADJ. **big, extensive, large, rich, wide** ◇ *English has a rich ~ and literature.* ◇ *Try to develop a wide ~.* | **limited, poor, restricted, small** | **active, expressive** | **passive, receptive** | **basic, essential, key** | **formal** | **everyday** | **new** | **business, musical, political, scientific** | **specialized, technical** | **common, shared**
VERB + VOCABULARY **have** | **acquire, learn** ◇ *Learners of languages acquire ~ through practice.* | **build, develop** | **broaden, enlarge, enrich, expand, extend, increase** ◇ *This book has been designed to help you expand your ~.* | **enter** ◇ *The expression 'think tank' entered the ~ (= became part of the language) in the 1960s.* | **use** ◇ *Specialized ~ is used in all the major disciplines.*
VOCABULARY + NOUN **item, word** (*AmE*) | **list** | **test** | **development**

PREP. **~ for, ~ of** ◇ *the essential ~ for tourism* ◇ *the ~ of science*
PHRASES **not in sb's ~** ◇ *The word 'failure' is not in his ~ (= for him, failure does not exist).*

vocal adj.

VERBS **be** | **become**
ADV. **extremely, fairly, very, etc.** | **highly** ◇ *a highly ~ opposition group* | **increasingly** ◇ *criticized by a small but increasingly ~ minority*
PREP. **about** ◇ *women who are very ~ about men's failings* | **in** ◇ *They have been very ~ in their opposition to the plan.*

vocation noun

ADJ. **true** | **Christian, religious**
VERB + VOCATION **find** ◇ *She struggled for years to find her true ~.* | **have** | **follow** (*esp. BrE*), **live** (*AmE*), **live out** (*AmE*), **pursue** ◇ *He is desperate to pursue his ~ as an artist.* ◇ *They are set on living out their ~ as priests.* | **miss** (*BrE*) ◇ *She feels that she missed her ~ by not working with children.*
PREP. **~ for** ◇ *She seems to have a ~ for healing.* | **~ to** ◇ *a ~ to the priesthood*
PHRASES **a sense of ~** ◇ *This is a job that demands a sense of ~.*

vogue noun

ADJ. **current**
VERB + VOGUE **enjoy** ◇ *Cycling enjoyed a ~ at the end of the 19th century.* | **come (back) into** ◇ *Scooters have recently come back into ~.*
PREP. **in ~** ◇ *the type of pop song in ~ at that time* | **out of ~** ◇ *Disaster movies are currently out of ~.* | **~ for** ◇ *the current ~ for Japanese food*

voice noun

1 sounds you make when speaking or singing

ADJ. **beautiful, fine, good, lovely, pleasant, sweet** ◇ *She has a beautiful singing ~.* | **big, booming, loud, ringing, sonorous, stentorian** (*formal*), **strong** | **light, little, small, thin, tiny, weak** | **low, soft** | **faint, inaudible, quiet** | **audible** | **deep, gravelly, gruff, hoarse, husky, rough** | **falsetto, high, high-pitched, shrill, squeaky** | **clear** | **muffled, muted** | **harsh, penetrating, scratchy, sharp** | **nasal** | **cracked, rasping, raspy, slurred** ◇ *I could tell from his slurred ~ that he'd been drinking.* | **mellifluous, rich, silky, smooth, velvet, velvety** | **sing-song** | **gentle, soothing** | **cheerful, cheery** | **friendly, warm** | **emotionless, matter-of-fact, unemotional** | **flat, monotone** | **calm, cool** | **firm, steady** | **shaky** | **urgent** | **authoritative, commanding** | **distinctive, unmistakable** | **familiar** | **raised** | **hushed** | **cold, icy** | **angry, annoyed** | **strained, tired** | **plaintive, sad** | **serious, stern** | **funny, silly** | **baby** | **annoying** | **whiny** | **mocking, sarcastic, teasing** | **excited** | **concerned, worried** | **distant** | **disembodied** | **inner** ◇ *An inner ~ told him that what he had done was wrong.* | **singing, speaking** | **alto, baritone, bass, contralto, soprano, tenor, treble** | **female, male** | **feminine, masculine**
VERB + VOICE **hear** ◇ *I could hear ~s in the next room.* | **raise** ◇ *She's a teacher who never has to raise her ~ to discipline the children.* | **drop, lower** ◇ *She dropped her ~ to a whisper.* ◇ *Please lower your ~!* | **project** ◇ *Try to project your ~ so that the people at the back of the room can hear you.* | **control** | **lose** ◇ *She's lost her ~ and won't be able to sing tonight.* | **strain** | **find** ◇ *He swallowed nervously as he tried to find his ~.* | **imitate, put on** ◇ *She put on a silly ~ as she imitated her boss.* | **disguise** | **know, recognize** | **silence**
VOICE + VERB **go up, rise** ◇ *His ~ rose in angry protest.* | **die away, drift away, drift off, drop, fade, tail off** (*esp. BrE*), **trail away, trail off** ◇ *'So he won't come…' her ~ trailed off in disappointment.* | **be filled with sth, be full of sth** ◇ *Her ~ was filled with emotion.* | **be laced with sth, be tinged with sth** | **sound angry, excited, sad, etc.** | **deepen, harden, soften, thicken** ◇ *His ~ suddenly thickened with*

emotion. | **echo** ◊ *Her ~ echoed through the silent house.* |
whisper ◊ *'Be quiet!' a ~ whispered in his ear.* | **hiss, purr** |
call, call out, cry, cry out ◊ *'Who is it?' a female ~ called out.*
| **scream, shout, yell** ◊ *She was dimly aware of ~s shouting.*
| **bellow, boom, boom out** | **resonate, reverberate, ring** |
come from sth | **cut through sth, pierce sth** ◊ *His deep ~
cut through the silence.* | **break, catch, catch in your throat,
crack** ◊ *His ~ broke with emotion.* ◊ *His ~ broke* (= became a
man's voice) *when he was 14.* | **ask** | **answer, reply** | **sing** |
falter, quaver, quiver, shake, tremble, waver ◊ *Her ~ shook
with fear.* | **drone, drone on** ◊ *The flat, unemotional ~
droned on.* | **be devoid of sth** | **be drowned out by sth** |
carry
VOICE + NOUN **coach, teacher** | **lessons** | **recognition** ◊ *the
computer's ~ recognition capability* | **mail** (usually *voice-
mail*), **mailbox, message, traffic** | **synthesizer** | **acting**
(= providing voices for animated film characters) | **actor**
(= who provides voices for animated film characters) |
command | **box** (usually *voicebox*)
PREP. **in a/your ~** ◊ *'Get out!' she shouted in a shrill ~.* ◊ *There
was fury in his ~ as he answered her.*
PHRASES **at the top of your ~** ◊ *I was shouting at the top of
my ~ but she couldn't hear me.* | **a babble of ~s, a hum of
~s, a murmur of ~s** ◊ *They could hear a loud babble of ~s
coming from the crowded bar.* | **in good ~** (*BrE*) ◊ *She was in
good ~* (= singing well) *at the concert tonight.* | **keep your ~
down** ◊ *Please keep your ~ down so as not to wake the
children.* | **keep your ~ level, keep your ~ steady** ◊ *He
managed to keep his ~ steady despite his feelings of panic.* |
~s in your head, ~s inside your head | **tone of ~** ◊ *'Do you
have to speak to me in that tone of ~?' she asked sadly.*

2 expression of ideas/opinions
ADJ. **critical, dissenting** ◊ *Dissenting ~s at the newspaper are
very rare.* | **lone** ◊ *a lone ~ of dissent* | **powerful** ◊ *Powerful
~s in the Senate are determined to bring down the president.*
| **distinctive** ◊ *a writer with a highly distinctive ~*
VERB + VOICE **find** ◊ *Refugees have been unable to find a ~ in
politics.* | **add, lend** ◊ *Many senior politicians have lent their
~s to the campaign.* | **give** ◊ *The magazine gave ~ to
hundreds of oppressed factory workers.* | **listen to**
PREP. **~ of** ◊ *to listen to the ~ of conscience*
PHRASES **make your ~ heard** ◊ *a society in which individuals
are able to make their ~s heard* | **speak with one ~** ◊ *The
teachers speak with one ~ when they demand an end to the
cuts.*

void *noun*
ADJ. **big, deep, great, large** | **endless, huge, massive** |
aching | **black, dark** | **empty**
VERB + VOID **create, leave** | **fill** ◊ *It seemed that nothing could
fill the aching black ~ left by Rachel's death.* | **feel**

volatile *adj.*
VERBS **be** | **become** | **remain**
ADV. **extremely, fairly, very, etc.** | **highly** ◊ *Edwards was a
highly ~ character.* | **increasingly** | **potentially** ◊ *a
potentially ~ situation* | **notoriously** | **politically** |
emotionally

volcano *noun*
ADJ. **active, dormant, extinct** | **erupting** | **submarine,
undersea, underwater**
…OF VOLCANOES **chain**
VOLCANO + VERB **erupt** ◊ *An active ~ may erupt at any time.* |
spew sth, spew sth out ◊ *a ~ spewing red hot lava*

volley *noun*
1 of stones, bullets, etc.
VERB + VOLLEY **fire, launch, unleash** ◊ *The police fired a ~ of
bullets over the heads of the crowd.*
PREP. **~ of**

2 in sports
ADJ. **backhand, forehand** (in tennis) | **left-foot, right-foot**
(in football/soccer) | **great, stunning, superb** (*esp. BrE*) ◊
*Williams took the set with a stunning backhand ~ down the
line.* | **30-yard, etc.**
VERB + VOLLEY **hit** ◊ *She hit a forehand ~ into the net.* | **lash**
(*BrE*), **strike, unleash** (all in football/soccer) ◊ *Cole lashed
home a 20-yard ~.*
PREP. **on the ~** (*BrE*) ◊ *Figo met the ball on the ~ and scored.*

voltage *noun*
ADJ. **high, low** | **constant** | **mains, supply** ◊ *Most house
lighting runs at the full mains ~ of 240 volts.* | **battery** |
input, output | **negative, positive**
VERB + VOLTAGE **increase** | **decrease, lower, reduce** | **adjust,
change** | **generate, produce** | **apply** ◊ *A ~ is then applied
across the cell electrodes.* | **measure**
PREP. **at a ~** ◊ *The motor operates at low ~s.* | **~ across** ◊ *a ~
applied across the two edges of a plate* | **~ of** ◊ *the ~ of a
battery*

volume *noun*
1 amount of space
ADJ. **total** ◊ *the total ~ of the containers* | **interior, internal**
VERB + VOLUME **calculate, measure**
PREP. **by ~** ◊ *They sell screws and nails by ~.* | **in ~** ◊ *two
gallons in ~*

2 quantity of sth
ADJ. **sheer** ◊ *The sheer ~ of fiction produced is staggering.* |
**considerable, enormous, great, heavy, high, huge, large,
substantial, vast** | **increased** | **increasing** | **low, small** |
decreased, reduced | **overall** | **production, sales** | **traffic**
VERB + VOLUME **increase** | **decrease, reduce** | **double in,
grow in, increase in, rise in** ◊ *Sales have doubled in ~.* |
decrease in, fall in | **determine, estimate**
VOLUME + VERB **double, grow, increase, rise** ◊ *Sales ~ has
doubled since 1999.* | **decrease, fall** | **exceed sth**

3 strength of sound that sth makes
ADJ. **high, loud** | **full, maximum** | **low**
VERB + VOLUME **increase, turn up** | **decrease, lower, turn
down** | **grow in, increase in, rise in** | **decrease in, fall in**
VOLUME + NOUN **control, dial, knob, setting** ◊ *the ~ control on
the television*
PREP. **at…~** ◊ *The car stereo was on at full ~.* | **~ on** ◊ *the ~
on the stereo*

4 book
ADJ. **bound, leather-bound** ◊ *a library full of bound ~s* |
companion ◊ *a companion ~ to the one on African wildlife* |
rare ◊ *Only a library would have this rare ~.* | **huge, large,
massive, substantial, thick** | **slender, slim, small** |
handsome | **dusty** | **old** | **single** | **separate** | **edited** |
published | **first, second, etc.** | **final** | **forthcoming**
…OF VOLUMES **series**
VERB + VOLUME **edit, illustrate, publish, write** | **read**
PREP. **in a/the ~** ◊ *Her poems are now available in a single ~.* |
~ of ◊ *a ~ of short stories* | **~ on** ◊ *a ~ on ancient history*
PHRASES **run to five, several, etc. ~s** ◊ *The encyclopedia is a
huge work, running to 20 ~s.*

volunteer *noun*
1 sb who offers to do sth
ADJ. **unpaid** ◊ *The office is staffed by unpaid ~s.* | **full-time,
part-time** | **committed, dedicated, enthusiastic, willing** |
qualified, trained | **potential, prospective** | **conservation**
(*BrE*), **hospital, Red Cross** | **church, community** | **local** |
healthy | **human** | **parent, student**
…OF VOLUNTEERS **army, band, group, network, team** ◊ *An
army of ~s cooked meals for the children.*
VERB + VOLUNTEER **appeal for, ask for, call for, look for** ◊ *The
charity is appealing for ~s to take elderly patients to and
from hospital.* | **find, get, recruit** ◊ *We can't get any ~s to
help in the kitchen.* | **become** | **train** | **provide** ◊ *The local
community provided ~s to repair the road.* | **could use** (*esp.
AmE*), **need, want** | **work as**

VOLUNTEER + VERB **come forward** (*esp. BrE*) ◊ *Hundreds of ~s have come forward to offer their help.* | **man sth, staff sth** | **run sth** | **carry sth out** | **participate (in sth)** | **provide support, support sb** ◊ *The support our ~s provide cannot be measured in purely practical terms.* | **work** | **help do sth**
VOLUNTEER + NOUN **staff, worker** | **labour/labor** | **group** | **coordinator, counsellor/counselor, driver, helper** (*BrE*) | **firefighter, fireman** | **organization** | **activity, effort, service, work** | **programme/program** | **vacation** (*AmE*)
PREP. **~ for** ◊ *He worked as a ~ for Oxfam.*

2 in the armed forces

ADJ. **army, civilian**
VERB + VOLUNTEER **recruit** | **serve as**
VOLUNTEER + NOUN **army, corps, force, regiment, unit** | **soldier** | **military** (*AmE*)

volunteer *verb*

ADV. **graciously** (*esp. AmE*), **kindly** ◊ *David graciously ~ed to model for the art class.* ◊ *Barbara has kindly ~ed to lead the session.*
PREP. **as** ◊ *We ~ed as witnesses.* | **for** ◊ *I ~ed for service in the Air Force.*

vomit *verb*

ADV. **violently** | **up** ◊ *He ~ed up all that he had eaten for lunch.*
VERB + VOMIT **want to** ◊ *The smell made me want to ~.* | **make sb** ◊ *They gave her salty water to make her ~.*
PHRASES **nausea and ~ing** ◊ *The symptoms include headaches, nausea and ~ing.* | **~ing and diarrhoea**

vote *noun*

1 choice/decision made by voting

ADJ. **electoral** | **majority** | **huge, massive** (*esp. BrE*), **overwhelming, resounding** (*esp. BrE*) ◊ *an overwhelming ~ in favour/favor of autonomy* | **unanimous** | **close, knife-edge** (*esp. BrE*), **narrow** (*esp. BrE*) | **two-thirds, two-to-one, etc.** | **democratic, direct, free** (*BrE*) ◊ *Members of Parliament will have a free ~ on this bill.* | **transferable** (*BrE*) ◊ *The single transferable ~ system operates.* | **fair** | **secret** | **national** | **popular** ◊ *The law was ratified by popular ~.* | **casting, decisive** | **final** | **crucial, important, key** | **affirmative, favourable/favorable, yes** | **negative, no** | **dissenting** | **protest** ◊ *He lost the election because of the protest ~.* | **tactical** (*BrE*) | **floating** (*BrE*), **swing** (*esp. AmE*) | **postal** (*BrE*), **proxy** | **invalid, valid** | **congressional, parliamentary, Senate** | **presidential** | **individual** | **block** ◊ *He won the seat thanks to Polish block ~s.* | **black, Hispanic, Jewish, etc.** ◊ *Ferrer got 84% of the Hispanic ~.* | **historic** | **first-place** | **confirmation, floor, recall, up-or-down** (= on which members vote yes or no), **voice** (*all AmE*) | **party-line** (*AmE*) | **Conservative, Republican, etc.**
VERB + VOTE **have, hold, put sth to the, take** ◊ *We should put the resolution to the ~.* ◊ *Let's take a ~ on the issue.* | **have** ◊ *The chairperson always has the casting ~.* | **cast, record** (*formal*) ◊ *You can cast your ~ at the local polling station.* ◊ *50% of the eligible voters recorded their ~.* | **gain, garner, get, obtain, poll, receive, secure, win** ◊ *Our candidate polled only 10% of the ~.* | **need, require** | **sway, swing** ◊ *factors that could swing the ~ against the president* | **influence** | **lose** | **court** ◊ *Bush had courted the military ~.* | **count, tally** ◊ *Votes are still being counted.* | **divide, split** ◊ *the party that split the Republican ~* | **schedule** | **delay, postpone** | **give sb** | **deny sb** | **suppress** | **throw away, waste**
VOTE + VERB **go to sb/sth** ◊ *My ~ will go to the party that addresses crime.* | **fall** ◊ *The party's ~ fell by 6%.* | **increase, rise** | **count** ◊ *Everyone's ~ counts.*
PREP. **by** ◊ *The bill was passed by a single ~.* ◊ *Members are elected by direct ~.* ◊ *Mr Olsen was approved by a ~ of 51–47.* | **~ against** | **~ for, ~ in favour/favor (of sth)** ◊ *a ~ for the government* | **~ on** ◊ *a ~ on the new law*
PHRASES **change your ~** ◊ *They want to persuade voters to change their ~.* | **force a ~ (on sth)** ◊ *Any senator can force a ~ on virtually any proposal.* | **a ~ of confidence, a ~ of no confidence** ◊ *The government received a massive ~ of confidence from the electorate.* | **a ~ of thanks** ◊ *A special ~ of thanks went to the organizer, Tom Woodhouse.* | **take a quick ~** ◊ *We took a quick ~ to decide on a leader.*
→ Special page at MEETING

2 the vote legal right to vote in elections

VERB + THE VOTE **have** ◊ *How many years is it since women have had the ~?* | **get** | **give sb**

vote *verb*

ADV. **overwhelmingly** | **unanimously** ◊ *The committee ~d unanimously to accept the plans.* | **narrowly** ◊ *The Senate ~d narrowly to continue funding the plan.* | **tactically** (*BrE*) | **online** | **consistently** | **down, in, out** ◊ *The proposal was ~d down.*
VERB + VOTE **be eligible to, be entitled to** ◊ *young people who are eligible to ~ for the first time* | **intend to**
PREP. **against** ◊ *They ~d overwhelmingly against the proposal.* | **for** ◊ *They all ~d for the new tax.* | **in** ◊ *She returned home in order to ~ in the elections.* | **in favour/favor of** ◊ *The committee ~d in favour/favor of the plan.* | **into** ◊ *the government that has just been ~d into power* | **off** ◊ *She was ~d off the committee.* | **on, upon** ◊ *Stockholders have the right to ~ on the proposal.* ◊ *Parliament is to ~ on tobacco advertising tomorrow.* | **out of** ◊ *He was ~d out of office.* | **(by)... to do sth** ◊ *They ~d 15 to 2 to accept the offer.* | **with** ◊ *Her party ~d with the government.*
PHRASES **the right to ~** ◊ *Everyone over 18 has the right to ~.* | **a round of voting** ◊ *She was elected on the second round of voting.* | **~ Conservative, Labour, Republican, etc.** | **~ no, ~ yes** ◊ *They ~d yes to the agreement.*

voter *noun*

ADJ. **eligible, registered** ◊ *Only a quarter of registered ~s actually voted in the election.* | **absentee** (*AmE*) | **overseas** | **floating** (*BrE*), **uncommitted, undecided** | **first-time, new** | **swing** | **likely, potential** | **ordinary** ◊ *the feelings of ordinary ~s* | **Labour, Republican, etc.** | **black, rural, young, etc.** | **primary** (*AmE*) | **state** (*AmE*)
VERB + VOTER **appeal to, attract, woo** ◊ *attempts to appeal to undecided ~s* | **persuade** | **convince, remind** | **urge, warn** | **influence, sway** | **register** | **disenfranchise**
VOTER + VERB **choose sb, elect sb, go for sb, pick sb** ◊ *In this election, ~s chose candidates who promised economic security.* | **back sb, favour/favor sb, prefer sb** | **participate in sth, turn out** ◊ *More than two million ~s participated in the election.* | **cast their vote, go to the polls, vote** | **want sth** | **approve sth, decide sth, pass sth, support sth** | **reject sth**
VOTER + NOUN **turnout** ◊ *Voter turnout was very low.* | **participation** | **registration** | **apathy, fatigue** | **intimidation** ◊ *The opposition alleged ~ intimidation by the army.* | **fraud** | **list, roll** (*AmE*)

voucher *noun*

ADJ. **food** | **travel** | **hotel** | **discount, money-off** (*both BrE*) | **gift, shopping** (*both BrE*) | **luncheon** (*BrE*) | **education, school** ◊ *the use of tax dollars for school ~s* | **housing** (*AmE*)
VERB + VOUCHER **give sb, issue (sb with)** (*esp. BrE*), **provide (sb with)** ◊ *The company issues travel ~s to all managers.* | **get, receive** ◊ *I got a credit ~ for £30.* ◊ *households that receive housing ~s to pay the rent* | **use** | **redeem, spend** (*both esp. BrE*)
VOUCHER + VERB **be worth sth** ◊ *a ~ worth £100* | **entitle sb to sth** (*esp. BrE*) ◊ *a ~ entitling you to a half-price meal* | **be redeemable** (*esp. BrE*) ◊ *a 50p money-off ~ redeemable against any future purchase of the product*
VOUCHER + NOUN **plan** (*AmE*), **program** (*AmE*), **scheme** (*BrE*), **system** | **school, student** (*both AmE*)
PREP. **~ for** ◊ *a ~ for children's glasses* ◊ *publicly financed ~s for education*

vow *noun*

ADJ. **solemn** | **marriage, wedding** | **monastic, religious,**

sacred | final ◇ *She decided to leave the convent before taking her final ~s.*
VERB + VOW **make, take** ◇ *He made a ~ to avenge his father's death.* | **keep** ◇ *She kept her ~ of silence until she died.* | **break** ◇ *Nothing will persuade me to break this ~.* | **exchange** ◇ *The couple exchanged ~s at the altar.* | **renew**
PREP. **~ of** ◇ *a ~ of poverty*
PHRASES **a ~ of celibacy, a ~ of chastity** ◇ *He took a lifelong ~ of celibacy.* | **a ~ of silence**

vow *verb*

ADV. **quietly, silently** ◇ *He silently ~ed vengeance on them all.*
PREP. **to** ◇ *She ~ed to herself that she would not show any emotion.*
PHRASES **~ never to do sth** ◇ *I ~ed never to drink so much again.* | **~ revenge, ~ revenge against sb, ~ revenge on sb**

vowel *noun*

ADJ. **long, short** | **open, rounded** | **back, front** | **weak** | **flat** | **final** | **accented, stressed** | **unaccented, unstressed**
VERB + VOWEL **begin with, contain, end in, end with** | **pronounce** ◇ *Americans pronounce this ~ like the one in 'may'.*
VOWEL + NOUN **sound** | **length** | **system**

voyage *noun*

ADJ. **epic, great, long** | **arduous** | **outward** | **homeward, return** | **first, maiden** | **final, last** | **ocean, sea** | **transatlantic** | **around-the-world** (*AmE*), **round-the-world** (*BrE*) | **solo**
VERB + VOYAGE **embark on, go on, make, set out on, undertake** | **complete** ◇ *The ship completed her maiden ~ in May.*
PREP. **during a/the ~** ◇ *Lady Franklin kept a journal during the ~.* | **on a/the ~** ◇ *There were mainly scientists on the ~.* | **~ from, ~ to** ◇ *The Titanic sank in April 1912 on its maiden ~ from Southampton to New York.*
PHRASES **a ~ of discovery** (*often figurative*) ◇ *Going to college can be a ~ of discovery.*

vulnerability *noun*

ADJ. **extreme, great** | **critical** | **potential** | **known, well-known** | **economic, financial, political** ◇ *the economic ~ of unskilled workers* | **security** | **software** | **genetic** ◇ *evidence of a genetic ~ to cancer* | **emotional, physical**
VERB + VULNERABILITY **demonstrate, discover, expose, highlight, identify, reveal, show** ◇ *The earthquake highlighted the ~ of elevated highways.* | **address** | **fix** (*computing*) ◇ *We attempt to fix security vulnerabilities as soon as possible.* | **decrease, reduce** | **increase** | **exploit, take advantage of** ◇ *The gang had taken advantage of the immigrants' ~.*
PREP. **~ to** ◇ *the extreme ~ of old people to crime*

vulnerable *adj.*

VERBS **be, prove** | **appear, feel, look, seem** ◇ *You must try not to appear ~.* | **become** | **remain** | **leave sb/sth, make sb/sth, render sb/sth** ◇ *The virus attacks the immune system, leaving your body ~ to infections.*
ADV. **extremely, fairly, very, etc.** ◇ *She is very sensitive and rather ~.* | **acutely, especially, highly, particularly** | **completely, totally** | **increasingly** | **potentially** | **peculiarly, uniquely** ◇ *Hippos are uniquely ~ to drought.* | **oddly** (*esp. AmE*), **strangely** (*esp. BrE*) ◇ *He smiled, making her suddenly feel oddly ~.* | **economically, politically** ◇ *The company is in an economically ~ position.* | **emotionally, psychologically**
PREP. **to** ◇ *These offices are highly ~ to terrorist attack.*

W w

wade *verb*

ADV. **slowly** | **ashore** ◇ *The men ~d ashore.* | **across, back, out**
PREP. **across, in, into, through, to** ◇ *We ~d across the stream.*
PHRASES **~ knee-deep, waist-deep, etc. in sth** ◇ *Rescuers had to ~ waist-deep in floodwater.*

waft *verb*

ADV. **gently, slowly** ◇ *The night air ~ed gently over them.* | **around, in, up** ◇ *A scent of honey ~ed up from the hives.*
PREP. **across, down, from, into, over, through, up** ◇ *Spicy smells ~ed through the air.*

wage (*also* wages) *noun*

ADJ. **competitive** (*esp. AmE*), **decent, fair, good, high** | **inadequate, low, meagre/meager** (*esp. BrE*), **poverty, small** ◇ *Women's ~s were lower than men's.* ◇ *He busked to supplement his meagre ~s.* | **falling, rising** | **annual, daily, hourly, regular, weekly, etc.** | **money** | **nominal, real** ◇ *Real ~s fell last year, when inflation is taken into account.* | **basic** (*esp. BrE*), **standard** ◇ *a basic ~ of £100 a week plus tips* | **livable** (*esp. AmE*), **living** ◇ *workers fighting for a living ~* | **minimum** ◇ *The Government this week raised the national minimum ~.* (*esp. BrE*) ◇ *They both work minimum-wage jobs.* (*esp. AmE*) | **prevailing** (*esp. AmE*) ◇ *The prevailing ~ is generally determined by local union rates.* | **average, median** (*esp. AmE*) | **back, lost, unpaid** ◇ *to receive reimbursement for lost ~s*
VERB + WAGE **pay** | **earn, make** (*esp. AmE*) ◇ *She earns a good ~ at the factory.* ◇ *15 million Americans make minimum ~.* ◇ *He made a good ~ as a trader.* | **live on** ◇ *How can you live on such a low ~?* | **demand** ◇ *Semi-skilled tradesmen began to demand higher ~s.* | **offer** ◇ *The store argues that it offers competitive ~s.* | **accept** | **receive** | **determine, set** ◇ *Markets set the ~s.* | **increase, push up, raise** ◇ *Full employment pushed up ~s.* | **cut, depress** (*esp. AmE*), **drive down, force down, hold down, keep down, keep low, lower** | **supplement** | **dock** ◇ *They docked his ~s for arriving at work two hours late.*
WAGE + VERB **increase, rise** | **fall**
WAGE + NOUN **earner** | **labour/labor, labourer/laborer** (*esp. AmE*), **workers** | **slave** (*figurative*) ◇ *my life as a corporate ~ slave* | **claim** ◇ *The union submitted a ~ claim for a 9% rise.* | **bargaining, negotiations** | **agreement, settlement** | **cut, reduction** | **cap, controls, freeze, restraint** ◇ *The government promised greater tax cuts in return for continued ~ restraints.* | **explosion, growth** (*esp. AmE*), **hike** (*esp. AmE*), **increase, inflation, rise** (*BrE*) | **bill** (*BrE*), **costs** | **structure, system** | **rate, scale** (*esp. AmE*) | **differential** (*esp. AmE*), **gap, inequality** ◇ *~ differentials between large and small companies* ◇ *the ~ gap between men and women* | **packet** (*BrE*) ◇ *He got his first ~ packet at fourteen years old.*
PHRASES **a cut in ~s, a decline in ~s, a fall in ~s** | **a downward pressure on ~s, an upward pressure on ~s** ◇ *Staff shortages have put an upward pressure on ~s.* | **growth in ~s, an increase in ~s, a rise in ~s** (*esp. BrE*)

wagon *noun*

1 vehicle pulled by animals

ADJ. **covered, open** | **horse-drawn** | **hay, supply** | **laden** | **chuck** (*AmE, old-fashioned*)
...OF WAGONS **train** ◇ *a long train of supply ~s*
VERB + WAGON **drive** | **draw, pull**
WAGON + VERB **roll** ◇ *covered ~s rolling across the prairies*
WAGON + NOUN **train** | **wheel**

2 (*BrE*) part of train → See also CAR

ADJ. **rail, railway** (*BrE*) | **coal, freight, goods**
VERB + WAGON **pull**

wail *noun*

ADJ. **loud | high-pitched | anguished, mournful, plaintive | banshee | distant** ◇ *We could just hear the distant ~ of a siren.*
VERB + WAIL **give, let out | hear**
PREP. **with a ~** ◇ *With a ~ he threw himself on the bed and buried his face in the pillow.* | **~ of** ◇ *She gave a ~ of anguish.*
→ Note at SOUND

waist *noun*

1 part around the middle of the body

ADJ. **narrow, slender, slim, small, thin, tiny | 34-inch, etc.**
VERB + WAIST **encircle** ◇ *Her arms encircled his ~.*
WAIST + NOUN **height**
PREP. **about the/sb's ~** (*esp. BrE*), **around the/sb's ~, round the/sb's ~** (*esp. BrE*) ◇ *She wore a broad belt around her ~.*
PHRASES **from the ~ down, from the ~ up** ◇ *A large towel covered him from the ~ down.* | **stripped to the ~ | wrap sth around sb's ~** ◇ *He wrapped his arms around her ~.*

2 part of a piece of clothing that goes around the waist

ADJ. **high, low | belted, drawstring, elastic** (*AmE*), **elasticated** (*BrE*) **| tight | 34-inch, etc.** ◇ *These jeans have a 32-inch ~.*
WAIST + NOUN **measurement, size**

waistcoat *noun* (*BrE*) → See also VEST

ADJ. **embroidered | leather, satin, velvet, etc.**
WAISTCOAT + NOUN **pocket**
→ Special page at CLOTHES

waistline *noun*

1 measurement of the body around the waist

ADJ. **expanding | 28-inch, 34-inch, etc.**
VERB + WAISTLINE **watch** ◇ *Low-fat foods are ideal for people who are watching their ~.*

2 part of a piece of clothing

ADJ. **high, low**

wait *noun*

ADJ. **endless, lengthy, long** ◇ *We had a long ~ to see the doctor.* | **short | agonizing, anxious, nail-biting, nerve-racking, nervous, worrying** (*all esp. BrE*) **| frustrating | boring, tedious | two-hour, one-month, three-year, etc.**
VERB + WAIT **face** (*esp. BrE*), **have** ◇ *The accused faces an agonizing ~ while the jury considers its verdict.*
PREP. **~ for** ◇ *a short ~ for an ambulance*
PHRASES **be worth the ~** ◇ *The dress was so beautiful when it arrived that it was well worth the ~.*

wait *verb*

ADV. **a while, long** ◇ *You might have to ~ a while before you get an answer.* ◇ *Have you been ~ing long?* | **forever** ◇ *We can't ~ forever.* | **in vain** ◇ *They ~ed in vain for a response.* | **quietly, silently | patiently, politely** ◇ *He ~ed patiently while she got ready.* | **anxiously, impatiently, nervously, tensely** ◇ *Their parents ~ed anxiously for news.* | **breathlessly, eagerly, expectantly, with bated breath** ◇ *I ~ed with bated breath for what would happen next.* | **about** (*esp. BrE*), **around**
VERB + WAIT **have to, must** ◇ *You'll have to ~ until you're older.* | **can hardly, cannot** ◇ *I could hardly ~ for the weekend.* ◇ *I can't ~ to see their new baby.*
PREP. **for** ◇ *I'm ~ing for a bus.* | **till, until** ◇ *We'll have to ~ until it stops raining.*
PHRASES **can't afford to ~** ◇ *We simply cannot afford to ~ any longer.* | **keep sb ~ing** ◇ *I'm sorry to have kept you ~ing.* | **~ and see** ◇ *You'll just have to ~ and see what you present is.* | **~ a long time** ◇ *She had to ~ a long time for the right man to come along.* | **~ a minute, moment, second, etc.** ◇ *Hey! Wait a minute! I'll come with you!* | **~ and see** ◇ *We'll ~ and see what the weather's like before we make a decision.* | **~ in line** (*esp. AmE*) ◇ *I had to ~ in line at the bank.* | **~ your turn** ◇ *You'll have to ~ your turn. These people all come before you.*

waiter, waitress *noun*

1 waiter/waitress

ADJ. **restaurant | passing** ◇ *She ordered a large vodka from a passing waiter.* | **friendly**
VERB + WAITER/WAITRESS **beckon, beckon to, call, call over, signal to, summon, wave over** (*esp. AmE*) ◇ *He casually waved over the waitress and settled the bill.* | **tip** ◇ *We ended up tipping our waiter 20%.*
WAITER/WAITRESS + VERB **arrive with sth, bring (sb) sth, serve (sb) sth** ◇ *A waitress arrived with the wine they had ordered.* | **come back, come over** ◇ *The waiter came to clear the plates.*
WAITER/WAITRESS + NOUN **service** ◇ *Lunch is a buffet meal, while dinner is waiter service.*
PHRASES **catch the waiter's/waitress's eye** ◇ *I tried to catch the waiter's eye to ask for our bill.*

2 waiter

ADJ. **head** ◇ *the head waiter in a large restaurant* | **drinks** (*BrE*), **wine** (*esp. BrE*) (usually *sommelier* in *AmE*) **| singing** ◇ *He worked as a singing waiter.*

3 waitress

ADJ. **diner** (*AmE*) **| cocktail**
→ Note at JOB

wake (also **wake up**) *verb*

1 stop being asleep

ADV. **early, late** ◇ *She had woken even earlier than usual.* | **suddenly | finally**
PREP. **from** ◇ *She had just woken up from a deep sleep.* | **to** ◇ *He woke to the sound of the sirens.* | **with** ◇ *I woke with a jolt.*
PHRASES **~ to find sth, ~ up to find sth** ◇ *Any minute now she'd ~ up to find herself at home safe in bed.* | **~ up with a start, ~ with a start** ◇ *She woke with a start from a terrible nightmare.*

2 make sb stop sleeping

ADV. **gently** ◇ *I woke him gently.*
VERB + WAKE **be careful not to, not want to, try not to** ◇ *Be careful not to ~ the children!*

walk *noun*

1 trip on foot

ADJ. **brief, little, short** ◇ *We took a brief ~ around the old quarter.* | **good, long, long-distance** (*BrE*), **marathon** (*BrE*) ◇ *It's a good* (= fairly long) *~ to the beach.* ◇ *We went for a long ~ after breakfast.* ◇ *He's done several long-distance ~s for charity.* | **three-minute, five minutes', etc.** ◇ *It's a five-minute ~ from the hotel to the restaurant.* ◇ *We live just a few minutes' ~ from the station.* | **brisk** ◇ *The doctor advised a brisk ~ every day.* | **easy, gentle** (*esp. BrE*), **leisurely | strenuous | lovely, pleasant | two-mile, etc. | daily | after-dinner, afternoon, evening, etc. | solitary** ◇ *She used to enjoy solitary ~s along the cliffs.* | **romantic | guided** (*esp. BrE*) ◇ *We went on a guided ~ of the city in the afternoon.* | **charity, sponsored** ◇ *She's doing a 200-mile charity ~ to raise money for cancer research.* | **circular** (*BrE*) **| coastal, country, forest, hill, lakeside, riverside, woodland** (*all esp. BrE*) **| nature | space, tightrope** ◇ *the anniversary of the first space ~*
VERB + WALK **do, go for, go on, have, take** ◇ *The book contains ~s you can do in half a day.* ◇ *We'll go for a ~ before lunch.* ◇ *We went on a ten-mile ~ along the coast.* | **take sb/sth for** ◇ *She takes her dog for a ~ every evening.* | **continue, resume**
WALK + VERB **take sb/sth** ◇ *The ~ takes two hours.* ◇ *The ~ takes you past a lot of interesting buildings.*
PREP. **on a/the ~** ◇ *He met her on one of his Sunday afternoon ~s.* | **within (a) ~** ◇ *All amenities are within an easy ~ of the hotel.* | **~ from, ~ to**
PHRASES **a ~ around** (*esp. BrE*) ◇ *I had a little ~ around to calm my nerves.*

2 style of walking

ADJ. **funny, silly** | **jaunty** (*esp. BrE*) | **ungainly** | **fast** | **sedate, slow, stately**
VERB + WALK **do, have** ◇ *She did a silly ~ to amuse her friends.* ◇ *He has an ungainly ~, fast with short steps.*

walk *verb*

ADV. **briskly, fast, quickly, swiftly** | **slowly** | **calmly, quietly** ◇ *I got up and ~ed calmly out into the early evening.* | **cautiously** | **barefoot** ◇ *She had no sandals and ~ed barefoot.* | **upright** ◇ *humans' ability to ~ upright* | **arm in arm, hand in hand** ◇ *The couple ~ed hand in hand along the beach.* | **with a limp** | **unaided** ◇ *Due to his illness, he can no longer ~ unaided.* | **with a cane** (*esp. AmE*), **with a stick** (*esp. BrE*) | **home** ◇ *He ~ed home from school.* | **downstairs, upstairs** | **offstage, onstage** ◇ *When she ~ed onstage, the audience started screaming.* | **ahead, around, away, back, backwards/backward, forward, in, off, on, out, together** ◇ *Jake was ~ing some way ahead.*
PREP. **along, down, into, out of, to, towards/toward, up,** etc. ◇ *She ~ed up the drive towards/toward the door.*
PHRASES **go ~ing** (*esp. BrE*) ◇ *We went ~ing by the waterfront.*

wall *noun*

ADJ. **high, low** | **long, short** | **thick, thin** | **massive** | **back, front, side** | **bare, blank** ◇ *to stare at a blank ~* | **exterior, external, outer, outside** | **inner, inside, interior, internal** | **adjoining** | **far, opposite** ◇ *A large window ran along the far ~.* | **dividing, partition, party** (*BrE*) | **boundary** (*esp. BrE*), **perimeter** | **curtain** | **load-bearing** ◇ *If a load-bearing ~ is weakened, the building could fall down.* | **retaining** ◇ *They built a retaining ~ around the pond.* | **panelled/paneled** | **bathroom, kitchen,** etc. | **brick, concrete, masonry, stone,** etc. | **castle, cave, city, garden, prison,** etc. | **harbour/harbor** (*esp. BrE*), **sea** | **cell, vessel** (*both biology*)
VERB + WALL **build, erect, put up** | **demolish, destroy, pull down** | **climb, climb over, scale** ◇ *The burglars must have scaled the side ~.* | **lean against** | **jump over** | **stare at** ◇ *She just sat there, staring at the ~.* | **adorn, decorate** | **be attached to, hang on** | **cover, line, paint, paper, plaster** ◇ *She covered her ~s with pictures of movie stars.* | **face** ◇ *She turned and faced the ~.*
WALL + VERB **stand** | **collapse, fall, fall down** | **enclose sth, surround sth** | **separate sth** ◇ *There was a ~ separating the two garages.* | **face sth** ◇ *the ~ facing the door*
WALL + NOUN **clock, light** | **plug** (*AmE*), **socket** | **unit** | **safe** | **art** (*esp. AmE*), **covering, decoration, hanging, painting, panel, tile** | **space**
PREP. **against a/the ~** ◇ *She leaned against the ~.* | **behind a/the ~** ◇ *Nobody can see behind the ~.* | **on a/the ~** ◇ *She hung the photos on the ~.* | **~ along** ◇ *the ~ along the seafront* | **~ around, ~ round** (*esp. BrE*) ◇ *high ~s around the prison* | **~ of** (*figurative*) ◇ *a solid ~ of fog*

wallet *noun*

ADJ. **bulging, fat** ◇ *He pulled a €50 note out of his fat ~.* | **empty** | **leather** | **CD**
VERB + WALLET **get out, pull out, take out** | **open** | **empty** | **put away** | **lose** | **steal**
WALLET + VERB **be stuffed with sth** ◇ *a ~ stuffed with fifty-dollar bills* | **contain** ◇ *a ~ containing more than £100*
PREP. **in a/the ~** ◇ *He carried a photo of his children in his ~.*

wallpaper *noun*

ADJ. **faded, peeling** | **floral, flowery, patterned, striped** | **flock** (*BrE*), **flocked** (*AmE*), **textured** | **aural** (*figurative*) ◇ *Ambient music is really just aural ~.* | **desktop** (*computing*) ◇ *You can download desktop ~.*
... OF WALLPAPER **roll** ◇ *six rolls of ~*
VERB + WALLPAPER **hang** | **be covered with, be hung with** | **strip, strip off**
WALLPAPER + VERB **peel off**
WALLPAPER + NOUN **paste**

wander *verb*

1 move slowly around a place/go from place to place

ADV. **slowly** | **aimlessly** | **disconsolately, restlessly** | **happily** | **at will, freely** ◇ *The cattle are allowed to ~ freely.* | **just, simply** ◇ *Simply ~ing is a pleasure in itself.* | **far, farther** (*esp. AmE*), **further** (*esp. BrE*), **further afield** (*esp. BrE*) ◇ *One day she ~ed further afield.* | **about** (*esp. BrE*), **across, along, around, away, back, in, off, out, over, round** (*esp. BrE*) ◇ *He just ~ed in one day and asked for a job.*
VERB + WANDER **be free to** ◇ *Visitors are free to ~ through the gardens and woods.* | **allow sb/sth to, let sb/sth** ◇ *How could you let him ~ off like that?*
PREP. **across, all over, along, among, around, down, in, into, out of, round** (*esp. BrE*), **through, towards/toward** ◇ *Don't go ~ing all over the house!* ◇ *He ~ed into a bar and ordered a drink.*
PHRASES **find sb ~ing** ◇ *They found him ~ing around aimlessly.*

2 stop concentrating

ADV. **a little**
VERB + WANDER **begin to** ◇ *His attention was beginning to ~.* | **allow sth to, let sth** ◇ *Lisa let her mind ~ a little.*
PREP. **from, to** ◇ *My thoughts ~ed from the exam questions to my interview the next day.*

wane *verb*

ADV. **a little, somewhat** ◇ *Her popularity was waning somewhat.* | **considerably** | **gradually** | **quickly, rapidly, soon**
VERB + WANE **begin to** ◇ *Her initial enthusiasm was clearly beginning to ~.*
PHRASES **wax and ~** (= grow and then decrease) ◇ *Public interest in the issue has waxed and ~d over the years.*

want *noun*

ADJ. **human** | **material**
VERB + WANT **meet, satisfy** ◇ *Society can't satisfy all human ~s.*
PREP. **for ~ of** ◇ *Refugees are dying for ~ of proper health care.* | **in ~** ◇ *Thousands of children are living in ~.*

want *verb*

ADV. **badly, desperately, really** | **just, only, simply** ◇ *I just ~ you to be happy.* | **genuinely, truly** ◇ *If you truly ~ to help, just do as I say.* | **always** ◇ *Thanks for the present—it's just what I've always ~ed.* | **never**
PHRASES **all you ~** ◇ *All I ~ is the truth.* | **exactly what you ~, just what you ~**

war *noun*

ADJ. **long, short** | **impending, ongoing** | **bloody** | **all-out, full-scale, total** ◇ *Six years of total ~ had left no citizen untouched.* | **limited** | **pre-emptive, preventative** (*AmE*) | **holy, just, religious** | **dirty** | **civil, global, world** | **air, guerrilla** | **atomic, nuclear** | **conventional** | **cold** | **economic, trade** | **drug** (*esp. AmE*) | **bidding, price** | **class, culture** (*esp. AmE*) | **turf** | **phoney** (*BrE*)
VERB + WAR **be in, fight in** ◇ *My grandfather fought in the Korean War.* | **fight, make, wage** ◇ *The two countries fought a short but bloody ~.* ◇ *The terrorists were charged with waging ~ against the state.* | **win** | **lose** | **declare** | **enter** ◇ *The United States entered the ~ in 1917.* | **launch, start** ◇ *They launched a trade ~ against France.* | **spark** ◇ *He fears the violence could spark a civil ~.* | **go to** ◇ *The country went to ~ in 1939.* | **end** | **avert, prevent** | **be devastated by, be ravaged by** | **be killed in**
WAR + VERB **approach, loom, threaten** | **begin, break out, come, erupt, start** | **escalate, spread** ◇ *talks to prevent the ~ from escalating* | **continue, drag on, go on, last, progress, rage, rage on** ◇ *The ~ raged for nearly two years.* | **come to an end, end**
WAR + NOUN **years** ◇ *the shortage of food during the ~ years* | **hero, veteran** | **chief, leader** | **casualties, victims** | **damage** | **correspondent** ◇ *the ~ correspondent of a daily newspaper* | **coverage** ◇ *critiques of the mainstream media's*

~ coverage | **artist, poet** (*both esp. BrE*) | **zone** | **effort** ◇ *Every available resource went towards/toward the ~ effort.* | **record** ◇ *Both candidates have distinguished ~ records.* | **wound** | **crime, criminal** | **cemetery, graves, memorial** | **plan** | **aims** | **game** | **chest** ◇ *The government has a $20-billion ~ chest to fight terrorism.* | **reparations** | **bride, widow** | **booty** | **cry, dance** | **machine** ◇ *the Soviet ~ machine*

PREP. **at ~** ◇ *a country at ~* | **between the ~s** (= between the First and Second World Wars), **in (a/the) ~** ◇ *killed in ~* ◇ *He took part in the Vietnam War.* | **~ against, ~ with** ◇ *the ~ against the French* ◇ *a ~ against drug abuse* | **~ between** ◇ *~ between Iran and Iraq* | **~ for** ◇ *the Greek ~ for independence* | **~ of** ◇ *a ~ of liberation* | **~ on** ◇ *The US declared ~ on Japan.* | **~ with** ◇ *a trade ~ with the United States*

PHRASES **the aftermath of the ~** ◇ *Unexploded mines were a big danger to civilians in the aftermath of the ~.* | **the brink of ~** ◇ *The crisis took Europe to the brink of ~.* | **the course of a/the ~** ◇ *He was wounded twice during the course of the ~.* | **a declaration of ~** ◇ *Congress has made a formal declaration of ~.* | **the horrors of ~** ◇ *The country had just emerged from the horrors of civil ~.* | **in a state of ~** ◇ *The country was now in a state of ~.* | **in time of ~, in times of ~** ◇ *In times of ~, troops were billeted in the mill.* | **on a ~ footing** ◇ *The army had been placed on a ~ footing.* | **the outbreak of ~** ◇ *At the outbreak of ~, most children were evacuated to the countryside.* | **the outcome of a/the ~** ◇ *The outcome of the ~ was far from certain.* | **a prisoner of ~** ◇ *He was held as a prisoner of ~.* | **a theatre/theater of ~** ◇ *The country has long been a theatre/theater of ~.* | **a ~ of attrition**

ward *noun*

ADJ. **open, public** (*both BrE*) | **private** (*BrE*) | **hospital** | **inpatient** (*esp. BrE*) | **isolation** (*esp. BrE*) | **maternity, psychiatric, surgical, etc.**

VERB + WARD **be admitted to** (*esp. BrE*) ◇ *He was admitted to the casualty ~.* | **be discharged from** (*esp. BrE*)

WARD + NOUN **nurse, sister, staff** (*all BrE*) | **round** (*BrE*) ◇ *The doctor was doing her morning ~ round.*

PREP. **in a/the ~** ◇ *She spent five days in the maternity ~.* | **on the ~** (*esp. BrE*) ◇ *How many midwives are on the ~?*

warden *noun*

ADJ. **deputy** | **church** (usually ***churchwarden***) (*esp. BrE*), **prison** (*esp. AmE*) | **park** (*esp. BrE*) | **game** ◇ *He is chief game ~ of the Masai Mara game reserve in Kenya.* | **community, neighbourhood, street** (*all BrE*) ◇ *Two neighbourhood ~s patrol the housing estate.* | **parking, traffic** (*both esp. BrE*) | **dog** (*BrE*)

→ Note at JOB

wardrobe *noun*

1 for storing clothes → See also CLOSET

ADJ. **built-in, fitted** (*both BrE*) | **double** (*BrE*) | **walk-in** (*BrE*)

VERB + WARDROBE **open** | **close**

WARDROBE + NOUN **door**

PREP. **in a/the ~** ◇ *She hung the dress up in the ~.*

PHRASES **the back of the ~, the bottom of the ~, the top of the ~** ◇ *I went through the pile of clothes at the back of my ~.*

2 sb's collection of clothes

ADJ. **new** | **extensive** | **whole** | **spring, summer, etc.**

VERB + WARDROBE **have** | **buy** ◇ *I want to buy a whole new summer ~.* | **build** ◇ *I want to build a ~ of classic, quality pieces.* | **change, revamp, update**

warehouse *noun*

ADJ. **30 000-square-foot, etc.** | **bonded** (*esp. BrE*) | **distribution, retail, wholesale** | **cotton, furniture, grain, wool, etc.** | **data** (*business*) | **abandoned, derelict, disused** (*esp. BrE*), **old** | **converted** ◇ *The offices are situated in a converted ~.* | **dockside**

VERB + WAREHOUSE **build** | **convert** ◇ *a residential district of ~s*

converted into lofts | **raid** ◇ *German police raided a ~ near Hamburg.*

WAREHOUSE + VERB **be filled with** ◇ *a ~ filled with crates*

WAREHOUSE + NOUN **manager, staff, worker** ◇ *He's a ~ manager for an import company.* | **district** (*esp. AmE*) ◇ *the ~ district of New Orleans* | **space** ◇ *The facility has over 6 905 square feet of ~ space.* | **store** (*AmE*) | **sale** (*AmE*)

wares *noun*

ADJ. **domestic, household**

VERB + WARES **sell** | **hawk, peddle, ply** ◇ *street traders hawking their ~* | **display, show, show off, showcase** | **shout** | **advertise, market, promote**

warfare *noun*

ADJ. **open** ◇ *Rivalry between football fans developed into open ~.* | **conventional, modern** | **biological, chemical, germ, nuclear** | **class, gang, internecine, tribal** | **guerrilla, siege, trench** | **aerial, air, naval, submarine** | **asymmetric, asymmetrical** ◇ *Terrorism is a response to asymmetric ~.* | **jungle, mountain, urban** | **economic, ideological, psychological** ◇ *a subtle form of psychological ~*

VERB + WARFARE **conduct, engage in, wage** ◇ *The rebels waged guerrilla ~ against the army.*

PREP. **~ against** ◇ *~ against other tribes* | **~ between** ◇ *~ between gangs*

warm *verb*

ADV. **properly, sufficiently, thoroughly** | **slightly** | **gently** | **gradually, slowly** | **instantly, quickly, rapidly, soon** ◇ *We soon ~ed up in front of the fire.* | **suddenly** ◇ *His voice suddenly ~ed.* | **through, up** ◇ *Return the bowl to the heat to ~ through.*

warm *adj.*

1 at a fairly high temperature

VERBS **be, feel, look, seem** | **become, get, grow, turn** ◇ *How can we get ~?* ◇ *She felt her face grow ~ at his remarks.* ◇ *The weather had turned ~.* | **keep, stay** ◇ *She tries to keep ~ by sitting right next to the fire.* ◇ *The bread should stay ~ for at least half an hour.* | **keep sb/sth, make sb/sth** ◇ *These will keep your feet ~.* | **serve sth** ◇ *Bake for 15 minutes and serve ~ with Greek yogurt.*

ADV. **extremely, fairly, very, etc.** | **exceptionally, particularly** | **almost** ◇ *It was a mild day, almost ~.* | **just** ◇ *Add the sour cream and cook, stirring, until just ~.* | **moderately, relatively** | **a little, slightly, etc.** | **enough, sufficiently** ◇ *Are you sure you'll be ~ enough dressed like that?* | **beautifully, comfortably, deliciously, pleasantly, wonderfully** ◇ *I slid further down into the pleasantly ~ bed* | **uncomfortably** ◇ *The room seemed uncomfortably ~.* | **surprisingly** | **unseasonably, unusually** ◇ *The night air was soft and unseasonably ~.*

PHRASES **nice (and) ~** ◇ *Come and have a nice ~ drink by the fire.* ◇ *That jacket looks nice and ~.* | **to the touch** ◇ *The machine may feel ~ to the touch.*

2 friendly

VERBS **be, sound** | **become**

ADV. **extremely, very** ◇ *an extremely ~ and friendly person* | **genuinely** | **surprisingly**

warmth *noun*

1 a fairly high temperature

ADJ. **comfortable, comforting, delicious, enveloping, glowing, pleasant** ◇ *the comforting ~ of her bed* ◇ *He moved closer to the pleasant ~ of the fire.* | **gentle** ◇ *the gentle ~ of the late summer sun* | **bodily** (*AmE*), **body** ◇ *This clothing maintains your body ~.*

VERB + WARMTH **feel** ◇ *She could feel the ~ of the child's hand in her own.* | **bask in, enjoy, revel in, savour/savor** ◇ *We lay on the beach, basking in the ~ of the hot sun.* | **add**

(*figurative*), **provide** ◇ *Browns and golds add ~ to a room.* | **retain** ◇ *Insulation will help retain the house's ~.*
WARMTH + VERB **radiate, spread** ◇ *She sat by the fire and felt the ~ spread through her body.*
PREP. **for ~** ◇ *They found the children huddled together for ~.* | **~ from** ◇ *~ from the radiator*

2 friendliness or kindness

ADJ. **great** | **genuine, real** | **emotional, human, personal** ◇ *She seems to be a person without human ~.*
VERB + WARMTH **bring, convey, exude, radiate, show** ◇ *a person who radiates ~ and kindness* | **lack**

warn *verb*

ADV. **clearly, explicitly** | **bluntly, firmly** ◇ *The chancellor bluntly ~ed the Cabinet to cut public spending or face higher taxes.* | **darkly, sternly** | **softly** ◇ *'Don't,' he ~ed softly.* | **specifically** ◇ *We were specifically ~ed against buying the house.* | **duly** ◇ *Having been duly ~ed that I would get nowhere with my application, I went right ahead and applied anyway.* | **always, constantly, repeatedly** ◇ *My mother constantly ~ed me not to go into teaching.* | **publicly**
VERB + WARN **had better, have to, must, should** ◇ *I must ~ you that some of these animals are extremely dangerous.* ◇ *I thought I should ~ her about it.* | **try to** ◇ *I did try to ~ you.* | **fail to** ◇ *She claimed doctors had failed to ~ her of the risks involved.*
PREP. **about** ◇ *No one had ~ed us about the unbearable heat.* | **against** ◇ *We were ~ed against drinking the local water.* | **of** ◇ *The report ~s of the dangers of obesity.* ◇ *They ~ed us of the risks involved.*
PHRASES **be ~ed** ◇ *You will get better—but be ~ed, it may be a long process.*

warning *noun*

ADJ. **dire, grim, ominous, stark** (*esp. BrE*), **stern, strong** ◇ *There were dire ~s about the dangers of watching too much TV.* | **repeated, urgent** | **adequate, advance, ample, due** (*esp. BrE*), **early, fair, prior** ◇ *I need advance ~ of how many people to cater for.* | **little** ◇ *There was little ~ of the coming disaster.* | **clear, specific** | **coded** (*BrE*) ◇ *The explosion came 20 minutes after a coded ~ to police.* | **first, initial, final, last** ◇ *The referee gave him a final ~.* | **formal, government, official** | **salutary** (*esp. BrE*), **timely** ◇ *The team's defeat is a salutary ~ before the World Cup.* | **friendly** | **veiled** ◇ *Her words sounded like a veiled ~.* | **audible, visual** ◇ *There is an audible ~ when a certain speed is exceeded.* | **verbal, written** (*both esp. BrE*) ◇ *His employers have placed him on final written ~.* | **intelligence** ◇ *intelligence ~s of terrorist attacks* | **air-raid, bomb, hazard, terror, terrorist, threat** (*AmE*) | **travel** (*esp. AmE*) | **fire, flood, gale, hurricane, storm, tornado, tsunami** ◇ *There are 39 severe flood ~s on 22 rivers across the country.* ◇ *A tropical storm ~ is in effect for the Gulf Coast.* | **health, safety** ◇ *Every cigarette packet carries a government health ~.* (*BrE*) | **profits** (*BrE*)
VERB + WARNING **give (sb), issue, post, send, send out** ◇ *The police have issued a ~ about pickpockets.* ◇ *Hurricane ~s have been posted on their website.* ◇ *The Institute has sent out a new ~ to all businesses.* | **provide** ◇ *The sensors provide early ~ of the approach of enemy troops.* | **shout, shout out, sound** ◇ *The sirens sound a ~ when fighter planes are sighted.* ◇ *The strike sounded a ~ to all employers in the industry.* | **reiterate, repeat** | **be, serve as** ◇ *Let this be a ~ to you not to trespass on my land again!* ◇ *What happened to him should serve as a ~ to all dishonest politicians.* | **get, have, receive** | **ignore** | **heed** ◇ *They failed to heed a ~ about the dangerous currents in the river.*
WARNING + VERB **come** ◇ *The ~ came just minutes before the bomb exploded.* | **sound** ◇ *On that day in 1916 air-raid ~s sounded throughout Edinburgh.*
WARNING + NOUN **label** (*esp. AmE*), **notice** (*esp. BrE*), **sign** ◇ *a campaign for health ~ labels on alcohol* ◇ *Red marks on the skin may be a ~ sign for this disease.* | **bell, light, signal, system**
PREP. **in ~** ◇ *The dog growled in ~ as we approached.* |

without ~ ◇ *He left his wife without ~.* | **~ about** ◇ *a ~ about teaching children to swim* | **~ against** ◇ *a ~ against complacency* | **~ of** ◇ *They sent us fair ~ of their arrival.* | **~ to** ◇ *The police issued a ~ to all drug users in the city.*
PHRASES **let that/this be a ~ (to you)** | **a word of ~** ◇ *He gave us a word of ~ about going out alone at night.*

warrant *noun*

ADJ. **arrest, death, search** ◇ *The king refused to sign the death ~ for his old friend.* | **royal** (*BrE*) | **outstanding** ◇ *He has an outstanding ~ for his arrest.* | **bench** (*AmE*) ◇ *The judge issued a bench ~.* | **criminal, judicial** (*both AmE*)
VERB + WARRANT **authorize, grant, issue, serve, sign** ◇ *The commissioner has issued a ~ for her arrest.* ◇ *The police served a ~ on him.* | **get, obtain** | **execute** ◇ *Police who executed a search ~ found a substantial amount of stolen property on the premises.* | **need, require** | **seek**
WARRANT + NOUN **card** (*BrE*)
PHRASES **without a ~** ◇ *In certain circumstances, police may enter premises without a ~.* | **~ for**

warranty *noun*

ADJ. **general** (*esp. BrE*) | **specific** (*esp. BrE*) ◇ *We can not give a specific ~ for the work done on your property.* | **six-month, two-year, year's** (*esp. BrE*), **etc.** | **extended, lifetime** ◇ *The tool comes with a lifetime ~.* | **limited**
VERB + WARRANTY **give, offer, provide** | **get** | **come with, have** ◇ *The computer comes with a year's ~ on all parts.* | **extend** ◇ *They've extended the ~ and the mileage.* | **carry** ◇ *The model carries a three-year ~.* | **void** (*esp. AmE*) ◇ *Manufacturers void their warranties if the labels have been tampered with.* | **buy, purchase**
WARRANTY + VERB **cover sth** ◇ *Corrosion is not covered by the ~.* | **expire, run out** | **cost**
WARRANTY + NOUN **period** | **claim** | **coverage** ◇ *The ~ coverage is 60 months.* | **repair, service, work** (*all esp. AmE*) | **cost** | **card** (*esp. AmE*) | **plan, policy** (*both esp. AmE*)
PREP. **under ~** ◇ *Is your car still under ~?* | **~ against** ◇ *a ~ against storm damage* | **~ on** ◇ *The ~ on my watch ran out just before it broke.*
PHRASES **breach of ~** ◇ *He took legal action against the company for breach of ~.*

warrior *noun*

ADJ. **fearless, fierce, formidable, great, mighty, noble, powerful** | **brave, valiant** | **famous, legendary, renowned** | **holy** ◇ *He views himself as a holy ~.* | **fellow** ◇ *He saved his fellow ~.* | **fallen** ◇ *the graves of the fallen ~s* | **seasoned, skilled, trained** | **armchair** ◇ *the armchair ~s at the Department of Defense* | **reluctant** | **ancient** ◇ *the last of the ancient ~s* | **weekend** (= person who exercises only at the weekend) (*AmE*) | **road** (= person who spends a lot of time driving) (*AmE*)
... OF WARRIORS **band**
WARRIOR + VERB **fight**

warship *noun*

ADJ. **modern** | **surface** | **naval** | **ironclad** | **enemy**
... OF WARSHIPS **fleet**
VERB + WARSHIP **build** | **command** | **sink** ◇ *A total of 18 ~s were sunk or heavily damaged.*
PREP. **aboard a ~, on a ~** ◇ *He is serving on a ~ in the Pacific.*

wary *adj.*

VERBS **be, feel, look, seem** | **become, get, grow** | **remain** | **make sb** ◇ *The strange look in his eyes made me ~ of accepting his offer.*
ADV. **extremely, fairly, very, etc.** | **decidedly, deeply** | **increasingly** | **especially, particularly** | **a little, slightly, etc.** | **instinctively, naturally** | **suddenly** ◇ *Paula frowned, suddenly ~.*
PREP. **about** ◇ *Be ~ about these so-called special offers.* | **of** ◇ *You should be very ~ of people offering cheap tickets.*
PHRASES **keep a ~ eye on sb/sth** (*often figurative*) ◇ *The chip manufacturers are keeping a ~ eye on the market.*

wash noun (esp. BrE)

ADJ. **good** | **quick** | **car** (BrE, AmE)
VERB + WASH **have** ◆ He had a quick ~ and shave. | **do** (BrE, AmE) ◆ I'm doing a dark ~ (= washing all the dark clothes together). | **could do with** (BrE), **could use** (AmE), **need** ◆ That car could do with a good ~.
PREP. **in the ~** (= being washed or waiting to be washed) (BrE, AmE) ◆ Your shirt's in the ~.
PHRASES **come out in the ~** (BrE, AmE, figurative) ◆ This will all come out in the ~ (= the truth will be revealed).

wash verb

ADV. **carefully, properly** (BrE), **thoroughly** | **gently** ◆ She gently ~ed and dressed the wound. | **quickly** | **frequently, regularly** ◆ Hands need to be ~ed regularly with hot water.
PHRASES **freshly ~ed, newly ~ed** ◆ the smell of freshly ~ed hair

washcloth noun (AmE)

ADJ. **damp, wet** | **cold** | **warm**
VERB + WASHCLOTH **wet** | **use** ◆ Use a damp ~ to clean the skin.
PREP. **with a ~** ◆ She wiped his forehead with a wet ~.

washing noun

1 cleaning sth with water

ADJ. **frequent, repeated** ◆ shampoo for frequent ~ | **good, thorough** ◆ After a thorough ~, I cut up the stalks and florets.
VERB + WASHING **do** (esp. BrE) ◆ I have some ~ to do today.
WASHING + NOUN **powder** (BrE)

2 (BrE) clothes

ADJ. **dirty**
... OF WASHING **line** ◆ A line of ~ fluttered in the breeze. | **pile** | piles of dirty ~
VERB + WASHING **hang out, put out** ◆ Can you hang the ~ out?
WASHING + NOUN **line**

washing machine noun

ADJ. **automatic**
VERB + WASHING MACHINE **load, put sth in** | **empty** | **run** ◆ How often do you run your ~? | **turn on**
PREP. **in a/the ~, into a/the ~** | **through a/the ~** (esp. AmE) ◆ I ran a load of laundry through the ~.

washing-up (BrE) noun

VERB + WASHING-UP **do** | **leave** ◆ Leave the washing-up—we can do it in the morning.
WASHING-UP + NOUN **bowl** | **liquid**

wasp noun

WASP + VERB **crawl, fly** | **sting sb** | **buzz**
WASP + NOUN **sting** | **nest** (AmE)
PHRASES **a wasp's nest**

wastage noun

ADJ. **excessive, high** | **natural** (BrE) ◆ Natural ~ will cut staff numbers to the required level. | **muscle** (BrE) ◆ Patients need exercise to prevent muscle ~.
VERB + WASTAGE **avoid, prevent** | **minimize** | **reduce** | **increase** | **allow for** ◆ Buy more paper than you need to allow for ~.

waste noun

1 missing an opportunity to do/use sth

ADJ. **absolute, complete, total, utter** ◆ The whole thing has been a complete ~ of time. | **big, colossal, enormous, great, huge, tremendous** | **awful, criminal, senseless, shocking, terrible** ◆ a criminal ~ of public money | **needless, pointless, unnecessary, useless** | **tragic** ◆ a tragic ~ of human life | **expensive** | **conspicuous**
VERB + WASTE **go to** ◆ If nobody comes all this food will go to ~. | **cause** | **avoid** ◆ Try to avoid unnecessary ~. | **cut, cut down on, reduce** | **minimize**
PREP. **~ of** ◆ a ~ of energy/resources

2 unwanted substances/things

ADJ. **dangerous, harmful, hazardous, poisonous, toxic** ◆ a dump containing hazardous ~ | **high-level, low-level** | **recyclable** (esp. BrE), **recycled** | **agricultural, commercial, industrial** | **domestic, household, kitchen** ◆ All household ~ should be disposed of in strong garbage bags. | **clinical** (BrE), **hospital, infectious** (esp. AmE), **medical** | **nuclear, radioactive** | **chemical** | **plastic** | **electronic** ◆ the vast amounts of electronic ~ being shipped to developing countries | **green, organic** | **animal, fish, hog** (AmE), **livestock, poultry** | **bodily, body, human** | **factory, mining, slaughterhouse** (esp. AmE) ◆ new regulations on the feeding of slaughterhouse ~ to cattle | **garden** (esp. BrE), **plant, vegetable, wood, yard** (AmE) | **municipal** | **liquid, solid** | **energy, food** | **building** (BrE), **construction** (AmE) ◆ Three quarters of all construction ~ was recycled.
VERB + WASTE **create, generate, produce** ◆ Tonnes of ~ are produced every year. | **dispose of, dump, get rid of** ◆ More people are dumping ~ illegally. | **clean up, remove** ◆ the highly expensive task of cleaning up toxic ~ | **burn, incinerate** ◆ an incinerator for burning hospital ~ | **bury, store** | **process, treat** ◆ facilities for processing radioactive ~ | **convert into sth, recycle** ◆ technology to convert solid ~ into renewable energy | **deal with, handle, manage** ◆ the best solutions for managing ~ | **cut, cut down on, minimize, reduce** | **eliminate** | **export, import** ◆ Industrialized countries continue to export their ~.
WASTE + VERB **contaminate sth, pollute sth** ◆ areas contaminated by industrial ~
WASTE + NOUN **collection** | **disposal, incineration** | **storage** | **processing, recycling** (BrE), **reprocessing** (BrE), **treatment** ◆ a ~ processing plant | **management** | **minimization, reduction** | **basket, bin** (BrE), **paper basket** (esp. BrE) | **dump, facility, repository** (esp. AmE), **site, tip** (BrE) ◆ The river was used for years as an industrial ~ dump. | **incinerator** | **pipe** (esp. BrE)

3 wastes areas of ground not lived in or cultivated

ADJ. **desert, frozen, icy** ◆ the frozen ~s of Antarctica

waste verb

ADV. **(not) completely, (not) entirely, (not) totally** ◆ In the end her efforts were not entirely ~d. | **just, simply** ◆ You're just wasting your breath. She never listens. | **largely**
VERB + WASTE **can't afford to, not want to** ◆ He didn't want to ~ valuable time in idle gossip. | **hate to** ◆ Their father hated to ~ energy. | **be a shame to, seem a shame to** ◆ It seems a shame to ~ this good food. | **not be going to, not intend to, refuse to** ◆ I'm not going to ~ any more time on the problem.
PREP. **on** ◆ Don't ~ your money on a hotel room.
PHRASES **no time to ~** ◆ Hurry up—there's no time to ~!

watch noun

1 instrument for telling the time

ADJ. **digital** | **analogue/analog, mechanical** (esp. AmE) | **pocket, wrist** (usually **wristwatch**) | **sports** | **designer** | **antique** | **quartz** | **diamond, gold, silver**
VERB + WATCH **check, consult, glance at, look at** | **reset, set** ◆ Don't forget to set your ~ to local time. | **synchronize** ◆ Let's synchronize our ~es. | **wind** ◆ Quartz ~es don't need winding. | **have on, wear** | **put on** | **take off**
WATCH + VERB **go, work** ◆ My ~ is ten years old and it's still going. | **stop** ◆ Sorry I'm late—my ~ has stopped. | **be slow, lose sth** ◆ My ~ loses a minute each day. | **be fast, gain sth** | **read sth** (esp. AmE), **say sth, show sth** ◆ My ~ says three o'clock. | **beep** ◆ Her wrist ~ beeped.
WATCH + NOUN **face** | **band** (usually **watchband**) (AmE), **strap** (BrE) | **battery**

2 guard

ADJ. **careful, close, vigilant** (esp. BrE) ◆ I kept a close ~ on my bag as I sat on the train. ◆ They kept a vigilant ~ for the enemy. | **constant** | **night** | **flood, hurricane** (esp. AmE), **storm, tornado** (esp. AmE) ◆ We have tornado ~es in effect

for a lot of Florida. | **suicide** ◇ *prisoners on suicide ~* |
neighbourhood/neighborhood
VERB + WATCH **keep, stand** ◇ *Two soldiers were ordered to keep ~ for enemy aircraft.* | **put** ◇ *The garrison commander had put an extra ~ on the prisoners.* | **post** ◇ *That night they posted ~es.* | **maintain** ◇ *The authorities maintained a careful ~ over the establishment.* | **issue** (*AmE*) ◇ *They're in charge of issuing the tornado ~es.*
WATCH + NOUN **committee** | **tower** | **list** (*AmE*) ◇ *the terrorist ~ list*
PREP. **on ~** ◇ *Some of the crew were sleeping, while others were on ~.* | **on the ~ for** ◇ *Cats are constantly on the ~ for mice or other small mammals.*
PHRASES **keep ~ over sb/sth, stand ~ over sb/sth** ◇ *She keeps ~ over the inmates.*

watch verb

ADV. **carefully, closely** ◇ *She ~ed the man closely to see where he would go.* | **attentively, avidly, eagerly, expectantly, intensely** (*esp. AmE*), **intently** | **curiously** ◇ *I could see Robby ~ing curiously.* | **absently, idly, lazily** | **calmly, impassively, numbly, passively** | **patiently** ◇ *I spent hours patiently ~ing the eagles.* | **anxiously, apprehensively, helplessly, nervously, warily** ◇ *She ~ed helplessly as her husband was dragged away.* | **open-mouthed** | **enviously** ◇ *He leant in and kissed her as I ~ed enviously.* | **amusedly** (*AmE*), **in amusement, with amusement** | **covertly, secretly** | **in silence, quietly, silently** | **just, merely, simply** ◇ *I love just ~ing the world go by.* | **religiously** ◇ *My father religiously ~ed the show every Friday night.*
VERB + WATCH **could only** ◇ *They could only ~ in silence as their possessions were taken away.* | **continue to** | **pause to, stay to, stop to** ◇ *They stopped to ~ the procession go by.* | **let sb** ◇ *He let me ~ while he assembled the model.*
PREP. **for** ◇ *We ~ed for any sign of change in the weather.* | **from** ◇ *They ~ed from an upstairs window.* | **in** ◇ *She ~ed in astonishment as he smashed the machine to pieces.* | **over** ◇ *Maria asked Amelia to ~ over her daughter.* | **with** ◇ *He ~ed with great interest how she coaxed the animals inside.*
PHRASES **sit and ~, stand and ~** ◇ *She stood and ~ed them walk off down the road.* | **~ and wait** ◇ *He couldn't get in touch with her, so he would just have to ~ and wait.* | **widely ~ed** ◇ *the most widely ~ed national news bulletins in the country*

watchdog noun

ADJ. **consumer** | **environmental, financial, health** (*BrE*), **industry, media** (*esp. AmE*), **nuclear, safety** | **privacy** (*esp. AmE*) | **government, independent, official, public**
VERB + WATCHDOG **act as, be**
WATCHDOG + NOUN **agency, body, group, organization** | **function, role** | **site, website** | **journalism** (*AmE*) ◇ *reporters who do the real work of ~ journalism*
PREP. **~ for** ◇ *an independent ~ for civil rights* | **~ of** ◇ *an unofficial ~ of pesticide use* | **~ on** ◇ *the government's official ~ on nature conservation* | **~ over** ◇ *The committee acts as an independent ~ over government spending.*

water noun
1 liquid

ADJ. **boiling, chilled, cold, cool, freezing, frigid** (*AmE*), **hot, ice-cold, icy, lukewarm, steaming, tepid, warm** ◇ *I could feel the icy ~ entering my lungs.* | **ice** (*AmE*), **iced** (*esp. BrE*) | **clean, clear, crystal-clear, pure** | **dirty** | **contaminated, polluted** | **fresh** | **brackish, salt** ◇ *These fish will quickly die in salt ~.* | **salted** ◇ *Cook the pasta in plenty of boiling salted ~.* | **soapy** ◇ *Alexis filled the sink with soapy ~.* | **hard, soft** | **dripping, flowing, pouring, running, rushing** ◇ *the fast-flowing ~ of the river* ◇ *All the rooms have hot and cold running ~.* | **lake, ocean** (*esp. AmE*), **river, sea** | **surface** ◇ *The surface ~ made the road treacherous for drivers.* | **ground** ◇ *areas which are dependent on ground ~* | **drinking, potable** (*esp. AmE*) | **tap** ◇ *Avoid drinking the tap*

~ *when you first arrive in the country.* | **well** ◇ *the purest well ~* | **bottled, mineral, sparkling, spring** | **soda** | **flavoured/flavored** | **boiled, distilled, filtered, sterile** | **deionized** | **waste** | **irrigation** ◇ *The farmers draw their irrigation ~ from the Colorado.* | **excess** ◇ *She dried off the excess ~ from her hair.* | **holy** ◇ *He kept sprinkling holy ~ on Mia.* | **scarce**
... OF WATER **drop** | **drink, sip** | **cup, glass**
VERB + WATER **drink, sip** | **gulp, gulp down** | **pour** | **slosh, spill, splash, spray, sprinkle, spurt, squirt** ◇ *Don't slosh too much ~ on the floor when you're having a bath.* ◇ *The burst pipe was spurting ~ everywhere.* | **filter, purify** | **contaminate, pollute** | **boil, heat** ◇ *Residents are being asked to boil their drinking ~.* | **bring, carry, fetch** ◇ *a woman fetching ~* | **pump** ◇ *How do you pump the ~ up here?* | **drain** ◇ *He twisted it to drain the excess ~.* | **absorb** ◇ *That causes the moss to absorb ~.* | **turn off, turn on** ◇ *They turned the ~ off for a few hours to do some work on the pipes.*
WATER + VERB **flow, pour, run** | **gush, rush, spurt** ◇ *Brown ~ gushed out of the rusty old tap.* | **drip, trickle** ◇ *There was ~ dripping from a hole in the ceiling.* | **lap, slosh, spill, splash, spray, squirt** ◇ *Water got into the boat and was sloshing around under our feet.* | **boil, cool, cool down, freeze** | **evaporate** ◇ *As the weather heats up, ~ evaporates.*
WATER + NOUN **vapour/vapor** | **temperature** | **pressure** | **supply** | **resources** | **quality** | **purification, treatment** | **filter** | **pipe** | **tank, tower** | **pump** | **pollution** | **shortage** | **level** | **table** ◇ *Building can be difficult where the ~ table lies close to the surface.* | **source** ◇ *the region's most important fresh ~ source* | **power** | **company, industry** | **conservation, management** (*esp. AmE*) | **bottle** | **cooler** (*esp. AmE*), **fountain** (*both esp. AmE*) | **heater** (*esp. AmE*) ◇ *household ~ heaters*

2 mass of water

ADJ. **deep, shallow** | **clear** | **muddy, murky, stagnant** | **calm, placid** (*esp. BrE*), **still** ◇ *the calm ~s of Lake Como* | **choppy, rough, stormy** | **dangerous, safe** ◇ *At last the boat reached safer ~s.* | **open** ◇ *large expanses of open ~* | **flood** (usually *floodwater*) ◇ *The floodwater had caused tremendous damage.* | **standing** ◇ *Some fields have areas with standing ~.* | **rising** ◇ *They climbed a tree to escape the rising ~.* | **bath, bathing** (*esp. BrE*) | **ballast** ◇ *the ballast ~ of ocean-going freighters*
WATER + VERB **rise** ◇ *The ~ was rising fast.* | **recede** ◇ *The ~ is now receding after the floods.*
WATER + NOUN **sports**
PREP. **by ~** ◇ *Goods were often transported by ~ in the 19th century.* | **in the ~** ◇ *I saw something large floating in the ~.* | **on the ~** ◇ *The swan landed gracefully on the ~.* | **through the ~** ◇ *The boat cut effortlessly through the ~.* | **under the ~** ◇ *An abandoned town lies under the ~ of the reservoir.*
PHRASES **the water's edge** ◇ *She crouched at the water's edge to wash her hands.*

3 waters sea

ADJ. **territorial** | **coastal** | **tropical** | **northern, southern** | **Antarctic, Arctic** | **Atlantic, Pacific, etc.** | **foreign, home, international** | **Japanese, etc.** | **uncharted** ◇ *The ship had drifted into uncharted ~s.* | **navigable** ◇ *inland navigable ~s* | **freezing, icy** ◇ *the icy ~s of the North Atlantic* | **shark-infested** ◇ *the shark-infested ~s off the coast of Florida*
PREP. **in...~, into...~** ◇ *The submarine had strayed into Russian ~s.*

waterfall noun

ADJ. **great, high** | **beautiful, impressive, magnificent, spectacular** | **cascading** | **small**
WATERFALL + VERB **cascade, fall, flow, pour down, tumble** ◇ *She watched the magnificent ~ cascade down the mountainside.* ◇ *The ~ fell about twenty feet to swirling rapids.*

watershed noun

ADJ. **historic, important, major** | **cultural, historical, political**
VERB + WATERSHED **be, mark, represent** | **reach**
WATERSHED + VERB **divide sth** ◇ *Darwin's theory of evolution was a ~ dividing the old way of thinking from the new.*

WATERSHED + NOUN **moment** ◊ *a ~ moment in recent music history* | **event** ◊ *The completion of this project was a ~ event in the company's history.* | **year** ◊ *a ~ year for Japan* | **project** | **decision**

PREP. **~ between** ◊ *The 19th century marked a ~ between the country's agricultural past and its industrial future.* | **~ for** ◊ *The granting of the vote represented a ~ for the rights of women.* | **~ in** ◊ *With the strike, a historical ~ in the development of the trade union movement was reached.*

wave *noun*

1 on water

ADJ. **big, enormous, giant, great, huge, mountainous** | **small, tiny** | **10-foot, 40-foot, etc.** | **gentle** ◊ *the gentle ~s of the bay* | **white-capped** | **incoming, oncoming** ◊ *He swam headlong into the oncoming ~.* | **breaking** | **crashing** | **rolling** | **lapping** | **ocean** ◊ *the roar of ocean ~s* | **tidal, tsunami** ◊ *Several villages have been destroyed by a huge tidal ~.* | **rogue** ◊ *These boats aren't strong enough to withstand rogue ~s.*

VERB + WAVE **ride** ◊ *Surfers flocked to the beach to ride the ~s.* | **surf** ◊ *She loved surfing the giant ~s of the sea.* | **catch** (*often figurative*) ◊ *How do we catch the next great ~ of innovation?*

WAVE + VERB **rise** | **break, fall, roll, roll in** ◊ *We watched the ~s breaking on the shore.* | **hit sth, pound sth, strike sth** ◊ *The ~s hit the rocks with huge energy.* | **lap** ◊ *the gentle sound of ~s lapping the sand* | **splash** ◊ *A huge ~ splashed over him.* | **crash, roar, smash** ◊ *I could hear the ~s crash against the rocks.*

WAVE + NOUN **energy, power**

PREP. **in the ~s** ◊ *children playing in the ~s* | **on the ~s** ◊ *There were seagulls bobbing on the ~s.*

PHRASES **the crash of the ~s, the crashing of the ~s, the lap of the ~s, the lapping of the ~s** ◊ *All you could hear was the lapping of the ~s.* | **the crest of a ~** (*often figurative*) ◊ *She is on the crest of a ~ at the moment following her Olympic success.*

2 movement of energy

ADJ. **acoustic, electromagnetic, gravitational, gravity, light, radio, seismic, shock, sound, ultrasonic**

VERB + WAVE **emit, generate** | **deflect** | **detect**

WAVE + VERB **travel** | **bounce off sth, travel** ◊ *Sound ~s bounce off objects in their path.*

3 increase/spread

ADJ. **big, enormous, great, huge, massive** | **fresh, new, next, recent** | **current** ◊ *the current ~ of business scandals* | **successive** ◊ *successive ~s of immigrants* | **first, second, etc.** ◊ *the first ~ of immigration in the 1950s* | **crime**

VERB + WAVE **send** ◊ *The news sent a ~ of relief through the crowd.* | **cause, generate, produce, prompt, spark, trigger** ◊ *This tendency has generated a new ~ of company mergers.* | **launch, unleash** ◊ *The attack unleashed a ~ of terror in the city.* | **feel** ◊ *I feel a ~ of panic flow through me.*

WAVE + VERB **sweep sth, sweep over sth, wash over sb/sth, wash through sb/sth** ◊ *With the fall of the Bastille in 1789, a ~ of euphoria swept Europe.* ◊ *A ~ of relief washed over him as he saw that the children were safe.*

PREP. **~ of** ◊ *a big ~ of refugees* | **on a ~** ◊ *swept along on a ~ of critical acclaim*

4 hand movement

ADJ. **quick** | **little, slight** (*esp. AmE*) | **cheery, friendly** | **farewell, goodbye** (*esp. AmE*), **parting** | **casual** | **dismissive** ◊ *She gave a dismissive ~ of her hand.* | **half-hearted**

VERB + WAVE **give (sb), return** ◊ *I returned his ~ and started to walk up to him.*

PREP. **with a ~** | **~ of** ◊ *He dismissed her thanks with a quick ~ of the hand.*

wave *verb*

ADV. **gently** ◊ *reeds waving gently in the breeze* | **vigorously** | **cheerfully, cheerily, happily** | **proudly** | **enthusiastically, excitedly, frantically, madly, wildly** ◊ *They stood by the side of the road and ~d frantically.* | **quickly** | **slightly** (*esp. AmE*) ◊ *She smiled and ~d slightly.* | **just, merely, simply** |

vaguely ◊ *He ~d a hand vaguely in the air.* | **casually** | **dismissively** | **half-heartedly** | **shyly** | **about** (*esp. BrE*), **around, aside, away, back, in, on, through** ◊ *She waved cheerfully and he ~d back.* ◊ *The guards ~d us on.*

VERB + WAVE **turn and, turn to** ◊ *He turned to ~ to his mother.*

PREP. **at** ◊ *We ~d at the people on the shore.* | **to** ◊ *They ~d to us as we passed.* ◊ *She ~d him to a seat.*

PHRASES **~ (sb) goodbye** ◊ *people waving goodbye to their friends and relatives*

wavelength *noun*

ADJ. **long, medium, short** | **infrared, ultraviolet** | **visible** | **radio**

VERB + WAVELENGTH **be tuned to**

PREP. **on a/the ~** ◊ *LPP Radio has broadcast on this ~ for years.*

PHRASES **on the same ~** (*figurative*) ◊ *My boss and I are just not on the same ~.*

way *noun*

1 method/style

ADJ. **convenient, easy, effective, efficient, good, ideal, practical, quick, simple, useful** ◊ *The best ~ to open it is with pliers.* | **appropriate, proper, right** | **wrong** | **normal** | **traditional** | **obvious** | **sure-fire** ◊ *a sure-fire ~ to get him to do whatever I want* | **important** ◊ *The most important ~ to stop accidental drownings is by education.* | **subtle** ◊ *There is no subtle ~ to tell someone that you no longer want them.* | **clever, ingenious** ◊ *I would think of some clever ~ to get myself out of this situation.* | **possible** ◊ *They've explored every possible ~ of dealing with the problem.* | **alternative, different** | **myriad, several, various** ◊ *Students develop those skills in myriad ~s.* | **same, similar** | **unique** ◊ *a unique ~ of settling disputes* | **new** | **old** | **old-fashioned** ◊ *We did it the old-fashioned ~.* | **funny, mysterious, odd, strange** ◊ *God works in mysterious ~s.* | **meaningful** ◊ *They have never contributed in any meaningful ~ to our civilization.* | **hard** ◊ *He learned about the dangers of drugs the hard ~.* | **friendly** | **winning** (*often figurative*) ◊ *The team got back to their winning ~s with a 2–1 victory.* ◊ *She isn't known for her winning ~s* (= *for being likeable*). | **creative, innovative** ◊ *We are searching for innovative and creative ~s to solve the many problems facing us.* | **cost-effective** ◊ *a cost-effective ~ to boost performance*

... OF WAYS **number** ◊ *There are a number of ~s to overcome this problem.*

VERB + WAY **have** ◊ *Fate has a ~ of changing the best of plans.* | **explore, look at, seek** ◊ *to look at ~s of improving language teaching* | **develop, devise, discover, figure out** (*esp. AmE*), **find, identify** ◊ *They believe he'll figure out a ~ to make it work.* | **create, invent** ◊ *Artists began to invent new ~s of painting.* | **change, mend** ◊ *Your father is unlikely to change his ~s now.* | **choose** ◊ *I chose a different ~ of collecting data.* | **react** ◊ *We expect computers to react a certain ~, in certain situations.* | **set in** ◊ *Grandma is so set in her ~s.*

PREP. **in a/the ~** ◊ *Can I help you in any ~?*

PHRASES **in a certain ~** ◊ *In a certain ~, all of that is true.* | **in a big ~** ◊ *He then started spending money in a big ~.* | **in every ~** ◊ *They're different in every ~.* | **in more ~s than one** ◊ *They're alike in more ~s than one.* | **in its/your own ~** ◊ *He was attractive in his own ~.* | **in some ~s** ◊ *It's more interesting, in some ~s, to watch what's going on behind the scenes here.* | **a ... kind of ~, a ... sort of ~** ◊ *He was a handsome man in a sinister sort of ~.* | **one ~ or another** ◊ *One ~ or another, I'm going to make it.* | **in one ~ or another** ◊ *Most people are creative in one ~ or another.* | **that's one ~ of putting it** ◊ *'She has a slightly abrasive manner.' 'Well, that's one ~ of putting it!'* | **put another ~** ◊ *Do you remember? Or, put another ~, do you know?* | **the ~ things are, the ~ things are going** ◊ *She is content with the ~ things are.* ◊ *The ~ things are going, I think that's achievable.* | **a ~ of life** ◊ *the beliefs and practices of the Hindu ~ of life* | **~s and means** ◊ *Newspapers have ~s and means of getting hold of secret information.*

2 route/road

ADJ. **best, quickest, right, shortest** | **wrong** | **own, separate** (*figurative*) ◇ *He's always gone his own ~ when it comes to design.* | **roundabout** ◇ *This is a roundabout ~ of saying that nothing has been accomplished.*

VERB + WAY **go** ◇ *I'm going your ~, so we can walk together.* ◇ *When we finished school, we all went our separate ~s.* (*figurative*) | **part** ◇ *We parted ~s once we went off to college.* | **go out of** (*figurative*) ◇ *She went out of her ~ to help them.* | **keep out of, stay out of** (*both figurative*) ◇ *Let's keep out of her ~ while she's in such a bad mood.* | **bar, block, get in, stand in** ◇ *A fallen tree blocked the ~.* ◇ *He wanted to go to college and would let nothing stand in his ~.* (*figurative*) | **clear, pave, prepare, smooth** (*all figurative*) ◇ *The withdrawal of troops should clear the ~ for a peace settlement.* | **give, make** (= allow sb/sth to go first or take your place) ◇ *Give ~ to traffic already on the roundabout.* (*BrE*) ◇ *The storm gave ~ to bright sunshine.* (*figurative*) ◇ *Make ~ for the guests!* ◇ *Tropical forest is felled to make ~ for grassland.* | **edge, feel, grope, inch, make, push, thread, weave, wend, wind, work** ◇ *He edged his ~ along the wall.* ◇ *The river wound its ~ through the valley.* | **claw, cut, elbow, fight, force, hack, pick, shoulder, shove** ◇ *She fought her ~ up to the top of the company.* (*figurative*) ◇ *We picked our ~ carefully over the jagged rocks.* | **bluff, talk, trick** (*figurative*) ◇ *She bluffed her ~ through the exam.* | **weasel, worm** ◇ *He had somehow wormed his ~ into her affections.* | **snake** ◇ *The procession snaked its ~ through the town.* | **lose** ◇ *She lost her ~ in the fog.* ◇ *This project seems to have lost its ~.* (*figurative*) | **find** ◇ *He couldn't find a ~ through the bracken.* ◇ *We will eventually find a ~ out of the crisis.* (*figurative*) | **manoeuvre/maneuver, navigate** ◇ *He had to navigate his ~ through the city's one-way streets.* | **ask (sb)** ◇ *She asked him the ~ to the station.* | **tell sb** | **know** ◇ *Do you know the ~?* | **come** (*figurative*) ◇ *Have any interesting articles come your ~ recently?*

PREP. **along the ~** ◇ *We saw a dreadful accident along the ~.* | **in the/your ~** ◇ *There were several rocks in the ~.* | **out of the/your ~** ◇ *Could you please get those boxes out of my ~?* | **on the/your ~** ◇ *We stopped for a snack on the ~ here.* | **out of the/your ~** ◇ *The library is slightly out of my ~.* | **~ across** ◇ *The ~ across the fields is longer but pleasanter.* | **~ from** | **~ out of** ◇ *Can you tell me the ~ out of here?* | **~ through** ◇ *The ~ through the woods is quicker.* | **~ to** ◇ *the easiest ~ from my house to yours*

PHRASES **take the easy ~ out** ◇ *He took the easy ~ out and paid someone to write the article for him.* | **the ~ back, the ~ forward** ◇ *On the ~ back, he invited me to his home for drinks.* | **the ~ down, the ~ up** | **the ~ here, the ~ over, the ~ there** | **the ~ home** ◇ *We stopped for a drink on the ~ home.* | **the ~ in, the ~ out** | **the ~ north, south, etc.** ◇ *We didn't stop on the ~ north.* | **on your merry ~** ◇ *Then he went off on his merry ~.*

3 direction/position

ADJ. **both** ◇ *Look both ~s before crossing the road.* | **opposite** ◇ *I went the opposite ~.* | **right** | **wrong** ◇ *They've gone the wrong ~.*

VERB + WAY **go** ◇ *Which ~ did she go?* | **lead, point, show** ◇ *He showed us the ~.* ◇ *There's a huge storm heading this ~.* | **walk** ◇ *Walk this ~, please.* | **look** ◇ *He looked my ~, but didn't seem to recognize me.*

PHRASES **the … way around, the … way round** (*esp. BrE*) ◇ *Try it the other ~ around.* | **the … way up** ◇ *Which ~ up does this box go?* | **~ to go!** (used to express approval) (*informal, esp. AmE*) ◇ *Way to go! I wish I could do that!*

4 distance in space/time

ADJ. **long** | **little, short**

VERB + WAY **come, go** ◇ *We had to go a long ~ before we found a place to eat.* ◇ *The study of genes has come a long ~ in recent years.* (*figurative*)

PREP. **~ from, ~ to** ◇ *It's quite a ~ from my house to the station.*

PHRASES **all the ~** ◇ *This bus doesn't go all the ~ so you'll have*

to change. | **the whole ~** (*AmE*) ◇ *the whole ~ to Arizona* | **the whole ~ through** ◇ *I watched the movie the whole ~ through.* | **quite a ~, some ~** ◇ *It's quite a ~ to walk to the station.* | **a … way ahead, a … way away, a … way off** ◇ *Your birthday is still some ~ off.*

weak adj.

VERBS **appear, be, feel, look, seem, sound** | **become, get, go, grow** | **remain** | **leave sb, make sb** ◇ *When the spasm passed, it left him ~ and sweating.*

ADV. **extremely, fairly, very, etc.** | **decidedly, especially, exceptionally, incredibly, particularly** | **a little, slightly, etc.** | **comparatively, relatively** | **fundamentally** | **curiously** ◇ *He complained of feeling curiously ~ and faint.* | **surprisingly** | **dangerously** | **notoriously** | **pathetically, pitifully** | **suddenly** ◇ *Her legs felt suddenly ~.* | **inherently** ◇ *The judge decided the evidence was inherently ~ and inconsistent.* | **economically, financially, mentally, militarily, morally, physically, politically**

PREP. **at** ◇ *She's rather ~ at languages.* | **from** ◇ *She was ~ from shock.* | **in** ◇ *He's ~ in English.* | **on** ◇ *The essay was rather ~ on detail.* | **with** ◇ *He was ~ with hunger.*

PHRASES **~ at the knees** ◇ *His sudden smile made her go ~ at the knees.*

weaken verb

ADV. **considerably, greatly, seriously, severely, significantly, substantially** | **badly** ◇ *The military was badly ~ed by the sanctions.* | **fatally** ◇ *The regime was fatally ~ed by the unrest and violence.* | **dramatically** ◇ *exchange rates that dramatically ~ed the dollar* | **further** | **slightly, somewhat** | **gradually, progressively, steadily** ◇ *Central authority has been progressively ~ed since the outbreak of the civil war.* | **permanently** | **eventually, ultimately** ◇ *The storm eventually ~ed.*

VERB + WEAKEN **begin to, start to** | **continue to** ◇ *The British pound continued to ~ against the dollar.* | **serve to** ◇ *The judgement serves to ~ public confidence in the courts.* | **attempt to, try to** | **tend to** | **threaten to** | **be designed to** ◇ *a move designed to ~ the rebels*

weakness noun

1 lack of strength

ADJ. **big, fundamental, great, major, profound, serious, significant** | **glaring** ◇ *The team doesn't have any glaring ~es.* | **fatal** ◇ *a fatal ~ in his theory* | **primary** | **small** | **physical** | **structural** | **methodological** | **personal** | **muscle, muscular** | **economic, political** | **apparent, perceived** ◇ *The criminals exploit apparent ~es in the system.* | **obvious** ◇ *She didn't seem to have any obvious ~es.* | **inherent, intrinsic** | **institutional** | **underlying** ◇ *the underlying ~ of the coalition's position* | **possible, potential** ◇ *Make companies aware of potential ~es so they know what steps to take.* | **relative** ◇ *a position of relative ~* | **human** | **moral**

VERB + WEAKNESS **have, suffer from** | **cause, create** | **exploit** | **assess, identify** | **address** ◇ *The management had to address specific ~es in training.* | **demonstrate, expose, highlight, point out, point to, reveal, show** | **acknowledge, admit, recognize** ◇ *business leaders who refuse to admit their ~es* | **hide** | **know** ◇ *They know their strengths and ~es.* | **minimize, overcome**

WEAKNESS + VERB **be, lie** ◇ *The greatest ~ of the plan lies in its lack of government support.*

PREP. **~ in** ◇ *Service conditions soon revealed the inherent ~es in the vehicle's design.*

PHRASES **a moment of ~** ◇ *In a moment of ~ I let him drive my car.* | **a sign of ~** ◇ *He saw compromise as a sign of ~.* | **strengths and ~es** ◇ *The appraisal system seeks to assess employees' strengths and ~es.*

2 liking for sth/sb

ADJ. **real**

VERB + WEAKNESS **have** ◇ *I have a real ~ for chocolate.* | **develop** | **overcome**

PREP. **~ for** ◇ *He can't overcome his ~ for fatty foods.*

wealth noun

1 money, property, etc.

ADJ. **considerable, enormous, fabulous, great, immense, incredible, tremendous, unimaginable, unprecedented, untold, vast** ◇ *It is a country of fabulous ~.* | **growing, increasing** | **relative** ◇ *the relative ~ of the nation* | **economic, financial, material, mineral, natural** ◇ *The country's strong economy was built on its mineral ~.* ◇ *The region possesses a vast natural ~, particularly of timber.* | **oil** ◇ *the great oil ~ of the region* | **net** ◇ *The average family increased its net ~ by 50% between 1989 and 2001.* | **corporate, national, personal, private** | **household** (*esp. AmE*) ◇ *Rising employment and household ~ are bolstering spending.* | **family, inherited** ◇ *a tax on inherited ~* | **new-found** ◇ *She wants to protect their new-found ~.* | **instant** ◇ *the pursuit of instant ~* | **new** ◇ *the kind of capital that generates new ~* | **accumulated** ◇ *the accumulated ~ from his business* | **total** ◇ *the total ~ of the global economy*
VERB + WEALTH **have, possess** | **accumulate, achieve, acquire, amass, build, gain, increase** | **inherit** | **lose** ◇ *He lost his ~ through poor investment.* | **transfer** | **create, generate, produce** | **distribute, share, spread** ◇ *He has no family with whom he can share his ~.* | **concentrate** | **display, flaunt** ◇ *He's never flaunted his ~.* | **enjoy** ◇ *She enjoys enormous ~ and material pleasures.*
PHRASES **a distribution of ~, a redistribution of ~** ◇ *a redistribution of ~ through taxation*

2 a wealth of a lot of

ADJ. **enormous, great, immense, incredible, tremendous, whole**
VERB + A WEALTH OF **have** ◇ *Switzerland has an enormous ~ of beautiful old buildings.* | **offer, provide** ◇ *The website provides a ~ of information.* | **bring** ◇ *He brings a ~ of experience to the cooperative.* | **contain** ◇ *This chapter contains a ~ of information in a very concise form.*
PREP. **of … ~** ◇ *She is a woman of untold ~.*

wealthy adj.

VERBS **be, look** | **become, grow**
ADV. **extremely, fairly, very, etc.** | **enormously, exceedingly, exceptionally, fabulously, immensely, incredibly, seriously** (*informal*) ◇ *He is now fabulously ~.* | **comparatively, reasonably, relatively** | **independently** ◇ *He is independently ~ and lives an unconventional lifestyle.*

wean verb

ADV. **gradually**
VERB + WEAN **attempt to, try to**
PREP. **(away) from** ◇ *Her parents are trying to ~ her away from gambling.* | **off** ◇ *They have gradually ~ed him off the drugs.* | **on** ◇ *younger men and women, ~ed on the Internet and email* | **onto** ◇ *to ~ a baby onto solid food*

weapon noun

ADJ. **deadly, lethal, potent, powerful** ◇ *He was charged with assault with a deadly ~.* | **non-lethal** | **dangerous** | **effective, useful** | **heavy, light** ◇ *The assault forces used heavy ~s, including rockets and mortars.* | **automatic, semi-automatic** | **atomic, biological, chemical, nuclear, thermonuclear** | **assault, offensive, strategic, tactical** ◇ *She pleaded guilty to carrying an offensive ~.* ◇ *a ban on the use of tactical nuclear ~s* | **loaded** | **conventional, unconventional** | **anti-aircraft, anti-tank** | **precision, precision-guided** | **concealed** ◇ *arrested for carrying a concealed ~* | **banned, illegal** | **murder** | **ultimate** (*often figurative*) ◇ *The workers' ultimate ~ was the strike.* | **secret** (*often figurative*) ◇ *The team's secret ~ was their new young defender.*
VERB + WEAPON **be armed with, carry, have, possess** | **acquire** ◇ *states that have acquired nuclear ~s* | **deploy, fire, use** | **use sth as** (*often figurative*) ◇ *She used wit as a ~ against her enemies.* | **load** ◇ *'Load your ~s!' Barrett ordered.* | **aim, point, raise** | **brandish, wield** ◇ *The guards began to draw their ~s.* | **holster** (*AmE*) | **drop** ◇ *Drop your ~s, or he dies!* | **lower** ◇ *The armed men lowered their ~s and stepped aside.* | **build, develop, produce** ◇ *states developing ~s of mass destruction* | **stockpile** | **smuggle**

WEAPONS + NOUN **system** | **technology** ◇ *the illegal transfer of ~s technology to hostile countries* | **cache** ◇ *A massive ~s cache was uncovered.* | **platform** ◇ *a sophisticated ~s platform* | **proliferation** ◇ *nuclear ~s proliferation* | **capability** | **facility** ◇ *a biological ~s facility* | **development**
PREP. **~ against** (*often figurative*) ◇ *This relaxation technique can serve as an effective ~ against stress.*

wear noun

1 use as clothing

ADJ. **daily, everyday, weekend** | **summer, winter**
PREP. **with ~** ◇ *New shoes get more comfortable with ~.*
PHRASES **years of ~** ◇ *This is a quality garment which should give years of ~.*

2 clothes

ADJ. **day, evening** | **designer, fashion** | **casual, leisure, outdoor, sports** (usually ***sportswear***) (= *casual clothes*) (*AmE*), **street** | **business** | **formal** | **bridal, maternity** | **active** (*AmE*), **athletic** (*AmE*), **sports** (usually ***sportswear***) (= *clothes for sports*) (*BrE*), **workout** (*AmE*) | **children's, men's, women's**

3 long use

ADJ. **hard, heavy**
VERB + WEAR **withstand** ◇ *This flooring can withstand years of hard ~.*
PREP. **with ~** ◇ *The stairs had become slippery with ~.*
PHRASES **centuries, years, etc. of ~** ◇ *The cathedral steps were polished smooth by centuries of ~.*

4 damage caused by long use

ADJ. **excessive** | **brake, engine, tyre/tire, etc.**
VERB + WEAR **show** ◇ *The cushions were beginning to show ~.* | **cause** | **minimize, reduce** | **prevent**
PREP. **~ on** ◇ *This new oil reduces ~ on the pump.*
PHRASES **signs of ~, ~ and tear**

wear verb

1 have a piece of clothing on

ADV. **proudly** ◇ *They came in, proudly ~ing their uniforms.* | **comfortably**
VERB + WEAR **tend to** ◇ *I tend to ~ a jacket to work.* | **prefer to** ◇ *Hannah preferred to ~ her hair short.* | **choose to, intend to, opt to** ◇ *I will probably choose to ~ jeans.* | **dare to** ◇ *the first time that I had ever dared to ~ something like this* | **refuse to** ◇ *She refused to ~ prison clothes.* | **forget to** ◇ *He had forgotten to ~ his gloves.* | **forbid sb to** | **be entitled to** ◇ *He is entitled to ~ the regimental tie.*

2 last for a long time

ADV. **badly, well** ◇ *Those curtains have worn very well.*

weariness noun

ADJ. **great** | **war**
VERB + WEARINESS **feel**
WEARINESS + VERB **overcome sb, overtake sb**
PREP. **in ~** ◇ *His eyes were half closing in ~.* | **~ in** ◇ *He detected a note of ~ in her voice.*

weary adj.

VERBS **be, feel, look, seem, sound** | **become, get, grow** ◇ *I've grown rather ~ of all your excuses.* | **make sb** ◇ *This war has made us all ~.*
ADV. **extremely, fairly, very, etc.** | **a little, slightly, etc.** ◇ *She looks a little ~.*
PREP. **of** ◇ *The people are ~ of war.*

weather noun

ADJ. **beautiful, excellent, fair, fine, glorious, good, great, ideal, lovely, nice, perfect, superb** (*esp. BrE*) | **adverse, appalling** (*esp. BrE*), **atrocious, awful, bad, dismal, dreadful** (*esp. BrE*), **foul, gloomy, grim** (*esp. BrE*), **horrible** (*esp. AmE*), **inclement, lousy, miserable, nasty, poor, rotten,** rough, terrible | hot, humid, muggy, sultry, warm | mild | bright, clear, sunny | calm | dry | reliable (*esp. BrE*), settled (*BrE*) | changeable (*esp. BrE*), fickle, uncertain, unpredictable, unsettled | extreme, fierce, harsh, severe, violent, wild | bitter, chilly, cold, freezing, frosty (*esp. BrE*), icy, wintry | cool | cloudy, grey/gray | damp, rainy, wet | foggy | blustery, stormy, windy | autumn (*esp. BrE*), fall (*AmE*), spring, summer, winter | unseasonable, unseasonably…, unseasonal (*esp. BrE*) ◇ *a spell of unseasonably warm ~.* | local

... OF WEATHER **spell**

VERB + WEATHER **enjoy** ◇ *I've been enjoying this beautiful ~.* | **have** ◇ *We've had great ~ all week.* | **brave** ◇ *Deciding to brave the ~, he grabbed his umbrella and went out.* | **forecast, predict** | **check** ◇ *I checked the ~ this morning.*

WEATHER + VERB **clear, clear up, improve, warm up** ◇ *We'll go just as soon as this ~ lets up.* | **hold, hold out** (*BrE*) ◇ *If the ~ holds out we could go swimming later.* | **keep up** ◇ *If the ~ holds out we could go swimming later.* | **threaten** ◇ *Bad ~ threatened.* | **break, deteriorate, worsen** ◇ *It was sunny until the weekend, but then the ~ broke.* | **become sth, get sth, turn sth** ◇ *Next day the ~ turned cold.* | **look sth** ◇ *The ~ looks beautiful today.* | **remain sth, stay sth** | **continue** | **close in** (*esp. BrE*), **set in** ◇ *The ~ closed in and the climbers had to take shelter.* ◇ *I wanted to mend the roof before the cold ~ set in.* | **come** ◇ *According to the forecast, there is a lot more wet ~ to come.* | **allow, permit** ◇ *I sat outside as often as the ~ allowed.* ◇ *We're having a barbecue next Saturday, ~ permitting.* (You cannot say 'weather allowing'.) | **prevent sth** ◇ *Stormy ~ prevented any play in today's tennis.* | **let sb down** (*BrE*) | **change** | **bring sth out** ◇ *The fine ~ brings out butterflies.*

WEATHER + NOUN **conditions** ◇ *The plane crashed into the sea in adverse ~ conditions.* | **patterns, system** ◇ *the effects of global warming on the world's ~ patterns* ◇ *Atlantic ~ systems* | **forecast, report** | **data, information, records** | **event** ◇ *an increase in extreme ~ events* | **satellite, station** | **centre/center** | **chart, map**

PHRASES **a change in the ~** ◇ *We hadn't bargained for such a dramatic change in the ~.* | **in all ~** (*esp. AmE*), **in all ~ conditions, in all ~s** (*BrE*), **whatever the ~** ◇ *The lifeboat crews go out in all ~(s).* ◇ *He swims in the sea every day, whatever the ~.* | **the vagaries of the ~** (*BrE*), **the vagaries of ~** (*AmE*) ◇ *She packed to cope with the vagaries of New York's ~.*

weather *verb*

1 pass safely through sth

ADV. **successfully, well** ◇ *Their company had ~ed the recession well.*

VERB + WEATHER **manage to** (*figurative*) ◇ *The company has managed to ~ the storm.*

2 change in appearance because of the sun/air/wind

ADV. **badly** ◇ *Some of the stone has ~ed badly.* | **naturally**

weave *verb*

ADV. **carefully, skilfully/skillfully** (*often figurative*) ◇ *Hall skilfully/skillfully ~s the historical research into a gripping narrative.* | **seamlessly** (*often figurative*) ◇ *The author seamlessly ~s together the stories of three people's lives.* | **inextricably, intricately** (*both figurative*) ◇ *Comedy and tragedy are inextricably woven into her fiction.* | **together** ◇ *The threads are woven together.*

PREP. **from** ◇ *a basket woven from strips of willow* | **into** ◇ *A pattern is woven into the fabric.*

web *noun*

1 that a spider makes

ADJ. **spider** (*esp. AmE*), **spider's** (*esp. BrE*)
VERB + WEB **build, make, spin, weave**

2 complicated series/network of sth

ADJ. **complex, complicated, dense, intricate, tangled** | **seamless**

VERB + WEB **create, form, weave** ◇ *The mass media form a ~ of communications.* | **be drawn into** ◇ *More and more people were drawn into his ~ of deceit.*

PHRASES **a ~ of deceit, a ~ of deception, a ~ of intrigue, a ~ of lies** | **a ~ of relationships**

3 the Web on the Internet

VERB + THE WEB **access** | **browse, search, surf** | **use** ◇ *Many people use the Web to make their travel plans.*

WEB + NOUN **page** | **address, link** | **browser, server** | **resource, service** | **mail** | **network, ring** | **design, development** | **publishing** | **designer, developer, editor, host, master** (usually *webmaster*), **user** | **directory, guide, index** | **connection** ◇ *a broadband Web connection* | **access** | **search** ◇ *A Web search brought up 900 hits.* | **content** | **application, tool**

PREP. **on the ~** ◇ *I found this survey on the Web.*

→ Special page at COMPUTER

website *noun* → See also SITE

ADJ. **Internet** | **official** ◇ *City College's official ~* | **favourite/favorite, popular** | **comedy, commercial, company, education, educational, government, news, personal, travel, etc.**

VERB + WEBSITE **search for** | **find** | **access, browse, check, check out, log onto, look at, read, see, visit** | **search** ◇ *I was searching this history ~ for something about Alexander the Great.* | **use** | **have** | **build, create, design, develop, make, set up** ◇ *We show you how to make your own ~ in ten simple steps.* | **launch** | **link to** | **upload sth to** | **host, maintain, run, update**

WEBSITE + VERB **contain sth, offer sth, provide sth** | **be dedicated to sth, be devoted to sth** ◇ *a ~ devoted to Rufus Wainwright* | **link to sth** | **be down, go down** ◇ *There were so many visitors to the ~ that it went down.*

WEBSITE + NOUN **address, URL** | **designer, owner** | **design**

PREP. **on a/the ~** ◇ *You can find details of all our products on our ~.*

PHRASES **a link to a ~** ◇ *This page includes lots of links to other ~s you may find interesting.*

→ Special page at COMPUTER

wedding *noun*

ADJ. **church, registry office** (*BrE*) | **traditional, white** | **big, lavish** | **small** | **gay, same-sex** | **Catholic, Jewish, etc.** | **royal** | **destination** (= in a place far from where you live) | **shotgun** (= where the bride is pregnant)

VERB + WEDDING **have** ◇ *They had a small ~ with close friends and family.* | **go through with** | **attend, come to, go to** | **celebrate** | **arrange, plan** | **invite sb to** | **conduct** (*esp. BrE*), **officiate at** ◇ *The ~ will be conducted by the local priest.* ◇ *The minister was asked to officiate at the ~.* | **call off, postpone, stop**

WEDDING + VERB **go ahead** (*esp. BrE*), **go off** (*esp. AmE*), **take place** ◇ *The ~ went off without a hitch.* ◇ *The ~ will take place in June.*

WEDDING + NOUN **day, night** | **invitation** | **plans, preparations** | **planner** | **date** ◇ *We haven't set a ~ date yet.* | **chapel** (*esp. AmE*), **venue** | **registry** | **dress, gown** | **attire** (*esp. AmE*), **clothes, outfit, suit** | **band, ring** ◇ *She had a plain ~ band on her third finger.* | **shower** (*AmE*) | **ceremony, service** | **vows** | **procession** | **march** | **party, reception** | **breakfast** (*BrE, formal*), **feast** | **celebrations** | **speech** (*esp. BrE*) | **cake** | **gift, present** | **list** (*BrE*) ◇ *We were choosing what present to buy from the ~ list they'd sent.* | **guests, party** | **singer** (*esp. AmE*) | **photographer** | **album, photographs, photos, pictures, video** | **anniversary** | **bells** (*figurative*) ◇ *After going out with her boyfriend for a year, she started talking about ~ bells.* | **industry** ◇ *I work in the ~ industry.*

PREP. **at a/the ~** ◇ *I met her at my brother's ~.*

wedge *verb*

ADV. **firmly, tightly**

PREP. **against, behind, between, into, under** ◇ *She ~d a chair firmly under the door handle.*

weighted

PHRASES ~ **sth in place,** ~ **sth open** ◇ *Someone had ~d the door open with a brick.*

Wednesday *noun* → Note at DAY

weed *noun*

ADJ. **annual, perennial** | **aquatic, water** | **noxious** (*esp. AmE*)
VERB + WEED **kill** | **clear, get rid of, pull up, remove** | **control, keep down, keep under control** ◇ *Fill the bed with annual flowers to keep the ~s down.*
WEED + VERB **grow, spread** | **spring up** ◇ *There were ~s springing up through the gravel.*
WEED + NOUN **control** | **killer** (usually **weedkiller**) | **trimmer** | **growth** | **seed, seedling**

week *noun*

ADJ. **last, past** | **previous** | **coming, following, next** | **consecutive, successive** ◇ *They won 1–0 for the fourth consecutive ~.* | **entire, full, whole** ◇ *It's the first time I've done a full week's work since the accident.* | **work** (*esp. AmE*) (usually **workweek** in AmE), **working** (*esp. BrE*) ◇ *a reduction in the working ~/workweek* | **busy, hard, tough** | **long** ◇ *It's been a long ~ and I'm very tired.* | **short** ◇ *This is a short ~ because of the public holiday.* ◇ *In just a few short ~s we'll be going home.* | **quiet** ◇ *It's been a very quiet ~ for me.* | **3-day, 40-hour, etc.** ◇ *He earns enough money to work a four-day ~.*
VERB + WEEK **spend** ◇ *We spent two ~s in Mexico last summer.* | **take** | **enter** ◇ *The strike has entered its second ~.*
WEEK + VERB **elapse, go by, pass** ◇ *The ~ passed very slowly.* | **drag**
PREP. **by the ~** ◇ *They're paid by the ~.* | **during the ~** ◇ *I go out most weekends, but rarely during the ~.* | **for a ~** ◇ *I haven't seen him for ~s.* | **in a ~** ◇ *We'll be back in a ~.* | **in ~s** ◇ *It hasn't rained in ~s.* | **over a ~, under a ~** ◇ *It's over a ~ since she called me.* | **per ~** ◇ *How much do you earn per ~?* | **within a/the ~** ◇ *I'll have the report finished within the next couple of ~s.*
PHRASES **a day of the ~** ◇ *Which day of the ~ was it?* | **twice, two days, etc. a ~** ◇ *She works three days a ~.*

weekend *noun*

ADJ. **long** ◇ *I took Friday off, and spent a long ~ visiting friends.* | **last, next** | **rainy, wet** (*esp. BrE*) ◇ *I spent the last rainy ~ cleaning the kitchen.* ◇ *It will be a wet ~ for much of England and Wales.*
VERB + WEEKEND **spend** ◇ *We spent the ~ in Paris.* | **have** ◇ *Did you have a nice ~?*
WEEKEND + NOUN **break, getaway** (*esp. AmE*), **trip, visit** | **home, house, retreat**
PREP. **at the ~** (*BrE*) ◇ *What are you doing at the ~?* | **at ~s** ◇ *What do you usually do at ~s?* | **on a ~** (*BrE, informal*) ◇ *The children play there on a ~.* | **on the ~** (*esp. AmE*) ◇ *He called me on the ~.* | **over the ~** ◇ *The office is closed over the ~.*
PHRASES **a ~ away, a ~ off**

weep *verb*

ADV. **quietly, silently, softly** | **loudly** | **openly** ◇ *The people wept openly when his death was announced.* | **bitterly** | **inconsolably** (*esp. BrE*), **uncontrollably** ◇ *His grandmother was ~ing uncontrollably.* | **copiously** (*esp. BrE*) | **almost, nearly** | **a little**
VERB + WEEP **begin to, start to** | **want to** | **make sb**
PREP. **at** ◇ *He wanted to ~ at the unfairness of it all.* | **for** ◇ *I felt I could have wept for joy.* ◇ *He was ~ing, in effect, for a lost age of innocence.* | **over** ◇ *We had wept over the death of our parents.* | **with** ◇ *She almost wept with happiness.*
PHRASES **break down and ~** ◇ *Several of the soldiers broke down and wept.* | **~ and wail** ◇ *The mourners followed the funeral procession, ~ing and wailing.* | **~ buckets** (= weep a lot) (*BrE, informal*)

weigh *verb*

1 consider sth carefully

ADV. **carefully** | **up** ◇ *The jury ~ed up the evidence carefully.*

PREP. **against** ◇ *We ~ed the cost of advertising against the likely gains from increased business.*

2 be considered important

ADV. **heavily, strongly**
PREP. **against** ◇ *His untidy appearance ~ed against him.* | **in favour/favor of** ◇ *This fact ~ed heavily in her favour/favor.* | **with** ◇ *His evidence ~ed strongly with the judge.*

weight *noun*

1 amount sth weighs

ADJ. **considerable, enormous, great, heavy, immense** | **light** | **extra** | **gross, net** | **total** | **average, mean** | **sheer** (*figurative*) ◇ *The sheer ~ of visitors is destroying this tourist attraction.*
VERB + WEIGHT **bear, carry, support** ◇ *The arch bears the ~ of the bridge above.* | **distribute**
PREP. **in ~** ◇ *It is about 76 pounds in ~.* | **beneath the ~, under the ~** ◇ *The boy was staggering beneath the ~ of a pile of boxes.* ◇ *Many buildings collapsed under the ~ of the ash.* ◇ *He was buckling under the ~ of his responsibilities.* (*figurative*)

2 weight of sb's body

ADJ. **low** | **ideal, right** | **healthy** | **excess** | **target** ◇ *I should soon be down to my target ~ of 70 kilos.* | **body** | **birth** ◇ *babies with a low birth ~*
VERB + WEIGHT **watch** ◇ *I won't have any cake—I have to watch my ~.* | **gain, put on** | **get down, get off, lose, reduce, shed** ◇ *He's lost a lot of ~.* | **keep down** | **maintain** | **bear, carry, hold, stand, support, take** ◇ *I was worried that the branch wouldn't take my ~.* | **put, rest** ◇ *The doctor told me not to put my ~ on this ankle for a month.* | **shift, transfer** ◇ *He nervously shifted his ~ from foot to foot.* | **distribute** ◇ *Stand with your legs apart and your ~ evenly distributed.* | **throw** ◇ *He threw his ~ at the door and it burst open.*
WEIGHT + VERB **go up, increase** | **come off, drop, fall, go down, plummet** (*esp. BrE*) | **fluctuate** ◇ *People's body ~ can fluctuate during the day.*
WEIGHT + NOUN **gain, loss** | **control** | **problem**

3 piece of metal

ADJ. **heavy, large** | **light** | **free**
VERB + WEIGHT **lift** ◇ *She did circuit training and lifted ~s to build her fitness.*
WEIGHT + NOUN **lifting, training** | **room**
PHRASES **~s and measures**

4 heavy object

ADJ. **heavy** | **dead** ◇ *With difficulty she managed to pull his dead ~ onto the bed.* | **leaden** (*figurative*) ◇ *A leaden ~ lay on her heart as she waved him goodbye.*
VERB + WEIGHT **lift** ◇ *Heavy ~s should be lifted with a straight back.*

5 importance/influence of sth

ADJ. **due, full, sufficient** ◇ *Environmental considerations were given due ~ in making the decision.* | **insufficient** (*esp. BrE*) | **considerable** | **little** | **added** | **sheer** ◇ *How can you ignore the sheer ~ of medical opinion?* | **economic, emotional, intellectual, political** ◇ *America's economic ~*
VERB + WEIGHT **attach, give, place** ◇ *They attach too much ~ to academic achievement.* | **carry** ◇ *Her opinion seemed to carry little ~ in the company.* | **add, lend** ◇ *The new evidence added considerable ~ to the prosecution's case.*
PHRASES **put your ~ behind sth, throw your ~ behind sth** | **~ of numbers** ◇ *The rebels were defeated by sheer ~ of numbers.*

weighted *adj.*

VERBS **be, seem**
ADV. **equally** ◇ *The exam consists of six equally ~ questions.* | **heavily**
PREP. **against** ◇ *This new legislation is ~ against the small farmer.* | **in favour/favor of** ◇ *The course is heavily ~ in*

favour/favor of engineering. | **towards/toward** ◇ *measures that are ~ towards/toward small investors*

weird *adj.*

VERBS **be, feel, seem, sound** ◇ *I started to feel quite ~.* | **get**
ADV. **extremely, fairly, very, etc.** ◇ *I started to feel really ~.* | **totally** (*esp. AmE*) | **a little, slightly, etc.** ◇ *It all sounds a little ~ to me.*
PHRASES **~ and wonderful** (*esp. BrE*) ◇ *Some of their clothes were really ~ and wonderful.*

welcome *noun*

ADJ. **big, enthusiastic, friendly, hearty** (*esp. AmE*), **great, rapturous** (*esp. BrE*), **rousing, special, tumultuous** (*esp. BrE*), **warm** ◇ *The audience gave the band a rousing ~.* | **broad** (*esp. BrE*) ◇ *The proposals have been given a broad ~ by green campaigners.* | **cautious, guarded, qualified** (*all esp. BrE*) | **official** | **hero's** ◇ *She got a hero's ~ on her return from the Olympics.*
VERB + WELCOME **get, receive** | **extend, give sb** | **outstay, overstay** ◇ *Sensing that he had outstayed his ~, he quickly left.*
WELCOME + VERB **await sb** (*BrE*) ◇ *A warm ~ awaits you at this family-run hotel.*
PREP. **in ~** ◇ *She held out her arms in ~.* | **~ from** ◇ *The proposal received a warm ~ from the committee.* | **~ to** ◇ *A big ~ to our special guest, James Greenan.* ◇ *They received a friendly ~ to their new home.*
PHRASES **words of ~** ◇ *Thank you for those words of ~.*

welcome *verb*

1 greet sb/be pleased sb has come

ADV. **heartily, warmly** ◇ *If you visit our town you will be warmly ~d.* | **gladly** (*esp. AmE*) | **formally** (*esp. BrE*), **officially** | **back** ◇ *The whole family turned out to ~ him back.*
VERB + WELCOME **be delighted to, be pleased to** | **prepare to, wait to** ◇ *The school is preparing to ~ the new intake of students.*
PREP. **into** ◇ *He ~d us into the club.* | **to** ◇ *We are delighted to ~ you to our company.*
PHRASES **look forward to welcoming sb, ~ sb with open arms** ◇ *They ~d the new volunteers with open arms (= with enthusiasm).*

2 be pleased about sth and support it

ADV. **enthusiastically, especially, greatly, particularly, really, warmly** ◇ *Many companies have warmly ~d these changes in legislation.* | **positively** (*esp. BrE*) ◇ *We positively ~ applications from all sections of the community.* | **broadly** (*esp. BrE*) | **cautiously** ◇ *Economists cautiously ~d the president's initiative.* | **initially**
PHRASES **be generally ~d, be universally ~d, be widely ~d** (*all esp. BrE*) ◇ *The proposals have been widely ~d.*

welcome *adj.*

VERBS **be, feel** | **make sb** ◇ *They made us very ~ in their home.*
ADV. **very** ◇ *The 1% rate cut is extremely ~.* | **especially, extremely, more than, most, particularly** ◇ *You would be a most ~ guest.* | **perfectly, quite** ◇ *You are perfectly ~ to stay here, if you don't mind the mess.* | **not entirely** ◇ *He made it plain that Holman's interest in his business affairs was not entirely ~.* | **always** ◇ *Visitors are always ~.*
PREP. **to** ◇ *New members are ~ to the club.*

welfare *noun*

1 good health and happiness

ADJ. **animal, child, community, family, human, personal** ◇ *people concerned about child ~* | **general, public**
VERB + WELFARE **improve, promote** ◇ *The government's policies will promote the ~ of all citizens.*

2 money, etc. from the government

ADJ. **state** | **social**
VERB + WELFARE **collect, receive** (*both AmE*) | **leave** (*AmE*) ◇ *financial incentives to leave ~*
WELFARE + NOUN **state** ◇ *the provision of services such as health through the ~ state* | **agency, authorities, department, office** (*esp. AmE*), **programme/program, provision, services, system** | **rolls** (*AmE*) ◇ *The government is trying to move more people off the ~ rolls into work.* | **officer** (*BrE*), **worker** | **benefits, payments** ◇ *lone parents living on ~ benefits* | **check** (*AmE*) ◇ *The ~ check never went far enough.* | **budget, costs, spending** | **cuts** | **policy, reform** | **recipient** | **mother** (*AmE*) | **fraud** ◇ *The new government promised to clamp down on ~ fraud.* | **dependency**
PREP. **on ~** (*esp. AmE*) ◇ *the number of families on ~*

well *noun*

1 for water

ADJ. **deep, shallow** | **dry** | **water** | **artesian** | **wishing**
VERB + WELL **dig, sink** | **fall down** ◇ *The dog fell down a ~.*
WELL + VERB **run dry**
PHRASES **at the bottom of a ~**

2 for oil

ADJ. **oil** | **new**
VERB + WELL **drill**

well-being *noun*

ADJ. **general, overall** | **emotional, mental, physical, psychological, social, spiritual** | **human, personal** | **economic, financial, material**
VERB + WELL-BEING **contribute to, enhance, ensure, improve, promote** ◇ *A better water supply would contribute dramatically to the people's ~.* | **threaten** | **affect**
PHRASES **health and ~** | **a sense of ~** ◇ *She was filled with a sense of ~.*

west *noun, adj.* → Note at DIRECTION

wet *adj.*

VERBS **be, feel, look** | **become, get, turn** ◇ *We got soaking ~ just going from the car to the house.* ◇ *The weather may turn ~ later on in the week.* | **get sth, make sth** ◇ *Mind you don't get your feet ~.*
ADV. **extremely, fairly, very, etc.** | **dripping, soaking, sopping** ◇ *His clothes were dripping ~.* | **a little, slightly, etc.** ◇ *It's still a little ~ outside.*
PREP. **with** ◇ *The grass was ~ with dew.*
PHRASES **~ through** ◇ *We were ~ through and cold.*

whale *noun*

ADJ. **beached, stranded** (*esp. BrE*)
... OF WHALES **pod, school**
VERB + WHALE **hunt, kill** | **harpoon** | **save**
WHALE + VERB **swim** | **dive** | **sing** | **blow (sth)** ◇ *We saw a ~ blowing a jet of spray high in the air.* | **breach (sth)** ◇ *Ahead, the ~ breached the surface of the water.* | **beach itself, be washed up, wash up**
WHALE + NOUN **hunter** | **watching** | **meat, oil** | **population, stocks** ◇ *management and conservation of ~ stocks* | **song**

wheat *noun*

ADJ. **ripe** | **cracked, whole** | **durum** | **spring, winter**
... OF WHEAT **ear, grain** | **bag, sack, sheaf** | **field**
VERB + WHEAT **grow** | **plant** (*esp. AmE*), **sow** | **cut, harvest** | **thresh** | **grind** | **eat**
WHEAT + VERB **grow**
WHEAT + NOUN **crop, harvest** | **field** | **bran, flour** | **bread** (*esp. AmE*) | **production**

wheel *noun*

1 on a bicycle, car, etc.

ADJ. **bicycle, car, etc.** | **spare** (*BrE*) | **front** | **back, rear** | **nearside, offside** (*both BrE*) | **alloy**

WHEEL + VERB **change**, **replace** ◇ *A tyre/tire blew and we had to change the ~.*

WHEEL + VERB **go around**, **go round** (*esp. BrE*), **spin**, **turn** ◇ *The ~s were still going around.* ◇ *The political ~ had turned full circle, and he was back in power.* (*figurative*) | **skid**, **slide**, **slip** ◇ *He braked suddenly, causing the front ~s to skid.* | **come off**, **fall off** | **lock** (*esp. BrE*) ◇ *She braked too hard and the ~s locked.*

WHEEL + NOUN **arch**, **base**, **bearings**, **hub**, **nut** (*BrE*), **rim**, **trim** (*BrE*), **well** (*esp. AmE*) | **clamp** (*BrE*)

PREP. **on ~s** ◇ *A child was pulling along a little dog on ~s.* | **under the ~s** ◇ *She fell under the ~s of a bus.*

2 (*also* **steering wheel**)

VERB + WHEEL **grip**, **hold** | **turn** ◇ *Turn the steering ~ hard to the right.* | **grab**, **take** ◇ *He grabbed the steering ~ from her to prevent the car going off the road.* ◇ *I drove the first 200 miles and then Steve took the ~.* | **lose control of**, **take control of**

WHEEL + NOUN **lock**

PREP. **at the ~** ◇ *The bus set off again with a fresh driver at the ~.* | **behind the ~** ◇ *I saw the car drive past, but didn't recognize the woman behind the ~.* ◇ *I spend a lot of time behind the ~* (= driving).

PHRASES **keep your hands on the steering ~**, **put your hands on the steering ~** | **take your hands off the steering ~**

wheelchair noun

ADJ. **electric**, **motorized**, **powered** (*esp. BrE*)

VERB + WHEELCHAIR **use** | **manoeuvre/maneuver** ◇ *Tony manoeuvred/maneuvered his ~ out from behind his desk.* | **push** | **be confined to** ◇ *He's been confined to a ~ since the accident.*

WHEELCHAIR + NOUN **access**, **accessibility** (*esp. AmE*), **ramp** | **user** ◇ *better access for ~ users* | **athlete**

PREP. **by ~** ◇ *In town, she gets around by ~.* | **in a/the ~** ◇ *It's hard to get around if you're in a ~.*

whereabouts noun

ADJ. **current**, **present** | **unknown** ◇ *The present ~ of the manuscript is unknown.* | **exact**

VERB + WHEREABOUTS **know** ◇ *She did not say where she was going, and nobody knows her ~.*

whiff noun

ADJ. **faint**, **slight** | **strong** | **unmistakable** (*often figurative*) ◇ *The unmistakable ~ of electoral blackmail could be detected.* | **deep**

VERB + WHIFF **catch**, **detect**, **get** ◇ *I caught the ~ of Scotch on his breath.* ◇ *Journalists caught a ~ of scandal and pursued the actress relentlessly.* (*figurative*) | **take** ◇ *She took a deep ~ of his aftershave.* | **have** (*often figurative*) ◇ *The proposal had the ~ of a hoax about it.*

PREP. **~ of** ◇ *a ~ of perfume*

PHRASES **at the faintest ~ of sth**, **at the first ~ of sth**, **at the merest ~ of sth** (*all figurative*) ◇ *He always retreated emotionally at the first ~ of conflict.*

while noun

ADJ. **brief**, **little**, **short** | **fair**, **good**, **long**, **some** ◇ *Things continued quiet for some ~.*

VERB + WHILE **take** ◇ *I'll mend it for you, but it could take a ~.*

PREP. **after a ~** ◇ *After a ~, I began to get bored with my job.* | **for a ~** ◇ *They chatted for a ~.* | **for the ~** (*BrE*) ◇ *There's no need to do anything for the ~.* | **in a ~** ◇ *I'll be back in a ~.*

PHRASES **all the ~** ◇ *The bird hopped across the lawn, keeping a sharp lookout all the ~.* | **once in a ~** ◇ *Everybody makes a mistake once in a ~.* | **(for) quite a ~** ◇ *He kept me waiting for quite a ~.* | **a ~ back** ◇ *The problems started a ~ back.*

whim noun

ADJ. **sudden** ◇ *The nest is vulnerable to the sudden ~s of the weather.* | **mere** | **personal** | **political** ◇ *Funding is subject to political ~.*

VERB + WHIM **cater to**, **follow**, **indulge**, **pander to** (*esp. BrE*), **satisfy** | **be subject to**, **be vulnerable to**, **depend on** ◇ *For years she had been subject to her husband's ~s.*

PREP. **at (sb's) ~** ◇ *They seem to be able to change the rules of the game at ~.* ◇ *Slaves could be bought and sold at the ~ of their masters.* | **on a ~** ◇ *He bought the jacket on a ~.*

PHRASES **your every ~** ◇ *The child's parents pandered to his every ~.*

whimper noun

ADJ. **little**, **slight** (*esp. AmE*), **small**, **soft** (*esp. AmE*) | **frightened** (*esp. AmE*), **pathetic**

VERB + WHIMPER **give**, **let out** ◇ *The animal gave a pathetic little ~.* ◇ *She let out a ~ of pain.* | **hear**

WHIMPER + VERB **escape sb/sth** ◇ *A small ~ escaped his lips.*

whimper verb

ADV. **quietly**, **softly** ◇ *The dog ~ed softly.* | **slightly** (*esp. AmE*) | **pathetically**

VERB + WHIMPER **begin to**, **start to** | **hear sb**

PREP. **in** ◇ *She was ~ing in fear.* | **with** ◇ *The boy was ~ing with pain.*

PHRASES **~ like a child** ◇ *He stirred in her arms, ~ing like a child.*

whine noun

ADJ. **high**, **high-pitched** | **nasal**

VERB + WHINE **give**, **let out** | **hear**

PREP. **with a ~** ◇ *She spoke with a ~.* | **~ of**

PHRASES **the ~ of an engine**, **the ~ of a motor**

→ Note at SOUND

whine verb

ADV. **softly** ◇ *The engines ~d softly in the background.* | **loudly** (*esp. AmE*) | **away**

whip noun

ADJ. **riding** | **bull**, **horse** (*usually* ***horsewhip***) | **leather**

VERB + WHIP **crack**, **flick** ◇ *He cracked the ~ and the horse leaped forward.* | **hold** | **use**

WHIP + VERB **crack** ◇ *A hound yelped briefly as a ~ cracked.* | **come down** (*esp. AmE*)

PHRASES **the crack of a ~**

whip verb

1 hit sb/sth with a whip

ADV. **soundly** ◇ *He was taken back to the jail and soundly whipped.*

2 mix sth until it is light and stiff

ADV. **lightly** ◇ *Lightly ~ the egg whites and add them to the mixture.* | **up**

whisky (*BrE*) (*AmE, IrishE* whiskey) noun

ADJ. **blended**, **malt**, **Scotch**, **single-malt** | **bourbon**, **rye** | **double**, **large** (*both esp. BrE*) | **single**, **small** (*both esp. BrE*) | **stiff** (*BrE*) | **neat** (*BrE*), **straight** (*AmE*) ◇ *a neat whisky* (*BrE*) ◇ *a straight whiskey* (*AmE*) | **fine**, **good** ◇ *a fine Irish whiskey* | **cheap** | **bootleg**

... OF WHISKY **drop** (*BrE*), **nip** (*esp. BrE*) ◇ *He added a drop of ~ to his coffee.* | **measure** (*BrE*), **shot**, **tot** (*esp. BrE*) ◇ *a large measure of ~* | **bottle**, **flask**, **glass**, **hip flask** (*BrE*)

VERB + WHISKY/WHISKEY **drink** ◇ *Do you drink ~?* | **have** ◇ *He had a ~ on the rocks.* | **pour (sb)** | **sip**, **down**, **finish** | **distil**, **make**, **produce** ◇ *the art of distilling ~*

WHISKY/WHISKEY + NOUN **drinker** | **bottle**, **decanter** | **glass**, **tumbler** (*esp. BrE*) | **barrel** | **sour** | **chaser** (*esp. BrE*) ◇ *He ordered a beer with a ~ chaser.* | **business**, **company**, **distiller** (*esp. BrE*), **distillery**, **industry**, **production**, **sales**

PHRASES **~ on the rocks** (= with ice)

whisper noun

ADJ. **barely audible**, **the barest**, **faint**, **gentle**, **hushed**, **low**, **mere**, **quiet**, **slight** (*esp. AmE*), **soft** ◇ *A barely audible ~ came from the closet.* ◇ *Jake got excited at the merest ~ of his lover.*

| **fierce, harsh** | **audible, loud, stage** ◇ *'I knew this would happen,' he said in a stage ~* (= one that he wanted everyone to hear). | **choked** (*esp. AmE*), **hoarse, husky** | **excited, urgent** | **conspiratorial**
VERB + WHISPER **hear**
PREP. **above a ~** ◇ *Their voices were very quiet, hardly above a ~.* | **in a ~** ◇ *They spoke in ~s.*

whisper *verb*

ADV. **gently, quietly, softly** | **loudly** | **hoarsely, huskily** | **fiercely, harshly, urgently** ◇ *'Come on,' he ~ed urgently.* | **brokenly, shakily** | **angrily, bitterly, furiously** | **conspiratorially** | **excitedly** | **almost, half** | **barely** (*esp. AmE*) | **back** ◇ *'Yes,' I ~ed back.*
VERB + WHISPER **can only** ◇ *He could only ~ in reply.* | **hear sb** ◇ *She heard him ~ her name.*
PREP. **about** ◇ *I felt that everyone was ~ing about me.* | **against** ◇ *'Hush!' he ~ed against her hair.* | **through** ◇ *'No!' he ~ed through gritted teeth.* | **to** ◇ *'Let's go,' she ~ed to Anne.*
PHRASES **~ sth in sb's ear, ~ sth into sb's ear**

whistle *noun*

1 small metal/plastic tube that you blow

ADJ. **dog, police, train** | **guard's, referee's, etc.** | **steam** | **penny, tin**
VERB + WHISTLE **blow, blow on, sound** ◇ *A train sounded its ~ in the distance.*
WHISTLE + VERB **blow, go, sound** ◇ *The referee's ~ went just before the ball crossed the line.*
PHRASES **a blast on a ~** ◇ *He gave a short blast on his ~.*

2 clear high-pitched sound

ADJ. **loud** | **high, high-pitched, piercing, sharp, shrill** | **low** | **long** | **short** | **silent** ◇ *He pursed his lips in a silent ~.* | **wolf** | **final** (*sports*) ◇ *From the opening to the final ~, Gray is relentless.*
VERB + WHISTLE **give, let out** | **hear**
PREP. **with a ~** ◇ *The train entered the tunnel with a shrill ~.* | **~ of** ◇ *She gave a low ~ of admiration.*
→ Note at SOUND

whistle *verb*

ADV. **loudly** | **softly, under your breath** | **through your teeth** ◇ *Norma looked at the letter and ~d softly through her teeth.* | **cheerfully, happily** | **tunelessly**
VERB + WHISTLE **begin to** | **hear sb**
PREP. **at** ◇ *Men ~d at her in the street.* | **in** ◇ *James ~d in amazement.* | **to** ◇ *William ~d to me from a distance.*

white *noun*

ADJ. **egg** ◇ *Whisk the egg ~s until stiff.*
VERB + WHITE **beat, whip, whisk**
PHRASES **the ~ of an egg** ◇ *Use the ~s of two eggs.*

white *adj., noun*

1 of the colour of snow or milk

ADJ. **dead, pure** | **bright, brilliant** | **creamy, icy, milky** | **dirty** | **plain**
→ Special page at COLOUR
PHRASES **as ~ as a ghost, as ~ as snow**

2 very pale because of illness or fear

VERBS **be, look** | **go, turn**
ADV. **extremely, very** | **rather**
PREP. **with** ◇ *He turned ~ with anger.*
PHRASES **as ~ as a sheet**

whole *noun*

1 all of sth

VERB + WHOLE **comprise, cover, embrace, encompass, involve, span** ◇ *The project involved the ~ of the university.* | **fill, occupy, take up** ◇ *The library takes up the ~ of the first floor.* | **permeate, pervade** ◇ *Technology permeates the ~ of our lives.*

2 complete thing

ADJ. **coherent, cohesive, harmonious, homogeneous, integrated, organized, seamless** ◇ *She was struggling to organize her ideas into a coherent ~.* | **one, single** | **larger** ◇ *The text must be seen as part of a larger ~.* | **complex** ◇ *The author examines each aspect of Roman society, then attempts to summarize the complex ~.* | **meaningful, satisfying** ◇ *At this age, babies do not yet combine sounds into a meaningful ~.* | **organic** | **collective, social**
VERB + WHOLE **form, make, make up** ◇ *He tried to fit the pieces of evidence together to make a coherent ~.*
PHRASES **as a ~** ◇ *Unemployment is higher in the north than in the country as a ~.*

wide *adj.*

1 covering a large area or range

VERBS **be, seem** | **become**
ADV. **extremely, fairly, very, etc.** ◇ *a very ~ range of clothing* | **enormously, exceptionally, extraordinarily, remarkably, unusually** | **increasingly** | **reasonably, relatively** | **sufficiently** | **surprisingly**
PHRASES **far and ~** ◇ *People came from far and ~ for the show.*

2 fully open

VERBS **be** | **go, grow** ◇ *His eyes grew ~.* | **fling sth, open sth, spread sth** ◇ *He stood up and flung ~ the door to the study.* ◇ *Open your mouth really ~.* ◇ *He spread his hands ~ in appeal.*
ADV. **extremely, really, very**
PREP. **with** ◇ *Their eyes were ~ with fear.*

3 not close

VERBS **be** | **fall, land**
ADV. **very** | **just**
PREP. **of** ◇ *Her shot fell just ~ of the target.*
PHRASES **~ of the mark** (= not accurate) (*esp. BrE*) ◇ *Their predictions turned out to be very ~ of the mark.*

widen *verb*

ADV. **considerably, dramatically, greatly, sharply, significantly** ◇ *The gap between rich and poor has ~ed considerably.* | **slightly** | **gradually, slowly** | **steadily** | **quickly, rapidly** | **suddenly** | **out** ◇ *The road gradually ~s out.*
PREP. **from, into** ◇ *At this point the river ~s into an estuary.* | **to** ◇ *The trade deficit had ~ed from £26 billion to £30 billion.* | **with** ◇ *Jasmine's eyes ~ed with disbelief.*

widespread *adj.*

VERBS **be** | **become** | **remain**
ADV. **extremely, fairly, very, etc.** | **remarkably** | **increasingly** | **relatively** | **sufficiently** | **geographically** ◇ *a geographically ~ species*
PREP. **among** ◇ *Illiteracy is ~ among the poor.*

widow *noun*

ADJ. **grieving** | **elderly, middle-aged, old, young** | **rich, wealthy** | **poor** | **war** | **football, golf, etc.** (= whose husband spends all his time playing or watching, golf, etc.)
VERB + WIDOW **become** ◇ *He died in March leaving a ~ and three children.* | **marry**
PHRASES **a widow's pension** (*BrE*)

width *noun*

ADJ. **great** ◇ *the great ~ of his shoulders* | **entire, full, overall, total, whole** | **narrow** ◇ *The fabric is only available in a narrow ~.* | **standard** | **varying** | **maximum, minimum**
VERB + WIDTH **have** ◇ *The windows have a ~ of six feet.* | **span** ◇ *a platform that spanned the ~ of the room* | **measure** ◇ *Measure the ~ of each side.* | **increase** | **decrease, narrow (to), reduce** ◇ *The snow had narrowed the ~ of the road to a single track.* ◇ *The road narrows to a ~ of just twelve feet.* | **vary in**
WIDTH + VERB **grow, increase** | **decrease** | **vary**
WIDTH + NOUN **measurement**

PREP. **across the ~** ◊ *The pattern goes across the full ~ of the material.* | **in ~** ◊ *The car is 1.775 m in ~.*

wife noun

ADJ. **new** | **future** | **former** (also **ex-wife**) | **first, second,** etc. | **deserted** | **divorced, estranged** | **common-law** | **dead, late** | **dependent** ◊ *With a dependent ~ and children, he can't afford to lose his job.* | **young** | **pregnant** | **beloved, dear, good, wonderful** | **attractive, beautiful, charming, lovely** | **dutiful, faithful, loving, loyal, supportive** | **long-suffering** ◊ *His long-suffering ~ had to put up with his numerous affairs.* | **unfaithful** | **jealous** | **domineering, nagging** | **battered** ◊ *a hostel for battered wives* | **trophy** (= an attractive younger wife) (*informal*) ◊ *She's a classic trophy wife—beautiful and half his age.*

VERB + WIFE **meet** ◊ *I first met my ~ at college.* | **marry** | **live with** | **desert, leave** | **be separated from** | **be unfaithful to, cheat on** | **batter, beat** | **accompany** ◊ *The general was accompanied by his ~.* | **survive** ◊ *Mr Thomas is survived by his ~, Muriel.*

WIFE + VERB **give birth** ◊ *His ~ has just given birth to a son.*

wig noun

ADJ. **blond** | **Afro, curly** | **powdered**

VERB + WIG **have on, sport, wear** ◊ *Do you think she was wearing a ~?* | **don, put on** | **remove, take off**

PREP. **in a/the ~** ◊ *Who's that man in the ~?*

wild adj.

1 animals/plants

VERBS **be, grow, live** ◊ *The flowers grow ~ in the mountains.* ◊ *The dogs live ~ on the streets.*

ADV. **truly** ◊ *This is truly ~ and unspoilt countryside.*

2 out of control

VERBS **be, look** ◊ *He looked ~ and dangerous.* | **go, run** ◊ *When the band appeared, the crowd went ~.* ◊ *They let their children run ~.* | **drive sb, make sb** ◊ *It makes me ~ (= very angry) to see such waste.*

ADV. **extremely, fairly, very,** etc. ◊ *Her hair was rather ~.* | **absolutely** | **a little, slightly,** etc.

PREP. **with** ◊ *The crowd was ~ with excitement.*

PHRASES **let your imagination run ~** ◊ *I just let my imagination run ~ and come up with as many ideas as I can.*

wilderness noun

ADJ. **last** | **great, vast** ◊ *Antarctica, the last great ~* | **barren, desert, desolate, howling** (*esp. AmE*) ◊ *He depicted the frontier as a howling ~ inhabited by uncivilized savages.* | **frozen** | **remote** | **trackless** (*esp. AmE*) | **uncharted** | **pristine, unspoiled** | **designated, protected** (*both AmE*) ◊ *The trail passes through a federally designated ~.* | **mountain** | **Alaskan, Arctic, Canadian,** etc. | **political** (*figurative*) ◊ *the man who brought the party back from the political ~*

VERB + WILDERNESS **tame, transform** ◊ *They transformed the ~ into a garden.* | **explore** ◊ *They set out to explore the continent's last great ~.* | **preserve, protect** (*both esp. AmE*)

WILDERNESS + NOUN **area** (*esp. AmE*) ◊ *officially designated ~ areas and wildlife refuges* | **preservation, protection** (*both esp. AmE*) | **years** (*figurative, esp. BrE*) ◊ *His ~ years (= when he was out of politics and the public eye) in the 1990s were spent in Canada.*

PREP. **in the ~** ◊ *We were hopelessly lost in the ~.*

wildlife noun

ADJ. **abundant** | **endangered, rare** | **indigenous, local, native** | **exotic** | **marine, urban, wetland**

VERB + WILDLIFE **conserve, preserve, protect, save** ◊ *They called on the government to help protect native ~.* | **attract, encourage** ◊ *The large variety of native plants attracts ~ to the area.* | **benefit** | **endanger, threaten** ◊ *The increasing use of pesticides threatens the ~ of the area.* | **damage, harm** | **disturb** ◊ *Do not allow your dog to disturb ~.* | **be (a) home for, be (a) home to, be rich in** ◊ *The forest is home to a wealth of ~.*

WILDLIFE + NOUN **habitat** | **area, garden** (*BrE*), **haven** (*esp.*

BrE), **park** (*esp. BrE*), **preserve** (*esp. BrE*), **refuge, reserve, sanctuary, site** (*BrE*) ◊ *The school has its own small ~ garden.* ◊ *the Wichita Mountains Wildlife Reserve in Texas* | **corridor** ◊ *~ corridors that tigers use to travel between reserves* | **conservation, management, protection** | **agency** (*esp. AmE*), **trust** (*BrE*) ◊ *data compiled by US and Canadian ~ agencies* | **biologist** (*AmE*), **conservationist, expert, manager** (*esp. AmE*), **officer** (*esp. BrE*), **official** (*esp. AmE*) ◊ *federal and state ~ officials* | **population, species** ◊ *The local fish and ~ population may be lost forever.* | **trade** ◊ *the illegal ~ trade* | **artist, film-maker, photographer** | **photography**

PHRASES **a diversity of ~, a wealth of ~** | **a/the impact on ~, a/the threat to ~** ◊ *The bacteria pose a real threat to ~.*

will noun

1 power to choose; desire

ADJ. **great, indomitable, iron, strong** ◊ *her indomitable ~ to win* ◊ *His unassuming manner concealed an iron ~.* | **weak** | **pure, sheer** ◊ *I was driven by the pure ~ to survive.* | **free** | **conscious** | **collective, general, majority, national, popular, public** ◊ *Is that the general ~, that we keep the present voting arrangements?* | **individual** | **human** | **divine** | **political** ◊ *The government lacked the political ~ to reform the tax system.* | **ill** ◊ *She bears them no ill ~.* (see also **goodwill**)

VERB + WILL **have** ◊ *She has a very strong ~.* | **lack** | **exercise, exert** | **lose** ◊ *She's lost the ~ to try and change things.* | **break, drain, sap** ◊ *Constant rejection has sapped her ~.* | **regain** ◊ *She usually manages to impose her ~ on the rest of the group.* | **bend (sb/sth) to, obey** ◊ *They were taught to obey their father's ~ without question.* | **go against** ◊ *My father didn't want me to leave home, and I didn't like to go against his ~.*

PREP. **against your ~** ◊ *Much against my ~, I let him go.* | **at ~** ◊ *She believes employers should have the right to hire and fire at ~.*

PHRASES **an act of ~** ◊ *It requires an act of ~ to make myself go running in the morning.* | **a battle of ~s, a clash of ~s** ◊ *The meeting turned out to be a clash of ~s.* | **an effort of ~** ◊ *With a great effort of ~ he resisted her pleas.* | **of your own free ~** ◊ *She left of her own free ~.* | **where there's a ~ there's a way** (= used to say that sth is possible if you really want it) | **the ~ to live** ◊ *She gradually regained the ~ to live.* | **God's ~, the ~ of God**

2 legal document

ADJ. **valid** ◊ *Two people must witness your signature or your ~ is not valid.* | **living** (= a record of your wishes regarding medical treatment at the end of your life)

VERB + WILL **draft, draw up, make, write** ◊ *His lawyer drew up the ~.* ◊ *Have you made your ~?* | **sign** | **leave** ◊ *She left no ~ and was unmarried.* | **read** | **alter, change** | **remember sb in** ◊ *My aunt remembered me in her ~.* | **administer, execute** | **challenge, contest** ◊ *The family decided to contest the ~ in court.* | **break, overturn, set aside** (*BrE*) ◊ *They succeeded in getting the ~ overturned.*

PREP. **by ~** ◊ *Some things cannot be given away by ~.* | **in a/the ~** ◊ *She left me some money in her ~.* | **under a/the ~** ◊ *Under her father's ~, she gets $5 000 a year.*

PHRASES **sb's last ~ and testament**

willing adj.

VERBS **appear, be, prove, seem** ◊ *They appear ~ to talk to us.* | **find sb** ◊ *She finally find someone ~ to lend her some money.* | **show yourself** ◊ *He showed himself ~ to take a risk.*

ADV. **more than, only too, really, very** ◊ *I'm more than ~ to get involved.* | **increasingly** | **perfectly, quite** ◊ *He's quite ~ to do the same for you.* | **enough** ◊ *He seemed ~ enough to listen.* | **apparently** | **certainly** | **always** ◊ *She is always ~ to help.* | **no longer**

PHRASES **ready and ~** ◊ *We're ready and ~ to do everything necessary to meet this challenge.* | **~ and able** ◊ *people who are ~ and able to work*

willingness noun

ADJ. **general** | **genuine** | **apparent** | **greater, increased** | **growing, increasing** | **new-found**
VERB + WILLINGNESS **demonstrate, display, indicate, show, signal** ◊ *The new government has shown a ~ to listen and learn.* | **announce, confirm, declare, express** ◊ *Workers' leaders have expressed their ~ to cooperate.* | **demand, depend on, require** ◊ *The success of this type of therapy depends on the patients' ~ to try to solve their problems.*
PREP. **in your ~** ◊ *In her ~ to help them, she quite forgot that she wasn't as strong as she had been.*

willpower noun

ADJ. **sheer** | **strong** | **all sb's** ◊ *It took all his ~ to stay in and study.*
VERB + WILLPOWER **have** ◊ *I'm no good at losing weight. The trouble is, I've no ~.* | **take** | **summon** ◊ *He tried to summon the ~ to get out of bed.*
PREP. **by ~** ◊ *She managed to finish the race by sheer ~.*

wilt verb

ADV. **visibly** (*esp. BrE*) ◊ *After a day spent shopping, she was visibly ~ing.*
VERB + WILT **begin to** ◊ *Some of the leaves were beginning to ~.*
PREP. **in** ◊ *The plants will ~ in direct sunlight.* | **under** ◊ *By half-time, the team was ~ing under the pressure.* | **with** ◊ *The passengers were visibly ~ing with the heat and movement of the bus.*

win noun

ADJ. **big, comfortable, convincing, decisive, easy, emphatic, handsome** (*esp. BrE*)**, resounding, runaway** (*BrE*) | **excellent, fine, great, impressive** | **thrilling** | **remarkable, shock** (*BrE*)**, unexpected, upset** (*AmE*) | **famous** ◊ *People still talk about the famous ~ against Brazil.* | **last-gasp** (*BrE*)**, narrow** ◊ *An extra-time penalty gave Barcelona a last-gasp ~ over Chelsea.* | **overtime** (*AmE*) | **hard-earned** (*esp. BrE*)**, hard-fought** | **come-from-behind** (*AmE*) | **deserved** (*BrE*) | **away, home** (*both BrE*) ◊ *The team claimed a 6–3 away ~ over Middlethorpe.* | **back-to-back, consecutive, straight** ◊ *The Red Sox opened the season with five straight ~s.* | **five-point, two-goal, etc.** | **cup-final** (in football/soccer)**, final-round, league, play-off, semi-final** | **Super Bowl™, World Series, etc.** | **Democrat, Labour, etc.**
VERB + WIN **chalk up, claim, clinch** (*esp. BrE*)**, earn, gain, get, have, notch, notch up, post** (*esp. AmE*)**, pull out** (*esp. AmE*)**, record, score** ◊ *We've had three successive ~s in the National League.* ◊ *Torino notched up a 2–1 ~ at Lazio.* | **cruise to, romp to** (*esp. BrE*) ◊ *Woods romped to a 12-shot ~ in the Open.* | **deserve, earn** | **give sb** | **celebrate**
WIN + VERB **come** ◊ *His only big ~ came in the French Open ten years ago.* | **keep sb, lift sb, put sb, take sb** ◊ *Williams's straight-sets ~ puts her through to the semi-final.*
PREP. **without a ~** ◊ *They've gone four games without a ~.* | **~ against, ~ over** ◊ *Liverpool gained a thrilling 5–4 ~ over Glenavon.*

win verb

ADV. **comfortably** (*esp. BrE*)**, convincingly, decisively, easily, handily** (*esp. AmE*)**, hands down, handsomely** (*esp. BrE*)**, outright** ◊ *The French team won hands down.* | **narrowly** ◊ *She narrowly won the first race.* | **nearly** | **duly** (*BrE*) ◊ *He duly won, but was then sidelined by a leg injury.* | **unexpectedly** | **eventually, finally, ultimately**
VERB + WIN **deserve to** ◊ *We didn't deserve to win—we played very badly.* | **hope to, want to** | **be expected to, be tipped to** (*BrE*)**, expect to** ◊ *The actress is tipped to ~ an Oscar for her performance.* | **be in a position to, be likely to** ◊ *He entered election day in a strong position to ~.* | **have yet to** ◊ *He has yet to ~ a major tournament.* | **go on to** ◊ *The movie was an instant success and went on to ~ five Academy Awards.* | **be going to** ◊ *Who do you think is going to ~?* | **manage to** | **try and, try to** ◊ *You have to try and ~ every*

race. | **fail to** ◊ *The far right party failed to ~ a single seat.* | **help (to), help sb (to)** ◊ *qualities which help ~ business and motivate staff*
PREP. **against** ◊ *They stand a good chance of winning against their league rivals.* | **at** ◊ *I never ~ at tennis.* | **by** ◊ *She won the race by 25 seconds.*
PHRASES **be capable of winning (sth)** ◊ *There are a lot of teams capable of winning the title.* | **be confident of winning (sth)** ◊ *We're confident of winning the title this year.* | **a chance of winning (sth), a chance to ~ sth, an opportunity to ~ sth** ◊ *the chance to ~ the trip of a lifetime* | **succeed in winning sth** ◊ *He succeeded in winning their confidence.* | **have, know, etc. what it takes to ~ sth** ◊ *Does he have what it takes to ~ the Tour?* | **~ by a landslide, ~ in a landslide** (*AmE*) ◊ *President Reagan won by a landslide.* | **~ or lose**

wince verb

ADV. **a little, slightly, etc.** | **inwardly** ◊ *He ~d inwardly at her harsh tone.* | **visibly**
VERB + WINCE **try not to** | **cause sb to, make sb** | **see sb**
PREP. **at, from, in, with** ◊ *She switched on the light, wincing at the sudden brightness.* ◊ *He ~d in pain.*

wind noun

ADJ. **fierce, harsh, high, stiff, strong** ◊ *Rain and high ~s are forecast.* ◊ *There was a stiff ~ blowing.* | **gale-force, hurricane-force, storm-force** | **blustery, gusty** | **light, moderate, slight** | **warm** | **biting, bitter, brisk, chill, chilly, cold, icy, winter** ◊ *The icy ~ cut right through us.* | **howling** | **fair, favourable/favorable, good** ◊ *They set sail the next morning with a fair ~.* | **adverse** ◊ *Adverse ~s swept the boat off course.* | **prevailing** ◊ *We tried to take advantage of the prevailing south-westerly ~s.* | **head, tail** ◊ *A tail ~ made the ride home very relaxing.* | **90 mile-an-hour, 100 mile-per-hour, etc.** | **east, north, etc.** | **easterly, northerly, south-westerly, etc.** | **trade** ◊ *The trade ~s originate in the South Pacific.* | **desert** | **solar** ◊ *The unmanned capsule will bring particles of solar ~ back to Earth.* | **political** (*figurative*)
...OF WIND **blast, gust** | **breath** ◊ *There wasn't a breath of ~ in the still air.*
VERB + WIND **brave** ◊ *Fans braved icy ~s to watch the match.* | **withstand** ◊ *The structure is able to withstand hurricane-force ~s.*
WIND + VERB **blow, come, gust** ◊ *The ~ came from the west.* ◊ *a northerly ~ gusting up to 80 mph* | **cut through sb/sth, rush through sth, sweep sth, sweep through sth** ◊ *A fierce ~ swept through the countryside.* | **howl, moan, roar, whistle** ◊ *The ~ roared through the tunnel.* | **buffet sth, rattle sth, whip sth, whip sth up** ◊ *The ~ whipped up the surface of the lake.* | **increase, pick up, rise** | **die down, drop** ◊ *Let's wait until the ~ drops before setting sail.* | **change** ◊ *The ~ suddenly changed and began blowing from the north.*
WIND + NOUN **conditions, direction, pressure, speed** | **chill** ◊ *The high ~ chill factor made it seem even colder.* | **energy, power** ◊ *renewable energies like solar and ~ power* | **farm, turbine** ◊ *the cost of generating electricity at offshore ~ farms* | **sock** (usually *windsock*) | **break** (usually *windbreak*) | **tunnel** ◊ *a ~ tunnel for testing new car designs* | **gauge** | **chimes** ◊ *I could hear the ~ chimes hanging in the window.*
PREP. **against the ~** ◊ *We were rowing against the ~.* | **in the ~** ◊ *a flag flapping in the ~* | **into the ~** ◊ *We were sailing into the ~.* | **out of ~** ◊ *Let's shelter out of the ~.*
PHRASES **the roar of the ~, the sound of the ~**

wind verb

ADV. **tight, tightly** | **carefully, neatly**
PREP. **around, round** (*esp. BrE*) ◊ *He wound the bandage tightly around his ankle.* | **into** ◊ *She wound the wool into a ball.*

windfall noun

ADJ. **unexpected** | **potential** | **cash** (*esp. BrE*) | **economic, financial, tax** | **$35 million, £3 million, etc.**
VERB + WINDFALL **get, have, reap, receive** ◊ *She had an unexpected ~ when a cousin died.*

window noun

1 in a building, car, etc.

ADJ. big, huge, large, long, tall, wide | narrow, small, tiny | panoramic | floor-to-ceiling | arched, bay, bow, casement, dormer, French, lattice, leaded, picture, rose, sash, skylight, stained-glass ◇ French ~s lead out onto the patio. ◇ The cathedral has a beautiful rose ~. | plate-glass | double-glazed | barred, curtained, shuttered ◇ All the ~s in the prison are barred. | curtainless | open | boarded-up | dark | bright, sunny | rain-streaked | draughty/drafty, ill-fitting | broken, cracked, shattered, smashed | dirty, dusty, filthy | clean | steamed-up | balcony, basement, bedroom, kitchen, etc. | back, front, rear, side, top, upstairs | first-floor, ground-floor (BrE), etc. | south-facing, etc. | display, shop (esp. BrE), store (esp. AmE), storefront (AmE) | car, carriage, train, etc. | back, driver's, passenger, rear, side | electric (BrE), power (AmE) | frosted, tinted ◇ a limousine with tinted ~s
VERB + WINDOW gaze out (of), glance out (of), look out (of), peer out (of), see out (of), stare out of ◇ It was raining so hard I could scarcely see out of the ~. | look in ◇ I found her looking in the ~ of a department store. | gaze (in) through, look (in) through, peer (in) through, see (sb/sth) through, stare through | lean out of, stick your head out of | knock on, rap on, tap on ◇ We tapped on the ~ to get their attention. | fling open, force (open), open, throw open ◇ There was evidence that the ~ had been forced. | roll down, wind down ◇ I rolled down the ~ to ask for directions. | close, roll up, shut | clean, wash | break, shatter, smash | blow out ◇ All the ~s were blown out with the force of the blast. | replace
WINDOW + VERB close, open ◇ How does the ~ open? | break, shatter, smash | flash, gleam, glint, glow, shine ◇ The ~s glinted in the sunlight. | steam up ◇ The ~s all steam up when you have a shower. | rattle ◇ The ~s rattle when a train goes past. | face sth, give a view of sth, look out on sth, overlook sth ◇ a studio with ~s looking out on the park
WINDOW + NOUN frame, ledge, pane, sill | blind, coverings (AmE), shade (AmE) | seat ◇ I always ask for a ~ seat when I fly. | cleaner ◇ He works as a ~ cleaner. | display | box ◇ floral displays such as ~ boxes and hanging baskets
PREP. at the ~ ◇ He was standing at the ~ waiting for us. | by the ~ ◇ I sat by the ~ to get some air. | in the ~ ◇ an advertisement in the ~ of the bakery ◇ We caught sight of him in the ~ as we passed. ◇ There was a vase of flowers in the ~. | out (of) ~ ◇ She gazed out of the ~ at the falling snow. | through ~ ◇ They threw a brick through the ~.

2 area on a computer screen

ADJ. active ◇ Click on the ~ to make it active. | pop-up | browser
VERB + WINDOW open | close ◇ If you close a couple of ~s, the screen will be less cluttered. | minimize, resize, shrink | drag, move | click on
WINDOW + VERB pop up
→ Special page at COMPUTER

windscreen (BrE) (AmE windshield) noun

ADJ. front, rear | car
VERB + WINDSCREEN/WINDSHIELD clean, scrape (sth off), wipe ◇ She scraped the ~ free of ice. | break, crack, shatter, smash (esp. BrE) | fit, replace | clear, defog (AmE), demist (BrE) ◇ She switched the wipers on to clear the ~.
WINDSCREEN/WINDSHIELD + VERB fog up (esp. AmE), mist up (BrE) | crack, shatter
WINDSCREEN/WINDSHIELD + NOUN wiper
PREP. on a/the ~ ◇ I came back to find a parking ticket on the ~. | through a/the ~ ◇ Bright evening sunlight glared through the ~.

wine noun

ADJ. red, white | fizzy (BrE), sparkling | dry | sweet | light ◇ He served a light white ~ with the lunch. | full-bodied, heady, strong | fruity | sour ◇ a cheap sour ~ | mature, young ◇ The younger ~s will be mature after about three years. | new, old ◇ some new ~s from South Africa | excellent, expensive, fine, good, great, quality, vintage | cheap, table | house ◇ The restaurant's house ~s are Australian. | dessert | fortified ◇ fortified ~s such as port and sherry | mulled, spiced | chilled ◇ chilled white ~ | dandelion, elderberry, rice, etc.
... OF WINE drop (esp. BrE) ◇ Would you like another drop of ~? | bottle, carafe, decanter, glass
VERB + WINE drink ◇ Do you drink ~? | have ◇ I'll have some ~, please. | taste ◇ He went to Chile to taste ~s. | sip, take a sip of ◇ She took a sip of her ~. | gulp, gulp down, swig | take a gulp of, take a swig of | pour (sb) ◇ The waiter went around pouring the ~. | make, produce ◇ The winery has been making ~ for 25 years. | age, mature ◇ ~ aged in the bottle | chill | order, serve | ply sb with ◇ They always ply their clients with ~ before getting down to business. | produce ◇ About 60% of Australia's ~ is produced in South Australia.
WINE + VERB flow (figurative) ◇ The ~ flowed freely at the party. | go to your head ◇ The ~ had gone to his head and he was starting to talk rubbish. | breathe ◇ Open the ~ an hour before the meal to let it breathe. | be corked | age, mature
WINE + NOUN bottle, glass | cooler (= for cooling wine) | list, selection ◇ The restaurant has an extensive ~ list. | rack ◇ I took another bottle from the ~ rack. | cellar | bar | shop (esp. BrE), store (esp. AmE) | cooler (= a drink) (AmE), spritzer | vinegar ◇ Add two tablespoons of white ~ vinegar. | grape ◇ Red ~ grapes grow well here. | tasting ◇ We hold occasional wine-tasting sessions. | drinker | grower, growing ◇ a wine-growing region | distributor (esp. AmE), importer, merchant (esp. BrE) | sales | business, industry | country, region ◇ a farm at the edge of northern California's ~ country
PHRASES ~ (sold) by the glass ◇ A good selection of ~ by the glass was on offer.

wing noun

1 of a bird/insect

ADJ. left, right | front ◇ The beetle's front ~s are small and are not used in flight. | back, hind | broad, long, narrow, pointed, short, stubby | delicate | leathery | broken, damaged ◇ a bird with a broken ~ | outspread, out-stretched | bat, butterfly, etc. ◇ the patterns on butterfly ~s | angel, fairy, etc. | Buffalo (AmE), chicken ◇ First, fry the chicken ~s in the oil until they begin to brown. | spicy
... OF WINGS pair
VERB + WING extend, flex, open, spread, stretch, unfold, unfurl | close, fold, tuck in | beat, flap, flutter ◇ It flapped its ~s and flew off. | clean | clip (often figurative) ◇ Mario felt he had had his ~s clipped when his car was impounded. | grow, sprout ◇ I wish I could sprout ~s and fly away.
WING + VERB beat, flap, flutter
WING + NOUN tip | feathers | span
PREP. on a/the ~ ◇ It had white markings on its ~s. | under a/the ~ ◇ The young birds were under the mother bird's ~. ◇ Simon's uncle had taken him under his ~. (figurative)

2 of a plane

ADJ. aircraft | left, port | right, starboard | fixed | folding
WING + NOUN tip

3 of a building

ADJ. north, south, etc. | private | hospital | maternity | high-security, maximum-security (= of a prison)
VERB + WING add, build
PREP. in a/the ~ ◇ Our rooms were in the west ~.

4 (BrE) of a car → See also FENDER

ADJ. nearside, offside | front, rear
VERB + WING damage, dent ◇ The nearside ~ was damaged in the accident. | mend, repair
WING + NOUN mirror
PREP. in a/the ~ ◇ There was a dent in one ~.

5 of an organization

ADJ. **left, right** | **conservative** | **liberal, progressive, reformist** | **extreme, radical** | **revolutionary** | **moderate** | **dissident** (*esp. BrE*) | **political** | **armed, military, para-military**
PREP. **on a/the ~** ◇ *They're on the left ~ of the party.*

wink *noun*

ADJ. **broad** | **little** | **conspiratorial, knowing, playful, sly**
VERB + WINK **give sb, throw sb** (*esp. AmE*)
PREP. **with a ~** ◇ *'Know what I mean?' he said with a ~.*

wink *verb*

ADV. **broadly** ◇ *He ~ed broadly at Lucinda.* | **cheekily** (*BrE*), **conspiratorially, flirtatiously, knowingly, mischievously, slyly, suggestively** ◇ *She ~ed knowingly at Jack.* | **back**
PREP. **at** ◇ *She ~ed at me, and I winked back.*

winner *noun*

ADJ. **overall** ◇ *She didn't win every race, but she was the overall ~.* | **outright** (*esp. BrE*) ◇ *With three teams finishing on 40 points, there was no outright ~.* | **eventual** | **joint** (*esp. BrE*) ◇ *They were joint ~s of the cup.* | **lucky** ◇ *She was the lucky ~ of that week's biggest lottery prize.* | **deserved, worthy** (*esp. BrE*) | **real** ◇ *Who are the real ~s in these elections?* | **clear, comfortable** (*esp. BrE*), **convincing** (*esp. BrE*), **easy, runaway** ◇ *She emerged as the clear ~.* | **impressive** | **big** ◇ *There were no big ~s in this week's lottery.* | **shock** (*BrE*), **surprise, unexpected, unlikely** | **likely, possible, potential** ◇ *She is the most likely ~ of the contest.* | **first-time, three-times, etc.** ◇ *Brazil, five-times ~s of the World Cup* | **consistent** (*esp. AmE*), **prolific** (*esp. BrE*), **regular** ◇ *She is a regular ~ in local road races.* | **award, championship, competition, contest, cup, election, jackpot, league, match, medal, prize** (usually *prizewinner*), **race, scholarship, title, tournament, trophy** ◇ *a bronze medal ~* | **Academy Award, Emmy, Grammy, etc.** | **Nobel Prize, Pulitzer Prize, etc.**
VERB + WINNER **emerge as** | **look** (*BrE*), **look like** (*esp. BrE*) ◇ *Barcelona look likely ~s of the League.* | **announce, declare (sb)** ◇ *The ~ of the competition will be announced this afternoon.* ◇ *Bush was declared the ~ of the election.* | **choose, pick, select** ◇ *The ~ will be chosen from the five architects who get through the first round.* ◇ *He's very good at picking ~s* (= at guessing who is going to win). | **decide, decide on, determine** | **back** ◇ *He backed the ~ and won £70.*
WINNER + VERB **get sth, receive sth** ◇ *The ~ will receive a prize of $500.*
PREP. **~ against, ~ over** ◇ *Uruguay were impressive 3–0 ~s over Japan.* | **~ of** ◇ *the ~ of the race*

winter *noun*

ADJ. **last, this past** (*esp. AmE*) | **the following, next, this, this coming** | **early, late** ◇ *It was impossible to walk the route in late ~.* | **long** | **bad, bitter, brutal** (*esp. AmE*), **cold, freezing, frigid** (*esp. AmE*), **hard, harsh, icy, severe, terrible** ◇ *one of the worst ~s we have ever had* | **bleak, dark, dreary, grey/gray** | **mild, warm** | **wet** | **nuclear**
WINTER + NOUN **conditions, temperature, weather** | **sun, sunlight, sunshine** | **cold** | **frost, rain, snow** ◇ *plants which are susceptible to ~ frosts* | **gale** (*esp. BrE*), **wind** | **landscape, scene, sky** ◇ *the artist's bleak ~ scene* | **solstice** | **term** | **break, holiday** (*BrE*), **vacation** (*AmE*) | **holidays** (= the time including Christmas, Hanukkah and New Year) (*BrE, AmE*) | **garden** | **crop** | **clothes, clothing, coat** | **collection** | **Olympics, sports**
PHRASES **go, fly, head, etc. south for the ~** ◇ *The birds fly south for the ~.* | **in the dead of ~, in the depths of ~** ◇ *a frigid midwestern city in the dead of ~*
→ Note at SEASON (for more collocates)

wipe *verb*

ADV. **carefully, gently** | **hastily, quickly** | **easily** ◇ *The plastic surface can be easily ~d.* | **just, simply** | **away, down, up** ◇ *I ~d up the spilled wine.*
PREP. **from** ◇ *She gently ~d the tears from her eyes.* | **off** ◇ *He ~d the marks off the wall.* | **on** ◇ *She ~d her hands on the towel.* | **with** ◇ *When you've finished with it, simply ~ it clean with a damp cloth.*
PHRASES **~ sth clean**

PHR V **wipe sth out**
ADV. **completely, totally** | **almost, nearly, practically, virtually** ◇ *The regiment was virtually ~d out in the first battle.* | **effectively** ◇ *The disease has been effectively ~d out.*
VERB + WIPE OUT **threaten to** ◇ *pollution that threatens to ~ out 100 000 fish*

wiper *noun*

ADJ. **windscreen** (*BrE*), **windshield** (*AmE*) | **rear**
VERB + WIPER **put on, switch on, turn on** | **turn off**
WIPER + VERB **be going, be on** ◇ *Cars were coming past with their ~s going.*
WIPER + NOUN **blade** | **fluid**

wire *noun*

1 metal as thin thread

ADJ. **taut** | **loose** | **fine, thin** | **thick** | **flexible, soft** | **stiff** | **rusty** | **metal, steel, etc.** | **baling** (*AmE*), **barbed, chicken** (= wire mesh used to make fences), **razor** | **piano** | **perimeter** | **trip** (usually *tripwire*) ◇ *The bomb was attached to a tripwire laid across the road.* | **high** (= in a circus) ◇ *One man rode a bicycle along the high ~ as the climax to the act.*
... OF WIRE **length, piece, strand** | **coil, roll** ◇ *coils of barbed ~*
VERB + WIRE **cut** ◇ *They cut the perimeter ~ and escaped.* | **bend, twist** | **stretch, string** ◇ *The ~ was stretched between two poles.* | **be surrounded by, be topped with, be wrapped in** ◇ *a fence topped with razor ~*
WIRE + NOUN **mesh, netting** (*esp. BrE*) | **basket, brush, cage, fence, fencing, frame, hanger, rack** ◇ *coat hangers* ◇ *Cool the cakes on a ~ rack.*
PREP. **behind a/the ~** ◇ *Behind the ~, the prisoners were exercising.* | **under a/the ~** ◇ *We got in under the ~.*

2 for electricity

ADJ. **electric, electrical, electricity** (*esp. BrE*) ◇ *Don't place carpets over electrical ~s.* | **overhead electricity ~s** | **earth** (*BrE*), **ground** (*AmE*), **live, neutral** ◇ *Don't touch that ~. It's live.* | **overhead** | **telegraph, telephone** | **fuse** | **bare, exposed** ◇ *Watch out for bare ~s.* | **insulated, plastic-coated** | **frayed** | **copper, silver, etc.** | **14-gauge, 20-gauge, etc.** (*esp. AmE*)
VERB + WIRE **attach, connect** ◇ *The ~ was attached to a pin in the plug.* | **disconnect** ◇ *He disconnected the ~ from the clock.* | **run** ◇ *The electrician ran a ~ from the kitchen to the bedroom.*
WIRE + VERB **go, lead, run, trail** ◇ *Where does this ~ go?* ◇ *There were ~s trailing everywhere.* | **dangle, protrude, stick out**
PREP. **along a/the ~, down a/the ~** ◇ *the flow of electrical current down a ~*
PHRASES **a tangle of ~s** ◇ *I found myself tripping over a tangle of ~s and cables.*

wire *verb*

ADV. **correctly, properly** ◇ *You should check that the socket is correctly ~d.* | **directly** | **together** ◇ *The components have to be ~d together in a certain way.* | **in, up** ◇ *She was ~d up to a heart monitor.* | **genetically** (*figurative*) ◇ *We're genetically ~d to love sugar.*
PREP. **for** ◇ *Many homes were ~d for lighting only.* | **into, to** ◇ *The Christmas tree lights are all ~d to one plug.*

wiring *noun*

ADJ. **electric, electrical** | **exposed, faulty** | **structured** (*AmE*) ◇ *a structured ~ network* | **mains** (*BrE*) | **house, phone, telephone** | **copper** | **brain, internal, neural** (*all figurative*)

◇ *Our internal ~ has not changed much since the time of our hairy ancestors.*
VERB + WIRING **install** | **replace** ◇ *The existing ~ will have to be replaced.* | **check**, **check over** ◇ *We'd better get an electrician to check the ~ before we start decorating.*
WIRING + NOUN **diagram** | **system**

wisdom *noun*

ADJ. **deep**, **great**, **profound** | **accepted**, **common**, **conventional**, **folk**, **perceived**, **popular**, **prevailing**, **received**, **traditional** ◇ *Conventional ~ has it that higher oil prices are bad for economic growth.* ◇ *The received ~ is that the book is always better than the film.* | **practical** | **homespun** ◇ *His journals are full of dubious pearls of homespun ~.* | **worldly** ◇ *He is too lacking in worldly ~ to be a politician.* | **accumulated**, **collective** ◇ *the accumulated ~ of generations* | **ancient** ◇ *A bridge between ancient ~ and modern insight is now being built.* | **innate**, **inner** | **political** | **divine**
VERB + WISDOM **challenge**, **doubt**, **have doubts about**, **question** ◇ *Many commentators doubted the political ~ of introducing a new tax.* | **accept** | **seek** ◇ *Those who seek ~ at the shrine will find it.* | **dispense**, **impart** ◇ *Do you have any ~ to impart on this subject?* | **prove** ◇ *The latest unemployment figures prove the ~ of the government's policy.*
WISDOM + VERB **dictate sth**, **have it that …** , **hold sth** (*esp. AmE*) ◇ *Popular ~ dictates that a father is essential in raising a son.*
PREP. **according to … ~**, **contrary to … ~** ◇ *Contrary to conventional ~, stress is not a bad thing.*
PHRASES **a fount of ~** (*formal or humorous*), **a source of ~** ◇ *Consultants are too often seen as the source of all ~.* | **in sb's ~** (*ironic*) ◇ *In their infinite ~, they closed the swimming pool at the busiest time of year.* | **pearls of ~** (*ironic*) ◇ *students eager to catch pearls of ~ from the professor's lips* | **wit and ~** ◇ *He entertained the audience for two hours with his wit and ~.* | **with the ~ of hindsight** ◇ *It's easy enough to see what we should have done, with the ~ of hindsight.* | **words of ~** ◇ *The former world champion imparted a few words of ~ to the young runners.*

wise *adj.*

VERBS **be**, **look**, **prove**, **seem** | **become**, **grow** | **consider sth**, **deem sth**, **think sth** ◇ *It was not considered ~ to move her to another hospital.*
ADV. **very** | **always** ◇ *It is always ~ to write down important points.*

wish *noun*

1 feeling that you want sth

ADJ. **dearest**, **deepest**, **desperate**, **fervent**, **fondest** (*esp. AmE*), **greatest**, **strong** | **conscious**, **unconscious** | **secret** | **express**, **expressed** | **dying**, **final**, **last** ◇ *He was denied his dying ~ to be reconciled with his son.* | **death** ◇ *Freud's theory of the death ~* | **personal** | **parental** ◇ *the child's detention against parental ~es*
VERB + WISH **have** ◇ *I have no ~ to cause any trouble among them.* | **express**, **make known** ◇ *She has expressed a ~ to seek asylum here.* | **fulfil/fulfill** ◇ *She fulfilled her deepest ~ when she flew solo for the first time.* | **get** ◇ *She's always wanted to be an actress, and I'm sure she'll get her ~.* | **grant (sb)** | **honour/honor**, **respect**, **take into account** ◇ *It is vital for schools to respect the ~es of parents.* | **carry out**, **comply with**, **meet** ◇ *We need to update our equipment if we are to meet customers' ~es.* | **obey** ◇ *She flew into a rage if the staff didn't obey her ~es.* | **deny sb** | **disregard**, **go against**, **ignore**, **override** (*esp. BrE*), **ride roughshod over** (*BrE*) ◇ *She eventually went against her family's ~es and published her autobiography.* ◇ *The Government blatantly ignored the ~es of the public.* ◇ *The committee rode roughshod over the ~es of union members.* | **reflect** ◇ *The change to the constitution reflects the ~es of the people who voted in the referendum.*
WISH + NOUN **fulfilment/fulfillment** | **list** ◇ *Draw up a ~ list, defining the requirements for your ideal home.*
PREP. **against sb's ~es** ◇ *Against his mother's ~es, he decided to quit school and look for a job.* | **in sb's ~** ◇ *In his ~ to be as helpful as possible, he was forever asking her what she*

wanted. | **in accordance with sb's ~s** ◇ *In accordance with his ~es, his ashes were scattered at sea.* | **~ for** ◇ *a ~ for peace*
2 saying secretly to yourself what you want to happen

VERB + WISH **have**, **make** ◇ *When you see a black cat, you have to make a ~.* | **get** ◇ *If you're the one who finds the hidden box, you get a ~.* | **grant** ◇ *The good fairy granted her three ~es.*
WISH + VERB **come true** ◇ *On Christmas Day their ~es came true.*

3 (usually **wishes**) hope that sb will be happy

ADJ. **best**, **good** ◇ *Give my best ~es to Alison.* | **well** (*AmE*) ◇ *Thanks to all those who sent well ~es.* | **heartfelt**, **sincere**
VERB + WISH **give sb**, **send (sb)**
PREP. **with … ~es** (at the end of a letter) ◇ *With best ~es for a happy birthday.* | **~ for** ◇ *Every good ~ for your future happiness together.*

wish *verb*

ADV. **dearly**, **desperately**, **devoutly** (*esp. AmE*), **fervently**, **heartily**, **really**, **sincerely** ◇ *I heartily ~ed that I had stayed at home.* ◇ *I really ~ I could go to America.* | **hard** ◇ *If you ~ really hard, maybe you'll get what you want.* | **secretly** | **just**, **merely**, **only**, **simply** ◇ *'Where is he now?' 'I only ~ I knew.'* | **sometimes** | **almost** ◇ *When I see the kids playing football, I almost ~ I was their age again.*
PREP. **for** ◇ *It's no use ~ing for the impossible.*

wit *noun*

1 clever use of words

ADJ. **great** | **quick**, **ready** | **acerbic**, **barbed**, **biting**, **caustic**, **dry**, **mordant**, **rapier**, **razor-sharp**, **sarcastic**, **sardonic**, **sharp**, **sly**, **wicked**, **wry** | **gentle**, **self-deprecating** | **dazzling** (*esp. BrE*), **sparkling** | **verbal**
VERB + WIT **have** ◇ *He has plenty of ~ and imagination.* ◇ *He had a dry ~.* (*BrE*)
PHRASES **~ and wisdom** ◇ *a book full of the ~ and wisdom of his 30 years in politics*

2 intelligence

ADJ. **native** ◇ *She had to use all her native ~ to convince the police.*
VERB + WIT **have** ◇ *I hope he has the ~ to take the key with him.* | **use**
PHRASES **beyond the ~ of man** (= impossible) (*esp. BrE*) ◇ *It should not be beyond the ~ of man to resolve this dispute.*

3 wits ability to think quickly

VERB + WITS **use** | **have** (*esp. AmE*) ◇ *I hope you had the ~s to apologize.* | **gather**, **recover** ◇ *She couldn't seem to gather her ~s and tell us what had happened.* | **sharpen** | **match** ◇ *The game allows you to match ~s with a computer criminal.*
PHRASES **a battle of ~s** ◇ *The strike developed into a battle of ~s between management and workers.* | **have your ~s about you**, **keep your ~s about you** ◇ *They do tough interviews, so you'll need to have your ~s about you.* | **pit your ~s against sb** (*esp. BrE*) ◇ *Celebrity teams pit their ~s against each other in this lively quiz show.* | **scare the ~s out of sb** ◇ *The latest news has scared the ~s out of investors.* ◇ *I was scared out of my ~s!* | **wits' end** ◇ *I'm at my wits' end trying to cope with his moods.*

withdraw *verb*

ADV. **altogether**, **completely** | **immediately**, **instantly** | **abruptly**, **hastily**, **promptly**, **quickly**, **soon** ◇ *She hastily withdrew her hand from his.* | **gradually**, **progressively** (*esp. BrE*) ◇ *Forces will be progressively withdrawn.* | **temporarily** | **immediately** | **subsequently** | **eventually** | **formally** ◇ *The US formally withdrew from the anti-ballistic missile treaty.* | **unilaterally** ◇ *the decision to unilaterally ~ from the occupied territories* | **voluntarily**
VERB + WITHDRAW **be forced to**, **be ordered to** ◇ *The troops were forced to ~ to their own borders.* ◇ *He was forced to ~ from the competition due to injury.* | **threaten to**, **wish to** |

withdrawal

944

choose to, decide to | persuade sb to | agree to ◇ *The government has agreed to ~ its troops.* | refuse to

PREP. **from** ◇ *Two thousand troops were withdrawn from the battle zone.* ◇ *They threatened to ~ their support from the government.* | **in favour/favor of** ◇ *He eventually withdrew in favour of Blair, thought to be the more popular candidate.* | **into** ◇ *She withdrew into her own world.*

withdrawal noun

1 removing/leaving

ADJ. eventual, imminent | abrupt, immediate, precipitous (*esp. BrE*), rapid, sudden | gradual, phased | complete, full, total, unconditional | partial | strategic, tactical | planned | voluntary | unilateral | ignominious (*formal*) ◇ *The UN were faced with an ignominious ~ or a long-term military presence.* | military, troop

VERB + WITHDRAWAL advocate, call for, demand ◇ *The party is calling for the phased ~ of troops from the island.* | agree to | order | announce | make ◇ *The police were forced to make a tactical ~.*

PREP. **~ by** ◇ *a ~ by government troops* | **~ from** ◇ *the army's ~ from the occupied territories*

2 from a bank account

ADJ. cash (*esp. BrE*) | ATM (*esp. AmE*)
VERB + WITHDRAWAL make
PREP. **~ from** ◇ *She made a ~ of £250 from her bank account.*

3 stopping

ADJ. abrupt | alcohol, caffeine, drug, nicotine
VERB + WITHDRAWAL go through, suffer
WITHDRAWAL + NOUN symptoms ◇ *He was suffering from ~ symptoms.*
PREP. **~ from** ◇ *She was still suffering ~ from nicotine.*

wither verb

ADV. simply ◇ *Their support had simply ~ed away.* (*figurative*) | slowly | away
PREP. into ◇ *His body slowly ~ed into dust.* | under ◇ *The grass ~ed under a scorching sun.*
PHRASES **~ and die** (*figurative*) ◇ *The business ~ed and eventually died.* | **~ on the vine** (*figurative*) ◇ *Without investment, home-grown industries are being allowed to ~ on the vine.*

withhold verb

ADV. deliberately, intentionally (*esp. AmE*)
VERB + WITHHOLD threaten to ◇ *The government was threatening to ~ future financial aid.* | decide to
PREP. from ◇ *He was accused of deliberately ~ing information from the police.*

withstand verb

VERB + WITHSTAND be able to, be unable to, can | manage to | be built to, be designed to, be made to ◇ *The wooden boat was built to ~ just about every weather condition at sea.* | be robust enough to, be strong enough to ◇ *The building is strong enough to ~ an earthquake.* | enable sth to, help sth (to)
PHRASES the ability to ~ sth, the strength to ~ sth | be capable of ~ing sth

witness noun

1 person who sees sth

ADJ. crucial (*esp. BrE*), key, material, vital (*esp. BrE*) ◇ *As the last person to see her alive, he was a material ~ in the case.* | independent (*esp. BrE*) | credible, reliable | unreliable | silent (*figurative*) ◇ *The ancient temples bear silent ~ to the passing dynasties.*
VERB + WITNESS appeal for (*esp. BrE*) ◇ *The police are appealing for ~es.* | trace ◇ *Police have so far failed to trace any ~es to the attack.*
WITNESS + VERB come forward ◇ *Two ~es came forward with*

evidence. | report ◇ *Witnesses reported that the suspect was a white male.*
WITNESS + NOUN account, statement (*esp. BrE*)
PREP. according to ~ ◇ *According to ~es, the thief escaped through the bedroom window.* | **~ to** ◇ *a ~ to murder*

2 in a court of law

ADJ. chief, main, principal (*esp. BrE*), star (*esp. AmE*) ◇ *the prosecution's chief ~* | potential | reluctant, unwilling | hostile | defence/defense, prosecution | federal, state, state's (*all AmE*) | expert | character | civilian, police (*BrE*)
VERB + WITNESS call, subpoena, summon (*esp. BrE*) ◇ *The defence called their first ~.* | be called as, be subpoenaed as, be summoned as (*esp. BrE*) ◇ *He was subpoenaed as a ~ in a bankruptcy case.* | appear as ◇ *She appeared as a character ~.* | swear in | cross-examine, examine, interrogate, interview, question | hear | discredit | intimidate, threaten ◇ *A judicial investigation was ordered, but ~es were threatened and none would testify.* | protect
WITNESS + VERB be sworn in, take the stand ◇ *The next ~ took the stand.* | give evidence, testify | state sth | identify sb ◇ *She was the only ~ to identify Peters as the attacker.*
WITNESS + NOUN box (*BrE*), stand (*AmE*) | summons (*BrE*) | testimony (*esp. AmE*) | intimidation (*esp. BrE*), tampering (*esp. AmE*) ◇ *The jury convicted him on two counts of ~ tampering.* | protection ◇ *She went into a ~ protection program.* (*AmE*) ◇ *He was placed on a ~ protection scheme.* (*BrE*)
PHRASES a ~ for the defence/defense, a ~ for the prosecution

3 of a signature

VERB + WITNESS act as
WITNESS + VERB sign
PREP. in front of ~ ◇ *the marriage contract is signed in front of ~es* | **~ to** ◇ *Would you be willing to act as a ~ to my signature when I sign my will?*

wolf noun

ADJ. lone ◇ *A lone ~ howled under the full moon.* | wild | hungry (*often figurative*) | ravening (*esp. BrE*), ravenous (*esp. AmE*) (*both usually figurative*) ◇ *She compared the media to a pack of ravening/ravenous wolves.* | big bad (*figurative*) ◇ *Labour groups are often seen as the big bad ~.*
... OF WOLVES pack
WOLF + VERB growl, howl | hunt | raise sb ◇ *a story of a young boy raised by wolves*
WOLF + NOUN cub | pack

woman noun

ADJ. young | middle-aged | elderly, old, older ◇ *The thief tricked his way into an elderly woman's home.* ◇ *Older women often have difficulty conceiving.* | adult, grown ◇ *The little girl she remembered was now a grown ~.* | married | single, unattached, unmarried | widowed | divorced | pregnant | childless | menopausal, post-menopausal | business (*usually businesswoman*), career, professional, working | average, ordinary | extraordinary, remarkable | attractive, beautiful, good-looking, handsome, pretty | desirable | plain, ugly | well-dressed | educated, intelligent, smart (*esp. AmE*) ◇ *highly educated women who are successful in business* | powerful, strong | successful | independent, modern | motherly | decent, good, kind, nice | evil, wicked | hysterical | battered ◇ *a hostel for battered women* | the other ◇ *She was the 'other woman' in this family drama* (= the one the husband was having an affair with).
VERB + WOMAN marry | depict, portray, present, show ◇ *We want to change the way women are depicted in the media.* | abuse, assault, rape
PHRASES the oppression of women, violence against women ◇ *a United Nations report on violence against women* | the position of women, the role of women, the status of women ◇ *There were important changes in the position of women in society.* | a ~ of a certain age (= not young) | women of childbearing age | a ~ of the world ◇ *He saw her as a ~ of the world who could offer him advice.* | women's liberation, the women's movement (*becoming*

old-fashioned) ◊ a symbol of women's liberation | **a women's group** | **women's rights** | **women's studies** ◊ a professor of women's studies

womb noun → See also UTERUS

ADJ. **barren** (formal, old-fashioned) | **artificial**
VERB + WOMB **come out of, emerge from** ◊ The baby's head was starting to emerge from the ~.
PREP. **in the/your ~, within the/your ~** ◊ the baby growing in her ~ ◊ A scan determines the position of the baby in the ~. ◊ the nine months for which we are carried in our mothers' ~s | **out of the/your ~**
PHRASES **the lining of the ~, the neck of the ~, the wall of the ~** (all esp. BrE) (usually ... **of the uterus** in AmE)

wonder noun

1 feeling of surprise/admiration

ADJ. **great** | **childlike, wide-eyed**
VERB + WONDER **feel** | **express** ◊ There aren't any words to express properly all the ~ that I feel. | **be filled with, be full of** ◊ The children's faces were full of ~ as they gazed up at the Christmas tree.
WONDER + NOUN **drug**
PREP. **in ~** ◊ Neville shook his head in ~ at it all ◊ She gazed down in ~ at the city spread below her. | **with ~** ◊ She held her breath with ~ and delight. | **~ at**
PHRASES **a feeling of ~, a sense of ~**

2 amazing thing/person

ADJ. **natural** ◊ Iceland is full hot springs and other natural ~s. | **architectural, technological, etc.** | **constant** ◊ It was a constant ~ to me that my father didn't die of exhaustion. | **nine days'** (esp. BrE), **seven-day** ◊ She was determined to prove she was no seven-day ~ whose promise would remain unfulfilled. | **boy** (humorous) ◊ the new boy ~ of French football | **one-hit** (humorous) ◊ The band was a one-hit ~ in the '80s—no one has heard of them since. | **chinless** (esp. BrE), **gutless** (esp. AmE) (both humorous) ◊ The public thinks we're a bunch of gutless ~s.
VERB + WONDER **discover, experience, explore** ◊ Now it is your turn to discover the ~ of Bermuda. | **appreciate**
PHRASES **do ~s (for sb/sth), work ~s (for sb/sth)** ◊ The change of diet has done ~s for my skin. ◊ A good night's sleep and a hearty breakfast worked ~s. | **is it any ~ (that) ... ?** | **(it's) little ~, (it's) no ~, (it's) small ~** ◊ No ~ you're still single—you never go out! | **a ~ to behold** ◊ The restored painting is a ~ to behold. | **the ~s of nature, the ~s of science, the ~s of technology** ◊ Thanks to the ~s of modern science, many common diseases will soon be things of the past. | **the ~s of the world** ◊ The palace has been described as the eighth ~ of the world.

wonder verb

ADV. **idly, vaguely** ◊ I ~ed vaguely whether Robert could be the murderer. | **briefly, fleetingly** | **uneasily** ◊ I ~ed uneasily if anything had happened to the children. | **irritably** | **aloud** ◊ 'Where's Natasha?' she ~ed aloud. | **just** ◊ 'Why do you ask?' 'I just ~ed.' | **always** ◊ I always ~ed why you never got married. | **often, sometimes** ◊ I sometimes ~ who's crazier, him or me. | **probably** ◊ You're probably ~ing what all the fuss is about.
VERB + WONDER **begin to, start to** ◊ I was just beginning to ~ where you were. | **cannot help but, can only, have to** ◊ I couldn't help but ~ what he was thinking. ◊ You have to ~ just what he sees in her. | **make sb** ◊ He's behaving so strangely. It makes you ~ whether he's in trouble somehow.
PREP. **about** ◊ We'd ~ed about you as a possible team member.
PHRASES **can't help ~ing** ◊ I can't help ~ing if he lost on purpose. | **keep ~ing**

wonderful adj.

VERBS **be, feel, look, smell, sound, taste**
ADV. **most, really** | **absolutely, just, perfectly, quite, simply, truly** ◊ The weather was absolutely ~. | **pretty, rather** (esp. BrE)
PHRASES **strange and ~** (esp. AmE), **weird and ~** (esp. BrE) ◊

the strange and ~ world of Chinese ghost stories ◊ She has a reputation for coming up with weird and ~ marketing ideas.

wood noun

1 what trees are made of

ADJ. **hard** | **soft** ◊ Pine is a soft ~. | **dark** ◊ The house had dark ~ floors. | **light, pale** | **green** ◊ The ~ was too green to burn. | **dead, rotten, rotting** ◊ She pruned the dead ~ from the tree. | **natural** ◊ varnish that retains the natural ~ look | **seasoned** | **rough, smooth** | **painted, polished, stained, varnished** | **carved** | **solid** | **laminated** | **charred** | **balsa, beech, cherry, pine, etc.**
... OF WOOD **bit, block, piece, plank, strip** ◊ I made a coffee table out of a few bits of ~. | **pile**
VERB + WOOD **carve, chop, cut, saw** | **be made from/in/of/ out of, carve sth from/in** ◊ The cabinet is made of cherry ~. | **paint, stain** ◊ She stained the ~ green. | **burn** | **gather** ◊ We gathered ~ for the fire.
WOOD + VERB **splinter** ◊ the sound of splintering ~ | **rot** ◊ Over the years, much of the ~ in the house had rotted. | **burn** ◊ Dry ~ burns easily.
WOOD + NOUN **chip, shavings** | **pulp** ◊ paper made from ~ pulp | **grain** ◊ The direction of the ~ grain influences the composition of the carving. | **carving** | **engraving** | **block** (usually **woodblock**) ◊ Japanese woodblock prints | **frame** | **floor, panel, panelling/paneling, plank** (esp. AmE) | **veneer** | **finish, trim** ◊ a wardrobe in a mahogany ~ finish | **fire** | **stove** (esp. AmE)
PREP. **in ~** ◊ The chapel has some interesting works in ~ and marble.
PHRASES **the grain of the ~** ◊ When using a plane, be sure to follow the grain of the ~.

2 (BrE) small forest

ADJ. **deep, dense, thick** | **dark** | **coniferous, deciduous** | **ancient** ◊ the largest ancient ~ in Scotland | **beech, birch, oak, etc.**
PREP. **in a/the ~, into a/the ~** ◊ a clearing in the ~ | **through a/the ~**

3 the woods area covered with trees

ADJ. **deep, dense, thick** | **dark**
PREP. **in the ~, into the ~** ◊ a walk in the ~s ◊ We came to a clearing in the ~s. | **through the ~** ◊ She wandered through the ~s.
PHRASES **deep in the ~s** ◊ a cabin deep in the ~s of Maine | **the edge of the ~s, the middle of the ~s**

woodwork noun

ADJ. **exterior, interior** | **carved** ◊ elaborately/intricately carved ~
VERB + WOODWORK **paint, varnish**
PREP. **in the ~** ◊ There were cracks in the ~.

wool noun

ADJ. **thick** | **fine** | **soft** | **rough** | **pure** | **raw** | **lamb's, sheep's** | **merino** (esp. BrE) | **knitting** (esp. BrE) | **cotton** (BrE), **mineral, steel, wire** (BrE)
... OF WOOL **ball** (esp. BrE), **skein**
VERB + WOOL **produce** | **spin** ◊ She spun ~ by hand to weave into clothing. | **card, comb** | **dye**
WOOL + NOUN **merchant** | **trade** (esp. BrE) | **shop** (BrE)

word noun

1 unit of language

ADJ. **two-letter, three-letter, etc.** | **monosyllabic, poly-syllabic** | **two-syllable, three-syllable, etc.** | **big, difficult, fancy, hard, long** ◊ He uses big ~s to impress people. ◊ 'Mendacity' is just a fancy ~ for 'lying'. | **polite** ◊ a more polite ~ for the same thing | **unfamiliar** | **simple** ◊ The book uses simple ~s and pictures to explain complex processes. | **compound, portmanteau** (esp. BrE) ◊ The portmanteau ~ 'synergy' combines 'synthesis' and 'energy'. | **native** | **borrowed, loan** ◊ When a new fruit is first imported, its name is usually also imported as a loan ~. | **foreign** | **Greek, Hebrew, Latin, etc.** ◊ *'Technology' comes from the Greek ~ 'techne'.* | **content, function** | **rhyming** ◊ *The children are asked to think of rhyming ~s.* | **exact, precise, very** ◊ *His exact ~s were, 'There's nothing we can do about it.'* ◊ *Those were her very ~s.* | **clear, plain** | **ambiguous** | **loaded** ◊ *She used loaded ~s like 'bully' when describing his actions.* | **abstract, concrete** | **everyday** ◊ *I find even everyday ~s difficult to spell.* | **archaic, obsolete** | **key** ◊ *He wrote down a few key ~s to help him remember what to say.* | **operative** ◊ *He seemed nice. But 'seemed' was the operative ~.* | **right, wrong** ◊ *You can't always find the right ~ when you're translating.* | **misspelled** ◊ *I found several misspelled ~s and grammatical errors.* | **bad, curse** (*AmE*), **cuss** (*AmE, informal*), **dirty, four-letter, naughty, obscene, rude, taboo** ◊ *The play is full of four-letter ~s.* ◊ *Work is a dirty ~ to Frank.* (*figurative*) (see also **swear word**) | **slang** ◊ *It's a slang ~ meaning 'boy' or 'person'.* | **household** ◊ *His name has become a household ~ since he first appeared in the series.* | **code** ◊ *The police use code ~s for their major operations.* | **buzz** (usually **buzzword**), **vogue** ◊ *E-marketing is the current buzzword.* | **magic** | **printed, spoken, written** ◊ *She combines visual images and the spoken ~ to great effect in her presentations.*

VERB + WORD **have** ◊ *Spanish has no ~ for 'understatement'.* | **use** ◊ *He uses lots of long ~s.* | **mention** ◊ *I daren't even mention the ~'money' to him.* | **form, make** ◊ *Rearrange the letters to form a ~.* | **pronounce** ◊ *How is this ~ pronounced?* | **mispronounce** | **spell** | **misuse** ◊ *a ~ that is often misused* | **know, speak, understand** ◊ *I don't speak a ~ of Swedish.* | **look up** ◊ *She looked the ~ up in the dictionary.* | **find** ◊ *I couldn't find the right ~ to express the concept.* | **choose, pick** ◊ *He chose his ~s carefully when commenting on her work.* | **translate** | **coin, invent** ◊ *The ~ 'e-commerce' was coined to refer to business done over the Internet.*

WORD + VERB **mean sth, signify sth** | **refer to sth, relate to sth** | **convey sth, describe sth, express sth** ◊ *~s describing body parts* ◊ *Words can't express how happy I am.* | **conjure sth up, evoke sth** ◊ *The ~ 'cruise' conjures up images of a luxury.* | **imply sth** | **denote sth** ◊ *Bold ~s denote chapter headings.* | **carry sth, have sth** ◊ *The same ~ can carry numerous meanings.* ◊ *The ~ has two meanings.* | **be derived from sth, come from sth, derive from sth** ◊ *'Window' derives from a Norse ~ meaning 'eye of the wind'.* | **begin with sth, end in sth, end with sth** ◊ *a ~ beginning with 'c'* | **rhyme** (**with sth**) ◊ *The ~s at the end of the lines all rhyme.* ◊ *I'm not sure what he said but the ~ sounded like 'bull'.* | **fail sb** ◊ *Words fail me* (= I cannot express how I feel).

WORD + NOUN **game, puzzle** | **identification, recognition** ◊ *These students have very poor word-recognition skills.* | **choice** | **association** | **formation** | **list**

PREP. **in sb's ~s** ◊ *The students had to retell the story in their own ~s.* | **~ for** ◊ *What's the French ~ for 'snail'?* | **~ in** ◊ *one of the most common ~s in the English language*

PHRASES **in all senses of the ~** ◊ *She was a true friend in all senses of the ~.* | **in other ~s** ◊ *They're letting me go—in other ~s, I've been sacked.* | **in so many ~s** ◊ *They told me in so many ~s* (= directly) *that I was no longer needed.* | **in the true sense of the ~** ◊ *People who overeat are not addicts in the true sense of the ~.* | **in ~s of one syllable** (= using very simple language) ◊ *Could you say that again in ~s of one syllable?*

2 a word that you say or write

ADJ. **angry, cross** (*esp. BrE*), **hard, harsh** ◊ *He never says a harsh ~ about his experiences.* | **hurtful, unkind** | **friendly, good, kind, nice** ◊ *He hasn't a good ~ to say for anybody.* | **final, last** (no plural) ◊ *The Chairman always has the last ~* (= the final decision) *on financial decisions.*

VERB + WORD **put in, say, speak, utter** ◊ *If you run into the boss, put in a good ~ for me!* ◊ *Nobody's uttered a ~ to me about it.* ◊ *Every ~ he utters is considered sacred.* | **give, say** ◊ *Just say the ~ and I'll go.* | **scream, shout, yell** ◊ *He kept shouting the ~ 'No!'* | **repeat** | **whisper** ◊ *He whispered*

the ~ to me.* | **slur** ◊ *I knew he'd been drinking because he was slurring his ~s.* | **enunciate** ◊ *He enunciated the ~ with extreme care.* | **not breathe** ◊ *Don't breathe a ~ to anyone about what I've told you!* | **type, write** | **scrawl, scribble** | **inscribe** | **hear, read** | **mishear, misread** ◊ *I misheard the ~ 'sick' as 'thick'.* | **cross out, delete, erase, rub out** (*BrE*) | **insert, substitute** ◊ *She deleted 'girl' and substituted the ~ 'woman'.* | **emphasize, stress** ◊ *By emphasizing particular ~s you can change the meaning.* | **hang on** ◊ *The journalists hung on his every ~ as he spoke of his ordeal.*

WORD + NOUN **count** ◊ *Don't waffle in your essay just to get the right ~ count.*

PREP. **in a ~** ◊ *'Would you like to help us?' 'In a ~* (= briefly), *no.'* | **without a ~** ◊ *She left without a ~.* | **~ about** ◊ *We never heard anyone say an unkind ~ about her.* | **~ from** ◊ *And now a ~ from our sponsors…* | **~ of** ◊ *a ~ of advice/warning*

PHRASES **get a ~ in, get a ~ in edgeways** (*BrE*), **get a ~ in edgewise** (*AmE*) ◊ *I wanted to tell you, but I couldn't get a ~ in.* | **a man of few ~s, a woman of few ~s** (= a person who speaks very little) | **sb never spoke a truer ~, never was a truer ~ spoken** ◊ *You said we were about to make a big mistake, and never was a truer ~ spoken!* (= you were right) | **not a single ~, not a ~** ◊ *Remember—not a ~ to* (= don't tell) *Peter about any of this.* ◊ *We didn't say a single ~ to each other all day.* | **not believe a ~** ◊ *I don't believe a ~ of what she said.* | **~ for ~** (= exactly) ◊ *He repeated ~ for ~ what the boy had said to him.* | **(by) ~ of mouth** ◊ *The restaurant does not advertise, but relies on ~ of mouth.* | **~s per minute, ~s per second** ◊ *He chatters away at about 200 ~s per minute.* ◊ *He types 80 ~s per minute.* | **a ~ to the wise** (= a piece of advice) ◊ *A ~ to the wise: just because it's a bargain doesn't mean you have to buy it.*

3 words what sb says; talk

ADJ. **few** ◊ *I want to say a few ~s* (= talk) *about Christina.* | **good, friendly, kind** ◊ *Thank you for those kind ~s.* | **unkind** | **angry, bitter, blunt, choice** (*ironic*), **cross, hard, harsh, strong** | **hurtful** | **polite** ◊ *She was charmed by his friendly smile and polite ~s.* | **flattering, honeyed** | **comforting, encouraging, soothing** ◊ *He tried to calm her with soothing ~s.* | **discouraging** | **empty, fine** (*ironic*), **meaningless** ◊ *Despite all their fine ~s, the council have never done anything to improve road safety.* | **weasel** ◊ *The government's promises on nurses' pay turned out to be weasel ~s* (= deliberately unclear). | **bold, brave** ◊ *Despite his brave ~s, I don't believe he can save the factory from closure.* | **wise** | **well-chosen** ◊ *He ruined her self-confidence with a few well-chosen ~s.* | **cautionary** | **soft, whispered** ◊ *They exchanged whispered ~s of love.* | **unspoken** ◊ *The look in her eyes filled in the unspoken ~s in her sentence.* | **dying, last** ◊ *Her last ~s were for her children.* | **parting** ◊ *Her parting ~s were 'I'll be back'.* | **famous, immortal** ◊ *the immortal ~s of Neil Armstrong as he stepped onto the moon* | **fateful, prophetic** ◊ *Seconds after uttering the fateful ~s 'this is easy!' he crashed.*

VERB + WORDS **have** ◊ *She had some harsh ~s to say about her colleagues.* | **say, speak** ◊ *Before we begin, I'd like to say a few ~s about who I am.* | **chant, intone, recite, sing** | **repeat** | **mouth** ◊ *The audience mouthed the ~s to all the songs.* | **whisper** ◊ *He whispered a few ~s of prayer.* | **blurt, blurt out** ◊ *She had blurted the ~s out before she realized it.* | **mumble, murmur, mutter** | **spit, spit out** ◊ *She was so furious, she almost spat the ~s out: 'You idiot!'* | **bandy, exchange, have** ◊ *I usually exchange a few ~s with him when I see him.* ◊ *Words were exchanged* (= there was an argument). | **memorize** ◊ *She had memorized all the ~s to the song.* | **recall, remember** ◊ *We recall the ~s of Martin Luther King, 'Free at last'.* | **heed** ◊ *She has given us a warning, and we should heed her ~s.* | **quote** | **distort, twist** ◊ *She felt angry at how the journalist had twisted her ~s.* | **borrow, echo** ◊ *In her speech she echoed the President's ~s.* | **regret** ◊ *She instantly regretted her ~s.* | **eat, take back** ◊ *When he told her she would fail, she swore she would make him eat his ~s.* | **drown, drown out** ◊ *Her ~s were drowned out by the roar of the engine.* | **not mince** ◊ *He doesn't mince his ~s when he talks about his ex-boss.*

WORDS + VERB **conjure sth up, evoke sth** ◊ *Her ~s conjured up* a strange picture in her mind. | **come, come out, emerge, leave sb's lips, leave sb's mouth** | **burst from sb, escape, fall, flow, pour out, slip out, spill out, tumble out** ◊ He was nervous, and his ~s came out in a rush. ◊ His ~s fell into the silence like stones. | **stick in your throat** ◊ He wanted to tell her how he felt about her, but the ~s stuck in his throat. | **drift, float, hang in the air** ◊ I let my ~s hang in the air. Maggie was no fool: she must realize I meant it. | **haunt sb, linger** ◊ Those mocking ~s haunted me for years. ◊ The ~s lingered in his mind long after they were spoken. | **echo, resonate, resound, reverberate, ring** ◊ Her teacher's ~s echoed in her ears. | **fade, fade away, tail away, tail off, trail away, trail off** ◊ His ~s faded to silence as he saw she didn't believe him. | **hit home, strike a chord, strike home, touch a chord** | **hurt, sting** | **sink in** ◊ She could feel her temper building as his ~s sank in.

PREP. **~s of** ◊ She whispered ~s of comfort in his ear. ◊ I listened to his ~s of wisdom.

PHRASES **(you) mark my ~s** (= believe me) ◊ Mark my ~s, this film will win an Oscar.

4 a word conversation

ADJ. **quick** | **quiet** ◊ The manager had a quiet ~ with Alison, and she gave him no more problems.

VERB + A WORD **have** ◊ I've had a few ~s with John, and he's quite happy for you to stay. ◊ I've had a ~ with John, and he's quite happy for you to stay.

PREP. **~ with** ◊ Can I have a quick ~ with you?

PHRASES **a ~ in sb's ear** (BrE) ◊ Can I have a ~ in your ear about tomorrow's presentation?

5 promise

ADJ. **solemn** ◊ She gave him her solemn ~ that she would give up drugs.

VERB + WORD **give sb** | **be as good as, be true to, keep** ◊ He promised to help and was as good as his ~. ◊ True to her ~, she returned next day. | **break, go back on** ◊ Once he has made a promise, he never goes back on his ~. | **believe, trust** ◊ She gave me a promise, and I'm willing to trust her ~. | **doubt** ◊ I'm sorry I doubted your ~.

PHRASES **have sb's ~ for sth** (esp. BrE) ◊ We only have her ~ for it that she sent the payment. | **a man of his ~, a woman of her ~** ◊ You needn't worry about him not paying you back—he's a man of his ~. | **take sb at their ~** ◊ He said I could stay at his house any time, so I took him at his ~. | **take sb's ~ for sth** ◊ I haven't seen his work, but I'll take his ~ for it that it's finished. | **your ~ against sb's** ◊ If it's your ~ against the police officer's, the jury are going to believe him. | **sb's ~ is their bond** | **~ of honour/honor** ◊ He gave me his ~ of honour/honor that he wouldn't tell anyone.

6 information/news

VERB + WORD **bring, get, send** ◊ He sent ~ to his family that his captors were treating him well. | **get, hear** ◊ We didn't get ~ of her arrest until the next day. | **spread**

WORD + VERB **get out, leak, leak out** ◊ If ~ gets out about the affair, he will have to resign. | **spread** ◊ Word that he had died spread fast. | **be, have it** ◊ The ~ is they've split up. ◊ Word has it that she's leaving.

PREP. **~ about** ◊ Health workers spread the ~ about the benefits of immunization. | **~ of** ◊ We soon got ~ of his arrival.

PHRASES **the ~ on the street is** (= people are saying) ◊ The ~ on the street is there's going to be a takeover. | **what's the ~?** (= what are people saying?)

word verb

ADV. **carefully, cautiously** ◊ We need to ~ our question carefully. | **ambiguously, vaguely** | **broadly, loosely** | **poorly** ◊ a poorly ~ed request that resulted in confusion | **strongly** ◊ He issued a very strongly ~ed statement denying any involvement in the plot. | **differently** ◊ It's the same sentiment, though ~ed rather differently.

wording noun

ADJ. **actual, careful, exact, precise, specific** | **original** ◊ I can't remember the original ~. | **clear** | **appropriate** | **vague** | **ambiguous** ◊ The ~ was deliberately ambiguous.

VERB + WORDING **alter, change** | **use** ◊ I understand, but I wouldn't use that exact ~. | **think about** ◊ We need to think carefully about the ~ of the request.

PREP. **~ of** ◊ What's the exact ~ of the clause?

work noun

1 effort/product of effort

ADJ. **hard** ◊ It's hard ~ trying to get him to do a few things for himself. ◊ It doesn't require skill—it's a matter of sheer hard ~. | **arduous, back-breaking, challenging, complicated, demanding, difficult, gruelling/grueling, intensive, labour-intensive/labor-intensive, tiring, tough** ◊ The show is the product of two years' intensive ~. | **tireless** ◊ Through their tireless ~, they proved his innocence. | **rewarding** | **heavy** ◊ They employ a couple of young men to do the heavy ~. | **donkey** (BrE, informal) ◊ I did the donkey ~ (= hard work requiring little skill) but I hired a professional for the hard part. | **grunt** (AmE, informal) ◊ He has done the grunt ~ (= the hard, boring part of a task), sifting through thousands of official records. | **light** ◊ She's only allowed to do a little light ~ because of her bad arm. | **easy** | **close** ◊ I need to wear glasses for close ~. | **physical** | **delicate** | **dangerous** | **dirty** ◊ Engine maintenance is dirty ~. ◊ The drugs gang used children to do their dirty ~ for them. (figurative) | **monotonous, repetitive, tedious** | **fascinating, interesting** | **purposeful** ◊ Many unemployed people welcome the chance to do purposeful ~, even if unpaid. | **valuable** ◊ The research institute needs funds in order to carry on its valuable ~. | **professional** | **men's, women's** ◊ They think that caring for children is women's ~. | **intellectual, mental** | **creative, imaginative** | **practical** (see also **fieldwork, paperwork**) | **detective, investigative** | **undercover** ◊ The scandal was revealed after months of undercover ~ by journalists. | **leg** (usually **legwork**) ◊ Her job as a market researcher involves a lot of legwork (= walking around to collect information). | **class, course** (usually **coursework**), **school** (usually **schoolwork**) ◊ She was getting distracted from her schoolwork. | **written** ◊ His written ~ is the best in the class. | **individual** | **group** | **project** | **collaborative, joint** ◊ classroom activities involving collaborative ~ between children ◊ The report is the joint ~ of an economist and a sociologist. | **remedial, restoration** ◊ The poorly designed bridge needs remedial ~ to make it safe. | **background, preliminary, preparatory** | **follow-up** | **extra** ◊ He's willing to do extra ~ to get the project finished on time. | **honest** ◊ He preferred to make his money from honest ~ rather than from gambling. | **excellent, good, nice** (informal), **outstanding, sterling** (esp. BrE) ◊ Nice ~, James! I'm impressed. ◊ In accepting the award, she mentioned the sterling ~ of her assistants. | **careful, meticulous, painstaking** | **poor, shoddy, sloppy** | **charitable, humanitarian** | **community, youth** | **missionary** | **groundbreaking, innovative, pioneering** ◊ He did pioneering ~ on microbes. | **empirical, experimental** | **theoretical** | **academic, commercial, educational, environmental, scientific** | **building, construction** | **cosmetic, dental** ◊ She's had a lot of dental ~ done. | **your own** ◊ Is this all your own ~ (= did you do it without help from others?)

... OF WORK **bit, piece** ◊ It was an interesting piece of ~.

VERB + WORK **carry out, do, put in** ◊ All the construction ~ was carried out in 2001. ◊ I had lots of ~ to do. ◊ She's put in a lot of ~ on the design. | **get done, have done** ◊ I think I'd better try and get some ~ done. ◊ We're going to have some building ~ done on the house. | **create, make** ◊ All these visitors make a lot of ~ for me. | **produce** ◊ Work produced on a computer tends to look more professional. | **get, have** ◊ We get far too much ~ at this time of year. | **take on, undertake** ◊ I've taken on more ~ than I have time to do. | **create, make** ◊ Small children make a lot of ~ for their parents. | **begin, commence, get down to, set about, set to, start** ◊ They began ~ on the project last year. ◊ Stop talking and get down to ~. ◊ We set to ~ on the outside of the house (= for example, painting it). | **go about** ◊ She went cheerfully about her ~. | **carry on, continue, resume** | **complete,** finish | **halt, hold up, stop** ◇ *Work on the project was halted.* | **lose** ◇ *They lost the ~ to a competitor.* | **undo** ◇ *The new president spent the first year undoing the ~ of his predecessor.* | **oversee, supervise** ◇ *The assistant manager supervises ~ on the factory floor.* | **check, inspect** | **admire, appreciate, value** ◇ *I really appreciate all your hard ~.* | **support** ◇ *We give grants to support the ~ of voluntary organizations.* | **set sb to** ◇ *She set them to ~ painting the fence.* | **require** ◇ *To carry out accurate market research requires a huge amount of ~.* | **hand in, submit** ◇ *We're supposed to hand in this ~ tomorrow.*

WORK + VERB come ◇ *The ~ comes in bursts according to the time of year.* | **wait** ◇ *That ~ can wait until tomorrow.* | **go** ◇ *How's the ~ going this morning?* | **involve sth** ◇ *What does the ~ involve?* | **begin, start** | **continue, go on** | **come to a halt, grind to a halt** ◇ *Work came to a complete halt in the summer.* | **cost** ◇ *How much will the ~ cost?*

WORK + NOUN ethic | **rate** ◇ *Her boss told her she had to increase her ~ rate.* | **habit** ◇ *Children can learn good ~ habits at school.* | **programme/program, schedule** | **crew** (*AmE*) ◇ *The construction company has three ~ crews of five men each.* | **load** (usually **workload**) ◇ *The instructor's ~ load was becoming increasingly heavy.* | **flow** ◇ *Her job is to manage the company's ~ flow.* | **surface** ◇ *Work surfaces should be left clear and clean.*

PREP. at ~ ◇ *He's been hard at ~ all morning.* | **~ on** ◇ *I have to do some ~ on the car before it'll be ready.* | **~ with** ◇ *She's done a lot of ~ with disadvantaged children.*

PHRASES a backlog of ~ ◇ *It will take a month to clear the backlog of ~.* | **keep up the good ~** ◇ *The hotel manager thanked the staff and told them to keep up the good ~.* | **your life's ~** ◇ *The art collection was his life's ~.* | **make light ~ of sth, make short ~ of sth** (= to do sth quickly and easily) ◇ *Mike made short ~ of fixing the engine.* | **not a stroke of ~** (*esp. BrE*) ◇ *She never does a stroke of ~.* | **pressure of ~** ◇ *Pressure of ~ forced him to cancel the cruise.* | **~ in progress** ◇ *The showroom has been designed so that people can see ~ in progress.*

2 job

ADJ. paid, unpaid ◇ *She is now looking for paid ~ outside the home.* | **lucrative, well-paid** | **badly paid** | **full-time, part-time** | **permanent** | **temporary** | **regular, steady** ◇ *He hasn't been in regular ~ since he left school.* | **casual** ◇ *During the college vacations he does casual ~ in the local hospital.* | **freelance** | **voluntary, volunteer** | **skilled** | **semi-skilled** | **unskilled** | **manual** | **indoor, outdoor** | **daily, day-to-day, everyday, routine** ◇ *People went about their daily ~ despite the war.* ◇ *Ambulance crews alternate between emergency and routine ~.* | **piece** ◇ *It's piece ~, so how much you earn depends on how fast you can work.* | **administrative, clerical, office, secretarial** | **managerial** | **domestic** | **social** | **research** | **agricultural, farm** | **building** | **nice** (*informal, humorous*) ◇ *A hundred grand for two days a week? Nice ~ if you can get it!*

VERB + WORK have ◇ *He has some freelance ~ at the moment.* | **look for** ◇ *He got laid off, so now he's looking for ~ again.* | **find, get** ◇ *Full-time ~ is hard to find.* | **go to** ◇ *I go to ~ by bus.* | **go out to** ◇ *Some mothers of young children choose not to go out to ~.* | **start** | **finish, knock off** (*informal*) ◇ *What time do you finish ~?* | **stop** ◇ *She stops ~ at the end of this month.* | **give up** ◇ *Just before he was sixty, he decided to give up ~.* | **go back to, return to** ◇ *She has just returned to ~ after the birth of her child.* | **allocate, give** | **outsource** | **coordinate** ◇ *Sales reps meet up monthly to coordinate their ~.* | **enjoy, love** ◇ *I'm lucky—I love my ~.*

WORK + VERB go ◇ *Work's going well at the moment.* | **start** ◇ *What time does ~ start in the morning?* | **finish** | **consist of sth, include sth, involve sth** ◇ *Her ~ consists of drawing up and coordinating schedules.*

WORK + NOUN day (*esp. AmE*), **hours, week** (*esp. AmE*) ◇ *Employees must not make personal calls during ~ hours.* | **force** (usually **workforce**) | **place** (usually **workplace**) | **area, environment, room** (usually **workroom**) | **station** (usually **workstation**) | **boots** (*esp. AmE*), **clothes** |

schedule | **experience** ◇ *The opportunities will depend on your ~ experience.* ◇ *He's doing a month's unpaid ~ experience with an engineering company.* (*BrE*) | **permit, visa** | **incentive** ◇ *High income tax can undermine ~ incentives.* | **practice** ◇ *An independent report has described some ~ practices in the industry as old-fashioned.* | **stoppage**

PREP. at ~ ◇ *'Where's Diane?' 'She's at ~.'* ◇ *We had a party at ~.* | **in (your) ~** ◇ *With so much unemployment, I'm lucky to be in ~.* (*BrE*) ◇ *It's important to be happy in your ~.* | **off ~** (*esp. BrE*) ◇ *She's been off ~ with a bad back since July.* | **out of ~** ◇ *He's been out of ~ since the factory closed.* | **through ~** ◇ *I met him through ~.*

PHRASES a line of ~ ◇ *'What line of ~ are you in?' 'Computing.'* | **a place of ~**

3 book/music/art

ADJ. classic, fine, great | **definitive, seminal** ◇ *Her book is still considered the definitive ~ on beetles.* | **best-known, well-known** | **important, influential** | **erudite, scholarly** | **ambitious** | **creative** | **literary** | **dramatic** | **critical** | **autobiographical, biographical** | **artistic** | **photographic** | **sculptural** | **art** (usually **artwork**) ◇ *The artwork in the book is superb.* | **untitled** | **completed, finished** ◇ *The finished ~ will be on view in the city art gallery.* | **unfinished** | **collaborative** | **solo** | **commissioned** ◇ *He does mainly commissioned portrait ~s.* | **abstract, figurative, graphic** | **choral, orchestral** | **guitar, piano, etc.** | **collected, complete** ◇ *the collected ~s of Stephen King* | **early** | **late, mature** ◇ *Picasso's mature ~s* | **latest, present, previous, recent** ◇ *These paintings are more abstract than her previous ~.* | **copyrighted** ◇ *People are using file-sharing to steal copyrighted ~s.* | **published** ◇ *Her portfolio includes published ~s in several magazines.* | **derivative** | **original**

...OF WORK series | **collection, exhibit** (*AmE*), **exhibition** (*esp. BrE*) ◇ *The gallery is staging a special exhibition of Monet's early ~s.*

VERB + WORK compose, create, produce, write ◇ *Beethoven composed his greatest ~s in the latter part of his life.* | **choreograph, conduct, translate** | **commission** | **perform, play** | **hear, read, see** ◇ *Her ~ can be seen in most of the major European galleries.* | **conduct, direct, edit, produce, publish, put on** ◇ *Over the next two years, the company is putting on the complete ~s of Brecht.* | **display, exhibit, feature, show, showcase** ◇ *The town hall is exhibiting ~s by local artists.* | **acclaim, admire, appreciate, praise** | **critique** (*esp. AmE*), **discuss, review** | **inform, inspire** ◇ *A love of landscape informs all his ~.*

WORK + VERB be called sth, be entitled sth, be titled sth (*esp. AmE*) ◇ *a ~ entitled 'The Sacrifice'* | **depict sth, describe sth, represent sth** ◇ *The ~ represents a synthesis of the natural and the artificial.* | **consist of sth** ◇ *a ~ consisting of twelve small blank canvases* | **appear, be on show, go on show** ◇ *Her ~ appears at the Museum of Contemporary Art this summer.*

PREP. in a/the ~ ◇ *She's studying the theme of death in the ~s of Beckett.* | **~ by** ◇ *a ~ by an unknown 18th-century writer*

PHRASES a ~ of art, a ~ of fiction, a ~ of literature ◇ *The building is hated by some and considered a ~ of art by others.* ◇ *They discovered that his report was a complete ~ of fiction.* (*humorous*) | **a ~ of genius** ◇ *Her latest novel is a ~ of genius.* → Note at ART

4 (*also* **works** *esp. BrE*) **building/repairing**

ADJ. extensive, major | **road** (usually **roadworks** in *BrE* and **roadwork** in *AmE*) | **maintenance, repair, restoration**

VERB + WORKS carry out ◇ *We are planning to carry out major ~s on the site.* | **plan** | **announce**

WORKS + VERB continue, go on ◇ *The ~s will continue until the end of July.* | **be completed, finish**

PREP. at the ~ (*BrE*) ◇ *A contraflow is in operation at the ~s near Junction 5.*

5 works (*esp. BrE*) **factory**

ADJ. brick, iron, steel (usually **brickworks**, etc.) | **railway** (*BrE*) | **sewage, treatment** ◇ *The smell is believed to have originated from the sewage ~s.* ◇ *Scotland's biggest water treatment ~s*

VERB + WORKS open | **close, close down, shut down**

WORKS + VERB **open** | **close, close down** ◇ *The steelworks closed in 1986.*
WORKS + NOUN **manager, supervisor** | **canteen** *(BrE)*
PREP. **at the** ~ ◇ *the night shift at the ~s*

work verb

1 do a job/task

ADV. **hard** ◇ *He had been ~ing hard all morning.* | **tirelessly** | **assiduously, busily, diligently, methodically** | **feverishly, frantically** | **steadily** | **slowly** | **quickly** | **around the clock, round the clock** *(esp. BrE)* ◇ *Emergency teams were ~ing around the clock to make the homes secure.* | **full-time, part-time** ◇ *A lot of mothers choose to ~ part-time.* | **illegally** ◇ *He was found to be ~ing illegally and was deported.* | **effectively, efficiently, productively** ◇ *I ~ more efficiently on my own.* | **actively** ◇ *We are actively ~ing to increase the number of women in science.* | **closely, collaboratively, cooperatively, together** ◇ *people who have ~ed closely together over a period of time* | **harmoniously** ◇ *We have proved that different groups can ~ harmoniously together.* | **alone, independently, individually** | **directly** ◇ *She ~s directly with customers.* | **primarily** ◇ *I ~ primarily with young children.* | **away** ◇ *We ~ed steadily away all morning.*
VERB + WORK **continue to** | **choose to, prefer to** ◇ *I prefer to ~ as part of a team.* | **motivate sb to** ◇ *Employees are motivated to ~ harder for a whole host of different reasons.* | **enable sb to** ◇ *I needed a job which would enable me to ~ at home.* | **refuse to**
PREP. **as** ◇ *He's ~ing as a teacher at the moment.* | **at** ◇ *I've spent three hours ~ing at this problem.* | **for** ◇ *She ~s for an oil company.* | **on** ◇ *We are ~ing on plans for a new swimming pool.* | **towards/toward** ◇ *They are all ~ing towards/toward a common goal.* | **with** ◇ *the people you ~ with* | **within** ◇ *An architect must ~ within the confines of the laws of physics.*

2 function; have a result/effect

ADV. **correctly, effectively, efficiently, properly, satisfactorily, well** ◇ *Everything ~ed very smoothly.* | **flawlessly, perfectly, seamlessly, smoothly** | **beautifully, brilliantly, splendidly** *(esp. BrE)*, **wonderfully** | **independently** ◇ *The fish's eyes can ~ independently of each other.* | **differently** | **synergistically** *(esp. AmE)*
VERB + WORK **seem to**
PHRASES **~ like a charm, ~ like magic** ◇ *Her strategy ~ed like a charm.* | **~ to sb's advantage, ~ to sb's disadvantage** ◇ *You can make your youth ~ to your advantage.*

PHR V **work out**

ADV. **beautifully, fine, great, perfectly, well** | **badly**
PREP. **as** ◇ *It all ~ed out as we planned.* | **between** ◇ *I told her I didn't think things would ~ out between us.* | **for** ◇ *Things ~ed out well for Janet in the end.* | **to** ◇ *This all ~s out to around $11 000.*

worker noun

ADJ. **good, hard, willing** | **productive** | **fast, quick** | **methodical, steady** | **slow** | **core, key** | **full-time, part-time** | **permanent** | **temporary** | **casual** ◇ *Casual ~s are usually paid by the hour.* | **shift** | **migrant, seasonal** | **freelance** | **self-employed** | **paid, salaried** | **voluntary** *(BrE)*, **volunteer** | **low-paid, low-wage** *(esp. AmE)*, **minimum-wage** *(AmE)* | **jobless** *(AmE)*, **laid-off, redundant** *(BrE)*, **unemployed** | **retired** | **female, male, woman** | **black, white** | **guest, immigrant** | **illegal, undocumented** *(AmE)* | **fellow** | **average** ◇ *One night in these hotels costs around the average worker's monthly wage.* | **skilled** | **low-skilled** *(AmE)*, **unskilled** | **semi-skilled** | **blue-collar, manual** | **clerical, office, white-collar** | **professional** | **shop-floor** | **unionized** | **non-union** | **private-sector, public-sector** | **council** *(BrE)*, **municipal** | **assembly-line, factory, garment** *(esp. AmE)*, **industrial, manufacturing, mill, production** | **construction** | **metal, steel, textile** | **auto** *(AmE)*, **car** | **maintenance** | **transit** *(AmE)*, **transport** *(esp. BrE)*, **transportation** *(AmE)* | **rail, railroad** *(AmE)*, **railway** *(BrE)* | **agricultural, farm, rural** | **health, health-care, hospital** | **care, childcare, community, day-care** *(AmE)*, **home-care** *(AmE)*, **outreach, social, welfare, youth** |

emergency, rescue | **aid, humanitarian, relief** | **charity** | **field, research** | **domestic** | **postal** | **sanitation** *(AmE)*
VERB + WORKER **employ, have** | **pay** | **engage, hire, recruit, take on** | **dismiss, fire, lay off, make redundant** *(BrE)*, **sack** *(esp. BrE)* | **exploit** ◇ *The union accused the company of exploiting its ~s.* | **educate, train** | **protect** | **organize, unionize**
WORKER + VERB **labour/labor, toil** *(literary)*, **work** | **earn sth** ◇ *These banana ~s earn about $7 000 per year.* | **run sth, staff sth** ◇ *The kitchen is staffed by three volunteers.* | **lose a job** ◇ *400 ~s have lost their jobs.* | **commute** ◇ *88% of the ~s commute by car.* | **demand sth** ◇ *Workers demanded fair wages and better working conditions.* | **vote** ◇ *The ~s voted for strike action.* | **(be on) strike, walk out** ◇ *The ~s walked out last month after a failure to agree terms.*
WORKER + NOUN **participation** ◇ *~ participation in decision-making* | **productivity** *(AmE)* | **compensation** *(AmE)* | **protection, rights** *(both AmE)* ◇ *The public are demanding more ~ protection.*
PHRASES **the exploitation of ~s** | **workers' demands, workers' rights**
→ Note at JOB

workforce noun

ADJ. **educated, qualified, skilled, trained, well-educated, well-trained** ◇ *a highly skilled ~* | **flexible, mobile, versatile** | **committed, dedicated, motivated** | **unionized** | **local** ◇ *A quarter of the local ~ is unemployed.* | **ageing/aging, declining, diminishing** ◇ *A declining ~ has to provide for an increasing number of retired people.* | **available, total** ◇ *The shipyard has a total ~ of 9 000.* | **entire, whole** ◇ *The new management decided to retrain the entire ~.* | **world-wide** | **large, small** | **reduced** | **2 000-strong, etc.** | **temporary** | **British, Japanese, US, etc.** | **female, male** | **diverse, multicultural** ◇ *Companies are under pressure to hire a more diverse ~.* | **industrial, manufacturing**
VERB + WORKFORCE **employ, have** ◇ *The company employs a ~ of nearly 5 000.* | **cut, downsize, halve, reduce, shrink, slash, slim, slim down, trim** | **double, expand, increase** | **educate, retrain, train** | **consult, consult with** ◇ *The management always consults with the ~ before introducing major changes.* | **enter, leave, re-enter** ◇ *The increase in the number of people entering the ~ has increased unemployment figures.*
WORKFORCE + VERB **fall** | **double, increase, rise** | **number sth, stand at sth** ◇ *The ~ numbers 500.*
PREP. **among a/the ~** ◇ *There is a change in the distribution of skills among the ~.* | **in a/the ~** ◇ *One person in the ~ is always responsible for the same job.*
PHRASES **a member of the ~**

workings noun

ADJ. **inner, internal** ◇ *the inner ~ of a watch* ◇ *the internal ~ of Congress* | **day-to-day** ◇ *the day-to-day ~ of the legal system* | **complex, detailed, intricate** | **financial**
VERB + WORKINGS **analyse/analyze, examine, explore, investigate, study** | **expose, lay bare, reveal** | **cast light on, shed light on** ◇ *Their research aims to shed light on the ~ of the human mind.* | **know** | **comprehend, understand** ◇ *It is hard to understand the complex ~ of the social security system.* | **explain**

workload noun

ADJ. **enormous, heavy, huge** | **excessive** | **additional, extra, increased** | **maximal, maximum** *(both AmE)* | **peak** | **lighter, reduced** | **administrative**
VERB + WORKLOAD **have** ◇ *She has an increased ~ this year.* | **expand, increase** | **ease, lighten, reduce** ◇ *An assistant one day a week would ease my ~.* | **distribute, share, spread** ◇ *We want to try and distribute the ~ more evenly.* | **cope with, handle, manage**
WORKLOAD + VERB **expand, increase** ◇ *Doctors are having to cope with an ever-expanding ~.*

workman noun

ADJ. **good, skilled | council** (*BrE*)
... OF WORKMEN **crew, gang** ◇ *A gang of workmen has been digging a hole in the road.*

workmanship noun

ADJ. **exquisite, fine, good, quality | bad, defective, faulty** (*esp. BrE*), **poor, shoddy**
VERB + WORKMANSHIP **admire** ◇ *I was admiring the exquisite ~ in the mosaic.* | **criticize**
PREP. **~ on** ◇ *He accused the garage of shoddy ~ on the bodywork.*
PHRASES **the quality of ~, the standard of ~**

workout noun

ADJ. **good | gruelling/grueling, hard, intense, strenuous, vigorous | light, low-impact | daily, morning, regular | forty-minute, two-hour, etc. | aerobic, cardio** (*informal, esp. AmE*), **cardiovascular | full-body, lower-body, upper-body | biceps, triceps, etc.**
VERB + WORKOUT **do, have** ◇ *When I do a good ~, I feel fine.* ◇ *The team had a hard ~ this morning.* | **complete, finish | miss, skip** (*AmE*) | **give sb/sth** ◇ *I went for a ride to give my new bike a ~.*
WORKOUT + NOUN **plan, programme/program, regimen** (*AmE*), **routine, schedule | session | clothes, gear, wear** (*all AmE*) | **buddy** (*informal*), **partner** (*both esp. AmE*) | **video**

workshop noun

1 room/building

ADJ. **craft, design, pottery | engineering, railway** (*BrE*) | **farm | carpenter's, stonemason's, etc.**
VERB + WORKSHOP **set up** ◇ *He set up a ~ for his carving.*
WORKSHOP + VERB **employ sb** ◇ *The ~ employs 25 full-time workers.*
PREP. **in a/the ~**

2 period of discussion/work

ADJ. **day-long, two-day, weekend, etc. | group | intensive | introductory | hands-on, practical | development, educational, professional, training** ◇ *The company holds regular skills development ~s.* | **skills** ◇ *Everyone in Personnel has attended a media skills ~.* | **research | dance, drama, music, poetry, theatre/theater, writing | actors', artists', children's, writers', etc.**
... OF WORKSHOPS **series** ◇ *We will be running a series of ~s for students.*
VERB + WORKSHOP **hold, host, offer, organize, put on, run, schedule** (*esp. AmE*), **sponsor** ◇ *The Institute will host a special two-day ~ on new building materials.* | **conduct, do, lead, present, teach | attend, go to, participate in, take part in**
WORKSHOP + VERB **cover sth, examine sth, focus on sth, look at sth** ◇ *The ~ covered a wide range of issues.* | **aim to, be aimed at sth, be designed to** ◇ *a ~ aimed at brainstorming new marketing ideas*
WORKSHOP + NOUN **discussion, session | leader, presenter | attendee** (*esp. AmE*), **member, participant**
PREP. **at a/the ~, during a/the ~** ◇ *During the ~, they each rehearsed their part in the performance.* | **in a/the ~** ◇ *In the one-day ~, she taught us the importance of breathing exercises.* | **~ for** ◇ *a ~ for teachers* | **~ on** ◇ *I learned these new skills at a ~ on databases.*
PHRASES **a member of a ~, a participant in a ~**

world noun

1 the earth/its people

ADJ. **known** ◇ *a medieval map of the known ~* | **entire, whole**
VERB + WORLD **create, make** ◇ *They believe that God created the ~.* | **destroy** ◇ *One of these days, humans will destroy the ~.* | **save | conquer, dominate, rule, take over** ◇ *Fast food outlets seem to be taking over the ~.* | **populate | explore, tour, travel | see** ◇ *As a young man, he wanted to see the ~*

before he settled down. | **lead** ◇ *Sweden leads the ~ in safety legislation.*
WORLD + VERB **end** ◇ *Many people imagine the ~ ending with an explosion.*
WORLD + NOUN **atlas, map | population | leader, power, superpower** ◇ *a meeting of the major ~ powers* | **economy | order** ◇ *the new ~ order marked by American dominance* | **recession, slump | market | trade | price** ◇ *World oil prices continue to rise.* | **domination** ◇ *A handful of Internet companies are battling for ~ domination.* | **empire** ◇ *He is at the head of a ~ media empire.* | **affairs, events, politics | attention, opinion** ◇ *The bombing alienated ~ opinion.* | **war | champ** (*informal*), **champion, record-holder** ◇ *He was easily beaten by the reigning ~ champion.* | **championship, cup, title | class** ◇ *The team is ~ class.* | **record** ◇ *She shattered the ~ record for the marathon.* | **rankings** ◇ *He has never before featured in the top ten ~ rankings.* | **renown** ◇ *scientists of ~ renown* | **religion** ◇ *the major ~ religions* | **cinema, music** (= from or influenced by cultures outside Europe and North America) | **premiere** ◇ *The movie had its ~ premiere at the Toronto Film Festival.* | **tour** ◇ *The band are about to embark on a six-month ~ tour.*
PREP. **across the ~** ◇ *Astronomers across the ~ will be watching the night sky.* | **around the ~, round the ~** (*esp. BrE*) ◇ *The ceremony was watched live by millions around the ~.* | **in the ~** ◇ *He felt he was the luckiest man in the whole ~.* | **throughout the ~** ◇ *People throughout the ~ will be watching the big game on television.*
PHRASES **all around the ~, all over the ~, all round the ~** (*esp. BrE*) ◇ *The ceremony was watched live by millions around the ~.* | **the end of the ~** (*figurative*) ◇ *It won't be the end of the ~ if you don't get the job.* | **on a ~ scale** ◇ *Communist parties were formed on a ~ scale after the Russian Revolution.* | **on the ~ stage** ◇ *The country became an important player on the ~ stage.* | **a part of the ~** ◇ *It's an interesting part of the ~.* | **rid the ~ of sth** ◇ *He is on a quest to rid the ~ of evil.* | **the ~ over** ◇ *Scientists the ~ over have been waiting for this breakthrough.*

2 part of the earth

ADJ. **Arab, English-speaking, Islamic, Muslim, Western, etc.** ◇ *Heads of state from all over the Arab ~ gathered for the conference.* | **civilized | free | developed, First, industrialized, rich** ◇ *First-World consumers will have to eat less meat.* | **developing, Third, underdeveloped | New, Old** ◇ *Machismo is a New World phenomenon with roots in Old World cultures.*
PREP. **in the ... ~** ◇ *In the Western ~, there is a different attitude to marriage.*

3 life/society

ADJ. **changing, chaotic, ever-changing, fast-changing, fast-paced | cruel, cut-throat, dog-eat-dog, hard, tough | alien, crazy, mad** (*esp. BrE*), **strange, topsy-turvy | ancient, medieval, Roman, etc. | contemporary, modern, post-modern, today's | globalized** ◇ *In today's globalized ~, telecommunications have broken down boundaries.* | **post-apocalyptic, post-war** ◇ *The movie is set in a bizarre post-apocalyptic ~.* | **brave new** ◇ *the architects' vision of a brave new ~ of pristine concrete* | **vanishing** ◇ *These tribesmen are proud survivors of a vanishing ~.* | **peaceful | ideal, perfect | imperfect** ◇ *This is an imperfect ~, and we have to compromise.* | **external, outer, outside, real** ◇ *Throughout his time in prison he had no contact with the outside ~.* ◇ *In the real ~ things don't always happen like they do in books.* | **day-to-day, everyday, mundane, workaday** ◇ *She has to deal with the day-to-day ~ of bills, schools, and problems.* | **dream, fantasy, fictional, imaginary, inner, make-believe, private** ◇ *She enjoys creating imaginary ~s for children.* ◇ *She lives in her own inner ~.* | **sb's own** ◇ *She lives in her own little ~.* | **alternative, parallel | material, physical | simulated, virtual | digital | spiritual | spirit** ◇ *Mediums claim to receive messages from the spirit ~.* | **secular | social | animal, insect, natural, plant** ◇ *I like living in the country because I'm interested in the natural ~.* | **academic, art, business, corporate, fashion, industrial, literary, medical, publishing, sports | different** ◇ *We come from different ~s.* | **whole, whole wide, wider** ◇ *She told him he was her only friend in the whole wide ~.* ◇ *The wider ~ learned of his* illness months after he told his family. | **small** ◊ I'm sure we'll meet again. It's a very small ~ in this profession.

VERB + WORLD **change, remake, reshape, revolutionize, shape, transform** ◊ Young people always think they are going to change the ~. ◊ Technology has remade the ~. | **have, inhabit, live in** ◊ Children often have their own private ~. | **look at, perceive, see, view** ◊ different ways of looking at the ~ | **create** ◊ Computer games create whole virtual ~s. | **imagine** ◊ Can you imagine a ~ without possessions? | **come into, enter, escape into** ◊ We come into the ~ with nothing. ◊ He entered the ~ of politics in 1997. ◊ Show business gave him the chance to escape into another ~. | **bring sb into** ◊ She had brought six children into the ~. | **divide** ◊ She tends to divide the ~ into 'winners' and 'losers'. | **escape from, shut yourself away from, shut out** ◊ He closed his eyes and tried to shut out the ~. | **face** ◊ For the first time since the death of her parents, she felt able to face the ~. | **take on** ◊ He felt ready to take on the ~ when he finished college. | **tell** ◊ He wanted to tell the ~ how happy he was. | **prove to, show** ◊ She was determined to show the ~ that she was no loser. | **rock, shake, shock, stun** ◊ The news of the assassination shook the ~.

WORLD + VERB **change** | **collapse, crumble, fall apart** ◊ His ~ fell apart when his wife died. | **revolve around sb/sth** ◊ She thinks the ~ revolves around her and her schedule. | **owe sb sth** ◊ He seems to think that the ~ owes him a living.

WORLD + NOUN **knowledge** | **view** ◊ Teachers influence the ~ view of their young students.

PREP. **in the … ~** ◊ He's well known in the fashion ~. | **~ about** (esp. BrE), **~ around** ◊ At this age, babies are starting to take an interest in the ~ around them. | **~ of** ◊ In the ~ of finance there is little room for sentiment. | **~ outside** ◊ Aren't you interested in the ~ outside your window?

PHRASES **sb's experience of the ~, sb's knowledge of the ~, sb's perception of the ~** | **the eyes of the ~** ◊ The eyes of the ~ are on the president. | **in an ideal ~, in a perfect ~** ◊ In an ideal ~, I'd like to work just three days a week. | **in a ~ of your own** ◊ I tapped on the window to get her attention but she was in a ~ of her own. | **the rest of the ~** ◊ He just wanted to shut himself away from the rest of the ~. | **take the ~ by storm** ◊ a young writer who is taking the ~ by storm | **watch the ~ go by** ◊ He likes to sit outside his front door and watch the ~ go by. | **a whole other ~** (informal) ◊ There is a whole other ~ outside school. | **the ways of the ~** ◊ He's too young to understand the ways of the ~. | **~s apart** ◊ Although they are twins, they are ~s apart in their attitude to life.

worm noun

WORM + VERB **burrow, crawl** ◊ Worms burrow down through the soil. | **wriggle, writhe** ◊ The ~ was wriggling on the hook.

WORM + NOUN **cast**

worried adj.

VERBS **be, feel, look, seem** | **get** ◊ I started to get ~ when they didn't arrive home.

ADV. **extremely, fairly, very, etc.** | **deeply, desperately, genuinely, particularly, seriously, terribly** | **increasingly** | **a little, slightly, etc.** | **clearly, obviously** ◊ 'What happened?' he asked, clearly ~.

PREP. **about** ◊ We were really ~ about you!

PHRASES **~ sick** ◊ She was ~ sick about her son.

worry noun

ADJ. **big, considerable, great, main, major, serious** ◊ Paying the mortgage is a big ~ for many people. ◊ Her mother's poor health caused her considerable ~. ◊ My greatest ~ is that he'll do something stupid. | **genuine, real** | **growing, increasing** | **slight** | **day-to-day** | **constant** ◊ The money side of things has been a constant ~. | **unnecessary** ◊ She gave her parents unnecessary ~ when she forgot to call them. | **immediate** ◊ My immediate ~ is money. | **nagging, niggling** ◊ I had a nagging ~ that we weren't going to get there. | **secret** ◊ It was a relief to share my secret worries with him. | **business, economic, financial, money** | **health**

VERB + WORRY **have** ◊ That year he had major health worries. |

be beset by ◊ She wanted to enjoy her retirement without being beset by financial worries. | **be frantic with, be out of your mind with, be sick with** ◊ I didn't know where he was and I was frantic with ~. | **express, voice** | **share** | **cause (sb), give sb** | **add to, increase** ◊ The fact that she heard nothing from him only increased her ~. | **forget** ◊ Try and forget your worries for a little while. | **alleviate, assuage, ease, soothe** | **remove, take away, take out of sth** ◊ Take the ~ out of flying with our travel insurance offer. | **dismiss** ◊ For years, the government has dismissed our worries as unfounded.

WORRY + VERB **disappear, melt** | **prove groundless, prove unfounded** ◊ Most of Nigel's worries proved groundless. | **plague sb** ◊ These worries plagued him constantly.

PREP. **amid worries** ◊ The dollar has fallen to a new low amid worries that the American economy is heading for trouble. | **~ about, ~ over** ◊ They will not have worries over money. | **~ to** ◊ His mother's health is an enormous ~ to him.

PHRASES **cause for ~** ◊ There is no immediate cause for ~. | **free from ~** | **have no worries on that score** (BrE) ◊ The staff all work very hard—we've no worries on that score. | **the least of your worries** ◊ At the moment, the car is the least of my worries. | **no worries!** (esp. BrE) ◊ No worries—there's plenty of time. | **a source of ~** ◊ Money is a constant source of ~.

worry verb

ADV. **a lot, particularly, really, terribly** ◊ She worries a lot about crime. ◊ What really worries me is what we do if there's nobody there. | **slightly** | **excessively, needlessly, too much, unduly, unnecessarily** ◊ You do ~ unnecessarily, you know. | **not too much** ◊ Don't ~ too much about it. | **constantly**

VERB + WORRY **not let sth, not need to** ◊ Don't let it ~ you unduly. | **begin to** | **tell sb not to**

PREP. **about** ◊ Don't ~ about me, I'll be fine. | **for** ◊ We can't help ~ing for your safety. | **with** ◊ Don't ~ the driver with unnecessary requests.

PHRASES **can't help ~ing** ◊ I can't help ~ing about the future. | **enough to ~ about, nothing to ~ about** ◊ Don't bother Harry—he has enough to ~ about as it is. | **stop ~ing** ◊ Stop ~ing, Dad, we'll be fine. | **~ yourself sick, ~ yourself to death** (both informal)

worrying adj.

VERBS **be**

ADV. **extremely, fairly, very, etc.** | **deeply, particularly, seriously, terribly** | **a little, slightly, etc.**

worse adj.

VERBS **be, feel, look, seem** ◊ I feel even ~ today! | **become, get, grow** ◊ The problem is getting ~ all the time. ◊ The pain grew ~. | **make sth** ◊ Ignoring the problem will make it ~.

ADV. **considerably, dramatically, far, a good deal, a great deal, infinitely, a lot, much, significantly** ◊ It's much ~ for the parents than it is for the child. ◊ The news got dramatically ~. ◊ Things were about to get very much ~. | **almost** ◊ The area seemed almost ~ than the city he had left. | **a little, rather, slightly, substantially** | **progressively, steadily** ◊ The problem became progressively ~. | **even, still** ◊ We've run out of coffee. Worse still, we can't get any more until tomorrow.

PHRASES **no, not any** ◊ He's no better and no ~ than yesterday.

worsen verb

ADV. **considerably, dramatically, markedly, significantly** ◊ The problem has ~ed considerably in recent months. | **gradually, progressively, steadily** | **rapidly** | **suddenly**

VERB + WORSEN **continue to** ◊ The economic recession has continued to ~. | **be expected to, be likely to**

worship noun

ADJ. **daily, regular** | **evening, morning** | **Sunday** | **public** |

collective (*esp. BrE*) | **religious** | **divine** | **Christian, Hindu, etc.** | **pagan** | **ancestor, nature, spirit, sun** | **idol** | **hero** ◇ *his hero ~ of the national team* | **devil**
VERB + WORSHIP **conduct, lead** ◇ *Our ~ today is led by the Reverend John Parker.* | **attend**
PREP. **in ~** ◇ *the use of music in ~* | **~ of** ◇ *the ~ of God*
PHRASES **an act of ~** | **forms of ~** | **freedom of ~** ◇ *Under the new regime, all religions enjoy freedom of ~.* | **a house of ~, a place of ~** ◇ *15% of the population attend a place of ~.* | **an object of ~**

worst *noun* **the worst**

ADJ. **absolute** (*esp. AmE*) ◇ *Christmas usually brings out the absolute ~ in sentimental platitudes.*
VERB + THE WORST **believe, think** ◇ *She always thinks the ~ of people.* | **anticipate, assume, expect** ◇ *It doesn't matter what I say. My mother always expects the ~.* | **fear, suspect** | **be prepared for, be ready for, prepare for** ◇ *Although all the votes have not yet been counted, the party is preparing for the ~.* | **confirm** ◇ *I had not expected to do well in my exams, and the letter confirmed the ~.* | **avoid, be spared, escape** ◇ *Scotland seemed to have escaped the ~ of the recession.* | **do your** ◇ *Let them do their ~ (= be as difficult as they can)—we'll fight them every inch of the way.*
THE WORST + VERB **be over** ◇ *He was still very ill, but the ~ seemed to be over.*
PREP. **at (sb/sth's) ~** ◇ *At ~, the drug can be fatal.* ◇ *At its ~, bullying is a kind of torture.* | **through the ~** ◇ *Her sister helped her through the ~ of her illness.*
PHRASES **bring out the ~ in sb** ◇ *Pressure can bring out the ~ in people.* | **the ~ of it** ◇ *If he got in a fight, he would get the ~ of it.* | **the ~ that can happen** ◇ *Don't worry—the ~ that can happen is that you'll get a fine.*

worth *noun*

ADJ. **real, true** ◇ *They don't appreciate her real ~.* | **inherent, intrinsic** ◇ *Study has an intrinsic ~, as well as helping you achieve your goals.* | **human, individual, own, personal, self** | **moral** | **proven** ◇ *They are looking for a new sales manager of proven ~.* | **economic, financial, market** ◇ *Some experts doubt the economic ~ of the project.* | **estimated** | **net** | **literary, musical**
VERB + WORTH **have** | **demonstrate, prove** ◇ *The emergency lighting has proved its ~ this year.* | **appreciate, determine, judge, know, measure** ◇ *They don't appreciate her true ~.* ◇ *She knows her own ~.* | **doubt, question** | **find out, learn, realize, recognize** ◇ *I only found out its real ~ when I tried to buy another one.* | **assess, estimate** | **increase** ◇ *Cutting out the debts will increase your net ~.*
PREP. **of ~** ◇ *He never contributed anything of ~ to the conversation.* | **~ to** ◇ *This necklace isn't worth anything in money terms, but its ~ to me is incalculable.*
PHRASES **a sense of (your own) ~** ◇ *She has no sense of her own ~.*

worth *adj.*

VERBS **be, prove** | **become** | **seem** | **make sth** | **find sth** | **consider sth, think sth** ◇ *Most of the candidates were not considered ~ interviewing.*
ADV. **really, well** ◇ *This book is well ~ reading.* | **certainly, definitely** | **barely, hardly, scarcely** ◇ *It's so unimportant it's hardly ~ mentioning.* | **almost** | **potentially** | **probably** | **reportedly** | **always** ◇ *It's always ~ seeing if you can get a cheap last-minute deal.*
PREP. **to** ◇ *This order is potentially ~ millions of pounds to the company.*

worthless *adj.*

VERBS **be, feel, prove, seem** | **become** | **make sth, render sth** ◇ *These contradictions made his evidence ~.* | **consider sth, discard sth as, dismiss sth as, regard sth as, see sth as** ◇ *The opinion polls were dismissed as ~.*
ADV. **absolutely, completely, quite, totally, utterly** | **almost, nearly, practically, virtually** | **essentially, largely**

PREP. **to** ◇ *The diseased plants are ~ to the farmer.*

worthwhile *adj.*

VERBS **be, seem** | **become** | **make sth** ◇ *Their gratitude made it all ~.* | **consider sth, find sth, think sth** ◇ *You might find it ~ to consult a lawyer.*
ADV. **extremely, particularly, really, truly, very, well** | **definitely** | **hardly** ◇ *The gamble seemed hardly ~.* | **financially, socially** ◇ *the pursuit of socially ~ goals*

worthy *adj.*

VERBS **be, prove (yourself), seem** | **consider sth, deem sth, judge sth, think sth**
ADV. **most, very, well** | **entirely, particularly, truly** | **equally** | **hardly** ◇ *The matter is hardly ~ of the managing director's time.* | **enough** ◇ *We thought it was a ~ enough objective.* | **morally** ◇ *a morally ~ action*
PREP. **of** ◇ *It's a matter ~ of our attention.*

wound *noun*

ADJ. **deep, serious, severe** | **fatal** ◇ *a fatal gunshot ~* | **minor** | **flesh** ◇ *Despite the large amount of blood, it was only a flesh ~.* | **clean** | **gaping, open** | **surgical** | **bleeding, festering** (*often figurative*), **infected** ◇ *The animal died from an infected ~.* | **face, head, leg, etc.** | **bullet, gunshot, knife, shrapnel, stab** | **multiple** ◇ *He had suffered multiple stab ~s to his chest.* | **entry, exit** ◇ *The exit ~ made by the bullet was much larger than the entry ~.* | **puncture, slash** ◇ *She suffered numerous slash and puncture ~s to her arms and upper body.* | **old** | **war** ◇ *His old war ~s still ached in certain weathers.* | **self-inflicted** (*often figurative*) ◇ *The President's self-inflicted ~s have called his credibility into question.* | **emotional, psychological**
VERB + WOUND **inflict** | **receive, suffer, suffer from** | **examine, probe** | **bandage, clean, cleanse, cover, dress, treat** | **nurse** | **heal** (*often figurative*) ◇ *They say that time heals all ~s.*
WOUND + VERB **close** | **heal** ◇ *It was a clean ~, and it healed quickly.* | **bleed**
WOUND + NOUN **care, healing**
PREP. **~ in** ◇ *He had deep ~s in his chest.* | **~ to** ◇ *He died of gunshot ~s to the head.*

wound *verb*

1 injure sb's body

ADV. **badly, critically, gravely, grievously, seriously, severely** | **fatally, mortally** ◇ *She was fatally ~ed in a car crash.* | **slightly**
PREP. **in** ◇ *One reporter was ~ed in the leg.*
PHRASES **the walking ~ed** (= people who have been wounded, but not so badly that they cannot walk)

2 hurt sb's feelings

ADV. **deeply** ◇ *She was deeply ~ed by his remarks.* | **emotionally**

woven *adj.*

1 making cloth

VERBS **be**
ADV. **closely, densely, finely, tightly** ◇ *very fine and closely ~ silk* | **delicately, intricately** | **coarsely, loosely**

2 connected as part of a story

VERBS **be**
ADV. **inextricably** ◇ *The theme of exploitation is inextricably ~ into the fabric of her fiction.* | **seamlessly** | **together** ◇ *The three short stories were ~ together into a movie.*
PREP. **into** ◇ *The moon is ~ into the story as a symbol of death.*

wrangle *noun*

ADJ. **bitter** | **lengthy, long-running** | **legal, planning** (*BrE*) ◇ *a lengthy planning ~ over the height of the building*
VERB + WRANGLE **be drawn into, have**
WRANGLE + VERB **ensue** | **continue** ◇ *The legal ~ continues.*
PREP. **in a/the ~** ◇ *The two countries fell out in a bitter ~ over imports.* | **~ between** ◇ *The ~ between the school and the*

wrap verb

ADV. **firmly, securely, tightly** | **loosely** | **carefully, neatly** | **individually** ◇ Each apple was individually wrapped in paper. | **up**
PREP. **around, round** (esp. BrE) ◇ He wrapped his arms tightly around her waist. | **in** ◇ She wrapped the child carefully in a blanket.

PHRV **wrap (sb) up**
ADV. **warm, warmly, well** ◇ Make sure you ~ up warmly if you're going out.
PREP. **against** ◇ We went outside, well wrapped up against the cold. | **in** ◇ Christine was wrapped up in one of the blankets.

wrapper noun

ADJ. **candy** (AmE), **candy-bar** (AmE), **chewing-gum, chocolate** (esp. BrE), **chocolate-bar** (esp. BrE), **gum, sweet** (BrE) | **food** | **Cellophane™, foil, paper, plastic** | **plain** ◇ The book arrived in a plain brown ~. | **empty**
VERB + WRAPPER **remove, take off, tear off** | **discard, drop, throw away, toss** (esp. AmE) ◇ He dropped the gum ~ on the floor.
WRAPPER + VERB **litter sth** ◇ Chocolate bar ~s littered the floor.
PREP. **in a/the ~, on a/the ~** ◇ There was a list of ingredients on the ~. | **out of a/the ~** ◇ She took the chocolate bar out of the foil ~.

wrath noun

ADJ. **full, great** | **divine, righteous** ◇ They saw the floods as a sign of divine ~.
VERB + WRATH **arouse, bring, bring down, draw** (esp. AmE), **earn, incur, provoke, unleash** ◇ This remark brought the judge's full ~ down on Sergeant Golding. ◇ He incurred Helen's ~ by arriving late. ◇ What had she done to provoke his ~? | **feel, suffer** ◇ This is the second hotel to feel the ~ of the bombers. | **fear** ◇ She feared her father's ~. | **brave, face, risk** ◇ If the President fails, he will face the ~ of the voters. | **appease, avoid, escape** ◇ They left gifts for the gods to appease their ~. ◇ He fled the country to escape the gang leader's ~. | **turn, vent** ◇ He vented his ~ on his colleagues.
PREP. **~ at** ◇ his ~ at the insult
PHRASES **God's ~, the ~ of God**

wreath noun

ADJ. **Christmas, festive, holiday** (AmE) | **funeral** | **holly, laurel, olive, poppy** (in the UK) ◇ Olive ~s were awarded to the Olympic victors. ◇ The princes laid a ~ at the Cenotaph.
VERB + WREATH **lay, place** ◇ The President laid a ~ at the war memorial. | **send** ◇ He didn't come to the funeral but he sent a ~. | **be crowned with, wear**
PREP. **~ of** ◇ She wore a ~ of roses around her head.

wreck noun

1 of a ship

VERB + WRECK **discover, find, locate** ◇ Divers were sent down to try and locate the ~. | **explore** | **raise, salvage** ◇ They're going to try and raise the ~ from the sea bed. | **salvage sth from**
PREP. **in a/the ~** ◇ They are worried about the oil still in the ~. | **on a/the ~** ◇ Heavy seas prevented salvage teams from landing on the ~. | **~ of** ◇ the ~ of the Titanic

2 of a car/plane

ADJ. **total** | **crumpled** | **blazing, burning** ◇ Explosions ripped through the blazing ~.
VERB + WRECK **be trapped in** ◇ Two passengers are still trapped in the ~. | **escape, escape from**

3 (esp. AmE) **accident**

ADJ. **car, train**
VERB + WRECK **cause** | **survive**
PHRASES **like watching a car ~, like watching a train ~** ◇ His attempts at damage control are like watching a car ~. | **a**

train ~ **waiting to happen** (= is likely to be a disaster) ◇ The campaign is a train ~ waiting to happen.

4 of a person

ADJ. **absolute, complete, total** | **emotional, nervous** ◇ The interview reduced him to a nervous ~. | **gibbering, quivering** ◇ I always turn into a gibbering ~ at interviews. | **physical**
VERB + WRECK **feel, look** (both esp. BrE) ◇ I hadn't slept for two days, and I felt a complete physical ~. | **reduce sb to** (esp. BrE)

wreck verb

ADV. **completely, totally** ◇ A bomb completely ~ed the building. | **almost, nearly** | **effectively** (esp. BrE)
VERB + WRECK **try to, want to** | **threaten to** ◇ a crisis that threatens to ~ the peace talks

wreckage noun

ADJ. **mangled, tangled** (esp. BrE), **twisted** | **blazing, burning, flaming, smoking, smoldering** | **aircraft, plane** | **human** ◇ the human ~ of the battlefield
... OF WRECKAGE **bit** (esp. BrE), **piece** ◇ Pieces of ~ have been found up to three miles away. | **pile**
VERB + WRECKAGE **scatter, spread** ◇ The crash left ~ spread over a wide area. | **be strewn with** ◇ The runway is still strewn with ~. | **survey** ◇ He surveyed the ~ of his expensive equipment. | **comb, comb through, search, sift through** ◇ Police are searching the ~ for clues to the cause of the accident. | **examine** | **clear** ◇ The ~ has now been cleared from the road. | **be buried beneath, be buried in, be trapped in** ◇ Several people are still trapped in the ~. | **crawl from** | **cut sb free from** (BrE), **cut sb from** (BrE), **free sb from, pull sb from** ◇ It took workers several minutes to free him from the ~. ◇ He had to be cut from the ~ by firemen. | **recover sth from, rescue sb/sth from, salvage sth from** ◇ Another body has been recovered from the ~. ◇ Could nothing be rescued from the ~ of her dreams? (figurative) | **emerge from** (figurative) ◇ A new leader emerged from the ~ of the election.
WRECKAGE + VERB **be strewn** ◇ Wreckage was strewn over a wide area.
PREP. **amidst the ~, among the ~** ◇ Bodies lay among the tangled ~. | **in the ~** ◇ Her body was discovered in the ~. | **~ from** ◇ A search is going on for ~ from the blazing aircraft.

wriggle verb

ADV. **uncomfortably** ◇ The children ~d uncomfortably in their seats. | **free** ◇ The dog ~d free of his grasp and ran off. | **about, around, away**
PREP. **out of** ◇ She ~d out of his grip. | **through** ◇ Pete attempted to ~ through the gap.
PHRASES **~ your way** ◇ She ~d her way under the heavy eiderdown.

wrinkle noun

ADJ. **fine** | **deep** ◇ He had deep ~s in his forehead. | **facial**
VERB + WRINKLE **have** | **get** | **prevent** ◇ Is there anything you can do to prevent ~s? | **erase, get rid of, smooth, smooth out** ◇ Botox temporarily erases ~s by acting on certain facial muscles. | **iron out, smooth, smooth out** ◇ I tried to iron out the ~s in my shirt. ◇ I went through my presentation to iron out any ~s. (figurative)
WRINKLE + VERB **appear, form** ◇ Fine ~s started to appear around her eyes.
PREP. **without a ~** ◇ Her skin was still without a ~.

wrist noun

ADJ. **bony, slender, small, thin, tiny** | **limp, weak** | **broken, fractured, injured, sore, sprained**
VERB + WRIST **catch (sb by), clasp, grab (sb by), grasp, grip, hold (sb by), seize, take sb by** ◇ 'Is it serious?' she asked, clasping the doctor's ~. ◇ I turned to leave but he grabbed me by the ~. | **grab hold of, take hold of** | **bend, twist** ◇ He

grabbed her ~ *but she twisted it free.* | **encircle, enclose** ◊ *Strong fingers encircled her tiny ~s.* | **rub** | **break, dislocate, fracture, sprain** | **bandage** | **bind, tie** ◊ *The burglars bound the family's ~s behind their backs.* | **slash, slit** ◊ *He slashed his ~s in a suicide attempt.*

WRIST + NOUN **watch** (usually *wristwatch*) | **band** (usually *wristband*), **strap** | **action** ◊ *The secret of making the ball spin is in the ~ action.* | **bone, joint** | **injury**

PREP. **around the/your ~, round the/your ~** (*esp. BrE*) ◊ *A policeman snapped handcuffs around his ~s.* | **by the ~, on the/your ~** ◊ *He wears weights on his ~s when he goes running.*

PHRASES **a flick of the ~** ◊ *She sent the ball flying over the net with a flick of the ~.*

writ noun

ADJ. **legal** | **High Court** (*in the UK*) | **libel, personal-injury** (*both BrE*)

VERB + WRIT **apply for, seek** | **obtain** ◊ *Creditors could obtain a ~ for the arrest of their debtors.* | **grant** ◊ *The Supreme Court granted a ~.* | **file, issue, serve** (*BrE*) ◊ *A ~ was filed in the High Court.* ◊ *The lawyer came to serve a ~ on him.* | **be served with** (*BrE*), **receive** ◊ *He has been served with a High Court ~.* | **suspend**

PREP. **in a/the ~** ◊ *22 defendants are named in the ~.* | **~ against** (*esp. BrE*) ◊ *The businessmen have issued a ~ against the authority for damages.* | **~ for** (*esp. BrE*) ◊ *a ~ for damages/libel* | **~ of** (*technical*) ◊ *a ~ of execution* (*BrE*)

PHRASES **an application for a ~ of …** (*BrE*), **a petition for a ~ of …** (*AmE*) ◊ *He can file a petition for a ~ of habeas corpus.*

write verb

1 form letters and words on paper

ADV. **clearly, neatly** ◊ *Children must learn to ~ neatly.* | **busily** ◊ *She was busily writing in a notebook.* | **down, out** ◊ *I'd better ~ this down, otherwise I'll forget it.*

VERB + WRITE **learn to** | **teach sb to** | **be able to, can, know how to**

PREP. **in** ◊ *The words were written in black ink.* | **on** ◊ *He wrote a list on the back of an old envelope.* | **with** ◊ *I ~ with an old fashioned pen.*

2 produce a piece of writing

ADV. **beautifully, eloquently, well** | **badly, poorly** | **clearly** ◊ *the ability to ~ clearly in plain English* | **at length, extensively** ◊ *He has written extensively on the subject.* | **frequently, regularly** ◊ *an art critic who ~s regularly in the French daily 'Le Figaro'* | **anonymously** | **specifically** ◊ *The role was written specifically for Rita Hayworth.* | **back** ◊ *She wrote back to him the next day.*

VERB + WRITE **commission sb to** ◊ *He has been commissioned to ~ a history of the town.* | **inspire sb to, prompt sb to** ◊ *She was inspired to ~ the poem by a visit to the cathedral.* | **set out to** ◊ *He set out to ~ a short book on taxation.* | **go on to** ◊ *After 'Tom Sawyer', Twain went on to ~ several other classic books.*

PREP. **about** ◊ *a journalist who ~s about problems in the developing world* | **for** ◊ *She ~s for 'The New York Times'.* | **from** ◊ *history written from the perspective of the losers* | **in** ◊ *She wrote in Arabic.* ◊ *He wrote in his journal.* | **into** ◊ *He had an extra clause written into his contract.* | **of** ◊ *She wrote of her life in Africa.* | **on** ◊ *He ~s on political issues.* | **to** ◊ *He wrote to the editor of the newspaper.* | **under** ◊ *Her novel was written under the pseudonym Currer Bell.* | **with** ◊ *Doris ~s with verve and wit.*

writer noun

ADJ. **celebrated, distinguished, eminent, famous, great, important, influential, leading, major, prominent, well-known** ◊ *one of the greatest ~s of all time* | **serious** | **award-winning** | **best-selling, popular, successful** | **favourite/favorite** | **prolific** ◊ *a very prolific crime ~* | **accomplished, creative, fine, gifted, good, talented** ◊ *one of the best ~s in journalism today* | **experienced, published** | **young** |

aspiring ◊ *a chance for aspiring ~s to get their work published* | **freelance, full-time, professional** | **contributing, senior, staff** (*all esp. AmE*) | **anonymous, ghost** (usually *ghostwriter*) | **contemporary, living, modern, recent** | **ancient, classical, Greek, Roman** | **Renaissance, Victorian, etc.** | **modernist, post-colonial** | **16th-century, etc.** | **early, later** ◊ *early ~s in sociology* | **black, female, gay, male, woman** ◊ *She gives talks about being a black woman ~.* | **Christian, communist, feminist, political, socialist** | **religious, spiritual** | **academic, technical** | **fiction, prose** | **comedy, crime, mystery, romance, science-fiction, sci-fi, thriller** | **baseball, cookbook** (*esp. AmE*), **cookery** (*BrE*), **fashion, food, football, golf, nature, science, sports, travel** | **copy** (usually *copywriter*), **editorial** (*esp. AmE*), **feature, headline, leader** (*BrE*), **magazine, newspaper** (*esp. AmE*), **speech** | **comic-book, short-story, textbook** | **film, screen** (usually *screenwriter*), **script** (usually *scriptwriter*) | **television, TV** | **music, song** (usually *songwriter*) | **software** | **letter, report** | **shorthand** (*BrE*) | **the present** (*written*) ◊ *The present ~* (= the person writing) *has no experience in microbiology.*

WRITER + VERB **write sth** ◊ *a popular ~ who has written over forty books* | **argue sth, describe sth, point sth out, put it, say sth, suggest sth** ◊ *Is political culture, as some ~s have suggested, in a state of collapse?* | **be interested in sth** | **draw on sth** ◊ *The ~ drew on his own experience to write this script.*

PREP. **as ~** ◊ *her career as a ~* | **~ for** ◊ *a freelance feature ~ for Time* | **~ of** ◊ *a ~ of children's books* | **~ on** ◊ *He is a prominent ~ on civil liberties.*

PHRASES **a group of ~s, a writer's group** | **a ~ in residence** ◊ *We have decided not to employ a ~ in residence after June.* | **a ~ of the day, period, time, etc.** ◊ *Unlike many ~s of the period, she is not preoccupied with morality.* | **writer's block** ◊ *He's just released a new album after two years of writer's block.*

→ Note at JOB

writing noun

1 activity/job of writing

ADJ. **effective** ◊ *The book aims to teach effective essay ~.* | **creative, descriptive, imaginative** | **clear, concise, sharp** | **academic, critical, editorial** (*AmE*), **scientific, technical** | **essay, feature** (*esp. AmE*), **fiction, journal** (*esp. AmE*), **letter, novel, prose, report, script, song** (usually *songwriting*) | **business, food, history, science, travel, etc.** | **opinion** (*esp. AmE*) | **developmental** (*AmE*) | **freelance, professional** | **student** (*esp. AmE*) ◊ *the evaluation of student ~*

… OF WRITING **piece**

VERB + WRITING **teach** | **improve**

WRITING + NOUN **skills** | **style** ◊ *His ~ style is well suited to this subject matter.*

PREP. **~ for** ◊ *the process of ~ for publication* | **~ in** ◊ *Students do most of their academic ~ in English.* | **~ of** ◊ *Housman's description of the ~ of poetry*

PHRASES **a style of ~**

2 written/printed words

VERB + WRITING **put sth in, put sth into** ◊ *The arrangement was never put into ~.*

PREP. **in ~** ◊ *This agreement has to be confirmed in ~.*

3 (often **writings**) books, etc.

ADJ. **fine, good, great** | **bad** | **influential** | **early, later** ◊ *His experiences in India influenced his later ~s.* | **ancient, contemporary** ◊ *Ancient ~s reinforce their claims to the land.* | **published, unpublished** | **prose** | **academic, autobiographical, critical, historical, philosophical, political, sacred, scholarly, scientific, theoretical** ◊ *Christians share some of their sacred ~s with the Jews.* | **popular** | **collected, selected** ◊ *Ruskin's collected ~s*

… OF WRITING **piece** | **anthology, collection** ◊ *an anthology of ~ about jazz*

VERB + WRITING **read** | **publish** ◊ *His ~s on the history of art were published by Greenway and Settle.*

WRITING + VERB **be about sth, deal with sth** ◊ *Her early ~ was concerned with the French Revolution.* | **include sth, range** ◊ *His ~s range from ancient to contemporary art.* | **indicate**

sth, provide sth, reflect sth, show sth, suggest sth ◇ *His ~s provide us with a first-hand account of the civil war.* ◇ *Her ~s reflect the breadth of her interests.* | **influence sb/sth, inspire sb/sth**
PREP. **in … ~** ◇ *You find more technical words in scientific ~.* | **through sb's ~** ◇ *Her influence has been greatest through her ~s.* | **~ about** ◇ *Her name crops up frequently in ~s about the Renaissance.* | **~ by** ◇ *a collection of ~s by artists* | **~ for** ◇ *the composer's fine ~ for the piano* | **~ on** ◇ *The book is a collection of ~s on death by various authors.*

4 putting words on paper
VERB + WRITING **do, practise/practice** ◇ *Every morning the children do ~.* | **improve**
WRITING + NOUN **paper** | **desk**
PHRASES **reading and ~**

5 handwriting → See also HANDWRITING
ADJ. **small, tiny** | **legible, neat** | **illegible** | **cursive** (*esp. AmE*), **joined-up** (*BrE*) | **childish** | **spidery**
VERB + WRITING **have** ◇ *He has very neat ~.* | **read** ◇ *I can't read your ~.* | **recognize** ◇ *I didn't recognize the ~.* | **decipher**
PREP. **in sb's ~** ◇ *The list was in Elizabeth's ~.*

wrong noun
ADJ. **great, terrible** | **past** | **moral** | **civil, criminal** ◇ *There are various kinds of civil ~s, or torts.*
VERB + WRONG **commit, do (sb), inflict** ◇ *If they do ~, they have to be punished.* ◇ *You are answerable in court for ~s done to individuals.* ◇ *the ~s inflicted on innocent people* ◇ *According to her, her son could do no ~.* | **compensate (sb) for, correct** (*esp. AmE*), **put right** (*esp. BrE*), **redress, right, undo** ◇ *How can we right these ~s?* | **suffer** ◇ *It's the job of the newspapers to expose the ~s suffered by such people.* | **forgive (sb for)** ◇ *The two communities must learn to forgive past ~s.* | **acknowledge, apologize for, recognize** | **see no** ◇ *I see no ~ in asking him to share the expenses.* | **expose** | **avenge**
PREP. **in the ~** ◇ *Although he knew he was in the ~, he wouldn't apologize.*
PHRASES **the difference between right and ~** ◇ *Children have to learn the difference between right and ~.* | **the rights and ~s (of sth)** ◇ *Whatever the rights and ~s of the situation, there's not a lot we can do.*

wrong adj.
VERBS **be, seem** | **go** ◇ *Things seemed to be going horribly ~.* | **get sth** ◇ *He got all his calculations ~.* | **find sth** ◇ *The doctor could find nothing ~ with him.* | **get sb** ◇ *Don't get me ~ (= don't misunderstand me)—I'm not asking for special treatment.* | **prove sb** ◇ *She was able to prove him ~.*
ADV. **all, badly, disastrously, drastically, dreadfully, hopelessly, horribly, seriously, spectacularly, terribly, tragically, very** ◇ *You've got it all ~. I never meant to imply that you were responsible.* | **absolutely, completely, dead, downright, entirely, fundamentally, plain** (*informal*), **quite, totally, utterly** ◇ *The authors are just plain ~ in their assessments.* | **just, simply** ◇ *She's simply ~ for this job.* | **not far** (*esp. BrE*) ◇ *They weren't far ~ with their estimate of 100 000.* | **not necessarily** | **clearly, obviously, plainly** | **ethically, morally** | **physically** ◇ *There is nothing physically ~ with him.*
PREP. **about** ◇ *You were completely ~ about Maurice. He's not leaving.* | **for** ◇ *She's all ~ for you.* | **in** ◇ *Everything was going ~ in my life.* | **with** ◇ *She was worried that there was something seriously ~ with her.*
PHRASES **there's nothing ~ with sth** ◇ *There's nothing inherently ~ with this type of nostalgia.* | **you can't go ~ (with sth)** ◇ *You can't go ~ with spaghetti—everyone likes it.*

X-ray noun
ADJ. **chest, foot, etc.** | **routine**
VERB + X-RAY **have** | **do, take** | **examine**
X-RAY + VERB **reveal sth, show sth** ◇ *The ~ showed a crack in one rib.*
X-RAY + NOUN **equipment, machine, plate** | **image, photography, picture** | **department** (*esp. BrE*), **unit** | **technician** | **eyes, vision**
PREP. **~ of** ◇ *The dentist took an ~ of my jaw.* | **~ on** ◇ *I had to have an ~ on my knee.*
PHRASES **the result of the ~** ◇ *The results of the ~ gave no cause for concern.*

yacht noun
ADJ. **luxury** | **private, royal** | **cruising, racing** | **motor, sailing** (*BrE*), **steam** (*esp. BrE*) | **land** | **60-foot, 110-foot, etc.**
VERB + YACHT **cruise on, sail** (*esp. BrE*) ◇ *They are cruising on a large motor ~.* | **moor** | **charter**
YACHT + VERB **sail** (*esp. BrE*), **set sail** (*BrE*)
YACHT + NOUN **race** | **club**
PREP. **aboard a/the ~, on a/the ~, on board a/the ~**

yard noun
1 piece of land next to a building
ADJ. **front** | **back** (usually ***backyard***), **rear** (*esp. BrE*) | **church** (usually ***churchyard***), **farm** (usually ***farmyard***), **kitchen** (*BrE*), **school** (*esp. AmE*) ◇ *kids playing in the school ~* | **livery** (*BrE*), **stable** | **exercise, prison** ◇ *The prisoners were taken to the exercise ~.*
VERB + YARD **enter, leave** ◇ *He entered the ~ through the back gate.* ◇ *I left our school ~ at recess and ran home.* | **enclose, surround** ◇ *The ~ was enclosed by a high wire fence.*
2 (*AmE*) **piece of land next to a house with grass** → See also GARDEN
ADJ. **back** (usually ***backyard***), **front, side** | **big, huge, large** | **small, tiny** | **fenced**
VERB + YARD **mow, rake, water** ◇ *My next-door neighbor was watering her ~.* | **landscape** ◇ *I've landscaped my tiny front ~ with tall grasses.* | **decorate** ◇ *The outside ~ was decorated with orange lights.* | **fence** ◇ *The front ~ is fenced for privacy.* | **cover** ◇ *Most of the ~ was covered with leaves.* | **cross** ◇ *We crossed the ~ to my house.* | **enter, leave** | **overlook** ◇ *the huge bay window overlooking the ~*
YARD + NOUN **sale** ◇ *I held a ~ sale to get rid of my old stuff.* | **sign** ◇ *The first Bush-Cheney ~ sign appeared on my street last week.*
PREP. **in ~** ◇ *She was standing in the ~.*
PHRASES **the corner of the ~, the edge of the ~, the middle of the ~, the side of the ~**
3 area used for a special purpose
ADJ. **lumber** (usually ***lumberyard***) (*AmE*), **timber** (*BrE*) ◇ *wood from a lumber ~* | **freight, marshalling** (*BrE*), **rail, railroad** (*AmE*), **railway** (*BrE*) | **boat** (usually ***boatyard***), **ship** (usually ***shipyard***), **shipbuilding** | **breaker's** (*BrE*), **junk** (usually ***junkyard***) (*esp. AmE*), **salvage** (*esp. AmE*), **scrap** (usually ***scrapyard***) (*esp. BrE*) ◇ *The steam tug was on her way to the breaker's ~ at the end of her naval service.* ◇

salvage ~s with cars that are being sold for parts | **repair**, **storage**

PHRASES **a builder's ~**, **the knacker's ~** (both BrE) ◇ a horse condemned to the knacker's ~ ◇ The company is heading for the knacker's ~. (figurative)

4 unit of measurement

→ Note at MEASURE

yardstick noun

ADJ. **good**, **reliable**, **useful** | **common** | **traditional** | **moral**
VERB + YARDSTICK **have** ◇ We don't have a common ~ by which to compare the two cases. | **apply**, **use (sth as)** | **give sb**, **provide (sb with)**, **serve as** | **measure sth against**, **measure sth by**
PREP. **against a ~** ◇ The new test provides a ~ against which to measure children's learning. | **by a ~** ◇ By any ~, that's a large amount of money. | **~ for** ◇ a ~ for measuring growth | **~ of** ◇ the ~ of success

yarn noun

1 thread

ADJ. **fine**, **thick** | **coloured/colored** | **cotton**, **synthetic**, **wool**, etc.
... OF YARN **length**, **piece** | **ball**
VERB + YARN **knit**, **knit with**, **spin**, **weave** ◇ The ~ is woven into a coarse fabric. | **thread** ◇ The ~ has to be threaded through the needle. | **dye** | **use**
PREP. **in a/the ~** ◇ There's a knot in the ~.

2 story

ADJ. **entertaining**, **good**, **gripping** (esp. BrE), **rattling** (BrE), **ripping** (BrE) ◇ He went on to spin an entertaining ~ about his army days. ◇ Galton's life makes a rattling good ~. | **adventure**, **seafaring**
VERB + YARN **spin (sb)**, **tell (sb)** ◇ He tried to spin us some ~ about how he was collecting for the church. It was all lies.
PREP. **~ about**

yawn noun

ADJ. **big**, **deep**, **huge** | **loud**, **noisy** | **stifled** | **collective** (figurative) ◇ The speech was greeted with a collective ~ from the press gallery.
VERB + YAWN **fight back**, **hold back**, **stifle**, **suppress** ◇ He struggled to stifle a ~. | **give**, **let out** ◇ The little boy gave a huge ~. | **conceal** ◇ He tried to conceal his ~ behind his hand.
YAWN + VERB **escape** ◇ A loud ~ escaped my lips.
PREP. **with a ~**

yawn verb

ADV. **hugely**, **widely** ◇ He sat up and ~ed hugely. | **loudly**
VERB + YAWN **make sb** | **hear sb**
PREP. **at** ◇ He got fed up with people ~ing at him when he talked about his job.
PHRASES **can't stop ~ing** ◇ I was so tired I couldn't stop ~ing.

year noun

1 period of 12 months; period from January till December

ADJ. **last**, **past** ◇ The chart shows our performance over the past ~. | **past**, **preceding**, **previous**, **recent** ◇ The event has not proved popular in past ~s. ◇ They had met once the previous ~. | **current** | **given**, **single** ◇ The death rate in any given ~. ◇ I paint the house every single ~. | **coming**, **ensuing**, **following**, **future**, **next**, **subsequent** ◇ We have high hopes for the coming ~. ◇ She died the following ~. ◇ We aim to do even better in future ~s. | **consecutive**, **straight**, **successive** ◇ She won the race for the third successive ~. | **alternate** | **new** ◇ We're going skiing early in the new ~. | **final** (esp. BrE) ◇ final-year university students | **entire**, **full**, **whole** | **long**, **short** ◇ We worked for five long ~s on this project. | **20-odd**, **30-odd**, etc. ◇ I visited Morocco 20-odd ~s ago. | **banner** (AmE), **golden**, **good**, **great**, **happy**, **profitable** ◇ the golden ~s of motoring | **big**, **memorable**,

momentous | **peak**, **record** ◇ a peak ~ for exports | **bad**, **hard**, **lean**, **poor**, **tough** | **calendar** | **leap** | **academic**, **school** | **freshman**, **junior**, **senior**, **sophomore** (all in the US) | **gap** (BrE) ◇ He was on a gap ~ before going to university. | **financial** (BrE), **fiscal** (esp. AmE), **tax** (esp. BrE) | **election** | **sabbatical** ◇ He spent his sabbatical ~ doing research in Moscow. | **rookie** (AmE, sports) | **light** (often figurative) ◇ The new range puts us light ~s ahead of the competition.
VERB + YEAR **spend** ◇ He spent last ~ trying to get a new job. | **take** ◇ It took him ten ~s to qualify as a vet. | **celebrate** ◇ Next month, they celebrate fifty ~s of marriage. | **put on**, **take off** ◇ His wife's death has put ~s on him (= made him look/feel much older). ◇ Careful make-up and styling can take ~s off you (= make you look much younger).
YEAR + VERB **begin**, **start** | **end**, **finish** | **elapse**, **go by**, **pass** ◇ A ~ elapsed before I heard from him again. ◇ The last ~ went by in flash. | **run from ... to ...** ◇ The academic ~ runs from October to June. | **see sth** ◇ That ~ saw the explosion of the Internet. | **mark sth** ◇ This ~ marks the 10th anniversary of her death.
PREP. **by the ~ ...** ◇ The reforms will be fully implemented by the ~ 2007. | **during the ~**, **over the ~** ◇ during the next academic ~ ◇ Over the past few ~s, we've made significant changes. ◇ Over the past several ~s, we've made significant changes. (AmE) | **for a/the ~** ◇ profit for the current ~ to December 31 ◇ We lived there for ten ~s. | **in a ~** ◇ I hope to retire in a ~/in a year's time. | **in a/the ~** ◇ in the next tax ~ ◇ Britain was invaded in the ~ 1066. ◇ In the past few ~s, she has become one of our top-selling authors. | **in ~s** ◇ It's the first time we've met in ~s (= for many years). | **over a ~**, **under a ~** ◇ We've been friends for over twenty ~s. | **per ~** ◇ Over 10 000 people per ~ are injured in this type of accident. | **throughout the ~** ◇ The global economy means that all types of fruit and vegetables are available throughout the ~. | **~s between ... and ...**, **~s from ... to ...** ◇ the boom ~s from 1993 to 2000 | **~ of** ◇ The book represents three ~s of hard work. ◇ That was in the ~ of the great flood.
PHRASES **after all these ~s**, **after all those ~s** ◇ They're still friends after all these ~s. | **all ~ long** ◇ I've been waiting for this moment all ~ long. | **all the ~ round** (BrE), **all ~ round** ◇ The city tour runs all the ~ round. | **the beginning of the ~**, **the end of the ~**, **the middle of the ~**, **the start of the ~** | **be six, etc. ~s of age**, **be six, etc. ~s old** ◇ She's only ten ~s old. | **early in the ~**, **late in the ~** | **a time of ~** ◇ It's usually much colder at this time of ~. | **the turn of the ~** (esp. BrE) ◇ The team has suffered a loss of form since the turn of the ~.

2 years period of time

ADJ. **intervening** ◇ He soon realized that a lot had changed in the intervening ~s. | **early**, **later** ◇ the early ~s of the 21st century ◇ In his later ~s, he drifted away from politics. | **college**, **high-school** (both AmE) | **inter-war**, **post-war**, **pre-war**, **war** ◇ The children spent the war ~s with relatives. | **childhood**, **early**, **formative**, **teen**, **teenage**, **tender** ◇ She was born in Spain but spent her formative ~s in Italy. ◇ children of tender ~s
VERB + YEARS **spend** ◇ His early ~s were spent in San Francisco.
PREP. **during the ... ~s** ◇ It happened during the Clinton ~s.

yearn verb

ADV. **secretly** | **desperately** | **still** | **always** ◇ I've always ~ed to go stock car racing.
PREP. **after** ◇ He still ~ed after her, even after all these years. | **for** ◇ She ~ed for children of her own.

yearning noun

ADJ. **deep**, **desperate**, **great**, **passionate** | **nostalgic**, **romantic**, **wistful** | **spiritual**
VERB + YEARNING **feel**, **have** | **find yourself** ◇ I found myself ~ for the end to come. | **express** | **satisfy**
PREP. **with (a) ~** ◇ He looked at her with ~. | **~ after** ◇ He felt a great ~ after his old job. | **~ for** ◇ They had a deep ~ for their homeland.

yell verb

ADV. **loudly** | **angrily, furiously, hysterically** | **excitedly, happily** (both esp. AmE) | **almost** | **back, out** ◊ She ~ed back at me to mind my own business.
VERB + YELL **hear sb**
PREP. **at** ◊ He ~ed at me furiously. | **for** ◊ He ~ed for help. | **in** ◊ She ~ed in pain as she touched the hot iron. | **with** ◊ The children were ~ing with delight.

yellow adj., noun

ADJ. **creamy, dirty, sickly** | **canary, golden, lemon, mustard, primrose** (esp. BrE), **sunny, sunshine**
→ Special page at COLOUR

yelp noun

ADJ. **startled, surprised** | **little, small** | **loud**
VERB + YELP **give, let out** | **hear**
PREP. **with a ~** | **~ of** ◊ She jumped back with a little ~ of surprise. ◊ a ~ of pain
→ Note at SOUND

yen noun → Note at CURRENCY

yes noun, exclamation

ADJ. **resounding** ◊ When the people were asked if they wanted the factory, the answer was a resounding ~. | **simple**
VERB + YES **answer, say** ◊ In reply to his question, most of them answered ~. ◊ Please say ~! | **vote**
YES + NOUN **vote**
PREP. **with a ~** ◊ He answered with a ~. | **~ to** ◊ They voted ~ to strike action.
PHRASES **~ or no** ◊ I need a simple ~ or no.

yield noun

ADJ. **good, high** ◊ savings products which offer high ~s ◊ This method of cultivation produces a higher ~. | **low, poor** ◊ Yields are very poor this year. | **bond, dividend** | **crop, grain**
VERB + YIELD **produce**
YIELD + VERB **jump, rise** | **decline, drop**

yoga noun

VERB + YOGA **do, practise/practice, take** (AmE) ◊ She does ~ for an hour a day. | **take up, try** | **teach**
YOGA + NOUN **exercise, position, posture, technique** | **mat** | **class, session** ◊ He attends regular ~ classes. ◊ I go to a ~ session on Thursdays. | **instructor, teacher** | **practice**

yogurt noun

ADJ. **natural** (esp. BrE), **plain** | **apricot, strawberry, etc.** | **fat-free, low-fat, non-fat** | **thick** | **frozen**
... OF YOGURT **carton** (AmE), **container** (AmE), **pot** (BrE)
YOGURT + NOUN **container** (AmE), **pot** (BrE) | **drink**

young adj.

VERBS **be, feel, look, seem** ◊ I felt ~ again. | **keep** ◊ All that exercise keeps her ~.
ADV. **extremely, fairly, very, etc.** ◊ She still looks very ~. | **relatively** ◊ He seemed relatively ~ to have so much responsibility. | **enough** ◊ She looked ~ enough to be his daughter.
PHRASES **~ at heart** ◊ He's over 70, but he's ~ at heart. | **~ for your age** ◊ He still looks ~ for his age.

youth noun

1 period of your life when you are young

ADJ. **early** | **lost** ◊ nostalgia for her lost ~ | **misspent** (often humorous) ◊ His lack of qualifications was taken as a sign of a misspent ~.
VERB + YOUTH **spend** ◊ She spent much of her ~ in Hong Kong. | **recapture, relive** ◊ She saw it as a chance to relive her misspent ~. | **waste** ◊ He wasted his ~ in front of a computer screen.
PREP. **during your ~** ◊ She contracted the disease during her

~. | **from ~** ◊ from ~ to maturity | **in your ~** ◊ He started going clubbing in his early ~. | **since your ~** ◊ I haven't danced since my ~! | **throughout your ~** ◊ He played football throughout his ~.
PHRASES **not in the first flush of ~** (esp. BrE) ◊ Though no longer in the first flush of ~ she's still remarkably energetic.

2 being young

ADJ. **comparative, extreme** (both esp. BrE) ◊ Her extreme ~ was against her. | **eternal** ◊ in search of eternal ~
VERB + YOUTH **have** ◊ You still have your youth—that's the main thing.
PHRASES **the fountain of ~** (figurative) ◊ The new cream is marketed as the fountain of ~.

3 young person

ADJ. **male** | **black, white** | **callow, impressionable, innocent** ◊ He was a callow ~ when he joined the newspaper. | **spotty** (BrE) ◊ She's going out with some spotty ~. | **fresh-faced** (esp. BrE) | **gangling** (esp. BrE), **gangly** (esp. AmE), **lanky** | **at-risk, high-risk, troubled**
... OF YOUTHS **gang** (esp. BrE), **group**

4 young people

ADJ. **modern** ◊ the aspirations of modern ~ | **local** | **inner-city, street** (AmE), **urban** | **working-class** | **immigrant** | **gay, Hispanic, Muslim** | **delinquent, disaffected** | **unemployed** | **educated** | **gilded** (BrE) | **privileged**
VERB + YOUTH **educate** ◊ a program to educate our ~ on the causes of health problems | **target** ◊ The website targets unemployed ~. | **corrupt**
YOUTH + NOUN **culture, subculture** | **centre/center, club, group, movement, organization** | **outreach** (esp. AmE), **programme/program** (esp. BrE), **scheme** (BrE), **work** (esp. BrE) ◊ ~ outreach programs run by the charity | **audience, market** | **sport** (esp. BrE), **sports** (esp. AmE) | **coach, team** | **basketball, football, hockey, etc.** | **band, orchestra** | **coordinator, leader, worker** | **minister, pastor** (both AmE) | **employment, training, unemployment** | **gang** | **violence** | **court, crime, custody** (BrE) ◊ a crackdown on ~ crime | **camp, hostel**
PHRASES **the country's ~, the nation's ~** | **the ~ of today, today's ~**

Z z

zeal noun

ADJ. **great** | **excessive** | **crusading, ideological** (esp. AmE), **missionary, reforming** (esp. BrE), **religious, revolutionary** ◊ a crusading ~ to eradicate drug abuse
VERB + ZEAL **burn with, have** ◊ He burned with a reforming ~. | **show**
PREP. **with ~** ◊ She went about the task with the ~ of an enthusiast. | **~ for** ◊ She had a true ~ for journalism. | **~ in** ◊ their ~ in the promotion of education

zest noun

ADJ. **great** | **added, infectious, youthful** ◊ Last month's victory has given him added ~ for the game.
VERB + ZEST **be full of, have** ◊ He is 74 years old but still full of ~. | **add, give sb/sth** ◊ The love affair added a little ~ to her life. | **lose**
PREP. **with ~** ◊ He campaigned with ~. | **~ for** ◊ a ~ for life

zip (BrE) (also zipper AmE, BrE) noun

VERB + ZIP/ZIPPER **pull** | **close, do up, pull up** | **open, pull down, undo** | **get caught in** ◊ The fabric got caught in the ~ and tore.
ZIP/ZIPPER + VERB **be stuck, get stuck, stick** ◊ The ~ on my bag has stuck. | **break** | **be open, be undone**

ZIP/ZIPPER + NOUN **closure** (*AmE*), **fastener** (*BrE*)
PREP. **with a ~** ◇ *a bag with a ~*
→ Special page at CLOTHES

zone *noun*

ADJ. **narrow, wide** | **marginal, peripheral, transition,
transitional, twilight** ◇ *a transition ~ between tropical and
arid vegetations* ◇ *the twilight ~ between living and merely
existing* | **border, frontier** | **neutral** | **battle, combat,
conflict, military, war** | **buffer, demilitarized, exclusion,
no-fly, no-go** ◇ *This area behind the station is a no-go ~ for
tourists.* | **occupation, occupied** | **free-fire** (*AmE, also
figurative*), **kill, target** ◇ *The Internet has become a free-fire ~
for conspiracy theories*(= *there are no restrictions*). ◇ *Our
truck was trapped in the kill ~* (= *where it can be attacked*).
| **danger** | **disaster** ◇ *The region has been declared an
ecological disaster ~.* | **safe, safety, security** ◇ *She stood
some distance away from him to maintain a safety ~.* | **drug-
free, nuclear-free, smoke-free, traffic-free, etc.** ◇ *Most of
the old town is a traffic-free ~.* | **northern, southern, etc.** |
central | **earthquake, fault, seismic** | **climate, climatic** |
temperate, tropical ◇ *the temperate and tropical ~s of South
America* | **coastal** | **dead** ◇ *an oxygen-depleted dead ~ at the
bottom of the sea* | **economic, enterprise, fishing, free-
trade, industrial** ◇ *an industrial ~ of factories, warehouses
and shipyards* | **autonomous** | **pedestrian** (*BrE*) | **school**
(*AmE*) | **time** ◇ *Vancouver is in the same time ~ as Los
Angeles.* | **erogenous** | **drop, landing** | **relegation** (*BrE*) ◇
*The team finds itself in the relegation ~ after a run of poor
results.* | **strike** (in baseball) | **end** (in American football) |
comfort ◇ *Students are unwilling to step outside their
comfort ~.*
VERB + ZONE **control, patrol** ◇ *The rebels control the southern
border ~.* | **create, declare sth, designate sth, establish** ◇
The area has been declared a closed military ~. | **enforce** ◇
Fighter planes are being sent to enforce the UN no-fly ~. |
violate ◇ *An enemy plane was shot down after it violated the
exclusion ~.* | **cross into, enter** ◇ *We were crossing into a
new time ~.* | **leave** ◇ *Aid workers were advised to leave the
danger ~.* | **divide sth into** ◇ *Europe is divided into
economic ~s.*
PREP. **in a/the ~, within a/the ~** ◇ *The plant grows only in
the temperate ~.* ◇ *Companies within enterprise ~s are given
special help.* | **into a/the ~** ◇ *We had accidentally strayed
into the war ~.* | **out of a/the ~** | **~ between** ◇ *the neutral ~
between the two countries*

zoo *noun*

ADJ. **petting** (*AmE*)
VERB + ZOO **go to, visit** | **escape from**
ZOO + NOUN **animals** | **keeper** (usually *zookeeper*)
PREP. **at a/the ~** ◇ *We saw a baby polar bear at the ~.* | **in a/
the ~** ◇ *These lions were born in the ~.*

zoology *noun* → Note at SUBJECT

KEY TO THE STUDY PAGES

S2 ideas into words

1 **a** constructive, positive **b** wacky **c** crackpot, crazy, mad, outlandish, wild **d** half-baked **e** grandiose

2 **a** come up with, dream up, hit on/upon, produce, think up **b** contribute, moot (*esp. BrE*), propose, put forward **c** promote, push (forward), sell **d** consider, entertain, flirt with, mull over, toy with, turn over **e** bounce around, bounce off sb, brainstorm, discuss, explore, talk about

3 **a** come into sb's brain/head/mind, come to sb, flash through sb's brain/mind, hit sb, occur to sb, pop into sb's head, strike sb **b** flow **c** emerge, evolve, form, grow **d** work (out) **e** come to nothing

4 the germ of an idea

S3–5 using a noun entry

Adjectives

1 a bewildering array of goods, a biting wind, a burning ambition, a convincing win, driving rain, a fighting chance, a gaping chasm, a staggering sum of money, a shining example, a crushing defeat, a haunting melody, a nagging pain, a piercing scream, a running battle, a sprawling suburb, a sweeping statement

Quantifiers

2 **a** *wisps* of cloud **b** *series/spate* of attacks **c** *bouts* of depression **d** *snatch* of their conversation **e** *stream* of traffic **f** *pack* of stray dogs **g** *hoots/howls* of laughter **h** *cloves* of garlic **i** *pang* of guilt **j** *glimmer* of hope

Verb + ...

3 **a** *got into/had* an argument **b** *clear/pay off* his debts **c** *came up with/put forward* the suggestion **d** *arrive at/draw* any firm conclusions **e** *agreed on/struck* a deal **f** a meeting has been *arranged/scheduled* **g** *accept/shoulder* the blame **h** *drummed/tapped* his fingers **i** *took/went on* a trip **j** *shade/shield* my eyes

... + verb

4 the wine had *flowed freely* ... my head was *throbbing* ... my stomach was *churning* ... the wind *howled* ... the rain *lashed* against the window ... my nerves were *on edge* ... I heard the *key turn/turning* ... my heart began to *hammer* in my chest ... footsteps *echoed* on the stairs ... my mind was *racing* ... the bedroom door *creaked* open ... my eyes *accustomed/adjusted* to the darkness ... the man's mouth *fell* open

... + noun

5 **a** beach resort **b** leg room **c** protest rally **d** traffic accident **e** famine relief **f** display case **g** shelf space **h** junk mail **i** crime wave **j** night shift

Prepositions

6 **a** *in* agony **b** *at* a disadvantage **c** confusion *over* ... **d** *above/over* the noise **e** *in* writing **f** *at* speed **g** *in* self-defence/self-defense **h** *in* this rain **i** *at(BrE)/on (esp.Ame)/over* the weekend **j** skill *at/in* ...

Phrases

7 a ... and *lend* a sympathetic ear. b I just couldn't *keep* a straight face.
c ..., he *pressed* his nose up against the glass. d ...the first time I *set* eyes on her.
e They really *put* their hearts into the task. f If this report *falls* into the wrong hands
g ..., I *felt* sick to stomach. h ...I vowed never to *set* foot in the place again.
i You must learn to *keep* your mouth shut. j ...she just *held/put* her head in her hands
and cried.

S6-7 using a verb entry

Adverbs

1 a argued *fiercely/heatedly* b *fiercely/passionately* defend c grinned *sheepishly/
wolfishly* d *categorically/flatly* denies e contrasted *markedly/starkly* f *brutally/
starkly* illustrates

Verb + ...

2 a *was happy to* accept b *failed to* comply c *serve to* highlight d *hasten to* add
e *take steps to* ensure f *offered to* resign g *was determined to* fight
h *can afford to* pay

Prepositions

3 a backfired *on* me b testify *against* a colleague c comment *on* their decision
d mistaking me *for* someone else e treated *for* sunstroke
f prejudice the jury *against* him g plotting *against* him h collaborated *on* many
projects i advise *against* drinking alcohol j appealed *for* calm

Phrases

4 a drink and drive b hire and fire c tossing and turning d mix and match
e hoping and praying f forgive and forget g braked to a halt h crack under the
strain i dawned bright and cold j grinning from ear to ear k pausing for breath

Collocations of phrasal verbs

5 I had *been left to* fend for myself . . . completely cut off *from* the rest of the world . . .
The water holes had dried up *completely* and I *was forced* to rely on cacti *for* water. I
tried to hang on *to* my sanity, clinging *desperately* to the hope . . . I pressed on *with*
my attempt . . . then *by chance* stumbled across an oasis. I *instantly* burst into load
cries of joy . . . and trees that blocked out the sun *completely*. I lay down in the shade
and *slowly* drifted off *to* sleep. I woke up *with* a start and l . . .

S8–9 using an adjective entry

Verbs

1 I nearly fell asleep. His mistake proved costly. The house smells damp. The house
stood empty. The crowd grew impatient. The roads run parallel. His mistake passed
unnoticed. The driver emerged unscathed.

2 a *drove* me crazy b *held* captive c *set* ablaze d *rendered* powerless e *deemed*
unsuitable f *beat* the security guard senseless g *regarded* him as eccentric h *jerked/
jolted* me awake

Adverbs

3 a painfully b mutually c fiercely d distinctly e wildly f grossly

4 a unduly concerned b justly proud c blissfully unaware
d conspicuously absent e depressingly familiar f outwardly composed
g eerily silent h downright dangerous

Prepositions

5 a damaging *to* the government b late *for* school c acquainted *with* the new software
d insistent *on/upon* maintaining her privacy e irresistible *to* women
f limited *to* two per person g conducive *to* economic growth h alarmed *at/by* the
latest crime statistics

Phrases

6 **a** alive and *well* **b** safe and *sound* **c** quick and *easy* **d** dazed and *confused*
e ready and *willing* **f** neat and *tidy* **g** worried *sick* **h** wet *through* **i** thrilled *to bits*
(BrE)/to pieces (AmE) **j** scared *out of my wits/stiff/to death* **k** bored *out of our brains*
(AmE)/out of our minds/rigid (BrE)/silly (BrE)/stiff/to death/to tears

S10–11 collocations with common verbs

The answers to the first three of these exercises are to some extent subjective. The aim is
to get you/your students thinking about how these verbs work. If, after working through
the exercises, you/they feel more confident about this area of collocation and more
familiar with some of these particular collocations, then the exercise has been successful.

1 **do** is the most usual verb for talking about tasks and duties, for example *do the
dishes, do the food for a party, do your homework, do your job, do research, do the/
some shopping, do a translation, do the washing/laundry*; exceptions could include
*make the bed, make dinner, make a photocopy; have a meeting; take an exam; give sth
a polish*

2 **do**: *damage, exercise, experiment, launder, operate, research, search, shop, sketch,
tour, translate, wash*
make: *argue, attempt, change, choose, connect, contribute, decide, film, guess, impact,
impress, mark, note, progress, promise, sketch, speak, state, suggest*
have: *argue, bath/bathe, break, breakfast, chat, drink, feel, guess, holiday(BrE),
impact, interest, look, meet, party, nap, shower, snack, swim, vacation(AmE)*
take: *act, bath/bathe, bite, break, breathe, decide, guess, holiday(BrE), look, nap,
note, notice, photograph, risk, shower, sip, swim, vacation(AmE), walk, X-ray*
give: *advise, answer, credit, cry, help, hug, instruct, kiss, lecture, opine, order, perform,
polish, prioritize, pull, push, shock, sigh, smile, speak, think, welcome*

3 **speaking**: *make a guess, make a promise, make a speech, make a statement, make a
suggestion, have an argument, have a chat, have a guess, take a (phone) call, give a
lecture, give your opinion, give an order, give a speech*
experiencing something *have an accident, have cancer, have a cold, have difficulty,
have fun, have a heart attack, have an operation, have problems, have a shock, have
trouble*

producing something using your hands, your mind or your skill *do the food for a
party, do a report, do a sketch, do a translation, make dinner, make a cake, make a
film/movie, make a sketch, take a picture/photo*

physical actions *do exercise, make a face, have a bath/shower, have a look, have a
nap, have a swim, take a bath/shower, take a bite, take a deep breath, take a nap, take
a pill, take a sip, take a swim, take a walk, give birth, give a cry of pain, give sb a hug,
give sb a kiss, give sb a lift/ride, give sth a polish, give sth a pull, give sb a push, give a
sigh, give a smile*

4 *do/take a course, do/take an exam, do/take French at school, do/make a sketch,
make/take a decision, make/have/take a guess, make/have an impact, make/take
notes, make/give a speech, have/take a bath/shower, have/take a break, have/take a
holiday/vacation, have/take a look, have/give a party, have/take a nap, have/take a
swim*

5/6 **a** *have/take a **close** look* **b** *do/take a test* **c** *give us a **warm** welcome*
d *have/take a nap* **e** *doing **odd** jobs* **f** *give **top** priority* **g** *have/take one more swim*
h *gave a short laugh* **i** *took an **instant** dislike* **j** *make any **rash** promises*
k *had/taken a **keen** interest* **l** *made her fortune* **m** *take (= a photo)/do (= a
drawing, etc.) a picture* **n** *making a terrible racket* **o** *made a **lasting** impression*
p *give the handle a **sharp** twist* **q** *have/make/take a **wild** guess* **r** *take the medicine*
s *making/taking **copious** notes* **t** *do/make a documentary*

natural disasters

a The famine has already *claimed* thousands of victims.
b The president visited the affected region in the *immediate* aftermath of the hurricane.
c Rescue *workers* are still looking for survivors.
d A massive relief *effort* is underway.
e Several villages have been *inundated* by the *severest* floods in decades.
f The city was *struck* by a *massive* earthquake shortly after midnight.
g The forest fires, *fanned* by warm winds, *raged* out of control for weeks.
h The volcano, which had been *dormant* for 50 years, began *erupting* late last night.

criminal justice

a ~~sent to~~ *remanded in (BrE)*, *taken into* custody **b** ~~did~~ *made* two arrests **c** ~~judged~~ *found* guilty **d** accused ~~with~~ *of* **e** ~~holds~~ *carries* a sentence **f** the judge ~~summarized~~ *summed up* **g** the jury ~~reported~~ *returned* a verdict **h** the original verdict was ~~squashed~~ *overturned, quashed (esp.BrE), reversed, set aside, thrown out (esp. AmE)*

education

a He got *full/~~maximum~~/top* marks in the listening test.
b I got a *failing/passing/~~winning~~* grade in math.
c We have to *do (BrE)/~~make~~/take* a vocabulary test every Friday.
d How many students have *joined/signed up for/~~undertaken~~* the course?
e She was always *~~losing~~/missing/skipping(AmE)* classes – no wonder she *~~crashed~~/failed/flunked (esp.AmE)* the exam.
f He suffers badly from exam *nerves/~~stress/worries~~*.
g The teacher *~~made up~~/set/wrote* a difficult exam but *checked/graded (AmE)/marked(BrE)* it leniently.
h We were supposed to *do/~~compose~~/write* an essay by Friday but I *~~delivered it~~/handed it in/turned it in (esp.AmE)* late.
i I *attended/~~visited~~/went to* a lecture on Japanese cinema.
j He went to Oxford where he *did/~~made~~/took* a degree *in/~~off~~/~~on~~* chemistry.

driving

a We drove down a narrow *~~curving~~/windy/winding* road and got stuck behind a truck *carrying/~~dragging~~/hauling/* timber.
b I *~~finished~~/ran out of/~~used up~~* the petrol/gas and had to *hitch/~~hitch-hike~~/thumb* a lift/ride to the nearest garage.
c There's always *busy/heavy/~~strong~~* traffic on the highway, so I usually take the *back/~~little~~/minor(esp. BrE)* roads.
d The car *~~pulled down~~/pulled over/pulled up* by the side of the road where there was a free parking *room/place/~~slot~~*
e I realized it was a *~~one-direction~~/one-way/~~single-way~~* street, so I had to *~~carry out~~/do/make* a U-turn.
f She *~~began~~/started/switched* on the engine to warm up the car and then started *~~rubbing~~/scraping/~~scratching~~* the ice off the windscreen/windshield.
g The demonstration *brought/reduced/~~slowed~~* traffic to a standstill, and some drivers began to *beep/~~bonk~~/honk* their horns in frustration.
h The car in front *~~cut down~~/slowed down/sped down* in order to let a police car *overtake/pass/~~take over~~*.
i I called a breakdown company to *haul away/~~pull away~~/tow away* my car as it had two *~~dead~~/~~empty~~/flat* tyres/tires.
j A car suddenly *pulled out/~~ran out~~/~~started out~~* in front of me and I had to *hit/slam on/~~tread on~~* the brakes.

politics

elections

a rigging, election b led, polls c launch, campaign d ran, office

government

e passed, bill f impose, ban g announced, plans h ruled out, possibility i hold, referendum j commission, report

opposition

k launched, attack l renewed, call m facing, backlash

international issues

n honour/honor, promise, o deploy, forces p issued, ultimatum q call, ceasefire

jobs

1   a a high-powered job b repetitive work c a competitive salary d flexible hours
     e her heavy workload f a short-term contract g a team meeting h a proven track
     record i in-house training j a skeleton staff

2   a *apply for* the job b *take* early retirement c *came out on (esp. BrE), went on* strike
     d *boost, enhance, improve* your job prospects e *fulfilling, reaching, realizing* her full
     potential, *handed in* her notice f *cancel, end, terminate* her contract, *missed* several
     important deadlines g *earn, make* her living, *achieved, fulfilled, realized* her
     ambition h *did* a brief stint, *do it for* a living

3   a brief stint b full potential c job prospects d wealth of experience

money

1   a an *awful* lot of money b doubled *in* value c *go up in, increase in, rise in* price
     d *facing* financial ruin e *lead to, mean, spell* economic ruin f *starting* salary
     g *went* bankrupt h *on a fixed, limited, low, modest, shoestring, small, tight* budget
     i *incurred, made, suffered, sustained, took* a loss *on* the deal j *arranged, got,
     obtained, raised (esp.BrE), took out* a large bank loan; had great difficulty *paying it
     off/back* k surge *in* demand; the company's stock has *hit, reached* an *all-time,* an
     historic, a *new,* a *record* high l *lost, made* a fortune *on* the stock market .
     m *placing, putting* a strain *on* the company's finances.

2   a small change b small fortune c healthy bank balance d take-home pay e false
     economy